California

EMPLOYMENT LAWS

2010

WEST®

A Thomson Reuters business

Mat #40814843

ISBN: 978–0–314–99761–6

SCOPE AND CONTENTS

Legislation

This pamphlet incorporates all laws through c. 632 of the 2009 portion of the 2009–2010 Regular Session, the end of the 2009–2010 First, Second and Fourth Extraordinary Sessions, and c. 29 of urgency legislation of the 2009–2010 Third Extraordinary Session, Governor's Reorganization Plan No. 1 of 2009, Prop. 1F, approved at the 5/19/2009 election, and propositions on the 6/8/2010 ballot received as of 10/1/2009. Federal statutes are current through P.L. 111–82, approved October 26, 2009, during the First Regular Session of the 111th Congress.

Regulations

The regulations incorporated in this pamphlet reflect all changes through Register 2009, No. 43.

Court Rules

The court rules incorporated in this pamphlet reflect all amendments available through November 1, 2009.

Ordinances

The text of Chapter 12B of the San Francisco Administrative Code incorporates all amendments approved through August 28, 2009.

Presentation of Changes

Additions or changes in statutes affected by 2009 legislation are indicated by underlining; deletions are indicated by asterisks. In court rules, additions or changes are indicated by underlining; deletions are indicated by strikethroughs.

Repealed Provisions

Repealed statutes and regulations are omitted.

Effective Dates of Legislation

All California legislative enactments in 2009 are effective January 1, 2010, unless indicated otherwise.

Election Results—May 19, 2009 Election

Propositions		Results
1A.	"Rainy Day" Budget Stabilization Fund. Initiative Constitutional Amendment.	Rejected
1B.	Education Funding. Payment Plan. Initiative Constitutional Amendment.	Rejected
1C.	Lottery Modernization Act. Initiative Constitutional Amendment and Statute.	Rejected
1D.	Children's Services Funding. Initiative Statute Amendment.	Rejected
1E.	Mental Health Funding. Initiative Statute Amendment.	Rejected
1F.	Elected Officials Salaries. Initiative Constitutional Amendment.	Approved

Veto Messages

Codified legislation which is subject to a governor's veto is followed by an italicized note indicating that fact. For the text of the message, please consult the Historical and Statutory Notes for the provision in *West's Annotated California Codes* or the material pertaining to the legislation affecting the provision in *West's California Legislative Service.*

*

TABLE OF SECTIONS AFFECTED

This table indicates sections affected by 2009 legislation

Employment Laws

LABOR CODE

Sec.	Effect	Chap.	Sec.
62.5	Amended	12(4X)	23
	Repealed	341	11
	Added	341	12
67	Added	12(4X)	24
87	Amended	140	135
273	Added	256	1
511	Amended	3(2X)	1
prec. 1500 (Pt. heading)	Added	242	1
1500	Added	242	1
1501	Added	242	1
1502	Added	242	1
1503	Added	242	1
1504	Added	242	1
1505	Added	242	1
1506	Added	242	1
1507	Added	242	1
prec. 1701 (Ch. heading)	Added	286	3
prec. 1701 (Art. heading)	Added	286	3
1701	Repealed	286	2
	Added	286	3
1701.1	Repealed	286	2
1701.2	Repealed	286	2
1701.4	Repealed	286	2
1701.5	Repealed	286	2
1701.8	Repealed	286	2
1701.10	Repealed	286	2
1701.12	Repealed	286	2
1701.13	Repealed	286	2
1701.15	Repealed	286	2
1701.16	Repealed	286	2
1701.17	Repealed	286	2
1701.18	Repealed	286	2
1701.19	Repealed	286	2
1701.20	Repealed	286	2
prec. 1702 (Art. heading)	Added	286	3
1702	Added	286	3
1702.1	Added	286	3
1702.3	Added	286	3
1702.4	Added	286	3
prec. 1703 (Art. heading)	Added	286	3
1703	Added	286	3
1703.1	Added	286	3
1703.3	Added	286	3
1703.4	Added	286	3
1703.5	Added	286	3
1703.6	Added	286	3

LABOR CODE

Sec.	Effect	Chap.	Sec.
prec. 1704 (Art. heading)	Added	286	3
1704	Added	286	3
1704.1	Added	286	3
1704.2	Added	286	3
1704.3	Added	286	3
prec. 1705 (Art. heading)	Added	286	3
1705	Added	286	3
1705.1	Added	286	3
1705.2	Added	286	3
1705.3	Added	286	3
1705.4	Added	286	3
1771.3	Added	7(2X)	5
1771.5	Amended	7(2X)	6
1771.55	Added	7(2X)	7
1771.7	Amended	7(2X)	8
1771.75	Added	7(2X)	9
1771.8	Amended	7(2X)	10
1771.85	Added	7(2X)	11
1771.9	Repealed	7(2X)	12
	Added	7(2X)	13
2051	Amended	224	1
2067	Amended	224	2
2699.5	Amended	140	136
3072	Amended	438	1
3600	Amended	272	1
3702.1	Amended	140	137
4352	Amended	12(4X)	25
4600	Amended	565	1
	Added	565	2
4610.3	Added	436	1
4850	Amended	389	1
7311.1	Amended	196	1
7311.25	Added	196	2

UNEMPLOYMENT INSURANCE CODE

Sec.	Effect	Chap.	Sec.
710.9	Added	437	1
822	Amended	9(3X)	20
1611	Amended	9(3X)	21
3001	Amended	9(3X)	22
4003	Amended	22(3X)	1
4004	Amended	22(3X)	2
4552	Amended	22(3X)	3
9801	Amended	95	1
9802.5	Amended	95	2
9808	Amended	95	3
10214.6	Added	12(4X)	32

TABLE OF SECTIONS AFFECTED

UNEMPLOYMENT INSURANCE CODE

Sec.	Effect	Chap.	Sec.
13019	Added	411	3
13020	Amended	15(4X)	5

UNEMPLOYMENT INSURANCE CODE

Sec.	Effect	Chap.	Sec.
14022	Added	12(4X)	33

RELATED PRODUCTS
FROM WEST

WITKIN TREATISES

Summary of California Law

California Procedure

California Evidence

California Criminal Law (with Norman Epstein)
[Also available on CD–ROM and Westlaw]

CALIFORNIA JURISPRUDENCE

[Also available on CD–ROM and Westlaw]

JURY INSTRUCTIONS

California Jury Instructions—Civil (BAJI & CACI)

California Jury Instructions—Criminal (CALJIC & CALCRIM)
[Also available in computer disc and looseleaf formats and on Westlaw]

CALIFORNIA CIVIL PRACTICE

Business Litigation

Civil Rights Litigation

Employment Litigation

Environmental Litigation

Family Law Litigation

Probate and Trust Proceedings

Procedure

Real Property Litigation

Torts

Workers' Compensation
[Also available on CD–ROM and Westlaw]

VIII

RELATED PRODUCTS

California Criminal Law
by Laurie L. Levenson and Alex Ricciardulli

California Insurance Law Dictionary and Desk Reference
by Bruce Cornblum

California Legal Filing Directory
by Patricia A. Britton

California Prejudgment Money Remedies
by Justice John Zebrowski, Barry Adler, and Paul Malingagio

California Search and Seizure
by Hon. Gregory M. Caskey

California Subpoena Handbook
by John M. Sink

Cohelan on California Class Actions
by Timothy D. Cohelan

Dunne on Depositions
by Kevin J. Dunne

Hanna and Van Atta on California Common Interest Developments
by John Paul Hanna and David Van Atta

Levenson on California Criminal Procedure
by Laurie L. Levenson

Mexican Legal Dictionary and Desk Reference
by Jorge Vargas

Overly on Electronic Evidence in California
by Michael R. Overly

Simons California Evidence Manual
by Justice Mark B. Simons

Younger on California Motions
by Judge Eric E. Younger (ret.) and Donald E. Bradley

REAL ESTATE PRACTICE

California Real Estate
by Harry D. Miller and Members of the Firm of Miller, Starr & Regalia

California Real Estate Forms 2d
by Alexander Hamilton

California Real Estate Digest

Miller & Starr Real Estate NewsAlert

California Construction Law Manual
by James Acret

California Construction Law Digests

XI

RELATED PRODUCTS

[Also available on CD–ROM]

WEST'S CALIFORNIA DIGEST

[Also available on CD–ROM]

WEST'S CALIFORNIA DESKTOP CODES
UNANNOTATED

California Civil Code

California Code of Civil Procedure

California Corporations Code

California Criminal and Motor Vehicle Law

California Education Code

California Elections Code

California Employment Laws

California Environmental Laws

California Evidence Code

California Family Laws and Rules

California Government Code

California Insurance Code

California Juvenile Laws and Rules

California Penal Code

California Penal and Evidence Codes

California Probate Code

California Revenue and Taxation Code

California Vehicle Code

California Water Code

ANNOTATED

California Business Statutes Annotated

California Civil Practice Statutes and Rules Annotated

Blumberg California Family Code Annotated

RELATED PRODUCTS

California Commercial Code Annotated

DiMugno and Glad California Insurance Laws Annotated

Dwyer & Bergsund California Environmental Laws Annotated

Imwinkelreid & Hallahan California Evidence Code Annotated

McGovern California Probate Code Annotated

Miller and Starr California Real Estate Laws Annotated

COURT RULES

California Rules of Court, State, Federal District and Federal Bankruptcy

Bay Area Local Court Rules—Superior Courts

Central California Local Court Rules—Superior Courts

Los Angeles County Court Rules—Superior Court

Northern California Local Court Rules—Superior Courts

Southern California Local Court Rules—Superior Courts

California KeyRules

JUDICIAL COUNCIL FORMS

California Judicial Council Forms

Legal Solutions Judicial Council and Local Forms Disc Products

---

STYLE MANUAL

California Style Manual
by Edward W. Jessen

Westlaw®

WestCheck.com™

WEST CD–ROM LIBRARIES™

RELATED PRODUCTS

To order any of these California practice tools, call your West Representative or **1–800–328–9352.**

NEED RESEARCH HELP?

You can get quality research results with free help—call the West Reference Attorneys when you have questions concerning Westlaw or West Publications at **1–800–REF–ATTY (1–800–733–2889)**.

INTERNET ACCESS

Contact the West Editorial Department directly with your questions and suggestions by e-mail at west.editor@thomson.com. Visit West's home page at west.thomson.com

WESTLAW ELECTRONIC RESEARCH GUIDE

Westlaw—Expanding the Reach of Your Library

Westlaw, West's online legal research service, provides you with the same quality and integrity that you have come to expect from West books. In addition, you have quick, easy access to West's vast collection of statutes, case law materials, public records, news and business information, and other legal and nonlegal resources. West's editorial enhancements, such as case headnotes and topic and key numbers, enable you to move quickly and easily between West print resources and Westlaw for your legal research.

Accessing Databases Using the Westlaw Directory

You can use the Westlaw Directory to view all the databases on Westlaw, as well as to link to detailed information about each database. To access the Westlaw Directory, click **Directory** at the top of any Westlaw page. Browse the directory by clicking the links for the headings or subheadings in the right frame. Click a database name to access a database. You can also type all or part of a database name in the *Search for a database* text box in the left frame and click **Go**. A list of databases is displayed. To access a database, click its name.

Retrieving a Specific Document

If you know the citation of a document, use the Find service on Westlaw to quickly retrieve the document. Click **Find&Print** at the top of any Westlaw page to display the Find a Document page. Type the citation in the *Find this document by citation* text box in the left frame and click **Go**.

Find templates are available for federal and state case law, the U.S. Constitution and state constitutions, federal and state statutes and regulations, and many other materials. If you are unsure of the correct citation format, simply type the publication abbreviation in the *Find this document by citation* text box and click **Go**. A fill-in-the-blank template is displayed. For example, to display a Find template for a state's statutes, type **xx st** (where xx is a state's two-letter postal abbreviation).

To retrieve a specific case when you know one or more parties' names, click **Find&Print**. Then click **Find a Case by Party Name** in the left frame. The Find a Case by Party Name search template is displayed.

Checking Citations in KeyCite®

KeyCite is the citation research service on Westlaw. KeyCite information is available for every case in West's® National Reporter System® and more than 1 million unpublished cases; federal statutes and regulations; statutes from all 50 states; administrative decisions from selected federal agencies; regulations and administrative decisions from selected states; and other materials.

You can use KeyCite to determine whether a case, statute, regulation, or administrative decision is good law. You can also use KeyCite to retrieve citing references to a document, including cases, administrative materials, secondary sources, and briefs and other court documents. KeyCite history for a statute includes citations to recent session laws that amend or repeal the section and proposed legislation.

Click **KeyCite** at the top of any Westlaw page to get a detailed explanation of the KeyCite status flags and depth of treatment stars. Depth of treatment stars help you focus on the most important citing references.

The KeyCite Alert service allows you to monitor the status of a case, statute, regulation, or administrative decision and sends you updates when its KeyCite result (i.e., history or citing references) changes.

United States Code Annotated® (USCA®)

The USCA contains the official text of the U.S. Code along with annotations that include notes of decisions, historical notes, research references, and cross-references.

State Statutes

Annotated state statutes are available for all 50 states and the District of Columbia.

Links Tab

When you are viewing a statute, the Links tab in the left frame allows you to view information related to the statute, including cases that cite the statute, legislative history, and prior versions of the statute.

- **Legislative History**

  Legislative history for federal statutes provides you with public laws, *Congressional Record* documents, committee reports, bill drafts, congressional testimony, congressional bills, and presidential messages. Legislative history for state statutes, available for 36 states and the District of Columbia, provides you with committee reports, legislative journals, transcripts of legislative proceedings, records of legislators' votes, and governors' messages.

- **Graphical Statutes®**

  This feature allows you to track changes to a statute in an easy-to-read graphical display, which includes enacting public laws, relevant legislative history materials, and prior versions.

- **Versions**

  You can view prior versions of the USCA and selected state statutes that were effective on a specific date.

- **50 State Surveys**

  These surveys allow you see how a particular legal topic has been addressed by comparable state statutes in any of the 50 states and the District of Columbia.

RegulationsPlus®

USCA® sections are linked to related **Code of Federal Regulations (CFR)** provisions to allow seamless viewing between the two Codes. Also featured are a CFR Index of more than 1 million references created by West attorney-editors, arranged by topic and linked directly to CFR sections, plus CFR Notes of Decisions, linked to the caselaw and to West Key Numbers and Topics.

ResultsPlus®

After you run a search in a statutes database, Westlaw automatically creates a ResultsPlus list of additional documents and West topic and key numbers that have a high statistical likelihood of matching the concepts in your search. Click a document title in the list to view the full text of the document.

Additional Information

Westlaw is available on the Web at westlaw.com.

For search assistance, call the West Reference Attorneys at
1–800–REF–ATTY (1–800–733–2889).

For technical assistance, call West Customer Technical Support at
1–800–WESTLAW (1–800–937–8529).

*

TABLE OF CONTENTS

CONSTITUTION

Page

Article

I. Declaration of Rights ---- 1

XIV. Labor Relations ---- 1

BUSINESS AND PROFESSIONS CODE

Division

2. Healing Arts ---- 3

  Chapter

  5. Medicine ---- 3

    Article

    3. License Required and Exemptions ---- 3

3. Professions and Vocations Generally ---- 4

  Chapter

  11.5 Private Security Services ---- 4

    Article

    4. Private Patrol Operators ---- 4

  21.5 Foreign Labor Contractors ---- 4

7. General Business Regulations ---- 5

  Part

  1. Licensing for Revenue and Regulation ---- 5

    Chapter

    4. Employment Activities ---- 5

  2. Preservation and Regulation of Competition ---- 6

    Chapter

    1. Contracts in Restraint of Trade ---- 6

CIVIL CODE

Division

1. Persons ---- 9

  Part

  2. Personal Rights ---- 9

  2.6 Confidentiality of Medical Information ---- 12

    Chapter

    2. Disclosure of Medical Information by Providers ---- 12

    3. Use and Disclosure of Medical Information by Employers ---- 17

    6. Relationship to Existing Law ---- 19

    7. Violations ---- 19

3. Obligations ---- 20

  Part

  2. Contract ---- 20

    Title

    4. Unlawful Contracts ---- 20

TABLE OF CONTENTS

Part

3. Obligations Imposed by Law 21
4. Obligations Arising from Particular Transactions 21

Title

1.6 Consumer Credit Reporting Agencies Act 21

Chapter

1. General Provisions 21
2. Obligations of Consumer Credit Reporting Agencies 23
3. Requirements on Users of Consumer Credit Reports 33

1.6A Investigative Consumer Reporting Agencies 34

Article

1. General Provisions 34
2. Obligations of Investigative Consumer Reporting Agencies 35
4. Remedies 41

1.8 Personal Data 43

Chapter

1. Information Practices Act of 1977 43

Article

1. General Provisions and Legislative Findings 43
2. Definitions 43
8. Access to Records and Administrative Remedies 44
9. Civil Remedies 44

2.91 Employment Agency, Employment Counseling, and Job Listing Services Act 46

Chapter

1. General Provisions 46
2. Employment Agencies 48
3. Employment Counseling Services 56
4. Job Listing Services 58
5. Records 62
6. Remedies and Enforcement 62
7. Nurses' Registries 63
8. Long–Term Care Facilities 66

15. Works of Improvement 67

Chapter

2. Mechanics' Liens 67

Article

2. Who is Entitled to Lien 67

Division

4. General Provisions 68

Part

1. Relief 68

Title

2. Compensatory Relief 68

Chapter

1. Damages in General 68

Article

3. Exemplary Damages 68

XX

TABLE OF CONTENTS

Chapter
2. Measure of Damages — 68

 Article
 2. Damages for Wrongs — 68

Title
3. Specific and Preventive Relief — 69

Chapter
2. Specific Relief — 69

 Article
 3. Specific Performance of Obligations — 69

7. Duty of Health Care Service Plans and Managed Care Entities — 69

CODE OF CIVIL PROCEDURE

Part
2 Of Civil Actions — 71

Title
2. Of the Time of Commencing Civil Actions — 71

Chapter
4. General Provisions as to the Time of Commencing Actions — 71

6.5 Attachment — 72

Chapter
7. Property Subject to Attachment — 72

7. Other Provisional Remedies in Civil Actions — 72

Chapter
3. Injunction — 72

9. Enforcement of Judgments — 80

Division
2. Enforcement of Money Judgments — 80

Chapter
5. Wage Garnishment — 80

 Article
 1. Short Title; Definitions — 80
 2. General Provisions — 80
 3. Restrictions on Earnings Withholding — 84
 4. Earnings Withholding Order for Taxes — 84
 5. Procedure for Earnings Withholding Orders and Exemption Claims — 87
 6. Forms; Employer's Instructions — 90
 7. Administration and Enforcement — 93

14. Miscellaneous Provisions — 93

Chapter
6. Of Costs — 93

3. Of Special Proceedings of a Civil Nature — 94

Title
4. Of the Enforcement of Liens — 94

Chapter
3. Certain Liens and Priorities for Salaries, Wages and Consumer Deposits — 94

9. Arbitration — 96

Chapter
1. General Provisions — 96
2. Enforcement of Arbitration Agreements — 96

XXI

TABLE OF CONTENTS

Title

10. Unclaimed Property 98

   Chapter

   7. Unclaimed Property Law 98

      Article

      1. Short Title; Definitions; Application 98

      2. Escheat of Unclaimed Personal Property 99

Part

4. Miscellaneous Provisions 100

   Title

   3. Of the Production of Evidence 100

      Chapter

      2. Means of Production 100

CORPORATIONS CODE

Title

4. Securities 103

   Division

   1. Corporate Securities Law of 1968 103

      Part

      3. Regulation and Notice Filing Requirements of Agents, Broker–Dealers, Investment Adviser Representatives, and Investment Advisers 103

         Chapter

         2. Licensing of Agents and Broker–Dealers 103

EDUCATION CODE

Title

1. General Education Code Provisions 105

   Division

   1. General Education Code Provisions 105

      Part

      6. Education Programs—State Master Plans 105

         Chapter

         2. Child Care and Development Services Act 105

            Article

            10. Administration 105

2. Elementary and Secondary Education 105

   Division

   3. Local Administration 105

      Part

      25. Employees 105

         Chapter

         1. Employees 105

            Article

            5. Reporting by School Employees of Improper Governmental Activities 105

   4. Instruction and Services 107

      Part

      28. General Instructional Programs 107

         Chapter

         17.5 California Career Resource Network 107

TABLE OF CONTENTS

Title
3. Postsecondary Education -- 109
   Division
   7. Community Colleges --- 109
      Part
      51. Employees --- 109
          Chapter
          1. Provisions Applying to All Employees ---------------- 109
             Article
             6. Reporting by Community College Employees of Improper Governmental Activities ------------------------------ 109
   8. California State University ----------------------------------- 111
      Part
      55. California State University ------------------------------ 111
          Chapter
          5. Personnel --- 111
             Article
             4. Investigation of Reported Improper Governmental Activities -- 111

ELECTIONS CODE

Division
12. Preelection Procedures --- 113
    Chapter
    4. Precinct Boards -- 113
       Article
       1. General Provisions -------------------------------------- 113
14. Election Day Procedures --- 113
    Chapter
    1. Privileges of Voters --- 113
    3. Procedure at Polls --- 113
       Article
       5. Provisional Voting ------------------------------------- 113

EVIDENCE CODE

Division
11. Writings -- 115
    Chapter
    2. Secondary Evidence of Writings ------------------------------ 115
       Article
       4. Production of Business Records ------------------------- 115

FAMILY CODE

Division
2.5 Domestic Partner Registration ----------------------------------- 117
    Part
    1. Definitions --- 117
    2. Registration -- 118
    3. Termination --- 120

Part

4.   Legal Effect 121

5.   Preemption 122

Division

3.   Marriage 122

Part

1.   Validity of Marriage 122

9.   Support 123

Part

1.   Definitions and General Provisions 123

Chapter

6.   Modification, Termination, or Set Aside of Support Orders 123

Article

2.   Discovery Before Commencing Modification or Termination Proceeding 123

7.   Health Insurance 123

Article

2.   Health Insurance Coverage Assignment 123

5.   Enforcement of Support Orders 126

Chapter

1.   General Provisions 126

8.   Earnings Assignment Order 127

Article

1.   Definitions 127

2.   General Provisions 128

6.   Information Concerning Address and Employment of Obligor 133

7.   Prohibited Practices 133

17.   Support Services 134

Chapter

2.   Child Support Enforcement 134

Article

2.   Collections and Enforcement 134

FINANCIAL CODE

Division

2.   Savings Association Law 135

Chapter

4.   Powers of Associations 135

Article

1.   General Powers 135

9.   California Finance Lenders Law 135

Chapter

1.   General Provisions 135

Article

4.   Regulations 135

20.   California Residential Mortgage Lending Act 136

Chapter

7.   Prohibited Practices and Penalties 136

TABLE OF CONTENTS

FOOD AND AGRICULTURAL CODE

Division

1. State Administration 137

   Part

   1. The Department of Food and Agriculture 137

      Chapter

      2. Fiscal Duties and Powers 137

         Article

         2. Department of Food and Agriculture Fund 137

GOVERNMENT CODE

Title

1. General 139

   Division

   4. Public Officers and Employees 139

      Chapter

      1. General 139

         Article

         2. Disqualification for Office or Employment 139

   7. Miscellaneous 140

      Chapter

      17. Employment of Veterans 140

      17.3 Enforcement Actions 142

2. Government of the State of California 143

   Division

   1. General 143

      Chapter

      5. Miscellaneous 143

      5.5 Drug–Free Workplace 144

         Article

         1. Definitions 144

         2. State Contractors and Grantees 144

      6.5 State Auditor 145

         Article

         3. California Whistleblower Protection Act 145

         3.5 Whistleblower Information 148

   2. Legislative Department 149

      Part

      1. Legislature 149

         Chapter

         4. Witnesses 149

   3. Executive Department 149

      Part

      1. State Departments and Agencies 149

         Chapter

         3.5 Administrative Regulations and Rulemaking 149

            Article

            5. Public Participation: Procedure for Adoption of Regulations 149

TABLE OF CONTENTS

Part

2. Constitutional Officers 150

Chapter

    5. Controller 150

Article

        2. Duties 150

    6. Attorney General 150

Article

        9. False Claims Actions 150

2.8 Department of Fair Employment and Housing 151

Chapter

    1. General Provisions 151

    3. Findings and Declarations of Policy 152

    4. Definitions 153

    5. Powers and Duties 157

Article

        1. The Department 157

        2. The Commission 159

    6. Discrimination Prohibited 159

Article

        1. Unlawful Practices, Generally 159

        2. Housing Discrimination 170

    7. Enforcement and Hearing Procedures 175

Article

        1. Unlawful Practices 175

        2. Housing Discrimination 183

    8. Nondiscrimination and Compliance Employment Programs 188

    9. Miscellaneous 189

Division

4. Fiscal Affairs 190

Part

2. State Funds 190

Chapter

    6. Prohibition on Use of State Funds and Facilities to Assist, Promote, or Deter Union Organizing 190

5. Personnel 193

Part

2.6. Personnel Administration 193

Chapter

    2. Administration of Salaries 193

Article

        3. Salary Classification 193

        4. Miscellaneous Compensation 193

3. Public Employees' Retirement System 193

Chapter

    1. General Provisions and Definitions 193

Article

        2. Definitions 193

    11. Service Credit 197

Article

        3. Computation of Service Credit 197

TABLE OF CONTENTS

Chapter

13. Retirement Benefits 197

    Article

    5. Disability Retirement Benefits 197

Title

3. Government of Counties 199

  Division

  4. Employees 199

    Part

    3. Retirement Systems 199

      Chapter

      3. County Employees Retirement Law of 1937 199

        Article

        8.6. Post–Employment Benefits 199

        10. Disability Retirement 201

5. Local Agencies 203

  Division

  1. Cities and Counties 203

    Part

    1. Powers and Duties Common to Cities and Counties 203

      Chapter

      1. General 203

        Article

        2. Powers and Duties of Legislative Bodies 203

8. The Organization and Government of Courts 203

  Chapter

  7. Trial Court Employment Protection and Governance Act 203

    Article

    3. Labor Relations 203

  7.5 Trial Court Interpreter Employment and Labor Relations Act 204

HEALTH AND SAFETY CODE

Division

2. Licensing Provisions 205

  Chapter

  2. Health Facilities 205

    Article

    3. Regulations 205

  2.2 Health Care Service Plans 206

    Article

    4.5 California COBRA Program 206

    5. Standards 213

13. Housing 215

  Part

  1. Employee Housing Act 215

    Chapter

    1. General Provisions and Definitions 215

    2. Application and Scope 218

    3. Permits and Fees 221

    4. Rules and Regulations 227

    5. Enforcement 228

    6. Violations 230

TABLE OF CONTENTS

Division

20. Miscellaneous Health and Safety Provisions ----- 237

   Chapter

   1. Enforcement Actions ----- 237
   6.5. Hazardous Waste Control ----- 237

      Article

      13. Management of Used Oil ----- 237

   10.4 Asbestos Notification ----- 238

103. Disease Prevention and Health Promotion ----- 242

   Part

   5. Environmental and Occupational Epidemiology ----- 242

      Chapter

      1. Occupational Health and Disease Control ----- 242
      2. Occupational Health and Disease Prevention ----- 242

         Article

         1. Occupational Health and Disease Prevention Program ----- 242
         2. Occupational Lead Poisoning Prevention ----- 243

105. Communicable Disease Prevention and Control ----- 246

   Part

   4. Human Immunodeficiency Virus (HIV) ----- 246

      Chapter

      7. Mandated Blood Testing and Confidentiality to Protect Public Health ---- 246

INSURANCE CODE

Division

1. General Rules Governing Insurance ----- 249

   Part

   2. The Business of Insurance ----- 249

      Chapter

      1. General Regulations ----- 249

         Article

         6.6 Insurance Information and Privacy Protection Act ----- 249

2. Classes of Insurance ----- 249

   Part

   2. Life and Disability Insurance ----- 249

      Chapter

      1. The Contract ----- 249

         Article

         1. General Provisions ----- 249
         1.7 California COBRA Program ----- 253

      4. Standard Provisions in Disability Policies ----- 261

         Article

         6. Interpretation of Policy ----- 261

   6.3 Access for Infants and Mothers ----- 261

      Chapter

      4. Subscriber Eligibility and Enrollment ----- 261

         Article

         2. Unfair Competition and Labor Practices ----- 261

TABLE OF CONTENTS

LABOR CODE

General Provisions --- 263

Division

1. Department of Industrial Relations --- 265

    Chapter

    1. General Powers and Duties --- 265
    1.5 Mediation --- 273
    2. Industrial Welfare Commission ------------------------------------- 274
    3. Commission on Health and Safety and Workers' Compensation ----- 274
    4. Division of Labor Standards Enforcement ------------------------- 276
    5. Division of Workers' Compensation ------------------------------- 288
    6. Occupational Safety and Health Standards Board ----------------- 309
    6.5 Occupational Safety and Health Appeals Board ------------------- 315
    7. Division of Labor Statistics and Research ------------------------- 316
    7.5 Division of Occupational Safety and Health ---------------------- 317

2. Employment Regulation and Supervision ----------------------------------- 318

    Part

    1. Compensation --- 318

        Chapter

        1. Payment of Wages --- 319

            Article

            1. General Occupations ------------------------------------ 319
            2. Seasonal Labor --- 338
            3. Special Occupations ------------------------------------ 339

        2. Assignment of Wages -------------------------------------- 342
        3. Privileges and Perquisites ------------------------------- 343

            Article

            1. Gratuities --- 343
            2. Bonds and Photographs ------------------------------- 344
            3. Contracts and Applications for Employment ------- 345
            4. Purchases --- 348

    2. Working Hours --- 348

        Chapter

        1. General --- 348
        2. Railroads -- 354
        3. Smelters and Underground Workings ------------------- 355
        4. Lumber Industries -- 357
        5. Pharmacies --- 357

    3. Privileges and Immunities -- 358

        Chapter

        1. Contracts Against Public Policy ------------------------- 358
        2. Solicitation of Employees by Misrepresentation ------ 359
        3. Class of Labor Employed; Labor Union Insignia ----- 359
        3.5 Contractors -- 361
        3.7 Alcohol and Drug Rehabilitation ----------------------- 362
        3.8 Lactation Accommodation -------------------------------- 362

XXIX

TABLE OF CONTENTS

Chapter

3.9	Employee Literacy Assistance	363
4.	Reemployment Privileges	363
4.5	Displaced Janitor Opportunity Act	364
4.6	Public Transit Service Contracts	366
5.	Political Affiliations	367
6.	Agreements in Connection with Trade Disputes	369
6.5	Peace Officers [Repealed]	369
7.	Jurisdictional Strikes	369
7.5	Collective Bargaining Agreements	370
8.	Professional Strikebreakers	371

Article

1.	Findings and Declarations	371
2.	Definitions	371
3.	Professional Strikebreakers	372
4.	Miscellaneous	372

9.	Public Transportation Labor Disputes	372
10.	Unlawful Acts During Labor Disputes	373

Part

3.5	Agricultural Labor Relations	374

Chapter

1.	General Provisions and Definitions	375
2.	Agricultural Labor Relations Board	376

Article

1.	Agricultural Labor Relations Board: Organization	376
2.	Investigatory Powers	378

3.	Rights of Agricultural Employees	378
4.	Unfair Labor Practices and Regulation of Secondary Boycotts	378
5.	Labor Representatives and Elections	383
6.	Prevention of Unfair Labor Practices and Judicial Review and Enforcement	385
6.5.	Contract Dispute Resolution	388
7.	Suits Involving Employers and Labor Organizations	390
8.	Limitations	390

4.

4.	Employees	391

Chapter

1.	Wages, Hours and Working Conditions	391
2.	Occupational Privileges and Restrictions	404

Article

1.	Female Employees [Repealed]	404
2.	Minors	404

3.	Working Hours	415

Article

1.	Female Employees [Repealed]	415
2.	Minors	415

4.	Relocations, Terminations, and Mass Layoffs	418
4.5	Fair Employment Practices [Repealed]	420
5.	Civil Air Patrol	420

TABLE OF CONTENTS

Part

6. Licensing... 421
   Chapter
   1. Athlete Agents [Repealed].. 421
   2. State Employment Bureaus [Repealed]... 421
   3. Farm Labor Contractors... 421
   4. Talent Agencies.. 432
      Article
      1. Scope and Definitions... 433
      2. Licenses.. 433
      3. Operation and Management.. 436
      4. California Entertainment Commission [Repealed]...................... 440
   4.5 Fee–Related Talent Services.. 440
      Article
      1. Definitions... 440
      2. Advance–Fee Talent Representation Service................................ 441
      3. Other Talent Services.. 442
      4. Remedies.. 446
      5. General Provisions... 446
      6. Remedies [Repealed]... 447
   5. Nurses Registries [Repealed]... 447

7. Public Works and Public Agencies.. 447
   Chapter
   1. Public Works... 447
      Article
      1. Scope and Operation... 447
      1.5 Right of Action.. 454
      2. Wages... 454
      3. Working Hours... 471
      4. Employment of Aliens [Repealed]... 471
      5. Securing Workers' Compensation.. 471
   2. Public Agencies.. 472
      Article
      1. Municipal Employees... 472
      2. Employment of Aliens [Repealed]... 472
      3. Loyalty of Employees [Repealed].. 472
   4. Firefighters... 472

8. Unemployment Relief... 473
   Chapter
   1. Extension of Public Works.. 473
   2. Unemployment Relief Camps [Repealed].. 474
   3. Public Service Districts [Repealed].. 474

8.5 Car Washes.. 474
   Chapter
   1. General Provisions... 474
   2. Registration.. 475
   3. Successorship... 477
   4. Operation.. 478
   5. Reporting.. 478

TABLE OF CONTENTS

Part

8.7   Employee Health Insurance [Rejected] 478

9.   Health 478

Chapter

0.5   Affordable Basic Health Care Act of 1992 [Rejected] 478

1.   Sanitary Conditions 478

Article

1.   Sanitary Standards 478

2.   Foundries and Metal Shops 478

3.   Factories and Business Establishments 479

4.   Camps [Repealed] 479

5.   General Health Provisions 479

2.   Employee Health Care Coverage [Repealed] 480

3.   Registration of Factories [Repealed] 480

4.   Employee Housing Act [Repealed] 480

10.   Industrial Homework 480

11.   Garment Manufacturing 484

Chapter

1.   General Provisions 484

2.   Registration 487

3.   Arbitration 492

12.   Sheepherders 493

13.   The Labor Code Private Attorneys General Act of 2004 495

Division

3.   Employment Relations 498

Chapter

1.   Scope of Division 498

2.   Employer and Employee 498

Article

1.   The Contract of Employment 498

2.   Obligations of Employer 499

3.   Obligations of Employee 504

3.5   Inventions Made by an Employee 505

4.   Termination of Employment 506

5.   Investigations of Employees 507

3.   Master and Servant [Repealed] 508

4.   Apprenticeship 508

4.   Workers' Compensation and Insurance 519

Part

1.   Scope and Operation 519

Chapter

1.   General Provisions 519

2.   Employers, Employees, and Dependents 538

Article

1.   Employers 538

2.   Employees 539

3.   Dependents 546

4.   Employee Notice 546

XXXII

TABLE OF CONTENTS

Chapter
3.	Conditions of Compensation Liability	547
4.	Compensation Insurance and Security	552

Article
1.	Insurance and Security	552
2.	Uninsured Employers Fund	562
2.5	Self–Insurers' Security Fund	574
3.	Insurance Rights and Privileges	576
4.	Construction Permit	578
5.	Workers' Compensation Misrepresentations	579

5.	Subrogation of Employer	580
6.	Hospital Inspection [Repealed]	583
7.	Medical Examinations	583

Article
1.	[Examination Requirements]	583
2.	Determination of Medical Issues	584

8.	Election to be Subject to Compensation Liability	591
9.	Economic Opportunity Programs	592

Article
1.	General Provisions	592
2.	Benefits	593
3.	Adjustment of Claims	593

10.	Disaster Service Workers	593
10.5	Disaster Service Workers [Renumbered]	595
11.	Asbestos Workers' Account	595

Article
1.	General Provisions	595
2.	Benefits	596
3.	Collections	598

Part
2.	Computation of Compensation	599

Chapter
1.	Average Earnings	599
2.	Compensation Schedules	603

Article
1.	General Provisions	603
2.	Medical and Hospital Treatment	605
2.3.	Medical Provider Networks	625
2.5	Medical–Legal Expenses	630
2.6	Vocational Rehabilitation [Repealed]	633
3.	Disability Payments	633
4.	Death Benefits	641
4.5	Public Official Death Benefits	645
5.	Subsequent Injuries Payments	647
6.	Special Payments to Certain Persons	648
7.	City Police and Firemen, Sheriffs, and Others	652

3.	Compensation Claims	655

TABLE OF CONTENTS

Chapter

1.	Payment and Assignment		655
2.	Compromise and Release		660
3.	Lump Sum Payments		661

Part

3.2 Workers' Compensation Health Care Provider Organization Act [Repealed] 663

3.5 Arbitration 663

4. Compensation Proceedings 664

Chapter

1. Jurisdiction 664

2. Limitations of Proceedings 671

2.3 Workers' Compensation—Truth in Advertising 675

2.5 Administrative Assistance 677

3. Applications and Answers 677

4. Attachments 683

5. Hearings 683

6. Findings and Awards 686

7. Reconsideration and Judicial Review 689

Article

1. Reconsideration 690

2. Judicial Review 691

3. Undertaking on Stay Order 693

Division

4.5 Workers' Compensation and Insurance: State Employees Not Otherwise Covered 693

Chapter

1. General Provisions 693

2. Direct Payments 693

3. Insurance 694

4. Benefits and Procedure 694

4.6 Workmen's Compensation Advisory Committee [Repealed] 696

4.7 Retraining and Rehabilitation 696

5. Safety in Employment 697

Part

1. Occupational Safety and Health 697

Chapter

1. Jurisdiction and Duties 697

2. Education and Research 709

2.5 Hazardous Substances Information and Training 714

Article

1. General Provisions 714

2. Definitions 714

3. Hazardous Substances 715

4. Duties 717

5. Liability and Remedies 720

6. Repeal [Repealed] 720

3. Responsibilities and Duties of Employers and Employees 720

4. Penalties 731

5. Temporary Variances 734

6. Permit Requirements 735

TABLE OF CONTENTS

Chapter

7. Appeal Proceedings 739
8. Enforcement of Civil Penalties 744
9. Miscellaneous Safety Provisions 745

Part

2. Safeguards on Railroads 748

    Chapter

    1. Jurisdiction 748
    2. Operation Personnel 749
    3. Safety Devices 751
    4. Trains 752

3. Safety on Buildings 752

    Chapter

    1. Buildings Under Construction or Repair 752

        Article

        1. Floors and Walls 752
        2. Scaffolding 753
        3. Construction Elevators 754
        4. Structural Steel Framed Buildings 754

    2. Elevators, Escalators, Platform and Stairway Chair Lifts, Dumbwaiters, Moving Walks, Automated People Movers, and Other Conveyances ... 756
    3. Safety Devices Upon Buildings to Safeguard Window Cleaners 767
    4. Aerial Passenger Tramways 768
    5. Cranes 770

        Article

        1. Permits for Tower Cranes 770
        2. Certification 771

4. Mining Industries 773

    Chapter

    1. Quartz Mines [Repealed] 773
    2. Coal Mines [Repealed] 773
    3. Underground Telephones 773

5. Ships and Vessels 773
6. Tanks and Boilers 774

    Chapter

    1. Scope of Chapter and General Provisions 774
    2. Administration 775
    3. Operation of Tanks and Boilers 775
    4. Inspection Fees 777
    5. Offenses 778
    6. Mismanagement of Steam Boilers 778

7. Volatile Flammable Liquids 778
7.5 Refinery and Chemical Plants 779

    Chapter

    1. General 779
    2. Process Safety Management Standards 779

8. Amusement Rides Safety Law 782
8.1 Permanent Amusement Ride Safety Inspection Program 785
9. Tunnel and Mine Safety 788

XXXV

TABLE OF CONTENTS

Chapter
1. Tunnels and Mines 788
2. Gassy and Extrahazardous Tunnels 790
3. Licensing and Penalties 793

Part
10. Use of Carcinogens 794
Chapter
1. General Provisions and Definitions 794
2. Exemptions 795
3. Standards and Administration 795
4. Reporting 797
5. Medical Examinations 798
6. Inspections 798
7. Penalties 798
11. Commercial Establishments 799
Chapter
1. Working Warehouses 799

Division
6. Construction and Repeals [Repealed] 799
10. Construction and Repeals [Repealed] 799

MILITARY AND VETERANS CODE

Division
1. Administration of Military and Veterans Affairs 801
Chapter
2. Department of Veterans Affairs 801
2. The Military Forces of the State 801
Part
1. The State Militia 801
Chapter
7. Privileges and Penalties 801

PENAL CODE

Part
1. Of Crimes and Punishments 811
Title
10. Of Crimes Against the Public Health and Safety 811
13. Of Crimes Against Property 812
Chapter
5. Larceny [Theft] 812
14. Malicious Mischief 813
15. Miscellaneous Crimes 817
Chapter
2. Of Other and Miscellaneous Offenses 817
3. Of Imprisonment and the Death Penalty 818
Title
1. Imprisonment of Male Prisoners in State Prisons 818
Chapter
7. Execution of Sentences of Imprisonment 818
Article
3. Blacklist or Extortion of Discharged Prisoner 818

XXXVI

TABLE OF CONTENTS

Chapter

9. Prison to Employment 818

Title

4. County Jails, Farms and Camps 818

Chapter

1. County Jails 818

Part

4. Prevention of Crimes and Apprehension of Criminals 818

Title

1. Investigation and Control of Crimes and Criminals 818

Chapter

1. Investigation, Identification, and Information Responsibilities of the Department of Justice 818

Article

3. Criminal Identification and Statistics 818

2. Control of Crimes and Criminals 821

Article

2. Reports of Injuries 821

2. Control of Deadly Weapons 822

Chapter

1. Firearms 822

Article

2. Unlawful Carrying and Possession of Weapons 822

PUBLIC UTILITIES CODE

Division

2.5 The Digital Infrastructure and Video Competition Act of 2006 827

4. Laws Relating to Utility Corporations and Their Employees 828

Chapter

1. Railroad Corporations 828

Article

7.3 Local Community Rail Security Act of 2006 828

3. Telegraph or Telephone Corporations 828

REVENUE AND TAXATION CODE

Division

2. Other Taxes 829

Part

10. Personal Income Tax 829

Chapter

2. Imposition of Tax 829

3. Computation of Taxable Income 846

Article

6. Deductions 846

10.2 Administration of Franchise and Income Tax Laws 854

Chapter

4. Payments and Assessments 854

Article

7. Penalties and Additions to Tax 854

10.3 Earned Income Tax Credit Information Act 854

XXXVII

TABLE OF CONTENTS

Part

11.   Corporation Tax Law 855

Chapter

3.5   Tax Credits 855

7.   Net Income 875

Article

2.   Special Deductions 875

3.   Items Not Deductible 883

UNEMPLOYMENT INSURANCE CODE

General Provisions 885

Division

1.   Unemployment and Disability Compensation 886

Part

1.   Unemployment Compensation 886

Chapter

1.   General Provisions 887

Article

1.   Policy and Interpretation 887

2.   General Definitions 887

2.   Administration 891

Article

1.   Employment Development Department 891

2.   State Advisory Council [Repealed] 897

3.   California Unemployment Insurance Appeals Board 897

4.   Interstate and Federal Cooperation 900

3.   Scope or Coverage 901

Article

1.   Employment 902

1.5   Employee 904

2.   Excluded Services 905

3.   Subject Employers 911

4.   Elective Coverage 916

5.   Elections for Financing Unemployment Insurance Coverage 926

6.   Financing Unemployment Insurance Coverage for Public School Employees 930

7.   Financing Unemployment Insurance Coverage for Local Public Entity Employees [Repealed] 933

4.   Contributions and Reports 933

Article

1.   Definitions 934

2.   "Wages," the Basis of the Contribution 934

3.   Contribution Rates 938

4.   Reserve Accounts 946

5.   Transfer of Reserve Accounts 950

6.   Records, Reports and Contribution Payments 952

7.   Payment of Reported Contributions 959

8.   Assessments 963

8.5   Employment Tax Amnesty [Repealed] 968

TABLE OF CONTENTS

Article

9. Refunds and Overpayments 968
10. Notice 971
11. Administrative Appellate Review 971
11.5 Taxpayer's Rights 973
12. Judicial Review 975

Chapter

5. Unemployment Compensation Benefits 976

Article

1. Eligibility and Disqualifications 976
1.5 Retraining Benefits 988
2. Computation (Amount and Duration) 991
2.2 Self–Employment Assistance Program 996
3. Filing, Determination, and Payment of Unemployment Compensation Benefit Claims 997
4. Overpayments 1001
5. Rights of Trainees [Repealed] 1004

5.4 Unemployment Compensation for Employees of the Legislature [Repealed] 1004
5.5 Between Terms Unemployment Compensation for Nonprofessional Employees of State Special Schools 1004
5.6 Unemployment Compensation for County Employees [Repealed] 1005
5.7 Unemployment Compensation for State Higher Education Employees [Repealed] 1005
5.8 Unemployment Compensation and Disability Benefits for Former Inmates of State Prisons or Institutions [Repealed] 1005
6. Financial Provisions 1005

Article

1. Deposit Account 1005
2. Unemployment Fund 1005
3. Administration Fund 1008
4. Contingent Fund 1010
4.1 Building Fund 1011
4.5 Benefit Audit Fund 1012
5. Investments in or Expenditures for Property 1012
6. Employment Training Fund 1012

7. Collections 1013

Article

1. Priority and Lien of Tax 1013
2. Liability of Successors, Officers and Fiduciaries 1014
3. Notices of Levy 1015
4. Warrant for Collection 1016
5. Summary Judgment 1016
6. Civil Action 1017
7. Additional Remedies 1018
8. Offers in Compromise 1019

8. Hearing Procedure 1020
9. Public Employment Offices 1022

XXXIX

TABLE OF CONTENTS

Chapter

9.5	Employment for Older Workers	1023
10.	Violations	1024

Part

2. Disability Compensation ... 1029

Chapter

1.	General Provisions	1030
2.	Disability Benefits	1032

Article

1.	Eligibility	1033
2.	Computation (Amount and Duration)	1036
3.	Disqualifications	1038
4.	Filing, Determination and Payment of Disability Benefit Claims	1039
5.	Overpayments	1044
6.	Rights of Trainees	1046
7.	Rights of Industrially Disabled Persons	1047

2.4	Nonindustrial Disability Insurance for State Employees	1048
3.	Additional Benefits [Repealed]	1048
3.5	Prorated Benefits [Repealed]	1048
4.	Contributions	1048
5.	Financial Provisions	1049

Article

1.	Disability Fund	1049
2.	Disability Administration Account	1052
3.	Disability Benefit Payment Account	1052
4.	Pregnancy Benefits [Repealed]	1052
5.	Investments in Buildings [Repealed]	1052
6.	Investments in Branch Office Buildings [Repealed]	1052

6.	Voluntary Plans	1052
7.	Paid Family Leave	1059

3. Extended Unemployment Compensation ... 1062

Chapter

1.	General Provisions	1062
2.	Extended Duration Benefits	1064

Article

1.	Eligibility and Disqualifications	1064
2.	Computation (Amount and Duration)	1065
3.	Filing, Determination, and Payment of Extended Duration Benefit Claims	1065
4.	Reserve Accounts	1067
5.	Overpayments	1068

3.	Additional Contributions [Repealed]	1068
4.	Retraining Benefits [Repealed]	1068

4. Federal–State Extended Compensation ... 1068

Chapter

1.	General Provisions	1068
2.	Federal–State Extended Benefits	1070

TABLE OF CONTENTS

Article

1. Eligibility and Disqualifications 1070
2. Computation (Amount and Duration) 1072
3. Filing, Determination, and Payment of Federal–State Extended Benefit Claims 1072
4. Reserve Accounts 1073
5. Overpayments 1074

Division

1.5 Automation of the Employment Development Department 1074

Chapter

1. Annual Reports 1074
2. Work Incentive Programs [Repealed] 1075
3. Employment Services Programs 1075

Part

1. Employment and Employability Services 1075

Chapter

1. General Provisions and Definitions 1076

Article

1. General Provisions 1076
2. Definitions 1077
3. Training for Energy–Related Jobs [Repealed] 1078

2. Employment Development Department 1078

Article

1. Administration 1078
2. Powers and Duties 1078
3. San Diego Multiuse Biotechnology Training Center 1083
4. California Youthbuild Program 1085
5. Jobs for California Graduates Program 1088
6. Employer Elder Care Benefits 1091

2.5 Youth Employment and Development [Repealed] 1091
2.7 California Work–Site Education and Training Act [Repealed] 1091
2.8 Displaced Worker Education and Training Act of 1982 [Repealed] 1091
2.9 Regional Employment Assessment, Job Search Assistance, and Placement Services for Displaced Workers [Repealed] 1091
3. Welfare–to–Work Grant Program [Repealed] 1091
3.5 Employment Training Panel 1091
4. Programs 1100

Article

1. Eligibility 1100

4.5 California Employment and Training Planning 1100

Article

1. Policies and Purposes 1100
2. General Provisions and Definitions 1101
2.5 California Workforce and Economic Information Program 1101
3. Coordination of Labor Market Information 1101

5. Employment Services for the Deaf and Hearing Impaired 1102
6. Regional Work Force Preparation and Economic Development Act [Repealed] 1103
7. Caregiver Training Initiative 1103

XLI

TABLE OF CONTENTS

Part

2. Employment Opportunities Act of 1971 [Repealed] ---------------------------------- 1106

Division

4. Career Opportunities Development [Repealed] ------------------------------------- 1106
5. Leisure Sharing --- 1106

Chapter

1. General Provisions --- 1106
2. Program Grants -- 1107
3. Technical Assistance -- 1109
4. Program Evaluation --- 1110
5. Miscellaneous --- 1110
6. Funding --- 1111

6. Withholding Tax on Wages -- 1112

Chapter

1. General Provisions --- 1112
2. Withholding and Payment of Tax --- 1117
3. Withholding Exemptions -- 1123
4. Reports, Returns, and Statements -- 1124
5. Collections -- 1126
6. Violations --- 1127

7. California Workforce Investment Act --- 1128

Chapter

1. General Provisions --- 1128
2. Definitions and Severability --- 1129
3. State Responsibilities -- 1129

   Article

   1. California Workforce Investment Board -------------------------------- 1129
   2. State Planning --- 1130

4. Local Service Delivery --- 1131

   Article

   1. Local Workforce Investment Board ------------------------------------ 1131
   2. Local Workforce Investment Plan ------------------------------------- 1133
   3. One–Stop Career Center System ------------------------------------- 1134

5. Educational Services -- 1135

8. California Green Collar Jobs Act of 2008 --------------------------------------- 1136
9. Calworks Program: Job Creation -- 1137
10. Employment Assistance for Workers with Disabilities --------------------------- 1138
15. Effective Date [Repealed] --- 1139

VEHICLE CODE

Division

6. Drivers' Licenses -- 1141

Chapter

7. Commercial Motor Vehicle Safety Program --------------------------------------- 1141

   Article

   7. Sanctions --- 1141

TABLE OF CONTENTS

WELFARE AND INSTITUTIONS CODE

Division
2.5 Youths --- 1143
  Chapter
  1. The Youth Authority --- 1143
    Article
    4. Powers and Duties of Youth Authority --- 1143
4.5. Services for the Developmentally Disabled --- 1143
  Chapter
  13. Habilitation Services for Persons with Developmental Disabilities --- 1143
  14. Employment --- 1143
9. Public Social Services --- 1144
  Part
  3. Aid and Medical Assistance --- 1144
    Chapter
    3 State Supplementary Program for Aged, Blind and Disabled --- 1144
      Article
      7. In–Home Supportive Services --- 1144
    5.5 County Administration of Refugee Social Services and Targeted Assistance Funds --- 1145
    7. Basic Health Care --- 1145
      Article
      3. Administration --- 1145
      4. The Medi–Cal Benefits Program --- 1147
    11. Elder Abuse and Dependent Adult Civil Protection Act --- 1148
      Article
      3. Mandatory and Nonmandatory Reports of Abuse --- 1148
      4. Confidentiality --- 1149
      10. Employee Statement --- 1151
      11. Criminal Record Reporting --- 1151

CALIFORNIA RULES OF COURT

Title
3. Civil Rules --- 1155
  Division
  11. Law and Motion --- 1155
    Chapter
    1. General Provisions --- 1155
    3. Provisional and Injunctive Relief --- 1155
      Article
      3. Injunctions --- 1155

RULES OF PROFESSIONAL CONDUCT OF THE STATE BAR OF CALIFORNIA

Chapter
2. Relationship Among Members --- 1157
3. Professional Relationship with Clients --- 1158

TABLE OF CONTENTS

CALIFORNIA CODE OF REGULATIONS

Title

2. Administration -- 1159
   Division
   4. Fair Employment and Housing Commission ----------------------------------- 1159
      Chapter
      1. Administration --- 1159
         Subchapter
         1. Administration -- 1159
         2. Powers and Duties of the Commission ------------------------ 1159
      2. Discrimination in Employment --------------------------------------- 1160
         Subchapter
         1. General Matters --- 1160
         2. Particular Employment Practices -------------------------- 1165
         3. Race and Color Discrimination (Reserved) --------------- 1171
         4. National Origin and Ancestry Discrimination ----------- 1171
         5. Ancestry Discrimination (Reserved) --------------------- 1171
         6. Sex Discrimination --- 1171
         6A. Sex Discrimination: Pregnancy, Childbirth or Related Medical Conditions --- 1173
         7. Marital Status Discrimination ---------------------------- 1182
         8. Religious Creed Discrimination -------------------------- 1182
         9. Disability Discrimination --------------------------------- 1183
         11. Age Discrimination -- 1187
         12. Family Care and Medical Leave ------------------------- 1190
      3. Discrimination In Housing (Reserved) ---------------------------- 1199
      4. Procedures of the Commission --------------------------------------- 1199
         Subchapter
         1. General Matters --- 1199
         3. Investigative Hearing (Reserved) ----------------------- 1216
         4. Advisory Agencies and Councils (Reserved) ----------- 1216
      5. Contractor Nondiscrimination and Compliance ----------------- 1216
         Subchapter
         1. General Matters --- 1216
         2. Regulations Applicable to Construction Contracts ----- 1221
         3. Regulations Applicable to Service and Supply Contracts -------- 1223
            Article
            1. Small Contracts -------------------------------------- 1223
            2. Regulated Contracts --------------------------------- 1224
         4. OCP Review Procedures ------------------------------------ 1224
         5. OCP Enforcement Proceedings ---------------------------- 1225
Title
8. Industrial Relations -- 1227
   Division
   1. Department of Industrial Relations --- 1227
      Chapter
      3.2 California Occupational Safety and Health Regulations (CAL/OSHA) ---- 1227

TABLE OF CONTENTS

Subchapter

1. Regulations of the Director of Industrial Relations 1227

   Article

   1. Definitions Under California Occupational Safety and Health Act of 1973 1227
   2. Advance Notice of Inspections 1227
   3. Citation, Notice, Special Order, Order to Take Special Action, Notice of No Violations After Investigation: Procedures 1228
   4. Proposed Penalty Procedure 1228
   4.5 Multi–Employer Worksites 1234
   5. Hazardous Substances Information and Training 1234
   6. Workers' Compensation Loss Control Consultation Services, Annual Health and Safety Loss Control Plan—Requirements and Procedures 1255

2. Regulations of the Division of Occupational Safety and Health 1260

   Article

   1. Employers' Obligation to Provide Information to Employees 1260
   1.5 Employer's Declaration of Abatement and Other Documentation of Abatement—Employee Notification—Posting Requirements 1261
   1.6 Adjudicative Hearings—General Rules of Practice and Procedure—Denial, Suspension or Revocation of Permits, Licenses, Certifications, Registrations or Other Authorizations and Orders Prohibiting Use, Issued by the Division of Occupational Safety and Health 1264
   2. Permits—Excavations, Trenches, Construction and Demolition and the Underground Use of Diesel Engines in Work in Mines and Tunnels 1268
   2.5 Registration—Asbestos–Related Work 1273
   2.6 Asbestos Consultants and Site Surveillance Technicians 1275
   2.7 Approval of Courses and Course Providers 1277
   3. Reporting Work–Connected Injuries 1296
   4. Aerial Passenger Tramway Inspection Fee Schedule 1296
   5. Boiler and Tank Permit and Inspection Fee Schedule 1297
   6. Permanent Amusement Rides 1298
   6.1 Amusement Ride Inspection Fee Schedule 1305
   7. Blaster's License 1305
   8. Elevator Inspection Fee Schedule 1306
   9. Correctional Industries 1307
   10. Civil and Criminal Enforcement Policy of the Division of Occupational Safety and Health 1308
   11. License Requirements—Crane and Derrick Certification 1308
   12. Tower Cranes—Operating Permit and Certification Requirements 1311
   13. Certification Requirements 1314

TABLE OF CONTENTS

Article

14. Limitations on Division Eligibility for Certifications, Licenses, and Registrations for Aliens 1315

Chapter

5. Industrial Welfare Commission 1320

Group

1. General Minimum Wage Order 1320

Article

1. Minimum Wage Order 1320

2. Industry and Occupation Orders 1321

Article

4. Professional, Technical, Clerical, Mechanical, and Similar .. 1321

6. Division of Labor Standards Enforcement 1331

Subchapter

1. Child Labor Orders—Prohibited Occupations 1331

Article

1. Prohibited Occupations 1331

2. Employment of Minors in the Entertainment Industry 1332

Article

1. Motion Picture Industries 1332

2.5 Child Labor Law Violations 1336

Article

1. Regulations Regarding Citation and Penalty Procedure for Violation of Child Labor Provisions 1336

3. Employment Agencies 1338

Article

1. General Rules and Regulations for Artists' Managers 1338

2. Controversies Submitted Under Section 1700.44, Labor Code 1341

5. Registration of Persons Who Unload Farm Products 1343

Article

1. Registration of Unloaders 1343

2. Registration of Producers 1343

3. Registration of Producer's Unloaders 1343

5.5 Unloading of Farm Products in the Markets of San Mateo, Alameda, and San Francisco 1344

Article

1. Unloading of Farm Products in the Markets of San Mateo, Alameda, and San Francisco 1344

6. Security for Wages 1345

Article

1. Logging and Sawmill Industry 1345

6.5 Hearings on Actions to Recover Wages, Penalties, and Other Demands for Compensation and on Claims from Holders of Dishonored Payroll Checks or Drafts 1345

Article

1. Rules of Practice and Procedure 1345

7. Industrial Homework 1349

TABLE OF CONTENTS

Article

1. Enforcement of Industrial Homework Act 1349
2. Prohibiting Industrial Homework in the Garment Manufacturing Industry 1349

Subchapter

8. Garment Manufacturers 1351
9. Labor Commissioner's Farm Labor Contractor Fund 1361
10. Registration of Employers, Transporters, and Supervisors of Minors Engaged in Door-to-Door Sales 1362
11. Car Washing and Polishing 1369
12. Collections 1375

SAN FRANCISCO ADMINISTRATIVE CODE

Chapter

12B. Nondiscrimination in Contracts 1377

APPENDICES

Industrial Welfare Commission Wage Orders; California and Federal Jury Instructions; Federal Labor and Employment Laws 1385

INDEX
(Page I–1)

*

CONSTITUTION
OF THE
STATE OF CALIFORNIA
1879

ARTICLE I. DECLARATION OF RIGHTS

Section
8. Business, profession, vocation or employment; sex, race, creed, color, or national or ethnic origin.
31. Discrimination based on race, sex, color, ethnicity, or national origin; gender-based qualifications in public employment, education, or contracting.

§ 8. Business, profession, vocation or employment; sex, race, creed, color, or national or ethnic origin

Sec. 8. A person may not be disqualified from entering or pursuing a business, profession, vocation, or employment because of sex, race, creed, color, or national or ethnic origin. *(Formerly Art. 20, § 18, amended Nov. 3, 1970. Renumbered Art. 1, § 8, Nov. 5, 1974.)*

§ 31. Discrimination based on race, sex, color, ethnicity, or national origin; gender-based qualifications in public employment, education, or contracting

Sec. 31. (a) The state shall not discriminate against, or grant preferential treatment to, any individual or group on the basis of race, sex, color, ethnicity, or national origin in the operation of public employment, public education, or public contracting.

(b) This section shall apply only to action taken after the section's effective date.

(c) Nothing in this section shall be interpreted as prohibiting bona fide qualifications based on sex which are reasonably necessary to the normal operation of public employment, public education, or public contracting.

(d) Nothing in this section shall be interpreted as invalidating any court order or consent decree which is in force as of the effective date of this section.

(e) Nothing in this section shall be interpreted as prohibiting action which must be taken to establish or maintain eligibility for any federal program, where ineligibility would result in a loss of federal funds to the state.

(f) For the purposes of this section, "state" shall include, but not necessarily be limited to, the state itself, any city, county, city and county, public university system, including the University of California, community college district, school district, special district, or any other political subdivision or governmental instrumentality of or within the state.

(g) The remedies available for violations of this section shall be the same, regardless of the injured party's race, sex, color, ethnicity, or national origin, as are otherwise available for violations of then-existing California antidiscrimination law.

(h) This section shall be self-executing. If any part or parts of this section are found to be in conflict with federal law or the United States Constitution, the section shall be implemented to the maximum extent that federal law and the United States Constitution permit. Any provision held invalid shall be severable from the remaining portions of this section. *(Added by Initiative Measure (Prop. 209, approved Nov. 5, 1996).)*

ARTICLE XIV. LABOR RELATIONS

Section
1. Minimum wages; general welfare of employees.
2. Public work; hours.
3. Mechanics' liens.
4. Workers' compensation.
5. Inmate labor programs; restrictions.

§ 1. Minimum wages; general welfare of employees

Section 1. The Legislature may provide for minimum wages and for the general welfare of employees and for those purposes may confer on a commission legislative, executive, and judicial powers. *(Adopted June 8, 1976.)*

§ 2. Public work; hours

Sec. 2. Worktime of mechanics or workers on public works may not exceed eight hours a day except in wartime or extraordinary emergencies that endanger life or property. The Legislature shall provide for enforcement of this section. *(Adopted June 8, 1976.)*

§ 3. Mechanics' liens

Sec. 3. Mechanics, persons furnishing materials, artisans, and laborers of every class, shall have a lien upon the property upon which they have bestowed labor or furnished material for the value of such labor done and material furnished; and the Legislature shall provide, by law, for the speedy and efficient enforcement of such liens. *(Adopted June 8, 1976.)*

§ 4. Workers' compensation

Sec. 4. The Legislature is hereby expressly vested with plenary power, unlimited by any provision of this Constitution, to create, and enforce a complete system of workers' compensation, by appropriate legislation, and in that behalf to create and enforce a liability on the part of any or all persons to compensate any or all of their workers for injury or disability, and their dependents for death incurred or sustained by the said workers in the course of their employment, irrespective of the fault of any party. A complete system of workers' compensation includes adequate provisions for the comfort, health and safety and general welfare of any and all workers and those dependent upon them for support to the extent of relieving from the consequences of any injury or death incurred or sustained by workers in the course of their employment, irrespective of the fault of any party; also full provision for securing safety in places of employment; full provision for such medical, surgical, hospital and other remedial treatment as is requisite to cure and relieve from the effects of such injury; full provision for adequate insurance coverage against liability to pay or furnish compensation; full provision for regulating such insurance coverage in all its aspects, including the establishment and management of a State compensation insurance fund; full provision for otherwise securing the payment of compensation; and full provision for vesting power, authority and jurisdiction in an administrative body with all the requisite governmental functions to determine any dispute or matter arising under such legislation, to the end that the administration of such legislation shall accomplish substantial justice in all cases expeditiously, inexpensively, and without incumbrance of any character; all of which matters are expressly declared to be the social public policy of this State, binding upon all departments of the State government.

The Legislature is vested with plenary powers, to provide for the settlement of any disputes arising under such legislation by arbitration, or by an industrial accident commission, by the courts, or by either, any, or all of these agencies, either separately or in combination, and may fix and control the method and manner of trial of any such dispute, the rules of evidence and the manner of review of decisions rendered by the tribunal or tribunals designated by it; provided, that all decisions of any such tribunal shall be subject to review by the appellate courts of this State. The Legislature may combine in one statute all the provisions for a complete system of workers' compensation, as herein defined.

The Legislature shall have power to provide for the payment of an award to the state in the case of the death, arising out of and in the course of the employment, of an employee without dependents, and such awards may be used for the payment of extra compensation for subsequent injuries beyond the liability of a single employer for awards to employees of the employer.

Nothing contained herein shall be taken or construed to impair or render ineffectual in any measure the creation and existence of the industrial accident commission of this State or the State compensation insurance fund, the creation and existence of which, with all the functions vested in them, are hereby ratified and confirmed. *(Adopted June 8, 1976.)*

§ 5. Inmate labor programs; restrictions

Sec. 5. (a) The Director of Corrections or any county Sheriff or other local government official charged with jail operations, may enter into contracts with public entities, nonprofit or for profit organizations, entities, or businesses for the purpose of conducting programs which use inmate labor. Such programs shall be operated and implemented pursuant to statutes enacted by or in accordance with the provisions of the Prison Inmate Labor Initiative of 1990, and by rules and regulations prescribed by the Director of Corrections and, for county jail programs, by local ordinances.

(b) No contract shall be executed with an employer that will initiate employment by inmates in the same job classification as non-inmate employees of the same employer who are on strike, as defined in Section 1132.6 of the Labor Code, as it reads on January 1, 1990, or who are subject to lockout, as defined in Section 1132.8 of the Labor Code, as it reads on January 1, 1990. Total daily hours worked by inmates employed in the same job classification as non-inmate employees of the same employer who are on strike, as defined in Section 1132.6 of the Labor Code, as it reads on January 1, 1990, or who are subject to lockout, as defined in Section 1132.8 of the Labor Code, as it reads on January 1, 1990, shall not exceed, for the duration of the strike, the average daily hours worked for the preceding six months, or if the program has been in operation for less than six months, the average for the period of operation.

(c) Nothing in this section shall be interpreted as creating a right of inmates to work. *(Added by Initiative Measure (Prop. 139), approved Nov. 6, 1990.)*

BUSINESS AND PROFESSIONS CODE

Division 2

HEALING ARTS

CHAPTER 5. MEDICINE

ARTICLE 3. LICENSE REQUIRED
AND EXEMPTIONS

Section
2056. Retaliation against physicians who advocate for medically appropriate health care for patients; prohibition; scope of protection.

§ 2056. Retaliation against physicians who advocate for medically appropriate health care for patients; prohibition; scope of protection

(a) The purpose of this section is to provide protection against retaliation for physicians who advocate for medically appropriate health care for their patients pursuant to Wickline v. State of California 192 Cal.App.3d 1630.

(b) It is the public policy of the State of California that a physician and surgeon be encouraged to advocate for medically appropriate health care for his or her patients. For purposes of this section, "to advocate for medically appropriate health care" means to appeal a payor's decision to deny payment for a service pursuant to the reasonable grievance or appeal procedure established by a medical group, independent practice association, preferred provider organization, foundation, hospital medical staff and governing body, or payer, or to protest a decision, policy, or practice that the physician, consistent with that degree of learning and skill ordinarily possessed by reputable physicians practicing according to the applicable legal standard of care, reasonably believes impairs the physician's ability to provide medically appropriate health care to his or her patients.

(c) The application and rendering by any person of a decision to terminate an employment or other contractual relationship with, or otherwise penalize, a physician and surgeon principally for advocating for medically appropriate health care consistent with that degree of learning and skill ordinarily possessed by reputable physicians

practicing according to the applicable legal standard of care violates the public policy of this state. No person shall terminate, retaliate against, or otherwise penalize a physician and surgeon for that advocacy, nor shall any person prohibit, restrict, or in any way discourage a physician and surgeon from communicating to a patient information in furtherance of medically appropriate health care.

(d) This section shall not be construed to prohibit a payer from making a determination not to pay for a particular medical treatment or service, or to prohibit a medical group, independent practice association, preferred provider organization, foundation, hospital medical staff, hospital governing body acting pursuant to Section 809.05, or payer from enforcing reasonable peer review or utilization review protocols or determining whether a physician has complied with those protocols.

(e) Medically appropriate health care in a hospital licensed pursuant to Section 1250 of the Health and Safety Code shall be defined by the hospital medical staff and approved by the governing body, consistent with that degree of learning and skill ordinarily possessed by reputable physicians practicing according to the applicable legal standard of care.

(f) Nothing in this section shall be construed to prohibit the governing body of a hospital from taking disciplinary actions against a physician and surgeon as authorized by Sections 809.05, 809.4, and 809.5.

(g) Nothing in this section shall be construed to prohibit the Medical Board of California from taking disciplinary actions against a physician and surgeon under Article 12 (commencing with Section 2220).

(h) For purposes of this section, "person" has the same meaning as set forth in Section 2032. (*Added by Stats.1993, c. 947 (A.B.1676), § 1. Amended by Stats. 1994, c. 1119 (A.B.3390), § 2; Stats.1996, c. 260 (S.B. 1847), § 1.*)

Division 3

PROFESSIONS AND VOCATIONS GENERALLY

CHAPTER 11.5 PRIVATE SECURITY SERVICES

ARTICLE 4. PRIVATE PATROL OPERATORS

Section
7583.46. Whistleblower protection.
7843. Geologist-in-training certificate; use of title.

§ 7583.46. Whistleblower protection

(a)(1) It shall be a violation of Section 1102.5 of the Labor Code for a private patrol operator to discharge, demote, threaten, or in any manner discriminate against an employee in the terms and conditions of his or her employment, for disclosing information or causing information to be disclosed, to a government or law enforcement agency, when the information is related to conduct proscribed in this chapter.

(2) A private patrol operator who intentionally violates this subdivision shall be liable in an action for damages brought against him or her by the injured party.

(b) A person who believes that he or she has been discharged, demoted, threatened, or in any other manner discriminated against in the terms and conditions of his or her employment, because that person disclosed or caused information to be disclosed to a government or law enforcement agency, may bring a claim against the private patrol operator within three years of the date of the discharge, demotion, threat, or discrimination.

(c) Neither the bureau nor the department is responsible for resolving claims under this section. *(Added by Stats.2002, c. 884 (A.B.2780), § 2.)*

§ 7843. Geologist-in-training certificate; use of title

(a) An applicant for certification as a geologist-in-training shall, upon making a passing grade in the National Association of State Boards of Geology's Fundamentals of Geology examination be issued a certificate as a geologist-in-training. A renewal or other fee, other than the application fee, may not be charged for this certification. The certificate shall become invalid when the holder has qualified as a professional geologist as provided in Section 7841.

(b) A geologist-in-training certificate does not authorize the holder thereof to practice or offer to practice geology, in his or her own right, or to use the title specified in Section 7804.

(c) It is unlawful for anyone other than the holder of a valid geologist-in-training certificate issued under this chapter to use the title of "geologist-in-training" or any abbreviation of that title. *(Added by Stats.2004, c. 865 (S.B.1914), § 25.)*

CHAPTER 21.5. FOREIGN LABOR CONTRACTORS

Section
9998. Application of chapter.
9998.1. Definitions.
9998.2. Employment services contracts; language; contents.
9998.3. False, fraudulent or misleading information; publication or circulation.
9998.4. Minors.
9998.5. Recruitment or inducement of foreign worker to proposed jobsite without bona fide job offer.
9998.6. Retaliatory action.
9998.7. Inducement to travel or accept employment by assurances of citizenship or permanent residency.
9998.8. Criminal penalties and civil actions.

§ 9998. Application of chapter

This chapter shall apply only to "nonagricultural workers" as defined by Section 1101(a)(15)(H)(ii)(b) of Title 8 of the federal Immigration and Nationality Act.[1] It shall not apply to any person duly licensed as a "farm labor contractor" as that term is defined in Section 1682 of the Labor Code nor shall it apply to any person exempt from the licensing requirement in Section 1682.5 of the Labor Code or to any employer employing agricultural workers as defined by Section 1101(a)(15)(H)(ii)(a) of Title 8 of the federal Immigration and Nationality Act.[2] *(Added by Stats.1988, c. 1450, § 1.)*

[1] 8 U.S.C.A. § 1101(a)(15)(H)(ii)(b).
[2] 8 U.S.C.A. § 1101(a)(15)(H)(ii)(a).

§ 9998.1. Definitions

The following definitions are applicable to this chapter:

(a) "Person" includes any natural person, company, firm, partnership, or joint venture, association, corporation, limited liability company, or sole proprietorship.

(b) "Compensation" means all forms of remuneration or consideration for the provision of employment services to foreign workers by a foreign labor contractor.

(c) "Employment services" includes, but is not limited to, procuring employment, marketing labor, or otherwise arranging the employment or transportation, housing, and other living accommodations for foreign workers either on behalf of those workers or on behalf of another party.

(d) "Foreign worker" means any person seeking employment who is not a United States citizen but who is authorized by the federal government to work in the United States, including a person who engages in temporary nonagricultural labor pursuant to Section 1101(a)(15)(H)(ii)(b) of Title 8 of the federal Immigration and Nationality Act.

(e) "Foreign labor contractor" means any person who for compensation agrees to assist in securing or who actually secures for or provides employment services to foreign workers. *(Added by Stats.1988, c. 1450, § 1. Amended by Stats.1994, c. 1010 (S.B.2053), § 18.)*

§ 9998.2. Employment services contracts; language; contents

Every contract for the provision of employment services to foreign workers shall be written in the primary language of the foreign worker and shall include all material terms including, but not limited to, any and all compensation or consideration to be provided to the foreign worker in exchange for that worker's labor or services, any wages, housing, transportation, other living accommodations, and other benefits which are to be provided. *(Added by Stats.1988, c. 1450, § 1. Amended by Stats.1989, c. 1360, § 6.)*

§ 9998.3. False, fraudulent or misleading information; publication or circulation

No foreign labor contractor shall make, publish, or circulate or cause to be made, published, or circulated, to any person any false, fraudulent, or misleading representation or information concerning the terms or conditions of employment at any place or places of employment. *(Added by Stats.1988, c. 1450, § 1.)*

§ 9998.4. Minors

No foreign labor contractor shall recruit for employment or cause any minor who is a foreign worker to be employed. *(Added by Stats.1988, c. 1450, § 1.)*

§ 9998.5. Recruitment or inducement of foreign worker to proposed jobsite without bona fide job offer

Any foreign labor contractor who recruits or solicits without a bona fide job order and who induces a foreign worker to be transported to a proposed jobsite and who does not then provide employment for the foreign worker shall pay wages to the foreign worker at the agreed rate of pay for the job to which the foreign worker was being transported and for the elapsed time from the point of recruitment to the jobsite to the point the worker returns to the place of original departure, and for any transportation costs incurred by the foreign worker in connection with the pursuit of the labor contractor's services. *(Added by Stats.1988, c. 1450, § 1.)*

§ 9998.6. Retaliatory action

No person shall take any action against a foreign worker in retaliation for the foreign worker's exercise of any right under this chapter. *(Added by Stats.1988, c. 1450, § 1.)*

§ 9998.7. Inducement to travel or accept employment by assurances of citizenship or permanent residency

No foreign labor contractor shall make promises or otherwise induce a foreign worker to travel or accept promises of employment by promising or providing assurances to the foreign worker that citizenship or permanent residency status in the United States shall be secured or pursued if the worker accepts the offer of services of the foreign labor contractor. *(Added by Stats.1988, c. 1450, § 1.)*

§ 9998.8. Criminal penalties and civil actions

(a) Any person who violates this chapter or who causes or induces another to violate this chapter is guilty of a misdemeanor punishable by a fine of not more than one thousand dollars ($1,000), or imprisonment in the county jail for not more than six months, or both.

(b) Any person aggrieved by a violation of this chapter may bring an action for injunctive relief or damages, or both. If the person aggrieved prevails on the action, this person shall recover damages, costs, and reasonable attorney's fees, but in no case shall recovery be less than five hundred dollars ($500). *(Added by Stats.1988, c. 1450, § 1.)*

Division 7

GENERAL BUSINESS REGULATIONS

Part 1

LICENSING FOR REVENUE AND REGULATION

CHAPTER 4. EMPLOYMENT ACTIVITIES

Section
16300. Prohibition against cities from requiring an employee to obtain business license or home business occupation permit for, or imposing business tax or registration fee based on, income earned for services performed for employer by employee in an employment relationship.

§ 16300. Prohibition against cities from requiring an employee to obtain business license or home business occupation permit for, or imposing business tax or registration fee based on, income earned for services performed for employer by employee in an employment relationship

(a) Notwithstanding any other provision of this part, Chapter 1.5 (commencing with Section 7284) of Part 1.7 of Division 2 of the Revenue and Taxation Code, or Chapter 3 (commencing with Section 37100) of Part 2 of Division 3 of Title 4 of the Government Code, no city, including a charter city, city and county, or county may require an employee to obtain a business license or home business occupation permit for, or impose a business tax or registration fee based on income earned for services performed for an employer by the employee in an employment relationship as determined by reference to the common law factors reflected in rulings or guidelines used by either the Internal Revenue Service or the Franchise Tax Board. When there is a dispute between a city, city and county, or county and a taxpayer, the manner in which a taxpayer reports or reported income to the Franchise Tax Board or the Internal Revenue Service shall create a presumption regarding whether the taxpayer performed services for an employer as an employee, or operated a business entity. For purposes of this section, "income" includes income paid currently or deferred and income that is fixed or contingent.

(b) Nothing in this section shall be interpreted to limit the authority of a city, city and county, or county to adopt and enforce zoning, health and safety ordinances, or regulations that define and limit activities that are permissible within its jurisdiction for the purposes of health, safety, welfare, and the provisions of applicable noise ordinances. *(Added by Stats.2001, c. 36 (A.B.205), § 1.)*

Part 2

PRESERVATION AND REGULATION OF COMPETITION

CHAPTER 1. CONTRACTS IN RESTRAINT OF TRADE

Section
16600. Void contracts.
16601. Sale of goodwill of business or ownership interest in or operating assets of business entity or division or subsidiary thereof; agreement not to compete.
16602. Partners; dissolution or dissociation; agreement not to compete.
16602.5. Non-compete agreement upon dissolution or sale of limited liability company.

§ 16600. Void contracts

Except as provided in this chapter, every contract by which anyone is restrained from engaging in a lawful profession, trade, or business of any kind is to that extent void. *(Added by Stats.1941, c. 526, § 1.)*

§ 16601. Sale of goodwill of business or ownership interest in or operating assets of business entity or division or subsidiary thereof; agreement not to compete

Any person who sells the goodwill of a business, or any owner of a business entity selling or otherwise disposing of all of his or her ownership interest in the business entity, or any owner of a business entity that sells (a) all or substantially all of its operating assets together with the goodwill of the business entity, (b) all or substantially all of the operating assets of a division or a subsidiary of the business entity together with the goodwill of that division or subsidiary, or (c) all of the ownership interest of any subsidiary, may agree with the buyer to refrain from carrying on a similar business within a specified geographic area in which the business so sold, or that of the business entity, division, or subsidiary has been carried on, so long as the buyer, or any person deriving title to the goodwill or ownership interest from the buyer, carries on a like business therein.

For the purposes of this section, "business entity" means any partnership (including a limited partnership or a limited liability partnership), limited liability company (including a series of a limited liability company formed under the laws of a jurisdiction that recognizes such a series), or corporation.

For the purposes of this section, "owner of a business entity" means any partner, in the case of a business entity that is a partnership (including a limited partnership or a limited liability partnership), or any member, in the case of a business entity that is a limited liability company (including a series of a limited liability company formed under the laws of a jurisdiction that recognizes such a series), or any owner of capital stock, in the case of a business entity that is a corporation.

For the purposes of this section, "ownership interest" means a partnership interest, in the case of a business entity that is a partnership (including a limited partnership a limited liability partnership), a membership interest, in the case of a business entity that is a limited liability company (including a series of a limited liability company formed under the laws of a jurisdiction that recognizes such a series), or a capital stockholder, in the case of a business entity that is a corporation.

For the purposes of this section, "subsidiary" means any business entity over which the selling business entity has voting control or from which the selling business entity has a right to receive a majority share of distributions upon dissolution or other liquidation of the business entity (or has both voting control and a right to receive these distributions.) *(Added by Stats.1941, c. 526, § 1. Amended by Stats.1941, c. 845, § 1; Stats.1945, c. 671, § 1; Stats.1963, c. 597, § 1; Stats.2002, c. 179 (A.B.601), § 1; Stats.2006, c. 495 (A.B.339), § 1.)*

§ 16602. Partners; dissolution or dissociation; agreement not to compete

(a) Any partner may, upon or in anticipation of any of the circumstances described in subdivision (b), agree that he or she will not carry on a similar business within a specified geographic area where the partnership business has been transacted, so long as any other member of the partnership, or any person deriving title to the business or its goodwill from any such other member of the partnership, carries on a like business therein.

(b) Subdivision (a) applies to either of the following circumstances:

(1) A dissolution of the partnership.

(2) Dissociation of the partner from the partnership.

(Added by Stats.1941, c. 526, p. 1834, § 1. Amended by Stats.1961, c. 1091, p. 2821, § 1; Stats.1996, c. 1003 (A.B.583), § 1; Stats.2002, c. 179 (A.B.601), § 2.)

§ 16602.5. Non-compete agreement upon dissolution or sale of limited liability company

Any member may, upon or in anticipation of a dissolution of, or the termination of his or her interest in, a limited liability company (including a series of a limited liability company formed under the laws of a jurisdiction recognizing such a series), agree that he or she or it will not carry on a similar business within a specified geographic area where the limited liability company business has been transacted, so long as any other member of the limited liability company, or any person deriving title to the business or its goodwill from any such other member of the limited liability company, carries on a like business therein. *(Added by Stats.1994, c. 1200 (S.B.469), § 1, eff. Sept. 30, 1994. Amended by Stats.2002, c. 179 (A.B.601), § 3; Stats.2006, c. 495 (A.B.339), § 2.)*

CIVIL CODE
Division 1
PERSONS

Part 2
PERSONAL RIGHTS

Section
47.   Privileged publication or broadcast.
49.   Personal relations, acts forbidden by.
51.   Unruh Civil Rights Act; equal rights; business establishments; violation.
51.1.   Mandatory service on State Solicitor General of each party's brief or petition and brief in causes of action based on violation of civil rights statutes.
51.7.   Freedom from violence or intimidation.
52.   Denial of civil rights or discrimination; damages; civil action by people or person aggrieved; intervention; unlawful practice complaint.
52.2.   Court of competent jurisdiction; defined; actions.
52.4.   Civil action for damages arising from gender violence.

§ 47.   Privileged publication or broadcast

A privileged publication or broadcast is one made:

(a) In the proper discharge of an official duty.

(b) In any (1) legislative proceeding, (2) judicial proceeding, (3) in any other official proceeding authorized by law, or (4) in the initiation or course of any other proceeding authorized by law and reviewable pursuant to Chapter 2 (commencing with Section 1084) of Title 1 of Part 3 of the Code of Civil Procedure, except as follows:

(1) An allegation or averment contained in any pleading or affidavit filed in an action for marital dissolution or legal separation made of or concerning a person by or against whom no affirmative relief is prayed in the action shall not be a privileged publication or broadcast as to the person making the allegation or averment within the meaning of this section unless the pleading is verified or affidavit sworn to, and is made without malice, by one having reasonable and probable cause for believing the truth of the allegation or averment and unless the allegation or averment is material and relevant to the issues in the action.

(2) This subdivision does not make privileged any communication made in furtherance of an act of intentional destruction or alteration of physical evidence undertaken for the purpose of depriving a party to litigation of the use of that evidence, whether or not the content of the communication is the subject of a subsequent publication or broadcast which is privileged pursuant to this section. As used in this paragraph, "physical evidence" means evidence specified in Section 250 of the Evidence Code or evidence that is property of any type specified in Chapter 14 (commencing with Section 2031.010) of Title 4 of Part 4 of the Code of Civil Procedure.

(3) This subdivision does not make privileged any communication made in a judicial proceeding knowingly concealing the existence of an insurance policy or policies.

(4) A recorded lis pendens is not a privileged publication unless it identifies an action previously filed with a court of competent jurisdiction which affects the title or right of possession of real property, as authorized or required by law.

(c) In a communication, without malice, to a person interested therein, (1) by one who is also interested, or (2) by one who stands in such a relation to the person interested as to afford a reasonable ground for supposing the motive for the communication to be innocent, or (3) who is requested by the person interested to give the information. This subdivision applies to and includes a communication concerning the job performance or qualifications of an applicant for employment, based upon credible evidence, made without malice, by a current or former employer of the applicant to, and upon request of, one whom the employer reasonably believes is a prospective employer of the applicant. This subdivision authorizes a current or former employer, or the employer's agent, to answer whether or not the employer would rehire a current or former employee. This subdivision shall not apply to a communication concerning the speech or activities of an applicant for employment if the speech or activities are constitutionally protected, or otherwise protected by Section 527.3 of the Code of Civil Procedure or any other provision of law.

(d)(1) By a fair and true report in, or a communication to, a public journal, of (A) a judicial, (B) legislative, or (C) other public official proceeding, or (D) of anything said in the course thereof, or (E) of a verified charge or complaint made by any person to a public official, upon which complaint a warrant has been issued.

(2) Nothing in paragraph (1) shall make privileged any communication to a public journal that does any of the following:

(A) Violates Rule 5–120 of the State Bar Rules of Professional Conduct.

(B) Breaches a court order.

(C) Violates any requirement of confidentiality imposed by law.

(e) By a fair and true report of (1) the proceedings of a public meeting, if the meeting was lawfully convened for a lawful purpose and open to the public, or (2) the publication of the matter complained of was for the public benefit. *(Enacted 1872. Amended by Code Am.1873–74, c. 612, p. 184, § 11; Stats.1895, c. 163, p. 167, § 1; Stats.1927, c. 866, p. 1881, § 1; Stats.1945, c. 1489, p. 2763, § 3; Stats.1979, c. 184, p. 403, § 1; Stats.1990, c. 1491 (A.B.3765), § 1; Stats.1991, c. 432 (A.B.529), § 1; Stats.1992, c. 615 (S.B.1804), § 1; Stats. 1994, c. 364 (A.B.2778), § 1; Stats.1994, c. 700 (S.B. 1457), § 2.5; Stats.1996, c. 1055 (S.B.1540), § 2; Stats. 2002, c. 1029 (A.B.2868), § 1, eff. Sept. 28, 2002; Stats. 2004, c. 182 (A.B.3081), § 4, operative July 1, 2005.)*

§ 49. Personal relations, acts forbidden by

The rights of personal relations forbid:

(a) The abduction or enticement of a child from a parent, or from a guardian entitled to its custody;

(b) The seduction of a person under the age of legal consent;

(c) Any injury to a servant which affects his ability to serve his master, other than seduction, abduction or criminal conversation. *(Enacted 1872. Amended by Stats.1905, c. 70, p. 68, § 1; Stats.1939, c. 128, p. 1245, § 1; Stats.1939, c. 1103, p. 3037, § 5.)*

§ 51. Unruh Civil Rights Act; equal rights; business establishments; violation

(a) This section shall be known, and may be cited, as the Unruh Civil Rights Act.

(b) All persons within the jurisdiction of this state are free and equal, and no matter what their sex, race, color, religion, ancestry, national origin, disability, medical condition, marital status, or sexual orientation are entitled to the full and equal accommodations, advantages, facilities, privileges, or services in all business establishments of every kind whatsoever.

(c) This section shall not be construed to confer any right or privilege on a person that is conditioned or limited by law or that is applicable alike to persons of every sex, color, race, religion, ancestry, national origin, disability, medical condition, marital status, or sexual orientation.

(d) Nothing in this section shall be construed to require any construction, alteration, repair, structural or otherwise, or modification of any sort whatsoever, beyond that construction, alteration, repair, or modification that is otherwise required by other provisions of law, to any new or existing establishment, facility, building, improvement, or any other structure, nor shall anything in this section be construed to augment, restrict, or alter in any way the authority of the State Architect to require construction, alteration, repair, or modifications that the State Architect otherwise possesses pursuant to other laws.

(e) For purposes of this section:

(1) "Disability" means any mental or physical disability as defined in Sections 12926 and 12926.1 of the Government Code.

(2) "Medical condition" has the same meaning as defined in subdivision (h) of Section 12926 of the Government Code.

(3) "Religion" includes all aspects of religious belief, observance, and practice.

(4) "Sex" has the same meaning as defined in subdivision (p) of Section 12926 of the Government Code.

(5) "Sex, race, color, religion, ancestry, national origin, disability, medical condition, marital status, or sexual orientation" includes a perception that the person has any particular characteristic or characteristics within the listed categories or that the person is associated with a person who has, or is perceived to have, any particular characteristic or characteristics within the listed categories.

(6) "Sexual orientation" has the same meaning as defined in subdivision (q) of Section 12926 of the Government Code.

(f) A violation of the right of any individual under the Americans with Disabilities Act of 1990 (Public Law 101–336) shall also constitute a violation of this section. *(Added by Stats.1905, c. 413, p. 553, § 1. Amended by Stats.1919, c. 210, p. 309, § 1; Stats.1923, c. 235, p. 485, § 1; Stats.1959, c. 1866, p. 4424, § 1; Stats.1961, c. 1187, p. 2920, § 1; Stats.1974, c. 1193, p. 2568, § 1; Stats.1987, c. 159, § 1; Stats.1992, c. 913 (A.B.1077), § 3; Stats.1998, c. 195 (A.B.2702), § 1; Stats.2000, c. 1049 (A.B.2222), § 2; Stats.2005, c. 420 (A.B.1400), § 3.)*

§ 51.1. Mandatory service on State Solicitor General of each party's brief or petition and brief in causes of action based on violation of civil rights statutes

If a violation of Section 51, 51.5, 51.7, 51.9, or 52.1 is alleged or the application or construction of any of these sections is in issue in any proceeding in the Supreme Court of California, a state court of appeal, or the appellate division of a superior court, each party shall serve a copy of the party's brief or petition and brief, on the State Solicitor General at the Office of the Attorney General. No brief may be accepted for filing unless the proof of service shows service on the State Solicitor General. Any party failing to comply with this requirement shall be given a reasonable opportunity to cure the failure before the court imposes any sanction and, in that instance, the court shall allow the Attorney General reasonable additional time to file a brief in the matter. *(Added by Stats.2002, c. 244 (A.B.2524), § 1.)*

§ 51.7. Freedom from violence or intimidation

(a) All persons within the jurisdiction of this state have the right to be free from any violence, or intimidation by threat of violence, committed against their persons or property because of political affiliation, or on account of any characteristic listed or defined in subdivision (b) or (e) of Section 51, or position in a labor dispute, or because another person perceives them to have one or more of those characteristics. The identification in this subdivision of particular bases of discrimination is illustrative rather than restrictive.

(b) This section does not apply to statements concerning positions in a labor dispute which are made during otherwise lawful labor picketing.

(Added by Stats.1976, c. 1293, p. 5778, § 2. Amended by Stats.1984, c. 1437, § 1; Stats.1985, c. 497, § 1; Stats.1987, c. 1277, § 2; Stats.1994, c. 407 (S.B.1595), § 1; Stats.2005, c. 420 (A.B.1400), § 5.)

§ 52. Denial of civil rights or discrimination; damages; civil action by people or person aggrieved; intervention; unlawful practice complaint

(a) Whoever denies, aids or incites a denial, or makes any discrimination or distinction contrary to Section 51, 51.5, or 51.6, is liable for each and every offense for the actual damages, and any amount that may be determined by a jury, or a court sitting without a jury, up to a maximum of three times the amount of actual damage but in no case less than four thousand dollars ($4,000), and any attorney's fees that may be determined by the court in addition thereto, suffered by any person denied the rights provided in Section 51, 51.5, or 51.6.

(b) Whoever denies the right provided by Section 51.7 or 51.9, or aids, incites, or conspires in that denial, is liable for each and every offense for the actual damages suffered by any person denied that right and, in addition, the following:

(1) An amount to be determined by a jury, or a court sitting without a jury, for exemplary damages.

(2) A civil penalty of twenty-five thousand dollars ($25,000) to be awarded to the person denied the right provided by Section 51.7 in any action brought by the person denied the right, or by the Attorney General, a district attorney, or a city attorney. An action for that penalty brought pursuant to Section 51.7 shall be commenced within three years of the alleged practice.

(3) Attorney's fees as may be determined by the court.

(c) Whenever there is reasonable cause to believe that any person or group of persons is engaged in conduct of resistance to the full enjoyment of any of the rights described in this section, and that conduct is of that nature and is intended to deny the full exercise of those rights, the Attorney General, any district attorney or city attorney, or any person aggrieved by the conduct may bring a civil action in the appropriate court by filing with it a complaint. The complaint shall contain the following:

(1) The signature of the officer, or, in his or her absence, the individual acting on behalf of the officer, or the signature of the person aggrieved.

(2) The facts pertaining to the conduct.

(3) A request for preventive relief, including an application for a permanent or temporary injunction, restrain-

ing order, or other order against the person or persons responsible for the conduct, as the complainant deems necessary to ensure the full enjoyment of the rights described in this section.

(d) Whenever an action has been commenced in any court seeking relief from the denial of equal protection of the laws under the Fourteenth Amendment to the Constitution of the United States on account of race, color, religion, sex, national origin, or disability, the Attorney General or any district attorney or city attorney for or in the name of the people of the State of California may intervene in the action upon timely application if the Attorney General or any district attorney or city attorney certifies that the case is of general public importance. In that action, the people of the State of California shall be entitled to the same relief as if it had instituted the action.

(e) Actions brought pursuant to this section are independent of any other actions, remedies, or procedures that may be available to an aggrieved party pursuant to any other law.

(f) Any person claiming to be aggrieved by an alleged unlawful practice in violation of Section 51 or 51.7 may also file a verified complaint with the Department of Fair Employment and Housing pursuant to Section 12948 of the Government Code.

(g) This section does not require any construction, alteration, repair, structural or otherwise, or modification of any sort whatsoever, beyond that construction, alteration, repair, or modification that is otherwise required by other provisions of law, to any new or existing establishment, facility, building, improvement, or any other structure, nor does this section augment, restrict, or alter in any way the authority of the State Architect to require construction, alteration, repair, or modifications that the State Architect otherwise possesses pursuant to other laws.

(h) For the purposes of this section, "actual damages" means special and general damages. This subdivision is declaratory of existing law. *(Added by Stats.1905, c. 413, p. 553, § 2. Amended by Stats.1919, c. 210, p. 309, § 2; Stats.1923, c. 235, p. 485, § 2; Stats.1959, c. 1866, p. 4424, § 2; Stats.1974, c. 1193, p. 2568, § 2; Stats.1976, c. 366, p. 1013, § 2; Stats.1976, c. 1293, p. 5778, § 2.5; Stats.1978, c. 1212, p. 3927, § 1; Stats.1981, c. 521, § 1, eff. Sept. 16, 1981; Stats.1986, c. 244, § 1; Stats.1987, c. 159, § 4; Stats.1989, c. 459, § 1; Stats.1991, c. 607 (S.B.98), § 2; Stats.1991, c. 839 (A.B.1169), § 2; Stats.1992, c. 913 (A.B.1077), § 3.6; Stats.1994, c. 535 (S.B.1288), § 1; Stats.1998, c. 195 (A.B.2702), § 4; Stats.1999, c; 964 (A.B.519), § 2; Stats.2000, c. 98 (A.B.2719), § 2; Stats. 2001, c. 261 (A.B.587), § 1; Stats.2005, c. 123 (A.B.378), § 1.)*

§ 52.2. Court of competent jurisdiction; defined; actions

An action pursuant to Section 52 or 54.3 may be brought in any court of competent jurisdiction. A "court of competent jurisdiction" shall include small claims court if the amount of the damages sought in the action does not exceed the jurisdictional limits stated in Sections 116.220 and 116.221 of the Code of Civil Procedure. *(Added by Stats.1998, c. 195 (A.B.2702), § 5. Amended by Stats.2006, c. 167 (A.B.2618), § 1.)*

§ 52.4. Civil action for damages arising from gender violence

(a) Any person who has been subjected to gender violence may bring a civil action for damages against any responsible party. The plaintiff may seek actual damages, compensatory damages, punitive damages, injunctive relief, any combination of those, or any other appropriate relief. A prevailing plaintiff may also be awarded attorney's fees and costs.

(b) An action brought pursuant to this section shall be commenced within three years of the act, or if the victim was a minor when the act occurred, within eight years after the date the plaintiff attains the age of majority or within three years after the date the plaintiff discovers or reasonably should have discovered the psychological injury or illness occurring after the age of majority that was caused by the act, whichever date occurs later.

(c) For purposes of this section, "gender violence," is a form of sex discrimination and means any of the following:

(1) One or more acts that would constitute a criminal offense under state law that has as an element the use, attempted use, or threatened use of physical force against the person or property of another, committed at least in part based on the gender of the victim, whether or not those acts have resulted in criminal complaints, charges, prosecution, or conviction.

(2) A physical intrusion or physical invasion of a sexual nature under coercive conditions, whether or not those acts have resulted in criminal complaints, charges, prosecution, or conviction.

(d) Notwithstanding any other laws that may establish the liability of an employer for the acts of an employee, this section does not establish any civil liability of a person because of his or her status as an employer, unless the employer personally committed an act of gender violence. *(Added by Stats.2002, c. 842 (A.B.1928), § 2.)*

Part 2.6

CONFIDENTIALITY OF MEDICAL INFORMATION

CHAPTER 2. DISCLOSURE OF MEDICAL INFORMATION BY PROVIDERS

Section
56.10.   Authorization; necessity; exceptions.
56.1007. Disclosure of medical information to specified persons involved with patient's care or health care payments; disclosure of medical information for other purposes.

Section
56.101.   Destruction of records.
56.102.   Disclosure of medical information by pharmaceutical company; authorizations, releases, consents, or waivers; exceptions.
56.103.   Disclosure of a minor's medical information; mental health condition.
56.104.   Patient's participation in outpatient treatment with psychotherapist; request; content; application.

§ 56.10. Authorization; necessity; exceptions

(a) No provider of health care, health care service plan, or contractor shall disclose medical information regarding a patient of the provider of health care or an enrollee or subscriber of a health care service plan without first obtaining an authorization, except as provided in subdivision (b) or (c).

(b) A provider of health care, a health care service plan, or a contractor shall disclose medical information if the disclosure is compelled by any of the following:

(1) By a court pursuant to an order of that court.

(2) By a board, commission, or administrative agency for purposes of adjudication pursuant to its lawful authority.

(3) By a party to a proceeding before a court or administrative agency pursuant to a subpoena, subpoena duces tecum, notice to appear served pursuant to Section 1987 of the Code of Civil Procedure, or any provision authorizing discovery in a proceeding before a court or administrative agency.

(4) By a board, commission, or administrative agency pursuant to an investigative subpoena issued under Article 2 (commencing with Section 11180) of Chapter 2 of Part 1 of Division 3 of Title 2 of the Government Code.

(5) By an arbitrator or arbitration panel, when arbitration is lawfully requested by either party, pursuant to a subpoena duces tecum issued under Section 1282.6 of the Code of Civil Procedure, or another provision authorizing discovery in a proceeding before an arbitrator or arbitration panel.

(6) By a search warrant lawfully issued to a governmental law enforcement agency.

(7) By the patient or the patient's representative pursuant to Chapter 1 (commencing with Section 123100) of Part 1 of Division 106 of the Health and Safety Code.

(8) By a coroner, when requested in the course of an investigation by the coroner's office for the purpose of identifying the decedent or locating next of kin, or when investigating deaths that may involve public health concerns, organ or tissue donation, child abuse, elder abuse, suicides, poisonings, accidents, sudden infant deaths, suspicious deaths, unknown deaths, or criminal deaths, or when otherwise authorized by the decedent's representative. Medical information requested by the coroner under this paragraph shall be limited to information regarding the patient who is the decedent and who is the

subject of the investigation and shall be disclosed to the coroner without delay upon request.

(9) When otherwise specifically required by law.

(c) A provider of health care or a health care service plan may disclose medical information as follows:

(1) The information may be disclosed to providers of health care, health care service plans, contractors, or other health care professionals or facilities for purposes of diagnosis or treatment of the patient. This includes, in an emergency situation, the communication of patient information by radio transmission or other means between emergency medical personnel at the scene of an emergency, or in an emergency medical transport vehicle, and emergency medical personnel at a health facility licensed pursuant to Chapter 2 (commencing with Section 1250) of Division 2 of the Health and Safety Code.

(2) The information may be disclosed to an insurer, employer, health care service plan, hospital service plan, employee benefit plan, governmental authority, contractor, or any other person or entity responsible for paying for health care services rendered to the patient, to the extent necessary to allow responsibility for payment to be determined and payment to be made. If (A) the patient is, by reason of a comatose or other disabling medical condition, unable to consent to the disclosure of medical information and (B) no other arrangements have been made to pay for the health care services being rendered to the patient, the information may be disclosed to a governmental authority to the extent necessary to determine the patient's eligibility for, and to obtain, payment under a governmental program for health care services provided to the patient. The information may also be disclosed to another provider of health care or health care service plan as necessary to assist the other provider or health care service plan in obtaining payment for health care services rendered by that provider of health care or health care service plan to the patient.

(3) The information may be disclosed to a person or entity that provides billing, claims management, medical data processing, or other administrative services for providers of health care or health care service plans or for any of the persons or entities specified in paragraph (2). However, information so disclosed shall not be further disclosed by the recipient in a way that would violate this part.

(4) The information may be disclosed to organized committees and agents of professional societies or of medical staffs of licensed hospitals, licensed health care service plans, professional standards review organizations, independent medical review organizations and their selected reviewers, utilization and quality control peer review organizations as established by Congress in Public Law 97–248 in 1982, contractors, or persons or organizations insuring, responsible for, or defending professional liability that a provider may incur, if the committees, agents, health care service plans, organizations, reviewers, contractors, or persons are engaged in reviewing the competence or qualifications of health care professionals or in reviewing health care services with respect to medical necessity, level of care, quality of care, or justification of charges.

(5) The information in the possession of a provider of health care or health care service plan may be reviewed by a private or public body responsible for licensing or accrediting the provider of health care or health care service plan. However, no patient-identifying medical information may be removed from the premises except as expressly permitted or required elsewhere by law, nor shall that information be further disclosed by the recipient in a way that would violate this part.

(6) The information may be disclosed to the county coroner in the course of an investigation by the coroner's office when requested for all purposes not included in paragraph (8) of subdivision (b).

(7) The information may be disclosed to public agencies, clinical investigators, including investigators conducting epidemiologic studies, health care research organizations, and accredited public or private nonprofit educational or health care institutions for bona fide research purposes. However, no information so disclosed shall be further disclosed by the recipient in a way that would disclose the identity of a patient or violate this part.

(8) A provider of health care or health care service plan that has created medical information as a result of employment-related health care services to an employee conducted at the specific prior written request and expense of the employer may disclose to the employee's employer that part of the information that:

(A) Is relevant in a lawsuit, arbitration, grievance, or other claim or challenge to which the employer and the employee are parties and in which the patient has placed in issue his or her medical history, mental or physical condition, or treatment, provided that information may only be used or disclosed in connection with that proceeding.

(B) Describes functional limitations of the patient that may entitle the patient to leave from work for medical reasons or limit the patient's fitness to perform his or her present employment, provided that no statement of medical cause is included in the information disclosed.

(9) Unless the provider of health care or health care service plan is notified in writing of an agreement by the sponsor, insurer, or administrator to the contrary, the information may be disclosed to a sponsor, insurer, or administrator of a group or individual insured or uninsured plan or policy that the patient seeks coverage by or benefits from, if the information was created by the provider of health care or health care service plan as the result of services conducted at the specific prior written request and expense of the sponsor, insurer, or administrator for the purpose of evaluating the application for coverage or benefits.

(10) The information may be disclosed to a health care service plan by providers of health care that contract with

the health care service plan and may be transferred among providers of health care that contract with the health care service plan, for the purpose of administering the health care service plan. Medical information shall not otherwise be disclosed by a health care service plan except in accordance with this part.

(11) This part does not prevent the disclosure by a provider of health care or a health care service plan to an insurance institution, agent, or support organization, subject to Article 6.6 (commencing with Section 791) of Chapter 1 of Part 2 of Division 1 of the Insurance Code, of medical information if the insurance institution, agent, or support organization has complied with all of the requirements for obtaining the information pursuant to Article 6.6 (commencing with Section 791) of Chapter 1 of Part 2 of Division 1 of the Insurance Code.

(12) The information relevant to the patient's condition, care, and treatment provided may be disclosed to a probate court investigator in the course of an investigation required or authorized in a conservatorship proceeding under the Guardianship–Conservatorship Law as defined in Section 1400 of the Probate Code, or to a probate court investigator, probation officer, or domestic relations investigator engaged in determining the need for an initial guardianship or continuation of an existing guardianship.

(13) The information may be disclosed to an organ procurement organization or a tissue bank processing the tissue of a decedent for transplantation into the body of another person, but only with respect to the donating decedent, for the purpose of aiding the transplant. For the purpose of this paragraph, "tissue bank" and "tissue" have the same meanings as defined in Section 1635 of the Health and Safety Code.

(14) The information may be disclosed when the disclosure is otherwise specifically authorized by law, including, but not limited to, the voluntary reporting, either directly or indirectly, to the federal Food and Drug Administration of adverse events related to drug products or medical device problems.

(15) Basic information, including the patient's name, city of residence, age, sex, and general condition, may be disclosed to a state-recognized or federally recognized disaster relief organization for the purpose of responding to disaster welfare inquiries.

(16) The information may be disclosed to a third party for purposes of encoding, encrypting, or otherwise anonymizing data. However, no information so disclosed shall be further disclosed by the recipient in a way that would violate this part, including the unauthorized manipulation of coded or encrypted medical information that reveals individually identifiable medical information.

(17) For purposes of disease management programs and services as defined in Section 1399.901 of the Health and Safety Code, information may be disclosed as follows: (A) to an entity contracting with a health care service plan or the health care service plan's contractors to monitor or administer care of enrollees for a covered benefit, if the disease management services and care are authorized by a treating physician, or (B) to a disease management organization, as defined in Section 1399.900 of the Health and Safety Code, that complies fully with the physician authorization requirements of Section 1399.902 of the Health and Safety Code, if the health care service plan or its contractor provides or has provided a description of the disease management services to a treating physician or to the health care service plan's or contractor's network of physicians. This paragraph does not require physician authorization for the care or treatment of the adherents of a well-recognized church or religious denomination who depend solely upon prayer or spiritual means for healing in the practice of the religion of that church or denomination.

(18) The information may be disclosed, as permitted by state and federal law or regulation, to a local health department for the purpose of preventing or controlling disease, injury, or disability, including, but not limited to, the reporting of disease, injury, vital events, including, but not limited to, birth or death, and the conduct of public health surveillance, public health investigations, and public health interventions, as authorized or required by state or federal law or regulation.

(19) The information may be disclosed, consistent with applicable law and standards of ethical conduct, by a psychotherapist, as defined in Section 1010 of the Evidence Code, if the psychotherapist, in good faith, believes the disclosure is necessary to prevent or lessen a serious and imminent threat to the health or safety of a reasonably foreseeable victim or victims, and the disclosure is made to a person or persons reasonably able to prevent or lessen the threat, including the target of the threat.

(20) The information may be disclosed as described in Section 56.103.

(21)(A) The information may be disclosed to an employee welfare benefit plan, as defined under Section 3(1) of the Employee Retirement Income Security Act of 1974 (29 U.S.C. Sec. 1002(1)), which is formed under Section 302(c)(5) of the Taft–Hartley Act (29 U.S.C. Sec. 186(c)(5)), to the extent that the employee welfare benefit plan provides medical care, and may also be disclosed to an entity contracting with the employee welfare benefit plan for billing, claims management, medical data processing, or other administrative services related to the provision of medical care to persons enrolled in the employee welfare benefit plan for health care coverage, if all of the following conditions are met:

(i) The disclosure is for the purpose of determining eligibility, coordinating benefits, or allowing the employee welfare benefit plan, or the contracting entity, to advocate on the behalf of a patient or enrollee with a provider, a health care service plan, or a state or federal regulatory agency.

(ii) The request for the information is accompanied by a written authorization for the release of the information submitted in a manner consistent with subdivision (a) and Section 56.11.

(iii) The disclosure is authorized by and made in a manner consistent with the Health Insurance Portability and Accountability Act of 1996 (Public Law 104–191).

(iv) Any information disclosed is not further used or disclosed by the recipient in any way that would directly or indirectly violate this part or the restrictions imposed by Part 164 of Title 45 of the Code of Federal Regulations, including the manipulation of the information in any way that might reveal individually identifiable medical information.

(B) For purposes of this paragraph, Section 1374.8 of the Health and Safety Code shall not apply.

(d) Except to the extent expressly authorized by a patient or enrollee or subscriber or as provided by subdivisions (b) and (c), a provider of health care, health care service plan, contractor, or corporation and its subsidiaries and affiliates shall not intentionally share, sell, use for marketing, or otherwise use medical information for a purpose not necessary to provide health care services to the patient.

(e) Except to the extent expressly authorized by a patient or enrollee or subscriber or as provided by subdivisions (b) and (c), a contractor or corporation and its subsidiaries and affiliates shall not further disclose medical information regarding a patient of the provider of health care or an enrollee or subscriber of a health care service plan or insurer or self-insured employer received under this section to a person or entity that is not engaged in providing direct health care services to the patient or his or her provider of health care or health care service plan or insurer or self-insured employer. *(Added by Stats.2000, c. 1068 (A.B.1836), § 1.16, operative Jan. 1, 2003. Amended by Stats.2002, c. 123 (A.B.1958), § 1, operative Jan. 1, 2003; Stats.2003, c. 562 (A.B.715), § 2; Stats.2006, c. 874 (S.B.1430), § 2; Stats.2007, c. 506 (A.B.1178), § 1; Stats.2007, c. 552 (A.B.1687), § 2; Stats.2007, c. 553 (A.B.1727), § 1.9; Stats.2008, c. 179 (S.B.1498), § 27; Stats.2009, c. 493 (A.B.952), § 1.)*

§ 56.1007. Disclosure of medical information to specified persons involved with patient's care or health care payments; disclosure of medical information for other purposes

(a) A provider of health care, health care service plan, or contractor may, in accordance with subdivision (c) or (d), disclose to a family member, other relative, domestic partner, or a close personal friend of the patient, or any other person identified by the patient, the medical information directly relevant to that person's involvement with the patient's care or payment related to the patient's health care.

(b) A provider of health care, health care service plan, or contractor may use or disclose medical information to notify, or assist in the notification of, including identifying or locating, a family member, a personal representative of the patient, a domestic partner, or another person responsible for the care of the patient of the patient's location, general condition, or death. Any use or disclosure of medical information for those notification purposes shall be in accordance with the provisions of subdivision (c), (d), or (e), as applicable.

(c)(1) Except as provided in paragraph (2), if the patient is present for, or otherwise available prior to, a use or disclosure permitted by subdivision (a) or (b) and has the capacity to make health care decisions, the provider of health care, health care service plan, or contractor may use or disclose the medical information if it does any of the following:

(A) Obtains the patient's agreement.

(B) Provides the patient with the opportunity to object to the disclosure, and the patient does not express an objection.

(C) Reasonably infers from the circumstances, based on the exercise of professional judgment, that the patient does not object to the disclosure.

(2) A provider of health care who is a psychotherapist, as defined in Section 1010 of the Evidence Code, may use or disclose medical information pursuant to this subdivision only if the psychotherapist complies with subparagraph (A) or (B) of paragraph (1).

(d) If the patient is not present, or the opportunity to agree or object to the use or disclosure cannot practicably be provided because of the patient's incapacity or an emergency circumstance, the provider of health care, health care service plan, or contractor may, in the exercise of professional judgment, determine whether the disclosure is in the best interests of the patient and, if so, disclose only the medical information that is directly relevant to the person's involvement with the patient's health care. A provider of health care, health care service plan, or contractor may use professional judgment and its experience with common practice to make reasonable inferences of the patient's best interest in allowing a person to act on behalf of the patient to pick up filled prescriptions, medical supplies, X-rays, or other similar forms of medical information.

(e) A provider of health care, health care service plan, or contractor may use or disclose medical information to a public or private entity authorized by law or by its charter to assist in disaster relief efforts, for the purpose of coordinating with those entities the uses or disclosures permitted by subdivision (b). The requirements in subdivisions (c) and (d) apply to those uses and disclosures to the extent that the provider of health care, health care service plan, or contractor, in the exercise of professional judgment, determines that the requirements do not interfere with the ability to respond to the emergency circumstances.

(f) Nothing in this section shall be construed to interfere with or limit the access authority of Protection and Advocacy, Inc., the Office of Patients' Rights, or any county patients' rights advocates to access medical information pursuant to any state or federal law. *(Added by Stats.2006, c. 833 (A.B.3013), § 1.)*

§ 56.101. Destruction of records

Every provider of health care, health care service plan, pharmaceutical company, or contractor who creates, maintains, preserves, stores, abandons, destroys, or disposes of medical records shall do so in a manner that preserves the confidentiality of the information contained therein. Any provider of health care, health care service plan, pharmaceutical company, or contractor who negligently creates, maintains, preserves, stores, abandons, destroys, or disposes of medical records shall be subject to the remedies and penalties provided under subdivisions (b) and (c) of Section 56.36. *(Added by Stats.1999, c. 526 (S.B.19), § 3. Amended by Stats.2000, c. 1067 (S.B.2094), § 4; Stats.2002, c. 853 (A.B.2191), § 2.)*

§ 56.102. Disclosure of medical information by pharmaceutical company; authorizations, releases, consents, or waivers; exceptions

(a) A pharmaceutical company may not require a patient, as a condition of receiving pharmaceuticals, medications, or prescription drugs, to sign an authorization, release, consent, or waiver that would permit the disclosure of medical information that otherwise may not be disclosed under Section 56.10 or any other provision of law, unless the disclosure is for one of the following purposes:

(1) Enrollment of the patient in a patient assistance program or prescription drug discount program.

(2) Enrollment of the patient in a clinical research project.

(3) Prioritization of distribution to the patient of a prescription medicine in limited supply in the United States.

(4) Response to an inquiry from the patient communicated in writing, by telephone, or by electronic mail.

(b) Except as provided in subdivision (a) or Section 56.10, a pharmaceutical company may not disclose medical information provided to it without first obtaining a valid authorization from the patient. *(Added by Stats. 2002, c. 853 (A.B.2191), § 3.)*

§ 56.103. Disclosure of a minor's medical information; mental health condition

(a) A provider of health care may disclose medical information to a county social worker, a probation officer, or any other person who is legally authorized to have custody or care of a minor for the purpose of coordinating health care services and medical treatment provided to the minor.

(b) For purposes of this section, health care services and medical treatment includes one or more providers of health care providing, coordinating, or managing health care and related services, including, but not limited to, a provider of health care coordinating health care with a third party, consultation between providers of health care

and medical treatment relating to a minor, or a provider of health care referring a minor for health care services to another provider of health care.

(c) For purposes of this section, a county social worker, a probation officer, or any other person who is legally authorized to have custody or care of a minor shall be considered a third party who may receive any of the following:

(1) Medical information described in Sections 56.05 and 56.10.

(2) Protected health information described in Section 160.103 of Title 45 of the Code of Federal Regulations.

(d) Medical information disclosed to a county social worker, probation officer, or any other person who is legally authorized to have custody or care of a minor shall not be further disclosed by the recipient unless the disclosure is for the purpose of coordinating health care services and medical treatment of the minor and the disclosure is authorized by law. Medical information disclosed pursuant to this section may not be admitted into evidence in any criminal or delinquency proceeding against the minor. Nothing in this subdivision shall prohibit identical evidence from being admissible in a criminal proceeding if that evidence is derived solely from lawful means other than this section and is permitted by law.

(e)(1) Notwithstanding Section 56.104, if a provider of health care determines that the disclosure of medical information concerning the diagnosis and treatment of a mental health condition of a minor is reasonably necessary for the purpose of assisting in coordinating the treatment and care of the minor, that information may be disclosed to a county social worker, probation officer, or any other person who is legally authorized to have custody or care of the minor. The information shall not be further disclosed by the recipient unless the disclosure is for the purpose of coordinating mental health services and treatment of the minor and the disclosure is authorized by law.

(2) As used in this subdivision, "medical information" does not include psychotherapy notes as defined in Section 164.501 of Title 45 of the Code of Federal Regulations.

(f) The disclosure of information pursuant to this section is not intended to limit the disclosure of information when that disclosure is otherwise required by law.

(g) For purposes of this section, "minor" means a minor taken into temporary custody or as to who a petition has been filed with the court, or who has been adjudged to be a dependent child or ward of the juvenile court pursuant to Section 300 or 601 of the Welfare and Institutions Code.

(h)(1) Except as described in paragraph (1) of subdivision (e), nothing in this section shall be construed to limit or otherwise affect existing privacy protections provided for in state or federal law.

(2) Nothing in this section shall be construed to expand the authority of a social worker, probation officer, or custodial caregiver beyond the authority provided under existing law to a parent or a patient representative regarding access to medical information. *(Added by Stats.2007, c. 552 (A.B.1687), § 3. Amended by Stats. 2008, c. 699 (S.B.1241), § 1; Stats.2008, c. 700 (A.B. 2352), § 1.)*

§ 56.104. Patient's participation in outpatient treatment with psychotherapist; request; content; application

(a) Notwithstanding subdivision (c) of Section 56.10, except as provided in * * * subdivision * * * (e), no provider of health care, health care service plan, or contractor may release medical information to persons or entities who have requested that information and who are authorized by law to receive that information pursuant to subdivision (c) of Section 56.10, if the requested information specifically relates to the patient's participation in outpatient treatment with a psychotherapist, unless the person or entity requesting that information submits to the patient pursuant to subdivision (b) and to the provider of health care, health care service plan, or contractor a written request, signed by the person requesting the information or an authorized agent of the entity requesting the information, that includes all of the following:

(1) The specific information relating to a patient's participation in outpatient treatment with a psychotherapist being requested and its specific intended use or uses.

(2) The length of time during which the information will be kept before being destroyed or disposed of. A person or entity may extend that timeframe, provided that the person or entity notifies the provider, plan, or contractor of the extension. Any notification of an extension shall include the specific reason for the extension, the intended use or uses of the information during the extended time, and the expected date of the destruction of the information.

(3) A statement that the information will not be used for any purpose other than its intended use.

(4) A statement that the person or entity requesting the information will destroy the information and all copies in the person's or entity's possession or control, will cause it to be destroyed, or will return the information and all copies of it before or immediately after the length of time specified in paragraph (2) has expired.

(b) The person or entity requesting the information shall submit a copy of the written request required by this section to the patient within 30 days of receipt of the information requested, unless the patient has signed a written waiver in the form of a letter signed and submitted by the patient to the provider of health care or health care service plan waiving notification.

(c) For purposes of this section, "psychotherapist" means a person who is both a "psychotherapist" as defined in Section 1010 of the Evidence Code and a "provider of health care" as defined in subdivision (i) of Section 56.05.

(d) This section does not apply to the disclosure or use of medical information by a law enforcement agency or a regulatory agency when required for an investigation of unlawful activity or for licensing, certification, or regulatory purposes, unless the disclosure is otherwise prohibited by law.

(e) This section shall not apply to either of the following:

(1) Information authorized to be disclosed pursuant to paragraph (1) of subdivision (c) of Section 56.10.

(2) Information requested by law enforcement or by the target of the threat subsequent to a disclosure authorized by paragraph (19) of subdivision (c) of Section 56.10, in which the additional information is clearly necessary to prevent the serious and imminent threat disclosed under that paragraph.

(f) Nothing in this section shall be construed to grant any additional authority to a provider of health care, health care service plan, or contractor to disclose information to a person or entity without the patient's consent. *(Added by Stats.1999, c. 527 (A.B.416), § 3. Amended by Stats.2004, c. 463 (S.B.598), § 1; Stats.2009, c. 464 (A.B.681), § 1.)*

CHAPTER 3. USE AND DISCLOSURE OF MEDICAL INFORMATION BY EMPLOYERS

Section
56.20. Confidentiality; prohibition of discrimination due to refusal to sign authorization; prohibition of disclosure; exceptions.
56.21. Authorization for disclosure by employer.
56.22. Copy of authorization to patient or signatory.
56.23. Communication of limitations of authorization to person to whom disclosure made.
56.24. Cancellation or modification of authorization.
56.245. Further disclosure by recipient of medical information.

§ 56.20. Confidentiality; prohibition of discrimination due to refusal to sign authorization; prohibition of disclosure; exceptions

(a) Each employer who receives medical information shall establish appropriate procedures to ensure the confidentiality and protection from unauthorized use and disclosure of that information. These procedures may include, but are not limited to, instruction regarding confidentiality of employees and agents handling files containing medical information, and security systems restricting access to files containing medical information.

(b) No employee shall be discriminated against in terms or conditions of employment due to that employee's refusal to sign an authorization under this part. However, nothing in this section shall prohibit an employer from taking such action as is necessary in the absence of medical information due to an employee's refusal to sign an authorization under this part.

(c) No employer shall use, disclose, or knowingly permit its employees or agents to use or disclose medical information which the employer possesses pertaining to its employees without the patient having first signed an authorization under Section 56.11 or Section 56.21 permitting such use or disclosure, except as follows:

(1) The information may be disclosed if the disclosure is compelled by judicial or administrative process or by any other specific provision of law.

(2) That part of the information which is relevant in a lawsuit, arbitration, grievance, or other claim or challenge to which the employer and employee are parties and in which the patient has placed in issue his or her medical history, mental or physical condition, or treatment may be used or disclosed in connection with that proceeding.

(3) The information may be used only for the purpose of administering and maintaining employee benefit plans, including health care plans and plans providing short-term and long-term disability income, workers' compensation and for determining eligibility for paid and unpaid leave from work for medical reasons.

(4) The information may be disclosed to a provider of health care or other health care professional or facility to aid the diagnosis or treatment of the patient, where the patient or other person specified in subdivision (c) of Section 56.21 is unable to authorize the disclosure.

(d) If an employer agrees in writing with one or more of its employees or maintains a written policy which provides that particular types of medical information shall not be used or disclosed by the employer in particular ways, the employer shall obtain an authorization for such uses or disclosures even if an authorization would not otherwise be required by subdivision (c). *(Added by Stats.1981, c. 782, § 2.)*

§ 56.21. Authorization for disclosure by employer

An authorization for an employer to disclose medical information shall be valid if it complies with all of the following:

(a) Is handwritten by the person who signs it or is in a typeface no smaller than 14–point type.

(b) Is clearly separate from any other language present on the same page and is executed by a signature that serves no purpose other than to execute the authorization.

(c) Is signed and dated by one of the following:

(1) The patient, except that a patient who is a minor may only sign an authorization for the disclosure of medical information obtained by a provider of health care in the course of furnishing services to which the minor could lawfully have consented under Part 1 (commencing with Section 25) or Part 2.7 (commencing with Section 60) of Division 1.

(2) The legal representative of the patient, if the patient is a minor or incompetent. However, authorization may not be given under this subdivision for the disclosure of medical information that pertains to a competent minor and that was created by a provider of health care in the course of furnishing services to which a minor patient could lawfully have consented under Part 1 (commencing with Section 25) or Part 2.7 (commencing with Section 60) of Division 1.

(3) The beneficiary or personal representative of a deceased patient.

(d) States the limitations, if any, on the types of medical information to be disclosed.

(e) States the name or functions of the employer or person authorized to disclose the medical information.

(f) States the names or functions of the persons or entities authorized to receive the medical information.

(g) States the limitations, if any, on the use of the medical information by the persons or entities authorized to receive the medical information.

(h) States a specific date after which the employer is no longer authorized to disclose the medical information.

(i) Advises the person who signed the authorization of the right to receive a copy of the authorization. *(Added by Stats.1981, c. 782, § 2. Amended by Stats.2003, c. 562 (A.B.715), § 5; Stats.2006, c. 538 (S.B.1852), § 39.)*

§ 56.22. Copy of authorization to patient or signatory

Upon demand by the patient or the person who signed an authorization, an employer possessing the authorization shall furnish a true copy thereof. *(Added by Stats.1981, c. 782, § 2.)*

§ 56.23. Communication of limitations of authorization to person to whom disclosure made

An employer that discloses medical information pursuant to an authorization required by this chapter shall communicate to the person or entity to which it discloses the medical information any limitations in the authorization regarding the use of the medical information. No employer that has attempted in good faith to comply with this provision shall be liable for any unauthorized use of the medical information by the person or entity to which the employer disclosed the medical information. *(Added by Stats.1981, c. 782, § 2.)*

§ 56.24. Cancellation or modification of authorization

Nothing in this part shall be construed to prevent a person who could sign the authorization pursuant to subdivision (c) of Section 56.21 from cancelling or modifying an authorization. However, the cancellation or modification shall be effective only after the employer actually receives written notice of the cancellation or modification. *(Added by Stats.1981, c. 782, § 2.)*

§ 56.245. Further disclosure by recipient of medical information

A recipient of medical information pursuant to an authorization as provided by this chapter may not further disclose such medical information unless in accordance with a new authorization that meets the requirements of Section 56.21, or as specifically required or permitted by other provisions of this chapter or by law. *(Added by Stats.1981, c. 782, § 2.)*

CHAPTER 6. RELATIONSHIP TO EXISTING LAW

Section
56.31.   Disclosure or use of medical information under subdivision (f) of Section 56.30; HIV infection or exposure; employment incident.

§ 56.31. Disclosure or use of medical information under subdivision (f) of Section 56.30; HIV infection or exposure; employment incident

Notwithstanding any other provision of law, nothing in subdivision (f) of Section 56.30 shall permit the disclosure or use of medical information regarding whether a patient is infected with or exposed to the human immunodeficiency virus without the prior authorization from the patient unless the patient is an injured worker claiming to be infected with or exposed to the human immunodeficiency virus through an exposure incident arising out of and in the course of employment. *(Added by Stats.1999, c. 766 (A.B.435), § 1.)*

CHAPTER 7. VIOLATIONS

Section
56.36.   Misdemeanors; violations; remedies.

§ 56.36. Misdemeanors; violations; remedies

(a) Any violation of the provisions of this part that results in economic loss or personal injury to a patient is punishable as a misdemeanor.

(b) In addition to any other remedies available at law, any individual may bring an action against any person or entity who has negligently released confidential information or records concerning him or her in violation of this part, for either or both of the following:

(1) Nominal damages of one thousand dollars ($1,000). In order to recover under this paragraph, it shall not be necessary that the plaintiff suffered or was threatened with actual damages.

(2) The amount of actual damages, if any, sustained by the patient.

(c)(1) In addition, any person or entity that negligently discloses medical information in violation of the provisions of this part shall also be liable, irrespective of the amount of damages suffered by the patient as a result of that violation, for an administrative fine or civil penalty not to exceed two thousand five hundred dollars ($2,500) per violation.

(2)(A) Any person or entity, other than a licensed health care professional, who knowingly and willfully obtains, discloses, or uses medical information in violation of this part shall be liable for an administrative fine or civil penalty not to exceed twenty-five thousand dollars ($25,000) per violation.

(B) Any licensed health care professional, who knowingly and willfully obtains, discloses, or uses medical information in violation of this part shall be liable on a first violation, for an administrative fine or civil penalty not to exceed two thousand five hundred dollars ($2,500) per violation, or on a second violation for an administrative fine or civil penalty not to exceed ten thousand dollars ($10,000) per violation, or on a third and subsequent violation for an administrative fine or civil penalty not to exceed twenty-five thousand dollars ($25,000) per violation. Nothing in this subdivision shall be construed to limit the liability of a health care service plan, a contractor, or a provider of health care that is not a licensed health care professional for any violation of this part.

(3)(A) Any person or entity, other than a licensed health care professional, who knowingly or willfully obtains or uses medical information in violation of this part for the purpose of financial gain shall be liable for an administrative fine or civil penalty not to exceed two hundred fifty thousand dollars ($250,000) per violation and shall also be subject to disgorgement of any proceeds or other consideration obtained as a result of the violation.

(B) Any licensed health care professional, who knowingly and willfully obtains, discloses, or uses medical information in violation of this part for financial gain shall be liable on a first violation, for an administrative fine or civil penalty not to exceed five thousand dollars ($5,000) per violation, or on a second violation for an administrative fine or civil penalty not to exceed twenty-five thousand dollars ($25,000) per violation, or on a third and subsequent violation for an administrative fine or civil penalty not to exceed two hundred fifty thousand dollars ($250,000) per violation and shall also be subject to disgorgement of any proceeds or other consideration obtained as a result of the violation. Nothing in this subdivision shall be construed to limit the liability of a health care service plan, a contractor, or a provider of health care that is not a licensed health care professional for any violation of this part.

(4) Nothing in this subdivision shall be construed as authorizing an administrative fine or civil penalty under both paragraphs (2) and (3) for the same violation.

(5) Any person or entity who is not permitted to receive medical information pursuant to this part and who knowingly and willfully obtains, discloses, or uses medical information without written authorization from the patient shall be liable for a civil penalty not to exceed two hundred fifty thousand dollars ($250,000) per violation.

(d) In assessing the amount of an administrative fine or civil penalty pursuant to subdivision (c), the Office of Health Information Integrity, licensing agency, or certifying board or court shall consider any one or more of the relevant circumstances presented by any of the parties to the case including, but not limited to, the following:

(1) Whether the defendant has made a reasonable, good faith attempt to comply with this part.

(2) The nature and seriousness of the misconduct.

(3) The harm to the patient, enrollee, or subscriber.

(4) The number of violations.

(5) The persistence of the misconduct.

(6) The length of time over which the misconduct occurred.

(7) The willfulness of the defendant's misconduct.

(8) The defendant's assets, liabilities, and net worth.

(e)(1) The civil penalty pursuant to subdivision (c) shall be assessed and recovered in a civil action brought in the name of the people of the State of California in any court of competent jurisdiction by any of the following:

(A) The Attorney General.

(B) Any district attorney.

(C) Any county counsel authorized by agreement with the district attorney in actions involving violation of a county ordinance.

(D) Any city attorney of a city.

(E) Any city attorney of a city and county having a population in excess of 750,000, with the consent of the district attorney.

(F) A city prosecutor in any city having a full-time city prosecutor or, with the consent of the district attorney, by a city attorney in any city and county.

(G) The Director of the Office of Health Information Integrity may recommend that any person described in subparagraphs (A) to (F), inclusive, bring a civil action under this section.

(2) If the action is brought by the Attorney General, one-half of the penalty collected shall be paid to the treasurer of the county in which the judgment was entered, and one-half to the General Fund. If the action is brought by a district attorney or county counsel, the penalty collected shall be paid to the treasurer of the county in which the judgment was entered. Except as provided in paragraph (3), if the action is brought by a city attorney or city prosecutor, one-half of the penalty collected shall be paid to the treasurer of the city in which the judgment was entered and one-half to the treasurer of the county in which the judgment was entered.

(3) If the action is brought by a city attorney of a city and county, the entire amount of the penalty collected shall be paid to the treasurer of the city and county in which the judgment was entered.

(4) Nothing in this section shall be construed as authorizing both an administrative fine and civil penalty for the same violation.

(5) Imposition of a fine or penalty provided for in this section shall not preclude imposition of any other sanctions or remedies authorized by law.

(6) Administrative fines or penalties issued pursuant to Section 1280.15 of the Health and Safety Code shall offset any other administrative fine or civil penalty imposed under this section for the same violation.

(f) For purposes of this section, "knowing" and "willful" shall have the same meanings as in Section 7 of the Penal Code.

(g) No person who discloses protected medical information in accordance with the provisions of this part shall be subject to the penalty provisions of this part.

(h) Paragraph (6) of subdivision (e) shall only become operative if Senate Bill 541 of the 2007–08 Regular Session[1] is enacted and becomes effective on or before January 1, 2009. *(Added by Stats.1981, c. 782, § 2. Amended by Stats.1999, c. 526 (S.B.19), § 8; Stats.2008, c. 602 (A.B.211), § 1.)*

[1] So enacted by Stats.2008, c. 605.

Division 3

OBLIGATIONS

Part 2

CONTRACT

Title 4

UNLAWFUL CONTRACTS

Section
1670.7.   Provision deducting from wages for cost of emigrating and transporting; void.

§ 1670.7. Provision deducting from wages for cost of emigrating and transporting; void

Any provision of a contract that purports to allow a deduction from a person's wages for the cost of emigrating and transporting that person to the United States is void as against public policy. *(Added by Stats.2008, c. 258 (A.B.1278), § 1. Amended by Stats.2009, c. 35 (S.B.174), § 2.)*

Part 3

OBLIGATIONS IMPOSED BY LAW

Section
1714.41. Knowingly assisting a child support obligor to escape, evade, or avoid paying child support; included actions.

§ 1714.41. Knowingly assisting a child support obligor to escape, evade, or avoid paying child support; included actions

(a) Any person or business entity that knowingly assists a child support obligor who has an unpaid child support obligation to escape, evade, or avoid paying court-ordered or court-approved child support shall be liable for three times the value of the assistance provided, such as the fair market value of the assets transferred or hidden, or the amount of the wages or other compensation paid to the child support obligor but not reported. The maximum liability imposed by this section shall not exceed the entire child support obligation due. Any funds or assets collected pursuant to this section shall be paid to the child support obligee, and shall not reduce the amount of the unpaid child support obligation. Upon the satisfaction of the unpaid child support obligation, this section shall not apply.

(b) For purposes of this section, actions taken to knowingly assist a child support obligor to escape, evade, or avoid paying court-ordered or court-approved child support include, but are not limited to, any of the following actions taken when the individual or entity knew or should have known of the child support obligation:

(1) Hiring or employing the child support obligor as an employee in a trade or business and failing to timely file a report of new employees with the California New Employee Registry maintained by the Employment Development Department.

(2) Engaging the child support obligor as a service provider and failing to timely file a report with the Employment Development Department as required by Section 1088.8 of the Unemployment Insurance Code.

(3) When engaged in a trade or business, paying wages or other forms of compensation for services rendered by a child support obligor that are not reported to the Employment Development Department as required, including, but not limited to, payment in cash or via barter or trade. *(Added by Stats.2006, c. 820 (A.B.2440), § 3.)*

Part 4

OBLIGATIONS ARISING FROM PARTICULAR TRANSACTIONS

Title 1.6

CONSUMER CREDIT REPORTING AGENCIES ACT

CHAPTER 1.　GENERAL PROVISIONS

Section
1785.1. Legislative findings and declaration.
1785.2. Short title.
1785.3. Definitions.
1785.4. Inapplicability to private detectives; exception.
1785.5. Assembly, evaluation or dissemination of information on checking account experiences of financial institution customers.
1785.6. Consumer notice or disclosure; California addresses.

§ 1785.1.　Legislative findings and declaration

The Legislature finds and declares as follows:

(a) An elaborate mechanism has been developed for investigating and evaluating the credit worthiness, credit standing, credit capacity, and general reputation of consumers.

(b) Consumer credit reporting agencies have assumed a vital role in assembling and evaluating consumer credit and other information on consumers.

(c) There is a need to insure that consumer credit reporting agencies exercise their grave responsibilities with fairness, impartiality, and a respect for the consumer's right to privacy.

(d) It is the purpose of this title to require that consumer credit reporting agencies adopt reasonable procedures for meeting the needs of commerce for consumer credit, personnel, insurance, hiring of a dwelling unit, and other information in a manner which is fair and equitable to the consumer, with regard to the confidentiality, accuracy, relevancy, and proper utilization of such information in accordance with the requirements of this title.

(e) The Legislature hereby intends to regulate consumer credit reporting agencies pursuant to this title in a manner which will best protect the interests of the people of the State of California.

(f) The extension of credit is a privilege and not a right. Nothing in this title shall preclude a creditor from denying credit to any applicant providing such denial is based on factors not inconsistent with present law.

(g) Any clauses in contracts which prohibit any action required by this title are not in the public interest and shall be considered unenforceable. This shall not invalidate the other terms of such a contract. *(Added by*

Stats.1975, c. 1271, p. 3369, § 1. Amended by Stats.1976, c. 666, p. 1638, § 1; Stats.1982, c. 1127, p. 4062, § 1.)

§ 1785.2. Short title

This act may be referred to as the Consumer Credit Reporting Agencies Act. *(Added by Stats.1975, c. 1271, p. 3369, § 1.)*

§ 1785.3. Definitions

The following terms as used in this title have the meaning expressed in this section:

(a) "Adverse action" means a denial or revocation of credit, a change in the terms of an existing credit arrangement which is adverse to the interests of the consumer, or a refusal to grant credit in substantially the amount or on substantially the terms requested. "Adverse action" includes all of the following:

(1) Any denial of, increase in any charge for, or reduction in the amount of, insurance for personal, family, or household purposes made in connection with the underwriting of insurance.

(2) Any denial of employment or any other decision made for employment purposes which adversely affects any current or prospective employee.

(3) Any action taken, or determination made, with respect to a consumer (A) for an application for an extension of credit, or an application for the hiring of a dwelling unit, and (B) that is adverse to the interests of the consumer.

"Adverse action" does not include (A) a refusal to extend additional credit to a consumer under an existing credit arrangement if (i) the applicant is delinquent or otherwise in default under that credit arrangement or (ii) the additional credit would exceed a credit limit previously established for the consumer or (B) a refusal or failure to authorize an account transaction at a point of sale.

(b) "Consumer" means a natural individual.

(c) "Consumer credit report" means any written, oral, or other communication of any information by a consumer credit reporting agency bearing on a consumer's credit worthiness, credit standing, or credit capacity, which is used or is expected to be used, or collected in whole or in part, for the purpose of serving as a factor in establishing the consumer's eligibility for: (1) credit to be used primarily for personal, family, or household purposes, or (2) employment purposes, or (3) hiring of a dwelling unit, as defined in subdivision (c) of Section 1940, or (4) other purposes authorized in Section 1785.11.

The term does not include (1) any report containing information solely as to transactions or experiences between the consumer and the person making the report, (2) any communication of that information or information from a credit application by a consumer that is internal within the organization that is the person making the report or that is made to an entity owned by, or affiliated by corporate control with, that person; provided that the consumer is informed by means of a clear and conspicuous written disclosure that information contained in the credit application may be provided to these persons; however, where a credit application is taken by telephone, disclosure shall initially be given orally at the time the application is taken, and a clear and conspicuous written disclosure shall be made to the consumer in the first written communication to that consumer after the application is taken, (3) any authorization or approval of a specific extension of credit directly or indirectly by the issuer of a credit card or similar device, (4) any report by a person conveying a decision whether to make a specific extension of credit directly or indirectly to a consumer in response to a request by a third party, if the third party advises the consumer of the name and address of the person to whom the request was made and the person makes the disclosures to the consumer required under Section 1785.20, (5) any report containing information solely on a consumer's character, general reputation, personal characteristics, or mode of living which is obtained through personal interviews with neighbors, friends, or associates of the consumer reported on, or others with whom he is acquainted or who may have knowledge concerning those items of information, (6) any communication about a consumer in connection with a credit transaction which is not initiated by the consumer, between persons who are affiliated (as defined in Section 150 of the Corporations Code) by common ownership or common corporate control (as defined by Section 160 of the Corporations Code), if either of those persons has complied with paragraph (2) of subdivision (b) of Section 1785.20.1 with respect to a prequalifying report from which the information communicated is taken and provided the consumer has consented to the provision and use of the prequalifying report in writing, or (7) any consumer credit report furnished for use in connection with a transaction which consists of an extension of credit to be used solely for a commercial purpose.

(d) "Consumer credit reporting agency" means any person who, for monetary fees, dues, or on a cooperative nonprofit basis, regularly engages in whole or in part in the business of assembling or evaluating consumer credit information or other information on consumers for the purpose of furnishing consumer credit reports to third parties, but does not include any governmental agency whose records are maintained primarily for traffic safety, law enforcement, or licensing purposes.

(e) "Credit transaction that is not initiated by the consumer" does not include the use of a consumer credit report by an assignee for collection or by a person with which the consumer has an account for purposes of (1) reviewing the account or (2) collecting the account. For purposes of this subdivision, "reviewing the account" includes activities related to account maintenance and monitoring, credit line increases, and account upgrades and enhancements.

(f) "Employment purposes," when used in connection with a consumer credit report, means a report used for the purpose of evaluating a consumer for employment, promotion, reassignment, or retention as an employee.

(g) "File," when used in connection with information on any consumer, means all of the information on that consumer recorded and retained by a consumer credit reporting agency, regardless of how the information is stored.

(h) "Firm offer of credit" means any offer of credit to a consumer that will be honored if, based on information in a consumer credit report on the consumer and other information bearing on the creditworthiness of the consumer, the consumer is determined to meet the criteria used to select the consumer for the offer and the consumer is able to provide any real property collateral specified in the offer. For purposes of this subdivision, the phrase "other information bearing on the creditworthiness of the consumer" means information that the person making the offer is permitted to consider pursuant to any rule, regulation, or formal written policy statement relating to the federal Fair Credit Reporting Act, as amended (15 U.S.C. Sec. 1681 et seq.), promulgated by the Federal Trade Commission or any federal bank regulatory agency.

(i) "Item of information" means any of one or more informative entries in a credit report which causes a creditor to deny credit to an applicant or increase the cost of credit to an applicant or deny an applicant a checking account with a bank or other financial institution.

(j) "Person" means any individual, partnership, corporation, trust, estate, cooperative, association, government or governmental subdivision or agency, or other entity.

(k) "Prequalifying report" means a report containing the limited information permitted under paragraph (2) of subdivision (b) of Section 1785.11.

(*l*) "State or local child support enforcement agency" means the Department of Child Support Services or local child support agency acting pursuant to Division 17 (commencing with Section 17000) of the Family Code to establish, enforce or modify child support obligations, and any state or local agency or official that succeeds to these responsibilities under a successor statute. (*Added by Stats.1975, c. 1271, p. 3369, § 1. Amended by Stats. 1976, c. 666, p. 1638, § 2; Stats.1982, c. 1127, p. 4062, § 2; Stats.1990, c. 1144 (S.B.2751), § 1; Stats.1992, c. 1194 (A.B.1629), § 1, operative July 1, 1993; Stats.1993, c. 285 (A.B.1340), § 1, eff. Aug. 2, 1993; Stats.1994, c. 225 (S.B.1483), § 1; Stats.1994, c. 1010 (S.B.2053), § 35; Stats.2000, c. 808 (A.B.1358), § 3, eff. Sept. 28, 2000.*)

§ 1785.4. Inapplicability to private detectives; exception

Nothing in this title shall apply to any person licensed pursuant to the provisions of Chapter 11 (commencing with Section 7500) of Division 3 of the Business and Professions Code, or to any employee of such person, unless such person is employed directly by a consumer credit reporting agency. (*Added by Stats.1975, c. 1271, p. 3370, § 1.*)

§ 1785.5. Assembly, evaluation or dissemination of information on checking account experiences of financial institution customers

Any person who, for monetary fees, dues, or on a cooperative nonprofit basis, regularly engages in whole or in part in the practice of assembling, evaluating, or disseminating information on the checking account experiences of consumer customers of banks or other financial institutions is, with the exception of compliance with the requirements of Section 1785.10, subdivisions (c), (d), and (e), only with regard to the provision of the address and telephone number, subject to the same laws which govern consumer credit reporting agencies. (*Added by Stats.1990, c. 1144 (S.B.2751), § 2. Amended by Stats. 2001, c. 236 (A.B.488), § 1, operative Jan. 1, 2003.*)

§ 1785.6. Consumer notice or disclosure; California addresses

The notices and disclosures to consumers provided for in this title shall be required to be made only to those consumers who have a mailing address in California. (*Added by Stats.1993, c. 285 (A.B.1340), § 2, eff. Aug. 2, 1993.*)

CHAPTER 2. OBLIGATIONS OF CONSUMER CREDIT REPORTING AGENCIES

Section
1785.10. Inspection of files by consumer; advice to consumer; coded files; availability of information; disclosure of recipients of credit reports and inquiries; reselling report or information; exemptions.
1785.11. Furnishing consumer report; circumstances.
1785.11.1. Security alerts in credit reports.
1785.11.2. Security freeze on credit report.
1785.11.3. Official information in consumer credit report requiring written confirmation where there is a security freeze on the report; security alerts and copies.
1785.11.4. Application of specified provisions to consumer credit reporting agency that acts only as a reseller of credit information; honoring security freezes.
1785.11.6. Entities not required to place in credit report either a security alert or security freeze.
1785.11.8. Election by consumer to remove name from list that consumer credit reporting agency furnishes for credit card solicitations.
1785.12. Report to governmental agency.
1785.13. Items of information prohibited; exceptions.
1785.135. Consumer credit reports; documents acting as lien or encumbrance.
1785.14. Agency procedures; record of purposes; disclosure to consumer; notice to supplier of information regarding obligations under title.
1785.15. Supplying files and information; right to information.
1785.15.1. Credit scores supplied upon request by consumer; key factors.
1785.15.2. Credit scoring model.
1785.18. Matters of public record; source; reports for employment purposes; prohibited information.

§ 1785.10. Inspection of files by consumer; advice to consumer; coded files; availability of information; disclosure of recipients of credit reports and inquiries; reselling report or information; exemptions

(a) Every consumer credit reporting agency shall, upon request and proper identification of any consumer, allow the consumer to visually inspect all files maintained regarding that consumer at the time of the request.

(b) Every consumer reporting agency, upon contact by a consumer by telephone, mail, or in person regarding information which may be contained in the agency files regarding that consumer, shall promptly advise the consumer of his or her rights under Sections 1785.11.8, 1785.19, and 1785.19. 5, and of the obligation of the agency to provide disclosure of the files in person, by mail, or by telephone pursuant to Section 1785.15, including the obligation of the agency to provide a decoded written version of the file or a written copy of the file with an explanation of any code, including any credit score used, and the key factors, as defined in Section 1785.15.1, if the consumer so requests that copy. The disclosure shall be provided in the manner selected by the consumer, chosen from among any reasonable means available to the consumer credit reporting agency.

The agency shall determine the applicability of subdivision (1) of Section 1785.17 and, where applicable, the agency shall inform the consumer of the rights under that section.

(c) All information on a consumer in the files of a consumer credit reporting agency at the time of a request for inspection under subdivision (a), shall be available for inspection, including the names, addresses and, if provided by the sources of information, the telephone numbers identified for customer service for the sources of information.

(d)(1) The consumer credit reporting agency shall also disclose the recipients of any consumer credit report on the consumer which the consumer credit reporting agency has furnished:

(A) For employment purposes within the two-year period preceding the request.

(B) For any other purpose within the 12–month period preceding the request.

(2) Disclosure of recipients of consumer credit reports for purposes of this subdivision shall include the name of the recipient or, if applicable, the fictitious business name under which the recipient does business disclosed in full. The identification shall also include the address and, if provided by the recipient, the telephone number identified for customer service for the recipient.

(e) The consumer credit reporting agency shall also disclose a record of all inquiries received by the agency in the 12–month period preceding the request that identified the consumer in connection with a credit transaction which is not initiated by the consumer. This record of inquiries shall include the name, address and, if provided by the recipient, the telephone number identified for customer service for each recipient making an inquiry.

(f) Any consumer credit reporting agency when it is subject to the provisions of Section 1785.22 is exempted from the requirements of subdivisions (c), (d), and (e), only with regard to the provision of the address and telephone number.

(g) Any consumer credit reporting agency, that provides a consumer credit report to another consumer credit reporting agency that procures the consumer credit report for the purpose of resale and is subject to Section 1785.22, is exempted from the requirements of subdivisions (d) and (e), only with regard to the provision of the address and telephone number regarding each prospective user to which the consumer credit report was sold.

(h) This section shall become operative on January 1, 2003. *(Added by Stats.2002, c. 9 (A.B.1531), § 2, eff. Feb. 19, 2002, operative Jan. 1, 2003.)*

§ 1785.11. Furnishing consumer report; circumstances

(a) A consumer credit reporting agency shall furnish a consumer credit report only under the following circumstances:

(1) In response to the order of a court having jurisdiction to issue an order.

(2) In accordance with the written instructions of the consumer to whom it relates.

(3) To a person whom it has reason to believe:

(A) Intends to use the information in connection with a credit transaction, or entering or enforcing an order of a court of competent jurisdiction for support, involving the consumer as to whom the information is to be furnished and involving the extension of credit to, or review or collection of an account of, the consumer; or

(B) Intends to use the information for employment purposes; or

(C) Intends to use the information in connection with the underwriting of insurance involving the consumer, or for insurance claims settlements; or

(D) Intends to use the information in connection with a determination of the consumer's eligibility for a license or other benefit granted by a governmental instrumentality required by law to consider the applicant's financial responsibility or status; or

(E) Intends to use the information in connection with the hiring of a dwelling unit, as defined in subdivision (c) of Section 1940; or

(F) Otherwise has a legitimate business need for the information in connection with a business transaction involving the consumer.

(b) A consumer credit reporting agency may furnish information for purposes of a credit transaction specified in subparagraph (A) of paragraph (3) of subdivision (a), where it is a credit transaction that is not initiated by the consumer, only under the circumstances specified in paragraph (1) or (2), as follows:

(1) The consumer authorizes the consumer credit reporting agency to furnish the consumer credit report to the person.

(2) The proposed transaction involves a firm offer of credit to the consumer, the consumer credit reporting agency has complied with subdivision (d), and the consumer has not elected pursuant to paragraph (1) of subdivision (d) to have the consumer's name excluded from lists of names provided by the consumer credit reporting agency for purposes of reporting in connection with the potential issuance of firm offers of credit. A consumer credit reporting agency may provide only the following information pursuant to this paragraph:

(A) The name and address of the consumer.

(B) Information pertaining to a consumer that is not identified or identifiable with a particular consumer.

(c) Except as provided in paragraph (3) of subdivision (a) of Section 1785.15, a consumer credit reporting agency shall not furnish to any person a record of inquiries solely resulting from credit transactions that are not initiated by the consumer.

(d)(1) A consumer may elect to have his or her name and address excluded from any list provided by a consumer credit reporting agency pursuant to paragraph (2) of subdivision (b) by notifying the consumer credit reporting agency, by telephone or in writing, through the notification system maintained by the consumer credit reporting agency pursuant to subdivision (e), that the consumer does not consent to any use of consumer credit reports relating to the consumer in connection with any transaction that is not initiated by the consumer.

(2) An election of a consumer under paragraph (1) shall be effective with respect to a consumer credit reporting agency, and any affiliate of the consumer credit reporting agency, on the date on which the consumer notifies the consumer credit reporting agency.

(3) An election of a consumer under paragraph (1) shall terminate and be of no force or effect following notice from the consumer to the consumer credit reporting agency, through the system established pursuant to subdivision (e), that the election is no longer effective.

(e) Each consumer credit reporting agency that furnishes a prequalifying report pursuant to subdivision (b) in connection with a credit transaction not initiated by the consumer shall establish and maintain a notification system, including a toll-free telephone number, that permits any consumer, with appropriate identification and for which the consumer credit reporting agency has a file, to notify the consumer credit reporting agency of the consumer's election to have the consumer's name removed from any list of names and addresses provided by the consumer credit reporting agency, and by any affiliated consumer credit reporting agency, pursuant to paragraph (2) of subdivision (b). Compliance with the requirements of this subdivision by a consumer credit reporting agency shall constitute compliance with those requirements by any affiliate of that consumer credit reporting agency.

(f) Each consumer credit reporting agency that compiles and maintains files on consumers on a nationwide basis shall establish and maintain a notification system under paragraph (1) of subdivision (e) jointly with its affiliated consumer credit reporting agencies. *(Added by Stats.1975, c. 1271, p. 3371, § 1. Amended by Stats.1982, c. 1127, p. 4063, § 3; Stats.1992, c. 1194 (A.B.1629), § 3, operative July 1, 1993; Stats.1993, c. 285 (A.B.1340), § 4, eff. Aug. 2, 1993; Stats.1994, c. 146 (A.B.3601), § 11; Stats.2000, c. 1012 (S.B.2166), § 1; Stats.2002, c. 664 (A.B.3034), § 40.)*

§ 1785.11.1. Security alerts in credit reports

(a) A consumer may elect to place a security alert in his or her credit report by making a request in writing or by telephone to a consumer credit reporting agency. "Security alert" means a notice placed in a consumer's credit report, at the request of the consumer, that notifies a recipient of the credit report that the consumer's identity may have been used without the consumer's consent to fraudulently obtain goods or services in the consumer's name.

(b) A consumer credit reporting agency shall notify each person requesting consumer credit information with respect to a consumer of the existence of a security alert in the credit report of that consumer, regardless of whether a full credit report, credit score, or summary report is requested.

(c) Each consumer credit reporting agency shall maintain a toll-free telephone number to accept security alert requests from consumers 24 hours a day, seven days a week.

(d) The toll-free telephone number shall be included in any written disclosure by a consumer credit reporting agency to any consumer pursuant to Section 1785.15 and shall be printed in a clear and conspicuous manner.

(e) A consumer credit reporting agency shall place a security alert on a consumer's credit report no later than five business days after receiving a request from the consumer.

(f) The security alert shall remain in place for at least 90 days, and a consumer shall have the right to request a renewal of the security alert.

(g) Any person who uses a consumer credit report in connection with the approval of credit based on an application for an extension of credit, or with the purchase, lease, or rental of goods or non-credit-related services and who receives notification of a security alert pursuant to subdivision (a) may not lend money, extend credit, or complete the purchase, lease, or rental of goods or non-credit-related services without taking reasonable steps to verify the consumer's identity, in order to ensure that the application for an extension of credit or for the purchase, lease, or rental of goods or non-credit-related services is not the result of identity theft. If the consumer has placed a statement with the security alert in his or her file requesting that identity be verified by calling a specified telephone number, any person who receives that statement with the security alert in a consumer's file pursuant to subdivision (a) shall take reasonable steps to verify the identity of the consumer by contacting the consumer using the specified telephone number prior to lending money, extending credit, or completing the purchase, lease, or rental of goods or non-credit-related services. If a person uses a consumer credit report to facilitate the extension of credit or for another permissible purpose on behalf of a subsidiary, affiliate, agent, assignee, or prospective assignee, that person may verify a consumer's identity under this section in lieu of the subsidiary, affiliate, agent, assignee, or prospective assignee.

(h) For purposes of this section, "extension of credit" does not include an increase in the dollar limit of an existing open-end credit plan, as defined in Regulation Z issued by the Board of Governors of the Federal Reserve System (12 C.F.R. 226.2), or any change to, or review of, an existing credit account.

(i) If reasonable steps are taken to verify the identity of the consumer pursuant to subdivision (b) of Section 1785.20.3, those steps constitute compliance with the requirements of this section, except that if a consumer has placed a statement including a telephone number with the security alert in his or her file, his or her identity shall be verified by contacting the consumer using that telephone number as specified pursuant to subdivision (g).

(j) A consumer credit reporting agency shall notify each consumer who has requested that a security alert be placed on his or her consumer credit report of the expiration date of the alert.

(k) Notwithstanding Section 1785.19, any consumer credit reporting agency that recklessly, willfully, or intentionally fails to place a security alert pursuant to this section shall be liable for a penalty in an amount of up to two thousand five hundred dollars ($2,500) and reasonable attorneys' fees. *(Added by Stats.2001, c. 720 (S.B. 168), § 1, operative July 1, 2002. Amended by Stats.2003, c. 533 (S.B.602), § 2; Stats.2003, c. 907 (S.B.25), § 1.5, operative July 1, 2004.)*

§ 1785.11.2. Security freeze on credit report

(a) A consumer may elect to place a security freeze on his or her credit report by making a request in writing by mail to a consumer credit reporting agency. "Security freeze" means a notice placed in a consumer's credit report, at the request of the consumer, and subject to certain exceptions, that prohibits the consumer credit reporting agency from releasing the consumer's credit report or any information from it without the express authorization of the consumer. If a security freeze is in place, information from a consumer's credit report may not be released to a third party without prior express authorization from the consumer. This subdivision does not prevent a consumer credit reporting agency from advising a third party that a security freeze is in effect with respect to the consumer's credit report.

(b) A consumer credit reporting agency shall place a security freeze on a consumer's credit report no later than three business days after receiving a written request from the consumer.

(c) The consumer credit reporting agency shall send a written confirmation of the security freeze to the consumer within 10 business days and shall provide the consumer with a unique personal identification number or password to be used by the consumer when providing authorization for the release of his or her credit for a specific party or period of time.

(d) If the consumer wishes to allow his or her credit report to be accessed for a specific party or period of time while a freeze is in place, he or she shall contact the consumer credit reporting agency, request that the freeze be temporarily lifted, and provide the following:

(1) Proper identification, as defined in subdivision (c) of Section 1785.15.

(2) The unique personal identification number or password provided by the credit reporting agency pursuant to subdivision (c).

(3) The proper information regarding the third party who is to receive the credit report or the time period for which the report shall be available to users of the credit report.

(e) A consumer credit reporting agency that receives a request from a consumer to temporarily lift a freeze on a credit report pursuant to subdivision (d) shall comply with the request no later than three business days after receiving the request.

(f) A consumer credit reporting agency may develop procedures involving the use of telephone, fax, the Internet, or other electronic media to receive and process a request from a consumer to temporarily lift a freeze on a credit report pursuant to subdivision (d) in an expedited manner.

(g) A consumer credit reporting agency shall remove or temporarily lift a freeze placed on a consumer's credit report only in the following cases:

(1) Upon consumer request, pursuant to subdivision (d) or (j).

(2) If the consumer's credit report was frozen due to a material misrepresentation of fact by the consumer. If a consumer credit reporting agency intends to remove a freeze upon a consumer's credit report pursuant to this paragraph, the consumer credit reporting agency shall notify the consumer in writing prior to removing the freeze on the consumer's credit report.

(h) A third party who requests access to a consumer credit report in connection with an application for credit or any other use may treat the application as incomplete if a security freeze is in effect and the consumer does not allow his or her credit report to be accessed for that specific party or period of time.

(i) If a consumer requests a security freeze, the consumer credit reporting agency shall disclose the process of placing and temporarily lifting a freeze and the process for allowing access to information from the consumer's credit report for a specific party or period of time while the freeze is in place.

(j) A security freeze shall remain in place until the consumer requests that the security freeze be removed. A consumer credit reporting agency shall remove a security freeze within three business days of receiving a request for removal from the consumer if the consumer provides both of the following:

(1) Proper identification, as defined in subdivision (c) of Section 1785.15.

(2) The unique personal identification number or password provided by the credit reporting agency pursuant to subdivision (c).

(k) A consumer credit reporting agency shall require proper identification, as defined in subdivision (c) of Section 1785.15, of the person making a request to place or remove a security freeze.

(l) The provisions of this section do not apply to the use of a consumer credit report by any of the following:

(1)(A)(i) A person or entity with which the consumer has or had, prior to any assignment, an account or contract, including a demand deposit account, or to which the consumer issued a negotiable instrument, for the purpose of reviewing the account or collecting the financial obligation owing for the account, contract, or negotiable instrument.

(ii) A subsidiary, affiliate, or agent of a person or entity described in clause (i), an assignee of a financial obligation owing by the consumer to such a person or entity, or a prospective assignee of a financial obligation owing by the consumer to such a person or entity in conjunction with the proposed purchase of the financial obligation, for the purpose of reviewing the account or collecting the financial obligation owing for the account, contract, or negotiable instrument.

(B) For purposes of this paragraph, "reviewing the account" includes activities related to account maintenance, monitoring, credit line increases, and account upgrades and enhancements.

(2) A subsidiary, affiliate, agent, assignee, or prospective assignee of a person to whom access has been granted under subdivision (d) for purposes of facilitating the extension of credit or other permissible use.

(3) Any state or local agency, law enforcement agency, trial court, or private collection agency acting pursuant to a court order, warrant, or subpoena.

(4) A child support agency acting pursuant to Chapter 2 (commencing with Section 17400) of Division 17 of the Family Code or Title IV–D of the Social Security Act (42 U.S.C. et seq.).

(5) The State Department of Health Care Services or its agents or assigns acting to investigate Medi–Cal fraud.

(6) The Franchise Tax Board or its agents or assigns acting to investigate or collect delinquent taxes or unpaid court orders or to fulfill any of its other statutory responsibilities.

(7) The use of credit information for the purposes of prescreening as provided for by the federal Fair Credit Reporting Act.

(8) Any person or entity administering a credit file monitoring subscription service to which the consumer has subscribed.

(9) Any person or entity for the purpose of providing a consumer with a copy of his or her credit report upon the consumer's request.

(m)(1) Except as provided in paragraph (2), this title does not prevent a consumer credit reporting agency from charging a fee of no more than ten dollars ($10) to a consumer for the placement of each freeze, the removal of the freeze, the temporary lift of the freeze for a period of time, or the temporary lift of the freeze for a specific party, regarding access to a consumer credit report, except that a consumer credit reporting agency may not charge a fee to a victim of identity theft who has submitted a valid police report or valid Department of Motor Vehicles investigative report that alleges a violation of Section 530.5 of the Penal Code.

(2) With respect to a consumer who is 65 years of age or older and who has provided identification confirming his or her age, a consumer credit reporting agency may charge a fee not to exceed five dollars ($5) for the placement of each freeze, the removal of the freeze, the temporary lift of the freeze for a period of time, or the temporary lift of the freeze for a specific party.

(n) Regardless of the existence of a security freeze, a consumer reporting agency may disclose public record information lawfully obtained by, or for, the consumer reporting agency from an open public record to the extent otherwise permitted by law. This subdivision does not prohibit a consumer reporting agency from electing to apply a valid security freeze to the entire contents of a credit report. *(Added by Stats.2001, c. 720 (S.B.168), § 2, operative Jan. 1, 2003. Amended by Stats.2002, c. 664 (A.B.3034), § 41; Stats.2002, c. 786 (S.B.1730), § 1; Stats.2003, c. 533 (S.B.602), § 3; Stats.2007, c. 699 (A.B.1298), § 2; Stats.2008, c. 151 (A.B.372), § 1.)*

Validity

A prior version of this section was held unconstitutional as violating free speech in the decision of U.D. Registry, Inc. v. State (App. 2 Dist. 2006) 50 Cal.Rptr.3d 647, 144 Cal.App.4th 405, modified on denial of rehearing, review denied.

§ 1785.11.3. Official information in consumer credit report requiring written confirmation where there is a security freeze on the report; security alerts and copies

(a) If a security freeze is in place, a consumer credit reporting agency shall not change any of the following official information in a consumer credit report without sending a written confirmation of the change to the consumer within 30 days of the change being posted to the consumer's file: name, date of birth, social security number, and address. Written confirmation is not required for technical modifications of a consumer's official information, including name and street abbreviations, complete spellings, or transposition of numbers or letters. In the case of an address change, the written confirmation shall be sent to both the new address and to the former address.

(b) If a consumer has placed a security alert, a consumer credit reporting agency shall provide the consumer, upon request, with a free copy of his or her credit report at the time the 90–day security alert period expires. *(Added by Stats.2001, c. 720 (S.B.168), § 3, operative Jan. 1, 2003.)*

§ 1785.11.4. Application of specified provisions to consumer credit reporting agency that acts only as a reseller of credit information; honoring security freezes

The provisions of Sections 1785.11.1, 1785.11.2, and 1785.11.3 do not apply to a consumer credit reporting agency that acts only as a reseller of credit information pursuant to Section 1785.22 by assembling and merging information contained in the data base of another consumer credit reporting agency or multiple consumer credit reporting agencies, and does not maintain a permanent data base of credit information from which new consumer credit reports are produced. However, a consumer credit reporting agency acting pursuant to Section 1785.22 shall honor any security freeze placed on a consumer credit report by another consumer credit reporting agency. *(Added by Stats.2001, c. 720 (S.B.168), § 4.)*

§ 1785.11.6. Entities not required to place in credit report either a security alert or security freeze

The following entities are not required to place in a credit report either a security alert, pursuant to Section 1785.11.1, or a security freeze, pursuant to Section 1785.11.2:

(a) A check services or fraud prevention services company, which issues reports on incidents of fraud or authorizations for the purpose of approving or processing negotiable instruments, electronic funds transfers, or similar methods of payments.

(b) A deposit account information service company, which issues reports regarding account closures due to fraud, substantial overdrafts, ATM abuse, or similar negative information regarding a consumer, to inquiring banks or other financial institutions for use only in reviewing a consumer request for a deposit account at the inquiring bank or financial institution. *(Added by Stats. 2001, c. 720 (S.B.168), § 5. Amended by Stats.2002, c. 786 (S.B.1730), § 2; Stats.2003, c. 907 (S.B.25), § 2.)*

§ 1785.11.8. Election by consumer to remove name from list that consumer credit reporting agency furnishes for credit card solicitations

A consumer may elect that his or her name shall be removed from any list that a consumer credit reporting agency furnishes for credit card solicitations, by notifying the consumer credit reporting agency, by telephone or in writing, pursuant to the notification system maintained by the consumer credit reporting agency pursuant to subdivision (d) of Section 1785.11. The election shall be effective for a minimum of two years, unless otherwise specified by the consumer. *(Added by Stats.2001, c. 354 (A.B.655), § 2.)*

§ 1785.12. Report to governmental agency

Notwithstanding the provisions of Section 1785.11, a consumer credit reporting agency may furnish to a governmental agency a consumer's name, address, former address, places of employment, or former places of employment. *(Added by Stats.1975, c. 1271, p. 3371, § 1.)*

§ 1785.13. Items of information prohibited; exceptions

(a) No consumer credit reporting agency shall make any consumer credit report containing any of the following items of information:

(1) Bankruptcies that, from the date of * * * the order for relief, antedate the report by more than 10 years.

(2) Suits and judgments that, from the date of entry or renewal, antedate the report by more than seven years or until the governing statute of limitations has expired, whichever is the longer period.

(3) Unlawful detainer actions, unless the lessor was the prevailing party. For purposes of this paragraph, the lessor shall be deemed to be the prevailing party only if (A) final judgment was awarded to the lessor (i) upon entry of the tenant's default, (ii) upon the granting of the lessor's motion for summary judgment, or (iii) following trial, or (B) the action was resolved by a written settlement agreement between the parties that states that the unlawful detainer action may be reported. In any other instance in which the action is resolved by settlement agreement, the lessor shall not be deemed to be the prevailing party for purposes of this paragraph.

(4) Paid tax liens that, from the date of payment, antedate the report by more than seven years.

(5) Accounts placed for collection or charged to profit and loss that antedate the report by more than seven years.

(6) Records of arrest, indictment, information, misdemeanor complaint, or conviction of a crime that, from the date of disposition, release, or parole, antedate the report

by more than seven years. These items of information shall no longer be reported if at any time it is learned that in the case of a conviction a full pardon has been granted, or in the case of an arrest, indictment, information, or misdemeanor complaint a conviction did not result.

(7) Any other adverse information that antedates the report by more than seven years.

(b) The seven-year period specified in paragraphs (5) and (7) of subdivision (a) shall commence to run, with respect to any account that is placed for collection (internally or by referral to a third party, whichever is earlier), charged to profit and loss, or subjected to any similar action, upon the expiration of the 180–day period beginning on the date of the commencement of the delinquency that immediately preceded the collection activity, charge to profit and loss, or similar action. Where more than one of these actions is taken with respect to a particular account, the seven-year period specified in paragraphs (5) and (7) shall commence concurrently for all these actions on the date of the first of these actions.

(c) Any consumer credit reporting agency that furnishes a consumer credit report containing information regarding any case involving a consumer arising under the bankruptcy provisions of Title 11 of the United States Code shall include an identification of the chapter of Title 11 of the United States Code under which the case arose if that can be ascertained from what was provided to the consumer credit reporting agency by the source of the information.

(d) A consumer credit report shall not include any adverse information concerning a consumer antedating the report by more than 10 years or that otherwise is prohibited from being included in a consumer credit report.

(e) If a consumer credit reporting agency is notified by a furnisher of credit information that an open-end credit account of the consumer has been closed by the consumer, any consumer credit report thereafter issued by the consumer credit reporting agency with respect to that consumer, and that includes information respecting that account, shall indicate the fact that the consumer has closed the account. For purposes of this subdivision, "open-end credit account" does not include any demand deposit account, such as a checking account, money market account, or share draft account.

(f) Consumer credit reporting agencies shall not include medical information in their files on consumers or furnish medical information for employment, insurance, or credit purposes in a consumer credit report without the consent of the consumer.

(g) A consumer credit reporting agency shall include in any consumer credit report information, if any, on the failure of the consumer to pay overdue child or spousal support, where the information either was provided to the consumer credit reporting agency pursuant to Section 4752 or has been provided to the consumer credit

reporting agency and verified by another federal, state, or local governmental agency. *(Added by Stats.1975, c. 1271, p. 3371, § 1. Amended by Stats.1982, c. 1127, p. 4064, § 4; Stats.1988, c. 900, § 1; Stats.1991, c. 965 (A.B.1796), § 1; Stats.1991, c. 1145 (A.B.2032), § 1.1; Stats.1992, c. 1194 (A.B.1629), § 4, operative July 1, 1993; Stats.1993, c. 285 (A.B.1340), § 5, eff. Aug. 2, 1993; Stats.1994, c. 146 (A.B.3601), § 12; Stats.2000, c. 1012 (S.B.2166), § 2; Stats.2009, c. 500 (A.B.1059), § 10.)*

Validity

A prior version of this section was held unconstitutional as a violation of the First Amendment in the decision of U.D. Registry, Inc. v. State of California (App. 2 Dist. 1995) 40 Cal.Rptr.2d 228, 34 Cal.App.4th 107.

§ 1785.135. Consumer credit reports; documents acting as lien or encumbrance

No consumer credit reporting agency shall make any consumer credit report with respect to a document which acts as a lien or other encumbrance, including, but not limited to, a notice of lis pendens, but which has together with it a court order striking or releasing the lien or other encumbrance pursuant to Section 765.030 of the Code of Civil Procedure. *(Added by Stats.1998, c. 779 (S.B.1759), § 1.)*

§ 1785.14. Agency procedures; record of purposes; disclosure to consumer; notice to supplier of information regarding obligations under title

(a) Every consumer credit reporting agency shall maintain reasonable procedures designed to avoid violations of Section 1785.13 and to limit furnishing of consumer credit reports to the purposes listed under Section 1785.11. These procedures shall require that prospective users of the information identify themselves, certify the purposes for which the information is sought and certify that the information will be used for no other purposes. From the effective date of this act the consumer credit reporting agency shall keep a record of the purposes as stated by the user. Every consumer credit reporting agency shall make a reasonable effort to verify the identity of a new prospective user and the uses certified by the prospective user prior to furnishing the user a consumer report. No consumer credit reporting agency may furnish a consumer credit report to any person unless the consumer credit reporting agency has reasonable grounds for believing that the consumer credit report will be used by the person for the purposes listed in Section 1785.11. A consumer credit reporting agency does not have reasonable grounds for believing that a consumer credit report will be used by the person for the purposes listed in Section 1785.11 unless all of the following requirements are met:

(1) If the prospective user is a retail seller, as defined in Section 1802.3, and intends to issue credit to a consumer who appears in person on the basis of an application for credit submitted in person, the consumer

credit reporting agency shall, with a reasonable degree of certainty, match at least three categories of identifying information within the file maintained by the consumer credit reporting agency on the consumer with the information provided to the consumer credit reporting agency by the retail seller. The categories of identifying information may include, but are not limited to, first and last name, month and date of birth, driver's license number, place of employment, current residence address, previous residence address, or social security number. The categories of information shall not include mother's maiden name.

(2) If the prospective user is a retail seller, as defined in Section 1802.3, and intends to issue credit to a consumer who appears in person on the basis of an application for credit submitted in person, the retail seller certifies, in writing, to the consumer credit reporting agency that it instructs its employees and agents to inspect a photo identification of the consumer at the time the application was submitted in person. This paragraph does not apply to an application for credit submitted by mail.

(3) If the prospective user intends to extend credit by mail pursuant to a solicitation by mail, the extension of credit shall be mailed to the same address as on the solicitation unless the prospective user verifies any address change by, among other methods, contacting the person to whom the extension of credit will be mailed.

(b) Whenever a consumer credit reporting agency prepares a consumer credit report, it shall follow reasonable procedures to assure maximum possible accuracy of the information concerning the individual about whom the report relates. These reasonable procedures shall include, but not be limited to, permanent retention by the consumer credit reporting agency in the consumer's file, or a separately individualized file, of that portion of the data in the file that is used by the consumer credit reporting agency to identify the individual consumer pursuant to paragraph (1) of subdivision (a). This permanently retained data shall be available for use in either a reinvestigation pursuant to subdivision (a) of Section 1785.16, an investigation where the consumer has filed a police report pursuant to subdivision (k) of Section 1785.16, or a restoration of a file involving the consumer. If the permanently retained identifying information is retained in a consumer's file, it shall be clearly identified in the file in order for an individual who reviews the file to easily distinguish between the permanently stored identifying information and any other identifying information that may be a part of the file. This retention requirement shall not apply to data that is reported in error, that is obsolete, or that is found to be inaccurate through the results of a reinvestigation initiated by a consumer pursuant to subdivision (a) of Section 1785.16.

(c) No consumer credit reporting agency may prohibit any user of any consumer credit report furnished by the consumer credit reporting agency from disclosing the contents of the consumer credit report to the consumer who is the subject of the report if adverse action may be taken by the user based in whole or in part on the consumer credit report. The act of disclosure to the consumer by the user of the contents of a consumer credit report shall not be a basis for liability of the consumer credit reporting agency or the user under Section 1785.31.

(d) A consumer credit reporting agency shall provide a written notice to any person who regularly and in the ordinary course of business supplies information to the consumer credit reporting agency concerning any consumer or to whom a consumer credit report is provided by the consumer credit reporting agency. The notice shall specify the person's obligations under this title. Copies of the appropriate code sections shall satisfy the requirement of this subdivision. *(Added by Stats.1975, c. 1271, p. 3372, § 1. Amended by Stats.1992, c. 1194 (A.B.1629), § 5, operative July 1, 1993; Stats.1993, c. 285 (A.B.1340), § 6, eff. Aug. 2, 1993; Stats.1997, c. 768 (A.B.156), § 1, operative July 1, 1998.)*

§ 1785.15. Supplying files and information; right to information

(a) A consumer credit reporting agency shall supply files and information required under Section 1785.10 during normal business hours and on reasonable notice. In addition to the disclosure provided by this chapter and any disclosures received by the consumer, the consumer has the right to request and receive all of the following:

(1) Either a decoded written version of the file or a written copy of the file, including all information in the file at the time of the request, with an explanation of any code used.

(2) A credit score for the consumer, the key factors, and the related information, as defined in and required by Section 1785.15.1.

(3) A record of all inquiries, by recipient, that result in the provision of information concerning the consumer in connection with a credit transaction not initiated by the consumer and that were received by the consumer credit reporting agency in the 12–month period immediately preceding the request for disclosure under this section.

(4) The recipients, including end users specified in Section 1785.22, of any consumer credit report on the consumer which the consumer credit reporting agency has furnished:

(A) For employment purposes within the two-year period preceding the request.

(B) For any other purpose within the 12–month period preceding the request.

Identification for purposes of this paragraph shall include the name of the recipient or, if applicable, the fictitious business name under which the recipient does business disclosed in full. If requested by the consumer, the identification shall also include the address of the recipient.

(b) Files maintained on a consumer shall be disclosed promptly as follows:

(1) In person, at the location where the consumer credit reporting agency maintains the trained personnel required by subdivision (d), if he or she appears in person and furnishes proper identification.

(2) By mail, if the consumer makes a written request with proper identification for a copy of the file or a decoded written version of that file to be sent to the consumer at a specified address. A disclosure pursuant to this paragraph shall be deposited in the United States mail, postage prepaid, within five business days after the consumer's written request for the disclosure is received by the consumer credit reporting agency. Consumer credit reporting agencies complying with requests for mailings under this section shall not be liable for disclosures to third parties caused by mishandling of mail after the mailings leave the consumer credit reporting agencies.

(3) A summary of all information contained in files on a consumer and required to be provided by Section 1785.10 shall be provided by telephone, if the consumer has made a written request, with proper identification for telephone disclosure.

(4) Information in a consumer's file required to be provided in writing under this section may also be disclosed in another form if authorized by the consumer and if available from the consumer credit reporting agency. For this purpose, a consumer may request disclosure in person pursuant to Section 1785.10, by telephone upon disclosure of proper identification by the consumer, by electronic means if available from the consumer credit reporting agency, or by any other reasonable means that is available from the consumer credit reporting agency.

(c) "Proper identification," as used in subdivision (b) means that information generally deemed sufficient to identify a person. Only if the consumer is unable to reasonably identify himself or herself with the information described above may a consumer credit reporting agency require additional information concerning the consumer's employment and personal or family history in order to verify his or her identity.

(d) The consumer credit reporting agency shall provide trained personnel to explain to the consumer any information furnished him or her pursuant to Section 1785.10.

(e) The consumer shall be permitted to be accompanied by one other person of his or her choosing, who shall furnish reasonable identification. A consumer credit reporting agency may require the consumer to furnish a written statement granting permission to the consumer credit reporting agency to discuss the consumer's file in that person's presence.

(f) Any written disclosure by a consumer credit reporting agency to any consumer pursuant to this section shall include a written summary of all rights the consumer has under this title and, in the case of a consumer credit reporting agency that compiles and maintains consumer credit reports on a nationwide basis, a toll-free telephone number that the consumer can use to communicate with the consumer credit reporting agency. The written summary of rights required under this subdivision is sufficient if in substantially the following form:

"You have a right to obtain a copy of your credit file from a consumer credit reporting agency. You may be charged a reasonable fee not exceeding eight dollars ($8). There is no fee, however, if you have been turned down for credit, employment, insurance, or a rental dwelling because of information in your credit report within the preceding 60 days. The consumer credit reporting agency must provide someone to help you interpret the information in your credit file.

You have a right to dispute inaccurate information by contacting the consumer credit reporting agency directly. However, neither you nor any credit repair company or credit service organization has the right to have accurate, current, and verifiable information removed from your credit report. Under the Federal Fair Credit Reporting Act, the consumer credit reporting agency must remove accurate, negative information from your report only if it is over seven years old. Bankruptcy information can be reported for 10 years.

If you have notified a consumer credit reporting agency in writing that you dispute the accuracy of information in your file, the consumer credit reporting agency must then, within 30 business days, reinvestigate and modify or remove inaccurate information. The consumer credit reporting agency may not charge a fee for this service. Any pertinent information and copies of all documents you have concerning an error should be given to the consumer credit reporting agency.

If reinvestigation does not resolve the dispute to your satisfaction, you may send a brief statement to the consumer credit reporting agency to keep in your file, explaining why you think the record is inaccurate. The consumer credit reporting agency must include your statement about disputed information in a report it issues about you.

You have a right to receive a record of all inquiries relating to a credit transaction initiated in 12 months preceding your request. This record shall include the recipients of any consumer credit report.

You may request in writing that the information contained in your file not be provided to a third party for marketing purposes.

You have a right to place a "security alert" in your credit report, which will warn anyone who receives information in your credit report that your identity may have been used without your consent. Recipients of your credit report are required to take reasonable steps, including contacting you at the telephone number you may provide with your security alert, to verify your identity prior to lending money, extending credit, or completing the purchase, lease, or rental of goods or services. The security alert may prevent credit, loans, and services from being approved in your name without your consent. However, you should be aware that taking advantage of this right may delay or interfere with the timely approval of any subsequent request or application you make regarding a new loan, credit, mortgage, or cellular phone or other new account, including an extension of credit at point of sale. If you place a security alert on your credit report, you have a right to obtain a free copy of your credit report at the time the 90–day security alert period expires. A security alert may be requested by calling the following toll-free telephone number: (Insert applicable toll-free telephone number). California consumers also have the right to obtain a "security freeze."

You have a right to place a "security freeze" on your credit report, which will prohibit a consumer credit reporting agency from releasing any information in your credit report without your express authorization. A security freeze must be requested in writing by mail. The security freeze is designed to prevent credit, loans, and services from being approved in your name without your consent. However, you should be aware that using a security freeze to take control over who gets access to the personal and financial information in your credit report may delay, interfere with, or prohibit the timely approval of any subsequent request or application you make regarding a new loan, credit, mortgage, or cellular phone or other new account, including an extension of credit at point of sale. When you place a security freeze on your credit report, you will be provided a personal identification number or password to use if you choose to remove the freeze on your credit report or authorize the release of your credit report for a specific party or period of time after the freeze is in place. To provide that authorization you must contact the consumer credit reporting agency and provide all of the following:

(1) The personal identification number or password.

(2) Proper identification to verify your identity.

(3) The proper information regarding the third party who is to receive the credit report or the period of time for which the report shall be available to users of the credit report.

A consumer credit reporting agency must authorize the release of your credit report no later than three business days after receiving the above information.

A security freeze does not apply when you have an existing account and a copy of your report is requested by your existing creditor or its agents or affiliates for certain types of account review, collection, fraud control, or similar activities.

If you are actively seeking credit, you should understand that the procedures involved in lifting a security freeze may slow your application for credit. You should plan ahead and lift a freeze, either completely if you are shopping around, or specifically for a certain creditor, before applying for new credit.

A consumer credit reporting agency may not charge a fee to a consumer for placing or removing a security freeze if the consumer is a victim of identity theft and submits a copy of a valid police report or valid Department of Motor Vehicles investigative report. A person 65 years of age or older with proper identification may be charged a fee of no more than $5 for placing, lifting, or removing a security freeze. All other consumers may be charged a fee of no more than $10 for each of these steps.

You have a right to bring civil action against anyone, including a consumer credit reporting agency, who improperly obtains access to a file, knowingly or willfully misuses file data, or fails to correct inaccurate file data.

If you are a victim of identity theft and provide to a consumer credit reporting agency a copy of a valid police report or a valid investigative report made by a Department of Motor Vehicles investigator with peace officer status describing your circumstances, the following shall apply:

(1) You have a right to have any information you list on the report as allegedly fraudulent promptly blocked so that the information cannot be reported. The information will be unblocked only if (A) the information you provide is a material misrepresentation of the facts, (B) you agree that the information is blocked in error, or (C) you knowingly obtained possession of goods, services, or moneys as result of the blocked transactions. If blocked information is unblocked, you will be promptly notified.

(2) Beginning July 1, 2003, you have a right to receive, free of charge and upon request, one copy of your credit report each month for up to 12 consecutive months." *(Added by Stats.1975, c. 1271, p. 3373, § 1. Amended by Stats.1976, c. 666, p. 1639, § 3; Stats.1980, c. 1113, p. 3580, § 2; Stats.1992, c. 1194 (A.B.1629), § 6, operative July 1, 1993; Stats.2000, c. 978 (S.B.1607), § 2, operative July 1, 2001; Stats.2001, c. 720 (S.B.168), § 6; Stats.2002, c. 860 (S.B.1239), § 1; Stats.2003, c. 907 (S.B.25), § 3; Stats.2008, c. 151 (A.B.372), § 2.)*

§ 1785.15.1. Credit scores supplied upon request by consumer; key factors

(a) Upon the consumer's request for a credit score, a consumer credit reporting agency shall supply to a consumer a notice which shall include the information described in paragraphs (1) to (5), inclusive, and a statement indicating that the information and credit scoring model may be different than the credit score that may be used by the lender. However, if the consumer requests the credit file and not the credit score, then the consumer shall receive the credit file and a statement that he or she may request and obtain a credit score.

(1) The consumer's current credit score or the consumer's most recent credit score that was previously calculated by the credit reporting agency for a purpose related to the extension of credit.

(2) The range of possible credit scores under the model used.

(3) All the key factors that adversely affected the consumer's credit score in the model used, the total number of which shall not exceed four.

(4) The date the credit score was created.

(5) The name of the person or entity that provided the credit score or credit file upon which the credit score was created.

(b) For purposes of this act, "credit score" means a numerical value or a categorization derived from a statistical tool or modeling system used by a person who makes or arranges a loan to predict the likelihood of certain credit behaviors, including default. The numerical value or the categorization derived from this analysis may also be referred to as a "risk predictor" or "risk score." "Credit score" does not include any mortgage score or rating of an automated underwriting system that considers one or more factors in addition to credit information, including, but not limited to, the loan to value ratio, the amount of down payment, or a consumer's financial assets. "Credit score" does not include other elements of the underwriting process or underwriting decision.

(c) For the purposes of this section, "key factors" means all relevant elements or reasons adversely affecting the credit score for the particular individual listed in the order of their importance based on their effect on the credit score.

(d) The information required by this section shall be provided in the same timeframe and manner as the information described in Section 1785.15.

(e) This section shall not be construed to compel a consumer reporting agency to develop or disclose a score if the agency does not (1) distribute scores that are used in connection with residential real property loans, or (2) develop scores that assist credit providers in understanding a consumer's general credit behavior and predicting his or her future credit behavior.

(f) This section shall not be construed to require a consumer credit reporting agency that distributes credit scores developed by another person or entity to provide a further explanation of them, or to process a dispute arising pursuant to subdivision (a) of Section 1785.16, except that the consumer credit reporting agency shall provide the consumer with the name and address and website for contacting the person or entity who developed the score or developed the methodology of the score. This subdivision does not apply to a consumer credit reporting agency that develops or modifies scores that are developed by another person or entity.

(g) This section shall not be construed to require a consumer reporting agency to maintain credit scores in its files. *(Added by Stats.2000, c. 978 (S.B.1607), § 3, operative July 1, 2001.)*

§ 1785.15.2. Credit scoring model

(a) In complying with Section 1785.15.1, a consumer credit reporting agency shall supply the consumer with a credit score that is derived from a credit scoring model that is widely distributed to users by that consumer credit reporting agency in connection with residential real property loans or with a credit score that assists the consumer in understanding the credit scoring assessment of his or her credit behavior and predictions about his or her future credit behavior, and a statement indicating that the information and credit scoring model may be different than that used by the lender.

(b) A consumer credit reporting agency may charge a reasonable fee for providing the information required under Section 1785.15.1. *(Added by Stats.2000, c. 978 (S.B.1607), § 4, operative July 1, 2001.)*

§ 1785.18. Matters of public record; source; reports for employment purposes; prohibited information

(a) Each consumer credit reporting agency which compiles and reports items of information concerning consumers which are matters of public record, shall specify in any report containing public record information the source from which that information was obtained, including the particular court, if there be such, and the date that the information was initially reported or publicized.

(b) A consumer credit reporting agency which furnishes a consumer credit report for employment purposes, and which for that purpose compiles and reports items of information on consumers which are matters of public record and are likely to have an adverse effect upon a consumer's ability to obtain employment shall, in addition, maintain strict procedures designed to ensure that whenever public record information which is likely to have an adverse effect on a consumer's ability to obtain employment is reported it is complete and up to date. For purposes of this paragraph, items of public record relating to arrests, indictments, convictions, suits, tax liens, and outstanding judgments shall be considered up to date if the current public record status of the item at the time of the report is reported.

(c) No consumer credit reporting agency which furnishes a consumer credit report for employment purposes shall report information on the age, marital status, race, color, or creed of any consumer. *(Added by Stats.1975, c. 1271, p. 3375, § 1. Amended by Stats.1991, c. 971 (A.B.1102), § 1.)*

CHAPTER 3. REQUIREMENTS ON USERS OF CONSUMER CREDIT REPORTS

Section
1785.20.5. Report for employment purposes; prior notice to person involved; contemporaneous copies for user and subject; denial of employment; identity of reporter; notice by user to consumer; liability.

§ 1785.20.5. Report for employment purposes; prior notice to person involved; contemporaneous copies for user and subject; denial of employment; identity of reporter; notice by user to consumer; liability

(a) Prior to requesting a consumer credit report for employment purposes, the user of the report shall provide written notice to the person involved. The notice shall inform the person that a report will be used and the source of the report, and shall contain a box that the person may check off to receive a copy of the credit report. If the consumer indicates that he or she wishes to receive a copy of the report, the user shall request that a copy be provided to the person when the user requests its copy from the credit reporting agency. The report to the user and to the subject person shall be provided contemporaneously and at no charge to the subject person.

(b) Whenever employment involving a consumer is denied either wholly or partly because of information contained in a consumer credit report from a consumer credit reporting agency, the user of the consumer credit report shall so advise the consumer against whom the adverse action has been taken and supply the name and address or addresses of the consumer credit reporting agency making the report. No person shall be held liable for any violation of this section if he or she shows by a preponderance of the evidence that, at the time of the alleged violation, he or she maintained reasonable procedures to assure compliance with this section. *(Added by Stats.1976, c. 666, p. 1643, § 7.5. Amended by Stats.1991, c. 971 (A.B.1102), § 2.)*

Title 1.6A

INVESTIGATIVE CONSUMER REPORTING AGENCIES

Article 1. GENERAL PROVISIONS

Section
1786.   Legislative findings and declaration.
1786.1.   Short title.
1786.2.   Definitions.

§ 1786. Legislative findings and declaration

The Legislature finds and declares as follows:

(a) Investigative consumer reporting agencies have assumed a vital role in collecting, assembling, evaluating, compiling, reporting, transmitting, transferring, or communicating information on consumers for employment and insurance purposes, and for purposes relating to the hiring of dwelling units, subpoenas and court orders, licensure, and other lawful purposes.

(b) There is a need to insure that investigative consumer reporting agencies exercise their grave responsibilities with fairness, impartiality, and a respect for the consumer's right to privacy.

(c) The crime of identity theft in this new computer era has exploded to become the fastest growing white collar crime in America.

(d) The unique nature of this crime means it can often go undetected for years without the victim being aware his identity has been misused.

(e) Because notice of identity theft is critical before the victim can take steps to stop and prosecute this crime,

consumers are best protected if they are automatically given copies of any investigative consumer reports made on them.

(f) It is the purpose of this title to require that investigative consumer reporting agencies adopt reasonable procedures for meeting the needs of commerce for employment, insurance information, and information relating to the hiring of dwelling units in a manner which is fair and equitable to the consumer, with regard to the confidentiality, accuracy, relevancy, and proper utilization of the information in accordance with the requirements of this title.

(g) The Legislature hereby intends to regulate investigative consumer reporting agencies pursuant to this title in a manner which will best protect the interests of the people of the State of California. *(Added by Stats.1975, c. 1272, p. 3378, § 1. Amended by Stats.1982, c. 1127, p. 4065, § 6; Stats.2001, c. 354 (A.B.655), § 6.)*

§ 1786.1. Short title

This title may be referred to as the Investigative Consumer Reporting Agencies Act. *(Added by Stats. 1975, c. 1272, p. 3378, § 1.)*

§ 1786.2. Definitions

The following terms as used in this title have the meaning expressed in this section:

(a) The term "person" means any individual, partnership, corporation, limited liability company, trust, estate, cooperative, association, government or governmental subdivision or agency, or other entity. The term "person" as used in this title shall not be construed to require duplicative reporting by any individual, corporation, trust, estate, cooperative, association, government, or governmental subdivision or agency, or other entity involved in the same transaction.

(b) The term "consumer" means a natural individual who has made application to a person for employment purposes, for insurance for personal, family, or household purposes, or the hiring of a dwelling unit, as defined in subdivision (c) of Section 1940.

(c) The term "investigative consumer report" means a consumer report in which information on a consumer's character, general reputation, personal characteristics, or mode of living is obtained through any means. The term does not include a consumer report or other compilation of information that is limited to specific factual information relating to a consumer's credit record or manner of obtaining credit obtained directly from a creditor of the consumer or from a consumer reporting agency when that information was obtained directly from a potential or existing creditor of the consumer or from the consumer. Notwithstanding the foregoing, for transactions between investigative consumer reporting agencies and insurance institutions, agents, or insurance-support organizations subject to Article 6.6 (commencing with Section 791) of Chapter 1 of Part 2 of Division 1 of the Insurance Code, the term "investigative consumer report" shall have the meaning set forth in subdivision (n) of Section 791.02 of the Insurance Code.

(d) The term "investigative consumer reporting agency" means any person who, for monetary fees or dues, engages in whole or in part in the practice of collecting, assembling, evaluating, compiling, reporting, transmitting, transferring, or communicating information concerning consumers for the purposes of furnishing investigative consumer reports to third parties, but does not include any governmental agency whose records are maintained primarily for traffic safety, law enforcement, or licensing purposes, or any licensed insurance agent, insurance broker, or solicitor, insurer, or life insurance agent.

(e) The term "file," when used in connection with information on any consumer, means all of the information on that consumer recorded and retained by an investigative consumer reporting agency regardless of how the information is stored.

(f) The term "employment purposes," when used in connection with an investigative consumer report, means a report used for the purpose of evaluating a consumer for employment, promotion, reassignment, or retention as an employee.

(g) The term "medical information" means information on a person's medical history or condition obtained directly or indirectly from a licensed physician, medical practitioner, hospital, clinic, or other medical or medically related facility. *(Added by Stats.1975, c. 1272, p. 3378, § 1. Amended by Stats.1976, c. 1150, p. 5209, § 1; Stats.1982, c. 1127, p. 4066, § 7; Stats.1994, c. 1010 (S.B.2053), § 36; Stats.1998, c. 988 (S.B.1454), § 1; Stats.2001, c. 354 (A.B.655), § 7.)*

Article 2

OBLIGATIONS OF INVESTIGATIVE CONSUMER REPORTING AGENCIES

Section
1786.10. Inspection of files by consumer; availability; sources; discovery; identification of recipients; disclosure.
1786.11. Availability of report to consumer.
1786.12. Furnishing consumer report; circumstances.
1786.14. Report to governmental agency.
1786.16. Procurement or preparation of report; conditions; insurance; employment; dwelling unit hiring; disclosure of nature and scope of investigation.
1786.18. Items of information prohibited.
1786.20. Agency reporting procedures; records; identity of user and uses to be made of reports.
1786.22. Supplying files and information; time; methods.
1786.24. Disputes as to completeness and accuracy of file; reinvestigation; notice to sources; contents; frivolous or irrelevant dispute; deletion and reinsertion of information; notice to consumer; statement of dispute.
1786.26. Allowable fees charged to consumer by an investigative consumer reporting agency for making disclosures to consumer; other disclosures without charge.
1786.28. Matters of public record; source; reports for employment purposes.
1786.29. Notices to be provided by investigative consumer reporting agency.
1786.30. Subsequent reports; verification.
1786.40. Consumer insurance request denied; notice to consumer of adverse action.

§ 1786.10. Inspection of files by consumer; availability; sources; discovery; identification of recipients; disclosure

(a) Every investigative consumer reporting agency shall, upon request and proper identification of any consumer, allow the consumer to visually inspect all files maintained regarding the consumer at the time of the request.

(b)(1) All items of information shall be available for inspection, except that the sources of information, other than public records and records from databases available for sale, acquired solely for use in preparing an investigative consumer report and actually used for no other purpose need not be disclosed. However, if an action is brought under this title, those sources shall be available to the consumer under appropriate discovery procedures in the court in which the action is brought.

(2) This title shall not be interpreted to mean that investigative consumer reporting agencies are required to divulge to consumers the sources of investigative consumer reports, except in appropriate discovery procedures as outlined in this title.

(c) The investigative consumer reporting agency shall also identify the recipients of any investigative consumer report on the consumer that the investigative consumer reporting agency has furnished for either of the following purposes:

(1) For employment or insurance purposes within the three-year period preceding the request.

(2) For any other purpose within the three-year period preceding the request.

(d) The identification of a recipient under subdivision (c) shall include the name of the recipient or, if applicable, the trade name (written in full) under which the recipient conducts business and, upon request of the consumer, the address and telephone number of the recipient.

(e) The investigative consumer reporting agency shall also disclose the dates, original payees, and amounts of any checks or charges upon which is based any adverse characterization of the consumer, included in the file at the time of the disclosure. *(Added by Stats.1975, c. 1272, p. 3379, § 1. Amended by Stats.1998, c. 988 (S.B.1454), § 2; Stats.2001, c. 354 (A.B.655), § 8; Stats.2006, c. 538 (S.B.1852), § 45.)*

§ 1786.11. Availability of report to consumer

Every investigative consumer reporting agency that provides an investigative consumer report to a person other than the consumer shall make a copy of that report available, upon request and proper identification, to the consumer for at least two years after the date that the report is provided to the other person. *(Added by Stats.1998, c. 988 (S.B.1454), § 3. Amended by Stats. 2001, c. 354 (A.B.655), § 9; Stats.2002, c. 1029 (A.B. 2868), § 3, eff. Sept. 28, 2002.)*

§ 1786.12. Furnishing consumer report; circumstances

An investigative consumer reporting agency shall only furnish an investigative consumer report under the following circumstances:

(a) In response to the order of a court having jurisdiction to issue the order.

(b) In compliance with a lawful subpoena issued by a court of competent jurisdiction.

(c) In accordance with the written instructions of the consumer to whom it relates.

(d) To a person that it has reason to believe:

(1) Intends to use the information for employment purposes; or

(2) Intends to use the information serving as a factor in determining a consumer's eligibility for insurance or the rate for any insurance; or

(3) Intends to use the information in connection with a determination of the consumer's eligibility for a license or other benefit granted by a governmental instrumentality required by law to consider the applicant's financial responsibility or status; or

(4) Intends to use the information in connection with an order of a court of competent jurisdiction to provide support where the imposition or enforcement of the order involves the consumer; or

(5) Intends to use the information in connection with the hiring of a dwelling unit, as defined in subdivision (c) of Section 1940.

(e) An investigative consumer reporting agency shall not prepare or furnish an investigative consumer report to a person described in subdivision (d) unless the agency has received the certification under paragraph (4) of subdivision (a) of Section 1786.16 from the person requesting the report.

(f) An investigative consumer reporting agency shall not furnish an investigative consumer report to a person described in subdivision (d) if that report contains medical information about a consumer, unless the consumer consents to the furnishing of the report. *(Added by Stats.1975, c. 1272, p. 3380, § 1. Amended by Stats. 1976, c. 1150, p. 5210, § 2; Stats.1982, c. 1127, p. 4067, § 8; Stats.1998, c. 988 (S.B.1454), § 4.)*

§ 1786.14. Report to governmental agency

Notwithstanding the provisions of Section 1786.12 an investigative consumer reporting agency may furnish to a governmental agency a consumer's name, address, former address, places of employment, or former places of employment. *(Added by Stats.1975, c. 1272, p. 3380, § 1.)*

§ 1786.16. Procurement or preparation of report; conditions; insurance; employment; dwelling unit hiring; disclosure of nature and scope of investigation

(a) Any person described in subdivision (d) of Section 1786.12 shall not procure or cause to be prepared an investigative consumer report unless the following applicable conditions are met:

(1) If an investigative consumer report is sought in connection with the underwriting of insurance, it shall be clearly and accurately disclosed in writing at the time the application form, medical form, binder, or similar document is signed by the consumer that an investigative consumer report regarding the consumer's character, general reputation, personal characteristics, and mode of living may be made. If no signed application form, medical form, binder, or similar document is involved in the underwriting transaction, the disclosure shall be made to the consumer in writing and mailed or otherwise delivered to the consumer not later than three days after the report was first requested. The disclosure shall include the name and address of any investigative consumer reporting agency conducting an investigation, plus the nature and scope of the investigation requested, and a summary of the provisions of Section 1786.22.

(2) If, at any time, an investigative consumer report is sought for employment purposes other than suspicion of wrongdoing or misconduct by the subject of the investigation, the person seeking the investigative consumer report may procure the report, or cause the report to be made, only if all of the following apply:

(A) The person procuring or causing the report to be made has a permissible purpose, as defined in Section 1786.12.

(B) The person procuring or causing the report to be made provides a clear and conspicuous disclosure in writing to the consumer at any time before the report is procured or caused to be made in a document that consists solely of the disclosure, that:

(i) An investigative consumer report may be obtained.

(ii) The permissible purpose of the report is identified.

(iii) The disclosure may include information on the consumer's character, general reputation, personal characteristics, and mode of living.

(iv) Identifies the name, address, and telephone number of the investigative consumer reporting agency conducting the investigation.

(v) Notifies the consumer in writing of the nature and scope of the investigation requested, including a summary of the provisions of Section 1786.22.

(C) The consumer has authorized in writing the procurement of the report.

(3) If an investigative consumer report is sought in connection with the hiring of a dwelling unit, as defined in subdivision (c) of Section 1940, the person procuring or causing the request to be made shall, not later than three days after the date on which the report was first requested, notify the consumer in writing that an investigative consumer report will be made regarding the consumer's character, general reputation, personal characteristics, and mode of living. The notification shall also include the name and address of the investigative consumer reporting agency that will prepare the report and a summary of the provisions of Section 1786.22.

(4) The person procuring or causing the request to be made shall certify to the investigative consumer reporting agency that the person has made the applicable disclosures to the consumer required by this subdivision and that the person will comply with subdivision (b).

(5) The person procuring the report or causing it to be prepared agrees to provide a copy of the report to the subject of the investigation, as provided in subdivision (b).

(b) Any person described in subdivision (d) of Section 1786.12 who requests an investigative consumer report, in accordance with subdivision (a) regarding that consumer, shall do the following:

(1) Provide the consumer a means by which the consumer may indicate on a written form, by means of a box to check, that the consumer wishes to receive a copy of any report that is prepared. If the consumer wishes to receive a copy of the report, the recipient of the report shall send a copy of the report to the consumer within three business days of the date that the report is provided to the recipient, who may contract with any other entity to send a copy to the consumer. The notice to request the report may be contained on either the disclosure form, as required by subdivision (a), or a separate consent form. The copy of the report shall contain the name, address, and telephone number of the person who issued the report and how to contact them.

(2) Comply with Section 1786.40, if the taking of adverse action is a consideration.

(c) Subdivisions (a) and (b) do not apply to an investigative consumer report procured or caused to be prepared by an employer, if the report is sought for employment purposes due to suspicion held by an employer of wrongdoing or misconduct by the subject of the investigation.

(d) Those persons described in subdivision (d) of Section 1786.12 constitute the sole and exclusive class of persons who may cause an investigative consumer report to be prepared. *(Added by Stats.1975, c. 1272, p. 3380, § 1. Amended by Stats.1976, c. 1150, p. 5210, § 3; Stats.1982, c. 1127, p. 4067, § 9; Stats.1998, c. 988 (S.B.1454), § 5; Stats.2001, c. 354 (A.B.655), § 10; Stats. 2002, c. 1030 (A.B.1068), § 3, eff. Sept. 28, 2002.)*

§ 1786.18. Items of information prohibited

(a) Except as authorized under subdivision (b), an investigative consumer reporting agency may not make or furnish any investigative consumer report containing any of the following items of information:

(1) Bankruptcies that, from the date of * * * the order for relief, antedate the report by more than 10 years.

(2) Suits that, from the date of filing, and satisfied judgments that, from the date of entry, antedate the report by more than seven years.

(3) Unsatisfied judgments that, from the date of entry, antedate the report by more than seven years.

(4) Unlawful detainer actions where the defendant was the prevailing party or where the action is resolved by settlement agreement.

(5) Paid tax liens that, from the date of payment, antedate the report by more than seven years.

(6) Accounts placed for collection or charged to profit and loss that antedate the report by more than seven years.

(7) Records of arrest, indictment, information, misdemeanor complaint, or conviction of a crime that, from the date of disposition, release, or parole, antedate the report by more than seven years. These items of information shall no longer be reported if at any time it is learned that, in the case of a conviction, a full pardon has been granted or, in the case of an arrest, indictment, information, or misdemeanor complaint, a conviction did not result; except that records of arrest, indictment, information, or misdemeanor complaints may be reported pending pronouncement of judgment on the particular subject matter of those records.

(8) Any other adverse information that antedates the report by more than seven years.

(b) The provisions of subdivision (a) are not applicable in either of the following circumstances:

(1) If the investigative consumer report is to be used in the underwriting of life insurance involving, or that may reasonably be expected to involve, an amount of two hundred fifty thousand dollars ($250,000) or more.

(2) If the investigative consumer report is to be used by an employer who is explicitly required by a governmental regulatory agency to check for records that are prohibited by subdivision (a) when the employer is reviewing a consumer's qualification for employment.

(c) Except as otherwise provided in Section 1786.28, an investigative consumer reporting agency shall not furnish an investigative consumer report that includes information that is a matter of public record and that relates to an arrest, indictment, conviction, civil judicial action, tax lien, or outstanding judgment, unless the agency has verified the accuracy of the information during the 30-day period ending on the date on which the report is furnished.

(d) An investigative consumer reporting agency shall not prepare or furnish an investigative consumer report on a consumer that contains information that is adverse to the interest of the consumer and that is obtained through a personal interview with a neighbor, friend, or associate of the consumer or with another person with whom the consumer is acquainted or who has knowledge of the item of information, unless either (1) the investigative consumer reporting agency has followed reasonable procedures to obtain confirmation of the information, from an additional source that has independent and direct knowledge of the information, or (2) the person interviewed is the best possible source of the information. *(Added by Stats.1975, c. 1272, p. 3381, § 1. Amended by Stats.1982, c. 1127, p. 4068, § 10; Stats.1991, c. 965 (A.B.1796), § 2; Stats.1998, c. 988 (S.B.1454), § 6; Stats. 2001, c. 354 (A.B.655), § 11; Stats.2002, c. 1029 (A.B. 2868), § 4, eff. Sept. 28, 2002; Stats.2009, c. 500 (A.B. 1059), § 11.)*

§ 1786.20. Agency reporting procedures; records; identity of user and uses to be made of reports

(a) An investigative consumer reporting agency shall maintain reasonable procedures designed to avoid violations of Section 1786.18 and to limit furnishing of investigative consumer reports for the purposes listed under Section 1786.12. These procedures shall require that prospective users of the information identify themselves, certify the purposes for which the information is sought and that the information will be used for no other purposes, and make the certifications described in paragraph (4) of subdivision (a) of Section 1786.16. From the effective date of this title, the investigative consumer reporting agency shall keep a record of the purposes for which information is sought, as stated by the user. The investigative consumer reporting agency may assume that the purpose for which a user seeks information remains the same as that which a user has previously stated. The investigative consumer reporting agency shall inform the user that the user is obligated to notify the agency of any change in the purpose for which information will be used. An investigative consumer reporting agency shall make a reasonable effort to verify the identity of a new prospective user and the uses certified by the prospective user prior to furnishing the user any investigative consumer reports. An investigative consumer reporting agency may not furnish an investigative consumer report to a person unless it has a written agreement that the investigative consumer reports will be used by that person only for purposes listed in Section 1786.12.

(b) Whenever an investigative consumer reporting agency prepares an investigative consumer report, it shall follow reasonable procedures to assure maximum possible accuracy of the information concerning the individual about whom the report relates. An investigative consumer reporting agency shall retain the investigative consumer report for two years after the report is provided.

(c) An investigative consumer reporting agency may not make an inquiry for the purpose of preparing an investigative consumer report on a consumer for employment purposes if the making of the inquiry by an employer or prospective employer of the consumer would violate applicable federal or state equal employment opportunity law or regulation.

(Added by Stats.1975, c. 1272, p. 3381, § 1. Amended by Stats.1998, c. 988 (S.B.1454), § 7; Stats.2001, c. 354 (A.B.655), § 12; Stats.2002, c. 1029 (A.B.2868), § 5, eff. Sept. 28, 2002; Stats.2003, c. 146 (A.B.1399), § 1.)

§ 1786.22. Supplying files and information; time; methods

(a) An investigative consumer reporting agency shall supply files and information required under Section 1786.10 during normal business hours and on reasonable notice.

(b) Files maintained on a consumer shall be made available for the consumer's visual inspection, as follows:

(1) In person, if he appears in person and furnishes proper identification. A copy of his file shall also be available to the consumer for a fee not to exceed the actual costs of duplication services provided.

(2) By certified mail, if he makes a written request, with proper identification, for copies to be sent to a specified addressee. Investigative consumer reporting agencies complying with requests for certified mailings under this section shall not be liable for disclosures to third parties caused by mishandling of mail after such mailings leave the investigative consumer reporting agencies.

(3) A summary of all information contained in files on a consumer and required to be provided by Section 1786.10 shall be provided by telephone, if the consumer has made a written request, with proper identification for telephone disclosure, and the toll charge, if any, for the telephone call is prepaid by or charged directly to the consumer.

(c) The term "proper identification" as used in subdivision (b) shall mean that information generally deemed sufficient to identify a person. Such information includes documents such as a valid driver's license, social security account number, military identification card, and credit cards. Only if the consumer is unable to reasonably identify himself with the information described above, may an investigative consumer reporting agency require additional information concerning the consumer's employment and personal or family history in order to verify his identity.

(d) The investigative consumer reporting agency shall provide trained personnel to explain to the consumer any information furnished him pursuant to Section 1786.10.

(e) The investigative consumer reporting agency shall provide a written explanation of any coded information contained in files maintained on a consumer. This written explanation shall be distributed whenever a file is provided to a consumer for visual inspection as required under Section 1786.22.

(f) The consumer shall be permitted to be accompanied by one other person of his choosing, who shall furnish reasonable identification. An investigative consumer reporting agency may require the consumer to furnish a written statement granting permission to the consumer reporting agency to discuss the consumer's file in such person's presence. *(Added by Stats.1975, c. 1272, p. 3382, § 1. Amended by Stats.1976, c. 666, p. 1645, § 16.)*

§ 1786.24. Disputes as to completeness and accuracy of file; reinvestigation; notice to sources; contents; frivolous or irrelevant dispute; deletion and reinsertion of information; notice to consumer; statement of dispute

(a) If the completeness or accuracy of any item of information contained in his or her file is disputed by a consumer, and the dispute is conveyed directly to the investigative consumer reporting agency by the consumer, the investigative consumer reporting agency shall, without charge, reinvestigate and record the current status of the disputed information or delete the item from the file in accordance with subdivision (c), before the end of the 30–day period beginning on the date on which the agency receives the notice of the dispute from the consumer.

(b) The agency shall notify any person who provided information in dispute at the address and in the manner specified by that person. The notice shall include all relevant information regarding the dispute that the investigative consumer reporting agency has received from the consumer. The agency shall also promptly provide to the person who provided the information in dispute all relevant information regarding the dispute that is received by the agency from the consumer during the reinvestigation.

(c) In conducting a reinvestigation, the investigative consumer reporting agency shall review and consider all relevant information submitted by the consumer with respect to the disputed item of information.

(d) Notwithstanding subdivision (a), an investigative consumer reporting agency may terminate a reinvestigation of information disputed by a consumer if the investigative consumer reporting agency reasonably determines that the dispute is frivolous or irrelevant, including by reason of a failure by a consumer to provide sufficient information to investigate the disputed information. Upon making a determination that a dispute is frivolous or irrelevant, the investigative consumer reporting agency shall notify the consumer, by mail or, if authorized by the consumer for that purpose, by any other means available to the agency. In this notification, the investigative consumer reporting agency shall state the specific reasons why it has determined that the consumer's dispute is frivolous or irrelevant and provide a description of any information required to investigate the disputed information, that may consist of a standardized form describing the general nature of the required information.

(e) If a reinvestigation is made and, after reinvestigation, the disputed item of information is found to be inaccurate, incomplete, or cannot be verified by the evidence submitted, the investigative consumer reporting agency shall promptly delete that information from the consumer's file or modify the information, as appropriate, based on the results of the reinvestigation, and shall notify the consumer that the information has been deleted or modified. The consumer reporting agency shall also notify any and all sources from which the disputed information was obtained and inform them in writing of the reasons and results of the reinvestigation, and send a copy of this notification to the consumer. In accordance with subdivision (b) of Section 1786.10, the copy of the notification sent to the consumer need not reveal the identity of the source of information, unless otherwise required by law.

(f) No information may be reinserted in the file of a consumer after having been deleted pursuant to this section, unless the person who furnished the information verifies that the information is complete and accurate. If any information deleted from the file of a consumer is reinserted in the file, the investigative consumer reporting agency shall promptly notify the consumer of the reinsertion in writing or, if authorized by the consumer for that purpose, by any other means available to the agency. As part of, or in addition to, this notice, the investigative consumer reporting agency shall provide to the consumer in writing (1) a statement that the disputed information has been reinserted, (2) the name, address, and telephone number of any furnisher of information contacted or that contacted the investigative consumer reporting agency in connection with the reinsertion, and the telephone number of the furnisher, if reasonably available, and (3) a notice that the consumer has the right to a reinvestigation of the information reinserted by the investigative consumer reporting agency and to add a statement to his or her file disputing the accuracy or completeness of the information.

(g) An investigative consumer reporting agency shall provide notice to the consumer of the results of any reinvestigation under this section by mail or, if authorized by the consumer for that purpose, by other means available to the agency. The notice shall include (1) a statement that the reinvestigation is completed, (2) an investigative consumer report that is based on the consumer's file as that file is revised as a result of the reinvestigation, (3) a description or indication of any changes made in the investigative consumer report as a result of those revisions to the consumer's file, (4) a notice that, if requested by the consumer, a description of the procedure used to determine the accuracy and completeness of the information shall be provided to the consumer by the investigative consumer reporting agency, including the name, business address, and telephone number of any furnisher of information contacted in connection with that information, (5) a notice that the consumer has the right to add a statement to the consumer's file disputing the accuracy or completeness of the information, and (6) a notice that the consumer has the right to request that the investigative consumer reporting agency furnish notifications under subdivision (k).

(h) The presence of information in the consumer's file that contradicts the contention of the consumer shall not, in and of itself, constitute reasonable grounds for believing the dispute is frivolous or irrelevant.

(i) If the investigative consumer reporting agency determines that the dispute is frivolous or irrelevant, or if the reinvestigation does not resolve the dispute, or if the information is reinserted into the file of a consumer pursuant to subdivision (f), the consumer may file a brief statement setting forth the nature of the dispute. The investigative consumer reporting agency may limit these statements to not more than 500 words if it provides the consumer with assistance in writing a clear summary of the dispute.

(j) If a statement of dispute is filed, the investigative consumer reporting agency shall, in any subsequent investigative consumer report containing the information in question, clearly note that the information is disputed by the consumer and shall include in the report either the statement of the consumer or a clear and accurate summary thereof.

(k) Following the deletion of information from the file of a consumer pursuant to this section, or following the filing of a dispute pursuant to subdivision (i), the investigative consumer reporting agency shall, at the request of the consumer, furnish notification that the item of information has been deleted or that the item of information is disputed. In the case of disputed information, the notification shall include the statement or summary of the dispute filed pursuant to subdivision (i). This notification shall be furnished to any person who has, within two years prior to the deletion or the filing of the dispute, received an investigative consumer report concerning the consumer for employment purposes, or who has, within one year of the deletion or the filing of the dispute, received an investigative consumer report concerning the consumer for any other purpose, if these investigative consumer reports contained the deleted or disputed information, unless the consumer specifically requests in writing that this notification not be given to all persons or to any specified persons. The investigative consumer reporting agency shall clearly and conspicuously disclose to the consumer his or her rights to make a request that this notification not be made.

(*l*) An investigative consumer reporting agency shall maintain reasonable procedures designed to prevent the reappearance in the file of a consumer and in investigative consumer reports information that has been deleted pursuant to this section and not reinserted pursuant to subdivision (f).

(m) If the dispute of a consumer is resolved by deletion of the disputed information within three business days, beginning with the day the investigative consumer reporting agency receives notice of the dispute in accor-

dance with subdivision (a), the investigative consumer reporting agency is exempt from requirements for further action under subdivisions (g), (i), and (j), if the agency: (1) provides prompt notice of the deletion to the consumer by telephone, (2) provides written confirmation of the deletion and a copy of an investigative consumer report of the consumer that is based on the file of a consumer after the deletion, and (3) includes, in the telephone notice or in a written notice that accompanies the confirmation and report, a statement of the consumer's right to request under subdivision (k) that the agency not furnish notifications under that subdivision.

(n) Any investigative consumer reporting agency that compiles and maintains files on consumers on a nationwide basis, as defined in the federal Fair Credit Reporting Act, as amended (15 U.S.C. Sec. 1681 et seq.), shall implement an automated system through which furnishers of information to that agency may report the results of a reinvestigation that finds incomplete or inaccurate information in the file of a consumer to other investigative consumer reporting agencies.

(*o*) All actions to be taken by an investigative consumer reporting agency under this section are governed by the applicable time periods specified in Section 611 of the federal Fair Credit Reporting Act, as amended (15 U.S.C. Sec. 1681i). *(Added by Stats.1975, c. 1272, p. 3383, § 1. Amended by Stats.1998, c. 988 (S.B.1454), § 8; Stats.2001, c. 354 (A.B.655), § 13; Stats.2002, c. 1029 (A.B.2868), § 6, eff. Sept. 28, 2002; Stats.2002, c. 1030 (A.B.1068), § 4, eff. Sept. 28, 2002; Stats.2004, c. 183 (A.B.3082), § 32.)*

§ 1786.26. Allowable fees charged to consumer by an investigative consumer reporting agency for making disclosures to consumer; other disclosures without charge

(a) Except as otherwise provided in subdivision (c), an investigative consumer reporting agency may charge a consumer a fee not exceeding eight dollars ($8) for making disclosures to the consumer pursuant to Sections 1786.10, 1786.11, and 1786.22. Any charges shall be indicated to the consumer prior to disclosure.

(b) An investigative consumer reporting agency shall not impose any charge for providing notice to a consumer required under Section 1786.24, furnishing an investigative consumer report pursuant to Section 1786.24, or notifying a person pursuant to subdivision (k) of Section 1786.24 of the deletion of information that is found to be inaccurate or that cannot be verified.

(c) Upon the request of the consumer, an investigative consumer reporting agency shall make all disclosures pursuant to Section 1786.10 and 1786.22 once during any 12–month period without charge to that consumer if the consumer certifies in writing that he or she (1) is unemployed and intends to apply for employment in the 60–day period beginning on the date the certification is made, (2) is a recipient of public welfare assistance, or (3) has reason to believe that the file on the consumer at the investigative consumer reporting agency contains inaccurate information due to fraud.

(d) An investigative consumer reporting agency shall not impose any charge on a consumer for providing any notification or making any disclosure required by this title, except as authorized by this section. *(Added by Stats.1975, c. 1272, p. 3384, § 1. Amended by Stats.1976, c. 666, p. 1646, § 17; Stats.1977, c. 579, p. 1838, § 31; Stats.1998, c. 988 (S.B.1454), § 9; Stats.2001, c. 354 (A.B.655), § 14.)*

§ 1786.28. Matters of public record; source; reports for employment purposes

(a) Each investigative consumer reporting agency that collects, assembles, evaluates, compiles, reports, transmits, transfers, or communicates items of information concerning consumers which are matters of public record shall specify in any report containing public record information the source from which this information was obtained, including the particular court, if applicable, and the date that this information was initially reported or publicized.

(b) A consumer reporting agency which furnishes a consumer report for employment purposes and which for that purpose compiles, collects, assembles, evaluates, reports, transmits, transfers, or communicates items of information on consumers which are matters of public record and are likely to have an adverse effect upon a consumer's ability to obtain employment shall in addition maintain strict procedures designed to insure that whenever public record information which is likely to have an adverse effect on a consumer's ability to obtain employment is reported it is complete and up to date. For purposes of this paragraph, items of public record relating to arrests, indictments, convictions, suits, tax liens, and outstanding judgments shall be considered up to date if the current public record status of the item at the time of the report is reported. *(Added by Stats.1975, c. 1272, p. 3384, § 1. Amended by Stats.2001, c. 354 (A.B.655), § 15.)*

§ 1786.29. Notices to be provided by investigative consumer-reporting agency

An investigative consumer reporting agency shall provide the following notices on the first page of an investigative consumer report:

(a) A notice in at least 12–point boldface type setting forth that the report does not guarantee the accuracy or truthfulness of the information as to the subject of the investigation, but only that it is accurately copied from public records, and information generated as a result of identity theft, including evidence of criminal activity, may be inaccurately associated with the consumer who is the subject of the report.

(b) An investigative consumer reporting agency shall provide a consumer seeking to obtain a copy of a report or making a request to review a file, a written notice in simple, plain English and Spanish setting forth the terms

and conditions of his or her right to receive all disclosures, as provided in Section 1786.26. *(Added by Stats. 2001, c. 354 (A.B.655), § 16. Amended by Stats.2002, c. 1030 (A.B.1068), § 5, eff. Sept. 28, 2002.)*

§ 1786.30. Subsequent reports; verification

Whenever an investigative consumer reporting agency prepares an investigative consumer report, no adverse information in the report (other than information that is a matter of public record, the status of which has been updated pursuant to Section 1786.28) may be included in a subsequent investigative consumer report unless that adverse information has been verified in the process of making the subsequent investigative consumer report, or the adverse information was received within the three-month period preceding the date the subsequent report is furnished. *(Added by Stats.1975, c. 1272, p. 3385, § 1. Amended by Stats.1998, c. 988 (S.B.1454), § 10.)*

§ 1786.40. Consumer insurance request denied; notice to consumer of adverse action

(a) Whenever insurance for personal, family, or household purposes, employment, or the hiring of a dwelling unit involving a consumer is denied, or the charge for that insurance or the hiring of a dwelling unit is increased, under circumstances in which a report regarding the consumer was obtained from an investigative consumer reporting agency, the user of the investigative consumer report shall so advise the consumer against whom the adverse action has been taken and supply the name and address of the investigative consumer reporting agency making the report.

(b) Whenever insurance for personal, family, or household purposes involving a consumer is denied or the charge for that insurance is increased, either wholly or in part because of information bearing upon the consumer's general reputation, personal characteristics, or mode of living, that was obtained from a person other than an investigative consumer reporting agency, the consumer, or another person related to the consumer and acting on the consumer's behalf, the user of the information shall, within a reasonable period of time, and upon the consumer's written request for the reasons for the adverse action received within 60 days after learning of the adverse action, disclose the nature and substance of the information to the consumer. The user of the information shall clearly and accurately disclose to the consumer his or her right to make this written request at the time the adverse action is communicated to the consumer. *(Added by Stats.2002, c. 1030 (A.B.1068), § 6, eff. Sept. 28, 2002.)*

Article 4. REMEDIES

Section
1786.50. Liability of reporter or user to consumer; actual and punitive damages; costs.
1786.52. Actions for invasion of privacy or defamation; limitations; discovery of misrepresentation.

Section
1786.53. Personal information obtained regarding consumer in lieu of using services of an investigative consumer reporting agency; disclosure; definitions; copy of information to consumer.
1786.55. Information obtained by an employer or employment agency without use of investigative consumer reporting agency; attorney-client communications or attorney work product.

§ 1786.50. Liability of reporter or user to consumer; actual and punitive damages; costs

(a) An investigative consumer reporting agency or user of information that fails to comply with any requirement under this title with respect to an investigative consumer report is liable to the consumer who is the subject of the report in an amount equal to the sum of all the following:

(1) Any actual damages sustained by the consumer as a result of the failure or, except in the case of class actions, ten thousand dollars ($10,000), whichever sum is greater.

(2) In the case of any successful action to enforce any liability under this chapter, the costs of the action together with reasonable attorney's fees as determined by the court.

(b) If the court determines that the violation was grossly negligent or willful, the court may, in addition, assess, and the consumer may recover, punitive damages.

(c) Notwithstanding subdivision (a), an investigative consumer reporting agency or user of information that fails to comply with any requirement under this title with respect to an investigative consumer report shall not be liable to a consumer who is the subject of the report where the failure to comply results in a more favorable investigative consumer report than if there had not been a failure to comply. *(Added by Stats.1975, c. 1272, p. 3386, § 1. Amended by Stats.1998, c. 988 (S.B.1454), § 12; Stats.2001, c. 354 (A.B.655), § 18; Stats.2002, c. 1029 (A.B.2868), § 7, eff. Sept. 28, 2002; Stats.2003, c. 146 (A.B.1399), § 2.)*

§ 1786.52. Actions for invasion of privacy or defamation; limitations; discovery of misrepresentation

Nothing in this chapter shall in any way affect the right of any consumer to maintain an action against an investigative consumer reporting agency, a user of an investigative consumer report, or an informant for invasion of privacy or defamation.

An action to enforce any liability created under this title may be brought in any appropriate court of competent jurisdiction within two years from the date of discovery.

(a) Any investigative consumer reporting agency or user of information against whom an action brought pursuant to Section 1681n or 1681o of Title 15 of the United States Code is pending shall not be subject to suit for the same act or omission under Section 1786.50.

(b) The entry of a final judgment against the investigative consumer reporting agency or user of information in

an action brought pursuant to the provisions of Section 1681n or 1681o of Title 15 of the United States Code shall be a bar to the maintenance of any action based on the same act or omission which might be brought under this title. *(Added by Stats.1975, c. 1272, p. 3386, § 1. Amended by Stats.2001, c. 354 (A.B.655), § 19.)*

§ 1786.53. Personal information obtained regarding consumer in lieu of using services of an investigative consumer reporting agency; disclosure; definitions; copy of information to consumer

(a) Any person who collects, assembles, evaluates, compiles, reports, transmits, transfers, or communicates information on a consumer's character, general reputation, personnel characteristics, or mode of living, for employment purposes, which are matters of public record, and does not use the services of an investigative consumer reporting agency, shall provide that information to the consumer pursuant to subdivision (b). For purposes of this section:

(1) "Adverse action," as relating to employment, means a denial of employment or any decision made for an employment purpose that adversely affects any current or prospective employee.

(2) The term "person" does not include an agency subject to the Information Practices Act of 1977 (Chapter 1 (commencing with Section 1798) of Title 1.8).

(3) "Public records" means records documenting an arrest, indictment, conviction, civil judicial action, tax lien, or outstanding judgment.

(b)(1) Any person described in subdivision (a), or any person who receives information pursuant to subdivision (a), shall provide a copy of the related public record to the consumer within seven days after receipt of the information, regardless of whether the information is received in a written or oral form.

(2) Any person shall provide on any job application form, or any other written form, a box that, if checked by the consumer, permits the consumer to waive his or her right to receive a copy of any public record obtained pursuant to this section.

(3) If any person obtains a public record pursuant to this section for the purpose of conducting an investigation for suspicion of wrongdoing or misconduct by the subject of the investigation, the person may withhold the information until the completion of the investigation. Upon completion, the person shall provide a copy of the public record pursuant to paragraph (1), unless the consumer waived his or her rights pursuant to paragraph (2).

(4) If any person takes any adverse action as a result of receiving information pursuant to subdivision (a), the person shall provide to the consumer a copy of the public record, regardless of whether the consumer waived his or her rights pursuant to paragraph (2).

(c) Nothing in subdivision (a) or (b) requires any person to provide the same information to any consumer on more than one occasion. *(Added by Stats.2001, c. 354*

(A.B.655), § 20. Amended by Stats.2002, c. 1030 (A.B. 1068), § 7, eff. Sept. 28, 2002.)

§ 1786.55. Information obtained by an employer or employment agency without use of investigative consumer reporting agency; attorney-client communications or attorney work product

Nothing in this chapter is intended to modify Section 1198.5 of the Labor Code or existing law concerning information obtained by an employer or employment agency without the use of the services of an investigative consumer reporting agency for employment reference checks, background investigations, credential verifications, or employee investigations, except as provided in Section 1786.53. Nothing in this chapter is intended to change or supersede existing law related to privileged attorney-client communications or attorney work product, or require the production or disclosure of that information. (Added by Stats.2002, c. 1030 (A.B.1068), § 8, eff. Sept. 28, 2002.)

Title 1.8

PERSONAL DATA

CHAPTER 1. INFORMATION PRACTICES ACT OF 1977

ARTICLE 1. GENERAL PROVISIONS AND LEGISLATIVE FINDINGS

Section
1798.   Citation of chapter.
1798.1. Legislative declaration and findings.

§ 1798. Citation of chapter

This chapter shall be known and may be cited as the Information Practices Act of 1977. (Added by Stats.1977, c. 709, p. 2269, § 1, operative July 1, 1978.)

§ 1798.1. Legislative declaration and findings

The Legislature declares that the right to privacy is a personal and fundamental right protected by Section 1 of Article I of the Constitution of California and by the United States Constitution and that all individuals have a right of privacy in information pertaining to them. The Legislature further makes the following findings:

(a) The right to privacy is being threatened by the indiscriminate collection, maintenance, and dissemination of personal information and the lack of effective laws and legal remedies.

(b) The increasing use of computers and other sophisticated information technology has greatly magnified the potential risk to individual privacy that can occur from the maintenance of personal information.

(c) In order to protect the privacy of individuals, it is necessary that the maintenance and dissemination of

personal information be subject to strict limits. (Added by Stats.1977, c. 709, p. 2269, § 1, operative July 1, 1978.)

ARTICLE 2. DEFINITIONS

Section
1798.3. Definitions.

§ 1798.3. Definitions

As used in this chapter:

(a) The term "personal information" means any information that is maintained by an agency that identifies or describes an individual, including, but not limited to, his or her name, social security number, physical description, home address, home telephone number, education, financial matters, and medical or employment history. It includes statements made by, or attributed to, the individual.

(b) The term "agency" means every state office, officer, department, division, bureau, board, commission, or other state agency, except that the term agency shall not include:

(1) The California Legislature.

(2) Any agency established under Article VI of the California Constitution.

(3) The State Compensation Insurance Fund, except as to any records which contain personal information about the employees of the State Compensation Insurance Fund.

(4) A local agency, as defined in subdivision (a) of Section 6252 of the Government Code.

(c) The term "disclose" means to disclose, release, transfer, disseminate, or otherwise communicate all or any part of any record orally, in writing, or by electronic or any other means to any person or entity.

(d) The term "individual" means a natural person.

(e) The term "maintain" includes maintain, acquire, use, or disclose.

(f) The term "person" means any natural person, corporation, partnership, limited liability company, firm, or association.

(g) The term "record" means any file or grouping of information about an individual that is maintained by an agency by reference to an identifying particular such as the individual's name, photograph, finger or voice print, or a number or symbol assigned to the individual.

(h) The term "system of records" means one or more records, which pertain to one or more individuals, which is maintained by any agency, from which information is retrieved by the name of an individual or by some identifying number, symbol or other identifying particular assigned to the individual.

(i) The term "governmental entity," except as used in Section 1798.26, means any branch of the federal government or of the local government.

(j) The term "commercial purpose" means any purpose which has financial gain as a major objective. It does not include the gathering or dissemination of newsworthy facts by a publisher or broadcaster.

(k) The term "regulatory agency" means the Department of Financial Institutions, the Department of Corporations, the Department of Insurance, the Department of Real Estate, and agencies of the United States or of any other state responsible for regulating financial institutions. *(Added by Stats.1977, c. 709, p. 2269, § 1, operative July 1, 1978. Amended by Stats.1978, c. 874, p. 2741, § 1, eff. Sept. 19, 1978; Stats.1979, c. 143, p. 330, § 1, eff. June 22, 1979; Stats.1980, c. 174, p. 391, § 1; Stats.1982, c. 604, p. 2579, § 1; Stats.1985, c. 595, § 2; Stats.1987, c. 1453, § 1; Stats.1994, c. 1010 (S.B.2053), § 40; Stats.1996, c. 1064 (A.B.3351), § 4, operative July 1, 1997; Stats.2005, c. 677 (S.B.512), § 1, eff. Oct. 7, 2005.)*

ARTICLE 8. ACCESS TO RECORDS AND ADMINISTRATIVE REMEDIES

Section

1798.38. Promises or understandings concerning confidentiality of source; specified information in possession of agencies; protection of identity.

1798.40. Nondisclosure of personal information to individual to whom information pertains; criteria.

§ 1798.38. Promises or understandings concerning confidentiality of source; specified information in possession of agencies; protection of identity

If information, including letters of recommendation, compiled for the purpose of determining suitability, eligibility, or qualifications for employment, advancement, renewal of appointment or promotion, status as adoptive parents, or for the receipt of state contracts, or for licensing purposes, was received with the promise or, prior to July 1, 1978, with the understanding that the identity of the source of the information would be held in confidence and the source is not in a supervisory position with respect to the individual to whom the record pertains, the agency shall fully inform the individual of all personal information about that individual without identification of the source. This may be done by providing a copy of the text of the material with only such deletions as are necessary to protect the identity of the source or by providing a comprehensive summary of the substance of the material. Whichever method is used, the agency shall insure that full disclosure is made to the subject of any personal information that could reasonably in any way reflect or convey anything detrimental, disparaging, or threatening to an individual's reputation, rights, benefits, privileges, or qualifications, or be used by an agency to make a determination that would affect an individual's rights, benefits, privileges, or qualifications. In institutions of higher education, "supervisory positions" shall not be deemed to include chairpersons of academic departments. *(Added by Stats.1977, c. 709, p. 2269, § 1,*

operative July 1, 1978. Amended by Stats.1985, c. 595, § 16.)

§ 1798.40. Nondisclosure of personal information to individual to whom information pertains; criteria

This chapter shall not be construed to require an agency to disclose personal information to the individual to whom the information pertains, if the information meets any of the following criteria:

(a) Is compiled for the purpose of identifying individual criminal offenders and alleged offenders and consists only of identifying data and notations of arrests, the nature and disposition of criminal charges, sentencing, confinement, release, and parole and probation status.

(b) Is compiled for the purpose of a criminal investigation of suspected criminal activities, including reports of informants and investigators, and associated with an identifiable individual.

(c) Is contained in any record which could identify an individual and which is compiled at any stage of the process of enforcement of the criminal laws, from the arrest or indictment stage through release from supervision and including the process of extradition or the exercise of executive clemency.

(d) Is maintained for the purpose of an investigation of an individual's fitness for licensure or public employment, or of a grievance or complaint, or a suspected civil offense, so long as the information is withheld only so as not to compromise the investigation, or a related investigation. The identities of individuals who provided information for the investigation may be withheld pursuant to Section 1798.38.

(e) Would compromise the objectivity or fairness of a competitive examination for appointment or promotion in public service, or to determine fitness for licensure, or to determine scholastic aptitude.

(f) Pertains to the physical or psychological condition of the individual, if the agency determines that disclosure would be detrimental to the individual. The information shall, upon the individual's written authorization, be disclosed to a licensed medical practitioner or psychologist designated by the individual.

(g) Relates to the settlement of claims for work related illnesses or injuries and is maintained exclusively by the State Compensation Insurance Fund.

(h) Is required by statute to be withheld from the individual to whom it pertains.

This section shall not be construed to deny an individual access to information relating to him or her if access is allowed by another statute or decisional law of this state. *(Added by Stats.1985, c. 595, § 18.)*

ARTICLE 9. CIVIL REMEDIES

Section

1798.45. Civil actions against agencies; grounds.

Section
1798.46. Actions for refusal to comply with requests for inspection; injunctions; proceedings de novo; in camera examination of records; attorney fees and costs.
1798.47. Injunctions; orders and judgments.
1798.48. Failure to maintain records properly; noncompliance with provisions of chapter and rules; actual damages; costs; attorney fees.
1798.49. Jurisdiction; limitation of actions; nonexclusive rights and remedies.
1798.50. Personnel actions; qualifications of individuals; subjective opinions; liability.
1798.51. Lapse of time; corrections to records.
1798.53. Invasion of privacy; intentional disclosure of personal information; state or federal records; exemplary damages; attorney fees and costs.

§ 1798.45. Civil actions against agencies; grounds

An individual may bring a civil action against an agency whenever such agency does any of the following:

(a) Refuses to comply with an individual's lawful request to inspect pursuant to subdivision (a) of Section 1798.34.

(b) Fails to maintain any record concerning any individual with such accuracy, relevancy, timeliness, and completeness as is necessary to assure fairness in any determination relating to the qualifications, character, rights, opportunities of, or benefits to the individual that may be made on the basis of such record, if, as a proximate result of such failure, a determination is made which is adverse to the individual.

(c) Fails to comply with any other provision of this chapter, or any rule promulgated thereunder, in such a way as to have an adverse effect on an individual. *(Added by Stats.1977, c. 709, p. 2269, § 1, operative July 1, 1978.)*

§ 1798.46. Actions for refusal to comply with requests for inspection; injunctions; proceedings de novo; in camera examination of records; attorney fees and costs

In any suit brought under the provisions of subdivision (a) of Section 1798.45:

(a) The court may enjoin the agency from withholding the records and order the production to the complainant of any agency records improperly withheld from the complainant. In such a suit the court shall determine the matter de novo, and may examine the contents of any agency records in camera to determine whether the records or any portion thereof may be withheld as being exempt from the individual's right of access and the burden is on the agency to sustain its action.

(b) The court shall assess against the agency reasonable attorney's fees and other litigation costs reasonably incurred in any suit under this section in which the complainant has prevailed. A party may be considered to have prevailed even though he or she does not prevail on all issues or against all parties. *(Added by Stats.1977,* c. 709, p. 2269, § 1, operative July 1, 1978. Amended by Stats.1985, c. 595, § 22.)*

§ 1798.47. Injunctions; orders and judgments

Any agency that fails to comply with any provision of this chapter may be enjoined by any court of competent jurisdiction. The court may make any order or judgment as may be necessary to prevent the use or employment by an agency of any practices which violate this chapter.

Actions for injunction under this section may be prosecuted by the Attorney General, or any district attorney in this state, in the name of the people of the State of California whether upon his or her own complaint, or of a member of the general public, or by any individual acting in his or her own behalf. *(Added by Stats.1977, c. 709, p. 2269, § 1, operative July 1, 1978. Amended by Stats.1991–1992, 1st Ex.Sess., c. 21 (A.B.66), § 33.7, eff. March 1, 1993.)*

§ 1798.48. Failure to maintain records properly; noncompliance with provisions of chapter and rules; actual damages; costs; attorney fees

In any suit brought under the provisions of subdivision (b) or (c) of Section 1798.45, the agency shall be liable to the individual in an amount equal to the sum of:

(a) Actual damages sustained by the individual, including damages for mental suffering.

(b) The costs of the action together with reasonable attorney's fees as determined by the court. *(Added by Stats.1977, c. 709, p. 2269, § 1, operative July 1, 1978.)*

§ 1798.49. Jurisdiction; limitation of actions; nonexclusive rights and remedies

An action to enforce any liability created under Sections 1798.45 to 1798.48, inclusive, may be brought in any court of competent jurisdiction in the county in which the complainant resides, or has his principal place of business, or in which the defendant's records are situated, within two years from the date on which the cause of action arises, except that where a defendant has materially and willfully misrepresented any information required under this section to be disclosed to an individual who is the subject of the information and the information so misrepresented is material to the establishment of the defendant's liability to that individual under this section, the action may be brought at any time within two years after discovery by the complainant of the misrepresentation. Nothing in Sections 1798.45 to 1798.48, inclusive, shall be construed to authorize any civil action by reason of any injury sustained as the result of any information practice covered by this chapter prior to July 1, 1978.

The rights and remedies set forth in this chapter shall be deemed to be nonexclusive and are in addition to all those rights and remedies which are otherwise available under any other provision of law. *(Added by Stats.1977, c. 709, p. 2269, § 1, operative July 1, 1978.)*

§ 1798.50. Personnel actions; qualifications of individuals; subjective opinions; liability

A civil action shall not lie under this article based upon an allegation that an opinion which is subjective in nature, as distinguished from a factual assertion, about an individual's qualifications, in connection with a personnel action concerning such an individual, was not accurate, relevant, timely, or complete. *(Added by Stats.1977, c. 709, p. 2269, § 1, operative July 1, 1978.)*

§ 1798.51. Lapse of time; corrections to records

Where a remedy other than those provided in Articles 8 and 9 is provided by law but is not available because of lapse of time an individual may obtain a correction to a record under this chapter but such correction shall not operate to revise or restore a right or remedy not provided by this chapter that has been barred because of lapse of time. *(Added by Stats.1977, c. 709, p. 2269, § 1, operative July 1, 1978.)*

§ 1798.53. Invasion of privacy; intentional disclosure of personal information; state or federal records; exemplary damages; attorney fees and costs

Any person, other than an employee of the state or of a local government agency acting solely in his or her official capacity, who intentionally discloses information, not otherwise public, which they know or should reasonably know was obtained from personal information maintained by a state agency or from "records" within a "system of records" (as these terms are defined in the Federal Privacy Act of 1974 (P.L. 93–579; 5 U.S.C. 552a)) maintained by a federal government agency, shall be subject to a civil action, for invasion of privacy, by the individual to whom the information pertains.

In any successful action brought under this section, the complainant, in addition to any special or general damages awarded, shall be awarded a minimum of two thousand five hundred dollars ($2,500) in exemplary damages as well as attorney's fees and other litigation costs reasonably incurred in the suit.

The right, remedy, and cause of action set forth in this section shall be nonexclusive and is in addition to all other rights, remedies, and causes of action for invasion of privacy, inherent in Section 1 of Article I of the California Constitution. *(Added by Stats.1977, c. 709, p. 2269, § 1, operative July 1, 1978. Amended by Stats.1985, c. 595, § 23.)*

Title 2.91

EMPLOYMENT AGENCY, EMPLOYMENT COUNSELING, AND JOB LISTING SERVICES ACT

CHAPTER 1. GENERAL PROVISIONS

Section
1812.500.   Citation of title.

Section
1812.501.   Definitions.
1812.502.   Application of title; person charging employer exclusively; nonprofit corporation; labor organization; nursing, business, or vocational school; job listing service.

§ 1812.500. Citation of title

This title shall be known and cited as the Employment Agency, Employment Counseling, and Job Listing Services Act. *(Added by Stats.1989, c. 704, § 2.)*

§ 1812.501. Definitions

(a)(1) "Employment agency" or "agency" means:

(A) Any person who, for a fee or other valuable consideration to be paid, directly or indirectly by a jobseeker, performs, offers to perform, or represents it can or will perform any of the following services:

(i) Procures, offers, promises, or attempts to procure employment or engagements for others or employees for employers.

(ii) Registers persons seeking to procure or retain employment or engagement.

(iii) Gives information as to where and from whom this help, employment, or engagement may be procured.

(iv) Provides employment or engagements.

(B) Any person who offers, as one of its main objects or purposes, to procure employment for any person who will pay for its services, or that collects dues, tuition, or membership or registration fees of any sort, if the main object of the person paying those fees is to secure employment.

(C) Any person who, for a fee or other valuable consideration, procures, offers, promises, provides, or attempts to procure babysitting or domestic employment for others or domestics or babysitters for others.

(2) "Employment agency" or "agency" shall not include any employment counseling service or any job listing service.

(b)(1) "Employment counseling service" means any person who offers, advertises, or represents it can or will provide any of the following services for a fee: career counseling, vocational guidance, aptitude testing, executive consulting, personnel consulting, career management, evaluation, or planning, or the development of résumés and other promotional materials relating to the preparation for employment. "Employment counseling service" shall not include persons who provide services strictly on an hourly basis with no financial obligation required of the consumer beyond the hourly fee for services rendered. An "employment counseling service" does not include the functions of an "employment agency" as defined in subdivision (a).

(2) "Employment counseling service" does not include:

(A) Businesses that are retained by, act solely on behalf of, and are compensated solely by prior or current employers that do not require any "customer" to sign a contract and do not in any way hold any "customer" liable for fees.

(B)(i) Any provider of vocational rehabilitation in which the counseling services are paid for by insurance benefits, if the counseling is provided as a result of marital dissolution or separation proceedings to prepare one of the spouses for reentry into the job market and if the fees are paid by some party other than the person receiving the counseling services.

(ii) The exemption provided in this subparagraph does not apply to any vocational rehabilitation counselor who receives any payments directly from the individual customer receiving the counseling.

(C) Any person who engages solely in the preparation of résumés and cover letters, provided that the résumé writing service does not advertise or hold itself out as offering other job seeking or placement services and does not charge more than three hundred dollars ($300) for any résumé, cover letter, or combination of both to any single customer in any individual transaction.

(D) Any public educational institution.

(E) Any private educational institution established solely for educational purposes that, as a part of its curriculum, offers employment counseling to its student body and conforms to the requirements of Article 3.5 (commencing with Section 94760) of Chapter 7 of Part 59 of the Education Code.

(F) A psychologist or psychological corporation licensed pursuant to Chapter 6.6 (commencing with Section 2900) of Division 2 of the Business and Professions Code, providing psychological assessment, career or occupational counseling, or consultation and related professional services within his, her, or its scope of practice.

(G) An educational psychologist licensed pursuant to Article 5 (commencing with Section 4986) of Chapter 13 of Division 2 of the Business and Professions Code, providing counseling services within his or her scope of practice.

(c) "Job listing service" means any person who provides, offers, or represents it can or will provide any of the following services, for a fee or other valuable consideration to be paid, directly or indirectly, by the jobseeker in advance of, or contemporaneously with, performance of these services: matches jobseekers with employment opportunities, providing or offering to provide jobseekers lists of employers or lists of job openings or like publications, or preparing résumés or lists of jobseekers for distribution to potential employers.

(d) A "nurses' registry" as defined in subdivision (b) of Section 1812.524 is an employment agency. However, unless otherwise provided for in this title, a nurses' registry shall not be required to comply with Chapter 2 (commencing with Section 1812.503) regulating employment agencies but, instead, shall be required to comply with Chapter 7 (commencing with Section 1812.524).

(e) "Jobseeker" means a person seeking employment.

(f) "Employer" means any individual, company, partnership, association, corporation, agent, employee, or representative for whom or for which an employment agency or job listing service attempts to obtain an employee or to place a jobseeker.

(g) "Job order" means any written or oral instruction, direction, or permission granted by an employer or its agent to an employment agency or job listing service to refer jobseekers for a specified job.

(h) "Domestic agency" means any agency that provides, or attempts to provide, employment by placement of domestic help in private homes.

(i) "Deposit" means any money or valuable consideration received by an employment agency or job listing service from a jobseeker for referring the jobseeker to a position of employment prior to the jobseeker's acceptance of a position.

(j) "Fee" means:

(1) Any money or other valuable consideration paid, or promised to be paid, for services rendered or to be rendered by any person conducting an employment agency, employment counseling service, or job listing service under this title.

(2) Any money received by any person in excess of that which has been paid out by him or her for transportation, transfer of baggage, or board and lodging for any applicant for employment.

(k) "Registration fee" means any charge made, or attempted to be made, by an employment agency for registering or listing an applicant for employment, for letter writing, or any charge of a like nature made, or attempted to be made without having a bona fide order for the placement of the applicant in a position.

(*l*) "Person" means any individual, corporation, partnership, limited liability company, trust, association, or other organization.

(m) This section shall become operative on January 1, 1997. *(Added by Stats.1995, c. 758 (A.B.446), § 8.5, operative Jan. 1, 1997. Amended by Stats.2006, c. 538 (S.B.1852), § 52.)*

§ 1812.502. Application of title; person charging employer exclusively; nonprofit corporation; labor organization; nursing, business, or vocational school; job listing service

(a) This title does not apply to any person who provides any of the services described in subdivision (a) of Section 1812.501 and who charges fees exclusively to employers for those services. The exemption from regulation provided by this subdivision does not apply to any person who provides babysitting or domestic employment for others. This subdivision does not apply to an employment counseling service as defined in subdivision (b) of Section 1812.501.

47

(b) This title shall not apply to any nonprofit corporation, organized for the purpose of economic adjustment, civic betterment, and the giving of vocational guidance and placement to its members, or others, including employment counseling services, when all of the following conditions exist:

(1) None of the directors, officers, or employees thereof receive any profit other than a nominal salary for services performed for the organization or corporation.

(2) No fee is charged for those services, though a voluntary contribution may be requested.

(3) Membership dues or fees charged are used solely for maintenance of the organization or corporation.

(c) Nothing in this title shall apply to a nonprofit corporation which has been formed in good faith for the promotion and advancement of the general professional interests of its members and which maintains a placement service principally engaged in securing employment for such members with the state or any county, city, district or other public agency under contracts providing employment for one year or longer, or any nonprofit corporation exempted by subdivision (b).

(d) This title shall not apply to a labor organization as defined in Section 1117 of the Labor Code, a newspaper of general circulation, bona fide newsletter, magazine, trade or professional journal, or other publication of general circulation, the main purpose of which is dissemination of news, reports, trade or professional information, or information not intended to assist in locating, securing, or procuring employment or assignments for others.

(e) As used in this title, "employment agency" or "agency" does not include a nursing school, business school, or vocational school, except that if such a school charges a fee for placement, the school shall be an employment agency within the meaning of this title.

(f)(1) A job listing service which meets the requirements specified in paragraph (2) or (3) shall not be subject to any of the following: Sections 1812.515, 1812.516, 1812.517, and 1812.518; subdivisions (a) and (b), and paragraph (3) of subdivision (c), and subdivision (d) of Section 1812.519; paragraph (2) of subdivision (b), and subdivisions (c), (d), (e), and (f) of Section 1812.520; and Section 1812.521.

(2) A job listing service shall be exempt pursuant to paragraph (1) if it complies with all of the following:

(A) Does not provide, offer, or imply the offer of, services related to employment.

(B) Does not offer or sell lists of employers or job openings to jobseekers on an in-person basis.

(C) Maintains records of all its advertisements, identified by date and publication, and the sources of information used for the preparation of lists of employers and job openings, from which can be determined the accuracy of any statistics regarding success rate or similar statistics

used in its advertising, promotional materials, or oral or written statements to jobseekers.

(D) Identifies, on each list of employers and job openings, its general source of information for jobs included on that list when the source of information is a publication or other public record.

(E) Provides, at or before the time of delivery of the list, a prominent written statement to the jobseeker granting the jobseeker a right to return the list for an immediate refund of the purchase price during a stated period of time which expires not less than 10 days from the date of delivery of the list. The list shall be deemed returned upon delivery to the address from which it was obtained or upon deposit in the mail properly addressed to that address, with postage prepaid.

(3) A job listing service shall be exempt pursuant to paragraph (1) if it complies with all of the following:

(A) A majority interest in the job listing service is owned by one or more colleges or universities, or alumni associations affiliated therewith, and each college or university is accredited by both (i) an accrediting agency recognized as such by the United States Department of Education and (ii) a member organization of the Council of Postsecondary Accreditation.

(B) The job listing service provides services related to employment exclusively for jobseekers who are the alumni of colleges or universities specified in subparagraph (A).

(C) The job listing service does not require, as a condition to receiving employment services, that the applicant have completed courses or examinations beyond the requirements for graduation from the college or university specified in subparagraph (A).

(D) More than 50 percent of the annual revenues received by the job listing service are derived from paid subscriptions of prospective employers. *(Added by Stats. 1989, c. 704, § 2. Amended by Stats.1990, c. 1256 (A.B.2649), § 4.)*

CHAPTER 2. EMPLOYMENT AGENCIES

Section
1812.503. Bond; deposit in lieu of bond.
1812.504. Contract.
1812.505. Fees; schedule; payment terms; notice; change; confession of judgment, note, or wage assignment as payment; deposit; termination of employment; interagency disputes; splitting; employer interest in agency.
1812.506. Fees; deposit; return; delay; notice; permanent employment; termination of employment; refusal to refund.
1812.507. Job order; referring jobseeker.
1812.508. False or misleading representations; advertisements; name, address, and telephone number; designation in name; fee; records.
1812.509. Employment of minors; notification required to be given to jobseekers; necessity of personal interview.

Section
1812.5093. Child care provider referral; disclosure.
1812.5095. Domestic worker; relationship with employment agency; agency referral authority and duties.

§ 1812.503. Bond; deposit in lieu of bond

(a) Every employment agency subject to this title shall maintain a bond issued by a surety company admitted to do business in this state. The principal sum of the bond shall be three thousand dollars ($3,000). A copy of the bond shall be filed with the Secretary of State.

(b) The bond required by this section shall be in favor of, and payable to, the people of the State of California and shall be conditioned that the person obtaining the bond will comply with this title and will pay all sums due any individual or group of individuals when the person or his or her representative, agent, or employee has received those sums. The bond shall be for the benefit of any person or persons damaged by any violation of this title or by fraud, dishonesty, misstatement, misrepresentation, deceit, unlawful acts or omissions, or failure to provide the services of the employment agency in performance of the contract with the jobseeker, by the employment agency or its agents, representatives, or employees while acting within the scope of their employment.

(c)(1) No employment agency shall conduct any business without having a current surety bond in the amount prescribed by this title and filing a copy of the bond with the Secretary of State.

(2) Thirty days prior to the cancellation or termination of any surety bond required by this section, the surety shall send a written notice of that cancellation or termination to both the employment agency and the Secretary of State, identifying the bond and the date of cancellation or termination.

(3) If any employment agency fails to obtain a new bond and file a copy of that bond with the Secretary of State by the effective date of the cancellation or termination of the former bond, the employment agency shall cease to conduct any business unless and until a new surety bond is obtained and a copy of that bond is filed with the Secretary of State.

(d) When a deposit has been made in lieu of the bond pursuant to Section 995.710 of the Code of Civil Procedure, the person asserting a claim against the deposit shall, in lieu of Section 996.430 of the Code of Civil Procedure, establish the claim by furnishing evidence to the Secretary of State of a money judgment entered by a court together with evidence that the claimant is a person described in subdivision (b).

(e) When a claimant has established the claim with the Secretary of State, the Secretary of State shall review and approve the claim and enter the date of approval thereon. The claim shall be designated an "approved claim."

(f) When the first claim against a particular deposit has been approved, it shall not be paid until the expiration of a period of 240 days after the date of its approval by the Secretary of State. Subsequent claims that are approved by the Secretary of State within the same 240–day period shall similarly not be paid until the expiration of the 240–day period. Upon the expiration of the 240–day period, the Secretary of State shall pay all approved claims from that 240–day period in full unless the deposit is insufficient, in which case each approved claim shall be paid a pro rata share of the deposit.

(g) When the Secretary of State approves the first claim against a particular deposit after the expiration of a 240–day period, the date of approval of that claim shall begin a new 240–day period to which subdivision (f) shall apply with respect to any amount remaining in the deposit.

(h) After a deposit is exhausted, no further claims shall be paid by the Secretary of State. Claimants who have had their claims paid in full or in part pursuant to subdivision (f) or (g) shall not be required to return funds received from the deposit for the benefit of other claimants.

(i) When a deposit has been made in lieu of a bond, the amount of the deposit shall not be subject to attachment, garnishment, or execution with respect to an action or judgment against the employment agency, other than as to an amount as no longer needed or required for the purpose of this title that would otherwise be returned to the employment agency by the Secretary of State.

(j) The Secretary of State shall retain a cash deposit for two years from the date the Secretary of State receives written notification from the assignor of the deposit that the assignor has ceased to engage in the business of an employment agency or has filed a bond pursuant to subdivision (a), provided that there are no outstanding claims against the deposit. This written notice shall include all of the following: (1) name, address, and telephone number of the assignor; (2) name, address, and telephone number of the bank at which the deposit is located; (3) account number of the deposit; and (4) a statement whether the assignor is ceasing to engage in the business of an employment agency or has filed a bond with the Secretary of State. The Secretary of State shall forward an acknowledgment of receipt of the written notice to the assignor at the address indicated therein, specifying the date of receipt of the written notice and anticipated date of release of the deposit, provided there are no outstanding claims against the deposit.

(k) A judge of a superior court may order the return of the deposit prior to the expiration of two years upon evidence satisfactory to the judge that there are no outstanding claims against the deposit or order the Secretary of State to retain the deposit for a sufficient period beyond the two years pursuant to subdivision (j) to resolve outstanding claims against the deposit account.

(*l*) The Secretary of State shall charge a filing fee not to exceed the cost of filing the bond or deposit filed in lieu of a bond as set forth in Section 995.710 of the Code of Civil Procedure.

(m) The Secretary of State shall enforce the provisions of this chapter that govern the filing and maintenance of bonds and deposits in lieu of bonds. *(Added by Stats. 1989, c. 704, § 2. Amended by Stats.1996, c. 633 (S.B. 1978), § 11; Stats.1998, c. 829 (S.B.1652), § 11; Stats. 2002, c. 784 (S.B.1316), § 15.)*

§ 1812.504. Contract

(a) Every employment agency shall give a written contract to every jobseeker from whom a fee or deposit is to be received, whether directly or indirectly. The original of the contract shall be given to the jobseeker at the time the jobseeker signs the contract and before the employment agency accepts any fee or deposit or the jobseeker becomes obligated to pay any such fee or deposit. The contract shall contain all of the following:

(1) The name, address, and telephone number of the employment agency, and, if the employment agency has more than one office or location, the address and telephone number of the principal office or location providing services to the jobseeker.

(2) The name and address of the person giving the order for help, the date and consecutive number of the receipt of the order by the agency, and its manner of transmission.

(3) The name of the jobseeker, the name and address of the person to whom the jobseeker is sent for employment, and the address where the jobseeker is to report for employment.

(4) The date and consecutive number of the contract.

(5) The amount of the fee to be charged and to be collected from the jobseeker, including a statement that if the employment is terminated, the fee may not exceed gross earnings of the jobseeker in that employment, and the amount of the fee paid or advanced by the prospective employer and by whom paid or advanced.

(6) The kind of work or employment.

(7) The daily hours of work; the wages or salary, including any consideration or privilege; the benefits; and any other conditions of employment.

(8) If any labor trouble exists at the place of employment, that fact shall be stated in the contract.

(9) A contract expiration date which shall not be later than 180 days from the date of the referral or signing of the contract, whichever occurs first; however, a domestic agency operating as a registry may enter into a continuing contract subject to termination by written notice by either the domestic worker or the agency.

(10) Any other term, condition, or understanding agreed upon between the agency and the jobseeker.

(11) The following statement, with the caption in type no smaller than 10–point boldfaced type and the remainder in a size no smaller than that generally used throughout the contract, and in full capitals, boldface, or italics:

RIGHT TO REFUND

"If you pay all or any portion of a fee and fail to accept employment, the employment agency shall, upon your request, return the amount paid to you within 48 hours after your request for a refund.

"If you leave employment for just cause or are discharged for reasons other than misconduct connected with your work within 90 days from the starting date of employment, the agency shall reduce your fee to that payable for temporary employment and shall refund any excess paid within 10 days of your request for a refund.

"No fee larger than that for temporary employment may be charged to you for employment lasting 90 days or less unless the agency's fee schedules, contracts, and agreements provide for a further charge if you leave employment without just cause or are discharged for misconduct in connection with your work.

"If any refund due is not made within the time limits set forth above, the employment agency shall pay you an additional sum equal to the amount of the refund."

(b) All contracts shall be dated and shall be made and numbered consecutively, both copies to be signed by the jobseeker and the person acting for the employment agency. The original shall be given to the jobseeker and one copy shall be kept on file at the employment agency.

(c) The full agreement between the parties shall be contained in a single document containing those elements set forth in this section.

(d) When a referral is made by telephone the agency shall execute the contract or receipt in triplicate and shall mail the original and duplicate to the jobseeker on the day the referral is made, with instructions that they be signed by the jobseeker and the duplicate returned to the agency. The date of mailing the contract or receipt to the jobseeker shall be entered thereon by the agency. The same contract or receipt shall not be used for more than one referral.

(e) For purposes of this section, a "domestic agency operating as a registry" means a domestic agency that engages in the business of obtaining and filling commitments for domestic help. *(Added by Stats.1989, c. 704, § 2. Amended by Stats.1996, c. 102 (S.B.2030), § 1.)*

§ 1812.505. Fees; schedule; payment terms; notice; change; confession of judgment, note, or wage assignment as payment; deposit; termination of employment; interagency disputes; splitting; employer interest in agency

(a)(1) An employment agency shall provide a copy of the agency's jobseeker fee schedule and payment terms to any jobseeker from whom a fee or deposit is to be received, prior to the jobseeker being interviewed by a counselor. The jobseeker fee schedule shall indicate the percentage of both the projected annual and first month's total gross earnings represented by those fees.

(2) In the schedule, the various employments or salary ranges by which the fee is to be computed or determined shall be classified, and in each class the maximum fee shall be fixed and shall include the charges of every kind rendered by the agency in each case or transaction on behalf of the prospective employee. Changes in the schedule may be made, but no change shall become effective until posted for not less than seven days in a conspicuous place in the agency.

(3) A copy of the schedule in effect shall be kept posted in the employment agency in a conspicuous place, and the posted schedule and the changes therein shall be in lettering or printing of not less than standard pica capitals. The date of the taking effect of the schedule and of each change therein shall appear on the posted copies.

(4) A copy of all fee schedules, and of all changes therein, shall be kept on file at the employment agency, retrospectively, for a period of one year.

(b) No fee charged or collected shall be in excess of the fee as scheduled.

(c) No employment agency shall accept, directly or indirectly, a registration fee of any kind.

(d) No employment agency may take from a jobseeker a confession of judgment, a promissory note or notes, or an assignment of wages to cover its fees.

(e) The employment agency shall give a receipt to every jobseeker from whom a deposit is received. No other deposit or prepayment of any kind may be required by an agency. If the jobseeker accepts employment, the deposit shall be applied to the fee to be paid by the jobseeker.

(f)(1) If a jobseeker leaves employment for just cause or is discharged for reasons other than misconduct connected with the jobseeker's work within 90 days from the starting date of employment, the agency shall reduce the fee payable by the jobseeker to that payable for temporary employment under subdivision (g) and shall refund any fee paid in excess of that amount.

(2) No charge may be made to or obligation to pay incurred by any jobseeker beyond that authorized by subdivision (g) for employment lasting 90 days or less, unless the agency's fee schedules, contracts, and agreements specifically provide for a further charge if the jobseeker leaves employment without just cause or is discharged for misconduct in connection with his or her work, and then only if lack of just cause or misconduct exists. Otherwise, the agency shall retain or charge only the fee for temporary employment for any employment lasting 90 days or less from the starting date of employment.

(3) Notwithstanding subdivision (a) and this subdivision, in no instance in which the employment accepted is subsequently terminated shall the fee charged or obligation to pay incurred by a jobseeker be greater than the total gross earnings of the jobseeker in that employment.

This provision shall be stated in all agency contracts issued pursuant to Section 1812.504.

(g) The fee payable by the jobseeker for temporary employment shall not exceed 1/90 of the fee for permanent employment for each consecutive calendar day during the period that the jobseeker is employed or compensated as though employed.

(h)(1) If a jobseeker accepts employment in which the jobseeker is to be paid on the basis of straight commissions, or a drawing account against commissions, or either a drawing account or salary plus commissions, the fee payable by the jobseeker may be predicated upon the projected total gross earnings during the first year of employment as estimated by the employer.

(2) Upon the conclusion of a jobseeker's first 12 months of employment, a computation of his or her actual total gross earnings may be provided by the jobseeker to the agency, and, predicated upon appropriate proof of earnings, an adjustment in the fee shall be made in which either the agency shall refund to the jobseeker any excess fee paid by him or her or the jobseeker shall pay to the agency any deficiency thereon.

(3) If the jobseeker's employment is terminated prior to the conclusion of the first 12 months of employment, the actual total gross earnings of the jobseeker for the period of employment shall be projected to 12 months on a pro rata basis as though the jobseeker had been employed for the entire period of 12 months, and a computation shall be made thereon. The fee paid or payable by the jobseeker shall be predicated upon that computation as though the jobseeker had been so employed.

(i) If an employment agency sends a jobseeker for employment and the jobseeker accepts employment other than that position specified in the bona fide order for employment to which the jobseeker was sent, but with the same employer, then the agency shall be entitled to a fee for the employment of the jobseeker, payable by the jobseeker, computed under the terms of the fee schedule in effect in the agency at the time of referral, provided that the jobseeker accepts employment within 180 days of the date of referral. The expiration date of the referral shall be stated in the contract.

In interagency disputes concerning the earning of a fee for placement of a jobseeker, the fee shall be earned by the agency responsible for the jobseeker being placed. A reasonable effort shall be made by the billing agency that it is entitled to the fee. The jobseeker shall be responsible for only one full fee for any single placement, and that fact shall be so stated in the contract.

(j)(1) No employment agency shall divide fees with an employer, an agent, or other employee of an employer or person to whom help is furnished.

(2) No employment agency shall charge any jobseeker a fee for accepting employment with such employment agency or any subsidiary of that agency.

(3) No employment agency shall charge any jobseeker a fee when help is furnished to an employer, an agent, any employee of an employer, a member, or person who has a financial interest in the employment agency. *(Added by Stats. 1989, c. 704, § 2.)*

§ 1812.506. Fees; deposit; return; delay; notice; permanent employment; termination of employment; refusal to refund

(a) If a jobseeker paying or becoming obligated to pay a fee, or making a deposit on a fee for placement fails to accept employment, the employment agency shall, upon request by the jobseeker, repay the amount of the deposit or fee to the jobseeker. Unless the deposit is returned within 48 hours after request, the employment agency shall pay to the jobseeker an additional sum equal to the amount of the deposit. A notice to this effect shall be inserted in all contracts between the agency and the jobseeker, and in all receipts given to the jobseeker for cash payment in advance of employment, and in the schedule of fees posted in the office of the agency.

(b)(1) All employment provided by any employment agency to any jobseeker from whom a fee is to be received shall be considered permanent only if it lasts longer than 90 days. If a jobseeker leaves the job or is discharged within the first 90 days of employment, the agency shall make a refund or reduction of the fee to the temporary fee amount unless the agency's fee schedules, contracts, and agreements specifically provide for a further charge if the jobseeker leaves employment without just cause or is discharged for misconduct in connection with his or her work.

(2) "Just cause" or "discharge for reasons other than misconduct" includes, but is not limited to, the following:

(A) Wages or salary less than that agreed upon between the jobseeker and the employer.

(B) Receiving a payroll check which is not honored by the bank upon which it was drawn.

(C) Working hours, working days, or working shifts significantly different than those agreed upon between the jobseeker and the employer.

(D) Receiving a work assignment, subsequent to accepting the job, which is substantially different from that agreed upon between the jobseeker and the employer.

(E) Being assigned to a job location different from that which was agreed upon between the jobseeker and the employer.

(F) The jobseeker's lack of physical ability to perform duties connected with the position agreed upon between the jobseeker and the employer unless the provisions of subparagraph (E) of paragraph (3) apply.

(G) A lockout or strike causing loss of pay.

(H) The jobseeker's lack of physical ability to perform duties connected with the position unless the provisions of subparagraph (E) of paragraph (3) apply.

(J)[1] The jobseeker's entry into active service in the armed forces.

(K) Physical or economic destruction of the business.

(L) The death of the jobseeker (any refund in that case shall be paid to the estate of the jobseeker).

(3) "Lack of just cause" or a discharge for "misconduct" includes, but is not limited to:

(A) Abandonment of the job by the jobseeker.

(B) Conviction of the jobseeker, subsequent to employment, of a crime when conviction temporarily or permanently prevents the jobseeker from fulfilling the terms of employment.

(C) Willful violation of lawful company policies or rules by the jobseeker.

(D) Willful failure to perform lawful duties appropriate to employment by the jobseeker.

(E) Acts of the jobseeker constituting misrepresentation or withholding of information directly related to education, work experience, responsibility, physical ability, or training, that would have caused the employer to refuse employment.

(c)(1) Except as otherwise provided in subdivision (a), a refund when due shall be made within 10 working days after request therefor from the jobseeker.

(2) Alternatively, if the decision of the agency is not to make a refund, the agency shall notify the jobseeker in writing, within the 10-day working period specified in paragraph (1), as to the specific reasons why the refund is not being made.

(3) If the agency fails to properly notify the jobseeker pursuant to paragraph (2) or fails to tender a refund within the time allowed, the agency shall be liable to the jobseeker in the amount of an additional sum equal to the amount of the refund. *(Added by Stats. 1989, c. 704, § 2.)*

[1] No (I) in enrolled copy.

§ 1812.507. Job order; referring jobseeker

(a) No employment agency shall accept a fee from any jobseeker, or send any jobseeker for employment, without having obtained, orally or in writing, a bona fide job order for employment.

(b) An agency shall identify itself as an employment agency to the employer in all instances in which it contacts an employer for the purpose of soliciting a job order. All job orders shall be recorded in writing. A job order for employment shall be considered to have been given by an employer to an employment agency under the following conditions:

(1) The employer, or his or her agent, orally or in writing, registers a request or gives permission that the agency recruit or refer jobseekers who meet the employer's stated job specifications and the employer furnishes such information as required by subdivision (a) of Section 1812.504. A job order is valid for the referral of any qualified jobseeker until it is filled or canceled by the

employer, and may serve as the basis for agency advertising. The agency is required to recontact the employer within 30 days to ensure that the position is still vacant prior to any additional advertising or referral of jobseekers.

(2) When an agency has brought the qualifications of a specific jobseeker to the attention of an employer and the employer has expressed interest in that jobseeker either by agreeing to interview the jobseeker, or by requesting that the agency furnish him or her with the jobseeker's resumé or other written history or data, or by initiating direct contact with the jobseeker as a result of information furnished by the agency, that action by the employer shall constitute a job order only for the jobseeker discussed and is not valid for advertisement, unless the contact by the agency resulted in a job order for a specific position sufficient under paragraph (1). If the employer has no position open but merely wishes to explore the possible employment of the jobseeker and the jobseeker is to be responsible for the placement fee, that fact shall be indicated on the jobseeker's referral contract.

(c) No employment agency shall refer a jobseeker to a job knowing or having reason to know that:

(1) The job does not exist or the jobseeker is not qualified for the job.

(2) The job has been described or advertised by or on behalf of the agency in a false, misleading, or deceptive manner.

(3) The agency has not obtained written or oral permission to list the job from the employer or an authorized agent of the employer. *(Added by Stats.1989, c. 704, § 2.)*

§ 1812.508. False or misleading representations; advertisements; name, address, and telephone number; designation in name; fee; records

(a) No employment agency shall make, or cause to be made, any false, misleading, or deceptive advertisements or representations concerning the services that the agency will provide to jobseekers.

(b)(1) No employment agency shall publish or cause to be published any false, fraudulent, or misleading information, representation, notice, or advertisements.

(2) All advertisements of an employment agency shall contain the correct name of the employment agency and one of the following:

(A) The street address of the agency's place of business.

(B) The correct telephone number of the agency at its place of business.

(3) Every employment agency, except a nurses' registry shall use, as part of its name, either the designation "agency" or "personnel service."

(4) No employment agency shall give any false information or make any false promises or representations concerning an engagement or employment to any job-seeker who registers or applies for an engagement or employment or help.

(5) No employment agency shall, by its name, advertisement, or any other representation, represent itself to be a home health agency, as defined by subdivision (a) of Section 1727 of the Health and Safety Code, or to perform the services of a home health agency. An employment agency shall provide a written disclosure to each individual receiving nursing services in his or her place of residence stating that it does not perform the services of a home health agency and clearly describing that it is an employment agency only and that any complaints against personnel providing nursing services who are neither licensed nor certified shall be submitted to the local district attorney, complaints against certified nursing assistants and certified home health aides providing nursing services shall be submitted to the local district attorney and the State Department of Health Services, and complaints against licensed personnel providing nursing services shall be submitted to the local district attorney and the Department of Consumer Affairs. The address and telephone number of each agency and board to which complaints are required to be submitted shall be provided by the employment agency to all patients prior to the time they are under the care of any nursing services personnel.

(6) Any person may refer complaints concerning employment agencies to the proper law enforcement agency for action.

(c)(1) Where an employment agency job advertisement includes a description of the placement fee associated with the advertised job, the employment agency shall describe the placement fee in a manner which either clearly indicates whether or not a jobseeker shall be responsible for the placement fee or in accordance with the following terms and provisions:

(A) "FEE" means the jobseeker pays the entire placement fee.

(B) "NO FEE" means the jobseeker pays no portion of the placement fee.

(2) Where "NO FEE" jobs are advertised and the agency also administers placement for "FEE" jobs, the advertisement shall state "ALSO FEE JOBS" in type of equal size, prominence, and boldness as "NO FEE" notations.

(3) A group job advertisement which includes a description of the placement fee shall describe the placement fee either separately for each job, or by use of the proper term as a heading under which all applicable jobs shall be listed. All those headings shall be in type and of the same size, prominence, and boldness.

(d) Special requirements not usually associated with a job shall be specified in any advertisement. When the location of the position advertised is more than 50 miles from the employment agency office responsible for the advertisement, it shall state either the location or that the job is "nonlocal." Special benefits of the job, if advertised, shall be specifically described and substitute terms or symbols such as "extras" or "+" shall not be sufficient.

(e) An advertised salary shall be based upon the starting salary contained in the job order. An advertised range of starting salaries shall be specified by preceding the minimum salary and maximum salary by the terms "from" and "to" respectively. When the job order contains only the maximum amount of a salary range, that advertised salary shall be preceded by the word "to." If a maximum salary is dependent upon the jobseeker's experience, the advertised salary may be described by listing the minimum salary and the term "up Depending on Experience" or "up D.O.E." The words "open" and "negotiable" or words or symbols of like import shall not be used as a substitute for the salary. If an advertised salary is based in whole or in part on commissions, that fact shall be indicated in the advertisement.

(f) All employment agencies shall maintain a record of all advertised jobs, correlated to show the date and the publication in which the advertisement appeared and the job order number of each job advertised, retrospectively for a period of one year. *(Added by Stats.1989, c. 704, § 2. Amended by Stats.1990, c. 761 (A.B.3924), § 1.)*

§ 1812.509. Employment of minors; notification required to be given to jobseekers; necessity of personal interview

(a) No employment agency shall, when employment would be in violation of Chapter 1 (commencing with Section 1171) of Part 4 of Division 2 of the Labor Code or Part 27 (commencing with Section 48000) of the Education Code, accept any application for employment made by, or on behalf of, any minor, or place or assist in placing any minor in that employment.

(b) Every employment agency shall notify each jobseeker before sending the jobseeker in response to a request for employment whether a labor contract is in existence at the establishment to which the jobseeker is being sent, and whether union membership is required.

(c) No employment agency shall send a jobseeker to any place where a strike, lockout, or other labor trouble exists without notifying the jobseeker of that fact and shall in addition thereto enter a statement of those conditions upon the contract or receipt given to the jobseeker.

(d) No babysitting, domestic, or other employment agency which procures babysitting or domestic employment for employers shall refer babysitters or domestics for any employment without first conducting a personal interview of the jobseeker and making a reasonable effort to verify the experience or training of the jobseeker.

(e) No employment agency that procures temporary employment for long-term health care employers shall refer certified nurse assistants or licensed nursing staff as defined in Section 1812.540, for any employment without first conducting a personal interview of the individual, verifying the experience, training, and references of the individual, and verifying that the individual is in good standing with the appropriate licensing or certification board, including verification that the individual has successfully secured a criminal record clearance. *(Added by Stats.1989, c. 704, § 2. Amended by Stats.1990, c. 1256 (A.B.2649), § 5; Stats.2001, c. 326 (A.B.1643), § 1.)*

§ 1812.5093. Child care provider referral; disclosure

(a) Every employment agency that refers a child care provider to an employer who is not required to be a licensed child day care facility pursuant to Section 1596.792 of the Health and Safety Code shall provide the employer with all the following:

(1) A description of the child care provider trustline registry established pursuant to Chapter 3.35 (commencing with Section 1596.60) of Division 2 of the Health and Safety Code that provides criminal history checks on child care providers.

(2) An explanation of how an employer may obtain more information about the child care provider trustline registry.

(3) A statement that an employment agency is prohibited by law from placing a child care provider unless the provider is a trustline applicant or a registered child care provider.

(4) An explanation of how the employer may verify the prospective child care provider's trustline registry registration.

(b) Receipt of the information required to be provided pursuant to subdivision (a) shall be verified in writing by the employer. *(Added by Stats.1998, c. 287 (A.B.2001), § 1.)*

§ 1812.5095. Domestic worker; relationship with employment agency; agency referral authority and duties

(a) For purposes of this section, the term "employment agency" means an employment agency, as defined in paragraph (3) of subdivision (a) of Section 1812.501, or a domestic agency, as defined in subdivision (h) of Section 1812.501.

(b) An employment agency is not the employer of a domestic worker for whom it procures, offers, refers, provides, or attempts to provide work, if all of the following factors characterize the nature of the relationship between the employment agency and the domestic worker for whom the agency procures, offers, refers, provides, or attempts to provide domestic work:

(1) There is a signed contract or agreement between the employment agency and the domestic worker that contains, at a minimum, provisions that specify all of the following:

(A) That the employment agency shall assist the domestic worker in securing work.

(B) How the employment agency's referral fee shall be paid.

(C) That the domestic worker is free to sign an agreement with other employment agencies and to perform domestic work for persons not referred by the employment agency.

(2) The domestic worker informs the employment agency of any restrictions on hours, location, conditions, or type of work he or she will accept and the domestic worker is free to select or reject any work opportunity procured, offered, referred, or provided by the employment agency.

(3) The domestic worker is free to renegotiate with the person hiring him or her the amount proposed to be paid for the work.

(4) The domestic worker does not receive any training from the employment agency with respect to the performance of domestic work. However, an employment agency may provide a voluntary orientation session in which the relationship between the employment agency and the domestic worker, including the employment agency's administrative and operating procedures, and the provisions of the contract or agreement between the employment agency and the domestic worker are explained.

(5) The domestic worker performs domestic work without any direction, control, or supervision exercised by the employment agency with respect to the manner and means of performing the domestic work. An employment agency shall not be deemed to be exercising direction, control, or supervision when it takes any of the following actions:

(A) Informs the domestic worker about the services to be provided and the conditions of work specified by the person seeking to hire a domestic worker.

(B) Contacts the person who has hired the domestic worker to determine whether that person is satisfied with the agency's referral service.

(C) Informs the domestic worker of the time during which new referrals are available.

(D) Requests the domestic worker to inform the employment agency if the domestic worker is unable to perform the work accepted.

(6) The employment agency does not provide tools, supplies, or equipment necessary to perform the domestic work.

(7) The domestic worker is not obligated to pay the employment agency's referral fee, and the employment agency is not obligated to pay the domestic worker if the person for whom the services were performed fails or refuses to pay for the domestic work.

(8) Payments for domestic services are made directly to either the domestic worker or to the employment agency. Payments made directly to the employment agency shall be deposited into a trust account until payment can be made to the domestic worker.

(9) The relationship between a domestic worker and the person for whom the domestic worker performs services may only be terminated by either of those parties and not by the employment agency that referred the domestic worker. However, an employment agency may decline to make additional referrals to a particular domestic worker, and the domestic worker may decline to accept a particular referral.

(c) The fee charged by an employment agency for its services shall be reasonable, negotiable, and based on a fixed percentage of the job cost.

(d) An employment agency referring a domestic worker to a job shall inform that domestic worker, in writing, on or before the signing of the contract pursuant to paragraph (1) of subdivision (b), that the domestic worker may be obligated to obtain business permits or licenses, where required by any state or local law, ordinance, or regulation, and that he or she is not eligible for unemployment insurance, state disability insurance, social security, or workers' compensation benefits through an employment agency complying with subdivision (b). The employment agency referring a domestic worker shall also inform that domestic worker, if the domestic worker is self-employed, that he or she is required to pay self-employment tax, state tax, and federal income taxes.

(e) An employment agency referring a domestic worker to a job shall verify the worker's legal status or authorization to work prior to providing referral services in accordance with procedures established under federal law.

(f) An employment agency referring a domestic worker to a job shall orally communicate to the person seeking domestic services the disclosure set forth below prior to the referral of the domestic worker the following disclosure statement:

"(Name of agency) is not the employer of the domestic worker it referred to you. Depending on your arrangement with the domestic worker, you may have employer responsibilities."

Within three business days after the employment agency refers a domestic worker to the person seeking domestic services, the following statement printed in not less than 10-point type shall be mailed to the person seeking domestic services:

"(Name of agency) is not the employer of the domestic worker it referred to you. The domestic worker may be your employee or an independent contractor depending on the relationship you have with him or her. If you direct and control the manner and means by which the domestic worker performs his or her work you may have employer responsibilities, including employment taxes and workers' compensation, under state and federal law. For additional information contact your local Employment Development Department and the Internal Revenue Service."

(g) An employment agency referring a domestic worker to a job shall not specify that a worker is self-employed or an independent contractor in any notice, advertisement, or brochure provided to either the worker or the customer.

(h) Every employment agency referring a domestic worker to a job and who is not the employer of the domestic worker being referred, shall in any paid telephone directory advertisement or any other promotional literature or advertising distributed or placed by such an employment agency, on or after January 1, 1995, insert the following statement, in no less than 6-point type which shall be in print which contrasts with the background of the advertisement so as to be easily legible:

"(Name of agency) is a referral agency."

(i) An employment agency may not refer, in its advertising, soliciting, or other presentments to the public, to any bond required to be filed pursuant to this chapter.

(j) An employment agency may not refer, in its advertising, soliciting, or other presentments to the public, to any licensure acquired by the agency.

(k) Any violation of this section with the intent to directly or indirectly mislead the public on the nature of services provided by an employment agency shall constitute unfair competition which includes any unlawful, unfair, or fraudulent business acts or practices and unfair, deceptive, untrue, or misleading advertising. Any person or entity that engages in unfair competition shall be liable for a civil penalty not to exceed two thousand five hundred dollars ($2,500) for each violation. *(Added by Stats.1993, c. 1275 (A.B.1370), § 1. Amended by Stats. 1994, c. 1081 (S.B.1418), § 1.)*

CHAPTER 3. EMPLOYMENT COUNSELING SERVICES

Section
1812.510. Bond; deposit in lieu of bond.
1812.511. Contract; cancellation.
1812.512. Fees; schedule; payment terms; notice; change; confession of judgment, note, or wage assignment as payment.
1812.513. False or misleading representations; advertisements; name, address, and telephone number; guarantee; records.

§ 1812.510. Bond; deposit in lieu of bond

(a) Every employment counseling service subject to this title shall maintain a bond issued by a surety company admitted to do business in this state. The principal sum of the bond shall be ten thousand dollars ($10,000). A copy of the bond shall be filed with the Secretary of State.

(b) The bond required by this section shall be in favor of, and payable to, the people of the State of California, and shall be conditioned that the person obtaining the bond will comply with this title and will pay all sums due any individual or group of individuals when the person or his or her representative, agent, or employee has received those sums. The bond shall be for the benefit of any person or persons damaged by any violation of this title or by fraud, dishonesty, misstatement, misrepresentation,

deceit, unlawful acts or omissions, or failure to provide the services of the employment counseling service in performance of the contract with the customer by the employment counseling service or its agents, representatives, or employees while acting within the scope of their employment.

(c)(1) No employment counseling service shall conduct any business without having a current surety bond in the amount prescribed by this title and filing a copy of the bond with the Secretary of State.

(2) Thirty days prior to the cancellation or termination of any surety bond required by this section, the surety shall send a written notice of that cancellation or termination to both the employment counseling service and the Secretary of State, identifying the bond and the date of cancellation or termination.

(3) If any employment counseling service fails to obtain a new bond and file a copy of that bond with the Secretary of State by the effective date of the cancellation or termination of the former bond, the employment counseling service shall cease to conduct any business unless and until a new surety bond is obtained and a copy of that bond is filed with the Secretary of State.

(d) When a deposit has been made in lieu of the bond pursuant to Section 995.710 of the Code of Civil Procedure, the person asserting a claim against the deposit shall, in lieu of Section 996.430 of the Code of Civil Procedure, establish the claim by furnishing evidence to the Secretary of State of a money judgment entered by a court together with evidence that the claimant is a person described in subdivision (b).

(e) When a person has established the claim with the Secretary of State, the Secretary of State shall immediately review and approve the claim and enter the date of approval on the claim. The claim shall be designated an "approved claim."

(f) When the first claim against a particular deposit has been approved, it shall not be paid until the expiration of a period of 240 days after the date of its approval by the Secretary of State. Subsequent claims that are approved by the Secretary of State within the same 240-day period shall similarly not be paid until the expiration of the 240-day period. Upon the expiration of the 240-day period, the Secretary of State shall pay all approved claims from that 240-day period in full unless the deposit is insufficient, in which case each approved claim shall be paid a pro rata share of the deposit.

(g) When the Secretary of State approves the first claim against a particular deposit account after the expiration of the 240-day period, the date of approval of that claim shall begin a new 240-day period to which subdivision (f) shall apply with respect to the amount remaining in the deposit account.

(h) After a deposit account is exhausted, no further claims shall be paid by the Secretary of State. Claimants who have had their claims paid in full or in part pursuant to subdivisions (f) and (g) shall not be required to return funds received from the deposit for the benefit of other claimants.

(i) When a deposit has been made in lieu of a bond, the amount of the deposit shall not be subject to attachment, garnishment, or execution with respect to an action or judgment against the employment counseling service, other than as to an amount as no longer needed or required for the purpose of this title that would otherwise be returned to the employment counseling service by the Secretary of State.

(j) The Secretary of State shall retain a cash deposit for two years from the date the Secretary of State receives written notification from the assignor of the deposit that the assignor has ceased to engage in the business of a counseling service or has filed a bond pursuant to subdivision (a), provided that there are no outstanding claims against the deposit. Written notification to the Secretary of State shall include all of the following: (1) name, address, and telephone number of the assignor; (2) name, address, and telephone number of the bank at which the deposit is located; (3) account number of the deposit; and (4) a statement whether the assignor is ceasing to engage in the business of a counseling service or has filed a bond with the Secretary of State. The Secretary of State shall forward an acknowledgment of receipt of the written notice to the assignor at the address indicated in the notice, specifying the date of receipt of the written notice and anticipated date of release of the deposit, provided there are no outstanding claims against the deposit account.

(k) A judge of a superior court may order the return of the deposit prior to the expiration of two years upon evidence satisfactory to the judge that there are no outstanding claims against the deposit or order the Secretary of State to retain the deposit for a sufficient period beyond the two years pursuant to subdivision (j) to resolve outstanding claims against the deposit account.

(*l*) The Secretary of State shall charge a filing fee not to exceed the cost of filing the bond or the deposit filed in lieu of a bond pursuant to Section 995.710 of the Code of Civil Procedure.

(m) The Secretary of State shall enforce the provisions of this chapter that govern the filing and maintenance of bonds and deposits in lieu of bonds. (*Added by Stats. 1989, c. 704, § 2. Amended by Stats.1996, c. 633 (S.B. 1978), § 12; Stats.1998, c. 829 (S.B.1652), § 12; Stats. 2002, c. 784 (S.B.1316), § 16.*)

§ 1812.511. Contract; cancellation

(a) Every contract for employment counseling services shall be in writing. An original and one copy of the contract shall be given to the customer at the time the customer signs the contract and before the employment counseling service accepts any fee or deposit or the customer becomes obligated to pay any such fee or deposit. The contract shall contain all of the following:

(1) The name, address, and telephone number of the employment counseling service.

(2) The name and address of the person signing the contract and the person to whom the employment counseling services are to be provided.

(3) A description of the services to be provided; a statement when those services are to be provided; the duration of the contract; and refund provisions as appropriate, to be applicable if the described services are not provided according to the contract.

(4) The amount of the fee to be charged to or collected from the person receiving the services or any other person, and the date or dates when that fee is required to be paid.

(5) The following statement, in type no smaller than 10-point boldfaced type:

"No verbal or written promise or guarantee of any job or employment is made or implied under the terms of this contract."

(6) The following statement, in immediate proximity to the space reserved for the customer's signature, in type no smaller than 10-point boldfaced type:

YOUR RIGHT TO CANCEL

/enter date of transaction/

"You may cancel this contract for employment counseling services, without any penalty or obligation, if notice of cancellation is given, in writing, within three business days from the above date.

"To cancel this contract, just mail or deliver a signed and dated copy of the following cancellation notice or any other written notice of cancellation, or send a telegram containing a notice of cancellation, to (name of employment counseling service) at (address of its place of business) NOT LATER THAN MIDNIGHT OF /date/."

CANCELLATION NOTICE

I hereby cancel this contract.

Dated: _____

_____ Customer's Signature"

Until the employment counseling service has complied with this section the customer may cancel the employment counseling services contract.

(b) All contracts shall be dated and shall be made and numbered consecutively in triplicate, the original and each copy to be signed by the customer and the person acting for the employment counseling service. The original and one copy shall be given to the customer and the other copy shall be kept on file at the employment counseling service.

(c) The full agreement between the parties shall be contained in a single document containing those elements set forth in this section. (*Added by Stats.1989, c. 704, § 2.*)

§ 1812.512. Fees; schedule; payment terms; notice; change; confession of judgment, note, or wage assignment as payment

(a)(1) An employment counseling service shall provide a copy of its fee schedule and payment terms to any customer from whom a fee or deposit is to be received, prior to the customer being interviewed by a counselor, agent, or employee.

(2) In the schedule, the maximum fee shall be fixed and shall include the charges of every kind rendered by the employment counseling service in each case or transaction on behalf of the prospective employee. Changes in the fee schedule may be made, but no change shall become effective until posted for not less than seven days in a conspicuous place in the employment counseling service.

(3) A copy of the schedule in effect shall be kept posted in the employment counseling service in a conspicuous place, and the posted schedule and the changes therein shall be in lettering or printing of not less than standard pica capitals. The date of the taking effect of the schedule and of each change therein shall appear on the posted copies.

(4) A copy of all fee schedules, and of all changes therein, shall be kept on file at the employment counseling service, retrospectively for a period of one year.

(b) No fee charged or collected shall be in excess of the fee as scheduled.

(c) No employment counseling service shall accept, directly or indirectly, a registration fee of any kind.

(d) No employment counseling service may take from a customer a confession of judgment, a promissory note or notes, or an assignment of wages to cover its fees. *(Added by Stats.1989, c. 704, § 2.)*

§ 1812.513. False or misleading representations; advertisements; name, address, and telephone number; guarantee; records

(a) No employment counseling service shall make or cause to be made any false, misleading, or deceptive advertisements or representations concerning the services that the employment counseling service will provide to customers.

(b)(1) No employment counseling service shall publish or cause to be published any false, fraudulent, or misleading information, representation, notice, or advertisements.

(2) All advertisements of an employment counseling service shall contain the correct name of the employment counseling service and one of the following:

(A) The street address of the employment counseling service's place of business.

(B) The correct telephone number of the employment counseling service at its place of business.

(c) No employment counseling service shall give any false information or make any false promises or represen-tations concerning engagement or employment to any customer, or make any verbal or written promise or guarantee of any job or employment.

(d) An employment counseling service shall maintain a record of all advertisements for the service, correlated to show the date and the publication in which the advertisement appeared, retrospectively, for a period of one year.

(e) No employment counseling service shall, by its choice of name or by advertisement or representation, represent itself to be an employment agency or to perform the job placement services of an employment agency. *(Added by Stats.1989, c. 704, § 2.)*

CHAPTER 4. JOB LISTING SERVICES

Section
1812.515. Bond; deposit in lieu of bond.
1812.516. Contracts; cancellation.
1812.517. Fees; schedule; payment terms; notice; change; confession of judgment, note, or wage assignment as payment; splitting.
1812.518. Refunds; failure to meet contract specifications; job not obtained or lasting less than 90 days; penalty.
1812.519. Job order; prerequisite to fee acceptance; conditions; referrals; exchange with employment agency.
1812.520. False or misleading representations; advertisements; contents; records.
1812.521. Illegal employment; minors; labor contract; union membership; labor trouble; notice.

§ 1812.515. Bond; deposit in lieu of bond

(a) Every job listing service subject to this title shall maintain a bond issued by a surety company admitted to do business in this state. The principal sum of the bond shall be ten thousand dollars ($10,000) for each location. A copy of the bond shall be filed with the Secretary of State.

(b) The bond required by this section shall be in favor of, and payable to, the people of the State of California, and shall be conditioned that the person obtaining the bond will comply with this title and will pay all sums due any individual or group of individuals when the person or his or her representative, agent, or employee has received those sums. The bond shall be for the benefit of any person or persons damaged by any violation of misrepresentation, deceit, unlawful acts of omissions, or failure to provide the services of the job listing service in performance of the contract with the jobseeker, by the job listing service or its agent, representatives, or employees while acting within the scope of their employment.

(c)(1) No job listing service shall conduct any business without having a current surety bond in the amount prescribed by this chapter and filing a copy of the bond with the Secretary of State, identifying the bond and the date of cancellation or termination.

(2) Thirty days prior to the cancellation or termination of any surety bond required by this section, the surety

shall send a written notice of that cancellation or termination to both the job listing service and the Secretary of State, identifying the bond and the date of cancellation or termination.

(3) If any job listing service fails to obtain a new bond and file a copy of that bond with the Secretary of State by the effective date of the cancellation or termination of the former bond, the job listing service shall cease to conduct any business unless and until a new surety bond is obtained and a copy of that bond is filed with the Secretary of State.

(d) When a deposit has been made in lieu of a bond pursuant to Section 995.710 of the Code of Civil Procedure, the person asserting a claim against the deposit shall, in lieu of Section 996.430 of the Code of Civil Procedure, establish the claim by furnishing evidence to the Secretary of State of a money judgment entered by a court together with evidence that the claimant is a person described in subdivision (b).

(e) When a person has established the claim with the Secretary of State, the Secretary of State shall review and approve the claim and enter the date of approval on the claim. The claim shall be designated an "approved claim."

(f) When the first claim against a particular deposit has been approved, it shall not be paid until the expiration of a period of 240 days after the date of its approval by the Secretary of State. Subsequent claims that are approved by the Secretary of State within the same 240–day period shall similarly not be paid until the expiration of the 240–day period. Upon the expiration of the 240–day period, the Secretary of State shall pay all approved claims from that 240–day period in full unless the deposit is insufficient, in which case each approved claim shall be paid in a pro rata share of the deposit.

(g) When the Secretary of State approves the first claim against a particular deposit after the expiration of the 240–day period, the date of approval of that claim shall begin a new 240–day period to which subdivision (f) shall apply with respect to the amount remaining in the deposit.

(h) After a deposit is exhausted, no further claims shall be paid by the Secretary of State. Claimants who have had their claims paid in full or in part pursuant to subdivisions (f) and (g) shall not be required to return funds received from the deposit for the benefit of other claimants.

(i) When a deposit has been made in lieu of a bond, the amount of the deposit shall not be subject to attachment, garnishment, or execution with respect to an action or judgment against the job listing service, other than as to an amount as no longer needed or required for the purpose of this title that would otherwise be returned to the job listing service by the Secretary of State.

(j) The Secretary of State shall retain a cash deposit for two years from the date the Secretary of State receives written notification from the assignor of the deposit that the assignor has ceased to engage in the business of a job listing service or has filed a bond pursuant to subdivision (a), provided that there are no outstanding claims against the deposit. Written notification to the Secretary of State shall include all of the following: (1) name, address, and telephone number of the assignor; (2) name, address, and telephone number of the bank at which the deposit is located; (3) account number of the deposit; and (4) a statement whether the assignor is ceasing to engage in the business of a job listing service or has filed a bond with the Secretary of State. The Secretary of State shall forward an acknowledgment of receipt of the written notice to the assignor at the address indicated therein, specifying the date of receipt of the written notice and anticipated date of release of the deposit, provided there are no outstanding claims against the deposit.

(k) A judge of a superior court may order the return of the deposit prior to the expiration of two years upon evidence satisfactory to the judge that there are no outstanding claims against the deposit or order the Secretary of State to retain the deposit for a specified period beyond the two years pursuant to subdivision (j) to resolve outstanding claims against the deposit account.

(*l*) The Secretary of State shall charge a filing fee not to exceed the cost of filing the bond or deposit filed in lieu of a bond pursuant to Section 995.710 of the Code of Civil Procedure.

(m) The Secretary of State shall enforce the provisions of this chapter that govern the filing and maintenance of bonds and deposits in lieu of bonds. *(Added by Stats. 1989, c. 704, § 2. Amended by Stats.1996, c. 633 (S.B. 1978), § 13; Stats.1998, c. 829 (S.B.1652), § 13; Stats. 2002, c. 784 (S.B.1316), § 17.)*

§ 1812.516. Contracts; cancellation

(a) Every job listing service shall give a written contract to every jobseeker from whom a fee or deposit is to be received, whether directly or indirectly. The original and one copy of the contract shall be given to the jobseeker at the time the jobseeker signs the contract and before the job listing service accepts any fee or deposit or the jobseeker becomes obligated to pay any such fee or deposit. The contract shall contain all of the following:

(1) The name of the job listing service and the addresses and telephone numbers of the principal office of the job listing service and the location providing the listing services to the jobseeker.

(2) The amount of the fee to be charged and to be collected from the jobseeker.

(3) A description of the service to be performed by the job listing service, including significant conditions, restrictions, and limitations where applicable.

(4) A description of the jobseeker's specifications for the employment opportunity in clear language understandable to the jobseeker, including, but not limited to, the following:

(A) Kind of work or employment.

59

(B) Interests of jobseeker.

(C) Qualifications of jobseeker.

(D) Daily hours of work, the wages or salary, benefits, and other conditions of employment.

(E) Location of job.

(5) The contract expiration date, which shall not be later than 90 days from the date of execution of the contract.

(6) The following statement, in immediate proximity to the space reserved for the jobseeker's signature, in type no smaller than 10-point boldfaced type:

YOUR RIGHT TO CANCEL

/enter date of transaction/

"You may cancel this contract for job listing services without any penalty or obligation, if notice of cancellation is given, in writing, within three business days from the above date.

"To cancel this contract, just mail or deliver a signed and dated copy of the following cancellation notice or any other written notice of cancellation, to (name of job listing service) at (address of its place of business), NOT LATER THAN MIDNIGHT OF /date/."

CANCELLATION NOTICE

I hereby cancel this contract.

Dated: _____

_____ Customer's Signature"

Until the job listing service has complied with this section the jobseeker may cancel the job listing service's contract.

(7) The following statement, with the caption in type no smaller than 10-point boldfaced type and the remainder in a size no smaller than that generally used throughout the contract, and in full capitals, boldface, or italics:

"RIGHT TO REFUND"

"If, within seven business days after payment of a fee or deposit, the job listing service has not supplied you with at least three available employment opportunities meeting the specifications of the contract as to type of job; interests of jobseeker; qualifications of jobseeker; hours, salary, benefits, and other conditions of employment; location of job; and any other specifications expressly set forth in the contract, the full amount of the fee or deposit paid shall be refunded to you upon your request.

"If you do not obtain a job through the services of the job listing service, or if you obtain employment which lasts less than 90 days, any amount paid in fees or deposits in excess of a twenty-five dollar ($25) service charge shall be refunded to you, upon your request after expiration of the contract.

"Any refund due must be made to you within 10 days of your request. If the refund is not made in that time, the job listing service must pay to you an additional sum equal to the amount of your fee or deposit."

(8) If any labor trouble exists at the place of employment, that fact shall be stated in the listing of that employment provided to the jobseeker.

(b) All contracts shall be dated and shall be made and numbered consecutively in triplicate, the original and each copy to be signed by the jobseeker and the person acting for the job listing service. The original and one copy shall be given to the jobseeker and the other copy shall be kept on file at the job listing service.

(c) The full agreement between the parties shall be contained in a single document containing those elements set forth in this section. *(Added by Stats.1989, c. 704, § 2. Amended by Stats.1990, c. 1256 (A.B.2649), § 6.)*

§ 1812.517. Fees; schedule; payment terms; notice; change; confession of judgment, note, or wage assignment as payment; splitting

(a)(1) A job listing service shall provide a copy of the service's fee schedule and payment terms to any jobseeker from whom a fee or deposit is to be received, prior to the jobseeker being interviewed by a counselor or other agent or employee.

(2) In the schedule, the maximum fee shall be fixed and shall include the charges of every kind rendered by the job listing service in each case or transaction on behalf of the prospective employee. Changes in the fee schedule may be made, but no change shall become effective until posted for not less than seven days in a conspicuous place in the job listing service.

(3) A copy of the schedule in effect shall be kept posted in the job listing service in a conspicuous place, and the posted schedule and the changes therein shall be in lettering or printing of not less than standard pica capitals. The date of the taking effect of the schedule and of each change therein shall appear on the posted copies.

(4) A copy of all fee schedules, and of all changes therein, shall be kept on file at the job listing service, retrospectively, for a period of one year.

(b) No fee charged or collected shall be in excess of the fee as scheduled.

(c) No job listing service may take from a jobseeker a confession of judgment, a promissory note or notes, or an assignment of wages to cover its fees.

(d) The fee charged shall not be based on a portion or percentage of the salary or wages earned or to be earned in the employment obtained through use of the job listing service.

(e)(1) No job listing service shall divide fees with an employer, an agent, or other employee of any employer or person to whom help is furnished.

(2) No job listing service shall charge any jobseeker a fee for accepting employment with that job listing service or any subsidiary of that service.

(3) No job listing service shall charge any jobseeker a fee when help is furnished to an employer, an agent, any employee of any employer, a member, or person who has a financial interest in the job listing service. *(Added by Stats.1989, c. 704, § 2.)*

§ 1812.518. Refunds; failure to meet contract specifications; job not obtained or lasting less than 90 days; penalty

(a)(1) A job listing service shall refund in full any advance fee paid and cancel any other obligation incurred by the jobseeker if the job listing service does not, within seven business days after execution of the contract, supply at least three employment opportunities then available to the jobseeker and meeting the specifications of the contract.

(2) A job listing service will be deemed to have supplied information meeting the specifications of the jobseeker if the information supplied meets the contract specifications with reference to: type of job; interests of jobseeker; qualifications of jobseeker; hours, salary, benefits, and other conditions of employment; location of job; and any other specifications expressly set forth in the contract.

(b) A job listing service shall refund any amount over and above a twenty-five dollar ($25) service charge and cancel any other obligation incurred by the jobseeker if the jobseeker does not obtain a job, or if employment, once obtained, lasts less than 90 days.

(c) A job listing service shall make all refunds required under this section within 10 days after the jobseeker requests such refund. Unless the refund is made within that time, the job listing service shall pay the jobseeker an additional sum equal to the amount of the deposit. *(Added by Stats.1989, c. 704, § 2.)*

§ 1812.519. Job order; prerequisite to fee acceptance; conditions; referrals; exchange with employment agency

(a) No job listing service shall accept a fee from any jobseeker, or send any jobseeker for employment, without having obtained, in writing, a bona fide job order for employment.

(b) A job listing service shall identify itself as a job listing service to the employer in all instances in which it contacts an employer for the purposes of soliciting a job order. All job orders shall be recorded in writing. A job order for employment shall be considered to have been given by an employer to a job listing service under the following conditions:

(1) The employer, or his or her agent, in writing, registers a request or gives permission that the job listing service recruit or refer jobseekers who meet the employer's stated job specifications and the employer furnishes such information as required by subdivision (a) of Section 1812.516.

(2) A job order is valid for the referral of any qualified jobseeker until it is filled or canceled by the employer, and may serve as the basis for job listing service advertising. The job listing service is required to recontact the employer within the four-day period immediately preceding dissemination of the job listing information to ensure that the position is still vacant prior to any additional advertising or referral of jobseekers.

(c) No job listing service shall refer a jobseeker to a job knowing or having reason to know that:

(1) The job does not exist or the jobseeker is not qualified for the job.

(2) The job has been described or advertised by or on behalf of the job listing service in a false, misleading, or deceptive manner.

(3) The job listing service has not obtained written permission to list the job from the employer or an authorized agent of the employer.

(d) No job listing service shall exchange job orders with an employment agency which charges a placement fee. *(Added by Stats.1989, c. 704, § 2. Amended by Stats.1991, c. 654 (A.B.1893), § 51.)*

§ 1812.520. False or misleading representations; advertisements; contents; records

(a) No job listing service shall make or cause to be made any false, misleading or deceptive advertisements or representations concerning the services that the job listing service will provide to jobseekers.

(b)(1) No job listing service shall publish or cause to be published any false, fraudulent, or misleading information, representation, notice, or advertisements.

(2) All advertisements of a job listing service shall contain the correct name of the job listing service and one of the following:

(A) The street address of the job listing service's place of business.

(B) The correct telephone number of the job listing service at its place of business.

(3) No job listing service shall give any false information or make any false promises or representations concerning an engagement or employment to any jobseeker.

(4) No job listing service shall, by its choice of name or by advertisement or representation, represent itself to be an employment agency or to perform the services of an employment agency.

(c) Special requirements not usually associated with a job shall be specified in any advertisement. When the location of the position advertised is more than 50 miles from the job listing service office responsible for the advertisement, it shall state either the location or that the job is "nonlocal." Special benefits of the job, if advertised, shall be specifically described and substitute terms or symbols such as "extras" or " + " shall not be sufficient.

(d) An advertised salary shall be based upon the starting salary contained in the job order. An advertised range of starting salaries shall be specified by preceding the minimum salary and maximum salary by terms "from" and "to" respectively. When the job order contains only the maximum amount of a salary range, that advertised salary shall be preceded by the word "to." If a maximum salary is dependent upon the jobseeker's experience, the advertised salary may be described by listing the minimum salary and the term "up Depending on Experience" or "up D.O.E." The words "open" and "negotiable" or words or symbols of like import shall not be used as a substitute for the salary. If an advertised salary is based in whole or in part on commissions, that fact shall be indicated in the advertisement.

(e) All job listing services shall maintain a record of all advertised jobs, correlated to show the date and the publication in which the advertisement appeared and the job order number of each job advertised, retrospectively for a period of one year. *(Added by Stats.1989, c. 704, § 2. Amended by Stats.1990, c. 1256, (A.B.2649), § 7.)*

§ 1812.521. Illegal employment; minors; labor contract; union membership; labor trouble; notice

(a) No job listing service shall, when employment would be in violation of Chapter 1 (commencing with Section 1171) of Part 4 of Division 2 of the Labor Code or Part 27 (commencing with Section 48000) of the Education Code, accept any application for employment made by, or on behalf of, any minor, or place or assist in placing any minor in that employment.

(b) Every job listing service shall notify each jobseeker before sending the jobseeker in response to a request for employment whether a labor contract is in existence at the establishment to which the jobseeker is being sent, and whether union membership is required.

(c) No job listing service shall send a jobseeker to any place where a strike, lockout, or other labor trouble exists without notifying the jobseeker of that fact and shall in addition thereto enter a statement of those conditions upon the contract or receipt given to the jobseeker. *(Added by Stats.1989, c. 704, § 2. Amended by Stats.1990, c. 1256, (A.B.2649), § 8.)*

CHAPTER 5.   RECORDS

Section
1812.522. Inspection; reports; separation from records of other business.

§ 1812.522. Inspection; reports; separation from records of other business

(a) All books, records, files, the schedules, and other papers required by this title to be kept by any employment agency, employment counseling service, or job listing service shall be open at all reasonable hours to the inspection of the representative of the Attorney General, any district attorney, or any city attorney. Every employment agency, employment counseling service, and job listing service shall furnish to the representative of the Attorney General, any district attorney, or any city attorney upon request a true copy of those books, records, files, the schedules, and papers or any portion thereof, and shall make such reports as the Attorney General prescribes.

(b) If any employment agency, employment counseling service, or job listing service also engages in any other business which is not subject to this title, the records of the agency or service pertaining to matters under the jurisdictions of this title shall be kept separate and apart from the records of that other business. *(Added by Stats.1989, c. 704, § 2.)*

CHAPTER 6.   REMEDIES AND ENFORCEMENT

Section
1812.523. Misdemeanors; civil actions and proceedings; false or misleading representation voiding contract; refund; damages; attorney fees; costs; other laws; waiver of provisions; severability.

§ 1812.523. Misdemeanors; civil actions and proceedings; false or misleading representation voiding contract; refund; damages; attorney fees; costs; other laws; waiver of provisions; severability

(a) Any person who violates any provision of this title is guilty of a misdemeanor. The Attorney General, any district attorney, or any city attorney may prosecute misdemeanor actions.

(b) Actions for violation of this title, including, but not limited to, equity proceedings to restrain and enjoin such a violation, may be instituted by the Attorney General, any district attorney, or any city attorney. This section shall not be deemed to prohibit the enforcement by any person of any right provided by this or any other law.

(c) If any person uses any untrue or misleading statement, information, or advertisement to sell its services or fails to comply with the applicable provisions of this title, or the contract does not comply with the applicable provisions of this title, then the contract shall be void and unenforceable as contrary to public policy and the jobseeker, customer, or nurse shall be entitled to the return of all sums paid.

(d) Any person who is injured by any violation of this title or by the breach of a contract subject to this title may bring an action for the recovery of damages, an equity proceeding to restrain and enjoin those violations, or both. The amount awarded may be up to three times the damages actually incurred, but in no event less than the amount paid by the jobseeker, customer, or nurse to the person subject to this title. If the person subject to this title refuses or is unwilling to pay the damages awarded, the amount awarded may be satisfied out of the security required by this title. If the plaintiff prevails, the plaintiff shall be awarded a reasonable attorney's fee and costs. If the court determines that the breach or violation was willful, by clear and convincing evidence, the court, in its discretion, may award punitive damages in addition to the amounts set forth above.

(e) The provisions of this title are not exclusive and do not relieve the parties subject to this title from the duty to comply with all other applicable laws.

(f) The remedies provided in this title are not exclusive and shall be in addition to any other remedies or procedures provided in any other law.

(g) Any waiver by the consumer, jobseeker, or nurse of the provisions of this title shall be deemed contrary to public policy and shall be void and unenforceable. Any attempt by a person subject to this title to have a jobseeker, customer, or nurse waive rights given by this title shall constitute a violation of this title.

(h) If any provisions of this title or the application thereof to any person or circumstances is held unconstitutional, the remainder of the title and the application of that provision to other persons and circumstances shall not be affected thereby. (Added by Stats.1989, c. 704, § 2.)

CHAPTER 7. NURSES' REGISTRIES

Section
1812.524. Definitions.
1812.525. Bond; deposit in lieu of bond.
1812.526. Continuing contract; contents.
1812.527. Fees; schedule; payment terms; notice; change.
1812.528. Experience, training, license; verification.
1812.529. Records.
1812.530. Registration fee; confession of judgment, note, or wage assignment as fee payment.
1812.531. Splitting fees.
1812.532. Failure to obtain or be paid for assignment; refund, delay, penalty.
1812.533. False or misleading representations; advertisements; contents.

§ 1812.524. Definitions

(a) "Nursing service" means the assignment of a nurse, as a private duty, self-employed, licensed registered nurse, licensed vocational nurse, or practical nurse to render service to a patient under the direction or supervision of a physician or surgeon registered to practice in this state.

(b) "Nurses' registry" means a person who engages in the business of obtaining and filling commitments for nursing service. A nurses' registry which makes or plans to make referrals for nurses' employment other than private duty nursing shall comply with Chapters 1 (commencing with Section 1812.500) and 2 (commencing with Section 1812.503) of this title with respect to those referrals.

(c) "Private duty nurse" means a self-employed nurse rendering service in the care of either a physically or mentally ill patient under the direction of a physician or surgeon, but who is paid by either the patient or the designated agent of the patient and who accepts the responsibilities of a self-employed private contractor. (Added by Stats.1989, c. 704, § 2. Amended by Stats.1990, c. 1256, (A.B.2649), § 9.)

§ 1812.525. Bond; deposit in lieu of bond

(a) Every nurses' registry subject to this title shall maintain a bond issued by a surety company admitted to do business in this state. The principal sum of the bond shall be three thousand dollars ($3,000). A copy of the bond shall be filed with the Secretary of State.

(b) The bond required by this section shall be in favor of, and payable to, the people of the State of California, and shall be conditioned that the person obtaining the bond will comply with this title and will pay all sums due any individual or group of individuals when the person or his or her representative, agent, or employee has received those sums. The bond shall be for the benefit of any person or persons damaged by any violation of this title or by fraud, dishonesty, misstatement, misrepresentation, deceit, unlawful acts or omissions, or failure to provide the services of the nurses' registry in performance of the contract with the nurse by the nurses' registry or its agents, representatives, or employees while acting within the scope of their employment.

(c)(1) No nurses' registry shall conduct any business without having a current surety bond in the amount prescribed by this title and filing a copy of the bond with the Secretary of State.

(2) Thirty days prior to the cancellation or termination of any surety bond required by this section, the surety shall send a written notice of that cancellation or termination to both the nurses' registry and the Secretary of State, identifying the bond and the date of cancellation or termination.

(3) If any nurses' registry fails to obtain a new bond and file a copy of that bond with the Secretary of State by the effective date of the cancellation or termination of the former bond, the nurses' registry shall cease to conduct any business unless and until a new surety bond is obtained and a copy of that bond is filed with the Secretary of State.

(d) When a deposit has been made in lieu of a bond pursuant to Section 995.710 of the Code of Civil Procedure, the person asserting a claim against the deposit shall, in lieu of Section 996.430 of the Code of Civil Procedure, establish the claim by furnishing evidence to the Secretary of State of a money judgment entered by a court together with evidence that the claimant is a person described in subdivision (b).

(e) When a person has established the claim with the Secretary of State, the Secretary of State shall review and approve the claim and enter the date of approval on the claim. The claim shall be designated an "approved claim."

(f) When the first claim against a particular deposit has been approved, it shall not be paid until the expiration of a period of 240 days after the date of its approval by the Secretary of State. Subsequent claims that are approved by the Secretary of State within the same 240–day period shall similarly not be paid until the expiration of the 240–day period. Upon the expiration of the 240–day period, the Secretary of State shall pay all approved claims from that 240–day period in full unless the deposit is insufficient, in which case each approved claim shall be paid a pro rata share of the deposit.

(g) When the Secretary of State approves the first claim against a particular deposit after the expiration of a 240–day period, the date of approval of that claim shall begin a new 240–day period to which subdivision (f) shall apply with respect to the amount remaining in the deposit.

(h) After a deposit is exhausted, no further claims shall be paid by the Secretary of State. Claimants who have had their claims paid in full or in part pursuant to subdivisions (f) and (g) shall not be required to return funds received from the deposit for the benefit of other claimants.

(i) When a deposit has been made in lieu of a bond, the amount of the deposit shall not be subject to attachment, garnishment, or execution with respect to an action or judgment against the nurses' registry, other than as to an amount as no longer needed or required for the purpose of this title that would otherwise be returned to the nurses' registry by the Secretary of State.

(j) The Secretary of State shall retain a cash deposit for two years from the date the Secretary of State receives written notification from the assignor of the deposit that the assignor has ceased to engage in the business of a nurses' registry or has filed a bond pursuant to subdivision (a), provided that there are no outstanding claims against the deposit. The written notice to the Secretary of State shall include all of the following: (1) name, address, and telephone number of the assignor; (2) name, address, and telephone number of the bank at which the deposit is located; (3) account number of the deposit; and (4) a statement whether the assignor is ceasing to engage in the business of a nurses' registry or has filed a bond with the Secretary of State. The Secretary of State shall forward an acknowledgment of receipt of the written notice to the assignor at the address indicated therein, specifying the date of receipt of the written notice and anticipated date of release of the deposit, provided there are no outstanding claims against the deposit.

(k) A judge of a superior court may order the return of the deposit prior to the expiration of two years upon evidence satisfactory to the judge that there are no outstanding claims against the deposit or order the Secretary of State to retain the deposit for a specified period beyond the two years pursuant to subdivision (j) to resolve outstanding claims against the deposit.

(*l*) The Secretary of State shall charge a filing fee not to exceed the cost of filing the bond or deposit filed in lieu of a bond pursuant to Section 995.710 of the Code of Civil Procedure.

(m) The Secretary of State shall enforce the provisions of this chapter that govern the filing and maintenance of bonds and deposits in lieu of bonds. *(Added by Stats. 1989, c. 704, § 2. Amended by Stats.1996, c. 633 (S.B. 1978), § 14; Stats.1998, c. 829 (S.B.1652), § 14; Stats. 2002, c. 784 (S.B.1316), § 18.)*

§ 1812.526. Continuing contract; contents

Nurses' registries may enter into a continuing contract with private duty nurses covering the assignment of those nurses by the nurses' registries. The continuing contract shall state:

(a) The name, address, and telephone number of the nurses' registry.

(b) The name, address, and telephone number of the nurse.

(c) The current fee schedule of the nurses' registry.

(d) The date of its execution by the nurses' registry and the nurse.

(e) The contract shall specify that the provisions thereof are to govern only the assignment of private duty nurses and shall do all of the following:

(1) Designate the nurses' registry as the continuous agent of the nurse for purposes of assignment.

(2) Provide that the contract in effect may be terminated at any time by written notice given by one to the other for any future assignment.

(3) Provide for delivery to the nurse at the time of the execution of the contract a written schedule of the rates of nurses' charges currently agreed to between the nurses' registry and the nurse for the nurse's services to the patient.

(4) State that the nurses' registry will immediately notify the nurse in writing of all subsequent changes in the rates to be charged the patient for services, and that the nurse shall agree to abide by these rates.

(5) Contain express undertakings by the nurses' registry that it shall continuously maintain true and correct records of orders and assignments as provided in this title.

(6) Provide that the nurses' registry shall periodically and at least once each month render to the nurse a written statement of all fees claimed to be due the nurses' registry, and further that the statement shall adequately identify each assignment as to the inception date and period of service covered by the claim, including the name of the patient and the amount of service fee claimed.

(7) Contain appropriate wording advising the nurse of his or her right to dispute the correctness of any service fee claimed by the nurses' registry in the written state-

ment referred to above, and that in the absence of objections within a reasonable time, any such service fee may be presumed to be correctly charged.

(8) Include any other term, condition, or understanding agreed upon between the nurses' registry and the nurse.

(f) Each contract shall be numbered consecutively in original and duplicate, both to be signed by the nurse and the nurses' registry. The original shall be given to the nurse and the duplicate shall be kept on file at the nurses' registry within the nurse's records.

(g) The full agreement between the parties shall be contained in a single document containing those elements set forth in this section. *(Added by Stats.1989, c. 704, § 2. Amended by Stats.1990, c. 1256, (A.B.2649), § 10.)*

§ 1812.527. Fees; schedule; payment terms; notice; change

(a)(1)[1] A nurses' registry shall provide a copy of the registry's fee schedule and payment terms to any nurse from whom a fee or deposit is to be received, prior to the nurse being interviewed by the registry.

(2) In the schedule, the maximum fee shall be fixed and shall include the charges of every kind rendered by the nurses' registry in each case or transaction on behalf of the nurse. Changes in the fee schedule may be made, but no change shall become effective until posted for not less than seven days in a conspicuous place in the nurses' registry.

(3) A copy of the schedule in effect shall be kept posted in the nurses' registry in a conspicuous place, and the posted schedule and the changes therein shall be in lettering or printing of not less than standard pica capitals. The date of the taking effect of the schedule and of each change therein shall appear on the posted copies.

(4) A copy of all fee schedules, and of all changes therein, shall be kept on file at the nurses' registry, retrospectively for a period of one year. *(Added by Stats.1989, c. 704, § 2.)*

[1] So in enrolled bill.

§ 1812.528. Experience, training, license; verification

It shall be the duty of the nurses' registry to verify in writing the claims as to the experience or training listed on the application and to keep a file of those records in the nurse's folder within the nurses' registry. It shall also be the duty of the person interviewing the jobseeker to require the jobseeker to exhibit his or her license as issued by the Board of Registered Nursing or the Board of Vocational Nurse and Psychiatric Technician Examiners, with a notation to be made on the application by the interviewer that the license has been inspected and the date of expiration of the license. *(Added by Stats.1989, c. 704, § 2.)*

§ 1812.529. Records

Each nurses' registry shall continuously maintain in its offices true and correct permanent log sheets and other records which shall disclose, in addition to the other information required, the date and hour of the receipt by the nurses' registry of each order for a private duty nurse, and the date and hour of the making or giving of each assignment to the nurse by the nurses' registry, the name of the nurse assigned, the name of the patient and the address where the nurse is assigned, the name of the attending physician, the date the assignment is to start, the period of actual service for each assignment, and the amount of the fee charged for each assignment. No nurses' registry, his or her agent or employees, shall make any false entry in those records. The nurses' registry shall maintain the log sheets and records required by this section respectively for a period of one year. *(Added by Stats.1989. c. 704, § 2.)*

§ 1812.530. Registration fee; confession of judgment, note, or wage assignment as fee payment

(a) No nurses' registry shall accept, directly or indirectly, a registration fee of any kind.

(b) No nurses' registry may take from a nurse a confession of judgment, or promissory note, or an assignment of wages to cover its fees. *(Added by Stats.1989, c. 704, § 2.)*

§ 1812.531. Splitting fees

No nurses' registry shall divide fees with any physician and surgeon, nurse, hospital, patient, or any agent or employee of any of these. *(Added by Stats.1989, c. 704, § 2.)*

§ 1812.532. Failure to obtain or be paid for assignment; refund; delay; penalty

In the event that a nurses' registry collects from a nurse a fee or expenses for an assignment, and the nurse fails to obtain the assignment, or the nurse fails to be paid for the assignment, the nurses' registry shall upon demand therefor, repay to the nurse the fee and expenses so collected. Unless repayment is made within 48 hours after demand, the nurses' registry shall pay to the nurse an additional sum equal to the amount of the fee. *(Added by Stats.1989, c. 704, § 2.)*

§ 1812.533. False or misleading representations; advertisements; contents

(a) No nurses' registry shall make, or cause to be made, any false, misleading, or deceptive advertisements or representations concerning the services that registry will provide to nurses.

(b)(1) No nurses' registry shall publish or cause to be published any false, fraudulent, or misleading information, representation, notice, or advertisements.

(2) All advertisements of a nurses' registry shall contain the correct name of the nurses' registry and one of the following:

(A) The street address of the registry's place of business.

(B) The correct telephone number of the registry at its place of business.

(3) No nurses' registry shall give any false information or make any false promises or representations concerning an assignment or employment to any nurse who registers or applies for an assignment or employment.

(4) No nurses' registry shall, by its name, advertisement, or any other representation, represent itself to be a home health agency, as defined by subdivision (a) of Section 1727 of the Health and Safety Code, or to perform the services of a home health agency. A nurses' registry shall provide a written disclosure to each individual receiving nursing services, as defined in subdivision (a) of Section 1812.524, in his or her place of residence stating that it does not perform the services of a home health agency and clearly describing that it is a nurses' registry only and that any complaints against licensed personnel providing a nursing service shall be brought to the local district attorney and the Department of Consumer Affairs. The address and telephone number of each agency and board to which complaints are required to be submitted shall be provided to all patients prior to the time they are under the care of any nursing services personnel.

(5) Any person may refer complaints concerning nurses' registries to the proper law enforcement agency for action.

(c) Every nurses' registry shall maintain a record of all advertisements, correlated to show the date and the publication in which the advertisement appeared, retrospectively for a period of one year. *(Added by Stats.1989, c. 704, § 2. Amended by Stats.1990, c. 761, (A.B.3924), § 2.)*

CHAPTER 8.　LONG–TERM CARE FACILITIES

Section
1812.540.　Definitions.
1812.541.　Information or material to be provided to long-term health care facility with respect to the referral of a temporary certified nurse assistant.
1812.542.　Information or material to be provided to long-term health care facility with respect to the referral of a temporary licensed nursing staff.
1812.543.　Adoption of policies and procedures by employment agency regarding prevention of resident or patient abuse by temporary staff.
1812.544.　Maintaining records of all advertisements by employment agencies making referrals of licensed nursing staff or certified nurse assistants for temporary employment in a long-term health care facility.

§ 1812.540.　Definitions

For purposes of this chapter, the following definitions shall apply:

(a) "Direct care service" means the temporary assignment of certified nurse assistants to render basic care services directed at the safety, comfort, personal hygiene, or protection of a patient who is a resident of a long-term health care facility.

(b) "Nursing service" means the temporary assignment of a licensed registered nurse, licensed vocational nurse, or psychiatric technician to render nursing and basic care services to a patient who is a resident of a long-term health care facility.

(c) "Licensed nursing staff" means a licensed registered nurse, licensed vocational nurse, or psychiatric technician.

(d) "Long-term health care facility" means a licensed facility, as defined in Section 1418 of the Health and Safety Code. *(Added by Stats.2001, c. 326 (A.B.1643), § 2.)*

§ 1812.541.　Information or material to be provided to long-term health care facility with respect to the referral of a temporary certified nurse assistant

Every employment agency that refers temporary certified nurse assistants to an employer that is a long-term health care facility shall provide the employer with all of the following:

(a) Written verification that the employment agency has verified that any certified nurse assistant referred by the agency is registered on the state registry of certified nurse assistants and is in good standing. The employment agency shall provide to the employer the certified nurse assistant's professional certification number and date of expiration.

(b) A statement that the certified nurse assistant has at least six months of experience working in a long-term health care facility.

(c) A statement that the certified nurse assistant has had a health examination within 90 days prior to employment with the employment agency or seven days after employment with the employment agency and at least annually thereafter by a person lawfully authorized to perform that procedure. Each examination shall include a medical history and physical evaluation. The employment agency shall also provide verification that the individual has had tuberculosis screening within 90 days prior to employment and annually thereafter.

(d) A statement that the certified nurse assistant will participate in the facility's orientation program and any in-service training programs at the request of the long-term health care employer.

(e) A statement that a certified nurse assistant is in compliance with the in-service training requirements of paragraph (1) of subdivision (a) of Section 1337.6 of the Health and Safety Code. *(Added by Stats.2001, c. 326 (A.B.1643), § 2.)*

§ 1812.542. Information or material to be provided to long-term health care facility with respect to the referral of a temporary licensed nursing staff

Every employment agency that refers temporary licensed nursing staff to an employer who is a licensed long-term health care facility shall provide the employer with all of the following:

(a) Written verification that the individual is in good standing with the Board of Registered Nursing or the Board of Vocational Nursing and Psychiatric Technicians, as applicable, and has successfully secured a criminal record clearance. The employment agency shall provide to the employer the individual's professional license and registration number and date of expiration.

(b) A statement that the licensed nursing staff person has had a health examination within 90 days prior to employment with the employment agency or seven days after employment with the employment agency and at least annually thereafter by a person lawfully authorized to perform that procedure. Each examination shall include a medical history and physical evaluation. The employment agency shall also provide verification that the individual has had tuberculosis screening within 90 days prior to employment and annually thereafter. *(Added by Stats.2001, c. 326 (A.B.1643), § 2.)*

§ 1812.543. Adoption of policies and procedures by employment agency regarding prevention of resident or patient abuse by temporary staff

(a) An employment agency that makes referrals of licensed nursing staff or certified nurse assistants for temporary employment in a long-term health care facility shall adopt policies and procedures regarding prevention of resident or patient abuse by temporary staff.

(b) The employment agency shall provide written verification to the long-term health care facility that any certified nurse assistants or licensed nursing staff referred by the agency do not have any unresolved allegations against them involving the mistreatment, neglect, or abuse of a patient, including injuries of unknown source and misappropriation of resident property.

(c) No temporary staff person referred by an employment agency may be solely responsible for a unit unless that person has received a full orientation to the facility and the applicable unit for which he or she is assigned.

(d) Upon the request of the State Department of Health Services, an employment agency shall provide a list of temporary employees who have been referred to a specified facility during the period in which the facility is involved in a labor action.

(e) An employment agency shall require that any employee referred to a long-term care facility be identified as a temporary staff person in the facility's daily staffing levels required to be posted in accordance with the standards set forth in Section 941 of Appendix F of Public Law 106–554 (42 U.S.C. Sec. 1395i–3(b)(8) and 42 U.S.C. Sec. 1395r(b)(8)). *(Added by Stats.2001, c. 326 (A.B.1643), § 2.)*

§ 1812.544. Maintaining records of all advertisements by employment agencies making referrals of licensed nursing staff or certified nurse assistants for temporary employment in a long-term health care facility

(a) Every employment agency that makes referrals of licensed nursing staff or certified nurse assistants for temporary employment in a long-term health care facility shall maintain a record of all advertisements, showing the date of publication and the publication in which the advertisement appeared, for a period of one year from the date of the advertisement.

(b) No employment agency that makes referrals for employment to a long-term health care facility shall, by its name, advertisement, or any other representation, represent itself to be a home health agency, as defined by subdivision (a) of Section 1727 of the Health and Safety Code, or to perform the services of a home health agency. The employment agency shall provide a written disclosure to each employer stating that it does not perform the services of a home health agency and clearly describing that it is an employment agency only.

(c) Any facility or individual may refer complaints concerning employment agencies which place licensed nursing staff or certified nurse assistants in long-term health care facilities to the appropriate licensing, certification, ombudsman, adult protective services, or proper law enforcement agency for action. *(Added by Stats.2001, c. 326 (A.B.1643), § 2.)*

Title 15

WORKS OF IMPROVEMENT

CHAPTER 2. MECHANICS' LIENS

ARTICLE 2. WHO IS ENTITLED TO LIEN

Section
3111. Trust fund lien under labor agreement.

§ 3111. Trust fund lien under labor agreement

For the purposes of this chapter, an express trust fund to which a portion of a laborer's total compensation is to be paid pursuant to an applicable employment agreement or a collective bargaining agreement for the provision of benefits, including, but not limited to, employer payments described in Section 1773.1 of the Labor Code and regulations thereunder, shall be entitled to assert the same rights and claims as laborers performing labor upon, or bestowing skill or other necessary services on, a work of improvement, to the extent of the compensation agreed to be paid to that express trust fund for labor on that improvement only. *(Added by Stats.1969, c. 1362, p. 2761, § 2, operative Jan. 1, 1971. Amended by Stats.1999, c. 795 (S.B.914), § 7.)*

Division 4

GENERAL PROVISIONS

Part 1

RELIEF

Title 2

COMPENSATORY RELIEF

CHAPTER 1. DAMAGES IN GENERAL

ARTICLE 3. EXEMPLARY DAMAGES

Section
3294. Exemplary damages; when allowable; definitions.

§ 3294. Exemplary damages; when allowable; definitions

(a) In an action for the breach of an obligation not arising from contract, where it is proven by clear and convincing evidence that the defendant has been guilty of oppression, fraud, or malice, the plaintiff, in addition to the actual damages, may recover damages for the sake of example and by way of punishing the defendant.

(b) An employer shall not be liable for damages pursuant to subdivision (a), based upon acts of an employee of the employer, unless the employer had advance knowledge of the unfitness of the employee and employed him or her with a conscious disregard of the rights or safety of others or authorized or ratified the wrongful conduct for which the damages are awarded or was personally guilty of oppression, fraud, or malice. With respect to a corporate employer, the advance knowledge and conscious disregard, authorization, ratification or act of oppression, fraud, or malice must be on the part of an officer, director, or managing agent of the corporation.

(c) As used in this section, the following definitions shall apply:

(1) "Malice" means conduct which is intended by the defendant to cause injury to the plaintiff or despicable conduct which is carried on by the defendant with a willful and conscious disregard of the rights or safety of others.

(2) "Oppression" means despicable conduct that subjects a person to cruel and unjust hardship in conscious disregard of that person's rights.

(3) "Fraud" means an intentional misrepresentation, deceit, or concealment of a material fact known to the defendant with the intention on the part of the defendant of thereby depriving a person of property or legal rights or otherwise causing injury.

(d) Damages may be recovered pursuant to this section in an action pursuant to Chapter 4 (commencing with Section 377.10) of Title 3 of Part 2 of the Code of Civil Procedure based upon a death which resulted from a homicide for which the defendant has been convicted of a felony, whether or not the decedent died instantly or survived the fatal injury for some period of time. The procedures for joinder and consolidation contained in Section 377.62 of the Code of Civil Procedure shall apply to prevent multiple recoveries of punitive or exemplary damages based upon the same wrongful act.

(e) The amendments to this section made by Chapter 1498 of the Statutes of 1987 apply to all actions in which the initial trial has not commenced prior to January 1, 1988. *(Enacted 1872. Amended by Stats.1905, c. 463, p. 621, § 1; Stats.1980, c. 1242, p. 4217, § 1; Stats.1982, c. 174, § 1; Stats.1983, c. 408, § 1; Stats.1987, c. 1498, § 5; Stats.1988, c. 160, § 17; Stats.1992, c. 178 (S.B.1496), § 5.)*

CHAPTER 2. MEASURE OF DAMAGES

ARTICLE 2. DAMAGES FOR WRONGS

Section
3339. Legislative findings, declarations and intent; immigration status; severability.

§ 3339. Legislative findings, declarations and intent; immigration status; severability

The Legislature finds and declares the following:

(a) All protections, rights, and remedies available under state law, except any reinstatement remedy prohibited by federal law, are available to all individuals regardless of immigration status who have applied for employment, or who are or who have been employed, in this state.

(b) For purposes of enforcing state labor, employment, civil rights, and employee housing laws, a person's immigration status is irrelevant to the issue of liability, and in proceedings or discovery undertaken to enforce those state laws no inquiry shall be permitted into a person's immigration status except where the person seeking to make this inquiry has shown by clear and convincing evidence that this inquiry is necessary in order to comply with federal immigration law.

(c) The provisions of this section are declaratory of existing law.

(d) The provisions of this section are severable. If any provision of this section or its application is held invalid, that invalidity shall not affect other provisions or applications that can be given effect without the invalid provision or application. *(Added by Stats.2002, c. 1071 (S.B.1818), § 1.)*

Title 3

SPECIFIC AND PREVENTIVE RELIEF

CHAPTER 2. SPECIFIC RELIEF

ARTICLE 3. SPECIFIC PERFORMANCE OF OBLIGATIONS

Section
3390. Obligations not specifically enforceable.

§ 3390. Obligations not specifically enforceable

The following obligations cannot be specifically enforced:

1. An obligation to render personal service;

2. An obligation to employ another in personal service;

3. An agreement to perform an act which the party has not power lawfully to perform when required to do so;

4. An agreement to procure the act or consent of the wife of the contracting party, or of any other third person; or,

5. An agreement, the terms of which are not sufficiently certain to make the precise act which is to be done clearly ascertainable. *(Enacted 1872. Amended by Stats. 1961, c. 461, p. 1551, § 5.)*

Title 7

DUTY OF HEALTH CARE SERVICE PLANS AND MANAGED CARE ENTITIES

Section
3428. Duty of ordinary care; indemnity; liability; waiver; damages; exhaustion of procedures under medical review system.

§ 3428. Duty of ordinary care; indemnity; liability; waiver; damages; exhaustion of procedures under medical review system

(a) For services rendered on or after January 1, 2001, a health care service plan or managed care entity, as described in subdivision (f) of Section 1345 of the Health and Safety Code, shall have a duty of ordinary care to arrange for the provision of medically necessary health care service to its subscribers and enrollees, where the health care service is a benefit provided under the plan, and shall be liable for any and all harm legally caused by its failure to exercise that ordinary care when both of the following apply:

(1) The failure to exercise ordinary care resulted in the denial, delay, or modification of the health care service recommended for, or furnished to, a subscriber or enrollee.

(2) The subscriber or enrollee suffered substantial harm.

(b) For purposes of this section: (1) substantial harm means loss of life, loss or significant impairment of limb or bodily function, significant disfigurement, severe and chronic physical pain, or significant financial loss; (2) health care services need not be recommended or furnished by an in-plan provider, but may be recommended or furnished by any health care provider practicing within the scope of his or her practice; and (3) health care services shall be recommended or furnished at any time prior to the inception of the action, and the recommendation need not be made prior to the occurrence of substantial harm.

(c) Health care service plans and managed care entities are not health care providers under any provision of law, including, but not limited to, Section 6146 of the Business and Professions Code, Sections 3333.1 or 3333.2 of this code, or Sections 340.5, 364, 425.13, 667.7, or 1295 of the Code of Civil Procedure.

(d) A health care service plan or managed care entity shall not seek indemnity, whether contractual or equitable, from a provider for liability imposed under subdivision (a). Any provision to the contrary in a contract with providers is void and unenforceable.

(e) This section shall not create any liability on the part of an employer or an employer group purchasing organization that purchases coverage or assumes risk on behalf of its employees or on behalf of self funded employee benefit plans.

(f) Any waiver by a subscriber or enrollee of the provisions of this section is contrary to public policy and shall be unenforceable and void.

(g) This section does not create any new or additional liability on the part of a health care service plan or managed care entity for harm caused that is attributable to the medical negligence of a treating physician or other treating health care provider.

(h) This section does not abrogate or limit any other theory of liability otherwise available at law.

(i) This section shall not apply in instances where subscribers or enrollees receive treatment by prayer, consistent with the provisions of subdivision (a) of Section 1270 of the Health and Safety Code, in lieu of medical treatment.

(j) Damages recoverable for a violation of this section include, but are not limited to, those set forth in Section 3333.

(k)(1) A person may not maintain a cause of action pursuant to this section against any entity required to comply with any independent medical review system or independent review system required by law unless the person or his or her representative has exhausted the procedures provided by the applicable independent review system.

(2) Compliance with paragraph (1) is not required in a case where either of the following applies:

(A) Substantial harm, as defined in subdivision (b), has occurred prior to the completion of the applicable review.

(B) Substantial harm, as defined, in subdivision (b), will imminently occur prior to the completion of the applicable review.

(3) This subdivision shall become operative only if Senate Bill 189 and Assembly Bill 55 of the 1999–2000 Regular Session are also enacted and enforceable.

(*l*) If any provision of this section or the application thereof to any person or circumstance is held to be unconstitutional or otherwise invalid or unenforceable, the remainder of the section and the application of those provisions to other persons or circumstances shall not be affected thereby. *(Added by Stats.1999, c. 536 (S.B.21), § 3.)*

CODE OF CIVIL PROCEDURE

Part 2

OF CIVIL ACTIONS

Title 2

OF THE TIME OF COMMENCING CIVIL ACTIONS

CHAPTER 4. GENERAL PROVISIONS AS TO THE TIME OF COMMENCING ACTIONS

Section
354.45. Armenian Genocide victims; deposited and looted assets; waiver of statute of limitations.
354.7. Braceros, heirs or beneficiaries of braceros; right of action for recovery of savings fund amounts; limitations; severability of provisions

§ 354.45. Armenian Genocide victims; deposited and looted assets; waiver of statute of limitations

(a) For purposes of this section, the following terms have the following meanings:

(1) "Armenian Genocide victim" means any person of Armenian or other ancestry living in the Ottoman Empire during the period of 1890 to 1923, inclusive, who died, was injured in person or property, was deported, or escaped to avoid persecution during that period.

(2) "Bank" means any banking or financial institution, including any institution that issued bonds, that conducted business in Ottoman Turkey at any time during the period of 1890 to 1923, inclusive.

(3) "Deposited assets" means any and all cash, securities, bonds, gold, jewels or jewelry, or any other tangible or intangible items of personal property, or any documents indicating ownership or possessory interests in real, personal, or intangible property, that were deposited with and held by a bank.

(4) "Looted assets" means any and all personal, commercial, real, and intangible property, including cash, securities, gold, jewelry, businesses, artwork, equipment, and intellectual property, that was taken from the ownership or control of an individual, organization, or entity, by theft, forced transfer, or exploitation, during the period of 1890 to 1923, inclusive, by any person, organization, or entity acting on behalf of, or in furtherance of the acts of, the Turkish Government, that were received by and deposited with a bank.

(b) Notwithstanding any other law, any Armenian Genocide victim, or heir or beneficiary of an Armenian Genocide victim, who resides in this state and has a claim arising out of a failure of a bank to pay or turn over deposited assets, or to turn over looted assets, may bring an action or may continue a pending action, to recover on that claim in any court of competent jurisdiction in this state, which court shall be deemed the proper forum for that action until its completion or resolution.

(c) Any action, including any pending action brought by an Armenian Genocide victim, or the heir or beneficiary of an Armenian Genocide victim, who resides in this state, seeking payment for, or the return of, deposited assets, or the return of looted assets, shall not be dismissed for failure to comply with the applicable statute of limitation, if the action is filed on or before December 31, 2016.

(d) The provisions of this section are severable. If any provision of this section or its application is held invalid, that invalidity shall not affect other provisions or applications that can be given effect without the invalid provision or application. *(Added by Stats.2006, c. 443 (S.B.1524), § 2.)*

Validity

This section was recognized as preempted for conflicting with the federal government's resolution of wartime claims arising out of World War I in the decision of Deirmenjian v. Deutsche Bank, A.G., C.D.Cal.2007, 526 F.Supp.2d 1068.

§ 354.7. Braceros, heirs or beneficiaries of braceros; right of action for recovery of savings fund amounts; limitations; severability of provisions

(a) The following definitions govern the construction of this section:

(1) "Bracero" means any person who participated in the labor importation program known as the Bracero program between January 1, 1942, and January 1, 1950, pursuant to agreements between the United States and Mexico.

(2) "Savings fund" means funds withheld from the wages of braceros as savings to be paid to braceros upon their return to Mexico.

(b) Notwithstanding any other provision of law, any bracero, or heir or beneficiary of a bracero, who has a claim arising out of a failure to pay or turn over savings fund amounts may bring a legal action or may continue a pending legal action to recover on that claim in any court of competent jurisdiction in this state, which court shall be deemed a proper forum for that action until its completion or resolution.

(c) Notwithstanding any other provision of law, any action brought by a bracero, or heir or beneficiary of a bracero, arising out of a failure to pay or turn over savings fund amounts shall not be dismissed for failure to comply with the otherwise applicable statute of limitations, provided the action is filed on or before December 31, 2005.

(d) The provisions of this section are severable. If any provision of this section or its application is held invalid, that invalidity shall not affect other provisions or applications that can be given effect without the invalid provision or application. *(Added by Stats.2002, c. 1070 (A.B.2913), § 2, eff. Sept. 29, 2002.)*

Title 6.5

ATTACHMENT

CHAPTER 7.   PROPERTY SUBJECT TO ATTACHMENT

Section
487.020.   Exempt property.

§ 487.020.   Exempt property

Except as provided in paragraph (2) of subdivision (a) of Section 3439.07 of the Civil Code, the following property is exempt from attachment:

(a) All property exempt from enforcement of a money judgment.

(b) Property which is necessary for the support of a defendant who is a natural person or the family of such defendant supported in whole or in part by the defendant.

(c) "Earnings" as defined by Section 706.011.

(d) All property not subject to attachment pursuant to Section 487.010. *(Added by Stats.1974, c. 1516, p. 3354, § 9, operative Jan. 1, 1977. Amended by Stats.1976, c. 437, p. 1128, § 25; Stats.1982, c. 1198, p. 4288, § 47, operative July 1, 1983; Stats.1986, c. 383, § 7.)*

Title 7

OTHER PROVISIONAL REMEDIES IN CIVIL ACTIONS

CHAPTER 3.   INJUNCTION

Section
527.3.   Labor disputes; jurisdiction of court.
527.6.   Harassment; temporary restraining order and injunction; procedure; domestic violence; support person; costs and attorney fees; punishment.
527.8.   Employees subject to unlawful violence or threat of violence at the workplace; temporary restraining order; injunction; constitutional protections for speech and activities.
527.85.   Officers authorized to maintain order on school campus or facility; threat of violence made off school campus; temporary restraining order and injunction; violation of restraining order.
527.9.   Relinquishment of firearms; persons subject to protective orders.

§ 527.3.   Labor disputes; jurisdiction of court

(a) In order to promote the rights of workers to engage in concerted activities for the purpose of collective bargaining, picketing or other mutual aid or protection, and to prevent the evils which frequently occur when courts interfere with the normal processes of dispute resolution between employers and recognized employee organizations, the equity jurisdiction of the courts in cases involving or growing out of a labor dispute shall be no broader than as set forth in subdivision (b) of this section, and the provisions of subdivision (b) of this section shall be strictly construed in accordance with existing law governing labor disputes with the purpose of avoiding any unnecessary judicial interference in labor disputes.

(b) The acts enumerated in this subdivision, whether performed singly or in concert, shall be legal, and no court nor any judge nor judges thereof, shall have jurisdiction to issue any restraining order or preliminary or permanent injunction which, in specific or general terms, prohibits any person or persons, whether singly or in concert, from doing any of the following:

(1) Giving publicity to, and obtaining or communicating information regarding the existence of, or the facts involved in, any labor dispute, whether by advertising, speaking, patrolling any public street or any place where any person or persons may lawfully be, or by any other method not involving fraud, violence or breach of the peace.

(2) Peaceful picketing or patrolling involving any labor dispute, whether engaged in singly or in numbers.

(3) Assembling peaceably to do any of the acts specified in paragraphs (1) and (2) or to promote lawful interests.

(4) Except as provided in subparagraph (iv), for purposes of this section, "labor dispute" is defined as follows:

(i) A case shall be held to involve or to grow out of a labor dispute when the case involves persons who are engaged in the same industry, trade, craft, or occupation; or have direct or indirect interests therein; or who are employees of the same employer; or who are members of the same or an affiliated organization of employers or employees; whether such dispute is (a) between one or more employers or associations of employers and one or more employees or associations of employees; (b) between one or more employers or associations of employers and one or more employers or associations of employers; or (c) between one or more employees or associations of employees and one or more employees or associations of employees; or when the case involves any conflicting or competing interests in a "labor dispute" of "persons participating or interested" therein (as defined in subparagraph (ii)).

(ii) A person or association shall be held to be a person participating or interested in a labor dispute if relief is sought against him or it, and if he or it is engaged in the same industry, trade, craft, or occupation in which such dispute occurs, or has a direct or indirect interest therein, or is a member, officer, or agent of any association composed in whole or in part of employers or employees engaged in such industry, trade, craft, or occupation.

(iii) The term "labor dispute" includes any controversy concerning terms or conditions of employment, or concerning the association or representation of persons in negotiating, fixing, maintaining, changing, or seeking to arrange terms or conditions of employment regardless of whether or not the disputants stand in the proximate relation of employer and employee.

(iv) The term "labor dispute" does not include a jurisdictional strike as defined in Section 1118 of the Labor Code.

(c) Nothing contained in this section shall be construed to alter or supersede the provisions of Chapter 1 of the 1975–76 Third Extraordinary Session [1], and to the extent of any conflict between the provisions of this act and that chapter, the provisions of the latter shall prevail.

(d) Nothing contained in this section shall be construed to alter the legal rights of public employees or their employers, nor shall this section alter the rights of parties to collective-bargaining agreements under the provisions of Section 1126 of the Labor Code.

(e) It is not the intent of this section to permit conduct that is unlawful including breach of the peace, disorderly conduct, the unlawful blocking of access or egress to premises where a labor dispute exists, or other similar unlawful activity. *(Added by Stats.1975, c. 1156, p. 2845, § 2.)*

[1] Labor Code § 1140 et seq.

§ 527.6. Harassment; temporary restraining order and injunction; procedure; domestic violence; support person; costs and attorney fees; punishment

(a) A person who has suffered harassment as defined in subdivision (b) may seek a temporary restraining order and an injunction prohibiting harassment as provided in this section.

(b) For the purposes of this section, "harassment" is unlawful violence, a credible threat of violence, or a knowing and willful course of conduct directed at a specific person that seriously alarms, annoys, or harasses the person, and that serves no legitimate purpose. The course of conduct must be such as would cause a reasonable person to suffer substantial emotional distress, and must actually cause substantial emotional distress to the plaintiff.

As used in this subdivision:

(1) "Unlawful violence" is any assault or battery, or stalking as prohibited in Section 646.9 of the Penal Code, but shall not include lawful acts of self-defense or defense of others.

(2) "Credible threat of violence" is a knowing and willful statement or course of conduct that would place a reasonable person in fear for his or her safety, or the safety of his or her immediate family, and that serves no legitimate purpose.

(3) "Course of conduct" is a pattern of conduct composed of a series of acts over a period of time, however short, evidencing a continuity of purpose, including following or stalking an individual, making harassing telephone calls to an individual, or sending harassing correspondence to an individual by any means, including, but not limited to, the use of public or private mails, interoffice mail, fax, or computer e-mail. Constitutionally protected activity is not included within the meaning of "course of conduct."

(c) Upon filing a petition for an injunction under this section, the plaintiff may obtain a temporary restraining order in accordance with Section 527, except to the extent this section provides a rule that is inconsistent. A temporary restraining order may be issued with or without notice upon an affidavit that, to the satisfaction of the court, shows reasonable proof of harassment of the plaintiff by the defendant, and that great or irreparable harm would result to the plaintiff. In the discretion of the court, and on a showing of good cause, a temporary restraining order or injunction, issued under this section may include other named family or household members who reside with the plaintiff. A temporary restraining order issued under this section shall remain in effect, at the court's discretion, for a period not to exceed 15 days, or, if the court extends the time for hearing under subdivision (d), not to exceed 22 days, unless otherwise modified or terminated by the court.

(d) Within 15 days, or, if good cause appears to the court, 22 days from the date the temporary restraining order is issued, a hearing shall be held on the petition for the injunction. The defendant may file a response that explains, excuses, justifies, or denies the alleged harassment or may file a cross-complaint under this section. At the hearing, the judge shall receive any testimony that is relevant, and may make an independent inquiry. If the judge finds by clear and convincing evidence that unlawful harassment exists, an injunction shall issue prohibiting the harassment. An injunction issued pursuant to this section shall have a duration of not more than three years. At any time within the three months before the expiration of the injunction, the plaintiff may apply for a renewal of the injunction by filing a new petition for an injunction under this section.

(e) This section does not preclude either party from representation by private counsel or from appearing on the party's own behalf.

(f) In a proceeding under this section if there are allegations or threats of domestic violence, a support person may accompany a party in court and, if the party is not represented by an attorney, may sit with the party at the table that is generally reserved for the party and the party's attorney. The support person is present to provide moral and emotional support for a person who alleges he or she is a victim of domestic violence. The support person is not present as a legal adviser and may not provide legal advice. The support person may assist the person who alleges he or she is a victim of domestic violence in feeling more confident that he or she will not be injured or threatened by the other party during the proceedings if the person who alleges he or she is a victim of domestic violence and the other party are required to be present in close proximity. This subdivision does not preclude the court from exercising its discretion to remove the support person from the courtroom if the court believes the support person is prompting, swaying, or influencing the party assisted by the support person.

(g) Upon the filing of a petition for an injunction under this section, the defendant shall be personally served with a copy of the petition, temporary restraining order, if any, and notice of hearing of the petition. Service shall be made at least five days before the hearing. The court may for good cause, on motion of the plaintiff or on its own motion, shorten the time for service on the defendant.

(h) The court shall order the plaintiff or the attorney for the plaintiff to deliver a copy of each temporary restraining order or injunction, or modification or termination thereof, granted under this section, by the close of the business day on which the order was granted, to the law enforcement agencies within the court's discretion as are requested by the plaintiff. Each appropriate law enforcement agency shall make available information as to the existence and current status of these orders to law enforcement officers responding to the scene of reported harassment.

An order issued under this section shall, on request of the plaintiff, be served on the defendant, whether or not the defendant has been taken into custody, by any law enforcement officer who is present at the scene of reported harassment involving the parties to the proceeding. The plaintiff shall provide the officer with an endorsed copy of the order and a proof of service that the officer shall complete and send to the issuing court.

Upon receiving information at the scene of an incident of harassment that a protective order has been issued under this section, or that a person who has been taken into custody is the subject of an order, if the protected person cannot produce a certified copy of the order, a law enforcement officer shall immediately attempt to verify the existence of the order.

If the law enforcement officer determines that a protective order has been issued, but not served, the officer shall immediately notify the defendant of the terms of the order and shall at that time also enforce the order. Verbal notice of the terms of the order shall constitute service of the order and is sufficient notice for the purposes of this section and for the purposes of Section 273.6 and subdivision (g) of Section 12021 of the Penal Code.

(i) The prevailing party in any action brought under this section may be awarded court costs and attorney's fees, if any.

(j) Any willful disobedience of any temporary restraining order or injunction granted under this section is punishable pursuant to Section 273.6 of the Penal Code.

(k)(1) A person subject to a protective order issued under this section shall not own, possess, purchase, receive, or attempt to purchase or receive a firearm while the protective order is in effect.

(2) The court shall order a person subject to a protective order issued under this section to relinquish any firearms he or she owns or possesses pursuant to Section 527.9.

(3) Every person who owns, possesses, purchases or receives, or attempts to purchase or receive a firearm while the protective order is in effect is punishable pursuant to subdivision (g) of Section 12021 of the Penal Code.

(*l*) This section does not apply to any action or proceeding covered by Title 1.6C (commencing with Section 1788) of the Civil Code or by Division 10 (commencing with Section 6200) of the Family Code. This section does not preclude a plaintiff from using other existing civil remedies.

(m) The Judicial Council shall promulgate forms and instructions therefor, and rules for service of process, scheduling of hearings, and any other matters required by this section. The petition and response forms shall be simple and concise, and their use by parties in actions brought pursuant to this section shall be mandatory.

(n) A temporary restraining order or injunction relating to harassment or domestic violence issued by a court pursuant to this section shall be issued on forms adopted by the Judicial Council of California and that have been approved by the Department of Justice pursuant to subdivision (i) of Section 6380 of the Family Code. However, the fact that an order issued by a court pursuant to this section was not issued on forms adopted by the Judicial Council and approved by the Department of Justice shall not, in and of itself, make the order unenforceable.

(*o*) Information on any temporary restraining order or injunction relating to harassment or domestic violence issued by a court pursuant to this section shall be transmitted to the Department of Justice in accordance with subdivision (b) of Section 6380 of the Family Code.

(p) There is no filing fee for a petition that alleges that a person has inflicted or threatened violence against the petitioner, or stalked the petitioner, or acted or spoken in any other manner that has placed the petitioner in reasonable fear of violence, and that seeks a protective or restraining order or injunction restraining stalking or future violence or threats of violence, in any action brought pursuant to this section. No fee shall be paid for a subpoena filed in connection with a petition alleging these acts. No fee shall be paid for filing a response to a petition alleging these acts.

(q)(1) Subject to paragraph (4) of subdivision (b) of Section 6103.2 of the Government Code, there shall be no fee for the service of process of a protective order, restraining order, or injunction to be issued, if any of the following conditions apply:

(A) The protective order, restraining order, or injunction issued pursuant to this section is based upon stalking, as prohibited by Section 646.9 of the Penal Code.

(B) The protective order, restraining order, or injunction issued pursuant to this section is based upon a credible threat of violence.

(C) The protective order, restraining order, or injunction is issued pursuant to Section 6222 of the Family Code.

(2) The Judicial Council shall prepare and develop application forms for applicants who wish to avail themselves of the services described in this subdivision. *(Added by Stats.2002, c. 1009 (A.B.2030), § 2, operative Jan. 1, 2007. Amended by Stats.2003, c. 498 (S.B.226), § 2, operative Jan. 1, 2007, Stats.2006, c. 476 (A.B.2695), § 1.)*

§ 527.8. Employees subject to unlawful violence or threat of violence at the workplace; temporary restraining order; injunction; constitutional protections for speech and activities

(a) Any employer, whose employee has suffered unlawful violence or a credible threat of violence from any individual, that can reasonably be construed to be carried out or to have been carried out at the workplace, may seek a temporary restraining order and an injunction on behalf of the employee and, at the discretion of the court, any number of other employees at the workplace, and, if appropriate, other employees at other workplaces of the employer.

(b) For the purposes of this section:

(1) "Unlawful violence" is any assault or battery, or stalking as prohibited in Section 646.9 of the Penal Code, but shall not include lawful acts of self-defense or defense of others.

(2) "Credible threat of violence" is a knowing and willful statement or course of conduct that would place a reasonable person in fear for his or her safety, or the safety of his or her immediate family, and that serves no legitimate purpose.

(3) "Course of conduct" is a pattern of conduct composed of a series of acts over a period of time, however short, evidencing a continuity of purpose, including following or stalking an employee to or from the place of work; entering the workplace; following an employee during hours of employment; making telephone calls to an employee; or sending correspondence to an employee by any means, including, but not limited to, the use of the public or private mails, interoffice mail, fax, or computer e-mail.

(c) This section does not permit a court to issue a temporary restraining order or injunction prohibiting speech or other activities that are constitutionally protected, or otherwise protected by Section 527.3 or any other provision of law.

(d) For purposes of this section, the terms "employer" and "employee" mean persons defined in Section 350 of the Labor Code. "Employer" also includes a federal agency, the state, a state agency, a city, county, or district, and a private, public, or quasi-public corporation, or any public agency thereof or therein. "Employee" also includes the members of boards of directors of private, public, and quasi-public corporations and elected and appointed public officers. For purposes of this section only, "employee" also includes a volunteer or independent contractor who performs services for the employer at the employer's worksite.

(e) Upon filing a petition for an injunction under this section, the plaintiff may obtain a temporary restraining order in accordance with subdivision (a) of Section 527, if the plaintiff also files an affidavit that, to the satisfaction of the court, shows reasonable proof that an employee has suffered unlawful violence or a credible threat of violence by the defendant, and that great or irreparable harm would result to an employee. In the discretion of the court, and on a showing of good cause, a temporary restraining order or injunction issued under this section may include other named family or household members who reside with the employee, or other persons employed at his or her workplace or workplaces.

A temporary restraining order granted under this section shall remain in effect, at the court's discretion, for a period not to exceed 15 days, unless otherwise modified or terminated by the court.

(f) Within 15 days of the filing of the petition, a hearing shall be held on the petition for the injunction. The defendant may file a response that explains, excuses, justifies, or denies the alleged unlawful violence or credible threats of violence or may file a cross-complaint under this section. At the hearing, the judge shall receive any testimony that is relevant and may make an independent inquiry. Moreover, if the defendant is a current employee of the entity requesting the injunction, the judge shall receive evidence concerning the employer's decision to retain, terminate, or otherwise discipline the defendant. If the judge finds by clear and convincing evidence that the defendant engaged in unlawful violence or made a credible threat of violence, an injunction shall issue prohibiting further unlawful violence or threats of violence. An injunction issued pursuant to this section shall have a duration of not more than three years. At any time within the three months before the expiration of the injunction, the plaintiff may apply for a renewal of the injunction by filing a new petition for an injunction under this section.

(g) This section does not preclude either party from representation by private counsel or from appearing on his or her own behalf.

(h) Upon filing of a petition for an injunction under this section, the defendant shall be personally served with a copy of the petition, temporary restraining order, if any, and notice of hearing of the petition. Service shall be made at least five days before the hearing. The court may, for good cause, on motion of the plaintiff or on its own motion, shorten the time for service on the defendant.

(i)(1) The court shall order the plaintiff or the attorney for the plaintiff to deliver a copy of each temporary restraining order or injunction, or modification or termination thereof, granted under this section, by the close of the business day on which the order was granted, to the law enforcement agencies within the court's discretion as are requested by the plaintiff. Each appropriate law enforcement agency shall make available information as to the existence and current status of these orders to law enforcement officers responding to the scene of reported unlawful violence or a credible threat of violence.

(2) At the request of the plaintiff, an order issued under this section shall be served on the defendant, regardless of whether the defendant has been taken into custody, by any law enforcement officer who is present at the scene of reported unlawful violence or a credible threat of violence involving the parties to the proceedings. The plaintiff shall provide the officer with an endorsed copy of the order and proof of service that the officer shall complete and send to the issuing court.

(3) Upon receiving information at the scene of an incident of unlawful violence or a credible threat of violence that a protective order has been issued under this section, or that a person who has been taken into custody is the subject of an order, if the plaintiff or the protected person cannot produce an endorsed copy of the order, a law enforcement officer shall immediately attempt to verify the existence of the order.

(4) If the law enforcement officer determines that a protective order has been issued, but not served, the officer shall immediately notify the defendant of the terms of the order and obtain the defendant's address. The law enforcement officer shall at that time also enforce the order, but may not arrest or take the defendant into custody for acts in violation of the order that were committed prior to the verbal notice of the terms and conditions of the order. The law enforcement officer's verbal notice of the terms of the order shall constitute service of the order and constitutes sufficient notice for the purposes of this section and for the purposes of Section 273.6 and subdivision (g) of Section 12021 of the Penal Code. The plaintiff shall mail an endorsed copy of the order to the defendant's mailing address provided to the law enforcement officer within one business day of the reported incident of unlawful violence or a credible threat of violence at which a verbal notice of the terms of the order was provided by a law enforcement officer.

(j)(1) A person subject to a protective order issued under this section shall not own, possess, purchase, receive, or attempt to purchase or receive a firearm while the protective order is in effect.

(2) The court shall order a person subject to a protective order issued under this section to relinquish any firearms he or she owns or possesses pursuant to Section 527.9.

(3) Every person who owns, possesses, purchases or receives, or attempts to purchase or receive a firearm while the protective order is in effect is punishable pursuant to subdivision (g) of Section 12021 of the Penal Code.

(k) Any intentional disobedience of any temporary restraining order or injunction granted under this section is punishable pursuant to Section 273.6 of the Penal Code.

(l) Nothing in this section may be construed as expanding, diminishing, altering, or modifying the duty, if any, of an employer to provide a safe workplace for employees and other persons.

(m) The Judicial Council shall develop forms, instructions, and rules for scheduling of hearings and other procedures established pursuant to this section. The forms for the petition and response shall be simple and concise, and their use by parties in actions brought pursuant to this section shall be mandatory.

(n) A temporary restraining order or injunction relating to harassment or domestic violence issued by a court pursuant to this section shall be issued on forms adopted by the Judicial Council of California and that have been approved by the Department of Justice pursuant to subdivision (i) of Section 6380 of the Family Code. However, the fact that an order issued by a court pursuant to this section was not issued on forms adopted by the Judicial Council and approved by the Department of Justice shall not, in and of itself, make the order unenforceable.

(o) Information on any temporary restraining order or injunction relating to harassment or domestic violence issued by a court pursuant to this section shall be transmitted to the Department of Justice in accordance with subdivision (b) of Section 6380 of the Family Code.

(p) There is no filing fee for a petition that alleges that a person has inflicted or threatened violence against an employee of the petitioner, or stalked the employee, or acted or spoken in any other manner that has placed the employee in reasonable fear of violence, and that seeks a protective or restraining order or injunction restraining stalking or future violence or threats of violence, in any action brought pursuant to this section. No fee shall be paid for a subpoena filed in connection with a petition alleging these acts. No fee shall be paid for filing a response to a petition alleging these acts.

(q)(1) Subject to paragraph (4) of subdivision (b) of Section 6103.2 of the Government Code, there shall be no fee for the service of process of a temporary restraining order or injunction to be issued pursuant to this section if either of the following conditions apply:

(A) The temporary restraining order or injunction issued pursuant to this section is based upon stalking, as prohibited by Section 646.9 of the Penal Code.

(B) The temporary restraining order or injunction issued pursuant to this section is based upon a credible threat of violence.

(2) The Judicial Council shall prepare and develop application forms for applicants who wish to avail themselves of the services described in this subdivision. *(Added by Stats.1993–94, 1st Ex.Sess., c. 29 (A.B.68), § 2. Amended by Stats.1998, c. 581 (A.B.2801), § 3; Stats. 1999, c. 661 (A.B.825), § 2; Stats.2000, c. 688 (A.B.1669), § 6; Stats.2002, c. 1008 (A.B.3028), § 3; Stats.2003, c. 498 (S.B.226), § 3; Stats.2005, c. 467 (A.B.429), § 1; Stats.2006, c. 476 (A.B.2695), § 2.)*

§ 527.85. Officers authorized to maintain order on school campus or facility; threat of violence made off school campus; temporary restraining order and injunction; violation of restraining order

(a) Any chief administrative officer of a postsecondary educational institution, or an officer or employee designated by the chief administrative officer to maintain order on the school campus or facility, a student of which has suffered a credible threat of violence made off the school campus or facility from any individual, which can reasonably be construed to be carried out or to have been carried out at the school campus or facility, may, with the written consent of the student, seek a temporary restraining order and an injunction, on behalf of the student and, at the discretion of the court, any number of other students at the campus or facility who are similarly situated.

(b) For the purposes of this section, the following definitions shall apply:

(1) "Chief administrative officer" means the principal, president, or highest ranking official of the postsecondary educational institution.

(2) "Course of conduct" means a pattern of conduct composed of a series of acts over a period of time, however short, evidencing a continuity of purpose, including any of the following:

(A) Following or stalking a student to or from school.

(B) Entering the school campus or facility.

(C) Following a student during school hours.

(D) Making telephone calls to a student.

(E) Sending correspondence to a student by any means, including, but not limited to, the use of the public or private mails, interoffice mail, fax, or computer e-mail.

(3) "Credible threat of violence" means a knowing and willful statement or course of conduct that would place a reasonable person in fear for his or her safety, or the safety of his or her immediate family, and that serves no legitimate purpose.

(4) "Postsecondary educational institution" means a private institution of vocational, professional, or postsecondary education.

(5) "Student" means an adult currently enrolled in or applying for admission to a postsecondary educational institution.

(6) "Unlawful violence" means any assault or battery, or stalking as prohibited in Section 646.9 of the Penal Code, but shall not include lawful acts of self-defense or defense of others.

(c) This section does not permit a court to issue a temporary restraining order or injunction prohibiting speech or other activities that are constitutionally protected, or otherwise protected by Section 527.3 or any other provision of law.

(d) Upon filing a petition for an injunction under this section, the plaintiff may obtain a temporary restraining order in accordance with subdivision (a) of Section 527, if the plaintiff also files an affidavit that, to the satisfaction of the court, shows reasonable proof that a student has suffered a credible threat of violence made off the school campus or facility by the defendant, and that great or irreparable harm would result to the student. In the discretion of the court, and on a showing of good cause, a temporary restraining order or injunction issued under this section may include other named family or household members who reside with the student, or other students at the campus or facility. A temporary restraining order granted under this section shall remain in effect, at the court's discretion, for a period not to exceed 15 days, unless otherwise modified or terminated by the court.

(e) Within 15 days of the filing of the petition, a hearing shall be held on the petition for the injunction. The defendant may file a response that explains, excuses, justifies, or denies the alleged credible threats of violence or may file a cross complaint under this section. At the hearing, the judge shall receive any testimony that is relevant and may make an independent inquiry. Moreover, if the defendant is a current student of the entity requesting the injunction, the judge shall receive evidence concerning the decision of the postsecondary educational institution decision to retain, terminate, or otherwise discipline the defendant. If the judge finds by clear and convincing evidence that the defendant made a credible threat of violence off the school campus or facility, an injunction shall be issued prohibiting further threats of violence. An injunction issued pursuant to this section shall have a duration of not more than three years. At any time within three months before the expiration of the injunction, the plaintiff may apply for a renewal of the injunction by filing a new petition for an injunction under this section.

(f) This section does not preclude either party from representation by private counsel or from appearing on his or her own behalf.

(g) Upon filing of a petition for an injunction under this section, the defendant shall be personally served with a copy of the petition, temporary restraining order, if any, and notice of hearing of the petition. Service shall be made at least five days before the hearing. The court may, for good cause, on motion of the plaintiff or on its own motion, shorten the time for service on the defendant.

(h)(1) The court shall order the plaintiff or the attorney for the plaintiff to deliver a copy of each temporary restraining order or injunction, or modification or termination thereof, granted under this section, by the close of the business day on which the order was granted, to the law enforcement agencies within the court's discretion as are requested by the plaintiff. Each appropriate law enforcement agency shall make available information as to the existence and current status of these orders to law enforcement officers responding to the scene of reported unlawful violence or a credible threat of violence.

(2) At the request of the plaintiff, an order issued under this section shall be served on the defendant, regardless of whether the defendant has been taken into custody, by any law enforcement officer who is present at the scene of reported unlawful violence or a credible threat of violence involving the parties to the proceedings. The plaintiff shall provide the officer with an endorsed copy of the order and proof of service that the officer shall complete and send to the issuing court.

(3) Upon receiving information at the scene of an incident of unlawful violence or a credible threat of violence that a protective order has been issued under this section, or that a person who has been taken into custody is the subject of an order, if the plaintiff or the protected person cannot produce an endorsed copy of the order, a law enforcement officer shall immediately attempt to verify the existence of the order.

(4) If the law enforcement officer determines that a protective order has been issued, but not served, the officer shall immediately notify the defendant of the terms of the order and obtain the defendant's address. The law enforcement officer shall at that time also enforce the order, but may not arrest or take the defendant into custody for acts in violation of the order that were committed prior to the verbal notice of the terms and conditions of the order. The law enforcement officer's verbal notice of the terms of the order shall constitute service of the order and constitutes sufficient notice for the purposes of this section, and Section 273.6 and subdivision (g) of Section 12021 of the Penal Code. The plaintiff shall mail an endorsed copy of the order to the defendant's mailing address provided to the law enforcement officer within one business day of the reported incident of unlawful violence or a credible threat of violence at which a verbal notice of the terms of the order was provided by a law enforcement officer.

(i)(1) A person subject to a protective order issued under this section shall not own, possess, purchase, receive, or attempt to purchase or receive a firearm while the protective order is in effect.

(2) The court shall order a person subject to a protective order issued under this section to relinquish any firearms he or she owns or possesses pursuant to Section 527.9.

(3) Every person who owns, possesses, purchases, or receives, or attempts to purchase or receive a firearm while the protective order is in effect is punishable pursuant to subdivision (g) of Section 12021 of the Penal Code.

(j) Any intentional disobedience of any temporary restraining order or injunction granted under this section is punishable pursuant to Section 273.6 of the Penal Code.

(k) Nothing in this section may be construed as expanding, diminishing, altering, or modifying the duty, if any, of a postsecondary educational institution to provide a safe environment for students and other persons.

(l) The Judicial Council shall develop forms, instructions, and rules for scheduling of hearings and other procedures established pursuant to this section. The forms for the petition and response shall be simple and concise, and their use by parties in actions brought pursuant to this section shall be mandatory.

(m) A temporary restraining order or injunction relating to harassment or domestic violence issued by a court pursuant to this section shall be issued on forms adopted by the Judicial Council and that have been approved by the Department of Justice pursuant to subdivision (i) of Section 6380 of the Family Code. However, the fact that an order issued by a court pursuant to this section was not issued on forms adopted by the Judicial Council and approved by the Department of Justice shall not, in and of itself, make the order unenforceable.

(n) Information on any temporary restraining order or injunction relating to harassment or domestic violence issued by a court pursuant to this section shall be transmitted to the Department of Justice in accordance with subdivision (b) of Section 6380 of the Family Code.

(o) There is no filing fee for a petition that alleges that a person has threatened violence against a student of the petitioner, or stalked the student, or acted or spoken in any other manner that has placed the student in reasonable fear of violence, and that seeks a protective or restraining order or injunction restraining stalking or future threats of violence, in any action brought pursuant to this section. No fee shall be paid for a subpoena filed in connection with a petition alleging these acts. No fee shall be paid for filing a response to a petition alleging these acts.

(p)(1) Subject to paragraph (4) of subdivision (b) of Section 6103.2 of the Government Code, there shall be no fee for the service of process of a temporary restraining order or injunction to be issued pursuant to this section if either of the following conditions apply:

(A) The temporary restraining order or injunction issued pursuant to this section is based upon stalking, as prohibited by Section 646.9 of the Penal Code.

(B) The temporary restraining order or injunction issued pursuant to this section is based upon a credible threat of violence.

(2) The Judicial Council shall prepare and develop application forms for applicants who wish to avail themselves of the services described in this subdivision. *(Added by Stats.2009, c. 566 (S.B.188), § 1.)*

§ 527.9. Relinquishment of firearms; persons subject to protective orders

(a) A person subject to a temporary restraining order or injunction issued pursuant to Section 527.6 or 527.8 of the Code of Civil Procedure, or subject to a restraining order issued pursuant to Section 136.2 of the Penal Code, or Section 15657.03 of the Welfare and Institutions Code, shall relinquish the firearm pursuant to this section.

(b) Upon the issuance of a protective order pursuant to subdivision (a), the court shall order the person to relinquish any firearm in that person's immediate possession or control, or subject to that person's immediate possession or control, within 24 hours of being served with the order, either by surrendering the firearm to the control of local law enforcement officials, or by selling the firearm to a licensed gun dealer, as specified in Section 12071 of the Penal Code. A person ordered to relinquish any firearm pursuant to this subdivision shall file with the court a receipt showing the firearm was surrendered to the local law enforcement agency or sold to a licensed gun dealer within 48 hours after receiving the order. In the event that it is necessary to continue the date of any hearing due to a request for a relinquishment order pursuant to this section, the court shall ensure that all applicable protective orders described in Section 6218 of the Family Code remain in effect or bifurcate the issues and grant the permanent restraining order pending the date of the hearing.

(c) A local law enforcement agency may charge the person subject to the order or injunction a fee for the storage of any firearm relinquished pursuant to this section. The fee shall not exceed the actual cost incurred by the local law enforcement agency for the storage of the firearm. For purposes of this subdivision, "actual cost" means expenses directly related to taking possession of a firearm, storing the firearm, and surrendering possession of the firearm to a licensed dealer as defined in Section 12071 of the Penal Code or to the person relinquishing the firearm.

(d) The restraining order requiring a person to relinquish a firearm pursuant to subdivision (b) shall state on its face that the respondent is prohibited from owning, possessing, purchasing, or receiving a firearm while the protective order is in effect and that the firearm shall be relinquished to the local law enforcement agency for that jurisdiction or sold to a licensed gun dealer, and that proof of surrender or sale shall be filed with the court within a specified period of receipt of the order. The order shall also state on its face the expiration date for relinquishment. Nothing in this section shall limit a respondent's right under existing law to petition the court at a later date for modification of the order.

(e) The restraining order requiring a person to relinquish a firearm pursuant to subdivision (b) shall prohibit the person from possessing or controlling any firearm for the duration of the order. At the expiration of the order, the local law enforcement agency shall return possession of any surrendered firearm to the respondent, within five days after the expiration of the relinquishment order, unless the local law enforcement agency determines that (1) the firearm has been stolen, (2) the respondent is prohibited from possessing a firearm because the respondent is in any prohibited class for the possession of firearms, as defined in Sections 12021 and 12021.1 of the Penal Code and Sections 8100 and 8103 of the Welfare and Institutions Code, or (3) another successive restraining order is used against the respondent under this section. If the local law enforcement agency determines that the respondent is the legal owner of any firearm deposited with the local law enforcement agency and is prohibited from possessing any firearm, the respondent shall be entitled to sell or transfer the firearm to a licensed dealer as defined in Section 12071 of the Penal Code. If the firearm has been stolen, the firearm shall be restored to the lawful owner upon his or her identification of the firearm and proof of ownership.

(f) The court may, as part of the relinquishment order, grant an exemption from the relinquishment requirements of this section for a particular firearm if the respondent can show that a particular firearm is necessary as a condition of continued employment and that the current employer is unable to reassign the respondent to another position where a firearm is unnecessary. If an exemption is granted pursuant to this subdivision, the order shall provide that the firearm shall be in the physical possession of the respondent only during scheduled work hours and during travel to and from his or her place of employment. In any case involving a peace officer who as a condition of employment and whose personal safety depends on the ability to carry a firearm, a court may allow the peace officer to continue to carry a firearm, either on duty or off duty, if the court finds by a preponderance of the evidence that the officer does not pose a threat of harm. Prior to making this finding, the court shall require a mandatory psychological evaluation of the peace officer and may require the peace officer to enter into counseling or other remedial treatment program to deal with any propensity for domestic violence.

(g) During the period of the relinquishment order, a respondent is entitled to make one sale of all firearms that are in the possession of a local law enforcement agency pursuant to this section. A licensed gun dealer, who presents a local law enforcement agency with a bill of sale indicating that all firearms owned by the respondent that are in the possession of the local law enforcement agency have been sold by the respondent to the licensed gun dealer, shall be given possession of those firearms, at the location where a respondent's firearms are stored, within five days of presenting the local law enforcement agency with a bill of sale.　*(Added by Stats.2003, c. 498 (S.B.226), § 4.　Amended by Stats.2006, c. 474 (A.B.2129), § 1.)*

Title 9

ENFORCEMENT OF JUDGMENTS

Division 2

ENFORCEMENT OF MONEY JUDGMENTS

CHAPTER 5.　WAGE GARNISHMENT

ARTICLE 1.　SHORT TITLE; DEFINITIONS

Section
706.010.　Short title.
706.011.　Definitions.

§ 706.010.　Short title

This chapter shall be known and may be cited as the "Wage Garnishment Law."　*(Added by Stats.1982, c. 1364, p. 5172, § 2, operative July 1, 1983.)*

§ 706.011.　Definitions

As used in this chapter:

(a) "Earnings" means compensation payable by an employer to an employee for personal services performed by such employee, whether denominated as wages, salary, commission, bonus, or otherwise.

(b) "Earnings assignment order for support" means an order, made pursuant to Chapter 8 (commencing with Section 5200) of Part 5 of Division 9 of the Family Code or Section 3088 of the Probate Code, which requires an employer to withhold earnings for support.

(c) "Employee" means a public officer and any individual who performs services subject to the right of the employer to control both what shall be done and how it shall be done.

(d) "Employer" means a person for whom an individual performs services as an employee.

(e) "Judgment creditor," as applied to the state, means the specific state agency seeking to collect a judgment or tax liability.

(f) "Judgment debtor" includes a person from whom the state is seeking to collect a tax liability under Article 4 (commencing with Section 706.070), whether or not a judgment has been obtained on such tax liability.

(g) "Person" includes an individual, a corporation, a partnership or other unincorporated association, a limited liability company, and a public entity. *(Added by Stats.1982, c. 1364, p. 5172, § 2, operative July 1, 1983. Amended by Stats.1990, c. 1493 (A.B.3974), § 30.5; Stats. 1992, c. 163 (A.B.2641), § 45, operative Jan. 1, 1994; Stats.1994, c. 1010 (S.B.2053), § 61.)*

ARTICLE 2.　GENERAL PROVISIONS

Section
706.020.　Application of chapter.
706.021.　Procedure for levy of execution upon employee earnings.
706.022.　Withholding period, defined; amount withheld; employer liability for amounts withheld and paid prior to service of order.
706.023.　Multiple earnings withholding orders.
706.024.　Amount required to satisfy earnings withholding order; discretionary notice; accrual of interest.
706.025.　Payments to levying officer.
706.026.　Levying officer; receipt, accounting, and payment of amounts; amounts collected under earnings withholding orders; filing account.
706.027.　Notice of satisfaction of judgment.
706.028.　Final earnings withholding order for costs and interest.
706.029.　Service of order creating lien; duration.
706.030.　Withholding order for support; operation with earnings withholding order.
706.031.　Earnings assignment order for support; operation with earnings withholding order.
706.032.　Termination of earnings withholding orders.
706.033.　Return of writ before earnings withholding order terminates; supplemental return on writ.
706.034.　Deduction from employee earnings for payments made in accordance with earnings withholding order.

§ 706.020.　Application of chapter

Except for an earning assignment order for support, the earnings of an employee shall not be required to be withheld by an employer for payment of a debt by means of any judicial procedure other than pursuant to this chapter.　*(Added by Stats.1982, c. 1364, p. 5173, § 2, operative July 1, 1983.　Amended by Stats.1992, c. 163 (A.B.2641), § 46, operative Jan. 1, 1994.)*

§ 706.021.　Procedure for levy of execution upon employee earnings

Notwithstanding any other provision of this title, a levy of execution upon the earnings of an employee shall be made by service of an earnings withholding order upon the employer in accordance with this chapter.　*(Added by Stats.1982, c. 1364, p. 5173, § 2, operative July 1, 1983.)*

§ 706.022.　Withholding period, defined; amount withheld; employer liability for amounts withheld and paid prior to service of order

(a) As used in this section, "withholding period" means the period which commences on the 10th day after service of an earnings withholding order upon the employer and which continues until the earliest of the following dates:

(1) The date the employer has withheld the full amount required to satisfy the order.

(2) The date of termination specified in a court order served on the employer.

(3) The date of termination specified in a notice of termination served on the employer by the levying officer.

(4) The date of termination of a dormant or suspended earnings withholding order as determined pursuant to Section 706.032.

(b) Except as otherwise provided by statute, an employer shall withhold the amounts required by an earnings withholding order from all earnings of the employee payable for any pay period of the employee which ends during the withholding period.

(c) An employer is not liable for any amounts withheld and paid over to the levying officer pursuant to an earnings withholding order prior to service upon the employer pursuant to paragraph (2) or (3) of subdivision (a). *(Added by Stats.1982, c. 1364, p. 5173, § 2, operative July 1, 1983. Amended by Stats.1989, c. 263, § 1; Stats. 1992, c. 283 (S.B.1372), § 5, eff. July 21, 1992.)*

§ 706.023. Multiple earnings withholding orders

Except as otherwise provided in this chapter:

(a) An employer shall comply with the first earnings withholding order served upon the employer.

(b) If the employer is served with two or more earnings withholding orders on the same day, the employer shall comply with the order issued pursuant to the judgment first entered. If two or more orders served on the same day are based on judgments entered upon the same day, the employer shall comply with whichever one of such orders the employer selects.

(c) If an earnings withholding order is served while an employer is required to comply with another earnings withholding order with respect to the earnings of the same employee, the subsequent order is ineffective and the employer shall not withhold earnings pursuant to the subsequent order. *(Added by Stats.1982, c. 1364, p. 5173, § 2, operative July 1, 1983.)*

§ 706.024. Amount required to satisfy earnings withholding order; discretionary notice; accrual of interest

(a) The amount required to satisfy an earnings withholding order is the total amount required to satisfy the writ of execution on the date the order is issued, with the following additions and subtractions:

(1) The addition of the statutory fee for service of the order and any other statutory fees for performing duties under the order.

(2) The addition of costs added to the order pursuant to Section 685.090.

(3) The subtraction of the amount of any partial satisfactions.

(4) The addition of daily interest accruing after issuance of the order, as adjusted for partial satisfactions.

(b) From time to time the levying officer, in the levying officer's discretion, may give written notice to the employer of the amount required to satisfy the earnings withholding order and the employer shall determine the total amount to withhold based upon the levying officer's notice, notwithstanding a different amount stated in the order originally served on the employer.

(c) If the full amount required to satisfy the earnings withholding order as stated in the order or in the levying officer's notice under subdivision (b) is withheld from the judgment debtor's earnings, interest ceases to accrue on that amount. *(Added by Stats.1992, c. 283 (S.B.1372), § 6, eff. July 21, 1992.)*

§ 706.025. Payments to levying officer

(a) Except as provided in subdivision (b), the amount required to be withheld pursuant to an earnings withholding order shall be paid monthly to the levying officer not later than the 15th day of each month. The initial monthly payment shall include all amounts required to be withheld from the earnings of the employee during the preceding calendar month up to the close of the employee's pay period ending closest to the last day of that month, and thereafter each monthly payment shall include amounts withheld from the employee's earnings for services rendered in the interim up to the close of the employee's pay period ending closest to the last day of the preceding calendar month.

(b) The employer may elect to pay the amounts withheld to the levying officer more frequently than monthly. If the employer so elects, payment of the amount withheld from the employee's earnings for each pay period shall be made not later than 10 days after the close of the pay period. *(Added by Stats.1982, c. 1364, p. 5173, § 2, operative July 1, 1983.)*

§ 706.026. Levying officer; receipt, accounting, and payment of amounts; amounts collected under earnings withholding orders; filing account

(a) The levying officer shall receive and account for all amounts paid by the employer pursuant to Section 706.025 and shall pay the amounts so received over to the person entitled thereto at least once every 30 days.

(b) At least once every two years, the levying officer shall file an account with the court for all amounts collected under the earnings withholding order, including costs and interest added to the amount due. *(Added by Stats.1982, c. 1364, p. 5174, § 2, operative July 1, 1983. Amended by Stats.1992, c. 283 (S.B.1372), § 7, eff. July 21, 1992.)*

§ 706.027. Notice of satisfaction of judgment

If the judgment pursuant to which the earnings withholding order is issued is satisfied before the order otherwise terminates pursuant to Section 706.022, the judgment creditor shall promptly notify the levying officer who shall promptly terminate the order by serving a notice of termination on the employer. *(Added by Stats.1982, c. 1364, p. 5174, § 2, operative July 1, 1983.)*

§ 706.028. Final earnings withholding order for costs and interest

(a) "Final earnings withholding order for costs and interest" means an earnings withholding order for the collection only of unsatisfied costs and interest, which is issued after an earlier earnings withholding order has been returned satisfied.

(b) After the amount stated as owing in a prior earnings withholding order is paid, the judgment creditor may obtain a final earnings withholding order for costs and interest to collect amounts of costs and interest that were not collected under the prior earnings withholding order.

(c) A final earnings withholding order for costs and interest shall be enforced in the same manner as other earnings withholding orders.

(d) Satisfaction of the amount stated as owing in a final earnings withholding order for costs and interest is equivalent to satisfaction of the money judgment. For this purpose, interest ceases to accrue on the date of issuance of the final earnings withholding order and no additional costs may be added after that date, except for the statutory fee for service of the order and any other statutory fees for performing duties under the order. *(Added by Stats.1992, c. 283 (S.B.1372), § 9, eff. July 21, 1992.)*

§ 706.029. Service of order creating lien; duration

Service of an earnings withholding order creates a lien upon the earnings of the judgment debtor that are required to be withheld pursuant to the order and upon all property of the employer subject to the enforcement of a money judgment in the amount required to be withheld pursuant to such order. The lien continues for a period of one year from the date the earnings of the judgment debtor become payable unless the amount required to be withheld pursuant to the order is paid as required by law. *(Added by Stats.1982, c. 1364, p. 5174, § 2, operative July 1, 1983.)*

§ 706.030. Withholding order for support; operation with earnings withholding order

(a) A "withholding order for support" is an earnings withholding order issued on a writ of execution to collect delinquent amounts payable under a judgment for the support of a child, or spouse or former spouse, of the judgment debtor. A withholding order for support shall be denoted as such on its face.

(b) The local child support agency may issue a withholding order for support on a notice of levy pursuant to Section 17522 of the Family Code to collect a support obligation.

(1) When the local child support agency issues a withholding order for support, a reference in this chapter to a levying officer is deemed to mean the local child support agency who issues the withholding order for support.

(2) Service of a withholding order for support issued by the local child support agency may be made by first-class mail or in any other manner described in Section 706.101. Service of a withholding order for support issued by the local child support agency is complete when it is received by the employer or a person described in paragraph (1) or (2) of subdivision (a) of Section 706.101, or if service is by first-class mail, service is complete as specified in Section 1013.

(3) The local child support agency shall serve upon the employer the withholding order for support, a copy of the order, and a notice informing the support obligor of the effect of the order and of his or her right to hearings and remedies provided in this chapter and in the Family Code. The notice shall be accompanied by the forms necessary to obtain an administrative review and a judicial hearing and instructions on how to file the forms. Within 10 days from the date of service, the employer shall deliver to the support obligor a copy of the withholding order for support, the forms to obtain an administrative review and judicial hearing, and the notice. If the support obligor is no longer employed by the employer and the employer does not owe the support obligor any earnings, the employer shall inform the local child support agency that the support obligor is no longer employed by the employer.

(4) An employer who fails to comply with paragraph (3) shall be subject to a civil penalty of five hundred dollars ($500) for each occurrence.

(5) The local child support agency shall provide for an administrative review to reconsider or modify the amount to be withheld for arrearages pursuant to the withholding order for support, if the support obligor requests a review at any time after service of the withholding order. The local child support agency shall provide the review in the same manner and timeframes provided for resolution of a complaint pursuant to Section 17800 of the Family Code. The local child support agency shall notify the employer if the review results in any modifications to the withholding order for support. If the local child support agency cannot complete the administrative review within 30 calendar days of receipt of the complaint, the local child support agency shall notify the employer to suspend withholding any disputed amount pending the completion of the review and the determination by the local child support agency.

(6) Nothing in this section prohibits the support obligor from seeking a judicial determination of arrearages pursuant to subdivision (c) of Section 17256 of the Family Code or from filing a motion for equitable division of earnings pursuant to Section 706.052 either prior to or after the administrative review provided by this section. Within five business days after receiving notice of the obligor having filed for judicial relief pursuant to this section, the local child support agency shall notify the employer to suspend withholding any disputed amount pending a determination by the court. The employer shall then adjust the withholding within not more than

nine days of receiving the notice from the local child support agency.

(c) Notwithstanding any other provision of this chapter:

(1) An employer shall continue to withhold pursuant to a withholding order for support until the earliest of the dates specified in paragraph (1), (2), or (3) of subdivision (a) of Section 706.022, except that a withholding order for support shall automatically terminate one year after the employment of the employee by the employer terminates.

(2) A withholding order for support has priority over any other earnings withholding order. An employer upon whom a withholding order for support is served shall withhold and pay over earnings of the employee pursuant to that order notwithstanding the requirements of another earnings withholding order.

(3) Subject to paragraph (2) and to Article 3 (commencing with Section 706.050), an employer shall withhold earnings pursuant to both a withholding order for support and another earnings withholding order simultaneously.

(4) An employer who willfully fails to withhold and forward support pursuant to a valid earnings withholding order for support issued and served upon the employer pursuant to this chapter is liable to the support obligee, as defined in Section 5214 of the Family Code, for the amount of support not withheld, forwarded, or otherwise paid to the support obligee.

(5) Notwithstanding any other provision of law, an employer shall send all earnings withheld pursuant to a withholding order for support to the levying officer or the State Disbursement Unit as described in Section 17309 of the Family Code within the time period specified by federal law.

(6) Once the State Disbursement Unit as described in Section 17309 of the Family Code is operational, all support payments made pursuant to an earnings withholding order shall be made to that unit.

(7) Earnings withheld pursuant to an earnings withholding order for support shall be credited toward satisfaction of a support judgment as specified in Section 695.221. *(Added by Stats.1982, c. 1364, p. 5174, § 2, operative July 1, 1983. Amended by Stats.1992, c. 283 (S.B.1372), § 10, eff. July 21, 1992; Stats.1997, c. 599 (A.B.573), § 5; Stats.2000, c. 808 (A.B.1358), § 17, eff. Sept. 28, 2000; Stats.2001, c. 755 (S.B.943), § 1, eff. Oct. 12, 2001; Stats.2003, c. 387 (A.B.739), § 1.)*

§ 706.031. Earnings assignment order for support; operation with earnings withholding order

(a) Nothing in this chapter affects an earnings assignment order for support.

(b) An earnings assignment order for support shall be given priority over any earnings withholding order. An employer upon whom an earnings assignment order for support is served shall withhold and pay over the earnings of the employee pursuant to the assignment order notwithstanding the requirements of any earnings withholding order. When an employer is required to cease withholding earnings pursuant to an earnings withholding order, the employer shall notify the levying officer who served the earnings withholding order that a supervening earnings assignment order for support is in effect.

(c) Subject to subdivisions (b), (d), and (e), an employer shall withhold earnings of an employee pursuant to both an earnings assignment order for support and an earnings withholding order.

(d) The employer shall withhold pursuant to an earnings withholding order only to the extent that the sum of the amount withheld pursuant to any earnings assignment order for support and the amount withheld pursuant to the earnings withholding order does not exceed the amount that may be withheld under Article 3 (commencing with Section 706.050).

(e) The employer shall withhold pursuant to an earnings withholding order for taxes only to the extent that the sum of the amount withheld pursuant to any earnings assignment order for support and the amount withheld pursuant to the earnings withholding order for taxes does not exceed the amount that may be withheld under Article 4 (commencing with Section 706.070). *(Added by Stats.1982, c. 1364, p. 5175, § 2, operative July 1, 1983. Amended by Stats.1992, c. 163 (A.B.2641), § 47, operative Jan. 1, 1994.)*

§ 706.032. Termination of earnings withholding orders

(a) Except as otherwise provided by statute:

(1) If withholding under an earnings withholding order ceases because the judgment debtor's employment has terminated, the earnings withholding order terminates at the conclusion of a continuous 180-day period during which no amounts are withheld under the order.

(2) If withholding under an earnings withholding order ceases because the judgment debtor's earnings are subject to an order or assignment with higher priority, the earnings withholding order terminates at the conclusion of a continuous two-year period during which no amounts are withheld under the order.

(b) If an earnings withholding order has terminated pursuant to subdivision (a), the employer shall return the order to the levying officer along with a statement of the reasons for returning the order. *(Added by Stats.1992, c. 283 (S.B.1372), § 11, eff. July 21, 1992.)*

§ 706.033. Return of writ before earnings withholding order terminates; supplemental return on writ

If the writ is returned before the earnings withholding order terminates, on termination of the earnings withholding order the levying officer shall make a supplemental return on the writ. The supplemental return shall contain the same information as an original return pursuant to Section 699.560. *(Added by Stats.1992, c. 283 (S.B.1372), § 12, eff. July 21, 1992.)*

§ 706.034. Deduction from employee earnings for payments made in accordance with earnings withholding order

The employer may deduct from the earnings of the employee the sum of one dollar and fifty cents ($1.50) for each payment made in accordance with an earnings withholding order issued pursuant to this chapter. *(Added by Stats.1997, c. 137 (A.B.519), § 1. Amended by Stats.2004, c. 520 (A.B.2530), § 1.)*

ARTICLE 3. RESTRICTIONS ON EARNINGS WITHHOLDING

Section
706.050. Amount of employee earnings exempt.
706.051. Amount necessary for support of judgment debtor or family; exemption.
706.052. Disposable earnings and earnings withheld pursuant to earning assignment order for support; exemption; equitable division of earnings by court.

§ 706.050. Amount of employee earnings exempt

Except as otherwise provided in this chapter, the amount of earnings of a judgment debtor exempt from the levy of an earnings withholding order shall be that amount that may not be withheld from the judgment debtor's earnings under federal law in Section 1673(a) of Title 15 of the United States Code. *(Added by Stats.1982, c. 1364, p. 5175, § 2, operative July 1, 1983.)*

§ 706.051. Amount necessary for support of judgment debtor or family; exemption

(a) For the purposes of this section, "family of the judgment debtor" includes the spouse or former spouse of the judgment debtor.

(b) Except as provided in subdivision (c), the portion of the judgment debtor's earnings which the judgment debtor proves is necessary for the support of the judgment debtor or the judgment debtor's family supported in whole or in part by the judgment debtor is exempt from levy under this chapter.

(c) The exemption provided in subdivision (b) is not available if any of the following exceptions applies:

(1) The debt was incurred for the common necessaries of life furnished to the judgment debtor or the family of the judgment debtor.

(2) The debt was incurred for personal services rendered by an employee or former employee of the judgment debtor.

(3) The order is a withholding order for support under Section 706.030.

(4) The order is one governed by Article 4 (commencing with Section 706.070) (state tax order). *(Added by Stats.1982, c. 1364, p. 5175, § 2, operative July 1, 1983.)*

§ 706.052. Disposable earnings and earnings withheld pursuant to earning assignment order for support; exemption; equitable division of earnings by court

(a) Except as provided in subdivision (b), one-half of the disposable earnings (as defined by Section 1672 of Title 15 of the United States Code) of the judgment debtor, plus any amount withheld from the judgment debtor's earnings pursuant to any earnings assignment order for support, is exempt from levy under this chapter where the earnings withholding order is a withholding order for support under Section 706.030.

(b) Except as provided in subdivision (c), upon motion of any interested party, the court shall make an equitable division of the judgment debtor's earnings that takes into account the needs of all the persons the judgment debtor is required to support and shall effectuate such division by an order determining the amount to be withheld from the judgment debtor's earnings pursuant to the withholding order for support.

(c) An order made under subdivision (b) may not authorize the withholding of an amount in excess of the amount that may be withheld for support under federal law under Section 1673 of Title 15 of the United States Code. *(Added by Stats.1982, c. 1364, p. 5176, § 2, operative July 1, 1983. Amended by Stats.1992, c. 163 (A.B.2641), § 48, operative Jan. 1, 1994.)*

ARTICLE 4. EARNINGS WITHHOLDING ORDER FOR TAXES

Section
706.070. Definitions.
706.071. Limitations on state's right to collect state tax liability.
706.072. Withholding order for taxes, defined; issuance requirements; notice of proposed issuance.
706.073. Application of chapter and article to withholding order for taxes; levying officer, defined.
706.074. Issuance of withholding order by state; contents; amount.
706.075. Service and delivery of copy of order and notice; hearing; employer liability.
706.076. Withholding amounts in excess of order issued under section 706.074; application to court for order; setting for hearing and notice; issuance of order; temporary earnings holding order.
706.077. Employer withholding; prior earnings withholding orders.
706.078. Pay periods to which withholding order applicable; jeopardy withholding order for taxes; termination of order.
706.080. Manner of service of order, notice or other document.
706.081. Form of order, notice or other document.
706.082. Court proceedings for review of taxpayer's liability.
706.084. Warrant, notice of levy or notice or order to withhold.

§ 706.070. Definitions

As used in this article:

(a) "State" means the State of California and includes any officer, department, board, or agency thereof.

(b) "State tax liability" means an amount for which the state has a state tax lien as defined in Section 7162 of the Government Code excluding a state tax lien created pursuant to the Fish and Game Code. *(Added by Stats.1982, c. 1364, p. 5176, § 2, operative July 1, 1983.)*

§ 706.071. Limitations on state's right to collect state tax liability

This chapter does not limit the state's right to collect a state tax liability except that (a) no levy upon earnings of an employee held by an employer is effective unless such levy is made in accordance with the provisions of this chapter and (b) other methods of collection may not be used to require an employer to withhold earnings of an employee in payment of a state tax liability. *(Added by Stats.1982, c. 1364, p. 5176, § 2, operative July 1, 1983.)*

§ 706.072. Withholding order for taxes, defined; issuance requirements; notice of proposed issuance

(a) A "withholding order for taxes" is an earnings withholding order issued pursuant to this article to collect a state tax liability and shall be denoted as a withholding order for taxes on its face.

(b) A withholding order for taxes may only be issued under one of the following circumstances:

(1) The existence of the state tax liability appears on the face of the taxpayer's return, including a case where such tax liability is disclosed from the taxpayer's return after errors in mathematical computations in the return have been corrected.

(2) The state tax liability has been assessed or determined as provided by statute and the taxpayer had notice of the proposed assessment or determination and had available an opportunity to have the proposed assessment or determination reviewed by appropriate administrative procedures. If the taxpayer makes a timely request for review of the assessment or determination, the state shall not issue a withholding order for taxes until the administrative review procedure is completed. If the taxpayer is given notice of the proposed assessment or determination but does not make a timely request for review, the state may issue a withholding order for taxes.

(c) In any case where a state tax liability has been assessed or determined prior to July 1, 1983, and the state determines that the requirement of subdivision (b) may not have been satisfied, the state may send a "Notice of Proposed Issuance of Withholding Order for Taxes" to the taxpayer at the taxpayer's last known address by first-class mail, postage prepaid. The notice shall advise the taxpayer that the taxpayer may have the assessment or determination reviewed by appropriate administrative procedures and state how such a review may be obtained. If the taxpayer is sent such a notice and requests such a review within 30 days from the date the notice was mailed to the taxpayer, the state shall provide appropriate administrative procedures for review of the assessment or

determination and shall not issue the withholding order for taxes until the administrative review procedure is completed. If the taxpayer is sent such a notice and does not request such a review within 30 days from the date the notice was mailed to the taxpayer, the state may issue the withholding order for taxes.

(d) A withholding order for taxes may be issued whether or not the state tax liability has been reduced to judgment. *(Added by Stats.1982, c. 1364, p. 5176, § 2, operative July 1, 1983.)*

§ 706.073. Application of chapter and article to withholding order for taxes; levying officer, defined

Except as otherwise provided in this article, the provisions of this chapter govern the procedures and proceedings concerning a withholding order for taxes. For the purposes of this article, a reference in this chapter to a "levying officer" shall be deemed to mean the specific state agency seeking to collect a state tax liability under this article. *(Added by Stats.1982, c. 1364, p. 5177, § 2, operative July 1, 1983.)*

§ 706.074. Issuance of withholding order by state; contents; amount

(a) The state may itself issue a withholding order for taxes under this section to collect a state tax liability. The order shall specify the total amount required to be withheld pursuant to the order (unpaid tax liability including any penalties, accrued interest, and costs).

(b) Unless a lesser amount is specified in the order, the amount to be withheld by the employer each pay period pursuant to an order issued under this section is the amount required to be withheld under Section 1673(a) of Title 15 of the United States Code, and is not subject to the exception provided in Section 1673(b) of Title 15 of the United States Code. *(Added by Stats.1982, c. 1364, p. 5177, § 2, operative July 1, 1983.)*

§ 706.075. Service and delivery of copy of order and notice; hearing; employer liability

(a) This section applies to any withholding order for taxes issued under this article.

(b) Together with the withholding order for taxes, the state shall serve upon the employer an additional copy of the order and a notice informing the taxpayer of the effect of the order and of his right to hearings and remedies provided in this chapter. Within 10 days from the date of service, the employer shall deliver to the taxpayer a copy of the order and the notice, except that immediate delivery shall be made where a jeopardy withholding order for taxes has been served. If the taxpayer is no longer employed by the employer and the employer does not owe the taxpayer any earnings, the employer is not required to make such delivery.

(c) The state shall provide for an administrative hearing to reconsider or modify the amount to be withheld pursuant to the withholding order for taxes, and the taxpayer may request such a hearing at any time after service of the order. If the taxpayer requests a hearing, the hearing shall be provided, and the matter shall be determined, within 15 days after the request is received by the state. The determination of the amount to be withheld is subject to the standard provided in subdivision (b) of Section 706.051. Judicial review of the determination made pursuant to this subdivision by the state may be had only if a petition for a writ of mandate pursuant to Section 1094.5 is filed within 90 days from the date that written notice of the state's determination was delivered or mailed to the taxpayer.

(d) The employer is not subject to any civil liability for failure to comply with subdivision (b). Nothing in this subdivision limits the power of a court to hold the employer in contempt of court for failure to comply with subdivision (b). *(Added by Stats.1982, c. 1364, p. 5178, § 2, operative July 1, 1983.)*

§ 706.076. Withholding amounts in excess of order issued under section 706.074; application to court for order; setting for hearing and notice; issuance of order; temporary earnings holding order

(a) A withholding order for taxes may be issued pursuant to this section requiring the employer of the taxpayer to withhold an amount in excess of the amount that may be required to be withheld pursuant to an order issued under Section 706.074.

(b) The state may, at any time, apply to a court of record in the county where the taxpayer was last known to reside for the issuance of a withholding order for taxes under this section to collect a state tax liability.

(c) The application for the order shall include a statement under oath that the state has served upon the taxpayer both of the following:

(1) A copy of the application.

(2) A notice informing the taxpayer of the purpose of the application and the right of the taxpayer to appear at the court hearing on the application.

(d) Upon the filing of the application, the court shall immediately set the matter for hearing and the court clerk shall send a notice of the time and place of the hearing by first-class mail, postage prepaid, to the state and the taxpayer. The notice shall be deposited in the mail at least 10 days before the day set for the hearing.

(e) After hearing, the court shall issue a withholding order for taxes which shall require the taxpayer's employer to withhold and pay over all earnings of the taxpayer other than that amount which the taxpayer proves is exempt under subdivision (b) of Section 706.051, but in no event shall the amount to be withheld be less than that permitted to be withheld under Section 706.050.

(f) The state may issue a temporary earnings holding order, which shall be denoted as such on its face, in any case where the state intends to apply for a withholding order for taxes under this section and has determined that the collection of the state tax liability will be jeopardized in whole or in part if the temporary earnings holding order is not issued. The temporary earnings holding order shall be directed to the taxpayer's employer and shall require the employer to retain in the employer's possession or under the employer's control all or such portion of the earnings of the taxpayer then or thereafter due as is specified in the order. Together with the temporary earnings holding order, the state shall serve upon the employer an additional copy of the order and a notice informing the taxpayer of the effect of the order and of the right to the remedies provided in this chapter. Upon receipt of the order, the employer shall deliver to the taxpayer a copy of the order and notice. If the taxpayer is no longer employed by the employer and the employer does not owe the taxpayer any earnings, the employer is not required to make such delivery. The temporary earnings holding order expires 15 days from the date it is served on the employer unless it is extended by the court on ex parte application for good cause shown. If a temporary earnings holding order is served on an employer, the state may not thereafter, for a period of six months, serve on the same employer another temporary earnings holding order for the same employee unless the court for good cause shown otherwise orders. Sections 706.153 and 706.154 apply to temporary earnings holding orders issued under this section. *(Added by Stats.1982, c. 1364, p. 5178, § 2, operative July 1, 1983.)*

§ 706.077. Employer withholding; prior earnings withholding orders

(a) Subject to subdivision (b), an employer upon whom a withholding order for taxes is served shall withhold and pay over earnings of the employee pursuant to such order and shall cease to withhold earnings pursuant to any prior earnings withholding order except that a withholding order for support shall be given priority as provided in Section 706.030. When an employer is required to cease withholding earnings pursuant to an earlier earnings withholding order, the employer shall notify the levying officer who served the earlier earnings withholding order that a supervening withholding order for taxes is in effect.

(b) An employer shall not withhold earnings of an employee pursuant to a withholding order for taxes if a prior withholding order for taxes is in effect, and, in such case, the subsequent withholding order for taxes is ineffective. *(Added by Stats.1982, c. 1364, p. 5179, § 2, operative July 1, 1983.)*

§ 706.078. Pay periods to which withholding order applicable; jeopardy withholding order for taxes; termination of order

(a) Except as provided in subdivision (b), the employer shall not withhold pursuant to a withholding order for taxes from earnings of the employee payable for any pay period of such employee that ends prior to the 10th day after service of the order.

(b) A "jeopardy withholding order for taxes," which shall be denoted as such on its face, is a withholding order for taxes that requires that the employer withhold pursuant to the order from earnings due to the employee at the time of service of the order on the employer and from earnings thereafter due. A jeopardy withholding order for taxes may be issued only where the state has determined that the collection of a state tax liability will be jeopardized in whole or in part by delaying the time when withholding from earnings commences.

(c) An employer shall continue to withhold pursuant to a withholding order for taxes until the amount specified in the order has been paid in full or the order is withdrawn, except that the order automatically terminates one year after the employment of the employee by the employer terminates. The state shall promptly serve on the employer a notice terminating the withholding order for taxes if the state tax liability for which the withholding order for taxes was issued is satisfied before the employer has withheld the full amount specified in the order, and the employer shall discontinue withholding in compliance with such notice. *(Added by Stats.1982, c. 1364, p. 5180, § 2, operative July 1, 1983.)*

§ 706.080. Manner of service of order, notice or other document

Service of a withholding order for taxes or of any other notice or document required under this chapter in connection with a withholding order for taxes may be made by the state by first-class mail, postage prepaid, or by any authorized state employee. Service of a withholding order for taxes is complete when it is received by the employer or a person described in paragraph (1) or (2) of subdivision (a) of Section 706.101. Service of, or the providing of, any other notice or document required to be served or provided under this chapter in connection with a withholding order for taxes is complete when the notice or document is deposited in the mail addressed to the last known address of the person on whom it is served or to whom it is to be provided. *(Added by Stats.1982, c. 1364, p. 5180, § 2, operative July 1, 1983.)*

§ 706.081. Form of order, notice or other document

Except for the forms referred to in Section 706.076, the state shall prescribe the form of any order, notice, or other document required by this chapter in connection with a withholding order for taxes notwithstanding Sections 706.100 and 706.120, and any form so prescribed is deemed to comply with this chapter. *(Added by Stats. 1982, c. 1364, p. 5180, § 2, operative July 1, 1983.)*

§ 706.082. Court proceedings for review of taxpayer's liability

No review of the taxpayer's tax liability shall be permitted in any court proceedings under this chapter. *(Added by Stats.1982, c. 1364, p. 5180, § 2, operative July 1, 1983.)*

§ 706.084. Warrant, notice of levy or notice or order to withhold

Where a warrant, notice of levy, or notice or order to withhold is served on the employer to enforce a state tax liability of a person who is an employee of that employer,

it shall be deemed to be a withholding order for taxes as to any earnings that are subject to the provisions of this chapter if both of the following requirements are satisfied:

(a) The form provides notice on its face that it is to be treated as a withholding order for taxes as to any earnings that are subject to the provisions of this chapter.

(b) The form provides all the information provided in a withholding order for taxes. *(Added by Stats.1982, c. 1364, p. 5180, § 2, operative July 1, 1983.)*

ARTICLE 5. PROCEDURE FOR EARNINGS WITHHOLDING ORDERS AND EXEMPTION CLAIMS

Section
706.100. Practice and procedure in proceedings under this chapter; rules.
706.101. Service of order by delivery; earnings withholding order.
706.102. Issuance of earnings withholding order where writ of execution issued and time for levy on property under writ not yet expired.
706.103. Service of documents by levying officer on employer.
706.104. Delivery of copy of order and notice to employee; completion of employer return.
706.105. Claim of exemption under § 706.051.
706.106. Findings in court proceedings.
706.108. Earnings withholding order; filing requirement; duties of levying officer.
706.109. Earnings withholding order; issuance against spouse of judgment debtor.

§ 706.100. Practice and procedure in proceedings under this chapter; rules

Notwithstanding any other provision of law, the Judicial Council may provide by rule for the practice and procedure in proceedings under this chapter except for the state's administrative hearings provided by Article 4 (commencing with Section 706.070). *(Added by Stats. 1982, c. 1364, p. 5181, § 2, operative July 1, 1983.)*

§ 706.101. Service of order by delivery; earnings withholding order

(a) An earnings withholding order shall be served by the levying officer upon the employer by delivery of the order to any of the following:

(1) The managing agent or person in charge, at the time of service, of the branch or office where the employee works or the office from which the employee is paid. In the case of a state employee, the office from which the employee is paid does not include the Controller's office unless the employee works directly for the Controller's office.

(2) Any person to whom a copy of the summons and of the complaint may be delivered to make service on the employer under Article 4 (commencing with Section 416.10) of Chapter 4 of Title 5.

(b) Service of an earnings withholding order shall be made by personal delivery as provided in Section 415.10 or 415.20 or by delivery by registered or certified mail, postage prepaid, with return receipt requested. When service is made by mail, service is complete at the time the return receipt is executed by or on behalf of the recipient. If the levying officer attempts service by mail under this subdivision and does not receive a return receipt within 15 days from the date of deposit in the mail of the earnings withholding order, the levying officer shall make service as provided in Article 3 (commencing with Section 415.10) of Chapter 4 of Title 5.

(c) The state may issue an earnings withholding order directly, without the use of a levying officer, for purposes of collecting overpayments of unemployment compensation or disability benefits pursuant to Article 4 (commencing with Section 1375) of Chapter 5 of Part 1 of, and Article 5 (commencing with Section 2735) of Chapter 2 of Part 2 of, Division 1 of the Unemployment Insurance Code. The earnings withholding order shall be served by registered or certified mail, postage prepaid, with return receipt requested. Service is deemed complete at the time the return receipt is executed by, or on behalf of, the recipient. If the state does not receive a return receipt within 15 days from the date of deposit in the mail of the withholding order, the state shall refer the earnings withholding order to a levying officer for service in accordance with subdivision (b).

(d) Except as provided in subdivision (b) or (c), service of any notice or document under this chapter may be made by first-class mail, postage prepaid. If service is made on the employer after the employer's return has been received by the levying officer, the service shall be made by first- class mail, postage prepaid, on the person designated in the employer's return to receive notices and at the address indicated in the employer's return, whether or not that address is within the county. This subdivision does not preclude service by personal delivery (1) on the employer before the employer's return has been received by the levying officer or (2) on the person designated in the employer's return after its receipt.

(e) Notwithstanding subdivision (b), if the judgment creditor so requests, the levying officer shall make service of the earnings withholding order by personal delivery as provided in Section 415.10 or 415.20. *(Added by Stats. 1982, c. 1364, p. 5181, § 2.2, operative July 1, 1983. Amended by Stats.1984, c. 538, § 28; Stats.1989, c. 1416, § 24; Stats.2002, c. 890 (A.B.2929), § 1.)*

§ 706.102. Issuance of earnings withholding order where writ of execution issued and time for levy on property under writ not yet expired

(a) If a writ of execution has been issued to the county where the judgment debtor's employer is to be served and the time specified in subdivision (b) of Section 699.530 for levy on property under the writ has not expired, a judgment creditor may apply for the issuance of an earnings withholding order by filing an application with a

levying officer in such county who shall promptly issue an earnings withholding order.

(b) This section does not apply where the earnings withholding order is a withholding order for taxes. *(Added by Stats.1982, c. 1364, p. 5182, § 2, operative July 1, 1983.)*

§ 706.103. Service of documents by levying officer on employer

(a) The levying officer shall serve upon the designated employer all of the following:

(1) The original and one copy of the earnings withholding order.

(2) The form for the employer's return.

(3) The notice to employee of earnings withholding order.

(b) At the time the levying officer makes service pursuant to subdivision (a), the levying officer shall provide the employer with a copy of the employer's instructions referred to in Section 706.127. The Judicial Council may adopt rules prescribing the circumstances when compliance with this subdivision is not required.

(c) No earnings withholding order shall be served upon the employer after the time specified in subdivision (b) of Section 699.530. *(Added by Stats.1982, c. 1364, p. 5182, § 2, operative July 1, 1983.)*

§ 706.104. Delivery of copy of order and notice to employee; completion of employer return

Any employer who is served with an earnings withholding order shall:

(a) Deliver to the judgment debtor a copy of the earnings withholding order and the notice to employee of earnings withholding within 10 days from the date of service. If the judgment debtor is no longer employed by the employer and the employer does not owe the employee any earnings, the employer is not required to make such delivery. The employer is not subject to any civil liability for failure to comply with this subdivision. Nothing in this subdivision limits the power of a court to hold the employer in contempt of court for failure to comply with this subdivision.

(b) Complete the employer's return on the form provided by the levying officer and mail it by first-class mail, postage prepaid, to the levying officer within 15 days from the date of service. If the earnings withholding order is ineffective, the employer shall state in the employer's return that the order will not be complied with for this reason and shall return the order to the levying officer with the employer's return. *(Added by Stats.1982, c. 1364, p. 5182, § 2, operative July 1, 1983.)*

§ 706.105. Claim of exemption under § 706.051

(a) A judgment debtor may claim an exemption under Section 706.051 under either of the following circumstances:

(1) No prior hearing has been held with respect to the earnings withholding order.

(2) There has been a material change in circumstances since the time of the last prior hearing on the earnings withholding order.

(b) A claim of exemption shall be made by filing with the levying officer an original and one copy of (1) the judgment debtor's claim of exemption and (2) the judgment debtor's financial statement.

(c) Upon filing of the claim of exemption, the levying officer shall promptly send to the judgment creditor, at the address stated in the application for the earnings withholding order, by first-class mail, postage prepaid, all of the following:

(1) A copy of the claim of exemption.

(2) A copy of the financial statement.

(3) A notice of claim of exemption. The notice shall state that the claim of exemption has been filed and that the earnings withholding order will be terminated, or modified to reflect the amount of earnings claimed to be exempt in the claim of exemption, unless a notice of opposition to the claim of exemption is filed with the levying officer by the judgment creditor within 10 days after the date of the mailing of the notice of claim of exemption.

(d) A judgment creditor who desires to contest a claim of exemption shall, within 10 days after the date of the mailing of the notice of claim of exemption, file with the levying officer a notice of opposition to the claim of exemption.

(e) If a notice of opposition to the claim of exemption is filed with the levying officer within the 10–day period, the judgment creditor is entitled to a hearing on the claim of exemption. If the judgment creditor desires a hearing on the claim of exemption, the judgment creditor shall file a notice of motion for an order determining the claim of exemption with the court within 10 days after the date the levying officer mailed the notice of claim of exemption. If the notice of motion is so filed, the hearing on the motion shall be held not later than 30 days from the date the notice of motion was filed unless continued by the court for good cause. At the time prescribed by subdivision (b) of Section 1005, the judgment creditor shall give written notice of the hearing to the levying officer and shall serve a notice of the hearing and a copy of the notice of opposition to the claim of exemption on the judgment debtor and, if the claim of exemption so requested, on the attorney for the judgment debtor. Service is deemed made when the notice of the hearing and a copy of the notice of opposition to the claim of exemption are deposited in the mail, postage prepaid, addressed to the judgment debtor at the address stated in the claim of exemption and, if service on the attorney for the judgment debtor was requested in the claim of exemption, to the attorney at the address stated in the claim of exemption. The judgment creditor shall file proof of the service with the court. After receiving the notice of the hearing and before the date set for the hearing, the levying officer shall file the claim of exemption and the notice of opposition to the claim of exemption with the court.

(f) If the levying officer does not receive a notice of opposition to the claim of exemption within the 10–day period after the date of mailing of the notice of claim of exemption and a notice of the hearing not later than 10 days after the filing of the notice of opposition to the claim of exemption, the levying officer shall serve on the employer one of the following:

(1) A notice that the earnings withholding order has been terminated if all of the judgment debtor's earnings were claimed to be exempt.

(2) A modified earnings withholding order that reflects the amount of earnings claimed to be exempt in the claim of exemption if only a portion of the judgment debtor's earnings was claimed to be exempt.

(g) If, after hearing, the court orders that the earnings withholding order be modified or terminated, the clerk shall promptly transmit a certified copy of the order to the levying officer who shall promptly serve on the employer of the judgment debtor (1) a copy of the modified earnings withholding order or (2) a notice that the earnings withholding order has been terminated. The court may order that the earnings withholding order be terminated as of a date that precedes the date of hearing. If the court determines that any amount withheld pursuant to the earnings withholding order shall be paid to the judgment debtor, the court shall make an order directing the person who holds that amount to pay it promptly to the judgment debtor.

(h) If the earnings withholding order is terminated by the court, unless the court otherwise orders or unless there is a material change of circumstances since the time of the last prior hearing on the earnings withholding order, the judgment creditor may not apply for another earnings withholding order directed to the same employer with respect to the same judgment debtor for a period of 100 days following the date of service of the earnings withholding order or 60 days after the date of the termination of the order, whichever is later.

(i) If an employer has withheld and paid over amounts pursuant to an earnings withholding order after the date of termination of the order but prior to the receipt of notice of its termination, the judgment debtor may recover those amounts only from the levying officer if the levying officer still holds those amounts or, if those amounts have been paid over to the judgment creditor, from the judgment creditor. If the employer has withheld amounts pursuant to an earnings withholding order after termination of the order but has not paid over those amounts to the levying officer, the employer shall promptly pay those amounts to the judgment debtor.

(j) An appeal lies from any court order under this section denying a claim of exemption or modifying or terminating an earnings withholding order. An appeal by the judgment creditor from an order modifying or terminating the earnings withholding order does not stay the order from which the appeal is taken. Notwithstanding the appeal, until the order modifying or terminating the earnings withholding order is set aside or modified, the order allowing the claim of exemption in whole or in part shall be given the same effect as if the appeal had not been taken.

(k) This section does not apply to a withholding order for support or a withholding order for taxes. *(Added by Stats.1982, c. 1364, p. 5183, § 2, operative July 1, 1983. Amended by Stats.1989, c. 693, § 3; Stats.1998, c. 931 (S.B.2139), § 94, eff. Sept. 28, 1998.)*

§ 706.106. Findings in court proceedings

No findings are required in court proceedings under this chapter. *(Added by Stats.1982, c. 1364, p. 5185, § 2, operative July 1, 1983.)*

§ 706.108. Earnings withholding order; filing requirement; duties of levying officer

(a) If a writ of execution has been issued to the county where the judgment debtor's employer is to be served and the time specified in subdivision (b) of Section 699.530 for levy on property under the writ has not expired, a judgment creditor may deliver an application for issuance of an earnings withholding order to a registered process server who may then issue an earnings withholding order.

(b) If the registered process server has issued the earnings withholding order, the registered process server, before serving the earnings withholding order, shall deposit with the levying officer a copy of the writ of execution, the application for issuance of an earnings withholding order, and a copy of the earnings withholding order, and shall pay the fee provided by Section 26750 of the Government Code.

(c) A registered process server may serve an earnings withholding order on an employer whether the earnings withholding order was issued by a levying officer or by a registered process server, but no earnings withholding order may be served after the time specified in subdivision (b) of Section 699.530. In performing this function, the registered process server shall serve upon the designated employer all of the following:

(1) The original and one copy of the earnings withholding order.

(2) The form for the employer's return.

(3) The notice to the employee of the earnings withholding order.

(4) A copy of the employer's instructions referred to in Section 706.127, except as otherwise prescribed in rules adopted by the Judicial Council.

(d) Within five court days after service under this section, all of the following shall be filed with the levying officer:

(1) The writ of execution, if it is not already in the hands of the levying officer.

(2) Proof of service on the employer of the papers listed in subdivision (c).

(3) Instructions in writing, as required by the provisions of Section 687.010.

(e) If the fee provided by Section 26750 of the Government Code has been paid, the levying officer shall perform all other duties required by this chapter as if the levying officer had served the earnings withholding order. If the registered process server does not comply with subdivisions (b), where applicable, and (d), the service of the earnings withholding order is ineffective and the levying officer is not required to perform any duties under the order and may terminate the order and may release any withheld earnings to the judgment debtor.

(f) The fee for services of a registered process server under this section shall be allowed as a recoverable cost pursuant to Section 1033.5. *(Added by Stats.1984, c. 538, § 29. Amended by Stats.1987, c. 1080, § 6; Stats.2002, c. 197 (A.B.2493), § 4; Stats.2009, c. 54 (S.B.544), § 6.)*

§ 706.109. Earnings withholding order; issuance against spouse of judgment debtor

An earnings withholding order may not be issued against the earnings of the spouse of the judgment debtor except by court order upon noticed motion. *(Added by Stats.1984, c. 1671, § 20.)*

ARTICLE 6. FORMS; EMPLOYER'S INSTRUCTIONS

Section
706.120. Form of documents.
706.121. Application for issuance of earnings withholding order; form and contents.
706.122. Notice to employee of earnings withholding order; form and contents.
706.123. Judgment debtor's claim of exemption; form and contents.
706.124. Judgment debtor's financial statement; form and contents.
706.125. Earnings withholding order; contents.
706.126. Employer's return; form and contents.
706.127. Employer's instructions; preparation, revision and supplementation; supplying to levying officers.
706.128. Judgment creditor's notice of opposition to claim of exemption; form and contents.
706.129. Copies of forms available from levying officers.

§ 706.120. Form of documents

Except as provided in Section 706.081, the Judicial Council shall prescribe the form of the applications, notices, claims of exemption, orders, and other documents required by this chapter as provided in Section 681.030, and only such forms may be used to implement this chapter. *(Added by Stats.1982, c. 1364, p. 5185, § 2, operative July 1, 1983.)*

§ 706.121. Application for issuance of earnings withholding order; form and contents

The "application for issuance of earnings withholding order" shall be executed under oath and shall include all of the following:

(a) The name, the last known address, and, if known, the social security number of the judgment debtor.

(b) The name and address of the judgment creditor.

(c) The court where the judgment was entered and the date the judgment was entered.

(d) The date of issuance of a writ of execution to the county where the earnings withholding order is sought.

(e) The total amount required to satisfy the order on the date of issuance (which may not exceed the amount required to satisfy the writ of execution on the date of issuance of the order plus the levying officer's statutory fee for service of the order).

(f) The name and address of the employer to whom the order will be directed.

(g) The name and address of the person to whom the withheld money is to be paid by the levying officer. *(Added by Stats.1982, c. 1364, p. 5185, § 2, operative July 1, 1983. Amended by Stats.1992, c. 283 (S.B.1372), § 14, eff. July 21, 1992.)*

§ 706.122. Notice to employee of earnings withholding order; form and contents

The "notice to employee of earnings withholding order" shall contain a statement that informs the employee in simple terms of the nature of a wage garnishment, the right to an exemption, the procedure for claiming an exemption, and any other information the Judicial Council determines would be useful to the employee and appropriate for inclusion in the notice, including all of the following:

(a) The named employer has been ordered to withhold from the earnings of the judgment debtor the amounts required to be withheld under Section 706.050, or such other amounts as are specified in the earnings withholding order, and to pay these amounts over to the levying officer for transmittal to the person specified in the order in payment of the judgment described in the order.

(b) The manner of computing the amounts required to be withheld pursuant to Section 706.050.

(c) The judgment debtor may be able to keep more or all of the judgment debtor's earnings if the judgment debtor proves that the additional earnings are necessary for the support of the judgment debtor or the judgment debtor's family supported in whole or in part by the judgment debtor.

(d) If the judgment debtor wishes a court hearing to prove that amounts should not be withheld from the judgment debtor's earnings because they are necessary for the support of the judgment debtor or the judgment debtor's family supported in whole or in part by the judgment debtor, the judgment debtor shall file with the levying officer an original and one copy of the "judgment debtor's claim of exemption" and an original and one copy of the "judgment debtor's financial statement." The notice shall also advise the judgment debtor that the claim of exemption form and the financial statement form may be obtained without charge at the office of the levying officer. *(Added by Stats.1982, c. 1364, p. 5186, § 2, operative July 1, 1983.)*

§ 706.123. Judgment debtor's claim of exemption; form and contents

The "judgment debtor's claim of exemption" shall be executed under oath. The claim of exemption shall indicate how much the judgment debtor believes should be withheld from the judgment debtor's earnings each pay period by the employer pursuant to the earnings withholding order and shall state the judgment debtor's present mailing address. *(Added by Stats.1982, c. 1364, p. 5186, § 2, operative July 1, 1983.)*

§ 706.124. Judgment debtor's financial statement; form and contents

The "judgment debtor's financial statement" shall be executed as provided in Section 703.530 and contain all of the information required by that section and the following additional information:

(a) Whether any earnings withholding orders are in effect with respect to the earnings of the judgment debtor or the spouse or dependents of the judgment debtor.

(b) Whether any earnings assignment orders for support are in effect with respect to the earnings of the judgment debtor or the spouse or dependents of the judgment debtor. *(Added by Stats.1982, c. 1364, p. 5186, § 2, operative July 1, 1983. Amended by Stats.1992, c. 163 (A.B.2641), § 49, operative Jan. 1, 1994.)*

§ 706.125. Earnings withholding order; contents

The "earnings withholding order" shall include all of the following:

(a) The name, address, and, if known, the social security number of the judgment debtor.

(b) The name and address of the employer to whom the order is directed.

(c) The court where the judgment was entered, the date the judgment was entered, and the name of the judgment creditor.

(d) The date of issuance of the writ of execution to the county where the earnings withholding order is sought.

(e) The total amount required to satisfy the order on the date of issuance (which may not exceed the amount required to satisfy the writ of execution on the date of issuance of the order plus the levying officer's statutory fee for service of the order).

(f) A description of the withholding period and an order to the employer to withhold from the earnings of the judgment debtor for each pay period the amount required to be withheld under Section 706.050 or the amount specified in the order subject to Section 706.024, as the case may be, for the pay periods ending during the withholding period.

(g) An order to the employer to pay over to the levying officer at a specified address the amount required to be withheld and paid over pursuant to the order in the manner and within the times provided by law.

(h) An order that the employer fill out the "employer's return" and return it by first-class mail, postage prepaid, to the levying officer at a specified address within 15 days after service of the earnings withholding order.

(i) An order that the employer deliver to the judgment debtor a copy of the earnings withholding order and the "notice to employee of earnings withholding order" within 10 days after service of the earnings withholding order; but, if the judgment debtor is no longer employed by the employer and the employer does not owe the employee any earnings, the employer is not required to make such delivery.

(j) The name and address of the levying officer. *(Added by Stats.1982, c. 1364, p. 5187, § 2, operative July 1, 1983. Amended by Stats.1992, c. 283 (S.B.1372), § 15, eff. July 21, 1992.)*

§ 706.126.　Employer's return; form and contents

(a) The "employer's return" shall be executed under oath. The form for the return provided to the employer shall state all of the following information:

(1) The name and address of the levying officer to whom the form is to be returned.

(2) A direction that the form be mailed to the levying officer by first-class mail, postage prepaid, no later than 15 days after the date of service of the earnings withholding order.

(3) The name, the address, and, if known, the social security number of the judgment debtor.

(b) In addition, the employer's return form shall require the employer to supply all of the following information:

(1) The date the earnings withholding order was served on the employer.

(2) Whether the judgment debtor is employed by the employer or whether the employer otherwise owes earnings to the employee.

(3) If the judgment debtor is employed by the employer or the employer otherwise owes earnings to the employee, the amount of the employee's earnings for the last pay period and the length of this pay period.

(4) Whether the employer was required on the date of service to comply with an earlier earnings withholding order and, if so, the name of the judgment creditor who secured the earlier order, the levying officer who served such order, the date it was issued, the date it was served, the expiration date of such order, and which of the earnings withholding orders the employer is required to comply with under the applicable statutory rules concerning the priority of such orders.

(5) Whether the employer was required on the date of service to comply with an earnings assignment order for support and, if so, the court which issued such assignment order and the date it was issued and any other information the Judicial Council determines is needed to identify the order.

(6) The name and address of the person to whom notices to the employer are to be sent. *(Added by Stats.1982, c. 1364, p. 5187, § 2, operative July 1, 1983. Amended by Stats.1992, c. 163 (A.B.2641), § 50, operative Jan. 1, 1994.)*

§ 706.127.　Employer's instructions; preparation, revision and supplementation; supplying to levying officers

(a) The Judicial Council shall prepare "employer's instructions" for employers and revise or supplement these instructions to reflect changes in the law or rules regulating the withholding of earnings.

(b) Except to the extent that they are included in the forms required to be provided by the employer to the levying officer, the Judicial Council shall publish and provide to the levying officers copies of the employer's instructions. *(Added by Stats.1982, c. 1364, p. 5188, § 2, operative July 1, 1983.)*

§ 706.128.　Judgment creditor's notice of opposition to claim of exemption; form and contents

The "judgment creditor's notice of opposition to the claim of exemption" shall be executed under oath and shall include all of the following:

(a) The name, last known address, and, if known, the social security number of the judgment debtor.

(b) The name and address of the judgment creditor.

(c) The date of mailing of the notice of claim of exemption.

(d) The amount of the judgment debtor's claim of exemption which the judgment creditor claims is not exempt.

(e) The factual and legal grounds for the judgment creditor's opposition to the claim of exemption. *(Added by Stats.1982, c. 1364, p. 5188, § 2, operative July 1, 1983.)*

§ 706.129.　Copies of forms available from levying officers

The levying officer shall have copies of the forms for the "judgment debtor's claim of exemption" and "judgment debtor's financial statement" available at the levying officer's office for distribution without charge to a person who desires to make a claim of exemption under Section 706.051. *(Added by Stats.1982, c. 1364, p. 5188, § 2, operative July 1, 1983.)*

ARTICLE 7. ADMINISTRATION AND ENFORCEMENT

Section
706.151. Acts required as conditions to exemption from provisions of federal consumer credit protection act.
706.152. Withholding with intent to defraud.
706.153. Deferral or acceleration of payments to employee; civil actions.
706.154. Failure of employer to withhold or pay over; liability for compliance with orders or notices purporting to be in accordance with chapter provisions.

§ 706.151. Acts required as conditions to exemption from provisions of federal consumer credit protection act

The Judicial Council may perform all acts required by the Administrator of the Wage and Hour Division of the United States Department of Labor as conditions to exemption of this state from the earnings garnishment provisions of the Consumer Credit Protection Act of 1968 (15 U.S.C. Secs. 1671–1677), including, but not limited to:

(a) Representing and acting on behalf of the state in relation to the Administrator of the Wage and Hour Division and the administrator's representatives with regard to any matter relating to, or arising out of, the application, interpretation, and enforcement of the laws of this state regulating withholding of earnings.

(b) Submitting to the Administrator of the Wage and Hour Division in duplicate and on a current basis, a certified copy of every statute of this state affecting earnings withholding, and a certified copy of any decision in any case involving any of those statutes, made by the Supreme Court of this state.

(c) Submitting to the Administrator of the Wage and Hour Division any information relating to the enforcement of earnings withholding laws of this state which the administrator may request. *(Added by Stats.1982, c. 1364, p. 5189, § 2, operative July 1, 1983.)*

§ 706.152. Withholding with intent to defraud

If an employer withholds earnings pursuant to this chapter and, with the intent to defraud either the judgment creditor or the judgment debtor, fails to pay such withheld earnings over to the levying officer, the employer is guilty of a misdemeanor. *(Added by Stats. 1982, c. 1364, p. 5189, § 2, operative July 1, 1983.)*

§ 706.153. Deferral or acceleration of payments to employee; civil actions

(a) No employer shall defer or accelerate any payment of earnings to an employee with the intent to defeat or diminish the judgment creditor's rights under an earnings withholding order issued pursuant to the procedures provided by this chapter.

(b) If an employer violates this section, the judgment creditor may bring a civil action against the employer to recover the amount that would have been withheld and paid over pursuant to this chapter had the employer not violated this section. The remedy provided by this subdivision is not exclusive. *(Added by Stats.1982, c. 1364, p. 5189, § 2, operative July 1, 1983.)*

§ 706.154. Failure of employer to withhold or pay over; liability for compliance with orders or notices purporting to be in accordance with chapter provisions

(a) If an employer fails to withhold or to pay over the amount the employer is required to withhold and pay over pursuant to this chapter, the judgment creditor may bring a civil action against the employer to recover such amount. The remedy provided by this subdivision is not exclusive.

(b) Notwithstanding subdivision (a), an employer who complies with any written order or written notice which purports to be given or served in accordance with the provisions of this chapter is not subject to any civil or criminal liability for such compliance unless the employer has actively participated in a fraud. *(Added by Stats.1982, c. 1364, p. 5189, § 2, operative July 1, 1983.)*

Title 14

MISCELLANEOUS PROVISIONS

CHAPTER 6. OF COSTS

Section
1031. Actions for recovery of wages for labor performed.

§ 1031. Actions for recovery of wages for labor performed

In actions for the recovery of wages for labor performed, where the amount of the demand, exclusive of interest, does not exceed three hundred dollars ($300), the court shall add, as part of the cost, in any judgment recovered by the plaintiff or cross-complainant, an attorney's fee not exceeding 20 percent of the amount recovered. *(Added by Stats.1933, c. 744, p. 1901, § 190. Amended by Stats.1939, c. 647, p. 2075, § 1; Stats.1945, c. 1149, p. 2189, § 1; Stats.1951, c. 1737, p. 4134, § 138, operative Jan. 1, 1952; Stats.1968, c. 71, p. 219, § 1; Stats.1973, c. 818, p. 1464, § 1; Stats.1986, c. 377, § 4.)*

Part 3

OF SPECIAL PROCEEDINGS OF A CIVIL NATURE

Title 4

OF THE ENFORCEMENT OF LIENS

CHAPTER 3. CERTAIN LIENS AND PRIORITIES FOR SALARIES, WAGES AND CONSUMER DEPOSITS

Section
1204. Assignments for benefit of creditors; preferred labor claims; payments; pro rata distribution; presentation of claims; disputed claims; receivership actions.
1206. Writ of attachment or execution; preferred labor claims; verification; filing; notation on writ of execution or abstract of judgment; inclusion of claims in execution; payment; disputed claims; costs; hearing; appeal; retention of proceeds.
1207. Disputed claims; admission of part of claim; costs.
1208. Pro rata distribution of proceeds of writ; costs; proceedings by claimants against property levied upon; notice of intention to release.

§ 1204. Assignments for benefit of creditors; preferred labor claims; payments; pro rata distribution; presentation of claims; disputed claims; receivership actions

When any assignment, whether voluntary or involuntary, and whether formal or informal, is made for the benefit of creditors of the assignor, or results from any proceeding in insolvency or receivership commenced against him or her, or when any property is turned over to the creditors of a person, firm, association or corporation, or to a receiver or trustee for the benefit of creditors, the following claims have priority in the following order:

(a) Allowed unsecured claims, but only to the extent of four thousand three hundred dollars ($4,300) for each individual or corporation, as the case may be, earned within 90 days before the date of the making of such assignment or the taking over of the property or the commencement of the court proceeding or the date of the cessation of the debtor's business, whichever occurs first, for either of the following:

(1) Wages, salaries, or commissions, including vacation, severance and sick leave pay earned by an individual.

(2) Sales commissions earned by an individual, or by a corporation with only one employee, acting as an independent contractor in the sale of goods or services of the debtor in the ordinary course of the debtor's business if, and only if, during the 12 months preceding the date of the making of the assignment or the taking over of the property or the commencement of the proceeding or the date of the cessation of the debtor's business, whichever occurs first, at least 75 percent of the amount that the individual or corporation earned by acting as an independent contractor in the sale of goods or services was earned from the debtor.

(b) Allowed unsecured claims for contributions to employee benefit plans arising from services rendered within 180 days before the date of the making of the assignment or the taking over of the property or the commencement of the court proceeding or the date of the cessation of the debtor's business, whichever occurs first; but only for each employee benefit plan, to the extent of the number of employees covered by the plan multiplied by four thousand three hundred dollars ($4,300), less the aggregate amount paid to the employees under subdivision (a), plus the aggregate amount paid by the estate on behalf of the employees to any other employee benefit plan.

(c) The above claims shall be paid by the trustee, assignee or receiver before the claim of any other creditor of the assignor, insolvent, or debtor whose property is so turned over, and shall be paid as soon as the money with which to pay same becomes available. If there is insufficient money to pay all the labor claims in full, the money available shall be distributed among the claimants in proportion to the amount of their respective claims. The trustee, receiver or assignee for the benefit of creditors shall have the right to require sworn claims to be presented and shall have the right to refuse to pay any such preferred claim, either in whole or in part, if he or she has reasonable cause to believe that a claim is not valid but shall pay any part thereof that is not disputed, without prejudice to the claimant's rights, as to the balance of his or her claim, and withhold sufficient money to cover the disputed portion until the claimant in question has a reasonable opportunity to establish the validity of his or her claim by court action, either in his or her own name or through an assignee.

(d) This section is binding upon all the courts of this state and in all receivership actions the court shall order the receiver to pay promptly out of the first receipts and earnings of the receivership, after paying the current operating expenses, such preferred labor claims. *(Added by Stats.1907, c. 256, p. 321, § 1. Amended by Stats.1931, c. 820, p. 1699, § 1; Stats.1933, c. 175, p. 621, § 1; Stats.1945, c. 1192, p. 2244, § 1; Stats.1951, c. 476, p. 1613, § 1; Stats.1961, c. 1082, p. 2813, § 1; Stats.1979, c. 394, p. 1465, § 3, eff. July 27, 1979, operative Oct. 1, 1979; Stats.1999, c. 202 (S.B.219), § 1.)*

§ 1206. Writ of attachment or execution; preferred labor claims; verification; filing; notation on writ of execution or abstract of judgment; inclusion of claims in execution; payment; disputed claims; costs; hearing; appeal; retention of proceeds

(a) Upon the levy under a writ of attachment or execution not founded upon a claim for labor, any miner, mechanic, salesman, servant, clerk, laborer or other person who has performed work or rendered personal services for the defendant within 90 days prior to the levy may file a verified statement of the claim with the officer executing the writ, file a copy with the court that issued the writ, and give copies, containing his or her address, to the plaintiff and the defendant, or any attorney, clerk or agent representing them, or mail copies to them by registered mail at their last known address, return of which by the post office undelivered shall be deemed a sufficient service if no better address is available, and that claim, not exceeding nine hundred dollars ($900), unless disputed, shall be paid by the officer, immediately upon the expiration of the time for dispute of the claim as prescribed in Section 1207, from the proceeds of the levy remaining in the officer's hands at the time of the filing of the statement or collectible by the officer on the basis of the writ.

(b) The court issuing the writ shall make a notation in the register of actions of every preferred labor claim of which it receives a copy and shall endorse on any writ of execution or abstract of judgment issued subsequently in the case that it is issued subject to the rights of a preferred labor claimant or claimants and giving the names and amounts of all preferred labor claims of which it has notice. In levying under any writ of execution the officer making the levy shall include in the amount due under the execution all preferred labor claims that have been filed in the action and of which the officer has notice, except any claims that may have been finally disallowed by the court under this procedure and of which disallowance the officer has actual notice. The amount due on preferred labor claims that have not been finally disallowed by the court shall be considered a part of the sum due under any writ of attachment or execution in augmentation of that amount and any person, firm, association, or corporation on whom a writ of attachment or execution is levied shall immediately pay to the levying officer the amount of the preferred labor claims, out of any money belonging to the defendant in the action, before paying the principal sum called for in the writ.

(c) If any claim is disputed within the time, and in the manner prescribed in Section 1207, and a copy of the dispute is mailed by registered mail to the claimant or the claimant's attorney at the address given in the statement of claim and the registry receipt is attached to the original of the dispute when it is filed with the levying officer, or is handed to the claimant or the claimant's attorney, the claimant, or the claimant's assignee, must within 10 days after the copy is deposited in the mail or is handed to the claimant or the claimant's attorney, petition the court having jurisdiction of the action on which the writ is based, for a hearing before it to determine the claim for priority, or the claim to priority is barred. If more than one attachment or execution is involved, the petition shall be filed in the court having jurisdiction over the senior attachment or execution. The hearing shall be held within 20 days from the filing of the petition, unless the court continues it for good cause. Ten days' notice of the hearing shall be given by the petitioner to the plaintiff, the defendant, and all parties claiming an interest in the property, or their attorneys. The notice may be informal and need specify only the name of the court, the names of the principal parties to the senior attachment or execution, and the name of the wage claimant or claimants on whose behalf it is filed but shall specify that the hearing is for the purpose of determining the claim for priority. The plaintiff, the defendant, or any other party claiming an interest may contest the amount or validity of the claim in spite of any confession of judgment or failure to appear or to contest the claim on the part of any other person.

(d) There shall be no cost for filing or hearing the petition. The hearing on the petition shall be informal but all parties testifying shall be sworn. Any claimant may appear on the claimant's own behalf at the hearing and may call and examine witnesses to substantiate his or her claim. An appeal may be taken from a judgment in a proceeding under this section in the manner provided for appeals from judgments of the court where the proceeding occurred, in an action of the same jurisdictional classification.

(e) The officer shall keep, until the determination of the claim for priority, any amount of the proceeds of the writ necessary to satisfy the claim. If the claim for priority is allowed, the officer shall pay the amount due, including the claimant's cost of suit, from those proceeds, immediately after the order allowing the claim becomes final. *(Added by Stats.1907, c. 256, p. 321, § 1. Amended by Stats.1929, c. 230, p. 432, § 1; Stats.1931, c. 822, p. 1702, § 1; Stats.1935, c. 557, p. 1644, § 1; Stats.1951, c. 476, p. 1613, § 2; Stats.1961, c. 1085, p. 2815, § 1; Stats.1982, c. 497, p. 2171, § 77, operative July 1, 1983; Stats.1998, c. 931 (S.B.2139), § 121, eff. Sept. 28, 1998; Stats.2001, c. 44 (S.B.562), § 7; Stats.2002, c. 664 (A.B. 3034), § 51.)*

§ 1207. Disputed claims; admission of part of claim; costs

Within five days after receiving a copy of the statement provided for in the next preceding section, either the plaintiff or the defendant in the action in which the writ issued may file with the officer a sworn statement denying that any part of such claim is due for services rendered within ninety days next preceding the levy of the writ, or denying that any part of such claim, beyond a sum specified, is so due. Such sworn statement can not be made on information and belief unless the party swearing to same has actual information and belief that the wage claim, or the portion thereof that is contested, is not justly due, and in such case the nature and source of the information must be given. If a part of the claim is admitted to be due, and the claimant nevertheless files a petition for hearing and the court does not allow more than the amount so admitted, he can not recover costs but the costs must be adjudged against him, and the amount thereof deducted from the sum found due him. *(Added by Stats.1907, c. 256, p. 322, § 1. Amended by Stats.1931, c. 822, p. 1703, § 2; Stats.1935, c. 557, p. 1645, § 2.)*

§ 1208. Pro rata distribution of proceeds of writ; costs; proceedings by claimants against property levied upon; notice of intention to release

If the claims presented under Section 1206 and not disputed, or, if disputed, established by judgment, exceed the proceeds of the writ not disposed of before their presentation, such proceeds shall be distributed among the claimants in proportion to the amount of their respective claims after the costs incurred by the senior attaching plaintiff or judgment creditor in such action have first been taken care of.

If sufficient money to pay in full all preferred labor claims filed under an attachment or execution does not become available immediately upon the expiration of the time for dispute of such claims under Section 1207, any of the claimants, or their assignees, have the right to proceed directly against the money or other property levied on in individual or joint actions by themselves or their assignees against the defendant, and the attachment or execution under which the preferred claims were filed shall be considered set aside as far as such claimants, or their assignees, are concerned so as to enable them, or any of them, or any of their assignees, to proceed directly against any or all of the money or other property in question by means of their own attachments or executions; provided, however, that any money collected on behalf of any such labor claimant, or his or her assignee, on the basis of such new attachment or execution shall be shared in by the other preferred labor claimants who have filed claims that have not been disputed, or, if disputed, established by judgment, in proportion to the amount of their respective claims, deducting only the costs in the action brought by the said labor claimant, or his or her assignee, and the costs in the original action brought by the senior attaching plaintiff or judgment creditor.

If such senior attaching plaintiff or judgment creditor requests a release of his or her original attachment or execution, and the preferred labor claims filed under same are not released, the officer who levied the writ must first mail notices of such request to release to each of the labor claimants who have filed claims, or their attorneys, which notices must specify that unless the claimants bring attachment actions of their own and levy on the money or property in question within five days from the date thereof the money or property will be released from the attachment or execution; provided, however, that such officer may instead collect sufficient money on the basis of the original writ to pay off the preferred labor claims in full and then release the attachment or execution, but in no case shall the officer release the attachment or execution without first taking care of the labor claims until the five-day period has expired, unless the officer's costs, keepers' fees or storage charges have not been immediately taken care of by some of the parties involved. In any case it shall be lawful for a garnishee to pay over to the officer levying the writ any money held by the garnishee without waiting for execution to be levied and the officer's receipt for the money shall be a sufficient quittance, and the officer shall collect such money and immediately pay off the established preferred labor claims in all cases where it is possible to do so without additional court proceedings on the officer's part. *(Added by Stats.1907, c. 256, p. 322, § 1. Amended by Stats.1931, c. 822, p. 1703, § 3; Stats.1982, c. 497, p. 2172, § 78, operative July 1, 1983.)*

Title 9

ARBITRATION

CHAPTER 1. GENERAL PROVISIONS

Section
1280. Definitions.

§ 1280. Definitions

As used in this title:

(a) "Agreement" includes but is not limited to agreements providing for valuations, appraisals and similar proceedings and agreements between employers and employees or between their respective representatives.

(b) "Award" includes but is not limited to an award made pursuant to an agreement not in writing.

(c) "Controversy" means any question arising between parties to an agreement whether such question is one of law or of fact or both.

(d) "Neutral arbitrator" means an arbitrator who is (1) selected jointly by the parties or by the arbitrators selected by the parties or (2) appointed by the court when the parties or the arbitrators selected by the parties fail to select an arbitrator who was to be selected jointly by them.

(e) "Party to the arbitration" means a party to the arbitration agreement:

(1) Who seeks to arbitrate a controversy pursuant to the agreement;

(2) Against whom such arbitration is sought pursuant to the agreement; or

(3) Who is made a party to such arbitration by order of the neutral arbitrator upon such party's application, upon the application of any other party to the arbitration or upon the neutral arbitrator's own determination.

(f) "Written agreement" shall be deemed to include a written agreement which has been extended or renewed by an oral or implied agreement. *(Added by Stats.1961, c. 461, p. 1540, § 2.)*

CHAPTER 2. ENFORCEMENT OF ARBITRATION AGREEMENTS

Section
1281. Validity, enforceability and irrevocability of agreements.

Section
1281.1. Requests to arbitrate.
1281.12. Tolling arbitration time period.
1281.2. Order to arbitrate controversy; petition; determination of court.
1281.3. Consolidation of separate arbitration proceedings; petition; grounds; procedure.
1281.4. Stay of pending actions or proceedings.

§ 1281. Validity, enforceability and irrevocability of agreements

A written agreement to submit to arbitration an existing controversy or a controversy thereafter arising is valid, enforceable and irrevocable, save upon such grounds as exist for the revocation of any contract. *(Added by Stats.1961, c. 461, p. 1541, § 2.)*

§ 1281.1. Requests to arbitrate

For the purposes of this article, any request to arbitrate made pursuant to subdivision (a) of Section 1299.4 shall be considered as made pursuant to a written agreement to submit a controversy to arbitration. *(Added by Stats. 2000, c. 906 (S.B.402), § 1.)*

§ 1281.12. Tolling arbitration time period

If an arbitration agreement requires that arbitration of a controversy be demanded or initiated by a party to the arbitration agreement within a period of time, the commencement of a civil action by that party based upon that controversy, within that period of time, shall toll the applicable time limitations contained in the arbitration agreement with respect to that controversy, from the date the civil action is commenced until 30 days after a final determination by the court that the party is required to arbitrate the controversy, or 30 days after the final termination of the civil action that was commenced and initiated the tolling, whichever date occurs first. *(Added by Stats.2006, c. 266 (A.B.1553), § 1.)*

§ 1281.2. Order to arbitrate controversy; petition; determination of court

On petition of a party to an arbitration agreement alleging the existence of a written agreement to arbitrate a controversy and that a party thereto refuses to arbitrate such controversy, the court shall order the petitioner and the respondent to arbitrate the controversy if it determines that an agreement to arbitrate the controversy exists, unless it determines that:

(a) The right to compel arbitration has been waived by the petitioner; or

(b) Grounds exist for the revocation of the agreement.

(c) A party to the arbitration agreement is also a party to a pending court action or special proceeding with a third party, arising out of the same transaction or series of related transactions and there is a possibility of conflicting rulings on a common issue of law or fact. For purposes of this section, a pending court action or special proceeding includes an action or proceeding initiated by the party refusing to arbitrate after the petition to compel arbitration has been filed, but on or before the date of the hearing on the petition. This subdivision shall not be applicable to an agreement to arbitrate disputes as to the professional negligence of a health care provider made pursuant to Section 1295.

If the court determines that a written agreement to arbitrate a controversy exists, an order to arbitrate such controversy may not be refused on the ground that the petitioner's contentions lack substantive merit.

If the court determines that there are other issues between the petitioner and the respondent which are not subject to arbitration and which are the subject of a pending action or special proceeding between the petitioner and the respondent and that a determination of such issues may make the arbitration unnecessary, the court may delay its order to arbitrate until the determination of such other issues or until such earlier time as the court specifies.

If the court determines that a party to the arbitration is also a party to litigation in a pending court action or special proceeding with a third party as set forth under subdivision (c) herein, the court (1) may refuse to enforce the arbitration agreement and may order intervention or joinder of all parties in a single action or special proceeding; (2) may order intervention or joinder as to all or only certain issues; (3) may order arbitration among the parties who have agreed to arbitration and stay the pending court action or special proceeding pending the outcome of the arbitration proceeding; or (4) may stay arbitration pending the outcome of the court action or special proceeding. *(Added by Stats.1961, c. 461, p. 1541, § 2. Amended by Stats.1978, c. 260, p. 543, § 1.)*

§ 1281.3. Consolidation of separate arbitration proceedings; petition; grounds; procedure

A party to an arbitration agreement may petition the court to consolidate separate arbitration proceedings, and the court may order consolidation of separate arbitration proceedings when:

(1) Separate arbitration agreements or proceedings exist between the same parties; or one party is a party to a separate arbitration agreement or proceeding with a third party; and

(2) The disputes arise from the same transactions or series of related transactions; and

(3) There is common issue or issues of law or fact creating the possibility of conflicting rulings by more than one arbitrator or panel of arbitrators.

If all of the applicable arbitration agreements name the same arbitrator, arbitration panel, or arbitration tribunal, the court, if it orders consolidation, shall order all matters to be heard before the arbitrator, panel, or tribunal agreed to by the parties. If the applicable arbitration agreements name separate arbitrators, panels, or tribunals, the court, if it orders consolidation, shall, in the absence of an agreed method of selection by all parties to

97

the consolidated arbitration, appoint an arbitrator in accord with the procedures set forth in Section 1281.6.

In the event that the arbitration agreements in consolidated proceedings contain inconsistent provisions, the court shall resolve such conflicts and determine the rights and duties of the various parties to achieve substantial justice under all the circumstances.

The court may exercise its discretion under this section to deny consolidation of separate arbitration proceedings or to consolidate separate arbitration proceedings only as to certain issues, leaving other issues to be resolved in separate proceedings.

This section shall not be applicable to an agreement to arbitrate disputes as to the professional negligence of a health care provider made pursuant to Section 1295. *(Added by Stats.1978, c. 260, p. 549, § 2.)*

§ 1281.4. Stay of pending actions or proceedings

If a court of competent jurisdiction, whether in this State or not, has ordered arbitration of a controversy which is an issue involved in an action or proceeding pending before a court of this State, the court in which such action or proceeding is pending shall, upon motion of a party to such action or proceeding, stay the action or proceeding until an arbitration is had in accordance with the order to arbitrate or until such earlier time as the court specifies.

If an application has been made to a court of competent jurisdiction, whether in this State or not, for an order to arbitrate a controversy which is an issue involved in an action or proceeding pending before a court of this State and such application is undetermined, the court in which such action or proceeding is pending shall, upon motion of a party to such action or proceeding, stay the action or proceeding until the application for an order to arbitrate is determined and, if arbitration of such controversy is ordered, until an arbitration is had in accordance with the order to arbitrate or until such earlier time as the court specifies.

If the issue which is the controversy subject to arbitration is severable, the stay may be with respect to that issue only. *(Added by Stats.1961, c. 461, p. 1541, § 2.)*

Title 10

UNCLAIMED PROPERTY

CHAPTER 7. UNCLAIMED PROPERTY LAW

ARTICLE 1. SHORT TITLE; DEFINITIONS; APPLICATION

Section
1501. Definitions.

§ 1501. Definitions

As used in this chapter, unless the context otherwise requires:

(a) "Apparent owner" means the person who appears from the records of the holder to be entitled to property held by the holder.

(b) "Banking organization" means any national or state bank, trust company, banking company, land bank, savings bank, safe-deposit company, private banker, or any similar organization.

(c) "Business association" means any private corporation, joint stock company, business trust, partnership, or any association for business purposes of two or more individuals, whether or not for profit, including, but not by way of limitation, a banking organization, financial organization, life insurance corporation, and utility.

(d) "Financial organization" means any federal or state savings and loan association, building and loan association, credit union, investment company, or any similar organization.

(e) "Holder" means any person in possession of property subject to this chapter belonging to another, or who is trustee in case of a trust, or is indebted to another on an obligation subject to this chapter.

(f) "Life insurance corporation" means any association or corporation transacting the business of insurance on the lives of persons or insurance appertaining thereto, including, but not by way of limitation, endowments, and annuities.

(g) "Owner" means a depositor in case of a deposit, a beneficiary in case of a trust, or creditor, claimant, or payee in case of other choses in action, or any person having a legal or equitable interest in property subject to this chapter, or his or her legal representative.

(h) "Person" means any individual, business association, government or governmental subdivision or agency, two or more persons having a joint or common interest, or any other legal or commercial entity, whether that person is acting in his or her own right or in a representative or fiduciary capacity.

(i) "Employee benefit plan distribution" means any money, life insurance, endowment or annuity policy or proceeds thereof, securities or other intangible property, or any tangible property, distributable to a participant, former participant, or the beneficiary or estate or heirs of a participant or former participant or beneficiary, from a trust or custodial fund established under a plan to provide health and welfare, pension, vacation, severance, retirement benefit, death benefit, stock purchase, profit sharing, employee savings, supplemental unemployment insurance benefits or similar benefits, or which is established under a plan by a business association functioning as or in conjunction with a labor union which receives for distribution residuals on behalf of employees working under collective-bargaining agreements.

(j) "Residuals" means payments pursuant to a collective bargaining agreement of additional compensation for domestic and foreign uses of recorded materials. *(Added by Stats.1959, c. 1809, p. 4296, § 2. Amended by Stats. 1968, c. 356, p. 739, § 5, operative Jan. 1, 1969; Stats.1972,*

c. 856, p. 1523, § 2, operative Jan. 1, 1973; Stats.1976, c. 582, p. 1421, § 1; Stats.1977, c. 579, p. 1843, § 36; Stats.1982, c. 786, p. 3046, § 1; Stats.1984, c. 899, § 1; Stats.1990, c. 450 (S.B.57), § 2, eff. July 31, 1990.)

ARTICLE 2.   ESCHEAT OF UNCLAIMED PERSONAL PROPERTY

Section
1510.   Escheat of intangible personal property.
1521.   Employee benefit plan distributions, income and other increments; conditions; exception; claim for residuals.

§ 1510.   Escheat of intangible personal property

Unless otherwise provided by statute of this state, intangible personal property escheats to this state under this chapter if the conditions for escheat stated in Sections 1513 through 1521 exist, and if:

(a) The last known address, as shown on the records of the holder, of the apparent owner is in this state.

(b) No address of the apparent owner appears on the records of the holder and:

(1) The last known address of the apparent owner is in this state; or

(2) The holder is domiciled in this state and has not previously paid the property to the state of the last known address of the apparent owner; or

(3) The holder is a government or governmental subdivision or agency of this state and has not previously paid the property to the state of the last known address of the apparent owner.

(c) The last known address, as shown on the records of the holder, of the apparent owner is in a state that does not provide by law for the escheat of such property and the holder is (1) domiciled in this state or (2) a government or governmental subdivision or agency of this state.

(d) The last known address, as shown on the records of the holder, of the apparent owner is in a foreign nation and the holder is (1) domiciled in this state or (2) a government or governmental subdivision or agency of this state. (Added by Stats.1968, c. 356, p. 742, § 11, operative

Jan. 1, 1969.   Amended by Stats.1972, c. 856, p. 1524, § 3, operative Jan. 1, 1973; Stats.1978, c. 1183, p. 3826, § 17.)

§ 1521.   Employee benefit plan distributions, income and other increments; conditions; exception; claim for residuals

(a) Except as provided in subdivision (b), and subject to Section 1510, all employee benefit plan distributions and any income or other increment thereon escheats to the state if the owner has not, within three years after it becomes payable or distributable, accepted the distribution, corresponded in writing concerning the distribution, or otherwise indicated an interest as evidenced by a memorandum or other record on file with the fiduciary of the trust or custodial fund or administrator of the plan under which the trust or fund is established. As used in this section, "fiduciary" means any person exercising any power, authority, or responsibility of management or disposition with respect to any money or other property of a retirement system or plan, and "administrator" means the person specifically so designated by the plan, trust agreement, contract, or other instrument under which the retirement system or plan is operated, or if none is designated, the employer.

(b) Except as provided in subdivision (c), an employee benefit plan distribution and any income or other increment thereon shall not escheat to this state if, at the time the distribution shall become payable to a participant in an employee benefit plan, the plan contains a provision for forfeiture or expressly authorizes the administrator to declare a forfeiture of a distribution to a beneficiary thereof who cannot be found after a period of time specified in the plan, and the trust or fund established under the plan has not terminated prior to the date on which the distribution would become forfeitable in accordance with the provision.

(c) A participant entitled to an employee benefit plan distribution in the form of residuals shall be relieved from a forfeiture declared under subdivision (b) upon the making of a claim therefor. (Added by Stats.1972, c. 856, p. 1524, § 4, operative Jan. 1, 1973. Amended by Stats. 1982, c. 786, p. 3050, § 4; Stats.1984, c. 899, § 2; Stats.1988, c. 286, § 10; Stats.1990, c. 450 (S.B.57), § 12, eff. July 31, 1990.)

Part 4

MISCELLANEOUS PROVISIONS

Title 3

OF THE PRODUCTION OF EVIDENCE

CHAPTER 2.   MEANS OF PRODUCTION

Section
1985.6.   Employment records; subpoena duces tecum or production of records; notice and service; motion to quash or modify subpoena.
2017.220.   Sexual harassment, assault or battery allegations; monetary sanctions.

§ 1985.6.   Employment records; subpoena duces tecum or production of records; notice and service; motion to quash or modify subpoena

(a) For purposes of this section, the following terms have the following meanings:

(1) "Deposition officer" means a person who meets the qualifications specified in Section 2020.420.

(2) "Employee" means any individual who is or has been employed by a witness subject to a subpoena duces tecum. "Employee" also means any individual who is or has been represented by a labor organization that is a witness subject to a subpoena duces tecum.

(3) "Employment records" means the original or any copy of books, documents, other writings, or electronic data pertaining to the employment of any employee maintained by the current or former employer of the employee, or by any labor organization that has represented or currently represents the employee.

(4) "Labor organization" has the meaning set forth in Section 1117 of the Labor Code.

(5) "Subpoenaing party" means the person or persons causing a subpoena duces tecum to be issued or served in connection with any civil action or proceeding, but does not include the state or local agencies described in Section 7465 of the Government Code, or any entity provided for under Article VI of the California Constitution in any proceeding maintained before an adjudicative body of that entity pursuant to Chapter 4 (commencing with Section 6000) of Division 3 of the Business and Professions Code.

(b) Prior to the date called for in the subpoena duces tecum of the production of employment records, the subpoenaing party shall serve or cause to be served on the employee whose records are being sought a copy of: the subpoena duces tecum; the affidavit supporting the issuance of the subpoena, if any; the notice described in subdivision (e); and proof of service as provided in paragraph (1) of subdivision (c). This service shall be made as follows:

(1) To the employee personally, or at his or her last known address, or in accordance with Chapter 5 (commencing with Section 1010) of Title 14 of Part 2, or, if he or she is a party, to his or her attorney of record. If the employee is a minor, service shall be made on the minor's parent, guardian, conservator, or similar fiduciary, or if one of them cannot be located with reasonable diligence, then service shall be made on any person having the care or control of the minor, or with whom the minor resides, and on the minor if the minor is at least 12 years of age.

(2) Not less than 10 days prior to the date for production specified in the subpoena duces tecum, plus the additional time provided by Section 1013 if service is by mail.

(3) At least five days prior to service upon the custodian of the employment records, plus the additional time provided by Section 1013 if service is by mail.

(c) Prior to the production of the records, the subpoenaing party shall either:

(1) Serve or cause to be served upon the witness a proof of personal service or of service by mail attesting to compliance with subdivision (b).

(2) Furnish the witness a written authorization to release the records signed by the employee or by his or her attorney of record. The witness may presume that the attorney purporting to sign the authorization on behalf of the employee acted with the consent of the employee, and that any objection to the release of records is waived.

(d) A subpoena duces tecum for the production of employment records shall be served in sufficient time to allow the witness a reasonable time, as provided in Section 2020.410, to locate and produce the records or copies thereof.

(e) Every copy of the subpoena duces tecum and affidavit served on an employee or his or her attorney in accordance with subdivision (b) shall be accompanied by a notice, in a typeface designed to call attention to the notice, indicating that (1) employment records about the employee are being sought from the witness named on the subpoena; (2) the employment records may be protected by a right of privacy; (3) if the employee objects to the witness furnishing the records to the party seeking the records, the employee shall file papers with the court prior to the date specified for production on the subpoena; and (4) if the subpoenaing party does not agree in writing to cancel or limit the subpoena, an attorney should be consulted about the employee's interest in protecting his or her rights of privacy. If a notice of taking of deposition is also served, that other notice may be set forth in a single document with the notice required by this subdivision.

(f)(1) Any employee whose employment records are sought by a subpoena duces tecum may, prior to the date for production, bring a motion under Section 1987.1 to quash or modify the subpoena duces tecum. Notice of the bringing of that motion shall be given to the witness and the deposition officer at least five days prior to production. The failure to provide notice to the deposition officer does not invalidate the motion to quash or modify the subpoena duces tecum but may be raised by the deposition officer as an affirmative defense in any action for liability for improper release of records.

(2) Any nonparty employee whose employment records are sought by a subpoena duces tecum may, prior to the date of production, serve on the subpoenaing party, the deposition officer, and the witness a written objection that cites the specific grounds on which production of the employment records should be prohibited.

(3) No witness or deposition officer shall be required to produce employment records after receipt of notice that the motion has been brought by an employee, or after receipt of a written objection from a nonparty employee, except upon order of the court in which the action is pending or by agreement of the parties, witnesses, and employees affected.

(4) The party requesting an employee's employment records may bring a motion under subdivision (c) of Section 1987 to enforce the subpoena within 20 days of service of the written objection. The motion shall be accompanied by a declaration showing a reasonable and good faith attempt at informal resolution of the dispute between the party requesting the employment records and the employee or the employee's attorney.

(g) Upon good cause shown and provided that the rights of witnesses and employees are preserved, a subpoenaing party shall be entitled to obtain an order shortening the time for service of a subpoena duces tecum or waiving the requirements of subdivision (b) if due diligence by the subpoenaing party has been shown.

(h) This section may not be construed to apply to any subpoena duces tecum that does not request the records of any particular employee or employees and that requires a custodian of records to delete all information that would in any way identify any employee whose records are to be produced.

(i) This section does not apply to proceedings conducted under Division 1 (commencing with Section 50), Division 4 (commencing with Section 3200), Division 4.5 (commencing with Section 6100), or Division 4.7 (commencing with Section 6200), of the Labor Code.

(j) Failure to comply with this section shall be sufficient basis for the witness to refuse to produce the employment records sought by subpoena duces tecum.

(k) If the subpoenaing party is the employee, and the employee is the only subject of the subpoenaed records, notice to the employee, and delivery of the other documents specified in subdivision (b) to the employee, are not required under this section. *(Added by Stats. 1995, c. 299 (A.B.617), § 1. Amended by Stats.1996, c. 679 (S.B.1821), § 2; Stats.1997, c. 442 (A.B.758), § 11; Stats.1998, c. 932 (A.B.1094), § 20; Stats.1999, c. 444 (A.B.794), § 2; Stats.2004, c. 182 (A.B.3081), § 19, operative July 1, 2005; Stats.2004, c. 101 (S.B.1465), § 1; Stats.2005, c. 22 (S.B.1108), § 20; Stats.2005, c. 294 (A.B.333), § 5; Stats.2005, c. 300 (A.B.496), § 7.5; Stats. 2006, c. 538 (S.B.1852), § 76.)*

§ 2017.220. Sexual harassment, assault or battery allegations; monetary sanctions

(a) In any civil action alleging conduct that constitutes sexual harassment, sexual assault, or sexual battery, any party seeking discovery concerning the plaintiff's sexual conduct with individuals other than the alleged perpetrator shall establish specific facts showing that there is good cause for that discovery, and that the matter sought to be discovered is relevant to the subject matter of the action and reasonably calculated to lead to the discovery of admissible evidence. This showing shall be made by a noticed motion, accompanied by a meet and confer declaration under Section 2016.040, and shall not be made or considered by the court at an ex parte hearing.

(b) The court shall impose a monetary sanction under Chapter 7 (commencing with Section 2023.010) against any party, person, or attorney who unsuccessfully makes or opposes a motion for discovery under subdivision (a), unless it finds that the one subject to the sanction acted with substantial justification or that other circumstances make the imposition of the sanction unjust. *(Added by Stats.2004, c. 182 (A.B.3081), § 23, operative July 1, 2005.)*

CORPORATIONS CODE

Title 4

SECURITIES

Division 1

CORPORATE SECURITIES LAW OF 1968

Part 3

REGULATION AND NOTICE FILING REQUIREMENTS OF AGENTS, BROKER–DEALERS, INVESTMENT ADVISER REPRESENTATIVES, AND INVESTMENT ADVISERS

CHAPTER 2. LICENSING OF AGENTS AND BROKER–DEALERS

Section
25221. Criminal history record checks; submission to Department of Justice of fingerprints of an applicant for employment.

§ 25221. Criminal history record checks; submission to Department of Justice of fingerprints of an applicant for employment

(a) Notwithstanding any other provision of law, a broker-dealer, or any affiliate thereof, licensed under this chapter, or any officer or employee thereof, may submit to the Department of Justice fingerprints of an applicant for employment for the purpose of obtaining information as to the existence and nature of a record of a conviction and of an arrest for which the Department of Justice establishes that the applicant was released on bail or on his or her own recognizance pending trial. Fingerprints taken pursuant to this section include fingerprints taken by the use of fingerprint live-scan technology, as described in Section 1596.871 of the Health and Safety Code.

(b) The Department of Justice shall provide the following information to the broker-dealer, affiliate, or officer or employee thereof pursuant to subdivision (a):

(1) Every conviction rendered against the applicant.

(2) Every arrest for which the Department of Justice establishes that the applicant was released on bail or on his or her own recognizance pending trial. *(Added by Stats.2001, c. 547 (A.B.119), § 1.)*

EDUCATION CODE

Title 1

GENERAL EDUCATION CODE PROVISIONS

Division 1

GENERAL EDUCATION CODE PROVISIONS

Part 6

EDUCATION PROGRAMS— STATE MASTER PLANS

CHAPTER 2. CHILD CARE AND DEVELOPMENT SERVICES ACT

ARTICLE 10. ADMINISTRATION

Section
8264.7. Staffing; basis of approval of programs.

§ 8264.7. Staffing; basis of approval of programs

The Superintendent of Public Instruction shall establish rules and regulations for the staffing of all center-based child care and development programs under contract with the department.

Priority shall be given by the department to the employment of persons in child development programs with ethnic backgrounds which are similar to those of the child for whom child development services are provided.

For purposes of staffing child care and development programs, the role of a teacher in child supervision means direct supervision of the children as well as supervision of aides and groups of children.

Family child care homes shall operate pursuant to adult/child ratios prescribed in Chapter 7 (commencing with Section 86001) of Division 6 of Title 22 of the California Code of Regulations.

Approval by the Superintendent of Public Instruction of any ongoing or new programs seeking to operate under the ratios and standards established by the Superintendent of Public Instruction under this chapter shall be based upon the following considerations:

(a) The type of facility in which care is being or is to be provided.

(b) The ability of the Superintendent of Public Instruction to implement a funding source change.

(c) The proportion of nonsubsidized children enrolled or to be enrolled by the agency.

(d) The most cost-effective ratios possible for the type of services provided or to be provided by the agency.

The Superintendent of Public Instruction shall apply for such waivers of federal requirements as are necessary to carry out this section. *(Formerly § 8287, added by Stats.1980, c. 798, p. 2490, § 19, eff. July 28, 1980. Renumbered § 8264.7 and amended by Stats.2004, c. 896 (A.B.2525), § 18, eff. Sept. 29, 2004.)*

Title 2

ELEMENTARY AND SECONDARY EDUCATION

Division 3

LOCAL ADMINISTRATION

Part 25

EMPLOYEES

CHAPTER 1. EMPLOYEES

ARTICLE 5. REPORTING BY SCHOOL EMPLOYEES OF IMPROPER GOVERNMENTAL ACTIVITIES

Section
44110. Short title.
44111. Legislative intent.
44112. Definitions.
44113. Use or attempt to use official authority or influence to interfere with protected disclosures; prohibitions; civil liability.
44114. Written complaints; filing with local law enforcement agency; penalties; other rights and remedies.

§ 44110. Short title

This article shall be known and may be referred to as the Reporting by School Employees of Improper Governmental Activities Act. *(Added by Stats.2000, c. 531 (A.B.2472), § 1.)*

§ 44111. Legislative intent

It is the intent of the Legislature that school employees and other persons disclose, to the extent not expressly prohibited by law, improper governmental activities. *(Added by Stats.2000, c. 531 (A.B.2472), § 1.)*

§ 44112. Definitions

For the purposes of this article, the following terms have the following meanings:

(a) "Employee" means a public school employee as defined in subdivision (j) of Section 3540.1 of the Government Code.

(b) "Illegal order" means any directive to violate or assist in violating a federal, state, or local law, rule, or regulation or an order to work or cause others to work in conditions outside of their line of duty that would unreasonably threaten the health or safety of employees or the public.

(c) "Improper governmental activity" means an activity by a public school agency or by an employee that is undertaken in the performance of the employee's official duties, whether or not that activity is within the scope of his or her employment, and that meets either of the following descriptions:

(1) The activity violates a state or federal law or regulation, including, but not limited to, corruption, malfeasance, bribery, theft of government property, fraudulent claims, fraud, coercion, conversion, malicious prosecution, misuse of government property, or willful omission to perform duty.

(2) The activity is economically wasteful or involves gross misconduct, incompetency, or inefficiency.

(d) "Person" means any individual, corporation, trust, association, any state or local government, or any agency or instrumentality of any of the foregoing.

(e) "Protected disclosure" means a good faith communication that discloses or demonstrates an intention to disclose information that may evidence either of the following:

(1) An improper governmental activity.

(2) Any condition that may significantly threaten the health or safety of employees or the public if the disclosure or intention to disclose was made for the purpose of remedying that condition.

(f) "Public school employer" has the same meaning as in subdivision (k) of Section 3540.1 of the Government Code. *(Added by Stats.2000, c. 531 (A.B.2472), § 1.)*

§ 44113. Use or attempt to use official authority or influence to interfere with protected disclosures; prohibitions; civil liability

(a) An employee may not directly or indirectly use or attempt to use the official authority or influence of the employee for the purpose of intimidating, threatening, coercing, commanding, or attempting to intimidate, threaten, coerce, or command any person for the purpose of interfering with the right of that person to disclose to an official agent matters within the scope of this article.

(b) For the purpose of subdivision (a), "use of official authority or influence" includes promising to confer or conferring any benefit; affecting or threatening to affect any reprisal; or taking, directing others to take, recommending, processing, or approving any personnel action, including, but not limited to appointment, promotion, transfer, assignment, performance evaluation, suspension, or other disciplinary action.

(c) For the purpose of subdivision (a), "official agent" includes a school administrator, member of the governing board of a school district or county board of education, county superintendent of schools, or the Superintendent of Public Instruction.

(d) An employee who violates subdivision (a) may be liable in an action for civil damages brought against the employee by the offended party.

(e) Nothing in this section shall be construed to authorize an individual to disclose information otherwise prohibited by or under law. *(Added by Stats.2000, c. 531 (A.B.2472), § 1.)*

§ 44114. Written complaints; filing with local law enforcement agency; penalties; other rights and remedies

(a) A public school employee or applicant for employment with a public school employer who files a written complaint with his or her supervisor, a school administrator, or the public school employer alleging actual or attempted acts of reprisal, retaliation, threats, coercion, or similar improper acts prohibited by Section 44113 for having disclosed improper governmental activities or for refusing to obey an illegal order may also file a copy of the written complaint with the local law enforcement agency together with a sworn statement that the contents of the written complaint are true, or are believed by the affiant to be true, under penalty of perjury. The complaint filed with the local law enforcement agency shall be filed within 12 months of the most recent act of reprisal that is the subject of the complaint.

(b) A person who intentionally engages in acts of reprisal, retaliation, threats, coercion, or similar acts against a public school employee or applicant for employment with a public school employer for having made a protected disclosure is subject to a fine not to exceed ten thousand dollars ($10,000) and imprisonment in the county jail for a period not to exceed one year. Any public school employee, officer, or administrator who intentionally engages in that conduct shall also be subject to discipline by the public school employer. If no adverse action is instituted by the public school employer and it is determined that there is reasonable cause to believe that an act of reprisal, retaliation, threats, coercion, or similar acts prohibited by Section 44113 occurred, the local law enforcement agency may report the nature and details of the activity to the governing board of the school district or county board of education, as appropriate.

(c) In addition to all other penalties provided by law, a person who intentionally engages in acts of reprisal, retaliation, threats, coercion, or similar acts against a public school employee or applicant for employment with a public school employer for having made a protected disclosure shall be liable in an action for damages brought against him or her by the injured party. Punitive damages may be awarded by the court where the acts of the offending party are proven to be malicious. Where liability has been established, the injured party shall also be entitled to reasonable attorney's fees as provided by law. However, an action for damages shall not be available to the injured party unless the injured party has first filed a complaint with the local law enforcement agency.

(d) This section is not intended to prevent a public school employer, school administrator, or supervisor from taking, failing to take, directing others to take, recommending, or approving a personnel action with respect to a public school employee or applicant for employment with a public school employer if the public school employer, school administrator, or supervisor reasonably believes the action or inaction is justified on the basis of evidence separate and apart from the fact that the person has made a protected disclosure as defined in subdivision (e) of Section 44112.

(e) In any civil action or administrative proceeding, once it has been demonstrated by a preponderance of evidence that an activity protected by this article was a contributing factor in the alleged retaliation against a former, current, or prospective public school employee, the burden of proof shall be on the supervisor, school administrator, or public school employer to demonstrate by clear and convincing evidence that the alleged action would have occurred for legitimate, independent reasons even if the public school employee had not engaged in protected disclosures or refused an illegal order. If the supervisor, school administrator, or public school employer fails to meet this burden of proof in an adverse action against the public school employee in any administrative review, challenge, or adjudication in which retaliation has been demonstrated to be a contributing factor, the public school employee shall have a complete affirmative defense in the adverse action.

(f) Nothing in this article shall be deemed to diminish the rights, privileges, or remedies of a public school employee under any other federal or state law or under an employment contract or collective bargaining agreement.

(g) If the provisions of this section are in conflict with the provisions of a memorandum of understanding reached pursuant to Chapter 10.7 (commencing with Section 3540) of Division 4 of Title 1 of the Government Code, the memorandum of understanding shall be controlling without further legislative action. *(Added by Stats.2000, c. 531 (A.B.2472), § 1. Amended by Stats. 2001, c. 159 (S.B.662), § 68.)*

Division 4

INSTRUCTION AND SERVICES

Part 28

GENERAL INSTRUCTIONAL PROGRAMS

CHAPTER 17.5. CALIFORNIA CAREER RESOURCE NETWORK

Section
53086. Creation of California Career Resource Network; mission; duties.
53086. Creation of California Career Resource Network Program; mission; duties; information and resources; State Agency Partners Committee; establishment and membership.

§ 53086. Creation of California Career Resource Network; mission; duties

Section operative until July 1, 2010. See, also, section operative July 1, 2010.

(a) There is in state government the California Career Resource Network, formerly called the California Occupational Information Coordinating Committee, composed of the Director of Employment Development, the Superintendent, the Chancellor of the California Community Colleges, the Director of Rehabilitation, the Director of Social Services, the Executive Director of the California Workforce Investment Board, the Executive Secretary of the Bureau for Private Postsecondary and Vocational Education, the Director of the California Youth Authority, the Director of the Department of Corrections, and the Director of the Department of Developmental Services, or their designees. This committee is established for the purposes of Section 2328 of Title 20 of the United States Code, for the purposes of this article, and for other purposes authorized by the Legislature.

(b) The mission of the California Career Resource Network is to provide all persons in California with career development information and resources to enable them to reach their career goals.

(c) The primary duty of the California Career Resource Network is to distribute career information, resources, and training materials to middle school and high school counselors, educators, and administrators, in order to ensure that middle schools and high schools have the necessary information available to provide a pupil with guidance and instruction on education and job requirements necessary for career development.

(d) Information and resources distributed by the California Career Resource Network shall provide all of the following:

(1) Encouragement to completing a secondary education.

(2) Career exploration tools, provided in written and multimedia format, that offer an introduction to the nature of career planning, self-assessment, methods of investigating the work world, methods of identifying and meeting education and training needs, and methods of creating a career action plan.

(3) Relevant information on the labor market and career opportunities.

(4) Assistance to a pupil in the acquisition and development of career competencies including the appropriate skills, attitudes, and knowledge to allow a pupil to successfully manage his or her career.

(e) The network shall perform its duties only upon funding provided in the annual Budget Act. *(Added by Stats.2005, c. 208 (S.B.665), § 2.)*

§ 53086. Creation of California Career Resource Network Program; mission; duties; information and resources; State Agency Partners Committee; establishment and membership

Section operative July 1, 2010. See, also, section operative until July 1, 2010.

(a) There is in * * * the department the California Career Resource Network Program, formerly called the California Occupational Information Coordinating Committee * * *. This program is established for the purposes of Section 2328 of Title 20 of the United States Code, for the purposes of this article, and for other purposes authorized by the Legislature.

(b) The mission of the * * * program is to provide all persons in California with career development information and resources to enable them to reach their career goals.

(c) The primary duty of the * * * program is to distribute career information, resources, and training materials to middle school and high school counselors, educators, and administrators, in order to ensure that middle schools and high schools have the necessary information available to provide a pupil with guidance and instruction on education and job requirements necessary for career development.

(d) Information and resources distributed by the * * * program shall provide all of the following:

(1) Encouragement to completing a secondary education.

(2) Career exploration tools, provided in written and multimedia format, that offer an introduction to the nature of career planning, self-assessment, methods of investigating the work world, methods of identifying and meeting education and training needs, and methods of creating a career action plan.

(3) Relevant information on the labor market and career opportunities.

(4) Assistance to a pupil in the acquisition and development of career competencies including the appropriate skills, attitudes, and knowledge to allow a pupil to successfully manage his or her career.

(e)(1) There is hereby established the State Agency Partners Committee composed of the following members or their designees:

(A) The Director of Employment Development.

(B) The Superintendent of Public Instruction.

(C) The Chancellor of the California Community Colleges.

(D) The Director of Rehabilitation.

(E) The Director of Social Services.

(F) The Executive Director of the California Workforce Investment Board.

(G) The Chief Deputy Secretary for Adult Operations of the Department of Corrections and Rehabilitation.

(H) The Chief Deputy Secretary of Juvenile Justice in the Department of Corrections and Rehabilitation.

(I) The Director of Developmental Services.

(2) The State Agency Partners Committee shall coordinate the use of network information and resources in programs that are implemented by the entities that the members of the committee represent.

(f) The program shall perform its duties only upon funding provided in the annual Budget Act. *(Added by Stats.2005, c. 208 (S.B.665), § 2. Amended by Stats.2009, c.32 (S.B.123), § 1, operative July 1, 2010.)*

Title 3

POSTSECONDARY EDUCATION

Division 7

COMMUNITY COLLEGES

Part 51

EMPLOYEES

CHAPTER 1. PROVISIONS APPLYING TO ALL EMPLOYEES

ARTICLE 6. REPORTING BY COMMUNITY COLLEGE EMPLOYEES OF IMPROPER GOVERNMENTAL ACTIVITIES

Section
87160. Short title.
87161. Legislative intent.
87162. Definitions.
87163. Use or attempt to use official authority or influence to interfere with protected disclosures; prohibitions; civil liability.
87164. Written complaints; filing with local law enforcement agency; penalties; other rights and remedies.

§ 87160. Short title

This article shall be known and may be referred to as the Reporting by Community College Employees of Improper Governmental Activities Act. *(Added by Stats. 2000, c. 531 (A.B.2472), § 2.)*

§ 87161. Legislative intent

It is the intent of the Legislature that community college employees and other persons disclose, to the extent not expressly prohibited by law, improper governmental activities. *(Added by Stats.2000, c. 531 (A.B. 2472), § 2.)*

§ 87162. Definitions

For the purposes of this article, the following terms have the following meanings:

(a) "Employee" means a public school employee as defined in subdivision (j) of Section 3540.1 of the Government Code as construed to include community college employees.

(b) "Illegal order" means any directive to violate or assist in violating a federal, state, or local law, rule, or regulation or an order to work or cause others to work in conditions outside of their line of duty that would unreasonably threaten the health or safety of employees or the public.

(c) "Improper governmental activity" means an activity by a community college or by an employee that is undertaken in the performance of the employee's official duties, whether or not that activity is within the scope of his or her employment, and that meets either of the following descriptions:

(1) The activity violates a state or federal law or regulation, including, but not limited to, corruption, malfeasance, bribery, theft of government property, fraudulent claims, fraud, coercion, conversion, malicious prosecution, misuse of government property, or willful omission to perform duty.

(2) The activity is economically wasteful or involves gross misconduct, incompetency, or inefficiency.

(d) "Person" means any individual, corporation, trust, association, any state or local government, or any agency or instrumentality of any of the foregoing.

(e) "Protected disclosure" means a good faith communication that discloses or demonstrates an intention to disclose information that may evidence either of the following:

(1) An improper governmental activity.

(2) Any condition that may significantly threaten the health or safety of employees or the public if the disclosure or intention to disclose was made for the purpose of remedying that condition.

(f) "Public school employer" has the same meaning as in subdivision (k) of Section 3540.1 of the Government Code as construed to include community college districts. *(Added by Stats.2000, c. 531 (A.B.2472), § 2.)*

§ 87163. Use or attempt to use official authority or influence to interfere with protected disclosures; prohibitions; civil liability

(a) An employee may not directly or indirectly use or attempt to use the official authority or influence of the employee for the purpose of intimidating, threatening, coercing, commanding, or attempting to intimidate, threaten, coerce, or command any person for the purpose of interfering with the right of that person to disclose to an official agent matters within the scope of this article.

(b) For the purpose of subdivision (a), "use of official authority or influence" includes promising to confer or conferring any benefit; affecting or threatening to affect any reprisal; or taking, directing others to take, recommending, processing, or approving any personnel action, including, but not limited to appointment, promotion, transfer, assignment, performance evaluation, suspension, or other disciplinary action.

(c) For the purpose of subdivision (a), "official agent" includes a community college administrator, member of the governing board of a community college district, or the Chancellor of the California Community Colleges.

(d) An employee who violates subdivision (a) may be liable in an action for civil damages brought against the employee by the offended party.

(e) Nothing in this section shall be construed to authorize an individual to disclose information otherwise prohibited by or under law. *(Added by Stats.2000, c. 531 (A.B.2472), § 2.)*

§ 87164. Written complaints; filing with local law enforcement agency; penalties; other rights and remedies

(a) An employee or applicant for employment with a public school employer who files a written complaint with his or her supervisor, a community college administrator, or the public school employer alleging actual or attempted acts of reprisal, retaliation, threats, coercion, or similar improper acts prohibited by Section 87163 for having disclosed improper governmental activities or for refusing to obey an illegal order may also file a copy of the written complaint with the local law enforcement agency, together with a sworn statement that the contents of the written complaint are true, or are believed by the affiant to be true, under penalty of perjury. The complaint filed with the local law enforcement agency shall be filed within 12 months of the most recent act of reprisal that is the subject of the complaint.

(b) A person who intentionally engages in acts of reprisal, retaliation, threats, coercion, or similar acts against an employee or applicant for employment with a public school employer for having made a protected disclosure is subject to a fine not to exceed ten thousand dollars ($10,000) and imprisonment in the county jail for a period not to exceed one year. An employee, officer, or administrator who intentionally engages in that conduct shall also be subject to discipline by the public school employer. If no adverse action is instituted by the public school employer, and it is determined that there is reasonable cause to believe that an act of reprisal, retaliation, threats, coercion, or similar acts prohibited by Section 87163, the local law enforcement agency may report the nature and details of the activity to the governing board of the community college district.

(c)(1) The State Personnel Board shall initiate a hearing or investigation of a written complaint of reprisal or retaliation as prohibited by Section 87163 within 10 working days of its submission. The executive officer of the State Personnel Board shall complete findings of the hearing or investigation within 60 working days thereafter, and shall provide a copy of the findings to the complaining employee or applicant for employment with a public school employer and to the appropriate supervisors, administrator, or employer. This hearing shall be conducted in accordance with Section 18671.2 of the Government Code, this part, and the rules of practice and procedure of the State Personnel Board. When the allegations contained in a complaint of reprisal or retaliation are the same as, or similar to, those contained in another appeal, the executive officer may consolidate the

appeals into the most appropriate format. In these cases, the time limits described in this paragraph shall not apply.

(2) Notwithstanding Section 18671.2 of the Government Code, no costs associated with hearings of the State Personnel Board conducted pursuant to paragraph (1) shall be charged to the board of governors. Instead, all of the costs associated with hearings of the State Personnel Board conducted pursuant to paragraph (1) shall be charged directly to the community college district that employs the complaining employee, or with whom the complaining applicant for employment has filed his or her employment application.

(d) If the findings of the executive officer of the State Personnel Board set forth acts of alleged misconduct by the supervisor, community college administrator, or public school employer, the supervisor, administrator, or employer may request a hearing before the State Personnel Board regarding the findings of the executive officer. The request for hearing and any subsequent determination by the board shall be made in accordance with the board's usual rules governing appeals, hearings, investigations, and disciplinary proceedings.

(e) If, after the hearing, the State Personnel Board determines that a violation of Section 87163 occurred, or if no hearing is requested and the findings of the executive officer conclude that improper activity has occurred, the board may order any appropriate relief, including, but not limited to, reinstatement, back pay, restoration of lost service credit if appropriate, and the expungement of any adverse records of the employee or applicant for employment with a public school employer who was the subject of the alleged acts of misconduct prohibited by Section 87163.

(f) Whenever the State Personnel Board determines that a supervisor, community college administrator, or public school employer has violated Section 87163, it shall cause an entry to that effect to be made in the supervisor's, community college administrator's, or public school employer's official personnel records.

(g) In order for the Governor and the Legislature to determine the need to continue or modify personnel procedures as they relate to the investigations of reprisals or retaliation for the disclosure of information by employees, the State Personnel Board, by June 30 of each year, shall submit a report to the Governor and the Legislature regarding complaints filed, hearings held, and legal actions taken pursuant to this section.

(h) In addition to all other penalties provided by law, a person who intentionally engages in acts of reprisal, retaliation, threats, coercion, or similar acts against an employee or applicant for employment with a public school employer for having made a protected disclosure shall be liable in an action for damages brought against him or her by the injured party. Punitive damages may be awarded by the court where the acts of the offending party are proven to be malicious. Where liability has been established, the injured party shall also be entitled to reasonable attorney's fees as provided by law. However, an action for damages shall not be available to the injured party unless the injured party has first filed a complaint with the local law enforcement agency. Nothing in this subdivision requires an injured party to file a complaint with the State Personnel Board prior to seeking relief for damages in a court of law.

(i) This section is not intended to prevent a public school employer, school administrator, or supervisor from taking, failing to take, directing others to take, recommending, or approving a personnel action with respect to an employee or applicant for employment with a public school employer if the public school employer, school administrator, or supervisor reasonably believes an action or inaction is justified on the basis of evidence separate and apart from the fact that the person has made a protected disclosure as defined in subdivision (e) of Section 87162.

(j) In any civil action or administrative proceeding, once it has been demonstrated by a preponderance of evidence that an activity protected by this article was a contributing factor in the alleged retaliation against a former, current, or prospective employee, the burden of proof shall be on the supervisor, school administrator, or public school employer to demonstrate by clear and convincing evidence that the alleged action would have occurred for legitimate, independent reasons even if the employee had not engaged in protected disclosures or refused an illegal order. If the supervisor, school administrator, or public school employer fails to meet this burden of proof in an adverse action against the employee in any administrative review, challenge, or adjudication in which retaliation has been demonstrated to be a contributing factor, the employee shall have a complete affirmative defense in the adverse action.

(k) Nothing in this article shall be deemed to diminish the rights, privileges, or remedies of an employee under any other federal or state law or under an employment contract or collective bargaining agreement.

(*l*) If the provisions of this section are in conflict with the provisions of a memorandum of understanding reached pursuant to Chapter 10.7 (commencing with Section 3540) of Division 4 of Title 1 of the Government Code, the memorandum of understanding shall be controlling without further legislative action. *(Added by Stats.2000, c. 531 (A.B.2472), § 2. Amended by Stats. 2001, c. 159 (S.B.662), § 84; Stats.2001, c. 416 (A.B.647), § 1; Stats.2002, c. 81 (A.B.2034), § 1.)*

Division 8

CALIFORNIA STATE UNIVERSITY

Part 55

CALIFORNIA STATE UNIVERSITY

CHAPTER 5. PERSONNEL

ARTICLE 4. INVESTIGATION OF REPORTED IMPROPER GOVERNMENTAL ACTIVITIES

Section
89570. Title of article.

Section
89571. Legislative intent.
89572. Definitions.
89573. Duties and authority of administrator upon receipt of protected written disclosure; confidentiality of identity of complainant.
89574. Confidentiality of investigative audit; limitations.

§ 89570. Title of article

This article shall be known and may be referred to as the California State University Investigation of Reported Improper Governmental Activities Act. *(Added by Stats. 2005, c. 310 (A.B.706), § 1.)*

§ 89571. Legislative intent

It is the intent of the Legislature that employees of, and applicants for employment at, the California State University should be free to report improper governmental activities and significant threats to health or safety and that their identities and the privacy rights of those affected by investigations of the protected disclosures be properly safeguarded. *(Added by Stats.2005, c. 310 (A.B.706), § 1.)*

§ 89572. Definitions

For the purposes of this article:

(a) "Applicant for employment" means an individual who has completed and submitted an application form for a specific, available position at a campus of the California State University or at the Office of the Chancellor of the California State University.

(b) "Complainant" means an employee or applicant for employment who files a report and makes a protected disclosure in accordance with established procedures of the California State University.

(c) "Employee" means any person employed by the California State University.

(d) "Improper governmental activity" has the same meaning as set forth in subdivision (b) of Section 8547.2 of the Government Code.

(e) "Protected disclosure" means any good faith communication, as defined by subdivision (d) of Section 8547.2 of the Government Code, that is made in accordance with established procedures of the California State University. *(Added by Stats.2005, c. 310 (A.B.706), § 1.)*

§ 89573. Duties and authority of administrator upon receipt of protected written disclosure; confidentiality of identity of complainant

(a) Upon receiving a protected disclosure in writing, the administrator designated in accordance with established procedures of the California State University shall acknowledge receipt of the written disclosure to the complainant. The administrator may conduct or cause to be conducted an investigative audit of the matter, and determine what action, if any, is necessary.

(b) The administrator shall issue a formal response to the complainant that contains a summary of the allegations, a summary of the investigation, whether the allegations were substantiated, and what actions, if any, were taken in response to the complaint. This response shall be issued in a timely fashion and in a manner that is consistent with the privacy interests of each person who is involved in the situation addressed by the response. This response shall be subject to disclosure in accordance with Chapter 3.5 (commencing with Section 6250) of Division 7 of Title 1 of the Government Code.

(c) The identity of the person providing the protected disclosure shall not be disclosed without the written permission of that person unless the disclosure is to a law enforcement agency that is conducting a criminal investigation or to the State Auditor. *(Added by Stats.2005, c. 310 (A.B.706), § 1.)*

§ 89574. Confidentiality of investigative audit; limitations

(a) Notwithstanding Chapter 3.5 (commencing with Section 6250) of Division 7 of Title 1 of the Government Code, every investigative audit undertaken under this article shall be kept confidential, except that the California State University may issue any report of an investigation that has substantiated an allegation made by the complainant, keeping confidential the identity of the individual or individuals involved, or release any findings resulting from an investigation conducted pursuant to Section 89045 that the trustees deem necessary to serve the interests of the state.

(b) This article shall not be construed to limit any authority conferred by law upon the Attorney General or any other department or agency of government to investigate any matter. *(Added by Stats.2005, c. 310 (A.B.706), § 1.)*

ELECTIONS CODE

Division 12

PREELECTION PROCEDURES

CHAPTER 4. PRECINCT BOARDS

ARTICLE 1. GENERAL PROVISIONS

Section
12312. Discharge for acting as election officer prohibited.

§ 12312. Discharge for acting as election officer prohibited

No person shall be suspended or discharged from any service or employment because of absence while serving as an election officer on election day. *(Stats.1994, c. 920 (S.B.1547), § 2.)*

Division 14

ELECTION DAY PROCEDURES

CHAPTER 1. PRIVILEGES OF VOTERS

Section
14000. Employees' time off to vote.
14001. Employers' notice; posting.
14002. Public employees' time off to vote; posting of notice.

§ 14000. Employees' time off to vote

(a) If a voter does not have sufficient time outside of working hours to vote at a statewide election, the voter may, without loss of pay, take off enough working time that, when added to the voting time available outside of working hours, will enable the voter to vote.

(b) No more than two hours of the time taken off for voting shall be without loss of pay. The time off for voting shall be only at the beginning or end of the regular working shift, whichever allows the most free time for voting and the least time off from the regular working shift, unless otherwise mutually agreed.

(c) If the employee on the third working day prior to the day of election, knows or has reason to believe that time off will be necessary to be able to vote on election day, the employee shall give the employer at least two working days' notice that time off for voting is desired, in accordance with this section. *(Stats.1994, c. 920 (S.B. 1547), § 2.)*

§ 14001. Employers' notice; posting

Not less than 10 days before every statewide election, every employer shall keep posted conspicuously at the place of work, if practicable, or elsewhere where it can be seen as employees come or go to their place of work, a notice setting forth the provisions of Section 14000. *(Stats.1994, c. 920 (S.B.1547), § 2.)*

§ 14002. Public employees' time off to vote; posting of notice

Sections 14000 and 14001 shall apply to all public agencies and the employees thereof, as well as to employers and employees in private industry. *(Stats. 1994, c. 920 (S.B.1547), § 2.)*

CHAPTER 3. PROCEDURES AT POLLS

ARTICLE 5. PROVISIONAL VOTING

Section
14313. States of emergency; issuance of provisional ballots for emergency workers; requirements.

§ 14313. States of emergency; issuance of provisional ballots for emergency workers; requirements

(a) Upon the declaration of a state of emergency by the Governor and the issuance of an executive order authorizing an emergency worker to cast a ballot outside of his or her home precinct, elections officials in the counties included in the executive order shall, upon demand, issue to an emergency worker a provisional ballot that may be identical to the provisional ballot offered to other voters in the county, using a process to be determined by the elections official. The elections official shall transmit for processing any ballot cast, including any materials necessary to process the ballot, pursuant to this section to the elections official in the county where the voter is registered to vote.

(b) To be counted, a ballot cast pursuant to this section shall satisfy both of the following requirements:

(1) Be cast by the voter no later than the close of the polls on election day.

(2) Be received by the county elections official where the voter is registered on or before the 10th day following the date of the election.

(c) Upon receipt of the returned ballot, the elections official shall process the ballot pursuant to the procedures in subdivision (c) of Section 14310.

(d) If the requirements in subdivisions (b) and (c) are met and the ballot is eligible to be counted, the ballot shall be duplicated and all other materials preserved according to the procedures set forth in this code.

(e) "Emergency worker" for the purposes of this section means a person who is officially engaged in responding to the proclaimed state of emergency and whose vocation has been identified in an executive order relating to the state of emergency. *(Added by Stats.2009, c. 395 (A.B.1440), § 1.)*

EVIDENCE CODE

Division 11

WRITINGS

CHAPTER 2. SECONDARY EVIDENCE
OF WRITINGS

ARTICLE 4. PRODUCTION OF
BUSINESS RECORDS

Section
1567. Employee income and benefit information; forms completed by employer; support modification or termination proceedings.

§ 1567. Employee income and benefit information; forms completed by employer; support modification or termination proceedings

A completed form described in Section 3664 of the Family Code for income and benefit information provided by the employer may be admissible in a proceeding for modification or termination of an order for child, family, or spousal support if both of the following requirements are met:

(a) The completed form complies with Sections 1561 and 1562.

(b) A copy of the completed form and notice was served on the employee named therein pursuant to Section 3664 of the Family Code. *(Added by Stats.1995, c. 506 (A.B.413), § 1.)*

FAMILY CODE

Division 2.5

DOMESTIC PARTNER REGISTRATION

Part 1

DEFINITIONS

Section
297.   Domestic partners and partnership; establishment.
297.5. Rights, protections and benefits; responsibilities; obligations and duties under law; date of registration as equivalent of date of marriage.

§ 297. Domestic partners and partnership; establishment

(a) Domestic partners are two adults who have chosen to share one another's lives in an intimate and committed relationship of mutual caring.

(b) A domestic partnership shall be established in California when both persons file a Declaration of Domestic Partnership with the Secretary of State pursuant to this division, and, at the time of filing, all of the following requirements are met:

(1) Both persons have a common residence.

(2) Neither person is married to someone else or is a member of another domestic partnership with someone else that has not been terminated, dissolved, or adjudged a nullity.

(3) The two persons are not related by blood in a way that would prevent them from being married to each other in this state.

(4) Both persons are at least 18 years of age.

(5) Either of the following:

(A) Both persons are members of the same sex.

(B) One or both of the persons meet the eligibility criteria under Title II of the Social Security Act as defined in 42 U.S.C. Section 402(a) for old-age insurance benefits or Title XVI of the Social Security Act as defined in 42 U.S.C. Section 1381 for aged individuals. Notwithstanding any other provision of this section, persons of opposite sexes may not constitute a domestic partnership unless one or both of the persons are over the age of 62.

(6) Both persons are capable of consenting to the domestic partnership.

(c) "Have a common residence" means that both domestic partners share the same residence. It is not necessary that the legal right to possess the common residence be in both of their names. Two people have a common residence even if one or both have additional residences. Domestic partners do not cease to have a common residence if one leaves the common residence but intends to return.

(Added by Stats.1999, c. 588 (A.B.26), § 2. Amended by Stats.2001, c. 893 (A.B.25), § 3; Stats.2003, c. 421 (A.B.205), § 3, operative Jan. 1, 2005.)

§ 297.5. Rights, protections and benefits; responsibilities; obligations and duties under law; date of registration as equivalent of date of marriage

(a) Registered domestic partners shall have the same rights, protections, and benefits, and shall be subject to the same responsibilities, obligations, and duties under law, whether they derive from statutes, administrative regulations, court rules, government policies, common law, or any other provisions or sources of law, as are granted to and imposed upon spouses.

(b) Former registered domestic partners shall have the same rights, protections, and benefits, and shall be subject to the same responsibilities, obligations, and duties under law, whether they derive from statutes, administrative regulations, court rules, government policies, common law, or any other provisions or sources of law, as are granted to and imposed upon former spouses.

(c) A surviving registered domestic partner, following the death of the other partner, shall have the same rights, protections, and benefits, and shall be subject to the same responsibilities, obligations, and duties under law, whether they derive from statutes, administrative regulations, court rules, government policies, common law, or any other provisions or sources of law, as are granted to and imposed upon a widow or a widower.

(d) The rights and obligations of registered domestic partners with respect to a child of either of them shall be the same as those of spouses. The rights and obligations of former or surviving registered domestic partners with respect to a child of either of them shall be the same as those of former or surviving spouses.

(e) To the extent that provisions of California law adopt, refer to, or rely upon, provisions of federal law in a way that otherwise would cause registered domestic partners to be treated differently than spouses, registered domestic partners shall be treated by California law as if federal law recognized a domestic partnership in the same manner as California law.

(f) Registered domestic partners shall have the same rights regarding nondiscrimination as those provided to spouses.

(g) No public agency in this state may discriminate against any person or couple on the ground that the

117

person is a registered domestic partner rather than a spouse or that the couple are registered domestic partners rather than spouses, except that nothing in this section applies to modify eligibility for long-term care plans pursuant to Chapter 15 (commencing with Section 21660) of Part 3 of Division 5 of Title 2 of the Government Code.

(h) This act does not preclude any state or local agency from exercising its regulatory authority to implement statutes providing rights to, or imposing responsibilities upon, domestic partners.

(i) This section does not amend or modify any provision of the California Constitution or any provision of any statute that was adopted by initiative.

(j) Where necessary to implement the rights of registered domestic partners under this act, gender-specific terms referring to spouses shall be construed to include domestic partners.

(k)(1) For purposes of the statutes, administrative regulations, court rules, government policies, common law, and any other provision or source of law governing the rights, protections, and benefits, and the responsibilities, obligations, and duties of registered domestic partners in this state, as effectuated by this section, with respect to community property, mutual responsibility for debts to third parties, the right in particular circumstances of either partner to seek financial support from the other following the dissolution of the partnership, and other rights and duties as between the partners concerning ownership of property, any reference to the date of a marriage shall be deemed to refer to the date of registration of a domestic partnership with the state.

(2) Notwithstanding paragraph (1), for domestic partnerships registered with the state before January 1, 2005, an agreement between the domestic partners that the partners intend to be governed by the requirements set forth in Sections 1600 to 1620, inclusive, and which complies with those sections, except for the agreement's effective date, shall be enforceable as provided by Sections 1600 to 1620, inclusive, if that agreement was fully executed and in force as of June 30, 2005. *(Added by Stats.2003, c. 421 (A.B.205), § 4, operative Jan. 1, 2005. Amended by Stats.2004, c. 947 (A.B.2580), § 2; Stats. 2006, c. 802 (S.B.1827), § 2.)*

Part 2

REGISTRATION

Section
298.　　Declaration of Domestic Partnership and Notice of Termination of Domestic Partnership forms.
298.5.　Filing of Declaration of Domestic Partnership forms; registration.
298.6.　Parties to registered domestic partnership; names; procedure for change of name.

§ 298. Declaration of Domestic Partnership and Notice of Termination of Domestic Partnership forms

(a)(1) The Secretary of State shall prepare forms entitled " Declaration of Domestic Partnership" and "Notice of Termination of Domestic Partnership" to meet the requirements of this division. These forms shall require the signature and seal of an acknowledgment by a notary public to be binding and valid.

(2) When funding allows, the Secretary of State shall include on the form notice that a lesbian, gay, bisexual, and transgender specific domestic abuse brochure is available upon request.

(b)(1) The Secretary of State shall distribute these forms to each county clerk. These forms shall be available to the public at the office of the Secretary of State and each county clerk.

(2) The Secretary of State shall, by regulation, establish fees for the actual costs of processing each of these forms, and the cost for preparing and sending the mailings and notices required pursuant to Section 299.3, and shall charge these fees to persons filing the forms.

(3) There is hereby established a fee of twenty-three dollars ($23) to be charged in addition to the existing fees established by regulation to persons filing domestic partner registrations pursuant to Section 297 for development and support of a lesbian, gay, bisexual, and transgender curriculum for training workshops on domestic violence, conducted pursuant to Section 13823.15 of the Penal Code, and for the support of a grant program to promote healthy nonviolent relationships in the lesbian, gay, bisexual, and transgender community. This paragraph shall not apply to persons of opposite sexes filing a domestic partnership registration and who meet the qualifications described in subparagraph (B) of paragraph (5) of subdivision (b) of Section 297.

(4) The fee established by paragraph (3) shall be deposited in the Equality in Prevention and Services for Domestic Abuse Fund, which is hereby established. The fund shall be administered by the Office of Emergency Services, and expenditures from the fund shall be used to support the purposes of paragraph (3).

(c) The Declaration of Domestic Partnership shall require each person who wants to become a domestic partner to (1) state that he or she meets the requirements of Section 297 at the time the form is signed, (2) provide a mailing address, (3) state that he or she consents to the jurisdiction of the Superior Courts of California for the purpose of a proceeding to obtain a judgment of dissolution or nullity of the domestic partnership or for legal separation of partners in the domestic partnership, or for any other proceeding related to the partners' rights and obligations, even if one or both partners ceases to be a resident of, or to maintain a domicile in, this state, (4) sign the form with a declaration that representations made therein are true, correct, and contain no material omissions of fact to the best knowledge and belief of the applicant, and (5) have a notary public acknowledge his or her signature. Both partners' signatures shall be affixed to one Declaration of Domestic Partnership form, which form shall then be transmitted to the Secretary of State according to the instructions provided on the form. Filing an intentionally and materially false Declaration of Domestic Partnership shall be punishable as a misdemeanor.

(d) The Declaration of Domestic Partnership form shall contain an optional section for either party or both parties to indicate a change in name pursuant to Section 298.6. The optional section shall require a party indicating a change in name to provide his or her date of birth. *(Added by Stats.1999, c. 588 (A.B.26), § 2. Amended by Stats.2003, c. 421 (A.B.205), § 5, operative Jan. 1, 2005; Stats.2006, c. 856 (A.B.2051), § 2; Stats.2007, c. 179 (S.B.86), § 7, eff. Aug. 24, 2007; Stats.2007, c. 567 (A.B.102), § 4.)*

§ 298.5. Filing of Declaration of Domestic Partnership forms; registration

(a) Two persons desiring to become domestic partners may complete and file a Declaration of Domestic Partnership with the Secretary of State.

(b) The Secretary of State shall register the Declaration of Domestic Partnership in a registry for those partnerships, and shall return a copy of the registered form and a Certificate of Registered Domestic Partnership and, except for those opposite sex domestic partners who meet the qualifications described in subparagraph (B) of paragraph (5) of subdivision (b) of Section 297, a copy of the brochure that is made available to county clerks and the Secretary of State by the State Department of Public Health pursuant to Section 358 and distributed to individuals receiving a confidential marriage license pursuant to Section 503, to the domestic partners at the mailing address provided by the domestic partners.

(c) No person who has filed a Declaration of Domestic Partnership may file a new Declaration of Domestic Partnership or enter a civil marriage with someone other than their registered domestic partner unless the most recent domestic partnership has been terminated or a final judgment of dissolution or nullity of the most recent domestic partnership has been entered. This prohibition does not apply if the previous domestic partnership ended because one of the partners died.

(d) When funding allows, the Secretary of State shall print and make available upon request, pursuant to Section 358, a lesbian, gay, bisexual, and transgender specific domestic abuse brochure developed by the State Department of Public Health and made available to the Secretary of State to domestic partners who qualify pursuant to Section 297.

(e) The Certificate of Registered Domestic Partnership shall include the name used by each party before registration of the domestic partnership and the new name, if any, selected by each party upon registration of the domestic partnership. *(Added by Stats.1999, c. 588 (A.B.26), § 2. Amended by Stats.2003, c. 421 (A.B.205),* § 6, operative Jan. 1, 2005; Stats.2006, c. 856 (A.B.2051), § 3; Stats.2007, c. 483 (S.B.1039), § 8; Stats.2007, c. 567 (A.B.102), § 5.)*

§ 298.6. Parties to registered domestic partnership; names; procedure for change of name

(a) Parties to a registered domestic partnership shall not be required to have the same name. Neither party shall be required to change his or her name. A person's name shall not change upon registration as a domestic partner unless that person elects to change his or her name pursuant to subdivision (b).

(b)(1) One party or both parties to a registered domestic partnership may elect to change the middle or last names by which that party wishes to be known after registration of the domestic partnership by entering the new name in the space provided on the Declaration of Domestic Partnership form without intent to defraud.

(2) A person may adopt any of the following middle or last names pursuant to paragraph (1):

(A) The current last name of the other domestic partner.

(B) The last name of either domestic partner given at birth.

(C) A name combining into a single last name all or a segment of the current last name or the last name of either domestic partner given at birth.

(D) A hyphenated combination of last names.

(3)(A) An election by a person to change his or her name pursuant to paragraph (1) shall serve as a record of the name change. A certified copy of the Certificate of Registered Domestic Partnership containing the new name, or retaining the former name, shall constitute proof that the use of the new name or retention of the former name is lawful.

(B) A certified copy of a Certificate of Registered Domestic Partnership shall be accepted as identification establishing a true, full name for purposes of Section 12800.7 of the Vehicle Code.

(C) Nothing in this section shall be construed to prohibit the Department of Motor Vehicles from accepting as identification other documents establishing a true, full name for purposes of Section 12800.7 of the Vehicle Code. Those documents may include, without limitation, a certified copy of a document that is substantially equivalent to a Certificate of Registered Domestic Partnership that records either of the following:

(i) A legal union of two persons that was validly formed in another jurisdiction and is recognized as a valid domestic partnership in this state pursuant to Section 299.2.

(ii) A legal union of domestic partners as defined by a local jurisdiction pursuant to Section 299.6.

(D) This section shall be applied in a manner consistent with the requirements of Sections 1653.5 and 12801 of the Vehicle Code.

(4) The adoption of a new name, or the choice not to adopt a new name, by means of a Declaration of Domestic Partnership pursuant to paragraph (1) shall not abrogate the right of either party to adopt a different name through usage at a future date, or to petition the superior court for a change of name pursuant to Title 8 (commencing with Section 1275) of Part 3 of the Code of Civil Procedure.

(c) Nothing in this section shall be construed to abrogate the common law right of any person to change his or her name, or the right of any person to petition the superior court for a change of name pursuant to Title 8 (commencing with Section 1275) of Part 3 of the Code of Civil Procedure. *(Added by Stats.2007, c. 567 (A.B.102), § 6.)*

Part 3

TERMINATION

Section
299.   Termination of registered domestic partnership; filing of Notice of Termination of Domestic Partnership; conditions; effective date; setting aside termination; jurisdiction.

§ 299. Termination of registered domestic partnership; filing of Notice of Termination of Domestic Partnership; conditions; effective date; setting aside termination; jurisdiction

(a) A registered domestic partnership may be terminated without filing a proceeding for dissolution of domestic partnership by the filing of a Notice of Termination of Domestic Partnership with the Secretary of State pursuant to this section, provided that all of the following conditions exist at the time of the filing:

(1) The Notice of Termination of Domestic Partnership is signed by both registered domestic partners.

(2) There are no children of the relationship of the parties born before or after registration of the domestic partnership or adopted by the parties after registration of the domestic partnership, and neither of the registered domestic partners, to their knowledge, is pregnant.

(3) The registered domestic partnership is not more than five years in duration.

(4) Neither party has any interest in real property wherever situated, with the exception of the lease of a residence occupied by either party which satisfies the following requirements:

(A) The lease does not include an option to purchase.

(B) The lease terminates within one year from the date of filing of the Notice of Termination of Domestic Partnership.

(5) There are no unpaid obligations in excess of the amount described in paragraph (6) of subdivision (a) of Section 2400, as adjusted by subdivision (b) of Section 2400, incurred by either or both of the parties after registration of the domestic partnership, excluding the amount of any unpaid obligation with respect to an automobile.

(6) The total fair market value of community property assets, excluding all encumbrances and automobiles, including any deferred compensation or retirement plan, is less than the amount described in paragraph (7) of subdivision (a) of Section 2400, as adjusted by subdivision (b) of Section 2400, and neither party has separate property assets, excluding all encumbrances and automobiles, in excess of that amount.

(7) The parties have executed an agreement setting forth the division of assets and the assumption of liabilities of the community property, and have executed any documents, title certificates, bills of sale, or other evidence of transfer necessary to effectuate the agreement.

(8) The parties waive any rights to support by the other domestic partner.

(9) The parties have read and understand a brochure prepared by the Secretary of State describing the requirements, nature, and effect of terminating a domestic partnership.

(10) Both parties desire that the domestic partnership be terminated.

(b) The registered domestic partnership shall be terminated effective six months after the date of filing of the Notice of Termination of Domestic Partnership with the Secretary of State pursuant to this section, provided that neither party has, before that date, filed with the Secretary of State a notice of revocation of the termination of domestic partnership, in the form and content as shall be prescribed by the Secretary of State, and sent to the other party a copy of the notice of revocation by first-class mail, postage prepaid, at the other party's last known address. The effect of termination of a domestic partnership pursuant to this section shall be the same as, and shall be treated for all purposes as, the entry of a judgment of dissolution of a domestic partnership.

(c) The termination of a domestic partnership pursuant to subdivision (b) does not prejudice nor bar the rights of either of the parties to institute an action in the superior court to set aside the termination for fraud, duress, mistake, or any other ground recognized at law or in equity. A court may set aside the termination of domestic partnership and declare the termination of the domestic partnership null and void upon proof that the parties did not meet the requirements of subdivision (a) at the time of the filing of the Notice of Termination of Domestic Partnership with the Secretary of State.

(d) The superior courts shall have jurisdiction over all proceedings relating to the dissolution of domestic partnerships, nullity of domestic partnerships, and legal separation of partners in a domestic partnership. The dissolution of a domestic partnership, nullity of a domestic partnership, and legal separation of partners in a domestic partnership shall follow the same procedures, and the partners shall possess the same rights, protections, and benefits, and be subject to the same responsibilities, obligations, and duties, as apply to the dissolution of marriage, nullity of marriage, and legal separation of spouses in a marriage, respectively, except as provided in subdivision (a), and except that, in accordance with the consent acknowledged by domestic partners in the Declaration of Domestic Partnership form, proceedings for dissolution, nullity, or legal separation of a domestic partnership registered in this state may be filed in the superior courts of this state even if neither domestic partner is a resident of, or maintains a domicile in, the state at the time the proceedings are filed. *(Added by Stats.2003, c. 421 (A.B.205), § 8, operative Jan. 1, 2005. Amended by Stats.2004, c. 947 (A.B.2580), § 3.)*

Part 4

LEGAL EFFECT

Section

299.2.   Recognizing same sex unions from another jurisdiction as a valid domestic partnership.

299.3.   Letter to be sent each registered domestic partner from Secretary of State; notice to potential domestic partner registrants.

§ 299.2. Recognizing same sex unions from another jurisdiction as a valid domestic partnership

A legal union of two persons of the same sex, other than a marriage, that was validly formed in another jurisdiction, and that is substantially equivalent to a domestic partnership as defined in this part, shall be recognized as a valid domestic partnership in this state regardless of whether it bears the name domestic partnership. *(Added by Stats.2003, c. 421 (A.B.205), § 9, operative Jan. 1, 2005.)*

§ 299.3. Letter to be sent each registered domestic partner from Secretary of State; notice to potential domestic partner registrants

(a) On or before June 30, 2004, and again on or before December 1, 2004, and again on or before January 31, 2005, the Secretary of State shall send the following letter to the mailing address on file of each registered domestic partner who registered more than one month prior to each of those dates:

"Dear Registered Domestic Partner:

This letter is being sent to all persons who have registered with the Secretary of State as a domestic partner.

Effective January 1, 2005, California's law related to the rights and responsibilities of registered domestic partners will change (or, if you are receiving this letter after that date, the law has changed, as of January 1, 2005). With this new legislation, for purposes of California law, domestic partners will have a great many new rights and responsibilities, including laws governing community property, those governing property transfer, those

regarding duties of mutual financial support and mutual responsibilities for certain debts to third parties, and many others. The way domestic partnerships are terminated is also changing. After January 1, 2005, under certain circumstances, it will be necessary to participate in a dissolution proceeding in court to end a domestic partnership.

Domestic partners who do not wish to be subject to these new rights and responsibilities MUST terminate their domestic partnership before January 1, 2005. Under the law in effect until January 1, 2005, your domestic partnership is automatically terminated if you or your partner marry or die while you are registered as domestic partners. It is also terminated if you send to your partner or your partner sends to you, by certified mail, a notice terminating the domestic partnership, or if you and your partner no longer share a common residence. In all cases, you are required to file a Notice of Termination of Domestic Partnership.

If you do not terminate your domestic partnership before January 1, 2005, as provided above, you will be subject to these new rights and responsibilities and, under certain circumstances, you will only be able to terminate your domestic partnership, other than as a result of your domestic partner's death, by the filing of a court action.

Further, if you registered your domestic partnership with the state prior to January 1, 2005, you have until June 30, 2005, to enter into a written agreement with your domestic partner that will be enforceable in the same manner as a premarital agreement under California law, if you intend to be so governed.

If you have any questions about any of these changes, please consult an attorney. If you cannot find an attorney in your locale, please contact your county bar association for a referral.

Sincerely,

The Secretary of State"

(b) From January 1, 2004, to December 31, 2004, inclusive, the Secretary of State shall provide the following notice with all requests for the Declaration of Domestic Partnership form. The Secretary of State also shall attach the Notice to the Declaration of Domestic Partnership form that is provided to the general public on the Secretary of State's Web site:

"NOTICE TO POTENTIAL DOMESTIC PARTNER REGISTRANTS

As of January 1, 2005, California's law of domestic partnership will change.

Beginning at that time, for purposes of California law, domestic partners will have a great many new rights and responsibilities, including laws governing community property, those governing property transfer, those regarding duties of mutual financial support and mutual responsibilities for certain debts to third parties, and many others. The way domestic partnerships are terminated will also change. Unlike current law, which allows partners to end their partnership simply by filing a "Termination of Domestic Partnership" form with the Secretary of State, after January 1, 2005, it will be necessary under certain circumstances to participate in a dissolution proceeding in court to end a domestic partnership.

If you have questions about these changes, please consult an attorney. If you cannot find an attorney in your area, please contact your county bar association for a referral." *(Added by Stats.2003, c. 421 (A.B.205), § 10. Amended by Stats.2004, c. 947 (A.B.2580), § 4; Stats. 2005, c. 22 (S.B.1108), § 59.)*

Part 5

PREEMPTION

Section
299.6.   Preemption of local ordinances or laws.

§ 299.6.   Preemption of local ordinances or laws

(a) Any local ordinance or law that provides for the creation of a "domestic partnership" shall be preempted on and after July 1, 2000, except as provided in subdivision (c).

(b) Domestic partnerships created under any local domestic partnership ordinance or law before July 1, 2000, shall remain valid. On and after July 1, 2000, domestic partnerships previously established under a local ordinance or law shall be governed by this division and the rights and duties of the partners shall be those set out in this division, except as provided in subdivision (c), provided a Declaration of Domestic Partnership is filed by the domestic partners under Section 298.5.

(c) Any local jurisdiction may retain or adopt ordinances, policies, or laws that offer rights within that jurisdiction to domestic partners as defined by Section 297 or as more broadly defined by the local jurisdiction's ordinances, policies, or laws, or that impose duties upon third parties regarding domestic partners as defined by Section 297 or as more broadly defined by the local jurisdiction's ordinances, policies, or laws, that are in addition to the rights and duties set out in this division, and the local rights may be conditioned upon the agreement of the domestic partners to assume the additional obligations set forth in this division. *(Added by Stats.1999, c. 588 (A.B.26), § 2.)*

Division 3

MARRIAGE

Part 1

VALIDITY OF MARRIAGE

Section
308.5.   Between man and woman only.

§ 308.5.   Between man and woman only

Only marriage between a man and a woman is valid or recognized in California. *(Added by Initiative Measure (Prop.22, § 2, eff. March 8, 2000).)*

Validity

This section was held unconstitutional as a violation of the equal protection clause in the decision of In re Marriage Cases (2008) 76 Cal.Rptr.3d 683, 43 Cal.4th 757, 183 P.3d 384, rehearing denied, on subsequent appeal 2009 WL 2515727, unpublished.

Division 9

SUPPORT

Part 1

DEFINITIONS AND GENERAL PROVISIONS

CHAPTER 6.   MODIFICATION, TERMINATION, OR SET ASIDE OF SUPPORT ORDERS

ARTICLE 2.   DISCOVERY BEFORE COMMENCING MODIFICATION OR TERMINATION PROCEEDING

Section
3664.   Requests for current income and expense declaration; authorized forms; requests to employer for income and benefit information; service.

§ 3664.   Requests for current income and expense declaration; authorized forms; requests to employer for income and benefit information; service

(a) At any time following a judgment of dissolution of marriage or legal separation of the parties, or a determination of paternity, that provides for payment of support, either the party ordered to pay support or the party to whom support was ordered to be paid or that party's assignee, without leave of court, may serve a request on the other party for the production of a completed current income and expense declaration in the form adopted by the Judicial Council.

(b) If there is no response within 35 days of service of the request or if the responsive income and expense declaration is incomplete as to any wage information, including the attachment of pay stubs and income tax returns, the requesting party may serve a request on the employer of the other party for information limited to the income and benefits provided to the party in the form adopted by the Judicial Council. The employer may require the requesting party to pay the reasonable costs of copying this information for the requesting party. The date specified in the request served on the employer for the production of income and benefit information shall not be less than 15 days from the date this request is issued.

(c) The requesting party shall serve or cause to be served on the employee described in this section or on his or her attorney a copy of the request served on the employer prior to the date specified in the request served on the employer for the production of income and benefit information. This copy shall be accompanied by a notice that, in a typeface that is intended to call attention to its terms, indicates all of the following:

(1) That information limited to the income and benefits provided to the employee by his or her employer is being sought from the employer named in the request for production.

(2) That the information may be protected by right of privacy.

(3) That, if the employee objects to the production of this information by the employer to the requesting party, the employee shall notify the court, in writing, of this objection prior to the date specified in the request served on the employer for the production of income and benefit information.

(4) That, if the requesting party does not agree, in writing, to cancel or narrow the scope of the request for the production of this information by the employer, the employee should consult an attorney regarding the employee's right to privacy and how to protect this right.

(d) The employee described in this section may, prior to the date specified in the request served on the employer for the production of income and benefit information, bring a motion pursuant to Section 1987.1 of the Code of Civil Procedure to quash or modify this request in the same manner as a subpoena duces tecum. Notice of this motion shall be given to the employer prior to the date specified in the request served on the employer for the production of income and benefit information. No employer shall be required to produce information limited to the income and benefits of the employee, except upon order of the court or upon agreement of the parties, employers, and employee affected.

(e) Service of a request for production of an income and expense declaration or for income and benefit information pursuant to this section or a copy thereof shall be by certified mail, postage prepaid, return receipt requested, to the last known address of the party to be served, or by personal service.

(f) The form adopted by the Judicial Council for purposes of the request on an employer described in subdivision (b) shall state that compliance with the request is voluntary, except upon order of the court or upon agreement of the parties, employers, and employee affected. *(Stats.1992, c. 162 (A.B.2650), § 10, operative Jan. 1, 1994. Amended by Stats.1995, c. 506 (A.B.413), § 2.)*

CHAPTER 7.   HEALTH INSURANCE

ARTICLE 2.   HEALTH INSURANCE COVERAGE ASSIGNMENT

Section
3760.   Definitions.
3761.   Application for health insurance coverage assignment; assignment order.
3762.   Denial of health insurance coverage assignment order; findings of court.

Section

3763. Time for order of health insurance coverage assign-
      ment order; modification.
3764. Effective date of assignment; copy of order and
      information to obligor; service of assignment order.
3765. Motion to quash assignment; grounds.
3766. Commencement of coverage; selection of plan.
3767. Duties of employer or health insurance provider.
3768. Failure to comply with a valid assignment order;
      liability.
3769. Discrimination prohibited; violation; penalty.
3770. Termination of assignment order; grounds.
3771. Information provided to the local child support agency.
3772. Forms; adoption by judicial council.
3773. Title IV–D cases where support enforcement services
      are provided by local child support agency.

§ 3760. Definitions

As used in this article, unless the provision or context otherwise requires:

(a) "Employer" includes the United States government and any public entity as defined in Section 811.2 of the Government Code.

(b) "Health insurance," "health insurance plan," "health insurance coverage," "health care services," or "health insurance coverage assignment" includes vision care and dental care coverage whether the vision care or dental care coverage is part of existing health insurance coverage or is issued as a separate policy or plan.

(c) "Health insurance coverage assignment" or "assignment order" means an order made under Section 3761.

(d) "National medical support notice" means the notice required by Section 666(a)(19) of Title 42 of the United States Code with respect to an order made pursuant to Section 3773. *(Stats.1992, c. 162 (A.B.2650), § 10, operative Jan. 1, 1994. Amended by Stats.2000, c. 119 (S.B.2045), § 1.)*

§ 3761. Application for health insurance coverage assignment; assignment order

(a) Upon application by a party or local child support agency in any proceeding where the court has ordered either or both parents to maintain health insurance coverage under Article 1 (commencing with Section 3750), the court shall order the employer of the obligor parent or other person providing health insurance to the obligor to enroll the supported child in the health insurance plan available to the obligor through the employer or other person and to deduct the appropriate premium or costs, if any, from the earnings of the obligor unless the court makes a finding of good cause for not making the order.

(b)(1) The application shall state that the party or local child support agency seeking the assignment order has given the obligor a written notice of the intent to seek a health insurance coverage assignment order in the event of a default in instituting coverage required by court order on behalf of the parties' child and that the notice

was transmitted by first-class mail, postage prepaid, or personally served at least 15 days before the date of the filing of the application for the order. The written notice of the intent to seek an assignment order required by this subdivision may be given at the time of filing a petition or complaint for support or at any later time, but shall be given at least 15 days before the date of filing the application under this section. The obligor may at any time waive the written notice required by this subdivision.

(2) The party or local child support agency seeking the assignment order shall file a certificate of service showing the method and date of service of the order and the statements required under Section 3772 upon the employer or provider of health insurance.

(c) The total amount that may be withheld from earnings for all obligations, including health insurance assignments, is limited by subdivision (a) of Section 706.052 of the Code of Civil Procedure or Section 1673 of Title 15 of the United States Code, whichever is less. *(Stats.1992, c. 162 (A.B.2650), § 10, operative Jan. 1, 1994. Amended by Stats.1993, c. 219 (A.B.1500), § 127; Stats. 1994, c. 1269 (A.B.2208), § 37; Stats.2000, c. 808 (A.B. 1358), § 31, eff. Sept. 28, 2000.)*

§ 3762. Denial of health insurance coverage assignment order; findings of court

Good cause for not making a health insurance coverage assignment order shall be limited to either of the following:

(a) The court finds that one of the conditions listed in subdivision (a) of Section 3765 or in Section 3770 exists.

(b) The court finds that the health insurance coverage assignment order would cause extraordinary hardship to the obligor. The court shall specify the nature of the extraordinary hardship and, whenever possible, a date by which the obligor shall obtain health insurance coverage or be subject to a health insurance coverage assignment. *(Stats.1992, c. 162 (A.B.2650), § 10, operative Jan. 1, 1994. Amended by Stats.1994, c. 1269 (A.B.2208), § 38.)*

§ 3763. Time for order of health insurance coverage assignment order; modification

(a) The health insurance coverage assignment order may be ordered at the time of trial or entry of a judgment ordering health insurance coverage. The order operates as an assignment and is binding on any existing or future employer of the obligor parent, or other person providing health insurance to the obligor, upon whom a copy of the order has been served.

(b) The order of assignment may be modified at any time by the court. *(Stats.1992, c. 162 (A.B.2650), § 10, operative Jan. 1, 1994. Amended by Stats.1994, c. 1269 (A.B.2208), § 39.)*

§ 3764. Effective date of assignment; copy of order and information to obligor; service of assignment order

(a) A health insurance coverage assignment order does not become effective until 20 days after service by the applicant of the assignment order on the employer.

(b) Within 10 days after service of the order, the employer or other person providing health insurance to the obligor shall deliver a copy of the order to the obligor, together with a written statement of the obligor's rights and the relevant procedures under the law to move to quash the order.

(c) Service of a health insurance coverage assignment order on any employer or other person providing health insurance may be made by first class mail in the manner prescribed in Section 1013 of the Code of Civil Procedure. *(Stats.1992, c. 162 (A.B.2650), § 10, operative Jan. 1, 1994. Amended by Stats.1994, c. 1269 (A.B.2208), § 40.)*

§ 3765. Motion to quash assignment; grounds

(a) The obligor may move to quash a health insurance coverage assignment order as provided in this section if the obligor declares under penalty of perjury that there is error on any of the following grounds:

(1) No order to maintain health insurance has been issued under Article 1 (commencing with Section 3750).

(2) The amount to be withheld for premiums is greater than that permissible under Article 1 (commencing with Section 3750) or greater than the amount otherwise ordered by the court.

(3) The amount of the increased premium is unreasonable.

(4) The alleged obligor is not the obligor from whom health insurance coverage is due.

(5) The child is or will be otherwise provided health care coverage.

(6) The employer's choice of coverage is inappropriate.

(b) The motion and notice of motion to quash the assignment order, including the declaration required by subdivision (a), shall be filed with the court issuing the assignment order within 15 days after delivery of a copy of the order to the obligor pursuant to subdivision (b) of Section 3764. The court clerk shall set the motion for hearing not less than 15 days, nor more than 30 days, after receipt of the notice of motion. The clerk shall, within five days after receipt of the notice of motion, deliver a copy of the notice of motion to (1) the district attorney personally or by first-class mail, and (2) the applicant and the employer or other person providing health insurance, at the appropriate addresses contained in the application, by first-class mail.

(c) Upon a finding of error described in subdivision (a), the court shall quash the assignment. *(Stats.1992, c. 162 (A.B.2650), § 10, operative Jan. 1, 1994. Amended by Stats.1994, c. 1269 (A.B.2208), § 41.)*

§ 3766. Commencement of coverage; selection of plan

(a) The employer, or other person providing health insurance, shall take steps to commence coverage, consistent with the order for the health insurance coverage assignment, within 30 days after service of the assignment order upon the obligor under Section 3764 unless the employer or other person providing health insurance coverage receives an order issued pursuant to Section 3765 to quash the health insurance coverage assignment. The employer, or the person providing health insurance, shall commence coverage at the earliest possible time and, if applicable, consistent with the group plan enrollment rules.

(b) If the obligor has made a selection of health coverage prior to the issuance of the court order, the selection shall not be superseded unless the child to be enrolled in the plan will not be provided benefits or coverage where the child resides or the court order specifically directs other health coverage.

(c) If the obligor has not enrolled in an available health plan, there is a choice of coverage, and the court has not ordered coverage by a specific plan, the employer or other person providing health insurance shall enroll the child in the plan that will provide reasonable benefits or coverage where the child resides. If that coverage is not available, the employer or other person providing health insurance shall, within 20 days, return the assignment order to the attorney or person initiating the assignment.

(d) If an assignment order is served on an employer or other person providing health insurance and no coverage is available for the supported child, the employer or other person shall, within 20 days, return the assignment to the attorney or person initiating the assignment. *(Stats.1992, c. 162 (A.B.2650), § 10, operative Jan. 1, 1994. Amended by Stats.1994, c. 1269 (A.B.2208), § 42; Stats.2002, c. 927 (A.B.3032), § 2.)*

§ 3767. Duties of employer or health insurance provider

The employer or other person providing health insurance shall do all of the following:

(a) Notify the applicant for the assignment order or notice of assignment of the commencement date of the coverage of the child.

(b) Provide evidence of coverage and any information necessary for the child to obtain benefits through the coverage to both parents or the person having custody of the child and to the local child support agency when requested by the local child support agency.

(c) Upon request by the parents or person having custody of the child, provide all forms and other documentation necessary for the purpose of submitting claims to the insurance carrier which the employer or other person providing health insurance usually provides to insureds. *(Stats.1992, c. 162 (A.B.2650), § 10, operative Jan. 1, 1994. Amended by Stats.1996, c. 1062 (A.B.1832), § 3; Stats.1997, c. 599 (A.B.573), § 8; Stats.2001, c. 755 (S.B.943), § 3, eff. Oct. 12, 2001.)*

§ 3768. Failure to comply with a valid assignment order; liability

(a) An employer or other person providing health insurance who willfully fails to comply with a valid health insurance coverage assignment order entered and served on the employer or other person pursuant to this article is liable to the applicant for the amount incurred in health care services that would otherwise have been covered under the insurance policy but for the conduct of the employer or other person that was contrary to the assignment order.

(b) Willful failure of an employer or other person providing health insurance to comply with a health insurance coverage assignment order is punishable as contempt of court under Section 1218 of the Code of Civil Procedure. *(Stats.1992, c. 162 (A.B.2650), § 10, operative Jan. 1, 1994. Amended by Stats.1994, c. 1269 (A.B.2208), § 43.)*

§ 3769. Discrimination prohibited; violation; penalty

No employer shall use a health insurance coverage assignment order as grounds for refusing to hire a person or for discharging or taking disciplinary action against an employee. An employer who violates this section may be assessed a civil penalty of a maximum of five hundred dollars ($500). *(Stats.1992, c. 162 (A.B.2650), § 10, operative Jan. 1, 1994. Amended by Stats.1994, c. 1269 (A.B.2208), § 44.)*

§ 3770. Termination of assignment order; grounds

Upon notice of motion by the obligor, the court shall terminate a health insurance coverage assignment order if any of the following conditions exist:

(a) A new order has been issued under Article 1 (commencing with Section 3750) that is inconsistent with the existing assignment.

(b) The employer or other person providing health insurance has discontinued that coverage to the obligor.

(c) The court determines that there is good cause, consistent with Section 3762, to terminate the assignment.

(d) The death or emancipation of the child for whom the health insurance has been obtained. *(Stats.1992, c. 162 (A.B.2650), § 10, operative Jan. 1, 1994. Amended by Stats.1994, c. 1269 (A.B.2208), § 45.)*

§ 3771. Information provided to the local child support agency

Upon request of the local child support agency the employer shall provide the following information to the local child support agency within 30 days:

(a) The social security number of the absent parent.

(b) The home address of the absent parent.

(c) Whether the absent parent has a health insurance policy and, if so, the policy names and numbers, and the names of the persons covered.

(d) Whether the health insurance policy provides coverage for dependent children of the absent parent who do not reside in the absent parent's home.

(e) If there is a subsequent lapse in health insurance coverage, the employer shall notify the local child support agency, giving the date the coverage ended, the reason for the lapse in coverage and, if the lapse is temporary, the date upon which coverage is expected to resume. *(Stats. 1992, c. 162 (A.B.2650), § 10, operative Jan. 1, 1994. Amended by Stats.2000, c. 808 (A.B.1358), § 32, eff. Sept. 28, 2000.)*

§ 3772. Forms; adoption by judicial council

The Judicial Council shall adopt forms for the health insurance coverage assignment required or authorized by this article, including, but not limited to, the application, the order, the statement of the obligor's rights, and an employer's return form which shall include information on the limitations on the total amount that may be withheld from earnings for obligations, including health insurance assignments, under subdivision (a) of Section 706.052 of the Code of Civil Procedure and Section 1673 of Title 15 of the United States Code, and the information required by Section 3771. The parties and child shall be sufficiently identified on the forms by the inclusion of birth dates, social security numbers, and any other information the Judicial Council determines is necessary. *(Stats.1992, c. 162 (A.B.2650), § 10, operative Jan. 1, 1994. Amended by Stats.1994, c. 1269 (A.B.2208), § 46.)*

§ 3773. Title IV–D cases where support enforcement services are provided by local child support agency

(a) This section applies only to Title IV–D cases where support enforcement services are being provided by the local child support agency pursuant to Section 17400.

(b) After the court has ordered that a parent provide health insurance coverage, the local child support agency shall serve on the employer a national medical support notice in lieu of the health insurance coverage assignment order. The national medical support notice may be combined with the order/notice to withhold income for child support that is authorized by Section 5246.

(c) A national medical support notice shall have the same force and effect as a health insurance coverage assignment order.

(d) The obligor shall have the same right to move to quash or terminate a national medical support notice as provided in this article for a health insurance coverage assignment order.

(Added by Stats.1997, c. 599 (A.B.573), § 9. Amended by Stats.1998, c. 858 (A.B.2169), § 1; Stats.2000, c. 119 (S.B.2045), § 2.)

Part 5

ENFORCEMENT OF SUPPORT ORDERS

CHAPTER 1.   GENERAL PROVISIONS

Section
4505.   Default due to unemployment; allegation by parent; list of places applied for employment; San Mateo County pilot project.

Section
4505. Default due to unemployment; allegation by parent; list of places applied for employment.

§ 4505. Default due to unemployment; allegation by parent; list of places applied for employment; San Mateo County pilot project

Text of section operative until Jan. 1, 2011.

(a) A court may require a parent who alleges that the parent's default in a child or family support order is due to the parent's unemployment to submit to the appropriate child support enforcement agency or any other entity designated by the court, including, but not limited to, the court itself, each two weeks, or at a frequency deemed appropriate by the court, a list of at least five different places the parent has applied for employment.

(b)(1) The Superior Court of the County of San Mateo may order a parent, concurrent with an initial order for the parent to pay child support, to submit to the appropriate child support enforcement agency or any other entity designated by the court, each two weeks, or at a frequency deemed appropriate by the court, a list of at least five different places the parent has applied for employment during the previous two-week period or other designated interval. The court may issue that order only upon the filing of a declaration by a child support enforcement officer of the local child support enforcement agency satisfying the following conditions:

(A) The declaration states that the child support enforcement officer has conducted an evaluation of the income and earning ability of the parent.

(B) The declaration details the communication, if any, between the obligor and the child support enforcement officer or the San Mateo County child support enforcement agency.

(C) The declaration states both of the following:

(i) The child support enforcement officer believes that, unless ordered by the court to seek employment under this subdivision, the parent would ignore the child support order and would be likely to default on his or her child support obligation.

(ii) The reasons for that belief.

(2) The Superior Court of the County of San Mateo shall not issue a citation for contempt for the failure of a parent to comply with an order issued pursuant to paragraph (1) unless the parent has become delinquent in his or her child support payments.

(3) The San Mateo County child support enforcement agency shall report to the department and the appropriate committees of the Legislature, on or before January 1, 2010, on the cost and performance of the pilot program described in this subdivision, including both of the following:

(A) The number of parents issued contempt citations and the effect of the citation on their employment status and support payments.

(B) The unemployment rate of, and the amount of support collected from, parents who are ordered to seek work pursuant to this subdivision compared with the unemployment rate of, and amount of support collected from, parents who are not subject to these orders.

(4) All costs related to the pilot program established in this subdivision shall be borne by the County of San Mateo.

(c) This section shall remain in effect only until January 1, 2011, and as of that date is repealed, unless a later enacted statute, that is enacted before January 1, 2011, deletes or extends that date. *(Stats.1992, c. 162 (A.B.2650), § 10, operative Jan. 1, 1994. Amended by Stats.2007, c. 249 (S.B.523), § 1.)*

Repeal

For repeal of this section, see its terms.

For text of section operative Jan. 1, 2011, see Family Code § 4505, post.

§ 4505. Default due to unemployment; allegation by parent; list of places applied for employment

Text of section operative Jan. 1, 2011.

(a) A court may require a parent who alleges that the parent's default in a child or family support order is due to the parent's unemployment to submit to the appropriate child support enforcement agency or any other entity designated by the court, including, but not limited to, the court itself, each two weeks, or at a frequency deemed appropriate by the court, a list of at least five different places the parent has applied for employment.

(b) This section shall become operative on January 1, 2011. *(Added by Stats.2007, c. 249 (S.B.523), § 2, operative Jan. 1, 2011.)*

For text of section operative until Jan. 1, 2011, see Family Code § 4505, ante.

CHAPTER 8. EARNINGS ASSIGNMENT ORDER

ARTICLE 1. DEFINITIONS

Section
5200. Construction of chapter.
5201. Arrearage; arrearages.
5202. Assignment order; earnings assignment order for support.
5204. Due date of support payments.
5206. Earnings.
5208. Earnings assignment order for support.
5210. Employer.
5212. IV-D Case.
5214. Obligee; assigned obligee.
5216. Obligor.
5220. Timely payment.

§ 5200. Construction of chapter

Unless the provision or context otherwise requires, the definitions in this article govern the construction of this chapter. *(Stats.1992, c. 162 (A.B.2650), § 10, operative Jan. 1, 1994.)*

§ 5201. Arrearage; arrearages

"Arrearage" or "arrearages" is the amount necessary to satisfy a support judgment or order pursuant to Section 695.210 of the Code of Civil Procedure. *(Added by Stats.1997, c. 599 (A.B.573), § 21.)*

§ 5202. Assignment order; earnings assignment order for support

"Assignment order" has the same meaning as "earnings assignment order for support." *(Stats.1992, c. 162 (A.B.2650), § 10, operative Jan. 1, 1994.)*

§ 5204. Due date of support payments

"Due date of support payments" is the date specifically stated in the order of support or, if no date is stated in the support order, the last day of the month in which the support payment is to be paid. *(Stats.1992, c. 162 (A.B.2650), § 10, operative Jan. 1, 1994.)*

§ 5206. Earnings

"Earnings," to the extent that they are subject to an earnings assignment order for support under Chapter 4 (commencing with Section 703.010) of Division 2 of Title 9 of Part 2 of the Code of Civil Procedure, include:

(a) Wages, salary, bonus, money, and benefits described in Sections 704.110, 704.113, and 704.115 of the Code of Civil Procedure.

(b) Payments due for services of independent contractors, interest, dividends, rents, royalties, residuals, patent rights, or mineral or other natural resource rights.

(c) Payments or credits due or becoming due as a result of written or oral contracts for services or sales whether denominated as wages, salary, commission, bonus, or otherwise.

(d) Payments due for workers' compensation temporary disability benefits.

(e) Payments due as a result of disability from benefits described in Section 704.130 of the Code of Civil Procedure.

(f) Any other payments or credits due or becoming due, regardless of source. *(Stats.1992, c. 162 (A.B.2650), § 10, operative Jan. 1, 1994. Amended by Stats.1993, c. 219 (A.B.1500), § 152.5; Stats.1997, c. 599 (A.B.573), § 22.)*

§ 5208. Earnings assignment order for support

(a) "Earnings assignment order for support" means an order that assigns to an obligee a portion of the earnings of a support obligor due or to become due in the future.

(b) Commencing January 1, 2000, all earnings assignment orders for support in any action in which child support or family support is ordered shall be issued on an "order/notice to withhold income for child support" mandated by Section 666 of Title 42 of the United States

Code. *(Stats.1992, c. 162 (A.B.2650), § 10, operative Jan. 1, 1994. Amended by Stats.1999, c. 480 (S.B.542), § 1.)*

§ 5210. Employer

"Employer" includes all of the following:

(a) A person for whom an individual performs services as an employee, as defined in Section 706.011 of the Code of Civil Procedure.

(b) The United States government and any public entity as defined in Section 811.2 of the Government Code.

(c) Any person or entity paying earnings as defined under Section 5206. *(Stats.1992, c. 162 (A.B.2650), § 10, operative Jan. 1, 1994.)*

§ 5212. IV–D Case

"IV–D Case" means any case being established, modified, or enforced by the local child support agency pursuant to Section 654 of Title 42 of the United States Code (Section 454 of the Social Security Act). *(Stats. 1992, c. 162 (A.B.2650), § 10, operative Jan. 1, 1994. Amended by Stats.1999, c. 480 (S.B.542), § 2.)*

§ 5214. Obligee; assigned obligee

"Obligee" or "assigned obligee" means either the person to whom support has been ordered to be paid, the local child support agency, or other person designated by the court to receive the payment. The local child support agency is the obligee for all Title IV–D cases as defined under Section 5212 or in which an application for services has been filed under Part D (commencing with Section 651) and Part E (commencing with Section 670) of Subchapter IV of Chapter 7 of Title 42 of the United States Code (Title IV–D or IV–E of the Social Security Act). *(Stats.1992, c. 162 (A.B.2650), § 10, operative Jan. 1, 1994. Amended by Stats.2000, c. 808 (A.B.1358), § 57, eff. Sept. 28, 2000; Stats.2001, c. 755 (S.B.943), § 7, eff. Oct. 12, 2001.)*

§ 5216. Obligor

"Obligor" means a person owing a duty of support. *(Stats.1992, c. 162 (A.B.2650), § 10, operative Jan. 1, 1994.)*

§ 5220. Timely payment

"Timely payment" means receipt of support payments by the obligee or assigned obligee within five days of the due date. *(Stats.1992, c. 162 (A.B.2650), § 10, operative Jan. 1, 1994.)*

ARTICLE 2.   GENERAL PROVISIONS

Section
5230.   Support orders; inclusion of earnings assignment order.
5230.1. Earning assignment or income withholding order of another state; enforceability; applicable law.
5230.5. Allegation of child support arrearage amount; perjury.

Section
5231. Binding effect of assignment order upon employers.
5232. Service of order on employer.
5233. Commencement of withholding.
5234. Delivery to obligor by employer; copy of order; statement of rights.
5235. Duties of employer; withholding and forwarding of support; liability.
5236. Simplification of wage withholding.
5237. Notice of obligee of change of address; effect of failure to notify.
5238. Assignments including both current support and arrearages; priority; multiple assignment orders for the same employee; proration of withheld payments.
5239. Arrearages of payment; computation.
5240. Payment of past due support; termination of service of order of assignment; grounds.
5241. Wilful failure to withhold or forward support, penalties; actions to collect withheld sums not forwarded; electronic transfer and employer awareness.
5242. Lien on earnings; service of order.
5243. Priority of order.
5244. Local child support agency; enforcement or collection duties.
5245. Enforcement of support obligations; authority of local child support agency to use civil and criminal remedies.
5246. Assignment of earnings; notice to employer; employer's duties; application of section.
5247. Civil liability of local child support agency or employer.

§ 5230. Support orders; inclusion of earnings assignment order

(a) When the court orders a party to pay an amount for support or orders a modification of the amount of support to be paid, the court shall include in its order an earnings assignment order for support that orders the employer of the obligor to pay to the obligee that portion of the obligor's earnings due or to become due in the future as will be sufficient to pay an amount to cover both of the following:

(1) The amount ordered by the court for support.

(2) An amount which shall be ordered by the court to be paid toward the liquidation of any arrearage.

(b) An earnings assignment order for support shall be issued, and shall be effective and enforceable pursuant to Section 5231, notwithstanding the absence of the name, address, or other identifying information regarding the obligor's employer. *(Stats.1992, c. 162 (A.B.2650), § 10, operative Jan. 1, 1994. Amended by Stats.1993, c. 876 (S.B.1068), § 22.5, eff. Oct. 6, 1993, operative Jan. 1, 1994; Stats.1997, c. 599 (A.B.573), § 23; Stats.2000, c. 808 (A.B.1358), § 57.3, eff. Sept. 28, 2000.)*

§ 5230.1. Earning assignment or income withholding order of another state; enforceability; applicable law

(a) An earnings assignment or income withholding order for support issued by a court or administrative agency of another state is binding upon an employer of the obligor to the same extent as an earnings assignment order made by a court of this state.

(b) When an employer receives an earnings assignment order or an income withholding order for support from a court or administrative agency in another state, all of the provisions of this chapter shall apply. *(Added by Stats.1997, c. 599 (A.B.573), § 24.)*

§ 5230.5. Allegation of child support arrearage amount; perjury

Any obligee alleging arrearages in child support shall specify the amount thereof under penalty of perjury. *(Added by Stats.1994, c. 1140 (S.B.279), § 2.)*

§ 5231. Binding effect of assignment order upon employers

Unless stayed pursuant to Article 4 (commencing with Section 5260), an assignment order is effective and binding upon any existing or future employer of the obligor upon whom a copy of the order is served in compliance with Sections 5232 and 5233, notwithstanding the absence of the name, address, or other identifying information regarding the obligor's employer, or the inclusion of incorrect information regarding the support obligor's employer. *(Stats.1992, c. 162 (A.B.2650), § 10, operative Jan. 1, 1994. Amended by Stats.2000, c. 808 (A.B.1358), § 57.5, eff. Sept. 28, 2000.)*

§ 5232. Service of order on employer

Service on an employer of an assignment order may be made by first-class mail in the manner prescribed in Section 1013 of the Code of Civil Procedure. The obligee shall serve the documents specified in Section 5234. *(Stats.1992, c. 162 (A.B.2650), § 10, operative Jan. 1, 1994. Amended by Stats.1997, c. 599 (A.B.573), § 25.)*

§ 5233. Commencement of withholding

Unless the order states a later date, beginning as soon as possible after service of the order on the employer but not later than 10 days after service of the order on the employer, the employer shall commence withholding pursuant to the assignment order from all earnings payable to the employee. *(Stats.1992, c. 162 (A.B.2650), § 10, operative Jan. 1, 1994.)*

§ 5234. Delivery to obligor by employer; copy of order; statement of rights

Within 10 days of service of an assignment order or an order/notice to withhold income for child support on an employer, the employer shall deliver both of the following to the obligor:

(a) A copy of the assignment order or the order/notice to withhold income for child support.

(b) A written statement of the obligor's rights under the law to seek to quash, modify, or stay service of the earnings assignment order, together with a blank form that the obligor can file with the court to request a hearing to quash, modify, or stay service of the earnings assignment order with instructions on how to file the form and obtain a hearing date.

(Stats.1992, c. 162 (A.B.2650), § 10, operative Jan. 1, 1994. Amended by Stats.1997, c. 599 (A.B.573), § 26; Stats.1999, c. 480 (S.B.542), § 3.)

§ 5235. Duties of employer; withholding and forwarding of support; liability

(a) The employer shall continue to withhold and forward support as required by the assignment order until served with notice terminating the assignment order. If an employer withholds support as required by the assignment order, the obligor shall not be held in contempt or subject to criminal prosecution for nonpayment of the support that was withheld by the employer but not received by the obligee. If the employer withheld the support but failed to forward the payments to the obligee, the employer shall be liable for the payments, including interest, as provided in Section 5241.

(b) Within 10 days of service of a substitution of payee on the employer, the employer shall forward all subsequent support to the governmental entity or other payee that sent the substitution.

(c) The employer shall send the amounts withheld to the obligee within the timeframe specified in federal law and shall report to the obligee the date on which the amount was withheld from the obligor's wages.

(d) The employer may deduct from the earnings of the employee the sum of one dollar and fifty cents ($1.50) for each payment made pursuant to the order.

(e) Once the State Disbursement Unit as required by Section 17309 is operational, the employer shall send all earnings withheld pursuant to this chapter to the State Disbursement Unit instead of the obligee. *(Stats.1992, c. 162 (A.B.2650), § 10, operative Jan. 1, 1994. Amended by Stats.1993, c. 876 (S.B.1068), § 23, eff. Oct. 6, 1993, operative Jan. 1, 1994; Stats.1994, c. 1269 (A.B.2208), § 50.2; Stats.1997, c. 599 (A.B.573), § 27; Stats.1998, c. 854 (A.B.960), § 4; Stats.2000, c. 808 (A.B.1358), § 58, eff. Sept. 28, 2000; Stats.2003, c. 387 (A.B.739), § 5; Stats.2004, c. 520 (A.B.2530), § 3.)*

§ 5236. Simplification of wage withholding

The state agency or the local agency, designated to enforce support obligations as required by federal law, shall allow employers to simplify the process of assignment order withholding by forwarding, as ordered by the court, the amounts of support withheld under more than one order in a consolidated check, accompanied by an itemized accounting providing names, social security number or other identifying number, and the amount attributable to each obligor. *(Stats.1992, c. 162 (A.B. 2650), § 10, operative Jan. 1, 1994.)*

§ 5237. Notice of obligee of change of address; effect of failure to notify

(a) Except as provided in subdivisions (b) and (c), the obligee shall notify the employer of the obligor, by first-class mail, postage prepaid, of any change of address within a reasonable period of time after the change.

(b) Where payments have been ordered to be made to a county officer designated by the court, the obligee who is the parent, guardian, or other person entitled to receive payment through the designated county officer shall notify the designated county officer by first-class mail, postage prepaid, of any address change within a reasonable period of time after the change.

(c) If the obligee is receiving support payments from the State Disbursement Unit as required by Section 17309, the obligee shall notify the State Disbursement Unit instead of the employer of the obligor as provided in subdivision (a).

(d)(1) Except as set forth in paragraph (2), if the employer, designated county officer, or the State Disbursement Unit is unable to deliver payments under the assignment order for a period of six months due to the failure of the obligee to notify the employer, designated county officer, or State Disbursement Unit, of a change of address, the employer, designated county officer, or State Disbursement Unit shall not make any further payments under the assignment order and shall return all undeliverable payments to the obligor.

(2) If payments are being directed to the State Disbursement Unit pursuant to subdivision (e) of Section 5235, but the case is not otherwise receiving services from the Title IV–D agency, and the State Disbursement Unit is unable to deliver payments under the assignment order for a period of 45 days due to the failure of the obligee to notify the employer, designated county officer, or State Disbursement Unit of a change of address, the Title IV–D agency shall take the following actions:

(A) Immediately return the undeliverable payments to the obligor if the obligee cannot be located.

(B) Notify the employer to suspend withholding pursuant to the wage assignment until the employer or Title IV–D agency is notified of the obligee's whereabouts. *(Stats.1992, c. 162 (A.B.2650), § 10, operative Jan. 1, 1994. Amended by Stats.1997, c. 599 (A.B.573), § 28; Stats. 2000, c. 808 (A.B.1358), § 59, eff. Sept. 28, 2000; Stats. 2003, c. 387 (A.B.739), § 6; Stats.2004, c. 806 (A.B.2358), § 1.)*

§ 5238. Assignments including both current support and arrearages; priority; multiple assignment orders for the same employee; proration of withheld payments

(a) Where an assignment order or assignment orders include both current support and payments towards the liquidation of arrearages, priority shall be given first to the current child support obligation, then the current spousal support obligation, and thereafter to the liquidation of child and then spousal support arrearages.

(b) Where there are multiple assignment orders for the same employee, the employer shall prorate the withheld payments as follows:

(1) If the obligor has more than one assignment for support, the employer shall add together the amount of support due for each assignment.

(2) If 50 percent of the obligor's net disposable earnings will not pay in full all of the assignments for support, the employer shall prorate it first among all of the current support assignments in the same proportion that each assignment bears to the total current support owed.

(3) The employer shall apply any remainder to the assignments for arrearage support in the same proportion that each assignment bears to the total arrearage owed. *(Stats.1992, c. 162 (A.B.2650), § 10, operative Jan. 1, 1994. Amended by Stats.1997, c. 599 (A.B.573), § 29.)*

§ 5239. Arrearages of payment; computation

Arrearages of support payments shall be computed on the basis of the payments owed and unpaid on the date that the obligor has been given notice of the assignment order as required by Section 5234. *(Stats.1992, c. 162 (A.B.2650), § 10, operative Jan. 1, 1994.)*

§ 5240. Payment of past due support; termination of service of order of assignment; grounds

Upon the filing and service of a motion and a notice of motion by the obligor, the court shall terminate the service of an assignment order if past due support has been paid in full, including any interest due, and if any of the following conditions exist:

(a) With regard to orders for spousal support, the death or remarriage of the spouse to whom support is owed.

(b) With regard to orders for child support, the death or emancipation of the child for whom support is owed.

(c) The court determines that there is good cause, as defined in Section 5260, to terminate the assignment order. This subdivision does not apply if there has been more than one application for an assignment order.

(d) The obligor meets the conditions of an alternative arrangement specified in paragraph (2) of subdivision (b) of Section 5260, and a wage assignment has not been previously terminated and subsequently initiated.

(e) There is no longer a current order for support.

(f) The termination of the stay of an assignment order under Section 5261 was improper, but only if that termination was based upon the obligor's failure to make timely support payments as described in subdivision (b) of Section 5261.

(g) The employer or agency designated to provide services under Title IV–D of the Social Security Act or the State Disbursement Unit is unable to deliver payment for a period of six months due to the failure of the obligee to notify that employer or agency or the State Disbursement Unit of a change in the obligee's address. *(Stats. 1992, c. 162 (A.B.2650), § 10, operative Jan. 1, 1994. Amended by Stats.1993, c. 876 (S.B.1068), § 24, eff. Oct. 6,*

1993, operative Jan. 1, 1994; Stats.1997, c. 599 (A.B.573), § 30; Stats.2003, c. 387 (A.B.739), § 7.)

§ 5241. Wilful failure to withhold or forward support; penalties; actions to collect withheld sums not forwarded; electronic transfer and employer awareness

(a) An employer who willfully fails to withhold and forward support pursuant to a currently valid assignment order entered and served upon the employer pursuant to this chapter is liable to the obligee for the amount of support not withheld, forwarded, or otherwise paid to the obligee, including any interest thereon.

(b) If an employer withholds support as required by the assignment order, the obligor shall not be held in contempt or subject to criminal prosecution for nonpayment of the support that was withheld by the employer but not received by the obligee. In addition, the employer is liable to the obligee for any interest incurred as a result of the employer's failure to timely forward the withheld support pursuant to an assignment earnings order.

(c) In addition to any other penalty or liability provided by law, willful failure by an employer to comply with an assignment order is punishable as a contempt pursuant to Section 1218 of the Code of Civil Procedure.

(d) If an employer withholds support, as required by the assignment order, but fails to forward the support to the obligee, the local child support agency shall take appropriate action to collect the withheld sums from the employer. The child support obligee or the local child support agency upon application may obtain an order requiring payment of support by electronic transfer from the employer's bank account if the employer has willfully failed to comply with the assignment order or if the employer has failed to comply with the assignment order on three separate occasions within a 12 month period. Where a court finds that an employer has willfully failed to comply with the assignment order or has otherwise failed to comply with the assignment order on three separate occasions within a 12–month period, the court may impose a civil penalty, in addition to any other penalty required by law, of up to 50 percent of the support amount that has not been received by the obligee.

(e) To facilitate employer awareness, the local child support agency shall make reasonable efforts to notify any employer subject to an assignment order pursuant to this chapter of the electronic fund transfer provision and enhanced penalties provided by this act.

(f) Notwithstanding any other provision of law, any penalty payable pursuant to this subdivision shall be payable directly to the obligee. The local child support agency shall not be required to establish or collect this penalty on behalf of the obligee. The penalty shall not be included when determining the income of the obligee for the purpose of determining the eligibility of the obligee for benefits payable pursuant to state supplemental income programs. A court may issue the order requiring payment of support by electronic transfer from the employer's bank account and impose the penalty described in this subdivision, after notice and hearing. This provision shall not be construed to expand or limit the duties and obligations of the Labor Commissioner, as set forth in Section 200 and following of the Labor Code. *(Stats.1992, c. 162 (A.B.2650), § 10, operative Jan. 1, 1994. Amended by Stats.1993, c. 745 (S.B.788), § 2; Stats.1993, c. 876 (S.B.1068), § 25, eff. Oct. 6, 1993, operative Jan. 1, 1994; Stats.1998, c. 854 (A.B.960), § 5; Stats.2000, c. 808 (A.B.1358), § 60, eff. Sept. 28, 2000; Stats.2001, c. 371 (A.B.1426), § 1; Stats.2003, c. 308 (A.B.738), § 2.)*

§ 5242. Lien on earnings; service of order

Service of the assignment order creates a lien on the earnings of the employee and the property of the employer to the same extent as the service of an earnings withholding order as provided in Section 706.029 of the Code of Civil Procedure. *(Stats.1992, c. 162 (A.B.2650), § 10, operative Jan. 1, 1994.)*

§ 5243. Priority of order

An assignment order for support has priority as against any attachment, execution, or other assignment as specified in Section 706.031 of the Code of Civil Procedure. *(Stats.1992, c. 162 (A.B.2650), § 10, operative Jan. 1, 1994. Amended by Stats.1993, c. 876 (S.B.1068), § 26, eff. Oct. 6, 1993, operative Jan. 1, 1994.)*

§ 5244. Local child support agency; enforcement or collection duties

A reference to the local child support agency in this chapter applies only when the local child support agency is otherwise ordered or required to act pursuant to law. Nothing in this chapter shall be deemed to mandate additional enforcement or collection duties upon the local child support agency beyond those otherwise imposed by law. *(Stats.1992, c. 162 (A.B.2650), § 10, operative Jan. 1, 1994. Amended by Stats.2000, c. 808 (A.B.1358), § 61, eff. Sept. 28, 2000.)*

§ 5245. Enforcement of support obligations; authority of local child support agency to use civil and criminal remedies

Nothing in this chapter limits the authority of the local child support agency to use any other civil and criminal remedies to enforce support obligations, regardless of whether or not the child or the obligee who is the parent, guardian, or other person entitled to receive payment is the recipient of welfare moneys. *(Stats.1992, c. 162 (A.B.2650), § 10, operative Jan. 1, 1994. Amended by Stats.1993, c. 219 (A.B.1500), § 153; Stats.2000, c. 808 (A.B.1358), § 62, eff. Sept. 28, 2000.)*

§ 5246. Assignment of earnings; notice to employer; employer's duties; application of section

(a) This section applies only to Title IV–D cases where support enforcement services are being provided by the local child support agency pursuant to Section 17400.

(b) In lieu of an earnings assignment order signed by a judicial officer, the local child support agency may serve on the employer a notice of assignment in the manner specified in Section 5232. An order/notice to withhold income for child support shall have the same force and effect as an earnings assignment order signed by a judicial officer. An order/notice to withhold income for child support, when used under this section, shall be considered a notice and shall not require the signature of a judicial officer.

(c) Pursuant to Section 666 of Title 42 of the United States Code, the federally mandated order/notice to withhold income for child support shall be used for the purposes described in this section.

(d)(1) An order/notice to withhold income may not reduce the current amount withheld for court-ordered child support.

(2) If the underlying court order for support does not provide for an arrearage payment, or if an additional arrearage accrues after the date of the court order for support, the local child support agency may send an order/notice to withhold income for child support that shall be used for the purposes described in this section directly to the employer which specifies the updated arrearage amount and directs the employer to withhold an additional amount to be applied towards liquidation of the arrearages not to exceed the maximum amount permitted by Section 1673(b) of Title 15 of the United States Code.

(3) Notwithstanding paragraph (2), if an obligor is disabled, meets the SSI resource test, and is receiving Supplemental Security Income/State Supplementary Payments (SSI/SSP) or, but for excess income as described in Section 416.1100 et seq. of Part 416 of Title 20 of the Code of Federal Regulations, would be eligible to receive SSI/SSP, pursuant to Section 12200 of the Welfare and Institutions Code, and the obligor has supplied the local child support agency with proof of his or her eligibility for and, if applicable, receipt of, SSI/SSP or Social Security Disability Insurance benefits, then the order/notice to withhold income issued by the local child support agency for the liquidation of the arrearage shall not exceed 5 percent of the obligor's total monthly Social Security Disability payments under Title II of the Social Security Act.

(e) If the obligor requests a hearing, a hearing date shall be scheduled within 20 days of the filing of the request with the court. The clerk of the court shall provide notice of the hearing to the local child support agency and the obligor no later than 10 days prior to the hearing.

(1) If at the hearing the obligor establishes that he or she is not the obligor or good cause or an alternative arrangement as provided in Section 5260, the court may order that service of the order/notice to withhold income for child support be quashed. If the court quashes service of the order/notice to withhold income for child

support, the local child support agency shall notify the employer within 10 days.

(2) If the obligor contends at the hearing that the payment of arrearages at the rate specified in the order/notice to withhold income for child support is excessive or that the total arrearages owing is incorrect, and if it is determined that payment of the arrearages at the rate specified in this section creates an undue hardship upon the obligor or that the withholding would exceed the maximum amount permitted by Section 1673(b) of Title 15 of the United States Code Annotated, the rate at which the arrearages must be paid shall be reduced to a rate that is fair and reasonable considering the circumstances of the parties and the best interest of the child. If it is determined at a hearing that the total amount of arrearages calculated is erroneous, the court shall modify the amount calculated to the correct amount. If the court modifies the total amount of arrearages owed or reduces the monthly payment due on the arrearages, the local child support agency shall serve the employer with an amended order/notice to withhold income for child support within 10 days.

(f) If an obligor's current support obligation has terminated by operation of law, the local child support agency may serve an order/notice to withhold income for child support on the employer which directs the employer to continue withholding from the obligor's earnings an amount to be applied towards liquidation of the arrearages, not to exceed the maximum amount permitted by Section 1673(b) of Title 15 of the United States Code, until such time that the employer is notified by the local child support agency that the arrearages have been paid in full. The employer shall provide the obligor with a copy of the order/notice to withhold income for child support and a blank form that the obligor may file with the court to request a hearing to modify or quash the assignment with instructions on how to file the form and obtain a hearing date. The obligor shall be entitled to the same rights to a hearing as specified in subdivision (e).

(g) The local child support agency shall retain a copy of the order/notice to withhold income for child support and shall file a copy with the court whenever a hearing concerning the order/notice to withhold income for child support is requested.

(h) The local child support agency may transmit an order/notice to withhold income for child support and other forms required by this section to the employer through electronic means. *(Added by Stats.1996, c. 957 (A.B.1058), § 8. Amended by Stats.1997, c. 599 (A.B. 573), § 31; Stats.1999, c. 480 (S.B.542), § 4; Stats.2000, c. 808 (A.B.1358), § 62.3, eff. Sept. 28, 2000; Stats.2001, c. 111 (A.B.429), § 1, eff. July 30, 2001; Stats.2001, c. 651 (A.B.891), § 2.)*

§ 5247. Civil liability of local child support agency or employer

Neither the local child support agency nor an employer shall be subject to any civil liability for any amount withheld and paid to the obligee, the local child support agency, or the State Disbursement Unit pursuant to an earnings assignment order or notice of assignment. *(Added by Stats.1997, c. 599 (A.B.573), § 32. Amended by Stats.2000, c. 808 (A.B.1358), § 63, eff. Sept. 28, 2000; Stats.2003, c. 387 (A.B.739), § 8.)*

ARTICLE 6. INFORMATION CONCERNING ADDRESS AND EMPLOYMENT OF OBLIGOR

Section
5280. Obligor's whereabouts or identity of employer unknown; duties of local child support agency.
5281. Duty of obligor to inform obligee of change of employment.
5282. Duty of employer to inform obligee of obligor's change of employment.

§ 5280. Obligor's whereabouts or identity of employer unknown; duties of local child support agency

If the obligee making the application under this chapter also states that the whereabouts of the obligor or the identity of the obligor's employer is unknown to the party to whom support has been ordered to be paid, the local child support agency shall do both of the following:

(a) Contact the California parent locator service maintained by the Department of Justice in the manner prescribed in Section 17506.

(b) Upon receiving the requested information, notify the court of the last known address of the obligor and the name and address of the obligor's last known employer. *(Stats.1992, c. 162 (A.B.2650), § 10, operative Jan. 1, 1994. Amended by Stats.2000, c. 808 (A.B.1358), § 67, eff. Sept. 28, 2000.)*

§ 5281. Duty of obligor to inform obligee of change of employment

An assignment order required or authorized by this chapter shall include a requirement that the obligor notify the obligee of any change of employment and of the name and address of the obligor's new employer within 10 days of obtaining new employment. *(Stats.1992, c. 162 (A.B.2650), § 10, operative Jan. 1, 1994.)*

§ 5282. Duty of employer to inform obligee of obligor's change of employment

After the obligor has left employment with the employer, the employer, at the time the next payment is due on the assignment order, shall notify the obligee designated in the assignment order by first-class mail, postage prepaid, to the last known address of the obligee that the obligor has left employment. *(Stats.1992, c. 162 (A.B. 2650), § 10, operative Jan. 1, 1994.)*

ARTICLE 7. PROHIBITED PRACTICES

Section
5290. Use of assignment order under chapter as basis of adverse employment action; violations; civil penalty.

§ 5290. Use of assignment order under chapter as basis of adverse employment action; violations; civil penalty

No employer shall use an assignment order authorized by this chapter as grounds for refusing to hire a person, or for discharging, taking disciplinary action against, denying a promotion to, or for taking any other action adversely affecting the terms and conditions of employment of, an employee. An employer who engages in the conduct prohibited by this section may be assessed a civil penalty of a maximum of five hundred dollars ($500). *(Stats. 1992, c. 162 (A.B.2650), § 10, operative Jan. 1, 1994. Amended by Stats.2004, c. 369 (A.B.1706), § 1.)*

Division 17

SUPPORT SERVICES

CHAPTER 2. CHILD SUPPORT ENFORCEMENT

ARTICLE 2. COLLECTIONS AND ENFORCEMENT

Section
17522.5. Issuance of levy or notice to withhold; liquidation of asset by person, financial institution, or securities intermediary in possession or control of financial asset; manner of liquidation and transfer of proceeds; value of financial assets exceeding total amount of support due; instructions for liquidation by obligor.

§ 17522.5. Issuance of levy or notice to withhold; liquidation of asset by person, financial institution, or securities intermediary in possession or control of financial asset; manner of liquidation and transfer of proceeds; value of financial assets exceeding total amount of support due; instructions for liquidation by obligor

(a) Notwithstanding Section 8112 of the Commercial Code and Section 700.130 of the Code of Civil Procedure, when a local child support agency pursuant to Section 17522, or the Franchise Tax Board pursuant to Section 18670 or 18670.5 of the Revenue and Taxation Code, or the department pursuant to Section 17454 or 17500, issues a levy upon, or requires by notice any employer, person, political officer or entity, or depository institution to withhold the amount of, as applicable, a financial asset for the purpose of collecting a delinquent child support obligation, the person, financial institution, or securities intermediary (as defined in Section 8102 of the Commercial Code) in possession or control of the financial asset shall liquidate the financial asset in a commercially reasonable manner within 20 days of the issuance of the levy or the notice to withhold. Within five days of liquidation, the person, financial institution, or securities intermediary shall transfer to the local child support agency, the Franchise Tax Board, or the department, as applicable, the proceeds of the liquidation, less any reasonable commissions or fees, or both, which are charged in the normal course of business.

(b) If the value of the financial assets exceed the total amount of support due, the obligor may, within 10 days after the service of the levy or notice to withhold upon the person, financial institution, or securities intermediary, instruct the person, financial institution, or securities intermediary who possesses or controls the financial assets as to which financial assets are to be sold to satisfy the obligation for delinquent support. If the obligor does not provide instructions for liquidation, the person, financial institution, or securities intermediary who possesses or controls the financial assets shall liquidate the financial assets in a commercially reasonable manner and in an amount sufficient to cover the obligation for delinquent child support, and any reasonable commissions or fees, or both, which are charged in the normal course of business, beginning with the financial assets purchased most recently.

(c) For the purposes of this section, a financial asset shall include, but not be limited to, an uncertificated security, certificated security, or security entitlement (as defined in Section 8102 of the Commercial Code), security (as defined in Section 8103 of the Commercial Code), or a securities account (as defined in Section 8501 of the Commercial Code). *(Added by Stats.2003, c. 225 (A.B.1752), § 5, eff. Aug. 11, 2003. Amended by Stats. 2004, c. 806 (A.B.2358), § 8.)*

FINANCIAL CODE

Division 2

SAVINGS ASSOCIATION LAW

CHAPTER 4. POWERS OF ASSOCIATIONS

ARTICLE 1. GENERAL POWERS

Section
6525. Delivery of fingerprints to law enforcement agencies; criminal history information.

§ 6525. Delivery of fingerprints to law enforcement agencies; criminal history information

(a) Notwithstanding the provisions of Sections 1051, 1052, and 1054 of the Labor Code and Section 2947 of the Penal Code, an association, a subsidiary or affiliate of an association, or any officer or employee thereof may deliver fingerprints taken of a director, an officer, an employee, or an applicant for employment to local, state, or federal law enforcement agencies for the purpose of obtaining information as to the existence and nature of a criminal record, if any, of the person fingerprinted relating to convictions, and to any arrest for which that person is released on bail or on his or her own recognizance pending trial, for the commission or attempted commission of a crime involving robbery, burglary, theft, embezzlement, fraud, forgery, bookmaking, receiving stolen property, counterfeiting, or involving checks or credit cards or using computers.

(b) The Department of Justice shall, pursuant to Section 11105 of the Penal Code, and a local agency may pursuant to Section 13300 of the Penal Code, furnish to the officer of the association or subsidiary or affiliate thereof responsible for the final decision regarding employment of the person fingerprinted, or to his or her designees having responsibilities for personnel or security decisions in the usual scope and course of their employment with the association, subsidiary, or affiliate summary criminal history information when requested pursuant to this section. If, upon evaluation of the criminal history information received pursuant to this section, the association, subsidiary, or affiliate determines that employment of the person fingerprinted would constitute an unreasonable risk to the association, subsidiary, or affiliate or its customers, the person fingerprinted may be denied employment.

(c) A request for records pursuant to this section made of the Department of Justice shall be on a form approved by the department. The department may charge a fee to be paid by the requesting association, subsidiary, or affiliate pursuant to subdivision (e) of Section 11105 of the Penal Code. No request shall be submitted without the written consent of the person fingerprinted.

(d) Any criminal history information obtained pursuant to this section is confidential and no recipient shall disclose its contents other than for the purpose for which it was acquired.

(e) "Affiliate," as used in this section, means any corporation controlling, controlled by, or under common control with, a savings association, whether directly, indirectly, or through one or more intermediaries. (Added by Stats.1983, c. 1091, § 2. Amended by Stats.1989, c. 868, § 6, eff. Sept. 26, 1989.)

Division 9

CALIFORNIA FINANCE LENDERS LAW

CHAPTER 1. GENERAL PROVISIONS

ARTICLE 4. REGULATIONS

Section
22168. Misleading the public regarding qualifications or experience; suspension or bar from employment; notice; hearing.

§ 22168. Misleading the public regarding qualifications or experience; suspension or bar from employment; notice; hearing

(a) The commissioner may, after appropriate notice and opportunity for hearing, suspend for a period not to exceed 12 months or bar a person from any position of employment with a licensee if the commissioner finds that the person has willfully used or claimed without authority a designation or certification of special education, practice, or skill that the person has not attained, or willfully held out to the public a confusingly similar designation or certification for the purpose of misleading the public regarding his or her qualifications or experience.

(b) Within 15 days from the date of a notice of intention to issue an order pursuant to subdivision (a), the person may request a hearing under the Administrative Procedure Act (Chapter 5 (commencing with Section 11500) of Part 1 of Division 3 of Title 2 of the

135

Government Code). Upon receiving a request, the matter shall be set for hearing to commence within 30 days after receipt unless the person subject to this division consents to a later date. If no hearing is requested within 15 days after the mailing or service of the notice and none is ordered by the commissioner, the failure to request a hearing shall constitute a waiver of the right to a hearing.

(c) Upon receipt of a notice of intention to issue an order pursuant to subdivision (a), the person who is the subject of the proposed order is immediately prohibited from engaging in any activities subject to licensure under this division.

(d) Persons suspended or barred under this section are prohibited from participating in any business activity of a licensed finance lender, broker, or mortgage loan originator, and from engaging in any business activity on the premises where a licensed finance lender, broker, or mortgage loan originator is conducting its business. This subdivision shall not be construed to prohibit suspended or barred persons from having their personal transactions processed by a licensed finance lender, broker, or mortgage loan originator. *(Added by Stats.2006, c. 201 (A.B.2890), § 1. Amended by Stats.2007, c. 130 (A.B. 299), § 95; Stats.2009, c. 160 (S.B.36), § 39, eff. Oct. 11, 2009.)*

Division 20

CALIFORNIA RESIDENTIAL MORTGAGE LENDING ACT

CHAPTER 7. PROHIBITED PRACTICES AND PENALTIES

Section
50511. Misleading the public regarding qualifications or experience; suspension or bar from employment.

§ 50511. Misleading the public regarding qualifications or experience; suspension or bar from employment

The commissioner may, subject to the requirements of subdivisions (b), (c), and (d) of Section 50318, suspend for a period not to exceed 12 months or bar a person from any position of employment with a licensee if the commissioner finds that the person has willfully used or claimed without authority a designation or certification of special education, practice, or skill that the person has not attained, or willfully held out to the public a confusingly similar designation or certification for the purpose of misleading the public regarding his or her qualifications or experience. *(Added by Stats.2006, c. 201 (A.B.2890), § 2.)*

FOOD AND AGRICULTURAL CODE

Division 1

STATE ADMINISTRATION

Part 1

THE DEPARTMENT OF FOOD AND AGRICULTURE

CHAPTER 2.   FISCAL DUTIES AND POWERS

ARTICLE 2.   DEPARTMENT OF FOOD AND AGRICULTURE FUND

Section
221.1.   Permanent positions with Controller's office; establishment; report to Legislature.

§ 221.1.   Permanent positions with Controller's office; establishment; report to Legislature

(a) Notwithstanding Section 221, the department shall establish all permanent positions with the Controller's office, pursuant to standard state administrative practices.

(b) The department shall report to the chairs of the fiscal committees of the Legislature and to the Legislative Analyst's office on or before January 10, 2005, on the positions established pursuant to subdivision (a) that have been funded by the department's general authority.   The report shall include a description of the positions by program, classification, and source of funding, as well as a complete description of the workload for the positions. *(Added by Stats.2004, c. 227 (S.B.1102), § 18, eff. Aug. 16, 2004.)*

GOVERNMENT CODE
Title 1
GENERAL

Division 4
PUBLIC OFFICERS AND EMPLOYEES
CHAPTER 1. GENERAL
ARTICLE 2. DISQUALIFICATION FOR OFFICE OR EMPLOYMENT

Section
1031.1.   Background investigations of peace officers; disclosure of employment information; immunities; penalties; confidentiality.
1041.   Requiring fingerprint images and associated information from prospective employees whose duties include access to medical information; application of requirement to contractors and others; requests for information; other investigations.
1042.   California Gambling Control Commission; requirement of fingerprint images; fees.

§ 1031.1.   Background Investigations of peace officers; disclosure of employment information; immunities; penalties; confidentiality

(a) For purposes of performing a thorough background investigation for applicants not currently employed as a peace officer, as required by subdivision (d) of Section 1031, an employer shall disclose employment information relating to a current or former employee, upon request of a law enforcement agency, if all of the following conditions are met:

(1) The request is made in writing.

(2) The request is accompanied by a notarized authorization by the applicant releasing the employer of liability.

(3) The request and the authorization are presented to the employer by a sworn officer or other authorized representative of the employing law enforcement agency.

(b) In the absence of fraud or malice, no employer shall be subject to any civil liability for any relevant cause of action by virtue of releasing employment information required pursuant to this section. Nothing in this section is intended to, nor does in any way or manner, abrogate or lessen the existing common law or statutory privileges and immunities of an employer.

(c) For purposes of this section, "employment information" includes written information in connection with job applications, performance evaluations, attendance records, disciplinary actions, eligibility for rehire, and other information relevant to peace officer performance, except information prohibited from disclosure by any other state or federal law or regulation.

(d) An employer's refusal to disclose information to a law enforcement agency in accordance with this section shall constitute grounds for a civil action for injunctive relief requiring disclosure on the part of an employer.

(e) Employment information disclosed by an employer to an initial requesting law enforcement agency shall be deemed confidential. However, the initial requesting law enforcement agency may disclose this information to another authorized law enforcement agency that is also conducting a peace officer background investigation. Whenever this information is disclosed to another law enforcement agency, that agency shall utilize the information for investigative leads only and the information shall be independently verified by that agency in order to be used in determining the suitability of a peace officer applicant.

(f) An employer may charge reasonable fees to cover actual costs incurred in copying and furnishing documents to law enforcement agencies as required by this section. *(Added by Stats.1993, c. 135 (S.B.1097), § 3.)*

§ 1041.   Requiring fingerprint images and associated information from prospective employees whose duties include access to medical information; application of requirement to contractors and others; requests for information; other investigations

(a)(1) The Department of Managed Health Care may require fingerprint images and associated information from a prospective employee whose duties would include access to medical information.

(2) The department shall require that any services contract or interagency agreement that may include review of medical information for compliance with the Knox–Keene Health Care Service Plan Act of 1975 (Chapter 2.2 (commencing with Section 1340) of Division 2 of the Health and Safety Code), and entered into, renewed, or amended after January 1, 2006, shall include a provision requiring the contractor to agree to permit the department to run criminal background checks on its employees, contractors, agents, or subcontractors that will have access to this information as part of their contract with the department.

(b) The fingerprint images and associated information of a prospective employee, contractor, agent, subcontractor, or employee of a contractor of the Department of Managed Health Care whose duties include or would include access to the information specified in subdivision (a), or any person who assumes those duties, may be furnished to the Department of Justice for the purpose of obtaining information as to the existence and nature of a record of state or federal level convictions and state or federal level arrests for which the Department of Justice establishes that the applicant was released on bail or on his or her own recognizance pending trial. Requests for federal level criminal offender record information, received by the Department of Justice, pursuant to this section, shall be forwarded to the Federal Bureau of Investigation by the Department of Justice.

(c) The Department of Justice shall respond to the Department of Managed Health Care with information as provided under subdivision (p) of Section 11105 of the Penal Code.

(d) The Department of Managed Health Care shall request subsequent arrest notification, from the Department of Justice, as provided under Section 11105.2 of the Penal Code, for applicants described in subdivision (a).

(e) The Department of Justice may assess a fee sufficient to cover the processing costs required under this section, as authorized pursuant to subdivision (e) of Section 11105 of the Penal Code.

(f) This section does not apply to an employee of the Department of Managed Health Care whose appointment occurred prior to January 1, 2006.

(g) The Department of Managed Health Care may investigate the criminal history for crimes involving moral turpitude of persons applying for employment in order to make a final determination of that person's fitness to perform duties that would include any access to confidential information. *(Added by Stats.2005, c. 339 (A.B.1517), § 1.)*

§ 1042. California Gambling Control Commission; requirement of fingerprint images; fees

(a)(1) The California Gambling Control Commission may require fingerprint images and associated information from a prospective employee if the employee's duties include, or would include, access to any of the following:

(A) Information that is required to be kept confidential under the Gambling Control Act (Chapter 5 (commencing with Section 19800) of Division 8 of the Business and Professions Code) or any tribal-state gaming compact, including, but not limited to, applications for licenses or findings of suitability, and information provided by or received from a tribe in connection with a tribal-state gaming compact.

(B) Access to state summary criminal history information, as defined in Section 11105 of the Penal Code, whether in full or in summary.

(C) Access to cash, checks, or other accountable items.

(2) The commission shall require that any services contract that is entered into, renewed, or amended on or after January 1, 2009, include a provision requiring the contractor to agree to permit the commission to require fingerprint images and associated information from the contractor's employees, contractors, agents, or subcontractors, whose duties include, or would include, access to information and accountable items under paragraph (1) as part of a contract with the commission, in order for the

commission to request criminal background checks on those individuals.

(b) The fingerprint images and associated information of a prospective employee, contractor, agent, subcontractor, or employee of a contractor of the California Gambling Control Commission whose duties include, or would include, access to the information or accountable items specified under paragraph (1) of subdivision (a), or any person who assumes duties that include access to that information or those accountable items, may be furnished to the Department of Justice for the purpose of obtaining information as to the existence and nature of a record of state or federal level convictions and state or federal level arrests for which the Department of Justice establishes that the applicant was released on bail or on his or her own recognizance pending trial. Requests for federal level criminal offender record information received by the Department of Justice pursuant to this section shall be forwarded to the Federal Bureau of Investigation by the Department of Justice.

(c) The Department of Justice shall respond to the California Gambling Control Commission with information as provided under subdivision (p) of Section 11105 of the Penal Code.

(d) The California Gambling Control Commission shall request subsequent arrest notification from the Department of Justice, as provided under Section 11105.2 of the Penal Code, for individuals described in subdivision (a) hired on or after January 1, 2009.

(e) The Department of Justice may assess a fee sufficient to cover the processing costs required under this section, as authorized pursuant to subdivision (e) of Section 11105 of the Penal Code.

(f) This section does not apply to an employee of the California Gambling Control Commission whose appointment occurred prior to January 1, 2009.

(g) The executive director of the California Gambling Control Commission may investigate the criminal history of persons applying for employment and prospective service contractors and their agents, subcontractors, or employees, in order to make a final determination of a person's fitness to perform duties that would include access to any information or accountable items specified under paragraph (1) of subdivision (a). Under no circumstances shall a person who would be disqualified from holding a state gambling license pursuant to subdivisions (c) to (f), inclusive, of Section 19859 of the Business and Professions Code be selected, appointed, or hired in a position that would include any duties involving access to information or accountable items specified under paragraph (1) of subdivision (a). *(Added by Stats.2008, c. 77 (A.B.2524), § 1.)*

Division 7

MISCELLANEOUS

CHAPTER 17. EMPLOYMENT OF VETERANS

Section
7280.   Short title.

Section
7280.1. Legislative finding and declaration.
7280.2. Veteran.
7280.3. Reimbursement of employers.
7280.4. Payments to employers.
7280.6. Administration of chapter.
7280.8. Certification of trainees.
7280.9. Certified trainee; standards.
7281. Restrictions on certification; findings of director; regulations.
7281.2. Restrictions on reimbursement of employers.
7281.4. Information to employers; costs.

§ 7280. Short title

This act shall be known and may be cited as the "Burton-Stull Vietnam Veterans Employment Act." *(Added by Stats.1974, c. 122, p. 244, § 1, eff. April 2, 1974.)*

§ 7280.1. Legislative finding and declaration

The Legislature hereby finds and declares that the employment of veterans of the Vietnam conflict after their separation from the armed forces is of prime public concern, and that to encourage employers in the private sector to hire such veterans, this chapter has been enacted. *(Added by Stats.1974, c. 122, p. 244, § 1, eff. April 2, 1974.)*

§ 7280.2. Veteran

For the purposes of this chapter "veteran" means any person (1) who served in the active military, naval, or air service of the United States for a period not less than 90 consecutive days or was discharged from the service due to a service-connected disability within such 90-day period, any portion of which was on or after August 5, 1964, and prior to a future date to be established by Proclamation of the Governor, (2) who was honorably discharged from the military service, and (3) who was, at the time of his entry into active duty, a native of or a bona fide resident of this state, or who, if a minor at such time, entered active duty while in the State of California and had lived in this state for six months immediately preceding his entry into active duty. *(Added by Stats. 1974, c. 122, p. 245, § 1, eff. April 2, 1974.)*

§ 7280.3. Reimbursement of employers

Each employer in private employment who hires an unemployed veteran of the Vietnam conflict at not less than the then-current federal minimum wage, or not less than the prevailing wage rate for the industry and occupation at that time, whichever is higher, shall be reimbursed by the state, pursuant to this chapter, in an amount equal to 50 percent of the cost to the employer for any salary or wages paid to such veteran. The maximum duration of the reimbursements to employers provided for by this section shall be 18 months for each veteran employed. *(Added by Stats.1974, c. 122, p. 245, § 1, eff. April 2, 1974.)*

§ 7280.4. Payments to employers

Such payments for reimbursement pursuant to Section 7280.3 shall be made to an employer who hires such a veteran as soon as possible after the veteran commences training. *(Added by Stats.1974, c. 122, p. 245, § 1, eff. April 2, 1974. Amended by Stats.1974, c. 845, p. 1810, § 1, eff. Sept. 18, 1974.)*

§ 7280.6. Administration of chapter

The provisions of this chapter shall be administered by, and payments shall be disbursed through, the Department of Employment Development, in addition to any other functions or duties which are imposed upon it by law. *(Added by Stats.1974, c. 122, p. 245, § 1, eff. April 2, 1974. Amended by Stats.1974, c. 845, p. 1810, § 2, eff. Sept. 18, 1974.)*

§ 7280.8. Certification of trainees

The Director of the Department of Employment Development, or his designee, shall certify to employers such veterans as certified trainees under this chapter as he or his designee shall deem to be qualified for training in employment by such employer. The director or his designee, when certifying trainees to employers, shall make every effort to insure that at least 50 percent of the certified trainees reside in economically disadvantaged areas, as such term is defined in Section 9111 of the Unemployment Insurance Code. *(Added by Stats.1974, c. 122, p. 245, § 1, eff. April 2, 1974. Amended by Stats. 1974, c. 845, p. 1810, § 3, eff. Sept. 18, 1974.)*

§ 7280.9. Certified trainee; standards

(a) For the purposes of this chapter, "certified trainee" means a person who both (1) meets the criteria of Section 7280.2 and (2) has entered into a written agreement called an "apprentice agreement" or a "trainee agreement" with a program sponsor to train under the provisions of such apprenticeship or training standards as are approved under Chapter 4 (commencing with Section 3070) of Division 3 of the Labor Code.

(b) Training standards shall be developed in accordance with Chapter 4 (commencing with Section 3070) of Division 3 of the Labor Code and Chapter 2 (commencing with Section 200) of Title 8 of the California Administrative Code. *(Added by Stats.1974, c. 122, p. 245, § 1, eff. April 2, 1974.)*

§ 7281. Restrictions on certification; findings of director; regulations

No veteran shall be certified under Section 7280.8 if any of the following occur:

(a) The director or his designee finds that the employer does not have a reasonable expectation of at least six months continuous full-time employment for each certified trainee certified to him.

(b) The director or his designee finds that there is reasonable cause to believe that the employer will demote, discharge, or lay off persons now employed by him and replace such persons with certified trainees.

(c) The employer is engaged in a labor dispute.

(d) The employment of certified trainees by the employer would constitute a breach of a collective bargaining agreement entered into by the employer.

(e) The director or his designee finds that there is no substantial likelihood that the employment offered by the employer to the certified trainee will result in either substantially permanent full-time employment or an upgrading of the certified trainee's job skills to a level at which reasonably permanent full-time employment may be expected to be available to him in the community.

(f) The director or his designee finds that, as to any person or class of persons or employer or class of employers to whom eligible veterans may otherwise be certified as certified trainees, such certification would result in any of the following:

(1) Employment involving any condition of wages, hours, conditions of employment, or safety prohibited by law or by a collective bargaining agreement entered into by the employer.

(2) A surplus of persons who will be unemployed as a result of such certification.

(3) The unlawful employment of minors or the violation of any laws relating to compulsory school attendance.

(4) Detriment to the health or welfare of any person.

(5) When it is found that the existing prevailing conditions in the area and industry would in any way be lowered or adversely affected.

(g) The employer is a party to any contract or agreement to receive federal reimbursement for training the individual veteran.

The director may, pursuant to Chapter 4.5 (commencing with Section 11371) of Part 1 of Division 3 of Title 2 of this code, make all necessary and reasonable regulations to prevent any abuses of the reimbursement program established under this chapter and for the administration of this section and Section 7280.8, and may obtain the assistance of any public or private agencies in finding and encouraging suitable employers to offer employment pursuant to this chapter. *(Added by Stats.1974, c. 122, p. 246, § 1, eff. April 2, 1974. Amended by Stats.1974, c. 845, p. 1811, § 4, eff. Sept. 18, 1974.)*

§ 7281.2. Restrictions on reimbursement of employers

No employer may receive any reimbursement for costs specified in this chapter if the veteran whom he hires as a trainee is a person whom the employer had previously employed, or a member of the employer's immediate family or related within the first degree. *(Added by Stats.1974, c. 122, p. 246, § 1, eff. April 2, 1974. Amended by Stats.1974, c. 845, p. 1811, § 5, eff. Sept. 18, 1974.)*

§ 7281.4. Information to employers; costs

Such portion of the funds appropriated each year by the Legislature for the purposes of this chapter as the Director of the Department of Employment Development shall determine may be used for advertising and mailing costs to inform employers in the state of the provisions of this chapter and any other programs for unemployed Vietnam veterans. *(Added by Stats.1974, c. 122, p. 247, § 1, eff. April 2, 1974.)*

CHAPTER 17.3.   ENFORCEMENT ACTIONS

Section
7285. Legislative findings and declarations; immigration status; severability.

§ 7285. Legislative findings and declarations; immigration status; severability

The Legislature finds and declares the following:

(a) All protections, rights, and remedies available under state law, except any reinstatement remedy prohibited by federal law, are available to all individuals regardless of immigration status who have applied for employment, or who are or who have been employed, in this state.

(b) For purposes of enforcing state labor, employment, civil rights, and employee housing laws, a person's immigration status is irrelevant to the issue of liability, and in proceedings or discovery undertaken to enforce those state laws no inquiry shall be permitted into a person's immigration status except where the person seeking to make the inquiry has shown by clear and convincing evidence that the inquiry is necessary in order to comply with federal immigration law.

(c) The provisions of this section are declaratory of existing law.

(d) The provisions of this section are severable. If any provision of this section or its application is held invalid, that invalidity shall not affect other provisions or applications that can be given effect without the invalid provision or application. *(Added by Stats.2002, c. 1071 (S.B.1818), § 2.)*

Title 2

GOVERNMENT OF THE STATE OF CALIFORNIA

Division 1

GENERAL

CHAPTER 5. MISCELLANEOUS

Section

8315. "Racial discrimination" and "discrimination on the basis of race" defined; International Convention on the Elimination of All Forms of Racial Discrimination; private causes of action and requiring government to prove racial discrimination pursuant to Section 31 of Article I of California Constitution.

§ 8315. "Racial discrimination" and "discrimination on the basis of race" defined; International Convention on the Elimination of All Forms of Racial Discrimination; private causes of action and requiring government to prove racial discrimination pursuant to Section 31 of Article I of California Constitution

(a) "Racial discrimination" or "discrimination on the basis of race" for the purposes of Section 31 of Article I of the California Constitution shall have the same meaning as the term "racial discrimination" as defined and used in paragraphs 1 and 4 of Article 1 of Part I of the International Convention on the Elimination of All Forms of Racial Discrimination, as adopted by the United Nations General Assembly on December 21, 1965, signed on behalf of the United States on September 28, 1966, and ratified by the United States Senate as Treaty Number 95–18 by United States Senate on June 24, 1994. The language contained in the pertinent provisions of the International Convention on the Elimination of All Forms of Racial Discrimination is set forth in subdivision (b).

(b) The International Convention on the Elimination of All Forms of Racial Discrimination, provides in paragraphs 1 and 4 of Article 1 of Part I, respectively, as follows:

"1. In this Convention, the term 'racial discrimination' shall mean any distinction, exclusion, restriction or preference based on race, colour, descent, or national or ethnic origin which has the purpose or effect of nullifying or impairing the recognition, enjoyment or exercise, on an equal footing, of human rights and fundamental freedoms in the political, economic, social, cultural or any other field of public life."

"4. Special measures taken for the sole purpose of securing adequate advancement of certain racial or ethnic groups or individuals requiring such protection as may be necessary in order to ensure such groups or individuals equal enjoyment or exercise of human rights and fundamental freedoms shall not be deemed racial discrimina-tion, provided, however, that such measures do not, as a consequence, lead to the maintenance of separate rights for different racial groups and that they shall not be continued after the objectives for which they were taken have been achieved."

(c) To allow the state to assist the United States Government in fulfilling its international obligation to pursue a policy to eliminate all forms of racial discrimination pursuant to paragraph 1 of Article 2 of Part I of the International Convention on the Elimination of All Forms of Racial Discrimination, as set forth in subdivision (d), the following provisions shall be used to interpret and implement Section 31 of Article I of the California Constitution:

(1) Section 31 of Article I of the California Constitution, except as to its prohibition of granting preferential treatment, shall not be interpreted as granting an individual a private cause of action to challenge any special measures undertaken for the purpose of securing adequate advancement of those racial groups requiring the protection pursuant to paragraph 1 of Article 2 of Part I of the International Convention on the Elimination of All Forms of Racial Discrimination. Special measures shall not be interpreted as preferential treatment.

(2) Section 31 of Article I of the California Constitution shall not be construed as requiring the government to prove racial discrimination before undertaking special measures for the purpose of securing adequate advancement of those racial minority groups needing that protection pursuant to paragraph 1 of Article 2 of Part I of the International Convention on the Elimination of All Forms of Racial Discrimination.

(d) Paragraph 1 of Article 2 of Part I of the International Convention on the Elimination of All Forms of Racial Discrimination provides as follows:

"1. States Parties (member nations that have adopted the International Convention on the Elimination of All Forms of Racial Discrimination) condemn racial discrimination to pursue by all appropriate means and without delay a policy of eliminating racial discrimination in all its forms and promoting the understanding among all races, and to this end:

"(a) Each State Party undertakes to engage in no act or practice of racial discrimination against persons, groups of persons or institutions and to ensure that all public authorities and public institutions, national and local, shall act in conformity with this obligation.

"(b) Each State Party undertakes not to sponsor, defend or support racial discrimination by any persons or organizations.

"(c) Each State Party shall take effective measures to review governmental, national and local policies, and to amend, rescind or nullify any laws and regulations which have the effect of creating or perpetuating racial discrimination wherever it exists.

"(d) Each State Party shall prohibit and bring to an end, by all appropriate means, including legislation as required by circumstances, racial discrimination by any persons, group or organization.

"(e) Each State Party undertakes to encourage, where appropriate, integrationist multiracial organizations and movements and other means of eliminating barriers between races, and to discourage anything which tends to strengthen racial division."   *(Added by Stats.2003, c. 211 (A.B.703), § 2.)*

Validity

This section, in its definition of and exceptions to "discrimination" and "preference", was held to conflict with constitutional provisions, in the decision of C & C Const., Inc. v. Sacramento Mun. Utility Dist. (App. 3 Dist. 2004) 18 Cal.Rptr.3d 715, 122 Cal.App.4th 284, rehearing denied, review denied.

CHAPTER 5.5.   DRUG–FREE WORKPLACE

ARTICLE 1.   DEFINITIONS

Section
8350.   Short title.
8351.   Definitions.

§ 8350.   Short title

This chapter shall be known, and may be cited, as the Drug-Free Workplace Act of 1990.   *(Added by Stats.1990, c. 1170 (S.B.1120), § 1.)*

§ 8351.   Definitions

As used in this chapter:

(a) "Drug-free workplace" means a site for the performance of work done in connection with a specific grant or contract described in Article 2 (commencing with Section 8355) of an entity at which employees of the entity are prohibited from engaging in the unlawful manufacture, distribution, dispensation, possession, or use of a controlled substance in accordance with the requirements of this chapter.

(b) "Employee" means the employee of a grantee or contractor directly engaged in the performance of work pursuant to the grant or contract described in Article 2 (commencing with Section 8355)[1]

(c) "Controlled substance" means a controlled substance in schedules I through V of Section 202 of the Controlled Substances Act (21 U.S.C. Sec. 812).

(d) "Grantee" means the department, division, or other unit of a person or organization responsible for performance under the grant.

(e) "Contractor" means the department, division, or other unit of a person or organization responsible for the performance under the contract.   *(Added by Stats.1990, c. 1170 (S.B.1120), § 1.)*

[1] So in chaptered copy.

ARTICLE 2.   STATE CONTRACTORS AND GRANTEES

Section
8355.   Certification to contracting or granting agency; requirements; exemption for certain credit card purchases.
8356.   Suspension of payments; termination of contract or grant; list of canceled awards.
8357.   Subcontractors.

§ 8355.   Certification to contracting or granting agency; requirements; exemption for certain credit card purchases

(a) Every person or organization awarded a contract or a grant for the procurement of any property or services from any state agency shall certify to the contracting or granting agency that it will provide a drug- free workplace by doing all of the following:

(1) Publishing a statement notifying employees that the unlawful manufacture, distribution, dispensation, possession, or use of a controlled substance is prohibited in the person's or organization's workplace and specifying the actions that will be taken against employees for violations of the prohibition.

(2) Establishing a drug-free awareness program to inform employees about all of the following:

(A) The dangers of drug abuse in the workplace.

(B) The person's or organization's policy of maintaining a drug-free workplace.

(C) Any available drug counseling, rehabilitation, and employee assistance programs.

(D) The penalties that may be imposed upon employees for drug abuse violations.

(3) Requiring that each employee engaged in the performance of the contract or grant be given a copy of the statement required by subdivision (a) and that, as a condition of employment on the contract or grant, the employee agrees to abide by the terms of the statement.

(b)(1) The certification requirement set forth in subdivision (a) does not apply to a credit card purchase of goods of two thousand five hundred dollars ($2,500) or less.

(2) The total amount of exemption authorized herein shall not exceed seven thousand five hundred dollars ($7,500) per year for each company from which a state agency is purchasing goods by credit card.   It shall be the responsibility of each state agency to monitor the use of this exemption and adhere to these restrictions on these purchases.   *(Added by Stats.1990, c. 1170 (S.B.1120), § 1. Amended by Stats.2005, c. 381 (S.B.828), § 1.)*

§ 8356. Suspension of payments; termination of contract or grant; list of canceled awards

(a) Each contract or grant awarded by a state agency may be subject to suspension of payments under the contract or grant or termination of the contract or grant, or both, and the contractor or grantee thereunder may be subject to debarment, in accordance with the requirements of this article, if the contracting or granting agency determines that any of the following has occurred:

(1) The contractor or grantee has made a false certification under Section 8355.

(2) The contractor or grantee violates the certification by failing to carry out the requirements of subdivisions (a) to (c), inclusive, of Section 8355.

(b) The Department of General Services shall establish and maintain a list of individuals and organizations whose contracts or grants have been canceled due to failure to comply with this chapter. This list shall be updated monthly and published each month. No state agency shall award a contract or grant to a person or organization on the published list until that person or organization has complied with this chapter.

(c) Every state agency that directly awards grants without review by the Department of General Services shall immediately notify the department of any individual or organization that has an award canceled on the basis of violation of this chapter. (Added by Stats.1990, c. 1170 (S.B.1120), § 1.)

§ 8357. Subcontractors

This chapter shall not be construed to require any contractor or grantee to ensure that other businesses with which it subcontracts also provide drug-free workplaces. (Added by Stats.1990, c. 1170 (S.B.1120), § 1.)

CHAPTER 6.5. STATE AUDITOR

ARTICLE 3. CALIFORNIA WHISTLEBLOWER PROTECTION ACT

Section
8547.2. Definitions.
8547.3. Use or attempt to use official authority or influence to interfere with disclosure of information; prohibition; civil liability.
8547.8. Reprisals or other improper acts for making a protected disclosure; complaints; limitation of actions; civil and criminal penalties; burden of proof; other rights and remedies.
8547.10. University of California employees; complaints of reprisals or other improper acts for making a protected disclosure; civil and criminal penalties; burden of proof; other rights and remedies.
8547.12. California State University employees; complaints alleging reprisals or other actual or attempted acts in response to making a protected disclosure; civil and criminal penalties; burden of proof; other rights and remedies; conflict with memorandum of understanding.

§ 8547.2. Definitions

For the purposes of this article, the following terms have the following meanings:

(a) "Employee" means any individual appointed by the Governor or employed or holding office in a state agency as defined by Section 11000, including, for purposes of Sections 8547.3 to 8547.7, inclusive, any employee of the California State University or an individual appointed by the Legislature to a state board or commission and who is not a Member or employee of the Legislature. "Employee" includes any former employee who met the criteria of this subdivision during his or her employment.

(b) "Improper governmental activity" means any activity by a state agency or by an employee that is undertaken in the performance of the employee's * * * duties, undertaken inside a state office, or, if undertaken outside a state office by the employee, directly relates to state government, whether or not that activity is within the scope of his or her employment, and that (1) is in violation of any state or federal law or regulation, including, but not limited to, corruption, malfeasance, bribery, theft of government property, fraudulent claims, fraud, coercion, conversion, malicious prosecution, misuse of government property, or willful omission to perform duty, or (2) is economically wasteful, or involves gross misconduct, incompetency, or inefficiency. For purposes of Sections 8547.4, 8547.5, 8547.10, and 8547.11, "improper governmental activity" includes any activity by the University of California or by an employee, including an officer or faculty member, who otherwise meets the criteria of this subdivision.

(c) "Person" means any individual, corporation, trust, association, any state or local government, or any agency or instrumentality of any of the foregoing.

(d) "Protected disclosure" means any good faith communication, including any communication based on, or when carrying out, job duties, that discloses or demonstrates an intention to disclose information that may evidence (1) an improper governmental activity or (2) any condition that may significantly threaten the health or safety of employees or the public if the disclosure or intention to disclose was made for the purpose of remedying that condition. Protected disclosure specifically includes any good faith communication to the Bureau of State Audits alleging an improper governmental activity and any evidence delivered to the Bureau of State Audits in support of the allegation.

(e) "Illegal order" means any directive to violate or assist in violating a federal, state, or local law, rule, or regulation or any order to work or cause others to work in conditions outside of their line of duty that would unreasonably threaten the health or safety of employees or the public.

(f) "State agency" is defined by Section 11000. "State agency" includes the University of California for purposes of Sections 8547.5 to 8547.7, inclusive, and the

California State University for purposes of Sections 8547.3 to 8547.7, inclusive. *(Added by Stats.1993, c. 12 (S.B.37), § 8, eff. May 7, 1993. Amended by Stats.1999, c. 673 (S.B.951), § 4; Stats.2009, c. 452 (A.B.567), § 5.)*

§ 8547.3. Use or attempt to use official authority or influence to interfere with disclosure of information; prohibition; civil liability

(a) An employee may not directly or indirectly use or attempt to use the official authority or influence of the employee for the purpose of intimidating, threatening, coercing, commanding, or attempting to intimidate, threaten, coerce, or command any person for the purpose of interfering with the rights conferred pursuant to this article.

(b) For the purpose of subdivision (a), "use of official authority or influence" includes promising to confer, or conferring, any benefit; effecting, or threatening to effect, any reprisal; or taking, or directing others to take, or recommending, processing, or approving, any personnel action, including, but not limited to, appointment, promotion, transfer, assignment, performance evaluation, suspension, or other disciplinary action.

(c) Any employee who violates subdivision (a) may be liable in an action for civil damages brought against the employee by the offended party.

(d) Nothing in this section shall be construed to authorize an individual to disclose information otherwise prohibited by or under law. *(Added by Stats.1993, c. 12 (S.B.37), § 8, eff. May 7, 1993. Amended by Stats.1999, c. 673 (S.B.951), § 5.)*

§ 8547.8. Reprisals or other improper acts for making a protected disclosure; complaints; limitation of actions; civil and criminal penalties; burden of proof; other rights and remedies

(a) A state employee or applicant for state employment who files a written complaint with his or her supervisor, manager, or the appointing power alleging actual or attempted acts of reprisal, retaliation, threats, coercion, or similar improper acts prohibited by Section 8547.3, may also file a copy of the written complaint with the State Personnel Board, together with a sworn statement that the contents of the written complaint are true, or are believed by the affiant to be true, under penalty of perjury. The complaint filed with the board, shall be filed within 12 months of the most recent act of reprisal complained about.

(b) Any person who intentionally engages in acts of reprisal, retaliation, threats, coercion, or similar acts against a state employee or applicant for state employment for having made a protected disclosure, is subject to a fine not to exceed ten thousand dollars ($10,000) and imprisonment in the county jail for a period not to exceed one year. Pursuant to Section 19683, any state civil service employee who intentionally engages in that conduct shall be disciplined by adverse action as provided by Section 19572.

146

(c) In addition to all other penalties provided by law, any person who intentionally engages in acts of reprisal, retaliation, threats, coercion, or similar acts against a state employee or applicant for state employment for having made a protected disclosure shall be liable in an action for damages brought against him or her by the injured party. Punitive damages may be awarded by the court where the acts of the offending party are proven to be malicious. Where liability has been established, the injured party shall also be entitled to reasonable attorney's fees as provided by law. However, any action for damages shall not be available to the injured party unless the injured party has first filed a complaint with the State Personnel Board pursuant to subdivision (a), and the board has issued, or failed to issue, findings pursuant to Section 19683.

(d) This section is not intended to prevent an appointing power, manager, or supervisor from taking, directing others to take, recommending, or approving any personnel action or from taking or failing to take a personnel action with respect to any state employee or applicant for state employment if the appointing power, manager, or supervisor reasonably believes any action or inaction is justified on the basis of evidence separate and apart from the fact that the person has made a protected disclosure as defined in subdivision (b) of Section 8547.2.

(e) In any civil action or administrative proceeding, once it has been demonstrated by a preponderance of evidence that an activity protected by this article was a contributing factor in the alleged retaliation against a former, current, or prospective employee, the burden of proof shall be on the supervisor, manager, or appointing power to demonstrate by clear and convincing evidence that the alleged action would have occurred for legitimate, independent reasons even if the employee had not engaged in protected disclosures or refused an illegal order. If the supervisor, manager, or appointing power fails to meet this burden of proof in an adverse action against the employee in any administrative review, challenge, or adjudication in which retaliation has been demonstrated to be a contributing factor, the employee shall have a complete affirmative defense in the adverse action.

(f) Nothing in this article shall be deemed to diminish the rights, privileges, or remedies of any employee under any other federal or state law or under any employment contract or collective bargaining agreement. *(Added by Stats.1993, c. 12 (S.B.37), § 8, eff. May 7, 1993. Amended by Stats.1999, c. 673 (S.B.951), § 6; Stats.2001, c. 883 (S.B.413), § 3.)*

§ 8547.10. University of California employees; complaints of reprisals or other improper acts for making a protected disclosure; civil and criminal penalties; burden of proof; other rights and remedies

(a) A University of California employee, including an officer or faculty member, or applicant for employment may file a written complaint with his or her supervisor or manager, or with any other university officer designated for that purpose by the regents, alleging actual or attempted acts of reprisal, retaliation, threats, coercion, or similar improper acts for having made a protected disclosure, together with a sworn statement that the contents of the written complaint are true, or are believed by the affiant to be true, under penalty of perjury. The complaint shall be filed within 12 months of the most recent act of reprisal complained about.

(b) Any person who intentionally engages in acts of reprisal, retaliation, threats, coercion, or similar acts against a University of California employee, including an officer or faculty member, or applicant for employment for having made a protected disclosure, is subject to a fine not to exceed ten thousand dollars ($10,000) and imprisonment in the county jail for up to a period of one year. Any university employee, including an officer or faculty member, who intentionally engages in that conduct shall also be subject to discipline by the university.

(c) In addition to all other penalties provided by law, any person who intentionally engages in acts of reprisal, retaliation, threats, coercion, or similar acts against a university employee, including an officer or faculty member, or applicant for employment for having made a protected disclosure shall be liable in an action for damages brought against him or her by the injured party. Punitive damages may be awarded by the court where the acts of the offending party are proven to be malicious. Where liability has been established, the injured party shall also be entitled to reasonable attorney's fees as provided by law. However, any action for damages shall not be available to the injured party unless the injured party has first filed a complaint with the university officer identified pursuant to subdivision (a), and the university has failed to reach a decision regarding that complaint within the time limits established for that purpose by the regents.

(d) This section is not intended to prevent a manager or supervisor from taking, directing others to take, recommending, or approving any personnel action or from taking or failing to take a personnel action with respect to any university employee, including an officer or faculty member, or applicant for employment if the manager or supervisor reasonably believes any action or inaction is justified on the basis of evidence separate and apart from the fact that the person has made a protected disclosure.

(e) In any civil action or administrative proceeding, once it has been demonstrated by a preponderance of the evidence that an activity protected by this article was a contributing factor in the alleged retaliation against a former, current, or prospective employee, the burden of proof shall be on the supervisor, manager, or appointing power to demonstrate by clear and convincing evidence that the alleged action would have occurred for legitimate, independent reasons even if the employee had not engaged in protected disclosures or refused an illegal order. If the supervisor, manager, or appointing power fails to meet this burden of proof in an adverse action against the employee in any administrative review, challenge, or adjudication in which retaliation has been demonstrated to be a contributing factor, the employee shall have a complete affirmative defense in the adverse action.

(f) Nothing in this article shall be deemed to diminish the rights, privileges, or remedies of any employee under any other federal or state law or under any employment contract or collective bargaining agreement. *(Added by Stats.1993, c. 12 (S.B.37), § 8, eff. May 7, 1993. Amended by Stats.1999, c. 673 (S.B.951), § 7.)*

§ 8547.12. California State University employees; complaints alleging reprisals or other actual or attempted acts in response to making a protected disclosure; civil and criminal penalties; burden of proof; other rights and remedies; conflict with memorandum of understanding

(a) A California State University employee, including an officer or faculty member, or applicant for employment may file a written complaint with his or her supervisor or manager, or with any other university officer designated for that purpose by the trustees, alleging actual or attempted acts of reprisal, retaliation, threats, coercion, or similar improper acts for having made a protected disclosure, together with a sworn statement that the contents of the written complaint are true, or are believed by the affiant to be true, under penalty of perjury. The complaint shall be filed within 12 months of the most recent act of reprisal complained about.

(b) Any person who intentionally engages in acts of reprisal, retaliation, threats, coercion, or similar acts against a California State University employee, including an officer or faculty member, or applicant for employment for having made a protected disclosure, is subject to a fine not to exceed ten thousand dollars ($10,000) and imprisonment in the county jail for up to a period of one year. Any university employee, including an officer or faculty member, who intentionally engages in that conduct shall also be subject to discipline by the university.

(c) In addition to all other penalties provided by law, any person who intentionally engages in acts of reprisal, retaliation, threats, coercion, or similar acts against a university employee, including an officer or faculty member, or applicant for employment for having made a protected disclosure shall be liable in an action for damages brought against him or her by the injured party. Punitive damages may be awarded by the court where the acts of the offending party are proven to be malicious. Where liability has been established, the injured party shall also be entitled to reasonable attorney's fees as provided by law. However, any action for damages shall not be available to the injured party unless the injured party has first filed a complaint with the university officer identified pursuant to subdivision (a), and the university

147

has failed to reach a decision regarding that complaint within the time limits established for that purpose by the trustees. Nothing in this section is intended to prohibit the injured party from seeking a remedy if the university has not satisfactorily addressed the complaint within 18 months.

(d) This section is not intended to prevent a manager or supervisor from taking, directing others to take, recommending, or approving any personnel action, or from taking or failing to take a personnel action with respect to any university employee, including an officer or faculty member, or applicant for employment if the manager or supervisor reasonably believes any action or inaction is justified on the basis of evidence separate and apart from the fact that the person has made a protected disclosure.

(e) In any civil action or administrative proceeding, once it has been demonstrated by a preponderance of the evidence that an activity protected by this article was a contributing factor in the alleged retaliation against a former, current, or prospective employee, the burden of proof shall be on the supervisor, manager, or appointing power to demonstrate by clear and convincing evidence that the alleged action would have occurred for legitimate, independent reasons even if the employee had not engaged in protected disclosures or refused an illegal order. If the supervisor, manager, or appointing power fails to meet this burden of proof in an adverse action against the employee in any administrative review, challenge, or adjudication in which retaliation has been demonstrated to be a contributing factor, the employee shall have a complete affirmative defense in the adverse action.

(f) Nothing in this article shall be deemed to diminish the rights, privileges, or remedies of any employee under any other federal or state law or under any employment contract or collective bargaining agreement.

(g) If the provisions of this section are in conflict with the provisions of a memorandum of understanding reached pursuant to Chapter 12 (commencing with Section 3560) of Division 4 of Title 1, the memorandum of understanding shall be controlling without further legislative action. *(Added by Stats.1994, c. 834 (S.B.2097), § 1. Amended by Stats.1999, c. 673 (S.B.951), § 8.)*

ARTICLE 3.5. WHISTLEBLOWER INFORMATION

Section
8548.   State agency.
8548.1.   Written explanation of Whistleblower Protection Act for state employees.
8548.2.   Notice regarding written explanation.
8548.3.   Provision of information by electronic mail.
8548.4.   Posting of information on web site.
8548.5.   Failure to comply with this article.

§ 8548. State agency

For purposes of this article, "state agency" means every state office, officer, department, division, bureau, board, and commission, including the California State University and the University of California. *(Added by Stats.2001, c. 883 (S.B.413), § 4.)*

§ 8548.1. Written explanation of Whistleblower Protection Act for state employees

No later than April 1, 2002, the State Auditor shall prepare for state employees a written explanation of the California Whistleblower Protection Act contained in Article 3 (commencing with Section 8547). The explanation shall include, but not be limited to, the following information:

(a) Instructions on how to contact the State Auditor by mail or telephone.

(b) A general overview of improper governmental activities and examples of three of the most common types of improper governmental activities that may be reported to the State Auditor.

(c) Examples of two of the most commonly reported governmental activities that the State Auditor does not have authority to investigate.

(d) An explanation of whistleblower protection available to state employees who report improper governmental activities to the State Auditor.

(e) The requirement that the State Auditor protect the anonymity of a person who reports improper governmental activity to the State Auditor.

(f) The State Auditor's authority in connection with violations of law discovered during an investigation of improper governmental activities. *(Added by Stats.2001, c. 883 (S.B.413), § 4.)*

§ 8548.2. Notice regarding written explanation

The State Auditor shall prepare for distribution to each state agency in an electronic format a notice containing the information in the written explanation prepared pursuant to Section 8548.1. No later than July 1, 2002, each state agency shall print and post this notice at its state office or offices in a location or locations where employee notices are maintained. A state agency shall not edit the written text of the notice but it may publish the notice in a manner it chooses, and it may include its own introductory language in the notice, provided that the language and the format selected do not alter the meaning of the notice. *(Added by Stats.2001, c. 883 (S.B.413), § 4.)*

§ 8548.3. Provision of information by electronic mail

On July 1, 2002, and annually thereafter, every state agency shall send the information contained in the notice by electronic mail to its employees who have authorized access to electronic mail from the agency. *(Added by Stats.2001, c. 883 (S.B.413), § 4.)*

§ 8548.4. Posting of information on web site

The State Auditor shall post the information described in Section 8548.1 on the Web site of the Bureau of State Audits. *(Added by Stats.2001, c. 883 (S.B.413), § 4.)*

§ 8548.5. Failure to comply with this article

The intentional failure of a state agency to comply with any provision of this article shall constitute an improper governmental activity for purposes of Article 3 (commencing with Section 8547). *(Added by Stats.2001, c. 883 (S.B.413), § 4.)*

Division 2

LEGISLATIVE DEPARTMENT

Part 1

LEGISLATURE

CHAPTER 4. WITNESSES

Section
9414. Misdemeanors.

§ 9414. Misdemeanors

(a) Any person who does any of the following is guilty of a misdemeanor:

(1) Coerces or attempts to coerce any person not to appear as a witness before any committee.

(2) Deprives, attempts to deprive, or threatens to deprive any other person, or requests any employer to deprive any employee, of lawful employment, when such deprivation, attempt, threat, or request is motivated by the fact that the other person or employee is, was, or may become a witness before a committee.

(b) Any employer or person acting on behalf of an employer who, directly or indirectly, harasses any person employed by that employer, when the harassment is motivated by the fact that the employee is, was, or may be a witness before a committee, is guilty of a misdemeanor.

(c) This section shall not be construed to prevent any employer from discharging an employee for cause nor shall it be construed to prevent a labor union or an agent thereof from requesting the dismissal of an employee when the request is motivated by a cause other than that specified herein. *(Added by Stats.1955, c. 680, p. 1170, § 1. Amended by Stats.1988, c. 1512, § 1.)*

Division 3

EXECUTIVE DEPARTMENT

Part 1

STATE DEPARTMENTS AND AGENCIES

CHAPTER 3.5. ADMINISTRATIVE REGULATIONS AND RULEMAKING

ARTICLE 5. PUBLIC PARTICIPATION: PROCEDURE FOR ADOPTION OF REGULATIONS

Section
11346.3. Action with potential or significant adverse economic impact on California business enterprises and

Section
individuals; potential cost impact; exemption from reporting.

§ 11346.3. Action with potential or significant adverse economic impact on California business enterprises and individuals; potential cost impact; exemption from reporting

(a) State agencies proposing to adopt, amend, or repeal any administrative regulation shall assess the potential for adverse economic impact on California business enterprises and individuals, avoiding the imposition of unnecessary or unreasonable regulations or reporting, recordkeeping, or compliance requirements. For purposes of this subdivision, assessing the potential for adverse economic impact shall require agencies, when proposing to adopt, amend, or repeal a regulation, to adhere to the following requirements, to the extent that these requirements do not conflict with other state or federal laws:

(1) The proposed adoption, amendment, or repeal of a regulation shall be based on adequate information concerning the need for, and consequences of, proposed governmental action.

(2) The state agency, prior to submitting a proposal to adopt, amend, or repeal a regulation to the office, shall consider the proposal's impact on business, with consideration of industries affected including the ability of California businesses to compete with businesses in other states. For purposes of evaluating the impact on the ability of California businesses to compete with businesses in other states, an agency shall consider, but not be limited to, information supplied by interested parties.

It is not the intent of this section to impose additional criteria on agencies, above that which exists in current law, in assessing adverse economic impact on California business enterprises, but only to assure that the assessment is made early in the process of initiation and development of a proposed adoption, amendment, or repeal of a regulation.

(b)(1) All state agencies proposing to adopt, amend, or repeal any administrative regulations shall assess whether and to what extent it will affect the following:

(A) The creation or elimination of jobs within the State of California.

(B) The creation of new businesses or the elimination of existing businesses within the State of California.

(C) The expansion of businesses currently doing business within the State of California.

(2) This subdivision does not apply to the University of California, the Hastings College of the Law, or the Fair Political Practices Commission.

(3) Information required from state agencies for the purpose of completing the assessment may come from existing state publications.

(c) No administrative regulation adopted on or after January 1, 1993, that requires a report shall apply to businesses, unless the state agency adopting the regulation makes a finding that it is necessary for the health, safety, or welfare of the people of the state that the regulation apply to businesses. *(Added by Stats.1994, c. 1039 (A.B.2531), § 24. Amended by Stats.2000, c. 1059 (A.B.505), § 10; Stats.2000, c. 1060 (A.B.1822), § 23.)*

Part 2

CONSTITUTIONAL OFFICERS

CHAPTER 5. CONTROLLER

ARTICLE 2. DUTIES

Section
12432. 21st Century Project; implementation of human resource management system; assessment of costs; collection from federal funds; appropriations.

§ 12432. 21st Century Project; implementation of human resource management system; assessment of costs; collection from federal funds; appropriations

(a) The Legislature hereby finds and declares that it is essential for the state to replace the current automated human resource/payroll systems operated by the Controller to ensure that state employees continue to be paid accurately and on time and that the state may take advantage of new capabilities and improved business practices. To achieve this replacement of the current systems, the Controller is authorized to procure, modify, and implement a new human resource management system that meets the needs of a modern state government. This replacement effort is known as the 21st Century Project.

(b) Notwithstanding any other provision of law, beginning with the 2004–05 fiscal year, the Controller may assess the special and nongovernmental cost funds in sufficient amounts to pay for the authorized 21st Century Project costs that are attributable to those funds. Assessments in support of the expenditures for the 21st Century Project shall be made quarterly, and the total amount assessed from these funds annually may not exceed the total expenditures incurred by the Controller for the 21st Century Project that are attributable to those funds in that fiscal year. Appropriations for this purpose shall be made in the annual Budget Act.

(c) To the extent permitted by law, beginning with the 2004–05 fiscal year, the Controller shall establish agreements with various agencies and departments for the collection from federal funds of costs that are attributable to federal funds. The total amount collected from those agencies and departments annually may not exceed the total expenditures incurred by the Controller for the 21st Century Project that are attributable to federal funds in that fiscal year. Appropriations for that purpose shall be made in the annual Budget Act.

(d) It is the intent of the Legislature that, beginning not earlier than the 2006–07 fiscal year, future annual

Budget Acts include General Fund appropriations in sufficient amounts for expenditures for the 21st Century Project that are attributable to the General Fund. It is the Legislature's intent that the share of the total project costs paid for by the General Fund shall be equivalent to the share of the total project costs paid for from special and nongovernmental cost fund assessments and collections from federal funds.

(e) This section shall remain in effect only until June 30, 2011, and as of that date is repealed, unless a later enacted statute, that is enacted before June 30, 2011, deletes or extends that date. *(Added by Stats.2004, c. 227 (S.B.1102), § 38, eff. Aug. 16, 2004.)*

Repeal

For repeal of this section, see its terms.

CHAPTER 6. ATTORNEY GENERAL

ARTICLE 9. FALSE CLAIMS ACTIONS

Section
12650. Short title; definitions.
12653. Employer interference with employee disclosures, etc.; liability of employer; remedies of employee.

§ 12650. Short title; definitions

(a) This article shall be known and may be cited as the False Claims Act.

(b) For purposes of this article:

(1) "Claim" means any request or demand, whether under a contract or otherwise, for money, property, or services * * *, and whether or not the state or * * * a political subdivision * * * has title to the money, property, or services * * * that meets either of the following conditions:

(A) Is presented to an officer, employee, or agent of the state or of a political subdivision.

(B) Is made to a contractor, grantee, or other recipient, if the money, property, or service is to be spent or used on a state or any political subdivision program or interest, and if the state or political subdivision meets either of the following conditions:

(i) Provides or has provided any portion of the money, property, or service requested or demanded.

(ii) Reimburses the contractor, grantee, or other recipient for any portion of the money, property, or service that is requested or demanded.

(2) "Claim" does not include requests or demands for money, property, or services that the state or a political subdivision has paid to an individual as compensation for employment with the state or political subdivision or as an income subsidy with no restrictions on that individual's use of the money, property, or services.

(3) "Knowing" and "knowingly" mean that a person, with respect to information, does any of the following:

(A) Has actual knowledge of the information.

(B) Acts in deliberate ignorance of the truth or falsity of the information.

(C) Acts in reckless disregard of the truth or falsity of the information.

Proof of specific intent to defraud is not required.

(4) "Material" means having a natural tendency to influence, or be capable of influencing, the payment or receipt of money, property, or services.

(5) "Political subdivision" includes any city, city and county, county, tax or assessment district, or other legally authorized local governmental entity with jurisdictional boundaries.

(6) "Political subdivision funds" means funds that are the subject of a claim presented to an officer, employee, or agent of a political subdivision or where the political subdivision provides, has provided, or will reimburse any portion of the money, property, or service requested or demanded.

(7) "Prosecuting authority" refers to the county counsel, city attorney, or other local government official charged with investigating, filing, and conducting civil legal proceedings on behalf of, or in the name of, a particular political subdivision.

(8) "Person" includes any natural person, corporation, firm, association, organization, partnership, limited liability company, business, or trust.

(9) "State funds" mean funds that are the subject of a claim presented to an officer, employee, or agent of the state or where the state provides, has provided, or will reimburse any portion of the money, property, or service requested or demanded. *(Added by Stats.1987, c. 1420, § 1. Amended by Stats.1994, c. 1010 (S.B.2053), § 141; Stats.1997, c. 300 (A.B.1586), § 3, eff. Aug. 18, 1997; Stats.2009, c. 277 (A.B.1196), § 1.)*

§ 12653. Employer interference with employee disclosures, etc.; liability of employer; remedies of employee

(a) No employer shall make, adopt, or enforce any rule, regulation, or policy preventing an employee from disclosing information to a government or law enforcement agency or from acting in furtherance of a false claims action, including investigating, initiating, testifying, or assisting in an action filed or to be filed under Section 12652.

(b) No employer shall discharge, demote, suspend, threaten, harass, deny promotion to, or in any other manner discriminate against, an employee in the terms and conditions of employment because of lawful acts done by the employee on behalf of the employee or others in disclosing information to a government or law enforcement agency or in furthering a false claims action, including investigation for, initiation of, testimony for, or assistance in, an action filed or to be filed under Section 12652.

(c) An employer who violates subdivision (b) shall be liable for all relief necessary to make the employee whole, including reinstatement with the same seniority status that the employee would have had but for the discrimination, two times the amount of back pay, interest on the back pay, compensation for any special damage sustained as a result of the discrimination, and, where appropriate, punitive damages. In addition, the defendant shall be required to pay litigation costs and reasonable attorneys' fees. An employee may bring an action in the appropriate superior court of the state for the relief provided in this subdivision.

(d) An employee who is discharged, demoted, suspended, harassed, denied promotion, or in any other manner discriminated against in the terms and conditions of employment by his or her employer because of participation in conduct which directly or indirectly resulted in a false claim being submitted to the state or a political subdivision shall be entitled to the remedies under subdivision (c) if, and only if, both of the following occur:

(1) The employee voluntarily disclosed information to a government or law enforcement agency or acted in furtherance of a false claims action, including investigation for, initiation of, testimony for, or assistance in an action filed or to be filed.

(2) The employee had been harassed, threatened with termination or demotion, or otherwise coerced by the employer or its management into engaging in the fraudulent activity in the first place. *(Added by Stats.1987, c. 1420, § 1.)*

Part 2.8

DEPARTMENT OF FAIR EMPLOYMENT AND HOUSING

CHAPTER 1. GENERAL PROVISIONS

Section
12900.   Short title.
12901.   Department; executive officer; appointment; salary.
12902.   Director as department head; law governing.
12903.   Commission; membership; appointment; chairperson; term.
12904.   Commission; vacancies; quorum.
12905.   Commission; compensation; expenses.
12906.   Commission; removal of members; grounds.

§ 12900. Short title

This part may be known and referred to as the "California Fair Employment and Housing Act." *(Added by Stats.1980, c. 992, § 4.)*

§ 12901. Department; executive officer; appointment; salary

There is in the state government, in the State and Consumer Services Agency, the Department of Fair Employment and Housing. The department is under the

151

direction of an executive officer known as the Director of Fair Employment and Housing, who is appointed by the Governor, subject to confirmation by the Senate, and who holds office at the pleasure of the Governor. The annual salary of the director is provided for by Chapter 6 (commencing with Section 11550) of Part 1 of Division 3 of Title 2. *(Added by Stats.1980, c. 992, § 4.)*

§ 12902. Director as department head; law governing

The provisions of Chapter 2 (commencing with Section 11150) of Part 1 of Division 3 of Title 2 apply to the director and the director is the head of a department within the meaning of such chapter. *(Added by Stats. 1980, c. 992, § 4.)*

§ 12903. Commission; membership; appointment; chairperson; term

There is in the State and Consumer Services Agency the Fair Employment and Housing Commission. The commission shall consist of seven members, to be known as commissioners, who shall be appointed by the Governor, by and with the advice and consent of the Senate, and one of whom shall be designated as chairperson by the Governor. The term of office of each member of the commission shall be for four years. *(Added by Stats. 1980, c. 992, § 4. Amended by Stats.1981, c. 625, p. 2379, § 1; Stats.2004, c. 647 (A.B.2870), § 1.)*

§ 12904. Commission; vacancies; quorum

Any member chosen to fill a vacancy on the commission occurring otherwise than by expiration of term shall be appointed for the unexpired term of the member whom he or she is to succeed. Four members of the commission shall constitute a quorum for the purpose of conducting the business thereof. *(Added by Stats.1980, c. 992, § 4. Amended by Stats.1985, c. 278, § 1.)*

§ 12905. Commission; compensation; expenses

Each member of the commission shall serve without compensation but shall receive one hundred dollars ($100) for each day actually spent in the performance of his or her duties under this part and shall also be entitled to his or her expenses actually and necessarily incurred in the performance of his or her duties. *(Added by Stats. 1980, c. 992, § 4. Amended by Stats.1985, c. 278, § 2.)*

§ 12906. Commission; removal of members; grounds

Any member of the commission may be removed by the Governor for inefficiency, for neglect of duty, misconduct or malfeasance in office, after being given a written statement of the charges and an opportunity to be heard thereon. *(Added by Stats.1980, c. 992, § 4.)*

CHAPTER 3. FINDINGS AND DECLARATIONS OF POLICY

Section
12920.   Public policy; employment rights and opportunities; housing; purpose; police power.

Section
12920.5.   Effective remedies; Legislature's authority.
12921.   Civil rights; employment and housing without discrimination.
12922.   Restrictions on eligibility for employment; religious corporations.

§ 12920. Public policy; employment rights and opportunities; housing; purpose; police power

It is hereby declared as the public policy of this state that it is necessary to protect and safeguard the right and opportunity of all persons to seek, obtain, and hold employment without discrimination or abridgment on account of race, religious creed, color, national origin, ancestry, physical disability, mental disability, medical condition, marital status, sex, age, or sexual orientation.

It is recognized that the practice of denying employment opportunity and discriminating in the terms of employment for these reasons foments domestic strife and unrest, deprives the state of the fullest utilization of its capacities for development and advancement, and substantially and adversely affects the interest of employees, employers, and the public in general.

Further, the practice of discrimination because of race, color, religion, sex, marital status, national origin, ancestry, familial status, disability, or sexual orientation in housing accommodations is declared to be against public policy.

It is the purpose of this part to provide effective remedies that will eliminate these discriminatory practices.

This part shall be deemed an exercise of the police power of the state for the protection of the welfare, health, and peace of the people of this state. *(Added by Stats.1980, c. 992, § 4. Amended by Stats.1992, c. 182 (S.B.1234), § 2; Stats.1992, c. 912 (A.B.1286), § 1; Stats. 1992, c. 913 (A.B.1077), § 19; Stats.1999, c. 592 (A.B. 1001), § 1.5.)*

§ 12920.5. Effective remedies; Legislature's authority

In order to eliminate discrimination, it is necessary to provide effective remedies that will both prevent and deter unlawful employment practices and redress the adverse effects of those practices on aggrieved persons. To that end, this part shall be deemed an exercise of the Legislature's authority pursuant to Section 1 of Article XIV of the California Constitution. *(Added by Stats. 1992, c. 911 (A.B.311), § 2.)*

§ 12921. Civil rights; employment and housing without discrimination

(a) The opportunity to seek, obtain and hold employment without discrimination because of race, religious creed, color, national origin, ancestry, physical disability, mental disability, medical condition, marital status, sex, age, or sexual orientation is hereby recognized as and declared to be a civil right.

(b) The opportunity to seek, obtain, and hold housing without discrimination because of race, color, religion, sex, sexual orientation, marital status, national origin, ancestry, familial status, disability, or any other basis prohibited by Section 51 of the Civil Code is hereby recognized as and declared to be a civil right. *(Added by Stats.1980, c. 992, § 4. Amended by Stats.1992, c. 912 (A.B.1286), § 2; Stats.1992, c. 913 (A.B.1077), § 20; Stats.1999, c. 591 (A.B.1670), § 4; Stats.1999, c. 592 (A.B.1001), § 2.5.)*

§ 12922. Restrictions on eligibility for employment; religious corporations

Notwithstanding any other provision of this part, an employer that is a religious corporation may restrict eligibility for employment in any position involving the performance of religious duties to adherents of the religion for which the corporation is organized. *(Added by Stats.1999, c. 913 (A.B.1541), § 1.)*

CHAPTER 4. DEFINITIONS

Section
12925.   Commission; commissioner; department; director; person.
12926.   Additional definitions.
12926.1.   Legislative findings and declarations; disability, mental disability, and medical condition; broad coverage under state law; interaction in determining reasonable accommodation.
12926.2.   Unlawful practices; religious corporation, religious duties defined; exception for nonprofit benefit corporations.
12927.   Housing accommodations; definitions.
12928.   Identity of employer; rebuttable presumption.

§ 12925. Commission; commissioner; department; director; person

As used in this part, unless a different meaning clearly appears from the context:

(a) "Commission" means the Fair Employment and Housing Commission and "commissioner" means a member of the commission.

(b) "Department" means the Department of Fair Employment and Housing.

(c) "Director" means the Director of Fair Employment and Housing.

(d) "Person" includes one or more individuals, partnerships, associations, corporations, limited liability companies, legal representatives, trustees, trustees in bankruptcy, and receivers or other fiduciaries. *(Added by Stats.1980, c. 992, § 4. Amended by Stats.1994, c. 1010 (S.B.2053), § 142.)*

§ 12926. Additional definitions

As used in this part in connection with unlawful practices, unless a different meaning clearly appears from the context:

(a) "Affirmative relief" or "prospective relief" includes the authority to order reinstatement of an employee, awards of backpay, reimbursement of out-of-pocket expenses, hiring, transfers, reassignments, grants of tenure, promotions, cease and desist orders, posting of notices, training of personnel, testing, expunging of records, reporting of records, and any other similar relief that is intended to correct unlawful practices under this part.

(b) "Age" refers to the chronological age of any individual who has reached his or her 40th birthday.

(c) "Employee" does not include any individual employed by his or her parents, spouse, or child, or any individual employed under a special license in a nonprofit sheltered workshop or rehabilitation facility.

(d) "Employer" includes any person regularly employing five or more persons, or any person acting as an agent of an employer, directly or indirectly, the state or any political or civil subdivision of the state, and cities, except as follows:

"Employer" does not include a religious association or corporation not organized for private profit.

(e) "Employment agency" includes any person undertaking for compensation to procure employees or opportunities to work.

(f) "Essential functions" means the fundamental job duties of the employment position the individual with a disability holds or desires. "Essential functions" does not include the marginal functions of the position.

(1) A job function may be considered essential for any of several reasons, including, but not limited to, any one or more of the following:

(A) The function may be essential because the reason the position exists is to perform that function.

(B) The function may be essential because of the limited number of employees available among whom the performance of that job function can be distributed.

(C) The function may be highly specialized, so that the incumbent in the position is hired for his or her expertise or ability to perform the particular function.

(2) Evidence of whether a particular function is essential includes, but is not limited to, the following:

(A) The employer's judgment as to which functions are essential.

(B) Written job descriptions prepared before advertising or interviewing applicants for the job.

(C) The amount of time spent on the job performing the function.

(D) The consequences of not requiring the incumbent to perform the function.

(E) The terms of a collective bargaining agreement.

(F) The work experiences of past incumbents in the job.

(G) The current work experience of incumbents in similar jobs.

(g) "Labor organization" includes any organization that exists and is constituted for the purpose, in whole or in part, of collective bargaining or of dealing with employers concerning grievances, terms or conditions of employment, or of other mutual aid or protection.

(h) "Medical condition" means either of the following:

(1) Any health impairment related to or associated with a diagnosis of cancer or a record or history of cancer.

(2) Genetic characteristics. For purposes of this section, "genetic characteristics" means either of the following:

(A) Any scientifically or medically identifiable gene or chromosome, or combination or alteration thereof, that is known to be a cause of a disease or disorder in a person or his or her offspring, or that is determined to be associated with a statistically increased risk of development of a disease or disorder, and that is presently not associated with any symptoms of any disease or disorder.

(B) Inherited characteristics that may derive from the individual or family member, that are known to be a cause of a disease or disorder in a person or his or her offspring, or that are determined to be associated with a statistically increased risk of development of a disease or disorder, and that are presently not associated with any symptoms of any disease or disorder.

(i) "Mental disability" includes, but is not limited to, all of the following:

(1) Having any mental or psychological disorder or condition, such as mental retardation, organic brain syndrome, emotional or mental illness, or specific learning disabilities, that limits a major life activity. For purposes of this section:

(A) "Limits" shall be determined without regard to mitigating measures, such as medications, assistive devices, or reasonable accommodations, unless the mitigating measure itself limits a major life activity.

(B) A mental or psychological disorder or condition limits a major life activity if it makes the achievement of the major life activity difficult.

(C) "Major life activities" shall be broadly construed and shall include physical, mental, and social activities and working.

(2) Any other mental or psychological disorder or condition not described in paragraph (1) that requires special education or related services.

(3) Having a record or history of a mental or psychological disorder or condition described in paragraph (1) or (2), which is known to the employer or other entity covered by this part.

(4) Being regarded or treated by the employer or other entity covered by this part as having, or having had, any mental condition that makes achievement of a major life activity difficult.

(5) Being regarded or treated by the employer or other entity covered by this part as having, or having had, a mental or psychological disorder or condition that has no present disabling effect, but that may become a mental disability as described in paragraph (1) or (2).

"Mental disability" does not include sexual behavior disorders, compulsive gambling, kleptomania, pyromania, or psychoactive substance use disorders resulting from the current unlawful use of controlled substances or other drugs.

(j) "On the bases enumerated in this part" means or refers to discrimination on the basis of one or more of the following: race, religious creed, color, national origin, ancestry, physical disability, mental disability, medical condition, marital status, sex, age, or sexual orientation.

(k) "Physical disability" includes, but is not limited to, all of the following:

(1) Having any physiological disease, disorder, condition, cosmetic disfigurement, or anatomical loss that does both of the following:

(A) Affects one or more of the following body systems: neurological, immunological, musculoskeletal, special sense organs, respiratory, including speech organs, cardiovascular, reproductive, digestive, genitourinary, hemic and lymphatic, skin, and endocrine.

(B) Limits a major life activity. For purposes of this section:

(i) "Limits" shall be determined without regard to mitigating measures such as medications, assistive devices, prosthetics, or reasonable accommodations, unless the mitigating measure itself limits a major life activity.

(ii) A physiological disease, disorder, condition, cosmetic disfigurement, or anatomical loss limits a major life activity if it makes the achievement of the major life activity difficult.

(iii) "Major life activities" shall be broadly construed and includes physical, mental, and social activities and working.

(2) Any other health impairment not described in paragraph (1) that requires special education or related services.

(3) Having a record or history of a disease, disorder, condition, cosmetic disfigurement, anatomical loss, or health impairment described in paragraph (1) or (2), which is known to the employer or other entity covered by this part.

(4) Being regarded or treated by the employer or other entity covered by this part as having, or having had, any physical condition that makes achievement of a major life activity difficult.

(5) Being regarded or treated by the employer or other entity covered by this part as having, or having had, a disease, disorder, condition, cosmetic disfigurement, anatomical loss, or health impairment that has no present

disabling effect but may become a physical disability as described in paragraph (1) or (2).

(6) "Physical disability" does not include sexual behavior disorders, compulsive gambling, kleptomania, pyromania, or psychoactive substance use disorders resulting from the current unlawful use of controlled substances or other drugs.

(l) Notwithstanding subdivisions (i) and (k), if the definition of "disability" used in the Americans with Disabilities Act of 1990 (Public Law 101–336) would result in broader protection of the civil rights of individuals with a mental disability or physical disability, as defined in subdivision (i) or (k), or would include any medical condition not included within those definitions, then that broader protection or coverage shall be deemed incorporated by reference into, and shall prevail over conflicting provisions of, the definitions in subdivisions (i) and (k).

(m) "Race, religious creed, color, national origin, ancestry, physical disability, mental disability, medical condition, marital status, sex, age, or sexual orientation" includes a perception that the person has any of those characteristics or that the person is associated with a person who has, or is perceived to have, any of those characteristics.

(n) "Reasonable accommodation" may include either of the following:

(1) Making existing facilities used by employees readily accessible to, and usable by, individuals with disabilities.

(2) Job restructuring, part-time or modified work schedules, reassignment to a vacant position, acquisition or modification of equipment or devices, adjustment or modifications of examinations, training materials or policies, the provision of qualified readers or interpreters, and other similar accommodations for individuals with disabilities.

(o) "Religious creed," "religion," "religious observance," "religious belief," and "creed" include all aspects of religious belief, observance, and practice.

(p) "Sex" includes, but is not limited to, pregnancy, childbirth, or medical conditions related to pregnancy or childbirth. "Sex" also includes, but is not limited to, a person's gender, as defined in Section 422.56 of the Penal Code.

(q) "Sexual orientation" means heterosexuality, homosexuality, and bisexuality.

(r) "Supervisor" means any individual having the authority, in the interest of the employer, to hire, transfer, suspend, lay off, recall, promote, discharge, assign, reward, or discipline other employees, or the responsibility to direct them, or to adjust their grievances, or effectively to recommend that action, if, in connection with the foregoing, the exercise of that authority is not of a merely routine or clerical nature, but requires the use of independent judgment.

(s) "Undue hardship" means an action requiring significant difficulty or expense, when considered in light of the following factors:

(1) The nature and cost of the accommodation needed.

(2) The overall financial resources of the facilities involved in the provision of the reasonable accommodations, the number of persons employed at the facility, and the effect on expenses and resources or the impact otherwise of these accommodations upon the operation of the facility.

(3) The overall financial resources of the covered entity, the overall size of the business of a covered entity with respect to the number of employees, and the number, type, and location of its facilities.

(4) The type of operations, including the composition, structure, and functions of the workforce of the entity.

(5) The geographic separateness, administrative, or fiscal relationship of the facility or facilities. *(Added by Stats.1980, c. 992, § 4. Amended by Stats.1985, c. 1151, § 1; Stats.1990, c. 15 (S.B.1027), § 1; Stats.1992, c. 911 (A.B.311), § 3; Stats.1992, c. 912 (A.B.1286), § 3; Stats. 1992, c. 913 (A.B.1077), § 21.3; Stats.1993, c. 1214 (A.B.551), § 5; Stats.1998, c. 99 (S.B.654), § 1; Stats. 1999, c. 311 (S.B.1185), § 2; Stats.1999, c. 591 (A.B. 1670), § 5.1; Stats.1999, c. 592 (A.B.1001), § 3.7; Stats. 2000, c. 1049 (A.B.2222), § 5; Stats.2003, c. 164 (A.B. 196), § 1; Stats.2004, c. 700 (S.B.1234), § 4.)*

§ 12926.1. Legislative findings and declarations; disability, mental disability, and medical condition; broad coverage under state law; interaction in determining reasonable accommodation

The Legislature finds and declares as follows:

(a) The law of this state in the area of disabilities provides protections independent from those in the federal Americans with Disabilities Act of 1990 (Public Law 101–336). Although the federal act provides a floor of protection, this state's law has always, even prior to passage of the federal act, afforded additional protections.

(b) The law of this state contains broad definitions of physical disability, mental disability, and medical condition. It is the intent of the Legislature that the definitions of physical disability and mental disability be construed so that applicants and employees are protected from discrimination due to an actual or perceived physical or mental impairment that is disabling, potentially disabling, or perceived as disabling or potentially disabling.

(c) Physical and mental disabilities include, but are not limited to, chronic or episodic conditions such as HIV/ AIDS, hepatitis, epilepsy, seizure disorder, diabetes, clinical depression, bipolar disorder, multiple sclerosis, and heart disease. In addition, the Legislature has determined that the definitions of "physical disability" and "mental disability" under the law of this state require

155

a "limitation" upon a major life activity, but do not require, as does the Americans with Disabilities Act of 1990, a "substantial limitation." This distinction is intended to result in broader coverage under the law of this state than under that federal act. Under the law of this state, whether a condition limits a major life activity shall be determined without respect to any mitigating measures, unless the mitigating measure itself limits a major life activity, regardless of federal law under the Americans with Disabilities Act of 1990. Further, under the law of this state, "working" is a major life activity, regardless of whether the actual or perceived working limitation implicates a particular employment or a class or broad range of employments.

(d) Notwithstanding any interpretation of law in Cassista v. Community Foods (1993) 5 Cal.4th 1050, the Legislature intends (1) for state law to be independent of the Americans with Disabilities Act of 1990, (2) to require a "limitation" rather than a "substantial limitation" of a major life activity, and (3) by enacting paragraph (4) of subdivision (i) and paragraph (4) of subdivision (k) of Section 12926, to provide protection when an individual is erroneously or mistakenly believed to have any physical or mental condition that limits a major life activity.

(e) The Legislature affirms the importance of the interactive process between the applicant or employee and the employer in determining a reasonable accommodation, as this requirement has been articulated by the Equal Employment Opportunity Commission in its interpretive guidance of the Americans with Disabilities Act of 1990. *(Added by Stats.2000, c. 1049 (A.B.2222), § 6.)*

§ 12926.2. Unlawful practices; religious corporation, religious duties defined; exception for nonprofit benefit corporations

As used in this part in connection with unlawful practices, unless a different meaning clearly appears from the context:

(a) "Religious corporation" means any corporation formed under, or otherwise subject to, Part 4 (commencing with Section 9110) or Part 6 (commencing with Section 10000) of Division 2 of Title 1 of the Corporations Code, and also includes a corporation that is formed primarily or exclusively for religious purposes under the laws of any other state to administer the affairs of an organized religious group and that is not organized for private profit.

(b) "Religious duties" means duties of employment connected with carrying on the religious activities of a religious corporation or association.

(c) Notwithstanding subdivision (d) of Section 12926 and except as otherwise provided in subdivision (d) of this section, "employer" includes a religious corporation or association with respect to persons employed by the religious association or corporation to perform duties, other than religious duties, at a health care facility operated by the religious association or corporation for

156

the provision of health care that is not restricted to adherents of the religion that established the association or corporation.

(d) "Employer" does not include a religious corporation with respect to either the employment, including promotion, of an individual of a particular religion, or the application of the employer's religious doctrines, tenets, or teachings, in any work connected with the provision of health care.

(e) Notwithstanding subdivision (d) of Section 12926, "employer" does not include a nonprofit public benefit corporation incorporated to provide health care on behalf of a religious organization under Part 2 (commencing with Section 5110) of Division 2 of Title 1 of the Corporations Code, with respect to employment, including promotion, of an individual of a particular religion in an executive or pastoral-care position connected with the provision of health care.

(f)(1) Notwithstanding any other provision of law, a nonprofit public benefit corporation formed by, or affiliated with, a particular religion and that operates an educational institution as its sole or primary activity, may restrict employment, including promotion, in any or all employment categories to individuals of a particular religion.

(2) Notwithstanding paragraph (1) or any other provision of law, employers that are nonprofit public benefit corporations specified in paragraph (1) shall be subject to the provisions of this part in all other respects, including, but not limited to, the prohibitions against discrimination made unlawful employment practices by this part. *(Added by Stats.1999, c. 913 (A.B.1541), § 2. Amended by Stats.2001, c. 910 (S.B.504), § 1.)*

§ 12927. Housing accommodations; definitions

As used in this part in connection with housing accommodations, unless a different meaning clearly appears from the context:

(a) "Affirmative actions" means any activity for the purpose of eliminating discrimination in housing accommodations because of race, color, religion, sex, marital status, national origin, ancestry, familial status, or disability.

(b) "Conciliation council" means a nonprofit organization, or a city or county human relations commission, which provides education, factfinding, and mediation or conciliation services in resolution of complaints of housing discrimination.

(c)(1) "Discrimination" includes refusal to sell, rent, or lease housing accommodations; includes refusal to negotiate for the sale, rental, or lease of housing accommodations; includes representation that a housing accommodation is not available for inspection, sale, or rental when that housing accommodation is in fact so available; includes any other denial or withholding of housing accommodations; includes provision of inferior terms, conditions, privileges, facilities, or services in connection with those housing accommodations; includes harassment in connection with those housing accommodations; includes the cancellation or termination of a sale or rental agreement; includes the provision of segregated or separated housing accommodations; includes the refusal to permit, at the expense of the disabled person, reasonable modifications of existing premises occupied or to be occupied by the disabled person, if the modifications may be necessary to afford the disabled person full enjoyment of the premises, except that, in the case of a rental, the landlord may, where it is reasonable to do so condition permission for a modification on the renter's agreeing to restore the interior of the premises to the condition that existed before the modification (other than for reasonable wear and tear), and includes refusal to make reasonable accommodations in rules, policies, practices, or services when these accommodations may be necessary to afford a disabled person equal opportunity to use and enjoy a dwelling.

(2) "Discrimination" does not include either of the following:

(A) Refusal to rent or lease a portion of an owner-occupied single-family house to a person as a roomer or boarder living within the household, provided that no more than one roomer or boarder is to live within the household, and the owner complies with subdivision (c) of Section 12955, which prohibits discriminatory notices, statements, and advertisements.

(B) Where the sharing of living areas in a single dwelling unit is involved, the use of words stating or tending to imply that the housing being advertised is available only to persons of one sex.

(d) "Housing accommodation" means any building, structure, or portion thereof that is occupied as, or intended for occupancy as, a residence by one or more families and any vacant land that is offered for sale or lease for the construction thereon of any building, structure, or portion thereof intended to be so occupied.

(e) "Owner" includes the lessee, sublessee, assignee, managing agent, real estate broker or salesperson, or any person having any legal or equitable right of ownership or possession or the right to rent or lease housing accommodations, and includes the state and any of its political subdivisions and any agency thereof.

(f) "Person" includes all individuals and entities that are described in Section 3602(d) of Title 42 of the United States Code, and in the definition of "owner" in subdivision (e) of this section, and all institutional third parties, including the Federal Home Loan Mortgage Corporation.

(g) "Aggrieved person" includes any person who claims to have been injured by a discriminatory housing practice or believes that the person will be injured by a discriminatory housing practice that is about to occur.

(h) "Real estate-related transactions" include any of the following:

(1) The making or purchasing of loans or providing other financial assistance that is for the purpose of purchasing, constructing, improving, repairing, or maintaining a dwelling, or that is secured by residential real estate.

(2) The selling, brokering, or appraising of residential real property.

(3) The use of territorial underwriting requirements, for the purpose of requiring a borrower in a specific geographic area to obtain earthquake insurance, required by an institutional third party on a loan secured by residential real property. *(Added by Stats.1980, c. 992, § 4. Amended by Stats.1992, c. 182 (S.B.1234), § 3; Stats.1993, c. 1277 (A.B.2244), § 3; Stats.1995, c. 169 (S.B.391), § 1; Stats.1995, c. 924 (S.B.1325), § 1, eff. Oct. 16, 1995; Stats.1999, c. 591 (A.B.1670), § 6.)*

§ 12928. Identity of employer; rebuttable presumption

Notwithstanding any other provision of this part, there is a rebuttable presumption that "employer," as defined by subdivision (d) of Section 12926, includes any person or entity identified as the employer on the employee's Federal Form W–2 (Wage and Tax Statement). *(Added by Stats.1999, c. 797 (S.B.211), § 1. Amended by Stats. 2004, c. 647 (A.B.2870), § 2.)*

CHAPTER 5. POWERS AND DUTIES

ARTICLE 1. THE DEPARTMENT

Section
12930. Functions, powers and duties.
12931. Assistance to communities and persons; resolutions of disputes, disagreements and difficulties relating to discriminatory practices; requests.
12932. Legislative recognition; employment of disabled persons; conciliation assistance; confidentiality; disciplinary action.
12933. Liaison with human relations commissions.

§ 12930. Functions, powers and duties

The department shall have the following functions, powers, and duties:

(a) To establish and maintain a principal office and any other offices within the state as are necessary to carry out the purposes of this part.

(b) To meet and function at any place within the state.

(c) To appoint attorneys, investigators, conciliators, and other employees as it may deem necessary, fix their compensation within the limitations provided by law, and prescribe their duties.

(d) To obtain upon request and utilize the services of all governmental departments and agencies and, in addition, with respect to housing discrimination, of conciliation councils.

(e) To adopt, promulgate, amend, and rescind suitable rules and regulations to carry out the functions and duties of the department pursuant to this part.

(f)(1) To receive, investigate, and conciliate complaints alleging practices made unlawful pursuant to Chapter 6 (commencing with Section 12940).

(2) To receive, investigate, and conciliate complaints alleging a violation of Section 51, 51.5, 51.7, 54, 54.1, or 54.2 of the Civil Code. The remedies and procedures of this part shall be independent of any other remedy or procedure that might apply.

(g) In connection with any matter under investigation or in question before the department pursuant to a complaint filed under Section 12960, 12961, or 12980:

(1) To issue subpoenas to require the attendance and testimony of witnesses and the production of books, records, documents, and physical materials.

(2) To administer oaths, examine witnesses under oath and take evidence, and take depositions and affidavits.

(3) To issue written interrogatories.

(4) To request the production for inspection and copying of books, records, documents, and physical materials.

(5) To petition the superior courts to compel the appearance and testimony of witnesses, the production of books, records, documents, and physical materials, and the answering of interrogatories.

(h) To issue accusations pursuant to Section 12965 or 12981 and to prosecute those accusations before the commission.

(i) To issue those publications and those results of investigations and research as in its judgment will tend to promote good will and minimize or eliminate discrimination in employment on the bases enumerated in this part and discrimination in housing because of race, religious creed, color, sex, marital status, national origin, ancestry, familial status, disability, or sexual orientation.

(j) To investigate, approve, certify, decertify, monitor, and enforce nondiscrimination programs proposed by a contractor to be engaged in pursuant to Section 12990.

(k) To render annually to the Governor and to the Legislature a written report of its activities and of its recommendations. *(Added by Stats.1980, c. 992, § 4. Amended by Stats.1980, c. 1023, § 1; Stats.1981, c. 899, p. 3423, § 1; Stats.1992, c. 182 (S.B.1234), § 4; Stats.1992, c. 911 (A.B.311), § 4; Stats.1999, c. 591 (A.B.1670), § 7; Stats.1999, c. 592 (A.B.1001), § 4.5.)*

§ 12931. Assistance to communities and persons; resolutions of disputes, disagreements and difficulties relating to discriminatory practices; requests

The department may also provide assistance to communities and persons therein in resolving disputes, disagreements, or difficulties relating to discriminatory practices based on race, religious creed, color, national origin, ancestry, physical disability, mental disability, medical condition, marital status, sex, familial status, age, or sexual orientation that impair the rights of persons in those communities under the Constitution or laws of the United States or of this state. The services of the department may be made available in cases of these disputes, disagreements, or difficulties only when, in its judgment, peaceful relations among the citizens of the community involved are threatened thereby. The department's services are to be made available only upon the request of an appropriate state or local public body, or upon the request of any person directly affected by any such dispute, disagreement, or difficulty.

The assistance of the department pursuant to this section shall be limited to endeavors at investigation, conference, conciliation, and persuasion. *(Added by Stats.1980, c. 992, § 4. Amended by Stats.1992, c. 182 (S.B.1234), § 5; Stats.1992, c. 912 (A.B.1286), § 4; Stats. 1992, c. 913 (A.B.1077), § 22; Stats.1999, c. 592 (A.B. 1001), § 5.)*

§ 12932. Legislative recognition; employment of disabled persons; conciliation assistance; confidentiality; disciplinary action

(a) The Legislature recognizes that the avoidance of discriminatory practices in the employment of disabled persons is most effectively achieved through the ongoing efforts of state agencies involved in the vocational rehabilitation and job placement of the disabled. The department may utilize the efforts and experience of the Department of Rehabilitation in the development of job opportunities for the disabled by requesting the Department of Rehabilitation to foster good will and to conciliate on employment policies with employers who, in the judgment of the department, have employment practices or policies that discriminate against disabled persons. Nothing contained in this paragraph shall be construed to transfer any of the functions, powers, or duties from the department to the Department of Rehabilitation.

(b) The activities of the department in providing conciliation assistance shall be conducted in confidence and without publicity, and the department shall hold confidential any information acquired in the regular performance of its duties upon the understanding that it would be so held.

(c) No employee of the department shall engage in the performance of investigative or prosecuting functions of any department or agency in any litigation arising out of a dispute in which he or she acted on behalf of the department. Any employee of the department, who makes public in any manner whatever any information in violation of this subdivision, is guilty of a misdemeanor and, if a member of the state civil service, shall be subject to disciplinary action under the State Civil Service Act (Part 2 (commencing with Section 18500) of Division 5 of Title 2).

(d) When contacted by the department, employers, labor organizations, or employment agencies shall be informed whether a particular discussion, or portion thereof, constitutes either of the following:

(1) Endeavors at conference, conciliation, and persuasion which may not be disclosed by the department or

received in evidence in any formal hearing or court action.

(2) Investigative processes, which are not so protected. *(Added by Stats.1980, c. 992, § 4. Amended by Stats.1989, c. 1309, § 2.)*

§ 12933. Liaison with human relations commissions

The department shall maintain liaison with the human relations commissions of cities, counties, and any city and county, and shall provide any information not designated by law as confidential to such commissions on request. *(Added by Stats.1980, c. 992, § 4.)*

ARTICLE 2. THE COMMISSION

Section
12935. Functions, powers and duties.

§ 12935. Functions, powers and duties

The commission shall have the following functions, powers, and duties:

(a) To adopt, promulgate, amend, and rescind suitable rules, regulations, and standards (1) to interpret, implement, and apply all provisions of this part, (2) to regulate the conduct of hearings held pursuant to Sections 12967 and 12981, and (3) to carry out all other functions and duties of the commission pursuant to this part.

(b) To conduct hearings pursuant to Sections 12967 and 12981.

(c) To conduct mediations at the request of the department at any time after a complaint is filed pursuant to Section 12960, 12961, or 12980. The department may withdraw a request for mediation at any time to pursue an investigation.

(d) To establish and maintain a principal office within the state and to meet and function at any place within the state.

(e) To appoint an executive secretary, and any attorneys and other employees as it may deem necessary, fix their compensation within the limitations provided by law, and prescribe their duties.

(f) To hold hearings, subpoena witnesses, compel their attendance, administer oaths, examine any person under oath and, in connection therewith, to require the production of any books or papers relating to any matter under investigation or in question before the commission.

(g) To create or provide financial or technical assistance to any advisory agencies and conciliation councils, local or otherwise, as in its judgment will aid in effectuating the purposes of this part, and to empower them to study the problems of discrimination in all or specific fields of human relationships or in particular instances of employment discrimination on the bases enumerated in this part or in specific instances of housing discrimination because of race, religious creed, color, national origin, ancestry, familial status, disability, marital status, sex, or sexual orientation and to foster, through community effort or otherwise, good will, cooperation, and conciliation among the groups and elements of the population of the state and to make recommendations to the commission for the development of policies and procedures in general. These advisory agencies and conciliation councils shall be composed of representative citizens, serving without pay.

(h) With respect to findings and orders made pursuant to this part, to establish a system of published opinions that shall serve as precedent in interpreting and applying the provisions of this part. Commission findings, orders, and opinions in an adjudicative proceeding are subject to Section 11425.60.

(i) To issue publications and results of inquiries and research that in its judgment will tend to promote good will and minimize or eliminate unlawful discrimination. These publications shall include an annual report to the Governor and the Legislature of its activities and recommendations.

(j) Notwithstanding Sections 11370.3 and 11502, to appoint administrative law judges, as it may deem necessary, to conduct hearings and mediations. Each administrative law judge shall possess the qualifications established by the State Personnel Board for the particular class of position involved. The hearing officers of the commission shall become administrative law judges on the effective date of this subdivision. [1] *(Added by Stats. 1980, c. 992, § 4. Amended by Stats.1981, c. 625, p. 2379, § 2; Stats.1992, c. 182 (S.B.1234), § 6; Stats.1992, c. 910 (A.B.2392), § 2.5; Stats.1995, c. 938 (S.B.523), § 53, operative July 1, 1997; Stats.1999, c. 592 (A.B.1001), § 6; Stats.2004, c. 647 (A.B.2870), § 3.)*

[1] Stats.2004, c. 647 (A.B.2870).

CHAPTER 6. DISCRIMINATION PROHIBITED

ARTICLE 1. UNLAWFUL PRACTICES, GENERALLY

Section
12940.   Employers, labor organizations, employment agencies and other persons; unlawful employment practice; exceptions.
12940.1. Individuals with heart trouble; firefighting or law enforcement activities; presumption of inability to perform; burden of proof to overcome presumption.
12940.3. Americans with Disabilities Act; study; cost of compliance; analysis of benefits; legislative intent.
12941.   Age discrimination; use of salary as method of differentiating between employees.
12942.   Continuation of employment beyond normal retirement date; effect on pension or retirement plans; compulsory retirement.
12943.   School districts; unlawful employment practice based on pregnancy or temporary disability.
12944.   Licensing boards; unlawful acts based on examinations and qualifications; determination of unlaw-

Section

fulness; inquiries; reasonable accommodations; records.

12945.   Pregnancy; childbirth or related medical condition; unlawful practice by employers; benefits and leaves of absence; transfer of position.

12945.1. Moore-Brown-Roberti Family Rights Act.

12945.2. Family care and medical leave; definitions; conditions; unlawful employment practices.

12945.5. Unlawful employment practice; sterilization.

12946.   Retention of applications, records and files for two years; failure to retain as unlawful practice by employers, labor organization and employment agencies.

12947.   Child care services for employees and members; not an unlawful practice.

12947.5. Prohibition on wearing of pants based on sex; unlawful employment practice; exemptions.

12948.   Denial of civil rights as unlawful practice.

12949.   Requirement to adhere to reasonable workplace appearance.

12950.   Sexual harassment; amendment of poster; distribution of information sheet; contents of information sheet; violations.

12950.1. Sexual harassment training and education requirements for new supervisory employees; contents of training and education; definitions; employer liability; violation of requirements.

12951.   Unlawful employment practice for employer to adopt or enforce policy that limits or prohibits use of language; conditions; business necessity.

§ 12940. Employers, labor organizations, employment agencies and other persons; unlawful employment practice; exceptions

It shall be an unlawful employment practice, unless based upon a bona fide occupational qualification, or, except where based upon applicable security regulations established by the United States or the State of California:

(a) For an employer, because of the race, religious creed, color, national origin, ancestry, physical disability, mental disability, medical condition, marital status, sex, age, or sexual orientation of any person, to refuse to hire or employ the person or to refuse to select the person for a training program leading to employment, or to bar or to discharge the person from employment or from a training program leading to employment, or to discriminate against the person in compensation or in terms, conditions, or privileges of employment.

(1) This part does not prohibit an employer from refusing to hire or discharging an employee with a physical or mental disability, or subject an employer to any legal liability resulting from the refusal to employ or the discharge of an employee with a physical or mental disability, where the employee, because of his or her physical or mental disability, is unable to perform his or her essential duties even with reasonable accommodations, or cannot perform those duties in a manner that would not endanger his or her health or safety or the health or safety of others even with reasonable accommodations.

(2) This part does not prohibit an employer from refusing to hire or discharging an employee who, because of the employee's medical condition, is unable to perform his or her essential duties even with reasonable accommodations, or cannot perform those duties in a manner that would not endanger the employee's health or safety or the health or safety of others even with reasonable accommodations. Nothing in this part shall subject an employer to any legal liability resulting from the refusal to employ or the discharge of an employee who, because of the employee's medical condition, is unable to perform his or her essential duties, or cannot perform those duties in a manner that would not endanger the employee's health or safety or the health or safety of others even with reasonable accommodations.

(3) Nothing in this part relating to discrimination on account of marital status shall do either of the following:

(A) Affect the right of an employer to reasonably regulate, for reasons of supervision, safety, security, or morale, the working of spouses in the same department, division, or facility, consistent with the rules and regulations adopted by the commission.

(B) Prohibit bona fide health plans from providing additional or greater benefits to employees with dependents than to those employees without or with fewer dependents.

(4) Nothing in this part relating to discrimination on account of sex shall affect the right of an employer to use veteran status as a factor in employee selection or to give special consideration to Vietnam era veterans.

(5) Nothing in this part prohibits an employer from refusing to employ an individual because of his or her age if the law compels or provides for that refusal. Promotions within the existing staff, hiring or promotion on the basis of experience and training, rehiring on the basis of seniority and prior service with the employer, or hiring under an established recruiting program from high schools, colleges, universities, or trade schools do not, in and of themselves, constitute unlawful employment practices.

(b) For a labor organization, because of the race, religious creed, color, national origin, ancestry, physical disability, mental disability, medical condition, marital status, sex, age, or sexual orientation of any person, to exclude, expel or restrict from its membership the person, or to provide only second-class or segregated membership or to discriminate against any person because of the race, religious creed, color, national origin, ancestry, physical disability, mental disability, medical condition, marital status, sex, age, or sexual orientation of the person in the election of officers of the labor organization or in the selection of the labor organization's staff or to discriminate in any way against any of its members or against any employer or against any person employed by an employer.

(c) For any person to discriminate against any person in the selection or training of that person in any

160

apprenticeship training program or any other training program leading to employment because of the race, religious creed, color, national origin, ancestry, physical disability, mental disability, medical condition, marital status, sex, age, or sexual orientation of the person discriminated against.

(d) For any employer or employment agency to print or circulate or cause to be printed or circulated any publication, or to make any non-job-related inquiry of an employee or applicant, either verbal or through use of an application form, that expresses, directly or indirectly, any limitation, specification, or discrimination as to race, religious creed, color, national origin, ancestry, physical disability, mental disability, medical condition, marital status, sex, age, or sexual orientation, or any intent to make any such limitation, specification or discrimination. Nothing in this part prohibits an employer or employment agency from inquiring into the age of an applicant, or from specifying age limitations, where the law compels or provides for that action.

(e)(1) Except as provided in paragraph (2) or (3), for any employer or employment agency to require any medical or psychological examination of an applicant, to make any medical or psychological inquiry of an applicant, to make any inquiry whether an applicant has a mental disability or physical disability or medical condition, or to make any inquiry regarding the nature or severity of a physical disability, mental disability, or medical condition.

(2) Notwithstanding paragraph (1), an employer or employment agency may inquire into the ability of an applicant to perform job-related functions and may respond to an applicant's request for reasonable accommodation.

(3) Notwithstanding paragraph (1), an employer or employment agency may require a medical or psychological examination or make a medical or psychological inquiry of a job applicant after an employment offer has been made but prior to the commencement of employment duties, provided that the examination or inquiry is job-related and consistent with business necessity and that all entering employees in the same job classification are subject to the same examination or inquiry.

(f)(1) Except as provided in paragraph (2), for any employer or employment agency to require any medical or psychological examination of an employee, to make any medical or psychological inquiry of an employee, to make any inquiry whether an employee has a mental disability, physical disability, or medical condition, or to make any inquiry regarding the nature or severity of a physical disability, mental disability, or medical condition.

(2) Notwithstanding paragraph (1), an employer or employment agency may require any examinations or inquiries that it can show to be job-related and consistent with business necessity. An employer or employment agency may conduct voluntary medical examinations, including voluntary medical histories, which are part of an employee health program available to employees at that worksite.

(g) For any employer, labor organization, or employment agency to harass, discharge, expel, or otherwise discriminate against any person because the person has made a report pursuant to Section 11161.8 of the Penal Code that prohibits retaliation against hospital employees who report suspected patient abuse by health facilities or community care facilities.

(h) For any employer, labor organization, employment agency, or person to discharge, expel, or otherwise discriminate against any person because the person has opposed any practices forbidden under this part or because the person has filed a complaint, testified, or assisted in any proceeding under this part.

(i) For any person to aid, abet, incite, compel, or coerce the doing of any of the acts forbidden under this part, or to attempt to do so.

(j)(1) For an employer, labor organization, employment agency, apprenticeship training program or any training program leading to employment, or any other person, because of race, religious creed, color, national origin, ancestry, physical disability, mental disability, medical condition, marital status, sex, age, or sexual orientation, to harass an employee, an applicant, or a person providing services pursuant to a contract. Harassment of an employee, an applicant, or a person providing services pursuant to a contract by an employee, other than an agent or supervisor, shall be unlawful if the entity, or its agents or supervisors, knows or should have known of this conduct and fails to take immediate and appropriate corrective action. An employer may also be responsible for the acts of nonemployees, with respect to sexual harassment of employees, applicants, or persons providing services pursuant to a contract in the workplace, where the employer, or its agents or supervisors, knows or should have known of the conduct and fails to take immediate and appropriate corrective action. In reviewing cases involving the acts of nonemployees, the extent of the employer's control and any other legal responsibility which the employer may have with respect to the conduct of those nonemployees shall be considered. An entity shall take all reasonable steps to prevent harassment from occurring. Loss of tangible job benefits shall not be necessary in order to establish harassment.

(2) The provisions of this subdivision are declaratory of existing law, except for the new duties imposed on employers with regard to harassment.

(3) An employee of an entity subject to this subdivision is personally liable for any harassment prohibited by this section that is perpetrated by the employee, regardless of whether the employer or covered entity knows or should have known of the conduct and fails to take immediate and appropriate corrective action.

(4)(A) For purposes of this subdivision only, "employer" means any person regularly employing one or more persons or regularly receiving the services of one or more persons providing services pursuant to a contract, or any person acting as an agent of an employer, directly or indirectly, the state, or any political or civil subdivision of the state, and cities. The definition of "employer" in subdivision (d) of Section 12926 applies to all provisions of this section other than this subdivision.

(B) Notwithstanding subparagraph (A), for purposes of this subdivision, "employer" does not include a religious association or corporation not organized for private profit, except as provided in Section 12926.2.

(C) For purposes of this subdivision, "harassment" because of sex includes sexual harassment, gender harassment, and harassment based on pregnancy, childbirth, or related medical conditions.

(5) For purposes of this subdivision, "a person providing services pursuant to a contract" means a person who meets all of the following criteria:

(A) The person has the right to control the performance of the contract for services and discretion as to the manner of performance.

(B) The person is customarily engaged in an independently established business.

(C) The person has control over the time and place the work is performed, supplies the tools and instruments used in the work, and performs work that requires a particular skill not ordinarily used in the course of the employer's work.

(k) For an employer, labor organization, employment agency, apprenticeship training program, or any training program leading to employment, to fail to take all reasonable steps necessary to prevent discrimination and harassment from occurring.

(*l*) For an employer or other entity covered by this part to refuse to hire or employ a person or to refuse to select a person for a training program leading to employment or to bar or to discharge a person from employment or from a training program leading to employment, or to discriminate against a person in compensation or in terms, conditions, or privileges of employment because of a conflict between the person's religious belief or observance and any employment requirement, unless the employer or other entity covered by this part demonstrates that it has explored any available reasonable alternative means of accommodating the religious belief or observance, including the possibilities of excusing the person from those duties that conflict with his or her religious belief or observance or permitting those duties to be performed at another time or by another person, but is unable to reasonably accommodate the religious belief or observance without undue hardship on the conduct of the business of the employer or other entity covered by this part. Religious belief or observance, as used in this section, includes, but is not limited to, observance of a Sabbath or other religious holy day or days, and reasonable time necessary for travel prior and subsequent to a religious observance.

162

(m) For an employer or other entity covered by this part to fail to make reasonable accommodation for the known physical or mental disability of an applicant or employee. Nothing in this subdivision or in paragraph (1) or (2) of subdivision (a) shall be construed to require an accommodation that is demonstrated by the employer or other covered entity to produce undue hardship to its operation.

(n) For an employer or other entity covered by this part to fail to engage in a timely, good faith, interactive process with the employee or applicant to determine effective reasonable accommodations, if any, in response to a request for reasonable accommodation by an employee or applicant with a known physical or mental disability or known medical condition.

(*o*) For an employer or other entity covered by this part, to subject, directly or indirectly, any employee, applicant, or other person to a test for the presence of a genetic characteristic. *(Added by Stats.1980, c. 992, § 4. Amended by Stats.1981, c. 11, p. 24, § 1; Stats.1981, c. 270, p. 1363, § 1; Stats.1982, c. 1184, p. 4219, § 1; Stats.1982, c. 1193, p. 4258, § 2; Stats.1984, c. 1754, § 2; Stats.1985, c. 1151, § 2; Stats.1987, c. 605, § 1; Stats. 1989, c. 1309, § 3; Stats.1992, c. 912 (A.B.1286), § 5; Stats.1992, c. 913 (A.B.1077), § 23.1; Stats.1993, c. 711 (A.B.675), § 2; Stats.1998, c. 485 (A.B.2803), § 85; Stats.1999, c. 591 (A.B.1670), § 8; Stats.1999, c. 592 (A.B.1001), § 7.5; Stats.2000, c. 1047 (A.B.1856), § 1; Stats.2000, c. 1049 (A.B.2222), § 7.5; Stats.2001, c. 909 (A.B.1475), § 1; Stats.2002, c. 664 (A.B.3034), § 94; Stats.2002, c. 525 (A.B.1599), § 1; Stats.2003, c. 671 (A.B.76), § 1.)*

§ 12940.1. Individuals with heart trouble; firefighting or law enforcement activities; presumption of inability to perform; burden of proof to overcome presumption

For the purposes of paragraph (1) of subdivision (a) of Section 12940, it shall be presumed that an individual with heart trouble, as referred to in Section 3212 of the Labor Code, applying for either a firefighter position or participation in an apprenticeship training program leading to employment in that position, where the actual duties require physical, active fire suppression, or a law enforcement position, the principal duties of which clearly consist of active law enforcement, could not perform his or her duties in a manner which would not endanger his or her health or safety or the health or safety of others. This presumption may be overcome by the applicant or the department proving, by a preponderance of the evidence, that the applicant would be able to safely perform the job. Law enforcement, for the purposes of this section, means police officer, deputy sheriff, or sheriff whose principal duties consist of active law enforcement service. *(Added by Stats.1984, c. 380, § 1.)*

§ 12940.3. Americans with Disabilities Act; study; cost of compliance; analysis of benefits; legislative intent

Prior to January 1, 1996, a study or survey of the costs, including litigation and reasonable accommodation expenses and other impacts on California employers of 15 or more employees, resulting from compliance with Title I of the Americans with Disabilities Act of 1990 (Public Law 101–336),[1] shall be undertaken jointly by the California Chamber of Commerce, the Department of Fair Employment and Housing, Protection and Advocacy, Inc., and the State Department of Rehabilitation. The study shall also include an analysis of the benefits of the requirements of Title I of the Americans with Disabilities Act of 1990 (Public Law 101–336) to persons with disabilities. The results of the study shall be submitted to the Commission on Special Education for their review and recommendations. The study shall provide a basis for a recommendation to the Legislature and the Governor concerning whether the hardships imposed upon businesses outweigh the benefits to persons with disabilities when the requirements of Title I of the Americans with Disabilities Act of 1990 (Public Law 101–336) are extended to California employers of 5 to 14, inclusive, employees by amending the Fair Employment and Housing Act to include people with mental disabilities as a protected class. In conducting the study and making a recommendation, the parties shall consider whether the additional requirements or consequences of being subject to the additional requirements will impose a significant hardship on employers of 5 to 14, inclusive, employees.

It is the intent to the Legislature that if, at the conclusion of the study and report to the Legislature, it is determined that employers of between 5 and 14 employees would not have a significant hardship in implementing the requirements of Title I of the Americans with Disabilities Act of 1990 (Public Law 101–336), legislation should be introduced to require that employers with between 5 and 14 employees are covered by the requirements of Title I of the Americans with Disabilities Act of 1990 (Public Law 101–336).

The Legislature intends that all employers, including employers of 5 to 14, inclusive, employees, voluntarily comply with the requirements of Title I of the Americans with Disabilities Act of 1990 (Public Law 101–336) so that persons with mental disabilities can participate fully in the employment opportunities provided to all Californians. However, it is the intent of the Legislature that existing employment discrimination provisions covering employers of 5 to 14, inclusive, employees shall not be altered by amendments to this part that become effective on January 1, 1993. *(Added by Stats.1992, c. 913 (A.B. 1077), § 23.5.)*

[1] 42 U.S.C.A. § 12101 et seq.

§ 12941. Age discrimination; use of salary as method of differentiating between employees

The Legislature hereby declares its rejection of the court of appeal opinion in Marks v. Loral Corp. (1997) 57 Cal.App.4th 30, and states that the opinion does not affect existing law in any way, including, but not limited to, the law pertaining to disparate treatment. The Legislature declares its intent that the use of salary as the basis for differentiating between employees when terminating employment may be found to constitute age discrimination if use of that criterion adversely impacts older workers as a group, and further declares its intent that the disparate impact theory of proof may be used in claims of age discrimination. The Legislature further reaffirms and declares its intent that the courts interpret the state's statutes prohibiting age discrimination in employment broadly and vigorously, in a manner comparable to prohibitions against sex and race discrimination, and with the goal of not only protecting older workers as individuals, but also of protecting older workers as a group, since they face unique obstacles in the later phases of their careers. Nothing in this section shall limit the affirmative defenses traditionally available in employment discrimination cases including, but not limited to, those set forth in Section 7286.7 of Title 2 of the California Code of Regulations. *(Formerly § 12941.1, added by Stats.1999, c. 222 (S.B.26), § 2. Renumbered § 12941 and amended by Stats.2002, c. 525 (A.B.1599), § 3.)*

§ 12942. Continuation of employment beyond normal retirement date; effect on pension or retirement plans; compulsory retirement

(a) Every employer in this state shall permit any employee who indicates in writing a desire in a reasonable time and can demonstrate the ability to do so, to continue his or her employment beyond any retirement date contained in any private pension or retirement plan.

This employment shall continue so long as the employee demonstrates his or her ability to perform the functions of the job adequately and the employer is satisfied with the quality of work performed.

(b) Any employee indicating this desire and continuing the employment shall give the employer written notice in reasonable time, of intent to retire or terminate when the retirement or termination occurs after the employee's retirement date.

(c) Nothing in this section or Section 12941 shall be construed to prohibit any of the following:

(1) To prohibit an institution of higher education, as defined by Section 1001 of Title 20 of the United States Code, from imposing a retirement policy for tenured faculty members, provided that the institution has a policy permitting reemployment of these individuals on a year-to-year basis.

(2) To prohibit compulsory retirement of any employee who has attained 70 years of age and is a physician employed by a professional medical corporation, the articles or bylaws of which provide for compulsory retirement.

(3) To prohibit compulsory retirement of any employee who has attained 65 years of age and who for the two-year period immediately before retirement was employed

163

in a bona fide executive or a high policymaking position, if that employee is entitled to an immediate nonforfeitable annual retirement benefit from a pension, profit-sharing, savings, or deferred compensation plan, or any combination of those plans, of the employer for the employee, which equals in the aggregate at least twenty-seven thousand dollars ($27,000). *(Added by Stats.1980, c. 992, § 4. Amended by Stats.1981, c. 146, p. 944, § 1; Stats.1983, c. 666, § 8; Stats.1989, c. 1309, § 7; Stats. 2004, c. 647 (A.B.2870), § 4.)*

§ 12943. School districts; unlawful employment practice based on pregnancy or temporary disability

It shall be an unlawful employment practice unless based upon a bona fide occupational qualification:

(a) For the governing board of any school district, because of the pregnancy of any female person, to refuse to hire or employ her, or to refuse to select her for a training program leading to employment, or to bar or to discharge her from employment or from a training program leading to employment, or to discriminate against her in compensation or in terms, conditions, or privileges of employment.

(b) For the governing board of any school district to terminate any employee who is temporarily disabled, pursuant to or on the basis of an employment policy under which insufficient or no leave is available, if the policy has a disparate impact on employees of one sex and is not justified by necessity of the public schools. *(Added by Stats.1980, c. 992, § 4.)*

§ 12944. Licensing boards; unlawful acts based on examinations and qualifications; determination of unlawfulness; inquiries; reasonable accommodations; records

(a) It shall be unlawful for a licensing board to require any examination or establish any other qualification for licensing that has an adverse impact on any class by virtue of its race, creed, color, national origin or ancestry, sex, age, medical condition, physical disability, mental disability, or sexual orientation, unless the practice can be demonstrated to be job related.

Where the commission, after hearing, determines that an examination is unlawful under this subdivision, the licensing board may continue to use and rely on the examination until such time as judicial review by the superior court of the determination is exhausted.

If an examination or other qualification for licensing is determined to be unlawful under this section, that determination shall not void, limit, repeal, or otherwise affect any right, privilege, status, or responsibility previously conferred upon any person by the examination or by a license issued in reliance on the examination or qualification.

(b) It shall be unlawful for a licensing board to fail or refuse to make reasonable accommodation to an individual's mental or physical disability or medical condition.

(c) It shall be unlawful for any licensing board, unless specifically acting in accordance with federal equal employment opportunity guidelines or regulations approved by the commission, to print or circulate or cause to be printed or circulated any publication, or to make any non-job-related inquiry, either verbal or through use of an application form, which expresses, directly or indirectly, any limitation, specification, or discrimination as to race, religious creed, color, national origin, ancestry, physical disability, mental disability, medical condition, sex, age, or sexual orientation or any intent to make any such limitation, specification, or discrimination. Nothing in this subdivision shall prohibit any licensing board from making, in connection with prospective licensure or certification, an inquiry as to, or a request for information regarding, the physical fitness of applicants if that inquiry or request for information is directly related and pertinent to the license or the licensed position the applicant is applying for. Nothing in this subdivision shall prohibit any licensing board, in connection with prospective examinations, licensure, or certification, from inviting individuals with physical or mental disabilities to request reasonable accommodations or from making inquiries related to reasonable accommodations.

(d) It is unlawful for a licensing board to discriminate against any person because the person has filed a complaint, testified, or assisted in any proceeding under this part.

(e) It is unlawful for any licensing board to fail to keep records of applications for licensing or certification for a period of two years following the date of receipt of the applications.

(f) As used in this section, "licensing board" means any state board, agency, or authority in the State and Consumer Services Agency that has the authority to grant licenses or certificates which are prerequisites to employment eligibility or professional status. *(Added by Stats. 1980, c. 992, § 4. Amended by Stats.1992, c. 912 (A.B. 1286), § 6; Stats.1992, c. 913 (A.B.1077), § 24; Stats. 1999, c. 592 (A.B.1001), § 8.)*

§ 12945. Pregnancy; childbirth or related medical condition; unlawful practice by employers; benefits and leaves of absence; transfer of position

In addition to the provisions that govern pregnancy, childbirth, or related medical conditions in Sections 12926 and 12940, it shall be an unlawful employment practice, unless based upon a bona fide occupational qualification:

(a) For an employer to refuse to allow a female employee disabled by pregnancy, childbirth, or related medical conditions to take a leave for a reasonable period of time not to exceed four months and thereafter return to work, as set forth in the commission's regulations. The employee shall be entitled to utilize any accrued vacation leave during this period of time. Reasonable period of time means that period during which the female employee is disabled on account of pregnancy, childbirth, or related medical conditions.

An employer may require an employee who plans to take a leave pursuant to this subdivision to give the employer reasonable notice of the date the leave shall commence and the estimated duration of the leave.

(b)(1) For an employer to refuse to provide reasonable accommodation for an employee for conditions related to pregnancy, childbirth, or related medical conditions, if she so requests, with the advice of her health care provider.

(2) For an employer who has a policy, practice, or collective bargaining agreement requiring or authorizing the transfer of temporarily disabled employees to less strenuous or hazardous positions for the duration of the disability to refuse to transfer a pregnant female employee who so requests.

(3) For an employer to refuse to temporarily transfer a pregnant female employee to a less strenuous or hazardous position for the duration of her pregnancy if she so requests, with the advice of her physician, where that transfer can be reasonably accommodated. However, no employer shall be required by this section to create additional employment that the employer would not otherwise have created, nor shall the employer be required to discharge any employee, transfer any employee with more seniority, or promote any employee who is not qualified to perform the job.

(c) This section shall not be construed to affect any other provision of law relating to sex discrimination or pregnancy, or in any way to diminish the coverage of pregnancy, childbirth, or medical conditions related to pregnancy or childbirth under any other provisions of this part, including subdivision (a) of Section 12940.

(Added by Stats.1980, c. 992, § 4. Amended by Stats.1990, c. 15 (S.B.1027), § 2; Stats.1992, c. 907 (A.B.2865), § 1; Stats.1999, c. 591 (A.B.1670), § 9; Stats.2004, c. 647 (A.B.2870), § 5.)

§ 12945.1. Moore-Brown-Roberti Family Rights Act

Sections 12945.2 and 19702.3 shall be known, and may be cited, as the Moore-Brown-Roberti Family Rights Act. *(Added by Stats.1993, c. 580 (S.B.193), § 1.)*

§ 12945.2. Family care and medical leave; definitions; conditions; unlawful employment practices

(a) Except as provided in subdivision (b), it shall be an unlawful employment practice for any employer, as defined in paragraph (2) of subdivision (c), to refuse to grant a request by any employee with more than 12 months of service with the employer, and who has at least 1,250 hours of service with the employer during the previous 12-month period, to take up to a total of 12 workweeks in any 12-month period for family care and medical leave. Family care and medical leave requested pursuant to this subdivision shall not be deemed to have been granted unless the employer provides the employee, upon granting the leave request, a guarantee of employ-

ment in the same or a comparable position upon the termination of the leave. The commission shall adopt a regulation specifying the elements of a reasonable request.

(b) Notwithstanding subdivision (a), it shall not be an unlawful employment practice for an employer to refuse to grant a request for family care and medical leave by an employee if the employer employs less than 50 employees within 75 miles of the worksite where that employee is employed.

(c) For purposes of this section:

(1) "Child" means a biological, adopted, or foster child, a stepchild, a legal ward, or a child of a person standing in loco parentis who is either of the following:

(A) Under 18 years of age.

(B) An adult dependent child.

(2) "Employer" means either of the following:

(A) Any person who directly employs 50 or more persons to perform services for a wage or salary.

(B) The state, and any political or civil subdivision of the state and cities.

(3) "Family care and medical leave" means any of the following:

(A) Leave for reason of the birth of a child of the employee, the placement of a child with an employee in connection with the adoption or foster care of the child by the employee, or the serious health condition of a child of the employee.

(B) Leave to care for a parent or a spouse who has a serious health condition.

(C) Leave because of an employee's own serious health condition that makes the employee unable to perform the functions of the position of that employee, except for leave taken for disability on account of pregnancy, childbirth, or related medical conditions.

(4) "Employment in the same or a comparable position" means employment in a position that has the same or similar duties and pay that can be performed at the same or similar geographic location as the position held prior to the leave.

(5) "FMLA" means the federal Family and Medical Leave Act of 1993 (P.L. 103-3).

(6) "Health care provider" means any of the following:

(A) An individual holding either a physician's and surgeon's certificate issued pursuant to Article 4 (commencing with Section 2080) of Chapter 5 of Division 2 of the Business and Professions Code, an osteopathic physician's and surgeon's certificate issued pursuant to Article 4.5 (commencing with Section 2099.5) of Chapter 5 of Division 2 of the Business and Professions Code, or an individual duly licensed as a physician, surgeon, or osteopathic physician or surgeon in another state or jurisdiction, who directly treats or supervises the treatment of the serious health condition.

(B)　Any other person determined by the United States Secretary of Labor to be capable of providing health care services under the FMLA.

(7)　"Parent" means a biological, foster, or adoptive parent, a stepparent, a legal guardian, or other person who stood in loco parentis to the employee when the employee was a child.

(8)　"Serious health condition" means an illness, injury, impairment, or physical or mental condition that involves either of the following:

(A)　Inpatient care in a hospital, hospice, or residential health care facility.

(B)　Continuing treatment or continuing supervision by a health care provider.

(d)　An employer shall not be required to pay an employee for any leave taken pursuant to subdivision (a), except as required by subdivision (e).

(e)　An employee taking a leave permitted by subdivision (a) may elect, or an employer may require the employee, to substitute, for leave allowed under subdivision (a), any of the employee's accrued vacation leave or other accrued time off during this period or any other paid or unpaid time off negotiated with the employer. If an employee takes a leave because of the employee's own serious health condition, the employee may also elect, or the employer may also require the employee, to substitute accrued sick leave during the period of the leave. However, an employee shall not use sick leave during a period of leave in connection with the birth, adoption, or foster care of a child, or to care for a child, parent, or spouse with a serious health condition, unless mutually agreed to by the employer and the employee.

(f)(1)　During any period that an eligible employee takes leave pursuant to subdivision (a) or takes leave that qualifies as leave taken under the FMLA, the employer shall maintain and pay for coverage under a "group health plan," as defined in Section 5000(b)(1) of the Internal Revenue Code of 1986, for the duration of the leave, not to exceed 12 workweeks in a 12-month period, commencing on the date leave taken under the FMLA commences, at the level and under the conditions coverage would have been provided if the employee had continued in employment continuously for the duration of the leave. Nothing in the preceding sentence shall preclude an employer from maintaining and paying for coverage under a "group health plan" beyond 12 workweeks. An employer may recover the premium that the employer paid as required by this subdivision for maintaining coverage for the employee under the group health plan if both of the following conditions occur:

(A)　The employee fails to return from leave after the period of leave to which the employee is entitled has expired.

(B)　The employee's failure to return from leave is for a reason other than the continuation, recurrence, or onset of a serious health condition that entitles the employee to

leave under subdivision (a) or other circumstances beyond the control of the employee.

(2)　Any employee taking leave pursuant to subdivision (a) shall continue to be entitled to participate in employee health plans for any period during which coverage is not provided by the employer under paragraph (1), employee benefit plans, including life, short-term, or long-term disability or accident insurance, pension and retirement plans, and supplemental unemployment benefit plans to the same extent and under the same conditions as apply to an unpaid leave taken for any purpose other than those described in subdivision (a). In the absence of these conditions an employee shall continue to be entitled to participate in these plans and, in the case of health and welfare employee benefit plans, including life, short-term, or long-term disability or accident insurance, or other similar plans, the employer may, at his or her discretion, require the employee to pay premiums, at the group rate, during the period of leave not covered by any accrued vacation leave, or other accrued time off, or any other paid or unpaid time off negotiated with the employer, as a condition of continued coverage during the leave period. However, the nonpayment of premiums by an employee shall not constitute a break in service, for purposes of longevity, seniority under any collective bargaining agreement, or any employee benefit plan.

For purposes of pension and retirement plans, an employer shall not be required to make plan payments for an employee during the leave period, and the leave period shall not be required to be counted for purposes of time accrued under the plan. However, an employee covered by a pension plan may continue to make contributions in accordance with the terms of the plan during the period of the leave.

(g)　During a family care and medical leave period, the employee shall retain employee status with the employer, and the leave shall not constitute a break in service, for purposes of longevity, seniority under any collective bargaining agreement, or any employee benefit plan. An employee returning from leave shall return with no less seniority than the employee had when the leave commenced, for purposes of layoff, recall, promotion, job assignment, and seniority-related benefits such as vacation.

(h)　If the employee's need for a leave pursuant to this section is foreseeable, the employee shall provide the employer with reasonable advance notice of the need for the leave.

(i)　If the employee's need for leave pursuant to this section is foreseeable due to a planned medical treatment or supervision, the employee shall make a reasonable effort to schedule the treatment or supervision to avoid disruption to the operations of the employer, subject to the approval of the health care provider of the individual requiring the treatment or supervision.

(j)(1)　An employer may require that an employee's request for leave to care for a child, a spouse, or a parent who has a serious health condition be supported by a certification issued by the health care provider of the individual requiring care. That certification shall be sufficient if it includes all of the following:

(A) The date on which the serious health condition commenced.

(B) The probable duration of the condition.

(C) An estimate of the amount of time that the health care provider believes the employee needs to care for the individual requiring the care.

(D) A statement that the serious health condition warrants the participation of a family member to provide care during a period of the treatment or supervision of the individual requiring care.

(?) Upon expiration of the time estimated by the health care provider in subparagraph (C) of paragraph (1), the employer may require the employee to obtain recertification, in accordance with the procedure provided in paragraph (1), if additional leave is required.

(k)(1) An employer may require that an employee's request for leave because of the employee's own serious health condition be supported by a certification issued by his or her health care provider. That certification shall be sufficient if it includes all of the following:

(A) The date on which the serious health condition commenced.

(B) The probable duration of the condition.

(C) A statement that, due to the serious health condition, the employee is unable to perform the function of his or her position.

(2) The employer may require that the employee obtain subsequent recertification regarding the employee's serious health condition on a reasonable basis, in accordance with the procedure provided in paragraph (1), if additional leave is required.

(3)(A) In any case in which the employer has reason to doubt the validity of the certification provided pursuant to this section, the employer may require, at the employer's expense, that the employee obtain the opinion of a second health care provider, designated or approved by the employer, concerning any information certified under paragraph (1).

(B) The health care provider designated or approved under subparagraph (A) shall not be employed on a regular basis by the employer.

(C) In any case in which the second opinion described in subparagraph (A) differs from the opinion in the original certification, the employer may require, at the employer's expense, that the employee obtain the opinion of a third health care provider, designated or approved jointly by the employer and the employee, concerning the information certified under paragraph (1).

(D) The opinion of the third health care provider concerning the information certified under paragraph (1)

shall be considered to be final and shall be binding on the employer and the employee.

(4) As a condition of an employee's return from leave taken because of the employee's own serious health condition, the employer may have a uniformly applied practice or policy that requires the employee to obtain certification from his or her health care provider that the employee is able to resume work. Nothing in this paragraph shall supersede a valid collective bargaining agreement that governs the return to work of that employee.

(l) It shall be an unlawful employment practice for an employer to refuse to hire, or to discharge, fine, suspend, expel, or discriminate against, any individual because of any of the following:

(1) An individual's exercise of the right to family care and medical leave provided by subdivision (a).

(2) An individual's giving information or testimony as to his or her own family care and medical leave, or another person's family care and medical leave, in any inquiry or proceeding related to rights guaranteed under this section.

(m) This section shall not be construed to require any changes in existing collective bargaining agreements during the life of the contract, or until January 1, 1993, whichever occurs first.

(n) The amendments made to this section by the act adding this subdivision shall not be construed to require any changes in existing collective bargaining agreements during the life of the contract, or until February 5, 1994, whichever occurs first.

(o) The provisions of this section shall be construed as separate and distinct from those of Section 12945.

(p) Leave provided for pursuant to this section may be taken in one or more periods. The 12-month period during which 12 workweeks of leave may be taken under this section shall run concurrently with the 12-month period under the FMLA, and shall commence the date leave taken under the FMLA commences.

(q) In any case in which both parents entitled to leave under subdivision (a) are employed by the same employer, the employer shall not be required to grant leave in connection with the birth, adoption, or foster care of a child that would allow the parents family care and medical leave totaling more than the amount specified in subdivision (a).

(r)(1) Notwithstanding subdivision (a), an employer may refuse to reinstate an employee returning from leave to the same or a comparable position if all of the following apply:

(A) The employee is a salaried employee who is among the highest paid 10 percent of the employer's employees who are employed within 75 miles of the worksite at which that employee is employed.

167

(B) The refusal is necessary to prevent substantial and grievous economic injury to the operations of the employer.

(C) The employer notifies the employee of the intent to refuse reinstatement at the time the employer determines the refusal is necessary under subparagraph (B).

(2) In any case in which the leave has already commenced, the employer shall give the employee a reasonable opportunity to return to work following the notice prescribed by subparagraph (C).

(s) Leave taken by an employee pursuant to this section shall run concurrently with leave taken pursuant to the FMLA, except for any leave taken under the FMLA for disability on account of pregnancy, childbirth, or related medical conditions. The aggregate amount of leave taken under this section or the FMLA, or both, except for leave taken for disability on account of pregnancy, childbirth, or related medical conditions, shall not exceed 12 workweeks in a 12-month period. An employee is entitled to take, in addition to the leave provided for under this section and the FMLA, the leave provided for in Section 12945, if the employee is otherwise qualified for that leave. *(Added by Stats.1991, c. 462 (A.B.77), § 4. Amended by Stats.1992, c. 427 (A.B.3355), § 49; Stats.1993, c. 827 (A.B.1460), § 1, eff. Oct. 5, 1993; Stats.1994, c. 146 (A.B.3601), § 68.)*

§ 12945.5. Unlawful employment practice; sterilization

It shall be an unlawful employment practice for an employer to require any employee to be sterilized as a condition of employment. *(Added by Stats.1980, c. 619, § 1.)*

§ 12946. Retention of applications, records and files for two years; failure to retain as unlawful practice by employers, labor organization and employment agencies

It shall be an unlawful practice for employers, labor organizations, and employment agencies subject to the provisions of this part to fail to maintain and preserve any and all applications, personnel, membership, or employment referral records and files for a minimum period of two years after the records and files are initially created or received, or for employers to fail to retain personnel files of applicants or terminated employees for a minimum period of two years after the date of the employment action taken. For the purposes of this section, the State Personnel Board is exempt from the two-year retention requirement and shall instead, maintain the records and files for a period of one year. Upon notice that a verified complaint against it has been filed under this part, any such employer, labor organization, or employment agency shall maintain and preserve any and all records and files until the complaint is fully and finally disposed of and all appeals or related proceedings terminated. The commission shall adopt suitable rules, regulations, and standards to carry out the purposes of this section. Where necessary, the department, pursuant

to its powers under Section 12974, may seek temporary or preliminary judicial relief to enforce this section. *(Added by Stats.1980, c. 992, § 4. Amended by Stats.1987, c. 605, § 3.)*

§ 12947. Child care services for employees and members; not an unlawful practice

It shall not be an unlawful practice under this part for an employer or labor organization to provide or make financial provision for child care services of a custodial or other nature for its employees or members who are responsible for minor children. *(Added by Stats.1980, c. 992, § 4.)*

§ 12947.5. Prohibition on wearing of pants based on sex; unlawful employment practice; exemptions

(a) It shall be an unlawful employment practice for an employer to refuse to permit an employee to wear pants on account of the sex of the employee.

(b) Nothing in this section shall prohibit an employer from requiring employees in a particular occupation to wear a uniform.

(c) Nothing in this section shall prohibit an employer from requiring an employee to wear a costume while that employee is portraying a specific character or dramatic role.

(d) The commission may exempt an employer from the requirements of this section for good cause shown and shall adopt standards and procedures for granting exemptions. *(Added by Stats.1994, c. 535 (S.B.1288), § 2.)*

§ 12948. Denial of civil rights as unlawful practice

It is an unlawful practice under this part for a person to deny or to aid, incite, or conspire in the denial of the rights created by Section 51, 51.5, 51.7, 54, 54.1, or 54.2 of the Civil Code. *(Added by Stats.1980, c. 992, § 4. Amended by Stats.1996, c. 498 (S.B.1687), § 5.5; Stats. 1999, c. 591 (A.B.1670), § 10.)*

§ 12949. Requirement to adhere to reasonable workplace appearance

Nothing in this part relating to gender-based discrimination affects the ability of an employer to require an employee to adhere to reasonable workplace appearance, grooming, and dress standards not precluded by other provisions of state or federal law, provided that an employer shall allow an employee to appear or dress consistently with the employee's gender identity. *(Added by Stats.2003, c. 164 (A.B.196), § 2.)*

§ 12950. Sexual harassment; amendment of poster; distribution of information sheet; contents of information sheet; violations

In addition to employer responsibilities set forth in subdivisions (j) and (k) of Section 12940 and in rules adopted by the department and the commission, every employer shall act to ensure a workplace free of sexual harassment by implementing the following minimum requirements:

(a) The department shall amend its current poster on discrimination in employment to include information relating to the illegality of sexual harassment. This amended poster shall be distributed to employers when the supply of the current poster is exhausted. One copy of the amended poster shall be provided by the department to an employer upon request. The amended poster shall be available at each office of the department, and shall be mailed if the request includes a self-addressed envelope with postage affixed. Multiple copies of the amended poster shall be made available online by the Department of Fair Employment and Housing. Each employer shall post the amended poster in a prominent and accessible location in the workplace.

(b) Each employer shall obtain from the department its information sheet on sexual harassment, which the department shall make available to employers for reproduction and distribution to employees. One copy of the information sheet shall be provided by the department to an employer upon request. The information sheets shall be available at each office of the department, and shall be mailed if the request includes a self-addressed envelope with postage affixed. Multiple copies of the information sheet shall be made available online by the Department of Fair Employment and Housing. Each employer shall distribute this information sheet to its employees, unless the employer provides equivalent information to its employees that contains, at a minimum, components on the following:

(1) The illegality of sexual harassment.

(2) The definition of sexual harassment under applicable state and federal law.

(3) A description of sexual harassment, utilizing examples.

(4) The internal complaint process of the employer available to the employee.

(5) The legal remedies and complaint process available through the department and the commission.

(6) Directions on how to contact the department and the commission.

(7) The protection against retaliation provided by Section 7287.8 of Title 2 of the California Code of Regulations for opposing the practices prohibited by this article or for filing a complaint with, or otherwise participating in an investigation, proceeding, or hearing conducted by, the department or the commission.

(c) The information sheet or information required to be distributed to employees pursuant to subdivision (b) shall be delivered in a manner that ensures distribution to each employee, such as including the information sheet or information with an employee's pay.

(d) Notwithstanding subdivisions (j) and (k) of Section 12940, a claim that the information sheet or information required to be distributed pursuant to this section did not

reach a particular individual or individuals shall not in and of itself result in the liability of any employer to any present or former employee or applicant in any action alleging sexual harassment. Conversely, an employer's compliance with this section does not insulate the employer from liability for sexual harassment of any current or former employee or applicant.

(e) If an employer violates the requirements of this section, the commission shall issue an order requiring the employer to comply with these requirements. *(Added by Stats.1992, c. 908 (A.B.2264), § 1. Amended by Stats. 2002, c. 490 (S.B.1945), § 1; Stats.2006, c. 69 (A.B.1806), § 5, eff. July 12, 2006.)*

§ 12950.1. **Sexual harassment training and education requirements for new supervisory employees; contents of training and education; definitions; employer liability; violation of requirements**

(a) By January 1, 2006, an employer having 50 or more employees shall provide at least two hours of classroom or other effective interactive training and education regarding sexual harassment to all supervisory employees in California who are employed as of July 1, 2005, and to all new supervisory employees within six months of their assumption of a supervisory position. Any employer who has provided this training and education to a supervisory employee after January 1, 2003, is not required to provide training and education by the January 1, 2006, deadline. After January 1, 2006, each employer covered by this section shall provide sexual harassment training and education to each supervisory employee in California once every two years. The training and education required by this section shall include information and practical guidance regarding the federal and state statutory provisions concerning the prohibition against and the prevention and correction of sexual harassment and the remedies available to victims of sexual harassment in employment. The training and education shall also include practical examples aimed at instructing supervisors in the prevention of harassment, discrimination, and retaliation, and shall be presented by trainers or educators with knowledge and expertise in the prevention of harassment, discrimination, and retaliation.

(b) The state shall incorporate the training required by subdivision (a) into the 80 hours of training provided to all new supervisory employees pursuant to subdivision (b) of Section 19995.4, using existing resources.

(c) For purposes of this section only, "employer" means any person regularly employing 50 or more persons or regularly receiving the services of 50 or more persons providing services pursuant to a contract, or any person acting as an agent of an employer, directly or indirectly, the state, or any political or civil subdivision of the state, and cities.

(d) Notwithstanding subdivisions (j) and (k) of Section 12940, a claim that the training and education required by this section did not reach a particular individual or individuals shall not in and of itself result in the liability of any employer to any present or former employee or applicant in any action alleging sexual harassment. Conversely, an employer's compliance with this section does not insulate the employer from liability for sexual harassment of any current or former employee or applicant.

(e) If an employer violates this section, the commission shall issue an order requiring the employer to comply with these requirements.

(f) The training and education required by this section is intended to establish a minimum threshold and should not discourage or relieve any employer from providing for longer, more frequent, or more elaborate training and education regarding workplace harassment or other forms of unlawful discrimination in order to meet its obligations to take all reasonable steps necessary to prevent and correct harassment and discrimination. *(Added by Stats.2004, c. 933 (A.B.1825), § 1. Amended by Stats.2006, c. 737 (A.B.2095), § 1.)*

§ 12951. Unlawful employment practice for employer to adopt or enforce policy that limits or prohibits use of language; conditions; business necessity

(a) It is an unlawful employment practice for an employer, as defined in subdivision (d) of Section 12926, to adopt or enforce a policy that limits or prohibits the use of any language in any workplace, unless both of the following conditions exist:

(1) The language restriction is justified by a business necessity.

(2) The employer has notified its employees of the circumstances and the time when the language restriction is required to be observed and of the consequences for violating the language restriction.

(b) For the purposes of this section, "business necessity" means an overriding legitimate business purpose such that the language restriction is necessary to the safe and efficient operation of the business, that the language restriction effectively fulfills the business purpose it is supposed to serve, and there is no alternative practice to the language restriction that would accomplish the business purpose equally well with a lesser discriminatory impact. *(Added by Stats.2001, c. 295 (A.B.800), § 2.)*

ARTICLE 2. HOUSING DISCRIMINATION

Section
12955.　　Unlawful practices.
12955.1.　Discrimination; disabled persons; design and construction of multifamily dwellings; building standards; adoption of regulations.
12955.1.1.　Covered multifamily dwellings and multistory dwelling unit defined.
12955.2.　Familial status.
12955.3.　Disability.
12955.4.　Religious organizations; preference to persons of same religion; restrictions.
12955.5.　Discriminatory housing practices; collecting information.
12955.6.　Construction with other laws.

Section
12955.7.　Coercion, intimidation, threats, or interference with rights.
12955.8.　Unlawful practices; proof; business establishment.
12955.9.　Housing for older persons; application.
12956.　Retention of records upon notice of complaint.
12956.1.　Restrictive covenants based on discriminatory grounds; notice on copy of document; penalty for adding racially restrictive covenant.
12956.2.　Restrictive covenants based on discriminatory grounds; recording of modification; submission to county counsel, filing, and public access; unauthorized modifications.

§ 12955. Unlawful practices

It shall be unlawful:

(a) For the owner of any housing accommodation to discriminate against or harass any person because of the race, color, religion, sex, sexual orientation, marital status, national origin, ancestry, familial status, source of income, or disability of that person.

(b) For the owner of any housing accommodation to make or to cause to be made any written or oral inquiry concerning the race, color, religion, sex, sexual orientation, marital status, national origin, ancestry, familial status, or disability of any person seeking to purchase, rent or lease any housing accommodation.

(c) For any person to make, print, or publish, or cause to be made, printed, or published any notice, statement, or advertisement, with respect to the sale or rental of a housing accommodation that indicates any preference, limitation, or discrimination based on race, color, religion, sex, sexual orientation, marital status, national origin, ancestry, familial status, source of income, or disability or an intention to make that preference, limitation, or discrimination.

(d) For any person subject to the provisions of Section 51 of the Civil Code, as that section applies to housing accommodations, to discriminate against any person on the basis of sex, sexual orientation, color, race, religion, ancestry, national origin, familial status, marital status, disability, source of income, or on any other basis prohibited by that section.

(e) For any person, bank, mortgage company or other financial institution that provides financial assistance for the purchase, organization, or construction of any housing accommodation to discriminate against any person or group of persons because of the race, color, religion, sex, sexual orientation, marital status, national origin, ancestry, familial status, source of income, or disability in the terms, conditions, or privileges relating to the obtaining or use of that financial assistance.

(f) For any owner of housing accommodations to harass, evict, or otherwise discriminate against any person in the sale or rental of housing accommodations when the owner's dominant purpose is retaliation against a person who has opposed practices unlawful under this section, informed law enforcement agencies of practices believed unlawful under this section, has testified or assisted in any proceeding under this part, or has aided or encouraged a person to exercise or enjoy the rights secured by this part. Nothing herein is intended to cause or permit the delay of an unlawful detainer action.

(g) For any person to aid, abet, incite, compel, or coerce the doing of any of the acts or practices declared unlawful in this section, or to attempt to do so.

(h) For any person, for profit, to induce any person to sell or rent any dwelling by representations regarding the entry or prospective entry into the neighborhood of a person or persons of a particular race, color, religion, sex, sexual orientation, marital status, ancestry, disability, source of income, familial status, or national origin.

(i) For any person or other organization or entity whose business involves real estate-related transactions to discriminate against any person in making available a transaction, or in the terms and conditions of a transaction, because of race, color, religion, sex, sexual orientation, marital status, national origin, ancestry, source of income, familial status, or disability.

(j) To deny a person access to, or membership or participation in, a multiple listing service, real estate brokerage organization, or other service because of race, color, religion, sex, sexual orientation, marital status, ancestry, disability, familial status, source of income, or national origin.

(k) To otherwise make unavailable or deny a dwelling based on discrimination because of race, color, religion, sex, sexual orientation, familial status, source of income, disability, or national origin.

(l) To discriminate through public or private land use practices, decisions, and authorizations because of race, color, religion, sex, sexual orientation, familial status, marital status, disability, national origin, source of income, or ancestry. Discrimination includes, but is not limited to, restrictive covenants, zoning laws, denials of use permits, and other actions authorized under the Planning and Zoning Law (Title 7 (commencing with Section 65000)), that make housing opportunities unavailable.

Discrimination under this subdivision also includes the existence of a restrictive covenant, regardless of whether accompanied by a statement that the restrictive covenant is repealed or void. This paragraph shall become operative on January 1, 2001.

(m) As used in this section, "race, color, religion, sex, sexual orientation, marital status, national origin, ancestry, familial status, source of income, or disability" includes a perception that the person has any of those characteristics or that the person is associated with a person who has, or is perceived to have, any of those characteristics.

(n) To use a financial or income standard in the rental of housing that fails to account for the aggregate income of persons residing together or proposing to reside together on the same basis as the aggregate income of married persons residing together or proposing to reside together.

(o) In instances where there is a government rent subsidy, to use a financial or income standard in assessing eligibility for the rental of housing that is not based on the portion of the rent to be paid by the tenant.

(p)(1) For the purposes of this section, "source of income" means lawful, verifiable income paid directly to a tenant or paid to a representative of a tenant. For the purposes of this section, a landlord is not considered a representative of a tenant.

(2) For the purposes of this section, it shall not constitute discrimination based on source of income to make a written or oral inquiry concerning the level or source of income.

(Added by Stats.1980, c. 992, § 4. Amended by Stats.1992, c. 182 (S.B.1234), § 7; Stats.1993, c. 1277 (A.B.2244), § 4; Stats.1999, c. 589 (S.B.1148), § 2; Stats. 1999, c. 590 (S.B.1098), § 4; Stats.1999, c. 591 (A.B. 1670), § 11.4; Stats.1999, c; 592 (A.B.1001), § 9.7; Stats.2004, c. 568 (S.B.1145), § 8.)

§ **12955.1. Discrimination; disabled persons; design and construction of multifamily dwellings; building standards; adoption of regulations**

(a) For purposes of Section 12955, "discrimination" includes, but is not limited to, a failure to design and construct a covered multifamily dwelling in a manner that allows access to, and use by, disabled persons by providing, at a minimum, the following features:

(1) All covered multifamily dwellings shall have at least one building entrance on an accessible route, unless it is impracticable to do so because of the terrain or unusual characteristics of the site. The burden of establishing impracticability because of terrain or unusual site characteristics is on the person or persons who designed or constructed the housing facility.

(2) All covered multifamily dwellings with a building entrance on an accessible route shall be designed and constructed in a manner that complies with all of the following:

(A) The public and common areas are readily accessible to and usable by persons with disabilities.

(B) All the doors designed to allow passage into and within all premises are sufficiently wide to allow passage by persons in wheelchairs.

(C) All premises within covered multifamily dwelling units contain the following features of adaptable design:

(i) An accessible route into and through the covered dwelling unit.

(ii) Light switches, electrical outlets, thermostats, and other environmental controls in accessible locations.

(iii) Reinforcements in bathroom walls to allow later installation of grab bars around the toilet, tub, shower stall, and shower seat, where those facilities are provided.

171

(iv) Useable kitchens and bathrooms so that an individual in a wheelchair can maneuver about the space.

(b)(1) For purposes of Section 12955, "discrimination" includes, but is not limited to, a failure to design and construct 10 percent of the multistory dwelling units in buildings without an elevator that consist of at least four condominium dwelling units or at least three rental apartment dwelling units in a manner that incorporates an accessible route to the primary entry level entrance and that meets the requirements of paragraph (2) of subdivision (a) with respect to the ground floor, at least one bathroom on the primary entry level and the public and common areas. Any fraction thereof shall be rounded up to the next whole number. For purposes of this subdivision, "elevator" does not include an elevator that serves only the first ground floor or any nonresidential area. In multistory dwelling units in these buildings without elevators, the "primary entry level entrance" means the principal entrance through which most people enter the dwelling unit, as designated by the California Building Standards Code or, if not designated by California Building Standards Code, by the building official. To determine the total number of multistory dwelling units subject to this subdivision, all multistory dwelling units in the buildings subject to this subdivision on a site shall be considered collectively. This subdivision shall not be construed to require an elevator within an individual multistory dwelling unit or within a building subject to this subdivision. This subdivision shall apply only to multistory dwelling units in a building subject to this subdivision for which an application for a construction permit is submitted on or after July 1, 2005.

(2) Notwithstanding subdivision (c), the Division of the State Architect and the Department of Housing and Community Development may adopt regulations to clarify, interpret, or implement this subdivision, if either of them deem it necessary and appropriate.

(c) Notwithstanding Section 12935, regulations adopting building standards necessary to implement, interpret, or make specific the provisions of this section shall be developed by the Division of the State Architect for public housing and by the Department of Housing and Community Development for all other residential occupancies, and shall be adopted pursuant to Chapter 4 (commencing with Section 18935) of Part 2.5 of the Health and Safety Code. Prior to the effective date of regulations adopted pursuant to this subdivision, existing federal accessibility standards that provide, to persons with disabilities, greater protections than existing state accessibility regulations shall apply. After regulations pursuant to this subdivision become effective, particular state regulations shall apply if they provide, to persons with disabilities, the same protections as, or greater protections than, the federal standards. If particular federal regulations provide greater protections than state regulations, then those federal standards shall apply. If the United States Department of Housing and Urban Development determines that any portion of the state regulations are not equivalent to the federal standards, the federal standards shall, as to those portions, apply to the design and construction of covered multifamily dwellings until the state regulations are brought into compliance with the federal standards. The appropriate state agency shall provide notice pursuant to the Administrative Procedure Act (Chapter 5 (commencing with Section 11500) of Part 5 of Division 3 of Title 2) of that determination.

(d) In investigating discrimination complaints, the department shall apply the building standards contained in the California Building Standards Code to determine whether a covered multifamily dwelling is designed and constructed for access to and use by disabled persons in accordance with this section.

(e) The building standard requirements for persons with disabilities imposed by this section shall meet or exceed the requirements under the federal Fair Housing Amendments Act of 1988 (P.L. 100–430) and its implementing regulations (24 C.F.R. 100.1 et seq.) and the existing state law building standards contained in the California Building Standards Code. *(Added by Stats. 1992, c. 182 (S.B.1234), § 8. Amended by Stats.1993, c. 1277 (A.B.2244), § 5; Stats.2003, c. 642 (S.B.1025), § 1.)*

§ 12955.1.1. Covered multifamily dwellings and multistory dwelling unit defined

For purposes of Section 12955.1, the following definitions shall apply:

(a) "Covered multifamily dwellings" means both of the following:

(1) Buildings that consist of at least four condominium dwelling units or at least three rental apartment dwelling units if the buildings have at least one elevator. For purposes of this definition, dwelling units within a single structure separated by firewalls do not constitute separate buildings.

(2) The ground floor dwelling units in buildings that consist of at least four condominium dwelling units or at least three rental apartment dwelling units if the buildings do not have an elevator. For purposes of this definition, dwelling units within a single structure separated by firewalls do not constitute separate buildings.

(b) "Multistory dwelling unit" means a condominium dwelling unit or rental apartment with finished living space on one floor and the floor immediately above or below it or, if applicable, the floors immediately above and below it. *(Added by Stats.2003, c. 642 (S.B.1025), § 2.)*

§ 12955.2. Familial status

For purposes of this part, "familial status" means one or more individuals under 18 years of age who reside with a parent, another person with care and legal custody of that individual, a person who has been given care and custody of that individual by a state or local governmental agency that is responsible for the welfare of children, or the designee of that parent or other person with legal custody of any individual under 18 years of age by written consent of the parent or designated custodian. The protections afforded by this part against discrimination on the basis of familial status also apply to any individual who is pregnant, who is in the process of securing legal custody of any individual under 18 years of age, or who is in the process of being given care and custody of any individual under 18 years of age by a state or local governmental agency responsible for the welfare of children. *(Added by Stats.1992, c. 182, (S.B.1234), § 9.)*

§ 12955.3. Disability

For purposes of this part, "disability" includes, but is not limited to, any physical or mental disability as defined in Section 12926.

(Added by Stats.1992, c. 182 (S.B.1234), § 10. Amended by Stats.2000, c. 1049 (A.B.2222), § 8.)

§ 12955.4. Religious organizations; preference to persons of same religion; restrictions

Nothing in this part shall prohibit a religious organization, association or society, or any nonprofit institution or organization operated, supervised, or controlled by or in conjunction with a religious organization, association, or society, from limiting the sale, rental, or occupancy of dwellings that it owns or operates for other than a commercial purpose to persons of the same religion or from giving preference to those persons, unless membership in that religion is restricted on account of race, color, or national origin. *(Added by Stats.1992, c. 182 (S.B. 1234), § 11.)*

§ 12955.5. Discriminatory housing practices; collecting information

Nothing in this part shall preclude the government from establishing programs to collect information relating to discriminatory housing practices. *(Added by Stats. 1992, c. 182 (S.B.1234), § 12.)*

§ 12955.6. Construction with other laws

Nothing in this part shall be construed to afford to the classes protected under this part, fewer rights or remedies than the federal Fair Housing Amendments Act of 1988 (P.L. 100-430) and its implementing regulations (24 C.F.R. 100.1 et seq.), or state law relating to fair employment and housing as it existed prior to the effective date of this section. Any state law that purports to require or permit any action that would be an unlawful practice under this part shall to that extent be invalid. This part may be construed to afford greater rights and remedies to an aggrieved person than those afforded by federal law and other state laws.

(Added by Stats.1992, c. 182 (S.B.1234), § 13. Amended by Stats.1993, c. 1277 (A.B.2244), § 5.5.)

§ 12955.7. Coercion, intimidation, threats, or interference with rights

It shall be unlawful to coerce, intimidate, threaten, or interfere with any person in the exercise or enjoyment of, or on account of that person having exercised or enjoyed, or on account of that person having aided or encouraged any other person in the exercise or enjoyment of, any right granted or protected by Section 12955 or 12955.1. *(Added by Stats.1993, c. 1277 (A.B.2244), § 6.)*

§ 12955.8. Unlawful practices; proof; business establishment

For purposes of this article, in connection with unlawful practices:

(a) Proof of an intentional violation of this article includes, but is not limited to, an act or failure to act that is otherwise covered by this part, that demonstrates an intent to discriminate in any manner in violation of this part. A person intends to discriminate if race, color, religion, sex, sexual orientation, familial status, marital status, disability, national origin, or ancestry is a motivating factor in committing a discriminatory housing practice even though other factors may have also motivated the practice. An intent to discriminate may be established by direct or circumstantial evidence.

(b) Proof of a violation causing a discriminatory effect is shown if an act or failure to act that is otherwise covered by this part, and that has the effect, regardless of intent, of unlawfully discriminating on the basis of race, color, religion, sex, sexual orientation, familial status, marital status, disability, national origin, or ancestry. A business establishment whose action or inaction has an unintended discriminatory effect shall not be considered to have committed an unlawful housing practice in violation of this part if the business establishment can establish that the action or inaction is necessary to the operation of the business and effectively carries out the significant business need it is alleged to serve. In cases that do not involve a business establishment, the person whose action or inaction has an unintended discriminatory effect shall not be considered to have committed an unlawful housing practice in violation of this part if the person can establish that the action or inaction is necessary to achieve an important purpose sufficiently compelling to override the discriminatory effect and effectively carries out the purpose it is alleged to serve.

(1) Any determination of a violation pursuant to this subdivision shall consider whether or not there are feasible alternatives that would equally well or better accomplish the purpose advanced with a less discriminatory effect.

(2) For purposes of this subdivision, the term "business establishment" shall have the same meaning as in Section 51 of the Civil Code. *(Added by Stats.1993, c. 1277 (A.B.2244), § 7. Amended by Stats.1999, c. 592 (A.B.1001), § 10.)*

§ 12955.9. Housing for older persons; application

(a) The provisions of this part relating to discrimination on the basis of familial status shall not apply to housing for older persons.

(b) As used in this section, "housing for older persons" means any of the following:

(1) Housing provided under any state or federal program that the Secretary of Housing and Urban Development determines is specifically designed and operated to assist elderly persons, as defined in the state or federal program.

(2) Housing that meets the standards for senior housing in Sections 51.2, 51.3, and 51.4 of the Civil Code, except to the extent that those standards violate the prohibition of familial status discrimination in the federal Fair Housing Amendments Act of 1988 (P.L. 100-430) and implementing regulations.

(3) Mobilehome parks that meet the standards for "housing for older persons" as defined in the federal Fair Housing Amendments Act of 1988 and implementing regulations.

(c) For purposes of this section, the burden of proof shall be on the owner to prove that the housing qualifies as housing for older persons. *(Added by Stats.1993, c. 1277, (A.B.2244), § 8.)*

§ 12956. Retention of records upon notice of complaint

Upon notice that a verified complaint against it has been filed under this part, any owner of housing accommodations shall maintain and preserve any and all rental records or any other written materials relevant to the complaint, until the complaint is fully and finally disposed of and all appeals or related proceedings terminated. *(Added by Stats.1987, c. 605, § 5.)*

§ 12956.1. Restrictive covenants based on discriminatory grounds; notice on copy of document; penalty for adding racially restrictive covenant

(a) As used in this section, "association," "governing documents," and "declaration" have the same meanings as set forth in Section 1351 of the Civil Code.

(b)(1) A county recorder, title insurance company, escrow company, real estate broker, real estate agent, or association that provides a copy of a declaration, governing document, or deed to any person shall place a cover page or stamp on the first page of the previously recorded document or documents stating, in at least 14–point boldface type, the following:

"If this document contains any restriction based on race, color, religion, sex, sexual orientation, familial status, marital status, disability, national origin, source of income as defined in subdivision (p) of Section 12955, or ancestry, that restriction violates state and federal fair housing laws and is void, and may be removed pursuant to Section 12956.2 of the Government Code. Lawful restrictions under state and federal law on the age of occupants in senior housing or housing for older persons shall not be construed as restrictions based on familial status."

(2) The requirements set forth in paragraph (1) shall not apply to documents being submitted for recordation to a county recorder.

(c) Any person who records a document for the express purpose of adding a racially restrictive covenant is guilty of a misdemeanor. The county recorder shall not incur any liability for recording the document. Notwithstanding any other provision of law, a prosecution for a violation of this subdivision shall commence within three years after the discovery of the recording of the document.

(Added by Stats.1999, c. 589 (S.B.1148), § 3. Amended by Stats.2000, c. 291 (A.B.1493), § 1, eff. Sept. 5, 2000; Stats.2002, c. 803 (A.B.1926), § 1; Stats.2005, c. 297 (A.B.394), § 1.)

§ 12956.2. Restrictive covenants based on discriminatory grounds; recording of modification; submission to county counsel, filing, and public access; unauthorized modifications

(a) A person who holds an ownership interest of record in property that he or she believes is the subject of an unlawfully restrictive covenant in violation of subdivision (*l*) of Section 12955 may record a document titled Restrictive Covenant Modification. The county recorder may choose to waive the fee prescribed for recording and indexing instruments pursuant to Section 27361 in the case of the modification document provided for in this section. The modification document shall include a complete copy of the original document containing the unlawfully restrictive language with the unlawfully restrictive language stricken.

(b) Before recording the modification document, the county recorder shall submit the modification document and the original document to the county counsel who shall determine whether the original document contains an unlawful restriction based on race, color, religion, sex, sexual orientation, familial status, marital status, disability, national origin, source of income as defined in subdivision (p) of Section 12955, or ancestry. The county counsel shall return the documents and inform the county recorder of its determination. The county recorder shall refuse to record the modification document if the county counsel finds that the original document does not contain an unlawful restriction as specified in this paragraph.

(c) The modification document shall be indexed in the same manner as the original document being modified. It shall contain a recording reference to the original document in the form of a book and page or instrument number, and date of the recording.

(d) Subject to covenants, conditions, and restrictions that were recorded after the recording of the original document that contains the unlawfully restrictive language and subject to covenants, conditions, and restrictions that will be recorded after the Restrictive Covenant Modification, the restrictions in the Restrictive Covenant Modification, once recorded, are the only restrictions having effect on the property. The effective date of the terms and conditions of the modification document shall be the same as the effective date of the original document.

(e) The county recorder shall make available to the public Restrictive Covenant Modification forms.

(f) If the holder of an ownership interest of record in property causes to be recorded a modified document pursuant to this section that contains modifications not authorized by this section, the county recorder shall not incur liability for recording the document. The liability that may result from the unauthorized recordation is the sole responsibility of the holder of the ownership interest of record who caused the modified recordation.

(g) This section does not apply to persons holding an ownership interest in property that is part of a common interest development as defined in subdivision (c) of Section 1351 of the Civil Code if the board of directors of that common interest development is subject to the requirements of subdivision (b) of Section 1352.5 of the Civil Code. *(Added by Stats.2005, c. 297 (A.B.394), § 2.)*

CHAPTER 7. ENFORCEMENT AND HEARING PROCEDURES

ARTICLE 1. UNLAWFUL PRACTICES

Section
12960. Procedure for prevention and elimination of unlawful employment practices; application of article; complaints; limitations.
12961. Class action.
12962. Service of complaint filed for investigation.
12963. Investigation by department after filing of complaint.
12963.1. Subpoenas; issuance; attendance of witnesses; production of books, records, etc.; service.
12963.2. Written interrogatories; issuance and service; written answers; inspection, compilations, abstracts, etc., of records.
12963.3. Deposition; issuance and service of subpoena; notice; procedure for taking.
12963.4. Requests for production of books, records, documents, etc.; issuance and service; identification; written response.
12963.5. Jurisdiction; petition to compel compliance; contents; order; review; mandamus; contempt.
12963.7. Elimination of unlawful employment practice by conference, conciliation and persuasion; confidentiality; disclosure as misdemeanor.
12964. Agreement based on conference, conciliation and persuasion; reduction to writing; compliance review; injunction; civil action.
12965. Written accusation by department; group or class complaint; civil action; transfer to court; relief; damages; tolling of statute of limitations.
12966. Accused as state contractor or supplier of goods and services to state; notice to and report by awarding agency.
12967. Hearings; determination of issues.
12968. Hearings; time.

Section
12969. Presentation by department of case in support of accusation; participation by members of commission.
12970. Findings; order; remedies; administrative fine; civil penalty; report to agency; dismissal; appeal rights; copy to district attorney.
12971. Withdrawal of complaint, dismissal by department or termination or closure of investigation; notice to respondent and complainant.
12972. Actions and procedures; procedural regulations; deposition by each party.
12973. Compliance review of final order or decision; time for review; judgment; fine or penalty; attorney's fees.
12974. Civil action for relief pending final disposition of complaint; temporary or preliminary relief; venue.
12975. Willful interference with duties of department or commission or willful violation of orders of commission relating to employment; misdemeanor; punishment.
12976. Willful violation of recordkeeping requirements; misdemeanor; punishment.

§ 12960. Procedure for prevention and elimination of unlawful employment practices; application of article; complaints; limitations

(a) The provisions of this article govern the procedure for the prevention and elimination of practices made unlawful pursuant to Article 1 (commencing with Section 12940) of Chapter 6.

(b) Any person claiming to be aggrieved by an alleged unlawful practice may file with the department a verified complaint, in writing, that shall state the name and address of the person, employer, labor organization, or employment agency alleged to have committed the unlawful practice complained of, and that shall set forth the particulars thereof and contain other information as may be required by the department. The director or his or her authorized representative may in like manner, on his or her own motion, make, sign, and file a complaint.

(c) Any employer whose employees, or some of them, refuse or threaten to refuse to cooperate with the provisions of this part may file with the department a verified complaint asking for assistance by conciliation or other remedial action.

(d) No complaint may be filed after the expiration of one year from the date upon which the alleged unlawful practice or refusal to cooperate occurred, except that this period may be extended as follows:

(1) For a period of time not to exceed 90 days following the expiration of that year, if a person allegedly aggrieved by an unlawful practice first obtained knowledge of the facts of the alleged unlawful practice after the expiration of one year from the date of their occurrence.

(2) For a period of time not to exceed one year following a rebutted presumption of the identity of the person's employer under Section 12928, in order to allow

a person allegedly aggrieved by an unlawful practice to make a substitute identification of the actual employer.

(3) For a period of time, not to exceed one year from the date the person aggrieved by an alleged violation of Section 51.7 of the Civil Code becomes aware of the identity of a person liable for the alleged violation, but in no case exceeding three years from the date of the alleged violation if during that period the aggrieved person is unaware of the identity of any person liable for the alleged violation.

(4) For a period of time not to exceed one year from the date that a person allegedly aggrieved by an unlawful practice attains the age of majority. *(Added by Stats. 1980, c. 992, § 4. Amended by Stats.1982, c. 1193, p. 4260, § 3; Stats.1999, c. 797 (S.B.211), § 2; Stats.2002, c. 490 (S.B.1945), § 2; Stats.2005, c. 642 (A.B.1669), § 1.)*

§ 12961.   Class action

Where an unlawful practice alleged in a verified complaint adversely affects, in a similar manner, a group or class of persons of which the aggrieved person filing the complaint is a member, or where such an unlawful practice raises questions of law or fact which are common to such a group or class, the aggrieved person or the director may file the complaint on behalf and as representative of such a group or class. Any complaint so filed may be investigated as a group or class complaint, and, if in the judgment of the director circumstances warrant, shall be treated as such for purposes of conciliation and accusation. Where an accusation is issued as a group or class accusation, the case shall be treated as a group or class case for all other purposes of this part, including, but not limited to, hearing, determination, reconsideration, and judicial proceedings. *(Added by Stats.1980, c. 992, § 4.)*

§ 12962.   Service of complaint filed for investigation

(a) The department shall cause any verified complaint filed for investigation under the provisions of this part to be served, either personally or by certified mail with return receipt requested, upon the person, employer, labor organization, or employment agency alleged to have committed the unlawful practice complained of.

(b) Notwithstanding subdivision (a), where a person claiming to be aggrieved by an alleged unlawful practice hires or retains private counsel for purposes of representation of the claim, the private counsel, and not the department, shall cause the verified complaint filed under the provisions of this part to be served, either personally or by certified mail with return receipt requested, upon the person, employer, labor organization, or employment agency alleged to have committed the unlawful practice.

(c) Service shall be made at the time of initial contact with the person, employer, labor organization, or employment agency or the agents thereof, or within 60 days, whichever first occurs. At the discretion of the director, the complaint may not contain the name of the complaining party unless the complaint is filed by the director or

his or her authorized representative. *(Added by Stats. 1980, c. 992, § 4. Amended by Stats.2003, c. 447 (A.B. 1536), § 1.)*

§ 12963.   Investigation by department after filing of complaint

After the filing of any complaint alleging facts sufficient to constitute a violation of any of the provisions of this part, the department shall make prompt investigation in connection therewith. *(Added by Stats.1980, c. 992, § 4. Amended by Stats.1980, c. 1023, § 2.)*

§ 12963.1.   Subpoenas; issuance; attendance of witnesses; production of books, records, etc.; service

Upon the filing of a complaint under Section 12960, 12961, or 12980:

(a) The department may issue and serve upon an individual, corporation, partnership, association, public entity, or other organization subpoenas to require the attendance and testimony of witnesses by deposition or otherwise, and in connection therewith, to require the production of books, records, documents, and physical materials in the possession of, or under the control of, the individual or organization named on the subpoena.

(b) A subpoena shall be served by delivering a copy of the subpoena to the individual named on the subpoena or to any person who would be eligible to receive service of summons on behalf of the individual or organization named on the subpoena, as provided in Sections 416.10 through 416.90 of the Code of Civil Procedure. A subpoena issued to a person, employer, labor organization, employment agency, or public entity alleged to have committed an unlawful practice in a complaint filed under Section 12960 or 12961 may also be delivered to the agent or representative who has responded to the department concerning the complaint on behalf of such person, employer, labor organization, employment agency, or public entity. The copy of the subpoena may be delivered by personal service, by substituted service in accordance with Section 415.20 of the Code of Civil Procedure, or by certified mail. The affidavit of the individual serving the subpoena setting forth the manner of such service, along with the return post office receipt in the case of mail service, shall be sufficient proof of such service.

(c) A subpoena for appearance and production of books, records, documents, and physical materials shall identify with reasonable particularity the things that are to be produced. The subpoena need not be accompanied by an affidavit showing good cause or the materiality of the things sought to be produced.

(d) A subpoena for appearance and testimony at a deposition or other proceeding issued to a corporation, partnership, association, public entity, or other organization shall state with reasonable particularity the matters on which testimony is sought. The organization served with such a subpoena shall have the obligation of producing as a witness one or more officers, directors, managing agents, or other individuals to testify on its behalf as to the matters specified in the subpoena.

(e) Service of a subpoena shall be made so as to allow the recipient of the subpoena a reasonable time for compliance. No individual named on a subpoena shall be obliged to attend as a witness before the department at a place out of the county in which that person resides, unless the distance is less than 150 miles from the individual's place of residence or good cause appears why attendance of the witness at greater distance should be required. Each witness who has appeared pursuant to a subpoena shall, upon demand, be paid by the department the same fees and mileage allowed by law to witnesses in civil cases. *(Added by Stats.1980, c. 1023, § 3.)*

§ 12963.2. Written interrogatories; issuance and service; written answers; inspection, compilations, abstracts, etc., of records

Upon the filing of a complaint under Section 12960, 12961, or 12980:

(a) The department may issue and serve written interrogatories on the same individuals and organizations and in the same manner as subpoenas may be issued and served under Section 12963.1. Any corporation, partnership, association, public entity, or other organization to which interrogatories are issued has the obligation of designating one or more officers, directors, managing agents, or other individuals to answer the interrogatories on the organization's behalf.

(b) Within 30 days after the service of the interrogatories, or such longer time as the department may permit, the recipient of the interrogatories shall serve on the department written answers either responding fully or stating any objection to each interrogatory separately. The answers shall be made under oath and shall be signed by each individual making them, and the answers shall identify which individual has responded to each interrogatory.

(c) When in order to answer an interrogatory it is necessary to make a compilation, abstract, audit, or summary of the business records of the recipient of the interrogatory and such a compilation, abstract, audit, or summary does not exist or is not in the possession or under the control of the recipient, it shall be a sufficient answer to the interrogatory to so state and to specify the records from which the answer may be derived or ascertained and to afford the department reasonable opportunity to inspect and copy or make compilations, abstracts, or summaries from such records. *(Added by Stats.1980, c. 1023, § 4.)*

§ 12963.3. Deposition; issuance and service of subpoena; notice; procedure for taking

(a) Depositions taken by the department shall be noticed by issuance and service of a subpoena pursuant to Section 12963.1. If, in the course of the investigation of a complaint, a subpoena is issued and served on an individual or organization not alleged in the complaint to

have committed an unlawful practice, written notice of the deposition shall also be mailed by the department to each individual or organization alleged in the complaint to have committed an unlawful practice.

(b) A deposition may be taken before any officer of the department who has been authorized by the director to administer oaths and take testimony, or before any other person before whom a deposition may be taken in a civil action pursuant to Section 2025.320 or subdivision (d) of Section 2026.010 of the Code of Civil Procedure. The person before whom the deposition is to be taken shall put the witness on oath and shall personally, or by someone acting under the person's direction and in the person's presence, record the testimony of the witness. The testimony shall be taken stenographically and transcribed unless the parties agree otherwise. All objections made at the time of the examination shall be noted on the deposition by the person before whom the deposition is taken, and evidence objected to shall be taken subject to the objections. *(Added by Stats.1980, c. 1023, § 5. Amended by Stats.1981, c. 899, p. 3424, § 2; Stats.2004, c. 647 (A.B.2870), § 6; Stats.2005, c. 294 (A.B.333), § 19.)*

§ 12963.4. Requests for production of books, records, documents, etc.; issuance and service; identification; written response

(a) The department may issue and serve requests for production for inspection and copying of books, records, documents, and physical materials in the possession or under the control of an individual or organization. A request for production may be issued and served on the same individuals and organizations and in the same manner as subpoenas may be issued and served under Section 12963.1.

(b) A request for production shall identify with reasonable particularity the things that are to be inspected and shall specify a reasonable time, place, and manner of making the inspection and performing the copying, and may prescribe such terms and conditions as are just.

(c) Within 15 days after service of a request for production or such longer time as the department may permit, the recipient of the request shall serve on the department a written response with respect to each item requested, either stating that inspection and copying will be permitted as requested or objecting to the request and stating the grounds of the objection. Unless a request for production is objected to, the recipient of the request shall thereafter permit the inspection and copying requested by the department. *(Added by Stats.1980, c. 1023, § 6.)*

§ 12963.5. Jurisdiction; petition to compel compliance; contents; order; review; mandamus; contempt

(a) The superior courts shall have jurisdiction to compel the attendance and testimony of witnesses, the production of books, records, documents, and physical materials, and the answering of interrogatories. If an individual or organization fails to comply with a subpoena, interrogatory, request for production, or examination under oath by refusing to respond fully or objecting thereto, or by obstructing any proceeding before the department, the department may file with a superior court a petition for an order compelling compliance, naming as respondent the individual or organization that has failed to comply. Such an action may be brought in any county in which the department's investigation or inquiry takes place, but if the respondent is not found within any such county, such an action may be brought in the county of the respondent's residence or principal office.

(b) The petition shall describe the inquiry or investigation before the department, the basis for its jurisdiction therein, and state facts showing that the subpoena, interrogatory, request for production, or examination under oath was issued or carried out in accordance with the requirements of this part, that the information sought was identified with sufficient particularity to permit response and is reasonably relevant to the inquiry or investigation before the department, and that the respondent has failed to comply. If the petition sets forth good cause for relief, the court shall issue an order to show cause to the respondent; otherwise the court shall enter an order denying the petition. The order to show cause shall be served, along with the department's petition, on the respondent in the same manner as summons must be served in civil actions, and the order shall be returnable not less than 10 days from its issuance nor later than 45 days after the filing of the petition. The respondent shall have the right to serve and file a written answer or other response to the petition and order to show cause.

(c) Unless otherwise stipulated by the parties, the court shall no later than 30 days after the filing of the petition file its order granting or denying the petition. However, the court may on its own motion for good cause extend such time an additional 30 days. If the order grants the petition in whole or part, the order shall set forth the manner in which the respondent shall comply and the period of time following the effective date of the order within which such compliance is required. A copy of the order shall be served by mail by the clerk upon the parties. If the order grants the petition in whole or in part, the order shall not become effective until 10 days after it is served. If the order denies the petition, it shall become effective on the date it is served.

(d) The order of the superior court shall be final and not subject to review by appeal. A party aggrieved by such order, or any part thereof, may within 15 days after the service of the superior court's order, serve and file in the appropriate court of appeal a petition for a writ of mandamus to compel the superior court to set aside or otherwise modify its order. If or whenever such review is sought from an order granting discovery, the order of the trial court shall be stayed upon the filing of the petition for a writ of mandamus, provided, however, the court of appeal may dissolve or modify the stay thereafter if it is in the public interest to do so. If or whenever such review is sought from a denial of discovery, the trial court's order shall not be stayed by the court of appeal except upon a clear showing of probable error.

(e) Within 15 days after the end of the compliance period specified in the final order of the superior court, after the exhaustion of any challenges to the order in higher courts, the department shall in writing certify to the court either that the order has been complied with or that the respondent has failed to comply. A copy of the certified statement shall be served on the respondent by personal delivery or certified mail. After receipt of a certified statement indicating the respondent's failure to comply with the order, the court may compel obedience to its order by contempt proceedings, and by making such additional orders as may be appropriate. Following such proceedings, the department shall, within 15 days after the respondent complies with the original order of the court, certify in writing to the court that such order has been complied with. A copy of the certified statement shall be served on the respondent by personal delivery or certified mail.

(f) The period of time within which the department is directed to file an accusation by Section 12965 shall be extended by the length of the period between the filing of a petition under this section and either (1) the final effective date, after the exhaustion of any challenges to the original order in higher courts, of an order of the superior court denying the petition, or (2) the filing by the department of a certified statement, pursuant to subdivision (e), indicating the respondent's compliance with the order of the superior court granting the petition in whole or in part, whichever occurs later. *(Added by Stats.1980, c. 1023, § 7.)*

§ 12963.7. Elimination of unlawful employment practice by conference, conciliation and persuasion; confidentiality; disclosure as misdemeanor

(a) If the department determines after investigation that the complaint is valid, the department shall immediately endeavor to eliminate the unlawful employment practice complained of by conference, conciliation, and persuasion. The staff of the department shall not disclose what has transpired in the course of any endeavors to eliminate the unlawful employment practice through conference, conciliation, and persuasion.

(b) Any member of the staff of the department who discloses information in violation of the requirements of this section is guilty of a misdemeanor. Such disclosure by an employee subject to civil service shall be cause for disciplinary action under the State Civil Service Act. *(Added by Stats.1980, c. 1023, § 8.)*

§ 12964. Agreement based on conference, conciliation and persuasion; reduction to writing; compliance review; injunction; civil action

Any agreement entered into by conference, conciliation and persuasion shall be reduced to writing, signed by all parties, and approved by the director or the authorized representative of the director. Within one year of the effective date of every agreement, the department shall conduct a compliance review to determine whether the agreement has been fully obeyed and implemented. Whenever the department believes, on the basis of evidence presented to it, that any person is violating or about to violate any agreement, the department may bring an action in the superior court against the person to enjoin him or her from continuing or engaging in the violation, or from doing anything in furtherance of the violation. In the action an order or judgment may be entered awarding a temporary restraining order or a preliminary or final injunction as may be proper. The action may be brought in any county in which actions may be brought under subdivision (b) of Section 12965. In resolving allegedly unlawful practices through conciliation the resolutions may be in the nature of, but are not limited to, types of remedies that might be ordered after accusation and hearing. *(Added by Stats.1980, c. 992, § 4. Amended by Stats.1986, c. 656, § 1.)*

§ 12965. Written accusation by department; group or class complaint; civil action; transfer to court; relief; damages; tolling of statute of limitations

(a) In the case of failure to eliminate an unlawful practice under this part through conference, conciliation, or persuasion, or in advance thereof if circumstances warrant, the director in his or her discretion may cause to be issued in the name of the department a written accusation. The accusation shall contain the name of the person, employer, labor organization, or employment agency accused, which shall be known as the respondent, shall set forth the nature of the charges, shall be served upon the respondent together with a copy of the verified complaint, as amended, and shall require the respondent to answer the charges at a hearing.

For any complaint treated by the director as a group or class complaint for purposes of investigation, conciliation, and accusation pursuant to Section 12961, an accusation shall be issued, if at all, within two years after the filing of the complaint. For any complaint alleging a violation of Section 51.7 of the Civil Code, an accusation shall be issued, if at all, within two years after the filing of the complaint. For all other complaints, an accusation shall be issued, if at all, within one year after the filing of a complaint. If the director determines, pursuant to Section 12961, that a complaint investigated as a group or class complaint under Section 12961 is to be treated as a group or class complaint for purposes of conciliation and accusation as well, that determination shall be made and shall be communicated in writing within one year after the filing of the complaint to each person, employer, labor organization, employment agency, or public entity alleged in the complaint to have committed an unlawful practice.

(b) If an accusation is not issued within 150 days after the filing of a complaint, or if the department earlier determines that no accusation will issue, the department shall promptly notify, in writing, the person claiming to be aggrieved that the department shall issue, on his or her request, the right-to-sue notice. This notice shall indicate that the person claiming to be aggrieved may bring a civil action under this part against the person, employer, labor organization, or employment agency named in the verified complaint within one year from the date of that notice. If the person claiming to be aggrieved does not request a right-to-sue notice, the department shall issue the notice upon completion of its investigation, and not later than one year after the filing of the complaint. A city, county, or district attorney in a location having an enforcement unit established on or before March 1, 1991, pursuant to a local ordinance enacted for the purpose of prosecuting HIV/AIDS discrimination claims, acting on behalf of any person claiming to be aggrieved due to HIV/AIDS discrimination, may also bring a civil action under this part against the person, employer, labor organization, or employment agency named in the notice. The superior courts of the State of California shall have jurisdiction of those actions, and the aggrieved person may file in these courts. An action may be brought in any county in the state in which the unlawful practice is alleged to have been committed, in the county in which the records relevant to the practice are maintained and administered, or in the county in which the aggrieved person would have worked or would have had access to the public accommodation but for the alleged unlawful practice, but if the defendant is not found within any of these counties, an action may be brought within the county of the defendant's residence or principal office. A copy of any complaint filed pursuant to this part shall be served on the principal offices of the department and of the commission. The remedy for failure to send a copy of a complaint is an order to do so. Those actions may not be filed as class actions or may not be maintained as class actions by the person or persons claiming to be aggrieved where those persons have filed a civil class action in the federal courts alleging a comparable claim of employment discrimination against the same defendant or defendants. In actions brought under this section, the court, in its discretion, may award to the prevailing party reasonable attorney's fees and costs, including expert witness fees, except where the action is filed by a public agency or a public official, acting in an official capacity.

(c)(1) If an accusation includes a prayer either for damages for emotional injuries as a component of actual damages, or for administrative fines, or for both, or if an accusation is amended for the purpose of adding a prayer either for damages for emotional injuries as a component of actual damages, or for administrative fines, or both, the respondent may within 30 days after service of the accusation or amended accusation, elect to transfer the proceedings to a court in lieu of a hearing pursuant to subdivision (a) by serving a written notice to that effect on the department, the commission, and the person claiming to be aggrieved. The commission shall prescribe the form and manner of giving written notice.

179

(2) No later than 30 days after the completion of service of the notice of election pursuant to paragraph (1), the department shall dismiss the accusation and shall, either itself or, at its election, through the Attorney General, file in the appropriate court an action in its own name on behalf of the person claiming to be aggrieved as the real party in interest. In this action, the person claiming to be aggrieved shall be the real party in interest and shall have the right to participate as a party and be represented by his or her own counsel. Complaints filed pursuant to this section shall be filed in the superior court in any county in which unlawful practices are alleged to have been committed, in the county in which records relevant to the alleged unlawful practices are maintained and administered, or in the county in which the person claiming to be aggrieved would have worked or would have had access to public accommodation, but for the alleged unlawful practices. If the defendant is not found in any of these counties, the action may be brought within the county of the defendant's residence or principal office. Those actions shall be assigned to the court's delay reduction program, or otherwise given priority for disposition by the court in which the action is filed.

(3) A court may grant as relief in any action filed pursuant to this subdivision any relief a court is empowered to grant in a civil action brought pursuant to subdivision (b), in addition to any other relief that, in the judgment of the court, will effectuate the purpose of this part. This relief may include a requirement that the employer conduct training for all employees, supervisors, and management on the requirements of this part, the rights and remedies of those who allege a violation of this part, and the employer's internal grievance procedures.

(4) The department may amend an accusation to pray for either damages for emotional injury or for administrative fines, or both, provided that the amendment is made within 30 days of the issuance of the original accusation.

(d)(1) Notwithstanding subdivision (b), the one-year statute of limitations, commencing from the date of the right-to-sue notice by the Department of Fair Employment and Housing, to the person claiming to be aggrieved, shall be tolled when all of the following requirements have been met:

(A) A charge of discrimination or harassment is timely filed concurrently with the Equal Employment Opportunity Commission and the Department of Fair Employment and Housing.

(B) The investigation of the charge is deferred by the Department of Fair Employment and Housing to the Equal Employment Opportunity Commission.

(C) A right-to-sue notice is issued to the person claiming to be aggrieved upon deferral of the charge by the Department of Fair Employment and Housing to the Equal Employment Opportunity Commission.

(2) The time for commencing an action for which the statute of limitations is tolled under paragraph (1) expires when the federal right-to-sue period to commence a civil

action expires, or one year from the date of the right-to-sue notice by the Department of Fair Employment and Housing, whichever is later.

(3) This subdivision is intended to codify the holding in Downs v. Department of Water and Power of City of Los Angeles (1997) 58 Cal.App.4th 1093.

(e)(1) Notwithstanding subdivision (b), the one-year statute of limitations, commencing from the date of the right-to-sue notice by the Department of Fair Employment and Housing, to the person claiming to be aggrieved, shall be tolled when all of the following requirements have been met:

(A) A charge of discrimination or harassment is timely filed concurrently with the Equal Employment Opportunity Commission and the Department of Fair Employment and Housing.

(B) The investigation of the charge is deferred by the Equal Employment Opportunity Commission to the Department of Fair Employment and Housing.

(C) After investigation and determination by the Department of Fair Employment and Housing, the Equal Employment Opportunity Commission agrees to perform a substantial weight review of the determination of the department or conducts its own investigation of the claim filed by the aggrieved person.

(2) The time for commencing an action for which the statute of limitations is tolled under paragraph (1) shall expire when the federal right-to-sue period to commence a civil action expires, or one year from the date of the right-to-sue notice by the Department of Fair Employment and Housing, whichever is later. *(Added by Stats. 1980, c. 992, § 4. Amended by Stats.1980, c. 1023, § 9; Stats.1984, c. 217, § 1; Stats.1984, c. 420, § 1.5; Stats. 1992, c. 911 (A.B.311), § 5; Stats.1992, c. 912 (A.B.1286), § 7.1; Stats.1998, c. 931 (S.B.2139), § 183, eff. Sept. 28, 1998; Stats.1999, c. 591 (A.B.1670), § 12; Stats.2000, c. 189 (A.B.2062), § 1; Stats.2001, c. 813 (A.B.276), § 1; Stats.2002, c. 664 (A.B.3034), § 94.5; Stats.2002, c. 294 (A.B.1146), § 1; Stats.2003, c. 62 (S.B.600), § 118; Stats. 2007, c. 43 (S.B.649), § 16.)*

§ 12966. Accused as state contractor or supplier of goods and services to state; notice to and report by awarding agency

Where the department issues an accusation, or is about to do so, and the respondent accused of engaging in unlawful practices under this part is a state contractor or is a supplier of goods and services to the state, the director shall send a written notice of the issuance of the accusation and a copy of the accusation to the appropriate awarding agency and request a report of any action which the awarding agency takes in response to the department's notification and issuance of accusation. *(Added by Stats.1980, c. 992, § 4.)*

§ 12967. Hearings; determination of issues

The commission shall hold hearings on accusations issued pursuant to Section 12965 and shall determine the issues raised therein. *(Added by Stats.1980, c. 992, § 4.)*

§ 12968. Hearings; time

Hearings shall take place not more than 90 days after the issuance of the accusation upon which they are based. *(Added by Stats.1980, c. 992, § 4.)*

§ 12969. Presentation by department of case in support of accusation; participation by members of commission

The case in support of the accusation shall be presented before the commission by the attorneys or agents of the department. Any commissioner who, in regard to a particular case, shall have previously been assigned to engage in investigation or conciliation endeavors or shall otherwise have been or be personally or professionally connected with the parties or factual situation of the original complaint upon which the accusation is based, shall not participate in the hearing except as a witness and shall not give his or her opinion of the merits of the case, nor shall he or she participate in the deliberations of the commission in such case. In connection with complaints initiated by the director, the personal or professional association of the commissioners with the director shall not prohibit the commissioners from participating in the deliberations of such cases. In any hearing, the content of discussions or endeavors at conciliation shall not be received in evidence. *(Added by Stats.1980, c. 992, § 4.)*

§ 12970. Findings; order; remedies; administrative fine; civil penalty; report to agency; dismissal; appeal rights; copy to district attorney

(a) If the commission finds that a respondent has engaged in any unlawful practice under this part, it shall state its findings of fact and determination and shall issue and cause to be served on the parties an order requiring the respondent to cease and desist from the unlawful practice and to take action, including, but not limited to, any of the following:

(1) The hiring, reinstatement, or upgrading of employees, with or without backpay.

(2) The admission or restoration to membership in any respondent labor organization.

(3) The payment of actual damages as may be available in civil actions under this part, except as otherwise provided in this section. Actual damages include, but are not limited to, damages for emotional injuries if the accusation or amended accusation prays for those damages. Actual damages awarded under this section for emotional pain, suffering, inconvenience, mental anguish, loss of enjoyment of life, and other nonpecuniary losses shall not exceed, in combination with the amounts of any administrative fines imposed pursuant to subdivision (c), one hundred fifty thousand dollars ($150,000) per aggrieved person per respondent.

(4) Notwithstanding paragraph (3), the payment of actual damages up to one hundred fifty thousand dollars ($150,000) assessed against a respondent for a violation of Section 51.7 of the Civil Code, as an unlawful practice under this part.

(5) Affirmative or prospective relief to prevent the recurrence of the unlawful practice.

(6) A report to the commission as to the manner of compliance with the commission's order.

(b) An unlawful practice under this part alone is not sufficient to sustain an award of actual damages pursuant to this section. The department is required to prove, by a preponderance of the evidence, that an aggrieved person has sustained actual injury. In determining whether to award damages for emotional injuries, and the amount of any award for these damages, the commission shall consider relevant evidence of the effects of discrimination on the aggrieved person with respect to any or all of the following:

(1) Physical and mental well-being.

(2) Personal integrity, dignity, and privacy.

(3) Ability to work, earn a living, and advance in his or her career.

(4) Personal and professional reputation.

(5) Family relationships.

(6) Access to the job and ability to associate with peers and coworkers.

The commission shall also consider the duration of the emotional injury, and whether that injury was caused or exacerbated by an aggrieved person's knowledge of a respondent's failure to respond adequately to, or to correct, the discriminatory practice or by the egregiousness of the discriminatory practice.

(c) In addition to the foregoing, in order to vindicate the purposes and policies of this part, the commission may assess against the respondent, if the accusation or amended accusation so prays, an administrative fine per aggrieved person per respondent, the amount of which shall be determined in accordance with the combined amount limitation of paragraph (3) of subdivision (a).

(d) In determining whether to assess an administrative fine pursuant to this section, the commission shall find that the respondent has been guilty of oppression, fraud, or malice, expressed or implied, as required by Section 3294 of the Civil Code. In determining the amount of fines, the commission shall consider relevant evidence of, including, but not limited to, the following:

(1) Willful, intentional, or purposeful conduct.

(2) Refusal to prevent or eliminate discrimination.

(3) Conscious disregard for the rights of employees.

(4) Commission of unlawful conduct.

(5) Intimidation or harassment.

(6) Conduct without just cause or excuse.

(7) Multiple violations of the Fair Employment and Housing Act.

The moneys derived from an administrative fine assessed pursuant to this subdivision shall be deposited in the General Fund. No administrative fine shall be assessed against a public entity. The commission shall have no authority to award punitive damages as a remedy for a finding of employment discrimination.

(e) In addition to the foregoing, in order to vindicate the purposes and policies of this part, the commission may assess against the respondent if the accusation or amended accusation so prays, a civil penalty of up to twenty-five thousand dollars ($25,000) to be awarded to a person denied any right provided for by Section 51.7 of the Civil Code, as an unlawful practice prohibited under this part.

(f) If the commission finds the respondent has engaged in an unlawful practice under this part, and the respondent is licensed or granted a privilege by an agency of the state to do business, provide a service, or conduct activities, and the unlawful practice is determined to have occurred in connection with the exercise of that license or privilege, the commission shall provide the licensing or privilege granting agency with a copy of its decision or order.

(g) If the commission finds that a respondent has not engaged in an unlawful practice under this part, the commission shall state its findings of fact and determination and issue and cause to be served on the parties an order dismissing the accusation as to that respondent.

(h) Any findings and determination made or any order issued pursuant to this section shall be written and shall indicate the identity of the members of the commission who participated therein.

(i) Any order issued by the commission shall have printed on its face references to the rights of appeal of any party to the proceeding to whose position the order is adverse.

(j) If the commission finds that a respondent has engaged in an unlawful practice under this part, and it appears that this practice consisted of acts described in Section 243.4, 261, 262, 286, 288, 288a, or 289 of the Penal Code, the commission, with the consent of the complainant, shall provide the local district attorney's office with a copy of its decision and order.

(k) Notwithstanding Section 12960, if the commission finds that a respondent has engaged in unlawful discrimination in housing under Section 12948, the remedies afforded in Section 12987 or any other provision in this part pertaining to housing discrimination, shall apply. *(Added by Stats.1980, c. 992, § 4. Amended by Stats.1984, c. 492, § 1; Stats.1984, c. 1754, § 3; Stats.1992, c. 911 (A.B.311), § 6; Stats.1996, c. 1075 (S.B.1444), § 12; Stats.1999, c. 591 (A.B.1670), § 13.)*

182

§ 12971. Withdrawal of complaint, dismissal by department or termination or closure of investigation; notice to respondent and complainant

If, at any time during the proceedings described in this part, after a complaint has been served on a respondent, the complaint is withdrawn by the complainant or dismissed by the department, or an investigation is terminated or closed by the department, notice of this fact shall be given to the respondent and the complainant without undue delay. *(Added by Stats.1980, c. 992, § 4.)*

§ 12972. Actions and procedures; procedural regulations; deposition by each party

(a) The commission shall conduct all actions and procedures in accordance with its procedural regulations.

(b)(1) If the commission does not have a procedural regulation on a particular issue, the commission shall rely upon pertinent provisions of the Administrative Procedure Act (Chapter 4 (commencing with Section 11370) of Part 1).

(2) Notwithstanding paragraph (1), the Administrative Adjudication Bill of Rights set forth in Article 6 (commencing with Section 11425.10) of Chapter 4.5 of Part 1, and the rules for judicial review set forth in Section 11523, shall apply to the commission.

(c) In addition to the discovery available to each party pursuant to subdivision (a), the department and the respondent may each cause a single deposition to be taken in the manner prescribed by law for depositions in civil actions in the superior courts of this state under Title 4 (commencing with Section 2016.010) of Part 4 of the Code of Civil Procedure. *(Added by Stats.1980, c. 992, § 4. Amended by Stats.1992, c. 910 (A.B.2392), § 3; Stats.1992, c. 911 (A.B.311), § 7.5; Stats.1998, c. 931 (S.B.2139), § 184, eff. Sept. 28, 1998; Stats.2004, c. 182 (A.B.3081), § 43, operative July 1, 2005; Stats.2004, c. 647 (A.B.2870), § 7; Stats.2005, c. 294 (A.B.333), § 20.)*

§ 12973. Compliance review of final order or decision; time for review; judgment; fine or penalty; attorney's fees

(a) Within one year of the effective date of every final order or decision issued pursuant to this part, the department shall conduct a compliance review to determine whether the order or decision has been fully obeyed and implemented.

(b) If the time for judicial review of a final commission order or decision has lapsed, or if all means of judicial review have been exhausted, the department may apply to the superior court in any county in which an action could have been brought under subdivision (b) of Section 12965 for the enforcement of the order or decision or order as modified in accordance with a decision on judicial review. If, after a hearing, the court determines that an order or decision has been issued by the commission and that either the time limits for judicial review have lapsed, or the order or decision was upheld in whole or in part on judicial review, the court shall issue a judgment and order enforcing the order or decision or order as modified in accordance with a decision on judicial review. The court shall not review the merits of the order or decision. The court's judgment shall be nonappealable and shall have the same force and effect as, and shall be subject to all the provisions of law relating to, a judgment in a civil action.

(c) Notwithstanding subdivisions (a) and (b), where the reviewing court denies a petition for writ of mandate seeking review of a commission order or decision, the court shall enter judgment denying the petition and enforcing the commission's final order or decision.

(d) If the commission has found that a respondent has engaged in an unlawful practice under this part and is liable for actual damages, an administrative fine, or a civil penalty, any amount due to that respondent by a state agency may be offset to satisfy the commission's final order or decision.

(e) Notwithstanding any other provision of law, the commission is not liable for attorney's fees of parties to the administrative adjudication of cases brought before the commission, including proceedings brought pursuant to Section 11523 of this code and Section 1094.5 of the Code of Civil Procedure. *(Added by Stats.1980, c. 992, § 4. Amended by Stats.1986, c. 656, § 2; Stats.2004, c. 647 (A.B.2870), § 8.)*

§ 12974. Civil action for relief pending final disposition of complaint; temporary or preliminary relief; venue

Whenever a complaint is filed with the department and the department concludes on the basis of a preliminary investigation that prompt judicial action is necessary to carry out the purposes of this part, the director or his authorized representative may bring a civil action for appropriate temporary or preliminary relief pending final disposition of such complaint. Any temporary restraining order or other order granting preliminary or temporary relief shall be issued in accordance with Section 527 of the Code of Civil Procedure. An action seeking such temporary or preliminary relief may be brought in any county in which actions may be brought under subdivision (b) of Section 12965. *(Added by Stats.1980, c. 992, § 4.)*

§ 12975. Willful interference with duties of department or commission or willful violation of orders of commission relating to employment; misdemeanor; punishment

Any person who shall willfully resist, prevent, impede or interfere with any member of the department or the commission or any of its agents or employees in the performance of duties pursuant to the provisions of this part relating to employment discrimination, or who shall in any manner willfully violate an order of the commission relating to such matter, is guilty of a misdemeanor, punishable by imprisonment in a county jail, not exceeding six months, or by a fine not exceeding one thousand dollars ($1,000), or both. *(Added by Stats.1980, c. 992,*

§ 4. Amended by Stats.1983, c. 1092, § 133, eff. Sept. 27, 1983, operative Jan. 1, 1984.)

§ 12976. Willful violation of recordkeeping requirements; misdemeanor; punishment

Any person who willfully violates Section 12946 concerning recordkeeping is guilty of a misdemeanor, punishable by imprisonment in a county jail, not exceeding six months, or by a fine not exceeding one thousand dollars ($1,000), or both. *(Added by Stats.1980, c. 992, § 4. Amended by Stats.1983, c. 1092, § 134, eff. Sept. 27, 1983, operative Jan. 1, 1984.)*

ARTICLE 2. HOUSING DISCRIMINATION

Section
12980. Procedure for prevention and elimination of discrimination in housing; application of article; complaint; other remedies; time; civil action.
12981. Departmental accusation upon failure of conference, conciliation or persuasion; application; housing discrimination action; hearings; compliance review; civil action; judgment and order.
12981.1. Dismissal of complaint or accusation.
12983. Actions to enjoin property owner from taking further action regarding property.
12984. Privilege of conference, conciliation or persuasion efforts; disclosure; misdemeanor; discipline.
12985. Contacts by department following filing of complaint; disclosure of nature of contact; privilege.
12986. Service of complaint on respondent.
12987. Findings by commission; order to cease and desist; other remedies; civil penalty; waiver; dismissal of accusation.
12987.1. Review of final order of relief; intervention as matter of right; enforcement decree; denial of petition.
12988. Affirmative actions.
12989. Civil action in lieu of administrative proceeding.
12989.1. Commencement of civil actions; statute of limitations; procedure.
12989.2. Relief; damages; fees and costs.
12989.3. Civil actions commenced by Attorney General.

§ 12980. Procedure for prevention and elimination of discrimination in housing; application of article; complaint; other remedies; time; civil action

This article governs the procedure for the prevention and elimination of discrimination in housing made unlawful pursuant to Article 2 (commencing with Section 12955) of Chapter 6.

(a) Any person claiming to be aggrieved by an alleged violation of Section 12955, 12955.1, or 12955.7 may file with the department a verified complaint in writing that shall state the name and address of the person alleged to have committed the violation complained of, and that shall set forth the particulars of the alleged violation and contain any other information required by the department.

The filing of a complaint and pursuit of conciliation or remedy under this part shall not prejudice the complainant's right to pursue effective judicial relief under other applicable laws, but if a civil action has been filed under Section 52 of the Civil Code, the department shall terminate proceedings upon notification of the entry of final judgment unless the judgment is a dismissal entered at the complainant's request.

(b) The Attorney General or the director may, in a like manner, make, sign, and file complaints citing practices that appear to violate the purpose of this part or any specific provisions of this part relating to housing discrimination.

No complaint may be filed after the expiration of one year from the date upon which the alleged violation occurred or terminated.

(c) The department may thereupon proceed upon the complaint in the same manner and with the same powers as provided in this part in the case of an unlawful practice, except that where the provisions of this article provide greater rights and remedies to an aggrieved person than the provisions of Article 1 (commencing with Section 12960), the provisions of this article shall prevail.

(d) Upon the filing of a complaint, the department shall serve notice upon the complainant of the time limits, rights of the parties, and choice of forums provided for under the law.

(e) The department shall commence proceedings with respect to a complaint within 30 days of filing of the complaint.

(f) An investigation of allegations contained in any complaint filed with the department shall be completed within 100 days after receipt of the complaint, unless it is impracticable to do so. If the investigation is not completed within 100 days, the complainant and respondent shall be notified, in writing, of the department's reasons for not doing so.

(g) Upon the conclusion of each investigation, the department shall prepare a final investigative report containing all of the following:

(1) The names of any witnesses and the dates of any contacts with those witnesses.

(2) A summary of the dates of any correspondence or other contacts with the aggrieved persons or the respondent.

(3) A summary of witness statements.

(4) Answers to interrogatories.

(5) A summary description of other pertinent records.

A final investigative report may be amended if additional evidence is later discovered.

(h) If an accusation is not issued within 100 days after the filing of a complaint, or if the department earlier determines that no accusation will issue, the department shall promptly notify the person claiming to be aggrieved. This notice shall, in any event, be issued no more than 30 days after the date of the determination or 30 days after the date of the expiration of the 100–day period, whichev-

er date first occurs. The notice shall indicate that the person claiming to be aggrieved may bring a civil action under this part against the person named in the verified complaint within the time period specified in Section 12989.1. The notice shall also indicate, unless the department has determined that no accusation will be issued, that the person claiming to be aggrieved has the option of continuing to seek redress for the alleged discrimination through the procedures of the department if he or she does not desire to file a civil action. The superior courts of the State of California shall have jurisdiction of these actions, and the aggrieved person may file in these courts. The action may be brought in any county in the state in which the violation is alleged to have been committed, or in the county in which the records relevant to the alleged violation are maintained and administered, but if the defendant is not found within that county, the action may be brought within the county of the defendant's residence or principal office. A copy of any complaint filed pursuant to this part shall be served on the principal offices of the department and of the commission. The remedy for failure to send a copy of a complaint is an order to do so. In a civil action brought under this section, the court, in its discretion, may award to the prevailing party reasonable attorney's fees.

(i) All agreements reached in settlement of any housing discrimination complaint filed pursuant to this section shall be made public, unless otherwise agreed by the complainant and respondent, and the department determines that the disclosure is not required to further the purposes of the act.

(j) All agreements reached in settlement of any housing discrimination complaint filed pursuant to this section shall be agreements between the respondent and complainant, and shall be subject to approval by the department. *(Added by Stats.1980, c. 992, § 4. Amended by Stats.1982, c. 454, p. 1847, § 45; Stats.1984, c. 217, § 2; Stats.1984, c. 420, § 2.5; Stats.1987, c. 605, § 6; Stats. 1992, c. 182 (S.B.1234), § 14; Stats.1993, c. 1277 (A.B. 2244), § 9; Stats.1998, c. 931 (S.B.2139), § 185, eff. Sept. 28, 1998; Stats.2003, c. 447 (A.B.1536), § 2; Stats.2007, c. 43 (S.B.649), § 17.)*

§ 12981. Departmental accusation upon failure of conference, conciliation or persuasion; application; housing discrimination action; hearings; compliance review; civil action; judgment and order

(a) In the case of failure to eliminate a violation of Section 12955, 12955.1, or 12955.7 that has occurred, or is about to occur, through conference, conciliation, and persuasion, or in advance thereof if circumstances warrant, the director shall cause to be issued in the name of the department, notwithstanding Section 12971, a written accusation, in the same manner and with the same powers as provided in Section 12965, except that where the provisions of this article provide greater rights and remedies to an aggrieved person than Section 12965, the provisions of this article shall prevail. An accusation alleging an unfair housing practice shall be issued within 100 days after the filing of a complaint unless it is impracticable to do so. The accusation shall require the respondent to answer the charges at an administrative hearing or civil trial as elected by the parties pursuant to Section 12989. Any aggrieved person may intervene as a matter of right in the proceeding, and the appeal or other judicial review of that proceeding.

(b) If the department determines that an allegation concerns the legality of any zoning or other land use law or ordinance, the department or the Attorney General shall take appropriate action with respect to the complaint according to the procedures established in this part for other complaints of housing discrimination.

(c) The commission shall hold hearings on accusations issued pursuant to subdivision (a) in the same manner and with the same powers as provided in Sections 12967 to 12972, inclusive, except that where the provisions of this article provide greater rights and remedies to an aggrieved person than do Sections 12967 to 12972, inclusive, the provisions of this article shall prevail. The commission shall make final administrative disposition of a complaint alleging unfair housing practices within one year of the date of filing of the complaint, unless it is impracticable to do so. If the department is unable to make final administrative disposition of a complaint within one year, it shall notify the complainant and the respondent, in writing, of its reasons for not doing so.

(d) Within one year of the effective date of every final order or decision issued pursuant to this part, the department shall conduct a compliance review to determine whether the order or decision has been fully obeyed and implemented.

(e) Whenever the department has reasonable cause to believe that a respondent has breached a conciliation agreement, the department shall refer the matter to the Attorney General with a recommendation that a civil action be filed for the enforcement of the agreement.

(f) If the time for judicial review of a final commission order or decision has lapsed, or if all means of judicial review have been exhausted, the department may apply to the superior court in any county in which an action could have been brought under subdivision (b) of Section 12965 for the enforcement of the order or decision or order as modified in accordance with a decision on judicial review. If, after a hearing, the court determines that an order or decision has been issued by the commission and that either the time limits for judicial review have lapsed, or the order or decision was upheld in whole or in part on judicial review, the court shall issue a judgment and order enforcing the order or decision or order as modified in accordance with a decision on judicial review. The court shall not review the merits of the order or decision. The court's judgment shall be nonappealable and shall have the same force and effect as, and shall be subject to all the provisions of law relating to, a judgment in a civil action.

(Added by Stats.1980, c. 992, § 4. Amended by Stats.1986, c. 656, § 3; Stats.1992, c. 182 (S.B.1234), § 15; Stats.1993, c. 1277 (A.B.2244), § 10; Stats.2003, c. 447 (A.B.1536), § 3.)

§ 12981.1. Dismissal of complaint or accusation

The department shall not dismiss a complaint or an accusation unless the complainant withdraws the complaint or the department determines after a thorough investigation that, based on the facts, no reasonable cause exists to believe that an unlawful housing practice, as prohibited by this part, has occurred or is about to occur. *(Added by Stats.1993, c. 1277 (A.B.2244), § 11.)*

§ 12983. Actions to enjoin property owner from taking further action regarding property

The department, or at its election the Attorney General, at any time after a complaint is filed with it and it has been determined that probable cause exists for believing that the allegations of the complaint are true and constitute a violation of this part, may bring an action in the superior court to enjoin the owner of the property from taking further action with respect to the rental, lease, or sale of the property, as well as to require compliance with Section 12956, until the department has completed its investigation and made its determination; but a temporary restraining order obtained under this section shall not, in any event, be in effect for more than 20 days. In this action an order or judgment may be entered awarding the temporary restraining order or the preliminary or final injunction in accordance with Section 527 of the Code of Civil Procedure. *(Added by Stats. 1980, c. 992, § 4. Amended by Stats.1987, c. 605, § 8; Stats.2003, c. 447 (A.B.1536), § 4.)*

§ 12984. Privilege of conference, conciliation or persuasion efforts; disclosure; misdemeanor; discipline

Except as provided in Section 12980, all matters connected with any conference, conciliation, or persuasion efforts under this part are privileged and may not be received in evidence. Except as provided in Section 12980, the members of the department and its staff shall not disclose to any person what has transpired in the course of such endeavors to conciliate. Every member of the department or its staff who discloses information in violation of this section is guilty of a misdemeanor. Such disclosure by an employee subject to civil service shall be cause for disciplinary action under the State Civil Service Act. *(Added by Stats.1980, c. 992, § 4. Amended by Stats.1992, c. 182 (S.B.1234), § 16.)*

§ 12985. Contacts by department following filing of complaint; disclosure of nature of contact; privilege

When a person is contacted by the department, a commissioner, or a member of the department's staff, following the filing of a complaint against that person, the person shall be informed whether the contact is for the purpose of investigation or conference, conciliation, or persuasion; and if it is for conference, conciliation, or

185

persuasion, the person shall be informed that all matters relating thereto are privileged. *(Added by Stats.1980, c. 992, § 4.)*

§ 12986. Service of complaint on respondent

The department shall within 10 days cause a copy of the verified complaint that has been filed under the provisions of this part to be served upon or mailed to the respondent alleged to have committed the violation complained of and shall advise the respondent in writing of his or her procedural rights and obligations. The respondent may file an answer to the complaint. *(Added by Stats.1980, c. 992, § 4. Amended by Stats.1987, c. 605, § 9; Stats.1992, c. 182 (S.B.1234), § 17.)*

§ 12987. Findings by commission; order to cease and desist; other remedies; civil penalty; waiver; dismissal of accusation

(a) If the commission, after hearing, finds that a respondent has engaged in any unlawful practice as defined in this part, the commission shall state its findings of fact and shall issue and cause to be served on the respondent an order requiring the respondent to cease and desist from the practice and to take those actions, as, in the judgment of the commission, will effectuate the purpose of this part, including, but not limited to, any of the following:

(1) The sale or rental of the housing accommodation if it is still available, or the sale or rental of a like housing accommodation, if one is available, or the provision of financial assistance, terms, conditions, or privileges previously denied in violation of subdivision (f) of Section 12955 in the purchase, organization, or construction of the housing accommodation, if available.

(2) Affirmative or prospective relief, including injunctive or other equitable relief.

(3) The payment to the complainant of a civil penalty against any named respondent, not to exceed ten thousand dollars ($10,000), unless, in a separate accusation, the respondent has been adjudged to have, with intent, committed a prior violation of Section 12955. If the respondent has, in a separate accusation, been adjudged to have committed a prior violation of Section 12955 within the five years preceding the filing of the complaint, the amount of the civil penalty may exceed ten thousand dollars ($10,000), but may not exceed twenty-five thousand dollars ($25,000). If the respondent, in separate accusations, has been adjudged to have, with intent, violated Section 12955 two or more times within the seven-year period preceding the filing of the complaint, the civil penalty may exceed twenty-five thousand dollars ($25,000), but may not exceed fifty thousand dollars ($50,000). All civil penalties awarded under this provision shall be collected by the department. The commission may award the prevailing party, other than the state, reasonable attorney's fees and costs against any party other than the state, including expert witness fees.

(4) The payment of actual damages to the complainant.

(b) In determining whether to assess a civil penalty pursuant to this section, the commission shall find that the respondent has been guilty of oppression, fraud, or malice, expressed or implied, as required by Section 3294 of the Civil Code. In determining the amount of a civil penalty, the commission shall consider Section 12955.6 and relevant evidence of, including, but not limited to, the following:

(1) Willful, intentional, or purposeful conduct.

(2) Refusal to prevent or eliminate discrimination.

(3) Conscious disregard for fair housing rights.

(4) Commission of unlawful conduct.

(5) Intimidation or harassment.

(6) Conduct without just cause or excuse.

(7) Multiple violations of the Fair Employment and Housing Act.

(c) If the commission finds that the respondent has engaged in an unlawful practice under this part, and the respondent is licensed or granted a privilege by an agency of the state or the federal government to do business, provide a service, or conduct activities, and the unlawful practice is determined to have occurred in connection with the exercise of that license or privilege, the commission shall provide the licensing or privilege granting agency with a copy of its decision or order.

(d) If the commission finds that the respondent has engaged in an unlawful practice under this part and is liable for actual damages or a civil penalty, any amount due to the respondent by a state agency may be offset to satisfy the commission's final order or decision.

(e) No remedy shall be available to the aggrieved person unless the aggrieved person waives any and all rights or claims under Section 52 of the Civil Code prior to receiving a remedy, and signs a written waiver to that effect.

(f) The commission may require a report of the manner of compliance.

(g) If the commission finds that a respondent has not engaged in any practice which constitutes a violation of this part, the commission shall state its findings of fact and shall issue and cause to be served on the complainant an order dismissing the accusation as to that respondent.

(h) Any order issued by the commission shall have printed on its face references to the provisions of the Administrative Procedure Act which prescribe the rights of appeal of any party to the proceeding to whose position the order is adverse. *(Added by Stats.1980, c. 992, § 4. Amended by Stats.1981, c. 899, p. 3424, § 3; Stats.1992, c. 182 (S.B.1234), § 18; Stats.2000, c. 189 (A.B.2062), § 2; Stats.2004, c. 647 (A.B.2870), § 9.)*

§ 12987.1.   Review of final order of relief; intervention as matter of right; enforcement decree; denial of petition

(a) Any party aggrieved by the commission's final order for relief may obtain a review of that order in accordance with the provisions of Section 11523 of this code and Section 1094.5 of the Code of Civil Procedure except that the limitations on the court's remedial powers as described in subdivision (f) of Section 1094.5 of the Code of Civil Procedure shall not apply.

(b) The superior court, in reviewing the commission's final order, may award the following relief:

(1) Grant to the petitioner, or any other party, temporary relief, including, but not limited to, a restraining order, or other order as the court deems just and proper.

(2) Affirm, modify, or set aside, in whole or in part, the order, or remand the order for further proceedings, and enforce the order to the extent that it is affirmed or modified.

(c) Any party to the proceeding before the commission or aggrieved person may intervene as a matter of right in the superior court proceeding.

(d) When the time for petitioning a court for review of the commission's order has expired, the department or any party to the commission proceeding may petition a court for a decree enforcing the commission's order. The court may grant any relief necessary to ensure compliance with the commission's order.

(e) Notwithstanding subdivisions (a) to (d), inclusive, where the reviewing court denies a petition for writ of mandate seeking review of a commission order or decision, the court shall enter judgment denying the petition and enforcing the commission's order or decision. *(Added by Stats.1993, c. 1277 (A.B.2244), § 12. Amended by Stats.2004, c. 647 (A.B.2870), § 10.)*

§ 12988.   Affirmative actions

The commission and the department may engage in affirmative actions with owners in furtherance of the purpose of this part as expressed in Section 12920. *(Added by Stats.1980, c. 992, § 4. Amended by Stats.1989, c. 1309, § 9.)*

§ 12989.   Civil action in lieu of administrative proceeding

(a) If an accusation is issued under Section 12981, a complainant, a respondent, or an aggrieved person on whose behalf a complaint is filed may elect, in lieu of an administrative proceeding under Section 12981, to have the claims asserted in the charge adjudicated in a civil action under this part.

(b) An election under this section may be made within 20 days after the service of the accusation, and not later than 20 days after service of the complaint to the respondent. A notice of election shall be filed with the department, and the department shall serve a copy of the notice to the director, the respondent, and the aggrieved person on whose behalf the complaint is filed. The notice shall be filed and served on all parties to the complaint in accordance with the procedures established by Section 12962.

(c) If either party serves a notice of election upon the department, as prescribed, the department shall, within 30 days after service of the notice of the election, dismiss the accusation. The department shall itself, or at its election through the Attorney General, within 30 days of receipt of the notice of election, file a civil action with the proper superior court in its name or on behalf of the aggrieved person as a real party in interest. In bringing a civil or administrative action, or pursuing subsequent appeals of those actions, the department or the Attorney General shall, in its representation of an aggrieved person's interests, comply with the Rules of Professional Conduct of the State Bar of California. The action may be filed in any county in the state in which the unlawful practice is alleged to have been committed, in the county in which the records relevant to that practice are maintained and administered, or in the county in which the aggrieved person would have resided in the housing accommodation. If the respondent is not found within that county, the action may be filed in the county of the respondent's residence or principal office.

(d) Any person aggrieved with respect to the issues to be determined in a civil action filed under this part may intervene as of right in that civil action.

(e) If an election is not made pursuant to this section, the director shall maintain an administrative proceeding based on the charges in the complaint in accordance with the procedures set forth in Section 12981.

(f) The director or his or her designated representative shall be available for consultation concerning any legal issues raised by the Attorney General that relate to evidentiary or tactical matters relevant to any civil action brought under this part. *(Added by Stats.1992, c. 182 (S.B.1234), § 19. Amended by Stats.1993, c. 1277 (A.B. 2244), § 13; Stats.2002, c. 784 (S.B.1316), § 128.)*

§ 12989.1.   Commencement of civil actions; statute of limitations; procedure

An aggrieved person may commence a civil action in an appropriate court not later than two years after the occurrence or the termination of an alleged discriminatory housing practice, or the breach of a conciliation agreement entered into, whichever occurs last, to obtain appropriate relief with respect to the discriminatory housing practice or breach. The computation of the two-year period shall not include any time during which an administrative proceeding under this part was pending with respect to a complaint or accusation under this part based upon the discriminatory housing practice or breach.

An aggrieved person may commence a civil action whether or not a complaint has been filed under this part and without regard to the status of any complaint. Any aggrieved person who is aggrieved with respect to the issues to be determined in a civil action filed under this part, may intervene in that civil action. However, if the department has obtained a conciliation agreement with the consent of an aggrieved person, no action may be filed under this part by the aggrieved person with respect to the alleged discriminatory housing practice that forms the basis for the complaint, except for the purpose of enforcing the terms of the agreement.

An aggrieved person may not commence a civil action with respect to an alleged discriminatory housing practice that forms the basis of an accusation issued by the department if the department has commenced a hearing on the accusation. *(Added by Stats.1992, c. 182 (S.B. 1234), § 20.)*

§ 12989.2. Relief; damages; fees and costs

(a) In a civil action brought under Section 12989 or 12989.1, if the court finds that a discriminatory housing practice has occurred or is about to occur, the court may award the plaintiff or complainant actual and punitive damages and may grant other relief, including the issuance of a temporary or permanent injunction, or temporary restraining order, or other order, as it deems appropriate to prevent any defendant from engaging in or continuing to engage in an unlawful practice. The court may, at its discretion, award the prevailing party, other than the state, reasonable attorney's fees and costs, including expert witness fees, against any party other than the state.

(b) Notwithstanding any other provision of law, the commission is not liable for the attorney's fees of parties to the administrative adjudication of cases brought before the commission, including proceedings under Sections 11523 and 12987.1 of this code and Section 1094.5 of the Code of Civil Procedure. *(Added by Stats.1992, c. 182 (S.B.1234), § 21. Amended by Stats.1993, c. 1277 (A.B. 2244), § 14; Stats.1999, c. 591 (A.B.1670), § 14; Stats. 2004, c. 647 (A.B.2870), § 11.)*

§ 12989.3. Civil actions commenced by Attorney General

(a) Whenever the Attorney General has reasonable cause to believe that any person or group of persons is engaged in a pattern or practice of denying to others the full enjoyment of any of the rights granted by this article, or that any group of persons has been denied any of the rights granted by this article and that denial raises an issue of general public importance, the Attorney General shall commence a civil action in any court.

(b) Upon referral from the department, the Attorney General may commence a civil action in any appropriate court for appropriate relief with respect to a discriminatory housing practice referred to the Attorney General by the department under subdivision (b) of Section 12981.

(c) A civil action under this section may be commenced not later than the expiration of 18 months after the date of the occurrence or termination of the alleged discriminatory housing practice.

188

(d) The Attorney General shall commence a civil action in any appropriate court for appropriate relief with respect to breach of a conciliation agreement referred to the Attorney General by the department. A civil action shall be commenced under this paragraph not later than the expiration of 90 days after the referral of the alleged breach.

(e) The Attorney General, on behalf of the department or other party at whose request a subpoena is issued, under this article, shall enforce that subpoena in appropriate proceedings in the court for the judicial district in which the person to whom the subpoena was addressed resides, was served, or transacts business.

(f) In a civil action under this section, the court may award any of the following:

(1) Preventive relief, including a permanent or temporary injunction, restraining order, or other order against the person responsible for a violation of this title as is necessary to assure the full enjoyment of the rights granted by this title.

(2) Other relief as the court deems appropriate, including monetary damages to persons aggrieved.

(3) A civil penalty in an amount not exceeding fifty thousand dollars ($50,000), for a first violation, and in an amount not exceeding one hundred thousand dollars ($100,000), for any subsequent violation.

(g) In a civil action under this section, the court, in its discretion, may allow the prevailing party, reasonable attorney's fees and costs, including expert witness fees, against any party other than the state.

(h) Upon timely application, any person may intervene in a civil action commenced by the Attorney General under this section that involves an alleged discriminatory housing practice with respect to which that person is an aggrieved person or a conciliation agreement to which that person is a party. The court may grant appropriate relief to any intervening party as is authorized to be granted to a plaintiff in a civil action under Section 12989.2. *(Added by Stats.1992, c. 182 (S.B.1234), § 22. Amended by Stats.1999, c. 591 (A.B.1670), § 15; Stats. 2003, c. 159 (A.B.1759), § 7, eff. Aug. 2, 2003.)*

CHAPTER 8. NONDISCRIMINATION AND COMPLIANCE EMPLOYMENT PROGRAMS

Section
12990. Contractors and subcontractors for state public works, goods and services; nondiscrimination program and clauses; exemption for certain credit card purchases; rules and regulations; federal programs as state compliance; sanctions to awarding agency.

§ 12990. Contractors and subcontractors for state public works, goods and services; nondiscrimination program and clauses; exemption for certain credit card purchases; rules and regulations; federal programs as state compliance; sanctions to awarding agency

(a) Any employer who is, or wishes to become, a contractor with the state for public works or for goods or services is subject to the provisions of this part relating to discrimination in employment and to the nondiscrimination requirements of this section and any rules and regulations that implement it.

(b) Prior to becoming a contractor or subcontractor with the state, an employer may be required to submit a nondiscrimination program to the department for approval and certification and may be required to submit periodic reports of its compliance with that program.

(c) Every state contract and subcontract for public works or for goods or services shall contain a nondiscrimination clause prohibiting discrimination on the bases enumerated in this part by contractors or subcontractors. The nondiscrimination clause shall contain a provision requiring contractors and subcontractors to give written notice of their obligations under that clause to labor organizations with which they have a collective bargaining or other agreement. These contractual provisions shall be fully and effectively enforced. This subdivision does not apply to a credit card purchase of goods of two thousand five hundred dollars ($2,500) or less. The total amount of exemption authorized herein shall not exceed seven thousand five hundred dollars ($7,500) per year for each company from which a state agency is purchasing goods by credit card. It shall be the responsibility of each state agency to monitor the use of this exemption and adhere to these restrictions on these purchases.

(d) The department shall periodically develop rules and regulations for the application and implementation of this section, and submit them to the commission for consideration and adoption in accordance with the provisions of Chapter 3.5 (commencing with Section 11340) of Part 1. Those rules and regulations shall describe and include, but not be limited to, all of the following:

(1) Procedures for the investigation, approval, certification, decertification, monitoring, and enforcement of nondiscrimination programs.

(2) The size of contracts or subcontracts below which any particular provision of this section shall not apply.

(3) The circumstances, if any, under which a contractor or subcontractor is not subject to this section.

(4) Criteria for determining the appropriate plant, region, division, or other unit of a contractor's or subcontractor's operation for which a nondiscrimination program is required.

(5) Procedures for coordinating the nondiscrimination requirements of this section and its implementing rules and regulations with the California Plan for Equal Opportunity in Apprenticeship, with the provisions and implementing regulations of Article 9.5 (commencing with Section 11135) of Chapter 1 of Part 1, and with comparable federal laws and regulations concerning nondiscrimination, equal employment opportunity, and affirmative action by those who contract with the United States.

(6) The basic principles and standards to guide the department in administering and implementing this section.

(e) Where a contractor or subcontractor is required to prepare an affirmative action, equal employment, or nondiscrimination program subject to review and approval by a federal compliance agency, that program may be filed with the department, instead of any nondiscrimination program regularly required by this section or its implementing rules and regulations. Such a program shall constitute a prima facie demonstration of compliance with this section. Where the department or a federal compliance agency has required the preparation of an affirmative action, equal employment, or nondiscrimination program subject to review and approval by the department or a federal compliance agency, evidence of such a program shall also constitute prima facie compliance with an ordinance or regulation of any city, city and county, or county that requires an employer to submit such a program to a local awarding agency for its approval prior to becoming a contractor or subcontractor with that agency.

(f) Where the department determines and certifies that the provisions of this section or its implementing rules and regulations are violated or where the commission, after hearing an accusation pursuant to Section 12967, determines a contractor or subcontractor is engaging in practices made unlawful under this part, the department or the commission may recommend appropriate sanctions to the awarding agency. Any such recommendation shall take into account the severity of the violation or violations and any other penalties, sanctions, or remedies previously imposed. *(Added by Stats.1980, c. 992, § 4. Amended by Stats.1982, c. 454, p. 1848, § 46; Stats.2005, c. 381 (S.B.828), § 2.)*

CHAPTER 9. MISCELLANEOUS

Section
12993. Construction of part; continuation of Civil Rights Law and other laws relating to discrimination; effect on retirement, pension and other plans; Unruh Civil Rights Act.
12993.5. Construction with Civil Code § 51.7.
12995. Construction; title or other interest; postsecondary student housing; selection on non-protected basis; preferential or quota basis; public nuisance law enforcement.
12996. Severability.

§ 12993. Construction of part; continuation of Civil Rights Law and other laws relating to discrimination; effect on retirement, pension and other plans; Unruh Civil Rights Act

(a) The provisions of this part shall be construed liberally for the accomplishment of the purposes of this part. Nothing contained in this part shall be deemed to repeal any of the provisions of the Civil Rights Law or of any other law of this state relating to discrimination because of race, religious creed, color, national origin,

189

ancestry, physical disability, mental disability, medical condition, marital status, sex, age, or sexual orientation, unless those provisions provide less protection to the enumerated classes of persons covered under this part.

(b) Nothing contained in this part relating to discrimination in employment on account of sex or medical condition shall be deemed to affect the operation of the terms or conditions of any bona fide retirement, pension, employee benefit, or insurance plan, provided the terms or conditions are in accordance with customary and reasonable or actuarially sound underwriting practices.

(c) While it is the intention of the Legislature to occupy the field of regulation of discrimination in employment and housing encompassed by the provisions of this part, exclusive of all other laws banning discrimination in employment and housing by any city, city and county, county, or other political subdivision of the state, nothing contained in this part shall be construed, in any manner or way, to limit or restrict the application of Section 51 of the Civil Code. *(Added by Stats.1980, c. 992, § 4. Amended by Stats.1992, c. 912 (A.B.1286), § 8; Stats.1992, c. 913 (A.B.1077), § 25; Stats.1993, c. 1277 (A.B.2244), § 15; Stats.1999, c; 592 (A.B.1001), § 11.)*

§ 12993.5. Construction with Civil Code § 51.7

Notwithstanding Section 12993, nothing contained in this part shall be construed, in any manner or way, to limit or restrict the application of Section 51.7 of the Civil Code. *(Added by Stats.1992, c. 911 (A.B.311), § 8.)*

§ 12995. Construction; title or other interest; postsecondary student housing; selection on non-protected basis; preferential or quota basis; public nuisance law enforcement

(a) Nothing contained in this part relating to discrimination in housing shall be construed to:

(1) Affect the title or other interest of a person who, prior to the granting of relief, purchases, leases, or takes an encumbrance on a housing accommodation in good faith and without either knowledge or actual notice of the filing of a complaint with the department or of a civil action.

(2) Prohibit any postsecondary educational institution, whether private or public, from providing housing accommodations reserved for either male or female students so long as no individual person is denied equal access to housing accommodations, or from providing separate housing accommodations reserved primarily for married students or for students with minor dependents who reside with them.

(3) Prohibit selection based upon factors other than race, color, religion, sex, marital status, national origin, ancestry, familial status, disability, or other basis prohibited by the Unruh Civil Rights Act.

(4) Promote housing accommodations on a preferential or quota basis.

(b) Nothing contained in this part relating to discrimination in housing shall affect the nondiscriminatory enforcement of state and local public nuisance laws, provided that those laws do not otherwise conflict with the provisions of this part. *(Added by Stats.1980, c. 992, § 4. Amended by Stats.1992, c. 182 (S.B.1234), § 23; Stats.1993, c. 830 (S.B.137), § 3, eff. Oct. 6, 1993; Stats.1993, c. 1277 (A.B.2244), § 16.)*

§ 12996. Severability

If any clause, sentence, paragraph, or part of this part relating to discrimination in employment or the application thereof to any person or circumstance, shall, for any reason, be adjudged by a court of competent jurisdiction to be invalid, such judgment shall not affect, impair, or invalidate the remainder of this part and the application thereof to other persons or circumstances, but shall be confined in its operation to the clause, sentence, paragraph, or part thereof directly involved in the controversy in which such judgment shall have been rendered and to the person or circumstances involved. *(Added by Stats. 1980, c. 992, § 4.)*

Division 4

FISCAL AFFAIRS

Part 2

STATE FUNDS

CHAPTER 6. PROHIBITION ON USE OF STATE FUNDS AND FACILITIES TO ASSIST, PROMOTE, OR DETER UNION ORGANIZING

Section
16645. Definitions.
16645.1. Prohibition; requests for reimbursements; records; violations; penalties.
16645.2. Grant recipients; accounting for use of state funds; violations; penalties.
16645.3. State contractors; prohibitions; service contracts for state or state agencies; violations; penalties.
16645.4. State contractors in receipt of state funds in excess of a certain amount pursuant to contracts with state or state agencies; prohibition; records; violations; penalties.
16645.5. Employers conducting business on state property pursuant to contracts or concession agreements; meeting prohibitions; violations; penalties.
16645.6. Public employers receiving state funds; prohibition; violations.
16645.7. Private employers receiving state funds in excess of a certain amount; certification requirements; records; violations; penalties.
16645.8. Prosecution of civil actions; notice requirements; intervention; attorney's fees and costs.
16646. Treatment of expenditures; accounting for expenditures.
16647. Exemptions.
16648. Retroactive application.
16649. Severability.

§ 16645. Definitions

For purposes of this chapter, the following terms have the following meanings:

(a) "Assist, promote, or deter union organizing" means any attempt by an employer to influence the decision of its employees in this state or those of its subcontractors regarding either of the following:

(1) Whether to support or oppose a labor organization that represents or seeks to represent those employees.

(2) Whether to become a member of any labor organization.

(b) "Employer" means any individual, corporation, unincorporated association, partnership, government agency or body, or other legal entity that employs more than one person in the state.

(c) "State contractor" means any employer that receives state funds for supplying goods or services pursuant to a written contract with the state or any of its agencies. "State contractor" includes an employer that receives state funds pursuant to a contract specified in paragraph (2) of subdivision (d). For purposes of this chapter, the contract shall be deemed to be a contract with a state agency.

(d)(1) "State funds" means any money drawn from the State Treasury or any special or trust fund of the state.

(2) "State funds" includes any money appropriated by the state and transferred to any public agency, including a special district, that is used by the public agency to fund, in whole or in part, a service contract in excess of two hundred fifty thousand dollars ($250,000).

(e) "State property" means any property or facility owned or leased by the state or any state agency. *(Added by Stats.2000, c. 872 (A.B.1889), § 2.)*

§ 16645.1. Prohibition; requests for reimbursements, records; violations; penalties

(a) No state funds shall be used to reimburse a state contractor for any costs incurred to assist, promote, or deter union organizing.

(b) Every request for reimbursement from state funds by a state contractor shall include a certification that the contractor is not seeking reimbursement for costs incurred to assist, promote, or deter union organizing. A state contractor that incurs costs to assist, promote, or deter union organizing shall maintain records sufficient to show that no reimbursement from state funds has been sought for those costs. The state contractor shall provide those records to the Attorney General upon request.

(c) A state contractor is liable to the state for the amount of any funds obtained in violation of subdivision (a) plus a civil penalty equal to twice the amount of those funds.

(d) This section does not apply to a fixed-price contract or to any other arrangement by which the amount of the payment of state funds does not depend on the costs incurred by the state contractor. *(Added by Stats.2000, c. 872 (A.B.1889), § 2.)*

§ 16645.2. Grant recipients; accounting for use of state funds; violations; penalties

(a) The recipient of a grant of state funds, including state funds disbursed as a grant by a public agency, shall not use the funds to assist, promote, or deter union organizing.

(b) For purposes of this section, each recipient of a grant of state funds shall account for those funds as follows:

(1) State funds designated by the grantor for use for a specific expenditure of the recipient shall be accounted for as allocated to that expenditure.

(2) State funds that are not designated as described in paragraph (1) shall be allocated on a pro rata basis to all expenditures by the recipient that support the program for which the grant is made.

(c) Prior to the disbursement of a grant of state funds, the recipient shall provide a certification to the state that none of the funds will be used to assist, promote, or deter union organizing. Any recipient that makes expenditures to assist, promote, or deter union organizing shall maintain records sufficient to show that state funds have not been used for those expenditures. The grant recipient shall provide those records to the Attorney General upon request.

(d) A grant recipient is liable to the state for the amount of any funds expended in violation of subdivision (a) plus a civil penalty equal to twice the amount of those funds. *(Added by Stats.2000, c. 872 (A.B.1889), § 2.)*

Validity

This section was held preempted by the National Labor Relations Act (NLRA) in the decision of Chamber of Commerce of U.S. v. Brown, 2008, 128 S.Ct. 2408, 171 L.Ed.2d 264, on remand 543 F.3d 1117.

§ 16645.3. State contractors; prohibitions; service contracts for state or state agencies; violations; penalties

(a) No state contractor shall assist, promote, or deter union organizing by employees who are performing work on a service contract, including a public works contract, for the state or a state agency.

(b) A state contractor that violates subdivision (a) is liable for a civil penalty of one thousand dollars ($1,000) per employee per violation. *(Added by Stats.2000, c. 872 (A.B.1889), § 2.)*

§ 16645.4. State contractors in receipt of state funds in excess of a certain amount pursuant to contracts with state or state agencies; prohibition; records; violations; penalties

(a) A state contractor that receives state funds in excess of fifty thousand dollars ($50,000) pursuant to a contract with the state or a state agency shall not use

191

those state funds to assist, promote, or deter union organizing during the life of the contract, including any extensions or renewals of the contract. The dollar threshold in this subdivision, however, does not limit the application of other provisions of this chapter that restrict the use of state funds.

(b) All contracts in excess of fifty thousand dollars ($50,000) and that are awarded by the state or a state agency shall contain the prohibition stated in subdivision (a).

(c) A state contractor who is subject to subdivision (a) and who makes expenditures to assist, promote, or deter union organizing shall maintain records sufficient to show that no state funds were used for those expenditures. The state contractor shall provide those records to the Attorney General upon request.

(d) A state contractor is liable to the state for the amount of any funds expended made in violation of subdivision (a) plus a civil penalty equal to twice the amount of those funds. *(Added by Stats.2000, c. 872 (A.B.1889), § 2.)*

§ 16645.5. Employers conducting business on state property pursuant to contracts or concession agreements; meeting prohibitions; violations; penalties

(a) An employer conducting business on state property pursuant to a contract or concession agreement with the state or a state agency, or a subcontractor on such a contract or agreement, shall not use state property to hold a meeting with any employees or supervisors if the purpose of the meeting is to assist, promote, or deter union organizing. This section does not apply if the state property is equally available, without charge, to the general public for holding a meeting.

(b) An employer that violates subdivision (a) shall be liable to the state for a civil penalty equal to one thousand dollars ($1,000) per employee per meeting. *(Added by Stats.2000, c. 872 (A.B.1889), § 2.)*

Validity

The negative treatment of this statute was vacated in the decision of Chamber of Commerce of U.S. v. Lockyer, C.A.9 (Cal.) 2005, 422 F.3d 973, rehearing en banc granted 435 F.3d 999, opinion withdrawn on rehearing 2006 WL 302357.

§ 16645.6. Public employers receiving state funds; prohibition; violations

(a) A public employer receiving state funds shall not use any of those funds to assist, promote, or deter union organizing.

(b) Any public official who knowingly authorizes the use of state funds in violation of subdivision (a) shall be liable to the state for the amount of those funds. *(Added by Stats.2000, c. 872 (A.B.1889), § 2.)*

§ 16645.7. Private employers receiving state funds in excess of a certain amount; certification requirements; records; violations; penalties

(a) A private employer receiving state funds in excess of ten thousand dollars ($10,000) in any calendar year on

192

account of its participation in a state program shall not use any of those funds to assist, promote, or deter union organizing.

(b) As a condition of participating in a state program pursuant to which it will receive state funds in excess of ten thousand dollars ($10,000) in any calendar year, a private employer shall provide a certification to the state that none of those funds will be used to assist, promote, or deter union organizing.

(c) A private employer who is subject to subdivision (a) and who makes expenditures to assist, promote, or deter union organizing shall maintain records sufficient to show that no state funds were used for those expenditures. The private employer shall provide those records to the Attorney General upon request.

(d) A private employer is liable to the state for any funds expended in violation of subdivision (a) plus a civil penalty equal to twice the amount of those funds. *(Added by Stats.2000, c. 872 (A.B.1889), § 2.)*

Validity

This section was held preempted by the National Labor Relations Act (NLRA) in the decision of Chamber of Commerce of U.S. v. Brown, 2008, 128 S.Ct. 2408, 171 L.Ed.2d 264, on remand 543 F.3d 1117.

§ 16645.8. Prosecution of civil actions; notice requirements; intervention; attorney's fees and costs

(a) A civil action for a violation of this chapter may be brought by the Attorney General, or by any state taxpayer, on behalf of the people of the State of California, for injunctive relief, damages, civil penalties, and other appropriate equitable relief. All damages and civil penalties collected pursuant to this chapter shall be paid to the State Treasury.

(b) Before filing an action under this section, a taxpayer shall give written notice to the Attorney General of the alleged violation and the intent to bring suit. If the Attorney General commences a civil action for the same alleged violation within 60 days of receiving the notice, a separate action by the taxpayer shall be barred.

(c) A taxpayer may intervene as a plaintiff in any action brought under this section.

(d) A prevailing plaintiff in any action under this section is entitled to recover reasonable attorney's fees and costs. A prevailing taxpayer intervenor who makes a substantial contribution to an action under this section is entitled to recover reasonable attorney's fees and costs. *(Added by Stats.2000, c. 872 (A.B.1889), § 2.)*

§ 16646. Treatment of expenditures; accounting for expenditures

(a) For purposes of this chapter, any expense, including legal and consulting fees and salaries of supervisors and employees, incurred for research for, or preparation, planning, or coordination of, or carrying out, an activity to assist, promote, or deter union organizing shall be treated as paid or incurred for that activity.

(b) For purposes of accounting for expenditures, if state funds and other funds are commingled, any expenditures to assist, promote, or deter union organizing shall be allocated between state funds and other funds on a pro rata basis. *(Added by Stats.2000, c. 872 (A.B.1889), § 2.)*

§ 16647. Exemptions

This chapter does not apply to an activity performed, or to an expense incurred, in connection with any of the following:

(a) Addressing a grievance or negotiating or administering a collective bargaining agreement.

(b) Allowing a labor organization or its representatives access to the employer's facilities or property.

(c) Performing an activity required by federal or state law or by a collective bargaining agreement.

(d) Negotiating, entering into, or carrying out a voluntary recognition agreement with a labor organization. *(Added by Stats.2000, c. 872 (A.B.1889), § 2.)*

§ 16648. Retroactive application

This chapter does not apply to an expenditure made prior to January 1, 2001, or to a grant or contract awarded prior to January 1, 2001, unless the grant or contract is modified, extended, or renewed after January 1, 2001. Nothing in this chapter requires employers to maintain records in any particular form. *(Added by Stats.2000, c. 872 (A.B.1889), § 2.)*

§ 16649. Severability

The provisions of this chapter are severable. If any section or portion of this chapter, or any application thereof, is held invalid, in whole or in part, that invalidity shall not effect any other section, portion, or application that can be given effect. *(Added by Stats.2000, c. 872 (A.B.1889), § 2.)*

Division 5

PERSONNEL

Part 2.6

PERSONNEL ADMINISTRATION

CHAPTER 2. ADMINISTRATION OF SALARIES

ARTICLE 3. SALARY CLASSIFICATION

Section
19825.5. Departmental setting and adjusting of annual compensation of officers and employees listed in §§ 11550, 11552 and 11554.

§ 19825.5. Departmental setting and adjusting of annual compensation of officers and employees listed in §§ 11550, 11552 and 11554

(a) Notwithstanding Sections 11550, 11552, and 11554, the department shall set and adjust, as needed, the annual compensation of the officers and employees listed in Sections 11550, 11552, and 11554.

(b) When setting or adjusting the annual compensation of the employees described in subdivision (a), the department shall consider the size and scope of the organization, compensation paid to other similar positions in other public jurisdictions, the scope of responsibility of the position, the need to avoid salary compaction, and other factors appropriate to the determination of compensation necessary to recruit and retain qualified employees in leadership positions for the state. The compensation shall not exceed 125 percent of the compensation recommended to be paid to the Governor of the State of California by the California Citizens Compensation Commission.

(c) The department shall notify the Legislature of the compensation level implemented for any of the employees described in subdivision (a) within 30 days of the effective date of the proposed compensation adjustment. *(Added by Stats.2006, c. 240 (A.B.2936), § 5, eff. Sept. 13, 2006.)*

ARTICLE 4. MISCELLANEOUS COMPENSATION

Section
19844.1. Computing overtime compensation; leave time; conflicts with other law.

§ 19844.1. Computing overtime compensation; leave time; conflicts with other law

(a) Notwithstanding any other provision of law, personal leave, sick leave, annual leave, vacation, bereavement leave, holiday leave, and any other paid or unpaid leave, shall not be considered as time worked by the employee for the purpose of computing cash compensation for overtime or compensating time off for overtime.

(b) If subdivision (a) is in conflict with the provisions of a memorandum of understanding reached or amended pursuant to Section 3517.5 on or after February 1, 2009, or the date that the act adding this section takes effect, whichever is later, that memorandum of understanding shall be controlling without further legislative action, except that if those provisions of the memorandum of understanding require the expenditure of funds, the provisions shall not become effective unless approved by the Legislature in the annual Budget Act. *(Added by Stats.2009–2010, 3rd Ex.Sess., c. 4 (S.B.8), § 5, eff. Feb. 20, 2009.)*

Part 3

PUBLIC EMPLOYEES' RETIREMENT SYSTEM

CHAPTER 1. GENERAL PROVISIONS AND DEFINITIONS

ARTICLE 2. DEFINITIONS

Section
20035.5. Final compensation; determinations with respect to members who retire or die on or after January 1, 2000.

Section

20035.6.   Final compensation for members of State Bargaining Unit 19 whose salary was reduced by five percent; application of section.

20037.6.   Final compensation; state membership beginning on or after July 1, 2006; persons represented by State Bargaining Unit 2; application.

20037.7.   Final compensation; state members represented by State Bargaining Units 1, 3, 4, 11, 14, 15, 17, 20, or 21; application.

20037.8.   Final compensation; state members represented by State Bargaining Units 12 or 13; application.

20037.9.   Final compensation; state membership beginning on or after Jan. 1, 2007; persons represented by State Bargaining Units 16 or 19; application.

20037.10.   Final compensation; state membership beginning on or after Jan. 1, 2007; persons represented by State Bargaining Unit 7; application.

20037.11.   Final compensation; state membership beginning on or after Jan. 1, 2007; persons represented by State Bargaining Unit 10; application.

20037.12.   Final compensation; state membership beginning on or after Jan. 1, 2007; persons represented by State Bargaining Unit 18; application.

20037.13.   Final compensation; members appointed to career executive assignment.

§ 20035.5.   Final compensation; determinations with respect to members who retire or die on or after January 1, 2000

Notwithstanding Section 20037, "final compensation" for the purposes of determining any pension or benefit with respect to a school member who retires or dies on or after January 1, 2000, and with respect to benefits based on service with a school employer, means the highest annual compensation that was earnable by the school member during the consecutive 12–month period of employment immediately preceding the effective date of his or her retirement or the date of his or her last separation from service if earlier or during any other period of 12 consecutive months during his or her membership in this system that the member designates on the application for retirement. *(Added by Stats.1999, c. 555 (S.B.400), § 1.)*

§ 20035.6.   Final compensation for members of State Bargaining Unit 19 whose salary was reduced by five percent; application of section

Notwithstanding Sections 20035 and 20037, "final compensation," for the purpose of determining any pension or benefit with respect to a member who retires or dies on or after July 1, 2003, who was a member of State Bargaining Unit 19, and whose monthly salary range that was to be effective July 1, 2003, was reduced by 5 percent pursuant to a memorandum of understanding entered during the 2003–04 fiscal year, means the highest annual compensation the member would have earned as of July 1, 2003, if that 5–percent reduction had not occurred. This section shall apply only if the period during which the member's salary was reduced would have otherwise been included in determining his or her final compensation. The increased costs, if any, that may result from the

application of the definition of "final compensation" provided in this section shall be paid by the employer in the same manner as other retirement benefits are funded. *(Formerly § 20035.5, added by Stats.2003, c. 615 (A.B. 375), § 6. Renumbered § 20035.6 and amended by Stats. 2004, c. 183 (A.B.3082), § 160; Stats.2004, c. 231 (S.B. 1603), § 1. Amended by Stats.2006, c. 538 (S.B.1852), § 290.)*

§ 20037.6.   Final compensation; state membership beginning on or after July 1, 2006; persons represented by State Bargaining Unit 2; application

(a) Notwithstanding Sections 20035 and 20037, final compensation for a person who is employed by the state for the first time and becomes a state member of the system on or after July 1, 2006, and is represented by State Bargaining Unit 2, means the highest average annual compensation earnable by the member during the consecutive 36–month period immediately preceding the effective date of his or her retirement, or the date of his or her last separation from state service if earlier, or during any other period of 36 consecutive months during his or her state membership that the member designates on the application for retirement.

(b) This section applies to service credit accrued while a member of State Bargaining Unit 2.

(c) This section does not apply to:

(1) Former state employees who return to state employment on or after July 1, 2006.

(2) State employees hired prior to July 1, 2006, who were subject to Section 20281.5 during the first 24 months of state employment.

(3) State employees hired prior to July 1, 2006, who become subject to representation by State Bargaining Unit 2 on or after July 1, 2006.

(4) State employees on an approved leave of absence who return to active employment on or after July 1, 2006. *(Added by Stats.2006, c. 28 (A.B.146), § 6, eff. May 18, 2006. Amended by Stats.2009, c. 130 (A.B.966), § 2.)*

§ 20037.7.   Final compensation; state members represented by State Bargaining Units 1, 3, 4, 11, 14, 15, 17, 20, or 21; application

(a) Notwithstanding Sections 20035 and 20037, final compensation for a person who is employed by the state for the first time and becomes a state member of the system on or after January 1, 2007, and is represented by State Bargaining Unit 1, 3, 4, 11, 14, 15, 17, 20, or 21, means the highest average annual compensation earnable by the member during the consecutive 36–month period immediately preceding the effective date of his or her retirement, or the date of his or her last separation from state service if earlier, or during any other period of 36 consecutive months during his or her state membership that the member designates on the application for retirement.

(b) This section applies to service credit accrued while a member of State Bargaining Unit 1, 3, 4, 11, 14, 15, 17, 20, or 21.

(c) This section does not apply to:

(1) Former state employees previously employed before January 1, 2007, who return to state employment on or after January 1, 2007.

(2) State employees hired prior to January 1, 2007, who were subject to Section 20281.5 during the first 24 months of state employment.

(3) State employees hired prior to January 1, 2007, who become subject to representation by State Bargaining Unit 1, 3, 4, 11, 14, 15, 17, 20, or 21 on or after January 1, 2007.

(4) State employees on an approved leave of absence employed before January 1, 2007, who return to active employment on or after January 1, 2007. *(Added by Stats.2006, c. 209 (A.B.1369), § 5, eff. Sept. 6, 2006. Amended by Stats.2007, c. 130 (A.B.299), § 121; Stats. 2009, c. 130 (A.B.966), § 3.)*

§ 20037.8. Final compensation; state members represented by State Bargaining Units 12 or 13; application

(a) Notwithstanding Sections 20035 and 20037, final compensation for a person who is employed by the state for the first time and becomes a state member of the system on or after January 1, 2007, and is represented by State Bargaining Unit 12 or 13, means the highest average annual compensation earnable by the member during the consecutive 36–month period immediately preceding the effective date of his or her retirement, or the date of his or her last separation from state service if earlier, or during any other period of 36 consecutive months during his or her state membership that the member designates on the application for retirement.

(b) This section applies to service credit accrued while a member of State Bargaining Unit 12 or 13.

(c) This section does not apply to:

(1) Former state employees previously employed before January 1, 2007, who return to state employment on or after January 1, 2007.

(2) State employees hired prior to January 1, 2007, who were subject to Section 20281.5 during the first 24 months of state employment.

(3) State employees hired prior to January 1, 2007, who become subject to representation by State Bargaining Unit 12 or 13 on or after January 1, 2007.

(4) State employees on an approved leave of absence employed before January 1, 2007, who return to active employment on or after January 1, 2007. *(Added by Stats.2006, c. 210 (S.B.357), § 5, eff. Sept. 6, 2006. Amended by Stats.2009, c. 130 (A.B.966), § 4.)*

§ 20037.9. Final compensation; state membership beginning on or after Jan. 1, 2007; persons represented by State Bargaining Units 16 or 19; application

(a) Notwithstanding Sections 20035 and 20037, final compensation for a person who is employed by the state for the first time and becomes a state member of the system on or after January 1, 2007, and is represented by State Bargaining Unit 16 or 19, means the highest average annual compensation earnable by the member during the consecutive 36–month period immediately preceding the effective date of his or her retirement, or the date of his or her last separation from state service if earlier, or during any other period of 36 consecutive months during his or her state membership that the member designates on the application for retirement.

(b) This section applies to service credit accrued while a member of State Bargaining Unit 16 or 19.

(c) This section does not apply to:

(1) Former state employees previously employed before January 1, 2007, who return to state employment on or after January 1, 2007.

(2) State employees hired prior to January 1, 2007, who were subject to Section 20281.5 during the first 24 months of state employment.

(3) State employees hired prior to January 1, 2007, who become subject to representation by State Bargaining Unit 16 or 19 on or after January 1, 2007.

(4) State employees on an approved leave of absence employed before January 1, 2007, who return to active employment on or after January 1, 2007. *(Added by Stats.2006, c. 237 (A.B.386), § 5, eff. Sept. 13, 2006. Amended by Stats.2009, c. 130 (A.B.966), § 5.)*

§ 20037.10. Final compensation; state membership beginning on or after Jan. 1, 2007; persons represented by State Bargaining Unit 7; application

(a) Notwithstanding Sections 20035 and 20037, final compensation for a person who is employed by the state for the first time and becomes a state member of the system on or after January 1, 2007, and is represented by State Bargaining Unit 7, means the highest average annual compensation earnable by the member during the consecutive 36–month period immediately preceding the effective date of his or her retirement, or the date of his or her last separation from state service if earlier, or during any other period of 36 consecutive months during his or her state membership that the member designates on the application for retirement.

(b) This section applies to service credit accrued while a member of State Bargaining Unit 7.

(c) This section does not apply to:

(1) Service credit accrued while classified as a state peace officer/firefighter while a member of Bargaining Unit 7.

(2) Former state employees previously employed before January 1, 2007, who return to state employment on or after January 1, 2007.

(3) State employees hired prior to January 1, 2007, who were subject to Section 20281.5 during the first 24 months of state employment.

(4) State employees hired prior to January 1, 2007, who become subject to representation by State Bargaining Unit 7 on or after January 1, 2007.

(5) State employees on an approved leave of absence employed before January 1, 2007, who return to active employment on or after January 1, 2007. *(Added by Stats.2006, c. 239 (A.B.2930), § 5, eff. Sept. 13, 2006. Amended by Stats.2009, c. 130 (A.B.966), § 6.)*

§ 20037.11. Final compensation; state membership beginning on or after Jan. 1, 2007; persons represented by State Bargaining Unit 10; application

(a) Notwithstanding Sections 20035 and 20037, final compensation for a person who is employed by the state for the first time and becomes a state member of the system on or after January 1, 2007, and is represented by State Bargaining Unit 10, means the highest average annual compensation earnable by the member during the consecutive 36–month period immediately preceding the effective date of his or her retirement, or the date of his or her last separation from state service if earlier, or during any other period of 36 consecutive months during his or her state membership that the member designates on the application for retirement.

(b) This section applies to service credit accrued while a member of State Bargaining Unit 10.

(c) This section does not apply to:

(1) Former state employees previously employed before January 1, 2007, who return to state employment on or after January 1, 2007.

(2) State employees hired prior to January 1, 2007, who were subject to Section 20281.5 during the first 24 months of state employment.

(3) State employees hired prior to January 1, 2007, who become subject to representation by State Bargaining Unit 10 on or after January 1, 2007.

(4) State employees on an approved leave of absence employed before January 1, 2007, who return to active employment on or after January 1, 2007. *(Added by Stats.2006, c. 238 (A.B.1458), § 5, eff. Sept. 13, 2006. Amended by Stats.2009, c. 130 (A.B.966), § 7.)*

§ 20037.12. Final compensation; state membership beginning on or after Jan. 1, 2007; persons represented by State Bargaining Unit 18; application

(a) Notwithstanding Sections 20035 and 20037, final compensation for a person who is employed by the state for the first time and becomes a state member of the system on or after January 1, 2007, and is represented by State Bargaining Unit 18, means the highest average annual compensation earnable by the member during the consecutive 36–month period immediately preceding the effective date of his or her retirement, or the date of his or her last separation from state service if earlier, or during any other period of 36 consecutive months during his or her state membership that the member designates on the application for retirement.

(b) This section applies to service credit accrued while a member of State Bargaining Unit 18.

(c) This section does not apply to:

(1) Former state employees previously employed before January 1, 2007, who return to state employment on or after January 1, 2007.

(2) State employees hired prior to January 1, 2007, who were subject to Section 20281.5 during the first 24 months of state employment.

(3) State employees hired prior to January 1, 2007, who become subject to representation by State Bargaining Unit 18 on or after January 1, 2007.

(4) State employees on an approved leave of absence employed before January 1, 2007, who return to active employment on or after January 1, 2007. *(Added by Stats.2006, c. 238 (A.B.1458), § 6, eff. Sept. 13, 2006. Amended by Stats.2009, c. 130 (A.B.966), § 8.)*

§ 20037.13. Final compensation; members appointed to career executive assignment

(a) Notwithstanding Sections 20035 and 20037, for the purposes of determining any pension or benefit with respect to benefits based on service with the state, "final compensation" means the highest annual compensation that was earnable by the state member during the consecutive 36–month period of employment immediately preceding the effective date of his or her retirement or the date of his or her last separation from state service or during any other period of 36 consecutive months during his or her membership in this system that the member designates on the application for retirement.

(b) This section shall only apply to a member appointed to a career executive assignment, as defined in Section 18546, who at the time of appointment meets one or more of the following criteria:

(1) He or she previously had, but does not currently have, permanent status in the civil service.

(2) He or she is a person described in Section 18990 who was not, within the past 12 months, employed by the Legislature for two or more consecutive years.

(3) He or she is a person described in Sections 18992 who was not, within the past 12 months, holding a nonelected exempt position in the executive branch.

(c) A state entity that employs a person described in subdivision (b) in a career executive assignment shall notify the Controller of this person's employment status and the Controller shall forward this information to the system. *(Added by Stats.2008, c. 353 (S.B.1472), § 9.)*

CHAPTER 11. SERVICE CREDIT

ARTICLE 3. COMPUTATION OF SERVICE CREDIT

Section
20969.   State employees subject to mandatory furloughs; credit based on amount that would have been credited without furloughs; terms and conditions of furlough reported by employer.
20969.1. Trial court employees subject to mandatory furloughs; credit based on amount of service that would have been credited without furloughs; furlough terms and conditions.

§ 20969. State employees subject to mandatory furloughs; credit based on amount that would have been credited without furloughs, terms and conditions of furlough reported by employer

(a) For all retirement purposes, including benefit eligibility and calculations of retirement allowances for members employed by the state that are subject to mandatory furloughs, credit for service and compensation earnable shall be based on the amount that would have been credited had the employee not been subject to mandatory furloughs.

(b) For the purposes of this section, "mandatory furloughs" means time during which a member identified below is directed to be absent from work without pay as a consequence of an Executive order in the 2008–09 and 2009–10 fiscal years:

(1) A state employee subject to an Executive order requiring a mandatory furlough for state employees.

(2) A person who is excepted from the definition of "state employee" in subdivision (c) of Section 3513, or who is an officer or employee of the executive branch of state government who is not a member of the civil service, and who is subject to an Executive order requiring a mandatory furlough for state employees.

(3) A state employee, a person who is excepted from the definition of "state employee" in subdivision (c) of Section 3513, or a person who is an officer or employee of the executive branch of state government who is not a member of the civil service, and whose employer is not under the direct executive authority of the Governor, and who is subject to a mandatory furlough imposed by his or her employer in response to encouragement in an Executive order.

(c) An employer of an employee identified in subdivision (b) shall notify the board of the terms and conditions of any mandatory furlough, including, but not limited to, the amount of mandatory furlough time imposed on employees during a reporting period and the date on which the mandatory furlough ends. The employer and the Controller shall provide any additional information as the board may require to implement this section. *(Added by Stats.2009, c. 240 (A.B.399), § 3.)*

§ 20969.1. Trial court employees subject to mandatory furloughs; credit based on amount of service that would have been credited without furloughs; furlough terms and conditions

(a) For all retirement purposes, including benefit eligibility and calculations of retirement allowances for members employed by a trial court that are subject to mandatory furloughs, as defined in subdivision (c), credit for service and compensation earnable shall be based on the amount of service that would have been credited had the employee not been subject to mandatory furloughs.

(b) A trial court shall notify the board of the terms and conditions of any mandatory furlough, including, but not limited to, the amount of mandatory furlough time imposed on employees during a reporting period, and the date on which the mandatory furlough ends. A trial court and a county in which the trial court is located that participates in this system by joint contract pursuant to Section 20460.1 shall provide that additional information as the board may require to implement this section.

(c) For the purposes of this section, "mandatory furloughs" is limited to the time during which a trial court employee is directed to be absent from work without pay in the 2009–10 fiscal year on the day designated by the Judicial Council for closure of the courts as authorized in Section 68106.

(d) For purposes of this section, "trial court employee" means a trial court employee, as that term is defined in Section 71601, whose employer has contracted for its employees to become members of the California Public Employees' Retirement System. *(Added by Stats.2009, c. 342 (S.B.75), § 1.)*

CHAPTER 13. RETIREMENT BENEFITS

Operative Effect

Operation of provisions of Part 3 which are not in conformity with Internal Revenue Code § 415, see Government Code § 21762.

ARTICLE 5. DISABILITY RETIREMENT BENEFITS

Section
21428.1. Allowance upon retirement of a patrol member for industrial disability as result of single event resulting in serious bodily injury.

Operative Effect

Operation of provisions of Part 3 which are not in conformity with Internal Revenue Code § 415, see Government Code § 21762.

§ 21428.1. Allowance upon retirement of a patrol member for industrial disability as result of single event resulting in serious bodily injury

(a) Upon retirement of a patrol member for industrial disability as the result of a single event that results in serious bodily injury, the member shall receive the higher of the allowance provided by Section 21406, or, the disability allowance otherwise provided pursuant to this section equal to 3 percent of his or her final compensation multiplied by the number of years of patrol service credited to him or her plus an annuity purchased with his or her accumulated additional contributions, if any. This section shall not apply to a disability that manifests more than six months after the effective date for the industrial disability retirement. This section does not entitle the member to an industrial disability retirement if the member would not otherwise be eligible for an industrial disability retirement.

(b) This section shall apply only to serious bodily injuries, and shall not be applied to disabilities that are the result of any of the following:

(1) Cumulative trauma.

(2) Cumulative injuries, including, but not limited to, heart conditions, stroke, stress, anxiety, or diabetes.

(3) Presumptive injuries or illnesses as described in Chapter 1 (commencing with Section 3200) of Part 1 of Division 4 of the Labor Code.

(4) Stress–related disabilities.

(5) Physical disability having mental origin.

(c) If a patrol member has other service credit as a state peace officer/firefighter member, state safety member, local safety member, state miscellaneous, state industrial, or local miscellaneous member under this system, the cumulative benefit pursuant to this section, including an annuity purchased with his or her accumulated contributions, shall not exceed 90 percent of final compensation.

(d) For purposes of this section, "serious bodily injury" includes any of the following:

(1) Total loss of sight in one or both eyes.

(2) Total loss of hearing in both ears.

(3) Amputation or total loss of function in a hand, arm, foot, or leg.

(4) A spinal cord injury resulting in paralysis which causes the complete loss of function in a hand, arm, foot, or leg.

(5) Physical injury to the brain resulting in serious cognitive disorders or paralysis which causes the complete loss of function in a hand, arm, foot, or leg.

(6) Injury to a major internal organ which substantially limits one or more "major life activities." Major life activities are functions such as caring for oneself, performing manual tasks, walking, seeing, hearing, breathing, learning, and performing substantial gainful employment.

(7) Any other serious physical injury that results in the inability to perform substantial gainful employment.

(e) This section applies only to those patrol members who are described by at least one of the following:

(1) Employed in a state bargaining unit for which a memorandum of understanding has been agreed to by the state employer and the recognized employee organization to become subject to this section.

(2) Excluded from the definition of state employee in subdivision (c) of Section 3513.

(3) Employed by the executive branch of government and not a member of the civil service.

(f) In the event of a dispute regarding the applicability of this section, the board shall proceed with retirement pursuant to any other section that may apply and with the payment of any benefits that are payable pursuant to any other section when this section is not applicable. If the board subsequently determines that this section is applicable, an amount equal to the benefits paid shall be deducted from the benefits payable pursuant to this section because of the determination. *(Added by Stats. 2006, c. 240 (A.B.2936), § 7, eff. Sept. 13, 2006.)*

Title 3

GOVERNMENT OF COUNTIES

Division 4

EMPLOYEES

Part 3

RETIREMENT SYSTEMS

CHAPTER 3. COUNTY EMPLOYEES RETIREMENT LAW OF 1937

ARTICLE 8.6. POST–EMPLOYMENT BENEFITS

Section

31694. Post-Employment Benefits Trust Account; establishment; purpose; contributions; use of funds.

31694.1. Post-Employment Benefits Trust Account; accounting; authority, roles, and responsibilities of board of retirement, or board of investments, and participating employers; agreement between employer and board; termination of participation or account.

31694.2. Employers electing to participate in Post-Employment Benefits Trust Account; responsibilities; delegation of responsibilities.

31694.3. Establishment of trust by county board of supervisors or district governing body for funding post-employment benefits; role of board; trust agreement establishing roles and responsibilities and providing manner and method of payment of investment and administrative expenses; contracting for outside trustee, third-party administrator, or investment manager.

31694.4. Application of article.

31694.5. Obligations created under other contracts.

Operative Effect

For operative effect of certain provisions of this chapter, see Government Code § 31899.6.

§ 31694. Post-Employment Benefits Trust Account; establishment; purpose; contributions; use of funds

(a) The board of supervisors of a county or the governing body of a district or other public entity may, by ordinance or resolution and with the agreement of the board of retirement, provide for the contribution of funds by the county, a district, or other public entity into a Post–Employment Benefits Trust Account. The retirement system may establish the Post–Employment Benefits Trust Account as a part of the retirement fund. The Post–Employment Benefits Trust Account shall be established for the sole purpose of funding the benefits provided under a post-employment group health, life, welfare, or other supplemental benefits plan or plans established and maintained by the county or district, which plan or plans may provide for self-insured coverage or the payment of all or a portion of the premiums on one or more insurance contracts or health care service plan contracts for retired employees of the participating county, district, or other public entity, and their qualified spouses, dependents and beneficiaries.

(b) Contributions to the Post–Employment Benefits Trust Account may include the proceeds of debt issued by the county, a district, or other public entity solely for the purpose of funding post-employment health, life, welfare, or other supplemental benefits.

(c) The post-employment benefits provided with the funds contributed to the Post–Employment Benefits Trust Account are in addition to any other benefits provided under this chapter.

(d)(1) Except as described in subdivision (b) of Section 31694.1, the assets of the retirement fund may not be used, directly or indirectly, to pay the cost of any benefits provided through the Post–Employment Benefits Trust Account or, except to the extent allowed by federal tax law, to pay any direct or indirect cost of administering the Post–Employment Benefits Trust Fund.

(2) Except as described in subdivision (c) of Section 31694.1, funds in the Post–Employment Benefits Trust Account may not be used, directly or indirectly, to pay the cost of any other benefits provided under this chapter. *(Added by Stats.2006, c. 846 (A.B.2863), § 6, eff. Sept. 30, 2006. Amended by Stats.2007, c. 327 (A.B.1124), § 4.)*

Operative Effect

For operative effect of certain provisions of this chapter, see Government Code § 31899.6.

§ 31694.1. Post-Employment Benefits Trust Account; accounting; authority, roles, and responsibilities of board of retirement, or board of investments, and participating employers; agreement between employer and board; termination of participation or account

(a) The retirement system shall separately account for the funds contributed to the Post–Employment Benefits Trust Account by each participating employer and the earnings and expenses related to the investment and administration of those funds.

(b) The board of retirement, or a board of investments in a county in which a board of investments has been established pursuant to Section 31520.2, shall have sole, exclusive, and plenary authority and fiduciary responsibility over the investment of the funds in the Post–Employment Benefits Trust Account, consistent with Sections 31594 and 31595, and as provided for in Section 17 of Article XVI of the California Constitution. The board of retirement or board of investments may invest funds in the Post–Employment Benefits Trust Account with those of the retirement system, to the extent allowed by federal tax laws. The investment earnings and investment expenses attributable to the investment activity of the Post–Employment Benefits Trust Account shall be accounted for separately from the investment earnings and expenses of the retirement fund.

(c) The funds in and investment earnings of the Post–Employment Benefits Trust Account shall be used to pay the reasonable costs related to investment expenses and administration of the Post–Employment Benefits Trust Account to the extent allowed by federal tax law. Those expenses shall not be deemed to be an investment or administrative expense of a retirement system under this chapter.

(d) The board of retirement, or a board of investments in a county in which a board of investments has been established pursuant to Section 31520.2, may establish rules and procedures governing the investments and administration of the Post–Employment Benefits Trust Account. The board of retirement or the board of investments shall determine the rate of interest to credit the funds in the Post–Employment Benefits Trust Account.

(e) The board of retirement, or a board of investments in a county in which a board of investments has been established pursuant to Section 31520.2, is authorized to take any and all actions necessary to establish and administer the Post–Employment Benefits Trust Account in compliance with applicable federal tax laws or other legal requirements.

(f) The board of retirement, or the board of retirement acting jointly with a board of investments in a county in which a board of investments has been established pursuant to Section 31520.2, and a participating employer in the Post–Employment Benefits Trust Account shall establish, by written agreement, the respective roles and responsibilities of the retirement system and the participating employer with respect to the administration and investment of the Post–Employment Benefits Trust Account, consistent with Section 17 of Article XVI of the California Constitution. That agreement shall include, but is not limited to, funding, distribution, expenditure, actuarial, accounting, and reporting considerations, and any applicable investment parameters. The board may, in its discretion, authorize an employer to transfer assets into or out of the Post–Employment Retirement Account, however, any transfer of assets shall comply with the terms of the contract between the employer and the board, satisfy requirements under applicable rules of the Governmental Accounting Standards Board, and satisfy the requirements of federal tax law. Once the investment parameters are established, the board of retirement, or a board of investments in a county in which a board of investments has been established pursuant to Section 31520.2, shall have sole control over the investment activity of the Post–Employment Benefits Trust Account as described in subdivision (b). Upon agreement and

authorization of the board of retirement and the governing body of a participating employer, the retirement system may administer a post-employment health, life, welfare, or other supplemental benefit plan sponsored by the participating employer and funded through the Post–Employment Benefits Trust Account.

(g) In accordance with procedures established in the written agreement described in subdivision (f), the participating employer may elect to terminate participation in the Post–Employment Benefits Trust and instruct the retirement system to either (1) transfer the funds held in the Post–Employment Benefits Trust Account to a successor trustee named by the employer, or (2) disburse the trust assets in accordance with subdivision (i). In addition, the board of retirement may terminate the participation of a participating employer in the Post–Employment Benefits Trust Account if either:

(1) The board of retirement finds that the participating employer is unable to satisfy the terms and conditions required by this article, the rules and procedures established by the board, or the participation agreement between the participating employer and the board of retirement.

(2) The board of retirement elects to terminate the Post–Employment Benefits Trust Account.

(h) If the board of retirement terminates the participation of an employer in the Post–Employment Benefits Trust Account, as described in paragraph (1) or (2) of subdivision (g), the funds attributable to that employer shall remain in the Post–Employment Benefits Trust Account, for the continued payment of post-employment benefits for current and future participants and the costs of administration and investment.

(i) If the board of retirement elects to terminate the Post–Employment Benefits Trust Account, the retirement system shall disburse the funds in Post–Employment Benefits Trust Account in the following order and manner:

(1) The retirement system shall retain an amount sufficient to pay for the post-employment benefits for participants in the post-employment benefits plan or plans provided by the former participating employer.

(2) The retirement system shall retain an amount sufficient to pay reasonable administrative and investment costs described in this section.

(3) After the amounts in paragraphs (1) and (2) have been retained or disbursed, the retirement system shall pay any remaining funds to the former participating employer or employers. *(Added by Stats.2006, c. 846 (A.B.2863), § 6, eff. Sept. 30, 2006. Amended by Stats. 2007, c. 327 (A.B.1124), § 5.)*

Operative Effect

For operative effect of certain provisions of this chapter, see Government Code § 31899.6.

§ 31694.2. Employers electing to participate in Post–Employment Benefits Trust Account; responsibilities; delegation of responsibilities

An employer who elects to participate in the Post–Employment Benefits Trust Account shall be required to establish, fund, and apply distributions from the Post–Employment Benefits Trust Account, and administer a post-employment health, life, welfare, or other supplemental benefit plan or plans funded through the Post–Employment Benefits Trust Account, pursuant to applicable federal tax requirements or other legal provisions. An employer may expressly delegate its responsibilities under this section to the retirement system as described in subdivision (f) of Section 31694.1, to the extent allowed by federal tax laws. *(Added by Stats.2006, c. 846 (A.B. 2863), § 6, eff. Sept. 30, 2006. Amended by Stats.2007, c. 327 (A.B.1124), § 6.)*

Operative Effect

For operative effect of certain provisions of this chapter, see Government Code § 31899.6.

§ 31694.3. Establishment of trust by county board of supervisors or district governing body for funding post-employment benefits; role of board; trust agreement establishing roles and responsibilities and providing manner and method of payment of investment and administrative expenses; contracting for outside trustee, third-party administrator, or investment manager

(a) The board of supervisors of a county, or the governing body of a district, may establish, by resolution or ordinance, its own trust for the sole purpose of funding any post-employment benefits provided under a group health, life, or other welfare benefits plan or plans established and maintained by that county or district.

(b) The board of retirement and, if applicable, the board of investments, may, with the agreement of the county or district, act as one or more of the following for that employer-established trust: trustee, third-party administrator, or investment manager. The board of retirement and, if applicable, the board of investments, may enter a trust agreement, third-party administrative services agreement, investment manager agreement, or other appropriate agreement with the county or district, which shall establish the respective roles and responsibilities of the parties with respect to the administration and investment of the employer-established trust. That agreement shall provide for the manner and method of payment for the reasonable costs related to investment expenses for, and administration of, the employer-established trust. Those expenses shall not be deemed to be an investment or administrative expense of a retirement system under this chapter.

(c) The county or district may contract with an entity other than the board of retirement or board of investments to act as trustee, third-party administrator, or investment manager for the trust.

(d) Contributions to the employer-established trust may include the proceeds of debt issued by the county or district solely for the purpose of funding post-employment health, life, or other welfare benefits. *(Added by Stats.2006, c. 846 (A.B.2863), § 6, eff. Sept. 30, 2006.)*

Operative Effect

For operative effect of certain provisions of this chapter, see Government Code § 31899.6.

§ 31694.4. Application of article

This article shall not apply to a county, district, or other public entity in a county of the first class as defined by Section 28020 until the provisions of this article are funded pursuant to the provisions of a ratified collective bargaining agreement by that county, district, or other public entity. *(Added by Stats.2006, c. 846 (A.B.2863), § 6, eff. Sept. 30, 2006.)*

Operative Effect

For operative effect of certain provisions of this chapter, see Government Code § 31899.6.

§ 31694.5. Obligations created under other contracts

A contract entered into between a public employer and a board of retirement or board of investments as described in Section 31694.1 shall not change the obligations of a public employer, board of retirement, or board of investments that are created under other contracts, laws, ordinances, regulations, or similar actions to provide benefits for employees or retired employees of a participating county, district, or other public entity, or their qualified spouses, dependents, and beneficiaries. *(Added by Stats.2006, c. 846 (A.B.2863), § 6, eff. Sept. 30, 2006.)*

Operative Effect

For operative effect of certain provisions of this chapter, see Government Code § 31899.6.

ARTICLE 10. DISABILITY RETIREMENT

Section
31725.65. Incapacitated service members and performance of duties; ability to perform other duties; vacant positions; reemployment plans; compensation; disability retirement allowance; application of section.

Operative Effect

For operative effect of certain provisions of this chapter, see Government Code § 31899.6.

§ 31725.65. Incapacitated service members and performance of duties; ability to perform other duties; vacant positions; reemployment plans; compensation; disability retirement allowance; application of section

(a) When the board finds, based on medical advice, that a member in county service is incapacitated for the

201

performance of the member's duties, the board shall determine, based upon that medical advice, whether the member may be capable of performing other duties. If the board determines that a member, although incapacitated for the performance of the member's duties, is capable of performing other duties, the board shall notify the appropriate agency in county service of its findings.

(b) When the appropriate agency in county service receives that notification from the board, the agency shall immediately inform the member of any vacant county positions that may be suitable for the member, consistent with his or her disability, and shall consult with the member in an effort to develop a reemployment plan that shall identify what position, if any, in county service would be compatible with the member's aptitudes, interests, and abilities.

(c) Upon approval by the member of the reemployment plan, the appropriate agency in county service shall notify the board that the agency is proceeding to implement the approved reemployment plan.

(d) Upon commencement of service by the member in the position specified in the approved reemployment plan, the member shall not be paid the disability retirement allowance to which the member would otherwise be entitled during the entire period that the member remains in county service. However, if the compensation rate of the position specified in the approved reemployment plan is less than the compensation rate of the position for which the member was incapacitated, the board shall, in lieu of the disability retirement allowance, pay to the member a supplemental disability allowance in an amount equal to the difference between the compensation rate of the position for which the member was incapacitated, applicable on the date of the commencement of service by the member in the position specified in the approved reemployment plan, and the compensation rate of the position specified in the plan, applicable on the same date. The supplemental disability allowance shall be adjusted annually to equal the difference between the current compensation rate of the position for which the member was incapacitated and the current compensation of the position specified in the approved reemployment plan. The supplemental disability allowance payments shall commence upon suspension of the disability retirement allowance and the amount of the payments shall not be greater than the disability retirement allowance to which the member would otherwise be entitled. Supplemental disability allowance payments made pursuant to this section shall be considered as a charge against the county advance reserve for current service, and all of these payments received by a member shall be considered as a part of the member's compensation within the meaning of Section 31460.

(e) From the time that the member is eligible to receive a disability retirement allowance until the appropriate agency is able to provide the position in county service specified in the approved reemployment plan, and the member has commenced service in that position, the disability retirement allowance to which the member is entitled under this article shall be paid. Upon commencement of service by the member in the position specified in the approved reemployment plan, the period during which the member was receiving disability retirement payments shall not be considered as breaking the continuity of the member's service, and the rate of the member's contributions shall continue to be based on the same age at entrance into the retirement system on which the member's rates were based prior to the date of the member's disability. The member's accumulated contributions shall not be reduced as a result of the member receiving the disability retirement payments, but shall be increased by the amount of interest that would have accrued had the member not been retired.

(f) Notwithstanding Section 31560, a member whose principal duties, while serving in the position for which the member was incapacitated, consisted of activities defined in Section 31469.3 shall, upon commencement of service by the member in the position specified in the approved reemployment plan, continue to be considered as satisfying the requirements of Section 31560, notwithstanding the actual duties performed during the entire period that the member remains in county service.

(g) This section shall apply only to members who are incapacitated for the performance of the member's duties on or after January 1, 2004, and who are eligible to retire for service-connected disability. *(Added by Stats.2004, c. 379 (A.B.2982), § 2, eff. Aug. 30, 2004. Amended by Stats.2005, c. 22 (S.B.1108), § 90.)*

Operative Effect

For operative effect of certain provisions of this chapter, see Government Code § 31899.6.

Title 5

LOCAL AGENCIES

Division 1

CITIES AND COUNTIES

Part 1

POWERS AND DUTIES COMMON TO CITIES AND COUNTIES

CHAPTER 1. GENERAL

ARTICLE 2. POWERS AND DUTIES OF LEGISLATIVE BODIES

Section
50026. Earnings tax; imposition; construction of section.

§ 50026. Earnings tax; imposition; construction of section

The legislative body of any local agency, chartered or general law, which is otherwise authorized by law or charter to impose any tax on the privilege of earning a livelihood by an employee or any other tax, fee or charge on or measured by the earnings, or any part thereof, of any employee, shall not impose any such tax, fee or charge on the earnings of any employee, when such employee is not a resident of the taxing jurisdiction, unless exactly the same tax, fee or charge at the same rate, with the same credits and deductions, is imposed on the earnings of all residents of the taxing jurisdiction who are employed therein.

This section shall not be construed as authorizing any tax prohibited by Section 17041.5 of the Revenue and Taxation Code or any other provision of law, nor shall it be construed so as to prohibit the levy or collection of any otherwise authorized tax upon a business measured by or according to gross receipts. *(Added by Stats.1968, c. 559, p. 1225, § 1.)*

Title 8

THE ORGANIZATION AND GOVERNMENT OF COURTS

CHAPTER 7. TRIAL COURT EMPLOYMENT PROTECTION AND GOVERNANCE ACT

ARTICLE 3. LABOR RELATIONS

Section
71639.1 Public Employment Relations Board; powers and duties; unfair practice charges; enforcement of rules; management employees; violation of rule or regulation.

§ 71639.1. Public Employment Relations Board; powers and duties; unfair practice charges; enforcement of rules; management employees; violation of rule or regulation

(a) As used in this article, "board" means the Public Employment Relations Board established pursuant to Section 3541.

(b) The powers and duties of the board described in Section 3541.3 shall also apply, as appropriate, to this article and shall include the authority as set forth in subdivisions (c) and (d). Included among the appropriate powers of the board are the power to order elections, to conduct any election the board orders, and to adopt rules to apply in areas where a trial court has no rule.

(c) A complaint alleging any violation of this article or of any rules and regulations adopted by a trial court pursuant to Section 71636 shall be processed as an unfair practice charge by the board. The initial determination as to whether the charge of unfair practice is justified and, if so, the appropriate remedy necessary to effectuate the purposes of this article, shall be a matter within the exclusive jurisdiction of the board. The board shall apply and interpret unfair labor practices consistent with existing judicial interpretations of this article and Section 71639.3. The board shall not issue a complaint in respect of any charge based upon an alleged unfair practice occurring more than six months prior to the filing of the charge, except that if the rules and regulations adopted by a trial court require exhaustion of a remedy prior to filing an unfair practice charge or the charging party chooses to exhaust a trial court's remedy prior to filing an unfair practice charge, the six-month limitation set forth in this subsection shall be tolled during such reasonable amount of time it takes the charging party to exhaust the remedy, but nothing herein shall require a charging party to exhaust a remedy when that remedy would be futile.

(d) The board shall enforce and apply rules adopted by a trial court concerning unit determinations, representation, recognition, and elections.

(e) This section does not apply to employees designated as management employees under Section 71637.1.

(f) The board shall not find it an unfair practice for an employee organization to violate a rule or regulation adopted by a trial court if that rule or regulation is itself in violation of this article. *(Added by Stats.2004, c. 227 (S.B.1102), § 68, eff. Aug. 16, 2004.)*

203

CHAPTER 7.5.   TRIAL COURT INTERPRETER EMPLOYMENT AND LABOR RELATIONS ACT

Section
71825. Public Employment Relations Board; powers and duties; unfair practice charges; enforcement of rules; management employees; violation of rule or regulation.

§ 71825.   Public Employment Relations Board; powers and duties; unfair practice charges; enforcement of rules; management employees; violation of rule or regulation

(a) As used in this section, "board" means the Public Employment Relations Board established pursuant to Section 3541.

(b) The powers and duties of the board described in Section 3541.3 shall also apply, as appropriate, to this chapter and shall include the authority as set forth in subdivisions (c) and (d). Included among the appropriate powers of the board are the power to order elections, to conduct any election the board orders, and to adopt rules to apply in areas where a regional court interpreter employment relations committee has no rule.

(c) A complaint alleging any violation of this chapter or of any rules and regulations adopted by a regional court interpreter employment relations committee pursuant to Section 71823 shall be processed as an unfair practice charge by the board. The initial determination as to whether the charge of unfair practice is justified and, if so, the appropriate remedy necessary to effectuate the purposes of this chapter, shall be a matter within the exclusive jurisdiction of the board. The board shall apply and interpret unfair labor practices consistent with existing judicial interpretations of this chapter and Section 71826(b). The board shall not issue a complaint in respect of any charge based upon an alleged unfair practice occurring more than six months prior to the filing of the charge, except that if the rules and regulations adopted by a regional court interpreter employment relations committee require exhaustion of a remedy prior to filing an unfair practice charge or the charging party chooses to exhaust a regional court interpreter employment relations committee's remedy prior to filing an unfair practice charge, the six-month limitation set forth in this subsection shall be tolled during such reasonable amount of time it takes the charging party to exhaust the remedy, but nothing herein shall require a charging party to exhaust a remedy when that remedy would be futile.

(d) The board shall enforce and apply rules adopted by a regional court interpreter employment relations committee concerning unit determinations, representation, recognition, and elections.

(e) This section does not apply to employees designated as management employees.

(f) The board shall not find it an unfair practice for an employee organization to violate a rule or regulation adopted by a regional court interpreter employment relations committee if that rule or regulation is itself in violation of this chapter. *(Added by Stats.2004, c. 227 (S.B.1102), § 74, eff. Aug. 16, 2004.)*

HEALTH AND SAFETY CODE

Division 2

LICENSING PROVISIONS

CHAPTER 2.   HEALTH FACILITIES

ARTICLE 3.   REGULATIONS

Section
1278.5.   Whistleblower protections.

§ 1278.5.   Whistleblower protections

(a) The Legislature finds and declares that it is the public policy of the State of California to encourage patients, nurses, members of the medical staff, and other health care workers to notify government entities of suspected unsafe patient care and conditions. The Legislature encourages this reporting in order to protect patients and in order to assist those accreditation and government entities charged with ensuring that health care is safe. The Legislature finds and declares that whistleblower protections apply primarily to issues relating to the care, services, and conditions of a facility and are not intended to conflict with existing provisions in state and federal law relating to employee and employer relations.

(b)(1) No health facility shall discriminate or retaliate, in any manner, against any patient, employee, member of the medical staff, or any other health care worker of the health facility because that person has done either of the following:

(A) Presented a grievance, complaint, or report to the facility, to an entity or agency responsible for accrediting or evaluating the facility, or the medical staff of the facility, or to any other governmental entity.

(B) Has initiated, participated, or cooperated in an investigation or administrative proceeding related to, the quality of care, services, or conditions at the facility that is carried out by an entity or agency responsible for accrediting or evaluating the facility or its medical staff, or governmental entity.

(2) No entity that owns or operates a health facility, or which owns or operates any other health facility, shall discriminate or retaliate against any person because that person has taken any actions pursuant to this subdivision.

(3) A violation of this section shall be subject to a civil penalty of not more than twenty-five thousand dollars ($25,000). The civil penalty shall be assessed and recovered through the same administrative process set forth in Chapter 2.4 (commencing with Section 1417) for long-term health care facilities.

(c) Any type of discriminatory treatment of a patient by whom, or upon whose behalf, a grievance or complaint has been submitted, directly or indirectly, to a governmental entity or received by a health facility administrator within 180 days of the filing of the grievance or complaint, shall raise a rebuttable presumption that the action was taken by the health facility in retaliation for the filing of the grievance or complaint.

(d)(1) There shall be a rebuttable presumption that discriminatory action was taken by the health facility, or by the entity that owns or operates that health facility, or that owns or operates any other health facility, in retaliation against an employee, member of the medical staff, or any other health care worker of the facility, if responsible staff at the facility or the entity that owns or operates the facility had knowledge of the actions, participation, or cooperation of the person responsible for any acts described in paragraph (1) of subdivision (b), and the discriminatory action occurs within 120 days of the filing of the grievance or complaint by the employee, member of the medical staff or any other health care worker of the facility.

(2) For purposes of this section, discriminatory treatment of an employee, member of the medical staff, or any other health care worker includes, but is not limited to, discharge, demotion, suspension, or any unfavorable changes in, or breach of, the terms or conditions of a contract, employment, or privileges of the employee, member of the medical staff, or any other health care worker of the health care facility, or the threat of any of these actions.

(e) The presumptions in subdivisions (c) and (d) shall be presumptions affecting the burden of producing evidence as provided in Section 603 of the Evidence Code.

(f) Any person who willfully violates this section is guilty of a misdemeanor punishable by a fine of not more than twenty thousand dollars ($20,000).

(g) An employee who has been discriminated against in employment pursuant to this section shall be entitled to reinstatement, reimbursement for lost wages and work benefits caused by the acts of the employer, and the legal costs associated with pursuing the case, or to any remedy deemed warranted by the court pursuant to this chapter or any other applicable provision of statutory or common law. A health care worker who has been discriminated against pursuant to this section shall be entitled to reimbursement for lost income and the legal costs associated with pursuing the case, or to any remedy deemed warranted by the court pursuant to this chapter or other applicable provision of statutory or common law. A member of the medical staff who has been discriminated against pursuant to this section shall be entitled to reinstatement, reimbursement for lost income resulting from any change in the terms or conditions of his or her privileges caused by the acts of the facility or the entity that owns or operates a health facility or any other health facility that is owned or operated by that entity, and the legal costs associated with pursuing the case, or to any remedy deemed warranted by the court pursuant to this chapter or any other applicable provision of statutory or common law.

(h) The medical staff of the health facility may petition the court for an injunction to protect a peer review committee from being required to comply with evidentiary demands on a pending peer review hearing from the member of the medical staff who has filed an action pursuant to this section, if the evidentiary demands from the complainant would impede the peer review process or endanger the health and safety of patients of the health facility during the peer review process. Prior to granting an injunction, the court shall conduct an in camera review of the evidence sought to be discovered to determine if a peer review hearing, as authorized in Section 805 and Sections 809 to 809.5, inclusive, of the Business and Professions Code, would be impeded. If it is determined that the peer review hearing will be impeded, the injunction shall be granted until the peer review hearing is completed. Nothing in this section shall preclude the court, on motion of its own or by a party, from issuing an injunction or other order under this subdivision in the interest of justice for the duration of the peer review process to protect the person from irreparable harm.

(i) For purposes of this section, "health facility" means any facility defined under this chapter, including, but not limited to, the facility's administrative personnel, employees, boards, and committees of the board, and medical staff.

(j) This section shall not apply to an inmate of a correctional facility or juvenile facility of the Department of Corrections and Rehabilitation, or to an inmate housed in a local detention facility including a county jail or a juvenile hall, juvenile camp, or other juvenile detention facility.

(k) This section shall not apply to a health facility that is a long-term health care facility, as defined in Section 1418. A health facility that is a long-term health care facility shall remain subject to Section 1432.

(*l*) Nothing in this section shall be construed to limit the ability of the medical staff to carry out its legitimate peer review activities in accordance with Sections 809 to 809.5, inclusive, of the Business and Professions Code.

(m) Nothing in this section abrogates or limits any other theory of liability or remedy otherwise available at law. (*Added by Stats.1999, c. 155 (S.B.97), § 1. Amended by Stats.2007, c. 683 (A.B.632), § 1.*)

CHAPTER 2.2. HEALTH CARE SERVICE PLANS

ARTICLE 4.5.   CALIFORNIA COBRA PROGRAM

Section
1366.20.   California Continuation Benefits Replacement Act (COBRA).
1366.21.   Definitions.
1366.22.   Continuation coverage requirements; exclusions from article.
1366.23.   Health care service plan; group benefit plan; continuation coverage.
1366.24.   Health care service plan; evidence of coverage; disclosure of continuation coverage.
1366.25.   Qualifying event; notification; termination of coverage; contracting for administrative services; premium assistance.
1366.26.   Qualified beneficiary electing continuation coverage; payments to plan.
1366.27.   Termination of continuation coverage.
1366.28.   Obligation to provide continuation coverage; exclusions.
1366.29.   Exhaustion of federal coverage; continuation up to 36 months.

§ 1366.20.   California Continuation Benefits Replacement Act (COBRA)

(a) This article shall be known as the California Continuation Benefits Replacement Act, or "Cal–COBRA."

(b) It is the intent of the Legislature that continued access to health insurance coverage is provided to employees, and their dependents, of employers with 2 to 19 eligible employees who are not currently offered continuation coverage under the Consolidated Omnibus Budget Reconciliation Act of 1985.

(c) It is the intent of the Legislature that any federal assistance that is or may become available to qualified beneficiaries under this article be effectively and promptly implemented by the department.

(d) The director, in consultation with the Insurance Commissioner, may adopt emergency regulations to implement this article in accordance with Chapter 3.5 (commencing with Section 11340) of Part 1 of Division 3 of Title 2 of the Government Code by making a finding of emergency and demonstrating the need for immediate action in the event that any federal assistance is or becomes available to qualified beneficiaries under this article. The adoption of these regulations shall be considered by the Office of Administrative Law to be necessary to avoid serious harm to the public peace, health, safety, or general welfare. Any regulations adopted pursuant to this subdivision shall be substantially similar to those adopted by the Insurance Commissioner under subdivision (d) of Section 10128.50 of the Insurance Code. (*Added by Stats.1997, c. 665 (S.B.719), § 1. Amended by Stats.2009, c. 3 (A.B.23), § 1, eff. May 12, 2009.*)

§ 1366.21. Definitions

The definitions contained in this section govern the construction of this article.

(a) "Continuation coverage" means extended coverage under the group benefit plan in which an eligible employee or eligible dependent is currently enrolled, or, in the case of a termination of the group benefit plan or an employer open enrollment period, extended coverage under the group benefit plan currently offered by the employer.

(b) "Group benefit plan" means any health care service plan contract provided pursuant to Article 3.1 (commencing with Section 1357) to an employer with 2 to 19 eligible employees, as defined in Section 1357, as well as a specialized health care service plan contract provided to an employer with 2 to 19 eligible employees, as defined in Section 1357.

(c)(1) "Qualified beneficiary" means any individual who, on the day before the qualifying event, is an enrollee in a group benefit plan offered by a health care service plan pursuant to Article 3.1 (commencing with Section 1357) and has a qualifying event, as defined in subdivision (d).

(2) "Qualified beneficiary eligible for premium assistance under Title III of Division B of the American Recovery and Reinvestment Act of 2009 (Public Law 111–5)" means a qualified beneficiary, as defined in paragraph (1), who (A) was or is eligible for continuation coverage as a result of the involuntary termination of the covered employee's employment during the period that begins with September 1, 2008, and ends with December 31, 2009, (B) elects continuation coverage, and (C) meets the definition of "qualified beneficiary" set forth in paragraph (3) of Section 1167 of Title 29 of the United States Code, as used in subparagraph (E) of paragraph (1) of subdivision (a) of Section 3001 of Title III of Division B of the American Recovery and Reinvestment Act of 2009 (Public Law 111–5) or any subsequent rules or regulations issued pursuant to that law.

(d) "Qualifying event" means any of the following events that, but for the election of continuation coverage under this article, would result in a loss of coverage under the group benefit plan to a qualified beneficiary:

(1) The death of the covered employee.

(2) The termination of employment or reduction in hours of the covered employee's employment, except that termination for gross misconduct does not constitute a qualifying event.

(3) The divorce or legal separation of the covered employee from the covered employee's spouse.

(4) The loss of dependent status by a dependent enrolled in the group benefit plan.

(5) With respect to a covered dependent only, the covered employee's entitlement to benefits under Title XVIII of the United States Social Security Act (Medicare).

(e) "Employer" means any employer that meets the definition of "small employer" as set forth in Section 1357 and (1) employed 2 to 19 eligible employees on at least 50 percent of its working days during the preceding calendar year, or, if the employer was not in business during any part of the preceding calendar year, employed 2 to 19 eligible employees on at least 50 percent of its working days during the preceding calendar quarter, (2) has contracted for health care coverage through a group benefit plan offered by a health care service plan, and (3) is not subject to Section 4980B of the United States Internal Revenue Code [1] or Chapter 18 of the Employee Retirement Income Security Act, 29 U.S.C. Section 1161 et seq.

(f) "Core coverage" means coverage of basic health care services, as defined in subdivision (b) of Section 1345, and other hospital, medical, or surgical benefits provided by the group benefit plan that a qualified beneficiary was receiving immediately prior to the qualifying event, other than noncore coverage.

(g) "Noncore coverage" means coverage for vision and dental care. *(Added by Stats.1997, c. 665 (S.B.719), § 1. Amended by Stats.1998, c. 107 (A.B.112), § 6, eff. July 6, 1998; Stats.2009, c. 3 (A.B.23), § 2, eff. May 12, 2009.)*

[1] Internal Revenue Code sections are in Title 26 of the U.S.C.A.

§ 1366.22. Continuation coverage requirements; exclusions from article

The continuation coverage requirements of this article do not apply to the following individuals:

(a) Individuals who are entitled to Medicare benefits or become entitled to Medicare benefits pursuant to Title XVIII of the United States Social Security Act, as amended or superseded. Entitlement to Medicare Part A only constitutes entitlement to benefits under Medicare.

(b) Individuals who have other hospital, medical, or surgical coverage or who are covered or become covered under another group benefit plan, including a self-insured employee welfare benefit plan, that provides coverage for individuals and that does not impose any exclusion or limitation with respect to any preexisting condition of the individual, other than a preexisting condition limitation or exclusion that does not apply to or is satisfied by the qualified beneficiary pursuant to Sections 1357 and 1357.06. A group conversion option under any group benefit plan shall not be considered as an arrangement under which an individual is or becomes covered.

(c) Individuals who are covered, become covered, or are eligible for federal COBRA coverage pursuant to Section 4980B of the United States Internal Revenue Code [1] or Chapter 18 of the Employee Retirement Income Security Act, 29 U.S.C. Section 1161 et seq.

(d) Individuals who are covered, become covered, or are eligible for coverage pursuant to Chapter 6A of the

207

Public Health Service Act, 42 U.S.C. Section 300bb–1 et seq.

(e) Qualified beneficiaries who fail to meet the requirements of subdivision (b) of Section 1366.24 or subdivision (h) of Section 1366.25 regarding notification of a qualifying event or election of continuation coverage within the specified time limits.

(f) Qualified beneficiaries who fail to submit the correct premium amount required by subdivision (b) of Section 1366.24 and Section 1366.26, in accordance with the terms and conditions of the plan contract, or fail to satisfy other terms and conditions of the plan contract. *(Added by Stats.1997, c. 665 (S.B.719), § 1. Amended by Stats.1998, c. 107 (A.B.112), § 7, eff. July 6, 1998; Stats.2009, c. 3 (A.B.23), § 3, eff. May 12, 2009.)*

[1] Internal Revenue Code sections are in Title 26 of the U.S.C.A.

§ 1366.23. Health care service plan; group benefit plan; continuation coverage

(a) Every health care service plan, including a specialized health care service plan contract, that provides coverage under a group benefit plan to an employer, as defined in Section 1366.21, shall offer continuation coverage, pursuant to this section, to a qualified beneficiary under the contract upon a qualifying event without evidence of insurability. The qualified beneficiary shall, upon election, be able to continue his or her coverage under the group benefit plan, subject to the contract's terms and conditions, and subject to the requirements of this article. Except as otherwise provided in this article, continuation coverage shall be provided under the same terms and conditions that apply to similarly situated individuals under the group benefit plan.

(b) Every health care service plan shall also offer the continuation coverage to a qualified beneficiary who (1) elects continuation coverage under a group benefit plan, as defined in this article or in Section 10128.51 of the Insurance Code, but whose continuation coverage is terminated pursuant to subdivision (b) of Section 1366.27, prior to any other termination date specified in Section 1366.27, or (2) who elects coverage through the health care service plan during any employer open enrollment, and the employer has contracted with the health care service plan to provide coverage to the employer's active employees. This continuation coverage shall be provided only for the balance of the period that the qualified beneficiary would have remained covered under the prior group benefit plan had the employer not terminated the group contract with the previous health care service plan or insurer.

(c) Every health care service plan or specialized health care service plan shall offer a qualified beneficiary the ability to elect the same core, noncore, or core and noncore coverage that the qualified beneficiary had immediately prior to the qualifying event.

(d) Any child who is born to a former employee who is a qualified beneficiary who has elected continuation coverage pursuant to this article or a child who is placed for adoption with a former employee who is a qualified beneficiary who has elected continuation coverage pursuant to this article during the period of continuation coverage provided by this article shall be considered a qualified beneficiary entitled to receive benefits pursuant to this article for the remainder of the period that the former employee is covered pursuant to this article, if the child is enrolled under a group benefit plan as a dependent of that former employee who is a qualified beneficiary within 30 days of the child's birth or placement for adoption.

(e) An individual who becomes a qualified beneficiary pursuant to this article shall continue to receive coverage pursuant to this article until continuation coverage is terminated at the qualified beneficiary's election or pursuant to Section 1366.27, whichever comes first, even if the employer that sponsored the group benefit plan that is continued subsequently becomes subject to Section 4980B of the United States Internal Revenue Code or Chapter 18 of the Employee Retirement Income Security Act, 29 U.S.C. Sec. 1161 et seq.

(f) A qualified beneficiary electing coverage pursuant to this section shall be considered part of the group contract and treated as similarly situated employees for contract purposes, unless otherwise specified in this article. *(Added by Stats.1997, c. 665 (S.B.719), § 1. Amended by Stats.1998, c. 107 (A.B.112), § 8, eff. July 6, 1998.)*

§ 1366.24. Health care service plan; evidence of coverage; disclosure of continuation coverage

(a) Every health care service plan evidence of coverage, provided for group benefit plans subject to this article, that is issued, amended, or renewed on or after January 1, 1999, shall disclose to covered employees of group benefit plans subject to this article the ability to continue coverage pursuant to this article, as required by this section.

(b) This disclosure shall state that all enrollees who are eligible to be qualified beneficiaries, as defined in subdivision (c) of Section 1366.21, shall be required, as a condition of receiving benefits pursuant to this article, to notify, in writing, the health care service plan, or the employer if the employer contracts to perform the administrative services as provided for in Section 1366.25, of all qualifying events as specified in paragraphs (1), (3), (4), and (5) of subdivision (d) of Section 1366.21 within 60 days of the date of the qualifying event. This disclosure shall inform enrollees that failure to make the notification to the health care service plan, or to the employer when under contract to provide the administrative services, within the required 60 days will disqualify the qualified beneficiary from receiving continuation coverage pursuant to this article. The disclosure shall further state that a qualified beneficiary who wishes to continue coverage under the group benefit plan pursuant to this article must request the continuation in writing and deliver the written request, by first-class mail, or other reliable means of delivery, including personal delivery, express mail, or private courier company, to the health care service plan, or to the employer if the plan has contracted with the employer for administrative services pursuant to subdivision (d) of Section 1366.25, within the 60–day period following the later of (1) the date that the enrollee's coverage under the group benefit plan terminated or will terminate by reason of a qualifying event, or (2) the date the enrollee was sent notice pursuant to subdivision (e) of Section 1366.25 of the ability to continue coverage under the group benefit plan. The disclosure required by this section shall also state that a qualified beneficiary electing continuation shall pay to the health care service plan, in accordance with the terms and conditions of the plan contract, which shall be set forth in the notice to the qualified beneficiary pursuant to subdivision (d) of Section 1366.25, the amount of the required premium payment, as set forth in Section 1366.26. The disclosure shall further require that the qualified beneficiary's first premium payment required to establish premium payment be delivered by first-class mail, certified mail, or other reliable means of delivery, including personal delivery, express mail, or private courier company, to the health care service plan, or to the employer if the employer has contracted with the plan to perform the administrative services pursuant to subdivision (d) of Section 1366.25, within 45 days of the date the qualified beneficiary provided written notice to the health care service plan or the employer, if the employer has contracted to perform the administrative services, of the election to continue coverage in order for coverage to be continued under this article. This disclosure shall also state that the first premium payment must equal an amount sufficient to pay any required premiums and all premiums due, and that failure to submit the correct premium amount within the 45–day period will disqualify the qualified beneficiary from receiving continuation coverage pursuant to this article.

(c) The disclosure required by this section shall also describe separately how qualified beneficiaries whose continuation coverage terminates under a prior group benefit plan pursuant to subdivision (b) of Section 1366.27 may continue their coverage for the balance of the period that the qualified beneficiary would have remained covered under the prior group benefit plan, including the requirements for election and payment. The disclosure shall clearly state that continuation coverage shall terminate if the qualified beneficiary fails to comply with the requirements pertaining to enrollment in, and payment of premiums to, the new group benefit plan within 30 days of receiving notice of the termination of the prior group benefit plan.

(d) Prior to August 1, 1998, every health care service plan shall provide to all covered employees of employers subject to this article a written notice containing the disclosures required by this section, or shall provide to all covered employees of employers subject to this section a new or amended evidence of coverage that includes the disclosures required by this section. Any specialized health care service plan that, in the ordinary course of business, maintains only the addresses of employer group purchasers of benefits and does not maintain addresses of covered employees, may comply with the notice requirements of this section through the provision of the notices to its employer group purchasers of benefits.

(e) Every plan disclosure form issued, amended, or renewed on and after January 1, 1999, for a group benefit plan subject to this article shall provide a notice that, under state law, an enrollee may be entitled to continuation of group coverage and that additional information regarding eligibility for this coverage may be found in the plan's evidence of coverage.

(f) Every disclosure issued, amended, or renewed on and after July 1, 2006, for a group benefit plan subject to this article shall include the following notice:

"Please examine your options carefully before declining this coverage. You should be aware that companies selling individual health insurance typically require a review of your medical history that could result in a higher premium or you could be denied coverage entirely." *(Added by Stats.1997, c. 665 (S.B.719), § 1. Amended by Stats.1998, c. 107 (A.B.112), § 8.5, eff. July 6, 1998; Stats.2005, c. 526 (A.B.356), § 2.)*

§ 1366.25. Qualifying event; notification; termination of coverage; contracting for administrative services; premium assistance

(a) Every group contract between a health care service plan and an employer subject to this article that is issued, amended, or renewed on or after July 1, 1998, shall require the employer to notify the plan, in writing, of any employee who has had a qualifying event, as defined in paragraph (2) of subdivision (d) of Section 1366.21, within 30 days of the qualifying event. The group contract shall also require the employer to notify the plan, in writing, within 30 days of the date, when the employer becomes subject to Section 4980B of the United States Internal Revenue Code [1] or Chapter 18 of the Employee Retirement Income Security Act, 29 U.S.C. Sec. 1161 et seq.

(b) Every group contract between a plan and an employer subject to this article that is issued, amended, or renewed on or after July 1, 1998, shall require the employer to notify qualified beneficiaries currently receiving continuation coverage, whose continuation coverage will terminate under one group benefit plan prior to the end of the period the qualified beneficiary would have remained covered, as specified in Section 1366.27, of the qualified beneficiary's ability to continue coverage under a new group benefit plan for the balance of the period the qualified beneficiary would have remained covered under the prior group benefit plan. This notice shall be provided either 30 days prior to the termination or when all enrolled employees are notified, whichever is later.

Every health care service plan and specialized health care service plan shall provide to the employer replacing

209

a health care service plan contract issued by the plan, or to the employer's agent or broker representative, within 15 days of any written request, information in possession of the plan reasonably required to administer the notification requirements of this subdivision and subdivision (c).

(c) Notwithstanding subdivision (a), the group contract between the health care service plan and the employer shall require the employer to notify the successor plan in writing of the qualified beneficiaries currently receiving continuation coverage so that the successor plan, or contracting employer or administrator, may provide those qualified beneficiaries with the necessary premium information, enrollment forms, and instructions consistent with the disclosure required by subdivision (c) of Section 1366.24 and subdivision (e) of this section to allow the qualified beneficiary to continue coverage. This information shall be sent to all qualified beneficiaries who are enrolled in the plan and those qualified beneficiaries who have been notified, pursuant to Section 1366.24, of their ability to continue their coverage and may still elect coverage within the specified 60–day period. This information shall be sent to the qualified beneficiary's last known address, as provided to the employer by the health care service plan or disability insurer currently providing continuation coverage to the qualified beneficiary. The successor plan shall not be obligated to provide this information to qualified beneficiaries if the employer or prior plan or insurer fails to comply with this section.

(d) A health care service plan may contract with an employer, or an administrator, to perform the administrative obligations of the plan as required by this article, including required notifications and collecting and forwarding premiums to the health care service plan. Except for the requirements of subdivisions (a), (b), and (c), this subdivision shall not be construed to permit a plan to require an employer to perform the administrative obligations of the plan as required by this article as a condition of the issuance or renewal of coverage.

(e) Every health care service plan, or employer or administrator that contracts to perform the notice and administrative services pursuant to this section, shall, within 14 days of receiving a notice of a qualifying event, provide to the qualified beneficiary the necessary benefits information, premium information, enrollment forms, and disclosures consistent with the notice requirements contained in subdivisions (b) and (c) of Section 1366.24 to allow the qualified beneficiary to formally elect continuation coverage. This information shall be sent to the qualified beneficiary's last known address.

(f) Every health care service plan, or employer or administrator that contracts to perform the notice and administrative services pursuant to this section, shall, during the 180–day period ending on the date that continuation coverage is terminated pursuant to paragraphs (1), (3), and (5) of subdivision (a) of Section 1366.27, notify a qualified beneficiary who has elected continuation coverage pursuant to this article of the date that his or her coverage will terminate, and shall notify

the qualified beneficiary of any conversion coverage available to that qualified beneficiary. This requirement shall not apply when the continuation coverage is terminated because the group contract between the plan and the employer is being terminated.

(g)(1) A health care service plan shall provide to a qualified beneficiary who has a qualifying event between September 1, 2008, and December 31, 2009, inclusive, a written notice containing information on the availability of premium assistance under Title III of Division B of the American Recovery and Reinvestment Act of 2009 (Public Law 111–5). This notice shall be sent to the qualified beneficiary's last known address. The notice shall include clear and easily understandable language to inform the qualified beneficiary that changes in federal law provide a new opportunity to elect continuation coverage with a 65–percent premium subsidy and shall include all of the following:

(A) The amount of the premium the person will pay. For qualified beneficiaries who had a qualifying event between September 1, 2008, and the effective date of this subdivision, inclusive, if a health care service plan is unable to provide the correct premium amount in the notice, the notice may contain the last known premium amount and an opportunity for the qualified beneficiary to request, through a toll-free telephone number, the correct premium that would apply to the beneficiary.

(B) Enrollment forms and any other information required to be included pursuant to subdivision (e) to allow the qualified beneficiary to elect continuation coverage. This information shall not be included in notices sent to qualified beneficiaries currently enrolled in continuation coverage.

(C) A description of the option to enroll in different coverage as provided in subparagraph (B) of paragraph (1) of subdivision (a) of Section 3001 of Title III of Division B of the American Recovery and Reinvestment Act of 2009 (Public Law 111–5). This description shall advise the qualified beneficiary to contact the covered employee's former employer for prior approval to choose this option.

(D) The eligibility requirements for premium assistance in the amount of 65 percent of the premium under Section 3001 of Title III of Division B of the American Recovery and Reinvestment Act of 2009 (Public Law 111–5).

(E) The duration of premium assistance available under Title III of Division B of the American Recovery and Reinvestment Act of 2009 (Public Law 111–5).

(F) A statement that a qualified beneficiary eligible for premium assistance under Title III of Division B of the American Recovery and Reinvestment Act of 2009 (Public Law 111–5) may elect continuation coverage no later than 60 days of the date of the notice.

(G) A statement that a qualified beneficiary eligible for premium assistance under Title III of Division B of the American Recovery and Reinvestment Act of 2009

(Public Law 111–5) who rejected or discontinued continuation coverage prior to receiving the notice required by this subdivision has the right to withdraw that rejection and elect continuation coverage with the premium assistance.

(H) A statement that reads as follows:

IF YOU ARE HAVING ANY DIFFICULTIES READING OR UNDERSTANDING THIS NOTICE, PLEASE CONTACT [name of health plan] at [insert appropriate telephone number].

(2) With respect to qualified beneficiaries who had a qualifying event between September 1, 2008, and the effective date of this subdivision, inclusive, the notice described in this subdivision shall be provided within the later of 14 calendar days of the effective date of this subdivision or seven business days after the date the plan receives notice of the qualifying event.

(3) With respect to qualified beneficiaries who had or have a qualifying event between the day after the effective date of this subdivision, and December 31, 2009, inclusive, the notice described in this subdivision shall be provided within the period of time specified in subdivision (e).

(4) For purposes of compliance with the notice requirements of this subdivision, the department may designate a model notice or notices that may be used by health care service plans. Use of the model notice or notices shall not require prior approval by the department. Any model notice or notices designated by the department for purposes of this subdivision shall not be subject to the Administrative Procedure Act (Chapter 3.5 (commencing with Section 11340) of Part 1 of Division 3 of Title 2 of the Government Code).

(5) Nothing in this section shall be construed to require a health care service plan to provide the plan's evidence of coverage as a part of the notice required by this subdivision, and nothing in this section shall be construed to require a health care service plan to amend its existing evidence of coverage to comply with the changes made to this section by the act amending this section during the first year of the 2009–10 Regular Session.

(h)(1) Notwithstanding any other provision of law, a qualified beneficiary eligible for premium assistance under Title III of Division B of the American Recovery and Reinvestment Act of 2009 (Public Law 111–5) may elect continuation coverage no later than 60 days after the date of the notice required by subdivision (g).

(2) For a qualified beneficiary who elects to continue coverage pursuant to paragraph (1), the period beginning on the date of the qualifying event and ending on the effective date of the continuation coverage shall be disregarded for purposes of calculating a break in coverage in determining whether a preexisting condition provision applies under subdivision (c) of Section 1357.06 or subdivision (e) of Section 1357.51.

(3) For a qualified beneficiary who had a qualifying event between September 1, 2008, and February 16, 2009, inclusive, and who elects continuation coverage pursuant to paragraph (1), the continuation coverage shall commence on the first day of the month following the election.

(4) For a qualified beneficiary who had a qualifying event between February 17, 2009, and the effective date of this subdivision, inclusive, and who elects continuation coverage pursuant to paragraph (1), the effective date of the continuation coverage shall be either of the following, at the option of the beneficiary, provided that the beneficiary pays the applicable premiums:

(A) The date of the qualifying event.

(B) The first day of the month following the election.

(i) Notwithstanding any other provision of law, a qualified beneficiary eligible for premium assistance under Title III of Division B of the American Recovery and Reinvestment Act of 2009 (Public Law 111–5) may elect to enroll in different coverage subject to the criteria provided under subparagraph (B) of paragraph (1) of subdivision (a) of Section 3001 of Title III of Division B of the American Recovery and Reinvestment Act of 2009 (Public Law 111–5).

(j) A qualified beneficiary enrolled in continuation coverage as of February 17, 2009, who is eligible for premium assistance under Title III of Division B of the American Recovery and Reinvestment Act of 2009 (Public Law 111–5) may request application of the premium assistance as of March 1, 2009, or later, consistent with Title III of Division B of the American Recovery and Reinvestment Act of 2009 (Public Law 111–5).

(k) A health care service plan that receives an election notice from a qualified beneficiary eligible for premium assistance under Title III of Division B of the American Recovery and Reinvestment Act of 2009 (Public Law 111–5), pursuant to subdivision (h), shall be considered a person entitled to reimbursement, as defined in Section 6432(b)(3) of the Internal Revenue Code, as amended by paragraph (12) of subdivision (a) of Section 3001 of Title III of Division B of the American Recovery and Reinvestment Act of 2009 (Public Law 111–5).

(l)(1) For purposes of compliance with Title III of Division B of the American Recovery and Reinvestment Act of 2009 (Public Law 111–5), in the absence of guidance from, or if specifically required for state-only continuation coverage by, the United States Department of Labor, the Internal Revenue Service, or the Centers for Medicare and Medicaid Services, a health care service plan may request verification of the involuntary termination of a covered employee's employment from the covered employee's former employer or the qualified beneficiary seeking premium assistance under Title III of Division B of the American Recovery and Reinvestment Act of 2009 (Public Law 111–5).

(2) A health care service plan that requests verification pursuant to paragraph (1) directly from a covered em-

ployee's former employer shall do so by providing a written notice to the employer. This written notice shall be sent by mail or facsimile to the covered employee's former employer within seven business days from the date the plan receives the qualified beneficiary's election notice pursuant to subdivision (h). Within 10 calendar days of receipt of written notice required by this paragraph, the former employer shall furnish to the health care service plan written verification as to whether the covered employee's employment was involuntarily terminated.

(3) A qualified beneficiary requesting premium assistance under Title III of Division B of the American Recovery and Reinvestment Act of 2009 (Public Law 111–5) may furnish to the health care service plan a written document or other information from the covered employee's former employer indicating that the covered employee's employment was involuntarily terminated. This document or information shall be deemed sufficient by the health care service plan to establish that the covered employee's employment was involuntarily terminated for purposes of Title III of Division B of the American Recovery and Reinvestment Act of 2009 (Public Law 111–5), unless the plan makes a reasonable and timely determination that the documents or information provided by the qualified beneficiary are legally insufficient to establish involuntary termination of employment.

(4) If a health care service plan requests verification pursuant to this subdivision and cannot verify involuntary termination of employment within 14 business days from the date the employer receives the verification request or from the date the plan receives documentation or other information from the qualified beneficiary pursuant to paragraph (3), the health care service plan shall either provide continuation coverage with the federal premium assistance to the qualified beneficiary or send the qualified beneficiary a denial letter which shall include notice of his or her right to appeal that determination pursuant to Title III of Division B of the American Recovery and Reinvestment Act of 2009 (Public Law 111–5).

(5) No person shall intentionally delay verification of involuntary termination of employment under this subdivision.

(m) The provision of information and forms related to the premium assistance available pursuant to Title III of Division B of the American Recovery and Reinvestment Act of 2009 (Public Law 111–5) to individuals by a health care service plan prior to the effective date of this subdivision shall not be considered a violation of this chapter provided that the plan complies with all of the requirements of this article. *(Added by Stats.1997, c. 665 (S.B.719), § 1. Amended by Stats.1998, c. 107 (A.B.112), § 9, eff. July 6, 1998; Stats.2009, c. 3 (A.B.23), § 4, eff. May 12, 2009.)*

[1] Internal Revenue Code sections are in Title 26 of the U.S.C.A.

§ 1366.26. Qualified beneficiary electing continuation coverage; payments to plan

A qualified beneficiary electing continuation coverage shall pay to the health care service plan, on or before the due date of each payment but not more frequently than on a monthly basis, not more than 110 percent of the applicable rate charged for a covered employee or, in the case of dependent coverage, not more than 110 percent of the applicable rate charged to a similarly situated individual under the group benefit plan being continued under the group contract. In the case of a qualified beneficiary who is determined to be disabled pursuant to Title II or Title XVI of the United States Social Security Act, the qualified beneficiary shall be required to pay to the health care service plan an amount no greater than 150 percent of the group rate after the first 18 months of continuation coverage provided pursuant to this section. In no case shall a health care service plan charge an employer an additional fee for administering Cal–COBRA other than those incorporated in the risk adjusted employee risk rate as provided for in subdivision (i) of Section 1357. *(Added by Stats.1997, c. 665 (S.B.719), § 1. Amended by Stats.1998, c. 107 (A.B.112), § 10, eff. July 6, 1998.)*

§ 1366.27. Termination of continuation coverage

(a) The continuation coverage provided pursuant to this article shall terminate at the first to occur of the following:

(1) In the case of a qualified beneficiary who is eligible for continuation coverage pursuant to paragraph (2) of subdivision (d) of Section 1366.21, the date 36 months after the date the qualified beneficiary's benefits under the contract would otherwise have terminated because of a qualifying event.

(2) The end of the period for which premium payments were made, if the qualified beneficiary ceases to make payments or fails to make timely payments of a required premium, in accordance with the terms and conditions of the plan contract. In the case of nonpayment of premiums, reinstatement shall be governed by the terms and conditions of the plan contract.

(3) In the case of a qualified beneficiary who is eligible for continuation coverage pursuant to paragraph (1), (3), (4), or (5) of subdivision (d) of Section 1366.21, the date 36 months after the date the qualified beneficiary's benefits under the contract would otherwise have terminated by reason of a qualifying event.

(4) The requirements of this article no longer apply to the qualified beneficiary pursuant to the provisions of Section 1366.22.

(5) In the case of a qualified beneficiary who is eligible for continuation coverage pursuant to paragraph (2) of subdivision (d) of Section 1366.21, and determined, under Title II or Title XVI of the Social Security Act, to be disabled at any time during the first 60 days of continuation coverage, and the spouse or dependent who has elected coverage pursuant to this article, the date 36

months after the date the qualified beneficiary's benefits under the contract would otherwise have terminated because of a qualifying event. The qualified beneficiary shall notify the plan, or the employer or administrator that contracts to perform administrative services, of the social security determination within 60 days of the date of the determination letter and prior to the end of the original 36–month continuation coverage period in order to be eligible for coverage pursuant to this subdivision. If the qualified beneficiary is no longer disabled under Title II or Title XVI of the Social Security Act, the benefits provided in this paragraph shall terminate on the later of the date provided by paragraph (1), or the month that begins more than 31 days after the date of the final determination under Title II or Title XVI of the United States Social Security Act that the qualified beneficiary is no longer disabled. A qualified beneficiary eligible for 36 months of continuation coverage as a result of a disability shall notify the plan, or the employer or administrator that contracts to perform the notice and administrative services, within 30 days of a determination that the qualified beneficiary is no longer disabled.

(6) In the case of a qualified beneficiary who is initially eligible for and elects continuation coverage pursuant to paragraph (2) of subdivision (d) of Section 1366.21, but who has another qualifying event, as described in paragraph (1), (3), (4), or (5) of subdivision (d) of Section 1366.21, within 36 months of the date of the first qualifying event, and the qualified beneficiary has notified the plan, or the employer or administrator under contract to provide administrative services, of the second qualifying event within 60 days of the date of the second qualifying event, the date 36 months after the date of the first qualifying event.

(7) The employer, or any successor employer or purchaser of the employer, ceases to provide any group benefit plan to his or her employees.

(8) The qualified beneficiary moves out of the plan's service area or the qualified beneficiary commits fraud or deception in the use of plan services.

(b) If the group contract between the plan and the employer is terminated prior to the date the qualified beneficiary's continuation coverage would terminate pursuant to this section, coverage under the prior plan shall terminate and the qualified beneficiary may elect continuation coverage under the subsequent group benefit plan, if any, pursuant to the requirements of subdivision (b) of Section 1366.23 and subdivision (c) of Section 1366.24.

(c) The amendments made to this section by Assembly Bill 1401 of the 2001–02 Regular Session [1] shall apply to individuals who begin receiving continuation coverage under this article on or after January 1, 2003. *(Added by Stats.1997, c. 665 (S.B.719), § 1. Amended by Stats.1998, c. 107 (A.B.112), § 11, eff. July 6, 1998; Stats.2002, c. 794 (A.B.1401), § 3.)*

[1] Stats.2002, c. 794 (A.B.1401), § 3.

§ 1366.28. Obligation to provide continuation coverage; exclusions

A health care service plan subject to this article shall not be obligated to provide continuation coverage to a qualified beneficiary pursuant to this article if an enrollee fails to make the notification required by Section 1366.24, or if the employer of the enrollee fails to comply with Section 1366.25. *(Added by Stats.1997, c. 665 (S.B.719), § 1.)*

§ 1366.29. Exhaustion of federal coverage; continuation up to 36 months

(a) A health care service plan shall offer an enrollee who has exhausted continuation coverage under COBRA the opportunity to continue coverage for up to 36 months from the date the enrollee's continuation coverage began, if the enrollee is entitled to less than 36 months of continuation coverage under COBRA. The health care service plan shall offer coverage pursuant to the terms of this article, including the rate limitations contained in Section 1366.26.

(b) Notification of the coverage available under this section shall be included in the notice of the pending termination of COBRA coverage that is required to be provided to COBRA beneficiaries and that is required to be provided under Section 1366.24.

(c) For purposes of this section, "COBRA" means Section 4980B of Title 26 of the United States Code, Sections 1161 et seq. of Title 29 of the United States Code, and Section 300bb of Title 42 of the United States Code.

(d) This section shall not apply to specialized health care service plans providing noncore coverage, as defined in subdivision (g) of Section 1366.21.

(e) This section shall become operative on September 1, 2003, and shall apply to individuals who begin receiving COBRA coverage on or after January 1, 2003. *(Added by Stats.2002, c. 794 (A.B.1401), § 4, operative Sept. 1, 2003.)*

ARTICLE 5. STANDARDS

Section
1367.46. Coverage for HIV testing.
1367.25. Prescription contraceptive method; contract coverage; religious employer exemption.
1367.26. List of contracting providers within enrollee's or prospective enrollee's general geographic area; contents; presentment and availability of information.
1374.58. Domestic partners; coverage.

§ 1367.46. Coverage for HIV testing

Every individual or group health care service plan contract that is issued, amended, or renewed on or after January 1, 2009, that covers hospital, medical, or surgery expenses shall provide coverage for human immunodeficiency virus (HIV) testing, regardless of whether the testing is related to a primary diagnosis. *(Added by Stats.2008, c. 631 (A.B.1894), § 1.)*

213

§ 1367.25. Prescription contraceptive method; contract coverage; religious employer exemption

(a) Every group health care service plan contract, except for a specialized health care service plan contract, that is issued, amended, renewed, or delivered on or after January 1, 2000, and every individual health care service plan contract that is amended, renewed, or delivered on or after January 1, 2000, except for a specialized health care service plan contract, shall provide coverage for the following, under general terms and conditions applicable to all benefits:

(1) A health care service plan contract that provides coverage for outpatient prescription drug benefits shall include coverage for a variety of federal Food and Drug Administration approved prescription contraceptive methods designated by the plan. In the event the patient's participating provider, acting within his or her scope of practice, determines that none of the methods designated by the plan is medically appropriate for the patient's medical or personal history, the plan shall also provide coverage for another federal Food and Drug Administration approved, medically appropriate prescription contraceptive method prescribed by the patient's provider.

(2) Outpatient prescription benefits for an enrollee shall be the same for an enrollee's covered spouse and covered nonspouse dependents.

(b) Notwithstanding any other provision of this section, a religious employer may request a health care service plan contract without coverage for federal Food and Drug Administration approved contraceptive methods that are contrary to the religious employer's religious tenets. If so requested, a health care service plan contract shall be provided without coverage for contraceptive methods.

(1) For purposes of this section, a "religious employer" is an entity for which each of the following is true:

(A) The inculcation of religious values is the purpose of the entity.

(B) The entity primarily employs persons who share the religious tenets of the entity.

(C) The entity serves primarily persons who share the religious tenets of the entity.

(D) The entity is a nonprofit organization as described in Section 6033(a)(2)(A)i or iii, of the Internal Revenue Code of 1986, as amended.

(2) Every religious employer that invokes the exemption provided under this section shall provide written notice to prospective enrollees prior to enrollment with the plan, listing the contraceptive health care services the employer refuses to cover for religious reasons.

(c) Nothing in this section shall be construed to exclude coverage for prescription contraceptive supplies ordered by a health care provider with prescriptive authority for reasons other than contraceptive purposes, such as decreasing the risk of ovarian cancer or eliminat-

ing symptoms of menopause, or for prescription contraception that is necessary to preserve the life or health of an enrollee.

(d) Nothing in this section shall be construed to deny or restrict in any way the department's authority to ensure plan compliance with this chapter when a plan provides coverage for prescription drugs.

(e) Nothing in this section shall be construed to require an individual or group health care service plan to cover experimental or investigational treatments. *(Added by Stats.1999, c. 532 (A.B.39), § 2. Amended by Stats.2000, c. 857 (A.B.2903), § 32; Stats.2002, c. 791 (S.B.842), § 4.)*

§ 1367.26. List of contracting providers within enrollee's or prospective enrollee's general geographic area; contents; presentment and availability of information

(a) A health care service plan shall provide, upon request, a list of the following contracting providers, within the enrollee's or prospective enrollee's general geographic area:

(1) Primary care providers.

(2) Medical groups.

(3) Independent practice associations.

(4) Hospitals.

(5) All other available contracting physicians, psychologists, acupuncturists, optometrists, podiatrists, chiropractors, licensed clinical social workers, marriage and family therapists, and nurse midwives to the extent their services may be accessed and are covered through the contract with the plan.

(b) This list shall indicate which providers have notified the plan that they have closed practices or are otherwise not accepting new patients at that time.

(c) The list shall indicate that it is subject to change without notice and shall provide a telephone number that enrollees can contact to obtain information regarding a particular provider. This information shall include whether or not that provider has indicated that he or she is accepting new patients.

(d) A health care service plan shall provide this information in written form to its enrollees or prospective enrollees upon request. A plan may, with the permission of the enrollee, satisfy the requirements of this section by directing the enrollee or prospective enrollee to the plan's provider listings on its website. Plans shall ensure that the information provided is updated at least quarterly. A plan may satisfy this update requirement by providing an insert or addendum to any existing provider listing. This requirement shall not mandate a complete republishing of a plan's provider directory.

(e) Each plan shall make information available, upon request, concerning a contracting provider's professional degree, board certifications and any recognized subspeciality[1] qualifications a specialist may have.

(f) Nothing in this section shall prohibit a plan from requiring its contracting providers, contracting provider groups, or contracting specialized health care plans to satisfy these requirements. If a plan delegates the responsibility of complying with this section to its contracting providers, contracting provider groups, or contracting specialized health care plans, the plan shall ensure that the requirements of this section are met.

(g) Every health care service plan shall allow enrollees to request the information required by this section through their toll-free telephone number or in writing. *(Added by Stats.2001, c. 817 (A.B.938), § 3, operative July 1, 2002.)*

[1] So in chaptered copy.

§ 1374.58. Domestic partners; coverage

(a) A group health care service plan that provides hospital, medical, or surgical expense benefits shall provide equal coverage to employers or guaranteed associations, as defined in Section 1357, for the registered domestic partner of an employee or subscriber to the same extent, and subject to the same terms and conditions, as provided to a spouse of the employee or subscriber, and shall inform employers and guaranteed associations of this coverage. A plan may not offer or provide coverage for a registered domestic partner that is not equal to the coverage provided to the spouse of an employee or subscriber.

(b) If an employer or guaranteed association has purchased coverage for spouses and registered domestic partners pursuant to subdivision (a), a health care service plan that provides hospital, medical, or surgical expense benefits for employees or subscribers and their spouses shall enroll, upon application by the employer or group administrator, a registered domestic partner of an employee or subscriber in accordance with the terms and conditions of the group contract that apply generally to all spouses under the plan, including coordination of benefits.

(c) For purposes of this section, the term "domestic partner" shall have the same meaning as that term is used in Section 297 of the Family Code.

(d)(1) A health care service plan may require that the employee or subscriber verify the status of the domestic partnership by providing to the plan a copy of a valid Declaration of Domestic Partnership filed with the Secretary of State pursuant to Section 298 of the Family Code or an equivalent document issued by a local agency of this state, another state, or a local agency of another state under which the partnership was created. The plan may also require that the employee or subscriber notify the plan upon the termination of the domestic partnership.

(2) Notwithstanding paragraph (1), a health care service plan may require the information described in that paragraph only if it also requests from the employee or subscriber whose spouse is provided coverage, verification of marital status and notification of dissolution of the marriage.

(e) Nothing in this section shall be construed to expand the requirements of Section 4980B of Title 26 of the United States Code, Section 1161, and following, of Title 29 of the United States Code, or Section 300bb-1, and following, of Title 42 of the United States Code, as added by the Consolidated Omnibus Budget Reconciliation Act of 1985 (Public Law 99–272), and as those provisions may be later amended.

(f) A plan subject to this section that is issued, amended, delivered, or renewed in this state on or after January 2, 2005, shall be deemed to provide coverage for registered domestic partners that is equal to the coverage provided to a spouse of an employee or subscriber. *(Added by Stats.2001, c. 893 (A.B.25), § 10. Amended by Stats.2004, c. 488 (A.B.2208), § 2.)*

Division 13
HOUSING

Part 1
EMPLOYEE HOUSING ACT
CHAPTER 1. GENERAL PROVISIONS AND DEFINITIONS

Section
17000. Short title.
17001. Compliance with building standards and regulations; local standards.
17002. Use of material, appliance, etc., not prescribed by this part; approval of alternate; ordinances.
17003. Commission.
17003.5. Reference to commission of housing and community development deemed to be to department of housing and community development; exercise of powers and duties.

Section
17004. Department.
17005. Employee; exclusions.
17005.5. Employee community housing.
17006. Resident-employment housing.
17007. Enforcement agency.
17008. Employee housing.
17009. Labor supply employee housing.
17009.5. Person.
17010. Temporary employee housing; seasonal employee housing; permanent employee housing; permanent single-family employee housing.
17011. Sleeping place.

§ 17000. Short title

This part shall be known as the Employee Housing Act. *(Added by Stats.1979, c. 62, p. 146, § 1, eff. May 14, 1979.)*

§ 17001. Compliance with building standards and regulations; local standards

Buildings used for human habitation, and buildings accessory thereto, within employee housing shall comply with the building standards published in the State Building Standards Code relating to employee housing and with the other regulations adopted pursuant to this part, unless a local ordinance prescribing minimum standards adopted in accordance with Sections 17958.5 and 17958.7 which is equal to such regulations is applicable. Notwithstanding the provisions of Section 17050, if such a local ordinance is applicable to buildings used for human habitation, and buildings accessory thereto, within employee housing, these buildings shall comply with the construction and erection provisions of the ordinance. *(Added by Stats.1979, c. 62, p. 146, § 1, eff. May 14, 1979. Amended by Stats.1979, c. 1152, p. 4249, § 45; Stats.1992, c. 1298 (A.B.3526), § 4.)*

§ 17002. Use of material, appliance, etc., not prescribed by this part; approval of alternate; ordinances

The provisions of this part are not intended to prevent the use of any material, appliance, installation, device, arrangement, or method of construction not specifically prescribed by this part if such alternate has been approved by the Department of Housing and Community Development.

The Department of Housing and Community Development may approve any such alternate if it finds that the proposed design is satisfactory and that the material, appliance, installation, device, arrangement, or method of construction offered is, for the purpose intended, at least the equivalent of that prescribed in this part in quality, strength, effectiveness, fire resistance, durability and safety, for the protection of life and health.

This section shall not apply to a local ordinance which is applicable pursuant to Section 17001. *(Added by Stats.1979, c. 62, p. 146, § 1, eff. May 14, 1979.)*

§ 17003. Commission

"Commission," as used in this part, means the Commission of Housing and Community Development. *(Added by Stats.1979, c. 62, p. 146, § 1, eff. May 14, 1979.)*

§ 17003.5. Reference to commission of housing and community development deemed to be to department of housing and community development; exercise of powers and duties

Any reference in this division to the Commission of Housing and Community Development shall be deemed to be to the Department of Housing and Community Development and the department may exercise all the powers and shall perform all the duties of the commission. *(Added by Stats.1981, c. 996, p. 3840, § 1.)*

216

§ 17004. Department

"Department," as used in this part, means the Department of Housing and Community Development. *(Added by Stats.1979, c. 62, p. 146, § 1, eff. May 14, 1979.)*

§ 17005. Employee; exclusions

"Employee," as used in this part, does not include any of the following:

(a) A person engaged in household domestic service.

(b) A person employed under circumstances in which his wages are incidental to professional training and where the employer is exempt from taxation under subdivision (b) of Section 4 of Article XIII of the California Constitution.

(c) A person employed incidental to training for, or in furtherance of, a religious vocation and where the employer is exempt from taxation under subdivision (f) of Section 3 of Article XIII of the California Constitution. *(Added by Stats.1979, c. 62, p. 146, § 1, eff. May 14, 1979.)*

§ 17005.5. Employee community housing

(a) "Employee community housing" means a community of single family detached dwellings which meet all of the following requirements:

(1) Each dwelling has a minimum of four rooms, including a separate kitchen and a separate bathroom.

(2) Each dwelling is owned or operated by an employer, and maintained by such employer in compliance with the provisions of the State Housing Law,[1] and the regulations adopted pursuant thereto, which materially affect health and safety.

(3) Each dwelling is inhabited by not more than one family, which includes at least one permanent year-round employee of the employer who owns or operates the dwelling.

(4) Each dwelling has direct access to a publicly owned and maintained road.

(5) Each dwelling is located within a community, as defined in subdivision (b).

(b) "Community" means not less than 200 single family detached dwellings meeting the requirements of subdivision (a), which are adjacent or in close proximity to each other, and which have maintenance services available to the residents of the dwelling units provided by persons employed by the employer for the express purpose of providing such services. *(Added by Stats.1979, c. 1031, p. 3555, § 2.)*

[1] Health and Safety Code § 17910 et seq.

§ 17006. Resident-employment housing

"Resident-employment housing," as used in this part, means apartment houses, hotels, motels, or dwellings, where living quarters are provided for five or more employees employed in the management, maintenance, or operation of an apartment house, hotel, motel, or dwellings. *(Added by Stats.1979, c. 62, p. 146, § 1, eff.*

May 14, 1979. Amended by Stats.1992, c. 1298 (A.B. 3526), § 5.)

§ 17007. Enforcement agency

"Enforcement agency," as used in this part, means the Department of Housing and Community Development, or any city, county, or city and county which has assumed responsibility for the enforcement of this part, pursuant to Section 17050. (Added by Stats.1979, c. 62, p. 146, § 1, eff. May 14, 1979.)

§ 17008. Employee housing

(a) "Employee housing," as used in this part, means any portion of any housing accommodation, or property upon which a housing accommodation is located, if all of the following factors exist:

(1) The accommodations consist of any living quarters, dwelling, boardinghouse, tent, bunkhouse, maintenance-of-way car, mobilehome, manufactured home, recreational vehicle, travel trailer, or other housing accommodations, maintained in one or more buildings or one or more sites, and the premises upon which they are situated or the area set aside and provided for parking of mobilehomes or camping of five or more employees by the employer.

(2) The accommodations are maintained in connection with any work or place where work is being performed, whether or not rent is involved.

(b)(1) "Employee housing," as used in this part, also includes any portion of any housing accommodation or property upon which housing accommodations are located, if all of the following factors exist:

(A) The housing accommodations or property are located in any rural area, as defined by Section 50101.

(B) The housing accommodations or property are not maintained in connection with any work or workplace.

(C) The housing accommodations or property are provided by someone other than an agricultural employer, as defined in Section 1140.4 of the Labor Code.

(D) The housing accommodations or property are used by five or more agricultural employees of any agricultural employer or employers for any of the following:

(i) Temporary or seasonal residency.

(ii) Permanent residency, if the housing accommodation is a mobilehome, manufactured home, travel trailer, or recreational vehicle.

(iii) Permanent residency, if the housing accommodation is subject to the State Housing Law and is more than 30 years old and at least 51 percent of the structures in the housing accommodation, or 51 percent of the accommodation if not separated into units, are occupied by agricultural employees.

(E) "Employee housing" does not include a hotel, motel, inn, tourist hotel, multifamily dwelling, or single-family house if all of the following factors exist:

(i) The housing is offered and rented to nonagricultural employees on the same terms that it is offered and rented to agricultural employees.

(ii) None of the occupants of the housing are employed by the owner or property manager of the housing or any party with an interest in the housing.

(iii) None of the occupants of the housing have rent deducted from their wages.

(iv) The owner or property manager of the housing is not an agricultural employer as defined in Section 1140.4 of the Labor Code, or an agent, as it relates to the housing in question, of an agricultural employer.

(v) Negotiation of the terms of occupancy of the housing is conducted between each occupant and the owner of the housing or between each occupant and a manager of the property who is employed by the owner of the housing.

(vi) The occupants are not required to live in the housing as a condition of employment or of securing employment and the occupants are not referred to live in the housing by the employer of the occupants, the agent of the employer of the occupants, or an agricultural employer as defined in Section 1140.4 of the Labor Code.

(vii) The housing accommodation was not at any time prior to January 1, 1984, employee housing as defined in subdivision (a).

(2) "Employee housing," as defined by this subdivision, does not include a hotel, motel, inn, tourist hotel, or permanent housing as defined by subdivision (d) of Section 17010, which has not been maintained, prior to January 1, 1984, or is not maintained on or after that date, as employee housing, as defined in subdivision (a).

(3) If at any time prior to January 1, 1984, a housing accommodation was employee housing, as defined in subdivision (a), and on or after January 1, 1984, was employee housing, as defined in this subdivision, the owner and operator shall comply with all requirements of this part. The owner and operator of any other housing accommodation which is employee housing pursuant to this subdivision shall be subject to the licensing and inspection provisions of this part and shall comply with all other provisions of this part, except that if any portion of the housing accommodation is held out for rent or lease to the general public, the construction and physical maintenance standards of the housing accommodation shall be consistent with the applicable provisions of the State Housing Law, Part 1.5 (commencing with Section 17910), the Mobilehome-Manufactured Homes Act, Part 2 (commencing with Section 18000); or the Mobilehome Parks Act, Part 2.1 (commencing with Section 18200). The owner or operator of the employee housing shall designate all units or spaces which are employee housing, as defined in this subdivision, for the purpose of inspection and licensing by the enforcement agency, subject to confirmation by the enforcement agency, based on all relevant evidence.

(c) "Employee housing" does not include employee community housing, as defined by Section 17005.5, which has been granted an exemption pursuant to Section 17031.3; housing, and the premises upon which it is situated, owned by a public entity; or privately owned housing, including ownership by a nonprofit entity, and the premises upon which it is situated, financed with public funds equaling 50 percent or more of the original development or purchase cost.

(d) "Employee housing" means the same as "labor camp," as that term may be used in this or other codes and, notwithstanding any local ordinance to the contrary in a general law or charter city, county, or city and county, shall be deemed a residential use if it exists in structures that are single-family houses or apartment houses as those terms are used in the State Housing Law (Part 1.5 (commencing with Section 17910)). *(Added by Stats. 1979, c. 62, p. 146, § 1, eff. May 14, 1979. Amended by Stats.1979, c. 1031, p. 3555, § 1; Stats.1983, c. 777, § 1; Stats.1985, c. 900, § 2; Stats.1992, c. 1298 (A.B.3526), § 6; Stats.1995, c. 561 (S.B.851), § 1.)*

§ 17009. Labor supply employee housing

"Labor supply employee housing," as used in this part, means any place, area, or piece of land where housing is provided for five or more employees or prospective employees of another by any individual, firm, partnership, association, or corporation that, for a fee or in-kind payment, employs persons to render personal services for, or under the direction of, a third person, or that recruits, solicits, supplies, or hires persons on behalf of an employer, and that, for a fee or in-kind payment, provides in connection therewith one or more of the following services:

(a) Furnishes board, lodging, or transportation for such employees or prospective employees.

(b) Supervises, times, checks, counts, weighs, or otherwise directs or measures the work of such employees.

(c) Disburses wage payments to such employees. *(Added by Stats.1979, c. 62, p. 146, § 1, eff. May 14, 1979. Amended by Stats.1992, c. 1298 (A.B.3526), § 7.)*

§ 17009.5. Person

(a) "Person," as used in this part, includes any natural person, firm, association, organization, partnership, business trust, company, joint stock company, corporation, limited liability company, joint venture, or other organizations of persons.

(b) "Person," as used in this part, may be used interchangeably with "tenant" or "employee," and those terms are used interchangeably when the context does not imply an employer or an owner of employee housing. *(Added by Stats.1992, c. 1298 (A.B.3526), § 8. Amended by Stats.1994, c. 1010 (S.B.2053), § 160.)*

§ 17010. Temporary employee housing; seasonal employee housing; permanent employee housing; permanent single-family employee housing

(a) "Temporary employee housing," as used in this part, means a labor camp which is not operated on the same site annually and which is established for one operation and is then removed.

(b) "Seasonal employee housing," as used in this part, means any camp which is operated annually on the same site and which is occupied for not more than 180 days in any calendar year.

(c) "Permanent employee housing," as used in this part, means any labor camp which is not temporary or seasonal.

(d) "Permanent single-family employee housing," as used in this part, means single-family detached dwellings, mobilehomes, as defined in Section 18008, manufactured homes, as defined in Section 18007, or factory-built housing, as defined in Section 19971, constructed and maintained in accordance with applicable state or federal laws, including required permits and inspections. Each dwelling shall be inhabited by only one family, which includes at least one permanent year-round employee. "Permanent single-family employee housing" does not include housing accommodations or property, as defined in subparagraph (D) of paragraph (1) of subdivision (b) of Section 17008. *(Added by Stats.1979, c. 62, p. 146, § 1, eff. May 14, 1979. Amended by Stats.1979, c. 385, p. 1449, § 1; Stats.1985, c. 674, § 1.3; Stats.1992, c. 1298 (A.B. 3526), § 9.)*

§ 17011. Sleeping place

"Sleeping place," as used in this part, means a dwelling, bunkhouse, tent, mobilehome, or other structure or shelter in which employees are housed in any employee housing. *(Added by Stats.1979, c. 62, p. 146, § 1, eff. May 14, 1979. Amended by Stats.1992, c. 1298 (A.B.3526), § 10.)*

CHAPTER 2. APPLICATION AND SCOPE

Section

17020.   Supremacy over local ordinances or regulations; continuation of existing rules and regulations; duration of building standards.

17021.   Reservation to local jurisdiction for local use zones, fire zones, property lines, water supply and sewage disposal; exception for construction or improvement to agricultural employee housing; compliance with California Environmental Quality Act; recovery of costs incurred for review of application or permit denial.

17021.5. Single-family structure with residential land use designation; treatment of employee housing; definition.

17021.6. Agricultural land use designation for employee housing; exemption from certain fees and taxes; definition; failure to maintain permit.

Section
17021.7.   Mobilehomes and recreational vehicles used to house agricultural employees; maintenance requirement.
17022.   Occupational safety and health standards; enforcement.
17022.5.   Model or prototype plans for employee housing.
17023.   Application of rules and regulations; duration of building standards.
17024.   Housing for faculty or employees of schools, colleges, or universities.

§ 17020. Supremacy over local ordinances or regulations; continuation of existing rules and regulations; duration of building standards

(a) Except as otherwise provided in this part, the provisions of this part, building standards published in the State Building Standards Code relating to employee housing, and the other rules and regulations promulgated pursuant to the provisions of this part which relate to labor camps apply in all parts of the state and supersede any ordinance or regulations enacted by any city, county, or city and county applicable to labor camps. Rules and regulations adopted or continued in effect prior to January 1, 1980, by former Chapter 4 (commencing with Section 2610) of Part 9 of Division 2 of the Labor Code are hereby continued in effect as rules and regulations under this part until amended or repealed by the Department of Housing and Community Development.

(b) Building standards, as defined by Section 18909, shall remain in effect only until January 1, 1985, or until adopted, amended, or superseded by provisions published in the State Building Standards Code relating to employee housing pursuant to Chapter 4 (commencing with Section 18935) of Part 2.5, whichever occurs sooner. *(Added by Stats.1979, c. 62, p. 146, § 1, eff. May 14, 1979. Amended by Stats.1979, c. 1152, p. 4249, § 46; Stats.1983, c. 101, § 117; Stats.1992, c. 1298 (A.B.3526), § 12.)*

§ 17021. Reservation to local jurisdiction for local use zones, fire zones, property lines, water supply and sewage disposal; exception for construction or improvement to agricultural employee housing; compliance with California Environmental Quality Act; recovery of costs incurred for review of application or permit denial

(a) Except as provided in Sections 17021.5 and 17021.6, local use zone requirements, local fire zones, property line, source of water supply and method of sewage disposal requirements are hereby specifically and entirely reserved to the local jurisdictions.

(b) Notwithstanding any other provision of law, with respect to a building permit, grading permit, or other approval from a city or county building department for the rehabilitation of real property improvements that are or will be employee housing for agricultural employees, or from a city or county health department for the operation, construction, or repair of a water system or waste disposal system servicing employee housing for agricultural employees, all of the following processing requirements shall apply:

(1) The local building or health department shall have up to 60 calendar days to approve or deny a complete application or permit request accompanied by applicable fees, or a shorter time period if required by the Permit Streamlining Act (Chapter 4.5 (commencing with Section 65920) of Division 1 of Title 7 of the Government Code). An application or permit request may be denied on procedural grounds only if the denial occurs within 30 calendar days and the denial includes an itemization of the procedural defects. An application or permit request may be denied on substantive grounds if the denial includes an itemization of all substantive defects.

(2) If the application or permit request is not approved or denied by the local building or health department within the period prescribed by paragraph (1), then the Department of Housing and Community Development may approve the application or permit request if it determines that the plans are consistent with all applicable building codes and health and safety requirements. At that time, the applicant may initiate any work consistent with the application or permit approved pursuant to this subdivision. Upon completion of the work, any other state or local agency shall accept the improvements as if they had been approved by the local building or health department. However, if that other local agency identifies any defects that would have resulted in that agency's disapproval of the improvements or plans thereto, those defects may be identified by the agency and shall be corrected by the applicant. The local building or health department shall inspect the plans and improvements prior to and during rehabilitation and issue a certificate of completion if the work is consistent with the plans and all applicable building codes and health and safety requirements.

(c) Nothing in this section shall be construed to exempt an application or permit request from complying with the California Environmental Quality Act (Division 13 (commencing with Section 21000) of the Public Resources Code).

(d) For purposes of this section, "agricultural employee" has the same meaning specified in subdivision (b) of Section 1140.4 of the Labor Code.

(e) The Department of Housing and Community Development may recover from a local building or health department costs incurred to review an application or permit request in compliance with paragraph (2) of subdivision (b). The amount recoverable may not exceed the applicable plan check fee published by the International Conference of Building Officials. *(Added by Stats.1979, c. 62, p. 146, § 1, eff. May 14, 1979. Amended by Stats.1992, c. 1298 (A.B.3526), § 13; Stats.2000, c. 702 (S.B.1545), § 1; Stats.2001, c. 118 (S.B.742), § 15, eff. July 30, 2001.)*

§ 17021.5. Single-family structure with residential land use designation; treatment of employee housing; definition

(a) Any employee housing which has qualified, or is intended to qualify, for a permit to operate pursuant to this part may invoke the provisions of this section.

(b) Any employee housing providing accommodations for six or fewer employees shall be deemed a single-family structure with a residential land use designation for the purposes of this section. For the purpose of all local ordinances, employee housing shall not be included within the definition of a boarding house, rooming house, hotel, dormitory, or other similar term that implies that the employee housing is a business run for profit or differs in any other way from a family dwelling. No conditional use permit, zoning variance, or other zoning clearance shall be required of employee housing that serves six or fewer employees that is not required of a family dwelling of the same type in the same zone. Use of a family dwelling for purposes of employee housing serving six or fewer persons shall not constitute a change of occupancy for purposes of Part 1.5 (commencing with Section 17910) or local building codes.

(c) Except as otherwise provided in this part, employee housing that serves six or fewer employees shall not be subject to any business taxes, local registration fees, use permit fees, or other fees to which other family dwellings of the same type in the same zone are not likewise subject. Nothing in this subdivision shall be construed to forbid the imposition of local property taxes, fees for water services and garbage collection, fees for normal inspections, local bond assessments, and other fees, charges, and assessments to which other family dwellings of the same type in the same zone are likewise subject. Neither the State Fire Marshal nor any local public entity shall charge any fee to the owner, operator or any resident for enforcing fire inspection regulations pursuant to state law or regulation or local ordinance, with respect to employee housing which serves six or fewer persons.

(d) For the purposes of any contract, deed, or covenant for the transfer of real property, employee housing which serves six or fewer employees shall be considered a residential use of property and a use of property by a single household, notwithstanding any disclaimers to the contrary. For purposes of this section, "employee housing" includes employee housing defined in subdivision (b) of Section 17008, even if the housing accommodations or property are not located in a rural area, as defined by Section 50101.

(e) The Legislature hereby declares that it is the policy of this state that each county and city shall permit and encourage the development and use of sufficient numbers and types of employee housing facilities as are commensurate with local needs. This section shall apply equally to any charter city, general law city, county, city and county, district and any other local public entity. (Added by Stats.1992, c. 1298 (A.B.3526), § 14. Amended by Stats.1993, c. 952 (A.B.2011), § 1.)

220

§ 17021.6. Agricultural land use designation for employee housing; exemption from certain fees and taxes; definition; failure to maintain permit

(a) The owner of any employee housing who has qualified or intends to qualify for a permit to operate pursuant to this part may invoke this section.

(b) Any employee housing consisting of no more than 36 beds in a group quarters or 12 units or spaces designed for use by a single family or household shall be deemed an agricultural land use designation for the purposes of this section. For the purpose of all local ordinances, employee housing shall not be deemed a use that implies that the employee housing is an activity that differs in any other way from an agricultural use. No conditional use permit, zoning variance, or other zoning clearance shall be required of this employee housing that is not required of any other agricultural activity in the same zone. The permitted occupancy in employee housing in an agricultural zone shall include agricultural employees who do not work on the property where the employee housing is located.

(c) Except as otherwise provided in this part, employee housing consisting of no more than 36 beds in a group quarters or 12 units or spaces designed for use by a single family or household shall not be subject to any business taxes, local registration fees, use permit fees, or other fees to which other agricultural activities in the same zone are not likewise subject. This subdivision does not forbid the imposition of local property taxes, fees for water services and garbage collection, fees for normal inspections, local bond assessments, and other fees, charges, and assessments to which other agricultural activities in the same zone are likewise subject. Neither the State Fire Marshal nor any local public entity shall charge any fee to the owner, operator, or any resident for enforcing fire inspection regulation pursuant to state law or regulations or local ordinance, with respect to employee housing consisting of no more than 36 beds in a group quarters or 12 units or spaces designed for use by a single family or household.

(d) For the purposes of any contract, deed, or covenant for the transfer of real property, employee housing consisting of no more than 36 beds in a group quarters or 12 units or spaces designed for use by a single family or household shall be considered an agricultural use of property, notwithstanding any disclaimers to the contrary. For purposes of this section, "employee housing" includes employee housing defined in subdivision (b) of Section 17008, even if the housing accommodations or property are not located in a rural area, as defined by Section 50101.

(e) The Legislature hereby declares that it is the policy of this state that each county and city shall permit and encourage the development and use of sufficient numbers and types of employee housing facilities as are commensurate with local need. This section shall apply equally to any charter city, general law city, county, city and county, district, and any other local public entity.

(f) If any owner who invokes the provisions of this section fails to maintain a permit to operate pursuant to this part throughout the first 10 consecutive years following the issuance of the original certificate of occupancy, both of the following shall occur:

(1) The enforcement agency shall notify the appropriate local government entity.

(2) The public agency that has waived any taxes, fees, assessments, or charges for employee housing pursuant to this section may recover the amount of those taxes, fees, assessments, or charges from the landowner, less 10 percent of that amount for each year that a valid permit has been maintained.

(g) Subdivision (f) shall not apply to an owner of any prospective, planned, or unfinished employee housing facility who has applied to the appropriate state and local public entities for a permit to construct or operate pursuant to this part prior to January 1, 1996. *(Added by Stats.1992, c. 1298 (A.B.3526), § 15. Amended by Stats. 1993, c. 952 (A.B.2011), § 2; Stats.1995, c. 376 (S.B.305), § 1; Stats.2004, c. 818 (S.B.1777), § 2; Stats.2006, c. 538 (S.B.1852), § 373; Stats.2006, c. 520 (S.B.1802), § 1.)*

§ 17021.7. Mobilehomes and recreational vehicles used to house agricultural employees; maintenance requirement

Notwithstanding subdivision (b) of Section 18214, subdivision (b) of Section 18862.39, and subdivision (b) of Section 18862.47, mobilehomes and recreational vehicles used to house agricultural employees shall be maintained in conformity with the applicable requirements of the Mobilehome Parks Act (Part 2.1 (commencing with Section 18200)). *(Added by Stats.1994, c. 896 (A.B.3735), § 1. Amended by Stats.2003, c. 814 (S.B.306), § 1.)*

§ 17022. Occupational safety and health standards; enforcement

Enforcement of occupational safety and health standards established pursuant to Chapter 6 (commencing with Section 140) of Division 1 of the Labor Code is hereby specifically and entirely reserved to the Division of Industrial Safety. *(Added by Stats.1979, c. 62, p. 146, § 1, eff. May 14, 1979.)*

§ 17022.5. Model or prototype plans for employee housing

The department shall adopt, and make available to the public, model or prototype plans for several types of employee housing, including, but not limited to, barracks, seasonal housing, family housing, and recreational vehicle parks. Any person intending to construct employee housing may adopt one or more of these models as the plans for the proposed housing. *(Added by Stats.1986, c. 1495, § 2.)*

§ 17023. Application of rules and regulations; duration of building standards

(a) Rules and regulations adopted or continued in effect pursuant to the provisions of this part relating to the erection or construction of buildings or structures within employee housing shall not apply to existing buildings or structures or to buildings and structures as to which construction is commenced or approved prior to the effective date of the rules and regulations, except by act of the Legislature, but regulations relating to use, maintenance, and occupancy shall apply to all employee housing approved for construction and operation before or after the effective date of these rules and regulations.

(b) Building standards, as defined in Section 18909, shall remain in effect only until January 1, 1985, or until adopted, amended, or superseded by provisions published in the State Building Standards Code pursuant to Chapter 4 (commencing with Section 18935) of Part 2.5, whichever occurs sooner. *(Added by Stats.1979, c. 62, p. 146, § 1, eff. May 14, 1979. Amended by Stats.1979, c. 1152, p. 4249, § 48; Stats.1992, c. 1298 (A.B.3526), § 16.)*

§ 17024. Housing for faculty or employees of schools, colleges, or universities

This part does not apply to resident-employment housing provided for faculty or employees of any public or privately operated school, college, or university. This part does not apply to any employee housing owned, operated, and maintained by any of the following:

(a) The federal government.

(b) The state.

(c) Any agency or political subdivision of the state.

(d) Any city, county, or city and county. *(Added by Stats.1979, c. 62, p. 146, § 1, eff. May 14, 1979. Amended by Stats.1984, c. 1342, § 4, eff. Sept. 26, 1984, operative Jan. 1, 1985; Stats.1992, c. 1298 (A.B.3526), § 17.)*

CHAPTER 3. PERMITS AND FEES

Section
17030. Permit required; exemptions; enforcement for railroad corporations.
17030.5. Permanent single-family housing; duration of permit; findings.
17031. Permanent housing; exemption from annual permit requirement; procedure; conditions; findings; revocation.
17031.3. Permit for employee community housing; exemptions.
17031.4. Local enforcement agency; information to department.
17031.5. Employee housing; termination or modification of tenancy; tenants' rights.
17031.6. Eviction proceedings; defenses; payment of reasonable monthly rental value to court in cases of delay or continuance.
17031.7. Retaliatory employment action.
17031.8. Local enforcement agencies; submission of information.

Section

17032.   Applications; time; contents; amended permits.
17033.   Railroad corporations; permits to operate employee housing.
17034.   Violations.
17035.   Roster.
17036.   Regulations; fees.
17037.   Compliance with requirements; failure to obtain permit; penalty fees.
17037.5. Certificate of non-operation; submittal to enforcement agency; requirements.
17038.   Compliance; appointment of responsible person; emergency telephone number.
17039.   Compliance; maintenance and sanitation; application of violation provisions.

§ 17030. Permit required; exemptions; enforcement for railroad corporations

(a) Every person operating employee housing shall obtain a permit to operate that employee housing from the enforcement agency, unless otherwise exempted by this part. It shall be unlawful for any person to operate employee housing without a valid permit to operate issued by the enforcement agency, as required by this part. Permits to operate shall be issued annually by the enforcement agency, except as provided in this section and Section 17030.5.

(b) Employee housing on a dairy farm which meets the requirements of Section 32505 of the Food and Agricultural Code, consisting only of permanent single-family employee housing, may be exempted from the requirement of obtaining a permit to operate employee housing, as provided in Section 17031. This housing shall meet the requirements of the State Housing Law [1] before an exemption is granted.

(c) A permit to operate shall be valid from the date of issuance through December 31 of the year of issuance, or December 31 of the year designated by the enforcement agency for permanent single-family employee housing. Permits to operate employee housing may prescribe conditions on the use or occupancy of the employee housing.

(d) The Department of Housing and Community Development shall be the enforcement agency for any employee housing owned or operated by a railroad corporation. *(Added by Stats.1979, c. 62, p. 146, § 1, eff. May 14, 1979. Amended by Stats.1979, c. 385, p. 1449, § 2; Stats.1980, c. 45, p. 119, § 1, eff. March 20, 1980; Stats.1992, c. 1298 (A.B.3526), § 18.)*

[1] Health and Safety Code § 17910 et seq.

§ 17030.5. Permanent single-family housing; duration of permit; findings

(a) A permit to operate employee housing consisting only of permanent single-family housing may, when approved by the enforcement agency, be issued for a longer period of time not to exceed five years.

(b) No permit to operate employee housing shall be issued for a period of time longer than one year during the first year of operation of the employee housing, or if within the previous two years the employee housing has been found to be in violation of this part or the regulations adopted pursuant thereto. Whenever the enforcement agency issues a permit for a period of time longer than one year, it shall make written findings indicating the reasons for issuing such a permit.

(c) The findings of the enforcement agency pursuant to subdivision (b) shall include, but not be limited to, the following information:

(1) The year the dwellings in the employee housing were constructed.

(2) The number of years the employee housing has been operated with a valid permit to operate.

(3) The number and character of any complaints received during the time the employee housing has been operating either with or without a permit.

(4) Any violations cited in the last inspection of the employee housing. *(Added by Stats.1980, c. 45, p. 119, § 2, eff. March 20, 1980. Amended by Stats.1992, c. 1298 (A.B.3526), § 19.)*

§ 17031. Permanent housing; exemption from annual permit requirement; procedure; conditions; findings; revocation

(a)(1) The operator of employee housing on a dairy farm that meets the requirements of Section 32505 of the Food and Agricultural Code, consisting only of permanent single-family employee housing, may request an exemption from the requirement of obtaining an annual permit to operate. The employee housing camp operator shall notify each tenant of the permanent single-family employee housing in writing that such an exemption is being requested. The request for exemption shall be made in writing to the enforcement agency.

(2) An exemption shall be granted to permanent single-family employee housing unless the housing is in violation of the State Housing Law [1], building standards published in the California Building Standards Code [2] relating to employee housing, or the other regulations adopted pursuant to the State Housing Law [1] in a manner that materially affects the health and safety of the occupants, or in the case of a mobilehome or manufactured home, is in violation of the National Manufactured Housing Construction and Safety Standards Act of 1974 (42 U.S.C. Secs. 5401, et seq.) or regulations of the department pursuant to Section 18028 in a manner that materially affects the health and safety of the occupants, or has been found in violation of this chapter within the previous two years.

(b) Whenever the enforcement agency issues an exemption from the requirement of obtaining a permit to operate, it shall make written findings indicating the reasons for issuing the exemption. Exemptions shall be reviewed annually by the enforcement agency.

The findings of the enforcement agency shall include, but not be limited to, all of the following information:

(1) The year the dwellings in the employee housing were constructed.

(2) The number of years the employee housing has been operated with a valid permit to operate.

(3) The number and character of any complaints received during the time the employee housing has been operating either with or without a permit.

(4) Any violations cited in the last inspection of the employee housing.

(c) Failure to maintain any permanent housing in accordance with the State Housing Law, or, in the case of mobilehomes or manufactured homes, failure to maintain these mobilehomes or manufactured homes in accordance with the provisions of Part 2.1 (commencing with Section 18200) of Division 13, and the regulations adopted pursuant thereto, in a manner which materially affects the health and safety of the occupants, shall be considered cause for revocation of an exemption. *(Added by Stats.1979, c. 62, p. 146, § 1, eff. May 14, 1979. Amended by Stats.1979, c. 385, p. 1449, § 3; Stats.1979, c. 1152, p. 4250, § 49; Stats.1983, c. 101, § 118; Stats.1992, c. 1298 (A.B.3526), § 20; Stats.2000, c. 471 (A.B.2008), § 3.)*

[1] Health and Safety Code § 17910 et seq.

[2] Health and Safety Code § 18935 et seq.

§ 17031.3. Permit for employee community housing; exemptions

(a) Every person operating or owning employee community housing shall obtain a permit to operate such housing as a labor camp pursuant to this part unless an exemption is granted by the enforcement agency pursuant to this section. A request for an exemption for each community shall be made in writing to the enforcement agency. The person requesting the exemption shall give written notice to each employee/tenant of the employee community housing that an exemption is being requested. The notice shall state the address and telephone number of the enforcement agency, and shall state that any employee/tenant may inform the enforcement agency of violations of health and safety standards within his or her dwelling unit.

(b) The enforcement agency, after a review of all relevant facts, shall grant an exemption to the owner or operator of the employee community housing unless it finds any of the following:

(1) The housing is in violation of provisions of the State Housing Law [1] or the regulations adopted pursuant thereto in a manner which materially affects the health and safety of the residents of the housing.

(2) The housing, within the previous two years, has been found in violation of the provisions of this part or the regulations adopted pursuant thereto in a manner which materially affects the health and safety of the residents of the housing.

(3) The housing does not meet the requirements of employee community housing as defined by Section 17005.5.

(c) An exemption granted for employee community housing in one community shall not apply to employee community housing in other communities operated or owned by the same person.

(d) Employee community housing granted an exemption pursuant to this section, during the period of such exemption, shall be subject to the provisions of the State Housing Law. During this period, any notice of violation of such law and verification of corrective action shall be forwarded to the department. Not less than once every 10 years after an exemption is granted pursuant to this part, every person operating or owning employee community housing shall give written notice to each employee/tenant of the employee community housing which shall state the address and telephone number of the enforcement agency, and shall state that any employee/tenant may inform the enforcement agency of violations of health and safety standards within his or her dwelling unit.

(e) The exemption granted pursuant to this section shall be rescinded by the enforcement agency if the employee community housing is not operated or maintained in substantial compliance with Section 17005.5. *(Added by Stats.1979, c. 1031, p. 3556, § 3.)*

[1] Health and Safety Code § 17910 et seq.

§ 17031.4. Local enforcement agency; information to department

When the enforcement agency is a local agency, upon granting an exemption pursuant to Section 17031.3, the enforcement agency shall submit the following information to the department:

(a) The year the housing was constructed.

(b) The number of years, if any, the housing has been operated as employee housing with a valid permit to operate.

(c) The number and character of any complaints received during the time the housing has been operated as employee housing.

(d) Any violations of the provisions of this part and the State Housing Law [1] which materially affect health and safety cited in the last inspection of the housing.

(e) That the employee community housing has been exempted pursuant to Section 17031.3, and conforms with the requirements of Section 17005.5. *(Added by Stats. 1979, c. 1031, p. 3556, § 4. Amended by Stats.1992, c. 1298 (A.B.3526), § 21.)*

[1] Health and Safety Code § 17910 et seq.

§ 17031.5. Employee housing; termination or modification of tenancy; tenants' rights

(a) No person operating employee housing shall terminate or modify a tenancy by increasing rent, decreasing services, threatening to bring or bringing an action to

223

evict, refusing to renew a tenancy, or in any other way intimidating, threatening, restraining, coercing, blacklisting, or discharging an employee or tenant because of the tenant's exercise of any of the following acts:

(1) Complaining in good faith, orally or in writing, to the operator, landlord, or employer about tenantability or about any right provided by this part.

(2) Exercising any legal right with respect to the housing provided by this part.

(3) Complaining in good faith, orally or in writing, to any applicable enforcement agency about tenantability or about any right provided by this part.

(4) Bringing an action to enforce any rights provided for by this part or Chapter 2 (commencing with Section 1940) of Title 5 of Part 4 of Division 3 of the Civil Code.

(5) Bringing an action under Section 1942.5 of the Civil Code.

(b) The tenant shall have a defense of retaliation in any action for possession if the employer or landlord acted in violation of this section. If the employer or landlord acts to discharge an employee or tenant or to modify or terminate a tenancy within six months after the employee or tenant has exercised any of the acts enumerated in subdivision (a), there is a rebuttable presumption affecting the burden of proof that the employer's or landlord's action was retaliatory.

(c) No tenant shall have a defense of retaliation in an action for possession where tenantability is an issue of fact and the untenantable condition was caused by the deliberate or negligent act or omission of the tenant or a member of his or her family, or other persons on the premises with his or her consent. *(Added by Stats.1979, c. 385, p. 1450, § 4. Amended by Stats.1985, c. 900, § 3; Stats.1991, c. 786 (A.B.923), § 1; Stats.1992, c. 1298 (A.B.3526), § 22.)*

§ 17031.6. Eviction proceedings; defenses; payment of reasonable monthly rental value to court in cases of delay or continuance

(a) In any action brought pursuant to Chapter 4 (commencing with Section 1159) of Title 3 of Part 3 of the Code of Civil Procedure, in order to evict a tenant from employee housing, this section shall apply to that proceeding, notwithstanding any other provision of law including, but not limited to, Section 1170.5 of the Code of Civil Procedure.

(b) If, in an action subject to this section, a tenant alleges both of the following in an answer or other response to an unlawful detainer action, the trial on that action shall be set not earlier than 30 days from the date of filing the answer, and in no event prior to the completion of reasonable and diligently pursued discovery, as determined by the court, unless both parties stipulate to an earlier date:

(1) The tenant is not guilty of unlawful detainer because he or she has engaged in protected activity pursuant to Section 1942.5 of the Civil Code or Section 17031.5 of this code.

(2) The landlord's claim that the eviction is to allow the landlord to remove the subject rental unit from use as employee housing or from the market in order to rehabilitate or demolish it is a pretext to retaliate against the tenant.

(c) If, in an action subject to this section, a tenant alleged that he or she is not guilty of unlawful detainer because he or she has engaged in protected activity pursuant to Section 1942.5 of the Civil Code or Section 17031.5, and the landlord alleges or introduces evidence at trial that the purpose of the eviction is to allow the landlord to remove the subject rental unit from use as employee housing or from the market in order to rehabilitate or demolish it, the court shall immediately continue the trial for not less than 30 days, unless both parties stipulate to a waiver of this requirement.

(d) (1) If, pursuant to this section, a trial is delayed or continued, the court, may, upon a noticed motion for a payment order by the lessor, order the monthly payment of the reasonable monthly rental value to the court, if rent were otherwise due, as a condition of issuing the delay or continuance order.

(2) "Reasonable monthly rental value," as used in this subdivision, means the amount determined by the court after deducting from the contract rent any set offs, including, but not limited to, a reduction in the rent because the dwelling is partially or completely untenantable or rent abatements due to the tenant or lessee. In addition, in determining whether to order the payment of a reasonable monthly rental value to the court, or in ascertaining its amount, the court shall consider the probability of the tenant or lessee prevailing in the trial, the financial ability of the tenant or lessee to maintain this action, and any other factor relevant to the proposed payment order. *(Added by Stats.1985, c. 900, § 4. Amended by Stats.1992, c. 1298 (A.B.3526), § 23.)*

§ 17031.7. Retaliatory employment action

(a) No person operating employee community housing that has been granted an exemption pursuant to Section 17031.3, or who is in the process of applying for such exemption, shall take any retaliatory employment action against an employee/tenant because of the employee/tenant's exercise of any of the following acts:

(1) Exercising any legal right with respect to the housing.

(2) Complaining, orally or in writing, to the landlord or employer about tenantability of the housing.

(3) Complaining, orally or in writing, to any applicable agency about tenantability of the housing.

(4) Bringing an action to enforce any rights provided for by this part or Chapter 2 (commencing with Section 1940) of Title 5 of Part 4 of Division 3 of the Civil Code.

(b) "Retaliatory employment action" includes discharge from employment, wage decrease, demotion, or any other action detrimental to the employee/tenant's employment status because of the employee/tenant's exercise of the enumerated acts.

(c) Any person subject to this section shall also be subject to the provisions of Section 1942.5 of the Civil Code. *(Added by Stats.1979, c. 1031, p. 3557, § 5.)*

§ 17031.8. Local enforcement agencies; submission of information

(a) An agency that exercises the responsibility for the enforcement of this part pursuant to Section 17050 shall submit to the Department of Housing and Community Development, on forms provided by the department, the information specified in subdivision (c) by March 31 of each year regarding the previous calendar year.

(b) The Department of Housing and Community Development shall gather the information specified in subdivision (c) for all permittees for which it acts as the enforcement agency and include a summary of the information from the permittees and enforcement agencies in the annual report submitted pursuant to Section 50408 regarding housing programs administered by the department. This subdivision shall be inoperative from July 1, 2009, to June 30, 2012, inclusive.

(c) The following information shall be provided for purposes of subdivisions (a) and (b) for the reporting year:

(1) The number and location of employee housing accommodations, including the number of permits to operate issued for employee housing accommodations.

(2) The number and location of inactive employee housing accommodations.

(3) The number and location of employee housing accommodations found operating without a permit.

(4) The number of employees occupying employee housing accommodations with a permit.

(5) The number of employees occupying accommodations found to be operating without a permit.

(6) The number and types of inspections and reinspections performed.

(7) A schedule of fees charged, the amount of fees collected for each type of fee charged and the total amount of fees collected.

(8) The number of complaints received during the reporting year and the character of any violations found for each accommodation operating under permit, operating without a permit, or inactive.

(9) The number and character of violations of this part and regulations adopted pursuant to this part found during inspection of each accommodation operating under permit, or operating without a permit.

(10) The number of violations of this part and regulations adopted pursuant to this part that resulted in civil citations.

(11) The number of cases referred to prosecutorial agencies such as the Attorney General or local district attorneys, the number of cases filed to enforce this part, and the amounts of all fines and civil penalties collected as a result of the enforcement of this part.

(12) The number of staff hours dedicated to the implementation of the Employee Housing Act (Part 1 (commencing with Section 17000)).

(13) The number and location of employee housing receiving an exemption pursuant to Section 17031, 17031.3, 17031.4, or 17033.

(d) The information specified in subdivision (c) shall be maintained by the department and provided to members of the public who have requested it in writing. *(Added by Stats.2009, c. 341 (S.B.73), § 2.)*

§ 17032. Applications; time; contents; amended permits

Application for a permit to operate shall be made to the enforcement agency at least 45 days prior to the date of initial occupancy and shall be on the forms supplied by the enforcement agency and shall contain at least the following information:

(a) The name and address and telephone numbers of the employee housing owner and operator.

(b) The location of the employee housing.

(c) Approximate number of occupants to be housed.

(d) A description of the facilities comprising the employee housing.

(e) Approximate dates of occupancy.

The operator shall obtain an amended permit to operate when there is any change in the foregoing information applicable to the employee housing. *(Added by Stats.1979, c. 62, p. 146, § 1, eff. May 14, 1979. Amended by Stats.1992, c. 1298 (A.B.3526), § 25.)*

§ 17033. Railroad corporations; permits to operate employee housing

Section 17032 shall not apply to employee housing owned or operated by railroad corporations. Application for a permit to operate employee housing owned or operated by a railroad corporation shall be made to the Department of Housing and Community Development within 30 days of initial occupancy and shall contain at least the following information:

(a) The name and address and telephone numbers of the employee housing owner and operator.

(b) The present location of the employee housing.

(c) The present approximate number of occupants to be housed.

(d) A description of the present facilities comprising the employee housing.

(e) Approximate dates of present occupancy. An amended permit shall not be required if there is any change in the foregoing information applicable to the railroad employee housing, provided, however, the railroad corporation shall make this information available to the department upon reasonable request. *(Added by Stats.1979, c. 62, p. 146, § 1, eff. May 14, 1979. Amended by Stats.1992, c. 1298 (A.B.3526), § 26; Stats.1993, c. 589 (A.B.2211), § 94.)*

§ 17034. Violations

If any person who holds an annual permit to operate employee housing violates any of the provisions of this part, building standards published in the State Building Standards Code relating to employee housing, the other regulations adopted pursuant to the provisions of this part, or conditions of the permit, the enforcement agency shall proceed according to Section 17055 immediately upon discovery of such a violation. *(Added by Stats.1979, c. 62, p. 146, § 1, eff. May 14, 1979. Amended by Stats.1979, c. 1152, p. 4251, § 50; Stats.1992, c. 1298 (A.B.3526), § 27.)*

§ 17035. Roster

The department shall establish and maintain a roster of all employee housing having a valid permit to operate. *(Added by Stats.1979, c. 62, p. 146, § 1, eff. May 14, 1979. Amended by Stats.1992, c. 1298 (A.B.3526), § 28.)*

§ 17036. Regulations; fees

(a) Except as provided in Section 18930, the department shall adopt regulations that it determines are necessary for the administration and enforcement of this part. The regulations adopted, amended, or repealed shall prescribe reasonable requirements for issuance of permits and establish procedures for suspension of permits, including appeal procedures.

(b) The department shall establish a schedule of fees to pay for the cost of administration and enforcement of this part, that includes, but is not limited to, the following minimum permit fees:

(1) A two-hundred-dollar ($200) issuance fee for a permit to operate employee housing for each employee housing facility.

(2) A twenty-seven-dollar ($27) permit operation fee for each employee the operator intends to house where that housing is supplied by the operator, and at least twenty-seven dollars ($27) for each lot or site provided for parking or the placement of manufactured homes, mobilehomes, or recreational vehicles or other accommodations by employees.

(c) On or after January 1, 2010, the department may increase the fees established pursuant to subdivision (b), if necessary, to finance the costs of administration and enforcement of this part.

(d) The department may adopt additional regulations to facilitate the development of employee housing pursuant to Sections 17021.5 and 17021.6. *(Added by Stats. 2009, c. 341 (S.B.73), § 4.)*

§ 17037. Compliance with requirements; failure to obtain permit; penalty fees

Every person, or the agent or officer thereof, constructing, operating, or maintaining employee housing shall comply with the requirements of this part, with building standards published in the State Building Standards Code relating to employee housing, and with the other regulations adopted pursuant to this part.

(a) Any person operating or maintaining employee housing without first having obtained a permit to operate from the enforcement agency shall pay double the fees prescribed for the permit to operate the employee housing.

(b) Any person found for a second or subsequent time within a five-year period to be operating or maintaining employee housing without first having obtained a permit to operate from the enforcement agency shall pay 10 times the fees prescribed for the permit to operate the employee housing. The two or more violations referenced in this paragraph may be with regard either to the same enforcement agency or to two or more different enforcement agencies. *(Added by Stats.1979, c. 62, p. 146, § 1, eff. May 14, 1979. Amended by Stats.1979, c. 1152, p. 4251, § 52; Stats.1983, c. 1210, § 1; Stats.1986, c. 1495, § 4; Stats.1991, c. 790 (A.B.1816), § 2; Stats.1991, c. 795 (A.B.2164), § 1; Stats.1992, c. 1298 (A.B.3526), § 30.)*

§ 17037.5. Certificate of non-operation; submittal to enforcement agency; requirements

(a) Any person who ceases to operate or maintain employee housing that is subject to the permit requirement pursuant to this part shall be required to annually complete and submit a Certificate of Non-Operation to the enforcement agency. The Certificate of Non-Operation shall be submitted for two years following the discontinuation of the use of any area on the property as employee housing. The Certificate of Non-Operation shall attest under penalty of perjury that the employee housing has been destroyed, or is no longer owned or operated, or has not been and shall not be occupied by five or more employees during the calendar year.

(b) The Certificate of Non-Operation shall include the owner's name and address, the operator's name and address, the employee housing name and location, the maximum number of employees who have occupied or shall occupy the employee housing during the calendar year, and any other information considered relevant by the enforcement agency. The Certificate of Non-Operation shall be completed and submitted to the enforcement agency no later than 30 calendar days after the enforcement agency provides the form to the owner or operator. *(Added by Stats.1991, c. 795 (A.B.2164), § 2. Amended by Stats.1992, c. 1298 (A.B.3526), § 31; Stats.2004, c. 183 (A.B.3082), § 196.)*

§ 17038. Compliance; appointment of responsible person; emergency telephone number

At all employee housing, a responsible person shall be appointed by the operator to maintain the employee housing in compliance with the use, maintenance, and occupancy requirements of this part and the regulations adopted pursuant thereto. In addition, at all employee housing, an operating telephone number shall be posted conspicuously for the purposes of emergencies and complaints. *(Added by Stats.1979, c. 62, p. 146, § 1, eff. May 14, 1979. Amended by Stats.1992, c. 1298 (A.B.3526), § 32.)*

§ 17039. Compliance; maintenance and sanitation; application of violation provisions

(a) Every occupant of employee housing shall properly use the facilities furnished and shall comply with the relevant maintenance and sanitation provisions of this part.

(b) The provisions of Chapter 6 (commencing with Section 17060) do not apply to this section. *(Added by Stats.1997, c. 49 (A.B.359), § 1.)*

CHAPTER 4. RULES AND REGULATIONS

Section
17040. Duties of department; enforcement of building standards; adoption and submission of building standards.
17041. Consistency with accepted standards and practices; fee schedule; waiver or reduction of fees.
17042. Building standards; restrictions on department.
17043. Overcrowding of accommodations; notice; proceedings; appeal; vacation of accommodations; alternative housing.
17043. Overcrowding of accommodations; notice; proceedings; appeal; vacation of accommodations; alternative housing.

§ 17040. Duties of department; enforcement of building standards; adoption and submission of building standards

(a) Except as provided in Section 18930, the department shall adopt, amend, or repeal rules and regulations for the protection of the public health, safety, and general welfare of employees and the public, governing the erection, construction, enlargement, conversion, alteration, repair, occupancy, use, sanitation, ventilation, and maintenance of all employee housing.

(b) The appropriate enforcement agency shall enforce building standards published in the State Building Standards Code relating to employee housing and other regulations of the department promulgated pursuant to subdivision (a), including, but not limited to, processing violations in accordance with Sections 17274 and 24436.5 of the Revenue and Taxation Code.

(c) The department shall adopt and submit building standards for approval pursuant to Chapter 4 (commencing with Section 18935) of Part 2.5 for the purposes described in this chapter. *(Added by Stats.1979, c. 62, p. 146, § 1, eff. May 14, 1979. Amended by Stats.1979, c. 1152, p. 4251, § 53; Stats.1983, c. 101, § 120; Stats.1992, c. 1298 (A.B.3526), § 33.)*

§ 17041. Consistency with accepted standards and practices; fee schedule; waiver or reduction of fees

(a) Except as provided in Section 17011, the rules and regulations adopted, amended, or repealed from time to time pursuant to this part shall be consistent with accepted standards and practices reasonably applicable to permanent and temporary employee housing and the utilization of housing or camping facilities. In promulgating rules and regulations, the department shall consider, among other things, geographic, topographic, and climatic conditions. The department may establish a schedule of fees for the construction and operation of employee housing wherever the department is the enforcing agency.

(b) The department may provide for the waiver or reduction of fees during construction or substantial rehabilitation that is not the result of a notice by an enforcement agency where funding is received from a public entity. The department shall provide for a waiver of the fees for an operating permit during the first three years of operation after new construction or substantial rehabilitation of employee housing that is not the result of a notice by an enforcement agency. *(Added by Stats.1979, c. 62, p. 146, § 1, eff. May 14, 1979. Amended by Stats.1983, c. 101, § 121; Stats.1992, c. 1298 (A.B. 3526), § 34.)*

§ 17042. Building standards; restrictions on department

Notwithstanding any other provision of this code or of law, and except as provided in the State Building Standards Law, Part 2.5 (commencing with Section 18900), on and after January 1, 1980, the department shall not adopt or publish a building standard as defined in Section 18909, unless the provisions of Sections 18930, 18933, 18938, 18940, 18943, 18944, and 18945 are expressly excepted in the statute under which the authority to adopt rules, regulations, or orders is delegated. Any building standard adopted in violation of this section shall have no force or effect. Any building standard adopted before January 1, 1980, or continued in effect, pursuant to this part and not expressly excepted by statute from the provisions of the State Building Standards Law, shall remain in effect only until January 1, 1985, or until adopted, amended, or superseded by provisions published in the State Building Standards Code, whichever occurs sooner. *(Added by Stats.1979, c. 1152, p. 4252, § 54. Amended by Stats.1983, c. 101, § 122.)*

§ 17043. Overcrowding of accommodations; notice; proceedings; appeal; vacation of accommodations; alternative housing

Text of section as added by Stats.1986, c. 1002, § 3, eff. Sept. 22, 1986.

Notwithstanding any other provision of law, if the condition rendering any of the accommodations in a labor camp substandard is the overcrowding of the accommodations, the enforcement agency shall provide notice to the affected residents of the condition and shall give the residents of the accommodations a reasonable opportunity to correct the violation prior to the commencement of any action or proceeding pursuant to this part. If the enforcement agency determines to institute proceedings to correct the overcrowded condition, the residents may appear and be heard at a hearing convened as part of the proceedings. If the enforcement agency permits the owner or operator of the labor camp to appeal the initial notice of violation or order to abate, the residents shall also be permitted to appeal the initial notice of violation or order to abate. On appeal, if the enforcement agency determines that the only means of abatement is the vacation of the accommodations, the enforcement agency shall consider the availability of alternative housing for the residents, and shall, if alternative housing is not available, grant the residents a reasonable period of time, as determined by the enforcement agency, to find alternative housing. *(Added by Stats.1986, c. 1002, § 3, eff. Sept. 22, 1986.)*

For another section of the same number, added by Stats.1986, c. 1495, § 5 and amended by Stats.1992, c. 1298 (A.B.3526), § 35, see Health and Safety Code § 17043, post.

§ 17043. Overcrowding of accommodations; notice; proceedings; appeal; vacation of accommodations; alternative housing

Text of section as added by Stats.1986, c. 1495, § 5 and amended by Stats.1992, c. 1298 (A.B. 3526), § 35.

(a) Notwithstanding any other provision of law, if the condition rendering any of the accommodations in employee housing substandard is the overcrowding of the accommodations, the enforcement agency shall provide notice to the affected residents of the condition and shall give the residents of the accommodations a reasonable opportunity to correct the violation prior to the commencement of any action or proceeding pursuant to this part. If the enforcement agency determines to institute proceedings to correct the overcrowded condition, the residents may appear and be heard at a hearing convened as part of the proceedings. If the enforcement agency permits the owner or operator of the employee housing to appeal the initial notice of violation or order to abate, the residents shall also be permitted to appeal the initial notice of violation or order to abate.

(b) On appeal, if the enforcement agency determines that the only means of abatement is the vacation of the accommodations, the enforcement agency shall consider the availability of alternative housing for the residents, and shall, if alternative housing is not available, grant the residents a reasonable period of time, as determined by the enforcement agency, to find alternative housing.

(Added by Stats.1986, c. 1495, § 5. Amended by Stats. 1992, c. 1298 (A.B.3526), § 35.)

For another section of the same number, added by Stats.1986, c. 1002, § 3, eff. Sept. 22, 1986, see Health and Safety Code § 17043, ante.

CHAPTER 5.   ENFORCEMENT

Section
17050.   Local enforcement; assumption of enforcement by department; powers of enforcement agency.
17051.   Service of process or notice.
17052.   Annual inspections; exceptions.
17053.   Complaint and information file; public record; availability to local enforcement agencies; district attorneys, and attorney general.
17054.   Attorney general; investigations; powers; prosecutions.
17055.   Administrative complaint; civil action.
17056.   Prosecution of serious violators; implementation of part; bilingual civil service employees; report.

§ 17050.   Local enforcement; assumption of enforcement by department; powers of enforcement agency

(a) Except as provided in Section 18930, the Department of Housing and Community Development may promulgate rules and regulations to interpret and make specific this part. When adopted, those rules and regulations shall apply to all parts of the state.

(b) Upon written notice to the Department of Housing and Community Development, any city, county, or city and county may assume the responsibility for the enforcement of this part, for the building standards published in the California Building Standards Code relating to employee housing, and for the other regulations adopted pursuant to this part following approval by the department for that assumption.

(c) The Department of Housing and Community Development shall adopt regulations which shall set forth the conditions for assumption and may include required qualifications of local enforcement agencies. When assumption is approved, the department shall transfer the responsibility for enforcement to the city, county, or city and county, together with all records of active and inactive employee housing within its jurisdiction.

(d) A city, county, or city and county may, by ordinance, establish a schedule of fees for the operation of employee housing not to exceed that which is established by the department. In no event may fees be charged to residents of employee housing.

(e)(1) In the event of nonenforcement of this part, of the building standards published in the California Building Standards Code relating to employee housing, or of the other rules and regulations adopted pursuant to this part, the department shall enforce this part, the building standards published in the California Building Standards Code relating to employee housing, and the rules and regulations adopted pursuant to this part in any city, county, or city and county after the department has given written notice to the governing body of the city, county, or city and county, setting forth in what respects the city, county, or city and county has failed to discharge its responsibility, and has failed to initiate corrective measures to carry out its responsibility within 30 days of the date of the notice.

(2) On or after January 1, 1987, in the event the local enforcement agency has failed to initiate adequate and reasonable corrective measures to carry out its responsibility, as determined by the department, within 30 days of the date of notice of one or more specific examples of nonenforcement, the department, at its option, may undertake investigation and enforcement of the alleged violations of this part within the local enforcement agency's jurisdiction, and the local enforcement agency shall be liable to the department and the Attorney General for the actual costs of the investigation and enforcement by these state agencies.

(f)(1) The department shall conduct an annual evaluation of the enforcement of this part, of the building standards published in the California Building Standards Code relating to employee housing, and of the other regulations adopted pursuant to this part by each city, county, or city and county which has assumed responsibility for enforcement. The department shall submit a written summary of the evaluation conducted pursuant to this subdivision with the report required by Section 50408.

(2) The department, in consultation with interested persons, including housing advocates and farming organizations, shall conduct an evaluation of the definition of "rural" as used in paragraph (1) of subdivision (b) of Section 17008 and submit a written summary of the evaluation with the report required in calendar year 1996 by Section 17031.8.

(g) Except as provided in Section 18945, the department shall be sole judge as to whether the local enforcement agency is properly enforcing the provisions. Except as provided in Section 18945, the local enforcement agency shall have the right to appeal the decision to the department.

(h)(1) Any city, county, or city and county may cancel its assumption of responsibility for the enforcement of these provisions by providing written notice of cancellation to the department. The department shall assume the responsibility within 90 days after receipt of the notice.

(2) A local enforcement agency that has been approved by the department to enforce the provisions of this chapter and cancels its assumption of responsibility and returns enforcement to the department under paragraph (1) shall remit to the department the fees established and collected under Section 17036 and subdivision (d) that have not been expended pursuant to this chapter and the regulations adopted thereunder. For the purpose of this paragraph, the local enforcement agency shall either identify the actual expenditures and pay to the department the balance of fees collected, or shall pay the

department a sum equal to the percentage of the years remaining before outstanding permits to operate expire.

(i) The enforcement agency may:

(1) Enter public or private properties to determine whether there exists any employee housing to which this part applies.

(2) Enter and inspect all employee housing wheresoever situated, and inspect all accommodations, equipment, or paraphernalia connected therewith.

(3) Enter and inspect the land adjacent to the employee housing to determine whether the sanitary and other requirements of this part, the building standards published in the California Building Standards Code relating to employee housing, and the other rules and regulations adopted pursuant to this part have been or are being complied with. *(Added by Stats.1979, c. 62, p. 146, § 1, eff. May 14, 1979. Amended by Stats.1979, c. 1152, p. 4252, § 55; Stats.1983, c. 101, § 123; Stats.1986, c. 1495, § 5.5; Stats.1991, c. 790 (A.B.1816), § 3; Stats.1992, c. 1298 (A.B.3526), § 36; Stats.1995, c. 561 (S.B.851), § 2; Stats.2008, c. 138 (A.B.2554), § 1.)*

§ 17051. Service of process or notice

For the purpose of securing compliance with this part, the officers and agents of the enforcement agency may serve any process or notice throughout its jurisdiction. *(Added by Stats.1979, c. 62, p. 146, § 1, eff. May 14, 1979.)*

§ 17052. Annual inspections; exceptions

The enforcement agency shall annually enter and inspect, and reinspect as necessary, all employee housing accommodations for compliance with the provisions of this part and regulations adopted pursuant to this part, except:

(a) Accommodations for employee housing consisting only of permanent single family housing that have been granted an exemption as provided in Section 17031.

(b) Accommodations for employee housing that have been issued a multiyear permit to operate pursuant to Section 17030.5.

(c) Accommodations for employee housing that are inactive.

(d) Accommodations for employee housing inspected in the prior calendar year with no violations identified or complaints received by the enforcement agency, which shall be inspected at least biennially.

The enforcement agency shall make every effort to complete the inspection prior to the occupancy of the employee housing. *(Added by Stats.1979, c. 62, p. 146, § 1, eff. May 14, 1979. Amended by Stats.1979, c. 385, p. 1451, § 5; Stats.1979, c. 1152, p. 4253, § 56; Stats.1980, c. 45, p. 120, § 3, eff. March 20, 1980; Stats.1992, c. 1298 (A.B.3526), § 37; Stats.1995, c. 561 (S.B.851), § 3.)*

§ 17053. Complaint and information file; public record; availability to local enforcement agencies; district attorneys, and attorney general

The department shall maintain a file of all reports of complaint or other significant information regarding employee housing maintenance and operation. Each file and information shall be available to local enforcement agencies, district attorneys, and the Attorney General. This material shall be a matter of public record. *(Added by Stats.1979, c. 62, p. 146, § 1, eff. May 14, 1979. Amended by Stats.1992, c. 1298 (A.B.3526), § 38.)*

§ 17054. Attorney general; investigations; powers; prosecutions

The Attorney General, upon the request of the Director of Housing and Community Development, shall conduct such investigations as may be necessary to determine whether any violation of any provision of this part has occurred. For such purpose, the Attorney General shall have the powers specified in Section 17050.

The Attorney General shall conduct such prosecutions of violations of this part as the director may request. *(Added by Stats.1979, c. 62, p. 146, § 1, eff. May 14, 1979.)*

§ 17055. Administrative complaint; civil action

(a) Any person residing in employee housing subject to this part may file an administrative complaint orally or in writing with the enforcement agency. The enforcement agency shall deliver a summary or copy of the complaint, by mail or in person, to the owner or operator, at the time of filing the complaint.

(b) If a civil action under this part has not been filed by the enforcement agency within 21 days after receipt of the complaint, the complainant may bring a civil action for injunctive or declaratory relief and appropriate statutory damages, civil penalties, actual damages, penalties, and other remedies which arise from any violation of this part, building standards published in the State Building Standards Code relating to employee housing, regulations adopted pursuant to this part, or conditions of the permit.

(c) In any civil action under this section, if the enforcement agency certifies that the employee housing is in compliance with this part, building standards published in the State Building Standards Code relating to employee housing, regulations adopted pursuant to this part, and conditions of the permit, no injunctive relief related to mandatory repairs shall be granted with respect to any alleged violation covered by the certificate.

(d) In any civil action brought by a private person or entity under this section, the private person or entity may be granted reasonable attorney's fees and costs, in addition to any other remedy granted, if the private person or entity prevails, and if the trier of fact finds that the violations involve retaliation or are so extensive and of such a nature that the immediate health and safety of residents or the public is endangered or has been endangered.

230

(e) If a complainant alleges, and the court finds, that residents of the employee housing were in imminent peril as a result of serious violations of this part, the complainant may immediately proceed with the filing of a civil action without regard to the 21-day waiting period specified in subdivision (b). *(Added by Stats.1979, c. 62, p. 146, § 1, eff. May 14, 1979. Amended by Stats.1979, c. 1152, p. 4253, § 57; Stats.1992, c. 1298 (A.B.3526), § 39; Stats.2000, c. 702 (S.B.1545), § 2.)*

§ 17056. Prosecution of serious violators; implementation of part; bilingual civil service employees; report

(a) In every part of the state, notwithstanding assumption of responsibilities by local enforcement agencies pursuant to Section 17050, the department shall establish procedures and devote resources to locating and prosecuting the most serious violators of this part and those who refuse to apply for or obtain permits to operate pursuant to this part, as determined by the department.

(b) The department shall maximize the efforts of personnel implementing this part by seeking to use new resources and nontraditional means, by coordinating with state, local, and federal agencies and by training and coordinating with local health and building departments.

(c) All of the requirements of this part shall be performed by civil service employees of the department who, to the extent feasible, shall be bilingual in Spanish and English.

(Added by Stats.1986, c. 1495, § 6. Amended by Stats.1991, c. 790 (A.B.1816), § 4; Stats.1992, c. 1296 (S.B.986), § 14, eff. Sept. 30, 1992; Stats.1992, c. 1298 (A.B.3526), § 40; Stats.1993, c. 952 (A.B.2011), § 4; Stats.1995, c. 561 (S.B.851), § 4.)

CHAPTER 6. VIOLATIONS

Section
17060.   Nuisance; health or safety hazards; jurisdiction; service of summons; lis pendens; recordation.
17060.2. Orders or notices of violation; vacating of accommodations; relocation ordinances; attorney's fees and costs; deferral of orders of abatement.
17060.5. Transfer to third party; continuance of action or proceeding; subjection of new owner to order for correction.
17061.   Misdemeanor; punishment; civil penalty.
17061.5. Multiple convictions; penalties.
17061.7. House confinement; costs.
17061.9. Citation; assessment of civil penalties; aggravating circumstances; enforcement procedures.
17062.   Reimbursement for investigative and legal costs; fines and penalties; appointment of receiver; conditions endangering residents; relocation compensation.
17062.5. Fines, civil penalties, and damages; disbursement.

§ 17060. Nuisance; health or safety hazards; jurisdiction; service of summons; lis pendens; recordation

(a) Any employee housing which does not conform to this part, building standards published in the State Building Standards Code relating to employee housing, the other regulations adopted pursuant to this part, or conditions of the permit, is a public nuisance and, if not made to conform within five days or within a longer period of time, not to exceed 30 days, which may be allowed by the enforcement agency after written notice, shall be abated by proper action brought in the superior court of the county in which the employee housing or greater portion thereof is situated. Where inspection verifies that the owner or operator of employee housing is proceeding with reasonable diligence, or where conditions beyond the control of the owner or operator prevent conformance, the enforcement agency may grant time extensions not to exceed 30 days in duration. No more than two of these extensions shall be allowed by the enforcement agency prior to initiation of action to abate the public nuisance.

(b) Any violation of this part, building standards published in the State Building Standards Code relating to employee housing, the other regulations adopted pursuant to this part, or the provisions of the permit which constitute an immediate or material hazard to the health or safety of the occupants of employee housing, shall be remedied within five days after written notice by the enforcement agency, or shorter time in case of emergency. In the event of failure to comply with this section, the Attorney General, or the attorney for the enforcement agency, shall, by verified complaint setting forth the facts, apply to the superior court for an order granting the relief for which the action or proceeding is brought until the entry of a final judgment or order.

(c) The superior court may make any order for which application is made pursuant to this section.

(d) In any action or proceeding brought pursuant to this part, service of summons is sufficient if served in the manner provided in the Code of Civil Procedure.

(e)(1) Any enforcement agency which institutes an action or proceeding pursuant to this section shall, at the time of filing the action or proceeding, record in the office of the recorder of the county or counties in which the property affected by the action or proceeding is situated, a notice of the pendency of the action or proceeding.

(2) The enforcement agency may charge the property owner for any costs involved in recording the notice and shall reimburse the owner for any amount charged if the action or proceeding is dismissed or if judgment is rendered for the property owner.

(f) The notice recorded pursuant to subdivision (e) shall be withdrawn by the enforcement agency by recording in the office of the county recorder, in the county or counties in which the notice was recorded, a notice of withdrawal within five days following satisfaction of a court order or other resolution of the action or proceeding.

(g) In any action or proceeding brought pursuant to this part, it is not necessary for the complainant to provide or file any undertaking or bond for the issuance of any preliminary or permanent injunction. In addition, it is not necessary for a complainant to allege or prove actual damages or the threat thereof, or actual injury or the threat thereof, to the plaintiff, so long as a violation of this part is alleged and proven. *(Added by Stats.1979, c. 62, p. 146, § 1, eff. May 14, 1979. Amended by Stats.1979, c. 1152, p. 4254, § 58; Stats.1983, c. 1210, § 2; Stats.1992, c. 1298 (A.B.3526), § 41; Stats.1993, c. 589 (A.B.2211), § 95.)*

§ 17060.2. Orders or notices of violation; vacating of accommodations; relocation ordinances; attorney's fees and costs; deferral of orders of abatement

(a) Notwithstanding any other provision of law, the operator of employee housing shall provide a resident of every unit in the employee housing with a written copy in English and Spanish of every order or notice of violation issued by an enforcement agency accompanied by an explanation of the owner's or operator's anticipated response to the order or notice. Each notice shall also advise the occupants of the right to a hardship deferral and the procedure for obtaining this, as set forth in subdivision (c). These copies may be provided by first-class mail or by posting a copy of the notice in a prominent place on each residential unit.

(b)(1)(A) The enforcement agency shall not require the vacating of all or any part of an accommodation unless it concurrently orders the operator to provide for the relocation of the tenants consistent with the requirements of Section 17062 prior to the date the vacating is required and requires expeditious demolition or repair to comply with this part, the building standards related to employee housing, or other rules and regulations adopted pursuant to this part. Any local government may, prior to January 1, 1994, enact a local relocation ordinance that imposes requirements more stringent than those contained in this section. The tenant or tenant association may enforce the relocation remedies of this section, and the enforcement agency, to the extent feasible, shall cooperate in these efforts. The enforcement agency may require vacation and demolition or itself vacate the building, repair or demolish the building, or institute any other appropriate action or proceeding, if either of the following occurs:

(i) The repair work is not done as scheduled or cannot be completed within a reasonable period of time.

(ii) There is a significant threat to the residents' or public health and safety.

(B) In any civil action brought by a private person or entity to obtain relocation assistance pursuant to subparagraph (A), following an enforcement agency's order to vacate all or any part of an accommodation, and the failure to comply with the agency's order to provide for

231

the relocation of the tenants, the private person or entity, if he, she, or it is the prevailing party, may be granted reasonable attorney's fees and costs, in addition to any other remedy granted.

(2) Prior to vacating and demolishing the accommodation, the public agency shall exert every reasonable effort to obtain or cause repairs. In addition, to the extent feasible, if the public entity causes vacation of the accommodation, it shall cooperate in efforts to obtain compensation from the owner or operator to compensate the displaced residents for their relocation expenses, including rent differentials.

(c) The enforcement agency or a court of competent jurisdiction may, in cases of extreme hardship to tenants of employee housing, provide for deferral of the effective date of orders of abatement. Any deferral of the effective date of any order of abatement shall include conditions, including, but not limited to, payment of rent to an appropriate receiver, which will ensure progress towards correcting defects, or assist in relocation of tenants prior to closure of the employee housing. (Added by Stats.1986, c. 1495, § 7. Amended by Stats.1992, c. 1298 (A.B.3526), § 42; Stats.1993, c. 952 (A.B.2011), § 5; Stats.1994, c. 1250 (A.B.2571), § 1; Stats.1995, c. 91 (S.B.975), § 63.)

§ 17060.5. Transfer to third party; continuance of action or proceeding; subjection of new owner to order for correction

(a) The sale or other transfer of property to a third party shall not render moot an action or proceeding brought pursuant to this chapter and instituted by an enforcement agency against the owner of record on the date a citation for a violation of this part was issued.

(b) Any person who obtains an ownership interest in any property after a notice of an action or proceeding has been recorded with respect to the property pursuant to Section 17060, and where there has been no withdrawal of the notice, shall be subject to any order to correct a violation, including any time limitations, specified in a citation issued pursuant to Section 17060. (Added by Stats.1983, c. 1210, § 3.)

§ 17061. Misdemeanor; punishment; civil penalty

(a) Any person who violates, or causes another person to violate, any provision of this part is guilty of a misdemeanor, punishable by a fine of not more than two thousand dollars ($2,000), or imprisonment for not more than 180 days, or both, for each violation of this part, provided that the violation does not cause personal injury to any person.

(b) Any person who willfully violates, or causes another person to violate, any provision of this part, provided that the violation causes personal injury to any person, is punishable by imprisonment in the state prison for two, three, or four years, or in a county jail not exceeding one year, or by a fine of not less than four thousand dollars ($4,000), but not exceeding ten thousand dollars ($10,-

000), or by both fine and imprisonment for each violation, or each day of a continuing violation, causing personal injury. This subdivision shall not be construed to preclude, or in any way limit, the applicability of any other law in any criminal prosecution.

(c) Any person who violates any provision of this part shall be liable for a civil penalty of not less than three hundred dollars ($300), nor more than one thousand dollars ($1,000), for each violation or for each day of a continuing violation. The amount of the civil penalty may be doubled, to a limit of not more than ten thousand dollars ($10,000), for each violation or for each day of a continuing violation if the court determines that the violation was willful, or if the court finds that the person received notice from an enforcement agency within the prior three years regarding any employee housing owned or operated by that person, and the violations are so extensive and of such a nature that the immediate health and safety of the residents or the public is endangered or has been endangered. The enforcement agency, or any person or entity affected by the violation, may institute or maintain an action in the appropriate court to collect any civil penalty arising under this subdivision and may be awarded reasonable costs and attorney's fees incurred in proving the existence of each violation and the liability for the civil penalties. (Added by Stats.1979, c. 62, p. 148, § 1, eff. May 14, 1979. Amended by Stats.1991, c. 790 (A.B.1816), § 5; Stats.1992, c. 1298 (A.B.3526), § 43.)

§ 17061.5. Multiple convictions; penalties

(a) Any person who is convicted pursuant to Section 17061 for a second or subsequent time within a five-year period or is convicted pursuant to subdivision (d) for a first or subsequent time within a five-year period after issuance of an injunction enforcing this chapter shall be punishable by a fine not to exceed six thousand dollars ($6,000) or by imprisonment not exceeding six months, or both the fine and imprisonment for each violation or day of a continuing violation.

(b) Any person found in contempt of a court order or injunction pursuant to Section 17060 within a five-year period from its issuance may be subject to a judgment for reasonable enforcement costs, including investigative costs, court costs, and attorney's fees, and civil penalties not to exceed six thousand dollars ($6,000) or by imprisonment not exceeding six months, or both the civil penalty and imprisonment, for each violation or day of a continuing violation.

(c) (1) If an injunction enforcing this chapter is issued within a five-year period after a conviction pursuant to subdivision (a), a finding of contempt pursuant to subdivision (b), or a prior injunction enforcing this chapter, the injunction shall provide for a civil penalty not to exceed six thousand dollars ($6,000) for each violation or day of a continuing violation and all costs of enforcement, including, but not limited to, investigative costs, inspection costs, enforcement costs, attorney's fees or costs, and all other costs of prosecution.

(2) The court may also order the owner not to claim any deduction with respect to state taxes for interest, taxes, expenses, depreciation, or amortization paid or incurred, with respect to the cited structure or structures, and related real property, in the taxable year of the initial order or notice. Within 90 days after issuing the order, the court shall mail to the Franchise Tax Board a written notice of its order prohibiting the owner from claiming deductions with respect to the cited structure or structures, and related real property, in lieu of the processing of a violation by the enforcement agency in accordance with Sections 17274 and 24436.5 of the Revenue and Taxation Code.

(3) The Franchise Tax Board shall examine the tax return of the owner of the cited structure or structures, and related real property, for the taxable year of the initial order or notice issued pursuant to paragraph (2). Notwithstanding Sections 19282 and 26451 of the Revenue and Taxation Code, the Franchise Tax Board shall notify the issuing court regarding the owner's compliance with the court order prohibiting the claiming of deductions with respect to the cited structure or structures, and related real property.

(d) Any person found in contempt of a court order or injunction pursuant to Section 17060, or who is convicted pursuant to Section 17061, for a second or subsequent time within a five-year period after a prior finding of contempt, a prior conviction, or the prior issuance of an injunction relating to the enforcement of this chapter, where there are violations that are determined by the trier of fact to be so extensive and of such a nature that the immediate health and safety of residents or the public is endangered and where the extent and nature of the violations are due to the defendant's habitual neglect of customary maintenance and display a flagrant lack of concern for the health and safety of residents or the public, may be subject to a judgment for reasonable enforcement costs, including investigative costs, court costs, and attorney's fees, and punishable by a fine not exceeding six thousand dollars ($6,000) and by imprisonment for not less than six months, but not exceeding one year, for each violation or day of a continuing violation, if the trier of fact finds at least three serious violations of the following categories of violations are involved:

(1) Termination, extended interruption, or serious defects of gas, water, or electric utility systems, if the interruption or termination is not caused by the tenant's failure to pay gas, water, or electric bills.

(2) Serious defects or lack of adequate space and water heating.

(3) Serious rodent, vermin, or insect infestation.

(4) Severe deterioration, rendering significant portions of the structure unsafe or unsanitary.

(5) Inadequate numbers of garbage receptacles or service.

(6) Unsanitary conditions affecting a significant portion of the structure as a result of faulty plumbing or sewage disposal.

(e) The remedies provided in subdivisions (a) to (d), inclusive, for second or subsequent violations shall apply without regard to whether the violations involved the same or different properties, or the same or different locations within a property, owned or operated by the person committing the violation. *(Added by Stats.1983, c. 1210, § 4. Amended by Stats.1986, c. 1495, § 8; Stats. 1991, c. 790 (A.B.1816), § 6; Stats.1992, c. 1298 (A.B. 3526), § 44.)*

§ 17061.7. House confinement; costs

(a) Any person found in contempt of a court order or injunction pursuant to Section 17060, or who is convicted pursuant to Section 17061, for a second or subsequent time within a five-year period after a prior finding of contempt, after a prior conviction, or after the prior issuance of an injunction relating to the enforcement of this chapter, may, in lieu of any penalties ordered pursuant to Section 17061.5 or any other provision of law, be ordered by the court, on its own motion or pursuant to a trial by jury on that issue if that is requested by the defendant, to be placed in house confinement in the employee housing or any accommodation within the employee housing that is the subject of the court action. The house confinement ordered pursuant to this section shall be for a period not to exceed one year.

(b) A defendant ordered to house confinement pursuant to this section may also be ordered by the court to pay the cost of having a police officer or guard stand guard outside the area in which the defendant has been confined under house confinement if it has been determined by the court that the defendant is able to pay these costs. No defendant shall be ordered, pursuant to this subdivision, to pay an amount exceeding two thousand dollars ($2,000) for any period of house confinement. *(Added by Stats.1991, c. 786 (A.B.923), § 2. Amended by Stats.1992, c. 1298 (A.B.3526), § 45.)*

§ 17061.9. Citation; assessment of civil penalties; aggravating circumstances; enforcement procedures

(a) In addition to other remedies provided in this part, the Director of the Department of Housing and Community Development or his or her designee or an employee authorized by a local enforcement agency which has assumed jurisdiction pursuant to Section 17050, may issue a citation which assesses a civil penalty to any owner or operator, or both, of employee housing violating this part, or regulations promulgated hereunder, if the owner or operator, or both, has permitted the continuation of a violation for at least 30 days after issuance of an order to correct the violation or violations from the enforcement agency. Each citation and related civil penalty assessment shall be issued no later than seven months after issuance of the order to correct which is the basis of the citation. The civil penalties provided for in this section

233

are not in addition to the penalties established in subdivision (b) of Section 17037.

(b) The amount of any civil penalty assessed pursuant to subdivision (a) shall not exceed three hundred dollars ($300) for each violation. The civil penalties assessed pursuant to this section shall be payable to the enforcement agency, notwithstanding any other provision of law. Whether or not the violation or violations, if applicable, giving cause for the citation are corrected, payment of the civil penalty shall be remitted to the enforcement agency within 45 days of the issuance of the citation.

(c) The amount of the civil penalty shall be increased to an amount not to exceed five hundred dollars ($500) for a violation if all the following circumstances exist:

(1) The citation is for a second or subsequent violation of this part, or the regulations promulgated hereunder, for which an order to correct was issued within one year prior to issuance of the new citation; and

(2) The original violation has continued to exist for at least six months from the date the order to correct the violation was issued or has recurred within six months from the date the order to correct the violation was issued.

(d) Any person or entity served a citation pursuant to this section may petition the director or his or her designee or the officially authorized representative of the local enforcement agency, where applicable. The petition shall be a written request briefly stating the grounds of the request. Any petition to be considered, shall be received by the department or the local enforcement agency within 30 days of the date of issuance of the citation.

(e) Upon receipt of a timely and complying petition, the enforcement agency shall suspend enforcement of the citation and set a time and place for the informal hearing and shall give the recipient of the citation written notice thereof. The hearing shall commence no later than 30 days following receipt of the petition or at another time scheduled by the enforcement agency pursuant to a request by the petitioner or the enforcement agency if the enforcement agency determines that good and sufficient cause exists. If the petitioner fails to appear at the time and place scheduled for the hearing, the enforcement agency may notify the petitioner in writing that the petition is dismissed and that compliance with the terms of the citation shall occur within 10 days after receipt of the notification.

(f) The enforcement agency shall notify the petitioner in writing of its decision and the reasons therefor within 30 days following conclusion of the informal hearing held pursuant to this section. If the decision upholds the citation, in whole or in part, the petitioner shall comply with the citation in accordance with the decision within 30 days after the decision is mailed by the enforcement agency. *(Added by Stats.1991, c. 795 (A.B.2164), § 3. Amended by Stats.1992, c. 1298 (A.B.3526), § 46.)*

234

§ 17062. Reimbursement for investigative and legal costs; fines and penalties; appointment of receiver; conditions endangering residents; relocation compensation

(a) Any state or local agency which participated in the investigation and enforcement pursuant to this part shall be reimbursed for its investigative and legal costs prior to and subsequent to the judgment.

(b) Notwithstanding any other provision of law, upon motion by the enforcement agency, the operator, or the tenants, the court may issue an order which would result in correction of defects, rather than closure of the employee housing. The order may provide, notwithstanding subdivision (a), that fines and penalties be paid for improvements, or that a lien be levied against the property to pay the costs of an independent receiver to complete repairs, or any other just and reasonable procedures.

(c)(1)(A) If employee housing is maintained in a manner that violates any provision of this part, including any rule, standard, or regulation promulgated pursuant to this part, and the violation is so extensive and of such a nature that the health and safety of residents or the public is substantially endangered, and if the owner or operator does not, within a reasonable time after issuance of the notice or order by the enforcement agency, correct the condition that is the cause of the violation, the enforcement agency, tenant, or tenant association or organization may, in addition to any other remedies provided by law, seek the appointment of a receiver pursuant to this subdivision.

(B) In its petition to the court, the enforcement agency, tenant, or tenant association or organization shall include proof that notice of the petition was served not less than five days prior to filing the petition, pursuant to Article 3 (commencing with Section 415.10) of Chapter 4 of Title 5 of Part 2 of the Code of Civil Procedure, to all persons with a recorded interest in the real property upon which the substandard employee housing exists.

(C) In appointing a receiver, the court shall consider whether the owner has been afforded a reasonable opportunity to correct the conditions cited in the notice of violation. The court shall not appoint any person as a receiver unless the person has demonstrated to the court his or her capacity, willingness, and expertise to develop and supervise a viable financial and construction plan for the satisfactory rehabilitation of the employee housing. If a receiver is appointed, the owner and his or her agent of the substandard employee housing shall be enjoined from collecting rents from the tenants, interfering with the receiver in the operation of the substandard employee housing, and encumbering or transferring the substandard employee housing or real property upon which the employee housing is situated.

(2) Any receiver appointed pursuant to this section shall have all of the following powers and duties in the order of priority listed in this paragraph, unless the court otherwise permits:

(A) To take full and complete control of the substandard employee housing.

(B) To manage the substandard employee housing and pay expenses of the operation of the substandard employee housing and real property upon which the employee housing is located, including taxes, insurance, utilities, general maintenance, and debt secured by an interest in the real property. However, the receiver shall not operate the employee housing for a longer period each year than the period it previously was operated as employee housing each year by the operator or owner.

(C) To secure a cost estimate and construction plan from a licensed contractor for the repairs necessary to correct the conditions cited in the notice of violation.

(D) To enter into contracts and employ a licensed contractor as necessary to correct the conditions cited in the notice of violation.

(E) To collect all rents and income from the substandard employee housing.

(F) To use all rents and income from the substandard employee housing to pay for the cost of rehabilitation and repairs determined by the court as necessary to correct the conditions cited in the notice of violation.

(G) To borrow funds to pay for repairs necessary to correct the conditions cited in the notice of violation and to borrow funds to pay for any relocation benefits authorized by paragraph (4) and secure that debt, with court approval, with a lien on the real property upon which the substandard employee housing is located. The lien shall be recorded in the county recorder's office in the county within which the employee housing is located.

(H) To exercise the powers granted receivers under Section 568 of the Code of Civil Procedure.

(3) The receiver shall be entitled to the same fees, commissions, and necessary expenses as receivers in actions to foreclose mortgages.

(4) If the conditions of the employee housing or the repair or rehabilitation thereof significantly affect the safe and sanitary use of the substandard employee housing by any tenant, to the extent that the tenant cannot safely reside in his or her unit, then the receiver shall provide relocation benefits in accordance with paragraph (3) of subdivision (d).

(5) The relocation compensation provided for in this section shall not preempt any local ordinance that provides for greater relocation assistance.

(6) In addition to any reporting required by the court, the receiver shall prepare monthly reports to the state or local enforcement agency which shall contain information on at least the following items:

(A) The total amount of rent payment received.

(B) Nature and amount of contracts negotiated relative to the operation or repair of the property.

(C) Payments made toward the repair of the premises.

(D) Progress of necessary repairs.

(E) Other payments made relative to the operation of the employee housing.

(F) Amount of tenant relocation benefits paid.

(7) The receiver shall be discharged when the conditions cited in the notice of violation have been remedied in accordance with the court order or judgment and a complete accounting of all costs and repairs has been delivered to the court. Upon removal of the condition, the owner, the mortgagee, or any lienor of record may apply for the discharge of all moneys not used by the receiver for removal of the condition and all other costs authorized by this section.

(8) The prevailing party in an action pursuant to this section shall at the court's equitable discretion be entitled to reasonable attorney's fees and court costs as may be fixed by the court.

(9) The county recorder may charge and collect fees for the recording of all notices and other documents required by this section pursuant to Article 5 (commencing with Section 27360) of Chapter 6 of Division 2 of Title 3 of the Government Code.

(10) Nothing in this section shall be construed to limit those rights available to tenants and owners under any other provision of the law.

(11) Nothing in this section shall be construed to deprive an owner of substandard employee housing of all procedural due process rights guaranteed by the California Constitution and the United States Constitution, including, but not limited to, receipt of notice of the violation claimed and an adequate and reasonable period of time to comply with any orders that are issued by the enforcement agency or the court.

(d) If the court finds that the employee housing is in a condition that substantially endangers the health and safety of residents pursuant to subdivision (a) of Section 17980.6, upon the entry of any order or judgment, the court shall do all of the following:

(1) Order the owner to pay all reasonable and actual costs of the enforcement agency including, but not limited to, inspection costs, investigation costs, enforcement costs, attorney's fees or costs, and all costs of prosecution.

(2) Order that the local enforcement agency shall provide the tenants with notice of the court order or judgment.

(3) Order that, if the owner undertakes repairs or rehabilitation as a result of being cited for a notice under this chapter, and if the conditions of the premises or the repair or rehabilitation thereof significantly affect the safe and sanitary use of the premises by any lawful tenant, so that the tenant cannot safely reside in the premises, then the owner shall provide or pay relocation benefits to each lawful tenant as specified in subdivision (b) of Section 17060.2. These benefits shall consist of actual reasonable moving and storage costs and relocation compensation. The actual moving and storage costs shall consist of all the following:

(A) Transportation of the tenant's personal property to the new location. The new location shall be in close proximity to the substandard premises, except where relocation to a new location beyond a close proximity is determined by the court to be justified.

(B) Packing, crating, unpacking, and uncrating the tenant's personal property.

(C) Insurance of the tenant's property while in transit.

(D) The reasonable replacement value of property lost, stolen, or damaged (not through the fault or negligence of the displaced person, his or her agent, or his or her employee) in the process of moving, where insurance covering the loss, theft, or damage is not reasonably available.

(E) The cost of disconnecting, dismantling, removing, reassembling, reconnecting, and reinstalling machinery, equipment, or other personal property of the tenant, including connection charges imposed by utility companies for starting utility service.

(e)(1) The relocation compensation shall be an amount equal to the differential between the contract rent and the fair market rental value determined by the United States Department of Housing and Urban Development for a unit of comparable size within the area for the period that the unit is being repaired, not to exceed 120 days or the duration that the camp is open, or the term of employment, whichever is less.

(2)(A) If the court finds that a tenant has been substantially responsible for causing or substantially contributing to the substandard conditions, then the relocation benefits of this section shall not be paid to this tenant. Each other tenant on the premises who has been ordered to relocate due to the substandard conditions and who is not substantially responsible for causing or contributing to the conditions shall be paid these benefits and moving costs at the time that he or she actually relocates.

(B) The court shall determine the date when the tenant is to relocate, and order the tenant to notify the enforcement agency and the owner of the address of the premises to which he or she has relocated, within five days after the relocation.

(C)(i) The court shall order that the owner shall offer the first right to occupancy of the premises to each tenant who received benefits pursuant to paragraph (3) of subdivision (d), before letting the unit for rent to a third party. The owner's offer on the first right to occupancy to the tenant shall be in writing, and sent by first-class certified mail to the address given by the tenant at the time of relocation. If the owner has not been provided the tenant's address by the tenant as prescribed by this section, the owner shall not be required to provide notice under this section or offer the tenant the right to return to occupancy.

236

(ii) The tenant shall notify the owner in writing that he or she will occupy the unit. The notice shall be sent by first-class certified mail no later than 10 days after the notice has been mailed by the owner.

(D) The court shall order that failure to comply with any abatement order under this chapter shall be punishable by civil contempt penalties under Chapter 6 (commencing with Section 17995) of Part 1.5, and any other penalties and fines as are available.

(f) The initiation of a proceeding or entry of a judgment pursuant to this section or Section 17980.6 shall be deemed to be a "proceeding" or "judgment" as provided by paragraph (4) or (5) of subdivision (a) of Section 1942.5 of the Civil Code.

(g) The term "owner," for the purposes of this section, shall include the owner, including any public entity that owns residential real property, at the time of the initial notice or order and any successor in interest who had actual or constructive knowledge of the notice, order, or prosecution.

(h) The remedies authorized by this section shall be in addition to those provided by any other law.

(i) Nothing in this section or in Section 17980.6 shall impair the rights of an owner exercising his or her rights established pursuant to Chapter 12.75 (commencing with Section 7060) of Division 7 of Title 1 of the Government Code. *(Added by Stats.1983, c. 1210, § 5. Amended by Stats.1986, c. 1495, § 9; Stats.1992, c. 1298 (A.B.3526), § 47; Stats.1993, c. 952 (A.B.2011), § 6.)*

§ 17062.5. Fines, civil penalties, and damages; disbursement

All fines, civil penalties, and damages awarded pursuant to this part shall be paid as provided in this section. The court order shall direct payment of these moneys for the costs authorized by subdivision (a) of Section 17062 or subdivision (d) of Section 17055. Thereafter, 50 percent of the balance of the total award shall be paid to the agency, person, or entity to which subdivision (a) of Section 17062 or subdivision (d) of Section 17055 is applicable. The balance of the award, if at least one thousand dollars ($1,000) is paid to that agency, person, or entity, shall be deposited in the Farmworker Housing Grant Fund, created pursuant to Section 50517.5, for expenditure by the department without further appropriation in a manner consistent with the other requirements of Section 50517.5, for any of the following purposes:

(a) Rental housing that serves lower and very low income households, as defined in Sections 50079.5 and 50105, respectively, who are agricultural employees.

(b) Rental dormitories for unaccompanied men or women who are agricultural employees.

(c) Rehabilitation or replacement of existing employee housing for seasonal use. *(Added by Stats.1993, c. 952 (A.B.2011), § 7.)*

Division 20

MISCELLANEOUS HEALTH AND SAFETY PROVISIONS

CHAPTER 1. ENFORCEMENT ACTIONS

Section
24000.   Legislative findings and declarations; immigration status; severability.

§ 24000. Legislative findings and declarations; immigration status; severability

The Legislature finds and declares the following:

(a) All protections, rights, and remedies available under state law, except any reinstatement remedy prohibited by federal law, are available to all individuals regardless of immigration status who have applied for employment, or who are or who have been employed, in this state.

(b) For purposes of enforcing state labor and employment laws, a person's immigration status is irrelevant to the issue of liability, and in proceedings or discovery undertaken to enforce those state laws no inquiry shall be permitted into a person's immigration status except where the person seeking to make this inquiry has shown by clear and convincing evidence that the inquiry is necessary in order to comply with federal immigration law.

(c) The provisions of this section are declaratory of existing law.

(d) The provisions of this section are severable. If any provision of this section or its application is held invalid, that invalidity shall not affect other provisions or applications that can be given effect without the invalid provision or application. *(Added by Stats.2002, c. 1071 (S.B.1818), § 3.)*

CHAPTER 6.5. HAZARDOUS WASTE CONTROL

ARTICLE 13. MANAGEMENT OF USED OIL

Section
25250.29.   Testing and analysis of used oil prior to shipping; exceptions; records; reports.
25250.30.   Out-of-state used oil recycling facilities; testing and reporting agreements; reimbursement.

§ 25250.29. Testing and analysis of used oil prior to shipping; exceptions; records; reports

(a) Except as provided in subdivisions (b) and (g), before a load of used oil is shipped to a transfer facility, recycling facility, or facility located out of the state, the used oil shall be tested and analyzed by a laboratory accredited by the State Department of Public Health pursuant to Article 3 (commencing with Section 100825) of Chapter 4 of Part 1 of Division 101, to ensure that the used oil meets all of the following characteristics:

(1) A flashpoint above 100 degrees Fahrenheit.

(2) A polychlorinated biphenyls (PCB) concentration of less than 5 ppm.

(3) A concentration of total halogens of 1000 ppm or less, unless the presumption in subclause (I) of clause (v) of subparagraph (C) of paragraph (1) of subdivision (a) of Section 25250.1 has been rebutted pursuant to subclause (II) of clause (v) of subparagraph (C) of paragraph (1) of subdivision (a) of Section 25250.1.

(b) The testing and analysis required pursuant to subdivision (a) shall be accomplished by a registered hazardous waste transporter prior to acceptance at a transfer facility or recycling facility, or shipment out of the state, except the transporter is not required to perform the testing and analysis if the transporter can do any of the following:

(1)(A) Demonstrate that testing and analysis has been performed by the generator of the used oil prior to shipment.

(B) Subparagraph (A) does not require the generator of the used oil to perform the testing and analysis required by this section.

(2) Provide documentation that the testing will be performed by a transfer facility or a recycling facility issued a permit by the department pursuant to this chapter.

(3) If shipped to an out-of-state facility, provide documentation certifying that the out-of-state facility receiving the used oil has entered into an agreement with the department that meets the requirements of Section 25250.30.

(c)(1) A transporter shall not require a used oil collection center to test tanks or containers that contain only used lubricating oil or oil filters accepted from the public as a condition of accepting the oil for shipment.

(2) A transporter shall not require a generator to test used oil as a condition of accepting that used oil for shipment.

(3) This subdivision does not alter a generator's responsibility to comply with regulations adopted by the department that govern the operation of a generator, and a transporter shall not be required to transport untested used oil.

(d) This section does not affect or limit a testing requirement that the department may impose on a used oil transfer facility or used oil recycling facility as a condition of a permit issued by the department, including, but not limited to, a test required pursuant to a facility's waste analysis plan.

(e) The person performing a test required by subdivision (a) shall maintain records of tests performed for used oil for at least three years and is subject to audit and verification by the department.

(f) The registered hazardous waste transporter who is listed as the transporter on the Uniform Hazardous Waste Manifest used to ship used oil out of state shall submit a report, on or before March 1 of each year, to the department, containing all of the following information for the preceding year:

(1) Total volume of used oil shipped out of state.

(2) Information pertaining to the out-of-state facility to which the used oil was shipped, including the facility name, facility address, and facility EPA ID number.

(3) Any other information that the department may require to ensure that the same data gathered for used oil managed within the state is gathered for used oil shipped out of state.

(g)(1) This section does not apply to a load for shipment that consists exclusively of used lubricating oil accepted by a used oil collection center from the public, including, but not limited to, used lubricating oil accepted by a publicly funded certified or uncertified used oil collection center located in a small rural county.

(2) This section does not require a generator to test used oil for dielectric oil derived from highly refined mineral oil used in oil filled electrical equipment. Nothing in this section exempts that oil from any testing requirement required by any other law.

(3) This section does not prohibit the transportation of used oil to a facility located outside the state, or impose liability other than compliance with the requirements of this section upon, or in another way affect the liability of, a generator whose used oil is transported to a facility located outside the state. *(Added by Stats.2009, c. 353 (S.B.546), § 1.)*

§ 25250.30. Out-of-state used oil recycling facilities; testing and reporting agreements; reimbursement

A used oil recycling facility located out of state that is registered or certified in accordance with Section 48662 of the Public Resources Code may enter into a testing and reporting agreement with the department. The agreement shall include a requirement on the out-of-state used oil recycling facility that is equivalent to the current testing and testing-related reporting requirements of a used oil recycling facility permit. As part of the agreement, the out-of-state used oil recycling facility shall agree to reimburse the department's full reasonable costs associated with the agreement, including any inspections the department deems necessary to ensure compliance with this provision. *(Added by Stats.2009, c. 353 (S.B. 546), § 2.)*

CHAPTER 10.4. ASBESTOS NOTIFICATION

Section
25915.   Buildings constructed prior to 1979; notice to employees of known asbestos-containing building

Section
         materials; contents and form of notice; exceptions.
25915.1. Asbestos management plans.
25915.2. Written notice to employees, other owners and employees of contractors; exceptions.
25915.5. Notice to persons having privity of contract with owner; effect of notice or lack of notice; method of delivery; liability of owner; owners within a residential common interest development or association.
25916.   Construction, maintenance or other work in area of asbestos-containing materials; posted warning.
25916.5. Designated owner to prepare notice; use by other owners.
25917.   Asbestos survey and monitoring data and asbestos management plans; review by other owners or employees; time and place for review.
25917.5. Asbestos information system or statewide asbestos register established pursuant to § 25927; requirements.
25918.   Asbestos.
25919.   Asbestos-containing construction material.
25919.2. Building.
25919.3. Employee.
25919.4. Employee's representative.
25919.5. Owner.
25919.6. Agent.
25919.7. Violations; operative date of section.

§ 25915. Buildings constructed prior to 1979; notice to employees of known asbestos-containing building materials; contents and form of notice; exceptions

(a) Notwithstanding any other provision of law, the owner of any building constructed prior to 1979, who knows that the building contains asbestos-containing construction materials, shall provide notice to all employees of that owner working within the building concerning all of the following:

(1) The existence of, conclusions from, and a description or list of the contents of, any survey known to the owner conducted to determine the existence and location of asbestos-containing construction materials within the building, and information describing when and where the results of the survey are available pursuant to Section 25917.

(2) Specific locations within the building known to the owner, or identified in a survey known to the owner, where asbestos-containing construction materials are present in any quantity.

(3) General procedures and handling restrictions necessary to prevent, and, if appropriate, to minimize disturbance, release, and exposure to the asbestos. If detailed handling instructions are necessary to ensure employee safety, the notice required by this section shall indicate where those instructions can be found.

(4) A summary of the results of any bulk sample analysis, or air monitoring, or monitoring conducted pursuant to Section 5208 of Title 8 of the California Code of Regulations, conducted for or by the owner or within the owner's control, including reference to sampling and

laboratory procedures utilized, and information describing when and where the specific monitoring data and sampling procedures are available pursuant to Section 25917.

(5) Potential health risks or impacts that may result from exposure to the asbestos in the building as identified in surveys or tests referred to in this section, or otherwise known to the owner.

The notice may contain a description and explanation of the health action levels or exposure standards established by the state or federal government. However, if the notice contains this description, the notice shall include, at least, a description and explanation of the no significant risk level established pursuant to Chapter 6.6 (commencing with Section 25249.5) of Division 20, and specified in Section 12711 of Title 22 of the California Code of Regulations, the school abatement clearance level specified in Section 49410.7 of the Education Code, and the action levels established by state and federal Occupational Safety and Health Act regulations.

The notice requirements specified in this subdivision shall not apply to an owner who elects to prepare an asbestos management plan pursuant to Section 25915.1. In those cases, the notice requirements specified in Section 25915.1 shall apply.

(b) If the owner has no special knowledge of the information required pursuant to paragraphs (3) and (5), of subdivision (a), the owner shall specifically inform his or her employees in the notice required by this section, that he or she lacks knowledge regarding handling instructions necessary to prevent and minimize release of, and exposure to, asbestos and the potential health impacts resulting from exposure to asbestos in the building, and shall encourage employees to contact local or state public health agencies.

(Added by Stats. 1988, c. 1502, § 1. Amended by Stats.1989, c. 948, § 1, eff. Sept. 27, 1989.)

§ 25915.1. Asbestos management plans

(a) An owner may elect to prepare an asbestos management plan for any building subject to this chapter, and in that case may, upon implementation of that plan, comply with the notification requirements of this chapter by providing notice to other owners and all employees of that owner working within the building of the following:

(1) The specific locations within the building where asbestos-containing construction materials are present in any quantity.

(2) Potential health risks or impacts that may result from exposure to the asbestos.

(3) Information to convey that moving, drilling, boring, or otherwise disturbing the asbestos-containing construction material identified may present a health risk and, consequently, should not be attempted by an employee who is not qualified to handle asbestos-containing construction material.

(4) The existence and availability of the management plan and a description of its contents.

(b) For purposes of this chapter, an asbestos management plan shall be designed to minimize the potential for release of asbestos fibers and to outline a schedule of actions to be undertaken with respect to the asbestos. The plan shall be prepared by a person accredited to prepare management plans for schools pursuant to Section 2646 of Title 15 of the United States Code and shall contain all of the following:

(1) The information specified in paragraphs (1) to (5), inclusive, of subdivision (a) of Section 25915.

(2) A description of an ongoing operations and maintenance program which shall include, but not be limited to, periodic reinspection and surveillance, suggested fiber release episode procedures, measures to minimize potential fiber releases, and information and training programs for building engineering and maintenance staff.

(3) Recordkeeping procedures to demonstrate implementation of the plan which shall be maintained for the life of the building to which they apply. *(Added by Stats.1989, c. 948, § 2, eff. Sept. 27, 1989.)*

§ 25915.2. Written notice to employees, other owners and employees of contractors; exceptions

(a) Notice provided pursuant to this chapter shall be provided in writing to each individual employee, and shall be mailed to other owners designated to receive the notice pursuant to subdivision (a) of Section 25915.5, within 15 days of the first receipt by the owner of information identifying the presence or location of asbestos-containing construction materials in the building. This notice shall be provided annually thereafter. In addition, if new information regarding those items specified in paragraphs (1) to (5), inclusive, of subdivision (a) of Section 25915 has been obtained within 90 days after the notice required by this subdivision is provided or any subsequent 90-day period, then a supplemental notice shall be provided within 15 days of the close of that 90-day period.

(b) Notice provided pursuant to this chapter shall be provided to new employees within 15 days of commencement of work in the building.

(c) Notice provided pursuant to this chapter shall be mailed to any new owner designated to receive the notice pursuant to subdivision (a) of Section 25915.5 within 15 days of the effective date of the agreement under which a person becomes a new owner.

(d) Subdivisions (a) and (c) shall not be construed to require owners of a building or part of a building within a residential common interest development to mail written notification to other owners of a building or part of a building within the residential common interest development, if all the following conditions are met:

(1) The association conspicuously posts, in each building or part of a building known to contain asbestos-containing materials, a large sign in a prominent location

239

that fully informs persons entering each building or part of a building within the common interest development that the association knows the building contains asbestos-containing materials.

The sign shall also inform persons of the location where further information, as required by this chapter, is available about the asbestos-containing materials known to be located in the building.

(2) The owners or association disclose, as soon as practicable before the transfer of title of a separate interest in the common interest development, to a transferee the existence of asbestos-containing material in a building or part of a building within the common interest development.

Failure to comply with this section shall not invalidate the transfer of title of real property. This paragraph shall only apply to transfers of title of separate interests in the common interest development of which the owners have knowledge. As used in this section, "association" and "common interest development" are defined in Section 1351 of the Civil Code.

(e) If a person contracting with an owner receives notice pursuant to this chapter, that contractor shall provide a copy of the notice to his or her employees or contractors working within the building.

(f) If the asbestos-containing construction material in the building is limited to an area or areas within the building that meet all the following criteria:

(1) Are unique and physically defined.

(2) Contain asbestos-containing construction materials in structural, mechanical, or building materials which are not replicated throughout the building.

(3) Are not connected to other areas through a common ventilation system; then, an owner required to give notice to his or her employees pursuant to subdivision (a) of Section 25915 or 25915.1 may provide that notice only to the employees working within or entering that area or those areas of the building meeting the conditions above.

(g) If the asbestos-containing construction material in the building is limited to an area or areas within the building that meet all the following criteria:

(1) Are accessed only by building maintenance employees or contractors and are not accessed by tenants or employees in the building, other than on an incidental basis.

(2) Contain asbestos-containing construction materials in structural, mechanical, or building materials which are not replicated in areas of the building which are accessed by tenants and employees.

(3) The owner knows that no asbestos fibers are being released or have the reasonable possibility to be released from the material; then, as to that asbestos-containing construction material, an owner required to give notice to his or her employees pursuant to subdivision (a) of Section 25915 or Section 25915.1 may provide that notice

240

only to its building maintenance employees and contractors who have access to that area or those areas of the building meeting the conditions above.

(h) In those areas of a building where the asbestos-containing construction material is composed only of asbestos fibers which are completely encapsulated, if the owner knows that no asbestos fibers are being released or have the reasonable possibility to be released from that material in its present condition and has no knowledge that other asbestos-containing material is present, then an owner required to give notice pursuant to subdivision (a) of Section 25915 shall provide the information required in paragraph (2) of subdivision (a) of Section 25915 and may substitute the following notice for the requirements of paragraphs (1), (3), (4), and (5) of subdivision (a) of Section 25915:

(1) The existence of, conclusions from, and a description or list of the contents of, that portion of any survey conducted to determine the existence and location of asbestos-containing construction materials within the building that refers to the asbestos materials described in this subdivision, and information describing when and where the results of the survey are available pursuant to Section 25917.

(2) Information to convey that moving, drilling, boring, or otherwise disturbing the asbestos-containing construction material identified may present a health risk and, consequently, should not be attempted by an unqualified employee. The notice shall identify the appropriate person the employee is required to contact if the condition of the asbestos-containing construction material deteriorates. *(Added by Stats.1989, c. 948, § 3, eff. Sept. 27, 1989. Amended by Stats.1991, c. 731 (A.B.1940), § 1; Stats.1992, c. 427 (A.B.3355), § 104.)*

§ 25915.5. Notice to persons having privity of contract with owner; effect of notice or lack of notice; method of delivery; liability of owner; owners within a residential common interest development or association

(a) An owner required to give notice to employees pursuant to this chapter, in addition to notifying his or her employees, shall mail, in accordance with this subdivision, a copy of that notice to all other persons who are owners of the building or part of the building, with whom the owner has privity of contract. Receipt of a notice pursuant to this section by an owner, lessee or operator shall constitute knowledge that the building contains asbestos-containing construction materials for purposes of this chapter. Notice to an owner shall be delivered by first-class mail addressed to the person and at the address designated for the receipt of notices under the lease, rental agreement, or contract with the owner.

(b) The delivery of notice under this section or negligent failure to provide that notice shall not constitute a breach of any covenant under the lease or rental agreement, and nothing in this chapter enlarges or diminishes any rights or duties respecting constructive eviction.

(c) No owner who, in good faith, complies with the provisions of this section shall be liable to any other owner for any damages alleged to have resulted from his or her compliance with the provisions of this section.

(d) This section shall not be construed to apply to owners of a building or part of a building within a residential common interest development or association, if the owners comply with the provisions of subdivision (d) of Section 25915.2. For purposes of this section, "association" and "common interest development" are defined in Section 1351 of the Civil Code. *(Added by Stats. 1988, c. 1502, § 1. Amended by Stats.1991, c. 731 (A.B.1940), § 2.)*

§ 25916. Construction, maintenance or other work in area of asbestos-containing materials; posted warning

If any construction, maintenance, or remodeling is conducted in an area of the building area where there is the potential for employees to come into contact with, or release or disturb, asbestos or asbestos-containing construction materials, the owner responsible for the performance of, or contracting for, any construction, maintenance, or remodeling in the area shall post that area with a clear and conspicuous warning notice. The posted warning notice shall read, in print which is readily visible because of its large size and bright color, as specified in either subdivision (a) or (b).

(a) "CAUTION. ASBESTOS. CANCER AND LUNG DISEASE HAZARD. DO NOT DISTURB WITHOUT PROPER TRAINING AND EQUIPMENT."

(b) "DANGER. ASBESTOS. CANCER AND LUNG DISEASE HAZARD. AUTHORIZED PERSONNEL ONLY. RESPIRATORS AND PROTECTIVE CLOTHING ARE REQUIRED IN THIS AREA." *(Added by Stats. 1988, c. 1502, § 1. Amended by Stats.1989, c. 948, § 4, eff. Sept. 27, 1989.)*

§ 25916.5. Designated owner to prepare notice; use by other owners

(a) When there is more than one owner of a building or part of a building subject to this chapter, the owners may agree in writing to designate one particular owner to prepare any notice required pursuant to this chapter.

(b) Any owner, other than the owner preparing the notice, may use a notice prepared by another owner to satisfy the requirements of this chapter if all of the following are satisfied:

(1) The notice fully complies with that owner's obligations under this chapter.

(2) That owner does not know that the notice contains false or misleading information.

(3) That owner does not know that the owner who prepared the notice has failed to comply with this chapter. *(Added by Stats.1989, c. 948, § 5, eff. Sept. 27, 1989.)*

§ 25917. Asbestos survey and monitoring data and asbestos management plans; review by other owners or employees; time and place for review

An owner shall make available, for review and photocopying, to other owners and all of his or her employees or those employees' representatives at an accessible place and time, all existing asbestos survey and monitoring data and any asbestos management plan which has been prepared, specific to the building. This place shall be within the building, or another building which is leased or also owned by the owner, located on the same property as the building, and accessible and convenient to employees, and shall be available during employee working hours, including lunch and break periods, if any owner maintains an office or similar facility in the building; if not, the survey, data, and asbestos management plan shall be available at another place, and at a time accessible and convenient to employees and their representatives. Any owner may enter into an agreement with another owner to provide the location where the survey, data, and asbestos management plan is available to employees within one building pursuant to this section. *(Added by Stats. 1988, c. 1502, § 1. Amended by Stats.1989, c. 948, § 6, eff. Sept. 27, 1989.)*

§ 25917.5. Asbestos information system or statewide asbestos register established pursuant to § 25927; requirements

If an asbestos information system or statewide asbestos register, or both, is established subsequent to the designing of the system and register pursuant to paragraphs (5) and (6) of subdivision (a) of Section 25927, the system or register, or both, as the case may be, shall integrate, be consistent with, and, at a minimum, include all of the requirements of this chapter. *(Added by Stats. 1988, c. 1502, § 1.)*

§ 25918. Asbestos

"Asbestos," as used in this chapter, has the same meaning as defined in Section 6501.7 of the Labor Code. *(Added by Stats. 1988, c. 1502, § 1.)*

§ 25919. Asbestos-containing construction material

"Asbestos-containing construction material," as used in this chapter, means any manufactured construction material, including structural, mechanical and building material, which contains more than one-tenth of 1 percent asbestos by weight. *(Added by Stats. 1988, c. 1502, § 1.)*

§ 25919.2. Building

"Building," as used in this chapter, means all or part of any "public and commercial building," as defined in Section 2642 of Title 15 of the United States Code, as that section reads on January 1, 1989, except that "building" shall not mean residential dwellings. *(Formerly § 25920, added by Stats.1988, c. 1502, § 1. Amended by Stats.1989, c. 948, § 7, eff. Sept. 27, 1989. Renumbered § 25919.2 and amended by Stats.1990, c. 216 (S.B.2510), § 69.)*

§ 25919.3. Employee

"Employee," as used in this chapter, means every person who is required or directed by any employer, to engage in any employment, and who performs that employment other than on a casual or incidental basis in any building subject to this chapter, or any person contracting with an owner who is required or directed to perform services, other than on a casual or incidental basis, in any building subject to this chapter. *(Formerly § 25921, added by Stats.1988, c. 1502, § 1. Renumbered § 25919.3 and amended by Stats.1990, c. 216 (S.B.2510), § 70.)*

§ 25919.4. Employee's representative

"Employee's representative," as used in this chapter, means an employee's union representative, a member of the employee's immediate family, a nonrelated member of the employee's household, and an employee's attorney or a person with power of attorney. *(Formerly § 25922, added by Stats.1988, c. 1502, § 1. Renumbered § 25919.4 and amended by Stats.1990, c. 216 (S.B.2510), § 71.)*

§ 25919.5. Owner

"Owner," as used in this chapter, means an owner, lessee, sublessee, or agent of the owner of a building or part of a building, including, but not limited to, the state or another public entity. *(Formerly § 25923, added by Stats.1988, c. 1502, § 1. Renumbered § 25919.5 and amended by Stats.1990, c. 216 (S.B.2510), § 72.)*

§ 25919.6. Agent

"Agent," as used in this chapter, means a person acting in accordance with Title 9 (commencing with Section 2295) of Part 4 of Division 3 of the Civil Code for purposes of managing, operating, leasing, or performing a similar function with respect to a building subject to this chapter. *(Formerly § 25923.1, added by Stats.1989, c. 948, § 8, eff. Sept. 27, 1989. Renumbered § 25919.6 and amended by Stats.1990, c. 216 (S.B.2510), § 73.)*

§ 25919.7. Violations; operative date of section

Any owner who knowingly or intentionally fails to comply with this chapter, or who knowingly or intentionally presents any false or misleading information to employees or any other owner, is guilty of a misdemeanor punishable by a fine of up to one thousand dollars ($1,000) or up to one year in the county jail, or both. This section shall become operative on July 1, 1989. *(Formerly § 25924, added by Stats.1988, c. 1502, § 1, operative July 1, 1989. Amended by Stats.1989, c. 948, § 9, eff. Sept. 27, 1989. Renumbered § 25919.7 and amended by Stats.1990, c. 216 (S.B.2510), § 74.)*

Division 103

DISEASE PREVENTION AND HEALTH PROMOTION

Part 5

ENVIRONMENTAL AND OCCUPATIONAL EPIDEMIOLOGY

CHAPTER 1. OCCUPATIONAL HEALTH AND DISEASE CONTROL

Section
105150. Local health departments; provision of services.

§ 105150. Local health departments; provision of services

(a) Local health departments, as defined in Section 101185, shall provide services in occupational health to promote the health of employed persons, including educational, consultative, statistical, investigative, and other activities appropriate thereto.

(b) This section shall become operative on July 1, 1994. *(Added by Stats.1995, c. 415 (S.B.1360), § 5.)*

CHAPTER 2. OCCUPATIONAL HEALTH AND DISEASE PREVENTION

ARTICLE 1. OCCUPATIONAL HEALTH AND DISEASE PREVENTION PROGRAM

Section
105175. Program; repository of hazardous substances capability; monitoring data; access to business.
105180. Avoidance of duplication.

§ 105175. Program; repository of hazardous substances capability; monitoring data; access to business

(a) The department shall maintain a program on occupational health and occupational disease prevention, including, but not limited to, the following:

(1) Investigations into the causes of morbidity and mortality from work-induced diseases.

(2) Development of recommendations for improved control of work-induced diseases.

(3) Maintenance of a thorough knowledge of the effects of industrial chemicals and work practices on the health of California workers.

(4) Provision of technical assistance in matters of occupational disease prevention and control to the De-

partment of Industrial Relations and other governmental and nongovernmental agencies, organizations, and private individuals.

(5) Collection and summarization of statistics describing the causes and prevalence of work-induced diseases in California.

(b) The functions provided for in subdivision (a) are intended to implement within the department a continuing research and development capability and a repository of hazardous substances capability which will reinforce and strengthen the administration of the California Occupational Safety and Health Act of 1973, Part 1 (commencing with Section 6300) of Division 5 of the Labor Code, including the capability to recommend occupational health standards to the California Occupational Safety and Health Standards Board. Whenever the repository identifies data gaps for any chemical regulated by the California Occupational Safety and Health Act of 1973, the department shall notify the Division of Occupational Safety and Health of the Department of Industrial Relations of its finding.

(c) Upon the request of the department, and in furtherance of the goals of the occupational disease prevention program, employers shall provide to the department the results of monitoring data, both exposure and medical, which has been collected pursuant to Cal–OSHA standards and regulations.

(d) The state department shall have access without delay to any place of employment during regular working hours and at other reasonable times to conduct investigations necessary to carry out the purposes of this article and Article 2 (commencing with Section 105185), including, but not limited to, research, health hazard evaluation, and epidemiological surveillance. In connection with the investigation, the department may question privately any employer, owner, operator, agent, or employee and review and copy records collected pursuant to Cal–OSHA standards and regulations, and other related records.

(e) The repository maintained pursuant to this section and Section 147.2 of the Labor Code shall contain the report issued pursuant to former Sections 13124 and 13125 of the Food and Agricultural Code. Whenever a request for toxicity information is received concerning a chemical discussed in that report, the department shall notify the requestor of the nature and extent of any data gaps identified in the report with respect to that chemical. Whenever the repository receives a request about toxicity information on any other chemical, in addition to providing available information about the known toxic effects of exposure to the chemical, the repository shall also notify the requester of a determination by any state agency or federal agency that the chronic health effects testing data on the chemical is inadequate or incomplete. State agencies that maintain information on the toxic effects of chemicals shall provide the repository with access to that information. *(Added by Stats.1995, c. 415 (S.B.1360), § 5. Amended by Stats.2004, c. 193 (S.B.111), § 116.)*

§ 105180. Avoidance of duplication

In any situation where these activities may duplicate or overlap the activities of another state department or agency such as the Department of Industrial Relations or Division of Industrial Safety, the department shall avoid duplication. *(Added by Stats.1995, c. 415 (S.B.1360), § 5.)*

ARTICLE 2. OCCUPATIONAL LEAD POISONING PREVENTION

Section
105185. Establishment of program; scope.
105190. Annual fee payable by employers; determination of category; amounts; adjustments; exemptions; deposits; expenditures.
105191. Legislative findings and declarations; regulations defining de minimis amounts of lead; exemptions from payment.
105195. Industries to which program applies; additions and deletions.
105197. Program to meet requirements of Residential Lead-Based Paint Hazard Reduction Act of 1992 and Title X of the Housing and Community Development Act of 1992; regulations regarding accreditation of training providers.

§ 105185. Establishment of program; scope

(a) The department shall establish and maintain an occupational lead poisoning prevention program, including, but not limited to, the following:

(1) Developing a system for monitoring laboratory reports of cases of adult lead toxicity, to create an occupational lead poisoning registry.

(2) Following up reported cases of occupational lead poisoning to ascertain the source of lead exposure.

(3) Conducting investigations in cases where take home exposure may be occurring, where there is a likelihood of identifying additional cases, or where a previously unidentified risk factor may be present.

(4) Conducting training of employers, employees, and health professionals regarding prevention of occupational lead poisoning.

(5) Making recommendations for the prevention of lead poisoning.

(b) In any situation where the activities specified in subdivision (a) may duplicate or overlap the activities of any other state department or agency, including the Department of Industrial Relations, the department shall coordinate with the other departments or agency and take actions to avoid program and service duplication.

(c) The department may adopt regulations to implement this section and Sections 105190 and 105195. Any regulations adopted shall be considered and adopted as emergency regulations in accordance with Section 11346.1 of the Government Code. *(Added by Stats.1995, c. 415 (S.B.1360), § 5.)*

§ 105190. Annual fee payable by employers; determination of category; amounts; adjustments; exemptions; deposits; expenditures

(a) A fee shall be paid annually to the State Board of Equalization by employers in industries identified by the four-digit Standard Industrial Classification (S.I.C., 1987 Edition) established by the United States Department of Commerce and for which the State Board of Equalization has received information from the department of documented evidence of potential occupational lead poisoning.

(b) The department shall provide to the State Board of Equalization on or before the first day of November of each year, all information for the prior three-year period obtained by the California Blood Lead Registry, regarding evidence of potential occupational lead poisoning by the Standard Industrial Classification. Based on this information, the State Board of Equalization shall determine whether an employer is within Category A of the Standard Industrial Classification or within Category B of the Standard Industrial Classification and shall implement the fee schedule set forth in subdivision (c). For the purpose of this subdivision and subdivision (c), a Category A Standard Industrial Classification code is a Standard Industrial Classification code listed in Section 105195 for which there have been fewer than 20 persons with elevated blood lead levels reported to the California Blood Lead Registry in the prior three-year period. A Category B Standard Industrial Classification code is a Standard Industrial Classification code listed in Section 105195 for which there have been 20 or more persons with elevated blood lead levels reported to the California Blood Lead Registry in the prior three-year period. An elevated blood lead level is a level greater than or equal to 25 micrograms of lead per deciliter of blood.

(c) For employers with 10 or more employees, but less than 100 employees, in a Category A Standard Industrial Classification code, the annual fee shall be one hundred ninety-five dollars ($195). For employers with 100 or more employees, but fewer than 500 employees, in a Category A Standard Industrial Classification code, the annual fee shall be three hundred ninety dollars ($390). For employers with 500 or more employees in a Category A Standard Industrial Classification code, the annual fee shall be nine hundred seventy-five dollars ($975). For employers with 10 or more employees, but fewer than 100 employees, in a Category B Standard Industrial Classification code, the annual fee shall be two hundred seventy-nine dollars ($279). For employers with 100 or more employees, but fewer than 500 employees, in a Category B Standard Industrial Classification code, the annual fee shall be seven hundred eighty-one dollars ($781). For employers with 500 or more employees in a Category B Standard Industrial Classification code, the annual fee shall be two thousand two hundred thirty-two dollars ($2,232). For the purpose of this subdivision, an employer is any person defined in Section 25118 of the Health

and Safety Code. Employers with fewer than 10 employees are not subject to any fees pursuant to this section.

(d) The fees imposed in subdivision (c) are the rates for calendar year 1995 and shall be adjusted annually by the State Board of Equalization to reflect increases or decreases in the cost of living during the prior fiscal year as measured by the Consumer Price Index issued by the Department of Industrial Relations, or a successor agency. This adjustment of fees shall not be subject to the requirements of Chapter 2.5 (commencing with Section 11340) of Part 1 of Division 3 of Title 2 of the Government Code.

(e) In no event shall the annual fee exceed the cost of the program described in Section 105185. The department may exempt from payment of fees those employers who demonstrate that lead is not present in their places of employment. The cost of the program described in Section 105185 shall not exceed the amount of revenue collected from the annual fee.

(f) The fee imposed pursuant to subdivision (b) shall be paid by each employer which is identified in the schedule in accordance with Part 22 (commencing with Section 43001) of Division 2 of the Revenue and Taxation Code and shall be deposited in the Occupational Lead Poisoning Prevention Account of the General Fund, which is hereby created, to be expended for the purposes of the Occupational Lead Poisoning Prevention Program, including the cost of administering the fees by the State Board of Equalization, upon appropriation by the Legislature. *(Formerly § 429.14, added by Stats.1991, c. 798 (S.B.240), § 3. Amended by Stats.1995, c. 630 (A.B.1964), § 1. Renumbered § 105190 and amended by Stats.1996, c. 1023 (S.B.1497), § 137, eff. Sept. 29, 1996; Stats.1996, c. 720 (A.B.1195), § 1, eff. July 29, 1996.)*

§ 105191. Legislative findings and declarations; regulations defining de minimis amounts of lead; exemptions from payment

(a) The Legislature finds and declares all of the following:

(1) There are some employers who use or disturb very small amounts of lead in ways that pose a very minimal potential for lead poisoning of employees.

(2) These users of de minimis amounts of lead are not currently eligible for a waiver of the Occupational Lead Poisoning Fee.

(b) The State Department of Health Services shall adopt regulations that define a de minimis amount of lead use or disturbance. Any employer who is within the requirements of this definition shall be exempt from payment of the Occupational Lead Poisoning Fee. *(Added by Stats.1996, c. 720 (A.B.1195), § 2.)*

§ 105195. Industries to which program applies; additions and deletions

(a) Sections 105185 and 105190 shall apply to the following industries:

(1) 1622 Bridges, tunnels, and elevated highways.

(2) 1721 Painting, paper hanging, and decorating.

(3) 1791 Structural steel erection.

(4) 1795 Wrecking and demolition work.

(5) 2759 Commercial printing.

(6) 2816 Inorganic pigments manufacture.

(7) 2819 Industrial inorganic chemicals.

(8) 2821 Plastics materials and resins.

(9) 2892 Explosives manufacture.

(10) 2899 Chemical preparations.

(11) 3069 Fabricated rubber products.

(12) 3087 Custom compounding of purchased plastics resins.

(13) 3089 Plastic products.

(14) 3229 Pressed and blown glass.

(15) 3231 Products of purchased glass.

(16) 3253 Ceramic walls and floor tiles.

(17) 3262 Vitreous china food utensils.

(18) 3269 Pottery products.

(19) 3313 Electrometallurgical products.

(20) 3331 Primary copper.

(21) 3339 Primary nonferrous metals, except copper and aluminum.

(22) 3341 Secondary nonferrous metals.

(23) 3356 Nonferrous rolling, drawing, extruding.

(24) 3363 Aluminum die castings.

(25) 3364 Nonferrous die castings.

(26) 3365 Aluminum foundries.

(27) 3366 Copper foundries.

(28) 3369 Nonferrous foundries.

(29) 3399 Primary metal products.

(30) 3411 Metal cans manufacture.

(31) 3431 Metal sanitary ware.

(32) 3432 Plumbing fittings and brass goods.

(33) 3441 Fabricated structural metal.

(34) 3484 Small arms.

(35) 3491 Industrial valves.

(36) 3492 Fluid power valves and hose fittings.

(37) 3494 Valves and pipe fittings.

(38) 3496 Miscellaneous fabricated wire products.

(39) 3497 Metal foil and leaf.

(40) 3585 Refrigeration and heating equipment.

(41) 3599 Machinery, except electrical.

(42) 3624 Carbon and graphite products.

(43) 3661 Telephone and telegraph apparatus.

(44) 3662 Radio and television communication equipment.

(45) 3663 Radio and television equipment.

(46) 3669 Communications equipment.

(47) 3674 Semiconductors and related devices.

(48) 3691 Storage batteries.

(49) 3692 Primary batteries, dry and wet.

(50) 3699 Electrical equipment and supplies.

(51) 3711 Motor vehicles and car bodies.

(52) 3714 Motor vehicle parts and accessories.

(53) 3721 Aircraft.

(54) 3953 Marking devices.

(55) 3812 Search and navigation equipment.

(56) 3829 Measuring and controlling devices.

(57) 5064 Electrical appliances, television, and radios.

(58) 5093 Scrap and waste materials.

(59) 7538 General automotive repair shops.

(60) 7539 Automotive repair shops.

(61) 7997 Membership sports and recreation clubs.

(62) 7999 Amusement and recreation.

(b)(1) If the department determines that the potential for occupational lead poisoning exists in industries not covered by this section, based on new evidence, the department shall have the authority to add Standard Industrial Classification codes by regulation. Multiple case reports of occupational lead toxicity shall be a criterion for adding Standard Industrial Classification codes covered by this section for the purpose of fee assessment.

(2) If the department determines that lead use and lead exposure no longer exist in an industry covered by this section, based on new evidence, the department shall delete the Standard Industrial Classification code or individual industries within a Standard Industrial Classification code by regulation. If the department otherwise determines that the potential for occupational lead poisoning no longer exists in an industry covered by this section, based on new evidence, the department shall have the authority to delete Standard Industrial Classification codes or individual industries with a Standard Industrial Classification code by regulation. If the department determines that lead use and lead exposure no longer exist in the operations of an employer in an industry covered by this section, based on evidence submitted by the employer, the department may waive the fee of that employer. *(Added by Stats.1995, c. 415 (S.B.1360), § 5. Amended by Stats.2006, c. 538 (S.B. 1852), § 416.)*

§ 105197. **Program to meet requirements of Residential Lead-Based Paint Hazard Reduction Act of 1992 and Title X of the Housing and Community Development Act of 1992; regulations regarding accreditation of training providers**

(a) A program is hereby established within the department to meet the requirements of the Residential Lead–Based Paint Hazard Reduction Act of 1992 (42 U.S.C. Sec. 4851 and following) and Title X of the Housing and Community Development Act of 1992 (P.L. 102–550).

(b) The department shall implement and administer the program. The department shall have powers and authority consistent with the intent of, and shall promulgate regulations to establish the program as an authorized state program pursuant to, Title IV, Section 402 to 404, inclusive, of the Toxic Substances Control Act (15 U.S.C. Sec. 2601 and following).

(c) Regulations regarding accreditation of training providers that are promulgated pursuant to subdivision (b) shall include, but not be limited to, provisions governing accreditation of providers of health and safety training to employees who engage in or supervise lead-related construction work as defined in Section 6716 of the Labor Code, and certification of employees who have successfully completed that training. Regulations regarding accreditation of training providers shall, as a condition of accreditation, require providers to offer training that meets the requirements of Section 6717 of the Labor Code. The department shall, not later than August 1, 1994, adopt regulations establishing fees for the accreditation of training providers, the certification of individuals, and the licensing of entities engaged in lead-related occupations. The fees imposed under this subdivision shall be established at levels not exceeding an amount sufficient to cover the costs of administering and enforcing the standards and regulations promulgated under this section. The fees established pursuant to this subdivision shall not be imposed on any state or local government or nonprofit training program.

(d) All regulations affecting the training of employees shall be adopted in consultation with the Division of Occupational Safety and Health. The regulations shall include provisions for allocating to the division an appropriate portion of funds to be expended for the program for the division's cost of enforcing compliance with training and certification requirements. The department shall adopt regulations to establish the program on or before August 1, 1994.

(e) The department shall review and amend its training, certification, and accreditation regulations promulgated under this section as is necessary to ensure continued eligibility for federal and state funding of lead-hazard reduction activities in the state. *(Added by Stats.1995, c. 415 (S.B.1360), § 5.)*

Division 105

COMMUNICABLE DISEASE PREVENTION AND CONTROL

Part 4

HUMAN IMMUNODEFICIENCY VIRUS (HIV)

CHAPTER 7. MANDATED BLOOD TESTING AND CONFIDENTIALITY TO PROTECT PUBLIC HEALTH

Section
120980. Unauthorized disclosures; penalties; damages; prohibited uses of results; disclosure pursuant to state reporting requirements; monthly reports; definitions.

§ 120980. **Unauthorized disclosures; penalties; damages; prohibited uses of results; disclosure pursuant to state reporting requirements; monthly reports; definitions**

(a) Any person who negligently discloses results of an HIV test, as defined in subdivision (c) of Section 120775, to any third party, in a manner that identifies or provides identifying characteristics of the person to whom the test results apply, except pursuant to a written authorization, as described in subdivision (g), or except as provided in Section 1603.1, 1603.3, or 121022 or any other statute that expressly provides an exemption to this section, shall be assessed a civil penalty in an amount not to exceed two thousand five hundred dollars ($2,500) plus court costs, as determined by the court, which penalty and costs shall be paid to the subject of the test.

(b) Any person who willfully or maliciously discloses the results of an HIV test, as defined in subdivision (c) of Section 120775, to any third party, in a manner that identifies or provides identifying characteristics of the person to whom the test results apply, except pursuant to a written authorization, as described in subdivision (g), or except as provided in Section 1603.1, 1603.3, or 121022 or any other statute that expressly provides an exemption to this section, shall be assessed a civil penalty in an amount not less than five thousand dollars ($5,000) and not more than ten thousand dollars ($10,000) plus court costs, as determined by the court, which penalty and costs shall be paid to the subject of the test.

(c) Any person who willfully, maliciously, or negligently discloses the results of an HIV test, as defined in subdivision (c) of Section 120775, to a third party, in a manner that identifies or provides identifying characteristics of the person to whom the test results apply, except pursuant to a written authorization, as described in subdivision (g), or except as provided in Section 1603.1, 1603.3, or 121022 or any other statute that expressly provides an exemption to this section, that results in economic, bodily, or psychological harm to the subject of the test, is guilty of a misdemeanor, punishable by imprisonment in the county jail for a period not to exceed one year, or a fine of not to exceed twenty-five thousand dollars ($25,000), or both.

(d) Any person who commits any act described in subdivision (a) or (b) shall be liable to the subject for all actual damages, including damages for economic, bodily, or psychological harm that is a proximate result of the act.

(e) Each disclosure made in violation of this chapter is a separate and actionable offense.

(f) Except as provided in Article 6.9 (commencing with Section 799) of Chapter 1 of Part 2 of Division 1 of the Insurance Code, the results of an HIV test, as defined in subdivision (c) of Section 120775, that identifies or provides identifying characteristics of the person to whom the test results apply, shall not be used in any instance for the determination of insurability or suitability for employment.

(g) "Written authorization," as used in this section, applies only to the disclosure of test results by a person responsible for the care and treatment of the person subject to the test. Written authorization is required for each separate disclosure of the test results, and shall include to whom the disclosure would be made.

(h) Nothing in this section limits or expands the right of an injured subject to recover damages under any other applicable law. Nothing in this section shall impose civil liability or criminal sanction for disclosure of the results of tests performed on cadavers to public health authorities or tissue banks.

(i) Nothing in this section imposes liability or criminal sanction for disclosure of an HIV test, as defined in subdivision (c) of Section 120775, in accordance with any reporting requirement for a case of HIV infection, including AIDS by the department or the Centers for Disease Control and Prevention under the United States Public Health Service.

(j) The department may require blood banks and plasma centers to submit monthly reports summarizing statistical data concerning the results of tests to detect the presence of viral hepatitis and HIV. This statistical summary shall not include the identity of individual donors or identifying characteristics that would identify individual donors.

(k) "Disclosed," as used in this section, means to disclose, release, transfer, disseminate, or otherwise communicate all or any part of any record orally, in writing, or by electronic means to any person or entity.

(l) When the results of an HIV test, as defined in subdivision (c) of Section 120775, are included in the medical record of the patient who is the subject of the test, the inclusion is not a disclosure for purposes of this section. (Added by Stats.1995, c. 415 (S.B.1360), § 7. Amended by Stats.2006, c. 20 (S.B.699), § 4, eff. April 17, 2006.)

INSURANCE CODE

Division 1

GENERAL RULES GOVERNING INSURANCE

Part 2

THE BUSINESS OF INSURANCE

CHAPTER 1.   GENERAL REGULATIONS

ARTICLE 6.6.   INSURANCE INFORMATION
AND PRIVACY PROTECTION ACT

Section
791.27.   Release of information to employers; authorizations;
exceptions.

§ 791.27.   Release of information to employers; authorizations; exceptions

A disability insurer that provides coverage for hospital, medical, or surgical expenses shall not release any information to an employer that would directly or indirectly indicate to the employer that an employee is receiving or has received services from a health care provider covered by the plan unless authorized to do so by the employee.   An insurer that has, pursuant to an agreement, assumed the responsibility to pay compensation pursuant to Article 3 (commencing with Section 3750) of Chapter 4 of Part 1 of Division 4 of the Labor Code, shall not be considered an employer for the purposes of this section.   Nothing in this section prohibits a disability insurer from releasing relevant information described in this section for the purposes set forth in Chapter 12 (commencing with Section 1871) of Part 2 of Division 1.   *(Added by Stats.1994, c. 614 (S.B.1832), § 9.)*

Division 2

CLASSES OF INSURANCE

Part 2

LIFE AND DISABILITY INSURANCE

CHAPTER 1.   THE CONTRACT

ARTICLE 1.   GENERAL PROVISIONS

Section
10110.1.   Insurable interest; employers; trusts and special
purpose entities; time of requirement; charitable organizations.
10110.5.   Provision for waiver of premium payments in
event of involuntary unemployment of insured;
additional reserves; additional reports.
10116.   Continuance of group life or disability policies
during labor dispute; individual contributions.
10116.5.   Employee-sponsored group plan; disability policy; continuation coverage for certain qualified
beneficiaries; rates charged to employer.
10121.7.   Domestic partners; coverage.
10123.196.   Disability insurance; contraceptive coverage.

§ 10110.1.   Insurable interest; employers; trusts and special purpose entities; time of requirement; charitable organizations

(a) An insurable interest, with reference to life and disability insurance, is an interest based upon a reasonable expectation of pecuniary advantage through the continued life, health, or bodily safety of another person and consequent loss by reason of that person's death or disability or a substantial interest engendered by love and affection in the case of individuals closely related by blood or law.

(b) An individual has an unlimited insurable interest in his or her own life, health, and bodily safety and may lawfully take out a policy of insurance on his or her own life, health, or bodily safety and have the policy made payable to whomsoever he or she pleases, regardless of whether the beneficiary designated has an insurable interest.

(c) Except as provided in Section 10110.4, an employer has an insurable interest, as referred to in subdivision (a), in the life or physical or mental ability of any of its directors, officers, or employees or the directors, officers, or employees of any of its subsidiaries or any other person whose death or physical or mental disability might cause financial loss to the employer; or, pursuant to any contractual arrangement with any shareholder concerning the reacquisition of shares owned by the shareholder at the time of his or her death or disability, on the life or physical or mental ability of that shareholder for the purpose of carrying out the contractual arrangement; or, pursuant to any contract obligating the employer as part of compensation arrangements or pursuant to a contract obligating the employer as guarantor or surety, on the life of the principal obligor.   The trustee of an employer or trustee of a pension, welfare benefit plan, or trust established by an employer providing life, health, disability, retirement, or similar benefits to employees and retired employees of the employer or its affiliates and acting in a fiduciary capacity with respect to those employees, retired employees, or their dependents or beneficiaries has an insurable interest in the lives of employees and retired employees for whom those benefits are to be provided. The employer shall obtain the written consent of the individual being insured.

(d) Trusts and special purpose entities that are used to apply for and initiate the issuance of policies of insurance for investors, where one or more beneficiaries of those trusts or special purpose entities do not have an insurable interest in the life of the insured, violate the insurable interest laws and the prohibition against wagering on life.

(e) Any device, scheme, or artifice designed to give the appearance of an insurable interest where there is no legitimate insurable interest violates the insurable interest laws.

(f) An insurable interest shall be required to exist at the time the contract of life or disability insurance becomes effective, but need not exist at the time the loss occurs.

(g) Any contract of life or disability insurance procured or caused to be procured upon another individual is void unless the person applying for the insurance has an insurable interest in the individual insured at the time of the application.

(h) Notwithstanding subdivisions (a), (f), and (g), a charitable organization that meets the requirements of Section 214 or 23701d of the Revenue and Taxation Code may effectuate life or disability insurance on an insured who consents to the issuance of that insurance.

(i) This section shall not be interpreted to define all instances in which an insurable interest exists. *(Added by Stats.1990, c. 1418 (S.B.2281), § 1.5. Amended by Stats. 1994, c. 177 (S.B.1340), § 1; Stats.2003, c. 328 (A.B.226), § 1; Stats.2009, c. 343 (S.B.98), § 1.)*

§ 10110.5. Provision for waiver of premium payments in event of involuntary unemployment of insured; additional reserves; additional reports

A policy or endorsement issued by an admitted life and disability insurer may contain a provision for a waiver of premium payments in the event of involuntary unemployment of the insured. Insurers issuing policies or endorsements which contain that provision shall establish any additional reserves and file any additional financial reports that the commissioner may require. *(Added by Stats.2005, c. 67 (A.B.837), § 1.)*

§ 10116. Continuance of group life or disability policies during labor dispute; individual contributions

No group life insurance policy or disability insurance policy shall be issued or delivered in this State where the premiums or any part thereof is paid or is to be paid in whole or in part by an employer pursuant to the terms of a collective bargaining agreement unless the policy provides that in the event of a cessation of work by the employees covered by the policy as the result of a labor dispute the policy, upon timely payment of the premium, shall continue in effect with respect to all employees insured by the policy on the date of the cessation of work who continue to pay their individual contribution, and who assume and pay the contribution due from the employer, for the period of cessation of work, under the following conditions:

(a) If the policyholder is not a trustee or the trustees of a fund established or maintained in whole or in part by the employer, the policy shall provide that the employee's individual contribution shall be the rate in the policy, on the date cessation of work occurs, applicable to an individual in the class to which the employee belongs as set forth in the policy. If the policy does not provide for a rate applicable to individuals, the policy shall provide that the employee's individual contribution shall be an amount equal to the amount determined by dividing (1) the total monthly premium in effect under the policy at the date of cessation of work by (2) the total number of persons insured under the policy at such date.

(b) If the policyholder is a trustee or the trustees of a fund established or maintained in whole or in part by the employer, the employee's contribution shall be the amount which he and his employer would have been required to contribute to the trust for such employee if (1) the cessation of work had not occurred and (2) the agreement requiring the employer to make contributions to the trust were in full force.

(c) The policy may provide that the continuation of insurance is contingent upon the collection of individual contributions by the union or unions representing the employees for policies referred to in subdivision (a) above, and by the policyholder or the policyholder's agent with respect to policies referred to in subdivision (b) above.

(d) The policy may provide that the continuation of insurance on each employee is contingent upon timely payment of contributions by the individual and timely payment of the premium by the entity responsible for collecting the individual contributions.

(e) The policy may provide that each individual premium rate shall be increased by any amount up to twenty percent (20%), or any higher percent which may be approved by the commissioner, of that otherwise shown in the policy during the period of cessation of work in order to provide sufficient compensation to the insurer to cover increased administrative costs and increased mortality and morbidity. If the policy does provide for such an increase, this shall have the effect of increasing the employee's contribution by a like percent.

(f) Nothing in this section shall be deemed to limit any right which the insurer may have in accordance with the terms of the policy to increase or decrease the premium rates before, during or after such cessation of work if, in fact, the insurer would have had the right to increase the premium rate had the cessation of work not occurred. If such a premium rate change is made, it shall be effective, notwithstanding any other provisions of this section, on such date as the insurer shall determine in accordance with the terms of the policy.

(g) The policy may contain such other provisions with respect to such continuation of insurance as the commissioner may approve.

(h) The policy may provide that, if a premium is unpaid at the date of cessation of work and such premium became due prior to such cessation of work, the continuation of insurance is contingent upon payment of such premium prior to the date the next premium becomes due under the terms of the policy.

Nothing herein shall be deemed to require the continuation of any loss of time payments included in any such group disability policy, nor of any other coverages beyond the time that seventy-five percent (75%) of the employees continue such coverage or as to any individual employee beyond the time that he takes full-time employment with another employer; nor shall anything herein be deemed to require continuation of coverage more than six (6) months after the cessation of work.

Nothing in this section shall be construed as modifying or in any way affecting the operation and effect of the provisions of Part 2 of Division 1 of the Unemployment Insurance Code.[1] *(Added by Stats.1961, c. 2097, p. 4360, § 1.)*

[1] Unemployment Insurance Code § 2601 et seq.

§ 10116.5. Employee-sponsored group plan; disability policy; continuation coverage for certain qualified beneficiaries; rates charged to employer

(a) Every policy of disability insurance that is issued, amended, delivered, or renewed in this state on or after January 1, 1999, that provides hospital, medical, or surgical expense coverage under an employer-sponsored group plan for an employer subject to COBRA, as defined in subdivision (e), or an employer group for which the disability insurer is required to offer Cal–COBRA coverage, as defined in subdivision (f), including a carrier providing replacement coverage under Section 10128.3, shall further offer the former employee the opportunity to continue benefits as required under subdivision (b), and shall further offer the former spouse of an employee or former employee the opportunity to continue benefits as required under subdivision (c).

(b)(1) If a former employee worked for the employer for at least five years prior to the date of termination of employment and is 60 years of age or older on the date employment ends is entitled to and so elects to continue benefits under COBRA or Cal–COBRA for himself or herself and for any spouse, the employee or spouse may further continue benefits beyond the date coverage under COBRA or Cal–COBRA ends, as set forth in paragraph (2). Except as otherwise specified in this section, continuation coverage shall be under the same benefit terms and conditions as if the continuation coverage under COBRA or Cal–COBRA had remained in force. For the employee or spouse, continuation coverage following the end of COBRA or Cal–COBRA is subject to payment

of premiums to the insurer. Individuals ineligible for COBRA or Cal–COBRA or who are eligible but have not elected or exhausted continuation coverage under federal COBRA or Cal–COBRA are not entitled to continuation coverage under this section. Premiums for continuation coverage under this section shall be billed by, and remitted to, the insurer in accordance with subdivision (d). Failure to pay the requisite premiums may result in termination of the continuation coverage in accordance with the applicable provisions in the insurer's group contract with the employer.

(2) The employer shall notify the former employee or spouse or both, or the former spouse of the employee or former employee, of the availability of the continuation benefits under this section in accordance with Section 2800.2 of the Labor Code. To continue health care coverage pursuant to this section, the individual shall elect to do so by notifying the insurer in writing within 30 calendar days prior to the date continuation coverage under COBRA or Cal–COBRA is scheduled to end. Every disability insurer shall provide to the employer replacing a group benefit plan policy issued by the insurer, or to the employer's agent or broker representative, within 15 days of any written request, information in possession of the insurer reasonably required to administer the requirements of Section 2800.2 of the Labor Code.

(3) The continuation coverage shall end automatically on the earlier of (A) the date the individual reaches age 65, (B) the date the individual is covered under any group health plan not maintained by the employer or any other insurer or health care service plan, regardless of whether that coverage is less valuable, (C) the date the individual becomes entitled to Medicare under Title XVIII of the Social Security Act, (D) for a spouse, five years from the date on which continuation coverage under COBRA or Cal–COBRA was scheduled to end for the spouse, or (E) the date on which the employer terminates its group contract with the insurer and ceases to provide coverage for any active employees through that insurer, in which case the insurer shall notify the former employee or spouse, or both, of the right to a conversion policy.

(c)(1) If a former spouse of an employee or former employee was covered as a qualified beneficiary under COBRA or Cal–COBRA, the former spouse may further continue benefits beyond the date coverage under COBRA or Cal–COBRA ends, as set forth in paragraph (2) of subdivision (b). Except as otherwise specified in this section, continuation coverage shall be under the same benefit terms and conditions as if the continuation coverage under COBRA or Cal–COBRA had remained in force. Continuation coverage following the end of COBRA or Cal–COBRA is subject to payment of premiums to the insurer. Premiums for continuation coverage under this section shall be billed by, and remitted to, the insurer in accordance with subdivision (d). Failure to pay the requisite premiums may result in termination of the continuation coverage in accordance

251

with the applicable provisions in the insurer's group contract with the employer or former employer.

(2) The continuation coverage for the former spouse shall end automatically on the earlier of (A) the date the individual reaches 65 years of age, (B) the date the individual is covered under any group health plan not maintained by the employer or any other health care service plan or insurer, regardless of whether that coverage is less valuable, (C) the date the individual becomes entitled to Medicare under Title XVIII of the Social Security Act, (D) five years from the date on which continuation coverage under COBRA or Cal–COBRA was scheduled to end for the former spouse, or (E) the date on which the employer or former employer terminates its group contract with the insurer and ceases to provide coverage for any active employees through that insurer, in which case the insurer shall notify the former spouse of the right to a conversion policy.

(d)(1) If the premium charged to the employer for a specific employee or dependent eligible under this section is adjusted for the age of the specific employee, or eligible dependent, on other than a composite basis, the rate for continuation coverage under this section shall not exceed 102 percent of the premium charged by the insurer to the employer for an employee of the same age as the former employee electing continuation coverage in the case of an individual who was eligible for COBRA, and 110 percent in the case of an individual who was eligible for Cal–COBRA. If the coverage continued is that of a former spouse, the premium charged shall not exceed 102 percent of the premium charged by the plan to the employer for an employee of the same age as the former spouse selecting continuation coverage in the case of an individual who was eligible for COBRA, and 110 percent in the case of an individual who was eligible for Cal–COBRA.

(2) If the premium charged to the employer for a specific employee or dependent eligible under this section is not adjusted for age of the specific employee, or eligible dependent, then the rate for continuation coverage under this section shall not exceed 213 percent of the applicable current group rate. For purposes of this section, the "applicable current group rate" means the total premiums charged by the insurer for coverage for the group, divided by the relevant number of covered persons.

(3) However, in computing the premiums charged to the specific employer group, the insurer shall not include consideration of the specific medical care expenditures for beneficiaries receiving continuation coverage pursuant to this section.

(e) For purposes of this section, "COBRA" means Section 4980B of Title 26, Section 1161 and following of Title 29, and Section 300bb of Title 42 of the United States Code, as added by the Consolidated Omnibus Budget Reconciliation Act of 1985 (P.L. 99–272), and as amended.

(f) For purposes of this section, "Cal-COBRA" means the continuation coverage that must be offered pursuant to Article 1.7 (commencing with Section 10128.50), or Article 4.5 (commencing with Section 1366.20) of Chapter 2.2 of Division 2 of the Health and Safety Code.

(g) For the purposes of this section, "former spouse" means either an individual who is divorced from an employee or former employee or an individual who was married to an employee or former employee at the time of the death of the employee or former employee.

(h) Every group benefit plan evidence of coverage that is issued, amended, or renewed after January 1, 1999, shall contain a description of the provisions and eligibility requirements for the continuation coverage offered pursuant to this section.

(i) This section shall take effect on January 1, 1999.

(j) This section does not apply to any individual who is not eligible for its continuation coverage prior to January 1, 2005. *(Added by Stats.1997, c. 665 (S.B.719), § 5, operative Jan. 1, 1999. Amended by Stats.1998, c. 107 (A.B.112), § 14, eff. July 6, 1998, operative Jan. 1, 1999; Stats.1999, c. 83 (S.B.966), § 122; Stats.2004, c. 64 (A.B.254), § 2.)*

Effective Date

For effective date of this section, see its terms.

§ 10121.7. Domestic partners; coverage

(a) A policy of group health insurance that provides hospital, medical, or surgical expense benefits shall provide equal coverage to employers or guaranteed associations, as defined in Section 10700, for the registered domestic partner of an employee, insured, or policyholder to the same extent, and subject to the same terms and conditions, as provided to a spouse of the employee, insured, or policyholder, and shall inform employers and guaranteed associations of this coverage. A policy may not offer or provide coverage for a registered domestic partner that is not equal to the coverage provided to the spouse of an employee, insured, or policyholder.

(b) If an employer or guaranteed association has purchased coverage for spouses and registered domestic partners pursuant to subdivision (a), a health insurer that provides hospital, medical, or surgical expense benefits for employees, insureds, or policyholders and their spouses shall enroll, upon application by the employer or group administrator, a registered domestic partner of the employee, insured, or policyholder in accordance with the terms and conditions of the group contract that apply generally to all spouses under the policy, including coordination of benefits.

(c) For purposes of this section, the term "domestic partner" shall have the same meaning as that term is used in Section 297 of the Family Code.

(d)(1) A policy of group health insurance may require that the employee, insured, or policyholder verify the status of the domestic partnership by providing to the insurer a copy of a valid Declaration of Domestic Partnership filed with the Secretary of State pursuant to Section 298 of the Family Code or an equivalent document issued by a local agency of this state, another state, or a local agency of another state under which the partnership was created. The policy may also require that the employee, insured, or policyholder notify the insurer upon the termination of the domestic partnership.

(2) Notwithstanding paragraph (1), a policy may require the information described in that paragraph only if it also requests from the employee, insured, or policyholder whose spouse is provided coverage, verification of marital status and notification of dissolution of the marriage.

(e) Nothing in this section shall be construed to expand the requirements of Section 4980B of Title 26 of the United States Code, Section 1161, and following, of Title 29 of the United States Code, or Section 300bb–1, and following, of Title 42 of the United States Code, as added by the Consolidated Omnibus Budget Reconciliation Act of 1985 (Public Law 99–272), and as those provisions may be later amended.

(f) A group health insurance policy subject to this section that is issued, amended, delivered, or renewed in this state on or after January 2, 2005, shall be deemed to provide coverage for registered domestic partners that is equal to the coverage provided to a spouse of an employee, insured, or policyholder. *(Added by Stats. 2001, c. 893 (A.B.25), § 11. Amended by Stats.2004, c. 488 (A.B.2208), § 4.)*

§ 10123.196. Disability insurance; contraceptive coverage

(a) Every individual and group policy of disability insurance issued, amended, renewed, or delivered on or after January 1, 2000, that provides coverage for hospital, medical, or surgical expenses, shall provide coverage for the following, under the same terms and conditions as applicable to all benefits:

(1) A disability insurance policy that provides coverage for outpatient prescription drug benefits shall include coverage for a variety of federal Food and Drug Administration (FDA) approved prescription contraceptive methods, as designated by the insurer. If an insured's health care provider determines that none of the methods designated by the disability insurer is medically appropriate for the insured's medical or personal history, the insurer shall, in the alternative, provide coverage for some other FDA approved prescription contraceptive method prescribed by the patient's health care provider.

(2) Outpatient prescription coverage with respect to an insured shall be identical for an insured's covered spouse and covered nonspouse dependents.

(b) Nothing in this section shall be construed to deny or restrict in any way any existing right or benefit provided under law or by contract.

(c) Nothing in this section shall be construed to require an individual or group disability insurance policy to cover experimental or investigational treatments.

(d) Notwithstanding any other provision of this section, a religious employer may request a disability insurance policy without coverage for contraceptive methods that are contrary to the religious employer's religious tenets. If so requested, a disability insurance policy shall be provided without coverage for contraceptive methods.

(1) For purposes of this section, a "religious employer" is an entity for which each of the following is true:

(A) The inculcation of religious values is the purpose of the entity.

(B) The entity primarily employs persons who share the religious tenets of the entity.

(C) The entity serves primarily persons who share the religious tenets of the entity.

(D) The entity is a nonprofit organization pursuant to Section 6033(a)(2)(A)(i) or (iii) of the Internal Revenue Code of 1986, as amended.

(2) Every religious employer that invokes the exemption provided under this section shall provide written notice to any prospective employee once an offer of employment has been made, and prior to that person commencing that employment, listing the contraceptive health care services the employer refuses to cover for religious reasons.

(e) Nothing in this section shall be construed to exclude coverage for prescription contraceptive supplies ordered by a health care provider with prescriptive authority for reasons other than contraceptive purposes, such as decreasing the risk of ovarian cancer or eliminating symptoms of menopause, or for prescription contraception that is necessary to preserve the life or health of an insured.

(f) This section shall only apply to disability insurance policies or contracts that are defined as health benefit plans pursuant to subdivision (a) of Section 10198.6, except that for accident only, specified disease, or hospital indemnity coverage, coverage for benefits under this section shall apply to the extent that the benefits are covered under the general terms and conditions that apply to all other benefits under the policy or contract. Nothing in this section shall be construed as imposing a new benefit mandate on accident only, specified disease, or hospital indemnity insurance. *(Added by Stats.1999, c. 538 (S.B.41), § 2.)*

ARTICLE 1.7. CALIFORNIA COBRA PROGRAM

Section
10128.50. California Continuation Benefits Replacement Act (Cal–COBRA).
10128.51. Definitions.
10128.52. Continuation coverage requirements; exclusions from article.

Section

10128.53.   Disability insurer; group benefit plan coverage; continuation coverage; qualified beneficiaries.

10128.54.   Disclosure of continuation coverage; policyholders or contractholders.

10128.55.   Qualifying event; notification to insurer; qualified beneficiaries; contracting for administrative services; premium assistance.

10128.56.   Qualified beneficiary electing continuation coverage; payments to disability insurer.

10128.57.   Termination of continuation coverage.

10128.58.   Obligation to provide continuation coverage; exclusions.

10128.59.   Exhaustion of federal coverage; continuation up to 36 months.

§ 10128.50. California Continuation Benefits Replacement Act (Cal–COBRA)

(a) This article shall be known as the California Continuation Benefits Replacement Act, or "Cal–COBRA."

(b) It is the intent of the Legislature that continued access to health insurance coverage is provided to employees, and their dependents, of employers with 2 to 19 eligible employees who are not currently offered continuation coverage under the Consolidated Omnibus Budget Reconciliation Act of 1985.

(c) It is the intent of the Legislature that any federal assistance that is or may become available to qualified beneficiaries under this article be effectively and promptly implemented by the department.

(d) The commissioner, in consultation with the Director of the Department of Managed Health Care, may adopt emergency regulations to implement this article in accordance with Chapter 3.5 (commencing with Section 11340) of Part 1 of Division 3 of Title 2 of the Government Code by making a finding of emergency and demonstrating the need for immediate action in the event that any federal assistance is or becomes available to qualified beneficiaries under this article. The adoption of these regulations shall be considered by the Office of Administrative Law to be necessary to avoid serious harm to the public peace, health, safety, or general welfare. Any regulations adopted pursuant to this subdivision shall be substantially similar to those adopted by the Director of the Department of Managed Health Care under subdivision (d) of Section 1366.20 of the Health and Safety Code. *(Added by Stats.1997, c. 665 (S.B.719), § 6. Amended by Stats.2009, c. 3 (A.B.23), § 5, eff. May 12, 2009.)*

§ 10128.51. Definitions

(a) "Continuation coverage" means extended coverage under the group benefit plan under which an eligible employee or eligible dependent is currently covered, or, in the case of a termination of the group benefit plan or an employer open enrollment period, extended coverage under the group benefit plan currently offered by the employer.

(b) "Group benefit plan" has the same meaning as "health benefit plan" defined in Section 10700, including group policies of vision-only and dental-only coverage, provided pursuant to Chapter 8 (commencing with Section 10700) to an employer with 2 to 19 eligible employees, as defined in Section 10700.

(c)(1) "Qualified beneficiary" means any individual who, on the day before the qualifying event, is covered under a group benefit plan offered by a disability insurer pursuant to Article 1 (commencing with Section 10700) of Chapter 8, and has a qualifying event, as defined in subdivision (d).

(2) "Qualified beneficiary eligible for premium assistance under Title III of Division B of the American Recovery and Reinvestment Act of 2009 (Public Law 111–5)" means a qualified beneficiary, as defined in paragraph (1), who (A) was or is eligible for continuation coverage as a result of the involuntary termination of the covered employee's employment during the period that begins with September 1, 2008, and ends with December 31, 2009, (B) elects continuation coverage, and (C) meets the definition of "qualified beneficiary" set forth in paragraph (3) of Section 1167 of Title 29 of the United States Code, as used in subparagraph (E) of paragraph (1) of subdivision (a) of Section 3001 of Title III of Division B of the American Recovery and Reinvestment Act of 2009 (Public Law 111–5) or any subsequent rules or regulations issued pursuant to that law.

(d) "Qualifying event" means any of the following events that, but for the election of continuation coverage under this article, would result in a loss of coverage under the group benefit plan to a qualified beneficiary:

(1) The death of the covered employee.

(2) The termination of employment or reduction in hours of the covered employee's employment, except that termination for gross misconduct does not constitute a qualifying event.

(3) The divorce or legal separation of the covered employee from the covered employee's spouse.

(4) The loss of dependent status by a dependent enrolled in the group benefit plan.

(5) With respect to a covered dependent only, the covered employee's entitlement to benefits under Title XVIII of the United States Social Security Act (Medicare).

(e) "Employer" means any employer that meets the definition of "small employer" as set forth in Section 10700 and (1) employed 2 to 19 eligible employees on at least 50 percent of its working days during the preceding calendar year, or, if the employer was not in business during any part of the preceding calendar year, employed 2 to 19 eligible employees on at least 50 percent of its working days during the preceding calendar quarter, (2) has contracted for health care coverage through a group benefit plan offered by a disability insurer, and (3) is not subject to Section 4980B of the United States Internal

Revenue Code [1] or Chapter 18 of the Employee Retirement Income Security Act, 29 U.S.C. Section 1161 et seq.

(f) "Core coverage" means coverage for hospital, medical, or surgical benefits provided under the group benefit plan that a qualified beneficiary was receiving immediately prior to the qualifying event, other than noncore coverage.

(g) "Noncore coverage" means coverage for vision and dental care. *(Added by Stats.1997, c. 665 (S.B.719), § 6. Amended by Stats.1998, c. 107 (A.B.112), § 15, eff. July 6, 1998; Stats.2009, c. 3 (A.B.23), § 6, eff. May 12, 2009.)*

[1] Internal Revenue Code sections are in Title 26 of the U.S.C.A.

§ 10128.52. Continuation coverage requirements; exclusions from article

The continuation coverage requirements of this article do not apply to the following individuals:

(a) Individuals who are entitled to Medicare benefits or become entitled to Medicare benefits pursuant to Title XVIII of the United States Social Security Act, as amended or superseded. Entitlement to Medicare Part A only constitutes entitlement to benefits under Medicare.

(b) Individuals who have other hospital, medical, or surgical coverage, or who are covered or become covered under another group benefit plan, including a self-insured employee welfare benefit plan, that provides coverage for individuals and that does not impose any exclusion or limitation with respect to any preexisting condition of the individual, other than a preexisting condition limitation or exclusion that does not apply to or is satisfied by the qualified beneficiary pursuant to Sections 10198.6 and 10198.7. A group conversion option under any group benefit plan shall not be considered as an arrangement under which an individual is or becomes covered.

(c) Individuals who are covered, become covered, or are eligible for federal COBRA coverage pursuant to Section 4980B of the United States Internal Revenue Code [1] or Chapter 18 of the Employee Retirement Income Security Act, 29 U.S.C. Section 1161 et seq.

(d) Individuals who are covered, become covered, or are eligible for coverage pursuant to Chapter 6A of the Public Health Service Act, 42 U.S.C. Section 300bb–1 et seq.

(e) Qualified beneficiaries who fail to meet the requirements of subdivision (b) of Section 10128.54 or subdivision (h) of Section 10128.55 regarding notification of a qualifying event or election of continuation coverage within the specified time limits.

(f) Qualified beneficiaries who fail to submit the correct premium amount required by subdivision (b) of Section 10128.55 and Section 10128.57, in accordance with the terms and conditions of the policy or contract, or fail to satisfy other terms and conditions of the policy or contract. *(Added by Stats.1997, c. 665 (S.B.719), § 6.*

Amended by Stats.1998, c. 107 (A.B.112), § 16, eff. July 6, 1998; Stats.2009, c. 3 (A.B.23), § 7, eff. May 12, 2009.)

[1] Internal Revenue Code sections are in Title 26 of the U.S.C.A.

§ 10128.53. Disability insurer; group benefit plan coverage; continuation coverage; qualified beneficiaries

(a) Every disability insurer, that provides coverage under a group benefit plan to an employer, including those policies and contracts that provide vision-only and dental-only benefits, as defined in Section 10128.51, shall offer continuation coverage, pursuant to this section, to a qualified beneficiary under the contract upon a qualifying event without evidence of insurability. The qualified beneficiary shall, upon election, be able to continue his or her coverage under the group benefit plan, subject to the contract's terms and conditions, and subject to the requirements of this section. Except as otherwise provided in this section, continuation coverage shall be provided under the same terms and conditions that apply to similarly situated individuals under the group benefit plan.

(b) Every disability insurer shall also offer the continuation coverage to a qualified beneficiary who (1) elects continuation coverage under a group benefit plan as defined in this article or in Section 1366.21 of the Health and Safety Code, but whose continuation coverage is terminated under the group benefit plan pursuant to subdivision (b) of Section 10128.57, prior to any other termination date specified in Section 10128.57, or (2) who elects coverage through the disability insurer during any employer open enrollment, and the employer has contracted with the disability insurer to provide coverage to the employer's active employees. This continuation coverage shall be provided only for the balance of the period that the qualified beneficiary would have remained covered under the prior group benefit plan had the employer not terminated the contract with the previous insurer or health care service plan.

(c) Every disability insurer shall offer a qualified beneficiary the ability to elect the same core, noncore, or core and noncore coverage that the qualified beneficiary had immediately prior to the qualifying event.

(d) Any child who is born to a former employee who is a qualified beneficiary who has elected continuation coverage pursuant to this section, or a child who is placed for adoption with a former employee who is a qualified beneficiary who has elected continuation coverage pursuant to this article during the period of continuation coverage provided by this article shall be considered a qualified beneficiary entitled to receive benefits pursuant to this article for the remainder of the period that the former employee is covered pursuant to this article, if the child is enrolled under a group benefit plan as a dependent of that former employee who is a qualified beneficiary within 30 days of the child's birth or placement for adoption.

(e) An individual who becomes a qualified beneficiary pursuant to this article shall continue to receive coverage pursuant to this article until continuation coverage is terminated at the qualified beneficiary's election or pursuant to Section 10128.57, whichever comes first, even if the employer that sponsored the group benefit plan that is continued subsequently becomes subject to Section 4980B of the United States Internal Revenue Code of Chapter 18 of the Employee Retirement Income Security Act, 29 U.S.C. Sec. 1161 et seq.

(f) A qualified beneficiary electing coverage pursuant to this section shall be considered part of the group benefit plan and treated as similarly situated employees for contract purposes, unless otherwise specified in this article. *(Added by Stats.1997, c. 665 (S.B.719), § 6. Amended by Stats.1998, c. 107 (A.B.112), § 17, eff. July 6, 1998.)*

§ 10128.54. Disclosure of continuation coverage; policyholders or contractholders

(a) Every insurer's evidence of coverage for group benefit plans subject to this article, that is issued, amended, or renewed on or after January 1, 1999, shall disclose to covered employees of group benefit plans subject to this article the ability to continue coverage pursuant to this article, as required by this section.

(b) This disclosure shall state that all insureds who are eligible to be qualified beneficiaries, as defined in subdivision (c) of Section 10128.51, shall be required, as a condition of receiving benefits pursuant to this article, to notify, in writing, the insurer, or the employer if the employer contracts to perform the administrative services as provided for in Section 10128.55, of all qualifying events as specified in paragraphs (1), (3), (4), and (5) of subdivision (d) of Section 10128.51 within 60 days of the date of the qualifying event. This disclosure shall inform insureds that failure to make the notification to the insurer, or to the employer when under contract to provide the administrative services, within the required 60 days will disqualify the qualified beneficiary from receiving continuation coverage pursuant to this article. The disclosure shall further state that a qualified beneficiary who wishes to continue coverage under the group benefit plan pursuant to this article must request the continuation in writing and deliver the written request, by first-class mail, or other reliable means of delivery, including personal delivery, express mail, or private courier company, to the disability insurer, or to the employer if the plan has contracted with the employer for administrative services pursuant to subdivision (d) of Section 10128.55, within the 60–day period following the later of (1) the date that the insured's coverage under the group benefit plan terminated or will terminate by reason of a qualifying event, or (2) the date the insured was sent notice pursuant to subdivision (e) of Section 10128.55 of the ability to continue coverage under the group benefit plan. The disclosure required by this section shall also state that a qualified beneficiary electing continuation shall pay to the disability insurer, in accordance with the terms and conditions of the policy or contract, which shall be set forth in the notice to the qualified beneficiary pursuant to subdivision (d) of Section 10128.55, the amount of the required premium payment, as set forth in Section 10128.56. The disclosure shall further require that the qualified beneficiary's first premium payment required to establish premium payment be delivered by first-class mail, certified mail, or other reliable means of delivery, including personal delivery, express mail, or private courier company, to the disability insurer, or to the employer if the employer has contracted with the insurer to perform the administrative services pursuant to subdivision (d) of Section 10128.55, within 45 days of the date the qualified beneficiary provided written notice to the insurer or the employer, if the employer has contracted to perform the administrative services, of the election to continue coverage in order for coverage to be continued under this article. This disclosure shall also state that the first premium payment must equal an amount sufficient to pay all required premiums and all premiums due, and that failure to submit the correct premium amount within the 45–day period will disqualify the qualified beneficiary from receiving continuation coverage pursuant to this article.

(c) The disclosure required by this section shall also describe separately how qualified beneficiaries whose continuation coverage terminates under a prior group benefit plan pursuant to Section 10128.57 may continue their coverage for the balance of the period that the qualified beneficiary would have remained covered under the prior group benefit plan, including the requirements for election and payment. The disclosure shall clearly state that continuation coverage shall terminate if the qualified beneficiary fails to comply with the requirements pertaining to enrollment in, and payment of premiums to, the new group benefit plan within 30 days of receiving notice of the termination of the prior group benefit plan.

(d) Prior to August 1, 1998, every insurer shall provide to all covered employees of employers subject to this article written notice containing the disclosures required by this section, or shall provide to all covered employees of employers subject to this article a new or amended evidence of coverage that includes the disclosures required by this section. Any insurer that, in the ordinary course of business, maintains only the addresses of employer group purchasers of benefits, and does not maintain addresses of covered employees, may comply with the notice requirements of this section through the provision of the notices to its employer group purchases of benefits.

(e) Every disclosure form issued, amended, or renewed on and after January 1, 1999, for a group benefit plan subject to this article shall provide a notice that, under state law, an insured may be entitled to continuation of group coverage and that additional information regarding eligibility for this coverage may be found in the evidence of coverage.

(f) Every disclosure form issued, amended, or renewed on and after July 1, 2006, for a group benefit plan subject to this article shall include the following notice:

"Please examine your options carefully before declining this coverage. You should be aware that companies selling individual health insurance typically require a review of your medical history that could result in a higher premium or you could be denied coverage entirely." *(Added by Stats.1997, c. 665 (S.B.719), § 6. Amended by Stats.1998, c. 107 (A.B.112), § 18, eff. July 6, 1998; Stats.2005, c. 526 (A.B.356), § 7.)*

§ 10128.55. Qualifying event; notification to insurer; qualified beneficiaries; contracting for administrative services; premium assistance

(a) Every group benefit plan contract between a disability insurer and an employer subject to this article that is issued, amended, or renewed on or after July 1, 1998, shall require the employer to notify the insurer in writing of any employee who has had a qualifying event, as defined in paragraph (2) of subdivision (d) of Section 10128.51, within 30 days of the qualifying event. The group contract shall also require the employer to notify the insurer, in writing, within 30 days of the date when the employer becomes subject to Section 4980B of the United States Internal Revenue Code [1] or Chapter 18 of the Employee Retirement Income Security Act, 29 U.S.C. Sec. 1161 et seq.

(b) Every group benefit plan contract between a disability insurer and an employer subject to this article that is issued, amended, or renewed after July 1, 1998, shall require the employer to notify qualified beneficiaries currently receiving continuation coverage, whose continuation coverage will terminate under one group benefit plan prior to the end of the period the qualified beneficiary would have remained covered, as specified in Section 10128.57, of the qualified beneficiary's ability to continue coverage under a new group benefit plan for the balance of the period the qualified beneficiary would have remained covered under the prior group benefit plan. This notice shall be provided either 30 days prior to the termination or when all enrolled employees are notified, whichever is later.

Every disability insurer shall provide to the employer replacing a group benefit plan policy issued by the insurer, or to the employer's agent or broker representative, within 15 days of any written request, information in possession of the insurer reasonably required to administer the notification requirements of this subdivision and subdivision (c).

(c) Notwithstanding subdivision (a), the group benefit plan contract between the insurer and the employer shall require the employer to notify the successor plan in writing of the qualified beneficiaries currently receiving continuation coverage so that the successor plan, or contracting employer or administrator, may provide those qualified beneficiaries with the necessary premium information, enrollment forms, and instructions consistent with the disclosure required by subdivision (c) of Section 10128.54 and subdivision (e) of this section to allow the qualified beneficiary to continue coverage. This information shall be sent to all qualified beneficiaries who are enrolled in the group benefit plan and those qualified beneficiaries who have been notified, pursuant to Section 10128.54 of their ability to continue their coverage and may still elect coverage within the specified 60–day period. This information shall be sent to the qualified beneficiary's last known address, as provided to the employer by the health care service plan or, disability insurer currently providing continuation coverage to the qualified beneficiary. The successor insurer shall not be obligated to provide this information to qualified beneficiaries if the employer or prior insurer or health care service plan fails to comply with this section.

(d) A disability insurer may contract with an employer, or an administrator, to perform the administrative obligations of the plan as required by this article, including required notifications and collecting and forwarding premiums to the insurer. Except for the requirements of subdivisions (a), (b), and (c), this subdivision shall not be construed to permit an insurer to require an employer to perform the administrative obligations of the insurer as required by this article as a condition of the issuance or renewal of coverage.

(e) Every insurer, or employer or administrator that contracts to perform the notice and administrative services pursuant to this section, shall, within 14 days of receiving a notice of a qualifying event, provide to the qualified beneficiary the necessary premium information, enrollment forms, and disclosures consistent with the notice requirements contained in subdivisions (b) and (c) of Section 10128.54 to allow the qualified beneficiary to formally elect continuation coverage. This information shall be sent to the qualified beneficiary's last known address.

(f) Every insurer, or employer or administrator that contracts to perform the notice and administrative services pursuant to this section, shall, during the 180–day period ending on the date that continuation coverage is terminated pursuant to paragraphs (1), (3), and (5) of subdivision (a) of Section 10128.57, notify a qualified beneficiary who has elected continuation coverage pursuant to this article of the date that his or her coverage will terminate, and shall notify the qualified beneficiary of any conversion coverage available to that qualified beneficiary. This requirement shall not apply when the continuation coverage is terminated because the group contract between the insurer and the employer is being terminated.

(g)(1) An insurer shall provide to a qualified beneficiary who has a qualifying event between September 1, 2008, and December 31, 2009, inclusive, a written notice containing information on the availability of premium assistance under Title III of Division B of the American Recovery and Reinvestment Act of 2009 (Public Law 111–5). This notice shall be sent to the qualified

257

beneficiary's last known address. The notice shall include clear and easily understandable language to inform the qualified beneficiary that changes in federal law provide a new opportunity to elect continuation coverage with a 65–percent premium subsidy and shall include all of the following:

(A) The amount of the premium the person will pay. For qualified beneficiaries who had a qualifying event between September 1, 2008, and the effective date of this subdivision, inclusive, if an insurer is unable to provide the correct premium amount in the notice, the notice may contain the last known premium amount and an opportunity for the qualified beneficiary to request, through a toll-free telephone number, the correct premium that would apply to the beneficiary.

(B) Enrollment forms and any other information required to be included pursuant to subdivision (e) to allow the qualified beneficiary to elect continuation coverage. This information shall not be included in notices sent to qualified beneficiaries currently enrolled in continuation coverage.

(C) A description of the option to enroll in different coverage as provided in subparagraph (B) of paragraph (1) of subdivision (a) of Section 3001 of Title III of Division B of the American Recovery and Reinvestment Act of 2009 (Public Law 111–5). This description shall advise the qualified beneficiary to contact the covered employee's former employer for prior approval to choose this option.

(D) The eligibility requirements for premium assistance in the amount of 65 percent of the premium under Section 3001 of Title III of Division B of the American Recovery and Reinvestment Act of 2009 (Public Law 111–5).

(E) The duration of premium assistance available under Title III of Division B of the American Recovery and Reinvestment Act of 2009 (Public Law 111–5).

(F) A statement that a qualified beneficiary eligible for premium assistance under Title III of Division B of the American Recovery and Reinvestment Act of 2009 (Public Law 111–5) may elect continuation coverage no later than 60 days of the date of the notice.

(G) A statement that a qualified beneficiary eligible for premium assistance under Title III of Division B of the American Recovery and Reinvestment Act of 2009 (Public Law 111–5) who rejected or discontinued continuation coverage prior to receiving the notice required by this subdivision has the right to withdraw that rejection and elect continuation coverage with the premium assistance.

(H) A statement that reads as follows:

IF YOU ARE HAVING ANY DIFFICULTIES READING OR UNDERSTANDING THIS NOTICE, PLEASE CONTACT [name of insurer] at [insert appropriate telephone number].

(2) With respect to qualified beneficiaries who had a qualifying event between September 1, 2008, and the effective date of this subdivision, inclusive, the notice described in this subdivision shall be provided within the later of 14 calendar days of the effective date of this subdivision or seven business days after the date the insurer receives notice of the qualifying event.

(3) With respect to qualified beneficiaries who had or have a qualifying event between the day after the effective date of this subdivision, and December 31, 2009, inclusive, the notice described in this subdivision shall be provided within the period of time specified in subdivision (e).

(4) Nothing in this section shall be construed to require an insurer to provide the insurer's evidence of coverage as a part of the notice required by this subdivision, and nothing in this section shall be construed require an insurer to amend its existing evidence of coverage to comply with the changes made to this section by the act amending this section during the first year of the 2009–10 Regular Session.

(h)(1) Notwithstanding any other provision of law, a qualified beneficiary eligible for premium assistance under Title III of Division B of the American Recovery and Reinvestment Act of 2009 (Public Law 111–5) may elect continuation coverage no later than 60 days after the date of the notice required by subdivision (g).

(2) For a qualified beneficiary who elects to continue coverage pursuant to paragraph (1), the period beginning on the date of the qualifying event and ending on the effective date of the continuation coverage shall be disregarded for purposes of calculating a break in coverage in determining whether a preexisting condition provision applies under subdivision (e) of Section 10198.7 or subdivision (c) of Section 10708.

(3) For a qualified beneficiary who had a qualifying event between September 1, 2008, and February 16, 2009, inclusive, and who elects continuation coverage pursuant to paragraph (1), the continuation coverage shall commence on the first day of the month following the election.

(4) For a qualified beneficiary who had a qualifying event between February 17, 2009, and the effective date of this subdivision, inclusive, and who elects continuation coverage pursuant to paragraph (1), the effective date of the continuation coverage shall be either of the following, at the option of the beneficiary, provided that the beneficiary pays the applicable premiums:

(A) The date of the qualifying event.

(B) The first day of the month following the election.

(i) Notwithstanding any other provision of law, a qualified beneficiary eligible for premium assistance under Title III of Division B of the American Recovery and Reinvestment Act of 2009 (Public Law 111–5) may elect to enroll in different coverage subject to the criteria provided under subparagraph (B) of paragraph (1) of subdivision (a) of Section 3001 of Title III of Division B of the American Recovery and Reinvestment Act of 2009 (Public Law 111–5).

(j) A qualified beneficiary enrolled in continuation coverage as of February 17, 2009, who is eligible for premium assistance under Title III of Division B of the American Recovery and Reinvestment Act of 2009 (Public Law 111–5) may request application of the premium assistance as of March 1, 2009, or later, consistent with Title III of Division B of the American Recovery and Reinvestment Act of 2009 (Public Law 111–5).

(k) An insurer that receives an election notice from a qualified beneficiary eligible for premium assistance under Title III of Division B of the American Recovery and Reinvestment Act of 2009 (Public Law 111–5), pursuant to subdivision (h), shall be considered a person entitled to reimbursement, as defined in Section 6432(b)(3) of the Internal Revenue Code, as amended by paragraph (12) of subdivision (a) of Section 3001 of Title III of Division B of the American Recovery and Reinvestment Act of 2009 (Public Law 111–5).

(*l*)(1) For purposes of compliance with Title III of Division B of the American Recovery and Reinvestment Act of 2009 (Public Law 111–5), in the absence of guidance from, or if specifically required for state-only continuation coverage by, the United States Department of Labor, the Internal Revenue Service, or the Centers for Medicare and Medicaid Services, an insurer may request verification of the involuntary termination of a covered employee's employment from the covered employee's former employer or the qualified beneficiary seeking premium assistance under Title III of Division B of the American Recovery and Reinvestment Act of 2009 (Public Law 111–5).

(2) An insurer that requests verification pursuant to paragraph (1) directly from a covered employee's former employer shall do so by providing a written notice to the employer. This written notice shall be sent by mail or facsimile to the covered employee's former employer within seven business days from the date the insurer receives the qualified beneficiary's election notice pursuant to subdivision (h). Within 10 calendar days of receipt of written notice required by this paragraph, the former employer shall furnish to the insurer written verification as to whether the covered employee's employment was involuntarily terminated.

(3) A qualified beneficiary requesting premium assistance under Title III of Division B of the American Recovery and Reinvestment Act of 2009 (Public Law 111–5) may furnish to the insurer a written document or other information from the covered employee's former employer indicating that the covered employee's employment was involuntarily terminated. This document or information shall be deemed sufficient by the insurer to establish that the covered employee's employment was involuntarily terminated for purposes of Title III of Division B of the American Recovery and Reinvestment Act of 2009 (Public Law 111–5), unless the insurer makes a reasonable and timely determination that the documents or information provided by the qualified beneficiary are legally insufficient to establish involuntary termination of employment.

(4) If an insurer requests verification pursuant to this subdivision and cannot verify involuntary termination of employment within 14 business days from the date the employer receives the verification request or from date the insurer receives documentation or other information from the qualified beneficiary pursuant to paragraph (3), the insurer shall either provide continuation coverage with the federal premium assistance to the qualified beneficiary or send the qualified beneficiary a denial letter which shall include notice of his or her right to appeal that determination pursuant to Title III of Division B of the American Recovery and Reinvestment Act of 2009 (Public Law 111–5).

(5) No person shall intentionally delay verification of involuntary termination of employment under this subdivision. *(Added by Stats.1997, c. 665 (S.B.719), § 6. Amended by Stats.1998, c. 107 (A.B.112), § 19, eff. July 6, 1998; Stats.2009, c. 3 (A.B.23), § 8, eff. May 12, 2009.)*

[1] Internal Revenue Code sections are in Title 26 of the U.S.C.A.

§ 10128.56. Qualified beneficiary electing continuation coverage; payments to disability insurer

A qualified beneficiary electing continuation coverage shall pay to the disability insurer, on or before the due date of each payment but not more frequently than on a monthly basis, not more than 110 percent of the applicable rate charged for a covered employee or, in the case of dependent coverage, not more than 110 percent of the applicable rate charged to a similarly situated individual under the group benefit plan being continued under the group contract. In the case of a qualified beneficiary who is determined to be disabled pursuant to Title II or Title XVI of the United States Social Security Act, the qualified beneficiary shall be required to pay to the insurer an amount no greater than 150 percent of the group rate after the first 18 months of continuation coverage provided pursuant to this section. In no case shall an insurer charge an employer an additional fee for administering Cal–COBRA other than those incorporated in the risk adjusted employee risk rate as provided for in subdivision (t) of Section 10700. *(Added by Stats.1997, c. 665 (S.B.719), § 6. Amended by Stats.1998, c. 107 (A.B.112), § 20, eff. July 6, 1998.)*

§ 10128.57. Termination of continuation coverage

(a) The continuation coverage provided pursuant to this article shall terminate at the first to occur of the following:

(1) In the case of a qualified beneficiary who is eligible for continuation coverage pursuant to paragraph (2) of subdivision (d) of Section 10128.51, the date 36 months after the date the qualified beneficiary's benefits under the contract would otherwise have terminated because of a qualifying event.

(2) The end of the period for which premium payments were made, if the qualified beneficiary ceases to make payments or fails to make timely payments of a required premium, in accordance with the terms and conditions of the policy or contract. In the case of nonpayment of premiums, reinstatement shall be governed by the terms and conditions of the plan contract.

(3) In the case of a qualified beneficiary who is eligible to continuation coverage pursuant to paragraph (1), (3), (4), or (5) of subdivision (d) of Section 10116.51, the date 36 months after the date the qualified beneficiary's benefits under the contract would otherwise have terminated by reason of a qualifying event.

(4) The requirements of this article no longer apply to the qualified beneficiary pursuant to the provisions of Section 10128.52.

(5) In the case of a qualified beneficiary who is eligible for continuation coverage pursuant to paragraph (2) of subdivision (d) of Section 10128.51, and determined, under Title II or Title XVI of the Social Security Act, to be disabled any time during the first 60 days of continuation coverage, and the spouse or dependent who has elected coverage pursuant to this article, the date 36 months after the date the qualified beneficiary's benefits under the contract would otherwise have terminated because of a qualifying event. The qualified beneficiary shall notify the insurer, or the employer or administrator that contracts to perform administrative services, of the social security determination within 60 days of the date of the determination letter and prior to the end of the original 36–month continuation coverage period in order to be eligible for coverage pursuant to this subdivision. If the qualified beneficiary is no longer disabled under Title II or Title XVI of the Social Security Act, the benefits provided in this paragraph shall terminate on the later of the date provided by paragraph (1), or the month that begins more than 31 days after the date of the final determination under Title II or Title XVI of the United States Social Security Act that the qualified beneficiary is no longer disabled. A qualified beneficiary eligible for 36 months of continuation coverage as a result of a disability shall notify the insurer, or the employer or administrator that contracts to perform the notice and administrative services, within 30 days of a determination that the qualified beneficiary is no longer disabled.

(6) In the case of a qualified beneficiary who is initially eligible for and elects continuation coverage pursuant to paragraph (2) of subdivision (d) of Section 10128.51, but who has another qualifying event, as described in paragraph (1), (3), (4), or (5) of subdivision (d) of Section 10128.51, within 36 months of the date of the first qualifying event, and has notified the insurer, or employer or administrator under contract to provide administrative services, of the second qualifying event within 60 days of the date of the second qualifying event, the date 36 months after the date of the first qualifying event.

260

(7) The employer, or any successor employer or purchaser of the employer, ceases to provide any group benefit plan to his or her employees.

(8) The qualified beneficiary moves out of the insurer's service area, or the qualified beneficiary commits fraud or deception in the use of benefits.

(b) If the group benefits contracts between the insurer and the employer is terminated prior to the date the qualified beneficiary's continuation coverage would terminate pursuant to this section, coverage under the prior plan shall terminate and the qualified beneficiary may elect continuation coverage under the subsequent group benefit plan, if any, pursuant to the requirements of subdivision (b) of Section 10128.53 and subdivision (c) of Section 10128.54.

(c) The amendments made to this section by Assembly Bill 1401 of the 2001–02 Regular Session [1] shall apply to individuals who begin receiving continuation coverage under this article on or after January 1, 2003. *(Added by Stats.1997, c. 665 (S.B.719), § 6. Amended by Stats.1998, c. 107 (A.B.112), § 21, eff. July 6, 1998; Stats.2002, c. 794 (A.B.1401), § 12.)*

[1] Stats.2002, c. 794 (A.B.1401)

§ 10128.58. Obligation to provide continuation coverage; exclusions

A disability insurer subject to this article shall not be obligated to provide continuation coverage to a qualified beneficiary pursuant to this article if an insured fails to make the notification required by Section 10128.54, or if the employer of the insured fails to comply with Section 10128.55. *(Added by Stats.1997, c. 665 (S.B.719), § 6. Amended by Stats.1998, c. 107 (A.B.112), § 22, eff. July 6, 1998.)*

§ 10128.59. Exhaustion of federal coverage; continuation up to 36 months

(a) A health insurer that provides coverage under a group benefit plan to an employer shall offer an insured who has exhausted continuation coverage under COBRA the opportunity to continue coverage for up to 36 months from the date the insured's continuation coverage began if the insured is entitled to less than 36 months of continuation coverage under COBRA. The health insurer shall offer coverage pursuant to terms of this article, including the rate limitations contained in Section 10128.56.

(b) Notification of the coverage available under this section shall be included in the notice of the pending termination of COBRA coverage that is required to be provided to COBRA beneficiaries and that is required to be provided under Section 10128.54.

(c) For purposes of this section, "COBRA" means Section 4980B of Title 26 of the United States Code, Sections 1161 et seq. of Title 29 of the United States Code, and Section 300bb of Title 42 of the United States Code.

(d) This section shall not apply to accident-only, specified disease, hospital indemnity, CHAMPUS supplement, long-term care, Medicare supplement, dental-only, or vision-only insurance policies.

(e) This section shall become operative on September 1, 2003, and shall apply to individuals who begin receiving COBRA coverage on or after January 1, 2003. *(Added by Stats.2002, c. 794 (A.B.1401), § 13, operative Sept. 1, 2003.)*

CHAPTER 4. STANDARD PROVISIONS IN DISABILITY POLICIES

ARTICLE 6. INTERPRETATION OF POLICY

Section
10385. Disability insurers; employees or contractors; compensation and performance expectations.

§ 10385. Disability insurers; employees or contractors; compensation and performance expectations

Compensation of a person or entity employed by, or contracted with, a disability insurer shall not be based on, or related in any way to, the number of policies or certificates for health insurance that the person or entity has caused or recommended to be rescinded, canceled, or limited, or the resulting cost savings to the insurer. A disability insurer shall not set performance goals or quotas, or provide compensation to any person or entity employed by, or contracted with, the insurer, based on the number of persons whose health insurance coverage is rescinded or any financial savings to the insurer associated with rescission of coverage. *(Added by Stats. 2008, c. 188 (A.B.1150), § 2.)*

Part 6.3

ACCESS FOR INFANTS AND MOTHERS

CHAPTER 4. SUBSCRIBER ELIGIBILITY AND ENROLLMENT

ARTICLE 2. UNFAIR COMPETITION AND LABOR PRACTICES

Section
12698.50. Insurers, insurance agents or brokers; referral of employee or dependent for purpose of separating person from group health coverage; enforcement actions.
12698.52. Employers; referral of employee or dependent for purpose of separating person from group health coverage; enforcement actions.
12698.54. Employers; change of share-of-cost ratio or maternity care coverage; enforcement actions.
12698.56. Group health coverage defined.

§ 12698.50. Insurers, insurance agents or brokers; referral of employee or dependent for purpose of separating person from group health coverage; enforcement actions

(a) It shall constitute unfair competition for purposes of Chapter 5 (commencing with Section 17200) of Part 2 of Division 7 of the Business and Professions Code for an insurer, an insurance agent or broker, or an administrator, as defined in Section 1759, to refer an individual employee or employee's dependent to the program, or arrange for an individual employee or employee's dependent to apply to the program, for the purpose of separating that employee or employee's dependent from group health coverage provided in connection with the employee's employment.

(b) Any employee described in subdivision (a) shall have a personal right of action to enforce subdivision (a). *(Added by Stats.1991, c. 278, (A.B.99), § 11.1, eff. July 30, 1991. Amended by Stats.2006, c. 538 (S.B.1852), § 474.)*

§ 12698.52. Employers; referral of employee or dependent for purpose of separating person from group health coverage; enforcement actions

It shall constitute an unfair labor practice contrary to public policy, and enforceable under Section 95 of the Labor Code, for any employer to refer an individual employee or employee's dependent to the program, or to arrange for an individual employee or employee's dependent to apply to the program, for the purpose of separating that employee or employee's dependent from group health coverage provided in connection with the employee's employment. *(Added by Stats.1991, c. 278, (A.B.99), § 11.1, eff. July 30, 1991.)*

§ 12698.54. Employers; change of share-of-cost ratio or maternity care coverage; enforcement actions

It shall constitute an unfair labor practice contrary to public policy and enforceable under Section 95 of the Labor Code for any employer to change the employee-employer share-of-cost ratio or to make any other modification of maternity care coverage for employees or employees' dependents that results in the enrollment of the employees or employees' dependents in the program established pursuant to this part. *(Added by Stats.1991, c. 278, (A.B.99), § 11.1, eff. July 30, 1991. Amended by Stats.2006, c. 538 (S.B.1852), § 475.)*

§ 12698.56. Group health coverage defined

For purposes of this article, "group health coverage" includes any nonprofit hospital service plan, health care service plan, self-insured employee welfare benefit plan, or disability insurance providing medical or hospital benefits. *(Added by Stats.1991, c. 278, (A.B.99), § 11.1, eff. July 30, 1991.)*

261

LABOR CODE

Division		Section
	General Provisions	1
1.	Department of Industrial Relations	50
1.5.	California Commission on Manpower, Automation and Technology [Repealed]	
2.	Employment Regulation and Supervision	200
3.	Employment Relations	2700
4.	Workers' Compensation and Insurance	3200

Division		Section
4.5.	Workers' Compensation and Insurance: State Employees Not Otherwise Covered	6100
4.6.	Workmen's Compensation Advisory Committee [Repealed]	
4.7.	Retraining and Rehabilitation	6200
5.	Safety in Employment	6300
6.	Construction and Repeals [Repealed]	
10.	Construction and Repeals [Repealed]	

GENERAL PROVISIONS

Section

1. Title of code.
2. Continuation of existing law.
3. Persons continued in office.
4. Savings clause; procedure.
5. Construction.
6. Headings.
7. Delegation of powers and duties.
8. Writing requirement; use of certified mail.
9. Statutes incorporated by reference; subsequent amendments.
10. Section defined.
11. Tenses.
12. Gender.
12.1. Man or men as person or persons.
13. Number.
14. County defined.
15. Shall; may.
16. Oath defined.
17. Signature and subscription defined.
18. Person defined.
18.5. Agency defined.
19. Department defined.
19.5. Secretary defined.
20. Director defined.
21. Labor Commissioner defined.
22. Violation defined.
23. Penalty for misdemeanor.
24. Severability of code provisions.
25. Sheriff defined.
26. Effects of certificate of rehabilitation, termination of probation, and dismissal of information or accusation.
27. Workers' compensation judge; workers' compensation referee; workers' compensation administrative law judge.
28. Independent medical examiner defined.
29. Medical director defined.
29.5. Workers' Memorial Day; proclamation.

§ 1. Title of code

This act shall be known as the Labor Code. *(Stats. 1937, c. 90, p. 185, § 1.)*

§ 2. Continuation of existing law

The provisions of this code, in so far as they are substantially the same as existing provisions relating to the same subject matter, shall be construed as restatements and continuations thereof and not as new enactments. *(Stats.1937, c. 90, p. 185, § 2.)*

§ 3. Persons continued in office

All persons who, at the time this code goes into effect, hold office under any of the acts repealed by this code, which offices are continued by this code, continue to hold the same according to the former tenure thereof. *(Stats. 1937, c. 90, p. 185, § 3.)*

§ 4. Savings clause; procedure

No action or proceeding commenced before this code takes effect, and no right accrued, is affected by the provisions of this code, but all procedure thereafter taken therein shall conform to the provisions of this code so far as possible. *(Stats.1937, c. 90, p. 185, § 4.)*

§ 5. Construction

Unless the context otherwise requires, the general provisions hereinafter set forth shall govern the construction of this code. *(Stats.1937, c. 90, p. 185, § 5.)*

§ 6. Headings

Division, part, chapter, article, and section headings contained herein shall not be deemed to govern, limit, modify or in any manner affect the scope, meaning, or intent of the provisions of any division, part, chapter, article, or section hereof. *(Stats.1937, c. 90, p. 185, § 6.)*

§ 7. Delegation of powers and duties

Whenever, by the provisions of this code, an administrative power is granted to a public officer or a duty imposed upon such an officer, the power may be exercised or the duty performed by a deputy of the officer or by a person authorized pursuant to law. *(Stats.1937, c. 90, p. 185, § 7.)*

§ 8. Writing requirement; use of certified mail

Writing includes any form of recorded message capable of comprehension by ordinary visual means. Whenever any notice, report, statement or record is required by this code, it shall be made in writing.

Wherever any notice or other communication is required by this code to be mailed by registered mail by or to any person or corporation, the mailing of such notice or other communication by certified mail shall be deemed to be a sufficient compliance with the requirements of law. *(Stats.1937, c. 90, p. 186, § 8. Amended by Stats. 1959, c. 400, p. 2333, § 5; Stats.1959, c. 426, p. 2365, § 6; Stats.1984, c. 1089, § 1.)*

§ 9. Statutes incorporated by reference; subsequent amendments

Whenever any reference is made to any portion of this code or of any other law of this State, such reference shall apply to all amendments and additions thereto now or hereafter made. *(Stats.1937, c. 90, p. 186, § 9.)*

§ 10. Section defined

"Section" means a section of this code unless some other statute is specifically mentioned. *(Stats.1937, c. 90, p. 186, § 10.)*

§ 11. Tenses

The present tense includes the past and future tenses; and the future, the present. *(Stats.1937, c. 90, p. 186, § 11.)*

§ 12. Gender

The masculine gender includes the feminine and neuter. *(Stats.1937, c. 90, p. 186, § 12.)*

§ 12.1. Man or men as person or persons

The Legislature hereby declares its intent that the terms "man" or "men" where appropriate shall be deemed "person" or "persons" and any references to the terms "man" or "men" in sections of this code be changed to "person" or "persons" when such code sections are being amended for any purpose. This section is declaratory and not amendatory of existing law. *(Added by Stats.1976, c. 1171, p. 5250, § 20.)*

§ 13. Number

The singular number includes the plural, and the plural the singular. *(Stats.1937, c. 90, p. 186, § 13.)*

§ 14. County defined

"County" includes "city and county." *(Stats.1937, c. 90, p. 186, § 14.)*

§ 15. Shall; may

"Shall" is mandatory and "may" is permissive. *(Stats. 1937, c. 90, p. 186, § 15.)*

§ 16. Oath defined

"Oath" includes affirmation. *(Stats.1937, c. 90, p. 186, § 16.)*

§ 17. Signature and subscription defined

"Signature" or "subscription" includes mark when the signer or subscriber can not write, such signer's or subscriber's name being written near the mark by a witness who writes his own name near the signer's or subscriber's name; but a signature or subscription by mark can be acknowledged or can serve as a signature or subscription to a sworn statement only when two witnesses so sign their own names thereto. *(Stats.1937, c. 90, p. 186, § 17.)*

§ 18. Person defined

"Person" means any person, association, organization, partnership, business trust, limited liability company, or corporation. *(Stats.1937, c. 90, p. 186, § 18. Amended by Stats.1994, c. 1010 (S.B.2053), § 178.)*

§ 18.5. Agency defined

"Agency" means the Labor and Workforce Development Agency. *(Added by Stats.2002, c. 859 (S.B.1236), § 9.)*

§ 19. Department defined

"Department" means Department of Industrial Relations. *(Stats.1937, c. 90, p. 186, § 19.)*

§ 19.5. Secretary defined

"Secretary" means the Secretary of Labor and Workforce Development. *(Added by Stats.2002, c. 859 (S.B. 1236), § 10.)*

§ 20. Director defined

"Director" means Director of Industrial Relations. *(Stats.1937, c. 90, p. 186, § 20.)*

§ 21. Labor Commissioner defined

"Labor Commissioner" means Chief of the Division of Labor Standards Enforcement. *(Stats.1937, c. 90, p. 186, § 21. Amended by Stats.1945, c. 1431, p. 2684, § 1; Stats.1976, c. 746, p. 1776, § 1.)*

§ 22. Violation defined

"Violation" includes a failure to comply with any requirement of the code. *(Stats.1937, c. 90, p. 186, § 22.)*

§ 23. Penalty for misdemeanor

Except in cases where a different punishment is prescribed, every offense declared by this code to be a misdemeanor is punishable by imprisonment in a county jail, not exceeding six months, or by a fine not exceeding one thousand dollars ($1,000), or both. *(Stats.1937, c. 90, p. 186, § 23. Amended by Stats.1983, c. 1092, § 187, eff. Sept. 27, 1983, operative Jan. 1, 1984.)*

§ 24. Severability of code provisions

If any provision of this code, or the application thereof to any person or circumstances, is held invalid the remainder of the code, and the application of its provisions to other persons or circumstances, shall not be affected thereby. *(Stats.1937, c. 90, p. 186, § 24.)*

§ 25. Sheriff defined

"Sheriff" includes "marshal." *(Added by Stats.1969, c. 525, p. 1141, § 1. Amended by Stats.1996, c. 872 (A.B. 3472), § 102.)*

§ 26. Effects of certificate of rehabilitation, termination of probation, and dismissal of information or accusation

Notwithstanding any other provision of this code, no person who has not previously obtained a license regulated by this code shall be denied a license solely on the basis that he has been convicted of a crime if he has obtained a certificate of rehabilitation under Section 4852.01 and following of the Penal Code, and if his probation has been terminated and the information or accusation has been dismissed pursuant to Section 1203.4 of the Penal Code. *(Added by Stats.1970, c. 947, p. 2109, § 6.)*

§ 27. Workers' compensation judge; workers' compensation referee; workers' compensation administrative law judge

Whenever the term "workers' compensation judge" or "workers' compensation referee" is used in this code in connection with the workers' compensation law, the term shall mean "workers' compensation administrative law judge." *(Added by Stats.1985, c. 326, § 1. Amended by Stats.1990, c. 1550 (A.B.2910), § 4; Stats.1993, c. 121 (A.B.110), § 12, eff. July 16, 1993; Stats.1998, c. 448 (S.B.453), § 1.)*

§ 28. Independent medical examiner defined

For injuries occurring on and after January 1, 1991, whenever the term "independent medical examiner" is used in this code, the term shall mean "qualified medical evaluator." *(Added by Stats.1989, c. 892, § 8.5. Amended by Stats.1990, c. 1550 (A.B.2910), § 5.)*

§ 29. Medical director defined

"Medical director" means the physician appointed by the administrative director pursuant to Section 122. *(Added by Stats.1990, c. 1550 (A.B.2910), § 6. Amended by Stats.2003, c. 639 (S.B.228), § 2.)*

§ 29.5. Workers' Memorial Day; proclamation

The Governor shall annually issue a proclamation declaring April 28 as Workers' Memorial Day in remembrance of the courage and integrity of American workers, and recommending that the day be observed in an appropriate manner. *(Added by Stats.1992, c. 571 (S.B. 1388), § 2.)*

Division 1

DEPARTMENT OF INDUSTRIAL RELATIONS

Chapter	Section
1. General Powers and Duties	50
1.5. Mediation	65
2. Industrial Welfare Commission	70
3. Division of Housing [Repealed]	
3. Commission on Health and Safety and Workers' Compensation	75
4. Division of Labor Standards Enforcement	79
5. Division of Workers' Compensation	110
6. Occupational Safety and Health Standards Board	140
6.5. Occupational Safety and Health Appeals Board	148
7. Division of Labor Statistics and Research	150
7.5. Division of Occupational Safety and Health	175

CHAPTER 1. GENERAL POWERS AND DUTIES

Section
50. Department of Industrial Relations in Labor and Workforce Development Agency.
50.5. Function.
50.6. Fair Labor Standards Act enforcement.
50.7. Occupational safety and health standards; state agency; budget; federal funding; state plan.
50.8. Occupational health and medicine; long range program; centers.
50.9. Impact of actions or projects proposed by public agencies on opportunities for profitable employment; comments.
51. Director of industrial relations; appointment; salary.
52. Conduct of department; applicability of Government Code.
53. Head of the department.
54. Powers and duties of director.
54.5. Attorney.
55. Organization of department; law enforcement; rules and regulations; exclusions.
56. Divisions.
57. Division chiefs.
57.1. Division of Occupational Safety and Health; chief; salary; officers and employees; appointment; deputy chiefs; salaries.
57.5. Administration of state compensation insurance fund; board of directors.
58. Possession, control, and title to property for use of department.
59. Administration and enforcement of laws.
60. Administration and enforcement.
60.5. Division of Occupational Safety and Health; administrative duties; transfer of powers and duties; regulations; references.
60.6. Division of Occupational Safety and Health; civil service personnel; transfer.
60.7. Division of occupational safety and health; records, books, papers, offices, etc.; transfer.

Section

60.8. Division of Occupational Safety and Health; authority to make expenditures.

60.9. Division of Occupational Safety and Health; health, safety, and carcinogen control units; laboratory services and personnel; agreements.

61. Division of Labor Standards Enforcement; administrative duties.

62. Expenditures.

62.5. Workers' Compensation Administration Revolving Fund; Uninsured Employers Benefits Trust Fund; Subsequent Injuries Benefits Trust Fund; Occupational Safety and Health Fund; Labor Enforcement and Compliance Fund; creation; separate surcharges.

62.6. Levy and collection of assessments; rules and regulations.

62.7. Cal-OSHA Targeted Inspection and Consultation Fund; components of fund; assessments.

62.9. Levy and collection of assessments; schedule; collection of delinquent assessments and penalties.

63. Refunds.

64. Reciprocal agreements for collection of wages.

64.5. Transmittal of information to State Board of Equalization regarding retail establishments operating without a seller's permit.

§ 50. Department of Industrial Relations in Labor and Workforce Development Agency

There is in the Labor and Workforce Development Agency the Department of Industrial Relations. *(Stats. 1937, c. 90, p. 186, § 50. Amended by Stats.1969, c. 138, p. 338, § 183, eff. Sept. 11, 1969; Stats.1972, c. 957, p. 1732, § 4; Stats.1977, c. 662, p. 2178, § 8; Stats.2002, c. 859 (S.B.1236), § 11.)*

§ 50.5. Function

One of the functions of the Department of Industrial Relations is to foster, promote, and develop the welfare of the wage earners of California, to improve their working conditions, and to advance their opportunities for profitable employment. *(Added by Stats.1939, c. 276, p. 1532, § 1.)*

§ 50.6. Fair Labor Standards Act enforcement

The Department of Industrial Relations may assist and cooperate with the Wage and Hour Division, and the Children's Bureau, United States Department of Labor, in the enforcement within this State of the Fair Labor Standards Act of 1938,[1] and, subject to the regulations of the Administrator of the Wage and Hour Division, or the Chief of the Children's Bureau, and subject to the laws of the State applicable to the receipt and expenditures of money, may be reimbursed by the division or the bureau for the reasonable cost of such assistance and cooperation. *(Added by Stats.1953, c. 31, p. 633, § 1.)*

[1] 29 U.S.C.A. § 201 et seq.

§ 50.7. Occupational safety and health standards; state agency; budget; federal funding; state plan

(a) The Department of Industrial Relations is the state agency designated to be responsible for administering the state plan for the development and enforcement of occupational safety and health standards relating to issues covered by corresponding standards promulgated under the federal Occupational Safety and Health Act of 1970 (Public Law 91–596).[1] The state plan shall be consistent with the provisions of state law governing occupational safety and health, including, but not limited to, Chapter 6 (commencing with Section 140) and Chapter 6.5 (commencing with Section 148) of Division 1, and Division 5 (commencing with Section 6300), of this code.

(b) The budget and budget bill submitted pursuant to Article IV, Section 12 of the California Constitution shall include in the item for the support of the Department of Industrial Relations amounts sufficient to fully carry out the purposes and provisions of the state plan and this code in a manner which assures that the risk of industrial injury, exposure to toxic substances, illness and death to employees will be minimized.

(c) Because Federal grants are available, maximum Federal funding shall be sought and, to the extent possible, the cost of administering the state plan shall be paid by funds obtained from federal grants.

(d) The Governor and the Department of Industrial Relations shall take all steps necessary to prevent withdrawal of approval for the state plan by the Federal government. If Federal approval of the state plan has been withdrawn before passage of this initiative, or if it is withdrawn at any time after passage of this initiative, the Governor shall submit a new state plan immediately so that California shall be approved and shall continue to have access to Federal funds. *(Added by Stats.1977, c. 81, p. 489, § 2. Amended by Initiative Measure, approved by the electors, Nov. 8, 1988.)*

[1] 29 U.S.C.A. § 651 et seq.

§ 50.8. Occupational health and medicine; long range program; centers

The department shall develop a long range program for upgrading and expanding the resources of the State of California in the area of occupational health and medicine. The program shall include a contractual agreement with the University of California for the creation of occupational health centers affiliated with regional schools of medicine and public health. One such occupational health center shall be situated in the northern part of the state and one in the southern part. The primary function of these occupational health centers shall be the training of occupational physicians and nurses, toxicologists, epidemiologists, and industrial hygienists. In addition, the centers shall serve as referral centers for occupational illnesses and shall engage in research on the causes, diagnosis, and prevention of occupational illnesses.

The centers shall also inform the Division of Occupational Safety and Health of the Department of Industrial Relations, State Department of Health Services, the Office of Environmental Health Hazard Assessment, and the Department of Pesticide Regulation of their clinical and research findings. *(Added by Stats.1978, c. 1245, p. 4057, § 1. Amended by Gov.Reorg.Plan No. 1 of 1991, § 148, eff. July 17, 1991.)*

§ 50.9. Impact of actions or projects proposed by public agencies on opportunities for profitable employment; comments

In furtherance of the provisions of Section 50.5, the director, or the Director of Employment Development, may comment on the impact of actions or projects proposed by public agencies on opportunities for profitable employment, and such agencies shall consider such comments in their decisions. *(Added by Stats.1979, c. 880, p. 3065, § 1.)*

§ 51. Director of industrial relations; appointment; salary

The department shall be conducted under the control of an executive officer known as Director of Industrial Relations. The Director of Industrial Relations shall be appointed by the Governor with the advice and consent of the Senate and hold office at the pleasure of the Governor and shall receive an annual salary provided for by Chapter 6 (commencing with Section 11550) of Part 1 of Division 3 of Title 2 of the Government Code. *(Stats.1937, c. 90, p. 186, § 51. Amended by Stats.1945, c. 1431, p. 2684, § 2; Stats.1947, c. 1442, p. 3010, § 12; Stats.1951, c. 1613, p. 3631, § 33; Stats.1983, c. 142, § 97.)*

§ 52. Conduct of department; applicability of Government Code

Except as otherwise prescribed in this code, the provisions of the Government Code [1] relating to departments of the State shall govern and apply to the conduct of the department. *(Stats.1937, c. 90, p. 187, § 52. Amended by Stats.1949, c. 211, p. 440, § 1.)*

[1] Government Code § 8100 et seq.

§ 53. Head of the department

Whenever in Section 1001 or in Part 1 (commencing with Section 11000) of Division 3 of Title 2 of the Government Code "head of the department" or similar designation occurs, the same shall, for the purposes of this code, mean the director, except that in respect to matters which by the express provisions of this code are committed to or retained under the jurisdiction of the Division of Workers' Compensation, the State Compensation Insurance Fund, the Occupational Safety and Health Standards Board, the Occupational Safety and Health Appeals Board, or the Industrial Welfare Commission the designation shall mean the Division of Workers' Compensation, the Administrative Director of the Division of Workers' Compensation, the Workers' Compensation Appeals Board, the State Compensation Insurance Fund, the Occupational Safety and Health Standards Board, the Occupational Safety and Health Appeals Board, or the Industrial Welfare Commission, as the case may be. *(Stats.1937, c. 90, p. 187, § 53.*

Amended by Stats.1945, c. 1431, p. 2684, § 3; Stats.1949, c. 211, p. 440, § 2; Stats.1965, c. 1513, p. 3555, § 1, operative Jan. 15, 1966; Stats.1973, c. 993, p. 1918, § 6, eff. Oct. 1, 1973; Stats.1981, c. 21, p. 46, § 1, eff. April 18, 1981; Stats.1994, c. 146 (A.B.3601), § 133; Stats.1994, c. 1097 (S.B.1803), § 2.)

§ 54. Powers and duties of director

The director shall perform all duties, exercise all powers and jurisdiction, assume and discharge all responsibilities, and carry out and effect all purposes vested by law in the department, except as otherwise expressly provided by this code. *(Stats.1937, c. 90, p. 187, § 54.)*

§ 54.5. Attorney

The director may appoint an attorney and assistants licensed to practice law in this state. In the absence of an appointment, the attorney for the Division of Workers' Compensation shall also perform legal services for the department as the Director of Industrial Relations may direct. *(Formerly § 143, added by Stats.1945, c. 1431, p. 2688, § 28. Renumbered § 54.5 and amended by Stats. 1953, c. 1757, p. 3515, § 9; Stats.1965, c. 1513, p. 3556, § 2, operative Jan. 15, 1966. Amended by Stats.1994, c. 146 (A.B.3601), § 134; Stats.1994, c. 1097 (S.B.1803), § 3.)*

§ 55. Organization of department; law enforcement; rules and regulations; exclusions

For the purpose of administration the director shall organize the department subject to the approval of the Governor, in the manner he deems necessary properly to segregate and conduct the work of the department. Notwithstanding any provision in this code to the contrary, the director may require any division in the department to assist in the enforcement of any or all laws within the jurisdiction of the department. Except as provided in Section 18930 of the Health and Safety Code, the director may, in accordance with the provisions of Chapter 4.5 (commencing with Section 11371), Part 1, Division 3, Title 2 of the Government Code, make rules and regulations that are reasonably necessary to carry out the provisions of this chapter and to effectuate its purposes. The provisions of this section, however, shall not apply to the Division of Workers' Compensation or the State Compensation Insurance Fund, except as to any power or jurisdiction within those divisions as may have been specifically conferred upon the director by law. *(Stats.1937, c. 90, p. 187, § 55. Amended by Stats.1953, c. 1757, p. 3514, § 1; Stats.1957, c. 2034, p. 3606, § 7; Stats.1973, c. 993, p. 1918, § 7, eff. Oct. 1, 1973; Stats. 1979, c. 1152, p. 4315, § 203; Stats.1994, c. 146 (A.B. 3601), § 135; Stats.1994, c. 1097 (S.B.1803), § 4.)*

§ 56. Divisions

The work of the department shall be divided into at least six divisions known as the Division of Workers' Compensation, the Division of Occupational Safety and Health, the Division of Labor Standards Enforcement, the Division of Labor Statistics and Research, the Division of Apprenticeship Standards, and the State Compensation Insurance Fund. *(Stats.1937, c. 90, p. 187, § 56. Amended by Stats.1945, c. 1431, p. 2685, § 4; Stats.1959, c. 121, p. 2005, § 2; Stats.1965, c. 1222, § 4; Stats.1976, c. 746, p. 1776, § 2; Stats.1979, c. 72, p. 176, § 12; Stats.1980, c. 992, p. 3166, § 9; Stats.1994, c. 146 (A.B. 3601), § 136; Stats.1994, c. 1097 (S.B.1803), § 5.)*

§ 57. Division chiefs

Each division shall be in charge of a chief who shall be appointed by the Governor and shall receive a salary fixed in accordance with law, and shall serve at the pleasure of the director. *(Stats.1937, c. 90, p. 187, § 57. Amended by Stats.1945, c. 1431, p. 2685, § 5; Stats.1947, c. 1330, p. 2885, § 1; Stats.1955, c. 1415, p. 2586, § 1; Stats.1961, c. 603, p. 1751, § 11; Stats.1973, c. 993, p. 1918, § 8, eff. Oct. 1, 1973.)*

§ 57.1. Division of Occupational Safety and Health; chief; salary; officers and employees; appointment; deputy chiefs; salaries

(a) The Chief of the Division of Occupational Safety and Health shall receive an annual salary as provided by Chapter 6 (commencing with Section 11550) of Part 1 of Division 3 of Title 2 of the Government Code.

(b) All officers or employees of the Division of Occupational Safety and Health employed after the operative date of this section shall be appointed by the director in accordance with the provisions of the State Civil Service Act. Notwithstanding the foregoing, two deputy chiefs of the Division of Occupational Safety and Health shall be appointed by the Governor, with the advice of the Director of Industrial Relations, to serve at the pleasure of the Director of Industrial Relations. The two deputy chiefs shall be exempt from civil service. The annual salaries of the two exempted deputy chiefs shall be fixed by the Director of Industrial Relations, subject to the approval of the Director of Finance. *(Added by Stats. 1973, c. 993, p. 1918, § 9, eff. Oct. 1, 1973. Amended by Stats.1979, c. 72, p. 176, § 13.)*

§ 57.5. Administration of state compensation insurance fund; board of directors

All duties, powers, and jurisdiction relating to the administration of the State Compensation Insurance Fund shall be vested in the Board of Directors of the State Compensation Insurance Fund. *(Added by Stats. 1945, c. 1431, p. 2685, § 6.)*

§ 58. Possession, control, and title to property for use of department

The department shall have possession and control of all records, books, papers, offices, equipment, supplies, moneys, funds, appropriations, land, and other property, real or personal, held for the benefit or use of all commissions, divisions, and offices of the department and the title to all such property held for the use and benefit of the State is hereby transferred to the State. *(Stats.1937, c. 90, p. 187, § 58.)*

§ 59. Administration and enforcement of laws

The department through its appropriate officers shall administer and enforce all laws imposing any duty, power, or function upon the offices or officers of the department. *(Stats.1937, c. 90, p. 188, § 59.)*

§ 60. Administration and enforcement

Except as otherwise provided, the provisions of Divisions 4 and 4.5 of this code [1] shall be administered and enforced by the Division of Workers' Compensation. *(Stats.1937, c. 90, p. 188, § 60. Amended by Stats.1945, c. 1431, p. 2685, § 7; Stats.1953, c. 1757, p. 3514, § 2; Stats.1965, c. 1513, p. 3556, § 3, operative Jan. 15, 1966; Stats.1994, c. 146 (A.B.3601), § 137.)*

[1] Labor Code §§ 3200 et seq., 6100 et seq.

§ 60.5. Division of Occupational Safety and Health; administrative duties; transfer of powers and duties; regulations; references

(a) The provisions of Part 1 of Division 5 of this code [1] shall be administered and enforced by the department through the Division of Occupational Safety and Health, subject to the direction of the director pursuant to Section 50.7.

(b) The Division of Occupational Safety and Health succeeds to, and is vested with, all of the powers, duties, purposes, responsibilities, and jurisdiction of the Division of Industrial Safety, which is hereby abolished, and any other jurisdiction conferred by law.

(c) All powers, duties, and responsibilities of the Chief of the Division of Industrial Safety are hereby transferred to the Chief of the Division of Occupational Safety and Health.

(d) Any regulation or other action made, prescribed, issued, granted, or performed by the abolished Division of Industrial Safety in the administration of a function transferred pursuant to subdivision (b) shall remain in effect and shall be deemed to be a regulation or action of the Division of Occupational Safety and Health unless and until repealed, modified, or rescinded by such division.

(e) Whenever any reference is made in any law to the abolished Division of Industrial Safety, it shall be deemed to be a reference to, and to mean, the Division of Occupational Safety and Health. *(Added by Stats.1945, c. 1431, p. 2685, § 8. Amended by Stats.1979, c. 72, p. 177, § 14.)*

[1] Labor Code § 6300 et seq.

§ 60.6. Division of Occupational Safety and Health; civil service personnel; transfer

All persons serving in the state civil service in the Division of Industrial Safety or in the Occupational Health Branch of the State Department of Health Services, and engaged in the performance of a function transferred to the Division of Occupational Safety and Health shall, in accordance with Section 19370 of the Government Code, remain in the state civil service and are hereby transferred to the Department of Industrial Relations. The status, positions, and rights of such persons shall not be affected by their transfer and shall continue to be retained by them pursuant to the State Civil Service Act, except as to positions the duties of which are vested in a position that is exempt from civil service. *(Added by Stats.1979, c. 72 p. 177, § 15.)*

§ 60.7. Division of occupational safety and health; records, books, papers, offices, etc.; transfer

The Division of Occupational Safety and Health shall have possession and control of all records, books, papers, offices, equipment, supplies, moneys, funds, appropriations, land, licenses, permits, agreements, contracts, claims, judgments, and other property, real or personal, held for the benefit or use of the Division of Industrial Safety and the Occupational Health Branch of the State Department of Health Services with respect to the functions of those organizations that are transferred to the Division of Occupational Safety and Health. *(Added by Stats.1979, c. 72, p. 177, § 16.)*

§ 60.8. Division of Occupational Safety and Health; authority to make expenditures

The Division of Occupational Safety and Health may expend money appropriated for the administration of the laws the enforcement of which is committed to the division. Such expenditures by the division shall be made in accordance with law in carrying out the purposes for which the appropriations were made. *(Added by Stats. 1979, c. 72, p. 178, § 17.)*

§ 60.9. Division of Occupational Safety and Health; health, safety, and carcinogen control units; laboratory services and personnel; agreements

There is within the Division of Occupational Safety and Health an occupational health unit and an occupational safety unit, which shall assist in the performance of occupational health functions and occupational safety functions, respectively, assigned to the division by law. There is also within the occupational health unit an occupational carcinogen control unit responsible for implementing the division's obligations pursuant to the Occupational Carcinogens Control Act of 1976 (Part 10 (commencing with Sec. 9000)). The division, in performing its responsibilities under this code, shall provide for laboratory services and service personnel with respect to occupational health matters by interagency agreement with the State Department of Health Services or another public entity, by contract with a private sector laboratory, or by establishment of a laboratory within the division, or by a combination thereof. In the event that the division contracts with the private sector for laboratory services, the division shall enter into an interagency agreement with the State Department of Health Services for quality control and performance evaluation of the contract

laboratory as well as analysis of nonroutine laboratory samples. *(Added by Stats.1979, c. 72, p. 178, § 18. Amended by Stats.1989, c. 299, § 1.)*

§ 61. Division of Labor Standards Enforcement; administrative duties

The provisions of Chapter 1 (commencing with Section 1171) of Part 4 of Division 2 shall be administered and enforced by the department through the Division of Labor Standards Enforcement. *(Stats.1937, c. 90, p. 188, § 61. Amended by Stats.1976, c. 746, p. 1776, § 3.)*

§ 62. Expenditures

The department may expend money appropriated for the administration of the provisions of the laws, the enforcement of which is committed to the department. The department may expend such money for the use, support, or maintenance of any commission or office of the department. Such expenditures by the department shall be made in accordance with law in carrying on the work for which such appropriations were made. *(Stats. 1937, c. 90, p. 188, § 62.)*

§ 62.5. Workers' Compensation Administration Revolving Fund; Uninsured Employers Benefits Trust Fund; Subsequent Injuries Benefits Trust Fund; Occupational Safety and Health Fund; Labor Enforcement and Compliance Fund; creation; separate surcharges

(a)(1) The Workers' Compensation Administration Revolving Fund is hereby created as a special account in the State Treasury. Money in the fund may be expended by the department, upon appropriation by the Legislature, for all of the following purposes, and may not be used or borrowed for any other purpose:

(A) For the administration of the workers' compensation program set forth in this division and Division 4 (commencing with Section 3200), other than the activities financed pursuant to Section 3702.5.

(B) For the Return-to-Work Program set forth in Section 139.48.

(C) For the enforcement of the insurance coverage program established and maintained by the Labor Commissioner pursuant to Section 90.3.

(2) The fund shall consist of surcharges made pursuant to paragraph (1) of subdivision (f).

(b)(1) The Uninsured Employers Benefits Trust Fund is hereby created as a special trust fund account in the State Treasury, of which the director is trustee, and its sources of funds are as provided in paragraph (1) of subdivision (f). Notwithstanding Section 13340 of the Government Code, the fund is continuously appropriated for the payment of nonadministrative expenses of the workers' compensation program for workers injured while employed by uninsured employers in accordance with Article 2 (commencing with Section 3710) of Chapter 4 of Part 1 of Division 4, and shall not be used for any other purpose. All moneys collected shall be retained in

269

the trust fund until paid as benefits to workers injured while employed by uninsured employers. Nonadministrative expenses include audits and reports of services prepared pursuant to subdivision (b) of Section 3716.1. The surcharge amount for this fund shall be stated separately.

(2) Notwithstanding any other provision of law, all references to the Uninsured Employers Fund shall mean the Uninsured Employers Benefits Trust Fund.

(3) Notwithstanding paragraph (1), in the event that budgetary restrictions or impasse prevent the timely payment of administrative expenses from the Workers' Compensation Administration Revolving Fund, those expenses shall be advanced from the Uninsured Employers Benefits Trust Fund. Expense advances made pursuant to this paragraph shall be reimbursed in full to the Uninsured Employers Benefits Trust Fund upon enactment of the annual Budget Act.

(4) Any moneys from penalties collected pursuant to Section 3722 as a result of the insurance coverage program established under Section 90.3 shall be deposited in the State Treasury to the credit of the Workers' Compensation Administration Revolving Fund created under this section, to cover expenses incurred by the director under the insurance coverage program. The amount of any penalties in excess of payment of administrative expenses incurred by the director for the insurance coverage program established under Section 90.3 shall be deposited in the State Treasury to the credit of the Uninsured Employers Benefits Trust Fund for nonadministrative expenses, as prescribed in paragraph (1), and notwithstanding paragraph (1), shall only be available upon appropriation by the Legislature.

(c)(1) The Subsequent Injuries Benefits Trust Fund is hereby created as a special trust fund account in the State Treasury, of which the director is trustee, and its sources of funds are as provided in paragraph (1) of subdivision (f). Notwithstanding Section 13340 of the Government Code, the fund is continuously appropriated for the nonadministrative expenses of the workers' compensation program for workers who have suffered serious injury and who are suffering from previous and serious permanent disabilities or physical impairments, in accordance with Article 5 (commencing with Section 4751) of Chapter 2 of Part 2 of Division 4, and Section 4 of Article XIV of the California Constitution, and shall not be used for any other purpose. All moneys collected shall be retained in the trust fund until paid as benefits to workers who have suffered serious injury and who are suffering from previous and serious permanent disabilities or physical impairments. Nonadministrative expenses include audits and reports of services pursuant to subdivision (c) of Section 4755. The surcharge amount for this fund shall be stated separately.

(2) Notwithstanding any other law, all references to the Subsequent Injuries Fund shall mean the Subsequent Injuries Benefits Trust Fund.

(3) Notwithstanding paragraph (1), in the event that budgetary restrictions or impasse prevent the timely payment of administrative expenses from the Workers' Compensation Administration Revolving Fund, those expenses shall be advanced from the Subsequent Injuries Benefits Trust Fund. Expense advances made pursuant to this paragraph shall be reimbursed in full to the Subsequent Injuries Benefits Trust Fund upon enactment of the annual Budget Act.

(d) The Occupational Safety and Health Fund is hereby created as a special account in the State Treasury. Moneys in the account may be expended by the department, upon appropriation by the Legislature, for support of the Division of Occupational Safety and Health, the Occupational Safety and Health Standards Board, and the Occupational Safety and Health Appeals Board, and the activities these entities perform as set forth in this division, and Division 5 (commencing with Section 6300).

(e) The Labor Enforcement and Compliance Fund is hereby created as a special account in the State Treasury. Moneys in the fund may be expended by the department, upon appropriation by the Legislature, for the support of the activities that the Division of Labor Standards Enforcement performs pursuant to this division and Division 2 (commencing with Section 200), Division 3 (commencing with Section 2700), and Division 4 (commencing with Section 3200). The fund shall consist of surcharges imposed pursuant to paragraph (3) of subdivision (f).

(f)(1) Separate surcharges shall be levied by the director upon all employers, as defined in Section 3300, for purposes of deposit in the Workers' Compensation Administration Revolving Fund, the Uninsured Employers Benefits Trust Fund, the Subsequent Injuries Benefits Trust Fund, and the Occupational Safety and Health Fund. The total amount of the surcharges shall be allocated between self-insured employers and insured employers in proportion to payroll respectively paid in the most recent year for which payroll information is available. The director shall adopt reasonable regulations governing the manner of collection of the surcharges. The regulations shall require the surcharges to be paid by self-insurers to be expressed as a percentage of indemnity paid during the most recent year for which information is available, and the surcharges to be paid by insured employers to be expressed as a percentage of premium. In no event shall the surcharges paid by insured employers be considered a premium for computation of a gross premium tax or agents' commission. In no event shall the total amount of the surcharges paid by insured and self-insured employers exceed the amounts reasonably necessary to carry out the purposes of this section.

(2) The surcharge levied by the director for the Occupational Safety and Health Fund, pursuant to paragraph (1), shall not generate revenues in excess of fifty-two million dollars ($52,000,000) on and after the 2009–10 fiscal year, adjusted for each fiscal year as appropriate

to reconcile any over/under assessments from previous fiscal years pursuant to Sections 15606 and 15609 of Title 8 of the California Code of Regulations, and may increase by not more than the state-local government deflator each year thereafter through July 1, 2013, and, as appropriate, to reconcile any over/under assessments from previous fiscal years. For the 2013–14 fiscal year, the surcharge level shall return to the level in place on June 30, 2009, adjusted for inflation based on the state-local government deflator.

(3) A separate surcharge shall be levied by the director upon all employers, as defined in Section 3300, for purposes of deposit in the Labor Enforcement and Compliance Fund. The total amount of the surcharges shall be allocated between employers in proportion to payroll respectively paid in the most recent year for which payroll information is available. The director shall adopt reasonable regulations governing the manner of collection of the surcharges. In no event shall the total amount of the surcharges paid by employers exceed the amounts reasonably necessary to carry out the purposes of this section.

(4) The surcharge levied by the director for the Labor Enforcement and Compliance Fund shall not exceed thirty-seven million dollars ($37,000,000) in the 2009–10 fiscal year, adjusted as appropriate to reconcile any over/under assessments from previous fiscal years, and shall not be adjusted each year thereafter by more than the state-local government deflator, and, as appropriate, to reconcile any over/under assessments from previous fiscal years pursuant to Sections 15606 and 15609 of Title 8 of the California Code of Regulations.

(5) The regulations adopted pursuant to paragraph (1) to (4), inclusive, shall be exempt from the rulemaking provisions of the Administrative Procedure Act (Chapter 3.5 (commencing with Section 11340) of Part 1 of Division 3 of Title 2 of the Government Code).

(g) On and after July 1, 2013, subdivision (e) and paragraphs (2) to (4), inclusive, of subdivision (f) are inoperative, unless a later enacted statute, that is enacted before July 1, 2013, deletes or extends that date. *(Added by Stats.2009, c. 341 (S.B.73), § 12.)*

§ 62.6. Levy and collection of assessments; rules and regulations

(a) The director shall levy and collect assessments from employers in accordance with subdivision (b), as necessary, to collect the aggregate amount determined by the Fraud Assessment Commission pursuant to Section 1872.83 of the Insurance Code. Revenues derived from the assessments shall be deposited in the Workers' Compensation Fraud Account in the Insurance Fund and shall only be expended, upon appropriation by the Legislature, for the investigation and prosecution of workers' compensation fraud and the willful failure to secure payment of workers' compensation, as prescribed by Section 1872.83 of the Insurance Code.

(b) Assessments shall be levied by the director upon all employers as defined in Section 3300. The total amount of the assessment shall be allocated between self-insured employers and insured employers in proportion to payroll respectively paid in the most recent year for which payroll information is available. The director shall promulgate reasonable rules and regulations governing the manner of collection of the assessment. The rules and regulations shall require the assessment to be paid by self-insurers to be expressed as a percentage of indemnity paid during the most recent year for which information is available, and the assessment to be paid by insured employers to be expressed as a percentage of premium. In no event shall the assessment paid by insured employers be considered a premium for computation of a gross premium tax or agents' commission. *(Added by Stats.1991, c. 116 (S.B. 1218), § 22. Amended by Stats.1991, c. 934 (A.B.1673), § 13; Stats.2002, c. 6 (A.B.749), § 18.)*

§ 62.7. Cal-OSHA Targeted Inspection and Consultation Fund; components of fund; assessments

(a) The Cal-OSHA Targeted Inspection and Consultation Fund is hereby created as a special account in the State Treasury. Proceeds of the fund may be expended by the department, upon appropriation by the Legislature, for the costs of the Cal-OSHA targeted inspection program provided by Section 6314.1 and the costs of the Cal-OSHA targeted consultation program provided by subdivision (a) of Section 6354, and for costs related to assessments levied and collected pursuant to Section 62.9.

(b) The fund shall consist of the assessments made pursuant to Section 62.9 and other moneys transferred to the fund.

(Added by Stats.1993, c. 121 (A.B.110), § 14, eff. July 16, 1993. Amended by Stats.1993, c. 1241 (S.B.147), § 1; Stats.1993, c. 1242 (S.B.223), § 15; Stats.1995, c. 33 (S.B.996), § 1, eff. June 30, 1995; Stats.1995, c. 556 (S.B.1051), § 3.)

§ 62.9. Levy and collection of assessments; schedule; collection of delinquent assessments and penalties

(a)(1) The director shall levy and collect assessments from employers in accordance with this section. The total amount of the assessment collected shall be the amount determined by the director to be necessary to produce the revenue sufficient to fund the programs specified by Section 62.7, except that the amount assessed in any year for those purposes shall not exceed 50 percent of the amounts appropriated from the General Fund for the support of the occupational safety and health program for the 1993–94 fiscal year, adjusted for inflation. The director also shall include in the total assessment amount the department's costs for administering the assessment, including the collections process and the cost of reimbursing the Franchise Tax Board for its cost of collection activities pursuant to subdivision (c).

(2) The insured employers and private sector self-insured employers that, pursuant to subdivision (b), are

subject to assessment shall be assessed, respectively, on the basis of their annual payroll subject to premium charges or their annual payroll that would be subject to premium charges if the employer were insured, as follows:

(A) An employer with a payroll of less than two hundred fifty thousand dollars ($250,000) shall be assessed one hundred dollars ($100).

(B) An employer with a payroll of two hundred fifty thousand dollars ($250,000) or more, but not more than five hundred thousand dollars ($500,000), shall be assessed two hundred dollars ($200).

(C) An employer with a payroll of more than five hundred thousand dollars ($500,000), but not more than seven hundred fifty thousand dollars ($750,000), shall be assessed four hundred dollars ($400).

(D) An employer with a payroll of more than seven hundred fifty thousand dollars ($750,000), but not more than one million dollars ($1,000,000), shall be assessed six hundred dollars ($600).

(E) An employer with a payroll of more than one million dollars ($1,000,000), but not more than one million five hundred thousand dollars ($1,500,000), shall be assessed eight hundred dollars ($800).

(F) An employer with a payroll of more than one million five hundred thousand dollars ($1,500,000), but not more than two million dollars ($2,000,000), shall be assessed one thousand dollars ($1,000).

(G) An employer with a payroll of more than two million dollars ($2,000,000), but not more than two million five hundred thousand dollars ($2,500,000), shall be assessed one thousand five hundred dollars ($1,500).

(H) An employer with a payroll of more than two million five hundred thousand dollars ($2,500,000), but not more than three million five hundred thousand dollars ($3,500,000), shall be assessed two thousand dollars ($2,000).

(I) An employer with a payroll of more than three million five hundred thousand dollars ($3,500,000), but not more than four million five hundred thousand dollars ($4,500,000), shall be assessed two thousand five hundred dollars ($2,500).

(J) An employer with a payroll of more than four million five hundred thousand dollars ($4,500,000), but not more than five million five hundred thousand dollars ($5,500,000), shall be assessed three thousand dollars ($3,000).

(K) An employer with a payroll of more than five million five hundred thousand dollars ($5,500,000), but not more than seven million dollars ($7,000,000), shall be assessed three thousand five hundred dollars ($3,500).

(L) An employer with a payroll of more than seven million dollars ($7,000,000), but not more than twenty million dollars ($20,000,000), shall be assessed six thousand seven hundred dollars ($6,700).

(M) An employer with a payroll of more than twenty million dollars ($20,000,000) shall be assessed ten thousand dollars ($10,000).

(b)(1) In the manner as specified by this section, the director shall identify those insured employers having a workers' compensation experience modification rating of 1.25 or more, and private sector self-insured employers having an equivalent experience modification rating of 1.25 or more as determined pursuant to subdivision (e).

(2) The assessment required by this section shall be levied annually, on a calendar year basis, on those insured employers and private sector self-insured employers, as identified pursuant to paragraph (1), having the highest workers' compensation experience modification ratings or equivalent experience modification ratings, that the director determines to be required numerically to produce the total amount of the assessment to be collected pursuant to subdivision (a).

(c) The director shall collect the assessment from insured employers as follows:

(1) Upon the request of the director, the Department of Insurance shall direct the licensed rating organization designated as the department's statistical agent to provide to the director, for purposes of subdivision (b), a list of all insured employers having a workers' compensation experience rating modification of 1.25 or more, according to the organization's records at the time the list is requested, for policies commencing the year preceding the year in which the assessment is to be collected.

(2) The director shall determine the annual payroll of each insured employer subject to assessment from the payroll that was reported to the licensed rating organization identified in paragraph (1) for the most recent period for which one full year of payroll information is available for all insured employers.

(3) On or before September 1 of each year, the director shall determine each of the current insured employers subject to assessment, and the amount of the total assessment for which each insured employer is liable. The director immediately shall notify each insured employer, in a format chosen by the insurer, of the insured's obligation to submit payment of the assessment to the director within 30 days after the date the billing was mailed, and warn the insured of the penalties for failure to make timely and full payment as provided by this subdivision.

(4) The director shall identify any insured employers that, within 30 days after the mailing of the billing notice, fail to pay, or object to, their assessments. The director shall mail to each of these employers a notice of delinquency and a notice of the intention to assess penalties, advising that, if the assessment is not paid in full within 15 days after the mailing of the notices, the director will levy against the employer a penalty equal to 25 percent of the employer's assessment, and will refer the assessment and penalty to the Franchise Tax Board or another agency for collection. The notices required by

this paragraph shall be sent by United States first-class mail.

(5) If an assessment is not paid by an insured employer within 15 days after the mailing of the notices required by paragraph (4), the director shall refer the delinquent assessment and the penalty to the Franchise Tax Board, or another agency, as deemed appropriate by the director, for collection pursuant to Section 19290.1 of the Revenue and Taxation Code.

(d) The director shall collect the assessment directly from private sector self-insured employers. The failure of any private sector self-insured employer to pay the assessment as billed constitutes grounds for the suspension or termination of the employer's certificate to self-insure.

(e) The director shall adopt regulations implementing this section that include provision for a method of determining experience modification ratings for private sector self-insured employers that is generally equivalent to the modification ratings that apply to insured employers and is weighted by both severity and frequency.

(f) The director shall determine whether the amount collected pursuant to any assessment exceeds expenditures, as described in subdivision (a), for the current year and shall credit the amount of any excess to any deficiency in the prior year's assessment or, if there is no deficiency, against the assessment for the subsequent year. *(Added by Stats.1995, c. 33 (S.B.996), § 2, eff. June 30, 1995. Amended by Stats.1998, c. 814 (A.B.1957), § 1; Stats.1999, c. 469 (A.B.1655), § 2; Stats.2008, c. 751 (A.B.1389), § 60, eff. Sept. 30, 2008.)*

§ 63. Refunds

The Director may authorize the refund of moneys received or collected by the department in payment of license fees or for other services in cases where the license can not lawfully be issued or the service rendered to the applicant. *(Added by Stats.1941, c. 947, p. 2542, § 1.)*

§ 64. Reciprocal agreements for collection of wages

The Labor Commissioner may enter into reciprocal agreements with the labor department or corresponding agency of any other state or with the person, board, officer, or commission authorized to act for and on behalf of that department or agency, for the collection in that other state of claims or judgments for wages and other demands based upon claims previously assigned to the Division of Labor Standards Enforcement. *(Added by Stats.1953, c. 877, p. 2232, § 1. Amended by Stats.1976, c. 746, p. 1776, § 4; Stats.1988, c. 96, § 1.)*

§ 64.5. Transmittal of information to State Board of Equalization regarding retail establishments operating without a seller's permit

When requested by the State Board of Equalization, the department may permit any duly authorized representative of that agency to transmit to the State Board of Equalization information available in the department's records that indicates a retail establishment is operating without a seller's permit required by the State Board of Equalization, to assist the State Board of Equalization in determining compliance with the Sales and Use Tax Law (Part 1 (commencing with Section 6001) of Division 2 of the Revenue and Taxation Code). *(Added by Stats.2008, c. 306 (A.B.3079), § 1.)*

CHAPTER 1.5. MEDIATION

Section
65. Powers and duties of department.
66. Mediation and conciliation service; unit of department.
67. Reimbursement.

§ 65. Powers and duties of department

The department may investigate and mediate labor disputes providing any bona fide party to this type of dispute requests intervention by the department and the department may proffer its services to both parties when work stoppage is threatened and neither party requests intervention. In the interest of preventing labor disputes the department shall endeavor to promote sound union-employer relationships. The department may arbitrate or arrange for the selection of boards of arbitration on such terms as all of the bona fide parties to the dispute may agree upon. Any decision or award arising out of an arbitration conducted pursuant to this section is a public record. Section 703.5 and Chapter 2 (commencing with Section 1115) of Division 9 of the Evidence Code apply to a mediation conducted by the California State Mediation and Conciliation Service, and any person conducting the mediation. All other records of the department relating to labor disputes are confidential. *(Added by Stats.1939, c. 810, p. 2368, § 1. Amended by Stats.1947, c. 1049, p. 2450, § 1; Stats.1949, c. 568, p. 1058, § 1; Stats.1997, c. 772 (A.B.939), § 11.)*

§ 66. Mediation and conciliation service; unit of department

The services of the department pursuant to Section 65 shall be conducted by a unit within the department to be known as the California State Mediation and Conciliation Service. *(Added by Stats.1978, c. 133, p. 352, § 1.)*

§ 67. Reimbursement

(a) Notwithstanding any other law, the director may seek and collect reimbursement from private and public sector employers, labor unions, and employee organizations for election, arbitration, and training and facilitation services provided by the California State Mediation and Conciliation Service pursuant to Section 65 and for representation services, including the provision of hearing officers, related to public transit labor relations provided by the California State Mediation and Conciliation Service pursuant to the Public Utilities Code.

(b) The director shall adopt regulations implementing this section. *(Added by Stats.2009–2010, 4th Ex.Sess., c. 12 (A.B.12), § 24, eff. July 28, 2009.)*

CHAPTER 2. INDUSTRIAL WELFARE COMMISSION

Section
70. Creation; members; appointment.
70.1. Industrial welfare commission; membership; composition.
71. Terms of commission members; vacancies.
72. Compensation and expenses of commission members.
73. Employment of personnel; appointment; supervision.
74. Subpoenas; administration of oaths; examination of witnesses.

§ 70. Creation; members; appointment

There is in the Department of Industrial Relations the Industrial Welfare Commission which consists of five members. The members of the commission shall be appointed by the Governor, with the consent of the Senate. *(Stats.1937, c. 90, p. 188, § 70. Amended by Stats.1976, c. 214, p. 399, § 1; Stats.1976, c. 746, p. 1776, § 6; Stats.1980, c. 1083, p. 3464, § 1.)*

§ 70.1. Industrial welfare commission; membership; composition

The Industrial Welfare Commission shall be composed of two representatives of organized labor who are members of recognized labor organizations, two representatives of employers, and one representative of the general public. The membership shall include members of both sexes. *(Added by Stats.1976, c. 214, p. 399, § 2. Amended by Stats.1990, c. 437 (A.B.2679), § 1; Stats.1990, c. 513 (S.B.1915), § 1.)*

§ 71. Terms of commission members; vacancies

The term of office of the members of the Industrial Welfare Commission shall be four years and they shall hold office until the appointment and qualification of their successors. The terms of the members of the commission in office at the time this code takes effect shall expire on January 15th of that year which for the particular member has heretofore been determined. Vacancies shall be filled by appointment for the unexpired terms. *(Stats.1937, c. 90, p. 188, § 71.)*

§ 72. Compensation and expenses of commission members

The members of the commission shall receive one hundred dollars ($100) for each day's actual attendance at meetings and other official business of the commission and shall receive their actual and necessary expenses incurred in the performance of their duties. *(Stats.1937, c. 90, p. 188, § 72. Amended by Stats.1945, c. 1431, p. 2686, § 9.5; Stats.1968, c. 109, p. 326, § 1; Stats.1969, c. 460, p. 1020, § 2; Stats.1976, c. 746, p. 1776, § 8; Stats.1980, c. 1083, p. 3464, § 2.)*

§ 73. Employment of personnel; appointment; supervision

The Industrial Welfare Commission may employ necessary assistants, officers, experts, and such other employees as it deems necessary. All such personnel of the commission shall be under the supervision of the chairman or an executive officer to whom the chairman delegates such responsibility. All such personnel shall be appointed pursuant to the State Civil Service Act (Part 1 (commencing with Section 18000) of Division 5 of Title 2 of the Government Code), except for the one exempt deputy or employee allowed by subdivision (e) of Section 4 of Article VII of the California Constitution. *(Added by Stats.1980, c. 1083, p. 3464, § 4.)*

§ 74. Subpoenas; administration of oaths; examination of witnesses

The Chief of the Division of Labor Standards Enforcement, for the purpose of enforcing Industrial Welfare Commission orders and provisions of this code, may issue subpoenas to compel the attendance of witnesses and production of books, papers, and records. Obedience to subpoenas issued by the chief of the division shall be enforced by the courts.

The Chief and enforcement deputies of the Division of Labor Standards Enforcement may administer oaths and examine witnesses under oath for the purpose of enforcing Industrial Welfare Commission orders and provisions of this code. *(Added by Stats.1949, c. 1184, p. 2104, § 1; Amended by Stats.1976, c. 746, p. 1777, § 10.)*

Chapter 3

COMMISSION ON HEALTH AND SAFETY AND WORKERS' COMPENSATION

Section
75. Creation of commission; membership and positions; meetings; compensation.
76. Personnel of the commission.
77. Study of workers' compensation system; succession of powers and duties of former Health and Safety Commission.
77.5. Survey and evaluation of standards of care; report.
77.7. Study of causes of insolvencies among workers' compensation insurers; scope and content of study; availability of required data; costs; disclosure of confidential information.
78. Prevention program grants; funding.

§ 75. Creation of commission; membership and positions; meetings; compensation

(a) There is in the department the Commission on Health and Safety and Workers' Compensation. The commission shall be composed of eight voting members. Four voting members shall represent organized labor, and four voting members shall represent employers. Not more than one employer member shall represent public agencies. Two of the employer and two of the labor members shall be appointed by the Governor. The

Senate Committee on Rules and the Speaker of the Assembly shall each appoint one employer and one labor representative. The public employer representative shall be appointed by the Governor. No action of the commission shall be valid unless agreed to by a majority of the membership and by not less than two members representing organized labor and two members representing employers.

(b) The commission shall select one of the members representing organized labor to chair the commission during the 1994 calendar year, and thereafter the commission shall alternatively select an employer and organized labor representative to chair the commission for one-year terms.

(c) The initial terms of the members of the commission shall be four years, and they shall hold office until the appointment of a successor. However, the initial terms of one employer and one labor member appointed by the Governor shall expire on December 31, 1995; the initial terms of the members appointed by the Senate Committee on Rules shall expire December 31, 1996; the initial terms of the members appointed by the Speaker of the Assembly shall expire on December 31, 1997; and the initial term of one employer and one labor member appointed by the Governor shall expire on December 31, 1998. Any vacancy shall be filled by appointment to the unexpired term.

(d) The commission shall meet every other month and upon the call of the chair. Meetings shall be open to the public. Members of the commission shall receive one hundred dollars ($100) for each day of their actual attendance at meetings of the commission and other official business of the commission and shall also receive their actual and necessary traveling expenses incurred in the performance of their duty as a member. Payment of per diem and traveling expenses shall be made from the Workers' Compensation Administration Revolving Fund, when appropriated by the Legislature. *(Added by Stats. 1993, c. 227 (S.B.1005), § 2. Amended by Stats.2002, c. 6 (A.B.749), § 19.)*

§ 76. Personnel of the commission

The commission may employ officers, assistants, experts, and other employees it deems necessary. All personnel of the commission shall be under the supervision of the chair or an executive officer to whom he or she delegates this responsibility. All personnel shall be appointed pursuant to the State Civil Service Act (Part 2 (commencing with Section 18500) of Division 5 of Title 2 of the Government Code), except for the one exemption allowed by subdivision (e) of Section 4 of Article VII of the California Constitution. *(Added by Stats.1993, c. 227 (S.B.1005), § 2.)*

§ 77. Study of workers' compensation system; succession of powers and duties of former Health and Safety Commission

(a) The commission shall conduct a continuing examination of the workers' compensation system, as defined in Section 4 of Article XIV of the California Constitution, and of the state's activities to prevent industrial injuries and occupational diseases. The commission may conduct or contract for studies it deems necessary to carry out its responsibilities. In carrying out its duties, the commission shall examine other states' workers' compensation programs and activities to prevent industrial injuries and occupational diseases. All state departments and agencies, and any rating organization licensed by the Insurance Commissioner pursuant to Article 3 (commencing with Section 11750) of Chapter 3 of Part 3 of Division 2 of the Insurance Code, shall cooperate with the commission and upon reasonable request provide information and data in their possession that the commission deems necessary for the purpose of carrying out its responsibilities. The commission shall issue an annual report on the state of the workers' compensation system, including recommendations for administrative or legislative modifications which would improve the operation of the system. The report shall be made available to the Governor, the Legislature, and the public on request.

(b) On or before July 1, 2003, and periodically thereafter as it deems necessary, the commission shall issue a report and recommendations on the improvement and simplification of the notices required to be provided by insurers and self-insured employers.

(c) The commission succeeds to, and is vested with, all of the powers, duties, purposes, responsibilities, and jurisdiction of the Health and Safety Commission which is hereby abolished, including the administration of grants to assist in establishing effective occupational injury and illness prevention programs. *(Added by Stats.1993, c. 227 (S.B.1005), § 2. Amended by Stats.2002, c. 6 (A.B.749), § 20.)*

§ 77.5. Survey and evaluation of standards of care; report

(a) On or before July 1, 2004, the commission shall conduct a survey and evaluation of evidence-based, peer-reviewed, nationally recognized standards of care, including existing medical treatment utilization standards, including independent medical review, as used in other states, at the national level, and in other medical benefit systems. The survey shall be updated periodically.

(b) On or before October 1, 2004, the commission shall issue a report of its findings and recommendations to the administrative director for purposes of the adoption of a medical treatment utilization schedule. *(Added by Stats.2003, c. 639 (S.B.228), § 3.)*

§ 77.7. Study of causes of insolvencies among workers' compensation insurers; scope and content of study; availability of required data; costs; disclosure of confidential information

(a) A study shall be undertaken to examine the causes of the number of insolvencies among workers' compensation insurers within the past 10 years. The study shall be conducted by an independent research organization under the direction of the commission. Not later than July 1, 2009, the commission and the department shall publish the report of the study on its Internet Web site and shall inform the Legislature and the Governor of the availability of the report.

(b) The study shall include an analysis of the following: the access to capital for workers' compensation insurance from all sources between 1993 and 2003; the availability, source, and risk assumed of reinsurers during this period; the use of deductible policies and their effect on solvency regulation; market activities by insurers and producers that affected market concentration; activities, including financial oversight of insurers, by insurance regulators and the National Association of Insurance Commissioners during this period; the quality of data reporting to the commissioner's designated statistical agent and the accuracy of recommendations provided by the commissioner's designated statistical agent during this period of time; and underwriting, claims adjusting, and reserving practices of insolvent insurers. The study shall also include a survey of reports of other state agencies analyzing the insurance market response to rising system costs within the applicable time period.

(c) Data reasonably required for the study shall be made available by the California Insurance Guarantee Association, Workers' Compensation Insurance Rating Bureau, third-party administrators for the insolvent insurers, whether prior to or after the insolvency, the State Compensation Insurance Fund, and the Department of Insurance. The commission shall also include a survey of reports by the commission and other state agencies analyzing the insurance market response to rising system costs within the applicable period of time.

(d) The cost of the study is not to exceed one million dollars ($1,000,000). Confidential information identifiable to a natural person or insurance company held by an agency, organization, association, or other person or entity shall be released to researchers upon satisfactory agreement to maintain confidentiality. Information or material that is not subject to subpoena from the agency, organization, association, or other person or entity shall not be subject to subpoena from the commission or the contracted research organization.

(e) The costs of the study shall be borne one-half by the commission from funds derived from the Workers' Compensation Administration Revolving Fund and one-half by insurers from assessments allocated to each insurer based on the insurer's proportionate share of the market as shown by the Market Share Report for Calendar Year 2006 published by the Department of Insurance.

(f) In order to protect individual company trade secrets, this study shall not lead to the disclosure of, either directly or indirectly, the business practices of a company that provides data pursuant to this section. This prohibition shall not apply to insurance companies that have been ordered by a court of competent jurisdiction to be placed in liquidation under the supervision of a liquidator

or other authority. *(Added by Stats.2007, c. 431 (S.B. 316), § 3. Amended by Stats.2008, c. 179 (S.B.1498), § 174.)*

§ 78. Prevention program grants; funding

(a) The commission shall review and approve applications from employers and employee organizations, as well as applications submitted jointly by an employer organization and an employee organization, for grants to assist in establishing effective occupational injury and illness prevention programs. The commission shall establish policies for the evaluation of these applications and shall give priority to applications proposing to target high-risk industries and occupations, including those with high injury or illness rates, and those in which employees are exposed to one or more hazardous substances or conditions or where there is a demonstrated need for research to determine effective strategies for the prevention of occupational illnesses or injuries.

(b) Civil and administrative penalties assessed and collected pursuant to Sections 129.5 and 4628 shall be deposited in the Workers' Compensation Administration Revolving Fund. Moneys in the fund, when appropriated by the Legislature to fund the grants under subdivision (a) and other activities and expenses of the commission set forth in this code, shall be expended by the department, upon approval by the commission. *(Added by Stats.1993, c. 227 (S.B.1005), § 2. Amended by Stats. 2002, c. 6 (A.B.749), § 21; Stats.2002, c. 866 (A.B.486), § 1.)*

CHAPTER 4. DIVISION OF LABOR STANDARDS ENFORCEMENT

Section
79.   Creation of division; chief.
80.   Headquarters.
81.   Employees; traveling expenses; location of offices.
82.   Powers, duties, etc.; transfer from division of labor law enforcement; commissioner; regulations.
83.   Powers, duties, etc.; transfer from division of industrial welfare; chief; regulations.
87.   Civil service; transferred employees; status.
88.   Personnel records; transferred employees.
89.   Transfer of property.
89.5.   Expenditure of appropriations and special funds.
90.   Access to places of labor; refusal of admission or information; misdemeanor; penalty.
90.3.   Identification of unlawfully uninsured employers; public policy; establishment and maintenance of program targeting employers; contact and inspection procedures and priorities.
90.5.   State policy; enforcement of minimum labor standards; field enforcement unit; offices; enforcement plan; report to legislature.
90.7.   Failure of employer to report all payroll of employees; request for audit of payroll.
91.   Impeding performance of duty; misdemeanor; penalty.
92.   Subpenas; oaths; examination of witnesses; proof of instruments; depositions; affidavits.

Section
93. Enforcement of subpoenas; disobedience; misdemeanor.
94. Office hours.
95. Enforcement; arrests; civil liability.
96. Assignment of claims.
96.3. Collective bargaining representatives, assignees of covered employees in filing claims for wages; employee option.
96.5. Claims against deposits of contractors; hearings.
96.6. Industrial relations unpaid wage fund; creation.
96.7. Collection of wages and benefits without assignment; commissioner as trustee; search; escheat; transfer to general fund at end of fiscal year.
97. Validity of assignments.
98. Employee complaints; investigations and hearings; pleadings; evidence.
98.1. Order, decision or award; appellate rights; interest on award.
98.2. Review; costs and attorney's fees; stay of execution; satisfaction of judgment.
98.3. Actions for collection of wages, etc., by labor commissioner; conditions.
98.4. Representation by commissioner of financially disabled persons in de novo proceedings.
98.5. Intervention by labor commissioner.
98.6. Discharge or discrimination against employee or applicant for conduct delineated in this chapter or because employee or applicant has filed complaint or claim, instituted or caused to be instituted any proceeding under or relating to his or her rights or testified relating to the same on behalf of that person or another; reinstatement and reimbursement or employment entitlement for applicant; severability; applicability.
98.7. Persons allegedly discharged or otherwise discriminated against in violation of law; filing of complaint; investigation; report; remedies; dismissal; appeals.
98.75. Discrimination complaint reports.
98.8. Regulations and rules of practice and procedure.
98.9. Contractors; findings of deliberate Labor Code violations; delivery of findings to contractors' state license board.
99. Filing of claims and liens.
100. Joinder of claimants.
100.5. Preferred claims.
101. Court costs; fees.
101.5. Filing and recording fees.
102. Cost of sheriff or marshal; specification upon return of summons or process; inclusion in judgment.
103. Actions in other states for collection of claims; assignments for collection.
104. Claims assigned by other states; actions; collection.
105. Bilingual persons in public contact positions; interpreters; explanatory materials and forms in non-English languages.
106. Joint Enforcement Strike Force on the Underground Economy; employees; citations or penalty assessment orders; appeals.
107. Enforcement of Welfare and Institutions Code § 14110.65; exclusion of claims made under that section.

§ 79. Creation of division; chief

There is in the Department of Industrial Relations the Division of Labor Standards Enforcement. The Division of Labor Standards Enforcement shall be under the direction of an executive officer known as the Chief, Division of Labor Standards Enforcement, who shall be appointed by the Governor, subject to confirmation of the Senate, and shall hold office at the pleasure of the Director of Industrial Relations. The annual salary of the chief shall be determined by the Department of Finance. *(Added by Stats.1976, c. 746, p. 1777, § 13.)*

§ 80. Headquarters

The headquarters of the Division of Labor Standards Enforcement, hereafter in this chapter referred to as the division, shall be located in San Francisco. *(Added by Stats.1976, c. 746, p. 1777, § 14.)*

§ 81. Employees; traveling expenses; location of offices

The employees of the division shall devote their full time to the work of the division and shall receive their actual necessary traveling expenses. The division shall maintain offices in San Francisco, Los Angeles, Sacramento, San Diego, Oakland, Fresno, San Jose, and in such other places as the Labor Commissioner may deem necessary. *(Added by Stats.1976, c. 746, p. 1777, § 15.)*

§ 82. Powers, duties, etc.; transfer from division of labor law enforcement; commissioner; regulations

(a) The Division of Labor Standards Enforcement succeeds to, and is vested with, all of the powers, duties, purposes, responsibilities, and jurisdiction of the Division of Labor Law Enforcement, which is hereby abolished.

(b) All powers, duties, purposes, and responsibilities of the Labor Commissioner, who is Chief of the Division of Labor Law Enforcement, are hereby transferred to the Labor Commissioner who is the Chief of the Division of Labor Standards Enforcement.

(c) Any regulation or other action made, prescribed, issued, granted, or performed by the abolished Division of Labor Law Enforcement in the administration, performance, or implementation of a function transferred pursuant to subdivision (a) of this section shall remain in effect and shall be deemed to be a regulation or action of the Division of Labor Standards Enforcement unless and until repealed, modified, or rescinded by such division.

(d) Whenever any reference is made in any law to the abolished Division of Labor Law Enforcement, it shall be deemed to be a reference to, and to mean, the Division of Labor Standards Enforcement. *(Added by Stats.1976, c. 746, p. 1777, § 16.)*

§ 83. Powers, duties, etc.; transfer from division of industrial welfare; chief; regulations

(a) The Division of Labor Standards Enforcement succeeds to, and is vested with, all of the powers, duties, purposes, responsibilities, and jurisdiction of the Division of Industrial Welfare, which is hereby abolished.

(b) All powers, duties, purposes, and responsibilities of the Chief, Division of Industrial Welfare are hereby transferred to the Chief of the Division of Labor Standards Enforcement.

(c) Any regulation or other action made, prescribed, issued, granted, or performed by the abolished Division of Industrial Welfare in the administration, performance, or implementation of a function transferred pursuant to subdivision (a) of this section shall remain in effect and shall be deemed to be a regulation or action of the Division of Labor Standards Enforcement unless and until repealed, modified, or rescinded by such division.

(d) Whenever any reference is made in any law to the abolished Division of Industrial Welfare it shall be deemed to be a reference to, and to mean, the Division of Labor Standards Enforcement. *(Added by Stats.1976, c. 746, p. 1778, § 17.)*

§ 87. Civil service; transferred employees; status

All persons, other than temporary employees, serving in the state civil service and engaged in the performance of a function transferred pursuant to this chapter, or engaged in the administration of a law, the administration of which is transferred pursuant to this chapter, shall, in accordance with Section 19050.9 of the Government Code, remain in the state civil service and are hereby transferred to the Division of Labor Standards Enforcement. The status, positions, and rights of those persons shall not be affected by their transfer and shall continue to be retained by them pursuant to the State Civil Service Act (Part 2 (commencing with Section 18500) of Division 5 of Title 5 of the Government Code), except as to positions the duties of which are vested in a position that is exempt from civil service. *(Added by Stats.1976, c. 746, p. 1778, § 18. Amended by Stats.2009, c. 140 (A.B.1164), § 135.)*

§ 88. Personnel records; transferred employees

The personnel records of all employees transferred pursuant to Section 87 shall remain in the Department of Industrial Relations. *(Added by Stats.1976, c. 746, p. 1779, § 19.)*

§ 89. Transfer of property

The Division of Labor Standards Enforcement shall have possession and control of all records, books, papers, offices, equipment, supplies, moneys, funds, appropriations, land, and other property, real or personal, held for the benefit or use of the Division of Labor Law Enforcement and the Division of Industrial Welfare with respect to the functions transferred pursuant to this chapter. *(Added by Stats.1976, c. 746, p. 1779, § 21.)*

§ 89.5. Expenditure of appropriations and special funds

The Division of Labor Standards Enforcement may expend the money in any appropriation or in any special fund in the State Treasury made available by law for the administration of the statutes the administration of which is committed to it pursuant to this chapter, or for the use, support, or maintenance of any board, bureau, commis-

sion, department, office, or officer whose duties, powers, and functions have been transferred to, and conferred upon, the Division of Labor Standards Enforcement pursuant to this chapter. Such expenditures by the Division of Labor Standards Enforcement shall be made in accordance with law in carrying out the purposes for which the appropriations were made or the special funds created. *(Added by Stats.1976, c. 746, p. 1779, § 22.)*

§ 90. Access to places of labor; refusal of admission or information; misdemeanor; penalty

The Labor Commissioner, his deputies and agents, shall have free access to all places of labor. Any person, or agent or officer thereof, who refuses admission to the Labor Commissioner or his deputy or agent or who, upon request, willfully neglects or refuses to furnish them any statistics or information, pertaining to their lawful duties, which are in his possession or under his control, is guilty of a misdemeanor, punishable by a fine of not more than one thousand dollars ($1,000). *(Stats.1937, c. 90, p. 190, § 90. Amended by Stats.1976, c. 1190, p. 5368, § 1; Stats.1983, c. 1092, § 188, eff. Sept. 27, 1983, operative Jan. 1, 1984.)*

§ 90.3. Identification of unlawfully uninsured employers; public policy; establishment and maintenance of program targeting employers; contact and inspection procedures and priorities

(a) It is the policy of this state to vigorously enforce the laws requiring employers to secure the payment of compensation as required by Section 3700 and to protect employers who comply with the law from those who attempt to gain a competitive advantage at the expense of their workers by failing to secure the payment of compensation.

(b) In order to ensure that the laws requiring employers to secure the payment of compensation are adequately enforced, the Labor Commissioner shall establish and maintain a program that systematically identifies unlawfully uninsured employers. The Labor Commissioner, in consultation with the Administrative Director of the Division of Workers' Compensation and the director, may prioritize targets for the program in consideration of available resources. The employers shall be identified from data from the Uninsured Employers' Fund, the Employment Development Department, the rating organizations licensed by the Insurance Commissioner pursuant to Article 3 (commencing with Section 11750) of Chapter 3 of Part 3 of Division 2 of the Insurance Code, and any other sources deemed likely to lead to the identification of unlawfully uninsured employers. All state departments and agencies and any rating organization licensed by the Insurance Commissioner pursuant to Article 3 (commencing with Section 11750) of Chapter 3 of Part 3 of Division 2 of the Insurance Code shall cooperate with the Labor Commissioner and on reasonable request provide information and data in their possession reasonably necessary to carry out the program.

(c) As part of the program, the Labor Commissioner shall establish procedures for ensuring that employers with payroll but with no record of workers' compensation coverage are contacted and, if no valid reason for the lack of record of coverage is shown, inspected on a priority basis.

(d) The Labor Commissioner shall annually, not later than March 1, prepare a report concerning the effectiveness of the program, publish it on the Labor Commissioner's Web site, as well as notify the Legislature, the Governor, the Insurance Commissioner, and the Administrative Director of the Division of Workers' Compensation of the report's availability. The report shall include, but not be limited to, all of the following:

(1) The number of employers identified from records of the Employment Development Department who were screened for matching records of insurance coverage or self-insurance.

(2) The number of employers identified from records of the Employment Development Department that were matched to records of insurance coverage or self-insurance.

(3) The number of employers identified from records of the Employment Development Department that were notified that there was no record of their insurance coverage.

(4) The number of employers responding to the notices, and the nature of the responses, including the number of employers who failed to provide satisfactory proof of workers' compensation coverage and including information about the reasons that employers who provided satisfactory proof of coverage were not appropriately recognized in the comparison performed under subdivision (b). The report may include recommendations to improve the accuracy and efficiency of the program in screening for unlawfully uninsured employers.

(5) The number of employers identified as unlawfully uninsured from records of the Uninsured Employers' Benefits Trust Fund or from records of the Division of Workers' Compensation, and the number of those employers that are also identifiable from the records of the Employment Development Department. These statistics shall be reported in a manner to permit analysis and estimation of the percentage of unlawfully uninsured employers that do not report wages to the Employment Development Department.

(6) The number of employers inspected.

(7) The number and amount of penalties assessed pursuant to Section 3722 as a result of the program.

(8) The number and amount of penalties collected pursuant to Section 3722 as a result of the program.

(e) The allocation of funds from the Workers' Compensation Administration Revolving Fund pursuant to subdivision (a) of Section 62.5 shall not increase the total amount of surcharges pursuant to subdivision (e) of Section 62.5. Startup costs for this program shall be allocated from the fiscal year 2007–08 surcharges collected. The total amount allocated for this program under subdivision (a) of Section 62.5 in subsequent years shall not exceed the amount of penalties collected pursuant to Section 3722 as a result of the program. *(Added by Stats.2002, c. 6 (A.B.749), § 22. Amended by Stats.2007, c. 662 (S.B.869), § 2.)*

§ 90.5. State policy; enforcement of minimum labor standards; field enforcement unit; offices; enforcement plan; report to legislature

(a) It is the policy of this state to vigorously enforce minimum labor standards in order to ensure employees are not required or permitted to work under substandard unlawful conditions or for employers that have not secured the payment of compensation, and to protect employers who comply with the law from those who attempt to gain a competitive advantage at the expense of their workers by failing to comply with minimum labor standards.

(b) In order to ensure that minimum labor standards are adequately enforced, the Labor Commissioner shall establish and maintain a field enforcement unit, which shall be administratively and physically separate from offices of the division that accept and determine individual employee complaints. The unit shall have offices in Los Angeles, San Francisco, San Jose, San Diego, Sacramento, and any other locations that the Labor Commissioner deems appropriate. The unit shall have primary responsibility for administering and enforcing those statutes and regulations most effectively enforced through field investigations, including Sections 226, 1021, 1021.5, 1193.5, 1193.6, 1194.5, 1197, 1198, 1771, 1776, 1777.5, 2651, 2673, 2675, and 3700, in accordance with the plan adopted by the Labor Commissioner pursuant to subdivision (c). Nothing in this section shall be construed to limit the authority of this unit in enforcing any statute or regulation in the course of its investigations.

(c) The Labor Commissioner shall adopt an enforcement plan for the field enforcement unit. The plan shall identify priorities for investigations to be undertaken by the unit that ensure the available resources will be concentrated in industries, occupations, and areas in which employees are relatively low paid and unskilled, and those in which there has been a history of violations of the statutes cited in subdivision (b), and those with high rates of noncompliance with Section 3700.

(d) The Labor Commissioner shall annually report to the Legislature, not later than March 1, concerning the effectiveness of the field enforcement unit. The report shall include, but not be limited to, all of the following:

(1) The enforcement plan adopted by the Labor Commissioner pursuant to subdivision (c), and the rationale for the priorities identified in the plan.

(2) The number of establishments investigated by the unit, and the number of types of violations found.

(3) The amount of wages found to be unlawfully withheld from workers, and the amount of unpaid wages recovered for workers.

(4) The amount of penalties and unpaid wages transferred to the General Fund as a result of the efforts of the unit. *(Added by Stats.1983, c. 323, § 60.36, eff. July 21, 1983. Amended by Stats.2001, c. 159 (S.B.662), § 155; Stats.2002, c. 6 (A.B.749), § 23.)*

§ 90.7. Failure of employer to report all payroll of employees; request for audit of payroll

When the division determines that an employer has violated Section 226.2, 1021, 1021.5, 1197, or 1771, or otherwise determines that an employer may have failed to report all the payroll of the employer's employees as required by law, the division shall advise the Insurance Commissioner and request that an audit be ordered pursuant to Section 11736.5 of the Insurance Code. *(Added by Stats.1987, c. 1386, § 2.)*

§ 91. Impeding performance of duty; misdemeanor; penalty

Any person who willfully impedes or prevents the Labor Commissioner or his deputies or agents in the performance of duty, is guilty of a misdemeanor, punishable by a fine of not less than one hundred dollars ($100) nor more than one thousand dollars ($1,000), or imprisonment for not less than seven nor more than 30 days in the county jail, or both. *(Stats.1937, c. 90, p. 190, § 91. Amended by Stats.1976, c. 1190, p. 5368, § 2; Stats.1983, c. 1092, § 189, eff. Sept. 27, 1983, operative Jan. 1, 1984.)*

§ 92. Subpenas; oaths; examination of witnesses; proof of instruments; depositions; affidavits

The Labor Commissioner, his deputies and agents, may issue subpenas to compel the attendance of witnesses and parties and the production of books, papers and records; administer oaths; examine witnesses under oath; take the verification, acknowledgment, or proof of written instruments; and take depositions and affidavits for the purpose of carrying out the provisions of this code and all laws which the division is to enforce. *(Stats.1937, c. 90, p. 191, § 92. Amended by Stats.1951, c. 960, p. 2577, § 1.)*

§ 93. Enforcement of subpoenas; disobedience; misdemeanor

Obedience to subpoenas issued by the Labor Commissioner, or his deputies or agents shall be enforced by the courts. It is a misdemeanor to ignore willfully such a subpoena if it calls for an appearance at a distance from the place of service of 100 miles, or less. *(Stats.1937, c. 90, p. 191, § 93. Amended by Stats.1939, c. 1114, p. 3059, § 1; Stats.1976, c. 1190, p. 5368, § 3.)*

§ 94. Office hours

The office of the division shall be open for business from 9 o'clock a.m. until 5 o'clock p.m. every day except nonjudicial days, and the officers thereof shall give to all

persons requesting it all needed information which they may possess. *(Stats.1937, c. 90, p. 191, § 94.)*

§ 95. Enforcement; arrests; civil liability

(a) The division may enforce the provisions of this code and all labor laws of the state the enforcement of which is not specifically vested in any other officer, board or commission. Except as provided in subdivision (d), in the enforcement of such provisions and laws, the director, deputy director, and such officers and employees as the director may designate, shall only have the authority, as public officers, to arrest without a warrant, any person who, in his presence, has violated or as to whom there is probable cause to believe has violated any of such provisions and laws.

In any case in which an arrest authorized by this subdivision is made for an offense declared to be a misdemeanor, and the person arrested does not demand to be taken before a magistrate, the arresting officer may, instead of taking such person before a magistrate, follow the procedure prescribed by Chapter 5C (commencing with Section 853.6) of Title 3 of Part 2 of the Penal Code. The provisions of such chapter shall thereafter apply with reference to any proceeding based upon the issuance of a citation pursuant to this authority.

(b) There shall be no civil liability on the part of and no cause of action shall arise against any person, acting pursuant to this section and within the scope of his authority, for false arrest or false imprisonment arising out of any arrest which is lawful or which the arresting officer, at the time of such arrest, had reasonable cause to believe was lawful. No such officer shall be deemed an aggressor or lose his right to self-defense by the use of reasonable force to effect the arrest or to prevent escape or to overcome resistance.

(c) The director, deputy director, and such officers and employees as the director may designate, may serve all processes and notices throughout the state.

(d) With respect to the enforcement of the provisions of this code and other labor laws as provided in subdivision (a), all officers and employees designated by the Labor Commissioner as investigators, shall have the authority of peace officers to make arrests, and may serve processes and notices as provided in subdivision (c). *(Stats.1937, c. 90, p. 191, § 95. Amended by Stats.1968, c. 1222, p. 2315, § 49; Stats.1971, c. 701, p. 1358, § 1.)*

§ 96. Assignment of claims

The Labor Commissioner and his or her deputies and representatives authorized by him or her in writing shall, upon the filing of a claim therefor by an employee, or an employee representative authorized in writing by an employee, with the Labor Commissioner, take assignments of:

(a) Wage claims and incidental expense accounts and advances.

(b) Mechanics' and other liens of employees.

(c) Claims based on "stop orders" for wages and on bonds for labor.

(d) Claims for damages for misrepresentations of conditions of employment.

(e) Claims for unreturned bond money of employees.

(f) Claims for penalties for nonpayment of wages.

(g) Claims for the return of workers' tools in the illegal possession of another person.

(h) Claims for vacation pay, severance pay, or other compensation supplemental to a wage agreement.

(i) Awards for workers' compensation benefits in which the Workers' Compensation Appeals Board has found that the employer has failed to secure payment of compensation and where the award remains unpaid more than 10 days after having become final.

(j) Claims for loss of wages as the result of discharge from employment for the garnishment of wages.

(k) Claims for loss of wages as the result of demotion, suspension, or discharge from employment for lawful conduct occurring during nonworking hours away from the employer's premises. *(Stats.1937, c. 90, p. 191, § 96. Amended by Stats.1939, c. 468, p. 1816, § 1; Stats.1945, c. 1336, p. 2506, § 1; Stats.1951, c. 478, p. 1616, § 1; Stats.1953, c. 555, p. 1813, § 1; Stats.1965, c. 1513, p. 3556, § 3.5, operative Jan. 15, 1966; Stats.1969, c. 1529, p. 3122, § 1; Stats.1970, c. 243, p. 503, § 1; Stats.1971, c. 1607, p. 3459, § 1; Stats.1972, c. 1421, p. 3103, § 1; Stats.1978, c. 1253, p. 4070, § 1; Stats.1982, c. 454, p. 1874, § 127; Stats.1999, c. 692 (A.B.1689), § 2.)*

§ 96.3. Collective bargaining representatives, assignees of covered employees in filing claims for wages; employee option

In cases where employees are covered by a collective bargaining agreement, the collective bargaining representative by virtue of such agreement may be the assignee of all such covered employees for purposes of filing claims for wages with the Labor Commissioner, subject to the option of the employee to reject such representation and to represent himself or herself. *(Added by Stats.1976, c. 1029, p. 4618, § 1.)*

§ 96.5. Claims against deposits of contractors; hearings

The Labor Commissioner shall conduct such hearings as may be necessary for the purpose of Section 7071.11 of the Business and Professions Code. In any action to recover upon a cash deposit after a determination made under Section 7071.11, the Labor Commissioner shall certify in writing to the appropriate court that he has heard and determined the validity of claims and demands and that the sum specified therein is the amount found due and payable. The certificate of the commissioner shall be considered by the court but shall not, by itself, be sufficient evidence to support a judgment. *(Added by Stats.1974, c. 201, p. 395, § 2.)*

§ 96.6. Industrial relations unpaid wage fund; creation

The Industrial Relations Unpaid Wage Fund is hereby created as a special fund in the State Treasury, which is continuously appropriated for the purposes of subdivision (c) of Section 96.7. *(Added by Stats.1975, c. 714, p. 1705, § 1.)*

§ 96.7. Collection of wages and benefits without assignment; commissioner as trustee; search; escheat; transfer to general fund at end of fiscal year

The Labor Commissioner, after investigation and upon determination that wages or monetary benefits are due and unpaid to any worker in the State of California, may collect such wages or benefits on behalf of the worker without assignment of such wages or benefits to the commissioner.

(a) The Labor Commissioner shall act as trustee of all such collected unpaid wages or benefits, and shall deposit such collected moneys in the Industrial Relations Unpaid Wage Fund.

(b) The Labor Commissioner shall make a diligent search to locate any worker for whom the Labor Commissioner has collected unpaid wages or benefits.

(c) All wages or benefits collected under this section shall be remitted to the worker, his lawful representative, or to any trust or custodial fund established under a plan to provide health and welfare, pension, vacation, retirement, or similar benefits from the Industrial Relations Unpaid Wage Fund.

(d) Any unpaid wages or benefits collected by the Labor Commissioner pursuant to this section shall be retained in the Industrial Relations Unpaid Wage Fund until remitted pursuant to subdivision (c), or until deposited in the General Fund.

(e) The Controller shall, at the end of each fiscal year, transfer to the General Fund the unencumbered balance, less six months of expenditures as determined by the Director of Finance, in the Industrial Relations Unpaid Wage Fund.

(f) All wages or benefits collected under this section which cannot be remitted from the Industrial Relations Unpaid Wage Fund pursuant to subdivision (c) because money has been transmitted to the General Fund shall be paid out of the General Fund from funds appropriated for that purpose. *(Added by Stats.1975, c. 714, p. 1705, § 2. Amended by Stats.1981, c. 562, p. 2214, § 1, eff. Sept. 19, 1981; Stats.2005, c. 74 (A.B.139), § 54, eff. July 19, 2005.)*

§ 97. Validity of assignments

The Labor Commissioner, his deputies and representatives shall not be bound by any rule requiring the consent of the spouse of a married claimant, the filing of a lien for record before it is assigned, or prohibiting the assignment of a claim for penalty before the claim has been incurred or any other technical rule with reference to the validity of assignments. *(Stats.1937, c. 90, p. 191, § 97. Amended by Stats.1939, c. 1114, p. 3059, § 2.)*

§ 98. Employee complaints; investigations and hearings; pleadings; evidence

(a) The Labor Commissioner shall have the authority to investigate employee complaints. The Labor Commissioner may provide for a hearing in any action to recover wages, penalties, and other demands for compensation properly before the division or the Labor Commissioner, including orders of the Industrial Welfare Commission, and shall determine all matters arising under his or her jurisdiction. It shall be within the jurisdiction of the Labor Commissioner to accept and determine claims from holders of payroll checks or payroll drafts returned unpaid because of insufficient funds, if, after a diligent search, the holder is unable to return the dishonored check or draft to the payee and recover the sums paid out. Within 30 days of the filing of the complaint, the Labor Commissioner shall notify the parties as to whether a hearing will be held, whether action will be taken in accordance with Section 98.3, or whether no further action will be taken on the complaint. If the determination is made by the Labor Commissioner to hold a hearing, the hearing shall be held within 90 days of the date of that determination. However, the Labor Commissioner may postpone or grant additional time before setting a hearing if the Labor Commissioner finds that it would lead to an equitable and just resolution of the dispute.

It is the intent of the Legislature that hearings held pursuant to this section be conducted in an informal setting preserving the right of the parties.

(b) When a hearing is set, a copy of the complaint, which shall include the amount of compensation requested, together with a notice of time and place of the hearing, shall be served on all parties, personally or by certified mail, or in the manner specified in Section 415.20 of the Code of Civil Procedure.

(c) Within 10 days after service of the notice and the complaint, a defendant may file an answer with the Labor Commissioner in any form as the Labor Commissioner may prescribe, setting forth the particulars in which the complaint is inaccurate or incomplete and the facts upon which the defendant intends to rely.

(d) No pleading other than the complaint and answer of the defendant or defendants shall be required. Both shall be in writing and shall conform to the form and the rules of practice and procedure adopted by the Labor Commissioner.

(e) Evidence on matters not pleaded in the answer shall be allowed only on terms and conditions the Labor Commissioner shall impose. In all these cases, the claimant shall be entitled to a continuance for purposes of review of the new evidence.

(f) If the defendant fails to appear or answer within the time allowed under this chapter, no default shall be taken against him or her, but the Labor Commissioner shall hear the evidence offered and shall issue an order, decision, or award in accordance with the evidence. A defendant failing to appear or answer, or subsequently contending to be aggrieved in any manner by want of notice of the pendency of the proceedings, may apply to the Labor Commissioner for relief in accordance with Section 473 of the Code of Civil Procedure. The Labor Commissioner may afford this relief. No right to relief, including the claim that the findings or award of the Labor Commissioner or judgment entered thereon are void upon their face, shall accrue to the defendant in any court unless prior application is made to the Labor Commissioner in accordance with this chapter.

(g) All hearings conducted pursuant to this chapter are governed by the division and by the rules of practice and procedure adopted by the Labor Commissioner.

(h)(1) Whenever a claim is filed under this chapter against a person operating or doing business under a fictitious business name, as defined in Section 17900 of the Business and Professions Code, which relates to the person's business, the division shall inquire at the time of the hearing whether the name of the person is the legal name under which the business or person has been licensed, registered, incorporated, or otherwise authorized to do business.

(2) The division may amend an order, decision, or award to conform to the legal name of the business or the person who is the defendant to a wage claim, if it can be shown that proper service was made on the defendant or his or her agent, unless a judgment had been entered on the order, decision, or award pursuant to subdivision (d) of Section 98.2. The Labor Commissioner may apply to the clerk of the superior court to amend a judgment that has been issued pursuant to a final order, decision, or award to conform to the legal name of the defendant, if it can be shown that proper service was made on the defendant or his or her agent. *(Stats.1937, c. 90, p. 191, § 98. Amended by Stats.1939, c. 468, p. 1816, § 2; Stats.1975, c. 144, p. 272, § 11; Stats.1976, c. 1190, p. 5368, § 4; Stats.1988, c. 5, § 1; Stats.1990, c. 1040 (S.B.240), § 1; Stats.1998, c. 931 (S.B.2139), § 345, eff. Sept. 28, 1998; Stats.2002, c. 784 (S.B.1316), § 520; Stats.2005, c. 405 (A.B.1311), § 1; Stats.2006, c. 538 (S.B.1852), § 477.)*

§ 98.1. Order, decision or award; appellate rights; interest on award

(a) Within 15 days after the hearing is concluded, the Labor Commissioner shall file in the office of the division a copy of the order, decision, or award. The order, decision, or award shall include a summary of the hearing and the reasons for the decision. Upon filing of the order, decision, or award, the Labor Commissioner shall serve a copy of the decision personally, by first-class mail, or in the manner specified in Section 415.20 of the Code of Civil Procedure on the parties. The notice shall also advise the parties of their right to appeal the decision or award and further advise the parties that failure to do so within the period prescribed by this chapter shall result in the decision or award becoming final and enforceable as a judgment by the superior court.

(b) For the purpose of this section, an award shall include any sums found owing, damages proved, and any penalties awarded pursuant to this code.

(c) All awards granted pursuant to a hearing under this chapter shall accrue interest on all due and unpaid wages at the same rate as prescribed by subdivision (b) of Section 3289 of the Civil Code. The interest shall accrue until the wages are paid from the date that the wages were due and payable as provided in Part 1 (commencing with Section 200) of Division 2. *(Added by Stats.1976, c. 1190, p. 5369, § 5. Amended by Stats.1979, c. 107, p. 244, § 1, eff. June 12, 1979; Stats.1981, c. 714, p. 2719, § 313; Stats.1985, c. 454, § 1; Stats.1988, c. 96, § 2; Stats.2000, c. 876 (A.B.2509), § 1; Stats.2002, c. 784 (S.B.1316), § 521; Stats.2005, c. 405 (A.B.1311), § 2.)*

§ 98.2. Review; costs and attorney's fees; stay of execution; satisfaction of judgment

(a) Within 10 days after service of notice of an order, decision, or award the parties may seek review by filing an appeal to the superior court, where the appeal shall be heard de novo. The court shall charge the first paper filing fee under Section 70611 of the Government Code to the party seeking review. The fee shall be distributed as provided in Section 68085.3 of the Government Code. A copy of the appeal request shall be served upon the Labor Commissioner by the appellant. For purposes of computing the 10-day period after service, Section 1013 of the Code of Civil Procedure is applicable.

(b) Whenever an employer files an appeal pursuant to this section, the employer shall post an undertaking with the reviewing court in the amount of the order, decision, or award. The undertaking shall consist of an appeal bond issued by a licensed surety or a cash deposit with the court in the amount of the order, decision, or award. The employer shall provide written notification to the other parties and the Labor Commissioner of the posting of the undertaking. The undertaking shall be on the condition that, if any judgment is entered in favor of the employee, the employer shall pay the amount owed pursuant to the judgment, and if the appeal is withdrawn or dismissed without entry of judgment, the employer shall pay the amount owed pursuant to the order, decision, or award of the Labor Commissioner unless the parties have executed a settlement agreement for payment of some other amount, in which case the employer shall pay the amount that the employer is obligated to pay under the terms of the settlement agreement. If the employer fails to pay the amount owed within 10 days of entry of the judgment, dismissal, or withdrawal of the appeal, or the execution of a settlement agreement, a portion of the undertaking equal to the amount owed, or the entire undertaking if the amount owed exceeds the undertaking, is forfeited to the employee.

(c) If the party seeking review by filing an appeal to the superior court is unsuccessful in the appeal, the court shall determine the costs and reasonable attorney's fees incurred by the other parties to the appeal, and assess that amount as a cost upon the party filing the appeal. An employee is successful if the court awards an amount greater than zero.

(d) If no notice of appeal of the order, decision, or award is filed within the period set forth in subdivision (a), the order, decision, or award shall, in the absence of fraud, be deemed the final order.

(e) The Labor Commissioner shall file, within 10 days of the order becoming final pursuant to subdivision (d), a certified copy of the final order with the clerk of the superior court of the appropriate county unless a settlement has been reached by the parties and approved by the Labor Commissioner. Judgment shall be entered immediately by the court clerk in conformity therewith. The judgment so entered has the same force and effect as, and is subject to all of the provisions of law relating to, a judgment in a civil action, and may be enforced in the same manner as any other judgment of the court in which it is entered. Enforcement of the judgment shall receive court priority.

(f)(1) In order to ensure that judgments are satisfied, the Labor Commissioner may serve upon the judgment debtor, personally or by first-class mail at the last known address of the judgment debtor listed with the division, a form similar to, and requiring the reporting of the same information as, the form approved or adopted by the Judicial Council for purposes of subdivision (a) of Section 116.830 of the Code of Civil Procedure to assist in identifying the nature and location of any assets of the judgment debtor.

(2) The judgment debtor shall complete the form and cause it to be delivered to the division at the address listed on the form within 35 days after the form has been served on the judgment debtor, unless the judgment has been satisfied. In case of willful failure by the judgment debtor to comply with this subdivision, the division or the judgment creditor may request the court to apply the sanctions provided in Section 708.170 of the Code of Civil Procedure.

(g) Notwithstanding subdivision (e), the Labor Commissioner may stay execution of any judgment entered upon an order, decision, or award that has become final upon good cause appearing therefor and may impose the terms and conditions of the stay of execution. A certified copy of the stay of execution shall be filed with the clerk entering the judgment.

(h) When a judgment is satisfied in fact, other than by execution, the Labor Commissioner may, upon the motion of either party or on its own motion, order entry of satisfaction of judgment. The clerk of the court shall enter a satisfaction of judgment upon the filing of a certified copy of the order.

(i) The Labor Commissioner shall make every reasonable effort to ensure that judgments are satisfied, including taking all appropriate legal action and requiring the employer to deposit a bond as provided in Section 240.

(j) The judgment creditor, or the Labor Commissioner as assignee of the judgment creditor, is entitled to court costs and reasonable attorney's fees for enforcing the judgment that is rendered pursuant to this section. *(Added by Stats.1976, c. 1190, p. 5370, § 6. Amended by Stats.1979, c. 107, p. 244, § 2, eff. June 12, 1979; Stats. 1980, c. 453, p. 960, § 1; Stats.1986, c. 628, § 1; Stats.1988, c. 96, § 3; Stats.1990, c. 1040 (S.B.240), § 2; Stats.1998, c. 931 (S.B.2139), § 346, eff. Sept. 28, 1998; Stats.2000, c. 876 (A.B.2509), § 2; Stats.2002, c. 784 (S.B.1316), § 522; Stats.2003, c. 62 (S.B.600), § 202; Stats.2003, c. 93 (A.B.223), § 2; Stats.2004, c. 183 (A.B. 3082), § 253; Stats.2005, c. 22 (S.B.1108), § 139; Stats. 2005, c. 75 (A.B.145), § 146, eff. July 19, 2005, operative Jan. 1, 2006; Stats.2007, c. 738 (A.B.1248), § 40.)*

§ 98.3. Actions for collection of wages, etc., by labor commissioner; conditions

(a) The Labor Commissioner may prosecute all actions for the collection of wages, penalties, and demands of persons who in the judgment of the Labor Commissioner are financially unable to employ counsel and the Labor Commissioner believes have claims which are valid and enforceable.

The Labor Commissioner may also prosecute actions for the return of worker's tools which are in the illegal possession of another person.

(b) The Labor Commissioner may prosecute action for the collection of wages and other moneys payable to employees or to the state arising out of an employment relationship or order of the Industrial Welfare Commission.

(c) The Labor Commissioner may also prosecute actions for wages or other monetary benefits that are due the Industrial Relations Unpaid Wage Fund. *(Added by Stats.1976, c. 1190, p. 5370, § 7.)*

§ 98.4. Representation by commissioner of financially disabled persons in de novo proceedings

The Labor Commissioner may, upon the request of a claimant financially unable to afford counsel, represent such claimant in the de novo proceedings provided for in Section 98.2. In the event that such claimant is attempting to uphold the amount awarded by the Labor Commissioner and is not objecting to any part of the Labor Commissioner's final order, the Labor Commissioner shall represent the claimant. *(Added by Stats.1976, c. 1190, p. 5370, § 8.)*

§ 98.5. Intervention by labor commissioner

The Labor Commissioner shall have the right to intervene in any court proceedings conducted pursuant to Section 98.2 where questions of the interpretation of

statutes or administrative regulations are present. *(Added by Stats.1976, c. 1190, p. 5371, § 10.)*

§ 98.6. Discharge or discrimination against employee or applicant for conduct delineated in this chapter or because employee or applicant has filed complaint or claim, instituted or caused to be instituted any proceeding under or relating to his or her rights or testified relating to the same on behalf of that person or another; reinstatement and reimbursement or employment entitlement for applicant; severability; applicability

(a) No person shall discharge an employee or in any manner discriminate against any employee or applicant for employment because the employee or applicant engaged in any conduct delineated in this chapter, including the conduct described in subdivision (k) of Section 96, and Chapter 5 (commencing with Section 1101) of Part 3 of Division 2, or because the employee or applicant for employment has filed a bona fide complaint or claim or instituted or caused to be instituted any proceeding under or relating to his or her rights, which are under the jurisdiction of the Labor Commissioner, or because the employee has initiated any action or notice pursuant to Section 2699, or has testified or is about to testify in any such proceeding or because of the exercise by the employee or applicant for employment on behalf of himself, herself, or others of any rights afforded him or her.

(b) Any employee who is discharged, threatened with discharge, demoted, suspended, or in any other manner discriminated against in the terms and conditions of his or her employment because the employee engaged in any conduct delineated in this chapter, including the conduct described in subdivision (k) of Section 96, and Chapter 5 (commencing with Section 1101) of Part 3 of Division 2, or because the employee has made a bona fide complaint or claim to the division pursuant to this part, or because the employee has initiated any action or notice pursuant to Section 2699 shall be entitled to reinstatement and reimbursement for lost wages and work benefits caused by those acts of the employer. Any employer who willfully refuses to hire, promote, or otherwise restore an employee or former employee who has been determined to be eligible for rehiring or promotion by a grievance procedure, arbitration, or hearing authorized by law, is guilty of a misdemeanor.

(c)(1) Any applicant for employment who is refused employment, who is not selected for a training program leading to employment, or who in any other manner is discriminated against in the terms and conditions of any offer of employment because the applicant engaged in any conduct delineated in this chapter, including the conduct described in subdivision (k) of Section 96, and Chapter 5 (commencing with Section 1101) of Part 3 of Division 2, or because the applicant has made a bona fide complaint or claim to the division pursuant to this part, or because the employee has initiated any action or notice pursuant to Section 2699 shall be entitled to employment and reimbursement for lost wages and work benefits caused by the acts of the prospective employer.

(2) This subdivision shall not be construed to invalidate any collective bargaining agreement that requires an applicant for a position that is subject to the collective bargaining agreement to sign a contract that protects either or both of the following as specified in subparagraphs (A) and (B), nor shall this subdivision be construed to invalidate any employer requirement of an applicant for a position that is not subject to a collective bargaining agreement to sign an employment contract that protects either or both of the following:

(A) An employer against any conduct that is actually in direct conflict with the essential enterprise-related interests of the employer and where breach of that contract would actually constitute a material and substantial disruption of the employer's operation.

(B) A firefighter against any disease that is presumed to arise in the course and scope of employment, by limiting his or her consumption of tobacco products on and off the job.

(d) The provisions of this section creating new actions or remedies that are effective on January 1, 2002, to employees or applicants for employment do not apply to any state or local law enforcement agency, any religious association or corporation specified in subdivision (d) of Section 12926 of the Government Code, except as provided in Section 12926.2 of the Government Code, or any person described in Section 1070 of the Evidence Code. *(Added by Stats.1978, c. 1250, p. 4064, § 1. Amended by Stats.2001, c. 820 (A.B.1015), § 2; Stats. 2004, c. 221 (S.B.1809), § 1, eff. Aug. 11, 2004; Stats.2005, c. 22 (S.B.1108), § 140.)*

§ 98.7. Persons allegedly discharged or otherwise discriminated against in violation of law; filing of complaint; investigation; report; remedies; dismissal; appeals

(a) Any person who believes that he or she has been discharged or otherwise discriminated against in violation of any law under the jurisdiction of the Labor Commissioner may file a complaint with the division within six months after the occurrence of the violation. The six-month period may be extended for good cause. The complaint shall be investigated by a discrimination complaint investigator in accordance with this section. The Labor Commissioner shall establish procedures for the investigation of discrimination complaints. A summary of the procedures shall be provided to each complainant and respondent at the time of initial contact. The Labor Commissioner shall inform complainants charging a violation of Section 6310 or 6311, at the time of initial contact, of his or her right to file a separate, concurrent complaint with the United States Department of Labor within 30 days after the occurrence of the violation.

(b) Each complaint of unlawful discharge or discrimination shall be assigned to a discrimination complaint investigator who shall prepare and submit a report to the Labor Commissioner based on an investigation of the complaint. The Labor Commissioner may designate the chief deputy or assistant Labor Commissioner or the chief counsel to receive and review the reports. The investigation shall include, where appropriate, interviews with the complainant, respondent, and any witnesses who may have information concerning the alleged violation, and a review of any documents that may be relevant to the disposition of the complaint. The identity of a witness shall remain confidential unless the identification of the witness becomes necessary to proceed with the investigation or to prosecute an action to enforce a determination. The investigation report submitted to the Labor Commissioner or designee shall include the statements and documents obtained in the investigation, and the findings of the investigator concerning whether a violation occurred. The Labor Commissioner may hold an investigative hearing whenever the Labor Commissioner determines, after review of the investigation report, that a hearing is necessary to fully establish the facts. In the hearing the investigation report shall be made a part of the record and the complainant and respondent shall have the opportunity to present further evidence. The Labor Commissioner shall issue, serve, and enforce any necessary subpoenas.

(c) If the Labor Commissioner determines a violation has occurred, he or she shall notify the complainant and respondent and direct the respondent to cease and desist from the violation and take any action deemed necessary to remedy the violation, including, where appropriate, rehiring or reinstatement, reimbursement of lost wages and interest thereon, payment of reasonable attorney's fees associated with any hearing held by the Labor Commissioner in investigating the complaint, and the posting of notices to employees. If the respondent does not comply with the order within 10 working days following notification of the Labor Commissioner's determination, the Labor Commissioner shall bring an action promptly in an appropriate court against the respondent. If the Labor Commissioner fails to bring an action in court promptly, the complainant may bring an action against the Labor Commissioner in any appropriate court for a writ of mandate to compel the Labor Commissioner to bring an action in court against the respondent. If the complainant prevails in his or her action for a writ, the court shall award the complainant court costs and reasonable attorney's fees, notwithstanding any other law. Regardless of any delay in bringing an action in court, the Labor Commissioner shall not be divested of jurisdiction. In any action, the court may permit the claimant to intervene as a party plaintiff to the action and shall have jurisdiction, for cause shown, to restrain the violation and to order all appropriate relief. Appropriate relief includes, but is not limited to, rehiring or reinstatement of the complainant, reimbursement of lost wages and interest thereon, and any other compensation or equitable relief as is appropriate under the circumstances of the case. The Labor Commissioner shall petition the court for appropriate temporary relief or restraining order unless he or she determines good cause exists for not doing so.

(d)(1) If the Labor Commissioner determines no violation has occurred, he or she shall notify the complainant and respondent and shall dismiss the complaint. The Labor Commissioner may direct the complainant to pay reasonable attorney's fees associated with any hearing held by the Labor Commissioner if the Labor Commissioner finds the complaint was frivolous, unreasonable, groundless, and was brought in bad faith. The complainant may, after notification of the Labor Commissioner's determination to dismiss a complaint, bring an action in an appropriate court, which shall have jurisdiction to determine whether a violation occurred, and if so, to restrain the violation and order all appropriate relief to remedy the violation. Appropriate relief includes, but is not limited to, rehiring or reinstatement of the complainant, reimbursement of lost wages and interest thereon, and other compensation or equitable relief as is appropriate under the circumstances of the case. When dismissing a complaint, the Labor Commissioner shall advise the complainant of his or her right to bring an action in an appropriate court if he or she disagrees with the determination of the Labor Commissioner, and in the case of an alleged violation of Section 6310 or 6311, to file a complaint against the state program with the United States Department of Labor.

(2) The filing of a timely complaint against the state program with the United States Department of Labor shall stay the Labor Commissioner's dismissal of the division complaint until the United States Secretary of Labor makes a determination regarding the alleged violation. Within 15 days of receipt of that determination, the Labor Commissioner shall notify the parties whether he or she will reopen the complaint filed with the division or whether he or she will reaffirm the dismissal.

(e) The Labor Commissioner shall notify the complainant and respondent of his or her determination under subdivision (c) or paragraph (1) of subdivision (d), not later than 60 days after the filing of the complaint. Determinations by the Labor Commissioner under subdivision (c) or (d) may be appealed by the complainant or respondent to the Director of Industrial Relations within 10 days following notification of the Labor Commissioner's determination. The appeal shall set forth specifically and in full detail the grounds upon which the appealing party considers the Labor Commissioner's determination to be unjust or unlawful, and every issue to be considered by the director. The director may consider any issue relating to the initial determination and may modify, affirm, or reverse the Labor Commissioner's determination. The director's determination shall be the determination of the Labor Commissioner. The director shall notify the complainant and respondent of his or her determination within 10 days of receipt of the appeal.

(f) The rights and remedies provided by this section do not preclude an employee from pursuing any other rights and remedies under any other law. *(Added by Stats.1985,*

c. 1479, § 2. Amended by Stats.1999, c. 615 (A.B.1127), § 1; Stats.2001, c. 134 (A.B.1069), § 1; Stats.2002, c. 664 (A.B.3034), § 158.)*

§ 98.75.   Discrimination complaint reports

The Labor Commissioner shall submit a report to the Legislature by February 15, 1987, and annually thereafter by February 15, providing the following information with respect to discrimination complaints for the previous calendar year:

(a) The number of complaints filed pursuant to Section 98.7 or 1197.5, grouped according to the section of the Labor Code allegedly violated.

(b) The number of determinations issued, the number of investigative hearings held, the number of complaints dismissed, and the number of complaints found to be valid, grouped by the year in which the complaints were filed.

(c) The number of cases in which the respondent complied with the Labor Commissioner's order to remedy unlawful discrimination, the number of these orders with which respondents failed to comply, the number of court actions brought by the Labor Commissioner to remedy unlawful discrimination, and the results of those court actions. If the Labor Commissioner did not bring an action in court within 10 days against a respondent who failed to comply with his or her order, the report shall specify the reasons for not bringing action in court. *(Added by Stats.1985, c. 1479, § 3.)*

§ 98.8.   Regulations and rules of practice and procedure

The Labor Commissioner shall promulgate all regulations and rules of practice and procedure necessary to carry out the provisions of this chapter. *(Added by Stats.1976, c. 1190, p. 5371, § 11.)*

§ 98.9.   Contractors; findings of deliberate Labor Code violations; delivery of findings to contractors' state license board

Upon a finding by the Labor Commissioner that a willful or deliberate violation of any of the provisions of the Labor Code, within the jurisdiction of the Labor Commissioner, has been committed by a person licensed as a contractor pursuant to Chapter 9 (commencing with Section 7000) of Division 3 of the Business and Professions Code, in the course of such licensed activity, the Labor Commissioner shall immediately, upon expiration of the period for review specified in Section 98.2, or other applicable section, deliver a certified copy of the finding of the violation to the registrar of the Contractors' State License Board. *(Added by Stats.1978, c. 1247, p. 4059, § 2.)*

§ 99.   Filing of claims and liens

The division may file preferred claims, mechanics' liens, and other liens of employees in the name of the Labor Commissioner, his deputy or representative or in the names of the employees, whenever the facts have been investigated and found to support the claims. A statement that such facts have been found shall be alleged in the preferred claim or lien if it is filed in the name of the Labor Commissioner, his deputy or representative. *(Stats.1937, c. 90, p. 192, § 99.)*

§ 100. Joinder of claimants

The division may join various claimants in one preferred claim or lien as well as list them with the data regarding their claims in an exhibit and join them, in case of suit, in one cause of action in cases where no valid reason exists for making separate causes of action for each individual employee. *(Stats.1937, c. 90, p. 192, § 100.)*

§ 100.5. Preferred claims

Preferred claims for work performed or personal services rendered are provided for in Sections 1204, 1205, 1206, 1207, and 1208 of the Code of Civil Procedure, and Part 9 (commencing with Section 11400) of Division 7 of the Probate Code. *(Added by Stats.1943, c. 1006, p. 2920, § 1. Amended by Stats.1965, c. 157, p. 1114, § 1; Stats.1988, c. 1199, § 22.5, operative July 1, 1989.)*

§ 101. Court costs; fees

No court costs of any nature shall be payable by the division, in any civil action to which the division is a party. Any sheriff or marshal requested by the Labor Commissioner or a deputy or representative of the Labor Commissioner shall serve the summons in the action upon any person within the jurisdiction of the sheriff or marshal or levy under a writ of attachment or execution in the action upon the property of any defendant without cost to the division except for keeper's fees, service fees, and storage charges. *(Stats.1937, c. 90, p. 192, § 101. Amended by Stats.1959, c. 210, p. 2119, § 1; Stats.1982, c. 497, p. 2200, § 130, operative July 1, 1983; Stats.1996, c. 872 (A.B.3472), § 103.)*

§ 101.5. Filing and recording fees

No fees shall be payable for the filing or recording of any document or paper in the performance of any official service by the Labor Commissioner. The amount ordinarily charged for such filing or recording shall be made a part of any judgment recovered by the Labor Commissioner and shall be paid by the Labor Commissioner if sufficient money is collected over and above the wages, penalties, or demands actually due the claimants. *(Added by Stats.1951, c. 1136, p. 2904, § 1; Amended by Stats.1976, c. 1190, p. 5371, § 12.)*

§ 102. Cost of sheriff or marshal; specification upon return of summons or process; inclusion in judgment

The sheriff or marshal shall specify when the summons or process is returned, what costs he or she would ordinarily have been entitled to for such service, and those costs and the other regular court costs that would have accrued if the action was not by the Labor Commis-

sioner shall be made a part of any judgment recovered by the Labor Commissioner and shall be paid by the Labor Commissioner if sufficient money is collected over and above the wages, penalties, or demands actually due the claimants. *(Stats.1937, c. 90, p. 192, § 102. Amended by Stats.1976, c. 1190, p. 5371, § 13; Stats.1996, c. 872 (A.B.3472), § 104.)*

§ 103. Actions in other states for collection of claims; assignments for collection

The Labor Commissioner shall, to the extent provided for by any reciprocal agreement entered into pursuant to Section 64, or by the laws of any other state, maintain actions in the courts of the other state for the collection of the claims for wages, judgments, and other demands and may assign the claims, judgments, and demands to the labor department or agency of the other state for collection to the extent that they may be permitted or provided for by the laws of that state or by reciprocal agreement. *(Added by Stats.1953, c. 877, p. 2233, § 2. Amended by Stats.1976, c. 1190, p. 5371, § 14; Stats.1983, c. 142, § 98.)*

§ 104. Claims assigned by other states; actions; collection

The Labor Commissioner shall, upon the written request of the labor department or other corresponding agency of any other state or of any person, board, officer or commission of such state authorized to act for and on behalf of such labor department or corresponding agency, maintain actions in the courts of this state upon assigned claims for wages, judgments and demands arising in such other state in the same manner and to the same extent that such actions by the Labor Commissioner are authorized when arising in this state; provided, however, that such actions may be commenced and maintained only in those cases where such other state by appropriate legislation or by reciprocal agreement extends a like comity to cases arising in this state. *(Added by Stats.1953, c. 877, p. 2233, § 3. Amended by Stats.1976, c. 1190, p. 5371, § 15.)*

§ 105. Bilingual persons in public contact positions; interpreters; explanatory materials and forms in non-English languages

(a) The Labor Commissioner shall provide qualified bilingual persons in public contact positions or as interpreters to assist those in such positions to provide information and services in the language of a limited- or non-English-speaking person, with the primary effort being exerted towards the largest segments of the non-English-speaking persons in this state.

(b) The Labor Commissioner shall provide that an interpreter be present at all hearings and interviews where appropriate.

(c) The Labor Commissioner shall prepare and distribute to the public, through its local offices, materials explaining services available in non-English languages, as well as in English. In addition, the commissioner shall prepare and use written materials in non-English languages as well as in English for use by local offices if the local office serves a substantial number of non-English-speaking people, as defined in Section 7296.2 of the Government Code. The commissioner shall prepare and use such complaint processing forms and form letters in the language of non-English-speaking people as the commissioner deems necessary and appropriate for the filing, investigation, and resolution of wage claims, giving due consideration to the rights and obligations of all parties. The commissioner may, from time to time, at his or her discretion, eliminate, modify, amend, or add to the complaint processing forms and form letters which are the subject of bilingual or multilingual treatment or application. *(Added by Stats.1976, c. 1190, p. 5372, § 16. Amended by Stats.1984, c. 1089, § 2.)*

§ 106. Joint Enforcement Strike Force on the Underground Economy; employees; citations or penalty assessment orders; appeals

(a) The Labor Commissioner may authorize an employee of any of the agencies that participate in the Joint Enforcement Strike Force on the Underground Economy, as defined in Section 329 of the Unemployment Insurance Code, to issue citations pursuant to Sections 226.4 and 1022 and issue and serve a penalty assessment order pursuant to subdivision (a) of Section 3722.

(b) No employees shall issue citations or penalty assessment orders pursuant to this section unless they have been specifically designated, authorized, and trained by the Labor Commissioner for this purpose. Appeals of all citations or penalty assessment orders shall follow the procedures prescribed in Section 226.5, 1023, or 3725, whichever is applicable.

(Added by Stats.1994, c. 1117 (S.B.1490), § 1. Amended by Stats.1999, c. 306 (S.B.319), § 1; Stats.2004, c. 685 (A.B.3020), § 1.)

§ 107. Enforcement of Welfare and Institutions Code § 14110.65; exclusion of claims made under that section

(a) The enforcement of Section 14110.65 of the Welfare and Institutions Code is vested with the State Department of Health Services.

(b) Any claim made under Section 14110.65 of the Welfare and Institutions Code shall not constitute a wage claim as provided in subdivision (a) of Section 96, and shall not be subject to this chapter. *(Added by Stats.2002, c. 898 (S.B.1536), § 18.)*

CHAPTER 5. DIVISION OF WORKERS' COMPENSATION

Section
110.   Definitions.
111.   Appeals Board; members; powers; administrative director's powers.
112.   Appointment of members; term; qualifications; salary.

Section
113.   Designation of chairman; acting chairman.
115.   Majority decision; assignment of cases.
116.   Seal of appeals board.
117.   Appointment of attorney.
119.   Duties of attorney.
120.   Secretary and assistant secretaries; appointment and duties.
121.   Deputy appeals board members.
122.   Appointment of medical director and assistants.
123.   Employees; salaries of judges.
123.3.   Official reporter; stenographic or clerical assistance.
123.5.   Workers' compensation administrative law judges; eligible lists; qualifications.
123.6.   Workers' compensation administrative law judges; ethics.
123.7.   Pro tempore workers' compensation judge.
124.   Administration and enforcement of division; bilingual forms and notices.
125.   Blank forms.
126.   Records; minutes of proceedings.
127.   Fees; amount; disposition; publications.
127.5.   Additional duties of court administrator.
127.6.   Study of medical treatment provided to workers with industrial injuries and illnesses.
128.   Appointment of commissioner under federal law; payment of expenses; powers.
129.   Audits; deficiencies; notice of assessment and order to pay; appeals; reports.
129.5.   Penalties; schedule of violations; notice of assessment; violations found to be general business practice; proceedings.
130.   Administration of oaths; certification of official acts; issuance of subpoenas.
131.   Fees and mileage of witnesses.
132.   Judicial enforcement of subpoena; procedure.
132a.   Discrimination against workers injured in course of employment or testifying before appeals board; penalties.
133.   Incidental powers and jurisdiction.
134.   Insurance, extent, and service of process; fees.
135.   Destruction of old files.
138.   Absences; appointment of deputy.
138.1.   Appointments; tenure; salary.
138.2.   Headquarters of Division; base of operations for appeals board; meetings.
138.3.   Notice of possible benefits, rules.
138.4.   Injuries involving loss of time; duties of administrative director.
138.5.   Child support obligations; cooperation in enforcement; workers' compensation notification project.
138.6.   Workers' compensation information system.
138.65.   Study of effect of 2003 and 2004 legislative reforms on workers' compensation.
138.7.   Individually identifiable information; access by nonparties; worker's compensation information system; privilege.
139.2.   Appointment and reappointment of qualified medical evaluators; requirements for and qualifications of evaluators; suspension or termination of evaluator and review thereof; agreements with respect to cases assigned to evaluators; assignment of panels and notice to employees; review of evaluations; regulations; fees.
139.3.   Referrals for medical diagnosis or treatment; financial interests of physician; prohibitions; penalties.

Section
139.31. Referrals to which prohibition of § 139.3 do not apply.
139.4. Advertising by medical evaluators and physicians; review for deceptive claims or statements; penalty.
139.43. Services or benefits to injured workers; false statements or advertising; penalty; exemptions.
139.45. Regulations governing advertising; characteristics of false or misleading advertising.
139.47. Return-to-Work Program.
139.48. Establishment of Return–to–Work Program and Workers' Compensation Return–to–Work Fund; workplace modification expense reimbursement; employment preference prohibited; regulations.
139.6. Information and assistance program.

§ 110. Definitions

As used in this chapter:

(a) "Appeals board" means the Workers' Compensation Appeals Board. The title of a member of the board is "commissioner."

(b) "Administrative director" means the Administrative Director of the Division of Workers' Compensation.

(c) "Division" means the Division of Workers' Compensation.

(d) "Medical director" means the physician appointed by the administrative director pursuant to Section 122.

(e) "Qualified medical evaluator" means physicians appointed by the administrative director pursuant to Section 139.2.

(f) "Court administrator" means the administrator of the workers' compensation adjudicatory process at the trial level. *(Added by Stats.1965, c. 1513, p. 3556, § 5, operative Jan. 15, 1966. Amended by Stats.1967, c. 1462, p. 3404, § 1; Stats.1981, c. 21, p. 46, § 2, eff. April 18, 1981; Stats.1989, c. 892, § 10; Stats.1990, c. 1550 (A.B. 2910), § 8; Stats.1993, c. 121 (A.B.110), § 15, eff. July 16, 1993, Stats.2002, c. 6 (A.B.749), § 24, Stats.2003, c. 639 (S.B.228), § 4.)*

§ 111. Appeals Board; members; powers; administrative director's powers

(a) The Workers' Compensation Appeals Board, consisting of seven members, shall exercise all judicial powers vested in it under this code. In all other respects, the Division of Workers' Compensation is under the control of the administrative director and, except as to those duties, powers, jurisdiction, responsibilities, and purposes as are specifically vested in the appeals board, the administrative director shall exercise the powers of the head of a department within the meaning of Article 1 (commencing with Section 11150) of Chapter 2 of Part 1 of Division 3 of Title 2 of the Government Code with respect to the Division of Workers' Compensation which shall include supervision of, and responsibility for, personnel, and the coordination of the work of the division, except personnel of the appeals board.

(b) The administrative director shall prepare and submit, on March 1 of each year, a report to the Governor and the Legislature covering the activities of the division during the prior year. The report shall include recommendations for improvement and the need, if any, for legislation to enhance the delivery of compensation to injured workers. The report shall include data on penalties imposed on employers or insurers due to delays in compensation or notices, or both, by category of penalty imposed. *(Added by Stats.1965, c. 1513, p. 3557, § 7, operative Jan. 15, 1966. Amended by Stats.1981, c. 21, p. 46, § 3, eff. April 18, 1981; Stats.1989, c. 892, § 11.)*

§ 112. Appointment of members; term; qualifications; salary

The members of the appeals board shall be appointed by the Governor with the advice and consent of the Senate. The term of office of the members appointed prior to January 1, 1990, shall be four years, and the term of office of members appointed on or after January 1, 1990, shall be six years and they shall hold office until the appointment and qualification of their successors.

Five of the members of the appeals board shall be experienced attorneys at law admitted to practice in the State of California. The other two members need not be attorneys at law. All members shall be selected with due consideration of their judicial temperament and abilities. Each member shall receive the salary provided for by Chapter 6 (commencing with Section 11550) of Part 1 of Division 3 of Title 2 of the Government Code. *(Stats. 1937, c. 90, p. 192, § 112. Amended by Stats.1945, c. 1431, p. 2687, § 19; Stats.1947, c. 1389, p. 2953, § 1; Stats.1951, c. 1613, p. 3631, § 37; Stats.1965, c. 1513, p. 3557, § 8, operative Jan. 15, 1966; Stats.1970, c. 242, p. 502, § 1; Stats.1983, c. 803, § 38; Stats.1989, c. 892, § 12; Stats.1990, c. 1550 (A.B.2910), § 8.5.)*

§ 113. Designation of chairman; acting chairman

The Governor shall designate the chairman of the appeals board from the membership of the appeals board. The person so designated shall hold the office of chairman at the pleasure of the Governor.

The chairman may designate in writing one of the other members of the appeals board to act as chairman during such time as he may be absent from the state on official business, on vacation, or absent due to illness. *(Added by Stats.1965, c. 1513, p. 3557, § 10, operative Jan. 15, 1966.)*

§ 115. Majority decision; assignment of cases

Actions of the appeals board shall be taken by decision of a majority of the appeals board except as otherwise expressly provided.

The chairman shall assign pending cases in which reconsideration is sought to any three members thereof for hearing, consideration and decision. Assignments by the chairman of members to such cases shall be rotated on a case-by-case basis with the composition of the members so assigned being varied and changed to assure that there shall never be a fixed and continued composition of members. Any such case assigned to any three members in which the finding, order, decision or award is made and filed by any two or more of such members shall be the action of the appeals board unless reconsideration is had in accordance with the provisions of Article 1 (commencing with Section 5900), Chapter 7, Part 4, Division 4 of this code. Any case assigned to three members shall be heard and decided only by them, unless the matter has been reassigned by the chairman on a majority vote of the appeals board to the appeals board as a whole in order to achieve uniformity of decision, or in cases presenting novel issues. *(Added by Stats.1965, c. 1513, p. 3557, § 13, operative Jan. 15, 1966.)*

§ 116. Seal of appeals board

The seal of the appeals board bearing the inscription "Workers' Compensation Appeals Board, Seal" shall be affixed to all writs and authentications of copies of records and to such other instruments as the appeals board directs. *(Added by Stats.1965, c. 1513, p. 3558, § 15, operative Jan. 15, 1966. Amended by Stats.1981, c. 21, p. 46, § 4, eff. April 18, 1981.)*

§ 117. Appointment of attorney

The administrative director may appoint an attorney licensed to practice law in the state as counsel to the division. *(Added by Stats.1965, c. 1513, p. 3558, § 17, operative Jan. 15, 1966. Amended by Stats.1989, c. 892, § 13.)*

§ 119. Duties of attorney

The attorney shall:

(a) Represent and appear for the state and the Division of Workers' Compensation and the appeals board in all actions and proceedings arising under any provision of this code administered by the division or under any order or act of the division or the appeals board and, if directed so to do, intervene, if possible, in any action or proceeding in which any such question is involved.

(b) Commence, prosecute, and expedite the final determination of all actions or proceedings, directed or authorized by the administrative director or the appeals board.

(c) Advise the administrative director and the appeals board and each member thereof, upon request, in regard to the jurisdiction, powers or duties of the administrative director, the appeals board and each member thereof.

(d) Generally perform the duties and services as attorney to the Division of Workers' Compensation and the appeals board which are required of him or her. *(Added by Stats.1965, c. 1513, p. 3558, § 20, operative Jan. 15, 1966. Amended by Stats.1994, c. 146 (A.B.3601), § 138; Stats.1994, c. 1097 (S.B.1803), § 6.)*

§ 120. Secretary and assistant secretaries; appointment and duties

The administrative director and the chairman of the appeals board may each respectively appoint a secretary and assistant secretaries to perform such services as shall

be prescribed. *(Added by Stats.1965, c. 1513, p. 3558, § 22, operative Jan. 15, 1966.)*

§ 121. Deputy appeals board members

The chairman of the appeals board may authorize its secretary and any two assistant secretaries to act as deputy appeals board members and may delegate authority and duties to these deputies. Not more than three deputies may act as appeals board members at any one time. No act of any deputy shall be valid unless it is concurred in by at least one member of the appeals board. *(Added by Stats.1965, c. 1513, p. 3559, § 24, operative Jan. 15, 1966. Amended by Stats.1981, c. 1150, p. 4587, § 1.)*

§ 122. Appointment of medical director and assistants

The administrative director shall appoint a medical director who shall possess a physician's and surgeon's certificate granted under Chapter 5 (commencing with Section 2000) of Division 2 of the Business and Professions Code. The medical director shall employ medical assistants who shall also possess physicians' and surgeons' certificates and other staff necessary to the performance of his or her duties. The salaries for the medical director and his or her assistants shall be fixed by the Department of Personnel Administration, commensurate with the salaries paid by private industry to medical directors and assistant medical directors. *(Added by Stats.1953, c. 1858, p. 3649, § 1. Amended by Stats.1965, c. 1513, p. 3559, § 25, operative Jan. 15, 1966; Stats.1989, c. 892, § 14; Stats.2003, c. 639 (S.B.228), § 5.)*

§ 123. Employees; salaries of judges

The administrative director may employ necessary assistants, officers, experts, statisticians, actuaries, accountants, workers' compensation administrative law judges, stenographic shorthand reporters, legal secretaries, disability evaluation raters, program technicians, and other employees to implement new, efficient court management systems. The salaries of the workers' compensation administrative law judges shall be fixed by the Department of Personnel Administration for a class of positions which perform judicial functions. *(Stats.1937, c. 90, p. 194, § 123. Amended by Stats.1951, c. 1613, p. 3634, § 54; Stats.1953, c. 1757, p. 3515, § 6; Stats.1965, c. 1513, p. 3559, § 27, operative Jan. 15, 1966; Stats.1985, c. 326, § 2; Stats.2002, c. 6 (A.B.749), § 25.)*

§ 123.3. Official reporter; stenographic or clerical assistance

Any official reporter employed by the administrative director shall render stenographic or clerical assistance as directed by the presiding workers' compensation administrative law judge of the office to which the reporter is assigned, when the presiding workers' compensation administrative law judge determines that the reporter is not engaged in the performance of any other duty imposed by law. *(Added by Stats.1981, c. 1150, p. 4587,*

§ 2. Amended by Stats.1985, c. 326, § 3; Stats.2002, c. 6 (A.B.749), § 26.)

§ 123.5. Workers' compensation administrative law judges; eligible lists; qualifications

(a) Workers' compensation administrative law judges employed by the administrative director and supervised by the court administrator pursuant to this chapter shall be taken from an eligible list of attorneys licensed to practice law in this state, who have the qualifications prescribed by the State Personnel Board. In establishing eligible lists for this purpose, state civil service examinations shall be conducted in accordance with the State Civil Service Act (Part 2 (commencing with Section 18500) of Division 5 of Title 2 of the Government Code). Every workers' compensation judge shall maintain membership in the State Bar of California during his or her tenure.

A workers' compensation administrative law judge may not receive his or her salary as a workers' compensation administrative law judge while any cause before the workers' compensation administrative law judge remains pending and undetermined for 90 days after it has been submitted for decision.

(b) All workers' compensation administrative law judges appointed on or after January 1, 2003, shall be attorneys licensed to practice law in California for five or more years prior to their appointment and shall have experience in workers' compensation law. *(Added by Stats.1967, c. 1453, p. 3388, § 1. Amended by Stats.1980, c. 414, p. 817, § 1; Stats.1985, c. 326, § 4; Stats.1989, c. 892, § 15; Stats.1990, c. 1550 (A.B.2910), § 9; Stats.2002, c. 6 (A.B.749), § 27; Stats.2002, c. 866 (A.B.486), § 2.)*

§ 123.6. Workers' compensation administrative law judges; ethics

(a) All workers' compensation administrative law judges employed by the administrative director and supervised by the court administrator shall subscribe to the Code of Judicial Ethics adopted by the Supreme Court pursuant to subdivision (m) of Section 18 of Article VI of the California Constitution for the conduct of judges and shall not otherwise, directly or indirectly, engage in conduct contrary to that code or to the commentary to the Code of Judicial Ethics.

In consultation with both the court administrator and the Commission on Judicial Performance, the administrative director shall adopt regulations to enforce this section. Existing regulations shall remain in effect until new regulations based on the recommendations of the court administrator and the Commission on Judicial Performance have become effective. To the extent possible, the rules shall be consistent with the procedures established by the Commission on Judicial Performance for regulating the activities of state judges and, to the extent possible, with the gift, honoraria, and travel restrictions on legislators contained in the Political Reform Act of 1974 (Title 9 (commencing with Section

81000) of the Government Code). The court administrator shall have the authority to enforce the rules adopted by the administrative director.

(b) Honoraria or travel allowed by the court administrator, and not otherwise prohibited by this section in connection with any public or private conference, convention, meeting, social event, or like gathering, the cost of which is significantly paid for by attorneys who practice before the board, may not be accepted unless the court administrator has provided prior approval in writing to the workers' compensation administrative law judge allowing him or her to accept those payments. *(Added by Stats.1980, c. 402, p. 788, § 1. Amended by Stats.1985, c. 326, § 5; Stats.1990, c. 1550 (A.B.2910), § 10; Stats.1993, c. 483 (A.B.1252), § 1, eff. Sept. 27, 1993; Stats.1998, c. 95 (A.B.2164), § 2; Stats.1998, c. 448 (S.B.453), § 2; Stats. 2002, c. 6 (A.B.749), § 28; Stats.2002, c. 866 (A.B.486), § 3; Stats.2005, c. 706 (A.B.1742), § 35.)*

Application

For application of 2005 amendment, see Stats.2005, c. 706 (A.B.1742), § 41.

§ 123.7. Pro tempore workers' compensation judge

The appeals board may, by rule or regulation, establish procedures whereby attorneys who are either certified specialists in workers' compensation by the California State Bar, or are eligible for this certification, may be appointed by the presiding workers' compensation judge of each board office to serve as a pro tempore workers' compensation judge in a particular case, upon the stipulation of the employee or his or her representative, and the employer or the insurance carrier. Service in this capacity by an attorney shall be voluntary and without pay. It is the intent of the Legislature that the use of pro tempore workers' compensation judges pursuant to this section shall not result in a reduction of the number of permanent civil service employees or the number of authorized full-time equivalent positions. *(Added by Stats.1981, c. 1150, p. 4587, § 3. Amended by Stats.1985, c. 326, § 6.)*

§ 124. Administration and enforcement of division; bilingual forms and notices

(a) In administering and enforcing this division and Division 4 (commencing with Section 3200), the division shall protect the interests of injured workers who are entitled to the timely provision of compensation.

(b) Forms and notices required to be given to employees by the division shall be in English and Spanish. *(Added by Stats.1989, c. 892, § 17. Amended by Stats. 1993, c. 1241 (S.B.147), § 1.5; Stats.2002, c. 6 (A.B.749), § 29; Stats.2003, c. 639 (S.B.228), § 6.)*

§ 125. Blank forms

The administrative director shall cause to be printed and furnished free of charge to any person blank forms that may facilitate or promote the efficient performance of the duties of the Division of Workers' Compensation. *(Stats.1937, c. 90, p. 194, § 125. Amended by Stats.1965, c. 1513, p. 3560, § 28, operative Jan. 15, 1966; Stats.1994, c. 146 (A.B.3601), § 139.)*

§ 126.   Records; minutes of proceedings

The Division of Workers' Compensation, including the administrative director and the appeals board, shall keep minutes of all their proceedings and other books or records requisite for proper and efficient administration. All records shall be kept in their respective offices. *(Stats.1937, c. 90, p. 194, § 126. Amended by Stats.1965, c. 1513, p. 3560, § 29, operative Jan. 15, 1966; Stats.1994, c. 146 (A.B.3601), § 140.)*

§ 127.   Fees; amount; disposition; publications

The administrative director and court administrator may:

(a) Charge and collect fees for copies of papers and records, for certified copies of official documents and orders or of the evidence taken or proceedings had, for transcripts of testimony, and for inspection of case files not stored in the place where the inspection is requested. The administrative director shall fix those fees in an amount sufficient to recover the actual costs of furnishing the services. No fees for inspection of case files shall be charged to an injured employee or his or her representative.

(b) Publish and distribute from time to time, in addition to the reports to the Governor, further reports and pamphlets covering the operations, proceedings, and matters relative to the work of the division.

(c) Prepare, publish, and distribute an office manual, for which a reasonable fee may be charged, and to which additions, deletions, amendments, and other changes from time to time may be adopted, published, and distributed, for which a reasonable fee may be charged for the revision, or for which a reasonable fee may be fixed on an annual subscription basis.

(d) Fix and collect reasonable charges for publications issued. *(Stats.1937, c. 90, p. 194, § 127. Amended by Stats.1957, c. 1825, p. 3222, § 1; Stats.1959, c. 1587, p. 3918, § 2; Stats.1965, c. 1513, p. 3560, § 30, operative Jan. 15, 1966; Stats.1973, c. 751, p. 1354, § 1; Stats.2002, c. 6 (A.B.749), § 30.)*

§ 127.5.   Additional duties of court administrator

In the exercise of his or her functions, the court administrator shall further the interests of uniformity and expedition of proceedings before workers' compensation administrative law judges, assure that all workers' compensation administrative law judges are qualified and adhere to deadlines mandated by law or regulations, and manage district office procedural matters at the trial level. *(Added by Stats.2002, c. 6 (A.B.749), § 31.)*

292

§ 127.6.   Study of medical treatment provided to workers with industrial injuries and illnesses

(a) The administrative director shall, in consultation with the Commission on Health and Safety and Workers' Compensation, other state agencies, and researchers and research institutions with expertise in health care delivery and occupational health care service, conduct a study of medical treatment provided to workers who have sustained industrial injuries and illnesses. The study shall focus on, but not be limited to, all of the following:

(1) Factors contributing to the rising costs and utilization of medical treatment and case management in the workers' compensation system.

(2) An evaluation of case management procedures that contribute to or achieve early and sustained return to work within the employee's temporary and permanent work restrictions.

(3) Performance measures for medical services that reflect patient outcomes.

(4) Physician utilization, quality of care, and outcome measurement data.

(5) Patient satisfaction.

(b) The administrative director shall begin the study on or before July 1, 2003, and shall report and make recommendations to the Legislature based on the results of the study on or before July 1, 2004.

(c) In implementing this section, the administrative director shall ensure the confidentiality and protection of patient-specific data. *(Added by Stats.2002, c. 6 (A.B. 749), § 32. Amended by Stats.2003, c. 639 (S.B.228), § 7.)*

§ 128.   Appointment of commissioner under federal law; payment of expenses; powers

The appeals board may accept appointment as deputy commissioner under, or any delegation of authority to enforce, the United States Longshoremen's and Harbor Worker's Compensation Act.[1] The appeals board may enter into arrangements with the United States, subject to the approval of the Department of Finance, for the payment of any expenses incurred in the performance of services under said act. In the performance of any duties under said act, appointment, or authority, the appeals board may, subject to the provisions thereof, exercise any authority conferred upon the appeals board by the laws of this state. *(Stats.1937, c. 90, p. 195, § 128. Amended by Stats.1965, c. 1513, p. 3560, § 31, operative Jan. 15, 1966.)*

[1] 33 U.S.C.A. § 901 et seq.

§ 129.   Audits; deficiencies; notice of assessment and order to pay; appeals; reports

(a) To make certain that injured workers, and their dependents in the event of their death, receive promptly and accurately the full measure of compensation to which they are entitled, the administrative director shall audit insurers, self-insured employers, and third-party administrators to determine if they have met their obligations under this code. Each audit subject shall be audited at least once every five years. The audit subjects shall be selected and the audits conducted pursuant to subdivision (b). The results of audits of insurers shall be provided to the Insurance Commissioner, and the results of audits of self- insurers and third-party administrators shall be provided to the Director of Industrial Relations. Nothing in this section shall restrict the authority of the Director of Industrial Relations or the Insurance Commissioner to audit their licensees.

(b) The administrative director shall schedule and conduct audits as follows:

(1) A profile audit review of every audit subject shall be conducted once every five years and on additional occasions indicated by target audit criteria. The administrative director shall annually establish a profile audit review performance standard that will identify the poorest performing audit subjects.

(2) A full compliance audit shall be conducted of each profile audited subject failing to meet or exceed the profile audit review performance standard. The full compliance audit shall be a comprehensive and detailed evaluation of the audit subject's performance. The administrative director shall annually establish a full compliance audit performance standard that will identify the audit subjects that are performing satisfactorily. Any full compliance audit subject that fails to meet or exceed the full compliance audit performance standard shall be audited again within two years.

(3) A targeted profile audit review or a full compliance audit may be conducted at any time in accordance with target audit criteria adopted by the administrative director. The target audit criteria shall be based on information obtained from benefit notices, from information and assistance officers, and from other reliable sources providing factual information that indicates an insurer, self insured employer, or third party administrator is failing to meet its obligations under this division or Division 4 (commencing with Section 3200) or the regulations of the administrative director.

(c) If, as a result of a profile audit review or a full compliance audit, the administrative director determines that any compensation, interest, or penalty is due and unpaid to an employee or dependent, the administrative director shall issue and cause to be served upon the insurer, self-insured employer, or third-party administrator a notice of assessment detailing the amounts due and unpaid in each case, and shall order the amounts paid to the person entitled thereto. The notice of assessment shall be served personally or by registered mail in accordance with subdivision (c) of Section 11505 of the Government Code. A copy of the notice of assessment shall also be sent to the affected employee or dependent.

If the amounts are not paid within 30 days after service of the notice of assessment, the employer shall also be liable for reasonable attorney's fees necessarily incurred by the employee or dependent to obtain amounts due. The administrative director shall advise each employee or dependent still owed compensation after this 30–day period of his or her rights with respect to the commencement of proceedings to collect the compensation owed. Amounts unpaid because the person entitled thereto cannot be located shall be paid to the Workers' Compensation Administration Revolving Fund. The Director of Industrial Relations shall promulgate rules and regulations establishing standards and procedures for the payment of compensation from moneys deposited in the Workers' Compensation Administration Revolving Fund whenever the person entitled thereto applies for compensation.

(d) A determination by the administrative director that an amount is or is not due to an employee or dependent shall not in any manner limit the jurisdiction or authority of the appeals board to determine the issue.

(e) Annually, commencing on April 1, 1991, the administrative director shall publish a report detailing the results of audits conducted pursuant to this section during the preceding calendar year. The report shall include the name of each insurer, self-insured employer, and third-party administrator audited during that period. For each insurer, self-insured employer, and third-party administrator audited, the report shall specify the total number of files audited, the number of violations found by type and amount of compensation, interest and penalties payable, and the amount collected for each violation. The administrative director shall also publish and make available to the public on request a list ranking all insurers, self-insured employers, and third-party administrators audited during the period according to their performance measured by the profile audit review and full compliance audit performance standards.

These reports shall not identify the particular claim file that resulted in a particular violation or penalty. Except as required by this subdivision or other provisions of law, the contents of individual claim files and auditor's working papers shall be confidential. Disclosure of claim information to the administrative director pursuant to an audit shall not waive the provisions of the Evidence Code relating to privilege.

(f) A profile audit review of the adjustment of claims against the Uninsured Employers Fund by the claims and collections unit of the Division of Workers' Compensation shall be conducted at least every five years. The results of this profile audit review shall be included in the report required by subdivision (e). *(Added by Stats.1965, c. 1513, p. 3561, § 32.5, operative Jan. 15, 1966. Amended by Stats.1978, c. 1379, p. 4570, § 1; Stats.1989, c. 892, § 18; Stats.1990, c. 1550 (A.B.2910), § 11; Stats.1993, c. 1241 (S.B.147), § 2; Stats.2001, c. 159 (S.B.662), § 156; Stats.2002, c. 6 (A.B.749), § 33.)*

§ 129.5. Penalties; schedule of violations; notice of assessment; violations found to be general business practice; proceedings

(a) The administrative director may assess an administrative penalty against an insurer, self-insured employer, or third-party administrator for any of the following:

293

(1) Failure to comply with the notice of assessment issued pursuant to subdivision (c) of Section 129 within 15 days of receipt.

(2) Failure to pay when due the undisputed portion of an indemnity payment, the reasonable cost of medical treatment of an injured worker, or a charge or cost implementing an approved vocational rehabilitation plan.

(3) Failure to comply with any rule or regulation of the administrative director.

(b) The administrative director shall promulgate regulations establishing a schedule of violations and the amount of the administrative penalty to be imposed for each type of violation. The schedule shall provide for imposition of a penalty of up to one hundred dollars ($100) for each violation of the less serious type and for imposition of penalties in progressively higher amounts for the most serious types of violations to be set at up to five thousand dollars ($5,000) per violation. The administrative director is authorized to impose penalties pursuant to rules and regulations which give due consideration to the appropriateness of the penalty with respect to the following factors:

(1) The gravity of the violation.

(2) The good faith of the insurer, self-insured employer, or third-party administrator.

(3) The history of previous violations, if any.

(4) The frequency of the violations.

(5) Whether the audit subject has met or exceeded the profile audit review performance standard.

(6) Whether a full compliance audit subject has met or exceeded the full compliance audit performance standard.

(7) The size of the audit subject location.

(c) The administrative director shall assess penalties as follows:

(1) If, after a profile audit review, the administrative director determines that the profile audit subject met or exceeded the profile audit review performance standard, no penalties shall be assessed under this section, but the audit subject shall be required to pay any compensation due and penalties due under subdivision (d) of Section 4650 as provided in subdivision (c) of Section 129.

(2) If, after a full compliance audit, the administrative director determines that the audit subject met or exceeded the full compliance audit performance standards, penalties for unpaid or late paid compensation, but no other penalties under this section, shall be assessed. The audit subject shall be required to pay any compensation due and penalties due under subdivision (d) of Section 4650 as provided in subdivision (c) of Section 129.

(3) If, after a full compliance audit, the administrative director determines that the audit subject failed to meet the full compliance audit performance standards, penalties shall be assessed as provided in a full compliance audit failure penalty schedule to be adopted by the administrative director. The full compliance audit failure penalty schedule shall adjust penalty levels relative to the size of the audit location to mitigate inequality between total penalties assessed against small and large audit subjects. The penalty amounts provided in the full compliance audit failure penalty schedule for the most serious type of violations shall not be limited by subdivision (b), but in no event shall the penalty for a single violation exceed forty thousand dollars ($40,000).

(d) The notice of penalty assessment shall be served personally or by registered mail in accordance with subdivision (c) of Section 11505 of the Government Code. The notice shall be in writing and shall describe the nature of the violation, including reference to the statutory provision or rule or regulation alleged to have been violated. The notice shall become final and the assessment shall be paid unless contested within 15 days of receipt by the insurer, self-insured employer, or third-party administrator.

(e) In addition to the penalty assessments permitted by subdivisions (a), (b), and (c), the administrative director may assess a civil penalty, not to exceed one hundred thousand dollars ($100,000), upon finding, after hearing, that an employer, insurer, or third-party administrator for an employer has knowingly committed or performed with sufficient frequency so as to indicate a general business practice any of the following:

(1) Induced employees to accept less than compensation due, or made it necessary for employees to resort to proceedings against the employer to secure compensation.

(2) Refused to comply with known and legally indisputable compensation obligations.

(3) Discharged or administered compensation obligations in a dishonest manner.

(4) Discharged or administered compensation obligations in a manner as to cause injury to the public or those dealing with the employer or insurer.

Any employer, insurer, or third-party administrator that fails to meet the full compliance audit performance standards in two consecutive full compliance audits shall be rebuttably presumed to have engaged in a general business practice of discharging and administering its compensation obligations in a manner causing injury to those dealing with it.

Upon a second or subsequent finding, the administrative director shall refer the matter to the Insurance Commissioner or the Director of Industrial Relations and request that a hearing be conducted to determine whether the certificate of authority, certificate of consent to self-insure, or certificate of consent to administer claims of self-insured employers, as the case may be, shall be revoked.

(f) An insurer, self-insured employer, or third-party administrator may file a written request for a conference with the administrative director within seven days after receipt of a notice of penalty assessment issued pursuant to subdivision (a) or (c). Within 15 days of the conference, the administrative director shall issue a notice of findings and serve it upon the contesting party by registered or certified mail. Any amount found due by the administrative director shall become due and payable 30 days after receipt of the notice of findings. The 30–day period shall be tolled during any appeal. A writ of mandate may be taken from the findings to the appropriate superior court upon the execution by the contesting party of a bond to the state in the principal sum that is double the amount found due and ordered by the administrative director, on the condition that the contesting party shall pay any judgment and costs rendered against it for the amount.

(g) An insurer, self-insured employer, or third-party administrator may file a written request for a hearing before the Workers' Compensation Appeals Board within seven days after receipt of a notice of penalty assessment issued pursuant to subdivision (e). Within 30 days of the hearing, the appeals board shall issue findings and orders and serve them upon the contesting party in the manner provided in its rules. Any amount found due by the appeals board shall become due and payable 45 days after receipt of the notice of findings. Judicial review of the findings and order shall be had in the manner provided by Article 2 (commencing with Section 5950) of Chapter 7 of Part 4 of Division 4. The 45–day period shall be tolled during appellate proceedings upon execution by the contesting party of a bond to the state in a principal sum that is double the amount found due and ordered by the appeals board on the condition that the contesting party shall pay the amount ultimately determined to be due and any costs awarded by an appellate court.

(h) Nothing in this section shall create nor eliminate a civil cause of action for the employee and his or her dependents.

(i) All moneys collected under this section shall be deposited in the State Treasury and credited to the Workers' Compensation Administration Revolving Fund. *(Added by Stats.1989, c. 892, § 19. Amended by Stats. 1990, c. 1550 (A.B.2910), § 12; Stats.1993, c. 1241 (S.B.147), § 3; Stats.2002, c. 6 (A.B.749), § 34.)*

§ 130. Administration of oaths; certification of official acts; issuance of subpoenas

The appeals board and each of its members, its secretary, assistant secretaries, and workers' compensation judges, may administer oaths, certify to all official acts, and issue subpoenas for the attendance of witnesses and the production of papers, books, accounts, documents and testimony in any inquiry, investigation, hearing or proceeding in any part of the state. *(Stats.1937, c. 90, p. 195, § 130. Amended by Stats.1965, c. 1513, p. 3561, § 33, operative Jan. 15, 1966; Stats.1985, c. 326, § 8.)*

§ 131. Fees and mileage of witnesses

Each witness who appears by order of the appeals board or any of its members, or a workers' compensation judge, shall receive, if demanded, for his or her attendance the same fees and mileage allowed by law to a witness in civil cases, paid by the party at whose request the witness is subpoenaed, unless otherwise ordered by the appeals board. When any witness who has not been required to attend at the request of any party is subpoenaed by the appeals board, his or her fees and mileage may be paid from the funds appropriated for the use of the appeals board in the same manner as other expenses of the appeals board are paid. Any witness subpoenaed, except one whose fees and mileage are paid from the funds of the appeals board, may, at the time of service, demand the fee to which he or she is entitled for travel to and from the place at which he or she is required to appear, and one day's attendance. If a witness demands his or her fees at the time of service, and they are not at that time paid or tendered, he or she shall not be required to attend as directed in the subpoena. All fees and mileage to which any witness is entitled under this section may be collected by action therefor instituted by the person to whom the fees are payable. *(Stats.1937, c. 90, p. 195, § 131. Amended by Stats.1965, c. 1513, p. 3561, § 34, operative Jan. 15, 1966; Stats.1985, c. 326, § 9.)*

§ 132. Judicial enforcement of subpoena; procedure

The superior court in and for the county in which any proceeding is held by the appeals board or a workers' compensation judge may compel the attendance of witnesses, the giving of testimony and the production of papers, including books, accounts, and documents, as required by any subpoena regularly issued hereunder. In case of the refusal of any witness to obey the subpoena the appeals board or the workers' compensation judge, before whom the testimony is to be given or produced, may report to the superior court in and for the county in which the proceeding is pending, by petition, setting forth that due notice has been given of the time and place of attendance of the witness, or the production of the papers, that the witness has been subpoenaed in the prescribed manner, and that the witness has failed and refused to obey the subpoena, or has refused to answer questions propounded to him or her in the course of the proceeding, and ask an order of the court, compelling the witness to attend and testify or produce the papers before the appeals board. The court shall thereupon enter an order directing the witness to appear before the court at a time and place fixed in the order, the time to be not more than 10 days from the date of the order, and then and there show cause why he or she had not attended and testified or produced the papers before the appeals board or the workers' compensation judge. A copy of the order shall be served upon the witness. If it appears to the court that the subpoena was regularly issued hereunder and that the witness was legally bound to comply therewith, the court shall thereupon enter an order that the witness appear before the appeals board or the workers' compensation judge at a time and place fixed in the order, and testify or produce the required papers, and upon failure to obey the order, the witness shall be dealt with as for contempt of court. The remedy provided in this section is cumulative, and shall not impair or interfere with the power of the appeals board or a member thereof to enforce the attendance of witnesses and the production of papers, and to punish for contempt in the same manner and to the same extent as courts of record. *(Stats.1937, c. 90, p. 196, § 132. Amended by Stats.1965, c. 1513, p. 3561, § 35, operative Jan. 15, 1966; Stats.1985, c. 326, § 10.)*

§ 132a. Discrimination against workers injured in course of employment or testifying before appeals board; penalties

It is the declared policy of this state that there should not be discrimination against workers who are injured in the course and scope of their employment.

(1) Any employer who discharges, or threatens to discharge, or in any manner discriminates against any employee because he or she has filed or made known his or her intention to file a claim for compensation with his or her employer or an application for adjudication, or because the employee has received a rating, award, or settlement, is guilty of a misdemeanor and the employee's compensation shall be increased by one-half, but in no event more than ten thousand dollars ($10,000), together with costs and expenses not in excess of two hundred fifty dollars ($250). Any such employee shall also be entitled to reinstatement and reimbursement for lost wages and work benefits caused by the acts of the employer.

(2) Any insurer that advises, directs, or threatens an insured under penalty of cancellation or a raise in premium or for any other reason, to discharge an employee because he or she has filed or made known his or her intention to file a claim for compensation with his or her employer or an application for adjudication, or because the employee has received a rating, award, or settlement, is guilty of a misdemeanor and subject to the increased compensation and costs provided in paragraph (1).

(3) Any employer who discharges, or threatens to discharge, or in any manner discriminates against any employee because the employee testified or made known his or her intentions to testify in another employee's case before the appeals board, is guilty of a misdemeanor, and the employee shall be entitled to reinstatement and reimbursement for lost wages and work benefits caused by the acts of the employer.

(4) Any insurer that advises, directs, or threatens an insured employer under penalty of cancellation or a raise in premium or for any other reason, to discharge or in any manner discriminate against an employee because the employee testified or made known his or her intention to testify in another employee's case before the appeals board, is guilty of a misdemeanor.

Proceedings for increased compensation as provided in paragraph (1), or for reinstatement and reimbursement for lost wages and work benefits, are to be instituted by filing an appropriate petition with the appeals board, but these proceedings may not be commenced more than one year from the discriminatory act or date of termination of the employee. The appeals board is vested with full power, authority, and jurisdiction to try and determine finally all matters specified in this section subject only to judicial review, except that the appeals board shall have no jurisdiction to try and determine a misdemeanor charge. The appeals board may refer and any worker may complain of suspected violations of the criminal misdemeanor provisions of this section to the Division of Labor Standards Enforcement, or directly to the office of the public prosecutor. *(Added by Stats.1972, c. 874, p. 1545, § 1. Amended by Stats.1978, c. 1250, p. 4065, § 3; Stats.1982, c. 922, p. 3363, § 1; Stats.1989, c. 892, § 20; Stats.1990, c. 1550 (A.B.2910), § 13.)*

§ 133. Incidental powers and jurisdiction

The Division of Workers' Compensation, including the administrative director, the court administrator, and the appeals board, shall have power and jurisdiction to do all things necessary or convenient in the exercise of any power or jurisdiction conferred upon it under this code. *(Stats.1937, c. 90, p. 196, § 133. Amended by Stats.1965, c. 1513, p. 3562, § 37, operative Jan. 15, 1966; Stats.1994, c. 146 (A.B.3601), § 141; Stats.1994, c. 1097 (S.B.1803), § 7; Stats.2002, c. 6 (A.B.749), § 35.)*

§ 134. Insurance, extent, and service of process; fees

The appeals board or any member thereof may issue writs or summons, warrants of attachment, warrants of commitment and all necessary process in proceedings for contempt, in like manner and to the same extent as courts of record. The process issued by the appeals board or any member thereof shall extend to all parts of the state and may be served by any persons authorized to serve process of courts of record or by any person designated for that purpose by the appeals board or any member thereof. The person executing process shall receive compensation allowed by the appeals board, not to exceed the fees prescribed by law for similar services. Such fees shall be paid in the same manner as provided herein for the fees of witnesses. *(Stats.1937, c. 90, p. 196, § 134. Amended by Stats.1965, c. 1513, p. 3563, § 38, operative Jan. 15, 1966.)*

§ 135. Destruction of old files

In accordance with rules of practice and procedure that it may adopt, the appeals board may, with the approval of the Department of Finance, destroy or otherwise dispose of any file kept by it in connection with any proceeding under Division 4 (commencing with Section 3200) or Division 4.5 (commencing with Section 6100). *(Added by Stats.1955, c. 1700, p. 3125, § 1. Amended by Stats.1965, c. 371, p. 1582, § 234; Stats.1965, c. 1513, p. 3563, § 39, operative Jan. 15, 1966; Stats.1982, c. 454, p. 1876, § 128; Stats.1995, c. 556 (S.B.1051), § 4.)*

§ 138. Absences; appointment of deputy

The administrative director and the court administrator may each appoint a deputy to act during that time as he or she may be absent from the state due to official business, vacation, or illness. *(Added by Stats.1965, c. 1513, p. 3563, § 42, operative Jan. 15, 1966. Amended by Stats.2002, c. 6 (A.B.749), § 36.)*

§ 138.1. Appointments; tenure; salary

(a) The administrative director shall be appointed by the Governor with the advice and consent of the Senate and shall hold office at the pleasure of the Governor. He or she shall receive the salary provided for by Chapter 6 (commencing with Section 11550) of Part 1 of Division 3 of Title 2 of the Government Code.

(b) The court administrator shall be appointed by the Governor with the advice and consent of the Senate. The court administrator shall hold office for a term of five years. The court administrator shall receive the salary provided for by Chapter 6 (commencing with Section 11550) of Part 1 of Division 3 of Title 2 of the Government Code. *(Added by Stats.1965, c. 1513, p. 3563, § 42.2, operative Jan. 15, 1966. Amended by Stats.1983, c. 803, § 39; Stats.2002, c. 6 (A.B.749), § 37; Stats.2003, c. 639 (S.B.228), § 7.5.)*

§ 138.2. Headquarters of Division; base of operations for appeals board; meetings

(a) The headquarters of the Division of Workers' Compensation shall be based at and operated from a centrally located city.

The administrative director and the court administrator shall have an office in that city with suitable rooms, necessary office furniture, stationery, and supplies, and may rent quarters in other places for the purpose of establishing branch or service offices, and for that purpose may provide those offices with necessary furniture, stationery and supplies.

(b) The administrative director shall provide suitable rooms, with necessary office furniture, stationery and supplies, for the appeals board at the centrally located city in which the board shall be based and from which it shall operate, and may rent quarters in other places for the purpose of establishing branch or service offices for the appeals board, and for that purpose may provide those offices with necessary furniture, stationery, and supplies.

(c) All meetings held by the administrative director shall be open and public. Notice thereof shall be published in papers of general circulation not more than 30 days and not less than 10 days prior to each meeting in Sacramento, San Francisco, Fresno, Los Angeles and San Diego. Written notice of all meetings shall be given to all persons who request in writing directed to the administrative director that they be given notice. *(Added by Stats.1965, c. 1513, p. 3563, § 42.4, operative Jan. 15, 1966. Amended by Stats.1994, c. 146 (A.B.3601), § 142;*

Stats.1994, c. 1097 (S.B.1803), § 8; Stats.2002, c. 6 (A.B.749), § 38.)

§ 138.3. Notice of possible benefits, rules

The administrative director shall, with respect to all injuries, prescribe, pursuant to Section 5402, reasonable rules and regulations requiring the employer to serve notice on the injured employee that he may be entitled to benefits under this division. *(Added by Stats.1975, c. 1099, p. 2670, § 1.)*

§ 138.4. Injuries involving loss of time; duties of administrative director

(a) For the purpose of this section, "claims administrator" means a self-administered workers' compensation insurer; or a self-administered self-insured employer; or a self-administered legally uninsured employer; or a self-administered joint powers authority; or a third-party claims administrator for an insurer, a self-insured employer, a legally uninsured employer, or a joint powers authority.

(b) With respect to injuries resulting in lost time beyond the employee's work shift at the time of injury or medical treatment beyond first aid:

(1) If the claims administrator obtains knowledge that the employer has not provided a claim form or a notice of potential eligibility for benefits to the employee, it shall provide the form and notice to the employee within three working days of its knowledge that the form or notice was not provided.

(2) If the claims administrator cannot determine if the employer has provided a claim form and notice of potential eligibility for benefits to the employee, the claims administrator shall provide the form and notice to the employee within 30 days of the administrator's date of knowledge of the claim.

(c) The administrative director shall prescribe reasonable rules and regulations for serving on the employee (or employee's dependents, in the case of death), notices dealing with the payment, nonpayment, or delay in payment of temporary disability, permanent disability, and death benefits and the provision of vocational rehabilitation services, notices of any change in the amount or type of benefits being provided, the termination of benefits, the rejection of any liability for compensation, and an accounting of benefits paid. *(Added by Stats.1965, c. 1513, p. 3564, § 43, operative Jan. 15, 1966. Amended by Stats.1987, c. 1019, § 1; Stats.1999, c. 83 (S.B.966), § 130; Stats.2002, c. 6 (A.B.749), § 39.)*

§ 138.5. Child support obligations; cooperation in enforcement; workers' compensation notification project

The Division of Workers' Compensation shall cooperate in the enforcement of child support obligations. At the request of the Department of Child Support Services, the administrative director shall assist in providing to the State Department of Child Support Services information concerning persons who are receiving permanent disability benefits or who have filed an application for adjudication of a claim which the Department of Child Support Services determines is necessary to carry out its responsibilities pursuant to Section 17510 of the Family Code.

The process of sharing information with regard to applicants for and recipients of permanent disability benefits required by this section shall be known as the Workers' Compensation Notification Project. *(Added by Stats.1984, c. 1463, § 2, eff. Sept. 26, 1984. Amended by Stats.1994, c. 146 (A.B.3601), § 143; Stats.1994, c. 1097 (S.B.1803), § 9; Stats.2000, c. 808 (A.B.1358), § 110, eff. Sept. 28, 2000.)*

§ 138.6. Workers' compensation information system

(a) The administrative director, in consultation with the Insurance Commissioner and the Workers' Compensation Insurance Rating Bureau, shall develop a cost-efficient workers' compensation information system, which shall be administered by the division. The administrative director shall adopt regulations specifying the data elements to be collected by electronic data interchange.

(b) The information system shall do the following:

(1) Assist the department to manage the workers' compensation system in an effective and efficient manner.

(2) Facilitate the evaluation of the efficiency and effectiveness of the benefit delivery system.

(3) Assist in measuring how adequately the system indemnifies injured workers and their dependents.

(4) Provide statistical data for research into specific aspects of the workers' compensation program.

(c) The data collected electronically shall be compatible with the Electronic Data Interchange System of the International Association of Industrial Accident Boards and Commissions. The administrative director may adopt regulations authorizing the use of other nationally recognized data transmission formats in addition to those set forth in the Electronic Data Interchange System for the transmission of data required pursuant to this section. The administrative director shall accept data transmissions in any authorized format. If the administrative director determines that any authorized data transmission format is not in general use by claims administrators, conflicts with the requirements of state or federal law, or is obsolete, the administrative director may adopt regulations eliminating that data transmission format from those authorized pursuant to this subdivision. *(Added by Stats.1993, c. 121 (A.B.110), § 16, eff. July 16, 1993. Amended by Stats.1993, c. 1242 (S.B.223), § 16; Stats. 1997, c. 729 (S.B.450), § 1; Stats.2000, c. 318 (S.B.1785), § 1.)*

§ 138.65. Study of effect of 2003 and 2004 legislative reforms on workers' compensation

(a) The administrative director, after consultation with the Insurance Commissioner, shall contract with a quali-

fied organization to study the effects of the 2003 and 2004 legislative reforms on workers' compensation insurance rates. The study shall do, but not be limited to, all of the following:

(1) Identify and quantify the savings generated by the reforms.

(2) Review workers' compensation insurance rates to determine the extent to which the reform savings were reflected in rates. When reviewing the rates, consideration shall be given to an insurer's premium revenue, claim costs, and surplus levels.

(3) Assess the effect of the reform savings on replenishing surpluses for workers' compensation insurance coverage.

(4) Review the effects of the reforms on the workers' compensation insurance rates, marketplace, and competition.

(5) Review the adequacy and accuracy of the pure premium rate as recommended by the Workers' Compensation Insurance Bureau and the pure premium rate adopted by the Insurance Commissioner.

(b) Insurers shall submit to the contracting organization premium revenue, claims costs, and surplus levels in different timing aggregates as established by the contracting organization, but at least quarterly and annually. The contracting organization may also request additional materials when appropriate. The contracting organization and the commission shall maintain strict confidentiality of the data. An insurer that fails to comply with the reporting requirements of this subdivision is subject to Section 11754 of the Insurance Code.

(c) The administrative director shall submit to the Governor, the Insurance Commissioner, and the President pro Tempore of the Senate, the Speaker of the Assembly, and the chairs of the appropriate policy committees of the Legislature, a progress report on the study on January 1, 2005, and July 1, 2005, and the final study on or before January 1, 2006. The Governor and the Insurance Commissioner shall review the results of the study and make recommendations as to the appropriateness of regulating insurance rates. If, after reviewing the study, the Governor and the Insurance Commissioner determine that the rates do not appropriately reflect the savings and the timing of the savings associated with the 2003 and 2004 reforms, the Governor and the Insurance Commissioner may submit proposals to the Legislature. The proposals shall take into consideration how rates should be regulated, and by whom. In no event shall the proposals unfairly penalize insurers that have properly reflected the 2003 and 2004 reforms in their rates, or can verify that they have not received any cost savings as a result of the reforms.

(d) The cost of the study shall be borne by the insurers up to one million dollars ($1,000,000). The cost of the study shall be allocated to an insurer based on the insurer's proportionate share of the market. *(Added by Stats.2004, c. 34 (S.B.899), § 1.5, eff. April 19, 2004.)*

Operative Effect

Section 47 of Stats.2004, c. 34 (S.B.899) provides that "[t]he amendment, addition, or repeal of, any provision of law made by this act shall apply prospectively from the date of enactment of this act, regardless of the date of injury, unless otherwise specified, but shall not constitute good cause to reopen or rescind, alter, or amend any existing order, decision, or award of the Workers' Compensation Appeals Board."

§ 138.7. Individually identifiable information; access by nonparties; worker's compensation information system; privilege

(a) Except as expressly permitted in subdivision (b), a person or public or private entity not a party to a claim for workers' compensation benefits may not obtain individually identifiable information obtained or maintained by the division on that claim. For purposes of this section, "individually identifiable information" means any data concerning an injury or claim that is linked to a uniquely identifiable employee, employer, claims administrator, or any other person or entity.

(b)(1) The administrative director, or a statistical agent designated by the administrative director, may use individually identifiable information for purposes of creating and maintaining the workers' compensation information system as specified in Section 138.6.

(2) The State Department of Health Services may use individually identifiable information for purposes of establishing and maintaining a program on occupational health and occupational disease prevention as specified in Section 105175 of the Health and Safety Code.

(3)(A) Individually identifiable information may be used by the Division of Workers' Compensation, the Division of Occupational Safety and Health, and the Division of Labor Statistics and Research as necessary to carry out their duties. The administrative director shall adopt regulations governing the access to the information described in this subdivision by these divisions. Any regulations adopted pursuant to this subdivision shall set forth the specific uses for which this information may be obtained.

(B) Individually identifiable information maintained in the workers' compensation information system and the Division of Workers' Compensation may be used by researchers employed by or under contract to the Commission on Health and Safety and Workers' Compensation as necessary to carry out the commission's research. The administrative director shall adopt regulations governing the access to the information described in this subdivision by commission researchers. These regulations shall set forth the specific uses for which this information may be obtained and include provisions guaranteeing the confidentiality of individually identifiable information. Individually identifiable information obtained under this subdivision shall not be disclosed to commission members. No individually identifiable information obtained by researchers under contract to the commission pursuant to this subparagraph may be disclosed to any other person or entity, public or private, for a use other than that research project for which the information was obtained. Within a reasonable period of time after the research for which the information was obtained has been completed, the data collected shall be modified in a manner so that the subjects cannot be identified, directly or through identifiers linked to the subjects.

(4) The administrative director shall adopt regulations allowing reasonable access to individually identifiable information by other persons or public or private entities for the purpose of bona fide statistical research. This research shall not divulge individually identifiable information concerning a particular employee, employer, claims administrator, or any other person or entity. The regulations adopted pursuant to this paragraph shall include provisions guaranteeing the confidentiality of individually identifiable information. Within a reasonable period of time after the research for which the information was obtained has been completed, the data collected shall be modified in a manner so that the subjects cannot be identified, directly or through identifiers linked to the subjects.

(5) This section shall not operate to exempt from disclosure any information that is considered to be a public record pursuant to the California Public Records Act (Chapter 3.5 (commencing with Section 6250) of Division 7 of Title 1 of the Government Code) contained in an individual's file once an application for adjudication has been filed pursuant to Section 5501.5.

However, individually identifiable information shall not be provided to any person or public or private entity who is not a party to the claim unless that person identifies himself or herself or that public or private entity identifies itself and states the reason for making the request. The administrative director may require the person or public or private entity making the request to produce information to verify that the name and address of the requester is valid and correct. If the purpose of the request is related to preemployment screening, the administrative director shall notify the person about whom the information is requested that the information was provided and shall include the following in 12–point type:

"IT MAY BE A VIOLATION OF FEDERAL AND STATE LAW TO DISCRIMINATE AGAINST A JOB APPLICANT BECAUSE THE APPLICANT HAS FILED A CLAIM FOR WORKERS' COMPENSATION BENEFITS."

Any residence address is confidential and shall not be disclosed to any person or public or private entity except to a party to the claim, a law enforcement agency, an office of a district attorney, any person for a journalistic purpose, or other governmental agency.

Nothing in this paragraph shall be construed to prohibit the use of individually identifiable information for purposes of identifying bona fide lien claimants.

(c) Except as provided in subdivision (b), individually identifiable information obtained by the division is privileged and is not subject to subpoena in a civil proceeding unless, after reasonable notice to the division and a hearing, a court determines that the public interest and the intent of this section will not be jeopardized by disclosure of the information. This section shall not operate to restrict access to information by any law enforcement agency or district attorney's office or to limit admissibility of that information in a criminal proceeding.

(d) It shall be unlawful for any person who has received individually identifiable information from the division pursuant to this section to provide that information to any person who is not entitled to it under this section. *(Added by Stats.1997, c. 674 (S.B.1141), § 1. Amended by Stats.1998, c. 624 (S.B.1430), § 2; Stats.2001, c. 792 (A.B.1681), § 1.)*

§ 139.2. Appointment and reappointment of qualified medical evaluators; requirements for and qualifications of evaluators; suspension or termination of evaluator and review thereof; agreements with respect to cases assigned to evaluators; assignment of panels and notice to employees; review of evaluations; regulations; fees

(a) The administrative director shall appoint qualified medical evaluators in each of the respective specialties as required for the evaluation of medical-legal issues. The appointments shall be for two-year terms.

(b) The administrative director shall appoint or reappoint as a qualified medical evaluator a physician, as defined in Section 3209.3, who is licensed to practice in this state and who demonstrates that he or she meets the requirements in paragraphs (1), (2), (6), and (7), and, if the physician is a medical doctor, doctor of osteopathy, doctor of chiropractic, or a psychologist, that he or she also meets the applicable requirements in paragraph (3), (4), or (5).

(1) Prior to his or her appointment as a qualified medical evaluator, passes an examination written and administered by the administrative director for the purpose of demonstrating competence in evaluating medical-legal issues in the workers' compensation system. Physicians shall not be required to pass an additional examination as a condition of reappointment. A physician seeking appointment as a qualified medical evaluator on or after January 1, 2001, shall also complete prior to appointment, a course on disability evaluation report writing approved by the administrative director. The administrative director shall specify the curriculum to be covered by disability evaluation report writing courses, which shall include, but is not limited to, 12 or more hours of instruction.

(2) Devotes at least one-third of total practice time to providing direct medical treatment, or has served as an agreed medical evaluator on eight or more occasions in the 12 months prior to applying to be appointed as a qualified medical evaluator.

(3) Is a medical doctor or doctor of osteopathy and meets one of the following requirements:

(A) Is board certified in a specialty by a board recognized by the administrative director and either the Medical Board of California or the Osteopathic Medical Board of California.

(B) Has successfully completed a residency training program accredited by the American College of Graduate Medical Education or the osteopathic equivalent.

(C) Was an active qualified medical evaluator on June 30, 2000.

(D) Has qualifications that the administrative director and either the Medical Board of California or the Osteopathic Medical Board of California, as appropriate, both deem to be equivalent to board certification in a specialty.

(4) Is a doctor of chiropractic and meets either of the following requirements:

(A) Has completed a chiropractic postgraduate specialty program of a minimum of 300 hours taught by a school or college recognized by the administrative director, the Board of Chiropractic Examiners and the Council on Chiropractic Education.

(B) Has been certified in California workers' compensation evaluation by a provider recognized by the administrative director. The certification program shall include instruction on disability evaluation report writing that meets the standards set forth in paragraph (1).

(5) Is a psychologist and meets one of the following requirements:

(A) Is board certified in clinical psychology by a board recognized by the administrative director.

(B) Holds a doctoral degree in psychology, or a doctoral degree deemed equivalent for licensure by the Board of Psychology pursuant to Section 2914 of the Business and Professions Code, from a university or professional school recognized by the administrative director and has not less than five years' postdoctoral experience in the diagnosis and treatment of emotional and mental disorders.

(C) Has not less than five years' postdoctoral experience in the diagnosis and treatment of emotional and mental disorders, and has served as an agreed medical evaluator on eight or more occasions prior to January 1, 1990.

(6) Does not have a conflict of interest as determined under the regulations adopted by the administrative director pursuant to subdivision (*o*).

(7) Meets any additional medical or professional standards adopted pursuant to paragraph (6) of subdivision (j).

(c) The administrative director shall adopt standards for appointment of physicians who are retired or who hold teaching positions who are exceptionally well qualified to serve as a qualified medical evaluator even though they do not otherwise qualify under paragraph (2) of subdivision (b). In no event shall a physician whose full-time practice is limited to the forensic evaluation of disability be appointed as a qualified medical evaluator under this subdivision.

(d) The qualified medical evaluator, upon request, shall be reappointed if he or she meets the qualifications of subdivision (b) and meets all of the following criteria:

(1) Is in compliance with all applicable regulations and evaluation guidelines adopted by the administrative director.

(2) Has not had more than five of his or her evaluations that were considered by a workers' compensation administrative law judge at a contested hearing rejected by the workers' compensation administrative law judge or the appeals board pursuant to this section during the most recent two-year period during which the physician served as a qualified medical evaluator. If the workers' compensation administrative law judge or the appeals board rejects the qualified medical evaluator's report on the basis that it fails to meet the minimum standards for those reports established by the administrative director or the appeals board, the workers' compensation administrative law judge or the appeals board, as the case may be, shall make a specific finding to that effect, and shall give notice to the medical evaluator and to the administrative director. Any rejection shall not be counted as one of the five qualifying rejections until the specific finding has become final and time for appeal has expired.

(3) Has completed within the previous 24 months at least 12 hours of continuing education in impairment evaluation or workers' compensation-related medical dispute evaluation approved by the administrative director.

(4) Has not been terminated, suspended, placed on probation, or otherwise disciplined by the administrative director during his or her most recent term as a qualified medical evaluator.

If the evaluator does not meet any one of these criteria, the administrative director may in his or her discretion reappoint or deny reappointment according to regulations adopted by the administrative director. In no event may a physician who does not currently meet the requirements for initial appointment or who has been terminated under subdivision (e) because his or her license has been revoked or terminated by the licensing authority be reappointed.

(e) The administrative director may, in his or her discretion, suspend or terminate a qualified medical evaluator during his or her term of appointment without a hearing as provided under subdivision (k) or (l) whenever either of the following conditions occurs:

(1) The evaluator's license to practice in California has been suspended by the relevant licensing authority so as to preclude practice, or has been revoked or terminated by the licensing authority.

(2) The evaluator has failed to timely pay the fee required by the administrative director pursuant to subdivision (n).

(f) The administrative director shall furnish a physician, upon request, with a written statement of its reasons for termination of, or for denying appointment or reappointment as, a qualified medical evaluator. Upon receipt of a specific response to the statement of reasons, the administrative director shall review his or her decision not to appoint or reappoint the physician or to terminate the physician and shall notify the physician of its final decision within 60 days after receipt of the physician's response.

(g) The administrative director shall establish agreements with qualified medical evaluators to assure the expeditious evaluation of cases assigned to them for comprehensive medical evaluations.

(h)(1) When requested by an employee or employer pursuant to Section 4062.1, the medical director appointed pursuant to Section 122 shall assign three-member panels of qualified medical evaluators within five working days after receiving a request for a panel. If a panel is not assigned within 15 working days, the employee shall have the right to obtain a medical evaluation from any qualified medical evaluator of his or her choice. The medical director shall use a random selection method for assigning panels of qualified medical evaluators. The medical director shall select evaluators who are specialists of the type requested by the employee. The medical director shall advise the employee that he or she should consult with his or her treating physician prior to deciding which type of specialist to request.

(2) The administrative director shall promulgate a form that shall notify the employee of the physicians selected for his or her panel after a request has been made pursuant to Section 4062.1 or 4062.2. The form shall include, for each physician on the panel, the physician's name, address, telephone number, specialty, number of years in practice, and a brief description of his or her education and training, and shall advise the employee that he or she is entitled to receive transportation expenses and temporary disability for each day necessary for the examination. The form shall also state in a clear and conspicuous location and type: "You have the right to consult with an information and assistance officer at no cost to you prior to selecting the doctor to prepare your evaluation, or you may consult with an attorney. If your claim eventually goes to court, the workers' compensation administrative law judge will consider the evaluation prepared by the doctor you select to decide your claim."

(3) When compiling the list of evaluators from which to select randomly, the medical director shall include all qualified medical evaluators who meet all of the following criteria:

(A) He or she does not have a conflict of interest in the case, as defined by regulations adopted pursuant to subdivision (o).

301

(B) He or she is certified by the administrative director to evaluate in an appropriate specialty and at locations within the general geographic area of the employee's residence.

(C) He or she has not been suspended or terminated as a qualified medical evaluator for failure to pay the fee required by the administrative director pursuant to subdivision (n) or for any other reason.

(4) When the medical director determines that an employee has requested an evaluation by a type of specialist that is appropriate for the employee's injury, but there are not enough qualified medical evaluators of that type within the general geographic area of the employee's residence to establish a three-member panel, the medical director shall include sufficient qualified medical evaluators from other geographic areas and the employer shall pay all necessary travel costs incurred in the event the employee selects an evaluator from another geographic area.

(i) The medical director appointed pursuant to Section 122 shall continuously review the quality of comprehensive medical evaluations and reports prepared by agreed and qualified medical evaluators and the timeliness with which evaluation reports are prepared and submitted. The review shall include, but not be limited to, a review of a random sample of reports submitted to the division, and a review of all reports alleged to be inaccurate or incomplete by a party to a case for which the evaluation was prepared. The medical director shall submit to the administrative director an annual report summarizing the results of the continuous review of medical evaluations and reports prepared by agreed and qualified medical evaluators and make recommendations for the improvement of the system of medical evaluations and determinations.

(j) After public hearing pursuant to Section 5307.3, the administrative director shall adopt regulations concerning the following issues:

(1)(A) Standards governing the timeframes within which medical evaluations shall be prepared and submitted by agreed and qualified medical evaluators. Except as provided in this subdivision, the timeframe for initial medical evaluations to be prepared and submitted shall be no more than 30 days after the evaluator has seen the employee or otherwise commenced the medical evaluation procedure. The administrative director shall develop regulations governing the provision of extensions of the 30–day period in both of the following cases:

(i) When the evaluator has not received test results or consulting physician's evaluations in time to meet the 30–day deadline.

(ii) To extend the 30–day period by not more than 15 days when the failure to meet the 30–day deadline was for good cause.

(B) For purposes of subparagraph (A), "good cause" means any of the following:

(i) Medical emergencies of the evaluator or evaluator's family.

(ii) Death in the evaluator's family.

(iii) Natural disasters or other community catastrophes that interrupt the operation of the evaluator's business.

(C) The administrative director shall develop timeframes governing availability of qualified medical evaluators for unrepresented employees under Sections 4061 and 4062. These timeframes shall give the employee the right to the addition of a new evaluator to his or her panel, selected at random, for each evaluator not available to see the employee within a specified period of time, but shall also permit the employee to waive this right for a specified period of time thereafter.

(2) Procedures to be followed by all physicians in evaluating the existence and extent of permanent impairment and limitations resulting from an injury in a manner consistent with Section 4660.

(3) Procedures governing the determination of any disputed medical treatment issues in a manner consistent with Section 5307.27.

(4) Procedures to be used in determining the compensability of psychiatric injury. The procedures shall be in accordance with Section 3208. 3 and shall require that the diagnosis of a mental disorder be expressed using the terminology and criteria of the American Psychiatric Association's Diagnostic and Statistical Manual of Mental Disorders, Third Edition–Revised, or the terminology and diagnostic criteria of other psychiatric diagnostic manuals generally approved and accepted nationally by practitioners in the field of psychiatric medicine.

(5) Guidelines for the range of time normally required to perform the following:

(A) A medical-legal evaluation that has not been defined and valued pursuant to Section 5307.6. The guidelines shall establish minimum times for patient contact in the conduct of the evaluations, and shall be consistent with regulations adopted pursuant to Section 5307.6.

(B) Any treatment procedures that have not been defined and valued pursuant to Section 5307.1.

(C) Any other evaluation procedure requested by the Insurance Commissioner, or deemed appropriate by the administrative director.

(6) Any additional medical or professional standards that a medical evaluator shall meet as a condition of appointment, reappointment, or maintenance in the status of a medical evaluator.

(k) Except as provided in this subdivision, the administrative director may, in his or her discretion, suspend or terminate the privilege of a physician to serve as a qualified medical evaluator if the administrative director, after hearing pursuant to subdivision (l), determines, based on substantial evidence, that a qualified medical evaluator:

(1) Has violated any material statutory or administrative duty.

(2) Has failed to follow the medical procedures or qualifications established pursuant to paragraph (2), (3), (4), or (5) of subdivision (j).

(3) Has failed to comply with the timeframe standards established pursuant to subdivision (j).

(4) Has failed to meet the requirements of subdivision (b) or (c).

(5) Has prepared medical-legal evaluations that fail to meet the minimum standards for those reports established by the administrative director or the appeals board.

(6) Has made material misrepresentations or false statements in an application for appointment or reappointment as a qualified medical evaluator.

No hearing shall be required prior to the suspension or termination of a physician's privilege to serve as a qualified medical evaluator when the physician has done either of the following:

(A) Failed to timely pay the fee required pursuant to subdivision (n).

(B) Had his or her license to practice in California suspended by the relevant licensing authority so as to preclude practice, or had the license revoked or terminated by the licensing authority.

(*l*) The administrative director shall cite the qualified medical evaluator for a violation listed in subdivision (k) and shall set a hearing on the alleged violation within 30 days of service of the citation on the qualified medical evaluator. In addition to the authority to terminate or suspend the qualified medical evaluator upon finding a violation listed in subdivision (k), the administrative director may, in his or her discretion, place a qualified medical evaluator on probation subject to appropriate conditions, including ordering continuing education or training. The administrative director shall report to the appropriate licensing board the name of any qualified medical evaluator who is disciplined pursuant to this subdivision.

(m) The administrative director shall terminate from the list of medical evaluators any physician where licensure has been terminated by the relevant licensing board, or who has been convicted of a misdemeanor or felony related to the conduct of his or her medical practice, or of a crime of moral turpitude. The administrative director shall suspend or terminate as a medical evaluator any physician who has been suspended or placed on probation by the relevant licensing board. If a physician is suspended or terminated as a qualified medical evaluator under this subdivision, a report prepared by the physician that is not complete, signed, and furnished to one or more of the parties prior to the date of conviction or action of the licensing board, whichever is earlier, shall not be admissible in any proceeding before the appeals board nor shall there be any liability for payment for the report and any expense incurred by the physician in connection with the report.

(n) Each qualified medical evaluator shall pay a fee, as determined by the administrative director, for appointment or reappointment. These fees shall be based on a sliding scale as established by the administrative director. All revenues from fees paid under this subdivision shall be deposited into the Workers' Compensation Administration Revolving Fund and are available for expenditure upon appropriation by the Legislature, and shall not be used by any other department or agency or for any purpose other than administration of the programs the Division of Workers' Compensation related to the provision of medical treatment to injured employees.

(*o*) An evaluator may not request or accept any compensation or other thing of value from any source that does or could create a conflict with his or her duties as an evaluator under this code. The administrative director, after consultation with the Commission on Health and Safety and Workers' Compensation, shall adopt regulations to implement this subdivision. *(Added by Stats.1989, c. 892, § 23. Amended by Stats.1990, c. 1550 (A.B.2910), § 16; Stats.1992, c. 1352 (A.B.3660), § 4.5, eff. Sept. 30, 1992; Stats.1993, c. 4 (S.B.31), § 1, eff. April 3, 1993; Stats.1993, c. 121 (A.B.110), § 18, eff. July 16, 1993; Stats.1993, c. 1242 (S.B.223), § 18; Stats.1994, c. 301 (S.B.1004), § 2, eff. July 21, 1994; Stats.1994, c. 1118 (S.B.1768), § 2; Stats.1995, c. 319 (A.B.1968), § 1; Stats.2000, c. 54 (A.B.776), § 1; Stats.2003, c. 228 (A.B. 1756), § 27, eff. Aug. 11, 2003; Stats.2003, c. 639 (S.B. 228), § 10; Stats.2004, c. 34 (S.B.899), § 2, eff. April 19, 2004.)*

Operative Effect

Section 47 of Stats.2004, c. 34 (S.B.899) provides that "[t]he amendment, addition, or repeal of, any provision of law made by this act shall apply prospectively from the date of enactment of this act, regardless of the date of injury, unless otherwise specified, but shall not constitute good cause to reopen or rescind, alter, or amend any existing order, decision, or award of the Workers' Compensation Appeals Board."

§ 139.3. Referrals for medical diagnosis or treatment; financial interests of physician; prohibitions; penalties

(a) Notwithstanding any other provision of law, to the extent those services are paid pursuant to Division 4 (commencing with Section 3200), it is unlawful for a physician to refer a person for clinical laboratory, diagnostic nuclear medicine, radiation oncology, physical therapy, physical rehabilitation, psychometric testing, home infusion therapy, outpatient surgery, or diagnostic imaging goods or services whether for treatment or medical-legal purposes if the physician or his or her immediate family, has a financial interest with the person or in the entity that receives the referral.

(b) For purposes of this section and Section 139.31, the following shall apply:

(1) "Diagnostic imaging" includes, but is not limited to, all X-ray, computed axial tomography magnetic resonance imaging, nuclear medicine, positron emission tomography, mammography, and ultrasound goods and services.

(2) "Immediate family" includes the spouse and children of the physician, the parents of the physician, and the spouses of the children of the physician.

(3) "Physician" means a physician as defined in Section 3209.3.

(4) A "financial interest" includes, but is not limited to, any type of ownership, interest, debt, loan, lease, compensation, remuneration, discount, rebate, refund, dividend, distribution, subsidy, or other form of direct or indirect payment, whether in money or otherwise, between a licensee and a person or entity to whom the physician refers a person for a good or service specified in subdivision (a). A financial interest also exists if there is an indirect relationship between a physician and the referral recipient, including, but not limited to, an arrangement whereby a physician has an ownership interest in any entity that leases property to the referral recipient. Any financial interest transferred by a physician to, or otherwise established in, any person or entity for the purpose of avoiding the prohibition of this section shall be deemed a financial interest of the physician.

(5) A "physician's office" is either of the following:

(A) An office of a physician in solo practice.

(B) An office in which the services or goods are personally provided by the physician or by employees in that office, or personally by independent contractors in that office, in accordance with other provisions of law. Employees and independent contractors shall be licensed or certified when that licensure or certification is required by law.

(6) The "office of a group practice" is an office or offices in which two or more physicians are legally organized as a partnership, professional corporation, or not-for-profit corporation licensed according to subdivision (a) of Section 1204 of the Health and Safety Code for which all of the following are applicable:

(A) Each physician who is a member of the group provides substantially the full range of services that the physician routinely provides, including medical care, consultation, diagnosis, or treatment, through the joint use of shared office space, facilities, equipment, and personnel.

(B) Substantially all of the services of the physicians who are members of the group are provided through the group and are billed in the name of the group and amounts so received are treated as receipts of the group, and except that in the case of multispecialty clinics, as defined in subdivision (*l*) of Section 1206 of the Health and Safety Code, physician services are billed in the name

304

of the multispecialty clinic and amounts so received are treated as receipts of the multispecialty clinic.

(C) The overhead expenses of, and the income from, the practice are distributed in accordance with methods previously determined by members of the group.

(7) Outpatient surgery includes both of the following:

(A) Any procedure performed on an outpatient basis in the operating rooms, ambulatory surgery rooms, endoscopy units, cardiac catheterization laboratories, or other sections of a freestanding ambulatory surgery clinic, whether or not licensed under paragraph (1) of subdivision (b) of Section 1204 of the Health and Safety Code.

(B) The ambulatory surgery itself.

(c)(1) It is unlawful for a licensee to enter into an arrangement or scheme, such as a cross-referral arrangement, that the licensee knows, or should know, has a principal purpose of ensuring referrals by the licensee to a particular entity that, if the licensee directly made referrals to that entity, would be in violation of this section.

(2) It shall be unlawful for a physician to offer, deliver, receive, or accept any rebate, refund, commission, preference, patronage dividend, discount, or other consideration, whether in the form of money or otherwise, as compensation or inducement for a referred evaluation or consultation.

(d) No claim for payment shall be presented by an entity to any individual, third-party payor, or other entity for any goods or services furnished pursuant to a referral prohibited under this section.

(e) A physician who refers to or seeks consultation from an organization in which the physician has a financial interest shall disclose this interest to the patient or if the patient is a minor, to the patient's parents or legal guardian in writing at the time of the referral.

(f) No insurer, self-insurer, or other payor shall pay a charge or lien for any goods or services resulting from a referral in violation of this section.

(g) A violation of subdivision (a) shall be a misdemeanor. The appropriate licensing board shall review the facts and circumstances of any conviction pursuant to subdivision (a) and take appropriate disciplinary action if the licensee has committed unprofessional conduct. Violations of this section may also be subject to civil penalties of up to five thousand dollars ($5,000) for each offense, which may be enforced by the Insurance Commissioner, Attorney General, or a district attorney. A violation of subdivision (c), (d), (e), or (f) is a public offense and is punishable upon conviction by a fine not exceeding fifteen thousand dollars ($15,000) for each violation and appropriate disciplinary action, including revocation of professional licensure, by the Medical Board of California or other appropriate governmental agency. *(Added by Stats.1993, c. 121 (A.B.110), § 20, eff. July 16, 1993. Amended by Stats.1993, c. 1242 (S.B.223), § 19; Stats. 2003, c. 639 (S.B.228), § 11.)*

§ 139.31. Referrals to which prohibition of § 139.3 do not apply

The prohibition of Section 139.3 shall not apply to or restrict any of the following:

(a) A physician may refer a patient for a good or service otherwise prohibited by subdivision (a) of Section 139.3 if the physician's regular practice is where there is no alternative provider of the service within either 25 miles or 40 minutes traveling time, via the shortest route on a paved road. A physician who refers to, or seeks consultation from, an organization in which the physician has a financial interest under this subdivision shall disclose this interest to the patient or the patient's parents or legal guardian in writing at the time of referral.

(b) A physician who has one or more of the following arrangements with another physician, a person, or an entity, is not prohibited from referring a patient to the physician, person, or entity because of the arrangement:

(1) A loan between a physician and the recipient of the referral, if the loan has commercially reasonable terms, bears interest at the prime rate or a higher rate that does not constitute usury, is adequately secured, and the loan terms are not affected by either party's referral of any person or the volume of services provided by either party.

(2) A lease of space or equipment between a physician and the recipient of the referral, if the lease is written, has commercially reasonable terms, has a fixed periodic rent payment, has a term of one year or more, and the lease payments are not affected by either party's referral of any person or the volume of services provided by either party.

(3) A physician's ownership of corporate investment securities, including shares, bonds, or other debt instruments that were purchased on terms that are available to the general public through a licensed securities exchange or NASDAQ, do not base profit distributions or other transfers of value on the physician's referral of persons to the corporation, do not have a separate class or accounting for any persons or for any physicians who may refer persons to the corporation, and are in a corporation that had, at the end of the corporation's most recent fiscal year, total gross assets exceeding one hundred million dollars ($100,000,000).

(4) A personal services arrangement between a physician or an immediate family member of the physician and the recipient of the referral if the arrangement meets all of the following requirements:

(A) It is set out in writing and is signed by the parties.

(B) It specifies all of the services to be provided by the physician or an immediate family member of the physician.

(C) The aggregate services contracted for do not exceed those that are reasonable and necessary for the legitimate business purposes of the arrangement.

(D) A written notice disclosing the existence of the personal services arrangement and including information on where a person may go to file a complaint against the

licensee or the immediate family member of the licensee, is provided to the following persons at the time any services pursuant to the arrangement are first provided:

(i) An injured worker who is referred by a licensee or an immediate family member of the licensee.

(ii) The injured worker's employer, if self-insured.

(iii) The injured worker's employer's insurer, if insured.

(iv) If the injured worker is known by the licensee or the recipient of the referral to be represented, the injured worker's attorney.

(E) The term of the arrangement is for at least one year.

(F) The compensation to be paid over the term of the arrangement is set in advance, does not exceed fair market value, and is not determined in a manner that takes into account the volume or value of any referrals or other business generated between the parties, except that if the services provided pursuant to the arrangement include medical services provided under Division 4, compensation paid for the services shall be subject to the official medical fee schedule promulgated pursuant to Section 5307.1 or subject to any contract authorized by Section 5307.11.

(G) The services to be performed under the arrangement do not involve the counseling or promotion of a business arrangement or other activity that violates any state or federal law.

(c)(1) A physician may refer a person to a health facility as defined in Section 1250 of the Health and Safety Code, to any facility owned or leased by a health facility, or to an outpatient surgical center, if the recipient of the referral does not compensate the physician for the patient referral, and any equipment lease arrangement between the physician and the referral recipient complies with the requirements of paragraph (2) of subdivision (b).

(2) Nothing shall preclude this subdivision from applying to a physician solely because the physician has an ownership or leasehold interest in an entire health facility or an entity that owns or leases an entire health facility.

(3) A physician may refer a person to a health facility for any service classified as an emergency under subdivision (a) or (b) of Section 1317.1 of the Health and Safety Code. For nonemergency outpatient diagnostic imaging services performed with equipment for which, when new, has a commercial retail price of four hundred thousand dollars ($400,000) or more, the referring physician shall obtain a service preauthorization from the insurer, or self-insured employer. Any oral authorization shall be memorialized in writing within five business days.

(d) A physician compensated or employed by a university may refer a person to any facility owned or operated by the university, or for a physician service, to another physician employed by the university, provided that the facility or university does not compensate the referring physician for the patient referral. For nonemergency diagnostic imaging services performed with equipment that, when new, has a commercial retail price of four hundred thousand dollars ($400,000) or more, the referring physician shall obtain a service preauthorization from the insurer or self-insured employer. An oral authorization shall be memorialized in writing within five business days. In the case of a facility which is totally or partially owned by an entity other than the university, but which is staffed by university physicians, those physicians may not refer patients to the facility if the facility compensates the referring physician for those referrals.

(e) The prohibition of Section 139.3 shall not apply to any service for a specific patient that is performed within, or goods that are supplied by, a physician's office, or the office of a group practice. Further, the provisions of Section 139.3 shall not alter, limit, or expand a physician's ability to deliver, or to direct or supervise the delivery of, in-office goods or services according to the laws, rules, and regulations governing his or her scope of practice. With respect to diagnostic imaging services performed with equipment that, when new, had a commercial retail price of four hundred thousand dollars ($400,000) or more, or for physical therapy services, or for psychometric testing that exceeds the routine screening battery protocols, with a time limit of two to five hours, established by the administrative director, the referring physician obtains a service preauthorization from the insurer or self-insured employer. Any oral authorization shall be memorialized in writing within five business days.

(f) The prohibition of Section 139.3 shall not apply where the physician is in a group practice as defined in Section 139.3 and refers a person for services specified in Section 139.3 to a multispecialty clinic, as defined in subdivision (*l*) of Section 1206 of the Health and Safety Code. For diagnostic imaging services performed with equipment that, when new, had a commercial retail price of four hundred thousand dollars ($400,000) or more, or physical therapy services, or psychometric testing that exceeds the routine screening battery protocols, with a time limit of two to five hours, established by the administrative director, performed at the multispecialty facility, the referring physician shall obtain a service preauthorization from the insurer or self-insured employer. Any oral authorization shall be memorialized in writing within five business days.

(g) The requirement for preauthorization in Sections (c), (e), and (f) shall not apply to a patient for whom the physician or group accepts payment on a capitated risk basis.

(h) The prohibition of Section 139.3 shall not apply to any facility when used to provide health care services to an enrollee of a health care service plan licensed pursuant to the Knox–Keene Health Care Service Plan Act of 1975 (Chapter 2.2 (commencing with Section 1340) of Division 2 of the Health and Safety Code).

(i) The prohibition of Section 139.3 shall not apply to an outpatient surgical center, as defined in paragraph (7)

of subdivision (b) of Section 139.3, where the referring physician obtains a service preauthorization from the insurer or self-insured employer after disclosure of the financial relationship. *(Added by Stats.1993, c. 121 (A.B.110), § 21, eff. July 16, 1993. Amended by Stats. 1993, c. 1242 (S.B.223), § 20; Stats.2002, c. 309 (S.B. 1907), § 2; Stats.2003, c. 639 (S.B.228), § 12.)*

§ 139.4. Advertising by medical evaluators and physicians; review for deceptive claims or statements; penalty

(a) The administrative director may review advertising copy to ensure compliance with Section 651 of the Business and Professions Code and may require qualified medical evaluators to maintain a file of all advertising copy for a period of 90 days from the date of its use. Any file so required to be maintained shall be available to the administrative director upon the administrative director's request for review.

(b) No advertising copy shall be used after its use has been disapproved by the administrative director and the qualified medical evaluator has been notified in writing of the disapproval.

(c) A qualified medical evaluator who is found by the administrative director to have violated any provision of this section may be terminated, suspended, or placed on probation.

(d) Proceedings to determine whether a violation of this section has occurred shall be conducted pursuant to Chapter 4 (commencing with Section 11370) of Part 1 of Division 3 of Title 2 of the Government Code.

(e) The administrative director shall adopt regulations governing advertising by physicians with respect to industrial injuries or illnesses.

(f) Subdivision (a) shall not be construed to alter the application of Section 651 of the Business and Professions Code. *(Added by Stats.1991, c. 116 (S.B.1218), § 23. Amended by Stats.2003, c. 639 (S.B.228), § 13.)*

§ 139.43. Services or benefits to injured workers; false statements or advertising; penalty; exemptions

(a) No person or entity shall advertise, print, display, publish, distribute, or broadcast, or cause or permit to be advertised, printed, displayed, published, distributed, or broadcast in any manner, any statement concerning services or benefits to be provided to an injured worker, that is paid for directly or indirectly by that person or entity and is false, misleading, or deceptive, or that omits material information necessary to make the statement therein not false, misleading, or deceptive.

(b) As soon as reasonably possible, but not later than January 1, 1994, the administrative director shall adopt regulations governing advertising by persons or entities other than physicians and attorneys with respect to services or benefits for injured workers. In promulgating regulations pursuant to this subdivision, the administrative director shall review existing regulations, including those adopted by the State Bar, to identify those regulatory approaches that may serve as a model for regulations required by this subdivision.

(c) A violation of subdivision (a) is a misdemeanor, punishable by incarceration in the county jail for not more than one year, or by a fine not exceeding ten thousand dollars ($10,000), or both.

(d) This section shall not apply to physicians or attorneys. It is the intent of the Legislature to exempt physicians and attorneys from this section because the conduct regulated by this section, with respect to physicians and attorneys, is governed by other provisions of law. *(Added by Stats.1991, c. 116 (S.B.1218), § 24. Amended by Stats.1992, c. 1352 (A.B.3660), § 5, eff. Sept. 30, 1992; Stats.2004, c. 193 (S.B.111), § 138.)*

§ 139.45. Regulations governing advertising; characteristics of false or misleading advertising

(a) In promulgating regulations pursuant to Sections 139.4 and 139.43, the administrative director shall take particular care to preclude any advertisements with respect to industrial injuries or illnesses that are false or mislead the public with respect to workers' compensation. In promulgating rules with respect to advertising, the State Bar and physician licensing boards shall also take particular care to achieve the same goal.

(b) For purposes of subdivision (a), false or misleading advertisements shall include advertisements that do any of the following:

(1) Contain an untrue statement.

(2) Contain any matter, or present or arrange any matter in a manner or format that is false, deceptive, or that tends to confuse, deceive, or mislead.

(3) Omit any fact necessary to make the statement made, in the light of the circumstances under which the statement is made, not misleading.

(4) Are transmitted in any manner that involves coercion, duress, compulsion, intimidation, threats, or vexatious or harassing conduct.

(5) Entice a person to respond by the offering of any consideration, including a good or service but excluding free medical evaluations or treatment, that would be provided either at no charge or for less than market value. No free medical evaluation or treatment shall be offered for the purpose of defrauding any entity. *(Added by Stats.1991, c. 116 (S.B.1218), § 25. Amended by Stats.1992, c. 1352 (A.B.3660), § 6, eff. Sept. 30, 1992; Stats.2003, c. 639 (S.B.228), § 14.)*

§ 139.47. Return-to-Work Program

The Director of Industrial Relations shall establish and maintain a program to encourage, facilitate, and educate employers to provide early and sustained return to work after occupational injury or illness. The program shall do both of the following:

(a) Develop educational materials and guides, in easily understandable language in both print and electronic form, for employers, health care providers, employees,

and labor unions. These materials shall address issues including, but not limited to, early return to work, assessment of functional abilities and limitations, development of appropriate work restrictions, job analysis, worksite modifications, assistive equipment and devices, and available resources.

(b) Conduct training for employee and employer organizations and health care providers concerning the accommodation of injured employees and the prevention of reinjury. *(Added by Stats.2002, c. 6 (A.B.749), § 40.)*

§ 139.48. Establishment of Return–to–Work Program and Workers' Compensation Return–to–Work Fund; workplace modification expense reimbursement; employment preference prohibited; regulations

(a)(1) The administrative director shall establish the Return–to–Work Program in order to promote the early and sustained return to work of the employee following a work-related injury or illness.

(2) This section shall be implemented to the extent funds are available.

(b) Upon submission by eligible employers of documentation in accordance with regulations adopted pursuant to subdivision (h), the administrative director shall pay the workplace modification expense reimbursement allowed under this section.

(c) The administrative director shall reimburse an eligible employer for expenses incurred to make workplace modifications to accommodate the employee's return to modified or alternative work, as follows:

(1) The maximum reimbursement to an eligible employer for expenses to accommodate each temporarily disabled injured worker is one thousand two hundred fifty dollars ($1,250).

(2) The maximum reimbursement to an eligible employer for expenses to accommodate each permanently disabled worker who is a qualified injured worker is two thousand five hundred dollars ($2,500). If the employer received reimbursement under paragraph (1), the amount of the reimbursement under paragraph (1) and this paragraph shall not exceed two thousand five hundred dollars ($2,500).

(3) The modification expenses shall be incurred in order to allow a temporarily disabled worker to perform modified or alternative work within physician-imposed temporary work restrictions, or to allow a permanently disabled worker who is an injured worker to return to sustained modified or alternative employment with the employer within physician-imposed permanent work restrictions.

(4) Allowable expenses may include physical modifications to the worksite, equipment, devices, furniture, tools, or other necessary costs for accommodation of the employee's restrictions.

(d) This section shall not create a preference in employment for injured employees over noninjured employees. It shall be unlawful for an employer to discriminatorily terminate, lay off, demote, or otherwise displace an employee in order to return an industrially injured employee to employment for the purpose of obtaining the reimbursement set forth in subdivision (c).

(e) For purposes of this section, the following definitions apply:

(1) "Eligible employer" means any employer, except the state or an employer eligible to secure the payment of compensation pursuant to subdivision (c) of Section 3700, who employs 50 or fewer full-time employees on the date of injury.

(2) "Employee" means a worker who has suffered a work-related injury or illness on or after July 1, 2004.

(f) The administrative director shall adopt regulations to carry out this section. Regulations allocating budget funds that are insufficient to implement the workplace modification expense reimbursement provided for in this section shall include a prioritization schema.

(g) The Workers' Compensation Return–to–Work Fund is hereby created as a special fund in the State Treasury. The fund shall consist of all penalties collected pursuant to Section 5814.6 and transfers made by the administrative director from the Workers' Compensation Administration Revolving Fund established pursuant to Section 62.5. The fund shall be administered by the administrative director. Moneys in the fund may be expended by the administrative director, upon appropriation by the Legislature, only for purposes of implementing this section.

(h) This section shall be operative on July 1, 2004.

(i) This section shall remain in effect only until January 1, 2010, and as of that date is repealed, unless a later enacted statute, that is enacted before January 1, 2010, deletes or extends that date. *(Added by Stats.2002, c. 6 (A.B.749), § 41, operative July 1, 2004. Amended by Stats.2004, c. 34 (S.B.899), § 3, eff. April 19, 2004, operative July 1, 2004; Stats.2008, c. 751 (A.B.1389), § 61, eff. Sept. 30, 2008.)*

Implementation

Implementation of this section is contingent upon availability of funding, by its own terms.

Operative Effect

Section 47 of Stats.2004, c. 34 (S.B.899) provides that "[t]he amendment, addition, or repeal of, any provision of law made by this act shall apply prospectively from the date of enactment of this act, regardless of the date of injury, unless otherwise specified, but shall not constitute good cause to reopen or rescind, alter, or amend any existing order, decision, or award of the Workers' Compensation Appeals Board."

Repeal

For repeal of this section, see its terms.

§ 139.6.　Information and assistance program

(a) The administrative director shall establish and effect within the Division of Workers' Compensation a continuing program to provide information and assistance concerning the rights, benefits, and obligations of the workers' compensation law to employees and employers subject thereto. The program shall include, but not be limited to, the following:

(1) The preparation, publishing, and as necessary, updating, of guides to the California workers' compensation system for employees and employers. The guides shall detail, in easily understandable language, the rights and obligations of employees and employers, the procedures for obtaining benefits, and the means provided for resolving disputes. Separate guides may be prepared for employees and employers. The appropriate guide shall be provided to all labor and employer organizations known to the administrative director, and to any other person upon request.

(2) The preparation, publishing, and as necessary, updating, of a pamphlet advising injured workers of their basic rights under workers' compensation law, and informing them of rights under the Americans with Disabilities Act, and the provisions of the Fair Employment and Housing Act relating to individuals with a disability. The pamphlet shall be written in easily understandable language. The pamphlet shall be available in both English and Spanish, and shall include basic information concerning the circumstances under which injured employees are entitled to the various types of workers' compensation benefits, the protections against discrimination because of an injury, the procedures for resolving any disputes which arise, and the right to seek information and advice from an information and assistance officer or an attorney.

(b) In each district office of the division, the administrative director shall appoint an information and assistance officer, and any other deputy information and assistance officers as the work of the district office may require. The administrative director shall provide office facilities and clerical support appropriate to the functions of these information and assistance officers.

(c) Each information and assistance officer shall be responsible for the performance of the following duties:

(1) Providing continuing information concerning rights, benefits, and obligations under workers' compensation laws to injured workers, employers, lien claimants, and other interested parties.

(2) Upon request by the injured worker, assisting in the prompt resolution of misunderstanding, disputes, and controversies arising out of claims for compensation, without formal proceedings, in order that full and timely compensation benefits shall be furnished. In performing this duty, information and assistance officers shall not be responsible for reviewing applications for adjudication or declarations of readiness to proceed. This function shall be performed by workers' compensation judges. This

function may also be performed by settlement conference referees upon delegation by the appeals board.

(3) Distributing any information pamphlets in English and Spanish as are prepared and approved by the administrative director to all inquiring injured workers and any other parties that may request copies of these pamphlets.

(4) Establishing and maintaining liaison with the persons located in the geographic area served by the district office, with other affected state agencies, and with organizations representing employees, employers, insurers, and the medical community. (Added by Stats.1976, c. 1017, p. 4594, § 2. Amended by Stats.1987, c. 1019, § 2; Stats.1990, c. 1550 (A.B.2910), § 19; Stats.1993, c. 121 (A.B.110), § 23, eff. July 16, 1993.)

CHAPTER 6. OCCUPATIONAL SAFETY AND HEALTH STANDARDS BOARD

Section
140. Members; appointment; qualifications; term; chairman; references to industrial safety board.
141. Term of members; compensation.
142. Enforcement of standards; continuation of orders previously adopted.
142.1. Meetings.
142.2. Consideration of proposed new orders or standards.
142.3. Adoption, amendment or repeal of standards and orders; publication of standards; contents of standards and orders; results of examinations and tests.
142.4. Method of adopting, amending and repealing orders and standards; emergency regulations.
142.7. Hazardous substance removal; occupational safety and health standard; safety and health conference.
143. Permanent variances.
143.1. Hearings on applications for permanent variances.
143.2. Rules of practice and procedure.
144. Enforcement agreements.
144.5. Division of occupational safety and health; enforcement of standards; powers and duties.
144.6. Standards for toxic materials and harmful physical agents; bases; considerations; criteria.
144.7. Bloodborne pathogen standard regulation; contents; list of existing needleless systems and needles with engineered sharps injury protection; availability for employers.
145. Personnel; law governing.
145.1. Powers of head of department.
146. Variance hearings; evidence and procedure.
147. References for evaluation of proposed standards or variances.
147.1. Division of occupational safety and health; development and promulgation of standards; powers and duties.
147.2. Toxic materials and harmful physical agents; data repository; function; reports.

§ 140. Members; appointment; qualifications; term; chairman; references to industrial safety board

(a) There is in the Department of Industrial Relations, the Occupational Safety and Health Standards Board which consists of seven members who shall be appointed by the Governor. Two members shall be from the field of management, two members shall be from the field of labor, one member shall be from the field of occupational health, one member shall be from the field of occupational safety and one member shall be from the general public. Members representing occupational safety and health fields and the public member shall be selected from other than the fields of management or labor.

(b) Terms of office for members of the Industrial Safety Board shall expire 60 days after the effective date of the amendment of this section enacted at the 1973–74 Regular Session. Newly appointed members of the Occupational Safety and Health Standards Board shall assume their duties upon that date.

(c) The Governor shall designate the chairman of the board from the membership of the board. The person so designated shall hold the office of chairman at the pleasure of the Governor. The chairman shall designate a member of the board to act as chairman in his absence.

(d) As used in this chapter, "board" means the Occupational Safety and Health Standards Board.

(e) All references in this or any other code to the Industrial Safety Board shall be deemed to mean the Occupational Safety and Health Standards Board. (Added by Stats.1945, c. 1431, p. 2668, § 28. Amended by Stats.1973, c. 993, p. 1919, § 11, eff. Oct. 1, 1973.)

§ 141. Term of members; compensation

(a) The terms of office of the members of the board shall be four years and they shall hold office until the appointment and qualification of a successor. The terms of the members of the board first appointed shall expire as follows: three members, one representative from management, one representative from labor, and one representative from occupational health, on June 1, 1974; three members, one representative from management, one representative from labor, and one representative from occupational safety, on June 1, 1975; one member June 1, 1976. The terms shall thereafter expire in the same relative order. Vacancies occurring shall be filled by appointment to the unexpired term.

(b) Each member of the board shall receive one hundred dollars ($100) for each day of his or her actual attendance at meetings of the board, and other official business of the board, and his or her actual and necessary traveling expenses incurred in the performance of his or her duty as a member. (Added by Stats.1945, c. 1431, p. 2688, § 28. Amended by Stats.1969, c. 460, p. 1020, § 3; Stats.1973, c. 993, p. 1919, § 12, eff. Oct. 1, 1973; Stats.2004, c. 183 (A.B.3082), § 254.)

§ 142. Enforcement of standards; continuation of orders previously adopted

The Division of Occupational Safety and Health shall enforce all occupational safety and health standards adopted pursuant to this chapter, and those heretofore adopted by the Industrial Accident Commission or the Industrial Safety Board. General safety orders heretofore adopted by the Industrial Accident Commission or the Industrial Safety Board shall continue to remain in effect, but they may be amended or repealed pursuant to this chapter. *(Added by Stats.1945, c. 1431, p. 2688, § 28. Amended by Stats.1973, c. 993, p. 1920, § 13, eff. Oct. 1, 1973; Stats.1979, c. 72, p. 178, § 19; Stats.1979, c. 1152, p. 4315, § 204; Stats.2002, c. 1124 (A.B.3000), § 40, eff. Sept. 30, 2002.)*

§ 142.1. Meetings

The board shall meet at least monthly. The meetings shall be rotated throughout the state at locations designated by the chairman. All meetings held by the board shall be open and public. Written notice of all meetings and a proposed agenda shall be given to all persons who make request for the notice in writing to the board. *(Added by Stats.1973, c. 993, p. 2311, § 14, eff. Oct. 1, 1973. Amended by Stats.1974, c. 1284, p. 2779, § 2; Stats.1985, c. 657, § 1.)*

§ 142.2. Consideration of proposed new orders or standards

At each of its meetings, the board shall make time available to interested persons to propose new or revised orders or standards appropriate for adoption pursuant to this chapter or other items concerning occupational safety and health. The board shall consider such proposed orders or standards and report its decision no later than six months following receipt of such proposals. *(Added by Stats.1973, c. 993, p. 1920, § 15, eff. Oct. 1, 1973.)*

§ 142.3. Adoption, amendment or repeal of standards and orders; publication of standards; contents of standards and orders; results of examinations and tests

(a)(1) The board, by an affirmative vote of at least four members, may adopt, amend or repeal occupational safety and health standards and orders. The board shall be the only agency in the state authorized to adopt occupational safety and health standards.

(2) The board shall adopt standards at least as effective as the federal standards for all issues for which federal standards have been promulgated under Section 6 of the Occupational Safety and Health Act of 1970 (P.L. 91–596) within six months of the promulgation date of the federal standards and which, when applicable to products which are distributed or used in interstate commerce, are required by compelling local conditions and do not unduly burden interstate commerce.

(3) No standard or amendment to any standard adopted by the board that is substantially the same as a federal standard shall be subject to Article 5 (commencing with Section 11346) and Article 6 (commencing with Section 11349) of Chapter 3.5 of Part 1 of Division 3 of Title 2 of the Government Code. For purposes of this subdivision, "substantially the same" means identical to the federal standard with the exception of editorial and format differences needed to conform to other state laws and standards.

(4) If a federal standard is promulgated and no state standard that is at least as effective as the federal standard is adopted by the board within six months of the date of promulgation of the federal standard, the following provisions shall apply unless adoption of the state standard is imminent:

(A) If there is no existing state standard covering the same issues, the federal standard shall be deemed to be a standard adopted by the board and enforceable by the division pursuant to Section 6317. This standard shall not be subject to Article 5 (commencing with Section 11346) and Article 6 (commencing with Section 11349) of Chapter 3.5 of Part 1 of Division 3 of Title 2 of the Government Code.

(B) If a state standard is in effect at the time a federal standard is promulgated covering the same issue or issues, the board may adopt the federal standard, or a portion thereof, as a standard enforceable by the division pursuant to Section 6317; provided, however, if a federal standard or portion thereof is adopted which replaces an existing state standard or portion thereof, the federal standard shall be as effective as the state standard or portion thereof. No adoption of or amendment to any federal standard, or portion thereof shall be subject to Article 5 (commencing with Section 11346) and Article 6 (commencing with Section 11349) of Chapter 3.5 of Part 1 of Division 3 of Title 2 of the Government Code.

(C) Any state standard adopted pursuant to subparagraph (A) or (B) shall become effective at the time the standard is filed with the Secretary of State, unless otherwise provided, but shall not take effect before the effective date of the equivalent federal standard and shall remain in effect for six months unless readopted by the board for an additional six months or superseded by a standard adopted by the board pursuant to paragraph (2) of subdivision (a).

(D) Any standard adopted pursuant to subparagraph (A), (B), or (C), shall be published in Title 8 of the California Code of Regulations in a manner similar to any other standards adopted pursuant to paragraphs (1) and (2) of subdivision (a) of this section.

(b) The State Building Standards Commission shall codify and publish in a semiannual supplement to the California Building Standards Code, or in a more frequent supplement if required by federal law, all occupational safety and health standards that would otherwise meet the definition of a building standard described in Section 18909 of the Health and Safety Code adopted by the board in the State Building Standards Code without reimbursement from the board. These occupational safety and health standards may also be published by the Occupational Safety and Health Standards Board in other provisions in Title 8 of the California Code of Regulations prior to publication in the California Building Standards Code if that other publication includes an appropriate identification of occupational safety and health standards contained in the other publication.

(c) Any occupational safety or health standard or order promulgated under this section shall prescribe the use of labels or other appropriate forms of warning as are necessary to ensure that employees are apprised of all hazards to which they are exposed, relevant symptoms and appropriate emergency treatment, and proper conditions and precautions for safe use or exposure. Where appropriate, these standards or orders shall also prescribe suitable protective equipment and control or technological procedures to be used in connection with these hazards and shall provide for monitoring or measuring employee exposure at such locations and intervals and in a manner as may be necessary for the protection of employees. In addition, where appropriate, the occupational safety or health standard or order shall prescribe the type and frequency of medical examinations or other tests which shall be made available, by the employer or at his or her cost, to employees exposed to such hazards in order to most effectively determine whether the health of such employee is adversely affected by this exposure.

(d) The results of these examinations or tests shall be furnished only to the Division of Occupational Safety and Health, the State Department of Health Services, any other authorized state agency, the employer, the employee, and, at the request of the employee, to his or her physician. *(Added by Stats.1973, c. 993, p. 1920, § 16, eff. Oct. 1, 1973. Amended by Stats.1976, c. 963, p. 2204, § 1; Stats.1978, c. 429, p. 1413, § 157.1, eff. July 17, 1978, operative July 1, 1978; Stats.1979, c. 72, p. 178, § 20; Stats.1979, c. 1152, p. 4315, § 205; Stats.1981, c. 817, p. 3168, § 8; Stats.1992, c. 1214 (A.B.2968), § 1; Stats.2002, c. 1124 (A.B.3000), § 41, eff. Sept. 30, 2002.)*

§ 142.4. Method of adopting, amending and repealing orders and standards; emergency regulations

(a) Occupational safety and health standards and orders shall be adopted, amended, or repealed as provided in Chapter 3.5 (commencing with Section 11340) of Part 1 of Division 3 of Title 2 of the Government Code, except as modified by this chapter.

(b) If an emergency regulation is based upon an emergency temporary standard published in the Federal Register by the Secretary of Labor pursuant to Section 6(c)(1) of the Federal Occupational Safety and Health Act of 1970 (P.L. 91–596; 29 U.S.C. Sec. 655(c)(1)), the 120–day period specified in Section 11346.1 of the Government Code shall be deemed not to expire until 120 days after a permanent standard is promulgated by the Secretary of Labor pursuant to Section 6(c)(3) of the Federal Occupational Safety and Health Act of 1970 (29 U.S.C. Sec. 655(c)(3)). *(Added by Stats.1973, c. 993, p. 1921, § 17, eff. Oct. 1, 1973. Amended by Stats.1982, c. 454, p. 1876, § 129; Stats.2006, c. 538 (S.B.1852), § 478.)*

§ 142.7. Hazardous substance removal; occupational safety and health standard; safety and health conference

(a) On or before October 1, 1987, the board shall adopt an occupational safety and health standard concerning hazardous substance removal work, so as to protect most effectively the health and safety of employees. The standard shall include, but not be limited to, requirements for all of the following:

(1) Specific work practices.

(2) Certification of all employees engaged in hazardous substance removal-related work, except that no certification shall be required for an employee whose only activity is the transportation of hazardous substances which are subject to the requirement for a certificate under Section 12804.1 of the Vehicle Code.

(3) Certification of supervisors with sufficient experience and authority to be responsible for hazardous substance removal work.

(4) Designation of a qualified person who shall be responsible for scheduling any air sampling, laboratory calibration of sampling equipment, evaluation of soil or other contaminated materials sampling results, and for conducting any equipment testing and evaluating the results of the tests.

(5) Requiring that a safety and health conference be held for all hazardous substance removal jobs before the start of actual work. The conference shall include representatives of the owner or contracting agency, the contractor, the employer, employees, and employee representatives, and shall include a discussion of the employer's safety and health program and the means, methods, devices, processes, practices, conditions, or operations which the employer intends to use in providing a safe and healthy place of employment.

(b) For purposes of this section, "hazardous substance removal work" means cleanup work at any of the following:

(1) A site where removal or remedial action is taken pursuant to either of the following:

(A) Chapter 6.8 (commencing with Section 25300) of Division 20 of the Health and Safety Code, regardless of whether the site is listed pursuant to Section 25356 of the Health and Safety Code.

(B) The federal Comprehensive Environmental Response, Compensation, and Liability Act of 1980 (42 U.S.C. Sec. 9601 et seq.).

(2) A site where corrective action is taken pursuant to Section 25187 or 25200.10 of the Health and Safety Code or the federal Resource Conservation and Recovery Act of 1976 (42 U.S.C. Sec. 6901 et seq.).

(3) A site where cleanup of a discharge of a hazardous substance is required pursuant to Division 7 (commencing with Section 13000) of the Water Code.

(4) A site where removal or remedial action is taken because a hazardous substance has been discharged or released in an amount that is reportable pursuant to Section 13271 of the Water Code or the federal Comprehensive Environmental Response, Compensation, and Liability Act of 1980 (42 U.S.C. Sec. 9601 et seq.).

"Hazardous substance removal work" does not include work related to a hazardous substance spill on a highway.

(c) Until the occupational safety and health standard required by subdivision (a) is adopted by the board and becomes effective, the occupational safety and health standard concerning hazardous substance removal work shall be the standard adopted by the federal government and codified in Section 1910.120 of Title 29 of the Code of Federal Regulations. In addition, before actual work is started on a hazardous substance removal job, a safety and health conference shall be held that shall include the participants and involve a discussion of the subjects described in paragraph (5) of subdivision (a). *(Added by Stats.1986, c. 1443, § 5, eff. Sept. 30, 1986. Amended by Stats.1990, c. 1188 (A.B.3018), § 1, eff. Sept. 24, 1990.)*

§ 143. Permanent variances

(a) Any employer may apply to the board for a permanent variance from an occupational safety and health standard, order, special order, or portion thereof, upon a showing of an alternate program, method, practice, means, device, or process which will provide equal or superior safety for employees.

(b) The board shall issue such variance if it determines on the record, after opportunity for an investigation where appropriate and a hearing, that the proponent of the variance has demonstrated by a preponderance of the evidence that the conditions, practices, means, methods, operations, or processes used or proposed to be used by an employer will provide employment and places of employment to his employees which are as safe and healthful as those which would prevail if he complied with the standard. The variance so issued shall prescribe the conditions the employer must maintain, and the practices, means, methods, operations, and processes which he must adopt and utilize to the extent they differ from the standard in question.

(c) The board is authorized to grant a variance from any standard or portion thereof whenever it determines such variance is necessary to permit an employer to participate in an experiment approved by the director designed to demonstrate or validate new and improved techniques to safeguard the health or safety of workers.

(d) A permanent variance may be modified or revoked upon application by an employer, employees, or the division, or by the board on its own motion, in the manner prescribed for its issuance under this section at any time. *(Added by Stats.1973, c. 993, p. 1921, § 19, eff. Oct. 1, 1973. Amended by Stats.1974, c. 1284, p. 2779, § 4.)*

§ 143.1. Hearings on applications for permanent variances

The board shall conduct hearings on such requests for a permanent variance after employees or employee representatives are properly notified and given an opportunity to appear. All board decisions on permanent variance requests shall be final except for any rehearing or judicial review provided for by law. *(Added by Stats.1973, c. 993, p. 1922, § 20, eff. Oct. 1, 1973.)*

§ 143.2. Rules of practice and procedure

The board, acting as a whole, may adopt, amend, or repeal rules of practice and procedure pertaining to hearings on applications for permanent variances, variance appeals, and other matters within its jurisdiction. All rules of practice and procedure amendments thereto, or repeal thereof, shall be made in accordance with the provisions of Chapter 3.5 (commencing with Section 11340) of Part 1 of Division 3 of Title 2 of the Government Code. *(Added by Stats.1973, c. 993, p. 1922, § 21, eff. Oct. 1, 1973. Amended by Stats.2004, c. 183 (A.B.3082), § 255.)*

§ 144. Enforcement agreements

(a) The authority of any agency, department, division, bureau or any other political subdivision other than the Division of Occupational Safety and Health to assist in the administration or enforcement of any occupational safety or health standard, order, or rule adopted pursuant to this chapter shall be contained in a written agreement with the Department of Industrial Relations or an agency authorized by the department to enter into such agreement.

(b) No such agreement shall deprive the Division of Occupational Safety and Health or other state agency to which authority has been delegated of any power or authority of the state agency.

(c) Such an agreement may provide for the right of access of an authorized representative of the designated agency to enter any place of employment which is under the jurisdiction of the Division of Occupational Safety and Health.

(d) If any representative of an agency operating under such an agreement becomes aware of an imminent hazard, he shall notify the employer and affected employees of the hazard and immediately notify the Division of Occupational Safety and Health.

(e) Nothing in this section shall affect or limit the authority of any state or local agency as to any matter other than the enforcement of occupational safety and health standards adopted by the board; however, nothing herein shall limit or reduce the authority of local agencies to adopt and enforce higher standards relating to occupational safety and health for their own employees. *(Added by Stats.1973, c. 993, p. 1922, § 23, eff. Oct. 1, 1973. Amended by Stats.1979, c. 72, p. 179, § 21.)*

§ 144.5. Division of occupational safety and health; enforcement of standards; powers and duties

(a) The Division of Occupational Safety and Health in connection with the enforcement of occupational safety and health standards adopted pursuant to this chapter shall do all of the following:

(1) Conduct inspections or investigations related to specific workplaces for the evaluation of occupational

health problems or environmental conditions which may be harmful to the health of employees.

(2) Upon request of any employer or employee, or on its own initiative, conduct special investigations or studies of occupational health problems which are unrelated to a specific enforcement action to the extent the circumstances indicate and priorities permit.

(3) Provide a continuing program of training for safety engineers of the Division of Occupational Safety and Health in the recognition of health hazards, in dealing with such hazards that do not require specialized competence or equipment and in acquainting them with the skills available from the State Department of Health Services and local health agencies.

(b)(1) When requested by a local health department, the Division of Occupational Safety and Health shall enter into a written agreement with such local health department to conduct inspections and evaluations of occupational health problems, including environmental and sanitary conditions, in places of employment.

(2) Any such agreement shall be subject to the provisions of Section 144. It shall be entered into only after a finding that the local health department can meet the necessary standards of performance for inspections and evaluations to be conducted pursuant to the agreement.

(3) Such agreement shall not be binding upon either party unless and until it has been fully approved by the United States Department of Labor.

(4) Such agreements shall be completed by the Division of Occupational Safety and Health and submitted for approval to the United States Department of Labor not later than six months from the date of request by the local health department.

(5) Inspection services performed under the agreement shall be conducted pursuant to the occupational safety and health standards adopted pursuant to this chapter. *(Added by Stats.1973, c. 993, p. 1922, § 24, eff. Oct. 1, 1973. Amended by Stats.1974, c. 1284, p. 2780, § 5; Stats.1977, c. 341, p. 928, § 1; Stats.1978, c. 429, p. 1414, § 157.2, eff. July 17, 1978, operative July 1, 1978; Stats.1979, c. 72, p. 179, § 22.)*

§ 144.6. Standards for toxic materials and harmful physical agents; bases; considerations; criteria

In promulgating standards dealing with toxic materials or harmful physical agents, the board shall adopt that standard which most adequately assures, to the extent feasible, that no employee will suffer material impairment of health or functional capacity even if such employee has regular exposure to a hazard regulated by such standard for the period of his working life. Development of standards under this section shall be based upon research, demonstrations, experiments, and such other information as may be appropriate. In addition to the attainment of the highest degree of health and safety protection for the employee, other considerations shall be the latest available scientific data in the field, the reasonableness of the

standards, and experience gained under this and other health and safety laws. Whenever practicable, the standard promulgated shall be expressed in terms of objective criteria and of the performance desired. *(Added by Stats.1973, c. 993, p. 1923, § 24.5, eff. Oct. 1, 1973. Amended by Stats.1976, c. 963, p. 2204, § 3.)*

§ 144.7. Bloodborne pathogen standard regulation; contents; list of existing needleless systems and needles with engineered sharps injury protection; availability for employers

(a) The board shall, no later than January 15, 1999, adopt an emergency regulation revising the bloodborne pathogen standard currently set forth in Section 5193 of Title 8 of the California Code of Regulations in accordance with subdivision (b). Following adoption of the emergency regulation, the board shall complete the regulation adoption process and shall formally adopt a regulation embodying a bloodborne pathogen standard meeting the requirements of subdivision (b), which regulation shall become operative no later than August 1, 1999. Notwithstanding Section 11346.1 of the Government Code, the emergency regulation adopted pursuant to this subdivision shall remain in effect until the nonemergency regulation becomes operative or until August 1, 1999, whichever first occurs.

(b) The board shall adopt a standard, as described in subdivision (a), to be developed by the Division of Occupational Safety and Health. The standard shall include, but not be limited to, the following:

(1) A revised definition of "engineering controls" that includes sharps injury prevention technology including, but not limited to, needleless systems and needles with engineered sharps injury protection, which shall be defined in the standard.

(2) A requirement that sharps injury prevention technology specified in paragraph (1) be included as engineering or work practice controls, except in cases where the employer or other appropriate party can demonstrate circumstances in which the technology does not promote employee or patient safety or interferes with a medical procedure. Those circumstances shall be specified in the standard, and shall include, but not be limited to, circumstances where the technology is medically contraindicated or not more effective than alternative measures used by the employer to prevent exposure incidents.

(3) A requirement that written exposure control plans include an effective procedure for identifying and selecting existing sharps injury prevention technology of the type specified in paragraph (1).

(4) A requirement that written exposure control plans be updated when necessary to reflect progress in implementing the sharps injury prevention technology specified in paragraph (1).

(5) A requirement that information concerning exposure incidents be recorded in a sharps injury log, including, but not limited to, the type and brand of device involved in the incident.

(c) The Division of Occupational Safety and Health may consider and propose for adoption by the board additional revisions to the bloodborne pathogen standards to prevent sharps injuries or exposure incidents including, but not limited to, training requirements and measures to increase vaccinations.

(d) The Division of Occupational Safety and Health and the State Department of Health Services shall jointly compile and maintain a list of existing needleless systems and needles with engineered sharps injury protection, which shall be available to assist employers in complying with the requirements of the bloodborne pathogen standard adopted pursuant to this section. The list may be developed from existing sources of information, including, but not limited to, the federal Food and Drug Administration, the federal Centers for Disease Control, the National Institute of Occupational Safety and Health, and the United States Department of Veterans Affairs. *(Added by Stats.1998, c. 999 (A.B.1208), § 1. Amended by Stats.2001, c. 370 (A.B.1046), § 2.)*

§ 145. Personnel; law governing

The board may employ necessary assistants, officers, experts, and such other employees as it deems necessary. All such personnel of the board shall be under the supervision of the chairman of the board or an executive officer to whom he delegates such responsibility. All such personnel shall be appointed pursuant to the State Civil Service Act (Part 1 (commencing with Section 18000) of Division 5 of Title 2 of the Government Code), except for the one exempt deputy or employee allowed by subdivision (e) of Section 4 of Article XXIV of the California Constitution[1]. *(Added by Stats.1973, c. 993, p. 1923, § 26, eff. Oct. 1, 1973.)*

[1] Repealed.

§ 145.1. Powers of head of department

The board and its duly authorized representatives in the performance of its duties shall have the powers of a head of a department as set forth in Article 2 (commencing with Section 11180) of Chapter 2 of Part 1 of Division 3 of Title 2 of the Government Code. *(Added by Stats.1973, c. 993, p. 1924, § 27, eff. Oct. 1, 1973.)*

§ 146. Variance hearings; evidence and procedure

In the conduct of hearings related to permanent variances, the board and its representatives are not bound by common law or statutory rules of evidence or by technical or formal rules of procedure but shall conduct the hearings in accordance with Article 8 (commencing with Section 11435.05) of Chapter 4.5 of Part 1 of Division 3 of Title 2 of, and Section 11513 of, the Government Code. A full and complete record shall be kept of all proceedings. *(Added by Stats.1973, c. 993, p. 1924, § 29, eff. Oct. 1, 1973. Amended by Stats.1995, c. 938 (S.B.523), § 72.8, operative July 1, 1997.)*

§ 147. References for evaluation of proposed standards or variances

The board shall refer to the Division of Occupational Safety and Health for evaluation any proposed occupational safety or health standard or variance from adopted standards received by the board from sources other than the division. The division shall submit a report on the proposed standard or variance within 60 days of receipt thereof. *(Added by Stats.1973, c. 993, p. 1924, § 31, eff. Oct. 1, 1973. Amended by Stats.1978, c. 429, p. 1415, § 157.3, eff. July 17, 1978, operative July 1, 1978; Stats. 1979, c. 72, p. 180, § 23.)*

§ 147.1. Division of occupational safety and health; development and promulgation of standards; powers and duties

In connection with the development and promulgation of occupational health standards the Division of Occupational Safety and Health shall perform all of the following functions:

(a) Analyze proposed and new federal occupational health standards, evaluate their impact on California, determine any necessity for their modification, and present proposed standards to the board in sufficient time for the board to conduct hearings and adopt standards within the time required.

(b) Maintain liaison with the National Institute of Occupational Safety and Health and the federal Occupational Safety and Health Administration in the development of recommended federal standards and when appropriate provide representation on federal advisory committees dealing with the development of occupational health standards.

(c) On occupational health issues not covered by federal standards maintain surveillance, determine the necessity for standards, develop and present proposed standards to the board.

(d) Evaluate any proposed occupational health standard or application for a variance of an occupational health standard received by the board, and submit a report to the board on the proposed standard or variance within 60 days of receipt thereof.

(e) Appear and testify at board hearings and other public proceedings involving occupational health matters. *(Added by Stats.1973, c. 993, p. 1924, § 32, eff. Oct. 1, 1973. Amended by Stats.1978, c. 429, p. 1415, § 157.4, eff. July 17, 1978, operative July 1, 1978; Stats.1979, c. 72, p. 180, § 24.)*

§ 147.2. Toxic materials and harmful physical agents; data repository; function; reports

In accordance with Chapter 2 (commencing with Section 6350) of Part 1 of Division 5 of this code and Section 105175 of the Health and Safety Code, the Department of Industrial Relations shall, by interagency agreement with the State Department of Health Services, establish a repository of current data on toxic materials and harmful physical agents in use or potentially in use in places of employment in the state.

The repository shall fulfill all of the following functions:

(1) Provide reliable information of practical use to employers, employees, representatives of employees, and other governmental agencies on the possible hazards to employees of exposure to toxic materials or harmful physical agents.

(2) Collect and evaluate toxicological and epidemiological data and any other information that may be pertinent to establishing harmful effects on health of exposure to toxic materials or harmful physical agents. Nothing in this subdivision shall be construed as authorizing the repository to require employers to report any information not otherwise required by law.

(3) Recommend to the Chief of the Division of Occupational Safety and Health Administration that an occupational safety and health standard be developed whenever it has been determined that a substance in use or potentially in use in places of employment is potentially toxic at the concentrations or under the conditions used.

(4) Notify the Director of Food and Agriculture of any information developed by the repository that is relevant to carrying out his or her responsibilities under Chapters 2 (commencing with Section 12751) and 3 (commencing with Section 14001) of Division 7 of the Food and Agricultural Code.

The Director of Industrial Relations shall appoint an Advisory Committee to the repository. The Advisory Committee shall consist of four representatives from labor, four representatives from management, four active practitioners in the occupational health field, and three persons knowledgeable in biomedical statistics or information storage and retrieval systems. The Advisory Committee shall meet on a regular basis at the request of the director. The committee shall be consulted by, and shall advise the director at each phase of the structuring and functioning of the repository and alert system with regard to, the procedures, methodology, validity, and practical utility of collecting, evaluating, and disseminating information concerning hazardous substances, consistent with the primary goals and objectives of the repository.

Nothing in this section shall be construed to limit the ability of the State Department of Health Services to propose occupational safety and health standards to the Occupational Safety and Health Standards Board.

Policies and procedures shall be developed to assure, to the extent possible, that the repository uses and does not duplicate the resources of the federal government and other states.

On or before December 31 of each year, the Department of Industrial Relations shall submit a report to the Legislature detailing the implementation and operation of the repository including, but not limited to, the amount and source of funds allocated and spent on repository activities, the toxic materials and harmful physical agents investigated during the past year and recommendations made concerning them, actions taken to inform interested persons of the possible hazards of exposure to toxic materials and harmful physical agents, and any recommendations for legislative changes relating to the functions of the repository. *(Added by Stats.1978, c. 1244, p. 4055, § 1. Amended by Stats.1996, c. 1023 (S.B.1497), § 379, eff. Sept. 29, 1996.)*

CHAPTER 6.5. OCCUPATIONAL SAFETY AND HEALTH APPEALS BOARD

Section
148. Members; chairman; salary.
148.1. Term of office.
148.2. Personnel.
148.4. Decisions and orders.
148.5. Finality of decision.
148.6. Binding effect of decision; right to judicial review.
148.7. Rules of practice and procedure.
148.8. Powers of head of department.
148.9. Decisions by majority.
149. Executive officer as deputy member; delegation of authority and duties.
149.5. Costs, award, rules of practice and procedure; payment.

§ 148. Members; chairman; salary

(a) There is in the Department of Industrial Relations the Occupational Safety and Health Appeals Board, consisting of three members appointed by the Governor, subject to the approval of the Senate. One member shall be from the field of management, one shall be from the field of labor and one member shall be from the general public. The public member shall be chosen from other than the fields of management and labor. Each member of the appeals board shall devote his full time to the performance of his duties.

(b) The chairman and each member of the appeals board shall receive the annual salary provided for by Chapter 6 (commencing with Section 11550) of Part 1 of Division 3 of Title 2 of the Government Code.

(c) The Governor shall designate the chairman of the appeals board from the membership of the appeals board. The person so designated shall hold the office of chairman at the pleasure of the Governor. The chairman shall designate a member of the appeals board to act as chairman in his absence. *(Added by Stats.1973, c. 993, p. 1925, § 33, eff. Oct. 1, 1973.)*

§ 148.1. Term of office

Each member of the appeals board shall serve for a term of four years and until his successor is appointed and qualifies. The terms of the first three members appointed to the appeals board shall expire on the second, third, and fourth January 15th following the date of the appointment of the first appointed member. A vacancy shall be filled by the Governor, subject to the approval of the Senate by appointment for the unexpired term. *(Added by Stats.1973, c. 993, p. 1925, § 33, eff. Oct. 1, 1973.)*

§ 148.2. Personnel

The appeals board may employ necessary assistants, officers, experts, hearing officers, and such other employees as it deems necessary. All such personnel of the appeals board shall be under the supervision of the chairman of the appeals board or an executive officer to whom the chairman delegates such responsibility. All such personnel shall be appointed pursuant to the State Civil Service Act (Part 2 (commencing with Section 18500) of Division 5 of Title 2 of the Government Code), except for the one exempt deputy or employee allowed by subdivision (e) of Section 4 of Article XXIV of the California Constitution[1]. The salaries of the hearing officers shall be fixed by the State Personnel Board at a rate comparable to that of other referees or hearing officers in state service whose duties and responsibilities are comparable, without regard to whether such other positions have membership in the State Bar of California as a prerequisite to appointment. *(Added by Stats.1973, c. 993, p. 1925, § 33, eff. Oct. 1, 1973.)*

[1] Repealed.

§ 148.4. Decisions and orders

All decisions and orders of the appeals board shall be in writing. *(Added by Stats.1973, c. 993, p. 1925, § 33, eff. Oct. 1, 1973.)*

§ 148.5. Finality of decision

A decision of the appeals board is final, except for any rehearing or judicial review as permitted by Chapter 4 (commencing with Section 6600) of Part 1 of Division 5. *(Added by Stats.1973, c. 993, p. 1925, § 33, eff. Oct. 1, 1973.)*

§ 148.6. Binding effect of decision; right to judicial review

A decision of the appeals board is binding on the director and the Division of Occupational Safety and Health with respect to the parties involved in the particular appeal. The director shall have the right to seek judicial review of an appeals board decision irrespective of whether or not he or she appeared or participated in the appeal to the appeals board or its hearing officer. *(Added by Stats.1973, c. 993, p. 1926, § 33, eff. Oct. 1, 1973. Amended by Stats.1989, c. 1360, § 101.)*

§ 148.7. Rules of practice and procedure

The appeals board, acting as a whole, may adopt, amend, or repeal rules of practice and procedure pertaining to hearing appeals and other matters falling within its jurisdiction. All such rules, amendments thereto, or repeals thereof shall be made in accordance with the provisions of Chapter 3.5 (commencing with Section 11340) of Part 1 of Division 3 of Title 2 of the Government Code. *(Added by Stats.1973, c. 993, p. 1926,*

§ 33, eff. Oct. 1, 1973. Amended by Stats.1982, c. 454, p. 1876, § 130.)*

§ 148.8. Powers of head of department

The appeals board and its duly authorized representatives in the performance of its duties shall have the powers of a head of a department as set forth in Article 2 (commencing with Section 11180) of Chapter 2 of Part 1 of Division 3 of Title 2 of the Government Code, except for Section 11185 of the Government Code. *(Added by Stats.1973, c. 993, p. 1926, § 33, eff. Oct. 1, 1973.)*

§ 148.9. Decisions by majority

Decisions of the appeals board shall be made by a majority of the appeals board, except as otherwise expressly provided. *(Added by Stats.1973, c. 993, p. 1926, § 33, eff. Oct. 1, 1973.)*

§ 149. Executive officer as deputy member; delegation of authority and duties

The chairman of the appeals board may authorize its executive officer to act as deputy appeals board member, and may delegate authority and duties to the executive officer in the event of the absence of a member of the appeals board. *(Added by Stats.1973, c. 993, p. 1926, § 33, eff. Oct. 1, 1973.)*

§ 149.5. Costs; award; rules of practice and procedure; payment

The appeals board may award reasonable costs, including attorney's fees, consultant's fees, and witness' fees, not to exceed five thousand dollars ($5,000) in the aggregate, to any employer who appeals a citation resulting from an inspection or investigation conducted on or after January 1, 1980, issued for violation of an occupational safety and health standard, rule, order, or regulation established pursuant to Chapter 6 (commencing with Section 140) of Division 1, if (1) either the employer prevails in the appeal, or the citation is withdrawn, and (2) the appeals board finds that the issuance of the citation was the result of arbitrary or capricious action or conduct by the division.

The appeals board shall adopt rules of practice and procedure to implement this section.

The payment of costs pursuant to this section shall be from funds in the regular operating budget of the division. The division shall show in its proposed budget for each fiscal year the following information with respect to the prior fiscal year:

(a) The total costs paid.

(b) The number of cases in which costs were paid. *(Added by Stats.1979, c. 1077, p. 3854, § 1.)*

CHAPTER 7. DIVISION OF LABOR STATISTICS AND RESEARCH

Section
150. Duties; performance of department statistical functions.

Section
151. Annual survey of ethnic derivation; data gathering; limitation.
152. Powers and duties.
153. Names of informants in reports; misdemeanor.
156. Annual report.

§ 150. Duties; performance of department statistical functions

The Division of Labor Statistics and Research, hereafter in this chapter referred to as the division, shall collect, compile and present facts and statistics relating to the condition of labor in the state, including information as to cost of living, labor supply and demand, industrial relations, industrial disputes, industrial accidents and safety, labor productivity, sanitary and other conditions, prison labor, and such other matters in relation to labor as the Director of Industrial Relations deems desirable. Except for statistics relating to internal administration, all statistical functions of the department shall be performed by the division. *(Added by Stats.1945, c. 1431, p. 2689, § 29. Amended by Stats.1973, c. 845, p. 1511, § 1.)*

§ 151. Annual survey of ethnic derivation; data gathering; limitation

The division shall conduct an annual survey of the ethnic derivation of the individuals who are parties to apprentice agreements described in Section 3077 of this code. In conducting this survey, the division shall use any pertinent data which the federal government may provide to avoid duplication of effort.

The Division of Apprenticeship Standards shall cooperate in the accomplishment of the survey required by this section as the division may request. The occasion of this survey may be used to gather such additional current data as may be of benefit to apprenticeship programs.

Data gathered pursuant to this section shall not be evidence per se of an unlawful employment practice.

Nothing in this section shall be construed to authorize any state agency to require an employer to employ a specified percentage of individuals of any particular ethnic derivation irrespective of such individuals' qualifications for employment. *(Added by Stats.1967, c. 1592, p. 3818, § 2, eff. Aug. 30, 1967.)*

§ 152. Powers and duties

The Chief of the Division of Labor Statistics and Research and employees of the division authorized by him may issue subpoenas to compel the attendance of witnesses and production of books, papers and records; administer oaths; examine witnesses under oath; take the verification or proof of written instruments; and take depositions and affidavits for the purpose of carrying out the provisions of this code and performing the duties which the division is required to perform. They shall have free access to all places of labor. Any person, or agent or officer thereof, who willfully neglects or refuses to furnish statistics requested by the division, which are in his possession, or under his control, or who refuses to admit the chief or his authorized employee to a place of labor, is guilty of a misdemeanor. The Director of Industrial Relations may direct the chief and the employees of other divisions of the department to transmit to the Division of Labor Statistics and Research any statistical information in their possession, or to conduct investigations and otherwise assist the Division of Labor Statistics and Research in the gathering of whatever statistics the director deems desirable. *(Formerly § 151, added by Stats.1945, c. 1431, p. 2689, § 29. Renumbered § 152 and amended by Stats.1967, c. 1592, p. 3818, § 1, eff. Aug. 30, 1967.)*

§ 153. Names of informants in reports; misdemeanor

Except as provided in Section 151 no use shall be made in the reports of the division of the names of persons supplying the information required under this code. Any agent or employee of the division who violates this section is guilty of a misdemeanor. *(Formerly § 152, added by Stats.1945, c. 1431, p. 2689, § 29. Renumbered § 153 and amended by Stats.1967, c. 1592, p. 3819, § 3, eff. Aug. 30, 1967.)*

§ 156. Annual report

An annual report containing statistics on California work injuries and occupational diseases and fatalities by industry classifications shall be completed and published by the Division of Labor Statistics and Research no later than December 31 of the following calendar year. All of the reports and statistics shall be available to the public. *(Added by Stats.1973, c. 993, p. 1926, § 35, eff. Oct. 1, 1973. Amended by Stats.1992, c. 386 (S.B.1976), § 2.)*

CHAPTER 7.5. DIVISION OF OCCUPATIONAL SAFETY AND HEALTH

Section
175. Liquefied petroleum gas storage facilities; lead agency; jurisdiction.
176. Legislative findings and declarations concerning the Dymally-Alatorre Bilingual Services Act; definitions; progress report.

§ 175. Liquefied petroleum gas storage facilities; lead agency; jurisdiction

The Division of Occupational Safety and Health shall be the lead agency in providing for public health and safety as well as worker health and safety in the construction, maintenance, and operation of any liquefied petroleum gas storage facility, other than a facility owned or maintained by a public utility, having a capacity of 100,000 barrels or more, including storage vessels, and related piping, pumping, distribution, and transfer apparatus. As the lead agency, the division shall request any state or local agency having statutory public health and safety jurisdiction over any part of the construction, maintenance, or operation of any such liquefied petroleum gas storage facility, other than a facility owned or maintained by a public utility, to exercise its statutory jurisdiction in relation to such facility, and shall report to the Legislature any instance in which such jurisdiction was not exercised. *(Added by Stats.1978, c. 976, p. 3041, § 1. Amended by Stats.1980, c. 676, p. 1966, § 212.)*

§ 176. Legislative findings and declarations concerning the Dymally-Alatorre Bilingual Services Act; definitions; progress report

(a) The Legislature hereby finds and declares that the Dymally–Alatorre Bilingual Services Act, Chapter 17.5 (commencing with Section 7290) of Division 7 of Title 1 of the Government Code, was enacted in 1973 to provide for the removal of language barriers that prevent the people of this state who are not proficient in English from effectively accessing government services and otherwise communicating with their government.

The Legislature further finds and declares that limited-English-proficient individuals will benefit from increased language-based access to the programs and services of the Division of Occupational Safety and Health.

The Legislature further finds and declares that federal statistics show that from 1996 to 2000, while overall worker fatalities dropped 14 percent, immigrant worker fatalities rose 17 percent. Immigrant workers die on the job at higher rates because they frequently work in more dangerous industries with little or no training. Language barriers compound the problem because training and warning signs are often only in English.

(b) As used in this section, a "public contact position" means any position responsible for responding to telephone or in-office inquiries or taking complaints from the general public regarding matters pertaining to occupational safety and health.

(c) As used in the section, an "investigative position" means any position responsible for investigating complaints, injuries, or deaths related to occupational safety and health.

(d) As used in this section, "limited-English-proficient" refers to persons who speak English less than "very well," in accordance with United States Census data.

(e) The division shall make all efforts to ensure that limited-English-proficient persons can communicate effectively with the division. Examples of potential measures include, but are not limited to, the hiring of bilingual persons in public contact positions and investigative positions, the use of contract based interpreters, and the use of telephone-based interpretation services. Nothing contained in this section relieves the division of its separate obligations under the Dymally–Alatorre Bilingual Services Act, Chapter 17.5 (commencing with Section 7290) of Division 7 of Title 1 of the Government Code, or any other state or federal laws requiring the provision of its services in languages other than English.

(f) On July 30, 2004, the Division of Occupational Safety and Health shall issue a progress report to the Legislature on the implementation of this section that shall, at a minimum, include all of the following:

(1) The most recent information provided to the California State Personnel Board pursuant to Section 7299.4 of the Government Code.

(2) The number of bilingual employees in public contact and investigative positions in each local office of the division and the languages they speak, other than English.

(3) A description of any centralized system or other resources for providing translation and interpretation services within the division.

(4) A description of any quality control measures or evaluations undertaken by the division to evaluate whether limited-English-proficient persons are able to communicate effectively with the division.

(5) A description of any means, such as contracted interpreters, telephone-based interpretation services, or video conferencing, used by the division to communicate with individuals who are limited-English-proficient in the event that bilingual employees in public contact or investigative positions are not available, and the frequency in which these services were used by the division during the most recent fiscal year. *(Added by Stats.2002, c. 885 (A.B.2837), § 2. Amended by Stats.2003, c. 62 (S.B.600), § 203.)*

Division 2

EMPLOYMENT REGULATION AND SUPERVISION

Part		Section
1.	Compensation	200
2.	Working Hours	510
3.	Privileges and Immunities	920
3.5.	Agricultural Labor Relations	1140
4.	Employees	1171
4.5	Fair Employment Practices [Repealed]	
5.	Civil Air Patrol	1500
6.	Licensing	1500
7.	Public Works and Public Agencies	1720
8.	Unemployment Relief	2010
8.5.	Car Washes	2050
8.7.	Employee Health Insurance [Rejected]	
9.	Health	2260

Part		Section
10.	Industrial Homework	2650
11.	Garment Manufacturing	2670
12.	Sheepherders	12695.1
13.	The Labor Code Private Attorneys General Act of 2004	2698

Part 1

COMPENSATION

Chapter		Section
1.	Payment of Wages	200

EMPLOYMENT REGULATION AND SUPERVISION

Chapter		Section
2.	Assignment of Wages	300
3.	Privileges and Perquisites	350

CHAPTER 1. PAYMENT OF WAGES

Article		Section
1.	General Occupations.........................	200
2.	Seasonal Labor	250
3.	Special Occupations	270

ARTICLE 1. GENERAL OCCUPATIONS

Section

200.   Definitions.
201.   Immediate payment of wages upon discharge or layoff; treatment of related benefits.
201.3. Temporary services employers; definitions; time for payment of employee wages; penalties.
201.5. Employee engaged in production or broadcasting of motion pictures; termination of employment; entitlement to payment of wages by next regular payday; definitions.
201.7. Oil drilling business; layoff; payment within reasonable time.
201.9. Employees employed at venue that hosts live theatrical or concerts events; collective bargaining agreement; establishment of time limits for payment of wages after discharge or layoff.
202.   Immediate payment of wages upon resignation; treatment of related benefits.
203.   Failure to make payment within required time; penalty; employee avoiding payment; limitation of actions.
203.1. Payment of wages or fringe benefits with bad check; penalty.
203.5. Failure of bonding company to pay verified claim for wages.
204.   Semimonthly payments; exceptions.
204a.   Employees of several employers; plan for central place of payment; notice to labor commissioner.
204b.   Weekly payments.
204c.   Semimonthly payments; exception of certain executive, administrative, or professional employees.
204.1. Employees of vehicle dealers; commission wages; monthly payment.
204.2. Executive, administrative, and professional employees.
204.3. Compensating time off in lieu of overtime compensation; limits.
205.   Agricultural and domestic employment; payment periods.
205.5. Agricultural employees; payment period and dates.
206.   Payment of undisputed amount; failure to pay determined amount; treble damages.
206.5. Execution of release of claim or right on account of wages due.
207.   Posting of notice of regular pay days.
208.   Place of payment.
209.   Payment in event of strike.
210.   Civil penalty for failure to make payments; action for recovery; disposition of money recovered.
211.   Actions to recover civil penalties; fees for service of summons; joinder of causes of action; demand for payment.

Section

212.   Prohibited forms of payment; instruments protested or dishonored; effect of notice.
213.   Exceptions.
214.   Place of prosecution for illegal form of payment.
215.   Violations; misdemeanor.
216.   Refusal to make payment; false denial of amount or validity of wages; misdemeanor.
217.   Enforcement.
218.   Authority of district attorney and wage claimant.
218.5. Actions for nonpayment of wages, fringe benefits, or health and welfare or pension fund contributions; award of attorney's fees to prevailing party; application of section.
218.6. Actions for nonpayment of wages; award of interest.
219.   Payment of wages at more frequent intervals, or in greater amounts, or in full when or before due; private agreements; state employers.
220.   Public employees.
220.2. Public employees; benefits; contributions; payments by employing agencies.
221.   Repayment of wages to employer.
222.   Withholding of part of wage.
222.5. Cost of pre-employment physical examination or physical examination required by law.
223.   Payment of less than statutory or contractual wage scale.
224.   Authorized deductions.
225.   Violations; misdemeanor.
225.5. Unlawful withholding of wages; civil penalty; action for recovery; disposition of money recovered.
226.   Itemized statements; contents; records; inspection of records; compliance with inspection request; limitation of application.
226.3. Civil penalties; itemized statements by employers; inadvertent mistakes.
226.4. Citation; issuance; service; contents; itemized statement.
226.5. Hearing on citation or assessment of civil penalty; decision; service on parties; amount due; writ of mandate; payment of citation amount; judgment; interest on judgment.
226.6. Violation of §§ 226 or 226.2; persons having control or disposition of wages; penalty.
226.7. Mandated meal or rest periods; requirement to work prohibited.
227.   Health, welfare or pension fund or vacation plan; failure to make agreed payments; offense.
227.3. Vested vacation wages; payment upon termination.
227.5. Annual statement of payments to employee benefit funds.
228.   Payments to apprenticeship funds.
229.   Actions to enforce payment of wages; effect of arbitration agreements.
230.   Jury duty; legal actions by domestic violence and sexual assault victims; right to time off; reinstatement and reimbursement; misdemeanor; right to file complaint with Division of Labor Standards Enforcement.
230.1. Employers with 25 or more employees; domestic violence and sexual assault victims; right to time off.
230.2. Victims of crime; work absences for judicial proceedings; covered employees.
230.3. Volunteer firefighter; reserve peace officer; emergency rescue personnel; time off; discrimination.
230.4. Volunteer firefighter; leaves of absence for training.

Section

230.7. Discharge or discrimination against employee for taking time off to appear in school on behalf of child.

230.8. Discharge of or discrimination against employee for taking time off to visit child's school or day care facility; use of vacation, personal leave, compensatory time off or time off without pay; documentation of participation; reinstatement and reimbursement.

231. Physical examination for driver's license required in employment; payment of costs.

232. Amount of wages; prohibition of sanctions against employee disclosure.

232.5. Working conditions; prohibition of sanctions against employee disclosure.

233. Sick leave; use to attend to illness in family.

234. Sick leave to attend to illness in family; employer absence control policy; legal and equitable relief.

240. Deposit of bond by employer; violation of article or judgment for nonpayment of wages; injunction.

243. Second offense by employer; temporary restraining order against doing business; bond; third offense; trial date; labor commissioner duties.

§ 200. Definitions

As used in this article: (a) "Wages" includes all amounts for labor performed by employees of every description, whether the amount is fixed or ascertained by the standard of time, task, piece, commission basis, or other method of calculation.

(b) "Labor" includes labor, work, or service whether rendered or performed under contract, subcontract, partnership, station plan, or other agreement if the labor to be paid for is performed personally by the person demanding payment. *(Stats.1937, c. 90, p. 197, § 200.)*

§ 201. Immediate payment of wages upon discharge or layoff; treatment of related benefits

(a) If an employer discharges an employee, the wages earned and unpaid at the time of discharge are due and payable immediately. An employer who lays off a group of employees by reason of the termination of seasonal employment in the curing, canning, or drying of any variety of perishable fruit, fish or vegetables, shall be deemed to have made immediate payment when the wages of said employees are paid within a reasonable time as necessary for computation and payment thereof; provided, however, that the reasonable time shall not exceed 72 hours, and further provided that payment shall be made by mail to any employee who so requests and designates a mailing address therefor.

(b) Notwithstanding any other provision of law, the state employer shall be deemed to have made an immediate payment of wages under this section for any unused or accumulated vacation, annual leave, holiday leave, or time off to which the employee is entitled by reason of previous overtime work where compensating time off was given by the appointing power, provided, at least five workdays prior to his or her final day of employment, the employee submits a written election to his or her appointing power authorizing the state employer to tender payment for any or all leave to be contributed on a pretax basis to the employee's account in a state-sponsored supplemental retirement plan as described under Sections 401(k), 403(b), or 457 of the Internal Revenue Code provided the plan allows those contributions. The contribution shall be tendered for payment to the employee's 401(k), 403(b), or 457 plan account no later than 45 days after the employee's discharge from employment. Nothing in this section is intended to authorize contributions in excess of the annual deferral limits imposed under federal and state law or the provisions of the supplemental retirement plan itself.

(c) Notwithstanding any other provision of law, when the state employer discharges an employee, the employee may, at least five workdays prior to his or her final day of employment, submit a written election to his or her appointing power authorizing the state employer to defer into the next calendar year payment of any or all of the employee's unused or accumulated vacation, annual leave, holiday leave, or time off to which the employee is entitled by reason of previous overtime work where compensating time off was given by the appointing power. To qualify for the deferral of payment under this section, only that portion of leave that extends past the November pay period for state employees shall be deferred into the next calendar year. An employee electing to defer payment into the next calendar year under this section may do any of the following:

(1) Contribute the entire payment to his or her 401(k), 403(b), or 457 plan account.

(2) Contribute any portion of the deferred payment to his or her 401(k), 403(b), or 457 plan account and receive cash payment for the remaining noncontributed unused leave.

(3) Receive a lump-sum payment for all of the deferred unused leave as described above.

Payments shall be tendered under this section no later than February 1 in the year following the employee's last day of employment. Nothing in this section is intended to authorize contributions in excess of the annual deferral limits imposed under federal and state law or the provisions of the supplemental retirement plan itself. *(Stats.1937, c. 90, p. 197, § 201. Amended by Stats.1947, c. 769, p. 1849, § 1; Stats.2002, c. 40 (A.B.1684), § 6, eff. May 16, 2002.)*

§ 201.3. Temporary services employers; definitions; time for payment of employee wages; penalties

(a) For purposes of this section, the following definitions apply:

(1) "Temporary services employer" means an employing unit that contracts with clients or customers to supply workers to perform services for the clients or customers and that performs all of the following functions:

(A) Negotiates with clients and customers for matters such as the time and place where the services are to be

320

provided, the type of work, the working conditions, and the quality and price of the services.

(B) Determines assignments or reassignments of workers, even if workers retain the right to refuse specific assignments.

(C) Retains the authority to assign or reassign a worker to another client or customer when the worker is determined unacceptable by a specific client or customer.

(D) Assigns or reassigns workers to perform services for clients or customers.

(E) Sets the rate of pay of workers, whether or not through negotiation.

(F) Pays workers from its own account or accounts.

(G) Retains the right to hire and terminate workers.

(2) "Temporary services employer" does not include any of the following:

(A) A bona fide nonprofit organization that provides temporary service employees to clients.

(B) A farm labor contractor, as defined in subdivision (b) of Section 1682.

(C) A garment manufacturing employer, which, for purposes of this section, has the same meaning as "contractor," as defined in subdivision (d) of Section 2671.

(3) "Employing unit" has the same meaning as defined in Section 135 of the Unemployment Insurance Code.

(4) "Client" and "customer" means the person with whom a temporary services employer has a contractual relationship to provide the services of one or more individuals employed by the temporary services employer.

(b)(1) Except as provided in paragraphs (2) to (5), inclusive, if an employee of a temporary services employer is assigned to work for a client, that employee's wages are due and payable no less frequently than weekly, regardless of when the assignment ends, and wages for work performed during any calendar week shall be due and payable not later than the regular payday of the following calendar week. A temporary services employer shall be deemed to have timely paid wages upon completion of an assignment if wages are paid in compliance with this subdivision.

(2) If an employee of a temporary services employer is assigned to work for a client on a day-to-day basis, that employee's wages are due and payable at the end of each day, regardless of when the assignment ends, if each of the following occurs:

(A) The employee reports to or assembles at the office of the temporary services employer or other location.

(B) The employee is dispatched to a client's worksite each day and returns to or reports to the office of the temporary services employer or other location upon completion of the assignment.

(C) The employee's work is not executive, administrative, or professional, as defined in the wage orders of the Industrial Welfare Commission, and is not clerical.

(3) If an employee of a temporary services employer is assigned to work for a client engaged in a trade dispute, that employee's wages are due and payable at the end of each day, regardless of when the assignment ends.

(4) If an employee of a temporary services employer is assigned to work for a client and is discharged by the temporary services employer or leasing employer, wages are due and payable as provided in Section 201.

(5) If an employee of a temporary services employer is assigned to work for a client and quits his or her employment with the temporary services employer, wages are due and payable as provided in Section 202.

(6) If an employee of a temporary services employer is assigned to work for a client for over 90 consecutive calendar days, this section shall not apply unless the temporary services employer pays the employee weekly in compliance with paragraph (1) of subdivision (b).

(c) A temporary services employer who violates this section shall be subject to the civil penalties provided for in Section 203, and to any other penalties available at law.

(d) Nothing in this section shall be interpreted to limit any rights or remedies otherwise available under state or federal law. *(Added by Stats.2008, c. 169 (S.B.940), § 1.)*

§ 201.5. Employee engaged in production or broadcasting of motion pictures; termination of employment; entitlement to payment of wages by next regular payday; definitions

(a) For purposes of this section, the following definitions apply:

(1) "An employee engaged in the production or broadcasting of motion pictures" means an employee to whom both of the following apply:

(A) The employee's job duties relate to or support the production or broadcasting of motion pictures or the facilities or equipment used in the production or broadcasting of motion pictures.

(B) The employee is hired for a period of limited duration to render services relating to or supporting a particular motion picture production or broadcasting project, or is hired on the basis of one or more daily or weekly calls.

(2) "Daily or weekly call" means an employment that, by its terms, will expire at the conclusion of one day or one week, unless renewed.

(3) "Next regular payday" means the day designated by the employer, pursuant to Section 204, for payment of wages earned during the payroll period in which the termination occurs.

(4) "Production or broadcasting of motion pictures" means the development, creation, presentation, or broadcasting of theatrical or televised motion pictures, television programs, commercial advertisements, music videos,

321

or any other moving images, including, but not limited to, productions made for entertainment, commercial, religious, or educational purposes, whether these productions are presented by means of film, tape, live broadcast, cable, satellite transmission, Web cast, or any other technology that is now in use or may be adopted in the future.

(b) An employee engaged in the production or broadcasting of motion pictures whose employment terminates is entitled to receive payment of the wages earned and unpaid at the time of the termination by the next regular payday.

(c) The payment of wages to employees covered by this section may be mailed to the employee or made available to the employee at a location specified by the employer in the county where the employee was hired or performed labor. The payment shall be deemed to have been made on the date that the employee's wages are mailed to the employee or made available to the employee at the location specified by the employer, whichever is earlier.

(d) For purposes of this section, an employment terminates when the employment relationship ends, whether by discharge, lay off, resignation, completion of employment for a specified term, or otherwise.

(e) Nothing in this section prohibits the parties to a valid collective bargaining agreement from establishing alternative provisions for final payment of wages to employees covered by this section if those provisions do not exceed the time limitation established in Section 204. *(Added by Stats.2006, c. 824 (A.B.3051), § 2.)*

§ 201.7. Oil drilling business; layoff; payment within reasonable time

An employer who lays off an employee or a group of employees engaged in the business of oil drilling shall be deemed to have made immediate payment within the meaning of Section 201 if the wages of such employees are paid within such reasonable time as may be necessary for computation or payment thereof; provided, however, that such reasonable time shall not exceed 24 hours after discharge excluding Saturdays, Sundays, and holidays; and provided further, such payment may be mailed and the date of mailing is the date of payment.

The Legislature finds and determines that special provision must be made for the payment of wages on discharge of employees engaged in oil drilling because their employment at various locations is often far removed from the employer's principal administrative offices, which makes the computation and payment of wages on an immediate basis unduly burdensome. *(Added by Stats.1980, c. 440, p. 925, § 1.)*

§ 201.9. Employees employed at venue that hosts live theatrical or concerts events; collective bargaining agreement; establishment of time limits for payment of wages after discharge or layoff

Notwithstanding subdivision (a) of Section 201, if employees are employed at a venue that hosts live theatrical or concert events and are enrolled in and routinely dispatched to employment through a hiring hall or other system of regular short-term employment established in accordance with a bona fide collective bargaining agreement, these employees and their employers may establish by express terms in their collective bargaining agreement the time limits for payment of wages to an employee who is discharged or laid off. *(Added by Stats.2006, c. 685 (S.B.1719), § 1.)*

§ 202. Immediate payment of wages upon resignation; treatment of related benefits

(a) If an employee not having a written contract for a definite period quits his or her employment, his or her wages shall become due and payable not later than 72 hours thereafter, unless the employee has given 72 hours previous notice of his or her intention to quit, in which case the employee is entitled to his or her wages at the time of quitting. Notwithstanding any other provision of law, an employee who quits without providing a 72–hour notice shall be entitled to receive payment by mail if he or she so requests and designates a mailing address. The date of the mailing shall constitute the date of payment for purposes of the requirement to provide payment within 72 hours of the notice of quitting.

(b) Notwithstanding any other provision of law, the state employer shall be deemed to have made an immediate payment of wages under this section for any unused or accumulated vacation, annual leave, holiday leave, sick leave to which the employee is otherwise entitled due to a disability retirement, or time off to which the employee is entitled by reason of previous overtime work where compensating time off was given by the appointing power, provided at least five workdays prior to his or her final day of employment, the employee submits a written election to his or her appointing power authorizing the state employer to tender payment for any or all leave to be contributed on a pretax basis to the employee's account in a state-sponsored supplemental retirement plan as described under Sections 401(k), 403(b), or 457 of the Internal Revenue Code provided the plan allows those contributions. The contribution shall be tendered for payment to the employee's 401(k), 403(b), or 457 plan account no later than 45 days after the employee's last day of employment. Nothing in this section is intended to authorize contributions in excess of the annual deferral limits imposed under federal and state law or the provisions of the supplemental retirement plan itself.

(c) Notwithstanding any other provision of law, when a state employee quits, retires, or disability retires from his or her employment with the state, the employee may, at least five workdays prior to his or her final day of employment, submit a written election to his or her appointing power authorizing the state employer to defer into the next calendar year payment of any or all of the employee's unused or accumulated vacation, annual leave, holiday leave, sick leave to which the employee is otherwise entitled due to a disability, retirement, or time off to which the employee is entitled by reason of previous overtime work where compensating time off was given by the appointing power. To qualify for the deferral of payment under this section, only that portion of leave that extends past the November pay period for state employees shall be deferred into the next calendar year under this section may do any of the following:

(1) Contribute the entire payment to his or her 401(k), 403(b), or 457 plan account.

(2) Contribute any portion of the deferred payment to his or her 401(k), 403(b), or 457 plan account and receive cash payment for the remaining noncontributed unused leave.

(3) Receive a lump-sum payment for all of the deferred unused leave as described above.

Payments shall be tendered under this section no later than February 1 in the year following the employee's last day of employment. Nothing in this section is intended to authorize contributions in excess of the annual deferral limits imposed under federal and state law or the provisions of the supplemental retirement plan itself. *(Stats.1937, c. 90, p. 197, § 202. Amended by Stats.1990, c. 440 (S.B.2109), § 1; Stats.2002, c. 40 (A.B.1684), § 7, eff. May 16, 2002.)*

§ 203. Failure to make payment within required time; penalty; employee avoiding payment; limitation of actions

(a) If an employer willfully fails to pay, without abatement or reduction, in accordance with Sections 201, 201.3, 201.5, 202, and 205.5, any wages of an employee who is discharged or who quits, the wages of the employee shall continue as a penalty from the due date thereof at the same rate until paid or until an action therefor is commenced; but the wages shall not continue for more than 30 days. An employee who secretes or absents himself or herself to avoid payment to him or her, or who refuses to receive the payment when fully tendered to him or her, including any penalty then accrued under this section, is not entitled to any benefit under this section for the time during which he or she so avoids payment.

(b) Suit may be filed for these penalties at any time before the expiration of the statute of limitations on an action for the wages from which the penalties arise. *(Stats.1937, c. 90, p. 197, § 203. Amended by Stats.1939, c. 1096, p. 3026, § 1; Stats.1975, c. 43, p. 75, § 1; Stats.1997, c. 92 (S.B.1071), § 1; Stats.2008, c. 169 (S.B.940), § 2.)*

§ 203.1. Payment of wages or fringe benefits with bad check; penalty

If an employer pays an employee in the regular course of employment or in accordance with Section 201, 201.3, 201.5, 201.7, or 202 any wages or fringe benefits, or both, by check, draft or voucher, which check, draft or voucher is subsequently refused payment because the employer or maker has no account with the bank, institution, or person on which the instrument is drawn, or has insuffi-

cient funds in the account upon which the instrument is drawn at the time of its presentation, so long as the same is presented within 30 days of receipt by the employee of the check, draft or voucher, those wages or fringe benefits, or both, shall continue as a penalty from the due date thereof at the same rate until paid or until an action therefor is commenced. However, those wages and fringe benefits shall not continue for more than 30 days and this penalty shall not apply if the employer can establish to the satisfaction of the Labor Commissioner or an appropriate court of law that the violation of this section was unintentional. This penalty also shall not apply in any case in which an employee recovers the service charge authorized by Section 1719 of the Civil Code in an action brought by the employee thereunder. *(Added by Stats.1963, c. 846, p. 2072, § 1. Amended by Stats.2000, c. 876 (A.B.2509), § 3; Stats.2008, c. 169 (S.B.940), § 3.)*

§ 203.5. Failure of bonding company to pay verified claim for wages

(a) If a bonding company issuing a bond which secures the payment of wages for labor or the surety on a bond willfully fails to pay, without abatement or reduction, any verified claim made for wages found to be due and payable, the claim for wages shall continue as a penalty against the bonding company or surety from the date on which demand for payment was made at the same rate until paid as the wages upon which the claim is based, except that the claim shall not continue as a penalty for more than 30 days.

(b) This section shall not apply to contractor's bonds required pursuant to Section 7071.6 of the Business and Professions Code. *(Added by Stats.1965, c. 638, p. 1984, § 1. Amended by Stats.1975, c. 321, p. 769, § 1; Stats. 1989, c. 1281, § 1.)*

§ 204. Semimonthly payments; exceptions

(a) All wages, other than those mentioned in Section 201, 201.3, 202, 204.1, or 204.2, earned by any person in any employment are due and payable twice during each calendar month, on days designated in advance by the employer as the regular paydays. Labor performed between the 1st and 15th days, inclusive, of any calendar month shall be paid for between the 16th and the 26th day of the month during which the labor was performed, and labor performed between the 16th and the last day, inclusive, of any calendar month, shall be paid for between the 1st and 10th day of the following month. However, salaries of executive, administrative, and professional employees of employers covered by the Fair Labor Standards Act, as set forth pursuant to Section 13(a)(1) of the Fair Labor Standards Act, as amended through March 1, 1969, in Part 541 of Title 29 of the Code of Federal Regulations, as that part now reads or may be amended to read at any time hereafter, may be paid once a month on or before the 26th day of the month during which the labor was performed if the entire month's salaries, including the unearned portion between

323

the date of payment and the last day of the month, are paid at that time.

(b)(1) Notwithstanding any other provision of this section, all wages earned for labor in excess of the normal work period shall be paid no later than the payday for the next regular payroll period.

(2) An employer is in compliance with the requirements of subdivision (a) of Section 226 relating to total hours worked by the employee, if hours worked in excess of the normal work period during the current pay period are itemized as corrections on the paystub for the next regular pay period. Any corrections set out in a subsequently issued paystub shall state the inclusive dates of the pay period for which the employer is correcting its initial report of hours worked.

(c) However, when employees are covered by a collective bargaining agreement that provides different pay arrangements, those arrangements shall apply to the covered employees.

(d) The requirements of this section shall be deemed satisfied by the payment of wages for weekly, biweekly, or semimonthly payroll if the wages are paid not more than seven calendar days following the close of the payroll period. *(Stats.1937, c. 90, p. 197, § 204. Amended by Stats.1967, c. 1170, p. 2859, § 1; Stats.1969, c. 599, p. 1229, § 1; Stats.1970, c. 1237, p. 2225, § 3; Stats.1970, c. 1260, p. 2279, § 2; Stats.1985, c. 785, § 1; Stats.1989, c. 469, § 1; Stats.2006, c. 737 (A.B.2095), § 2; Stats.2008, c. 169 (S.B.940), § 4.)*

§ 204a. Employees of several employers; plan for central place of payment; notice to labor commissioner

When workers are engaged in an employment that normally involves working for several employers in the same industry interchangeably, and the several employers, or some of them, cooperate to establish a plan for the payment of wages at a central place or places and in accordance with a unified schedule of pay days, all the provisions of this chapter except 201, 202, and 208 shall apply. All such workers, including those who have been discharged and those who quit, shall receive their wages at such central place or places.

This section shall not apply to any such plan until 10 days after notice of their intention to set up such a plan shall have been given to the Labor Commissioner by the employers who cooperate to establish the plan. Having once been established, no such plan can be abandoned except after notice of their intention to abandon such plan has been given to the Labor Commissioner by the employers intending to abandon the plan. *(Added by Stats.1941, c. 11, p. 422, § 1, eff. Jan. 30, 1941.)*

§ 204b. Weekly payments

Section 204 shall be inapplicable to employees paid on a weekly basis on a regular day designated by the employer in advance of the rendition of services as the regular payday.

Labor performed by a weekly-paid employee during any calendar week and prior to or on the regular payday shall be paid for not later than the regular payday of the employer for such weekly-paid employee falling during the following calendar week.

Labor performed by a weekly-paid employee during any calendar week and subsequent to the regular payday shall be paid for not later than seven days after the regular payday of the employer for such weekly-paid employee falling during the following calendar week. *(Added by Stats.1959, c. 1564, p. 3898, § 1.)*

§ 204c. Semimonthly payments; exception of certain executive, administrative, or professional employees

Section 204 shall be inapplicable to executive, administrative or professional employees who are not covered by any collective bargaining agreement, who are not subject to the Fair Labor Standards Act,[1] whose monthly remuneration does not include overtime pay, and who are paid within seven days of the close of their monthly payroll period. *(Added by Stats.1971, c. 343, p. 682, § 1.)*

[1] 29 U.S.C.A. § 201 et seq.

§ 204.1. Employees of vehicle dealers; commission wages; monthly payment

Commission wages paid to any person employed by an employer licensed as a vehicle dealer by the Department of Motor Vehicles are due and payable once during each calendar month on a day designated in advance by the employer as the regular payday. Commission wages are compensation paid to any person for services rendered in the sale of such employer's property or services and based proportionately upon the amount or value thereof.

The provisions of this section shall not apply if there exists a collective bargaining agreement between the employer and his employees which provides for the date on which wages shall be paid. *(Added by Stats.1967, c. 1170, p. 2859, § 2.)*

§ 204.2. Executive, administrative, and professional employees

Salaries of executive, administrative, and professional employees of employers covered by the Fair Labor Standards Act,[1] as set forth pursuant to Section 13(a)(1) of the Fair Labor Standards Act of 1938, as amended through March 1, 1969, (Title 29, Section 213(a)(1), United States Code) in Part 541 of Title 29 of the Code of Federal Regulations, as that part now reads, earned for labor performed in excess of 40 hours in a calendar week are due and payable on or before the 26th day of the calendar month immediately following the month in which such labor was performed. However, when such employees are covered by a collective bargaining agreement that provides different pay arrangements, those arrangements will apply to the covered employees. *(Added by Stats.1970, c. 1237, p. 2225, § 2.)*

[1] 29 U.S.C.A. § 201 et seq.

§ 204.3. Compensating time off in lieu of overtime compensation; limits

(a) An employee may receive, in lieu of overtime compensation, compensating time off at a rate of not less than one and one-half hours for each hour of employment for which overtime compensation is required by law. If an hour of employment would otherwise be compensable at a rate of more than one and one-half times the employee's regular rate of compensation, then the employee may receive compensating time off commensurate with the higher rate.

(b) An employer may provide compensating time off under subdivision (a) if the following four conditions are met:

(1) The compensating time off is provided pursuant to applicable provisions of a collective bargaining agreement, memorandum of understanding, or other written agreement between the employer and the duly authorized representative of the employer's employees; or, in the case of employees not covered by the aforementioned agreement or memorandum of understanding, pursuant to a written agreement entered into between the employer and employee before the performance of the work.

(2) The employee has not accrued compensating time in excess of the limit prescribed by subdivision (c).

(3) The employee has requested, in writing, compensating time off in lieu of overtime compensation.

(4) The employee is regularly scheduled to work no less than 40 hours in a workweek.

(c)(1) An employee may not accrue more than 240 hours of compensating time off. Any employee who has accrued 240 hours of compensating time off shall, for any additional overtime hours of work, be paid overtime compensation.

(2) If compensation is paid to an employee for accrued compensating time off, the compensation shall be paid at the regular rate earned by the employee at the time the employee receives payment.

(d) An employee who has accrued compensating time off authorized to be provided under subdivision (a) shall, upon termination of employment, be paid for the unused compensating time at a rate of compensation not less than the average regular rate received by the employee during the last three years of the employee's employment, or the final regular rate received by the employee, whichever is higher.

(e)(1) An employee who has accrued compensating time off authorized to be provided under subdivision (a), and who has requested the use of that compensating time, shall be permitted by the employee's employer to use the time within a reasonable period after making the request, if the use of the compensating time does not unduly disrupt the operations of the employer.

(2) Upon the request of an employee, the employer shall pay overtime compensation in cash in lieu of compensating time off for any compensating time off that has accrued for at least two pay periods.

(3) For purposes of determining whether a request to use compensating time has been granted within a reasonable period, the following factors shall be relevant:

(A) The normal schedule of work.

(B) Anticipated peak workloads based on past experience.

(C) Emergency requirements for staff and services.

(D) The availability of qualified substitute staff.

(f) Every employer shall keep records that accurately reflect compensating time earned and used.

(g) For purposes of this section, the terms "compensating time" and "compensating time off" mean hours during which an employee is not working, which are not counted as hours worked during the applicable workweek or other work period for purposes of overtime compensation, and for which the employee is compensated at the employee's regular rate.

(h) This section shall not apply to any employee exempt from the overtime provisions of the California wage orders.

(i) This section shall not apply to any employee who is subject to the following wage orders of the Industrial Welfare Commission: Orders No. 8-80, 13-80, and 14-80 (affecting industries handling products after harvest, industries preparing agricultural products for market on the farm, and agricultural occupations), Order No. 3-80 (affecting the canning, freezing, and preserving industry), Orders No. 5-89 and 10-89 (affecting the public housekeeping and amusement and recreation industries), and Order No. 1-89 (affecting the manufacturing industry). *(Added by Stats.1993, c. 544 (A.B.2092), § 1.)*

§ 205. Agricultural and domestic employment; payment periods

In agricultural, viticultural, and horticultural pursuits, in stock or poultry raising, and in household domestic service, when the employees in such employments are boarded and lodged by the employer, the wages due any employee remaining in such employment shall become due and payable once in each calendar month on a day designated in advance by the employer as the regular payday. No two successive paydays shall be more than 31 days apart, and the payment shall include all wages up to the regular payday. Notwithstanding the provisions of this section, wages of workers employed by a farm labor contractor shall be paid on payroll periods at least once every week on a business day designated in advance by the farm labor contractor. Payment on such payday shall include all wages earned up to and including the fourth day before such payday. *(Stats.1937, c. 90, p. 197, § 205. Amended by Stats.1951, c. 1746, p. 4160, § 1; Stats.1976, c. 1041, p. 4653, § 1.)*

§ 205.5. Agricultural employees; payment period and dates

All wages, other than those mentioned in Sections 201 and 202, earned by any agricultural employee, as defined in Section 1140.4, are due and payable twice during each calendar month, on days designated in advance by the agricultural employer as the regular paydays. Labor performed between the 1st and the 15th days, inclusive, of any calendar month shall be paid between the 16th and the 22nd day of the month during which the labor was performed. Labor performed between the 16th and the last day, inclusive, of any calendar month shall be paid between the first and the seventh day of the following month. Agricultural employees, as used in this section, shall not include those employees who are covered by Section 205. *(Added by Stats.1976, c. 1041, p. 4653, § 1.5. Amended by Stats.1997, c. 92 (S.B.1071), § 2.)*

§ 206. Payment of undisputed amount; failure to pay determined amount; treble damages

(a) In case of a dispute over wages, the employer shall pay, without condition and within the time set by this article, all wages, or parts thereof, conceded by him to be due, leaving to the employee all remedies he might otherwise be entitled to as to any balance claimed.

(b) If, after an investigation and hearing, the Labor Commissioner has determined the validity of any employee's claim for wages, the claim is due and payable within 10 days after receipt of notice by the employer that such wages are due. Any employer having the ability to pay who willfully fails to pay such wages within 10 days shall, in addition to any other applicable penalty, pay treble the amount of any damages accruing to the employee as a direct and foreseeable consequence of such failure to pay. *(Stats.1937, c. 90, p. 198, § 206. Amended by Stats.1975, c. 312, p. 759, § 1.)*

§ 206.5. Execution of release of claim or right on account of wages due

(a) An employer shall not require the execution of a release of a claim or right on account of wages due, or to become due, or made as an advance on wages to be earned, unless payment of those wages has been made. A release required or executed in violation of the provisions of this section shall be null and void as between the employer and the employee. Violation of this section by the employer is a misdemeanor.

(b) For purposes of this section, "execution of a release" includes requiring an employee, as a condition of being paid, to execute a statement of the hours he or she worked during a pay period which the employer knows to be false. *(Added by Stats.1959, c. 1066, p. 3127, § 1. Amended by Stats.2008, c. 224 (A.B.2075), § 1.)*

§ 207. Posting of notice of regular pay days

Every employer shall keep posted conspicuously at the place of work, if practicable, or otherwise where it can be seen as employees come or go to their places of work, or at the office or nearest agency for payment kept by the employer, a notice specifying the regular pay days and the time and place of payment, in accordance with this article. *(Stats.1937, c. 90, p. 198, § 207.)*

§ 208. Place of payment

Every employee who is discharged shall be paid at the place of discharge, and every employee who quits shall be paid at the office or agency of the employer in the county where the employee has been performing labor. All payments shall be made in the manner provided by law. *(Stats.1937, c. 90, p. 198, § 208.)*

§ 209. Payment in event of strike

In the event of any strike, the unpaid wages earned by striking employees shall become due and payable on the next regular pay day, and the payment or settlement thereof shall include all amounts due the striking employees without abatement or reduction. The employer shall return to each striking employee any deposit, money, or other guaranty required by him from the employee for the faithful performance of the duties of the employment. *(Stats.1937, c. 90, p. 198, § 209.)*

§ 210. Civil penalty for failure to make payments; action for recovery; disposition of money recovered

(a) In addition to, and entirely independent and apart from, any other penalty provided in this article, every person who fails to pay the wages of each employee as provided in Sections 201.3, 204, 204b, 204.1, 204.2, 205, 205.5, and 1197.5, shall be subject to a civil penalty as follows:

(1) For any initial violation, one hundred dollars ($100) for each failure to pay each employee.

(2) For each subsequent violation, or any willful or intentional violation, two hundred dollars ($200) for each failure to pay each employee, plus 25 percent of the amount unlawfully withheld.

(b) The penalty shall be recovered by the Labor Commissioner as part of a hearing held to recover unpaid wages and penalties pursuant to this chapter or in an independent civil action. The action shall be brought in the name of the people of the State of California and the Labor Commissioner and the attorneys thereof may proceed and act for and on behalf of the people in bringing these actions. Twelve and one-half percent of the penalty recovered shall be paid into a fund within the Labor and Workforce Development Agency dedicated to educating employers about state labor laws, and the remainder shall be paid into the State Treasury to the credit of the General Fund. *(Stats.1937, c. 90, p. 198, § 210. Amended by Stats.1945, c. 1431, p. 2690, § 30; Stats.1961, c. 209, p. 1219, § 1; Stats.1976, c. 1190, p. 5372, § 17; Stats.1983, c. 1096, § 1; Stats.2003, c. 329 (A.B.276), § 1; Stats.2008, c. 169 (S.B.940), § 5.)*

§ 211. Actions to recover civil penalties; fees for service of summons; joinder of causes of action; demand for payment

When action to recover such penalties is brought, no court costs shall be payable by the state or the division. Any sheriff or marshal who serves the summons in the action upon any defendant within his or her jurisdiction shall do so without cost to the division. The sheriff or marshal shall specify in the return what costs he or she would ordinarily have been entitled to for such service, and those costs and the other regular court costs that would have accrued were the action not on behalf of the state shall be made a part of any judgment recovered by the plaintiff and shall be paid out of the first money recovered on the judgment. Several causes of action for the penalties may be united in the same action without being separately stated. A demand is a prerequisite to the bringing of any action under this section or Section 210. The division on behalf of the state may accept and receipt for any penalties so paid, with or without suit. *(Stats.1937, c. 90, p. 198, § 211. Amended by Stats.1996, c. 872 (A.B.3472), § 105.)*

§ 212. Prohibited forms of payment; instruments protested or dishonored; effect of notice

(a) No person, or agent or officer thereof, shall issue in payment of wages due, or to become due, or as an advance on wages to be earned:

(1) Any order, check, draft, note, memorandum, or other acknowledgment of indebtedness, unless it is negotiable and payable in cash, on demand, without discount, at some established place of business in the state, the name and address of which must appear on the instrument, and at the time of its issuance and for a reasonable time thereafter, which must be at least 30 days, the maker or drawer has sufficient funds in, or credit, arrangement, or understanding with the drawee for its payment.

(2) Any scrip, coupon, cards, or other thing redeemable, in merchandise or purporting to be payable or redeemable otherwise than in money.

(b) Where an instrument mentioned in subdivision (a) is protested or dishonored, the notice or memorandum of protest or dishonor is admissible as proof of presentation, nonpayment and protest and is presumptive evidence of knowledge of insufficiency of funds or credit with the drawee.

(c) Notwithstanding paragraph (1) of subdivision (a), if the drawee is a bank, the bank's address need not appear on the instrument and, in that case, the instrument shall be negotiable and payable in cash, on demand, without discount, at any place of business of the drawee chosen by the person entitled to enforce the instrument. *(Stats. 1937, c. 90, p. 199, § 212. Amended by Stats.1947, c. 395, p. 968, § 1; Stats.1971, c. 438, p. 893, § 136; Stats.1997, c. 352 (S.B.496), § 1.)*

§ 213. Exceptions

Nothing contained in Section 212 shall:

(a) Prohibit an employer from guaranteeing the payment of bills incurred by an employee for the necessaries of life or for the tools and implements used by the employee in the performance of his or her duties.

(b) Apply to counties, municipal corporations, quasi-municipal corporations, or school districts.

(c) Apply to students of nonprofit schools, colleges, universities, and other nonprofit educational institutions.

(d) Prohibit an employer from depositing wages due or to become due or an advance on wages to be earned in an account in any bank, savings and loan association, or credit union of the employee's choice with a place of business located in this state, provided that the employee has voluntarily authorized that deposit. If an employer discharges an employee or the employee quits, the employer may pay the wages earned and unpaid at the time the employee is discharged or quits by making a deposit authorized pursuant to this subdivision, provided that the employer complies with the provisions of this article relating to the payment of wages upon termination or quitting of employment. *(Stats.1937, c. 90, p. 199, § 213. Amended by Stats.1939, c. 1075, p. 2999, § 1; Stats.1972, c. 223, p. 466, § 1, eff. June 30, 1972; Stats. 1973, c. 263, p. 660, § 1; Stats.2005, c. 149 (A.B.1093), § 1.)*

§ 214. Place of prosecution for illegal form of payment

Prosecution under section 212 may be brought either at the place where the alleged illegal order, check, draft, note, memorandum or other acknowledgment of wage indebtedness is issued or at the place where it is made payable. *(Stats.1937, c. 90, p. 199, § 214.)*

§ 215. Violations; misdemeanor

Any person, or the agent, manager, superintendent or officer thereof, who violates any provision of Section 201.3, 204, 204b, 205, 207, 208, 209, or 212 is guilty of a misdemeanor. Any failure to keep posted any notice required by Section 207 is prima facie evidence of a violation of these sections. *(Stats.1937, c. 90, p. 199, § 215. Amended by Stats.1961, c. 139, p. 1146, § 1; Stats.2008, c. 169 (S.B.940), § 6.)*

§ 216. Refusal to make payment; false denial of amount or validity of wages; misdemeanor

In addition to any other penalty imposed by this article, any person, or an agent, manager, superintendent, or officer thereof is guilty of a misdemeanor, who:

(a) Having the ability to pay, willfully refuses to pay wages due and payable after demand has been made.

(b) Falsely denies the amount or validity thereof, or that the same is due, with intent to secure for himself, his employer or other person, any discount upon such indebtedness, or with intent to annoy, harass, oppress, hinder, delay, or defraud, the person to whom such indebtedness is due. *(Stats.1937, c. 90, p. 199, § 216. Amended by Stats.1959, c. 1358, p. 3629, § 1.)*

§ 217. Enforcement

The Division of Labor Law Enforcement shall inquire diligently for any violations of this article, and, in cases which it deems proper, shall institute the actions for the penalties provided for in this article and shall enforce this article. *(Stats.1937, c. 90, p. 200, § 217. Amended by Stats.1945, c. 1431, p. 2690, § 31.)*

§ 218. Authority of district attorney and wage claimant

Nothing in this article shall limit the authority of the district attorney of any county or prosecuting attorney of any city to prosecute actions, either civil or criminal, for violations of this article or to enforce the provisions thereof independently and without specific direction of the division. Nothing in this article shall limit the right of any wage claimant to sue directly or through an assignee for any wages or penalty due him under this article. *(Stats.1937, c. 90, p. 200, § 218.)*

§ 218.5. Actions for nonpayment of wages, fringe benefits, or health and welfare or pension fund contributions; award of attorney's fees to prevailing party; application of section

In any action brought for the nonpayment of wages, fringe benefits, or health and welfare or pension fund contributions, the court shall award reasonable attorney's fees and costs to the prevailing party if any party to the action requests attorney's fees and costs upon the initiation of the action. This section shall not apply to an action brought by the Labor Commissioner. This section shall not apply to a surety issuing a bond pursuant to Chapter 9 (commencing with Section 7000) of Division 3 of the Business and Professions Code or to an action to enforce a mechanics lien brought under Chapter 2 (commencing with Section 3109) of Title 15 of Part 4 of Division 3 of the Civil Code.

This section does not apply to any action for which attorney's fees are recoverable under Section 1194. *(Added by Stats.1986, c. 1211, § 1. Amended by Stats. 2000, c. 876 (A.B.2509), § 4.)*

§ 218.6. Actions for nonpayment of wages; award of interest

In any action brought for the nonpayment of wages, the court shall award interest on all due and unpaid wages at the rate of interest specified in subdivision (b) of Section 3289 of the Civil Code, which shall accrue from the date that the wages were due and payable as provided in Part 1 (commencing with Section 200) of Division 2. *(Added by Stats.2000, c. 876 (A.B.2509), § 5.)*

§ 219. Payment of wages at more frequent intervals, or in greater amounts, or in full when or before due; private agreements; state employers

(a) Nothing in this article shall in any way limit or prohibit the payment of wages at more frequent intervals, or in greater amounts, or in full when or before due, but no provision of this article can in any way be contravened or set aside by a private agreement, whether written, oral, or implied.

(b) The state employer does not violate this section by authorizing employees who quit, or are discharged from, their employment with the state to take payment for any unused or accumulated vacation, annual leave, holiday leave, sick leave to which the employee is otherwise entitled due to a disability retirement, or time off to which the employee is entitled by reason of previous overtime work where compensating time off was given by the appointing power, as provided in Section 201 or 202. *(Stats.1937, c. 90, p. 200, § 219. Amended by Stats.2002, c. 40 (A.B.1684), § 8, eff. May 16, 2002.)*

§ 220. Public employees

(a) Sections 201.3, 201.5, 201.7, 203.1, 203.5, 204, 204a, 204b, 204c, 204.1, 205, and 205.5 do not apply to the payment of wages of employees directly employed by the State of California. Except as provided in subdivision (b), all other employment is subject to these provisions.

(b) Sections 200 to 211, inclusive, and Sections 215 to 219, inclusive, do not apply to the payment of wages of employees directly employed by any county, incorporated city, or town or other municipal corporation. All other employments are subject to these provisions. *(Stats.1937, c. 90, p. 200, § 220. Amended by Stats.2000, c. 885 (A.B.2410), § 1; Stats.2008, c. 169 (S.B.940), § 7.)*

§ 220.2. Public employees; benefits; contributions; payments by employing agencies

Contributions to vacation allowances, pension or retirement funds, sick leave, and health and welfare benefits on behalf of persons employed by any county, political subdivision, incorporated city or town or other municipal corporations may be made in the same manner and on the same basis as made by private employers.

Payments made by the employing agency to any such fund on behalf of any employee shall be in lieu of benefits such as vacation allowance, pension or retirement fund, sick leave, and health and welfare benefits which are now or may hereafter be granted directly by the employing agency in accordance with law.

This section shall only apply to nonpermanent laborers, workmen, and mechanics employed on an hourly or per diem basis.

The employing agency is empowered to determine the equitable application of this section to insure that the employees receive benefits comparable to, but not in excess of those provided in comparable private employment.

The employing agency shall make payments only to plans which meet the following standards:

1. A plan office is located within the State of California.

2. Any fund connected with the plan is required to be audited at least annually by an independent, licensed certified public accountant.

3. Each trustee or administrator of the fund or plan authorized to receive, handle, deal with or draw upon the assets of the fund or plan is required to be bonded. *(Added by Stats.1959, c. 2051, p. 4746, § 1. Amended by Stats.1969, c. 1230, p. 2383, § 1.)*

§ 221. Repayment of wages to employer

It shall be unlawful for any employer to collect or receive from an employee any part of wages theretofore paid by said employer to said employee. *(Added by Stats.1937, c. 357, p. 774.)*

§ 222. Withholding of part of wage

It shall be unlawful, in case of any wage agreement arrived at through collective bargaining, either wilfully or unlawfully or with intent to defraud an employee, a competitor, or any other person, to withhold from said employee any part of the wage agreed upon. *(Added by Stats.1937, c. 357, p. 774. Amended by Stats.1939, c. 1062, p. 2990, § 1.)*

§ 222.5. Cost of pre-employment physical examination or physical examination required by law

No person shall withhold or deduct from the compensation of any employee, or require any prospective employee or applicant for employment to pay, any fee for, or cost of, any pre-employment medical or physical examination taken as a condition of employment, nor shall any person withhold or deduct from the compensation of any employee, or require any employee to pay any fee for, or costs of, medical or physical examinations required by any law or regulation of federal, state or local governments or agencies thereof. *(Added by Stats.1945, c. 1911, p. 2244, § 1. Amended by Stats.1957, c. 1113, p. 2414, § 1.)*

§ 223. Payment of less than statutory or contractual wage scale

Where any statute or contract requires an employer to maintain the designated wage scale, it shall be unlawful to secretly pay a lower wage while purporting to pay the wage designated by statute or by contract. *(Added by Stats.1937, c. 357, p. 774.)*

§ 224. Authorized deductions

The provisions of Sections 221, 222 and 223 shall in no way make it unlawful for an employer to withhold or divert any portion of an employee's wages when the employer is required or empowered so to do by state or federal law or when a deduction is expressly authorized in writing by the employee to cover insurance premiums, hospital or medical dues, or other deductions not amounting to a rebate or deduction from the standard wage arrived at by collective bargaining or pursuant to wage agreement or statute, or when a deduction to cover health and welfare or pension plan contributions is expressly authorized by a collective bargaining or wage agreement.

Nothing in this section or any other provision of law shall be construed as authorizing an employer to withhold or divert any portion of an employee's wages to pay any tax, fee or charge prohibited by Section 50026 of the Government Code, whether or not the employee authorizes such withholding or diversion. *(Added by Stats.1937, c. 357, p. 774. Amended by Stats.1955, c. 496, p. 968, § 1; Stats.1968, c. 559, p. 1226, § 2.)*

§ 225. Violations; misdemeanor

The violation of any provision of Sections 221, 222, 222.5, or 223 is a misdemeanor. *(Added by Stats.1937, c. 357, p. 774. Amended by Stats.1945, c. 1191, p. 2244, § 2.)*

§ 225.5. Unlawful withholding of wages; civil penalty; action for recovery; disposition of money recovered

In addition to, and entirely independent and apart from, any other penalty provided in this article, every person who unlawfully withholds wages due any employee in violation of Section 212, 216, 221, 222, or 223 shall be subject to a civil penalty as follows:

(a) For any initial violation, one hundred dollars ($100) for each failure to pay each employee.

(b) For each subsequent violation, or any willful or intentional violation, two hundred dollars ($200) for each failure to pay each employee, plus 25 percent of the amount unlawfully withheld.

The penalty shall be recovered by the Labor Commissioner as part of a hearing held to recover unpaid wages and penalties or in an independent civil action. The action shall be brought in the name of the people of the State of California and the Labor Commissioner and attorneys thereof may proceed and act for and on behalf of the people in bringing the action. Twelve and one-half percent of the penalty recovered shall be paid into a fund within the Labor and Workforce Development Agency dedicated to educating employers about state labor laws, and the remainder shall be paid into the State Treasury to the credit of the General Fund. *(Added by Stats.1983, c. 1096, § 2. Amended by Stats.2003, c. 329 (A.B.276), § 2.)*

§ 226. Itemized statements; contents; records; inspection of records; compliance with inspection request; limitation of application

(a) Every employer shall, semimonthly or at the time of each payment of wages, furnish each of his or her employees, either as a detachable part of the check, draft, or voucher paying the employee's wages, or separately when wages are paid by personal check or cash, an accurate itemized statement in writing showing (1) gross wages earned, (2) total hours worked by the employee, except for any employee whose compensation is solely based on a salary and who is exempt from payment of overtime under subdivision (a) of Section 515 or any applicable order of the Industrial Welfare Commission, (3) the number of piece-rate units earned and any applicable piece rate if the employee is paid on a piece-rate basis, (4) all deductions, provided that all deductions made on written orders of the employee may be aggregated and shown as one item, (5) net wages earned, (6) the inclusive dates of the period for which the employee is paid, (7) the name of the employee and his or her social security number, except that by January 1, 2008, only the last four digits of his or her social security number or an employee identification number other than a social security number may be shown on the itemized statement, (8) the name and address of the legal entity that is the employer, and (9) all applicable hourly rates in effect during the pay period and the corresponding number of hours worked at each hourly rate by the employee. The deductions made from payments of wages shall be recorded in ink or other indelible form, properly dated, showing the month, day, and year, and a copy of the statement or a record of the deductions shall be kept on file by the employer for at least three years at the place of employment or at a central location within the State of California.

(b) An employer that is required by this code or any regulation adopted pursuant to this code to keep the information required by subdivision (a) shall afford current and former employees the right to inspect or copy the records pertaining to that current or former employee, upon reasonable request to the employer. The employer may take reasonable steps to assure the identity of a current or former employee. If the employer provides copies of the records, the actual cost of reproduction may be charged to the current or former employee.

(c) An employer who receives a written or oral request to inspect or copy records pursuant to subdivision (b) pertaining to a current or former employee shall comply with the request as soon as practicable, but no later than 21 calendar days from the date of the request. A violation of this subdivision is an infraction. Impossibility of performance, not caused by or a result of a violation of law, shall be an affirmative defense for an employer in any action alleging a violation of this subdivision. An employer may designate the person to whom a request under this subdivision will be made.

(d) This section does not apply to any employer of any person employed by the owner or occupant of a residential dwelling whose duties are incidental to the ownership, maintenance, or use of the dwelling, including the care and supervision of children, or whose duties are personal and not in the course of the trade, business, profession, or occupation of the owner or occupant.

(e) An employee suffering injury as a result of a knowing and intentional failure by an employer to comply with subdivision (a) is entitled to recover the greater of all actual damages or fifty dollars ($50) for the initial pay period in which a violation occurs and one hundred dollars ($100) per employee for each violation in a subsequent pay period, not exceeding an aggregate penalty of four thousand dollars ($4,000), and is entitled to an award of costs and reasonable attorney's fees.

(f) A failure by an employer to permit a current or former employee to inspect or copy records within the time set forth in subdivision (c) entitles the current or former employee or the Labor Commissioner to recover a seven-hundred-fifty-dollar ($750) penalty from the employer.

(g) An employee may also bring an action for injunctive relief to ensure compliance with this section, and is entitled to an award of costs and reasonable attorney's fees.

(h) This section does not apply to the state, to any city, county, city and county, district, or to any other governmental entity, except that if the state or a city, county, city and county, district, or other governmental entity furnishes its employees with a check, draft, or voucher paying the employee's wages, the state or a city, county, city and county, district, or other governmental entity shall, by January 1, 2008, use no more than the last four digits of the employee's social security number or shall use an employee identification number other than the social security number on the itemized statement provided with the check, draft, or voucher. (*Added by Stats.1943, c. 1027, p. 2965, § 1. Amended by Stats.1945, c. 1140, p. 2179, § 1; Stats.1963, c. 1080, p. 2540, § 1; Stats.1976, c. 832, p. 1899, § 1; Stats.1978, c. 1247, p. 4059, § 3, operative Jan. 1, 1980; Stats.1982, c. 454, p. 1876, § 131; Stats.1982, c. 327, p. 1470, § 124, eff. June 30, 1982; Stats.1984, c. 486, § 1, operative Jan. 1, 1986; Stats.1987, c. 976, § 1; Stats.1988, c. 827, § 1, eff. Sept. 12, 1988; Stats.2000, c. 876 (A.B.2509), § 6; Stats.2002, c. 933 (A.B.2412), § 1; Stats.2003, c. 329 (A.B.276), § 3; Stats. 2004, c. 860 (S.B.1618), § 1; Stats.2005, c. 103 (S.B.101), § 1, eff. July 21, 2005.*)

§ 226.3. Civil penalties; itemized statements by employers; inadvertent mistakes

Any employer who violates subdivision (a) of Section 226 shall be subject to a civil penalty in the amount of two hundred fifty dollars ($250) per employee per violation in an initial citation and one thousand dollars ($1,000) per employee for each violation in a subsequent citation, for which the employer fails to provide the employee a wage deduction statement or fails to keep the records required in subdivision (a) of Section 226. The civil penalties provided for in this section are in addition to any other penalty provided by law. In enforcing this section, the Labor Commissioner shall take into consideration whether the violation was inadvertent, and in his or her discretion, may decide not to penalize an employer for a first violation when that violation was due to a clerical error or inadvertent mistake. (*Added by Stats.1979, c. 1050, p. 3703, § 3. Amended by Stats.1987, c. 976, § 4; Stats.1990, c. 838 (A.B.2693), § 1; Stats.1992, c. 424 (A.B.3123), § 1.*)

§ 226.4. Citation; issuance; service; contents; itemized statement

If, upon inspection or investigation, the Labor Commissioner determines that an employer is in violation of subdivision (a) of Section 226, the Labor Commissioner may issue a citation to the person in violation. The citation may be served personally or by registered mail in accordance with subdivision (c) of Section 11505 of the Government Code. Each citation shall be in writing and shall describe the nature of the violation, including reference to the statutory provision alleged to have been violated. *(Added by Stats.1979, c. 1050, p. 3703, § 4. Amended by Stats.1982, c. 327, § 125, eff. June. 30, 1982; Stats.1987, c. 976, § 5; Stats.2006, c. 538 (S.B.1852), § 479.)*

§ 226.5. Hearing on citation or assessment of civil penalty; decision; service on parties; amount due; writ of mandate; payment of citation amount; judgment; interest on judgment

(a) If a person desires to contest a citation or the proposed assessment of a civil penalty therefor, he or she shall within 15 business days after service of the citation notify the office of the Labor Commissioner which appears on the citation of his or her request for an informal hearing. The Labor Commissioner or his or her deputy or agent shall, within 30 days, hold a hearing at the conclusion of which the citation or proposed assessment of a civil penalty shall be affirmed, modified, or dismissed. The decision of the Labor Commissioner shall consist of a notice of findings, findings, and order which shall be served on all parties to the hearing within 15 days after the hearing by regular first-class mail at the last known address of the party on file with the Labor Commissioner. Service shall be completed pursuant to Section 1013 of the Code of Civil Procedure. Any amount found due by the Labor Commissioner as a result of a hearing shall become due and payable 45 days after notice of the findings and written findings and order have been mailed to the party assessed. A writ of mandate may be taken from this finding to the appropriate superior court, as long as the party agrees to pay any judgment and costs ultimately rendered by the court against the party for the assessment. The writ shall be taken within 45 days of service of the notice of findings, findings, and order thereon.

(b) A person to whom a citation has been issued shall, in lieu of contesting a citation pursuant to this section, transmit to the office of the Labor Commissioner designated on the citation the amount specified for the violation within 15 business days after issuance of the citation.

(c) When no petition objecting to a citation or the proposed assessment of a civil penalty is filed, a certified copy of the citation or proposed civil penalty may be filed by the Labor Commissioner in the office of the clerk or the superior court in any county in which the person assessed has or had a place of business. The clerk, immediately upon the filing, shall enter judgment for the state against the person assessed in the amount shown on the citation or proposed assessment of a civil penalty.

(d) When findings and the order thereon are made affirming or modifying a citation or proposed assessment of a civil penalty after hearing, a certified copy of these findings and the order entered thereon may be entered by the Labor Commissioner in the office of the clerk of the superior court in any county in which the person assessed has property or in which the person assessed has or had a place of business. The clerk, immediately upon the filing, shall enter judgment for the state against the person assessed in the amount shown on the certified order.

(e) A judgment entered pursuant to this section shall bear the same rate of interest and shall have the same effect as other judgments and be given the same preference allowed by the law on other judgments rendered for claims for taxes. The clerk shall make no charge for the service provided by this section to be performed by him or her. *(Added by Stats.1979, c. 1050, p. 3704, § 5. Amended by Stats.1988, c. 96, § 4.)*

§ 226.6. Violation of §§ 226 or 226.2; persons having control or disposition of wages; penalty

Any employer who knowingly and intentionally violates the provisions of Section 226 or 226.2, or any officer, agent, employee, fiduciary, or other person who has the control, receipt, custody, or disposal of, or pays, the wages due any employee, and who knowingly and intentionally participates or aids in the violation of any provision of Section 226 or 226.2 is guilty of a misdemeanor and, upon conviction thereof, shall be fined not more than one thousand dollars ($1,000) or be imprisoned not to exceed one year, or both, at the discretion of the court. That fine or imprisonment, or both, shall be in addition to any other penalty provided by law. *(Added by Stats.1984, c. 1490, § 3, eff. Sept. 27, 1984.)*

§ 226.7. Mandated meal or rest periods; requirement to work prohibited

(a) No employer shall require any employee to work during any meal or rest period mandated by an applicable order of the Industrial Welfare Commission.

(b) If an employer fails to provide an employee a meal period or rest period in accordance with an applicable order of the Industrial Welfare Commission, the employer shall pay the employee one additional hour of pay at the employee's regular rate of compensation for each work day that the meal or rest period is not provided. *(Added by Stats.2000, c. 876 (A.B.2509), § 7.)*

§ 227. Health, welfare or pension fund or vacation plan; failure to make agreed payments; offense

Whenever an employer has agreed with any employee to make payments to a health or welfare fund, pension fund or vacation plan, or other similar plan for the benefit of the employees, or a negotiated industrial promotion fund, or has entered into a collective bargaining agreement providing for these payments, it shall be unlawful for that employer willfully or with intent to defraud to fail to make the payments required by the terms of that agreement. A violation of any provision of this section where the amount the employer failed to pay into the fund or funds exceeds five hundred dollars ($500) shall be punishable by imprisonment in the state prison, or in a county jail for a period of not more than one year, by a fine of not more than one thousand dollars ($1,000), or by both that imprisonment and fine. All other violations shall be punishable as a misdemeanor. *(Added by Stats.1955, c. 1570, p. 2850, § 1. Amended by Stats.1959, c. 824, p. 2843, § 1; Stats.1974, c. 1033, p. 2232, § 1; Stats.1975, c. 678, p. 1489, § 52; Stats.2008, c. 699 (S.B.1241), § 8.)*

§ 227.3. Vested vacation wages; payment upon termination

Unless otherwise provided by a collective-bargaining agreement, whenever a contract of employment or employer policy provides for paid vacations, and an employee is terminated without having taken off his vested vacation time, all vested vacation shall be paid to him as wages at his final rate in accordance with such contract of employment or employer policy respecting eligibility or time served; provided, however, that an employment contract or employer policy shall not provide for forfeiture of vested vacation time upon termination. The Labor Commissioner or a designated representative, in the resolution of any dispute with regard to vested vacation time, shall apply the principles of equity and fairness. *(Added by Stats.1972, c. 1321, p. 2628, § 1. Amended by Stats.1976, c. 1041, p. 4653, § 2.)*

§ 227.5. Annual statement of payments to employee benefit funds

Whenever an employer has agreed with any employee to make payments to a health or welfare fund, pension fund or vacation plan, or such other plan for the benefit of the employee, or has entered into a collective bargaining agreement providing for such payments, the employer upon written request of the employee shall furnish such employee annually a statement indicating whether or not such payments have been made and for what periods. *(Added by Stats.1963, c. 898, p. 2141, § 1.)*

§ 228. Payments to apprenticeship funds

The payments under Section 227 of this code shall be deemed to include payments to apprenticeship funds.

This amendment is hereby declared to be merely a clarification of the original intention of the Legislature and is not a substantive change. *(Added by Stats.1961, c. 1218, p. 2955, § 1.)*

§ 229. Actions to enforce payment of wages; effect of arbitration agreements

Actions to enforce the provisions of this article for the collection of due and unpaid wages claimed by an individual may be maintained without regard to the existence of any private agreement to arbitrate. This section shall not apply to claims involving any dispute concerning the interpretation or application of any collective bargaining agreement containing such an arbitration agreement. *(Added by Stats.1959, c. 1939, p. 4532, § 1.)*

§ 230. Jury duty; legal actions by domestic violence and sexual assault victims; right to time off; reinstatement and reimbursement; misdemeanor; right to file complaint with Division of Labor Standards Enforcement

(a) An employer may not discharge or in any manner discriminate against an employee for taking time off to serve as required by law on an inquest jury or trial jury, if the employee, prior to taking the time off, gives reasonable notice to the employer that he or she is required to serve.

(b) An employer may not discharge or in any manner discriminate or retaliate against an employee, including, but not limited to, an employee who is a victim of a crime, for taking time off to appear in court to comply with a subpoena or other court order as a witness in any judicial proceeding.

(c) An employer may not discharge or in any manner discriminate or retaliate against an employee who is a victim of domestic violence or a victim of sexual assault for taking time off from work to obtain or attempt to obtain any relief, including, but not limited to, a temporary restraining order, restraining order, or other injunctive relief, to help ensure the health, safety, or welfare of the victim or his or her child.

(d)(1) As a condition of taking time off for a purpose set forth in subdivision (c), the employee shall give the employer reasonable advance notice of the employee's intention to take time off, unless the advance notice is not feasible.

(2) When an unscheduled absence occurs, the employer shall not take any action against the employee if the employee, within a reasonable time after the absence, provides a certification to the employer. Certification shall be sufficient in the form of any of the following:

(A) A police report indicating that the employee was a victim of domestic violence or sexual assault.

(B) A court order protecting or separating the employee from the perpetrator of an act of domestic violence or sexual assault, or other evidence from the court or prosecuting attorney that the employee has appeared in court.

(C) Documentation from a medical professional, domestic violence advocate or advocate for victims of sexual assault, health care provider, or counselor that the employee was undergoing treatment for physical or mental injuries or abuse resulting in victimization from an act of domestic violence or sexual assault.

(3) To the extent allowed by law, the employer shall maintain the confidentiality of any employee requesting leave under subdivision (c).

(e) Any employee who is discharged, threatened with discharge, demoted, suspended, or in any other manner discriminated or retaliated against in the terms and conditions of employment by his or her employer because the employee has taken time off for a purpose set forth in subdivision (a), (b), or (c) shall be entitled to reinstatement and reimbursement for lost wages and work benefits caused by the acts of the employer. Any employer who willfully refuses to rehire, promote, or otherwise restore an employee or former employee who has been determined to be eligible for rehiring or promotion by a grievance procedure or hearing authorized by law is guilty of a misdemeanor.

(f)(1) Any employee who is discharged, threatened with discharge, demoted, suspended, or in any other manner discriminated or retaliated against in the terms and conditions of employment by his or her employer because the employee has exercised his or her rights as set forth in subdivision (a), (b), or (c) may file a complaint with the Division of Labor Standards Enforcement of the Department of Industrial Relations pursuant to Section 98.7.

(2) Notwithstanding any time limitation in Section 98.7, an employee filing a complaint with the division based upon a violation of subdivision (c) shall have one year from the date of occurrence of the violation to file his or her complaint.

(g) An employee may use vacation, personal leave, or compensatory time off that is otherwise available to the employee under the applicable terms of employment, unless otherwise provided by a collective bargaining agreement, for time taken off for a purpose specified in subdivision (a), (b), or (c). The entitlement of any employee under this section shall not be diminished by any collective bargaining agreement term or condition.

(h) For purposes of this section:

(1) "Domestic violence" means any of the types of abuse set forth in Section 6211 of the Family Code, as amended

(2) "Sexual assault" means any of the crimes set forth in Section 261, 261.5, 262, 265, 266, 266a, 266b, 266c, 266g, 266j, 267, 269, 273.4, 285, 286, 288, 288a, 288.5, 289, or 311.4 of the Penal Code, as amended. *(Added by Stats.1968, c. 1270, p. 2395, § 1. Amended by Stats.1978, c. 161, p. 392, § 1; Stats.1999, c. 340 (S.B.56), § 1; Stats.2000, c. 487 (A.B.2357), § 2; Stats.2002, c. 275 (A.B.2195), § 1.)*

§ 230.1. Employers with 25 or more employees; domestic violence and sexual assault victims; right to time off

(a) In addition to the requirements and prohibitions imposed on employees pursuant to Section 230, an employer with 25 or more employees may not discharge or in any manner discriminate or retaliate against an employee who is a victim of domestic violence or a victim of sexual assault for taking time off from work to attend to any of the following:

(1) To seek medical attention for injuries caused by domestic violence or sexual assault.

(2) To obtain services from a domestic violence shelter, program, or rape crisis center as a result of domestic violence or sexual assault.

(3) To obtain psychological counseling related to an experience of domestic violence or sexual assault.

(4) To participate in safety planning and take other actions to increase safety from future domestic violence or sexual assault, including temporary or permanent relocation.

(b)(1) As a condition of taking time off for a purpose set forth in subdivision (a), the employee shall give the employer reasonable advance notice of the employee's intention to take time off, unless the advance notice is not feasible.

(2) When an unscheduled absence occurs, the employer may not take any action against the employee if the employee, within a reasonable time after the absence, provides a certification to the employer. Certification shall be sufficient in the form of any of the following:

(A) A police report indicating that the employee was a victim of domestic violence or sexual assault.

(B) A court order protecting or separating the employee from the perpetrator of an act of domestic violence or sexual assault, or other evidence from the court or prosecuting attorney that the employee appeared in court.

(C) Documentation from a medical professional, domestic violence advocate or advocate for victims of sexual assault, health care provider, or counselor that the employee was undergoing treatment for physical or mental injuries or abuse resulting in victimization from an act of domestic violence or sexual assault.

(3) To the extent allowed by law, employers shall maintain the confidentiality of any employee requesting leave under subdivision (a).

(c) Any employee who is discharged, threatened with discharge, demoted, suspended, or in any other manner discriminated or retaliated against in the terms and conditions of employment by his or her employer because the employee has taken time off for a purpose set forth in subdivision (a) is entitled to reinstatement and reimbursement for lost wages and work benefits caused by the acts of the employer. Any employer who willfully refuses to rehire, promote, or otherwise restore an employee or former employee who has been determined to be eligible for rehiring or promotion by a grievance procedure or hearing authorized by law is guilty of a misdemeanor.

(d)(1) Any employee who is discharged, threatened with discharge, demoted, suspended, or in any other manner discriminated or retaliated against in the terms and conditions of employment by his or her employer because the employee has exercised his or her rights as set forth in subdivision (a) may file a complaint with the Division of Labor Standards Enforcement of the Department of Industrial Relations pursuant to Section 98. 7.

(2) Notwithstanding any time limitation in Section 98.7, an employee filing a complaint with the division based upon a violation of subdivision (a) has one year from the date of occurrence of the violation to file his or her complaint.

(e) An employee may use vacation, personal leave, or compensatory time off that is otherwise available to the employee under the applicable terms of employment, unless otherwise provided by a collective bargaining agreement, for time taken off for a purpose specified in subdivision (a). The entitlement of any employee under this section may not be diminished by any collective bargaining agreement term or condition.

(f) This section does not create a right for an employee to take unpaid leave that exceeds the unpaid leave time allowed under, or is in addition to the unpaid leave time permitted by, the federal Family and Medical Leave Act of 1993 (29 U.S.C. Sec. 2601 et seq.).

(g) For purposes of this section:

(1) "Domestic violence" means any of the types of abuse set forth in Section 6211 of the Family Code, as amended.

(2) "Sexual assault" means any of the crimes set forth in Section 261, 261.5, 262, 265, 266, 266a, 266b, 266c, 266g, 266j, 267, 269, 273.4, 285, 286, 288, 288a, 288.5, 289, or 311.4 of the Penal Code, as amended. *(Added by Stats.2000, c. 487 (A.B.2357), § 3. Amended by Stats. 2001, c. 159 (S.B.662), § 157; Stats.2002, c. 664 (A.B. 3034), § 159; Stats.2002, c. 275 (A.B.2195), § 2; Stats. 2003, c. 62 (S.B.600), § 204.)*

§ 230.2. Victims of crime; work absences for judicial proceedings; covered employees

(a) As used in this section:

(1) "Immediate family member" means spouse, child, stepchild, brother, stepbrother, sister, stepsister, mother, stepmother, father, or stepfather.

(2) "Registered domestic partner" means a domestic partner, as defined in Section 297 of the Family Code, and registered pursuant to Part 2 (commencing with Section 298) of Division 2.5 of the Family Code.

(3) "Victim" means a person against whom one of the following crimes has been committed:

(A) A violent felony, as defined in subdivision (c) of Section 667.5 of the Penal Code.

(B) A serious felony, as defined in subdivision (c) of Section 1192.7 of the Penal Code.

(C) A felony provision of law proscribing theft or embezzlement.

(b) An employer, and any agent of an employer, shall allow an employee who is a victim of a crime, an immediate family member of a victim, a registered domestic partner of a victim, or the child of a registered domestic partner of a victim to be absent from work in order to attend judicial proceedings related to that crime.

(c) Before an employee may be absent from work pursuant to subdivision (b), the employee shall give the employer a copy of the notice of each scheduled proceeding that is provided to the victim by the agency responsible for providing notice, unless advance notice is not feasible. When advance notice is not feasible or an unscheduled absence occurs, the employer shall not take any action against the employee if the employee, within a reasonable time after the absence, provides the employer with documentation evidencing the judicial proceeding from any of the following entities:

(1) The court or government agency setting the hearing.

(2) The district attorney or prosecuting attorney's office.

(3) The victim/witness office that is advocating on behalf of the victim.

(d) An employee who is absent from work pursuant to subdivision (b) may elect to use the employee's accrued paid vacation time, personal leave time, sick leave time, compensatory time off that is otherwise available to the employee, or unpaid leave time, unless otherwise provided by a collective bargaining agreement, for an absence pursuant to subdivision (b). The entitlement of any employee under this section shall not be diminished by any collective bargaining agreement term or condition.

(e) An employer shall keep confidential any records regarding the employee's absence from work pursuant to subdivision (b).

(f) An employer may not discharge from employment or in any manner discriminate against an employee, in compensation or other terms, conditions, or privileges of employment, including, but not limited to the loss of seniority or precedence, because the employee is absent from work pursuant to this section.

(g)(1) Any employee who is discharged, threatened with discharge, demoted, suspended, or in any other manner discriminated or retaliated against in the terms and conditions of employment by his or her employer because the employee has exercised his or her rights as set forth in subdivision (b) may file a complaint with the Division of Labor Standards Enforcement of the Department of Industrial Relations pursuant to Section 98. 7.

(2) Notwithstanding any time limitation in Section 98.7, an employee filing a complaint with the division based upon a violation of subdivision (b) shall have one year from the date of occurrence of the violation to file his or her complaint.

(h) District attorney and victim/witness offices are encouraged to make information regarding this section available for distribution at their offices. *(Added by Stats.2003, c. 630 (S.B.478), § 1.)*

§ 230.3. Volunteer firefighter; reserve peace officer; emergency rescue personnel; time off; discrimination

(a) No employer shall discharge or in any manner discriminate against an employee for taking time off to perform emergency duty as a volunteer firefighter, a reserve peace officer, or emergency rescue personnel.

(b) Any employee who is discharged, threatened with discharge, demoted, suspended, or in any other manner discriminated against in the terms and conditions of employment by his or her employer because the employee has taken time off to perform emergency duty as a volunteer firefighter, a reserve peace officer, or emergency rescue personnel shall be entitled to reinstatement and reimbursement for lost wages and work benefits caused by the acts of the employer. Any employer who willfully refuses to rehire, promote, or otherwise restore an employee or former employee who has been determined to be eligible for rehiring or promotion by a grievance procedure, arbitration, or hearing authorized by law, is guilty of a misdemeanor.

(c) Subdivisions (a) and (b) of this section shall not apply to any public safety agency or provider of emergency medical services when, as determined by the employer, the employee's absence would hinder the availability of public safety or emergency medical services.

(d)(1) For purposes of this section, "volunteer firefighter" shall have the same meaning as the term "volunteer" in subdivision (m) of Section 50952 of the Government Code.

(2) For purposes of this section, "emergency rescue personnel" means any person who is an officer, employee, or member of a fire department or fire protection or firefighting agency of the federal government, the State of California, a city, county, city and county, district, or other public or municipal corporation or political subdivision of this state, or of a sheriff's department, police department, or a private fire department, whether that person is a volunteer or partly paid or fully paid, while he or she is actually engaged in providing emergency services as defined by subdivision (e) of Section 1799.107 of the Health and Safety Code. *(Added by Stats.1989, c. 167, § 1. Amended by Stats.2000, c. 244 (S.B.1353), § 1.)*

§ 230.4. Volunteer firefighter; leaves of absence for training

(a) An employee who is a volunteer firefighter, and works for an employer employing 50 or more employees, shall be permitted to take temporary leaves of absence, not to exceed an aggregate of 14 days per calendar year, for the purpose of engaging in fire or law enforcement training.

(b) An employee who works for an employer employing 50 or more employees who is discharged, threatened with discharge, demoted, suspended, or in any other manner discriminated against in the terms and conditions of employment by his or her employer because the employee has taken time off to engage in fire or law enforcement training as provided in subdivision (a), is entitled to reinstatement and reimbursement for lost wages and work benefits caused by the acts of the employer.

(c) An employee seeking reinstatement and reimbursement pursuant to this section may file a complaint with the Division of Labor Standards Enforcement in accordance with Section 98.7, and upon receipt of such a complaint, the Labor Commissioner shall proceed as provided in that section. *(Added by Stats.2000, c. 361 (A.B.2535), § 1.)*

§ 230.7. Discharge or discrimination against employee for taking time off to appear in school on behalf of child

(a) No employer shall discharge or in any manner discriminate against an employee who is the parent or guardian of a pupil for taking time off to appear in the school of a pupil pursuant to a request made under Section 48900.1 of the Education Code, if the employee, prior to taking the time off, gives reasonable notice to the employer that he or she is requested to appear in the school.

(b) Any employee who is discharged, threatened with discharge, demoted, suspended, or in any other manner discriminated against in the terms and conditions of employment by his or her employer because the employee has taken time off to appear in the school of a pupil pursuant to a request made under Section 48900.1 of the Education Code shall be entitled to reinstatement and reimbursement for lost wages and work benefits caused by those acts of the employer. *(Added by Stats.1989, c. 213, § 2.)*

§ 230.8. Discharge of or discrimination against employee for taking time off to visit child's school or day care facility; use of vacation, personal leave, compensatory time off or time off without pay; documentation of participation; reinstatement and reimbursement

(a)(1) No employer who employs 25 or more employees working at the same location shall discharge or in any way discriminate against an employee who is a parent, guardian, or grandparent having custody, of one or more children in kindergarten or grades 1 to 12, inclusive, or attending a licensed child day care facility, for taking off up to 40 hours each year, not exceeding eight hours in any calendar month of the year, to participate in activities of the school or licensed child day care facility of any of his or her children, if the employee, prior to taking the time off, gives reasonable notice to the employer of the planned absence of the employee.

(2) If both parents of a child are employed by the same employer at the same worksite, the entitlement under paragraph (1) of a planned absence as to that child applies, at any one time, only to the parent who first gives notice to the employer, such that the other parent may take a planned absence simultaneously as to that same

child under the conditions described in paragraph (1) only if he or she obtains the employer's approval for the requested time off.

(b)(1) The employee shall utilize existing vacation, personal leave, or compensatory time off for purposes of the planned absence authorized by this section, unless otherwise provided by a collective bargaining agreement entered into before January 1, 1995, and in effect on that date. An employee also may utilize time off without pay for this purpose, to the extent made available by his or her employer. The entitlement of any employee under this section shall not be diminished by any collective bargaining agreement term or condition that is agreed to on or after January 1, 1995.

(2) Notwithstanding paragraph (1), in the event that all permanent, full-time employees of an employer are accorded vacation during the same period of time in the calendar year, an employee of that employer may not utilize that accrued vacation benefit at any other time for purposes of the planned absence authorized by this section.

(c) The employee, if requested by the employer, shall provide documentation from the school or licensed child day care facility as proof that he or she participated in school or licensed child day care facility activities on a specific date and at a particular time. For purposes of this subdivision, "documentation" means whatever written verification of parental participation the school or licensed child day care facility deems appropriate and reasonable.

(d) Any employee who is discharged, threatened with discharge, demoted, suspended, or in any other manner discriminated against in terms and conditions of employment by his or her employer because the employee has taken time off to participate in school or licensed child day care facility activities as described in this section shall be entitled to reinstatement and reimbursement for lost wages and work benefits caused by the acts of the employer. Any employer who willfully refuses to rehire, promote, or otherwise restore an employee or former employee who has been determined to be eligible for rehiring or promotion by a grievance procedure, arbitration, or hearing authorized by law shall be subject to a civil penalty in an amount equal to three times the amount of the employee's lost wages and work benefits. *(Added by Stats.1990, c. 859 (A.B.3782), § 2. Amended by Stats.1994, c. 1290 (A.B.2590), § 3; Stats.1997, c. 157 (A.B.47), § 1.)*

§ 231. Physical examination for driver's license required in employment; payment of costs

Any employer who requires, as a condition of employment, that an employee have a driver's license shall pay the cost of any physical examination of the employee which may be required for issuance of such license, except where the physical examination was taken prior to the time the employee applied for such employment with the employer. *(Added by Stats.1971, c. 1279, p. 2506, § 1.)*

336

§ 232. Amount of wages; prohibition of sanctions against employee disclosure

No employer may do any of the following:

(a) Require, as a condition of employment, that an employee refrain from disclosing the amount of his or her wages.

(b) Require an employee to sign a waiver or other document that purports to deny the employee the right to disclose the amount of his or her wages.

(c) Discharge, formally discipline, or otherwise discriminate against an employee who discloses the amount of his or her wages. *(Added by Stats.1984, c. 814, § 1. Amended by Stats.2002, c. 934 (A.B.2895), § 1.)*

§ 232.5. Working conditions; prohibition of sanctions against employee disclosure

No employer may do any of the following:

(a) Require, as a condition of employment, that an employee refrain from disclosing information about the employer's working conditions.

(b) Require an employee to sign a waiver or other document that purports to deny the employee the right to disclose information about the employer's working conditions.

(c) Discharge, formally discipline, or otherwise discriminate against an employee who discloses information about the employer's working conditions.

(d) This section is not intended to permit an employee to disclose proprietary information, trade secret information, or information that is otherwise subject to a legal privilege without the consent of his or her employer. *(Added by Stats.2002, c. 934 (A.B.2895), § 2.)*

§ 233. Sick leave; use to attend to illness in family

(a) Any employer who provides sick leave for employees shall permit an employee to use in any calendar year the employee's accrued and available sick leave entitlement, in an amount not less than the sick leave that would be accrued during six months at the employee's then current rate of entitlement, to attend to an illness of a child, parent, spouse, or domestic partner of the employee. All conditions and restrictions placed by the employer upon the use by an employee of sick leave also shall apply to the use by an employee of sick leave to attend to an illness of his or her child, parent, spouse, or domestic partner. This section does not extend the maximum period of leave to which an employee is entitled under Section 12945.2 of the Government Code or under the federal Family and Medical Leave Act of 1993 (29 U.S.C. Sec. 2606 et seq.), regardless of whether the employee receives sick leave compensation during that leave.

(b) As used in this section:

(1) "Child" means a biological, foster, or adopted child, a stepchild, a legal ward, a child of a domestic partner, or a child of a person standing in loco parentis.

(2) "Employer" means any person employing another under any appointment or contract of hire and includes the state, political subdivisions of the state, and municipalities.

(3) "Parent" means a biological, foster, or adoptive parent, a stepparent, or a legal guardian.

(4) "Sick leave" means accrued increments of compensated leave provided by an employer to an employee as a benefit of the employment for use by the employee during an absence from the employment for any of the following reasons:

(A) The employee is physically or mentally unable to perform his or her duties due to illness, injury, or a medical condition of the employee.

(B) The absence is for the purpose of obtaining professional diagnosis or treatment for a medical condition of the employee.

(C) The absence is for other medical reasons of the employee, such as pregnancy or obtaining a physical examination.

"Sick leave" does not include any benefit provided under an employee welfare benefit plan subject to the federal Employee Retirement Income Security Act of 1974 (Public Law 93–406, as amended) [1] and does not include any insurance benefit, workers' compensation benefit, unemployment compensation disability benefit, or benefit not payable from the employer's general assets.

(c) No employer shall deny an employee the right to use sick leave or discharge, threaten to discharge, demote, suspend, or in any manner discriminate against an employee for using, or attempting to exercise the right to use, sick leave to attend to an illness of a child, parent, spouse, or domestic partner of the employee.

(d) Any employee aggrieved by a violation of this section shall be entitled to reinstatement and actual damages or one day's pay, whichever is greater, and to appropriate equitable relief.

(e) Upon the filing of a complaint by an employee, the Labor Commissioner shall enforce the provisions of this section in accordance with the provisions of Chapter 4 (commencing with Section 79) of Division 1, including, but not limited to, Sections 92, 96.7, 98, and 98.1 to 98.8, inclusive. Alternatively, an employee may bring a civil action for the remedies provided by this section in a court of competent jurisdiction. If the employee prevails, the court may award reasonable attorney's fees.

(f) The rights and remedies specified in this section are cumulative and nonexclusive and are in addition to any other rights or remedies afforded by contract or under other provisions of law. *(Added by Stats.1999, c. 164 (A.B.109), § 1. Amended by Stats.2001, c. 893 (A.B.25), § 12.)*

[1] 29 U.S.C.A. § 1001 et seq.

§ 234. Sick leave to attend to illness in family; employer absence control policy; legal and equitable relief

An employer absence control policy that counts sick leave taken pursuant to Section 233 as an absence that may lead to or result in discipline, discharge, demotion, or suspension is a per se violation of Section 233. An employee working under this policy is entitled to appropriate legal and equitable relief pursuant to Section 233. *(Added by Stats.2002, c. 1107 (S.B.1471), § 1.)*

§ 240. Deposit of bond by employer; violation of article or judgment for nonpayment of wages; injunction

(a) If any employer has been convicted of a violation of any provision of this article, or if any judgment against an employer for nonpayment of wages remains unsatisfied for a period of 10 days after the time to appeal therefrom has expired, and no appeal therefrom is then pending, the Labor Commissioner may require the employer to deposit a bond in such sum as the Labor Commissioner may deem sufficient and adequate in the circumstances, to be approved by the Labor Commissioner. The bond shall be payable to the Labor Commissioner and shall be conditioned that the employer shall, for a definite future period, not exceeding six months, pay the employees in accordance with the provisions of this article, and shall be further conditioned upon the payment by the employer of any judgment which may be recovered against the employer pursuant to the provisions of this article.

(b) If within 10 days after demand for the bond, which demand may be made by mail, the employer fails to deposit the bond, the Labor Commissioner may bring an action in the name and on behalf of the people of the State of California against the employer in a court of competent jurisdiction to compel the employer to furnish the bond or to cease doing business until the employer has done so. The employer has the burden of proving either that the bond is unnecessary or that the amount demanded is excessive. If the court finds that there is just cause for requiring the bond, and that the bond is reasonably necessary or proper to secure prompt payment of the wages of the employees of the employer and the employer's compliance with the provisions of this article, the court may enjoin the employer, whether an individual, partnership, corporation, company, trust, or association, and such other person or persons as may have been or may be concerned with or in any way participating in the failure to pay the wages resulting in the conviction or in the judgment, from doing business until the requirement is met, and make other and further orders appropriate to compel compliance with the requirement. *(Added by Stats.1975, c. 445, p. 940, § 1. Amended by Stats.1982, c. 517, p. 2401, § 298.)*

§ 243. Second offense by employer; temporary restraining order against doing business; bond; third offense; trial date; labor commissioner duties

(a) If, within 10 years of either a conviction for a violation of this article or failing to satisfy a judgment for nonpayment of wages, or of both, it is alleged that an employer on a second occasion has been convicted of again violating this article or is failing to satisfy a judgment for nonpayment of wages, an employee or the employee's legal representative, an attorney licensed to practice law in this state, may, on behalf of himself or herself and others, bring an action in a court of competent jurisdiction for a temporary restraining order prohibiting the employer from doing business in this state unless the employer deposits with the court a bond to secure compliance by the employer with this article or to satisfy the judgment for nonpayment of wages.

(b) Upon the filing of an affidavit that, to the satisfaction of the court, shows reasonable proof that an employer, for the second time within 10 years, has been convicted of violating this article or has failed to satisfy a judgment for the nonpayment of wages, or both, the court, pursuant to Section 527 of the Code of Civil Procedure, may grant a temporary restraining order that prohibits the employer within 30 days from conducting any business within the state, unless the employer deposits a bond payable to the Labor Commissioner that is conditioned on the employer making wage payments in accordance with this article, or upon satisfaction by the employer of any judgment for nonpayment of wages, or both. The court shall order that the bond be deposited with the court by the employer at any point in time that, within a five-year period from the date of the order, the employer employs more than 10 employees. The court shall order that the bond be in an amount equal to twenty-five thousand dollars ($25,000) or 25 percent of the weekly gross payroll of the employer at the time of the posting of the bond, whichever is greater, and that the term of the bond be for the duration of the service of the employee who brought the action, until past due wages have been paid, or until satisfaction of a judgment for nonpayment of wages.

(c) For purposes of subdivision (b), an employer shall be deemed to have been convicted of having violated this article or to have failed to satisfy a judgment for the second time within 10 years if, to secure labor or personal services in connection with his or her business, the employer uses the services of an agent, contractor, or subcontractor who is convicted of a violation of this article or fails to satisfy a judgment for wages respecting those employees, or both, but only if the employer had actual knowledge of the person's failure to pay wages. In issuing a temporary restraining order pursuant to this section, the court, in determining the amount and term of the bond, shall count the agent's, contractor's, or subcontractor's employees as part of the employer's total work force. This subdivision shall not apply where a temporary restraining order against the agent, contractor, or subcontractor as an employer has been issued pursuant to subdivision (b).

(d) An employer who, for the third time within 10 years of the first occurrence, is alleged to have violated this article or to have failed to satisfy a judgment for

338

nonpayment of wages, or both, shall be deemed by the court to have commenced a new five-year period for which the posting of a bond may be ordered in accordance with subdivision (b), except that the court may, in its discretion, require the posting of a bond in a greater amount as it determines appropriate under the circumstances.

(e) A former employee who was a party to an earlier action against an employer in which a judgment for the payment of wages was obtained, and who alleges that the employer has failed to satisfy the judgment for the payment of wages, in addition to any other available remedy, may petition the court pursuant to subdivision (b) for a temporary restraining order against the employer to cease doing business in this state unless the employer posts a bond with the court.

(f) Actions brought pursuant to this section shall be set for trial at the earliest possible date, and shall take precedence over all other cases, except older matters of the same character and matters to which special precedence may be given by law.

(g) Nothing in this section shall be construed to impose any mandatory duties on the Labor Commissioner. *(Added by Stats.1989, c. 945, § 1. Amended by Stats.2006, c. 538 (S.B.1852), § 480.)*

ARTICLE 2.   SEASONAL LABOR

Section
250.   Seasonal labor defined.
251.   Seamen's wages; wage payments regulated by federal statute.
252.   Payment in presence of labor commissioner.
253.   Hearing of wage disputes; decision.
254.   Findings and award.
255.   Effect of award; judicial review.
256.   Civil penalty.
257.   Statutes incorporated by reference.

§ 250.   Seasonal labor defined

As used in this article "seasonal labor" means all labor performed by any person hired in this State to perform services outside of this State for a period greater than one month, where the wages are to be paid in this State, not at fixed intervals, but at the termination of such employment. *(Stats.1937, c. 90, p. 201, § 250.)*

§ 251.   Seamen's wages; wage payments regulated by federal statute

This article shall not apply to wages earned by seamen or other persons, where payment is regulated by Federal statute. *(Stats.1937, c. 90, p. 201, § 251.)*

§ 252.   Payment in presence of labor commissioner

Upon application of either the employer or the employee, the wages earned in seasonal labor shall be paid in the presence of the Labor Commissioner, or his deputy or agent. *(Stats.1937, c. 90, p. 201, § 252.)*

§ 253. Hearing of wage disputes; decision

The Labor Commissioner shall hear and decide all wage disputes arising in connection with seasonal labor and shall allow or reject any deductions made from such wages. He shall reject all deductions made for gambling and liquor debts incurred by the employee during such employment. *(Stats.1937, c. 90, p. 201, § 253.)*

§ 254. Findings and award

After a final hearing by the Labor Commissioner, he shall file in the office of his division a copy of the findings of fact and his award. *(Stats.1937, c. 90, p. 201, § 254.)*

§ 255. Effect of award; judicial review

The amount of the award of the Labor Commissioner shall, in the absence of fraud, be conclusively presumed to be the amount of the wages due and unpaid to the employee at the time of the termination of the employment but shall be subject to review by the courts in the manner provided by the Code of Civil Procedure. *(Stats. 1937, c. 90, p. 201, § 255.)*

§ 256. Civil penalty

The Labor Commissioner shall impose a civil penalty in an amount not exceeding 30 days pay as waiting time under the terms of Section 203. *(Stats.1937, c. 90, p. 201, § 256. Amended by Stats.1983, c. 1096, § 3.)*

§ 257. Statutes incorporated by reference

All provisions of Article 1 of this chapter [1], except sections 204, 205, 207, 208, 209, 210, 211 and 215 are applicable to this article. *(Stats.1937, c. 90, p. 201, § 257.)*

[1] Section 200 et seq. of this chapter.

ARTICLE 3.   SPECIAL OCCUPATIONS

Section
270. Mining; required deposit; violation; misdemeanor.
270.5. Logging; operating saw mill; required deposit; violation; misdemeanor.
270.6. Door-to-door selling or telephone solicitation; required deposit; violation; misdemeanor.
271. Theatrical enterprises; required deposit; violation; misdemeanor.
272. Notice of place of deposit; effect of violation.
273. Unpaid wages of farm laborers or garment workers; statement regarding satisfaction of final judgments prerequisite to licensure as farm labor contractor, registration as garment manufacturer, or renewal or reinstatement of license or registration; fines and penalties for fraud.

§ 270. Mining; required deposit; violation; misdemeanor

No person, or agent or officer thereof, engaged in the business of extracting or of extracting and refining or reducing minerals other than petroleum, except persons having a free and unencumbered title to the fee of the property being worked and except mining partnerships in respect to the members of the partnership, shall fail or neglect, before commencing work in any period for which a single payment of wages is made, to have on hand or on deposit with a bank or trust company, in the county where such property is located or if there is no bank or trust company in the county, then in the bank or trust company nearest the property, cash or readily salable securities of a market value sufficient to pay the wages of every person employed on the mining property, or in connection therewith, for such period.

Any person, or agent or officer thereof, who violates this section is guilty of a misdemeanor. *(Added by Stats.1945, c. 628, p. 1155, § 3.)*

§ 270.5. Logging; operating saw mill; required deposit; violation; misdemeanor

(a) No person, agent or officer thereof, or logging contractor, or sawmill operations contractor, engaged in the business of logging or operating a sawmill for converting logs into lumber, except in the case of logging or sawmill operations of persons having a free and unencumbered title to the fee of real property in this state, of a market value sufficient to pay the wages of every person employed in connection with such operations in any period for which a single payment of wages is made, shall fail or neglect, before commencing work in any period for which such single payment of wages is made, or for four calendar weeks, whichever is the longer, to do one of the following:

(1) Have on hand or on deposit with a bank or trust company, in the county where such business is conducted, or if there is no bank or trust company in the county, then in the bank or trust company nearest such operations, cash or readily salable securities of a market value sufficient to pay the wages of every person employed in connection with such operations for such period.

(2) Deposit with the Labor Commissioner the bond of a surety company authorized to do business within the state, acceptable to the Labor Commissioner, conditioned upon the payment of all wages found by the Labor Commissioner to be due and unpaid in connection with such operations.

(b) The cash and securities on deposit referred to in subdivision (a) shall not be commingled with other deposits, securities or property of the employer and shall be held in trust and shall not be used for any other purpose than paying the wages due employees. Such moneys so held in trust are not subject to the enforcement of a money judgment by any other creditor of the employer.

(c) Any person, agent or officer thereof, or logging contractor, or sawmill operations contractor, who violates this section is guilty of a misdemeanor. *(Added by Stats.1957, c. 593, p. 1690, § 1. Amended by Stats.1961, c. 318, p. 1359, § 1; Stats.1963, c. 178, p. 911, § 1; Stats.1982, c. 497, p. 2201, § 131, operative July 1, 1983.)*

§ 270.6. Door-to-door selling or telephone solicitation; required deposit; violation; misdemeanor

(a) No person, or agent or officer thereof, without a permanent and fixed place of business or residence in this state who uses or employs any person in the door-to-door selling of any merchandise, in any similar itinerant activity, or in any telephone solicitation, shall fail or neglect, before commencing work in any period for which any single payment of wages is made or for four calendar weeks, whichever is longer, to do any one of the following:

(1) Have on hand or on deposit with a bank or trust company in the county where the business is conducted, or if there is no bank or trust company in the county, then in the bank or trust company nearest these operations, cash or readily salable securities of a market value sufficient to pay the wages of every person employed in connection with these operations for that period described in this subdivision.

(2) Deposit with the Labor Commissioner the bond of a surety company authorized to do business within the state, acceptable to the Labor Commissioner, conditioned upon the payment of all wages found to be due and unpaid in connection with these operations under any provision of this code.

(3) Deposit with the Labor Commissioner a time certificate of deposit indicating that the person, agent, or officer subject to this section has deposited with a bank or trust company cash payable to the order of the Labor Commissioner sufficient to pay the wages of every person employed in connection with these operations for that period described in this subdivision.

(b) The cash and securities on deposit referred to in subdivision (a) shall not be commingled with other deposits, securities, or property of the employer and shall be held in trust and shall not be used for any other purpose than paying the wages due employees. The moneys so held in trust are not subject to enforcement of a money judgment by any other creditor of the employer.

(c) Any person, or agent or officer thereof, who violates this section is guilty of a misdemeanor. *(Added by Stats.1965, c. 329, p. 1437, § 1. Amended by Stats. 1982, c. 497, p. 2201, § 132, operative July 1, 1983; Stats.2006, c. 538 (S.B.1852), § 481.)*

§ 271. Theatrical enterprises; required deposit; violation; misdemeanor

No person, or agent or officer thereof, engaged in the business of promoting a theatrical enterprise where living individuals are used or employed in the presentation, except persons having a free and unencumbered title to the fee of the property on which the theatrical enterprise is produced, shall fail or neglect, before producing such enterprise in any period for which a single payment of wages is made, to have on hand or on deposit with a bank or trust company, in the county in which such enterprise is to be produced, or if there is no bank or trust company in the county, then in the bank or trust company nearest the place where such enterprise is produced, cash or readily salable securities of a market value sufficient to pay the wages of every individual used or employed in the production of such enterprise, or in connection therewith for such period. The provisions of this section shall not apply to the use or employment of individuals by a radio or television broadcasting enterprise; provided, there is on hand or on deposit with a bank or trust company in this State cash or readily salable securities of a market value sufficient to pay the wages of every individual used or employed in such enterprise, or in connection therewith.

Theatrical enterprise as used in this section means the production of any circus, vaudeville, carnival, revues, variety shows, musical comedies, operettas, opera, drama, theatrical, endurance contest, walkathon, marathon, derby, or other entertainments, exhibitions, or performances.

Any person, or agent or officer thereof, who violates this section is guilty of a misdemeanor. *(Added by Stats.1945, c. 628, p. 1155, § 3.)*

§ 272. Notice of place of deposit; effect of violation

Every person, agent, or officer thereof engaged in the businesses specified in Section 270, 270.5, 270.6, or 271, shall keep conspicuously posted upon the premises where persons are employed, a notice specifying the name and address of the bank or trust company where the required cash or readily salable securities are on deposit, or the name of the surety or sureties on the bond deposited pursuant to Section 270.5 or 270.6. Failure to keep the notice conspicuously posted is prima facie evidence of a violation of Section 270, 270.5, 270.6, or 271. *(Added by Stats.1951, c. 774, p. 2264, § 1. Amended by Stats.1957, c. 593, p. 1690, § 2; Stats.1965, c. 329, p. 1438, § 2.)*

§ 273. Unpaid wages of farm laborers or garment workers; statement regarding satisfaction of final judgments prerequisite to licensure as farm labor contractor, registration as garment manufacturer, or renewal or reinstatement of license or registration; fines and penalties for fraud

(a) The following definitions apply for purposes of this section:

(1) "All activities relating to an adverse license or registration action" includes, but is not limited to, all of the following which occur as a result of a failure to comply with this section:

(A) Denial of a new application or a renewal application for licensure or registration.

(B) Denial of reinstatement of a license or registration.

(C) Suspension of a license or registration.

(D) Assessment and recovery of civil penalties for knowingly providing false information in the statement required by paragraph (1) of subdivision (b).

(2) "Farm labor contractor" has the same meaning as set forth in Section 1682.

(3) "Final judgment issued by a court" means a judgment with respect to which all possibility of a direct attack, by way of appeal, motion for a new trial, or motion pursuant to Section 663 of the Code of Civil Procedure to vacate the judgment, has been exhausted and also includes any final arbitration award where the time to file a petition for a trial de novo or a petition to vacate or correct the arbitration award has expired, and no petition is pending.

(4) "Garment manufacturer" means a person engaged in garment manufacturing as described in Section 2671.

(5) "Involving unpaid wages" means all amounts required to be paid by a final judgment, order, or accord involving a failure of the licensee or registrant to pay required wages.

(6) "Licensee" has the same meaning as set forth in Section 1682.

(7) "Registrant" means a person who holds a valid and unrevoked garment manufacturer registration.

(b)(1) The Labor Commissioner shall require an applicant for any of the following to submit a statement as to whether the applicant has satisfied all requirements imposed by a final judgment issued by a court or by a final order issued by the Labor Commissioner or by an accord involving unpaid wages:

(A) Licensure as a farm labor contractor.

(B) Registration as a garment manufacturer.

(C) Renewal or reinstatement of a farm labor contractor license or a garment manufacturer registration.

(D) A change in the persons identified pursuant to Section 1689 or subparagraph (B) of paragraph (1) of subdivision (a) of Section 2675.

(2) A person who knowingly provides false information in the statement submitted pursuant to this subdivision shall be subject to a civil penalty of no less than one thousand dollars ($1,000) nor more than twenty-five thousand dollars ($25,000), in addition to any civil remedies available to the Labor Commissioner. The penalty shall be recovered by the Labor Commissioner as part of a hearing relating to a denial of an application for a license or registration, a hearing relating to a denial of a renewal or reinstatement of a license or registration, a hearing to contest the civil penalties assessed under this section by the Labor Commissioner, or in an independent civil action. The action shall be brought in the name of the people of the State of California and the Labor Commissioner and the attorneys thereof may proceed and act for and on behalf of the people in bringing these actions.

(c) Notwithstanding any other provision of law, the Labor Commissioner shall not approve an application described in subdivision (b) if the statement submitted with it shows that the applicant has failed to satisfy all requirements imposed by a final judgment issued by a court or by a final order issued by the Labor Commissioner or by an accord involving unpaid wages, as described in subdivision (b), unless the applicant submits either of the following to the Labor Commissioner:

(1) A bond or a cash deposit, in addition to any required by Section 240, 1684, 1688, 2675, or 2679, in an amount sufficient to guarantee payment of all amounts due under a final judgment issued by a court or by a final order issued by the Labor Commissioner involving unpaid wages.

(2) A notarized accord between the applicant and the other parties to the judgment, order, or accord demonstrating that the applicant has satisfied all requirements imposed by the judgment, order, or accord involving unpaid wages.

(d) Notwithstanding any other provision of law, if the Labor Commissioner determines after granting an application described in subdivision (b), that the applicant made a false representation on the statement he or she submitted, the Labor Commissioner shall suspend the farm labor contractor license or garment manufacturer registration effective on the date of its issuance, renewal, or reinstatement. The license or registration shall remain suspended until the applicant satisfies either of the following requirements:

(1) Documents to the satisfaction of the Labor Commissioner that he or she has satisfied all requirements imposed by a final judgment issued by a court or by a final order of the Labor Commissioner or by an accord involving unpaid wages.

(2) Files with the Labor Commissioner a notarized accord as described in paragraph (2) of subdivision (c).

(e)(1) A licensee or registrant shall notify the Labor Commissioner in writing within 90 days of the date of a final judgment issued by a court, a final order issued by the Labor Commissioner, or an accord that imposes on the licensee or registrant requirements involving unpaid wages. If the licensee or registrant fails to comply with this notification requirement, the Labor Commissioner shall suspend the license or registration on the date that the Labor Commissioner is informed, or is made aware of, the judgment, order, or accord. The suspension shall remain in effect until the licensee or registrant satisfies either of the requirements described in subdivision (d).

(2) A licensee or registrant who notifies the Labor Commissioner of a judgment, order, or accord pursuant to paragraph (1), shall file with the notice a bond or a cash deposit meeting the criteria of paragraph (1) of subdivision (c).

(f)(1) The Labor Commissioner may reduce the amount of a bond or cash deposit required by this section upon proof, to the satisfaction of the Labor Commissioner, of partial satisfaction of the requirements imposed by a final judgment issued by a court, a final order issued by the Labor Commissioner, or an accord involving unpaid wages. The Labor Commissioner shall not reduce the bond or cash deposit amount below the balance of the entire amount involving unpaid wages. Upon full satisfaction of the requirements involving unpaid wages, the

Labor Commissioner may terminate the bond or cash deposit requirement.

(2) Notwithstanding paragraph (1), within one year from the date of filing the bond or cash deposit pursuant to paragraph (1) of subdivision (c) or paragraph (2) of subdivision (e), a licensee or registrant shall submit a notarized accord between the licensee or registrant and the other parties to the judgment, order, or accord demonstrating satisfaction of all requirements imposed by the judgment, order, or accord involving unpaid wages. The Labor Commissioner shall suspend the license or registration of a person who fails to file the notarized accord within that timeframe. Notwithstanding paragraph (1) of subdivision (c), a person who has failed to file a notarized accord within the timeframe required by this subdivision shall have his or her license or registration reinstated only after demonstrating that he or she has satisfied all requirements imposed by a final judgment, order, or accord involving unpaid wages. As an alternative to payment in full of all debts involving unpaid wages, a person may submit a notarized copy of an accord between the licensee or registrant and the other parties to the accord.

(g) The failure of a licensee or registrant to maintain a bond required by this section or to abide by all requirements imposed on a licensee or registrant by an accord involving unpaid wages between the licensee or registrant and the other parties to the accord shall result in the automatic suspension of his or her license or registration.

(h)(1) A licensee or registrant shall not allow a person who is a judgment debtor in a final judgment issued by a court or in a final order issued by the Labor Commissioner involving unpaid wages that imposes requirements that have not been satisfied in their entirety to serve in a capacity described in Section 1689 or subparagraph (B) of paragraph (1) of subdivision (a) of Section 2675.

(2) The Labor Commissioner shall suspend the license of a farm labor contractor or the registration of a garment manufacturer who violates the provisions of paragraph (1). The Labor Commissioner shall reinstate the license or registration upon the resignation of the person named as a judgment debtor or complete satisfaction of the unpaid wages requirements.

(i) A person whose license or registration is suspended pursuant to this section, who is denied issuance or reinstatement of a license or registration, or who has been assessed a civil penalty for knowingly providing false information in the statement required by paragraph (1) of subdivision (b) shall pay to the Labor Commissioner all reasonable costs incurred by the Labor Commissioner in all activities relating to the adverse license or registration action, commencing with the first notice issued by the Labor Commissioner that he or she has taken any adverse action under this section relative to a license or registration. The Labor Commissioner shall not reinstate a license or registration unless the person has paid all costs assessed by the Labor Commissioner or has entered into

an accord with the Labor Commissioner that establishes a payment plan.

(j) This section shall not apply to an applicant for a farm labor contractor license or a garment manufacturer registration or to a licensee or registrant when the unpaid wages, as described by this section, have been discharged in a bankruptcy proceeding. *(Added by Stats.2009, c. 256 (A.B.854), § 1.)*

CHAPTER 2. ASSIGNMENT OF WAGES

Section
300. Validity and exceptions.

§ 300. Validity and exceptions

(a) As used in this section, the phrase "assignment of wages" includes the sale or assignment of, or giving of an order for, wages or salary but does not include an order or assignment made pursuant to Chapter 8 (commencing with Section 5200) of Part 5 of Division 9 of the Family Code or Section 3088 of the Probate Code.

(b) No assignment of wages, earned or to be earned, is valid unless all of the following conditions are satisfied:

(1) The assignment is contained in a separate written instrument, signed by the person by whom the wages or salary have been earned or are to be earned, and identifying specifically the transaction to which the assignment relates.

(2) Where the assignment is made by a married person, the written consent of the spouse of the person making the assignment is attached to the assignment. No such consent is required of any married person (A) after entry of a judgment decreeing a legal separation from such person's spouse or (B) if the married person and the spouse of the married person are living separate and apart after entry of an interlocutory judgment of dissolution of their marriage, if a written statement by the person making the assignment, setting forth such facts, is attached to or included in the assignment.

(3) Where the assignment is made by a minor, the written consent of a parent or guardian of the minor is attached to the assignment.

(4) Where the assignment is made by a person who is unmarried or who is an adult or who is both unmarried and an adult, a written statement by the person making the assignment, setting forth such facts, is attached to or included in the assignment.

(5) No other assignment exists in connection with the same transaction or series of transactions and a written statement by the person making the assignment to that effect is attached to or included in the assignment.

(6) A copy of the assignment and of the written statement provided for in paragraphs (2), (4), and (5), authenticated by a notary public, is filed with the employer, accompanied by an itemized statement of the amount then due to the assignee.

(7) At the time the assignment is filed with the employer, no other assignment of wages of the employee is subject to payment and no earnings withholding order against the employee's wages or salary is in force.

(c) Under any assignment of wages, a sum not to exceed 50 per centum of the assignor's wages or salary shall be withheld by, and be collectible from, the assignor's employer at the time of each payment of such wages or salary.

(d) The employer is entitled to rely upon the statements of fact in the written statement provided for in paragraphs (2), (4), and (5) of subdivision (b), without the necessity of inquiring into the truth thereof, and the employer shall incur no liability whatsoever by reason of any payments made by the employer to an assignee under any assignment in reliance upon the facts so stated.

(e) An assignment of wages to be earned is revocable at any time by the maker thereof. Any power of attorney to assign or collect wages or salary is revocable at any time by the maker thereof. No revocation of such an assignment or power of attorney is effective as to the employer until the employer receives written notice of revocation from the maker.

(f) No assignment of wages, earned or to be earned, is valid under any circumstances if the wages or salary earned or to be earned are paid under a plan for payment at a central place or places established under the provisions of Section 204a.

(g) This section does not apply to deductions which the employer may be requested by the employee to make for the payment of life, retirement, disability or unemployment insurance premiums, for the payment of taxes owing from the employee, for contribution to funds, plans or systems providing for death, retirement, disability, unemployment, or other benefits, for the payment for goods or services furnished by the employer to the employee or the employee's family at the request of the employee, or for charitable, educational, patriotic or similar purposes.

(h) No assignment of wages is valid unless at the time of the making thereof, such wages or salary have been earned, except for necessities of life and then only to the person or persons furnishing such necessities of life directly and then only for the amount needed to furnish such necessities. *(Stats.1937, c. 90, p. 202, § 300. Amended by Stats.1941, c. 529, p. 1851, § 5; Stats.1943, c. 1048, p. 2988, § 1; Stats.1974, c. 1516, p. 3388, § 31, operative Jan. 1, 1977; Stats.1978, c. 1133, p. 3483, § 9, operative Jan. 1, 1980; Stats.1982, c. 497, p. 2202, § 132.5, operative July 1, 1983; Stats.1992, c. 163 (A.B.2641), § 99, operative Jan. 1, 1994.)*

CHAPTER 3. PRIVILEGES AND PERQUISITES

Article   Section
1. Gratuities 350
2. Bonds and Photographs 400
3. Contracts and Applications for Employment 430
4. Purchases 450

ARTICLE 1. GRATUITIES

Section
350. Definitions.
351. Gratuities; disposition.
353. Records of gratuities received by employer; inspection.
354. Violation; misdemeanor; penalty.
355. Enforcement agency; disposition of fines.
356. Legislative declaration.

§ 350. Definitions

As used in this article, unless the context indicates otherwise:

(a) "Employer" means every person engaged in any business or enterprise in this state that has one or more persons in service under any appointment, contract of hire, or apprenticeship, express or implied, oral or written, irrespective of whether the person is the owner of the business or is operating on a concessionaire or other basis.

(b) "Employee" means every person, including aliens and minors, rendering actual service in any business for an employer, whether gratuitously or for wages or pay, whether the wages or pay are measured by the standard of time, piece, task, commission, or other method of calculation, and whether the service is rendered on a commission, concessionaire, or other basis.

(c) "Employing" includes hiring, or in any way contracting for, the services of an employee.

(d) "Agent" means every person other than the employer having the authority to hire or discharge any employee or supervise, direct, or control the acts of employees.

(e) "Gratuity" includes any tip, gratuity, money, or part thereof that has been paid or given to or left for an employee by a patron of a business over and above the actual amount due the business for services rendered or for goods, food, drink, or articles sold or served to the patron. Any amounts paid directly by a patron to a dancer employed by an employer subject to Industrial Welfare Commission Order No. 5 or 10 shall be deemed a gratuity.

(f) "Business" means any business establishment or enterprise, regardless of where conducted. *(Stats.1937, c. 90, p. 202, § 350. Amended by Stats.2000, c. 876 (A.B. 2509), § 8.)*

§ 351. Gratuities; disposition

No employer or agent shall collect, take, or receive any gratuity or a part thereof that is paid, given to, or left for an employee by a patron, or deduct any amount from wages due an employee on account of a gratuity, or require an employee to credit the amount, or any part thereof, of a gratuity against and as a part of the wages due the employee from the employer. Every gratuity is hereby declared to be the sole property of the employee or employees to whom it was paid, given, or left for. An employer that permits patrons to pay gratuities by credit card shall pay the employees the full amount of the gratuity that the patron indicated on the credit card slip, without any deductions for any credit card payment processing fees or costs that may be charged to the employer by the credit card company. Payment of gratuities made by patrons using credit cards shall be made to the employees not later than the next regular payday following the date the patron authorized the credit card payment. *(Stats.1937, c. 90, p. 203, § 351. Amended by Stats.1965, c. 686, p. 2062, § 1; Stats.1973, c. 879, p. 1610, § 1; Stats.1974, c. 552, p. 1375, § 1; Stats.1975, c. 324, p. 771, § 1; Stats.2000, c. 876 (A.B. 2509), § 9.)*

§ 353. Records of gratuities received by employer; inspection

Every employer shall keep accurate records of all gratuities received by him, whether received directly from the employee or indirectly by means of deductions from the wages of the employee or otherwise. Such records shall be open to inspection at all reasonable hours by the department. *(Stats.1937, c. 90, p. 203, § 353.)*

§ 354. Violation; misdemeanor; penalty

Any employer who violates any provision of this article is guilty of a misdemeanor, punishable by a fine not exceeding one thousand dollars ($1,000) or by imprisonment for not exceeding 60 days, or both. *(Stats.1937, c. 90, p. 203, § 354. Amended by Stats.1983, c. 1092, § 190, eff. Sept. 27, 1983, operative Jan. 1, 1984.)*

§ 355. Enforcement agency; disposition of fines

The Department of Industrial Relations shall enforce the provisions of this article. All fines collected under this article shall be paid into the State treasury and credited to the general fund. *(Stats.1937, c. 90, p. 203, § 355.)*

§ 356. Legislative declaration

The Legislature expressly declares that the purpose of this article is to prevent fraud upon the public in connection with the practice of tipping and declares that this article is passed for a public reason and can not be contravened by a private agreement. As a part of the social public policy of this State, this article is binding upon all departments of the State. *(Stats.1937, c. 90, p. 203, § 356.)*

ARTICLE 2. BONDS AND PHOTOGRAPHS

Section
400. Applicant defined.
401. Payment of cost.
402. Cash bond.
403. Deposit in savings bank; withdrawal; written agreement between employer and employee.

Section
404. Enforcement of money judgments; return of cash; bond.
405. Prohibited use of property put up as bond; commingling with employer's property; violation.
406. Property put up as part of employment contract.
407. Investment in business in connection with employment.
408. Violations; misdemeanor; penalty.
409. Disposition of fines.
410. Enforcement officer.

§ 400. Applicant defined

As used in this article, "applicant" means an applicant for employment. *(Stats.1937, c. 90, p. 203, § 400.)*

§ 401. Payment of cost

If a bond or photograph of an employee or applicant is required by any employer, the cost thereof shall be paid by the employer. *(Stats.1937, c. 90, p. 203, § 401.)*

§ 402. Cash bond

No employer shall demand, exact, or accept any cash bond from any employee or applicant unless:

(a) The employee or applicant is entrusted with property of an equivalent value, or

(b) The employer advances regularly to the employee goods, wares, or merchandise to be delivered or sold by the employee, and for which the employer is reimbursed by the employee at regular periodic intervals, and the employer limits the cash bond to an amount sufficient to cover the value of the goods, wares, or merchandise so advanced during the period prior to the payment therefor. *(Stats.1937, c. 90, p. 203, § 402.)*

§ 403. Deposit in savings bank; withdrawal; written agreement between employer and employee

If cash is received as a bond it shall be deposited in a savings account in a bank authorized to do business in this State, and may be withdrawn only upon the joint signatures of the employer and the employee or applicant.

Cash put up as a bond shall be accompanied by an agreement in writing made by the employer and employee or applicant, setting forth the conditions under which the bond is given. *(Stats.1937, c. 90, p. 204, § 403.)*

§ 404. Enforcement of money judgments; return of cash; bond

Any money put up as a bond under Sections 401, 402 and 403:

(a) Is not subject to enforcement of a money judgment except in an action between the employer and the employee or applicant, or their successors or assigns.

(b) Shall be returned to the employee or applicant together with accrued interest thereon, immediately upon the return of the money or property entrusted to the employee or applicant and upon the fulfillment of the agreement, subject only to the deduction necessary to balance accounts between the employer and employee or applicant. *(Stats.1937, c. 90, p. 204, § 404. Amended by Stats.1974, c. 1516, p. 3389, § 32, operative Jan. 1, 1977; Stats.1982, c. 497, p. 2203, § 133, operative July 1, 1983.)*

§ 405. Prohibited use of property put up as bond; commingling with employer's property; violation

Any property put up by any employee or applicant as a bond shall not be used for any purpose other than liquidating accounts between the employer and employee or for return to the employee or applicant and shall be held in trust for this purpose and not mingled with the property of the employer. No contract between the employer and employee or applicant shall abrogate the provisions of this section. Any employer or prospective employer, or agent or officer thereof, who misappropriates any such property, mingles it with his own, or uses it for any other purpose than that herein set forth is guilty of theft and shall be punished in accordance with the provisions of the Penal Code relating to theft. *(Stats. 1937, c. 90, p. 204, § 405.)*

§ 406. Property put up as part of employment contract

Any property put up by an employee, or applicant as a part of the contract of employment, directly or indirectly, shall be deemed to be put up as a bond and is subject to the provisions of this article whether the property is put up on a note or as a loan or an investment and regardless of the wording of the agreement under which it is put up. *(Stats.1937, c. 90, p. 204, § 406.)*

§ 407. Investment in business in connection with employment

Investments and the sale of stock or an interest in a business in connection with the securing of a position are illegal as against the public policy of the State and shall not be advertised or held out in any way as a part of the consideration for any employment. *(Stats.1937, c. 90, p. 204, § 407.)*

§ 408. Violations; misdemeanor; penalty

Any person or agent or officer thereof, who violates any provision of this article, except the provisions of Section 405, is guilty of a misdemeanor, punishable by a fine of not less than fifty dollars ($50) and not exceeding one thousand dollars ($1,000), or imprisonment for not exceeding six months, or both. *(Stats.1937, c. 90, p. 204, § 408. Amended by Stats.1983, c. 1092, § 191, eff. Sept. 27, 1983, operative Jan. 1, 1984.)*

§ 409. Disposition of fines

All fines imposed and collected under this article shall be paid into the State treasury and credited to the general fund. *(Stats.1937, c. 90, p. 205, § 409.)*

§ 410. Enforcement officer

The Labor Commissioner shall enforce this article. *(Stats.1937, c. 90, p. 205, § 410.)*

ARTICLE 3. CONTRACTS AND APPLICATIONS FOR EMPLOYMENT

Section
430. Applicant defined.
432. Delivery of copy of instrument to employee.
432.2. Polygraph or lie detector test as condition of employment; advice of rights.
432.5. Unlawful terms and conditions.
432.7. Disclosure of arrest or detention not resulting in conviction or referral or participation in diversion programs; violations; remedies; exception; screening prospective concessionaires.
432.8. Limitations on employers and penalties for certain convictions.
433. Violation; misdemeanor.
434. Applications for employment by railroads.
435. Audio or video recording of employee restroom, locker room, or changing room; prohibition; use of recordings in violation of section.

§ 430. Applicant defined

As used in this article "applicant" means an applicant for employment. *(Stats.1937, c. 90, p. 205, § 430.)*

§ 432. Delivery of copy of instrument to employee

If an employee or applicant signs any instrument relating to the obtaining or holding of employment, he shall be given a copy of the instrument upon request. *(Stats.1937, c. 90, p. 205, § 432. Amended by Stats.1969, c. 714, p. 1409, § 1.)*

§ 432.2. Polygraph or lie detector test as condition of employment; advice of rights

(a) No employer shall demand or require any applicant for employment or prospective employment or any employee to submit to or take a polygraph, lie detector or similar test or examination as a condition of employment or continued employment. The prohibition of this section does not apply to the federal government or any agency thereof or the state government or any agency or local subdivision thereof, including, but not limited to, counties, cities and counties, cities, districts, authorities, and agencies.

(b) No employer shall request any person to take such a test, or administer such a test, without first advising the person in writing at the time the test is to be administered of the rights guaranteed by this section. *(Added by Stats.1963, c. 1881, p. 3866, § 1. Amended by Stats.1981, c. 316, p. 1456, § 1.)*

§ 432.5. Unlawful terms and conditions

No employer, or agent, manager, superintendent, or officer thereof, shall require any employee or applicant for employment to agree, in writing, to any term or condition which is known by such employer, or agent, manager, superintendent, or officer thereof to be prohibited by law. *(Added by Stats.1963, c. 559, p. 1440, § 1.)*

§ 432.7. Disclosure of arrest or detention not resulting in conviction or referral or participation in diversion programs; violations; remedies; exception; screening prospective concessionaires

(a) No employer, whether a public agency or private individual or corporation, shall ask an applicant for employment to disclose, through any written form or verbally, information concerning an arrest or detention that did not result in conviction, or information concerning a referral to, and participation in, any pretrial or posttrial diversion program, nor shall any employer seek from any source whatsoever, or utilize, as a factor in determining any condition of employment including hiring, promotion, termination, or any apprenticeship training program or any other training program leading to employment, any record of arrest or detention that did not result in conviction, or any record regarding a referral to, and participation in, any pretrial or posttrial diversion program. As used in this section, a conviction shall include a plea, verdict, or finding of guilt regardless of whether sentence is imposed by the court. Nothing in this section shall prevent an employer from asking an employee or applicant for employment about an arrest for which the employee or applicant is out on bail or on his or her own recognizance pending trial.

(b) Nothing in this section shall prohibit the disclosure of the information authorized for release under Sections 13203 and 13300 of the Penal Code, to a government agency employing a peace officer. However, the employer shall not determine any condition of employment other than paid administrative leave based solely on an arrest report. The information contained in an arrest report may be used as the starting point for an independent, internal investigation of a peace officer in accordance with Chapter 9.7 (commencing with Section 3300) of Division 4 of Title 1 of the Government Code.

(c) In any case where a person violates this section, or Article 6 (commencing with Section 11140) of Chapter 1 of Title 1 of Part 4 of the Penal Code, the applicant may bring an action to recover from that person actual damages or two hundred dollars ($200), whichever is greater, plus costs, and reasonable attorney's fees. An intentional violation of this section shall entitle the applicant to treble actual damages, or five hundred dollars ($500), whichever is greater, plus costs, and reasonable attorney's fees. An intentional violation of this section is a misdemeanor punishable by a fine not to exceed five hundred dollars ($500).

(d) The remedies under this section shall be in addition to and not in derogation of all other rights and remedies that an applicant may have under any other law.

(e) Persons seeking employment or persons already employed as peace officers or persons seeking employment for positions in the Department of Justice or other criminal justice agencies as defined in Section 13101 of the Penal Code are not covered by this section.

(f) Nothing in this section shall prohibit an employer at a health facility, as defined in Section 1250 of the Health and Safety Code, from asking an applicant for employment either of the following:

(1) With regard to an applicant for a position with regular access to patients, to disclose an arrest under any section specified in Section 290 of the Penal Code.

(2) With regard to an applicant for a position with access to drugs and medication, to disclose an arrest under any section specified in Section 11590 of the Health and Safety Code.

(g) (1) No peace officer or employee of a law enforcement agency with access to criminal offender record information maintained by a local law enforcement criminal justice agency shall knowingly disclose, with intent to affect a person's employment, any information contained therein pertaining to an arrest or detention or proceeding that did not result in a conviction, including information pertaining to a referral to, and participation in, any pretrial or posttrial diversion program, to any person not authorized by law to receive that information.

(2) No other person authorized by law to receive criminal offender record information maintained by a local law enforcement criminal justice agency shall knowingly disclose any information received therefrom pertaining to an arrest or detention or proceeding that did not result in a conviction, including information pertaining to a referral to, and participation in, any pretrial or posttrial diversion program, to any person not authorized by law to receive that information.

(3) No person, except those specifically referred to in Section 1070 of the Evidence Code, who knowing he or she is not authorized by law to receive or possess criminal justice records information maintained by a local law enforcement criminal justice agency, pertaining to an arrest or other proceeding that did not result in a conviction, including information pertaining to a referral to, and participation in, any pretrial or posttrial diversion program, shall receive or possess that information.

(h) "A person authorized by law to receive that information," for purposes of this section, means any person or public agency authorized by a court, statute, or decisional law to receive information contained in criminal offender records maintained by a local law enforcement criminal justice agency, and includes, but is not limited to, those persons set forth in Section 11105 of the Penal Code, and any person employed by a law enforcement criminal justice agency who is required by that employment to receive, analyze, or process criminal offender record information.

(i) Nothing in this section shall require the Department of Justice to remove entries relating to an arrest or detention not resulting in conviction from summary criminal history records forwarded to an employer pursuant to law.

(j) As used in this section, "pretrial or posttrial diversion program" means any program under Chapter 2.5 (commencing with Section 1000) or Chapter 2.7 (commencing with Section 1001) of Title 6 of Part 2 of the

Penal Code, Section 13201 or 13352.5 of the Vehicle Code, or any other program expressly authorized and described by statute as a diversion program.

(k) (1) Subdivision (a) shall not apply to any city, city and county, county, or district, or any officer or official thereof, in screening a prospective concessionaire, or the affiliates and associates of a prospective concessionaire for purposes of consenting to, or approving of, the prospective concessionaire's application for, or acquisition of, any beneficial interest in a concession, lease, or other property interest.

(2) For purposes of this subdivision the following terms have the following meanings:

(A) "Screening" means a written request for criminal history information made to a local law enforcement agency.

(B) "Prospective concessionaire" means any individual, general or limited partnership, corporation, trust, association, or other entity that is applying for, or seeking to obtain, a public agency's consent to, or approval of, the acquisition by that individual or entity of any beneficial ownership interest in any public agency's concession, lease, or other property right whether directly or indirectly held. However, "prospective concessionaire" does not include any of the following:

(i) A lender acquiring an interest solely as security for a bona fide loan made in the ordinary course of the lender's business and not made for the purpose of acquisition.

(ii) A lender upon foreclosure or assignment in lieu of foreclosure of the lender's security.

(C) "Affiliate" means any individual or entity that controls, or is controlled by, the prospective concessionaire, or who is under common control with the prospective concessionaire.

(D) "Associate" means any individual or entity that shares a common business purpose with the prospective concessionaire with respect to the beneficial ownership interest that is subject to the consent or approval of the city, county, city and county, or district.

(E) "Control" means the possession, direct or indirect, of the power to direct, or cause the direction of, the management or policies of the controlled individual or entity.

(l) (1) Nothing in subdivision (a) shall prohibit a public agency, or any officer or official thereof, from denying consent to, or approval of, a prospective concessionaire's application for, or acquisition of, any beneficial interest in a concession, lease, or other property interest based on the criminal history information of the prospective concessionaire or the affiliates or associates of the prospective concessionaire that show any criminal conviction for offenses involving moral turpitude. Criminal history information for purposes of this subdivision includes any criminal history information obtained pursuant to Section 11105 or 13300 of the Penal Code.

(2) In considering criminal history information, a public agency shall consider the crime for which the prospective concessionaire or the affiliates or associates of the prospective concessionaire was convicted only if that crime relates to the specific business that is proposed to be conducted by the prospective concessionaire.

(3) Any prospective concessionaire whose application for consent or approval to acquire a beneficial interest in a concession, lease, or other property interest is denied based on criminal history information shall be provided a written statement of the reason for the denial.

(4) (A) If the prospective concessionaire submits a written request to the public agency within 10 days of the date of the notice of denial, the public agency shall review its decision with regard to any corrected record or other evidence presented by the prospective concessionaire as to the accuracy or incompleteness of the criminal history information utilized by the public agency in making its original decision.

(B) The prospective concessionaire shall submit the copy or the corrected record or any other evidence to the public agency within 90 days of a request for review. The public agency shall render its decision within 20 days of the submission of evidence by the prospective concessionaire. *(Added by Stats.1975, c. 1043, p. 2457, § 2. Amended by Stats.1975, c. 1117, p. 2710, § 3; Stats.1977, c. 574, p. 1817, § 1, eff. Sept. 3, 1977; Stats.1981, c. 1103, p. 4312, § 1; Stats.1983, c. 1092, § 192, eff. Sept. 27, 1983, operative Jan. 1, 1984; Stats.1983, c. 1297, § 2; Stats.1984, c. 216, § 4; Stats.1981, c. 1103, p. 4312, § 1, operative Aug. 31, 1984; Stats.1990, c. 769 (A.B.4311), § 1; Stats. 1992, c. 1026 (S.B.1769), § 3.)*

§ 432.8. Limitations on employers and penalties for certain convictions

The limitations on employers and the penalties provided for in Section 432.7 shall apply to a conviction for violation of subdivision (b) or (c) of Section 11357 of the Health and Safety Code or a statutory predecessor thereof, or subdivision (c) of Section 11360 of the Health and Safety Code, or Section 11364, 11365, or 11550 of the Health and Safety Code as they related to marijuana prior to January 1, 1976, or a statutory predecessor thereof, two years from the date of such a conviction. *(Added by Stats.1976, c. 952, p. 2180, § 3.)*

§ 433. Violation; misdemeanor

Any person violating this article is guilty of a misdemeanor. *(Stats.1937, c. 90, p. 205, § 433.)*

§ 434. Applications for employment by railroads

The provisions of this article shall not apply to applications for employment filed with common carriers by railroad subject to the act of Congress known as the Railway Labor Act.[1] *(Stats.1937, c. 90, p. 205, § 434.)*

[1] 45 U.S.C.A. § 151 et seq.

§ 435. Audio or video recording of employee restroom, locker room, or changing room; prohibition; use of recordings in violation of section

(a) No employer may cause an audio or video recording to be made of an employee in a restroom, locker room, or room designated by an employer for changing clothes, unless authorized by court order.

(b) No recording made in violation of this section may be used by an employer for any purpose. This section applies to a private or public employer, except the federal government.

(c) A violation of this section constitutes an infraction. *(Added by Stats.1998, c. 515 (A.B.2303), § 1.)*

ARTICLE 4. PURCHASES

Section
450. Coercion.
451. Violation; penalty.
452. Uniforms.

§ 450. Coercion

(a) No employer, or agent or officer thereof, or other person, may compel or coerce any employee, or applicant for employment, to patronize his or her employer, or any other person, in the purchase of any thing of value.

(b) For purposes of this section, to compel or coerce the purchase of any thing of value includes, but is not limited to, instances where an employer requires the payment of a fee or consideration of any type from an applicant for employment for any of the following purposes:

(1) For an individual to apply for employment orally or in writing.

(2) For an individual to receive, obtain, complete, or submit an application for employment.

(3) For an employer to provide, accept, or process an application for employment. *(Stats.1937, c. 90, p. 205, § 450. Amended by Stats.1998, c. 442 (A.B.1570), § 1.)*

§ 451. Violation; penalty

Any person, or agent or officer thereof, who violates this article is guilty of a misdemeanor. *(Stats.1937, c. 90, p. 205, § 451.)*

§ 452. Uniforms

Nothing in this article shall prohibit an employer from prescribing the weight, color, quality, texture, style, form and make of uniforms required to be worn by his employees. *(Stats.1937, c. 90, p. 205, § 452.)*

Part 2

WORKING HOURS

Chapter   Section
 1. General 510

Chapter   Section
 2. Railroads 600
 3. Smelters and Underground Workings 750
 4. Lumber Industries 800
 5. Pharmacies 850

CHAPTER 1. GENERAL

Section
500.   Definitions.
510.   Day's work; overtime; commuting time.
511.   Alternative workweek schedules.
512.   Meal periods.
512.5. Adoption or amendment by Industrial Welfare Commission of order applying to employee of public agency who operates a commercial motor vehicle; exemption of employee relating to meal or rest periods.
513.   Makeup work time.
514.   Employees covered by collective bargaining agreements; application of §§ 551 and 552.
515.   Exemptions.
515.5. Computer software field employees; exemption; requirements.
515.6. Licensed physicians and surgeons; exemption from § 510.
515.8. Teachers at private elementary or secondary academic institutions; Section 510 not applicable; exemptions.
516.   Adoption or amendment of working condition orders.
517.   Industrial Welfare Commission; adoption of wage, hours, and working conditions orders; review of wages, hours, and working conditions in certain industries; publication of wage orders and other regulations.
550.   Day's rest defined.
551.   One day's rest in seven.
552.   Maximum consecutive working days.
553.   Violation; misdemeanor.
554.   Exemptions from §§ 551 and 552.
555.   Applicability to cities and counties.
556.   Application of §§ 551 and 552.
558.   Violations of chapter; civil penalties.

§ 500. Definitions

For purposes of this chapter, the following terms shall have the following meanings:

(a) "Workday" and "day" mean any consecutive 24-hour period commencing at the same time each calendar day.

(b) "Workweek" and "week" mean any seven consecutive days, starting with the same calendar day each week. "Workweek" is a fixed and regularly recurring period of 168 hours, seven consecutive 24-hour periods.

(c) "Alternative workweek schedule" means any regularly scheduled workweek requiring an employee to work more than eight hours in a 24-hour period. *(Added by Stats.1999, c. 134 (A.B.60), § 3.)*

§ 510. Day's work; overtime; commuting time

(a) Eight hours of labor constitutes a day's work. Any work in excess of eight hours in one workday and any work in excess of 40 hours in any one workweek and the first eight hours worked on the seventh day of work in any one workweek shall be compensated at the rate of no less than one and one-half times the regular rate of pay for an employee. Any work in excess of 12 hours in one day shall be compensated at the rate of no less than twice the regular rate of pay for an employee. In addition, any work in excess of eight hours on any seventh day of a workweek shall be compensated at the rate of no less than twice the regular rate of pay of an employee. Nothing in this section requires an employer to combine more than one rate of overtime compensation in order to calculate the amount to be paid to an employee for any hour of overtime work. The requirements of this section do not apply to the payment of overtime compensation to an employee working pursuant to any of the following:

(1) An alternative workweek schedule adopted pursuant to Section 511.

(2) An alternative workweek schedule adopted pursuant to a collective bargaining agreement pursuant to Section 514.

(3) An alternative workweek schedule to which this chapter is inapplicable pursuant to Section 554.

(b) Time spent commuting to and from the first place at which an employee's presence is required by the employer shall not be considered to be a part of a day's work, when the employee commutes in a vehicle that is owned, leased, or subsidized by the employer and is used for the purpose of ridesharing, as defined in Section 522 of the Vehicle Code.

(c) This section does not affect, change, or limit an employer's liability under the workers' compensation law. *(Stats.1937, c. 90, p. 205, § 510. Amended by Stats.1982, c. 185, p. 563, § 1; Stats.1999, c. 134 (A.B.60), § 4.)*

§ 511. Alternative workweek schedules

(a) Upon the proposal of an employer, the employees of an employer may adopt a regularly scheduled alternative workweek that authorizes work by the affected employees for no longer than 10 hours per day within a 40–hour workweek without the payment to the affected employees of an overtime rate of compensation pursuant to this section. A proposal to adopt an alternative workweek schedule shall be deemed adopted only if it receives approval in a secret ballot election by at least two-thirds of affected employees in a readily identifiable work unit. The regularly scheduled alternative workweek proposed by an employer for adoption by employees may be a single work schedule that would become the standard schedule for workers in the work unit, or a menu of work schedule options, from which each employee in the unit would be entitled to choose. Notwithstanding subdivision (c) of Section 500, the menu of work schedule options may include a regular schedule of eight-hour days that are compensated in accordance with subdivision (a) of Section 510. Employees who adopt a menu of work schedule options may, with employer consent, move from one schedule option to another on a weekly basis.

(b) An affected employee working longer than eight hours but not more than 12 hours in a day pursuant to an alternative workweek schedule adopted pursuant to this section shall be paid an overtime rate of compensation of no less than one and one-half times the regular rate of pay of the employee for any work in excess of the regularly scheduled hours established by the alternative workweek agreement and for any work in excess of 40 hours per week. An overtime rate of compensation of no less than double the regular rate of pay of the employee shall be paid for any work in excess of 12 hours per day and for any work in excess of eight hours on those days worked beyond the regularly scheduled workdays established by the alternative workweek agreement. Nothing in this section requires an employer to combine more than one rate of overtime compensation in order to calculate the amount to be paid to an employee for any hour of overtime work.

(c) An employer shall not reduce an employee's regular rate of hourly pay as a result of the adoption, repeal, or nullification of an alternative workweek schedule.

(d) An employer shall make a reasonable effort to find a work schedule not to exceed eight hours in a workday, in order to accommodate any affected employee who was eligible to vote in an election authorized by this section and who is unable to work the alternative schedule hours established as the result of that election. An employer shall be permitted to provide a work schedule not to exceed eight hours in a workday to accommodate any employee who was hired after the date of the election and who is unable to work the alternative schedule established as the result of that election. An employer shall explore any available reasonable alternative means of accommodating the religious belief or observance of an affected employee that conflicts with an adopted alternative workweek schedule, in the manner provided by subdivision (j) of Section 12940 of the Government Code.

(e) The results of any election conducted pursuant to this section shall be reported by an employer to the Division of Labor Statistics and Research within 30 days after the results are final.

(f) Any type of alternative workweek schedule that is authorized by this code and that was in effect on January 1, 2000, may be repealed by the affected employees pursuant to this section. Any alternative workweek schedule that was adopted pursuant to Wage Order Numbers 1, 4, 5, 7, or 9 of the Industrial Welfare Commission is null and void, except for an alternative workweek providing for a regular schedule of no more than 10 hours' work in a workday that was adopted by a two-thirds vote of affected employees in a secret ballot election pursuant to wage orders of the Industrial Welfare Commission in effect prior to 1998. This subdivision does not apply to exemptions authorized pursuant to Section 515.

(g) Notwithstanding subdivision (f), an alternative workweek schedule in the health care industry adopted by a two-thirds vote of affected employees in a secret ballot election pursuant to Wage * * * Order Numbers 4 and 5 in effect prior to 1998 that provided for workdays exceeding 10 hours but not exceeding 12 hours in a day without the payment of overtime compensation shall be valid until July 1, 2000. An employer in the health care industry shall make a reasonable effort to accommodate any employee in the health care industry who is unable to work the alternative schedule established as the result of a valid election held in accordance with provisions of Wage * * * Order Number 4 or 5 that were in effect prior to 1998.

(h) Notwithstanding subdivision (f), if an employee is voluntarily working an alternative workweek schedule providing for a regular work schedule of not more than 10 hours' work in a workday as of July 1, 1999, an employee may continue to work that alternative workweek schedule without the entitlement of the payment of daily overtime compensation for the hours provided in that schedule if the employer approves a written request of the employee to work that schedule.

(i) For purposes of this section, "work unit" includes a division, a department, a job classification, a shift, a separate physical location, or a recognized subdivision thereof. A work unit may consist of an individual employee as long as the criteria for an identifiable work unit in this section is met. *(Added by Stats.1999, c. 134 (A.B.60), § 5. Amended by Stats.2009–2010, 2nd Ex.Sess., c. 3 (A.B.5), § 1, eff. May 21, 2009.)*

§ 512.   Meal periods

(a) An employer may not employ an employee for a work period of more than five hours per day without providing the employee with a meal period of not less than 30 minutes, except that if the total work period per day of the employee is no more than six hours, the meal period may be waived by mutual consent of both the employer and employee. An employer may not employ an employee for a work period of more than 10 hours per day without providing the employee with a second meal period of not less than 30 minutes, except that if the total hours worked is no more than 12 hours, the second meal period may be waived by mutual consent of the employer and the employee only if the first meal period was not waived.

(b) Notwithstanding subdivision (a), the Industrial Welfare Commission may adopt a working condition order permitting a meal period to commence after six hours of work if the commission determines that the order is consistent with the health and welfare of the affected employees.

(c) Subdivision (a) does not apply to an employee in the wholesale baking industry who is subject to an Industrial Welfare Commission wage order and who is covered by a valid collective bargaining agreement that provides for a 35–hour workweek consisting of five seven-hour days, payment of 1 and½ the regular rate of pay for time worked in excess of seven hours per day, and a rest period of not less than 10 minutes every two hours. 350

(d) If an employee in the motion picture industry or the broadcasting industry, as those industries are defined in Industrial Welfare Commission Wage Orders 11 and 12, is covered by a valid collective bargaining agreement that provides for meal periods and includes a monetary remedy if the employee does not receive a meal period required by the agreement, then the terms, conditions, and remedies of the agreement pertaining to meal periods apply in lieu of the applicable provisions pertaining to meal periods of subdivision (a) of this section, Section 226.7, and Industrial Welfare Commission Wage Orders 11 and 12. *(Added by Stats.1999, c. 134 (A.B.60), § 6. Amended by Stats.2000, c. 492 (S.B.88), § 1, eff. Sept. 19, 2000; Stats.2003, c. 207 (A.B.330), § 1; Stats. 2005, c. 414 (A.B.1734), § 1.)*

§ 512.5.   Adoption or amendment by Industrial Welfare Commission of order applying to employee of public agency who operates a commercial motor vehicle; exemption of employee relating to meal or rest periods

(a) Notwithstanding any provision of this chapter, if the Industrial Welfare Commission adopts or amends an order that applies to an employee of a public agency who operates a commercial motor vehicle, it may exempt that employee from the application of the provisions of that order which relate to meal periods or rest periods, consistent with the health and welfare of that employee, if he or she is covered by a valid collective bargaining agreement.

(b) "Commercial motor vehicle" for the purposes of this section has the same meaning as provided in subdivision (b) of Section 15210 of the Vehicle Code.

(c) "Public agency" for the purposes of this section means the state and any political subdivision of the state, including any city, county, city and county, or special district. *(Added by Stats.2003, c. 327 (A.B.98), § 1.)*

§ 513.   Makeup work time

If an employer approves a written request of an employee to make up work time that is or would be lost as a result of a personal obligation of the employee, the hours of that makeup work time, if performed in the same workweek in which the work time was lost, may not be counted towards computing the total number of hours worked in a day for purposes of the overtime requirements specified in Section 510 or 511, except for hours in excess of 11 hours of work in one day or 40 hours in one workweek. An employee shall provide a signed written request for each occasion that the employee makes a request to make up work time pursuant to this section. An employer is prohibited from encouraging or otherwise soliciting an employee to request the employer's approval to take personal time off and make up the work hours within the same week pursuant to this section. *(Added by Stats.1999, c. 134 (A.B.60), § 7.)*

§ 514. Employees covered by collective bargaining agreements; application of §§ 551 and 552

Sections 510 and 511 do not apply to an employee covered by a valid collective bargaining agreement if the agreement expressly provides for the wages, hours of work, and working conditions of the employees, and if the agreement provides premium wage rates for all overtime hours worked and a regular hourly rate of pay for those employees of not less than 30 percent more than the state minimum wage. *(Added by Stats.1999, c. 134 (A.B.60), § 8. Amended by Stats.2001, c. 148 (S.B.1208), § 1.)*

§ 515. Exemptions

(a) The Industrial Welfare Commission may establish exemptions from the requirement that an overtime rate of compensation be paid pursuant to Sections 510 and 511 for executive, administrative, and professional employees, provided that the employee is primarily engaged in the duties that meet the test of the exemption, customarily and regularly exercises discretion and independent judgment in performing those duties, and earns a monthly salary equivalent to no less than two times the state minimum wage for full-time employment. The commission shall conduct a review of the duties that meet the test of the exemption. The commission may, based upon this review, convene a public hearing to adopt or modify regulations at that hearing pertaining to duties that meet the test of the exemption without convening wage boards. Any hearing conducted pursuant to this subdivision shall be concluded not later than July 1, 2000.

(b)(1) The commission may establish additional exemptions to hours of work requirements under this division where it finds that hours or conditions of labor may be prejudicial to the health or welfare of employees in any occupation, trade, or industry. This paragraph shall become inoperative on January 1, 2005.

(2) Except as otherwise provided in this section and in subdivision (g) of Section 511, nothing in this section requires the commission to alter any exemption from provisions regulating hours of work that was contained in any valid wage order in effect in 1997. Except as otherwise provided in this division, the commission may review, retain, or eliminate any exemption from provisions regulating hours of work that was contained in any valid wage order in effect in 1997.

(c) For the purposes of this section, "full-time employment" means employment in which an employee is employed for 40 hours per week.

(d) For the purpose of computing the overtime rate of compensation required to be paid to a nonexempt full-time salaried employee, the employee's regular hourly rate shall be 1/40th of the employee's weekly salary.

(e) For the purposes of this section, "primarily" means more than one-half of the employee's worktime.

(f)(1) In addition to the requirements of subdivision (a), registered nurses employed to engage in the practice of nursing shall not be exempted from coverage under any part of the orders of the Industrial Welfare Commission, unless they individually meet the criteria for exemptions established for executive or administrative employees.

(2) This subdivision does not apply to any of the following:

(A) A certified nurse midwife who is primarily engaged in performing duties for which certification is required pursuant to Article 2.5 (commencing with Section 2746) of Chapter 6 of Division 2 of the Business and Professions Code.

(B) A certified nurse anesthetist who is primarily engaged in performing duties for which certification is required pursuant to Article 7 (commencing with Section 2825) of Chapter 6 of Division 2 of the Business and Professions Code.

(C) A certified nurse practitioner who is primarily engaged in performing duties for which certification is required pursuant to Article 8 (commencing with Section 2834) of Chapter 6 of Division 2 of the Business and Professions Code.

(D) Nothing in this paragraph shall exempt the occupations set forth in subparagraphs (A), (B), and (C) from meeting the requirements of subdivision (a). *(Added by Stats.1999, c. 134 (A.B.60), § 9. Amended by Stats.2000, c. 492 (S.B.88), § 2, eff. Sept. 19, 2000.)*

§ 515.5. Computer software field employees; exemption; requirements

(a) Except as provided in subdivision (b), an employee in the computer software field shall be exempt from the requirement that an overtime rate of compensation be paid pursuant to Section 510 if all of the following apply:

(1) The employee is primarily engaged in work that is intellectual or creative and that requires the exercise of discretion and independent judgment.

(2) The employee is primarily engaged in duties that consist of one or more of the following:

(A) The application of systems analysis techniques and procedures, including consulting with users, to determine hardware, software, or system functional specifications.

(B) The design, development, documentation, analysis, creation, testing, or modification of computer systems or programs, including prototypes, based on and related to user or system design specifications.

(C) The documentation, testing, creation, or modification of computer programs related to the design of software or hardware for computer operating systems.

(3) The employee is highly skilled and is proficient in the theoretical and practical application of highly specialized information to computer systems analysis, programming, or software engineering. A job title shall not be determinative of the applicability of this exemption.

(4) The employee's hourly rate of pay is not less than thirty-six dollars ($36.00) or, if the employee is paid on a salaried basis, the employee earns an annual salary of not

351

less than seventy-five thousand dollars ($75,000) for full-time employment, which is paid at least once a month and in a monthly amount of not less than six thousand two hundred fifty dollars ($6,250). The Division of Labor Statistics and Research shall adjust both the hourly pay rate and the salary level described in this paragraph on October 1 of each year to be effective on January 1 of the following year by an amount equal to the percentage increase in the California Consumer Price Index for Urban Wage Earners and Clerical Workers.

(b) The exemption provided in subdivision (a) does not apply to an employee if any of the following apply:

(1) The employee is a trainee or employee in an entry-level position who is learning to become proficient in the theoretical and practical application of highly specialized information to computer systems analysis, programming, and software engineering.

(2) The employee is in a computer-related occupation but has not attained the level of skill and expertise necessary to work independently and without close supervision.

(3) The employee is engaged in the operation of computers or in the manufacture, repair, or maintenance of computer hardware and related equipment.

(4) The employee is an engineer, drafter, machinist, or other professional whose work is highly dependent upon or facilitated by the use of computers and computer software programs and who is skilled in computer-aided design software, including CAD/CAM, but who is not engaged in computer systems analysis, programming, or any other similarly skilled computer-related occupation.

(5) The employee is a writer engaged in writing material, including box labels, product descriptions, documentation, promotional material, setup and installation instructions, and other similar written information, either for print or for onscreen media or who writes or provides content material intended to be read by customers, subscribers, or visitors to computer-related media such as the World Wide Web or CD–ROMs.

(6) The employee is engaged in any of the activities set forth in subdivision (a) for the purpose of creating imagery for effects used in the motion picture, television, or theatrical industry. *(Added by Stats.2000, c. 492 (S.B.88), § 3, eff. Sept. 19, 2000. Amended by Stats.2005, c. 149 (A.B.1093), § 2; Stats.2007, c. 482 (S.B.929), § 1; Stats.2008, c. 753 (A.B.10), § 1, eff. Sept. 30, 2008.)*

§ 515.6. Licensed physicians and surgeons; exemption from § 510

(a) Section 510 shall not apply to any employee who is a licensed physician or surgeon, who is primarily engaged in duties that require licensure pursuant to Chapter 5 (commencing with Section 2000) of Division 2 of the Business and Professions Code, and whose hourly rate of pay is equal to or greater than fifty-five dollars ($55.00). The Division of Labor Statistics and Research shall adjust this threshold rate of pay each October 1, to be effective

the following January 1, by an amount equal to the percentage increase in the California Consumer Price Index for Urban Wage Earners and Clerical Workers.

(b) The exemption provided in subdivision (a) shall not apply to an employee employed in a medical internship or resident program or to a physician employee covered by a valid collective bargaining agreement pursuant to Section 514. *(Added by Stats.2001, c. 148 (S.B. 1208), § 3. Amended by Stats.2003, c. 884 (A.B.1719), § 1.)*

§ 515.8. Teachers at private elementary or secondary academic institutions; Section 510 not applicable; exemptions

(a) Section 510 does not apply to an individual employed as a teacher at a private elementary or secondary academic institution in which pupils are enrolled in kindergarten or any of grades 1 to 12, inclusive.

(b) For purposes of this section, "employed as a teacher" means that the employee meets all of the following requirements:

(1) The employee is primarily engaged in the duty of imparting knowledge to pupils by teaching, instructing, or lecturing.

(2) The employee customarily and regularly exercises discretion and independent judgment in performing the duties of a teacher.

(3) The employee earns a monthly salary equivalent to no less than two times the state minimum wage for full-time employment.

(4) The employee has attained at least one of the following levels of professional advancement:

(A) A baccalaureate or higher degree from an accredited institution of higher education.

(B) Current compliance with the requirements established by the California Commission on Teacher Credentialing, or the equivalent certification authority in another state, for obtaining a preliminary or alternative teaching credential.

(c) This section does not apply to any tutor, teaching assistant, instructional aide, student teacher, day care provider, vocational instructor, or other similar employee.

(d) The exemption established in subdivision (a) is in addition to, and does not limit or supersede, any exemption from overtime established by a Wage Order of the Industrial Welfare Commission for persons employed in a professional capacity, and does not affect any exemption from overtime established by that commission pursuant to subdivision (a) of Section 515 for persons employed in an executive or administrative capacity. *(Added by Stats.2006, c. 159 (A.B.2613), § 1.)*

§ 516. Adoption or amendment of working condition orders

Except as provided in Section 512, the Industrial Welfare Commission may adopt or amend working condition orders with respect to break periods, meal periods, and days of rest for any workers in California consistent with the health and welfare of those workers. *(Added by Stats.1999, c. 134 (A.B.60), § 10. Amended by Stats.2000, c. 492 (S.B.88), § 4, eff. Sept. 19, 2000.)*

§ 517. Industrial Welfare Commission; adoption of wage, hours, and working conditions orders; review of wages, hours, and working conditions in certain industries; publication of wage orders and other regulations

(a) The Industrial Welfare Commission shall, at a public hearing to be concluded by July 1, 2000, adopt wage, hours, and working conditions consistent with this chapter without convening wage boards, which orders shall be final and conclusive for all purposes. These orders shall include regulations necessary to provide assurances of fairness regarding the conduct of employee workweek elections, procedures for employees to petition for and obtain elections to repeal alternative workweek schedules, procedures for implementation of those schedules, conditions under which an adopted alternative workweek schedule can be repealed by the employer, employee disclosures, designations of work, and processing of workweek election petitions pursuant to Parts 2 and 4 of this division and in any wage order of the commission and such other regulations as may be needed to fulfill the duties of the commission pursuant to this part.

(b) Prior to July 1, 2000, the Industrial Welfare Commission shall conduct a review of wages, hours, and working conditions in the ski industry, commercial fishing industry, and health care industry, and for stable employees in the horseracing industry. Notwithstanding subdivision (a) and Sections 510 and 511, and consistent with its duty to protect the health, safety, and welfare of workers pursuant to Section 1173, the commission may, based upon this review, convene a public hearing to adopt or modify regulations at that hearing pertaining to the industries herein, without convening wage boards. Any hearing conducted pursuant to this subdivision shall be concluded not later than July 1, 2000.

(c) Notwithstanding subdivision (a) of Section 515, prior to July 1, 2000, the commission shall conduct a review of wages, hours, and working conditions of licensed pharmacists. The commission may, based upon this review, convene a public hearing to adopt or modify regulations at that hearing pertaining to licensed pharmacists without convening wage boards. Any hearing conducted pursuant to this subdivision shall be concluded not later than July 1, 2000.

(d) Notwithstanding sections 1171 and subdivision (a) of Section 515, the Industrial Welfare Commission shall conduct a review of wages, hours, and working conditions of outside salespersons. The commission may, based upon this review, convene a public hearing to adopt or modify regulations at that hearing pertaining to outside salespersons without convening wage boards. Any hear-

ing conducted pursuant to this subdivision shall be concluded not later than July 1, 2000.

(e) Nothing in this section is intended to restrict the Industrial Welfare Commission in its continuing duties pursuant to Section 1173.

(f) No action taken by the Industrial Welfare Commission pursuant to this section is subject to the requirements of Article 5 (commencing with Section 11346) of Chapter 3.5 of Part 1 of Division 3 of Title 2 of the Government Code.

(g) All wage orders and other regulations issued or adopted pursuant to this section shall be published in accordance with Section 1182.1. *(Added by Stats.1999, c. 134 (A.B.60), § 11.)*

§ 550. Day's rest defined

As used in this chapter "day's rest" applies to all situations whether the employee is engaged by the day, week, month, or year, and whether the work performed is done in the day or night time. *(Stats.1937, c. 90, p. 205, § 550.)*

§ 551. One day's rest in seven

Every person employed in any occupation of labor is entitled to one day's rest therefrom in seven. *(Stats.1937, c. 90, p. 205, § 551.)*

§ 552. Maximum consecutive working days

No employer of labor shall cause his employees to work more than six days in seven. *(Stats.1937, c. 90, p. 205, § 552.)*

§ 553. Violation; misdemeanor

Any person who violates this chapter is guilty of a misdemeanor. *(Stats.1937, c. 90, p. 205, § 553.)*

§ 554. Exemptions from §§ 551 and 552

(a) Sections 551 and 552 shall not apply to any cases of emergency nor to work performed in the protection of life or property from loss or destruction, nor to any common carrier engaged in or connected with the movement of trains. This chapter, with the exception of Section 558, shall not apply to any person employed in an agricultural occupation, as defined in Order No. 14–80 (operative January 1, 1998) of the Industrial Welfare Commission. Nothing in this chapter shall be construed to prevent an accumulation of days of rest when the nature of the employment reasonably requires that the employee work seven or more consecutive days, if in each calendar month the employee receives days of rest equivalent to one day's rest in seven. The requirement respecting the equivalent of one day's rest in seven shall apply, notwithstanding the other provisions of this chapter relating to collective bargaining agreements, where the employer and a labor organization representing employees of the employer have entered into a valid collective bargaining agreement respecting the hours of work of the employees, unless the agreement expressly provides otherwise.

(b) In addition to the exceptions specified in subdivision (a), the Chief of the Division of Labor Standards Enforcement may, when in his or her judgment hardship will result, exempt any employer or employees from the provisions of Sections 551 and 552. *(Stats.1937, c. 90, p. 205, § 554. Amended by Stats.1941, c. 1264, p. 3210, § 1; Stats.1945, c. 1431, p. 2690, § 33; Stats.1961, c. 839, p. 2121, § 1; Stats.1980, c. 676, p. 1966, § 215; Stats.1999, c. 134 (A.B.60), § 12; Stats.2001, c. 148 (S.B.1208), § 2.)*

§ 555. Applicability to cities and counties

Sections 550, 551, 552 and 554 of this chapter are applicable to cities which are cities and counties and to the officers and employees thereof. *(Added by Stats. 1941, c. 1184, p. 2943, § 1. Amended by Stats.1955, c. 624, p. 1124, § 69.)*

§ 556. Application of §§ 551 and 552

Sections 551 and 552 shall not apply to any employer or employee when the total hours of employment do not exceed 30 hours in any week or six hours in any one day thereof. *(Added by Stats.1941, c. 1267, p. 3212, § 1. Amended by Stats.1999, c. 134 (A.B.60), § 13.)*

§ 558. Violations of chapter; civil penalties

(a) Any employer or other person acting on behalf of an employer who violates, or causes to be violated, a section of this chapter or any provision regulating hours and days of work in any order of the Industrial Welfare Commission shall be subject to a civil penalty as follows:

(1) For any initial violation, fifty dollars ($50) for each underpaid employee for each pay period for which the employee was underpaid in addition to an amount sufficient to recover underpaid wages.

(2) For each subsequent violation, one hundred dollars ($100) for each underpaid employee for each pay period for which the employee was underpaid in addition to an amount sufficient to recover underpaid wages.

(3) Wages recovered pursuant to this section shall be paid to the affected employee.

(b) If upon inspection or investigation the Labor Commissioner determines that a person had paid or caused to be paid a wage for overtime work in violation of any provision of this chapter, or any provision regulating hours and days of work in any order of the Industrial Welfare Commission, the Labor Commissioner may issue a citation. The procedures for issuing, contesting, and enforcing judgments for citations or civil penalties issued by the Labor Commissioner for a violation of this chapter shall be the same as those set out in Section 1197.1.

(c) The civil penalties provided for in this section are in addition to any other civil or criminal penalty provided by law. *(Added by Stats.1999, c. 134 (A.B.60), § 14.)*

354

CHAPTER 2.   RAILROADS

Section
600. Definitions.
601. Maximum consecutive hours on duty.
602. Minimum consecutive hours off duty.
603. Maximum aggregate hours of duty in 24-hour period; minimum consecutive hours off duty.
604. Maximum hours of persons handling orders affecting train movements; emergencies.
605. Violation by railroad corporation; penalty; recovery.
606. Violation by officer or agent; misdemeanor; penalty.
607. Emergency exceptions.

§ 600. Definitions

As used in this chapter, unless the context otherwise indicates:

(a) "Railroad" means any steam railroad, electric railroad, or railway, operated in whole or in part in this State.

(b) "Railroad corporation" means a corporation or receiver operating a railroad.

(c) "Trainman" means a conductor, motorman, engineer, fireman, brakeman, train dispatcher, or telegraph operator, employed by or working in connection with a railroad. *(Stats.1937, c. 90, p. 205, § 600.)*

§ 601. Maximum consecutive hours on duty

No railroad corporation or any officer, agent or representative of such corporation shall require or knowingly permit any trainman to be on duty for a longer period than 12 consecutive hours. *(Stats.1937, c. 90, p. 206, § 601. Amended by Stats.1982, c. 896, p. 3323, § 1.)*

§ 602. Minimum consecutive hours off duty

Whenever any trainman has been continuously on duty for 12 hours he shall be relieved and not required or permitted again to go on duty or perform any work for the railroad corporation until he has had at least 10 consecutive hours off duty. *(Stats.1937, c. 90, p. 206, § 602. Amended by Stats.1982, c. 896, p. 3323, § 2.)*

§ 603. Maximum aggregate hours of duty in 24-hour period; minimum consecutive hours off duty

No trainman who has been on duty 12 hours in the aggregate in any 24-hour period shall be required or permitted to continue or again go on duty without having had at least 8 consecutive hours off duty. *(Stats.1937, c. 90, p. 206, § 603. Amended by Stats.1982, c. 896, p. 3323, § 3.)*

§ 604. Maximum hours of persons handling orders affecting train movements; emergencies

No person who by the use of the telegraph or telephone, dispatches, reports, transmits, receives or delivers orders pertaining to or affecting train movements shall be required or permitted to be on duty for a longer period than nine hours in any twenty-four hours, in towers, offices, places and stations continuously operated night and day, nor for a longer period than thirteen hours in towers, offices, places and stations operated only during the daytime. In case of emergency, however, the persons referred to in this section may be permitted to be on duty for four additional hours in a twenty-four hour period. Such additional duty shall not be required or permitted on more than three days in any week. *(Stats. 1937, c. 90, p. 206, § 604.)*

§ 605. Violation by railroad corporation; penalty; recovery

Any railroad corporation that violates any of the provisions of this chapter is liable to the state in a penalty of not less than five hundred dollars ($500) nor more than five thousand dollars ($5,000) for each offense. The penalty shall be recovered and suit therefor shall be brought in the name of the state in a court of competent jurisdiction in any county into or through which said railroad may pass. The suit may be brought either by the Attorney General of the state or under his or her direction by the district attorney of any county in the state into or through which said railroad passes. *(Stats.1937, c. 90, p. 206, § 605. Amended by Stats.2003, c. 329 (A.B. 276), § 4.)*

§ 606. Violation by officer or agent; misdemeanor; penalty

Any officer, agent or representative of any railroad corporation who violates any of the provisions of this chapter is guilty of a misdemeanor, punishable by a fine of not less than one hundred dollars ($100) nor more than one thousand dollars ($1,000) for each offense, or confinement in the county jail for not less than 10 nor more than 60 days, or both. Such person so offending may be prosecuted under this section, either in the county where he is at the time of commission of the offense, or in any county where such employee has been permitted or required to work in violation of this chapter. *(Stats.1937, c. 90, p. 206, § 606. Amended by Stats.1983, c. 1092, § 193, eff. Sept. 27, 1983, operative Jan. 1, 1984.)*

§ 607. Emergency exceptions

This chapter shall not apply in any case of casualty, unavoidable accident, or act of God; nor where the delay was the result of a cause not known to, and which could not have been foreseen by, the railroad corporation, or its officer or agent in charge of a trainman at the time the trainman left a terminal. This chapter shall not apply to the crews of wrecking, or relief trains. *(Stats.1937, c. 90, p. 207, § 607.)*

CHAPTER 3. SMELTERS AND UNDERGROUND WORKINGS

Section
750.   Maximum period of employment; consecutive hours; places and persons exempted.
750.5.   Working hours; collective-bargaining agreements; employee elections.
751.   Emergencies.
751.5.   Emergency repairs or replacements.

Section
751.8.   Overtime compensation.
752.   Employee complaints concerning elections; violations; penalties; remedies; employer retaliation.
752.5.   Severability of chapter.

§ 750. Maximum period of employment; consecutive hours; places and persons exempted

(a) Except as otherwise provided in this chapter, no employee may be employed for a period that exceeds eight hours within any 24–hour period and the hours of employment of any workday shall be consecutive, excluding intermissions for meals, for all persons who are employed or engaged in work in any of the following:

(1) Underground mines.

(2) Smelters and plants for the reduction or refining of ores or metals.

(b) No provision of this chapter applies to quarries or other operations for the extraction of nonmetallic minerals, including, but not limited to, sand, gravel, and rock.

(c) No provision of this chapter applies to an employee who is employed in an executive, administrative, or professional capacity, or employed as an outside salesperson. *(Stats.1937, c. 90, p. 207, § 750. Amended by Stats.1995, c. 903 (A.B.739), § 1.)*

§ 750.5. Working hours; collective-bargaining agreements; employee elections

Notwithstanding Section 750, an employee may be employed for a period that exceeds eight hours within a 24–hour period, under the circumstances specified in subdivision (a), (b), or (c), as follows:

(a) If the employer and a labor organization representing employees of the employer have entered into a valid collective bargaining agreement that expressly provides for the wages, hours of work, and working conditions of the employees.

(b) If a two-thirds majority of the affected employees of that employer whose hours are regulated by this chapter have voted in an election to adopt a policy that specifies periods of work that may exceed eight hours in a 24–hour period, and the employer adopts that policy, subject to all of the following conditions:

(1) The agreement adopted with respect to that policy reflects the results of the election.

(2) The election is conducted, at the expense of the employer, with the use of secret ballots, during regular working hours. Upon the written request of an employee to his or her employer, or to the Labor Commissioner, made no later than 10 days prior to the date set for the election, the employer shall cause the election to be conducted by a neutral third party with experience in conducting employee elections. If such a written request is made to the commissioner pursuant to this paragraph, the commissioner shall not disclose the identity of the employee and shall notify the employer, no later than five days prior to the date set for the election, that the

election is required to be conducted by a neutral third party. Such an election may be conducted by utilizing mail ballots.

(3) All employees of that employer whose hours are regulated by this chapter and who have become employed by that employer within 24 hours of the time the election is commenced are eligible to vote in the election.

(4) The policy shall be effective for the period specified therein, not exceeding 12 months.

(5) No later than 14 days prior to the date set for an election, the employer shall do all of the following:

(A) Provide a written notice to the affected employees that describes the effects the proposed work schedule would have on the employees' wages, hours, and benefits, and the employees' rights under this chapter, including the right to request that the election be conducted by a neutral third party pursuant to this section, and to file a complaint against the employer pursuant to this chapter.

(B) Provide a written statement to the affected employees, prepared by a neutral source knowledgeable in health and safety matters and unaffiliated with the employer, that explains any health and safety considerations of extended work shifts.

(C) Hold informational meetings for the affected employees on each shift during the regular working hours of the affected employees. At each of these meetings, the employer shall explain the effect of the proposed policy on the hours and compensation of the employees. Written notice of the time, date, place, and purpose of these informational meetings shall be conspicuously posted in at least three locations throughout the mine site for at least seven consecutive days before the date of the meetings. Written notice of the time, date, place, and purpose of the election shall be posted in the same manner and for the same period. Failure to comply with the procedural requirements of this paragraph shall void the results of the election for purposes of this section.

(6) Any employer that establishes a regular scheduled workday pursuant to this subdivision shall make a reasonable attempt to place an employee, who was eligible to participate in the election that authorized an extended workday schedule and who is unable or unwilling to work the extended schedule, in an alternative work assignment that the employee is capable of performing. An employer shall not be required to offer an alternative work assignment to an employee if an alternative work assignment that the employee is capable of performing is not available or if the employee commenced his or her employment after the election.

(c) On the day a scheduled change of shift takes effect. *(Added by Stats.1983, c. 36, § 1, eff. May 12, 1983. Amended by Stats.1995, c. 903 (A.B.739), § 2.)*

§ 751. Emergencies

In the case of an emergency where life or property is in imminent danger, the work shift may be extended during the continuance of the emergency. *(Stats.1937, c. 90, p.*

356

207, § 751. Amended by Stats.1995, c. 903 (A.B.739), § 3.)*

§ 751.5. Emergency repairs or replacements

Where emergency repairs to, or maintenance or replacement of, machinery or equipment are necessary for the continuous operation thereof, the hours that an employee may be engaged in performing the emergency repairs, maintenance, or replacement, may, during the pendency of the emergency, exceed the period specified in Section 750. *(Added by Stats.1963, c. 896, p. 2140, § 1. Amended by Stats.1995, c. 903 (A.B.739), § 4.)*

§ 751.8. Overtime compensation

(a) Notwithstanding Section 750, the period of employment may exceed eight hours in any 24–hour period if the employee is paid at the overtime rate of pay for hours worked in excess of that employee's regularly scheduled shift and for hours worked in excess of 40 hours in a seven-day period. Unless regularly scheduled shifts are established pursuant to Section 750.5, overtime rates of pay shall be paid for all hours worked in excess of those hours prescribed by Section 750 as the maximum allowable hours of employment.

(b) All work performed in any workday in excess of the scheduled hours established by an agreement pursuant to subdivision (b) of Section 750.5 up to and including 12 hours, or in excess of 40 hours in a workweek, shall be compensated at one and one-half times the employee's regular rate of compensation. All work performed in any workday in excess of 12 hours shall be compensated at double the employee's regular rate of compensation. No hours that are compensated at either one and one-half times, or double, the regular rate of compensation shall be included in determining the number of hours an employee has worked in a workweek for purposes of computing premium compensation. *(Added by Stats. 1995, c. 903 (A.B.739), § 5.)*

§ 752. Employee complaints concerning elections; violations; penalties; remedies; employer retaliation

(a) Any affected employee, or his or her representative, may file a complaint with the Labor Commissioner concerning the conduct of an election pursuant to subdivision (b) of Section 750.5 within 14 days following notice of the outcome of the election. The Labor Commissioner shall investigate the complaint and shall invalidate the election if the commissioner finds that misconduct has occurred that could have affected the outcome of the election. If the election is invalidated, the commissioner shall prohibit the employer from conducting a similar election for a period of 12 months.

(b) Any employer, or representative of an employer, that violates Section 750 or 751.8 shall be subject to a civil penalty as follows:

(1) For any initial violation that is intentionally committed, one hundred dollars ($100) for each affected employee for each violation for each pay period.

(2) For each subsequent violation for the same offense, two hundred dollars ($200) for each violation for each affected employee for each pay period, regardless of whether the initial violation is intentionally committed.

(c) If the Labor Commissioner determines that an employer has failed to comply with paragraph (6) of subdivision (b) of Section 750.5, the Labor Commissioner shall order the employer to comply. The order, in appropriate cases, shall include provisions for reinstatement and backpay.

(d) An employer shall not retaliate in any way against an employee for exercising any right pursuant to this chapter. *(Added by Stats.1995, c. 903 (A.B.739), § 7. Amended by Stats.2003, c. 329 (A.B.276), § 5.)*

§ 752.5. Severability of chapter

The provisions of this chapter are severable. If any provision of this chapter or its application is held invalid, that invalidity shall not affect other provisions or applications that can be given effect without the invalid provision or application. *(Added by Stats.1995, c. 903 (A.B.739), § 8.)*

CHAPTER 4. LUMBER INDUSTRIES

Section
800. Midday meal period.
801. Violation; misdemeanor; penalty.

§ 800. Midday meal period

Every person operating a sawmill, shakemill, shinglemill, logging camp, planing mill, veneer mill, plywood plant or any other type of plant or mill which processes or manufactures any lumber, lumber products or allied wood products, in this State shall allow his employees a period of not less than one-half hour for the midday meal, between the third and fifth hours of each day's shift after the start thereof. *(Stats.1937, c. 90, p. 207, § 800. Amended by Stats.1949, c. 485, p. 832, § 1; Stats.1959, c. 717, p. 2699, § 1.)*

§ 801. Violation; misdemeanor; penalty

Any person, or agent or officer thereof who violates any provision of this chapter is guilty of a misdemeanor, punishable by a fine of not less than one hundred dollars ($100) nor more than four hundred dollars ($400). *(Stats.1937, c. 90, p. 207, § 801. Amended by Stats.1983, c. 1092, § 195, eff. Sept. 27, 1983, operative Jan. 1, 1984.)*

CHAPTER 5. PHARMACIES

Section
850. Maximum hours and days of employment performed by employee.
851. Maximum hours and days of employment required or permitted by employer.
851.5. Consecutive hours of work; exemption of hospital employing one pharmacist.
852. Weekly day of rest.
853. Violation; misdemeanor; penalty.

Section
854. Emergency exemption; emergency defined.
855. Legislative declaration.
856. Enforcement officer.

§ 850. Maximum hours and days of employment performed by employee

No person employed to sell at retail drugs and medicines or to compound physicians' prescriptions shall perform any work in any store, dispensary, pharmacy, laboratory, or office for more than an average of nine hours per day, or for more than 108 hours in any two consecutive weeks or for more than 12 days in any two consecutive weeks, except that any registered pharmacist may be so employed and may perform such work for the full period of time permitted by this section. *(Stats.1937, c. 90, p. 207, § 850. Amended by Stats.1939, c. 567, p. 1970, § 1; Stats.1955, c. 435, p. 890, § 1.)*

§ 851. Maximum hours and days of employment required or permitted by employer

No person employing another person to sell at retail drugs and medicines or to compound physicians' prescriptions shall require or permit such employee to perform any work in any store, dispensary, pharmacy, laboratory, or office for more than an average of nine hours per day, or for more than 108 hours in any two consecutive weeks or for more than 12 days in any two consecutive weeks, except that any registered pharmacist may be so employed and may perform such work for the full period of time permitted by this section. *(Stats.1937, c. 90, p. 207, § 851. Amended by Stats.1939, c. 567, p. 1970, § 2; Stats.1955, c. 436, p. 890, § 1.)*

§ 851.5. Consecutive hours of work; exemption of hospital employing one pharmacist

Except on Sundays and holidays, and except for a period of time for meals, not to exceed one hour in length, the hours of work permitted per day by this chapter shall be consecutive. This section does not apply to hospitals employing only one person to compound physicians' prescriptions. *(Added by Stats.1939, c. 567, p. 1970, § 4.)*

§ 852. Weekly day of rest

The employer shall apportion the periods of rest to be taken by an employee so that the employee will have one complete day of rest during each week. *(Stats.1937, c. 90, p. 208, § 852. Amended by Stats.1939, c. 567, p. 1970, § 3.)*

§ 853. Violation; misdemeanor; penalty

Any person who violates any provision of this chapter is guilty of a misdemeanor punishable by a fine of not less than forty dollars ($40) nor more than one hundred dollars ($100) or by imprisonment for not exceeding 60 days, or both. *(Stats.1937, c. 90, p. 208, § 853. Amended by Stats.1983, c. 1092, § 196, eff. Sept. 27, 1983, operative Jan. 1, 1984.)*

§ 854. Emergency exemption; emergency defined

The provisions of this chapter shall not apply in any case of emergency. The word "emergency" shall be construed as being accident, death, sickness or epidemic. *(Stats.1937, c. 90, p. 208, § 854.)*

§ 855. Legislative declaration

The provisions of this chapter are enacted as a measure for the protection of the public health. *(Stats.1937, c. 90, p. 208, § 855.)*

§ 856. Enforcement officer

The Labor Commissioner shall enforce this chapter. *(Stats.1937, c. 90, p. 208, § 856.)*

Part 3

PRIVILEGES AND IMMUNITIES

Chapter	Section
1. Contracts against Public Policy	920
2. Solicitation of Employees by Misrepresentation	970
3. Class of Labor Employed; Labor Union Insignia	1010
3.5. Contractors	1020
3.7. Alcohol and Drug Rehabilitation	1025
3.8. Lactation Accommodation	1030
3.9. Employee Literacy Assistance	1040
4. Reemployment Privileges	1050
4.5. Displaced Janitor Opportunity Act	1060
4.6. Public Transit Service Contracts	1070
5. Political Affiliations	1100
6. Agreements in Connection with Trade Disputes	1110
6.5. Peace Officers [Repealed]	1112
7. Jurisdictional Strikes	1115
7.5. Collective Bargaining Agreements	1126
8. Professional Strikebreakers	1130
9. Public Transportation Labor Disputes	1137
10. Unlawful Acts During Labor Disputes	1138

CHAPTER 1. CONTRACTS AGAINST PUBLIC POLICY

Section
920. Promise defined.
921. Promises respecting membership in labor and employer organizations.
922. Coercion not to join labor organization; misdemeanor.
923. Declaration of public policy.

§ 920. Promise defined

As used in this chapter, unless the context otherwise indicates, "promise" includes promise, undertaking, contract, or agreement, whether written or oral, express or implied. *(Stats.1937, c. 90, p. 208, § 920.)*

358

§ 921. Promises respecting membership in labor and employer organizations

Every promise made after August 21, 1933, between any employee or prospective employee and his employer, prospective employer or any other person is contrary to public policy if either party thereto promises any of the following:

(a) To join or to remain a member of a labor organization or to join or remain a member of an employer organization,

(b) Not to join or not to remain a member of a labor organization or of an employer organization.

(c) To withdraw from an employment relation in the event that he joins or remains a member of a labor organization or of an employer organization.

Such promise shall not afford any basis for the granting of legal or equitable relief by any court against a party to such promise, or against any other persons who advise, urge, or induce, without fraud or violence or threat thereof, either party thereto to act in disregard of such promise. *(Stats.1937, c. 90, p. 208, § 921.)*

§ 922. Coercion not to join labor organization; misdemeanor

Any person or agent or officer thereof who coerces or compels any person to enter into an agreement, written or verbal, not to join or become a member of any labor organization, as a condition of securing employment or continuing in the employment of any such person is guilty of a misdemeanor. *(Stats.1937, c. 90, p. 208, § 922.)*

§ 923. Declaration of public policy

In the interpretation and application of this chapter, the public policy of this State is declared as follows:

Negotiation of terms and conditions of labor should result from voluntary agreement between employer and employees. Governmental authority has permitted and encouraged employers to organize in the corporate and other forms of capital control. In dealing with such employers, the individual unorganized worker is helpless to exercise actual liberty of contract and to protect his freedom of labor, and thereby to obtain acceptable terms and conditions of employment. Therefore it is necessary that the individual workman have full freedom of association, self-organization, and designation of representatives of his own choosing, to negotiate the terms and conditions of his employment, and that he shall be free from the interference, restraint, or coercion of employers of labor, or their agents, in the designation of such representatives or in self-organization or in other concerted activities for the purpose of collective bargaining or other mutual aid or protection. *(Stats.1937, c. 90, p. 208, § 923.)*

CHAPTER 2. SOLICITATION OF EMPLOYEES BY MISREPRESENTATION

Section
970. Misrepresentations.
971. Violations; misdemeanor; penalty.
972. Civil penalty.
973. Solicitation of employees during labor dispute; required statement and information.
974. Violation; misdemeanor.
976. Publishing advertisement offering employment as salesman, broker or agent; misrepresentation as to compensation or commissions.
977. Violation; misdemeanor.

§ 970. Misrepresentations

No person, or agent or officer thereof, directly or indirectly, shall influence, persuade, or engage any person to change from one place to another in this State or from any place outside to any place within the State, or from any place within the State to any place outside, for the purpose of working in any branch of labor, through or by means of knowingly false representations, whether spoken, written, or advertised in printed form, concerning either:

(a) The kind, character, or existence of such work;

(b) The length of time such work will last, or the compensation therefor;

(c) The sanitary or housing conditions relating to or surrounding the work;

(d) The existence or nonexistence of any strike, lockout, or other labor dispute affecting it and pending between the proposed employer and the persons then or last engaged in the performance of the labor for which the employee is sought. *(Stats.1937, c. 90, p. 209, § 970.)*

§ 971. Violations; misdemeanor; penalty

Any person, or agent or officer thereof, who violates Section 970 is guilty of a misdemeanor punishable by a fine of not less than fifty dollars ($50) nor more than one thousand dollars ($1,000) or imprisonment for not more than six months or both. *(Stats.1937, c. 90, p. 209, § 971. Amended by Stats.1983, c. 1092, § 197, eff. Sept. 27, 1983, operative Jan. 1, 1984.)*

§ 972. Civil penalty

In addition to such criminal penalty, any person, or agent or officer thereof who violates any provision of section 970 is liable to the party aggrieved, in a civil action, for double damages resulting from such misrepresentations. Such civil action may be brought by an aggrieved person or his assigns or successors in interest, without first establishing any criminal liability. *(Stats. 1937, c. 90, p. 209, § 972.)*

§ 973. Solicitation of employees during labor dispute; required statement and information

If any person advertises for, or seeks employees by means of newspapers, posters, letters, or otherwise, or solicits or communicates by letter or otherwise with persons to work for him or the person for whom he is acting, or to work at any shop, plant, or establishment while a strike, lockout, or other trade dispute is still in active progress at such shop, plant, or establishment, he shall plainly and explicitly mention in such advertisement or oral or written solicitations or communications that a strike, lockout, or other labor disturbance exists.

The person inserting any such advertisement, solicitation, or communication in a newspaper, on a poster, or otherwise, shall insert in such advertisement, solicitation or communication his own name and, if he is representing another, the name of the person he is representing and at whose direction and under whose authority he is inserting the advertisement, solicitation or communication. The appearance of this name in connection with such advertisement, solicitation or communication is prima facie evidence as to the person responsible for the advertisement, solicitation or communication. *(Stats.1937, c. 90, p. 209, § 973. Amended by Stats.1947, c. 281, p. 846, § 1.)*

§ 974. Violation; misdemeanor

Any person, or agent or officer thereof, who violates Section 973 is guilty of a misdemeanor. *(Stats.1937, c. 90, p. 210, § 974. Amended by Stats.1943, c. 1024, p. 2963, § 1.)*

§ 976. Publishing advertisement offering employment as salesman, broker or agent; misrepresentation as to compensation or commissions

No person shall publish or cause to be published any advertisement, solicitation or communication in any newspaper, poster or letter, offering employment as a salesman, broker or agent, whether as an employee or independent contractor, which advertisement, solicitation or communication (a) is willfully designed to mislead any person as to compensation or commissions which may be earned; or (b) falsely represents the compensation or commissions which may be earned.

This section shall not be applicable to any publisher of a newspaper, magazine, or other publication, who publishes an advertisement, solicitation or communication in good faith, without knowledge of its false, deceptive or misleading character. *(Added by Stats.1961, c. 1583, p. 3409, § 1. Amended by Stats.1970, c. 243, p. 503, § 2.)*

§ 977. Violation; misdemeanor

Any person, or agent or officer thereof, who violates Section 976 is guilty of a misdemeanor. *(Added by Stats.1961, c. 1583, p. 3409, § 2.)*

CHAPTER 3. CLASS OF LABOR EMPLOYED; LABOR UNION INSIGNIA

Section
1010. Label defined.
1011. Labor misrepresentation on label; misdemeanor; penalty.

Section
1012. False representation of manufacture or sale by union employees; misdemeanor; penalty.
1013. Forge defined.
1014. Registered union labels and trade-marks.
1015. Forgery; misdemeanor; penalty.
1016. Unauthorized use of union label, trademark, or insignia; misdemeanor; penalty.
1017. Unauthorized use of union card; misdemeanor.
1018. Unauthorized wearing of union button; misdemeanor; punishment.

§ 1010. Label defined

As used in this chapter "label" includes label, imprint, trade-mark, tag, stamp, inscription, or other device. *(Stats.1937, c. 90, p. 210, § 1010.)*

§ 1011. Labor misrepresentation on label; misdemeanor; penalty

A person engaged in the production, manufacture, or sale of any article of merchandise in this state, shall not, by any label placed or impressed upon such article, or upon its container, misrepresent or falsely state any of the following as to the production of such article:

(a) The kind, character, or nature of the labor employed.

(b) The extent of the labor employed.

(c) The number or kind of persons exclusively employed.

(d) That a particular or distinctive class or character of laborers was wholly and exclusively employed, when in fact another class, or character, or distinction of laborers was used or employed either jointly or in anywise supplementary to such exclusive class, character, or distinction of laborers.

Violation of any provision of this section is a misdemeanor punishable by a fine of not less than one hundred dollars ($100) nor more than one thousand dollars ($1,000), or by imprisonment for not less than 20 nor more than 90 days, or both. *(Stats.1937, c. 90, p. 210, § 1011. Amended by Stats.1983, c. 1092, § 198, eff. Sept. 27, 1983, operative Jan. 1, 1984.)*

§ 1012. False representation of manufacture or sale by union employees; misdemeanor; penalty

Any person engaged in the production, manufacture, or sale of any article of merchandise in this state, or any person engaged in the performance of any acts or services of a private, public, or quasi-public nature for profit, who willfully misrepresents or falsely states that members of trades unions, labor associations, or labor organizations were engaged or employed in the manufacture, production, or sale of such article or in the performance of such acts or services, is guilty of a misdemeanor punishable by a fine of not more than one thousand dollars ($1,000), or by imprisonment in the county jail for not more than 90 days, or both. *(Stats.1937, c. 90, p. 210, § 1012. Amended by Stats.1983, c. 1092, § 199, eff. Sept. 27, 1983, operative Jan. 1, 1984.)*

§ 1013. Forge defined

As used in this chapter "forge" means forge, reproduce, copy, imitate, or counterfeit. *(Stats.1937, c. 90, p. 210, § 1013.)*

§ 1014. Registered union labels and trade-marks

Any trade union, labor association, or labor organization, organized and existing in this State, which has adopted and registered a label or trademark in accordance with the law of this State, has the exclusive right to the ownership, use, and control of such label or trademark. *(Stats.1937, c. 90, p. 210, § 1014.)*

§ 1015. Forgery; misdemeanor; penalty

Any person who, without having an unrevoked written authority from such trade union, labor association or labor organization, willfully forges or procures to be forged such label or trademark, with intent to sell or assist other persons to sell, any goods to which such forged label is affixed as having been made, manufactured, or produced in whole or in part by labor, laborers, or employees who are members of, or allied or associated with, such trade union, labor association, or labor organization, is guilty of a misdemeanor, punishable by a fine not more than one thousand dollars ($1,000) or imprisonment for not more than 90 days, or both. *(Stats.1937, c. 90, p. 211, § 1015. Amended by Stats.1983, c. 1092, § 200, eff. Sept. 27, 1983, operative Jan. 1, 1984.)*

§ 1016. Unauthorized use of union label, trademark, or insignia; misdemeanor; penalty

Any person who willfully uses or displays the genuine label, trademark, insignia, seal, device, or form of advertisement of any association or labor union, in any manner not authorized by such association or labor organization or not in conformity with the bylaws thereof, is guilty of a misdemeanor punishable by a fine not exceeding two hundred dollars ($200) or imprisonment for not more than three months, or both. *(Stats.1937, c. 90, p. 211, § 1016. Amended by Stats.1983, c. 1092, § 201, eff. Sept. 27, 1983, operative Jan. 1, 1984.)*

§ 1017. Unauthorized use of union card; misdemeanor

Any person who wilfully uses the card of any labor union to obtain aid, assistance, or employment, unless entitled to use such card under the rules and regulations of a labor union within this State is guilty of a misdemeanor. *(Stats.1937, c. 90, p. 211, § 1017.)*

§ 1018. Unauthorized wearing of union button; misdemeanor; punishment

Any person who willfully wears the button of any labor union of this state, unless entitled to wear the button under the rules of such union, is guilty of a misdemeanor, and is punishable by imprisonment in the county jail for not more than 20 days or by a fine of not more than forty dollars ($40), or by both fine and imprisonment. *(Added by Stats.1953, c. 85, p. 807, § 1. Amended by Stats.1983, c. 1092, § 202, eff. Sept. 27, 1983, operative Jan. 1, 1984.)*

CHAPTER 3.5. CONTRACTORS

Section
1020. Legislative intent.
1021. Employment by unlicensed contractor; civil penalty for employer.
1021.5. Contract by licensed contractor with contractor or other who is not valid independent contractor; civil penalty for licensed contractor.
1022. Citation for violations; service; contents.
1023. Content of citation or civil penalty; notice; hearing; final order; payment of penalty; judgment; interest on judgment.
1024. Industrial relations construction industry enforcement fund; deposit of civil penalties; use of funds.

§ 1020. Legislative intent

It is the intent of the Legislature in enacting this chapter to establish a citation system for the imposition of prompt and effective civil sanctions against violators of the laws and regulations of this state relating to the employment of workers by unlicensed contractors and the utilization of unlicensed contractors and other persons who are not valid independent contractors by licensed contractors. *(Added by Stats.1979, c. 864, p. 3012, § 1. Amended by Stats.1982, c. 761, p. 3008, § 1.)*

§ 1021. Employment by unlicensed contractor; civil penalty for employer

Any person who does not hold a valid state contractor's license issued pursuant to Chapter 9 (commencing with Section 7000) of Division 3 of the Business and Professions Code, and who employs any worker to perform services for which a license is required, shall be subject to a civil penalty in the amount of two hundred dollars ($200) per employee for each day of employment. The civil penalties provided for by this section are in addition to any other penalty provided by law. *(Added by Stats.1979, c. 864, p. 3012, § 1. Amended by Stats.2003, c. 329 (A.B.276), § 6.)*

§ 1021.5. Contract by licensed contractor with contractor or other who is not valid independent contractor; civil penalty for licensed contractor

Any person who holds a valid state contractor's license issued pursuant to Chapter 9 (commencing with Section 7000) of Division 3 of the Business and Professions Code, and who willingly and knowingly enters into a contract with any person to perform services for which a license is required as an independent contractor, and that person does not meet the burden of proof of independent contractor status pursuant to Section 2750.5 or hold a valid state contractor's license, shall be subject to a civil penalty in the amount of two hundred dollars ($200) per person so contracted with for each day of the contract. The civil penalties provided for by this section are in addition to any other penalty provided by law. *(Added by Stats.1982, c. 761, p. 3008, § 2. Amended by Stats.2003, c. 329 (A.B.276), § 7.)*

§ 1022. Citation for violations; service; contents

If upon inspection or investigation the Labor Commissioner determines that any person is employing workers in violation of Section 1021 or 1021.5, he or she may issue a citation to the person in violation. The citation may be served personally or by registered mail in accordance with subdivision (c) of Section 11505 of the Government Code. Each citation shall be in writing and shall describe the nature of the violation, including reference to the statutory provision alleged to have been violated. *(Added by Stats.1979, c. 864, p. 3012, § 1. Amended by Stats.1982, c. 761, p. 3009, § 3.)*

§ 1023. Content of citation or civil penalty; notice; hearing; final order; payment of penalty; judgment; interest on judgment

(a) If a person desires to contest a citation or the proposed assessment of a civil penalty therefor, he or she shall within 15 business days after service of the citation notify the office of the Labor Commissioner which appears on the citation of his or her request for an informal hearing. The Labor Commissioner or his or her deputy or agent shall, within 30 days, hold a hearing at the conclusion of which the citation or proposed assessment of a civil penalty shall be affirmed, modified, or dismissed. The decision of the Labor Commissioner shall consist of a notice of findings, findings, and order which shall be served on all parties to the hearing within 15 days after the hearing by regular first-class mail at the last known address of the party on file with the Labor Commissioner. Service shall be completed pursuant to Section 1013 of the Code of Civil Procedure. Any amount found due by the Labor Commissioner as a result of a hearing shall become due and payable 45 days after notice of the findings and written findings and order have been mailed to the party assessed. A writ of mandate may be taken from that finding to the appropriate superior court, as long as the party agrees to pay any judgment and costs ultimately rendered by the court against the party for the assessment. The writ shall be taken within 45 days of service of the notice of findings, findings, and order thereon.

(b) A person to whom a citation has been issued, shall, in lieu of contesting a citation pursuant to this section, transmit to the office of the Labor Commissioner designated on the citation the amount specified for the violation within 15 business days after issuance of the citation.

(c) When no petition objecting to a citation or the proposed assessment of a civil penalty is filed, a certified copy of the citation or proposed civil penalty may be filed by the Labor Commissioner in the office of the clerk of the superior court in any county in which the person assessed has property or in which the person assessed has or had a place of business. The clerk, immediately upon the filing, shall enter judgment for the state against the person assessed in the amount shown on the citation or proposed assessment of a civil penalty.

(d) When findings and the order thereon are made affirming or modifying a citation or proposed assessment of a civil penalty after hearing, a certified copy of the findings and the order entered thereon may be entered by the Labor Commissioner in the office of the clerk of the superior court in any county in which the person assessed has property or in which the person assessed has or had a place of business. The clerk, immediately upon the filing, shall enter judgment for the state against the person assessed in the amount shown on the certified order.

(e) A judgment entered pursuant to this section shall bear the same rate of interest and shall have the same effect as other judgments and be given the same preference allowed by law on other judgments rendered for claims for taxes. The clerk shall make no charge for the service provided by this section to be performed by him or her. *(Added by Stats.1979, c. 864, p. 3012, § 1. Amended by Stats.1988, c. 96, § 5.)*

§ 1024. Industrial relations construction industry enforcement fund; deposit of civil penalties; use of funds

All civil penalties collected pursuant to this chapter shall be deposited in the Industrial Relations Construction Industry Enforcement Fund, which is hereby created. All moneys in the fund shall be used for the purpose of enforcing the provisions of this chapter, as appropriated by the Legislature.

It is the intent of the Legislature in enacting this section to provide for the prompt and effective enforcement of labor laws relating to the construction industry. *(Added by Stats.1981, c. 1172, p. 4719, § 1. Amended by Stats.2008, c. 55 (A.B.3060), § 1.)*

CHAPTER 3.7. ALCOHOL AND DRUG REHABILITATION

Section
1025. Accommodation of employee in alcohol or drug rehabilitation program; construction of chapter.
1026. Safeguarding employee privacy.
1027. Compensation not required; use of sick leave.
1028. Complaints by employees; applicable law.

§ 1025. Accommodation of employee in alcohol or drug rehabilitation program; construction of chapter

Every private employer regularly employing 25 or more employees shall reasonably accommodate any employee who wishes to voluntarily enter and participate in an alcohol or drug rehabilitation program, provided that this reasonable accommodation does not impose an undue hardship on the employer.

Nothing in this chapter shall be construed to prohibit an employer from refusing to hire, or discharging an employee who, because of the employee's current use of alcohol or drugs, is unable to perform his or her duties, or cannot perform the duties in a manner which would not endanger his or her health or safety or the health or

safety of others. *(Added by Stats.1984, c. 1103, § 1. Amended by Stats.1987, c. 506, § 2.)*

§ 1026. Safeguarding employee privacy

The employer shall make reasonable efforts to safeguard the privacy of the employee as to the fact that he or she has enrolled in an alcohol or drug rehabilitation program. *(Added by Stats.1984, c. 1103, § 1. Amended by Stats.1987, c. 506, § 3.)*

§ 1027. Compensation not required; use of sick leave

Nothing in this chapter shall be construed to require an employer to provide time off with pay, except that an employee may use sick leave to which he or she is entitled for the purpose of entering and participating in an alcohol or drug rehabilitation program. *(Added by Stats.1984, c. 1103, § 1. Amended by Stats.1987, c. 506, § 4.)*

§ 1028. Complaints by employees; applicable law

An employee may file a complaint with the Labor Commissioner if he or she believes that he or she has been denied reasonable accommodation as required by this chapter. Sections 98, 98.1, 98.2, 98.3, 98.4, 98.5, 98.6, and 98.7 shall be applicable to a complaint filed pursuant to this section. *(Added by Stats.1984, c. 1103, § 1.)*

CHAPTER 3.8. LACTATION ACCOMMODATION

Section
1030. Break time for employees to express breast milk; time issues.
1031. Use of room or location other than toilet stall.
1032. Provision of break time.
1033. Violation.

§ 1030. Break time for employees to express breast milk; time issues

Every employer, including the state and any political subdivision, shall provide a reasonable amount of break time to accommodate an employee desiring to express breast milk for the employee's infant child. The break time shall, if possible, run concurrently with any break time already provided to the employee. Break time for an employee that does not run concurrently with the rest time authorized for the employee by the applicable wage order of the Industrial Welfare Commission shall be unpaid. *(Added by Stats.2001, c. 821 (A.B.1025), § 1.)*

§ 1031. Use of room or location other than toilet stall

The employer shall make reasonable efforts to provide the employee with the use of a room or other location, other than a toilet stall, in close proximity to the employee's work area, for the employee to express milk in private. The room or location may include the place where the employee normally works if it otherwise meets the requirements of this section. *(Added by Stats.2001, c. 821 (A.B.1025), § 1.)*

§ 1032. Provision of break time

An employer is not required to provide break time under this chapter if to do so would seriously disrupt the operations of the employer. *(Added by Stats.2001, c. 821 (A.B.1025), § 1.)*

§ 1033. Violation

(a) An employer who violates any provision of this chapter shall be subject to a civil penalty in the amount of one hundred dollars ($100) for each violation.

(b) If, upon inspection or investigation, the Labor Commissioner determines that a violation of this chapter has occurred, the Labor Commissioner may issue a citation. The procedures for issuing, contesting, and enforcing judgments for citations or civil penalties issued by the Labor Commissioner for violations of this chapter shall be the same as those set forth in Section 1197.1.

(c) Notwithstanding any other provision of this code, violations of this chapter shall not be misdemeanors under this code. *(Added by Stats.2001, c. 821 (A.B.1025), § 1.)*

CHAPTER 3.9. EMPLOYEE LITERACY ASSISTANCE

Section
1040. Short title.
1041. Employer assistance.
1042. Privacy of employee.
1043. Time off with pay not required of employer.
1044. Termination of employment; prohibition.

§ 1040. Short title

This chapter shall be known and may be cited as the Employee Literacy Education Assistance Act. *(Added by Stats.1991, c. 339 (S.B.647), § 2.)*

§ 1041. Employer assistance

(a) Every private employer regularly employing 25 or more employees shall reasonably accommodate and assist any employee who reveals a problem of illiteracy and requests employer assistance in enrolling in an adult literacy education program, provided that this reasonable accommodation does not impose an undue hardship on the employer.

(b) For purposes of this section, employer assistance includes, but is not limited to, providing the employee with the locations of local literacy education programs or arranging for a literacy education provider to visit the jobsite. *(Added by Stats.1991, c. 339 (S.B.647), § 2.)*

§ 1042. Privacy of employee

The employer shall make reasonable efforts to safeguard the privacy of the employee as to the fact that he or she has a problem with illiteracy. *(Added by Stats.1991, c. 339 (S.B.647), § 2.)*

§ 1043. Time off with pay not required of employer

Nothing in this chapter shall be construed to require an employer to provide time off with pay for an employee to enroll and participate in an adult literacy education program. *(Added by Stats.1991, c. 339 (S.B.647), § 2.)*

§ 1044. Termination of employment; prohibition

An employee who reveals a problem of illiteracy and who satisfactorily performs his or her work shall not be subject to termination of employment because of the disclosure of illiteracy. *(Added by Stats.1991, c. 339 (S.B. 647), § 2.)*

CHAPTER 4. REEMPLOYMENT PRIVILEGES

Section
1050. Misrepresentation preventing employment of former employee; misdemeanor.
1051. Improper use of fingerprint or photograph; misdemeanor.
1052. Permitting violation; misdemeanor.
1053. Truthful statement of reasons for termination of employment.
1054. Violation; civil penalty.
1055. Public utility corporations; letter of service upon termination of employment.
1056. Violation by public utility; misdemeanor; penalty.
1057. Management company employee; fingerprints.

§ 1050. Misrepresentation preventing employment of former employee; misdemeanor

Any person, or agent or officer thereof, who, after having discharged an employee from the service of such person or after an employee has voluntarily left such service, by any misrepresentation prevents or attempts to prevent the former employee from obtaining employment, is guilty of a misdemeanor. *(Stats.1937, c. 90, p. 211, § 1050. Amended by Stats.1981, c. 513, p. 1874, § 1.)*

§ 1051. Improper use of fingerprint or photograph; misdemeanor

Except as provided in Section 1057, any person or agent or officer thereof, who requires, as a condition precedent to securing or retaining employment, that an employee or applicant for employment be photographed or fingerprinted by any person who desires his or her photograph or fingerprints for the purpose of furnishing the same or information concerning the same or concerning the employee or applicant for employment to any other employer or third person, and these photographs and fingerprints could be used to the detriment of the employee or applicant for employment is guilty of a misdemeanor. *(Stats.1937, c. 90, p. 211, § 1051. Amended by Stats.1987, c. 77, § 1.)*

§ 1052. Permitting violation; misdemeanor

Any person who knowingly causes, suffers, or permits an agent, superintendent, manager, or employee in his employ to commit a violation of sections 1050 and 1051,

363

or who fails to take all reasonable steps within his power to prevent such violation is guilty of a misdemeanor. *(Stats.1937, c. 90, p. 211, § 1052.)*

§ 1053. Truthful statement of reasons for termination of employment

Nothing in this chapter shall prevent an employer or an agent, employee, superintendent or manager thereof from furnishing, upon special request therefor, a truthful statement concerning the reason for the discharge of an employee or why an employee voluntarily left the service of the employer. If such statement furnishes any mark, sign, or other means conveying information different from that expressed by words therein, such fact, or the fact that such statement or other means of furnishing information was given without a special request therefor is prima facie evidence of a violation of sections 1050 to 1053. *(Stats.1937, c. 90, p. 211, § 1053.)*

§ 1054. Violation; civil penalty

In addition to and apart from the criminal penalty provided any person or agent or officer thereof, who violates any provision of sections 1050 to 1052, inclusive, is liable to the party aggrieved, in a civil action, for treble damages. Such civil action may be brought by such aggrieved person or his assigns, or successors in interest, without first establishing any criminal liability under this article. *(Stats.1937, c. 90, p. 212, § 1054.)*

§ 1055. Public utility corporations; letter of service upon termination of employment

Every public utility corporation shall, upon request by any employee leaving its service, give to such employee a letter stating the period of service and the kind of service rendered to the public utility corporation by the employee. *(Stats.1937, c. 90, p. 212, § 1055.)*

§ 1056. Violation by public utility; misdemeanor; penalty

Every public utility corporation violating Section 1055 is guilty of a misdemeanor punishable by a fine of not less than fifty dollars ($50) nor more than two hundred dollars ($200) for each offense, which fine shall be collected by the district attorney of the county in which the public utility corporation has its principal place of business. *(Stats.1937, c. 90, p. 212, § 1056. Amended by Stats.1983, c. 1092, § 203, eff. Sept. 27, 1983, operative Jan. 1, 1984.)*

§ 1057. Management company employee; fingerprints

Section 1051 shall not apply to any employee of a diversified or nondiversified management company, as defined in Section 80a–5 of Title 15 of the United States Code, and the affiliates thereof, as defined in Sections 80a–2(a)(2) and 80a–2(a)(3) of Title 15 of the United States Code, who is required to be fingerprinted pursuant to federal law. *(Added by Stats.1987, c. 77, § 2.)*

CHAPTER 4.5. DISPLACED JANITOR OPPORTUNITY ACT

Section
1060. Definitions.
1061. Notification of successor service contract; obligations of successor contractor or subcontractor.
1062. Remedies for violations; calculation of backpay.
1063. Application of chapter.
1064. Authority to enact ordinances imposing greater standards or additional enforcement provisions.
1065. Severability.

§ 1060. Definitions

The following definitions shall apply throughout this chapter:

(a) "Awarding authority" means any person that awards or otherwise enters into contracts for janitorial or building maintenance services performed within the State of California, including any subcontracts for janitorial or building maintenance services.

(b) "Contractor" means any person that employs 25 or more individuals and that enters into a service contract with the awarding authority.

(c) "Employee" means any person employed as a service employee of a contractor or subcontractor who works at least 15 hours per week and whose primary place of employment is in the State of California under a contract to provide janitorial or building maintenance services. "Employee" does not include a person who is a managerial, supervisory, or confidential employee, including those employees who would be so defined under the federal Fair Labor Standards Act.

(d) "Person" means any individual, proprietorship, partnership, joint venture, corporation, limited liability company, trust, association, or other entity that may employ individuals or enter into contracts.

(e) "Service contract" means any contract that has the principal purpose of providing services through the use of service employees.

(f) "Subcontractor" means any person who is not an employee who enters into a contract with a contractor to assist the contractor in performing a service contract.

(g) "Successor service contract" means a service contract for the performance of essentially the same services as were previously performed pursuant to a different service contract at the same facility that terminated within the previous 30 days. A service contract entered into more than 30 days after the termination of a predecessor service contract shall be considered a "successor service contract" if its execution was delayed for the purpose of avoiding application of this chapter. *(Added by Stats. 2001, c. 795 (S.B.20), § 1.)*

§ 1061. Notification of successor service contract; obligations of successor contractor or subcontractor

(a)(1) If an awarding authority notifies a contractor that the service contract between the awarding authority and the contractor has been terminated or will be terminated, the awarding authority shall indicate in that notification whether a successor service contract has been or will be awarded in its place and, if so, shall identify the name and address of the successor contractor. The terminated contractor shall, within three working days after receiving that notification, provide to the successor contractor identified by the awarding authority, the name, date of hire, and job classification of each employee employed at the site or sites covered by the terminated service contract at the time of the contract termination.

(2) If the terminated contractor has not learned the identity of the successor contractor, if any, the terminated contractor shall provide that information to the awarding authority, which shall be responsible for providing that information to the successor contractor as soon as that contractor has been selected.

(3) The requirements of this section shall be equally applicable to all subcontractors of a terminated contractor.

(b)(1) A successor contractor or successor subcontractor shall retain, for a 60 day transition employment period, employees who have been employed by the terminated contractor or its subcontractors, if any, for the preceding four months or longer at the site or sites covered by the successor service contract unless the successor contractor or successor subcontractor has reasonable and substantiated cause not to hire a particular employee based on that employee's performance or conduct while working under the terminated contract. This requirement shall be stated by awarding authorities in all initial bid packages that are governed by this chapter.

(2) The successor contractor or successor subcontractor shall make a written offer of employment to each employee, as required by this section, in the employee's primary language or another language in which the employee is literate. That offer shall state the time within which the employee must accept that offer, but in no case may that time be less than 10 days. Nothing in this section requires the successor contractor or successor subcontractor to pay the same wages or offer the same benefits as were provided by the prior contractor or prior subcontractor.

(3) If at any time the successor contractor or successor subcontractor determines that fewer employees are needed to perform services under the successor service contract or successor subcontract than were required by the terminated contractor under the terminated contract or terminated subcontract, the successor contractor or successor subcontractor shall retain employees by seniority within the job classification.

(c) The successor contractor or successor subcontractor, upon commencing service under the successor service contract, shall provide a list of its employees and a list of employees of its subcontractors providing services at the site or sites covered under that contract to the awarding authority. These lists shall indicate which of these employees were employed at the site or sites by the terminated contractor or terminated subcontractor. The successor contractor or successor subcontractor shall also provide a list of any of the terminated contractor's employees who were not retained either by the successor contractor or successor subcontractor, stating the reason these employees were not retained.

(d) During the 60–day transition employment period, the successor contractor or successor subcontractor shall maintain a preferential hiring list of eligible covered employees not retained by the successor contractor or successor subcontractor from which the successor contractor or successor subcontractor shall hire additional employees until such time as all of the terminated contractor's or terminated subcontractor's employees have been offered employment with the successor contractor or successor subcontractor.

(e) During the initial 60–day transition employment period, the successor contractor or successor subcontractor shall not discharge without cause an employee retained pursuant to this chapter. Cause shall be based only on the performance or conduct of the particular employee.

(f) At the end of the 60–day transition employment period, a successor contractor or successor subcontractor shall provide a written performance evaluation to each employee retained pursuant to this chapter. If the employee's performance during that 60–day period is satisfactory, the successor contractor or successor subcontractor shall offer the employee continued employment. Any employment after the 60–day transition employment period shall be at-will employment under which the employee may be terminated without cause. (Added by Stats.2001, c. 795 (S.B.20), § 1.)

§ 1062. Remedies for violations; calculation of backpay

(a) An employee, who was not offered employment or who has been discharged in violation of this chapter by a successor contractor or successor subcontractor, or an agent of the employee may bring an action against a successor contractor or successor subcontractor in any superior court of the State of California having jurisdiction over the successor contractor or successor subcontractor. Upon finding a violation of this chapter, the court shall award backpay, including the value of benefits, for each day during which the violation has occurred and continues to occur. The amount of backpay shall be calculated as the greater of either of the following:

(1) The average regular rate of pay received by the employee during the last three years of the employee's employment in the same occupation classification multiplied by the average hours worked during the last three years of the employee's employment.

(2) The final regular rate of pay received by the employee at the time of termination of the predecessor contract multiplied by the number of hours usually worked by the employee.

(b) The court may order a preliminary or permanent injunction to stop the continued violation of this chapter.

(c) If the employee is the prevailing party in the legal action, the court shall award the employee reasonable attorney's fees and costs as part of the costs recoverable.

(d) In the absence of a claim by an employee that he or she was terminated in violation of this chapter, an employee may not maintain a cause of action under this chapter solely for the failure of an employer to provide a written performance evaluation. *(Added by Stats.2001, c. 795 (S.B.20), § 1.)*

§ 1063. Application of chapter

(a) This chapter only applies to contracts entered into on or after January 1, 2002.

(b) Except for the obligations specified in subdivisions (a) and (b) of Section 1061, nothing in this chapter changes or increases the relationship or duties of a property owner or an awarding authority, or their agents, with respect to contractors, subcontractors, or their employees.

(c) Nothing in this chapter limits the right of a property owner or an awarding authority to terminate a service contract or to replace a contractor with another contractor or with the property owner's or awarding authority's own employees. *(Added by Stats.2001, c. 795 (S.B.20), § 1.)*

§ 1064. Authority to enact ordinances imposing greater standards or additional enforcement provisions

Nothing in this chapter shall prohibit a local government agency from enacting ordinances relating to displaced janitors that impose greater standards than, or establish additional enforcement provisions to, those prescribed by this chapter. *(Added by Stats.2001, c. 795 (S.B.20), § 1.)*

§ 1065. Severability

If any provision or provisions of this chapter or any application thereof is held invalid, that invalidity shall not affect any other provisions or applications of this chapter that can be given effect notwithstanding that invalidity. *(Added by Stats.2001, c. 795 (S.B.20), § 1.)*

CHAPTER 4.6. PUBLIC TRANSIT SERVICE CONTRACTS

Section
1070. Legislative findings and declarations.
1071. Definitions.
1072. Bidder declarations; preferences for employee retention; existing service contractor obligations; successor contractor and subcontractor obligations.
1073. Violations of chapter; injunctive relief; attorney's fees and costs.
1074. Termination of contract; conditions; post-termination bidding eligibility.

§ 1070. Legislative findings and declarations

The Legislature finds and declares all of the following:

(a) That when public transit agencies award contracts to operate bus and rail services to a new contractor, qualified employees of the prior contractor who are not reemployed by the successor contractor face significant economic dislocation as a result.

(b) That those displaced employees rely unnecessarily upon the unemployment insurance system, public social services, and health programs, increasing costs to these vital government programs and placing a significant burden upon both the government and the taxpayers.

(c) That it serves an important social purpose to establish incentives for contractors who bid public transit services contracts to retain qualified employees of the prior contractor to perform the same or similar work. *(Added by Stats.2003, c. 103 (S.B.158), § 1.)*

§ 1071. Definitions

The following definitions apply throughout this chapter:

(a) "Awarding authority" means any local government agency, including any city, county, special district, transit district, joint powers authority, or nonprofit corporation that awards or otherwise enters into contracts for public transit services performed within the State of California.

(b) "Bidder" means any person who submits a bid to an awarding agency for a public transit service contract or subcontract.

(c) "Contractor" means any person who enters into a public transit service contract with an awarding authority.

(d) "Employee" means any person who works for a contractor or subcontractor under a contract. "Employee" does not include an executive, administrative, or professional employee exempt from the payment of overtime compensation within the meaning of subdivision (a) of Section 515 or any person who is not an "employee" as defined under Section 2(3) of the National Labor Relations Act (29 U.S.C. Sec. 152(3)).

(e) "Person" means any individual, proprietorship, partnership, joint venture, corporation, limited liability company, trust, association, or other entity that may employ individuals or enter into contracts.

(f) "Public transit services" means the provision of passenger transportation services to the general public, including paratransit service.

(g) "Service contract" means any contract the principal purpose of which is to provide public transit services through the use of service employees.

(h) "Subcontractor" means any person who is not an employee who enters into a contract with a contractor to assist the contractor in performing a service contract. *(Added by Stats.2003, c. 103 (S.B.158), § 1.)*

§ 1072. Bidder declarations; preferences for employee retention; existing service contractor obligations; successor contractor and subcontractor obligations

(a) A bidder shall declare as part of the bid for a service contract whether or not he or she will retain the employees of the prior contractor or subcontractor for a period of not less than 90 days.

(b) An awarding authority letting a service contract out to bid shall give a 10 percent preference to any bidder who agrees to retain the employees of the prior contractor or subcontractor pursuant to subdivision (a).

(c)(1) If the awarding authority announces that it intends to let a service contract out to bid, the existing service contractor, within a reasonable time, shall provide to the awarding authority the number of employees who are performing services under the service contract and the wage rates, benefits, and job classifications of those employees. In addition, the existing service contractor shall make this information available to any entity that the awarding authority has identified as a bona fide bidder. If the successor service contract is awarded to a new contractor, the existing contractor shall provide the names, addresses, dates of hire, wages, benefit levels, and job classifications of employees to the successor contractor. The duties imposed by this subdivision shall be contained in all service contracts.

(2) A successor contractor or subcontractor who agrees to retain employees pursuant to subdivision (a) shall retain employees who have been employed by the prior contractor or subcontractors, except for reasonable and substantiated cause. That cause is limited to the particular employee's performance or conduct while working under the prior contract or the employee's failure of any controlled substances and alcohol test, physical examination, criminal background check required by law as a condition of employment, or other standard hiring qualification lawfully required by the successor contractor or subcontractor.

(3) The successor contractor or subcontractor shall make a written offer of employment to each employee to be rehired. That offer shall state the time within which the employee must accept that offer, but in no case less than 10 days. Nothing in this section requires the successor contractor or subcontractor to pay the same wages or offer the same benefits provided by the prior contractor or subcontractor.

(4) If, at any time, the successor contractor or subcontractor determines that fewer employees are required than were required under the prior contract or subcontract, he or she shall retain qualified employees by seniority within the job classification. In determining those employees who are qualified, the successor contractor or subcontractor may require an employee to possess any license that is required by law to operate the equipment that the employee will operate as an employee of the successor contractor or subcontractor. (Added by Stats.2003, c. 103 (S.B.158), § 1.)

§ 1073. Violations of chapter; injunctive relief; attorney's fees and costs

(a) An employee who was not offered employment or who has been discharged in violation of this chapter, or his or her agent, may bring an action against the successor contractor or subcontractor in any superior court having jurisdiction over the successor contractor or subcontractor. Upon finding a violation of this chapter, the court shall order reinstatement to employment with the successor contractor or subcontractor and award backpay, including the value of benefits, for each day of violation. A violation of this chapter continues for each day that the successor contractor or subcontractor fails to employ the employee, within the period agreed to pursuant to Section 1072.

(b) The court may preliminarily or permanently enjoin the continued violation of this chapter.

(c) If the employee prevails in an action brought under this chapter, the court shall award the employee reasonable attorney's fees and costs as part of the costs recoverable. (Added by Stats.2003, c. 103 (S.B.158), § 1.)

§ 1074. Termination of contract; conditions; post-termination bidding eligibility

(a) Upon its own motion or upon the request of any member of the public, an awarding authority may terminate any service contract made pursuant to Section 1072 if both of the following occur:

(1) The contractor or subcontractor has substantially breached the contract.

(2) The awarding authority holds a public hearing within 30 days of the receipt of the request or its announcement of its intention to terminate.

(b) A contractor or subcontractor terminated pursuant to subdivision (a) shall be ineligible to bid on or be awarded a service contract or subcontract with that awarding authority for a period of not less than one year and not more than three years, to be determined by the awarding authority. (Added by Stats.2003, c. 103 (S.B. 158), § 1.)

CHAPTER 5. POLITICAL AFFILIATIONS

Section
1101. Political activities of employees; prohibition of prevention or control by employer.
1102. Coercion of political activities of employees.
1102.5. Employer prohibition of disclosure of information by employee to government or law enforcement agency; suspected violation or noncompliance to federal or state law; employer retaliation; civil penalties.
1102.6. Civil actions or administrative proceedings; burden of proof for employer.
1102.7. Whistleblower hotline; confidential information; office of the Attorney General.
1102.8. Display of employees' rights and responsibilities under whistleblower laws; compliance with posting requirement.

Section
1103.   Violation; misdemeanor; penalty.
1104.   Responsibility of employer for actions of agents.
1105.   Employee's action for damages.
1106.   Employee.

§ 1101. Political activities of employees; prohibition of prevention or control by employer

No employer shall make, adopt, or enforce any rule, regulation, or policy:

(a) Forbidding or preventing employees from engaging or participating in politics or from becoming candidates for public office.

(b) Controlling or directing, or tending to control or direct the political activities or affiliations of employees. *(Stats.1937, c. 90, p. 212, § 1101.)*

§ 1102. Coercion of political activities of employees

No employer shall coerce or influence or attempt to coerce or influence his employees through or by means of threat of discharge or loss of employment to adopt or follow or refrain from adopting or following any particular course or line of political action or political activity. *(Stats.1937, c. 90, p. 212, § 1102.)*

§ 1102.5. Employer prohibition of disclosure of information by employee to government or law enforcement agency; suspected violation or noncompliance to federal or state law; employer retaliation; civil penalties

(a) An employer may not make, adopt, or enforce any rule, regulation, or policy preventing an employee from disclosing information to a government or law enforcement agency, where the employee has reasonable cause to believe that the information discloses a violation of state or federal statute, or a violation or noncompliance with a state or federal rule or regulation.

(b) An employer may not retaliate against an employee for disclosing information to a government or law enforcement agency, where the employee has reasonable cause to believe that the information discloses a violation of state or federal statute, or a violation or noncompliance with a state or federal rule or regulation.

(c) An employer may not retaliate against an employee for refusing to participate in an activity that would result in a violation of state or federal statute, or a violation or noncompliance with a state or federal rule or regulation.

(d) An employer may not retaliate against an employee for having exercised his or her rights under subdivision (a), (b), or (c) in any former employment.

(e) A report made by an employee of a government agency to his or her employer is a disclosure of information to a government or law enforcement agency pursuant to subdivisions (a) and (b).

(f) In addition to other penalties, an employer that is a corporation or limited liability company is liable for a civil penalty not exceeding ten thousand dollars ($10,000) for each violation of this section.

(g) This section does not apply to rules, regulations, or policies which implement, or to actions by employers against employees who violate, the confidentiality of the lawyer-client privilege of Article 3 (commencing with Section 950), the physician-patient privilege of Article 6 (commencing with Section 990) of Chapter 4 of Division 8 of the Evidence Code, or trade secret information. *(Added by Stats.1984, c. 1083, § 1. Amended by Stats. 2003, c. 484 (S.B.777), § 2.)*

§ 1102.6. Civil actions or administrative proceedings; burden of proof for employer

In a civil action or administrative proceeding brought pursuant to Section 1102.5, once it has been demonstrated by a preponderance of the evidence that an activity proscribed by Section 1102.5 was a contributing factor in the alleged prohibited action against the employee, the employer shall have the burden of proof to demonstrate by clear and convincing evidence that the alleged action would have occurred for legitimate, independent reasons even if the employee had not engaged in activities protected by Section 1102.5. *(Added by Stats.2003, c. 484 (S.B.777), § 3.)*

§ 1102.7. Whistleblower hotline; confidential information; office of the Attorney General

(a) The office of the Attorney General shall maintain a whistleblower hotline to receive calls from persons who have information regarding possible violations of state or federal statutes, rules, or regulations, or violations of fiduciary responsibility by a corporation or limited liability company to its shareholders, investors, or employees.

(b) The Attorney General shall refer calls received on the whistleblower hotline to the appropriate government authority for review and possible investigation.

(c) During the initial review of a call received pursuant to subdivision (a), the Attorney General or appropriate government agency shall hold in confidence information disclosed through the whistleblower hotline, including the identity of the caller disclosing the information and the employer identified by the caller.

(d) A call made to the whistleblower hotline pursuant to subdivision (a) or its referral to an appropriate agency under subdivision (b) may not be the sole basis for a time period under a statute of limitation to commence. This section does not change existing law relating to statutes of limitation. *(Added by Stats.2003, c. 484 (S.B.777), § 4.)*

§ 1102.8. Display of employees' rights and responsibilities under whistleblower laws; compliance with posting requirement

(a) An employer shall prominently display in lettering larger than size 14 point type a list of employees' rights and responsibilities under the whistleblower laws, including the telephone number of the whistleblower hotline described in Section 1102.7.

(b) Any state agency required to post a notice pursuant to Section 8548.2 of the Government Code or subdivision (b) of Section 6128 of the Penal Code shall be deemed in compliance with the posting requirement set forth in subdivision (a) if the notice posted pursuant to Section 8548.2 of the Government Code or subdivision (b) of Section 6128 of the Penal Code also contains the whistleblower hotline number described in Section 1102.7. *(Added by Stats.2003, c. 484 (S.B.777), § 5. Amended by Stats.2004, c. 820 (A.B.1127), § 1, eff. Sept. 27, 2004.)*

§ 1103. Violation; misdemeanor; penalty

Any employer who violates this chapter is guilty of a misdemeanor punishable, in the case of an individual, by imprisonment in the county jail not to exceed one year or a fine of not to exceed $1000 or both and, in the case of a corporation, by a fine of not to exceed $5000. *(Stats. 1937, c. 90, p. 212, § 1103.)*

§ 1104. Responsibility of employer for actions of agents

In all prosecutions under this chapter, the employer is responsible for the acts of his managers, officers, agents, and employees. *(Stats.1937, c. 90, p. 212, § 1104.)*

§ 1105. Employee's action for damages

Nothing in this chapter shall prevent the injured employee from recovering damages from his employer for injury suffered through a violation of this chapter. *(Stats.1937, c. 90, p. 212, § 1105.)*

§ 1106. Employee

For purposes of Sections 1102.5, 1102.6, 1102.7, 1102.8, 1104, and 1105, "employee" includes, but is not limited to, any individual employed by the state or any subdivision thereof, any county, city, city and county, including any charter city or county, and any school district, community college district, municipal or public corporation, political subdivision, or the University of California. *(Added by Stats.1992, c. 1230 (A.B.3486), § 1. Amended by Stats.2003, c. 484 (S.B.777), § 7.)*

CHAPTER 6. AGREEMENTS IN CONNECTION WITH TRADE DISPUTES

Section
1110. Agreements between two or more persons; legality.

§ 1110. Agreements between two or more persons; legality

No agreement, combination, or contract, by or between two or more persons to do or procure to be done, or not to do or procure not to be done, any act in contemplation or furtherance of any trade dispute between employers and employees in the State is criminal, if the same act committed by one person would not be punishable as a crime. This chapter does not authorize violence, or threats thereof. *(Stats.1937, c. 90, p. 213, § 1110.)*

CHAPTER 6.5. PEACE OFFICERS [REPEALED]

CHAPTER 7. JURISDICTIONAL STRIKES

Section
1115. Legislative declaration.
1116. Injunction; damages.
1117. Labor organization and person defined.
1118. Jurisdictional strike defined.
1119. Scope of chapter.
1120. Severability of chapter provisions.
1122. Employee group financed or dominated by employer; action for damages.

§ 1115. Legislative declaration

A jurisdictional strike as herein defined is hereby declared to be against the public policy of the State of California and is hereby declared to be unlawful. *(Added by Stats.1947, c. 1388, p. 2952, § 1.)*

§ 1116. Injunction; damages

Any person injured or threatened with injury by violation of any of the provisions hereof shall be entitled to injunctive relief therefrom in a proper case, and to recover any damages resulting therefrom in any court of competent jurisdiction. *(Added by Stats.1947, c. 1388, p. 2952, § 1.)*

§ 1117. Labor organization and person defined

As used herein, "labor organization" means any organization or any agency or employee representation committee or any local unit thereof in which employees participate, and exists for the purpose, in whole or in part, of dealing with employers concerning grievances, labor disputes, wages, hours of employment or conditions of work, which labor organization is not found to be or to have been financed in whole or in part, interfered with, dominated or controlled by the employer or any employer association within one year of the commencement of any proceeding brought under this chapter. The plaintiff shall have the affirmative of the issue with respect to establishing the existence of a "labor organization" as defined herein.

As used herein, "person" means any person, association, organization, partnership, corporation, limited liability company, unincorporated association, or labor organization. *(Added by Stats.1947, c. 1388, p. 2952 § 1. Amended by Stats.1955, c. 1417, p. 2587, § 1; Stats.1994, c. 1010 (S.B.2053), § 179.)*

§ 1118. Jurisdictional strike defined

As used in this chapter, "jurisdictional strike" means a concerted refusal to perform work for an employer or any other concerted interference with an employer's operation or business, arising out of a controversy between two or more labor organizations as to which of them has or should have the exclusive right to bargain collectively with an employer on behalf of his employees or any of them, or arising out of a controversy between two or more labor organizations as to which of them has or should have the exclusive right to have its members perform work for an employer. *(Added by Stats.1947, c. 1388, p. 2952, § 1.)*

§ 1119.   Scope of chapter

Nothing in this chapter shall be construed to interfere with collective bargaining subject to the prohibitions herein set forth, nor to prohibit any individual voluntarily becoming or remaining a member of a labor organization, or from personally requesting any other individual to join a labor organization. *(Added by Stats.1947, c. 1388, p. 2952, § 1.)*

§ 1120.   Severability of chapter provisions

If any provision of this chapter or the application of such provision to any person or circumstance shall be held invalid, the remainder of this chapter or the application of such provision to persons or circumstances other than those as to which it is held invalid, shall not be affected thereby. *(Added by Stats.1947, c. 1388, p. 2952, § 1.)*

§ 1122.   Employee group financed or dominated by employer; action for damages

Any person who organizes an employee group which is financed in whole or in part, interfered with or dominated or controlled by the employer or any employer association, as well as such employer or employer association, shall be liable to suit by any person who is injured thereby. Said injured party shall recover the damages sustained by him and the costs of suit. *(Added by Stats.1955, c. 1417, p. 2588, § 2.)*

CHAPTER 7.5.   COLLECTIVE BARGAINING AGREEMENTS

Section
1126.   Enforceability; remedies for breach.
1127.   Successor clause in collective bargaining agreement; force and effect.
1128.   Attorney's fees; action to compel arbitration; appeals of decision of arbitrator; application of section.

§ 1126.   Enforceability; remedies for breach

Any collective bargaining agreement between an employer and a labor organization shall be enforceable at law or in equity, and a breach of such collective bargaining agreement by any party thereto shall be subject to the same remedies, including injunctive relief, as are available on other contracts in the courts of this State. *(Added by Stats.1941, c. 1188, p. 2959, § 1.)*

§ 1127.   Successor clause in collective bargaining agreement; force and effect

(a) Where a collective bargaining agreement between an employer and a labor organization contains a successor clause, such clause shall be binding upon and enforceable against any successor employer who succeeds to the contracting employer's business until the expiration date of the agreement stated in the agreement. No such successor clause shall be binding upon or enforceable against any successor employer for more than three years from the effective date of the collective bargaining agreement between the contracting employer and the labor organization.

(b) As used in this section, "successor employer" means any purchaser, assignee, or transferee of a business the employees of which are subject to a collective bargaining agreement, if such purchaser, assignee, or transferee conducts or will conduct substantially the same business operation, or offer the same service, and use the same physical facilities, as the contracting employer.

(c) This section shall not apply to a receiver or trustee in bankruptcy of any contracting employer who has gone into receivership or bankruptcy, or to any employer who acquires a business from a receiver or trustee in bankruptcy, or to any employer which is a public entity, or to any employer who is subject to the National Labor Relations Act,[1] Agricultural Labor Relations Act of 1975,[2] or the Railway Labor Act.[3]

(d) An employer who is a party to a collective bargaining agreement containing a successor clause has the affirmative duty to disclose the existence of such agreement and such clause to any successor employer. Such disclosure requirement shall be satisfied by including in any contract of sale, agreement to purchase, or any similar instrument of conveyance, a statement that the successor employer is bound by such successor clause as provided for in the collective bargaining agreement. *(Added by Stats.1976, c. 1057, p. 4686, § 1.)*

[1] 29 U.S.C.A. § 151 et seq.
[2] Section 1140 et seq.
[3] 45 U.S.C.A. § 151 et seq.

§ 1128.   Attorney's fees; action to compel arbitration; appeals of decision of arbitrator; application of section

(a) Where a party to a collective bargaining agreement prevails in a court action to compel arbitration of disputes concerning the collective bargaining agreement, the court shall award attorney's fees to the prevailing party unless the other party has raised substantial and credible issues involving complex or significant questions of law or fact regarding whether or not the dispute is arbitrable under the agreement.

If the dispute is later found to be not arbitrable under the collective bargaining agreement, any award made pursuant to this subdivision shall be vacated and those sums paid to satisfy the award shall be reimbursed to the payor.

(b) Where a party to a collective bargaining agreement appeals the decision of an arbitrator regarding disputes concerning the collective bargaining agreement, the court shall award attorney's fees to the prevailing appellee unless the appellant has raised substantial issues involving complex or significant questions of law.

(c) Where a party to a collective bargaining agreement prevails in a court action to compel compliance with the decision or award of an arbitrator or a grievance panel regarding disputes concerning the collective bargaining agreement, the court shall award attorney's fees to the prevailing party unless the other party has raised substantial issues involving complex or significant questions of law.

(d) This section shall not apply to public employment. *(Added by Stats.1984, c. 672, § 1. Amended by Stats.1986, c. 1211, § 2.)*

CHAPTER 8. PROFESSIONAL STRIKEBREAKERS

Article	Section
1. Findings and Declarations	1130
2. Definitions	1132
3. Professional Strikebreakers	1134
4. Miscellaneous	1136

ARTICLE 1.   FINDINGS AND DECLARATIONS

Section
1130.   Legislative findings and declarations.

§ 1130.   Legislative findings and declarations

The Legislature hereby makes the following findings and declarations:

Relations between organized labor and management in this state have for many years been marked by a mature adherence to the principles of good faith, collective bargaining and mutual respect for the rights, interest and well-being of working people, business and industry. The importation or use in this state of professional strikebreakers as replacements during a strike or lockout endangers such sound and beneficial relations between labor and management.

Experience in this state and in other parts of this country demonstrates that the utilization of professional strikebreakers in labor disputes is inimical to the public welfare and good order, in that such practices tend to produce and prolong industrial strife, frustrate collective bargaining and encourage violence, crimes and other disorders.

The aforementioned evils are beyond the regulation of applicable federal law, and the mitigation and correction thereof requires the exercise of the police power of this state. *(Added by Stats.1976, c. 1079, p. 4868, § 50.)*

ARTICLE 2.   DEFINITIONS

Section
1132.   Construction of chapter.
1132.2. Employer.
1132.4. Employee.
1132.6. Strike.
1132.8. Lockout.
1133.   Professional strikebreaker.

§ 1132.   Construction of chapter

Unless provided otherwise, the definitions in this article govern the construction of this chapter. *(Added by Stats.1976, c. 1079, p. 4868, § 50.)*

§ 1132.2.   Employer

"Employer" means a person, partnership, firm, corporation, association, or other entity, which employs any person or persons to perform services for a wage or salary, and includes any person, partnership, firm, corporation, limited liability company, association or other entity acting as an agent of an employer, directly or indirectly. *(Added by Stats.1976, c. 1079, p. 4868, § 50. Amended by Stats.1994, c. 1010 (S.B.2053), § 180.)*

§ 1132.4.   Employee

"Employee" means any person who performs services for wages or salary under a contract of employment, express or implied, for an employer. *(Added by Stats. 1976, c. 1079, p. 4868, § 50.)*

§ 1132.6.   Strike

"Strike" means any concerted act of more than 50 percent of the bargaining unit employees in a lawful refusal of such employees under applicable state or federal law to perform work or services for an employer, other than work stoppages based on conflicting union jurisdictions or work stoppages unauthorized by the proper union governing body. *(Added by Stats.1976, c. 1079, p. 4868, § 50.)*

§ 1132.8.   Lockout

"Lockout" means any refusal by an employer to permit any group of five or more employees to work as a result of a dispute with such employees affecting wages, hours or other terms or conditions of employment of such employees. *(Added by Stats.1976, c. 1079, p. 4868, § 50.)*

§ 1133.   Professional strikebreaker

"Professional strikebreaker" means any person other than supervisorial personnel who have been in the employ of the employer before the commencement of the strike or lockout or members of the immediate family of the owner of the place of business:

(1) Who during a period of five years immediately preceding the acts described in subdivision (2) of this section has offered himself and has been accepted on repeated occasions to two or more employers at whose places of business a strike or lockout was currently in progress, for employment for the duration of such strike or lockout for the purpose of replacing an employee or employees involved in such strike or lockout, and

(2) Who currently offers himself to an employer at whose place of business a strike or lockout is presently in progress for employment for the purpose of replacing an employee or employees involved in such strike or lockout.

As used in this section:

(a) "Repeated occasions" means on three or more occasions (exclusive of any current offer for employment in connection with a current strike or lockout).

(b) "Employment for the duration of such strike or lockout" includes employment for all or part of the duration of such strike or lockout; and, in connection therewith, includes services during all or part of such strike or lockout which began no more than one month prior to the initiation thereof, or, in the alternative, which concluded not later than one month after the termination of such strike or lockout.

(c) "Employment" means services for an employer, whether compensated by wages, salary, or any other consideration not limited to the foregoing and whether secured, arranged or paid for by an employer or any other person, partnership, firm, corporation, association or other entity.

(d) "Supervisorial personnel" means those employees who have the authority to hire, fire, reward, or discipline other employees of the employer, or who have a history of having had the authority to effectively recommend such action. *(Added by Stats.1976, c. 1079, p. 4868, § 50.)*

ARTICLE 3.   PROFESSIONAL STRIKEBREAKERS

Section
1134.   Use of strikebreakers prohibited.
1134.2. Offer of self for employment or to replace employees.

§ 1134.   Use of strikebreakers prohibited

It shall be unlawful for any employer willingly and knowingly to utilize any professional strikebreaker to replace an employee or employees involved in a strike or lockout at a place of business located within this state. *(Added by Stats.1976, c. 1079, p. 4868, § 50.)*

§ 1134.2.   Offer of self for employment or to replace employees

It shall be unlawful for any professional strikebreaker willingly and knowingly to offer himself for employment or to replace an employee or employees involved in a strike or lockout at a place of business located within this state. *(Added by Stats.1976, c. 1079, p. 4868, § 50.)*

ARTICLE 4.   MISCELLANEOUS

Section
1136.   Violations, penalty.
1136.2. Severability.

§ 1136.   Violations, penalty

Any person, partnership, firm, corporation, association or other entity, or officer or agent thereof, who shall violate any of the provisions of this chapter shall upon conviction thereof be subject to a fine not to exceed one thousand dollars ($1,000), or imprisonment for a period not to exceed 90 days, or both such fine and imprisonment, in the discretion of the court. *(Added by Stats.*

1976, c. 1079, p. 4868, § 50. Amended by Stats.1983, c. 1092, § 204, eff. Sept. 27, 1983, operative Jan. 1, 1984.)*

§ 1136.2.   Severability

If any part of the provisions of this chapter, or the application thereof, to any person or circumstance is held invalid in the final judgment of a court of competent jurisdiction, the remainder of this chapter, including the application of such part or provision to other persons or circumstances, shall not be affected thereby, and this chapter shall otherwise continue in full force and effect and shall otherwise be fully operative. To this end, the provisions of this chapter, and each of them, are hereby declared to be severable. *(Added by Stats.1976, c. 1079, p. 4868, § 50.   Amended by Stats.1977, c. 579, p. 1901, § 146.)*

CHAPTER 9.   PUBLIC TRANSPORTATION LABOR DISPUTES

Section
1137.   Definitions.
1137.1. Disputes between exclusive bargaining representatives of public transit employees and local agencies; applicable provisions.
1137.2. Grounds for appointment of board of investigation; report; prohibition of strike or lockout.
1137.3. Composition and compensation of board of investigation; powers for purposes of hearings and investigations.
1137.4. Injunction to prevent or discontinue strike or lockout.
1137.5. Time period for negotiating or meeting and conferring process; application of chapter.
1137.6. Right to strike; construction of chapter.

§ 1137.   Definitions

The definitions set forth in this section shall govern the construction and meaning of the terms used in this chapter:

(a) "Local agency" means any city, county, special district, or other public entity in the state. It includes a charter city or a charter county.

(b) "Public transit employee" means an employee of any transit district of the state, an employee of the Golden Gate Bridge, Highway and Transportation District, and an employee of any local agency who is employed to work for transit service provided by such agency. *(Added by Stats.1981, c. 812, p. 3147, § 1.)*

§ 1137.1.   Disputes between exclusive bargaining representatives of public transit employees and local agencies; applicable provisions

Notwithstanding any other provision of law, the following provisions shall govern disputes between exclusive bargaining representatives of public transit employees and local agencies:

(a) Such disputes shall not be subject to any factfinding procedure otherwise provided by law.

(b) Each party shall exchange contract proposals not less than 90 days before the expiration of a contract, and shall be in formal collective bargaining not less than 60 days before such expiration.

(c) Each party shall supply to the other party such reasonable data as are requested by the other party.

(d) At the request of either party to a dispute, a conciliator from the State Conciliation Service shall be assigned to mediate the dispute and shall have access to all formal negotiations.

The provisions of this section shall not apply to any local agency subject to the provisions of Chapter 10 (commencing with Section 3500) of Division 4 of Title 1 of the Government Code. *(Added by Stats.1981, c. 812, p. 3147, § 1.)*

§ 1137.2. Grounds for appointment of board of investigation; report; prohibition of strike or lockout

(a) Whenever in the opinion of the Governor, a threatened or actual strike or lockout will, if permitted to occur or continue, significantly disrupt public transportation services and endanger the public's health, safety, or welfare, and upon the request of either party to the dispute, the Governor may appoint a board to investigate the issues involved in the dispute and to make a written report to him or her within seven days. Such report shall include a statement of the facts with respect to the dispute, including the respective positions of the parties, but shall not contain recommendations. Such report shall be made available to the public.

(b) Any strike or lockout during the period of investigation of the board appointed pursuant to this section is prohibited. *(Added by Stats.1981, c. 812, p. 3147, § 1.)*

§ 1137.3. Composition and compensation of board of investigation; powers for purposes of hearings and investigations

The board of investigation shall be composed of no more than five members, one of whom shall be designated by the Governor as chairperson. Members of the board shall receive one hundred dollars ($100) for each day actually spent by them in the work of the board and shall receive their actual and necessary expenses incurred in the performance of their duties.

The board may hold public hearings to ascertain the facts with respect to the causes and circumstances of the dispute. For the purpose of any hearing or investigation, the board may summon and subpoena witnesses, require the production of papers, books, accounts, reports, documents, records, and papers of any kind and description, to issue subpoenas, and to take all necessary means to compel the attendance of witnesses and procure testimony. *(Added by Stats.1981, c. 812, p. 3147, § 1.)*

§ 1137.4. Injunction to prevent or discontinue strike or lockout

Upon receiving a report from a board of investigation, the Governor may request the Attorney General to, and

he or she shall, petition any court of competent jurisdiction to enjoin such strike or lockout or the continuing thereof, for a period of 60 days. The court shall issue an order enjoining such strike or lockout, or the continuation thereof, if the court finds that such threatened or actual strike or lockout, if permitted to occur or continue, will significantly disrupt public transportation services and endanger the public's health, safety, or welfare. *(Added by Stats.1981, c. 812, p. 3147, § 1.)*

§ 1137.5. Time period for negotiating or meeting and conferring process; application of chapter

If the charter or establishing legislation of the local agency establishes a time period for the negotiating or meeting and conferring process which is shorter than 60 days, the provisions of this chapter shall not be applicable to any disputes which may arise between the exclusive bargaining representative of public transit employees and the local agency. *(Added by Stats.1981, c. 812, p. 3147, § 1.)*

§ 1137.6. Right to strike; construction of chapter

Except as expressly provided by subdivision (b) of Section 1137.2 and Section 1137.4, nothing in this chapter shall be construed to grant or deprive employees of a right to strike. *(Added by Stats.1981, c. 812, p. 3147, § 1.)*

CHAPTER 10. UNLAWFUL ACTS DURING LABOR DISPUTES

Section

1138.   Liability of officers or members of associations or organizations; labor disputes.
1138.1.   Issuance of temporary or permanent injunctions; state court's authority; findings of fact; hearing.
1138.2.   Restraining orders or injunction relief.
1138.3.   Restraining orders or temporary or permanent injunction.
1138.4.   Labor dispute.
1138.5.   Peace officers.

§ 1138. Liability of officers or members of associations or organizations; labor disputes

No officer or member of any association or organization, and no association or organization, participating or interested in a labor dispute, shall be held responsible or liable in any court of this state for the unlawful acts of individual officers, members, or agents, except upon clear proof of actual participation in, or actual authorization of those acts. *(Added by Stats.1999, c. 616 (A.B.1268), § 1.)*

§ 1138.1. Issuance of temporary or permanent injunctions; state court's authority; findings of fact; hearing

(a) No court of this state shall have authority to issue a temporary or permanent injunction in any case involving or growing out of a labor dispute, except after hearing the testimony of witnesses in open court, with opportunity for cross-examination, in support of the allegations of a complaint made under oath, and testimony in opposition thereto, if offered, and except after findings of fact by the court, of all of the following:

(1) That unlawful acts have been threatened and will be committed unless restrained or have been committed and will be continued unless restrained, but no injunction or temporary restraining order shall be issued on account of any threat or unlawful act excepting against the person or persons, association, or organization making the threat or committing the unlawful act or actually authorized those acts.

(2) That substantial and irreparable injury to complainant's property will follow.

(3) That as to each item of relief granted greater injury will be inflicted upon complainant by the denial of relief than will be inflicted upon defendants by the granting of relief.

(4) That complainant has no adequate remedy at law.

(5) That the public officers charged with the duty to protect complainant's property are unable or unwilling to furnish adequate protection.

(b) The hearing shall be held after due and personal notice thereof has been given, in the manner that the court shall direct, to all known persons against whom relief is sought, and also to the chief of those public officials of the county and city within which the unlawful acts have been threatened or committed charged with the duty to protect complainant's property. However, if a complainant also alleges that, unless a temporary restraining order is issued without notice, a substantial and irreparable injury to complainant's property will be unavoidable, such a temporary restraining order may be issued upon testimony under oath, sufficient, if sustained, to justify the court in issuing a temporary injunction upon a hearing after notice. Such a temporary restraining order shall be effective for no longer than five days and shall become void at the expiration of those five days. No temporary restraining order shall be issued unless the judicial officer issuing the temporary restraining order first hears oral argument from the opposing party or opposing party's attorney, except in the instances specified in subparagraphs (B) and (C) of paragraph (2) of subdivision (c) of Section 527 of the Code of Civil Procedure. No temporary restraining order or temporary injunction shall be issued except on the condition that the complainant first files an undertaking with adequate security in an amount to be fixed by the court sufficient to recompense those enjoined for any loss, expense, or damage caused by the improvident or erroneous issuance of the order or injunction, including all reasonable costs, together with a reasonable attorney's fee, and expense of defense against the order or against the granting of any injunctive relief sought in the same proceeding and subsequently denied by the court.

(c) The undertaking shall be an agreement entered into by the complainant and the surety upon which a decree may be rendered in the same suit or proceeding against the complainant and surety, upon a hearing to

374

assess damages of which hearing the complainant and surety shall have reasonable notice, the complainant and surety submitting themselves to the jurisdiction of the court for that purpose. Nothing contained in this section shall deprive any party having a claim or cause of action under or upon such undertaking from electing to pursue his or her ordinary remedy by suit at law or in equity. *(Added by Stats.1999, c. 616 (A.B.1268), § 1.)*

§ 1138.2.   Restraining orders or injunction relief

No restraining order or injunctive relief shall be granted to any complainant involved in the labor dispute in question who has failed to comply with any obligation imposed by law, or who has failed to make every reasonable effort to settle that dispute either by negotiation or with the aid of any available governmental machinery of mediation or voluntary arbitration. *(Added by Stats.1999, c. 616 (A.B.1268), § 1.)*

§ 1138.3.   Restraining orders or temporary or permanent injunctions

No restraining order or temporary or permanent injunction shall be granted in a case involving or growing out of a labor dispute, except on the basis of findings of fact made and filed by the court in the record of the case prior to the issuance of the restraining order or injunction; and every restraining order or injunction granted in a case involving or growing out of a labor dispute shall include only a prohibition of the specific act or acts as may be expressly complained of in the complaint or petition filed in such case and as shall be expressly included in findings of fact made and filed by the court. *(Added by Stats.1999, c. 616 (A.B.1268), § 1.)*

§ 1138.4.   Labor dispute

The term "labor dispute" as used in this chapter has the same meaning as set forth in clauses (i), (ii), and (iii) of paragraph (4) of subdivision (b) of Section 527.3 of the Code of Civil Procedure. *(Added by Stats.1999, c. 616 (A.B.1268), § 1.)*

§ 1138.5.   Peace officers

Sections 1138.1, 1138.2, and 1138.3 shall not apply to any peace officer as defined in Chapter 4.5 (commencing with Section 830) of Title 3 of Part 2 of the Penal Code. *(Added by Stats.1999, c. 616 (A.B.1268), § 1.)*

Part 3.5

AGRICULTURAL LABOR RELATIONS

Chapter		Section
1.	General Provisions and Definitions	1140
2.	Agricultural Labor Relations Board	1141
3.	Rights of Agricultural Employees	1152
4.	Unfair Labor Practices and Regulation of Secondary Boycotts	1153
5.	Labor Representatives and Elections	1156
6.	Prevention of Unfair Labor Practices and Judicial Review and Enforcement	1160

Chapter		Section
6.5.	Contract Dispute Resolution	1164
7.	Suits Involving Employers and Labor Organizations	1165
8.	Limitations	1166

CHAPTER 1. GENERAL PROVISIONS AND DEFINITIONS

Section
1140. Short title.
1140.2. State policy.
1140.4. Definitions.

§ 1140. Short title

This part shall be known and may be referred to as the Alatorre-Zenovich-Dunlap-Berman Agricultural Labor Relations Act of 1975. *(Added by Stats.1975, 3rd Ex. Sess., c. 1, p. 4013, § 2.)*

§ 1140.2. State policy

It is hereby stated to be the policy of the State of California to encourage and protect the right of agricultural employees to full freedom of association, self-organization, and designation of representatives of their own choosing, to negotiate the terms and conditions of their employment, and to be free from the interference, restraint, or coercion of employers of labor, or their agents, in the designation of such representatives or in self-organization or in other concerted activities for the purpose of collective bargaining or other mutual aid or protection. For this purpose this part is adopted to provide for collective-bargaining rights for agricultural employees. *(Added by Stats.1975, 3rd Ex. Sess., c. 1, p. 4013, § 2.)*

§ 1140.4. Definitions

As used in this part:

(a) The term "agriculture" includes farming in all its branches, and, among other things, includes the cultivation and tillage of the soil, dairying, the production, cultivation, growing, and harvesting of any agricultural or horticultural commodities (including commodities defined as agricultural commodities in Section 1141j(g) of Title 12 of the United States Code), the raising of livestock, bees, furbearing animals, or poultry, and any practices (including any forestry or lumbering operations) performed by a farmer or on a farm as an incident to or in conjunction with such farming operations, including preparation for market and delivery to storage or to market or to carriers for transportation to market.

(b) The term "agricultural employee" or "employee" shall mean one engaged in agriculture, as such term is defined in subdivision (a). However, nothing in this subdivision shall be construed to include any person other than those employees excluded from the coverage of the National Labor Relations Act, as amended, as agricultural employees, pursuant to Section 2(3) of the Labor Management Relations Act (Section 152(3), Title 29,

United States Code), and Section 3(f) of the Fair Labor Standards Act (Section 203(f), Title 29, United States Code).

Further, nothing in this part shall apply, or be construed to apply, to any employee who performs work to be done at the site of the construction, alteration, painting, or repair of a building, structure, or other work (as these terms have been construed under Section 8(e) of the Labor Management Relations Act, 29 U.S.C. Sec. 158(e)) or logging or timber-clearing operations in initial preparation of land for farming, or who does land leveling or only land surveying for any of the above.

As used in this subdivision, "land leveling" shall include only major land moving operations changing the contour of the land, but shall not include annual or seasonal tillage or preparation of land for cultivation.

(c) The term "agricultural employer" shall be liberally construed to include any person acting directly or indirectly in the interest of an employer in relation to an agricultural employee, any individual grower, corporate grower, cooperative grower, harvesting association, hiring association, land management group, any association of persons or cooperatives engaged in agriculture, and shall include any person who owns or leases or manages land used for agricultural purposes, but shall exclude any person supplying agricultural workers to an employer, any farm labor contractor as defined by Section 1682, and any person functioning in the capacity of a labor contractor. The employer engaging such labor contractor or person shall be deemed the employer for all purposes under this part.

(d) The term "person" shall mean one or more individuals, corporations, partnerships, limited liability companies, associations, legal representatives, trustees in bankruptcy, receivers, or any other legal entity, employer, or labor organization having an interest in the outcome of a proceeding under this part.

(e) The term "representatives" includes any individual or labor organization.

(f) The term "labor organization" means any organization of any kind, or any agency or employee representation committee or plan, in which employees participate and which exists, in whole or in part, for the purpose of dealing with employers concerning grievances, labor disputes, wages, rates of pay, hours of employment, or conditions of work for agricultural employees.

(g) The term "unfair labor practice" means any unfair labor practice specified in Chapter 4 (commencing with Section 1153) of this part.

(h) The term "labor dispute" includes any controversy concerning terms, tenure, or conditions of employment, or concerning the association or representation of persons in negotiating, fixing, maintaining, changing, or seeking to arrange terms or conditions of employment, regardless of whether the disputants stand in the proximate relation of employer and employee.

(i) The term "board" means Agricultural Labor Relations Board.

(j) The term "supervisor" means any individual having the authority, in the interest of the employer, to hire, transfer, suspend, lay off, recall, promote, discharge, assign, reward, or discipline other employees, or the responsibility to direct them, or to adjust their grievances, or effectively to recommend such action, if, in connection with the foregoing, the exercise of such authority is not of a merely routine or clerical nature, but requires the use of independent judgment. *(Added by Stats.1975, 3rd Ex. Sess., c. 1, p. 4013, § 2. Amended by Stats.1994, c. 1010 (S.B.2053), § 181.)*

CHAPTER 2. AGRICULTURAL LABOR RELATIONS BOARD

Article	Section
1. Agricultural Labor Relations Board: Organization	1141
2. Investigatory Powers	1151

ARTICLE 1. AGRICULTURAL LABOR RELATIONS BOARD: ORGANIZATION

Section
1141. Creation; membership; appointment; tenure; vacancies; removal.
1142. Principal office; regional offices; delegation of powers; review by board.
1142.5. 24-hour service; telephone messages; election petitions filed by bargaining unit on strike.
1143. Annual report.
1144. Rules and regulations.
1144.5. Applicable law; unfair labor practice charges.
1145. Officers and employees; appointment.
1146. Delegation of powers to members; vacancies; quorum.
1147. Compensation.
1148. Applicability of precedents of federal act.
1149. General counsel; power and duties.
1150. Reappointment; full-time occupation.

§ 1141. Creation; membership; appointment; tenure; vacancies; removal

(a) There is hereby created in the Labor and Workforce Development Agency the Agricultural Labor Relations Board, which shall consist of five members.

(b) The members of the board shall be appointed by the Governor with the advice and consent of the Senate. The term of office of the members shall be five years, and the terms shall be staggered at one-year intervals. Upon the initial appointment, one member shall be appointed for a term ending January 1, 1977, one member shall be appointed for a term ending January 1, 1978, one member shall be appointed for a term ending January 1, 1979, one member shall be appointed for a term ending January 1, 1980, and one member shall be appointed for a term ending January 1, 1981. Any individual appointed to fill a vacancy of any member shall be appointed only for the unexpired term of the member to whose term he or she is succeeding. The Governor shall designate one member to serve as chairperson of the board. Any member of the board may be removed by the Governor, upon notice and hearing, for neglect of duty or malfeasance in office, but for no other cause. *(Added by Stats.1975, 3rd Ex. Sess., c. 1, p. 4013, § 2. Amended by Stats.2002, c. 859 (S.B.1236), § 12.)*

§ 1142. Principal office; regional offices; delegation of powers; review by board

(a) The principal office of the board shall be in Sacramento, but it may meet and exercise any or all of its power at any other place in California.

(b) Besides the principal office in Sacramento, as provided in subdivision (a), the board may establish offices in such other cities as it shall deem necessary. The board may delegate to the personnel of these offices such powers as it deems appropriate to determine the unit appropriate for the purpose of collective bargaining, to investigate and provide for hearings, to determine whether a question of representation exists, to direct an election by a secret ballot pursuant to the provisions of Chapter 5 (commencing with Section 1156), and to certify the results of such election, and to investigate, conduct hearings and make determinations relating to unfair labor practices. The board may review any action taken pursuant to the authority delegated under this section upon a request for a review of such action filed with the board by an interested party. Any such review made by the board shall not, unless specifically ordered by the board, operate as a stay of any action taken. The entire record considered by the board in considering or acting upon any such request or review shall be made available to all parties prior to such consideration or action, and the board's findings and action thereon shall be published as a decision of the board. *(Added by Stats.1975, 3rd Ex. Sess., c. 1, p. 4013, § 2.)*

§ 1142.5. 24-hour service; telephone messages; election petitions filed by bargaining unit on strike

(a) The board shall maintain, at its principal office, a telephone line 24 hours a day, seven days a week, for the purpose of providing interested persons with information concerning their rights and responsibilities under this part, or for referring such persons to the appropriate agency or entity with the capacity to render advice or help in dealing with any situation arising out of agricultural labor disputes.

In order to carry out its responsibilities pursuant to this subdivision, the board may contract with an answering service to receive telephone messages during periods of time that its principal office is normally not open for business. Such messages shall be transmitted to the board on the board's next business day, or at such earlier time as the board specifies, or to its designated representative at the earliest possible time.

(b) Whenever a petition for an election has been filed in a bargaining unit in which a majority of the employees are engaged in a strike, the necessary and appropriate services of the board in the region in which the election will be held shall be available to the parties involved 24 hours a day until the election is held.　(Added by Stats.1978, c. 921, p. 2889, § 1. Amended by Stats.1979, c. 468, p. 1625, § 1.)

§ 1143. Annual report

The board shall, at the close of each fiscal year, make a report in writing to the Legislature and to the Governor stating in detail the cases it has heard, the decisions it has rendered, the names, salaries, and duties of all employees and officers in the employ or under the supervision of the board, and an account of all moneys it has disbursed. (Added by Stats.1975, 3rd Ex. Sess., c. 1, p. 4013, § 2.)

§ 1144. Rules and regulations

The board may from time to time make, amend, and rescind, in the manner prescribed in Chapter 3.5 (commencing with Section 11340) of Part 1 of Division 3 of Title 2 of the Government Code, such rules and regulations as may be necessary to carry out this part. (Added by Stats.1975, 3rd Ex. Sess., c. 1, p. 4013, § 2. Amended by Stats.1983, c. 142, § 99.)

§ 1144.5. Applicable law; unfair labor practice charges

(a) Notwithstanding Section 11425.10 of the Government Code, Chapter 4.5 (commencing with Section 11400) of Part 1 of Division 3 of Title 2 of the Government Code does not apply to a hearing by the board under this part, except a hearing to determine an unfair labor practice charge.

(b) Notwithstanding Sections 11425.30 and 11430.10 of the Government Code, in a hearing to determine an unfair labor practice charge, a person who has participated in a determination of probable cause, injunctive or other pre-hearing relief, or other equivalent preliminary determination in an adjudicative proceeding may serve as presiding officer or as a supervisor of the presiding officer or may assist or advise the presiding officer in the same proceeding. (Added by Stats.1995, c. 938 (S.B.523), § 73, operative July 1, 1997.)

§ 1145. Officers and employees; appointment

The board may appoint an executive secretary and such attorneys, hearing officers, administrative law officers, and other employees as it may from time to time find necessary for the proper performance of its duties. Attorneys appointed pursuant to this section may, at the discretion of the board, appear for and represent the board in any case in court. All employees appointed by the board shall perform their duties in an objective and impartial manner without prejudice toward any party subject to the jurisdiction of the board. (Added by Stats.1975, 3rd Ex.Sess., c. 1, p. 4013, § 2. Amended by Stats.1978, c. 1072, p. 3291, § 1.)

§ 1146. Delegation of powers to members; vacancies; quorum

The board is authorized to delegate to any group of three or more board members any or all the powers which it may itself exercise. A vacancy in the board shall not impair the right of the remaining members to exercise all the powers of the board, and three members shall at all times constitute a quorum. A vacancy shall be filled in the same manner as an original appointment. (Added by Stats.1975, 3rd Ex. Sess., c. 1, p. 4013, § 2.)

§ 1147. Compensation

Each member of the board shall receive the salary provided for by Chapter 6 (commencing with Section 11550) of Part 1 of Division 3 of Title 2 of the Government Code. (Added by Stats.1975, 3rd Ex. Sess., c. 1, p. 4013, § 2. Amended by Stats.1983, c. 803, § 40.)

§ 1148. Applicability of precedents of federal act

The board shall follow applicable precedents of the National Labor Relations Act, as amended.[1] (Added by Stats.1975, 3rd Ex. Sess., c. 1, p. 4013, § 2.)

[1] 29 U.S.C.A. § 151 et seq.

§ 1149. General counsel; power and duties

There shall be a general counsel of the board who shall be appointed by the Governor, subject to confirmation by a majority of the Senate, for a term of four years. The general counsel shall have the power to appoint such attorneys, administrative assistants, and other employees as necessary for the proper exercise of his duties. The general counsel of the board shall exercise general supervision over all attorneys employed by the board (other than administrative law officers and legal assistants to board members), and over the officers and employees in the regional offices. He shall have final authority, on behalf of the board, with respect to the investigation of charges and issuance of complaints under Chapter 6 (commencing with Section 1160) of this part, and with respect to the prosecution of such complaints before the board. He shall have such other duties as the board may prescribe or as may be provided by law. All employees appointed by the general counsel shall perform their duties in an objective and impartial manner without prejudice toward any party subject to the jurisdiction of the board. In case of a vacancy in the office of the general counsel, the Governor is authorized to designate the officer or employee who shall act as general counsel during such vacancy, but no person or persons so designated shall so act either (1) for more than 40 days when the Legislature is in session unless a nomination to fill such vacancy shall have been submitted to the Senate, or (2) after the adjournment sine die of the session of the Senate in which such nomination was submitted. (Added by Stats.1975, 3rd Ex. Sess., c. 1, p. 4013, § 2. Amended by Stats.1978, c. 1072, p. 3292, § 2.)

§ 1150. Reappointment; full-time occupation

Each member of the board and the general counsel of the board shall be eligible for reappointment, and shall not engage in any other business, vocation, or employment. *(Added by Stats.1975, 3rd Ex. Sess., c. 1, p. 4013, § 2.)*

ARTICLE 2. INVESTIGATORY POWERS

Section

1151.   Access to evidence and places of labor; subpoena power; enforcement.
1151.2.   Self-incrimination.
1151.3.   Right to counsel.
1151.4.   Process; service; witnesses; fees.
1151.5.   State departments and agencies; furnishing records, papers and information.
1151.6.   Resistance, interference, etc., with members, agents or agencies in performance of duties; misdemeanor; fine.

§ 1151. Access to evidence and places of labor; subpoena power; enforcement

For the purpose of all hearings and investigations, which, in the opinion of the board, are necessary and proper for the exercise of the powers vested in it by Chapters 5 (commencing with Section 1156) and 6 (commencing with Section 1160) of this part:

(a) The board, or its duly authorized agents or agencies, shall at all reasonable times have access to, for the purpose of examination, and the right to copy, any evidence of any person being investigated or proceeded against that relates to any matter under investigation or in question. The members of the board or their designees or their duly authorized agents shall have the right of free access to all places of labor. The board, or any member thereof, shall upon application of any party to such proceedings, forthwith issue to such party subpoenas requiring the attendance and testimony of witnesses or the production of any evidence in such proceeding or investigation requested in such application. Within five days after the service of a subpoena on any person requiring the production of any evidence in his possession or under his control, such person may petition the board to revoke, and the board shall revoke, such subpoena if in its opinion the evidence whose production is required does not relate to any matter under investigation, or any matter in question in such proceedings, or if in its opinion such subpoena does not describe with sufficient particularity the evidence whose production is required. Any member of the board, or any agent or agency designated by the board for such purposes, may administer oaths and affirmations, examine witnesses, and receive evidence. Such attendance of witnesses and the production of such evidence may be required from any place in the state at any designated place of hearing.

(b) In case of contumacy or refusal to obey a subpoena issued to any person, any superior court in any county within the jurisdiction of which the inquiry is carried on, or within the jurisdiction of which such person allegedly guilty of contumacy or refusal to obey is found or resides or transacts business, shall, upon application by the board, have jurisdiction to issue to such person an order requiring such person to appear before the board, its member, agent, or agency, there to produce evidence if so ordered, or there to give testimony touching the matter under investigation or in question. Any failure to obey such order of the court may be punished by such court as a contempt thereof. *(Added by Stats.1975, 3rd Ex. Sess., c. 1, p. 4013, § 2.)*

§ 1151.2. Self-incrimination

(a) No person shall be excused from attending and testifying, or from producing books, records, correspondence, documents, or other evidence in obedience to the subpoena of the board, on the ground that the testimony or evidence required of him may tend to incriminate him or subject him to a penalty or forfeiture. However, no individual shall be prosecuted or subjected to any penalty or forfeiture for or on account of any transaction, matter, or thing concerning which he is compelled, after having claimed his privilege against self-incrimination, to testify or produce evidence, except that such individual so testifying shall not be exempt from prosecution and punishment for perjury committed in so testifying.

(b) No individual shall be granted immunity pursuant to subdivision (a) unless, at least 10 calendar days prior thereto, the board has given written notice, by registered mail, to the district attorney of each county who may have reasonable grounds for objecting to such grant of immunity. Such notice shall specify the subject matter of the inquiries to which the witness' answers are to be immunized from use.

The board may not grant immunity in any case where it finds that a district attorney has reasonable grounds for objecting to such grant of immunity provided that the board may disregard objections that are not accompanied by the declaration of the district attorney that he or she is familiar with the notice and which sets forth the grounds for resisting such grant of immunity. *(Added by Stats. 1975, 3rd Ex.Sess., c. 1, p. 4013, § 2. Amended by Stats.1980, c. 1282, p. 4328, § 1.)*

§ 1151.3. Right to counsel

Any party shall have the right to appear at any hearing in person, by counsel, or by other representative. *(Added by Stats.1975, 3rd Ex. Sess., c. 1, p. 4013, § 2.)*

§ 1151.4. Process; service; witnesses; fees

(a) Complaints, orders, and other process and papers of the board, its members, agents, or agency, may be served either personally or by registered mail or by telegraph, or by leaving a copy thereof at the principal office or place of business of the person required to be served. The verified return by the individual so serving the same setting forth the manner of such service shall be proof of the same, and the return post office receipt or telegraph receipt therefor when registered and mailed or telegraphed as provided in this subdivision shall be proof of service of the same. Witnesses summoned before the board, its members, agents, or agency, shall be paid the same fees and mileage that are paid witnesses in the courts of the state, and witnesses whose depositions are taken and the persons taking the same shall severally be entitled to the same fees as are paid for like services in the courts of the state.

(b) All process of any court to which application may be made under this part may be served in the county where the defendant or other person required to be served resides or may be found. *(Added by Stats.1975, 3rd Ex.Sess., c. 1, p. 4013, § 2.)*

§ 1151.5. State departments and agencies; furnishing records, papers and information

The several departments and agencies of the state upon request by the board, shall furnish the board all records, papers, and information in their possession, not otherwise privileged, relating to any matter before the board. *(Added by Stats.1975, 3rd Ex. Sess., c. 1, p. 4013, § 2.)*

§ 1151.6. Resistance, interference, etc., with members, agents or agencies in performance of duties; misdemeanor; fine

Any person who shall willfully resist, prevent, impede, or interfere with any member of the board or any of its agents or agencies in the performance of duties pursuant to this part shall be guilty of a misdemeanor, and shall be punished by a fine of not more than five thousand ($5,000) dollars. *(Added by Stats.1975, 3rd Ex. Sess., c. 1, p. 4013, § 2.)*

CHAPTER 3. RIGHTS OF AGRICULTURAL EMPLOYEES

Section
1152. Enumeration.

§ 1152. Enumeration

Employees shall have the right to self-organization, to form, join, or assist labor organizations, to bargain collectively through representatives of their own choosing, and to engage in other concerted activities for the purpose of collective bargaining or other mutual aid or protection, and shall also have the right to refrain from any or all of such activities except to the extent that such right may be affected by an agreement requiring membership in a labor organization as a condition of continued employment as authorized in subdivision (c) of Section 1153. *(Added by Stats.1975, 3rd Ex. Sess., c. 1, p. 4013, § 2.)*

CHAPTER 4. UNFAIR LABOR PRACTICES AND REGULATION OF SECONDARY BOYCOTTS

Section
1153. Employer; unfair labor practices.
1154. Labor organization or agents; unfair labor practices.

Section
1154.5. Secondary boycotts.
1154.6. Employment for voting purposes only.
1155. Freedom of speech.
1155.2. Collective bargaining in good faith; extension of certification in absence of good faith.
1155.3. Termination or modification of existing contract; requirements.
1155.4. Employer, association, etc.; payment, loan or delivery of money or thing of value.
1155.5. Request, demand, receipt, etc., of payment, loan, or delivery of money or thing of value.
1155.6. Exemption of payments for employee compensation, satisfaction of judgments, awards, etc., sales in course of business, union dues, and certain trust funds.
1155.7. Nonagricultural employees; law governing.

§ 1153. Employer; unfair labor practices

It shall be an unfair labor practice for an agricultural employer to do any of the following:

(a) To interfere with, restrain, or coerce agricultural employees in the exercise of the rights guaranteed in Section 1152.

(b) To dominate or interfere with the formation or administration of any labor organization or contribute financial or other support to it. However, subject to such rules and regulations as may be made and published by the board pursuant to Section 1144, an agricultural employer shall not be prohibited from permitting agricultural employees to confer with him during working hours without loss of time or pay.

(c) By discrimination in regard to the hiring or tenure of employment, or any term or condition of employment, to encourage or discourage membership in any labor organization.

Nothing in this part, or in any other statute of this state, shall preclude an agricultural employer from making an agreement with a labor organization (not established, maintained, or assisted by any action defined in this section as an unfair labor practice) to require as a condition of employment, membership therein on or after the fifth day following the beginning of such employment, or the effective date of such agreement whichever is later, if such labor organization is the representative of the agricultural employees as provided in Section 1156 in the appropriate collective-bargaining unit covered by such agreement. No employee who has been required to pay dues to a labor organization by virtue of his employment as an agricultural worker during any calendar month, shall be required to pay dues to another labor organization by virtue of similar employment during such month. For purposes of this chapter, membership shall mean the satisfaction of all reasonable terms and conditions uniformly applicable to other members in good standing; provided, that such membership shall not be denied or terminated except in compliance with a constitution or bylaws which afford full and fair rights to speech, assembly, and equal voting and membership privileges for all members, and which contain adequate procedures to assure due process to members and applicants for membership.

(d) To discharge or otherwise discriminate against an agricultural employee because he has filed charges or given testimony under this part.

(e) To refuse to bargain collectively in good faith with labor organizations certified pursuant to the provisions of Chapter 5 (commencing with Section 1156) of this part.

(f) To recognize, bargain with, or sign a collective-bargaining agreement with any labor organization not certified pursuant to the provisions of this part. *(Added by Stats.1975, 3rd Ex. Sess., c. 1, p. 4013, § 2.)*

§ 1154. Labor organization or agents; unfair labor practices

It shall be an unfair labor practice for a labor organization or its agents to do any of the following:

(a) To restrain or coerce:

(1) Agricultural employees in the exercise of the rights guaranteed in Section 1152. This paragraph shall not impair the right of a labor organization to prescribe its own rules with respect to the acquisition or retention of membership therein.

(2) An agricultural employer in the selection of his representatives for the purposes of collective bargaining or the adjustment of grievances.

(b) To cause or attempt to cause an agricultural employer to discriminate against an employee in violation of subdivision (c) of Section 1153, or to discriminate against an employee with respect to whom membership in such organization has been denied or terminated for reasons other than failure to satisfy the membership requirements specified in subdivision (c) of Section 1153.

(c) To refuse to bargain collectively in good faith with an agricultural employer, provided it is the representative of his employees subject to the provisions of Chapter 5 (commencing with Section 1156) of this part.

(d) To do either of the following: (i) To engage in, or to induce or encourage any individual employed by any person to engage in, a strike or a refusal in the course of his employment to use, manufacture, process, transport, or otherwise handle or work on any goods, articles, materials, or commodities, or to perform any services; or (ii) to threaten, coerce, or restrain any person; where in either case (i) or (ii) an object thereof is any of the following:

(1) Forcing or requiring any employer or self-employed person to join any labor or employer organization or to enter into any agreement which is prohibited by Section 1154.5.

(2) Forcing or requiring any person to cease using, selling, transporting, or otherwise dealing in the products of any other producer, processor, or manufacturer, or to cease doing business with any other person, or forcing or requiring any other employer to recognize or bargain with a labor organization as the representative of his employ-

ees unless such labor organization has been certified as the representative of such employees. Nothing contained in this paragraph shall be construed to make unlawful, where not otherwise unlawful, any primary strike or primary picketing.

(3) Forcing or requiring any employer to recognize or bargain with a particular labor organization as the representative of his agricultural employees if another labor organization has been certified as the representative of such employees under the provisions of Chapter 5 (commencing with Section 1156) of this part.

(4) Forcing or requiring any employer to assign particular work to employees in a particular labor organization or in a particular trade, craft, or class, unless such employer is failing to conform to an order or certification of the board determining the bargaining representative for employees performing such work.

Nothing contained in this subdivision (d) shall be construed to prohibit publicity, including picketing for the purpose of truthfully advising the public, including consumers, that a product or products or ingredients thereof are produced by an agricultural employer with whom the labor organization has a primary dispute and are distributed by another employer, as long as such publicity does not have an effect of inducing any individual employed by any person other than the primary employer in the course of his employment to refuse to pick up, deliver, or transport any goods, or not to perform any services at the establishment of the employer engaged in such distribution, and as long as such publicity does not have the effect of requesting the public to cease patronizing such other employer.

However, publicity which includes picketing and has the effect of requesting the public to cease patronizing such other employer, shall be permitted only if the labor organization is currently certified as the representative of the primary employer's employees.

Further, publicity other than picketing, but including peaceful distribution of literature which has the effect of requesting the public to cease patronizing such other employer, shall be permitted only if the labor organization has not lost an election for the primary employer's employees within the preceding 12-month period, and no other labor organization is currently certified as the representative of the primary employer's employees.

Nothing contained in this subdivision (d) shall be construed to prohibit publicity, including picketing, which may not be prohibited under the United States Constitution or the California Constitution.

Nor shall anything in this subdivision (d) be construed to apply or be applicable to any labor organization in its representation of workers who are not agricultural employees. Any such labor organization shall continue to be governed in its intrastate activities for nonagricultural workers by Section 923 and applicable judicial precedents.

(e) To require of employees covered by an agreement authorized under subdivision (c) of Section 1153 the payment, as a condition precedent to becoming a member of such organization, of a fee in an amount which the board finds excessive or discriminatory under all circumstances. In making such a finding, the board shall consider, among other relevant factors, the practices and customs of labor organizations in the agriculture industry and the wages currently paid to the employees affected.

(f) To cause or attempt to cause an agricultural employer to pay or deliver, or agree to pay or deliver, any money or other thing of value, in the nature of an exaction, for services which are not performed or not to be performed.

(g) To picket or cause to be picketed, or threaten to picket or cause to be picketed, any employer where an object thereof is either forcing or requiring an employer to recognize or bargain with a labor organization as the representative of his employees, or forcing or requiring the employees of an employer to accept or select such labor organization as their collective-bargaining representative, unless such labor organization is currently certified as the representative of such employees, in any of the following cases:

(1) Where the employer has lawfully recognized in accordance with this part any other labor organization and a question concerning representation may not appropriately be raised under Section 1156.3.

(2) Where within the preceding 12 months a valid election under Chapter 5 (commencing with Section 1156) of this part has been conducted.

Nothing in this subdivision shall be construed to prohibit any picketing or other publicity for the purpose of truthfully advising the public (including consumers) that an employer does not employ members of, or have a contract with, a labor organization, unless an effect of such picketing is to induce any individual employed by any other person in the course of his employment, not to pick up, deliver, or transport any goods or not to perform any services.

Nothing in this subdivision (g) shall be construed to permit any act which would otherwise be an unfair labor practice under this section.

(h) To picket or cause to be picketed, or threaten to picket or cause to be picketed, any employer where an object thereof is either forcing or requiring an employer to recognize or bargain with the labor organization as a representative of his employees unless such labor organization is currently certified as the collective-bargaining representative of such employees.

(i) Nothing contained in this section shall be construed to make unlawful a refusal by any person to enter upon the premises of any agricultural employer, other than his own employer, if the employees of such employer are engaged in a strike ratified or approved by a representative of such employees whom such employer is required to recognize under this part. *(Added by Stats.1975, 3rd Ex. Sess., c. 1, p. 4013, § 2.)*

§ 1154.5. Secondary boycotts

It shall be an unfair labor practice for any labor organization which represents the employees of the employer and such employer to enter into any contract or agreement, express or implied, whereby such employer ceases or refrains, or agrees to cease or refrain, from handling, using, selling, transporting, or otherwise dealing in any of the products of any other employer, or to cease doing business with any other person, and any contract or agreement entered into heretofore or hereafter containing such an agreement shall be, to such extent, unenforceable and void. Nothing in this section shall apply to an agreement between a labor organization and an employer relating to a supplier of an ingredient or ingredients which are integrated into a product produced or distributed by such employer where the labor organization is certified as the representative of the employees of such supplier, but no collective-bargaining agreement between such supplier and such labor organization is in effect. Further, nothing in this section shall apply to an agreement between a labor organization and an agricultural employer relating to the contracting or subcontracting of work to be done at the site of the farm and related operations. Nothing in this part shall prohibit the enforcement of any agreement which is within the foregoing exceptions.

Nor shall anything in this section be construed to apply or be applicable to any labor organization in its representation of workers who are not agricultural employees. Any such labor organization shall continue to be governed in its intrastate activities for nonagricultural workers by Section 923 and applicable judicial precedents. *(Added by Stats.1975, 3rd Ex. Sess., c. 1, p. 4013, § 2.)*

§ 1154.6. Employment for voting purposes only

It shall be an unfair labor practice for an employer or labor organization, or their agents, willfully to arrange for persons to become employees for the primary purpose of voting in elections. *(Added by Stats.1975, 3rd Ex. Sess., c. 1, p. 4013, § 2.)*

§ 1155. Freedom of speech

The expressing of any views, arguments, or opinions, or the dissemination thereof, whether in written, printed, graphic, or visual form, shall not constitute evidence of an unfair labor practice under the provisions of this part, if such expression contains no threat of reprisal or force, or promise of benefit. *(Added by Stats.1975, 3rd Ex.Sess., c. 1, p. 4013, § 2.)*

§ 1155.2. Collective bargaining in good faith; extension of certification in absence of good faith

(a) For purposes of this part, to bargain collectively in good faith is the performance of the mutual obligation of the agricultural employer and the representative of the agricultural employees to meet at reasonable times and confer in good faith with respect to wages, hours, and other terms and conditions of employment, or the negotiation of an agreement, or any questions arising thereunder, and the execution of a written contract incorporating any agreement reached if requested by either party, but such obligation does not compel either party to agree to a proposal or require the making of a concession.

(b) Upon the filing by any person of a petition not earlier than the 90th day nor later than the 60th day preceding the expiration of the 12-month period following initial certification, the board shall determine whether an employer has bargained in good faith with the currently certified labor organization. If the board finds that the employer has not bargained in good faith, it may extend the certification for up to one additional year, effective immediately upon the expiration of the previous 12-month period following initial certification. *(Added by Stats.1975, 3rd Ex. Sess., c. 1, p. 4013, § 2.)*

§ 1155.3. Termination or modification of existing contract; requirements

(a) Where there is in effect a collective-bargaining contract covering agricultural employees, the duty to bargain collectively shall also mean that no party to such contract shall terminate or modify such contract, unless the party desiring such termination or modification does all of the following:

(1) Serves a written notice upon the other party to the contract of the proposed termination or modification not less than 60 days prior to the expiration date thereof, or, in the event such contract contains no expiration date, 60 days prior to the time it is proposed to make such termination or modification.

(2) Offers to meet and confer with the other party for the purpose of negotiating a new contract or a contract containing the proposed modifications.

(3) Notifies the Conciliation Service of the State of California within 30 days after such notice of the existence of a dispute, provided no agreement has been reached by that time.

(4) Continues in full force and effect, without resorting to strike or lockout, all the terms and conditions of the existing contract, for a period of 60 days after such notice is given, or until the expiration date of such contract, whichever occurs later.

(b) The duties imposed upon agricultural employers and labor organizations by paragraphs (2), (3), and (4) of subdivision (a) shall become inapplicable upon an intervening certification of the board that the labor organization or individual which is a party to the contract has been superseded as, or has ceased to be the representative of the employees, subject to the provisions of Chapter 5 (commencing with Section 1156) of this part, and the duties so imposed shall not be construed to require either party to discuss or agree to any modification of the terms and conditions contained in a contract for a fixed period, if such modification is to become effective before such

terms and conditions can be reopened under the provisions of the contract. Any agricultural employee who engages in a strike within the 60-day period specified in this section shall lose his status as an agricultural employee of the agricultural employer engaged in the particular labor dispute, for the purposes of Section 1153 to 1154 inclusive, and Chapters 5 (commencing with Section 1156) and 6 (commencing with Section 1160) of this part, but such loss of status for such employee shall terminate if and when he is reemployed by such employer. *(Added by Stats.1975, 3rd Ex. Sess., c. 1, p. 4013, § 2.)*

§ 1155.4. Employer, association, etc.; payment, loan or delivery of money or thing of value

It shall be unlawful for any agricultural employer or association of agricultural employers, or any person who acts as a labor relations expert, adviser, or consultant to an agricultural employer, or who acts in the interest of an agricultural employer, to pay, lend, or deliver, any money or other thing of value to any of the following:

(a) Any representative of any of his agricultural employees.

(b) Any agricultural labor organization, or any officer or employee thereof, which represents, seeks to represent, or would admit to membership, any of the agricultural employees of such employer.

(c) Any employee or group or committee of employees of such employer in excess of their normal compensation for the purpose of causing such employee or group or committee directly or indirectly to influence any other employees in the exercise of the right to organize and bargain collectively through representatives of their own choosing.

(d) Any officer or employee of an agricultural labor organization with intent to influence him in respect to any of his actions, decisions, or duties as a representative of agricultural employees or as such officer or employee of such labor organization. *(Added by Stats.1975, 3rd Ex. Sess., c. 1, p. 4013, § 2.)*

§ 1155.5. Request, demand, receipt, etc., of payment, loan, or delivery of money or thing of value

It shall be unlawful for any person to request, demand, receive, or accept, or agree to receive or accept, any payment, loan, or delivery of any money or other thing of value prohibited by Section 1155.4. *(Added by Stats.1975, 3rd Ex. Sess., c. 1, p. 4013, § 2.)*

§ 1155.6. Exemption of payments for employee compensation, satisfaction of judgments, awards, etc., sales in course of business, union dues, and certain trust funds

Nothing in Section 1155.4 or 1155.5 shall apply to any matter set forth in subsection (c) of Section 186 of Title 29 of the United States Code. *(Added by Stats.1975, 3rd Ex. Sess., c. 1, p. 4013, § 2.)*

§ 1155.7. Nonagricultural employees; law governing

Nothing in this chapter shall be construed to apply or be applicable to any labor organization in its representation of workers who are not agricultural employees. Any such labor organization shall continue to be governed in its intrastate activities for nonagricultural workers by Section 923 and applicable judicial precedents. *(Added by Stats.1975, 3rd Ex. Sess., c. 1, p. 4013, § 2.)*

CHAPTER 5. LABOR REPRESENTATIVES AND ELECTIONS

Section
1156.   Exclusive representatives; grievances.
1156.2.   Bargaining unit; determination of appropriate unit.
1156.3.   Petition; contents; representation election; objections; certification; decertification; procedure.
1156.4.   Petition; timeliness of filing; peak agricultural employment.
1156.5.   Direction of election after a valid election; limitation.
1156.6.   Direction of election after certification of unit; limitation.
1156.7.   Petition for election; agreements executed previously or under this chapter; decertification; question of representation; conditions.
1157.   Eligibility to vote; economic strikers; disputes prior to effective date of this part.
1157.2.   Runoff election.
1157.3.   Payroll lists; maintenance; availability.
1158.   Transcript; inclusions.
1159.   Parties to valid agreement; certified labor organizations.

§ 1156. Exclusive representatives; grievances

Representatives designated or selected by a secret ballot for the purposes of collective bargaining by the majority of the agricultural employees in the bargaining unit shall be the exclusive representatives of all the agricultural employees in such unit for the purpose of collective bargaining with respect to rates of pay, wages, hours of employment, or other conditions of employment. Any individual agricultural employee or a group of agricultural employees shall have the right at any time to present grievances to their agricultural employer and to have such grievances adjusted, without the intervention of the bargaining representative, as long as the adjustment is not inconsistent with the terms of a collective-bargaining contract or agreement then in effect, if the bargaining representative has been given opportunity to be present at such adjustment. *(Added by Stats.1975, 3rd Ex. Sess., c. 1, p. 4013, § 2.)*

§ 1156.2. Bargaining unit; determination of appropriate unit

The bargaining unit shall be all the agricultural employees of an employer. If the agricultural employees of the employer are employed in two or more noncontiguous geographical areas, the board shall determine the appropriate unit or units of agricultural employees in which a secret ballot election shall be conducted. *(Added by Stats.1975, 3rd Ex. Sess., c. 1, p. 4013, § 2.)*

§ 1156.3. Petition; contents; representation election; objections; certification; decertification; procedure

(a) A petition that is either signed by, or accompanied by authorization cards signed by, a majority of the currently employed employees in the bargaining unit, may be filed by an agricultural employee or group of agricultural employees, or any individual or labor organization acting on behalf of those agricultural employees, in accordance with any rules and regulations prescribed by the board. The petition shall allege all of the following:

(1) That the number of agricultural employees currently employed by the employer named in the petition, as determined from the employer's payroll immediately preceding the filing of the petition, is not less than 50 percent of the employer's peak agricultural employment for the current calendar year.

(2) That no valid election pursuant to this section has been conducted among the agricultural employees of the employer named in the petition within the 12 months immediately preceding the filing of the petition.

(3) That no labor organization is currently certified as the exclusive collective-bargaining representative of the agricultural employees of the employer named in the petition.

(4) That the petition is not barred by an existing collective-bargaining agreement.

(b) Upon receipt of a signed petition, as described in subdivision (a), the board shall immediately investigate the petition. If the board has reasonable cause to believe that a bona fide question of representation exists, it shall direct a representation election by secret ballot to be held, upon due notice to all interested parties and within a maximum of seven days of the filing of the petition. If, at the time the election petition is filed, a majority of the employees in a bargaining unit are engaged in a strike, the board shall, with all due diligence, attempt to hold a secret ballot election within 48 hours of the filing of the petition. The holding of elections under strike circumstances shall take precedence over the holding of other secret ballot elections.

(c) The board shall make available at any election held under this chapter ballots printed in English and Spanish. The board may also make available at the election ballots printed in any other language as may be requested by an agricultural labor organization or any agricultural employee eligible to vote under this part. Every election ballot, except ballots in runoff elections where the choice is between labor organizations, shall provide the employee with the opportunity to vote against representation by a labor organization by providing an appropriate space designated "No Labor Organizations."

(d) Any other labor organization shall be qualified to appear on the ballot if it presents authorization cards signed by at least 20 percent of the employees in the bargaining unit at least 24 hours prior to the election.

(e)(1) Within five days after an election, any person may file with the board a signed petition asserting that

383

allegations made in the petition filed pursuant to subdivision (a) were incorrect, asserting that the board improperly determined the geographical scope of the bargaining unit, or objecting to the conduct of the election or conduct affecting the results of the election.

(2) Upon receipt of a petition under this subdivision, the board, upon due notice, shall conduct a hearing to determine whether the election shall be certified. This hearing may be conducted by an officer or employee of a regional office of the board. The officer may not make any recommendations with respect to the certification of the election. The board may refuse to certify the election if it finds, on the record of the hearing, that any of the assertions made in the petition filed pursuant to this subdivision are correct, that the election was not conducted properly, or that misconduct affecting the results of the election occurred. The board shall certify the election unless it determines that there are sufficient grounds to refuse to do so.

(f) If no petition is filed pursuant to subdivision (e) within five days of the election, the board shall certify the election.

(g) The board shall decertify a labor organization if either of the following occur:

(1) The Department of Fair Employment and Housing finds that the labor organization engaged in discrimination on any basis listed in subdivision (a) of Section 12940 of the Government Code, as those bases are defined in Sections 12926 and 12926.1 of the Government Code, except as otherwise provided in Section 12940 of the Government Code.

(2) The United States Equal Employment Opportunity Commission finds, pursuant to Section 2000e–5 of Title 42 of the United States Code, that the labor organization engaged in discrimination on the basis of race, color, national origin, religion, sex, or any other arbitrary or invidious classification in violation of Subchapter VI of Chapter 21 of Title 42 of the United States Code [1] during the period of the labor organization's present certification. *(Added by Stats.1975, 3rd Ex. Sess., c. 1, p. 4013, § 2. Amended by Stats.2004, c. 788 (A.B.2900), § 13.)*

[1] 42 U.S.C.A. § 2000e et seq.

§ 1156.4. Petition; timeliness of filing; peak agricultural employment

Recognizing that agriculture is a seasonal occupation for a majority of agricultural employees, and wishing to provide the fullest scope for employees' enjoyment of the rights included in this part, the board shall not consider a representation petition or a petition to decertify as timely filed unless the employer's payroll reflects 50 percent of the peak agricultural employment for such employer for the current calendar year for the payroll period immediately preceding the filing of the petition.

In this connection, the peak agricultural employment for the prior season shall alone not be a basis for such determination, but rather the board shall estimate peak

employment on the basis of acreage and crop statistics which shall be applied uniformly throughout the State of California and upon all other relevant data. *(Added by Stats.1975, 3rd Ex.Sess., c. 1, p. 4013, § 2.)*

§ 1156.5. Direction of election after a valid election; limitation

The board shall not direct an election in any bargaining unit where a valid election has been held in the immediately preceding 12-month period. *(Added by Stats.1975, 3rd Ex.Sess., c. 1, p. 4013, § 2.)*

§ 1156.6. Direction of election after certification of unit; limitation

The board shall not direct an election in any bargaining unit which is represented by a labor organization that has been certified within the immediately preceding 12-month period or whose certification has been extended pursuant to subdivision (b) of Section 1155.2. *(Added by Stats.1975, 3rd Ex. Sess., c. 1, p. 4013, § 2.)*

§ 1156.7. Petition for election; agreements executed previously or under this chapter; decertification; question of representation; conditions

(a) No collective-bargaining agreement executed prior to the effective date of this chapter shall bar a petition for an election.

(b) A collective-bargaining agreement executed by an employer and a labor organization certified as the exclusive bargaining representative of his employees pursuant to this chapter shall be a bar to a petition for an election among such employees for the term of the agreement, but in any event such bar shall not exceed three years, provided that both the following conditions are met:

(1) The agreement is in writing and executed by all parties thereto.

(2) It incorporates the substantive terms and conditions of employment of such employees.

(c) Upon the filing with the board by an employee or group of employees of a petition signed by 30 percent or more of the agricultural employees in a bargaining unit represented by a certified labor organization which is a party to a valid collective-bargaining agreement, requesting that such labor organization be decertified, the board shall conduct an election by secret ballot pursuant to the applicable provisions of this chapter, and shall certify the results to such labor organization and employer.

However, such a petition shall not be deemed timely unless it is filed during the year preceding the expiration of a collective-bargaining agreement which would otherwise bar the holding of an election, and when the number of agricultural employees is not less than 50 percent of the employer's peak agricultural employment for the current calendar year.

(d) Upon the filing with the board of a signed petition by an agricultural employee or group of agricultural employees, or any individual or labor organization acting in their behalf, accompanied by authorization cards signed by a majority of the employees in an appropriate bargaining unit, and alleging all the conditions of paragraphs (1), (2), and (3), the board shall immediately investigate such petition and, if it has reasonable cause to believe that a bona fide question of representation exists, it shall direct an election by secret ballot pursuant to the applicable provisions of this chapter:

(1) That the number of agricultural employees currently employed by the employer named in the petition, as determined from his payroll immediately preceding the filing of the petition, is not less than 50 percent of his peak agricultural employment for the current calendar year.

(2) That no valid election pursuant to this section has been conducted among the agricultural employees of the employer named in the petition within the 12 months immediately preceding the filing thereof.

(3) That a labor organization, certified for an appropriate unit, has a collective-bargaining agreement with the employer which would otherwise bar the holding of an election and that this agreement will expire within the next 12 months. *(Added by Stats.1975, 3rd Ex. Sess., c. 1, p. 4013, § 2.)*

§ 1157. Eligibility to vote; economic strikers; disputes prior to effective date of this part

All agricultural employees of the employer whose names appear on the payroll applicable to the payroll period immediately preceding the filing of the petition of such an election shall be eligible to vote. An economic striker shall be eligible to vote under such regulations as the board shall find are consistent with the purposes and provisions of this part in any election, provided that the striker who has been permanently replaced shall not be eligible to vote in any election conducted more than 12 months after the commencement of the strike.

In the case of elections conducted within 18 months of the effective date of this part which involve labor disputes which commenced prior to such effective date, the board shall have the jurisdiction to adopt fair, equitable, and appropriate eligibility rules, which shall effectuate the policies of this part, with respect to the eligibility of economic strikers who were paid for work performed or for paid vacation during the payroll period immediately preceding the expiration of a collective-bargaining agreement or the commencement of a strike; provided, however, that in no event shall the board afford eligibility to any such striker who has not performed any services for the employer during the 36-month period immediately preceding the effective date of this part. *(Added by Stats.1975, 3rd Ex. Sess., c. 1, p. 4013, § 2.)*

§ 1157.2. Runoff election

In any election where none of the choices on the ballot receives a majority, a runoff shall be conducted, the ballot providing for a selection between the two choices receiving the largest and second largest number of valid votes cast in the election. *(Added by Stats.1975, 3rd Ex. Sess., c. 1, p. 4013, § 2.)*

§ 1157.3. Payroll lists; maintenance; availability

Employers shall maintain accurate and current payroll lists containing the names and addresses of all their employees, and shall make such lists available to the board upon request. *(Added by Stats.1975, 3rd Ex. Sess., c. 1, p. 4013, § 2.)*

§ 1158. Transcript; inclusions

Whenever an order of the board made pursuant to Section 1160.3 is based in whole or in part upon the facts certified following an investigation pursuant to Sections 1156.3 to 1157.2 inclusive, and there is a petition for review of such order, such certification and the record of such investigation shall be included in the transcript of the entire record required to be filed under Section 1160.8 and thereupon the decree of the court enforcing, modifying, or setting aside in whole or in part the order of the board shall be made and entered upon the pleadings, testimony, and proceedings set forth in such transcript. *(Added by Stats.1975, 3rd Ex. Sess., c. 1, p. 4013, § 2.)*

§ 1159. Parties to valid agreement; certified labor organizations

In order to assure the full freedom of association, self-organization, and designation of representatives of the employees own choosing, only labor organizations certified pursuant to this part shall be parties to a legally valid collective-bargaining agreement. *(Added by Stats.1975, 3rd Ex. Sess., c. 1, p. 4013, § 2.)*

CHAPTER 6. PREVENTION OF UNFAIR LABOR PRACTICES AND JUDICIAL REVIEW AND ENFORCEMENT

Section
1160. Authority of board.
1160.2. Complaint; contents; amendment; answer; limitations.
1160.3. Findings and orders; remedies.
1160.4. Petition to superior court for temporary relief or restraining order; notice; jurisdiction.
1160.5. Determination of dispute relating to assignment of particular work to particular organization, trade, craft or class; voluntary adjustment.
1160.6. Cases relating to forcing joinder of organization, use of secondary boycott, recognition, etc.; priority; injunctive relief.
1160.7. Discrimination cases; priority.
1160.8. Petition to modify or set aside board order; jurisdiction; procedure.
1160.9. Exclusive nature of this chapter.
1161. Agricultural Employee Relief Fund.

§ 1160. Authority of board

The board is empowered, as provided in this chapter, to prevent any person from engaging in any unfair labor practice, as set forth in Chapter 4 (commencing with

Section 1153) of this part. *(Added by Stats.1975, 3rd Ex. Sess., c. 1, p. 4013, § 2.)*

§ 1160.2. Complaint; contents; amendment; answer; limitations

Whenever it is charged that any person has engaged in or is engaging in any such unfair labor practice, the board, or any agent or agency designated by the board for such purposes, shall have power to issue and cause to be served upon such person a complaint stating the charges in that respect, and containing a notice of hearing before the board or a member thereof, or before a designated agency or agencies, at a place therein fixed, not less than five days after the serving of such complaint. No complaint shall issue based upon any unfair labor practice occurring more than six months prior to the filing of the charge with the board and the service of a copy thereof upon the person against whom such charge is made, unless the person aggrieved thereby was prevented from filing such charge by reason of service in the armed forces, in which event the six-month period shall be computed from the day of his discharge. Any such complaint may be amended by the member, agent, or agency conducting the hearing, or the board in its discretion, at any time prior to the issuance of an order based thereon. The person so complained against shall have the right to file an answer to the original or amended complaint and to appear in person or otherwise and give testimony at the place and time fixed in the complaint. In the discretion of the member, agent, or agency conducting the hearing or the board, any other person may be allowed to intervene in the proceeding and to present testimony. Any such proceeding shall, so far as practicable, be conducted in accordance with the Evidence Code. All proceedings shall be appropriately reported. *(Added by Stats.1975, 3rd Ex. Sess., c. 1, p. 4013, § 2.)*

§ 1160.3. Findings and orders; remedies

The testimony taken by such member, agent, or agency, or the board in such hearing shall be reduced to writing and filed with the board. Thereafter, in its discretion, the board, upon notice, may take further testimony or hear argument. If, upon the preponderance of the testimony taken, the board shall be of the opinion that any person named in the complaint has engaged in or is engaging in any such unfair labor practice, the board shall state its findings of fact and shall issue and cause to be served on such person an order requiring such person to cease and desist from such unfair labor practice, to take affirmative action, including reinstatement of employees with or without backpay, and making employees whole, when the board deems such relief appropriate, for the loss of pay resulting from the employer's refusal to bargain, and to provide such other relief as will effectuate the policies of this part. Where an order directs reinstatement of an employee, backpay may be required of the employer or labor organization, as the case may be, responsible for the discrimination suffered by him. Such order may further

require such person to make reports from time to time showing the extent to which it has complied with the order. If, upon the preponderance of the testimony taken, the board shall be of the opinion that the person named in the complaint has not engaged in or is not engaging in any unfair labor practice, the board shall state its findings of fact and shall issue an order dismissing the complaint. No order of the board shall require the reinstatement of any individual as an employee who has been suspended or discharged, or the payment to him of any backpay, if such individual was suspended or discharged for cause. In case the evidence is presented before a member of the board, or before an administrative law officer thereof, such member, or such administrative law officer, as the case may be, shall issue and cause to be served on the parties to the proceedings a proposed report, together with a recommended order, which shall be filed with the board, and, if no exceptions are filed within 20 days after service thereof upon such parties, or within such further period as the board may authorize, such recommended order shall become the order of the board and become effective as therein prescribed.

Until the record in a case shall have been filed in a court, as provided in this chapter, the board may, at any time upon reasonable notice and in such manner as it shall deem proper, modify or set aside, in whole or in part, any finding or order made or issued by it. *(Added by Stats.1975, 3rd Ex. Sess., c. 1, p. 4013, § 2.)*

§ 1160.4. Petition to superior court for temporary relief or restraining order; notice; jurisdiction

The board shall have power, upon issuance of a complaint as provided in Section 1160.2 charging that any person has engaged in or is engaging in an unfair labor practice, to petition the superior court in any county wherein the unfair labor practice in question is alleged to have occurred, or wherein such person resides or transacts business, for appropriate temporary relief or restraining order. Upon the filing of any such petition, the board shall cause notice thereof to be served upon such person, and thereupon the court shall have jurisdiction to grant to the board such temporary relief or restraining order as the court deems just and proper. *(Added by Stats.1975, 3rd Ex. Sess., c. 1, p. 4013, § 2.)*

§ 1160.5. Determination of dispute relating to assignment of particular work to particular organization, trade, craft or class; voluntary adjustment

Whenever it is charged that any person has engaged in an unfair labor practice within the meaning of paragraph (4) of subdivision (d) of Section 1154, the board is empowered and directed to hear and determine the dispute out of which such unfair labor practice shall have arisen, unless within 10 days after notice that such charge has been filed, the parties to such dispute submit to the board satisfactory evidence that they have adjusted, or agreed upon methods for the voluntary adjustment of the dispute. Upon compliance by the parties to the dispute with the decision of the board or upon such voluntary adjustment of the dispute, such charge shall be dismissed. *(Added by Stats.1975, 3rd Ex. Sess., c. 1, p. 4013, § 2.)*

§ 1160.6. Cases relating to forcing joinder of organization, use of secondary boycott, recognition, etc.; priority; injunctive relief

Whenever it is charged that any person has engaged in an unfair labor practice within the meaning of paragraph (1), (2), or (3) of subdivision (d), or of subdivision (g), of Section 1154, or of Section 1155, the preliminary investigation of such charge shall be made forthwith and given priority over all other cases except cases of like character in the office where it is filed or to which it is referred. If, after such investigation, the officer or regional attorney to whom the matter may be referred has reasonable cause to believe such charge is true and that a complaint should issue, he shall, on behalf of the board, petition the superior court in the county in which the unfair labor practice in question has occurred, is alleged to have occurred, or where the person alleged to have committed the unfair labor practice resides or transacts business, for appropriate injunctive relief pending the final adjudication of the board with respect to the matter. The officer or regional attorney shall make all reasonable efforts to advise the party against whom the restraining order is sought of his intention to seek such order at least 24 hours prior to doing so. In the event the officer or regional attorney has been unable to advise such party of his intent at least 24 hours in advance, he shall submit a declaration to the court under penalty of perjury setting forth in detail the efforts he has made. Upon the filing of any such petition, the superior court shall have jurisdiction to grant such injunctive relief or temporary restraining order as it deems just and proper. Upon the filing of any such petition, the board shall cause notice thereof to be served upon any person involved in the charge and such person, including the charging party, shall be given an opportunity to appear by counsel and present any relevant testimony. For the purposes of this section, the superior court shall be deemed to have jurisdiction of a labor organization either in the county in which such organization maintains its principal office, or in any county in which its duly authorized officers or agents are engaged in promoting or protecting the interests of employee members. The service of legal process upon such officer or agent shall constitute service upon the labor organization and make such organization a party to the suit. In situations where such relief is appropriate, the procedure specified herein shall apply to charges with respect to paragraph (4) of subdivision (d) of Section 1154. *(Added by Stats.1975, 3rd Ex. Sess., c. 1, p. 4013, § 2.)*

§ 1160.7. Discrimination cases; priority

Whenever it is charged that any person has engaged in an unfair labor practice within the meaning of subdivision (c) of Section 1153 or subdivision (b) of Section 1154, such charge shall be given priority over all other cases except cases of like character in the office where it is filed or to which it is referred and cases given priority under Section 1160.6. *(Added by Stats.1975, 3rd Ex. Sess., c. 1, p. 4013, § 2.)*

§ 1160.8. Petition to modify or set aside board order; jurisdiction; procedure

Any person aggrieved by the final order of the board granting or denying in whole or in part the relief sought may obtain a review of such order in the court of appeal having jurisdiction over the county wherein the unfair labor practice in question was alleged to have been engaged in, or wherein such person resides or transacts business, by filing in such court a written petition requesting that the order of the board be modified or set aside. Such petition shall be filed with the court within 30 days from the date of the issuance of the board's order. Upon the filing of such petition, the court shall cause notice to be served upon the board and thereupon shall have jurisdiction of the proceeding. The board shall file in the court the record of the proceeding, certified by the board within 10 days after the clerk's notice unless such time is extended by the court for good cause shown. The court shall have jurisdiction to grant to the board such temporary relief or restraining order it deems just and proper and in like manner to make and enter a decree enforcing, modifying and enforcing as so modified, or setting aside in whole or in part, the order of the board. The findings of the board with respect to questions of fact if supported by substantial evidence on the record considered as a whole shall in like manner be conclusive.

An order directing an election shall not be stayed pending review, but such order may be reviewed as provided in Section 1158.

If the time for review of the board order has lapsed, and the person has not voluntarily complied with the board's order, the board may apply to the superior court in any county in which the unfair labor practice occurred or wherein such person resides or transacts business for enforcement of its order. If after hearing, the court determines that the order was issued pursuant to procedures established by the board and that the person refuses to comply with the order, the court shall enforce such order by writ of injunction or other proper process. The court shall not review the merits of the order. *(Added by Stats.1975, 3rd Ex. Sess., c. 1, p. 4013, § 2.)*

§ 1160.9. Exclusive nature of this chapter

The procedures set forth in this chapter shall be the exclusive method of redressing unfair labor practices. *(Added by Stats.1975, 3rd Ex.Sess., c. 1, p. 4013, § 2.)*

§ 1161. Agricultural Employee Relief Fund

(a) The Agricultural Employee Relief Fund is hereby created as a special fund in the State Treasury and is continuously appropriated to the Agricultural Labor Relations Board for the purposes specified in subdivision (c). The board shall act as a trustee of all moneys deposited in the fund.

(b) Any monetary relief ordered by the board pursuant to this part to be paid by an employer to an employee shall be collected by the board on behalf of the employee. All monetary relief so collected by the board shall be remitted to the employee for whom the board collected the money.

(c)(1) Notwithstanding Section 1519 of the Code of Civil Procedure, if the board has made a diligent effort to locate an employee on whose behalf the board has collected monetary relief pursuant to this part, and is unable to locate the employee or the lawful representative of the employee for a period of two years after the date the board collected the monetary relief, the board shall deposit those moneys in the fund.

(2) Moneys in the fund shall be used by the board to pay employees the unpaid balance of any monetary relief ordered by the board to be paid by an employer to an employee. Prior to making any payment from the fund, the board first shall make a finding that, in an individual case, the collection of the full amount of the monetary relief ordered is not possible after reasonable efforts have been made to collect the balance from the employer.

(d) As used in this section, "fund" means the Agricultural Employee Relief Fund.

(e) On or before July 1, 2002, the board shall report to the Legislature on the status of the fund. *(Added by Stats.2001, c. 408 (S.B.1198), § 1. Amended by Stats. 2002, c. 664 (A.B.3034), § 160.)*

CHAPTER 6.5. CONTRACT DISPUTE RESOLUTION

Section
1164.   Declaration of failure to reach collective bargaining agreement; order for mandatory mediation and conciliation; selection of mediator; meetings; report; factors considered.
1164.3.   Review of report; procedure.
1164.5.   Judicial review; petition; scope.
1164.7.   Judicial review; procedure.
1164.9.   Judicial review; jurisdiction.
1164.11.   Criteria required prior to filing demand.
1164.12.   Limitation upon number of declarations allowed.
1164.13.   Severability.

§ 1164. Declaration of failure to reach collective bargaining agreement; order for mandatory mediation and conciliation; selection of mediator; meetings; report; factors considered

(a) An agricultural employer or a labor organization certified as the exclusive bargaining agent of a bargaining unit of agricultural employees may file with the board, at any time following (1) 90 days after a renewed demand to bargain by an agricultural employer or a labor organization certified prior to January 1, 2003, which meets the conditions specified in Section 1164.11 or (2) 180 days after an initial request to bargain by an agricultural employer or a labor organization certified after January 1, 2003, a declaration that the parties have failed to reach a

collective bargaining agreement and a request that the board issue an order directing the parties to mandatory mediation and conciliation of their issues. "Agricultural employer," for purposes of this chapter, means an agricultural employer, as defined in subdivision (c) of Section 1140.4, who has employed or engaged 25 or more agricultural employees during any calendar week in the year preceding the filing of a declaration pursuant to this subdivision.

(b) Upon receipt of a declaration pursuant to subdivision (a), the board shall immediately issue an order directing the parties to mandatory mediation and conciliation of their issues. The board shall request from the California State Mediation and Conciliation Service a list of nine mediators who have experience in labor mediation. The California State Mediation and Conciliation Service may include names chosen from its own mediators, or from a list of names supplied by the American Arbitration Association or the Federal Mediation Service. The parties shall select a mediator from the list within seven days of receipt of the list. If the parties cannot agree on a mediator, they shall strike names from the list until a mediator is chosen by process of elimination. If a party refuses to participate in selecting a mediator, the other party may choose a mediator from the list. The costs of mediation and conciliation shall be borne equally by the parties.

(c) Upon appointment, the mediator shall immediately schedule meetings at a time and location reasonably accessible to the parties. Mediation shall proceed for a period of 30 days. Upon expiration of the 30–day period, if the parties do not resolve the issues to their mutual satisfaction, the mediator shall certify that the mediation process has been exhausted. Upon mutual agreement of the parties, the mediator may extend the mediation period for an additional 30 days.

(d) Within 21 days, the mediator shall file a report with the board that resolves all of the issues between the parties and establishes the final terms of a collective bargaining agreement, including all issues subject to mediation and all issues resolved by the parties prior to the certification of the exhaustion of the mediation process. With respect to any issues in dispute between the parties, the report shall include the basis for the mediator's determination. The mediator's determination shall be supported by the record.

(e) In resolving the issues in dispute, the mediator may consider those factors commonly considered in similar proceedings, including:

(1) The stipulations of the parties.

(2) The financial condition of the employer and its ability to meet the costs of the contract in those instances where the employer claims an inability to meet the union's wage and benefit demands.

(3) The corresponding wages, benefits, and terms and conditions of employment in other collective bargaining

agreements covering similar agricultural operations with similar labor requirements.

(4) The corresponding wages, benefits, and terms and conditions of employment prevailing in comparable firms or industries in geographical areas with similar economic conditions, taking into account the size of the employer, the skills, experience, and training required of the employees, and the difficulty and nature of the work performed.

(5) The average consumer prices for goods and services according to the California Consumer Price Index, and the overall cost of living, in the area where the work is performed. *(Added by Stats.2002, c. 1145 (S.B.1156), § 2. Amended by Stats.2002, c. 1146 (A.B.2596), § 1; Stats.2003, c. 870 (S.B.75), § 1.)*

§ 1164.3. Review of report; procedure

(a) Either party, within seven days of the filing of the report by the mediator, may petition the board for review of the report. The petitioning party shall, in the petition, specify the particular provisions of the mediator's report for which it is seeking review by the board and shall specify the specific grounds authorizing review by the board. The board, within 10 days of receipt of a petition, may accept for review those portions of the petition for which a prima facie case has been established that (1) a provision of the collective bargaining agreement set forth in the mediator's report is unrelated to wages, hours, or other conditions of employment within the meaning of Section 1155.2, (2) a provision of the collective bargaining agreement set forth in the mediator's report is based on clearly erroneous findings of material fact, or (3) a provision of the collective bargaining agreement set forth in the mediator's report is arbitrary or capricious in light of the mediator's findings of fact.

(b) If it finds grounds exist to grant review within the meaning of subdivision (a), the board shall order the provisions of the report that are not the subject of the petition for review into effect as a final order of the board. If the board does not accept a petition for review or no petition for review is filed, then the mediator's report shall become a final order of the board.

(c) The board shall issue a decision concerning the petition and if it determines that a provision of the collective bargaining agreement contained in the mediator's report violates the provisions of subdivision (a), it shall, within 21 days, issue an order requiring the mediator to modify the terms of the collective bargaining agreement. The mediator shall meet with the parties for additional mediation for a period not to exceed 30 days. At the expiration of this mediation period, the mediator shall prepare a second report resolving any outstanding issues. The second report shall be filed with the board.

(d) Either party, within seven days of the filing of the mediator's second report, may petition the board for a review of the mediator's second report pursuant to the procedures specified in subdivision (a). If no petition is filed, the mediator's report shall take immediate effect as a final order of the board. If a petition is filed, the board shall issue an order confirming the mediator's report and order it into immediate effect, unless it finds that the report is subject to review for any of the grounds specified in subdivision (a), in which case the board shall determine the issues and shall issue a final order of the board.

(e) Either party, within seven days of the filing of the report by the mediator, may petition the board to set aside the report if a prima facie case is established that any of the following have occurred: (1) the mediator's report was procured by corruption, fraud, or other undue means, (2) there was corruption in the mediator, or (3) the rights of the petitioning party were substantially prejudiced by the misconduct of the mediator. For the sole purpose of interpreting the terms of paragraphs (1), (2), and (3), case law that interprets similar terms used in Section 1286.2 of the Code of Civil Procedure shall apply. If the board finds that any of these grounds exist, the board shall within 10 days vacate the report of the mediator and shall order the selection and appointment of a new mediator, and an additional mediation period of 30 days, pursuant to Section 1164.

(f) Within 60 days after the order of the board takes effect, either party or the board may file an action to enforce the order of the board, in the superior court for the County of Sacramento or in the county where either party's principal place of business is located. No final order of the board shall be stayed during any appeal under this section, unless the court finds that (1) the appellant will be irreparably harmed by the implementation of the board's order, and (2) the appellant has demonstrated a likelihood of success on appeal. *(Added by Stats.2002, c. 1145 (S.B.1156), § 2. Amended by Stats.2002, c. 1146 (A.B.2596), § 2; Stats.2003, c. 870 (S.B.75), § 2.)*

§ 1164.5. Judicial review; petition; scope

(a) Within 30 days after the order of the board takes effect, a party may petition for a writ of review in the court of appeal or the California Supreme Court. If the writ issues, it shall be made returnable at a time and place specified by court order and shall direct the board to certify its record in the case to the court within the time specified. The petition for review shall be served personally upon the executive director of the board and the nonappealing party personally or by service.

(b) The review by the court shall not extend further than to determine, on the basis of the entire record, whether any of the following occurred:

(1) The board acted without, or in excess of, its powers or jurisdiction.

(2) The board has not proceeded in the manner required by law.

(3) The order or decision of the board was procured by fraud or was an abuse of discretion.

(4) The order or decision of the board violates any right of the petitioner under the Constitution of the United States or the California Constitution.

(c) Nothing in this section shall be construed to permit the court to hold a trial de novo, to take evidence other than as specified by the California Rules of Court, or to exercise its independent judgment on the evidence. *(Added by Stats.2002, c. 1145 (S.B.1156), § 2.)*

§ 1164.7.   Judicial review; procedure

(a) The board and each party to the action or proceeding before the mediator may appear in the review proceeding. Upon the hearing, the court of appeal or the Supreme Court shall enter judgment either affirming or setting aside the order of the board.

(b) The provisions of the Code of Civil Procedure relating to writs of review shall, so far as applicable, apply to proceedings instituted under this chapter. *(Added by Stats.2002, c. 1145 (S.B.1156), § 2.)*

§ 1164.9.   Judicial review; jurisdiction

No court of this state, except the court of appeal or the Supreme Court, to the extent specified in this article, shall have jurisdiction to review, reverse, correct, or annul any order or decision of the board to suspend or delay the execution or operation thereof, or to enjoin, restrain, or interfere with the board in the performance of its official duties, as provided by law and the rules of court. *(Added by Stats.2002, c. 1145 (S.B.1156), § 2.)*

§ 1164.11.   Criteria required prior to filing demand

A demand made pursuant to paragraph (1) of subdivision (a) of Section 1164 may be made only in cases which meet all of the following criteria: (a) the parties have failed to reach agreement for at least one year after the date on which the labor organization made its initial request to bargain, (b) the employer has committed an unfair labor practice, and (c) the parties have not previously had a binding contract between them. *(Added by Stats.2002, c. 1145 (S.B.1156), § 2. Amended by Stats.2002, c. 1146 (A.B.2596), § 3.)*

§ 1164.12.   Limitation upon number of declarations allowed

To ensure an orderly implementation of the mediation process ordered by this chapter, a party may not file a total of more than 75 declarations with the board prior to January 1, 2008. In calculating the number of declarations so filed, the identity of the other party with respect to whom the declaration is filed, shall be irrelevant. *(Added by Stats.2002, c. 1146 (A.B.2596), § 4. Amended by Stats.2003, c. 870 (S.B.75), § 3.)*

§ 1164.13.   Severability

The provisions of this chapter are severable. If any provision of this chapter or its application is held invalid, that invalidity shall not affect other provisions or applications that can be given effect without the invalid provision

or application. *(Added by Stats.2002, c. 1145 (S.B.1156), § 2.)*

CHAPTER 7.   SUITS INVOLVING EMPLOYERS AND LABOR ORGANIZATIONS

Section
1165.   Right to sue; venue; amount; agency; liability.
1165.2. Jurisdiction of superior court.
1165.3. Service of process.
1165.4. Agency; authorized or ratified acts.

§ 1165.   Right to sue; venue; amount; agency; liability

(a) Suits for violation of contracts between an agricultural employer and an agricultural labor organization representing agricultural employees, as defined in this part, or between any such labor organizations, may be brought in any superior court having jurisdiction of the parties, without respect to the amount in controversy.

(b) Any agricultural labor organization which represents agricultural employees and any agricultural employer shall be bound by the acts of its agents. Any such labor organization may sue or be sued as an entity and in behalf of the employees whom it represents in the courts of this state. Any money judgment against a labor organization in a superior court shall be enforceable only against the organization as an entity and against its assets, and shall not be enforceable against any individual member or his assets. *(Added by Stats.1975, 3rd Ex. Sess., c. 1, p. 4013, § 2.)*

§ 1165.2.   Jurisdiction of superior court

For the purpose of this part, the superior court shall have jurisdiction over a labor organization in this state if such organization maintains its principal office in this state, or if its duly authorized officers or agents are engaged in representing or acting for employee members. *(Added by Stats.1975, 3rd Ex. Sess., c. 1, p. 4013, § 2.)*

§ 1165.3.   Service of process

The service of summons, subpoena, or other legal process of any superior court upon an officer or agent of a labor organization, in his capacity as such, shall constitute service upon the labor organization. *(Added by Stats.1975, 3rd Ex. Sess., c. 1, p. 4013, § 2.)*

§ 1165.4.   Agency; authorized or ratified acts

For the purpose of this part, in determining whether any person is acting as an agent of another person so as to make such other person responsible for his acts, the question of whether the specific acts performed were actually authorized or subsequently ratified shall not be controlling. *(Added by Stats.1975, 3rd Ex. Sess., c. 1, p. 4013, § 2.)*

CHAPTER 8.   LIMITATIONS

Section
1166.   Right to strike.

Section
1166.2. Supervisors; status.
1166.3. Severability.

§ 1166. Right to strike

Nothing in this part, except as specifically provided for herein, shall be construed so as either to interfere with or impede or diminish in any way the right to strike, or to affect the limitations or qualifications on such right. *(Added by Stats.1975, 3rd Ex. Sess., c. 1, p. 4013, § 2.)*

§ 1166.2. Supervisors; status

Nothing in this part shall prohibit any individual employed as a supervisor from becoming or remaining a member of a labor organization, but no employer subject to this part shall be compelled to deem individuals defined herein as supervisors as employees for the purpose of any law, either national or local, relating to collective bargaining. *(Added by Stats.1975, 3rd Ex. Sess., c. 1, p. 4013, § 2.)*

§ 1166.3. Severability

(a) If any provision of this part, or the application of such provision to any person or circumstances, shall be held invalid, the remainder of this part, or the application of such provision to persons or circumstances other than those as to which it is held invalid, shall not be affected thereby.

(b) If any other act of the Legislature shall conflict with the provisions of this part, this part shall prevail. *(Added by Stats.1975, 3rd Ex. Sess., c. 1, p. 4013, § 2.)*

Part 4

EMPLOYEES

Chapter   **Section**
1. Wages, Hours and Working Conditions 1171
2. Occupational Privileges and Restrictions..........1250
3. Working Hours 1350
4. Relocations, Terminations, and Mass Lay-
        offs......................................1400

CHAPTER 1. WAGES, HOURS AND WORKING CONDITIONS

Section
1171.   Scope of chapter.
1171.5.   Legislative findings and declarations; immigration
            status; severability.
1173.   Duties of industrial welfare commission.
1174.   Duties of employers.
1174.5.   Failure to maintain records; penalties.
1175.   Violation of employer's duties; misdemeanor.
1176.   Witnesses; subpenas; enforcement.
1176.1.   Petition; adoption, amendment, or repeal of a
            regulation.
1176.3.   Petition; notice to petitioner; consideration; writ-
            ten decision; reconsideration; final actions.
1177.   Rules of practice and procedure.
1178.   Investigation; findings; selection of wage board.

1178.5.   Inadequate wages, hours or conditions of labor;
            selection of wage board; report and recommenda-
            tion; proposed regulations; hearing.
1179.   Compensation and traveling expenses of wage board
            members; powers and jurisdiction of commission.
1180.   Record of wage board proceeding; admissibility in
            evidence.
1181.   Notice of hearing on order; publication; mailing;
            contents.
1182.   Amendment, rescission or promulgation of orders;
            order for increased minimum wage.
1182.1.   Publication of action taken pursuant to §§ 517 and
            1182.
1182.4.   Student employee, camp counselor or program
            counselor of organized camp; compensation; val-
            ue of meals and lodging.
1182.5.   Preexisting workweek arrangements; petition for
            review and modification; stay of order; condi-
            tions for certification.
1182.6.   Preexisting workweek arrangements; voluntary
            agreements for workweeks including 12-hour
            days; application of section; limitation.
1182.7.   Petitions for review and modification; orders regu-
            lating health care industry; procedure.
1182.8.   Resident apartment managers; charges for apart-
            ment supplied.
1182.11. Minimum wage for all industries; amount; adoption
            of minimum wage orders.
1182.12. Minimum wage as of January 1, 2007, and as of
            January 1, 2008.
1182.13. Permissible meals and lodging credit adjustment;
            amendment and republication of Industrial Wel-
            fare Commission's wage orders; employer posting
            of copy of amended republished order; finality
            and conclusiveness of amended and republished
            wage orders.
1183.   Delivery of copies of orders to employers; posting
            requirements.
1184.   Effective date of action taken pursuant to Section
            1182.
1185.   Validity and operation of orders.
1186.   Pharmacy practitioners; exemption from Industrial
            Welfare Commission orders.
1186.5.   Pharmacy practitioners employed in mercantile in-
            dustry; adoption of alternative workweek sched-
            ule.
1187.   Findings of fact.
1188.   Rehearing.
1190.   Judicial review.
1191.   Special license for mentally or physically handi-
            capped.
1191.5.   Sheltered workshop or rehabilitation facility; special
            license.
1192.   Special license for apprentices and learners.
1193.   Maximum number of employed special licensees.
1193.5.   Administration and enforcement; authority of au-
            thorized representatives; unpaid minimum or
            overtime wages; disposition.
1193.6.   Action to recover minimum wage compensation,
            interest, attorney's fees and costs by department
            or division.
1194.   Action to recover minimum wage, overtime compen-
            sation, interest, attorney's fees, and costs by
            employee.
1194.2.   Liquidated damages.

Section

1194.5.   Injunction against violation of laws governing wages, hours or working conditions.

1195.   Registration of complaints with division; investigation; enforcement of minimum wage.

1195.5.   Determination of computation and payment of wages in excess of minimum; examination of records; enforcement of payment of unpaid sums.

1197.   Payment of less than minimum wage.

1197.1.   Payment of less than minimum wage; civil penalty; citation; hearing; notice of decision; enforcement.

1197.5.   Equal wage rates for all employees; variations; enforcement.

1198.   Maximum hours of work; standard conditions of labor; employment in violation.

1198.3.   Mandatory days off requirements; exemption for hardship.

1198.4.   Enforcement policy statements or interpretations of orders; availability.

1198.5.   Right to inspect records.

1199.   Misdemeanors; punishment.

1199.5.   Misdemeanors; fines not more than $10,000; imprisonment not more than six months.

1200.   Presumption of lawfulness of minimum wages, maximum hours, and standard conditions.

1201.   Board of arbitration; commission.

1202.   Collection of statistics and investigations by division of labor statistics and research.

1203.   Publication of reports and bulletins.

1204.   Prerequisites to effectiveness of order.

1205.   Exercise of local police powers with respect to labor standards; state agencies and local jurisdictions.

§ 1171.   Scope of chapter

The provisions of this chapter shall apply to and include men, women and minors employed in any occupation, trade, or industry, whether compensation is measured by time, piece, or otherwise, but shall not include any individual employed as an outside salesman or any individual participating in a national service program carried out using assistance provided under Section 12571 of Title 42 of the United States Code.

Any individual participating in a national service program pursuant to Section 12571 of Title 42 of the United States Code shall be informed by the nonprofit, educational institution or other entity using his or her service, prior to the commencement of service of the requirement, if any, to work hours in excess of eight hours per day, or 40 hours per week, or both, and shall have the opportunity to opt out of that national service program at that time. Individuals participating in a national service program pursuant to Section 12571 of Title 42 of the United States Code shall not be discriminated against or be denied continued participation in the program for refusing to work overtime for a legitimate reason. *(Stats. 1937, c. 90, p. 213, § 1171. Amended by Stats.1972, c. 1122, p. 2153, § 2; Stats.2000, c. 365 (S.B.945), § 3.)*

§ 1171.5.   Legislative findings and declarations; immigration status; severability

The Legislature finds and declares the following:

(a) All protections, rights, and remedies available under state law, except any reinstatement remedy prohibited by federal law, are available to all individuals regardless of immigration status who have applied for employment, or who are or who have been employed, in this state.

(b) For purposes of enforcing state labor and employment laws, a person's immigration status is irrelevant to the issue of liability, and in proceedings or discovery undertaken to enforce those state laws no inquiry shall be permitted into a person's immigration status except where the person seeking to make this inquiry has shown by clear and convincing evidence that the inquiry is necessary in order to comply with federal immigration law.

(c) The provisions of this section are declaratory of existing law.

(d) The provisions of this section are severable. If any provision of this section or its application is held invalid, that invalidity shall not affect other provisions or applications that can be given effect without the invalid provision or application. *(Added by Stats.2002, c. 1071 (S.B.1818), § 4.)*

§ 1173.   Duties of industrial welfare commission

It is the continuing duty of the Industrial Welfare Commission, hereinafter referred to in this chapter as the commission, to ascertain the wages paid to all employees in this state, to ascertain the hours and conditions of labor and employment in the various occupations, trades, and industries in which employees are employed in this state, and to investigate the health, safety, and welfare of those employees.

The commission shall conduct a full review of the adequacy of the minimum wage at least once every two years. The commission may, upon its own motion or upon petition, amend or rescind any order or portion of any order or adopt an order covering any occupation, trade, or industry not covered by an existing order pursuant to this chapter.

Before adopting any new rules, regulations, or policies, the commission shall consult with the Occupational Safety and Health Standards Board to determine those areas and subject matters where the respective jurisdictions of the commission and the Occupational Safety and Health Standards Board overlap. This consultation need not take the form of a joint meeting. In the case of such overlapping jurisdiction, the Occupational Safety and Health Standards Board shall have exclusive jurisdiction, and rules, regulations, or policies of the commission on the same subject have no force or effect. *(Stats.1937, c. 90, p. 213, § 1173. Amended by Stats.1972, c. 1122, p. 2153, § 3; Stats.1973, c. 1007, p. 2002, § 1.5; Stats.1980, c. 676, p. 1967, § 216; Stats.1980, c. 1083, p. 3464, § 5; Stats.1998, c. 150 (A.B.1307), § 1.)*

§ 1174.   Duties of employers

Every person employing labor in this state shall:

(a) Furnish to the commission, at its request, reports or information that the commission requires to carry out this chapter. The reports and information shall be verified if required by the commission or any member thereof.

(b) Allow any member of the commission or the employees of the Division of Labor Standards Enforcement free access to the place of business or employment of the person to secure any information or make any investigation that they are authorized by this chapter to ascertain or make. The commission may inspect or make excerpts, relating to the employment of employees, from the books, reports, contracts, payrolls, documents, or papers of the person.

(c) Keep a record showing the names and addresses of all employees employed and the ages of all minors.

(d) Keep, at a central location in the state or at the plants or establishments at which employees are employed, payroll records showing the hours worked daily by and the wages paid to, and the number of piece-rate units earned by and any applicable piece rate paid to, employees employed at the respective plants or establishments. These records shall be kept in accordance with rules established for this purpose by the commission, but in any case shall be kept on file for not less than two years. *(Stats.1937, c. 90, p. 213, § 1174. Amended by Stats.1945, c. 1431, p. 2690, § 34; Stats.1972, c. 1122, p. 2153, § 4; Stats.1979, c. 373, p. 1346, § 227; Stats.1990, c. 1379 (A.B.119), § 1; Stats.2000, c. 876 (A.B.2509), § 10.)*

§ 1174.5. Failure to maintain records; penalties

Any person employing labor who willfully fails to maintain the records required by subdivision (c) of Section 1174 or accurate and complete records required by subdivision (d) of Section 1174, or to allow any member of the commission or employee of the division to inspect records pursuant to subdivision (b) of Section 1174, shall be subject to a civil penalty of five hundred dollars ($500). *(Added by Stats.1990, c. 1379 (A.B.119), § 2. Amended by Stats.2000, c. 135 (A.B.2539), § 123.)*

§ 1175. Violation of employer's duties; misdemeanor

Any person, or officer or agent thereof, is guilty of a misdemeanor who:

(a) Neglects or refuses to furnish the information requested under the provisions of Section 1174.

(b) Refuses access to his place of business or employment to any member of the commission or employee of the Division of Labor Standards Enforcement when administering or enforcing this chapter.

(c) Hinders such member, or employee in securing information authorized by Section 1174.

(d) Fails to keep any of the records required by Section 1174. *(Stats.1937, c. 90, p. 214, § 1175. Amended by Stats.1945, c. 1431, p. 2691, § 35; Stats.1979, c. 373, p. 1347, § 228.)*

§ 1176. Witnesses; subpenas; enforcement

The commission or any members thereof may subpena witnesses and administer oaths. All witnesses subpenaed by the commission shall be paid the fees and mileage fixed by law in civil cases. In case of the failure of a person to comply with an order or subpena of the commission or any member thereof, or in the case of the refusal of a witness to testify to any matter regarding which he may lawfully be interrogated before any wage board or the commission, it shall be the duty of the superior court or judge thereof, on the application of a member of the commission, to compel obedience in a manner by which such obedience could be compelled in a proceeding pending before the court. *(Formerly § 1177, Stats.1937, c. 90, p. 214, § 1177. Renumbered § 1176 and amended by Stats.1949, c. 1454, p. 2535, § 2.)*

§ 1176.1. Petition; adoption, amendment, or repeal of a regulation

Any interested party may petition the commission requesting the adoption, amendment, or repeal of a regulation. The petition shall state clearly and concisely all of the following:

(a) The substance or nature of the regulation, amendment, or repeal that is requested.

(b) The reason for the request.

(c) Reference to the commission's authority to take the action that is requested. *(Added by Stats.1987, c. 863, § 1.)*

§ 1176.3. Petition; notice to petitioner; consideration; written decision; reconsideration; final actions

(a) Within 120 days of the receipt of a petition requesting the adoption, amendment, or repeal of a regulation, the commission shall notify the petitioner in writing of the receipt of the petition, set the matter for consideration at a public meeting, and issue a written decision taking one of the following actions:

(1) Setting the matter for public hearing pursuant to Section 1178 or 1178.5.

(2) Denying the petition. A decision denying a petition shall include a statement explaining the reasons for the denial.

(b) The petitioner may request reconsideration of any part or all of a decision denying a petition pursuant to paragraph (2) of subdivision (a) of Section 1176.3. The commission's reconsideration of any matter relating to a petition shall be subject to subdivision (a), except that a decision to deny reconsideration shall be final.

(c) In cases where a petition is referred to a wage board, the commission shall complete its final actions on the petition within 90 days after completion of the public hearing process pursuant to subdivision (c) of Section 1178.5. *(Added by Stats.1987, c. 863, § 2.)*

§ 1177. Rules of practice and procedure

(a) The commission may make and enforce rules of practice and procedure and shall not be bound by the rules of evidence. Each order of the commission shall be concurred in by a majority of the commissioners.

(b) The commission shall prepare a statement as to the basis upon which an adopted or amended order is predicated. The statement shall be concurred in by a majority of the commissioners. The commission shall publish a copy of the statement with the order in the California Regulatory Notice Register. The commission also shall provide a copy of the statement to any interested party upon request. *(Formerly § 1178, Stats. 1937, c. 90, p. 214, § 1178. Renumbered § 1177 and amended by Stats.1949, c. 1454, p. 2535, § 3; Stats.1969, c. 1218, p. 2359, § 2. Amended by Stats.1998, c. 150 (A.B.1307), § 2.)*

§ 1178. Investigation; findings; selection of wage board

If after investigation the commission finds that in any occupation, trade, or industry, the wages paid to employees may be inadequate to supply the cost of proper living, or that the hours or conditions of labor may be prejudicial to the health, morals, or welfare of employees, the commission shall select a wage board to consider any of such matters and transmit to such wage board the information supporting its findings gathered in the investigation. Such investigation shall include at least one public hearing. *(Formerly § 1179, Stats.1937, c. 90, p. 214, § 1179. Renumbered § 1178 and amended by Stats. 1949, c. 1454, p. 2536, § 4; Stats.1965, c. 631, p. 1972, § 1; Stats.1972, c. 1122, p. 2153, § 5; Stats.1973, c. 1007, p. 2002, § 2; Stats.1980, c. 1083, p. 3465, § 6.)*

§ 1178.5. Inadequate wages, hours or conditions of labor; selection of wage board; report and recommendation; proposed regulations; hearing

(a) If the commission finds that wages paid to employees may be inadequate to supply the cost of proper living, it shall select one wage board composed of an equal number of representatives of employers and employees, and a nonvoting representative of the commission, designated by the commission, who shall act as chairperson. The wage board shall consider the findings of the commission and such other information it deems appropriate and report to the commission its recommendation of a minimum wage adequate to supply the necessary cost of proper living to, and maintain the health and welfare of employees in this state, and its recommendations on such other matters related to the minimum wage on which the commission has requested recommendations.

(b) If the commission finds that hours or conditions of labor may be prejudicial to the health or welfare of employees in any occupation, trade, or industry, it shall select a wage board composed of an equal number of representatives of employers and employees in the occupation, trade, or industry in question, and a nonvoting

representative of the commission, designated by the commission, who shall act as chairperson. The wage board shall consider the findings of the commission and such other information it deems appropriate and report to the commission its recommendation as to what action should be taken by the commission with respect to the matter under consideration.

(c) Prior to amending or rescinding any existing order or adopting any new order, and after receipt of the wage board report and recommendation, the commission shall prepare proposed regulations with respect to the matter under consideration. The proposed regulations shall include any recommendation of the wage board which received the support of at least two-thirds of the members of the wage board. A public hearing on the proposed regulations shall be held in each of at least three cities in this state, except when the proposed regulations would affect only an occupation, trade, or industry which is not statewide in scope, in which case a public hearing shall be held in the locality in which the occupation, trade, or industry prevails. The proceedings shall be recorded and transcribed and shall thereafter be a matter of public record. *(Added by Stats.1980, c. 1083, p. 3465, § 8.)*

§ 1179. Compensation and traveling expenses of wage board members; powers and jurisdiction of commission

The members of the wage board shall be allowed fifty dollars ($50) per diem and necessary traveling expenses while engaged in such conferences. The commission shall make rules governing the number and selection of the members and the mode of procedure of the wage board, and shall exercise exclusive jurisdiction over all questions as to the validity of the procedure. *(Formerly § 1180, enacted by Stats.1937, c. 90, p. 214, § 1180. Amended by Stats.1947, c. 1188, p. 2671, § 1.5. Renumbered § 1179 and amended by Stats.1949, c. 1454, p. 2536, § 5; Stats.1980, c. 1083, p. 3466, § 9.)*

§ 1180. Record of wage board proceeding; admissibility in evidence

The proceedings and deliberations of the wage board shall be made a matter of record for the use of the commission, and shall be admissible as evidence in any proceedings before the commission. *(Formerly § 1181, Stats.1937, c. 90, p. 214, § 1181. Renumbered § 1180 and amended by Stats.1949, c. 1454, p. 2536, § 6.)*

§ 1181. Notice of hearing on order; publication; mailing; contents

Upon the fixing of the time and place for the holding of a hearing for the purpose of considering and acting upon the proposed regulations or any matters referred to in Sections 1176 to 1180, inclusive, the commission shall:

(a) Give public notice thereof by advertisement in at least one newspaper published in each of the cities of Los Angeles, Oakland, Sacramento, San Jose, Fresno, Eureka, San Diego, Long Beach, Alameda, Berkeley, Stockton, San Bernardino, and San Francisco.

(b) Mail a copy of the notice and the proposed regulations to the clerk of the superior court of each county in the state to be posted at the courthouse; to each association of employers or employees which, in the opinion of the commission, would be affected by the hearing; and to any person or organization within this state filing with the commission a written request for notice of such hearing. Failure to mail such notice shall not invalidate any order of the commission issued after such hearing.

The notice shall also state the time and place fixed for the hearing, which shall not be less than 30 days from the date of publication and mailing of such notices. *(Formerly § 1183, enacted by Stats.1937, c. 90, p. 215, § 1183. Amended by Stats.1945, c. 1431, p. 2691, § 36. Renumbered § 1181 and amended by Stats.1949, c. 1454, p. 2537, § 8; Stats.1965, c. 631, p. 1972, § 2; Stats.1980, c. 1083, p. 3466, § 10. Amended by Stats.2002, c. 784 (S.B.1316), § 523.)*

§ 1182. Amendment, rescission or promulgation of orders; order for increased minimum wage

(a) After receipt of the wage board report and the public hearings on the proposed regulations, the commission may, upon its own motion, amend or rescind an existing order or promulgate a new order. However, with respect to proposed regulations based on recommendations supported by at least two-thirds of the members of the wage board, the commission shall adopt such proposed regulations, unless it finds there is no substantial evidence to support such recommendations.

(b) If at any time the federal minimum wage applicable to employees covered by the Fair Labor Standards Act of 1938, as amended, prior to February 1, 1967, is scheduled to exceed the minimum wage fixed by the commission, the provisions of Sections 1178 and 1178.5 pertaining to wage boards shall be waived and the commission shall, in a public meeting, adopt an order fixing a new minimum wage at the scheduled higher federal minimum wage. The effective date of such order shall be the same as the effective date of the federal minimum wage, and such order shall not become operative in the event the scheduled increase in the federal minimum wage does not become operative. *(Added by Stats.1980, c. 1083, p. 3466, § 12.)*

§ 1182.1. Publication of action taken pursuant to §§ 517 and 1182

Any action taken by the commission pursuant to Sections 517 and 1182 shall be published in at least one newspaper in each of the Cities of Los Angeles, Sacramento, Oakland, San Jose, Fresno, San Diego, and San Francisco. A summary of the action taken and notice of where the complete text of the new or amended order may be obtained may be published in lieu of the complete text when the commission determines such summary and notice will adequately inform the public. The statement as to the basis of the order need not be published.

(Added by Stats.1980, c. 1083, p. 3467, § 13. Amended by Stats.1999, c. 134 (A.B.60), § 15.)

§ 1182.4. Student employee, camp counselor or program counselor of organized camp; compensation; value of meals and lodging

(a) No student employee, camp counselor, or program counselor of an organized camp shall be subject to a minimum wage or maximum hour order of the commission if the student employee, camp counselor, or program counselor receives a weekly salary of at least 85 percent of the minimum wage for a 40-hour week, regardless of the number of hours per week the student employee, camp counselor, or program counselor might work at the organized camp. If the student employee, camp counselor, or program counselor works less than 40 hours per week, the student employee, camp counselor, or program counselor shall be paid at least 85 percent of the minimum hourly wage for each hour worked.

(b) An organized camp may deduct the value of meals and lodging from the salary of a student employee, camp counselor, or program counselor pursuant to appropriate orders of the commission.

(c) As used in this section, "organized camp" means an organized camp, as defined in Section 18897 of the Health and Safety Code, which meets the standards of the American Camping Association. *(Added by Stats.1979, c. 529, p. 1727, § 1, eff. Sept. 7, 1979. Amended by Stats.1980, c. 379, p. 755, § 1, eff. July 10, 1980.)*

§ 1182.5. Preexisting workweek arrangements; petition for review and modification; stay of order; conditions for certification

(a) The Legislature finds that the time permitted the Industrial Welfare Commission to consider daily overtime compensation petitions that are to be given priority attention by the commission pursuant to Section 20 of Chapter 1083 of the Statutes of 1980, has created unanticipated delays in the review and possible modification of applicable commission orders for preexisting workweek arrangements, as defined in subdivision (b). The Legislature finds further that legislation is necessary to provide redress of hardships resulting from these unanticipated delays by the enactment of special commission review procedures that augment, and do not limit in any way, the rights and privileges of parties before the Industrial Welfare Commission under this chapter.

(b) For purposes of this section only, a "preexisting workweek arrangement" is defined as, and limited to, a workweek arrangement that existed before November 1980, and had to be modified or abandoned by an employer because the workweek arrangement did not qualify for any exemption provided by the Industrial Welfare Commission from its daily overtime requirements for collectively bargained arrangements, and did not otherwise comply with the daily overtime requirements of an applicable commission order.

(c) An employer who has had in operation an established preexisting workweek arrangement may, prior to July 1, 1985, file a verified petition with the commission for review and modification of an applicable order and, upon filing this petition, shall simultaneously file a copy with the Labor Commissioner. Upon receipt of the petition by the Labor Commissioner a stay of enforcement of the applicable commission order as it would affect the workweek arrangement shall take effect. The Labor Commissioner may reject a petition that, on its face, cannot qualify as a preexisting workweek arrangement. Within three months of commencement of the stay the Labor Commissioner shall certify the preexisting workweek arrangement to the commission if, upon examination, the Labor Commissioner finds that all of the following conditions are met by the workweek arrangement:

(1) It was established by the petitioning employer and was in operation prior to November 1980.

(2) It had to be abandoned or modified by the employer because of noncompliance with the applicable order of the commission.

(3) It was established on a nondiscriminatory basis with the support of affected employees and it continues to have the support of two-thirds of the employees in the covered work group.

(4) It complied with all applicable standards of the commission, other than daily overtime requirements.

(5) It is found, after consultation with the Director of Industrial Relations when appropriate, not to be adverse to the health and welfare of affected employees.

In the course of examining a preexisting workweek arrangement and following certification, the Labor Commissioner shall not divert any of the resources of the Division of Labor Standards Enforcement for the purpose of investigating, prosecuting, or otherwise acting upon any alleged violations of the daily overtime provisions of an applicable commission order during any period in 1980 in which a court-issued stay of enforcement was in effect for these provisions; provided, the workweek arrangement involved was in operation during that period in good faith reliance by the employer upon the court-issued stay of enforcement and with the approval of two-thirds of the employer's affected employees.

(d) In the course of examining a petition for certification to the commission, the Labor Commissioner shall have access to all pertinent records of the petitioning employer and shall have the authority to converse with affected employees of the employer without the presence of management. Until the commission takes action on a petition, the Labor Commissioner shall retain the authority to withdraw a certification to the commission for cause.

(e) Upon receipt by the commission of the Labor Commissioner's certification of a preexisting workweek arrangement, the stay of enforcement shall continue as hereinafter provided beyond the three-month period for

396

certification until modified or rescinded by the commission. The modification or rescission shall not be made without an appropriate hearing and findings regarding the applicable order. If the commission undertakes review of the applicable order, the stay of enforcement shall continue through the review process and until any resulting modification of the applicable order, in which case, the modified order shall become applicable to the preexisting workweek arrangement. *(Added by Stats. 1981, c. 1060, p. 4086, § 1. Amended by Stats.1984, c. 869, § 1.)*

§ 1182.6. Preexisting workweek arrangements; voluntary agreements for workweeks including 12-hour days; application of section; limitation

(a) No employer who continuously operates a manufacturing facility 24 hours a day for seven days a week, and who has had in operation an established preexisting workweek arrangement, as defined in subdivision (b), shall be in violation of this code or any applicable wage order of the commission by instituting, pursuant to an agreement voluntarily executed by the employer and at least two-thirds of the affected employees before the performance of the work, a regularly scheduled workweek that includes three working days of not more than 12 hours a day, or regularly scheduled workweeks that include three working days of not more than 12 hours a day one week and four working days of not more than 12 hours a day in the following week for an average workweek of 42 hours over a two-week period.

(b) For purposes of this section only, a "preexisting workweek arrangement" is defined as, and limited to, a workweek arrangement that existed before November 1980, and had to be modified or abandoned by an employer because the workweek arrangement did not qualify for any exemption provided by the Industrial Welfare Commission from its daily overtime requirements for collectively bargained arrangements, and did not otherwise comply with the daily overtime requirements of an applicable commission order.

(c) The agreement described in subdivision (a) shall be confirmed by an affirmative vote by secret ballot by at least two-thirds of the affected employees, and may be rescinded at any time by a two-thirds vote of the affected employees. A new vote on whether the agreement described in subdivision (a) shall be continued shall be held every three years, and an affirmative vote by at least two-thirds of the affected employees shall be necessary to continue the agreement.

(d) The employer shall not be required to pay premium wage rates to employees working a schedule described in subdivision (a) unless the employee is required or permitted to work more than 12 hours in any workday, more than the scheduled three or four days in any workweek, or more than 40 hours in any workweek.

(e) This section shall not apply to any employer who is now, or in the future becomes, a party to a collective-bargaining agreement covering employees who would otherwise be covered by this section.

(f) No employee working a schedule described in subdivision (a) shall be required to work more than four consecutive days within seven consecutive days. *(Added by Stats.1982, c. 1365, p. 5237, § 1. Amended by Stats. 2006, c. 538 (S.B.1852), § 482.)*

§ 1182.7. Petitions for review and modification; orders regulating health care industry; procedure

(a) The Legislature finds that the time permitted the Industrial Welfare Commission to consider petitions, including, but not limited to, daily overtime compensation petitions that are to be given priority attention by the commission pursuant to Section 20 of Chapter 1083 of the Statutes of 1980, has created unanticipated and unwarranted delays in the review and possible modification of applicable commission orders. The Legislature finds further that legislation is necessary to provide redress of hardships resulting from these delays by the enactment of special commission review procedures that augment, and do not limit in any way, the rights and privileges of parties before the Industrial Welfare Commission under this chapter.

(b) Notwithstanding any other provisions of this chapter to the contrary, if a labor organization or a trade association recognized in the health care industry files or has filed a petition with the commission that requests an amendment to an order of the commission that would directly regulate only the health care industry, the petitioner may request that the ordinary procedure established by this chapter for the review of petitions of this nature not be used and that the procedure specified in subdivisions (c) and (d) be followed instead. If the request is made by the petitioner, the commission shall be required to follow the procedure specified in subdivisions (c) and (d).

(c) Upon the filing of a request under subdivision (b), the procedure to revise an order of the commission provided in Sections 1178 to 1182, inclusive, shall be waived. In lieu of that procedure, the commission shall propose the adoption of or may reject the petition, in whole or in part, without appointing a wage board. The commission shall act on the petition within 45 days of the date the petition is originally filed. If the commission rejects the petition, it shall state its reasons for rejection.

The commission shall thereafter conduct hearings on any proposal to adopt the petition in whole or in part in the manner specified in subdivision (c) of Section 1178.5 and publish the proposed action in the manner provided in Section 1181. However, the hearings shall be conducted within 90 days of the date the petition is originally filed.

(d) Not more than 30 days following the hearings specified in subdivision (c), the commission shall take final action with respect to its proposal. No later than 15 days following final action, notice of the action taken shall be given in the manner provided for in Sections

1182.1 and 1183. Any action adopting, amending, or repealing an order of the commission pursuant to this section shall take effect 60 days following the date of this notice.

(e) Notwithstanding any other provisions of this chapter, the commission shall not adopt, amend, or repeal a proposal which has been changed from that which has originally been made available to the public, unless the change is nonsubstantive in nature and the commission complies with the procedure specified in this subdivision.

If a substantive change is made to the original proposal after the close of the public hearing, the full text of the resulting change shall be noticed within five days and made available to the public for comments for at least 10 days before the commission adopts, amends, or repeals the regulation. No later than 10 days following the close of the public comment period, the commission shall take final action with respect to its modified proposal, and give notice of that action within 10 days in the manner provided in Sections 1182.1 and 1183. In no case shall any action adopting, amending, or repealing an order take effect more than 60 days following the close of the public comment period. *(Added by Stats.1982, c. 405, p. 1745, § 1. Amended by Stats.1986, c. 644, § 1; Stats. 1987, c. 460, § 1.)*

§ 1182.8. Resident apartment managers; charges for apartment supplied

No employer shall be in violation of any provision of any applicable order of the Industrial Welfare Commission relating to credit or charges for lodging for charging, pursuant to a voluntary written agreement, a resident apartment manager up to two-thirds of the fair market rental value of the apartment supplied to the manager, if no credit for the apartment is used to meet the employer's minimum wage obligation to the manager. *(Added by Stats.1982, c. 913, p. 3350, § 1.)*

§ 1182.11. Minimum wage for all industries; amount; adoption of minimum wage orders

Notwithstanding any other provision of this part, on and after March 1, 1997, the minimum wage for all industries shall not be less than five dollars ($5.00) per hour; on and after March 1, 1998, the minimum wage for all industries shall not be less than five dollars and seventy-five cents ($5.75) per hour. The Industrial Welfare Commission shall, at a public meeting, adopt minimum wage orders consistent with this section without convening wage boards, which wage orders shall be final and conclusive for all purposes. *(Added by Initiative Measure (Prop. 210, § 2, approved Nov. 5, 1996).)*

§ 1182.12. Minimum wage as of January 1, 2007, and as of January 1, 2008

Notwithstanding any other provision of this part, on and after January 1, 2007, the minimum wage for all industries shall be not less than seven dollars and fifty cents ($7.50) per hour, and on and after January 1, 2008, the minimum wage for all industries shall be not less than eight dollars ($8.00) per hour. *(Added by Stats.2006, c. 230 (A.B.1835), § 1.)*

§ 1182.13. Permissible meals and lodging credit adjustment; amendment and republication of Industrial Welfare Commission's wage orders; employer posting of copy of amended republished order; finality and conclusiveness of amended and republished wage orders

(a) The Department of Industrial Relations shall adjust upwards the permissible meals and lodging credits by the same percentage as the increase in the minimum wage made pursuant to Section 1182.12.

(b) The Department of Industrial Relations shall amend and republish the Industrial Welfare Commission's wage orders to be consistent with this section and Section 1182.12. The department shall make no other changes to the wage orders of the Industrial Welfare Commission that are in existence on the effective date of this section. The department shall meet the requirements set forth in Section 1183.

(c) Every employer that is subject to an amended republished order under this section shall post a copy of the order and keep it posted in a conspicuous location frequented by employees during the hours of the workday as required by Section 1183.

(d) Wage orders that are amended and republished as required under this section shall be final and conclusive for all purposes and dispositive of all pending petitions before the Industrial Welfare Commission as of the effective date of the act adding this section. Any amendment and republication pursuant to this section shall be exempt from the rulemaking provisions of the Administrative Procedure Act (Chapter 3.5 (commencing with Section 11340) of Part 1 of Division 3 of Title 2 of the Government Code), and from the procedures set forth in Sections 1177, 1178.5, 1181, 1182, and 1182.1. *(Added by Stats.2006, c. 230 (A.B.1835), § 2.)*

§ 1183. Delivery of copies of orders to employers; posting requirements

(a) So far as practicable, the commission, by mail, shall send a copy of the order authorized by Section 1182 to each employer in the occupation or industry in question, and each employer shall post a copy of the order in the building in which employees affected by the order are employed. The commission shall also send a copy of the order to each employer registering his or her name with the commission for that purpose, but failure to mail the order or notice of the order to any employer affected by the order shall not relieve the employer from the duty of complying with the order.

(b) The commission shall prepare a summary of the regulations contained in its orders. The summary shall be printed on the first page of the document containing the full text of the order. The summary shall include a brief description of the following subjects of the orders: minimum wage, hours and days of work, reporting time,

pay records, cash shortages and breakage, uniforms and equipment, meals and lodging, meal and rest periods, and seats. The summary shall also include information as to how to contact the field office of the Division of Labor Standards Enforcement, how to obtain a copy of the full text of the order and the statement as to the basis for the order, and any other information the commission deems necessary. The commission, at its discretion, may prepare a separate summary for each order or any combination of orders, or it may incorporate the regulations of all its orders into a single summary.

(c) A finding by the commission that there has been publication of any action taken by the commission as required by Section 1182.1 is conclusive as to the obligation of an employer to comply with the order.

(d) Every employer who is subject to an order of the commission shall post a copy of the order and keep it posted in a conspicuous location frequented by employees during the hours of the workday. *(Added by Stats. 1998, c. 150 (A.B.1307), § 4.)*

§ 1184. Effective date of action taken pursuant to Section 1182

Any action taken by the commission pursuant to Section 1182 shall be effective on the first day of the succeeding January or July and not less than 60 days from the date of publication pursuant to Section 1182.1. *(Added by Stats.1980, c. 1083, p. 3467, § 15. Amended by Stats.1998, c. 150 (A.B.1307), § 5.)*

§ 1185. Validity and operation of orders

The orders of the commission fixing minimum wages, maximum hours, and standard conditions of labor for all employees, when promulgated in accordance with the provisions of this chapter, shall be valid and operative and such orders are hereby expressly exempted from the provisions of Article 5 (commencing with Section 11346) of Chapter 3.5 of Part 1 of Division 3 of Title 2 of the Government Code. *(Added by Stats.1949, c. 1454, p. 2538, § 12. Amended by Stats.1969, c. 213, p. 542, § 1; Stats.1972, c. 1122, p. 2155, § 8; Stats.1973, c. 1007, p. 2003, § 4; Stats.1980, c. 676, p. 1967, § 217.)*

§ 1186. Pharmacy practitioners; exemption from Industrial Welfare Commission orders

A person employed in the practice of pharmacy is not exempt from coverage under any provision of the orders of the Industrial Welfare Commission unless he or she individually meets the criteria established for exemption as executive or administrative employees. No person employed in the practice of pharmacy may be subject to any exemption from coverage under the orders of the Industrial Welfare Commission established for professional employees. *(Added by Stats.1999, c. 190 (S.B.651), § 2.)*

§ 1186.5. Pharmacy practitioners employed in mercantile industry; adoption of alternative workweek schedule

Notwithstanding any other provision of law, pharmacists engaged in the practice of pharmacy who are employed in the mercantile industry, as defined by Wage Order 7 of the Industrial Welfare Commission, shall be permitted to adopt alternative workweek schedules allowed by the provisions of Wage Order 4, including the provisions for alternative workweeks that can be adopted by employees working in the health care industry. *(Added by Stats.2007, c. 480 (S.B.812), § 1.)*

§ 1187. Findings of fact

The findings of fact made by the commission are, in the absence of fraud, conclusive. *(Stats.1937, c. 90, p. 216, § 1187.)*

§ 1188. Rehearing

Any person aggrieved directly or indirectly by any final rule or regulation of the commission made under this chapter may apply to the commission for a rehearing in respect to any matters determined or covered therein and specified in the application for rehearing within 20 days after the publication thereof. The application for rehearing shall be verified and shall state fully the grounds upon which the application for rehearing is based. The commission upon considering an application for rehearing may grant the same by order and notice thereof given by mail to the party applying for the rehearing, and fix a time for the rehearing and reconsider its order, rule, or regulation. The commission may redetermine the matter upon the record before it and give notice of its redetermination in the same manner as provided for service of an original order, rule, or regulation. The commission may deny such rehearing upon the record before it, giving notice of its decision by mail to the applicant therefor. Such rehearing is deemed to be denied unless acted upon by the commission within thirty days after being filed. *(Stats.1937, c. 90, p. 216, § 1188.)*

§ 1190. Judicial review

Nothing in this chapter shall prevent a review or other action permitted by the Constitution and laws of this State by a court of competent jurisdiction with reference to any order, rule, or regulation of the commission under this chapter. *(Stats.1937, c. 90, p. 216, § 1190.)*

§ 1191. Special license for mentally or physically handicapped

For any occupation in which a minimum wage has been established, the commission may issue to an employee who is mentally or physically handicapped, or both, a special license authorizing the employment of the licensee for a period not to exceed one year from date of issue, at a wage less than the legal minimum wage. The commission shall fix a special minimum wage for the licensee. Such license may be renewed on a yearly basis.

(Stats.1937, c. 90, p. 217, § 1191. Amended by Stats.1961, c. 543, p. 1654, § 1; Stats.1972, c. 1122, p. 2155, § 9.)

§ 1191.5. Sheltered workshop or rehabilitation facility; special license

Notwithstanding the provisions of Section 1191, the commission may issue a special license to a nonprofit organization such as a sheltered workshop or rehabilitation facility to permit the employment of employees who have been determined by the commission to meet the requirements in Section 1191 without requiring individual licenses of such employees. The commission shall fix a special minimum wage for such employees. The special license for the nonprofit corporation shall be renewed on a yearly basis, or more frequently as determined by the commission. *(Added by Stats.1970, c. 1081, p. 1922, § 1. Amended by Stats.1973, c. 213, p. 631, § 1; Stats.1973, c. 1007, p. 2004, § 5.)*

§ 1192. Special license for apprentices and learners

For any occupation in which a minimum wage has been established, the commission may issue to an apprentice or learner a special license authorizing the employment of such apprentice or learner for the time and under the conditions which the commission determines and at a wage less than the legal minimum wage. The commission shall fix a special wage for such apprentice or learner. *(Stats.1937, c. 90, p. 217, § 1192.)*

§ 1193. Maximum number of employed special licensees

The commission may fix the maximum number of employees to be employed under the licenses provided for in Sections 1191 and 1192 in any occupation, trade, industry, or establishment in which a minimum wage has been established. *(Stats.1937, c. 90, p. 217, § 1193. Amended by Stats.1972, c. 1122, p. 2155, § 10.)*

§ 1193.5. Administration and enforcement; authority of authorized representatives; unpaid minimum or overtime wages; disposition

The provisions of this chapter shall be administered and enforced by the division. Any authorized representative of the division shall have authority to:

(a) Investigate and ascertain the wages of all employees, and the hours and working conditions of all employees employed in any occupation in the state;

(b) Supervise the payment of unpaid minimum wages or unpaid overtime compensation owing to any employee under the provisions of this chapter or the orders of the commission. Acceptance of payment of sums found to be due on demand of the division shall constitute a waiver on the part of the employee of his or her cause of action under Section 1194.

Unpaid minimum wages or unpaid overtime wages recovered by the division under the provisions of this section which for any reason cannot be delivered within six months from date of collection to the employee for whom such wages were collected shall be deposited into the Industrial Relations Unpaid Wage Fund in the State Treasury. *(Added by Stats.1961, c. 408, p. 1479, § 1. Amended by Stats.1965, c. 254, p. 1240, § 1; Stats.1968, c. 1343, p. 2563, § 1; Stats.1972, c. 1122, p. 2155, § 11; Stats.1973, c. 1007, p. 2004, § 6; Stats.1980, c. 1083, p. 3467, § 17.)*

§ 1193.6. Action to recover minimum wage compensation, interest, attorney's fees and costs by department or division

(a) The department or division may, with or without the consent of the employee or employees affected, commence and prosecute a civil action to recover unpaid minimum wages or unpaid overtime compensation, including interest thereon, owing to any employee under this chapter or the orders of the commission, and, in addition to these wages, compensation, and interest, shall be awarded reasonable attorney's fees, and costs of suit. The consent of any employee to the bringing of this action shall constitute a waiver on the part of the employee of his or her cause of action under Section 1194 unless the action is dismissed without prejudice by the department or the division.

(b) The amendments made to this section by Chapter 825 of the Statutes of 1991 shall apply only to civil actions commenced on or after January 1, 1992. *(Added by Stats.1961, c. 408, p. 1479, § 2. Amended by Stats.1972, c. 1122, p. 2155, § 12; Stats.1973, c. 1007, p. 2004, § 7; Stats.1991, c. 825 (S.B.955), § 1; Stats.1992, c. 427 (A.B.3355), § 119.)*

§ 1194. Action to recover minimum wage, overtime compensation, interest, attorney's fees, and costs by employee

(a) Notwithstanding any agreement to work for a lesser wage, any employee receiving less than the legal minimum wage or the legal overtime compensation applicable to the employee is entitled to recover in a civil action the unpaid balance of the full amount of this minimum wage or overtime compensation, including interest thereon, reasonable attorney's fees, and costs of suit.

(b) The amendments made to this section by Chapter 825 of the Statutes of 1991 shall apply only to civil actions commenced on or after January 1, 1992. *(Stats.1937, c. 90, p. 217, § 1194. Amended by Stats.1961, c. 408, p. 1479, § 3; Stats.1972, c. 1122, p. 2156, § 13; Stats.1973, c. 1007, p. 2004, § 8; Stats.1991, c. 825 (S.B.955), § 2; Stats.1992, c. 427 (A.B.3355), § 120.)*

§ 1194.2. Liquidated damages

(a) In any action under Section 1193.6 or Section 1194 to recover wages because of the payment of a wage less than the minimum wage fixed by an order of the commission, an employee shall be entitled to recover liquidated damages in an amount equal to the wages unlawfully unpaid and interest thereon. Nothing in this subdivision shall be construed to authorize the recovery

of liquidated damages for failure to pay overtime compensation.

(b) Notwithstanding subdivision (a), if the employer demonstrates to the satisfaction of the court that the act or omission giving rise to the action was in good faith and that the employer had reasonable grounds for believing that the act or omission was not a violation of any provision of the Labor Code relating to minimum wage, or an order of the commission, the court may, in its discretion, refuse to award liquidated damages or award any amount of liquidated damages not exceeding the amount specified in subdivision (a).

(c) This section only shall apply to civil actions commenced on or after January 1, 1992. *(Added by Stats. 1991, c. 825 (S.B.955), § 3.)*

§ 1194.5. Injunction against violation of laws governing wages, hours or working conditions

In any case in which a person employing an employee has willfully violated any of the laws, regulations, or orders governing the wages, hours of work, or working conditions of such employee, the division may seek, in a court of competent jurisdiction, and the court may grant, an injunction against any further violations of any such laws, regulations, or orders by such person. *(Added by Stats.1961, c. 408, p. 1479, § 4. Amended by Stats.1972, c. 1122, p. 2156, § 14.)*

§ 1195. Registration of complaints with division; investigation; enforcement of minimum wage

Any person may register with the Division of Labor Standards Enforcement a complaint that the wage paid to an employee for whom a minimum wage has been fixed by the commission is less than that rate. The division shall investigate the matter and take all proceedings necessary to enforce the payment of a wage not less than the minimum wage. *(Stats.1937, c. 90, p. 217, § 1195. Amended by Stats.1972, c. 1122, p. 2156, § 15; Stats.1979, c. 373, p. 1347, § 229.)*

§ 1195.5. Determination of computation and payment of wages in excess of minimum; examination of records; enforcement of payment of unpaid sums

The Division of Labor Standards Enforcement shall determine, upon request, whether the wages of employees, which exceed the minimum wages fixed by the commission, have been correctly computed and paid. For this purpose, the division may examine the books, reports, contracts, payrolls and other documents of the employer relative to the employment of employees. The division shall enforce the payment of any sums found, upon examination, to be due and unpaid to the employees. *(Added by Stats.1943, c. 425, p. 1961, § 1. Amended by Stats.1972, c. 1122, p. 2156, § 16; Stats.1976, c. 1184, p. 5288, § 1.)*

§ 1197. Payment of less than minimum wage

The minimum wage for employees fixed by the commission is the minimum wage to be paid to employees, and the payment of a less wage than the minimum so fixed is unlawful. *(Stats.1937, c. 90, p. 217, § 1197. Amended by Stats.1972, c. 1122, p. 2156, § 17.)*

§ 1197.1. Payment of less than minimum wage; civil penalty; citation; hearing; notice of decision; enforcement

(a) Any employer or other person acting either individually or as an officer, agent, or employee of another person, who pays or causes to be paid to any employee a wage less than the minimum fixed by an order of the commission shall be subject to a civil penalty as follows:

(1) For any initial violation that is intentionally committed, one hundred dollars ($100) for each underpaid employee for each pay period for which the employee is underpaid.

(2) For each subsequent violation for the same specific offense, two hundred fifty dollars ($250) for each underpaid employee for each pay period for which the employee is underpaid regardless of whether the initial violation is intentionally committed.

(b) If, upon inspection or investigation, the Labor Commissioner determines that a person has paid or caused to be paid a wage less than the minimum, the Labor Commissioner may issue a citation to the person in violation. The citation may be served personally or by registered mail in accordance with subdivision (c) of Section 11505 of the Government Code. Each citation shall be in writing and shall describe the nature of the violation, including reference to the statutory provision alleged to have been violated. The Labor Commissioner promptly shall take all appropriate action, in accordance with this section, to enforce the citation and to recover the civil penalty assessed in connection with the citation.

(c) If a person desires to contest a citation or the proposed assessment of a civil penalty therefor, the person shall, within 15 business days after service of the citation, notify the office of the Labor Commissioner that appears on the citation of his or her request for an informal hearing. The Labor Commissioner or his or her deputy or agent shall, within 30 days, hold a hearing at the conclusion of which the citation or proposed assessment of a civil penalty shall be affirmed, modified, or dismissed.

The decision of the Labor Commissioner shall consist of a notice of findings, findings, and an order, all of which shall be served on all parties to the hearing within 15 days after the hearing by regular first-class mail at the last known address of the party on file with the Labor Commissioner. Service shall be completed pursuant to Section 1013 of the Code of Civil Procedure. Any amount found due by the Labor Commissioner as a result of a hearing shall become due and payable 45 days after notice of the findings and written findings and order have been mailed to the party assessed. A writ of mandate may be taken from this finding to the appropriate superior court. The party shall pay any judgment and costs ultimately rendered by the court against the party

for the assessment. The writ shall be taken within 45 days of service of the notice of findings, findings, and order thereon.

(d) A person to whom a citation has been issued shall, in lieu of contesting a citation pursuant to this section, transmit to the office of the Labor Commissioner designated on the citation the amount specified for the violation within 15 business days after issuance of the citation.

(e) When no petition objecting to a citation or the proposed assessment of a civil penalty is filed, a certified copy of the citation or proposed civil penalty may be filed by the Labor Commissioner in the office of the clerk of the superior court in any county in which the person assessed has or had a place of business. The clerk, immediately upon the filing, shall enter judgment for the state against the person assessed in the amount shown on the citation or proposed assessment of a civil penalty.

(f) When findings and the order thereon are made affirming or modifying a citation or proposed assessment of a civil penalty after hearing, a certified copy of these findings and the order entered thereon may be entered by the Labor Commissioner in the office of the clerk of the superior court in any county in which the person assessed has property or in which the person assessed has or had a place of business. The clerk, immediately upon the filing, shall enter judgment for the state against the person assessed in the amount shown on the certified order.

(g) A judgment entered pursuant to this section shall bear the same rate of interest and shall have the same effect as other judgments and be given the same preference allowed by the law on other judgments rendered for claims for taxes. The clerk shall make no charge for the service provided by this section to be performed by him or her.

(h) The civil penalties provided for in this section are in addition to any other penalty provided by law.

(i) This section shall not apply to any order of the commission relating to household occupations. *(Added by Stats.1983, c. 1145, § 1. Amended by Stats.1995, c. 393 (A.B.1870), § 1; Stats.1997, c. 35 (A.B.1448), § 1; Stats. 2003, c. 329 (A.B.276), § 8.)*

§ 1197.5. Equal wage rates for all employees; variations; enforcement

(a) No employer shall pay any individual in the employer's employ at wage rates less than the rates paid to employees of the opposite sex in the same establishment for equal work on jobs the performance of which requires equal skill, effort, and responsibility, and which are performed under similar working conditions, except where the payment is made pursuant to a seniority system, a merit system, a system which measures earnings by quantity or quality of production, or a differential based on any bona fide factor other than sex.

401

(b) Any employer who violates subdivision (a) is liable to the employee affected in the amount of the wages, and interest thereon, of which the employee is deprived by reason of the violation, and in an additional equal amount as liquidated damages.

(c) The provisions of this section shall be administered and enforced by the Division of Labor Standards Enforcement. If the division finds that an employer has violated this section, it may supervise the payment of wages and interest found to be due and unpaid to employees under subdivision (a). Acceptance of payment in full made by an employer and approved by the division shall constitute a waiver on the part of the employee of the employee's cause of action under subdivision (g).

(d) Every employer shall maintain records of the wages and wage rates, job classifications, and other terms and conditions of employment of the persons employed by the employer. All of the records shall be kept on file for a period of two years.

(e) Any employee may file a complaint with the division that the wages paid are less than the wages to which the employee is entitled under subdivision (a). These complaints shall be investigated as provided in subdivision (b) of Section 98.7. The name of any employee who submits to the division a complaint regarding an alleged violation of subdivision (a) shall be kept confidential by the division until validity of the complaint is established by the division, or unless the confidentiality must be abridged by the division in order to investigate the complaint. The name of the complaining employee shall remain confidential if the complaint is withdrawn before the confidentiality is abridged by the division. The division shall take all proceedings necessary to enforce the payment of any sums found to be due and unpaid to these employees.

(f) The department or division may commence and prosecute, unless otherwise requested by the employee or affected group of employees, a civil action on behalf of the employee and on behalf of a similarly affected group of employees to recover unpaid wages and liquidated damages under subdivision (a), and in addition shall be entitled to recover costs of suit. The consent of any employee to the bringing of any action shall constitute a waiver on the part of the employee of the employee's cause of action under subdivision (g) unless the action is dismissed without prejudice by the department or the division, except that the employee may intervene in the suit or may initiate independent action if the suit has not been determined within 180 days from the date of the filing of the complaint.

(g) Any employee receiving less than the wage to which the employee is entitled under this section may recover in a civil action the balance of the wages, including interest thereon, and an equal amount as liquidated damages, together with the costs of the suit and reasonable attorney's fees, notwithstanding any agreement to work for a lesser wage.

(h) A civil action to recover wages under subdivision (a) may be commenced no later than two years after the cause of action occurs, except that a cause of action arising out of a willful violation may be commenced no later than three years after the cause of action occurs.

(i) If an employee recovers amounts due the employee under subdivision (b), and also files a complaint or brings an action under subdivision (d) of Section 206 of Title 29 of the United States Code which results in an additional recovery under federal law for the same violation, the employee shall return to the employer the amounts recovered under subdivision (b), or the amounts recovered under federal law, whichever is less. *(Added by Stats.1949, c. 804, p. 1541, § 1. Amended by Stats.1957, c. 2384, p. 4130, § 1; Stats.1965, c. 825, p. 2417, § 1; Stats.1968, c. 325, p. 705, § 1; Stats.1976, c. 1184, p. 5288, § 3; Stats.1982, c. 1116, p. 4034, § 1; Stats.1985, c. 1479, § 4.)*

§ 1198. Maximum hours of work; standard conditions of labor; employment in violation

The maximum hours of work and the standard conditions of labor fixed by the commission shall be the maximum hours of work and the standard conditions of labor for employees. The employment of any employee for longer hours than those fixed by the order or under conditions of labor prohibited by the order is unlawful. *(Stats.1937, c. 90, p. 217, § 1198. Amended by Stats.1973, c. 1007, p. 2005, § 9.)*

§ 1198.3. Mandatory days off requirements; exemption for hardship

(a) The Chief of the Division of Labor Standards Enforcement may, when in his or her judgment hardship will result, exempt any employer or employees from any mandatory day or days off requirement contained in any order of the commission. Any exemption granted by the chief pursuant to this section shall be only of sufficient duration to permit the employer or employees to comply with the requirements contained in the order of the commission, but not more than one year. The exemption may be renewed by the chief only after he or she has investigated and is satisfied that a good faith effort is being made to comply with the order of the commission.

(b) No employer shall discharge or in any other manner discriminate against any employee who refuses to work hours in excess of those permitted by the order of the commission. *(Added by Stats.1979, c. 1112, p. 4046, § 1, eff. Sept. 28, 1979. Amended by Stats.1980, c. 1083, p. 3467, § 18; Stats.1980, c. 1309, p. 4432, § 3; Stats.1983, c. 659, § 1; Stats.1985, c. 620, § 1.)*

§ 1198.4. Enforcement policy statements or interpretations of orders; availability

Upon request, the Chief of the Division of Labor Standards Enforcement shall make available to the public any enforcement policy statements or interpretations of orders of the Industrial Welfare Commission. Copies of such policy statements shall be furnished to the Industrial

Welfare Commission. *(Added by Stats.1980, c. 1083, p. 3468, § 19.)*

§ 1198.5. Right to inspect records

(a) Every employee has the right to inspect the personnel records that the employer maintains relating to the employee's performance or to any grievance concerning the employee.

(b) The employer shall make the contents of those personnel records available to the employee at reasonable intervals and at reasonable times. Except as provided in paragraph (3) of subdivision (c), the employer shall not be required to make those personnel records available at a time when the employee is actually required to render service to the employer.

(c) The employer shall do one of the following:

(1) Keep a copy of each employee's personnel records at the place where the employee reports to work.

(2) Make the employee's personnel records available at the place where the employee reports to work within a reasonable period of time following an employee's request.

(3) Permit the employee to inspect the personnel records at the location where the employer stores the personnel records, with no loss of compensation to the employee.

(d) The requirements of this section shall not apply to:

(1) Records relating to the investigation of a possible criminal offense.

(2) Letters of reference.

(3) Ratings, reports, or records that were:

(A) Obtained prior to the employee's employment.

(B) Prepared by identifiable examination committee members.

(C) Obtained in connection with a promotional examination.

(4) Employees who are subject to the Public Safety Officers Procedural Bill of Rights, Chapter 9.7 (commencing with Section 3300) of Division 4 of Title 1 of the Government Code.

(5) Employees of agencies subject to the Information Practices Act of 1977 (Title 1.8 (commencing with Section 1798) of Part 4 of Division 3 of the Civil Code).

(e) The Labor Commissioner may adopt regulations that determine the reasonable times and reasonable intervals for the inspection of records maintained by an employer that is not a public agency.

(f) If a public agency has established an independent employee relations board or commission, an employee shall first seek relief regarding any matter or dispute relating to this section from that board or commission before pursuing any available judicial remedy.

(g) In enacting this section, it is the intent of the Legislature to establish minimum standards for the inspection of personnel records by employees. Nothing in this section shall be construed to prevent the establishment of additional rules for the inspection of personnel records that are established as the result of agreements between an employer and a recognized employee organization. *(Added by Stats.2000, c. 886 (S.B.1327), § 11.)*

§ 1199. Misdemeanors; punishment

Every employer or other person acting either individually or as an officer, agent, or employee of another person is guilty of a misdemeanor and is punishable by a fine of not less than one hundred dollars ($100) or by imprisonment for not less than 30 days, or by both, who does any of the following:

(a) Requires or causes any employee to work for longer hours than those fixed, or under conditions of labor prohibited by an order of the commission.

(b) Pays or causes to be paid to any employee a wage less than the minimum fixed by an order of the commission.

(c) Violates or refuses or neglects to comply with any provision of this chapter or any order or ruling of the commission. *(Stats.1937, c. 90, p. 217, § 1199. Amended by Stats.1965, c. 825, p. 2418, § 2; Stats.1968, c. 325, p. 706, § 2; Stats.1972, c. 1122, p. 2157, § 18; Stats.1973, c. 1007, p. 2005, § 10; Stats.1982, c. 1116, p. 4036, § 2; Stats.1983, c. 1092, § 205, eff. Sept. 27, 1983, operative Jan. 1, 1984.)*

§ 1199.5. Misdemeanors; fines not more than $10,000; imprisonment not more than six months

Every employer or other person acting either individually or as an officer, agent, or employee of another person is guilty of a misdemeanor and is punishable by a fine of not more than ten thousand dollars ($10,000), or by imprisonment for not more than six months, or by both, who willfully does any of the following:

(a) Pays or causes to be paid any employee a wage less than the rate paid to an employee of the opposite sex as required by Section 1197.5.

(b) Reduces the wages of any employee in order to comply with Section 1197.5.

No person shall be imprisoned pursuant to this section except for an offense committed after the conviction of the person for a prior offense pursuant to this section. *(Added by Stats.1982, c. 1116, p. 4036, § 3.)*

§ 1200. Presumption of lawfulness of minimum wages, maximum hours, and standard conditions

In every prosecution for violation of any provision of this chapter, the minimum wage, the maximum hours of work, and the standard conditions of labor fixed by the commission shall be presumed to be reasonable and lawful. *(Stats.1937, c. 90, p. 218, § 1200.)*

§ 1201. Board of arbitration; commission

The commission shall not act as a board of arbitration during a strike or lockout. *(Stats.1937, c. 90, p. 218, § 1201.)*

§ 1202. Collection of statistics and investigations by division of labor statistics and research

Upon the request of the commission, the Division of Labor Statistics and Research shall cause such statistics and other data and information to be gathered, and investigations made, as the commission may require. The cost thereof shall be paid out of the appropriations made for the expenses of the commission. *(Stats.1937, c. 90, p. 218, § 1202. Amended by Stats.1945, c. 1431, p. 2691, § 38.)*

§ 1203. Publication of reports and bulletins

The commission may publish and distribute from time to time reports and bulletins covering its operations and proceedings under this chapter and such other matters relative thereto which it deems advisable. *(Stats.1937, c. 90, p. 218, § 1203.)*

§ 1204. Prerequisites to effectiveness of order

No order made by the commission under the provisions of Sections 1182 or 1184 of this chapter shall be effective unless and until compliance is had with the provisions of Section 1178 of this code. *(Added by Stats.1947, c. 1188, p. 2671, § 1. Amended by Stats.1953, c. 208, p. 1352, § 1.)*

§ 1205. Exercise of local police powers with respect to labor standards; state agencies and local jurisdictions

(a) As used in this section:

(1) "Local jurisdiction" means any city, county, district, or agency, or any subdivision or combination thereof.

(2) "State agency" means any state office, officer, department, division, bureau, board, commission, or agency, or any subdivision thereof.

(3) "Labor standards" means any legal requirements regarding wages paid, hours worked, and other conditions of employment.

(b) Nothing in this part shall be deemed to restrict the exercise of local police powers in a more stringent manner.

(c) When a local jurisdiction expends funds that have been provided to it by a state agency, operates a program that has received assistance from a state agency, or engages in an activity that has received assistance from a state agency, labor standards established by the local jurisdiction through exercise of local police powers or spending powers shall take effect with regard to that expenditure, program, or activity, so long as those labor standards are not in explicit conflict with, or explicitly preempted by, state law. A state agency may not require as a condition to the receipt of state funds or assistance that a local jurisdiction refrain from applying labor standards established by the local jurisdiction to expenditures, programs, or activities supported by the state funds or assistance in question. *(Added by Stats.1990, c. 1379 (A.B.119), § 3. Amended by Stats.2002, c. 298 (A.B. 2509), § 1.)*

CHAPTER 2. OCCUPATIONAL PRIVILEGES AND RESTRICTIONS

Article   Section
1. Female Employees [Repealed]
2. Minors 1290

ARTICLE 1. FEMALE EMPLOYEES [REPEALED]

ARTICLE 2. MINORS

Section
1285.   Legislative intent.
1286.   Definitions.
1287.   Citation for violation; contents; service.
1288.   Classification of citations; civil penalties.
1289.   Objections to citation and penalties; hearing; order; judgment; interest on judgment.
1290.   Employment of minors under 16.
1291.   Work for manufacturing establishment.
1292.   Tasks prohibited to minors under 16.
1293.   Tasks prohibited to minors under 16.
1293.1. Tasks prohibited to minors under 12.
1294.   Places of employment prohibited to minors under 16.
1294.1. Minors under 16 years of age and all minors; prohibited employment.
1294.3. Employment allowed minors 14 to 15 years of age.
1294.4. Delivery of newspapers; means of transportation.
1294.5. Gas service stations.
1295.   Courses of training; exception.
1295.5. Employment of minors; performance of sports-attending services.
1296.   Determination of additional employments dangerous to minors; prohibition; judicial review.
1297.   Messengers; minimum ages; hours of work.
1298.   Sale or distribution of newspapers, magazines, periodicals, or circulars.
1299.   Permits and certificates for employment of minors.
1300.   Return of certificates and permits; cancellation; grounds for cancellation.
1301.   Application of article to owners or controllers of realty.
1302.   Authority to enter places of employment; denial of entrance; report to commissioner.
1303.   Violation; misdemeanor; penalty.
1304.   Prima facie evidence of violation.
1305.   Disposition of fines.
1307.   Custody of minors illegally at work.
1308.   Occupations prohibited to minors; persons causing employment; penalties; exceptions.
1308.1. Minors under 6 or 16; door-to-door selling.
1308.2. Transportation, direction or supervision of minors more than 10 miles from minor's residence or facilitation of participation in door-to-door sales; registration with labor commissioner; conditions;

Section

renewal; proof of registration; temporary registration; violation; penalty.

1308.3.　Employment of minors under 16 years of age in door-to-door sales more than 10 miles from minor's residence; registration with labor commissioner; conditions; renewal; inspection; proof of registration; temporary registration; violation; penalty; application.

1308.4.　Revocation, suspension, or refusal to renew any registration.

1308.5.　Minors under 16; occupations requiring consent of commissioner; misdemeanor.

1308.6.　Prerequisites to commissioner's consent.

1308.7　Hours of employment of minor in entertainment industry; violations.

1308.8.　Employment of infants under the age of one month in the entertainment industry.

1308.9.　Labor Commissioner's written consent; effect of failure to timely establish "Coogan Trust Account" for minor; application for written consent to employ minor more than once in a six-month period.

1309　Employment of minors in prohibited occupations; penalties.

1309.5.　Films, photographs, slides, or magazines; depiction of minors under 18 engaged in sexual conduct; sales or distribution for resale; sources of material; maintenance of records; misdemeanor.

1309.6.　Violations of section 1309.5; civil penalties; disposition.

1310.　Exceptions; appearance in entertainment.

1311.　Enforcement agency.

1312.　Enforcement of article.

§ 1285.　Legislative intent

It is the intent of the Legislature in enacting Sections 1286 to 1289, inclusive, to establish a citation system for the imposition of prompt and effective civil sanctions against violators of the laws and regulations of this state relating to the employment of minors. The civil penalties provided for in this article are in addition to any other penalty provided by law. *(Added by Stats.1975, c. 144, p. 272, § 12.)*

§ 1286.　Definitions

As used in this article:

(a) "Director" means the Director of Industrial Relations or his or her designee.

(b) "Department" means the Department of Industrial Relations.

(c) "Minor" means any person under the age of 18 years who is required to attend school under Chapter 2 (commencing with Section 48200) and Chapter 3 (commencing with Section 48400) of Part 27 of the Education Code and any person under the age of six years. A person under the age of 18 years who is not required to attend school under Chapter 2 (commencing with Section 48200) and Chapter 3 (commencing with Section 48400) of Part 27 of the Education Code solely because that person is a nonresident of California shall still be considered a minor.

(d) "Labor Commissioner" means the Chief of the Division of Labor Law Enforcement, his or her deputies or agents, who shall have the authority to conduct informal hearings and determine the amount of civil penalties in accordance with this article.

(e) "Door–to–door sales" has the same meaning as "home solicitation contract or offer," as defined in subdivision (a) of Section 1689.5 of the Civil Code, except that "door-to-door sales" is not subject to the minimum monetary limitation set forth in that subdivision. *(Added by Stats.1975, c. 144, p. 272, § 13. Amended by Stats. 1989, c. 806, § 1; Stats.1994, c. 1175 (A.B.1900), § 5; Stats.1995, c. 887 (S.B.443), § 2.)*

§ 1287.　Citation for violation; contents; service

If upon inspection or investigation the director determines that a person is in violation of any statutory provision or rule or regulation relating to the employment of minors, he may issue a citation to the person in violation. The citation may be served personally or by registered mail in accordance with subdivision (c) of Section 11505 of the Government Code. Each citation shall be in writing and shall describe the nature of the violation, including reference to the statutory provisions, rule, or regulation alleged to have been violated. *(Added by Stats.1975, c. 144, p. 273, § 14.)*

§ 1288.　Classification of citations; civil penalties

Citations issued pursuant to this article shall be classified according to the nature of the violation, and shall indicate the classification on the face thereof, as follows:

(a) Class "A" violations are violations of Section 1290, 1292, 1293, 1293.1, 1294, 1294.1, 1294.5, 1308, 1308.1, or 1392, and any other violations that the director determines present an imminent danger to minor employees or a substantial probability that death or serious physical harm would result therefrom. The violation of Section 1391 for the third or subsequent time shall also constitute a class "A" violation. A physical condition or one or more practices, means, methods, or operations in use in a place of employment may constitute a violation. A class "A" violation is subject to a civil penalty in an amount not less than five thousand dollars ($5,000) and not exceeding ten thousand dollars ($10,000) for each and every violation. Willful or repeated violations shall receive higher civil penalties than those imposed for comparable nonwillful or first violations, not to exceed ten thousand dollars ($10,000).

(b) Class "B" violations are violations of Section 1299 or 1308.5, or a violation of Section 1391 for the first and second time, and those other violations that the director determines have a direct or immediate relationship to the health, safety, or security of minor employees, other than class "A" violations. A class "B" violation is subject to a civil penalty in an amount not less than five hundred dollars ($500) and not to exceed one thousand dollars ($1,000) for each and every violation. Willful or repeated violations shall receive higher civil penalties than those imposed for comparable nonwillful or first violations. A second violation of Section 1391 shall be subject to a civil penalty of one thousand dollars ($1,000).

(c) Nothing in this section shall preclude the imposition of criminal penalties provided for in this chapter. *(Added by Stats.1975, c. 144, p. 273, § 15. Amended by Stats.1977, c. 796, p. 2442, § 2; Stats.1994, c. 1175 (A.B.1900), § 6; Stats.1995, c. 887 (S.B.443), § 3.)*

§ 1289. Objections to citation and penalties; hearing; order; judgment; interest on judgment

(a) If a person desires to contest a citation or the proposed assessment of a civil penalty therefor, he or she shall within 15 business days after service of the citation notify the office of the Labor Commissioner that appears on the citation of his or her request for an informal hearing. The Labor Commissioner or the commissioner's deputy or agent shall, within 30 days, hold a hearing at the conclusion of which the citation or proposed assessment of a civil penalty shall be affirmed, modified, or dismissed. The decision of the Labor Commissioner shall consist of a notice of findings, findings, and order that shall be served on all parties to the hearing within 15 days after the hearing by regular first-class mail at the last known address of the party on file with the Labor Commissioner. Service shall be completed pursuant to Section 1013 of the Code of Civil Procedure. Any amount found due by the Labor Commissioner as a result of a hearing shall become due and payable 45 days after notice of the findings and written findings and order have been mailed to the party assessed. A writ of mandate may be taken from that finding to the appropriate superior court, as long as the party agrees to pay any judgment and costs ultimately rendered by the court against the party for the assessment. The writ shall be taken within 45 days of service of the notice of findings, findings, and order thereon.

(b) A person to whom a citation has been issued, shall, in lieu of contesting a citation pursuant to this section, transmit to the office of the Labor Commissioner designated on the citation the amount specified for the violation within 15 business days after issuance of the citation.

(c) When no petition objecting to a citation or the proposed assessment of a civil penalty is filed, a certified copy of the citation or proposed civil penalty may be filed by the Labor Commissioner in the office of the clerk of the superior court in any county in which the person assessed has property or in which the person assessed has or had a place of business. The clerk, immediately upon the filing, shall enter judgment for the state against the person assessed in the amount shown on the citation or proposed assessment of a civil penalty.

(d) When findings and the order thereon are made affirming or modifying a citation or proposed assessment of a civil penalty after hearing, a certified copy of the findings and the order entered thereon may be entered by the Labor Commissioner in the office of the clerk of the superior court in any county in which the person assessed has property or in which the person assessed has or had a place of business. The clerk, immediately upon the filing, shall enter judgment for the state against the person assessed in the amount shown on the certified order.

(e) A judgment entered pursuant to this section shall bear the same rate of interest and shall have the same effect as other judgments and be given the same preference allowed by law on other judgments rendered for claims for taxes. The clerk shall make no charge for the service provided by this section to be performed by him or her. *(Added by Stats.1975, c. 144, p. 273, § 16. Amended by Stats.1985, c. 658, § 1; Stats.1988, c. 96, § 6; Stats.2006, c. 538 (S.B.1852), § 483.)*

§ 1290. Employment of minors under 16

No minor under the age of 16 years shall be employed, permitted, or suffered to work in or in connection with any manufacturing establishment or other place of labor or employment at any time except as may be provided in this article or by the provisions of Part 27 (commencing with Section 48000) of the Education Code. *(Stats.1937, c. 90, p. 219, § 1290. Amended by Stats.1945, c. 627, p. 1154, § 1; Stats.1965, c. 157, p. 1114, § 2; Stats.1980, c. 676, p. 1967, § 218.)*

§ 1291. Work for manufacturing establishment

Work is done for a manufacturing establishment within the meaning of this article whenever it is done at any place upon the work of a manufacturing establishment, or upon any of the materials entering into the products of a manufacturing establishment, whether under contract or arrangement with any person in charge of or connected with a manufacturing establishment directly or indirectly through contractors or third persons. *(Stats.1937, c. 90, p. 219, § 1291.)*

§ 1292. Tasks prohibited to minors under 16

No minor under the age of sixteen years shall be employed or permitted to work in any capacity in:

(a) Adjusting any belt to any machinery.

(b) Sewing or lacing machine belts in any workshop or factory.

(c) Oiling, wiping, or cleaning machinery, or assisting therein. *(Stats.1937, c. 90, p. 219, § 1292.)*

§ 1293. Tasks prohibited to minors under 16

No minor under the age of sixteen years shall be employed, or permitted, to work in any capacity in operating or assisting in operating any of the following machines:

(a) Circular or band saws; wood shapers; wood-jointers; planers; sandpaper or wood-polishing machinery; wood turning or boring machinery.

(b) Picker machines or machines used in picking wool, cotton, hair, or other material; carding machines; leather-burnishing machines; laundry machinery.

(c) Printing-presses of all kinds; boring or drill presses; stamping machines used in sheet-metal and tinware, in paper and leather manufacturing, or in washer and nut factories; metal or paper-cutting machines; paper-lace machines.

(d) Corner-staying machines in paper-box factories; corrugating rolls, such as are used in corrugated paper, roofing or washboard factories.

(e) Dough brakes or cracker machinery of any description.

(f) Wire or iron straightening or drawing machinery; rolling-mill machinery; power punches or shears; washing, grinding or mixing machinery; calendar rolls in paper and rubber manufacturing; steam-boilers; in proximity to any hazardous or unguarded belts, machinery or gearing. *(Stats.1937, c. 90, p. 219, § 1293.)*

§ 1293.1. Tasks prohibited to minors under 12

(a) Except as provided in subdivision (c) of Section 1394, no minor under the age of 12 years may be employed or permitted to work, or accompany or be permitted to accompany an employed parent or guardian, in an agricultural zone of danger. As used in this section, "agricultural zone of danger" means any or all of the following:

(1) On or about moving equipment.

(2) In or about unprotected chemicals.

(3) In or about any unprotected water hazard.

The Department of Industrial Relations may, after hearing, determine other hazards that constitute an agricultural zone of danger.

(b) Except for employment described in subdivision (a) of Section 1394, no minor under the age of 12 years may be employed or permitted to work, or accompany an employed parent or guardian, in any of the occupations declared hazardous for employment of minors below 16 years of age in Section 570.71 of Title 29 of the Code of Federal Regulations, as that regulation may be amended from time to time. *(Added by Stats.1975, c. 144, p. 274, § 17. Amended by Stats.1994, c. 1175 (A.B.1900), § 7.)*

§ 1294. Places of employment prohibited to minors under 16

No minor under the age of 16 years shall be employed or permitted to work in any capacity:

(a) Upon any railroad, whether steam, electric, or hydraulic.

(b) Upon any vessel or boat engaged in navigation or commerce within the jurisdiction of this state.

(c) In, about, or in connection with any processes in which dangerous or poisonous acids are used, in the manufacture or packing of paints, colors, white or red lead, or in soldering.

(d) In occupations causing dust in injurious quantities, in the manufacture or use of dangerous or poisonous dyes, in the manufacture or preparation of compositions with dangerous or poisonous gases, or in the manufacture or use of compositions of lye in which the quantity thereof is injurious to health.

(e) On scaffolding, in heavy work in the building trades, in any tunnel or excavation, or in, about or in connection with any mine, coal breaker, coke oven or quarry.

(f) In assorting, manufacturing or packing tobacco.

(g) Operating any automobile, motorcar, or truck.

(h) In any occupation dangerous to the life or limb, or injurious to the health or morals of the minor. *(Stats. 1937, c. 90, p. 220, § 1294. Amended by Stats.1975, c. 144, p. 274, § 18; Stats.1976, c. 489, p. 1232, § 1; Stats.1994, c. 1175 (A.B.1900), § 8.)*

§ 1294.1. Minors under 16 years of age and all minors; prohibited employment

(a) No minor under the age of 16 years shall be employed or permitted to work in either of the following:

(1) Any occupation declared particularly hazardous for the employment of minors below the age of 16 years in Section 570.71 of Subpart E–1 of Part 570 of Title 29 of the Code of Federal Regulations, as that regulation may be revised from time to time.

(2) Any occupation excluded from the application of Subpart C of Part 570 of Title 29 of the Code of Federal Regulations, as set forth in Section 570.33 and paragraph (b) of Section 570.34 thereof, as those regulations may be revised from time to time.

(b) No minor shall be employed or permitted to work in any occupation declared particularly hazardous for the employment of minors between 16 and 18 years of age, or declared detrimental to their health or well-being, in Subpart E of Part 570 of Title 29 of the Code of Federal Regulations, as those regulations may be revised from time to time.

(c) Nothing in this section shall prohibit a minor engaged in the processing and delivery of newspapers from entering areas of a newspaper plant, other than areas where printing presses are located, for purposes related to the processing or delivery of newspapers. *(Added by Stats.1994, c. 1175 (A.B.1900), § 9. Amended by Stats.1995, c. 887 (S.B.443), § 4.)*

§ 1294.3. Employment allowed minors 14 to 15 years of age

Minors 14 and 15 years of age may be employed in occupations not otherwise prohibited by this chapter, including, but not limited to, the following:

(a) Office and clerical work, including the operation of office machines.

(b) Cashiering, selling, modeling, art work, work in advertising departments, window trimming, and comparative shopping.

(c) Price marking and tagging by hand or by machine, assembling orders, packing and shelving.

(d) Bagging and carrying out customers' orders.

(e) Errand and delivery work by foot, bicycle, and public transportation.

(f) Cleanup work, including the use of vacuum cleaners and floor waxers, and maintenance of grounds, but not including the use of power-driven mowers or cutters.

(g) Kitchen work and other work involved in preparing and serving food and beverages, including the operation of machines and devices used in the performance of this work, including, but not limited to, dishwashers, toasters, dumbwaiters, popcorn poppers, milkshake blenders, and coffee grinders.

(h) Cleaning vegetables and fruits, and wrapping, sealing, labeling, weighing, pricing, and stocking goods when performed in areas physically separate from areas where meat is prepared for sale and outside freezers or meat coolers. *(Added by Stats.1994, c. 1175 (A.B.1900), § 10. Amended by Stats.1995, c. 887 (S.B.443), § 5.)*

§ 1294.4. Delivery of newspapers; means of transportation

Nothing in this chapter shall be construed to prohibit a minor engaged in the delivery of newspapers to consumers from making deliveries by foot, bicycle, public transportation, or by an automobile driven by a person 16 years of age or older. *(Added by Stats.1994, c. 1175 (A.B.1900), § 11. Amended by Stats.1995, c. 887 (S.B. 443), § 6.)*

§ 1294.5. Gas service stations

(a) Minors 16 and 17 years of age may work in gas service stations in the following activities:

(1) Dispensing gas or oil.

(2) Courtesy service.

(3) Car cleaning, washing, and polishing.

(4) Activities specified in Section 1294.3.

(b) No minor 16 or 17 years of age may perform work in gas service stations that involves the use of pits, racks, or lifting apparatus, or that involves the inflation of any tire mounted on a rim equipped with a removable retaining ring.

(c) Minors under the age of 16 years may be employed in gas service stations to perform only those activities specified in Section 1294.3. *(Added by Stats.1994, c. 1175 (A.B.1900), § 12.)*

§ 1295. Courses of training; exception

(a) Sections 1292, 1293, 1294, and 1294.5 shall not apply to any of the following:

(1) Courses of training in vocational or manual training schools or in state institutions.

(2) Apprenticeship training provided in an apprenticeship training program established pursuant to Chapter 4 (commencing with Section 3070) of Division 3.

(3) Work experience education programs conducted pursuant to either or both Section 29007.5[1] and Article 5.5 (commencing with Section 5985)[2] of Chapter 6 of Division 6 of the Education Code, provided that the work experience coordinator determines that the students have been sufficiently trained in the employment or work otherwise prohibited by these sections, if parental approval is obtained, and the principal or the counselor of the student has determined that the progress of the student toward graduation will not be impaired.

(b) Section 1294.1 shall not apply to the following persons as provided by Section 570.72 of Title 29 of the Code of Federal Regulations:

(1) Student-learners in a bona fide vocational agriculture program working in the occupations specified in paragraph (1) of subdivision (a) of Section 1294.1 under a written agreement that provides that the student-learner's work is incidental to training, intermittent, for short periods of time, and under close supervision of a qualified person, and includes all of the following:

(A) Safety instructions given by the school and correlated with the student-learners's on-the-job training.

(B) A schedule of organized and progressive work processes for the student-learner.

(C) The name of the student-learner.

(D) The signature of the employer and a school authority, each of whom must keep copies of the agreement.

(2) Minors 14 or 15 years of age who hold certificates of completion of either a tractor operation or a machine operation program and who are working in the occupations for which they have been trained. These certificates are valid only for the occupations specified in paragraph (1) of subdivision (a) of Section 1294.1. Farmers employing minors who have completed this program shall keep a copy of the certificates of completion on file with the minor's records.

(3) Minors 14 and 15 years old who hold certificates of completion of either a tractor operation or a machine operation program of the United States Office of Education Vocational Agriculture Training Program and are working in the occupations for which they have been trained. These certificates are valid only for the occupations specified in paragraph (1) of subdivision (a) of Section 1294.1. Farmers employing minors who have completed this program shall keep a copy of the certificate of completion on file with the minor's records. *(Stats.1937, c. 90, p. 220, § 1295. Amended by Stats.1971,*

c. 1106, p. 2091, § 3; Stats.1994, c. 1175 (A.B.1900), § 13; Stats.1995, c. 91 (S.B.975), § 105.)

[1] So in enrolled bill.
[2] So in enrolled bill.

§ 1295.5. Employment of minors; performance of sports-attending services

(a) Notwithstanding Section 1391 of this code or Section 49116 of the Education Code, minors 14 years of age and older may be employed during the hours permitted by subdivision (b) to perform sports-attending services in professional baseball as enumerated in subsection (b) of Section 570.35 of Title 29 of the Code of Federal Regulations. No employer may employ a minor 14 or 15 years of age to perform sports-attending services in professional baseball without the prior written approval of either the school district of the school in which the minor is enrolled or the county board of education of the county in which that school district is located.

(b) Any minor 14 or 15 years of age who performs sports-attending services in professional baseball pursuant to subdivision (a) may be employed outside of school hours until 12:30 a.m. during any evening preceding a nonschoolday and until 10 p.m. during any evening preceding a schoolday. No employer may employ a minor 14 or 15 years of age to perform sports-attending services in professional baseball pursuant to subdivision (a) for more than five hours in any schoolday, for more than 18 hours in any week while school is in session, for more than eight hours in any nonschoolday, or for more than 40 hours in any week that school is not in session. An employer may employ a minor 16 or 17 years of age outside of school hours to perform sports-attending services in professional baseball pursuant to subdivision (a) for up to five hours in any schoolday.

(c) The school authority issuing the permit to the minor to perform sports-attending services in professional baseball shall both (1) provide the local office of the Division of Labor Standards Enforcement with a copy of the permit within five business days after the date the permit is issued and (2) monitor the academic achievement of the minor to ensure that the educational progress of the minor is being maintained or improves during the period of employment. (Added by Stats.1997, c. 763 (A.B.1363), § 1, eff. Oct. 8, 1997. Amended by Stats.1998, c. 485 (A.B.2803), § 120.)

§ 1296. Determination of additional employments dangerous to minors; prohibition; judicial review

The Division of Labor Standards Enforcement may, after a hearing, determine whether any particular trade, process of manufacture, or occupation, in which the employment of minors is not already forbidden by law, or whether any particular method of carrying on the trade, process of manufacture, or occupation is sufficiently dangerous to the lives or limbs or injurious to the health or morals of minors to justify their exclusion therefrom. No minor shall be employed or permitted to work in any occupation thus determined to be dangerous or injurious to minors. Any determination hereunder may be reviewed by the superior court. (Stats.1937, c. 90, p. 220, § 1296. Amended by Stats.1949, c. 127, p. 359, § 1; Stats.1980, c. 676, p. 1968, § 219; Stats.1994, c. 1175 (A.B.1900), § 14; Stats.1995, c. 91 (S.B.975), § 106.)

§ 1297. Messengers; minimum ages; hours of work

No minor under the age of 16 years shall be employed or permitted to work as a messenger for any telegraph, telephone, or messenger company, or for the United States government or any of its departments while operating a telegraph, telephone, or messenger service, in the distribution, transmission, or delivery of goods or messages in cities of more than 15,000 inhabitants; nor shall any minor under the age of 18 years be employed, permitted, or suffered to engage in such work before 6 o'clock in the morning or after 9 o'clock in the evening. Nothing in this section shall apply to any minor employed to deliver newspapers to consumers. (Stats.1937, c. 90, p. 220, § 1297. Amended by Stats.1975, c. 44, p. 76, § 1; Stats.1992, c. 1189 (A.B.662), § 3.)

§ 1298. Sale or distribution of newspapers, magazines, periodicals, or circulars

(a) Notwithstanding Section 1308.1, no minor under 12 years of age shall be employed or permitted to work at any time in or in connection with the occupation of selling or distributing newspapers, magazines, periodicals, or circulars.

(b) This section shall not apply to a minor who is at least 10 years of age and is engaged as a newspaper carrier on the effective date of the act adding this subdivision. (Stats.1937, c. 90, p. 221, § 1298. Amended by Stats.1975, c. 42, p. 75, § 1; Stats.1994, c. 1175 (A.B.1900), § 15.)

§ 1299. Permits and certificates for employment of minors

Every person, or agent or officer thereof, employing minors, either directly or indirectly through third persons, shall keep on file all permits and certificates, either to work or to employ, issued under this article or Part 27 (commencing with Section 48000) of the Education Code. The files shall be open at all times to the inspection of the school attendance and probation officers, the State Board of Education, and the officers of the Division of Labor Standards Enforcement. (Stats.1937, c. 90, p. 221, § 1299. Amended by Stats.1945, c. 627, p. 1154, § 2; Stats.1965, c. 157, p. 1115, § 3; Stats.1969, c. 1589, p. 3229, § 5; Stats.1972, c. 579, p. 1004, § 25; Stats.1980, c. 676, p. 1968, § 220; Stats.1981, c. 714, p. 2720, § 314; Stats.1988, c. 96, § 7.)

§ 1300. Return of certificates and permits; cancellation; grounds for cancellation

All certificates and permits to work or to employ shall be subject to cancellation at any time by the Labor Commissioner or by the issuing authority, whenever the commissioner or the issuing authority finds that the

409

conditions for the legal issuance of such certificate or permit no longer exist or have never existed. *(Stats.1937, c. 90, p. 221, § 1300. Amended by Stats.1972, c. 1441, p. 3158, § 7.)*

§ 1301. Application of article to owners or controllers of realty

(a) The provisions of this article concerning the employment of minors, and the civil penalties for violations of those provisions, shall be fully applicable to every person who owns or controls the real property upon which a minor is employed, whether or not that person is the minor's employer, if the minor's employment is for the benefit of the person, and the person has knowingly permitted the violation or continuation of violations.

(b) The posting of a notice pursuant to Section 49140 of the Education Code shall not operate to exempt any person from this article. *(Added by Stats.1975, c. 144, p. 275, § 20. Amended by Stats.2006, c. 538 (S.B.1852), § 484.)*

§ 1302. Authority to enter places of employment; denial of entrance; report to commissioner

The attendance supervisor, who is a full-time attendance supervisor performing no other duties, of any county, city and county, or school district in which any place of employment is situated, or the probation officer of the county, may at any time, enter the place of employment for the purpose of examining permits to work or to employ of all minors employed in the place of employment, or for the purpose of investigating violations of this article or of Chapter 2 (commencing with Section 48200), 3 (commencing with Section 48400), or 7 (commencing with Section 49100) of Part 27 of the Education Code. If an attendance supervisor or probation officer is denied entrance to the place of employment, or if any violations of laws relating to the employment of minors are found to exist, the attendance supervisor or probation officer shall report the denial of entrance or the violation to the Labor Commissioner. The report shall be made within 48 hours and shall be in writing, setting forth the fact that he or she has good cause to believe that these laws are being violated in the place of employment, and describing the nature of the violation. *(Stats.1937, c. 90, p. 221, § 1302. Amended by Stats.1945, c. 627, p. 1154, § 3; Stats.1965, c. 157, p. 1115, § 4; Stats.1975, c. 144, p. 275, § 21; Stats.2006, c. 538 (S.B.1852), § 485.)*

§ 1303. Violation; misdemeanor; penalty

Any person, or agent or officer thereof, employing either directly or indirectly through third persons, or any parent or guardian of a minor affected by this article who violates any provision hereof, or who employs, or permits any minor to be employed in violation hereof, is guilty of a misdemeanor, punishable by a fine of not less than one thousand dollars ($1,000) nor more than five thousand dollars ($5,000) or imprisonment in the county jail for not more than six months, or both. Any person who willfully violates this article shall, upon conviction, be subject to a fine of not more than ten thousand dollars ($10,000) or to imprisonment in the county jail for not more than six months, or both. No person shall be imprisoned under this section, except for an offense committed after the conviction of that person for a prior offense under this article. *(Stats.1937, c. 90, p. 222, § 1303. Amended by Stats.1983, c. 1092, § 206, eff. Sept. 27, 1983, operative Jan. 1, 1984; Stats.1987, c. 386, § 1; Stats.1994, c. 1175 (A.B.1900), § 16.)*

§ 1304. Prima facie evidence of violation

Failure to produce any permit or certificate either to work or to employ is prima facie evidence of the illegal employment of any minor whose permit or certificate is not so produced. Proof that any person was the manager or superintendent of any place of employment subject to the provisions of this article at the time any minor is alleged to have been employed therein in violation thereof, is prima facie evidence that the person employed, or permitted the minor so to work. The sworn statement of the Labor Commissioner or his deputy or agents as to the age of any child affected by this article is prima facie evidence of the age of such child. *(Stats.1937, c. 90, p. 222, § 1304. Amended by Stats.1969, c. 1589, p. 3229, § 6.)*

§ 1305. Disposition of fines

(a) All fines and penalties collected under this article, other than as the result of a judicial proceeding to enforce collection, shall be paid to the department in the form of remittances payable to the Department of Industrial Relations. The department shall transmit the payments to the State Treasury and the payments shall be credited to the General Fund.

(b) Notwithstanding Section 1463 of the Penal Code, all fines and penalties collected in judicial proceedings to enforce their collection, except for the civil penalties that are assessed and collected pursuant to Sections 1287, 1288, and 1289, shall be allocated pursuant to court order. The court shall direct that 50 percent of the fines and penalties assessed shall be transmitted to the county treasury, if prosecuted by the district attorney or the county counsel, or to the city treasury, if prosecuted by the city attorney, 25 percent of the fines and penalties assessed shall be transmitted to the Department of Industrial Relations to be available, upon appropriation by the Legislature, for the purpose of recovering costs incurred by the department pursuant to this chapter, and 25 percent of the fines and penalties assessed be transmitted to the Treasurer for deposit in the State Treasury to the credit of the General Fund. *(Stats.1937, c. 90, p. 222, § 1305. Amended by Stats.1949, c. 127, p. 360, § 3; Stats.1975, c. 144, p. 275, § 22; Stats.1994, c. 1175 (A.B.1900), § 17; Stats.1995, c. 887 (S.B.443), § 7.)*

§ 1307. Custody of minors illegally at work

All minors coming within the provisions of Division 9 (commencing with Section 10501)[1] of the Education Code shall be placed or delivered into the custody of the school district authorities of the county or city in which they are found illegally at work. *(Stats.1937, c. 90, p. 222, § 1307. Amended by Stats.1945, c. 627, p. 1154, § 4; Stats.1965, c. 157, p. 1115, § 5.)*

[1] Educ.C.1976, § 48001; repealed.

§ 1308. Occupations prohibited to minors; persons causing employment; penalties; exceptions

(a) Any person is guilty of a misdemeanor and is punishable by a fine of not less than one thousand dollars ($1,000) and not more than five thousand dollars ($5,000), imprisonment for not exceeding six months, or both, who, as parent, relative, guardian, employer, or otherwise having the care, custody, or control of any minor under the age of 16 years, exhibits, uses, or employs, or in any manner or under any pretense, sells, apprentices, gives away, lets out, or disposes of the minor to any person, under any name, title, or pretense for, or who causes, procures, or encourages the minor to engage in any of the following:

(1) Any business, exhibition, or vocation injurious to the health or dangerous to the life or limb of the minor.

(2) The vocation, occupation, service, or purpose of singing, playing on musical instruments, rope or wire walking, dancing, begging, or peddling, or as a gymnast, acrobat, contortionist, or rider, in any place whatsoever.

(3) Any obscene, indecent, or immoral purposes, exhibition, or practice whatsoever. Notwithstanding any other provision of law, this paragraph shall apply to a person with respect to any minor under the age of 18 years.

(4) Any mendicant or wandering business.

Any person who willfully violates this section shall, upon conviction, be subject to a fine of not more than ten thousand dollars ($10,000), or to imprisonment in the county jail for not more than six months, or both. No person shall be imprisoned under this section, except for an offense committed after the conviction of that person for a prior offense under this article.

(b) Nothing in this section applies to or affects any of the following:

(1) The employment or use of any minor as a singer or musician in any church, school, or academy, or the teaching or learning of the science or practice of music.

(2) The employment of any minor as a musician at any concert or other musical entertainment, or as a performer in any form of entertainment, on the written consent of the Labor Commissioner pursuant to Section 1308.5.

(3) The participation by any minor of any age, whether or not the minor receives payment for his or her services or receives money prizes, in any horseback riding exhibition, contest, or event other than a rough stock rodeo event, circus, or race. As used in this paragraph, "rough stock rodeo event" means any rodeo event operated for profit or operated by other than a nonprofit organization in which unbroken, little-trained, or imperfectly trained animals are ridden or handled by the participant, and shall include, but not be limited to, saddle bronc riding, bareback riding, and bull riding. As used in this paragraph, "race" means any speed contest between two or more animals that are on a course at the same time and that is operated for profit or operated other than by a nonprofit organization.

(4) The leading of livestock by a minor in nonprofit fairs, stock parades, livestock shows and exhibitions. *(Stats.1937, c. 90, p. 222, § 1308. Amended by Stats.1949, c. 447, p. 792, § 2; Stats.1961, c. 1808, p. 3844, § 1; Stats.1974, c. 523, p. 1207, § 3, eff. Aug. 20, 1974; Stats.1983, c. 1092, § 207, eff. Sept. 27, 1983, operative Jan. 1, 1984; Stats.1987, c. 386, § 2; Stats.1989, c. 806, § 2; Stats.1994, c. 1175 (A.B.1900), § 18; Stats.1995, c. 887 (S.B.443), § 8.)*

§ 1308.1. Minors under 6 or 16; door-to-door selling

(a) No minor under the age of 6 years shall be permitted to engage in the door-to-door sales or street sales of candy, cookies, flowers, or any other merchandise or commodities.

(b) No minor under 16 years of age, permitted by law to engage in door-to-door sales of newspaper or magazine subscriptions, or of candy, cookies, flowers, or other merchandise or commodities, shall be employed in those activities more than 50 miles from his or her place of residence. *(Added by Stats.1989, c. 806, § 3. Amended by Stats.1994, c. 1175 (A.B.1900), § 19.)*

§ 1308.2. Transportation, direction or supervision of minors more than 10 miles from minor's residence or facilitation of participation in door-to-door sales; registration with labor commissioner; conditions; renewal; proof of registration; temporary registration; violation; penalty

(a) Except as provided in subdivision (f), any person 18 years of age or older who transports, or provides direction or supervision during transportation of, a minor under 16 years of age to any location more than 10 miles from the minor's residence, or directs or supervises a minor, for the purpose of facilitating the minor's participation in door-to-door sales of any merchandise or commodity, shall register with the Labor Commissioner pursuant to this section. Registration may be renewed on an annual basis.

(b) The Labor Commissioner shall not register or renew registration of any person pursuant to this section unless all of the following conditions are satisfied:

(1) The person has executed a written application on a form prescribed by the Labor Commissioner, including all of the following:

(A) The name, address, social security number, and California driver's license number of the applicant and the name, address, and employer identification number of the organization from which the merchandise to be sold is purchased. The information provided pursuant to this

411

subparagraph shall be set forth in a declaration of the individual applicant under penalty of perjury.

(B) A statement by the applicant containing all facts required by the Labor Commissioner concerning the applicant's character, competency, responsibility, and the manner and method by which the applicant proposes to transport the minor or minors, the number of minors to be transported, methods and levels of adult supervision to be provided, the nature of the merchandise to be sold, the content of any promotional statement to be delivered by any minor, and a description of how the merchandise or commodity to be sold would be represented to the public.

(2) The Labor Commissioner, following an investigation thereof, is satisfied as to the character, competency, and responsibility of the applicant.

(3) Each application for initial registration shall be accompanied by a fee determined by the Labor Commissioner in an amount sufficient in the aggregate to defray the division's costs of administering the registration program, but which shall not exceed one hundred dollars ($100) for initial registration or fifty dollars ($50) for registration renewal.

(c) Any registrant under this section shall have proof of registration with the Labor Commissioner in his or her immediate possession at all times when engaged in any activity described in subdivision (a).

(d) Whenever an application for a registration or renewal is made, and application processing pursuant to this section has not been completed, the Labor Commissioner may, at his or her discretion, issue a temporary or provisional registration valid for a period not exceeding 90 days, and subject, where appropriate, to summary revocation by the Labor Commissioner. Otherwise, the conditions for issuance or renewal of registration shall meet the requirements of subdivision (b).

(e) Any person who violates subdivision (a) or (c) is guilty of a misdemeanor, punishable by a fine of one thousand dollars ($1,000) per affected minor upon the first conviction for a violation, two thousand five hundred dollars ($2,500) per affected minor for the second conviction for a violation, and ten thousand dollars ($10,000) per affected minor for a third or subsequent conviction for a violation.

(f) The following persons are not required to register under this section:

(1) A parent or the guardian of the minor.

(2) A person solely providing transportation for hire, who is not otherwise subject to the registration requirements of subdivision (a).

(3) A person acting on behalf of a trustee or charitable corporation, as defined in Sections 12582 and 12582.1, respectively, of the Government Code, or of any entity described in Section 12583 of the Government Code. (*Added by Stats.1994, c. 1175 (A.B.1900), § 20.*)

412

§ 1308.3. Employment of minors under 16 years of age in door-to-door sales more than 10 miles from minor's residence; registration with labor commissioner; conditions; renewal; inspection; proof of registration; temporary registration; violation; penalty; application

(a) Except as provided in subdivision (g), any individual, association, corporation, or other entity that employs or uses, either directly or indirectly through third persons, minors under 16 years of age in door-to-door sales at any location more than 10 miles from the minor's residence shall register with the Labor Commissioner pursuant to this section. Registration may be renewed on an annual basis.

(b) The Labor Commissioner shall not register or renew registration of any applicant pursuant to this section unless all of the following conditions are satisfied:

(1) The organization has executed a written application therefor on a form prescribed by the Labor Commissioner, including all of the following:

(A) The company's name, address, and employer identification number, and the names, addresses, and social security numbers of all adults employed to supervise, accompany, or transport minors who would be engaged in door-to-door sales. The information provided pursuant to this subparagraph shall be set forth in a declaration under penalty of perjury by the applicant if an individual, or an officer of an applicant that is an association, corporation, or other entity.

(B) A statement of all the facts required by the Labor Commissioner concerning the nature of the merchandise to be sold and a plan detailing the level and nature of adult supervision to be provided minors engaged in door-to-door sales. The information provided pursuant to this subparagraph shall be by declaration under penalty of perjury by the individual, or an officer of the association, corporation, or other entity.

(C) A copy of any written contract or other written agreement to be offered by the applicant to minors employed or used by the applicant in door-to-door sales.

(2) The Labor Commissioner, following an investigation thereof, is satisfied that the employer has not previously violated this article and does not propose to expose minors in its employ to hazardous or unsafe working conditions.

(3) Each application for initial registration shall be accompanied by a fee determined by the Labor Commissioner in an amount sufficient in the aggregate to defray the division's costs of administering the registration program, but which shall not exceed three hundred fifty dollars ($350) for initial registration or two hundred dollars ($200) for registration renewal.

(c) Any registrant under this section shall, upon request, make available for inspection by the Labor Commissioner all of its payroll records for any period.

(d) Any registrant under this section, or person acting on behalf of a registrant, shall have proof of registration with the Labor Commissioner in his or her immediate possession at all times when engaged in any activity described in subdivision (a).

(e) Whenever an application for a registration or renewal is made, and application processing pursuant to this section has not been completed, the Labor Commissioner may, at his or her discretion, issue a temporary or provisional registration valid for a period not exceeding 90 days, and subject, where appropriate, to summary revocation by the Labor Commissioner. Otherwise, the conditions for issuance or renewal of registration shall meet the requirements of subdivision (a).

(f) Any person or entity, or any agent or officer thereof, who violates subdivision (a) or (d), and any parent or guardian who knowingly permits a minor in his or her custody to be employed in door-to-door sales specified in subdivision (a) by an unregistered person or entity, or permits any minor to be employed in violation hereof, is guilty of a misdemeanor, punishable by a fine of one thousand dollars ($1,000) per affected minor for the first conviction for a violation, two thousand five hundred dollars ($2,500) per affected minor for the second conviction for a violation, and ten thousand dollars ($10,000) per affected minor for a third or subsequent conviction for a violation.

(g) This section does not apply to any trustee or charitable corporation, as defined in Sections 12582 and 12582.1, respectively, of the Government Code, or to any entity described in Section 12583 of the Government Code. *(Added by Stats.1994, c. 1175 (A.B.1900), § 21. Amended by Stats.1995, c. 887 (S.B.443), § 9.)*

§ 1308.4. Revocation, suspension, or refusal to renew any registration

The Labor Commissioner may revoke, suspend, or refuse to renew any registration under Section 1308.2 or 1308.3 when any of the following have occurred:

(a) The registrant or any agent of the registrant has violated or failed to comply with Section 1308.2 or 1308.3.

(b) The registrant has made any misrepresentation or false statement in his or her application for registration under Section 1308.2 or 1308.3.

(c) The registrant has operated in a manner substantially different from the conditions of operation stated in the application for registration.

(d) The registrant, or any agent of the registrant, has been found by a court of law or the Labor Commissioner to have violated, or willfully aided or abetted any person in the violation of, any law of this state regulating the employment of minors, the payment of wages to minors, or the conditions, terms, or places of employment affecting the health and safety of minors.

(e) The registrant has been found, by a court of law or the Secretary of Labor, to have violated any provision of the child labor provisions set forth in Section 12 of the federal Fair Labor Standards Act of 1938, as amended (29 U.S.C. Sec. 212). *(Added by Stats.1994, c. 1175 (A.B.1900), § 22.)*

§ 1308.5. Minors under 16; occupations requiring consent of commissioner; misdemeanor

(a) This section, with the exception of paragraph (4) of this subdivision, shall apply to all minors under the age of 16 years. The written consent of the Labor Commissioner is required for any minor, not otherwise exempted by this chapter, for any of the following:

(1) The employment of any minor, in the presentation of any drama, legitimate play, or in any radio broadcasting or television studio.

(2) The employment of any minor 12 years of age or over in any other performance, concert, or entertainment.

(3) The appearance of any minor over the age of eight years in any performance, concert, or entertainment during the public school vacation.

(4) Allowing any minor between the ages of 8 and 18 years, who is by any law of this state permitted to be employed as an actor, actress, or performer in a theater, motion picture studio, radio broadcasting studio, or television studio, before 10 o'clock p.m., in the presentation of a performance, play, or drama continuing from an earlier hour until after 10 o'clock, to continue his part in such presentation between the hours of 10 and 12 p.m.

(5) The appearance of any minor in any entertainment which is noncommercial in nature.

(6) The employment of any minor artist in the making of phonograph recordings.

(7) The employment of any minor as an advertising or photographic model.

(8) The employment or appearance of any minor pursuant to a contract approved by the superior court under Chapter 3 (commencing with Section 6750) of Part 3 of Division 11 of the Family Code.

(b) Any person, or the agent, manager, superintendent or officer thereof, employing either directly or indirectly through third persons, or any parent or guardian of a minor who employs, or permits any minor to be employed in violation of any of the provisions of this section is guilty of a misdemeanor. Failure to produce the written consent from the Labor Commissioner is prima facie evidence of the illegal employment of any minor whose written consent is not produced. *(Added by Stats.1975, c. 144, p. 275, § 24. Amended by Stats.1994, c. 1269 (A.B.2208), § 59.5.)*

§ 1308.6. Prerequisites to commissioner's consent

No consent shall be given at any time unless the officer giving it is satisfied that all of the following conditions are met:

(a) The environment in which the performance, concert, or entertainment is to be produced is proper for the minor.

(b) The conditions of employment are not detrimental to the health of the minor.

(c) The minor's education will not be neglected or hampered by his or her participation in the performance, concert, or entertainment.

The Labor Commissioner may require the authority charged with the issuance of age and schooling certificates to make the necessary investigation into the conditions covered by this section. *(Formerly § 1396, added by Stats.1937, c. 90, p. 225, § 1396. Renumbered § 1308.6 and amended by Stats.1988, c. 96, § 9.)*

§ 1308.7   Hours of employment of minor in entertainment industry; violations

(a) No minor shall be employed in the entertainment industry more than eight hours in one day of 24 hours, or more than 48 hours in one week, or before 5 a.m., or after 10 p.m. on any day preceding a schoolday. However, a minor may work the hours authorized by this section during any evening preceding a nonschoolday until 12:30 a.m. of the nonschoolday.

(b) For purposes of this section, "schoolday" means any day in which a minor is required to attend school for 240 minutes or more.

(c) Any person or the agent or officer thereof, or any parent or guardian, who directly or indirectly violates or causes or suffers the violation of this section, is guilty of a misdemeanor punishable by a fine of not less than five hundred dollars ($500) nor more than one thousand dollars ($1,000), or imprisonment in the county jail for not more than 60 days, or both. *(Added by Stats.1993, c. 570 (A.B.1837), § 1, eff. Sept. 28, 1993.)*

§ 1308.8.   Employment of infants under the age of one month in the entertainment industry

(a) No infant under the age of one month may be employed on any motion picture set or location unless a licensed physician and surgeon who is board-certified in pediatrics provides written certification that the infant is at least 15 days old and, in his or her medical opinion, the infant was carried to full term, was of normal birth weight, is physically capable of handling the stress of filmmaking, and the infant's lungs, eyes, heart, and immune system are sufficiently developed to withstand the potential risks.

(b) Any parent, guardian, or employer of a minor, and any officer or agent of an employer of a minor, who directly or indirectly violates subdivision (a), or who causes or suffers a violation of subdivision (a), with respect to that minor, is guilty of a misdemeanor punishable by a fine of not less than two thousand five hundred dollars ($2,500) nor more than five thousand dollars ($5,000), by imprisonment in the county jail for not more than 60 days, or by both that fine and imprisonment. *(Added by Stats.1998, c. 239 (A.B.744), § 1.)*

414

§ 1308.9.   Labor Commissioner's written consent; effect of failure to timely establish "Coogan Trust Account" for minor; application for written consent to employ minor more than once in a six-month period

(a) If the Labor Commissioner provides written consent pursuant to Section 1308.5 for the employment of a minor under a contract described in Section 6750 of the Family Code, that consent shall be void after the expiration of 10 business days from the date written consent was granted, unless it is attached to a true and correct copy of the trustee's statement evidencing the establishment on behalf of the minor of a "Coogan Trust Account" pursuant to Chapter 3 (commencing with Section 6750) of Part 3 of Division 11 of the Family Code. If the written consent is attached to a true and correct copy of that trustee's statement, the written consent shall be valid for a six-month period.

(b) A person may not apply for the written consent of the Labor Commissioner to employ the same minor under a contract described in Section 6750 of the Family Code more than once in any six-month period. If written consent is issued by the Labor Commissioner for the employment of the same minor more than once within any six-month period, the earliest dated written consent shall be valid and any other written consent issued during that six-month period shall be void. *(Added by Stats. 2003, c. 667 (S.B.210), § 4.)*

§ 1309.   Employment of minors in prohibited occupations; penalties

Every person who takes, receives, hires, employs, uses, exhibits, or has in custody, for any of the purposes mentioned in Section 1308, any minor under the age of 16, or under the age of 18, as specified in paragraph (3) of subdivision (a) of Section 1308, is guilty of a misdemeanor punishable by a fine of not less than one thousand dollars ($1,000) nor more than five thousand dollars ($5,000), or imprisonment for not more than six months, or both.

Any person who willfully violates this section shall, upon conviction, be subject to a fine of not more than ten thousand dollars ($10,000), or to imprisonment in the county jail for not more than six months, or both. No person shall be imprisoned under this section, except for an offense committed after the conviction of that person for a prior offense under this article. *(Stats.1937, c. 90, p. 223, § 1309. Amended by Stats.1983, c. 1092, § 208, eff. Sept. 27, 1983 operative Jan. 1, 1984; Stats.1987, c. 386, § 3; Stats.1989, c. 806, § 4; Stats.1994, c. 1175 (A.B. 1900), § 23.)*

§ 1309.5.   Films, photographs, slides, or magazines; depiction of minors under 18 engaged in sexual conduct; sales or distribution for resale; sources of material; maintenance of records; misdemeanor

(a) Every person who, with knowledge that a person is a minor under 18 years of age, or who, while in possession of these facts that he or she should reasonably know that the person is a minor under 18 years of age, knowingly sells or distributes for resale films, photographs, slides, or magazines which depict a minor under 18 years of age engaged in sexual conduct as defined in Section 311.4 of the Penal Code, shall determine the names and addresses of persons from whom this material is obtained, and shall keep a record of these names and addresses. These records shall be kept for a period of three years after the material is obtained, and shall be kept confidential except that they shall be available to law enforcement officers as described in Section 830.1 and subdivision (h) of Section 830.3 of the Penal Code upon request.

(b) Every retailer who knows or reasonably should know that films, photographs, slides, or magazines depict a minor under the age of 18 years engaged in sexual conduct as defined in Section 311.4 of the Penal Code, shall keep a record of the names and addresses of persons from whom this material is acquired. These records shall be kept for a period of three years after the material is acquired, and shall be kept confidential except that they shall be available to law enforcement officers as described in Section 830.1 and subdivision (h) of Section 830.3 of the Penal Code upon request.

(c) The failure to keep and maintain the records described in subdivisions (a) and (b) for a period of three years after the obtaining or acquisition of this material is a misdemeanor. Disclosure of these records by law enforcement officers, except in the performance of their duties, is a misdemeanor. *(Added by Stats.1977, c. 1148, p. 3687, § 1, eff. Sept. 29, 1977. Amended by Stats.1989, c. 806, § 5.)*

§ 1309.6. Violations of section 1309.5; civil penalties; disposition

(a) Any person who violates any provision of Section 1309.5 shall be liable for a civil penalty not to exceed seven thousand five hundred dollars ($7,500) for each violation, which shall be assessed and recovered in a civil action brought in the name of the people of the State of California by the Attorney General or by any district attorney, county counsel, or city attorney in any court of competent jurisdiction.

(b) If the action is brought by the Attorney General, one-half of the penalty collected shall be paid to the treasurer of the county in which the judgment was entered, and one-half to the State Treasurer. If brought by a district attorney or county counsel, the entire amount of penalty collected shall be paid to the treasurer of the county in which the judgment was entered. If brought by a city attorney or city prosecutor, one-half of the penalty shall be paid to the treasurer of the county and one-half to the city. *(Added by Stats.1977, c. 1148, p. 3687, § 2, eff. Sept. 29, 1977. Amended by Stats.1995, c. 887 (S.B.443), § 10.)*

§ 1310. Exceptions; appearance in entertainment

Nothing in this article or Article 2 (commencing with Section 1390) of Chapter 3 shall prohibit or prevent:

(a) The appearance of any minor in any church, public or religious school, or community entertainment.

(b) The appearance of any minor in any school entertainment or in any entertainment for charity or for children, for which no admission fee is charged.

(c) The appearance of any minor in any radio or television broadcasting exhibition, where the minor receives no compensation directly or indirectly therefor, and where the engagement of the minor is limited to a single appearance lasting not more than one hour, and where no admission fee is charged for the radio broadcasting or television exhibition.

(d) The appearance of any minor at any one event during a calendar year, occurring on a day on which school attendance is not required or on the day preceding such a day, lasting four hours or less, where a parent or guardian of the minor is present, for which the minor does not directly or indirectly receive any compensation. *(Formerly § 1394.5, added by Stats.1951, c. 1019, p. 2648, § 2. Renumbered § 1310 and amended by Stats.1988, c. 96, § 8. Amended by Stats.1992, c. 657 (A.B.3143), § 1.)*

§ 1311. Enforcement agency

The Division of Labor Standards Enforcement shall enforce this article. *(Stats.1937, c. 90, p. 223, § 1311. Amended by Stats.1949, c. 127, p. 360, § 5; Stats.1980, c. 676, p. 1968, § 221.)*

§ 1312. Enforcement of article

Nothing in this article shall limit the authority of the Attorney General or the district attorney of any county, either upon their own complaint or the complaint of any person acting for himself or the general public, to prosecute actions, either civil or criminal, for violations of this article, or to enforce the provisions thereof independently and without specific direction of the director. *(Added by Stats.1975, c. 144, p. 276, § 26.)*

CHAPTER 3. WORKING HOURS

Article	Section
1. Female Employees [Repealed]	
2. Minors	1390

ARTICLE 1. FEMALE EMPLOYEES [REPEALED]

ARTICLE 2. MINORS

Section
1390. Definitions.
1391. Hours of employment of minors; violation; misdemeanor; penalty.
1391.1. Minors 16 to 18 years of age enrolled in work experience or cooperative vocational education programs.

Section

1391.2.   Minors under 18 years of age; high school graduate
          or equivalent or possessing certificate of proficien-
          cy; same hours and pay as adults; exceptions.

1392.   Employment for more than eight hours in one day;
          misdemeanor.

1393.   Agricultural packing plants employing minors; ex-
          emptions; issuance; revocation; notice; applica-
          tion; posting.

1393.5.   Agricultural packing plants; employment of minors
          who are enrollees in Lake County schools; inspec-
          tion of agricultural packing plant by Labor Com-
          missioner; information to be included in written
          report to receive an exemption or a renewal of an
          exemption.

1394.   Employment of minors at agricultural, horticultural,
          viticultural, or domestic labor while not in school.

1398.   Enforcement agency.

1399.   Enforcement of article.

§ 1390. Definitions

As used in this article, unless the context otherwise indicates:

(a) "Horticultural" includes the curing and drying but not the canning of all varieties of fruit.

(b) "Drama" or "play" includes the production of motion picture plays. *(Stats.1937, c. 90, p. 224, § 1390.)*

§ 1391. Hours of employment of minors; violation; misdemeanor; penalty

(a) Except as provided in Sections 1297, 1298, and 1308.7:

(1) No employer shall employ a minor 15 years of age or younger for more than eight hours in one day of 24 hours, or more than 40 hours in one week, or before 7 a.m. or after 7 p.m., except that from June 1 through Labor Day, a minor 15 years of age or younger may be employed for the hours authorized by this section until 9 p.m. in the evening.

(2) Notwithstanding paragraph (1), while school is in session, no employer shall employ a minor 14 or 15 years of age for more than three hours in any schoolday, nor more than 18 hours in any week, nor during school hours, except that a minor enrolled in and employed pursuant to a school-supervised and school-administered work experience and career exploration program may be employed for no more than 23 hours, any portion of which may be during school hours.

(3) No employer shall employ a minor 16 or 17 years of age for more than eight hours in one day of 24 hours or more than 48 hours in one week, or before 5 a.m., or after 10 p.m. on any day preceding a schoolday. However, a minor 16 or 17 years of age may be employed for the hours authorized by this section during any evening preceding a nonschoolday until 12:30 a.m. of the non-schoolday.

(4) Notwithstanding paragraph (3), while school is in session, no employer shall employ a minor 16 or 17 years

416

of age for more than four hours in any schoolday, except as follows:

(A) The minor is employed in personal attendant occupations, as defined in the Industrial Welfare Commission Minimum Wage Order No. 15 (8 Cal. Code Regs. Sec. 11150), school-approved work experience, or cooperative vocational education programs.

(B) The minor has been issued a permit to work pursuant to subdivision (c) of Section 49112 and is employed in accordance with the provisions of that permit.

(b) For purposes of this section, "schoolday" means any day in which a minor is required to attend school for 240 minutes or more.

(c) Any person or the agent or officer thereof, or any parent or guardian, who directly or indirectly violates or causes or suffers the violation of this section is guilty of a misdemeanor punishable by a fine of not less than one thousand dollars ($1,000) nor more than five thousand dollars ($5,000), or imprisonment in the county jail for not more than 60 days, or both. Any person who willfully violates this section shall, upon conviction, be subject to a fine of not more than ten thousand dollars ($10,000) or to imprisonment in the county jail for not more than six months, or both. No person shall be imprisoned under this section, except for an offense committed after the conviction of that person for a prior offense under this article.

(d) Nothing in this section shall apply to any minor employed to deliver newspapers to consumers. *(Stats. 1937, c. 90, p. 224, § 1391. Amended by Stats.1971, c. 1317, p. 2619, § 1; Stats.1972, c. 579, p. 1004, § 26; Stats.1983, c. 1092, § 210, eff. Sept. 27, 1983, operative Jan. 1, 1984; Stats.1987, c. 386, § 4; Stats.1989, c. 66, § 1; Stats.1992, c. 1189 (A.B.662), § 4; Stats.1993, c. 570 (A.B.1837), § 2, eff. Sept. 28, 1993; Stats.1994, c. 1175 (A.B.1900), § 24; Stats.1995, c. 887 (S.B.443), § 11.)*

§ 1391.1. Minors 16 to 18 years of age enrolled in work experience or cooperative vocational education programs

Minors 16 years of age or older and under the age of 18 years enrolled in work experience or cooperative vocational education programs approved by the State Department of Education or in work experience education programs conducted by private schools may work after 10 p.m. but not later than 12:30 a.m., providing such employment is not detrimental to the health, education, or welfare of the minor and the approval of the parent and the work experience coordinator has been obtained. However, if any such minor works any time during the hours from 10 p.m. to 12:30 a.m., he or she shall be paid for work during that time at a rate which is not less than the minimum wage paid to adults. *(Added by Stats.1971, c. 1106, p. 2091, § 5. Amended by Stats.1978, c. 185, p. 415, § 1; Stats.1982, c. 231, p. 758, § 1.)*

§ 1391.2. Minors under 18 years of age; high school graduate or equivalent or possessing certificate of proficiency; same hours and pay as adults; exceptions

(a) Notwithstanding Sections 1391 and 1391.1, any minor under 18 years of age who has been graduated from a high school maintaining a four-year course above the eighth grade of the elementary schools, or who has had an equal amount of education in a private school or by private tuition, or who has been awarded a certificate of proficiency pursuant to Section 48412 of the Education Code, may be employed for the same hours as an adult may be employed in performing the same work.

(b) Notwithstanding the provisions of the orders of the Industrial Welfare Commission, no employer shall pay any minor described in this section in his employ at wage rates less than the rates paid to adult employees in the same establishment for the same quantity and quality of the same classification of work; provided, however, that nothing herein shall prohibit a variation of rates of pay for such minors and adult employees engaged in the same classification of work based upon a difference in seniority, length of service, ability, skill, difference in duties or services performed, whether regularly or occasionally, difference in the shift or time of day worked, hours of work, or other reasonable differentiation, when exercised in good faith. *(Added by Stats.1977, c. 765, p. 2388, § 1.)*

§ 1392. Employment for more than eight hours in one day; misdemeanor

Every person who has a minor under his or her control, as a ward or an apprentice, and who, except in household occupations, requires the minor to work more than eight hours in any one day, is guilty of a misdemeanor. *(Stats.1937, c. 90, p. 224, § 1392. Amended by Stats.1994, c. 1175 (A.B.1900), § 25.)*

§ 1393. Agricultural packing plants employing minors; exemptions; issuance; revocation; notice; application; posting

(a) Notwithstanding any other provision of this article and Article 2 (commencing with Section 49110) of Chapter 7 of Part 27 of Division 4 of Title 2 of the Education Code, the Labor Commissioner may issue an exemption from laws regulating the employment of minors to employers operating agricultural packing plants that employ minors 16 and 17 years of age during any day during which school is not in session, for up to 10 hours per day during the peak harvest season. These exemptions shall only be granted if they do not materially affect the safety and welfare of minor employees and will prevent undue hardship on the employer. The Labor Commissioner may require an inspection of an agricultural packing plant prior to issuing an exemption.

(b) Any exemption granted pursuant to subdivision (a) shall be in writing to be effective, and may be revoked after reasonable notice is given, in writing, by the Labor Commissioner. Any notice of revocation shall include the reason for the revocation.

(c) An application for an exemption under subdivision (a) shall be made by an employer on a form provided by the Labor Commissioner, and a copy of the application shall be posted at the employer's place of employment at the time the application is filed with the division. *(Added by Stats.1994, c. 1175 (A.B.1900), § 26. Amended by Stats.1995, c. 887 (S.B.443), § 12.)*

§ 1393.5. Agricultural packing plants; employment of minors who are enrollees in Lake County schools; inspection of agricultural packing plant by Labor Commissioner; information to be included in written report to receive an exemption or a renewal of an exemption

(a) Notwithstanding any other provision of this article or Article 2 (commencing with Section 49110) of Chapter 7 of Part 27 of the Education Code, an exemption issued pursuant to Section 1393 may authorize the employment during the peak harvest season of a minor, 16 or 17 years of age who resides in Lake County, during any day in which school is not in session for up to 10 hours per day and more than 48 hours but not more than 60 hours in any one week, only upon the prior written approval of the Lake County Office of Education.

(b) Each year, the Labor Commissioner, prior to issuing or renewing an exemption under this section, shall inspect the affected agricultural packing plant.

(c) As a condition of receiving an exemption or a renewal of an exemption under this section, an affected employer shall, on or before March 1 of each year, file a written report to the Labor Commissioner that contains the following employment information regarding the employer's prior year's payroll:

(1) The number of minors employed by that employer.

(2) A list of the age and hours worked on a weekly basis of each minor employed.

(d) Notwithstanding Chapter 24 (commencing with Section 7550) of Division 7 of Title 1 of the Government Code, the Labor Commissioner shall submit a written report to the Legislature, on or before March 1 of each year, that describes the general working conditions of minors employed in the agricultural packing industry during the past year, and that includes all of the following information:

(1) The number of minors employed in the agricultural packing industry.

(2) The number of exemptions issued, renewed, or denied pursuant to this section.

(3) A summary of the inspections conducted by the Labor Commissioner pursuant to this section.

(4) The number of workplace injuries that occurred to minors at agricultural packing plants.

(5) The number of violations of labor laws and regulations that occurred at agricultural packing plants.

417

(e) This section shall remain in effect only until January 1, 2012, and as of that date is repealed. *(Added by Stats.1996, c. 1117 (S.B.1988), § 1. Amended by Stats.1998, c. 237 (S.B.2054), § 1; Stats.2001, c. 345 (S.B.912), § 1; Stats.2004, c. 151 (S.B.1134), § 1; Stats. 2007, c. 296 (S.B.319), § 1.)*

Repeal

For repeal of this section, see its terms.

§ 1394. Employment of minors at agricultural, horticultural, viticultural, or domestic labor while not in school

Nothing in this article or Article 2 (commencing with Section 1285) of Chapter 2 shall prohibit or prevent either of the following:

(a) The employment of any minor at agricultural, horticultural, viticultural, or domestic labor during the time the public schools are not in session, or during other than school hours, when the work performed is for or under the control of his parent or guardian and is performed upon or in connection with premises owned, operated or controlled by the parent or guardian. However, nothing herein shall permit children under school-age to work at these occupations, while the public schools are in session.

(b) The full-time employment of minors who meet all other legal employment requirements, if they are exempt from compulsory school attendance under Section 48231 of the Education Code. *(Stats.1937, c. 90, p. 225, § 1394. Amended by Stats.1941, c. 287, p. 1420, § 1; Stats.1949, c. 447, p. 791, § 1; Stats.1951, c. 1019, p. 2648, § 1; Stats.1957, c. 1903, p. 3320, § 3, eff. July 10, 1957; Stats.1975, c. 144, p. 276, § 27; Stats.1977, c. 285, p. 1181, § 1, eff. July 8, 1977; Stats.1977, c. 1221, p. 4107, § 5; Stats.1979, c. 373, p. 1347, § 230; Stats.1994, c. 1175 (A.B.1900), § 27.)*

§ 1398. Enforcement agency

The Division of Labor Standards Enforcement shall enforce the provisions of this article. *(Stats.1937, c. 90, p. 226, § 1398. Amended by Stats.1949, c. 127, p. 360, § 6; Stats.1980, c. 676, p. 1968, § 224.)*

§ 1399. Enforcement of article

Nothing in this article shall limit the authority of the Attorney General or the district attorney of any county, either upon their own complaint or the complaint of any person acting for himself or the general public, to prosecute actions, either civil or criminal, for violations of this article, or to enforce the provisions thereof independently and without specific direction of the director. *(Added by Stats.1975, c. 144, p. 277, § 30.)*

CHAPTER 4. RELOCATIONS, TERMINATIONS, AND MASS LAYOFFS

Section

1400.   Construction of chapter; definitions; application of chapter.

Section

1401.   Notice requirements.
1402.   Failure to give required notice; liability of employer.
1402.5.   Exemption from notice requirements; conditions.
1403.   Civil penalty.
1404.   Civil actions against employer.
1405.   Reduction of penalties.
1406.   Authority of commissioner to examine books and records of employers.
1407.   Payments made by employers who fail to give required notice; construction; treatment of benefits.
1408.   Severability of chapter provisions.

§ 1400. Construction of chapter; definitions; application of chapter

The definitions set forth in this section shall govern the construction and meaning of the terms used in this chapter:

(a) "Covered establishment" means any industrial or commercial facility or part thereof that employs, or has employed within the preceding 12 months, 75 or more persons.

(b) "Employer" means any person, as defined by Section 18, who directly or indirectly owns and operates a covered establishment. A parent corporation is an employer as to any covered establishment directly owned and operated by its corporate subsidiary.

(c) "Layoff" means a separation from a position for lack of funds or lack of work.

(d) "Mass layoff" means a layoff during any 30–day period of 50 or more employees at a covered establishment.

(e) "Relocation" means the removal of all or substantially all of the industrial or commercial operations in a covered establishment to a different location 100 miles or more away.

(f) "Termination" means the cessation or substantial cessation of industrial or commercial operations in a covered establishment.

(g)(1) This chapter does not apply where the closing or layoff is the result of the completion of a particular project or undertaking of an employer subject to Wage Order 11, regulating the Broadcasting Industry, Wage Order 12, regulating the Motion Picture Industry, or Wage Order 16, regulating Certain On–Site Occupations in the Construction, Drilling, Logging and Mining Industries, of the Industrial Welfare Commission, and the employees were hired with the understanding that their employment was limited to the duration of that project or undertaking.

(2) This chapter does not apply to employees who are employed in seasonal employment where the employees were hired with the understanding that their employment was seasonal and temporary.

(h) "Employee" means a person employed by an employer for at least 6 months of the 12 months preceding the date on which notice is required. *(Added by Stats.2002, c. 780 (A.B.2957), § 1.)*

§ 1401. Notice requirements

(a) An employer may not order a mass layoff, relocation, or termination at a covered establishment unless, 60 days before the order takes effect, the employer gives written notice of the order to the following:

(1) The employees of the covered establishment affected by the order.

(2) The Employment Development Department, the local workforce investment board, and the chief elected official of each city and county government within which the termination, relocation, or mass layoff occurs.

(b) An employer required to give notice of any mass layoff, relocation, or termination under this chapter shall include in its notice the elements required by the federal Worker Adjustment and Retraining Notification Act (29 U.S.C. Sec. 2101 et seq.).

(c) Notwithstanding the requirements of subdivision (a), an employer is not required to provide notice if a mass layoff, relocation, or termination is necessitated by a physical calamity or act of war. *(Added by Stats.2002, c. 780 (A.B.2957), § 1.)*

§ 1402. Failure to give required notice; liability of employer

(a) An employer who fails to give notice as required by paragraph (1) of subdivision (a) of Section 1401 before ordering a mass layoff, relocation, or termination is liable to each employee entitled to notice who lost his or her employment for:

(1) Back pay at the average regular rate of compensation received by the employee during the last three years of his or her employment, or the employee's final rate of compensation, whichever is higher.

(2) The value of the cost of any benefits to which the employee would have been entitled had his or her employment not been lost, including the cost of any medical expenses incurred by the employee that would have been covered under an employee benefit plan.

(b) Liability under this section is calculated for the period of the employer's violation, up to a maximum of 60 days, or one-half the number of days that the employee was employed by the employer, whichever period is smaller.

(c) The amount of an employer's liability under subdivision (a) is reduced by the following:

(1) Any wages, except vacation moneys accrued prior to the period of the employer's violation, paid by the employer to the employee during the period of the employer's violation.

(2) Any voluntary and unconditional payments made by the employer to the employee that were not required to satisfy any legal obligation.

(3) Any payments by the employer to a third party or trustee, such as premiums for health benefits or payments to a defined contribution pension plan, on behalf of and

attributable to the employee for the period of the violation. *(Added by Stats.2002, c. 780 (A.B.2957), § 1.)*

§ 1402.5. Exemption from notice requirements; conditions

(a) An employer is not required to comply with the notice requirement contained in subdivision (a) of Section 1401 if the department determines that all of the following conditions exist:

(1) As of the time that notice would have been required, the employer was actively seeking capital or business.

(2) The capital or business sought, if obtained, would have enabled the employer to avoid or postpone the relocation or termination.

(3) The employer reasonably and in good faith believed that giving the notice required by subdivision (a) of Section 1401 would have precluded the employer from obtaining the needed capital or business.

(b) The department may not determine that the employer was actively seeking capital or business under subdivision (a) unless the employer provides the department with both of the following:

(1) A written record consisting of all documents relevant to the determination of whether the employer was actively seeking capital or business, as specified by the department.

(2) An affidavit verifying the contents of the documents contained in the record.

(c) The affidavit provided to the department pursuant to paragraph (2) of subdivision (b) shall contain a declaration signed under penalty of perjury stating that the affidavit and the contents of the documents contained in the record submitted pursuant to paragraph (1) of subdivision (b) are true and correct.

(d) This section does not apply to notice of a mass layoff as defined by subdivision (d) of Section 1400. *(Added by Stats.2002, c. 780 (A.B.2957), § 1.)*

§ 1403. Civil penalty

An employer who fails to give notice as required by paragraph (2) of subdivision (a) of Section 1401 is subject to a civil penalty of not more than five hundred dollars ($500) for each day of the employer's violation. The employer is not subject to a civil penalty under this section, however, if the employer pays to all applicable employees the amounts for which the employer is liable under Section 1402 within three weeks from the date the employer orders the mass layoff, relocation, or termination. *(Added by Stats.2002, c. 780 (A.B.2957), § 1.)*

§ 1404. Civil actions against employer

A person, including a local government or an employee representative, seeking to establish liability against an employer may bring a civil action on behalf of the person, other persons similarly situated, or both, in any court of competent jurisdiction. The court may award reasonable

419

attorney's fees as part of costs to any plaintiff who prevails in a civil action brought under this chapter. *(Added by Stats.2002, c. 780 (A.B.2957), § 1.)*

§ 1405. Reduction of penalties

If the court determines that an employer conducted a reasonable investigation in good faith, and had reasonable grounds to believe that its conduct was not a violation of this chapter, the court may reduce the amount of any penalty imposed against the employer under this chapter. *(Added by Stats.2002, c. 780 (A.B. 2957), § 1.)*

§ 1406. Authority of commissioner to examine books and records of employers

In any investigation or proceeding under this chapter, the Labor Commissioner has, in addition to all other powers granted by law, the authority to examine the books and records of an employer. *(Added by Stats.2002, c. 780 (A.B.2957), § 1.)*

§ 1407. Payments made by employers who fail to give required notice; construction; treatment of benefits

(a) Payments to a person under subdivision (a) of Section 1402 by an employer who has failed to provide the advance notice of facility closure required by this chapter or the federal Worker Adjustment and Retraining Notification Act (29 U.S.C. Sec. 2101 et seq.) may not be construed as wages or compensation for personal services under Article 2 (commencing with Section 926) of Chapter 4 of Part 1 of Division 1 of the Unemployment Insurance Code.

(b) Benefits payable under Chapter 5 (commencing with Section 1251) of Part 1 of Division 1 of the Unemployment Insurance Code may not be denied or reduced because of the receipt of payments related to an employer's violation of this chapter or the federal Worker Adjustment and Retraining Notification Act (29 U.S.C. Sec. 2101 et seq.). *(Added by Stats.2002, c. 780 (A.B. 2957), § 1.)*

§ 1408. Severability of chapter provisions

The provisions of this chapter are severable. If any provision of this chapter or its application is held invalid, that invalidity shall not affect other provisions or applications that can be given effect without the invalid provision or application. *(Added by Stats.2002, c. 780 (A.B.2957), § 1.)*

Part 4.5

FAIR EMPLOYMENT PRACTICES [REPEALED]

Part 5

CIVIL AIR PATROL

Section
1500.   Short title.

Section
1501.   Definitions.
1502.   Prohibited actions.
1503.   Civil Air Patrol unpaid leave; notice of intended leave dates; exhaustion of other leave not required; paid leave.
1504.   Restoration of employee to position; negotiation for maintenance of benefits.
1505.   Accrued employee benefits; collective bargaining.
1506.   Exercise of right.
1507.   Civil action; injunction and equitable relief.

§ 1500. Short title

This part shall be known and may be cited as the Civil Air Patrol Employment Protection Act. *(Added by Stats.2009, c. 242 (A.B.485), § 1.)*

§ 1501. Definitions

In this part, the following terms have the following meanings:

(a) "Civil Air Patrol leave" means leave requested by an employee who is a volunteer member of the California Wing of the civilian auxiliary of the United States Air Force commonly known as the Civil Air Patrol and who has been duly directed and authorized by the United States Air Force, the California Emergency Management Agency, or other political subdivision of the State of California that has the authority to authorize an emergency operational mission of the California Wing of the Civil Air Patrol, to respond to an emergency operational mission, within or outside of the state, of the California Wing of the Civil Air Patrol.

(b) "Employee" means a person who may be permitted, required, or directed by an employer for wages or pay to engage in any employment and who has been employed by that employer for at least a 90–day period immediately preceding the commencement of leave, if otherwise eligible for leave.

(c) "Employee benefits" means all benefits, other than salary and wages, provided or made available to an employee by an employer and includes group life insurance, health insurance, disability insurance, and pensions, regardless of whether benefits are provided by a policy or practice of an employer.

(d) "Employer" means any person, partnership, corporation, association, or other business entity; or the State of California, a municipality, or other unit of local government; that employs more than 15 employees. *(Added by Stats.2009, c. 242 (A.B.485), § 1.)*

§ 1502. Prohibited actions

An employer shall not discriminate against or discharge from employment a member of the Civil Air Patrol because of such membership and shall not hinder or prevent a member from performing service as part of the California Wing of the Civil Air Patrol during an emergency operational mission of the California Wing of the Civil Air Patrol for which a member is entitled to leave under this part. *(Added by Stats.2009, c. 242 (A.B.485), § 1.)*

§ 1503. Civil Air Patrol unpaid leave; notice of intended leave dates; exhaustion of other leave not required; paid leave

(a)(1) An employer shall provide not less than 10 days per calendar year of unpaid Civil Air Patrol leave to an employee responding to an emergency operational mission of the California Wing of the Civil Air Patrol. Civil Air Patrol leave for a single emergency operational mission shall not exceed three days, unless an extension of time is granted by the governmental entity that authorized the emergency operational mission, and the extension of the leave is approved by the employer.

(2) Notwithstanding paragraph (1), an employer is not required to grant Civil Air Patrol leave to an employee who is required to respond to either the same or other simultaneous emergency operational mission as a first responder or disaster service worker for a local, state, or federal agency.

(b)(1) An employee shall give the employer as much notice as possible of the intended dates upon which the Civil Air Patrol leave will begin and end.

(2) An employer may require certification from the proper Civil Air Patrol authority to verify the eligibility of the employee for the leave requested or taken. The employer may deny the leave to be taken as Civil Air Patrol leave if the employee fails to provide the required certification.

(c) An employee taking leave under this part shall not be required to exhaust all accrued vacation leave, personal leave, compensatory leave, sick leave, disability leave, and any other leave that may be available to the employee in order to take Civil Air Patrol leave.

(d) Nothing in this act prevents an employer from providing paid leave for leave taken pursuant to this part. *(Added by Stats.2009, c. 242 (A.B.485), § 1.)*

§ 1504. Restoration of employee to position; negotiation for maintenance of benefits

(a) An employer shall, upon expiration of a leave authorized by this part, restore an employee to the position held by him or her when the leave began or to a position with equivalent seniority status, employee benefits, pay, and other terms and conditions of employment. An employer may decline to restore an employee as required in this subdivision because of conditions unrelated to the exercise of rights under this part by the employee.

(b) An employer and an employee may negotiate for the employer to maintain the benefits of the employee at the expense of the employer during the leave. *(Added by Stats.2009, c. 242 (A.B.485), § 1.)*

§ 1505. Accrued employee benefits; collective bargaining

(a) Taking Civil Air Patrol leave under this part shall not result in the loss of an employee benefit accrued before the date on which the leave began.

(b) This part does not affect the obligation of an employer to comply with any collective bargaining agreement or employee benefit plan that provides greater leave rights to employees than the rights provided under this part.

(c) The rights provided under this part shall not be diminished by any collective bargaining agreement or employee benefit plan entered into on or after January 1, 2010.

(d) This part does not affect or diminish the contract rights or seniority status of an employee not entitled to Civil Air Patrol leave. *(Added by Stats.2009, c. 242 (A.B.485), § 1.)*

§ 1506. Exercise of right

(a) An employer shall not interfere with, restrain, or deny the exercise of the attempt to exercise a right established by this part.

(b) An employer shall not discharge, fine, suspend, expel, discipline, or in any other manner discriminate against an employee who does any of the following:

(1) Exercises a right provided under this part.

(2) Opposes a practice made unlawful by this part. *(Added by Stats.2009, c. 242 (A.B.485), § 1.)*

§ 1507. Civil action; injunction and equitable relief

(a) An employee may bring a civil action in the superior court of the appropriate county to enforce this part.

(b) The court may enjoin any act or practice that violates this part and may order any equitable relief necessary and appropriate to redress the violation or to enforce this part. *(Added by Stats.2009, c. 242 (A.B.485), § 1.)*

Part 6

LICENSING

Chapter		Section
1.	Athlete Agents [Repealed]	
2.	State Employment Bureaus [Repealed]	
3.	Farm Labor Contractors	1682
4.	Talent Agencies	1700
4.5.	Fee–Related Talent Services	1701
5.	Nurses Registries [Repealed]	

CHAPTER 1. ATHLETE AGENTS [REPEALED]

CHAPTER 2. STATE EMPLOYMENT BUREAUS [REPEALED]

CHAPTER 3. FARM LABOR CONTRACTORS

Section
1682.   Definitions.

Section
1682.3.   Day haulers.
1682.4.   Farm labor contractor.
1682.5.   Exclusions.
1682.7.   Examination and licensing of farm labor contractors; office in Fresno; suitable facilities.
1682.8.   Farm labor contractor special enforcement unit.
1683.   Requirement of license.
1684.   Prerequisites to issuance or renewal of license.
1684.3.   Temporary or provisional license.
1684.5.   Submission of licensee list to highway patrol.
1685.   Persons disqualified.
1686.   Refusal of license; conduct of proceedings; applicability of Government Code.
1687.   License; lamination; contents; size, format, hologram.
1688.   Expiration of license; renewal.
1689.   Renewal applications.
1690.   Grounds for revocation, suspension, and refusal of license.
1690.1.   Failure to remit worker contributions as grounds for refusal to issue or renew license.
1691.   License subject to two or more final judgments for failure to pay wages due; license suspension; telephone information line; "serious violation".
1692.   Hearing on revocation or suspension; conduct of proceedings; applicability of Government Code.
1692.5.   License; surrender on suspension or revocation.
1693.   Action on bond; assignment of claims to labor commissioner.
1694.   Service of process on licensee departing state.
1695.   Duties of licensee.
1695.5.   Payroll list of contractor's employees working for grower; furnishing grower; form; contents.
1695.55.   Payroll records for each farm laborer.
1695.6.   Contract with unlicensed farm labor contractor; prohibition.
1695.7.   Farm labor contractors; license requirements.
1695.8.   Performance of activity or service by persons after suspension, revocation or renew denial of license; time period; contracts and use of persons by farm labor contractors.
1695.9.   Responsibility of person contracted by farm labor contractor who is acting in capacity of farm labor contractor to provide copy of license; violations; retention period.
1696.   Prohibited acts of licensee.
1696.2.   Vehicles used by licensee for transportation of individuals; display of name and license number.
1696.3.   Licensee or employee operating bus or truck for transportation of individuals; chauffeurs' licenses.
1696.4.   Registration of vehicles used by licensee for transportation of individuals; evidence of insurance; rental of vehicles.
1696.5.   Itemized statement of wage deductions.
1696.6.   Bona fide order for employment as prerequisite to recruitment or solicitation and transportation.
1696.8.   Farm Labor Contractor Enforcement Unit.
1697.   Violations; misdemeanor; penalty; civil action by aggrieved employee; engaging in farm contracting activities after license suspension or revocation; penalties.
1697.1.   Transportation fees; false, fraudulent, or misleading representations; misdemeanor; civil actions.
1697.2.   Trials to be set for earliest possible date.

Section
1697.3.   Determination of failure to pay wages; order of payment.
1698.   Payments and deposits into Farmworker Remedial Account.
1698.1.   Transfer of interest of profits of agency.
1698.2.   Unlawful employment.
1698.3.   Acceptance of fee without employment order.
1698.4.   Referral of woman or minor to place of ill-repute.
1698.5.   Referral of minor to on-sale liquor establishment.
1698.6.   Permitting persons of bad character to frequent agency.
1698.7.   Unlawful employment of minors.
1698.8.   Division of fees with employer prohibited.
1699.   Rules and regulations.

§ 1682.   Definitions

As used in this chapter:

(a) "Person" includes any individual, firm, partnership, association, limited liability company, or corporation.

(b) "Farm labor contractor" designates any person who, for a fee, employs workers to render personal services in connection with the production of any farm products to, for, or under the direction of a third person, or who recruits, solicits, supplies, or hires workers on behalf of an employer engaged in the growing or producing of farm products, and who, for a fee, provides in connection therewith one or more of the following services: furnishes board, lodging, or transportation for those workers; supervises, times, checks, counts, weighs, or otherwise directs or measures their work; or disburses wage payments to these persons.

(c) "License" means a license issued by the Labor Commissioner to carry on the business, activities, or operations of a farm labor contractor under this chapter.

(d) "Licensee" means a farm labor contractor who holds a valid and unrevoked license under this chapter.

(e) "Fee" shall mean (1) the difference between the amount received by a labor contractor and the amount paid out by him or her to persons employed to render personal services to, for or under the direction of a third person; (2) any valuable consideration received or to be received by a farm labor contractor for or in connection with any of the services described above, and shall include the difference between any amount received or to be received by him or her, and the amount paid out by him or her, for or in connection with the rendering of such services. *(Added by Stats.1951, c. 1746, p. 4161, § 2. Amended by Stats.1955, c. 1834, p. 3377, § 1; Stats.1994, c. 1010 (S.B.2053), § 183.)*

§ 1682.3.   Day haulers

"Farm labor contractor" includes any "day hauler." "Day hauler" means any person who is employed by a farm labor contractor to transport, or who for a fee transports, by motor vehicle, workers to render personal services in connection with the production of any farm products to, for, or under the direction of a third person. *(Added by Stats.1957, c. 1704, p. 3081, § 1.)*

§ 1682.4. Farm labor contractor

"Farm labor contractor" does not include a commercial packing house engaged in both the harvesting and the packing of citrus fruit or soft fruit for a client or customer. *(Added by Stats.1985, c. 662, § 1.)*

§ 1682.5. Exclusions

This chapter does not apply to:

(a) A nonprofit corporation or organization with respect to services specified in subdivision (b) of Section 1682, which are performed for its members.

(b) Any person who performs the services specified in subdivision (b) of Section 1682 only within the scope of his employment by the third person on whose behalf he is so acting and not as an independent contractor. *(Added by Stats.1955, c. 1834, p. 3377, § 2.)*

§ 1682.7. Examination and licensing of farm labor contractors; office in Fresno; suitable facilities

The Labor Commissioner shall ensure that the office maintained in Fresno has suitable facilities and sufficient personnel for the examination and licensing of farm labor contractors and for the processing of complaints against farm labor contractors or any agent of a farm labor contractor. *(Added by Stats.2000, c. 877 (A.D.2707), § 1.)*

§ 1682.8. Farm labor contractor special enforcement unit

The Labor Commissioner may establish and maintain a Farm Labor Contractor Special Enforcement Unit within the Division of Labor Standards Enforcement office in Fresno of the Department of Industrial Relations for the hiring of additional agents to enforce the provisions of this chapter by revoking, suspending, or refusing to renew farm labor contractors' licenses pursuant to Section 1690. *(Added by Stats.2000, c. 917 (A.B.1338), § 1.)*

§ 1683. Requirement of license

No person shall act as a farm labor contractor until a license to do so has been issued to him by the Labor Commissioner, and unless such license is in full force and effect and is in his possession. The Labor Commissioner shall, by regulation, provide a means of issuing duplicate licenses in case of loss of the original license or any other appropriate instances. *(Added by Stats.1951, c. 1746, p. 4161, § 2.)*

§ 1684. Prerequisites to issuance or renewal of license

(a) The Labor Commissioner shall not issue to any person a license to act as a farm labor contractor, nor shall the Labor Commissioner renew that license, until all of the following conditions are satisfied:

(1) The person has executed a written application in a form prescribed by the Labor Commissioner, subscribed and sworn to by the person, and containing all of the following:

(A) A statement by the person of all facts required by the Labor Commissioner concerning the applicant's character, competency, responsibility, and the manner and method by which the person proposes to conduct operations as a farm labor contractor if the license is issued.

(B) The names and addresses of all persons, except bona fide employees on stated salaries, financially interested, either as partners, associates, or profit sharers, in the proposed operation as a farm labor contractor, together with the amount of their respective interests.

(C) A declaration consenting to the designation by a court of the Labor Commissioner as an agent available to accept service of summons in any action against the licensee if the licensee has left the jurisdiction in which the action is commenced or otherwise has become unavailable to accept service.

(2) The Labor Commissioner, after investigation, is satisfied as to the character, competency, and responsibility of the person.

(3) The person has deposited with the Labor Commissioner a surety bond in an amount based on the size of the person's annual payroll for all employees, as follows:

(A) For payrolls up to five hundred thousand dollars ($500,000), a twenty-five thousand dollar ($25,000) bond.

(B) For payrolls of five hundred thousand dollars ($500,000) to two million dollars ($2,000,000), a fifty thousand dollar ($50,000) bond.

(C) For payrolls greater than two million dollars ($2,000,000), a seventy-five thousand dollar ($75,000) bond.

Where the contractor has been the subject of a final judgment in a year in an amount equal to that of the bond required, he or she shall be required to deposit an additional bond within 60 days. The bond shall be payable to the people of the State of California and shall be conditioned that the farm labor contractor will comply with all the terms and provisions of this chapter and will pay all damages occasioned to any person by failure to do so, or by any violation of this chapter, or false statements or misrepresentations made in the procurement of the license. The bond shall also be payable for interest on wages and for any damages arising from violation of orders of the Industrial Welfare Commission, and for any other monetary relief awarded to an agricultural worker as a result of a violation of this code.

(4) The person has paid to the Labor Commissioner a license fee of five hundred dollars ($500) plus a filing fee of ten dollars ($10). However, where a timely application for renewal is filed, the ten dollar ($10) filing fee is not required. The Labor Commissioner shall deposit one hundred fifty dollars ($150) of each licensee's annual license fee into the Farmworker Remedial Account. Funds from this account shall be disbursed by the Labor Commissioner only to persons determined by the Labor Commissioner to have been damaged by any licensee when the damage exceeds the limits of the licensee's bond, or to persons determined by the Labor Commissioner to have been damaged by an unlicensed farm labor contractor. In making these determinations, the Labor

Commissioner shall disburse funds from the Farmworker Remedial Account to satisfy claims against farm labor contractors or unlicensed farm labor contractors, which shall also include interest on wages and any damages arising from the violation of orders of the Industrial Welfare Commission, and for any other monetary relief awarded to an agricultural worker as a result of a violation of this code. The Labor Commissioner may disburse funds from the Farmworker Remedial Account to farm labor contractors, for payment of farmworkers, where a contractor is unable to pay farmworkers due to the failure of a grower or packer to pay the contractor. Any disbursed funds subsequently recovered by the Labor Commissioner pursuant to Section 1693, or otherwise, shall be returned to the Farmworker Remedial Account.

(5) The person has taken a written examination that demonstrates an essential degree of knowledge of the current laws and administrative regulations concerning farm labor contractors as the Labor Commissioner deems necessary for the safety and protection of farmers, farmworkers, and the public. To successfully complete the examinations, the person must correctly answer at least 85 percent of the questions posed. The examination period shall not exceed four hours. The examination may only be taken a maximum of three times in a calendar year. The examinations shall include a demonstration of knowledge of the current laws and regulations regarding wages, hours, and working conditions, penalties, employee housing and transportation, collective bargaining, field sanitation, and safe work practices related to pesticide use, including all of the following subjects:

(A) Field reentry regulations.

(B) Worker pesticide safety training.

(C) Employer responsibility for safe working conditions.

(D) Symptoms and appropriate treatment of pesticide poisoning.

(6) The person has registered as a farm labor contractor pursuant to the federal Migrant and Seasonal Agricultural Worker Protection Act (29 U.S.C. 1801 et seq.), when registration is required pursuant to federal law.

(b)(1) The Labor Commissioner shall consult with the Director of Pesticide Regulation, the Department of the California Highway Patrol, the Department of Housing and Community Development, the Employment Development Department, the Department of Food and Agriculture, the Department of Motor Vehicles, and the Division of Occupational Safety and Health in preparing the examination required by paragraph (5) of subdivision (a) and the appropriate educational materials pertaining to the matters included in the examination, and may charge a fee of not more than one hundred dollars ($100) to cover the cost of administration of the examination.

(2) In addition, the person must enroll and participate in at least eight hours of relevant, educational classes each year. The classes shall be chosen from a list of approved classes prepared by the Labor Commissioner, in consultation with the persons and entities listed in paragraph (1) and county agricultural commissioners.

(c) The Labor Commissioner may renew a license without requiring the applicant for renewal to take the examination specified in paragraph (5) of subdivision (a) if the Labor Commissioner finds that the applicant meets all of the following criteria:

(1) Has satisfactorily completed the examination during the immediately preceding two years.

(2) Has not during the preceding year been found to be in violation of any applicable laws or regulations including, but not limited to, Division 7 (commencing with Section 12501) of the Food and Agricultural Code, Part 1 (commencing with Section 17000) of Division 13 of the Health and Safety Code, Division 2 (commencing with Section 200), Division 4 (commencing with Section 3200), and Division 5 (commencing with Section 6300) of this code, and Chapter 1 (commencing with Section 12500) of Division 6 of the Vehicle Code.

(3) Has, for each year since the license was obtained, enrolled and participated in at least eight hours of relevant, educational classes, chosen from a list of approved classes prepared by the Labor Commissioner.

(4) Has complied with all other requirements of this section. *(Added by Stats.1951, c. 1746, p. 4162, § 2. Amended by Stats.1959, c. 950, p. 2978, § 1; Stats.1963, c. 1992, p. 4073, § 1; Stats.1965, c. 570, p. 1895, § 1; Stats.1965, c. 1191, p. 3007, § 1.5; Stats.1967, c. 125, p. 1154, § 1; Stats.1968, c. 733, p. 1430, § 1; Stats.1969, c. 1094, p. 2095, § 1; Stats.1970, c. 1587, p. 3303, § 1; Stats.1970, c. 1588, p. 3305, § 1; Stats.1971, c. 278, p. 584, § 1, eff. July 7, 1971; Stats.1972, c. 271, p. 545, § 1; Stats.1976, c. 803, p. 1851, § 1; Stats. 1982, c. 517, p. 2402, § 299; Stats.1983, c. 685, § 1; Stats.1988, c. 1000, § 1; Stats.1991, c. 1197 (A.B.318), § 1; Gov.Reorg.Plan No. 1 of 1991, § 148.5, eff. July 17, 1991; Stats.1991, c. 1197 (A.B.318), § 1; Stats.1992, c. 1349 (A.B.3146), § 1; Stats.2000, c. 917 (A.B.1338), § 2; Stats.2001, c. 147 (S.B.1125), § 1; Stats.2006, c. 69 (A.B.1806), § 22, eff. July 12, 2006.)*

§ 1684.3. Temporary or provisional license

Whenever an application for a license or renewal is made, and application processing pursuant to this chapter has not been completed, the Labor Commissioner may, at his or her discretion, issue a temporary or provisional license valid for a period not exceeding 90 days, and subject, where appropriate, to the automatic and summary revocation by the Labor Commissioner. Otherwise, the conditions for issuance or renewal shall meet the requirements of Section 1684. *(Added by Stats.1984, c. 557, § 2.)*

§ 1684.5. Submission of licensee list to highway patrol

The Labor Commissioner shall quarterly submit to the Department of the California Highway Patrol a list of all licensees. *(Added by Stats.1974, c. 1447, p. 3159, § 1, eff.*

Sept. 26, 1974. Amended by Stats.2000, c. 917 (A.B.1338), § 3.)

§ 1685. Persons disqualified

No license to operate as a farm labor contractor shall be granted:

(a) To any person who sells or proposes to sell intoxicating liquors in a building or on premises where he operates or proposes to operate as a farm labor contractor.

(b) To a person whose license has been revoked within three (3) years from the date of application. *(Added by Stats.1951, c. 1746, p. 4162, § 2. Amended by Stats.1967, c. 125, p. 1154, § 2.)*

§ 1686. Refusal of license; conduct of proceedings; applicability of Government Code

The Labor Commissioner, upon proper notice and hearing, may refuse to grant a license. The proceedings shall be conducted in accordance with Chapter 5 of Part 1 of Division 3 of Title 2 of the Government Code [1] and the commissioner shall have all of the powers granted therein. *(Added by Stats.1951, c. 1746, p. 4162, § 2.)*

[1] Government Code § 11500 et seq.

§ 1687. License; lamination; contents; size, format, hologram

(a) Each laminated license shall contain, on the face thereof, all of the following:

(1) The name and address of the licensee and the fact that the licensee is licensed to act as a farm labor contractor for the period upon the face of the license only.

(2) The number, date of issuance, and date of expiration of the license.

(3) The amount of the surety bond deposited by the licensee.

(4) The fact that the license may not be transferred or assigned.

(5) A picture of the licensee taken at the time of application.

(b) The license shall be similar in size and format to a driver's license issued by the Department of Motor Vehicles, and shall contain a hologram and a signature to verify authenticity. The cost of the hologrammed license shall be appropriated from the license fee.

(c) The license shall contain on the back thereof the definition of a farm labor contractor, as defined by subdivision (b) of Section 1682. *(Added by Stats.1951, c. 1746, p. 4162, § 2. Amended by Stats.1970, c. 1587, p. 3304, § 2; Stats.1971, c. 438, p. 893, § 137; Stats.1982, c. 517, p. 2403, § 300; Stats.2000, c. 917 (A.B.1338), § 4.)*

§ 1688. Expiration of license; renewal

The license when first issued shall run to the next birthday of the applicant, and each license shall then be renewed within the 30 days preceding the licensee's birthday and shall run from birthday to birthday. In case the applicant is a partnership or corporation, the license for a partnership shall be renewed within the 30 days preceding the birthday of the oldest partner, and the license for a corporation shall be renewed within the 30 days preceding the anniversary of the date the corporation was lawfully formed. Renewal shall require the filing of an application for renewal, a renewal bond, and the payment of the annual license fee, but the Labor Commissioner may demand that a new application or a new bond be submitted. *(Added by Stats.1951, c. 1746, p. 4163, § 2. Amended by Stats.1953, c. 881, p. 2236, § 1, operative Jan. 1, 1954; Stats.1970, c. 1587, p. 3304, § 3; Stats.1970, c. 1588, p. 3305, § 2; Stats.1971, c. 278, p. 585, § 2, eff. July 7, 1971; Stats.1982, c. 517, p. 2404, § 301.)*

§ 1689. Renewal applications

All applications for renewal shall state the names and addresses of all persons, except bona fide employees on stated salaries, financially interested either as partners, associates or profit sharers in the operation of the farm labor contractor. *(Added by Stats.1951, c. 1746, p. 4163, § 2. Amended by Stats.1967, c. 125, p. 1154, § 3.)*

§ 1690. Grounds for revocation, suspension, and refusal of license

The Labor Commissioner may revoke, suspend, or refuse to renew any license when it is shown that any of the following have occurred:

(a) The licensee or any agent of the licensee has violated or failed to comply with any of the provisions of this chapter.

(b) The licensee has made any misrepresentations or false statements in his or her application for a license.

(c) The conditions under which the license was issued have changed or no longer exist.

(d) The licensee, or any agent of the licensee, has violated, or has willfully aided or abetted any person in the violation of, or failed to comply with, any law of the State of California regulating the employment of employees in agriculture, the payment of wages to farm employees, or the conditions, terms, or places of employment affecting the health and safety of farm employees, which is applicable to the business, activities, or operations of the licensee in his or her capacity as a farm labor contractor.

(e) The licensee, or any agent of the licensee, has failed to comply with any provisions of the Vehicle Code pertaining to a farm labor vehicle, as described in Sections 322 and 323 of the Vehicle Code, under the licensee's control, or has allowed a farm labor vehicle under his or her control to be operated by a driver without a valid driver's license and certificate required pursuant to Section 12519 of the Vehicle Code.

(f) The licensee has been found, by a court or the Secretary of Labor, to have violated any provision of the federal Migrant and Seasonal Agricultural Worker Pro-

425

tection Act (Chapter 20 (commencing with Section 1801), Title 29, United States Code), provided that the licensee is required to register as a farm labor contractor pursuant to federal law. *(Added by Stats.1951, c. 1746, p. 4163, § 2. Amended by Stats.1974, c. 1447, p. 3159, § 2, eff. Sept. 26, 1974; Stats.1976, c. 803, p. 1853, § 2; Stats.1988, c. 1000, § 2.)*

§ 1690.1. Failure to remit worker contributions as grounds for refusal to issue or renew license

If any licensee fails to remit the proper amount of worker contributions required by Chapter 4 (commencing with Section 901) of Part 1 of Division 1 of the Unemployment Insurance Code, or the Employment Development Department has made an assessment for such unpaid worker contributions against the licensee that is final, the Labor Commissioner shall, upon written notice by the Employment Development Department, refuse to issue or renew the license of such licensee until such licensee has fully paid the amount of delinquency for such unpaid worker contributions.

The Labor Commissioner shall not, however, refuse to renew the license of a licensee under this section until the assessment for unpaid worker contributions is final and unpaid, and the licensee has exhausted, or failed to seek, his right of administrative review of such final assessment, pursuant to Chapter 4 (commencing with Section 901) of Part 1 of Division 1 of the Unemployment Insurance Code. *(Added by Stats.1970, c. 1216, p. 2134, § 1. Amended by Stats.1973, c. 1206, p. 2614, § 35; Stats.1973, c. 1207, p. 2665, § 35; Stats.1973, c. 1212, p. 2754, § 64; Stats.1977, c. 1252, p. 4435, § 357, operative July 1, 1978.)*

§ 1691. License subject to two or more final judgments for failure to pay wages due; license suspension; telephone information line; "serious violation"

(a) If any licensee has been subject to two or more final judgments by a court for failure to pay wages due with respect to his or her agricultural employees within a five-year period, the Labor Commissioner shall suspend for one year the license of the licensee. The Labor Commissioner shall maintain a telephone information line for the purpose of advising potential or actual employees of farm labor contractors regarding the compliance of individual farm labor contractors with applicable laws and regulations.

(b) For purposes of this section, a "serious violation" shall have the same meaning as provided in paragraph (1) of subdivision (a) of Section 6130 of Title 3 of the California Code of Regulations. *(Added by Stats.1988, c. 1000, § 3. Amended by Stats.1992, c. 1349 (A.B.3146), § 2.)*

§ 1692. Hearing on revocation or suspension; conduct of proceedings; applicability of Government Code

Before revoking or suspending any license, the Labor Commissioner shall afford the holder of such license an opportunity to be heard in person or by counsel. The proceedings shall be conducted in accordance with Chap-

ter 5 of Part 1 of Division 3 of Title 2 of the Government Code,[1] and the commissioner shall have all the powers granted therein. *(Added by Stats.1951, c. 1746, p. 4163, § 2.)*

[1] Government Code § 11500 et seq.

§ 1692.5. License; surrender on suspension or revocation

A licensee whose license is suspended or revoked pursuant to the provisions of this chapter shall immediately surrender such license to the Labor Commissioner. *(Added by Stats.1970, c. 448, p. 897, § 1.)*

§ 1693. Action on bond; assignment of claims to labor commissioner

The Labor Commissioner and the deputies and representatives authorized by the Labor Commissioner in writing may take assignments of actions on the bond against licensees by persons damaged and may prosecute such actions on behalf of persons who, in the judgment of the Labor Commissioner, are financially unable to employ counsel, in the same manner that claims are prosecuted under Section 98. *(Added by Stats.1951, c. 1746, p. 4163, § 2. Amended by Stats.1970, c. 1587, p. 3304, § 4; Stats.1982, c. 517, p. 2404, § 304.)*

§ 1694. Service of process on licensee departing state

When a licensee has departed from the State with intent to defraud creditors or to avoid service of summons in any action brought under this chapter, service shall be made upon the surety as prescribed in the Code of Civil Procedure. A copy of the summons shall be mailed to the licensee at the last known post-office address of his residence, as shown by the records of the Labor Commissioner. Service is complete as to such licensee, after mailing, at the expiration of the time prescribed by the Code of Civil Procedure for service of summons in the particular court in which suit is brought. *(Added by Stats.1951, c. 1746, p. 4164, § 2.)*

§ 1695. Duties of licensee

(a) Every licensee shall do all of the following:

(1) Carry his or her license and proof of registration issued pursuant to paragraph (8) with him or her at all times and exhibit the same to all persons with whom he or she intends to deal in his or her capacity as a farm labor contractor prior to so dealing.

(2) File at the United States Post Office serving the address of the licensee, as noted on the face of his or her license, with the office of the Labor Commissioner, and with the agricultural commissioner of the county or counties in which the labor contractor has contracted with a grower, a correct change of address immediately upon each occasion the licensee permanently moves his or her address. The address shall also be the mailing address for purposes of notice required by the Labor Code or by any other applicable statute or regulations respecting service by mail.

(3) Promptly when due, pay or distribute to the individuals entitled thereto, all moneys or other things of value entrusted to the licensee by any third person for this purpose.

(4) Comply on his or her part with the terms and provisions of all legal and valid agreements and contracts entered into between licensee in his or her capacity as a farm labor contractor and third persons.

(5) Have available for inspection by his or her employees and by the grower with whom he or she has contracted, a written statement in English and Spanish showing the rate of compensation he or she receives from the grower and the rate of compensation he or she is paying to his or her employees for services rendered to, for, or under the control of the grower.

(6) Take out a policy of insurance with any insurance carrier authorized to do business in the State of California in an amount satisfactory to the commissioner, which insures the licensee against liability for damage to persons or property arising out of the licensee's operation of, or ownership of, any vehicle or vehicles for the transportation of individuals in connection with his or her business, activities, or operations as a farm labor contractor.

(7) Have displayed prominently at the site where the work is to be performed and on all vehicles used by the licensee for the transportation of employees, the rate of compensation the licensee is paying to his or her employees for their services, printed in both English and Spanish and in lettering of a size to be prescribed by the Department of Industrial Relations.

(8) Register annually with the agricultural commissioner of the county or counties in which the labor contractor has contracted with a grower.

(9) Provide information and training on applicable laws and regulations governing worker safety, including the requirements of Article 10.5 (commencing with Section 12980) of Chapter 2 of Division 7 of the Food and Agriculture Code, or regulating the terms and conditions of agricultural employment, to each crew leader, foreman, or other employee whose duties include the supervision, direction, or control of any agricultural worker on behalf of a licensee, or pursuant to, a contract or agreement for agricultural services entered into with a licensee.

(b) The board of supervisors of a county may establish fees to be charged each licensee for the recovery of the actual costs incurred by commissioners in the administration of registrations and change of address and the issuance of proofs of registration. *(Added by Stats.1951, c. 1746, p. 4164, § 2. Amended by Stats.1963, c. 265, p. 1023, § 1; Stats.1965, c. 1978, p. 4504, § 1; Stats.1972, c. 271, p. 546, § 2; Stats.1990, c. 661 (A.B.3550), § 3; Stats.1992, c. 1349 (A.B.3146), § 3.)*

§ 1695.5. Payroll list of contractor's employees working for grower; furnishing grower; form; contents

(a) Every farm labor contractor, upon request of any agricultural grower with whom he or she has a contract to supply farmworkers, shall immediately furnish the grower with a payroll list of all the contractor's employees working for the grower.

(b) The payroll list shall be on a uniform form approved by the Labor Commissioner, which shall include, but not be limited to, the employee's name, social security number, permanent and temporary address, telephone number, and length of employment with the grower.

(c) The requirements of this section are in addition to any requirements of federal law, including the federal Migrant and Seasonal Agricultural Worker Protection Act (Chapter 20 (commencing with Section 1801), Title 29, United States Code). *(Added by Stats.1976, c. 779, p. 1819, § 1. Amended by Stats.1988, c. 1000, § 4.)*

§ 1695.55. Payroll records for each farm laborer

(a) Every person acting in the capacity of a farm labor contractor shall provide any grower with whom he or she has contracted to supply farmworkers a payroll record for each farmworker providing labor under the contract. The payroll record shall include a disclosure of the wages and hours worked for each farmworker.

(b) Each grower entering into a contract with a farm labor contractor shall retain a copy of the payroll record provided by the contractor for the duration of the contract. *(Added by Stats.2000, c. 917 (A.B.1338), § 5.)*

§ 1695.6. Contract with unlicensed farm labor contractor; prohibition

No person shall knowingly enter into an agreement for the services of a farm labor contractor who is not licensed under this chapter. *(Added by Stats.1976, c. 805, p. 1853, § 3.)*

§ 1695.7. Farm labor contractors; license requirements

(a)(1) Prior to entering into any contract or agreement to supply agricultural labor or services to a grower, a farm labor contractor shall first provide to the grower a copy of his or her current valid state license. A failure to do so is a violation of this chapter. The grower shall keep a copy of the license for a period of three years following the termination of the contract or agreement.

(2) In the event that the licensee or prospective licensee has fulfilled all the requirements for a license, but the Labor Commissioner has not been able to timely issue or renew a license, the Labor Commissioner shall issue to the person applying for a license, or renewal of a license, a letter of authorization permitting that person to operate or continue to operate as a farm labor contractor. For purposes of this section, a "valid state license" shall include a letter of authorization issued pursuant to this paragraph.

(3)(A) No grower shall enter into a contract or agreement with a person acting in the capacity of a farm labor contractor who fails to provide a copy of his or her license. A grower has an affirmative obligation to inspect the license of any person contracted as a farm labor contractor, a copy of whose license is provided to the grower pursuant to paragraph (1), and to verify that the license is valid. The grower shall request verification from the license verification unit by the close of the third business day following the day on which the farm labor contractor is engaged. The grower may be supplied services by the farm labor contractor and shall not be liable under this section for an invalid license while awaiting verification from the verification unit. The verification received from the license verification unit shall serve as conclusive evidence of the grower's compliance with this subparagraph. The verification shall be valid until the farm labor contractor's license expires. Failure to comply with this subparagraph is a violation of this chapter.

(B) A farm labor contractor has an affirmative obligation to inspect the license of any person contracted by the farm labor contractor who is acting in the capacity of a farm labor contractor a copy of whose license is provided to the farm labor contractor pursuant to Section 1695.9, and to verify that the license is valid. The farm labor contractor shall request verification from the license verification unit by the close of the third business day following the day on which the individual who is acting as the farm labor contractor is engaged. The farm labor contractor may be supplied services by the acting farm labor contractor and shall not be liable under this section for an invalid license while awaiting verification from the verification unit. The verification received from the license verification unit shall serve as conclusive evidence of the farm labor contractor's compliance with this subparagraph. The verification shall be valid until the individual's license expires. Failure to comply with this subparagraph is a violation of this chapter.

(C) If a determination is made by the Labor Commissioner that the verification system is inoperable, no grower or farm labor contractor shall be liable under this section until seven business days after the Labor Commissioner determines the system is operable and has made public notice to affected parties.

(4)(A) If a contract or agreement entered into with a farm labor contractor extends beyond the expiration date of his or her license, or extends beyond the date contained in the letter of authorization to operate, the farm labor contractor shall provide to the grower, upon renewal of the license or issuance of the letter of authorization a copy of his or her current valid renewed license or a copy of a letter of authorization issued by the Labor Commissioner. In the event the farm labor contractor's license is not renewed, the farm labor contractor shall notify the grower within three days.

(B) If a contract or agreement entered into by a farm labor contractor with another farm labor contractor extends beyond the expiration date of his or her license, or extends beyond the date contained in the letter of authorization to operate, the other farm labor contractor shall provide to the farm labor contractor, upon renewal of the license or issuance of the letter of authorization a copy of his or her current valid renewed license or a copy of a letter of authorization issued by the Labor Commissioner. In the event the license of a person contracted by a farm labor contractor who is acting as farm labor contractor is not renewed, the person shall notify the farm labor contractor within three days.

(b) A failure by a farm labor contractor to provide a copy of his or her license to the grower shall not constitute a defense against liability under this section for a grower who subsequently fails to comply with the requirements of subparagraph (A) of paragraph (3) of subdivision (a). A failure by a person acting as a farm labor contractor who is contracted by a farm labor contractor to provide a copy of his or her license to the farm labor contractor shall not constitute a defense against liability under this section for a farm labor contractor who subsequently fails to comply with the requirements of subparagraph (B) of paragraph (3) of subdivision (a).

(c)(1) Any person who acts in the capacity of a farm labor contractor without first securing a license or while his or her license has been suspended or revoked is guilty of a misdemeanor punishable by a fine of not less than one thousand dollars ($1,000) nor more than five thousand dollars ($5,000), or imprisonment in the county jail for not more than six months, or both, and is subject to other sanctions under this chapter, including subdivisions (b) and (c) of Section 1697.

(2) Any grower or farm labor contractor who enters into a contract or agreement in violation of this section shall be subject to a civil action by an aggrieved worker for any claims arising from the contract or agreement that are a direct result of any violation of any state law regulating wages, housing, pesticides, or transportation committed by the unlicensed farm labor contractor. The court shall grant a prevailing plaintiff reasonable attorney's fees and costs.

(3) On or after January 1, 2003, any grower, farm labor contractor, or other person acting either individually or as an officer, agent, or employee of any grower or farm labor contractor who knowingly and willfully fails to pay, or causes the failure to pay, wages as set forth in subdivision (b) of Section 1199, or any higher wages that have been agreed to, is guilty of a misdemeanor punishable as set forth in subdivision (f). However, if the prosecutor elects to prosecute any grower, farm labor contractor, or other person pursuant to this paragraph and subdivision (f), multiple failures to pay wages within a single payroll and in a single pay period shall constitute one violation.

(4) Any aggrieved worker who, claims a violation of this section, may bring a civil action for injunctive relief and lost wages as provided in Section 218, and, upon

prevailing, shall recover reasonable attorney's fees and costs.

(d) As used in this section:

(1) "Business day" means any day on which the offices of the license verification unit are open to the public for the conducting of business.

(2) "Grower" means any person who owns or leases land used for the planting, cultivation, production, harvesting, or packing of any farm products, if he or she hires or uses persons acting as farm labor contractors, and includes a packing shed or a person or entity who farms the land on behalf of the land owner, whether or not he or she owns or leases the land.

(3) "Inspect," with regard to inspecting a license, means to examine the license to determine whether it reasonably appears on its face to be genuine.

(4) "License verification unit" means the Farm Labor Contractor License Verification Unit established pursuant to subdivision (e).

(5) "Verify," with respect to verifying a license, means to contact by telephone, facsimile, website, electronic mail, or other means as determined by the Labor Commissioner, the license verification unit to confirm the validity of a license and to record in the requester's files the unique verification number provided by the license verification unit to document that the requester confirmed the validity of the license of the farm labor contractor with whom he or she has entered into a contract or agreement to supply services.

(e) The Labor Commissioner shall establish and maintain a Farm Labor Contractor License Verification Unit commencing no later than July 1, 2002. The license verification unit shall, upon the request of a grower or farm labor contractor, certify the status of a state license issued to a farm labor contractor. The license verification unit shall assign a unique verification number to the request and the unit shall within 24 hours send by mail, or, if available, by facsimile or electronic mail, confirmation that will serve as conclusive evidence of compliance with the verification requirements of this section. The obligation under this section to verify licenses shall not become operative and the penalties for failure to verify a license shall not be applicable until three months after the license verification unit becomes operational, as certified by the State Auditor.

(f)(1) On or after January 1, 2003, a violation of paragraph (3) of subdivision (c) is a misdemeanor and is punishable as provided in subdivision (a) of Section 1697, except that the fine portion of the penalty shall be as follows:

(A) Upon conviction for a first violation, by a fine of not less than one thousand dollars ($1,000) nor more than five thousand dollars ($5,000), and is subject to other sanctions under this chapter, including subdivisions (b) and (c) of Section 1697. Upon conviction, the Labor Commissioner shall revoke the defendant's license and

the defendant shall be ineligible for a license for a period of one year from the date of revocation.

(B) Upon a conviction for a violation committed within three years after a conviction for a prior violation, by a fine of not less than ten thousand dollars ($10,000) and is subject to other sanctions under this chapter, including subdivisions (b) and (c) of Section 1697. Upon a second conviction, the Labor Commissioner shall revoke the defendant's license and the defendant shall be ineligible for a license for a period of two years from the date of revocation.

(C) Upon a conviction for a violation committed within five years after a second conviction pursuant to subparagraph (B), by a fine of not less than twenty-five thousand dollars ($25,000), and is subject to other sanctions under this chapter, including subdivisions (b) and (c) of Section 1697. Upon a third conviction, the Labor Commissioner shall revoke the defendant's license and the defendant shall not thereafter be eligible to obtain a license.

(2) If a person is prosecuted under this subdivision, that person may not be prosecuted under any other law if the prosecution would be based upon the same set of facts as the prosecution under this subdivision.

(g) A farm labor contractor, a person contracted by a farm labor contractor who is acting in the capacity of a farm labor contractor, or an employer of a farm labor contractor is subject to Section 98.6 and 1102.5. *(Added by Stats.1991, c. 1197 (A.B.318), § 2. Amended by Stats.1992, c. 421 (A.B.2878), § 1; Stats.2001, c. 157 (A.B.423), § 1.)*

§ 1695.8. Performance of activity or service by persons after suspension, revocation or renew denial of license; time period; contracts and use of persons by farm labor contractors

(a) No person whose license was suspended, revoked, or denied renewal by the Labor Commissioner shall perform any activity or service specified in subdivision (b) of Section 1682 or in Section 1682.3 to, for, or under the direction of a farm labor contractor, whether as an employee, independent contractor, or otherwise, for three years after the license is suspended, revoked, or denied renewal, or until the license is reinstated, whichever first occurs.

(b) No farm labor contractor shall knowingly contract with or use any person specified in subdivision (a), whether as an employee, independent contractor, or otherwise, to perform an activity or service specified in subdivision (b) of Section 1682 or in Section 1682.3 for three years after the license of the person is suspended, revoked, or denied renewal, or until the license is reinstated, whichever first occurs. *(Added by Stats.2001, c. 157 (A.B.423), § 2.)*

§ 1695.9. Responsibility of person contracted by farm labor contractor who is acting in capacity of farm labor contractor to provide copy of license; violations; retention period

Any person contracted by a farm labor contractor who is acting in the capacity of a farm labor contractor shall first provide to the farm labor contractor a copy of his or her current valid state license. A farm labor contractor is responsible for ensuring that every person who is performing farm labor contracting activities on behalf of the farm labor contractor has obtained a farm labor contractor license as required by Section 1683 prior to the person's engagement in any activity described in subdivision (b) of Section 1682. A farm labor contractor who utilizes the services of another farm labor contractor who is not his or her employee shall also comply with the provisions of this chapter. The farm labor contractor is responsible for any violations of this chapter committed by his or her employee, whether or not the employee has registered as required by this chapter. The farm labor contractor shall keep a copy of the license or licenses for a period of three years following the termination of the contract or agreement. *(Added by Stats.2001, c. 157 (A.B.423), § 3.)*

§ 1696. Prohibited acts of licensee

No licensee shall:

(1) Make any misrepresentation or false statement in his application for a license.

(2) Make or cause to be made, to any person, any false, fraudulent, or misleading representation, or publish or circulate or cause to be published or circulated any false, fraudulent, or misleading information concerning the terms or conditions or existence of employment at any place or places, or by any person or persons, or of any individual or individuals.

(3) Send or transport any worker to any place where the labor contractor knows a strike or lockout exists, without notifying the worker that such conditions exist.

(4) Do any act in his capacity as a farm labor contractor, or cause any act to be done, which constitutes a crime involving moral turpitude, or the effect of which causes any act to be done which constitutes a crime involving moral turpitude under any law of the State of California. *(Added by Stats.1951, c. 1746, p. 4164, § 2.)*

§ 1696.2. Vehicles used by licensee for transportation of individuals; display of name and license number

All vehicles used by a licensee for the transportation of individuals in his operations as a farm labor contractor shall have displayed prominently at the entrance of such vehicle the name of the farm labor contractor and the number of his license as issued by the Labor Commissioner pursuant to this chapter. *(Added by Stats.1957, c. 1705, p. 3081, § 1.)*

§ 1696.3. Licensee or employee operating bus or truck for transportation of individuals; chauffeurs' licenses

Any farm labor contractor or person employed by a farm labor contractor who operates a bus or truck in the transportation of individuals in connection with the business, activities, or operations of a farm labor contractor shall be licensed as required by Section 12519 of the Vehicle Code. *(Added by Stats.1957, c. 1706, p. 3081, § 1. Amended by Stats.1959, c. 330, p. 2256, § 1; Stats.1963, c. 209, p. 950, § 15, eff. April 29, 1963.)*

§ 1696.4. Registration of vehicles used by licensee for transportation of individuals; evidence of insurance; rental of vehicles

(a) All vehicles defined in Section 322 of the Vehicle Code, including those described in Section 1696.3, used by a farm labor contractor for the transportation of individuals in his or her operations as a farm labor contractor, including, but not limited to, vehicles not owned by that contractor, shall be registered with the Labor Commissioner. The registration shall include the name of the owner and driver of the vehicle, and the license number and description of the vehicle. The Labor Commissioner shall require, as a condition of registration, that the farm labor contractor submit evidence showing that the contractor has in effect an insurance policy applicable to the vehicle, as required by Section 1695.

(b) Commencing on April 1, 2000, and quarterly thereafter, the Labor Commissioner shall provide the Commissioner of the California Highway Patrol with a list of all vehicles registered pursuant to subdivision (a). *(Added by Stats.1957, c. 1703, p. 3080, § 1. Amended by Stats.1967, c. 125, p. 1155, § 4; Stats.1999, c. 556 (A.B. 555), § 1, eff. Sept. 29, 1999.)*

§ 1696.5. Itemized statement of wage deductions

Every licensee shall, at the time of each payment of wages, which shall be not less often than once every week as required by Section 205 of this code, furnish each of the workers employed by him either as a detachable part of the check, draft, or voucher paying the employee's wages, or separately, an itemized statement in writing showing in detail each and every deduction made from such wages. *(Added by Stats.1963, c. 1306, p. 2831, § 1. Amended by Stats.1972, c. 271, p. 547, § 3; Stats.1976, c. 1041, p. 4654, § 3.)*

§ 1696.6. Bona fide order for employment as prerequisite to recruitment or solicitation and transportation

(a) No licensee shall recruit or solicit and transport an employee for farmwork unless he has first obtained, either orally or in writing, a bona fide order for such employment.

(b) Any farm labor contractor who recruits or solicits a farmworker without a bona fide order and induces him to be transported to a proposed jobsite and does not then provide employment for him shall pay wages to such farmworker at the agreed rate of pay for the job to which he was being transported and for the elapsed time from the point of departure with return to the same place. *(Added by Stats.1965, c. 1979, p. 4505, § 1.)*

§ 1696.8.   Farm Labor Contractor Enforcement Unit

(a) The director shall establish a Farm Labor Contractor Enforcement Unit. The unit shall develop a program to provide technical assistance to a district attorney's office that establishes a local farm labor contractor enforcement unit. A local farm labor contractor enforcement unit established pursuant to this section shall, whenever possible, coordinate its enforcement efforts with the Rural Crime Prevention Program in its jurisdiction, if any, established pursuant to Section 14171 of the Penal Code. Any funds appropriated to the department for purposes of this section shall be administered and allocated by the director.

(b) A local farm labor contractor enforcement unit that receives technical assistance pursuant to this section shall concentrate enhanced prosecution efforts and resources on the prosecution of farm labor contractors who violate a state law regulating wages. For purposes of this subdivision, "enhanced prosecution efforts and resources" include, but are not limited to, all of the following:

(1) "Vertical" prosecutorial representation, whereby the prosecutor who makes the initial filing or appearance performs all subsequent court appearances on a particular case through its conclusion, including the sentencing phase.

(2) Assignment of highly qualified investigators and prosecutors to farm labor enforcement cases.

(3) Significant reduction of caseloads for investigators and prosecutors assigned to farm labor enforcement cases. *(Added by Stats.2001, c. 157 (A.B.423), § 4.)*

§ 1697.   Violations; misdemeanor; penalty; civil action by aggrieved employee; engaging in farm contracting activities after license suspension or revocation; penalties

(a) Any person who violates this chapter, or who causes or induces another to violate this chapter, is guilty of a misdemeanor punishable by a fine of not more than one thousand dollars ($1,000), or imprisonment in the county jail for not more than six months, or both.

(b) Any employee aggrieved by any violation of this chapter, other than acts and conduct also proscribed by Sections 1153, 1154, and 1155, may do all of the following:

(1) Bring a civil action for injunctive relief or damages, or both, against a farm labor contractor or unlicensed farm labor contractor who violates this chapter and, upon prevailing, shall recover reasonable attorney's fees.

(2) Enforce the liability on the farm labor contractor's bond.

(c) Any farm labor contractor who engages in farm labor contracting activities after his or her license has been suspended or revoked is guilty of an offense punishable by a fine of not less than one thousand dollars ($1,000) and not more than five thousand dollars ($5,000), or by imprisonment for not less than six months and not more than one year, or both. *(Added by Stats.1951, c. 1746, p. 4165, § 2. Amended by Stats.1976, c. 803, p. 1853, § 4; Stats.1982, c. 517, p. 2404, § 305; Stats.1983, c. 1092, § 212, eff. Sept. 27, 1983, operative Jan. 1, 1984; Stats.1988, c. 1000, § 5.)*

§ 1697.1.   Transportation fees; false, fraudulent, or misleading representations; misdemeanor; civil actions

(a) No person shall make, or cause to be made, false, fraudulent, or misleading representations that employment in the growing or producing of farm products, or an employee benefit related to that employment, will be jeopardized unless an individual or his or her family members pay a fee or other thing of value for transportation by that person to or from the business or worksite of an employer.

(b) Any person who violates this section, or who causes or induces another to violate this section, is guilty of a misdemeanor punishable by a fine of not more than five thousand dollars ($5,000) and not less than five hundred dollars ($500), or imprisonment in the county jail for not more than 30 days, or both.

(c) Any individual claiming to be aggrieved by a violation of this section may bring a civil action for injunctive relief, damages, or both. If the court finds that the defendant has violated this section, it shall award actual damages, plus an amount equal to treble the amount of actual damages, or five hundred dollars ($500) per violation, whichever is greater. The court shall also grant a prevailing plaintiff reasonable attorneys' fees and costs.

(d) Any other party who, upon information and belief, claims a violation of this section has been committed may bring a civil action for injunctive relief on behalf of the general public and, upon prevailing, shall recover reasonable attorneys' fees and costs. *(Added by Stats.1989, c. 476, § 1.)*

§ 1697.2.   Trials to be set for earliest possible date

Actions brought under this chapter shall be set for trial at the earliest possible date, and shall take precedence over all other cases, except older matters of the same character and matters to which special precedence may be given by law. *(Added by Stats.1988, c. 1000, § 6.)*

§ 1697.3.   Determination of failure to pay wages; order of payment

Upon the final determination of the Labor Commissioner that a grower, a farm labor contractor, or person acting in the capacity of a farm labor contractor has failed to pay wages to its employees, the grower, farm labor

431

contractor, or person acting in the capacity of a farm labor contractor shall immediately pay those wages. If payment is not made within 30 days of the final determination, the Labor Commissioner shall forward the matter for consideration of prosecution to the local district attorney's office. *(Added by Stats.2001, c. 157 (A.B.423), § 5.)*

§ 1698. Payments and deposits into Farmworker Remedial Account

All fines collected for violations of this chapter shall be paid into the Farmworker Remedial Account and shall be available, upon appropriation, for purposes of this chapter. Of the moneys collected for licenses issued pursuant to this chapter, one hundred fifty dollars ($150) of each annual license fee shall be deposited in the Farmworker Remedial Account pursuant to paragraph (4) of subdivision (a) of Section 1684, three hundred fifty dollars ($350) of each annual license fee shall be expended by the Labor Commissioner to fund the Farm Labor Contractor Enforcement Unit and the Farm Labor Contractor License Verification Unit, both within the department, and the remaining money shall be paid into the State Treasury and credited to the General Fund. *(Added by Stats.1967, c. 1505, p. 3571, § 4. Amended by Stats.2000, c. 917 (A.B.1338), § 6; Stats.2001, c. 157 (A.B.423), § 6; Stats. 2002, c. 787 (S.B.1798), § 6; Stats.2006, c. 69 (A.B.1806), § 23, eff. July 12, 2006.)*

§ 1698.1. Transfer of interest of profits of agency

No licensee shall sell, transfer or give away any interest in or the right to participate in the profits of said licensee's business without the written consent of the Labor Commissioner. A violation of this section shall constitute a misdemeanor, and shall be punishable by a fine of not less than two hundred dollars ($200) nor more than two thousand dollars ($2,000), or imprisonment for not more than 60 days, or both. *(Added by Stats.1967, c. 1505, p. 3572, § 5. Amended by Stats.1972, c. 271, p. 547, § 4; Stats.1983, c. 1092, § 213, eff. Sept. 27, 1983, operative Jan. 1, 1984; Stats.2000, c. 917 (A.B.1338), § 7.)*

§ 1698.2. Unlawful employment

No licensee shall knowingly issue a contract for employment containing any term or condition which, if complied with, would be in violation of law, or attempt to fill an order for help to be employed in violation of law. *(Added by Stats.1967, c. 1505, p. 3572, § 6.)*

§ 1698.3. Acceptance of fee without employment order

No licensee shall accept a fee from any applicant for employment, or send any applicant for employment without having obtained orally or in writing, a bona fide order therefor, and in no case shall such licensee accept, directly or indirectly, a registration fee of any kind. *(Added by Stats.1967, c. 1505, p. 3572, § 7.)*

§ 1698.4. Referral of woman or minor to place of ill-repute

No licensee shall send or cause to be sent, any woman or minor under the age of 18 years, as an employee to any house of ill fame, to any house or place of amusement for immoral purpose, to places resorted to for the purposes of prostitution, or to gambling houses, the character of which places the licensee could have ascertained upon reasonable inquiry. *(Added by Stats.1967, c. 1505, p. 3572, § 8. Amended by Stats.1972, c. 579, p. 1005, § 28; Stats.1972, c. 271, p. 547, § 5.)*

§ 1698.5. Referral of minor to on-sale liquor establishment

No licensee shall send any minor to any saloon or place where intoxicating liquors are sold to be consumed on the premises. *(Added by Stats.1967, c. 1505, p. 3572, § 9. Amended by Stats.1972, c. 579, p. 1005, § 29.)*

§ 1698.6. Permitting persons of bad character to frequent agency

No licensee shall knowingly permit any persons of bad character, prostitutes, gamblers, intoxicated persons, or procurers to frequent his premises. *(Added by Stats.1967, c. 1505, p. 3572, § 10.)*

§ 1698.7. Unlawful employment of minors

No licensee shall accept any application for employment made by or on behalf of any child, or shall place or assist in placing any such child in any employment whatever in violation of Part 4 (commencing with Section 1171) of this division. *(Added by Stats.1967, c. 1505, p. 3572, § 11.)*

§ 1698.8. Division of fees with employer prohibited

No licensee shall divide fees with an employer, an agent or other employee of an employer or person to whom help is furnished. *(Added by Stats.1967, c. 1505, p. 3572, § 12.)*

§ 1699. Rules and regulations

The Labor Commissioner may, in accordance with the provisions of Chapter 4.5 (commencing with Section 11371), Part 1, Division 3, Title 2 of the Government Code, adopt, amend, and repeal such rules and regulations as are reasonably necessary for the purpose of enforcing and administering this chapter and as are not inconsistent with this chapter. *(Added by Stats.1951, c. 1746, p. 4165, § 2. Amended by Stats.1957, c. 2034, p. 3605, § 5; Stats.1967, c. 125, p. 1155, § 5.)*

CHAPTER 4. TALENT AGENCIES

Article	Section
1. Scope and Definitions	1700
2. Licenses	1700.5
3. Operation and Management	1700.23
4. California Entertainment Commission [Repealed]	

ARTICLE 1. SCOPE AND DEFINITIONS

Section
1700.   "Person" defined.
1700.1. "Theatrical engagement," "motion picture engagement," and "emergency engagement" defined.
1700.2. Definitions.
1700.3. "License" and "licensee" defined.
1700.4. "Talent agency" and "artists" defined.

§ 1700. "Person" defined

As used in this chapter, "person" means any individual, company, society, firm, partnership, association, corporation, limited liability company, manager, or their agents or employees. *(Added by Stats.1959, c. 888, p. 2920, § 1. Amended by Stats.1994, c. 1010 (S.B.2053), § 184.)*

§ 1700.1. "Theatrical engagement," "motion picture engagement," and "emergency engagement" defined

As used in this chapter:

(a) "Theatrical engagement" means any engagement or employment of a person as an actor, performer, or entertainer in a circus, vaudeville, theatrical, or other entertainment, exhibition, or performance.

(b) "Motion picture engagement" means any engagement or employment of a person as an actor, actress, director, scenario, or continuity writer, camera man, or in any capacity concerned with the making of motion pictures.

(c) "Emergency engagement" means an engagement which has to be performed within 24 hours from the time when the contract for such engagement is made. *(Added by Stats.1959, c. 888, p. 2920, § 1.)*

§ 1700.2. Definitions

(a) As used in this chapter, "fee" means any of the following:

(1) Any money or other valuable consideration paid or promised to be paid for services rendered or to be rendered by any person conducting the business of a talent agency under this chapter.

(2) Any money received by any person in excess of that which has been paid out by him or her for transportation, transfer of baggage, or board and lodging for any applicant for employment.

(3) The difference between the amount of money received by any person who furnished employees, performers, or entertainers for circus, vaudeville, theatrical, or other entertainments, exhibitions, or performances, and the amount paid by him or her to the employee, performer, or entertainer.

(b) As used in this chapter, "registration fee" means any charge made, or attempted to be made, to an artist for any of the following purposes:

(1) Registering or listing an applicant for employment in the entertainment industry.

(2) Letter writing.

(3) Photographs, film strips, video tapes, or other reproductions of the applicant.

(4) Costumes for the applicant.

(5) Any activity of a like nature. *(Added by Stats.1959, c. 888, p. 2920, § 1. Amended by Stats.1978, c. 1382, p. 4575, § 4; Stats.1986, c. 488, § 1.)*

§ 1700.3. "License" and "licensee" defined

As used in this chapter:

(a) "License" means a license issued by the Labor Commissioner to carry on the business of a talent agency under this chapter.

(b) "Licensee" means a talent agency which holds a valid, unrevoked, and unforfeited license under this chapter. *(Added by Stats.1959, c. 888, p. 2921, § 1. Amended by Stats.1978, c. 1382, p. 4576, § 5.)*

§ 1700.4. "Talent agency" and "artists" defined

(a) "Talent agency" means a person or corporation who engages in the occupation of procuring, offering, promising, or attempting to procure employment or engagements for an artist or artists, except that the activities of procuring, offering, or promising to procure recording contracts for an artist or artists shall not of itself subject a person or corporation to regulation and licensing under this chapter. Talent agencies may, in addition, counsel or direct artists in the development of their professional careers.

(b) "Artists" means actors and actresses rendering services on the legitimate stage and in the production of motion pictures, radio artists, musical artists, musical organizations, directors of legitimate stage, motion picture and radio productions, musical directors, writers, cinematographers, composers, lyricists, arrangers, models, and other artists and persons rendering professional services in motion picture, theatrical, radio, television and other entertainment enterprises. *(Added by Stats.1982, c. 682, p. 2815, § 2, operative Jan. 1, 1986. Amended by Stats.1984, c. 553, § 2, eff. July 17, 1984, operative Jan. 1, 1986; Stats.1986, c. 488, § 2, operative January 1, 1986.)*

ARTICLE 2. LICENSES

Section
1700.5.   Necessity of talent agency license; posting an advertisement; renewal of prior licenses.
1700.6.   Application; contents; fingerprints; character affidavits.
1700.7.   Investigation of character and responsibility of applicant.
1700.8.   Refusal to grant license; hearing; conduct of proceedings; power of commissioner.
1700.9.   Places or persons not entitled to license.
1700.10. Duration of license; renewal; application; bond; fee; branch office license.
1700.11. Application for renewal; contents.
1700.12. Filing fee; annual fee.
1700.13. Application for consent to transfer or assign license; filing fee; consent to change location.

Section
1700.14.   Temporary or provisional license.
1700.15.   Surety bond; deposit with labor commissioner.
1700.16.   Payee of bond; conditions.
1700.18.   Disposition of fees and fines.
1700.19.   Contents of license.
1700.20.   Person and place covered by license; transferability.
1700.20a.   Estate certificate of convenience; grounds for issuance.
1700.20b.   Eligibility for estate certificate of convenience; duration; renewal.
1700.21.   Revocation or suspension of license; grounds.
1700.22.   Hearing; conduct of proceedings; powers of commissioner.

§ 1700.5. Necessity of talent agency license; posting an advertisement; renewal of prior licenses

No person shall engage in or carry on the occupation of a talent agency without first procuring a license therefor from the Labor Commissioner. The license shall be posted in a conspicuous place in the office of the licensee. The license number shall be referred to in any advertisement for the purpose of the solicitation of talent for the talent agency.

Licenses issued for talent agencies prior to the effective date of this chapter shall not be invalidated thereby, but renewals of those licenses shall be obtained in the manner prescribed by this chapter. *(Added by Stats.1959, c. 888, p. 2921, § 1. Amended by Stats.1978, c. 1382, p. 4576, § 7; Stats.1989, c. 480, § 1.)*

§ 1700.6. Application; contents; fingerprints; character affidavits

A written application for a license shall be made to the Labor Commissioner in the form prescribed by him or her and shall state:

(a) The name and address of the applicant.

(b) The street and number of the building or place where the business of the talent agency is to be conducted.

(c) The business or occupation engaged in by the applicant for at least two years immediately preceding the date of application.

(d) If the applicant is other than a corporation, the names and addresses of all persons, except bona fide employees on stated salaries, financially interested, either as partners, associates, or profit sharers, in the operation of the talent agency in question, together with the amount of their respective interests.

If the applicant is a corporation, the corporate name, the names, residential addresses, and telephone numbers of all officers of the corporation, the names of all persons exercising managing responsibility in the applicant or licensee's office, and the names and addresses of all persons having a financial interest of 10 percent or more in the business and the percentage of financial interest owned by those persons.

The application shall be accompanied by two sets of fingerprints of the applicant and affidavits of at least two reputable residents of the city or county in which the business of the talent agency is to be conducted who have known, or been associated with, the applicant for two years, that the applicant is a person of good moral character or, in the case of a corporation, has a reputation for fair dealing. *(Added by Stats.1959, c. 888, p. 2921, § 1. Amended by Stats.1978, c. 1382, p. 4576, § 8; Stats.1986, c. 488, § 3.)*

§ 1700.7. Investigation of character and responsibility of applicant

Upon receipt of an application for a license the Labor Commissioner may cause an investigation to be made as to the character and responsibility of the applicant and of the premises designated in such application as the place in which it is proposed to conduct the business of the talent agency. *(Added by Stats.1959, c. 888, p. 2922, § 1. Amended by Stats.1978, c. 1382, p. 4577, § 9.)*

§ 1700.8. Refusal to grant license; hearing; conduct of proceedings; power of commissioner

The commissioner upon proper notice and hearing may refuse to grant a license. The proceedings shall be conducted in accordance with Chapter 5 (commencing at Section 11500) of Part 1 of Division 3 of Title 2 of the Government Code and the commissioner shall have all the power granted therein. *(Added by Stats.1959, c. 888, p. 2922, § 1.)*

§ 1700.9. Places or persons not entitled to license

No license shall be granted to conduct the business of a talent agency:

(a) In a place that would endanger the health, safety, or welfare of the artist.

(b) To a person whose license has been revoked within three years from the date of application. *(Added by Stats.1959, c. 888, p. 2922, § 1. Amended by Stats.1978, c. 1382, p. 4577, § 10; Stats.1986, c. 488, § 4.)*

§ 1700.10. Duration of license; renewal; application; bond; fee; branch office license

The license when first issued shall run to the next birthday of the applicant, and each license shall then be renewed within the 30 days preceding the licensee's birthday and shall run from birthday to birthday. In case the applicant is a partnership, such license shall be renewed within the 30 days preceding the birthday of the oldest partner. If the applicant is a corporation, such license shall be renewed within the 30 days preceding the anniversary of the date the corporation was lawfully formed. Renewal shall require the filing of an application for renewal, a renewal bond, and the payment of the annual license fee, but the Labor Commissioner may demand that a new application or new bond be submitted.

If the applicant or licensee desires, in addition, a branch office license, he shall file an application in accordance with the provisions of this section as heretofore set forth. *(Added by Stats.1978, c. 1382, p. 4577, § 11.5.)*

§ 1700.11. Application for renewal; contents

All applications for renewal shall state the names and addresses of all persons, except bona fide employees on stated salaries, financially interested either as partners, associates or profit sharers, in the operation of the business of the talent agency. *(Added by Stats.1959, c. 888, p. 2922, § 1. Amended by Stats.1978, c. 1382, p. 4577, § 11.8.)*

§ 1700.12. Filing fee; annual fee

A filing fee of twenty-five dollars ($25) shall be paid to the Labor Commissioner at the time the application for issuance of a talent agency license is filed.

In addition to the filing fee required for application for issuance of a talent agency license, every talent agency shall pay to the Labor Commissioner annually at the time a license is issued or renewed:

(a) A license fee of two hundred twenty-five dollars ($225).

(b) Fifty dollars ($50) for each branch office maintained by the talent agency in this state. *(Added by Stats.1959, c. 888, p. 2922, § 1. Amended by Stats.1965, c. 234, p. 1206, § 1; Stats.1978, c. 1382, p. 4577, § 12; Stats.1983, c. 323, § 61, eff. July 21, 1983.)*

§ 1700.13. Application for consent to transfer or assign license; filing fee; consent to change location

A filing fee of twenty-five dollars ($25) shall be paid to the Labor Commissioner at the time application for consent to the transfer or assignment of a talent agency license is made but no license fee shall be required upon the assignment or transfer of a license.

The location of a talent agency shall not be changed without the written consent of the Labor Commissioner. *(Added by Stats.1959, c. 888, p. 2922, § 1. Amended by Stats.1978, c. 1382, p. 4578, § 13.)*

§ 1700.14. Temporary or provisional license

Whenever an application for a license or renewal is made, and application processing pursuant to this chapter has not been completed, the Labor Commissioner may, at his or her discretion, issue a temporary or provisional license valid for a period not exceeding 90 days, and subject, where appropriate, to the automatic and summary revocation by the Labor Commissioner. Otherwise, the conditions for issuance or renewal shall meet the requirements of Section 1700.6. *(Added by Stats.1984, c. 557, § 3.)*

§ 1700.15. Surety bond; deposit with labor commissioner

A talent agency shall also deposit with the Labor Commissioner, prior to the issuance or renewal of a license, a surety bond in the penal sum of fifty thousand dollars ($50,000). *(Added by Stats.1959, c. 888, p. 2923, § 1. Amended by Stats.1978, c. 1382, p. 4578, § 14; Stats.1986, c. 488, § 5; Stats.2005, c. 46 (S.B.184), § 1.)*

§ 1700.16. Payee of bond; conditions

Such surety bonds shall be payable to the people of the State of California, and shall be conditioned that the person applying for the license will comply with this chapter and will pay all sums due any individual or group of individuals when such person or his representative or agent has received such sums, and will pay all damages occasioned to any person by reason of misstatement, misrepresentation, fraud, deceit, or any unlawful acts or omissions of the licensed talent agency, or its agents or employees, while acting within the scope of their employment. *(Added by Stats.1959, c. 888, p. 2923, § 1. Amended by Stats.1978, c. 1382, p. 4578, § 15.)*

§ 1700.18. Disposition of fees and fines

All moneys collected for licenses and all fines collected for violations of the provisions of this chapter shall be paid into the State Treasury and credited to the General Fund. *(Added by Stats.1959, c. 888, p. 2923, § 1.)*

§ 1700.19. Contents of license

Each license shall contain all of the following:

(a) The name of the licensee.

(b) A designation of the city, street, and number of the premises in which the licensee is authorized to carry on the business of a talent agency.

(c) The number and date of issuance of the license. *(Added by Stats.1959, c. 888, p. 2923, § 1. Amended by Stats.1978, c. 1382, p. 4578, § 17; Stats.1986, c. 488, § 6.)*

§ 1700.20. Person and place covered by license; transferability

No license shall protect any other than the person to whom it is issued nor any places other than those designated in the license. No license shall be transferred or assigned to any person unless written consent is obtained from the Labor Commissioner. *(Added by Stats.1959, c. 888, p. 2923, § 1.)*

§ 1700.20a. Estate certificate of convenience; grounds for issuance

The Labor Commissioner may issue to a person eligible therefor a certificate of convenience to conduct the business of a talent agency where the person licensed to conduct such talent agency business has died or has had a conservator of the estate appointed by a court of competent jurisdiction. Such a certificate of convenience may be denominated an estate certificate of convenience. *(Added by Stats.1965, c. 252, p. 1238, § 1. Amended by*

435

Stats.1978, c. 1382, p. 4578, § 18; Stats.1979, c. 730, p. 2509, § 89, operative Jan. 1, 1981.)

§ 1700.20b. Eligibility for estate certificate of convenience; duration; renewal

To be eligible for a certificate of convenience, a person shall be either:

(a) The executor or administrator of the estate of a deceased person licensed to conduct the business of a talent agency.

(b) If no executor or administrator has been appointed, the surviving spouse or heir otherwise entitled to conduct the business of such deceased licensee.

(c) The conservator of the estate of a person licensed to conduct the business of a talent agency.

Such estate certificate of convenience shall continue in force for a period of not to exceed 90 days, and shall be renewable for such period as the Labor Commissioner may deem appropriate, pending the disposal of the talent agency license or the procurement of a new license under the provisions of this chapter. *(Added by Stats.1965, c. 252, p. 1239, § 2. Amended by Stats.1978, c. 1382, p. 4579, § 19; Stats.1979, c. 730, p. 2509, § 90, operative Jan. 1, 1981.)*

§ 1700.21. Revocation or suspension of license; grounds

The Labor Commissioner may revoke or suspend any license when it is shown that any of the following occur:

(a) The licensee or his or her agent has violated or failed to comply with any of the provisions of this chapter.

(b) The licensee has ceased to be of good moral character.

(c) The conditions under which the license was issued have changed or no longer exist.

(d) The licensee has made any material misrepresentation or false statement in his or her application for a license. *(Added by Stats.1959, c. 888, p. 2923, § 1. Amended by Stats.1986, c. 488, § 7.)*

§ 1700.22. Hearing; conduct of proceedings; powers of commissioner

Before revoking or suspending any license, the Labor Commissioner shall afford the holder of such license an opportunity to be heard in person or by counsel. The proceedings shall be conducted in accordance with Chapter 5 (commencing at Section 11500) of Part 1 of Division 3 of Title 2 of the Government Code, and the commissioner shall have all the powers granted therein. *(Added by Stats.1959, c. 888, p. 2924, § 1.)*

ARTICLE 3.   OPERATION AND MANAGEMENT

Section
1700.23. Approval of talent agency contracts; grounds for disapproval; required statements in contracts.

Section
1700.24. Filing and posting of talent agency fee schedule; changes in schedule.
1700.25. Trust funds; disbursements; records; disputes; penalties; attorney's fees.
1700.26. Records of talent agency; required entries.
1700.27. Inspection of books and records; furnishing copies to commissioner; reports.
1700.28. Posting copies of laws in office of talent agency.
1700.29. Rules and regulations.
1700.30. Sale or transfer of interest or rights to profit.
1700.31. Employment in violation of law.
1700.32. False, fraudulent or misleading information or advertisement.
1700.33. Sending artist to unsafe place prohibited.
1700.34. Sending minor to saloon or on-sale liquor establishment.
1700.35. Permitting persons of bad character to frequent or be employed in talent agency's place of business.
1700.36. Unlawful employment of minors.
1700.37. Judicially approved contract not disaffirmable by minor.
1700.38. Notice of labor dispute at place of employment.
1700.39. Fee-splitting.
1700.40. Registration fees; refunds; referrals; conflicts of interest.
1700.41. Reimbursement for traveling expenses.
1700.44. Dispute; hearing; determination; bond; certification of no controversy; failure to obtain license; limitations of actions.
1700.45. Arbitration; contract provisions.
1700.47. Unlawful discrimination.

§ 1700.23. Approval of talent agency contracts; grounds for disapproval; required statements in contracts

Every talent agency shall submit to the Labor Commissioner a form or forms of contract to be utilized by such talent agency in entering into written contracts with artists for the employment of the services of such talent agency by such artists, and secure the approval of the Labor Commissioner thereof. Such approval shall not be withheld as to any proposed form of contract unless such proposed form of contract is unfair, unjust and oppressive to the artist. Each such form of contract, except under the conditions specified in Section 1700.45, shall contain an agreement by the talent agency to refer any controversy between the artist and the talent agency relating to the terms of the contract to the Labor Commissioner for adjustment. There shall be printed on the face of the contract in prominent type the following: "This talent agency is licensed by the Labor Commissioner of the State of California." *(Added by Stats.1959, c. 888, p. 2924, § 1. Amended by Stats.1978, c. 1382, p. 4579, § 20.)*

§ 1700.24. Filing and posting of talent agency fee schedule; changes in schedule

Every talent agency shall file with the Labor Commissioner a schedule of fees to be charged and collected in the conduct of that occupation, and shall also keep a copy of the schedule posted in a conspicuous place in the office of the talent agency. Changes in the schedule may be made from time to time, but no fee or change of fee shall become effective until seven days after the date of filing thereof with the Labor Commissioner and until posted for not less than seven days in a conspicuous place in the office of the talent agency. *(Added by Stats.1959, c. 888, p. 2924, § 1. Amended by Stats.1978, c. 1382, p. 4579, § 21; Stats.1986, c. 488, § 8.)*

§ 1700.25. Trust funds; disbursements; records; disputes; penalties; attorney's fees

(a) A licensee who receives any payment of funds on behalf of an artist shall immediately deposit that amount in a trust fund account maintained by him or her in a bank or other recognized depository. The funds, less the licensee's commission, shall be disbursed to the artist within 30 days after receipt. However, notwithstanding the preceding sentence, the licensee may retain the funds beyond 30 days of receipt in either of the following circumstances:

(1) To the extent necessary to offset an obligation of the artist to the talent agency that is then due and owing.

(2) When the funds are the subject of a controversy pending before the Labor Commissioner under Section 1700.44 concerning a fee alleged to be owed by the artist to the licensee.

(b) A separate record shall be maintained of all funds received on behalf of an artist and the record shall further indicate the disposition of the funds.

(c) If disputed by the artist and the dispute is referred to the Labor Commissioner, the failure of a licensee to disburse funds to an artist within 30 days of receipt shall constitute a "controversy" within the meaning of Section 1700.44.

(d) Any funds specified in subdivision (a) that are the subject of a controversy pending before the Labor Commissioner under Section 1700.44 shall be retained in the trust fund account specified in subdivision (a) and shall not be used by the licensee for any purpose until the controversy is determined by the Labor Commissioner or settled by the parties.

(e) If the Labor Commissioner finds, in proceedings under Section 1700.44, that the licensee's failure to disburse funds to an artist within the time required by subdivision (a) was a willful violation, the Labor Commissioner may, in addition to other relief under Section 1700.44, order the following:

(1) Award reasonable attorney's fees to the prevailing artist.

(2) Award interest to the prevailing artist on the funds wrongfully withheld at the rate of 10 percent per annum during the period of the violation.

(f) Nothing in subdivision (c), (d), or (e) shall be deemed to supersede Section 1700.45 or to affect the enforceability of a contractual arbitration provision meeting the criteria of Section 1700.45. *(Added by Stats.1986,*

c. 488, § 10. Amended by Stats.1994, c. 1032 (A.B.1901), § 1.)

§ 1700.26. Records of talent agency; required entries

Every talent agency shall keep records in a form approved by the Labor Commissioner, in which shall be entered all of the following:

(1) The name and address of each artist employing the talent agency.

(2) The amount of fee received from the artist.

(3) The employments secured by the artist during the term of the contract between the artist and the talent agency, and the amount of compensation received by the artists pursuant thereto.

(4) Any other information which the Labor Commissioner requires.

No talent agency, its agent or employees, shall make any false entry in any records. *(Added by Stats.1959, c. 888, p. 2925, § 1. Amended by Stats.1978, c. 1382, p. 4580, § 23; Stats.1986, c. 488, § 11.)*

§ 1700.27. Inspection of books and records; furnishing copies to commissioner; reports

All books, records, and other papers kept pursuant to this chapter by any talent agency shall be open at all reasonable hours to the inspection of the Labor Commissioner and his agents. Every talent agency shall furnish to the Labor Commissioner upon request a true copy of such books, records, and papers or any portion thereof, and shall make such reports as the Labor Commissioner prescribes. *(Added by Stats.1959, c. 888, p. 2925, § 1. Amended by Stats.1978, c. 1382, p. 4580, § 24.)*

§ 1700.28. Posting copies of laws in office of talent agency

Every talent agency shall post in a conspicuous place in the office of such talent agency a printed copy of this chapter and of such other statutes as may be specified by the Labor Commissioner. Such copies shall also contain the name and address of the officer charged with the enforcement of this chapter. The Labor Commissioner shall furnish to talent agencies printed copies of any statute required to be posted under the provisions of this section. *(Added by Stats.1959, c. 888, p. 2925, § 1. Amended by Stats.1978, c. 1382, p. 4580, § 25.)*

§ 1700.29. Rules and regulations

The Labor Commissioner may, in accordance with the provisions of Chapter 4 (commencing at Section 11370), Part 1, Division 3, Title 2 of the Government Code, adopt, amend, and repeal such rules and regulations as are reasonably necessary for the purpose of enforcing and administering this chapter and as are not inconsistent with this chapter. *(Added by Stats.1959, c. 888, p. 2925, § 1.)*

§ 1700.30. Sale or transfer of interest or rights to profit

No talent agency shall sell, transfer, or give away to any person other than a director, officer, manager, employee, or shareholder of the talent agency any interest in or the right to participate in the profits of the talent agency without the written consent of the Labor Commissioner. *(Added by Stats.1959, c. 888, p. 2925, § 1. Amended by Stats.1978, c. 1382, p. 4580, § 26; Stats.1983, c. 1092, § 214, eff. Sept. 27, 1983, operative Jan. 1, 1984; Stats. 1986, c. 488, § 12.)*

§ 1700.31. Employment in violation of law

No talent agency shall knowingly issue a contract for employment containing any term or condition which, if complied with, would be in violation of law, or attempt to fill an order for help to be employed in violation of law. *(Added by Stats.1959, c. 888, p. 2926, § 1. Amended by Stats.1978, c. 1382, p. 4581, § 27.)*

§ 1700.32. False, fraudulent or misleading information or advertisement

No talent agency shall publish or cause to be published any false, fraudulent, or misleading information, representation, notice, or advertisement. All advertisements of a talent agency by means of cards, circulars, or signs, and in newspapers and other publications, and all letterheads, receipts, and blanks shall be printed and contain the licensed name and address of the talent agency and the words "talent agency." No talent agency shall give any false information or make any false promises or representations concerning an engagement or employment to any applicant who applies for an engagement or employment. *(Added by Stats.1959, c. 888, p. 2926, § 1. Amended by Stats.1978, c. 1382, p. 4581, § 28.)*

§ 1700.33. Sending artist to unsafe place prohibited

No talent agency shall send or cause to be sent, any artist to any place where the health, safety, or welfare of the artist could be adversely affected, the character of which place the talent agency could have ascertained upon reasonable inquiry. *(Added by Stats.1959, c. 888, p. 2926, § 1. Amended by Stats.1972, c. 579, p. 1005, § 30; Stats.1978, c. 1382, p. 4581, § 29; Stats.1986, c. 488, § 13.)*

§ 1700.34. Sending minor to saloon or on-sale liquor establishment

No talent agency shall send any minor to any saloon or place where intoxicating liquors are sold to be consumed on the premises. *(Added by Stats.1959, c. 888, p. 2926, § 1. Amended by Stats.1972, c. 579, p. 1005, § 31; Stats.1978, c. 1382, p. 4581, § 30.)*

§ 1700.35. Permitting persons of bad character to frequent or be employed in talent agency's place of business

No talent agency shall knowingly permit any persons of bad character, prostitutes, gamblers, intoxicated persons, or procurers to frequent, or be employed in, the place of business of the talent agency. *(Added by Stats.1959, c. 888, p. 2926, § 1. Amended by Stats.1978, c. 1382, p. 4581, § 31.)*

§ 1700.36. Unlawful employment of minors

No talent agency shall accept any application for employment made by or on behalf of any minor, as defined by subdivision (c) of Section 1286, or shall place or assist in placing any such minor in any employment whatever in violation of Part 4 (commencing with Section 1171). *(Added by Stats.1959, c. 888, p. 2926, § 1. Amended by Stats.1978, c. 1382, p. 4581, § 32; Stats.1983, c. 142, § 100.)*

§ 1700.37. Judicially approved contract not disaffirmable by minor

A minor cannot disaffirm a contract, otherwise valid, entered into during minority, either during the actual minority of the minor entering into such contract or at any time thereafter, with a duly licensed talent agency as defined in Section 1700.4 to secure him engagements to render artistic or creative services in motion pictures, television, the production of phonograph records, the legitimate or living stage, or otherwise in the entertainment field including, but without being limited to, services as an actor, actress, dancer, musician, comedian, singer, or other performer or entertainer, or as a writer, director, producer, production executive, choreographer, composer, conductor or designer, the blank form of which has been approved by the Labor Commissioner pursuant to Section 1700.23, where such contract has been approved by the superior court of the county where such minor resides or is employed.

Such approval may be given by the superior court on the petition of either party to the contract after such reasonable notice to the other party thereto as may be fixed by said court, with opportunity to such other party to appear and be heard. *(Added by Stats.1959, c. 888, p. 2926, § 1. Amended by Stats.1963, c. 1885, p. 3870, § 2; Stats.1978, c. 1382, p. 4581, § 33.)*

§ 1700.38. Notice of labor dispute at place of employment

No talent agency shall knowingly secure employment for an artist in any place where a strike, lockout, or other labor trouble exists, without notifying the artist of such conditions. *(Added by Stats.1959, c. 888, p. 2926, § 1. Amended by Stats.1978, c. 1382, p. 4582, § 34.*

§ 1700.39. Fee-splitting

No talent agency shall divide fees with an employer, an agent or other employee of an employer. *(Added by Stats.1959, c. 888, p. 2926, § 1. Amended by Stats.1978, c. 1382, p. 4582, § 35.)*

§ 1700.40. Registration fees; refunds; referrals; conflicts of interest

(a) No talent agency shall collect a registration fee. In the event that a talent agency shall collect from an artist a fee or expenses for obtaining employment for the artist, and the artist shall fail to procure the employment, or the artist shall fail to be paid for the employment, the talent agency shall, upon demand therefor, repay to the artist the fee and expenses so collected. Unless repayment thereof is made within 48 hours after demand therefor, the talent agency shall pay to the artist an additional sum equal to the amount of the fee.

(b) No talent agency may refer an artist to any person, firm, or corporation in which the talent agency has a direct or indirect financial interest for other services to be rendered to the artist, including, but not limited to, photography, audition tapes, demonstration reels or similar materials, business management, personal management, coaching, dramatic school, casting or talent brochures, agency-client directories, or other printing.

(c) No talent agency may accept any referral fee or similar compensation from any person, association, or corporation providing services of any type expressly set forth in subdivision (b) to an artist under contract with the talent agency. *(Added by Stats.1959, c. 888, p. 2927, § 1. Amended by Stats.1978, c. 1382, p. 4582, § 36; Stats.1986, c. 488, § 14; Stats.1994, c. 1032 (A.B.1901), § 2.)*

§ 1700.41. Reimbursement for traveling expenses

In cases where an artist is sent by a talent agency beyond the limits of the city in which the office of such talent agency is located upon the representation of such talent agency that employment of a particular type will there be available for the artist and the artist does not find such employment available, such talent agency shall reimburse the artist for any actual expenses incurred in going to and returning from the place where the artist has been so sent unless the artist has been otherwise so reimbursed. *(Added by Stats.1959, c. 888, p. 2927, § 1. Amended by Stats.1978, c. 1382, p. 4582, § 37.)*

§ 1700.44. Dispute; hearing; determination; bond; certification of no controversy; failure to obtain license; limitations of actions

(a) In cases of controversy arising under this chapter, the parties involved shall refer the matters in dispute to the Labor Commissioner, who shall hear and determine the same, subject to an appeal within 10 days after determination, to the superior court where the same shall be heard de novo. To stay any award for money, the party aggrieved shall execute a bond approved by the superior court in a sum not exceeding twice the amount of the judgment. In all other cases the bond shall be in a sum of not less than one thousand dollars ($1,000) and approved by the superior court.

The Labor Commissioner may certify without a hearing that there is no controversy within the meaning of this section if he or she has by investigation established that there is no dispute as to the amount of the fee due. Service of the certification shall be made upon all parties concerned by registered or certified mail with return receipt requested and the certification shall become conclusive 10 days after the date of mailing if no objection has been filed with the Labor Commissioner during that period.

(b) Notwithstanding any other provision of law to the contrary, failure of any person to obtain a license from the Labor Commissioner pursuant to this chapter shall not be considered a criminal act under any law of this state.

(c) No action or proceeding shall be brought pursuant to this chapter with respect to any violation which is alleged to have occurred more than one year prior to commencement of the action or proceeding.

(d) It is not unlawful for a person or corporation which is not licensed pursuant to this chapter to act in conjunction with, and at the request of, a licensed talent agency in the negotiation of an employment contract. *(Added by Stats.1982, c. 682, p. 2816, § 4, operative Jan. 1, 1986. Amended by Stats.1984, c. 553, § 4, eff. July 17, 1984, operative Jan. 1, 1986; Stats.1986, c. 488, § 15 operative Jan. 1, 1986.)*

Validity

This section was held preempted by the Federal Arbitration Act in the decision of Preston v. Ferrer, 2008, 128 S.Ct. 978, 169 L.Ed.2d 917.

§ 1700.45. Arbitration; contract provisions

Notwithstanding Section 1700.44, a provision in a contract providing for the decision by arbitration of any controversy under the contract or as to its existence, validity, construction, performance, nonperformance, breach, operation, continuance, or termination, shall be valid:

(a) If the provision is contained in a contract between a talent agency and a person for whom the talent agency under the contract undertakes to endeavor to secure employment, or

(b) If the provision is inserted in the contract pursuant to any rule, regulation, or contract of a bona fide labor union regulating the relations of its members to a talent agency, and

(c) If the contract provides for reasonable notice to the Labor Commissioner of the time and place of all arbitration hearings, and

(d) If the contract provides that the Labor Commissioner or his or her authorized representative has the right to attend all arbitration hearings.

Except as otherwise provided in this section, any arbitration shall be governed by the provisions of Title 9 (commencing with Section 1280) of Part 3 of the Code of Civil Procedure.

If there is an arbitration provision in a contract, the contract need not provide that the talent agency agrees to refer any controversy between the applicant and the talent agency regarding the terms of the contract to the

439

Labor Commissioner for adjustment, and Section 1700.44 shall not apply to controversies pertaining to the contract.

A provision in a contract providing for the decision by arbitration of any controversy arising under this chapter which does not meet the requirements of this section is not made valid by Section 1281 of the Code of Civil Procedure. *(Added by Stats.1959, c. 888, p. 2927, § 1. Amended by Stats.1961, c. 461, p. 1552, § 7; Stats.1978, c. 1382, p. 4582, § 39; Stats.1986, c. 488, § 16.)*

Validity

This section was held preempted by the Federal Arbitration Act in the decision of Preston v. Ferrer, 2008, 128 S.Ct. 978, 169 L.Ed.2d 917.

§ 1700.47. Unlawful discrimination

It shall be unlawful for any licensee to refuse to represent any artist on account of that artist's race, color, creed, sex, national origin, religion, or handicap. *(Added by Stats.1986, c. 488, § 18.)*

ARTICLE 4.   CALIFORNIA ENTERTAINMENT COMMISSION [REPEALED]

CHAPTER 4.5.   FEE–RELATED TALENT SERVICES

Article	Section
1. **Definitions**	1701
2. **Advance–Fee Talent Representation Service**	1702
3. **Other Talent Services**	1703
4. **Remedies**	1704
5. **General Provisions**	1705
6. **Remedies [Repealed]**	

ARTICLE 1.   DEFINITIONS

Section
1701.   Definitions.

§ 1701. Definitions

For purposes of this chapter, the following terms have the following meanings:

(a) "Artist" means a person who is or seeks to become an actor, actress, model, extra, radio artist, musical artist, musical organization, director, musical director, writer, cinematographer, composer, lyricist, arranger, or other person rendering professional services in motion picture, theatrical, radio, television, Internet, print media, or other entertainment enterprises or technologies.

(b) "Audition" means any activity for the purpose of obtaining employment, compensated or not, as an artist whereby an artist meets with, interviews or performs before, or displays his or her talent before, any person, including a producer, a director, or a casting director, or an associate, representative, or designee of a producer, director, or casting director, who has, or is represented to have, input into the decision to select an artist for an employment opportunity. An "audition" may be in-person or through electronic means, live or recorded, and

440

may include a performance or other display of the artist's promotional materials.

(c) "Employment opportunity" means the opportunity to obtain work as an artist, whether compensated or not.

(d) "Fee" means any money or other valuable consideration paid or promised to be paid by or on behalf of an artist for services rendered or to be rendered by any person conducting business under this chapter. "Fee" does not include the following:

(1) A fee calculated as a percentage of the income earned by the artist for his or her employment as an artist.

(2)(A) Reimbursements for out-of-pocket costs actually incurred by the payee on behalf of the artist for services rendered or goods provided to the artist by an independent third party if all of the following conditions are met:

(i) The payee has no direct or indirect financial interest in the third party.

(ii) The payee does not accept any referral fee, kickback, or other consideration for referring the artist.

(iii) The services rendered or goods provided for the out-of-pocket costs are not, and are not represented to be, a condition for the payee to register or list the artist with the payee.

(iv) The payee maintains adequate records to establish that the amount to be reimbursed was actually advanced or owed to a third party and that the third party is not a person with whom the payee has a direct or indirect financial interest or from whom the payee receives any consideration for referring the artist. To satisfy this condition, the payee shall maintain the records for at least three years and make them available for inspection and copying within 24 hours of a written request by the Labor Commissioner, the Attorney General, a district attorney, a city attorney, or a state or local enforcement agency.

(B) A person asserting a defense based upon this paragraph has the burden of producing evidence to support the defense.

(3) Appearances, marketing, or similar activities by an artist rendered in the context of promoting that artist's career.

(4) Royalties or profit participation from work or services as an artist payable under a bona fide contractual obligation.

(e) "Person" means an individual, company, society, firm, partnership, association, corporation, limited liability company, trust, or other organization.

(f) "Talent counseling service" means a person who does not manage or direct the development of an artist's career and who, for a fee from, or on behalf of, an artist, provides or offers to provide, or advertises or represents itself as providing, that artist, directly or by referral to another person, with career counseling, vocational guidance, aptitude testing, or career evaluation as an artist.

(g) "Talent listing service" means a person who, for a fee from, or on behalf of, an artist, provides or offers to provide, or advertises or represents itself as providing, an artist, directly or by referral to another person, with any of the following:

(1) A list of one or more auditions or employment opportunities.

(2) A list of talent agents or talent managers, including an associate, representative, or designee thereof.

(3) A search, or providing the artist with the ability to perform a self-directed search, of any database for an audition or employment opportunity, or a database of talent agents or talent managers, or an associate, representative, or designee thereof.

(4) Storage or maintenance for distribution or disclosure to a person represented as offering an audition or employment opportunity, or to a talent agent, talent manager, or an associate, representative, or designee of a talent agent or talent manager, of either of the following: (A) an artist's name, photograph, Internet Web site, filmstrip, videotape, audition tape, demonstration reel, résumé, portfolio, or other reproduction or promotional material of the artist or (B) an artist's schedule of availability for an audition or employment opportunity.

(h) "Talent scout" means an individual employed, appointed, or authorized by a talent service, who solicits or attempts to solicit an artist for the purpose of becoming a client of the service. The principals of a service are themselves talent scouts if they solicit on behalf of the service.

(i) "Talent service" means a talent counseling service, a talent listing service, or a talent training service.

(j) "Talent training service" means a person who, for a fee from, or on behalf of, an artist, provides or offers to provide, or advertises or represents itself as providing, an artist, directly or by referral to another person, with lessons, coaching, seminars, workshops, or similar training as an artist. *(Added by Stats.2009, c. 286 (A.B.1319), § 3.)*

ARTICLE 2. ADVANCE–FEE TALENT REPRESENTATION SERVICE

Section
1702.   Advance–fee talent representation service prohibited.
1702.1. "Advance-fee talent representation service" defined.
1702.3. Violations.
1702.4. Application of article.

§ 1702. Advance–fee talent representation service prohibited

No person shall own, operate, or act in the capacity of an advance-fee talent representation service or advertise, solicit for, or knowingly refer a person to, an advance-fee talent representation service. *(Added by Stats.2009, c. 286 (A.B.1319), § 3.)*

§ 1702.1. "Advance-fee talent representation service" defined

(a) "Advance-fee talent representation service" means a person who provides or offers to provide, or advertises or represents itself as providing, an artist, directly or by referral to another person, with one or more of the following services described below, provided that the person charges or receives a fee from or on behalf of an artist for photographs, Internet Web sites, or other reproductions or other promotional materials as an artist; lessons, coaching, seminars, workshops, or similar training for an artist; or for one or more of the following services:

(1) Procuring or attempting to procure an employment opportunity or an engagement as an artist.

(2) Procuring or attempting to procure an audition for an artist.

(3) Managing or directing the development of an artist's career.

(4) Procuring or attempting to procure a talent agent or talent manager, including an associate, representative, or designee of a talent agent or talent manager.

(b) "Advance-fee talent representation service" also means a person who charges or receives a fee from, or on behalf of, an artist for any product or service required for the artist to obtain, from or through the person, any of the services described in paragraphs (1) to (4), inclusive, of subdivision (a). *(Added by Stats.2009, c. 286 (A.B. 1319), § 3.)*

§ 1702.3. Violations

A person who violates Section 1702 is subject to the provisions of Article 4 (commencing with Section 1704). *(Added by Stats.2009, c. 286 (A.B.1319), § 3.)*

§ 1702.4 Application of article

This article does not apply to the following:

(a) A public educational institution.

(b) A nonprofit corporation, organized to achieve economic adjustment and civic betterment, give vocational guidance, including employment counseling services, and assist in the placement of its members or others, if all of the following conditions exist:

(1) None of the corporation's directors, officers, or employees receive any compensation other than a nominal salary for services performed for the corporation.

(2) The corporation does not charge a fee for its services, although it may request a voluntary contribution.

(3) The corporation uses any membership dues or fees solely for maintenance.

(c) A nonprofit corporation, formed in good faith for the promotion and advancement of the general professional interests of its members, that maintains a placement service principally engaged to secure employment for its members with the state or a county, city, district, or other public agency under contracts providing employment for one year or longer, or with a nonprofit corporation exempted by subdivision (b).

(d) A labor organization, as defined in Section 1117.

(e) A newspaper, bona fide newsletter, magazine, trade or professional journal, or other publication of general circulation, whether in print or on the Internet, that has as its main purpose the dissemination of news, reports, trade or professional information, or information not intended to assist in locating, securing, or procuring employment or assignments for others.

(f) A public institution. *(Added by Stats.2009, c. 286 (A.B.1319), § 3.)*

ARTICLE 3.   OTHER TALENT SERVICES

Section
1703.   Contract requirements.
1703.1.   Records.
1703.3.   Bond; deposit in lieu of bond.
1703.4.   Prohibited acts.
1703.5.   Exclusive use of name.
1703.6.   Application of article.

§ 1703.   Contract requirements

(a) Every contract and agreement between an artist and a talent service shall be in writing, in at least 10–point type, and contain all of the following provisions:

(1) The name, address, telephone number, fax number (if any), e-mail address (if any), and Internet Web site address (if any), of the talent service, the artist to whom services are to be provided, and the representative executing the contract on behalf of the talent service.

(2) A description of the services to be performed, a statement when those services are to be provided, and the duration of the contract.

(3) Evidence of compliance with applicable bonding requirements, including the name of the bonding company and the bond number, if any, and a statement that a bond in the amount of fifty thousand dollars ($50,000) must be posted with the Labor Commissioner.

(4) The amount of any fees to be charged to or collected from, or on behalf of, the artist receiving the services, and the date or dates when those fees are required to be paid.

(5) The following statements, in boldface type and in close proximity to the artist's signature:

"(Name of talent service) IS A TALENT COUNSELING SERVICE, TALENT LISTING SERVICE, OR TALENT TRAINING SERVICE (whichever is applicable). THIS IS NOT A TALENT AGENCY CONTRACT. ONLY A TALENT AGENT LICENSED PURSUANT TO SECTION 1700.5 OF THE LABOR CODE MAY ENGAGE IN THE OCCUPATION OF PROCURING, OFFERING, PROMISING, OR ATTEMPTING TO PROCURE EMPLOYMENT OR ENGAGEMENTS FOR AN ARTIST. (Name of talent service) IS PROHIBITED BY LAW FROM OFFER-

ING OR ATTEMPTING TO OBTAIN AUDITIONS OR EMPLOYMENT FOR YOU. IT MAY ONLY PROVIDE YOU WITH TRAINING, COUNSELING, OR LISTING INFORMATION (whichever is applicable). FOR MORE INFORMATION, CONSULT CHAPTER 4.5 (COMMENCING WITH SECTION 1701) OF PART 6 OF DIVISION 2 OF THE LABOR CODE. A DISPUTE ARISING OUT OF THE PERFORMANCE OF THE CONTRACT BY THE TALENT SERVICE THAT IS NOT RESOLVED TO THE SATISFACTION OF THE ARTIST SHOULD BE REFERRED TO A LOCAL CONSUMER AFFAIRS DEPARTMENT OR LOCAL LAW ENFORCEMENT, AS APPROPRIATE.

YOUR RIGHT TO CANCEL
(enter date of transaction)

You may cancel this contract and obtain a full refund, without any penalty or obligation, if notice of cancellation is given, in writing, within 10 business days from the above date or the date on which you commence utilizing the services under the contract, whichever is longer. For purposes of this section, business days are Monday through Friday.

To cancel this contract, mail or deliver or send by facsimile transmission a signed and dated copy of the following cancellation notice or any other written notice of cancellation to (name of talent service) at (address of its place of business), fax number (if any), e-mail address (if any), and Internet Web site address (if any), NOT LATER THAN MIDNIGHT OF (date) . If the contract was executed in part or in whole through the Internet, you may cancel the contract by sending the notification to: (e-mail address).

CANCELLATION NOTICE

I hereby cancel this contract.

Dated: _____

_____
Artist Signature.

If you cancel, all fees you have paid must be refunded to you within 10 business days after delivery of the cancellation notice to the talent service."

(6) A statement conspicuously disclosing whether the artist may or may not obtain a refund after the 10–day cancellation period described in paragraph (5) has expired.

(b) Except for contracts executed over the Internet, a contract subject to this section shall be dated and signed by the artist and the representative executing the contract on behalf of the talent service. In the case of a contract executed over the Internet, the talent service shall give the artist clear and conspicuous notice of the contract terms and provide to the artist the ability to acknowledge receipt of the terms before acknowledging agreement thereto. In any dispute regarding compliance with this subdivision, the talent service shall have the burden of proving that the artist received the terms and acknowledged agreement thereto.

(c) If the talent service offers to list or display information about an artist, including a photograph, on the service's Internet Web site, or on a Web site that the talent service has authority to design or alter, the contract shall contain a notice that the talent service will remove the listing and content within 10 days of a request by the artist or, in the case of a minor, the artist's parent or guardian. The contract shall include a valid telephone number, mailing address, and e-mail address for the talent service to which a request for removal may be made.

(d) A contract between an artist and a talent service shall be contained in a single document that includes the elements set forth in this section. A contract subject to this section that does not comply with subdivisions (a) to (f), inclusive, is voidable at the election of the artist and may be canceled by the artist at any time without any penalty or obligation.

(e)(1) An artist may cancel a contract or within 10 business days from the date he or she commences utilizing the services under the contract. An artist shall notify the talent service of the cancellation for talent services within 10 business days of the date he or she executed the contract by mailing, delivering, or sending by facsimile transmission to the talent service, a signed and dated copy of the cancellation notice or any other written notice of cancellation, or by sending a notice of cancellation via the Internet if the contract was executed in part or in whole through the Internet. A talent service shall refund all fees paid by, or on behalf of, an artist within 10 business days after delivery of the cancellation notice.

(2) Unless a talent service conspicuously discloses in the contract that cancellation is prohibited after the 10-day cancellation period described in paragraph (1), an artist may cancel a contract for talent services at any time after the 10-day cancellation period by mailing, delivering, or sending by facsimile transmission to the talent service a signed and dated copy of the cancellation notice or any other written notice of cancellation, or by sending a notice of cancellation via the Internet if the contract was executed in part or in whole through the Internet. Within 10 business days after delivery of the cancellation notice, the talent service shall refund to the artist on a pro rata basis all fees paid by, or on behalf of, the artist.

(f) A contract between an artist and a talent service shall have a term of not more than one year and shall not be renewed automatically.

(g) The talent service shall maintain the address set forth in the contract for receipt of cancellation and for removal of an Internet Web site or other listing, unless it furnishes the artist with written notice of a change of address. Written notice of a change of address may be done by e-mail if the artist designates an e-mail address in the contract for purposes of receiving written notice.

(h) The talent service shall advise a person inquiring about canceling a contract to follow the written procedures for cancellation set forth in the contract.

(i) Before the artist signs a contract and before the artist or any person acting on his or her behalf becomes obligated to pay or pays any fee, the talent service shall provide a copy of the contract to the artist for the artist to keep. If the contract was executed through the Internet, the talent service may provide a copy of the contract to the artist by making it available to be downloaded and printed through the Internet.

(j) The talent service shall maintain the original executed contract on file at its place of business. *(Added by Stats.2009, c. 286 (A.B.1319), § 3.)*

§ 1703.1. Records

(a) Every person engaging in the business of a talent service shall keep and maintain records of the talent service business, including the following:

(1) The name and address of each artist contracting with the talent service.

(2) The amount of the fees paid by or for the artist during the term of the contract with the talent service.

(3) Records described in clause (iv) of subparagraph (A) of paragraph (2) of subdivision (d) of Section 1701.

(4) Records described in paragraph (1) of subdivision (b) of Section 1703.6.

(5) Records described in subdivision (j) of Section 1703.

(6) Records described in paragraph (1) of subdivision (a) of Section 1703.4.

(7) Records described in paragraph (2) of subdivision (a) of Section 1703.4.

(8) Records described in paragraph (2) of subdivision (c) of Section 1703.4.

(9) The name, address, date of birth, social security number, federal tax identification number, and driver's license number and state of issuance thereof, of the owner of the talent service and of the corporate officers of the talent service, if it is owned by a corporation.

(10) The legal name, principal residence address, date of birth, and driver's license number and state of issuance thereof, of every talent scout and the name each talent scout uses while soliciting artists.

(11) Any other information that the Labor Commissioner requires.

(b) All books, records, and other papers kept pursuant to this chapter by a talent service shall be open for inspection during the hours between 9 a.m. and 5 p.m., inclusive, Monday to Friday, inclusive, except legal holidays, by a peace officer or a representative from the Labor Commissioner, the Attorney General, any district attorney, or any city attorney. Every talent service shall furnish to the Labor Commissioner, a law enforcement officer, the Attorney General, any district attorney, or any city attorney, upon request, a true copy of those books, records, and papers, or any portion thereof, and shall make reports as the Labor Commissioner requires. The inspecting party shall maintain the confidentiality of any personal identifying information contained in the records maintained pursuant to this section, and shall not share, sell, or transfer the information to any third party unless it is otherwise authorized by state or federal law.

A written or verbal solicitation or advertisement for an artist to perform or demonstrate any talent for the talent service, or to appear for an interview with the talent service, shall include the following clear and conspicuous statement: "This is not an audition for employment or for obtaining a talent agent or talent management." *(Added by Stats.2009, c. 286 (A.B.1319), § 3.)*

§ 1703.3. Bond; deposit in lieu of bond

(a) Prior to advertising or engaging in business, a talent service shall file with the Labor Commissioner a bond in the amount of fifty thousand dollars ($50,000) or a deposit in lieu of the bond pursuant to Section 995.710 of the Code of Civil Procedure. The bond shall be executed by a corporate surety qualified to do business in this state and conditioned upon compliance with this chapter. The total aggregate liability on the bond shall be limited to fifty thousand dollars ($50,000). The bond may be terminated pursuant to Section 995.440 of, or Article 13 (commencing with Section 996.310) of Chapter 2 of Title 14 of Part 2 of, the Code of Civil Procedure.

(b) The bond required by this section shall be in favor of, and payable to, the people of the State of California and shall be for the benefit of any person injured by any unlawful act, omission, or failure to provide the services of the talent service.

(c) The Labor Commissioner shall charge and collect a filing fee to cover the cost of filing the bond or deposit.

(d)(1) Whenever a deposit is made in lieu of the bond otherwise required by this section, the person asserting the claim against the deposit shall establish the claim by furnishing evidence to the Labor Commissioner of injury resulting from an unlawful act, omission, or failure to provide the services of the talent service or of a money judgment entered by a court.

(2) When a claimant has established the claim with the Labor Commissioner, the Labor Commissioner shall review and approve the claim and enter the date of the approval thereon. The claim shall be designated an approved claim.

(3) When the first claim against a particular deposit has been approved, it shall not be paid until the expiration of a period of 240 days after the date of its approval by the Labor Commissioner. Subsequent claims that are approved by the Labor Commissioner within the same 240-day period shall similarly not be paid until the expiration of that 240-day period. Upon the expiration of the 240-day period, the Labor Commission-

er shall pay all approved claims from that 240-day period in full unless the deposit is insufficient, in which case every approved claim shall be paid a pro rata share of the deposit.

(4) Whenever the Labor Commissioner approves the first claim against a particular deposit after the expiration of a 240-day period, the date of approval of that claim shall begin a new 240-day period to which paragraph (3) applies with respect to any amount remaining in the deposit.

(5) After a deposit is exhausted, no further claims shall be paid by the Labor Commissioner. Claimants who have had claims paid in full or in part pursuant to paragraph (3) or (4) shall not be required to return funds received from the deposit for the benefit of other claimants.

(6) Whenever a deposit has been made in lieu of a bond, the amount of the deposit shall not be subject to attachment, garnishment, or execution with respect to an action or judgment against the assignor of the deposit, other than as to an amount as no longer needed or required for the purposes of this chapter and that would otherwise be returned to the assignor of the deposit by the Labor Commissioner.

(7) The Labor Commissioner shall return a deposit two years from the date it receives written notification from the assignor of the deposit that the assignor has ceased to engage in the business or act in the capacity of a talent service or has filed a bond pursuant to subdivision (a), provided that there are no outstanding claims against the deposit. The written notice shall include all of the following:

(A) The name, address, and telephone number of the assignor.

(B) The name, address, and telephone number of the bank at which the deposit is located.

(C) The account number of the deposit.

(D) A statement that the assignor is ceasing to engage in the business or act in the capacity of a talent service or has filed a bond with the Labor Commissioner. The Labor Commissioner shall forward an acknowledgment of receipt of the written notice to the assignor at the address indicated therein, specifying the date of receipt of the written notice and the anticipated date of release of the deposit, provided that there are then no outstanding claims against the deposit.

(8) A superior court may order the return of the deposit prior to the expiration of two years upon evidence satisfactory to the court that there are no outstanding claims against the deposit, or order the Labor Commissioner to retain the deposit for a specified period beyond the two years to resolve outstanding claims against the deposit.

(9) This subdivision applies to all deposits retained by the Labor Commissioner. The Labor Commissioner

shall notify each assignor of a deposit it retains and of the applicability of this section.

(10) Compliance with Sections 1700.15 and 1700.16 of this code or Section 1812.503, 1812.510, or 1812.515 of the Civil Code shall not satisfy the requirements of this section. *(Added by Stats.2009, c. 286 (A.B.1319), § 3.)*

§ 1703.4. Prohibited acts

(a) A talent service, its owners, directors, officers, agents, and employees shall not do any of the following:

(1) Make or cause to be made any advertisement or representation expressly or impliedly offering the opportunity for an artist to meet with or audition before any producer, director, casting director, or any associate thereof, or any other person who makes, or is represented to make, decisions for the process of hiring artists for employment as an artist, or any talent agent or talent manager, or any associate, representative, or designee thereof, unless the talent service maintains for inspection and copying written evidence of the supporting facts, including the name, business address, and job title of all persons conducting the meeting or audition, and the title of the production and the name of the production company.

(2) Make or cause to be made any advertisement or representation that any artist, whether identified or not, has obtained an audition, employment opportunity, or employment as an artist in whole or in part by use of the talent service unless the talent service maintains for inspection written evidence of the supporting facts upon which the claim is based, including the name of the artist and the approximate dates the talent service was used by the artist.

(3) Charge or attempt to charge an artist for an audition or employment opportunity.

(4) Require an artist, as a condition for using the talent service or for obtaining an additional benefit or preferential treatment from the talent service, to pay a fee for creating or providing photographs, filmstrips, videotapes, audition tapes, demonstration reels, or other reproductions of the artist, Internet Web sites, casting or talent brochures, or other promotional materials for the artist.

(5) Charge or attempt to charge an artist any fee not disclosed pursuant to paragraph (4) of subdivision (a) of Section 1703.

(6) Refer an artist to a person who charges the artist a fee for any service or any product in which the talent service, its owners, directors, officers, agents, or employees have a direct or indirect financial interest, unless the fee and the financial interest are conspicuously disclosed in a separate writing provided to the artist to keep prior to his or her execution of the contract with the talent service.

(7) Require an artist, as a condition for using a talent service or for obtaining any additional benefit or preferential treatment from the talent service, to pay a fee to any other talent service in which the talent service, its owners, directors, officers, agents, or employees have a direct or indirect financial interest.

(8) Accept any compensation or other consideration for referring an artist to any person charging the artist a fee.

(9) Fail to remove information about, or photographs of, the artist displayed on the talent service's Internet Web site, or a Web site that the service has the authority to design or alter, within 10 days of delivery of a request made by telephone, mail, facsimile transmission, or electronic mail from the artist or from a parent or guardian of the artist if the artist is a minor.

(b) A talent training service and talent counseling service and the owners, officers, directors, agents, and employees of the talent training service or talent counseling service shall not own, operate, or have a direct or indirect financial interest in a talent listing service.

(c) A talent listing service and its owners, officers, directors, agents, and employees shall not do either of the following:

(1) Own, operate, or have a direct or indirect financial interest in a talent training service or a talent counseling service.

(2) Provide a listing of an audition, job, or employment opportunity without written permission for the listing. A talent listing service shall keep and maintain a copy of all original listings; the name, business address, and business telephone number of the person granting permission to the talent listing service to use the listing; and the date the permission was granted.

(3) Make or cause to be made an advertisement or representation that includes the trademark, logo, name, word, or phrase of a company or organization, including a studio, production company, network, broadcaster, talent agency licensed pursuant to Section 1700.5, labor union, or organization as defined in Section 1117, in any manner that falsely or misleadingly suggests the endorsement, sponsorship, approval, or affiliation of a talent service. *(Added by Stats.2009, c. 286 (A.B.1319), § 3.)*

§ 1703.5. Exclusive use of name

No talent scout shall use the same name as used by any other talent scout soliciting for the same talent service, and no talent service shall permit a talent scout to use the same name as used by any other talent scout soliciting for the talent service. *(Added by Stats.2009, c. 286 (A.B. 1319), § 3.)*

§ 1703.6. Application of article

This article does not apply to any of the following:

(a) An entity described in subdivisions (a), (b), (d), (e), and (f) of Section 1702.4.

(b)(1) A private educational institution established solely for educational purposes which, as a part of its curriculum, offers employment counseling to its student body and satisfies either of the following:

(A) The institution conforms to the requirements of Article 5 (commencing with Section 33190) of Chapter 2 of Part 20 of Division 2 of Title 2 of the Education Code.

(B) More than 90 percent of the students to whom instruction, training, or education is provided during any semester or other term of instruction have completed or terminated their secondary education or are beyond the age of compulsory high school attendance. A person claiming exemption under this subparagraph shall maintain adequate records to establish the age of its students, including the name, date of birth, principal residence address, principal telephone number, driver's license number and state of issuance thereof, and dates of attendance, and shall make them available for inspection and copying within 24 hours of a written request by the Labor Commissioner, the Attorney General, a district attorney, a city attorney, or a state or local law enforcement agency. The inspecting party shall maintain the confidentiality of any personal identifying information contained in the records maintained pursuant to this section, and shall not share, sell, or transfer the information to any third party unless it is otherwise authorized by state or federal law.

(2) A person claiming an exemption under this subdivision has the burden of producing evidence to establish the exemption.

(c) A psychologist or psychological corporation, licensed pursuant to Chapter 6.6 (commencing with Section 2900) of Division 2 of the Business and Professions Code, that provides psychological assessment, career or occupational counseling, or consultation and related professional services within the scope of its practice.

(d) An educational psychologist, licensed pursuant to Article 1 (commencing with Section 4980) of Chapter 13 of Division 2 of the Business and Professions Code, who provides counseling services within the scope of his or her practice.

(e) A talent listing service, if all of the following apply:

(1) A majority interest in the service is owned by one or more colleges or universities, or alumni associations affiliated therewith, and each of the colleges or universities is accredited by an accrediting agency recognized by the United States Department of Education and a member organization of the Council of Postsecondary Accreditation.

(2) The service provides services exclusively for artists who are the alumni of colleges or universities specified in paragraph (1).

(3) The service does not require, as a condition to receiving services, an applicant to have completed courses or examinations beyond the requirements for graduation from the applicant's college or university specified in paragraph (1).

(4) More than 50 percent of the annual revenues received by the service are derived from paid subscriptions of prospective employers.

(f) A public library. *(Added by Stats.2009, c. 286 (A.B.1319), § 3.)*

ARTICLE 4. REMEDIES

Section
1704.   Violations; punishment.
1704.1. Actions for a violation.
1704.2. Damages; recovery actions.
1704.3. Satisfaction of judgments; bond or deposit proceeds.

§ 1704. Violations; punishment

A person, including, an owner, officer, director, agent, or employee of a talent service, who willfully violates any provision of this chapter is guilty of a misdemeanor. Each violation is punishable by imprisonment in a county jail for not more than one year, by a fine not exceeding ten thousand dollars ($10,000), or by both that fine and imprisonment. However, payment of restitution to an artist shall take precedence over the payment of a fine. *(Added by Stats.2009, c. 286 (A.B.1319), § 3.)*

§ 1704.1. Actions for a violation

The Attorney General, a district attorney, or a city attorney may institute an action for a violation of this chapter, including an action to restrain and enjoin a violation. *(Added by Stats.2009, c. 286 (A.B.1319), § 3.)*

§ 1704.2. Damages; recovery actions

A person who is injured by a violation of this chapter or by the breach of a contract subject to this chapter may bring an action for recovery of damages or to restrain and enjoin a violation, or both. The court shall award to a plaintiff who prevails in an action under this chapter reasonable attorney's fees and costs. The amount awarded for damages for a violation of this chapter shall be not less than three times the amount paid by the artist, or on behalf of the artist, to the talent service or the advance-fee talent representation service. *(Added by Stats.2009, c. 286 (A.B.1319), § 3.)*

§ 1704.3. Satisfaction of judgments; bond or deposit proceeds

The Labor Commissioner shall use the proceeds of a bond or deposit posted by a person pursuant to this chapter to satisfy a judgment or restitution order resulting from the person's violation of a provision of this chapter, if the person fails to pay all amounts required by the judgment or restitution order. *(Added by Stats.2009, c. 286 (A.B.1319), § 3.)*

ARTICLE 5. GENERAL PROVISIONS

Section
1705.   Applicability of other laws.
1705.1. Availability of other remedies.
1705.2. Waiver of rights under this chapter.
1705.3. Effect of unconstitutional provisions.
1705.4. Chapter compliance.

§ 1705. Applicability of other laws

The provisions of this chapter are not exclusive and do not relieve a person subject to this chapter from the duty to comply with all other laws. *(Added by Stats.2009, c. 286 (A.B.1319), § 3.)*

§ 1705.1. Availability of other remedies

The remedies provided in this chapter are not exclusive and shall be in addition to any other remedies or procedures provided in any other law, including Section 17500 of the Business and Professions Code. *(Added by Stats.2009, c. 286 (A.B.1319), § 3.)*

§ 1705.2. Waiver of rights under this chapter

A waiver by an artist of the provisions of this chapter is deemed contrary to public policy and void and unenforceable. An attempt by a person or a talent service to have an artist waive his or her rights under this chapter is a violation of this chapter. *(Added by Stats.2009, c. 286 (A.B.1319), § 3.)*

§ 1705.3. Effect of unconstitutional provisions

If any provision of this chapter or the application thereof to any person or circumstances is held unconstitutional, the remainder of the chapter and the application of that provision to other persons and circumstances shall not be affected thereby. *(Added by Stats.2009, c. 286 (A.B.1319), § 3.)*

§ 1705.4. Chapter compliance

Compliance with this chapter does not satisfy and is not a substitute for the requirements mandated by any other applicable law, including the obligation to obtain a license under the Talent Agencies Act (Chapter 4 (commencing with Section 1700)), prior to procuring, offering, promising, or attempting to procure employment or engagements for artists. *(Added by Stats.2009, c. 286 (A.B. 1319), § 3.)*

ARTICLE 6. REMEDIES [REPEALED]

CHAPTER 5. NURSES REGISTRIES [REPEALED]

Part 7

PUBLIC WORKS AND PUBLIC AGENCIES

Chapter	Section
1. Public Works	1720
2. Public Agencies	1900
4. Firefighters	1960

CHAPTER 1. PUBLIC WORKS

Article	Section
1. Scope and Operation	1720
1.5. Right of Action	1750
2. Wages	1770
3. Working Hours	1810
4. Employment of Aliens [Repealed]	

Article	Section
5. Securing Workers' Compensation	1860

ARTICLE 1. SCOPE AND OPERATION

Section

1720. "Public works" defined; "paid for in whole or in part out of public funds" defined; exception for private residential projects; exclusions.

1720.2. Public works; private contracts; conditions.

1720.3. Public works; hauling refuse from public works site.

1720.4. Work performed by volunteers, volunteer coordinators, or conservation corps members; exemption from chapter; application; report to legislature; appropriation.

1721. Political subdivision defined.

1722. Awarding body and body awarding the contract defined.

1722.1. Contractor; subcontractor defined.

1723. Worker defined.

1724. Locality in which public work is performed defined.

1725. Alien defined.

1726. Cognizance of violations in execution of contracts; reports; withholding procedures; actions to recover wages; costs and attorneys fees.

1727. Withholding to satisfy wage and penalty assessments.

1728. Acceptance of cash in lieu of withholding.

1729. Withholding of amounts from subcontractors.

1734. Disposition of fines and penalties collected by court.

1735. Discrimination in employment.

1736. Investigations; confidentiality of names of employees reporting violations of this chapter.

1740. Public contracts; modification to comply with federal wage schedules without republication.

1741. Determination of violations; civil wage and penalty assessments; service interest on due and unpaid wages; list of violators.

1742. Review of wage and penalty assessments; hearing procedure.

1742.1. Liability of contractor, subcontractor, or surety; settlements.

1743. Joint and several liability; order of collection; application of amounts collected; payment of workers; bonding company liability.

§ 1720. "Public works" defined; "paid for in whole or in part out of public funds" defined; exception for private residential projects; exclusions

(a) As used in this chapter, "public works" means:

(1) Construction, alteration, demolition, installation, or repair work done under contract and paid for in whole or in part out of public funds, except work done directly by any public utility company pursuant to order of the Public Utilities Commission or other public authority. For purposes of this paragraph, "construction" includes work performed during the design and preconstruction phases of construction including, but not limited to, inspection and land surveying work.

(2) Work done for irrigation, utility, reclamation, and improvement districts, and other districts of this type. "Public work" does not include the operation of the irrigation or drainage system of any irrigation or reclama-

447

tion district, except as used in Section 1778 relating to retaining wages.

(3) Street, sewer, or other improvement work done under the direction and supervision or by the authority of any officer or public body of the state, or of any political subdivision or district thereof, whether the political subdivision or district operates under a freeholder's charter or not.

(4) The laying of carpet done under a building lease-maintenance contract and paid for out of public funds.

(5) The laying of carpet in a public building done under contract and paid for in whole or in part out of public funds.

(6) Public transportation demonstration projects authorized pursuant to Section 143 of the Streets and Highways Code.

(b) For purposes of this section, "paid for in whole or in part out of public funds" means all of the following:

(1) The payment of money or the equivalent of money by the state or political subdivision directly to or on behalf of the public works contractor, subcontractor, or developer.

(2) Performance of construction work by the state or political subdivision in execution of the project.

(3) Transfer by the state or political subdivision of an asset of value for less than fair market price.

(4) Fees, costs, rents, insurance or bond premiums, loans, interest rates, or other obligations that would normally be required in the execution of the contract, that are paid, reduced, charged at less than fair market value, waived, or forgiven by the state or political subdivision.

(5) Money loaned by the state or political subdivision that is to be repaid on a contingent basis.

(6) Credits that are applied by the state or political subdivision against repayment obligations to the state or political subdivision.

(c) Notwithstanding subdivision (b):

(1) Private residential projects built on private property are not subject to the requirements of this chapter unless the projects are built pursuant to an agreement with a state agency, redevelopment agency, or local public housing authority.

(2) If the state or a political subdivision requires a private developer to perform construction, alteration, demolition, installation, or repair work on a public work of improvement as a condition of regulatory approval of an otherwise private development project, and the state or political subdivision contributes no more money, or the equivalent of money, to the overall project than is required to perform this public improvement work, and the state or political subdivision maintains no proprietary interest in the overall project, then only the public improvement work shall thereby become subject to this chapter.

(3) If the state or a political subdivision reimburses a private developer for costs that would normally be borne by the public, or provides directly or indirectly a public subsidy to a private development project that is de minimis in the context of the project, an otherwise private development project shall not thereby become subject to the requirements of this chapter.

(4) The construction or rehabilitation of affordable housing units for low- or moderate-income persons pursuant to paragraph (5) or (7) of subdivision (e) of Section 33334.2 of the Health and Safety Code that are paid for solely with moneys from a Low and Moderate Income Housing Fund established pursuant to Section 33334.3 of the Health and Safety Code or that are paid for by a combination of private funds and funds available pursuant to Section 33334.2 or 33334.3 of the Health and Safety Code do not constitute a project that is paid for in whole or in part out of public funds.

(5) "Paid for in whole or in part out of public funds" does not include tax credits provided pursuant to Section 17053.49 or 23649 of the Revenue and Taxation Code.

(6) Unless otherwise required by a public funding program, the construction or rehabilitation of privately owned residential projects is not subject to the requirements of this chapter if one or more of the following conditions are met:

(A) The project is a self-help housing project in which no fewer than 500 hours of construction work associated with the homes are to be performed by the homebuyers.

(B) The project consists of rehabilitation or expansion work associated with a facility operated on a not-for-profit basis as temporary or transitional housing for homeless persons with a total project cost of less than twenty-five thousand dollars ($25,000).

(C) Assistance is provided to a household as either mortgage assistance, downpayment assistance, or for the rehabilitation of a single-family home.

(D) The project consists of new construction, or expansion, or rehabilitation work associated with a facility developed by a nonprofit organization to be operated on a not-for-profit basis to provide emergency or transitional shelter and ancillary services and assistance to homeless adults and children. The nonprofit organization operating the project shall provide, at no profit, not less than 50 percent of the total project cost from nonpublic sources, excluding real property that is transferred or leased. Total project cost includes the value of donated labor, materials, architectural, and engineering services.

(E) The public participation in the project that would otherwise meet the criteria of subdivision (b) is public funding in the form of below-market interest rate loans for a project in which occupancy of at least 40 percent of the units is restricted for at least 20 years, by deed or regulatory agreement, to individuals or families earning no more than 80 percent of the area median income.

(d) Notwithstanding any provision of this section to the contrary, the following projects shall not, solely by reason of this section, be subject to the requirements of this chapter:

(1) Qualified residential rental projects, as defined by Section 142 (d) of the Internal Revenue Code, financed in whole or in part through the issuance of bonds that receive allocation of a portion of the state ceiling pursuant to Chapter 11.8 of Division 1 (commencing with Section 8869.80) of the Government Code on or before December 31, 2003.

(2) Single-family residential projects financed in whole or in part through the issuance of qualified mortgage revenue bonds or qualified veterans' mortgage bonds, as defined by Section 143 of the Internal Revenue Code, or with mortgage credit certificates under a Qualified Mortgage Credit Certificate Program, as defined by Section 25 of the Internal Revenue Code, that receive allocation of a portion of the state ceiling pursuant to Chapter 11.8 of Division 1 (commencing with Section 8869.80) of the Government Code on or before December 31, 2003.

(3) Low-income housing projects that are allocated federal or state low- income housing tax credits pursuant to Section 42 of the Internal Revenue Code, Chapter 3.6 of Division 31 (commencing with Section 50199.4) of the Health and Safety Code, or Section 12206, 17058, or 23610.5 of the Revenue and Taxation Code, on or before December 31, 2003.

(e) If a statute, other than this section, or a regulation, other than a regulation adopted pursuant to this section, or an ordinance or a contract applies this chapter to a project, the exclusions set forth in subdivision (d) do not apply to that project.

(f) For purposes of this section, references to the Internal Revenue Code mean the Internal Revenue Code of 1986, as amended, and include the corresponding predecessor sections of the Internal Revenue Code of 1954, as amended.

(g) The amendments made to this section by either Chapter 938 of the Statutes of 2001 or the act adding this subdivision[1] shall not be construed to preempt local ordinances requiring the payment of prevailing wages on housing projects. *(Stats.1937, c. 90, p. 241, § 1720. Amended by Stats.1953, c. 1706, p. 3454, § 1; Stats.1972, c. 717, p. 1306, § 1; Stats.1973, c. 77, p. 129, § 19; Stats.1989, c. 278, § 1, eff. Aug. 7, 1989; Stats.2000, c. 881 (S.B.1999), § 1; Stats.2001, c. 938 (S.B.975), § 2; Stats. 2002, c. 1048 (S.B.972), § 1.)*

[1] Stats.2002, c. 1048 (S.B.972), § 1.

§ 1720.2. Public works; private contracts; conditions

For the limited purposes of Article 2 (commencing with Section 1770) of this chapter, "public works" also means any construction work done under private contract when all of the following conditions exist:

(a) The construction contract is between private persons.

(b) The property subject to the construction contract is privately owned, but upon completion of the construction

work, more than 50 percent of the assignable square feet of the property is leased to the state or a political subdivision for its use.

(c) Either of the following conditions exist:

(1) The lease agreement between the lessor and the state or political subdivision, as lessee, was entered into prior to the construction contract.

(2) The construction work is performed according to plans, specifications, or criteria furnished by the state or political subdivision, and the lease agreement between the lessor and the state or political subdivision, as lessee, is entered into during, or upon completion of, the construction work. *(Added by Stats.1974, c. 1027, p. 2228, § 1. Amended by Stats.1980, c. 962, p. 3054, § 1.)*

§ 1720.3. Public works; hauling refuse from public works site

For the limited purposes of Article 2 (commencing with Section 1770), "public works" also means the hauling of refuse from a public works site to an outside disposal location, with respect to contracts involving any state agency, including the California State University and the University of California, or any political subdivision of the state. *(Added by Stats.1976, c. 1084, p. 4907, § 1. Amended by Stats.1983, c. 143, § 201; Stats.1983, c. 142, § 101; Stats.1999, c. 220 (A.B.302), § 1.)*

§ 1720.4. Work performed by volunteers, volunteer coordinators, or conservation corps members; exemption from chapter; application; report to legislature; appropriation

(a) This chapter shall not apply to any of the following work:

(1) Any work performed by a volunteer. For purposes of this section, "volunteer" means an individual who performs work for civic, charitable, or humanitarian reasons for a public agency or corporation qualified under Section 501(c)(3) of the Internal Revenue Code [1] as a tax-exempt organization, without promise, expectation, or receipt of any compensation for work performed.

(A) An individual shall be considered a volunteer only when his or her services are offered freely and without pressure and coercion, direct or implied, from an employer.

(B) An individual may receive reasonable meals, lodging, transportation, and incidental expenses or nominal nonmonetary awards without losing volunteer status if, in the entire context of the situation, those benefits and payments are not a substitute form of compensation for work performed.

(C) An individual shall not be considered a volunteer if the person is otherwise employed for compensation at any time (i) in the construction, alteration, demolition, installation, repair, or maintenance work on the same project, or (ii) by a contractor, other than a corporation qualified under Section 501(c)(3) of the Internal Revenue Code as a tax-exempt organization, that is receiving

449

payment to perform construction, alteration, demolition, installation, repair, or maintenance work on the same project.

(2) Any work performed by a volunteer coordinator. For purposes of this section, "volunteer coordinator" means an individual paid by a corporation qualified under Section 501(c)(3) of the Internal Revenue Code as a tax-exempt organization, to oversee or supervise volunteers. An individual may be considered a volunteer coordinator even if the individual performs some nonsupervisory work on a project alongside the volunteers, so long as the individual's primary responsibility on the project is to oversee or supervise the volunteers rather than to perform nonsupervisory work.

(3) Any work performed by members of the California Conservation Corps or of Community Conservation Corps certified by the California Conservation Corps pursuant to Section 14507.5 of the Public Resources Code.

(b) This section shall apply retroactively to otherwise covered work concluded on or after January 1, 2002, to the extent permitted by law.

(c) On or before January 1, 2011, the director shall submit a written report to the Legislature that does both of the following:

(1) Describes the number and the nature of complaints received and investigations conducted involving the use of volunteers on public works projects subject to this chapter, that are projects as described in Section 21190 of the Public Resources Code.

(2) Provides an estimate of each of the following as they relate to public works projects that involve the acquisition, presentation, or restoration of natural areas, including parks or ecological reserves, or other public works projects that have one or more of the purposes, as described in Section 21190 of the Public Resources Code:

(A) The number of hours per year that volunteers work on public works projects.

(B) The cost per year of public works projects, that are projects as described in Section 21190 of the Public Resources Code, and the percentage of work performed by volunteers.

(C) The types of work done by volunteers on public works projects, that are projects as described in Section 21190 of the Public Resources Code.

(d) The sum of one hundred thousand dollars ($100,-000) is hereby appropriated from the Environmental License Plate Fund for the purposes of funding the report required pursuant to subdivision (c).

(e) This section shall remain in effect only until January 1, 2012, and as of that date is repealed, unless a later enacted statute, which is enacted before January 1, 2012, deletes or extends that date. *(Added by Stats.2004,*

c. 330 (A.B.2690), § 2, eff. Aug. 30, 2004. Amended by Stats.2008, c. 678 (A.B.2537), § 1.)

[1] Internal Revenue Code sections are in Title 26 of the U.S.C.A.

Repeal

For repeal of this section, see its terms.

§ 1721. Political subdivision defined

"Political subdivision" includes any county, city, district, public housing authority, or public agency of the state, and assessment or improvement districts. *(Stats. 1937, c. 90, p. 241, § 1721. Amended by Stats.1953, c. 1283, p. 2839, § 1; Stats.1985, c. 239, § 1.)*

§ 1722. Awarding body and body awarding the contract defined

"Awarding body" or "body awarding the contract" means department, board, authority, officer or agent awarding a contract for public work. *(Stats.1937, c. 90, p. 241, § 1722.)*

§ 1722.1. Contractor; subcontractor defined

For the purposes of this chapter, "contractor" and "subcontractor" include a contractor, subcontractor, licensee, officer, agent, or representative thereof, acting in that capacity, when working on public works pursuant to this article and Article 2 (commencing with Section 1770). *(Added by Stats.1978, c. 1249, p. 4061, § 1. Amended by Stats.1982, c. 454, p. 1877, § 132.)*

§ 1723. Worker defined

"Worker" includes laborer, worker, or mechanic. *(Stats.1937, c. 90, p. 241, § 1723. Amended by Stats.2000, c. 954 (A.B.1646), § 2, operative July 1, 2001.)*

§ 1724. Locality in which public work is performed defined

"Locality in which public work is performed" means the county in which the public work is done in cases in which the contract is awarded by the State, and means the limits of the political subdivision on whose behalf the contract is awarded in other cases. *(Stats.1937, c. 90, p. 241, § 1724.)*

§ 1725. Alien defined

"Alien" means any person who is not a born or fully naturalized citizen of the United States. *(Stats.1937, c. 90, p. 241, § 1725.)*

§ 1726. Cognizance of violations in execution of contracts; reports; withholding procedures; actions to recover wages; costs and attorneys fees

(a) The body awarding the contract for public work shall take cognizance of violations of this chapter committed in the course of the execution of the contract, and shall promptly report any suspected violations to the Labor Commissioner.

(b) If the awarding body determines as a result of its own investigation that there has been a violation of this chapter and withholds contract payments, the procedures in Section 1771.6 shall be followed.

(c) A contractor may bring an action in a court of competent jurisdiction to recover from an awarding body the difference between the wages actually paid to an employee and the wages that were required to be paid to an employee under this chapter, any penalties required to be paid under this chapter, and costs and attorney's fees related to this action, if either of the following is true:

(1) The awarding body previously affirmatively represented to the contractor in writing, in the call for bids, or otherwise, that the work to be covered by the bid or contract was not a "public work," as defined in this chapter.

(2) The awarding body received actual written notice from the Department of Industrial Relations that the work to be covered by the bid or contract is a "public work," as defined in this chapter, and failed to disclose that information to the contractor before the bid opening or awarding of the contract. *(Stats.1937, c. 90, p. 241, § 1726. Amended by Stats.2000, c. 954 (A.B.1646), § 3, operative July 1, 2001; Stats.2003, c. 804 (S.B.966), § 1.)*

§ 1727. Withholding to satisfy wage and penalty assessments

(a) Before making payments to the contractor of money due under a contract for public work, the awarding body shall withhold and retain therefrom all amounts required to satisfy any civil wage and penalty assessment issued by the Labor Commissioner under this chapter. The amounts required to satisfy a civil wage and penalty assessment shall not be disbursed by the awarding body until receipt of a final order that is no longer subject to judicial review.

(b) If the awarding body has not retained sufficient money under the contract to satisfy a civil wage and penalty assessment based on a subcontractor's violations, the contractor shall, upon the request of the Labor Commissioner, withhold sufficient money due the subcontractor under the contract to satisfy the assessment and transfer the money to the awarding body. These amounts shall not be disbursed by the awarding body until receipt of a final order that is no longer subject to judicial review. *(Stats.1937, c. 90, p. 241, § 1727. Amended by Stats.1945, c. 1431, p. 2692, § 50; Stats.1992, c. 1342 (S.B.222), § 1; Stats.2000, c. 954 (A.B.1646), § 4, operative July 1, 2001.)*

§ 1728. Acceptance of cash in lieu of withholding

In cases of contracts with assessment or improvement districts where full payment is made in the form of a single warrant, or other evidence of full payment, after completion and acceptance of the work, the awarding body shall accept from the contractor in cash a sum equal to, and in lieu of, any amount required to be withheld, retained, or forfeited under the provisions of this section, and said awarding body shall then release the final warrant or payment in full. *(Stats.1937, c. 90, p. 242, § 1728.)*

§ 1729. Withholding of amounts from subcontractors

It shall be lawful for any contractor to withhold from any subcontractor under him sufficient sums to cover any penalties withheld from him by the awarding body on account of the subcontractor's failure to comply with the terms of this chapter, and if payment has already been made to the subcontractor the contractor may recover from him the amount of the penalty or forfeiture in a suit at law. *(Stats.1937, c. 90, p. 242, § 1729.)*

§ 1734. Disposition of fines and penalties collected by court

Any court collecting any fines or penalties under the criminal provisions of this chapter or any of the labor laws pertaining to public works shall as soon as practicable after the receipt thereof deposit same with the county treasurer of the county in which such court is situated. Amounts so deposited shall be paid at least once a month by warrant of the county auditor drawn upon requisition of the judge or clerk of said court, to the State Treasurer for deposit in the General Fund. *(Stats.1937, c. 90, p. 243, § 1734. Amended by Stats.1953, c. 523, p. 1763, § 5.)*

§ 1735. Discrimination in employment

A contractor shall not discriminate in the employment of persons upon public works on any basis listed in subdivision (a) of Section 12940 of the Government Code, as those bases are defined in Sections 12926 and 12926.1 of the Government Code, except as otherwise provided in Section 12940 of the Government Code. Every contractor for public works who violates this section is subject to all the penalties imposed for a violation of this chapter. *(Added by Stats.1939, c. 643, p. 2068, § 1. Amended by Stats.1965, c. 283, p. 1284, § 7; Stats.1976, c. 1174, p. 5270, § 1; Stats.1980, c. 992, p. 3166, § 10; Stats.1992, c. 913 (A.B.1077), § 36; Stats.2004, c. 788 (A.B.2900), § 14.)*

§ 1736. Investigations; confidentiality of names of employees reporting violations of this chapter

During any investigation conducted under this part, the Division of Labor Standards Enforcement shall keep confidential the name of any employee who reports a violation of this chapter and any other information that may identify the employee. *(Added by Stats.1999, c. 302 (A.B.1395), § 1.)*

§ 1740. Public contracts; modification to comply with federal wage schedules without republication

Notwithstanding any other provision of this chapter or any other law of this State, except limitations imposed by the Constitution, the legislative body of a political subdivision which has received or is to receive a loan or grant of funds from the Federal Government or a federal department or agency for public works of that political subdivision, may provide in its call for bids in connection with such public works that all bid specifications and contracts and other procedures in connection with bids or contracts shall be subject to modification to comply with revisions in federal minimum wage schedules without the necessity of republication or duplication of other formal statutory requirements. *(Added by Stats.1957, c. 1992, p. 3545, § 1.)*

§ 1741. Determination of violations; civil wage and penalty assessments; service interest on due and unpaid wages; list of violators

(a) If the Labor Commissioner or his or her designee determines after an investigation that there has been a violation of this chapter, the Labor Commissioner shall with reasonable promptness issue a civil wage and penalty assessment to the contractor or subcontractor or both. The assessment shall be in writing and shall describe the nature of the violation and the amount of wages, penalties, and forfeitures due and shall include the basis for the assessment. The assessment shall be served not later than 180 days after the filing of a valid notice of completion in the office of the county recorder in each county in which the public work or some part thereof was performed, or not later than 180 days after acceptance of the public work, whichever occurs last. However, if the assessment is served after the expiration of this 180–day period, but before the expiration of an additional 180 days, and the awarding body has not yet made full payment to the contractor, the assessment is valid up to the amount of the funds retained. Service of the assessment shall be completed pursuant to Section 1013 of the Code of Civil Procedure by first-class and certified mail to the contractor, subcontractor, and awarding body. The assessment shall advise the contractor and subcontractor of the procedure for obtaining review of the assessment. The Labor Commissioner shall, to the extent practicable, ascertain the identity of any bonding company issuing a bond that secures the payment of wages covered by the assessment and any surety on a bond, and shall serve a copy of the assessment by certified mail to the bonding company or surety at the same time service is made to the contractor, subcontractor, and awarding body. However, no bonding company or surety shall be relieved of its responsibilities because it failed to receive notice from the Labor Commissioner.

(b) Interest shall accrue on all due and unpaid wages at the rate described in subdivision (b) of Section 3289 of the Civil Code. The interest shall accrue from the date that the wages were due and payable, as provided in Part 7 (commencing with Section 1720) of Division 2, until the wages are paid.

(c)(1) The Labor Commissioner shall maintain a public list of the names of each contractor and subcontractor who has been found to have committed a willful violation of Section 1775 or to whom a final order, which is no longer subject to judicial review, has been issued.

(2) The list shall include the date of each assessment, the amount of wages and penalties assessed, and the amount collected.

(3) The list shall be updated at least quarterly, and the contractor's or subcontractor's name shall remain on that list until the assessment is satisfied, or for a period of three years beginning from the date of the issuance of the assessment, whichever is later. *(Added by Stats.2000, c. 954 (A.B.1646), § 9, operative, July 1, 2001. Amended by Stats.2003, c. 849 (A.B.1418), § 2.)*

§ 1742. Review of wage and penalty assessments; hearing procedure

(a) An affected contractor or subcontractor may obtain review of a civil wage and penalty assessment under this chapter by transmitting a written request to the office of the Labor Commissioner that appears on the assessment within 60 days after service of the assessment. If no hearing is requested within 60 days after service of the assessment, the assessment shall become final.

(b) Upon receipt of a timely request, a hearing shall be commenced within 90 days before the director, who shall appoint an impartial hearing officer possessing the qualifications of an administrative law judge pursuant to subdivision (b) of Section 11502 of the Government Code. The appointed hearing officer shall be an employee of the department, but shall not be an employee of the Division of Labor Standards Enforcement. The contractor or subcontractor shall be provided an opportunity to review evidence to be utilized by the Labor Commissioner at the hearing within 20 days of the receipt of the written request for a hearing. Any evidence obtained by the Labor Commissioner subsequent to the 20–day cutoff shall be promptly disclosed to the contractor or subcontractor.

The contractor or subcontractor shall have the burden of proving that the basis for the civil wage and penalty assessment is incorrect. The assessment shall be sufficiently detailed to provide fair notice to the contractor or subcontractor of the issues at the hearing.

Within 45 days of the conclusion of the hearing, the director shall issue a written decision affirming, modifying, or dismissing the assessment. The decision of the director shall consist of a notice of findings, findings, and an order. This decision shall be served on all parties and the awarding body pursuant to Section 1013 of the Code of Civil Procedure by first-class mail at the last known address of the party on file with the Labor Commissioner. Within 15 days of the issuance of the decision, the director may reconsider or modify the decision to correct an error, except that a clerical error may be corrected at any time.

The director shall adopt regulations setting forth procedures for hearings under this subdivision.

(c) An affected contractor or subcontractor may obtain review of the decision of the director by filing a petition for a writ of mandate to the appropriate superior court pursuant to Section 1094.5 of the Code of Civil

Procedure within 45 days after service of the decision. If no petition for writ of mandate is filed within 45 days after service of the decision, the order shall become final. If it is claimed in a petition for writ of mandate that the findings are not supported by the evidence, abuse of discretion is established if the court determines that the findings are not supported by substantial evidence in the light of the whole record.

(d) A certified copy of a final order may be filed by the Labor Commissioner in the office of the clerk of the superior court in any county in which the affected contractor or subcontractor has property or has or had a place of business. The clerk, immediately upon the filing, shall enter judgment for the state against the person assessed in the amount shown on the certified order.

(e) A judgment entered pursuant to this section shall bear the same rate of interest and shall have the same effect as other judgments and shall be given the same preference allowed by law on other judgments rendered for claims for taxes. The clerk shall not charge for the service performed by him or her pursuant to this section.

(f) An awarding body that has withheld funds in response to a civil wage and penalty assessment under this chapter shall, upon receipt of a certified copy of a final order that is no longer subject to judicial review, promptly transmit the withheld funds, up to the amount of the certified order, to the Labor Commissioner.

(g) This section shall provide the exclusive method for review of a civil wage and penalty assessment by the Labor Commissioner under this chapter or the decision of an awarding body to withhold contract payments pursuant to Section 1771.5.

(Added by Stats.2000, c. 954 (A.B.1646), § 10, operative July 1, 2001. Amended by Stats.2004, c. 685 (A.B. 3020), § 2; Stats.2006, c. 828 (A.B.2907), § 1; Stats.2008, c. 402 (S.B.1352), § 1.)

§ 1742.1. Liability of contractor, subcontractor, or surety; settlements

(a) After 60 days following the service of a civil wage and penalty assessment under Section 1741 or a notice of withholding under subdivision (a) of Section 1771.6, the affected contractor, subcontractor, and surety on a bond or bonds issued to secure the payment of wages covered by the assessment or notice shall be liable for liquidated damages in an amount equal to the wages, or portion thereof, that still remain unpaid. If the assessment or notice subsequently is overturned or modified after administrative or judicial review, liquidated damages shall be payable only on the wages found to be due and unpaid.

Additionally, if the contractor or subcontractor demonstrates to the satisfaction of the director that he or she had substantial grounds for appealing the assessment or notice with respect to a portion of the unpaid wages covered by the assessment or notice, the director may exercise his or her discretion to waive payment of the liquidated damages with respect to that portion of the unpaid wages. Any liquidated damages shall be distributed to the employee along with the unpaid wages. Section 203.5 shall not apply to claims for prevailing wages under this chapter.

(b) Notwithstanding subdivision (a), there shall be no liability for liquidated damages if the full amount of the assessment or notice, including penalties, has been deposited with the Department of Industrial Relations, within 60 days following service of the assessment or notice, for the department to hold in escrow pending administrative and judicial review. The department shall release such funds, plus any interest earned, at the conclusion of all administrative and judicial review to the persons and entities who are found to be entitled to such funds.

(c) The Labor Commissioner shall, upon receipt of a request from the affected contractor or subcontractor within 30 days following the service of a civil wage and penalty assessment under Section 1741, afford the contractor or subcontractor the opportunity to meet with the Labor Commissioner or his or her designee to attempt to settle a dispute regarding the assessment without the need for formal proceedings. The awarding body shall, upon receipt of a request from the affected contractor or subcontractor within 30 days following the service of a notice of withholding under subdivision (a) of Section 1771.6, afford the contractor or subcontractor the opportunity to meet with the designee of the awarding body to attempt to settle a dispute regarding the notice without the need for formal proceedings. The settlement meeting may be held in person or by telephone and shall take place before the expiration of the 60-day period for seeking administrative review. No evidence of anything said or any admission made for the purpose of, in the course of, or pursuant to, the settlement meeting is admissible or subject to discovery in any administrative or civil proceeding. No writing prepared for the purpose of, in the course of, or pursuant to, the settlement meeting, other than a final settlement agreement, is admissible or subject to discovery in any administrative or civil proceeding. The assessment or notice shall advise the contractor or subcontractor of the opportunity to request a settlement meeting.

(d) This section shall become operative on January 1, 2007. *(Added by Stats.2000, c. 954 (A.B.1646), § 13, operative Jan. 1, 2005. Amended by Stats.2004, c. 685 (A.B.3020), § 5, operative Jan. 1, 2007; Stats.2008, c. 402 (S.B.1352), § 3.)*

§ 1743. Joint and several liability; order of collection; application of amounts collected; payment of workers; bonding company liability

(a) The contractor and subcontractor shall be jointly and severally liable for all amounts due pursuant to a final order under this chapter or a judgment thereon. The Labor Commissioner shall first exhaust all reasonable remedies to collect the amount due from the subcontractor before pursuing the claim against the contractor.

(b) From the amount collected, the wage claim shall be satisfied prior to the amount being applied to penalties. If insufficient money is recovered to pay each worker in full, the money shall be prorated among all workers.

(c) Wages for workers who cannot be located shall be placed in the Industrial Relations Unpaid Wage Fund and held in trust for the workers pursuant to Section 96.7. Penalties shall be paid into the General Fund.

(d) A final order under this chapter or a judgment thereon shall be binding, with respect to the amount found to be due, on a bonding company issuing a bond that secures the payment of wages and a surety on a bond. The limitations period of any action on a payment bond shall be tolled pending a final order that is no longer subject to judicial review. *(Added by Stats.2000, c. 954 (A.B.1646), § 14, operative July 1, 2001.)*

ARTICLE 1.5. RIGHT OF ACTION

Section
1750. Second lowest bidder or legal entity with contract with second lowest bidder; damage due to acceptance of successful bidder who violated provisions of workers' compensation or Unemployment Insurance Code; rebuttable presumption; costs and fees.

§ 1750. Second lowest bidder or legal entity with contract with second lowest bidder; damage due to acceptance of successful bidder who violated provisions of workers' compensation or Unemployment Insurance Code; rebuttable presumption; costs and fees

(a)(1) The second lowest bidder, and any person, firm, association, trust, partnership, labor organization, corporation, or other legal entity which has, prior to the letting of the bids on the public works project in question, entered into a contract with the second lowest bidder, that suffers damage as a proximate result of a competitive bid for a public works project, as defined in subdivision (b), not being accepted due to the successful bidder's violation, as evidenced by the conviction of the successful bidder therefor, of any provision of Division 4 (commencing with Section 3200) or of the Unemployment Insurance Code, may bring an action for damages in the appropriate state court against the violating person or legal entity.

(2) There shall be a rebuttable presumption that a successful bidder who has been convicted of a violation of any provision of Division 4 (commencing with Section 3200) of this code or of the Unemployment Insurance Code, or of both, was awarded the bid because that successful bidder was able to lower the bid due to this violation or these violations occurring on the contract for public work awarded by the public agency.

(b) For purposes of this article:

(1) "Public works project" means the construction, repair, remodeling, alteration, conversion, modernization,

improvement, rehabilitation, replacement, or renovation of a public building or structure.

(2) "Second lowest bidder" means the second lowest qualified bidder deemed responsive by the public agency awarding the contract for public work.

(3) The "second lowest bidder" and the "successful bidder" may include any person, firm, association, corporation, or other legal entity.

(c) In an action brought pursuant to this section, the court may award costs and reasonable attorney's fees, in an amount to be determined in the court's discretion, to the prevailing party.

(d) For purposes of an action brought pursuant to this section, employee status shall be determined pursuant to Division 4 (commencing with Section 3200) with respect to alleged violations of that division, pursuant to the Unemployment Insurance Code with respect to alleged violations of that code, and pursuant to Section 2750.5 with respect to alleged violations of either Division 4 (commencing with Section 3200) or of the Unemployment Insurance Code.

(e) The right of action established pursuant to this article shall not be construed to diminish rights of action established pursuant to Section 19102 of, and Article 1.8 (commencing with Section 20104.70) of Chapter 1 of Part 3 of Division 2 of, the Public Contract Code.

(f) A second lowest bidder who has been convicted of a violation of any provision of Division 4 (commencing with Section 3200) of the Labor Code or of the Unemployment Insurance Code, or both, within one year prior to filing the bid for public work, and who has failed to take affirmative steps to correct that violation or those violations, is prohibited from taking any action authorized by this section. *(Added by Stats.1991, c. 906 (A.B.1754), § 1.)*

ARTICLE 2. WAGES

Section
1770. Determination of general prevailing rate.
1771. Payment of general prevailing rate.
1771.2. Action by joint labor-management committee against employer that fails to pay prevailing wage to its employees.
1771.3. State Public Works Enforcement Fund; creation; assessment of fee to cover expenses of enforcing prevailing wage requirements; report to Legislature.
1771.5. Exemptions from general prevailing rate; labor compliance program; withholding contract payments for failure to comply; revocation of approval of labor compliance program; application.
1771.55. Exemptions from general prevailing rate requirements for awarding bodies electing to undertake specified criteria.
1771.6. Deposits of penalties or forfeitures withheld from contract payment.
1771.7. Awarding body choosing to use funds derived from Kindergarten–University Public Education Facili-

Section

ties Bond Act for public works project; initiating and enforcing labor compliance program.

1771.75. Awarding body choosing to use funds derived from Kindergarten–University Public Education Facilities Bond Act for public works project; payment of compliance fee.

1771.8. Adoption and enforcement of labor compliance program for application to public works project.

1771.85. Public works projects financed by Water Security, Clean Drinking Water, Coastal and Beach Protection Act funds; payment of compliance fee by awarding body.

1771.9. Public works projects financed by Safe, Reliable High–Speed Passenger Train Bond Act funds; payment of compliance fee by awarding body.

1772. Employees of contractors and subcontractors.

1773. Method of determining general prevailing rates; holidays; adoption of rates established by collective bargaining.

1773.1. Employer payments included in per diem wages.

1773.2. Specification of general wage rate in call for bids, in bid specifications and in contract; posting at job site.

1773.3. Contract awards; copy to division; notice to local committee; discrepancy in ratio.

1773.4. Review of determination of prevailing wages.

1773.5. Rules and regulations.

1773.6. Determination of change in prevailing wages during quarter; availability to awarding body.

1773.7. Exemption of special funds of state agencies from charges for services.

1773.9. General prevailing rate of per diem wages; method of determining; rates established by collective bargaining agreements.

1773.11. Private entity's employees; prevailing rate of per diem wages and holiday and overtime work; determinations.

1774. Payment of general prevailing rate.

1775. Penalties for violations.

1776. Payroll records; retention; inspection; noncompliance penalties; rules and regulations.

1777. Violation; misdemeanor.

1777.1. Violations with intent to defraud; willful violations.

1777.5. Employment of registered apprentices; wages; standards; number; apprenticeable craft or trade; exemptions; contributions.

1777.6. Discrimination against apprentices.

1777.7. Violations of § 1777.5; civil penalty; denial of right to bid on contracts; procedure; violations by subcontractors.

1778. Receipt of portion of wages of workman; felony.

1779. Fee for registering or placing person in public work; misdemeanor.

1780. Placement of order for employment of workman; misdemeanor.

1781. Actions to recover increased costs incurred; liability; public works; definitions; penalties.

§ 1770. Determination of general prevailing rate

The Director of the Department of Industrial Relations shall determine the general prevailing rate of per diem wages in accordance with the standards set forth in Section 1773, and the director's determination in the matter shall be final except as provided in Section 1773.4.

Nothing in this article, however, shall prohibit the payment of more than the general prevailing rate of wages to any workman employed on public work. Nothing in this act shall permit any overtime work in violation of Article 3 of this chapter. *(Stats.1937, c. 90, p. 243, § 1770. Amended by Stats.1953, c. 1706, p. 3455, § 2; Stats.1976, c. 281, p. 587, § 2.)*

§ 1771. Payment of general prevailing rate

Except for public works projects of one thousand dollars ($1,000) or less, not less than the general prevailing rate of per diem wages for work of a similar character in the locality in which the public work is performed, and not less than the general prevailing rate of per diem wages for holiday and overtime work fixed as provided in this chapter, shall be paid to all workers employed on public works.

This section is applicable only to work performed under contract, and is not applicable to work carried out by a public agency with its own forces. This section is applicable to contracts let for maintenance work. *(Stats. 1937, c. 90, p. 243, § 1771. Amended by Stats.1953, c. 1706, p. 3455, § 3; Stats.1974, c. 1202, p. 2593, § 1; Stats.1976, c. 861, p. 1969, § 2; Stats.1981, c. 449, p. 1697, § 1.)*

§ 1771.2. Action by joint labor-management committee against employer that fails to pay prevailing wage to its employees

A joint labor-management committee established pursuant to the federal Labor Management Cooperation Act of 1978 (Section 175a of Title 29 of the United States Code) may bring an action in any court of competent jurisdiction against an employer that fails to pay the prevailing wage to its employees, as required by this article. This action shall be commenced not later than 180 days after the filing of a valid notice of completion in the office of the county recorder in each county in which the public work or some part thereof was performed, or not later than 180 days after acceptance of the public work, whichever last occurs. *(Added by Stats.2001, c. 804 (S.B.588), § 1.)*

§ 1771.3. State Public Works Enforcement Fund; creation; assessment of fee to cover expenses of enforcing prevailing wage requirements; report to Legislature

(a)(1) The State Public Works Enforcement Fund is hereby created as a special fund in the State Treasury. Notwithstanding Section 13340 of the Government Code, moneys in the fund shall be continuously appropriated for the purposes the Department of Industrial Relations' enforcement of prevailing wage requirements applicable to public works pursuant to this chapter, and labor compliance enforcement as set forth in subdivision (b) of Section 1771.55, and shall not be used or borrowed for any other purpose.

(2) The Director of Industrial Relations, with the approval of the Director of Finance, shall determine and

assess a fee on any awarding body using funds derived from any bond issued by the state to fund public works projects, in an amount not to exceed one-fourth of 1 percent of the bond proceeds. The fee shall be set to cover the expenses of the Department of Industrial Relations for administering the prevailing wage requirements on public works projects using those bond funds. All fees collected pursuant to this subdivision section shall be deposited in the State Public Works Enforcement Fund, and shall be used only for enforcement of prevailing wage requirements on projects using bond funds and other projects for which awarding bodies pay into the fund. The administration and enforcement of prevailing wage requirements is an administrative expense associated with public works construction.

(b) The fee imposed by this section shall not apply to any contract awarded prior to the effective date of regulations adopted by the department pursuant to paragraph (2) of subdivision (b) of Section 1771.55.

(c) The department shall report to the Legislature, not later than March 1, 2011, on its administration of the State Public Works Enforcement Fund, and the prevailing wage enforcement activities undertaken by the department utilizing that funding. *(Added by Stats.2009–2010, 2nd Ex.Sess., c. 7 (S.B.9), § 5, eff. May 21, 2009.)*

§ 1771.5. Exemptions from general prevailing rate; labor compliance program; withholding contract payments for failure to comply; revocation of approval of labor compliance program; application

(a) Notwithstanding Section 1771, an awarding body may not require the payment of the general prevailing rate of per diem wages or the general prevailing rate of per diem wages for holiday and overtime work for any public works project of twenty-five thousand dollars ($25,000) or less when the project is for construction work, or for any public works project of fifteen thousand dollars ($15,000) or less when the project is for alteration, demolition, repair, or maintenance work, if the awarding body elects to initiate and enforce a labor compliance program pursuant to subdivision (b) for every public works project under the authority of the awarding body.

(b) For * * * purposes of this section, a labor compliance program shall include, but not be limited to, the following requirements:

(1) All bid invitations and public works contracts shall contain appropriate language concerning the requirements of this chapter.

(2) A prejob conference shall be conducted with the contractor and subcontractors to discuss federal and state labor law requirements applicable to the contract.

(3) Project contractors and subcontractors shall maintain and furnish, at a designated time, a certified copy of each weekly payroll containing a statement of compliance signed under penalty of perjury.

(4) The awarding body shall review, and, if appropriate, audit payroll records to verify compliance with this chapter.

(5) The awarding body shall withhold contract payments when payroll records are delinquent or inadequate.

(6) The awarding body shall withhold contract payments equal to the amount of underpayment and applicable penalties when, after investigation, it is established that underpayment has occurred.

(c) For purposes of this chapter, "labor compliance program" means a labor compliance program that is approved, as specified in state regulations, by the Director of the Department of Industrial Relations.

(d) For purposes of this chapter, the Director of the Department of Industrial Relations may revoke the approval of a labor compliance program in the manner specified in state regulations.

(e) This section shall not apply to contracts awarded after the latter of either the effective date of any fee adopted by the Department of Industrial Relations to be deposited in the State Public Works Enforcement Fund, pursuant to Sections 1771.3, 1771.55, 1771.75, 1771.85, and 1771.9 of this code, subdivision (d) of Section 17250.30 of, and subdivision (d) of Section 81704, of the Education Code, subdivision (f) of Section 6531 of the Government Code, and paragraph (3) of subdivision (b) of Section 20133 of, paragraph (5) of subdivision (b) of Section 20175.2 of, subdivision (b) of Section 20193 of, subdivision (c) of Section 20209.7 of, Section 20209.24 of, and subdivision (a) of Section 20919.3 of the Public Contract Code, or the effective date of the regulations adopted by the department pursuant to paragraph (2) of subdivision (b) of Section 1771.55. *(Added by Stats.1989, c. 1224, § 2. Amended by Stats.1999, c. 83 (S.B.966), § 132; Stats.2003, c. 834 (A.B.324), § 1; Stats.2009–2010, 2nd Ex.Sess., c. 7 (S.B.9), § 6, eff. May 21, 2009.)*

§ 1771.55. Exemptions from general prevailing rate requirements for awarding bodies electing to undertake specified criteria

(a) Notwithstanding Section 1771, an awarding body may not require the payment of the general prevailing rate of per diem wages or the general prevailing rate of per diem wages for holiday and overtime work for any public works project of twenty-five thousand dollars ($25,000) or less when the project is for construction work, or for any public works project of fifteen thousand dollars ($15,000) or less when the project is for alteration, demolition, repair, or maintenance work, if the awarding body elects to undertake all of the following for every public works project under the authority of the awarding body:

(1) Ensure that all bid invitations and public works contracts contain appropriate language concerning the requirements of this chapter.

(2) Conduct a prejob conference with the contractor and subcontractor to discuss federal and state labor law requirements applicable to contract.

(3) Pay a fee to the Department of Industrial Relations for the enforcement of prevailing wage obligations in an amount that the department shall establish, and as it may from time to time amend, in an amount not to exceed one-fourth of 1 percent of the total public works project costs, sufficient to support the department's costs in ensuring compliance with and enforcing prevailing wage requirements on the project. All fees collected pursuant to this subdivision shall be deposited in the State Public Works Enforcement Fund created by Section 1771.3, and shall be used only for enforcement of prevailing wage requirements on those projects.

(b) For all projects required to pay a fee into the State Public Works Enforcement Fund, the Department of Industrial Relations shall do the following:

(1) Review on a monthly basis, and if appropriate, audit payroll records to verify compliance with this chapter.

(2) Adopt reasonable regulations setting forth the manner in which the department will ensure compliance with and enforce prevailing wage requirements on the project. In adopting these regulations, the department shall give consideration to the duties of labor compliance programs as set forth in Sections 16421 to 16439, inclusive, of Title 8 of the California Code of Regulations.

(c) The department may waive the fee set forth in this section for an awarding body that has previously been granted approval by the director to initiate and operate a labor compliance program on the awarding body's projects, and that requests to continue to operate that labor compliance program on its projects in lieu of labor compliance by the department pursuant to subdivision (b). This fee shall not be waived for an awarding body that contracts with a third party to initiate and enforce labor compliance programs on the awarding body's projects.

(d) Subdivisions (a) and (c) of this section shall only apply to a contract awarded on or after both the effective date of the department's adoption of the fee set forth in subdivision (a) and of regulations pursuant to paragraph (2) of subdivision (b). *(Added by Stats.2009–2010, 2nd Ex.Sess., c. 7 (S.B.9), § 7, eff. May 21, 2009.)*

§ 1771.6. Deposits of penalties or forfeitures withheld from contract payment

(a) Any awarding body that enforces this chapter in accordance with Section 1726 or 1771.5 shall provide notice of the withholding of contract payments to the contractor and subcontractor, if applicable. The notice shall be in writing and shall describe the nature of the violation and the amount of wages, penalties, and forfeitures withheld. Service of the notice shall be completed pursuant to Section 1013 of the Code of Civil Procedure by first-class and certified mail to the contractor and

subcontractor, if applicable. The notice shall advise the contractor and subcontractor, if applicable, of the procedure for obtaining review of the withholding of contract payments.

The awarding body shall also serve a copy of the notice by certified mail to any bonding company issuing a bond that secures the payment of wages covered by the notice and to any surety on a bond, if their identities are known to the awarding body.

(b) The withholding of contract payments in accordance with Section 1726 or 1771.5 shall be reviewable under Section 1742 in the same manner as if the notice of the withholding was a civil penalty order of the Labor Commissioner under this chapter. If review is requested, the Labor Commissioner may intervene to represent the awarding body.

(c) Pending a final order, or the expiration of the time period for seeking review of the notice of the withholding, the awarding body shall not disburse any contract payments withheld.

(d) From the amount recovered, the wage claim shall be satisfied prior to the amount being applied to penalties. If insufficient money is recovered to pay each worker in full, the money shall be prorated among all workers.

(e) Wages for workers who cannot be located shall be placed in the Industrial Relations Unpaid Wage Fund and held in trust for the workers pursuant to Section 96.7. Penalties shall be paid into the General Fund of the awarding body that has enforced this chapter pursuant to Section 1771.5. *(Added by Stats.2000, c. 954 (A.B.1646), § 16, operative July 1, 2001.)*

§ 1771.7. Awarding body choosing to use funds derived from Kindergarten–University Public Education Facilities Bond Act for public works project; initiating and enforcing labor compliance program

(a)(1) An awarding body that chooses to use funds derived from either the Kindergarten–University Public Education Facilities Bond Act of 2002 [1] or the Kindergarten–University Public Education Facilities Bond Act of 2004 [2] for a public works project, shall initiate and enforce, or contract with a third party to initiate and enforce, a labor compliance program, as described in subdivision (b) of Section 1771.5, with respect to that public works project.

(2) If an awarding body described in paragraph (1) chooses to contract with a third party to initiate and enforce a labor compliance program for a project described in paragraph (1), that third party shall not review the payroll records of its own employees or the employees of its subcontractors, and the awarding body or an independent third party shall review these payroll records for purposes of the labor compliance program.

(b) This section applies to public works that commence on or after April 1, 2003. For purposes of this subdivision, work performed during the design and pre-

457

construction phases of construction, including, but not limited to, inspection and land surveying work, does not constitute the commencement of a public work.

(c)(1) For purposes of this section, if any campus of the California State University chooses to use the funds described in subdivision (a), then the "awarding body" is the Chancellor of the California State University. For purposes of this subdivision, if the chancellor is required by subdivision (a) to initiate and enforce, or to contract with a third party to initiate and enforce, the labor compliance program described in that subdivision, then in addition to the requirements imposed upon an awarding body by subdivision (b) of Section 1771.5, the Chancellor of the California State University shall review the payroll records described in paragraphs (3) and (4) of subdivision (b) of Section 1771.5 on at least a monthly basis to ensure the awarding body's compliance with the labor compliance program.

(2) For purposes of this subdivision, if an awarding body described in subdivision (a) is the University of California or any campus of that university, and that awarding body is required by subdivision (a) to initiate and enforce, or to contract with a third party to initiate and enforce, the labor compliance program described in that subdivision, then in addition to the requirements imposed upon an awarding body by subdivision (b) of Section 1771.5, the payroll records described in paragraphs (3) and (4) of subdivision (b) of Section 1771.5 shall be reviewed on at least a monthly basis to ensure the awarding body's compliance with the labor compliance program.

(d)(1) An awarding body described in subdivision (a) shall make a written finding that the awarding body has initiated and enforced, or has contracted with a third party to initiate and enforce, the labor compliance program described in subdivision (a).

(2)(A) If an awarding body described in subdivision (a) is a school district, the governing body of that district shall transmit to the State Allocation Board, in the manner determined by that board, a copy of the finding described in paragraph (1).

(B) The State Allocation Board shall not release the funds described in subdivision (a) to an awarding body that is a school district until the State Allocation Board has received the written finding described in paragraph (1).

(C) If the State Allocation Board conducts a postaward audit procedure with respect to an award of the funds described in subdivision (a) to an awarding body that is a school district, the State Allocation Board shall verify, in the manner determined by that board, that the school district has complied with the requirements of this subdivision.

(3) If an awarding body described in subdivision (a) is a community college district, the Chancellor of the California State University, or the office of the President of the University of California or any campus of the University of California, that awarding body shall transmit, in the manner determined by the Director of the Department of Industrial Relations, a copy of the finding described in paragraph (1) to the director of that department, or the director of any successor agency that is responsible for the oversight of employee wage and employee work hours laws.

(e) Notwithstanding Section 17070.63 of the Education Code, for purposes of this act, the State Allocation Board shall increase the grant amounts as described in Chapter 12.5 (commencing with Section 17070.10) of Part 10 of Division 1 of Title 1 of the Education Code to accommodate the state's share of the increased costs of a new construction or modernization project due to the initiation and enforcement of the labor compliance program.

(f) This section shall become inoperative upon the latter of the effective date of regulations adopted by the Department of Industrial Relations pursuant to paragraph (2) of subdivision (b) of Section 1771.55 or the effective date of the fees adopted by the department pursuant to Section 1771.75, and shall be repealed on the January 1 next following that date. *(Added by Stats.2002, c. 868 (A.B.1506), § 2, operative Nov. 5, 2002. Amended by Stats.2003, c. 834 (A.B.324), § 2; Stats.2005, c. 606 (A.B.414), § 1; Stats.2009–2010, 2nd Ex.Sess., c. 7 (S.B.9), § 8, eff. May 21, 2009.)*

[1] See Education Code § 100600 et seq.
[2] See Education Code § 100800 et seq.

Inoperative Date and Repeal

For inoperative date and repeal of this section, see its terms.

§ 1771.75. Awarding body choosing to use funds derived from Kindergarten–University Public Education Facilities Bond Act for public works project; payment of compliance fee

(a) An awarding body that chooses to use funds derived from either the Kindergarten–University Public Education Facilities Bond Act of 2002 [1] or the Kindergarten–University Public Education Facilities Bond Act of 2004 [2] for a public works project, shall pay a fee to the Department of Industrial Relations, in an amount that the department shall establish, and as it may from time to time amend, in an amount not to exceed one-fourth of 1 percent of the bond proceeds, sufficient to support the department's costs in ensuring compliance with and enforcing prevailing wage requirements on the project, and labor compliance enforcement as set forth in subdivision (b) of Section 1771.55. All fees collected pursuant to this subdivision shall be deposited in the State Public Works Enforcement Fund created by Section 1771.3, and shall be used only for enforcement of prevailing wage requirements on those projects. The department may waive the fee set forth in this section for an awarding body that has previously been granted approval by the director to initiate and operate a labor compliance program on the awarding body's projects, and requests to continue to operate that labor compliance program on its projects in lieu of labor compliance by the department pursuant to subdivision (b) of Section 1771.55. This fee shall not be waived for an awarding body that contracts with a third party to initiate and enforce labor compliance programs on the awarding body's projects.

(b) This section applies to public works that commence on or after April 1, 2003. For purposes of this subdivision, work performed during the design and pre-construction phases of construction, including, but not limited to, inspection and land surveying work, does not constitute the commencement of a public work.

(c)(1) For purposes of this section, if any campus of the California State University chooses to use the funds described in subdivision (a), then the awarding body is the Chancellor of the California State University and the chancellor is required by subdivision (a) to pay a fee to the Department of Industrial Relations.

(2) For purposes of this subdivision, if an awarding body described in subdivision (a) is the University of California or any campus of that university, and that awarding body is required by subdivision (a) to pay a fee to the Department of Industrial Relations, then the university shall review the payroll records on at least a monthly basis to ensure the university's compliance with prevailing wage obligations.

(d) The department shall notify the State Allocation Board of awarding bodies that have paid a fee as required by subdivision (a).

(e) Notwithstanding Section 17070.63 of the Education Code, for purposes of this section, the State Allocation Board shall increase the grant amounts as described in Chapter 12.5 (commencing with Section 17070.10) of Part 10 of Division 1 of Title 1 of the Education Code to accommodate the state's share of the increased costs of a new construction or modernization project due to the fee required to be paid to the Department of Industrial Relations to ensure compliance with and enforcement of prevailing wage laws on the project. All fees collected pursuant to this subdivision shall be deposited in the State Public Works Enforcement Fund created by Section 1771.3.

(f) This section shall only apply to a contract awarded on or after both the effective date of the department's adoption of the fee set forth in subdivision (a) and of regulations pursuant to paragraph (2) of subdivision (b) of Section 1771.55. *(Added by Stats.2009–2010, 2nd Ex.Sess., c. 7 (S.B.9), § 9, eff. May 21, 2009.)*

¹ See Education Code § 100600 et seq.
² See Education Code § 100800 et seq.

§ 1771.8. Adoption and enforcement of labor compliance program for application to public works project

(a) The body awarding any contract for a public works project financed in any part with funds made available by the Water Security, Clean Drinking Water, Coastal and Beach Protection Act of 2002 (Division 26.5 (commenc-

ing with Section 79500) of the Water Code) shall adopt and enforce, or contract with a third party to adopt and enforce, a labor compliance program pursuant to subdivision (b) of Section 1771.5 for application to that public works project.

(b) This section shall become operative only if the Water Security, Clean Drinking Water, Coastal and Beach Protection Act of 2002 (Division 26.5 (commencing with Section 79500) of the Water Code) is approved by the voters at the November 5, 2002, statewide general election.

(c) This section shall become inoperative on the latter of the effective date of the regulations adopted by the Department of Industrial Relations pursuant to paragraph (2) of subdivision (b) of Section 1771.55 or the effective date of the fees adopted by the department pursuant to Section 1771.85, and shall be repealed on the January 1 next following that date. *(Added by Stats.2002, c. 892 (S.B.278), § 2, operative Nov. 5, 2002. Amended by Stats.2009–2010, 2nd Ex.Sess., c. 7 (S.B.9), § 10, eff. May 21, 2009.)*

Inoperative Date and Repeal

For inoperative date and repeal of this section, see its terms.

§ 1771.85. Public works projects financed by Water Security, Clean Drinking Water, Coastal and Beach Protection Act funds; payment of compliance fee by awarding body

(a) The body awarding any contract for a public works project financed in any part with funds made available by the Water Security, Clean Drinking Water, Coastal and Beach Protection Act of 2002 (Division 26.5 (commencing with Section 79500) of the Water Code) shall pay a fee to the Department of Industrial Relations, in an amount that the department shall establish, and as it may from time to time amend, in an amount not to exceed one-fourth of 1 percent of the bond proceeds, sufficient to support the department's costs in ensuring compliance with and enforcing prevailing wage requirements on the project, and labor compliance enforcement as set forth in subdivision (b) of Section 1771.55. All fees collected pursuant to this subdivision shall be deposited in the State Public Works Enforcement Fund created by Section 1771.3, and shall be used only for enforcement of prevailing wage requirements on those projects. The department may waive the fee set forth in this section for an awarding body that has previously been granted approval by the director to initiate and operate a labor compliance program on the awarding body's projects, and requests to continue to operate that labor compliance program on its projects in lieu of labor compliance by the department pursuant to subdivision (b) of Section 1771.55. This fee shall not be waived for an awarding body that contracts with a third party to initiate and enforce labor compliance programs on the awarding body's projects.

(b) This section shall only apply to a contract awarded on or after both the effective date of the department's adoption of the fee set forth in subdivision (a) and of regulations pursuant to paragraph (2) of subdivision (b) of Section 1771.55. *(Added by Stats.2009–2010, 2nd Ex.Sess., c. 7 (S.B.9), § 11, eff. May 21, 2009.)*

§ 1771.9. Public works projects financed by Safe, Reliable High–Speed Passenger Train Bond Act funds; payment of compliance fee by awarding body

(a) The body awarding any contract for a public works project financed in any part with funds made available by the Safe, Reliable High–Speed Passenger Train Bond Act for the 21st Century (Chapter 20 (commencing with Section 2704) of Division 3 of the Streets and Highways Code) shall pay a fee to the Department of Industrial Relations, in an amount that the department shall establish, and as it may from time to time amend, in an amount not to exceed one-fourth of 1 percent of the bond proceeds, sufficient to support the department's costs in ensuring compliance with and enforcing prevailing wage requirements on the project, and labor compliance enforcement as set forth in subdivision (b) of Section 1771.55. All fees collected pursuant to this subdivision shall be deposited in the State Public Works Enforcement Fund created by Section 1771.3, and shall be used only for enforcement of prevailing wage requirements on those projects. The department may waive the fee set forth in this section for an awarding body that has previously been granted approval by the director to initiate and operate a labor compliance program on the awarding body's projects, and requests to continue to operate that labor compliance program on its projects in lieu of labor compliance by the department pursuant to subdivision (b) of Section 1771.55. This fee shall not be waived for an awarding body that contracts with a third party to initiate and enforce labor compliance programs on the awarding body's projects.

(b) This section shall apply only to a contract awarded on or after both the effective date of the department's adoption of the fee set forth in subdivision (a) and of regulations pursuant to paragraph (2) of subdivision (b) of Section 1771.55. *(Added by Stats.2009–2010, 2nd Ex.Sess., c. 7 (S.B.9), § 13, eff. May 21, 2009.)*

§ 1772. Employees of contractors and subcontractors

Workers employed by contractors or subcontractors in the execution of any contract for public work are deemed to be employed upon public work. *(Stats.1937, c. 90, p. 243, § 1772. Amended by Stats.1992, c. 1342 (S.B.222), § 7).)*

§ 1773. Method of determining general prevailing rates; holidays; adoption of rates established by collective bargaining

The body awarding any contract for public work, or otherwise undertaking any public work, shall obtain the general prevailing rate of per diem wages and the general prevailing rate for holiday and overtime work in the locality in which the public work is to be performed for each craft, classification, or type of worker needed to execute the contract from the Director of Industrial Relations. The holidays upon which those rates shall be paid need not be specified by the awarding body, but shall be all holidays recognized in the applicable collective bargaining agreement. If the prevailing rate is not based on a collectively bargained rate, the holidays upon which the prevailing rate shall be paid shall be as provided in Section 6700 of the Government Code.

In determining the rates, the Director of Industrial Relations shall ascertain and consider the applicable wage rates established by collective bargaining agreements and the rates that may have been predetermined for federal public works, within the locality and in the nearest labor market area. Where the rates do not constitute the rates actually prevailing in the locality, the director shall obtain and consider further data from the labor organizations and employers or employer associations concerned, including the recognized collective bargaining representatives for the particular craft, classification, or type of work involved. The rate fixed for each craft, classification, or type of work shall be not less than the prevailing rate paid in the craft, classification, or type of work.

If the director determines that the rate of prevailing wage for any craft, classification, or type of worker is the rate established by a collective bargaining agreement, the director may adopt that rate by reference as provided for in the collective bargaining agreement and that determination shall be effective for the life of the agreement or until the director determines that another rate should be adopted. *(Stats.1937, c. 90, p. 243, § 1773. Amended by Stats.1953, c. 1706, p. 3455, § 4; Stats.1968, c. 699, p. 1398, § 1, operative July 1, 1969; Stats.1971, c. 785, p. 1538, § 1; Stats.1976, c. 281, p. 588, § 3; Stats.1999, c. 30 (S.B.16), § 1.)*

§ 1773.1. Employer payments included in per diem wages

(a) Per diem wages, when the term is used in this chapter or in any other statute applicable to public works, shall be deemed to include employer payments for the following:

(1) Health and welfare.

(2) Pension.

(3) Vacation.

(4) Travel.

(5) Subsistence.

(6) Apprenticeship or other training programs authorized by Section 3093, so long as the cost of training is reasonably related to the amount of the contributions.

(7) Worker protection and assistance programs or committees established under the federal Labor Management Cooperation Act of 1978 (Section 175a of Title 29 of the United States Code), to the extent that the activities of the programs or committees are directed to

the monitoring and enforcement of laws related to public works.

(8) Industry advancement and collective bargaining agreements administrative fees, provided that these payments are required under a collective bargaining agreement pertaining to the particular craft, classification, or type of work within the locality or the nearest labor market area at issue.

(9) Other purposes similar to those specified in paragraphs (1) to (8), inclusive.

(b) Employer payments include all of the following:

(1) The rate of contribution irrevocably made by the employer to a trustee or third person pursuant to a plan, fund, or program.

(2) The rate of actual costs to the employer reasonably anticipated in providing benefits to workers pursuant to an enforceable commitment to carry out a financially responsible plan or program communicated in writing to the workers affected.

(3) Payments to the California Apprenticeship Council pursuant to Section 1777.5.

(c) Employer payments are a credit against the obligation to pay the general prevailing rate of per diem wages. However, no credit shall be granted for benefits required to be provided by other state or federal law. Credits for employer payments also shall not reduce the obligation to pay the hourly straight time or overtime wages found to be prevailing.

(d) The credit for employer payments shall be computed on an annualized basis where the employer seeks credit for employer payments that are higher for public works projects than for private construction performed by the same employer, except where one or more of the following occur:

(1) The employer has an enforceable obligation to make the higher rate of payments on future private construction performed by the employer.

(2) The higher rate of payments is required by a project labor agreement.

(3) The payments are made to the California Apprenticeship Council pursuant to Section 1777.5.

(4) The director determines that annualization would not serve the purposes of this chapter.

(e)(1) For the purpose of determining those per diem wages for contracts, the representative of any craft, classification, or type of worker needed to execute contracts shall file with the Department of Industrial Relations fully executed copies of the collective bargaining agreements for the particular craft, classification, or type of work involved. The collective bargaining agreements shall be filed after their execution and thereafter may be taken into consideration pursuant to Section 1773 whenever filed 30 days prior to the call for bids. If the collective bargaining agreement has not been formalized, a typescript of the final draft may be filed temporarily,

accompanied by a statement under penalty of perjury as to its effective date.

(2) Where a copy of the collective bargaining agreement has previously been filed, fully executed copies of all modifications and extensions of the agreement that affect per diem wages or holidays shall be filed.

(3) The failure to comply with filing requirements of this subdivision shall not be grounds for setting aside a prevailing wage determination if the information taken into consideration is correct. (Added by Stats.1959, c. 2173, p. 5291, § 1. Amended by Stats.1969, c. 1502, p. 3072, § 1; Stats.1976, c. 281, p. 588, § 4; Stats.1999, c. 30 (S.B.16), § 2; Stats.2000, c. 954 (A.B.1646), § 18, operative July 1, 2001; Stats.2003, c. 839 (A.B.807), § 1; Stats.2003, c. 905 (S.B.868), § 1.)

§ 1773.2. Specification of general wage rate in call for bids, in bid specifications and in contract; posting at job site

The body awarding any contract for public work, or otherwise undertaking any public work, shall specify in the call for bids for the contract, and in the bid specifications and in the contract itself, what the general rate of per diem wages is for each craft, classification, or type of worker needed to execute the contract.

In lieu of specifying the rate of wages in the call for bids, and in the bid specifications and in the contract itself, the awarding body may, in the call for bids, bid specifications, and contract, include a statement that copies of the prevailing rate of per diem wages are on file at its principal office, which shall be made available to any interested party on request. The awarding body shall also cause a copy of the determination of the director of the prevailing rate of per diem wages to be posted at each job site. (Added by Stats.1971, c. 785, p. 1538, § 2. Amended by Stats.1974, c. 876, p. 1869, § 1; Stats.1977, c. 423, p. 1435, § 1; Stats.1992, c. 1342 (S.B.222), § 8.)

§ 1773.3. Contract awards; copy to division; notice to local committee; discrepancy in ratio

An awarding agency whose public works contract falls within the jurisdiction of Section 1777.5 shall, within five days of the award, send a copy of the award to the Division of Apprenticeship Standards. When specifically requested by a local joint apprenticeship committee, the division shall notify the local joint apprenticeship committee regarding all such awards applicable to the joint apprenticeship committee making the request. Within five days of a finding of any discrepancy regarding the ratio of apprentices to journeymen, pursuant to the certificated fixed number of apprentices to journeymen, the awarding agency shall notify the Division of Apprenticeship Standards. (Formerly § 3098, added by Stats. 1972, c. 1399, p. 2922, § 2. Amended by Stats.1974, c. 1095, p. 2322, § 1. Renumbered § 1773.3 and amended by Stats.1978, c. 1249, p. 4063, § 6.)

§ 1773.4. Review of determination of prevailing wages

Any prospective bidder or his representative, any representative of any craft, classification or type of workman involved, or the awarding body may, within 20 days after commencement of advertising of the call for bids by the awarding body, file with the Director of Industrial Relations a verified petition to review the determination of any such rate or rates upon the ground that they have not been determined in accordance with the provision of Section 1773 of this code. Within two days thereafter, a copy of such petition shall be filed with the awarding body. The petition shall set forth the facts upon which it is based. The Director of Industrial Relations or his authorized representative shall, upon notice to the petitioner, the awarding body and such other persons as he deems proper, including the recognized collective bargaining representatives for the particular crafts, classifications or types of work involved, institute an investigation or hold a hearing. Within 20 days after the filing of such petition, or within such longer period as agreed upon by the director, the awarding body, and all the interested parties, he shall make a determination and transmit the same in writing to the awarding body and to the interested parties.

Such determination shall be final and shall be the determination of the awarding body. Upon receipt by it of the notice of the filing of such petition the body awarding the contract or authorizing the public work shall extend the closing date for the submission of bids or the starting of work until five days after the determination of the general prevailing rates of per diem wages pursuant to this section.

Upon the filing of any such petition, notice thereof shall be set forth in the next and all subsequent publications by the awarding body of the call for bids. No other notice need be given to bidders by the awarding body by publication or otherwise. The determination of the director shall be included in the contract. (Added by Stats.1953, c. 1706, p. 3455, § 4.5. Amended by Stats. 1968, c. 699, p. 1399, § 2, operative July 1, 1969; Stats. 1969, c. 301, p. 671, § 1.)

§ 1773.5. Rules and regulations

The Director of Industrial Relations may establish rules and regulations for the purpose of carrying out this chapter, including, but not limited to, the responsibilities and duties of awarding bodies under this chapter. (Added by Stats.1953, c. 1706, p. 3456, § 5. Amended by Stats.1989, c. 1224, § 5.)

§ 1773.6. Determination of change in prevailing wages during quarter; availability to awarding body

If during any quarterly period the Director of Industrial Relations shall determine that there has been a change in any prevailing rate of per diem wages in any locality he shall make such change available to the awarding body and his determination shall be final. Such determination by the Director of Industrial Relations shall not be

effective as to any contract for which the notice to bidders has been published. (Added by Stats.1953, c. 1706, p. 3456, § 6. Amended by Stats.1957, c. 1932, p. 3446, § 486; Stats.1963, c. 1786, p. 3592, § 68, operative Oct. 1, 1963; Stats.1976, c. 281, p. 588, § 6.)

§ 1773.7. Exemption of special funds of state agencies from charges for services

The provisions of Section 11250 of the Government Code shall not be applicable to Sections 1773, 1773.4, and 1773.6. (Added by Stats.1976, c. 281, p. 589, § 8.)

§ 1773.9. General prevailing rate of per diem wages; method of determining; rates established by collective bargaining agreements

(a) The Director of Industrial Relations shall use the methodology set forth in subdivision (b) to determine the general prevailing rate of per diem wages in the locality in which the public work is to be performed.

(b) The general prevailing rate of per diem wages includes all of the following:

(1) The basic hourly wage rate being paid to a majority of workers engaged in the particular craft, classification, or type of work within the locality and in the nearest labor market area, if a majority of the workers is paid at a single rate. If no single rate is being paid to a majority of the workers, then the single rate being paid to the greatest number of workers, or modal rate, is prevailing. If a modal rate cannot be determined, then the director shall establish an alternative rate, consistent with the methodology for determining the modal rate, by considering the appropriate collective bargaining agreements, federal rates, rates in the nearest labor market area, or other data such as wage survey data.

(2) Other employer payments included in per diem wages pursuant to Section 1773.1 and as included as part of the total hourly wage rate from which the basic hourly wage rate was derived. In the event the total hourly wage rate does not include any employer payments, the director shall establish a prevailing employer payment rate by the same procedure set forth in paragraph (1).

(3) The rate for holiday and overtime work shall be those rates specified in the collective bargaining agreement when the basic hourly rate is based on a collective bargaining agreement rate. In the event the basic hourly rate is not based on a collective bargaining agreement, the rate for holidays and overtime work, if any, included with the prevailing basic hourly rate of pay shall be prevailing.

(c)(1) If the director determines that the general prevailing rate of per diem wages is the rate established by a collective bargaining agreement, and that the collective bargaining agreement contains definite and predetermined changes during its term that will affect the rate adopted, the director shall incorporate those changes into the determination. Predetermined changes that are rescinded prior to their effective date shall not be enforced.

(2) When the director determines that there is a definite and predetermined change in the general prevailing rate of per diem wages as described in paragraph (1), but has not published, at the time of the effective date of the predetermined change, the allocation of the predetermined change as between the basic hourly wage and other employer payments included in per diem wages pursuant to Section 1773.1, a contractor or subcontractor may allocate payments of not less than the amount of the definite and predetermined change to either the basic hourly wage or other employer payments included in per diem wages for up to 60 days following the director's publication of the specific allocation of the predetermined change.

(3) When the director determines that there is a definite and predetermined change in the general prevailing rate of per diem wages as described in paragraph (1), but the allocation of that predetermined change as between the basic hourly wage and other employer payments included in per diem wages pursuant to Section 1773.1 is subsequently altered by the parties to a collective bargaining agreement described in paragraph (1), a contractor or subcontractor may allocate payments of not less than the amount of the definite and predetermined change in accordance with either the originally published allocation or the allocation as altered in the collective bargaining agreement. *(Added by Stats.1999, c. 30 (S.B.16), § 1. Amended by Stats.2007, c. 182 (S.B.929), § 2.)*

§ 1773.11. Private entity's employees; prevailing rate of per diem wages and holiday and overtime work; determinations

(a) Notwithstanding any other provision of law and except as otherwise provided by this section, if the state or a political subdivision thereof agrees by contract with a private entity that the private entity's employees receive, in performing that contract, the general prevailing rate of per diem wages and the general prevailing rate for holiday and overtime work, the director shall, upon a request by the state or the political subdivision, do both of the following:

(1) Determine, as otherwise provided by law, the wage rates for each craft, classification, or type of worker that are needed to execute the contract.

(2) Provide these wage rates to the state or political subdivision that requests them.

(b) This section does not apply to a contract for a public work, as defined in this chapter.

(c) The director shall determine and provide the wage rates described in this section in the order in which the requests for these wage rates were received and regardless of the calendar year in which they were received. If there are more than 20 pending requests in a calendar year, the director shall respond only to the first 20 requests in the order in which they were received. If the director determines that funding is available in any calendar year to determine and provide these wage rates

in response to more than 20 requests, the director shall respond to these requests in a manner consistent with this subdivision. *(Added by Stats.2003, c. 343 (A.B.852), § 1.)*

§ 1774. Payment of general prevailing rate

The contractor to whom the contract is awarded, and any subcontractor under him, shall pay not less than the specified prevailing rates of wages to all workmen employed in the execution of the contract. *(Stats.1937, c. 90, p. 243, § 1774.)*

§ 1775. Penalties for violations

(a)(1) The contractor and any subcontractor under the contractor shall, as a penalty to the state or political subdivision on whose behalf the contract is made or awarded, forfeit not more than fifty dollars ($50) for each calendar day, or portion thereof, for each worker paid less than the prevailing wage rates as determined by the director for the work or craft in which the worker is employed for any public work done under the contract by the contractor or, except as provided in subdivision (b), by any subcontractor under the contractor.

(2)(A) The amount of the penalty shall be determined by the Labor Commissioner based on consideration of both of the following:

(i) Whether the failure of the contractor or subcontractor to pay the correct rate of per diem wages was a good faith mistake and, if so, the error was promptly and voluntarily corrected when brought to the attention of the contractor or subcontractor.

(ii) Whether the contractor or subcontractor has a prior record of failing to meet its prevailing wage obligations.

(B)(i) The penalty may not be less than ten dollars ($10) for each calendar day, or portion thereof, for each worker paid less than the prevailing wage rate, unless the failure of the contractor or subcontractor to pay the correct rate of per diem wages was a good faith mistake and, if so, the error was promptly and voluntarily corrected when brought to the attention of the contractor or subcontractor.

(ii) The penalty may not be less than twenty dollars ($20) for each calendar day, or portion thereof, for each worker paid less than the prevailing wage rate, if the contractor or subcontractor has been assessed penalties within the previous three years for failing to meet its prevailing wage obligations on a separate contract, unless those penalties were subsequently withdrawn or overturned.

(iii) The penalty may not be less than thirty dollars ($30) for each calendar day, or portion thereof, for each worker paid less than the prevailing wage rate, if the Labor Commissioner determines that the violation was willful, as defined in subdivision (c) of Section 1777.1.

(C) When the amount due under this section is collected from the contractor or subcontractor, any outstanding wage claim under Chapter 1 (commencing with Section 1720) of Part 7 of Division 2 against that contractor or subcontractor shall be satisfied before applying that amount to the penalty imposed on that contractor or subcontractor pursuant to this section.

(D) The determination of the Labor Commissioner as to the amount of the penalty shall be reviewable only for abuse of discretion.

(E) The difference between the prevailing wage rates and the amount paid to each worker for each calendar day or portion thereof for which each worker was paid less than the prevailing wage rate shall be paid to each worker by the contractor or subcontractor, and the body awarding the contract shall cause to be inserted in the contract a stipulation that this section will be complied with.

(b) If a worker employed by a subcontractor on a public works project is not paid the general prevailing rate of per diem wages by the subcontractor, the prime contractor of the project is not liable for any penalties under subdivision (a) unless the prime contractor had knowledge of that failure of the subcontractor to pay the specified prevailing rate of wages to those workers or unless the prime contractor fails to comply with all of the following requirements:

(1) The contract executed between the contractor and the subcontractor for the performance of work on the public works project shall include a copy of the provisions of Sections 1771, 1775, 1776, 1777.5, 1813, and 1815.

(2) The contractor shall monitor the payment of the specified general prevailing rate of per diem wages by the subcontractor to the employees, by periodic review of the certified payroll records of the subcontractor.

(3) Upon becoming aware of the failure of the subcontractor to pay his or her workers the specified prevailing rate of wages, the contractor shall diligently take corrective action to halt or rectify the failure, including, but not limited to, retaining sufficient funds due the subcontractor for work performed on the public works project.

(4) Prior to making final payment to the subcontractor for work performed on the public works project, the contractor shall obtain an affidavit signed under penalty of perjury from the subcontractor that the subcontractor has paid the specified general prevailing rate of per diem wages to his or her employees on the public works project and any amounts due pursuant to Section 1813.

(c) The Division of Labor Standards Enforcement shall notify the contractor on a public works project within 15 days of the receipt by the Division of Labor Standards Enforcement of a complaint of the failure of a subcontractor on that public works project to pay workers the general prevailing rate of per diem wages. *(Added by Stats.1997, c. 757 (S.B.1328), § 2. Amended by Stats. 2000, c. 954 (A.B.1646), § 20, operative July 1, 2001; Stats.2003, c. 849 (A.B.1418), § 3.)*

464

§ 1776. Payroll records; retention; inspection; noncompliance penalties; rules and regulations

(a) Each contractor and subcontractor shall keep accurate payroll records, showing the name, address, social security number, work classification, straight time and overtime hours worked each day and week, and the actual per diem wages paid to each journeyman, apprentice, worker, or other employee employed by him or her in connection with the public work. Each payroll record shall contain or be verified by a written declaration that it is made under penalty of perjury, stating both of the following:

(1) The information contained in the payroll record is true and correct.

(2) The employer has complied with the requirements of Sections 1771, 1811, and 1815 for any work performed by his or her employees on the public works project.

(b) The payroll records enumerated under subdivision (a) shall be certified and shall be available for inspection at all reasonable hours at the principal office of the contractor on the following basis:

(1) A certified copy of an employee's payroll record shall be made available for inspection or furnished to the employee or his or her authorized representative on request.

(2) A certified copy of all payroll records enumerated in subdivision (a) shall be made available for inspection or furnished upon request to a representative of the body awarding the contract, the Division of Labor Standards Enforcement, and the Division of Apprenticeship Standards of the Department of Industrial Relations.

(3) A certified copy of all payroll records enumerated in subdivision (a) shall be made available upon request by the public for inspection or for copies thereof. However, a request by the public shall be made through either the body awarding the contract, the Division of Apprenticeship Standards, or the Division of Labor Standards Enforcement. If the requested payroll records have not been provided pursuant to paragraph (2), the requesting party shall, prior to being provided the records, reimburse the costs of preparation by the contractor, subcontractors, and the entity through which the request was made. The public may not be given access to the records at the principal office of the contractor.

(c) The certified payroll records shall be on forms provided by the Division of Labor Standards Enforcement or shall contain the same information as the forms provided by the division. The payroll records may consist of printouts of payroll data that are maintained as computer records, if the printouts contain the same information as the forms provided by the division and the printouts are verified in the manner specified in subdivision (a).

(d) A contractor or subcontractor shall file a certified copy of the records enumerated in subdivision (a) with the entity that requested the records within 10 days after receipt of a written request.

(e) Any copy of records made available for inspection as copies and furnished upon request to the public or any public agency by the awarding body, the Division of Apprenticeship Standards, or the Division of Labor Standards Enforcement shall be marked or obliterated to prevent disclosure of an individual's name, address, and social security number. The name and address of the contractor awarded the contract or the subcontractor performing the contract shall not be marked or obliterated. Any copy of records made available for inspection by, or furnished to, a joint labor-management committee established pursuant to the federal Labor Management Cooperation Act of 1978 (29 U.S.C. Sec. 175a) shall be marked or obliterated only to prevent disclosure of an individual's name and social security number. A joint labor management committee may maintain an action in a court of competent jurisdiction against an employer who fails to comply with Section 1774. The court may award restitution to an employee for unpaid wages and may award the joint labor management committee reasonable attorney's fees and costs incurred in maintaining the action. An action under this subdivision may not be based on the employer's misclassification of the craft of a worker on its certified payroll records. Nothing in this subdivision limits any other available remedies for a violation of this chapter.

(f) The contractor shall inform the body awarding the contract of the location of the records enumerated under subdivision (a), including the street address, city, and county, and shall, within five working days, provide a notice of a change of location and address.

(g) The contractor or subcontractor has 10 days in which to comply subsequent to receipt of a written notice requesting the records enumerated in subdivision (a). In the event that the contractor or subcontractor fails to comply within the 10-day period, he or she shall, as a penalty to the state or political subdivision on whose behalf the contract is made or awarded, forfeit twenty-five dollars ($25) for each calendar day, or portion thereof, for each worker, until strict compliance is effectuated. Upon the request of the Division of Apprenticeship Standards or the Division of Labor Standards Enforcement, these penalties shall be withheld from progress payments then due. A contractor is not subject to a penalty assessment pursuant to this section due to the failure of a subcontractor to comply with this section.

(h) The body awarding the contract shall cause to be inserted in the contract stipulations to effectuate this section.

(i) The director shall adopt rules consistent with the California Public Records Act (Chapter 3.5 (commencing with Section 6250) of Division 7 of Title 1 of the Government Code) and the Information Practices Act of 1977 (Title 1.8 (commencing with Section 1798) of Part 4 of Division 3 of the Civil Code) governing the release of these records, including the establishment of reasonable fees to be charged for reproducing copies of records required by this section. *(Added by Stats.1997, c. 757 (S.B.1328), § 4. Amended by Stats.2001, c. 804 (S.B.588), § 2; Stats.2002, c. 664 (A.B.3034), § 161; Stats.2002, c. 28 (A.B.1448), § 1; Stats.2003, c. 62 (S.B.600), § 205; Stats.2005, c. 500 (S.B.759), § 1.)*

§ 1777. Violation; misdemeanor

Any officer, agent, or representative of the State or of any political subdivision who wilfully violates any provision of this article, and any contractor, or subcontractor, or agent or representative thereof, doing public work who neglects to comply with any provision of section 1776 is guilty of a misdemeanor. *(Stats.1937, c. 90, p. 244, § 1777.)*

§ 1777.1. Violations with intent to defraud; willful violations

(a) Whenever a contractor or subcontractor performing a public works project pursuant to this chapter is found by the Labor Commissioner to be in violation of this chapter with intent to defraud, except Section 1777.5, the contractor or subcontractor or a firm, corporation, partnership, or association in which the contractor or subcontractor has any interest is ineligible for a period of not less than one year or more than three years to do either of the following:

(1) Bid on or be awarded a contract for a public works project.

(2) Perform work as a subcontractor on a public works project.

(b) Whenever a contractor or subcontractor performing a public works project pursuant to this chapter is found by the Labor Commissioner to be in willful violation of this chapter, except Section 1777.5, the contractor or subcontractor or a firm, corporation, partnership, or association in which the contractor or subcontractor has any interest is ineligible for a period up to three years for each second and subsequent violation occurring within three years of a separate and previous willful violation of this chapter to do either of the following:

(1) Bid on or be awarded a contract for a public works project.

(2) Perform work as a subcontractor on a public works project.

(c) A willful violation occurs when the contractor or subcontractor knew or reasonably should have known of his or her obligations under the public works law and deliberately fails or refuses to comply with its provisions.

(d) Not less than semiannually, the Labor Commissioner shall publish and distribute to awarding bodies a list of contractors who are ineligible to bid on or be awarded a public works contract, or to perform work as a subcontractor on a public works project pursuant to this chapter. The list shall contain the name of the contractor, the Contractor's State License Board license number of the contractor, and the effective period of debarment of the contractor. The commissioner shall also place advertisements in construction industry publications targeted to the contractors and subcontractors, chosen by the commissioner, that state the effective period of the debarment and the reason for debarment. The advertisements shall appear one time for each debarment of a contractor in each publication chosen by the commissioner. The debarred contractor or subcontractor shall be liable to the commissioner for the reasonable cost of the advertisements, not to exceed five thousand dollars ($5,000). The amount paid to the commissioner for the advertisements shall be credited against the contractor's or subcontractor's obligation to pay civil fines or penalties for the same willful violation of this chapter.

(e) For purposes of this section, "contractor or subcontractor" means a firm, corporation, partnership, or association and its responsible managing officer, as well as any supervisors, managers, and officers found by the Labor Commissioner to be personally and substantially responsible for the willful violation of this chapter.

(f) For the purposes of this section, the term "any interest" means an interest in the entity bidding or performing work on the public works project, whether as an owner, partner, officer, manager, employee, agent, consultant, or representative. "Any interest" includes, but is not limited to, all instances where the debarred contractor or subcontractor receives payments, whether cash or any other form of compensation, from any entity bidding or performing work on the public works project, or enters into any contracts or agreements with the entity bidding or performing work on the public works project for services performed or to be performed for contracts that have been or will be assigned or sublet, or for vehicles, tools, equipment, or supplies that have been or will be sold, rented, or leased during the period from the initiation of the debarment proceedings until the end of the term of the debarment period. "Any interest" does not include shares held in a publicly traded corporation if the shares were not received as compensation after the initiation of debarment from an entity bidding or performing work on a public works project.

(g) For the purposes of this section, the term "entity" is defined as a company, limited liability company, association, partnership, sole proprietorship, limited liability partnership, corporation, business trust, or organization.

(h) The Labor Commissioner shall adopt rules and regulations for the administration and enforcement of this section. *(Added by Stats.1989, c. 1224, § 10. Amended by Stats.1998, c. 443 (A.B.1569), § 1; Stats. 2000, c. 970 (A.B.2513), § 1.)*

§ 1777.5. Employment of registered apprentices; wages; standards; number; apprenticeable craft or trade; exemptions; contributions

(a) Nothing in this chapter shall prevent the employment of properly registered apprentices upon public works.

(b) Every apprentice employed upon public works shall be paid the prevailing rate of per diem wages for apprentices in the trade to which he or she is registered and shall be employed only at the work of the craft or trade to which he or she is registered.

(c) Only apprentices, as defined in Section 3077, who are in training under apprenticeship standards that have been approved by the Chief of the Division of Apprenticeship Standards and who are parties to written apprentice agreements under Chapter 4 (commencing with Section 3070) of Division 3 are eligible to be employed at the apprentice wage rate on public works. The employment and training of each apprentice shall be in accordance with either of the following:

(1) The apprenticeship standards and apprentice agreements under which he or she is training.

(2) The rules and regulations of the California Apprenticeship Council.

(d) When the contractor to whom the contract is awarded by the state or any political subdivision, in performing any of the work under the contract, employs workers in any apprenticeable craft or trade, the contractor shall employ apprentices in at least the ratio set forth in this section and may apply to any apprenticeship program in the craft or trade that can provide apprentices to the site of the public work for a certificate approving the contractor under the apprenticeship standards for the employment and training of apprentices in the area or industry affected. However, the decision of the apprenticeship program to approve or deny a certificate shall be subject to review by the Administrator of Apprenticeship. The apprenticeship program or programs, upon approving the contractor, shall arrange for the dispatch of apprentices to the contractor. A contractor covered by an apprenticeship program's standards shall not be required to submit any additional application in order to include additional public works contracts under that program. "Apprenticeable craft or trade," as used in this section, means a craft or trade determined as an apprenticeable occupation in accordance with rules and regulations prescribed by the California Apprenticeship Council. As used in this section, "contractor" includes any subcontractor under a contractor who performs any public works not excluded by subdivision (o).

(e) Prior to commencing work on a contract for public works, every contractor shall submit contract award information to an applicable apprenticeship program that can supply apprentices to the site of the public work. The information submitted shall include an estimate of journeyman hours to be performed under the contract, the number of apprentices proposed to be employed, and the approximate dates the apprentices would be employed. A copy of this information shall also be submitted to the awarding body if requested by the awarding body. Within 60 days after concluding work on the contract, each contractor and subcontractor shall submit to the awarding body, if requested, and to the apprenticeship program a verified statement of the journeyman and apprentice hours performed on the contract. The information under this subdivision shall be public. The apprenticeship programs shall retain this information for 12 months.

(f) The apprenticeship program that can supply apprentices to the area of the site of the public work shall ensure equal employment and affirmative action in apprenticeship for women and minorities.

(g) The ratio of work performed by apprentices to journeymen employed in a particular craft or trade on the public work may be no higher than the ratio stipulated in the apprenticeship standards under which the apprenticeship program operates where the contractor agrees to be bound by those standards, but, except as otherwise provided in this section, in no case shall the ratio be less than one hour of apprentice work for every five hours of journeyman work.

(h) This ratio of apprentice work to journeyman work shall apply during any day or portion of a day when any journeyman is employed at the jobsite and shall be computed on the basis of the hours worked during the day by journeymen so employed. Any work performed by a journeyman in excess of eight hours per day or 40 hours per week shall not be used to calculate the ratio. The contractor shall employ apprentices for the number of hours computed as above before the end of the contract or, in the case of a subcontractor, before the end of the subcontract. However, the contractor shall endeavor, to the greatest extent possible, to employ apprentices during the same time period that the journeymen in the same craft or trade are employed at the jobsite. Where an hourly apprenticeship ratio is not feasible for a particular craft or trade, the Chief of the Division of Apprenticeship Standards, upon application of an apprenticeship program, may order a minimum ratio of not less than one apprentice for each five journeymen in a craft or trade classification.

(i) A contractor covered by this section that has agreed to be covered by an apprenticeship program's standards upon the issuance of the approval certificate, or that has been previously approved for an apprenticeship program in the craft or trade, shall employ the number of apprentices or the ratio of apprentices to journeymen stipulated in the applicable apprenticeship standards, but in no event less than the 1–to–5 ratio required by subdivision (g).

(j) Upon proper showing by a contractor that he or she employs apprentices in a particular craft or trade in the state on all of his or her contracts on an annual average of not less than one hour of apprentice work for every five hours of labor performed by journeymen, the Chief of the Division of Apprenticeship Standards may grant a certificate exempting the contractor from the 1–to–5 hourly ratio, as set forth in this section for that craft or trade.

(k) An apprenticeship program has the discretion to grant to a participating contractor or contractor association a certificate, which shall be subject to the approval of the Administrator of Apprenticeship, exempting the contractor from the 1–to–5 ratio set forth in this section when it finds that any one of the following conditions is met:

(1) Unemployment for the previous three-month period in the area exceeds an average of 15 percent.

(2) The number of apprentices in training in the area exceeds a ratio of 1 to 5.

(3) There is a showing that the apprenticeable craft or trade is replacing at least one-thirtieth of its journeymen annually through apprenticeship training, either on a statewide basis or on a local basis.

(4) Assignment of an apprentice to any work performed under a public works contract would create a condition that would jeopardize his or her life or the life, safety, or property of fellow employees or the public at large, or the specific task to which the apprentice is to be assigned is of a nature that training cannot be provided by a journeyman.

(l) When an exemption is granted pursuant to subdivision (k) to an organization that represents contractors in a specific trade from the 1–to–5 ratio on a local or statewide basis, the member contractors shall not be required to submit individual applications for approval to local joint apprenticeship committees, if they are already covered by the local apprenticeship standards.

(m)(1) A contractor to whom a contract is awarded, who, in performing any of the work under the contract, employs journeymen or apprentices in any apprenticeable craft or trade shall contribute to the California Apprenticeship Council the same amount that the director determines is the prevailing amount of apprenticeship training contributions in the area of the public works site. A contractor may take as a credit for payments to the council any amounts paid by the contractor to an approved apprenticeship program that can supply apprentices to the site of the public works project. The contractor may add the amount of the contributions in computing his or her bid for the contract.

(2) At the conclusion of the 2002–03 fiscal year and each fiscal year thereafter, the California Apprenticeship Council shall distribute training contributions received by the council under this subdivision, less the expenses of the Division of Apprenticeship Standards for administering this subdivision, by making grants to approved apprenticeship programs for the purpose of training apprentices. The funds shall be distributed as follows:

(A) If there is an approved multiemployer apprenticeship program serving the same craft or trade and geographic area for which the training contributions were made to the council, a grant to that program shall be made.

(B) If there are two or more approved multiemployer apprenticeship programs serving the same craft or trade and geographic area for which the training contributions were made to the council, the grant shall be divided among those programs based on the number of apprentices registered in each program.

(C) All training contributions not distributed under subparagraphs (A) and (B) shall be used to defray the future expenses of the Division of Apprenticeship Standards.

(3) All training contributions received pursuant to this subdivision shall be deposited in the Apprenticeship Training Contribution Fund, which is hereby created in the State Treasury. Notwithstanding Section 13340 of the Government Code, all money in the Apprenticeship Training Contribution Fund is hereby continuously appropriated for the purpose of carrying out this subdivision and to pay the expenses of the Division of Apprenticeship Standards.

(n) The body awarding the contract shall cause to be inserted in the contract stipulations to effectuate this section. The stipulations shall fix the responsibility of compliance with this section for all apprenticeable occupations with the prime contractor.

(*o*) This section does not apply to contracts of general contractors or to contracts of specialty contractors not bidding for work through a general or prime contractor when the contracts of general contractors or those specialty contractors involve less than thirty thousand dollars ($30,000).

(p) All decisions of an apprenticeship program under this section are subject to Section 3081. (*Added by Stats.1937, c. 872, p. 2424. Amended by Stats.1939, c. 971, p. 2723, § 1; Stats.1957, c. 699, p. 1890, § 1; Stats.1968, c. 1411, p. 2772, § 1; Stats.1969, c. 1260, p. 2466, § 1, eff. Aug. 31, 1969; Stats.1972, c. 1087, p. 2026, § 1; Stats. 1972, c. 1399, § 1; Stats.1974, c. 965, p. 2011, § 1; Stats.1976, c. 538, p. 1372, § 1; Stats.1976, c. 1179, p. 5277, § 2, eff. Sept. 22, 1976; Stats.1989, c. 1224, § 11; Stats.1997, c. 17 (S.B.947), § 91; Stats.1999, c. 903 (A.B.921), § 2; Stats.2000, c. 135 (A.B.2539), § 124; Stats.2000, c. 875 (A.B.2481), § 1; Stats.2002, c. 1124 (A.B.3000), § 43, eff. Sept. 30, 2002; Stats.2003, c. 228 (A.B.1756), § 38, eff. Aug. 11, 2003.*)

§ 1777.6. Discrimination against apprentices

An employer or a labor union shall not refuse to accept otherwise qualified employees as registered apprentices on any public works on any basis listed in subdivision (a) of Section 12940 of the Government Code, as those bases are defined in Sections 12926 and 12926.1 of the Government Code, except as provided in Section 3077 of this code and Section 12940 of the Government Code. (*Added by Stats.1951, c. 1192, p. 3005, § 1; Amended by Stats.1965, c. 283, p. 1284, § 8 Stats.1971, c. 280, p. 586, § 1; Stats.1976, c. 1179, p. 5279, § 3, eff. Sept. 22, 1976; Stats.2004, c. 788 (A.B.2900), § 15.*)

§ 1777.7. Violations of § 1777.5; civil penalty; denial of right to bid on contracts; procedure; violations by subcontractors

(a)(1) A contractor or subcontractor that is determined by the Chief of the Division of Apprenticeship Standards to have knowingly violated Section 1777.5 shall

forfeit as a civil penalty an amount not exceeding one hundred dollars ($100) for each full calendar day of noncompliance. The amount of this penalty may be reduced by the Chief if the amount of the penalty would be disproportionate to the severity of the violation. A contractor or subcontractor that knowingly commits a second or subsequent violation of Section 1777.5 within a three-year period, where the noncompliance results in apprenticeship training not being provided as required by this chapter, shall forfeit as a civil penalty the sum of not more than three hundred dollars ($300) for each full calendar day of noncompliance. Notwithstanding Section 1727, upon receipt of a determination that a civil penalty has been imposed by the Chief, the awarding body shall withhold the amount of the civil penalty from contract progress payments then due or to become due.

(2) In lieu of the penalty provided for in this subdivision, the Chief may, for a first-time violation and with the concurrence of an apprenticeship program described in subdivision (d), order the contractor or subcontractor to provide apprentice employment equivalent to the work hours that would have been provided for apprentices during the period of noncompliance.

(b) In the event a contractor or subcontractor is determined by the Chief to have knowingly committed a serious violation of any provision of Section 1777.5, the Chief may also deny to the contractor or subcontractor, and to its responsible officers, the right to bid on or be awarded or perform work as a subcontractor on any public works contract for a period of up to one year for the first violation and for a period of up to three years for a second or subsequent violation. Each period of debarment shall run from the date the determination of noncompliance by the Chief becomes a final order of the Administrator of Apprenticeship.

(c)(1) An affected contractor, subcontractor, or responsible officer may obtain a review of the determination of the Chief imposing the debarment or civil penalty by transmitting a written request to the office of the Administrator within 30 days after service of the determination of debarment or civil penalty. A copy of this report shall also be served on the Chief. If the Administrator does not receive a timely request for review of the determination of debarment or civil penalty made by the Chief, the order shall become the final order of the Administrator.

(2) Within 20 days of the timely receipt of a request for review, the Chief shall provide the contractor, subcontractor, or responsible officer the opportunity to review any evidence the Chief may offer at the hearing. The Chief shall also promptly disclose any nonprivileged documents obtained after the 20-day time limit at a time set forth for exchange of evidence by the Administrator.

(3) Within 90 days of the timely receipt of a request for review, a hearing shall be commenced before the Administrator or an impartial hearing officer designated by the Administrator and possessing the qualifications of an administrative law judge pursuant to subdivision (b) of

Section 11502 of the Government Code. The affected contractor, subcontractor, or responsible officer shall have the burden of providing evidence of compliance with Section 1777.5.

(4) Within 45 days of the conclusion of the hearing, the Administrator shall issue a written decision affirming, modifying, or dismissing the determination of debarment or civil penalty. The decision shall contain a statement of the factual and legal basis for the decision and an order. This decision shall be served on all parties and the awarding body pursuant to Section 1013 of the Code of Civil Procedure by first-class mail at the last known address of the party that the party has filed with the Administrator. Within 15 days of issuance of the decision, the Administrator may reconsider or modify the decision to correct an error, except that a clerical error may be corrected at any time.

(5) An affected contractor, subcontractor, or responsible officer who has timely requested review and obtained a decision under paragraph (4) may obtain review of the decision of the Administrator by filing a petition for a writ of mandate to the appropriate superior court pursuant to Section 1094.5 of the Code of Civil Procedure within 45 days after service of the final decision. If no timely petition for a writ of mandate is filed, the decision shall become the final order of the Administrator. The decision of the Administrator shall be affirmed unless the petitioner shows that the Administrator abused his or her discretion. If the petitioner claims that the findings are not supported by the evidence, abuse of discretion is established if the court determines that the findings are not supported by substantial evidence in light of the entire record.

(6) The Chief may certify a copy of the final order of the Administrator and file it with the clerk of the superior court in any county in which the affected contractor or subcontractor has property or has or had a place of business. The clerk, immediately upon the filing, shall enter judgment for the state against the person assessed in the amount shown on the certified order. A judgment entered pursuant to this section shall bear the same rate of interest and shall have the same effect as other judgments and be given the same preference allowed by the law on other judgments rendered for claims for taxes. The clerk shall not charge for the service performed by him or her pursuant to this section. An awarding body that has withheld funds in response to a determination by the Chief imposing a penalty under this section shall, upon receipt of a certified copy of a final order of the Administrator, promptly transmit the withheld funds, up to the amount of the certified order, to the Administrator.

(d) If a subcontractor is found to have violated Section 1777.5, the prime contractor of the project is not liable for any penalties under subdivision (a), unless the prime contractor had knowledge of the subcontractor's failure to comply with the provisions of Section 1777.5 or unless the prime contractor fails to comply with any of the following requirements:

(1) The contract executed between the contractor and the subcontractor or the performance of work on the public works project shall include a copy of the provisions of Sections 1771, 1775, 1776, 1777.5, 1813, and 1815.

(2) The contractor shall continually monitor a subcontractor's use of apprentices required to be employed on the public works project pursuant to subdivision (d) of Section 1777.5, including, but not limited to, periodic review of the certified payroll of the subcontractor.

(3) Upon becoming aware of a failure of the subcontractor to employ the required number of apprentices, the contractor shall take corrective action, including, but not limited to, retaining funds due the subcontractor for work performed on the public works project until the failure is corrected.

(4) Prior to making the final payment to the subcontractor for work performed on the public works project, the contractor shall obtain a declaration signed under penalty of perjury from the subcontractor that the subcontractor has employed the required number of apprentices on the public works project.

(e) Any funds withheld by the awarding body pursuant to this section shall be deposited in the General Fund if the awarding body is a state entity, or in the equivalent fund of an awarding body if the awarding body is an entity other than the state.

(f) The Chief shall consider, in setting the amount of a monetary penalty, in determining whether a violation is serious, and in determining whether and for how long a party should be debarred for violating this section, all of the following circumstances:

(1) Whether the violation was intentional.

(2) Whether the party has committed other violations of Section 1777.5.

(3) Whether, upon notice of the violation, the party took steps to voluntarily remedy the violation.

(4) Whether, and to what extent, the violation resulted in lost training opportunities for apprentices.

(5) Whether, and to what extent, the violation otherwise harmed apprentices or apprenticeship programs.

If a party seeks review of a decision by the Chief to impose a monetary penalty or period of debarment, the Administrator shall decide de novo the appropriate penalty, by considering the same factors set forth above.

(g) The interpretation of Section 1777.5 and this section shall be in accordance with the regulations of the California Apprenticeship Council. The Administrator may adopt regulations to establish guidelines for the imposition of monetary penalties and periods of debarment and may designate precedential decisions under Section 11425.60 of the Government Code. (Added by Stats.1989, c. 1224, § 13. Amended by Stats.1999, c. 903

(A.B.921), § 3; Stats.2000, c. 135 (A.B.2539), § 125; Stats.2000, c. 875 (A.B.2481), § 2.)

§ 1778. Receipt of portion of wages of workman; felony

Every person, who individually or as a representative of an awarding or public body or officer, or as a contractor or subcontractor doing public work, or agent or officer thereof, who takes, receives, or conspires with another to take or receive, for his own use or the use of any other person any portion of the wages of any workman or working subcontractor, in connection with services rendered upon any public work is guilty of a felony. (Stats.1937, c. 90, p. 244, § 1778.)

§ 1779. Fee for registering or placing person in public work; misdemeanor

Any person or agent or officer thereof who charges, collects, or attempts to charge or collect, directly or indirectly, a fee or valuable consideration for registering any person for public work, or for giving information as to where such employment may be procured, or for placing, assisting in placing, or attempting to place, any person in public work, whether the person is to work directly for the State, or any political subdivision or for a contractor or subcontractor doing public work is guilty of a misdemeanor. (Stats.1937, c. 90, p. 244, § 1779.)

§ 1780. Placement of order for employment of workman; misdemeanor

Any person acting on behalf of the State or any political subdivision, or any contractor or subcontractor or agent or representative thereof, doing any public work who places any order for the employment of a workman on public work where the filling of the order for employment involves the charging of a fee, or the receiving of a valuable consideration from any applicant for employment is guilty of a misdemeanor. (Stats.1937, c. 90, p. 244, § 1780.)

§ 1781. Actions to recover increased costs incurred; liability; public works; definitions; penalties

(a)(1) Notwithstanding any other provision of law, a contractor may, subject to paragraphs (2) and (3), bring an action in a court of competent jurisdiction to recover from the body awarding a contract for a public work or otherwise undertaking any public work any increased costs incurred by the contractor as a result of any decision by the body, the Department of Industrial Relations, or a court that classifies, after the time at which the body accepts the contractor's bid or awards the contractor a contract in circumstances where no bid is solicited, the work covered by the bid or contract as a "public work," as defined in this chapter, to which Section 1771 applies, if that body, before the bid opening or awarding of the contract, failed to identify as a "public work," as defined in this chapter, in the bid specification or in the contract documents that portion of the work that the decision classifies as a "public work."

(2) The body awarding a contract for a public work or otherwise undertaking any public work is not liable for increased costs in an action described in paragraph (1) if all of the following conditions are met:

(A) The contractor did not directly submit a bid to, or directly contract with, that body.

(B) The body stated in the contract, agreement, ordinance, or other written arrangement by which it undertook the public work that the work described in paragraph (1) was a "public work," as defined in this chapter, to which Section 1771 applies, and obligated the party with whom the body makes its written arrangement to cause the work described in paragraph (1) to be performed as a "public work."

(C) The body fulfilled all of its duties, if any, under the Civil Code or any other provision of law pertaining to the body providing and maintaining bonds to secure the payment of contractors, including the payment of wages to workers performing the work described in paragraph (1).

(3) If a contractor did not directly submit a bid to, or directly contract with a body awarding a contract for, or otherwise undertaking a public work, the liability of that body in an action commenced by the contractor under subdivision (a) is limited to that portion of a judgment, obtained by that contractor against the body that solicited the contractor's bid or awarded the contract to the contractor, that the contractor is unable to satisfy. For purposes of this paragraph, a contractor may not be deemed to be unable to satisfy any portion of a judgment unless, in addition to other collection measures, the contractor has made a good faith attempt to collect that portion of the judgment against a surety bond, guarantee, or some other form of assurance.

(b) When construction has not commenced at the time a final decision by the Department of Industrial Relations or a court classifies all or part of the work covered by the bid or contract as a "public work," as defined in this chapter, the body that solicited the bid or awarded the contract shall rebid the "public work" covered by the contract as a "public work," any bid that was submitted and any contract that was executed for this work are null and void, and the contractor may not be compensated for any nonconstruction work already performed unless the body soliciting the bid or awarding the contract has agreed to compensate the contractor for this work.

(c) For purposes of this section:

(1) "Awarding body" does not include the Department of General Services, the Department of Transportation, or the Department of Water Resources.

(2) "Increased costs" includes, but is not limited to:

(A) Labor cost increases required to be paid to workers who perform or performed work on the "public work" as a result of the events described in subdivision (a).

(B) Penalties for a violation of this article for which the contractor is liable, and which violation is the result of the events described in subdivision (a). *(Added by Stats.2003, c. 804 (S.B.966), § 2.)*

ARTICLE 3. WORKING HOURS

Section
1810. Legal day's work.
1811. Maximum hours per day and per week.
1812. Record of hours of employment; inspection.
1813. Forfeiture for violations; contract stipulation; report of violations.
1814. Violation; misdemeanor.
1815. Overtime.

§ 1810. Legal day's work

Eight hours labor constitutes a legal day's work in all cases where the same is performed under the authority of any law of this State, or under the direction, or control, or by the authority of any officer of this State acting in his official capacity, or under the direction, or control or by the authority of any municipal corporation, or of any officer thereof. A stipulation to that effect shall be made a part of all contracts to which the State or any municipal corporation therein is a party. *(Stats.1937, c. 90, p. 245, § 1810.)*

§ 1811. Maximum hours per day and per week

The time of service of any workman employed upon public work is limited and restricted to 8 hours during any one calendar day, and 40 hours during any one calendar week, except as hereinafter provided for under Section 1815. *(Stats.1937, c. 90, p. 245, § 1811. Amended by Stats.1961, c. 238, p. 1256, § 1; Stats.1963, c. 964, p. 2222, § 1.)*

§ 1812. Record of hours of employment; inspection

Every contractor and subcontractor shall keep an accurate record showing the name of and actual hours worked each calendar day and each calendar week by each worker employed by him or her in connection with the public work. The record shall be kept open at all reasonable hours to the inspection of the awarding body and to the Division of Labor Standards Enforcement. *(Formerly § 1814, Stats.1937, c. 90, p. 245, § 1814. Amended by Stats.1945, c. 1431, p. 2692, § 51. Renumbered § 1812 and amended by Stats.1961, c. 238, p. 1256, § 4; Stats.1963, c. 964, p. 2222, § 2; Stats.1988, c. 160, § 123.)*

§ 1813. Forfeiture for violations; contract stipulation; report of violations

The contractor or subcontractor shall, as a penalty to the state or political subdivision on whose behalf the contract is made or awarded, forfeit twenty-five dollars ($25) for each worker employed in the execution of the contract by the respective contractor or subcontractor for each calendar day during which the worker is required or permitted to work more than 8 hours in any one calendar day and 40 hours in any one calendar week in violation of the provisions of this article. In awarding any contract for public work, the awarding body shall cause to be inserted in the contract a stipulation to this effect. The awarding body shall take cognizance of all violations of this article committed in the course of the execution of the contract, and shall report them to the Division of Labor Standards Enforcement.

(Added by Stats.1997, c. 757 (S.B.1328), § 6. Amended by Stats.2002, c. 28 (A.B.1448), § 3.)

§ 1814. Violation; misdemeanor

Any officer, agent, or representative of the State or any political subdivision who violates any provision of this article and any contractor or subcontractor or agent or representative thereof doing public work who neglects to comply with any provision of Section 1812 is guilty of a misdemeanor. *(Formerly § 1816, Stats.1937, c. 90, p. 246, § 1816. Renumbered § 1814 and amended by Stats.1961, c. 238, p. 1257, § 6.)*

§ 1815. Overtime

Notwithstanding the provisions of Sections 1810 to 1814, inclusive, of this code, and notwithstanding any stipulation inserted in any contract pursuant to the requirements of said sections, work performed by employees of contractors in excess of 8 hours per day, and 40 hours during any one week, shall be permitted upon public work upon compensation for all hours worked in excess of 8 hours per day at not less than 1½ times the basic rate of pay. *(Formerly § 1817, added by Stats.1941, c. 759, p. 2295, § 1. Renumbered § 1815 and amended by Stats.1961, c. 238, p. 1257, § 7; Stats.1963, c. 964, p. 2223, § 4.)*

ARTICLE 4. EMPLOYMENT OF ALIENS [REPEALED]

ARTICLE 5. SECURING WORKERS' COMPENSATION

Section
1860. Required contract provision.
1861. Certification by contractor.

§ 1860. Required contract provision

The awarding body shall cause to be inserted in every public works contract a clause providing that, in accordance with the provisions of Section 3700 of the Labor Code, every contractor will be required to secure the payment of compensation to his employees. *(Added by Stats.1965, c. 1000, p. 2630, § 2.)*

§ 1861. Certification by contractor

Each contractor to whom a public works contract is awarded shall sign and file with the awarding body the following certification prior to performing the work of the contract: "I am aware of the provisions of Section 3700 of the Labor Code which require every employer to be insured against liability for workers' compensation or to undertake self-insurance in accordance with the provisions of that code, and I will comply with such provisions before commencing the performance of the work of this contract." *(Added by Stats.1965, c. 1000, p. 2630, § 2. Amended by Stats.1979, c. 373, p. 1343, § 232.)*

CHAPTER 2.   PUBLIC AGENCIES

Article	Section
1. Municipal Employees	1900
2. Employment of Aliens [Repealed]	
3. Loyalty of Employees [Repealed]	

ARTICLE 1.   MUNICIPAL EMPLOYEES

Section
1900.   Employees entitled to time off for meals.
1901.   Violation; misdemeanor.

§ 1900.   Employees entitled to time off for meals

Every employee of a city whose hours of labor exceed 120 in a week is entitled to be off duty at least three hours during every twenty-four hours for the purpose of procuring meals. No deduction of salary shall be made by reason thereof. *(Stats.1937, c. 90, p. 247, § 1900.)*

§ 1901.   Violation; misdemeanor

Any officer or agent of a city having supervision and control of employees covered by this article who violates any provision hereof is guilty of a misdemeanor. *(Stats. 1937, c. 90, p. 247, § 1901.)*

ARTICLE 2.   EMPLOYMENT OF ALIENS [REPEALED]

ARTICLE 3.   LOYALTY OF EMPLOYEES [REPEALED]

CHAPTER 4.   FIREFIGHTERS

Section
1960.   Interference with right to join labor organization prohibited.
1961.   "Employees" defined.
1962.   Right of employees to organize; right to strike or to recognize picket line.
1963.   Construction of chapter.
1964.   Removal of volunteer firefighters; regulations; hearing, notice, charges, and review; probation.

§ 1960.   Interference with right to join labor organization prohibited

Neither the State nor any county, political subdivision, incorporated city, town, nor any other municipal corporation shall prohibit, deny or obstruct the right of firefighters to join any bona fide labor organization of their own choice. *(Added by Stats.1959, c. 723, p. 2711, § 1.)*

§ 1961.   "Employees" defined

As used in this chapter, the term "employees" means the employees of the fire departments and fire services of the State, counties, cities, cities and counties, districts, and other political subdivisions of the State. *(Added by Stats.1959, c. 723, p. 2711, § 1.)*

§ 1962.   Right of employees to organize; right to strike or to recognize picket line

Employees shall have the right to self-organization, to form, join, or assist labor organizations, to present grievances and recommendations regarding wages, salaries, hours, and working conditions to the governing body, and to discuss the same with such governing body, through such an organization, but shall not have the right to strike, or to recognize a picket line of a labor organization while in the course of the performance of their official duties. *(Added by Stats.1959, c. 723, p. 2711, § 1.)*

§ 1963.   Construction of chapter

The enactment of this chapter shall not be construed as making the provisions of Section 923 of this code applicable to public employees. *(Added by Stats.1959, c. 723, p. 2712, § 1.)*

§ 1964.   Removal of volunteer firefighters; regulations; hearing, notice, charges, and review; probation

(a) The governing body of any regularly organized volunteer fire department may, but shall not be required to, adopt regulations governing the removal of volunteer firefighters from the volunteer fire department.

(b) In the event that the governing body chooses to adopt these regulations, it shall have the discretion, after soliciting comments from the membership of the volunteer fire department, to adopt any reasonable regulations which may, but need not, include some or all of the following elements, in addition to other provisions:

(1) Members of the department shall not be removed from membership, except for incompetence, misconduct, or failure to comply with the rules and regulations of the department. Removals, except for absenteeism at fires or meetings, shall be made only after a hearing with due notice, with stated charges, and with the right of the member to a review.

(2) The charges shall be in writing and may be made by the governing body. The burden of proving incompetency or misconduct shall be on the person alleging it.

(3) Hearings on the charges shall be held by the officer or body having the power to remove the person, or by a deputy or employee of the officer or body designated in writing for that purpose.

In case a deputy or other employee is so designated, he or she shall for the purpose of the hearing be vested with all the powers of the officer or body, and shall make a record of the hearing which shall be referred to the officer or body for review with his or her recommendations.

(4) The notice of the hearing shall specify the time and place of the hearing and state the body or person before whom the hearing will be held. Notice and a copy of the charges shall be served personally upon the accused member at least 10 days but not more than 30 days before the date of the hearing.

(5) A stenographer may be employed for the purpose of taking testimony at the hearing.

(6) The officer or body having the power to remove the person may suspend the person after charges are filed and pending disposition of the charges, and after the hearing may remove the person or may suspend him or her for a period of time not to exceed one year.

(7) Volunteer firefighters shall serve a probationary period of a length to be specified by the governing board, not to exceed one year. A probationary volunteer firefighter may be removed from membership without specification of cause. The decision to remove a probationer shall not require notice or a hearing.

(c) The requirement of subdivision (b) to solicit comments from the membership shall not be deemed to create a duty to meet and confer with the membership.

(d) In the event that a governing body of a regularly organized volunteer fire department adopts regulations governing removal of volunteer firefighters, the regulations shall not be interpreted as creating a property right in the volunteer firefighter job or position.

(e) When regulations have been adopted, and where the regulations provide for a hearing and decision by the governing body, a volunteer firefighter may commence a proceeding in accordance with the provisions of Section 1094.5 of the Code of Civil Procedure to set aside the decision of the governing body on the ground that the decision is not supported by substantial evidence. The court shall not employ its independent judgment in reviewing the evidence. The proceeding shall be commenced within 90 days from the date that the governing body renders its decision. This remedy shall be the exclusive method for review of the governing body's decision. *(Added by Stats.1985, c. 499, § 1.)*

Part 8

UNEMPLOYMENT RELIEF

Chapter   **Section**
1. Extension of Public Works 2010
2. Unemployment Relief Camps [Repealed]
3. Public Service Districts [Repealed]

CHAPTER 1. EXTENSION OF PUBLIC WORKS

Section
2010. State agency defined.
2011. Tentative plans for extension of public works.
2012. Industrial conditions affecting employment of labor; inquiry; report to governor.

Section
2013. Apportionment of emergency fund for extension of public works.
2014. Lists of applicants for public employment.
2015. Preferences for employment.

§ 2010. State agency defined

As used in this chapter, "State agency" means any department, division, board, bureau, or commission of the State. *(Stats.1937, c. 90, p. 247, § 2010.)*

§ 2011. Tentative plans for extension of public works

The Department of Finance shall ascertain and secure from the several State agencies tentative plans for the extension of public works which are best adapted to supply increased opportunities for advantageous public labor during periods of temporary unemployment. Such plans shall include estimates of the amount, character, and duration of employment, the number of employees who could be profitably employed therein, together with rates of wages and other information which the Department of Finance deems necessary. *(Stats.1937, c. 90, p. 248, § 2011.)*

§ 2012. Industrial conditions affecting employment of labor; inquiry; report to governor

The Division of Labor Statistics and Research shall keep constantly advised of industrial conditions throughout the State as affecting the employment of labor. Whenever the Governor represents or the division has reason to believe, that a period of extraordinary unemployment caused by industrial depression exists in the State, it shall immediately hold an inquiry into the facts relating thereto, and report to the Governor whether, in fact, such condition exists. *(Stats.1937, c. 90, p. 248, § 2012. Amended by Stats.1945, c. 1431, p. 2693, § 53.)*

§ 2013. Apportionment of emergency fund for extension of public works

If the Division of Labor Statistics and Research reports to the Governor that a condition of extraordinary unemployment caused by industrial depression does exist within this State, the Department of Finance may apportion the available Emergency Fund among the several State agencies for the extension of the public works of the State under the charge or direction thereof, in the manner which the Department of Finance believes to be best adapted to advance the public interest by providing the maximum of public employment consistent with the most useful, permanent, and economic extension of public works. *(Stats.1937, c. 90, p. 248, § 2013. Amended by Stats.1945, c. 1431, p. 2693, § 54.)*

§ 2014. Lists of applicants for public employment

The Department of Employment Development immediately upon the publication of a finding under this chapter that a period of extraordinary unemployment due to industrial depression exists throughout this state shall prepare approved lists of applicants for public employment, secure full information as to their industrial qualifications, and shall submit the same to the Department of Finance for transmission to the state agencies which avail themselves of the provisions of this chapter. *(Stats.1937, c. 90, p. 248, § 2014. Amended by Stats.1945, c. 1431, p. 2693, § 55; Stats.1973, c. 1206, p. 2615, § 36; Stats.1973, c. 1207, p. 2665, § 36.)*

§ 2015. Preferences for employment

Preference for employment under this chapter shall be extended: First, to citizens of this State. Second, to citizens of other States within the United States, who are within the State at the time of making application. Third, to aliens who are within the State at the time of making application. *(Stats.1937, c. 90, p. 248, § 2015.)*

CHAPTER 2. UNEMPLOYMENT RELIEF CAMPS [REPEALED]

CHAPTER 3. PUBLIC SERVICE DISTRICTS [REPEALED]

Part 8.5

CAR WASHES

Chapter	Section
1. General Provisions	2050
2. Registration	2054
3. Successorship	2066
4. Operation	2067
5. Reporting	2068

Repeal

For repeal of Part 8.5, see Labor Code § 2067.

CHAPTER 1. GENERAL PROVISIONS

Section
2050. Purpose of part; exercise of police power of State.
2051. Definitions.
2052. Employment records; contents of records.
2053. Enforcement of chapter by Division of Labor Standards and Enforcement.

Repeal

For repeal of Part 8.5, see Labor Code § 2067.

§ 2050. Purpose of part; exercise of police power of State

The enactment of this part is an exercise of the police power of the State of California for the protection for the public welfare, prosperity, health, safety, and peace of its people. The civil penalties provided by this chapter are in addition to any other penalty provided by law. *(Added by Stats.2003, c. 825 (A.B.1688), § 2.)*

Repeal

For repeal of Part 8.5, see Labor Code § 2067.

§ 2051. Definitions

As used in this part:

(a) "Car washing and polishing" means washing, cleaning, drying, polishing, detailing, servicing, or otherwise providing cosmetic care to vehicles. "Car washing and polishing" does not include motor vehicle repair, as defined in Section 9880.1 of the Business and Professions Code.

(b)(1) "Employer" means any individual, partnership, corporation, limited liability company, joint venture, or association engaged in the business of car washing and polishing that engages any other individual in providing those services.

(2) "Employer" does not include any charitable, youth, service, veteran, or sports group, club, or association that conducts car washing and polishing on an intermittent basis to raise funds for charitable, education, or religious purposes. "Employer" does not include any licensed vehicle dealer or car rental agency * * * that conducts car washing and polishing ancillary to its primary business of selling, leasing, or servicing vehicles. "Employer" does not include either a new motor vehicle dealer, as defined in Section 426 of the Vehicle Code, that is primarily engaged in the business of selling, leasing, renting, or servicing vehicles or an automotive repair dealer, as defined by subdivision (a) of Section 9880.1 of the Business and Professions Code, who is primarily engaged in the business of repairing and diagnosing malfunctions of motor vehicles. "Employer" does not include any self-service car wash or automated car wash that has employees for cashiering or maintenance purposes only.

(c) "Employee" means any person, including an alien or minor, who renders actual car washing and polishing services in any business for an employer, whether for tips or for wages, and whether wages are calculated by time, piece, task, commission, or other method of calculation, and whether the services are rendered on a commission, concessionaire, or other basis.

(d) "Commissioner" means the Labor Commissioner. *(Added by Stats.2003, c. 825 (A.B.1688), § 2. Amended by Stats.2009, c. 224 (A.B.236), § 1.)*

Repeal

For repeal of Part 8.5, see Labor Code § 2067.

§ 2052. Employment records; contents of records

Every employer shall keep accurate records for three years, showing all of the following:

(a) The names and addresses of all employees engaged in rendering actual services for any business of the employer.

(b) The hours worked daily by each employee, including the times the employee begins and ends each work period.

(c) All gratuities received daily by the employer, whether received directly from the employee or indirectly by deduction from the wages of the employee or otherwise.

(d) The wage and wage rate paid each payroll period.

(e) The age of all minor employees.

(f) Any other conditions of employment. *(Added by Stats.2003, c. 825 (A.B.1688), § 2.)*

Repeal

For repeal of Part 8.5, see Labor Code § 2067.

§ 2053. Enforcement of chapter by Division of Labor Standards and Enforcement

The Division of Labor Standards and Enforcement shall enforce this chapter. The commissioner may adopt any regulations necessary to carry out the provisions of this chapter. *(Added by Stats.2003, c. 825 (A.B.1688), § 2.)*

Repeal

For repeal of Part 8.5, see Labor Code § 2067.

CHAPTER 2. REGISTRATION

Section
2054. Annual registration.
2055. Requirements for registration or renewal.
2056. Information to be made available to registrants upon issuance of certificate of registration.
2057. Proof of registration.
2058. Mailed renewal notices; defenses for failure to renew registration.
2059. Registration fee; Car Wash Worker Restitution Fund.
2060. Necessity of compliance with registration and bond requirements.
2061. Approval of registration by commissioner; conditions
2062. Circumstances where registration or renewal is prohibited.
2063. Posted list of registered car washing and polishing business on Department of Industrial Relations Web site.
2064. Civil fines for failure to register business.
2065. Establishment of Car Wash Worker Restitution Fund; disbursements of moneys from fund; regulations.

Repeal

For repeal of Part 8.5, see Labor Code § 2067.

§ 2054. Annual registration

Every employer shall register with the commissioner annually. *(Added by Stats.2003, c. 825 (A.B.1688), § 2.)*

Repeal

For repeal of Part 8.5, see Labor Code § 2067.

§ 2055. Requirements for registration or renewal

The commissioner may not permit any employer to register, nor may the commissioner permit any employer to renew registration until all of the following conditions are satisfied:

(a) The employer has applied for registration to the commissioner by presenting proof of compliance with the local government's business licensing or regional regulatory requirements.

(b) The employer has obtained a surety bond issued by a surety company admitted to do business in this state. The principal sum of the bond shall be not less than fifteen thousand dollars ($15,000). The employer shall file a copy of the bond with the commissioner.

(1) The bond required by this section shall be in favor of, and payable to the people of the State of California and shall be for the benefit of any employee damaged by his or her employer's failure to pay wages, interest on wages, or fringe benefits, or damaged by violation of Section 351 or 353.

(2) Thirty days prior to the cancellation or termination of any surety bond required by this section, the surety shall send written notice to both the employer and the commissioner, identifying the bond and the date of the cancellation or termination.

(3) An employer may not conduct any business until the employer obtains a new surety bond and files a copy of it with the commissioner.

(c) The employer has documented that a current workers' compensation insurance policy is in effect for the employees.

(d) The employer has paid the fees established pursuant to Section 2059. *(Added by Stats.2003, c. 825 (A.B.1688), § 2.)*

Repeal

For repeal of Part 8.5, see Labor Code § 2067.

§ 2056. Information to be made available to registrants upon issuance of certificate of registration

When a certificate of registration is originally issued or renewed under this chapter, the commissioner shall provide related and supplemental information to the registrant regarding business administration and applicable labor laws. *(Added by Stats.2003, c. 825 (A.B.1688), § 2.)*

Repeal

For repeal of Part 8.5, see Labor Code § 2067.

§ 2057. Proof of registration

Proof of registration shall be by an official Division of Labor Standards Enforcement registration form. Each employer shall post the registration form where it may be read by the employees during the workday. *(Added by Stats.2003, c. 825 (A.B.1688), § 2.)*

Repeal

For repeal of Part 8.5, see Labor Code § 2067.

§ 2058. Mailed renewal notices; defenses for failure to renew registration

At least 30 days prior to the expiration of each registrant's registration, the commissioner shall mail a renewal notice to the last known address of the registrant. However, omission of the commissioner to provide the renewal notice in accordance with this subdivision may not excuse a registrant from making timely application for renewal of registration, may not be a defense in any action or proceeding involving failure to renew registration, and may not subject the commissioner to any legal liability. *(Added by Stats.2003, c. 825 (A.B.1688), § 2.)*

Repeal

For repeal of Part 8.5, see Labor Code § 2067.

§ 2059. Registration fee; Car Wash Worker Restitution Fund

(a) The commissioner shall collect from employers a registration fee of two hundred fifty dollars ($250) for each branch location. The commissioner may periodically adjust the registration fee for inflation to ensure that the fee is sufficient to fund all costs to administer and enforce the provisions of this part.

(b) In addition to the fee specified in subdivision (a), each employer shall be assessed an annual fee of fifty dollars ($50) for each branch location which shall be deposited in the Car Wash Worker Restitution Fund. *(Added by Stats.2003, c. 825 (A.B.1688), § 2.)*

Repeal

For repeal of Part 8.5, see Labor Code § 2067.

§ 2060. Necessity of compliance with registration and bond requirements

No employer may conduct any business without complying with the registration and bond requirements of this chapter. *(Added by Stats.2003, c. 825 (A.B.1688), § 2.)*

Repeal

For repeal of Part 8.5, see Labor Code § 2067.

§ 2061. Approval of registration by commissioner; conditions

The commissioner may not approve the registration of any employer until all of the following conditions are satisfied:

(a) The employer has executed a written application, in a form prescribed by the commissioner, subscribed, and sworn by the employer containing the following:

(1) The name of the business entity and, if applicable, its fictitious or "doing business as" name.

(2) The form of the business entity and, if a corporation, all of the following:

(A) The date of incorporation.

(B) The state in which incorporated.

(C) If a foreign corporation, the date the articles of incorporation were filed with the California Secretary of State.

(D) Whether the corporation is in good standing with the Secretary of State.

(3) The federal employer identification number (FEIN) and the state employer identification number (SEIN) of the business.

(4) The business' address and telephone number and, if applicable, the addresses and telephone numbers of any branch locations.

(5) Whether the application is for a new or renewal registration and, if the application is for a renewal, the prior registration number.

(6) The names, residential addresses, telephone numbers, and Social Security numbers of the following persons:

(A) All corporate officers, if the business entity is a corporation.

(B) All persons exercising management responsibility in the applicant's office, regardless of form of business entity.

(C) All persons, except bona fide employees on regular salaries, who have a financial interest of 10 percent or more in the business, regardless of the form of business entity, and the actual percent owned by each of those persons.

(7) The policy number, effective date, expiration date, and name and address of the carrier of the applicant business' current workers' compensation coverage.

(8) Whether any persons named in response to subparagraphs (A), (B), or (C) of subparagraph (6) of this section presently:

(A) Owe any unpaid wages.

(B) Have unpaid judgments outstanding.

(C) Have any liens or suits pending in court against himself or herself.

(D) Owe payroll taxes, or personal, partnership, or corporate income taxes, Social Security taxes, or disability insurance.

An applicant who answers affirmatively to any item described in paragraph (8) shall provide, as part of the application, additional information on the unpaid amounts, including the name and address of the party owed, the amount owed, and any existing payment arrangements.

(9) Whether any persons named in response to subparagraphs (A), (B), or (C) of paragraph (6) of this section have ever been cited or assessed any penalty for violating any provision of the Labor Code.

An applicant who answers affirmatively to any item described in paragraph (9) shall provide additional information, as part of the application, on the date, nature of citation, amount of penalties assessed for each citation, and the disposition of the citation, if any. The application shall describe any appeal filed. If the citation was not appealed, or if it was upheld on appeal, the applicant shall state whether the penalty assessment was paid.

(b) The employer has paid a registration fee to the commissioner pursuant to subdivision (d) of Section 2055. *(Added by Stats.2003, c. 825 (A.B.1688), § 2.)*

Repeal

For repeal of Part 8.5, see Labor Code § 2067.

§ 2062. Circumstances where registration or renewal is prohibited

The commissioner may not register or renew the registration of an employer in any of the following circumstances:

(a) The employer has not fully satisfied any final judgment for unpaid wages due to an employee or former employee of a business for which the employer is required to register under this chapter.

(b) The employer has failed to remit the proper amount of contributions required by the Unemployment Insurance Code or the Employment Development Department had made an assessment for those unpaid contributions against the employer that has become final and the employer has not fully paid the amount of delinquency for those unpaid contributions.

(c) The employer has failed to remit the amount of Social Security and Medicare tax contributions required by the Federal Insurance Contributions Act (FICA) to the Internal Revenue Service and the employer has not fully paid the amount or delinquency for those unpaid contributions. *(Added by Stats.2003, c. 825 (A.B.1688), § 2.)*

Repeal

For repeal of Part 8.5, see Labor Code § 2067.

§ 2063. Posted list of registered car washing and polishing business on Department of Industrial Relations Web site

On the Web site of the Department of Industrial Relations the Labor Commissioner shall post a list of registered car washing and polishing businesses, including the name, address, registration number, and effective dates of registration. *(Added by Stats.2003, c. 825 (A.B.1688), § 2.)*

Repeal

For repeal of Part 8.5, see Labor Code § 2067.

§ 2064. Civil fines for failure to register business

An employer who fails to register pursuant to Section 2054 is subject to a civil fine of one hundred dollars ($100) for each calendar day, not to exceed ten thousand dollars ($10,000), the employer conducts car washing and polishing while unregistered. *(Added by Stats.2003, c. 825 (A.B.1688), § 2.)*

Repeal

For repeal of Part 8.5, see Labor Code § 2067.

§ 2065. Establishment of Car Wash Worker Restitution Fund; disbursements of moneys from fund; regulations

(a) The Car Wash Worker Restitution Fund is established in the State Treasury.

(1) The following moneys shall be deposited into this fund:

(A) The annual fee required pursuant to subdivision (b) of Section 2059.

(B) Fifty percent of the fines collected pursuant to Section 2064.

(C) Fifty dollars ($50) of the initial registration fee required pursuant to subdivision (a) of Section 2059.

(2) Upon appropriation by the Legislature, the moneys in the fund shall be disbursed by the commissioner only to persons determined by the commissioner to have been damaged by the failure to pay wages and penalties and other related damages by any employer, to ensure the payment of wages and penalties and other related damages. Any disbursed funds subsequently recovered by the commissioner shall be returned to the fund.

(b) The Car Wash Worker Fund is established in the State Treasury.

(1) The following moneys shall be deposited into this fund:

(A) Fifty percent of the fines collected pursuant to Section 2064.

(B) The initial registration fee required pursuant to subdivision (a) of Section 2059, less the amount specified in subparagraph (C) of paragraph (1) of subdivision (a).

(2) Upon appropriation by the Legislature, the moneys in this fund shall be applied to costs incurred by the commissioner in administering the provisions of this part and enforcement and investigation of the car washing and polishing industry.

(c) The Department of Industrial Relations may establish by regulation those procedures necessary to carry out the provisions of this section. *(Added by Stats.2003, c. 825 (A.B.1688), § 2. Amended by Stats.2004, c. 227 (S.B.1102), § 81, eff. Aug. 16, 2004.)*

Repeal

For repeal of Part 8.5, see Labor Code § 2067.

CHAPTER 3. SUCCESSORSHIP

Section
2066. Successor liability for owed wages and penalties; criteria.

§ 2066. Successor liability for owed wages and penalties; criteria

A successor to any employer that is engaged in car washing and polishing that owed wages and penalties to the predecessor's former employee or employees is liable for those wages and penalties if the successor meets any of the following criteria:

(a) Uses substantially the same facilities or workforce to offer substantially the same services as the predecessor employer.

(b) Shares in the ownership, management, control of the labor relations, or interrelations of business operations with the predecessor employer.

(c) Employs in a managerial capacity any person who directly or indirectly controlled the wages, hours, or working conditions of the affected employees of the predecessor employer.

(d) Is an immediate family member of any owner, partner, officer, or director of the predecessor employer of any person who had a financial interest in the predecessor employer. *(Added by Stats.2003, c. 825 (A.B.1688), § 2.)*

CHAPTER 4.   OPERATION

Section
2067.   Repeal of Part.

§ 2067. Repeal of Part

This part shall remain in effect only until January 1, 2014, and as of that date is repealed, unless a later enacted statute, that is enacted before January 1, 2014, deletes or extends that date. *(Added by Stats.2003, c. 825 (A.B.1688), § 2. Amended by Stats.2006, c. 656 (S.B. 1468), § 1; Stats.2009, c. 224 (A.B.236), § 2.)*

CHAPTER 5.   REPORTING

Section
2068.   Study and report on status of labor law violations and enforcement in car washing and policy industry.

§ 2068. Study and report on status of labor law violations and enforcement in car washing and policy industry

The commissioner shall study and report to the Legislature, not later than December 31, 2008, on the status of labor law violations and enforcement in the car washing

and polishing industry. *(Added by Stats.2006, c. 656 (S.B.1468), § 2.)*

Part 8.7

EMPLOYEE HEALTH INSURANCE [REJECTED]

Part 9

HEALTH

Chapter	Section
0.5. Affordable Basic Health Care Act of 1992 [Rejected]	
1. Sanitary Conditions	2260
2. Employee Health Care Coverage [Repealed]	
3. Registration of Factories [Repealed]	
4. Employee Housing Act [Repealed]	

CHAPTER 0.5.   AFFORDABLE BASIC HEALTH CARE ACT OF 1992 [REJECTED]

CHAPTER 1.   SANITARY CONDITIONS

Article	Section
1. Sanitary Standards	2260
2. Foundries and Metal Shops	2330
3. Factories and Business Establishments	2350
4. Camps [Repealed]	
5. General Health Provisions	2440

ARTICLE 1.   SANITARY STANDARDS

Section
2260.   Compliance with standards.

§ 2260. Compliance with standards

All employers shall comply with standards relating to sanitary facilities adopted by the Occupational Safety and Health Standards Board pursuant to Chapter 6 (commencing with Section 140) of Division 1. *(Added by Stats.1994, c. 486 (A.B.3416), § 2.)*

ARTICLE 2.   FOUNDRIES AND METAL SHOPS

Section
2330.   Water and toilet facilities for employees.
2331.   Ventilation.

§ 2330. Water and toilet facilities for employees

The owner or manager of every foundry or metal shop engaged in the casting, fabricating, or working over in any manner of any metal or compound, where one or more persons are employed, shall maintain for the use of the employees wash bowls, sinks or other appliances and a water closet connected with running water. *(Stats.1937, c. 90, p. 253, § 2330. Amended by Stats.1941, c. 349, p. 1637, § 1; Stats.1976, c. 1171, p. 5258, § 21.)*

§ 2331. Ventilation

The owner or manager of every foundry or metal shop engaged in the casting, fabricating, or working over in any manner of any metal or compound, where one or more persons are employed, shall comply with standards relating to mechanical ventilation systems adopted by the Occupational Safety and Health Standards Board pursuant to Chapter 6 (commencing with Section 140) of Division 1. *(Added by Stats.1994, c. 486 (A.B.3416), § 4.)*

ARTICLE 3. FACTORIES AND BUSINESS ESTABLISHMENTS

Section
2350. Toilet facilities.
2351. Ventilation.
2352. Use of condemned place.
2353. Exhaust fans and blowers.
2354. Violation; misdemeanor; penalty.
2355. Enforcement official.

§ 2350. Toilet facilities

Every factory, workshop, mercantile or other establishment in which one or more persons are employed, shall be kept clean and free from the effluvia arising from any drain or other nuisance, and shall be provided, within reasonable access, with a sufficient number of toilet facilities for the use of the employees. When there are five or more employees who are not all of the same gender, a sufficient number of separate toilet facilities shall be provided for the use of each sex, which shall be plainly so designated. *(Stats.1937, c. 90, p. 253, § 2350. Amended by Stats.1941, c. 349, p. 1638, § 2; Stats.1994, c. 186 (A.B.3416), § 7; Stats.1995, c. 91 (S.B.975), § 107.)*

§ 2351. Ventilation

Every factory or workshop in which one or more persons are employed shall be so ventilated while work is carried on that the air will not become injurious to the health of the employees, and shall also be so ventilated as to render harmless, as far as practicable, all injurious gases, vapors, dust, or other impurities generated in the course of the manufacturing process or handicraft carried on therein. *(Stats.1937, c. 90, p. 253, § 2351. Amended by Stats.1941, c. 349, p. 1638, § 3; Stats.1943, c. 899, p. 2746, § 1; Stats.1945, c. 800, p. 1496, § 5.)*

§ 2352. Use of condemned place

No place which the Labor Commissioner condemns as unhealthy and unsuitable, shall be used as a place of employment. *(Stats.1937, c. 90, p. 254, § 2352. Amended by Stats.1943, c. 486, p. 2030, § 1.)*

§ 2353. Exhaust fans and blowers

In any factory, workshop, or other establishment where dust, filaments, or injurious gases are produced or generated, which may be inhaled by employees, the person, under whose authority the work is carried on, shall cause to be provided and used, exhaust fans or blowers with pipes and hoods extending therefrom to each machine, contrivance or apparatus by which dust, filaments or injurious gases are produced or generated. The fans and blowers, and the pipes and hoods, shall be properly fitted and adjusted, and of power and dimensions sufficient to prevent the dust, filaments, or injurious gases from escaping into the atmosphere of any room where employees are at work. *(Stats.1937, c. 90, p. 254, § 2353.)*

§ 2354. Violation; misdemeanor; penalty

Any person violating this article is guilty of a misdemeanor, punishable by a fine of not less than one hundred dollars ($100) nor more than six hundred dollars ($600), or by imprisonment in the county jail for not less than 30 days nor more than 90 days, or both. *(Stats.1937, c. 90, p. 254, § 2354. Amended by Stats.1983, c. 1092, § 216, eff. Sept. 27, 1983, operative Jan. 1, 1984.)*

§ 2355. Enforcement official

The Labor Commissioner shall enforce this article. *(Stats.1937, c. 90, p. 254, § 2355.)*

ARTICLE 4. CAMPS [REPEALED]

ARTICLE 5. GENERAL HEALTH PROVISIONS

Section
2440. Medical services and first aid; compliance with standards.
2441. Drinking water; violations; enforcement.

§ 2440. Medical services and first aid; compliance with standards

All employers shall comply with standards relating to the ready availability of medical services and first aid adopted by the Occupational Safety and Health Standards Board, pursuant to Chapter 6 (commencing with Section 140) of Division 1. *(Added by Stats.1994, c. 486 (A.B.3416), § 9.)*

§ 2441. Drinking water; violations; enforcement

(a) Every employer of labor in this state shall, without making a charge therefor, provide fresh and pure drinking water to his or her employees during working hours. Access to the drinking water shall be permitted at reasonable and convenient times and places. Any violation of this section is punishable for each offense by a fine of not less than fifty dollars ($50), nor more than two hundred dollars ($200), or by imprisonment for not more than 30 days, or by both the fine and imprisonment.

(b) The State Department of Health Services and all health officers of counties, cities, and health districts shall enforce the provisions of this section pursuant to subdivision (b) of Section 118390 of the Health and Safety Code. The enforcement shall not be construed to abridge or limit in any manner the jurisdiction of the Division of Industrial Safety of the Department of Industrial Relations pursuant to Division 5 (commencing with Section 6300). *(Added by Stats.1953, c. 84, p. 806, § 1. Amended by Stats.1978, c. 926, p. 2896, § 2; Stats.1983, c. 1092, § 217, eff. Sept. 27, 1983, operative Jan. 1, 1984; Stats. 1996, c. 1023 (S.B.1497), § 380, eff. Sept. 29, 1996.)*

CHAPTER 2. EMPLOYEE HEALTH CARE COVERAGE [REPEALED]

CHAPTER 3. REGISTRATION OF FACTORIES [REPEALED]

CHAPTER 4. EMPLOYEE HOUSING ACT [REPEALED]

Part 10

INDUSTRIAL HOMEWORK

Section
2650.   Definitions.
2651.   Prohibited materials and articles for home manufacture.
2652.   Investigations.
2653.   Powers of division.
2654.   Order to discontinue industrial homework in industry.
2655.   Public hearing on order; notice; place.
2656.   Search warrants.
2658.   Employers' license; necessity; application; form; duration; renewal; fees; suspension and revocation; transferability.
2658.1. Unlicensed persons; failure to prevent taking articles or materials for home manufacture; misdemeanor; evidence.
2658.5. Unlicensed persons; employment of homeworkers; permitting home manufacture; misdemeanor; penalty.
2658.7. Goods constituting evidence of violation; confiscation; forfeiture; investigations.
2659.   Permitting home manufacture by person lacking license or permit.
2660.   Homeworker's permit; necessity; fee; duration; application; scope; waiver of fee.
2660.1. Duty of homeworker to furnish information to division.
2660.5. Home manufacture without permit; misdemeanor; penalty.
2661.   Qualifications for permit.
2662.   Revocation or suspension of permit; grounds.
2663.   Label of employer's name and address of industrial homework articles or materials.
2664.   Authority of division to confiscate articles and materials manufactured in violation of provisions; notice; contesting confiscation; procedure for appeal; decision of Labor Commissioner.
2665.   Duties of employers; compliance with labor standards; keeping records; furnishing reports or information.

Section
2666.   Enforcement agency; inspection and investigation; rules and regulations; powers of law enforcement officers.
2667.   Violations; misdemeanors; injunction.

§ 2650. Definitions

As used in this part:

(a) "To manufacture" means to make, process, prepare, alter, repair, or finish in whole or in part, or to assemble, inspect, wrap, or package any articles or materials.

(b) "Employer" means any person who, directly or indirectly or through an employee, agent, independent contractor, or any other person, employs an industrial homeworker.

(c) "Home" means any room, house, apartment, or other premises, whichever is most extensive, used in whole or in part as a place of dwelling; and includes outbuildings upon premises that are primarily used as a place of dwelling, where such outbuildings are under the control of the person dwelling on such premises.

(d) "Industrial homework" means any manufacture in a home of materials or articles for an employer when such articles or materials are not for the personal use of the employer or a member of his or her family.

(e) "Division" means the Division of Labor Standards Enforcement.

(f) "Industrial homeworker" means any person who does industrial homework.

(g) "To employ" means to engage, suffer or permit any person to do industrial homework, or to tolerate, suffer, or permit articles or materials under one's custody or control to be manufactured in a home by industrial homework.

(h) "Person" means any individual, partnership and each partner thereof, corporation, limited liability company, or association. *(Added by Stats.1939, c. 809, p. 2364, § 1. Amended by Stats.1957, c. 420, p. 1268, § 1; Stats.1980, c. 676, p. 1968, § 225; Stats.1994, c. 1010 (S.B.2053), § 185.)*

§ 2651. Prohibited materials and articles for home manufacture

The manufacture by industrial homework of any of the following materials or articles shall be unlawful, and no license or permit issued under this part shall be deemed to authorize such manufacture: articles of food or drink; articles for use in connection with the serving of food or drink; articles of wearing apparel; toys and dolls; tobacco; drugs and poisons; bandages and other sanitary goods; explosives, fireworks, and articles of like character; articles, the manufacture of which by industrial homework is determined by the division to be injurious to the health or welfare of the industrial homeworkers within the industry or to render unduly difficult the maintenance of existing labor standards or the enforcement of labor standards established by law or regulation for factory workers in the industry. *(Added by Stats.1939, c. 809, p. 2365, § 1. Amended by Stats.1957, c. 420, p. 1269, § 2; Stats.1975, c. 735, p. 1724, § 1.)*

§ 2652. Investigations

The division shall have the power to make an investigation of any industry not specifically exempted and made unlawful by Section 2651 which employs industrial homeworkers, in order to determine whether the wages and conditions of employment of industrial homeworkers in the industry are injurious to their health and welfare or whether the wages and conditions of employment of the industrial homeworkers have the effect of rendering unduly difficult the maintenance of existing labor standards or the enforcement of labor standards established by law or regulation for factory workers in the industry. *(Added by Stats.1939, c. 809, p. 2635, § 1. Amended by Stats.1975, c. 735, p. 1725, § 2.)*

§ 2653. Powers of division

To effectuate the provisions of this part, the division shall have the powers given by Article 2 (commencing with Section 11180) of Chapter 2, Part 1, Division 3, Title 2 of the Government Code to a head of a department. *(Added by Stats.1939, c. 809, p. 2365, § 1. Amended by Stats.1957, c. 48, p. 611, § 1; Stats.1957, c. 420, p. 1269, § 3.)*

§ 2654. Order to discontinue industrial homework in industry

If, on the basis of information in its possession, with or without an investigation, the division shall find that industrial homework cannot be continued within an industry without injuring the health and welfare of the industrial homeworkers within that industry, or without rendering unduly difficult the maintenance of existing labor standards or the enforcement of labor standards established by law or regulation for factory workers in that industry, the division shall by order declare such industrial homework to be unlawful and require all employers in the industry to discontinue manufacture by industrial homework. The order shall set forth the type or types of manufacturing which are prohibited after its effective date, and shall contain such terms and conditions as the division may deem necessary to carry out the purpose and intent of this part. *(Added by Stats.1939, c. 809, p. 2365, § 1. Amended by Stats.1957, c. 420, p. 1269, § 4; Stats.1975, c. 735, p. 1725, § 3.)*

§ 2655. Public hearing on order; notice; place

After making such order the division shall hold a public hearing or hearings at which an opportunity to be heard shall be afforded to any employer, or representative of employers, and any industrial homeworker, or representative of industrial homeworkers, and any other person having an interest in the subject matter of the hearing. A public notice of each hearing shall be given at least 30 days before the hearing is held and in such manner as may be determined by the division. The division shall send written notice of the hearing to every business and employer which the division believes may be adversely affected by the order. The hearing or hearings shall be in such place or places as the division deems most convenient to the employers and industrial homeworkers to be affected by the order. *(Added by Stats.1939, c. 809, p. 2365, § 1. Amended by Stats.1975, c. 735, p. 1725, § 4.)*

§ 2656. Search warrants

The division may seek a search warrant pursuant to the procedures set forth in Chapter 3 (commencing with Section 1523) of Title 12 of Part 2 of the Penal Code to enable it to have access to, and to inspect, the premises of any industrial homeworker or distributor in this state. *(Added by Stats.1975, c. 735, p. 1725, § 7.)*

§ 2658. Employers' license; necessity; application; form; duration; renewal; fees; suspension and revocation; transferability

No person shall employ an industrial homeworker in any industry not prohibited by Section 2651 unless the person employing an industrial homeworker has obtained a valid industrial homework license from the division.

Application for a license to employ industrial homeworkers shall be made to the division in such form as the division may by regulation prescribe. A license fee of one hundred dollars ($100) for each industrial homeworker employed shall be paid to the division and such license shall be valid for a period of one year from the date of issuance unless sooner revoked or suspended.

Renewal fees shall be at the same rate and conditions as the original license.

The division may revoke or suspend the license upon a finding that the person has violated this part or has failed to comply with the regulations of the division or with any provision of the license. The industrial homework license shall not be transferable.

All license fees received under this part shall be paid into the State Treasury. *(Added by Stats.1939, c. 809, p. 2366, § 1. Amended by Stats.1957, c. 420, p. 1269, § 5; Stats.1965, c. 430, p. 1739, § 1; Stats.1975, c. 735, p. 1726, § 9.)*

§ 2658.1. Unlicensed persons; failure to prevent taking articles or materials for home manufacture; misdemeanor; evidence

Every person who, without having in his possession a then valid industrial homework license issued to him by the Division of Labor Standards Enforcement, negligently fails to prevent articles or materials under his custody or control from being taken to a home for manufacture by industrial homework is guilty of a misdemeanor. Possession, control or custody of articles or materials for the purpose of manufacture by industrial homework by a person other than the owner or operator of a factory shall be presumptive evidence that said owner or operator has negligently failed to prevent articles or materials under his custody or control from being taken to a home for manufacture by industrial homework, where it is established that such owner or operator is entitled to possession, control or custody of such articles. *(Added by Stats.1957, c. 420, p. 1270, § 6. Amended by Stats.1980, c. 676, p. 1969, § 226.)*

§ 2658.5. Unlicensed persons; employment of homeworkers; permitting home manufacture; misdemeanor; penalty

Every person, which term shall be deemed to include manufacturers, contractors, jobbers and wholesalers, who, without having in his possession a then-valid industrial homework license issued to him by the Division of Labor Standards Enforcement, employs an industrial homeworker, or who tolerates, suffers, or permits articles or materials owned by him, or under his custody or control to be taken to a home for manufacture by industrial homework or who accepts and pays a person for the manufacture in a home of articles and materials by industrial homework, or who places an advertisement for industrial homework the performance of which is not permitted under this part is guilty of a misdemeanor which misdemeanor shall be punished for the first offense by a fine of not more than one thousand dollars ($1,000) or by imprisonment in the county jail for not more than 30 days, or by both such fine and imprisonment, and for a second conviction by a fine of not more than five thousand dollars ($5,000) or imprisonment in the county jail for not more than six months, or by both such fine and imprisonment. A person, which term shall be deemed to include manufacturers, contractors, jobbers and wholesalers, convicted for a third time, and any subsequent times, shall be guilty of a misdemeanor, and shall be punished by a fine of not more than thirty thousand dollars ($30,000) or by imprisonment in the county jail for not more than one year, or by both such fine and imprisonment. Upon a third conviction, in addition to any penalties or fines imposed, the business license of the manufacturer or owner of the goods, garments or products produced by industrial homework which is not permitted by this part shall be suspended for a period not to exceed three years. The court may suspend all or a part of any penalty imposed by this section on condition that the defendant refrains from any future or other violation of this part. *(Added by Stats.1957, c. 420, p. 1270, § 7. Amended by Stats.1975, c. 735, p. 1726, § 10; Stats.1980, c. 676, p. 1969, § 227.)*

§ 2658.7. Goods constituting evidence of violation; confiscation; forfeiture; investigations

Any goods, assembled or partially assembled, whether found in the homeworker's home, in transit to or from the home, or in the manufacturer's or his contractor's possession, pursuant to an order obtained under Section 2656, which constitute evidence of a violation of industrial homework laws, shall be confiscated by the division and properly marked and identified.

A determination or decision that a violation of Section 2651 has been committed shall carry with it, in addition to whatever other penalties are imposed as prescribed in this act, forfeiture of the aforementioned confiscated goods, garments or products identified as goods, garments or products produced by illegal industrial homework, and placed in the custody of the division, which shall be charged with the responsibility of disposing of them.

The division shall have the power to make an investigation of any industry in which the utilization of industrial homework has been made unlawful by Section 2651, in order to determine compliance with Section 2651. *(Added by Stats.1975, c. 735, p. 1727, § 11. Amended by Stats.1980, c. 612, p. 1693, § 1.)*

§ 2659. Permitting home manufacture by person lacking license or permit

No person shall engage, suffer or permit any person to do industrial homework, or tolerate, suffer or permit articles or materials under his custody or control to be manufactured by industrial homework by a person who is not in possession of either a valid employer's license or homeworker's permit issued in accordance with this part. *(Added by Stats.1939, c. 809, p. 2366, § 1. Amended by Stats.1957, c. 420, p. 1270, § 8.)*

§ 2660. Homeworker's permit; necessity; fee; duration; application; scope; waiver of fee

No person shall do industrial homework within this state unless he has in his possession a valid homeworker's permit issued to him by the division. The permit shall be issued for a fee of twenty-five dollars ($25), and shall be valid for industrial homework performed for the licensed employer of industrial homeworkers, named therein, for a period of one year from the date of its issuance unless sooner revoked or suspended. Application for a permit shall be made in such form as the division may by regulation prescribe. The permit shall be valid only for work performed by the applicant himself in his own home. The division may waive the fee for a homeworker's permit in cases where the applicant requests such waiver, and can establish that payments of the fee would result in financial hardship. *(Added by Stats.1939, c. 809, p. 2660, § 1. Amended by Stats.1957, c. 420, p. 1271, § 9; Stats.1975, c. 735, p. 1727, § 12.)*

§ 2660.1. Duty of homeworker to furnish information to division

Every person doing industrial homework, with or without a valid homeworker's permit issued by the division, shall reveal to the division, on demand, the name and address of the employer, the name and address of the owner or source of the articles or materials for industrial homework, the rate of compensation and any other information known to the homeworker and pertinent to the enforcement of this section. This information so revealed by the homeworker to the division shall not be used by the division in any action against or prosecution of the homeworker. *(Added by Stats.1957, c. 420, p. 1271, § 10.)*

§ 2660.5. Home manufacture without permit; misdemeanor; penalty

Every person who does industrial homework without having in his possession a valid homeworker's permit issued to him by the division is guilty of a misdemeanor which misdemeanor shall be punishable for the first offense by a fine of not more than fifty dollars ($50) and for the second offense by a fine of not more than one hundred dollars ($100). The court may suspend such fine on condition the industrial homeworker cooperates with the division in the lawful prosecutions of persons violating this part and to secure compliance with this part, or on condition the defendant refrains from any future violation of this part. *(Added by Stats.1957, c. 420, p. 1271, § 11. Amended by Stats.1975, c. 735, p. 1727, § 13.)*

§ 2661. Qualifications for permit

No homeworker's permit shall be issued to any person under the age of 16 years; or to any person suffering from an infectious, contagious, or communicable disease, or to any person living in a home that is not clean, sanitary, and free from infectious, contagious, or communicable disease. *(Added by Stats.1939, c. 809, p. 2367, § 1. Amended by Stats.1957, c. 48, p. 611, § 2; Stats. 1957, c. 420, p. 1271, § 12; Stats.1975, c. 735, p. 1728, § 14.)*

§ 2662. Revocation or suspension of permit; grounds

The division may revoke or suspend any homeworker's permit upon a finding that the industrial homeworker is performing industrial homework contrary to the conditions under which the permit was issued or in violation of this part or has permitted any person not holding a valid homeworker's permit to assist him in performing industrial homework or on expiration or revocation of the industrial homework license of the employer. *(Added by Stats.1939, c. 809, p. 2367, § 1. Amended by Stats.1957, c. 420, p. 1271, § 13.)*

§ 2663. Label of employer's name and address of industrial homework articles or materials

No person shall tolerate, suffer or permit any materials or articles to be manufactured by industrial homework unless there has been conspicuously affixed to each article or material or, if this is impossible, to the package or other container in which such goods are kept, a label or other mark of identification bearing the employer's name and address, printed or written legibly in English. *(Added by Stats.1939, c. 809, p. 2367, § 1. Amended by Stats.1957, c. 420, p. 1271, § 14.)*

§ 2664. Authority of division to confiscate articles and materials manufactured in violation of provisions; notice; contesting confiscation; procedure for appeal; decision of Labor Commissioner

(a) Any article or material which is being manufactured in a home in violation of any provision of this part may be confiscated by the division. Articles or material confiscated pursuant to this section shall be placed in the custody of the division, which shall be responsible for destroying or disposing of them pursuant to regulations adopted under Section 2666, provided that the articles or material shall not enter the mainstream of commerce and shall not be offered for sale. The division shall, by certified mail, give notice of the confiscation and the procedure for appealing the confiscation to the person whose name and address are affixed to the article or material as provided in this part. The notice shall state that failure to file a written notice of appeal with the Labor Commissioner within 15 days after service of the notice of confiscation shall result in the destruction or disposition of the confiscated article or material.

(b) To contest the confiscation of articles or material, a person shall, within 15 days after service of the notice of confiscation, file a written notice of appeal with the Office of the Labor Commissioner at the address that appears on the notice of confiscation. Within 30 days after the timely filing of a notice of appeal, the Labor Commissioner shall hold a hearing on the appeal. The hearing shall be recorded. Based on the evidence presented at the hearing, the Labor Commissioner may affirm, modify, or dismiss the confiscation, and may order the return of none, some, or all of the confiscated articles or material, under terms that the Labor Commissioner may specify. The decision of the Labor Commissioner shall consist of findings of fact, legal analysis, and an order. The decision shall be served by first-class mail on all parties to the hearing, to the last known address of the parties on file with the Labor Commissioner, within 15 days of the conclusion of the hearing. Service shall be complete pursuant to Section 1013 of the Code of Civil Procedure. Judicial review shall be by petition for writ of mandate, filed with the appropriate court, within 45 days of service of the decision. *(Added by Stats.1939, c. 809, p. 2367, § 1. Amended by Stats.1957, c. 420, p. 1272, § 15; Stats.1975, c. 735, p. 1728, § 15; Stats.1980, c. 612, p. 1693, § 2; Stats.2003, c. 214 (A.B.1132), § 1.)*

§ 2665. Duties of employers; compliance with labor standards; keeping records; furnishing reports or information

Every person who employs or otherwise avails himself of the services of industrial homeworkers in this State shall:

(a) Comply with the labor standards as provided in Chapter 1 (commencing with Section 1171) of Part 4 of Division 2 of the Labor Code.

(b) Keep in a manner approved by the division, accurate information as follows:

1. Full name and home address of each industrial homeworker employed by him;

2. Amount and description of materials delivered to each industrial homeworker employed by him with date of delivery, and rate of compensation;

3. Gross amount of compensation paid to each industrial homeworker employed by him and date of payment;

4. Names and addresses of all agents or independent contractors to whom he has delivered materials or articles for manufacture by industrial homework together with quantity, description of materials and date of delivery;

5. Names and addresses of all manufacturers or independent contractors from whom he has received articles or materials for industrial homework together with quantity, description of materials and date of receipt.

(c) Furnish to the division at its request reports or information which the division requires to carry out the provisions of this part. Such reports and information shall be verified as requested by the division. *(Added by Stats.1939, c. 809, p. 2367, § 1. Amended by Stats.1957, c. 420, p. 1272, § 16.)*

§ 2666. Enforcement agency; inspection and investigation; rules and regulations; powers of law enforcement officers

The Division of Labor Standards Enforcement shall enforce the provisions of this part. The division and the authorized representatives of the Department of Industrial Relations are authorized and directed to make all inspections and investigations necessary for the enforcement of this part. Every employer shall permit authorized employees of the division free access to his place of business for the purpose of making investigations authorized by this part or necessary to carry out its provisions and permit them to inspect and copy his payroll or other records or documents relating to the enforcement of this part, or interview his employees or agents. The division may make, in accordance with the provisions of Chapter 3.5 (commencing with Section 11340) of Part 1 of Division 3 of Title 2 of the Government Code, such rules and regulations as are reasonably necessary to carry out the provisions of this part. The violation of any such rule or regulation shall be deemed a violation of this part.

Every law enforcement officer of the state, any county, municipality, or other government entity who has reason to suspect any violation of this part shall have all the powers of an authorized representative of the Department of Industrial Relations, in the investigation of such suspected violation. *(Added by Stats.1939, c. 809, p. 2367, § 1. Amended by Stats.1957, c. 420, p. 1272, § 17; Stats.1957, c. 2034, p. 3605, § 2; Stats.1975, c. 735, p. 1728, § 16; Stats.1980, c. 676, p. 1970, § 228.)*

§ 2667. Violations; misdemeanors; injunction

Unless otherwise provided herein, every person acting either individually or as an officer, agent, employee or independent contractor for another person who violates or refuses or neglects to comply with any provision of this part, or any regulation of the division made in accordance with the provisions of this part is guilty of a misdemeanor.

Whenever the provisions of this part prohibit the employment of a person in certain work or under certain conditions, the employer shall not knowingly permit such person to work with or without compensation.

The Attorney General may seek appropriate injunctive relief consistent with, and in furtherance of the purposes of, this part. *(Added by Stats.1939, c. 809, p. 2368, § 1. Amended by Stats.1957, c. 420, p. 1273, § 18; Stats.1975, c. 735, p. 1728, § 17.)*

Part 11

GARMENT MANUFACTURING

Chapter	Section
1. General Provisions	2670
2. Registration	2675
3. Arbitration	2685

CHAPTER 1.   GENERAL PROVISIONS

Section
2670.   Legislative intent.
2671.   Definitions.
2672.   Regulations and rules.
2673.   Records.
2673.1.   Guarantee of payment of applicable minimum wage and overtime compensation; enforcement of guarantee; damages; costs; judicial review; other remedies; revocation of registration for failure to pay wages.
2674.   Enforcement of certain provisions.
2674.1.   Advisory committee.
2674.2.   Annual budget; statement of cost; funds.

§ 2670. Legislative intent

It is the intent of the Legislature, in enacting this part, to establish a system of registration, penalties, confiscation, bonding requirements, and misdemeanors for the imposition of prompt and effective criminal and civil sanctions against violations of, and especially patterns and practices of violations of, any of the laws as set forth herein and regulations of this state applicable to the employment of workers in the garment industry. The civil penalties provided for in this part are in addition to any other penalty provided by law. This part shall be deemed an exercise of the police power of the state for the protection of the public welfare, prosperity, health, safety, and peace of the people of the State of California. *(Added by Stats.1980, c. 633, p. 1731, § 1, operative July 1, 1981.)*

§ 2671. Definitions

As used in this part:

(a) "Person" means any individual, partnership, corporation, limited liability company, or association, and includes, but is not limited to, employers, manufacturers, jobbers, wholesalers, contractors, subcontractors, and any other person or entity engaged in the business of garment manufacturing.

"Person" does not include any person who manufactures garments by himself or herself, without the assis-

484

tance of a contractor, employee, or others; any person who engages solely in that part of the business engaged solely in cleaning, alteration, or tailoring; any person who engages in the activities herein regulated as an employee with wages as his or her sole compensation; or any person as provided by regulation.

(b) "Garment manufacturing" means sewing, cutting, making, processing, repairing, finishing, assembling, or otherwise preparing any garment or any article of wearing apparel or accessories designed or intended to be worn by any individual, including, but not limited to, clothing, hats, gloves, handbags, hosiery, ties, scarfs, and belts, for sale or resale by any person or any persons contracting to have those operations performed and other operations and practices in the apparel industry as may be identified in regulations of the Department of Industrial Relations consistent with the purposes of this part. The Department of Industrial Relations shall adopt, and may from time to time amend, regulations to clarify and refine this definition to be consistent with current and future industry practices, but the regulations shall not limit the scope of garment manufacturing, as defined in this subdivision.

(c) "Commissioner" means the Labor Commissioner.

(d) "Contractor" means any person who, with the assistance of employees or others, is primarily engaged in sewing, cutting, making, processing, repairing, finishing, assembling, or otherwise preparing any garment or any article of wearing apparel or accessories designed or intended to be worn by any individual, including, but not limited to, clothing, hats, gloves, handbags, hosiery, ties, scarfs, and belts, for another person. "Contractor" includes a subcontractor that is primarily engaged in those operations. *(Added by Stats.1980, c. 633, p. 1731, § 1, operative July 1, 1981. Amended by Stats.1984, c. 1564, § 1; Stats.1994, c. 1010 (S.B.2053), § 186; Stats.1999, c. 554 (A.B.633), § 1.)*

§ 2672. Regulations and rules

The commissioner shall promulgate all regulations and rules necessary to carry out the provisions of this part. The commissioner, upon good cause, may impose, in his or her discretion, the terms of penalties, the revocation of registrations, and the confiscation or disposal of goods in accordance with such rules and regulations. *(Added by Stats.1980, c. 633, p. 1732, § 1, operative July 1, 1981.)*

§ 2673. Records

Every employer engaged in the business of garment manufacturing shall keep accurate records for three years which show all of the following:

(a) The names and addresses of all garment workers directly employed by such person.

(b) The hours worked daily by employees, including the times the employees begin and end each work period.

(c) The daily production sheets, including piece rates.

(d) The wage and wage rates paid each payroll period.

(e) The contract worksheets indicating the price per unit agreed to between the contractor and manufacturer.

(f) The ages of all minor employees.

(g) Any other conditions of employment. *(Added by Stats.1980, c. 633, p. 1732, § 1, operative July 1, 1981.)*

§ 2673.1. Guarantee of payment of applicable minimum wage and overtime compensation; enforcement of guarantee; damages; costs; judicial review; other remedies; revocation of registration for failure to pay wages

(a) To ensure that employees are paid for all hours worked, a person engaged in garment manufacturing, as defined in Section 2671, who contracts with another person for the performance of garment manufacturing operations shall guarantee payment of the applicable minimum wage and overtime compensation, as required by law, that are due from that other person to its employees that perform those operations.

(b) Where the work of two or more persons is being performed at the same worksite during the same payroll period, the liability of each person under this guarantee shall be limited to his or her proportionate share, as determined by the Labor Commissioner pursuant to paragraph (3) or (4) of subdivision (d).

(c) Employees may enforce this guarantee solely by filing a claim with the Labor Commissioner against the contractor and the guarantor or guarantors, if known, to recover unpaid wages. Guarantors whose identity or existence is unknown at the time the claim is filed may be added to the claim pursuant to paragraph (2) of subdivision (d).

(d) Claims filed with the Labor Commissioner for payment of wages pursuant to subdivision (c) shall be subject to the following procedure:

(1) Within 10 business days of receiving a claim pursuant subdivision (c), the Labor Commissioner shall give written notice to the employee, the contractor, and persons that may be guarantors of the nature of the claim and the date of the meet-and-confer conference on the claim. Within 10 business days of receiving the claim, the Labor Commissioner shall issue a subpoena duces tecum requiring the contractor to submit to the Labor Commissioner those books and records as may be necessary to investigate the claim and determine the identity of any potential guarantors for the payment of the wage claim, including, but not limited to, invoices for work performed for any and all persons during the period included in the claim. Compliance with such a request for books and records, within 10 days of the mailing of the notice, shall be a condition of continued registration pursuant to Section 2675. At the request of any party, the Labor Commissioner shall provide to that party copies of all books and records received by the Labor Commissioner in conducting its investigation.

(2) Within 30 days of receiving a claim pursuant to subdivision (c), the Labor Commissioner shall send a

notice of the claim and of the meet-and-confer conference to any other persons who may be guarantors with respect to the claim.

(3) Within 60 days of receiving a claim pursuant to subdivision (c), the Labor Commissioner shall hold a meet-and-confer conference with the employee, the contractor, and all known potential guarantors to attempt to resolve the claim. Prior to the meet-and-confer conference, the Labor Commissioner shall conduct and complete an investigation of the claim, shall make a finding and assessment of the amount of wages owed, and shall conduct an investigation and determine each guarantor's proportionate share of liability. The investigation shall include, but not be limited to, interviewing the employee and his or her witnesses and making a finding and assessment of back wages due, if any, to the employee. An employee's claim of hours worked and back wages due shall be presumed valid and shall be the Labor Commissioner's assessment, unless the contractor provides specific, compelling, and reliable written evidence to the contrary and is able to produce records pursuant to subdivision (d) of Section 1174 or Section 2673 that are accurate and contemporaneous, itemized wage deduction statements pursuant to Section 226, bona fide complete and accurate payroll records, and evidence of the precise hours worked by the employee for each pay period during the period of the claim. If the Labor Commissioner finds falsification by the contractor of payroll records submitted for any pay period of the claim, any other payroll records submitted by the contractor shall be presumed false and disregarded.

The Labor Commissioner shall present his or her findings and assessment of the amount of wages owed and each guarantor's proportionate share thereof to the parties at the meet-and-confer conference and shall make a demand for payment of the amount of the assessment. If no resolution is reached, the Labor Commissioner shall, at the meet-and-confer conference, set the matter for hearing pursuant to paragraph (4). The Labor Commissioner's assessment, pursuant to this paragraph, of the amount of back wages due is solely for purposes of the meet-and-confer conference and shall not be admissible or be given any weight in the hearing conducted pursuant to paragraph (4). If the Labor Commissioner has not identified any potential guarantors after investigation and the matter is not resolved at the conclusion of the meet-and-confer conference, the Commissioner shall proceed against the contractor pursuant to Section 98.

(4) The hearing shall commence within 30 days of, and shall be completed within 45 days of, the date of the meet-and-confer conference. The hearing may be bifurcated, addressing first the question of liability of the contractor and the guarantor or guarantors, and immediately thereafter the proportionate responsibility of the guarantors. The Labor Commissioner shall present his or her proposed findings of the guarantor's proportionate share at the hearing. Any party may present evidence at the hearing to support or rebut the proposed findings.

Except as provided in this paragraph, the hearing shall be held in accordance with the procedure set forth in subdivisions (b) to (h), inclusive, of Section 98. It is the intent of the Legislature that these hearings be conducted in an informal setting preserving the rights of the parties.

(5) Within 15 days of the completion of the hearing, the Labor Commissioner shall issue an order, decision, or award with respect to the claim and shall file the order, decision, or award in accordance with Section 98.1.

(e) An employee shall be entitled to recover, from the contractor, liquidated damages in an amount equal to the wages unlawfully withheld, as set forth in Section 1194.2, and liquidated damages in an amount equal to unpaid overtime compensation due. A guarantor under subdivision (a) shall be liable for its proportionate share of those liquidated damages if the guarantor has acted in bad faith, including, but not limited to, failure to pay or unreasonably delaying payment to its contractor, unreasonably reducing payment to its contractor where it is established that the guarantor knew or reasonably should have known that the price set for the work was insufficient to cover the minimum wage and overtime pay owed by the contractor, asserting frivolous defenses, or unreasonably delaying or impeding the Labor Commissioner's investigation of the claim.

(f) If either the contractor or guarantor refuses to pay the assessment, and the employee prevails at the hearing, the party that refuses to pay shall pay the employee's reasonable attorney's fees and costs. If the employee rejects the assessment of the Labor Commissioner and prevails at the hearing, the employer shall pay the employee's reasonable attorney's fees and costs. The guarantor shall be jointly and severally liable for the contractor's share of the attorney's fees and costs awarded to an employee only if the Labor Commissioner determines that the guarantor acted in bad faith, including, but not limited to, failure to pay, unreasonably delaying payment to the contractor, unreasonably reducing payment to the contractor where it is established that the guarantor knew or reasonably should have known that the price set for the work was insufficient to cover the applicable minimum wage and overtime pay owed by the contractor, asserting frivolous defenses, or unreasonably delaying or impeding the Labor Commissioner's investigation of the claim.

(g) Any party shall have the right to judicial review of the order, decision, or award of the Labor Commissioner made pursuant to paragraph (5) of subdivision (d) as provided in Section 98.2. As a condition precedent to filing an appeal, the contractor or the guarantor, whichever appeals, shall post a bond with the Commissioner in an amount equal to one and one-half times the amount of the award. No bond shall be required of an employee filing an appeal pursuant to Section 98.2. At the employee's request, the Labor Commissioner shall represent the employee in the judicial review as provided in Section 98.4.

(h) If the contractor or guarantor appeals the order, decision, or award of the Labor Commissioner and the employee prevails on appeal, the court shall order the contractor or guarantor, as the case may be, to pay the reasonable attorney's fees and costs of the employee incurred in pursuing his or her claim. If the employee appeals the order, decision, or award of the Labor Commissioner and the contractor or guarantor prevails on appeal, the court may order the employee to pay the reasonable attorney's fees and costs of the contractor employer or guarantor only if the court determines that the employee acted in bad faith in bringing the claim.

(i) The rights and remedies provided by this section do not preclude an employee from pursuing any other rights and remedies under any other provision of state or federal law. If a finding and assessment is not issued as specified and within the time limits in paragraph (3) of subdivision (d), the employee may bring a civil action for the recovery of unpaid wages pursuant to any other rights and remedies under any other provision of the laws of this state unless, prior to the employee bringing the civil action, the guarantor files a petition for writ of mandate within 10 days of the date the assessment should have been issued. If findings and assessments are not made, or a hearing is not commenced or an order, decision, or award is not issued within the time limits specified in paragraphs (4) and (5) of subdivision (d), any party may file a petition for writ of mandate to compel the Labor Commissioner to issue findings and assessments, commence the hearing, or issue the order, decision, or award. All time requirements specified in this section shall be mandatory and shall be enforceable by a writ of mandate.

(j) The Labor Commissioner may enforce the wage guarantee described in this section in the same manner as a proceeding against the contractor. The Labor Commissioner may, with or without a complaint being filed by an employee, conduct an investigation as to whether all the employees of persons engaged in garment manufacturing are being paid minimum wage or overtime compensation and, with or without the consent of the employees affected, commence a civil action to enforce the wage guarantee. Prior to commencing such a civil action and pursuant to rules of practice and procedure adopted by the Labor Commissioner, the commissioner shall provide notice of the investigation to each guarantor and employee, issue findings and an assessment of the amount of wages due, hold a meet-and-confer conference with the guarantors and employees to attempt to resolve the matter, and provide for a hearing.

(k) Except as expressly provided in this section, this section shall not be deemed to create any new right to bring a civil action of any kind for unpaid minimum wages, overtime pay, penalties, wage assessments, attorney's fees, or costs against a registered garment manufacturer based on its use of any contractor that is also a registered garment manufacturer.

(l) The payment of the wage guarantee provided in this section shall not be used as a basis for finding that the registered garment manufacturer making the payment is a joint employer, coemployer, or single employer of any employees of a contractor that is also a registered garment manufacturer.

(m) The Labor Commissioner may, in his or her discretion, revoke the registration under this part of any registrant that fails to pay, on a timely basis, any wages awarded pursuant to this section, after the award has become final. *(Added by Stats.1999, c. 554 (A.B.633), § 2.)*

§ 2674. Enforcement of certain provisions

The Division of Labor Standards Enforcement shall enforce Section 2673 and Chapter 2 (commencing with Section 2675). *(Added by Stats.1980, c. 633, p. 1732, § 1, operative July 1, 1981.)*

§ 2674.1. Advisory committee

The commissioner shall appoint an advisory committee on garment manufacturing to advise him or her of common industry problems and to effect liaison between his or her office and various segments of the industry. The committee shall consist of a cross section of the industry and shall include representatives of unions, employees, contractor associations, jobbers, and manufacturers. *(Added by Stats.1980, c. 633, p. 1732, § 1, operative July 1, 1981.)*

§ 2674.2. Annual budget; statement of cost; funds

In the annual budget submitted to the Legislature pursuant to Section 12 of Article IV of the California Constitution, the Governor shall include a detailed statement of the cost of regulation and estimated revenues pursuant to the provisions of this part. The Legislature intends that the fees established and other revenue received pursuant to this part shall provide sufficient funds to meet all state costs incurred pursuant to this part. *(Added by Stats.1980, c. 633, p. 1732, § 1, operative July 1, 1981.)*

CHAPTER 2. REGISTRATION

Section
2675.   Applications and renewals; conditions; requirements.
2675.2.   Extension of registration pending renewal; conditions.
2675.5.   Annual registration fees; disposition.
2676.   Failure to register; misdemeanor.
2676.5.   Display of name, address, and registration number; waiver; application.
2676.7.   Local agency; requiring proof of registration; prior application for license or permit.
2677.   Manufacturer contracting with unregistered or unbonded employer; joint liability; civil actions by employees.
2677.5.   Business practices causing or likely to cause violation; prohibition.
2678.   Penalty.

Section
2679.   Additional penalty; deposit of bond; second and subsequent violations; revocation of registration; confiscation; notice.
2680.   Confiscation of garments or wearing apparel; disposal; notice; confiscation of manufacturing equipment and property.
2680.5.   Pricing and quality disputes between manufacturers and contractors; authority to investigate and mediate.
2681.   Contest of penalty or confiscation; payment in lieu of contest; petition for hearing; hearing; findings and order; writ of mandate; judgment; interest on judgment.
2682.   Application of moneys recovered.
2684.   Employer primarily engaged in sewing or assembly of garments for other persons; liability of successor employer for unpaid wages.

§ 2675. Applications and renewals; conditions; requirements

(a) For purposes of enforcing this part and Sections 204, 209, 212, 221, 222, 222.5, 223, 226, 227, and 227.5, Chapter 2 (commencing with Section 300) and Article 2 (commencing with Section 400) of Chapter 3 of Part 1 of this division, Sections 1195.5, 1197, 1197.5, and 1198, Division 4 (commencing with Section 3200) and Division 4.7 (commencing with Section 6200), every person engaged in the business of garment manufacturing, shall register with the commissioner.

The commissioner shall not permit any person to register, nor shall the commissioner allow any person to renew registration, until all the following conditions are satisfied:

(1) The person has executed a written application therefor in a form prescribed by the commissioner, subscribed and sworn by the person, and containing:

(A) A statement by the person of all facts required by the commissioner concerning the applicant's character, competency, responsibility, and the manner and method by which the person proposes to engage in the business of garment manufacturing if the registration is issued.

(B) The names and addresses of all persons, except bona fide employees on stated salaries, financially interested, either as partners, associates, or profit sharers, in the proposed business of garment manufacturing together with the amount of their respective interests, except that in the case of a publicly traded corporation a listing of principal officers shall suffice.

(2) The commissioner, after investigation, is satisfied as to the character, competency, and responsibility of the person.

(3) In the case of a person who has been cited and penalized within the prior three years under this part, the person has deposited or has on file a surety bond in the sum and form that the commissioner deems sufficient and adequate to ensure future compliance, not to exceed five thousand dollars ($5,000). The bond shall be payable to the people of California and shall be for the benefit of any employee of a registrant damaged by the registrant's failure to pay wages and fringe benefits, or for the benefit of any employee of a registrant damaged by a violation of Section 2677.5.

(4) The person has documented that a current workers' compensation insurance policy is in effect for the employees of the person seeking registration.

(5) The person has paid an initial or renewal registration fee to the commissioner. The fee for initial registration and for each registration renewal shall be established in an amount determined by the Labor Commissioner to be sufficient to defray the costs of administering this part and shall be based on the applicant's annual volume, but shall be not less than two hundred fifty dollars ($250) and shall be not more than one thousand dollars ($1,000) for contractors and two thousand five hundred dollars ($2,500) for all other registrants.

(b) At the time a certificate of registration is originally issued or renewed, the commissioner shall provide related and supplemental information regarding business administration and applicable labor laws. This related and supplemental information, as much as reasonably possible, shall be provided in the primary language of the garment manufacturer. The information shall include all subject matter on which persons seeking registration are examined pursuant to subdivision (c), and shall be available to persons seeking registration prior to taking this examination.

(c) Effective January 1, 1991, persons seeking registration under this section for the first time, and persons seeking to renew their registration pursuant to subdivision (f), shall comply with all of the following requirements:

(1) Demonstrate, by an oral or written examination, or both, knowledge of the pertinent laws and administrative regulations concerning garment manufacturing as the commissioner deems necessary for the safety and protection of garment workers.

(2) Demonstrate, by an oral or written examination, or both, knowledge of state laws and regulations relating to occupational safety and health which shall include, but not be limited to, the following:

(A) Section 3203 of Title 8 of the California Code of Regulations (Injury Prevention Program).

(B) Section 3220 of Title 8 of the California Code of Regulations (Emergency Action Plan).

(C) Section 3221 of Title 8 of the California Code of Regulations (Fire Prevention Plan).

(D) Section 6151 of Title 8 of the California Code of Regulations which provides for the placement, use, maintenance, and testing of portable fire extinguishers provided for the use of employees.

(3) Sign a statement which provides that he or she shall do all of the following:

(A) Comply with those regulations specified in paragraph (2) which establish minimum standards for securing safety in all places of employment.

(B) Ensure that all employees are made aware of the existence of these regulations and any other applicable laws and are instructed in how to implement the Injury Prevention Program, Emergency Action Plan, and Fire Prevention Plan, specified in paragraph (2), in the workplace.

(C) Ensure that all employees are instructed in the use of portable fire extinguishers.

(D) Post the Injury Prevention Program, Emergency Action Plan, and Fire Prevention Plan, specified in paragraph (2), in a prominent location in the workplace.

(d) The Division of Occupational Safety and Health shall assist the Division of Labor Standards Enforcement in developing the examination which shall include, but not be limited to, the state's occupational safety and health laws specified in paragraph (2) of subdivision (c).

(e) The commissioner shall charge a fee to persons taking the examinations required by subdivision (c) which is sufficient to pay for costs incurred in administering the examinations.

(f) A person seeking renewal of registration shall be required to take both of the examinations, and sign the statement, specified in subdivision (c). However, once a renewal of registration has been granted based on these examinations, subsequent examinations shall only be required at the discretion of the commissioner if, in the preceding year, the registrant has been found to be in violation of subdivision (a) or any of the sections enumerated in that subdivision.

(g) Proof of registration shall be by an official Division of Labor Standards Enforcement registration form. Every person, as set forth in Section 2671, shall post the registration form where it may be read by employees during the workday.

(h) At least 90 days prior to the expiration of each registrant's registration, the commissioner shall mail a renewal notice to the last known address of the registrant. The notice shall include all necessary application forms and complete instructions for registration renewal. However, omission of the commissioner to provide notice in accordance with this subdivision shall not excuse a registrant from making timely application for renewal of registration, shall not be a defense in any action or proceeding involving failure to renew registration, and shall not subject the commissioner to any legal liability under this section. *(Added by Stats.1980, c. 633, p. 1732, § 1, operative July 1, 1981. Amended by Stats.1984, c. 1564, § 2; Stats.1991, c. 7 (A.B.42), § 1, eff. Dec. 13, 1990, operative Jan. 1, 1991; Stats.1996, c. 619 (S.B.1112), § 1; Stats.1999, c. 554 (A.B.633), § 3.)*

§ 2675.2. Extension of registration pending renewal; conditions

Whenever an application for renewal of registration is received by the Labor Commissioner 30 days prior to the expiration of the registration, and the Labor Commissioner cannot process the application before the expiration date, the Labor Commissioner may extend the registration for no more than 90 days if the applicant has submitted a complete application, owes no outstanding penalties, owes no back wages, meets all applicable bonding requirements, and meets all other requirements for registration. Upon a showing of extenuating circumstances, the Labor Commissioner may provide such an extension with respect to a renewal application not received 30 or more days prior to expiration. *(Added by Stats.1996, c. 619 (S.B.1112), § 2.)*

§ 2675.5. Annual registration fees; disposition

(a) The commissioner shall deposit seventy-five dollars ($75) of each registrant's annual registration fee, required pursuant to paragraph (5) of subdivision (a) of Section 2675, into one separate account. Funds from the separate account shall be disbursed by the commissioner only to persons determined by the commissioner to have been damaged by the failure to pay wages and benefits by any garment manufacturer, jobber, contractor, or subcontractor after exhausting a bond, if any, to ensure the payment of wages and benefits. Any disbursed funds subsequently recovered by the commissioner shall be returned to the separate account.

(b) The remainder of each registrant's annual registration fee not deposited into the special account pursuant to subdivision (a) shall be deposited in a subaccount and applied to costs incurred by the commissioner in administering the provisions of Section 2673.1, Section 2675, and this section, upon appropriation by the Legislature. *(Added by Stats.1984, c. 1564, § 3. Amended by Stats. 1999, c. 554 (A.B.633), § 4; Stats.2000, c. 127 (A.B.2866), § 24, eff. July 10, 2000.)*

§ 2676. Failure to register; misdemeanor

Any person engaged in the business of garment manufacturing who is not registered is guilty of a misdemeanor, except as provided in subdivision (d) of Section 2678. *(Added by Stats.1980, c. 633, p. 1733, § 1, operative July 1, 1981. Amended by Stats.1998, c. 276 (S.B.1514), § 1.)*

§ 2676.5. Display of name, address, and registration number; waiver; application

(a) Every person registered as a garment manufacturer shall display on the front entrance of his or her business premise, and also, if the front entrance is within the interior of a building, on or near the main exterior entrance of the building in which his or her business premise is located, his or her name, address, and garment manufacturing registration number, all in letters not less than three inches high.

(b) The Labor Commissioner may waive the requirements of this section if he or she finds compliance to be unfeasible due to the design or layout of a business premise.

(c) This section shall not apply to a showroom or a building containing a showroom if no garment manufacturing or only incidental garment manufacturing is conducted in the showroom or the building.

(d) As used in this section, "showroom" means a room where merchandise is exposed for sale or where samples are displayed. *(Added by Stats.1989, c. 140, § 1.)*

§ 2676.7. Local agency; requiring proof of registration; prior application for license or permit

Any local agency which issues business licenses or permits shall require, as a condition of issuing any business license or permit for a garment manufacturing business, proof that the person applying for the license or permit is registered pursuant to this chapter. The official Division of Labor Standards Enforcement registration form issued pursuant to Section 2675 shall constitute proof of registration.

A person may apply for a business license or permit prior to registration with the commissioner. *(Added by Stats.1990, c. 172 (A.B.189), § 1.)*

§ 2677. Manufacturer contracting with unregistered or unbonded employer; joint liability; civil actions by employees

(a) Any person engaged in the business of garment manufacturing who contracts with any other person similarly engaged who has not registered with the commissioner or does not have a valid bond on file with the commissioner, as required by Section 2675, shall be deemed an employer, and shall be jointly liable with such other person for any violation of Section 2675 and the sections enumerated in that section.

(b) Any employee of a person or persons engaged in garment manufacturing who are not registered as required by this part may bring a civil action against any person deemed to be an employer pursuant to subdivision (a) to recover any wages, damages, or penalties to which the employee may be entitled because of a violation by the unregistered person or persons of any provision specified in subdivision (a) of Section 2675, or may file a claim with the Labor Commissioner pursuant to Section 2673.1. In any civil action brought pursuant to this subdivision, the court shall grant a prevailing plaintiff's reasonable attorney's fees and costs. *(Added by Stats. 1980, c. 633, p. 1733, § 1, operative July 1, 1981. Amended by Stats.1984, c. 1564, § 4; Stats.1999, c. 554 (A.B.633), § 5.)*

§ 2677.5. Business practices causing or likely to cause violation; prohibition

It shall be illegal for any person registered pursuant to this chapter and contracting with another registrant to engage in any business practice which causes or is likely

to cause a violation of this chapter. *(Added by Stats.1984, c. 1564, § 5.)*

§ 2678. Penalty

(a) A penalty, as provided in subdivision (c), may be imposed against any person for any of the following:

(1) Failure to comply within 15 days of any judgment due for violation of any labor laws applicable to garment industry workers.

(2) Failure to comply with the registration requirements of this part.

(3) Failure to comply with Section 2673 or any section enumerated in Section 2675.

(b) The order imposing the penalty may be served personally or by registered mail in accordance with subdivision (c) of Section 11505 of the Government Code. The order shall be in writing and shall describe the nature of the violation, including reference to the statutory provisions, rules, or regulations alleged to have been violated.

(c) The penalties shall be a civil penalty of one hundred dollars ($100) for each affected employee for the initial violation and a civil penalty of two hundred dollars ($200) for each affected employee for the second or subsequent violation.

(d) If a person is subject to civil penalties for a violation described in subdivision (a), but does not employ one or more workers, the civil penalty shall be five hundred dollars ($500), and the person shall not be guilty of a misdemeanor as specified in Section 2676. *(Added by Stats.1980, c. 633, p. 1733, § 1, operative July 1, 1981. Amended by Stats.1984, c. 1564, § 6; Stats.1998, c. 276 (S.B.1514), § 2.)*

§ 2679. Additional penalty; deposit of bond; second and subsequent violations; revocation of registration; confiscation; notice

(a) The commissioner, in addition to any civil penalty imposed pursuant to Section 2679, may require that as a condition of continued registration, such employer deposit with him or her within 10 days a bond to ensure payment of wages and benefits in such sum and form as the commissioner may deem sufficient and adequate in the circumstances but not to exceed ten thousand dollars ($10,000). The bond shall be payable to the commissioner and shall provide that the employer shall pay his or her employees in accordance with the provisions of Section 2675. In lieu of the deposit of a bond, the commissioner, in his or her discretion, may accept other evidence of financial security sufficient to guarantee payment of wages to affected employees.

(b) The commissioner, in addition to any civil penalty imposed, shall require a bond as set forth in subdivision (a) upon any second or subsequent violation within any two-year period. The commissioner may revoke the registration of any person for any period ranging from 30 days to one year upon a third or subsequent violation within any two-year period and may confiscate any garment or wearing apparel, assembled or partially assembled, if the violation relates to minimum wages, child labor, or maximum hours of labor. If the commissioner does exercise the authority to confiscate upon such a third or subsequent violation, the commissioner shall notify persons for whom assembly is performed and shall provide for the return of such garment owner's confiscated garments or wearing apparel upon such assumption and satisfaction of liability for the violation. *(Added by Stats.1980, c. 633, p. 1734, § 1, operative July 1, 1981.)*

§ 2680. Confiscation of garments or wearing apparel; disposal; notice; confiscation of manufacturing equipment and property

(a) Any garment or wearing apparel, assembled or partially assembled by or on behalf of any person who has not complied with the registration requirements of this part, may be confiscated by the Division of Labor Standards Enforcement. Garments and wearing apparel confiscated pursuant to this section shall be placed in the custody of the division, which shall be charged with the responsibility of destroying or disposing of them pursuant to regulations adopted under Section 2672, provided that the goods shall not enter the mainstream of commerce and shall not be offered for sale. The division shall, by registered mail and telephone, give notice of the removal and the location where the confiscated goods are held in custody to the known manufacturer and contractor.

(b) If the person from whom garments or wearing apparel are confiscated pursuant to subdivision (a) was providing the confiscated garments or wearing apparel as a contractor and has previously, within the immediately preceding five-year period, had garments or wearing apparel confiscated pursuant to subdivision (a), the Labor Commissioner may, in addition to the remedies set forth in subdivision (a), confiscate the means of production, including all manufacturing equipment and the property where the current unregistered garment manufacturing operations have taken place. This subdivision does not apply where nonregistration of the contractor was due to delayed renewal of registration.

(c) The proceeds from the sale of any equipment or property under subdivision (b) shall be deposited into a single account in the General Fund, to be known as the Back Wages and Taxes Account. At the Labor Commissioner's discretion, and upon appropriation by the Legislature, funds from that account may be disbursed to pay back wages owed to garment workers, including, but not limited to, workers of the unregistered contractor whose violation caused the confiscation, and for the payment of taxes. *(Added by Stats.1980, c. 633, p. 1734, § 1, operative July 1, 1981. Amended by Stats.1999, c. 554 (A.B.633), § 6.)*

§ 2680.5. Pricing and quality disputes between manufacturers and contractors; authority to investigate and mediate

The commissioner shall have the authority to investigate and mediate pricing and quality disputes arising out of written contracts between manufacturers and contractors in the garment industry. *(Added by Stats.1984, c. 1564, § 7.)*

§ 2681. Contest of penalty or confiscation; payment in lieu of contest; petition for hearing; hearing; findings and order; writ of mandate; judgment; interest on judgment

(a) Any person against whom a penalty is assessed or whose goods are confiscated shall, in lieu of contesting the penalty or the confiscation pursuant to this section, transmit to the office of the Labor Commissioner designated on the citation the amount specified for the violation within 15 business days after the issuance of the citation.

(b) If a person desires to contest an assessment of a penalty or the confiscation of goods, he or she shall, within 15 business days after service of the citation or confiscation of the goods, or both, petition, in writing, the office of the Labor Commissioner which appears on the citation or on the receipt for the confiscated goods of his or her request for an informal hearing. The Labor Commissioner or his or her deputy or agent shall, within 30 days, hold a hearing at the conclusion of which the penalty set forth in the citation or the issue of the confiscation of the goods, or both, shall be affirmed, modified, or dismissed. If confiscated goods are involved, the hearing shall be held within 10 days. The decision of the Labor Commissioner shall consist of a notice of findings, findings, and order which shall be served on all parties to the hearing within 15 days after the hearing by regular first-class mail at the last known address of the party on file with the Labor Commissioner. Service shall be completed pursuant to Section 1013 of the Code of Civil Procedure. Any amount found due by the Labor Commissioner as a result of a hearing shall become due and payable 45 days after notice of the findings and written findings and order have been mailed to the party assessed. A writ of mandate may be taken from this finding to the appropriate superior court, as long as the party agrees to pay any judgment and costs ultimately rendered by the court against the party for the assessment. The writ must be taken within 45 days of service of the notice of findings, findings, and order thereon.

(c) When no petition objecting to a citation or the proposed assessment of a civil penalty or confiscation of goods, or both, is filed, a certified copy of the citation or proposed civil penalty may be filed by the Labor Commissioner in the office of the clerk of the superior court in any county in which the person assessed has property or in which the person assessed has or had a place of business. The clerk, immediately upon the filing, shall enter judgment for the state against the person assessed in the amount shown on the citation or proposed assessment of a civil penalty.

(d) When findings and the order thereon are made affirming or modifying a citation or proposed assessment of a civil penalty after hearing, a certified copy of these findings and the order entered thereon may be entered by the Labor Commissioner in the office of the clerk of the superior court in any county in which the person assessed has property or in which the person assessed has or had a place of business. The clerk, immediately upon the filing, shall enter judgment for the state against the person assessed in the amount shown on the certified order.

(e) A judgment entered pursuant to this section shall bear the same rate of interest and shall have the same effect as other judgments and be given the same preference allowed by law on other judgments rendered for claims for taxes. The clerk shall make no charge for the service provided by this section to be performed by him or her. *(Added by Stats.1988, c. 96, § 12.)*

§ 2682. Application of moneys recovered

Moneys recovered under this chapter shall be applied first to payment of wages due affected employees. If insufficient funds are withheld or recovered, the money shall be prorated among all such workers. Any remainder shall be paid to the General Fund of the state. *(Added by Stats.1980, c. 633, p. 1735, § 1, operative July 1, 1981.)*

§ 2684. Employer primarily engaged in sewing or assembly of garments for other persons; liability of successor employer for unpaid wages

(a) The Legislature finds and declares that persons who are primarily engaged in sewing or assembly of garments for other persons engaged in garment manufacturing frequently close down their sewing shops to avoid paying their employees' wages and subsequently reopen under the conditions described in subdivision (b), and are more likely to do so than are other types of persons engaged in garment manufacturing.

(b) A successor to any employer that is primarily engaged in sewing or assembly of garments for other persons engaged in the business of garment manufacturing, as defined by subdivision (b) of Section 2671, that owes wages to the predecessor's former employee or employees is liable for those wages if the successor meets any of the following criteria:

(1) Uses substantially the same facilities or work force to produce substantially the same products for substantially the same type of customers as the predecessor employer.

(2) Shares in the ownership, management, control of labor relations, or interrelations of business operations with the predecessor employer.

(3) Has in its employ in a managerial capacity any person who directly or indirectly controlled the wages, hours, or working conditions of the affected employees of the predecessor employer.

(4) Is an immediate family member of any owner, partner, officer, or director of the predecessor employer

or of any person who had a financial interest in the predecessor employer.

This section does not impose liability upon a successor for the guarantee of unpaid minimum wages and overtime compensation set forth in subdivision (a) or (b) of Section 2673.1. *(Added by Stats.1999, c. 554 (A.B.633), § 7.)*

CHAPTER 3. ARBITRATION

Section
2685. Pricing and product quality disputes; arbitration procedures.
2686. Notice of dispute; appointment and composition of panel.
2687. Notice and time of hearing.
2688. Hearing; party not represented; appearance as waiver of notice defect.
2689. Hearing; procedures.
2690. Award; majority vote; signatures; notice.
2691. Compliance with award; time; filing proof; review; notice; trial de novo.
2692. Costs; attorneys' fees.

§ 2685. Pricing and product quality disputes; arbitration procedures

The commissioner shall establish, in accordance with the provisions of this chapter, procedures for mandatory arbitration of pricing and product quality disputes arising out of written contracts between manufacturers and contractors. *(Added by Stats.1980, c. 633, p. 1735, § 1, operative July 1, 1981.)*

§ 2686. Notice of dispute; appointment and composition of panel

Upon the written request of any manufacturer or contractor, the Conciliation Service of the Department of Industrial Relations shall notify the other party to the dispute of the request for arbitration and shall, within seven days of receipt of the request, appoint an arbitration panel to hear and render a decision regarding the dispute. The panel shall be constituted as follows:

(a) A management level representative from a manufacturer in the general geographic area in which the dispute arises, provided that insofar as possible the manufacturer shall not be a direct competitor of the manufacturer involved in the dispute to be arbitrated. This panel member also shall be selected in accordance with the terms of the written contract.

(b) A representative from the contractors' association whose membership encompasses the general geographic area in which the dispute arises. This panel member also shall be selected in accordance with the terms of the written contract.

(c) A third party to be chosen and agreed upon by the first two parties to the dispute from a list of arbitrators provided by the American Arbitration Association. This party shall act as chairperson of the panel. *(Added by*

Stats.1980, c. 633, p. 1735, § 1, operative July 1, 1981. Amended by Stats.2006, c. 538 (S.B.1852), § 486.)

§ 2687. Notice and time of hearing

Within seven days of appointment, the chairperson of the panel shall notify the parties in writing of the date, time, and location of the hearing before the panel. The hearing date shall be scheduled no later than 21 days after the filing of the request for arbitration, provided, however, that each party shall have no less than five days notice prior to the hearing date. *(Added by Stats.1980, c. 633, p. 1736, § 1, operative July 1, 1981.)*

§ 2688. Hearing; party not represented; appearance as waiver of notice defect

On the date and time specified in the hearing notice, the chairperson shall convene the hearing and shall determine whether each party is represented. If neither party is represented, the arbitration shall be terminated, with costs assigned to the party requesting arbitration, and the parties shall forfeit any further rights under this section relating to the dispute for which arbitration was requested. In the event only one party is in attendance, the arbitration shall proceed and the panel shall make its award based upon the evidence presented. Appearance at the hearing by a party shall be deemed to waive any alleged defect in notice. *(Added by Stats.1980, c. 633, p. 1736, § 1, operative July 1, 1981.)*

§ 2689. Hearing; procedures

To facilitate the conduct of the hearing, the following procedures shall govern:

(a) Upon good cause shown by a party, the chairperson shall be empowered to issue subpoenae duces tecum and ad testificandum.

(b) Each party may be represented by an attorney at the party's own expense.

(c) The formal rules of evidence shall not be applicable, but any relevant evidence shall be admitted if it is evidence upon which responsible persons would rely in the conduct of serious business affairs.

(d) All testimony shall be taken under oath.

(e) No formal written records shall be kept unless one or both parties agree to employ at their own expense a qualified court reporter for that purpose. In such case, a copy of the record shall be provided to the panel and a copy shall be made available to the other party at the standard cost for such additional copies.

(f) Those in attendance at the hearing shall be limited to the panel, the parties and their counsel, a court reporter, interpreters when requested by a party or the panel, and witnesses while testifying.

(g) Upon the request of a panel member, the panel may allow a period, not to exceed three days following the conclusion of the hearing, during which time a party may submit otherwise admissible evidence not available during the course of the hearing. *(Added by Stats.1980, c. 633, p. 1736, § 1, operative July 1, 1981.)*

§ 2690. Award; majority vote; signatures; notice

Within 15 days after the conclusion of the hearing, the panel shall make a written award, which shall determine all questions submitted for arbitration. All decisions of the panel shall be by majority vote and the award shall be signed by the members concurring therein. The panel immediately shall provide written notice of the award to the parties and to the commissioner. *(Added by Stats. 1980, c. 633, p. 1737, § 1, operative July 1, 1981.)*

§ 2691. Compliance with award; time; filing proof; review; notice; trial de novo

Within 10 days of receipt of notice of the award, the party or parties who are required to comply with the terms of the award shall so comply and file proof of such compliance with the commissioner or shall file a notice of appeal with the superior court for the county in which the hearing was held. Upon the filing of such an appeal, a trial de novo shall be held, provided, however, that the decision reached by the panel as stated in the award shall be received as evidence by the trial court. *(Added by Stats.1980, c. 633, p. 1737, § 1, operative July 1, 1981. Amended by Stats.2002, c. 784 (S.B.1316), § 525.)*

§ 2692. Costs; attorneys' fees

The basic costs of the arbitration proceeding, including interpreters requested by the panel, shall be borne equally by all parties to the proceeding, provided, however, that the panel may as a part of its award impose all such costs on the party requesting arbitration if a majority of the panel determines that the matter brought before it was frivolous. In addition, in the case of a frivolous claim the panel may impose upon the party requesting arbitration the costs of translators, court reporters, and reasonable attorneys fees incurred by the other party. *(Added by Stats.1980, c. 633, p. 1737, § 1, operative July 1, 1981.)*

Part 12

SHEEPHERDERS

Section
2695.1.   Legislative intent to codify certain labor protections for sheepherders; other remedies; construction of terms.
2695.2.   Amount of wages; tools or equipment requirements; meal and rest periods; housing and other services; violations; penalties.

§ 2695.1. Legislative intent to codify certain labor protections for sheepherders; other remedies; construction of terms

(a) In enacting this legislation, it is the intent of the Legislature to codify certain labor protections that should be afforded to sheepherders, as defined. The provisions of this section are in addition to, and are entirely independent from, any other statutory or legal protections, rights, or remedies that are or may be available under this code or any other state law or regulation to sheepherders either as individuals, employees, or persons.

(b) All terms used in this section and in Section 2695.2 have the meanings assigned to them by this code or any other state law or regulation. *(Added by Stats.2001, c. 948 (A.B.1675), § 1. Amended by Stats.2002, c. 664 (A.B.3034), § 162.5.)*

§ 2695.2. Amount of wages; tools or equipment requirements; meal and rest periods; housing and other services; violations; penalties

(a)(1) For a sheepherder employed on a regularly scheduled 24–hour shift on a seven-day-a-week "on-call" basis, an employer may, as an alternative to paying the minimum wage for all hours worked, instead pay no less than the monthly minimum wage adopted by the Industrial Welfare Commission on April 24, 2001. Any sheepherder who performs nonsheepherding, nonagricultural work on any workday shall be fully covered for that workweek by the provisions of any applicable laws or regulations relating to that work.

(2) After July 1, 2002, the amount of the monthly minimum wage permitted under paragraph (1) shall be increased each time that the state minimum wage is increased and shall become effective on the same date as any increase in the state minimum wage. The amount of the increase shall be determined by calculating the percentage increase of the new rate over the previous rate, and then by applying the same percentage increase to the minimum monthly wage rate.

(b)(1) When tools or equipment are required by the employer or are necessary to the performance of a job, the tools and equipment shall be provided and maintained by the employer, except that a sheepherder whose wages are at least two times the minimum wage provided herein, or if paid on a monthly basis, at least two times the monthly minimum wage, may be required to provide and maintain handtools and equipment customarily required by the trade or craft.

(2) A reasonable deposit may be required as security for the return of the items furnished by the employer under provisions of paragraph (1) upon issuance of a receipt to the sheepherder for the deposit. The deposits shall be made pursuant to Article 2 (commencing with Section 400) of Chapter 3. Alternatively, with the prior written authorization of the sheepherder, an employer may deduct from the sheepherder's last check the cost of any item furnished pursuant to paragraph (1) when the item is not returned. No deduction shall be made at any time for normal wear and tear. All items furnished by the employer shall be returned by the sheepherder upon completion of the job.

(c) No employer of sheepherders shall employ a sheepherder for a work period of more than five hours without a meal period of no less than 30 minutes, except that when a work period of not more than six hours will complete a day's work, the meal period may be waived by

the mutual consent of the employer and the sheepherder. An employer may be relieved of this obligation if a meal period of 30 minutes cannot reasonably be provided because no one is available to relieve a sheepherder tending flock alone on that day. Where a meal period of 30 minutes can be provided but not without interruption, a sheepherder shall be allowed to complete the meal period during that day.

(d) To the extent practicable, every employer shall authorize and permit all sheepherders to take rest periods. The rest period, insofar as is practicable, shall be in the middle of each work period. The authorized rest times shall be based on the total hours worked daily at the rate of 10 minutes net rest time per four hours, or major fraction thereof, of work. However, a rest period need not be authorized for sheepherders whose total daily worktime is less than three and one-half hours.

(e) When the nature of the work reasonably permits the use of seats, suitable seats shall be provided for sheepherders working on or at a machine.

(f) After January 1, 2003, during times when a sheepherder is lodged in mobile housing units where it is feasible to provide lodging that meets the minimum standards established by this section because there is practicable access for mobile housing units, the lodging provided shall include at a minimum all of the following:

(1) Toilets and bathing facilities, which may include portable toilets and portable shower facilities.

(2) Heating.

(3) Inside lighting.

(4) Potable hot and cold water.

(5) Adequate cooking facilities and utensils.

(6) A working refrigerator, which may include a butane or propane gas refrigerator, or for no more than a one-week period during which a nonworking refrigerator is repaired or replaced, a means of refrigerating perishable food items, which may include ice chests, provided that ice is delivered to the sheepherder, as needed, to maintain a continuous temperature required to retard spoilage and ensure food safety.

(g) After January 1, 2003, all sheepherders shall be provided with all of the following at each worksite:

(1) Regular mail service.

(2) A means of communication through telephone or radio solely for use in a medical emergency affecting the sheepherder or for an emergency relating to the herding operation. If the means of communication is provided by telephone, the sheepherder may be charged for the actual cost of nonemergency telephone use. Nothing in this subdivision shall preclude an employer from providing additional means of communication to the sheepherder which are appropriate because telephones or radios are out of range or otherwise inoperable.

(3) Visitor access to the housing.

(4) Upon request and to the extent practicable, access to transportation to and from the nearest locale where shopping, medical, or cultural facilities and services are available on a weekly basis.

(h) In addition to any other civil penalties provided by law, any employer or any other person acting on behalf of the employer who violates or causes to be violated the provisions of this section shall be subject to a civil penalty, as follows:

(1) For the initial violation, fifty dollars ($50) for each underpaid employee for each pay period during which the employee was underpaid, plus an amount sufficient to recover the unpaid wages.

(2) For any subsequent violation, one hundred dollars ($100) for each underpaid employee for each pay period during which the employee was underpaid, plus an amount sufficient to recover the unpaid wages.

(3) The affected employee shall receive payment of all wages recovered.

(i) If the application of any provision of any subdivision, sentence, clause, phrase, word, or portion of this legislation is held invalid, unconstitutional, unauthorized, or prohibited by statute, the remaining provisions thereof shall not be affected and shall continue to be given full force and effect as if the part held invalid or unconstitutional had not been included.

(j) Every employer of sheepherders shall post a copy of this part in an area frequented by sheepherders where it may be easily read during the workday. Where the location of work or other conditions make posting impractical, every employer shall make a copy of this part available to sheepherders upon request. Copies of this part shall be posted and made available in a language understood by the sheepherder. An employer is deemed to have complied with this subdivision if he or she posts where practical, or makes available upon request where posting is impractical, a copy of the Industrial Welfare Commission Order 14–2001, as adopted on April 24, 2001, relating to sheepherders, provided that the posted material includes a sufficient summary of each of the provisions of this part. *(Added by Stats.2001, c. 948 (A.B.1675), § 1. Amended by Stats.2002, c. 664 (A.B. 3034), § 163.)*

Part 13

THE LABOR CODE PRIVATE ATTORNEYS GENERAL ACT OF 2004

Section
2698.   Short title.
2699.   Actions brought by an aggrieved employee or on behalf of self or other current or former employees; authority; gap-filler penalties; attorneys fees; exclusion; distribution of recovered penalties.
2699.3.   Requirements for aggrieved employee to commence a civil action.
2699.5.   Application of subd. (a) of § 2699.3.

§ 2698. Short title

This part shall be known and may be cited as the Labor Code Private Attorneys General Act of 2004. *(Added by Stats.2003, c. 906 (S.B.796), § 2.)*

§ 2699. Actions brought by an aggrieved employee or on behalf of self or other current or former employees; authority; gap-filler penalties; attorneys fees; exclusion; distribution of recovered penalties

(a) Notwithstanding any other provision of law, any provision of this code that provides for a civil penalty to be assessed and collected by the Labor and Workforce Development Agency or any of its departments, divisions, commissions, boards, agencies, or employees, for a violation of this code, may, as an alternative, be recovered through a civil action brought by an aggrieved employee on behalf of himself or herself and other current or former employees pursuant to the procedures specified in Section 2699.3.

(b) For purposes of this part, "person" has the same meaning as defined in Section 18.

(c) For purposes of this part, "aggrieved employee" means any person who was employed by the alleged violator and against whom one or more of the alleged violations was committed.

(d) For purposes of this part, "cure" means that the employer abates each violation alleged by any aggrieved employee, the employer is in compliance with the underlying statutes as specified in the notice required by this part, and any aggrieved employee is made whole.

(e)(1) For purposes of this part, whenever the Labor and Workforce Development Agency, or any of its departments, divisions, commissions, boards, agencies, or employees, has discretion to assess a civil penalty, a court is authorized to exercise the same discretion, subject to the same limitations and conditions, to assess a civil penalty.

(2) In any action by an aggrieved employee seeking recovery of a civil penalty available under subdivision (a) or (f), a court may award a lesser amount than the maximum civil penalty amount specified by this part if, based on the facts and circumstances of the particular case, to do otherwise would result in an award that is unjust, arbitrary and oppressive, or confiscatory.

(f) For all provisions of this code except those for which a civil penalty is specifically provided, there is established a civil penalty for a violation of these provisions, as follows:

(1) If, at the time of the alleged violation, the person does not employ one or more employees, the civil penalty is five hundred dollars ($500).

(2) If, at the time of the alleged violation, the person employs one or more employees, the civil penalty is one hundred dollars ($100) for each aggrieved employee per pay period for the initial violation and two hundred dollars ($200) for each aggrieved employee per pay period for each subsequent violation.

(3) If the alleged violation is a failure to act by the Labor and Workplace Development Agency, or any of its departments, divisions, commissions, boards, agencies, or employees, there shall be no civil penalty.

(g)(1) Except as provided in paragraph (2), an aggrieved employee may recover the civil penalty described in subdivision (f) in a civil action pursuant to the procedures specified in Section 2699.3 filed on behalf of himself or herself and other current or former employees against whom one or more of the alleged violations was committed. Any employee who prevails in any action shall be entitled to an award of reasonable attorney's fees and costs. Nothing in this part shall operate to limit an employee's right to pursue or recover other remedies available under state or federal law, either separately or concurrently with an action taken under this part.

(2) No action shall be brought under this part for any violation of a posting, notice, agency reporting, or filing requirement of this code, except where the filing or reporting requirement involves mandatory payroll or workplace injury reporting.

(h) No action may be brought under this section by an aggrieved employee if the agency or any of its departments, divisions, commissions, boards, agencies, or employees, on the same facts and theories, cites a person within the timeframes set forth in Section 2699.3 for a violation of the same section or sections of the Labor Code under which the aggrieved employee is attempting to recover a civil penalty on behalf of himself or herself or others or initiates a proceeding pursuant to Section 98.3.

(i) Except as provided in subdivision (j), civil penalties recovered by aggrieved employees shall be distributed as follows: 75 percent to the Labor and Workforce Development Agency for enforcement of labor laws and education of employers and employees about their rights and responsibilities under this code, to be continuously appropriated to supplement and not supplant the funding to the agency for those purposes; and 25 percent to the aggrieved employees.

(j) Civil penalties recovered under paragraph (1) of subdivision (f) shall be distributed to the Labor and Workforce Development Agency for enforcement of labor laws and education of employers and employees about their rights and responsibilities under this code, to be continuously appropriated to supplement and not supplant the funding to the agency for those purposes.

(k) Nothing contained in this part is intended to alter or otherwise affect the exclusive remedy provided by the workers' compensation provisions of this code for liability against an employer for the compensation for any injury to or death of an employee arising out of and in the course of employment.

(l) The superior court shall review and approve any penalties sought as part of a proposed settlement agreement pursuant to this part.

(m) This section shall not apply to the recovery of administrative and civil penalties in connection with the workers' compensation law as contained in Division 1 (commencing with Section 50) and Division 4 (commencing with Section 3200), including, but not limited to, Sections 129.5 and 132a.

(n) The agency or any of its departments, divisions, commissions, boards, or agencies may promulgate regulations to implement the provisions of this part. *(Added by Stats.2003, c. 906 (S.B.796), § 2. Amended by Stats.2004, c. 34 (S.B.899), § 5.5, eff. April 19, 2004; Stats.2004, c. 221 (S.B.1809), § 3, eff. Aug. 11, 2004.)*

Operative Effect

Prior to amendment by § 3 of Stats.2004, c. 221 (S.B.1809), eff. Aug. 11, 2004, § 47 of Stats.2004, c. 34 (S.B.899), eff. April 19, 2004, had provided that "[t]he amendment, addition, or repeal of, any provision of law made by this act shall apply prospectively from the date of enactment of this act, regardless of the date of injury, unless otherwise specified, but shall not constitute good cause to reopen or rescind, alter, or amend any existing order, decision, or award of the Workers' Compensation Appeals Board."

§ 2699.3. Requirements for aggrieved employee to commence a civil action

(a) A civil action by an aggrieved employee pursuant to subdivision (a) or (f) of Section 2699 alleging a violation of any provision listed in Section 2699.5 shall commence only after the following requirements have been met:

(1) The aggrieved employee or representative shall give written notice by certified mail to the Labor and Workforce Development Agency and the employer of the specific provisions of this code alleged to have been violated, including the facts and theories to support the alleged violation.

(2)(A) The agency shall notify the employer and the aggrieved employee or representative by certified mail that it does not intend to investigate the alleged violation within 30 calendar days of the postmark date of the notice received pursuant to paragraph (1). Upon receipt of that notice or if no notice is provided within 33 calendar days of the postmark date of the notice given pursuant to paragraph (1), the aggrieved employee may commence a civil action pursuant to Section 2699.

(B) If the agency intends to investigate the alleged violation, it shall notify the employer and the aggrieved employee or representative by certified mail of its decision within 33 calendar days of the postmark date of the notice received pursuant to paragraph (1). Within 120 calendar days of that decision, the agency may investigate the alleged violation and issue any appropriate citation. If the agency determines that no citation will be issued, it shall notify the employer and aggrieved employee of that decision within five business days thereof by certified mail. Upon receipt of that notice or if no citation is issued by the agency within the 158–day period prescribed by subparagraph (A) and this subparagraph or if the agency fails to provide timely or any notification, the aggrieved employee may commence a civil action pursuant to Section 2699.

(C) Notwithstanding any other provision of law, a plaintiff may as a matter of right amend an existing complaint to add a cause of action arising under this part at any time within 60 days of the time periods specified in this part.

(b) A civil action by an aggrieved employee pursuant to subdivision (a) or (f) of Section 2699 alleging a violation of any provision of Division 5 (commencing with Section 6300) other than those listed in Section 2699.5 shall commence only after the following requirements have been met:

(1) The aggrieved employee or representative shall give notice by certified mail to the Division of Occupational Safety and Health and the employer, with a copy to the Labor and Workforce Development Agency, of the specific provisions of Division 5 (commencing with Section 6300) alleged to have been violated, including the facts and theories to support the alleged violation.

(2)(A) The division shall inspect or investigate the alleged violation pursuant to the procedures specified in Division 5 (commencing with Section 6300).

(i) If the division issues a citation, the employee may not commence an action pursuant to Section 2699. The division shall notify the aggrieved employee and employer in writing within 14 calendar days of certifying that the employer has corrected the violation.

(ii) If by the end of the period for inspection or investigation provided for in Section 6317, the division fails to issue a citation and the aggrieved employee disputes that decision, the employee may challenge that decision in the superior court. In such an action, the superior court shall follow precedents of the Occupational Safety and Health Appeals Board. If the court finds that the division should have issued a citation and orders the division to issue a citation, then the aggrieved employee may not commence a civil action pursuant to Section 2699.

(iii) A complaint in superior court alleging a violation of Division 5 (commencing with Section 6300) other than those listed in Section 2699.5 shall include therewith a copy of the notice of violation provided to the division and employer pursuant to paragraph (1).

(iv) The superior court shall not dismiss the action for nonmaterial differences in facts or theories between those contained in the notice of violation provided to the division and employer pursuant to paragraph (1) and the complaint filed with the court.

(B) If the division fails to inspect or investigate the alleged violation as provided by Section 6309, the provisions of subdivision (c) shall apply to the determination of the alleged violation.

(3)(A) Nothing in this subdivision shall be construed to alter the authority of the division to permit long-term abatement periods or to enter into memoranda of understanding or joint agreements with employers in the case of long-term abatement issues.

(B) Nothing in this subdivision shall be construed to authorize an employee to file a notice or to commence a civil action pursuant to Section 2699 during the period that an employer has voluntarily entered into consultation with the division to ameliorate a condition in that particular worksite.

(C) An employer who has been provided notice pursuant to this section may not then enter into consultation with the division in order to avoid an action under this section.

(4) The superior court shall review and approve any proposed settlement of alleged violations of the provisions of Division 5 (commencing with Section 6300) to ensure that the settlement provisions are at least as effective as the protections or remedies provided by state and federal law or regulation for the alleged violation. The provisions of the settlement relating to health and safety laws shall be submitted to the division at the same time that they are submitted to the court. This requirement shall be construed to authorize and permit the division to comment on those settlement provisions, and the court shall grant the division's commentary the appropriate weight.

(c) A civil action by an aggrieved employee pursuant to subdivision (a) or (f) of Section 2699 alleging a violation of any provision other than those listed in Section 2699.5 or Division 5 (commencing with Section 6300) shall commence only after the following requirements have been met:

(1) The aggrieved employee or representative shall give written notice by certified mail to the Labor and Workforce Development Agency and the employer of the specific provisions of this code alleged to have been violated, including the facts and theories to support the alleged violation.

(2)(A) The employer may cure the alleged violation within 33 calendar days of the postmark date of the notice. The employer shall give written notice by certified mail within that period of time to the aggrieved employee or representative and the agency if the alleged violation is cured, including a description of actions taken, and no civil action pursuant to Section 2699 may commence. If the alleged violation is not cured within the 33-day period, the employee may commence a civil action pursuant to Section 2699.

(B) No employer may avail himself or herself of the notice and cure provisions of this subdivision more than three times in a 12-month period for the same violation or violations contained in the notice, regardless of the location of the worksite.

(3) If the aggrieved employee disputes that the alleged violation has been cured, the aggrieved employee or

497

representative shall provide written notice by certified mail, including specified grounds to support that dispute, to the employer and the agency. Within 17 calendar days of the postmark date of that notice, the agency shall review the actions taken by the employer to cure the alleged violation, and provide written notice of its decision by certified mail to the aggrieved employee and the employer. The agency may grant the employer three additional business days to cure the alleged violation. If the agency determines that the alleged violation has not been cured or if the agency fails to provide timely or any notification, the employee may proceed with the civil action pursuant to Section 2699. If the agency determines that the alleged violation has been cured, but the employee still disagrees, the employee may appeal that determination to the superior court.

(d) The periods specified in this section are not counted as part of the time limited for the commencement of the civil action to recover penalties under this part. *(Added by Stats.2004, c. 221 (S.B.1809), § 4, eff. Aug. 11, 2004.)*

§ 2699.5. Application of subd. (a) of § 2699.3

The provisions of subdivision (a) of Section 2699.3 apply to any alleged violation of the following provisions: subdivision (k) of Section 96, Sections 98.6, 201, 201.3, 201.5, 201.7, 202, 203, 203.1, 203.5, 204, 204a, 204b, 204.1, 204.2, 205, 205.5, 206, 206.5, 208, 209, and 212, subdivision (d) of Section 213, Sections 221, 222, 222.5, 223, and 224, subdivision (a) of Section 226, Sections 226.7, 227, 227.3, 230, 230.1, 230.2, 230.3, 230.4, 230.7, 230.8, and 231, subdivision (c) of Section 232, subdivision (c) of Section 232.5, Sections 233, 234, 351, 353, and 403, subdivision (b) of Section 404, Sections 432.2, 432.5, 432.7, 435, 450, 510, 511, 512, 513, 551, 552, 601, 602, 603, 604, 750, 751.8, 800, 850, 851, 851.5, 852, 921, 922, 923, 970, 973, 976, 1021, 1021.5, 1025, 1026, 1101, 1102, 1102.5, and 1153, subdivisions (c) and (d) of Section 1174, Sections 1194, 1197, 1197.1, 1197.5, and 1198, subdivision (b) of Section 1198.3, Sections 1199, 1199.5, 1290, 1292, 1293, 1293.1, 1294, 1294.1, 1294.5, 1296, 1297, 1298, 1301, 1308, 1308.1, 1308.7, 1309, 1309.5, 1391, 1391.1, 1391.2, 1392, 1683, and 1695, subdivision (a) of Section 1695.5, Sections 1695.55, 1695.6, 1695.7, 1695.8, 1695.9, 1696, 1696.5, 1696.6, 1697.1, 1700.25, 1700.26, 1700.31, 1700.32, 1700.40, and 1700.47, paragraphs (1), (2), and (3) of subdivision (a) of, and subdivision (e) of, Section 1701.4, subdivision (a) of Section 1701.5, Sections 1701.8, 1701.10, 1701.12, 1735, 1771, 1774, 1776, 1777.5, 1811, 1815, 2651, and 2673, subdivision (a) of Section 2673.1, Sections 2695.2, 2800, 2801, 2802, 2806, and 2810, subdivision (b) of Section 2929, and Sections 3095, 6310, 6311, and 6399.7. *(Added by Stats.2004, c. 221 (S.B.1809), § 5, eff. Aug. 11, 2004. Amended by Stats.2005, c. 22 (S.B. 1108), § 141; Stats.2008, c. 169 (S.B.940), § 8; Stats. 2009, c. 140 (A.B.1164), § 136.)*

Division 3

EMPLOYMENT RELATIONS

Chapter	Section
1. Scope of Division	2700
2. Employer and Employee	2750
3. Master and Servant [Repealed]	
4. Apprenticeship	3070

Article	Section
2. Obligations of Employer	2800
3. Obligations of Employee	2850
3.5. Inventions Made By an Employee	2870
4. Termination of Employment	2920
5. Investigations of Employees	2930

CHAPTER 1. SCOPE OF DIVISION

Section
2700. Effect upon workmen's compensation and insurance provisions.

§ 2700. Effect upon workmen's compensation and insurance provisions

The provisions of this division shall not limit, change, or in any way qualify the provisions of Divisions 4 [1] and 4.5 [2] of this code, but shall be fully operative and effective in all cases where the provisions of Divisions 4 and 4.5 are not applicable. *(Stats.1937, c. 90, p. 258, § 2700. Amended by Stats.1957, c. 48, p. 611, § 3.)*

[1] Labor Code § 3201 et seq.
[2] Labor Code § 6100 et seq.

CHAPTER 2. EMPLOYER AND EMPLOYEE

Article	Section
1. The Contract of Employment	2750

ARTICLE 1. THE CONTRACT OF EMPLOYMENT

Section
2750. Definition.
2750.5. Contractors; presumption of employee status; proof of independent contractor status.
2750.6. Physician and surgeon as independent contractor; rebuttable presumption.
2751. Commission contracts; required provisions; formalities; definitions.
2752. Commission contracts; violations; triple damages.

§ 2750. Definition

The contract of employment is a contract by which one, who is called the employer, engages another, who is called the employee, to do something for the benefit of the employer or a third person. *(Stats.1937, c. 90, p. 258, § 2750.)*

§ 2750.5. Contractors; presumption of employee status; proof of independent contractor status

There is a rebuttable presumption affecting the burden of proof that a worker performing services for which a license is required pursuant to Chapter 9 (commencing with Section 7000) of Division 3 of the Business and Professions Code, or who is performing such services for a person who is required to obtain such a license is an employee rather than an independent contractor. Proof of independent contractor status includes satisfactory proof of these factors:

(a) That the individual has the right to control and discretion as to the manner of performance of the contract for services in that the result of the work and not the means by which it is accomplished is the primary factor bargained for.

(b) That the individual is customarily engaged in an independently established business.

(c) That the individual's independent contractor status is bona fide and not a subterfuge to avoid employee status. A bona fide independent contractor status is further evidenced by the presence of cumulative factors such as substantial investment other than personal services in the business, holding out to be in business for oneself, bargaining for a contract to complete a specific project for compensation by project rather than by time, control over the time and place the work is performed, supplying the tools or instrumentalities used in the work other than tools and instrumentalities normally and customarily provided by employees, hiring employees, performing work that is not ordinarily in the course of the principal's work, performing work that requires a particular skill, holding a license pursuant to the Business and Professions Code, the intent by the parties that the work relationship is of an independent contractor status, or that the relationship is not severable or terminable at will by the principal but gives rise to an action for breach of contract.

In addition to the factors contained in subdivisions (a), (b), and (c), any person performing any function or activity for which a license is required pursuant to Chapter 9 (commencing with Section 7000) of Division 3 of the Business and Professions Code shall hold a valid contractors' license as a condition of having independent contractor status.

For purposes of workers' compensation law, this presumption is a supplement to the existing statutory definitions of employee and independent contractor, and is not intended to lessen the coverage of employees under Division 4 and Division 5. *(Added by Stats.1978, c. 1246, p. 4058, § 1. Amended by Stats.1979, c. 605, p. 1879, § 1.)*

§ 2750.6. Physician and surgeon as independent contractor; rebuttable presumption

There is a rebuttable presumption affecting the burden of proof that a physician and surgeon, licensed pursuant to Division 2 (commencing with Section 500) of the Business and Professions Code, who enters into a contract for the performance of health services on behalf of a licensed primary care clinic, as defined in paragraph (1) of subdivision (a) of Section 1204 of the Health and Safety Code, is an independent contractor rather than an employee. Nothing in this section shall authorize the employment of a physician and surgeon to provide professional services when the employment would violate any other provision of law. *(Added by Stats.1984, c. 783, § 1.)*

§ 2751. Commission contracts; required provisions; formalities; definitions

Whenever any employer who has no permanent and fixed place of business in this State enters into a contract of employment with an employee for services to be rendered within this State and the contemplated method of payment of the employee involves commissions, the contract shall be in writing and shall set forth the method by which the commissions shall be computed and paid.

The employer shall give a signed copy of each such contract to every employee who is a party thereto and shall obtain a signed receipt for the contract from each employee.

As used in this section, "commissions" does not include short term productivity bonuses such as are paid to retail clerks; and it does not include bonus and profit-sharing plans, unless there has been an offer by the employer to pay a fixed percentage of sales or profits as compensation for work to be performed. *(Added by Stats.1963, c. 1088, p. 2549, § 1.)*

Validity

Labor Code §§ 2751 and 2752 were held unconstitutional, as violative of both the commerce clause and equal protection clause, in the decision of Lett v. Paymentech, Inc., N.D.Cal. 1999, 81 F.Supp.2d 992.

§ 2752. Commission contracts; violations; triple damages

Any employer who does not employ an employee pursuant to a written contract as required by Section 2751 shall be liable to the employee in a civil action for triple damages. *(Added by Stats.1963, c. 1088, p. 2549, § 2.)*

Validity

Labor Code §§ 2751 and 2752 were held unconstitutional, as violative of both the commerce clause and equal protection clause, in the decision of Lett v. Paymentech, Inc., N.D.Cal. 1999, 81 F.Supp.2d 992.

ARTICLE 2. OBLIGATIONS OF EMPLOYER

Section
2800. Losses caused by employer's negligence; indemnification.

Section

2800.1. Musical instruments of employees; precautions for protection; liability of employer.

2800.2. Medical or health insurance providers; notification of conversion privilege.

2800.3. Availability of conversion coverage.

2801. Employer's defenses to actions by employees.

2802. Indemnification for employee's expenses and losses in discharging duties; award interest; definition.

2803. Action by personal representative of deceased employee.

2803.4. Employee Retirement Income Security Act of 1974; health benefits; Medi-Cal or medicaid benefits exception prohibited; third party liability.

2803.5. Health care benefits; coverage of children.

2804. Invalidity of agreement waiving article provisions.

2806. Coverage for medical, surgical or hospital benefits; discontinuation; notice to employees.

2807. Notification to former employees of availability of continued medical, surgical, or hospital benefits.

2808. Description of benefit plan; provision to employees; notification of coverage options upon termination of employment.

2809. Employer-managed deferred compensation plans; pre-enrollment information; notice of financial risks; quarterly financial summaries; self-directed plans.

2810. Individuals contracting for labor or services with construction, farm labor, garment, janitorial or security guard contractors; necessity of funds sufficient to allow compliance with local, state and federal laws or regulations governing labor or services to be provided; rebuttable presumption; contents and copy of contract or agreement; violations and actions for damages.

§ 2800. Losses caused by employer's negligence; indemnification

An employer shall in all cases indemnify his employee for losses caused by the employer's want of ordinary care. *(Stats.1937, c. 90, p. 258, § 2800.)*

§ 2800.1. Musical instruments of employees; precautions for protection; liability of employer

An employer shall in all cases take reasonable and necessary precautions to safeguard musical instruments and equipment, belonging to an employed musician, located on premises under the employer's control. In the event such equipment is damaged or stolen as a result of the employer's failure or refusal to take such reasonable and necessary precautions, the employer shall be liable to the owner for repair or replacement thereof if the employed musician has taken reasonable and necessary precautions to safeguard the musical instruments and equipment.

For the purposes of this section: (a) "employer" includes a purchaser of services and the owner of premises upon which an employed musician is working; and (b) "employee" is any employed musician working on premises which are under an employer's control. *(Added by Stats.1973, c. 497, p. 972, § 1.)*

§ 2800.2. Medical or health insurance providers; notification of conversion privilege

(a) Any employer, employee association, or other entity otherwise providing hospital, surgical, or major medical benefits to its employees or members is solely responsible for notification of its employees or members of the conversion coverage made available pursuant to Part 6.1 (commencing with Section 12670) of Division 2 of the Insurance Code or Section 1373.6 of the Health and Safety Code.

(b) Any employer, employee association, or other entity, whether private or public, that provides hospital, medical, or surgical expense coverage that a former employee may continue under Section 4980B of Title 26 of the United States Code, Section 1161 et seq. of Title 29 of the United States Code, or Section 300bb of Title 42 of the United States Code, as added by the Consolidated Omnibus Budget Reconciliation Act of 1985 (Public Law 99–272), and as may be later amended (hereafter "COBRA"), shall, in conjunction with the notification required by COBRA that COBRA continuation coverage will cease and conversion coverage is available, and as a part of the notification required by subdivision (a), also notify the former employee, spouse, or former spouse of the availability of the continuation coverage under Section 1373.621 of the Health and Safety Code, and Sections 10116.5 and 11512.03 of the Insurance Code.

(c) On or after July 1, 2006, notification provided to employees, members, former employees, spouses, or former spouses under subdivisions (a) and (b) shall also include the following notification:

"Please examine your options carefully before declining this coverage. You should be aware that companies selling individual health insurance typically require a review of your medical history that could result in a higher premium or you could be denied coverage entirely." *(Added by Stats.1981, c. 1096, p. 4261, § 3, operative Jan. 1, 1983. Amended by Stats.1995, c. 489 (S.B.761), § 6; Stats.1996, c. 1118 (S.B.2043), § 15, eff. Sept. 30, 1996, operative Jan. 1, 1997; Stats.2005, c. 526 (A.B.356), § 8.)*

§ 2800.3. Availability of conversion coverage

Any employer, other than a self-insurer, employee association or other entity otherwise providing hospital, surgical or major medical benefits to its employees or members shall also make available conversion coverage which complies with the provisions of Part 6.1 (commencing with Section 12670) of Division 2 of the Insurance Code and Section 1373.6 of the Health and Safety Code. *(Added by Stats.1981, c. 1096, p. 4262, § 4, operative Jan. 1, 1983.)*

§ 2801. Employer's defenses to actions by employees

In any action to recover damages for a personal injury sustained within this State by an employee while engaged in the line of his duty or the course of his employment as such, or for death resulting from personal injury so sustained, in which recovery is sought upon the ground of want of ordinary or reasonable care of the employer, or of any officer, agent or servant of the employer, the fact that such employee has been guilty of contributory negligence shall not bar a recovery therein where his contributory negligence was slight and that of the employer was gross, in comparison, but the damages may be diminished by the jury in proportion to the amount of negligence attributable to such employee.

It shall be conclusively presumed that such employee was not guilty of contributory negligence in any case where the violation of any law enacted for the safety of employees contributed to such employee's injury.

It shall not be a defense that:

(a) The employee either expressly or impliedly assumed the risk of the hazard complained of.

(b) The injury or death was caused in whole or in part by the want of ordinary or reasonable care of a fellow servant.

No contract, or regulation, shall exempt the employer from any provisions of this section. *(Stats.1937, c. 90, p. 258, § 2801.)*

§ 2802. Indemnification for employee's expenses and losses in discharging duties; award interest; definition

(a) An employer shall indemnify his or her employee for all necessary expenditures or losses incurred by the employee in direct consequence of the discharge of his or her duties, or of his or her obedience to the directions of the employer, even though unlawful, unless the employee, at the time of obeying the directions, believed them to be unlawful.

(b) All awards made by a court or by the Division of Labor Standards Enforcement for reimbursement of necessary expenditures under this section shall carry interest at the same rate as judgments in civil actions. Interest shall accrue from the date on which the employee incurred the necessary expenditure or loss.

(c) For purposes of this section, the term "necessary expenditures or losses" shall include all reasonable costs, including, but not limited to, attorney's fees incurred by the employee enforcing the rights granted by this section. *(Stats.1937, c. 90, p. 258, § 2802. Amended by Stats.2000, c. 990 (S.B.1305), § 1.)*

§ 2803. Action by personal representative of deceased employee

When death, whether instantaneously or otherwise, results from an injury to an employee caused by the want of ordinary or reasonable care of an employer or of any officer, agent, a servant of the employer, the personal representative of such employee shall have a right of action therefor against such employer, and may recover damages in respect thereof, for and on behalf of the surviving spouse, children, dependent parents, and dependent brothers and sisters, in order of precedence as stated, but no more than one action shall be brought for such recovery. *(Stats.1937, c. 90, p. 258, § 2803. Amended by Stats.1976, c. 1171, p. 5258, § 22.)*

§ 2803.4. Employee Retirement Income Security Act of 1974; health benefits; Medi-Cal or medicaid benefits exception prohibited; third party liability

(a) Any employer providing health benefits under the Employee Retirement Income Security Act of 1974 (29 U.S.C. Sec. 1001, et seq.) shall not provide an exception for other coverage where the other coverage is entitlement to Medi-Cal benefits under Chapter 7 (commencing with Section 14000) or Chapter 8 (commencing with Section 14200) of Part 3 of Division 9 of the Welfare and Institutions Code, or medicaid benefits under Subchapter 19 (commencing with Section 1396) of Chapter 7 of Title 42 of the United States Code. Any employer providing health benefits under the Employee Retirement Income Security Act of 1974 shall not provide an exception for the Medi-Cal or medicaid benefits.

(b) Any employer providing health benefits under the Employee Retirement Income Security Act of 1974 shall not provide that the benefits payable are subject to reduction if the individual insured has entitlement to Medi-Cal or medicaid benefits.

(c) Any employer providing health benefits under the Employee Retirement Income Security Act of 1974 shall not provide an exception for enrollment for benefits because of an applicant's entitlement to Medi-Cal benefits under Chapter 7 (commencing with Section 14000) or Chapter 8 (commencing with Section 14200) of Part 3 of Division 9 of the Welfare and Institutions Code, or medicaid benefits under Subchapter 19 (commencing with Section 1396) of Chapter 7 of Title 42 of the United States Code.

(d) The State Department of Health Services shall consider health benefits available under the Employee Retirement Income Security Act of 1974 in determining legal liability of any third party for medical expenses incurred by a Medi-Cal or medicaid recipient under Section 14124.90 of the Welfare and Institutions Code and Subchapter 19 (commencing with Section 1396) of Chapter 7 of Title 42 of the United States Code. *(Added by Stats.1994, c. 147 (A.B.2377), § 16, eff. July 11, 1994.)*

§ 2803.5. Health care benefits; coverage of children

Any employer who offers health care coverage, including employers and insurers, shall comply with the standards set forth in Chapter 7 (commencing with Section 3750) of Part 1 of Division 9 of the Family Code and Section 14124.94 of the Welfare and Institutions Code. *(Added by Stats.1994, c. 147 (A.B.2377), § 17, eff. July 11, 1994. Amended by Stats.1996, c. 1062 (A.B.1832), § 28.)*

§ 2804. Invalidity of agreement waiving article provisions

Any contract or agreement, express or implied, made by any employee to waive the benefits of this article or any part thereof, is null and void, and this article shall not deprive any employee or his personal representative of any right or remedy to which he is entitled under the laws of this State. *(Stats.1937, c. 90, p. 259, § 2804.)*

§ 2806. Coverage for medical, surgical or hospital benefits; discontinuation; notice to employees

(a) No employer, whether private or public, shall discontinue coverage for medical, surgical, or hospital benefits for employees unless the employer has notified and advised all covered employees in writing of any discontinuation of coverage, inclusive of nonrenewal and cancellation, but not inclusive of employment termination or cases in which substitute coverage has been provided, at least 15 days in advance of such discontinuation.

(b) If coverage is provided by a third party, failure of the employer to give the necessary notice shall not require the third party to continue the coverage beyond the date it would otherwise terminate.

(c) This section shall not apply to any employee welfare benefit plan that is subject to the Employee Retirement Income Security Act of 1974. *(Added by Stats.1979, c. 222, p. 475, § 1. Amended by Stats.1992, c. 722 (S.B.485), § 8, eff. Sept. 15, 1992.)*

§ 2807. Notification to former employees of availability of continued medical, surgical, or hospital benefits

(a) All employers, whether private or public, shall provide notification to former employees, along with the notification required by federal law pursuant to the Consolidated Omnibus Budget Reconciliation Act of 1985 (Public Law 99–272), of the availability of continued coverage for medical, surgical, or hospital benefits, a standardized written description of the Health Insurance Premium Program established by the State Department of Health Services pursuant to Section 120835 of the Health and Safety Code and Section 14124.91 of the Welfare and Institutions Code. The employer shall utilize the standardized written description prepared by the State Department of Health Services pursuant to subdivision (b).

(b) The State Department of Health Services shall prepare and make available, on request, a standardized written description of the Health Insurance Premium Program, at cost. *(Added by Stats.1992, c. 722 (S.B.485), § 9, eff. Sept. 15, 1992. Amended by Stats.1996, c. 1023 (S.B.1497), § 381, eff. Sept. 29, 1996.)*

§ 2808. Description of benefit plan; provision to employees; notification of coverage options upon termination of employment

(a) It is the responsibility of all employers, whether public or private, to provide to all eligible employees an outline of coverage or similar explanation of all benefits provided under employer-sponsored health coverage, including, but not limited to, provider information for health maintenance organizations and preferred provider organizations.

(b) All employers, whether public or private, shall provide to employees, upon termination, notification of all continuation, disability extension, and conversion coverage options under any employer-sponsored coverage for which the employee may remain eligible after employment with that employer terminates. *(Added by Stats.1993, c. 1210 (A.B.1100), § 12.*

§ 2809. Employer-managed deferred compensation plans; pre-enrollment information; notice of financial risks; quarterly financial summaries; self-directed plans

(a) Any employer, whether private or public, that offers its employees an employer-managed deferred compensation plan shall provide to each employee, prior to the employee's enrollment in the plan, written notice of the reasonably foreseeable financial risks accompanying participation in the plan, historical information to date as to the performance of the investments or funds available under the plan, and an annual balance sheet, annual audit, or similar document that describes the employer's financial condition as of a date no earlier than the immediately preceding year.

(b) Within 30 days after the end of each quarter of the calendar year, the employer, who directly manages the investments of a deferred compensation plan, shall provide, to each employee enrolled in a deferred compensation plan offered by the employer, a written report summarizing the current financial condition of the employer, summarizing the financial performance during the preceding quarter of each investment or fund available under the plan, and describing the actual performance of the employee's funds that are invested in each investment or fund in the plan.

(c) The obligations described in subdivisions (a) and (b) may be performed by a plan manager designated by the employer, who may contract with an investment manager for that purpose.

(d) If an employee is enrolled in a deferred compensation plan that is self-directed through a financial institution, the requirements set forth in this section shall be deemed to have been met. *(Added by Stats.1996, c. 1160 (S.B.238), § 1.)*

§ 2810. Individuals contracting for labor or services with construction, farm labor, garment, janitorial or security guard contractors; necessity of funds sufficient to allow compliance with local, state and federal laws or regulations governing labor or services to be provided; rebuttable presumption; contents and copy of contract or agreement; violations and actions for damages

(a) A person or entity may not enter into a contract or agreement for labor or services with a construction, farm labor, garment, janitorial, or security guard contractor, where the person or entity knows or should know that the contract or agreement does not include funds sufficient to allow the contractor to comply with all applicable local, state, and federal laws or regulations governing the labor or services to be provided.

(b) There is a rebuttable presumption affecting the burden of proof that there has been no violation of subdivision (a) where the contract or agreement with a construction, farm labor, garment, janitorial, or security guard contractor meets all of the requirements in subdivision (d).

(c) Subdivision (a) does not apply to a person or entity who executes a collective bargaining agreement covering the workers employed under the contract or agreement, or to a person who enters into a contract or agreement for labor or services to be performed on his or her home residences, provided that a family member resides in the residence or residences for which the labor or services are to be performed for at least a part of the year.

(d) To meet the requirements of subdivision (b), a contract or agreement with a construction, farm labor, garment, janitorial, or security guard contractor for labor or services must be in writing, in a single document, and contain all of the following provisions, in addition to any other provisions that may be required by regulations adopted by the Labor Commissioner from time to time:

(1) The name, address, and telephone number of the person or entity and the construction, farm labor, garment, janitorial, or security guard contractor through whom the labor or services are to be provided.

(2) A description of the labor or services to be provided and a statement of when those services are to be commenced and completed.

(3) The employer identification number for state tax purposes of the construction, farm labor, garment, janitorial, or security guard contractor.

(4) The workers' compensation insurance policy number and the name, address, and telephone number of the insurance carrier of the construction, farm labor, garment, janitorial, or security guard contractor.

(5) The vehicle identification number of any vehicle that is owned by the construction, farm labor, garment, janitorial, or security guard contractor and used for transportation in connection with any service provided pursuant to the contract or agreement, the number of the vehicle liability insurance policy that covers the vehicle, and the name, address, and telephone number of the insurance carrier.

(6) The address of any real property to be used to house workers in connection with the contract or agreement.

(7) The total number of workers to be employed under the contract or agreement, the total amount of all wages to be paid, and the date or dates when those wages are to be paid.

(8) The amount of the commission or other payment made to the construction, farm labor, garment, janitorial, or security guard contractor for services under the contract or agreement.

(9) The total number of persons who will be utilized under the contract or agreement as independent contractors, along with a list of the current local, state, and federal contractor license identification numbers that the independent contractors are required to have under local, state, or federal laws or regulations.

(10) The signatures of all parties, and the date the contract or agreement was signed.

(e)(1) To qualify for the rebuttable presumption set forth in subdivision (b), a material change to the terms and conditions of a contract or agreement between a person or entity and a construction, farm labor, garment, janitorial, or security guard contractor must be in writing, in a single document, and contain all of the provisions listed in subdivision (d) that are affected by the change.

(2) If a provision required to be contained in a contract or agreement pursuant to paragraph (7) or (9) of subdivision (d) is unknown at the time the contract or agreement is executed, the best estimate available at that time is sufficient to satisfy the requirements of subdivision (d). If an estimate is used in place of actual figures in accordance with this paragraph, the parties to the contract or agreement have a continuing duty to ascertain the information required pursuant to paragraph (7) or (9) of subdivision (d) and to reduce that information to writing in accordance with the requirements of paragraph (1) once that information becomes known.

(f) A person or entity who enters into a contract or agreement referred to in subdivisions (d) or (e) shall keep a copy of the written contract or agreement for a period of not less than four years following the termination of the contract or agreement.

(g)(1) An employee aggrieved by a violation of subdivision (a) may file an action for damages to recover the greater of all of his or her actual damages or two hundred fifty dollars ($250) per employee per violation for an initial violation and one thousand dollars ($1,000) per employee for each subsequent violation, and, upon prevailing in an action brought pursuant to this section, may recover costs and reasonable attorney's fees. An action under this section may not be maintained unless it is pleaded and proved that an employee was injured as a result of a violation of a labor law or regulation in connection with the performance of the contract or agreement.

(2) An employee aggrieved by a violation of subdivision (a) may also bring an action for injunctive relief and, upon prevailing, may recover costs and reasonable attorney's fees.

(h) The phrase "construction, farm labor, garment, janitorial, or security guard contractor" includes any person, as defined in this code, whether or not licensed, who is acting in the capacity of a construction, farm labor, garment, janitorial, or security guard contractor.

(i)(1) The term "knows" includes the knowledge, arising from familiarity with the normal facts and circumstances of the business activity engaged in, that the contract or agreement does not include funds sufficient to allow the contractor to comply with applicable laws.

(2) The phrase "should know" includes the knowledge of any additional facts or information that would make a reasonably prudent person undertake to inquire whether, taken together, the contract or agreement contains sufficient funds to allow the contractor to comply with applicable laws.

(3) A failure by a person or entity to request or obtain any information from the contractor that is required by any applicable statute or by the contract or agreement between them, constitutes knowledge of that information for purposes of this section. *(Added by Stats.2003, c. 908 (S.B.179), § 1.)*

ARTICLE 3.   OBLIGATIONS OF EMPLOYEE

Section
2850.   Gratuitous service; performance; degree of care.
2851.   Service at own request; performance; relinquishment.
2852.   Written power of attorney; performance; notice of termination.
2853.   Service at own request for own advantage; degree of care.
2854.   Compensated service; degree of care.
2855.   Enforcement of contract to render personal service; time limit.
2856.   Compliance with employer's directions.
2857.   Conformance to usage of place of performance.
2858.   Degree of skill.
2859.   Use of skill possessed.
2860.   Ownership of things acquired by virtue of employment.
2861.   Accounts; notice of things received for account of employer.
2862.   Delivery of things received on account of employer.
2863.   Preference to performance of employer's business.
2864.   Liability for actions of substitute.
2865.   Liability for negligence; liability of employer for value of services rendered.
2866.   Joint services; performance by survivor.

§ 2850. Gratuitous service; performance; degree of care

One who, without consideration, undertakes to do a service for another, is not bound to perform the same but if he actually enters upon its performance, he shall use at least slight care and diligence therein. *(Stats.1937, c. 90, p. 259, § 2850.)*

§ 2851. Service at own request; performance; relinquishment

One who, by his own special request, induces another to intrust him with the performance of a service, shall perform the same fully. In other cases, one who undertakes a gratuitous service may relinquish it at any time. *(Stats.1937, c. 90, p. 259, § 2851.)*

§ 2852. Written power of attorney; performance; notice of termination

A gratuitous employee, who accepts a written power of attorney, shall act under it so long as it remains in force,

or until he gives notice to his employer that he will not do so. *(Stats.1937, c. 90, p. 259, § 2852.)*

§ 2853. Service at own request for own advantage; degree of care

One who is employed at his own request to do that which is more for his own advantage than for that of his employer, shall use great care and diligence therein to protect the interest of the employer. *(Stats.1937, c. 90, p. 259, § 2853.)*

§ 2854. Compensated service; degree of care

One who, for a good consideration, agrees to serve another, shall perform the service, and shall use ordinary care and diligence therein, so long as he is thus employed. *(Stats.1937, c. 90, p. 259, § 2854.)*

§ 2855. Enforcement of contract to render personal service; time limit

(a) Except as otherwise provided in subdivision (b), a contract to render personal service, other than a contract of apprenticeship as provided in Chapter 4 (commencing with Section 3070), may not be enforced against the employee beyond seven years from the commencement of service under it. Any contract, otherwise valid, to perform or render service of a special, unique, unusual, extraordinary, or intellectual character, which gives it peculiar value and the loss of which cannot be reasonably or adequately compensated in damages in an action at law, may nevertheless be enforced against the person contracting to render the service, for a term not to exceed seven years from the commencement of service under it. If the employee voluntarily continues to serve under it beyond that time, the contract may be referred to as affording a presumptive measure of the compensation.

(b) Notwithstanding subdivision (a):

(1) Any employee who is a party to a contract to render personal service in the production of phonorecords in which sounds are first fixed, as defined in Section 101 of Title 17 of the United States Code, may not invoke the provisions of subdivision (a) without first giving written notice to the employer in accordance with Section 1020 of the Code of Civil Procedure, specifying that the employee from and after a future date certain specified in the notice will no longer render service under the contract by reason of subdivision (a).

(2) Any party to a contract described in paragraph (1) shall have the right to recover damages for a breach of the contract occurring during its term in an action commenced during or after its term, but within the applicable period prescribed by law.

(3) If a party to a contract described in paragraph (1) is, or could contractually be, required to render personal service in the production of a specified quantity of the phonorecords and fails to render all of the required service prior to the date specified in the notice provided in paragraph (1), the party damaged by the failure shall have the right to recover damages for each phonorecord

as to which that party has failed to render service in an action that, notwithstanding paragraph (2), shall be commenced within 45 days after the date specified in the notice. *(Stats.1937, c. 90, p. 259, § 2855. Amended by Stats.1987, c. 591, § 1; Stats.2006, c. 538 (S.B.1852), § 487.)*

§ 2856. Compliance with employer's directions

An employee shall substantially comply with all the directions of his employer concerning the service on which he is engaged, except where such obedience is impossible or unlawful, or would impose new and unreasonable burdens upon the employee. *(Stats.1937, c. 90, p. 259, § 2856.)*

§ 2857. Conformance to usage of place of performance

An employee shall perform his service in conformity to the usage of the place of performance, unless otherwise directed by his employer, or unless it is impracticable or manifestly injurious to his employer to do so. *(Stats. 1937, c. 90, p. 260, § 2857.)*

§ 2858. Degree of skill

An employee is bound to exercise a reasonable degree of skill, unless his employer has notice, before employing him, of his want of skill. *(Stats.1937, c. 90, p. 260, § 2858.)*

§ 2859. Use of skill possessed

An employee is always bound to use such skill as he possesses, so far as the same is required, for the service specified. *(Stats.1937, c. 90, p. 260, § 2859.)*

§ 2860. Ownership of things acquired by virtue of employment

Everything which an employee acquires by virtue of his employment, except the compensation which is due to him from his employer, belongs to the employer, whether acquired lawfully or unlawfully, or during or after the expiration of the term of his employment. *(Stats.1937, c. 90, p. 260, § 2860.)*

§ 2861. Accounts; notice of things received for account of employer

An employee shall, on demand, render to his employer just accounts of all his transactions in the course of his service, as often as is reasonable, and shall, without demand, give prompt notice to his employer of everything which he receives for the account of the employer. *(Stats.1937, c. 90, p. 260, § 2861.)*

§ 2862. Delivery of things received on account of employer

An employee who receives anything on account of his employer, in any capacity other than that of a mere servant, is not bound to deliver it to the employer until demanded, and is not at liberty to send it to the employer from a distance, without demand, in any mode involving greater risk than its retention by the employee himself. *(Stats.1937, c. 90, p. 260, § 2862.)*

§ 2863. Preference to performance of employer's business

An employee who has any business to transact on his own account, similar to that intrusted to him by his employer, shall always give the preference to the business of the employer. *(Stats.1937, c. 90, p. 260, § 2863.)*

§ 2864. Liability for actions of substitute

An employee who is expressly authorized to employ a substitute is liable to his principal only for want of ordinary care in his selection. The substitute is directly responsible to the principal. *(Stats.1937, c. 90, p. 260, § 2864.)*

§ 2865. Liability for negligence; liability of employer for value of services rendered

An employee who is guilty of a culpable degree of negligence is liable to his employer for the damage thereby caused to the employer. The employer is liable to the employee if the service is not gratuitous, for the value of the services only as are properly rendered. *(Stats.1937, c. 90, p. 260, § 2865.)*

§ 2866. Joint services; performance by survivor

Where service is to be rendered by two or more persons jointly, and one of them dies, the survivor shall act alone, if the service to be rendered is such as he can rightly perform without the aid of the deceased person, but not otherwise. *(Stats.1937, c. 90, p. 260, § 2866.)*

ARTICLE 3.5. INVENTIONS MADE BY AN EMPLOYEE

Section
2870. Employment agreements; assignment of rights.
2871. Conditions of employment or continued employment; disclosure of inventions.
2872. Notice to employee; burden of proof.

§ 2870. Employment agreements; assignment of rights

(a) Any provision in an employment agreement which provides that an employee shall assign, or offer to assign, any of his or her rights in an invention to his or her employer shall not apply to an invention that the employee developed entirely on his or her own time without using the employer's equipment, supplies, facilities, or trade secret information except for those inventions that either:

(1) Relate at the time of conception or reduction to practice of the invention to the employer's business, or actual or demonstrably anticipated research or development of the employer; or

(2) Result from any work performed by the employee for the employer.

(b) To the extent a provision in an employment agreement purports to require an employee to assign an

505

invention otherwise excluded from being required to be assigned under subdivision (a), the provision is against the public policy of this state and is unenforceable. *(Added by Stats.1979, c. 1001, p. 3401, § 1. Amended by Stats.1986, c. 346, § 1; Stats.1991, c. 647 (S.B.879), § 5.)*

§ 2871. Conditions of employment or continued employment; disclosure of inventions

No employer shall require a provision made void and unenforceable by Section 2870 as a condition of employment or continued employment. Nothing in this article shall be construed to forbid or restrict the right of an employer to provide in contracts of employment for disclosure, provided that any such disclosures be received in confidence, of all of the employee's inventions made solely or jointly with others during the term of his or her employment, a review process by the employer to determine such issues as may arise, and for full title to certain patents and inventions to be in the United States, as required by contracts between the employer and the United States or any of its agencies. *(Added by Stats. 1979, c. 1001, p. 3401, § 1.)*

§ 2872. Notice to employee; burden of proof

If an employment agreement entered into after January 1, 1980, contains a provision requiring the employee to assign or offer to assign any of his or her rights in any invention to his or her employer, the employer must also, at the time the agreement is made, provide a written notification to the employee that the agreement does not apply to an invention which qualifies fully under the provisions of Section 2870. In any suit or action arising thereunder, the burden of proof shall be on the employee claiming the benefits of its provisions. *(Added by Stats. 1979, c. 1001, p. 3401, § 1.)*

ARTICLE 4. TERMINATION OF EMPLOYMENT

Section
2920. Events terminating employment.
2921. Notice of death or incapacity of employer.
2922. Termination at will upon notice; employment for a specified term.
2923. Continuation of service after notice of death or incapacity of employer; compensation for service.
2924. Employment for a specified term; grounds for termination by employer.
2925. Employment for specified term; grounds for termination by employee.
2926. Compensation for services rendered to time of dismissal.
2927. Compensation for services rendered to time of quitting.
2928. Deductions for tardiness of employee.
2929. Garnishment and wages defined; prohibition against discharge for threat of garnishment for payment of one judgment.

§ 2920. Events terminating employment

Every employment is terminated by any of the following:

(a) Expiration of its appointed term.

(b) Extinction of its subject.

(c) Death of the employee.

(d) The employee's legal incapacity to act as such. *(Stats.1937, c. 90, p. 260, § 2920.)*

§ 2921. Notice of death or incapacity of employer

Every employment in which the power of the employee is not coupled with an interest in its subject is terminated by notice to the employee of either of the following:

(a) The death of the employer.

(b) The legal incapacity of the employer to contract. *(Stats.1937, c. 90, p. 261, § 2921.)*

§ 2922. Termination at will upon notice; employment for a specified term

An employment, having no specified term, may be terminated at the will of either party on notice to the other. Employment for a specified term means an employment for a period greater than one month. *(Stats.1937, c. 90, p. 261, § 2922. Amended by Stats.1969, c. 1529, p. 3123, § 2; Stats.1971, c. 1580, p. 3186, § 1; Stats.1971, c. 1607, p. 3459, § 2.)*

§ 2923. Continuation of service after notice of death or incapacity of employer; compensation for service

An employee, unless the term of his service has expired or unless he has a right to discontinue it at any time without notice, shall continue his service after notice of the death or incapacity of his employer, so far as is necessary to protect from serious injury the interests of the employer's successor in interest, until a reasonable time after notice of the facts has been communicated to such successor. The successor shall compensate the employee for such service according to the terms of the contract of employment. *(Stats.1937, c. 90, p. 261, § 2923.)*

§ 2924. Employment for a specified term; grounds for termination by employer

An employment for a specified term may be terminated at any time by the employer in case of any willful breach of duty by the employee in the course of his employment, or in case of his habitual neglect of his duty or continued incapacity to perform it. *(Stats.1937, c. 90, p. 261, § 2924. Amended by Stats.1969, c. 1529, p. 3123, § 3; Stats.1971, c. 1580, p. 3186, § 2; Stats.1971, c. 1607, p. 3460, § 3.)*

§ 2925. Employment for specified term; grounds for termination by employee

An employment for a specified term may be terminated by the employee at any time in case of any wilful or permanent breach of the obligations of his employer to him as an employee. *(Stats.1937, c. 90, p. 261, § 2925.)*

§ 2926. Compensation for services rendered to time of dismissal

An employee who is not employed for a specified term and who is dismissed by his employer is entitled to compensation for services rendered up to the time of such dismissal. *(Stats.1937, c. 90, p. 261, § 2926.)*

§ 2927. Compensation for services rendered to time of quitting

An employee who is not employed for a specified term and who quits the service of his employer is entitled to compensation for services rendered up to the time of such quitting. *(Stats.1937, c. 90, p. 261, § 2927.)*

§ 2928. Deductions for tardiness of employee

No deduction from the wages of an employee on account of his coming late to work shall be made in excess of the proportionate wage which would have been earned during the time actually lost, but for a loss of time less than thirty minutes, a half hour's wage may be deducted. *(Stats.1937, c. 90, p. 261, § 2928.)*

§ 2929. Garnishment and wages defined; prohibition against discharge for threat of garnishment for payment of one judgment

(a) As used in this section:

(1) "Garnishment" means any judicial procedure through which the wages of an employee are required to be withheld for the payment of any debt.

(2) "Wages" has the same meaning as that term has under Section 200.

(b) No employer may discharge any employee by reason of the fact that the garnishment of his wages has been threatened. No employer may discharge any employee by reason of the fact that his wages have been subjected to garnishment for the payment of one judgment. A provision of a contract of employment that provides an employee with less protection than is provided by this subdivision is against public policy and void.

(c) Unless the employee has greater rights under the contract of employment, the wages of an employee who is discharged in violation of this section shall continue until reinstatement notwithstanding such discharge, but such wages shall not continue for more than 30 days and shall not exceed the amount of wages earned during the 30 calendar days immediately preceding the date of the levy of execution upon the employee's wages which resulted in his discharge. The employee shall give notice to his employer of his intention to make a wage claim under this subdivision within 30 days after being discharged; and, if he desires to have the Labor Commissioner take an assignment of his wage claim, the employee shall file a wage claim with the Labor Commissioner within 60 days after being discharged. The Labor Commissioner may, in his discretion, take assignment of wage claims under this subdivision as provided for in Section 96. A discharged employee shall not be permitted to recover wages under this subdivision if a criminal prosecution based on the same discharge has been commenced for violation of Section 304 of the Consumer Credit Protection Act of 1968 (15 U.S.C. Sec. 1674).

(d) Nothing in this section affects any other rights the employee may have against his employer.

(e) This section is intended to aid in the enforcement of the prohibition against discharge for garnishment of earnings provided in the Consumer Credit Protection Act of 1968 (15 U.S.C. Secs. 1671–1677) and shall be interpreted and applied in a manner which is consistent with the corresponding provisions of such act. *(Added by Stats.1971, c. 1607, p. 3460, § 4.)*

ARTICLE 5. INVESTIGATIONS OF EMPLOYEES

Section
2930. Discipline or discharge on basis of shopping investigator's report; copy to employee; exemption.

§ 2930. Discipline or discharge on basis of shopping investigator's report; copy to employee; exemption

(a) Any employer who disciplines or discharges an employee on the basis of a shopping investigator's report of the employee's conduct, performance, or honesty performed by a person licensed pursuant to Chapter 11 (commencing with Section 7500) of Division 3 of the Business and Professions Code shall provide the employee with a copy of the investigation report prior to discharging or disciplining the employee. Where an interview occurs which might result in the termination of an employee for dishonesty, the employee shall be handed a copy of the latest investigation report on which the interview was based during the course of the interview prior to its conclusion. This section shall not be applicable if the licensee conducting the investigation is employed exclusively and regularly by one employer in connection with the affairs of only that employer and where there exists an employer-employee relationship and the entire investigation is conducted solely for such employer by such licensee.

(b) For purposes of this section, a "shopping investigator" is a person who: shops in commercial, retail, and service establishments to test integrity of sales, warehouse, stockroom, and service personnel, and evaluates sales techniques and services rendered customers; reviews an establishment's policies and standards to ascertain employee performance requirements; buys merchandise, orders food, or utilizes services to evaluate sales technique and courtesy of employees, carries merchandise to check stand or sales counter and observes employees during sales transaction to detect irregularities in listing or calling prices, itemizing merchandise, or handling cash; or delivers purchases to an agency conducting shopping investigation service; and, following any one or more of the above activities, writes a report of investigations for each establishment visited. *(Added by Stats.1978, c. 1252, p. 4070, § 4. Amended by Stats.1980, c. 370, p. 739, § 1.)*

CHAPTER 3. MASTER AND SERVANT [REPEALED]

CHAPTER 4. APPRENTICESHIP

Section

3070. Apprenticeship council; composition; appointment; terms; compensation; traveling expenses.

3071. Report on activities of division and council; contents.

3072. Administrator of apprenticeship; appointment of assistants; labor compliance program enforcement actions; appeal; penalties.

3073. Chief of division of apprenticeship standards; duties.

3073.1. Random audits; reports.

3073.2. Adoption of industry-specific training criteria for apprenticeship programs; audits.

3073.3. Legislative intent with respect to women and ethnic minorities in apprenticeship programs.

3073.5. Report to legislature and public on activities of division and council.

3074. Duties of state and local boards for vocational education; payment of excess costs; instruction of isolated apprentices; application of equal opportunity.

3074.1. Availability of programs; information.

3074.3. Recognition of registration in apprenticeship programs.

3074.7. Fees.

3075. Apprenticeship programs; administration; necessary conditions.

3075.1. Apprenticeship as form of on-the-job training.

3076. Function of committees.

3076.3. Program sponsors; duties.

3076.5. Veteran applicants; additional credit.

3077. Apprentice and apprenticeship agreement defined; term of apprenticeship.

3077.5. Maximum age for apprentices.

3078. Apprenticeship agreement; required provisions.

3079. Approval and execution of agreement; agreement binding during majority of apprentice.

3080. Execution of agreement by employers' association and employees' organizations; required provisions.

3081. Investigation of violation of agreements; hearings.

3082. Appeal of administrator's determination to council.

3083. Decision of council; effect.

3084. Judicial review of questions of law.

3084.5. Injunction.

3085. Prerequisites to actions on agreement; exhaustion of administrative remedies.

3086. Collective bargaining agreements establishing apprenticeship standards.

3088. Severability of chapter provisions.

3089. Title of chapter.

3090. Applications for apprenticeship and on-the-job training; contracts with federal agencies.

3091. Acceptance into apprenticeship training program predicated on payment of fee.

3091.5. Sale of instructional material; special deposit fund account.

3092. Apprenticeship term credit for successful graduation from specified training program.

3093. On-the-job training programs.

3095. Discrimination as misdemeanor; penalty.

3097. Provision of services to employment development department; use of funds.

Section

3098. Employment as apprentice; employers that are party to apprenticeship agreement or standards.

3099. Electrician competency and training standards.

3099.2. Persons who perform work as electricians; certification requirements and categories; additional grounds for discipline.

3099.3. Duties of the Division of Apprenticeship Standards.

3099.4. On-the-job experience for certification; requirements.

3099.5. Electrician Certification Fund.

§ 3070. Apprenticeship council; composition; appointment; terms; compensation; traveling expenses

There is in the Division of Apprenticeship Standards the California Apprenticeship Council, which shall be appointed by the Governor, composed of six representatives each from employers or employer organizations and employee organizations, that sponsor apprenticeship programs under this chapter, respectively, geographically selected, and of two representatives of the general public. The Director of Industrial Relations, or his or her permanent and best qualified designee, and the Superintendent of Public Instruction, or his or her permanent and best qualified designee, and the Chancellor of the California Community Colleges, or his or her permanent and best qualified designee, shall also be members of the California Apprenticeship Council. The chairperson shall be elected by vote of the California Apprenticeship Council. Beginning with appointments in 1985, three representatives each of employers and employees, and one public representative shall serve until January 15, 1989. In 1987, three representatives each of the employers and employees, and one public representative shall serve until January 15, 1991. Any member whose term expires on January 15, 1986, shall continue to serve until January 15, 1987. Thereafter each member shall serve for a term of four years. Any member appointed to fill a vacancy occurring prior to the expiration of the term of his or her predecessor shall be appointed for the remainder of that term. Each member of the council shall receive the sum of one hundred dollars ($100) for each day of actual attendance at meetings of the council, for each day of actual attendance at hearings by the council or a committee thereof pursuant to Section 3082, and for each day of actual attendance at meetings of other committees established by the council and approved by the Director of Industrial Relations, together with his or her actual and necessary traveling expenses incurred in connection therewith. *(Added by Stats.1939, c. 220, p. 1472, § 2. Amended by Stats.1941, c. 974, p. 2611, § 1; Stats.1943, c. 513, p. 2057, § 1; Stats.1955, c. 1137, p. 2129, § 1; Stats.1969, c. 313, p. 680, § 1; Stats.1969, c. 460, p. 1023, § 9; Stats.1969, c. 1360, p. 2750, § 5; Stats.1976, c. 301, p. 609, § 2; Stats.1980, c. 1165, p. 3917, § 3; Stats.1984, c. 834, § 1; Stats.1999, c. 903 (A.B.921), § 4.)*

§ 3071. Report on activities of division and council; contents

The California Apprenticeship Council shall meet at the call of the Director of Industrial Relations and shall aid him or her in formulating policies for the effective administration of this chapter.

Thereafter, the California Apprenticeship Council shall meet quarterly at a designated date and special meetings may be held at the call of the chairman. The California Apprenticeship Council shall issue rules and regulations which establish standards for minimum wages, maximum hours, and working conditions for apprentice agreements, hereinafter in this chapter referred to as apprenticeship standards, which in no case shall be lower than those prescribed by this chapter; and shall issue rules and regulations governing equal opportunities in apprenticeship, affirmative action programs which include women and minorities in apprenticeship, and other on-the-job training, and criteria for selection procedures with a view particularly toward eliminating criteria not relevant to qualification for training employment or more stringent than is reasonably necessary.   *(Added by Stats.1939, c. 220, p. 1472, § 2. Amended by Stats.1967, c. 1704, p. 4264, § 1; Stats.1968, c. 1346, p. 2565, § 1; Stats.1969, c. 313, p. 681, § 2, Stats.1973, c. 1206, p. 2615, § 37; Stats.1973, c. 1207, p. 2665, § 37; Stats.1976, c. 1179, p. 5279, § 4, eff. Sept. 22, 1976; Stats.1984, c. 330, § 1; Stats.1985, c. 272, § 1; Stats.1991, c. 269 (S.B.411), § 1.)*

§ 3072. Administrator of apprenticeship; appointment of assistants; labor compliance program enforcement actions; appeal; penalties

(a) The Director of Industrial Relations is ex officio the Administrator of Apprenticeship and is authorized to appoint * * * assistants as * * * necessary to effectuate the purposes of this chapter.

(b) An awarding body, as defined in Section 1722, that implements an approved labor compliance program pursuant to subdivision (b) of Section 1771.5 may, upon mutual agreement with the Chief of the Division of Apprenticeship Standards and at his or her discretion, assist the director in the enforcement of Section 1777.5 through the operation of that approved labor compliance program under the terms and conditions prescribed by the Chief of the Division of Apprenticeship Standards.

(c) A contractor may appeal the result of a labor compliance program enforcement action related to Section 1777.5 through the procedures described in Section 1777.7.

(d) If the involvement of the Chief of the Division of Apprenticeship Standards in a labor compliance program enforcement action is limited to a review of an assessment and the matter is resolved without litigation by or against the chief, the awarding body that has implemented the labor compliance program shall enforce any applicable penalties, as specified in Section 1777.7, and shall deposit any penalties and forfeitures collected in its general fund.   *(Added by Stats.1939, c. 220, p. 1473, § 2. Amended by Stats.2009, c. 438 (A.B.395), § 1.)*

§ 3073. Chief of division of apprenticeship standards; duties

The Chief of the Division of Apprenticeship Standards, or his or her duly authorized representative, shall administer the provisions of this chapter; act as secretary of the California Apprenticeship Council; shall foster, promote, and develop the welfare of the apprentice and industry, improve the working conditions of apprentices, and advance their opportunities for profitable employment; shall ensure that selection procedures are impartially administered to all applicants for apprenticeship; shall gather and promptly disseminate information through apprenticeship and training information centers; shall maintain on public file in all high schools and field offices of the Employment Development Department the name and location of the local area apprenticeship committees, the filing date, and minimum requirements for application of all registered apprenticeship programs; shall cooperate in the development of apprenticeship programs and may advise with them on problems affecting apprenticeship standards; shall audit all selection and disciplinary proceedings of apprentices or prospective apprentices; may enter joint agreements with the Employment Development Department outreach education and employment programs, and educational institutions on the operation of apprenticeship information centers, including positive efforts to achieve information on equal opportunity and affirmative action programs for women and minorities; and shall supervise and recommend apprenticeship agreements as to these standards and perform such other duties associated therewith as the California Apprenticeship Council may recommend. The chief shall coordinate the exchange, by the California Apprenticeship Council, the apprenticeship program sponsors, the Fair Employment and Housing Commission, community organizations, and other interested persons, of information on available minorities and women who may serve as apprentices.   *(Added by Stats.1939, c. 220, p. 1473, § 2. Amended by Stats.1969, c. 313, p. 681, § 3; Stats.1976, c. 1179, p. 5280, § 5, eff. Sept. 22, 1976; Stats.1984, c. 316, § 1; Stats.1985, c. 272, § 2.)*

§ 3073.1. Random audits; reports

(a) The division shall randomly audit apprenticeship programs approved under this chapter during each five-year period commencing January 1, 2000, to ensure that the program is complying with its standards, that all on-the-job training is performed by journeymen, that all related and supplemental instruction required by the apprenticeship standards is being provided, that all work processes in the apprenticeship standards are being covered, and that graduates have completed the apprenticeship program's requirements. The division shall examine each apprenticeship program to determine whether apprentices are graduating from the program on schedule or dropping out and to determine whether

509

graduates of the program have obtained employment as journeymen. Every apprenticeship program sponsor shall have a duty to cooperate with the division in conducting an audit.

(b) Audit reports shall be presented to the California Apprenticeship Council and shall be made public, except that the division shall not make public information which would infringe on the privacy of individual apprentices. The division shall recommend remedial action to correct deficiencies recognized in the audit report, and the failure to correct deficiencies within a reasonable period of time shall be grounds for withdrawing state approval of a program. Nothing shall prevent the division from conducting more frequent audits of apprenticeship programs where deficiencies have been identified.

(c) The division shall give priority in conducting audits to programs that have been identified as having deficiencies. The division may conduct simplified audits for programs with fewer than five registered apprentices. *(Added by Stats.1999, c. 903 (A.B.921), § 5.)*

§ 3073.2. Adoption of industry-specific training criteria for apprenticeship programs; audits

(a) The California Apprenticeship Council may adopt industry-specific training criteria for use by apprenticeship programs subject to the requirements of this chapter. The adoption of those criteria, as established following notice and a workshop pursuant to Section 212.01 of Title 8 of the California Code of Regulations, is not subject to Chapter 3.5 (commencing with Section 11340) of Division 3 of Title 2 of the Government Code.

(b) Audits conducted by the division pursuant to Section 3073.1 shall ensure that any applicable training criteria established pursuant to this section are followed.

(c) This section shall remain in effect only until January 1, 2012, and as of that date is repealed, unless a later enacted statute, that is enacted before January 1, 2012, deletes or extends that date. *(Added by Stats.2003, c. 842 (A.B.1028), § 1. Amended by Stats.2006, c. 828 (A.B.2907), § 3.)*

Repeal

For repeal of this section, see its terms.

§ 3073.3. Legislative intent with respect to women and ethnic minorities in apprenticeship programs

It is the intent of the Legislature that the Department of Industrial Relations will encourage greater participation for women and ethnic minorities in apprenticeship programs. *(Added by Stats.2003, c. 842 (A.B.1028), § 2.)*

§ 3073.5. Report to legislature and public on activities of division and council

The Chief of the Division of Apprenticeship Standards and the California Apprenticeship Council shall annually report through the Director of Industrial Relations to the Legislature and the public on the activities of the division

and the council. The report shall contain information including, but not limited to, analyses of the following:

(a) The number of individuals, including numbers of women and minorities, registered in apprenticeship programs in this state for the current year and in each of the previous five years.

(b) The number and percentage of apprentices, including numbers and percentages of minorities and women, registered in each apprenticeship program having five or more apprentices, and the percentage of those apprentices who have completed their programs successfully in the current year and in each of the previous five years.

(c) Remedial actions taken by the division to assist those apprenticeship programs having difficulty in achieving affirmative action goals or having very low completion rates.

(d) The number of disputed issues with respect to individual apprenticeship agreements submitted to the Administrator of Apprenticeship for determination and the number of those issues resolved by the council on appeal.

(e) The number of apprenticeship program applications received by the division, the number approved, the number denied and the reason for those denials, the number being reviewed, and deficiencies, if any, with respect to those program applications being reviewed.

(f) The number of apprenticeship programs, approved by the Division of Apprenticeship Standards, that are disapproved by the California Apprenticeship Council, and the reasons for those disapprovals. *(Added by Stats.1991, c. 269 (S.B.411), § 2. Amended by Stats.1991, c. 806 (A.B.386), § 1.)*

§ 3074. Duties of state and local boards for vocational education; payment of excess costs; instruction of isolated apprentices; application of equal opportunity

The preparation of trade analyses and development of curriculum for instruction, and the administration and supervision of related and supplemental instruction for apprentices, coordination of instruction with job experiences, and the selection and training of teachers and coordinators for this instruction shall be the responsibility of, and shall be provided by, state and local boards responsible for vocational education upon agreement with the program sponsor. This responsibility shall not preclude the establishment of off-campus related and supplemental instruction when approved, developed, and operated in cooperation with state and local school boards responsible for vocational education, and when the instruction meets all other requirements of this chapter. It is the intent of this chapter that the instruction shall be made available to apprentices through classroom instruction, correspondence courses, self-study or other means of instruction approved by state and local public education agencies authorized to provide vocational education.

Pursuant to this chapter all excess costs incurred by local public education agencies exceeding state apportionments and local revenue earned by the attendance of apprentices shall be payable by the program sponsor, upon joint agreement between the sponsor and the local education agency. The State Board of Education and the Board of Governors of the California Community Colleges, and the Division of Apprenticeship Standards shall jointly issue regulations regarding calculation and payment provisions of excess costs to be borne by the program sponsors. All funds accrued by local education agencies from attendance in apprenticeship classes authorized by this section shall be expended or allocated for all such classes offered by the local education agency before excess costs may be claimed.

The Department of Education and the Board of Governors of the California Community Colleges may provide related and supplemental instruction to isolated apprentices as a direct instructional service, on a contractual basis with local school districts, by correspondence, or by a combination of these means. For the purpose of this section, an isolated apprentice is an apprentice registered with the Division of Apprenticeship Standards in the Department of Industrial Relations who cannot be enrolled in a class of related and supplementary instruction for apprentices because of the small number of apprentices available for an appropriate class or because there is no existing apprenticeship program within a reasonable travel distance.

Interested parties may file a complaint in accordance with Section 201 of Title 8 of the Administrative Code, when a community college or secondary education district is unable to reach agreement with program sponsors in providing related and supplemental instruction. In the process of securing an amicable adjustment, the administrator, or his or her representative, shall meet with the parties involved, including, but not limited to, the chancellor, or his or her representative, or the Superintendent of Public Instruction, or his or her representative.

Community colleges, and other public school districts, shall refuse to provide related and supplemental instruction to an apprenticeship program when it is determined by the Administrator of Apprenticeship that the program sponsor has been found to be in noncompliance with the State of California Plan for Equal Opportunity in Apprenticeship. *(Added by Stats.1939, c. 220, p. 1473, § 2. Amended by Stats.1963, c. 1561, p. 3144, § 1; Stats.1969, c. 1360, p. 2748, § 2; Stats.1971, c. 1046, p. 2002, § 1; Stats.1972, c. 1389, p. 2886, § 1; Stats.1975, c. 1051, p. 2485, § 1; Stats.1984, c. 330, § 2.)*

§ 3074.1. Availability of programs; information

In compliance with the affirmative action requirements of California's plan for equal opportunity in apprenticeship, school districts maintaining high schools, community colleges districts, and apprenticeship program sponsors, shall provide students with information as to the availability of apprenticeship programs. *(Added by Stats.1976, c. 1175, p. 5272, § 1.)*

§ 3074.3. Recognition of registration in apprenticeship programs

In providing related and supplemental instruction pursuant to Section 3074, and notwithstanding any provisions of the Education Code, the Superintendent of Public Instruction and the Chancellor of the California Community Colleges shall recognize registration in an apprenticeship program approved by the Division of Apprenticeship Standards in the Department of Industrial Relations as an acceptable prerequisite to enrollment into such related and supplemental classes. *(Added by Stats.1976, c. 1179, p. 5280, § 5.5, eff. Sept. 22, 1976. Amended by Stats.1984, c. 285, §1.)*

§ 3074.7. Fees

Notwithstanding any other provision of law, the governing board of a school district which offers classroom instruction in postgraduate and upgrading courses pursuant to subdivision (d) of Section 3093 of this code may impose a fee upon individuals receiving instruction in such postgraduate and upgrading courses. Such fee shall be not more than the amount necessary, as determined by the governing board, to cover the total cost of all such classroom instruction given the individuals. *(Added by Stats.1968, c. 961, p. 1847, § 2.)*

§ 3075. Apprenticeship programs; administration; necessary conditions

(a) An apprenticeship program may be administered by a joint apprenticeship committee, unilateral management or labor apprenticeship committee, or an individual employer. Programs may be approved by the chief in any trade in the state or in a city or trade area, whenever the apprentice training needs justify the establishment. Where a collective bargaining agreement exists, a program shall be jointly sponsored unless either party to the agreement waives its right to representation in writing. Joint apprenticeship committees shall be composed of an equal number of employer and employee representatives.

(b) For purposes of this section, the apprentice training needs in the building and construction trades shall be deemed to justify the approval of a new apprenticeship program only if any of the following conditions are met:

(1) There is no existing apprenticeship program approved under this chapter serving the same craft or trade and geographic area.

(2) Existing apprenticeship programs approved under this chapter that serve the same craft or trade and geographic area do not have the capacity, or neglect or refuse, to dispatch sufficient apprentices to qualified employers at a public works site who are willing to abide by the applicable apprenticeship standards.

(3) Existing apprenticeship programs approved under this chapter that serve the same trade and geographic area have been identified by the California Apprentice-

511

ship Council as deficient in meeting their obligations under this chapter.

(c) Notwithstanding subdivision (b), the California Apprenticeship Council may approve a new apprenticeship program if special circumstances, as established by regulation, justify the establishment of the program. *(Added by Stats.1939, c. 220, p. 1473, § 2. Amended by Stats.1976, c. 1179, p. 5281, § 6, eff. Sept. 22, 1976; Stats.1984, c. 330, § 3; Stats.1999, c. 903 (A.B.921), § 7.)*

§ 3075.1. Apprenticeship as form of on-the-job training

It is the public policy of this state to encourage the utilization of apprenticeship as a form of on-the-job training, when such training is cost-effective in developing skills needed to perform public services. State and local public agencies shall make a diligent effort to establish apprenticeship programs for apprenticeable occupations in their respective work forces. In furtherance of this policy, public agencies shall take into consideration (a) the extent to which a continuous supply of trained personnel is readily available to public agencies to meet their skill requirements in the various occupations which are determined to be apprenticeable, and (b) the application of established programs in the private sector, where appropriate. Public sector apprenticeship programs should be fully compatible with affirmative action goals for the participation of minorities and women in apprenticeship programs. *(Added by Stats.1976, c. 1179, p. 5281, § 7, eff. Sept. 22, 1976.)*

§ 3076. Function of committees

The function of a joint apprenticeship committee, when specific written authority is delegated by the parent organizations represented, shall be to establish work processes, wage rates, working conditions for apprentices, the number of apprentices which shall be employed in the trade under apprentice agreements, and aid in the adjustment of apprenticeship disputes in accordance with standards for apprenticeship set up by the California Apprenticeship Council. Disciplinary proceedings resulting from disputes shall be duly noticed to the involved individuals. *(Added by Stats.1939, c. 220, p. 1473, § 2. Amended by Stats.1963, c. 89, p. 718, § 1; Stats.1968, c. 1346, p. 2566, § 2; Stats.1969, c. 313, p. 681, § 4; Stats.1976, c. 1179, p. 5281, § 8, eff. Sept. 22, 1976; Stats.1984, c. 330, § 4; Stats.1985, c. 272, § 3.)*

§ 3076.3. Program sponsors; duties

Program sponsors shall establish selection procedures which specify minimum requirements for formal education or equivalency, physical examination, if any, subject matter of written tests and oral interviews, and any other criteria pertinent to the selection process; shall specify the relative weights of all factors which determine selection to an apprenticeship program; shall submit in writing to the chief an official statement of each selection procedure including the filing date and location of the program sponsor; shall make a copy of the selection procedures available to each applicant; shall provide in writing to each applicant not selected an official explanation setting forth the reason or reasons for the nonselection, copies of which shall be retained as a public record in the files of the program sponsor for a period of five years; and shall implement affirmative action programs for minorities and women in accordance with the rules, regulations, and guidelines of the California Apprenticeship Council. *(Added by Stats.1984, c. 330, § 4.5.)*

§ 3076.5. Veteran applicants; additional credit

A program sponsor may provide in its selection procedures for an additional 10 points credit in the selection of veteran applicants for apprenticeship.

"Veteran," as used in this section, means a veteran who has served in the armed forces of this country for at least 181 consecutive days since January 31, 1955, and who has been discharged or released under conditions other than dishonorable, but does not include any person who served only in auxiliary or reserve components of the armed forces whose services therein did not exempt him or her from the operation of the Selective Training and Service Act of 1940 (54 Stat. 885). *(Added by Stats.1974, c. 618, p. 1466, § 1, eff. Sept. 5, 1974. Amended by Stats.1984, c. 330, § 5.)*

§ 3077. Apprentice and apprenticeship agreement defined; term of apprenticeship

The term "apprentice" as used in this chapter, means a person at least 16 years of age who has entered into a written agreement, in this chapter called an "apprentice agreement," with an employer or program sponsor. The term of apprenticeship for each apprenticeable occupation shall be approved by the chief, and in no case shall provide for less than 2,000 hours of reasonably continuous employment for such person and for his or her participation in an approved program of training through employment and through education in related and supplemental subjects. *(Added by Stats.1939, c. 220, p. 1473, § 2. Amended by Stats.1951, c. 1074, p. 2804, § 1; Stats.1984, c. 330, § 6.)*

§ 3077.5. Maximum age for apprentices

A program sponsor administering an apprenticeship program under this chapter shall not provide a maximum age for apprentices. *(Added by Stats.1967, c. 1611, p. 3853, § 1. Amended by Stats.1968, c. 1123, p. 2139, § 1; Stats.1976, c. 1179, p. 5282, § 9, eff. Sept. 22, 1976; Stats.1984, c. 330, § 7.)*

§ 3078. Apprenticeship agreement; required provisions

Every apprentice agreement entered into under this chapter shall directly, or by reference, contain:

(a) The names of the contracting parties.

(b) The date of birth of the apprentice.

(c) A statement of the trade, craft, or business which the apprentice is to be taught, and the time at which the apprenticeship will begin and end.

(d) A statement showing the number of hours to be spent by the apprentice in work and the learning objectives to be accomplished through related and supplemental instruction, except as otherwise provided under Section 3074. These exceptions shall be subject to the appeal procedures established in Sections 3081, 3082, 3083, and 3084. A minimum of 144 hours of related and supplemental instruction for each year of apprenticeship is recommended; however, related instruction may be expressed in terms of units or other objectives to be accomplished. In no case shall the combined weekly hours of work and required related and supplemental instruction of the apprentice exceed the maximum number of hours of work prescribed by law for a person of the age of the apprentice.

(e) A statement setting forth a schedule of the processes in the trade or industry divisions in which the apprentice is to be taught and the approximate time to be spent at each process.

(f) A statement of the graduated scale of wages to be paid the apprentice and whether the required schooltime shall be compensated.

(g) A statement providing for a period of probation of not more than 1,000 hours of employment and not more than 72 hours of related instruction, during which time the apprentice agreement may be terminated by the program sponsor at the request in writing of either party, and providing that after the probationary period the apprentice agreement may be terminated by the administrator by mutual agreement of all parties thereto, or canceled by the administrator for good and sufficient reason.

(h) A provision that all controversies or differences concerning the apprentice agreement which cannot be adjusted locally, or which are not covered by collective-bargaining agreement, shall be submitted to the administrator for determination as provided for in Section 3081.

(i) A provision that an employer who is unable to fulfill his or her obligation under the apprentice agreement may, with approval of the administrator, transfer the contract to any other employer if the apprentice consents and the other employer agrees to assume the obligation of the apprentice agreement.

(j) Such additional terms and conditions as may be prescribed or approved by the California Apprenticeship Council, not inconsistent with the provisions of this chapter.

(k) A clause providing that there shall be no liability on the part of the other contracting party for an injury sustained by an apprentice engaged in schoolwork at a time when the employment of the apprentice has been temporarily or permanently terminated. (Added by Stats. 1939, c. 220, p. 1473, § 2. Amended by Stats.1963, c. 125, p. 798, § 1; Stats.1969, c. 313, p. 682, § 5; Stats.1975, c. 1051, p. 2486, § 2; Stats.1976, c. 301, p. 610, § 4; Stats.1984, c. 330, § 8.)

§ 3079. Approval and execution of agreement; agreement binding during majority of apprentice

Every apprentice agreement under this chapter shall be approved by the local joint apprenticeship committee or the parties to a collective bargaining agreement or, subject to review by the council, by the administrator where there is no collective bargaining agreement or joint committee, a copy of which shall be filed with the California Apprenticeship Council. Every apprentice agreement shall be signed by the employer, or his or her agent, or by a program sponsor, as provided in Section 3080, and by the apprentice, and if the apprentice is a minor, by the minor's parent or guardian. Where a minor enters into an apprentice agreement under this chapter for a period of training extending into his or her majority, the apprentice agreement shall likewise be binding for such a period as may be covered during the apprentice's majority. (Added by Stats.1939, c. 220, p. 1474, § 2. Amended by Stats.1947, c. 821, p. 1946, § 1; Stats.1969, c. 313, p. 683, § 6; Stats.1984, c. 330, § 9.)

§ 3080. Execution of agreement by employers' association and employees' organizations; required provisions

(a) For the purpose of providing greater diversity of training or continuity of employment, any apprentice agreement made under this chapter may in the discretion of the California Apprenticeship Council be signed by an association of employers or an organization of employees instead of by an individual employer. In that case, the apprentice agreement shall expressly provide that the association of employers or organization of employees does not assume the obligation of an employer but agrees to use its best endeavors to procure employment and training for an apprentice with one or more employers who will accept full responsibility, as herein provided, for all the terms and conditions of employment and training set forth in the agreement between the apprentice and employer association or employee organization during the period of the apprentice's employment. The apprentice agreement shall also expressly provide for the transfer of the apprentice, subject to the approval of the California Apprenticeship Council, to an employer or employers who shall sign a written agreement with the apprentice, and if the apprentice is a minor, with the apprentice's parent or guardian, as specified in Section 3079, contracting to employ the apprentice for the whole or a definite part of the total period of apprenticeship under the terms and conditions of employment and training set forth in the apprentice agreement.

(b) All apprenticeship programs with more than one employer or an association of employers shall include provisions sufficient to ensure meaningful representation of the interests of apprentices in the management of the program. (Added by Stats.1939, c. 220, p. 1475, § 2. Amended by Stats.1969, c. 313, p. 683, § 7; Stats.1984, c. 330, § 10; Stats.1999, c. 903 (A.B.921), § 8.)

§ 3081.   Investigation of violation of agreements; hearings

Upon the complaint of any interested person or upon his own initiative, the administrator may investigate to determine if there has been a violation of the terms of an apprentice agreement, made under this chapter, and he may hold hearings, inquiries, and other proceedings necessary to such investigations and determinations. The parties to such agreement shall be given a fair and impartial hearing, after reasonable notice thereof. All such hearings, investigations and determinations shall be made under authority of reasonable rules and procedures prescribed by the California Apprenticeship Council. *(Added by Stats.1939, c. 220, p. 1475, § 2. Amended by Stats.1969, c. 313, p. 684, § 8.)*

§ 3082.   Appeal of administrator's determination to council

The determination of the administrator shall be filed with the California Apprenticeship Council. If no appeal therefrom is filed with the California Apprenticeship Council within 10 days from the date the parties are given notification of the determination, in accordance with Section 1013a and Section 2015.5 of the Code of Civil Procedure, the determination shall become the order of the California Apprenticeship Council. Any person aggrieved by the determination or action of the administrator may appeal therefrom to the California Apprenticeship Council, which shall review the entire record and may hold a hearing thereon after due notice to the interested parties. *(Added by Stats.1939, c. 220, p. 1475, § 2. Amended by Stats.1969, c. 313, p. 684, § 9; Stats. 1984, c. 370, § 1.)*

§ 3083.   Decision of council; effect

The decision of the California Apprenticeship Council as to the facts shall be conclusive if supported by the evidence and all orders and decisions of the California Apprenticeship Council shall be prima facie lawful and reasonable. *(Added by Stats.1939, c. 220, p. 1476, § 2. Amended by Stats.1969, c. 313, p. 684, § 10.)*

§ 3084.   Judicial review of questions of law

Any party to an apprentice agreement aggrieved by an order or decision of the California Apprenticeship Council may maintain appropriate proceedings in the courts on questions of law. The decision of the California Apprenticeship Council shall be conclusive if the proceeding is not filed within 30 days after the date the aggrieved party is given notification of the decision. *(Added by Stats. 1939, c. 220, p. 1476, § 2. Amended by Stats.1969, c. 313, p. 684, § 11; Stats.1984, c. 370, § 2.)*

§ 3084.5.   Injunction

In any case in which a person or persons have willfully violated any of the laws, regulations, or orders governing applicants for apprenticeship or apprentices registered under this chapter, the Division of Apprenticeship Standards may obtain in a court of competent jurisdiction, an injunction against any further violations of any such laws, regulations, or orders by such person or persons. *(Added by Stats.1970, c. 1504, p. 2989, § 1.)*

§ 3085.   Prerequisites to actions on agreement; exhaustion of administrative remedies

No person shall institute any action for the enforcement of any apprentice agreement, or damages for the breach of any apprentice agreement, made under this chapter, unless he shall first have exhausted all administrative remedies provided by this chapter. *(Added by Stats.1939, c. 220, p. 1476, § 2.)*

§ 3086.   Collective bargaining agreements establishing apprenticeship standards

Nothing in this chapter or in any apprentice agreement approved under this chapter shall operate to invalidate any apprenticeship provision in any collective agreement between employers and employees setting up higher apprenticeship standards. *(Added by Stats.1939, c. 220, p. 1476, § 2.)*

§ 3088.   Severability of chapter provisions

If any provision of this chapter or the application thereof to any person or circumstances is held invalid, the remainder of the chapter and the application of such provision to other persons and circumstances, shall not be affected thereby. *(Added by Stats.1939, c. 220, p. 1476, § 2.)*

§ 3089.   Title of chapter

This chapter shall be known and may be cited as the Shelley-Maloney Apprentice Labor Standards Act of 1939. *(Added by Stats.1939, c. 220, p. 1476, § 2.)*

§ 3090.   Applications for apprenticeship and on-the-job training; contracts with federal agencies

The Division of Apprenticeship Standards shall investigate, approve or reject applications from establishments for apprenticeship and other on-the-job training, and for that purpose, may cooperate, or contract with, and receive reimbursements from the appropriate agencies of the Federal Government. *(Added by Stats.1947, c. 42, p. 528, § 1.)*

§ 3091.   Acceptance into apprenticeship training program predicated on payment of fee

Acceptance of an application for entrance into an apprenticeship training program shall not be predicated on the payment of any fee. Reasonable costs for expense incurred may be charged after an applicant has been accepted into the program. *(Added by Stats.1968, c. 1124, p. 2139, § 1.)*

§ 3091.5.   Sale of instructional material; special deposit fund account

Pursuant to Section 16370 of the Government Code, there is hereby authorized in the State Treasury a Special Deposit Fund Account, which shall consist of moneys collected from the sale of instructional material to persons enrolled in any apprenticeship training program under this chapter. All of the moneys collected are hereby appropriated without regard to fiscal year for the support of the Department of Education to be used for the development and production of apprenticeship instructional material. *(Added by Stats.1985, c. 1546, § 19.)*

§ 3092. Apprenticeship term credit for successful graduation from specified training program

A successful graduate of a training program in a particular apprenticeable occupation of a vocational education program meeting the standards of the California State Plan for Vocational Education may receive credit toward a term of apprenticeship if the program is jointly established and approved by a school district, a county superintendent of schools, a public entity conducting a regional occupational center or program, or a private postsecondary vocational school accredited by a regional or national accrediting agency recognized by the United States Office of Education and the program sponsor of the particular apprenticeable occupation. *(Added by Stats.1976, c. 1262, p. 5595, § 1. Amended by Stats.1984, c. 330, § 11.)*

§ 3093. On-the-job training programs

(a) This section applies only when voluntarily requested by the parties to a collective bargaining agreement or by an employer, his or her association, or a union, or its representative where there is no collective bargaining agreement.

(b) Nothing in this section may be construed in any way so as to compel, regulate, interfere with, or duplicate the provisions of any established training programs which are operated under the terms of any collective bargaining agreements or unilaterally by any employer or bona fide labor union.

(c) Services contemplated under this section may be provided only when voluntarily requested and shall be denied when it is found that existing prevailing conditions in the area and industry would in any way be lowered or adversely affected.

(d) The California Apprenticeship Council in cooperation with the Department of Education, the Employment Development Department, and the Board of Governors of the California Community Colleges may foster and promote on-the-job training programs other than apprenticeship as follows: (1) programs for journeymen in the apprenticeable occupations to keep them abreast of current techniques, methods, and materials and opportunities for advancement in their industries; (2) programs in other than apprenticeable occupations for workers entering the labor market for the first time or workers entering new occupations by reason of having been displaced from former occupations by reason of economic, industrial, technological scientific changes, or developments; (3) the programs shall be in accord with and agreed to by the parties to any applicable collective

bargaining agreements and where appropriate will include joint employer-employee cooperation in the programs.

(e) The Division of Apprenticeship Standards when requested may foster and promote voluntary on-the-job training programs in accordance with this section, and assist employers, employees and other interested persons and agencies in the development and carrying out of the programs. The Division of Apprenticeship Standards shall cooperate in these functions with the Department of Education, the Employment Development Department, and the Board of Governors of the California Community Colleges and other governmental agencies. The Division of Apprenticeship Standards may cooperate with the Department of Corrections and the Department of the Youth Authority in the development of training programs for inmates and releasees of correctional institutions.

(f) The programs, where appropriate, may include related and supplemental classroom instruction offered and administered by state and local boards responsible for vocational education.

(g) The activities and services of the Division of Apprenticeship Standards in training programs under this section shall be performed without curtailing or in any way interfering with the division's activities and services in apprenticeship.

(h) The Division of Apprenticeship Standards may contract with, and receive reimbursements from, appropriate federal, state, and other governmental agencies.

(i) The vocational education activities and services of the Department of Education, the Board of Governors of the California Community Colleges, and local public school districts shall not be abridged or abrogated through implementation of this section.

(j) "On-the-job training" as used in this section refers exclusively to training confined to the needs of a specific occupation and conducted at the jobsite for employed workers.

(k) "Journeyman," as used in this section, means a person who has either (1) completed an accredited apprenticeship in his craft, or (2) who has completed the equivalent of an apprenticeship in length and content of work experience and all other requirements in the apprenticeship standards for the craft which has workers classified as journeymen in an apprenticeable occupation.

(*l*) Nothing in this section shall be construed to require prior approval, ratification, or reference of any training program to the Division of Apprenticeship Standards or the Department of Industrial Relations. *(Added by Stats.1961, c. 1892, p. 3990, § 1. Amended by Stats.1969, c. 1360, p. 2748, § 4; Stats.1981, c. 714, p. 2720, § 315.)*

§ 3095. Discrimination as misdemeanor; penalty

Every person who willfully discriminates in any recruitment or apprenticeship program on any basis listed in subdivision (a) of Section 12940 of the Government

Code, as those bases are defined in Sections 12926 and 12926.1 of the Government Code, except as otherwise provided in Section 12940 of the Government Code, is guilty of a misdemeanor punishable by a fine of not more than one thousand dollars ($1,000) or by imprisonment for not more than six months, or both. *(Added by Stats.1965, c. 1449, p. 3398, § 1. Amended by Stats.1967, c. 325, p. 1520, § 1; Stats.1967, c. 1593, p. 3821, § 3; Stats.1971, c. 280, p. 586, § 2; Stats.2004, c. 788 (A.B. 2900), § 16.)*

§ 3097. Provision of services to employment development department; use of funds

The Department of Industrial Relations, Division of Apprenticeship Standards, may cooperate in the provision of, or provide, services to the Employment Development Department, and to service delivery areas, as designated pursuant to the Job Training Partnership Act (P.L. 97–300,[1] and Division 8 commencing with Section 15000 of the Unemployment Insurance Code). The Department of Industrial Relations, Division of Apprenticeship Standards may enter into any agreements as may be necessary for this purpose.

The Division of Apprenticeship Standards shall exert maximum effort to persuade sponsors of its registered, nonfederally funded, voluntary apprenticeship and on-the-job training programs to accept to the maximum possible extent the eligible persons as described in the Job Training Partnership Act (P.L. 97–300) and Division 8 (commencing with Section 15000) of the Unemployment Insurance Code. *(Added by Stats.1968, c. 1460, p. 2905, § 10. Amended by Stats.1981, c. 714, p. 2721, § 316; Stats.1985, c. 351, § 1.)*

[1] 29 U.S.C.A. § 1501 et seq.

§ 3098. Employment as apprentice; employers that are party to apprenticeship agreement or standards

An apprentice registered in an approved apprenticeship program in any of the building and construction trades shall be employed only as an apprentice when performing any construction work for an employer that is a party, individually or through an employer association, to any apprenticeship agreement or standards covering that individual. *(Added by Stats.1999, c. 903 (A.B.921), § 9.)*

§ 3099. Electrician competency and training standards

(a) The Division of Apprenticeship Standards shall do all of the following:

(1) On or before July 1, 2001, establish and validate minimum standards for the competency and training of electricians through a system of testing and certification.

(2) On or before March 1, 2000, establish an advisory committee and panels as necessary to carry out the functions under this section. There shall be contractor representation from both joint apprenticeship programs and unilateral nonunion programs in the electrical contracting industry.

(3) On or before July 1, 2001, establish fees necessary to implement this section.

(4) On or before July 1, 2001, establish and adopt regulations to enforce this section.

(5) Issue certification cards to electricians who have been certified pursuant to this section. Fees collected pursuant to paragraph (3) are continuously appropriated in an amount sufficient to pay the costs of issuing certification cards, and that amount may be expended for that purpose by the division.

(6) On or before July 1, 2003, establish an electrical certification curriculum committee comprised of representatives of the State Department of Education, the California Community Colleges, and the division. The electrical certification curriculum committee shall do all of the following:

(A) Establish written educational curriculum standards for enrollees in training programs established pursuant to Section 3099.4.

(B) If an educational provider's curriculum meets the written educational curriculum standards established in accordance with subparagraph (A), designate that curriculum as an approved curriculum of classroom instruction.

(C) At the committee's discretion, review the approved curriculum of classroom instruction of any designated educational provider. The committee may withdraw its approval of the curriculum if the educational provider does not continue to meet the established written educational curriculum standards.

(D) Require each designated educational provider to submit an annual notice to the committee stating whether the educational provider is continuing to offer the approved curriculum of classroom instruction and whether any material changes have been made to the curriculum since its approval.

(b) There shall be no discrimination for or against any person based on membership or nonmembership in a union.

(c) As used in this section, "electricians" includes all persons who engage in the connection of electrical devices for electrical contractors licensed pursuant to Section 7058 of the Business and Professions Code, specifically, contractors classified as electrical contractors in the Contractors' State License Board Rules and Regulations. This section does not apply to electrical connections under 100 volt-amperes. This section does not apply to persons performing work to which Section 7042.5 of the Business and Professions Code is applicable, or to electrical work ordinarily and customarily performed by stationary engineers. This section does not apply to electrical work in connection with the installation, operation, or maintenance of temporary or portable electrical equipment performed by technicians in the theatrical, motion picture production, television, hotel, exhibition, or trade show industries. *(Added by Stats. 1999, c. 781 (A.B.931), § 1. Amended by Stats.2000, c. 875 (A.B.2481), § 3; Stats.2002, c. 48 (A.B.1087), § 1;*

Stats.2004, c. 183 (A.B.3082), § 262; Stats.2006, c. 828 (A.B.2907), § 4.)

§ 3099.2. Persons who perform work as electricians; certification requirements and categories; additional grounds for discipline

(a)(1) Persons who perform work as electricians shall become certified pursuant to Section 3099 by the deadline specified in this subdivision. After the applicable deadline, uncertified persons shall not perform electrical work for which certification is required.

(2) The deadline for certification as a general electrician or fire/life safety technician is January 1, 2006, except that persons who applied for certification prior to January 1, 2006, have until January 1, 2007, to pass the certification examination. The deadline for certification as a residential electrician is January 1, 2007, and the deadline for certification as a voice data video technician or a nonresidential lighting technician is January 1, 2008. The California Apprenticeship Council may extend the certification date for any of these three categories of electricians up to January 1, 2009, if the council concludes that the existing deadline will not provide persons sufficient time to obtain certification, enroll in an apprenticeship or training program, or register pursuant to Section 3099.4.

(3) For purposes of any continuing education or recertification requirement, individuals who become certified prior to the deadline for certification shall be treated as having become certified on the first anniversary of their certification date that falls after the certification deadline.

(b)(1) Certification is required only for those persons who perform work as electricians for contractors licensed as class C–10 electrical contractors under the Contractors' State License Board Rules and Regulations.

(2) Certification is not required for persons performing work for contractors licensed as class C–7 low voltage systems or class C–45 electric sign contractors as long as the work performed is within the scope of the class C–7 or class C–45 license, including incidental and supplemental work as defined in Section 7059 of the Business and Professions Code, and regardless of whether the same contractor is also licensed as a class C–10 contractor.

(3) Certification is not required for work performed by a worker on a high-voltage electrical transmission or distribution system owned by a local publicly owned electric utility, as defined in Section 224.3 of the Public Utilities Code; an electrical corporation, as defined in Section 218 of the Public Utilities Code; a person, as defined in Section 205 of the Public Utilities Code; or a corporation, as defined in Section 204 of the Public Utilities Code; when the worker is employed by the utility or a licensed contractor principally engaged in installing or maintaining transmission or distribution systems.

(c) The division shall establish separate certifications for general electrician, fire/life safety technician, residential electrician, voice data video technician, and nonresidential lighting technician.

(d) Notwithstanding subdivision (a), certification is not required for registered apprentices performing electrical work as part of an apprenticeship program approved under this chapter, a federal Office of Apprenticeship program, or a state apprenticeship program authorized by the federal Office of Apprenticeship. An apprentice who is within one year of completion of his or her term of apprenticeship shall be permitted to take the certification examination and, upon passing the examination, shall be certified immediately upon completion of the term of apprenticeship.

(e) Notwithstanding subdivision (a), certification is not required for any person employed pursuant to Section 3099.4.

(f) Notwithstanding subdivision (a), certification is not required for a nonresidential lighting trainee (1) who is enrolled in an on-the-job instructional training program approved by the Chief of the Division of Apprenticeship Standards pursuant to Section 3090, and (2) who is under the onsite supervision of a nonresidential lighting technician certified pursuant to Section 3099.

(g) Notwithstanding subdivision (a), the qualifying person for a class C–10 electrical contractor license issued by the Contractors' State License Board need not also be certified pursuant to Section 3099 to perform electrical work for that licensed contractor or to supervise an uncertified person employed by that licensed contractor pursuant to Section 3099.4.

(h) Commencing July 1, 2009, the following shall constitute additional grounds for disciplinary proceedings, including suspension or revocation of the license of a class C–10 electrical contractor pursuant to Article 7 (commencing with Section 7090) of Chapter 9 of Division 3 of the Business and Professions Code.

(1) The contractor willfully employs one or more uncertified persons to perform work as electricians in violation of this section.

(2) The contractor willfully fails to provide the adequate supervision of uncertified workers required by paragraph (3) of subdivision (a) of Section 3099.4.

(3) The contractor willfully fails to provide adequate supervision of apprentices performing work pursuant to subdivision (d).

(i) The Chief of the Division of Apprenticeship Standards shall develop a process for referring cases to the Contractors' State License Board when it has been determined that a violation of this section has likely occurred. On or before July 1, 2009, the chief shall prepare and execute a memorandum of understanding with the Registrar of Contractors in furtherance of this section.

(j) Upon receipt of a referral by the Chief of the Division of Apprenticeship Standards alleging a violation under this section, the Registrar of Contractors shall open an investigation. Any disciplinary action against the licensee shall be initiated within 60 days of the receipt of the referral. The Registrar of Contractors may initiate disciplinary action against any licensee upon his or her own investigation, the filing of any complaint, or any finding that results from a referral from the Chief of the Division of Apprenticeship Standards alleging a violation under this section. Failure of the employer or employee to provide evidence of certification or trainee status shall create a rebuttable presumption of violation of this provision.

(k) For the purposes of this section, "electricians" has the same meaning as the definition set forth in Section 3099. *(Added by Stats.2002, c. 48 (A.B.1087), § 2. Amended by Stats.2003, c. 884 (A.B.1719), § 2; Stats. 2006, c. 828 (A.B.2907), § 5; Stats.2008, c. 558 (A.B. 3048), § 1; Stats.2008, c. 716 (S.B.1362), § 2.5.)*

§ 3099.3. Duties of the Division of Apprenticeship Standards

The Division of Apprenticeship Standards shall do all of the following:

(a) Make information about electrician certification available in non-English languages spoken by a substantial number of construction workers, as defined in Section 7296.2 of the Government Code.

(b) Provide for the administration of certification tests in Spanish and, to the extent practicable, other non-English languages spoken by a substantial number of applicants, as defined in Section 7296.2 of the Government Code, except insofar as the ability to understand warning signs, instructions, and certain other information in English is necessary for safety reasons.

(c) Ensure, in conjunction with the California Apprenticeship Council, that by no later than January 1, 2003, all electrician apprenticeship programs approved under this chapter that impose minimum formal education requirements as a condition of entry provide for reasonable alternative means of satisfying those requirements.

(d) Ensure, in conjunction with the California Apprenticeship Council, that by no later than January 1, 2003, all electrician apprenticeship programs approved under this chapter have adopted reasonable procedures for granting credit toward a term of apprenticeship for other vocational training and on-the-job training experience.

(e) Report to the Legislature, prior to the deadline for individuals to become certified, on the status of electrician certification, including all of the following:

(1) The number of persons who have been certified pursuant to Section 3099.

(2) The number of persons enrolled in electrician apprenticeship programs.

(3) The number of persons who have registered pursuant to Section 3099.4.

(4) The estimated number of individuals performing work for Class C–10 electrical contractors for which

certification will be required after the deadline for certification, who have not yet been certified and are not enrolled in apprenticeship programs or registered pursuant to Section 3099.4.

(5) Whether enforcement of the deadline for certification will cause a shortage of electricians in California.

(6) Whether persons who wish to become certified electricians will have an adequate opportunity to pass the certification exam, to register pursuant to Section 3099.4, or to enroll in an apprenticeship program prior to the deadline for certification. *(Added by Stats.2002, c. 48 (A.B.1087), § 3. Amended by Stats.2003, c. 62 (S.B.600), § 206; Stats.2003, c. 884 (A.B.1719), § 3; Stats.2005, c. 22 (S.B.1108), § 142.)*

§ 3099.4. On-the-job experience for certification; requirements

(a) After the deadline for certification, an uncertified person may perform electrical work for which certification is required under Section 3099 in order to acquire the necessary on-the-job experience for certification, if all of the following requirements are met:

(1) The person is registered with the Division of Apprenticeship Standards. A list of current registrants shall be maintained by the division and made available to the public upon request.

(2) The person either has completed or is enrolled in an approved curriculum of classroom instruction.

(3) The employer attests that the person shall be under the direct supervision of an electrician certified pursuant to Section 3099 who is responsible for supervising no more than one uncertified person. An employer who is found by the division to have failed to provide adequate supervision may be barred by the division from employing uncertified individuals pursuant to this section in the future.

(b) For purposes of this section, an "approved curriculum of classroom instruction" means a curriculum of classroom instruction approved by the electrician certification curriculum committee established pursuant to paragraph (6) of subdivision (a) of Section 3099 and provided under the jurisdiction of the State Department of Education, the Board of Governors of the California Community Colleges, or the Bureau for Private Postsecondary and Vocational Education.

(c) The curriculum committee may grant approval to an educational provider that presently offers only a partial curriculum if the educational provider intends in the future to offer, or to cooperate with other educational providers to offer, a complete curriculum for the type of certification involved. The curriculum committee may require an educational provider receiving approval for a partial curriculum to periodically renew its approval with the curriculum committee until a complete curriculum is offered and approved. A partial curriculum means a combination of classes that do not include all classroom educational components of the complete curriculum for one of the categories of certification established in accordance with subdivision (c) of Section 3099.2.

(d) An educational provider that receives approval for a partial curriculum must disclose in all communications to students and to the public that the educational provider has only received approval for a partial curriculum and shall not make any representations that the provider offers a complete approved curriculum of classroom instruction as established by subparagraph (A) of paragraph (6) of subdivision (a) of Section 3099.

(e) For purposes of this section, a person is "enrolled" in an approved curriculum of classroom instruction if the person is attending classes on a full-time or part-time basis toward the completion of an approved curriculum.

(f) Registration under this section shall be renewed annually and the registrant shall provide to the division certification of the classwork completed and on-the-job experience acquired since the prior registration.

(g) For purposes of verifying the information provided by a person registered with the division, an educational provider of an approved curriculum of classroom instruction shall, upon the division's request, provide the division with information regarding the enrollment status and instruction completed by a person registered. By registering with the division in accordance with this section, a person consents to the release of this information.

(h) The division shall establish registration fees necessary to implement this section, not to exceed twenty-five dollars ($25) for the initial registration. There shall be no fee for annual renewal of registration. Fees collected are continuously appropriated in an amount sufficient to administer this section and that amount may be expended by the division for this purpose.

(i) The division shall issue regulations to implement this section.

(j) For purposes of Section 1773, persons employed pursuant to this section do not constitute a separate craft, classification, or type of worker.

(k) Notwithstanding any other provision of law, an uncertified person who has completed an approved curriculum of classroom instruction and is currently registered with the division may take the certification examination. The person shall be certified upon passing the examination and satisfactorily completing the requisite number of on-the-job hours required for certification. A person who passes the examination prior to completing the requisite hours of on-the-job experience shall continue to comply with subdivision (f). *(Added by Stats.2002, c. 48 (A.B.1087), § 4. Amended by Stats.2003, c. 884 (A.B.1719), § 4; Stats.2006, c. 828 (A.B.2907), § 6.)*

§ 3099.5. Electrician Certification Fund

(a) The Electrician Certification Fund is hereby created as a special account in the State Treasury. Proceeds of the fund may be expended by the department, upon appropriation by the Legislature, for the costs of the Division of Apprenticeship Standards program to validate and certify electricians as provided by Section 3099, and shall not be used for any other purpose.

(b) The fund shall consist of the fees collected pursuant to Section 3099. *(Added by Stats.2000, c. 127 (A.B.2866), § 25, eff. July 10, 2000.)*

Division 4

WORKERS' COMPENSATION AND INSURANCE

Part		Section
1.	Scope and Operation	3200
2.	Computation of Compensation	4451
3.	Compensation Claims	4900
3.2.	Workers' Compensation Health Care Provider Organization Act [Repealed]	
3.5.	Arbitration	5270
4.	Compensation Proceedings	5300

Chapter		Section
9.	Economic Opportunity Programs	4201
10.	Disaster Service Workers	4351
10.5	Disaster Service Workers [Renumbered]	
11.	Asbestos Workers' Account	4401

Part 1

SCOPE AND OPERATION

Chapter		Section
1.	General Provisions	3200
2.	Employers, Employees, and Dependents	3300
3.	Conditions of Compensation Liability	3600
4.	Compensation Insurance and Security	3700
5.	Subrogation of Employer	3850
6.	Hospital Inspection	3950
7.	Medical Examinations	4050
8.	Election to be Subject to Compensation Liability	4150

CHAPTER 1. GENERAL PROVISIONS

Section	
3200.	Workmen's compensation as meaning workers' compensation; legislative intent.
3201.	Legislative declaration.
3201.5.	Collective bargaining agreements; construction; construction maintenance; other specified activities.
3201.7.	Labor-management agreements; permissible subjects.
3201.81.	Collective bargaining agreements; authorized negotiating organization.
3201.9.	Reports to include updated loss experience participating in specified programs.
3202.	Liberal construction.

519

LABOR CODE

Section

3202.5. Construction as to burden of proof; preponderance of the evidence.

3203. Employment in interstate commerce.

3204. Definitions.

3205. Division.

3205.5. Appeals board.

3206. Administrative director.

3207. Compensation.

3208. Injury.

3208.05. Injury; bloodborne disease; preventive care to health care worker; documentation; human immunodeficiency virus.

3208.1. Specific or cumulative injuries.

3208.2. Two or more injuries; separate determination of questions of fact and law.

3208.3. Psychiatric injuries; compensability; employment conditions; notice of termination or layoff; prevention programs; inmates.

3208.4. Injuries arising out of alleged sexual harassment, sexual assault, or sexual battery; discovery; evidence.

3209. Damages.

3209.3. Physician; psychologist; acupuncturist.

3209.4. Optometrists.

3209.5. Medical, surgical, and hospital treatment.

3209.6. Chiropractors.

3209.7. Treatment of injuries; agreement.

3209.8. Treatment by marriage, family and child counselors, and clinical social workers.

3209.9. Acupuncturist; representation as physician or surgeon with M.D. or D.O. degree.

3209.10. Provision of medical treatment for work-related injury by physician assistant or nurse practitioner; authority of the same to cosign report and to authorize time off from work for injuries.

3210. Person.

3211. Insurer.

3211.5. "Firefighter", "Firefighting member" and "Member of a fire department" defined.

3211.9. Disaster council.

3211.91. Accredited disaster council.

3211.92. Disaster service worker.

3211.93. Disaster service.

3211.93a. Disaster service; exclusion of activities for which disaster council receives fee.

3212. Members of sheriff's office or California Highway Patrol, district attorney's staff of inspectors and investigators or of police or fire departments; injury; inclusion of hernia, heart trouble and pneumonia.

3212.1. Active firefighters and peace officers; injury; inclusion of cancer; presumption.

3212.2. Injury; custodial, supervisory and security officers and employees; inclusion of heart trouble.

3212.3. Injury; peace officers of Department of California Highway Patrol.

3212.4. Injury; inclusion of heart trouble, hernia and pneumonia; member defined.

3212.5. Injury; inclusion of heart trouble and pneumonia; members defined.

3212.6. Members of police department, sheriff's office, California Highway Patrol or inspector or investigator in district attorney's office, etc.; injury; inclusion of tuberculosis; applicant testing.

Section

3212.7. Injury; inclusion of heart trouble, hernia, pneumonia or tuberculosis.

3212.8. Members of sheriff's office, police or fire departments, etc.; injury; inclusion of blood-borne infectious disease or methicillin-resistant Staphylococcus aureus skin infection.

3212.85. Peace officers and fire department members; injury; inclusion of exposure to biochemical substances; compensation; presumption that injury arose out of, and in course of, employment; definitions.

3212.9. Members of police department, sheriff's office, California Highway Patrol, or county probation officer or inspector or investigator in a district attorney's office, etc.; injury; inclusion of meningitis.

3212.10. Injury; member of Department of Corrections, officer or employee of Department of Youth Authority, and peace officers; inclusion of heart trouble, hernia, pneumonia, tuberculosis and meningitis; presumption.

3212.11. Lifeguards; skin cancer that develops or manifests itself during period of employment; compensation awarded for injury; months employed; rebuttable presumption.

3212.12. Peace officers, corpsmembers, and conservation corps employees; Lyme disease; compensation; presumption.

3213. Injury; University of California police department, police academy graduates; inclusion of heart trouble and pneumonia.

3213.2. Lower back impairments; law enforcement personnel.

3214. Early intervention program; policy and implementation; services; costs.

3215. Referral of clients or patients for compensation; penalty.

3217. Construction of referral provisions; violation of multiple provisions; sentence; exemptions.

3218. Violations of § 3215; penalties.

3219. Compensation, inducements or rewards given to adjuster of claims for the referral or settlement of a claim; offense; void contracts; fees and compensation.

§ 3200. Workmen's compensation as meaning workers' compensation; legislative intent

The Legislature hereby declares its intent that the term "workmen's compensation" shall hereafter also be known as "workers' compensation," and that the "Workmen's Compensation Appeals Board" shall hereafter be known as the "Workers' Compensation Appeals Board." In furtherance of this policy it is the desire of the Legislature that references to the terms "workmen's compensation" and "Workmen's Compensation Appeals Board" in this code or elsewhere be changed to "workers' compensation" and "Workers' Compensation Appeals Board" when such laws are being amended for any purpose. This act is declaratory and not amendatory of existing law. *(Added by Stats.1974, c. 1454, p. 3177, § 11. Amended by Stats.1981, c. 21, p. 46, § 5, eff. April 18, 1981.)*

520

§ 3201. Legislative declaration

This division and Division 5 (commencing with Section 6300) are an expression of the police power and are intended to make effective and apply to a complete system of workers' compensation the provisions of Section 4 of Article XIV of the California Constitution. *(Stats.1937, c. 90, p. 265, § 3201. Amended by Stats. 1984, c. 193, § 95; Stats.1986, c. 248, § 157.)*

§ 3201.5. Collective bargaining agreements; construction; construction maintenance; other specified activities

(a) Except as provided in subdivisions (b) and (c), the Department of Industrial Relations and the courts of this state shall recognize as valid and binding any provision in a collective bargaining agreement between a private employer or groups of employers engaged in construction, construction maintenance, or activities limited to rock, sand, gravel, cement and asphalt operations, heavy-duty mechanics, surveying, and construction inspection and a union that is the recognized or certified exclusive bargaining representative that establishes any of the following:

(1) An alternative dispute resolution system governing disputes between employees and employers or their insurers that supplements or replaces all or part of those dispute resolution processes contained in this division, including, but not limited to, mediation and arbitration. Any system of arbitration shall provide that the decision of the arbiter or board of arbitration is subject to review by the appeals board in the same manner as provided for reconsideration of a final order, decision, or award made and filed by a workers' compensation administrative law judge pursuant to the procedures set forth in Article 1 (commencing with Section 5900) of Chapter 7 of Part 4 of Division 4, and the court of appeals pursuant to the procedures set forth in Article 2 (commencing with Section 5950) of Chapter 7 of Part 4 of Division 4, governing orders, decisions, or awards of the appeals board. The findings of fact, award, order, or decision of the arbitrator shall have the same force and effect as an award, order, or decision of a workers' compensation administrative law judge. Any provision for arbitration established pursuant to this section shall not be subject to Sections 5270, 5270.5, 5271, 5272, 5273, 5275, and 5277.

(2) The use of an agreed list of providers of medical treatment that may be the exclusive source of all medical treatment provided under this division.

(3) The use of an agreed, limited list of qualified medical evaluators and agreed medical evaluators that may be the exclusive source of qualified medical evaluators and agreed medical evaluators under this division.

(4) Joint labor management safety committees.

(5) A light-duty, modified job or return-to-work program.

(6) A vocational rehabilitation or retraining program utilizing an agreed list of providers of rehabilitation services that may be the exclusive source of providers of rehabilitation services under this division.

(b)(1) Nothing in this section shall allow a collective bargaining agreement that diminishes the entitlement of an employee to compensation payments for total or partial disability, temporary disability, vocational rehabilitation, or medical treatment fully paid by the employer as otherwise provided in this division. The portion of any agreement that violates this paragraph shall be declared null and void.

(2) The parties may negotiate any aspect of the delivery of medical benefits and the delivery of disability compensation to employees of the employer or group of employers that are eligible for group health benefits and nonoccupational disability benefits through their employer.

(c) Subdivision (a) shall apply only to the following:

(1) An employer developing or projecting an annual workers' compensation insurance premium, in California, of two hundred fifty thousand dollars ($250,000) or more, or any employer that paid an annual workers' compensation insurance premium, in California, of two hundred fifty thousand dollars ($250,000) in at least one of the previous three years.

(2) Groups of employers engaged in a workers' compensation safety group complying with Sections 11656.6 and 11656.7 of the Insurance Code, and established pursuant to a joint labor management safety committee or committees, that develops or projects annual workers' compensation insurance premiums of two million dollars ($2,000,000) or more.

(3) Employers or groups of employers that are self-insured in compliance with Section 3700 that would have projected annual workers' compensation costs that meet the requirements of, and that meet the other requirements of, paragraph (1) in the case of employers, or paragraph (2) in the case of groups of employers.

(4) Employers covered by an owner or general contractor provided wrap-up insurance policy applicable to a single construction site that develops workers' compensation insurance premiums of two million dollars ($2,000,000) or more with respect to those employees covered by that wrap-up insurance policy.

(d) Employers and labor representatives who meet the eligibility requirements of this section shall be issued a letter by the administrative director advising each employer and labor representative that, based upon the review of all documents and materials submitted as required by the administrative director, each has met the eligibility requirements of this section.

(e) The premium rate for a policy of insurance issued pursuant to this section shall not be subject to the requirements of Section 11732 or 11732.5 of the Insurance Code.

(f) No employer may establish or continue a program established under this section until it has provided the administrative director with all of the following:

(1) Upon its original application and whenever it is renegotiated thereafter, a copy of the collective bargaining agreement and the approximate number of employees who will be covered thereby.

(2) Upon its original application and annually thereafter, a valid and active license where that license is required by law as a condition of doing business in the state within the industries set forth in subdivision (a) of Section 3201.5.

(3) Upon its original application and annually thereafter, a statement signed under penalty of perjury, that no action has been taken by any administrative agency or court of the United States to invalidate the collective bargaining agreement.

(4) The name, address, and telephone number of the contact person of the employer.

(5) Any other information that the administrative director deems necessary to further the purposes of this section.

(g) No collective bargaining representative may establish or continue to participate in a program established under this section unless all of the following requirements are met:

(1) Upon its original application and annually thereafter, it has provided to the administrative director a copy of its most recent LM–2 or LM–3 filing with the United States Department of Labor, along with a statement, signed under penalty of perjury, that the document is a true and correct copy.

(2) It has provided to the administrative director the name, address, and telephone number of the contact person or persons of the collective bargaining representative or representatives.

(h) Commencing July 1, 1995, and annually thereafter, the Division of Workers' Compensation shall report to the Director of the Department of Industrial Relations the number of collective bargaining agreements received and the number of employees covered by these agreements.

(i) By June 30, 1996, and annually thereafter, the Administrative Director of the Division of Workers' Compensation shall prepare and notify Members of the Legislature that a report authorized by this section is available upon request. The report based upon aggregate data shall include the following:

(1) Person hours and payroll covered by agreements filed.

(2) The number of claims filed.

(3) The average cost per claim shall be reported by cost components whenever practicable.

(4) The number of litigated claims, including the number of claims submitted to mediation, the appeals board, or the court of appeal.

(5) The number of contested claims resolved prior to arbitration.

(6) The projected incurred costs and actual costs of claims.

(7) Safety history.

(8) The number of workers participating in vocational rehabilitation.

(9) The number of workers participating in light-duty programs.

The division shall have the authority to require those employers and groups of employers listed in subdivision (c) to provide the data listed above.

(j) The data obtained by the administrative director pursuant to this section shall be confidential and not subject to public disclosure under any law of this state. However, the Division of Workers' Compensation shall create derivative works pursuant to subdivisions (h) and (i) based on the collective bargaining agreements and data. Those derivative works shall not be confidential, but shall be public. On a monthly basis the administrative director shall make available an updated list of employers and unions entering into collective bargaining agreements containing provisions authorized by this section. *(Added by Stats.1993, c. 117 (S.B.983), § 1, eff. July 16, 1993. Amended by Stats.1994, c. 963 (S.B.853), § 1, eff. Sept. 28, 1994; Stats.1995, c. 886 (S.B.619), § 3; Stats.2002, c. 866 (A.B.486), § 4; Stats.2004, c. 34 (S.B. 899), § 6, eff. April 19, 2004.)*

Operative Effect

Section 47 of Stats.2004, c. 34 (S.B.899) provides that "[t]he amendment, addition, or repeal of, any provision of law made by this act shall apply prospectively from the date of enactment of this act, regardless of the date of injury, unless otherwise specified, but shall not constitute good cause to reopen or rescind, alter, or amend any existing order, decision, or award of the Workers' Compensation Appeals Board."

§ 3201.7. Labor-management agreements; permissible subjects

(a) Except as provided in subdivision (b), the Department of Industrial Relations and the courts of this state shall recognize as valid and binding any labor-management agreement that meets all of the following requirements:

(1) The labor-management agreement has been negotiated separate and apart from any collective bargaining agreement covering affected employees.

(2) The labor-management agreement is restricted to the establishment of the terms and conditions necessary to implement this section.

(3) The labor-management agreement has been negotiated in accordance with the authorization of the administrative director pursuant to subdivision (d), between an employer or groups of employers and a union that is the recognized or certified exclusive bargaining representative that establishes any of the following:

(A) An alternative dispute resolution system governing disputes between employees and employers or their insurers that supplements or replaces all or part of those dispute resolution processes contained in this division, including, but not limited to, mediation and arbitration. Any system of arbitration shall provide that the decision of the arbiter or board of arbitration is subject to review by the appeals board in the same manner as provided for reconsideration of a final order, decision, or award made and filed by a workers' compensation administrative law judge pursuant to the procedures set forth in Article 1 (commencing with Section 5900) of Chapter 7 of Part 4 of Division 4, and the court of appeals pursuant to the procedures set forth in Article 2 (commencing with Section 5950) of Chapter 7 of Part 4 of Division 4, governing orders, decisions, or awards of the appeals board. The findings of fact, award, order, or decision of the arbitrator shall have the same force and effect as an award, order, or decision of a workers' compensation administrative law judge. Any provision for arbitration established pursuant to this section shall not be subject to Sections 5270, 5270.5, 5271, 5272, 5273, 5275, and 5277.

(B) The use of an agreed list of providers of medical treatment that may be the exclusive source of all medical treatment provided under this division.

(C) The use of an agreed, limited list of qualified medical evaluators and agreed medical evaluators that may be the exclusive source of qualified medical evaluators and agreed medical evaluators under this division.

(D) Joint labor management safety committees.

(E) A light-duty, modified job, or return-to-work program.

(F) A vocational rehabilitation or retraining program utilizing an agreed list of providers of rehabilitation services that may be the exclusive source of providers of rehabilitation services under this division.

(b)(1) Nothing in this section shall allow a labor-management agreement that diminishes the entitlement of an employee to compensation payments for total or partial disability, temporary disability, vocational rehabilitation, or medical treatment fully paid by the employer as otherwise provided in this division; nor shall any agreement authorized by this section deny to any employee the right to representation by counsel at all stages during the alternative dispute resolution process. The portion of any agreement that violates this paragraph shall be declared null and void.

(2) The parties may negotiate any aspect of the delivery of medical benefits and the delivery of disability compensation to employees of the employer or group of employers that are eligible for group health benefits and nonoccupational disability benefits through their employer.

(c) Subdivision (a) shall apply only to the following:

(1) An employer developing or projecting an annual workers' compensation insurance premium, in California, of fifty thousand dollars ($50,000) or more, and employing at least 50 employees, or any employer that paid an annual workers' compensation insurance premium, in California, of fifty thousand dollars ($50,000), and employing at least 50 employees in at least one of the previous three years.

(2) Groups of employers engaged in a workers' compensation safety group complying with Sections 11656.6 and 11656.7 of the Insurance Code, and established pursuant to a joint labor management safety committee or committees, that develops or projects annual workers' compensation insurance premiums of five hundred thousand dollars ($500,000) or more.

(3) Employers or groups of employers, including cities and counties, that are self-insured in compliance with Section 3700 that would have projected annual workers' compensation costs that meet the requirements of, and that meet the other requirements of, paragraph (1) in the case of employers, or paragraph (2) in the case of groups of employers.

(d) Any recognized or certified exclusive bargaining representative in an industry not covered by Section 3201.5, may file a petition with the administrative director seeking permission to negotiate with an employer or group of employers to enter into a labor-management agreement pursuant to this section. The petition shall specify the bargaining unit or units to be included, the names of the employers or groups of employers, and shall be accompanied by proof of the labor union's status as the exclusive bargaining representative. The current collective bargaining agreement or agreements shall be attached to the petition. The petition shall be in the form designated by the administrative director. Upon receipt of the petition, the administrative director shall promptly verify the petitioner's status as the exclusive bargaining representative. If the petition satisfies the requirements set forth in this subdivision, the administrative director shall issue a letter advising each employer and labor representative of their eligibility to enter into negotiations, for a period not to exceed one year, for the purpose of reaching agreement on a labor-management agreement pursuant to this section. The parties may jointly request, and shall be granted, by the administrative director, an additional one-year period to negotiate an agreement.

(e) No employer may establish or continue a program established under this section until it has provided the administrative director with all of the following:

(1) Upon its original application and whenever it is renegotiated thereafter, a copy of the labor-management agreement and the approximate number of employees who will be covered thereby.

(2) Upon its original application and annually thereafter, a statement signed under penalty of perjury, that no action has been taken by any administrative agency or court of the United States to invalidate the labor-management agreement.

(3) The name, address, and telephone number of the contact person of the employer.

(4) Any other information that the administrative director deems necessary to further the purposes of this section.

(f) No collective bargaining representative may establish or continue to participate in a program established under this section unless all of the following requirements are met:

(1) Upon its original application and annually thereafter, it has provided to the administrative director a copy of its most recent LM–2 or LM–3 filing with the United States Department of Labor, where such filing is required by law, along with a statement, signed under penalty of perjury, that the document is a true and correct copy.

(2) It has provided to the administrative director the name, address, and telephone number of the contact person or persons of the collective bargaining representative or representatives.

(g) Commencing July 1, 2005, and annually thereafter, the Division of Workers' Compensation shall report to the Director of Industrial Relations the number of labor-management agreements received and the number of employees covered by these agreements.

(h) By June 30, 2006, and annually thereafter, the administrative director shall prepare and notify Members of the Legislature that a report authorized by this section is available upon request. The report based upon aggregate data shall include the following:

(1) Person hours and payroll covered by agreements filed.

(2) The number of claims filed.

(3) The average cost per claim shall be reported by cost components whenever practicable.

(4) The number of litigated claims, including the number of claims submitted to mediation, the appeals board, or the court of appeal.

(5) The number of contested claims resolved prior to arbitration.

(6) The projected incurred costs and actual costs of claims.

(7) Safety history.

(8) The number of workers participating in vocational rehabilitation.

(9) The number of workers participating in light-duty programs.

(10) Overall worker satisfaction.

The division shall have the authority to require employers and groups of employers participating in labor-

management agreements pursuant to this section to provide the data listed above.

(i) The data obtained by the administrative director pursuant to this section shall be confidential and not subject to public disclosure under any law of this state. However, the Division of Workers' Compensation shall create derivative works pursuant to subdivisions (f) and (g) based on the labor-management agreements and data. Those derivative works shall not be confidential, but shall be public. On a monthly basis, the administrative director shall make available an updated list of employers and unions entering into labor-management agreements authorized by this section. *(Added by Stats.2003, c. 639 (S.B.228), § 14.7. Amended by Stats.2004, c. 34 (S.B. 899), § 7, eff. April 19, 2004.)*

Operative Effect

Section 47 of Stats.2004, c. 34 (S.B.899) provides that "[t]he amendment, addition, or repeal of, any provision of law made by this act shall apply prospectively from the date of enactment of this act, regardless of the date of injury, unless otherwise specified, but shall not constitute good cause to reopen or rescind, alter, or amend any existing order, decision, or award of the Workers' Compensation Appeals Board."

§ 3201.81. Collective bargaining agreements; authorized negotiating organization

In the horse racing industry, the organization certified by the California Horse Racing Board to represent the majority of licensed jockeys pursuant to subdivision (b) of Section 19612.9 of the Business and Professions Code is the labor organization authorized to negotiate the collective bargaining agreement establishing an alternative dispute resolution system for licensed jockeys pursuant to Section 3201.7. *(Added by Stats.2003, c. 884 (A.B.1719), § 5. Amended by Stats.2007, c. 130 (A.B.299), § 184.)*

§ 3201.9. Reports to include updated loss experience participating in specified programs

(a) On or before June 30, 2004, and biannually thereafter, the report required in subdivision (i) of Section 3201.5 and subdivision (h) of Section 3201.7 shall include updated loss experience for all employers and groups of employers participating in a program established under those sections. The report shall include updated data on each item set forth in subdivision (i) of Section 3201.5 and subdivision (h) of Section 3201.7 for the previous year for injuries in 2003 and beyond. Updates for each program shall be done for the original program year and for subsequent years. The insurers, the Department of Insurance, and the rating organization designated by the Insurance Commissioner pursuant to Article 3 (commencing with Section 11750) of Chapter 3 of Part 3 of Division 2 of the Insurance Code, shall provide the administrative director with any information that the administrative director determines is reasonably necessary to conduct the study.

(b) Commencing on and after June 30, 2004, the Insurance Commissioner, or the commissioner's designee, shall prepare for inclusion in the report required in subdivision (i) of Section 3201.5 and subdivision (h) of Section 3201.7 a review of both of the following:

(1) The adequacy of rates charged for these programs, including the impact of scheduled credits and debits.

(2) The comparative results for these programs with other programs not subject to Section 3201.5 or Section 3201.7.

(c) Upon completion of the report, the administrative director shall report the findings to the Legislature, the Department of Insurance, the designated rating organization, and the programs and insurers participating in the study.

(d) The data obtained by the administrative director pursuant to this section shall be confidential and not subject to public disclosure under any law of this state. *(Added by Stats.2002, c. 6 (A.B.749), § 42.5. Amended by Stats.2004, c. 34 (S.B.899), § 8, eff. April 19, 2004.)*

Operative Effect

Section 47 of Stats.2004, c. 34 (S.B.899) provides that "[t]he amendment, addition, or repeal of, any provision of law made by this act shall apply prospectively from the date of enactment of this act, regardless of the date of injury, unless otherwise specified, but shall not constitute good cause to reopen or rescind, alter, or amend any existing order, decision, or award of the Workers' Compensation Appeals Board."

§ 3202. Liberal construction

This division and Division 5 (commencing with Section 6300) shall be liberally construed by the courts with the purpose of extending their benefits for the protection of persons injured in the course of their employment. *(Stats.1937, c. 90, p. 265, § 3202. Amended by Stats. 1984, c. 193, § 96; Stats.1986, c. 248, § 158.)*

§ 3202.5. Construction as to burden of proof; preponderance of the evidence

All parties and lien claimants shall meet the evidentiary burden of proof on all issues by a preponderance of the evidence in order that all parties are considered equal before the law. "Preponderance of the evidence" means that evidence that, when weighed with that opposed to it, has more convincing force and the greater probability of truth. When weighing the evidence, the test is not the relative number of witnesses, but the relative convincing force of the evidence. *(Added by Stats.1982, c. 922, p. 3365, § 3. Amended by Stats.1993, c. 4 (S.B.31), § 1.5, eff. April 3, 1993; Stats.2004, c. 34 (S.B.899), § 9, eff. April 19, 2004.)*

Operative Effect

Section 47 of Stats.2004, c. 34 (S.B.899) provides that "[t]he amendment, addition, or repeal

of, any provision of law made by this act shall apply prospectively from the date of enactment of this act, regardless of the date of injury, unless otherwise specified, but shall not constitute good cause to reopen or rescind, alter, or amend any existing order, decision, or award of the Workers' Compensation Appeals Board."

§ 3203. Employment in interstate commerce

This division and Division 5 (commencing with Section 6300) do not apply to employers or employments which, according to law, are so engaged in interstate commerce as not to be subject to the legislative power of the state, nor to employees injured while they are so engaged, except in so far as these divisions are permitted to apply under the Constitution or laws of the United States. *(Stats.1937, c. 90, p. 265, § 3203. Amended by Stats. 1984, c. 193, § 97; Stats.1986, c. 248, § 159.)*

§ 3204. Definitions

Unless the context otherwise requires, the definitions hereinafter set forth in this chapter shall govern the construction and meaning of the terms and phrases used in this division. *(Stats.1937, c. 90, p. 265, § 3204.)*

§ 3205. Division

"Division" means the Division of Workers' Compensation. *(Added by Stats.1965, c. 1513, p. 3566, § 18, operative Jan. 15, 1966. Amended by Stats.1994, c. 146 (A.B.3601), § 145; Stats.1994, c. 1097 (S.B.1803), § 10.)*

§ 3205.5. Appeals board

"Appeals board" means the Workers' Compensation Appeals Board of the Division of Workers' Compensation. *(Added by Stats.1965, c. 1513, p. 3567, § 49, operative Jan. 15, 1966. Amended by Stats.1981, c. 21, p. 47, § 6, eff. April 18, 1981; Stats.1994, c. 146 (A.B.3601), § 146; Stats.1994, c. 1097 (S.B.1803), § 11.)*

§ 3206. Administrative director

"Administrative director" means the Director of the Division of Workers' Compensation. *(Added by Stats. 1965, c. 1513, p. 3567, § 51, operative Jan. 15, 1966. Amended by Stats.1994, c. 146 (A.B.3601), § 147; Stats. 1994, c. 1097 (S.B.1803), § 12.)*

§ 3207. Compensation

"Compensation" means compensation under this division and includes every benefit or payment conferred by this division upon an injured employee, or in the event of his or her death, upon his or her dependents, without regard to negligence. *(Stats.1937, c. 90, p. 266, § 3207. Amended by Stats.1965, c. 1513, p. 3567, § 52, operative Jan. 15, 1966; Stats.2004, c. 34 (S.B.899), § 10, eff. April 19, 2004.)*

Operative Effect

Section 47 of Stats.2004, c. 34 (S.B.899) provides that "[t]he amendment, addition, or repeal of, any provision of law made by this act shall apply prospectively from the date of enactment of this act, regardless of the date of injury, unless otherwise specified, but shall not constitute good cause to reopen or rescind, alter, or amend any existing order, decision, or award of the Workers' Compensation Appeals Board."

§ 3208. Injury

"Injury" includes any injury or disease arising out of the employment, including injuries to artificial members, dentures, hearing aids, eyeglasses and medical braces of all types; provided, however, that eyeglasses and hearing aids will not be replaced, repaired, or otherwise compensated for, unless injury to them is incident to an injury causing disability. *(Stats.1937, c. 90, p. 266, § 3208. Amended by Stats.1949, c. 1409, p. 2464, § 1; Stats.1951, c. 606, p. 1766, § 1; Stats.1953, c. 297, p. 1449, § 1; Stats.1971, c. 1064, p. 2025, § 1.)*

§ 3208.05. Injury; bloodborne disease; preventive care to health care worker; documentation; human immunodeficiency virus

(a) "Injury" includes a reaction to or a side effect arising from health care provided by an employer to a health care worker, which health care is intended to prevent the development or manifestation of any bloodborne disease, illness, syndrome, or condition recognized as occupationally incurred by Cal-OSHA, the Federal Centers for Disease Control, or other appropriate governmental entities. This section shall apply only to preventive health care that the employer provided to a health care worker under the following circumstances: (1) prior to an exposure because of risk of occupational exposure to such a disease, illness, syndrome, or condition, or (2) where the preventive care is provided as a consequence of a documented exposure to blood or bodily fluid containing blood that arose out of and in the course of employment. Such a disease, illness, syndrome, or condition includes, but is not limited to, hepatitis, and the human immunodeficiency virus. Such preventive health care, and any disability indemnity or other benefits required as a result of the preventive health care provided by the employer, shall be compensable under the workers' compensation system. The employer may require the health care worker to document that the employer provided the preventive health care and that the reaction or side effects arising from the preventive health care resulted in lost work time, health care costs, or other costs normally compensable under workers' compensation.

(b) The benefits of this section shall not be provided to a health care worker for a reaction to or side effect from health care intended to prevent the development of the human immunodeficiency virus if the worker claims a work-related exposure and if the worker tests positive within 48 hours of that exposure to a test to determine the presence of the human immunodeficiency virus.

(c) For purposes of this section, "health care worker" includes any person who is an employee of a provider of health care as defined in subdivision (d) of Section 56.05 of the Civil Code, and who is exposed to human blood or other bodily fluids contaminated with blood in the course of employment, including, but not limited to, a registered nurse, a licensed vocational nurse, a certified nurse aide, clinical laboratory technologist, dental hygienist, physician, janitor, and housekeeping worker. "Health care worker" does not include an employee who provides employee health services for an employer primarily engaged in a business other than providing health care. *(Added by Stats.1992, c. 1085 (S.B.890), § 1.)*

§ 3208.1. Specific or cumulative injuries

An injury may be either: (a) "specific," occurring as the result of one incident or exposure which causes disability or need for medical treatment; or (b) "cumulative," occurring as repetitive mentally or physically traumatic activities extending over a period of time, the combined effect of which causes any disability or need for medical treatment. The date of a cumulative injury shall be the date determined under Section 5412. *(Added by Stats.1968, c. 4, 1st Ex.Sess., p. 31, § 1, operative Jan. 1, 1969. Amended by Stats.1973, c. 1024, p. 2032, § 1.)*

§ 3208.2. Two or more injuries; separate determination of questions of fact and law

When disability, need for medical treatment, or death results from the combined effects of two or more injuries, either specific, cumulative, or both, all questions of fact and law shall be separately determined with respect to each such injury, including, but not limited to, the apportionment between such injuries of liability for disability benefits, the cost of medical treatment, and any death benefit. *(Added by Stats.1968, c. 4, 1st Ex.Sess., p. 31, § 2, operative Jan. 1, 1969.)*

§ 3208.3. Psychiatric injuries; compensability; employment conditions; notice of termination or layoff; prevention programs; inmates

(a) A psychiatric injury shall be compensable if it is a mental disorder which causes disability or need for medical treatment, and it is diagnosed pursuant to procedures promulgated under paragraph (4) of subdivision (j) of Section 139.2 or, until these procedures are promulgated, it is diagnosed using the terminology and criteria of the American Psychiatric Association's Diagnostic and Statistical Manual of Mental Disorders, Third Edition-Revised, or the terminology and diagnostic criteria of other psychiatric diagnostic manuals generally approved and accepted nationally by practitioners in the field of psychiatric medicine.

(b)(1) In order to establish that a psychiatric injury is compensable, an employee shall demonstrate by a preponderance of the evidence that actual events of employment were predominant as to all causes combined of the psychiatric injury.

(2) Notwithstanding paragraph (1), in the case of employees whose injuries resulted from being a victim of a violent act or from direct exposure to a significant

526

violent act, the employee shall be required to demonstrate by a preponderance of the evidence that actual events of employment were a substantial cause of the injury.

(3) For the purposes of this section, "substantial cause" means at least 35 to 40 percent of the causation from all sources combined.

(c) It is the intent of the Legislature in enacting this section to establish a new and higher threshold of compensability for psychiatric injury under this division.

(d) Notwithstanding any other provision of this division, no compensation shall be paid pursuant to this division for a psychiatric injury related to a claim against an employer unless the employee has been employed by that employer for at least six months. The six months of employment need not be continuous. This subdivision shall not apply if the psychiatric injury is caused by a sudden and extraordinary employment condition. Nothing in this subdivision shall be construed to authorize an employee, or his or her dependents, to bring an action at law or equity for damages against the employer for a psychiatric injury, where those rights would not exist pursuant to the exclusive remedy doctrine set forth in Section 3602 in the absence of the amendment of this section by the act adding this subdivision.

(e) Where the claim for compensation is filed after notice of termination of employment or layoff, including voluntary layoff, and the claim is for an injury occurring prior to the time of notice of termination or layoff, no compensation shall be paid unless the employee demonstrates by a preponderance of the evidence that actual events of employment were predominant as to all causes combined of the psychiatric injury and one or more of the following conditions exist:

(1) Sudden and extraordinary events of employment were the cause of the injury.

(2) The employer has notice of the psychiatric injury under Chapter 2 (commencing with Section 5400) prior to the notice of termination or layoff.

(3) The employee's medical records existing prior to notice of termination or layoff contain evidence of treatment of the psychiatric injury.

(4) Upon a finding of sexual or racial harassment by any trier of fact, whether contractual, administrative, regulatory, or judicial.

(5) Evidence that the date of injury, as specified in Section 5411 or 5412, is subsequent to the date of the notice of termination or layoff, but prior to the effective date of the termination or layoff.

(f) For purposes of this section, an employee provided notice pursuant to Sections 44948.5, 44949, 44951, 44955, 44955.6, 72411, 87740, and 87743 of the Education Code shall be considered to have been provided a notice of termination or layoff only upon a district's final decision not to reemploy that person.

(g) A notice of termination or layoff that is not followed within 60 days by that termination or layoff shall not be subject to the provisions of this subdivision, and this subdivision shall not apply until receipt of a later notice of termination or layoff. The issuance of frequent notices of termination or layoff to an employee shall be considered a bad faith personnel action and shall make this subdivision inapplicable to the employee.

(h) No compensation under this division shall be paid by an employer for a psychiatric injury if the injury was substantially caused by a lawful, nondiscriminatory, good faith personnel action. The burden of proof shall rest with the party asserting the issue.

(i) When a psychiatric injury claim is filed against an employer, and an application for adjudication of claim is filed by an employer or employee, the division shall provide the employer with information concerning psychiatric injury prevention programs.

(j) An employee who is an inmate, as defined in subdivision (e) of Section 3351, or his or her family on behalf of an inmate, shall not be entitled to compensation for a psychiatric injury except as provided in subdivision (d) of Section 3370. *(Added by Stats.1989, c. 892, § 25. Amended by Stats.1990, c. 1550 (A.B.2910), § 20; Stats. 1991, c. 115 (A.B.971), § 4, eff. July 16, 1991; Stats.1993, c. 118 (A.B.119), § 1, eff. July 16, 1993; Stats.1993, c. 1242 (S.B.223), § 22; Stats.1994, c. 497 (A.B.1269), § 1.)*

§ 3208.4. Injuries arising out of alleged sexual harassment, sexual assault, or sexual battery; discovery; evidence

In any proceeding under this division involving an injury arising out of alleged conduct that constitutes sexual harassment, sexual assault, or sexual battery, any party seeking discovery concerning sexual conduct of the applicant with any person other than the defendant, whether consensual or nonconsensual or prior or subsequent to the alleged act complained of, shall establish specific facts showing good cause for that discovery on a noticed motion to the appeals board. The motion shall not be made or considered at an ex parte hearing.

The procedures set forth in Section 783 of the Evidence Code shall be followed if evidence of sexual conduct of the applicant is offered to attack his or her credibility. Opinion evidence, evidence of reputation, and evidence of specific instances of sexual conduct of the applicant with any person other than the defendant, or any of such evidence, is not admissible by the defendant to prove consent by or the absence of injury to the applicant, unless the injury alleged by the applicant is in the nature of loss of consortium. *(Added by Stats.1993, c. 121 (A.B.110), § 24, eff. July 16, 1993.)*

§ 3209. Damages

"Damages" means the recovery allowed in an action at law as contrasted with compensation. *(Stats.1937, c. 90, p. 266, § 3209.)*

§ 3209.3. Physician; psychologist; acupuncturist

(a) "Physician" includes physicians and surgeons holding an M.D. or D.O. degree, psychologists, acupuncturists, optometrists, dentists, podiatrists, and chiropractic practitioners licensed by California state law and within the scope of their practice as defined by California state law.

(b) "Psychologist" means a licensed psychologist with a doctoral degree in psychology, or a doctoral degree deemed equivalent for licensure by the Board of Psychology pursuant to Section 2914 of the Business and Professions Code, and who either has at least two years of clinical experience in a recognized health setting or has met the standards of the National Register of the Health Service Providers in Psychology.

(c) When treatment or evaluation for an injury is provided by a psychologist, provision shall be made for appropriate medical collaboration when requested by the employer or the insurer.

(d) "Acupuncturist" means a person who holds an acupuncturist's certificate issued pursuant to Chapter 12 (commencing with Section 4925) of Division 2 of the Business and Professions Code.

(e) Nothing in this section shall be construed to authorize acupuncturists to determine disability for the purposes of Article 3 (commencing with Section 4650) of Chapter 2 of Part 2, or under Section 2708 of the Unemployment Insurance Code.

(Added by Stats.1945, c. 629, p. 1156, § 1. Amended by Stats.1947, c. 620, p. 1627, § 1; Stats.1947, c. 1404, p. 2965, § 1; Stats.1949, c. 644, p. 1152, § 1; Stats.1961, c. 215, p. 1235, § 40; Stats.1977, c. 1168, p. 3826, § 1; Stats.1985, c. 1156, § 1; Stats.1988, c. 1496, § 1; Stats. 1992, c. 824 (A.B.400), § 1; Stats.1994, c. 1118 (S.B. 1768), § 3; Stats.1996, c. 26 (A.B.1002), § 1; Stats.1997, c. 98 (S.B.212), § 1.)

§ 3209.4. Optometrists

The inclusion of optometrists in Section 3209.3 does not imply any right or entitle any optometrist to represent, advertise, or hold himself out as a physician. *(Added by Stats.1947, c. 1404, p. 2965, § 2.)*

§ 3209.5. Medical, surgical, and hospital treatment

Medical, surgical, and hospital treatment, including nursing, medicines, medical and surgical supplies, crutches, and apparatus, includes but is not limited to services and supplies by physical therapists, chiropractic practitioners, and acupuncturists, as licensed by California state law and within the scope of their practice as defined by law. *(Added by Stats.1945, c. 629, p. 1156, § 2. Amended by Stats.1971, c. 1490, p. 2943, § 4; Stats.1987, c. 898, § 2; Stats.1998, c. 440 (A.B.204), § 1.)*

§ 3209.6. Chiropractors

The inclusion of chiropractors in Sections 3209.3 and 3209.5 does not imply any right or entitle any chiroprac-

tor to represent, advertise, or hold himself out as a physician. *(Added by Stats.1945, c. 629, p. 1156, § 3.)*

§ 3209.7. Treatment of injuries; agreement

Treatment of injuries at the expense of the employer may also include, either in addition to or in place of medical, surgical, and hospital services, as specified in Section 3209.5, any other form of therapy, treatment, or healing practice agreed upon voluntarily in writing, between the employee and his employer. Such agreement may be entered into at any time after employment and shall be in a form approved by the Department of Industrial Relations, and shall include at least the following items:

(a) A description of the form of healing practice intended to be relied upon and designation of individuals and facilities qualified to administer it.

(b) The employee shall not by entering into such an agreement or by selecting such therapy, treatment or healing practice, waive any rights conferred upon him by law, or forfeit any benefits to which he might otherwise be entitled.

(c) The employer and the employee shall each reserve the right to terminate such agreement upon seven days written notice to the other party.

No liability shall be incurred by the employer under the provisions of this section, except as provided for in Chapter 3 (commencing with Section 3600), of this part. *(Added by Stats.1970, c. 1250, p. 2258, § 1.)*

§ 3209.8. Treatment by marriage, family and child counselors, and clinical social workers

Treatment reasonably required to cure or relieve from the effects of an injury shall include the services of marriage and family therapists and clinical social workers licensed by California state law and within the scope of their practice as defined by California state law if the injured person is referred to the marriage and family therapist or the clinical social worker by a licensed physician and surgeon, with the approval of the employer, for treatment of a condition arising out of the injury. Nothing in this section shall be construed to authorize marriage and family therapists or clinical social workers to determine disability for the purposes of Article 3 (commencing with Section 4650) of Chapter 2 of Part 2. The requirement of this section that the employer approve the referral by a licensed physician or surgeon shall not be construed to preclude reimbursement for self-procured treatment, found by the appeals board to be otherwise compensable pursuant to this division, where the employer has refused to authorize any treatment for the condition arising from the injury treated by the marriage and family therapist or clinical social worker. *(Added by Stats.1985, c. 1156, § 2. Amended by Stats. 1991, c. 234 (S.B.902), § 1; Stats.2002, c. 1013 (S.B.2026), § 94.)*

§ 3209.9. Acupuncturist; representation as physician or surgeon with M.D. or D.O. degree

The inclusion of acupuncturists in Section 3209.3 does not imply any right or entitle any acupuncturist to represent, advertise, or hold himself or herself out as a physician or surgeon holding an M.D. or D.O. degree. *(Added by Stats.1997, c. 98 (S.B.212), § 3.)*

§ 3209.10. Provision of medical treatment for work-related injury by physician assistant or nurse practitioner; authority of the same to cosign report and to authorize time off from work for injuries

(a) Medical treatment of a work-related injury required to cure or relieve the effects of the injury may be provided by a state licensed physician assistant or nurse practitioner, acting under the review or supervision of a physician and surgeon pursuant to standardized procedures or protocols within their lawfully authorized scope of practice. The reviewing or supervising physician and surgeon of the physician assistant or nurse practitioner shall be deemed to be the treating physician. For the purposes of this section, "medical treatment" includes the authority of the nurse practitioner or physician assistant to authorize the patient to receive time off from work for a period not to exceed three calendar days if that authority is included in a standardized procedure or protocol approved by the supervising physician. The nurse practitioner or physician assistant may cosign the Doctor's First Report of Occupational Injury or Illness. The treating physician shall make any determination of temporary disability and shall sign the report.

(b) The provision of subdivision (a) that requires the cosignature of the treating physician applies to this section only and it is not the intent of the Legislature that the requirement apply to any other section of law or to any other statute or regulation. Nothing in this section implies that a nurse practitioner or physician assistant is a physician as defined in Section 3209.3.

(Added by Stats.2001, c. 229 (A.B.1194), § 1. Amended by Stats.2004, c. 100 (A.B.2919), § 1.)

§ 3210. Person

"Person" includes an individual, firm, voluntary association, or a public, quasi public, or private corporation. *(Stats.1937, c. 90, p. 266, § 3210.)*

§ 3211. Insurer

"Insurer" includes the State Compensation Insurance Fund and any private company, corporation, mutual association, reciprocal or interinsurance exchange authorized under the laws of this State to insure employers against liability for compensation and any employer to whom a certificate of consent to self-insure has been issued. *(Stats.1937, c. 90, p. 266, § 3211.)*

§ 3211.5. "Firefighter", "Firefighting member" and "Member of a fire department" defined

For purposes of this division, whenever the term "firefighter," "firefighting member," and "member of a fire department" is used, the term shall include, but shall not be limited to, unless the context expressly provides otherwise, a person engaged in providing firefighting services who is an apprentice, volunteer, or employee on a partly paid or fully paid basis. *(Added by Stats.2002, c. 870 (A.B.1847), § 2.)*

§ 3211.9. Disaster council

"Disaster council" means a public agency established by ordinance which is empowered to register and direct the activities of disaster service workers within the area of the county, city, city and county, or any part thereof, and is thus, because of such registration and direction, acting as an instrumentality of the state in aid of the carrying out of the general governmental functions and policy of the state. *(Added by Stats.1946, 1st Ex.Sess. c. 104, p. 132, § 1, eff. March 8, 1946. Amended by Stats.1951, c. 1440, p. 3399, § 1; Stats.1971, c. 38, p. 53, § 17.)*

§ 3211.91. Accredited disaster council

"Accredited disaster council" means a disaster council that is certified by the Office of Emergency Services as conforming with the rules and regulations established by the office pursuant to Article 10 (commencing with Section 8610) of Chapter 7 of Division 1 of Title 2 of the Government Code. A disaster council remains accredited only while the certification of the Office of Emergency Services is in effect and is not revoked. *(Added by Stats.1946, 1st Ex.Sess., c. 104, p. 133, § 2, eff. March 8, 1946. Amended by Stats.1971, c. 438, p. 893, § 139; Stats.2006, c. 502 (A.B.1889), § 9.)*

§ 3211.92. Disaster service worker

(a) "Disaster service worker" means any natural person who is registered with an accredited disaster council or a state agency for the purpose of engaging in disaster service pursuant to the California Emergency Services Act without pay or other consideration.

(b) "Disaster service worker" includes public employees performing disaster work that is outside the course and scope of their regular employment without pay and also includes any unregistered person impressed into service during a state of war emergency, a state of emergency, or a local emergency by a person having authority to command the aid of citizens in the execution of his or her duties.

(c) Persons registered with a disaster council at the time that council becomes accredited need not reregister in order to be entitled to the benefits provided by Chapter 10 (commencing with Section 4351).

(d) "Disaster service worker" does not include any member registered as an active firefighting member of any regularly organized volunteer fire department, having official recognition, and full or partial support of the county, city, or district in which the fire department is located. *(Added by Stats.1946, 1st Ex.Sess. c. 104, p. 133, § 3, eff. March 8, 1946. Amended by Stats.1950, 3rd Ex.Sess. c. 30, p. 56, § 2, eff. Oct. 14, 1950; Stats.1951, c. 1440, p. 3400, § 2; Stats.1951, c. 1673, p. 3828, § 1; Stats.1957, c. 2056, p. 3651, § 1; Stats.1971, c. 38, p. 53, § 18; Stats.1974, c. 1158, p. 2466, § 5; Stats.1982, c. 454, p. 1877, § 133; Stats.2000, c. 506 (S.B.1350), § 33.)*

§ 3211.93.   Disaster service

"Disaster service" means all activities authorized by and carried on pursuant to the California Emergency Services Act, including training necessary or proper to engage in such activities. *(Added by Stats.1946, 1st Ex.Sess. c. 104, p. 133, § 4, eff. March 8, 1946. Amended by Stats.1951, c. 1440, p. 3400, § 3; Stats.1971, c. 438, p. 894, § 140.)*

§ 3211.93a.   Disaster service; exclusion of activities for which disaster council receives fee

"Disaster service" does not include any activities or functions performed by a person if the accredited disaster council with which that person is registered receives a fee or other compensation for the performance of those activities or functions by that person. *(Added by Stats. 1957, c. 1103, p. 2408, § 1.   Amended by Stats.1971, c. 438, p. 894, § 141; Stats.2000, c. 506 (S.B.1350), § 34.)*

§ 3212.   Members of sheriff's office or California Highway Patrol, district attorney's staff of inspectors and investigators or of police or fire departments; injury; inclusion of hernia, heart trouble and pneumonia

In the case of members of a sheriff's office or the California Highway Patrol, district attorney's staff of inspectors and investigators or of police or fire departments of cities, counties, cities and counties, districts or other public or municipal corporations or political subdivisions, whether those members are volunteer, partly paid, or fully paid, and in the case of active firefighting members of the Department of Forestry and Fire Protection whose duties require firefighting or of any county forestry or firefighting department or unit, whether voluntary, fully paid, or partly paid, and in the case of members of the warden service of the Wildlife Protection Branch of the Department of Fish and Game whose principal duties consist of active law enforcement service, excepting those whose principal duties are clerical or otherwise do not clearly fall within the scope of active law enforcement service such as stenographers, telephone operators, and other officeworkers, the term "injury" as used in this act includes hernia when any part of the hernia develops or manifests itself during a period while the member is in the service in the office, staff, division, department, or unit, and in the case of members of fire departments, except those whose principal duties are clerical, such as stenographers, telephone operators, and other officeworkers, and in the case of county forestry or firefighting departments, except those whose principal

duties are clerical, such as stenographers, telephone operators, and other officeworkers, and in the case of active firefighting members of the Department of Forestry and Fire Protection whose duties require firefighting, and in the case of members of the warden service of the Wildlife Protection Branch of the Department of Fish and Game whose principal duties consist of active law enforcement service, excepting those whose principal duties are clerical or otherwise do not clearly fall within the scope of active law enforcement service such as stenographers, telephone operators, and other officeworkers, the term "injury" includes pneumonia and heart trouble that develops or manifests itself during a period while the member is in the service of the office, staff, department, or unit.   In the case of regular salaried county or city and county peace officers, the term "injury" also includes any hernia that manifests itself or develops during a period while the officer is in the service.   The compensation that is awarded for the hernia, heart trouble, or pneumonia shall include full hospital, surgical, medical treatment, disability indemnity, and death benefits, as provided by the workers' compensation laws of this state.

The hernia, heart trouble, or pneumonia so developing or manifesting itself in those cases shall be presumed to arise out of and in the course of the employment.   This presumption is disputable and may be controverted by other evidence, but unless so controverted, the appeals board is bound to find in accordance with it.   The presumption shall be extended to a member following termination of service for a period of three calendar months for each full year of the requisite service, but not to exceed 60 months in any circumstance, commencing with the last date actually worked in the specified capacity.

The hernia, heart trouble, or pneumonia so developing or manifesting itself in those cases shall in no case be attributed to any disease existing prior to that development or manifestation. *(Stats.1937, c. 90, p. 266, § 3212. Amended by Stats.1939, c. 256, p. 1511, § 1; Stats.1945, c. 742, p. 1428, § 1;   Stats.1947, c. 1210, p. 2721, § 1; Stats.1949, c. 730, p. 1347, § 1;   Stats.1955, c. 797, p. 1398, § 1;   Stats.1959, c. 758, p. 2744, § 1;   Stats.1965, c. 1513, p. 3567, § 52.5, operative Jan. 15, 1966;   Stats.1965, c. 1690, p. 3817, § 1; Stats.1971, c. 562, p. 1076, § 1;   Stats.1976, c. 466, p. 1091, § 1;   Stats.1980, c. 676, p. 1970, § 229; Stats.1992, c. 427 (A.B.3355), § 121;   Stats.2001, c. 833 (A.B.196), § 2;   Stats.2002, c. 664 (A.B.3034), § 164.)*

§ 3212.1.   Active firefighters and peace officers; injury; inclusion of cancer; presumption

(a)   This section applies to all of the following:

(1)   Active firefighting members, whether volunteers, partly paid, or fully paid, of all of the following fire departments:

(A)   A fire department of a city, county, city and county, district, or other public or municipal corporation or political subdivision.

(B) A fire department of the University of California and the California State University.

(C) The Department of Forestry and Fire Protection.

(D) A county forestry or firefighting department or unit.

(2) Active firefighting members of a fire department that serves a United States Department of Defense installation and who are certified by the Department of Defense as meeting its standards for firefighters.

(3) Peace officers, as defined in Section 830.1, subdivision (a) of Section 830.2, and subdivisions (a) and (b) of Section 830.37, of the Penal Code, who are primarily engaged in active law enforcement activities.

(4)(A) Fire and rescue services coordinators who work for the Office of Emergency Services.

(B) For purposes of this paragraph, "fire and rescue services coordinator" means a coordinator with any of the following job classifications: coordinator, senior coordinator, or chief coordinator.

(b) The term "injury," as used in this division, includes cancer, including leukemia, that develops or manifests itself during a period in which any member described in subdivision (a) is in the service of the department or unit, if the member demonstrates that he or she was exposed, while in the service of the department or unit, to a known carcinogen as defined by the International Agency for Research on Cancer, or as defined by the director.

(c) The compensation that is awarded for cancer shall include full hospital, surgical, medical treatment, disability indemnity, and death benefits, as provided by this division.

(d) The cancer so developing or manifesting itself in these cases shall be presumed to arise out of and in the course of the employment. This presumption is disputable and may be controverted by evidence that the primary site of the cancer has been established and that the carcinogen to which the member has demonstrated exposure is not reasonably linked to the disabling cancer. Unless so controverted, the appeals board is bound to find in accordance with the presumption. This presumption shall be extended to a member following termination of service for a period of three calendar months for each full year of the requisite service, but not to exceed 60 months in any circumstance, commencing with the last date actually worked in the specified capacity.

(e) The amendments to this section enacted during the 1999 portion of the 1999–2000 Regular Session shall be applied to claims for benefits filed or pending on or after January 1, 1997, including, but not limited to, claims for benefits filed on or after that date that have previously been denied, or that are being appealed following denial. *(Added by Stats.1982, c. 1568, p. 6178, § 1. Amended by Stats. 1984, c. 114, § 1; Stats.1988, c. 1038, § 1; Stats. 1989, c. 1171, § 2; Stats.1999, c. 595 (A.B.539), § 1; Stats.2000, c. 887 (S.B.1820), § 1; Stats.2008, c. 747 (S.B.1271), § 1.)*

§ 3212.2. Injury; custodial, supervisory and security officers and employees; inclusion of heart trouble

In the case of officers and employees in the Department of Corrections having custodial duties, each officer and employee in the Department of Youth Authority having group supervisory duties, and each security officer employed at the Atascadero State Hospital, the term "injury" includes heart trouble which develops or manifests itself during a period while such officer or employee is in the service of such department or hospital.

The compensation which is awarded for such heart trouble shall include full hospital, surgical, medical treatment, disability indemnity, and death benefits, as provided by the workmen's compensation laws of this state.

Such heart trouble so developing or manifesting itself in such cases shall be presumed to arise out of and in the course of the employment. This presumption is disputable and may be controverted by other evidence, but unless so controverted, the appeals board is bound to find in accordance with it. This presumption shall be extended to a member following termination of service for a period of three calendar months for each full year of the requisite service, but not to exceed 60 months in any circumstance, commencing with the last date actually worked in the specified capacity. *(Added by Stats.1959, c. 1155, p. 3247, § 1. Amended by Stats.1965, c. 1513, p. 3568, § 53, operative Jan. 15, 1966; Stats.1976, c. 466, p. 1207, § 2.)*

§ 3212.3. Injury; peace officers of Department of California Highway Patrol

In the case of a peace officer who is designated under subdivision (a) of Section 2250.1 of the Vehicle Code and who has graduated from an academy certified by the Commission on Peace Officer Standards and Training, when that officer is employed upon a regular, full-time salary, the term "injury," as used in this division, includes heart trouble and pneumonia which develops or manifests itself during a period while that officer is in the service of the Department of the California Highway Patrol. The compensation which is awarded for the heart trouble or pneumonia shall include full hospital, surgical, medical treatment, disability indemnity, and death benefits as provided by this division.

The heart trouble or pneumonia so developing or manifesting itself shall be presumed to arise out of and in the course of the employment. However, a peace officer of the Department of the California Highway Patrol, as designated under subdivision (a) of Section 2250.1 of the Vehicle Code, shall have served five years or more in that capacity or as a peace officer with the former California State Police Division, or in both capacities, before the presumption shall arise as to the compensability of heart trouble so developing or manifesting itself. This presumption is disputable and may be controverted by other evidence, but unless so controverted, the appeals board is bound to find in accordance with it. This presumption shall be extended to a member following termination of service for a period of three calendar months for each full year of the requisite service, but not to exceed 60 months in any circumstance, commencing with the last date actually worked in the specified capacity.

The heart trouble or pneumonia so developing or manifesting itself in these cases shall in no case be attributed to any disease existing prior to that development or manifestation.

The term "peace officers" as used herein shall be limited to those employees of the Department of the California Highway Patrol who are designated as peace officers under subdivision (a) of Section 2250.1 of the Vehicle Code. (Added by Stats.1972, c. 1360, p. 2709, § 1. Amended by Stats.1976, c. 466, p. 1207, § 3; Gov.Reorg.Plan No. 1 of 1995, § 40, eff. July 12, 1995; Stats.1996, c. 305 (A.B.3103), § 41.)

§ 3212.4. Injury; inclusion of heart trouble, hernia and pneumonia; member defined

In the case of a member of a University of California fire department located at a campus or other facility administered by the Regents of University of California, when any such member is employed by such a department upon a regular, full-time salary, on a nonprobationary basis, the term "injury" as used in this division includes heart trouble, hernia, or pneumonia which develops or manifests itself during a period while such member is in the service of such a University of California fire department. The compensation which is awarded for such heart trouble, hernia, or pneumonia shall include full hospital, surgical, medical treatment, disability indemnity, and death benefits as provided by the provisions of this division.

Such heart trouble, hernia, or pneumonia so developing or manifesting itself shall be presumed to arise out of and in the course of the employment. This presumption is disputable and may be controverted by other evidence, but unless so controverted, the appeals board is bound to find in accordance with it. This presumption shall be extended to a member following termination of service for a period of three calendar months for each full year of the requisite service, but not to exceed 60 months in any circumstance, commencing with the last date actually worked in the specified capacity.

Such heart trouble, hernia, or pneumonia so developing or manifesting itself in such cases shall in no case be attributed to any disease existing prior to such development or manifestation.

The term "member" as used herein shall exclude those employees of a University of California fire department whose principal duties are those of a telephone operator, clerk, stenographer, machinist, mechanic, or otherwise, and whose functions do not clearly fall within the scope of active firefighting and prevention service. (Added by Stats.1972, c. 1149, p. 2243, § 1. Amended by Stats.1976, c. 466, p. 1208, § 4.)

532

§ 3212.5. Injury; inclusion of heart trouble and pneumonia; members defined

In the case of a member of a police department of a city or municipality, or a member of the State Highway Patrol, when any such member is employed upon a regular, full-time salary, and in the case of a sheriff or deputy sheriff, or an inspector or investigator in a district attorney's office of any county, employed upon a regular, full-time salary, the term "injury" as used in this division includes heart trouble and pneumonia which develops or manifests itself during a period while such member, sheriff, or deputy sheriff, inspector or investigator is in the service of the police department, the State Highway Patrol, the sheriff's office or the district attorney's office, as the case may be. The compensation which is awarded for such heart trouble or pneumonia shall include full hospital, surgical, medical treatment, disability indemnity, and death benefits as provided by the provisions of this division.

Such heart trouble or pneumonia so developing or manifesting itself shall be presumed to arise out of and in the course of the employment; provided, however, that the member of the police department, State Highway Patrol, the sheriff or deputy sheriff, or an inspector or investigator in a district attorney's office of any county shall have served five years or more in such capacity before the presumption shall arise as to the compensability of heart trouble so developing or manifesting itself. This presumption is disputable and may be controverted by other evidence, but unless so controverted, the appeals board is bound to find in accordance with it. This presumption shall be extended to a member following termination of service for a period of three calendar months for each full year of the requisite service, but not to exceed 60 months in any circumstance, commencing with the last date actually worked in the specified capacity.

Such heart trouble or pneumonia so developing or manifesting itself in such cases shall in no case be attributed to any disease existing prior to such development or manifestation.

The term "members" as used herein shall be limited to those employees of police departments, the California Highway Patrol and sheriffs' departments and inspectors and investigators of a district attorney's office who are defined as peace officers in Section 830.1, 830.2, or 830.3 of the Penal Code. (Added by Stats.1939, c. 627, p. 2047, § 1. Amended by Stats.1943, c. 255, p. 1168, § 1; Stats.1949, c. 693, p. 1189, § 1; Stats.1955, c. 797, p. 1399, § 2; Stats.1959, c. 758, p. 2745, § 2; Stats.1965, c. 940, p. 2551, § 1; Stats.1965, c. 1513, p. 3568, § 54, operative Jan. 15, 1966; Stats.1968, c. 1100, p. 2113, § 1; Stats.1971, c. 562, p. 1077, § 2; Stats.1972, c. 618, p. 1136, § 109; Stats.1976, c. 466, p. 1209, § 5.)

§ 3212.6. Members of police department, sheriff's office, California Highway Patrol or inspector or investigator in district attorney's office, etc.; injury; inclusion of tuberculosis; applicant testing

In the case of a member of a police department of a city or county, or a member of the sheriff's office of a county, or a member of the California Highway Patrol, or an inspector or investigator in a district attorney's office of any county whose principal duties consist of active law enforcement service, or a prison or jail guard or correctional officer who is employed by a public agency, when that person is employed upon a regular, full-time salary, or in the case of members of fire departments of any city, county, or district, or other public or municipal corporations or political subdivisions, when those members are employed on a regular fully paid basis, and in the case of active firefighting members of the Department of Forestry and Fire Protection whose duties require firefighting and first-aid response services, or of any county forestry or firefighting department or unit, where those members are employed on a regular fully paid basis, excepting those whose principal duties are clerical or otherwise do not clearly fall within the scope of active law enforcement, firefighting, or emergency first-aid response service such as stenographers, telephone operators, and other officeworkers, the term "injury" includes tuberculosis that develops or manifests itself during a period while that member is in the service of that department or office. The compensation that is awarded for the tuberculosis shall include full hospital, surgical, medical treatment, disability indemnity, and death benefits as provided by the provisions of this division.

The tuberculosis so developing or manifesting itself shall be presumed to arise out of and in the course of the employment. This presumption is disputable and may be controverted by other evidence, but unless so controverted, the appeals board is bound to find in accordance with it. This presumption shall be extended to a member following termination of service for a period of three calendar months for each full year of the requisite service, but not to exceed 60 months in any circumstance, commencing with the last date actually worked in the specified capacity.

A public entity may require applicants for employment in firefighting positions who would be entitled to the benefits granted by this section to be tested for infection for tuberculosis. *(Added by Stats.1957, c. 295, p. 938, § 1. Amended by Stats.1965, c. 1513, p. 3569, § 55, operative Jan. 15, 1966; Stats.1971, c. 562, p. 1078, § 3; Stats.1976, c. 466, p. 1209, § 6; Stats.1995, c. 683 (S.B.658), § 1; Stats.1996, c. 802 (A.B.521), § 1; Stats.2001, c. 833 (A.B.196), § 3.)*

§ 3212.7. Injury; inclusion of heart trouble, hernia, pneumonia or tuberculosis

In the case of an employee in the Department of Justice falling within the "state safety" class, when any such individual is employed under civil service upon a regular, full-time salary, the term "injury," as used in this division, includes heart trouble or hernia or pneumonia or tuberculosis which develops or manifests itself during the period while such individual is in the service of the Department of Justice. The compensation which is awarded for any such injury shall include full hospital, surgical, medical treatment, disability indemnity, and

death benefits as provided by the provisions of this division.

Such heart trouble, hernia, pneumonia, or tuberculosis so developing or manifesting itself shall be presumed to arise out of and in the course of the employment. This presumption is disputable and may be controverted by other evidence but unless so controverted, the appeals board is bound to find in accordance with it. This presumption shall be extended to a member following termination of service for a period of three calendar months for each full year of the requisite service, but not to exceed 60 months in any circumstance, commencing with the last date actually worked in the specified capacity.

Such heart trouble, hernia, pneumonia, or tuberculosis developing or manifesting itself in such cases shall in no case be attributed to any disease existing prior to such development or manifestation. *(Added by Stats.1961, c. 619, p. 1777, § 1. Amended by Stats.1965, c. 1513, p. 3569, § 56, operative Jan. 15, 1966; Stats.1972, c. 1377, p. 2829, § 66; Stats.1976, c. 466, p. 1210, § 7.)*

§ 3212.8. Members of sheriff's office, police or fire departments, etc.; injury; inclusion of blood-borne infectious disease or methicillin-resistant Staphylococcus aureus skin infection

(a) In the case of members of a sheriff's office, of police or fire departments of cities, counties, cities and counties, districts, or other public or municipal corporations or political subdivisions, or individuals described in Chapter 4.5 (commencing with Section 830) of Title 3 of Part 2 of the Penal Code, whether those persons are volunteer, partly paid, or fully paid, and in the case of active firefighting members of the Department of Forestry and Fire Protection, or of any county forestry or firefighting department or unit, whether voluntary, fully paid, or partly paid, excepting those whose principal duties are clerical or otherwise do not clearly fall within the scope of active law enforcement service or active firefighting services, such as stenographers, telephone operators, and other office workers, the term "injury" as used in this division, includes a blood-borne infectious disease or methicillin-resistant Staphylococcus aureus skin infection when any part of the blood-borne infectious disease or methicillin-resistant Staphylococcus aureus skin infection develops or manifests itself during a period while that person is in the service of that office, staff, division, department, or unit. The compensation that is awarded for a blood-borne infectious disease or methicillin-resistant Staphylococcus aureus skin infection shall include, but not be limited to, full hospital, surgical, medical treatment, disability indemnity, and death benefits, as provided by the workers' compensation laws of this state.

(b)(1) The blood-borne infectious disease or methicillin-resistant Staphylococcus aureus skin infection so developing or manifesting itself in those cases shall be presumed to arise out of and in the course of the

533

employment or service. This presumption is disputable and may be controverted by other evidence, but unless so controverted, the appeals board is bound to find in accordance with it.

(2) The blood-borne infectious disease presumption shall be extended to a person covered by subdivision (a) following termination of service for a period of three calendar months for each full year of service, but not to exceed 60 months in any circumstance, commencing with the last date actually worked in the specified capacity.

(3) Notwithstanding paragraph (2), the methicillin-resistant Staphylococcus aureus skin infection presumption shall be extended to a person covered by subdivision (a) following termination of service for a period of 90 days, commencing with the last day actually worked in the specified capacity.

(c) The blood-borne infectious disease or methicillin-resistant Staphylococcus aureus skin infection so developing or manifesting itself in those cases shall in no case be attributed to any disease or skin infection existing prior to that development or manifestation.

(d) For the purposes of this section, "blood-borne infectious disease" means a disease caused by exposure to pathogenic microorganisms that are present in human blood that can cause disease in humans, including those pathogenic microorganisms defined as blood-borne pathogens by the Department of Industrial Relations. *(Added by Stats.2000, c. 490 (S.B.32), § 1. Amended by Stats.2001, c. 833 (A.B.196), § 4; Stats.2008, c. 684 (A.B.2754), § 2.)*

§ 3212.85. Peace officers and fire department members; injury; inclusion of exposure to biochemical substances; compensation; presumption that injury arose out of, and in course of, employment; definitions

(a) This section applies to peace officers described in Sections 830.1 to 830.5, inclusive, of the Penal Code, and members of a fire department.

(b) The term "injury," as used in this division, includes illness or resulting death due to exposure to a biochemical substance that develops or occurs during a period in which any member described in subdivision (a) is in the service of the department or unit.

(c) The compensation that is awarded for injury pursuant to this section shall include full hospital, surgical, medical treatment, disability indemnity, and death benefits, as provided by this division.

(d) The injury that develops or manifests itself in these cases shall be presumed to arise out of, and in the course of, the employment. This presumption is disputable and may be controverted by other evidence. Unless controverted, the appeals board is bound to find in accordance with the presumption. This presumption shall be extended to a member following termination of service for a period of three calendar months for each full year of the requisite service, but not to exceed 60 months in any

534

circumstance, commencing with the last date actually worked in the specified capacity.

(e) For purposes of this section, the following definitions apply:

(1) "Biochemical substance" means any biological or chemical agent that may be used as a weapon of mass destruction, including, but not limited to, any chemical warfare agent, weaponized biological agent, or nuclear or radiological agent, as these terms are defined in Section 11417 of the Penal Code.

(2) "Members of a fire department" includes, but is not limited to, an apprentice, volunteer, partly paid, or fully paid member of any of the following:

(A) A fire department of a city, county, city and county, district, or other public or municipal corporation or political subdivision.

(B) A fire department of the University of California and the California State University.

(C) The Department of Forestry and Fire Protection.

(D) A county forestry or firefighting department or unit. *(Added by Stats.2002, c. 870 (A.B.1847), § 3.)*

§ 3212.9. Members of police department, sheriff's office, California Highway Patrol, or county probation officer or inspector or investigator in a district attorney's office, etc.; injury; inclusion of meningitis

In the case of a member of a police department of a city, county, or city and county, or a member of the sheriff's office of a county, or a member of the California Highway Patrol, or a county probation officer, or an inspector or investigator in a district attorney's office of any county whose principal duties consist of active law enforcement service, when that person is employed on a regular, full-time salary, or in the case of a member of a fire department of any city, county, or district, or other public or municipal corporation or political subdivision, or any county forestry or firefighting department or unit, when those members are employed on a regular full-time salary, excepting those whose principal duties are clerical or otherwise do not clearly fall within the scope of active law enforcement or firefighting, such as stenographers, telephone operators, and other officeworkers, the term "injury" includes meningitis that develops or manifests itself during a period while that person is in the service of that department, office, or unit. The compensation that is awarded for the meningitis shall include full hospital, surgical, medical treatment, disability indemnity, and death benefits as provided by the provisions of this division.

The meningitis so developing or manifesting itself shall be presumed to arise out of and in the course of the employment. This presumption is disputable and may be controverted by other evidence, but unless so controverted, the appeals board is bound to find in accordance with it. This presumption shall be extended to a person following termination of service for a period of three calendar months for each full year of the requisite service, but not to exceed 60 months in any circumstance, commencing with the last date actually worked in the specified capacity. *(Added by Stats.2000, c. 883 (A.B. 2043), § 1. Amended by Stats.2001, c. 833 (A.B.196), § 5.)*

§ 3212.10. Injury; member of Department of Corrections, officer or employee of Department of Youth Authority, and peace officers; inclusion of heart trouble, hernia, pneumonia, tuberculosis and meningitis; presumption

In the case of a peace officer of the Department of Corrections who has custodial or supervisory duties of inmates or parolees, or a peace officer of the Department of the Youth Authority who has custodial or supervisory duties of wards or parolees, or a peace officer as defined in Section 830.5 of the Penal Code and employed by a local agency, the term "injury" as used in this division includes heart trouble, pneumonia, tuberculosis, and meningitis that develops or manifests itself during a period in which any peace officer covered under this section is in the service of the department or unit. The compensation that is awarded for that injury shall include full hospital, surgical, medical treatment, disability indemnity, and death benefits as provided by the provisions of this division.

The heart trouble, pneumonia, tuberculosis, and meningitis so developing or manifesting itself shall be presumed to arise out of and in the course of employment. This presumption is disputable and may be controverted by other evidence, but unless so controverted, the appeals board is bound to find in accordance with it. This presumption shall be extended to a member following termination of service for a period of three calendar months for each full year of requisite service, but not to exceed 60 months in any circumstance, commencing with the last date actually worked in the specified capacity. *(Added by Stats.2001, c. 835 (S.B.1222), § 2. Amended by Stats.2002, c. 664 (A.B.3034), § 165.)*

§ 3212.11. Lifeguards; skin cancer that develops or manifests itself during period of employment; compensation awarded for injury; months employed; rebuttable presumption

This section applies to both of the following: (a) active lifeguards employed by a city, county, city and county, district, or other public or municipal corporation or political subdivision, and (b) active state lifeguards employed by the Department of Parks and Recreation. The term "injury," as used in this division, includes skin cancer that develops or manifests itself during the period of the lifeguard's employment. The compensation awarded for that injury shall include full hospital, surgical, and medical treatment, disability indemnity, and death benefits, as provided by the provisions of this division.

Skin cancer so developing or manifesting itself shall be presumed to arise out of and in the course of the employment. This presumption is disputable and may be controverted by other evidence, but unless so controverted, the appeals board shall find in accordance with it. This presumption shall be extended to a lifeguard following termination of service for a period of three calendar months for each full year of the requisite service, but not to exceed 60 months in any circumstance, commencing with the last date actually worked in the specified capacity.

Skin cancer so developing or manifesting itself in these cases shall not be attributed to any disease existing prior to that development or manifestation.

This section shall only apply to lifeguards employed for more than three consecutive months in a calendar year. *(Added by Stats.2001, c. 846 (A.B.663), § 1.)*

§ 3212.12. Peace officers, corpsmembers, and conservation corps employees; Lyme disease; compensation; presumption

(a) This section applies to peace officers, as defined in subdivision (b) of Section 830.1 of the Penal Code, subdivisions (e), (f), and (g) of Section 830.2 of the Penal Code, and corpsmembers, as defined by Section 14302 of the Public Resources Code, and other employees at the California Conservation Corps classified as any of the following:

Title	Class
Backcounty Trails Camp Supervisor, California Conservation Corps	1030
Conservationist I, California Conservation Corps	1029
Conservationist II, California Conservation Corps	1003
Conservationist II, Nursery, California Conservation Corps	7370

(b) The term "injury," as used in this division, includes Lyme disease that develops or manifests itself during a period in which any person described in subdivision (a) is in the service of the department.

(c) The compensation that is awarded for Lyme disease shall include full hospital, surgical, medical treatment, disability indemnity, and death benefits, as provided by this division.

(d) Lyme disease so developing or manifesting itself in these cases shall be presumed to arise out of and in the course of the employment. This presumption is disputable and may be controverted by evidence that the Lyme disease is not reasonably linked to the work performance. Unless so controverted, the appeals board shall find in accordance with the presumption. This presumption shall be extended to a person described in subdivision (a) following termination of service for a period of three calendar months for each full year of the requisite service, but not to exceed 60 months in any circumstance, commencing with the last date actually worked in the specified capacity. *(Added by Stats.2002, c. 876 (A.B. 2125), § 1.)*

§ 3213. Injury; University of California police department, police academy graduates; inclusion of heart trouble and pneumonia

In the case of a member of the University of California Police Department who has graduated from an academy certified by the Commission on Peace Officer Standards and Training, when he and all members of the campus department of which he is a member have graduated from such an academy, and when any such member is employed upon a regular, full-time salary, the term "injury" as used in this division includes heart trouble and pneumonia which develops or manifests itself during a period while such member is in the service of such campus department of the University of California Police Department. The compensation which is awarded for such heart trouble or pneumonia shall include full hospital, surgical, medical treatment, disability indemnity, and death benefits as provided by the provisions of this division.

Such heart trouble or pneumonia so developing or manifesting itself shall be presumed to arise out of and in the course of the employment; provided, however, that the member of the University of California Police Department shall have served five years or more in such capacity before the presumption shall arise as to the compensability of heart trouble so developing or manifesting itself. This presumption is disputable and may be controverted by other evidence, but unless so controverted, the appeals board is bound to find in accordance with it. This presumption shall be extended to a member following termination of service for a period of three calendar months for each full year of the requisite service, but not to exceed 60 months in any circumstance, commencing with the last date actually worked in the specified capacity.

Such heart trouble or pneumonia so developing or manifesting itself in such cases shall in no case be attributed to any disease existing prior to such development or manifestation.

As used in this section:

(a) "Members" shall be limited to those employees of the University of California Police Department who are defined as peace officers in Section 830.2 of the Penal Code.

(b) "Campus" shall include any campus or other installation maintained under the jurisdiction of the Regents of the University of California.

(c) "Campus department" means all members of the University of California Police Department who are assigned and serve on a particular campus. *(Added by Stats.1971, c. 918, p. 1801, § 1. Amended by Stats.1976, c. 466, p. 1210, § 8.)*

§ 3213.2. Lower back impairments; law enforcement personnel

(a) In the case of a member of a police department of a city, county, or city and county, or a member of the

sheriff's office of a county, or a peace officer employed by the Department of the California Highway Patrol, or a peace officer employed by the University of California, who has been employed for at least five years as a peace officer on a regular, full-time salary and has been required to wear a duty belt as a condition of employment, the term "injury," as used in this division, includes lower back impairments. The compensation that is awarded for lower back impairments shall include full hospital, surgical, medical treatment, disability indemnity, and death benefits as provided by the provisions of this division.

(b) The lower back impairment so developing or manifesting itself in the peace officer shall be presumed to arise out of and in the course of the employment. This presumption is disputable and may be controverted by other evidence, but unless so controverted, the appeals board is bound to find in accordance with it. This presumption shall be extended to a person following termination of service for a period of three calendar months for each full year of the requisite service, but not to exceed 60 months in any circumstance, commencing with the last date actually worked in the specified capacity.

(c) For purposes of this section, "duty belt" means a belt used for the purpose of holding a gun, handcuffs, baton, and other items related to law enforcement. *(Added by Stats.2001, c. 834 (S.B.424), § 1.)*

§ 3214. Early intervention program; policy and implementation; services; costs

(a) The Department of Corrections and the Department of the Youth Authority shall, in conjunction with all recognized employee representative associations, develop policy and implement the workers' compensation early intervention program by December 31, 1989, for all department employees who sustain an injury. The program shall include, but not be limited to, counseling by an authorized independent early intervention counselor and the services of an agreed medical panel to assist in timely decisions regarding compensability. Costs of services through early intervention shall be borne by the departments.

(b) It is the intent of the Legislature to reduce all costs associated with the delivery of workers' compensation benefits, in balance with the need to ensure timely and adequate benefits to the injured worker. Toward this goal the workers' compensation early intervention program was established in the Department of Corrections and the Department of the Youth Authority. The fundamental concept of the program is to settle disputes rather than to litigate them. This is a worthwhile concept in terms of cost control for the employer and timely receipt of benefits for the worker. To ascertain the effectiveness of the program is crucial in helping guide policy in this arena.

(Added by Stats.1988, c. 1233, § 2. Amended by Stats.1994, c. 1034 (A.B.2163), § 1, eff. Sept. 29, 1994; Stats.2001, c. 745 (S.B.1191), § 157, eff. Oct. 12, 2001.)

§ 3215. Referral of clients or patients for compensation; penalty

Except as otherwise permitted by law, any person acting individually or through his or her employees or agents, who offers, delivers, receives, or accepts any rebate, refund, commission, preference, patronage, dividend, discount or other consideration, whether in the form of money or otherwise, as compensation or inducement for referring clients or patients to perform or obtain services or benefits pursuant to this division, is guilty of a crime. *(Added by Stats.1991, c. 116 (S.B.1218), § 26.)*

§ 3217. Construction of referral provisions; violation of multiple provisions; sentence; exemptions

(a) Section 3215 shall not be construed to prevent the recommendation of professional employment where that recommendation is not prohibited by the Rules of Professional Conduct of the State Bar.

(b) Section 3215 shall not be construed to prohibit a public defender or assigned counsel from making known his or her availability as a criminal defense attorney to persons unable to afford legal counsel, whether or not those persons are in custody.

(c) Any person who commits an act that violates both Section 3215 and either Section 650 of the Business and Professions Code or Section 750 of the Insurance Code shall, upon conviction, have judgment and sentence imposed for only one violation for any act.

(d) Section 3215 shall not be construed to prohibit the payment or receipt of consideration or services that is lawful pursuant to Section 650 of the Business and Professions Code.

(e) Notwithstanding Sections 3215 and 3219, and Section 750 of the Insurance Code, nothing shall prevent an attorney at law or a law firm from providing any person or entity with legal advice, information, or legal services, including the providing of printed, copied, or written documents, either without charge or for an otherwise lawfully agreed upon attorney fee.

(f) Section 3215 shall not be construed to prohibit a workers' compensation insurer from offering, and an employer from accepting, a workers' compensation insurance policy with rates that reflect premium discounts based upon the employer securing coverage for occupational or nonoccupational illnesses or injuries from a health care service plan or disability insurer that is owned by, affiliated with, or has a contractual relationship with, the workers' compensation insurer. *(Added by Stats. 1991, c. 116 (S.B.1218), § 27. Amended by Stats.1993, c. 120 (A.B.1300), § 3.7, eff. July 16, 1993; Stats.1993, c. 1242 (S.B.223), § 23; Stats.1995, c. 886 (S.B.619), § 4.)*

§ 3218. Violations of § 3215; penalties

A violation of Section 3215 is a public offense punishable upon a first conviction by incarceration in the county jail for not more than one year, or by incarceration in the state prison, or by a fine not exceeding ten thousand dollars ($10,000), or by both incarceration and fine. A second or subsequent conviction is punishable by incarceration in state prison. *(Added by Stats.1991, c. 116 (S.B.1218), § 28.)*

§ 3219. Compensation, inducements or rewards given to adjuster of claims for the referral or settlement of a claim; offense; void contracts; fees and compensation

(a)(1) Except as otherwise permitted by law, any person acting individually or through his or her employees or agents, who offers or delivers any rebate, refund, commission, preference, patronage, dividend, discount, or other consideration to any adjuster of claims for compensation, as defined in Section 3207, as compensation, inducement, or reward for the referral or settlement of any claim, is guilty of a felony.

(2) Except as otherwise permitted by law, any adjuster of claims for compensation, as defined in Section 3207, who accepts or receives any rebate, refund, commission, preference, patronage, dividend, discount, or other consideration, as compensation, inducement, or reward for the referral or settlement of any claim, is guilty of a felony.

(b) Any contract for professional services secured by any medical clinic, laboratory, physician or other health care provider in this state in violation of Section 550 of the Penal Code, Section 1871.4 of the Insurance Code, Section 650 or 651 of the Business and Professions Code, or Section 3215 or subdivision (a) of Section 3219 of this code is void. In any action against any medical clinic, laboratory, physician, or other health care provider, or the owners or operators thereof, under Chapter 4 (commencing with Section 17000) or Chapter 5 (commencing with Section 17200) of Division 7 of the Business and Professions Code, any judgment shall include an order divesting the medical clinic, laboratory, physician, or other health care provider, and the owners and operators thereof, of any fees and other compensation received pursuant to any such void contract. Those fees and compensation shall be recoverable as additional civil penalties under Chapter 4 (commencing with Section 17000) or Chapter 5 (commencing with Section 17200) of Division 7 of the Business and Professions Code. The judgment may also include an order prohibiting the person from further participating in any manner in the entity in which that person directly or indirectly owned or operated for a time period that the court deems appropriate. For the purpose of this section, "operated" means participated in the management, direction, or control of the entity.

(c) Notwithstanding Section 17206 or any other provision of law, any fees recovered pursuant to subdivision (b) in an action involving professional services related to the provision of workers' compensation shall be allocated as follows: if the action is brought by the Attorney General, one-half of the penalty collected shall be paid to the State General Fund, and one-half of the penalty collected shall be paid to the Workers' Compensation Fraud Account in the Insurance Fund; if the action is brought by a district attorney, one-half of the penalty collected shall be paid to the treasurer of the county in which the judgment was entered, and one-half of the penalty collected shall be paid to the Workers' Compensation Fraud Account in the Insurance Fund; if the action is brought by a city attorney or city prosecutor, one-half of the penalty collected shall be paid to the treasurer of the city in which the judgment was entered, and one-half of the penalty collected shall be paid to the Workers' Compensation Fraud Account in the Insurance Fund. Moneys deposited into the Workers' Compensation Fraud Account pursuant to this subdivision shall be used in the investigation and prosecution of workers' compensation fraud, as appropriated by the Legislature. *(Added by Stats.1993, c. 120 (A.B.1300), § 4, eff. July 16, 1993.)*

CHAPTER 2. EMPLOYERS, EMPLOYEES, AND DEPENDENTS

Article	Section
1. Employers	3300
2. Employees	3350
3. Dependents	3500
4. Employee Notice	3550

ARTICLE 1.   EMPLOYERS

Section
3300. Employer defined.
3301. Exclusion of certain sponsors.
3302. Temporary employment agencies, referral services, labor contractors or other similar entities.

§ 3300.   Employer defined

As used in this division, "employer" means:

(a) The State and every State agency.

(b) Each county, city, district, and all public and quasi public corporations and public agencies therein.

(c) Every person including any public service corporation, which has any natural person in service.

(d) The legal representative of any deceased employer. *(Stats.1937, c. 90, p. 266, § 3300.)*

§ 3301.   Exclusion of certain sponsors

As used in this division, "employer" excludes the following:

(a) Any person while acting solely as the sponsor of a bowling team.

(b) Any private, nonprofit organization while acting solely as the sponsor of a person who, as a condition of

sentencing by a superior or municipal court, is performing services for the organization.

The exclusions of this section do not exclude any person or organization from the application of this division which is otherwise an employer for the purposes of this division. *(Added by Stats.1965, c. 365, p. 1474, § 1. Amended by Stats.1981, c. 21, p. 47, § 7, eff. April 18, 1981.)*

§ 3302.   Temporary employment agencies, referral services, labor contractors or other similar entities

(a)(1) When a licensed contractor enters an agreement with a temporary employment agency, employment referral service, labor contractor, or other similar entity for the entity to supply the contractor with an individual to perform acts or contracts for which the contractor's license is required under Chapter 9 (commencing with Section 7000) of Division 3 of the Business and Professions Code and the licensed contractor is responsible for supervising the employee's work, the temporary employment agency, employment referral service, labor contractor, or other similar entity shall pay workers' compensation premiums based on the contractor's experience modification rating.

(2) The temporary employment agency, employment referral service, labor contractor, or other similar entity described in paragraph (1) shall report to the insurer both of the following:

(A) Its payroll on a monthly basis in sufficient detail to allow the insurer to determine the number of workers provided and the wages paid to these workers during the period the workers were supplied to the licensed contractor.

(B) The licensed contractor's name, address, and experience modification factor as reported by the licensed contractor.

(C) The workers' compensation classifications associated with the payroll reported pursuant to subparagraph (A). Classifications shall be assigned in accordance with the rules set forth in the California Workers' Compensation Uniform Statistical Reporting Plan published by the Workers' Compensation Insurance Rating Bureau.

(b) The temporary employment agency, employment referral service, labor contractor, or other similar entity supplying the individual under the conditions specified in subdivision (a) shall be solely responsible for the individual's workers' compensation, as specified in subdivision (a).

(c) Nothing in this section is intended to change existing law in effect on December 31, 2002, as it relates to the sole remedy provisions of this division and the special employer provisions of Section 11663 of the Insurance Code.

(d) A licensed contractor that is using a temporary worker supplied pursuant to subdivision (a) shall notify the temporary employment agency, employment referral service, labor contractor, or other similar entity that supplied that temporary worker when either of the following occurs:

(1) The temporary worker is being used on a public works project.

(2) The contractor reassigns a temporary worker to a position other than the classification to which the worker was originally assigned.

(e) A temporary employment agency, employment referral service, labor contractor, or other similar entity may pass through to a licensed contractor any additional costs incurred as a result of this section. *(Added by Stats.2002, c. 1098 (A.B.2816), § 1.)*

ARTICLE 2. EMPLOYEES

Section
3350. Definitions.
3351. Employee; inclusions.
3351.5. Employee.
3352. Employee; exclusions.
3352.94. Disaster service worker as employee.
3353. Independent contractor.
3354. Employers of household employees; exemptions.
3355. Course of trade, business, profession, or occupation.
3356. Trade, business, profession, or occupation.
3357. Employee presumption.
3358. Watchmen for nonindustrial establishment paid by subscription.
3360. Workmen associated in partnership.
3361. Members of volunteer fire departments.
3361.5. Volunteer workers of recreation and park districts.
3362. Members of police departments.
3362.5. Reserve or auxiliary officers.
3363. Active member of reserve fish and game warden program.
3363.5. Persons performing voluntary services for public agency.
3363.6. Persons performing voluntary services for private nonprofit organization.
3364. Sheriff's reserve; volunteer, unsalaried members.
3364.5. Persons performing voluntary services for school districts.
3364.55. Workmen's compensation for ward of juvenile court injured in rehabilitation work.
3364.6. Juvenile traffic offenders or probationers engaged in rehabilitative work on public property; resolution.
3364.7. Ward of juvenile court committed to regional youth educational facility engaged in rehabilitative work without pay on public property; workers' compensation benefits.
3365. Persons engaged in suppressing fires.
3366. Persons engaged in law enforcement service as part of posse comitatus or assisting police officer; persons excluded.
3367. Persons rendering technical assistance; fire, explosion, or other hazardous occurrence; persons excluded.
3368. Work experience education; occupational training classes; apprentices.
3369. Inclusion within coverage of this division; effect on other coverage.
3370. Inmate of state penal or correctional institution; conditions.
3371. Workers' compensation attorneys list; representation before appeals board.

§ 3350. Definitions

Unless the context otherwise requires, the definitions set forth in this article shall govern the construction and meaning of the terms and phrases used in this division. *(Stats.1937, c. 90, p. 267, § 3350.)*

§ 3351. Employee; inclusions

"Employee" means every person in the service of an employer under any appointment or contract of hire or apprenticeship, express or implied, oral or written, whether lawfully or unlawfully employed, and includes:

(a) Aliens and minors.

(b) All elected and appointed paid public officers.

(c) All officers and members of boards of directors of quasi-public or private corporations while rendering actual service for the corporations for pay; provided that, where the officers and directors of the private corporation are the sole shareholders thereof, the corporation and the officers and directors shall come under the compensation provisions of this division only by election as provided in subdivision (a) of Section 4151.

(d) Except as provided in subdivision (h) of Section 3352, any person employed by the owner or occupant of a residential dwelling whose duties are incidental to the ownership, maintenance, or use of the dwelling, including the care and supervision of children, or whose duties are personal and not in the course of the trade, business, profession, or occupation of the owner or occupant.

(e) All persons incarcerated in a state penal or correctional institution while engaged in assigned work or employment as defined in paragraph (1) of subdivision (a) of Section 10021 of Title 8 of the California Code of Regulations, or engaged in work performed under contract.

(f) All working members of a partnership or limited liability company receiving wages irrespective of profits from the partnership or limited liability company; provided that where the working members of the partnership or limited liability company are general partners or managers, the partnership or limited liability company and the partners or managers shall come under the compensation provisions of this division only by election as provided in subdivision (a) of Section 4151. If a private corporation is a general partner or manager, "working members of a partnership or limited liability company" shall include the corporation and the officers and directors of the corporation, provided that the officers and directors are the sole shareholders of the corporation. If a limited liability company is a partner or member, "working members of the partnership or limited liability company" shall include the managers of the limited liability company.

(g) For the purposes of subdivisions (c) and (f), the persons holding the power to revoke a trust as to shares

539

of a private corporation or as to general partnership or limited liability company interests held in the trust, shall be deemed to be the shareholders of the private corporation, or the general partners of the partnership, or the managers of the limited liability company. *(Added by Stats.1977, c. 17, p. 30, § 17, eff. March 25, 1977. Amended by Stats.1978, c. 958, p. 2960, § 1; Stats.1985, c. 1156, § 3; Stats.1994, c. 497 (A.B.1269), § 2; Stats.1996, c. 57 (S.B.141), § 26, eff. June 6, 1996.)*

§ 3351.5. Employee

"Employee" includes:

(a) Any person whose employment training is arranged by the State Department of Rehabilitation with any employer. Such person shall be deemed an employee of such employer for workers' compensation purposes; provided that, the department shall bear the full amount of any additional workers' compensation insurance premium expense incurred by the employer due to the provisions of this section.

(b) Any person defined in subdivision (d) of Section 3351 who performs domestic service comprising in-home supportive services under Article 7 (commencing with Section 12300), Chapter 3, Part 3, Division 9 of the Welfare and Institutions Code. For purposes of Section 3352, such person shall be deemed an employee of the recipient of such services for workers' compensation purposes if the state or county makes or provides for direct payment to such person or to the recipient of in-home supportive services for the purchase of services, subject to the provisions of Section 12302.2 of the Welfare and Institutions Code.

(c) Any person while engaged by contract for the creation of a specially ordered or commissioned work of authorship in which the parties expressly agree in a written instrument signed by them that the work shall be considered a work made for hire, as defined in Section 101 of Title 17 of the United States Code, and the ordering or commissioning party obtains ownership of all the rights comprised in the copyright in the work. *(Added by Stats.1969, c. 1133, p. 2201, § 1. Amended by Stats.1978, c. 463, p. 1571, § 2, eff. July 18, 1978; Stats.1982, c. 1332, p. 4933, § 1.)*

§ 3352. Employee; exclusions

"Employee" excludes the following:

(a) Any person defined in subdivision (d) of Section 3351 who is employed by his or her parent, spouse, or child.

(b) Any person performing services in return for aid or sustenance only, received from any religious, charitable, or relief organization.

(c) Any person holding an appointment as deputy clerk or deputy sheriff appointed for his or her own convenience, and who receives no compensation from the county or municipal corporation or from the citizens thereof for his or her services as the deputy. This exclusion is operative only as to employment by the county or municipal corporation and does not deprive any person so deputized from recourse against a private person employing him or her for injury occurring in the course of and arising out of the employment.

(d) Any person performing voluntary services at or for a recreational camp, hut, or lodge operated by a nonprofit organization, exempt from federal income tax under Section 101(6) of the Internal Revenue Code, of which he or she or a member of his or her family is a member and who receives no compensation for those services other than meals, lodging, or transportation.

(e) Any person performing voluntary service as a ski patrolman who receives no compensation for those services other than meals or lodging or the use of ski tow or ski lift facilities.

(f) Any person employed by a ski lift operator to work at a snow ski area who is relieved of and not performing any prescribed duties, while participating in recreational activities on his or her own initiative.

(g) Any person, other than a regular employee, participating in sports or athletics who receives no compensation for the participation other than the use of athletic equipment, uniforms, transportation, travel, meals, lodgings, or other expenses incidental thereto.

(h) Any person defined in subdivision (d) of Section 3351 who was employed by the employer to be held liable for less than 52 hours during the 90 calendar days immediately preceding the date of the injury for injuries, as defined in Section 5411, or during the 90 calendar days immediately preceding the date of the last employment in an occupation exposing the employee to the hazards of the disease or injury for injuries, as defined in Section 5412, or who earned less than one hundred dollars ($100) in wages from the employer during the 90 calendar days immediately preceding the date of the injury for injuries, as defined in Section 5411, or during the 90 calendar days immediately preceding the date of the last employment in an occupation exposing the employee to the hazards of the disease or injury for injuries, as defined in Section 5412.

(i) Any person performing voluntary service for a public agency or a private, nonprofit organization who receives no remuneration for the services other than meals, transportation, lodging, or reimbursement for incidental expenses.

(j) Any person, other than a regular employee, performing officiating services relating to amateur sporting events sponsored by any public agency or private, nonprofit organization, who receives no remuneration for these services other than a stipend for each day of service no greater than the amount established by the Department of Personnel Administration as a per diem expense for employees or officers of the state. The stipend shall be presumed to cover incidental expenses involved in officiating, including, but not limited to, meals, transportation, lodging, rule books and courses, uniforms, and appropriate equipment.

(k) Any student participating as an athlete in amateur sporting events sponsored by any public agency, public or private nonprofit college, university or school, who receives no remuneration for the participation other than the use of athletic equipment, uniforms, transportation, travel, meals, lodgings, scholarships, grants-in-aid, or other expenses incidental thereto.

(*l*) Any law enforcement officer who is regularly employed by a local or state law enforcement agency in an adjoining state and who is deputized to work under the supervision of a California peace officer pursuant to paragraph (4) of subdivision (a) of Section 832.6 of the Penal Code.

(m) Any law enforcement officer who is regularly employed by the Oregon State Police, the Nevada Department of Motor Vehicles and Public Safety, or the Arizona Department of Public Safety and who is acting as a peace officer in this state pursuant to subdivision (a) of Section 830.32 of the Penal Code.

(n) Any person, other than a regular employee, performing services as a sports official for an entity sponsoring an intercollegiate or interscholastic sports event, or any person performing services as a sports official for a public agency, public entity, or a private nonprofit organization, which public agency, public entity, or private nonprofit organization sponsors an amateur sports event. For purposes of this subdivision, "sports official" includes an umpire, referee, judge, scorekeeper, timekeeper, or other person who is a neutral participant in a sports event.

(o) Any person who is an owner-builder, as defined in subdivision (a) of Section 50692 of the Health and Safety Code, who is participating in a mutual self-help housing program, as defined in Section 50087 of the Health and Safety Code, sponsored by a nonprofit corporation. *(Added by Stats.1977, c. 17, p. 30, § 18, eff. March 25, 1977 Amended by Stats.1978, c. 239, p. 504, § 1, eff. June 16, 1978; Stats.1978, c. 1303, p. 4258, § 1; Stats.1979, c. 76, p. 184, § 1; Stats.1981, c. 21, p. 47, § 8, eff. April 18, 1981; Stats.1988, c. 1482, § 1; Stats.1989, c. 594, § 2; Stats.1995, c. 725 (A.B.1655), § 1; Stats.1996, c. 872 (A.B.3472), § 106; Stats.1996, c. 320 (A.B.2160), § 30; Stats.1998, c. 931 (S.B.2139), § 347, eff. Sept. 28, 1998; Stats.2004, c. 83 (A.B.2649), § 1.)*

§ 3352.94. Disaster service worker as employee

"Employee" excludes a disaster service worker while performing services as a disaster service worker except as provided in Chapter 10 of this part.[1] "Employee" excludes any unregistered person performing like services as a disaster service worker without pay or other consideration, except as provided by Section 3211.92 of this code. *(Added by Stats.1946, 1st Ex.Sess., c. 104, p. 133, § 5, eff. March 8, 1946. Amended by Stats.1951, c. 1440, p. 3400, § 4.)*

[1] See Labor Code § 4351 et seq.

§ 3353. Independent contractor

"Independent contractor" means any person who renders service for a specified recompense for a specified result, under the control of his principal as to the result of his work only and not as to the means by which such result is accomplished. *(Stats.1937, c. 90, p. 267, § 3353.)*

§ 3354. Employers of household employees; exemptions

Employers of employees defined by subdivision (d) of Section 3351 shall not be subject to the provisions of Sections 3710, 3710.1, 3710.2, 3711, 3712, and 3722, or any other penalty provided by law, for failure to secure the payment of compensation for such employees.

This section shall not apply to employers of employees specified in subdivision (b) of Section 3715, with respect to such employees. *(Added by Stats.1977, c. 17, p. 31, § 19, eff. March 25, 1977.)*

§ 3355. Course of trade, business, profession, or occupation

As used in subdivision (d) of Section 3351, the term "course of trade, business, profession, or occupation" includes all services tending toward the preservation, maintenance, or operation of the business, business premises, or business property of the employer. *(Added by Stats.1977, c. 17, p. 31, § 20, eff. March 25, 1977.)*

§ 3356. Trade, business, profession, or occupation

As used in subdivision (d) of Section 3351 and in Section 3355, the term "trade, business, profession, or occupation" includes any undertaking actually engaged in by the employer with some degree of regularity, irrespective of the trade name, articles of incorporation, or principal business of the employer. *(Added by Stats.1977, c. 17, p. 31, § 21, eff. March 25, 1977.)*

§ 3357. Employee presumption

Any person rendering service for another, other than as an independent contractor, or unless expressly excluded herein, is presumed to be an employee. *(Stats.1937, c. 90, p. 268, § 3357.)*

§ 3358. Watchmen for nonindustrial establishment paid by subscription

Watchmen for nonindustrial establishments, paid by subscription by several persons, are not employees under this division. In other cases where watchmen, paid by subscription by several persons, have at the time of the injury sustained by them taken out and maintained in force insurance upon themselves as self-employing persons, conferring benefits equal to those conferred by this division, the employer is not liable under this division. *(Stats.1937, c. 90, p. 268, § 3358.)*

§ 3360. Workmen associated in partnership

Workmen associating themselves under a partnership agreement, the principal purpose of which is the performance of the labor on a particular piece of work are employees of the person having such work executed. In respect to injuries which occur while such workmen maintain in force insurance in an insurer, insuring to themselves and all persons employed by them benefits identical with those conferred by this division the person for whom such work is to be done is not liable as an employer under this division. *(Stats.1937, c. 90, p. 268, § 3360.)*

§ 3361.   Members of volunteer fire departments

Each member registered as an active firefighting member of any regularly organized volunteer fire department, having official recognition, and full or partial support of the government of the county, city, town, or district in which the volunteer fire department is located, is an employee of that county, city, town, or district for the purposes of this division, and is entitled to receive compensation from the county, city, town or district in accordance with the provisions thereof. *(Stats.1937, c. 90, p. 268, § 3361. Amended by Stats.1951, c. 1673, p. 3829, § 2; Stats.1973, c. 953, p. 1794, § 1; Stats. 1984, c. 114, § 3.)*

§ 3361.5.   Volunteer workers of recreation and park districts

Notwithstanding Section 3351, a volunteer, unsalaried person authorized by the governing board of a recreation and park district to perform volunteer services for the district shall, upon the adoption of a resolution of the governing board of the district so declaring, be deemed an employee of the district for the purposes of this division and shall be entitled to the workers' compensation benefits provided by this division for any injury sustained by him or her while engaged in the performance of any service under the direction and control of the governing board of the recreation and park district. *(Added by Stats.1973, c. 472, p. 947, § 1. Amended by Stats.1982, c. 454, p. 1877, § 134.)*

§ 3362.   Members of police departments

Each male or female member registered as an active policeman or policewoman of any regularly organized police department having official recognition and full or partial support of the government of the county, city, town or district in which such police department is located, shall, upon the adoption of a resolution by the governing body of the county, city, town or district so declaring, be deemed an employee of such county, city, town or district for the purpose of this division and shall be entitled to receive compensation from such county, city, town or district in accordance with the provisions thereof. *(Added by Stats.1959, c. 1650, p. 4027, § 1.)*

§ 3362.5.   Reserve or auxiliary officers

Whenever any qualified person is deputized or appointed by the proper authority as a reserve or auxiliary sheriff or city police officer, a deputy sheriff, or a reserve police officer of a regional park district or a transit district, and is assigned specific police functions by that authority, the person is an employee of the county, city, city and county, town, or district for the purposes of this division while performing duties as a peace officer if the person is not performing services as a disaster service worker for purposes of Chapter 10 (commencing with Section 4351). *(Added by Stats.1989, c. 892, § 25.5.)*

§ 3363.   Active member of reserve fish and game warden program

Each member registered with the Department of Fish and Game as an active member of the reserve fish and game warden program of the department is an employee of the department for the purposes of this division, and is entitled to receive compensation from the department in accordance with the provisions thereof. *(Added by Stats.1961, c. 1394, p. 3189, § 1.)*

§ 3363.5.   Persons performing voluntary services for public agency

(a) Notwithstanding Sections 3351, 3352, and 3357, a person who performs voluntary service without pay for a public agency, as designated and authorized by the governing body of the agency or its designee, shall, upon adoption of a resolution by the governing body of the agency so declaring, be deemed to be an employee of the agency for purposes of this division while performing such service.

(b) For purposes of this section, "voluntary service without pay" shall include services performed by any person, who receives no remuneration other than meals, transportation, lodging, or reimbursement for incidental expenses. *(Added by Stats.1971, c. 579, p. 1173, § 1. Amended by Stats.1974, c. 912, p. 1926, § 1; Stats.1979, c. 76, p. 185, § 2.)*

§ 3363.6.   Persons performing voluntary services for private nonprofit organization

(a) Notwithstanding Sections 3351, 3352, and 3357, a person who performs voluntary service without pay for a private, nonprofit organization, as designated and authorized by the board of directors of the organization, shall, when the board of directors of the organization, in its sole discretion, so declares in writing and prior to the injury, be deemed an employee of the organization for purposes of this division while performing such service.

(b) For purposes of this section, "voluntary service without pay" shall include the performance of services by a parent, without remuneration in cash, when rendered to a cooperative parent participation nursery school if such service is required as a condition of participation in the organization.

(c) For purposes of this section, "voluntary service without pay" shall include the performance of services by a person who receives no remuneration other than meals, transportation, lodging, or reimbursement for incidental expenses. *(Added by Stats.1974, c. 912, p. 1926, § 2. Amended by Stats.1976, c. 51, p. 81, § 1, eff. March 20,*

1976; Stats.1978, c. 239, p. 506, § 2, eff. June 16, 1978; Stats.1979, c. 76, p. 185, § 3.)

§ 3364. Sheriff's reserve; volunteer, unsalaried members

Notwithstanding subdivision (c) of Section 3352, a volunteer, unsalaried member of a sheriff's reserve in any county who is not deemed an employee of the county under Section 3362.5, shall, upon the adoption of a resolution of the board of supervisors declaring that the member is deemed an employee of the county for the purposes of this division, be entitled to the workers' compensation benefits provided by this division for any injury sustained by him or her while engaged in the performance of any active law enforcement service under the direction and control of the sheriff. *(Added by Stats.1961, c. 901, p. 2525, § 1. Amended by Stats.1989, c. 892, § 26; Stats.2006, c. 538 (S.B.1852), § 488.)*

§ 3364.5. Persons performing voluntary services for school districts

Notwithstanding Section 3351 of the Labor Code, a volunteer, unsalaried person authorized by the governing board of a school district or the county superintendent of schools to perform volunteer services for the school district or the county superintendent shall, upon the adoption of a resolution of the governing board of the school district or the county board of education so declaring, be deemed an employee of the district or the county superintendent for the purposes of this division and shall be entitled to the workmen's compensation benefits provided by this division for any injury sustained by him while engaged in the performance of any service under the direction and control of the governing board of the school district or the county superintendent. *(Added by Stats.1967, c. 345, p. 1544, § 2. Amended by Stats.1968, c. 1146, p. 2180, § 1.)*

§ 3364.55. Workmen's compensation for ward of juvenile court injured in rehabilitation work

A ward of the juvenile court engaged in rehabilitative work without pay, under an assignment by order of the juvenile court to a work project on public property within the jurisdiction of any governmental entity, including the federal government, shall, upon the adoption of a resolution of the board of supervisors declaring that such ward is deemed an employee of the county for purposes of this division, be entitled to the workers' compensation benefits provided by this division for injury sustained while in the performance of such assigned work project, provided:

(a) That such ward shall not be entitled to any temporary disability indemnity benefits.

(b) That in determining permanent disability benefits, average weekly earnings shall be taken at the minimum provided therefor in Section 4453. *(Added by Stats.1968, c. 1226, p. 2336, § 2. Amended by Stats.1972, c. 628, p. 1163, § 1; Stats.1976, c. 1347, p. 6137, § 3.)*

§ 3364.6. Juvenile traffic offenders or probationers engaged in rehabilitative work on public property; resolution

Notwithstanding Sections 3351 and 3352, juvenile traffic offenders pursuant to Section 564 of the Welfare and Institutions Code, or juvenile probationers pursuant to subdivision (a) of Section 725 of the Welfare and Institutions Code, engaged in rehabilitative work without pay, under an assignment by order of the juvenile court to a work project on public property within the jurisdiction of any governmental entity, including the federal government, shall, upon the adoption of a resolution of the board of supervisors declaring that such traffic offenders or probationers, or both such groups, shall be deemed employees of the county for purposes of this division, be entitled to the workers' compensation benefits provided by this division for injury sustained while in the performance of such assigned work project, provided:

(a) That such traffic offender or probationer shall not be entitled to any temporary disability indemnity benefits.

(b) That in determining permanent disability benefits, average weekly earnings shall be taken at the minimum provided therefor in Section 4453. *(Added by Stats.1976, c. 428, p. 1095, § 2.)*

§ 3364.7. Ward of juvenile court committed to regional youth educational facility engaged in rehabilitative work without pay on public property; workers' compensation benefits

Notwithstanding Sections 3351 and 3352, a ward of the juvenile court committed to a regional youth educational facility pursuant to Article 24.5 (commencing with Section 894), engaged in rehabilitative work without pay on public property within the jurisdiction of any governmental entity, including the federal government, shall, upon the adoption of a resolution of the board of supervisors declaring that such wards shall be deemed employees of the county for purposes of this division, be entitled to the workers' compensation benefits provided by this division for injury sustained while in the performance of such public work project, provided:

(a) That the ward shall not be entitled to any disability indemnity benefits.

(b) That in determining permanent disability benefits, average weekly earnings shall be taken at the minimum provided therefor in Section 4453. *(Added by Stats. 1984, c. 1455, § 4, eff. Sept. 26, 1984.)*

§ 3365. Persons engaged in suppressing fires

For the purposes of this division:

(a) Except as provided in subdivisions (b) and (c), each person engaged in suppressing a fire pursuant to Section 4153 or 4436 of the Public Resources Code, and each person (other than an independent contractor or an employee of an independent contractor) engaged in suppressing a fire at the request of a public officer or employee charged with the duty of preventing or suppressing fires, is deemed, except when the entity is the

543

United States or an agency thereof, to be an employee of the public entity that he is serving or assisting in the suppression of the fire, and is entitled to receive compensation from such public entity in accordance with the provisions of this division. When the entity being served is the United States or an agency thereof, the State Department of Corrections shall be deemed the employer and the cost of workers' compensation may be considered in fixing the reimbursement paid by the United States for the service of prisoners. A person is engaged in suppressing a fire only during the period he (1) is actually fighting the fire, (2) is being transported to or from the fire, or (3) is engaged in training exercises for fire suppression.

(b) A member of the armed forces of the United States while serving under military command in suppressing a fire is not an employee of a public entity.

(c) Neither a person who contracts to furnish aircraft with pilots to a public entity for fire prevention or suppression service, nor his employees, shall be deemed to be employees of the public entity; but a person who contracts to furnish aircraft to a public entity for fire prevention or suppression service and to pilot the aircraft himself shall be deemed to be an employee of the public entity. *(Added by Stats.1963, c. 1684, p. 3305, § 1. Amended by Stats.1969, c. 213, p. 542, § 2; Stats.1969, c. 1112, p. 2170, § 1, eff. Aug. 29, 1969; Stats.1976, c. 1347, p. 6137, § 4.)*

§ 3366. Persons engaged in law enforcement service as part of posse comitatus or assisting police officer; persons excluded

(a) For the purposes of this division, each person engaged in the performance of active law enforcement service as part of the posse comitatus or power of the county, and each person (other than an independent contractor or an employee of an independent contractor) engaged in assisting any peace officer in active law enforcement service at the request of such peace officer, is deemed to be an employee of the public entity that he or she is serving or assisting in the enforcement of the law, and is entitled to receive compensation from the public entity in accordance with the provisions of this division.

(b) Nothing in this section shall be construed to provide workers' compensation benefits to a person who is any of the following:

(1) A law enforcement officer who is regularly employed by a local or state law enforcement agency in an adjoining state and who is deputized to work under the supervision of a California peace officer pursuant to paragraph (4) of subdivision (a) of Section 832.6 of the Penal Code.

(2) A law enforcement officer who is regularly employed by the Oregon State Police, the Nevada Department of Motor Vehicles and Public Safety, or the Arizona Department of Public Safety and who is acting as a peace officer in this state pursuant to subdivision (a) of Section

830.32 of the Penal Code. *(Added by Stats.1963, c. 1684, p. 3306, § 2. Amended by Stats.1988, c. 1482, § 2; Stats.1989, c. 1360, § 102; Stats.1989, c. 594, § 3.)*

§ 3367. Persons rendering technical assistance; fire, explosion, or other hazardous occurrence; persons excluded

(a) For purposes of this division any person voluntarily rendering technical assistance to a public entity to prevent a fire, explosion, or other hazardous occurrence, at the request of a duly authorized fire or law enforcement officer of that public entity is deemed an employee of the public entity to whom the technical assistance was rendered, and is entitled to receive compensation benefits in accordance with the provisions of this division. Rendering technical assistance shall include the time that person is traveling to, or returning from, the location of the potentially hazardous condition for which he or she has been requested to volunteer his or her assistance.

(b) Nothing in this section shall be construed to provide workers' compensation benefits to a person who is any of the following:

(1) A law enforcement officer who is regularly employed by a local or state law enforcement agency in an adjoining state and who is deputized to work under the supervision of a California peace officer pursuant to paragraph (4) of subdivision (a) of Section 832.6 of the Penal Code.

(2) A law enforcement officer who is regularly employed by the Oregon State Police, the Nevada Department of Motor Vehicles and Public Safety, or the Arizona Department of Public Safety and who is acting as a peace officer in this state pursuant to subdivision (a) of Section 830.32 of the Penal Code. *(Added by Stats.1970, c. 884, p. 1618, § 1. Amended by Stats.1988, c. 1482, § 3; Stats. 1989, c. 1360, § 103; Stats.1989, c. 594, § 4.)*

§ 3368. Work experience education; occupational training classes; apprentices

Notwithstanding any provision of this code or the Education Code to the contrary, the school district, county superintendent of schools, or any school administered by the State Department of Education under whose supervision work experience education, cooperative vocational education, or community classrooms, as defined by regulations adopted by the Superintendent of Public Instruction, or student apprenticeship programs registered by the Division of Apprenticeship Standards for registered student apprentices, are provided, shall be considered the employer under Division 4 (commencing with Section 3200) of persons receiving this training unless the persons during the training are being paid a cash wage or salary by a private employer. However, in the case of students being paid a cash wage or salary by a private employer in supervised work experience education or cooperative vocational education, or in the case of registered student apprentices, the school district, county superintendent of schools, or any school administered by the State Department of Education may elect to provide workers' compensation coverage, unless the person or firm under whom the persons are receiving work experience or occupational training elects to provide workers' compensation coverage. If the school district or other educational agency elects to provide workers' compensation coverage for students being paid a cash wage or salary by a private employer in supervised work experience education or cooperative vocational education, it may only be for a transitional period not to exceed three months. A registered student apprentice is a registered apprentice who is (1) at least 16 years of age, (2) a full-time high school student in the 10th, 11th, or 12th grade, and (3) in an apprenticeship program for registered student apprentices registered with the Division of Apprenticeship Standards. An apprentice, while attending related and supplemental instruction classes, shall be considered to be in the employ of the apprentice's employer and not subject to this section, unless the apprentice is unemployed. Whenever this work experience education, cooperative vocational education, community classroom education, or student apprenticeship program registered by the Division of Apprenticeship Standards for registered student apprentices, is under the supervision of a regional occupational center or program operated by two or more school districts pursuant to Section 52301 of the Education Code, the district of residence of the persons receiving the training shall be deemed the employer for the purposes of this section. *(Added by Stats.1971, c. 1396, p. 2748, § 2. Amended by Stats.1974, c. 1008, p. 2185, § 2; Stats.1980, c. 1165, p. 3918, § 4; Stats.1997, c. 345 (S.B.952), § 2; Stats.1998, c. 541 (S.B.1817), § 1.)*

§ 3369. Inclusion within coverage of this division; effect on other coverage

The inclusion of any person or groups of persons within the coverage of this division shall not cause any such person or group of persons to be within the coverage of any other statute unless any other such statute expressly so provides. *(Added by Stats.1974, c. 966, p. 2014, § 2.)*

§ 3370. Inmate of state penal or correctional institution; conditions

(a) Each inmate of a state penal or correctional institution shall be entitled to the workers' compensation benefits provided by this division for injury arising out of and in the course of assigned employment and for the death of the inmate if the injury proximately causes death, subject to all of the following conditions:

(1) The inmate was not injured as the result of an assault in which the inmate was the initial aggressor, or as the result of the intentional act of the inmate injuring himself or herself.

(2) The inmate shall not be entitled to any temporary disability indemnity benefits while incarcerated in a state prison.

(3) No benefits shall be paid to an inmate while he or she is incarcerated. The period of benefit payment shall instead commence upon release from incarceration. If an inmate who has been released from incarceration, and has been receiving benefits under this section, is reincarcerated in a city or county jail, or state penal or correctional institution, the benefits shall cease immediately upon the inmate's reincarceration and shall not be paid for the duration of the reincarceration.

(4) This section shall not be construed to provide for the payment to an inmate, upon release from incarceration, of temporary disability benefits which were not paid due to the prohibition of paragraph (2).

(5) In determining temporary and permanent disability indemnity benefits for the inmate, the average weekly earnings shall be taken at not more than the minimum amount set forth in Section 4453.

(6) Where a dispute exists respecting an inmate's rights to the workers' compensation benefits provided herein, the inmate may file an application with the appeals board to resolve the dispute. The application may be filed at any time during the inmate's incarceration.

(7) After release or discharge from a correctional institution, the former inmate shall have one year in which to file an original application with the appeals board, unless the time of injury is such that it would allow more time under Section 5804 of the Labor Code.

(8) The percentage of disability to total disability shall be determined as for the occupation of a laborer of like age by applying the schedule for the determination of the percentages of permanent disabilities prepared and adopted by the administrative director.

(9) This division shall be the exclusive remedy against the state for injuries occurring while engaged in assigned work or work under contract. Nothing in this division shall affect any right or remedy of an injured inmate for injuries not compensated by this division.

(b) The Department of Corrections shall present to each inmate of a state penal or correctional institution, prior to his or her first assignment to work at the institution, a printed statement of his or her rights under this division, and a description of procedures to be followed in filing for benefits under this section. The statement shall be approved by the administrative director and be posted in a conspicuous place at each place where an inmate works.

(c) Notwithstanding any other provision of this division, the Department of Corrections shall have medical control over treatment provided an injured inmate while incarcerated in a state prison, except, that in serious cases, the inmate is entitled, upon request, to the services of a consulting physician.

(d) Paragraphs (2), (3), and (4) of subdivision (a) shall also be applicable to an inmate of a state penal or correctional institution who would otherwise be entitled to receive workers' compensation benefits based on an injury sustained prior to his or her incarceration. However, temporary and permanent disability benefits which, except for this subdivision, would otherwise be payable to an inmate during incarceration based on an injury sustained prior to incarceration shall be paid to the dependents of the inmate. If the inmate has no dependents, the temporary disability benefits which, except for this subdivision, would otherwise be payable during the inmate's incarceration shall be paid to the State Treasury to the credit of the Uninsured Employers Fund, and the permanent disability benefits which would otherwise be payable during the inmate's incarceration shall be held in trust for the inmate by the Department of Corrections during the period of incarceration.

For purposes of this subdivision, "dependents" means the inmate's spouse or children, including an inmate's former spouse due to divorce and the inmate's children from that marriage.

(e) Notwithstanding any other provision of this division, an employee who is an inmate, as defined in subdivision (e) of Section 3351 who is eligible for vocational rehabilitation services as defined in Section 4635 shall only be eligible for direct placement services. *(Added by Stats.1976, c. 1347, p. 6138, § 5. Amended by Stats.1988, c. 839, § 1; Stats.1994, c. 497 (A.B.1269), § 3.)*

§ 3371. Workers' compensation attorneys list; representation before appeals board

If the issues are complex or if the inmate applicant requests, the Department of Corrections shall furnish a list of qualified workers' compensation attorneys to permit the inmate applicant to choose an attorney to represent him or her before the appeals board. *(Added by Stats.1994, c. 497 (A.B.1269), § 5.)*

ARTICLE 3.   DEPENDENTS

Section
3501. Persons conclusively presumed wholly dependent.
3502. Determination of dependency questions; time of injury.
3503. Requisite relationship.

§ 3501. Persons conclusively presumed wholly dependent

(a) A child under the age of 18 years, or a child of any age found by any trier of fact, whether contractual, administrative, regulatory, or judicial, to be physically or mentally incapacitated from earning, shall be conclusively presumed to be wholly dependent for support upon a deceased employee-parent with whom that child is living at the time of injury resulting in death of the parent or for whose maintenance the parent was legally liable at the time of injury resulting in death of the parent, there being no surviving totally dependent parent.

(b) A spouse to whom a deceased employee is married at the time of death shall be conclusively presumed to be wholly dependent for support upon the deceased employee if the surviving spouse earned thirty thousand dollars

($30,000) or less in the twelve months immediately preceding the death. *(Added by Stats.1979, c. 749, p. 2600, § 2. Amended by Stats.1989, c. 892, § 26.5; Stats. 2002, c. 6 (A.B.749), § 43; Stats.2002, c. 866 (A.B.486), § 6.)*

§ 3502. Determination of dependency questions; time of injury

In all other cases, questions of entire or partial dependency and questions as to who are dependents and the extent of their dependency shall be determined in accordance with the facts as they exist at the time of the injury of the employee. *(Stats.1937, c. 90, p. 269, § 3502.)*

§ 3503. Requisite relationship

No person is a dependent of any deceased employee unless in good faith a member of the family or household of the employee, or unless the person bears to the employee the relation of husband or wife, child, posthumous child, adopted child or stepchild, grandchild, father or mother, father-in-law or mother-in-law, grandfather or grandmother, brother or sister, uncle or aunt, brother-in-law or sister-in-law, nephew or niece. *(Stats. 1937, c. 90, p. 269, § 3503. Amended by Stats.1979, c. 749, p. 2600, § 3.)*

ARTICLE 4.   EMPLOYEE NOTICE

Section
3550. Conspicuous location; contents; failure to keep notice as misdemeanor; exemption; form.
3551. Written notice to new employees.
3553. Workers' compensation eligibility; employee victims; crimes occurring at place of employment.

§ 3550. Conspicuous location; contents; failure to keep notice as misdemeanor; exemption; form

(a) Every employer subject to the compensation provisions of this division shall post and keep posted in a conspicuous location frequented by employees, and where the notice may be easily read by employees during the hours of the workday, a notice that states the name of the current compensation insurance carrier of the employer, or when such is the fact, that the employer is self-insured, and who is responsible for claims adjustment.

(b) Failure to keep any notice required by this section conspicuously posted shall constitute a misdemeanor, and shall be prima facie evidence of noninsurance.

(c) This section shall not apply with respect to the employment of employees as defined in subdivision (d) of Section 3351.

(d) The form and content of the notice required by this section shall be prescribed by the administrative director, after consultation with the Commission on Health and Safety and Workers' Compensation, and shall advise employees that all injuries should be reported to their employer. The notice shall be easily understandable. It shall be posted in both English and Spanish where there are Spanish-speaking employees. The notice shall include the following information:

(1) How to get emergency medical treatment, if needed.

(2) The kinds of events, injuries, and illnesses covered by workers' compensation.

(3) The injured employee's right to receive medical care.

(4) The rights of the employee to select and change the treating physician pursuant to the provisions of Section 4600.

(5) The rights of the employee to receive temporary disability indemnity, permanent disability indemnity, vocational rehabilitation services, and death benefits, as appropriate.

(6) To whom injuries should be reported.

(7) The existence of time limits for the employer to be notified of an occupational injury.

(8) The protections against discrimination provided pursuant to Section 132a.

(9) The location and telephone number of the nearest information and assistance officer.

(e) Failure of an employer to provide the notice required by this section shall automatically permit the employee to be treated by his or her personal physician with respect to an injury occurring during that failure.

(f) The form and content of the notice required to be posted by this section shall be made available to self-insured employers and insurers by the administrative director. Insurers shall provide this notice to each of their policyholders, with advice concerning the requirements of this section and the penalties for a failure to post this notice. *(Added by Stats. 1984, c. 1141, § 1. Amended by Stats.1987, c. 1019, § 3; Stats.2002, c. 6 (A.B.749), § 44.)*

§ 3551. Written notice to new employees

(a) Every employer subject to the compensation provisions of this code, except employers of employees defined in subdivision (d) of Section 3351, shall give every new employee, either at the time the employee is hired or by the end of the first pay period, written notice of the information contained in Section 3550. The content of the notice required by this section shall be prescribed by the administrative director after consultation with the Commission on Health and Safety and Workers' Compensation.

(b) The notice required by this section shall be easily understandable and available in both English and Spanish. In addition to the information contained in Section 3550, the content of the notice required by this section shall include:

(1) Generally, how to obtain appropriate medical care for a job injury.

(2) The role and function of the primary treating physician.

(3) A form that the employee may use as an optional method for notifying the employer of the name of the employee's "personal physician," as defined by Section 4600, or "personal chiropractor," as defined by Section 4601.

(c) The content of the notice required by this section shall be made available to employers and insurers by the administrative director. Insurers shall provide this notice to each of their policyholders, with advice concerning the requirements of this section and the penalties for a failure to provide this notice to all employees. *(Added by Stats. 1984, c. 1141, § 1. Amended by Stats.2002, c. 6 (A.B.749), § 45.)*

§ 3553. Workers' compensation eligibility; employee victims; crimes occurring at place of employment

Every employer subject to the compensation provisions of this code shall give any employee who is a victim of a crime that occurred at the employee's place of employment written notice that the employee is eligible for workers' compensation for injuries, including psychiatric injuries, that may have resulted from the place of employment crime. The employer shall provide this notice, either personally or by first-class mail, within one working day of the place of employment crime, or within one working day of the date the employer reasonably should have known of the crime. *(Added by Stats.1997, c. 527 (S.B.150), § 3.)*

CHAPTER 3. CONDITIONS OF COMPENSATION LIABILITY

Section
3600. Liability for compensation; conditions of compensation; credits against judgment or settlement; employee injured or killed by third party in course of employment
3600.1. Off-duty state firefighters.
3600.2. Off duty peace officers.
3600.3. Off-duty peace officer; department of forestry.
3600.4. Off-duty firemen.
3600.5. Injuries in extraterritorial employment.
3600.6. Disaster service workers.
3600.8. Alternative commute programs; sponsorship or mandate by governmental entity; actions within the course of employment; vanpools.
3601. Exclusive remedy against fellow employee; additional remedy in event of death.
3602. Exclusive remedy against employer; action for damages; conditions of employers's liability; security for payment of compensation.
3603. Discharge of compensation claims.
3604. Public employment in violation of law.
3605. Payment of compensation to minor.

§ 3600. Liability for compensation; conditions of compensation; credits against judgment or settlement; employee injured or killed by third party in course of employment

(a) Liability for the compensation provided by this division, in lieu of any other liability whatsoever to any

547

person except as otherwise specifically provided in Sections 3602, 3706, and 4558, shall, without regard to negligence, exist against an employer for any injury sustained by his or her employees arising out of and in the course of the employment and for the death of any employee if the injury proximately causes death, in those cases where the following conditions of compensation concur:

(1) Where, at the time of the injury, both the employer and the employee are subject to the compensation provisions of this division.

(2) Where, at the time of the injury, the employee is performing service growing out of and incidental to his or her employment and is acting within the course of his or her employment.

(3) Where the injury is proximately caused by the employment, either with or without negligence.

(4) Where the injury is not caused by the intoxication, by alcohol or the unlawful use of a controlled substance, of the injured employee. As used in this paragraph, "controlled substance" shall have the same meaning as prescribed in Section 11007 of the Health and Safety Code.

(5) Where the injury is not intentionally self-inflicted.

(6) Where the employee has not willfully and deliberately caused his or her own death.

(7) Where the injury does not arise out of an altercation in which the injured employee is the initial physical aggressor.

(8) Where the injury is not caused by the commission of a felony, or a crime which is punishable as specified in subdivision (b) of Section 17 of the Penal Code, by the injured employee, for which he or she has been convicted.

(9) Where the injury does not arise out of voluntary participation in any off-duty recreational, social, or athletic activity not constituting part of the employee's work-related duties, except where these activities are a reasonable expectancy of, or are expressly or impliedly required by, the employment. The administrative director shall promulgate reasonable rules and regulations requiring employers to post and keep posted in a conspicuous place or places a notice advising employees of the provisions of this subdivision. Failure of the employer to post the notice shall not constitute an expression of intent to waive the provisions of this subdivision.

(10) Except for psychiatric injuries governed by subdivision (e) of Section 3208.3, where the claim for compensation is filed after notice of termination or layoff, including voluntary layoff, and the claim is for an injury occurring prior to the time of notice of termination or layoff, no compensation shall be paid unless the employee demonstrates by a preponderance of the evidence that one or more of the following conditions apply:

(A) The employer has notice of the injury, as provided under Chapter 2 (commencing with Section 5400), prior to the notice of termination or layoff.

(B) The employee's medical records, existing prior to the notice of termination or layoff, contain evidence of the injury.

(C) The date of injury, as specified in Section 5411, is subsequent to the date of the notice of termination or layoff, but prior to the effective date of the termination or layoff.

(D) The date of injury, as specified in Section 5412, is subsequent to the date of the notice of termination or layoff.

For purposes of this paragraph, an employee provided notice pursuant to Sections 44948.5, 44949, 44951, 44955, * * * 72411, 87740, and 87743 of the Education Code shall be considered to have been provided a notice of termination or layoff only upon a district's final decision not to reemploy that person.

A notice of termination or layoff that is not followed within 60 days by that termination or layoff shall not be subject to the provisions of this paragraph, and this paragraph shall not apply until receipt of a later notice of termination or layoff. The issuance of frequent notices of termination or layoff to an employee shall be considered a bad faith personnel action and shall make this paragraph inapplicable to the employee.

(b) Where an employee, or his or her dependents, receives the compensation provided by this division and secures a judgment for, or settlement of, civil damages pursuant to those specific exemptions to the employee's exclusive remedy set forth in subdivision (b) of Section 3602 and Section 4558, the compensation paid under this division shall be credited against the judgment or settlement, and the employer shall be relieved from the obligation to pay further compensation to, or on behalf of, the employee or his or her dependents up to the net amount of the judgment or settlement received by the employee or his or her heirs, or that portion of the judgment as has been satisfied.

(c) For purposes of determining whether to grant or deny a workers' compensation claim, if an employee is injured or killed by a third party in the course of the employee's employment, no personal relationship or personal connection shall be deemed to exist between the employee and the third party based only on a determination that the third party injured or killed the employee solely because of the third party's personal beliefs relating to his or her perception of the employee's race, religious creed, color, national origin, age, gender, disability, sex, or sexual orientation. *(Stats.1937, c. 90, p. 269, § 3600. Amended by Stats.1961, c. 2170, p. 4493, § 1; Stats.1978, c. 1303, p. 4262, § 5; Stats.1982, c. 922, p. 3365, § 4; Stats.1986, c. 755, § 1; Stats.1990, c. 939 (A.B.4315), § 1; Stats.1993, c. 118 (A.B.119), § 2, eff. July 16, 1993; Stats.1993, c. 1242 (S.B.223), § 24; Stats.2009, c. 272 (A.B.1093), § 1.)*

§ 3600.1. Off-duty state firefighters

(a) Whenever any firefighter of the state, as defined in Section 19886 of the Government Code, is injured, dies, or is disabled from performing his or her duties as a firefighter by reason of his or her proceeding to or engaging in a fire-suppression or rescue operation, or the protection or preservation of life or property, anywhere in this state, including the jurisdiction in which he or she is employed, but is not at the time acting under the immediate direction of his or her employer, he or she or his or her dependents, as the case may be, shall be accorded by his or her employer all of the same benefits of this division that he, she, or they would have received had that firefighter been acting under the immediate direction of his or her employer. Any injury, disability, or death incurred under the circumstances described in this section shall be deemed to have arisen out of, and been sustained in, the course of employment for purposes of workers' compensation and all other benefits.

(b) Nothing in this section shall be deemed to do either of the following:

(1) Require the extension of any benefits to a firefighter who, at the time of his or her injury, death, or disability, is acting for compensation from one other than the state.

(2) Require the extension of any benefits to a firefighter employed by the state where by departmental regulation, whether now in force or hereafter enacted or promulgated, the activity giving rise to the injury, disability, or death is expressly prohibited.

(c) If the provisions of this section are in conflict with the provisions of a memorandum of understanding reached pursuant to Section 3517.5 of the Government Code, the memorandum of understanding shall be controlling without further legislative action, except that if the provisions of a memorandum of understanding require the expenditure of funds, the provisions shall not become effective unless approved by the Legislature in the annual Budget Act. (Added by Stats.1980, c. 407, p. 794, § 1. Amended by Stats.2004, c. 183 (A.B.3082), § 263; Stats.2005, c. 22 (S.B.1108), § 143.)

§ 3600.2.　Off-duty peace officers

(a) Whenever any peace officer, as defined in Section 50920 of the Government Code, is injured, dies, or is disabled from performing his duties as a peace officer by reason of engaging in the apprehension or attempted apprehension of law violators or suspected law violators, or protection or preservation of life or property, or the preservation of the peace anywhere in this state, including the local jurisdiction in which he is employed, but is not at the time acting under the immediate direction of his employer, he or his dependents, as the case may be, shall be accorded by his employer all of the same benefits, including the benefits of this division, which he or they would have received had that peace officer been acting under the immediate direction of his employer. Any injury, disability, or death incurred under the circumstances described in this section shall be deemed to have arisen out of and been sustained in the course of

employment for purposes of workers' compensation and all other benefits.

(b) Nothing in this section shall be deemed to:

(1) Require the extension of any benefits to a peace officer who at the time of his injury, death, or disability is acting for compensation from one other than the city, county, city and county, judicial district, or town of his primary employment.

(2) Require the extension of any benefits to a peace officer employed by a city, county, city and county, judicial district, or town which by charter, ordinance, or departmental regulation, whether now in force or hereafter enacted or promulgated, expressly prohibits the activity giving rise to the injury, disability, or death.

(3) Enlarge or extend the authority of any peace officer to make an arrest; provided, however, that illegality of the arrest shall not affect the extension of benefits by reason of this act if the peace officer reasonably believed that the arrest was not illegal. (Added by Stats.1980, c. 407, p. 795, § 2.)

§ 3600.3.　Off-duty peace officer; department of forestry

(a) For the purposes of Section 3600, an off-duty peace officer, as defined in subdivision (b), who is performing, within the jurisdiction of his or her employing agency, a service he or she would, in the course of his or her employment, have been required to perform if he or she were on duty, is performing a service growing out of and incidental to his or her employment and is acting within the course of his or her employment if, as a condition of his or her employment, he or she is required to be on call within the jurisdiction during off-duty hours.

(b) As used in subdivision (a), "peace officer" means those employees of the Department of Forestry and Fire Protection named as peace officers for purposes of subdivision (b) of Section 830.37 of the Penal Code.

(c) This section does not apply to any off-duty peace officer while he or she is engaged, either as an employee or as an independent contractor, in any capacity other than as a peace officer. (Added by Stats.1972, c. 1107, p. 2115, § 1. Amended by Stats.1973, c. 508, p. 982, § 1; Stats.1974, c. 631, p. 1481, § 1; Stats.1980, c. 676, p. 1971, § 230; Stats.1980, c. 407, p. 796, § 3; Stats.1981, c. 714, p. 2722, § 317; Stats.1989, c. 1165, § 14; Stats.1992, c. 427 (A.B.3355), § 122.)

§ 3600.4.　Off-duty firemen

(a) Whenever any firefighter of a city, county, city and county, district, or other public or municipal corporation or political subdivision, or any firefighter employed by a private entity, is injured, dies, or is disabled from performing his or her duties as a firefighter by reason of his or her proceeding to or engaging in a fire suppression or rescue operation, or the protection or preservation of life or property, anywhere in this state, including the local jurisdiction in which he or she is employed, but is not at the time acting under the immediate direction of his or

549

her employer, he or she or his or her dependents, as the case may be, shall be accorded by his or her employer all of the same benefits of this division which he or she or they would have received had that firefighter been acting under the immediate direction of his or her employer. Any injury, disability, or death incurred under the circumstances described in this section shall be deemed to have arisen out of and been sustained in the course of employment for purposes of workers' compensation and all other benefits.

(b) Nothing in this section shall be deemed to:

(1) Require the extension of any benefits to a firefighter who at the time of his or her injury, death, or disability is acting for compensation from one other than the city, county, city and county, district, or other public or municipal corporation or political subdivision, or private entity, of his or her primary employment or enrollment.

(2) Require the extension of any benefits to a firefighter employed by a city, county, city and county, district, or other public or municipal corporation or political subdivision, or private entity, which by charter, ordinance, departmental regulation, or private employer policy, whether now in force or hereafter enacted or promulgated, expressly prohibits the activity giving rise to the injury, disability, or death. However, this paragraph shall not apply to relieve the employer from liability for benefits for any injury, disability, or death of a firefighter when the firefighter is acting pursuant to Section 1799.107 of the Health and Safety Code. *(Added by Stats.1980, c. 407, p. 796, § 4. Amended by Stats. 1984, c. 114, § 4; Stats.1998, c. 617 (A.B.2173), § 2.)*

§ 3600.5.   Injuries in extraterritorial employment

(a) If an employee who has been hired or is regularly employed in the state receives personal injury by accident arising out of and in the course of such employment outside of this state, he, or his dependents, in the case of his death, shall be entitled to compensation according to the law of this state.

(b) Any employee who has been hired outside of this state and his employer shall be exempted from the provisions of this division while such employee is temporarily within this state doing work for his employer if such employer has furnished workmen's compensation insurance coverage under the workmen's compensation insurance or similar laws of a state other than California, so as to cover such employee's employment while in this state; provided, the extraterritorial provisions of this division are recognized in such other state and provided employers and employees who are covered in this state are likewise exempted from the application of the workmen's compensation insurance or similar laws of such other state. The benefits under the Workmen's Compensation Insurance Act or similar laws of such other state, or other remedies under such act or such laws, shall be the exclusive remedy against such employer for any injury, whether resulting in death or not, received by such employee while working for such employer in this state.

A certificate from the duly authorized officer of the appeals board or similar department of another state certifying that the employer of such other state is insured therein and has provided extraterritorial coverage insuring his employees while working within this state shall be prima facie evidence that such employer carries such workmen's compensation insurance. *(Added by Stats. 1955, c. 1813, p. 3352, § 1. Amended by Stats.1965, c. 1513, p. 3570, § 57, operative Jan. 15, 1966.)*

§ 3600.6.   Disaster service workers

Disaster service workers registered by a disaster council while performing services under the general direction of the disaster council shall be entitled to all of the same benefits of this division as any other injured employee, except as provided by Chapter 10 (commencing with Section 4351) of Part 1. For purposes of this section, an unregistered person impressed into performing service as a disaster service worker during a state of war emergency, a state of emergency, or a local emergency by a person having authority to command the aid of citizens in the execution of his or her duties shall also be deemed a disaster service worker and shall be entitled to the same benefits of this division as any other disaster service worker. *(Added by Stats.1986, c. 554, § 1.)*

§ 3600.8.   Alternative commute programs; sponsorship or mandate by governmental entity; actions within the course of employment; vanpools

(a) No employee who voluntarily participates in an alternative commute program that is sponsored or mandated by a governmental entity shall be considered to be acting within the course of his or her employment while utilizing that program to travel to or from his or her place of employment, unless he or she is paid a regular wage or salary in compensation for those periods of travel. An employee who is injured while acting outside the course of his or her employment, or his or her dependents in the event of the employee's death, shall not be barred from bringing an action at law for damages against his or her employer as a result of this section.

(b) Any alternative commute program provided, sponsored, or subsidized by an employee's employer in order to comply with any trip reduction mandates of an air quality management district or local government shall be considered a program mandated by a governmental entity. An employer's reimbursement of employee expenses or subsidization of costs related to an alternative commute program shall not be considered payment of a wage or salary in compensation for the period of travel. If an employer's salary is not based on the hours the employee works, payment of his or her salary shall not be considered to be in compensation for the period of travel unless there is a specific written agreement between the employer and the employee to that effect. If an employer elects to provide workers' compensation coverage for those employees who are passengers in a vehicle owned and operated by the employer or an agent thereof, those employees shall be considered to be within the course of their employment, provided the employer notifies employees in writing prior to participation of the employee or coverage becoming effective.

(c) As used in this section, "governmental entity" means a regional air district, air quality management district, congestion management agency, or other local jurisdiction having authority to enact air pollution or congestion management controls or impose them upon entities within its jurisdiction.

(d) Notwithstanding any other provision of law, vanpool programs may continue to provide workers' compensation benefits to employees who participate in an alternative commute program by riding in a vanpool, in the case in which the vanpool vehicle is owned or registered to the employer.

(e) Employees of the state who participate in an alternative commute program, while riding in a vanpool vehicle that is registered to or owned by the state, shall be deemed to be within the course and scope of employment for workers' compensation purposes only. *(Added by Stats.1994, c. 622 (S.B.1360), § 1.)*

§ 3601. Exclusive remedy against fellow employee; additional remedy in event of death

(a) Where the conditions of compensation set forth in Section 3600 concur, the right to recover such compensation, pursuant to the provisions of this division is, except as specifically provided in this section, the exclusive remedy for injury or death of an employee against any other employee of the employer acting within the scope of his or her employment, except that an employee, or his or her dependents in the event of his or her death, shall, in addition to the right to compensation against the employer, have a right to bring an action at law for damages against the other employee, as if this division did not apply, in either of the following cases:

(1) When the injury or death is proximately caused by the willful and unprovoked physical act of aggression of the other employee.

(2) When the injury or death is proximately caused by the intoxication of the other employee.

(b) In no event, either by legal action or by agreement whether entered into by the other employee or on his or her behalf, shall the employer be held liable, directly or indirectly, for damages awarded against, or for a liability incurred by the other employee under paragraph (1) or (2) of subdivision (a).

(c) No employee shall be held liable, directly or indirectly, to his or her employer, for injury or death of a coemployee except where the injured employee or his or her dependents obtain a recovery under subdivision (a). *(Stats.1937, c. 90, p. 269, § 3601. Amended by Stats.1959, c. 1189, p. 3275, § 1; Stats.1971, c. 1751, p. 3780, § 1, operative April 1, 1972; Stats. 1982, c. 922, p. 3366, § 5.)*

§ 3602. Exclusive remedy against employer; action for damages; conditions of employers's liability; security for payment of compensation

(a) Where the conditions of compensation set forth in Section 3600 concur, the right to recover such compensation is, except as specifically provided in this section and Sections 3706 and 4558, the sole and exclusive remedy of the employee or his or her dependents against the employer, and the fact that either the employee or the employer also occupied another or dual capacity prior to, or at the time of, the employee's industrial injury shall not permit the employee or his or her dependents to bring an action at law for damages against the employer.

(b) An employee, or his or her dependents in the event of his or her death, may bring an action at law for damages against the employer, as if this division did not apply, in the following instances:

(1) Where the employee's injury or death is proximately caused by a willful physical assault by the employer.

(2) Where the employee's injury is aggravated by the employer's fraudulent concealment of the existence of the injury and its connection with the employment, in which case the employer's liability shall be limited to those damages proximately caused by the aggravation. The burden of proof respecting apportionment of damages between the injury and any subsequent aggravation thereof is upon the employer.

(3) Where the employee's injury or death is proximately caused by a defective product manufactured by the employer and sold, leased, or otherwise transferred for valuable consideration to an independent third person, and that product is thereafter provided for the employee's use by a third person.

(c) In all cases where the conditions of compensation set forth in Section 3600 do not concur, the liability of the employer shall be the same as if this division had not been enacted.

(d) For the purposes of this division, including Sections 3700 and 3706, an employer may secure the payment of compensation on employees provided to it by agreement by another employer by entering into a valid and enforceable agreement with that other employer under which the other employer agrees to obtain, and has, in fact, obtained workers' compensation coverage for those employees. In those cases, both employers shall be considered to have secured the payment of compensation within the meaning of this section and Sections 3700 and 3706 if there is a valid and enforceable agreement between the employers to obtain that coverage, and that coverage, as specified in subdivision (a) or (b) of Section 3700, has been in fact obtained, and the coverage remains in effect for the duration of the employment providing legally sufficient coverage to the employee or employees who form the subject matter of the coverage. That agreement shall not be made for the purpose of avoiding an employer's appropriate experience rating as defined in subdivision (c) of Section 11730 of the Insurance Code.

Employers who have complied with this subdivision shall not be subject to civil, criminal, or other penalties for failure to provide workers' compensation coverage or tort liability in the event of employee injury, but may, in the absence of compliance, be subject to all three. *(Stats.1937, c. 90, p. 269, § 3602. Amended by Stats.1982, c. 922, p. 3367, § 6; Stats.1995, c. 800 (A.B.914), § 1.)*

§ 3603. Discharge of compensation claims

Payment of compensation in accordance with the order and direction of the appeals board shall discharge the employer from all claims therefor. *(Stats.1937, c. 90, p. 269, § 3603. Amended by Stats.1971, c. 438, p. 894, § 142.)*

§ 3604. Public employment in violation of law

It is not a defense to the State, any county, city, district or institution thereof, or any public or quasi-public corporation, that a person injured while rendering service for it was not lawfully employed by reason of the violation of any civil service or other law or regulation respecting the hiring of employees. *(Stats.1937, c. 90, p. 269, § 3604.)*

§ 3605. Payment of compensation to minor

The compensation due an injured minor may be paid to him until his parent or guardian gives the employer or the latter's compensation insurance carrier written notice that he claims such compensation.

Compensation paid to such injured minor prior to receipt of such written notice is in full release of the employer and insurance carrier for the amount so paid. The minor can not disaffirm such payment upon appointment of a guardian or coming of age. *(Added by Stats.1939, c. 648, p. 2076, § 1.)*

CHAPTER 4. COMPENSATION INSURANCE AND SECURITY

Article   **Section**
1.   **Insurance and Security** 3700
2.   **Uninsured Employers Fund** 3710
2.5. **Self-Insurers' Security Fund** 3740
3.   **Insurance Rights and Privileges** 3750
4.   **Construction Permit** 3800
5.   **Workers' Compensation Misrepresentations** ..3820

ARTICLE 1. INSURANCE AND SECURITY

Section
3700.   Security for payment of compensation.
3700.1. Definitions.
3700.5. Failure to secure payment of compensation; penalties.
3701.   Private self-insuring employer; annual renewal or deposit of new security for payment of compensation; minimum deposit; form of security; withdrawal; perfected security interest.
3701.3. Return of excess amounts of security to private self-insured employer.

Section
3701.5. Private self-insured, employer; failure to pay workers' compensation; utilization of security deposit; payment through Self-Insurers' Security Fund; audit; disputes; appeals.
3701.7. Self-insured employer; period of unlawful uninsurance; conditions for self-insurance.
3701.8. Self-Insurers' Security Fund; alternative security systems for private self-insuring employers; requirements set by director; composite deposits; deposit assessments and factors considered; right to appeal assessment; segregated cash portion of composite deposit.
3702.   Certificate of consent to self-insure; revocation.
3702.1. Third-party administrator; certificate of consent; estimate of liability for employer's annual report.
3702.2. Self-insurer's annual report; annual summary reports by director; release of information.
3702.3. Failure to submit reports or information; penalty.
3702.5. Cost of administration of self-insured programs; payment by certificate fees on self-insurers; other fees and penalties; self-insurance plans fund.
3702.6. Audit program for self-insurers.
3702.7. Revocation of certificate of consent; fines.
3702.8. Employers who have ceased to be self-insured; discharge of continuing obligations; proceedings on failure to comply.
3702.9. Additional penalties for violation of obligations relating to report, security deposit, or assessment; costs and attorney fee; fraud, bad faith, or repeated violation; waiver or remission of payments.
3702.10. Rules and regulations.
3703.   Administration of compensation benefits by self-insurer.
3705.   Preferred subrogation rights of self-insurers' security fund or surety.
3706.   Effect of failure to secure payment of compensation; action for damages.
3706.5. Application of article and certain sections to agency or organization performing officiating services relating to amateur sporting events.
3707.   Attachment of property of employer.
3708.   Presumption of employer's negligence; defenses abolished; applicability of section to household employees.
3708.5. Service of complaint; consolidation of actions.
3709.   Credit against judgment; liens; attorney fees; satisfaction of judgment.
3709.5. Satisfaction of judgment; payment of attorney fees; credit against liability for compensation.

§ 3700. Security for payment of compensation

Every employer except the state shall secure the payment of compensation in one or more of the following ways:

(a) By being insured against liability to pay compensation by one or more insurers duly authorized to write compensation insurance in this state.

(b) By securing from the Director of Industrial Relations a certificate of consent to self-insure either as an individual employer, or as one employer in a group of employers, which may be given upon furnishing proof satisfactory to the Director of Industrial Relations of ability to self-insure and to pay any compensation that may become due to his or her employees.

(c) For any county, city, city and county, municipal corporation, public district, public agency, or any political subdivision of the state, including each member of a pooling arrangement under a joint exercise of powers agreement (but not the state itself), by securing from the Director of Industrial Relations a certificate of consent to self-insure against workers' compensation claims, which certificate may be given upon furnishing proof satisfactory to the director of ability to administer workers' compensation claims properly, and to pay workers' compensation claims that may become due to its employees. On or before March 31, 1979, a political subdivision of the state which, on December 31, 1978, was uninsured for its liability to pay compensation, shall file a properly completed and executed application for a certificate of consent to self-insure against workers' compensation claims. The certificate shall be issued and be subject to the provisions of Section 3702.

For purposes of this section, "state" shall include the superior courts of California. *(Stats.1937, c. 90, p. 270, § 3700. Amended by Stats.1945, c. 1431, p. 2694, § 63; Stats.1946, 1st Ex.Sess. c. 7, p. 12, § 1; Stats.1978, c. 1379, p. 4571, § 2; Stats.1986, c. 1128, § 1, eff. Sept 25, 1986; Stats.1993, c. 121 (A.B.110), § 25, eff. July 16, 1993; Stats.2002, c. 905 (S.B.2011), § 10.)*

§ 3700.1. Definitions

As used in this article:

(a) "Director" means the Director of Industrial Relations.

(b) "Private self-insurer" means a private employer which has secured the payment of compensation pursuant to Section 3701.

(c) "Insolvent self-insurer" means a private self-insurer who has failed to pay compensation and whose security deposit has been called by the director pursuant to Section 3701.5.

(d) "Fund" means the Self-Insurers' Security Fund established pursuant to Section 3742.

(e) "Trustees" means the Board of Trustees of the Self-Insurers' Security Fund.

(f) "Member" means a private self-insurer which participates in the Self-Insurers' Security Fund.

(g) "Incurred liabilities for the payment of compensation" means the sum of an estimate of future compensation, as compensation is defined by Section 3207, plus an estimate of the amount necessary to provide for the administration of claims, including legal costs. *(Added by Stats.1986, c. 1128, § 2, eff. Sept. 25, 1986. Amended by Stats.1987, c. 169, § 1, eff. July 23, 1987.)*

§ 3700.5. Failure to secure payment of compensation; penalties

(a) The failure to secure the payment of compensation as required by this article by one who knew, or because of his or her knowledge or experience should be reasonably expected to have known, of the obligation to secure the payment of compensation, is a misdemeanor punishable by imprisonment in the county jail for up to one year, or by a fine of up to double the amount of premium, as determined by the court, that would otherwise have been due to secure the payment of compensation during the time compensation was not secured, but not less than ten thousand dollars ($ 10,000), or by both that imprisonment and fine.

(b) A second or subsequent conviction shall be punished by imprisonment in the county jail for a period not to exceed one year, by a fine of triple the amount of premium, or by both that imprisonment and fine, as determined by the court, that would otherwise have been due to secure the payment of compensation during the time payment was not secured, but not less than fifty thousand dollars ($50,000).

(c) Upon a first conviction of a person under this section, the person may be charged the costs of investigation at the discretion of the court. Upon a subsequent conviction, the person shall be charged the costs of investigation in addition to any other penalties pursuant to subdivision (b). The costs of investigation shall be paid only after the payment of any benefits that may be owed to injured workers, any reimbursement that may be owed to the director for benefits provided to the injured worker pursuant to Section 3717, and any other penalty assessments that may be owed. *(Added by Stats.1981, c. 894, p. 3408, § 1. Amended by Stats.1986, c. 1128, § 3, eff. Sept. 25, 1986; Stats.1999, c. 553 (A.B.279), § 1; Stats.2003–2004, 4th Ex.Sess., c. 2 (S.B.2), § 3, eff. March 1, 2005.)*

§ 3701. Private self-insuring employer; annual renewal or deposit of new security for payment of compensation, minimum deposit, form of security, withdrawal; perfected security interest

(a) Each year every private self-insuring employer shall secure incurred liabilities for the payment of compensation and the performance of the obligations of employers imposed under this chapter by renewing the prior year's security deposit or by making a new deposit of security. If a new deposit is made, it shall be posted within 60 days of the filing of the self-insured employer's annual report with the director, but in no event later than May 1.

(b) The minimum deposit shall be 125 percent of the private self-insurer's estimated future liability for compensation to secure payment of compensation plus 10 percent of the private self-insurer's estimated future liability for compensation to secure payment of all administrative and legal costs relating to or arising from the employer's self-insuring. In no event shall the security deposit for the incurred liabilities for compensation be less than two hundred twenty thousand dollars ($220,000).

(c) In determining the amount of the deposit required to secure incurred liabilities for the payment of compensation and the performance of obligations of a self-insured employer imposed under this chapter, the director shall offset estimated future liabilities for the same claims covered by a self-insured plan under the Longshore and Harbor Workers' Compensation Act (33 U.S.C. Sec. 901 et seq.), but in no event shall the offset exceed the estimated future liabilities for the claims under this chapter.

(d) The director may only accept as security, and the employer shall deposit as security, cash, securities, surety bonds, or irrevocable letters of credit in any combination the director, in his or her discretion, deems adequate security. The current deposit shall include any amounts covered by terminated surety bonds or excess insurance policies, as shall be set forth in regulations adopted by the director pursuant to Section 3702.10.

(e) Surety bonds, irrevocable letters of credit, and documents showing issuance of any irrevocable letter of credit shall be deposited with, and be in a form approved by, the director, shall be exonerated only according to its terms and, in no event, by the posting of additional security.

(f) The director may accept as security a joint security deposit that secures an employer's obligation under this chapter and that also secures that employer's obligations under the federal Longshore and Harbor Workers' Compensation Act.

(g) The liability of the Self-Insurers' Security Fund, with respect to any claims brought under both this chapter and under the federal Longshore and Harbor Workers' Compensation Act, to pay for shortfalls in a security deposit shall be limited to the amount of claim liability owing the employee under this chapter offset by the amount of any claim liability owing under the Longshore and Harbor Workers' Compensation Act, but in no event shall the liability of the fund exceed the claim liability under this chapter. The employee shall be entitled to pursue recovery under either or both the state and federal programs.

(h) Securities shall be deposited on behalf of the director by the self-insured employer with the Treasurer. Securities shall be accepted by the Treasurer for deposit and shall be withdrawn only upon written order of the director.

(i) Cash shall be deposited in a financial institution approved by the director, and in the account assigned to the director. Cash shall be withdrawn only upon written order of the director.

(j) Upon the sending by the director of a request to renew, request to post, or request to increase or decrease a security deposit, a perfected security interest is created in the private self-insured's assets in favor of the director to the extent of any then unsecured portion of the self-insured's incurred liabilities. That perfected security interest is transferred to any cash or securities thereafter posted by the private self-insured with the director and is released only upon either of the following:

(1) The acceptance by the director of a surety bond or irrevocable letter of credit for the full amount of the incurred liabilities for the payment of compensation.

(2) The return of cash or securities by the director.

The private self-insured employer loses all right, title, and interest in, and any right to control, all assets or obligations posted or left on deposit as security. The director may liquidate the deposit as provided in Section 3701.5 and apply it to the self-insured employer's incurred liabilities either directly or through the Self-Insurers' Security Fund. *(Stats.1937, c. 90, p. 270, § 3701. Amended by Stats.1945, c. 1431, p. 2694, § 64; Stats.1946, 1st Ex.Sess. c. 7, p. 13, § 2; Stats.1959, c. 951, p. 2979, § 1; Stats.1971, c. 1758, p. 3793, § 1; Stats.1973, c. 1040, p. 2063, § 1; Stats.1978, c. 1379, p. 4571, § 3; Stats.1984, c. 252, § 1, eff. June 27, 1984; Stats.1986, c. 1128, § 4, eff. Sept. 25, 1986; Stats.1987, c. 169, § 2, eff. July 23, 1987; Stats.1993, c. 917 (A.B.424), § 1; Stats. 1993, c. 1242 (S.B.223), § 24.5; Stats.1994, c. 56 (A.B. 968), § 1.)*

§ 3701.3. Return of excess amounts of security to private self-insured employer

The director shall return to a private self-insured employer all amounts determined, in the director's discretion, to be in excess of that needed to assure the administration of the employer's self insuring, including legal fees, and the payment of any future claims. *(Added by Stats.1986, c. 1128, § 5, eff. Sept. 25, 1986.)*

§ 3701.5. Private self-insured, employer; failure to pay workers' compensation; utilization of security deposit; payment through Self–Insurers' Security Fund; audit; disputes; appeals

(a) If the director determines that a private self-insured employer has failed to pay workers' compensation as required by this division, the security deposit shall be utilized to administer and pay the employer's compensation obligations.

(b) If the director determines the security deposit has not been immediately made available for the payment of compensation, the director shall determine the method of payment and claims administration as appropriate, which may include, but is not limited to, payment by a surety that issued the bond, or payment by an issuer of an irrevocable letter of credit, and administration by a surety or by an adjusting agency, or through the Self-Insurers' Security Fund, or any combination thereof.

(c) If the director determines the payment of benefits and claims administration shall be made through the Self-Insurers' Security Fund, the fund shall commence payment of the private self-insured employer's obligations for which it is liable under Section 3743 within 30 days of notification. Payments shall be made to claimants whose entitlement to benefits can be ascertained by the fund, with or without proceedings before the appeals board.

Upon the assumption of obligations by the fund pursuant to the director's determination, the fund shall have a right to immediate possession of any posted security and the custodian, surety, or issuer of any irrevocable letter of credit shall turn over the security to the fund together with the interest that has accrued since the date of the self-insured employer's default or insolvency.

(d) The director shall promptly audit an employer upon making a determination under subdivision (a) or (b). The employer, any excess insurer, and any adjusting agency shall provide any relevant information in their possession. If the audit results in a preliminary estimate that liabilities exceed the amount of the security deposit, the director shall direct the custodian of the security deposit to liquidate it and provide all proceeds to the Self-Insurers' Security Fund. If the preliminary estimate is that liabilities are less than the security deposit, the director shall ensure the administration and payment of compensation pursuant to subdivision (b).

(e) The payment of benefits by the Self-Insurers' Security Fund from security deposit proceeds shall release and discharge any custodian of the security deposit, surety, any issuer of a letter of credit, and the self-insured employer, from liability to fulfill obligations to provide those same benefits as compensation, but does not release any person from any liability to the fund for full reimbursement. Payment by a surety constitutes a full release of the surety's liability under the bond to the extent of that payment, and entitles the surety to full reimbursement by the principal or his or her estate. Full reimbursement includes necessary attorney fees and other costs and expenses, without prior claim or proceedings on the part of the injured employee or other beneficiaries. Any decision or determination made, or any settlement approved, by the director or by the appeals board under subdivision (g) shall conclusively be presumed valid and binding as to any and all known claims arising out of the underlying dispute, unless an appeal is made within the time limit specified in Section 5950.

(f) The director shall advise the Self-Insurers' Security Fund promptly after receipt of information indicating that a private self-insured employer may be unable to meet its compensation obligations. The director shall also advise the Self-Insurers' Security Fund of all determinations and directives made or issued pursuant to this section.

(g) Disputes concerning the posting, renewal, termination, exoneration, or return of all or any portion of the security deposit, or any liability arising out of the posting or failure to post security, or adequacy of the security or reasonableness of administrative costs, including legal fees, and arising between or among a surety, the issuer of an agreement of assumption and guarantee of workers' compensation liabilities, the issuer of a letter of credit, any custodian of the security deposit, a self-insured employer, or the Self-Insurers' Security Fund shall be resolved by the director. An appeal from the director's decision or determination may be taken to the appropriate superior court by petition for writ of mandate. Payment of claims from the security deposit or by the Self-Insurers' Security Fund shall not be stayed pending the resolution of the disputes unless and until the superior court issues a determination staying a payment of claims decision or determination of the director. *(Added by Stats.1984, c. 252, § 2, eff. June 27, 1984. Amended by Stats.1986, c. 1128, § 6, eff. Sept. 25, 1986; Stats.1989, c. 1258, § 2.)*

§ 3701.7. Self-insured employer; period of unlawful uninsurance; conditions for self-insurance

Where any employer requesting coverage under a new or existing certificate of consent to self-insure has had a period of unlawful uninsurance, either for an applicant in its entirety or for a subsidiary or member of a joint powers authority legally responsible for its own workers' compensation obligations, the following special conditions shall apply before the requesting employer can operate under a certificate of consent to self-insure:

(a) The director may require a deposit of not less than 200 percent of the outstanding liabilities remaining unpaid at the time of application, which had been incurred during the uninsurance period.

(b) At the discretion of the director, where a public or private employer has been previously totally uninsured for workers' compensation pursuant to Section 3700, the director may require an additional deposit not to exceed 100 percent of the total outstanding liabilities for the uninsured period, or the sum of two hundred fifty thousand dollars ($250,000), whichever is greater.

(c) In addition to the deposits required by subdivisions (a) and (b), a penalty shall be paid to the Uninsured Employers Fund of 10 percent per year of the remaining unpaid liabilities, for every year liabilities remain outstanding. In addition, an additional application fee, not to exceed one thousand dollars ($1,000), plus assessments, pursuant to Section 3702.5 and subdivision (b) of Section 3745, may be imposed by the director and the Self-Insurers' Security Fund, respectively, against private self-insured employers.

(d) An employer may retrospectively insure the outstanding liabilities arising out of the uninsured period, either before or after an application for self-insurance has been approved. Upon proof of insurance acceptable to the director, no deposit shall be required for the period of uninsurance.

The penalties to be paid to the Uninsured Employers Fund shall consist of a one-time payment of 20 percent of the outstanding liabilities for the period of uninsurance remaining unpaid at the time of application, in lieu of any other penalty for being unlawfully uninsured pursuant to this code.

(e) In the case of a subsidiary which meets all of the following conditions, a certificate shall issue without penalty:

(1) The subsidiary has never had a certificate revoked for reasons set forth in Section 3702.

(2) Employee injuries were reported to the Office of Self-Insurance Plans in annual reports.

(3) The security deposit of the certificate holder was calculated to include the entity's compensation liabilities.

(4) Application for a separate certificate or corrected certificate is made within 90 days and completed within 180 days of notice from the Office of Self-Insurance Plans. If the requirements of this subdivision are not met, all penalties pursuant to subdivision (b) of Section 3702.9 shall apply.

(f) The director may approve an application on the date the application is substantially completed, subject to completion requirements, and may make the certificate effective on an earlier date, covering a period of uninsurance, if the employer complies with the requirements of this section.

(g) Any decision by the director may be contested by an entity in the manner provided in Section 3701.5.

(h) Nothing in this section shall abrogate the right of an employee to bring an action against an uninsured employer pursuant to Section 3706.

(i) Nothing in this statute shall abrogate the right of a self-insured employer to insure against known or unknown claims arising out of the self-insurance period. *(Added by Stats.1989, c. 507, § 1. Amended by Stats.1990, c. 704 (A.B.3853), § 1.)*

§ 3701.8. Self–Insurers' Security Fund; alternative security systems for private self-insuring employers; requirements set by director; composite deposits; deposit assessments and factors considered; right to appeal assessment; segregated cash portion of composite deposit

(a) As an alternative to each private self-insuring employer securing its own incurred liabilities as provided in Section 3701, the director may provide by regulation for an alternative security system whereby all private self-insureds designated for full participation by the director shall collectively secure their aggregate incurred liabilities through the Self–Insurers' Security Fund. The regulations shall provide for the director to set a total security requirement for these participating self-insured employers based on a review of their annual reports and any other self-insurer information as may be specified by the director. The Self–Insurers' Security Fund shall propose to the director a combination of cash and securities, surety bonds, irrevocable letters of credit, insurance, or other financial instruments or guarantees satisfactory to the director sufficient to meet the security requirement set by the director. Upon approval by the director and posting by the Self–Insurers' Security Fund on or before the date set by the director, that combination shall be the composite deposit. The noncash elements of the composite deposit may be one-year or multiple-year instruments. If the Self–Insurers' Security Fund fails to post

the required composite deposit by the date set by the director, then within 30 days after that date, each private self-insuring employer shall secure its incurred liabilities in the manner required by Section 3701. Self–insured employers not designated for full participation by the director shall meet all requirements as may be set by the director pursuant to subdivision (g).

(b) In order to provide for the composite deposit approved by the director, the Self–Insurers' Security Fund shall assess, in a manner approved by the director, each fully participating private self-insuring employer a deposit assessment payable within 30 days of assessment. The amount of the deposit assessment charged each fully participating self-insured employer shall be set by the Self–Insurers' Security Fund, based on its reasonable consideration of all the following factors:

(1) The total amount needed to provide the composite deposit.

(2) The self-insuring employer's paid or incurred liabilities as reflected in its annual report.

(3) The financial strength and creditworthiness of the self-insured.

(4) Any other reasonable factors as may be authorized by regulation.

(5) In order to make a composite deposit proposal to the director and set the deposit assessment to be charged each fully participating self-insured, the Self–Insurers' Security Fund shall have access to the annual reports and other information submitted by all self-insuring employers to the director, under terms and conditions as may be set by the director, to preserve the confidentiality of the self-insured's financial information.

(c) Upon payment of the deposit assessment and except as provided herein, the self-insuring employer loses all right, title, and interest in the deposit assessment. To the extent that in any one year the deposit assessment paid by self-insurers is not exhausted in the purchase of securities, surety bonds, irrevocable letters of credit, insurance, or other financial instruments to post with the director as part of the composite deposit, the surplus shall remain posted with the director, and the principal and interest earned on that surplus shall remain as part of the composite deposit in subsequent years. In the event that in any one year the Self–Insurers' Security Fund fails to post the required composite deposit by the date set the by the director, and the director requires each private self-insuring employer to secure its incurred liabilities in the manner required by Section 3701, then any deposit assessment paid in that year shall be refunded to the self-insuring employer that paid the deposit assessment.

(d) If any private self-insuring employer objects to the calculation, posting, or any other aspect of its deposit assessment, upon payment of the assessment in the time provided, the employer shall have the right to appeal the assessment to the director, who shall have exclusive jurisdiction over this dispute. If any private self-insuring employer fails to pay the deposit assessment in the time provided, the director shall order the self-insuring employer to pay a penalty of not less than 10 percent of its deposit assessment, and to post a separate security deposit in the manner provided by Section 3701. The penalty shall be added to the composite deposit held by the director. The director may also revoke the certificate of consent to self-insure of any self-insuring employer who fails to pay the deposit assessment in the time provided.

(e) Upon the posting by the Self–Insurers' Security Fund of the composite deposit with the director, the deposit shall be held until the director determines that a private self-insured employer has failed to pay workers' compensation as required by this division, and the director orders the Self–Insurers' Security Fund to commence payment. Upon ordering the Self–Insurers' Security Fund to commence payment, the director shall make available to the fund that portion of the composite deposit necessary to pay the workers' compensation benefits of the defaulting self-insuring employer. In the event additional funds are needed in subsequent years to pay the workers' compensation benefits of any self-insuring employer who defaulted in earlier years, the director shall make available to the Self–Insurers' Security Fund any portions of the composite deposit as may be needed to pay those benefits. In making the deposit available to the Self–Insurers' Security Fund, the director shall also allow any amounts as may be reasonably necessary to pay for the administrative and other activities of the fund.

(f) The cash portion of the composite deposit shall be segregated from all other funds held by the director, and shall be invested by the director for the sole benefit of the Self–Insurers' Security Fund and the injured workers of private self-insured employers, and may not be used for any other purpose by the state. Alternatively, the director, in his discretion, may allow the Self–Insurers' Security Fund to hold, invest, and draw upon the cash portion of the composite deposit as prescribed by regulation.

(g) Notwithstanding any other provision of this section, the director shall, by regulation, set minimum credit, financial, or other conditions that a private self-insured must meet in order to be a fully participating self-insurer in the alternative security system. In the event any private self-insuring employer is unable to meet the conditions set by the director, or upon application of the Self–Insurers' Security Fund to exclude an employer for credit or financial reasons, the director shall exclude the self-insuring employer from full participation in the alternative security system. In the event a self-insuring employer is excluded from full participation, the nonfully participating private self-insuring employer shall post a separate security deposit in the manner provided by Section 3701 and pay a deposit assessment set by the director. Alternatively, the director may order that the nonfully participating private self-insuring employer post a separate security deposit to secure a portion of its incurred liabilities and pay a deposit assessment set by the director.

(h) An employer who self-insures through group self-insurance and an employer whose certificate to self-insure has been revoked may fully participate in the alternative security system if both the director and the Self–Insurers' Security Fund approve the participation of the self-insurer. If not approved for full participation, or if an employer is issued a certificate to self-insure after the composite deposit is posted, the employer shall satisfy the requirements of subdivision (g) for nonfully participating private self-insurers.

(i) At all times, a self-insured employer shall have secured its incurred workers' compensation liabilities either in the manner required by Section 3701 or through the alternative security system, and there shall not be any lapse in the security. *(Added by Stats.2002, c. 866 (A.B.486), § 7.)*

§ 3702. Certificate of consent to self-insure; revocation

(a) A certificate of consent to self-insure may be revoked by the director at any time for good cause after a hearing. Good cause includes, among other things, the impairment of the solvency of the employer to the extent that there is a marked reduction of the employer's financial strength, failure to maintain a security deposit as required by Section 3701, failure to pay assessments of the Self–Insurers' Security Fund, frequent or flagrant violations of state safety and health orders, the failure or inability of the employer to fulfill his or her obligations, or any of the following practices by the employer or his or her agent in charge of the administration of obligations under this division:

(1) Habitually and as a matter of practice and custom inducing claimants for compensation to accept less than the compensation due, or making it necessary for them to resort to proceedings against the employer to secure compensation due.

(2) Where liability for temporary disability indemnity is not in dispute, intentionally failing to pay temporary disability indemnity without good cause in order to influence the amount of permanent disability benefits due.

(3) Intentionally refusing to comply with known and legally indisputable compensation obligations.

(4) Discharging or administering his or her compensation obligations in a dishonest manner.

(5) Discharging or administering his or her compensation obligations in such a manner as to cause injury to the public or those dealing with the employer.

(b) Where revocation is in part based upon the director's finding of a marked reduction of the employer's financial strength or the failure or inability of the employer to fulfill his or her obligations, or a practice of discharging obligations in a dishonest manner, it is a condition precedent to the employer's challenge or appeal of the revocation that the employer have in effect insurance against liability to pay compensation.

(c) The director may hold a hearing to determine whether good cause exists to revoke an employer's certificate of consent to self-insure if the employer is cited for a willful, or repeat serious violation of the standard adopted pursuant to Section 6401.7 and the citation has become final. *(Stats.1937, c. 90, p. 270, § 3702. Amended by Stats.1945, c. 1431, p. 2695, § 65; Stats.1978, c. 1379, p. 4572, § 4; Stats.1984, c. 252, § 3, eff. May 27, 1984; Stats.1984, c. 1521, § 1, operative July 1, 1985; Stats.1989, c. 1369, § 2, eff. Oct. 2, 1989.)*

§ 3702.1. Third-party administrator; certificate of consent; estimate of liability for employer's annual report

(a) No person, firm, or corporation, other than an insurer admitted to transact workers' compensation insurance in this state, shall contract to administer claims of self-insured employers as a third-party administrator unless in possession of a certificate of consent to administer self-insured employers' workers' compensation claims.

(b) As a condition of receiving a certificate of consent, all persons given discretion by a third-party administrator to deny, accept, or negotiate a workers' compensation claim shall demonstrate their competency to the director by written examination, or other methods approved by the director.

(c) A separate certificate shall be required for each adjusting location operated by a third-party administrator. A third-party administrator holding a certificate of consent shall be subject to regulation only under this division with respect to the adjustment, administration, and management of workers' compensation claims for any self-insured employer.

(d) A third-party administrator retained by a self-insured employer to administer the employer's workers' compensation claims shall estimate the total accrued liability of the employer for the payment of compensation for the employer's annual report to the director and shall make the estimate both in good faith and with the exercise of a reasonable degree of care. The use of a third-party administrator shall not, however, discharge or alter the employer's responsibilities with respect to the report. *(Added by Stats.1984, c. 1521, § 2, operative July 1, 1985. Amended by Stats.1986, c. 1128, § 7, eff. Sept. 25, 1986; Stats.2009, c. 140 (A.B.1164), § 137.)*

§ 3702.2. Self-insurer's annual report; annual summary reports by director; release of information

(a) All self-insured employers shall file a self-insurer's annual report in a form prescribed by the director.

(b) To enable the director to determine the amount of the security deposit required by subdivision (c) of Section 3701, the annual report of a self-insured employer who has self-insured both state and federal workers' compensation liability shall also set forth (1) the amount of all compensation liability incurred, paid-to-date, and esti-

mated future liability under both this chapter and under the federal Longshore and Harbor Workers' Compensation Act (33 U.S.C. Sec. 901 et seq.), and (2) the identity and the amount of the security deposit securing the employer's liability under state and federal self-insured programs.

(c) The director shall annually prepare an aggregated summary of all self-insured employer liability to pay compensation reported on the self-insurers' employers annual reports, including a separate summary for public and private employer self-insurers. The summaries shall be in the same format as the individual self-insured employers are required to report that liability on the employer self-insurer's annual report forms prescribed by the director. The aggregated summaries shall be made available to the public on the self-insurance section of the department's Internet Web site. Nothing in this subdivision shall authorize the director to release or make available information that is aggregated by industry or business type, that identifies individual self-insured filers, or that includes any individually identifiable claimant information.

(d) The director may release a copy, or make available an electronic version, of the data contained in any public sector employer self-insurer's annual reports received from an individual public entity self-insurer or from a joint powers authority employer and its membership. However, the release of any annual report information by the director shall not include any portion of any listing of open indemnity claims that contains individually identifiable claimant information, or any portion of excess insurance coverage information that contains any individually identifiable claimant information. *(Added by Stats. 1986, c. 1128, § 8, eff. Sept. 25, 1986. Amended by Stats.1993, c. 917 (A.B.424), § 2; Stats.2006, c. 115 (A.B.2087), § 1.)*

§ 3702.3. Failure to submit reports or information; penalty

Failure to submit reports or information as deemed necessary by the director to implement the purposes of Section 3701, 3702, or 3702.2 may result in the assessment of a civil penalty as set forth in subdivision (a) of Section 3702.9. Moneys collected shall be used for the administration of self-insurance plans. *(Added by Stats.1978, c. 1379, p. 4572, § 6. Amended by Stats.1986, c. 1128, § 9, eff. Sept. 25, 1986; Stats.1992, c. 532 (A.B.2771), § 1.)*

§ 3702.5. Cost of administration of self-insured programs; payment by certificate fees on self-insurers; other fees and penalties; self-insurance plans fund

(a) The cost of administration of the public self-insured program by the Director of Industrial Relations shall be a General Fund item. The cost of administration of the private self-insured program by the Director of Industrial Relations shall be borne by the private self-insurers through payment of certificate fees which shall be established by the director in broad ranges based on the comparative numbers of employees insured by the private self-insurers and the number of adjusting locations. The director may assess other fees as necessary to cover the costs of special audits or services rendered to private self-insured employers. The director may assess a civil penalty for late filing as set forth in subdivision (a) of Section 3702.9.

(b) All revenues from fees and penalties paid by private self-insured employers shall be deposited into the Self-Insurance Plans Fund, which is hereby created for the administration of the private self-insurance program. Any unencumbered balance in subdivision (a) of Item 8350-001-001 of the Budget Act of 1983 shall be transferred to the Self-Insurance Plans Fund. The director shall annually eliminate any unused surplus in the Self-Insurance Plans Fund by reducing certificate fee assessments by an appropriate amount in the subsequent year. Moneys paid into the Self-Insurance Plans Fund for administration of the private self-insured program shall not be used by any other department or agency or for any purpose other than administration of the private self-insurance program. Detailed accountability shall be maintained by the director for any security deposit or other funds held in trust for the Self-Insurer's Security Fund in the Self-Insurance Plans Fund.

Moneys held by the director shall be invested in the Surplus Money Investment Fund. Interest shall be paid on all moneys transferred to the General Fund in accordance with Section 16310 of the Government Code. The Treasurer's and Controller's administrative costs may be charged to the interest earnings upon approval of the director. *(Added by Stats.1971, c. 1758, p. 3793, § 2. Amended by Stats.1978, c. 1379, p. 4572, § 7; Stats.1984, c. 1734, § 1, eff. Sept. 30, 1984, operative July 1, 1984; Stats.1992, c. 532 (A.B.2771), § 2.)*

§ 3702.6. Audit program for self-insurers

(a) The director shall establish an audit program addressing the adequacy of estimates of future liability of claims for all private self-insured employers, and shall ensure that all private self-insured employers are audited within a three-year cycle by the Office of Self Insurance Plans.

(b) Each public self-insurer shall advise its governing board within 90 days after submission of the self-insurer's annual report of the total liabilities reported and whether current funding of those workers' compensation liabilities is in compliance with the requirements of Government Accounting Standards Board Publication No. 10.

(c) The director shall, upon a showing of good cause, order a special audit of any public self-insured employer to determine the adequacy of estimates of future liability of claims.

(d) For purposes of this section, "good cause" means that there exists circumstances sufficient to raise concerns regarding the adequacy of estimates of future liability of claims to justify a special audit. *(Added by Stats.1971, c. 1758, p. 3793, § 3. Amended by Stats.1986, c. 1128, § 10,*

eff. Sept. 25, 1986; Stats.1989, c. 892, § 27; Stats.1992, c. 532 (A.B.2771), § 3.)

§ 3702.7. Revocation of certificate of consent; fines

A certificate of consent to administer claims of self-insured employers may be revoked by the director at any time for good cause after a hearing. Good cause includes, but is not limited to, the violation of subsection (1), (2), (3), (4), or (5) of subdivision (a) of Section 3702. In lieu of revocation of a certificate of consent, the director may impose a fine of not less than fifty dollars ($50) nor more than five hundred dollars ($500) for each violation. *(Added by Stats. 1984, c. 1521, § 4, operative July 1, 1985.)*

§ 3702.8. Employers who have ceased to be self-insured; discharge of continuing obligations; proceedings on failure to comply

(a) Employers who have ceased to be self-insured employers shall discharge their continuing obligations to secure the payment of workers' compensation that accrued during the period of self-insurance, for purposes of Sections 3700, 3700.5, 3706, and 3715, and shall comply with all of the following obligations of current certificate holders:

(1) Filing annual reports as deemed necessary by the director to carry out the requirements of this chapter.

(2) In the case of a private employer, depositing and maintaining a security deposit for accrued liability for the payment of any workers' compensation that may become due, pursuant to subdivision (b) of Section 3700 and Section 3701, except as provided in subdivision (c).

(3) Paying within 30 days all assessments of which notice is sent, pursuant to subdivision (b) of Section 3745, within 36 months from the last day the employer's certificate of self-insurance was in effect. Assessments shall be based on the benefits paid by the employer during the last full calendar year of self-insurance on claims incurred during that year.

(b) In addition to proceedings to establish liabilities and penalties otherwise provided, a failure to comply may be the subject of a proceeding before the director. An appeal from the director's determination shall be taken to the appropriate superior court by petition for writ of mandate.

(c) Notwithstanding subdivision (a), any employer who is currently self-insured or who has ceased to be self-insured may purchase a special excess workers' compensation policy to discharge any or all of the employer's continuing obligations as a self-insurer to pay compensation or to secure the payment of compensation.

(1) The special excess workers' compensation insurance policy shall be issued by an insurer authorized to transact workers' compensation insurance in this state.

(2) Each carrier's special excess workers' compensation policy shall be approved as to form and substance by the Insurance Commissioner, and rates for special excess

workers' compensation insurance shall be subject to the filing requirements set forth in Section 11735 of the Insurance Code.

(3) Each special excess workers' compensation insurance policy shall be submitted by the employer to the director. The director shall adopt and publish minimum insurer financial rating standards for companies issuing special excess workers' compensation policies.

(4) Upon acceptance by the director, a special excess workers' compensation policy shall provide coverage for all or any portion of the purchasing employer's claims for compensation arising out of injuries occurring during the period the employer was self-insured in accordance with Sections 3755, 3756, and 3757 of the Labor Code and Sections 11651 and 11654 of the Insurance Code. The director's acceptance shall discharge the Self–Insurer's Security Fund, without recourse or liability to the Self–Insurer's Security Fund, of any continuing liability for the claims covered by the special excess workers' compensation insurance policy.

(5) For public employers, no security deposit or financial guarantee bond or other security shall be required. The director shall set minimum financial rating standards for insurers issuing special excess workers' compensation policies for public employers.

(d)(1) In order for the special excess workers' compensation insurance policy to discharge the full obligations of a private employer to maintain a security deposit with the director for the payment of self-insured claims, applicable to the period to be covered by the policy, the special excess policy shall provide coverage for all claims for compensation arising out of that liability. The employer shall maintain the required deposit for the period covered by the policy with the director for a period of three years after the issuance date of the special excess policy.

(2) If the special workers' compensation insurance policy does not provide coverage for all of the continuing obligations for which the private self-insured employer is liable, to the extent the employer's obligations are not covered by the policy a private employer shall maintain the required deposit with the director. In addition, the employer shall maintain with the director the required deposit for the period covered by the policy for a period of three years after the issuance date of the special excess policy.

(e) The director shall adopt regulations pursuant to Section 3702.10 that are reasonably necessary to implement this section in order to reasonably protect injured workers, employers, the Self–Insurers' Security Fund, and the California Insurance Guarantee Association.

(f) The posting of a special excess workers' compensation insurance policy with the director shall discharge the obligation of the Self–Insurer's Security Fund pursuant to Section 3744 to pay claims in the event of an insolvency of a private employer to the extent of coverage of compensation liabilities under the special excess workers' compensation insurance policy. The California Insurance Guarantee Association shall be advised by the director whenever a special excess workers' compensation insurance policy is posted. *(Added by Stats.1986, c. 1128, § 11, eff. Sept. 25, 1986. Amended by Stats.1989, c. 1258, § 3; Stats.1990, c. 704 (A.B.3853), § 2; Stats.1999, c. 721 (A.B.1309), § 7.)*

§ 3702.9. Additional penalties for violation of obligations relating to report, security deposit, or assessment; costs and attorney fee; fraud, bad faith, or repeated violation; waiver or remission of payments

(a) In addition to remedies and penalties otherwise provided for a failure to secure the payment of compensation, the director may, after a determination that an obligation created in this article has been violated, also enter an order against any self-insured employer, including employers who are no longer self-insured, but who are required to comply with Section 3702.8, directing compliance, restitution for any losses, and a civil penalty in an amount not to exceed the following:

(1) For a failure to file a complete or timely annual report, an amount up to 5 percent of the incurred liabilities in the last report or one thousand five hundred dollars ($1,500), whichever is less, for each 30 days or portion thereof during which there is a failure.

(2) For failure to deposit and maintain a security deposit, an amount up to 10 percent of the increase not timely filed or five thousand dollars ($5,000), whichever is less, for each 30 days or portion thereof during which there is a failure.

(3) For a failure to timely or completely pay an assessment, an amount up to the assessment or two thousand five hundred dollars ($2,500), whichever is less, for each 30 days or portion thereof during which there is a failure.

(4) Where the failure was by an employer which knew or reasonably should have known of the obligation, the director shall, in addition, award reimbursement for all expenditures and costs by the fund or any intervening party, including a reasonable attorney fee.

(5) Where the failure was malicious, fraudulent, in bad faith, or a repeated violation, the director may award, as an additional civil penalty, liquidated damages of up to double the amounts assessed under paragraphs (1) to (4), inclusive, for deposit in the General Fund.

(b) An employer may deposit and maintain a security deposit or pay an assessment, reserving its right to challenge the amount or liability therefor at a hearing. If the director or the appeals board or a court, upon appeal, concludes that the employer is not liable or the amounts are excessive, then the director may waive, release, compromise, refund, or otherwise remit amounts which had been paid or deposited by an employer. The director may condition the waiver, release, compromise, refund, or remittance upon the present and continued future compliance with the obligations of subdivision (a) of Section 3702.8 for a period up to two years.

(c) Notwithstanding subdivision (b), where a violation has occurred, the director may waive, release, compromise, or otherwise reduce any civil penalty otherwise due upon a showing that a violation occurred through the employer's mistake, inadvertence, surprise, or excusable neglect. Neglect is not excusable within the meaning of this subdivision where the employer knew, or reasonably should have known, of the obligations. *(Added by Stats.1986, c. 1128, § 12, eff. Sept. 25, 1986.)*

§ 3702.10. Rules and regulations

The director, in accordance with Chapter 3.5 (commencing with Section 11340) of Part 1 of Division 3 of Title 2 of the Government Code, may adopt, amend, and repeal rules and regulations reasonably necessary to carry out the purposes of Section 129 and Article 1 (commencing with Section 3700), Article 2 (commencing with Section 3710), and Article 2.5 (commencing with Section 3740). This authorization includes, but is not limited to, the adoption of regulations to do all of the following:

(a) Specifying what constitutes ability to self-insure and to pay any compensation which may become due under Section 3700.

(b) Specifying what constitutes a marked reduction of an employer's financial strength.

(c) Specifying what constitutes a failure or inability to fulfill the employer's obligations under Section 3702.

(d) Interpreting and defining the terms used.

(e) Establishing procedures and standards for hearing and determinations, and providing for those determinations to be appealed to the appeals board.

(f) Specifying the standards, form, and content of agreements, forms, and reports between parties who have obligations pursuant to this chapter.

(g) Providing for the combinations and relative liabilities of security deposits, assumptions, and guarantees used pursuant to this chapter.

(h) Disclosing otherwise confidential financial information concerning self-insureds to courts or the Self-Insurers' Security Fund and specifying appropriate safeguards for that information.

(i) Requiring an amount to be added to each security deposit to secure the cost of administration of claims and to pay all legal costs.

(j) Authorizing and encouraging group self-insurance. *(Added by Stats.1986, c. 1128, § 13, eff. Sept. 25, 1986. Amended by Stats.1993, c. 121 (A.B.110), § 26, eff. July 16, 1993.)*

§ 3703. Administration of compensation benefits by self-insurer

So long as the certificate has not been revoked, and the self-insurer maintains on deposit the requisite bond or securities, the self-insurer shall not be required or obliged to pay into the State Compensation Insurance Fund any sums covering liability for compensation excepting life pensions; and the self-insurer may fully administer any compensation benefits assessed against the self-insurer. *(Stats.1937, c. 90, p. 270, § 3703. Amended by Stats.1959, c. 951, p. 2979, § 2.)*

§ 3705. Preferred subrogation rights of self-insurers' security fund or surety

The Self-Insurers' Security Fund or the surety making payment of compensation hereunder shall have the same preference over the other debts of the principal or his or her estate as is given by law to the person directly entitled to the compensation. *(Stats.1937, c. 90, p. 271, § 3705. Amended by Stats.1986, c. 1128, § 14, eff. Sept. 25, 1986.)*

§ 3706. Effect of failure to secure payment of compensation; action for damages

If any employer fails to secure the payment of compensation, any injured employee or his dependents may bring an action at law against such employer for damages, as if this division did not apply. *(Stats.1937, c. 90, p. 271, § 3706. Amended by Stats.1965, c. 1513, p. 3570, § 59, operative Jan. 15, 1966; Stats.1971, c. 1598, p. 3437, § 1.)*

§ 3706.5. Application of article and certain sections to agency or organization performing officiating services relating to amateur sporting events

The provisions of this article and Sections 4553, 4554, and 4555, and any other penalty provided by law for failure to secure the payment of compensation for employees, shall not apply to individual members of a board or governing body of a public agency or to members of a private, nonprofit organization, if the agency or organization performs officiating services relating to amateur sporting events and such members are excluded from the definition of "employee" pursuant to subdivision (j) of Section 3352. *(Added by Stats.1981, c. 21, p. 48, § 9, eff. April 18, 1981.)*

§ 3707. Attachment of property of employer

The injured employee or his dependents may in such action attach the property of the employer, at any time upon or after the institution of such action, in an amount fixed by the court, to secure the payment of any judgment which is ultimately obtained. The provisions of the Code of Civil Procedure, not inconsistent with this division, shall govern the issuance of, and proceedings upon such attachment. *(Stats.1937, c. 90, p. 271, § 3707.)*

§ 3708. Presumption of employer's negligence; defenses abolished; applicability of section to household employees

In such action it is presumed that the injury to the employee was a direct result and grew out of the negligence of the employer, and the burden of proof is upon the employer, to rebut the presumption of negligence. It is not a defense to the employer that the employee was guilty of contributory negligence, or assumed the risk of the hazard complained of, or that the injury was caused by the negligence of a fellow servant.

No contract or regulation shall restore to the employer any of the foregoing defenses.

This section shall not apply to any employer of an employee, as defined in subdivision (d) of Section 3351, with respect to such employee, but shall apply to employers of employees described in subdivision (b) of Section 3715, with respect to such employees. *(Stats.1937, c. 90, p. 271, § 3708. Amended by Stats.1977, c. 17, p. 31, § 22, eff. March 25, 1977.)*

§ 3708.5. Service of complaint; consolidation of actions

If an employee brings such an action for damages, the employee shall forthwith give a copy of the complaint to the Uninsured Employers Fund of the action by personal service or certified mail. Proof of such service shall be filed in such action. If a civil action has been initiated against the employer pursuant to Section 3717, the actions shall be consolidated. *(Added by Stats.1980, c. 1091, p. 3502, § 1.)*

§ 3709. Credit against judgment; liens; attorney fees; satisfaction of judgment

If, as a result of such action for damages, a judgment is obtained against the employer, any compensation awarded, paid, or secured by the employer shall be credited against the judgment. The court shall allow as a first lien against such judgment the amount of compensation paid by the director from the Uninsured Employers Fund pursuant to Section 3716.

Such judgment shall include a reasonable attorney's fee fixed by the court. The director, as administrator of the Uninsured Employers Fund, shall have a first lien against any proceeds of settlement in such action, before or after judgment, in the amount of compensation paid by the director from the Uninsured Employers Fund pursuant to Section 3716.

No satisfaction of a judgment in such action, in whole or in part, shall be valid as against the director without giving the director notice and a reasonable opportunity to perfect and satisfy his lien. *(Stats.1937, c. 90, p. 271, § 3709. Amended by Stats.1965, c. 1513, p. 3571, § 60, operative Jan. 15, 1966; Stats.1980, c. 1091, p. 3502, § 2.)*

§ 3709.5. Satisfaction of judgment; payment of attorney fees; credit against liability for compensation

After the payment of attorney's fees fixed by the court, the employer shall be relieved from the obligation to pay further compensation to or on behalf of the employee under this division up to the entire amount of the balance of the judgment, if satisfied, or such portion as has been satisfied.

After the satisfaction by the employer of the attorney's fees fixed by the court, the Uninsured Employers Fund shall be relieved from the obligation to pay further compensation to or on behalf of the employee pursuant to Section 3716, up to the entire amount of the balance of the judgment, if satisfied, or such portion as has been satisfied.

The appeals board shall allow as a credit to the employer and to the Uninsured Employers Fund, to be applied against the liability for compensation, the amount recovered by the employee in such action, either by settlement or after the judgment, as has not been applied to the expense of attorney's fees and costs. *(Added by Stats.1980, c. 1091, p. 3502, § 3.)*

ARTICLE 2.   UNINSURED EMPLOYERS FUND

Section
3710.   Enforcement; rules and regulations; "director" defined.
3710.1. Stop order for failure to secure payment of compensation; payment for time lost; protest; hearing; writ of mandate.
3710.2. Failure to observe stop order; failure to insure or self-insure; punishment; injunction.
3710.3. Stop order issued to carrier; transmittal to jurisdictional entity.
3711.   Furnishing written statement of name of employer's insurer or manner in which employer has complied with § 3700; failure to comply with request.
3712.   Conduct of business without security for payment of compensation; business strictures and penalties; prosecution of action.
3714.   Conference, mandatory settlement conference, standby conference, rating calendar; costs; filing.
3715.   Failure of employer to secure payment of compensation; employee application for compensation; filing; hearing; award; prima facie case; finding notice; appeal; resolution by director.
3716.   Uninsured employers benefits trust fund; payment of awards; liability; application and notice of lawsuit; identification of uninsured employers.
3716.1. Legal representation of director and state; costs; reimbursement; investigative and claims adjustment services; annual report to legislature and director.
3716.2. Payment of awarded benefits; penalties and interest; civil suits to enforce payment.
3716.3. Judgments against uninsured employers; enforcement by nonjudicial foreclosure.
3716.4. Judgment against carrier pursuant to § 3716.2; transmittal of copy to jurisdictional entity for enforcement.
3716.5. Job classification of employees paid from fund; designation; report.
3717.   Liquidated claim for damages against employer; actions; joint and several liability with corporation.
3717.1. Parties; substantial shareholders and parents of corporation; joinder; service of process.
3717.2. Status as substantial shareholder or parent; determination by appeals board.
3718.   Joinder of causes; credit against judgment; payment of amount recovered into state treasury.
3719.   Compromise of suit, action or proceeding or prosecution to final judgment.
3720.   Lien certificate: contents; recordation; duration of lien; aggrieved parties; amended certificate.
3720.1. Parents or substantial shareholders; prima facie evidence; hearing; writ of mandate.

Section
3721. Cancellation of lien.
3722. Penalty assessment order against uninsured employer.
3725. Contest of penalty assessment order; hearing; writ of mandate.
3726. Filing of assessment; entry and filing of judgment; interest; costs.
3727. Certificate of amount of penalty due from employer; filing; lien; effect of recording.
3727.1. Withdrawal of stop order or penalty assessment order.
3728. Cash revolving fund.
3730. Last day for filing falling on weekend or holiday.
3731. Service of orders.
3732. Recovery of damages from person or entity other than employer causing injury or death of employee.

§ 3710. Enforcement; rules and regulations; "director" defined

(a) The Director of Industrial Relations shall enforce the provisions of this article. The director may employ necessary investigators, clerks, and other employees, and make use of the services of any employee of the department whom he may assign to assist him in the enforcement of this article. Prosecutions for criminal violations of this division may be conducted by the appropriate public official of the county in which the offense is committed, by the Attorney General, or by any attorney in the civil service of the Department of Industrial Relations designated by the director for such purpose.

(b) The director, in accordance with the provisions of Chapter 4 (commencing at Section 11370) of Part 1 of Division 3 of Title 2 of the Government Code, may adopt, amend and repeal such rules and regulations as are reasonably necessary for the purpose of enforcing and administering this article and as are not inconsistent with law.

(c) As used in this article, "director" means the Director of Industrial Relations or the director's designated agents. *(Stats.1937, c. 90, p. 271, § 3710. Amended by Stats.1939, c. 649, p. 2076, § 1; Stats.1945, c. 1431, p. 2695, § 66; Stats.1951, c. 1436, p. 3394, § 1; Stats. 1953, c. 1757, p. 3516, § 11; Stats.1955, c. 323, p. 775, § 1; Stats.1980, c. 852, p. 2651, § 2.)*

§ 3710.1. Stop order for failure to secure payment of compensation; payment for time lost; protest; hearing; writ of mandate

Where an employer has failed to secure the payment of compensation as required by Section 3700, the director shall issue and serve on such employer a stop order prohibiting the use of employee labor by such employer until the employer's compliance with the provisions of Section 3700. Such stop order shall become effective immediately upon service. Any employee so affected by such work stoppage shall be paid by the employer for such time lost, not exceeding 10 days, pending compliance by the employer. Such employer may protest the stop order by making and filing with the director a written request for a hearing within 20 days after service of such stop order. Such hearing shall be held within 5 days from the date of filing such request. The director shall notify the employer of the time and place of the hearing by mail. At the conclusion of the hearing the stop order shall be immediately affirmed or dismissed, and within 24 hours thereafter the director shall issue and serve on all parties to the hearing by registered or certified mail a written notice of findings and findings. A writ of mandate may be taken from the findings to the appropriate superior court. Such writ must be taken within 45 days after the mailing of the notice of findings and findings. *(Added by Stats.1980, c. 852, p. 2652, § 4.)*

§ 3710.2. Failure to observe stop order; failure to insure or self-insure; punishment; injunction

Failure of an employer, officer, or anyone having direction, management, or control of any place of employment or of employees to observe a stop order issued and served upon him or her pursuant to Section 3710.1 is a misdemeanor punishable by imprisonment in the county jail not exceeding 60 days or by a fine not exceeding ten thousand dollars ($10,000), or both. Fines shall be paid into the State Treasury to the credit of the Uninsured Employers Fund. The director may also obtain injunctive and other relief from the courts to carry out the purposes of Section 3710.1. The failure to obtain a policy of workers' compensation insurance or a certificate of consent to self-insure as required by Section 3700 is a misdemeanor in accordance with Section 3700.5. *(Added by Stats.1951, c. 1436, p. 3394, § 3. Amended by Stats. 1955, c. 323, p. 775, § 3; Stats.1965, c. 1513, p. 3571, § 61, operative Jan. 15, 1966; Stats.1976, c. 1036, p. 4640, § 2, eff. Sept. 20, 1976; Stats.1980, c. 852, p. 2652, § 5; Stats.1989, c. 507, § 2; Stats.1991, c. 600 (A.B.1576), § 1.)*

§ 3710.3. Stop order issued to carrier; transmittal to jurisdictional entity

Whenever a stop order has been issued pursuant to Section 3710.1 to a motor carrier of property subject to the jurisdiction and control of the Department of Motor Vehicles or to a household goods carrier, passenger stage corporation, or charter-party carrier of passengers subject to the jurisdiction and control of the Public Utilities Commission, the director shall transmit the stop order to the Public Utilities Commission or the Department of Motor Vehicles, whichever has jurisdiction over the affected carrier, within 30 days. *(Added by Stats.1991, c. 1071 (A.B.410), § 1. Amended by Stats.1996, c. 1042 (A.B.1683), § 2.3, eff. Sept. 29, 1996; Stats.1998, c. 485 (A.B.2803), § 123.)*

§ 3711. Furnishing written statement of name of employer's insurer or manner in which employer has complied with § 3700; failure to comply with request

The director, an investigator for the Department of Insurance Fraud Bureau or its successor, or a district attorney investigator assigned to investigate workers' compensation fraud may, at any time, require an employer to furnish a written statement showing the name of his or her insurer or the manner in which the employer has complied with Section 3700. Failure of the employer for a period of 10 days to furnish the written statement is prima facie evidence that he or she has failed or neglected in respect to the matters so required. The 10–day period may not be construed to allow an uninsured employer, so found by the director, any extension of time from the application of the provisions of Section 3710.1. An insured employer who fails to respond to an inquiry respecting his or her status as to his or her workers' compensation security shall be assessed and required to pay a penalty of five hundred dollars ($500) to the director for deposit in the State Treasury to the credit of the Uninsured Employers Fund. In any prosecution under this article, the burden of proof is upon the defendant to show that he or she has secured the payment of compensation in one of the two ways set forth in Section 3700. (Stats.1937, c. 90, p. 271, § 3711. Amended by Stats.1945, c. 1431, p. 2695, § 67; Stats.1955, c. 323, p. 776, § 4; Stats.1976, c. 1036, p. 4640, § 3, eff. Sept. 20, 1976; Stats.1980, c. 852, p. 2652, § 6; Stats.1991, c. 600 (A.B.1576), § 2; Stats.1992, c. 1276 (A.B.3251), § 2; Stats.1993, c. 60 (S.B.452), § 7, eff. June 30, 1993; Stats.2003–2004, 4th Ex.Sess., c. 2 (S.B.2), § 4, eff. March 1, 2005.)

§ 3712. Conduct of business without security for payment of compensation; business strictures and penalties; prosecution of action

(a) The securing of the payment of compensation in a way provided in this division is essential to the functioning of the expressly declared social public policy of this state in the matter of workers' compensation. The conduct or operation of any business or undertaking without full compensation security, in continuing violation of social policy, shall be subject to imposition of business strictures and monetary penalties by the director, including, but not limited to, resort to the superior court of any county in which all or some part of the business is being thus unlawfully conducted or operated, for carrying out the intent of this article.

(b) In a proceeding before the superior court in matters concerned with this article, no filing fee shall be charged to the plaintiff; nor may any charge or cost be imposed for any act or service required of or done by any state or county officer or employee in connection with the proceeding. If the court or the judge before whom the order to show cause in the proceeding is made returnable, finds that the defendant is conducting or operating a business or undertaking without the full compensation security required, the court or judge shall forthwith, and without continuance, issue an order restraining the future or further conduct and operation of the business or undertaking so long as the violation of social public policy continues. The action shall be prosecuted by the Attorney General of California, the district attorney of the county in which suit is brought, the city attorney of any

city in which such a business or undertaking is being operated or conducted without full compensation security, or any attorney possessing civil service status who is an employee of the Department of Industrial Relations who may be designated by the director for that purpose. No finding made in the course of any such action is binding on the appeals board in any subsequent proceeding before it for benefits under this division. (Added by Stats.1939, c. 649, p. 2077, § 4. Amended by Stats.1945, c. 1431, p. 2695, § 68; Stats.1953, c. 1757, p. 3516, § 12; Stats.1955, c. 323, p. 776, § 5; Stats.1965, c. 1513, p. 3571, § 62, operative Jan. 15, 1966; Stats.1976, c. 1036, p. 4640, § 4, eff. Sept. 20, 1976; Stats.1980, c. 852, p. 2653, § 7; Stats.1982, c. 517, p. 2404, § 309.)

§ 3714. Conference, mandatory settlement conference, standby conference, rating calendar; costs; filing

(a) All cases involving the Uninsured Employers Fund or the Subsequent Injuries Fund as a party or involving death without dependents shall only be heard for conference, mandatory settlement conference pursuant to subdivision (d) of Section 5502, standby conference, or rating calendar at the district Workers' Compensation Appeals Board located in San Francisco, Los Angeles, Van Nuys, Anaheim, Sacramento, or San Diego, except for good cause shown and with the consent of the director. This subdivision shall not apply to trials or hearings pursuant to Section 5309 or to expedited hearings pursuant to subdivision (b) of Section 5502.

(b) For the cases specified in subdivision (a), the presiding judge of the Workers' Compensation Appeals Board located in San Francisco, Los Angeles, Van Nuys, Anaheim, Sacramento, or San Diego shall have the authority, either by standing order or on a case-by-case basis, to order a conference, mandatory settlement conference pursuant to subdivision (d) of Section 5502, standby conference, or rating calendar in which no testimony will be taken to be conducted by telephone conference call among the parties and their attorneys of record who do not reside in the county in which that appeals board is located. The cost of the scheduling of the conference call shall be charged against the appropriate fund of the department.

(c) Any filings of documents necessary for the proceedings specified in subdivisions (a) and (b) may be served on the appeals board and the parties by facsimile machine, but if so served, within five workings days service shall be made on the appeals board and the parties as required by regulation.

(d) This section shall remain in effect for two years commencing on the date that the administrative director certifies and publishes that the rearrangement of judicial resources required by this section, and conference call facilities required for this section are in place. The certification shall be published in the California Notice Register, but shall be required to have been posted in the office of each appeals board at least 30 days prior to that publication. Notwithstanding this section, with the permission of the presiding judge and under standards set by the administrative director, parties may be permitted to conclude existing cases where they were filed. This section shall cease to be operative at the end of that two-year period, and shall be repealed on January 1 following that date. *(Added by Stats.1992, c. 611 (A.B.3774), § 1.)*

Operative Effect

For operative effect and repeal of section, see its terms.

§ 3715. Failure of employer to secure payment of compensation; employee application for compensation; filing; hearing; award; prima facie case; finding notice; appeal; resolution by director

(a) Any employee, except an employee as defined in subdivision (d) of Section 3351, whose employer has failed to secure the payment of compensation as required by this division, or his or her dependents in case death has ensued, may, in addition to proceeding against his or her employer by civil action in the courts as provided in Section 3706, file his or her application with the appeals board for compensation and the appeals board shall hear and determine the application for compensation in like manner as in other claims and shall make the award to the claimant as he or she would be entitled to receive if the employer had secured the payment of compensation as required, and the employer shall pay the award in the manner and amount fixed thereby or shall furnish to the appeals board a bond, in any amount and with any sureties as the appeals board requires, to pay the employee the award in the manner and amount fixed thereby.

(b) Notwithstanding this section or any other provision of this chapter except Section 3708, any person described in subdivision (d) of Section 3351 who is (1) engaged in household domestic service who is employed by one employer for over 52 hours per week, (2) engaged as a part-time gardener in connection with a private dwelling, if the number of hours devoted to the gardening work for any individual regularly exceeds 44 hours per month, or (3) engaged in casual employment where the work contemplated is to be completed in not less than 10 working days, without regard to the number of persons employed, and where the total labor cost of the work is not less than one hundred dollars ($100) (which amount shall not include charges other than for personal services), shall be entitled, in addition to proceeding against his or her employer by civil action in the courts as provided in Section 3706, to file his or her application with the appeals board for compensation. The appeals board shall hear and determine the application for compensation in like manner as in other claims, and shall make the award to the claimant as he or she would be entitled to receive if the person's employer had secured the payment of compensation as required, and the employer shall pay the award in the manner and amount fixed thereby, or shall furnish to the appeals board a bond, in any amount and with any sureties as the appeals

board requires, to pay the employee the award in the manner and amount fixed thereby.

It is the intent of the Legislature that the amendments to this section by Chapter 17 of the Statutes of 1977, make no change in the law as it applied to those types of employees covered by this subdivision prior to the effective date of Chapter 1263 of the 1975 Regular Session.

(c) In any claim in which it is alleged that the employer has failed to secure the payment of compensation, the director, only for purposes of this section and Section 3720, shall determine, on the basis of the evidence available to him or her, whether the employer was prima facie illegally uninsured. A finding that the employer was prima facie illegally uninsured shall be made when the director determines that there is sufficient evidence to constitute a prima facie case that the employer employed an employee on the date of the alleged injury and had failed to secure the payment of compensation, and that the employee was injured arising out of, and occurring in the course of, the employment.

Failure of the employer to furnish within 10 days the written statement in response to a written demand for a written statement prescribed in Section 3711, addressed to the employer at its address as shown on the official address record of the appeals board, shall constitute in itself sufficient evidence for a prima facie case that the employer failed to secure the payment of compensation.

A written denial by the insurer named in the statement furnished by the employer as prescribed in Section 3711, that the employer was so insured as claimed, or the nonexistence of a valid certificate of consent to self-insure for the time of the claimed injury, if the statement furnished by the employer claims the employer was self-insured, shall constitute in itself sufficient evidence for a prima facie case that the employer had failed to secure the payment of compensation.

The nonexistence of a record of the employer's insurance with the Workers' Compensation Insurance Rating Bureau shall constitute in itself sufficient evidence for a prima facie case that the employer failed to secure the payment of compensation.

The unrebutted written declaration under penalty of perjury by the injured employee, or applicant other than the employee, that the employee was employed by the employer at the time of the injury, and that he or she was injured in the course of his or her employment, shall constitute, in itself, sufficient evidence for a prima facie case that the employer employed the employee at the time of the injury, and that the employee was injured arising out of, and occurring in the course of, the employment.

(d) When the director determines that an employer was prima facie illegally uninsured, the director shall mail a written notice of the determination to the employer at his or her address as shown on the official address record of the appeals board, and to any other more recent

565

address the director may possess. The notice shall advise the employer of its right to appeal the finding, and that a lien may be placed against the employer's and any parent corporation's property, or the property of substantial shareholders of a corporate employer as defined by Section 3717.

Any employer aggrieved by a finding of the director that it was prima facie illegally uninsured may appeal the finding by filing a petition before the appeals board. The petition shall be filed within 20 days after the finding is issued. The appeals board shall hold a hearing on the petition within 20 days after the petition is filed with the appeals board. The appeals board shall have exclusive jurisdiction to determine appeals of the findings by the director, and no court of this state has jurisdiction to review, annul, or suspend the findings or the liens created thereunder, except as provided by Article 2 (commencing with Section 5950) of Chapter 7 of Part 4 of Division 4.

(e) Any claim brought against an employer under this section may be resolved by the director by compromise and release or stipulated findings and award as long as the appeals board has acquired jurisdiction over the employer and the employer has been given notice and an opportunity to object.

Notice may be given by service on the employer of an appeals board notice of intention to approve the compromise and release or stipulated findings and award. The employer shall have 20 days after service of the notice of intention to file an objection with the appeals board and show good cause therefor.

If the employer objects, the appeals board shall determine if there is good cause for the objection.

If the appeals board finds good cause for the objection, the director may proceed with the compromise and release or stipulated findings and award if doing so best serves the interest of the Uninsured Employers Fund, but shall have no cause of action against the employer under Section 3717 unless the appeals board case is tried to its conclusion and the employer is found liable.

If the appeals board does not find good cause for the objection, and the compromise and release or stipulated findings and award is approved, the Uninsured Employers Fund shall have a cause of action against the employer pursuant to Section 3717.

(f) The director may adopt regulations to implement and interpret the procedures provided for in this section. *(Added by Stats.1971, c. 1598, p. 3437, § 3. Amended by Stats.1977, c. 17, p. 32, § 24, eff. March 25, 1977; Stats.1980, c. 852, p. 2655, § 10; Stats.1980, c. 1091, p. 3503, § 5; Stats.1985, c. 1547, § 2; Stats.1987, c. 202, § 1; Stats.1989, c. 461, § 1.)*

§ 3716. Uninsured employers benefits trust fund; payment of awards; liability; application and notice of lawsuit; identification of uninsured employers

(a) If the employer fails to pay the compensation required by Section 3715 to the person entitled thereto, or fails to furnish the bond required by Section 3715 within a period of 10 days after notification of the award, the award, upon application by the person entitled thereto, shall be paid by the director from the Uninsured Employers Benefits Trust Fund. The expenses of the director in administering these provisions, directly or by contract pursuant to Section 3716.1, shall be paid from the Workers' Compensation Administration Revolving Fund. Refunds may be paid from the Uninsured Employers Benefits Trust Fund for amounts remitted erroneously to the fund, or the director may authorize offsetting subsequent remittances to the fund.

(b) It is the intent of the Legislature that the Uninsured Employers Benefits Trust Fund is created to ensure that workers who happen to be employed by illegally uninsured employers are not deprived of workers' compensation benefits, and is not created as a source of contribution to insurance carriers, or self-insured, or legally insured employers. The Uninsured Employers Benefits Trust Fund has no liability for claims of occupational disease or cumulative injury unless no employer during the period of the occupational disease or cumulative injury during which liability is imposed under Section 5500.5 was insured for workers' compensation, was permissibly self-insured, or was legally uninsured. No employer has a right of contribution against the Uninsured Employers Benefits Trust Fund for the liability of an illegally uninsured employer under an award of benefits for occupational disease or cumulative injury, nor may an employee in a claim of occupational disease or cumulative injury elect to proceed against an illegally uninsured employer.

(c) The Uninsured Employers Benefits Trust Fund has no liability to pay for medical, surgical, chiropractic, hospital, or other treatment, the liability for which treatment is imposed upon the employer pursuant to Section 4600, and which treatment has been provided or paid for by the State Department of Health Services pursuant to the California Medical Assistance Program.

(d) The Uninsured Employers Benefits Trust Fund shall have no liability to pay compensation, nor shall it be joined in any appeals board proceeding, unless the employer alleged to be illegally uninsured shall first either have made a general appearance or have been served with the application specified in Section 3715 and with a special notice of lawsuit issued by the appeals board. The special notice of lawsuit shall be in a form to be prescribed by the appeals board, and it shall contain at least the information and warnings required by the Code of Civil Procedure to be contained in the summons issued in a civil action. The special notice of lawsuit shall also contain a notice that if the appeals board makes an award against the defendant that his or her house or other dwelling and other property may be taken to satisfy the award in a nonjudicial sale, with no exemptions from execution. The special notice of lawsuit shall, in addition, contain a notice that a lien may be imposed upon the defendant's property without further hearing and before the issuance of an award. The applicant shall identify a legal person or entity as the employer named in the special notice of lawsuit. The reasonable expense of serving the application and special notice of lawsuit, when incurred by the employee, shall be awarded as a cost. Proof of service of the special notice of lawsuit and application shall be filed with the appeals board.

(1) The application and special notice of lawsuit may be served, within or without this state, in the manner provided for service of summons in the Code of Civil Procedure. Thereafter, an employer, alleged to be illegally uninsured, shall notify the appeals board of the address at which it may be served with official notices and papers, and shall notify the appeals board of any changes in the address. No findings, order, decision, award, or other notice or paper need be served in this manner on an employer, alleged to be illegally uninsured, who has been served as provided in this section, and who has not filed an answer, otherwise made a general appearance, or furnished the appeals board with its address. The findings, orders, decisions, awards, or other notice or paper may be mailed to the employer as the board, by regulation, may provide.

(2) Notwithstanding paragraph (1), if the employer alleged to be illegally uninsured has not filed an answer, otherwise made a general appearance, or furnished the appeals board with its address, the appeals board shall serve any findings, order, decision, award, or other notice or paper on the employer by mail at the address the appeals board has for the employer. The failure of delivery at that address or the lack of personal service on an employer who has been served as provided in this section, of these findings, order, decision, award, or other notice or paper, shall not constitute grounds for reopening or invalidating any appeals board action pursuant to Section 5506, or for contesting the validity of any judgment obtained under Section 3716 or 5806, a lien under Section 3720, or a settlement under subdivision (e) of Section 3715.

(3) The board, by regulation, may provide for service procedures in cases where a request for new and further benefits is made after the issuance of any findings and award and a substantial period of time has passed since the first service or attempted service.

(4) The director, on behalf of the Uninsured Employers Benefits Trust Fund, shall furnish information as to the identities, legal capacities, and addresses of uninsured employers known to the director upon request of the board or upon a showing of good cause by the employee or the employee's representative. Good cause shall include a declaration by the employee's representative, filed under penalty of perjury, that the information is necessary to represent the employee in proceedings under this division. *(Added by Stats.1971, c. 1598, p. 3438, § 4. Amended by Stats.1977, c. 17, p. 33, § 24.5, eff. March 25, 1977; Stats.1980, c. 852, p. 2656, § 11; Stats.1981, c. 894, p. 3408, § 2; Stats.1990, c. 770 (S.B.*

241), § 1; Stats.1993, c. 1241 (S.B.147), § 5; Stats.2003, c. 228 (A.B.1756), § 28, eff. Aug. 11, 2003.)

§ 3716.1. Legal representation of director and state; costs; reimbursement; investigative and claims adjustment services; annual report to legislature and director

(a) In any hearing, investigation, or proceeding, the Attorney General, or attorneys of the Department of Industrial Relations, shall represent the director and the state. Expenses incident to representation of the director and the state, before the appeals board and in civil court, by the Attorney General or Department of Industrial Relations attorneys, shall be reimbursed from the Workers' Compensation Administration Revolving Fund. Expenses incident to representation by the Attorney General or attorneys of the Department of Industrial Relations incurred in attempts to recover moneys pursuant to Section 3717 of the Labor Code shall not exceed the total amounts recovered by the director on behalf of the Uninsured Employers Benefits Trust Fund pursuant to this chapter.

(b) The director shall assign investigative and claims' adjustment services respecting matters concerning uninsured employers injury cases. The director or his or her representative may make these service assignments within the department, or he or she may contract for these services with the State Compensation Insurance Fund, except insofar as these matters might conflict with the interests of the State Compensation Insurance Fund. The administrative costs associated with these services shall be reimbursed from the Workers' Compensation Administration Revolving Fund and the nonadministrative costs from the Uninsured Employers Benefits Trust Fund, except when a budget impasse requires advances as described in subdivision (c) of Section 62.5. To the extent permitted by state law, the director may contract for audits or reports of services under this section.

(c) Commencing November 1, 2004, the State Compensation Insurance Fund and the director shall report annually to the fiscal committees of both houses of the Legislature and the Director of Finance, regarding any of the following:

(1) The number of uninsured employers claims paid in the previous fiscal year, the total cost of those claims, and levels of reserves for incurred claims.

(2) The administrative costs associated with claims payment activities.

(3) Annual revenues to the Uninsured Employers Benefits Trust Fund from all of the following:

(A) Assessments collected pursuant to subdivision (c) of Section 62.5.

(B) Fines and penalties collected by the department.

(C) Revenues collected pursuant to Section 3717.

(4) Projected annual program and claims costs for the current and upcoming fiscal years. *(Added by Stats.1976, c. 1036, p. 4641, § 6, eff. Sept. 20, 1976. Amended by*

Stats.1980, c. 852, p. 2656, § 12; Stats.1981, c. 894, p. 3409, § 3; Stats.2003, c. 228 (A.B.1756), § 29, eff. Aug. 11, 2003.)

§ 3716.2. Payment of awarded benefits; penalties and interest; civil suits to enforce payment

Notwithstanding the precise elements of an award of compensation benefits, and notwithstanding the claim and demand for payment being made therefor to the director, the director, as administrator of the Uninsured Employers Fund, shall pay the claimant only such benefits allowed, recognizing proper liens thereon, that would have accrued against an employer properly insured for workers' compensation liability. The Uninsured Employers Fund shall not be liable for any penalties or for the payment of interest on any awards. However, in civil suits by the director to enforce payment of an award, including procedures pursuant to Section 3717, the total amount of the award, including interest, other penalties, and attorney's fees granted by the award, shall be sought. Recovery by the director, in a civil suit or by other means, of awarded benefits in excess of amounts paid to the claimant by the Uninsured Employers Fund shall be paid over to the injured employee or his representative, as the case may be. (Added by Stats.1976, c. 1036, p. 4642, § 7, eff. Sept. 20, 1976. Amended by Stats.1980, c. 852, p. 2656, § 13; Stats.1981, c. 894, p. 3409, § 4; Stats.1999, c. 83 (S.B.966), § 133.)

§ 3716.3. Judgments against uninsured employers; enforcement by nonjudicial foreclosure

(a) Notwithstanding any other provision of law to the contrary, when the director obtains a judgment against an uninsured employer, the director may, in addition to any other remedies provided by law, enforce the judgment by nonjudicial foreclosure. This enforcement shall not be subject to Chapter 4 (commencing with Section 703.010) of Division 2 of Title 9 of Part 2 of the Code of Civil Procedure relating to claiming exemptions after levy.

(b) To enforce the judgment by nonjudicial foreclosure, the director shall record with the county recorder of any county in which real property of the parties against whom the judgment is taken is located, a certified copy of the judgment together with the director's notice of intent to foreclose. The notice of intent to foreclose shall set forth all of the following:

(1) The name, address, and telephone number of the trustee authorized by the director to enforce the lien by sale.

(2) The legal description of the real property to be foreclosed upon.

(3) Proof of service by registered or certified mail on the following:

(A) The parties against whom the foreclosure is sought at their last known address as shown on the official records of the appeals board and as shown on the latest recorded deed, deed of trust, or mortgage affecting the real property which is the subject of the foreclosure.

(B) All of the owners of the real property which is subject to the foreclosure at their last address as shown on the latest equalized assessment roll.

(c) Upon the expiration of 20 days following recording of the judgment and notice of intent to foreclose, the trustee may proceed to sell the real property. Any sale by the trustee shall be conducted in accordance with Article 1 (commencing with Section 2920) of Chapter 2 of Title 14 of Part 4 of Division 3 of the Civil Code applicable to the exercise of powers of sale of property under powers created by mortgages and deeds of trust.

(d) The director may authorize any person, including an attorney, corporation, or other business entity, to act as trustee pursuant to subdivision (b).

(e) Except as provided in subdivision (f), this section shall apply to all judgments which the director has obtained or may obtain pursuant to Section 3717, 3726, or 5806.

(f) This section shall not apply to the principal residence of an employer if the appeals board finds that the employer, on the date of injury, employed 10 or fewer employees. An employer seeking this exemption shall provide proof of payment of tax withholding required pursuant to Division 6 (commencing with Section 13000) of the Unemployment Insurance Code, to assist in determining the number of employees on the date of injury. (Added by Stats.1990, c. 770 (S.B.241) § 2.)

§ 3716.4. Judgment against carrier pursuant to § 3716.2; transmittal of copy to jurisdictional entity for enforcement

Whenever a final judgment has been entered against a motor carrier of property subject to the jurisdiction and control of the Department of Motor Vehicles or a passenger stage corporation, charter-party carrier of passengers, or a household goods carrier subject to the jurisdiction and control of the Public Utilities Commission as a result of an award having been made pursuant to Section 3716.2, the director may transmit to the Public Utilities Commission or the Department of Motor Vehicles, whichever has jurisdiction over the affected carrier, a copy of the judgment along with the name and address of the regulated entity and any other persons, corporations, or entities named in the judgment which are jointly and severally liable for the debt to the State Treasury with a complaint requesting that the Public Utilities Commission or the Department of Motor Vehicles immediately revoke the carrier's Public Utilities Commission certificate of public convenience and necessity or Department of Motor Vehicles motor carrier permit. (Added by Stats.1991, c. 1071 (A.B.410), § 2. Amended by Stats. 1996, c. 1042 (A.B.1683), § 2.5, eff. Sept. 29, 1996.)

§ 3716.5. Job classification of employees paid from fund; designation; report

In the payment of workers' compensation benefits from the Uninsured Employers Fund, the director shall do the following:

(a) Designate the job classifications of employees who are paid compensation from the fund.

(b) Compile data on the job classifications of employees paid compensation from the fund and report this data to the Legislature by November 1, 1990, and annually thereafter. *(Added by Stats.1989, c. 827, § 1.)*

§ 3717. Liquidated claim for damages against employer; actions; joint and several liability with corporation

(a) A findings and award that is the subject of a demand on the Uninsured Employers Fund or an approved compromise and release or stipulated findings and award entered into by the director pursuant to subdivision (e) of Section 3715, or a decision and order of the rehabilitation unit of the Division of Workers' Compensation, that has become final, shall constitute a liquidated claim for damages against an employer in the amount so ascertained and fixed by the appeals board, and the appeals board shall certify the same to the director who may institute a civil action against the employer in the name of the director, as administrator of the Uninsured Employers Fund, for the collection of the award, or may obtain a judgment against the employer pursuant to Section 5806. In the event that the appeals board finds that a corporation is the employer of an injured employee, and that the corporation has not secured the payment of compensation as required by this chapter, the following persons shall be jointly and severally liable with the corporation to the director in the action:

(1) All persons who are a parent, as defined in Section 175 of the Corporations Code, of the corporation.

(2) All persons who are substantial shareholders, as defined in subdivision (b), of the corporation or its parent. In the action it shall be sufficient for plaintiff to set forth a copy of the findings and award of the appeals board relative to the claims as certified by the appeals board to the director and to state that there is due to plaintiff on account of the finding and award of the appeals board a specified sum which plaintiff claims with interest. The director shall be further entitled to costs and reasonable attorney fees, and to his or her investigation and litigation expenses for the appeals board proceedings, and a reasonable attorney fee for litigating the appeals board proceedings. A certified copy of the findings and award in the claim shall be attached to the complaint. The contents of the findings and award shall be deemed proved. The answer or demurrer to the complaint shall be filed within 10 days, the reply or demurrer to the answer within 20 days, and the demurrer to the reply within 30 days after the return day of the summons or service by publication. All motions and demurrers shall be submitted to the court within 10 days after they are filed. At the time the civil action filed pursuant to this section is at issue, it shall be placed at the head of the trial docket and shall be first in order for trial.

Nothing in this chapter shall be construed to preclude informal adjustment by the director of a claim for compensation benefits before the issuance of findings and award wherever it appears to the director that the employer is uninsured and that informal adjustment will facilitate the expeditious delivery of compensation benefits to the injured employee.

(b) As used in this section, "substantial shareholder" means a shareholder who owns at least 15 percent of the total value of all classes of stock, or, if no stock has been issued, who owns at least 15 percent of the beneficial interests in the corporation.

(c) For purposes of this section, in determining the ownership of stock or beneficial interest in the corporation, in the determination of whether a person is a substantial shareholder of the corporation, the rules of attribution of ownership of Section 17384 [1] of the Revenue and Taxation Code shall be applied.

(d) For purposes of this section, "corporation" shall not include:

(1) Any corporation which is the issuer of any security which is exempted by Section 25101 of the Corporations Code from Section 25130 of the Corporations Code.

(2) Any corporation which is the issuer of any security exempted by subdivision (c), (d), or (i) of Section 25100 of the Corporations Code from Sections 25110, 25120, and 25130 of the Corporations Code.

(3) Any corporation which is the issuer of any security which has qualified either by coordination, as provided by Section 25111 of the Corporations Code, or by notification, as provided by Section 25112 of the Corporations Code. *(Added by Stats.1971, c. 1598, p. 3438, § 5. Amended by Stats.1976, c. 1036, p. 4642, § 8, eff. Sept. 20, 1976; Stats.1980, c. 852, p. 2657, § 13.5; Stats.1981, c. 894, p. 3410, § 5; Stats.1987, c. 202, § 2; Stats.1989, c. 461, § 2; Stats.1994, c. 146 (A.B.3601), § 148.)*

[1] Repealed by Stats.1983, c. 488, 32, eff. July 28, 1983.

§ 3717.1. Parties; substantial shareholders and parents of corporation; joinder; service of process

In any claim in which an alleged uninsured employer is a corporation, the director may cause substantial shareholders and parents, as defined by Section 3717, to be joined as parties. Substantial shareholders may be served as provided in this division for service on adverse parties, or if they cannot be found with reasonable diligence, by serving the corporation. The corporation, upon this service, shall notify the shareholder of the service, and mail the served document to him or her at the shareholder's last address known to the corporation. *(Added by Stats.1985, c. 1547, § 3.)*

§ 3717.2. Status as substantial shareholder or parent; determination by appeals board

Upon request of the director, the appeals board shall make findings of whether persons are substantial shareholders or parents, as defined in Section 3717. The director may in his or her discretion proceed against substantial shareholders and parents pursuant to Section

3717 without those findings of the appeals board. *(Added by Stats.1985, c. 1547, § 4.)*

§ 3718. Joinder of causes; credit against judgment; payment of amount recovered into state treasury

The cause of action provided in Section 3717 and any cause of action arising out of Section 3722 may be joined in one action against an employer. The amount recovered in such action from such employer shall be paid into the State Treasury to the credit of the Uninsured Employers Fund. *(Added by Stats.1971, c. 1598, p. 3438, § 6. Amended by Stats.1976, c. 1036, p. 4643, § 9, eff. Sept. 20, 1976.)*

§ 3719. Compromise of suit, action or proceeding or prosecution to final judgment

Any suit, action, proceeding, or award brought or made against any employer under Section 3717 may be compromised by the director, or such suit, action, or proceeding may be prosecuted to final judgment as in the discretion of the director may best subserve the interests of the Uninsured Employers Fund. *(Added by Stats.1971, c. 1598, p. 3439, § 7. Amended by Stats.1980, c. 852, p. 2657, § 14.)*

§ 3720. Lien certificate: contents; recordation; duration of lien; aggrieved parties; amended certificate

(a) When the appeals board or the director determines under Section 3715 or 3716 that an employer has not secured the payment of compensation as required by this division or when the director has determined that the employer is prima facie illegally uninsured, the director may file for record in the office of the county recorder in the counties where the employer's property is possibly located, a certificate of lien showing the date that the employer was determined to be illegally uninsured or the date that the director has determined that the employer was prima facie illegally uninsured. The certificate shall show the name and address of the employer against whom it was filed, and the fact that the employer has not secured the payment of compensation as required by this division. Upon the recordation, the certificate shall constitute a valid lien in favor of the director, and shall have the same force, effect and priority as a judgment lien and shall continue for 10 years from the time of the recording of the certificate unless sooner released or otherwise discharged. A copy of the certificate shall be served upon the employer by mail, by the director. A facsimile signature of the director accompanied by the seal imprint of the department shall be sufficient for recording purposes of liens and releases or cancellations thereof considered herein. Certificates of liens may be filed in any or all counties of the state, depending upon the information the director obtains concerning the employer's assets.

(b) For purposes of this section, in the event the employer is a corporation, those persons in whom either the appeals board finds are the parent or the substantial shareholders of the corporation or its parent, or whom the director finds pursuant to Section 3720.1 to be prima facie the parent or the substantial shareholders of the corporation or its parent, as defined in Section 3717, shall be deemed to be the employer, and the director may file the certificates against those persons.

(c) A person who claims to be aggrieved by the filing of a lien against the property of an uninsured employer because he or she has the same or a similar name, may apply to the director to have filed an amended certificate of lien which shows that the aggrieved applicant is not the uninsured employer which is the subject of the lien. If the director finds that the aggrieved applicant is not the same as the uninsured employer, the director shall file an amended certificate of lien with the county recorder of the county in which the aggrieved applicant has property, which shall show, by reasonably identifying information furnished by the aggrieved applicant, that the uninsured employer and the aggrieved applicant are not the same. If the director does not file the amended certificate of lien within 60 days of application therefor, the applicant may appeal the director's failure to so find by filing a petition with the appeals board, which shall make a finding as to whether the applicant and the uninsured employer are the same.

(d) Liens filed under this section have continued existence independent of, and may be foreclosed upon independently of, any right of action arising out of Section 3717 or 5806. *(Added by Stats.1971, c. 1598, p. 3439, § 8. Amended by Stats.1974, c. 46, p. 96, § 3; Stats.1976, c. 1036, p. 4642, § 10, eff. Sept. 20, 1976; Stats.1980, c. 852, p. 2657, § 15; Stats.1985, c. 1547, § 5; Stats.1992, c. 1226 (A.B.3758), § 2.)*

§ 3720.1. Parents or substantial shareholders; prima facie evidence; hearing; writ of mandate

(a) In any claim in which the alleged uninsured employer is a corporation, for purposes of filing certificates of lien pursuant to Section 3720, the director may determine, according to the evidence available to him or her, whether a person is prima facie a parent or substantial shareholder, as defined in Section 3717. A finding that a person was prima facie a parent or substantial shareholder shall be made when the director determines that there is sufficient evidence to constitute a prima facie case that the person was a parent or substantial shareholder.

(b) Any person aggrieved by a finding of the director that he or she was prima facie a parent or substantial shareholder may request a hearing on the finding by filing a written request for hearing with the director. The director shall hold a hearing on the matter within 20 days of the receipt of the request for hearing, and shall mail a notice of time and place of hearing to the person requesting hearing at least 10 days prior to the hearing. The hearing officer shall hear and receive evidence, and within 10 days of the hearing, file his or her findings on whether there is sufficient evidence to constitute a prima facie case that the person was a substantial shareholder or parent. The hearing officer shall serve with his or her findings a summary of evidence received and relied upon, and the reasons for the findings. A party may at his or her own expense require that the hearing proceedings be recorded and transcribed.

(c) A party aggrieved by the findings of the hearing officer may within 20 days apply for a writ of mandate to the superior court. Venue shall lie in the county in which is located the office of the director which issued the findings after the hearing. *(Added by Stats.1985, c. 1547, § 6.)*

§ 3721. Cancellation of lien

The director shall provide the employer with a certificate of cancellation of lien after the employer has paid to the claimant or to the Uninsured Employers Fund the amount of the compensation or benefits which has been ordered paid to the claimant, or when the application has finally been denied after the claimant has exhausted the remedies provided by law in those cases, or when the employer has filed a bond in the amount and with such surety as the appeals board approves conditioned on the payment of all sums ordered paid to the claimant, or when, after a finding that the employer was prima facie illegally uninsured, it is finally determined that the finding was in error. The recorder shall make no charge for filing the certificates of lien, for filing amended certificates of lien, or for cancellation when liens are filed in error. Cancellation of lien certificates provided to the employer may be filed for recordation by the employer at his or her expense. *(Added by Stats.1971, c. 1598, p. 3439, § 9. Amended by Stats.1976, c. 1036, p. 4643, § 11, eff. Sept. 20, 1976; Stats.1985, c. 1547, § 7.)*

§ 3722. Penalty assessment order against uninsured employer

(a) At the time the stop order is issued and served pursuant to Section 3710.1, the director shall also issue and serve a penalty assessment order requiring the uninsured employer to pay to the director, for deposit in the State Treasury to the credit of the Uninsured Employers Fund, the sum of one thousand dollars ($1,000) per employee employed at the time the order is issued and served, as an additional penalty for being uninsured at that time.

(b) At any time that the director determines that an employer has been uninsured for a period in excess of one week during the calendar year preceding the determination, the director may issue and serve a penalty assessment order requiring the uninsured employer to pay to the director, for deposit in the State Treasury to the credit of the Uninsured Employers Fund, the greater of (1) twice the amount the employer would have paid in workers' compensation premiums during the period the employer was uninsured, determined according to subdivision (c), or (2) the sum of one thousand dollars ($1,000) per employee employed during the period the employer was uninsured. A penalty assessment issued and served by the director pursuant to this subdivision shall be in lieu of, and not in addition to, any other penalty issued and served by the director pursuant to subdivision (a).

(c) If the employer is currently insured, or becomes insured during the period during which the penalty under subdivision (b) is being determined, the amount an employer would have paid in workers' compensation premiums shall be calculated by prorating the current premium for the number of weeks the employer was uninsured. If the employer is uninsured at the time the penalty under subdivision (b) is being determined, the amount an employer would have paid in workers' compensation premiums shall be calculated by applying the weekly premium per employee calculated according to subdivision (d) of Section 11734 of the Insurance Code to the number of weeks the employer was uninsured. Each employee of the uninsured employer shall be assumed to be assigned to the governing classification for that employer as determined by the director after consultation with the Insurance Commissioner. If the employer contends that the assignment of the governing classification is incorrect, or that any employee should be assigned to a different classification, the employer has the burden to prove that the different classification should be utilized.

(d) If upon the filing of a claim for compensation under this division the Workers' Compensation Appeals Board finds that any employer has not secured the payment of compensation as required by this division and finds the claim either noncompensable or compensable, the appeals board shall mail a copy of their findings to the uninsured employer and the director, together with a direction to the uninsured employer to file a verified statement pursuant to subdivision (e).

After the time for any appeal has expired and the adjudication of the claim has become final, the uninsured employer shall be assessed and pay as a penalty either of the following:

(1) In noncompensable cases, two thousand dollars ($2,000) per each employee employed at the time of the claimed injury.

(2) In compensable cases, ten thousand dollars ($10,000) per each employee employed on the date of the injury.

(e) In order to establish the number of employees the uninsured employer had on the date of the claimed injury in noncompensable cases and on the date of injury in compensable cases, the employer shall submit to the director within 10 days after service of findings, awards, and orders of the Workers' Compensation Appeals Board a verified statement of the number of employees in his or her employ on the date of injury. If the employer fails to submit to the director this verified statement or if the director disputes the accuracy of the number of employees reported by the employer, the director shall use any information regarding the number of employees as the director may have or otherwise obtains.

(f) Except for penalties assessed under subdivision (b), the maximum amount of penalties which may be assessed pursuant to this section is one hundred thousand dollars ($100,000). Payment shall be transmitted to the director for deposit in the State Treasury to the credit of the Uninsured Employers Fund.

(g)(1) The Workers' Compensation Appeals Board may provide for a summary hearing on the sole issue of compensation coverage to effect the provisions of this section.

(2) In the event a claim is settled by the director pursuant to subdivision (e) of Section 3715 by means of a compromise and release or stipulations with request for award, the appeals board may also provide for a summary hearing on the issue of compensability. *(Added by Stats.1980, c. 852, p. 2658, § 17. Amended by Stats.1989, c. 507, § 3; Stats.1991, c. 600 (A.B.1576), § 3; Stats.2002, c. 6 (A.B.749), § 47.)*

§ 3725. Contest of penalty assessment order; hearing; writ of mandate

If an employer desires to contest a penalty assessment order, the employer shall file with the director a written request for a hearing within 15 days after service of the order. Upon receipt of the request, the director shall set the matter for a hearing within 30 days thereafter and shall notify the employer of the time and place of the hearing by mail at least 10 days prior to the date of the hearing. The decision of the director shall consist of a notice of findings and findings which shall be served on all parties to the hearing by registered or certified mail within 15 days after the hearing. Any amount found due by the director as a result of a hearing shall become due and payable 45 days after notice of the findings and written findings have been mailed by registered or certified mail to the party assessed. A writ of mandate may be taken from these findings to the appropriate superior court upon the execution by the party assessed of a bond to the state in double the amount found due and ordered paid by the director, as long as the party agrees to pay any judgment and costs rendered against the party for the assessment. The writ shall be taken within 45 days after mailing the notice of findings and findings. *(Added by Stats.1980, c. 852, p. 2659, § 20. Amended by Stats.1982, c. 454, p. 1877, § 135; Stats.1988, c. 96, § 13.)*

§ 3726. Filing of assessment; entry and filing of judgment; interest; costs

(a) When no petition objecting to a penalty assessment order is filed, a certified copy of the order may be filed by the director in the office of the clerk of the superior court in any county in which the employer has property or in which the employer has or had a place of business. The clerk, immediately upon such filing, shall enter judgment for the state against the employer in the amount shown on the penalty assessment order.

(b) When findings are made affirming or modifying a penalty assessment order after hearing, a certified copy of

such order and a certified copy of such findings may be filed by the director in the office of the clerk of the superior court in any county in which the employer has property or in which the employer has or had a place of business. The clerk, immediately upon such filing, shall enter judgment for the state against the employer in the amount shown on the penalty assessment order or in the amount shown in the findings if the order has been modified.

(c) A judgment entered pursuant to the provisions of this section may be filed by the clerk in a looseleaf book entitled "Special Judgments for State Uninsured Employers Fund." Such judgment shall bear the same rate of interest and shall have the same effect as other judgments and be given the same preference allowed by law on other judgments rendered for claims for taxes. The clerk shall make no charge for the service provided by this section to be performed by him. *(Added by Stats.1971, c. 1598, p. 3440, § 14. Amended by Stats.1976, c. 1036, p. 4645, § 17, eff. Sept. 20, 1976; Stats.1980, c. 852, p. 2659, § 21.)*

§ 3727. Certificate of amount of penalty due from employer; filing; lien; effect of recording

If the director determines pursuant to Section 3722 that an employer has failed to secure the payment of compensation as required by this division, the director may file with the county recorder of any counties in which such employer's property may be located his certificate of the amount of penalty due from such employer and such amount shall be a lien in favor of the director from the date of such filing against the real property and personal property of the employer within the county in which such certificate is filed. The recorder shall accept and file such certificate and record the same as a mortgage on real estate and shall file the same as a security interest and he shall index the same as mortgage on real estate and as a security interest. Certificates of liens may be filed in any and all counties of the state, depending upon the information the director obtains concerning the employer's assets. The recorder shall make no charge for the services provided by this section to be performed by him. Upon payment of the penalty assessment, the director shall issue a certificate of cancellation of penalty assessment, which may be recorded by the employer at his expense. *(Added by Stats.1971, c. 1598, p. 3441, § 15. Amended by Stats.1976, c. 1036, p. 4645, § 18, eff. Sept. 20, 1976; Stats.1980, c. 852, p. 2660, § 22.)*

§ 3727.1. Withdrawal of stop order or penalty assessment order

The director may withdraw a stop order or a penalty assessment order where investigation reveals the employer had secured the payment of compensation as required by Section 3700 on the date and at the time of service of such order. The director also may withdraw a penalty assessment order where investigation discloses that the employer was insured on the date and at the time of an injury or claimed injury, or where an insured employer responded in writing to a request to furnish the status of his workers' compensation coverage within the time prescribed. *(Added by Stats.1980, c. 852, p. 2660, § 23.)*

§ 3728. Cash revolving fund

(a) The director may draw from the State Treasury out of the Uninsured Employers Benefits Trust Fund for the purposes of Sections 3716 and 3716.1, without at the time presenting vouchers and itemized statements, a sum not to exceed in the aggregate the level provided for pursuant to Section 16400 of the Government Code, to be used as a cash revolving fund. The revolving fund shall be deposited in any banks and under any conditions as the Department of General Services determines. The Controller shall draw his or her warrants in favor of the Director of Industrial Relations for the amounts so withdrawn and the Treasurer shall pay these warrants.

(b) Expenditures made from the revolving fund in payment of claims for compensation due from the Uninsured Employers Benefits Trust Fund and from the Workers' Compensation Administration Revolving Fund for administrative and adjusting services rendered are exempted from the operation of Section 925.6 of the Government Code. Reimbursement of the revolving fund from the Uninsured Employers Benefits Trust Fund or the Workers' Compensation Administration Revolving Fund for expenditures shall be made upon presentation to the Controller of an abstract or statement of the expenditures. The abstract or statement shall be in any form as the Controller requires. *(Added by Stats.1976, c. 1036, p. 4645, § 19, eff. Sept. 20, 1976. Amended by Stats.1992, c. 100 (S.B.1992), § 1, eff. June 26, 1992; Stats.2003, c. 228 (A.B.1756), § 30, eff. Aug. 11, 2003.)*

§ 3730. Last day for filing falling on weekend or holiday

When the last day for filing any instrument or other document pursuant to this chapter falls upon a Saturday, Sunday or other holiday, such act may be performed upon the next business day with the same effect as if it had been performed upon the day appointed. *(Added by Stats.1980, c. 852, p. 2660, § 24.)*

§ 3731. Service of orders

Any stop order or penalty assessment order may be personally served upon the employer either by (1) manual delivery of the order to the employer personally or by (2) leaving signed copies of the order during usual office hours with the person who is apparently in charge of the office and by thereafter mailing copies of the order by first class mail, postage prepaid to the employer at the place where signed copies of the order were left. *(Added by Stats.1980, c. 852, p. 2660, § 25.)*

§ 3732. Recovery of damages from person or entity other than employer causing injury or death of employee

(a) If compensation is paid or becomes payable from the Uninsured Employers Fund, whether as a result of a findings and award, award based upon stipulations, compromise and release executed on behalf of the director, or payments voluntarily furnished by the director pursuant to Section 4903.3, the director may recover damages from any person or entity, other than the employer, whose tortious act or omission proximately caused the injury or death of the employee. The damages shall include any compensation, including additional compensation by way of interest or penalty, paid or payable by the director, plus the expense incurred by the director in investigating and litigating the workers' compensation claim and a reasonable attorney fee for litigating the workers' compensation claim. The director may compromise, or settle and release any claim, and may waive any claim, including the lien allowed by this section, in whole or in part, for the convenience of the director.

(b) Except as otherwise provided in this section, Chapter 5 (commencing with Section 3850) of Part 1 of Division 4 shall be applicable to these actions, the director being treated as an employer within the meaning of Chapter 5 to the extent not inconsistent with this section.

(c) Actions brought under this section shall be commenced within one year after the later of either the time the director pays or the time the director becomes obligated to pay any compensation from the Uninsured Employers Fund.

(d) In the trial of these actions, any negligence attributable to the employer shall not be imputed to the director or to the Uninsured Employers Fund, and the damages recoverable by the director shall not be reduced by any percentage of fault or negligence attributable to the employer or to the employee.

(e) In determining the credit to the Uninsured Employers Fund provided by Section 3861, the appeals board shall not take into consideration any negligence of the employer, but shall allow a credit for the entire amount of the employee's recovery either by settlement or after judgment, as has not theretofore been applied to the payment of expenses or attorney's fees.

(f) When an action or claim is brought by an employee, his or her guardian, conservator, personal representative, estate, survivors, or heirs against a third party who may be liable for causing the injury or death of the employee, any settlement or judgment obtained is subject to the director's claim for damages recoverable by the director pursuant to subdivision (a), and the director shall have a lien against any settlement in the amount of the damages.

(g) No judgment or settlement in any action or claim by an employee, his or her guardian, conservator, personal representative, survivors, or heirs to recover damages for injuries, where the director has an interest, shall be satisfied without first giving the director notice and a reasonable opportunity to perfect and satisfy his or her lien. The director shall be mailed a copy of the complaint in the third-party action as soon as reasonable after it is filed with the court.

(h) When the director has perfected a lien upon a judgment or settlement in favor of an employee, his or her guardian, conservator, personal representative, survivors or heirs against any third party, the director shall be entitled to a writ of execution as a lien claimant to enforce payment of the lien against the third party with interest and other accruing costs as in the case of other executions. In the event the amount of the judgment or settlement so recovered has been paid to the employee, his or her guardian, conservator, personal representative, survivors, or heirs, the director shall be entitled to a writ of execution against the employee, his or her guardian, conservator, personal representative, survivors, or heirs to the extent of the director's lien, with interest and other accruing costs as in the cost of other executions.

(i) Except as otherwise provided in this section, notwithstanding any other provision of law, the entire amount of any settlement of the action or claim of the employee, his or her guardian, conservator, personal representative, survivors, or heirs, with or without suit, is subject to the director's lien claim for the damages recoverable by the director pursuant to subdivision (a).

(j) Where the action or claim is brought by the employee, his or her guardian, conservator, personal representative, estate, survivors, or heirs, and the director has not joined in the action, and the employee, his or her guardian, conservator, personal representative, estate, survivors, or heirs incur a personal liability to pay attorney's fees and costs of litigation, the director's claim for damages shall be limited to the amount of the director's claim for damages less that portion of the costs of litigation expenses determined by multiplying the total cost of litigation expenses by the ratio of the full amount of the director's claim for damages to the full amount of the judgment, award, or settlement, and less 25 percent of the balance after subtracting the director's share of litigation expenses, which represents the director's reasonable share of attorney's fees incurred.

(k) In the trial of the director's action for damages, and in the allowance of his or her lien in an action by the employee, guardian, executor, personal representative, survivors, or heirs, the compensation paid from the Uninsured Employers Fund pursuant to an award as provided in Section 3716 is conclusively presumed to be reasonable in amount and to be proximately caused by the event or events which caused the employee's injury or death.

(*l*) In the action for damages the director shall be entitled to recover, if he or she prevails, the entire amount of the damages recoverable by the director pursuant to subdivision (a), regardless of whether the damages recoverable by the employee, guardian, conservator, personal representative, survivors, or heirs are of lesser amount. *(Added by Stats.1981, c. 894, p. 3411, § 6. Amended by Stats.1985, c. 666, § 1; Stats.1989, c. 461, § 3.)*

574

ARTICLE 2.5. SELF–INSURERS' SECURITY FUND

Section
3740.   Legislative intent.
3741.   Definitions.
3742.   Establishment of fund as nonprofit mutual benefit corporation; membership; board of trustees; by-laws; powers and duties of fund; confidential information.
3743.   Assumption of workers' compensation obligations of insolvent self-insurer; assessed penalties; party in interest in proceedings against insolvent self-insurer.
3744.   Reimbursement for obligations paid and assumed; right to action; party in interest in action for damages for failure to pay.
3745.   Maintenance of assets or line of credit to continue payment of compensation obligations; assessment for funding; collection of delinquent assessments.
3746.   Audit; annual report.
3747.   Young-La Follette Self-Insurers' Security Act.

§ 3740. Legislative intent

It is the intent of the Legislature in enacting this article and Article 1 (commencing with Section 3700) to provide for the continuation of workers' compensation benefits delayed due to the failure of a private self-insured employer to meet its compensation obligations when the employers' security deposit is either inadequate or not immediately accessible for the payment of benefits. With respect to the continued liability of a surety for claims that arose under a bond after termination of that bond and to a surety's liability for the cost of administration of claims, it is the intent of the Legislature to clarify existing law. The Legislature finds and declares that the establishment of the Self-Insurers' Security Fund is a necessary component of a complete system of workers' compensation, required by Section 4 of Article XIV of the California Constitution, to have adequate provisions for the comfort, health and safety, and general welfare of any and all workers and their dependents to the extent of relieving the consequences of any industrial injury or death, and full provision for securing the payment of compensation. *(Added by Stats. 1984, c. 252, § 5, eff. June 27, 1984. Amended by Stats.1986, c. 1128, § 15, eff. Sept. 25, 1986.)*

§ 3741. Definitions

As used in this article:

(a) "Director" means the Director of Industrial Relations.

(b) "Private self-insurer" means a private employer which has secured the payment of compensation pursuant to subdivision (b) of Section 3700.

(c) "Insolvent self-insurer" means a private self-insurer who has failed to pay compensation and whose security deposit has been called by the director pursuant to Section 3701.5.

(d) "Fund" means the Self-Insurers' Security Fund established pursuant to Section 3742.

(e) "Trustees" means the Board of Trustees of the Self-Insurers' Security Fund.

(f) "Member" means a private self-insurer which participates in the Self-Insurers' Security Fund. *(Added by Stats. 1984, c. 252, § 5, eff. June 27, 1984.)*

§ 3742. Establishment of fund as nonprofit mutual benefit corporation; membership; board of trustees; bylaws; powers and duties of fund; confidential information

(a) The Self–Insurers' Security Fund shall be established as a Nonprofit Mutual Benefit Corporation pursuant to Part 3 (commencing with Section 7110) of Division 2 of Title 1 of the Corporations Code and this article. If any provision of the Nonprofit Mutual Benefit Corporation Law conflicts with any provision of this article, the provisions of this article shall apply. Each private self-insurer shall participate as a member in the fund as a condition of maintaining its certificate of consent to self-insure.

(b) The fund shall be governed by a seven member board of trustees. The director shall hold ex officio status, with full powers equal to those of a trustee, except that the director shall not have a vote. The director, or a delegate authorized in writing to act as the director's representative on the board of trustees, shall carry out exclusively the responsibilities set forth in Division 1 (commencing with Section 50) through Division 4 (commencing with Section 3200) and shall not have the obligations of a trustee under the Nonprofit Mutual Benefit Corporation Law. The fund shall adopt bylaws to segregate the director from all matters that may involve fund litigation against the department or fund participation in legal proceedings before the director. Although not voting, the director or a delegate authorized in writing to represent the director, shall be counted toward a quorum of trustees. The remaining six trustees shall be representatives of private self-insurers. The self-insurer trustees shall be elected by the members of the fund, each member having one vote. Three of the trustees initially elected by the members shall serve two-year terms, and three shall serve four-year terms. Thereafter, trustees shall be elected to four-year terms, and shall serve until their successors are elected and assume office pursuant to the bylaws of the fund.

(c) The fund shall establish bylaws as are necessary to effectuate the purposes of this article and to carry out the responsibilities of the fund, including, but not limited to, any obligations imposed by the director pursuant to Section 3701.8. The fund may carry out its responsibilities directly or by contract, and may purchase services and insurance and borrow funds as it deems necessary for the protection of the members and their employees. The fund may receive confidential information concerning the financial condition of self-insured employers whose liabilities to pay compensation may devolve upon it and shall adopt bylaws to prevent dissemination of that information.

(d) The director may also require fund members to subscribe to financial instruments or guarantees to be posted with the director in order to satisfy the security requirements set by the director pursuant to Section 3701.8. *(Added by Stats. 1984, c. 252, § 5, eff. June 27, 1984. Amended by Stats.1986, c. 1128, § 16, eff. Sept. 25, 1986; Stats.2002, c. 866 (A.B.486), § 8.)*

§ 3743. Assumption of workers' compensation obligations of insolvent self-insurer; assessed penalties; party in interest in proceedings against insolvent self-insurer

(a) Upon order of the director pursuant to Section 3701.5, the fund shall assume the workers' compensation obligations of an insolvent self-insurer.

(b) Notwithstanding subdivision (a), the fund shall not be liable for the payment of any penalties assessed for any act or omission on the part of any person other than the fund, including, but not limited to, the penalties provided in Section 132a, 3706, 4553, 4554, 4556, 4557, 4558, 4601.5, 5814, or 5814.1.

(c) The fund shall be a party in interest in all proceedings involving compensation claims against an insolvent self-insurer whose compensation obligations have been paid or assumed by the fund. The fund shall have the same rights and defenses as the insolvent self-insurer, including, but not limited to, all of the following:

(1) To appear, defend, and appeal claims.

(2) To receive notice of, investigate, adjust, compromise, settle, and pay claims.

(3) To investigate, handle, and deny claims. *(Added by Stats. 1984, c. 252, § 5, eff. June 27, 1984.)*

§ 3744. Reimbursement for obligations paid and assumed; right to action; party in interest in action for damages for failure to pay

(a) The fund shall have the right and obligation to obtain reimbursement from an insolvent self-insurer up to the amount of the self-insurer's workers' compensation obligations paid and assumed by the fund, including reasonable administrative and legal costs. This right includes, but is not limited to, a right to claim for wages and other necessities of life advanced to claimants as subrogee of the claimants in any action to collect against the self-insured as debtor.

(b) The fund shall have the right and obligation to obtain from the security deposit of an insolvent self-insurer the amount of the self-insurer's compensation obligations, including reasonable administrative and legal costs, paid or assumed by the fund. Reimbursement of administrative costs, including legal costs, shall be subject to approval by a majority vote of the fund's trustees. The fund shall be a party in interest in any action to obtain the security deposit for the payment of compensation obligations of an insolvent self-insurer.

(c) The fund shall have the right to bring an action against any person to recover compensation paid and

575

liability assumed by the fund, including, but not limited to, any excess insurance carrier of the self-insured employer, and any person whose negligence or breach of any obligation contributed to any underestimation of the self-insured employer's total accrued liability as reported to the director.

(d) The fund may be a party in interest in any action brought by any other person seeking damages resulting from the failure of an insolvent self-insurer to pay workers' compensation required pursuant to this division. *(Added by Stats. 1984, c. 252, § 5, eff. June 27, 1984. Amended by Stats.1986, c. 1128, § 17, eff. Sept. 25, 1986.)*

§ 3745. Maintenance of assets or line of credit to continue payment of compensation obligations; assessment for funding; collection of delinquent assessments

(a) The fund shall maintain cash, readily marketable securities, or other assets, or a line of credit, approved by the director, sufficient to immediately continue the payment of the compensation obligations of an insolvent self-insurer pending assessment of the members. The director may establish the minimum amount to be maintained by, or immediately available to, the fund for this purpose.

(b) The fund may assess each of its members a pro rata share of the funding necessary to carry out the purposes of this article. However, no member shall be assessed at one time in excess of 1.5 percent of the benefits paid by the member for claims incurred during the previous calendar year as a self-insurer, and total annual assessments in any calendar year shall not exceed 2 percent of the benefits paid for claims incurred during the previous calendar year. Funds obtained by assessments pursuant to this subdivision may only be used for the purposes of this article.

(c) The trustees shall certify to the director the collection and receipt of all moneys from assessments, noting any delinquencies. The trustees shall take any action deemed appropriate to collect any delinquent assessments. *(Added by Stats. 1984, c. 252, § 5, eff. June 27, 1984. Amended by Stats.1986, c. 1128, § 18, eff. Sept. 25, 1986.)*

§ 3746. Audit; annual report

The trustees shall annually contract for an independent certified audit of the financial activities of the fund. An annual report on the financial status of the fund as of June 30 shall be submitted to the director and to each member. *(Added by Stats.1984, c. 252, § 5, eff. June 27, 1984.)*

§ 3747. Young-La Follette Self-Insurers' Security Act

This article shall be known and may be referred to as the "Young-La Follette Self-Insurers' Security Act." *(Added by Stats.1984, c. 252, § 5, eff. June 27, 1984.)*

576

ARTICLE 3.   INSURANCE RIGHTS AND PRIVILEGES

Section
3750. Scope of division.
3751. Contribution from or deduction from earnings of employee to cover cost of compensation; misdemeanor; collection of money for services to cure injury for which claim form filed; liability.
3752. Liability for compensation; effect of other benefits.
3753. Recovery of compensation from employer and insurer.
3754. Effect of payment of compensation by employer or insurer.
3755. Insurer's notice of assumption of liability; relief of employer from liability to claimant.
3756. Notice of insurer's agreement to pay compensation.
3757. Relief of employer from liability to claimant.
3758. Substitution of insurer in place of employer; continuance of proceedings against insurer.
3759. Order relieving employer from liability.
3760. Report of injuries to insurer; order to submit report; failure to comply with order; contempt.
3761. Claim filed directly with insurer; notice to employer; information from employer.
3762. Factors affecting employer's premium; disclosures by insurer.

§ 3750.   Scope of division

Nothing in this division shall affect:

(a) The organization of any mutual or other insurer.

(b) Any existing contract for insurance.

(c) The right of the employer to insure in mutual or other insurers, in whole or in part, against liability for the compensation provided by this division.

(d) The right to provide by mutual or other insurance, or by arrangement with his employees, or otherwise, for the payment to such employees, their families, dependents or representatives, of sick, accident, or death benefits, in addition to the compensation provided for by this division.

(e) The right of the employer to waive the waiting period provided for herein by insurance coverage. *(Stats. 1937, c. 90, p. 272, § 3750.)*

§ 3751.   Contribution from or deduction from earnings of employee to cover cost of compensation; misdemeanor; collection of money for services to cure injury for which claim form filed; liability

(a) No employer shall exact or receive from any employee any contribution, or make or take any deduction from the earnings of any employee, either directly or indirectly, to cover the whole or any part of the cost of compensation under this division. Violation of this subdivision is a misdemeanor.

(b) If an employee has filed a claim form pursuant to Section 5401, a provider of medical services shall not, with actual knowledge that a claim is pending, collect money directly from the employee for services to cure or relieve the effects of the injury for which the claim form was filed, unless the medical provider has received written notice that liability for the injury has been rejected by the employer and the medical provider has provided a copy of this notice to the employee. Any medical provider who violates this subdivision shall be liable for three times the amount unlawfully collected, plus reasonable attorney's fees and costs. *(Stats.1937, c. 90, p. 272, § 3751. Amended by Stats.1990, c. 997 (A.B.2695), § 1.)*

§ 3752. Liability for compensation; effect of other benefits

Liability for compensation shall not be reduced or affected by any insurance, contribution or other benefit whatsoever due to or received by the person entitled to such compensation, except as otherwise provided by this division. *(Stats.1937, c. 90, p. 272, § 3752.)*

§ 3753. Recovery of compensation from employer and insurer

The person entitled to compensation may, irrespective of any insurance or other contract, except as otherwise provided in this division, recover such compensation directly from the employer. In addition thereto, he may enforce in his own name, in the manner provided by this division the liability of any insurer either by making the insurer a party to the original application or by filing a separate application for any portion of such compensation. *(Stats.1937, c. 90, p. 272, § 3753.)*

§ 3754. Effect of payment of compensation by employer or insurer

Payment in whole or in part of compensation by either the employer or the insurer shall, to the extent thereof, be a bar to recovery against each of them of the amount so paid. *(Stats.1937, c. 90, p. 272, § 3754. Amended by Stats.1955, c. 1672, p. 3007, § 2.)*

§ 3755. Insurer's notice of assumption of liability; relief of employer from liability to claimant

If the employer is insured against liability for compensation, and if after the suffering of any injury the insurer causes to be served upon any compensation claimant a notice that it has assumed and agreed to pay any compensation to the claimant for which the employer is liable, such employer shall be relieved from liability for compensation to such claimant upon the filing of a copy of such notice with the appeals board. The insurer shall, without further notice, be substituted in place of the employer in any proceeding theretofore or thereafter instituted by such claimant to recover such compensation, and the employer shall be dismissed therefrom.

Such proceedings shall not abate on account of such substitution but shall be continued against such insurer. *(Stats.1937, c. 90, p. 272, § 3755. Amended by Stats.1965, c. 1513, p. 3572, § 64, operative Jan. 15, 1966.)*

§ 3756. Notice of insurer's agreement to pay compensation

If at the time of the suffering of a compensable injury, the employer is insured against liability for the full amount of compensation payable, he may cause to be served upon the compensation claimant and upon the insurer a notice that the insurer has agreed to pay any compensation for which the employer is liable. The employer may also file a copy of such notice with the appeals board. *(Stats.1937, c. 90, p. 272, § 3756. Amended by Stats.1965, c. 1513, p. 3572, § 65, operative Jan. 15, 1966.)*

§ 3757. Relief of employer from liability to claimant

If it thereafter appears to the satisfaction of the appeals board that the insurer has assumed the liability for compensation, the employer shall thereupon be relieved from liability for compensation to the claimant. The insurer shall, after notice, be substituted in place of the employer in any proceeding instituted by the claimant to recover compensation, and the employer shall be dismissed therefrom. *(Stats.1937, c. 90, p. 273, § 3757. Amended by Stats.1965, c. 1513, p. 3573, § 66, operative Jan. 15, 1966.)*

§ 3758. Substitution of insurer in place of employer; continuance of proceedings against insurer

A proceeding to obtain compensation shall not abate on account of substitution of the insurer in place of the employer and on account of the dismissal of the employer, but shall be continued against such insurer. *(Stats. 1937, c. 90, p. 273, § 3758.)*

§ 3759. Order relieving employer from liability

The appeals board may enter its order relieving the employer from liability where it appears from the pleadings, stipulations, or proof that an insurer joined as party to the proceeding is liable for the full compensation for which the employer in such proceeding is liable. *(Stats. 1937, c. 90, p. 273, § 3759. Amended by Stats.1965, c. 1513, p. 3573, § 67, operative Jan. 15, 1966.)*

§ 3760. Report of injuries to insurer; order to submit report; failure to comply with order; contempt

Every employer who is insured against any liability imposed by this division shall file with the insurer a complete report of every injury to each employee as specified in Section 6409.1. If not so filed, the insurer may petition the appeals board for an order, or the appeals board may of its own motion issue an order, directing the employer to submit a report of the injury within five days after service of the order. Failure of the employer to comply with the appeals board's order may be punished by the appeals board as a contempt. *(Added by Stats.1951, c. 893, p. 2414, § 1. Amended by Stats. 1965, c. 1513, p. 3573, § 68, operative Jan. 15, 1966; Stats.1967, c. 1364, p. 3202, § 1; Stats.1987, c. 1019, § 4.)*

§ 3761. Claim filed directly with insurer; notice to employer; information from employer

(a) An insurer securing an employer's liability under this division shall notify the employer, within 15 days, of each claim for indemnity filed against the employer directly with the insurer if the employer has not timely provided to the insurer a report of occupational injury or occupational illness pursuant to Section 6409.1. The insurer shall furnish an employer who has not filed this report with an opportunity to provide to the insurer, prior to the expiration of the 90-day period specified in Section 5402, all relevant information available to the employer concerning the claim.

(b) An employer shall promptly notify its insurer in writing at any time during the pendency of a claim when the employer has actual knowledge of any facts which would tend to disprove any aspect of the employee's claim. When an employer notifies its insurer in writing that, in the employer's opinion, no compensation is payable to an employee, at the employer's written request, to the appeals board, the appeals board may approve a compromise and release agreement, or stipulation, that provides compensation to the employee only where there is proof of service upon the employer by the insurer, to the employer's last known address, not less than 15 days prior to the appeals board action, of notice of the time and place of the hearing at which the compromise and release agreement or stipulation is to be approved. The insurer shall file proof of this service with the appeals board.

Failure by the insurer to provide the required notice shall not prohibit the board from approving a compromise and release agreement, or stipulation; however, the board shall order the insurer to pay reasonable expenses as provided in Section 5813.

(c) In establishing a reserve pursuant to a claim that affects premiums against an employer, an insurer shall provide the employer, upon request, a written report of the reserve amount established. The written report shall include, at a minimum, the following:

(1) Estimated medical-legal costs.

(2) Estimated vocational rehabilitation costs, if any.

(3) Itemization of all other estimated expenses to be paid from the reserve.

(d) When an employer properly provides notification to its insurer pursuant to subdivision (b), and the appeals board thereafter determines that no compensation is payable under this division, the insurer shall reimburse the employer for any premium paid solely due to the inclusion of the successfully challenged payments in the calculation of the employer's experience modification. The employee shall not be required to refund the challenged payment. *(Added by Stats.1991, c. 116 (S.B. 1218), § 29. Amended by Stats.1993, c. 121 (A.B.110), § 27, eff. July 16, 1993; Stats.1994, c. 1118 (S.B.1768), § 5.)*

578

§ 3762. Factors affecting employer's premium; disclosures by insurer

(a) Except as provided in subdivisions (b) and (c), the insurer shall discuss all elements of the claim file that affect the employer's premium with the employer, and shall supply copies of the documents that affect the premium at the employer's expense during reasonable business hours.

(b) The right provided by this section shall not extend to any document that the insurer is prohibited from disclosing to the employer under the attorney-client privilege, any other applicable privilege, or statutory prohibition upon disclosure, or under Section 1877.4 of the Insurance Code.

(c) An insurer, third-party administrator retained by a self-insured employer pursuant to Section 3702.1 to administer the employer's workers' compensation claims, and those employees and agents specified by a self-insured employer to administer the employer's workers' compensation claims, are prohibited from disclosing or causing to be disclosed to an employer, any medical information, as defined in subdivision (b) of Section 56.05 of the Civil Code, about an employee who has filed a workers' compensation claim, except as follows:

(1) Medical information limited to the diagnosis of the mental or physical condition for which workers' compensation is claimed and the treatment provided for this condition.

(2) Medical information regarding the injury for which workers' compensation is claimed that is necessary for the employer to have in order for the employer to modify the employee's work duties. *(Added by Stats.1993, c. 121 (A.B.110), § 28, eff. July 16, 1993. Amended by Stats. 1993, c. 1242 (S.B.223), § 25; Stats.1999, c. 766 (A.B. 435), § 2; Stats.2000, c. 135 (A.B.2539), § 126; Stats. 2002, c. 6 (A.B.749), § 48.)*

ARTICLE 4. CONSTRUCTION PERMIT

Section
3800.   Workers' compensation coverage; declarations; certificate.

§ 3800. Workers' compensation coverage; declarations; certificate

(a) Every county or city which requires the issuance of a permit as a condition precedent to the construction, alteration, improvement, demolition, or repair of any building or structure shall require that each applicant for the permit sign a declaration under penalty of perjury verifying workers' compensation coverage or exemption from coverage, as required by Section 19825 of the Health and Safety Code.

(b) At the time of permit issuance, contractors shall show their valid workers' compensation insurance certificate, or the city or county may verify the workers' compensation coverage by electronic means. *(Added by Stats.1941, c. 1010, p. 2642, § 1. Amended by Stats.1945, c. 1431, p. 2696, § 69.5; Stats.1953, c. 552, p. 1811, § 1; Stats.1959, c. 361, p. 2281, § 1; Stats.1963, c. 1140, p. 2616, § 2; Stats.1988, c. 160, § 124; Stats.1994, c. 178 (A.B.443), § 2; Stats.1999, c. 982 (A.B.1678), § 8.)*

ARTICLE 5. WORKERS' COMPENSATION MISREPRESENTATIONS

Section
3820. Legislative declarations; prohibited acts; penalties.
3822. Notice warning against committing workers' compensation fraud; contents.
3823. Protocols for fraudulent claims; civil liability, privileges and immunities.

§ 3820. Legislative declarations; prohibited acts; penalties

(a) In enacting this section, the Legislature declares that there exists a compelling interest in eliminating fraud in the workers' compensation system. The Legislature recognizes that the conduct prohibited by this section is, for the most part, already subject to criminal penalties pursuant to other provisions of law. However, the Legislature finds and declares that the addition of civil money penalties will provide necessary enforcement flexibility. The Legislature, in exercising its plenary authority related to workers' compensation, declares that these sections are both necessary and carefully tailored to combat the fraud and abuse that is rampant in the workers' compensation system.

(b) It is unlawful to do any of the following:

(1) Willfully misrepresent any fact in order to obtain workers' compensation insurance at less than the proper rate.

(2) Present or cause to be presented any knowingly false or fraudulent written or oral material statement in support of, or in opposition to, any claim for compensation for the purpose of obtaining or denying any compensation, as defined in Section 3207.

(3) Knowingly solicit, receive, offer, pay, or accept any rebate, refund, commission, preference, patronage, dividend, discount, or other consideration, whether in the form of money or otherwise, as compensation or inducement for soliciting or referring clients or patients to obtain services or benefits pursuant to Division 4 (commencing with Section 3200) unless the payment or receipt of consideration for services other than the referral of clients or patients is lawful pursuant to Section 650 of the Business and Professions Code or expressly permitted by the Rules of Professional Conduct of the State Bar.

(4) Knowingly operate or participate in a service that, for profit, refers or recommends clients or patients to obtain medical or medical-legal services or benefits pursuant to Division 4 (commencing with Section 3200).

(5) Knowingly assist, abet, solicit, or conspire with any person who engages in an unlawful act under this section.

(c) For the purposes of this section, "statement" includes, but is not limited to, any notice, proof of injury, bill for services, payment for services, hospital or doctor records, X-ray, test results, medical-legal expenses as defined in Section 4620, or other evidence of loss, expense, or payment.

(d) Any person who violates any provision of this section shall be subject, in addition to any other penalties that may be prescribed by law, to a civil penalty of not less than four thousand dollars ($4,000) nor more than ten thousand dollars ($10,000), plus an assessment of not more than three times the amount of the medical treatment expenses paid pursuant to Article 2 (commencing with Section 4600) and medical-legal expenses paid pursuant to Article 2.5 (commencing with Section 4620) for each claim for compensation submitted in violation of this section.

(e) Any person who violates subdivision (b) and who has a prior felony conviction of an offense set forth in Section 1871.1 or 1871.4 of the Insurance Code, or in Section 549 of the Penal Code, shall be subject, in addition to the penalties set forth in subdivision (d), to a civil penalty of four thousand dollars ($4,000) for each item or service with respect to which a violation of subdivision (b) occurred.

(f) The penalties provided for in subdivisions (d) and (e) shall be assessed and recovered in a civil action brought in the name of the people of the State of California by any district attorney.

(g) In assessing the amount of the civil penalty the court shall consider any one or more of the relevant circumstances presented by any of the parties to the case, including, but not limited to, the following: the nature and seriousness of the misconduct, the number of violations, the persistence of the misconduct, the length of time over which the misconduct occurred, the willfulness of the defendant's misconduct, and the defendant's assets, liabilities, and net worth.

(h) All penalties collected pursuant to this section shall be paid to the Workers' Compensation Fraud Account in the Insurance Fund pursuant to Section 1872.83 of the Insurance Code. All costs incurred by district attorneys in carrying out this article shall be funded from the Workers' Compensation Fraud Account. It is the intent of the Legislature that the program instituted by this article be supported entirely from funds produced by moneys deposited into the Workers' Compensation Fraud Account from the imposition of civil money penalties for workers' compensation fraud collected pursuant to this section. All moneys claimed by district attorneys as costs of carrying out this article shall be paid pursuant to a determination by the Fraud Assessment Commission established by Section 1872.83 of the Insurance Code and on appropriation by the Legislature. *(Added by Stats.1993, c. 120 (A.B.1300), § 4.5, eff. July 16, 1993. Amended by Stats.1993, c. 1242 (S.B.223), § 26; Stats.2002, c. 6 (A.B.749), § 49.)*

§ 3822. Notice warning against committing workers' compensation fraud; contents

The administrative director shall, on an annual basis, provide to every employer, claims adjuster, third party administrator, physician, and attorney who participates in the workers' compensation system, a notice that warns the recipient against committing workers' compensation fraud. The notice shall specify the penalties that are applied for committing workers' compensation fraud. The Fraud Assessment Commission, established by Section 1872.83 of the Insurance Code, shall provide the administrative director with all funds necessary to carry out this section. *(Added by Stats.2002, c. 6 (A.B.749), § 50.)*

§ 3823. Protocols for fraudulent claims; civil liability, privileges and immunities

(a) The administrative director shall, in coordination with the Bureau of Fraudulent Claims of the Department of Insurance, the Medi–Cal Fraud Task Force, and the Bureau of Medi–Cal Fraud and Elder Abuse of the Department of Justice, or their successor entities, adopt protocols, to the extent that these protocols are applicable to achieve the purpose of subdivision (b), similar to those adopted by the Department of Insurance concerning medical billing and provider fraud.

(b) Any insurer, self-insured employer, third-party administrator, workers' compensation administrative law judge, audit unit, attorney, or other person that believes that a fraudulent claim has been made by any person or entity providing medical care, as described in Section 4600, shall report the apparent fraudulent claim in the manner prescribed by subdivision (a).

(c) No insurer, self-insured employer, third-party administrator, workers' compensation administrative law judge, audit unit, attorney, or other person that reports any apparent fraudulent claim under this section shall be subject to any civil liability in a cause of action of any kind when the insurer, self-insured employer, third-party administrator, workers' compensation administrative law judge, audit unit, attorney, or other person acts in good faith, without malice, and reasonably believes that the action taken was warranted by the known facts, obtained by reasonable efforts. Nothing in this section is intended to, nor does in any manner, abrogate or lessen the existing common law or statutory privileges and immunities of any insurer, self-insured employer, third-party administrator, workers' compensation administrative law judge, audit unit, attorney, or other person. *(Added by Stats.2003, c. 639 (S.B.228), § 15. Amended by Stats. 2004, c. 34 (S.B.899), § 11, eff. April 19, 2004.)*

Operative Effect

Section 47 of Stats.2004, c. 34 (S.B.899) provides that "[t]he amendment, addition, or repeal of, any provision of law made by this act shall apply prospectively from the date of enactment of this act, regardless of the date of injury, unless otherwise specified, but shall not constitute good cause to reopen or rescind, alter, or amend any existing order, decision, or award of the Workers' Compensation Appeals Board."

CHAPTER 5. SUBROGATION OF EMPLOYER

Section
3850. Definitions.
3851. Survival of action.
3852. Action against third person; rights of employee and employer.
3853. Copy of complaint; proof of service; joinder of plaintiffs; consolidation of actions.
3854. Action by employer alone; evidence of compensation payments and liability.
3855. Action by employee; evidence of compensation payments and liability or of loss of employee's earning capacity; proof of other items of damage.
3856. Actions against third party; payment of excess recovery to employee; employer's lien against judgment; costs and fees.
3857. Further liens.
3858. Relief of employer from liability for compensation; notice to employer before satisfaction of judgment.
3859. Release or settlement of claim; consent of employer and employee.
3860. Notice before release or settlement; employer's claim for reimbursement; costs and fees.
3861. Credits against employer's liability for compensation; amount of recovery by employee.
3862. Enforcement of employer's lien against judgment.
3864. Liability to reimburse or hold third person harmless on judgment or settlement.
3865. Lien claims of Employment Development Department against judgment or settlement.

§ 3850. Definitions

As used in this chapter:

(a) "Employee" includes the person injured and any other person to whom a claim accrues by reason of the injury or death of the former.

(b) "Employer" includes insurer as defined in this division.

(c) "Employer" also includes the Self-Insurers' Security Fund, where the employer's compensation obligations have been assumed pursuant to Section 3743. *(Stats. 1937, c. 90, p. 273, § 3850. Amended by Stats.1984, c. 252, § 6, eff. June 27, 1984.)*

§ 3851. Survival of action

The death of the employee or of any other person, does not abate any right of action established by this chapter. *(Stats.1937, c. 90, p. 273, § 3851.)*

§ 3852. Action against third person; rights of employee and employer

The claim of an employee, including, but not limited to, any peace officer or firefighter, for compensation does not affect his or her claim or right of action for all damages proximately resulting from the injury or death against any person other than the employer. Any employer who pays, or becomes obligated to pay compensation, or who pays, or becomes obligated to pay salary in lieu of compensation, or who pays or becomes obligated to pay an amount to the Department of Industrial Relations pursuant to Section 4706.5, may likewise make a claim or bring an action against the third person. In the latter event the employer may recover in the same suit, in addition to the total amount of compensation, damages for which he or she was liable including all salary, wage, pension, or other emolument paid to the employee or to his or her dependents. The respective rights against the third person of the heirs of an employee claiming under Section 377.60 of the Code of Civil Procedure, and an employer claiming pursuant to this section, shall be determined by the court. *(Stats.1937, c. 90, p. 273, § 3852. Amended by Stats.1939, c. 902, p. 2519, § 2; Stats.1970, c. 242, p. 502, § 2; Stats.1981, c. 21, p. 48, § 10, eff. April 18, 1981; Stats.1982, c. 149, p. 492, § 1, eff. April 5, 1982; Stats.1982, c. 258, p. 836, § 2; Stats.1993, c. 589 (A.B.2211), § 108.)*

§ 3853. Copy of complaint; proof of service; joinder of plaintiffs; consolidation of actions

If either the employee or the employer brings an action against such third person, he shall forthwith give to the other a copy of the complaint by personal service or certified mail. Proof of such service shall be filed in such action. If the action is brought by either the employer or employee, the other may, at any time before trial on the facts, join as party plaintiff or shall consolidate his action, if brought independently. *(Stats.1937, c. 90, p. 273, § 3853. Amended by Stats.1980, c. 582, p. 1591, § 1.)*

§ 3854. Action by employer alone; evidence of compensation payments and liability

If the action is prosecuted by the employer alone, evidence of any amount which the employer has paid or become obligated to pay by reason of the injury or death of the employee is admissible, and such expenditures or liability shall be considered as proximately resulting from such injury or death in addition to any other items of damage proximately resulting therefrom. *(Stats.1937, c. 90, p. 273, § 3854. Amended by Stats.1949, c. 120, p. 355, § 1; Stats.1959, c. 1255, p. 3387, § 1.)*

§ 3855. Action by employee; evidence of compensation payments and liability or of loss of employee's earning capacity; proof of other items of damage

If the employee joins in or prosecutes such action, either the evidence of the amount of disability indemnity or death benefit paid or to be paid by the employer or the evidence of loss of earning capacity by the employee shall be admissible, but not both. Proof of all other items of damage to either the employer or employee proximately resulting from such injury or death is admissible and is part of the damages. *(Stats.1937, c. 90, p. 274, § 3855.)*

§ 3856. Actions against third party; payment of excess recovery to employee; employer's lien against judgment; costs and fees

In the event of suit against such third party:

(a) If the action is prosecuted by the employer alone, the court shall first order paid from any judgment for damages recovered the reasonable litigation expenses incurred in preparation and prosecution of such action, together with a reasonable attorney's fee which shall be based solely upon the services rendered by the employer's attorney in effecting recovery both for the benefit of the employer and the employee. After the payment of such expenses and attorney's fees, the court shall apply out of the amount of such judgment an amount sufficient to reimburse the employer for the amount of his expenditure for compensation together with any amounts to which he may be entitled as special damages under Section 3852 and shall order any excess paid to the injured employee or other person entitled thereto.

(b) If the action is prosecuted by the employee alone, the court shall first order paid from any judgment for damages recovered the reasonable litigation expenses incurred in preparation and prosecution of such action, together with a reasonable attorney's fee which shall be based solely upon the services rendered by the employee's attorney in effecting recovery both for the benefit of the employee and the employer. After the payment of such expenses and attorney's fee the court shall, on application of the employer, allow as a first lien against the amount of such judgment for damages, the amount of the employer's expenditure for compensation together with any amounts to which he may be entitled as special damages under Section 3852.

(c) If the action is prosecuted both by the employee and the employer, in a single action or in consolidated actions, and they are represented by the same agreed attorney or by separate attorneys, the court shall first order paid from any judgment for damages recovered, the reasonable litigation expenses incurred in preparation and prosecution of such action or actions, together with reasonable attorneys' fees based solely on the services rendered for the benefit of both parties where they are represented by the same attorney, and where they are represented by separate attorneys, based solely upon the service rendered in each instance by the attorney in effecting recovery for the benefit of the party represented. After the payment of such expenses and attorneys' fees the court shall apply out of the amount of such judgment for damages an amount sufficient to reimburse the employer for the amount of his expenditures for compensation together with any other amounts to which he may be entitled as special damages under Section 3852.

(d) The amount of reasonable litigation expenses and the amount of attorneys' fees under subdivisions (a), (b), and (c) of this section shall be fixed by the court. Where the employer and employee are represented by separate attorneys they may propose to the court, for its consideration and determination, the amount and division of such expenses and fees. *(Added by Stats.1959, c. 1255, p. 3387, § 3.)*

§ 3857.   Further liens

The court shall, upon further application at any time before the judgment is satisfied, allow as a further lien the amount of any expenditures of the employer for compensation subsequent to the original order. *(Stats.1937, c. 90, p. 274, § 3857.)*

§ 3858.   Relief of employer from liability for compensation; notice to employer before satisfaction of judgment

After payment of litigation expenses and attorneys' fees fixed by the court pursuant to Section 3856 and payment of the employer's lien, the employer shall be relieved from the obligation to pay further compensation to or on behalf of the employee under this division up to the entire amount of the balance of the judgment, if satisfied, without any deduction.   No satisfaction of such judgment in whole or in part, shall be valid without giving the employer notice and a reasonable opportunity to perfect and satisfy his lien. *(Stats.1937, c. 90, p. 274, § 3858. Amended by Stats.1959, c. 1255, p. 3388, § 4.)*

§ 3859.   Release or settlement of claim; consent of employer and employee

(a) No release or settlement of any claim under this chapter as to either the employee or the employer is valid without the written consent of both.   Proof of service filed with the court is sufficient in any action or proceeding where such approval is required by law.

(b) Notwithstanding anything to the contrary contained in this chapter, an employee may settle and release any claim he may have against a third party without the consent of the employer.   Such settlement or release shall be subject to the employer's right to proceed to recover compensation he has paid in accordance with Section 3852. *(Stats.1937, c. 90, p. 274, § 3859. Amended by Stats.1959, c. 1255, p. 3389, § 5; Stats.1971, c. 485, p. 969, § 1.)*

§ 3860.   Notice before release or settlement; employer's claim for reimbursement; costs and fees

(a) No release or settlement under this chapter, with or without suit, is valid or binding as to any party thereto without notice to both the employer and the employee, with opportunity to the employer to recover the amount of compensation he has paid or become obligated to pay and any special damages to which he may be entitled under Section 3852, and opportunity to the employee to recover all damages he has suffered and with provision for determination of expenses and attorney's fees as herein provided.

(b) Except as provided in Section 3859, the entire amount of such settlement, with or without suit, is subject to the employer's full claim for reimbursement for compensation he has paid or become obligated to pay

and any special damages to which he may be entitled under Section 3852, together with expenses and attorney fees, if any, subject to the limitations in this section set forth.

(c) Where settlement is effected, with or without suit, solely through the efforts of the employee's attorney, then prior to the reimbursement of the employer, as provided in subdivision (b) hereof, there shall be deducted from the amount of the settlement the reasonable expenses incurred in effecting such settlement, including costs of suit, if any, together with a reasonable attorney's fee to be paid to the employee's attorney, for his services in securing and effecting settlement for the benefit of both the employer and the employee.

(d) Where settlement is effected, with or without suit, solely through the efforts of the employer's attorney, then, prior to the reimbursement of the employer as provided in subdivision (b) hereof, there shall be deducted from the amount of the settlement the reasonable expenses incurred in effecting such settlement, including costs of suit, if any, together with a reasonable attorney's fee to be paid to the employer's attorney, for his services in securing and effecting settlement for the benefit of both the employer and the employee.

(e) Where both the employer and the employee are represented by the same agreed attorney or by separate attorneys in effecting a settlement, with or without suit, prior to reimbursement of the employer, as provided in subdivision (b) hereof, there shall be deducted from the amount of the settlement the reasonable expenses incurred by both the employer and the employee or on behalf of either, including costs of suit, if any, together with reasonable attorneys' fees to be paid to the respective attorneys for the employer and the employee, based upon the respective services rendered in securing and effecting settlement for the benefit of the party represented.   In the event both parties are represented by the same attorney, by agreement, the attorney's fee shall be based on the services rendered for the benefit of both.

(f) The amount of expenses and attorneys' fees referred to in this section shall, on settlement of suit, or on any settlement requiring court approval, be set by the court.   In all other cases these amounts shall be set by the appeals board.   Where the employer and the employee are represented by separate attorneys they may propose to the court or the appeals board, for consideration and determination, the amount and division of such expenses and fees. *(Added by Stats.1959, c. 1255, p. 3389, § 7. Amended by Stats.1965, c. 1513, p. 3573, § 69, operative Jan. 15, 1966; Stats.1971, c. 485, p. 970, § 2.)*

§ 3861.   Credits against employer's liability for compensation; amount of recovery by employee

The appeals board is empowered to and shall allow, as a credit to the employer to be applied against his liability for compensation, such amount of any recovery by the employee for his injury, either by settlement or after judgment, as has not theretofore been applied to the payment of expenses or attorneys' fees, pursuant to the provisions of Sections 3856, 3858, and 3860 of this code, or has not been applied to reimburse the employer. *(Stats.1937, c. 90, p. 274, § 3861. Amended by Stats.1949, c. 120, p. 356, § 3; Stats.1957, c. 615, p. 1826, § 2; Stats.1959, c. 1255, p. 3390, § 8; Stats.1965, c. 1513, p. 3574, § 70, operative Jan. 15, 1966).*

§ 3862. Enforcement of employer's lien against judgment

Any employer entitled to and who has been allowed and has perfected a lien upon the judgment or award in favor of an employee against any third party for damages occasioned to the same employer by payment of compensation, expenses of medical treatment, and any other charges under this act, may enforce payment of the lien against the third party, or, in case the damages recovered by the employee have been paid to the employee, against the employee to the extent of the lien, in the manner provided for enforcement of money judgments generally. *(Added by Stats.1937, c. 506, p. 1496. Amended by Stats.1982, c. 497, p. 2204, § 134, operative July 1, 1983.)*

§ 3864. Liability to reimburse or hold third person harmless on judgment or settlement

If an action as provided in this chapter prosecuted by the employee, the employer, or both jointly against the third person results in judgment against such third person, or settlement by such third person, the employer shall have no liability to reimburse or hold such third person harmless on such judgment or settlement in absence of a written agreement so to do executed prior to the injury. *(Added by Stats.1959, c. 955, p. 2986, § 1.)*

§ 3865. Lien claims of Employment Development Department against judgment or settlement

Any judgment or settlement of an action as provided for in this chapter is, upon notice to the court, subject to the same lien claims of the Employment Development Department as are provided for in Chapter 1 (commencing with Section 4900) of Part 3, and shall be allowed by the court as it determines necessary to avoid a duplication of payment as compensation to the employee for lost earnings. *(Added by Stats.1989, c. 1280, § 1.)*

CHAPTER 6. HOSPITAL INSPECTION [REPEALED]

CHAPTER 7. MEDICAL EXAMINATIONS

Article	Section
1. [Examination Requirements]	4050
2. Determination of Medical Issues	4061

ARTICLE 1. [EXAMINATION REQUIREMENTS]

Section
4050. Duty of employee to submit to examination.
4051. Request or order for examination.
4052. Presence of employee's physician at examination.
4053. Failure to comply with employer's request; suspension of right to maintain proceedings.
4054. Failure to comply with appeals board; barring of right to disability payments.
4055. Testimony of physician.
4055.2. Subpoenas of medical records; copy to parties of record.
4056. Death or disability caused by unreasonable refusal to submit to medical or surgical treatment.

Application

The heading of Article 1 was editorially supplied.

§ 4050. Duty of employee to submit to examination

Whenever the right to compensation under this division exists in favor of an employee, he shall, upon the written request of his employer, submit at reasonable intervals to examination by a practicing physician, provided and paid for by the employer, and shall likewise submit to examination at reasonable intervals by any physician selected by the administrative director or appeals board or referee thereof. *(Stats.1937, c. 90, p. 275, § 4050. Amended by Stats.1965, c. 1513, p. 3575, § 74, operative Jan. 15, 1966.)*

§ 4051. Request or order for examination

The request or order for the medical examination shall fix a time and place therefor, due consideration being given to the convenience of the employee and his physical condition and ability to attend at the time and place fixed. *(Stats.1937, c. 90, p. 276, § 4051.)*

§ 4052. Presence of employee's physician at examination

The employee may employ at his own expense a physician, to be present at any examination required by his employer. *(Stats.1937, c. 90, p. 276, § 4052.)*

§ 4053. Failure to comply with employer's request; suspension of right to maintain proceedings

So long as the employee, after written request of the employer, fails or refuses to submit to such examination or in any way obstructs it, his right to begin or maintain any proceeding for the collection of compensation shall be suspended. *(Stats.1937, c. 90, p. 276, § 4053.)*

§ 4054. Failure to comply with appeals board; barring of right to disability payments

If the employee fails or refuses to submit to examination after direction by the appeals board, or a referee thereof, or in any way obstructs the examination, his right to the disability payments which accrue during the period of such failure, refusal or obstruction, shall be barred. *(Stats.1937, c. 90, p. 276, § 4054. Amended by Stats.1965, c. 1513, p. 3575, § 75, operative Jan. 15, 1966.)*

§ 4055. Testimony of physician

Any physician who makes or is present at any such examination may be required to report or testify as to the results thereof. *(Stats.1937, c. 90, p. 276, § 4055.)*

§ 4055.2. Subpoenas of medical records; copy to parties of record

Any party who subpoenas records in any proceeding under this division shall concurrent with service of the subpoena upon the person who has possession of the records, send a copy of the subpoena to all parties of record in the proceeding. *(Added by Stats.1974, c. 783, p. 1708, § 1. Amended by Stats.1999, c. 444 (A.B.794), § 7.)*

§ 4056. Death or disability caused by unreasonable refusal to submit to medical or surgical treatment

No compensation is payable in case of the death or disability of an employee when his death is caused, or when and so far as his disability is caused, continued, or aggravated, by an unreasonable refusal to submit to medical treatment, or to any surgical treatment, if the risk of the treatment is, in the opinion of the appeals board, based upon expert medical or surgical advice, inconsiderable in view of the seriousness of the injury. *(Stats.1937, c. 90, p. 276, § 4056. Amended by Stats.1965, c. 1513, p. 3575, § 76, operative Jan. 15, 1966.)*

ARTICLE 2. DETERMINATION OF MEDICAL ISSUES

Section

4060.   Compensability of injury in dispute; medical-legal evaluation; notice requirements.

4061.   Notice of permanent disability indemnity; medical evaluation.

4061.5. Opinion of treating physician; treatment by more than one physician.

4062.   Notice of objections to medical determination by treating physician and employee objection to treatment recommendations; time limits and extensions; medical evaluation; objections to reports; second opinions.

4062.1. Agreements on medical evaluator and preparation by agreed medical evaluator of formal medical evaluation on issues in dispute where employee is not represented by attorney; requests for medical evaluation and submission of form; selection and appointment of physician; notice; expenses; participation of employee in evaluation; subsequent representation by an attorney.

4062.2. Obtaining a comprehensive medical evaluation on or after January 1, 2005 where an employee is represented by an attorney.

4062.3. Information available to evaluators; communications; disputed medical issues and findings; new medical issues.

4062.5. Failure of evaluator to complete evaluation on time; liability for costs.

4062.8. Development of educational materials for treating physicians and other providers.

4063.   Resolution of issues; duty of employer.

Section

4064.   Comprehensive medical-legal evaluation; cost; application for adjudication; attorney's fees.

4066.   Attorney's fees; contested evaluations.

4067.   Medical evaluations for continuing cases.

4067.5. Operative date of article.

4068.   Physician reports containing conjecture, inadequate evidence, or bias; notification to administrative agencies.

Operative Effect

Article 2 is operative for injuries occurring on and after Jan. 1, 1991. See Labor Code § 4067.5.

§ 4060. Compensability of injury in dispute; medical-legal evaluation; notice requirements

(a) This section shall apply to disputes over the compensability of any injury. This section shall not apply where injury to any part or parts of the body is accepted as compensable by the employer.

(b) Neither the employer nor the employee shall be liable for any comprehensive medical-legal evaluation performed by other than the treating physician, except as provided in this section. However, reports of treating physicians shall be admissible.

(c) If a medical evaluation is required to determine compensability at any time after the filing of the claim form, and the employee is represented by an attorney, a medical evaluation to determine compensability shall be obtained only by the procedure provided in Section 4062.2.

(d) If a medical evaluation is required to determine compensability at any time after the claim form is filed, and the employee is not represented by an attorney, the employer shall provide the employee with notice either that the employer requests a comprehensive medical evaluation to determine compensability or that the employer has not accepted liability and the employee may request a comprehensive medical evaluation to determine compensability. Either party may request a comprehensive medical evaluation to determine compensability. The evaluation shall be obtained only by the procedure provided in Section 4062.1.

(e)(1) Each notice required by subdivision (d) shall describe the administrative procedures available to the injured employee and advise the employee of his or her right to consult an information and assistance officer or an attorney. It shall contain the following language:

"Should you decide to be represented by an attorney, you may or may not receive a larger award, but, unless you are determined to be ineligible for an award, the attorney's fee will be deducted from any award you might receive for disability benefits. The decision to be represented by an attorney is yours to make, but it is voluntary and may not be necessary for you to receive your benefits."

(2) The notice required by subdivision (d) shall be accompanied by the form prescribed by the administrative director for requesting the assignment of a panel of qualified medical evaluators. *(Added by Stats.1993, c. 121 (A.B.110), § 29, eff. July 16, 1993. Amended by Stats. 1993, c. 1242 (S.B.223), § 27; Stats.2004, c. 34 (S.B.899), § 12, eff. April 19, 2004.)*

Operative Effect

Section 47 of Stats.2004, c. 34 (S.B.899) provides that "[t]he amendment, addition, or repeal of, any provision of law made by this act shall apply prospectively from the date of enactment of this act, regardless of the date of injury, unless otherwise specified, but shall not constitute good cause to reopen or rescind, alter, or amend any existing order, decision, or award of the Workers' Compensation Appeals Board."

§ 4061. Notice of permanent disability indemnity; medical evaluation

(a) Together with the last payment of temporary disability indemnity, the employer shall, in a form prescribed by the administrative director pursuant to Section 138.4, provide the employee one of the following:

(1) Notice either that no permanent disability indemnity will be paid because the employer alleges the employee has no permanent impairment or limitations resulting from the injury or notice of the amount of permanent disability indemnity determined by the employer to be payable. The notice shall include information concerning how the employee may obtain a formal medical evaluation pursuant to subdivision (c) or (d) if he or she disagrees with the position taken by the employer. The notice shall be accompanied by the form prescribed by the administrative director for requesting assignment of a panel of qualified medical evaluators, unless the employee is represented by an attorney. If the employer determines permanent disability indemnity is payable, the employer shall advise the employee of the amount determined payable and the basis on which the determination was made and whether there is need for continuing medical care.

(2) Notice that permanent disability indemnity may be or is payable, but that the amount cannot be determined because the employee's medical condition is not yet permanent and stationary. The notice shall advise the employee that his or her medical condition will be monitored until it is permanent and stationary, at which time the necessary evaluation will be performed to determine the existence and extent of permanent impairment and limitations for the purpose of rating permanent disability and to determine the need for continuing medical care, or at which time the employer will advise the employee of the amount of permanent disability indemnity the employer has determined to be payable. If an employee is provided notice pursuant to this paragraph and the employer later takes the position that the employee has no permanent impairment or limitations resulting from the injury, or later determines permanent disability indemnity is payable, the employer shall in either event, within 14 days of the determination to take either position, provide the employee with the notice specified in paragraph (1).

(b) Each notice required by subdivision (a) shall describe the administrative procedures available to the injured employee and advise the employee of his or her right to consult an information and assistance officer or an attorney. It shall contain the following language:

"Should you decide to be represented by an attorney, you may or may not receive a larger award, but, unless you are determined to be ineligible for an award, the attorney's fee will be deducted from any award you might receive for disability benefits. The decision to be represented by an attorney is yours to make, but it is voluntary and may not be necessary for you to receive your benefits."

(c) If the parties do not agree to a permanent disability rating based on the treating physician's evaluation, and the employee is represented by an attorney, a medical evaluation to determine permanent disability shall be obtained as provided in Section 4062.2.

(d) If the parties do not agree to a permanent disability rating based on the treating physician's evaluation, and if the employee is not represented by an attorney, the employer shall immediately provide the employee with a form prescribed by the medical director with which to request assignment of a panel of three qualified medical evaluators. Either party may request a comprehensive medical evaluation to determine permanent disability, and the evaluation shall be obtained only by the procedure provided in Section 4062.1.

(e) The qualified medical evaluator who has evaluated an unrepresented employee shall serve the comprehensive medical evaluation and the summary form on the employee, employer, and the administrative director. The unrepresented employee or the employer may submit the treating physician's evaluation for the calculation of a permanent disability rating. Within 20 days of receipt of the comprehensive medical evaluation, the administrative director shall calculate the permanent disability rating according to Section 4660 and serve the rating on the employee and employer.

(f) Any comprehensive medical evaluation concerning an unrepresented employee which indicates that part or all of an employee's permanent impairment or limitations may be subject to apportionment pursuant to Sections 4663 and 4664 shall first be submitted by the administrative director to a workers' compensation judge who may refer the report back to the qualified medical evaluator for correction or clarification if the judge determines the proposed apportionment is inconsistent with the law.

(g) Within 30 days of receipt of the rating, if the employee is unrepresented, the employee or employer may request that the administrative director reconsider the recommended rating or obtain additional information

585

from the treating physician or medical evaluator to address issues not addressed or not completely addressed in the original comprehensive medical evaluation or not prepared in accord with the procedures promulgated under paragraph (2) or (3) of subdivision (j) of Section 139.2. This request shall be in writing, shall specify the reasons the rating should be reconsidered, and shall be served on the other party. If the administrative director finds the comprehensive medical evaluation is not complete or not in compliance with the required procedures, the administrative director shall return the report to the treating physician or qualified medical evaluator for appropriate action as the administrative director instructs. Upon receipt of the treating physician's or qualified medical evaluator's final comprehensive medical evaluation and summary form, the administrative director shall recalculate the permanent disability rating according to Section 4660 and serve the rating, the comprehensive medical evaluation, and the summary form on the employee and employer.

(h)(1) If a comprehensive medical evaluation from the treating physician or an agreed medical evaluator or a qualified medical evaluator selected from a three-member panel resolves any issue so as to require an employer to provide compensation, the employer shall commence the payment of compensation or promptly commence proceedings before the appeals board to resolve the dispute.

(2) If the employee and employer agree to a stipulated findings and award as provided under Section 5702 or to compromise and release the claim under Chapter 2 (commencing with Section 5000) of Part 3, or if the employee wishes to commute the award under Chapter 3 (commencing with Section 5100) of Part 3, the appeals board shall first determine whether the agreement or commutation is in the best interests of the employee and whether the proper procedures have been followed in determining the permanent disability rating. The administrative director shall promulgate a form to notify the employee, at the time of service of any rating under this section, of the options specified in this subdivision, the potential advantages and disadvantages of each option, and the procedure for disputing the rating.

(i) No issue relating to the existence or extent of permanent impairment and limitations resulting from the injury may be the subject of a declaration of readiness to proceed unless there has first been a medical evaluation by a treating physician or an agreed or qualified medical evaluator. With the exception of an evaluation or evaluations prepared by the treating physician or physicians, no evaluation of permanent impairment and limitations resulting from the injury shall be obtained, except in accordance with Section 4062.1 or 4062.2. Evaluations obtained in violation of this prohibition shall not be admissible in any proceeding before the appeals board. *(Added by Stats.1989, c. 892, § 28, operative Jan. 1, 1991. Amended by Stats.1990, c. 1550 (A.B.2910), § 21; Stats. 1993, c. 121 (A.B.110), § 30, eff. July 16, 1993; Stats.1993,*

c. 1241 (S.B.147), § 6; Stats.1993, c. 1242 (S.B.223), § 28; Stats.2002, c. 6 (A.B.749), § 51; Stats.2003, c. 639 (S.B. 228), § 16; Stats.2004, c. 34 (S.B.899), § 13, eff. April 19, 2004.)

Operative Effect

Section 47 of Stats.2004, c. 34 (S.B.899) provides that "[t]he amendment, addition, or repeal of, any provision of law made by this act shall apply prospectively from the date of enactment of this act, regardless of the date of injury, unless otherwise specified, but shall not constitute good cause to reopen or rescind, alter, or amend any existing order, decision, or award of the Workers' Compensation Appeals Board."

§ 4061.5. Opinion of treating physician; treatment by more than one physician

The treating physician primarily responsible for managing the care of the injured worker or the physician designated by that treating physician shall, in accordance with rules promulgated by the administrative director, render opinions on all medical issues necessary to determine eligibility for compensation. In the event that there is more than one treating physician, a single report shall be prepared by the physician primarily responsible for managing the injured worker's care that incorporates the findings of the various treating physicians. *(Added by Stats.1993, c. 121 (A.B.110), § 31, eff. July 16, 1993.)*

§ 4062. Notice of objections to medical determination by treating physician and employee objection to treatment recommendations; time limits and extensions; medical evaluation; objections to reports; second opinions

(a) If either the employee or employer objects to a medical determination made by the treating physician concerning any medical issues not covered by Section 4060 or 4061 and not subject to Section 4610, the objecting party shall notify the other party in writing of the objection within 20 days of receipt of the report if the employee is represented by an attorney or within 30 days of receipt of the report if the employee is not represented by an attorney. Employer objections to the treating physician's recommendation for spinal surgery shall be subject to subdivision (b), and after denial of the physician's recommendation, in accordance with Section 4610. If the employee objects to a decision made pursuant to Section 4610 to modify, delay, or deny a treatment recommendation, the employee shall notify the employer of the objection in writing within 20 days of receipt of that decision. These time limits may be extended for good cause or by mutual agreement. If the employee is represented by an attorney, a medical evaluation to determine the disputed medical issue shall be obtained as provided in Section 4062.2, and no other medical evaluation shall be obtained. If the employee is not represented by an attorney, the employer shall immediately provide the employee with a form prescribed by the medical director with which to request assignment of a panel of three qualified medical evaluators, the evaluation shall be obtained as provided in Section 4062.1, and no other medical evaluation shall be obtained.

(b) The employer may object to a report of the treating physician recommending that spinal surgery be performed within 10 days of the receipt of the report. If the employee is represented by an attorney, the parties shall seek agreement with the other party on a California licensed board-certified or board-eligible orthopedic surgeon or neurosurgeon to prepare a second opinion report resolving the disputed surgical recommendation. If no agreement is reached within 10 days, or if the employee is not represented by an attorney, an orthopedic surgeon or neurosurgeon shall be randomly selected by the administrative director to prepare a second opinion report resolving the disputed surgical recommendation. Examinations shall be scheduled on an expedited basis. The second opinion report shall be served on the parties within 45 days of receipt of the treating physician's report. If the second opinion report recommends surgery, the employer shall authorize the surgery. If the second opinion report does not recommend surgery, the employer shall file a declaration of readiness to proceed. The employer shall not be liable for medical treatment costs for the disputed surgical procedure, whether through a lien filed with the appeals board or as a self-procured medical expense, or for periods of temporary disability resulting from the surgery, if the disputed surgical procedure is performed prior to the completion of the second opinion process required by this subdivision.

(c) The second opinion physician shall not have any material professional, familial, or financial affiliation, as determined by the administrative director, with any of the following:

(1) The employer, his or her workers' compensation insurer, third-party claims administrator, or other entity contracted to provide utilization review services pursuant to Section 4610.

(2) Any officer, director, or employee of the employer's health care provider, workers' compensation insurer, or third-party claims administrator.

(3) A physician, the physician's medical group, or the independent practice association involved in the health care service in dispute.

(4) The facility or institution at which either the proposed health care service, or the alternative service, if any, recommended by the employer's health care provider, workers' compensation insurer, or third-party claims administrator, would be provided.

(5) The development or manufacture of the principal drug, device, procedure, or other therapy proposed by the employee or his or her treating physician whose treatment is under review, or the alternative therapy, if any, recommended by the employer or other entity.

(6) The employee or the employee's immediate family.

(Added by Stats.2003, c. 639 (S.B.228), § 17. Amended by Stats.2004, c. 34 (S.B.899), § 14, eff. April 19, 2004.)

Operative Effect

Section 47 of Stats.2004, c. 34 (S.B.899) provides that "[t]he amendment, addition, or repeal of, any provision of law made by this act shall apply prospectively from the date of enactment of this act, regardless of the date of injury, unless otherwise specified, but shall not constitute good cause to reopen or rescind, alter, or amend any existing order, decision, or award of the Workers' Compensation Appeals Board."

§ 4062.1. Agreements on medical evaluator and preparation by agreed medical evaluator of formal medical evaluation on issues in dispute where employee is not represented by attorney; requests for medical evaluation and submission of form; selection and appointment of physician; notice; expenses; participation of employee in evaluation; subsequent representation by an attorney

(a) If an employee is not represented by an attorney, the employer shall not seek agreement with the employee on an agreed medical evaluator, nor shall an agreed medical evaluator prepare the formal medical evaluation on any issues in dispute.

(b) If either party requests a medical evaluation pursuant to Section 4060, 4061, or 4062, either party may submit the form prescribed by the administrative director requesting the medical director to assign a panel of three qualified medical evaluators in accordance with Section 139.2. However, the employer may not submit the form unless the employee has not submitted the form within 10 days after the employer has furnished the form to the employee and requested the employee to submit the form. The party submitting the request form shall designate the specialty of the physicians that will be assigned to the panel.

(c) Within 10 days of the issuance of a panel of qualified medical evaluators, the employee shall select a physician from the panel to prepare a medical evaluation, the employee shall schedule the appointment, and the employee shall inform the employer of the selection and the appointment. If the employee does not inform the employer of the selection within 10 days of the assignment of a panel of qualified medical evaluators, then the employer may select the physician from the panel to prepare a medical evaluation. If the employee informs the employer of the selection within 10 days of the assignment of the panel but has not made the appointment, or if the employer selects the physician pursuant to this subdivision, then the employer shall arrange the appointment. Upon receipt of written notice of the appointment arrangements from the employee, or upon giving the employee notice of an appointment arranged by the employer, the employer shall furnish payment of estimated travel expense.

587

(d) The evaluator shall give the employee, at the appointment, a brief opportunity to ask questions concerning the evaluation process and the evaluator's background. The unrepresented employee shall then participate in the evaluation as requested by the evaluator unless the employee has good cause to discontinue the evaluation. For purposes of this subdivision, "good cause" shall include evidence that the evaluator is biased against the employee because of his or her race, sex, national origin, religion, or sexual preference or evidence that the evaluator has requested the employee to submit to an unnecessary medical examination or procedure. If the unrepresented employee declines to proceed with the evaluation, he or she shall have the right to a new panel of three qualified medical evaluators from which to select one to prepare a comprehensive medical evaluation. If the appeals board subsequently determines that the employee did not have good cause to not proceed with the evaluation, the cost of the evaluation shall be deducted from any award the employee obtains.

(e) If an employee has received a comprehensive medical-legal evaluation under this section, and he or she later becomes represented by an attorney, he or she shall not be entitled to an additional evaluation. *(Added by Stats.1989, c. 892, § 28, operative Jan. 1, 1991. Amended by Stats.2004, c. 34 (S.B.899), § 16, eff. April 19, 2004.)*

Operative Effect

Section 47 of Stats.2004, c. 34 (S.B.899) provides that "[t]he amendment, addition, or repeal of, any provision of law made by this act shall apply prospectively from the date of enactment of this act, regardless of the date of injury, unless otherwise specified, but shall not constitute good cause to reopen or rescind, alter, or amend any existing order, decision, or award of the Workers' Compensation Appeals Board."

§ 4062.2. Obtaining a comprehensive medical evaluation on or after January 1, 2005 where an employee is represented by an attorney

(a) Whenever a comprehensive medical evaluation is required to resolve any dispute arising out of an injury or a claimed injury occurring on or after January 1, 2005, and the employee is represented by an attorney, the evaluation shall be obtained only as provided in this section.

(b) If either party requests a medical evaluation pursuant to Section 4060, 4061, or 4062, either party may commence the selection process for an agreed medical evaluator by making a written request naming at least one proposed physician to be the evaluator. The parties shall seek agreement with the other party on the physician, who need not be a qualified medical evaluator, to prepare a report resolving the disputed issue. If no agreement is reached within 10 days of the first written proposal that names a proposed agreed medical evaluator, or any additional time not to exceed 20 days agreed to by the parties, either party may request the assignment of a three-member panel of qualified medical evaluators to conduct a comprehensive medical evaluation. The party submitting the request shall designate the specialty of the medical evaluator, the specialty of the medical evaluator requested by the other party if it has been made known to the party submitting the request, and the specialty of the treating physician. The party submitting the request form shall serve a copy of the request form on the other party.

(c) Within 10 days of assignment of the panel by the administrative director, the parties shall confer and attempt to agree upon an agreed medical evaluator selected from the panel. If the parties have not agreed on a medical evaluator from the panel by the 10th day after assignment of the panel, each party may then strike one name from the panel. The remaining qualified medical evaluator shall serve as the medical evaluator. If a party fails to exercise the right to strike a name from the panel within three working days of gaining the right to do so, the other party may select any physician who remains on the panel to serve as the medical evaluator. The administrative director may prescribe the form, the manner, or both, by which the parties shall conduct the selection process.

(d) The represented employee shall be responsible for arranging the appointment for the examination, but upon his or her failure to inform the employer of the appointment within 10 days after the medical evaluator has been selected, the employer may arrange the appointment and notify the employee of the arrangements.

(e) If an employee has received a comprehensive medical-legal evaluation under this section, and he or she later ceases to be represented, he or she shall not be entitled to an additional evaluation. *(Added by Stats. 2004, c. 34 (S.B.899), § 18, eff. April 19, 2004.)*

Operative Effect

Section 47 of Stats.2004, c. 34 (S.B.899) provides that "[t]he amendment, addition, or repeal of, any provision of law made by this act shall apply prospectively from the date of enactment of this act, regardless of the date of injury, unless otherwise specified, but shall not constitute good cause to reopen or rescind, alter, or amend any existing order, decision, or award of the Workers' Compensation Appeals Board."

§ 4062.3. Information available to evaluators; communications; disputed medical issues and findings; new medical issues

(a) Any party may provide to the qualified medical evaluator selected from a panel any of the following information:

(1) Records prepared or maintained by the employee's treating physician or physicians.

(2) Medical and nonmedical records relevant to determination of the medical issue.

(b) Information that a party proposes to provide to the qualified medical evaluator selected from a panel shall be served on the opposing party 20 days before the information is provided to the evaluator. If the opposing party objects to consideration of nonmedical records within 10 days thereafter, the records shall not be provided to the evaluator. Either party may use discovery to establish the accuracy or authenticity of nonmedical records prior to the evaluation.

(c) If an agreed medical evaluator is selected, as part of their agreement on an evaluator, the parties shall agree on what information is to be provided to the agreed medical evaluator.

(d) In any formal medical evaluation, the agreed or qualified medical evaluator shall identify the following:

(1) All information received from the parties.

(2) All information reviewed in preparation of the report.

(3) All information relied upon in the formulation of his or her opinion.

(e) All communications with an agreed medical evaluator or a qualified medical evaluator selected from a panel before a medical evaluation shall be in writing and shall be served on the opposing party 20 days in advance of the evaluation. Any subsequent communication with the medical evaluator shall be in writing and shall be served on the opposing party when sent to the medical evaluator.

(f) Ex parte communication with an agreed medical evaluator or a qualified medical evaluator selected from a panel is prohibited. If a party communicates with the agreed medical evaluator or the qualified medical evaluator in violation of subdivision (e), the aggrieved party may elect to terminate the medical evaluation and seek a new evaluation from another qualified medical evaluator to be selected according to Section 4062.1 or 4062.2, as applicable, or proceed with the initial evaluation.

(g) The party making the communication prohibited by this section shall be subject to being charged with contempt before the appeals board and shall be liable for the costs incurred by the aggrieved party as a result of the prohibited communication, including the cost of the medical evaluation, additional discovery costs, and attorney's fees for related discovery.

(h) Subdivisions (e) and (f) shall not apply to oral or written communications by the employee or, if the employee is deceased, the employee's dependent, in the course of the examination or at the request of the evaluator in connection with the examination.

(i) Upon completing a determination of the disputed medical issue, the medical evaluator shall summarize the medical findings on a form prescribed by the administrative director and shall serve the formal medical evaluation and the summary form on the employee and the employer. The medical evaluation shall address all contested medical issues arising from all injuries reported on one or more claim forms prior to the date of the employee's initial appointment with the medical evaluator.

(j) If, after a medical evaluation is prepared, the employer or the employee subsequently objects to any new medical issue, the parties, to the extent possible, shall utilize the same medical evaluator who prepared the previous evaluation to resolve the medical dispute.

(k) No disputed medical issue specified in subdivision (a) may be the subject of declaration of readiness to proceed unless there has first been an evaluation by the treating physician or an agreed or qualified medical evaluator. *(Added by Stats.2004, c. 34 (S.B.899), § 19, eff. April 19, 2004.)*

Operative Effect

Section 47 of Stats.2004, c. 34 (S.B.899) provides that "[t]he amendment, addition, or repeal of, any provision of law made by this act shall apply prospectively from the date of enactment of this act, regardless of the date of injury, unless otherwise specified, but shall not constitute good cause to reopen or rescind, alter, or amend any existing order, decision, or award of the Workers' Compensation Appeals Board."

§ 4062.5. Failure of evaluator to complete evaluation on time; liability for costs

If a qualified medical evaluator selected from a panel fails to complete the formal medical evaluation within the timeframes established by the administrative director pursuant to paragraph (1) of subdivision (j) of Section 139.2, a new evaluation may be obtained upon the request of either party, as provided in Sections 4062.1 or 4062.2. Neither the employee nor the employer shall have any liability for payment for the formal medical evaluation which was not completed within the required timeframes unless the employee or employer, on forms prescribed by the administrative director, each waive the right to a new evaluation and elects to accept the original evaluation even though it was not completed within the required timeframes. *(Added by Stats.1989, c. 892, § 28, operative Jan. 1, 1991. Amended by Stats.1990, c. 1550 (A.B.2910), § 24; Stats.2003, c. 639 (S.B.228), § 19; Stats.2004, c. 34 (S.B.899), § 20, eff. April 19, 2004.)*

Operative Effect

Section 47 of Stats.2004, c. 34 (S.B.899) provides that "[t]he amendment, addition, or repeal of, any provision of law made by this act shall apply prospectively from the date of enactment of this act, regardless of the date of injury, unless otherwise specified, but shall not constitute good cause to reopen or rescind, alter, or amend any existing order, decision, or award of the Workers' Compensation Appeals Board."

§ 4062.8. Development of educational materials for treating physicians and other providers

The administrative director shall develop, not later than January 1, 2004, and periodically revise as necessary thereafter, educational materials to be used to provide treating physicians, as described in Section 3209.3, or other providers, as described in Section 3209.5, with information and training in basic concepts of workers' compensation, the role of the treating physician, the conduct of permanent and stationary evaluations, and report writing, as appropriate. *(Added by Stats.2004, c. 34 (S.B.899), § 21, eff. April 19, 2004.)*

Operative Effect

Section 47 of Stats.2004, c. 34 (S.B.899) provides that "[t]he amendment, addition, or repeal of, any provision of law made by this act shall apply prospectively from the date of enactment of this act, regardless of the date of injury, unless otherwise specified, but shall not constitute good cause to reopen or rescind, alter, or amend any existing order, decision, or award of the Workers' Compensation Appeals Board."

§ 4063. Resolution of issues; duty of employer

If a formal medical evaluation from an agreed medical evaluator or a qualified medical evaluator selected from a three member panel resolves any issue so as to require an employer to provide compensation, the employer shall commence the payment of compensation or file an application for adjudication of claim. *(Added by Stats. 1989, c. 892, § 28, operative Jan. 1, 1991.)*

§ 4064. Comprehensive medical-legal evaluation; cost; application for adjudication; attorney's fees

(a) The employer shall be liable for the cost of each reasonable and necessary comprehensive medical-legal evaluation obtained by the employee pursuant to Sections 4060, 4061, and 4062. Each comprehensive medical-legal evaluation shall address all contested medical issues arising from all injuries reported on one or more claim forms.

(b) For injuries occurring on or after January 1, 2003, if an unrepresented employee obtains an attorney after the evaluation pursuant to subdivision (d) of Section 4061 or subdivision (b) of Section 4062 has been completed, the employee shall be entitled to the same reports at employer expense as an employee who has been represented from the time the dispute arose and those reports shall be admissible in any proceeding before the appeals board.

(c) Subject to Section 4906, if an employer files an application for adjudication and the employee is unrepresented at the time the application is filed, the employer shall be liable for any attorney's fees incurred by the employee in connection with the application for adjudication.

590

(d) The employer shall not be liable for the cost of any comprehensive medical evaluations obtained by the employee other than those authorized pursuant to Sections 4060, 4061, and 4062. However, no party is prohibited from obtaining any medical evaluation or consultation at the party's own expense. In no event shall an employer or employee be liable for an evaluation obtained in violation of subdivision (b) of Section 4060. All comprehensive medical evaluations obtained by any party shall be admissible in any proceeding before the appeals board except as provided in subdivisions (d) and (m) of Section 4061 and subdivisions (b) and (e) of Section 4062. *(Added by Stats.1989, c. 892, § 28, operative Jan. 1, 1991; Stats.1989, c. 893, § 2. Amended by Stats.1990, c. 1550 (A.B.2910), § 25; Stats.1993, c. 121 (A.B.110), § 34, eff. July 16, 1993; Stats.1993, c. 1242 (S.B.223), § 30; Stats. 1998, c. 485 (A.B.2803), § 124; Stats.2002, c. 6 (A.B.749), § 54.)*

§ 4066. Attorney's fees; contested evaluations

When the employer files an application for adjudication of claim contesting the formal medical evaluation prepared by an agreed medical evaluator under this article, regardless of outcome, the workers' compensation judge or the appeals board shall assess the employee's attorney's fees against the employer, subject to Section 4906. *(Added by Stats.1989, c. 892, § 28, operative Jan. 1, 1991.)*

§ 4067. Medical evaluations for continuing cases

If the jurisdiction of the appeals board is invoked pursuant to Section 5803 upon the grounds that the effects of the injury have recurred, increased, diminished, or terminated, a formal medical evaluation shall be obtained pursuant to this article.

When an agreed medical evaluator or a qualified medical evaluator selected by an unrepresented employee from a three-member panel has previously made a formal medical evaluation of the same or similar issues, the subsequent or additional formal medical evaluation shall be conducted by the same agreed medical evaluator or qualified medical evaluator, unless the workers' compensation judge has made a finding that he or she did not rely on the prior evaluator's formal medical evaluation, any party contested the original medical evaluation by filing an application for adjudication, the unrepresented employee hired an attorney and selected a qualified medical evaluator to conduct another evaluation pursuant to subdivision (b) of Section 4064, or the prior evaluator is no longer qualified or readily available to prepare a formal medical evaluation, in which case Sections 4061 or 4062, as the case may be, shall apply as if there had been no prior formal medical evaluation. *(Added by Stats. 1989, c. 892, § 28, operative Jan. 1, 1991. Amended by Stats.1990, c. 1550 (A.B.2910), § 27; Stats.2002, c. 6 (A.B.749), § 56.)*

§ 4067.5. Operative date of article

This article shall become operative for injuries occurring on and after January 1, 1991. *(Added by Stats.1989, c. 892, § 28, operative Jan. 1991. Amended by Stats.1990, c. 1550 (A.B.2910), § 28.)*

§ 4068. Physician reports containing conjecture, inadequate evidence, or bias; notification to administrative agencies

(a) Upon determining that a treating physician's report contains opinions that are the result of conjecture, are not supported by adequate evidence, or that indicate bias, the appeals board shall so notify the administrative director in writing in a manner he or she has specified.

(b) If the administrative director believes that any treating physician's reports show a pattern of unsupported opinions, he or she shall notify in writing the physician's applicable licensing body of his or her findings. *(Added by Stats.1993, c. 121 (A.B.110), § 36, eff. July 16, 1993. Amended by Stats.2003, c. 639 (S.B.228), § 22.)*

CHAPTER 8. ELECTION TO BE SUBJECT TO COMPENSATION LIABILITY

Section
4150. Joint election of employer and employee.
4151. Manner of election by employer.
4152. Filing of statement of election; duration; renewal.
4153. Employees included in statement.
4154. Acceptance by employees.
4155. Public employment.
4156. Exemption from liability for compensation.
4157. Newspaper, magazine or periodical vendor, seller or delivery person; inclusion under compensation provisions by employer; status as independent contractor for other purposes.

§ 4150. Joint election of employer and employee

When an employer has in his employment any person not included within the term "employee" as defined by Article 2 of Chapter 2 of Part 1 of this division or a person not entitled to compensation under this division, such employer and such person employed by him may, by their joint election, come under the compensation provisions of this division in the manner hereinafter provided. *(Stats.1937, c. 90, p. 276, § 4150.)*

§ 4151. Manner of election by employer

Election on the part of the employer shall be made in one of the following ways:

(a) By insuring against liability for compensation, in which case he is deemed, as to all persons employed by him and covered by insurance, to have so elected during the period such insurance remains in force.

(b) By filing with the administrative director a statement to the effect that he accepts the compensation provisions of this division. *(Stats.1937, c. 90, p. 276,*

§ 4151. Amended by Stats.1965, c. 1513, p. 3575, § 77, operative Jan. 15, 1966.)

§ 4152. Filing of statement of election; duration; renewal

The statement, when filed, shall operate, within the meaning of Chapter 3 (commencing with Section 3600), to subject him or her to the compensation provisions thereof for the term of one year from the date of filing. Thereafter, without further act on his or her part, he or she shall be so subject for successive terms of one year each, unless at least 60 days prior to the expiration of such first or succeeding year, he or she files with the administrative director a notice that he or she withdraws his or her election. *(Stats.1937, c. 90, p. 277, § 4152. Amended by Stats.1965, c. 1513, p. 3576, § 78, operative Jan. 15, 1966; Stats.1982, c. 454, p. 1878, § 136.)*

§ 4153. Employees included in statement

Such statement of acceptance includes persons whose employment is both casual and not in the course of the trade, business, profession, or occupation of the employer, unless expressly excluded therefrom. *(Stats.1937, c. 90, p. 277, § 4153.)*

§ 4154. Acceptance by employees

Where any employer has made an election in either of the modes above prescribed, any person in his service is deemed to have accepted the compensation provisions of this division if, at the time of the injury for which liability is claimed:

(a) Such employer is subject to the compensation provisions of this division and;

(b) Such person in his service has not, either upon entering into the employment, or within five days after the filing of an election by the employer, given to such employer notice in writing that he elects not to be subject to the compensation provisions of this division.

In case of such acceptance, the person employed becomes subject to the compensation provisions at the time of the filing of the election or entry in the employment. *(Stats.1937, c. 90, p. 277, § 4154.)*

§ 4155. Public employment

The State and each county, city, district, and public agency thereof and all State institutions are conclusively presumed to have elected to come within the provisions of this division as to all employments otherwise excluded from this division. *(Stats.1937, c. 90, p. 277, § 4155.)*

§ 4156. Exemption from liability for compensation

No liability for compensation shall attach to any employer of a person excluded by subdivision (h) of Section 3352 from the definition of "employee" for an injury to or the death of a person so excluded which occurs on or after the effective date of this section if such employer elected to come under the compensation provisions of this division pursuant to subdivision (a) of

Section 4151 prior to the effective date of this section by purchasing or renewing a policy providing comprehensive personal liability insurance containing a provision for coverage against liability for the payment of compensation, as defined in Section 3207 of the Labor Code, to any person defined as an employee by subdivision (d) of Section 3351 of the Labor Code; provided, however, nothing in this section shall prohibit an employer from providing compensation pursuant to the provisions of this chapter. *(Added by Stats.1977, c. 17, p. 33, § 25, eff. March 25, 1977.)*

§ 4157. Newspaper, magazine or periodical vendor, seller or delivery person; inclusion under compensation provisions by employer; status as independent contractor for other purposes

Where any employer has made an election pursuant to this chapter to include under the compensation provisions of this division an independent contractor engaged in vending, selling, offering for sale, or delivering directly to the public any newspaper, magazine, or periodical, the status of such person as an independent contractor for all other purposes shall not be affected by such election. *(Added by Stats.1978, c. 672, p. 6162, § 1.)*

CHAPTER 9. ECONOMIC OPPORTUNITY PROGRAMS

Article   Section
1. General Provisions 4201
2. Benefits 4211
3. Adjustment of Claims 4226

ARTICLE 1. GENERAL PROVISIONS

Section
4201. Intent of chapter.
4202. Economic opportunity program defined.
4203. Enrollee defined.
4204. Sponsoring agency defined.
4205. Participating agency defined.
4206. Right of enrollee to receive compensation.
4207. Injury or death in course of duties for sponsoring agency; compensation; conditions.
4208. Exclusiveness of remedy for injury or death of enrollee.
4209. Applicability of division to enrollees.

§ 4201. Intent of chapter

It is the intent of this chapter to apply to all enrollees in economic opportunity programs, including, but not limited to, work training or work study authorized by or financed in whole or in part through provisions of Public Law 88–452 (Economic Opportunity Act of 1964). *(Added by Stats.1965, c. 1685, p. 3804, § 1.)*

§ 4202. Economic opportunity program defined

"Economic Opportunity Program" means any program adopted pursuant to Public Law 88–452, including, but not limited to, work training and work study. *(Added by Stats.1965, c. 1685, p. 3804, § 1.)*

§ 4203. Enrollee defined

"Enrollee" means any person enrolled in an economic opportunity program. *(Added by Stats.1965, c. 1685, p. 3804, § 1.)*

§ 4204. Sponsoring agency defined

"Sponsoring agency" means any agency, entity, or institution, public or private, receiving grants or financial assistance, either directly or as a subcontractor, pursuant to Public Law 88–452. *(Added by Stats.1965, c. 1685, p. 3804, § 1.)*

§ 4205. Participating agency defined

"Participating agency" means any agency, entity or institution, public or private, taking part in an economic opportunity program, other than a sponsoring agency. *(Added by Stats.1965, c. 1685, p. 3804, § 1.)*

§ 4206. Right of enrollee to receive compensation

Except as provided in this chapter, an enrollee within a given economic opportunity program shall have no right to receive compensation from sponsoring or participating agencies, entities, and institutions, public or private. *(Added by Stats.1965, c. 1685, p. 3804, § 1.)*

§ 4207. Injury or death in course of duties for sponsoring agency; compensation; conditions

Compensation shall be furnished an enrollee for injury or to dependents if injury causes death, suffered within or without the state occurring in the course of his duties for a sponsoring agency within an economic opportunity program if the following conditions occur:

(a) Where, at the time of injury, the enrollee is performing services and is acting within the scope of his duties as a recipient of aid within an economic opportunity program.

(b) Where injury is proximately caused by his service as an enrollee within an economic opportunity program either with or without negligence.

(c) Where injury is not caused by the intoxication of the injured enrollee.

(d) Where the injury is not intentionally self-inflicted. *(Added by Stats.1965, c. 1685, p. 3805, § 1.)*

§ 4208. Exclusiveness of remedy for injury or death of enrollee

Where the conditions of compensation exist, the right to recover such compensation pursuant to the provisions of this chapter is the exclusive remedy for injury or death of an enrollee against the sponsoring agency, or the participating agency. *(Added by Stats.1965, c. 1685, p. 3805, § 1.)*

§ 4209. Applicability of division to enrollees

Insofar as not inconsistent with the provisions of this chapter, all of the provisions of this division shall pertain to enrollees and their dependents and the furnishing of compensation benefits thereto. *(Added by Stats.1965, c. 1685, p. 3805, § 1.)*

ARTICLE 2. BENEFITS

Section
4211. Existence of liability; compensation.
4212. Average weekly earnings; determination; statutory minimum average weekly earnings for temporary disability indemnity.
4213. Permanent disability; percentage of disability to total disability; determination.
4214. Death benefit; burial expenses.

§ 4211. Existence of liability; compensation

Where liability for compensation exists, such compensation shall be provided as limited by this chapter. *(Added by Stats.1965, c. 1685, p. 3805, § 1.)*

§ 4212. Average weekly earnings; determination; statutory minimum average weekly earnings for temporary disability indemnity

If an enrollee suffers injury or death in the performance of his duties under an economic opportunity program, then, irrespective of his remuneration from this or other employment, his average weekly earnings for the purpose of determining temporary and permanent disability indemnity shall be determined in accordance with Section 4453, provided that for the purpose of this chapter only, there shall be no statutory minimum average weekly earnings for temporary disability indemnity. If the injury sustained by an enrollee causes death, death benefits shall be determined in accordance with Sections 4701 and 4702 of this code. *(Added by Stats. 1965, c. 1685, p. 3805, § 1.)*

§ 4213. Permanent disability; percentage of disability to total disability; determination

If the injury sustained by an enrollee causes permanent disability, the percentage of disability to total disability shall be determined for the occupation of a laborer of like age by applying the schedule for the determination of the percentage of permanent disabilities prepared and adopted by the appeals board. *(Added by Stats.1965, c. 1685, p. 3805, § 1. Amended by Stats.1967, c. 1364, p. 3203, § 3.)*

§ 4214. Death benefit; burial expenses

In addition to death benefit in the event of fatal injury, the reasonable expenses of the enrollee's burial shall be paid not to exceed six hundred dollars ($600). *(Added by Stats.1965, c. 1685, p. 3805, § 1.)*

ARTICLE 3. ADJUSTMENT OF CLAIMS

Section
4226. Benefits to enrollees from federal government; reduction of state monetary benefits.
4227. Medical treatment from federal government.

Section
4228. Medical treatment in form of reimbursement from federal government.
4229. Receipt of benefits under state law preventing receipt of benefits under federal statute.

§ 4226. Benefits to enrollees from federal government; reduction of state monetary benefits

Should the United States government or any agent thereof, pursuant to federal statute, rule or regulations furnish benefits to enrollees or dependents of enrollees under an economic opportunity program, then the amount of indemnity which an enrollee or his dependents are entitled to receive under this chapter shall be reduced by the amount of monetary benefits the enrollee or his dependents have and will receive from the above source as a result of injury. *(Added by Stats.1965, c. 1685, p. 3806, § 1.)*

§ 4227. Medical treatment from federal government

If the United States government or any agent thereof furnishes medical treatment to an injured enrollee, the enrollee will have no right to receive the same or similar treatment under this chapter. *(Added by Stats.1965, c. 1685, p. 3806, § 1.)*

§ 4228. Medical treatment in form of reimbursement from federal government

If the furnishing of medical treatment by the United States government or its agent takes the form of reimbursement of the enrollee, he shall have no right to receive the same or similar treatment under this chapter. *(Added by Stats.1965, c. 1685, p. 3806, § 1.)*

§ 4229. Receipt of benefits under state law preventing receipt of benefits under federal statute

If the furnishing of compensation benefits to an enrollee or his dependents under this chapter prevents such enrollee or his dependents from receiving benefits under the provisions of federal statute, rule or regulations, then the enrollee or his dependents shall have no right and shall not receive compensation benefits under this chapter. *(Added by Stats.1965, c. 1685, p. 3806, § 1.)*

CHAPTER 10. DISASTER SERVICE WORKERS

Section
4350. Administration of chapter.
4351. Exclusive remedy; liability for compensation.
4352. Payment of compensation from appropriated funds; liability; reserves.
4353. Average weekly earnings for determining disability indemnity.
4354. Permanent disability; determination of percentage of disability to total disability; amount of weekly payment.
4355. Federal assistance; entitlement to assistance under the Division.

§ 4350. Administration of chapter

The Office of Emergency Services shall administer this chapter as it relates to volunteer disaster service workers. *(Added by Stats.2003, c. 228 (A.B.1756), § 32, eff. Aug. 11, 2003.)*

§ 4351. Exclusive remedy; liability for compensation

Compensation provided by this division is the exclusive remedy of a disaster service worker, or his or her dependents, for injury or death arising out of, and in the course of, his or her activities as a disaster service worker as against the state, the disaster council with which he or she is registered, and the county or city which has empowered the disaster council to register and direct his or her activities. Liability for compensation provided by this division is in lieu of any other liability whatsoever to a disaster service worker or his or her dependents or any other person on his or her behalf against the state, the disaster council with which the disaster service worker is registered, and the county or city which has empowered the disaster council to register and direct his or her activities, for any injury or death arising out of, and in the course of, his or her activities as a disaster service worker. *(Added by Stats.1986, c. 554, § 3.)*

§ 4352. Payment of compensation from appropriated funds; liability; reserves

(a) No compensation shall be paid or furnished to a disaster service * * * worker or a dependent of a disaster service worker pursuant to this division * * * absent an initial appropriation of funds for the purpose of furnishing compensation to a disaster service * * * worker or a dependent of a disaster service worker. Liability for the initial payment or furnishing of compensation is dependent upon and limited to the availability of money so appropriated.

(b) Notwithstanding subdivision (a), when appropriated funds are temporarily unavailable for disbursement, the State Compensation Insurance Fund may provide compensation to an eligible claimant under this section whose injuries have previously either been accepted or found to be compensable by the Workers' Compensation Appeals Board.

(1) Compensation to, and benefits for, an eligible claimant provided for under this subdivision may include the issuance of checks by the State Compensation Insurance Fund.

(2) Within 30 days of the date funds that had been temporarily unavailable are appropriated, and therefore become available, the California Emergency Management Agency shall reimburse the State Compensation Insurance Fund for compensation paid to, or benefits paid for, a claimant pursuant to paragraph (1), in addition to any applicable interest, service fees, or charges.

(c) After all money * * * appropriated as described in subdivision (a) is expended or set aside in bookkeeping reserves for the payment or furnishing of compensation and reimbursing the State Compensation Insurance Fund

for its services, the payment or furnishing of compensation for an injury to a disaster service worker or his or her dependents is dependent upon there having been a reserve set up for the payment or furnishing of compensation to that disaster service worker or his or her dependents and for that injury, and liability is limited to the amount of the reserve. The excess in a reserve for the payment or furnishing of compensation or for reimbursing the State Compensation Insurance Fund for its compensation payments and services may be transferred to reserves of other disaster service workers for the payment or furnishing of compensation and reimbursing the State Compensation Insurance Fund, or may be used to set up reserves for other disaster service workers. *(Added by Stats.1986, c. 554, § 3. Amended by Stats. 2009–2010, 4th Ex.Sess., c. 12 (A.B.12), § 25, eff. July 28, 2009.)*

§ 4353. Average weekly earnings for determining disability indemnity

If a disaster service worker suffers injury or death while in the performance of duties as a disaster service worker, then, irrespective of his or her remuneration from this or other employment or from both, the average weekly earnings for the purposes of determining temporary and permanent disability indemnity shall be taken at the maximum fixed for each, respectively, in Section 4453. *(Added by Stats.1986, c. 554, § 3.)*

§ 4354. Permanent disability; determination of percentage of disability to total disability; amount of weekly payment

If the injury sustained by a disaster service worker causes permanent disability, the percentage of disability to total disability shall be determined as for the occupation of a laborer of like age by applying the schedule for the determination of the percentages of permanent disabilities prepared and adopted by the administrative director. The amount of the weekly payment for permanent disability shall be the same as the weekly benefit which would be paid for temporary total disability pursuant to Section 4353. *(Added by Stats.1986, c. 554, § 3.)*

§ 4355. Federal assistance; entitlement to assistance under the Division

(a) Should the United States Government or any agent thereof, in accordance with any federal statute, rule, or regulation, furnish monetary assistance, benefits, or other temporary or permanent relief to disaster service workers or to disaster service workers and their dependents for injuries arising out of and occurring in the course of their activities as disaster service workers, the amount of compensation that any disaster service worker or his or her dependents are otherwise entitled to receive from the State of California under this division for any injury shall be reduced by the amount of monetary assistance, benefits, or other temporary or permanent relief the disaster service worker or his or her dependents have received and will receive from the United States or any agent thereof as a result of the injury.

(b) If, in addition to monetary assistance, benefits, or other temporary or permanent relief, the United States Government or any agent thereof furnishes medical, surgical, or hospital treatment, or any combination thereof, to an injured disaster service worker, the disaster service worker has no right to receive similar medical, surgical, or hospital treatment under this division.

(c) If, in addition to monetary assistance, benefits, or other temporary or permanent relief, the United States Government or any agent thereof will reimburse a disaster service worker or his or her dependents for medical, surgical, or hospital treatment, or any combination thereof, furnished to the injured disaster service worker, the disaster service worker has no right to receive similar medical, surgical, or hospital treatment under this division.

(d) If the furnishing of compensation under this division to a disaster service worker or his or her dependents prevents the disaster service worker or his or her dependents from receiving assistance, benefits, or other temporary or permanent relief under a federal statute, rule, regulation, the disaster service worker and his or her dependents shall have no right to, and may not receive, any compensation from the State of California under this division for any injury for which the United States Government or any agent thereof will furnish assistance, benefits, or other temporary or permanent relief in the absence of the furnishing of compensation by the State of California. *(Added by Stats.2003, c. 228 (A.B.1756), § 34, eff. Aug. 11, 2003.)*

CHAPTER 10.5. DISASTER SERVICE WORKERS [RENUMBERED]

CHAPTER 11. ASBESTOS WORKERS' ACCOUNT

Article   Section
1. General Provisions...........................4401
2. Benefits 4407
3. Collections 4412

Operative Effect

For duration of provisions for payments and continuation of collection powers under Chapter 11, see Labor Code § 4418.

ARTICLE 1. GENERAL PROVISIONS

Section
4401. Public policy.
4402. Definitions.
4403. Creation of account; administration; appropriation.
4404. Application of division.
4405. Temporary remedy.
4406. Payments as advances on workers' compensation; conditions.

Operative Effect

For duration of provisions for payments and continuation of collection powers under Chapter 11, see Labor Code § 4418.

§ 4401. Public policy

It is the declared policy of the state that qualified injured workers with asbestosis which arises out of and occurs in the course of employment shall receive workers' compensation asbestos workers' benefits promptly and not be subjected to delays of litigation to determine the responsible employer. *(Added by Stats.1980, c. 1041, p. 3322, § 1. Amended by Stats.1982, c. 1077, p. 3897, § 1, eff. Sept. 15, 1982.)*

Operative Effect

For duration of provisions for payments and continuation of collection powers under Chapter 11, see Labor Code § 4418.

§ 4402. Definitions

(a) "Asbestosis" means any pathology, whether or not combined with preexisting pathology, which results in disability or need for medical treatment from inhalation of asbestos fibers.

(b) "Asbestos worker" means any person whose occupation subjected him or her to an exposure to asbestos fibers.

(c) "Asbestos workers' benefits" means temporary total disability benefits, permanent total disability benefits, death benefits, and medical benefits.

(d) "Dependents" means, and is limited to, a surviving spouse who at the time of injury was dependent on the deceased asbestos worker for half or more of his or her support, and minor children of the deceased asbestos worker. *(Added by Stats.1980, c. 1041, p. 3322, § 1. Amended by Stats.1982, c. 1077, p. 3897, § 1.5, eff. Sept. 15, 1982.)*

Operative Effect

For duration of provisions for payments and continuation of collection powers under Chapter 11, see Labor Code § 4418.

§ 4403. Creation of account; administration; appropriation

The Asbestos Workers' Account is hereby created in the Uninsured Employers Fund in the State Treasury, and shall be administered by the Director of Industrial Relations. The money in the Asbestos Workers' Account is hereby continuously appropriated for the purposes of this chapter, and to pay the expenses of the director in administering these provisions. *(Added by Stats.1980, c. 1041, p. 3322, § 1.)*

Operative Effect

For duration of provisions for payments and continuation of collection powers under Chapter 11, see Labor Code § 4418.

§ 4404. Application of division

Insofar as not inconsistent with the provisions of this chapter, all of the provisions of this division shall pertain to asbestos workers and their dependents for purposes of furnishing workers' compensation asbestos workers' benefits thereto. *(Added by Stats.1980, c. 1041, p. 3322, § 1. Amended by Stats.1982, c. 454, p. 1878, § 137; Stats.1982, c. 1077, p. 3898, § 2, eff. Sept. 15, 1982.)*

Operative Effect

For duration of provisions for payments and continuation of collection powers under Chapter 11, see Labor Code § 4418.

§ 4405. Temporary remedy

Where the conditions of compensation exist under this division the right to recover workers' compensation asbestos workers' benefits pursuant to the provisions of this chapter is a temporary remedy for injury to an asbestos worker against the Asbestos Workers' Account, and such asbestos worker or his or her dependents shall make all reasonable effort to establish the identity of the employer responsible for securing the payment of compensation. *(Added by Stats.1980, c. 1041, p. 3322, § 1. Amended by Stats.1982, c. 1077, p. 3898, § 3, eff. Sept. 15, 1982.)*

Operative Effect

For duration of provisions for payments and continuation of collection powers under Chapter 11, see Labor Code § 4418.

§ 4406. Payments as advances on workers' compensation; conditions

(a) Payments as advances on workers' compensation asbestos workers' benefits shall be furnished an asbestos worker for injury resulting in asbestosis, or the dependents of the asbestos worker in the case of his or her death due to asbestosis, subject to the provisions of this division, if all of the following conditions occur:

(1) The asbestos worker demonstrates to the account that at the time of exposure, the asbestos worker was performing services and was acting within the scope of his or her duties in an occupation that subjected the asbestos worker to the exposure to asbestos.

(2) The asbestos worker demonstrates to the account that he or she is suffering from asbestosis.

(3) The asbestos worker demonstrates to the account that he or she developed asbestosis from the employment.

(4) The asbestos worker is entitled to compensation for asbestosis as otherwise provided for in this division.

(b) The findings of the account with regard to the conditions in subdivision (a) shall not be evidence in any other proceeding.

(c) The account shall require the asbestos worker to submit to an independent medical examination unless the information and assistance officer, in consultation with the medical director or his or her designee, determines that there exists adequate medical evidence that the worker developed asbestosis from the employment. *(Added by Stats.1980, c. 1041, p. 3322, § 1. Amended by Stats.1982, c. 1077, p. 3898, § 4, eff. Sept. 15. 1982.)*

Operative Effect

For duration of provisions for payments and continuation of collection powers under Chapter 11, see Labor Code § 4418.

ARTICLE 2. BENEFITS

Section
4407.   Payments.
4407.3.   Death benefits; manner of payment.
4407.5.   Lump-sum payment.
4408.   Claim.
4409.   Investigative and claims adjustment services.
4409.5.   Workers' compensation judges; appointment; priorities.
4410.   Information and assistance officers.
4411.   Procedure.

Operative Effect

For duration of provisions for payments and continuation of collection powers under Chapter 11, see Labor Code § 4418.

§ 4407. Payments

When the account determines that the conditions in Section 4406 have occurred, payments as advances on workers' compensation asbestos workers' benefits shall be provided in accordance with this chapter, notwithstanding the right of the asbestos worker to secure compensation as otherwise provided for in this division. *(Added by Stats.1980, c. 1041, p. 3323, § 1. Amended by Stats.1982, c. 1077, p. 3898, § 5, eff. Sept. 15, 1982.)*

Operative Effect

For duration of provisions for payments and continuation of collection powers under Chapter 11, see Labor Code § 4418.

§ 4407.3. Death benefits; manner of payment

For purposes of this chapter, the death benefit shall be paid in installments in the same manner and amounts as temporary disability indemnity. *(Added by Stats.1982, c. 1077, p. 3899, § 6, eff. Sept. 15, 1982.)*

Operative Effect

For duration of provisions for payments and continuation of collection powers under Chapter 11, see Labor Code § 4418.

§ 4407.5. Lump-sum payment

Benefits provided by this chapter shall not be commuted into a lump-sum payment. *(Added by Stats.1982, c. 1077, p. 3899, § 7, eff. Sept. 15, 1982.)*

Operative Effect

For duration of provisions for payments and continuation of collection powers under Chapter 11, see Labor Code § 4418.

§ 4408. Claim

Prior to seeking compensation benefits under this chapter, the asbestos worker shall first make claim on the employer or its workers' compensation insurance carrier for payment of compensation under this division. If the asbestos worker is unable to locate the responsible employer or insurance carrier, or if the employer or insurance carrier fails to pay or denies liability for the compensation required by this division to the person entitled thereto, within a period of 30 days after the assertion of such a claim, the asbestos worker may seek payment of workers' compensation asbestos workers' benefits required by this division from the Asbestos Workers' Account. *(Added by Stats.1980, c. 1041, p. 3323, § 1. Amended by Stats.1982, c. 1077, p. 3899, § 8, eff. Sept. 15, 1982.)*

Operative Effect

For duration of provisions for payments and continuation of collection powers under Chapter 11, see Labor Code § 4418.

§ 4409. Investigative and claims adjustment services

The Director of Industrial Relations, or his or her representative, shall assign investigative and claims adjustment services respecting matters concerning Asbestos Workers' Account cases. Those assignments may be made within the department, including the Division of Workers' Compensation, and excluding the State Compensation Insurance Fund. *(Added by Stats.1980, c. 1041, p. 3323, § 1. Amended by Stats.1994, c. 146 (A.B.3601), § 149; Stats.1994, c. 1097 (S.B.1803), § 13.)*

Operative Effect

For duration of provisions for payments and continuation of collection powers under Chapter 11, see Labor Code § 4418.

§ 4409.5. Workers' compensation judges; appointment; priorities

The administrative director shall appoint workers' compensation judges and support staff who shall give priority to the processing of the claims of asbestos workers. *(Added by Stats.1980, c. 1041, p. 3323, § 1. Amended by Stats.1985, c. 326, § 12.)*

Operative Effect

For duration of provisions for payments and continuation of collection powers under Chapter 11, see Labor Code § 4418.

§ 4410. Information and assistance officers

The administrative director shall appoint at least two information and assistance officers who shall give priority to assisting asbestos workers pursuant to the provisions of this chapter. The information and assistance officer shall assist to the fullest extent possible any asbestos worker seeking benefits under this chapter. In assisting the asbestos worker, the information and assistance officer shall conduct necessary investigation and procure those records, reports, and information which are necessary to the early identification of responsible employers and insurance carriers, and to facilitate in the expediting of payments of benefits that may be due under this division. *(Added by Stats.1980, c. 1041, p. 3323, § 1.)*

Operative Effect

For duration of provisions for payments and continuation of collection powers under Chapter 11, see Labor Code § 4418.

§ 4411. Procedure

(a) When a claim is made against the Asbestos Workers' Account, the account shall secure appropriate information, adjust the claim, and pay benefits provided by this chapter in accordance with the provisions of this division.

(b) The asbestos worker shall, prior to the first payment of benefits by the Asbestos Workers' Account, file an application before the Workers' Compensation Appeals Board to determine the responsible employer for payment of compensation under this division.

(c) In every case before the Workers' Compensation Appeals Board in which a claim of injury from exposure to asbestos is alleged, the appeals board shall join the Asbestos Workers' Account as a party to the proceeding and serve the fund with copies of all decisions and orders, including findings and awards, and order approving compromise and release.

(d) Once a decision establishing the responsible employer or insurance carrier is agreed upon between the parties, or is issued by the Workers' Compensation Appeals Board, and becomes final, the Asbestos Workers' Account shall terminate payment of compensation benefits, notify all interested parties accordingly, and seek collection as provided for under this chapter. Responsibility for payment of all future compensation benefits shall be in accordance with such agreement, order, or decision.

(e) The account shall terminate the payment of benefits to any employee who fails to cooperate fully in determining the responsible employer or insurance carrier.

(f) The Asbestos Workers' Account may, at any time, commence or join in proceedings before the Workers' Compensation Appeals Board by filing an application on its own behalf. In any case in which the Asbestos Workers' Account has been joined as a party or has filed an application on its own behalf, the Asbestos Workers' Account shall have all of the rights and privileges of a party applicant. *(Added by Stats.1980, c. 1041, p. 3321, § 1.)*

Operative Effect

For duration of provisions for payments and continuation of collection powers under Chapter 11, see Labor Code § 4418.

ARTICLE 3. COLLECTIONS

Section
4412.   Action to recover benefits paid and costs; uninsured employer.
4413.   Limitation of time; exemption.
4414.   Lien for moneys expended.
4415.   Attorneys.
4416.   Notice to employer or insurance carrier of amount required to satisfy lien; time for payment; costs; interest; priority.
4417.   Actions against third parties; lien on recovery; effect on employer's liability.
4418.   Duration of provisions for payments; continuation of collection powers.

Operative Effect

For duration of provisions for payments and continuation of collection powers under Chapter 11, see Labor Code § 4418.

§ 4412. Action to recover benefits paid and costs; uninsured employer

The Asbestos Workers' Account shall take all reasonable and appropriate action to insure that recovery is made by the account for all moneys paid as compensation benefits and as costs.

In the event that the responsible employer is uninsured, the account shall not be entitled to reimbursement from the Uninsured Employers Fund. *(Added by Stats. 1980, c. 1041, p. 3324, § 1.)*

Operative Effect

For duration of provisions for payments and continuation of collection powers under Chapter 11, see Labor Code § 4418.

§ 4413. Limitation of time; exemption

No limitation of time provided by this division shall run against the Asbestos Workers' Account to initiate proceedings before the Workers' Compensation Appeals Board when the account has made any payment of moneys, incurred any costs for services, or encumbered any liability of the account. *(Added by Stats.1980, c. 1041,*

p. 3324, § 1. Amended by Stats.1982, c. 454, p. 1878, § 138.)*

Operative Effect

For duration of provisions for payments and continuation of collection powers under Chapter 11, see Labor Code § 4418.

§ 4414. Lien for moneys expended

Immediately following the receipt of knowledge of initiation of proceedings before the Workers' Compensation Appeals Board, or any other jurisdiction providing benefits for the same injury, the Asbestos Workers' Account shall file a lien and may invoke such other remedies as are available to recover moneys expended for compensation benefits. *(Added by Stats.1980, c. 1041, p. 3324, § 1.)*

Operative Effect

For duration of provisions for payments and continuation of collection powers under Chapter 11, see Labor Code § 4418.

§ 4415. Attorneys

In any hearing or proceeding, the Director of Industrial Relations may use attorneys from within the department, or the Attorney General, to represent the director and the state. *(Added by Stats.1980, c. 1041, p. 3324, § 1.)*

Operative Effect

For duration of provisions for payments and continuation of collection powers under Chapter 11, see Labor Code § 4418.

§ 4416. Notice to employer or insurance carrier of amount required to satisfy lien; time for payment; costs; interest; priority

Once an agreement as to the responsible employer is reached, or a decision is issued by the Workers' Compensation Appeals Board and becomes final, the Asbestos Workers' Account shall notify the responsible employer or insurance carrier of the amount of payment necessary to satisfy the lien in full. Full payment of the lien shall be made by the responsible employer or insurance carrier within 30 days of the issue of such notification. The account may grant a reasonable extension of time for payment of the lien beyond 30 days. This payment shall be for all moneys expended for compensation benefits, and for all recoverable costs including the cost of independent medical examination and all costs reasonably incidental thereto, including, but not limited to, costs of transportation, hospitalization, consultative evaluation, X-rays, laboratory tests, and other diagnostic procedures. The payment shall bear interest, as provided in Section 5800, from the date of the agreement or decision through the date of payment.

The lien of the Asbestos Workers' Account shall be allowed as a first lien against compensation, and shall have priority over all other liens. The lien of the

Asbestos Workers' Account may not be reduced by the Workers' Compensation Appeals Board or by the parties unless express written consent to the proposed reduction of the lien is given by the Asbestos Workers' Account and is filed in the record of proceedings before the Workers' Compensation Appeals Board. *(Added by Stats.1980, c. 1041, p. 3324, § 1.)*

Operative Effect

For duration of provisions for payments and continuation of collection powers under Chapter 11, see Labor Code § 4418.

§ 4417. Actions against third parties; lien on recovery; effect on employer's liability

Nothing in this chapter shall be construed to preclude the filing by an asbestos worker of a claim or suit for damages or indemnity against any person other than his or her employer. The Asbestos Workers' Account shall be entitled to recover from, and shall have a first lien against, any amount which is recoverable by the injured employee pursuant to civil judgment or settlement in relation to a claim for damages or indemnity for the effect of exposure to asbestos, for all compensation benefits paid to the injured employee by the Asbestos Workers' Account which have not previously been recovered from the responsible employer or employers by the Asbestos Workers' Account. Recovery by the Asbestos Workers' Account pursuant to the provisions of this section shall not have the effect of extinguishing or diminishing the liability of the responsible employer or employers to the injured employee for compensation payable under the provisions of this division. *(Added by Stats.1980, c. 1041, p. 3325, § 1.)*

Operative Effect

For duration of provisions for payments and continuation of collection powers under Chapter 11, see Labor Code § 4418.

§ 4418. Duration of provisions for payments; continuation of collection powers

The provisions of this chapter providing for the payment of workers' compensation asbestos workers' benefits from the Asbestos Workers' Account shall be operative only until January 1, 1989, and as of that date all payments from the fund shall be terminated, and the state shall have no further obligation to pay asbestos workers' benefits, unless a later enacted statute which is chaptered before January 1, 1989, deletes or extends that date. However, if no statute is enacted to delete or extend that date prior to January 1, 1989, the authority of the Asbestos Workers' Account under this chapter to recover the benefits and costs paid to asbestos workers prior to that date shall continue until the benefits and costs have been recovered. *(Added by Stats.1980, c. 1041, p. 3325, § 1. Amended by Stats.1982, c. 1077, p. 3899, § 9, eff. Sept. 15, 1982; Stats.1985, c. 1156, § 4.)*

Part 2

COMPUTATION OF COMPENSATION

Chapter	Section
1. Average Earnings	4451
2. Compensation Schedules	4550

CHAPTER 1. AVERAGE EARNINGS

Section
4451. Average annual earnings.
4452. Minimum and maximum.
4452.5. Permanent total disability and permanent partial disability defined.
4453. Average annual earnings; average weekly earnings; computation; minimum and maximum.
4453.5. Continuance of benefit payments for injury; effect of statutory changes.
4454. Items included and excluded in determination of average weekly earnings.
4455. Permanent injury to employees under 18 years; determination of average weekly earnings.
4456. Unemployment work relief employee; computation of disability payments.
4457. Unascertainable weekly earnings of workmen associated in partnership.
4458. Average weekly and annual earnings of volunteer fire department members and persons engaged in suppressing fires.
4458.2. Injury or death to peace officer or law enforcement officer; average earnings; maximum limits.
4458.5. Injury following active service and within period extending presumption that injury arose in course of employment; maximum earnings.
4459. Prior disability; effect; determination of average weekly earnings.

§ 4451. Average annual earnings

Average annual earnings shall be taken as fifty-two times the average weekly earnings referred to in this chapter. *(Stats.1937, c. 90, p. 278, § 4451.)*

§ 4452. Minimum and maximum

Four times the average annual earnings shall be taken at not less than four thousand eight hundred dollars and sixty-four cents ($4,800.64) nor more than fifteen thousand two hundred dollars and sixty-four cents ($15,-200.64) in disability cases, and in death cases shall be taken at not less than the minimum nor more than the maximum limits as provided in Section 4702 of this code. *(Stats.1937, c. 90, p. 278, § 4452. Amended by Stats.1939, c. 308, p. 1580, § 1; Stats.1947, c. 1033, p. 2304, § 2; Stats.1951, c. 606, p. 1766, § 2; Stats.1955, c. 956, p. 1851, § 1; Stats.1957, c. 1996, p. 3551, § 2.)*

§ 4452.5. Permanent total disability and permanent partial disability defined

As used in this division:

(a) "Permanent total disability" means a permanent disability with a rating of 100 percent permanent disability only.

599

(b) "Permanent partial disability" means a permanent disability with a rating of less than 100 percent permanent disability. *(Added by Stats.1973, c. 1023, p. 2028, § 1, operative April 1, 1974.)*

§ 4453. Average annual earnings; average weekly earnings; computation; minimum and maximum

(a) In computing average annual earnings for the purposes of temporary disability indemnity and permanent total disability indemnity only, the average weekly earnings shall be taken at:

(1) Not less than one hundred twenty-six dollars ($126) nor more than two hundred ninety-four dollars ($294), for injuries occurring on or after January 1, 1983.

(2) Not less than one hundred sixty-eight dollars ($168) nor more than three hundred thirty-six dollars ($336), for injuries occurring on or after January 1, 1984.

(3) Not less than one hundred sixty-eight dollars ($168) for permanent total disability, and, for temporary disability, not less than the lesser of one hundred sixty-eight dollars ($168) or 1.5 times the employee's average weekly earnings from all employers, but in no event less than one hundred forty-seven dollars ($147), nor more than three hundred ninety-nine dollars ($399), for injuries occurring on or after January 1, 1990.

(4) Not less than one hundred sixty-eight dollars ($168) for permanent total disability, and for temporary disability, not less than the lesser of one hundred eighty-nine dollars ($189) or 1.5 times the employee's average weekly earnings from all employers, nor more than five hundred four dollars ($504), for injuries occurring on or after January 1, 1991.

(5) Not less than one hundred sixty-eight dollars ($168) for permanent total disability, and for temporary disability, not less than the lesser of one hundred eighty-nine dollars ($189) or 1.5 times the employee's average weekly earnings from all employers, nor more than six hundred nine dollars ($609), for injuries occurring on or after July 1, 1994.

(6) Not less than one hundred sixty-eight dollars ($168) for permanent total disability, and for temporary disability, not less than the lesser of one hundred eighty-nine dollars ($189) or 1.5 times the employee's average weekly earnings from all employers, nor more than six hundred seventy-two dollars ($672), for injuries occurring on or after July 1, 1995.

(7) Not less than one hundred sixty-eight dollars ($168) for permanent total disability, and for temporary disability, not less than the lesser of one hundred eighty-nine dollars ($189) or 1.5 times the employee's average weekly earnings from all employers, nor more than seven hundred thirty-five dollars ($735), for injuries occurring on or after July 1, 1996.

(8) Not less than one hundred eighty-nine dollars ($189), nor more than nine hundred three dollars ($903), for injuries occurring on or after January 1, 2003.

(9) Not less than one hundred eighty-nine dollars ($189), nor more than one thousand ninety-two dollars ($1,092), for injuries occurring on or after January 1, 2004.

(10) Not less than one hundred eighty-nine dollars ($189), nor more than one thousand two hundred sixty dollars ($1,260), for injuries occurring on or after January 1, 2005. For injuries occurring on or after January 1, 2006, average weekly earnings shall be taken at not less than one hundred eighty-nine dollars ($189), nor more than one thousand two hundred sixty dollars ($1,260) or 1.5 times the state average weekly wage, whichever is greater. Commencing on January 1, 2007, and each January 1 thereafter, the limits specified in this paragraph shall be increased by an amount equal to the percentage increase in the state average weekly wage as compared to the prior year. For purposes of this paragraph, "state average weekly wage" means the average weekly wage paid by employers to employees covered by unemployment insurance as reported by the United States Department of Labor for California for the 12 months ending March 31 of the calendar year preceding the year in which the injury occurred.

(b) In computing average annual earnings for purposes of permanent partial disability indemnity, except as provided in Section 4659, the average weekly earnings shall be taken at:

(1) Not less than seventy-five dollars ($75), nor more than one hundred ninety-five dollars ($195), for injuries occurring on or after January 1, 1983.

(2) Not less than one hundred five dollars ($105), nor more than two hundred ten dollars ($210), for injuries occurring on or after January 1, 1984.

(3) When the final adjusted permanent disability rating of the injured employee is 15 percent or greater, but not more than 24.75 percent: (A) not less than one hundred five dollars ($105), nor more than two hundred twenty-two dollars ($222), for injuries occurring on or after July 1, 1994; (B) not less than one hundred five dollars ($105), nor more than two hundred thirty-one dollars ($231), for injuries occurring on or after July 1, 1995; (C) not less than one hundred five dollars ($105), nor more than two hundred forty dollars ($240), for injuries occurring on or after July 1, 1996.

(4) When the final adjusted permanent disability rating of the injured employee is 25 percent or greater, not less than one hundred five dollars ($105), nor more than two hundred twenty-two dollars ($222), for injuries occurring on or after January 1, 1991.

(5) When the final adjusted permanent disability rating of the injured employee is 25 percent or greater but not more than 69.75 percent: (A) not less than one hundred five dollars ($105), nor more than two hundred thirty-seven dollars ($237), for injuries occurring on or after July 1, 1994; (B) not less than one hundred five dollars ($105), nor more than two hundred forty-six dollars ($246), for injuries occurring on or after July 1,

1995; and (C) not less than one hundred five dollars ($105), nor more than two hundred fifty-five dollars ($255), for injuries occurring on or after July 1, 1996.

(6) When the final adjusted permanent disability rating of the injured employee is less than 70 percent: (A) not less than one hundred fifty dollars ($150), nor more than two hundred seventy-seven dollars and fifty cents ($277.50), for injuries occurring on or after January 1, 2003; (B) not less than one hundred fifty-seven dollars and fifty cents ($157.50), nor more than three hundred dollars ($300), for injuries occurring on or after January 1, 2004; (C) not less than one hundred fifty-seven dollars and fifty cents ($157.50), nor more than three hundred thirty dollars ($330), for injuries occurring on or after January 1, 2005; and (D) not less than one hundred ninety-five dollars ($195), nor more than three hundred forty-five dollars ($345), for injuries occurring on or after January 1, 2006.

(7) When the final adjusted permanent disability rating of the injured employee is 70 percent or greater, but less than 100 percent: (A) not less than one hundred five dollars ($105), nor more than two hundred fifty-two dollars ($252), for injuries occurring on or after July 1, 1994; (B) not less than one hundred five dollars ($105), nor more than two hundred ninety-seven dollars ($297), for injuries occurring on or after July 1, 1995; (C) not less than one hundred five dollars ($105), nor more than three hundred forty-five dollars ($345), for injuries occurring on or after July 1, 1996; (D) not less than one hundred fifty dollars ($150), nor more than three hundred forty-five dollars ($345), for injuries occurring on or after January 1, 2003; (E) not less than one hundred fifty-seven dollars and fifty cents ($157.50), nor more than three hundred seventy-five dollars ($375), for injuries occurring on or after January 1, 2004; (F) not less than one hundred fifty-seven dollars and fifty cents ($157.50), nor more than four hundred five dollars ($405), for injuries occurring on or after January 1, 2005; and (G) not less than one hundred ninety-five dollars ($195), nor more than four hundred five dollars ($405), for injuries occurring on or after January 1, 2006.

(c) Between the limits specified in subdivisions (a) and (b), the average weekly earnings, except as provided in Sections 4456 to 4459, shall be arrived at as follows:

(1) Where the employment is for 30 or more hours a week and for five or more working days a week, the average weekly earnings shall be the number of working days a week times the daily earnings at the time of the injury.

(2) Where the employee is working for two or more employers at or about the time of the injury, the average weekly earnings shall be taken as the aggregate of these earnings from all employments computed in terms of one week; but the earnings from employments other than the employment in which the injury occurred shall not be taken at a higher rate than the hourly rate paid at the time of the injury.

(3) If the earnings are at an irregular rate, such as piecework, or on a commission basis, or are specified to be by week, month, or other period, then the average weekly earnings mentioned in subdivision (a) shall be taken as the actual weekly earnings averaged for this period of time, not exceeding one year, as may conveniently be taken to determine an average weekly rate of pay.

(4) Where the employment is for less than 30 hours per week, or where for any reason the foregoing methods of arriving at the average weekly earnings cannot reasonably and fairly be applied, the average weekly earnings shall be taken at 100 percent of the sum which reasonably represents the average weekly earning capacity of the injured employee at the time of his or her injury, due consideration being given to his or her actual earnings from all sources and employments.

(d) Every computation made pursuant to this section beginning January 1, 1990, shall be made only with reference to temporary disability or the permanent disability resulting from an original injury sustained after January 1, 1990. However, all rights existing under this section on January 1, 1990, shall be continued in force. Except as provided in Section 4661.5, disability indemnity benefits shall be calculated according to the limits in this section in effect on the date of injury and shall remain in effect for the duration of any disability resulting from the injury. *(Added by Stats.1977, c. 17, p. 33, § 26, eff. March 25, 1977. Amended by Stats.1977, c. 1018, p. 3054, § 1; Stats.1980, c. 1042, p. 3328, § 1; Stats.1982, c. 922, p. 3367, § 7; Stats.1989, c. 892, § 29; Stats.1989, c. 893, § 3; Stats.1990, c. 1550 (A.B.2910), § 29; Stats.1993, c. 121 (A.B.110), § 37, eff. July 16, 1993; Stats.2002, c. 6 (A.B.749), § 57; Stats.2002, c. 866 (A.B.486), § 9.)*

§ 4453.5. Continuance of benefit payments for injury; effect of statutory changes

Benefits payable on account of an injury shall not be affected by a subsequent statutory change in amounts of indemnity payable under this division, and shall be continued as authorized, and in the amounts provided for, by the law in effect at the time the injury giving rise to the right to such benefits occurred. *(Added by Stats.1972, c. 460, p. 830, § 1.)*

§ 4454. Items included and excluded in determination of average weekly earnings

In determining average weekly earnings within the limits fixed in Section 4453, there shall be included overtime and the market value of board, lodging, fuel, and other advantages received by the injured employee as part of his remuneration, which can be estimated in money, but such average weekly earnings shall not include any sum which the employer pays to or for the injured employee to cover any special expenses entailed on the employee by the nature of his employment, nor shall there be included either the cost or the market value of any savings, wage continuation, wage replacement, or stock acquisition program or of any employee benefit

601

programs for which the employer pays or contributes to persons other than the employee or his family. *(Stats. 1937, c. 90, p. 279, § 4454. Amended by Stats.1968, 1st Ex.Sess., c. 4, p. 32, § 5, operative Jan. 1, 1969.)*

§ 4455. Permanent injury to employees under 18 years; determination of average weekly earnings

If the injured employee is under 18 years of age, and his or her incapacity is permanent, his or her average weekly earnings shall be deemed, within the limits fixed in Section 4453, to be the weekly sum that under ordinary circumstances he or she would probably be able to earn at the age of 18 years, in the occupation in which he or she was employed at the time of the injury or in any occupation to which he or she would reasonably have been promoted if he or she had not been injured. If the probable earnings at the age of 18 years cannot reasonably be determined, his or her average weekly earnings shall be taken at the maximum limit established in Section 4453. *(Stats.1937, c. 90, p. 279, § 4455. Amended by Stats.1945, c. 821, p. 1514, § 1; Stats.1949, c. 484, p. 831, § 1; Stats.1955, c. 956, p. 1852, § 3; Stats.1957, c. 1996, p. 3552, § 4; Stats.1959, c. 1189, p. 3277, § 3; Stats.1971, c. 1750, p. 3775, § 2, operative April 1, 1972; Stats.1972, c. 579, p. 1005, § 33; Stats.1974, c. 226, p. 425, § 2, eff. May 7, 1974; Stats.2001, c. 159 (S.B.662), § 158; Stats.2002, c. 6 (A.B.749), § 58.)*

§ 4456. Unemployment work relief employee; computation of disability payments

Where any employee is injured while engaged on any unemployment work relief program conducted by the State, or a political subdivision, or any State or governmental agency, the disability payments due under this division shall be determined solely on the monthly earnings or anticipated earnings of such person from such program, such payments to be within the minimum and maximum limits set forth in section 4453. *(Stats.1937, c. 90, p. 280, § 4456.)*

§ 4457. Unascertainable weekly earnings of workmen associated in partnership

In the event the average weekly earnings of workmen associating themselves under a partnership agreement, the principal purpose of which is the performance of labor on a particular piece of work, are not otherwise ascertainable, they shall be deemed to be forty dollars ($40). *(Stats.1937, c. 90, p. 280, § 4457. Amended by Stats.1961, c. 903, p. 2526, § 1.)*

§ 4458. Average weekly and annual earnings of volunteer fire department members and persons engaged in suppressing fires

If a member registered as an active firefighting member of any regularly organized volunteer fire department as described in Section 3361 suffers injury or death while in the performance of his duty as fireman, or if a person engaged in fire suppression as described in Section 3365 suffers injury or death while so engaged, then, irrespec-

tive of his remuneration from this or other employment or from both, his average weekly earnings for the purposes of determining temporary disability indemnity and permanent disability indemnity shall be taken at the maximum fixed for each, respectively, in Section 4453. Four times his average annual earnings in disability cases and in death cases shall be taken at the maximum limits provided in Sections 4452 and 4702 respectively. *(Stats. 1937, c. 90, p. 280, § 4458. Amended by Stats.1941, c. 362, p. 1647, § 1; Stats.1951, c. 606, p. 1767, § 4; Stats.1951, c. 1524, p. 3501, § 1; Stats.1963, c. 1684, p. 3306, § 3; Stats.1973, c. 953, p. 1794, § 2; Stats.1976, c. 1347, p. 6139, § 7.)*

§ 4458.2. Injury or death to peace officer or law enforcement officer; average earnings; maximum limits

If an active peace officer of any department as described in Section 3362 suffers injury or death while in the performance of his or her duties as a peace officer, or if a person engaged in the performance of active law enforcement service as described in Section 3366 suffers injury or death while in the performance of that active law enforcement service, or if a person registered as a reserve peace officer of any regularly organized police or sheriff's department as described in Section 3362.5 suffers injury or death while in the performance of his or her duties as a peace officer, then, irrespective of his or her remuneration from this or other employment or from both, his or her average weekly earnings for the purposes of determining temporary disability indemnity and permanent disability indemnity shall be taken at the maximum fixed for each, respectively, in Section 4453. Four times his or her average annual earnings in disability cases and in death cases shall be taken at the maximum limits provided in Sections 4452 and 4702 respectively. *(Added by Stats.1961, c. 1581, p. 3408, § 1. Amended by Stats.1963, c. 1684, p. 3306, § 4; Stats.1989, c. 892, § 30.5.)*

§ 4458.5. Injury following active service and within period extending presumption that injury arose in course of employment; maximum earnings

If a member suffers "an injury" following termination of active service, and within the time prescribed in Section 3212, 3212.2, 3212.3, 3212.4, 3212.5, 3212.6, 3212.7, or 3213, then, irrespective of his remuneration from any postactive service employment, his average weekly earnings for the purposes of determining temporary disability indemnity, permanent total disability indemnity, and permanent partial disability indemnity, shall be taken at the maximum fixed for each such disability, respectively, in Section 4453. *(Formerly § 4458, added by Stats.1976, c. 466, p. 1211, § 9. Renumbered § 4458.5 and amended by Stats.1978, c. 380, p. 1180, § 118.)*

§ 4459. Prior disability; effect; determination of average weekly earnings

The fact that an employee has suffered a previous disability, or received compensation therefor, does not preclude him from compensation for a later injury, or his dependents from compensation for death resulting therefrom, but in determining compensation for the later injury, or death resulting therefrom, his average weekly earnings shall be fixed at the sum which reasonably represents his earning capacity at the time of the later injury. *(Stats.1937, c. 90, p. 280, § 4459.)*

CHAPTER 2. COMPENSATION SCHEDULES

Article		Section
1.	General Provisions	4550
2.	Medical and Hospital Treatment	4600
2.3.	Medical Provider Networks	4616
2.5.	Medical-legal expenses	4620
2.6.	Vocational Rehabilitation [Repealed]	
3.	Disability Payments	4650
4.	Death Benefits	4700
4.5.	Public Official Death Benefits	4720
5.	Subsequent Injuries Payments	4750
6.	Special Payments to Certain Persons	4800
7.	City Police and Firemen, Sheriffs, and Others	4850

ARTICLE 1. GENERAL PROVISIONS

Section
4550. Payment by employer.
4551. Serious and willful misconduct of employee.
4552. Determination of employee's misconduct by appeals board.
4553. Serious and willful misconduct of employer.
4553.1. Required findings.
4554. Employer's failure to secure payment of compensation.
4555. Attorney's fees.
4555.5. Reduction of award; denial of petition; costs.
4556. Inapplicability of maximum limits on computation of average earnings.
4557. Illegally employed minor under 16 years.
4558. Removal or noninstallation of power press guards; definitions; actions for injury or death; proof required; contribution.

§ 4550. Payment by employer

Where liability for compensation exists under this division, such compensation shall be furnished or paid by the employer and shall be as provided in this chapter. *(Stats.1937, c. 90, p. 280, § 4550.)*

§ 4551. Serious and willful misconduct of employee

Where the injury is caused by the serious and willful misconduct of the injured employee, the compensation otherwise recoverable therefor shall be reduced one-half, except:

(a) Where the injury results in death.

(b) Where the injury results in a permanent disability of 70 percent or over.

(c) Where the injury is caused by the failure of the employer to comply with any provision of law, or any safety order of the Division of Occupational Safety and Health, with reference to the safety of places of employment.

(d) Where the injured employee is under 16 years of age at the time of injury. *(Stats.1937, c. 90, p. 280, § 4551. Amended by Stats.1965, c. 1513, p. 3576, § 80, operative Jan. 15, 1966; Stats.1980, c. 676, p. 1972, § 231.)*

§ 4552. Determination of employee's misconduct by appeals board

The reduction of compensation because of the serious and willful misconduct of an employee is not enforceable, valid, or binding in any respect until the appeals board has so determined by its findings and award as provided in Chapter 6 of Part 4 of this division. *(Stats.1937, c. 90, p. 281, § 4552. Amended by Stats.1965, c. 1513, p. 3576, § 81, operative Jan. 15, 1966.)*

§ 4553. Serious and willful misconduct of employer

The amount of compensation otherwise recoverable shall be increased one-half, together with costs and expenses not to exceed two hundred fifty dollars ($250), where the employee is injured by reason of the serious and willful misconduct of any of the following:

(a) The employer, or his managing representative.

(b) If the employer is a partnership, on the part of one of the partners or a managing representative or general superintendent thereof.

(c) If the employer is a corporation, on the part of an executive, managing officer, or general superintendent thereof. *(Stats.1937, c. 90, p. 281, § 4553. Amended by Stats.1949, c. 785, p. 1516, § 1; Stats.1959, c. 1189, p. 3277, § 5; Stats.1972, c. 1029, p. 1907, § 1; Stats.1982, c. 922, p. 3369, § 10.)*

§ 4553.1. Required findings

In order to support a holding of serious and willful misconduct by an employer based upon violation of a safety order, the appeals board must specifically find all of the following:

(1) The specific manner in which the order was violated.

(2) That the violation of the safety order did proximately cause the injury or death, and the specific manner in which the violation constituted the proximate cause.

(3) That the safety order, and the conditions making the safety order applicable, were known to, and violated by, a particular named person, either the employer, or a representative designated by Section 4553, or that the condition making the safety order applicable was obvious, created a probability of serious injury, and that the failure of the employer, or a representative designated by Section 4553, to correct the condition constituted a reckless disregard for the probable consequences. *(Added by Stats.1959, c. 1189, p. 3278, § 6. Amended by Stats.1965, c. 1513, p. 3576, § 82, operative Jan. 15, 1966; Stats.1982, c. 922, p. 3369, § 11.)*

§ 4554. Employer's failure to secure payment of compensation

In case of the willful failure by an employer to secure the payment of compensation, the amount of compensation otherwise recoverable for injury or death as provided in this division shall be increased 10 percent. Failure of the employer to secure the payment of compensation as provided in Article 1 (commencing at Section 3700) of Chapter 4 of Part 1 of this division is prima facie evidence of willfulness on his part. *(Stats.1937, c. 90, p. 281, § 4554. Amended by Stats.1959, c. 1189, p. 3278, § 7.)*

§ 4555. Attorney's fees

In case of failure by an employer to secure the payment of compensation, the appeals board may award a reasonable attorney's fee in addition to the amount of compensation recoverable. When a fee is awarded under this section no further fee shall be allowed under Section 4903 but the provisions of Section 4903 shall be applicable to secure the payment of any fee awarded under this section. *(Added by Stats.1945, c. 520, p. 1050, § 2. Amended by Stats.1965, c. 1513, p. 3577, § 83, operative Jan. 15, 1966.)*

§ 4555.5. Reduction of award; denial of petition; costs

Whenever a petition to reduce an award, based upon a permanent disability rating which has become final, is denied, the appeals board may order the petitioner to pay to the injured employee all costs incident to the furnishing of X-rays, laboratory services, medical reports, and medical testimony incurred by such employee in connection with the proceeding on such petition. *(Added by Stats.1959, c. 1189, p. 3278, § 8. Amended by Stats.1965, c. 1513, p. 3577, § 84, operative Jan. 15, 1966.)*

§ 4556. Inapplicability of maximum limits on computation of average earnings

The increases provided for by this article shall not be limited by the provisions of Chapter 1 of this part relating to maximum amounts in the computation of average earnings. *(Added by Stats.1945, c. 520, p. 1050, § 3.)*

§ 4557. Illegally employed minor under 16 years

Where the injury is to an employee under 16 years of age and illegally employed at the time of injury, the entire compensation otherwise recoverable shall be increased fifty percent (50%), and such additional sum shall be paid by the employer at the same time and in the same manner as the normal compensation benefits.

An employer shall not be held liable for the additional compensation provided by this section if such an employee is hired pursuant to a birth certificate, automobile driver's license, or other reasonable evidence of the fact the employee is over the age of 15 years, even though such evidence of age were falsely obtained by the employee. The additional compensation provided by this section shall not exceed the maximum sum specified by Section 4553 for additional compensation payable for serious and willful misconduct on the part of an employer. This section shall not apply to the State or any of its political subdivisions or districts. *(Added by Stats.1951, c. 1414, p. 3369, § 1. Amended by Stats.1961, c. 1621, p. 3515, § 1.)*

§ 4558. Removal or noninstallation of power press guards; definitions; actions for injury or death; proof required; contribution

(a) As used in this section:

(1) "Employer" means a named identifiable person who is, prior to the time of the employee's injury or death, an owner or supervisor having managerial authority to direct and control the acts of employees.

(2) "Failure to install" means omitting to attach a point of operation guard either provided or required by the manufacturer, when the attachment is required by the manufacturer and made known by him or her to the employer at the time of acquisition, installation, or manufacturer-required modification of the power press.

(3) "Manufacturer" means the designer, fabricator, or assembler of a power press.

(4) "Power press" means any material-forming machine that utilizes a die which is designed for use in the manufacture of other products.

(5) "Removal" means physical removal of a point of operation guard which is either installed by the manufacturer or installed by the employer pursuant to the requirements or instructions of the manufacturer.

(6) "Specifically authorized" means an affirmative instruction issued by the employer prior to the time of the employee's physical injury or death, but shall not mean any subsequent acquiescence in, or ratification of, removal of a point of operation safety guard.

(b) An employee, or his or her dependents in the event of the employee's death, may bring an action at law for damages against the employer where the employee's injury or death is proximately caused by the employer's knowing removal of, or knowing failure to install, a point of operation guard on a power press, and this removal or failure to install is specifically authorized by the employer under conditions known by the employer to create a probability of serious injury or death.

(c) No liability shall arise under this section absent proof that the manufacturer designed, installed, required, or otherwise provided by specification for the attachment of the guards and conveyed knowledge of the same to the employer. Proof of conveyance of this information to the employer by the manufacturer may come from any source.

(d) No right of action for contribution or indemnity by any defendant shall exist against the employer; however, a defendant may seek contribution after the employee secures a judgment against the employer pursuant to the provisions of this section if the employer fails to discharge his or her comparative share of the judgment. *(Added by Stats.1982, c. 922, p. 3369, § 12.)*

ARTICLE 2. MEDICAL AND HOSPITAL TREATMENT

Section

4600. Provision of treatment by employer; rights of employee.

4600. Provision of treatment by employer; rights of employee.

4600.1. Generic drug equivalents.

4600.2. Medicines and medical supplies required by this article; injured employees subject to specified contracts; period of time for which medicines and medical supplies are to be provided; adoption of standards.

4600.3. Contracts with health care organizations; notice to employees; employee's choice of health care provider; collective bargaining agreements.

4600.35. License requirements for specified reimbursements.

4600.4. Normal business day.

4600.5. Certification as health care organization; chiropractic care; acupuncture care.

4600.6. Applicants for certification as health care organizations under § 4600.5; rules and procedures.

4600.7. Workers' Compensation Managed Care Fund; creation; schedule of fees and revenues; General Fund loan repayment plan.

4601. Request for change of physician; chiropractor or acupuncturist.

4602. Certification of competency of consulting physician.

4603. Change of physician or chiropractor by employer.

4603.2. Notice of selection of physician; physician's report; payment for medical treatment; contested, denied or otherwise considered incomplete itemization; employer responsibility; interest or increase in compensation; itemization review.

4603.4. Rules and regulations; payment for medical treatment.

4603.5. Format and content of notices; reasonable geographic areas; time limits for notices and responses; notification of employees' rights.

4604. Determination of controversies by appeals board.

4604.5. Medical treatment utilization schedules; recommended guidelines; presumptions; limitation on number of visits per industrial injury occurring on or after January 1, 2004.

4605. Employee's right to personal physician.

4606. Public entities; self-insured employer under Workmen's Compensation, Insurance and Safety Act.

4607. Attorney fees; successful defense by injured employee.

4608. Pharmacy benefits; claim form reproductions.

4609. Sale, lease, or transfer of list of contracted health care providers and their reimbursement rates; disclosures and other requirements.

4610. Utilization review.

4610.1. Utilization review process; penalty for unreasonable delay in payment of compensation.

4610.3. Medical provider networks and health care organization contracts; employer authorized medical care; rescission or modification of treatment authorization.

4611. Contracts between health care providers and contracting agents; definitions.

4614. Fee limitations.

4614.1. Certified Knox-Keene health care service plans; payments.

§ 4600. Provision of treatment by employer; rights of employee

Section operative until Jan. 1, 2010. See, also, section operative Jan. 1, 2010.

(a) Medical, surgical, chiropractic, acupuncture, and hospital treatment, including nursing, medicines, medical and surgical supplies, crutches, and apparatuses, including orthotic and prosthetic devices and services, that is reasonably required to cure or relieve the injured worker from the effects of his or her injury shall be provided by the employer. In the case of his or her neglect or refusal reasonably to do so, the employer is liable for the reasonable expense incurred by or on behalf of the employee in providing treatment.

(b) As used in this division and notwithstanding any other provision of law, medical treatment that is reasonably required to cure or relieve the injured worker from the effects of his or her injury means treatment that is based upon the guidelines adopted by the administrative director pursuant to Section 5307.27 or, prior to the adoption of those guidelines, the updated American College of Occupational and Environmental Medicine's Occupational Medicine Practice Guidelines.

(c) Unless the employer or the employer's insurer has established a medical provider network as provided for in Section 4616, after 30 days from the date the injury is reported, the employee may be treated by a physician of his or her own choice or at a facility of his or her own choice within a reasonable geographic area.

(d)(1) If an employee has notified his or her employer in writing prior to the date of injury that he or she has a personal physician, the employee shall have the right to be treated by that physician from the date of injury if either of the following conditions exist:

(A) The employer provides nonoccupational group health coverage in a health care service plan, licensed pursuant to Chapter 2.2 (commencing with Section 1340) of Division 2 of the Health and Safety Code.

(B) The employer provides nonoccupational health coverage in a group health plan or a group health insurance policy as described in Section 4616.7.

(2) For purposes of paragraph (1), a personal physician shall meet all of the following conditions:

(A) The physician is the employee's regular physician and surgeon, licensed pursuant to Chapter 5 (commencing with Section 2000) of Division 2 of the Business and Professions Code.

(B) The physician is the employee's primary care physician and has previously directed the medical treatment of the employee, and who retains the employee's medical records, including his or her medical history. "Personal physician" includes a medical group, if the medical group is a single corporation or partnership composed of licensed doctors of medicine or osteopathy, which operates an integrated multispecialty medical

605

group providing comprehensive medical services predominantly for nonoccupational illnesses and injuries.

(C) The physician agrees to be predesignated.

(3) If the employer provides nonoccupational health care pursuant to Chapter 2.2 (commencing with Section 1340) of Division 2 of the Health and Safety Code, and the employer is notified pursuant to paragraph (1), all medical treatment, utilization review of medical treatment, access to medical treatment, and other medical treatment issues shall be governed by Chapter 2.2 (commencing with Section 1340) of Division 2 of the Health and Safety Code. Disputes regarding the provision of medical treatment shall be resolved pursuant to Article 5.55 (commencing with Section 1374.30) of Chapter 2.2 of Division 2 of the Health and Safety Code.

(4) If the employer provides nonoccupational health care, as described in Section 4616.7, all medical treatment, utilization review of medical treatment, access to medical treatment, and other medical treatment issues shall be governed by the applicable provisions of the Insurance Code.

(5) The insurer may require prior authorization of any nonemergency treatment or diagnostic service and may conduct reasonably necessary utilization review pursuant to Section 4610.

(6) An employee shall be entitled to all medically appropriate referrals by the personal physician to other physicians or medical providers within the nonoccupational health care plan. An employee shall be entitled to treatment by physicians or other medical providers outside of the nonoccupational health care plan pursuant to standards established in Article 5 (commencing with Section 1367) of Chapter 2.2 of Division 2 of the Health and Safety Code.

(7) The division shall conduct an evaluation of this program and present its findings to the Governor and the Legislature on or before December 31, 2008.

(8) This subdivision shall remain in effect only until December 31, 2009, and as of that date is repealed, unless a later enacted statute that is enacted before December 31, 2009, deletes or extends that date.

(e)(1) When at the request of the employer, the employer's insurer, the administrative director, the appeals board, or a workers' compensation administrative law judge, the employee submits to examination by a physician, he or she shall be entitled to receive, in addition to all other benefits herein provided, all reasonable expenses of transportation, meals, and lodging incident to reporting for the examination, together with one day of temporary disability indemnity for each day of wages lost in submitting to the examination.

(2) Regardless of the date of injury, "reasonable expenses of transportation" includes mileage fees from the employee's home to the place of the examination and back at the rate of twenty-one cents ($0.21) a mile or the mileage rate adopted by the Director of the Department of Personnel Administration pursuant to Section 19820 of

the Government Code, whichever is higher, plus any bridge tolls. The mileage and tolls shall be paid to the employee at the time he or she is given notification of the time and place of the examination.

(f) When at the request of the employer, the employer's insurer, the administrative director, the appeals board, or a workers' compensation administrative law judge, an employee submits to examination by a physician and the employee does not proficiently speak or understand the English language, he or she shall be entitled to the services of a qualified interpreter in accordance with conditions and a fee schedule prescribed by the administrative director. These services shall be provided by the employer. For purposes of this section, "qualified interpreter" means a language interpreter certified, or deemed certified, pursuant to Article 8 (commencing with Section 11435.05) of Chapter 4.5 of Part 1 of Division 3 of Title 2 of, or Section 68566 of, the Government Code.

(g) This section shall remain in effect only until January 1, 2010, and as of that date is repealed, unless a later enacted statute, that is enacted before January 1, 2010, deletes or extends that date. *(Added by Stats.1981, c. 1150, p. 4591, § 7, operative Jan. 1, 1984. Amended by Stats.1983, c. 1284, § 4, operative July 1, 1984; Stats.1984, c. 596, § 2, operative July 1, 1984; Stats.1989, c. 892, § 31.5; Stats.1990, c. 110 (S.B.1379), § 1; Stats.1990, c. 1550 (A.B.2910), § 30; Stats.1993, c. 121 (A.B.110), § 38, eff. July 16, 1993; Stats.1994, c. 477 (A.B.3077), § 1; Stats.1995, c. 938 (S.B.523), § 74, operative July 1, 1997; Stats.1998, c. 440 (A.B.204), § 2; Stats.2004, c. 34 (S.B. 899), § 23, eff. April 19, 2004; Stats.2006, c. 819 (A.B. 2068), § 2; Stats.2009, c. 565 (S.B.186), § 1.)*

Operative Effect

Section 47 of Stats.2004, c. 34 (S.B.899) provides that "[t]he amendment, addition, or repeal of, any provision of law made by this act shall apply prospectively from the date of enactment of this act, regardless of the date of injury, unless otherwise specified, but shall not constitute good cause to reopen or rescind, alter, or amend any existing order, decision, or award of the Workers' Compensation Appeals Board."

Repeal

For repeal of this section, see its terms.

§ 4600.   Provision of treatment by employer; rights of employee

Section operative Jan. 1, 2010. See, also, section operative until Jan. 1, 2010.

(a) Medical, surgical, chiropractic, acupuncture, and hospital treatment, including nursing, medicines, medical and surgical supplies, crutches, and apparatuses, including orthotic and prosthetic devices and services, that is reasonably required to cure or relieve the injured worker from the effects of his or her injury shall be provided by the employer. In the case of his or her neglect or refusal reasonably to do so, the employer is liable for the reasonable expense incurred by or on behalf of the employee in providing treatment.

(b) As used in this division and notwithstanding any other provision of law, medical treatment that is reasonably required to cure or relieve the injured worker from the effects of his or her injury means treatment that is based upon the guidelines adopted by the administrative director pursuant to Section 5307.27 or, prior to the adoption of those guidelines, the updated American College of Occupational and Environmental Medicine's Occupational Medicine Practice Guidelines.

(c) Unless the employer or the employer's insurer has established a medical provider network as provided for in Section 4616, after 30 days from the date the injury is reported, the employee may be treated by a physician of his or her own choice or at a facility of his or her own choice within a reasonable geographic area.

(d)(1) If an employee has notified his or her employer in writing prior to the date of injury that he or she has a personal physician, the employee shall have the right to be treated by that physician from the date of injury if either of the following conditions exist:

(A) The employer provides nonoccupational group health coverage in a health care service plan, licensed pursuant to Chapter 2.2 (commencing with Section 1340) of Division 2 of the Health and Safety Code.

(B) The employer provides nonoccupational health coverage in a group health plan or a group health insurance policy as described in Section 4616.7.

(2) For purposes of paragraph (1), a personal physician shall meet all of the following conditions:

(A) Be the employee's regular physician and surgeon, licensed pursuant to Chapter 5 (commencing with Section 2000) of Division 2 of the Business and Professions Code.

(B) Be the employee's primary care physician and has previously directed the medical treatment of the employee, and who retains the employee's medical records, including his or her medical history. "Personal physician" includes a medical group, if the medical group is a single corporation or partnership composed of licensed doctors of medicine or osteopathy, which operates an integrated multispecialty medical group providing comprehensive medical services predominantly for nonoccupational illnesses and injuries.

(C) The physician agrees to be predesignated.

(3) If the employer provides nonoccupational health care pursuant to Chapter 2.2 (commencing with Section 1340) of Division 2 of the Health and Safety Code, and the employer is notified pursuant to paragraph (1), all medical treatment, utilization review of medical treatment, access to medical treatment, and other medical treatment issues shall be governed by Chapter 2.2 (commencing with Section 1340) of Division 2 of the Health and Safety Code. Disputes regarding the provision of medical treatment shall be resolved pursuant to Article

5.55 (commencing with Section 1374.30) of Chapter 2.2 of Division 2 of the Health and Safety Code.

(4) If the employer provides nonoccupational health care, as described in Section 4616.7, all medical treatment, utilization review of medical treatment, access to medical treatment, and other medical treatment issues shall be governed by the applicable provisions of the Insurance Code.

(5) The insurer may require prior authorization of any nonemergency treatment or diagnostic service and may conduct reasonably necessary utilization review pursuant to Section 4610.

(6) An employee shall be entitled to all medically appropriate referrals by the personal physician to other physicians or medical providers within the nonoccupational health care plan. An employee shall be entitled to treatment by physicians or other medical providers outside of the nonoccupational health care plan pursuant to standards established in Article 5 (commencing with Section 1367) of Chapter 2.2 of Division 2 of the Health and Safety Code.

(e)(1) When at the request of the employer, the employer's insurer, the administrative director, the appeals board, or a workers' compensation administrative law judge, the employee submits to examination by a physician, he or she shall be entitled to receive, in addition to all other benefits herein provided, all reasonable expenses of transportation, meals, and lodging incident to reporting for the examination, together with one day of temporary disability indemnity for each day of wages lost in submitting to the examination.

(2) Regardless of the date of injury, "reasonable expenses of transportation" includes mileage fees from the employee's home to the place of the examination and back at the rate of twenty-one cents ($0.21) a mile or the mileage rate adopted by the Director of the Department of Personnel Administration pursuant to Section 19820 of the Government Code, whichever is higher, plus any bridge tolls. The mileage and tolls shall be paid to the employee at the time he or she is given notification of the time and place of the examination.

(f) When at the request of the employer, the employer's insurer, the administrative director, the appeals board, or a workers' compensation administrative law judge, an employee submits to examination by a physician and the employee does not proficiently speak or understand the English language, he or she shall be entitled to the services of a qualified interpreter in accordance with conditions and a fee schedule prescribed by the administrative director. These services shall be provided by the employer. For purposes of this section, "qualified interpreter" means a language interpreter certified, or deemed certified, pursuant to Article 8 (commencing with Section 11435.05) of Chapter 4.5 of Part 1 of Division 3 of Title 2 of, or Section 68566 of, the Government Code.

(g) This section shall become operative on January 1, 2010. *(Added by Stats.2009, c. 565 (S.B.186), § 2, operative Jan. 1, 2010.)*

§ 4600.1. Generic drug equivalents

(a) Subject to subdivision (b), any person or entity that dispenses medicines and medical supplies, as required by Section 4600, shall dispense the generic drug equivalent.

(b) A person or entity shall not be required to dispense a generic drug equivalent under either of the following circumstances:

(1) When a generic drug equivalent is unavailable.

(2) When the prescribing physician specifically provides in writing that a nongeneric drug must be dispensed.

(c) For purposes of this section, "dispense" has the same meaning as the definition contained in Section 4024 of the Business and Professions Code.

(d) Nothing in this section shall be construed to preclude a prescribing physician, who is also the dispensing physician, from dispensing a generic drug equivalent. *(Added by Stats.2003, c. 639 (S.B.228), § 24.)*

§ 4600.2. Medicines and medical supplies required by this article; injured employees subject to specified contracts; period of time for which medicines and medical supplies are to be provided; adoption of standards

(a) Notwithstanding Section 4600, when a self-insured employer, group of self-insured employers, insurer of an employer, or group of insurers contracts with a pharmacy, group of pharmacies, or pharmacy benefit network to provide medicines and medical supplies required by this article to be provided to injured employees, those injured employees that are subject to the contract shall be provided medicines and medical supplies in the manner prescribed in the contract for as long as medicines or medical supplies are reasonably required to cure or relieve the injured employee from the effects of the injury.

(b) Nothing in this section shall affect the ability of employee-selected physicians to continue to prescribe and have the employer provide medicines and medical supplies that the physicians deem reasonably required to cure or relieve the injured employee from the effects of the injury.

(c) Each contract described in subdivision (a) shall comply with standards adopted by the administrative director. In adopting those standards, the administrative director shall seek to reduce pharmaceutical costs and may consult any relevant studies or practices in other states. The standards shall provide for access to a pharmacy within a reasonable geographic distance from an injured employee's residence. *(Added by Stats.2002, c. 6 (A.B.749), § 60.)*

608

§ 4600.3. Contracts with health care organizations; notice to employees; employee's choice of health care provider; collective bargaining agreements

(a)(1) Notwithstanding Section 4600, when a self-insured employer, group of self-insured employers, or the insurer of an employer contracts with a health care organization certified pursuant to Section 4600. 5 for health care services required by this article to be provided to injured employees, those employees who are subject to the contract shall receive medical services in the manner prescribed in the contract, providing that the employee may choose to be treated by a personal physician, personal chiropractor, or personal acupuncturist that he or she has designated prior to the injury, in which case the employee shall not be treated by the health care organization. Every employee shall be given an affirmative choice at the time of employment and at least annually thereafter to designate or change the designation of a health care organization or a personal physician, personal chiropractor, or personal acupuncturist. The choice shall be memorialized in writing and maintained in the employee's personnel records. The employee who has designated a personal physician, personal chiropractor, or personal acupuncturist may change their designated caregiver at any time prior to the injury. Any employee who fails to designate a personal physician, personal chiropractor, or personal acupuncturist shall be treated by the health care organization selected by the employer. If the health care organization offered by the employer is the workers' compensation insurer that covers the employee or is an entity that controls or is controlled by that insurer, as defined by Section 1215 of the Insurance Code, this information shall be included in the notice of contract with a health care organization.

(2) Each contract described in paragraph (1) shall comply with the certification standards provided in Section 4600.5, and shall provide all medical, surgical, chiropractic, acupuncture, and hospital treatment, including nursing, medicines, medical and surgical supplies, crutches, and apparatus, including artificial members, that is reasonably required to cure or relieve the effects of the injury, as required by this division, without any payment by the employee of deductibles, copayments, or any share of the premium. However, an employee may receive immediate emergency medical treatment that is compensable from a medical service or health care provider who is not a member of the health care organization.

(3) Insured employers, a group of self-insured employers, or self-insured employers who contract with a health care organization for medical services shall give notice to employees of eligible medical service providers and any other information regarding the contract and manner of receiving medical services as the administrative director may prescribe. Employees shall be duly notified that if they choose to receive care from the health care organization they must receive treatment for all occupational injuries and illnesses as prescribed by this section.

(b) Notwithstanding subdivision (a), no employer which is required to bargain with an exclusive or certified bargaining agent which represents employees of the employer in accordance with state or federal employer-employee relations law shall contract with a health care organization for purposes of Section 4600.5 with regard to employees whom the bargaining agent is recognized or certified to represent for collective bargaining purposes pursuant to state or federal employer-employee relations law unless authorized to do so by mutual agreement between the bargaining agent and the employer. If the collective bargaining agreement is subject to the National Labor Relations Act, the employer may contract with a health care organization for purposes of Section 4600.5 at any time when the employer and bargaining agent have bargained to impasse to the extent required by federal law.

(c)(1) When an employee is not receiving or is not eligible to receive health care coverage for nonoccupational injuries or illnesses provided by the employer, if 90 days from the date the injury is reported the employee who has been receiving treatment from a health care organization or his or her physician, chiropractor, acupuncturist, or other agent notifies his or her employer in writing that he or she desires to stop treatment by the health care organization, he or she shall have the right to be treated by a physician, chiropractor, or acupuncturist or at a facility of his or her own choosing within a reasonable geographic area.

(2) When an employee is receiving or is eligible to receive health care coverage for nonoccupational injuries or illnesses provided by the employer, and has agreed to receive care for occupational injuries and illnesses from a health care organization provided by the employer, the employee may be treated for occupational injuries and diseases by a physician, chiropractor, or acupuncturist of his or her own choice or at a facility of his or her own choice within a reasonable geographic area if the employee or his or her physician, chiropractor, acupuncturist, or other agent notifies his or her employer in writing only after 180 days from the date the injury was reported, or upon the date of contract renewal or open enrollment of the health care organization, whichever occurs first, but in no case until 90 days from the date the injury was reported.

(3) For purposes of this subdivision, an employer shall be deemed to provide health care coverage for nonoccupational injuries and illnesses if the employer pays more than one-half the costs of the coverage, or if the plan is established pursuant to collective bargaining.

(d) An employee and employer may agree to other forms of therapy pursuant to Section 3209.7.

(e) An employee enrolled in a health care organization shall have the right to no less than one change of physician on request, and shall be given a choice of physicians affiliated with the health care organization. The health care organization shall provide the employee a choice of participating physicians within five days of receiving a request. In addition, the employee shall have the right to a second opinion from a participating physician on a matter pertaining to diagnosis or treatment from a participating physician.

(f) Nothing in this section or Section 4600.5 shall be construed to prohibit a self-insured employer, a group of self-insured employers, or insurer from engaging in any activities permitted by Section 4600.

(g) Notwithstanding subdivision (c), in the event that the employer, group of employers, or the employer's workers' compensation insurer no longer contracts with the health care organization that has been treating an injured employee, the employee may continue treatment provided or arranged by the health care organization. If the employee does not choose to continue treatment by the health care organization, the employer may control the employee's treatment for 30 days from the date the injury was reported. After that period, the employee may be treated by a physician of his or her own choice or at a facility of his or her own choice within a reasonable geographic area. *(Added by Stats.1993, c. 121 (A.B.110), § 39, eff. July 16, 1993. Amended by Stats.1993, c. 1242 (S.B.223), § 32; Stats.1998, c. 485 (A.B.2803), § 125; Stats.1998, c. 440 (A.B.204), § 3; Stats.2002, c. 6 (A.B. 749), § 61.)*

§ 4600.35. License requirements for specified reimbursements

Any entity seeking to reimburse health care providers for health care services rendered to injured workers on a capitated, or per person per month basis, shall be licensed pursuant to the Knox Keene Health Care Service Plan Act of 1975 (Chapter 2.2 (commencing with Section 1340) of Division 2 of the Health and Safety Code). *(Added by Stats.2002, c. 6 (A.B.749), § 61.5.)*

§ 4600.4. Normal business day

(a) A workers' compensation insurer, third-party administrator, or other entity that requires, or pursuant to regulation requires, a treating physician to obtain either utilization review or prior authorization in order to diagnose or treat injuries or diseases compensable under this article, shall ensure the availability of those services from 9 a.m. to 5:30 p.m. Pacific coast time of each normal business day.

(b) For purposes of this section "normal business day" means a business day as defined in Section 9 of the Civil Code. *(Added by Stats.1999, c. 124 (A.B.775), § 1.)*

§ 4600.5. Certification as health care organization; chiropractic care; acupuncture care

(a) Any health care service plan licensed pursuant to the Knox–Keene Health Care Service Plan Act, a disability insurer licensed by the Department of Insurance, or any entity, including, but not limited to, workers' compensation insurers and third-party administrators authorized by the administrative director under subdivision (e), may make written application to the administrative director to

609

become certified as a health care organization to provide health care to injured employees for injuries and diseases compensable under this article.

(b) Each application for certification shall be accompanied by a reasonable fee prescribed by the administrative director, sufficient to cover the actual cost of processing the application. A certificate is valid for the period that the director may prescribe unless sooner revoked or suspended.

(c) If the health care organization is a health care service plan licensed pursuant to the Knox–Keene Health Care Service Plan Act, and has provided the Managed Care Unit of the Division of Workers' Compensation with the necessary documentation to comply with this subdivision, that organization shall be deemed to be a health care organization able to provide health care pursuant to Section 4600.3, without further application duplicating the documentation already filed with the Department of Managed Health Care. These plans shall be required to remain in good standing with the Department of Managed Health Care, and shall meet the following additional requirements:

(1) Proposes to provide all medical and health care services that may be required by this article.

(2) Provides a program involving cooperative efforts by the employees, the employer, and the health plan to promote workplace health and safety, consultative and other services, and early return to work for injured employees.

(3) Proposes a timely and accurate method to meet the requirements set forth by the administrative director for all carriers of workers' compensation coverage to report necessary information regarding medical and health care service cost and utilization, rates of return to work, average time in medical treatment, and other measures as determined by the administrative director to enable the director to determine the effectiveness of the plan.

(4) Agrees to provide the administrative director with information, reports, and records prepared and submitted to the Department of Managed Health Care in compliance with the Knox–Keene Health Care Service Plan Act, relating to financial solvency, provider accessibility, peer review, utilization review, and quality assurance, upon request, if the administrative director determines the information is necessary to verify that the plan is providing medical treatment to injured employees in compliance with the requirements of this code.

Disclosure of peer review proceedings and records to the administrative director shall not alter the status of the proceedings or records as privileged and confidential communications pursuant to Sections 1370 and 1370.1 of the Health and Safety Code.

(5) Demonstrates the capability to provide occupational medicine and related disciplines.

(6) Complies with any other requirement the administrative director determines is necessary to provide medical services to injured employees consistent with the intent of this article, including, but not limited to, a written patient grievance policy.

(d) If the health care organization is a disability insurer licensed by the Department of Insurance, and is in compliance with subdivision (d) of Sections 10133 and 10133.5 of the Insurance Code, the administrative director shall certify the organization to provide health care pursuant to Section 4600.3 if the director finds that the plan is in good standing with the Department of Insurance and meets the following additional requirements:

(1) Proposes to provide all medical and health care services that may be required by this article.

(2) Provides a program involving cooperative efforts by the employees, the employer, and the health plan to promote workplace health and safety, consultative and other services, and early return to work for injured employees.

(3) Proposes a timely and accurate method to meet the requirements set forth by the administrative director for all carriers of workers' compensation coverage to report necessary information regarding medical and health care service cost and utilization, rates of return to work, average time in medical treatment, and other measures as determined by the administrative director to enable the director to determine the effectiveness of the plan.

(4) Agrees to provide the administrative director with information, reports, and records prepared and submitted to the Department of Insurance in compliance with the Insurance Code relating to financial solvency, provider accessibility, peer review, utilization review, and quality assurance, upon request, if the administrative director determines the information is necessary to verify that the plan is providing medical treatment to injured employees consistent with the intent of this article.

Disclosure of peer review proceedings and records to the administrative director shall not alter the status of the proceedings or records as privileged and confidential communications pursuant to subdivision (d) of Section 10133 of the Insurance Code.

(5) Demonstrates the capability to provide occupational medicine and related disciplines.

(6) Complies with any other requirement the administrative director determines is necessary to provide medical services to injured employees consistent with the intent of this article, including, but not limited to, a written patient grievance policy.

(e) If the health care organization is a workers' compensation insurer, third-party administrator, or any other entity that the administrative director determines meets the requirements of Section 4600.6, the administrative director shall certify the organization to provide health care pursuant to Section 4600.3 if the director finds that it meets the following additional requirements:

(1) Proposes to provide all medical and health care services that may be required by this article.

(2) Provides a program involving cooperative efforts by the employees, the employer, and the health plan to promote workplace health and safety, consultative and other services, and early return to work for injured employees.

(3) Proposes a timely and accurate method to meet the requirements set forth by the administrative director for all carriers of workers' compensation coverage to report necessary information regarding medical and health care service cost and utilization, rates of return to work, average time in medical treatment, and other measures as determined by the administrative director to enable the director to determine the effectiveness of the plan.

(4) Agrees to provide the administrative director with information, reports, and records relating to provider accessibility, peer review, utilization review, quality assurance, advertising, disclosure, medical and financial audits, and grievance systems, upon request, if the administrative director determines the information is necessary to verify that the plan is providing medical treatment to injured employees consistent with the intent of this article.

Disclosure of peer review proceedings and records to the administrative director shall not alter the status of the proceedings or records as privileged and confidential communications pursuant to subdivision (d) of Section 10133 of the Insurance Code.

(5) Demonstrates the capability to provide occupational medicine and related disciplines.

(6) Complies with any other requirement the administrative director determines is necessary to provide medical services to injured employees consistent with the intent of this article, including, but not limited to, a written patient grievance policy.

(7) Complies with the following requirements:

(A) An organization certified by the administrative director under this subdivision may not provide or undertake to arrange for the provision of health care to employees, or to pay for or to reimburse any part of the cost of that health care in return for a prepaid or periodic charge paid by or on behalf of those employees.

(B) Every organization certified under this subdivision shall operate on a fee-for-service basis. As used in this section, fee for service refers to the situation where the amount of reimbursement paid by the employer to the organization or providers of health care is determined by the amount and type of health care rendered by the organization or provider of health care.

(C) An organization certified under this subdivision is prohibited from assuming risk.

(f)(1) A workers' compensation health care provider organization authorized by the Department of Corporations on December 31, 1997, shall be eligible for certification as a health care organization under subdivision (e).

(2) An entity that had, on December 31, 1997, submitted an application with the Commissioner of Corporations under Part 3.2 (commencing with Section 5150)

shall be considered an applicant for certification under subdivision (e) and shall be entitled to priority in consideration of its application. The Commissioner of Corporations shall provide complete files for all pending applications to the administrative director on or before January 31, 1998.

(g) The provisions of this section shall not affect the confidentiality or admission in evidence of a claimant's medical treatment records.

(h) Charges for services arranged for or provided by health care service plans certified by this section and that are paid on a per-enrollee-periodic-charge basis shall not be subject to the schedules adopted by the administrative director pursuant to Section 5307.1.

(i) Nothing in this section shall be construed to expand or constrict any requirements imposed by law on a health care service plan or insurer when operating as other than a health care organization pursuant to this section.

(j) In consultation with interested parties, including the Department of Corporations and the Department of Insurance, the administrative director shall adopt rules necessary to carry out this section.

(k) The administrative director shall refuse to certify or may revoke or suspend the certification of any health care organization under this section if the director finds that:

(1) The plan for providing medical treatment fails to meet the requirements of this section.

(2) A health care service plan licensed by the Department of Managed Health Care, a workers' compensation health care provider organization authorized by the Department of Corporations, or a carrier licensed by the Department of Insurance is not in good standing with its licensing agency.

(3) Services under the plan are not being provided in accordance with the terms of a certified plan.

(l)(1) When an injured employee requests chiropractic treatment for work-related injuries, the health care organization shall provide the injured worker with access to the services of a chiropractor pursuant to guidelines for chiropractic care established by paragraph (2). Within five working days of the employee's request to see a chiropractor, the health care organization and any person or entity who directs the kind or manner of health care services for the plan shall refer an injured employee to an affiliated chiropractor for work-related injuries that are within the guidelines for chiropractic care established by paragraph (2). Chiropractic care rendered in accordance with guidelines for chiropractic care established pursuant to paragraph (2) shall be provided by duly licensed chiropractors affiliated with the plan.

(2) The health care organization shall establish guidelines for chiropractic care in consultation with affiliated chiropractors who are participants in the health care organization's utilization review process for chiropractic care, which may include qualified medical evaluators

611

knowledgeable in the treatment of chiropractic conditions. The guidelines for chiropractic care shall, at a minimum, explicitly require the referral of any injured employee who so requests to an affiliated chiropractor for the evaluation or treatment, or both, of neuromusculoskeletal conditions.

(3) Whenever a dispute concerning the appropriateness or necessity of chiropractic care for work-related injuries arises, the dispute shall be resolved by the health care organization's utilization review process for chiropractic care in accordance with the health care organization's guidelines for chiropractic care established by paragraph (2).

Chiropractic utilization review for work-related injuries shall be conducted in accordance with the health care organization's approved quality assurance standards and utilization review process for chiropractic care. Chiropractors affiliated with the plan shall have access to the health care organization's provider appeals process and, in the case of chiropractic care for work-related injuries, the review shall include review by a chiropractor affiliated with the health care organization, as determined by the health care organization.

(4) The health care organization shall inform employees of the procedures for processing and resolving grievances, including those related to chiropractic care, including the location and telephone number where grievances may be submitted.

(5) All guidelines for chiropractic care and utilization review shall be consistent with the standards of this code that require care to cure or relieve the effects of the industrial injury.

(m) Individually identifiable medical information on patients submitted to the division shall not be subject to the California Public Records Act (Chapter 3.5 (commencing with Section 6250) of Division 7 of Title 1 of the Government Code).

(n)(1) When an injured employee requests acupuncture treatment for work-related injuries, the health care organization shall provide the injured worker with access to the services of an acupuncturist pursuant to guidelines for acupuncture care established by paragraph (2). Within five working days of the employee's request to see an acupuncturist, the health care organization and any person or entity who directs the kind or manner of health care services for the plan shall refer an injured employee to an affiliated acupuncturist for work-related injuries that are within the guidelines for acupuncture care established by paragraph (2). Acupuncture care rendered in accordance with guidelines for acupuncture care established pursuant to paragraph (2) shall be provided by duly licensed acupuncturists affiliated with the plan.

(2) The health care organization shall establish guidelines for acupuncture care in consultation with affiliated acupuncturists who are participants in the health care organization's utilization review process for acupuncture care, which may include qualified medical evaluators.

The guidelines for acupuncture care shall, at a minimum, explicitly require the referral of any injured employee who so requests to an affiliated acupuncturist for the evaluation or treatment, or both, of neuromusculoskeletal conditions.

(3) Whenever a dispute concerning the appropriateness or necessity of acupuncture care for work-related injuries arises, the dispute shall be resolved by the health care organization's utilization review process for acupuncture care in accordance with the health care organization's guidelines for acupuncture care established by paragraph (2).

Acupuncture utilization review for work-related injuries shall be conducted in accordance with the health care organization's approved quality assurance standards and utilization review process for acupuncture care. Acupuncturists affiliated with the plan shall have access to the health care organization's provider appeals process and, in the case of acupuncture care for work-related injuries, the review shall include review by an acupuncturist affiliated with the health care organization, as determined by the health care organization.

(4) The health care organization shall inform employees of the procedures for processing and resolving grievances, including those related to acupuncture care, including the location and telephone number where grievances may be submitted.

(5) All guidelines for acupuncture care and utilization review shall be consistent with the standards of this code that require care to cure or relieve the effects of the industrial injury. *(Added by Stats.1993, c. 121 (A.B.110), § 40, eff. July 16, 1993. Amended by Stats.1993, c. 1242 (S.B.223), § 33; Stats.1994, c. 285 (A.B.2736), § 1; Stats. 1994, c. 1118 (S.B.1768), § 6; Stats.1997, c. 346 (S.B. 1063), § 1; Stats.1998, c. 440 (A.B.204), § 4; Stats.1999, c. 525 (A.B.78), § 190; Stats.2000, c. 857 (A.B.2903), § 77; Stats.2002, c. 6 (A.B.749), § 61.7; Stats.2002, c. 866 (A.B.486), § 10.)*

§ 4600.6. Applicants for certification as health care organizations under § 4600.5; rules and procedures

Any workers' compensation insurer, third-party administrator, or other entity seeking certification as a health care organization under subdivision (e) of Section 4600.5 shall be subject to the following rules and procedures:

(a) Each application for authorization as an organization under subdivision (e) of Section 4600.5 shall be verified by an authorized representative of the applicant and shall be in a form prescribed by the administrative director. The application shall be accompanied by the prescribed fee and shall set forth or be accompanied by each and all of the following:

(1) The basic organizational documents of the applicant, such as the articles of incorporation, articles of association, partnership agreement, trust agreement, or other applicable documents and all amendments thereto.

(2) A copy of the bylaws, rules, and regulations, or similar documents regulating the conduct of the internal affairs of the applicant.

(3) A list of the names, addresses, and official positions of the persons who are to be responsible for the conduct of the affairs of the applicant, which shall include, among others, all members of the board of directors, board of trustees, executive committee, or other governing board or committee, the principal officers, each shareholder with over 5 percent interest in the case of a corporation, and all partners or members in the case of a partnership or association, and each person who has loaned funds to the applicant for the operation of its business.

(4) A copy of any contract made, or to be made, between the applicant and any provider of health care, or persons listed in paragraph (3), or any other person or organization agreeing to perform an administrative function or service for the plan. The administrative director by rule may identify contracts excluded from this requirement and make provision for the submission of form contracts. The payment rendered or to be rendered to the provider of health care services shall be deemed confidential information that shall not be divulged by the administrative director, except that the payment may be disclosed and become a public record in any legislative, administrative, or judicial proceeding or inquiry. The organization shall also submit the name and address of each provider employed by, or contracting with, the organization, together with his or her license number.

(5) A statement describing the organization, its method of providing for health services, and its physical facilities. If applicable, this statement shall include the health care delivery capabilities of the organization, including the number of full-time and part-time physicians under Section 3209.3, the numbers and types of licensed or state-certified health care support staff, the number of hospital beds contracted for, and the arrangements and the methods by which health care will be provided, as defined by the administrative director under Sections 4600.3 and 4600.5.

(6) A copy of the disclosure forms or materials that are to be issued to employees.

(7) A copy of the form of the contract that is to be issued to any employer, insurer of an employer, or a group of self-insured employers.

(8) Financial statements accompanied by a report, certificate, or opinion of an independent certified public accountant. However, the financial statements from public entities or political subdivisions of the state need not include a report, certificate, or opinion by an independent certified public accountant if the financial statement complies with any requirements that may be established by regulation of the administrative director.

(9) A description of the proposed method of marketing the organization and a copy of any contract made with any person to solicit on behalf of the organization or a copy of the form of agreement used and a list of the contracting parties.

(10) A statement describing the service area or areas to be served, including the service location for each provider rendering professional services on behalf of the organization and the location of any other organization facilities where required by the administrative director.

(11) A description of organization grievance procedures to be utilized as required by this part, and a copy of the form specified by paragraph (3) of subdivision (j).

(12) A description of the procedures and programs for internal review of the quality of health care pursuant to the requirements set forth in this part.

(13) Evidence of adequate insurance coverage or self-insurance to respond to claims for damages arising out of the furnishing of workers' compensation health care.

(14) Evidence of adequate insurance coverage or self-insurance to protect against losses of facilities where required by the administrative director.

(15) Evidence of adequate workers' compensation coverage to protect against claims arising out of work-related injuries that might be brought by the employees and staff of an organization against the organization.

(16) Evidence of fidelity bonds in such amount as the administrative director prescribes by regulation.

(17) Other information that the administrative director may reasonably require.

(b)(1) An organization, solicitor, solicitor firm, or representative may not use or permit the use of any advertising or solicitation that is untrue or misleading, or any form of disclosure that is deceptive. For purposes of this chapter:

(A) A written or printed statement or item of information shall be deemed untrue if it does not conform to fact in any respect that is or may be significant to an employer or employee, or potential employer or employee.

(B) A written or printed statement or item of information shall be deemed misleading whether or not it may be literally true, if, in the total context in which the statement is made or the item of information is communicated, the statement or item of information may be understood by a person not possessing special knowledge regarding health care coverage, as indicating any benefit or advantage, or the absence of any exclusion, limitation, or disadvantage of possible significance to an employer or employee, or potential employer or employee.

(C) A disclosure form shall be deemed to be deceptive if the disclosure form taken as a whole and with consideration given to typography and format, as well as language, shall be such as to cause a reasonable person, not possessing special knowledge of workers' compensation health care, and the disclosure form therefor, to expect benefits, service charges, or other advantages that the disclosure form does not provide or that the organization issuing that disclosure form does not regularly make available to employees.

(2) An organization, solicitor, or representative may not use or permit the use of any verbal statement that is untrue, misleading, or deceptive or make any representations about health care offered by the organization or its cost that does not conform to fact. All verbal statements are to be held to the same standards as those for printed matter provided in paragraph (1).

(c) It is unlawful for any person, including an organization, subject to this part, to represent or imply in any manner that the person or organization has been sponsored, recommended, or approved, or that the person's or organization's abilities or qualifications have in any respect been passed upon, by the administrative director.

(d)(1) An organization may not publish or distribute, or allow to be published or distributed on its behalf, any advertisement unless (A) a true copy thereof has first been filed with the administrative director, at least 30 days prior to any such use, or any shorter period as the administrative director by rule or order may allow, and (B) the administrative director by notice has not found the advertisement, wholly or in part, to be untrue, misleading, deceptive, or otherwise not in compliance with this part or the rules thereunder, and specified the deficiencies, within the 30 days or any shorter time as the administrative director by rule or order may allow.

(2) If the administrative director finds that any advertisement of an organization has materially failed to comply with this part or the rules thereunder, the administrative director may, by order, require the organization to publish in the same or similar medium, an approved correction or retraction of any untrue, misleading, or deceptive statement contained in the advertising.

(3) The administrative director by rule or order may classify organizations and advertisements and exempt certain classes, wholly or in part, either unconditionally or upon specified terms and conditions or for specified periods, from the application of subdivision (a).

(e)(1) The administrative director shall require the use by each organization of disclosure forms or materials containing any information regarding the health care and terms of the workers' compensation health care contract that the administrative director may require, so as to afford the public, employers, and employees with a full and fair disclosure of the provisions of the contract in readily understood language and in a clearly organized manner. The administrative director may require that the materials be presented in a reasonably uniform manner so as to facilitate comparisons between contracts of the same or other types of organizations. The disclosure form shall describe the health care that is required by the administrative director under Sections 4600.3 and 4600.5, and shall provide that all information be in concise and specific terms, relative to the contract, together with any additional information as may be required by the administrative director, in connection with the organization or contract.

(2) All organizations, solicitors, and representatives of a workers' compensation health care provider organiza-

tion shall, when presenting any contract for examination or sale to a prospective employee, provide the employee with a properly completed disclosure form, as prescribed by the administrative director pursuant to this section for each contract so examined or sold.

(3) In addition to the other disclosures required by this section, every organization and any agent or employee of the organization shall, when representing an organization for examination or sale to any individual purchaser or the representative of a group consisting of 25 or fewer individuals, disclose in writing the ratio of premium cost to health care paid for contracts with individuals and with groups of the same or similar size for the organization's preceding fiscal year. An organization may report that information by geographic area, provided the organization identifies the geographic area and reports information applicable to that geographic area.

(4) Where the administrative director finds it necessary in the interest of full and fair disclosure, all advertising and other consumer information disseminated by an organization for the purpose of influencing persons to become members of an organization shall contain any supplemental disclosure information that the administrative director may require.

(f) When the administrative director finds it necessary in the interest of full and fair disclosure, all advertising and other consumer information disseminated by an organization for the purpose of influencing persons to become members of an organization shall contain any supplemental disclosure information that the administrative director may require.

(g)(1) An organization may not refuse to enter into any contract, or may not cancel or decline to renew or reinstate any contract, because of the age or any characteristic listed or defined in subdivision (b) or (e) of Section 51 of the Civil Code of any contracting party, prospective contracting party, or person reasonably expected to benefit from that contract as an employee or otherwise.

(2) The terms of any contract shall not be modified, and the benefits or coverage of any contract shall not be subject to any limitations, exceptions, exclusions, reductions, copayments, coinsurance, deductibles, reservations, or premium, price, or charge differentials, or other modifications because of the age or any characteristic listed or defined in subdivision (b) or (e) of Section 51 of the Civil Code of any contracting party, potential contracting party, or person reasonably expected to benefit from that contract as an employee or otherwise; except that premium, price, or charge differentials because of the sex or age of any individual when based on objective, valid, and up-to-date statistical and actuarial data are not prohibited. Nothing in this section shall be construed to permit an organization to charge different rates to individual employees within the same group solely on the basis of the employee's sex.

(3) It shall be deemed a violation of subdivision (a) for any organization to utilize marital status, living arrange-

ments, occupation, gender, beneficiary designation, ZIP Codes or other territorial classification, or any combination thereof for the purpose of establishing sexual orientation. Nothing in this section shall be construed to alter in any manner the existing law prohibiting organizations from conducting tests for the presence of human immunodeficiency virus or evidence thereof.

(4) This section shall not be construed to limit the authority of the administrative director to adopt or enforce regulations prohibiting discrimination because of sex, marital status, or sexual orientation.

(h)(1) An organization may not use in its name any of the words "insurance," "casualty," "health care service plan," "health plan," "surety," "mutual," or any other words descriptive of the health plan, insurance, casualty, or surety business or use any name similar to the name or description of any health care service plan, insurance, or surety corporation doing business in this state unless that organization controls or is controlled by an entity licensed as a health care service plan or insurer pursuant to the Health and Safety Code or the Insurance Code and the organization employs a name related to that of the controlled or controlling entity.

(2) Section 2415 of the Business and Professions Code, pertaining to fictitious names, does not apply to organizations certified under this section.

(3) An organization or solicitor firm may not adopt a name style that is deceptive, or one that could cause the public to believe the organization is affiliated with or recommended by any governmental or private entity unless this affiliation or endorsement exists.

(i) Each organization shall meet the following requirements:

(1) All facilities located in this state, including, but not limited to, clinics, hospitals, and skilled nursing facilities, to be utilized by the organization shall be licensed by the State Department of Health Services, if that licensure is required by law. Facilities not located in this state shall conform to all licensing and other requirements of the jurisdiction in which they are located.

(2) All personnel employed by or under contract to the organization shall be licensed or certified by their respective board or agency, where that licensure or certification is required by law.

(3) All equipment required to be licensed or registered by law shall be so licensed or registered and the operating personnel for that equipment shall be licensed or certified as required by law.

(4) The organization shall furnish services in a manner providing continuity of care and ready referral of patients to other providers at any time as may be appropriate and consistent with good professional practice.

(5) All health care shall be readily available at reasonable times to all employees. To the extent feasible, the organization shall make all health care readily accessible to all employees.

(6) The organization shall employ and utilize allied health manpower for the furnishing of health care to the extent permitted by law and consistent with good health care practice.

(7) The organization shall have the organizational and administrative capacity to provide services to employees. The organization shall be able to demonstrate to the department that health care decisions are rendered by qualified providers, unhindered by fiscal and administrative management.

(8) All contracts with employers, insurers of employers, and self-insured employers and all contracts with providers, and other persons furnishing services, equipment, or facilities to or in connection with the workers' compensation health care organization, shall be fair, reasonable, and consistent with the objectives of this part.

(9) Each organization shall provide to employees all workers' compensation health care required by this code. The administrative director shall not determine the scope of workers' compensation health care to be offered by an organization.

(j)(1) Every organization shall establish and maintain a grievance system approved by the administrative director under which employees may submit their grievances to the organization. Each system shall provide reasonable procedures in accordance with regulations adopted by the administrative director that shall ensure adequate consideration of employee grievances and rectification when appropriate.

(2) Every organization shall inform employees upon enrollment and annually thereafter of the procedures for processing and resolving grievances. The information shall include the location and telephone number where grievances may be submitted.

(3) Every organization shall provide forms for complaints to be given to employees who wish to register written complaints. The forms used by organizations shall be approved by the administrative director in advance as to format.

(4) The organization shall keep in its files all copies of complaints, and the responses thereto, for a period of five years.

(k) Every organization shall establish procedures in accordance with regulations of the administrative director for continuously reviewing the quality of care, performance of medical personnel, utilization of services and facilities, and costs. Notwithstanding any other provision of law, there shall be no monetary liability on the part of, and no cause of action for damages shall arise against, any person who participates in quality of care or utilization reviews by peer review committees that are composed chiefly of physicians, as defined by Section 3209.3, for any act performed during the reviews if the person acts without malice, has made a reasonable effort to obtain the facts of the matter, and believes that the action taken is warranted by the facts, and neither the proceedings nor the records of the reviews shall be subject to

615

discovery, nor shall any person in attendance at the reviews be required to testify as to what transpired thereat. Disclosure of the proceedings or records to the governing body of an organization or to any person or entity designated by the organization to review activities of the committees shall not alter the status of the records or of the proceedings as privileged communications.

The above prohibition relating to discovery or testimony does not apply to the statements made by any person in attendance at a review who is a party to an action or proceeding the subject matter of which was reviewed, or to any person requesting hospital staff privileges, or in any action against an insurance carrier alleging bad faith by the carrier in refusing to accept a settlement offer within the policy limits, or to the administrative director in conducting surveys pursuant to subdivision (o).

This section shall not be construed to confer immunity from liability on any workers' compensation health care organization. In any case in which, but for the enactment of the preceding provisions of this section, a cause of action would arise against an organization, the cause of action shall exist notwithstanding the provisions of this section.

(l) Nothing in this chapter shall be construed to prevent an organization from utilizing subcommittees to participate in peer review activities, nor to prevent an organization from delegating the responsibilities required by subdivision (i) as it determines to be appropriate, to subcommittees including subcommittees composed of a majority of nonphysician health care providers licensed pursuant to the Business and Professions Code, as long as the organization controls the scope of authority delegated and may revoke all or part of this authority at any time. Persons who participate in the subcommittees shall be entitled to the same immunity from monetary liability and actions for civil damages as persons who participate in organization or provider peer review committees pursuant to subdivision (i).

(m) Every organization shall have and shall demonstrate to the administrative director that it has all of the following:

(1) Adequate provision for continuity of care.

(2) A procedure for prompt payment and denial of provider claims.

(n) Every contract between an organization and an employer or insurer of an employer, and every contract between any organization and a provider of health care, shall be in writing.

(o)(1) The administrative director shall conduct periodically an onsite medical survey of the health care delivery system of each organization. The survey shall include a review of the procedures for obtaining health care, the procedures for regulating utilization, peer review mechanisms, internal procedures for assuring quality of care, and the overall performance of the organization in providing health care and meeting the health needs of employees.

(2) The survey shall be conducted by a panel of qualified health professionals experienced in evaluating the delivery of workers' compensation health care. The administrative director shall be authorized to contract with professional organizations or outside personnel to conduct medical surveys. These organizations or personnel shall have demonstrated the ability to objectively evaluate the delivery of this health care.

(3) Surveys performed pursuant to this section shall be conducted as often as deemed necessary by the administrative director to assure the protection of employees, but not less frequently than once every three years. Nothing in this section shall be construed to require the survey team to visit each clinic, hospital, office, or facility of the organization.

(4) Nothing in this section shall be construed to require the medical survey team to review peer review proceedings and records conducted and compiled under this section or in medical records. However, the administrative director shall be authorized to require onsite review of these peer review proceedings and records or medical records where necessary to determine that quality health care is being delivered to employees. Where medical record review is authorized, the survey team shall ensure that the confidentiality of the physician-patient relationship is safeguarded in accordance with existing law and neither the survey team nor the administrative director or the administrative director's staff may be compelled to disclose this information except in accordance with the physician-patient relationship. The administrative director shall ensure that the confidentiality of the peer review proceedings and records is maintained. The disclosure of the peer review proceedings and records to the administrative director or the medical survey team shall not alter the status of the proceedings or records as privileged and confidential communications.

(5) The procedures and standards utilized by the survey team shall be made available to the organizations prior to the conducting of medical surveys.

(6) During the survey, the members of the survey team shall offer such advice and assistance to the organization as deemed appropriate.

(7) The administrative director shall notify the organization of deficiencies found by the survey team. The administrative director shall give the organization a reasonable time to correct the deficiencies, and failure on the part of the organization to comply to the administrative director's satisfaction shall constitute cause for disciplinary action against the organization.

(8) Reports of all surveys, deficiencies, and correction plans shall be open to public inspection, except that no surveys, deficiencies or correction plans shall be made public unless the organization has had an opportunity to review the survey and file a statement of response within 30 days, to be attached to the report.

(p)(1) All records, books, and papers of an organization, management company, solicitor, solicitor firm, and any provider or subcontractor providing medical or other services to an organization, management company, solicitor, or solicitor firm shall be open to inspection during normal business hours by the administrative director.

(2) To the extent feasible, all the records, books, and papers described in paragraph (1) shall be located in this state. In examining those records outside this state, the administrative director shall consider the cost to the organization, consistent with the effectiveness of the administrative director's examination, and may upon reasonable notice require that these records, books, and papers, or a specified portion thereof, be made available for examination in this state, or that a true and accurate copy of these records, books, and papers, or a specified portion thereof, be furnished to the administrative director.

(q)(1) The administrative director shall conduct an examination of the administrative affairs of any organization, and each person with whom the organization has made arrangements for administrative, or management services, as often as deemed necessary to protect the interest of employees, but not less frequently than once every five years.

(2) The expense of conducting any additional or nonroutine examinations pursuant to this section, and the expense of conducting any additional or nonroutine medical surveys pursuant to subdivision (o) shall be charged against the organization being examined or surveyed. The amount shall include the actual salaries or compensation paid to the persons making the examination or survey, the expenses incurred in the course thereof, and overhead costs in connection therewith as fixed by the administrative director. In determining the cost of examinations or surveys, the administrative director may use the estimated average hourly cost for all persons performing examinations or surveys of workers' compensation health care organizations for the fiscal year. The amount charged shall be remitted by the organization to the administrative director.

(3) Reports of all examinations shall be open to public inspection, except that no examination shall be made public, unless the organization has had an opportunity to review the examination report and file a statement or response within 30 days, to be attached to the report. *(Added by Stats.1997, c. 346 (S.B.1063), § 2. Amended by Stats.2008, c. 682 (A.B.2654), § 9.)*

§ 4600.7. Workers' Compensation Managed Care Fund; creation; schedule of fees and revenues; General Fund loan repayment plan

(a) The Workers' Compensation Managed Care Fund is hereby created in the State Treasury for the administration of Sections 4600.3 and 4600.5 by the Division of Workers' Compensation. The administrative director shall establish a schedule of fees and revenues to be charged to certified health care organizations and applicants for certification to fully fund the administration of these provisions and to repay amounts received as a loan

from the General Fund. All fees and revenues shall be deposited in the Workers' Compensation Managed Care Fund and shall be used when appropriated by the Legislature solely for the purpose of carrying out the responsibilities of the Division of Workers' Compensation under Section 4600.3 or 4600.5.

(b) On and after July 1, 1998, no funds received as a loan from the General Fund shall be used to support the administration of Sections 4600.3 and 4600.5. The loan amount shall be repaid to the General Fund by assessing a surcharge on the enrollment fee for each of the next five fiscal years. In the event the surcharge does not produce sufficient revenue over this period, the surcharge shall be adjusted to fully repay the loan over the following three fiscal years, with the final assessment calculated by dividing the balance of the loan by the enrollees at the end of the final fiscal year. *(Added by Stats.1994, c. 152 (A.B.2395), § 1, eff. July 11, 1994. Amended by Stats. 1998, c. 282 (S.B.2101), § 1.)*

§ 4601. Request for change of physician; chiropractor or acupuncturist

(a) If the employee so requests, the employer shall tender the employee one change of physician. The employee at any time may request that the employer tender this one-time change of physician. Upon request of the employee for a change of physician, the maximum amount of time permitted by law for the employer or insurance carrier to provide the employee an alternative physician or, if requested by the employee, a chiropractor, or an acupuncturist shall be five working days from the date of the request. Notwithstanding the 30-day time period specified in Section 4600, a request for a change of physician pursuant to this section may be made at any time. The employee is entitled, in any serious case, upon request, to the services of a consulting physician, chiropractor, or acupuncturist of his or her choice at the expense of the employer. The treatment shall be at the expense of the employer.

(b) If an employee requesting a change of physician pursuant to subdivision (a) has notified his or her employer in writing prior to the date of injury that he or she has a personal chiropractor, the alternative physician tendered by the employer to the employee, if the employee so requests, shall be the employee's personal chiropractor. For the purpose of this article, "personal chiropractor" means the employee's regular chiropractor licensed pursuant to Chapter 2 (commencing with Section 1000) of Division 2 of the Business and Professions Code, who has previously directed treatment of the employee, and who retains the employee's chiropractic treatment records, including his or her chiropractic history.

(c) If an employee requesting a change of physician pursuant to subdivision (a) has notified his or her employer in writing prior to the date of injury that he or she has a personal acupuncturist, the alternative physician tendered by the employer to the employee, if the employee so requests, shall be the employee's personal acupuncturist. For the purpose of this article, "personal acupuncturist" means the employee's regular acupuncturist licensed pursuant to Chapter 12 (commencing with Section 4935) of Division 2 of the Business and Professions Code, who has previously directed treatment of the employee, and who retains the employee's acupuncture treatment records, including his or her acupuncture history. *(Added by Stats.1975, c. 1259, p. 3304, § 3. Amended by Stats.1985, c. 241, § 1; Stats.1990, c. 110 (S.B.1379), § 2; Stats.1998, c. 440 (A.B.204), § 5.)*

§ 4602. Certification of competency of consulting physician

If the employee so requests, the employer shall procure certification by either the administrative director or the appeals board as the case may be of the competency, for the particular case, of the consulting or additional physicians. *(Stats.1937, c. 90, p. 282, § 4602. Amended by Stats.1965, c. 1513, p. 3578, § 86, operative Jan. 15, 1966.)*

§ 4603. Change of physician or chiropractor by employer

If the employer desires a change of physicians or chiropractor, he may petition the administrative director who, upon a showing of good cause by the employer, may order the employer to provide a panel of five physicians, or if requested by the employee, four physicians and one chiropractor competent to treat the particular case, from which the employee must select one. *(Added by Stats. 1975, c. 1259, p. 3305, § 5.)*

§ 4603.2. Notice of selection of physician; physician's report; payment for medical treatment; contested, denied or otherwise considered incomplete itemization; employer responsibility; interest or increase in compensation; itemization review

(a) Upon selecting a physician pursuant to Section 4600, the employee or physician shall forthwith notify the employer of the name and address of the physician. The physician shall submit a report to the employer within five working days from the date of the initial examination and shall submit periodic reports at intervals that may be prescribed by rules and regulations adopted by the administrative director.

(b)(1) Except as provided in subdivision (d) of Section 4603.4, or under contracts authorized under Section 5307.11, payment for medical treatment provided or authorized by the treating physician selected by the employee or designated by the employer shall be made at reasonable maximum amounts in the official medical fee schedule, pursuant to Section 5307.1, in effect on the date of service. Payments shall be made by the employer within 45 working days after receipt of each separate, itemization of medical services provided, together with any required reports and any written authorization for services that may have been received by the physician. If the itemization or a portion thereof is contested, denied, or considered incomplete, the physician shall be notified,

in writing, that the itemization is contested, denied, or considered incomplete, within 30 working days after receipt of the itemization by the employer. A notice that an itemization is incomplete shall state all additional information required to make a decision. Any properly documented list of services provided not paid at the rates then in effect under Section 5307.1 within the 45–working-day period shall be increased by 15 percent, together with interest at the same rate as judgments in civil actions retroactive to the date of receipt of the itemization, unless the employer does both of the following:

(A) Pays the provider at the rates in effect within the 45–working-day period.

(B) Advises, in the manner prescribed by the administrative director, the physician, or another provider of the items being contested, the reasons for contesting these items, and the remedies available to the physician or the other provider if he or she disagrees. In the case of an itemization that includes services provided by a hospital, outpatient surgery center, or independent diagnostic facility, advice that a request has been made for an audit of the itemization shall satisfy the requirements of this paragraph.

An employer's liability to a physician or another provider under this section for delayed payments shall not affect its liability to an employee under Section 5814 or any other provision of this division.

(2) Notwithstanding paragraph (1), if the employer is a governmental entity, payment for medical treatment provided or authorized by the treating physician selected by the employee or designated by the employer shall be made within 60 working days after receipt of each separate itemization, together with any required reports and any written authorization for services that may have been received by the physician.

(c) Any interest or increase in compensation paid by an insurer pursuant to this section shall be treated in the same manner as an increase in compensation under subdivision (d) of Section 4650 for the purposes of any classification of risks and premium rates, and any system of merit rating approved or issued pursuant to Article 2 (commencing with Section 11730) of Chapter 3 of Part 3 of Division 2 of the Insurance Code.

(d)(1) Whenever an employer or insurer employs an individual or contracts with an entity to conduct a review of an itemization submitted by a physician or medical provider, the employer or insurer shall make available to that individual or entity all documentation submitted together with that itemization by the physician or medical provider. When an individual or entity conducting a itemization review determines that additional information or documentation is necessary to review the itemization, the individual or entity shall contact the claims administrator or insurer to obtain the necessary information or documentation that was submitted by the physician or medical provider pursuant to subdivision (b).

(2) An individual or entity reviewing an itemization of service submitted by a physician or medical provider shall not alter the procedure codes listed or recommend reduction of the amount of the payment unless the documentation submitted by the physician or medical provider with the itemization of service has been reviewed by that individual or entity. If the reviewer does not recommend payment for services as itemized by the physician or medical provider, the explanation of review shall provide the physician or medical provider with a specific explanation as to why the reviewer altered the procedure code or changed other parts of the itemization and the specific deficiency in the itemization or documentation that caused the reviewer to conclude that the altered procedure code or amount recommended for payment more accurately represents the service performed.

(3) The appeals board shall have jurisdiction over disputes arising out of this subdivision pursuant to Section 5304. *(Added by Stats.1975, c. 1259, p. 3305, § 6. Amended by Stats.1984, c. 909, § 2; Stats.1990, c. 770 (S.B.241), § 3; Stats.1999, c. 124 (A.B.775), § 2; Stats. 2000, c. 1069 (S.B.1732), § 4; Stats.2001, c. 240 (A.B. 1179), § 1; Stats.2003, c. 639 (S.B.228), § 25; Stats.2004, c. 34 (S.B.899), § 24, eff. April 19, 2004; Stats.2006, c. 69 (A.B.1806), § 24, eff. July 12, 2006.)*

Operative Effect

Section 47 of Stats.2004, c. 34 (S.B.899) provides that "[t]he amendment, addition, or repeal of, any provision of law made by this act shall apply prospectively from the date of enactment of this act, regardless of the date of injury, unless otherwise specified, but shall not constitute good cause to reopen or rescind, alter, or amend any existing order, decision, or award of the Workers' Compensation Appeals Board."

§ 4603.4 Rules and regulations; payment for medical treatment

(a) The administrative director shall adopt rules and regulations to do all of the following:

(1) Ensure that all health care providers and facilities submit medical bills for payment on standardized forms.

(2) Require acceptance by employers of electronic claims for payment of medical services.

(3) Ensure confidentiality of medical information submitted on electronic claims for payment of medical services.

(b) To the extent feasible, standards adopted pursuant to subdivision (a) shall be consistent with existing standards under the federal Health Insurance Portability and Accountability Act of 1996.

(c) The rules and regulations requiring employers to accept electronic claims for payment of medical services shall be adopted on or before January 1, 2005, and shall require all employers to accept electronic claims for payment of medical services on or before July 1, 2006.

(d) Payment for medical treatment provided or authorized by the treating physician selected by the employee or designated by the employer shall be made by the employer within 15 working days after electronic receipt of an itemized electronic billing for services at or below the maximum fees provided in the official medical fee schedule adopted pursuant to Section 5307.1. If the billing is contested, denied, or incomplete, payment shall be made in accordance with Section 4603.2. *(Added by Stats.2002, c. 6 (A.B.749), § 62. Amended by Stats.2003, c. 639 (S.B.228), § 26.)*

§ 4603.5. Format and content of notices; reasonable geographic areas; time limits for notices and responses; notification of employees' rights

The administrative director shall adopt rules pertaining to the format and content of notices required by this article; define reasonable geographic areas for the purposes of Section 4600; specify time limits for all such notices, and responses thereto; and adopt any other rules necessary to make effective the requirements of this article.

Employers shall notify all employees of their rights under this section. *(Added by Stats.1975, c. 1259, p. 3305, § 7.)*

§ 4604. Determination of controversies by appeals board

Controversies between employer and employee arising under this chapter shall be determined by the appeals board, upon the request of either party. *(Stats.1937, c. 90, p. 282, § 4604. Amended by Stats.1965, c. 1513, p. 3578, § 88, operative Jan. 15, 1966.)*

§ 4604.5. Medical treatment utilization schedules; recommended guidelines; presumptions; limitation on number of visits per industrial injury occurring on or after January 1, 2004

(a) Upon adoption by the administrative director of a medical treatment utilization schedule pursuant to Section 5307.27, the recommended guidelines set forth in the schedule shall be presumptively correct on the issue of extent and scope of medical treatment. The presumption is rebuttable and may be controverted by a preponderance of the scientific medical evidence establishing that a variance from the guidelines reasonably is required to cure or relieve the injured worker from the effects of his or her injury. The presumption created is one affecting the burden of proof.

(b) The recommended guidelines set forth in the schedule adopted pursuant to subdivision (a) shall reflect practices that are evidence and scientifically based, nationally recognized, and peer reviewed. The guidelines shall be designed to assist providers by offering an analytical framework for the evaluation and treatment of injured workers, and shall constitute care in accordance with Section 4600 for all injured workers diagnosed with industrial conditions.

(c) Three months after the publication date of the updated American College of Occupational and Environmental Medicine's Occupational Medicine Practice Guidelines, and continuing until the effective date of a medical treatment utilization schedule, pursuant to Section 5307.27, the recommended guidelines set forth in the American College of Occupational and Environmental Medicine's Occupational Medicine Practice Guidelines shall be presumptively correct on the issue of extent and scope of medical treatment, regardless of date of injury. The presumption is rebuttable and may be controverted by a preponderance of the evidence establishing that a variance from the guidelines reasonably is required to cure and relieve the employee from the effects of his or her injury, in accordance with Section 4600. The presumption created is one affecting the burden of proof.

(d)(1) Notwithstanding the medical treatment utilization schedule or the guidelines set forth in the American College of Occupational and Environmental Medicine's Occupational Medicine Practice Guidelines, for injuries occurring on and after January 1, 2004, an employee shall be entitled to no more than 24 chiropractic, 24 occupational therapy, and 24 physical therapy visits per industrial injury.

(2) Paragraph (1) shall not apply when an employer authorizes, in writing, additional visits to a health care practitioner for physical medicine services.

(3) Paragraph (1) shall not apply to visits for postsurgical physical medicine and postsurgical rehabilitation services provided in compliance with a postsurgical treatment utilization schedule established by the administrative director pursuant to Section 5307.27.

(e) For all injuries not covered by the American College of Occupational and Environmental Medicine's Occupational Medicine Practice Guidelines or the official utilization schedule after adoption pursuant to Section 5307.27, authorized treatment shall be in accordance with other evidence-based medical treatment guidelines that are recognized generally by the national medical community and scientifically based. *(Added by Stats.2003, c. 639 (S.B.228), § 27. Amended by Stats.2004, c. 34 (S.B.899), § 25, eff. April 19, 2004; Stats.2007, c. 621 (A.B.1073), § 1; Stats.2008, c. 179 (S.B.1498), § 175.)*

§ 4605. Employee's right to personal physician

Nothing contained in this chapter shall limit the right of the employee to provide, at his own expense, a consulting physician or any attending physicians whom he desires. *(Stats.1937, c. 90, p. 282, § 4605.)*

§ 4606. Public entities; self-insured employer under Workmen's Compensation, Insurance and Safety Act

Any county, city and county, city, school district, or other public corporation within the state which was a self-insured employer under the "Workmen's Compensation, Insurance and Safety Act," enacted by Chapter 176 of the

Statutes of 1913, may provide such medical, and hospital treatment, including nursing, medicines, medical and surgical supplies, crutches, and apparatus, including artificial members, which is reasonably required to cure or relieve from the effects of an injury to a former employee who was covered under such act, without regard to the 90-day limitation of subdivision (a) of Section 15 of such act for medical treatment. The provisions of this section shall not be operative in any such county, city and county, city, school district, or other public corporation unless adopted by a resolution of the governing body of such public entity. *(Added by Stats.1972, c. 451, p. 820, § 1, eff. July 21, 1972.)*

§ 4607. Attorney fees; successful defense by injured employee

Where a party to a proceeding institutes proceedings to terminate an award made by the appeals board to an applicant for continuing medical treatment and is unsuccessful in such proceedings, the appeals board may determine the amount of attorney's fees reasonably incurred by the applicant in resisting the proceeding to terminate the medical treatment, and may assess such reasonable attorney's fees as a cost upon the party instituting the proceedings to terminate the award of the appeals board. *(Added by Stats.1973, c. 663, p. 1215, § 1.)*

§ 4608. Pharmacy benefits; claim form reproductions

No workers' compensation insurer, self-insured employer, or agent of an insurer or self-insured employer, shall refuse to pay pharmacy benefits solely because the claim form utilized is reproduced by the person providing the pharmacy benefits, provided the reproduced form is an exact copy of that used by the insurer, self-insured employer, or agent. *(Added by Stats.1984, c. 137, § 1.)*

§ 4609. Sale, lease, or transfer of list of contracted health care providers and their reimbursement rates; disclosures and other requirements

(a) In order to prevent the improper selling, leasing, or transferring of a health care provider's contract, it is the intent of the Legislature that every arrangement that results in any payor paying a health care provider a reduced rate for health care services based on the health care provider's participation in a network or panel shall be disclosed by the contracting agent to the provider in advance and shall actively encourage employees to use the network, unless the health care provider agrees to provide discounts without that active encouragement.

(b) Beginning July 1, 2000, every contracting agent that sells, leases, assigns, transfers, or conveys its list of contracted health care providers and their contracted reimbursement rates to a payor, as defined in subparagraph (A) of paragraph (3) of subdivision (d), or another contracting agent shall, upon entering or renewing a provider contract, do all of the following:

(1) Disclose whether the list of contracted providers may be sold, leased, transferred, or conveyed to other

payors or other contracting agents, and specify whether those payors or contracting agents include workers' compensation insurers or automobile insurers.

(2) Disclose what specific practices, if any, payors utilize to actively encourage employees to use the list of contracted providers when obtaining medical care that entitles a payor to claim a contracted rate. For purposes of this paragraph, a payor is deemed to have actively encouraged employees to use the list of contracted providers if the employer provides information directly to employees during the period the employer has medical control advising them of the existence of the list of contracted providers through the use of a variety of advertising or marketing approaches that supply the names, addresses, and telephone numbers of contracted providers to employees; or in advance of a workplace injury, or upon notice of an injury or claim by an employee, the approaches may include, but are not limited to, the use of provider directories, the use of a list of all contracted providers in an area geographically accessible to the posting site, the use of wall cards that direct employees to a readily accessible listing of those providers at the same location as the wall cards, the use of wall cards that direct employees to a toll-free telephone number or Internet Web site address, or the use of toll-free telephone numbers or Internet Web site addresses supplied directly during the period the employer has medical control. However, Internet Web site addresses alone shall not be deemed to satisfy the requirements of this paragraph. Nothing in this paragraph shall prevent contracting agents or payors from providing only listings of providers located within a reasonable geographic range of an employee. A payor who otherwise meets the requirements of this paragraph is deemed to have met the requirements of this paragraph regardless of the employer's ability to control medical treatment pursuant to Sections 4600 and 4600.3.

(3) Disclose whether payors to which the list of contracted providers may be sold, leased, transferred, or conveyed may be permitted to pay a provider's contracted rate without actively encouraging the employees to use the list of contracted providers when obtaining medical care. Nothing in this subdivision shall be construed to require a payor to actively encourage the employees to use the list of contracted providers when obtaining medical care in the case of an emergency.

(4) Disclose, upon the initial signing of a contract, and within 15 business days of receipt of a written request from a provider or provider panel, a payor summary of all payors currently eligible to claim a provider's contracted rate due to the provider's and payor's respective written agreements with any contracting agent.

(5) Allow providers, upon the initial signing, renewal, or amendment of a provider contract, to decline to be included in any list of contracted providers that is sold, leased, transferred, or conveyed to payors that do not actively encourage the employees to use the list of contracted providers when obtaining medical care as described in paragraph (2). Each provider's election under this paragraph shall be binding on the contracting agent with which the provider has the contract and any other contracting agent that buys, leases, or otherwise obtains the list of contracted providers.

A provider shall not be excluded from any list of contracted providers that is sold, leased, transferred, or conveyed to payors that actively encourage the employees to use the list of contracted providers when obtaining medical care, based upon the provider's refusal to be included on any list of contracted providers that is sold, leased, transferred, or conveyed to payors that do not actively encourage the employees to use the list of contracted providers when obtaining medical care.

(6) If the payor's explanation of benefits or explanation of review does not identify the name of the network that has a written agreement signed by the provider whereby the payor is entitled, directly or indirectly, to pay a preferred rate for the services rendered, the contracting agent shall do the following:

(A) Maintain a Web site that is accessible to all contracted providers and updated at least quarterly and maintain a toll-free telephone number accessible to all contracted providers whereby providers may access payor summary information.

(B) Disclose through the use of an Internet Web site, a toll-free telephone number, or through a delivery or mail service to its contracted providers, within 30 days, any sale, lease assignment, transfer or conveyance of the contracted reimbursement rates to another contracting agent or payor.

(7) Nothing in this subdivision shall be construed to impose requirements or regulations upon payors, as defined in subparagraph (A) of paragraph (3) of subdivision (d).

(c) Beginning July 1, 2000, a payor, as defined in subparagraph (B) of paragraph (3) of subdivision (d), shall do all of the following:

(1) Provide an explanation of benefits or explanation of review that identifies the name of the network with which the payor has an agreement that entitles them to pay a preferred rate for the services rendered.

(2) Demonstrate that it is entitled to pay a contracted rate within 30 business days of receipt of a written request from a provider who has received a claim payment from the payor. The provider shall include in the request a statement explaining why the payment is not at the correct contracted rate for the services provided. The failure of the provider to include a statement shall relieve the payor from the responsibility of demonstrating that it is entitled to pay the disputed contracted rate. The failure of a payor to make the demonstration to a properly documented request of the provider within 30 business days shall render the payor responsible for the lesser of the provider's actual fee or, as applicable, any fee schedule pursuant to this division, which amount shall be due and payable within 10 days of receipt of written

notice from the provider, and shall bar the payor from taking any future discounts from that provider without the provider's express written consent until the payor can demonstrate to the provider that it is entitled to pay a contracted rate as provided in this subdivision. A payor shall be deemed to have demonstrated that it is entitled to pay a contracted rate if it complies with either of the following:

(A) Describes the specific practices the payor utilizes to comply with paragraph (2) of subdivision (b), and demonstrates compliance with paragraph (1).

(B) Identifies the contracting agent with whom the payor has a written agreement whereby the payor is not required to actively encourage employees to use the list of contracted providers pursuant to paragraph (5) of subdivision (b).

(d) For the purposes of this section, the following terms have the following meanings:

(1) "Contracting agent" means an insurer licensed under the Insurance Code to provide workers' compensation insurance, a health care service plan, including a specialized health care service plan, a preferred provider organization, or a self-insured employer, while engaged, for monetary or other consideration, in the act of selling, leasing, transferring, assigning, or conveying a provider or provider panel to provide health care services to employees for work-related injuries.

(2) "Employee" means a person entitled to seek health care services for a work-related injury.

(3)(A) For the purposes of subdivision (b), "payor" means a health care service plan, including a specialized health care service plan, an insurer licensed under the Insurance Code to provide disability insurance that covers hospital, medical, or surgical benefits, automobile insurance, or workers' compensation insurance, or a self-insured employer that is responsible to pay for health care services provided to beneficiaries.

(B) For the purposes of subdivision (c), "payor" means an insurer licensed under the Insurance Code to provide workers' compensation insurance, a self-insured employer, a third-party administrator or trust, or any other third party that is responsible to pay health care services provided to employees for work-related injuries, or an agent of an entity included in this definition.

(4) "Payor summary" means a written summary that includes the payor's name and the type of plan, including, but not limited to, a group health plan, an automobile insurance plan, and a workers' compensation insurance plan.

(5) "Provider" means any of the following:

(A) Any person licensed or certified pursuant to Division 2 (commencing with Section 500) of the Business and Professions Code.

(B) Any person licensed pursuant to the Chiropractic Initiative Act or the Osteopathic Initiative Act.

(C) Any person licensed pursuant to Chapter 2.5 (commencing with Section 1440) of Division 2 of the Health and Safety Code.

(D) A clinic, health dispensary, or health facility licensed pursuant to Division 2 (commencing with Section 1200) of the Health and Safety Code.

(E) Any entity exempt from licensure pursuant to Section 1206 of the Health and Safety Code.

(e) This section shall become operative on July 1, 2000. *(Added by Stats.1999, c. 545 (S.B.559), § 4, operative July 1, 2000. Amended by Stats.2000, c. 1069 (S.B. 1732), § 5; Stats.2001, c. 159 (S.B.662), § 159.)*

§ 4610.   Utilization review

(a) For purposes of this section, "utilization review" means utilization review or utilization management functions that prospectively, retrospectively, or concurrently review and approve, modify, delay, or deny, based in whole or in part on medical necessity to cure and relieve, treatment recommendations by physicians, as defined in Section 3209.3, prior to, retrospectively, or concurrent with the provision of medical treatment services pursuant to Section 4600.

(b) Every employer shall establish a utilization review process in compliance with this section, either directly or through its insurer or an entity with which an employer or insurer contracts for these services.

(c) Each utilization review process shall be governed by written policies and procedures. These policies and procedures shall ensure that decisions based on the medical necessity to cure and relieve of proposed medical treatment services are consistent with the schedule for medical treatment utilization adopted pursuant to Section 5307.27. Prior to adoption of the schedule, these policies and procedures shall be consistent with the recommended standards set forth in the American College of Occupational and Environmental Medicine Occupational Medical Practice Guidelines. These policies and procedures, and a description of the utilization process, shall be filed with the administrative director and shall be disclosed by the employer to employees, physicians, and the public upon request.

(d) If an employer, insurer, or other entity subject to this section requests medical information from a physician in order to determine whether to approve, modify, delay, or deny requests for authorization, the employer shall request only the information reasonably necessary to make the determination. The employer, insurer, or other entity shall employ or designate a medical director who holds an unrestricted license to practice medicine in this state issued pursuant to Section 2050 or Section 2450 of the Business and Professions Code. The medical director shall ensure that the process by which the employer or other entity reviews and approves, modifies, delays, or denies requests by physicians prior to, retrospectively, or concurrent with the provision of medical treatment services, complies with the requirements of this section. Nothing in this section shall be construed as restricting the existing authority of the Medical Board of California.

(e) No person other than a licensed physician who is competent to evaluate the specific clinical issues involved in the medical treatment services, and where these services are within the scope of the physician's practice, requested by the physician may modify, delay, or deny requests for authorization of medical treatment for reasons of medical necessity to cure and relieve.

(f) The criteria or guidelines used in the utilization review process to determine whether to approve, modify, delay, or deny medical treatment services shall be all of the following:

(1) Developed with involvement from actively practicing physicians.

(2) Consistent with the schedule for medical treatment utilization adopted pursuant to Section 5307.27. Prior to adoption of the schedule, these policies and procedures shall be consistent with the recommended standards set forth in the American College of Occupational and Environmental Medicine Occupational Medical Practice Guidelines.

(3) Evaluated at least annually, and updated if necessary.

(4) Disclosed to the physician and the employee, if used as the basis of a decision to modify, delay, or deny services in a specified case under review.

(5) Available to the public upon request. An employer shall only be required to disclose the criteria or guidelines for the specific procedures or conditions requested. An employer may charge members of the public reasonable copying and postage expenses related to disclosing criteria or guidelines pursuant to this paragraph. Criteria or guidelines may also be made available through electronic means. No charge shall be required for an employee whose physician's request for medical treatment services is under review.

(g) In determining whether to approve, modify, delay, or deny requests by physicians prior to, retrospectively, or concurrent with the provisions of medical treatment services to employees all of the following requirements must be met:

(1) Prospective or concurrent decisions shall be made in a timely fashion that is appropriate for the nature of the employee's condition, not to exceed five working days from the receipt of the information reasonably necessary to make the determination, but in no event more than 14 days from the date of the medical treatment recommendation by the physician. In cases where the review is retrospective, the decision shall be communicated to the individual who received services, or to the individual's designee, within 30 days of receipt of information that is reasonably necessary to make this determination.

(2) When the employee's condition is such that the employee faces an imminent and serious threat to his or her health, including, but not limited to, the potential loss of life, limb, or other major bodily function, or the normal timeframe for the decisionmaking process, as described in paragraph (1), would be detrimental to the employee's life or health or could jeopardize the employee's ability to regain maximum function, decisions to approve, modify, delay, or deny requests by physicians prior to, or concurrent with, the provision of medical treatment services to employees shall be made in a timely fashion that is appropriate for the nature of the employee's condition, but not to exceed 72 hours after the receipt of the information reasonably necessary to make the determination.

(3)(A) Decisions to approve, modify, delay, or deny requests by physicians for authorization prior to, or concurrent with, the provision of medical treatment services to employees shall be communicated to the requesting physician within 24 hours of the decision. Decisions resulting in modification, delay, or denial of all or part of the requested health care service shall be communicated to physicians initially by telephone or facsimile, and to the physician and employee in writing within 24 hours for concurrent review, or within two business days of the decision for prospective review, as prescribed by the administrative director. If the request is not approved in full, disputes shall be resolved in accordance with Section 4062. If a request to perform spinal surgery is denied, disputes shall be resolved in accordance with subdivision (b) of Section 4062.

(B) In the case of concurrent review, medical care shall not be discontinued until the employee's physician has been notified of the decision and a care plan has been agreed upon by the physician that is appropriate for the medical needs of the employee. Medical care provided during a concurrent review shall be care that is medically necessary to cure and relieve, and an insurer or self-insured employer shall only be liable for those services determined medically necessary to cure and relieve. If the insurer or self-insured employer disputes whether or not one or more services offered concurrently with a utilization review were medically necessary to cure and relieve, the dispute shall be resolved pursuant to Section 4062, except in cases involving recommendations for the performance of spinal surgery, which shall be governed by the provisions of subdivision (b) of Section 4062. Any compromise between the parties that an insurer or self-insured employer believes may result in payment for services that were not medically necessary to cure and relieve shall be reported by the insurer or the self-insured employer to the licensing board of the provider or providers who received the payments, in a manner set forth by the respective board and in such a way as to minimize reporting costs both to the board and to the insurer or self-insured employer, for evaluation as to possible violations of the statutes governing appropriate professional practices. No fees shall be levied upon insurers or self-insured employers making reports required by this section.

(4) Communications regarding decisions to approve requests by physicians shall specify the specific medical treatment service approved. Responses regarding decisions to modify, delay, or deny medical treatment services requested by physicians shall include a clear and concise explanation of the reasons for the employer's decision, a description of the criteria or guidelines used, and the clinical reasons for the decisions regarding medical necessity.

(5) If the employer, insurer, or other entity cannot make a decision within the timeframes specified in paragraph (1) or (2) because the employer or other entity is not in receipt of all of the information reasonably necessary and requested, because the employer requires consultation by an expert reviewer, or because the employer has asked that an additional examination or test be performed upon the employee that is reasonable and consistent with good medical practice, the employer shall immediately notify the physician and the employee, in writing, that the employer cannot make a decision within the required timeframe, and specify the information requested but not received, the expert reviewer to be consulted, or the additional examinations or tests required. The employer shall also notify the physician and employee of the anticipated date on which a decision may be rendered. Upon receipt of all information reasonably necessary and requested by the employer, the employer shall approve, modify, or deny the request for authorization within the timeframes specified in paragraph (1) or (2).

(h) Every employer, insurer, or other entity subject to this section shall maintain telephone access for physicians to request authorization for health care services.

(i) If the administrative director determines that the employer, insurer, or other entity subject to this section has failed to meet any of the timeframes in this section, or has failed to meet any other requirement of this section, the administrative director may assess, by order, administrative penalties for each failure. A proceeding for the issuance of an order assessing administrative penalties shall be subject to appropriate notice to, and an opportunity for a hearing with regard to, the person affected. The administrative penalties shall not be deemed to be an exclusive remedy for the administrative director. These penalties shall be deposited in the Workers' Compensation Administration Revolving Fund. *(Added by Stats. 2003, c. 639 (S.B.228), § 28.)*

§ 4610.1. Utilization review process; penalty for unreasonable delay in payment of compensation

An employee shall not be entitled to an increase in compensation under Section 5814 for unreasonable delay in the provision of medical treatment for periods of time necessary to complete the utilization review process in compliance with Section 4610. A determination by the appeals board that medical treatment is appropriate shall not be conclusive evidence that medical treatment was unreasonably delayed or denied for purposes of penalties

624

under Section 5814. In no case shall this section preclude an employee from entitlement to an increase in compensation under Section 5814 when an employer has unreasonably delayed or denied medical treatment due to an unreasonable delay in completion of the utilization review process set forth in Section 4610. *(Added by Stats.2003, c. 638 (A.B.1557), § 1.)*

§ 4610.3. Medical provider networks and health care organization contracts; employer authorized medical care; rescission or modification of treatment authorization

(a) Regardless of whether an employer has established a medical provider network pursuant to Section 4616 or entered into a contract with a health care organization pursuant to Section 4600.5, an employer that authorizes medical treatment shall not rescind or modify that authorization after the medical treatment has been provided based on that authorization for any reason, including, but not limited to, the employer's subsequent determination that the physician who treated the employee was not eligible to treat that injured employee. If the authorized medical treatment consists of a series of treatments or services, the employer may rescind or modify the authorization only for the treatments or services that have not already been provided.

(b) This section shall not be construed to expand or alter the benefits available under, or the terms and conditions of, any contract, including, but not limited to, existing medical provider network and health care organization contracts.

(c) This section shall not be construed to impact the ability of the employer to transfer treatment of an injured employee into a medical provider network or health care organization. This subdivision is declaratory of existing law.

(d) This section shall not be construed to establish that a provider of authorized medical treatment is the physician primarily responsible for managing the injured employee's care for purposes of rendering opinions on all medical issues necessary to determine eligibility for compensation. *(Added by Stats.2009, c. 436 (A.B.361), § 1.)*

§ 4611. Contracts between health care providers and contracting agents; definitions

(a) When a contracting agent sells, leases, or transfers a health provider's contract to a payor, the rights and obligations of the provider shall be governed by the underlying contract between the health care provider and the contracting agent.

(b) For purposes of this section, the following terms have the following meanings:

(1) "Contracting agent" has the meaning set forth in paragraph (2) of subdivision (d) of Section 4609.

(2) "Payor" has the meaning set forth in paragraph (3) of subdivision (d) of Section 4609. *(Formerly § 4610, added by Stats.2003, c. 203 (A.B.175), § 4. Renumbered*

§ 4611 and amended by Stats.2004, c. 183 (A.B.3082), § 264.)

§ 4614. Fee limitations

(a)(1) Notwithstanding Section 5307.1, where the employee's individual or organizational provider of health care services rendered under this division and paid on a fee-for-service basis is also the provider of health care services under contract with the employee's health benefit program, and the service or treatment provided is included within the range of benefits of the employee's health benefit program, and paid on a fee-for-service basis, the amount of payment for services provided under this division, for a work-related occurrence or illness, shall be no more than the amount that would have been paid for the same services under the health benefit plan, for a non-work-related occurrence or illness.

(2) A health care service plan that arranges for health care services to be rendered to an employee under this division under a contract, and which is also the employee's organizational provider for nonoccupational injuries and illnesses, with the exception of a nonprofit health care service plan that exclusively contracts with a medical group to provide or arrange for medical services to its enrollees in a designated geographic area, shall be paid by the employer for services rendered under this division only on a capitated basis.

(b)(1) Where the employee's individual or organizational provider of health care services rendered under this division who is not providing services under a contract is not the provider of health care services under contract with the employee's health benefit program or where the services rendered under this division are not within the benefits provided under the employer-sponsored health benefit program, the provider shall receive payment that is no more than the average of the payment that would have been paid by five of the largest preferred provider organizations by geographic region. Physicians, as defined in Section 3209.3, shall be reimbursed at the same averaged rates, regardless of licensure, for the delivery of services under the same procedure code. This subdivision shall not apply to a health care service plan that provides its services on a capitated basis.

(2) The administrative director shall identify the regions and the five largest carriers in each region. The carriers shall provide the necessary information to the administrative director in the form and manner requested by the administrative director. The administrative director shall make this information available to the affected providers on an annual basis.

(c) Nothing in this section shall prohibit an individual or organizational health care provider from being paid fees different from those set forth in the official medical fee schedule by an employer, insurance carrier, third-party administrator on behalf of employers, or preferred provider organization representing an employer or insurance carrier provided that the administrative director has determined that the alternative negotiated rates between the organizational or individual provider and a payer, a third-party administrator on behalf of employers, or a preferred provider organization will produce greater savings in the aggregate than if each item on billings were to be charged at the scheduled rate.

(d) For the purposes of this section, "organizational provider" means an entity that arranges for health care services to be rendered directly by individual caregivers. An organizational provider may be a health care service plan, disability insurer, health care organization, preferred provider organization, or workers' compensation insurer arranging for care through a managed care network or on a fee-for-service basis. An individual provider is either an individual or institution that provides care directly to the injured worker. *(Added by Stats.1993, c. 121 (A.B.110), § 41, eff. July 16, 1993. Amended by Stats.1993, c. 1242 (S.B.223), § 34; Stats.2002, c. 866 (A.B.486), § 11.)*

§ 4614.1. Certified Knox-Keene health care service plans; payments

Notwithstanding subdivision (f) of Section 1345 of the Health and Safety Code, a health care service plan licensed pursuant to the Knox-Keene Health Care Service Plan Act and certified by the administrative director pursuant to Section 4600.5 to provide health care pursuant to Section 4600.3 shall be permitted to accept payment from a self-insured employer, a group of self-insured employers, or the insurer of an employer on a fee-for-service basis for the provision of such health care as long as the health care service plan is not both the health care organization in which the employee is enrolled and the plan through which the employee receives regular health benefits. *(Added by Stats.1993, c. 121 (A.B.110), § 42, eff. July 16, 1993. Amended by Stats. 1993, c. 1242 (S.B.223), § 35.)*

ARTICLE 2.3. MEDICAL PROVIDER NETWORKS

Section
4616. Establishment or modification of networks; number and type of physicians; availability of treatment; approval of plan; compensation; authorization of treatment; regulations.
4616.1. Economic profiling; filing of policies and procedures; public disclosure; definitions.
4616.2. Continuity of care; filing written policies; revisions; notice, review and copies; completion of treatment by terminated providers for certain conditions.
4616.3. Initial medical evaluation and treatment; choice of physician in network; second or third opinions; out-of-network specialists.
4616.4. Independent medical reviews; contracts to perform; physician qualifications; review requirements and standards; submission of applications and relevant information; conduct of examinations; reports; decisions; treatment and costs.
4616.5. Employer defined.
4616.6. Additional examinations and reports inadmissible.

Section
4616.7.   Approval of health care organizations; health care
          service plans; group disability insurance policies;
          Taft–Hartley health and welfare funds.

§ 4616. Establishment or modification of networks; number and type of physicians; availability of treatment; approval of plan; compensation; authorization of treatment; regulations

(a)(1) On or after January 1, 2005, an insurer or employer may establish or modify a medical provider network for the provision of medical treatment to injured employees. The network shall include physicians primarily engaged in the treatment of occupational injuries and physicians primarily engaged in the treatment of nonoccupational injuries. The goal shall be at least 25 percent of physicians primarily engaged in the treatment of nonoccupational injuries. The administrative director shall encourage the integration of occupational and nonoccupational providers. The number of physicians in the medical provider network shall be sufficient to enable treatment for injuries or conditions to be provided in a timely manner. The provider network shall include an adequate number and type of physicians, as described in Section 3209.3, or other providers, as described in Section 3209.5, to treat common injuries experienced by injured employees based on the type of occupation or industry in which the employee is engaged, and the geographic area where the employees are employed.

(2) Medical treatment for injuries shall be readily available at reasonable times to all employees. To the extent feasible, all medical treatment for injuries shall be readily accessible to all employees. With respect to availability and accessibility of treatment, the administrative director shall consider the needs of rural areas, specifically those in which health facilities are located at least 30 miles apart.

(b) The employer or insurer shall submit a plan for the medical provider network to the administrative director for approval. The administrative director shall approve the plan if he or she determines that the plan meets the requirements of this section. If the administrative director does not act on the plan within 60 days of submitting the plan, it shall be deemed approved.

(c) Physician compensation may not be structured in order to achieve the goal of reducing, delaying, or denying medical treatment or restricting access to medical treatment.

(d) If the employer or insurer meets the requirements of this section, the administrative director may not withhold approval or disapprove an employer's or insurer's medical provider network based solely on the selection of providers. In developing a medical provider network, an employer or insurer shall have the exclusive right to determine the members of their network.

(e) All treatment provided shall be provided in accordance with the medical treatment utilization schedule established pursuant to Section 5307.27 or the American College of Occupational Medicine's Occupational Medicine Practice Guidelines, as appropriate.

(f) No person other than a licensed physician who is competent to evaluate the specific clinical issues involved in the medical treatment services, when these services are within the scope of the physician's practice, may modify, delay, or deny requests for authorization of medical treatment.

(g) On or before November 1, 2004, the administrative director, in consultation with the Department of Managed Health Care, shall adopt regulations implementing this article. The administrative director shall develop regulations that establish procedures for purposes of making medical provider network modifications. *(Added by Stats.2004, c. 34 (S.B.899), § 27, eff. April 19, 2004.)*

Operative Effect

Section 47 of Stats.2004, c. 34 (S.B.899) provides that "[t]he amendment, addition, or repeal of, any provision of law made by this act shall apply prospectively from the date of enactment of this act, regardless of the date of injury, unless otherwise specified, but shall not constitute good cause to reopen or rescind, alter, or amend any existing order, decision, or award of the Workers' Compensation Appeals Board."

§ 4616.1. Economic profiling; filing of policies and procedures; public disclosure; definitions

(a) An insurer or employer that offers a medical provider network under this division and that uses economic profiling shall file with the administrative director a description of any policies and procedures related to economic profiling utilized by the insurer or employer. The filing shall describe how these policies and procedures are used in utilization review, peer review, incentive and penalty programs, and in provider retention and termination decisions. The insurer or employer shall provide a copy of the filing to an individual physician, provider, medical group, or individual practice association.

(b) The administrative director shall make each insurer's or employer's filing available to the public upon request. The administrative director may not publicly disclose any information submitted pursuant to this section that is determined by the administrative director to be confidential pursuant to state or federal law.

(c) For the purposes of this article, "economic profiling" shall mean any evaluation of a particular physician, provider, medical group, or individual practice association based in whole or in part on the economic costs or utilization of services associated with medical care provided or authorized by the physician, provider, medical group, or individual practice association. *(Added by Stats.2004, c. 34 (S.B.899), § 27, eff. April 19, 2004.)*

Section 47 of Stats.2004, c. 34 (S.B.899) provides that "[t]he amendment, addition, or repeal of, any provision of law made by this act shall apply prospectively from the date of enactment of this act, regardless of the date of injury, unless otherwise specified, but shall not constitute good cause to reopen or rescind, alter, or amend any existing order, decision, or award of the Workers' Compensation Appeals Board."

§ 4616.2. Continuity of care; filing written policies; revisions; notice, review and copies; completion of treatment by terminated providers for certain conditions

(a) An insurer or employer that arranges for care for injured employees through a medical provider network shall file a written continuity of care policy with the administrative director.

(b) If approved by the administrative director, the provisions of the written continuity of care policy shall replace all prior continuity of care policies. The insurer or employer shall file a revision of the continuity of care policy with the administrative director if it makes a material change to the policy.

(c) The insurer or employer shall provide to all employees entering the workers' compensation system notice of its written continuity of care policy and information regarding the process for an employee to request a review under the policy and shall provide, upon request, a copy of the written policy to an employee.

(d)(1) An insurer or employer that offers a medical provider network shall, at the request of an injured employee, provide the completion of treatment as set forth in this section by a terminated provider.

(2) The completion of treatment shall be provided by a terminated provider to an injured employee who, at the time of the contract's termination, was receiving services from that provider for one of the conditions described in paragraph (3).

(3) The insurer or employer shall provide for the completion of treatment for the following conditions subject to coverage through the workers' compensation system:

(A) An acute condition. An acute condition is a medical condition that involves a sudden onset of symptoms due to an illness, injury, or other medical problem that requires prompt medical attention and that has a limited duration. Completion of treatment shall be provided for the duration of the acute condition.

(B) A serious chronic condition. A serious chronic condition is a medical condition due to a disease, illness, or other medical problem or medical disorder that is serious in nature and that persists without full cure or worsens over an extended period of time or requires ongoing treatment to maintain remission or prevent deterioration. Completion of treatment shall be provided for a period of time necessary to complete a course of treatment and to arrange for a safe transfer to another provider, as determined by the insurer or employer in consultation with the injured employee and the terminated provider and consistent with good professional practice. Completion of treatment under this paragraph shall not exceed 12 months from the contract termination date.

(C) A terminal illness. A terminal illness is an incurable or irreversible condition that has a high probability of causing death within one year or less. Completion of treatment shall be provided for the duration of a terminal illness.

(D) Performance of a surgery or other procedure that is authorized by the insurer or employer as part of a documented course of treatment and has been recommended and documented by the provider to occur within 180 days of the contract's termination date.

(4)(A) The insurer or employer may require the terminated provider whose services are continued beyond the contract termination date pursuant to this section to agree in writing to be subject to the same contractual terms and conditions that were imposed upon the provider prior to termination. If the terminated provider does not agree to comply or does not comply with these contractual terms and conditions, the insurer or employer is not required to continue the provider's services beyond the contract termination date.

(B) Unless otherwise agreed by the terminated provider and the insurer or employer, the services rendered pursuant to this section shall be compensated at rates and methods of payment similar to those used by the insurer or employer for currently contracting providers providing similar services who are practicing in the same or a similar geographic area as the terminated provider. The insurer or provider is not required to continue the services of a terminated provider if the provider does not accept the payment rates provided for in this paragraph.

(5) An insurer or employer shall ensure that the requirements of this section are met.

(6) This section shall not require an insurer or employer to provide for completion of treatment by a provider whose contract with the insurer or employer has been terminated or not renewed for reasons relating to a medical disciplinary cause or reason, as defined in paragraph (6) of subdivision (a) of Section 805 of the Business and Profession Code, or fraud or other criminal activity.

(7) Nothing in this section shall preclude an insurer or employer from providing continuity of care beyond the requirements of this section.

(e) The insurer or employer may require the terminated provider whose services are continued beyond the contract termination date pursuant to this section to agree in writing to be subject to the same contractual terms and conditions that were imposed upon the provider prior to termination. If the terminated provider does not agree to comply or does not comply with these contractual terms and conditions, the insurer or employer is not required to continue the provider's services beyond the contract termination date. *(Added by Stats.2004, c. 34 (S.B.899), § 27, eff. April 19, 2004.)*

Operative Effect

Section 47 of Stats.2004, c. 34 (S.B.899) provides that "[t]he amendment, addition, or repeal of, any provision of law made by this act shall apply prospectively from the date of enactment of this act, regardless of the date of injury, unless otherwise specified, but shall not constitute good cause to reopen or rescind, alter, or amend any existing order, decision, or award of the Workers' Compensation Appeals Board."

§ 4616.3. Initial medical evaluation and treatment; choice of physician in network; second or third opinions; out-of-network specialists

(a) When the injured employee notifies the employer of the injury or files a claim for workers' compensation with the employer, the employer shall arrange an initial medical evaluation and begin treatment as required by Section 4600.

(b) The employer shall notify the employee of his or her right to be treated by a physician of his or her choice after the first visit from the medical provider network established pursuant to this article, and the method by which the list of participating providers may be accessed by the employee.

(c) If an injured employee disputes either the diagnosis or the treatment prescribed by the treating physician, the employee may seek the opinion of another physician in the medical provider network. If the injured employee disputes the diagnosis or treatment prescribed by the second physician, the employee may seek the opinion of a third physician in the medical provider network.

(d)(1) Selection by the injured employee of a treating physician and any subsequent physicians shall be based on the physician's specialty or recognized expertise in treating the particular injury or condition in question.

(2) Treatment by a specialist who is not a member of the medical provider network may be permitted on a case-by-case basis if the medical provider network does not contain a physician who can provide the approved treatment and the treatment is approved by the employer or the insurer. *(Added by Stats.2004, c. 34 (S.B.899), § 27, eff. April 19, 2004.)*

Operative Effect

Section 47 of Stats.2004, c. 34 (S.B.899) provides that "[t]he amendment, addition, or repeal of, any provision of law made by this act shall apply prospectively from the date of enactment of this act, regardless of the date of injury, unless otherwise specified, but shall not constitute good cause to reopen or rescind, alter, or amend any

existing order, decision, or award of the Workers' Compensation Appeals Board."

§ 4616.4. Independent medical reviews; contracts to perform; physician qualifications; review requirements and standards; submission of applications and relevant information; conduct of examinations; reports; decisions; treatment and costs

(a)(1) The administrative director shall contract with individual physicians, as described in paragraph (2), or an independent medical review organization to perform independent medical reviews pursuant to this section.

(2) Only physicians licensed pursuant to Chapter 5 (commencing with Section 2000) of the Business and Professions Code may be independent medical reviewers.

(3) The administrative director shall ensure that the independent medical reviewers or those within the review organization shall do all of the following:

(A) Be appropriately credentialed and privileged.

(B) Ensure that the reviews provided by the medical professionals are timely, clear, and credible, and that reviews are monitored for quality on an ongoing basis.

(C) Ensure that the method of selecting medical professionals for individual cases achieves a fair and impartial panel of medical professionals who are qualified to render recommendations regarding the clinical conditions consistent with the medical utilization schedule established pursuant to Section 5307.27, or the American College of Occupational and Environmental Medicine's Occupational Medicine Practice Guidelines.

(D) Ensure that confidentiality of medical records and the review materials, consistent with the requirements of this section and applicable state and federal law.

(E) Ensure the independence of the medical professionals retained to perform the reviews through conflict-of-interest policies and prohibitions, and ensure adequate screening for conflicts of interest.

(4) Medical professionals selected by the administrative director or the independent medical review organizations to review medical treatment decisions shall be physicians, as specified in paragraph (2) of subdivision (a), who meet the following minimum requirements:

(A) The medical professional shall be a clinician knowledgeable in the treatment of the employee's medical condition, knowledgeable about the proposed treatment, and familiar with guidelines and protocols in the area of treatment under review.

(B) Notwithstanding any other provision of law, the medical professional shall hold a nonrestricted license in any state of the United States, and for physicians, a current certification by a recognized American medical specialty board in the area or areas appropriate to the condition or treatment under review.

(C) The medical professional shall have no history of disciplinary action or sanctions, including, but not limited to, loss of staff privileges or participation restrictions taken or pending by any hospital, government, or regulatory body.

(b) If, after the third physician's opinion, the treatment or diagnostic service remains disputed, the injured employee may request independent medical review regarding the disputed treatment or diagnostic service still in dispute after the third physician's opinion in accordance with Section 4616.3. The standard to be utilized for independent medical review is identical to that contained in the medical treatment utilization schedule established in Section 5307.27, or the American College of Occupational and Environmental Medicine's Occupational Medicine Practice Guidelines, as appropriate.

(c) Applications for independent medical review shall be submitted to the administrative director on a one-page form provided by the administrative director entitled "Independent Medical Review Application." The form shall contain a signed release from the injured employee, or a person authorized pursuant to law to act on behalf of the injured employee, authorizing the release of medical and treatment information. The injured employee may provide any relevant material or documentation with the application. The administrative director or the independent medical review organization shall assign the independent medical reviewer.

(d) Following receipt of the application for independent medical review, the employer or insurer shall provide the independent medical reviewer, assigned pursuant to subdivision (c), with all information that was considered in relation to the disputed treatment or diagnostic service, including both of the following:

(1) A copy of all correspondence from, and received by, any treating physician who provided a treatment or diagnostic service to the injured employee in connection with the injury.

(2) A complete and legible copy of all medical records and other information used by the physicians in making a decision regarding the disputed treatment or diagnostic service.

(e) Upon receipt of information and documents related to the application for independent medical review, the independent medical reviewer shall conduct a physical examination of the injured employee at the employee's discretion. The reviewer may order any diagnostic tests necessary to make his or her determination regarding medical treatment. Utilizing the medical treatment utilization schedule established pursuant to Section 5307.27, or the American College of Occupational and Environmental Medicine's Occupational Medicine Practice Guidelines, as appropriate, and taking into account any reports and information provided, the reviewer shall determine whether the disputed health care service was consistent with Section 5307.27 or the American College of Occupational and Environmental Medicine's Occupational Medicine Practice Guidelines based on the specific medical needs of the injured employee.

(f) The independent medical reviewer shall issue a report to the administrative director, in writing, and in layperson's terms to the maximum extent practicable, containing his or her analysis and determination whether the disputed health care service was consistent with the medical treatment utilization schedule established pursuant to Section 5307.27, or the American College of Occupational and Environmental Medicine's Occupational Medicine Practice Guidelines, as appropriate, within 30 days of the examination of the injured employee, or within less time as prescribed by the administrative director. If the disputed health care service has not been provided and the independent medical reviewer certifies in writing that an imminent and serious threat to the health of the injured employee may exist, including, but not limited to, serious pain, the potential loss of life, limb, or major bodily function, or the immediate and serious deterioration of the injured employee, the report shall be expedited and rendered within three days of the examination by the independent medical reviewer. Subject to the approval of the administrative director, the deadlines for analyses and determinations involving both regular and expedited reviews may be extended by the administrative director for up to three days in extraordinary circumstances or for good cause.

(g) The independent medical reviewer's analysis shall cite the injured employee's medical condition, the relevant documents in the record, and the relevant findings associated with the documents or any other information submitted to the reviewer in order to support the determination.

(h) The administrative director shall immediately adopt the determination of the independent medical reviewer, and shall promptly issue a written decision to the parties.

(i) If the determination of the independent medical reviewer finds that the disputed treatment or diagnostic service is consistent with Section 5307.27 or the American College of Occupational and Environmental Medicine's Occupational Medicine Practice Guidelines, the injured employee may seek the disputed treatment or diagnostic service from a physician of his or her choice from within or outside the medical provider network. Treatment outside the medical provider network shall be provided consistent with Section 5307.27 or the American College of Occupational and Environmental Medicine's Occupational Practice Guidelines. The employer shall be liable for the cost of any approved medical treatment in accordance with Section 5307.1 or 5307.11. (*Added by Stats.2004, c. 34 (S.B.899), § 27, eff. April 19, 2004.*)

Operative Effect

Section 47 of Stats.2004, c. 34 (S.B.899) provides that "[t]he amendment, addition, or repeal of, any provision of law made by this act shall apply prospectively from the date of enactment of this act, regardless of the date of injury, unless otherwise specified, but shall not constitute good cause to reopen or rescind, alter, or amend any existing order, decision, or award of the Workers' Compensation Appeals Board."

§ 4616.5. Employer defined

For purposes of this article, "employer" means a self-insured employer, joint powers authority, or the state. *(Added by Stats.2004, c. 34 (S.B.899), § 27, eff. April 19, 2004.)*

Operative Effect

Section 47 of Stats.2004, c. 34 (S.B.899) provides that "[t]he amendment, addition, or repeal of, any provision of law made by this act shall apply prospectively from the date of enactment of this act, regardless of the date of injury, unless otherwise specified, but shall not constitute good cause to reopen or rescind, alter, or amend any existing order, decision, or award of the Workers' Compensation Appeals Board."

§ 4616.6. Additional examinations and reports inadmissible

No additional examinations shall be ordered by the appeals board and no other reports shall be admissable to resolve any controversy arising out of this article. *(Added by Stats.2004, c. 34 (S.B.899), § 27, eff. April 19, 2004.)*

Operative Effect

Section 47 of Stats.2004, c. 34 (S.B.899) provides that "[t]he amendment, addition, or repeal of, any provision of law made by this act shall apply prospectively from the date of enactment of this act, regardless of the date of injury, unless otherwise specified, but shall not constitute good cause to reopen or rescind, alter, or amend any existing order, decision, or award of the Workers' Compensation Appeals Board."

§ 4616.7. Approval of health care organizations; health care service plans; group disability insurance policies; Taft–Hartley health and welfare funds

(a) A health care organization certified pursuant to Section 4600.5 shall be deemed approved pursuant to this article if it meets the percentage required for physicians primarily engaged in nonoccupational medicine specified in subdivision (a) of Section 4616 and all the other requirements of this article are met, as determined by the administrative director.

(b) A health care service plan, licensed pursuant to Chapter 2.2 (commencing with Section 1340) of Division 2 of the Health and Safety Code, shall be deemed approved for purposes of this article if it has a reasonable number of physicians with competency in occupational medicine, as determined by the administrative director.

(c) A group disability insurance policy, as defined in subdivision (b) of Section 106 of the Insurance Code, that covers hospital, surgical, and medical care expenses shall be deemed approved for purposes of this article if it has a

reasonable number of physicians with competency in occupational medicine, as determined by the administrative director. For the purposes of this section, a group disability insurance policy shall not include Medicare supplement, vision-only, dental-only, and Champus-supplement insurance. For purposes of this section, a group disability insurance policy shall not include hospital indemnity, accident-only, and specified disease insurance that pays benefits on a fixed benefit, cash-payment-only basis.

(d) Any Taft–Hartley health and welfare fund shall be deemed approved for purposes of this article if it has a reasonable number of physicians with competency in occupational medicine, as determined by the administrative director. *(Added by Stats.2004, c. 34 (S.B.899), § 27, eff. April 19, 2004.)*

Operative Effect

Section 47 of Stats.2004, c. 34 (S.B.899) provides that "[t]he amendment, addition, or repeal of, any provision of law made by this act shall apply prospectively from the date of enactment of this act, regardless of the date of injury, unless otherwise specified, but shall not constitute good cause to reopen or rescind, alter, or amend any existing order, decision, or award of the Workers' Compensation Appeals Board."

ARTICLE 2.5. MEDICAL–LEGAL EXPENSES

Section
4620. Definition of medical-legal expense; contested claims; costs incidental to production of medical report.
4621. Reimbursements; commencement of medical-legal evaluations; additional benefits.
4622. Payment of expenses; time; penalty and interest; notice of employer contest; rules and regulations.
4625. Prompt payment; petition for reimbursement.
4626. Billing procedures.
4627. Rules and regulations.
4628. Examination of employee; preparation of medical-legal report; charges for services; failure to comply; penalties; physician's curriculum vitae.

§ 4620. Definition of medical-legal expense; contested claims; costs incidental to production of medical report

(a) For purposes of this article, a medical-legal expense means any costs and expenses incurred by or on behalf of any party, the administrative director, the board, or a referee for X-rays, laboratory fees, other diagnostic tests, medical reports, medical records, medical testimony, and, as needed, interpreter's fees, for the purpose of proving or disproving a contested claim.

(b) A contested claim exists when the employer knows or reasonably should know that the employee is claiming entitlement to any benefit arising out of a claimed industrial injury and one of the following conditions exists:

(1) The employer rejects liability for a claimed benefit.

(2) The employer fails to accept liability for benefits after the expiration of a reasonable period of time within which to decide if it will contest the claim.

(3) The employer fails to respond to a demand for payment of benefits after the expiration of any time period fixed by statute for the payment of indemnity.

(c) Costs of medical evaluations, diagnostic tests, and interpreters incidental to the production of a medical report do not constitute medical-legal expenses unless the medical report is capable of proving or disproving a disputed medical fact, the determination of which is essential to an adjudication of the employee's claim for benefits. In determining whether a report meets the requirements of this subdivision, a judge shall give full consideration to the substance as well as the form of the report, as required by applicable statutes and regulations. *(Added by Stats.1984, c. 596, § 4, eff. July 19, 1984. Amended by Stats.1985, c. 428, § 1, eff. July 30, 1985; Stats.1993, c. 4 (S.B.31), § 2, eff. April 3, 1993.)*

§ 4621. Reimbursements; commencement of medical-legal evaluations; additional benefits

(a) In accordance with the rules of practice and procedure of the appeals board, the employee, or the dependents of a deceased employee, shall be reimbursed for his or her medical-legal expenses and reasonably, actually, and necessarily incurred, except as provided in Section 4064. The reasonableness of, and necessity for, incurring these expenses shall be determined with respect to the time when the expenses were actually incurred. Costs for medical evaluations, diagnostic tests, and interpreters' services incidental to the production of a medical report shall not be incurred earlier than the date of receipt by the employer, the employer's insurance carrier, or, if represented, the attorney of record, of all reports and documents required by the administrative director incidental to the services. This subdivision is not applicable unless there has been compliance with Section 4620.

(b) Except as provided in subdivision (c) and Sections 4061 and 4062, no comprehensive medical-legal evaluations, except those at the request of an employer, shall be performed during the first 60 days after the notice of claim has been filed pursuant to Section 5401, and neither the employer nor the employee shall be liable for any expenses incurred for comprehensive medical-legal evaluations performed within the first 60 days after the notice of claim has been filed pursuant to Section 5401.

(c) Comprehensive medical-legal evaluations may be performed at any time after the claim form has been filed pursuant to Section 5401 if the employer has rejected the claim.

(d) Where, at the request of the employer, the employer's insurance carrier, the administrative director, the appeals board, or a referee, the employee submits to examination by a physician, he or she shall be entitled to receive, in addition to all other benefits herein provided, all reasonable expenses of transportation, meals, and lodging incident to reporting for the examination to the same extent and manner as provided for in Section 4600. *(Added by Stats.1984, c. 596, § 4, eff. July 19, 1984. Amended by Stats.1993, c. 4 (S.B.31), § 3, eff. April 3, 1993; Stats.1993, c. 121 (A.B.110), § 43, eff. July 16, 1993.)*

§ 4622. Payment of expenses; time; penalty and interest; notice of employer contest; rules and regulations

All medical-legal expenses for which the employer is liable shall, upon receipt by the employer of all reports and documents required by the administrative director incident to the services, be paid to whom the funds and expenses are due, as follows:

(a) Except as provided in subdivision (b), within 60 days after receipt by the employer of each separate, written billing and report, and where payment is not made within this period, that portion of the billed sum then unreasonably unpaid shall be increased by 10 percent, together with interest thereon at the rate of 7 percent per annum retroactive to the date of receipt of the bill and report by the employer. Where the employer, within the 60-day period, contests the reasonableness and necessity for incurring the fees, services, and expenses, payment shall be made within 20 days of the filing of an order of the appeals board directing payment.

The penalty provided for in this subdivision shall not apply if (1) the employer pays the provider that portion of his or her charges which do not exceed the amount deemed reasonable pursuant to subdivision (c) of Section 4624 within 60 days of receipt of the report and itemized billing, and, (2) the appeals board sustains the employer's position in contesting the reasonableness or necessity for incurring the expenses. If the employer prevails before the appeals board, the referee shall order the physician to reimburse the employer for the amount of the paid charges found to be unreasonable.

(b) Where requested by the employee, or the dependents of a deceased employee, within 20 days from the filing of an order of the appeals board directing payment, and where payment is not made within that period, that portion of the billed sum then unpaid shall be increased by 10 percent, together with interest thereon at the rate of 7 percent per annum retroactive to the date of the filing of the order of the board directing payment.

(c) The employer shall notify, in writing, the provider of the services, the employee, or if represented, his or her attorney, if the employer contests the reasonableness or necessity of incurring these expenses, and shall indicate the reasons therefor.

The appeals board shall promulgate all necessary and reasonable rules and regulations to insure compliance with this section, and shall take such further steps as may be necessary to guarantee that the rules and regulations are enforced.

The provisions of Sections 5800 and 5814 shall not apply to this section.

(d) Nothing contained in this section shall be construed to create a rebuttable presumption of entitlement to payment of an expense upon receipt by the employer of the required reports and documents. This section is not applicable unless there has been compliance with Sections 4620 and 4621. *(Added by Stats.1984, c. 596, § 4, eff. July 19, 1984. Amended by Stats.1993, c. 4 (S.B.31), § 4, eff. April 3, 1993.)*

§ 4625. Prompt payment; petition for reimbursement

(a) Notwithstanding subdivision (d) of Section 4628, all charges for medical-legal expenses for which the employer is liable that are not in excess of those set forth in the official medical-legal fee schedule adopted pursuant to Section 5307.6 shall be paid promptly pursuant to Section 4622.

(b) If the employer contests the reasonableness of the charges it has paid, the employer may file a petition with the appeals board to obtain reimbursement of the charges from the physician that are considered to be unreasonable. *(Added by Stats.1984, c. 596, § 4, eff. July 19, 1984. Amended by Stats.1985, c. 428, § 4, eff. July 30, 1985; Stats.1990, c. 1550 (A.B.2910), § 33; Stats.1993, c. 4 (S.B.31), § 7, eff. April 3, 1993.)*

§ 4626. Billing procedures

All charges for X-rays, laboratory services, and other diagnostic tests provided in connection with an industrial medical-legal evaluation shall be billed in accordance with the official medical fee schedule adopted by the administrative director pursuant to Section 5307.1 and shall be itemized separately in accordance with rules promulgated by the administrative director. *(Added by Stats.1984, c. 596, § 4, eff. July 19, 1984.)*

§ 4627. Rules and regulations

The board and the administrative director may promulgate such reasonable rules and regulations as may be necessary to interpret this article and compel compliance with its provisions. *(Added by Stats.1984, c. 596, § 4, eff. July 19, 1984.)*

§ 4628. Examination of employee; preparation of medical-legal report; charges for services; failure to comply; penalties; physician's curriculum vitae

(a) Except as provided in subdivision (c), no person, other than the physician who signs the medical-legal report, except a nurse performing those functions routinely performed by a nurse, such as taking blood pressure, shall examine the injured employee or participate in the nonclerical preparation of the report, including all of the following:

(1) Taking a complete history.

(2) Reviewing and summarizing prior medical records.

(3) Composing and drafting the conclusions of the report.

(b) The report shall disclose the date when and location where the evaluation was performed; that the physician or physicians signing the report actually performed the evaluation; whether the evaluation performed and the time spent performing the evaluation was in compliance with the guidelines established by the administrative director pursuant to paragraph (5) of subdivision (j) of Section 139.2 or Section 5307.6 and shall disclose the name and qualifications of each person who performed any services in connection with the report, including diagnostic studies, other than its clerical preparation. If the report discloses that the evaluation performed or the time spent performing the evaluation was not in compliance with the guidelines established by the administrative director, the report shall explain, in detail, any variance and the reason or reasons therefor.

(c) If the initial outline of a patient's history or excerpting of prior medical records is not done by the physician, the physician shall review the excerpts and the entire outline and shall make additional inquiries and examinations as are necessary and appropriate to identify and determine the relevant medical issues.

(d) No amount may be charged in excess of the direct charges for the physician's professional services and the reasonable costs of laboratory examinations, diagnostic studies, and other medical tests, and reasonable costs of clerical expense necessary to producing the report. Direct charges for the physician's professional services shall include reasonable overhead expense.

(e) Failure to comply with the requirements of this section shall make the report inadmissible as evidence and shall eliminate any liability for payment of any medical-legal expense incurred in connection with the report.

(f) Knowing failure to comply with the requirements of this section shall subject the physician to a civil penalty of up to one thousand dollars ($1,000) for each violation to be assessed by a workers' compensation judge or the appeals board. All civil penalties collected under this section shall be deposited in the Workers' Compensation Administration Revolving Fund.

(g) A physician who is assessed a civil penalty under this section may be terminated, suspended, or placed on probation as a qualified medical evaluator pursuant to subdivisions (k) and (*l*) of Section 139.2.

(h) Knowing failure to comply with the requirements of this section shall subject the physician to contempt pursuant to the judicial powers vested in the appeals board.

(i) Any person billing for medical-legal evaluations, diagnostic procedures, or diagnostic services performed by persons other than those employed by the reporting physician or physicians, or a medical corporation owned by the reporting physician or physicians shall specify the amount paid or to be paid to those persons for the evaluations, procedures, or services. This subdivision shall not apply to any procedure or service defined or valued pursuant to Section 5307.1.

(j) The report shall contain a declaration by the physician signing the report, under penalty of perjury, stating:

"I declare under penalty of perjury that the information contained in this report and its attachments, if any, is true and correct to the best of my knowledge and belief, except as to information that I have indicated I received from others. As to that information, I declare under penalty of perjury that the information accurately describes the information provided to me and, except as noted herein, that I believe it to be true."

The foregoing declaration shall be dated and signed by the reporting physician and shall indicate the county wherein it was signed.

(k) The physician shall provide a curriculum vitae upon request by a party and include a statement concerning the percent of the physician's total practice time that is annually devoted to medical treatment. *(Added by Stats. 1989, c. 892, § 32.5. Amended by Stats.1990, c. 1550 (A.B.2910), § 34; Stats.1992, c. 1352 (A.B.3660), § 7, eff. Sept. 30, 1992; Stats.1993, c. 120 (A.B.1300), § 5, eff. July 16, 1993; Stats.2002, c. 6 (A.B.749), § 62.5; Stats.2003, c. 639 (S.B.228), § 29.)*

ARTICLE 2.6. VOCATIONAL REHABILITATION [REPEALED]

ARTICLE 3. DISABILITY PAYMENTS

Section
4650. Commencement; late payments; reimbursement of insurers for increases.
4650.5. Injury resulting from criminal act; time of commencement.
4651. Manner of payment.
4651.1. Petition alleging decrease or termination of disability; presumption of continuance of disability; service of copy of petition on employer.
4651.2. Petition of injured workman pursuing rehabilitation plan.
4651.3. Denial of petition alleging decrease or termination of disability; assessment of attorney's fees.
4652. Waiting period.
4653. Temporary total disability.
4654. Temporary partial disability.
4655. Temporary total and partial disability.
4656. Maximum aggregate disability payments and periods.
4657. Weekly loss in wages during temporary partial disability; computation of probable earnings.
4658. Permanent disability; schedule.
4658.1. "Regular work", "modified work" and "alternative work" defined; determining equivalency of wages and compensation; waiver of distance condition.
4658.5. Supplemental job displacement benefit; voucher for retraining or skill enhancement.
4658.6. Exceptions to liability for supplemental job displacement benefit.
4659. Computation of payments for permanent disability of 70 percent or over.
4660. Determination of percentages of permanent disability; nature of the physical injury or disfigurement;

Section
employee's diminished future earning capacity; schedule; regulations.
4661. Payment for temporary and permanent disabilities; computation.
4661.5. Temporary total disability indemnity; payments made two years or more from the date of injury.
4662. Disabilities presumed to be total.
4663. Apportionment of permanent disability; causation; physician's report and apportionment determination.
4664. Liability of employer for percentage of permanent disability directly caused by injury arising out of and occurring in course of employment; prior award presumption; accumulation of permanent disability awards; regions of body.

§ 4650. Commencement; late payments; reimbursement of insurers for increases

(a) If an injury causes temporary disability, the first payment of temporary disability indemnity shall be made not later than 14 days after knowledge of the injury and disability, on which date all indemnity then due shall be paid, unless liability for the injury is earlier denied.

(b) If the injury causes permanent disability, the first payment shall be made within 14 days after the date of last payment of temporary disability indemnity. When the last payment of temporary disability indemnity has been made pursuant to subdivision (c) of Section 4656, and regardless of whether the extent of permanent disability can be determined at that date, the employer nevertheless shall commence the timely payment required by this subdivision and shall continue to make these payments until the employer's reasonable estimate of permanent disability indemnity due has been paid, and if the amount of permanent disability indemnity due has been determined, until that amount has been paid.

(c) Payment of temporary or permanent disability indemnity subsequent to the first payment shall be made as due every two weeks on the day designated with the first payment.

(d) If any indemnity payment is not made timely as required by this section, the amount of the late payment shall be increased 10 percent and shall be paid, without application, to the employee, unless the employer continues the employee's wages under a salary continuation plan, as defined in subdivision (g). No increase shall apply to any payment due prior to or within 14 days after the date the claim form was submitted to the employer under Section 5401. No increase shall apply when, within the 14–day period specified under subdivision (a), the employer is unable to determine whether temporary disability indemnity payments are owed and advises the employee, in the manner prescribed in rules and regulations adopted pursuant to Section 138.4, why payments cannot be made within the 14–day period, what additional information is required to make the decision whether temporary disability indemnity payments are owed, and when the employer expects to have the information required to make the decision.

(e) If the employer is insured for its obligation to provide compensation, the employer shall be obligated to reimburse the insurer for the amount of increase in indemnity payments, made pursuant to subdivision (d), if the late payment which gives rise to the increase in indemnity payments, is due less than seven days after the insurer receives the completed claim form from the employer. Except as specified in this subdivision, an employer shall not be obligated to reimburse an insurer nor shall an insurer be permitted to seek reimbursement, directly or indirectly, for the amount of increase in indemnity payments specified in this section.

(f) If an employer is obligated under subdivision (e) to reimburse the insurer for the amount of increase in indemnity payments, the insurer shall notify the employer in writing, within 30 days of the payment, that the employer is obligated to reimburse the insurer and shall bill and collect the amount of the payment no later than at final audit. However, the insurer shall not be obligated to collect, and the employer shall not be obligated to reimburse, amounts paid pursuant to subdivision (d) unless the aggregate total paid in a policy year exceeds one hundred dollars ($100). The employer shall have 60 days, following notice of the obligation to reimburse, to appeal the decision of the insurer to the Department of Insurance. The notice of the obligation to reimburse shall specify that the employer has the right to appeal the decision of the insurer as provided in this subdivision.

(g) For purposes of this section, "salary continuation plan" means a plan that meets both of the following requirements:

(1) The plan is paid for by the employer pursuant to statute, collective bargaining agreement, memorandum of understanding, or established employer policy.

(2) The plan provides the employee on his or her regular payday with salary not less than the employee is entitled to receive pursuant to statute, collective bargaining agreement, memorandum of understanding, or established employer policy and not less than the employee would otherwise receive in indemnity payments. (Stats. 1937, c. 90, p. 282, § 4650. Amended by Stats.1947, c. 1033, p. 2305, § 5; Stats.1949, c. 408, p. 751, § 1; Stats.1949, c. 705, p. 1295, § 1; Stats.1959, c. 1189, p. 3279, § 11; Stats.1971, c. 1750, p. 3776, § 4, operative April 1, 1972; Stats.1973, c. 1021, p. 2025, § 1, operative April 1, 1974; Stats.1989, c. 892, § 34; Stats.1990, c. 1550 (A.B.2910), § 41; Stats.2004, c. 34 (S.B.899), § 28, eff. April 19, 2004.)

Operative Effect

Section 47 of Stats.2004, c. 34 (S.B.899) provides that "[t]he amendment, addition, or repeal of, any provision of law made by this act shall apply prospectively from the date of enactment of this act, regardless of the date of injury, unless otherwise specified, but shall not constitute good cause to reopen or rescind, alter, or amend any existing order, decision, or award of the Workers' Compensation Appeals Board."

§ 4650.5. Injury resulting from criminal act; time of commencement

Notwithstanding Section 4650, in the case of state civil service employees, employees of the Regents of the University of California, and employees of the Board of Trustees of the California State University, the disability payment shall be made from the first day the injured employee leaves work as a result of the injury, if the injury is the result of a criminal act of violence against the employee. (Added by Stats.1981, c. 1052, p. 4064, § 2. Amended by Stats.1983, c. 142, § 102.)

§ 4651.   Manner of payment

(a) No disability indemnity payment shall be made by any written instrument unless it is immediately negotiable and payable in cash, on demand, without discount at some established place of business in the state.

Nothing in this section shall prohibit an employer from depositing the disability indemnity payment in an account in any bank, savings and loan association or credit union of the employee's choice in this state, provided the employee has voluntarily authorized the deposit, nor shall it prohibit an employer from electronically depositing the disability indemnity payment in an account in any bank, savings and loan association, or credit union, that the employee has previously authorized to receive electronic deposits of payroll, unless the employee has requested, in writing, that disability indemnity benefits not be electronically deposited in the account.

(b) It is not a violation of this section if a delay in the negotiation of a written instrument is caused solely by the application of state or federal banking laws or regulations.

(c) On or before July 1, 2004, the administrative director shall present to the Governor recommendations on how to provide better access to funds paid to injured workers in light of the requirements of federal and state laws and regulations governing the negotiability of disability indemnity payments. The administrative director shall make specific recommendations regarding payments to migratory and seasonal farmworkers. The Commission on Health and Safety and Workers' Compensation and the Employment Development Department shall assist the administrative director in the completion of this report. (Stats.1937, c. 90, p. 282, § 4651. Amended by Stats.1947, c. 945, p. 2217, § 1; Stats.1965, c. 1513, p. 3578, § 89, operative Jan. 15, 1966; Stats.1971, c. 569, p. 1092, § 1; Stats.1972, c. 223, p. 466, § 2, eff. June 30, 1972; Stats.1973, c. 263, p. 660, § 2; Stats.1989, c. 892, § 35; Stats.2002, c. 6 (A.B.749), § 65.)

§ 4651.1. Petition alleging decrease or termination of disability; presumption of continuance of disability; service of copy of petition on employer

Where a petition is filed with the appeals board concerning a continuing award of such appeals board, in which it is alleged that the disability has decreased or terminated, there shall be a rebuttable presumption that such temporary disability continues for at least one week following the filing of such petition. In such case, payment for such week shall be made in accordance with the provisions of Sections 4650 and 4651 of this code.

Where the employee has returned to work at or prior to the date of such filing, however, no such presumption shall apply.

Service of a copy of such petition on the employee shall be made as provided by Section 5316 of this code. *(Added by Stats.1947, c. 1128, p. 2566, § 1. Amended by Stats.1965, c. 1513, p. 3579, § 90, operative Jan. 15, 1966.)*

§ 4651.2. Petition of injured workman pursuing rehabilitation plan

No petitions filed under Section 4651.1 shall be granted while the injured workman is pursuing a rehabilitation plan under Section 139.5 of this code. *(Added by Stats.1965, c. 1513, p. 3579, § 90.5, operative Jan. 15, 1966.)*

§ 4651.3. Denial of petition alleging decrease or termination of disability; assessment of attorney's fees

Where a petition is filed with the appeals board pursuant to the provisions of Section 4651.1, and is subsequently denied wholly by the appeals board, the board may determine the amount of attorney's fees reasonably incurred by the applicant in resisting the petition and may assess such reasonable attorney's fees as a cost upon the party filing the petition to decrease or terminate the award of the appeals board. *(Added by Stats.1971, c. 1558, p. 3082, § 1.)*

§ 4652. Waiting period

Except as otherwise provided by Section 4650.5, no temporary disability indemnity is recoverable for the disability suffered during the first three days after the employee leaves work as a result of the injury unless temporary disability continues for more than 14 days or the employee is hospitalized as an inpatient for treatment required by the injury, in either of which cases temporary disability indemnity shall be payable from the date of disability. For purposes of calculating the waiting period, the day of the injury shall be included unless the employee was paid full wages for that day. *(Stats.1937, c. 90, p. 282, § 4652. Amended by Stats.1949, c. 705, p. 1296, § 2; Stats.1973, c. 1021, p. 2026, § 2, operative April 1, 1974; Stats.1981, c. 1052, p. 4064, § 3; Stats.1989, c. 892, § 36.)*

§ 4653. Temporary total disability

If the injury causes temporary total disability, the disability payment is two-thirds of the average weekly earnings during the period of such disability, consideration being given to the ability of the injured employee to compete in an open labor market. *(Stats.1937, c. 90, p. 282, § 4653. Amended by Stats.1973, c. 1023, p. 2029, § 4, operative April 1, 1974.)*

§ 4654. Temporary partial disability

If the injury causes temporary partial disability, the disability payment is two-thirds of the weekly loss in wages during the period of such disability. However, such disability payment shall be reduced by the sum of unemployment compensation benefits and extended duration benefits received by the employee during the period of temporary partial disability. *(Stats.1937, c. 90, p. 282, § 4654. Amended by Stats.1967, c. 1721, p. 4289, § 1; Stats.1973, c. 1023, p. 2029, § 5, operative April 1, 1974.)*

§ 4655. Temporary total and partial disability

If the injury causes temporary disability which is at times total and at times partial, the weekly disability payment during the period of each total or partial disability is in accordance with sections 4653 and 4654 respectively. *(Stats.1937, c. 90, p. 282, § 4655.)*

§ 4656. Maximum aggregate disability payments and periods

(a) Aggregate disability payments for a single injury occurring prior to January 1, 1979, causing temporary disability shall not extend for more than 240 compensable weeks within a period of five years from the date of the injury.

(b) Aggregate disability payments for a single injury occurring on or after January 1, 1979, and prior to April 19, 2004, causing temporary partial disability shall not extend for more than 240 compensable weeks within a period of five years from the date of the injury.

(c)(1) Aggregate disability payments for a single injury occurring on or after April 19, 2004, causing temporary disability shall not extend for more than 104 compensable weeks within a period of two years from the date of commencement of temporary disability payment.

(2) Aggregate disability payments for a single injury occurring on or after January 1, 2008, causing temporary disability shall not extend for more than 104 compensable weeks within a period of five years from the date of injury.

(3) Notwithstanding paragraphs (1) and (2), for an employee who suffers from the following injuries or conditions, aggregate disability payments for a single injury occurring on or after April 19, 2004, causing temporary disability shall not extend for more than 240 compensable weeks within a period of five years from the date of the injury:

(A) Acute and chronic hepatitis B.

(B) Acute and chronic hepatitis C.

(C) Amputations.

(D) Severe burns.

(E) Human immunodeficiency virus (HIV).

(F) High–velocity eye injuries.

(G) Chemical burns to the eyes.

(H) Pulmonary fibrosis.

(I) Chronic lung disease. *(Stats.1937, c. 90, p. 282, § 4656. Amended by Stats.1947, c. 1033, p. 2305, § 4; Stats.1955, c. 956, p. 1852, § 5; Stats.1959, c. 1189, p. 3279, § 12; Stats.1978, c. 937, p. 2913, § 1; Stats.2004, c. 34 (S.B.899), § 29, eff. April 19, 2004; Stats.2007, c. 595 (A.B.338), § 1.)*

§ 4657. Weekly loss in wages during temporary partial disability; computation of probable earnings

In case of temporary partial disability the weekly loss in wages shall consist of the difference between the average weekly earnings of the injured employee and the weekly amount which the injured employee will probably be able to earn during the disability, to be determined in view of the nature and extent of the injury. In computing such probable earnings, due regard shall be given to the ability of the injured employee to compete in an open labor market. If evidence of exact loss of earnings is lacking, such weekly loss in wages may be computed from the proportionate loss of physical ability or earning power caused by the injury. *(Stats.1937, c. 90, p. 282, § 4657.)*

§ 4658. Permanent disability; schedule

(a) For injuries occurring prior to January 1, 1992, if the injury causes permanent disability, the percentage of disability to total disability shall be determined, and the disability payment computed and allowed, according to paragraph (1). However, in no event shall the disability payment allowed be less than the disability payment computed according to paragraph (2).

(1)

Column 1—Range of percentage of permanent disability incurred:	Column 2—Number of weeks for which two thirds of average weekly earnings allowed for each 1 percent of permanent disability within percentage range:
Under 10	3
10–19.75	4
20–29.75	5
30–49.75	6
50–69.75	7
70–99.75	8

The number of weeks for which payments shall be allowed set forth in column 2 above based upon the percentage of permanent disability set forth in column 1 above shall be cumulative, and the number of benefit weeks shall increase with the severity of the disability. The following schedule is illustrative of the computation of the number of benefit weeks:

Column 1—Percentage of permanent disability incurred:	Column 2—Cumulative number of benefit weeks:
5	15.00
10	30.25

15	50.25
20	70.50
25	95.50
30	120.75
35	150.75
40	180.75
45	210.75
50	241.00
55	276.00
60	311.00
65	346.00
70	381.25
75	421.25
80	461.25
85	501.25
90	541.25
95	581.25
100	for life

(2) Two–thirds of the average weekly earnings for four weeks for each 1 percent of disability, where, for the purposes of this subdivision, the average weekly earnings shall be taken at not more than seventy-eight dollars and seventy-five cents ($78.75).

(b) This subdivision shall apply to injuries occurring on or after January 1, 1992. If the injury causes permanent disability, the percentage of disability to total disability shall be determined, and the disability payment computed and allowed, according to paragraph (1). However, in no event shall the disability payment allowed be less than the disability payment computed according to paragraph (2).

(1)

Column 1—Range of percentage of permanent disability incurred:	Column 2—Number of weeks for which two thirds of average weekly earnings allowed for each 1 percent of permanent disability within percentage range:
Under 10	3
10–19.75	4
20–24.75	5
25–29.75	6
30–49.75	7
50–69.75	8
70–99.75	9

The numbers set forth in column 2 above are based upon the percentage of permanent disability set forth in column 1 above and shall be cumulative, and shall increase with the severity of the disability in the manner illustrated in subdivision (a).

(2) Two–thirds of the average weekly earnings for four weeks for each 1 percent of disability, where, for the purposes of this subdivision, the average weekly earnings shall be taken at not more than seventy-eight dollars and seventy-five cents ($78.75).

(c) This subdivision shall apply to injuries occurring on or after January 1, 2004. If the injury causes permanent disability, the percentage of disability to total disability shall be determined, and the disability payment computed and allowed as follows:

Column 1—Range of percentage of permanent disability incurred:	Column 2—Number of weeks for which two thirds of average weekly earnings allowed for each 1 percent of permanent disability within percentage range:
Under 10	4
10–19.75	5
20–24.75	5
25–29.75	6
30–49.75	7
50–69.75	8
70–99.75	9

The numbers set forth in column 2 above are based upon the percentage of permanent disability set forth in column 1 above and shall be cumulative, and shall increase with the severity of the disability in the manner illustrated in subdivision (a).

(d)(1) This subdivision shall apply to injuries occurring on or after the effective date of the revised permanent disability schedule adopted by the administrative director pursuant to Section 4660. If the injury causes permanent disability, the percentage of disability to total disability shall be determined, and the basic disability payment computed as follows:

Column 1—Range of percentage of permanent disability incurred:	Column 2—Number of weeks for which two thirds of average weekly earnings allowed for each 1 percent of permanent disability within percentage range:
0.25–9.75	3
10–14.75	4
15–24.75	5
25–29.75	6
30–49.75	7
50–69.75	8
70–99.75	16

The numbers set forth in column 2 above are based upon the percentage of permanent disability set forth in column 1 above and shall be cumulative, and shall increase with the severity of the disability in the manner illustrated in subdivision (a).

(2) If, within 60 days of a disability becoming permanent and stationary, an employer does not offer the injured employee regular work, modified work, or alternative work, in the form and manner prescribed by the administrative director, for a period of at least 12 months, each disability payment remaining to be paid to the injured employee from the date of the end of the 60–day period shall be paid in accordance with paragraph (1) and increased by 15 percent. This paragraph shall not apply to an employer that employs fewer than 50 employees.

(3)(A) If, within 60 days of a disability becoming permanent and stationary, an employer offers the injured employee regular work, modified work, or alternative work, in the form and manner prescribed by the administrative director, for a period of at least 12 months, and regardless of whether the injured employee accepts or rejects the offer, each disability payment remaining to be paid to the injured employee from the date the offer was made shall be paid in accordance with paragraph (1) and decreased by 15 percent.

(B) If the regular work, modified work, or alternative work is terminated by the employer before the end of the period for which disability payments are due the injured employee, the amount of each of the remaining disability payments shall be paid in accordance with paragraph (1) and increased by 15 percent. An employee who voluntarily terminates employment shall not be eligible for payment under this subparagraph. This paragraph shall not apply to an employer that employs fewer than 50 employees.

(4) For compensable claims arising before April 30, 2004, the schedule provided in this subdivision shall not apply to the determination of permanent disabilities when there has been either a comprehensive medical-legal report or a report by a treating physician, indicating the existence of permanent disability, or when the employer is required to provide the notice required by Section 4061 to the injured worker. (Stats.1937, c. 90, p. 283, § 4658. Amended by Stats.1949, c. 1583, p. 2883, § 1; Stats.1959, c. 1189, p. 3280, § 13; Stats.1971, c. 1750, p. 3776, § 5, operative April 1, 1972; Stats 1973, c. 1023, p. 2029, § 6, operative April 1, 1974; Stats.1989, c. 892, § 37; Stats. 1989, c. 893, § 4; Stats.2002, c. 6 (A.B.749), § 66; Stats.2004, c. 34 (S.B.899), § 30, eff. April 19, 2004.)

Operative Effect

Section 47 of Stats.2004, c. 34 (S.B.899) provides that "[t]he amendment, addition, or repeal of, any provision of law made by this act shall apply prospectively from the date of enactment of this act, regardless of the date of injury, unless otherwise specified, but shall not constitute good cause to reopen or rescind, alter, or amend any existing order, decision, or award of the Workers' Compensation Appeals Board."

§ 4658.1. "Regular work", "modified work" and "alternative work" defined; determining equivalency of wages and compensation; waiver of distance condition

As used in this article, the following definitions apply:

(a) "Regular work" means the employee's usual occupation or the position in which the employee was engaged at the time of injury and that offers wages and compensation equivalent to those paid to the employee at the time of injury, and located within a reasonable commuting distance of the employee's residence at the time of injury.

(b) "Modified work" means regular work modified so that the employee has the ability to perform all the functions of the job and that offers wages and compensation that are at least 85 percent of those paid to the employee at the time of injury, and located within a reasonable commuting distance of the employee's residence at the time of injury.

(c) "Alternative work" means work that the employee has the ability to perform, that offers wages and compensation that are at least 85 percent of those paid to the employee at the time of injury, and that is located within reasonable commuting distance of the employee's residence at the time of injury.

(d) For the purpose of determining whether wages and compensation are equivalent to those paid at the time of injury, the wages and compensation for any increase in working hours over the average hours worked at the time of injury shall not be considered.

(e) For the purpose of determining whether wages and compensation are equivalent to those paid at the time of injury, actual wages and compensation shall be determined without regard to the minimums and maximums set forth in Chapter 1 (commencing with Section 4451).

(f) The condition that regular work, modified work, or alternative work be located within a reasonable distance of the employee's residence at the time of injury may be waived by the employee. The condition shall be deemed to be waived if the employee accepts the regular work, modified work, or alternative work and does not object to the location within 20 days of being informed of the right to object. The condition shall be conclusively deemed to be satisfied if the offered work is at the same location and the same shift as the employment at the time of injury. *(Added by Stats.2004, c. 34 (S.B.899), § 31, eff. April 19, 2004.)*

Operative Effect

Section 47 of Stats.2004, c. 34 (S.B.899) provides that "[t]he amendment, addition, or repeal of, any provision of law made by this act shall apply prospectively from the date of enactment of this act, regardless of the date of injury, unless otherwise specified, but shall not constitute good cause to reopen or rescind, alter, or amend any existing order, decision, or award of the Workers' Compensation Appeals Board."

§ 4658.5. Supplemental job displacement benefit; voucher for retraining or skill enhancement

(a) Except as provided in Section 4658.6, if the injury causes permanent partial disability and the injured employee does not return to work for the employer within 60 days of the termination of temporary disability, the injured employee shall be eligible for a supplemental job displacement benefit in the form of a nontransferable voucher for education-related retraining or skill enhancement, or both, at state-approved or accredited schools, as follows:

(1) Up to four thousand dollars ($4,000) for permanent partial disability awards of less than 15 percent.

(2) Up to six thousand dollars ($6,000) for permanent partial disability awards between 15 and 25 percent.

(3) Up to eight thousand dollars ($8,000) for permanent partial disability awards between 26 and 49 percent.

(4) Up to ten thousand dollars ($10,000) for permanent partial disability awards between 50 and 99 percent.

(b) The voucher may be used for payment of tuition, fees, books, and other expenses required by the school for retraining or skill enhancement. No more than 10 percent of the voucher moneys may be used for vocational or return-to-work counseling. The administrative director shall adopt regulations governing the form of payment, direct reimbursement to the injured employee upon presentation to the employer of appropriate documentation and receipts, and other matters necessary to the proper administration of the supplemental job displacement benefit.

(c) Within 10 days of the last payment of temporary disability, the employer shall provide to the employee, in the form and manner prescribed by the administrative director, information that provides notice of rights under this section. This notice shall be sent by certified mail.

(d) This section shall apply to injuries occurring on or after January 1, 2004. *(Added by Stats.2003, c. 635 (A.B.227), § 14.4. Amended by Stats.2005, c. 22 (S.B. 1108), § 144; Stats.2008, c. 179 (S.B.1498), § 176.)*

§ 4658.6. Exceptions to liability for supplemental job displacement benefit

The employer shall not be liable for the supplemental job displacement benefit if the employer meets either of the following conditions:

(a) Within 30 days of the termination of temporary disability indemnity payments, the employer offers, and the employee rejects, or fails to accept, in the form and manner prescribed by the administrative director, modified work, accommodating the employee's work restrictions, lasting at least 12 months.

(b) Within 30 days of the termination of temporary disability indemnity payments, the employer offers, and the employee rejects, or fails to accept, in the form and manner prescribed by the administrative director, alternative work meeting all of the following conditions:

(1) The employee has the ability to perform the essential functions of the job provided.

(2) The job provided is in a regular position lasting at least 12 months.

(3) The job provided offers wages and compensation that are within 15 percent of those paid to the employee at the time of injury.

(4) The job is located within reasonable commuting distance of the employee's residence at the time of injury. *(Added by Stats.2003, c. 635 (A.B.227), § 15.)*

§ 4659. Computation of payments for permanent disability of 70 percent or over

(a) If the permanent disability is at least 70 percent, but less than 100 percent, 1.5 percent of the average weekly earnings for each 1 percent of disability in excess of 60 percent is to be paid during the remainder of life, after payment for the maximum number of weeks specified in Section 4658 has been made. For the purposes of this subdivision only, average weekly earnings shall be taken at not more than one hundred seven dollars and sixty-nine cents ($107.69). For injuries occurring on or after July 1, 1994, average weekly wages shall not be taken at more than one hundred fifty-seven dollars and sixty-nine cents ($157.69). For injuries occurring on or after July 1, 1995, average weekly wages shall not be taken at more than two hundred seven dollars and sixty-nine cents ($207.69). For injuries occurring on or after July 1, 1996, average weekly wages shall not be taken at more than two hundred fifty-seven dollars and sixty-nine cents ($257.69). For injuries occurring on or after January 1, 2006, average weekly wages shall not be taken at more than five hundred fifteen dollars and thirty-eight cents ($515.38).

(b) If the permanent disability is total, the indemnity based upon the average weekly earnings determined under Section 4453 shall be paid during the remainder of life.

(c) For injuries occurring on or after January 1, 2003, an employee who becomes entitled to receive a life pension or total permanent disability indemnity as set forth in subdivisions (a) and (b) shall have that payment increased annually commencing on January 1, 2004, and each January 1 thereafter, by an amount equal to the percentage increase in the "state average weekly wage" as compared to the prior year. For purposes of this subdivision, "state average weekly wage" means the average weekly wage paid by employers to employees covered by unemployment insurance as reported by the United States Department of Labor for California for the 12 months ending March 31 of the calendar year preceding the year in which the injury occurred. *(Added by Stats.1971, c. 1750, p. 3777, § 5.7, operative April 1, 1972. Amended by Stats.1973, c. 1023, p. 2030, § 7, operative April 1, 1974; Stats.1993, c. 121 (A.B.110), § 52.5, eff. July 16, 1993, Stats.2002, c. 6 (A.B.749), § 67.)*

§ 4660. Determination of percentages of permanent disability; nature of the physical injury or disfigurement; employee's diminished future earning capacity; schedule; regulations

(a) In determining the percentages of permanent disability, account shall be taken of the nature of the physical injury or disfigurement, the occupation of the injured employee, and his or her age at the time of the injury, consideration being given to an employee's diminished future earning capacity.

(b)(1) For purposes of this section, the "nature of the physical injury or disfigurement" shall incorporate the descriptions and measurements of physical impairments and the corresponding percentages of impairments published in the American Medical Association (AMA) Guides to the Evaluation of Permanent Impairment (5th Edition).

(2) For purposes of this section, an employee's diminished future earning capacity shall be a numeric formula

based on empirical data and findings that aggregate the average percentage of long-term loss of income resulting from each type of injury for similarly situated employees. The administrative director shall formulate the adjusted rating schedule based on empirical data and findings from the Evaluation of California's Permanent Disability Rating Schedule, Interim Report (December 2003), prepared by the RAND Institute for Civil Justice, and upon data from additional empirical studies.

(c) The administrative director shall amend the schedule for the determination of the percentage of permanent disability in accordance with this section at least once every five years. This schedule shall be available for public inspection and, without formal introduction in evidence, shall be prima facie evidence of the percentage of permanent disability to be attributed to each injury covered by the schedule.

(d) The schedule shall promote consistency, uniformity, and objectivity. The schedule and any amendment thereto or revision thereof shall apply prospectively and shall apply to and govern only those permanent disabilities that result from compensable injuries received or occurring on and after the effective date of the adoption of the schedule, amendment or revision, as the fact may be. For compensable claims arising before January 1, 2005, the schedule as revised pursuant to changes made in legislation enacted during the 2003–04 Regular and Extraordinary Sessions shall apply to the determination of permanent disabilities when there has been either no comprehensive medical-legal report or no report by a treating physician indicating the existence of permanent disability, or when the employer is not required to provide the notice required by Section 4061 to the injured worker.

(e) On or before January 1, 2005, the administrative director shall adopt regulations to implement the changes made to this section by the act that added this subdivision. *(Stats.1937, c. 90, p. 283, § 4660. Amended by Stats.1951, c. 1688, p. 3880, § 1; Stats.1965, c. 1513, p. 3579, § 91, operative Jan. 15, 1966; Stats.1993, c. 121 (A.B.110), § 53, eff. July 16, 1993; Stats.2004, c. 34 (S.B.899), § 32, eff. April 19, 2004.)*

Operative Effect

Section 47 of Stats.2004, c. 34 (S.B.899) provides that "[t]he amendment, addition, or repeal of, any provision of law made by this act shall apply prospectively from the date of enactment of this act, regardless of the date of injury, unless otherwise specified, but shall not constitute good cause to reopen or rescind, alter, or amend any existing order, decision, or award of the Workers' Compensation Appeals Board."

§ 4661. Payment for temporary and permanent disabilities; computation

Where an injury causes both temporary and permanent disability, the injured employee is entitled to compensation for any permanent disability sustained by him in addition to any payment received by such injured employee for temporary disability.

Every computation made pursuant to this section shall be made only with reference to disability resulting from an original injury sustained after this section as amended during the 1949 Regular Session of the Legislature becomes effective; provided, however, that all rights presently existing under this section shall be continued in force. *(Stats.1937, c. 90, p. 284, § 4661. Amended by Stats.1945, c. 1335, p. 2506, § 1; Stats.1947, c. 1132, p. 2572, § 1; Stats.1949, c. 107, p. 346, § 1.)*

§ 4661.5. Temporary total disability indemnity; payments made two years or more from the date of injury

Notwithstanding any other provision of this division, when any temporary total disability indemnity payment is made two years or more from the date of injury, the amount of this payment shall be computed in accordance with the temporary disability indemnity average weekly earnings amount specified in Section 4453 in effect on the date each temporary total disability payment is made unless computing the payment on this basis produces a lower payment because of a reduction in the minimum average weekly earnings applicable under Section 4453. *(Added by Stats.1974, c. 1294, p. 2818, § 1. Amended by Stats.1978, c. 247, p. 519, § 1; Stats.1989, c. 892, § 38.)*

§ 4662. Disabilities presumed to be total

Any of the following permanent disabilities shall be conclusively presumed to be total in character:

(a) Loss of both eyes or the sight thereof.

(b) Loss of both hands or the use thereof.

(c) An injury resulting in a practically total paralysis.

(d) An injury to the brain resulting in incurable mental incapacity or insanity.

In all other cases, permanent total disability shall be determined in accordance with the fact. *(Stats.1937, c. 90, p. 284, § 4662. Amended by Stats.2007, c. 31 (A.B. 1640), § 2.)*

§ 4663. Apportionment of permanent disability; causation; physician's report and apportionment determination

(a) Apportionment of permanent disability shall be based on causation.

(b) Any physician who prepares a report addressing the issue of permanent disability due to a claimed industrial injury shall in that report address the issue of causation of the permanent disability.

(c) In order for a physician's report to be considered complete on the issue of permanent disability, the report must include an apportionment determination. A physician shall make an apportionment determination by finding what approximate percentage of the permanent disability was caused by the direct result of injury arising

out of and occurring in the course of employment and what approximate percentage of the permanent disability was caused by other factors both before and subsequent to the industrial injury, including prior industrial injuries. If the physician is unable to include an apportionment determination in his or her report, the physician shall state the specific reasons why the physician could not make a determination of the effect of that prior condition on the permanent disability arising from the injury. The physician shall then consult with other physicians or refer the employee to another physician from whom the employee is authorized to seek treatment or evaluation in accordance with this division in order to make the final determination.

(d) An employee who claims an industrial injury shall, upon request, disclose all previous permanent disabilities or physical impairments.

(e) Subdivisions (a), (b), and (c) shall not apply to injuries or illnesses covered under Sections 3212, 3212.1, 3212.2, 3212.3, 3212.4, 3212.5, 3212.6, 3212.7, 3212.8, 3212.85, 3212.9, 3212.10, 3212.11, 3212.12, 3213, and 3213.2. *(Added by Stats.2004, c. 34 (S.B.899), § 34, eff. April 19, 2004. Amended by Stats.2006, c. 836 (A.B.1368), § 1.)*

Operative Effect

Section 47 of Stats.2004, c. 34 (S.B.899) provides that "[t]he amendment, addition, or repeal of, any provision of law made by this act shall apply prospectively from the date of enactment of this act, regardless of the date of injury, unless otherwise specified, but shall not constitute good cause to reopen or rescind, alter, or amend any existing order, decision, or award of the Workers' Compensation Appeals Board."

§ 4664. Liability of employer for percentage of permanent disability directly caused by injury arising out of and occurring in course of employment; prior award presumption; accumulation of permanent disability awards; regions of body

(a) The employer shall only be liable for the percentage of permanent disability directly caused by the injury arising out of and occurring in the course of employment.

(b) If the applicant has received a prior award of permanent disability, it shall be conclusively presumed that the prior permanent disability exists at the time of any subsequent industrial injury. This presumption is a presumption affecting the burden of proof.

(c)(1) The accumulation of all permanent disability awards issued with respect to any one region of the body in favor of one individual employee shall not exceed 100 percent over the employee's lifetime unless the employee's injury or illness is conclusively presumed to be total in character pursuant to Section 4662. As used in this section, the regions of the body are the following:

(A) Hearing.

(B) Vision.

(C) Mental and behavioral disorders.

(D) The spine.

(E) The upper extremities, including the shoulders.

(F) The lower extremities, including the hip joints.

(G) The head, face, cardiovascular system, respiratory system, and all other systems or regions of the body not listed in subparagraphs (A) to (F), inclusive.

(2) Nothing in this section shall be construed to permit the permanent disability rating for each individual injury sustained by an employee arising from the same industrial accident, when added together, from exceeding 100 percent. *(Added by Stats.2004, c. 34 (S.B.899), § 35, eff. April 19, 2004.)*

Operative Effect

Section 47 of Stats.2004, c. 34 (S.B.899) provides that "[t]he amendment, addition, or repeal of, any provision of law made by this act shall apply prospectively from the date of enactment of this act, regardless of the date of injury, unless otherwise specified, but shall not constitute good cause to reopen or rescind, alter, or amend any existing order, decision, or award of the Workers' Compensation Appeals Board."

ARTICLE 4. DEATH BENEFITS

Section
4700. Effect of death on liability, accrued compensation; payment.
4701. Liability of employer for burial expenses and death benefits.
4702. Death benefit.
4703. Allocation of death benefit.
4703.5. Continued payments for totally dependent minor children.
4703.6. Application of § 4703.5 to totally dependent minor child of designated safety and patrol members.
4704. Power of appeals board to adjust allocation; payment of benefit.
4705. Application of benefit payment.
4706. Death of dependent beneficiary without surviving dependent.
4706.5. Death of employee without surviving dependent; payment to department for subsequent injuries.
4707. Death of active member of public employee's retirement system; exceptions.
4708. Determination of cause of death of member of retirement system.
4709. Scholarships for dependents of peace officers, officers or employees of departments of corrections or youth authority, and firefighters.

§ 4700. Effect of death on liability, accrued compensation; payment

The death of an injured employee does not affect the liability of the employer under Articles 2 (commencing with Section 4600) and 3 (commencing with Section 4650). Neither temporary nor permanent disability pay-ments shall be made for any period of time subsequent to the death of the employee. Any accrued and unpaid compensation shall be paid to the dependents, or, if there are no dependents, to the personal representative of the deceased employee or heirs or other persons entitled thereto, without administration. *(Stats.1937, c. 90, p. 284, § 4700. Amended by Stats.1969, c. 850, p. 1682, § 1; Stats.1972, c. 1334, p. 2666, § 1; Stats.1983, c. 142, § 103.)*

§ 4701. Liability of employer for burial expenses and death benefits

When an injury causes death, either with or without disability, the employer shall be liable, in addition to any other benefits provided by this division, for all of the following:

(a) Reasonable expenses of the employee's burial, not exceeding two thousand dollars ($2,000) and for injuries occurring on and after January 1, 1991, not exceeding five thousand dollars ($5,000).

(b) A death benefit, to be allowed to the dependents when the employee leaves any person dependent upon him or her for support. *(Stats.1937, c. 90, p. 284, § 4701. Amended by Stats.1943, c. 678, p. 2433, § 1; Stats.1949, c. 321, p. 609, § 1; Stats.1959, c. 1189, p. 3280, § 15; Stats.1968, 1st Ex.Sess., c. 4, p. 32, § 7, operative Jan. 1, 1969; Stats.1978, c. 487, p. 1616, § 1; Stats.1985, c. 1567, § 1; Stats.1988, c. 584, § 1; Stats.1989, c. 892, § 39.)*

§ 4702. Death benefit

(a) Except as otherwise provided in this section and Sections 4553, 4554, 4557, and 4558, and notwithstanding any amount of compensation paid or otherwise owing to the surviving dependent, personal representative, heir, or other person entitled to a deceased employee's accrued and unpaid compensation, the death benefit in cases of total dependency shall be as follows:

(1) In the case of two total dependents and regardless of the number of partial dependents, for injuries occurring before January 1, 1991, ninety-five thousand dollars ($95,000), for injuries occurring on or after January 1, 1991, one hundred fifteen thousand dollars ($115,000), for injuries occurring on or after July 1, 1994, one hundred thirty-five thousand dollars ($135,000), for injuries occurring on or after July 1, 1996, one hundred forty-five thousand dollars ($145,000), and for injuries occurring on or after January 1, 2006, two hundred ninety thousand dollars ($290,000).

(2) In the case of one total dependent and one or more partial dependents, for injuries occurring before January 1, 1991, seventy thousand dollars ($70,000), for injuries occurring on or after January 1, 1991, ninety-five thousand dollars ($95,000), for injuries occurring on or after July 1, 1994, one hundred fifteen thousand dollars ($115,000), for injuries occurring on or after July 1, 1996, one hundred twenty-five thousand dollars ($125,000), and for injuries occurring on or after January 1, 2006, two hundred fifty thousand dollars ($250,000), plus four times

the amount annually devoted to the support of the partial dependents, but not more than the following: for injuries occurring before January 1, 1991, a total of ninety-five thousand dollars ($95,000), for injuries occurring on or after January 1, 1991, one hundred fifteen thousand dollars ($115,000), for injuries occurring on or after July 1, 1994, one hundred twenty-five thousand dollars ($125,-000), for injuries occurring on or after July 1, 1996, one hundred forty-five thousand dollars ($145,000), and for injuries occurring on or after January 1, 2006, two hundred ninety thousand dollars ($290,000).

(3) In the case of one total dependent and no partial dependents, for injuries occurring before January 1, 1991, seventy thousand dollars ($70,000), for injuries occurring on or after January 1, 1991, ninety-five thousand dollars ($95,000), for injuries occurring on or after July 1, 1994, one hundred fifteen thousand dollars ($115,000), for injuries occurring on or after July 1, 1996, one hundred twenty-five thousand dollars ($125,000), and for injuries occurring on or after January 1, 2006, two hundred fifty thousand dollars ($250,000).

(4)(A) In the case of no total dependents and one or more partial dependents, for injuries occurring before January 1, 1991, four times the amount annually devoted to the support of the partial dependents, but not more than seventy thousand dollars ($70,000), for injuries occurring on or after January 1, 1991, a total of ninety-five thousand dollars ($95,000), for injuries occurring on or after July 1, 1994, one hundred fifteen thousand dollars ($115,000), and for injuries occurring on or after July 1, 1996, but before January 1, 2006, one hundred twenty-five thousand dollars ($125,000).

(B) In the case of no total dependents and one or more partial dependents, eight times the amount annually devoted to the support of the partial dependents, for injuries occurring on or after January 1, 2006, but not more than two hundred fifty thousand dollars ($250,000).

(5) In the case of three or more total dependents and regardless of the number of partial dependents, one hundred fifty thousand dollars ($150,000), for injuries occurring on or after July 1, 1994, one hundred sixty thousand dollars ($160,000), for injuries occurring on or after July 1, 1996, and three hundred twenty thousand dollars ($320,000), for injuries occurring on or after January 1, 2006.

(6)(A) In the case of a police officer who has no total dependents and no partial dependents, for injuries occurring on or after January 1, 2003, and prior to January 1, 2004, two hundred fifty thousand dollars ($250,000) to the estate of the deceased police officer.

(B) For injuries occurring on or after January 1, 2004, in the case of no total dependents and no partial dependents, two hundred fifty thousand dollars ($250,-000) to the estate of the deceased employee.

(b) A death benefit in all cases shall be paid in installments in the same manner and amounts as temporary total disability indemnity would have to be made to

642

the employee, unless the appeals board otherwise orders. However, no payment shall be made at a weekly rate of less than two hundred twenty-four dollars ($224).

(c) Disability indemnity shall not be deducted from the death benefit and shall be paid in addition to the death benefit when the injury resulting in death occurs after September 30, 1949.

(d) All rights under this section existing prior to January 1, 1990, shall be continued in force. *(Stats.1937, c. 90, p. 284, § 4702. Amended by Stats.1939, c. 308, p. 1581, § 3; Stats.1947, c. 1031, p. 2302, § 1; Stats.1949, c. 410, p. 752, § 1; Stats.1949, c. 1414, p. 2466, § 1; Stats.1951, c. 606, p. 1768, § 7; Stats.1951, c. 1437, p. 3395, § 2; Stats.1955, c. 956, p. 1852, § 6; Stats.1957, c. 1996, p. 3553, § 6; Stats.1959, c. 1189, p. 3280, § 16; Stats.1965, c. 1513, p. 3579, § 92, operative Jan. 15, 1966; Stats.1968, 1st Ex.Sess., c. 4, p. 33, § 8, operative Jan. 1, 1969; Stats.1969, c. 65, p. 187, § 1, eff. May 1, 1969; Stats.1971, c. 1750, p. 3777, § 6, operative April 1, 1972; Stats.1972, c. 1151, p. 2267, § 1; Stats.1973, c. 1022, p. 2026, § 1; Stats.1976, c. 1017, p. 4595, § 6; Stats.1979, c. 749, p. 2600, § 4; Stats.1980, c. 1042, p. 3329, § 4; Stats. 1982, c. 922, p. 3370, § 13; Stats.1983, c. 142, § 104; Stats.1989, c. 892, § 40; Stats.1990, c. 1550 (A.B.2910), § 42; Stats.1993, c. 121 (A.B.110), § 53.5, eff. July 16, 1993; Stats.1994, c. 1097 (S.B.1803), § 18; Stats.2002, c. 6 (A.B.749), § 68; Stats.2002, c. 866 (A.B.486), § 12; Stats.2004, c. 92 (A.B.1840), § 1; Stats.2006, c. 119 (A.B.2292), § 2.)*

Validity

This statute was held unconstitutional in the decision of Six Flags, Inc. v. W.C.A.B. (App. 2 Dist. 2006) 51 Cal.Rptr.3d 377, 145 Cal.App.4th 91.

Operative Effect

Section 2 of Stats.2004, c. 92 (A.B.1840) provides that the intent of the Legislature is that the amendment to this section shall have retroactive effect.

§ 4703. Allocation of death benefit

Subject to the provisions of Section 4704, this section shall determine the right to a death benefit.

If there is any person wholly dependent for support upon a deceased employee, that person shall receive a full death benefit as set forth in Section 4702 for one total dependent, and any additional partial dependents shall receive a death benefit as set forth in subdivision (b) of Section 4702 to a maximum aggregate amount of twenty-five thousand dollars ($25,000).

If there are two or more persons wholly dependent for support upon a deceased employee, those persons shall receive the death benefit set forth in subdivision (a) of Section 4702, and any person partially dependent shall receive no part thereof.

If there is more than one person wholly dependent for support upon a deceased employee, the death benefit shall be divided equally among them.

If there is more than one person partially dependent for support upon a deceased employee, and no person wholly dependent for support, the amount allowed as a death benefit shall be divided among the persons so partially dependent in proportion to the relative extent of their dependency. *(Stats.1937, c. 90, p. 285, § 4703. Amended by Stats.1981, c. 210, p. 1130, § 1.)*

§ 4703.5. Continued payments for totally dependent minor children

In the case of one or more totally dependent minor children, as defined in Section 3501, after payment of the amount specified in Section 4702, and notwithstanding the maximum limitations specified in Sections 4702 and 4703, payment of death benefits shall continue until the youngest child attains age 18, or until the death of a child physically or mentally incapacitated from earning, in the same manner and amount as temporary total disability indemnity would have been paid to the employee, except that no payment shall be made at a weekly rate of less than two hundred twenty-four dollars ($224). *(Added by Stats.1989, c. 892, § 41. Amended by Stats.1990, c. 1550 (A.B.2910), § 43; Stats.2002, c. 6 (A.B.749), § 69.)*

§ 4703.6. Application of § 4703.5 to totally dependent minor child of designated safety and patrol members

The provisions of Section 4703.5 shall also apply to a totally dependent minor child of a local safety member as defined in Article 4 (commencing with Section 20420) of Chapter 4 of Part 3 of Division 5 of Title 2 of the Government Code, or a safety member as defined in Section 31469.3 of the Government Code, other than a member performing duties related to juvenile hall group counseling and group supervision, or a safety member subject to any public retirement system, or a patrol member as defined in Section 20390 of the Government Code, if that member was killed in the line of duty prior to January 1, 1990, and the totally dependent minor child is otherwise entitled to benefits under Section 4703.5. *(Added by Stats.2001, c. 589 (A.B.262), § 1. Amended by Stats.2002, c. 296 (A.B.2008), § 1, eff. Aug. 28, 2002.)*

Operative Effect

Section 2 of Stats.2002, c. 296 (A.B.2008) provides that the provisions of that act shall apply retroactively to January 1, 2002.

§ 4704. Power of appeals board to adjust allocation; payment of benefit

The appeals board may set apart or reassign the death benefit to any one or more of the dependents in accordance with their respective needs and in a just and equitable manner, and may order payment to a dependent subsequent in right, or not otherwise entitled thereto, upon good cause being shown therefor. The death benefit shall be paid to such one or more of the dependents of the deceased or to a trustee appointed by the appeals board for the benefit of the person entitled thereto, as determined by the appeals board. *(Stats.1937, c. 90, p. 285, § 4704. Amended by Stats.1965, c. 1513, p. 3580, § 93, operative Jan. 15, 1966.)*

§ 4705. Application of benefit payment

The person to whom the death benefit is paid for the use of the several beneficiaries shall apply it in compliance with the findings and directions of the appeals board. *(Stats.1937, c. 90, p. 285, § 4705. Amended by Stats.1965, c. 1513, p. 3580, § 94, operative Jan. 15, 1966.)*

§ 4706. Death of dependent beneficiary without surviving dependent

(a) If a dependent beneficiary of any deceased employee dies and there is no surviving dependent, the payments of the death benefit accrued and payable at the time of the death of the sole remaining dependent shall be paid upon the order of the appeals board to the heirs of the dependent or, if none, to the heirs of the deceased employee, without administration.

(b) In the event there is no surviving dependent and no surviving heir, the appeals board may order the burial expense of the deceased employee, not to exceed the amount specified in Section 4701, paid to the proper person, without administration. *(Stats.1937, c. 90, p. 285, § 4706. Amended by Stats.1957, c. 1996, p. 3551, § 1; Stats.1965, c. 1513, p. 3580, § 95, operative Jan. 15, 1966; Stats.1972, c. 1334, p. 2666, § 2.)*

§ 4706.5. Death of employee without surviving dependent; payment to department for subsequent injuries

(a) Whenever any fatal injury is suffered by an employee under circumstances that would entitle the employee to compensation benefits, but for his or her death, and the employee does not leave surviving any person entitled to a dependency death benefit, the employer shall pay a sum to the Department of Industrial Relations equal to the total dependency death benefit that would be payable to a surviving spouse with no dependent minor children.

(b) When the deceased employee leaves no surviving dependent, personal representative, heir, or other person entitled to the accrued and unpaid compensation referred to in Section 4700, the accrued and unpaid compensation shall be paid by the employer to the Department of Industrial Relations.

(c) The payments to be made to the Department of Industrial Relations, as required by subdivisions (a) and (b), shall be deposited in the General Fund and shall be credited, as a reimbursement, to any appropriation to the Department of Industrial Relations for payment of the additional compensation for subsequent injury provided in Article 5 (commencing with Section 4751), in the fiscal year in which the Controller's receipt is issued.

(d) The payments to be made to the Department of Industrial Relations, as required by subdivision (a), shall be paid to the department in a lump sum in the manner provided in subdivision (b) of Section 5101.

(e) The Department of Industrial Relations shall keep a record of all payments due the state under this section, and shall take any steps as may be necessary to collect those amounts.

(f) Each employer, or the employer's insurance carrier, shall notify the administrative director, in any form as the administrative director may prescribe, of each employee death, except when the employer has actual knowledge or notice that the deceased employee left a surviving dependent.

(g) When, after a reasonable search, the employer concludes that the deceased employee left no one surviving who is entitled to a dependency death benefit, and concludes that the death was under circumstances that would entitle the employee to compensation benefits, the employer may voluntarily make the payment referred to in subdivision (a). Payments so made shall be construed as payments made pursuant to an appeals board findings and award. Thereafter, if the appeals board finds that the deceased employee did in fact leave a person surviving who is entitled to a dependency death benefit, upon that finding, all payments referred to in subdivision (a) that have been made shall be forthwith returned to the employer, or if insured, to the employer's workers' compensation carrier that indemnified the employer for the loss.

(h) This section does not apply where there is no surviving person entitled to a dependency death benefit or accrued and unpaid compensation if a death benefit is paid to any person under paragraph (6) of subdivision (a) of Section 4702. *(Added by Stats.1972, c. 1334, p. 2666, § 3. Amended by Stats.1973, c. 21, p. 37, § 1, eff. April 12, 1973, operative March 7, 1973; Stats.1974, c. 854, p. 1819, § 1; Stats.1978, c. 471, p. 1587, § 1, operative July 1, 1979; Stats.1983, c. 142, § 105; Stats.2004, c. 34 (S.B.899), § 36, eff. April 19, 2004; Stats.2006, c. 119 (A.B.2292), § 3.)*

Operative Effect

Section 47 of Stats.2004, c. 34 (S.B.899) provides that "[t]he amendment, addition, or repeal of, any provision of law made by this act shall apply prospectively from the date of enactment of this act, regardless of the date of injury, unless otherwise specified, but shall not constitute good cause to reopen or rescind, alter, or amend any existing order, decision, or award of the Workers' Compensation Appeals Board."

§ 4707. Death of active member of public employee's retirement system; exceptions

(a) Except as provided in subdivision (b), no benefits, except reasonable expenses of burial not exceeding one thousand dollars ($1,000), shall be awarded under this division on account of the death of an employee who is an active member of the Public Employees' Retirement System unless it is determined that a special death

benefit, as defined in the Public Employees' Retirement Law, or the benefit provided in lieu of the special death benefit in Sections 21547 and 21548 of the Government Code, will not be paid by the Public Employees' Retirement System to the surviving spouse or children under 18 years of age, of the deceased, on account of the death, but if the total death allowance paid to the surviving spouse and children is less than the benefit otherwise payable under this division the surviving spouse and children are entitled, under this division, to the difference.

The amendments to this section during the 1977–78 Regular Session shall be applied retroactively to July 1, 1976.

(b) The limitation prescribed by subdivision (a) shall not apply to local safety members, or patrol members, as defined in Section 20390 of the Government Code, of the Public Employees' Retirement System. This subdivision shall be applied retroactively. *(Added by Stats.1947, c. 310, p. 868, § 1. Amended by Stats.1951, c. 376, p. 1180, § 1; Stats.1963, c. 1467, p. 3033, § 1; Stats.1968, 1st Ex.Sess., c. 4, p. 33, § 9, operative Jan. 1, 1969; Stats.1969, c. 639, p. 1290, § 1; Stats.1976, c. 341, p. 936, § 12.5, eff. July 7, 1976, operative July 1, 1976; Stats.1977, c. 468, p. 1528, § 4; Stats.1989, c. 478, § 1; Stats.1998, c. 770 (A.B.2342), § 1; Stats.1999, c. 83 (S.B.966), § 134; Stats. 2001, c. 589 (A.B.262), § 2.)*

§ 4708. Determination of cause of death of member of retirement system

Upon application of any party in interest for a death benefit provided by this division on the death of an employee member of the Public Employees' Retirement System, the latter shall be joined as a defendant, and the appeals board shall determine whether the death resulted from injury or illness arising out of and in the course of his employment, for the purpose of enabling the appeals board to apply the provision of this division and the board of administration to apply the provisions of the Public Employees' Retirement Law. *(Added by Stats.1951, c. 1359, p. 3273, § 1. Amended by Stats.1965, c. 1513, p. 3580, § 96, operative Jan. 15, 1966; Stats.1969, c. 639, p. 1291, § 2.)*

§ 4709. Scholarships for dependents of peace officers, officers or employees of departments of corrections or youth authority, and firefighters

(a) Notwithstanding any other provisions of law, a dependent of a peace officer, as defined in Section 830.1, 830.2, 830.3, 830.31, 830.32, 830.33, 830.34, 830.35, 830.36, 830.37, 830.38, 830.39, 830.4, 830.5, or 830.6 of the Penal Code, who is killed in the performance of duty or who dies or is totally disabled as a result of an accident or an injury caused by external violence or physical force, incurred in the performance of duty, when the death, accident, or injury is compensable under this division or Division 4.5 (commencing with Section 6100) shall be entitled to a scholarship at any institution described in subdivision (*l*) of Section 69535 of the Education Code. The scholarship shall be in an amount equal to the amount provided a student who has been awarded a Cal Grant scholarship as specified in Article 3 (commencing with Section 69530) of Chapter 2 of Part 42 of the Education Code.

(b) A dependent of an officer or employee of the Department of Corrections or the Department of the Youth Authority described in Section 20017.77 of the Government Code who is killed in the performance of duty, or who dies or is totally disabled as a result of an accident or an injury incurred in the performance of duty, when the death, accident, or injury is caused by the direct action of an inmate, and is compensable under this division or Division 4.5 (commencing with Section 6100), shall also be entitled to a scholarship specified in this section.

(c) Notwithstanding any other provisions of law, a dependent of a firefighter employed by a county, city, city and county, district, or other political subdivision of the state, who is killed in the performance of duty or who dies or is totally disabled as a result of an accident or injury incurred in the performance of duty, when the death, accident, or injury is compensable under this division or Division 4.5 (commencing with Section 6100), shall also be entitled to a scholarship specified in this section.

(d) Nothing in this section shall be interpreted to allow the admittance of the dependent into a college or university unless the dependent is otherwise qualified to gain admittance to the college or university.

(e) The scholarship provided for by this section shall be paid out of funds annually appropriated in the Budget Act to the Student Aid Commission established by Article 2 (commencing with Section 69510) of Chapter 2 of Part 42 of the Education Code.

(f) The receipt of a scholarship provided for by this section shall not preclude a dependent from receiving a Cal Grant award pursuant to Article 3 (commencing with Section 69530) of Chapter 2 of Part 42 of the Education Code, any other grant, or any fee waivers that may be provided by an institution of higher education. The receipt of a Cal Grant award pursuant to Article 3 (commencing with Section 69530) of Chapter 2 of Part 42 of the Education Code, any other grant, or any fee waivers that may be provided by an institution of higher education shall not preclude a dependent from receiving a scholarship provided for by this section.

(g) The amendments made to this section during the 1995 portion of the 1995–96 Regular Session shall apply to a student receiving a scholarship on the effective date of the amendments unless that application would result in the student receiving a scholarship on less favorable terms or in a lesser amount, in which case the student shall continue to receive the scholarship on the same terms and conditions in effect prior to the effective date of the amendments.

(h) As used in this section, "dependent" means the children (natural or adopted) or spouse, at the time of the death or injury, of the peace officer, law enforcement officer, or firefighter.

(i) Eligibility for a scholarship under this section shall be limited to a person who demonstrates financial need as determined by the Student Aid Commission pursuant to Article 1.5 (commencing with Section 69503) of Chapter 2 of Part 42 of the Education Code. For purposes of determining financial need, the proceeds of death benefits received by the dependent, including, but not limited to, a continuation of income received from the Public Employees' Retirement System, the proceeds from the federal Public Safety Officers' Benefits Act, life insurance policies, proceeds from Sections 4702 and 4703.5, any private scholarship where receipt is predicated upon the recipient being the survivor of a deceased public safety officer, the scholarship awarded pursuant to Section 68120 of the Education Code, and any interest received from these benefits, shall not be considered. *(Added by Stats.1969, c. 1616, p. 3409, § 1. Amended by Stats.1971, c. 919, p. 1803, § 1; Stats.1971, c. 920, p. 1805, § 1, eff. Oct. 6, 1971; Stats.1973, c. 290, p. 698, § 1; Stats.1974, c. 292, p. 566, § 5; Stats.1988, c. 1557, § 1; Stats.1989, c. 173, § 1; Stats.1990, c. 552 (A.B.3033), § 1; Stats.1995, c. 646 (A.B.812), § 2; Stats.2001, c. 806 (S.B.730), § 1.)*

ARTICLE 4.5. PUBLIC OFFICIAL DEATH BENEFITS

Section
4720. Definitions.
4721. Right to special death benefit.
4722. Persons entitled to benefit.
4723. Choice of benefits.
4724. Claim.
4725. Disbursing agent; fee.
4726. Rules and regulations.
4727. Ineligibility.
4728. Educational scholarships; amounts.

§ 4720. Definitions

As used in this article:

(a) "Elected public official" means any person other than the President or Vice President of the United States who holds any federal, state, local, or special district elective office as a result of winning election in California to such office or being appointed to fill a vacancy in such office.

(b) "Assassination" means the killing of an elected public official as a direct result of an intentional act perpetrated by an individual or individuals acting to prevent, or retaliate for, the performance of official duties, acting because of the public position held by the official, or acting because of pathological reasons. *(Added by Stats.1979, c. 983, p. 3362, § 1.)*

§ 4721. Right to special death benefit

The surviving spouse or dependent minor children of an elected public official who is killed by assassination shall be entitled to a special death benefit which shall be in addition to any other benefits provided for by this division or Division 4.5 (commencing with Section 6100). *(Added by Stats.1979, c. 983, p. 3362, § 1. Amended by Stats.1983, c. 142, § 106.)*

§ 4722. Persons entitled to benefit

If the deceased elected public official is survived by a spouse with or without dependent minor children, such special death benefit shall be payable to the surviving spouse. If the deceased elected public official leaves no surviving spouse but one or more dependent minor children, benefits shall be paid to a guardian ad litem and trustee for such child or children appointed by the Workers' Compensation Appeals Board. In the absence of a surviving spouse and dependent minor children, the benefit shall be payable to any legally recognized dependent parent of the deceased elected public official. *(Added by Stats.1979, c. 983, p. 3362, § 1.)*

§ 4723. Choice of benefits

The person or persons to whom the special death benefit is payable pursuant to Section 4722 shall, within one year of the date of death of the elected public official, choose either of the following benefits:

(a) An annual benefit equal to one-half of the average annual salary paid to the elected public official in his or her elected capacity, less credit for any other death benefit provided for under existing law or by public funds, except benefits payable pursuant to this division or Division 4.5 (commencing with Section 6100). Payments shall be paid not less frequently than monthly, and shall be paid from the date of death until the spouse dies or remarries, or until the youngest minor dependent child reaches the age of 18 years, whichever occurs last. If payments are being made to a dependent parent or parents they shall continue during dependency.

(b) A lump-sum benefit of one hundred fifty thousand dollars ($150,000), less any other death benefit provided for under existing law or by public funds, except benefits payable pursuant to this division or Division 4.5 (commencing with Section 6100). *(Added by Stats.1979, c. 983, p. 3362, § 1. Amended by Stats.1983, c. 142, § 107.)*

§ 4724. Claim

The person or persons to whom the special death benefit is payable pursuant to Section 4722 shall file a claim therefor with the State Board of Control, which shall be processed pursuant to the provisions of Chapter 3 (commencing with Section 900) of Part 2 of Division 3.6 of Title 1 of the Government Code. *(Added by Stats. 1979, c. 983, p. 3362, § 1. Amended by Stats.1981, c. 714, p. 2722, § 318.)*

§ 4725. Disbursing agent; fee

The State Compensation Insurance Fund shall be the disbursing agent for payments made pursuant to this article and shall receive a fee for its services to be negotiated by the State Board of Control. Unless otherwise provided herein, payments shall be made in accordance with the provisions of this division. *(Added by Stats.1979, c. 983, p. 3362, § 1.)*

§ 4726. Rules and regulations

The State Board of Control and the Administrative Director of the Division of Workers' Compensation shall jointly adopt rules and regulations as may be necessary to carry out the provisions of this article. *(Added by Stats.1979, c. 983, p. 3362, § 1. Amended by Stats.1994, c. 146 (A.B.3601), § 150.)*

§ 4727. Ineligibility

Any person who is convicted of any crime in connection with the assassination of an elected public official shall not be eligible for any benefits pursuant to this article. *(Added by Stats.1979, c. 983, p. 3362, § 1.)*

§ 4728. Educational scholarships; amounts

(a) A dependent of an elected public official, who was intentionally killed while holding office, in retaliation for, or to prevent the performance of, an official duty, shall be entitled to a scholarship at any institution described in subdivision (k) of Section 69535 of the Education Code. The scholarship shall be in an amount equal to the amount provided a student who has been awarded a Cal Grant scholarship as specified in Article 3 (commencing with Section 69530) of Chapter 2 of Part 42 of the Education Code. Eligibility for a scholarship under this section shall be limited to a person who demonstrates financial need as determined by the Student Aid Commission pursuant to Article 1.5 (commencing with Section 69503) of Chapter 2 of Part 42 of the Education Code.

(b) The scholarship provided for by this section shall be paid out of funds annually appropriated in the Budget Act to the Student Aid Commission established by Article 2 (commencing with Section 69510) of Chapter 2 of Part 42 of the Education Code.

(c) The receipt of a scholarship provided for by this section shall not preclude a dependent from receiving a Cal Grant award pursuant to Article 3 (commencing with Section 69530) of Chapter 2 of Part 42 of the Education Code, any other grant, or any fee waivers that may be provided by an institution of higher education. The receipt of a Cal Grant award pursuant to Article 3 (commencing with Section 69530) of Chapter 2 of Part 42 of the Education Code, any other grant, or any fee waivers that may be provided by an institution of higher education shall not preclude a dependent from receiving a scholarship provided for by this section.

(d) This section shall apply to a student receiving a scholarship on the effective date of the section unless that application would result in the student receiving a scholarship on less favorable terms or in a lesser amount, in which case the student shall continue to receive the scholarship on the same terms and conditions in effect prior to the effective date of this section.

(e) As used in this section, "dependent" means the children (natural or adopted) or spouse, at the time of the death or injury, of the elected public official. *(Added by Stats.1995, c. 646 (A.B.812), § 3.)*

ARTICLE 5. SUBSEQUENT INJURIES PAYMENTS

Section
4751. Combined permanent partial disabilities; additional compensation.
4753. Reduction of additional compensation.
4753.5. Representation of state at hearing, investigation or proceeding; reimbursement of expenses.
4754. Payment of additional compensation; use of appropriated funds; reimbursement of state compensation insurance fund for cost of payment services.
4754.5. Compromise and release agreements.
4755. Cash revolving fund for payment of additional compensation; reimbursement; assignment of claims adjustment services and legal representation services; annual report to the legislature and director.

§ 4751. Combined permanent partial disabilities; additional compensation

If an employee who is permanently partially disabled receives a subsequent compensable injury resulting in additional permanent partial disability so that the degree of disability caused by the combination of both disabilities is greater than that which would have resulted from the subsequent injury alone, and the combined effect of the last injury and the previous disability or impairment is a permanent disability equal to 70 percent or more of total, he shall be paid in addition to the compensation due under this code for the permanent partial disability caused by the last injury compensation for the remainder of the combined permanent disability existing after the last injury as provided in this article; provided, that either (a) the previous disability or impairment affected a hand, an arm, a foot, a leg, or an eye, and the permanent disability resulting from the subsequent injury affects the opposite and corresponding member, and such latter permanent disability, when considered alone and without regard to, or adjustment for, the occupation or age of the employee, is equal to 5 percent or more of total, or (b) the permanent disability resulting from the subsequent injury, when considered alone and without regard to or adjustment for the occupation or the age of the employee, is equal to 35 percent or more of total. *(Added by Stats.1945, c. 1161, p. 2209, § 2. Amended by Stats.1949, c. 1525, p. 2711, § 1; Stats.1955, c. 1092, p. 2076, § 1; Stats.1959, c. 1034, p. 3055, § 1.)*

§ 4753. Reduction of additional compensation

Such additional compensation is not in addition to but shall be reduced to the extent of any monetary payments received by the employee, from any source whatsoever, for or on account of such preexisting disability or impairment, except as to payments being made to the employee or to which he is entitled as a pension or other compensation for disability incurred in service in the armed forces of the United States, and except as to payments being made to him or to which he is entitled as assistance under the provisions of Chapter 2 (commencing with Section 11200), Chapter 3 (commencing with Section 12000), Chapter 4 (commencing with Section 12500), Chapter 5 (commencing with Section 13000), or Chapter 6 (commencing with Section 13500) of Part 3, or Part 5 (commencing with Section 17000), of Division 9 of the Welfare and Institutions Code, and excluding from such monetary payments received by the employee for or on account of such preexisting disability or impairment a sum equal to all sums reasonably and necessarily expended by the employee for or on account of attorney's fees, costs and expenses incidental to the recovery of such monetary payments.

All cases under this section and under Section 4751 shall be governed by the terms of this section and Section 4751 as in effect on the date of the particular subsequent injury. *(Added by Stats.1945, c. 1161, p. 2210, § 3. Amended by Stats.1949, c. 786, p. 1517, § 1; Stats.1949, c. 1525, p. 2711, § 2; Stats.1951, c. 646, p. 1823, § 1; Stats.1955, c. 1092, p. 2076, § 2; Stats.1957, c. 2061, p. 3656, § 1; Stats.1959, c. 1034, p. 3055, § 2; Stats.1971, c. 438, p. 897, § 149.)*

§ 4753.5. Representation of state at hearing, investigation or proceeding; reimbursement of expenses

In any hearing, investigation, or proceeding, the state shall be represented by the Attorney General, or the attorneys of the Department of Industrial Relations, as appointed by the director. Expenses incident to representation, including costs for investigation, medical examinations, other expert reports, fees for witnesses, and other necessary and proper expenses, but excluding the salary of any of the Attorney General's deputies, shall be reimbursed from the Workers' Compensation Administration Revolving Fund. No witness fees or fees for medical services shall exceed those fees prescribed by the appeals board for the same services in those cases where the appeals board, by rule, has prescribed fees. Reimbursement pursuant to this section shall be in addition to, and in augmentation of, any other appropriations made or funds available for the use or support of the legal representation. *(Added by Stats.1949, c. 1525, p. 2711, § 3. Amended by Stats.1965, c. 1513, p. 3580, § 97, operative Jan. 15, 1966; Stats.1981, c. 894, p. 3412, § 7; Stats.1994, c. 146 (A.B.3601), § 151; Stats.2003, c. 228 (A.B.1756), § 36, eff. Aug. 11, 2003; Stats.2006, c. 538 (S.B.1852), § 489.)*

§ 4754. Payment of additional compensation; use of appropriated funds; reimbursement of state compensation insurance fund for cost of payment services

The appeals board shall fix and award the amounts of special additional compensation to be paid under this article, and shall direct the State Compensation Insurance Fund to pay the additional compensation so awarded. Such additional compensation may be paid only from funds appropriated for such purpose. Out of any such appropriation the fund may reimburse itself for the cost of service rendered in payment of compensation awards pursuant to this article and maintenance of accounts and records pertaining thereto, which cost shall not exceed 5 percent of the amount of award paid. *(Added by Stats.1945, c. 1161, p. 2210, § 4. Amended by Stats.1947, c. 1505, p. 3104, § 1; Stats.1965, c. 1513, p. 3581, § 98, operative Jan. 15, 1966.)*

§ 4754.5. Compromise and release agreements

Nothing in this article shall impair the right of the Attorney General or the Department of Industrial Relations to release by compromise any claims brought under the provisions of this article. No such compromise and release agreement is valid unless it is approved by the appeals board; however, the provisions of Sections 5000 to 5004, inclusive, of this code, shall not apply to such compromise and release agreements. *(Added by Stats. 1959, c. 1730, p. 4181, § 1. Amended by Stats.1965, c. 1513, p. 3581, § 99, operative Jan. 15, 1966; Stats.1968, c. 1253, p. 2370, § 1; Stats.1981, c. 894, p. 3412, § 8.)*

§ 4755. Cash revolving fund for payment of additional compensation; reimbursement; assignment of claims adjustment services and legal representation services; annual report to the legislature and director

(a) The State Compensation Insurance Fund may draw from the State Treasury out of the Subsequent Injuries Benefits Trust Fund for the purposes specified in Section 4751, without at the time presenting vouchers and itemized statements, a sum not to exceed in the aggregate fifty thousand dollars ($50,000), to be used as a cash revolving fund. The revolving fund shall be deposited in any banks and under any conditions as the Department of Finance determines. The Controller shall draw his or her warrants in favor of the State Compensation Insurance Fund for the amounts so withdrawn and the Treasurer shall pay these warrants.

(b) Expenditures made from the revolving fund in payments on claims for any additional compensation and for adjusting services are exempted from the operation of Section 16003 of the Government Code. Reimbursement of the revolving fund for these expenditures shall be made upon presentation to the Controller of an abstract or statement of the expenditures. The abstract or statement shall be in any form as the Controller requires.

(c) The director shall assign claims adjustment services and legal representation services respecting matters concerning subsequent injuries. The director or his or her representative may make these service assignments within the department, or he or she may contract for these services with the State Compensation Insurance Fund, for a fee in addition to that authorized by Section 4754, except insofar as these matters might conflict with the interests of the State Compensation Insurance Fund. The administrative costs associated with these services shall be reimbursed from the Workers' Compensation Administration Revolving Fund, except when a budget

impasse requires advances as provided in subdivision (d) of Section 62.5. To the extent permitted by state law, the director may contract for audits or reports of services under this section.

(d) Commencing November 1, 2004, the State Compensation Insurance Fund and the director shall report annually to the fiscal committees of both houses of the Legislature and the Director of Finance, regarding all of the following:

(1) The number of subsequent injuries claims paid in the previous fiscal year, the total costs of those claims, and the levels of reserves on incurred claims.

(2) The administrative costs associated with claims payment activities.

(3) Annual revenues to the Subsequent Injuries Benefits Trust Fund from both of the following:

(A) Assessments collected pursuant to subdivision (d) of Section 62.5.

(B) Other revenues collected by the department.

(4) Projected annual program and claims costs for the current and upcoming fiscal years. *(Added by Stats.1947, c. 1505, p. 3105, § 2. Amended by Stats.1965, c. 371, p. 1582, § 235; Stats.1974, c. 1221, p. 2650, § 36; Stats.2003, c. 228 (A.B.1756), § 37, eff. Aug. 11, 2003.)*

ARTICLE 6. SPECIAL PAYMENTS TO CERTAIN PERSONS

Section

4800.   Department of Justice members; leave of absence with pay in lieu of disability payments.

4800.5.   Highway patrol members; leave of absence with pay in lieu of disability payments.

4801.   Determination of disability; out of and in course of duty; cessation.

4802.   Medical, surgical and hospital benefits.

4803.   Disability continuing for more than one year.

4804.   Double indemnity prohibited.

4804.1.   Firefighting and prevention service members of University of California fire department.

4804.2.   Determination of disability by appeals board; duration.

4804.3.   Medical, surgical and hospital benefits.

4804.4.   Disability continuing for more than one year.

4804.5.   Double indemnity prohibited.

4806.   Law enforcement members of University of California police department.

4807.   Determination of disability by appeals board; duration.

4808.   Medical, surgical and hospital benefits.

4809.   Disability continuing for more than one year.

4810.   Double indemnity prohibited.

4816.   California State University Police Department; collective bargaining agreement; enhanced industrial disability leave; application.

4817.   Appeals board; disability determination.

4819.   Extended disability; applicable provisions.

4820.   Disability indemnity; concurrent salary payments.

§ 4800. Department of Justice members; leave of absence with pay in lieu of disability payments

Whenever any member of the Department of Justice falling within the "state peace officer/firefighter" class is disabled by injury arising out of and in the course of his or her duties, he or she shall become entitled, regardless of his or her period of service with the Department of Justice to leave of absence while so disabled without loss of salary, in lieu of disability payments under this chapter, for a period of not exceeding one year. This section shall apply only to members of the Department of Justice whose principal duties consist of active law enforcement and shall not apply to persons employed in the Department of Justice whose principal duties are those of telephone operator, clerk, stenographer, machinist, mechanic or otherwise clearly not falling within the scope of active law enforcement service, even though this person is subject to occasional call or is occasionally called upon to perform duties within the scope of active law enforcement service.

This section shall apply to harbor policemen employed by the San Francisco Port Commission who are described in Section 20017.76 of the Government Code.

This section shall not apply to periods of disability which occur subsequent to termination of employment by resignation, retirement or dismissal. When this section does not apply, the employee shall be eligible for those benefits which would apply if this section had not been enacted. *(Stats.1937, c. 90, p. 285, § 4800. Amended by Stats.1967, c. 1553, p. 3725, § 5, operative Dec. 1, 1967; Stats.1969, c. 213, p. 543, § 3, Stats.1969, c. 1402, p. 2848, § 1; Stats.1971, c. 1089, p. 2066, § 2; Stats.1972, c. 1377, p. 2829, § 67; Stats.1980, c. 451, p. 958, § 1; Stats.1994, c. 762 (A.B.2801), § 7, eff. Sept. 23, 1994.)*

§ 4800.5. Highway patrol members; leave of absence with pay in lieu of disability payments

(a) Whenever any sworn member of the Department of the California Highway Patrol is disabled by a single injury, excluding disabilities that are the result of cumulative trauma or cumulative injuries, arising out of and in the course of his or her duties, he or she shall become entitled, regardless of his or her period of service with the patrol, to leave of absence while so disabled without loss of salary, in lieu of disability payments under this chapter, for a period of not exceeding one year. This section shall apply only to members of the Department of the California Highway Patrol whose principal duties consist of active law enforcement and shall not apply to persons employed in the Department of the California Highway Patrol whose principal duties are those of telephone operator, clerk, stenographer, machinist, mechanic, or otherwise clearly not falling within the scope of active law enforcement service, even though this person is subject to occasional call or is occasionally called upon to perform the duties of active law enforcement service.

(b) Benefits payable for eligible sworn members of the Department of the California Highway Patrol whose disability is solely the result of cumulative trauma or injury shall be limited to the actual period of temporary disability or entitlement to maintenance allowance, or for one year, whichever is less.

(c) This section shall not apply to periods of disability that occur subsequent to termination of employment by resignation, retirement, or dismissal. When this section does not apply, the employee shall be eligible for those benefits that would apply had this section not been enacted.

(d) The appeals board may determine, upon request of any party, whether or not the disability referred to in this section arose out of and in the course of duty. In any action in which a dispute exists regarding the nature of the injury or the period of temporary disability or entitlement to maintenance allowance, or both, and upon the request of any party thereto, the appeals board shall determine when the disability commenced and ceased, and the amount of benefits provided by this division to which the employee is entitled during the period of this disability. The appeals board shall have the jurisdiction to award and enforce payment of these benefits, subject to subdivision (a) or (b), pursuant to Part 4 (commencing with Section 5300). A decision issued by the appeals board under this section is final and binding upon the parties subject to the rights of appeal contained in Chapter 7 (commencing with Section 5900) of Part 4.

(e) Except as provided in subdivision (g), this section shall apply for periods of disability commencing on or after January 1, 1995.

(f) This section does not apply to peace officers designated under subdivision (a) of Section 2250.1 of the Vehicle Code.

(g) Peace officers of the California State Police Division who become sworn members of the Department of the California Highway Patrol as a result of the Governor's Reorganization Plan No. 1 of 1995, other than those officers described in subdivision (f), shall be eligible for injury benefits accruing to sworn members of the Department of the California Highway Patrol under this division only for injuries occurring on or after July 12, 1995. *(Added by Stats.1994, c. 762 (A.B.2801), § 8, eff. Sept. 23, 1994. Amended by Stats.1995, c. 91 (S.B.975), § 108; Gov.Reorg.Plan No. 1 of 1995, § 41, eff. July 12, 1995; Stats.1996, c. 305 (A.B.3103), § 42.)*

§ 4801. Determination of disability; out of and in course of duty; cessation

It shall be the duty of the appeals board to determine in the case of members of the California Highway Patrol, upon request of the Department of the California Highway Patrol or Department of Justice, and, in the case of the harbor policemen, upon the request of the San Francisco Port Commission, whether or not the disability referred to in Section 4800 arose out of and in the course of duty. The appeals board shall, also, in any disputed case, determine when such disability ceases. *(Stats.1937, c. 90, p. 286, § 4801. Amended by Stats.1965, c. 1513, p.*

3581, § 100, operative Jan. 15, 1966; Stats.1967, c. 1553, p. 3725, § 6, operative Dec. 1, 1967; Stats.1969, c. 213, p. 543, § 4; Stats.1969, c. 1402, p. 2849, § 2; Stats.1971, c. 1089, p. 2067, § 3.)

§ 4802. Medical, surgical and hospital benefits

Any such member of the California Highway Patrol or Department of Justice, or any such harbor policeman, so disabled is entitled from the date of injury and regardless of retirement under the Public Employees' Retirement System, to the medical, surgical and hospital benefits prescribed by this division as part of the compensation for persons injured in the course of and arising out of their employment, at the expense of the Department of the California Highway Patrol, the Department of Justice, or the San Francisco Port Commission, as the case may be, and such expense shall be charged upon the fund out of which the compensation of the member is paid. (Stats. 1937, c. 90, p. 286, § 4802. Amended by Stats.1937, c. 848, p. 2366; Stats.1967, c. 1553, p. 3725, § 7, operative Dec. 1, 1967; Stats.1969, c. 213, p. 543, § 5; Stats.1969, c. 1402, p. 2849, § 3; Stats.1971, c. 1089, p. 2067, § 4; Stats.1972, c. 1377, p. 2830, § 68.)

§ 4803. Disability continuing for more than one year

Whenever such disability of such member of the California Highway Patrol, or Department of Justice, or of such harbor policeman, continues for a period beyond one year, such member or harbor policeman shall thereafter be subject, as to disability indemnity, to the provisions of this division other than Section 4800, which refers to temporary disability only, during the remainder of the disability, except that such compensation shall be paid out of funds available for the support of the Department of the California Highway Patrol, the Department of Justice, or the San Francisco Port Commission, as the case may be, and the leave of absence shall continue. (Stats.1937, c. 90, p. 286, § 4803. Amended by Stats.1937, c. 848, p. 2366; Stats.1939, c. 902, p. 2519, § 3; Stats.1943, c. 1137, p. 3082, § 1; Stats.1967, c. 1553, p. 3726, § 8, operative Dec. 1, 1967; Stats.1969, c. 213, p. 544, § 6; Stats.1969, c. 1402, p. 2849, § 4; Stats.1971, c. 1089, p. 2067, § 5; Stats.1972, c. 1377, p. 2830, § 69.)

§ 4804. Double indemnity prohibited

No disability indemnity shall be paid to said member of the California Highway Patrol or harbor policeman as temporary disability concurrently with wages or salary payments. (Added by Stats.1937, c. 848, p. 2366. Amended by Stats.1939, c. 902, p. 2519, § 4; Stats.1943, c. 1137, p. 3082, § 2; Stats.1967, c. 1553, p. 3726, § 9, operative Dec. 1, 1967.)

§ 4804.1. Firefighting and prevention service members of University of California fire department

Whenever any member of a University of California fire department specified in Section 3212.4 falling within the active "firefighting and prevention service" class is disabled by injury arising out of and in the course of his duties, he shall become entitled, regardless of his period of service with a University of California fire department, to leave of absence while so disabled without loss of salary, in lieu of disability payments under this chapter, for a period of not exceeding one year. This section shall apply only to members of a University of California fire department whose principal duties consist of active firefighting and prevention service and shall not apply to persons employed in a University of California fire department whose principal duties are those of telephone operator, clerk, stenographer, machinist, mechanic, or otherwise clearly not falling within the scope of active firefighting and prevention service, even though such person is subject to occasional call or is occasionally called upon to perform duties within the scope of active firefighting and prevention service. (Added by Stats.1972, c. 1149, p. 2244, § 2.)

§ 4804.2. Determination of disability by appeals board; duration

It shall be the duty of the appeals board to determine in the case of members of a University of California fire department specified in Section 4804.1, upon request of the Regents of the University of California, whether or not the disability referred to in Section 4804.1 arose out of and in the course of duty. The appeals board shall, also in any disputed case, determine when such disability ceases. (Added by Stats.1972, c. 1149, p. 2244, § 3.)

§ 4804.3. Medical, surgical and hospital benefits

Any such member of a University of California fire department specified in Section 4804.1, so disabled is entitled from the date of injury and regardless of retirement under the Public Employees' Retirement System, or other retirement system, to the medical, surgical, and hospital benefits prescribed by this division as part of the compensation for persons injured in the course of and arising out of their employment, at the expense of the Regents of the University of California, and such expense shall be charged upon the fund out of which the compensation of the member is paid. (Added by Stats.1972, c. 1149, p. 2244, § 4.)

§ 4804.4. Disability continuing for more than one year

Whenever such disability of such member of a University of California fire department, specified in Section 4804.1, continues for a period beyond one year, such member shall thereafter be subject, as to disability indemnity, to the provisions of this division other than Section 4804.1, which refers to temporary disability only, during the remainder of the disability, except that such compensation shall be paid out of funds available for the support of the Regents of the University of California, and the leave of absence shall continue. (Added by Stats.1972, c. 1149, p. 2245, § 5.)

§ 4804.5. Double indemnity prohibited

No disability indemnity shall be paid to said member of a University of California fire department, specified in

Section 4804.1, as temporary disability concurrently with wages or salary payments. *(Added by Stats.1972, c. 1149, p. 2245, § 6.)*

§ 4806. Law enforcement members of University of California police department

Whenever any member of the University of California Police Department falling within the "law enforcement" class is disabled by injury arising out of and in the course of his duties, he shall become entitled, regardless of his period of service with the police department, to leave of absence while so disabled without loss of salary, in lieu of disability payments under this chapter, for a period of not exceeding one year. This section shall apply only to members of the University of California Police Department whose principal duties consist of active law enforcement, and shall not apply to persons employed in the University of California Police Department whose principal duties are those of telephone operator, clerk, stenographer, machinist, mechanic or otherwise clearly not falling within the scope of active law enforcement service, even though such person is subject to occasional call or is occasionally called upon to perform duties within the scope of active law enforcement service.

This section shall apply only to those members of the University of California Police Department specified in Section 3213. *(Added by Stats.1971, c. 918, p. 1802, § 3.)*

§ 4807. Determination of disability by appeals board; duration

It shall be the duty of the appeals board to determine, in the case of members of the University of California Police Department, upon the request of the Regents of the University of California, whether or not the disability referred to in Section 4806 arose out of and in the course of duty. The appeals board shall, also in any disputed case, determine when such disability ceases. *(Added by Stats 1971, c 918, p 1803, § 4)*

§ 4808. Medical, surgical and hospital benefits

Any such member of the University of California Police Department so disabled is entitled from the date of injury, and regardless of retirement under either the University of California Retirement System or Public Employees' Retirement System, to the medical, surgical, and hospital benefits prescribed by this division as part of the compensation for persons injured in the course of and arising out of their employment, at the expense of the Regents of the University of California, and such expense shall be charged upon the fund out of which the compensation of the member is paid. *(Added by Stats. 1971, c. 918, p. 1803, § 5.)*

§ 4809. Disability continuing for more than one year

Whenever such disability of such member of the University of California Police Department continues for a period beyond one year, such member shall thereafter be subject, as to disability indemnity, to the provisions of this division other than Section 4806, which refers to temporary disability only, during the remainder of the disability, except that such compensation shall be paid out of funds available for the support of the Regents of the University of California and the leave of absence shall continue. *(Added by Stats.1971, c. 918, p. 1803, § 6.)*

§ 4810. Double indemnity prohibited

No disability indemnity shall be paid to such member of the University of California Police Department as temporary disability concurrently with wages or salary payments. *(Added by Stats.1971, c. 918, p. 1803, § 7.)*

§ 4816. California State University Police Department; collective bargaining agreement; enhanced industrial disability leave; application

Pursuant to a collective bargaining agreement applicable to members of the California State University Police Department, whenever any member of that police department falling within the "law enforcement" class is disabled by injury or illness arising out of and in the course of his or her duties, he or she shall become entitled, regardless of his or her period of service with the police department, to enhanced industrial disability leave equivalent to the injured employee's net take home salary on the date of occurrence of the injury. For the purposes of this section, "net take home salary" means the amount of salary received after federal income tax, state income tax, and the employee's retirement contribution has been deducted from the employee's gross salary, in lieu of disability payments under this chapter, for a period of not exceeding one year. No benefits shall be paid under this section for any psychiatric disability or any physical disability arising from a psychiatric injury.

This section shall apply only to members of the California State University Police Department whose principal duties consist of active law enforcement, and shall not apply to persons employed in the California State University Police Department whose principal duties are those of telephone operator, clerk, stenographer, machinist, mechanic, or otherwise clearly not falling within the scope of active law enforcement service, even though the person is subject to occasional call or is occasionally called upon to perform duties within the scope of active law enforcement service. *(Added by Stats.1994, c. 50 (S.B.1034), § 1.)*

§ 4817. Appeals board; disability determination

It shall be the duty of the appeals board to determine, in the case of members of the California State University Police Department, upon the request of the Board of Trustees of the California State University, whether or not the disability referred to in Section 4816 arose out of and in the course of duty. The appeals board shall, also in any disputed case, determine when such disability ceases. *(Added by Stats.1994, c. 50 (S.B.1034), § 2.)*

§ 4819. Extended disability; applicable provisions

Whenever the disability of a member of the California State University Police Department continues for a

651

period beyond one year, that member shall thereafter be subject, as to disability indemnity, to the provisions of this division other than Section 4816, which refers to temporary disability only, during the remainder of the disability. *(Added by Stats.1994, c. 50 (S.B.1034), § 3.)*

§ 4820. Disability indemnity; concurrent salary payments

No disability indemnity shall be paid to a member of the California State University Police Department as temporary disability concurrently with wages or salary payments. *(Added by Stats.1994, c. 50 (S.B.1034), § 4.)*

ARTICLE 7. CITY POLICE AND FIREMEN, SHERIFFS, AND OTHERS

Section
4850.   Police officers, firefighters, sheriff's officers, and other personnel; leave of absence with salary in lieu of temporary disability or maintenance payments.
4850.3.   Local safety officers; advanced disability pension payments.
4850.4.   Advanced disability pension payments; exceptions; time for payments; continuance of payments; employee requirements; tolling of time period; repayment of any advanced disability pension payments.
4850.5.   San Luis Obispo county; benefits for public safety officers not in public employees' retirement system or subject to county employees retirement law of 1937.
4850.7.   Firefighters not covered by state or county retirement provisions; entitlement to benefits; resolution.
4851.   Determination of disability; out of and in course of duty; commencement and cessation of disability; benefit amount; jurisdiction of appeals board.
4852.   Medical, surgical, and hospital benefits.
4853.   Continuation of disability for more than one year.
4854.   Prohibition of double indemnity.
4855.   Reserve public safety employees.
4856.   Spouses of employees or employers killed in performance of duty; choice of monthly or lump-sum benefits; minor dependents; addition of new spouse or stepchildren as family members.

§ 4850. Police officers, firefighters, sheriff's officers, and other personnel; leave of absence with salary in lieu of temporary disability or maintenance payments

(a) Whenever any person listed in subdivision (b), who is * * * employed on a regular, full-time basis, and is disabled, whether temporarily or permanently, by injury or illness arising out of and in the course of his or her duties, he or she shall become entitled, regardless of his or her period of service with the city, county, or district, to a leave of absence while so disabled without loss of salary in lieu of temporary disability payments or maintenance allowance payments under Section 139.5, if any, that would be payable under this chapter, for the period of the disability, but not exceeding one year, or until that earlier date as he or she is retired on permanent disability

pension, and is actually receiving disability pension payments, or advanced disability pension payments pursuant to Section 4850.3.

(b) The persons eligible under subdivision (a) include all of the following:

(1) City police officers.

(2) City, county, or district firefighters.

(3) Sheriffs.

(4) Officers or employees of any sheriff's offices.

(5) Inspectors, investigators, detectives, or personnel with comparable titles in any district attorney's office.

(6) County probation officers, group counselors, or juvenile services officers.

(7) Officers or employees of a probation office.

(8) Peace officers under Section 830.31 of the Penal Code employed on a regular, full-time basis by a county of the first class.

(9) Lifeguards employed year round on a regular, full-time basis by a county of the first class.

(10) Airport law enforcement officers under subdivision (d) of Section 830.33 of the Penal Code.

(11) Harbor or port police officers, wardens, or special officers of a harbor or port district or city or county harbor department under subdivision (a) of Section 830.1 or subdivision (b) of Section 830.33 of the Penal Code.

(12) Police officers of the Los Angeles Unified School District.

(c) This section shall apply only to persons listed in subdivision (b) who meet the requirements of subdivision (a), and shall not include any of the following:

(1) Employees of a police department whose principal duties are those of a telephone operator, clerk, stenographer, machinist, mechanic, or otherwise, and whose functions do not clearly fall within the scope of active law enforcement service.

(2) Employees of a county sheriff's office whose principal duties are those of a telephone operator, clerk, stenographer, machinist, mechanic, or otherwise, and whose functions do not clearly come within the scope of active law enforcement service.

(3) Employees of a county probation office whose principal duties are those of a telephone operator, clerk, stenographer, machinist, mechanic, or otherwise, and whose functions do not clearly come within the scope of active law enforcement service.

(4) Employees of a city fire department, county fire department, or fire district whose principal duties are those of a telephone operator, clerk, stenographer, machinist, mechanic, or otherwise, and whose functions do not clearly fall within the scope of active firefighting and prevention service.

(d) If the employer is insured, the payments that, except for this section, the insurer would be obligated to make as disability indemnity to the injured, the insurer may pay to the insured.

(e) No leave of absence taken pursuant to this section by a peace officer, as defined by Chapter 4.5 (commencing with Section 830) of Title 3 of Part 2 of the Penal Code, or by a city, county, or district firefighter, shall be deemed to constitute family care and medical leave, as defined in Section 12945.2 of the Government Code, or to reduce the time authorized for family care and medical leave by Section 12945.2 of the Government Code.

(f) This section shall not apply to any persons described in subdivision (b) who are employees of the City and County of San Francisco. *(Added by Stats.1983, c. 762, § 2. Amended by Stats.1984, c. 114, § 5.5; Stats. 1989, c. 1464, § 10, eff. Oct. 2, 1989, operative Jan. 1, 1990; Stats.1990, c. 1550 (A.B.2910), § 44; Stats.1995, c. 474 (A.B.509), § 1; Stats.1999, c. 270 (A.B.224), § 1; Stats. 1999, c. 970 (A.B.1387), § 1.5; Stats.2000, c. 920 (A.B. 1883), § 1; Stats.2000, c. 929 (S.B.2081), § 3; Stats.2001, c. 791 (A.B.1374), § 1; Stats.2009, c. 389 (A.B.1227), § 1.)*

§ 4850.3. Local safety officers; advanced disability pension payments

A city, county, special district, or harbor district that is a member of the Public Employees' Retirement System, is subject to the County Employees Retirement Law of 1937, or is subject to the Los Angeles City Employees' Retirement System, may make advanced disability pension payments to any local safety officer who has qualified for benefits under Section 4850 and is approved for a disability allowance. The payments shall be no less than 50 percent of the estimated highest average annual compensation earnable by the local safety officer during the three consecutive years of employment immediately preceding the effective date of his or her disability retirement, unless the local safety officer chooses an optional settlement in the permanent disability retirement application process which would reduce the pension allowance below 50 percent. In the case where the local safety officer's choice lowers the disability pension allowance below 50 percent of average annual compensation as calculated, the advanced pension payments shall be set at an amount equal to the disability pension allowance . If a local agency has an adopted policy of paying for any accumulated sick leave after the safety officer is eligible for a disability allowance, the advanced disability pension payments under this section may only be made when the local safety officer has exhausted all sick leave payments. Advanced disability pension payments shall not be considered a salary under this or any other provision of law. All advanced disability pension payments made by a local agency with membership in the Public Employees' Retirement System shall be reimbursed by the Public Employees' Retirement System pursuant to Section 21293.1 of the Government Code. *(Added by Stats.1985, c. 1254, § 7, eff. Sept. 30, 1985. Amended by Stats.1989, c. 1464, § 11, eff. Oct. 2, 1989; Stats.2000, c. 920 (A.B.1883), § 2.)*

§ 4850.4. Advanced disability pension payments; exceptions; time for payments; continuance of payments; employee requirements; tolling of time period; repayment of any advanced disability pension payments

(a) A city, county, special district, or harbor district that is a member of the Public Employees' Retirement System, is subject to the County Employees Retirement Law of 1937, or is subject to the Los Angeles City Employees' Retirement Systems, shall make advanced disability pension payments in accordance with Section 4850.3 unless any of the following is applicable:

(1) After an examination of the employee by a physician, the physician determines that there is no discernable injury to, or illness of, the employee.

(2) The employee was incontrovertibly outside the course of his or her employment duties when the injury occurred.

(3) There is proof of fraud associated with the filing of the employee's claim.

(b) Any employer described in subdivision (a) who is required to make advanced disability pension payments, shall make the payments commencing no later than 30 days from the date of issuance of the last disbursed of the following:

(1) The employee's last regular payment of wages or salary.

(2) The employee's last payment of benefits under Section 4850.

(3) The employee's last payment for sick leave.

(c) The advanced disability payments shall continue until the claimant is approved or disapproved for a disability allowance pursuant to final adjudication as provided by law.

(d) An employer described in subdivision (a) shall be required to make advanced disability pension payments only if the employee does all of the following:

(1) Files an application for disability retirement at least 60 days prior to the payment of benefits pursuant to subdivision (a).

(2) Fully cooperates in providing the employer with medical information and in attending all statutorily required medical examinations and evaluations set by the employer.

(3) Fully cooperates with the evaluation process established by the retirement plan.

(e) The 30–day period for the commencement of payments pursuant to subdivision (b) shall be tolled by whatever period of time is directly related to the employee's failure to comply with the provisions of subdivision (d).

(f) After final adjudication, if an employee's disability application is denied, the local agency and the employee shall arrange for the employee to repay any advanced disability pension payments received by the employee pursuant to this subdivision. The repayment plan shall take into account the employee's ability to repay the advanced disability payments received. Absent an agreement on repayment, the matter shall be submitted for a local agency administrative appeals remedy that includes an independent level of resolution to determine a reasonable repayment plan. If repayment is not made according to the repayment plan, the local agency may take reasonable steps, including litigation, to recover the payments advanced. *(Added by Stats.2002, c. 189 (A.B. 1982), § 1. Amended by Stats.2002, c. 877 (A.B.2131), § 3.)*

§ 4850.5.   San Luis Obispo county; benefits for public safety officers not in public employees' retirement system or subject to county employees retirement law of 1937

Any firefighter employed by the County of San Luis Obispo, and the sheriff or any officer or employee of the sheriff's office of the County of San Luis Obispo, and any county probation officer, group counselor, or juvenile services officer, or any officer or employee of a probation office, employed by the County of San Luis Obispo, shall, upon the adoption of a resolution of the board of supervisors so declaring, be entitled to the benefits of this article, if otherwise entitled to these benefits, even though the employee is not a member of the Public Employees' Retirement System or subject to the County Employees Retirement Law of 1937 (Chapter 3 (commencing with Section 31450) of Part 3 of Division 4 of Title 3 of the Government Code). *(Added by Stats.1980, c. 703, p. 2106, § 1. Amended by Stats.1984, c. 114, § 6; Stats. 1999, c. 970 (A.B.1387), § 2.)*

§ 4850.7.   Firefighters not covered by state or county retirement provisions; entitlement to benefits; resolution

(a) Any firefighter employed by a dependent or independent fire district may be entitled to the benefits of this article, if otherwise entitled to these benefits, even though the employee is not a member of the Public Employees' Retirement System or subject to the County Employees Retirement Law of 1937 (Chapter 3 (commencing with Section 31450) of Part 3 of Division 4 of Title 3 of the Government Code).

(b) The issue of whether the firefighters employed by a fire district are entitled to the benefits of this article is subject to Article 10 (commencing with Section 3500) of Chapter 3 of Division 4 of Title 1 of the Government Code.

(c) If the governing body of the district agrees that the benefits shall apply, it shall adopt a resolution to that effect. *(Added by Stats.1990, c. 905 (S.B.2075), § 1.)*

§ 4851.   Determination of disability; out of and in course of duty; commencement and cessation of disability; benefit amount; jurisdiction of appeals board

The governing body of any city, county, or city and county, in addition to anyone else properly entitled,

including the Public Employees' Retirement System, may request the appeals board to determine in any case, and the appeals board shall determine, whether or not the disability referred to in Section 4850 arose out of and in the course of duty. The appeals board shall also, in any disputed case, determine when the disability commenced and ceased, and the amount of benefits provided by this division to which the employee is entitled during the period of the disability. The appeals board shall have jurisdiction to award and enforce payment of these benefits pursuant to Part 4 (commencing with Section 5300). *(Added by Stats.1939, c. 926, p. 2604, § 1. Amended by Stats.1949, c. 1143, p. 2043, § 2; Stats.1965, c. 1513, p. 3581, § 101, operative Jan. 15, 1966; Stats.1969, c. 639, p. 1292, § 4; Stats.1977, c. 382, p. 1370, § 1; Stats.1985, c. 1050, § 1.)*

§ 4852.   Medical, surgical, and hospital benefits

The provisions of this article do not diminish or affect the right of any such officer or employee to the medical, surgical, and hospital benefits prescribed by this division. *(Added by Stats.1939, c. 926, p. 2604, § 1. Amended by Stats.1949, c. 1143, p. 2043, § 3.)*

§ 4853.   Continuation of disability for more than one year

Whenever such disability of any such officer or employee continues for a period beyond one year, such member shall thereafter be subject as to disability indemnity to the provisions of this division other than Section 4850 during the remainder of the period of said disability or until the effective date of his retirement under the Public Employees' Retirement Act, and the leave of absence shall continue. *(Added by Stats.1939, c. 926, p. 2604. Amended by Stats.1949, c. 1143, p. 2403, § 4; Stats.1951, c. 1378, p. 3300, § 2; Stats.1969, c. 639, p. 1292, § 5.)*

§ 4854.   Prohibition of double indemnity

No disability indemnity shall be paid to any such officer or employee concurrently with wages or salary payments. *(Added by Stats.1939, c. 926, p. 2604, § 1. Amended by Stats.1949, c. 1143, p. 2403, § 5; Stats.1951, c. 1378, p. 3300, § 3.)*

§ 4855.   Reserve public safety employees

This article shall not be applicable to individuals who are appointed as reserve public safety employees and are deemed to be employees of a county, city, town or district for workmen's compensation purposes pursuant to Section 3362. *(Added by Stats.1968, c. 1178, p. 2238, § 1.)*

§ 4856.   Spouses of employees or employers killed in performance of duty; choice of monthly or lumpsum benefits; minor dependents; addition of new spouse or stepchildren as family members

(a) Whenever any local employee who is a firefighter, or peace officer as described in Chapter 4.5 (commencing with Section 830) of Title 3 of Part 2 of the Penal Code, is killed in the performance of his or her duty or dies as a result of an accident or injury caused by external violence or physical force incurred in the performance of his or her duty, the employer shall continue providing health benefits to the deceased employee's spouse under the same terms and conditions provided prior to the death, or prior to the accident or injury that caused the death, of the employee unless the surviving spouse elects to receive a lump-sum survivors benefit in lieu of monthly benefits. Minor dependents shall continue to receive benefits under the coverage provided the surviving spouse or, if there is no surviving spouse, until the age of 21 years. However, pursuant to Section 22822 of the Government Code, the surviving spouse may not add the new spouse or stepchildren as family members under the continued health benefits coverage of the surviving spouse.

(b) Subdivision (a) also applies to the employer of any local employee who is a firefighter, or peace officer as described in Chapter 4.5 (commencing with Section 830) of Title 3 of Part 2 of the Penal Code, who was killed in the performance of his or her duty or who died as a result of an accident or injury caused by external violence or physical force incurred in the performance of his or her duty prior to September 30, 1996. *(Added by Stats.1996, c. 1120 (A.B.3478), § 5, eff. Sept. 30, 1996. Amended by Stats.1997, c. 193 (S.B.563), § 1; Stats.2004, c. 69 (S.B. 626), § 34, eff. June 24, 2004.)*

Part 3

COMPENSATION CLAIMS

Chapter	Section
1. **Payment and Assignment**	4900
2. **Compromise and Release**	5000
3. **Lump Sum Payments**	5100

CHAPTER 1. PAYMENT AND ASSIGNMENT

Section
4900. Nonassignability.
4901. Exemption from debts.
4902. Prohibition against payment to attorney or agent.
4903. Allowable liens.
4903.1. Reimbursement for benefits paid or services providing; filing of liens.
4903.2. Attorney's fee.
4903.3. Discretionary compensation in cases to which director is a party before the issuance of award; lien.
4903.4. Resolution of disputes concerning liens.
4903.5. Lien claims for expenses; filing requirements; application.
4903.6. Lien claims, applications for adjudication, or declarations of readiness to proceed; filing requirements; adoption of regulations; application of prohibitions.
4904. Notice of lien; approval by appeals board; determination of amount; effect of determination; payment; approval of compromise and release agreement.
4904.1. Effect of payment of liens upon immediate payment of balance of award.

Section
4905. Order for payment of claim without notice.
4906. Reasonableness of claim for legal and medical services; attorney fee agreements; disclosures and statements.
4907. Suspension of privilege of appearing as representative of party to proceedings.
4908. Priority of compensation claim.
4909. Payment and acceptance of payment of amount not due or pending dispute of right compensation.
4909.1. Representatives of departments of correction and youth authority authorized to request payments, allowances, or benefits described in § 4909.

§ 4900. Nonassignability

No claim for compensation, except as provided in Section 96, is assignable before payment, but this provision does not affect the survival thereof. *(Stats.1937, c. 90, p. 287, § 4900. Amended by Stats.1953, c. 555, p. 1814, § 2.)*

§ 4901. Exemption from debts

No claim for compensation nor compensation awarded, adjudged, or paid, is subject to be taken for the debts of the party entitled to such compensation except as hereinafter provided. *(Stats.1937, c. 90, p. 287, § 4901.)*

§ 4902. Prohibition against payment to attorney or agent

No compensation, whether awarded or voluntarily paid, shall be paid to any attorney at law or in fact or other agent, but shall be paid directly to the claimant entitled thereto unless otherwise ordered by the appeals board. No payment made to an attorney at law or in fact or other agent in violation of this section shall be credited to the employer. *(Stats.1937, c. 90, p. 287, § 4902. Amended by Stats.1965, c. 1513, p. 3582, § 102, operative Jan. 15, 1966.)*

§ 4903. Allowable liens

The appeals board may determine, and allow as liens against any sum to be paid as compensation, any amount determined as hereinafter set forth in subdivisions (a) through (i). If more than one lien is allowed, the appeals board may determine the priorities, if any, between the liens allowed. The liens that may be allowed hereunder are as follows:

(a) A reasonable attorney's fee for legal services pertaining to any claim for compensation either before the appeals board or before any of the appellate courts, and the reasonable disbursements in connection therewith. No fee for legal services shall be awarded to any representative who is not an attorney, except with respect to those claims for compensation for which an application, pursuant to Section 5501, has been filed with the appeals board on or before December 31, 1991, or for which a disclosure form, pursuant to Section 4906, has been sent to the employer, or insurer or third-party administrator, if either is known, on or before December 31, 1991.

(b) The reasonable expense incurred by or on behalf of the injured employee, as provided by Article 2 (commencing with Section 4600) and, to the extent the employee is entitled to reimbursement under Section 4621, medical-legal expenses as provided by Article 2.5 (commencing with Section 4620) of Chapter 2 of Part 2.

(c) The reasonable value of the living expenses of an injured employee or of his or her dependents, subsequent to the injury.

(d) The reasonable burial expenses of the deceased employee, not to exceed the amount provided for by Section 4701.

(e) The reasonable living expenses of the spouse or minor children of the injured employee, or both, subsequent to the date of the injury, where the employee has deserted or is neglecting his or her family. These expenses shall be allowed in the proportion that the appeals board deems proper, under application of the spouse, guardian of the minor children, or the assignee, pursuant to subdivision (a) of Section 11477 of the Welfare and Institutions Code, of the spouse, a former spouse, or minor children. A collection received as a result of a lien against a workers' compensation award imposed pursuant to this subdivision for payment of child support ordered by a court shall be credited as provided in Section 695.221 of the Code of Civil Procedure.

(f) The amount of unemployment compensation disability benefits that have been paid under or pursuant to the Unemployment Insurance Code in those cases where, pending a determination under this division there was uncertainty whether the benefits were payable under the Unemployment Insurance Code or payable hereunder; provided, however, that any lien under this subdivision shall be allowed and paid as provided in Section 4904.

(g) The amount of unemployment compensation benefits and extended duration benefits paid to the injured employee for the same day or days for which he or she receives, or is entitled to receive, temporary total disability indemnity payments under this division; provided, however, that any lien under this subdivision shall be allowed and paid as provided in Section 4904.

(h) The amount of family temporary disability insurance benefits that have been paid to the injured employee pursuant to the Unemployment Insurance Code for the same day or days for which that employee receives, or is entitled to receive, temporary total disability indemnity payments under this division, provided, however, that any lien under this subdivision shall be allowed and paid as provided in Section 4904.

(i) The amount of indemnification granted by the California Victims of Crime Program pursuant to Article 1 (commencing with Section 13959) of Chapter 5 of Part 4 of Division 3 of Title 2 of the Government Code.

(j) The amount of compensation, including expenses of medical treatment, and recoverable costs that have been paid by the Asbestos Workers' Account pursuant to the provisions of Chapter 11 (commencing with Section

4401) of Part 1. *(Stats.1937, c. 90, p. 287, § 4903. Amended by Stats.1945, c. 507, p. 1007, § 1; Stats.1947, c. 833, p. 1998, § 1; Stats.1949, c. 488, p. 837, § 1; Stats.1957, c. 1977, p. 3524, § 1; Stats.1963, c. 1556, p. 3140, § 1; Stats.1965, c. 1513, p. 3582, § 103, operative Jan. 15, 1966; Stats.1967, c. 1721, p. 4289, § 2; Stats.1980, c. 1041, p. 3325, § 2; Stats.1980, c. 1370, p. 4970, § 5.1, eff. Oct. 1, 1980; Stats.1981, c. 809, p. 3141, § 1, eff. Sept. 25, 1981; Stats.1984, c. 1463, § 2.5, eff. Sept. 26, 1984; Stats.1987, c. 1434, § 1; Stats.1991, c. 116 (S.B.1218), § 30; Stats.1991, c. 934 (A.B.1673), § 14; Stats.1993, c. 876 (S.B.1068), § 28, eff. Oct. 6, 1993; Stats.1994, c. 75 (A.B.1702), § 4, eff. May 20, 1994; Stats.1996, c. 1077 (A.B.2898), § 12; Stats.2003, c. 797 (S.B.727), § 1.)*

Operative Effect

For operative effect of Stats.2003, c. 797 (S.B. 727) upon benefits payable for family temporary disability insurance claims, see section 28 of that act.

§ 4903.1.   Reimbursement for benefits paid or services providing; filing of liens

(a) The appeals board, arbitrator, or settlement conference referee, before issuing an award or approval of any compromise of claim, shall determine, on the basis of liens filed with it pursuant to subdivision (b) or (c), whether any benefits have been paid or services provided by a health care provider, a health care service plan, a group disability policy, including a loss of income policy, a self-insured employee welfare benefit plan, or a hospital service contract, and its award or approval shall provide for reimbursement for benefits paid or services provided under these plans as follows:

(1) When the referee issues an award finding that an injury or illness arises out of and in the course of employment, but denies the applicant reimbursement for self-procured medical costs solely because of lack of notice to the applicant's employer of his need for hospital, surgical, or medical care, the appeals board shall nevertheless award a lien against the employee's recovery, to the extent of benefits paid or services provided, for the effects of the industrial injury or illness, by a health care provider, a health care service plan, a group disability policy, a self-insured employee welfare benefit plan, or a hospital service contract.

(2) When the referee issues an award finding that an injury or illness arises out of and in the course of employment, and makes an award for reimbursement for self-procured medical costs, the appeals board shall allow a lien, to the extent of benefits paid or services provided, for the effects of the industrial injury or illness, by a health care provider, a health care service plan, a group disability policy, a self-insured employee welfare benefit plan, or a hospital service contract.

(3) When the referee issues an award finding that an injury or illness arises out of and in the course of employment and makes an award for temporary disability

indemnity, the appeals board shall allow a lien as living expense under Section 4903, for benefits paid by a group disability policy providing loss of time benefits. Such lien shall be allowed to the extent that benefits have been paid for the same day or days for which temporary disability indemnity is awarded and shall not exceed the award for temporary disability indemnity. No lien shall be allowed hereunder unless the group disability policy provides for reduction, exclusion, or coordination of loss of time benefits on account of workers' compensation benefits.

(4) When the parties propose that the case be disposed of by way of a compromise and release agreement, in the event the lien claimant, other than a health care provider, does not agree to the amount allocated to it, then the referee shall determine the potential recovery and reduce the amount of the lien in the ratio of the applicant's recovery to the potential recovery in full satisfaction of its lien claim.

(b) When a compromise of claim or an award is submitted to the appeals board, arbitrator, or settlement conference referee for approval, the parties shall file with the appeals board, arbitrator, or settlement conference referee any liens served on the parties.

(c) Any lien claimant under Section 4903 or this section shall file its lien with the appeals board in writing upon a form approved by the appeals board. The lien shall be accompanied by a full statement or itemized voucher supporting the lien and justifying the right to reimbursement and proof of service upon the injured worker, or if deceased, upon the worker's dependents, the employer, the insurer, and the respective attorneys or other agents of record.

(d) The appeals board shall file liens required by subdivision (c) immediately upon receipt. Numbers shall be assigned pursuant to subdivision (c) of Section 5500. *(Added by Stats.1975, c. 1109, p. 2686, § 1. Amended by Stats.1979, c. 855, p. 2963, § 1; Stats.1990, c. 1550 (A.B.2910), § 45.)*

§ 4903.2. Attorney's fee

Where a lien claimant is reimbursed pursuant to subdivision (f) or (g) of Section 4903 or Section 4903.1, for benefits paid or services provided, the appeals board may award an attorney's fee to the applicant's attorney out of the lien claimant's recovery if the appeals board determines that all of the following occurred:

(a) The lien claimant received notice of all hearings following the filing of the lien and received notice of intent to award the applicant's attorney a fee.

(b) An attorney or other representative of the lien claimant did not participate in the proceedings before the appeals board with respect to the lien claim.

(c) There were bona fide issues respecting compensability, or respecting allowability of the lien, such that the services of an attorney were reasonably required to effectuate recovery on the claim of lien and were instrumental in effecting the recovery.

(d) The case was not disposed of by compromise and release.

The amount of the attorney's fee out of the lien claimant's recovery shall be based on the extent of applicant's attorney's efforts on behalf of the lien claimant. The ratio of the amount of the attorney's fee awarded against the lien claimant's recovery to that recovery shall not exceed the ratio of the amount of the attorney's fee awarded against the applicant's award to that award. *(Added by Stats.1980, c. 417, p. 821, § 1. Amended by Stats.1983, c. 142, § 108.)*

§ 4903.3. Discretionary compensation in cases to which director is a party before the issuance of award; lien

The director, as administrator of the Uninsured Employers Fund, may, in his discretion, provide compensation, including medical treatment, from the Uninsured Employers Fund in cases to which the director is a party before the issuance of any award, if such compensation is not being provided to the applicant.

The appeals board shall determine and allow as a first lien against any sum to be paid as compensation the amount of compensation, including the cost of medical treatment, provided by the director pursuant to this section. *(Added by Stats.1981, c. 894, p. 3412, § 9.)*

§ 4903.4. Resolution of disputes concerning liens

When a dispute arises concerning a lien for expenses incurred by or on behalf of the injured employee as provided by Article 2 (commencing with Section 4600) of Chapter 2 of Part 2, the appeals board may resolve the dispute in a separate proceeding, which may include binding arbitration upon agreement of the employer, lien claimant, and the employee, if the employee remains a party to the dispute, according to the rules of practice and procedure. *(Added by Stats.1989, c. 892, § 42. Amended by Stats.1990, c. 1550 (A.B.2910), § 46.)*

§ 4903.5. Lien claims for expenses; filing requirements; application

(a) No lien claim for expenses as provided in subdivision (b) of Section 4903 may be filed after six months from the date on which the appeals board or a workers' compensation administrative law judge issues a final decision, findings, order, including an order approving compromise and release, or award, on the merits of the claim, after five years from the date of the injury for which the services were provided, or after one year from the date the services were provided, whichever is later.

(b) Notwithstanding subdivision (a), any health care provider, health care service plan, group disability insurer, employee benefit plan, or other entity providing medical benefits on a nonindustrial basis, may file a lien claim for expenses as provided in subdivision (b) of Section 4903 within six months after the person or entity first has knowledge that an industrial injury is being claimed.

(c) The injured worker shall not be liable for any underlying obligation if a lien claim has not been filed and served within the allowable period. Except when the lien claimant is the applicant as provided in Section 5501, a lien claimant shall not file a declaration of readiness to proceed in any case until the case-in-chief has been resolved.

(d) This section shall not apply to civil actions brought under the Cartwright Act (Chapter 2 (commencing with Section 16700) of Part 2 of Division 7 of the Business and Professions Code), the Unfair Practices Act (Chapter 4 (commencing with Section 17000) of Part 2 of Division 7 of the Business and Professions Code), or the federal Racketeer Influenced and Corrupt Organization Act (Chapter 96 (commencing with Section 1961) of Title 18 of the United States Code) based on concerted action with other insurers that are not parties to the case in which the lien or claim is filed. *(Added by Stats.2002, c. 6 (A.B.749), § 70.)*

§ 4903.6. Lien claims, applications for adjudication, or declarations of readiness to proceed; filing requirements; adoption of regulations; application of prohibitions

(a) Except as necessary to meet the requirements of Section 4903.5, no lien claim or application for adjudication shall be filed under subdivision (b) of Section 4903 until the expiration of one of the following:

(1) Sixty days after the date of acceptance or rejection of liability for the claim, or expiration of the time provided for investigation of liability pursuant to subdivision (b) of Section 5402, whichever date is earlier.

(2) The time provided for payment of medical treatment bills pursuant to Section 4603.2.

(3) The time provided for payment of medical-legal expenses pursuant to Section 4622.

(b) No declaration of readiness to proceed shall be filed for a lien under subdivision (b) of Section 4903 until the underlying case has been resolved or where the applicant chooses not to proceed with his or her case.

(c) The appeals board shall adopt reasonable regulations to ensure compliance with this section, and shall take any further steps as may be necessary to enforce the regulations, including, but not limited to, impositions of sanctions pursuant to Section 5813.

(d) The prohibitions of this section shall not apply to lien claims, applications for adjudication, or declarations of readiness to proceed filed by or on behalf of the employee, or to the filings by or on behalf of the employer. *(Added by Stats.2006, c. 69 (A.B.1806), § 26, eff. July 12, 2006.)*

§ 4904. Notice of lien; approval by appeals board; determination of amount; effect of determination; payment; approval of compromise and release agreement

(a) If notice is given in writing to the insurer, or to the employer if uninsured, setting forth the nature and extent of any claim that is allowable as a lien, the claim is a lien against any amount thereafter payable as compensation, subject to the determination of the amount and approval of the lien by the appeals board. When the Employment Development Department has served an insurer or employer with a lien claim, the insurer or employer shall notify the Employment Development Department, in writing, as soon as possible, but in no event later than 15 working days after commencing disability indemnity payments. When a lien has been served on an insurer or an employer by the Employment Development Department, the insurer or employer shall notify the Employment Development Department, in writing, within 10 working days of filing an application for adjudication, a stipulated award, or a compromise and release with the appeals board.

(b)(1) In determining the amount of lien to be allowed for unemployment compensation disability benefits under subdivision (f) of Section 4903, the appeals board shall allow the lien in the amount of benefits which it finds were paid for the same day or days of disability for which an award of compensation for any permanent disability indemnity resulting solely from the same injury or illness or temporary disability indemnity, or both, is made and for which the employer has not reimbursed the Employment Development Department pursuant to Section 2629.1 of the Unemployment Insurance Code.

(2) In determining the amount of lien to be allowed for unemployment compensation benefits and extended duration benefits under subdivision (g) of Section 4903, the appeals board shall allow the lien in the amount of benefits which it finds were paid for the same day or days for which an award of compensation for temporary total disability is made.

(3) In determining the amount of lien to be allowed for family temporary disability insurance benefits under subdivision (h) of Section 4903, the appeals board shall allow the lien in the amount of benefits that it finds were paid for the same day or days for which an award of compensation for temporary total disability is made and for which the employer has not reimbursed the Employment Development Department pursuant to Section 2629.1 of the Unemployment Insurance Code.

(c) In the case of agreements for the compromise and release of a disputed claim for compensation, the applicant and defendant may propose to the appeals board, as part of the compromise and release agreement, an amount out of the settlement to be paid to any lien claimant claiming under subdivision (f), (g), or (h) of Section 4903. If the lien claimant objects to the amount proposed for payment of its lien under a compromise and release settlement or stipulation, the appeals board shall determine the extent of the lien claimant's entitlement to reimbursement on its lien and make and file findings on all facts involved in the controversy over this issue in accordance with Section 5313. The appeals board may approve a compromise and release agreement or stipulation which proposes the disallowance of a lien, in whole or in part, only where there is proof of service upon the lien claimant by the defendant, not less than 15 days prior to the appeals board action, of all medical and rehabilitation documents and a copy of the proposed compromise and release agreement or stipulation. The determination of the appeals board, subject to petition for reconsideration and to the right of judicial review, as to the amount of lien allowed under subdivision (f), (g), or (h) of Section 4903, whether in connection with an award of compensation or the approval of a compromise and release agreement, shall be binding on the lien claimant, the applicant, and the defendant, insofar as the right to benefits paid under the Unemployment Insurance Code for which the lien was claimed. The appeals board may order the amount of any lien claim, as determined and allowed by it, to be paid directly to the person entitled, either in a lump sum or in installments.

(d) Where unemployment compensation disability benefits, including family temporary disability insurance benefits, have been paid pursuant to the Unemployment Insurance Code while reconsideration of an order, decision, or award is pending, or has been granted, the appeals board shall determine and allow a final amount on the lien as of the date the board is ready to issue its decision denying a petition for reconsideration or affirming, rescinding, altering or amending the original findings, order, decision, or award.

(e) The appeals board may not be prohibited from approving a compromise and release agreement on all other issues and deferring to subsequent proceedings the determination of a lien claimant's entitlement to reimbursement if the defendant in any of these proceedings agrees to pay the amount subsequently determined to be due under the lien claim. *(Stats.1937, c. 90, p. 288, § 4904. Amended by Stats.1957, c. 1977, p. 3524, § 2; Stats.1965, c. 157, p. 1116, § 6; Stats.1965, c. 691, p. 2073, § 1; Stats.1965, c. 1513, p. 3582, § 104, operative Jan. 15, 1966; Stats.1967, c. 125, p. 1155, § 6; Stats.1967, c. 1721, p. 4290, § 3; Stats.1970, c. 985, p. 1757, § 1; Stats.1989, c. 1280, § 2; Stats.1990, c. 1550 (A.B.2910), § 47; Stats. 1993, c. 748 (S.B.4), § 1; Stats.2003, c. 797 (S.B.727), § 2.)*

Operative Effect

For operative effect of Stats.2003, c. 797 (S.B. 727) upon benefits payable for family temporary disability insurance claims, see section 28 of that act.

§ 4904.1. Effect of payment of liens upon immediate payment of balance of award

The payment of liens as provided in Section 4904, shall in no way affect the commencement of immediate payments on any balance of the award to the injured claimant where an installment payment for his disability has been determined. *(Added by Stats.1957, c. 1241, p. 2548, § 1.)*

§ 4905. Order for payment of claim without notice

Where it appears in any proceeding pending before the appeals board that a lien should be allowed if it had been duly requested by the party entitled thereto, the appeals board may, without any request for such lien having been made, order the payment of the claim to be made directly to the person entitled, in the same manner and with the same effect as though the lien had been regularly requested, and the award to such person shall constitute a lien against unpaid compensation due at the time of service of the award. *(Stats.1937, c. 90, p. 288, § 4905. Amended by Stats.1965, c. 1513, p. 3583, § 105, operative Jan. 15, 1966.)*

§ 4906. Reasonableness of claim for legal and medical services; attorney fee agreements; disclosures and statements

(a) No charge, claim, or agreement for the legal services or disbursements mentioned in subdivision (a) of Section 4903, or for the expense mentioned in subdivision (b) of Section 4903, is enforceable, valid, or binding in excess of a reasonable amount. The appeals board may determine what constitutes a reasonable amount.

(b) No attorney or agent shall demand or accept any fee from an employee or dependent of an employee for the purpose of representing the employee or dependent of an employee in any proceeding of the division, appeals board, or any appellate procedure related thereto until the amount of the fee has been approved or set by the appeals board.

(c) Any fee agreement shall be submitted to the appeals board for approval within 10 days after the agreement is made.

(d) In establishing a reasonable attorney's fee, consideration shall be given to the responsibility assumed by the attorney, the care exercised in representing the applicant, the time involved, and the results obtained.

(e) At the initial consultation, an attorney shall furnish the employee a written disclosure form promulgated by the administrative director which shall clearly and prominently describe the procedures available to the injured employee or his or her dependents. The disclosure form shall describe this section, the range of attorney's fees customarily approved by the appeals board, and the attorney's fees provisions of Section 4064 and the extent to which an employee may receive compensation without incurring attorney's fees. The disclosure form shall include the telephone number of the administrative director together with the statement that the employee may receive answers at that number to questions concerning entitlement to compensation or the procedures to follow to receive compensation. A copy of the disclosure form shall be signed by the employee and the attorney and sent to the employer, or insurer or third-party administrator, if either is known, by the attorney within 15 days of the employee's and attorney's execution thereof.

(f) The disclosure form set forth in subdivision (e) shall contain, prominently stated, the following statement:

"Any person who makes or causes to be made any knowingly false or fraudulent material statement or representation for the purpose of obtaining or denying worker's compensation benefits or payments is guilty of a felony."

(g) The employee, the insurer, the employer, and the attorneys for each party shall sign and file with the board a statement, with the application or answer, under penalty of perjury that they have not violated Section 139.3 and that they have not offered, delivered, received, or accepted any rebate, refund, commission, preference, patronage dividend, discount, or other consideration, whether in the form of money or otherwise, as compensation or inducement for any referred examination or evaluation. *(Stats.1937, c. 90, p. 288, § 4906. Amended by Stats.1965, c. 1513, p. 3583, § 106, operative Jan. 15, 1966; Stats.1989, c. 892, § 43; Stats.1990, c. 1550 (A.B. 2910), § 48; Stats.1991, c. 934 (A.B.1673), § 15; Stats. 1993, c. 120 (A.B.1300), § 6, eff. July, 16, 1993; Stats.1993, c. 1241 (S.B.147), § 15.)*

§ 4907. Suspension of privilege of appearing as representative of party to proceedings

The privilege of any person, including attorneys admitted to practice in the Supreme Court of the state to appear in any proceeding as a representative of any party before the appeals board, or any of its referees, may, after a hearing, be removed, denied, or suspended by the appeals board for a violation of this chapter or for other good cause. *(Stats.1937, c. 90, p. 288, § 4907. Amended by Stats.1965, c. 1513, p. 3583, § 107, operative Jan. 15, 1966.)*

§ 4908. Priority of compensation claim

A claim for compensation for the injury or death of any employee, or any award or judgment entered thereon, has the same preference over the other debts of the employer, or his estate and of the insurer which is given by the law to claims for wages. Such preference is for the entire amount of the compensation to be paid. This section shall not impair the lien of any previous award. *(Stats. 1937, c. 90, p. 288, § 4908. Amended by Stats.1939, c. 649, p. 2076, § 2.)*

§ 4909. Payment and acceptance of payment of amount not due or pending dispute of right compensation

Any payment, allowance, or benefit received by the injured employee during the period of his incapacity, or by his dependents in the event of his death, which by the terms of this division was not then due and payable or when there is any dispute or question concerning the right to compensation, shall not, in the absence of any agreement, be an admission of liability for compensation on the part of the employer, but any such payment, allowance, or benefit may be taken into account by the appeals board in fixing the amount of the compensation

to be paid. The acceptance of any such payment, allowance, or benefit shall not operate as a waiver of any right or claim which the employee or his dependents has against the employer. *(Stats.1937, c. 90, p. 288, § 4909. Amended by Stats.1965, c. 1513, p. 3583, § 108, operative Jan. 15, 1966.)*

§ 4909.1. Representatives of departments of correction and youth authority authorized to request payments, allowances, or benefits described in § 4909

Authorized representatives of the Department of Corrections, and the Department of the Youth Authority may request the State Compensation Insurance Fund to provide any payment, allowance, or benefit as described in Section 4909. When requested by an authorized representative, the State Compensation Insurance Fund shall administer the benefits in a timely fashion. *(Added by Stats.1988, c. 1233, § 3.)*

CHAPTER 2. COMPROMISE AND RELEASE

Section
5000. Exemption of employer from liability for compensation prohibited; authority to compromise and release claims.
5001. Compensation defined; approval of release or compromise.
5002. Filing of copy; entry of award based on release or compromise.
5003. Execution and contents.
5004. Contents in case of death.
5005. Claim of occupational disease or cumulative injury.
5006. Collateral estoppel; effect of appeals board determinations.

§ 5000. Exemption of employer from liability for compensation prohibited; authority to compromise and release claims

No contract, rule, or regulation shall exempt the employer from liability for the compensation fixed by this division, but nothing in this division shall:

(a) Impair the right of the parties interested to compromise, subject to the provisions herein contained, any liability which is claimed to exist under this division on account of injury or death.

(b) Confer upon the dependents of any injured employee any interest which the employee may not release by compromise or for which he, or his estate is in the event of such compromise by him accountable to dependents. *(Stats.1937, c. 90, p. 289, § 5000.)*

§ 5001. Compensation defined; approval of release or compromise

Compensation is the measure of the responsibility which the employer has assumed for injuries or deaths which occur to employees in his employment when subject to this division. No release of liability or compromise agreement is valid unless it is approved by the appeals board or referee. *(Stats.1937, c. 90, p. 289, § 5001. Amended by Stats.1947, c. 1014, p. 2280, § 1;*

Stats.1951, c. 778, p. 2267, § 2; Stats.1955, c. 1822, p. 3365, § 4; Stats.1965, c. 1513, p. 3584, § 109, operative Jan. 15, 1966.)

§ 5002. Filing of copy; entry of award based on release or compromise

A copy of the release or compromise agreement signed by both parties shall forthwith be filed with the appeals board. Upon filing with and approval by the appeals board, it may, without notice, of its own motion or on the application of either party, enter its award based upon the release or compromise agreement. *(Stats.1937, c. 90, p. 289, § 5002. Amended by Stats.1965, c. 1513, p. 3584, § 110, operative Jan. 15, 1966.)*

§ 5003. Execution and contents

Every release or compromise agreement shall be in writing and duly executed, and the signature of the employee or other beneficiary shall be attested by two disinterested witnesses or acknowledged before a notary public. The document shall specify:

(a) The date of the accident.

(b) The average weekly wages of the employee, determined according to Chapter 1 of Part 2 of this division.

(c) The nature of the disability, whether total or partial, permanent or temporary.

(d) The amount paid, or due and unpaid, to the employee up to the date of the release or agreement or death, and the amount of the payment or benefits then or thereafter to be made.

(e) The length of time such payment or benefit is to continue.

(f) In the event a claim of lien under subdivision (f) or (g) of Section 4903 has been filed, the number of days and the amount of temporary disability indemnity which should be allowed to the lien claimant. *(Stats.1937, c. 90, p. 289, § 5003. Amended by Stats.1945, c. 1510, p. 2821, § 1; Stats.1953, c. 554, p. 1812, § 1; Stats.1957, c. 1977, p. 3525, § 3; Stats.1967, c. 1721, p. 4291, § 4.)*

§ 5004. Contents in case of death

In case of death there shall also be stated in the release or compromise agreement:

(a) The date of death.

(b) The name of the widow.

(c) The names and ages of all children.

(d) The names of all other dependents.

(e) Whether the dependents are total or partial.

(f) The amount paid or to be paid as a death benefit and to whom payment is to be made. *(Stats.1937, c. 90, p. 289, § 5004.)*

§ 5005. Claim of occupational disease or cumulative injury

In any case involving a claim of occupational disease or cumulative injury, as set forth in Section 5500.5, the employee and any employer, or any insurance carrier for any employer, may enter into a compromise and release agreement settling either all or any part of the employee's claim, including a part of his claim against any employer. Such compromise and release agreement, upon approval by the appeals board or a referee, shall be a total release as to such employer or insurance carrier for the portion or portions of the claim released, but shall not constitute a bar to a recovery from any one or all of the remaining employers or insurance carriers for the periods of exposure not so released.

In any case where a compromise and release agreement of a portion of a claim has been made and approved, the employee may elect to proceed as provided in Section 5500.5 against any one or more of the remaining employers, or against an employer for that portion of his exposure not so released; in any such proceeding after election following compromise and release, that portion of liability attributable to the portion or portions of the exposure so released shall be assessed and deducted from the liability of the remaining defendant or defendants, but any such defendant shall receive no credit for any moneys paid by way of compromise and release in excess of the liability actually assessed against the released employments and the employee shall not receive any further benefits from the released employments for any liability assessed to them above what was paid by way of compromise and release.

In approving a compromise and release agreement under this section, the appeals board or referee shall determine the adequacy of the compromise and release agreement as it shall then reflect the potential liability of the released exposure after apportionment, but need not make a final actual determination of the potential liability of the employer or employers for that portion of the exposure being released. *(Added by Stats.1974, c. 1164, p. 2493, § 1.)*

§ 5006. Collateral estoppel; effect of appeals board determinations

A determination of facts by the appeals board under this chapter has no collateral estoppel effect on a subsequent criminal prosecution and does not preclude litigation of those same facts in the criminal proceeding. *(Added by Stats.1995, c. 158 (A.B.891), § 1.)*

CHAPTER 3. LUMP SUM PAYMENTS

Section
5100. Commutation of compensation; payment in lump sum; conditions.
5100.5. Restriction on commutation.
5100.6. Commutation or settlement of compensation of indemnity payments of employee under rehabilitation.
5101. Computation of amount.
5102. Manner of payment; deposit in trust.
5103. Payments by trustee.
5104. Appointment of trustee.
5105. Receipt for payment of lump sum; certificate of appeals board; filing of certificate.

Section
5106. Uninsured employer; order for payment of present
         worth of future installments into uninsured employ-
         ers fund; future payments.

§ 5100. Commutation of compensation; payment in lump sum; conditions

At the time of making its award, or at any time thereafter, the appeals board, on its own motion either upon notice, or upon application of either party with due notice to the other, may commute the compensation payable under this division to a lump sum and order it to be paid forthwith or at some future time if any of the following conditions appear:

(a) That such commutation is necessary for the protection of the person entitled thereto, or for the best interest of the applicant. In determining what is in the best interest of the applicant, the appeals board shall consider the general financial condition of the applicant, including but not limited to, the applicant's ability to live without periodic indemnity payments and to discharge debts incurred prior to the date of injury.

(b) That commutation will avoid inequity and will not cause undue expense or hardship to the applicant.

(c) That the employer has sold or otherwise disposed of the greater part of his assets or is about to do so.

(d) That the employer is not a resident of this state. *(Stats.1937, c. 90, p. 290, § 5100. Amended by Stats.1963, c. 2123, p. 4408, § 1; Stats.1965, c. 1513, p. 3584, § 111, operative Jan. 15, 1966; Stats.1976, c. 1403, p. 6322, § 1; Stats.1982, c. 1015, p. 3718, § 1.)*

§ 5100.5. Restriction on commutation

Notwithstanding the provisions of Section 5100, the appeals board shall not commute the compensation payable under this division to a lump sum when such compensation is payable under Section 4751 of the Labor Code. *(Added by Stats.1955, c. 1093, p. 2077, § 1. Amended by Stats.1965, c. 1513, p. 3584, § 112, operative Jan. 15, 1966.)*

§ 5100.6. Commutation or settlement of compensation of indemnity payments of employee under rehabilitation

Notwithstanding the provisions of Section 5100, the appeals board shall not permit the commutation or settlement of prospective compensation or indemnity payments or other benefits to which the employee is entitled under vocational rehabilitation. *(Added by Stats. 1965, c. 1513, p. 3584, § 113, operative Jan. 15, 1966. Amended by Stats.1976, c. 1079, p. 4870, § 51; Stats.1998, c. 524 (S.B.1965), § 2.)*

§ 5101. Computation of amount

The amount of the lump sum shall be determined as follows:

(a) If the injury causes temporary disability, the appeals board shall estimate the probable duration thereof and the probable amount of the temporary disability payments therefor, in accordance with Chapter 2 of Part 2 [1] of this division, and shall fix the lump sum at the amount so determined.

(b) If the injury causes permanent disability or death, the appeals board shall fix the total amount of the permanent disability payment or death benefit payable therefor in accordance with Chapter 2 of Part 2 of this division, and shall estimate the present value thereof, assuming interest at the rate of 3 percent per annum and disregarding the probability of the beneficiary's death in all cases except where the percentage of permanent disability is such as to entitle the beneficiary to a life pension, and then taking into consideration the probability of the beneficiary's death only in estimating the present value of such life pension. *(Stats.1937, c. 90, p. 290, § 5101. Amended by Stats.1945, c. 1253, p. 2368, § 1; Stats.1965, c. 1513, p. 3584, § 114, operative Jan. 15, 1966.)*

[1] Section 4550 et seq.

§ 5102. Manner of payment; deposit in trust

The appeals board may order the lump sum paid directly to the injured employee or his dependents, or deposited with any savings bank or trust company authorized to transact business in this state, which agrees to accept the same as a deposit bearing interest; or the appeals board may order the lump sum deposited with the State Compensation Insurance Fund. Any lump sum so deposited, together with all interest derived therefrom, shall thereafter be held in trust for the injured employee, or in the event of his death, for his dependents. In the event of the employee's death, his dependents shall have no further recourse against the employer under this chapter. *(Stats.1937, c. 90, p. 290, § 5102. Amended by Stats.1965, c. 1513, p. 3585, § 115, operative Jan. 15, 1966.)*

§ 5103. Payments by trustee

Payments from the lump sum so deposited shall be made by the trustee only in the amounts and at the time fixed by order of the appeals board and until the lump sum and interest thereon are exhausted. *(Stats.1937, c. 90, p. 290, § 5103. Amended by Stats.1965, c. 1513, p. 3585, § 116, operative Jan. 15, 1966.)*

§ 5104. Appointment of trustee

In the appointment of the trustee, preference may be given to the choice of the injured employee or his dependents. *(Stats.1937, c. 90, p. 291, § 5104.)*

§ 5105. Receipt for payment of lump sum; certificate of appeals board; filing of certificate

Upon the payment of a lump sum, the employer shall present to the appeals board a proper receipt evidencing the same, executed either by the injured employee or his dependents, or by the trustee. The appeals board shall thereupon issue its certificate in proper form evidencing such payment. Such certificate, upon filing with the clerk of the superior court in which any judgment upon an award has been entered, operates as a satisfaction of the award and fully discharges the employer from any further liability on account thereof. *(Stats.1937, c. 90, p. 291, § 5105. Amended by Stats.1965, c. 1513, p. 3585, § 117, operative Jan. 15, 1966.)*

§ 5106. Uninsured employer; order for payment of present worth of future installments into uninsured employers fund; future payments

The appeals board shall, upon the request of the Director of Industrial Relations, where the employer is uninsured and the installments of compensation awarded are to be paid in the future, determine the present worth of the future payments, discounted at the rate of 3 percent per annum, and order the present worth paid into the Uninsured Employers Fund, which fund shall thereafter pay to the beneficiaries of the award the future payments as they become due. *(Stats.1937, c. 90, p. 291, § 5106. Amended by Stats.1965, c. 1513, p. 3585, § 118, operative Jan. 15, 1966; Stats.1987, c. 202, § 3.)*

Part 3.2

WORKERS' COMPENSATION HEALTH CARE PROVIDER ORGANIZATION ACT [REPEALED]

Part 3.5

ARBITRATION

Section
5270.   Application of part.
5270.5. Eligible arbitrators; qualifications.
5271.   Selection of arbitrator.
5272.   Duties and responsibilities of arbitrator.
5273.   Costs.
5275.   Disputes subject to arbitration.
5276.   Commencement of proceedings; service of documents.
5277.   Findings and award; failure to submit decision within specified time.
5278.   Disclosure of settlement offers; ex parte communications.

§ 5270. Application of part

This part shall not apply in cases where an injured employee or dependent is involved unless the employee or dependent is represented by an attorney. *(Added by Stats.1989, c. 892, § 44. Amended by Stats.1990, c. 1550 (A.B.2910), § 49.)*

§ 5270.5. Eligible arbitrators; qualifications

(a) The presiding workers' compensation judge at each district office shall prepare a list of all eligible attorneys who apply to be placed on the list of eligible arbitrators. Attorneys are eligible to become arbitrators if they are active members of the California State Bar Association and are one of the following:

(1) A certified specialist in workers' compensation, or eligible to become certified.

(2) A retired workers' compensation judge.

(3) A retired appeals board member.

(4) An attorney who has been certified to serve as a judge pro tempore.

(b) No attorney shall be included in a panel of arbitrators, if he or she has served as a judge in any proceeding involving the same case, or has represented, or whose firm has represented, any party in the same case. *(Added by Stats.1989, c. 892, § 44.)*

§ 5271. Selection of arbitrator

(a) The parties to a dispute submitted for arbitration may select any eligible attorney from the list prepared by the presiding workers' compensation judge to serve as arbitrator. However, when the disputed issue involves insurance coverage, the parties may select any attorney as arbitrator upon agreement of the parties.

(b) If the parties cannot select an arbitrator by agreement, either party may request the presiding workers' compensation judge to assign a panel of five arbitrators selected at random from the list of eligible attorneys. No more than three arbitrators on a five-member panel may be defense attorneys, no more than three may be applicant's attorneys, and no more than two may be retired workers' compensation judges or appeals board commissioners.

(c) For each party in excess of one party in the capacity of employer and one party in the capacity of injured employee or lien claimant, the presiding judge shall randomly select two additional arbitrators to add to the panel. For each additional party in the capacity of employer, the presiding judge shall assign a retired workers' compensation judge or retired appeals board commissioner and an applicant's attorney. For each additional party in the capacity of injured employee or lien claimant, the presiding judge shall assign a retired workers' compensation judge or retired appeals board commissioner and a defense attorney. For each additional other party, the presiding judge shall assign two arbitrators to the panel, in order of rotation from case to case, as follows: a retired workers' compensation judge or retired appeals board commissioner, an applicant's attorney, a defense attorney.

(d) A party may petition the presiding workers' compensation judge to remove a member from the panel pursuant to Section 170.1 of the Code of Civil Procedure. The presiding workers' compensation judge shall assign another eligible attorney to replace any member removed under this subdivision.

(e) Each party or lien claimant shall strike two members from the panel, and the remaining attorney shall serve as arbitrator. *(Added by Stats.1989, c. 892, § 44. Amended by Stats.1990, c. 1550 (A.B.2910), § 50.)*

§ 5272. Duties and responsibilities of arbitrator

Arbitrators shall have all of the statutory and regulatory duties and responsibilities of a workers' compensation judge, as set forth in Chapter 1 (commencing with Section 5300) of Part 4, except for the following:

(a) Arbitrators shall have no power to order the injured worker to be examined by a qualified medical evaluator pursuant to Sections 5701 and 5703.5.

(b) Arbitrators shall not have power of contempt. *(Added by Stats.1989, c. 892, § 44. Amended by Stats. 1990, c. 1550 (A.B.2910), § 51.)*

§ 5273. Costs

(a) In disputes between an employee and an employer, the employer shall pay all costs related to the arbitration proceeding, including use of facilities, hearing reporter per diems and transcript costs.

(b) In all other disputes, the costs of the arbitration proceedings, including the arbitrator's compensation, shall be paid as follows:

(1) By the parties equally in any dispute between an employer and an insurer, or an employer and a lien claimant.

(2) By the parties equally in proceedings subject to Section 5500.5.

(3) By the dependents in accordance with their proportionate share of death benefits, where there is no dispute as to the injury causing death.

(c) Disputes regarding the costs or fees for arbitration shall be within the exclusive jurisdiction of the appeals board, and shall be determined initially by the presiding judge of the district office. *(Added by Stats.1989, c. 892, § 44. Amended by Stats.1990, c. 1550 (A.B.2910), § 52.)*

§ 5275. Disputes subject to arbitration

(a) Disputes involving the following issues shall be submitted for arbitration:

(1) Insurance coverage.

(2) Right of contribution in accordance with Section 5500.5.

(b) By agreement of the parties, any issue arising under Division 1 (commencing with Section 50) or Division 4 (commencing with Section 3200) may be submitted for arbitration, regardless of the date of injury. *(Added by Stats.1989, c. 892, § 44. Amended by Stats. 1990, c. 1550 (A.B.2910), § 53; Stats.1993, c. 121 (A.B. 110), § 55, eff. July 16, 1993; Stats.1994, c. 470 (A.B. 1811), § 1; Stats.2002, c. 6 (A.B.749), § 70.5.)*

§ 5276. Commencement of proceedings; service of documents

(a) Arbitration proceedings may commence at any place and time agreed upon by all parties.

(b) If the parties cannot agree on a time or place to commence arbitration proceedings, the arbitrator shall order the date, time and place for commencement of the

proceeding. Unless all parties agree otherwise, arbitration proceedings shall commence not less than 30 days nor more than 60 days from the date an arbitrator is selected.

(c) Ten days before the arbitration, each party shall submit to the arbitrator and serve on the opposing party reports, records and other documentary evidence on which that party intends to rely. If a party intends to rely upon excerpts of records or depositions, only copies of the excerpts shall be submitted to the arbitrator. *(Added by Stats.1989, c. 892, § 44.)*

§ 5277. Findings and award; failure to submit decision within specified time

(a) The arbitrator's findings and award shall be served on all parties within 30 days of submission of the case for decision.

(b) The arbitrator's award shall comply with Section 5313 and shall be filed with the appeals board office pursuant to venue rules published by the appeals board.

(c) The findings of fact, award, order, or decision of the arbitrator shall have the same force and effect as an award, order, or decision of a workers' compensation judge.

(d) Use of an arbitrator for any part of a proceeding or any issue shall not bind the parties to the use of the same arbitrator for any subsequent issues or proceedings.

(e) Unless all parties agree to a longer period of time, the failure of the arbitrator to submit the decision within 30 days shall result in forfeiture of the arbitrator's fee and shall vacate the submission order and all stipulations.

(f) The presiding workers' compensation judge may submit supplemental proceedings to arbitration pursuant to this part. *(Added by Stats.1989, c. 892, § 44. Amended by Stats.2006, c. 538 (S.B.1852), § 490.)*

§ 5278. Disclosure of settlement offers; ex parte communications

(a) No disclosure of any offers of settlement made by any party shall be made to the arbitrator prior to the filing of the award.

(b) Article 7 (commencing with Section 11430.10) of Chapter 4.5 of Part 1 of Division 3 of Title 2 of the Government Code applies to a communication to the arbitrator or a potential arbitrator. *(Added by Stats.1990, c. 1550 (A.B.2910), § 54. Amended by Stats.1995, c. 938 (S.B.523), § 75, operative July 1, 1997.)*

Part 4

COMPENSATION PROCEEDINGS

Chapter		Section
1.	Jurisdiction	5300
2.	Limitations of Proceedings	5400
2.3.	Workers' Compensation—Truth in Advertising	5430
2.5.	Administrative Assistance	5450

Chapter		Section
3.	Applications and Answers	5500
4.	Attachments	5600
5.	Hearings	5700
6.	Findings and Awards	5800
7.	Reconsideration and Judicial Review	5900

CHAPTER 1. JURISDICTION

Section
5300. Exclusive jurisdiction of appeals board.
5301. Jurisdiction of appeals board.
5302. Presumption of lawfulness of order, rules, findings, decisions and awards of appeals board.
5303. Single cause of action for each injury; joinder of claims.
5304. Controversies relating to medical, surgical, and hospital treatment.
5305. Controversies arising out of injuries suffered outside the state.
5306. Proceedings against employer's estate.
5307. Practice and procedure; change of rules or regulations; hearings.
5307.1. Medical fee schedule.
5307.11. Contract between health care provider or licensed health facility and contracting agent for reimbursement rates different from fee schedule in § 5307.1.
5307.2. Annual study of access to medical treatment.
5307.27. Medical treatment utilization schedule.
5307.3. Regulation of administrative director; adoption, amendment or rescission; hearing.
5307.4. Notice of proposed rule or regulation; participation.
5307.5 Trustees and guardians; joinder of parties.
5307.6. Medical-legal expenses schedule; additional compensation prohibited.
5308. Controversies over insurance policies issued to self-employed persons; arbitration.
5309. Trial of issues; hearings.
5310. Workers' compensation judges.
5311. Objections to reference.
5311.5. Continuing education requirements for workers' compensation administrative law judges.
5312. Oath of workers' compensation judge.
5313. Findings; award, order, or decision.
5315. Adoption, modification or vacation of workers' compensation judge's action.
5316. Service of notice, order, or decision.
5317. Service upon public officers.
5318. Implantable medical devices, hardware, and instrumentation.

§ 5300. Exclusive jurisdiction of appeals board

All the following proceedings shall be instituted before the appeals board and not elsewhere, except as otherwise provided in Division 4:

(a) For the recovery of compensation, or concerning any right or liability arising out of or incidental thereto.

(b) For the enforcement against the employer or an insurer of any liability for compensation imposed upon the employer by this division in favor of the injured employee, his or her dependents, or any third person.

(c) For the determination of any question as to the distribution of compensation among dependents or other persons.

(d) For the determination of any question as to who are dependents of any deceased employee, or what persons are entitled to any benefit under the compensation provisions of this division.

(e) For obtaining any order which by Division 4 the appeals board is authorized to make.

(f) For the determination of any other matter, jurisdiction over which is vested by Division 4 in the Division of Workers' Compensation, including the administrative director and the appeals board. *(Stats.1937, c. 90, p. 291, § 5300. Amended by Stats.1951, c. 27, p. 156, § 1; Stats.1965, c. 1513, p. 3585, § 119, operative Jan. 15, 1966; Stats.1994, c. 146 (A.B.3601), § 152.)*

§ 5301. Jurisdiction of appeals board

The appeals board is vested with full power, authority and jurisdiction to try and determine finally all the matters specified in Section 5300 subject only to the review by the courts as specified in this division. *(Stats. 1937, c. 90, p. 291, § 5301. Amended by Stats.1945, c. 1431, p. 2697, § 70; Stats.1951, c. 778, p. 2267, § 3; Stats.1965, c. 1513, p. 3586, § 120, operative Jan. 15, 1966.)*

§ 5302. Presumption of lawfulness of order, rules, findings, decisions and awards of appeals board

All orders, rules, findings, decisions, and awards of the appeals board shall be prima facie lawful and conclusively presumed to be reasonable and lawful, until and unless they are modified or set aside by the appeals board or upon a review by the courts within the time and in the manner specified in this division. *(Stats.1937, c. 90, p. 291, § 5302. Amended by Stats.1965, c. 1513, p. 3586, § 121, operative Jan. 15, 1966.)*

§ 5303. Single cause of action for each injury; joinder of claims

There is but one cause of action for each injury coming within the provisions of this division. All claims brought for medical expense, disability payments, death benefits, burial expense, liens, or any other matter arising out of such injury may, in the discretion of the appeals board, be joined in the same proceeding at any time; provided, however, that no injury, whether specific or cumulative, shall, for any purpose whatsoever, merge into or form a part of another injury; nor shall any award based on a cumulative injury include disability caused by any specific injury or by any other cumulative injury causing or contributing to the existing disability, need for medical treatment or death. *(Stats.1937, c. 90, p. 292, § 5303. Amended by Stats.1947, c. 1034, p. 2306, § 1; Stats.1965, c. 1513, p. 3586, § 122, operative Jan. 15, 1966; Stats.1968, 1st Ex.Sess., c. 4, p. 34, § 10, operative Jan. 1, 1969.)*

§ 5304. Controversies relating to medical, surgical, and hospital treatment

The appeals board has jurisdiction over any controversy relating to or arising out of Sections 4600 to 4605 inclusive, unless an express agreement fixing the amounts to be paid for medical, surgical or hospital treatment as such treatment is described in those sections has been made between the persons or institutions rendering such treatment and the employer or insurer. *(Stats.1937, c. 90, p. 292, § 5304. Amended by Stats.1965, c. 1513, p. 3586, § 123, operative Jan. 15, 1966.)*

§ 5305. Controversies arising out of injuries suffered outside the state

The Division of Workers' Compensation, including the administrative director, and the appeals board have jurisdiction over all controversies arising out of injuries suffered outside the territorial limits of this state in those cases where the injured employee is a resident of this state at the time of the injury and the contract of hire was made in this state. Any employee described by this section, or his or her dependents, shall be entitled to the compensation or death benefits provided by this division. *(Stats.1937, c. 90, p. 292, § 5305. Amended by Stats.1965, c. 1513, p. 3587, § 124, operative Jan. 15, 1966; Stats.1994, c. 146 (A.B.3601), § 153; Stats.2002, c. 6 (A.B.749), § 71.)*

§ 5306. Proceedings against employer's estate

The death of an employer subsequent to the sustaining of an injury by an employee shall not impair the right of the employee to proceed before the appeals board against the estate of the employer, and the failure of the employee or his dependents to cause the claim to be presented to the executor or administrator of the estate shall not in any way bar or suspend such right. *(Stats. 1937, c. 90, p. 292, § 5306. Amended by Stats.1965, c. 1513, p. 3587, § 125, operative Jan. 15, 1966.)*

§ 5307. Practice and procedure; change of rules or regulations; hearings

(a) Except for those rules and regulations within the authority of the court administrator regarding trial level proceedings as defined in subdivision (c), the appeals board may by an order signed by four members:

(1) Adopt reasonable and proper rules of practice and procedure.

(2) Regulate and provide the manner in which, and by whom, minors and incompetent persons are to appear and be represented before it.

(3) Regulate and prescribe the kind and character of notices, where not specifically prescribed by this division, and the service thereof.

(4) Regulate and prescribe the nature and extent of the proofs and evidence.

(b) No rule or regulation of the appeals board pursuant to this section shall be adopted, amended, or rescinded without public hearings. Any written request filed

with the appeals board seeking a change in its rules or regulations shall be deemed to be denied if not set by the appeals board for public hearing to be held within six months of the date on which the request is received by the appeals board.

(c) The court administrator shall adopt reasonable, proper, and uniform rules for district office procedure regarding trial level proceedings of the workers' compensation appeals board. These rules shall include, but not be limited to, all of the following:

(1) Rules regarding conferences, hearings, continuances, and other matters deemed reasonable and necessary to expeditiously resolve disputes.

(2) The kind and character of forms to be used at all trial level proceedings.

All rules and regulations adopted by the court administrator pursuant to this subdivision shall be subject to the requirements of the rulemaking provisions of the Administrative Procedure Act (Chapter 3.5 (commencing with Section 11340) of Part 1 of Division 3 of Title 2 of the Government Code). *(Stats.1937, c. 90, p. 292, § 5307. Amended by Stats.1945, c. 1431, p. 2697, § 71; Stats.1955, c. 1822, p. 3364, § 2; Stats.1961, c. 2217, p. 4566, § 1; Stats.1965, c. 1513, p. 3587, § 126, operative Jan. 15, 1966; Stats.1977, c. 517, p. 1658, § 1); Stats.2002, c. 6 (A.B.749), § 72.)*

§ 5307.1. Medical fee schedule

(a) The administrative director, after public hearings, shall adopt and revise periodically an official medical fee schedule that shall establish reasonable maximum fees paid for medical services other than physician services, drugs and pharmacy services, health care facility fees, home health care, and all other treatment, care, services, and goods described in Section 4600 and provided pursuant to this section. Except for physician services, all fees shall be in accordance with the fee-related structure and rules of the relevant Medicare and Medi–Cal payment systems, provided that employer liability for medical treatment, including issues of reasonableness, necessity, frequency, and duration, shall be determined in accordance with Section 4600. Commencing January 1, 2004, and continuing until the time the administrative director has adopted an official medical fee schedule in accordance with the fee-related structure and rules of the relevant Medicare payment systems, except for the components listed in subdivision (j), maximum reasonable fees shall be 120 percent of the estimated aggregate fees prescribed in the relevant Medicare payment system for the same class of services before application of the inflation factors provided in subdivision (g), except that for pharmacy services and drugs that are not otherwise covered by a Medicare fee schedule payment for facility services, the maximum reasonable fees shall be 100 percent of fees prescribed in the relevant Medi–Cal payment system. Upon adoption by the administrative director of an official medical fee schedule pursuant to this section, the maximum reasonable fees paid shall not exceed 120 percent of estimated aggregate fees prescribed in the Medicare payment system for the same class of services before application of the inflation factors provided in subdivision (g). Pharmacy services and drugs shall be subject to the requirements of this section, whether furnished through a pharmacy or dispensed directly by the practitioner pursuant to subdivision (b) of Section 4024 of the Business and Professions Code.

(b) In order to comply with the standards specified in subdivision (f), the administrative director may adopt different conversion factors, diagnostic related group weights, and other factors affecting payment amounts from those used in the Medicare payment system, provided estimated aggregate fees do not exceed 120 percent of the estimated aggregate fees paid for the same class of services in the relevant Medicare payment system.

(c) Notwithstanding subdivisions (a) and (d), the maximum facility fee for services performed in an ambulatory surgical center, or in a hospital outpatient department, may not exceed 120 percent of the fee paid by Medicare for the same services performed in a hospital outpatient department.

(d) If the administrative director determines that a medical treatment, facility use, product, or service is not covered by a Medicare payment system, the administrative director shall establish maximum fees for that item, provided that the maximum fee paid shall not exceed 120 percent of the fees paid by Medicare for services that require comparable resources. If the administrative director determines that a pharmacy service or drug is not covered by a Medi–Cal payment system, the administrative director shall establish maximum fees for that item. However, the maximum fee paid shall not exceed 100 percent of the fees paid by Medi–Cal for pharmacy services or drugs that require comparable resources.

(e) Prior to the adoption by the administrative director of a medical fee schedule pursuant to this section, for any treatment, facility use, product, or service not covered by a Medicare payment system, including acupuncture services, or, with regard to pharmacy services and drugs, for a pharmacy service or drug that is not covered by a Medi–Cal payment system, the maximum reasonable fee paid shall not exceed the fee specified in the official medical fee schedule in effect on December 31, 2003.

(f) Within the limits provided by this section, the rates or fees established shall be adequate to ensure a reasonable standard of services and care for injured employees.

(g)(1)(A) Notwithstanding any other provision of law, the official medical fee schedule shall be adjusted to conform to any relevant changes in the Medicare and Medi–Cal payment systems no later than 60 days after the effective date of those changes, provided that both of the following conditions are met:

(i) The annual inflation adjustment for facility fees for inpatient hospital services provided by acute care hospitals and for hospital outpatient services shall be determined solely by the estimated increase in the hospital

market basket for the 12 months beginning October 1 of the preceding calendar year.

(ii) The annual update in the operating standardized amount and capital standard rate for inpatient hospital services provided by hospitals excluded from the Medicare prospective payment system for acute care hospitals and the conversion factor for hospital outpatient services shall be determined solely by the estimated increase in the hospital market basket for excluded hospitals for the 12 months beginning October 1 of the preceding calendar year.

(B) The update factors contained in clauses (i) and (ii) of subparagraph (A) shall be applied beginning with the first update in the Medicare fee schedule payment amounts after December 31, 2003.

(2) The administrative director shall determine the effective date of the changes, and shall issue an order, exempt from Sections 5307.3 and 5307.4 and the rulemaking provisions of the Administrative Procedure Act (Chapter 3.5 (commencing with Section 11340) of Part 1 of Division 3 of Title 2 of the Government Code), informing the public of the changes and their effective date. All orders issued pursuant to this paragraph shall be published on the Internet Web site of the Division of Workers' Compensation.

(3) For the purposes of this subdivision, the following definitions apply:

(A) "Medicare Economic Index" means the input price index used by the federal Centers for Medicare and Medicaid Services to measure changes in the costs of a providing physician and other services paid under the resource-based relative value scale.

(B) "Hospital market basket" means the input price index used by the federal Centers for Medicare and Medicaid Services to measure changes in the costs of providing inpatient hospital services provided by acute care hospitals that are included in the Medicare prospective payment system.

(C) "Hospital market basket for excluded hospitals" means the input price index used by the federal Centers for Medicare and Medicaid Services to measure changes in the costs of providing inpatient services by hospitals that are excluded from the Medicare prospective payment system.

(h) Nothing in this section shall prohibit an employer or insurer from contracting with a medical provider for reimbursement rates different from those prescribed in the official medical fee schedule.

(i) Except as provided in Section 4626, the official medical fee schedule shall not apply to medical-legal expenses, as that term is defined by Section 4620.

(j) The following Medicare payment system components may not become part of the official medical fee schedule until January 1, 2005:

(1) Inpatient skilled nursing facility care.

(2) Home health agency services.

(3) Inpatient services furnished by hospitals that are exempt from the prospective payment system for general acute care hospitals.

(4) Outpatient renal dialysis services.

(k) Notwithstanding subdivision (a), for the calendar years 2004 and 2005, the existing official medical fee schedule rates for physician services shall remain in effect, but these rates shall be reduced by 5 percent. The administrative director may reduce fees of individual procedures by different amounts, but in no event shall the administrative director reduce the fee for a procedure that is currently reimbursed at a rate at or below the Medicare rate for the same procedure.

(*l*) Notwithstanding subdivision (a), the administrative director, commencing January 1, 2006, shall have the authority, after public hearings, to adopt and revise, no less frequently than biennially, an official medical fee schedule for physician services. If the administrative director fails to adopt an official medical fee schedule for physician services by January 1, 2006, the existing official medical fee schedule rates for physician services shall remain in effect until a new schedule is adopted or the existing schedule is revised.

(m)(1) Notwithstanding subdivisions (a), (b), (f), and (g), commencing January 1, 2008, the administrative director, after public hearings, may adopt and revise, no less frequently than biennially, an official medical fee schedule for inpatient facility fees for burn cases in accordance with this subdivision. Until the date that the administrative director adopts a fee schedule pursuant to this subdivision, the inpatient fee schedule adopted and revised in accordance with subdivisions (a) and (g) shall continue to apply to inpatient facility fees for burn cases.

(2) In order to establish inpatient facility fees for burn cases that are adequate to ensure a reasonable standard of services and care, the administrative director may do any of the following:

(A) Adopt a fee schedule in accordance with the Medicare payment system, or adopt different conversion factors, diagnostic related group weights, and other factors affecting payment amounts from those used in the Medicare payment system.

(B) Adopt a fee schedule utilizing payment methodologies other than those utilized by the Medicare payment system.

(C) Adopt a fee schedule that utilizes both Medicare and non–Medicare methodologies.

(3) Inpatient facility fees for burn cases may exceed 120 percent, but in no case shall exceed 180 percent, of the fees paid by Medicare. Inpatient facility fees for burn cases shall be excluded from the calculation of estimated aggregate fees for purposes of other subdivisions of this section.

(4) The changes to this section made by this subdivision shall remain in effect only until January 1, 2011. *(Added by Stats.2003, c. 639 (S.B.228), § 35. Amended by*

668

Stats.2006, c. 538 (S.B.1852), § 491; Stats.2007, c. 697 (A.B.1269), § 1.)

§ 5307.11.   Contract between health care provider or licensed health facility and contracting agent for reimbursement rates different from fee schedule in § 5307.1

A health care provider or health facility licensed pursuant to Section 1250 of the Health and Safety Code, and a contracting agent, employer, or carrier may contract for reimbursement rates different from those in the fee schedule adopted and revised pursuant to Section 5307.1. When a health care provider or health facility licensed pursuant to Section 1250 of the Health and Safety Code, and a contracting agent, employer, or carrier contract for reimbursement rates different from those in the fee schedule, the medical fee schedule for that health care provider or health facility licensed pursuant to Section 1250 of the Health and Safety Code shall not apply to the contracted reimbursement rates. Except as provided in subdivision (b) of Section 5307.1, the official medical fee schedule shall establish maximum reimbursement rates for all medical services for injuries subject to this division provided by a health care provider or health care facility licensed pursuant to Section 1250 of the Health and Safety Code other than those specified in contracts subject to this section. *(Added by Stats.2001, c. 252 (A.B.1177), § 1.)*

§ 5307.2.   Annual study of access to medical treatment

The administrative director shall contract with an independent consulting firm, to the extent permitted by state law, to perform an annual study of access to medical treatment for injured workers. The study shall analyze whether there is adequate access to quality health care and products, including prescription drugs and pharmacy services, for injured workers and make recommendations to ensure continued access. If the administrative director determines, based on this study, that there is insufficient access to quality health care or products for injured workers, including access to prescription drugs and pharmacy services, the administrative director may make appropriate adjustments to medical, prescription drugs and pharmacy services, and facilities' fees. When there has been a determination that substantial access problems exist, the administrative director may, in accordance with the notification and hearing requirements of Section 5307.1, adopt fees in excess of 120 percent of the applicable Medicare payment system fee, or in excess of 100 percent of the fees prescribed in the relevant Medi–Cal payment system, for the applicable services or products. *(Added by Stats.2003, c. 639 (S.B.228), § 37. Amended by Stats.2008, c. 193 (A.B.2091), § 1.)*

§ 5307.27.   Medical treatment utilization schedule

On or before December 1, 2004, the administrative director, in consultation with the Commission on Health and Safety and Workers' Compensation, shall adopt, after public hearings, a medical treatment utilization schedule, that shall incorporate the evidence-based, peer-reviewed, nationally recognized standards of care recommended by the commission pursuant to Section 77.5, and that shall address, at a minimum, the frequency, duration, intensity, and appropriateness of all treatment procedures and modalities commonly performed in workers' compensation cases. *(Added by Stats.2003, c. 639 (S.B.228), § 41.)*

§ 5307.3. Regulation of administrative director; adoption, amendment or rescission; hearing

The administrative director may adopt, amend, or repeal any rules and regulations that are reasonably necessary to enforce this division, except where this power is specifically reserved to the appeals board or the court administrator.

No rule or regulation of the administrative director pursuant to this section shall be adopted, amended, or rescinded without public hearings. Any written request filed with the administrative director seeking a change in its rules or regulations shall be deemed to be denied if not set by the administrative director for public hearing to be held within six months of the date on which the request is received by the administrative director. *(Added by Stats.1965, c. 1513, p. 3587, § 128, operative Jan. 15, 1966. Amended by Stats.1977, c. 517, p. 1658, § 2; Stats.1989, c. 892, § 44.5; Stats.2003, c. 639 (S.B.228), § 42.)*

§ 5307.4. Notice of proposed rule or regulation; participation

(a) Public hearings required under Sections 5307 and 5307.3 shall be subject to the provisions of this section except to the extent that there is involved a matter relating to the management, or to personnel, or to public property, loans, grants, benefits, or to contracts, of the appeals board or the administrative director.

(b) Notice of the rule or regulation proposed to be adopted, amended, or rescinded, shall be given to such business and labor organizations and firms or individuals who have requested notice thereof. The notice shall include all the following:

(1) A statement of the time, place, and nature of the public hearings.

(2) Reference to the legal authority under which the rule is proposed.

(3) Either the terms or substance of the proposed rule, or a description of the subjects and the issues involved.

(c) Except where the proposed rule or regulation has a significant impact on the public, this section shall not apply to interpretive rules, general statements of policy, or rules of agency organization.

(d) After notice required by this section, the appeals board or the administrative director shall give interested persons the opportunity to participate in the rulemaking through submission of written data, views, or arguments, with opportunity for oral presentation. If, after consideration of the relevant matter presented, the appeals board

or the administrative director adopts a rule, it or he shall publish a concise, general statement of reasons for the adoption of the rule. The rule and statement of reasons shall be given to the same individuals and organizations who have requested notice of hearings.

(e) The notice required under this section shall be made not less than 30 days prior to the public hearing date. *(Added by Stats.1977, c. 517, p. 1658, § 3.)*

§ 5307.5. Trustees and guardians; joinder of parties

The appeals board or a workers' compensation judge may:

(a) Appoint a trustee or guardian ad litem to appear for and represent any minor or incompetent upon the terms and conditions which it deems proper. The guardian or trustee shall, if required by the appeals board, give a bond in the form and of the character required by law from a guardian appointed by a superior court and in the amount which the appeals board determines. The bond shall be approved by the appeals board, and the guardian or trustee shall not be discharged from liability until he or she files an account with the appeals board or with the superior court and the account is approved. The trustee or guardian shall receive the compensation for his or her services fixed and allowed by the appeals board or by the superior court.

(b) Provide for the joinder in the same proceeding of all persons interested therein, whether as employer, insurer, employee, dependent, creditor, or otherwise. *(Added by Stats.1945, c. 1431, p. 2697, § 72. Amended by Stats.1965, c. 1513, p. 3588, § 129, operative Jan. 15, 1966; Stats.1985, c. 326, § 13.)*

§ 5307.6. Medical-legal expenses schedule; additional compensation prohibited

(a) The administrative director shall adopt and revise a fee schedule for medical-legal expenses as defined by Section 4620, which shall be prima facie evidence of the reasonableness of fees charged for medical-legal expenses at the same time he or she adopts and revises the medical fee schedule pursuant to Section 5307.1.

The schedule shall consist of a series of procedure codes, relative values, and a conversion factor producing fees which provide remuneration to physicians performing medical-legal evaluations at a level equivalent to that provided to physicians for reasonably comparable work, and which additionally recognizes the relative complexity of various types of evaluations, the amount of time spent by the physician in direct contact with the patient, and the need to prepare a written report.

(b) A provider shall not be paid fees in excess of those set forth in the fee schedule established under this section unless the provider provides an itemization and explanation of the fee that shows that it is both a reasonable fee and that extraordinary circumstances relating to the medical condition being evaluated justify a higher fee; provided, however, that in no event shall a provider charge in excess of his or her usual fee. The employer

669

and employee shall have standing to contest fees in excess of those set forth in the fee schedule.

(c) In the event of a dispute between the provider and the employer, employee, or carrier concerning the fees charged, the provider may be allowed a reasonable fee for testimony if the provider testified pursuant to the employer's or carrier's subpoena and the judge or referee determines that the fee charged was reasonable and justified by extraordinary circumstances.

(d)(1) No provider may request nor accept any compensation, including, but not limited to, any kind of remuneration, discount, rebate, refund, dividend, distribution, subsidy, or other form of direct or indirect payment, whether in money or otherwise, from any source for medical-legal expenses if such compensation is in addition to the fees authorized by this section. In addition to being subject to discipline pursuant to the provisions of subdivision (k) of Section 139.2, any provider violating this subdivision is subject to disciplinary action by the appropriate licensing board.

(2) This subdivision does not apply to medical-legal expenses for which the administrative director has not adopted a fee schedule. *(Added by Stats.1993, c. 4 (S.B.31), § 8, eff. April 3, 1993. Amended by Stats.1993, c. 121 (A.B.110), § 57, eff. July 16, 1993; Stats.1993, c. 1242 (S.B.223), § 38.)*

§ 5308.   Controversies over insurance policies issued to self-employed persons; arbitration

The appeals board has jurisdiction to determine controversies arising out of insurance policies issued to self-employing persons, conferring benefits identical with those prescribed by this division.

The appeals board may try and determine matters referred to it by the parties under the provisions of Title 9 (commencing with Section 1280) of Part 3 of the Code of Civil Procedure, with respect to controversies arising out of insurance issued to self-employing persons under the provisions of this division. Such controversies may be submitted to it by the signed agreement of the parties, or by the application of one party and the submission of the other to its jurisdiction, with or without an express request for arbitration.

The State Compensation Insurance Fund, when the consent of the other party is obtained, shall submit to the appeals board all controversies susceptible of being arbitrated under this section.

In acting as arbitrator under this section, the appeals board has all the powers which it may lawfully exercise in compensation cases, and its findings and award upon such arbitration have the same conclusiveness and are subject to the same mode of reopening, review, and enforcement as in compensation cases. No fee or cost shall be charged by the appeals board for arbitrating the issues presented under this section. *(Stats.1937, c. 90, p. 293, § 5308. Amended by Stats.1965, c. 157, p. 1116, § 7; Stats.1965, c. 1513, p. 3589, § 130, operative Jan. 15, 1966; Stats.1967, c. 125, p. 1156, § 7.)*

§ 5309.   Trial of issues; hearings

The appeals board may, in accordance with rules of practice and procedure which it shall adopt and upon the agreement of the parties, on the application of either, or of its own motion, and with or without notice, direct and order a workers' compensation judge:

(a) To try the issues in any proceeding before it, whether of fact or of law, and make and file a finding, order, decision, or award based thereon.

(b) To hold hearings and ascertain facts necessary to enable the appeals board to determine any proceeding or to make any order, decision, or award that the appeals board is authorized to make under Divisions 4 or 5, or necessary for the information of the appeals board.

(c) To issue writs or summons, warrants of attachment, warrants of commitment, and all necessary process in proceedings for direct and hybrid contempt in a like manner and to the same extent as courts of record. For the purposes of this section, "hybrid contempt" means a charge of contempt which arises from events occurring in the immediate presence of the workers' compensation judge for reasons which occur outside the presence of the workers' compensation judge. *(Stats.1937, c. 90, p. 293, § 5309. Amended by Stats.1951, c. 778, p. 2267, § 4; Stats.1965, c. 1513, p. 3589, § 131, operative Jan. 15, 1966; Stats.1985, c. 326, § 14; Stats.1988, c. 222, § 1.)*

§ 5310.   Workers' compensation judges

The appeals board may appoint one or more workers' compensation administrative law judges in any proceeding, as it may deem necessary or advisable, and may refer, remove to itself, or transfer to a workers' compensation administrative law judge the proceedings on any claim. The administrative director, after consideration of the recommendation of the court administrator, may appoint workers' compensation administrative law judges. Any workers' compensation administrative law judge appointed by the administrative director has the powers, jurisdiction, and authority granted by law, by the order of appointment, and by the rules of the appeals board. *(Stats.1937, c. 90, p. 293, § 5310. Amended by Stats.1951, c. 778, p. 2267, § 5; Stats.1953, c. 1757, p. 3517, § 13; Stats.1965, c. 1513, p. 3589, § 132, operative Jan. 15, 1966; Stats.1985, c. 326, § 15; Stats.2002, c. 6 (A.B.749), § 75.)*

§ 5311.   Objections to reference

Any party to the proceeding may object to the reference of the proceeding to a particular workers' compensation judge upon any one or more of the grounds specified in Section 641 of the Code of Civil Procedure and the objection shall be heard and disposed of by the appeals board. Affidavits may be read and witnesses examined as to the objections. *(Stats.1937, c. 90, p. 293, § 5311. Amended by Stats.1965, c. 1513, p. 3589, § 133, operative Jan. 15, 1966; Stats.1985, c. 326, § 16.)*

§ 5311.5. Continuing education requirements for workers' compensation administrative law judges

The administrative director or the court administrator shall require all workers' compensation administrative law judges to participate in continuing education to further their abilities as workers' compensation administrative law judges, including courses in ethics and conflict of interest. The director may coordinate the requirements with those imposed upon attorneys by the State Bar in order that the requirements may be consistent. *(Added by Stats.1993, c. 483 (A.B.1252), § 2, eff. Sept. 27, 1993. Amended by Stats.2002, c. 6 (A.B.749), § 76.)*

§ 5312. Oath of workers' compensation judge

Before entering upon his or her duties, the workers' compensation judge shall be sworn, before an officer authorized to administer oaths, faithfully and fairly to hear and determine the matters and issues referred to him or her, to make just findings and to report according to his or her understanding. *(Stats.1937, c. 90, p. 294, § 5312. Amended by Stats.1985, c. 326, § 17.)*

§ 5313. Findings; award, order, or decision

The appeals board or the workers' compensation judge shall, within 30 days after the case is submitted, make and file findings upon all facts involved in the controversy and an award, order, or decision stating the determination as to the rights of the parties. Together with the findings, decision, order or award there shall be served upon all the parties to the proceedings a summary of the evidence received and relied upon and the reasons or grounds upon which the determination was made. *(Added by Stats.1951, c. 778, p. 2267, § 7. Amended by Stats.1953, c. 1256, p. 2814, § 1; Stats.1965, c. 1513, p. 3589, § 134, operative Jan. 15, 1966; Stats.1985, c. 326, § 18.)*

§ 5315. Adoption, modification or vacation of workers' compensation judge's action

Within 60 days after the filing of the findings, decision, order or award, the appeals board may confirm, adopt, modify or set aside the findings, order, decision, or award of a workers' compensation judge and may, with or without further proceedings, and with or without notice, enter its order, findings, decision, or award based upon the record in the case. *(Stats.1937, c. 90, p. 294, § 5315. Amended by Stats.1951, c. 778, p. 2267, § 8; Stats.1953, c. 1256, p. 2814, § 2; Stats.1965, c. 1513, p. 3589, § 135, operative Jan. 15, 1966; Stats.1985, c. 326, § 19.)*

§ 5316. Service of notice, order, or decision

Any notice, order, or decision required by this division to be served upon any person either before, during, or after the institution of any proceeding before the appeals board, may be served in the manner provided by Chapter 5, Title 14 of Part 2 of the Code of Civil Procedure, unless otherwise directed by the appeals board. In the latter event the document shall be served in accordance with the order or direction of the appeals board. The appeals board may, in the cases mentioned in the Code of Civil Procedure, order service to be made by publication of notice of time and place of hearing. Where service is ordered to be made by publication the date of the hearing may be fixed at more than 30 days from the date of filing the application. *(Stats.1937, c. 90, p. 294, § 5316. Amended by Stats.1965, c. 1513, p. 3589, § 136, operative Jan. 15, 1966.)*

§ 5317. Service upon public officers

Any such notice, order or decision affecting the State or any county, city, school district, or public corporation therein, shall be served upon the person upon whom the service of similar notices, orders, or decisions is authorized by law. *(Stats.1937, c. 90, p. 294, § 5317.)*

§ 5318. Implantable medical devices, hardware, and instrumentation

(a) Implantable medical devices, hardware, and instrumentation for Diagnostic Related Groups (DRGs) 004, 496, 497, 498, 519, and 520 shall be separately reimbursed at the provider's documented paid cost, plus an additional 10 percent of the provider's documented paid cost, not to exceed a maximum of two hundred fifty dollars ($250), plus any sales tax and shipping and handling charges actually paid.

(b) This section shall be operative only until the administrative director adopts a regulation specifying separate reimbursement, if any, for implantable medical hardware or instrumentation for complex spinal surgeries. *(Added by Stats.2003, c. 639 (S.B.228), § 44.)*

CHAPTER 2. LIMITATIONS OF PROCEEDINGS

Section
5400.	Notice of injury or death; time for service upon employer.
5401.	Claim forms; notification and filing.
5401.7.	Form contents; notice of penalty for false statement.
5402.	Knowledge as equivalent to service; presumption of compensable injury; employer responsibility with respect to treatment.
5403.	Effect of failure to give or of defects in notice.
5404.	Failure to institute proceedings within time limited; effect of timely filing of application for any part of compensation.
5404.5.	Dismissal of claim; notice.
5405.	Medical, surgical, hospital and disability benefits.
5406.	Death benefits.
5406.5.	Death benefits for asbestos workers and firefighters from asbestosis; limitation of actions.
5406.6.	Death from HIV-related disease; limitation of actions for proceedings for death benefits.
5407.	Employer's serious and willful misconduct.
5407.5.	Reduction of compensation for misconduct.
5408.	Minors and incompetents.
5409.	Affirmative defenses.
5410.	New and further disability.
5410.1.	Proceedings to reduce amount of permanent disability; attorneys' fees for unsuccessful applicant.
5411.	Date of injury.
5412.	Date of injury for occupational disease or cumulative injuries.

Section

5413.   Collateral estoppel; effect of appeals board determinations.

§ 5400. Notice of injury or death; time for service upon employer

Except as provided by sections 5402 and 5403, no claim to recover compensation under this division shall be maintained unless within thirty days after the occurrence of the injury which is claimed to have caused the disability or death, there is served upon the employer notice in writing, signed by the person injured or someone in his behalf, or in case of the death of the person injured, by a dependent or someone in the dependent's behalf. *(Stats. 1937, c. 90, p. 294, § 5400.)*

§ 5401. Claim forms; notification and filing

(a) Within one working day of receiving notice or knowledge of injury under Section 5400 or 5402, which injury results in lost time beyond the employee's work shift at the time of injury or which results in medical treatment beyond first aid, the employer shall provide, personally or by first-class mail, a claim form and a notice of potential eligibility for benefits under this division to the injured employee, or in the case of death, to his or her dependents. As used in this subdivision, "first aid" means any one-time treatment, and any followup visit for the purpose of observation of minor scratches, cuts, burns, splinters, or other minor industrial injury, which do not ordinarily require medical care. This one-time treatment, and followup visit for the purpose of observation, is considered first aid even though provided by a physician or registered professional personnel. "Minor industrial injury" shall not include serious exposure to a hazardous substance as defined in subdivision (i) of Section 6302. The claim form shall request the injured employee's name and address, social security number, the time and address where the injury occurred, and the nature of and part of the body affected by the injury. Claim forms shall be available at district offices of the Employment Development Department and the division. Claim forms may be made available to the employee from any other source.

(b) Insofar as practicable, the notice of potential eligibility for benefits required by this section and the claim form shall be a single document and shall instruct the injured employee to fully read the notice of potential eligibility. The form and content of the notice and claim form shall be prescribed by the administrative director after consultation with the Commission on Health and Safety and Workers' Compensation. The notice shall be easily understandable and available in both English and Spanish. The content shall include, but not be limited to, the following:

(1) The procedure to be used to commence proceedings for the collection of compensation for the purposes of this chapter.

(2) A description of the different types of workers' compensation benefits.

(3) What happens to the claim form after it is filed.

(4) From whom the employee can obtain medical care for the injury.

(5) The role and function of the primary treating physician.

(6) The rights of an employee to select and change the treating physician pursuant to subdivision (e) of Section 3550 and Section 4600.

(7) How to get medical care while the claim is pending.

(8) The protections against discrimination provided pursuant to Section 132a.

(9) The following written statements:

(A) You have a right to disagree with decisions affecting your claim.

(B) You can obtain free information from an information and assistance officer of the state Division of Workers' Compensation, or you can hear recorded information and a list of local offices by calling [applicable information and assistance telephone number(s)].

(C) You can consult an attorney. Most attorneys offer one free consultation. If you decide to hire an attorney, his or her fee will be taken out of some of your benefits. For names of workers' compensation attorneys, call the State Bar of California at [telephone number of the State Bar of California's legal specialization program, or its equivalent].

(c) The completed claim form shall be filed with the employer by the injured employee, or, in the case of death, by a dependent of the injured employee, or by an agent of the employee or dependent. Except as provided in subdivision (d), a claim form is deemed filed when it is personally delivered to the employer or received by the employer by first-class or certified mail. A dated copy of the completed form shall be provided by the employer to the employer's insurer and to the employee, dependent, or agent who filed the claim form.

(d) The claim form shall be filed with the employer prior to the injured employee's entitlement to late payment supplements under subdivision (d) of Section 4650, or prior to the injured employee's request for a medical evaluation under Section 4060, 4061, or 4062. Filing of the claim form with the employer shall toll, for injuries occurring on or after January 1, 1994, the time limitations set forth in Sections 5405 and 5406 until the claim is denied by the employer or the injury becomes presumptively compensable pursuant to Section 5402. For purposes of this subdivision, a claim form is deemed filed when it is personally delivered to the employer or mailed to the employer by first-class or certified mail. *(Added by Stats.1989, c. 892, § 46. Amended by Stats. 1990, c. 1550 (A.B.2910), § 54.7; Stats.1993, c. 121 (A.B.110), § 58, eff. July 16, 1993; Stats.1993, c. 1242 (S.B.223), § 39; Stats.1994, c. 1118 (S.B.1768), § 8; Stats.2002, c. 6 (A.B.749), § 77.)*

§ 5401.7. Form contents; notice of penalty for false statement

The claim form shall contain, prominently stated, the following statement:

"Any person who makes or causes to be made any knowingly false or fraudulent material statement or material representation for the purpose of obtaining or denying workers' compensation benefits or payments is guilty of a felony."

The statements required to be printed or displayed pursuant to Sections 1871.2 and 1879.2 of the Insurance Code may, but are not required to, appear on the claim form. *(Added by Stats.1991, c. 116 (S.B.1218), § 31. Amended by Stats.1991, c. 934 (A.B.1673), § 16; Stats. 1993, c. 121 (A.B.110), § 61, eff. July 16, 1993; Stats.1997, c. 346 (S.B.1063), § 4.)*

§ 5402. Knowledge as equivalent to service; presumption of compensable injury; employer responsibility with respect to treatment

(a) Knowledge of an injury, obtained from any source, on the part of an employer, his or her managing agent, superintendent, foreman, or other person in authority, or knowledge of the assertion of a claim of injury sufficient to afford opportunity to the employer to make an investigation into the facts, is equivalent to service under Section 5400.

(b) If liability is not rejected within 90 days after the date the claim form is filed under Section 5401, the injury shall be presumed compensable under this division. The presumption of this subdivision is rebuttable only by evidence discovered subsequent to the 90–day period.

(c) Within one working day after an employee files a claim form under Section 5401, the employer shall authorize the provision of all treatment, consistent with Section 5307.27 or the American College of Occupational and Environmental Medicine's Occupational Medicine Practice Guidelines, for the alleged injury and shall continue to provide the treatment until the date that liability for the claim is accepted or rejected. Until the date the claim is accepted or rejected, liability for medical treatment shall be limited to ten thousand dollars ($10,-000).

(d) Treatment provided under subdivision (c) shall not give rise to a presumption of liability on the part of the employer. *(Stats.1937, c. 90, p. 295, § 5402. Amended by Stats.1975, c. 1099, p. 2670, § 2; Stats.1989, c. 892, § 47; Stats.1990, c. 1550 (A.B.2910), § 57; Stats.2000, c. 883 (A.B.2043), § 2; Stats.2004, c. 34 (S.B.899), § 40, eff. April 19, 2004.)*

Operative Effect

Section 47 of Stats.2004, c. 34 (S.B.899) provides that "[t]he amendment, addition, or repeal of, any provision of law made by this act shall apply prospectively from the date of enactment of this act, regardless of the date of injury, unless otherwise specified, but shall not constitute good cause to reopen or rescind, alter, or amend any existing order, decision, or award of the Workers' Compensation Appeals Board."

§ 5403. Effect of failure to give or of defects in notice

The failure to give notice under section 5400, or any defect or inaccuracy in a notice is not a bar to recovery under this division if it is found as a fact in the proceedings for the collection of the claim that the employer was not in fact misled or prejudiced by such failure. *(Stats.1937, c. 90, p. 295, § 5403.)*

§ 5404. Failure to institute proceedings within time limited; effect of timely filing of application for any part of compensation

Unless compensation is paid within the time limited in this chapter for the institution of proceedings for its collection, the right to institute such proceedings is barred. The timely filing of an application with the appeals board by any party in interest for any part of the compensation defined by Section 3207 renders this chapter inoperative as to all further claims by such party against the defendants therein named for compensation arising from that injury, and the right to present such further claims is governed by Sections 5803 to 5805, inclusive. *(Stats.1937, c. 90, p. 295, § 5404. Amended by Stats.1947, c. 1034, p. 2306, § 2; Stats.1965, c. 1513, p. 3590, § 137, operative Jan. 15, 1966.)*

§ 5404.5. Dismissal of claim; notice

(a) Where a claim form has been filed prior to January 1, 1994, and where the claim is denied by the employer, the claim may be dismissed if there has been no activity for the previous 180 days and if the claims adjuster has served notice pursuant to Article 3 (commencing with Section 415.10) of Chapter 4 of Title 5 of the Code of Civil Procedure. The notice shall specify that the claim will be dismissed by operation of law unless an application for adjudication of the claim is filed within 180 days of service of the notice.

(b) Where a claim form has been filed prior to January 1, 1994, and where benefits have been furnished by the employer, the claim may be dismissed if there has been no activity for the previous 180 days and if the claims adjuster has served notice pursuant to Article 3 (commencing with Section 415.10) of Chapter 4 of Title 5 of the Code of Civil Procedure. The notice shall specify that the claim will be dismissed by operation of law unless an application for adjudication of the claim is filed within five years of the date of injury or within one year of the last furnishing of benefits, whichever is later.

(c) The administrative director may adopt rules of practice and procedure consistent with this section.

(d) The provisions of subdivisions (a) and (b) do not limit the jurisdiction of the appeals board.

(e) This section is applicable to injuries occurring before January 1, 1994. *(Added by Stats.1993, c. 121*

673

(A.B.110), § 62, eff. July 16, 1993. Amended by Stats. 1993, c. 1242 (S.B.223), § 40.)

§ 5405. Medical, surgical, hospital and disability benefits

The period within which proceedings may be commenced for the collection of the benefits provided by Article 2 (commencing with Section 4600) or Article 3 (commencing with Section 4650), or both, of Chapter 2 of Part 2 is one year from any of the following:

(a) The date of injury.

(b) The expiration of any period covered by payment under Article 3 (commencing with Section 4650) of Chapter 2 of Part 2.

(c) The last date on which any benefits provided for in Article 2 (commencing with Section 4600) of Chapter 2 of Part 2 were furnished. *(Stats.1937, c. 90, p. 295, § 5405. Amended by Stats.1947, c. 1034, p. 2307, § 3; Stats.2002, c. 6 (A.B.749), § 78.)*

§ 5406. Death benefits

Except as provided in Section 5406.5 or 5406.6, the period within which may be commenced proceedings for the collection of the benefits provided by Article 4 (commencing with Section 4700) of Chapter 2 of Part 2 is one year from:

(a) The date of death where death occurs within one year from date of injury; or

(b) The date of last furnishing of any benefits under Chapter 2 (commencing with Section 4550) of Part 2, where death occurs more than one year from the date of injury; or

(c) The date of death, where death occurs more than one year after the date of injury and compensation benefits have been furnished.

No such proceedings may be commenced more than one year after the date of death, nor more than 240 weeks from the date of injury. *(Stats.1937, c. 90, p. 295, § 5406. Amended by Stats.1947, c. 1034, p. 2307, § 4; Stats.1959, c. 1959, p. 4564, § 1; Stats.1961, c. 1588, p. 3415, § 1; Stats.1980, c. 1041, p. 3326, § 3); Stats.1999, c. 358 (S.B.77), § 3.)*

§ 5406.5. Death benefits for asbestos workers and firefighters from asbestosis; limitation of actions

In the case of the death of an asbestos worker or firefighter from asbestosis, the period within which proceedings may be commenced for the collection of the benefits provided by Article 4 (commencing with Section 4700) of Chapter 2 of Part 2 is one year from the date of death. *(Added by Stats.1980, c. 1041, p. 3327, § 4. Amended by Stats.2003, c. 831 (A.B.149), § 1.)*

§ 5406.6. Death from HIV-related disease; limitation of actions for proceedings for death benefits

(a) In the case of the death of a health care worker, a worker described in Section 3212, or a worker described

674

in Section 830.5 of the Penal Code from an HIV-related disease, the period within which proceedings may be commenced for the collection of benefits provided by Article 4 (commencing with Section 4700) of Chapter 2 of Part 2 is one year from the date of death, providing that one or more of the following events has occurred:

(1) A report of the injury or exposure was made to the employer or to a governmental agency authorized to administer industrial injury claims, within one year of the date of the injury.

(2) The worker has complied with the notice provisions of this chapter and the claim has not been finally determined to be noncompensable.

(3) The employer provided, or was ordered to provide, workers' compensation benefits for the injury prior to the date of death.

(b) For the purposes of this section, "health care worker" means an employee who has direct contact, in the course of his or her employment, with blood or other bodily fluids contaminated with blood, or with other bodily fluids identified by the Division of Occupational Safety and Health as capable of transmitting HIV, who is either (1) any person who is an employee of a provider of health care, as defined in subdivision (d) of Section 56.05 of the Civil Code, including, but not limited to, a registered nurse, licensed vocational nurse, certified nurse aide, clinical laboratory technologist, dental hygienist, physician, janitor, or housekeeping worker, or (2) an employee who provides direct patient care. *(Added by Stats.1999, c. 358 (S.B.77), § 4.)*

§ 5407. Employer's serious and willful misconduct

The period within which may be commenced proceedings for the collection of compensation on the ground of serious and willful misconduct of the employer, under provisions of Section 4553, is as follows:

Twelve months from the date of injury. This period shall not be extended by payment of compensation, agreement therefor, or the filing of application for compensation benefits under other provisions of this division. *(Stats.1937, c. 90, p. 296, § 5407. Amended by Stats.1972, c. 618, p. 1137, § 110.)*

§ 5407.5. Reduction of compensation for misconduct

The period within which may be commenced proceedings for the reduction of compensation on the ground of serious and willful misconduct of the employee, under provisions of Section 4551, is as follows:

Twelve months from the date of injury. However, this limitation shall not apply in any case where the employee has commenced proceedings for the increase of compensation on the ground of serious and willful misconduct of the employer. *(Added by Stats.1953, c. 572, p. 1823, § 1. Amended by Stats.1972, c. 618, p. 1137, § 111.)*

§ 5408. Minors and incompetents

If an injured employee or, in the case of the employee's death, any of the employee's dependents, is under 18 years of age or incompetent at any time when any right or privilege accrues to such employee or dependent under this division, a guardian or conservator of the estate appointed by the court, or a guardian ad litem or trustee appointed by the appeals board, may, on behalf of the employee or dependent, claim and exercise any right or privilege with the same force and effect as if no disability existed.

No limitation of time provided by this division shall run against any person under 18 years of age or any incompetent unless and until a guardian or conservator of the estate or trustee is appointed. The appeals board may determine the fact of the minority or incompetency of any injured employee and may appoint a trustee to receive and disburse compensation payments for the benefit of such minor or incompetent and his family. *(Stats.1937, c. 90, p. 296, § 5408. Amended by Stats.1965, c. 1513, p. 3590, § 138, operative Jan. 15, 1966; Stats.1971, c. 822, p. 1624, § 1; Stats.1971, c. 1748, p. 3760, § 49; Stats.1979, c. 730, p. 2510, § 91, operative Jan. 1, 1981.)*

§ 5409. Affirmative defenses

The running of the period of limitations prescribed by this chapter is an affirmative defense and operates to bar the remedy and not to extinguish the right of the employee. Such defense may be waived. Failure to present such defense prior to the submission of the cause for decision is a sufficient waiver. *(Stats.1937, c. 90, p. 296, § 5409.)*

§ 5410. New and further disability

Nothing in this chapter shall bar the right of any injured worker to institute proceedings for the collection of compensation, including vocational rehabilitation services, within five years after the date of the injury upon the ground that the original injury has caused new and further disability or that the provision of vocational rehabilitation services has become feasible because the employee's medical condition has improved or because of other factors not capable of determination at the time the employer's liability for vocational rehabilitation services otherwise terminated. The jurisdiction of the appeals board in these cases shall be a continuing jurisdiction within this period. This section does not extend the limitation provided in Section 5407. *(Stats.1937, c. 90, p. 296, § 5410. Amended by Stats.1949, c. 677, p. 1174, § 1; Stats.1965, c. 1513, p. 3590, § 139, operative Jan. 15, 1966; Stats.1982, c. 922, p. 3371, § 15; Stats.1989, c. 892, § 49.)*

§ 5410.1. Proceedings to reduce amount of permanent disability; attorneys' fees for unsuccessful applicant

Should any party to a proceeding institute proceedings to reduce the amount of permanent disability awarded to an applicant by the appeals board and be unsuccessful in such proceeding, the board may make a finding as to the amount of a reasonable attorney's fee incurred by the applicant in resisting such proceeding to reduce permanent disability benefits previously awarded by the appeals board and assess the same as costs upon the party

instituting the proceeding for the reduction of permanent disability benefits. *(Added by Stats.1971, c. 1558, p. 3082, § 2.)*

§ 5411. Date of injury

The date of injury, except in cases of occupational disease or cumulative injury, is that date during the employment on which occurred the alleged incident or exposure, for the consequences of which compensation is claimed. *(Added by Stats.1947, c. 1034, p. 2307, § 5. Amended by Stats.1973, c. 1024, p. 2032, § 2.)*

§ 5412. Date of injury for occupational disease or cumulative injuries

The date of injury in cases of occupational diseases or cumulative injuries is that date upon which the employee first suffered disability therefrom and either knew, or in the exercise of reasonable diligence should have known, that such disability was caused by his present or prior employment. *(Added by Stats.1947, c. 1034, p. 2307, § 6. Amended by Stats.1973, c. 1024, p. 2032, § 3.)*

§ 5413. Collateral estoppel; effect of appeals board determinations

A determination of facts by the appeals board under this chapter has no collateral estoppel effect on a subsequent criminal prosecution and does not preclude litigation of those same facts in the criminal proceeding. *(Added by Stats.1995, c. 158 (A.B.891), § 2.)*

CHAPTER 2.3. WORKERS' COMPENSATION— TRUTH IN ADVERTISING

Section
5430. Short title.
5431. Purpose.
5432. Advertisement to solicit workers' compensation claims; mandatory notice or statement.
5433. Advertisements and lead generating devices; mandatory disclosure; deceptive or misleading names or advertising techniques.
5434. Violation; misdemeanor.

§ 5430. Short title

This chapter shall be known and may be cited as the Workers' Compensation Truth in Advertising Act of 1992. *(Added by Stats.1992, c. 904 (A.B.2329), § 1.)*

§ 5431. Purpose

The purpose of this chapter is to assure truthful and adequate disclosure of all material and relevant information in the advertising which solicits persons to file workers' compensation claims or to engage or consult counsel or a medical care provider or clinic to consider a workers' compensation claim. *(Added by Stats.1992, c. 904 (A.B.2329), § 1.)*

§ 5432. Advertisement to solicit workers' compensation claims; mandatory notice or statement

(a) Any advertisement which solicits persons to file workers' compensation claims or to engage or consult counsel or a medical care provider or clinic to consider a workers' compensation claim in any newspaper, magazine, circular, form letter, or open publication, published, distributed, or circulated in this state, or on any billboard, card, label, transit advertisement or other written advertising medium shall state at the top or bottom on the front side or surface of the document in at least 12-point roman boldface type font, except for any billboard which shall be in type whose letters are 12 inches in height or any transit advertisement which shall be in type whose letters are seven inches in height and for any television announcement which shall be in 12-point roman boldface type font and appear in a dark background and remain on the screen for a minimum of five seconds and for any radio announcement which shall be read at an understandable pace with no loud music or sound effects, or both, to compete for the listener's attention, the following:

NOTICE

Making a false or fraudulent workers' compensation claim is a felony subject to up to 5 years in prison or a fine of up to $50,000 or double the value of the fraud, whichever is greater, or by both imprisonment and fine.

(b) Any television or radio announcement published or disseminated in this state which solicits persons to file workers' compensation claims or to engage or consult counsel to consider a workers' compensation claim under this code shall include the following spoken statement by the announcer of the advertisement:

"Making a false or fraudulent workers' compensation claim is a felony subject to up to 5 years in prison or a fine of up to $50,000 or double the value of the fraud, whichever is greater, or by both imprisonment and fine."

(c) This chapter does not supersede or repeal any regulation which governs advertising under this code and those regulations shall continue to be in force in addition to this chapter.

(d) For purposes of subdivisions (a) and (b), the notice or statement shall be written or spoken in English. In those cases where the preponderance of the listening or reading public receives information other than in the English language, the written notice or spoken statement shall be in those other languages. *(Added by Stats.1992, c. 904 (A.B.2329), § 1.)*

§ 5433. Advertisements and lead generating devices; mandatory disclosure; deceptive or misleading names or advertising techniques

(a) Any advertisement or other device designed to produce leads based on a response from a person to file a workers' compensation claim or to engage or consult counsel or a medical care provider or clinic shall disclose that an agent may contact the individual if that is the fact. In addition, an individual who makes contact with a person as a result of acquiring that individual's name from a lead generating device shall disclose that fact in the initial contact with that person.

(b) No person shall solicit persons to file a workers' compensation claim or to engage or consult counsel or a medical care provider or clinic to consider a workers' compensation claim through the use of a true or fictitious name which is deceptive or misleading with regard to the status, character, or proprietary or representative capacity of the entity or person, or to the true purpose of the advertisement.

(c) For purposes of this section, an advertisement includes a solicitation in any newspaper, magazine, circular, form letter, or open publication, published, distributed, or circulated in this state, or on any billboard, card, label, transit advertisement, or other written advertising medium, and includes envelopes, stationery, business cards, or other material designed to encourage the filing of a workers' compensation claim.

(d) Advertisements shall not employ words, initials, letters, symbols, or other devices which are so similar to those used by governmental agencies, a nonprofit or charitable institution, or other entity that they could have the capacity or tendency to mislead the public. Examples of misleading materials include, but are not limited to, those that imply any of the following:

(1) The advertisement is in some way provided by or is endorsed by a governmental agency or charitable institution.

(2) The advertiser is the same as, is connected with, or is endorsed by a governmental agency or charitable institution.

(e) Advertisements may not use the name of a state or political subdivision thereof in an advertising solicitation.

(f) Advertisements may not use any name, service mark, slogan, symbol, or any device in any manner which implies that the advertiser, or any person or entity associated with the advertiser, or that any agency who may call upon the person in response to the advertisement, is connected with a governmental agency.

(g) Advertisements may not imply that the reader, listener, or viewer may lose a right or privilege or benefits under federal, state, or local law if he or she fails to respond to the advertisement. *(Added by Stats.1992, c. 904 (A.B.2329), § 1. Amended by Stats.1998, c. 485 (A.B.2803), § 126; Stats.1999, c. 83 (S.B.966), § 135.)*

§ 5434. Violation; misdemeanor

(a) Any advertiser who violates Section 5431 or 5432 is guilty of a misdemeanor.

(b) For the purposes of this chapter, "advertiser" means any person who provides workers' compensation claims services which are described in the written or broadcast advertisements, any person to whom persons solicited by the advertisements are directed to for inquiries or the provision of workers' compensation claims related services, or any person paying for the preparation, broadcast, printing, dissemination, or placement of the advertisements. *(Added by Stats.1992, c. 904 (A.B.2329), § 1.)*

CHAPTER 2.5. ADMINISTRATIVE ASSISTANCE

Section
5450. Assistance and advice to be informally provided.
5451. Information and assistance officers; duties.
5453. Recommendations.
5454. Tolling of limitations period.
5455. Application for benefits not prohibited; admissibility of evidence.

§ 5450. Assistance and advice to be informally provided

The Division of Workers' Compensation shall make available to employees, employers and other interested parties information, assistance, and advice to assure the proper and timely furnishing of benefits and to assist in the resolution of disputes on an informal basis. *(Added by Stats.1976, c. 1017, p. 4596, § 8. Amended by Stats. 1994, c. 146 (A.B.3601), § 154; Stats.1994, c. 1097 (S.B.1803), § 19.)*

§ 5451. Information and assistance officers; duties

Any party may consult with, or seek the advice of, an information and assistance officer within the Division of Workers' Compensation as designated by the administrative director. If no application is filed, if the employee is not represented, or upon agreement of the parties, the information and assistance officer shall consider the contentions of the parties and may refer the matter to the appropriate bureau or unit within the Division of Workers' Compensation for review and recommendations. The information and assistance officer shall advise the employer and the employee of their rights, benefits, and obligations under this division. Upon making a referral, the information and assistance officer shall arrange for a copy of any pertinent material submitted to be served upon the parties or their representatives, if any. The procedures to be followed by the information and assistance officer shall be governed by the rules and regulations of the administrative director adopted after public hearings. *(Added by Stats.1976, c. 1017, p. 4596, § 8. Amended by Stats.1979, c. 828, p. 2872, § 1; Stats.1994, c. 146 (A.B.3601), § 155; Stats.1994, c. 1097 (S.B.1803), § 20.)*

§ 5453. Recommendations

After consideration of the information submitted, including the reports of any bureau or unit within the Division of Workers' Compensation which have been received, the information and assistance officer shall make a recommendation which shall be served on the parties or their representatives, if any. *(Added by Stats. 1976, c. 1017, p. 4596, § 8. Amended by Stats.1994, c. 146 (A.B.3601), § 157; Stats.1994, c. 1097 (S.B.1803), § 22.)*

§ 5454. Tolling of limitations period

Submission of any matter to an information and assistance officer of the Division of Workers' Compensation shall toll any applicable statute of limitations for the period that the matter is under consideration by the information and assistance officer, and for 60 days following the issuance of his or her recommendation. *(Added by Stats.1976, c. 1017, p. 4596, § 8. Amended by Stats.1994, c. 146 (A.B.3601), § 158; Stats.1994, c. 1097 (S.B.1803), § 23.)*

§ 5455. Application for benefits not prohibited; admissibility of evidence

Nothing in this chapter shall prohibit any party from filing an application for benefits under this division. In any proceeding pursuant to such application, the admissibility of written evidence or reports submitted by any party pursuant to this chapter, or Section 5502, shall be governed by Chapter 5 (commencing with Section 5700). *(Added by Stats.1976, c. 1017, p. 4596, § 8. Amended by Stats.1983, c. 142, § 109.)*

CHAPTER 3. APPLICATIONS AND ANSWERS

Section
5500. Pleadings; form and content; establishment of appeals board jurisdiction; commencement of proceedings.
5500.3. Uniform district office and court procedures, forms, time of court settings; establishment; violation.
5500.5. Occupational disease or cumulative injury arising out of more than one employment.
5500.6. Occupational disease or cumulative injury to household employees.
5501. Application; filing; service of copy.
5501.5. Application for adjudication of claim; place of filing.
5501.6. Change of venue.
5502. Time for hearing; required forms; calendar priorities; expedited hearings; mandatory settlement conferences; application of section.
5502.5. Continuances.
5503. Designations of parties.
5504. Service of notice of hearing.
5505. Answer, form and contents, service; evidence on matters not pleaded.
5506. Failure to answer and appear.
5507. Dismissal of application.

§ 5500. Pleadings; form and content; establishment of appeals board jurisdiction; commencement of proceedings

No pleadings other than the application and answer shall be required. Both shall be in writing and shall conform to forms prescribed by the appeals board in its rules of practice and procedure, simply but clearly and completely delineating all relevant matters of agreement and all issues of disagreement within the jurisdiction of the appeals board, and providing for the furnishing of any additional information as the appeals board may properly determine necessary to expedite its hearing and determination of the claim.

The amendment of this section made during the 1993 portion of the 1993–94 Regular Session shall apply to all applications filed on or after January 1, 1994.

Notwithstanding Section 5401, except where a claim form has been filed for an injury occurring on or after January 1, 1990, and before January 1, 1994, the filing of an application for adjudication and not the filing of a claim form shall establish the jurisdiction of the appeals board and shall commence proceedings before the appeals board for the collection of benefits. *(Stats.1937, c. 90, p. 296, § 5500. Amended by Stats.1963, c. 1575, p. 5157, § 1; Stats.1965, c. 1513, p. 3590, § 140, operative Jan. 15, 1966; Stats.1989, c. 892, § 50; Stats.1990, c. 1550 (A.B.2910), § 58; Stats.1993, c. 121, § 63, eff. July 16, 1993; Stats.1994, c. 1118 (S.B.1768), § 9.)*

§ 5500.3. Uniform district office and court procedures, forms, time of court settings; establishment; violation

(a) The court administrator shall establish uniform district office procedures, uniform forms, and uniform time of court settings for all district offices of the appeals board. No district office of the appeals board or workers' compensation administration law judge shall require forms or procedures other than as established by the court administrator. The court administrator shall take reasonable steps to ensure enforcement of this section. A workers' compensation administrative law judge who violates this section may be subject to disciplinary proceedings.

(b) The appeals board shall establish uniform court procedures and uniform forms for all other proceedings of the appeals board. No district office of the appeals board or workers' compensation administrative law judge shall require forms or procedures other than as established by the appeals board. *(Added by Stats.1989, c. 1443, § 2. Amended by Stats.2002, c. 6 (A.B.749), § 79.)*

§ 5500.5. Occupational disease or cumulative injury arising out of more than one employment

(a) Except as otherwise provided in Section 5500.6, liability for occupational disease or cumulative injury claims filed or asserted on or after January 1, 1978, shall be limited to those employers who employed the employee during a period of four years immediately preceding either the date of injury, as determined pursuant to Section 5412, or the last date on which the employee was employed in an occupation exposing him or her to the hazards of the occupational disease or cumulative injury, whichever occurs first. Commencing January 1, 1979, and thereafter on the first day of January for each of the next two years, the liability period for occupational disease or cumulative injury shall be decreased by one year so that liability is limited in the following manner:

For claims filed or asserted on or after:	The period shall be:
January 1, 1979	three years
January 1, 1980	two years
January 1, 1981 and thereafter	one year

In the event that none of the employers during the above referenced periods of occupational disease or cumulative injury are insured for workers' compensation coverage or an approved alternative thereof, liability shall be imposed upon the last year of employment exposing the employee to the hazards of the occupational disease or cumulative injury for which an employer is insured for workers' compensation coverage or an approved alternative thereof.

Any employer held liable for workers' compensation benefits as a result of another employer's failure to secure the payment of compensation as required by this division shall be entitled to reimbursement from the employers who were unlawfully uninsured during the last year of the employee's employment, and shall be subrogated to the rights granted to the employee against the unlawfully uninsured employers under the provisions of Article 1 (commencing with Section 3700) of Chapter 4 of Part 1 of Division 4.

If, based upon all the evidence presented, the appeals board or workers' compensation judge finds the existence of cumulative injury or occupational disease, liability for the cumulative injury or occupational disease shall not be apportioned to prior or subsequent years; however, in determining the liability, evidence of disability due to specific injury, disability due to nonindustrial causes, or disability previously compensated for by way of a findings and award or order approving compromise and release, or a voluntary payment of disability, may be admissible for purposes of apportionment.

(b) Where a claim for compensation benefits is made on account of an occupational disease or cumulative injury which may have arisen out of more than one employment, the application shall state the names and addresses of all employers liable under subdivision (a), the places of employment, and the approximate periods of employment where the employee was exposed to the hazards of the occupational disease or cumulative injury. If the application is not so prepared or omits necessary and proper employers, any interested party, at or prior to the first hearing, may request the appeals board to join as defendant any necessary or proper party. If the request is made prior to the first hearing on the application, the appeals board shall forthwith join the employer as a party defendant and cause a copy of the application together with a notice of the time and place of hearing to be served upon the omitted employer; provided, the notice can be given within the time specified in this division. If the notice cannot be timely given or if the motion for joinder is made at the time of the first hearing, then the appeals board or the workers' compensation judge before whom the hearing is held, if it is found that the omitted employer named is a necessary or proper party, may order a joinder of the party and continue the hearing so that proper notice may be given to the party or parties so joined. Only one continuance shall be allowed for the purpose of joining additional parties. Subsequent to the first hearing the appeals board shall join as a party defendant any additional employer when it appears that the employer is a proper party, but the liability of the employer shall not be determined until supplemental proceedings are instituted.

(c) In any case involving a claim of occupational disease or cumulative injury occurring as a result of more than one employment within the appropriate time period set forth in subdivision (a), the employee making the claim, or his or her dependents, may elect to proceed against any one or more of the employers. Where such an election is made, the employee must successfully prove his or her claim against any one of the employers named, and any award which the appeals board shall issue awarding compensation benefits shall be a joint and several award as against any two or more employers who may be held liable for compensation benefits. If, during the pendency of any claim wherein the employee or his or her dependents has made an election to proceed against one or more employers, it should appear that there is another proper party not yet joined, the additional party shall be joined as a defendant by the appeals board on the motion of any party in interest, but the liability of the employer shall not be determined until supplemental proceedings are instituted. Any employer joined as a defendant subsequent to the first hearing or subsequent to the election provided herein shall not be entitled to participate in any of the proceedings prior to the appeal board's final decision, nor to any continuance or further proceedings, but may be permitted to ascertain from the employee or his or her dependents such information as will enable the employer to determine the time, place, and duration of the alleged employment. On supplemental proceedings, however, the right of the employer to full and complete examination or cross-examination shall not be restricted.

(d)(1) In the event a self-insured employer which owns and operates a work location in the State of California, sells or has sold the ownership and operation of the work location pursuant to a sale of a business or all or part of the assets of a business to another self-insured person or entity after January 1, 1974, but before January 1, 1978, and all the requirements of subparagraphs (A) to (D), inclusive, exist, then the liability of the employer-seller and employer-buyer, respectively, for cumulative injuries suffered by employees employed at the work location immediately before the sale shall, until January 1, 1986, be governed by the provisions of this section which were in effect on the date of that sale.

(A) The sale constitutes a material change in ownership of such work location.

(B) The person or entity making the purchase continues the operation of the work location.

(C) The person or entity becomes the employer of substantially all of the employees of the employer-seller.

(D) The agreement of sale makes no special provision for the allocation of liabilities for workers' compensation between the buyer and the seller.

(2) For purposes of this subdivision:

(A) "Work location" shall mean any fixed place of business, office, or plant where employees regularly work in the trade or business of the employer.

(B) A "material change in ownership" shall mean a change in ownership whereby the employer-seller does not retain, directly or indirectly, through one or more corporate entities, associations, trusts, partnerships, joint ventures, or family members, a controlling interest in the work location.

(3) This subdivision shall have no force or effect on or after January 1, 1986, unless otherwise extended by the Legislature prior to that date, and it shall not have any force or effect as respects an employee who, subsequent to the sale described in paragraph (1) and prior to the date of his or her application for compensation benefits has been filed, is transferred to a different work location by the employer-buyer.

(4) If any provision of this subdivision or the application thereof to any person or circumstances is held invalid, that invalidity shall not affect other provisions or applications of this subdivision which can be given effect without the invalid provision or application, and to this end the provisions of this subdivision are severable.

(e) At any time within one year after the appeals board has made an award for compensation benefits in connection with an occupational disease or cumulative injury, any employer held liable under the award may institute proceedings before the appeals board for the purpose of determining an apportionment of liability or right of contribution. The proceeding shall not diminish, restrict, or alter in any way the recovery previously allowed the employee or his or her dependents, but shall be limited to a determination of the respective contribution rights, interest or liabilities of all the employers joined in the proceeding, either initially or supplementally; provided, however, if the appeals board finds on supplemental proceedings for the purpose of determining an apportionment of liability or of a right of contribution that an employer previously held liable in fact has no liability, it may dismiss the employer and amend its original award in such manner as may be required.

(f) If any proceeding before the appeals board for the purpose of determining an apportionment of liability or of a right of contribution where any employee incurred a disability or death resulting from silicosis in underground metal mining operations, the determination of the respective rights and interests of all of the employers joined in the proceedings either initially or supplementally shall be as follows:

(1) All employers whose underground metal mining operations resulted in a silicotic exposure during the period of the employee's employment in those operations shall be jointly and severally liable for the payment of compensation and of medical, surgical, legal and hospital expense which may be awarded to the employee or his or

her estate or dependents as the result of disability or death resulting from or aggravated by the exposure.

(2) In making its determination in the supplemental proceeding for the purpose of determining an apportionment of liability or of a right of contribution of percentage liabilities of the various employers engaged in underground metal mining operations the appeals board shall consider as a rebuttal presumption that employment in underground work in any mine for a continuous period of more than three calendar months will result in a silicotic exposure for the employee so employed during the period of employment if the underground metal mine was driven or sunk in rock having a composition which will result in dissemination of silica or silicotic dust particles when drilled, blasted, or transported.

(g) Any employer shall be entitled to rebut the presumption by showing to the satisfaction of the appeals board, or the workers' compensation judge, that the mining methods used by the employer in the employee's place of employment did not result during his or her employment in the creation of silica dust in sufficient amount or concentration to constitute a silicotic hazard. Dust counts, competently made, at intervals and in locations as meet the requirements of the Division of Occupational Safety and Health for safe working conditions may be received as evidence of the amount and concentration of silica dust in the workings where the counts have been made at the time when they were made. The appeals board may from time to time, as its experience may indicate proper, promulgate orders as to the frequency with which dust counts shall be taken in different types of workings in order to justify their acceptance as evidence of the existence or nonexistence of a silicotic hazard in the property where they have been taken.

(h) The amendments to this section adopted at the 1959 Regular Session of the Legislature [1] shall operate retroactively, and shall apply retrospectively to any cases pending before the appeals board or courts. From and after the date this section becomes effective no payment shall be made out of the fund used for payment of the additional compensation provided for in Section 4751, or out of any other state funds, in satisfaction of any liability heretofore incurred or hereafter incurred, except awards which have become final without regard to the continuing jurisdiction of the appeals board on that effective date, and the state and its funds shall be without liability therefor. This subdivision shall not in any way effect a reduction in any benefit conferred or which may be conferred upon any injured employee or his dependents.

(i) The amendments to this section adopted at the 1977 Regular Session of the Legislature shall apply to any claims for benefits under this division which are filed or asserted on or after January 1, 1978, unless otherwise specified in this section. *(Added by Stats.1977, c. 17, p. 35, § 29, eff. March 25, 1977. Amended by Stats.1977, c.*

680

360, p. 1334, § 1; Stats.1980, c. 676, p. 1972, § 232; Stats.1985, c. 326, § 20.)

[1] Former § 5500.5, from which this section was derived, was so amended.

§ 5500.6. Occupational disease or cumulative injury to household employees

Liability for occupational disease or cumulative injury which results from exposure solely during employment as an employee, as defined in subdivision (d) of Section 3351, shall be limited to those employers in whose employment the employee was exposed to the hazards of the occupational disease or cumulative injury during the last day on which the employee was employed in an occupation exposing the employee to the hazards of the disease or injury. In the event that none of the employers of the last day of hazardous employment is insured for workers' compensation liability, that liability, shall be imposed upon the last employer exposing the employee to the hazards of the occupational disease or cumulative injury who has secured workers' compensation insurance coverage or an approved alternative thereto. If, based upon all the evidence presented, the appeals board or the workers' compensation judge finds the existence of cumulative injury or occupational disease, liability for the cumulative injury or occupational disease shall not be apportioned to prior employers. However, in determining liability, evidence of disability due to specific injury, disability due to non-work-related causes, or disability previously compensated for by way of a findings and award or order approving compromise and release, or a voluntary payment of disability, may be admissible for purposes of apportionment. *(Added by Stats.1977, c. 17, p. 38, § 30, eff. March 25, 1977. Amended by Stats.1985, c. 326, § 21.)*

§ 5501. Application; filing; service of copy

The application may be filed with the appeals board by any party in interest, his attorney, or other representative authorized in writing. A representative who is not an attorney licensed by the State Bar of this state shall notify the appeals board in writing that he or she is not an attorney licensed by the State Bar of this state. Upon the filing of the application, the appeals board shall, where the applicant is represented by an attorney or other representative, serve a conformed copy of the application showing the date of filing and the case number upon applicant's attorney or representative. The applicant's attorney or representative shall, upon receipt of the conformed copy, forthwith serve a copy of the conformed application upon all other parties to the claim. If the applicant is unrepresented, a copy thereof shall forthwith be served upon all adverse parties by the appeals board. *(Stats.1937, c. 90 p. 296, § 5501. Amended by Stats.1965, c. 1513, p. 3593, § 142, operative Jan. 15, 1966; Stats.1971, c. 393, p. 761, § 1; Stats.1979, c. 828, p. 2872, § 2; Stats.1991, c. 934 (A.B.1673), § 17.)*

§ 5501.5. Application for adjudication of claim; place of filing

(a) The application for adjudication of claim shall be filed in any of the following locations:

(1) In the county where the injured employee or dependent of a deceased employee resides on the date of filing.

(2) In the county where the injury allegedly occurred, or, in cumulative trauma and industrial disease claims, where the last alleged injurious exposure occurred.

(3) In the county where the employee's attorney maintains his or her principal place of business, if the employee is represented by an attorney.

(b) If the county selected for filing has more than one office of the appeals board, the application shall be filed at any location of the appeals board within that county that meets the criteria specified in subdivision (a). The written consent of the employee, or dependent of a deceased employee, to the selected venue site shall be filed with the application.

(c) If the venue site where the application is to be filed is the county where the employee's attorney maintains his or her principal place of business, the attorney for the employee shall indicate that venue site when forwarding the information request form required by Section 5401.5. The employer shall have 30 days from receipt of the information request form to object to the selected venue site. Where there is an employer objection to a venue site under paragraph (3) of subdivision (a), then the application shall be filed pursuant to either paragraph (1) or (2) of subdivision (a).

(d) If there is no appeals board office in the county where venue is permitted under subdivision (a), the application shall be filed at the appeals board office nearest the residence on the date of filing of the injured employee or dependent of a deceased employee, or the nearest place where the injury allegedly occurred, or, in cumulative trauma and industrial disease claims, where the last injurious exposure occurred, or nearest the location where the attorney of the employee maintains his or her principal place of business, unless the employer objects under subdivision (c). *(Added by Stats.1990, c. 1550 (A.B.2910), § 59.)*

§ 5501.6. Change of venue

(a) An applicant or defendant may petition the appeals board for a change of venue and a change of venue shall be granted for good cause. The reasons for the change of venue shall be specifically set forth in the request for change of venue.

(b) If a change of venue is requested for the convenience of witnesses, the names and addresses of these witnesses and the substance of their testimony shall be specifically set forth in the request for change of venue. *(Added by Stats.1990, c. 1550 (A.B.2910), § 60.)*

§ 5502. Time for hearing; required forms; calendar priorities; expedited hearings; mandatory settlement conferences; application of section

(a) Except as provided in subdivisions (b) and (d), the hearing shall be held not less than 10 days, and not more than 60 days, after the date a declaration of readiness to proceed, on a form prescribed by the court administrator, is filed. If a claim form has been filed for an injury occurring on or after January 1, 1990, and before January 1, 1994, an application for adjudication shall accompany the declaration of readiness to proceed.

(b) The court administrator shall establish a priority calendar for issues requiring an expedited hearing and decision. A hearing shall be held and a determination as to the rights of the parties shall be made and filed within 30 days after the declaration of readiness to proceed is filed if the issues in dispute are any of the following:

(1) The employee's entitlement to medical treatment pursuant to Section 4600.

(2) The employee's entitlement to, or the amount of, temporary disability indemnity payments.

(3) The employee's entitlement to vocational rehabilitation services, or the termination of an employer's liability to provide these services to an employee.

(4) The employee's entitlement to compensation from one or more responsible employers when two or more employers dispute liability as among themselves.

(5) Any other issues requiring an expedited hearing and determination as prescribed in rules and regulations of the administrative director.

(c) The court administrator shall establish a priority conference calendar for cases in which the employee is represented by an attorney and the issues in dispute are employment or injury arising out of employment or in the course of employment. The conference shall be conducted by a workers' compensation administrative law judge within 30 days after the declaration of readiness to proceed. If the dispute cannot be resolved at the conference, a trial shall be set as expeditiously as possible, unless good cause is shown why discovery is not complete, in which case status conferences shall be held at regular intervals. The case shall be set for trial when discovery is complete, or when the workers' compensation administrative law judge determines that the parties have had sufficient time in which to complete reasonable discovery. A determination as to the rights of the parties shall be made and filed within 30 days after the trial.

(d) The court administrator shall report quarterly to the Governor and to the Legislature concerning the frequency and types of issues which are not heard and decided within the period prescribed in this section and the reasons therefor.

(e)(1) In all cases, a mandatory settlement conference shall be conducted not less than 10 days, and not more than 30 days, after the filing of a declaration of readiness to proceed. If the dispute is not resolved, the regular hearing shall be held within 75 days after the declaration of readiness to proceed is filed.

(2) The settlement conference shall be conducted by a workers' compensation administrative law judge or by a referee who is eligible to be a workers' compensation administrative law judge or eligible to be an arbitrator under Section 5270.5. At the mandatory settlement conference, the referee or workers' compensation administrative law judge shall have the authority to resolve the dispute, including the authority to approve a compromise and release or issue a stipulated finding and award, and if the dispute cannot be resolved, to frame the issues and stipulations for trial. The appeals board shall adopt any regulations needed to implement this subdivision. The presiding workers' compensation administrative law judge shall supervise settlement conference referees in the performance of their judicial functions under this subdivision.

(3) If the claim is not resolved at the mandatory settlement conference, the parties shall file a pretrial conference statement noting the specific issues in dispute, each party's proposed permanent disability rating, and listing the exhibits, and disclosing witnesses. Discovery shall close on the date of the mandatory settlement conference. Evidence not disclosed or obtained thereafter shall not be admissible unless the proponent of the evidence can demonstrate that it was not available or could not have been discovered by the exercise of due diligence prior to the settlement conference.

(f) In cases involving the Director of the Department of Industrial Relations in his or her capacity as administrator of the Uninsured Employers Fund, this section shall not apply unless proof of service, as specified in paragraph (1) of subdivision (d) of Section 3716 has been filed with the appeals board and provided to the Director of Industrial Relations, valid jurisdiction has been established over the employer, and the fund has been joined.

(g) Except as provided in subdivision (a) and in Section 4065, the provisions of this section shall apply irrespective of the date of injury. *(Added by Stats.1989, c. 892, § 52. Amended by Stats.1990, c. 1550 (A.B.2910), § 61; Stats.1992, c. 1226 (A.B.3758), § 3; Stats.1993, c. 121 (A.B.110), § 64, eff. July 16, 1993; Stats.1994, c. 1118 (S.B.1768), § 10; Stats.2002, c. 6 (A.B.749), § 80; Stats. 2002, c. 866 (A.B.486), § 14.)*

§ 5502.5.　Continuances

A continuance of any conference or hearing required by Section 5502 shall not be favored, but may be granted by a workers' compensation judge upon any terms as are just upon a showing of good cause. When determining a request for continuance, the workers' compensation judge shall take into consideration the complexity of the issues, the diligence of the parties, and the prejudice incurred on the part of any party by reasons of granting or denying a continuance. *(Added by Stats.1990, c. 1550 (A.B.2910), § 62.)*

682

§ 5503.　Designations of parties

The person so applying shall be known as the applicant and the adverse party shall be known as the defendant. *(Stats.1937, c. 90, p. 297, § 5503.)*

§ 5504.　Service of notice of hearing

A notice of the time and place of hearing shall be served upon the applicant and all adverse parties and may be served either in the manner of service of a summons in a civil action or in the same manner as any notice that is authorized or required to be served under the provisions of this division. *(Stats.1937, c. 90, p. 297, § 5504. Amended by Stats.1971, c. 393, p. 762, § 3.)*

§ 5505.　Answer, form and contents, service; evidence on matters not pleaded

If any defendant desires to disclaim any interest in the subject matter of the claim in controversy, or considers that the application is in any respect inaccurate or incomplete, or desires to bring any fact, paper, or document to the attention of the appeals board as a defense to the claim or otherwise, he may, within 10 days after the service of the application upon him, file with or mail to the appeals board his answer in such form as the appeals board may prescribe, setting forth the particulars in which the application is inaccurate or incomplete, and the facts upon which he intends to rely. A copy of the answer shall be forthwith served upon all adverse parties. Evidence upon matters not pleaded by answer shall be allowed only upon the terms and conditions imposed by the appeals board or referee holding the hearing. *(Stats. 1937, c. 90, p. 297, § 5505. Amended by Stats.1941, c. 984, p. 2621, § 1; Stats.1963, c. 1575, p. 3158, § 2; Stats.1965, c. 1513, p. 3593, § 143, operative Jan. 15, 1966.)*

§ 5506.　Failure to answer and appear

If the defendant fails to appear or answer, no default shall be taken against him, but the appeals board shall proceed to the hearing of the matter upon the terms and conditions which it deems proper. A defendant failing to appear or answer, or subsequently contending that no service was made upon him, or claiming to be aggrieved in any other manner by want of notice of the pendency of the proceedings, may apply to the appeals board for relief substantially in accordance with the provisions of Section 473 of the Code of Civil Procedure. The appeals board may afford such relief. No right to relief, including the claim that the findings and award of the appeals board or judgment entered thereon are void upon their face, shall accrue to such defendant in any court unless prior application is made to the appeals board in accordance with this section. In no event shall any petition to any court be allowed except as prescribed in Sections 5950 and 5951. *(Stats.1937, c. 90, p. 297, § 5506. Amended by Stats.1965, c. 1513, p. 3594, § 144, operative Jan. 15, 1966.)*

§5507. Dismissal of application

If an application shows upon its face that the applicant is not entitled to compensation, the appeals board may, after opportunity to the applicant to be heard orally or to submit his claim or argument in writing dismiss the application without any hearing thereon. Such dismissal may be upon the motion of the appeals board or upon motion of the adverse party. The pendency of such motion or notice of intended dismissal shall not, unless otherwise ordered by the appeals board, delay the hearing on the application upon its merits. *(Stats.1937, c. 90, p. 297, § 5507. Amended by Stats.1965, c. 1513, p. 3594, § 145, operative Jan. 15, 1966.)*

CHAPTER 4. ATTACHMENTS

Section
5600. Issuance; grounds; amounts.
5601. Proceedings; applicability of Code of Civil Procedure.
5602. Prerequisites to issuance; discharge.
5603. Preference to realty of employer.

§5600. Issuance; grounds; amounts

The appeals board may, upon the filing of an application by or on behalf of an injured employee, the employee's dependents, or any other party in interest, direct the clerk of the superior court of any county to issue writs of attachment authorizing the sheriff to attach the property of the defendant as security for the payment of any compensation which may be awarded in any of the following cases:

(a) In any case mentioned in Section 415.50 of the Code of Civil Procedure.

(b) Where the employer has failed to secure the payment of compensation as required by Article 1 (commencing with Section 3700) of Chapter 4 of Part 1.

The attachment shall be in an amount fixed by the appeals board, not exceeding the greatest probable award against the defendant in the matter. *(Stats.1937, c. 90, p. 298, § 5600. Amended by Stats.1965, c. 1513, p. 3594, § 146, operative Jan. 15, 1966; Stats.1974, c. 544, p. 1258, § 36; Stats.1974, c. 1516, p. 3390, § 33, operative Jan. 1, 1977; Stats.1983, c. 142, § 110; Stats.2002, c. 784 (S.B. 1316), § 526.)*

§5601. Proceedings; applicability of Code of Civil Procedure

The provisions of Title 6.5 (commencing with Section 481.010) of Part 2 of the Code of Civil Procedure, as far as applicable, shall govern the proceedings upon attachment, the appeals board being substituted therein for the proper court. *(Stats.1937, c. 90, p. 298, § 5601. Amended by Stats.1965, c. 1513, p. 3594, § 147, operative Jan. 15, 1966; Stats.1974, c. 1516, p. 3390, § 34, operative Jan. 1, 1977.)*

§5602. Prerequisites to issuance; discharge

No writ of attachment shall be issued except upon the order of the appeals board. Such order shall not be made where it appears from the application or affidavit in support thereof that the employer was, at the time of the injury to the employee, insured against liability imposed by this division by any insurer. If, at any time after the levying of an attachment, it appears that such employer was so insured, and the requisites for dismissing the employer from the proceeding and substituting the insurer as defendant under any method prescribed by this division are established, the appeals board shall forthwith discharge the attachment. *(Stats.1937, c. 90, p. 298, § 5602. Amended by Stats.1965, c. 1513, p. 3595, § 148, operative Jan. 15, 1966.)*

§5603. Preference to realty of employer

In levying attachments preference shall be given to the real property of the employer. *(Stats.1937, c. 90, p. 298, § 5603.)*

CHAPTER 5. HEARINGS

Section
5700. Adjournment and continuance; presence of parties; right to present testimony.
5701. Power of appeals board to procure evidence.
5702. Stipulation of facts.
5703. Admissible evidence.
5703.5. Examination by medical evaluator; cost; report.
5704. Service of transcripts of testimony and other matters added to record outside open hearing.
5705. Burden of proof; affirmative defenses.
5706. Autopsies.
5707. Autopsy of body not in possession of coroner; refusal to allow autopsy; presumption.
5708. Conduct of hearings and investigations; rules of evidence and procedure; reporter.
5709. Effect of informality in proceedings and admission of evidence.
5710. Depositions.

§5700. Adjournment and continuance; presence of parties; right to present testimony

The hearing on the application may be adjourned from time to time and from place to place in the discretion of the appeals board or the workers' compensation judge holding the hearing. Any hearing adjourned by the workers' compensation judge shall be continued to be heard by and shall be concluded and the decision made by the workers' compensation judge who previously heard it. Either party may be present at any hearing, in person, by attorney, or by any other agent, and may present testimony pertinent under the pleadings. *(Stats.1937, c. 90, p. 298, § 5700. Amended by Stats.1945, c. 1431, p. 2697, § 73; Stats.1965, c. 1513, p. 3595, § 149, operative Jan. 15, 1966; Stats.1985, c. 326, § 22.)*

§5701. Power of appeals board to procure evidence

The appeals board may, with or without notice to either party, cause testimony to be taken, or inspection of

683

the premises where the injury occurred to be made, or the timebooks and payroll of the employer to be examined by any member of the board or a workers' compensation judge appointed by the appeals board. The appeals board may also from time to time direct any employee claiming compensation to be examined by a regular physician. The testimony so taken and the results of any inspection or examination shall be reported to the appeals board for its consideration. *(Stats.1937, c. 90, p. 298, § 5701. Amended by Stats.1965, c. 1513, p. 3595, § 150, operative Jan. 15, 1966; Stats.1985, c. 326, § 23.)*

§ 5702. Stipulation of facts

The parties to a controversy may stipulate the facts relative thereto in writing and file such stipulation with the appeals board. The appeals board may thereupon make its findings and award based upon such stipulation, or may set the matter down for hearing and take further testimony or make the further investigation necessary to enable it to determine the matter in controversy. *(Stats. 1937, c. 90, p. 299, § 5702. Amended by Stats.1965, c. 1513, p. 3595, § 151, operative Jan. 15, 1966.)*

§ 5703. Admissible evidence

The appeals board may receive as evidence either at or subsequent to a hearing, and use as proof of any fact in dispute, the following matters, in addition to sworn testimony presented in open hearing:

(a) Reports of attending or examining physicians.

(1) Statements concerning any bill for services are admissible only if made under penalty of perjury that they are true and correct to the best knowledge of the physician.

(2) In addition, reports are admissible under this subdivision only if the physician has further stated in the body of the report that there has not been a violation of Section 139.3 and that the contents of the report are true and correct to the best knowledge of the physician. The statement shall be made under penalty of perjury.

(b) Reports of special investigators appointed by the appeals board or a workers' compensation judge to investigate and report upon any scientific or medical question.

(c) Reports of employers, containing copies of timesheets, book accounts, reports, and other records properly authenticated.

(d) Properly authenticated copies of hospital records of the case of the injured employee.

(e) All publications of the Division of Workers' Compensation.

(f) All official publications of the State of California and United States governments.

(g) Excerpts from expert testimony received by the appeals board upon similar issues of scientific fact in other cases and the prior decisions of the appeals board upon similar issues.

(h) Relevant portions of medical treatment protocols published by medical specialty societies. To be admissible, the party offering such a protocol or portion of a protocol shall concurrently enter into evidence information regarding how the protocol was developed, and to what extent the protocol is evidence-based, peer-reviewed, and nationally recognized. If a party offers into evidence a portion of a treatment protocol, any other party may offer into evidence additional portions of the protocol. The party offering a protocol, or portion thereof, into evidence shall either make a printed copy of the full protocol available for review and copying, or shall provide an Internet address at which the entire protocol may be accessed without charge.

(i) The medical treatment utilization schedule in effect pursuant to Section 5307.27 or the guidelines in effect pursuant to Section 4604.5. *(Stats.1937, c. 90, 299, § 5703. Amended by Stats.1965, c. 1513, p. 3595, § 152, operative Jan. 15, 1966; Stats.1985, c. 326, § 24; Stats. 1993, c. 120 (A.B.1300), § 7, eff. July 16, 1993; Stats.1994, c. 146 (A.B.3601), § 159; Stats.2003, c. 639 (S.B.228), § 45; Stats.2004, c. 34 (S.B.899), § 41, eff. April 19, 2004.)*

Operative Effect

Section 47 of Stats.2004, c. 34 (S.B.899) provides that "[t]he amendment, addition, or repeal of, any provision of law made by this act shall apply prospectively from the date of enactment of this act, regardless of the date of injury, unless otherwise specified, but shall not constitute good cause to reopen or rescind, alter, or amend any existing order, decision, or award of the Workers' Compensation Appeals Board."

§ 5703.5. Examination by medical evaluator; cost; report

(a) The appeals board, at any time after an application is filed and prior to the expiration of its jurisdiction may, upon the agreement of a party to pay the cost, direct an unrepresented employee to be examined by a qualified medical evaluator selected by the appeals board, within the scope of the qualified medical evaluator's professional training, upon any clinical question then at issue before the appeals board.

(b) The administrative director or his or her designees, upon the submission of a matter to an information and assistance officer, may, upon the agreement of a party to pay the cost, and with the consent of an unrepresented employee direct the injured employee to be examined by a qualified medical evaluator selected by the medical director, within the scope of the qualified medical evaluator's professional training, upon any clinical question, other than those issues specified in Section 4061, then pertinent to the investigation of the information and assistance officer.

(c) The 1989 and 1990 amendments to this section shall become operative for injuries occurring on and after January 1, 1991. *(Added by Stats.1963, c. 2181, p. 4568,*

§ 1. Amended by Stats.1965, c. 1513, p. 3596, § 153, operative Jan. 15, 1966; Stats.1978, c. 198, p. 437, § 2; Stats.1989, c. 892, § 53; Stats.1989, c. 893, § 5; Stats. 1990, c. 1550 (A.B.2910), § 63.)

§ 5704. Service of transcripts of testimony and other matters added to record outside open hearing

Transcripts of all testimony taken without notice and copies of all reports and other matters added to the record, otherwise than during the course of an open hearing, shall be served upon the parties to the proceeding, and an opportunity shall be given to produce evidence in explanation or rebuttal thereof before decision is rendered. *(Stats.1937, c. 90, p. 299, § 5704. Amended by Stats.1951, c. 1003, p. 2637, § 1.)*

§ 5705. Burden of proof; affirmative defenses

The burden of proof rests upon the party or lien claimant holding the affirmative of the issue. The following are affirmative defenses, and the burden of proof rests upon the employer to establish them:

(a) That an injured person claiming to be an employee was an independent contractor or otherwise excluded from the protection of this division where there is proof that the injured person was at the time of his or her injury actually performing service for the alleged employer.

(b) Intoxication of an employee causing his or her injury.

(c) Willful misconduct of an employee causing his or her injury.

(d) Aggravation of disability by unreasonable conduct of the employee.

(e) Prejudice to the employer by failure of the employee to give notice, as required by Sections 5400 and 5401. *(Stats.1937, c. 90, p. 299, § 5705. Amended by Stats.1993, c. 4 (S.B.31), § 9, eff. April 3, 1993.)*

§ 5706. Autopsies

Where it is represented to the appeals board, either before or after the filing of an application, that an employee has died as a result of injuries sustained in the course of his employment, the appeals board may require an autopsy. The report of the physician performing the autopsy may be received in evidence in any proceedings theretofore or thereafter brought. If at the time the autopsy is requested, the body of the employee is in the custody of the coroner, the coroner shall, upon the request of the appeals board or of any party interested, afford reasonable opportunity for the attendance of any physicians named by the appeals board at any autopsy ordered by him. If the coroner does not require, or has already performed the autopsy, he shall permit an autopsy or reexamination to be performed by physicians named by the appeals board. No fee shall be charged by the coroner for any service, arrangement, or permission given by him. *(Stats.1937, c. 90, p. 300, § 5706. Amended by Stats.1965, c. 1513, p. 3596, § 154, operative Jan. 15, 1966.)*

§ 5707. Autopsy of body not in possession of coroner; refusal to allow autopsy; presumption

If the body of a deceased employee is not in the custody of the coroner, the appeals board may authorize the performance of such autopsy and, if necessary, the exhumation of the body therefor. If the dependents, or a majority thereof, of any such deceased employee, having the custody of the body refuse to allow the autopsy, it shall not be performed. In such case, upon the hearing of any application for compensation it is a disputable presumption that the injury or death was not due to causes entitling the claimants to benefits under this division. *(Stats.1937, c. 90, p. 300, § 5707. Amended by Stats.1965, c. 1513, p. 3596, § 155, operative Jan. 15, 1966.)*

§ 5708. Conduct of hearings and investigations; rules of evidence and procedure; reporter

All hearings and investigations before the appeals board or a workers' compensation judge are governed by this division and by the rules of practice and procedures adopted by the appeals board. In the conduct thereof they shall not be bound by the common law or statutory rules of evidence and procedure, but may make inquiry in the manner, through oral testimony and records, which is best calculated to ascertain the substantial rights of the parties and carry out justly the spirit and provisions of this division. All oral testimony, objections, and rulings shall be taken down in shorthand by a competent phonographic reporter. *(Stats.1937, c. 90, p. 300, § 5708. Amended by Stats.1945, c. 1431, p. 2697, § 74; Stats.1965, c. 1513, p. 3596, § 156, operative Jan. 15, 1966; Stats.1985, c. 326, § 25.)*

§ 5709. Effect of informality in proceedings and admission of evidence

No informality in any proceeding or in the manner of taking testimony shall invalidate any order, decision, award, or rule made and filed as specified in this division. No order, decision, award, or rule shall be invalidated because of the admission into the record, and use as proof of any fact in dispute, of any evidence not admissible under the common law or statutory rules of evidence and procedure. *(Stats.1937, c. 90, p. 300, § 5709. Amended by Stats.1945, c. 1431, p. 2698, § 75; Stats.1951, c. 778, p. 2268, § 9.)*

§ 5710. Depositions

(a) The appeals board, a workers' compensation judge, or any party to the action or proceeding, may, in any investigation or hearing before the appeals board, cause the deposition of witnesses residing within or without the state to be taken in the manner prescribed by law for like depositions in civil actions in the superior courts of this state under Title 4 (commencing with Section 2016.010) of Part 4 of the Code of Civil Procedure. To that end the attendance of witnesses and the production of records may be required. Depositions may be taken outside the state before any officer authorized to administer oaths.

The appeals board or a workers' compensation judge in any proceeding before the appeals board may cause evidence to be taken in other jurisdictions before the agency authorized to hear workers' compensation matters in those other jurisdictions.

(b) Where the employer or insurance carrier requests a deposition to be taken of an injured employee, or any person claiming benefits as a dependent of an injured employee, the deponent is entitled to receive in addition to all other benefits:

(1) All reasonable expenses of transportation, meals, and lodging incident to the deposition.

(2) Reimbursement for any loss of wages incurred during attendance at the deposition.

(3) A copy of the transcript of the deposition, without cost.

(4) A reasonable allowance for attorney's fees for the deponent, if represented by an attorney licensed by the State Bar of this state. The fee shall be discretionary with, and, if allowed, shall be set by, the appeals board, but shall be paid by the employer or his or her insurer.

(5) A reasonable allowance for interpreter's fees for the deponent, if interpretation services are needed and provided by a language interpreter certified or deemed certified pursuant to Article 8 (commencing with Section 11435.05) of Chapter 4.5 of Part 1 of Division 3 of Title 2 of, or Section 68566 of, the Government Code. The fee shall be in accordance with the fee schedule set by the administrative director and paid by the employer or his or her insurer. Payment for interpreter's services shall be allowed for deposition of a non-English-speaking injured worker, and for any other deposition-related events as permitted by the administrative director. *(Stats.1937, c. 90, p. 300, § 5710. Amended by Stats.1945, c. 168, p. 651, § 1; Stats.1945, c. 1431, p. 2698, 76; Stats.1965, c. 1513, p. 3597, § 157, operative Jan. 15, 1966; Stats.1971, c. 1416, p. 2818, § 1; Stats.1972, c. 1316, p. 2620, § 1; Stats.1979, c. 603, p. 1876, § 1; Stats.1985, c. 326, § 26; Stats.1991, c. 116 (S.B.1218), § 32; Stats.1993, c. 121 (A.B.110), § 65, eff. July 16, 1993; Stats.1995, c. 938 (S.B.523), § 76, operative July 1, 1997; Stats.1998, c. 931 (S.B.2139), § 348, eff. Sept. 28, 1998; Stats.2004, c. 182 (A.B.3081), § 47, operative July 1, 2005.)*

CHAPTER 6.   FINDINGS AND AWARDS

Section
5800.   Interest on awards.
5800.5. Thirty day period.
5801.   Amount and manner of payment; supplemental award for attorney's fee.
5802.   Award for future disability.
5803.   Continuing jurisdiction of appeals board.
5803.5. Conviction of making false or fraudulent statements to obtain or deny workers' compensation; reconsideration of order or decision.
5804.   Rescission, alteration, or amendment of award after five years from date of injury.
5805.   Effect of rescission, alteration, or amendment.

Section
5806.   Filing of certified copy; entry of judgment.
5807.   Judgment roll.
5808.   Stay of execution of judgment; order of appeals board; filing; stay of order, decision or award of appeals board.
5809.   Entry of satisfaction of judgment.
5810.   Judicial review.
5811.   Fees of clerk; allowance of costs; interpreters.
5813.   Bad-faith actions or tactics; liability for expenses, attorney's fees and costs.
5814.   Penalty for unreasonable delay or refusal of payment of compensation; self-imposed penalties; settlement of accrued claims; reduction of payment; other liability issues.
5814.1. Unreasonable delay or refusal to make payment; discretionary compensation; payment of penalty by employer.
5814.5. Delayed or refused payment of compensation; attorneys fees in enforcement proceedings.
5814.6. Penalty for knowingly violating § 5814 with a frequency indicating general business practice.
5815.   Determination of all issues raised.
5816.   Collateral estoppel; effect of appeals board determinations.

§ 5800.   Interest on awards

All awards of the appeals board either for the payment of compensation or for the payment of death benefits, shall carry interest at the same rate as judgments in civil actions on all due and unpaid payments from the date of the making and filing of said award. Such interest shall run from the date of making and filing of an award, as to amounts which by the terms of the award are payable forthwith. As to amounts which under the terms of the award subsequently become due in installments or otherwise, such interest shall run from the date when each such amount becomes due and payable. *(Added by 1937, c. 90, p. 301, § 5800. Amended by Stats.1945, c. 695, p. 1380, § 1; Stats.1951, c. 778, p. 2268, § 10; Stats.1965, c. 1513, p. 3597, § 158, operative Jan. 15, 1966.)*

§ 5800.5.   Thirty day period

The 30-day period specified in Section 5313, shall run from the date of the submission of the application for decision and the provisions requiring the decision within such 30-day period shall be deemed mandatory and not merely directive. *(Added by Stats.1949, c. 1455, p. 2538, § 1. Amended by Stats.1953, c. 1256, p. 2814, § 3.)*

§ 5801.   Amount and manner of payment; supplemental award for attorney's fee

The appeals board in its award may fix and determine the total amount of compensation to be paid and specify the manner of payment, or may fix and determine the weekly disability payment to be made and order payment thereof during the continuance of disability.

In the event the injured employee or the dependent of a deceased employee prevails in any petition by the employer for a writ of review from an award of the appeals board and the reviewing court finds that there is no reasonable basis for the petition, it shall remand the cause to the appeals board for the purpose of making a supplemental award awarding to the injured employee or his attorney, or the dependent of a deceased employee or his attorney a reasonable attorney's fee for services rendered in connection with the petition for writ of review. Any such fee shall be in addition to the amount of compensation otherwise recoverable and shall be paid as part of the award by the party liable to pay such award. *(Stats.1937, c. 90, p. 301, § 5801. Amended by Stats.1949, c. 223, p. 446, § 1; Stats.1953, c. 553, p. 1812, § 1; Stats.1965, c. 1513, p. 3597, § 159, operative Jan. 15, 1966.)*

§ 5802. Award for future disability

If, in any proceeding under this division, it is proved that an injury has been suffered for which the employer would be liable to pay compensation if disability had resulted therefrom, but it is not proved that any disability has resulted, the appeals board may, instead of dismissing the application, award a nominal disability indemnity, if it appears that disability is likely to result at a future time. *(Stats.1937, c. 90, p. 301, § 5802. Amended by Stats.1965, c. 1513, p. 3597, § 160, operative Jan. 15, 1966.)*

§ 5803. Continuing jurisdiction of appeals board

The appeals board has continuing jurisdiction over all its orders, decisions, and awards made and entered under the provisions of this division, and the decisions and orders of the rehabilitation unit established under Section 139.5. At any time, upon notice and after an opportunity to be heard is given to the parties in interest, the appeals board may rescind, alter, or amend any order, decision, or award, good cause appearing therefor.

This power includes the right to review, grant or regrant, diminish, increase, or terminate, within the limits prescribed by this division, any compensation awarded, upon the grounds that the disability of the person in whose favor the award was made has either recurred, increased, diminished, or terminated. *(Stats.1937, c. 90, p. 301, § 5803. Amended by Stats.1965, c. 1513, p. 3598, § 161, operative Jan. 15, 1966; Stats.1982, c. 922, p. 3372, § 16.)*

§ 5803.5. Conviction of making false or fraudulent statements to obtain or deny workers' compensation; reconsideration of order or decision

Any conviction pursuant to Section 1871.4 of the Insurance Code that materially affects the basis of any order, decision, or award of the appeals board shall be sufficient grounds for a reconsideration of that order, decision, or award. *(Added by Stats.1991, c. 116 (S.B. 1218), § 33.)*

§ 5804. Rescission, alteration, or amendment of award after five years from date of injury

No award of compensation shall be rescinded, altered, or amended after five years from the date of the injury except upon a petition by a party in interest filed within such five years and any counterpetition seeking other relief filed by the adverse party within 30 days of the original petition raising issues in addition to those raised by such original petition. Provided, however, that after an award has been made finding that there was employment and the time to petition for a rehearing or reconsideration or review has expired or such petition if made has been determined, the appeals board upon a petition to reopen shall not have the power to find that there was no employment. *(Stats.1937, c. 90, p. 301, § 5804. Amended by Stats.1949, c. 677, p. 1174, § 2; Stats.1951, c. 1287, p. 3176, § 1; Stats.1963, c. 1866, p. 3851, § 1; Stats.1965, c. 1513, p. 3598, § 162, operative Jan. 15, 1966.)*

§ 5805. Effect of rescission, alteration, or amendment

Any order, decision, or award rescinding, altering or amending a prior order, decision, or award shall have the effect herein provided for original orders, decisions, and awards. *(Stats.1937, c. 90, p. 301, § 5805.)*

§ 5806. Filing of certified copy; entry of judgment

Any party affected thereby may file a certified copy of the findings and order, decision, or award of the appeals board with the clerk of the superior court of any county. Judgment shall be entered immediately by the clerk in conformity therewith. The words "any party affected thereby" include the Uninsured Employers Fund. In any case in which the findings and order, decision, or award of the appeals board is against an employer that has failed to secure the payment of compensation, the State of California on behalf of the Uninsured Employers Fund shall be entitled to have judgment entered not only against the employer, but also against any person found to be parents or substantial shareholders under Section 3717. *(Stats.1937, c. 90, p. 301, § 5806. Amended by Stats.1965, c. 1513, p. 3598, § 163, operative Jan. 15, 1966; Stats.1992, c. 1226 (A.B.3758), § 4.)*

§ 5807. Judgment roll

The certified copy of the findings and order, decision, or award of the appeals board and a copy of the judgment constitute the judgment-roll. The pleadings, all orders of the appeals board, its original findings and order, decision, or award, and all other papers and documents filed in the cause shall remain on file in the office of the appeals board. *(Stats.1937, c. 90, p. 301, § 5807. Amended by Stats.1965, c. 1513, p. 3598, § 164, operative Jan. 15, 1966.)*

§ 5808. Stay of execution of judgment; order of appeals board; filing; stay of order, decision or award of appeals board

The appeals board or a member thereof may stay the execution of any judgment entered upon an order, decision, or award of the appeals board, upon good cause appearing therefor and may impose the terms and conditions of the stay of execution. A certified copy of such order shall be filed with the clerk entering judgment.

Where it is desirable to stay the enforcement of an order, decision, or award and a certified copy thereof and of the findings has not been issued, the appeals board or a member thereof may order the certified copy to be withheld with the same force and under the same conditions as it might issue a stay of execution if the certified copy had been issued and judgment entered thereon. *(Stats.1937, c. 90, p. 302, § 5805. Amended by Stats.1945, c. 1431, p. 2698, § 77; Stats.1965, c. 1513, p. 3598, § 165, operative Jan. 15, 1966.)*

§ 5809. Entry of satisfaction of judgment

When a judgment is satisfied in fact, otherwise than upon an execution, the appeals board may, upon motion of either party or of its own motion, order the entry of satisfaction of the judgment. The clerk shall enter satisfaction of judgment only upon the filing of a certified copy of such order. *(Stats.1937, c. 90, p. 302, § 5809. Amended by Stats.1965, c. 1513, p. 3599, § 166, operative Jan. 15, 1966.)*

§ 5810. Judicial review

The orders, findings, decisions, or awards of the appeals board made and entered under this division may be reviewed by the courts specified in Sections 5950 to 5956 within the time and in the manner therein specified and not otherwise. *(Stats.1937, c. 90, p. 302, § 5810. Amended by Stats.1965, c. 1513, p. 3599, § 167, operative Jan. 15, 1966.)*

§ 5811. Fees of clerk; allowance of costs; interpreters

(a) No fees shall be charged by the clerk of any court for the performance of any official service required by this division, except for the docketing of awards as judgments and for certified copies of transcripts thereof. In all proceedings under this division before the appeals board, costs as between the parties may be allowed by the appeals board.

(b) It shall be the responsibility of any party producing a witness requiring an interpreter to arrange for the presence of a qualified interpreter. A qualified interpreter is a language interpreter who is certified, or deemed certified, pursuant to Article 8 (commencing with Section 11435.05) of Chapter 4.5 of Part 1 of Division 3 of Title 2 of, or Section 68566 of, the Government Code.

Interpreter fees which are reasonably, actually, and necessarily incurred shall be allowed as cost under this section, provided they are in accordance with the fee schedule set by the administrative director.

A qualified interpreter may render services during the following:

(1) A deposition.

(2) An appeals board hearing.

(3) During those settings which the administrative director determines are reasonably necessary to ascertain the validity or extent of injury to an employee who cannot communicate in English. *(Stats.1937, c. 90, p. 302, § 5811. Amended by Stats.1945, c. 802, p. 1497, § 1;*

Stats.1965, c. 1513, p. 3599, § 168, operative Jan. 15, 1966; Stats.1993, c. 121 (A.B.110), § 65.5, eff. July 16, 1993; Stats.1995, c. 938 (S.B.523), § 77, operative July 1, 1997.)

§ 5813. Bad-faith actions or tactics; liability for expenses, attorney's fees and costs

(a) The workers' compensation referee or appeals board may order a party, the party's attorney, or both, to pay any reasonable expenses, including attorney's fees and costs, incurred by another party as a result of bad-faith actions or tactics that are frivolous or solely intended to cause unnecessary delay. In addition, a workers' compensation referee or the appeals board, in its sole discretion, may order additional sanctions not to exceed two thousand five hundred dollars ($2,500) to be transmitted to the General Fund.

(b) The determination of sanctions shall be made after written application by the party seeking sanctions or upon the appeal board's own motion.

(c) This section shall apply to all applications for adjudication that are filed on or after January 1, 1994. *(Added by Stats.1993, c. 121 (A.B.110), § 66, eff. July 16, 1993. Amended by Stats.1993, c. 1242 (S.B.223), § 41.)*

§ 5814. Penalty for unreasonable delay or refusal of payment of compensation; self-imposed penalties; settlement of accrued claims; reduction of payment; other liability issues

(a) When payment of compensation has been unreasonably delayed or refused, either prior to or subsequent to the issuance of an award, the amount of the payment unreasonably delayed or refused shall be increased up to 25 percent or up to ten thousand dollars ($10,000), whichever is less. In any proceeding under this section, the appeals board shall use its discretion to accomplish a fair balance and substantial justice between the parties.

(b) If a potential violation of this section is discovered by the employer prior to an employee claiming a penalty under this section, the employer, within 90 days of the date of the discovery, may pay a self-imposed penalty in the amount of 10 percent of the amount of the payment unreasonably delayed or refused, along with the amount of the payment delayed or refused. This self-imposed penalty shall be in lieu of the penalty in subdivision (a).

(c) Upon the approval of a compromise and release, findings and awards, or stipulations and orders by the appeals board, it shall be conclusively presumed that any accrued claims for penalty have been resolved, regardless of whether a petition for penalty has been filed, unless the claim for penalty is expressly excluded by the terms of the order or award. Upon the submission of any issue for determination at a regular trial hearing, it shall be conclusively presumed that any accrued claim for penalty in connection with the benefit at issue has been resolved, regardless of whether a petition for penalty has been filed, unless the issue of penalty is also submitted or is expressly excluded in the statement of issues being submitted.

(d) The payment of any increased award pursuant to subdivision (a) shall be reduced by any amount paid under subdivision (d) of Section 4650 on the same unreasonably delayed or refused benefit payment.

(e) No unreasonable delay in the provision of medical treatment shall be found when the treatment has been authorized by the employer in a timely manner and the only dispute concerns payment of a billing submitted by a physician or medical provider as provided in Section 4603.2.

(f) Nothing in this section shall be construed to create a civil cause of action.

(g) Notwithstanding any other provision of law, no action may be brought to recover penalties that may be awarded under this section more than two years from the date the payment of compensation was due.

(h) This section shall apply to all injuries, without regard to whether the injury occurs before, on, or after the operative date of this section.

(i) This section shall become operative on June 1, 2004. *(Added by Stats.2004, c. 34 (S.B.899), § 43, eff. April 19, 2004, operative June 1, 2004.)*

Operative Effect

Section 47 of Stats.2004, c. 34 (S.B.899) provides that "[t]he amendment, addition, or repeal of, any provision of law made by this act shall apply prospectively from the date of enactment of this act, regardless of the date of injury, unless otherwise specified, but shall not constitute good cause to reopen or rescind, alter, or amend any existing order, decision, or award of the Workers' Compensation Appeals Board."

§ 5814.1. Unreasonable delay or refusal to make payment; discretionary compensation; payment of penalty by employer

When the payment of compensation has been unreasonably delayed or refused prior to the issuance of an award, and the director has provided discretionary compensation pursuant to Section 4903.3, the appeals board shall award to the director a penalty to be paid by the employer in the amount of 10 percent of the compensation so provided by the director, such penalty to be in addition to the penalty imposed by Section 5814. The question of delay and the reasonableness of the cause therefor shall be determined by the appeals board in accordance with the facts. *(Added by Stats.1981, c. 894, p. 3413, § 10.)*

§ 5814.5. Delayed or refused payment of compensation; attorneys fees in enforcement proceedings

When the payment of compensation has been unreasonably delayed or refused subsequent to the issuance of an award by an employer that has secured the payment of compensation pursuant to Section 3700, the appeals board shall, in addition to increasing the order, decision, or award pursuant to Section 5814, award reasonable attorneys' fees incurred in enforcing the payment of compensation awarded. *(Added by Stats.1984, c. 806, § 1. Amended by Stats.2002, c. 6 (A.B.749), § 82.)*

§ 5814.6. Penalty for knowingly violating § 5814 with a frequency indicating general business practice

(a) Any employer or insurer that knowingly violates Section 5814 with a frequency that indicates a general business practice is liable for administrative penalties of not to exceed four hundred thousand dollars ($400,000). Penalty payments shall be imposed by the administrative director and deposited into the Return-to-Work Fund established pursuant to Section 139.48.

(b) The administrative director may impose a penalty under either this section or subdivision (e) of Section 129.5.

(c) This section shall become operative on June 1, 2004. *(Added by Stats.2004, c. 34 (S.B.899), § 44, eff. April 19, 2004, operative June 1, 2004.)*

Operative Effect

Section 47 of Stats.2004, c. 34 (S.B.899) provides that "[t]he amendment, addition, or repeal of, any provision of law made by this act shall apply prospectively from the date of enactment of this act, regardless of the date of injury, unless otherwise specified, but shall not constitute good cause to reopen or rescind, alter, or amend any existing order, decision, or award of the Workers' Compensation Appeals Board."

§ 5815. Determination of all issues raised

Every order, decision or award, other than an order merely appointing a trustee or guardian, shall contain a determination of all issues presented for determination by the appeals board prior thereto and not theretofore determined. Any issue not so determined will be deemed decided adversely as to the party in whose interest such issue was raised. *(Added by Stats.1963, c. 1575, p. 3158, § 3. Amended by Stats.1965, c. 1513, p. 3599, § 170, operative Jan. 15, 1966.)*

§ 5816. Collateral estoppel; effect of appeals board determinations

A determination of facts by the appeals board under this chapter has no collateral estoppel effect on a subsequent criminal prosecution and does not preclude litigation of those same facts in the criminal proceeding. *(Added by Stats.1995, c. 158 (A.B.891), § 3.)*

CHAPTER 7. RECONSIDERATION AND JUDICIAL REVIEW

Article	Section
1. Reconsideration	5900
2. Judicial Review	5950
3. Undertaking on Stay Order	6000

ARTICLE 1. RECONSIDERATION

Section
5900. Petition of aggrieved person; motion of appeals board.
5901. Prerequisites to court action.
5902. Petition for reconsideration.
5903. Time for filing; grounds.
5904. Waiver of matters not specified in petition.
5905. Service of petition; answer.
5906. Action of appeals board on petition.
5907. Reconsideration without further proceedings.
5908. Action of appeals board after reconsideration; referral of fraudulent claims.
5908.5. Decision of appeals board on petition; contents; effect on judicial review.
5909. Effect of failure of appeals board to act on petition.
5910. Stay of proceedings.
5911. Reconsideration of board decision.

§ 5900. Petition of aggrieved person; motion of appeals board

(a) Any person aggrieved directly or indirectly by any final order, decision, or award made and filed by the appeals board or a workers' compensation judge under any provision contained in this division, may petition the appeals board for reconsideration in respect to any matters determined or covered by the final order, decision, or award, and specified in the petition for reconsideration. The petition shall be made only within the time and in the manner specified in this chapter.

(b) At any time within 60 days after the filing of an order, decision, or award made by a workers' compensation judge and the accompanying report, the appeals board may, on its own motion, grant reconsideration. *(Stats.1937, c. 90, p. 302, § 5900. Amended by Stats.1951, c. 778, p. 2268, § 13; Stats.1965, c. 1513, p. 3599, § 171, operative Jan. 15, 1966; Stats.1985, c. 326, § 27.)*

§ 5901. Prerequisites to court action

No cause of action arising out of any final order, decision or award made and filed by the appeals board or a workers' compensation judge shall accrue in any court to any person until and unless the appeals board on its own motion sets aside the final order, decision, or award and removes the proceeding to itself or if the person files a petition for reconsideration, and the reconsideration is granted or denied. Nothing herein contained shall prevent the enforcement of any final order, decision, or award, in the manner provided in this division. *(Stats. 1937, c. 90, p. 302, § 5901. Amended by Stats.1951, c. 778, p. 2268, § 14; Stats.1965, c. 1513, p. 3600, § 172, operative Jan. 15, 1966; Stats.1985, c. 326, § 28.)*

§ 5902. Petition for reconsideration

The petition for reconsideration shall set forth specifically and in full detail the grounds upon which the petitioner considers the final order, decision or award made and filed by the appeals board or a workers' compensation judge to be unjust or unlawful, and every issue to be considered by the appeals board. The petition shall be verified upon oath in the manner required for verified pleadings in courts of record and shall contain a general statement of any evidence or other matters upon which the applicant relies in support thereof. *(Stats.1937, c. 90, p. 303, § 5902. Amended by Stats.1951, c. 778, p. 2269, § 15; Stats.1965, c. 1513, p. 3600, § 173, operative Jan. 15, 1966; Stats.1985, c. 326, § 29.)*

§ 5903. Time for filing; grounds

At any time within 20 days after the service of any final order, decision, or award made and filed by the appeals board or a workers' compensation judge granting or denying compensation, or arising out of or incidental thereto, any person aggrieved thereby may petition for reconsideration upon one or more of the following grounds and no other:

(a) That by the order, decision, or award made and filed by the appeals board or the workers' compensation judge, the appeals board acted without or in excess of its powers.

(b) That the order, decision, or award was procured by fraud.

(c) That the evidence does not justify the findings of fact.

(d) That the petitioner has discovered new evidence material to him or her, which he or she could not, with reasonable diligence, have discovered and produced at the hearing.

(e) That the findings of fact do not support the order, decision, or award.

Nothing contained in this section shall limit the grant of continuing jurisdiction contained in Sections 5803 to 5805, inclusive. *(Stats.1937, c. 90, p. 303, § 5903. Amended by Stats.1951, c. 778, p. 2269, § 16; Stats.1965, c. 1513, p. 3600, § 174, operative Jan. 15, 1966; Stats.1985, c. 326, § 30.)*

§ 5904. Waiver of matters not specified in petition

The petitioner for reconsideration shall be deemed to have finally waived all objections, irregularities, and illegalities concerning the matter upon which the reconsideration is sought other than those set forth in the petition for reconsideration. *(Stats.1937, c. 90, p. 303, § 5904. Amended by Stats.1951, c. 778, p. 2269, § 17.)*

§ 5905. Service of petition; answer

A copy of the petition for reconsideration shall be served forthwith upon all adverse parties by the person petitioning for reconsideration. Any adverse party may file an answer thereto within 10 days thereafter. Such answer shall likewise be verified. The appeals board may require the petition for reconsideration to be served on other persons designated by it. *(Stats.1937, c. 90, p. 303, § 5905. Amended by Stats.1951, c. 778, p. 2269, § 18; Stats.1965, c. 1513, p. 3600, § 175, operative Jan. 15, 1966.)*

§ 5906. Action of appeals board on petition

Upon the filing of a petition for reconsideration, or having granted reconsideration upon its own motion, the appeals board may, with or without further proceedings and with or without notice affirm, rescind, alter, or amend the order, decision, or award made and filed by the appeals board or the workers' compensation judge on the basis of the evidence previously submitted in the case, or may grant reconsideration and direct the taking of additional evidence. Notice of the time and place of any hearing on reconsideration shall be given to the petitioner and adverse parties and to other persons as the appeals board orders. *(Added by Stats.1951, c. 778, p. 2269, § 20. Amended by Stats.1965, c. 1513, p. 3601, § 176, operative Jan. 15, 1966; Stats.1985, c. 326, § 31.)*

§ 5907. Reconsideration without further proceedings

If, at the time of granting reconsideration, it appears to the satisfaction of the appeals board that no sufficient reason exists for taking further testimony, the appeals board may affirm, rescind, alter, or amend the order, decision, or award made and filed by the appeals board or the workers' compensation judge and may, without further proceedings, without notice, and without setting a time and place for further hearing, enter its findings, order, decision, or award based upon the record in the case. *(Stats.1937, c. 90, p. 303, § 5907. Amended by Stats.1951, c. 778, p. 2270, § 21; Stats.1965, c. 1513, p. 3601, § 177, operative Jan. 15, 1966; Stats.1985, c. 326, § 32; Stats.2006, c. 538 (S.B.1852), § 492.)*

§ 5908. Action of appeals board after reconsideration; referral of fraudulent claims

(a) After the taking of additional evidence and a consideration of all of the facts the appeals board may affirm, rescind, alter, or amend the original order, decision, or award. An order, decision, or award made following reconsideration which affirms, rescinds, alters, or amends the original order, decision, or award shall be made by the appeals board but shall not affect any right or the enforcement of any right arising from or by virtue of the original order, decision, or award, unless so ordered by the appeals board.

(b) In any case where the appeals board rescinds or reduces an order, decision, or award on the grounds specified in paragraph (b) of Section 5903, the appeals board shall refer the case to the Bureau of Fraudulent Claims pursuant to Article 4 (commencing with Section 12990) of Chapter 2 of Division 3 of the Insurance Code, if the employer is insured, or to the district attorney of the county in which the fraud occurred if the employer is self-insured. *(Added by Stats.1951, c. 778, p. 2270, § 23. Amended by Stats.1965, c. 1513, p. 3601, § 178, operative Jan. 15, 1966; Stats.1989, c. 892, § 54.)*

§ 5908.5. Decision of appeals board on petition; contents; effect on judicial review

Any decision of the appeals board granting or denying a petition for reconsideration or affirming, rescinding, altering, or amending the original findings, order, decision, or award following reconsideration shall be made by the appeals board and not by a workers' compensation judge and shall be in writing, signed by a majority of the appeals board members assigned thereto, and shall state the evidence relied upon and specify in detail the reasons for the decision.

The requirements of this section shall in no way be construed so as to broaden the scope of judicial review as provided for in Article 2 (commencing with Section 5950) of this chapter. *(Added by Stats.1951, c. 778, p. 2270, § 24. Amended by Stats.1953, c. 1256, p. 2814, § 4; Stats.1955, c. 1822, p. 3363, § 1; Stats.1965, c. 1513, p. 3601, § 179, operative Jan. 15, 1966; Stats.1969, c. 918, p. 1849, § 1; Stats.1985, c. 326, § 33.)*

§ 5909. Effect of failure of appeals board to act on petition

A petition for reconsideration is deemed to have been denied by the appeals board unless it is acted upon within 60 days from the date of filing. *(Stats.1937, c. 90, p. 304, § 5909. Amended by Stats.1951, c. 778, p. 2270, § 25; Stats.1965, c. 1513, p. 3601, § 180, operative Jan. 15, 1966; Stats.1992, c. 1226 (A.B.3758), § 5.)*

§ 5910. Stay of proceedings

The filing of a petition for reconsideration shall suspend for a period of 10 days the order, decision, or award affected, insofar as it applies to the parties to the petition, unless otherwise ordered by the appeals board. The appeals board upon the terms and conditions which it by order directs, may stay, suspend, or postpone the order, decision, or award during the pendency of the reconsideration. *(Stats.1937, c. 90, p. 304, § 5910. Amended by Stats.1951, c. 778, p. 2270, § 26; Stats.1965, c. 1513, p. 3601, § 181, operative Jan. 15, 1966.)*

§ 5911. Reconsideration of board decision

Nothing contained in this article shall be construed to prevent the appeals board, on petition of an aggrieved party or on its own motion, from granting reconsideration of an original order, decision, or award made and filed by the appeals board within the same time specified for reconsideration of an original order, decision, or award. *(Added by Stats.1951, c. 778, p. 2270, § 27. Amended by Stats.1965, c. 1513, p. 3602, § 182, operative Jan. 15, 1966.)*

ARTICLE 2. JUDICIAL REVIEW

Section
5950. Application for writ; time.
5951. Return day; prohibition of new and additional evidence.
5952. Scope of review.
5953. Findings and conclusions of appeals board on questions; appearances; judgment.
5954. Applicability of Code of Civil Procedure; service of pleadings.
5955. Review jurisdiction of courts.

Section
5956.   Stay and suspension of order, rule, decision or award of
        appeals board.

§ 5950.   Application for writ; time

Any person affected by an order, decision, or award of the appeals board may, within the time limit specified in this section, apply to the Supreme Court or to the court of appeal for the appellate district in which he resides, for a writ of review, for the purpose of inquiring into and determining the lawfulness of the original order, decision, or award or of the order, decision, or award following reconsideration. The application for writ of review must be made within 45 days after a petition for reconsideration is denied, or, if a petition is granted or reconsideration is had on the appeal board's own motion, within 45 days after the filing of the order, decision, or award following reconsideration. *(Added by Stats.1951, c. 778, p. 2271, § 29. Amended by Stats.1965, c. 1513, p. 3602, § 183, operative Jan. 15, 1966; Stats.1967, c. 17, p. 847, § 103; Stats.1978, c. 661, p. 2123, § 1.)*

§ 5951.   Return day; prohibition of new and additional evidence

The writ of review shall be made returnable at a time and place then or thereafter specified by court order and shall direct the appeals board to certify its record in the case to the court within the time therein specified. No new or additional evidence shall be introduced in such court, but the cause shall be heard on the record of the appeals board, as certified to by it. *(Stats.1937, c. 90, p. 304, § 5951. Amended by Stats.1963, c. 461, p. 1310, § 5; Stats.1965, c. 1513, p. 3602, § 184, operative Jan. 15, 1966.)*

§ 5952.   Scope of review

The review by the court shall not be extended further than to determine, based upon the entire record which shall be certified by the appeals board, whether:

(a) The appeals board acted without or in excess of its powers.

(b) The order, decision, or award was procured by fraud.

(c) The order, decision, or award was unreasonable.

(d) The order, decision, or award was not supported by substantial evidence.

(e) If findings of fact are made, such findings of fact support the order, decision, or award under review.

Nothing in this section shall permit the court to hold a trial de novo, to take evidence, or to exercise its independent judgment on the evidence. *(Stats.1937, c. 90, p. 304, § 5952. Amended by Stats.1951, c. 606, p. 1769, § 8; Stats.1953, c. 94, p. 815, § 1; Stats.1965, c. 1513, p. 3602, § 185, operative Jan. 15, 1966.)*

§ 5953.   Findings and conclusions of appeals board on questions; appearances; judgment

The findings and conclusions of the appeals board on questions of fact are conclusive and final and are not subject to review. Such questions of fact shall include ultimate facts and the findings and conclusions of the appeals board. The appeals board and each party to the action or proceeding before the appeals board shall have the right to appear in the review proceeding. Upon the hearing, the court shall enter judgment either affirming or annulling the order, decision, or award, or the court may remand the case for further proceedings before the appeals board. *(Stats.1937, c. 90, p. 305, § 5953. Amended by Stats.1965, c. 1513, p. 3602, § 186, operative Jan. 15, 1966.)*

§ 5954.   Applicability of Code of Civil Procedure; service of pleadings

The provisions of the Code of Civil Procedure relating to writs of review shall, so far as applicable, apply to proceedings in the courts under the provisions of this article. A copy of every pleading filed pursuant to the terms of this article shall be served on the appeals board and upon every party who entered an appearance in the action before the appeals board and whose interest therein is adverse to the party filing such pleading. *(Stats.1937, c. 90, p. 305, § 5954. Amended by Stats.1945, c. 1509, p. 2821, § 1; Stats.1965, c. 1513, p. 3603, § 187, operative Jan. 15, 1966.)*

§ 5955.   Review jurisdiction of courts

No court of this state, except the Supreme Court and the courts of appeal to the extent herein specified, has jurisdiction to review, reverse, correct, or annul any order, rule, decision, or award of the appeals board, or to suspend or delay the operation or execution thereof, or to restrain, enjoin, or interfere with the appeals board in the performance of its duties but a writ of mandate shall lie from the Supreme Court or a court of appeal in all proper cases. *(Stats.1937, c. 90, p. 305, § 5955. Amended by Stats.1965, c. 1513, p. 3603, § 188, operative Jan. 15, 1966; Stats.1967, c. 17, p. 847, § 104.)*

§ 5956.   Stay and suspension of order, rule, decision or award of appeals board

The filing of a petition for, or the pendency of, a writ of review shall not of itself stay or suspend the operation of any order, rule, decision, or award of the appeals board, but the court before which the petition is filed may stay or suspend, in whole or in part, the operation of the order, decision, or award of the appeals board subject to review, upon the terms and conditions which it by order directs, except as provided in Article 3 of this chapter [1]. *(Stats. 1937, c. 90, p. 305, § 5956. Amended by Stats.1965, c. 1513, p. 3603, § 189, operative Jan. 15, 1966.)*

[1] § 6000 et seq.

ARTICLE 3. UNDERTAKING ON STAY ORDER

Section
6000. Undertaking required.
6001. Terms and conditions of undertaking.
6002. Filing with appeals board.

§ 6000. Undertaking required

The operation of any order, decision, or award of the appeals board under the provisions of this division or any judgment entered thereon, shall not at any time be stayed by the court to which petition is made for a writ of review, unless an undertaking is executed on the part of the petitioner. *(Stats.1937, c. 90, p. 305, § 6000. Amended by Stats.1965, c. 1513, p. 3603, § 190, operative Jan. 15, 1966; Stats.1982, c. 517, p. 2405, § 310.)*

§ 6001. Terms and conditions of undertaking

The undertaking shall provide that:

(a) The petitioner and sureties are bound in double the amount named in such order, decision, or award.

(b) If the order, decision, or award appealed from, or any part thereof, is affirmed, or the proceeding upon review is dismissed, the petitioner will pay the amount directed to be paid by the order, decision, or award or the part of such amount as to which the order, decision, or award is affirmed, and all damages and costs which are awarded against the petitioner.

(c) If the petitioner does not make such payment within 30 days after the filing with the appeals board of the remittitur from the reviewing court, judgment in favor of the adverse party may be entered on motion of the adverse party, and the undertaking shall apply to any judgment entered thereon. Such judgment may be entered in any superior court in which a certified copy of the order, decision, or award is filed, against the sureties for such amount, together with interest that is due thereon, and the damages and costs which are awarded against the petitioner. The provisions of the Code of Civil Procedure, except insofar as they are inconsistent with this division, are applicable to the undertaking. *(Stats.1937, c. 90, p. 305, § 6001. Amended by Stats.1965, c. 1513, p. 3603, § 191, operative Jan. 15, 1966.)*

§ 6002. Filing with appeals board

The undertaking shall be filed with the appeals board. The certificate of the appeals board, or any proper officer thereof, of the filing and approval of such undertaking, is sufficient evidence of the compliance of the petitioner with the provisions of this article. *(Stats.1937, c. 90, p. 305, § 6002. Amended by Stats.1965, c. 1513, p. 3604, § 192, operative Jan. 15, 1966.)*

Division 4.5

WORKERS' COMPENSATION AND INSURANCE: STATE EMPLOYEES NOT OTHERWISE COVERED

Chapter   Section
1. General Provisions 6100
2. Direct Payments 6110
3. Insurance 6130
4. Benefits and Procedure 6140

CHAPTER 1. GENERAL PROVISIONS

Section
6100. Purpose of division.
6101. Definitions.

§ 6100. Purpose of division

The purpose of this division is to effect economy, efficiency, and continuity in the public service by providing means for increasing the willingness of competent persons to assume the risk of injuries or death in State employment and for restoring experienced employees to productive work at the earliest possible moment following injury in the course of and arising out of State employment, irrespective of fault, in circumstances which make the injury or resulting death noncompensable under the provisions of Division 4 of this code[1]. *(Added by Stats.1943, c. 45, p. 259, § 1, eff. Feb. 10, 1943.)*

[1] § 3200 et seq.

§ 6101. Definitions

Unless the context otherwise requires, as used in this division:

(a) "State agency" means any agency, department, division, commission, board, bureau, officer, or other authority of the State of California.

(b) "Fund" means State Compensation Insurance Fund.

(c) "Appeals board" means the Workers' Compensation Appeals Board. *(Added by Stats.1943, c. 45, p. 259, § 1, eff. Feb. 10, 1943. Amended by Stats.1965, c. 1513, p. 3604, § 193, operative Jan. 15, 1966; Stats.1981, c. 21, p. 49, § 11, eff. April 18, 1981.)*

CHAPTER 2. DIRECT PAYMENTS

Section
6110. Powers of state agency.
6111. Master agreement for services of state compensation insurance fund.
6112. Provision for uniform rates for services to all state agencies.
6113. Expenditures from fund.

Section
6114.   Reimbursement of fund by state agency.
6115.   Action against third persons.

§ 6110. Powers of state agency

Any State agency may, by appropriate action, undertake to provide hospitalization, medical treatment and indemnity, including death benefits, to its employees and to their dependents for injury or death suffered from accident, irrespective of fault, occurring in the course of and arising out of the employment with such State agency, where the injury or death is not compensable under the provisions of Division 4 of this code [1]. (*Added by Stats.1943, c. 45, p. 259, § 1, eff. Feb. 10, 1943.*)

[1] § 3200 et seq.

§ 6111. Master agreement for services of state compensation insurance fund

The State Compensation Insurance Fund may enter into a master agreement with the State Department of Finance to render services in accordance with the agreement in the adjustment and disposition of claims against any State agency arising under this chapter. (*Added by Stats.1943, c. 45, p. 259, § 1, eff. Feb. 10, 1943.*)

§ 6112. Provision for uniform rates for services to all state agencies

The master agreement shall provide for the rendition of services at a uniform rate to all State agencies. (*Added by Stats.1943, c. 45, p. 260, § 1, eff. Feb. 10, 1943.*)

§ 6113. Expenditures from fund

The fund may make all expenditures, including payments to claimants for medical care or for adjustment or settlement of claims. (*Added by Stats.1943, c. 45, p. 260, § 1, eff. Feb. 10, 1943.*)

§ 6114. Reimbursement of fund by state agency

The agreement shall provide that the State agency whose officer or employee is a claimant shall reimburse the fund for the expenditures and for the actual cost of services rendered. (*Added by Stats.1943, c. 45, p. 260, § 1, eff. Feb. 10, 1943.*)

§ 6115. Action against third persons

The fund may in its own name, or in the name of the State agency for which services are performed, do any and all things necessary to recover on behalf of the State agency any and all amounts which an employer might recover from third persons under Chapter 5 of Part 1 of Division 4 of this code [1], or which an insurer might recover pursuant to Section 11662 of the Insurance Code, including the rights to commence and prosecute actions or to intervene in other court proceedings, or to compromise claims before or after commencement of suit. (*Added by Stats.1943, c. 45, p. 260, § 1, eff. Feb. 10, 1943.*)

[1] § 3850 et seq.

694

CHAPTER 3. INSURANCE

Section
6130.   State insurance in lieu of direct payments from fund.
6131.   Payment of premiums by state agency.

§ 6130. State insurance in lieu of direct payments from fund

In lieu of direct payments pursuant to Chapter 2 of this division, any State agency may obtain by insurance from the State Compensation Insurance Fund, if the fund accepts the risk when the application for insurance is made, otherwise from any other insurer, hospitalization, medical treatment, and indemnity, including death benefits, on behalf of its employees and of their dependents for injury or death suffered from accident, irrespective of fault, occurring in the course of and arising out of the employment with such State agency, where the injury or death is not compensable under the provisions of Division 4 of this code. (*Added by Stats.1943, c. 45, p. 260, § 1, eff. Feb. 10, 1943.*)

§ 6131. Payment of premiums by state agency

The premium for such insurance shall be a proper charge against any moneys appropriated for the support of or expenditure by such State agency. In case such State agency is supported by or authorized to expend moneys appropriated out of more than one fund, it may, with the approval of the Director of Finance, determine the proportion of such premium to be paid out of each such fund. (*Added by Stats.1943, c. 45, p. 260, § 1, eff. Feb. 10, 1943.*)

CHAPTER 4. BENEFITS AND PROCEDURE

Section
6140.   Benefits.
6141.   Procedure and limitations; incorporation of Division 4 by reference.
6142.   Sections excepted from incorporation by reference.
6143.   Powers of appeals board.
6144.   Determination of controversies submitted to appeals board.
6145.   Requirement of state submission of controversies.
6146.   Arbitration powers of appeals board.
6147.   Written agreement of claimant; prerequisite to direct payment of benefit.
6148.   Written agreement of claimant; contents; prerequisite to payment of benefit by insurer.
6149.   Negotiation of agreement before injury.

§ 6140. Benefits

The hospitalization, medical treatment, and indemnity, including death benefits, provided pursuant to this division shall be the same as provided by Division 4 of this code for employees entitled to the benefits of that division. (*Added by Stats.1943, c. 45, p. 260, § 1, eff. Feb. 10, 1943.*)

§ 6141. Procedure and limitations; incorporation of Division 4 by reference

Except as otherwise provided in this chapter, the provisions of Division 4 of this code, relating to benefits, procedure, and limitations, and all other provisions of that division, so far as they are consistent with the intent and purpose of this division, are made a part hereof the same as if set forth herein verbatim. *(Added by Stats. 1943, c. 45, p. 260, § 1, eff. Feb. 10, 1943.)*

§ 6142. Sections excepted from incorporation by reference

The provisions of Sections 3212, 3212.5, 3361, 4458, and 4800 to 4855, inclusive, of this code, as well as of other sections of Division 4 of this code, which are restrictive to particular persons or occupations, are excepted from this division and its operation. *(Added by Stats.1943, c. 45, p. 261, § 1, eff. Feb. 10, 1943.)*

§ 6143. Powers of appeals board

The appeals board is vested with all power not inconsistent with Article VI of the Constitution of the State of California to hear and determine any dispute or matter arising out of an obligation under this division to provide directly, or through the medium of insurance, benefits identical with those prescribed by Division 4 of this code, with such limitations as are authorized, in the case of insurance, by Section 11657 of the Insurance Code. *(Added by Stats. 1943, c. 45, p. 261, § 1, eff. Feb. 10, 1943. Amended by Stats.1965, c. 1513, p. 3604, § 194, operative Jan. 15, 1966.)*

§ 6144. Determination of controversies submitted to appeals board

The appeals board may try and determine controversies under this division referred to it by the parties under the provisions of Title 9 (commencing with Section 1280) of Part 3 of the Code of Civil Procedure, when such controversies are submitted to it by the signed agreement of the parties, or by the application of one party and the submission of the other to its jurisdiction, with or without an express request for arbitration. *(Added by Stats.1943, c. 45, p. 261, § 1, eff. Feb. 10, 1943. Amended by Stats.1965, c. 1513, p. 3604, § 195, operative Jan. 15, 1966; Stats.1977, c. 579, p. 1901, § 148.)*

§ 6145. Requirement of state submission of controversies

The state, acting by or through any state agency, or when the consent of the opposing party is obtained, shall submit to the appeals board all controversies under this division susceptible of being arbitrated. *(Added by Stats.1943, c. 45, p. 261, § 1, eff. Feb. 10, 1943. Amended by Stats.1965, c. 1513, p. 3604, § 196, operative Jan. 15, 1966.)*

§ 6146. Arbitration powers of appeals board

In acting as arbitrator, the appeals board has all the powers which it has in compensation cases, and its findings and award upon an arbitration have the same conclusiveness and are subject to the same mode of reopening, review, and enforcement as in compensation cases.

No fee or cost shall be charged by the appeals board for acting as arbitrator. *(Added by Stats.1943, c. 45, p. 261, § 1, eff. Feb. 10, 1943. Amended by Stats.1965, c. 1513, p. 3604, § 197, operative Jan. 15, 1966.)*

§ 6147. Written agreement of claimant; prerequisite to direct payment of benefit

No state agency, either directly or through its adjusting agency, the State Compensation Insurance Fund, shall pay or provide any benefit authorized by this division unless and until the claimant makes and delivers to such state agency or to the fund an agreement in writing that if he, or his dependents in the event of his death, elects or elect to bring suit against the state with respect to the injury or death, except an action before the appeals board pursuant to the provisions of this division, or an action against the state for damages resulting from the negligence of an employee of another state agency, he or they will allow, and take all proper measures to effect, a credit to the reasonable value of all benefits which he or they have received under the provisions of this division, deductible from any verdict or judgment obtained in such suit, and from the date of commencement of suit will forego further benefits under this division. *(Added by Stats.1943, c. 45, p. 261, § 1, eff. Feb. 10, 1943. Amended by Stats.1965, c. 1513, p. 3605, § 198, operative Jan. 15, 1966.)*

§ 6148. Written agreement of claimant; contents; prerequisite to payment of benefit by insurer

The insurer, when insurance exists, shall not pay or provide any benefit authorized by this division unless and until the claimant makes and delivers to the insurer an agreement in writing that if he, or his dependents in the event of his death, elects or elect to bring suit against the state or the insurer with respect to the injury or death, except an action before the appeals board pursuant to the provisions of this division, or an action against the state for damages resulting from the negligence of an employee of another state agency, he or they will allow, and take all proper measures to effect, a credit to the reasonable value of all benefits which he or they have received under the provisions of this division, deductible from any verdict or judgment obtained in such suit, and from the date of commencement of suit will forego further benefits under such insurance. *(Added by Stats.1943, c. 45, p. 261, § 1, eff. Feb. 10, 1943. Amended by Stats.1965, c. 1513, p. 3605, § 199, operative Jan. 15, 1966.)*

§ 6149. Negotiation of agreement before injury

Nothing shall preclude an employee from negotiating the agreement mentioned in Sections 6147 and 6148 prior to the occurrence of injury. *(Added by Stats.1943, c. 45, p. 262, § 1, eff. Feb. 10, 1943.)*

Division 4.6

WORKMEN'S COMPENSATION ADVISORY COMMITTEE [REPEALED]

Division 4.7

RETRAINING AND REHABILITATION

Section
6200. Procedures for selection and referral of injured full-time public employees; purpose.
6201. Notice of availability of services.
6202. Initiation of plan.
6203. Subsistence allowance.
6204. Employee's cooperation; unreasonable refusal.
6205. Submission of plan.
6206. Extent of services.
6207. Additional benefit.
6208. Voluntary acceptance of program.

§ 6200. Procedures for selection and referral of injured full-time public employees; purpose

Every public agency, its insurance carrier, and the State Department of Rehabilitation shall jointly formulate procedures for the selection and orderly referral of injured full-time public employees who may be benefited by rehabilitation services and retrained for other positions in public service. The State Department of Rehabilitation shall cooperate in both designing and monitoring results of rehabilitation programs for the disabled employees. The primary purpose of this division is to encourage public agencies to reemploy their injured employees in suitable and gainful employment. *(Added by Stats.1971, c. 1506, p. 2976, § 1.)*

§ 6201. Notice of availability of services

The employer or insurance carrier shall notify the injured employee of the availability of rehabilitation services in those cases where there is continuing disability of 28 days and beyond. Notification shall be made at the time the employee is paid retroactively for the first day of disability (in cases of 28 days of continuing disability or hospitalization) which has previously been uncompensated. A copy of said notification shall be forwarded to the State Department of Rehabilitation. *(Added by Stats. 1971, c. 1506, p. 2976, § 1.)*

§ 6202. Initiation of plan

The initiation of a rehabilitation plan shall be the joint responsibility of the injured employee, and the employer or the insurance carrier. *(Added by Stats.1971, c. 1506, p. 2977, § 1.)*

§ 6203. Subsistence allowance

If a rehabilitation plan requires an injured employee to attend an educational or medical facility away from his home, the injured employee shall be paid a reasonable and necessary subsistence allowance in addition to temporary disability indemnity. The subsistence allowance shall be regarded neither as indemnity nor as replacement for lost earnings, but rather as an amount reasonable and necessary to sustain the employee. The determination of need in a particular case shall be established as part of the rehabilitation plan. *(Added by Stats.1971, c. 1506, p. 2977, § 1. Amended by Stats.1972, c. 715, p. 1303, § 1.)*

§ 6204. Employee's cooperation; unreasonable refusal

An injured employee agreeing to a rehabilitation plan shall cooperate in carrying it out. On his unreasonable refusal to comply with the provisions of the rehabilitation plan, the injured employee's rights to further subsistence shall be suspended until compliance is obtained, except that the payment of temporary or permanent disability indemnity, which would be payable regardless of the rehabilitation plan, shall not be suspended. *(Added by Stats.1971, c. 1506, p. 2977, § 1. Amended by Stats.1972, c. 715, p. 1303, § 2.)*

§ 6205. Submission of plan

The injured employee may agree with his employer or insurance carrier upon a rehabilitation plan without submission of such plan for approval to the State Department of Rehabilitation. Provision of service under such plans shall be at no cost to the State General Fund. *(Added by Stats.1971, c. 1506, p. 2977, § 1.)*

§ 6206. Extent of services

The injured employee shall receive such medical and vocational rehabilitative services as may be reasonably necessary to restore him to suitable employment. *(Added by Stats.1971, c. 1506, p. 2977, § 1.)*

§ 6207. Additional benefit

The injured employee's rehabilitation benefit is an additional benefit and shall not be converted to or replace any workmen's compensation benefit available to him. *(Added by Stats.1971, c. 1506, p. 2977, § 1.)*

§ 6208. Voluntary acceptance of program

The initiation and acceptance of a rehabilitation program shall be voluntary and not compulsory upon the employer, the insurance carrier, or the injured employee. *(Added by Stats.1972, c. 715, p. 1304, § 3.)*

Division 5

SAFETY IN EMPLOYMENT

Part		Section
1.	Occupational Safety and Health	6300
2.	Safeguards on Railroads	6800
3.	Safety on Buildings	7100
4.	Mining Industries	7400
5.	Ships and Vessels	7600
6.	Tanks and Boilers	7620
7.	Volatile Flammable Liquids	7800
7.5.	Refinery and Chemical Plants	7850
8.	Amusement Rides Safety Law	7900
8.1.	Permanent Amusement Ride Safety Inspection Program	7920
9.	Tunnel and Mine Safety	7950
10.	Use of Carcinogens	9000
11.	Commercial Establishments	9100

Part 1

OCCUPATIONAL SAFETY AND HEALTH

Chapter		Section
1.	Jurisdiction and Duties	6300
2.	Education and Research	6350
2.5.	Hazardous Substances Information and Training	6360
3.	Responsibilities and Duties of Employers and Employees	6400
4.	Penalties	6423
5.	Temporary Variances	6450
6.	Permit Requirements	6500
7.	Appeal Proceedings	6600
8.	Enforcement of Civil Penalties	6650
9.	Miscellaneous Safety Provisions	6700

CHAPTER 1. JURISDICTION AND DUTIES

Section

6300. Purpose.

6301. Construction of part.

6302. Director; department; insurer; division; standards board; appeals board; aquaculture; serious injury or illness; serious exposure.

6303. Place of employment; employment.

6303.5. No limit on state jurisdiction if federal law authorizes concurrent state jurisdiction over safety and health issues.

6304. Employer.

6304.1. Employee.

6304.2. State prisoners; department of corrections; employee and employer.

6304.3. Correctional industry safety committees; duties and functions; complaints concerning working conditions; inspections or investigations.

6304.4. Appeal proceedings; status of prisoners.

6304.5. Applicability of division to proceedings on employee safety; evidence in personal injury and wrongful death actions.

6305. Occupational safety and health standards and orders; special order.

Section

6306. Safe; safety; health; safety devise; safeguard.

6307. Division; power, jurisdiction and supervision.

6307.1. Asbestos spraying; enforcement of prohibitions.

6308. Division; enforcement powers.

6308.5. Hearings; opportunity to submit facts or arguments.

6309. Investigations; response to complaints; protection of complainants.

6310. Retaliation for filing complaint prohibited; offenses.

6311. Retaliation for refusal to work in violation of health and safety standards; action for wages.

6312. Discrimination complaint.

6313. Investigation of industrial accidents, serious exposures, or occupational illnesses; corrective orders.

6313.5. Transmittal to registrar of contractors copies of investigation reports.

6314. Authority to enter premises; investigation, inspection and photography; refusal; inspection warrant; subpoenas; observers; preservation of materials and accident site; violation; punishment.

6314.1. High hazardous industries; priority inspection plans.

6314.5. Evaluations conducted during inspections.

6315. Bureau of investigations.

6315.3. Annual report.

6315.5. Evidence; admissibility of standards, orders, regulations, findings and decisions; presumption.

6316. Powers and jurisdiction of local governing bodies.

6317. Citation or notice, abatement; civil penalties; limitations; records.

6317.5. Falsified materials; posting or distribution in workplace; citation; cumulative sanctions and remedies.

6317.7. Failure to find violations upon inspection; notice to employer.

6318. Posting citations.

6319. Notice of citation or order and right to contest; appeal; civil penalty regulations.

6319.3. New employers; violations of injury prevention program standards; assessment of civil penalties.

6319.5. Incomplete abatement; hearing; affirmance or modification of requirements.

6320. Reinspection.

6321. Advance notice of inspection or investigation; offense.

6322. Confidential information; trade secrets.

6323. Injunction against use or operation of dangerous machine, apparatus or equipment.

6324. Temporary restraining order; sufficiency of showing.

6325. Dangerous condition; notice of prohibited use.

6325.5. Friable asbestos in workplace; prohibited use.

6326. Violation against prohibition of use; offense.

6327. Prohibited entry or use; contest by employer.

6327.5. Mandamus to compel division to act.

6328. Notice relating to safety rules and right to report unsafe conditions, etc.; posting.

6329. Disposition of funds collected for violations.

6330. Annual report.

6331. Tests to define safety standards for use of positive pressure, closed circuit, breathing apparatus in interior structural fires.

Section
6332.   Record of violence against community health care
          workers.

§ 6300. Purpose

The California Occupational Safety and Health Act of 1973 is hereby enacted for the purpose of assuring safe and healthful working conditions for all California working men and women by authorizing the enforcement of effective standards, assisting and encouraging employers to maintain safe and healthful working conditions, and by providing for research, information, education, training, and enforcement in the field of occupational safety and health. *(Added by Stats.1973, c. 993, p. 1927, § 40, eff. Oct. 1, 1973.)*

§ 6301. Construction of part

The definitions set forth in this chapter shall govern the construction and interpretation of this part. *(Added by Stats.1973, c. 993, p. 1927, § 42, eff. Oct. 1, 1973.)*

§ 6302. Director; department; insurer; division; standards board; appeals board; aquaculture; serious injury or illness; serious exposure

As used in this division:

(a) "Director" means the Director of Industrial Relations.

(b) "Department" means the Department of Industrial Relations.

(c) "Insurer" includes the State Compensation Insurance Fund and any private company, corporation, mutual association, and reciprocal or interinsurance exchange, authorized under the laws of this state to insure employers against liability for compensation under this part and under Division 4 (commencing with Section 3201), and any employer to whom a certificate of consent to self-insure has been issued.

(d) "Division" means the Division of Occupational Safety and Health.

(e) "Standards board" means the Occupational Safety and Health Standards Board, within the department.

(f) "Appeals board" means the Occupational Safety and Health Appeals Board, within the department.

(g) "Aquaculture" means a form of agriculture as defined in Section 17 of the Fish and Game Code.

(h) "Serious injury or illness" means any injury or illness occurring in a place of employment or in connection with any employment which requires inpatient hospitalization for a period in excess of 24 hours for other than medical observation or in which an employee suffers a loss of any member of the body or suffers any serious degree of permanent disfigurement, but does not include any injury or illness or death caused by the commission of a Penal Code violation, except the violation of Section 385 of the Penal Code, or an accident on a public street or highway.

698

(i) "Serious exposure" means any exposure of an employee to a hazardous substance when the exposure occurs as a result of an incident, accident, emergency, or exposure over time and is in a degree or amount sufficient to create a substantial probability that death or serious physical harm in the future could result from the exposure. *(Added by Stats.1973, c. 993, p. 1927, § 44, eff. Oct. 1, 1973. Amended by Stats.1979, c. 72, p. 181, § 25; Stats.1982, c. 1486, p. 5732, § 27; Stats.1983, c. 131, § 29, eff. June 27, 1983; Stats.1984, c. 1317, § 1.)*

§ 6303. Place of employment; employment

(a) "Place of employment" means any place, and the premises appurtenant thereto, where employment is carried on, except a place where the health and safety jurisdiction is vested by law in, and actively exercised by, any state or federal agency other than the division.

(b) "Employment" includes the carrying on of any trade, enterprise, project, industry, business, occupation, or work, including all excavation, demolition, and construction work, or any process or operation in any way related thereto, in which any person is engaged or permitted to work for hire, except household domestic service.

(c) "Employment," for purposes of this division only, also includes volunteer firefighting when covered by Division 4 (commencing with Section 3200) pursuant to Section 3361.

(d) Subdivision (c) shall become operative on January 1, 2004. *(Added by Stats.1973, c. 993, p. 1927, § 46, eff. Oct. 1, 1973. Amended by Stats.1978, c. 1248, p. 4060, § 1; Stats.2001, c. 807 (S.B.1207), § 1; Stats.2002, c. 368 (A.B.2118), § 1, eff. Sept. 5, 2002.)*

§ 6303.5. No limit on state jurisdiction if federal law authorizes concurrent state jurisdiction over safety and health issues

Nothing in this division shall be construed to limit the jurisdiction of the state over any employment or place of employment by reason of the exercise of occupational safety and health jurisdiction by any federal agency if federal jurisdiction is being exercised under a federal law which expressly authorizes concurrent state jurisdiction over occupational safety or health issues. *(Added by Initiative Measure (Prop. 97), approved by the electors, Nov. 8, 1988.)*

§ 6304. Employer

"Employer" shall have the same meaning as in Section 3300. *(Stats.1937, c. 90, p. 306, § 6304. Amended by Stats.1971, c. 1751, p. 3780, § 2, operative April 1, 1972.)*

§ 6304.1. Employee

(a) "Employee" means every person who is required or directed by any employer to engage in any employment or to go to work or be at any time in any place of employment.

(b) "Employee" also includes volunteer firefighters covered by Division 4 (commencing with Section 3200) pursuant to Section 3361.

(c) Subdivision (b) shall become operative on January 1, 2004.

(d) This act does not affect claims that arose pursuant to Division 5 of this code between January 1, 2002, and the effective date of this act. *(Added by Stats.1973, c. 993, p. 1928, § 47, eff. Oct. 1, 1973. Amended by Stats.2001, c. 807 (S.B.1207), § 2; Stats.2002, c. 368 (A.B.2118), § 2, eff. Sept. 5, 2002.)*

§ 6304.2. State prisoners; department of corrections; employee and employer

Notwithstanding Section 6413, and except as provided in Sections 6304.3 and 6304.4, any state prisoner engaged in correctional industry, as defined by the Department of Corrections, shall be deemed to be an "employee," and the Department of Corrections shall be deemed to be an "employer," with regard to such prisoners for the purposes of this part. *(Added by Stats.1977, c. 1215, p. 4901, § 1.)*

§ 6304.3. Correctional industry safety committees; duties and functions; complaints concerning working conditions; inspections or investigations

(a) A Correctional Industry Safety Committee shall be established in accordance with Department of Corrections administrative procedures at each facility maintaining a correctional industry, as defined by the Department of Corrections. The Division of Occupational Safety and Health shall promulgate, and the Department of Corrections shall implement, regulations concerning the duties and functions which shall govern the operation of each such committee.

(b) All complaints alleging unsafe or unhealthy working conditions in a correctional industry shall initially be directed to the Correctional Industry Safety Committee of the facility prison. The committee shall attempt to resolve all complaints.

If a complaint is not resolved by the committee within 15 calendar days, the complaint shall be referred by the committee to the division where it shall be reviewed. When the division receives a complaint which, in its determination, constitutes a bona fide allegation of a safety or health violation, the division shall summarily investigate the same as soon as possible, but not later than three working days after receipt of a complaint charging a serious violation, as defined in Section 6309, and not later than 14 calendar days after receipt of a complaint charging a nonserious violation.

(c) Except as provided in subdivision (b) and in Section 6313, the inspection or investigation of a facility maintaining a correctional industry, as defined by the Department of Corrections, shall be discretionary with the division.

(d) Notwithstanding Section 6321, the division may give advance notice of an inspection or investigation and may postpone the same if such action is necessary for the maintenance of security at the facility where the inspection or investigation is to be held, or for insuring the safety and health of the division's representative who will be conducting such inspection or investigation. *(Added by Stats.1977, c. 1215, p. 4091, § 2. Amended by Stats. 1980, c. 676, p. 1976, § 233.)*

§ 6304.4. Appeal proceedings; status of prisoners

A prisoner engaged in correctional industry, as defined by the Department of Corrections, shall not be considered an employee for purposes of the provisions relating to appeal proceedings set forth in Chapter 7 (commencing with Section 6600). *(Added by Stats.1977, c. 1215, p. 4092, § 3. Amended by Stats.1983, c. 142, § 111.)*

§ 6304.5. Applicability of division to proceedings on employee safety; evidence in personal injury and wrongful death actions

It is the intent of the Legislature that the provisions of this division, and the occupational safety and health standards and orders promulgated under this code, are applicable to proceedings against employers for the exclusive purpose of maintaining and enforcing employee safety.

Neither the issuance of, or failure to issue, a citation by the division shall have any application to, nor be considered in, nor be admissible into, evidence in any personal injury or wrongful death action, except as between an employee and his or her own employer. Sections 452 and 669 of the Evidence Code shall apply to this division and to occupational safety and health standards adopted under this division in the same manner as any other statute, ordinance, or regulation. The testimony of employees of the division shall not be admissible as expert opinion or with respect to the application of occupational safety and health standards. It is the intent of the Legislature that the amendments to this section enacted in the 1999–2000 Regular Session shall not abrogate the holding in Brock v. State of California (1978) 81 Cal.App.3d 752. *(Added by Stats.1971, c. 1751, p. 3780, § 3, operative April 1, 1972. Amended by Stats.1999, c. 615 (A.B.1127), § 2.)*

§ 6305. Occupational safety and health standards and orders; special order

(a) "Occupational safety and health standards and orders" means standards and orders adopted by the standards board pursuant to Chapter 6 (commencing with Section 140) of Division 1 and general orders heretofore adopted by the Industrial Safety Board or the Industrial Accident Commission.

(b) "Special order" means any order written by the chief or the chief's authorized representative to correct an unsafe condition, device, or place of employment which poses a threat to the health or safety of an employee and which cannot be made safe under existing standards or orders of the standards board. These orders shall have the same effect as any other standard or order of the standards board, but shall apply only to the employment or place of employment described in the written order of the chief's authorized representative. *(Added by Stats.1973, c. 993, p. 1928, § 49, eff. Oct. 1, 1973. Amended by Stats.1974, c. 1284, p. 2781, § 6; Stats.1980, c. 676, p. 1977, § 234; Stats.1981, c. 714, p. 2722, § 319.)*

§ 6306. Safe; safety; health; safety devise; safeguard

(a) "Safe," "safety," and "health" as applied to an employment or a place of employment mean such freedom from danger to the life, safety, or health of employees as the nature of the employment reasonably permits.

(b) "Safety device" and "safeguard" shall be given a broad interpretation so as to include any practicable method of mitigating or preventing a specific danger, including the danger of exposure to potentially injurious levels of ionizing radiation or potentially injurious quantities of radioactive materials. *(Added by Stats.1973, c. 993, p. 1928, § 51, eff. Oct. 1, 1973.)*

§ 6307. Division; power, jurisdiction and supervision

The division has the power, jurisdiction, and supervision over every employment and place of employment in this state, which is necessary to adequately enforce and administer all laws and lawful standards and orders, or special orders requiring such employment and place of employment to be safe, and requiring the protection of the life, safety, and health of every employee in such employment or place of employment. *(Added by Stats. 1973, c. 993, p. 1928, § 53, eff. Oct. 1, 1973.)*

§ 6307.1. Asbestos spraying; enforcement of prohibitions

The State Department of Health Services shall assist the division in the enforcement of Section 25910 of the Health and Safety Code in the manner prescribed by a written agreement between the State Department of Health Services and the Department of Industrial Relations, pursuant to Section 144. *(Added by Stats.1977, c. 62, p. 459, § 2, eff. May 18, 1977. Amended by Stats.1980, c. 676, p. 1977, § 235.)*

§ 6308. Division; enforcement powers

The division, in enforcing occupational safety and health standards and orders and special orders may do any of the following:

(a) Declare and prescribe what safety devices, safeguards, or other means or methods of protection are well adapted to render the employees of every employment and place of employment safe as required by law or lawful order.

(b) Enforce Section 25910 of the Health and Safety Code and standards and orders adopted by the standards board pursuant to Chapter 6 (commencing with Section 140) of Division 1 of the Labor Code, for the installation, use, maintenance, and operation of reasonable uniform

safety devices, safeguards, and other means or methods of protection, which are necessary to carry out all laws and lawful standards or special orders relative to the protection of the life and safety of employees in employments and places of employment.

(c) Require the performance of any other act which the protection of the life and safety of the employees in employments and places of employment reasonably demands.

An employer may request a hearing on a special order or action ordered pursuant to this section, at which the employer, owner, or any other person may appear. The appeals board shall conduct the hearing at the earliest possible time.

All orders, rules, regulations, findings, and decisions of the division made or entered under this part, except special orders and action orders, may be reviewed by the Supreme Court and the courts of appeal as may be provided by law. *(Added by Stats.1973, c. 993, p. 1928, § 55, eff. Oct. 1, 1973. Amended by Stats.1977, c. 62, p. 459, § 3, eff. May 18, 1977; Stats.1984, c. 1138, § 1.)*

§ 6308.5. Hearings; opportunity to submit facts or arguments

Hearings conducted by the division pursuant to this part shall give any affected employer or other affected person the opportunity to submit facts or arguments, but may be conducted informally, either orally or in writing. *(Added by Stats.1974, c. 1284, p. 2781, § 7.)*

§ 6309. Investigations; response to complaints; protection of complainants

If the division learns or has reason to believe that an employment or place of employment is not safe or is injurious to the welfare of an employee, it may, on its own motion, or upon complaint, summarily investigate the same with or without notice or hearings. However, if the division receives a complaint from an employee, an employee's representative, including, but not limited to, an attorney, health or safety professional, union representative, or government agency representative, or an employer of an employee directly involved in an unsafe place of employment, that his or her employment or place of employment is not safe, it shall, with or without notice or hearing, summarily investigate the complaint as soon as possible, but not later than three working days after receipt of a complaint charging a serious violation, and not later than 14 calendar days after receipt of a complaint charging a nonserious violation. The division shall attempt to determine the period of time in the future that the complainant believes the unsafe condition may continue to exist, and shall allocate inspection resources so as to respond first to those situations in which time is of the essence. For purposes of this section, a complaint is deemed to allege a serious violation if the division determines that the complaint charges that there is a substantial probability that death or serious physical harm could result from a condition which exists, or from one or more practices, means, methods, operations, or processes which have been adopted or are in use in a place of employment. When a complaint charging a serious violation is received from a state or local prosecutor, or a local law enforcement agency, the division shall summarily investigate the employment or place of employment within 24 hours of receipt of the complaint. All other complaints are deemed to allege nonserious violations. The division may enter and serve any necessary order relative thereto. The division is not required to respond to a complaint within this period where, from the facts stated in the complaint, it determines that the complaint is intended to willfully harass an employer or is without any reasonable basis.

The division shall keep complete and accurate records of all complaints, whether verbal or written, and shall inform the complainant, whenever his or her identity is known, of any action taken by the division in regard to the subject matter of the complaint, and the reasons for the action, within 14 calendar days of taking any action. The records of the division shall include the dates on which any action was taken on the complaint, or the reasons for not taking any action on the complaint. The division shall, pursuant to authorized regulations, conduct an informal review of any refusal by a representative of the division to issue a citation with respect to an alleged violation. The division shall furnish the employee or the representative of employees requesting the review a written statement of the reasons for the division's final disposition of the case.

The name of a person who submits to the division a complaint regarding the unsafe condition of an employment or place of employment shall be kept confidential by the division, unless that person requests otherwise.

The division shall annually compile and release on its Web site data pertaining to complaints received and citations issued.

The requirements of this section do not relieve the division of its requirement to inspect and assure that all places of employment are safe and healthful for employees. The division shall maintain the capability to receive and act upon complaints at all times. *(Added by Stats. 1973, c. 993, p. 1929, § 57, eff. Oct. 1, 1973. Amended by Stats.1974, c. 544, p. 1258, § 37; Stats.1974, c. 1284, p. 2781, § 8; Stats.1976, c. 13, p. 10, § 1; Stats.1976, c. 544, p. 1381, § 1; Stats.1985, c. 1479, § 5; Stats.1999, c. 615 (A.B.1127), § 3; Stats.2002, c. 885 (A.B.2837), § 2; Stats.2003, c. 884 (A.B.1719), § 6.)*

§ 6310. Retaliation for filing complaint prohibited; offenses

(a) No person shall discharge or in any manner discriminate against any employee because the employee has done any of the following:

(1) Made any oral or written complaint to the division, other governmental agencies having statutory responsibility for or assisting the division with reference to employee safety or health, his or her employer, or his or her representative.

(2) Instituted or caused to be instituted any proceeding under or relating to his or her rights or has testified or is about to testify in the proceeding or because of the exercise by the employee on behalf of himself, herself, or others of any rights afforded him or her.

(3) Participated in an occupational health and safety committee established pursuant to Section 6401.7.

(b) Any employee who is discharged, threatened with discharge, demoted, suspended, or in any other manner discriminated against in the terms and conditions of employment by his or her employer because the employee has made a bona fide oral or written complaint to the division, other governmental agencies having statutory responsibility for or assisting the division with reference to employee safety or health, his or her employer, or his or her representative, of unsafe working conditions, or work practices, in his or her employment or place of employment, or has participated in an employer-employee occupational health and safety committee, shall be entitled to reinstatement and reimbursement for lost wages and work benefits caused by the acts of the employer. Any employer who willfully refuses to rehire, promote, or otherwise restore an employee or former employee who has been determined to be eligible for rehiring or promotion by a grievance procedure, arbitration, or hearing authorized by law, is guilty of a misdemeanor. *(Added by Stats.1973, c. 993, p. 1930, § 59, eff. Oct. 1, 1973. Amended by Stats.1974, c. 1284, p. 2782, § 9; Stats.1977, c. 460, p. 1515, § 1; Stats.1989, c. 1369, § 3, eff. Oct. 2, 1989.)*

§ 6311. Retaliation for refusal to work in violation of health and safety standards; action for wages

No employee shall be laid off or discharged for refusing to perform work in the performance of which this code, including Section 6400, any occupational safety or health standard or any safety order of the division or standards board will be violated, where the violation would create a real and apparent hazard to the employee or his or her fellow employees. Any employee who is laid off or discharged in violation of this section or is otherwise not paid because he or she refused to perform work in the performance of which this code, any occupational safety or health standard or any safety order of the division or standards board will be violated and where the violation would create a real and apparent hazard to the employee or his or her fellow employees shall have a right of action for wages for the time the employee is without work as a result of the layoff or discharge. *(Added by Stats.1973, c. 993, p. 1930, § 61, eff. Oct. 1, 1973. Amended by Stats.1982, c. 1384, p. 5281, § 1; Stats.1985, c. 1479, § 6.)*

§ 6312. Discrimination complaint

Any employee who believes that he or she has been discharged or otherwise discriminated against by any person in violation of Section 6310 or 6311 may file a

701

complaint with the Labor Commissioner pursuant to Section 98.7. *(Added by Stats.1973, c. 993, p. 1930, § 63, eff. Oct. 1, 1973. Amended by Stats.1980, c. 676, p. 1978, § 236; Stats.1984, c. 1317, § 2; Stats.1985, c. 1479, § 7.)*

§ 6313. Investigation of industrial accidents, serious exposures, or occupational illnesses; corrective orders

(a) The division shall investigate the causes of any employment accident that is fatal to one or more employees or that results in a serious injury or illness, or a serious exposure, unless it determines that an investigation is unnecessary. If the division determines that an investigation of an accident is unnecessary, it shall summarize the facts indicating that the accident need not be investigated and the means by which the facts were determined. The division shall establish guidelines for determining the circumstances under which an investigation of these accidents and exposures is unnecessary.

(b) The division may investigate the causes of any other industrial accident or occupational illness which occurs within the state in any employment or place of employment, or which directly or indirectly arises from or is connected with the maintenance or operation of the employment or place of employment, and shall issue any orders necessary to eliminate the causes and to prevent reoccurrence. The orders may not be admitted as evidence in any action for damages, or any proceeding to recover compensation, based on or arising out of injury or death caused by the accident or illness. *(Added by Stats.1973, c. 993, p. 1931, § 65, eff. Oct. 1, 1973. Amended by Stats.1979, c. 889, p. 3078, § 2, eff. Sept. 22, 1979; Stats.1984, c. 1317, § 3; Stats.2002, c. 885 (A.B. 2837), § 3.)*

§ 6313.5. Transmittal to registrar of contractors copies of investigation reports

The division shall transmit to the Registrar of Contractors copies of any reports made in any investigation conducted pursuant to subdivision (a) of Section 6313, and may, upon its own motion or at the request of the Registrar of Contractors, transmit copies of any other reports made in any investigation conducted pursuant to subdivision (b) of Section 6313 involving a contractor licensed pursuant to the Contractors License Law (Chapter 9 (commencing with Section 7000) of Division 3 of the Business and Professions Code). *(Added by Stats.1973, c. 993, p. 1931, § 66, eff. Oct. 1, 1973.)*

§ 6314. Authority to enter premises; investigation, inspection and photography; refusal; inspection warrant; subpoenas; observers; preservation of materials and accident site; violation; punishment

(a) To make an investigation or inspection, the chief of the division and all qualified divisional inspectors and investigators authorized by him or her shall, upon presenting appropriate credentials to the employer, have free access to any place of employment to investigate and inspect during regular working hours, and at other

reasonable times when necessary for the protection of safety and health, and within reasonable limits and in a reasonable manner. The chief or his or her authorized representative may, during the course of any investigation or inspection, obtain any statistics, information, or any physical materials in the possession of the employer that are directly related to the purpose of the investigation or inspection, conduct any tests necessary to the investigation or inspection, and take photographs. Photographs taken by the division during the course of any investigation or inspection shall be considered to be confidential information pursuant to the provisions of Section 6322, and shall not be deemed to be public records for purposes of the California Public Records Act.

(b) If permission to investigate or inspect the place of employment is refused, or the facts or circumstances reasonably justify the failure to seek permission, the chief or his or her authorized representative may obtain an inspection warrant pursuant to the provisions of Title 13 (commencing with Section 1822.50) of the Code of Civil Procedure. Cause for the issuance of a warrant shall be deemed to exist if there has been an industrial accident, injury, or illness reported, if any complaint that violations of occupational safety and health standards exist at the place of employment has been received by the division, or if the place of employment to be inspected has been chosen on the basis of specific neutral criteria contained in a general administrative plan for the enforcement of this division.

(c) The chief and his or her authorized representatives may issue subpoenas to compel the attendance of witnesses and the production of books, papers, records, and physical materials, administer oaths, examine witnesses under oath, take verification or proof of written materials, and take depositions and affidavits for the purpose of carrying out the duties of the division.

(d) In the course of any investigation or inspection of an employer or place of employment by an authorized representative of the division, a representative of the employer and a representative authorized by his or her employees shall have an opportunity to accompany him or her on the tour of inspection. Any employee or employer, or their authorized representatives, shall have the right to discuss safety and health violations or safety and health problems with the inspector privately during the course of an investigation or inspection. Where there is no authorized employee representative, the chief or his or her authorized representatives shall consult with a reasonable number of employees concerning matters of health and safety of the place of employment.

(e) During any investigation of an industrial accident or occupational illness conducted by the division pursuant to the provisions of Section 6313, the chief or his or her authorized representative may issue an order to preserve physical materials or the accident site as they were at the time the accident or illness occurred if, in the opinion of the division, it is necessary to do so in order to determine the cause or causes of the accident or illness, and the evidence is in potential danger of being removed, altered, or tampered with. Under these circumstances, the division shall issue that order in a manner that will avoid, to the extent possible, any interference with normal business operations.

A conspicuous notice that an order has been issued shall be prepared by the division and shall be posted by the employer in the area or on the article to be preserved. The order shall be limited to the immediate area and the machines, devices, apparatus, or equipment directly associated with the accident or illness.

Any person who knowingly violates an order issued by the division pursuant to this subdivision shall, upon conviction, be punished by a fine of not more than five thousand dollars ($5,000). *(Added by Stats.1973, c. 993, p. 1931, § 68, eff. Oct. 1, 1973. Amended by Stats.1979, c. 241, p. 503, § 1, eff. July 10, 1979; Stats.1984, c. 1317, § 4; Stats.1993, c. 998 (A.B.2016), § 1.)*

§ 6314.1. High hazardous industries; priority inspection plans

(a) The division shall establish a program for targeting employers in high hazardous industries with the highest incidence of preventable occupational injuries and illnesses and workers' compensation losses. The employers shall be identified from any or all of the following data sources: the California Work Injury and Illness program, the Occupational Injuries and Illness Survey, the federal hazardous employers' list, experience modification and other relevant data maintained and furnished by all rating organizations as defined in Section 11750.1 of the Insurance Code, histories of violations of Occupational Safety and Health Act standards, and any other source deemed to be appropriate that identifies injury and illness rates.

(b) The division shall establish procedures for ensuring that the highest hazardous employers in the most hazardous industries are inspected on a priority basis. The division may send a letter to the high hazard employers who are identified pursuant to this section informing them of their status and directing them to submit a plan, including the establishment of joint labor-management health and safety committees, within a time determined by the division for reducing their occupational injury and illness rates. Employers who submit plans that meet the requirements of the division may be placed on a secondary inspection schedule. Employers on that schedule shall be inspected on a random basis as determined by the division. Employers who do not submit plans meeting the requirements of the division within the time specified by the division shall be placed on the primary inspection list. Every employer on the primary inspection list shall be subject to an inspection. The division shall employ sufficient personnel to meet minimum federal targeted inspection standards.

(c) The division shall establish and maintain regional plans for allocating the division's resources for the targeted inspection program in addition to the inspections required or authorized in Sections 6309, 6313, and 6320. Each regional plan shall focus on industries selected from the targeted inspection program as well as any other scheduled inspections that the division determines to be appropriate to the region, including the cleanup of hazardous waste sites. All targeted inspections shall be conducted on a priority basis, targeting the worst employers first.

(d) In order to maximize the impact of the regional plans, the division shall coordinate its education, training, and consulting services with the priorities established in the regional plans. *(Added by Stats.1993, c. 121 (A.B. 110), § 68, eff. July 16, 1993.)*

§ 6314.5. Evaluations conducted during inspections

(a) Every inspection conducted by the division shall include an evaluation of the employer's injury prevention program established pursuant to Section 6401.7. The division shall evaluate injury prevention programs using the criteria for substantial compliance determined by the standards board. The evaluation shall include interviews with a sample of employees and the members of any employer-employee occupational safety and health committee. In any inspection which includes work for which a permit is required pursuant to Section 6500 and for which a permit has been issued pursuant to Section 6502, the evaluation of the employer's injury prevention program shall be limited to the implementation of the plan approved by the division in the issuance of the permit. Before any inspection is concluded, the division shall notify the employer of the services available from the department to assist the employer to establish, maintain, improve, and evaluate the employer's injury prevention program.

(b) Inspections also shall include an evaluation of the following:

(1) The condition or conditions alleged in the complaint if the inspection is conducted pursuant to Section 6309.

(2) The condition or conditions involved in the accident if the inspection is conducted pursuant to Section 6313.

(3) The condition or conditions involving work for which a permit is required pursuant to Section 6500, for which notification of asbestos related work is required pursuant to Section 6501.5, or for which a report of use of a carcinogen is required pursuant to Section 9030.

(4) The condition or conditions related to significant safety or health hazards in the industries identified in the regional plans developed pursuant to Section 6314.1.

(5) The condition or conditions involved in abatement of previous violations, special orders, or action orders if the inspection is conducted pursuant to Section 6320.

(c) The scope of any inspection may be expanded beyond the evaluations specified in subdivisions (a) and (b) whenever, in the opinion of the division, a more complete inspection is warranted. *(Added by Stats.1989, c. 1369, § 5, eff. Oct. 2, 1989.)*

§ 6315. Bureau of investigations

(a) There is within the division a Bureau of Investigations. The bureau is responsible for directing accident investigations involving violations of standards, orders, special orders, or Section 25910 of the Health and Safety Code, in which there is a serious injury to five or more employees, death, or request for prosecution by a division representative. The bureau shall review inspection reports involving a serious violation where there have been serious injuries to one to four employees or a serious exposure, and may investigate those cases in which the bureau finds criminal violations may have occurred. The bureau is responsible for preparing cases for the purpose of prosecution, including evidence and findings.

(b) The division shall provide the bureau with all of the following:

(1) All initial accident reports.

(2) The division's inspection report for any inspection involving a serious violation where there is a fatality, and the reports necessary for the bureau's review required pursuant to subdivision (a).

(3) Any other documents in the possession of the division requested by the bureau for its review or investigation of any case or which the division determines will be helpful to the bureau in its investigation of the case.

(c) The supervisor of the bureau is the administrative chief of the bureau, and shall be an attorney.

(d) The bureau shall be staffed by as many attorneys and investigators as are necessary to carry out the purposes of this chapter. To the extent possible, the attorneys and investigators shall be experienced in criminal law.

(e) The supervisor of the bureau and bureau representatives designated by the supervisor have a right of access to all places of employment necessary to the investigation, may collect any evidence or samples they deem necessary to an investigation, and have all of the powers enumerated in Section 6314.

(f) The supervisor of the bureau and bureau representatives designated by the supervisor may serve all processes and notices throughout the state.

(g) In any case where the bureau is required to conduct an investigation, and in which there is a serious injury or death, the results of the investigation shall be referred in a timely manner by the bureau to the appropriate prosecuting authority having jurisdiction for appropriate action, unless the bureau determines that there is legally insufficient evidence of a violation of the law. If the bureau determines that there is legally insufficient evidence of a violation of the law, the bureau shall notify the appropriate prosecuting authority, if the prosecuting authority requests notice.

(h) The bureau may communicate with the appropriate prosecuting authority at any time the bureau deems appropriate.

(i) Upon the request of a county district attorney, the department may develop a protocol for the referral of cases that may involve criminal conduct to the appropriate prosecuting authority in lieu of or in cooperation with an investigation by the bureau. The protocol shall provide for the voluntary acceptance of referrals after a review of the case by the prosecuting authority. In cases accepted for investigation by the prosecuting authority, the protocol shall provide for cooperation between the prosecuting authority, the division, and the bureau. Where a referral is declined by the prosecuting authority, the bureau shall comply with subdivisions (a) to (h), inclusive. *(Added by Stats.1973, c. 993, p. 1932, § 70, eff. Oct. 1, 1973. Amended by Stats.1974, c. 1284, p. 2782, § 10; Stats.1977, c. 62, p. 460, § 4, eff. May 18, 1977; Stats.1978, c. 1224, p. 3956, § 1; Stats.1984, c. 1317, § 5; Stats.2002, c. 885 (A.B.2837), § 4; Stats.2003, c. 884 (A.B.1719), § 7.)*

§ 6315.3. Annual report

The bureau shall, not later than February 15, annually submit to the division for submission to the director a report on the activities of the bureau, including, but not limited to, the following:

(a) Totals of each type of report provided the bureau under each category in subdivision (b) of Section 6315.

(b) Totals of each type of case reflecting the number of investigations and court cases in progress at the start of the calendar year being reported, investigations completed in the calendar year, cases referred to appropriate prosecuting authorities in the calendar year, and investigations and court cases in progress at the end of the calendar year. The types of cases shall include the following:

(1) Those that the bureau is required to investigate, divided into fatalities, serious injuries to five or more employees, and requests for prosecution from a division representative.

(2) Those that were initiated by the bureau following the review required in subdivision (a) of Section 6315, divided into serious injuries to fewer than five employees and serious exposures.

(c) A summary of the dispositions in the calendar year of cases referred by the bureau to appropriate prosecuting authorities. The summary shall be divided into the types of cases, as described in subdivision (b), and shall show at least the violation, the statute for which the case was referred for prosecution, and the dates of referral to the bureau for investigation, referral from the bureau for prosecution, and the final court action if the case was prosecuted.

(d) A summary of investigations completed in the calendar year that did not result in a referral for prosecution, divided into the types of cases as described in subdivision (b), showing the violation and the reasons for nonreferral.

(e) A summary of the use of the bureau's resources in accomplishing the bureau's mission. *(Added by Stats. 1984, c. 1317, § 6. Amended by Stats.2006, c. 538 (S.B.1852), § 493.)*

§ 6315.5. Evidence; admissibility of standards, orders, regulations, findings and decisions; presumption

All occupational safety and health standards and orders, rules, regulations, findings, and decisions of the division made and entered pursuant to this part are admissible as evidence in any prosecution for the violation of any provision of this part, and shall, in every such prosecution, be presumed to be reasonable and lawful and to fix a reasonable and proper standard and requirement of safety unless, prior to the institution of the prosecution for such violation, proceedings for a hearing on a special order are instituted, or a petition is filed under Section 11426 of the Government Code [1]. *(Added by Stats.1973, c. 993, p. 1933, § 70.5, eff. Oct. 1, 1973.)*

[1] Repealed.

§ 6316. Powers and jurisdiction of local governing bodies

Except as limited by Chapter 6 (commencing with Section 140) of Division 1, nothing in this part shall deprive the governing body of any county, city, or public corporation, board, or department, of any power or jurisdiction over or relative to any place of employment. *(Added by Stats.1973, c. 993, p. 1933, § 72, eff. Oct. 1, 1973.)*

§ 6317. Citation or notice, abatement; civil penalties; limitations; records

If, upon inspection or investigation, the division believes that an employer has violated Section 25910 of the Health and Safety Code or any standard, rule, order, or regulation established pursuant to Chapter 6 (commencing with Section 140) of Division 1 of the Labor Code, or any standard, rule, order, or regulation established pursuant to this part, it shall with reasonable promptness issue a citation to the employer. Each citation shall be in writing and shall describe with particularity the nature of the violation, including a reference to the provision of the code, standard, rule, regulation, or order alleged to have been violated. In addition, the citation shall fix a reasonable time for the abatement of the alleged violation. The period specified for abatement shall not commence running until the date the citation or notice is received by certified mail and the certified mail receipt is signed, or if not signed, the date the return is made to the post office. If the division officially and directly delivers the citation or notice to the employer, the period specified for abatement shall commence running on the date of the delivery.

A "notice" in lieu of citation may be issued with respect to violations found in an inspection or investigation which meet either of the following requirements:

(1) The violations do not have a direct relationship upon the health or safety of an employee.

(2) The violations do not have an immediate relationship to the health or safety of an employee, and are of a general or regulatory nature. A notice in lieu of a citation may be issued only if the employer agrees to correct the violations within a reasonable time, as specified by the division, and agrees not to appeal the finding of the division that the violations exist. A notice issued pursuant to this paragraph shall have the same effect as a citation for purposes of establishing repeat violations or a failure to abate. Every notice shall clearly state the abatement period specified by the division, that the notice may not be appealed, and that the notice has the same effect as a citation for purposes of establishing a repeated violation or a failure to abate. The employer shall indicate agreement to the provisions and conditions of the notice by his or her signature on the notice.

Under no circumstances shall a notice be issued in lieu of a citation if the violations are serious, repeated, willful, or arise from a failure to abate.

The director shall prescribe guidelines for the issuance of these notices.

The division may impose a civil penalty against an employer as specified in Chapter 4 (commencing with Section 6423) of this part. A notice in lieu of a citation may not be issued if the number of first instance violations found in the inspection (other than serious, willful, or repeated violations) is 10 or more violations.

No citation or notice shall be issued by the division for a given violation or violations after six months have elapsed since occurrence of the violation.

The director shall prescribe procedures for the issuance of a citation or notice.

The division shall prepare and maintain records capable of supplying an inspector with previous citations and notices issued to an employer. *(Added by Stats.1973, c. 993, p. 1933, § 74, eff. Oct. 1, 1973. Amended by Stats.1976, c. 963, p. 2205, § 1; Stats.1977, c. 62, p. 160, § 5, eff. May 18, 1977; Stats.1978, c. 759, p. 2371, § 1; Stats.1985, c. 1269, § 1; Stats.1991, c. 599 (A.B.1545), § 1, eff. Oct. 7, 1991.)*

§ 6317.5. Falsified materials; posting or distribution in workplace; citation; cumulative sanctions and remedies

(a) If, upon inspection or investigation, the division finds that an employer has falsified any materials posted in the workplace or distributed to employees related to the California Occupational Safety and Health Act, the division shall issue a citation to the employer.

(b) Each citation issued pursuant to this section, or a copy or copies thereof, shall be prominently posted, as prescribed in regulations issued by the director.

(c) Any employer served with a citation pursuant to subdivision (a) may appeal to the appeals board pursuant to the provisions of Chapter 7 (commencing with Section 6600). The appeal shall be subject to the timeframes and procedures set forth in that chapter.

(d) The provisions of this section are in addition to, and not in lieu of, all other criminal penalties and civil remedies that may be applicable to any act leading to issuance of a citation pursuant to this section. *(Added by Stats.1993, c. 580 (S.B.193), § 2.)*

§ 6317.7. Failure to find violations upon inspection; notice to employer

If, upon inspection or investigation, the division finds no violations pursuant to this chapter, the division with reasonable promptness shall issue a written notice to the employer specifying the areas inspected and stating that no violations were found.

The director shall prescribe procedures for the issuance of this notice. *(Added by Stats.1993, c. 580 (S.B.193), § 3.)*

§ 6318. Posting citations

(a) Each citation issued under Section 6317, and each special order or action ordered pursuant to Section 6308, or a copy or copies thereof, shall be prominently posted, as prescribed in regulations issued by the director, at or near each place a violation referred to in the citation or order occurred. All postings shall be maintained for three working days, or until the unsafe condition is abated, whichever is longer. Following each investigation of an industrial accident or occupational illness, if no violations are found, the employer shall post a notice prepared by the division so indicating for three working days.

(b) When the division verifies abatement of a serious violation or an order at the time of inspection or upon reinspection, the employer shall post a notice prepared by the division so indicating for three working days. In all other cases of abatement of serious violations, the employer shall post the signed statement confirming abatement prepared pursuant to Section 6320. *(Added by Stats.1973, c. 993, p. 1933, § 76, eff. Oct. 1, 1973. Amended by Stats.1984, c. 1138, § 2; Stats.1984, c. 1317, § 7.5; Stats.1989, c. 1369, § 6, eff. Oct. 2, 1989.)*

§ 6319. Notice of citation or order and right to contest; appeal; civil penalty regulations

(a) If, after an inspection or investigation, the division issues a citation pursuant to Section 6317 or an order pursuant to Section 6308, it shall, within a reasonable time after the termination of the inspection or investigation, notify the employer by certified mail of the citation or order, and that the employer has 15 working days from receipt of the notice within which to notify the appeals board that he or she wishes to contest the citation or order for any reason set forth in Section 6600 or 6600.5.

(b) Any employer served by certified mail with a notice of civil penalty may appeal to the appeals board within 15 working days from receipt of that notice for any reason set forth in Section 6600. If the citation is issued for a violation involving the condition or operation of any machine, device, apparatus, or equipment, and a person

other than the employer is obligated to the employer to repair the machine, device, apparatus, or equipment and to pay any penalties assessed against the employer, the other person may appeal to the appeals board within 15 working days of the receipt of the citation by the employer for any reasons set forth in Section 6600.

(c) The director shall promulgate regulations covering the assessment of civil penalties under this chapter which give due consideration to the appropriateness of the penalty with respect to the following factors:

(1) The size of the business of the employer being charged.

(2) The gravity of the violation.

(3) The good faith of the employer, including timely abatement.

(4) The history of previous violations.

(d) Notwithstanding subdivision (c), if serious injury, illness, exposure, or death is caused by any serious, willful, or repeated violation, or by any failure to correct a serious violation within the time permitted for its correction, the penalty shall not be reduced for any reason other than the size of the business of the employer being charged. Whenever the division issues a citation for a violation covered by this subdivision, it shall notify the employer of its determination that serious injury, illness, exposure or death was caused by the violation and shall, upon request, provide the employer with a copy of the inspection report.

(e) The employer shall not be liable for a civil penalty under this part for any citation issued by a division representative providing consulting services pursuant to Sections 6354 and 6355.

(f) Whenever a citation of a self-insured employer for a willful, or repeat serious violation of the standard adopted pursuant to Section 6401.7 becomes final, the division shall notify the director so that a hearing may be held to determine whether good cause exists to revoke the employer's certificate of consent to self-insure as provided in Section 3702.

(g) Based upon the evidence, the division may propose appropriate modifications concerning the characterization of violations and corresponding modifications to civil penalties as a result thereof. *(Added by Stats.1973, c. 993, p. 1934, § 78, eff. Oct. 1, 1973. Amended by Stats.1974, c. 1284, p. 2783, § 11; Stats.1976, c. 1404, p. 6323, § 1; Stats.1984, c. 1138, § 3; Stats.1989, c. 1369, § 7, eff. Oct. 2, 1989.)*

§ 6319.3. New employers; violations of injury prevention program standards; assessment of civil penalties

(a) Except as provided in subdivision (b) of this section and subdivision (j) of Section 6401.7, no civil penalty shall be assessed against any new employer in the state for a violation of any standard developed pursuant to subdivision (a) of Section 6401.7 for a period of one year after the date the new employer establishes a business in the state.

(b) Subdivision (a) shall only apply to an employer who has made a good faith effort to comply with any standard developed pursuant to subdivision (a) of Section 6401.7, but shall not apply if the employer is found to have committed a serious, willful, or repeated violation of that standard, or fails to abate the violation and is assessed a penalty pursuant to Section 6430. *(Added by Stats.1993, c. 928 (A.B.395), § 1.)*

§ 6319.5. Incomplete abatement; hearing; affirmance or modification of requirements

Upon a showing by an employer of a good-faith effort to comply with the abatement requirement of a citation, and that abatement has not been completed because of factors beyond his reasonable control, the division, after an opportunity for a hearing, shall issue an order affirming or modifying the abatement requirements in such citation. *(Added by Stats.1973, c. 993, p. 1934, § 78.5, eff. Oct. 1, 1973).*

§ 6320. Reinspection

(a) If, after inspection or investigation, the division issues a special order, order to take special action, or a citation for a serious violation, and if at the time of inspection the order is not complied with or the violation is not abated, the division shall conduct a reinspection in the following cases:

(1) All inspections or investigations involving a serious violation of a standard adopted pursuant to Section 6401.7, a special order or order to take special action, serious violations of those orders, and serious violations characterized as repeat or willful or with abatement periods of less than six days. These reinspections shall be conducted at the end of the period fixed for compliance with the order or abatement of the violation or within 30 days thereafter.

(2) At least 20 percent of the inspections or investigations involving a serious violation not otherwise scheduled for reinspection. These inspections shall be randomly selected and shall be conducted at the end of the period fixed for abatement of the violation or within a reasonable time thereafter.

(b) Whenever a serious violation is not abated at the time of the initial or subsequent inspection, the division shall require the employer to submit a signed statement under penalty of perjury that he or she has complied with the abatement terms within the period fixed for abatement of the violation. If the statement is not received by the division within 10 working days after the end of the period fixed for abatement, the division shall revoke any adjustments to the civil penalty based on abatement of the violation. The division shall include on the initial notice of civil penalty a clear warning of reinspection and automatic revocation of any civil penalty adjustments based on abatement for failure to submit the required statement in the time allotted, and of an additional, potentially substantial monetary penalty for failure to abate the violation. If the division fails to receive evidence of abatement or the statement within 10 working days after the end of the abatement period, the division shall notify the employer that the additional civil penalty for failure to abate, as provided in Section 6430, will be assessed retroactive to the end of the abatement period unless the employer can provide sufficient evidence that the violation was abated prior to that date. The division shall conduct a reinspection of serious violations within 45 days following the end of the abatement period whenever it still has no evidence of abatement. *(Added by Stats.1973, c. 993, p. 1934, § 80, eff. Oct. 1, 1973. Amended by Stats.1988, c. 1152, § 1; Stats.1989, c. 1369, § 8, eff. Oct. 2, 1989.)*

§ 6321. Advance notice of inspection or investigation; offense

No person or employer shall be given advance warning of an inspection or investigation by any authorized representative of the division unless authorized under provisions of this part.

Only the chief or, in the case of his absence, his authorized representatives shall have the authority to permit advance notice of an inspection or investigation. The director shall, as soon as practicable, set down limitations under which an employer may be granted advance notice by the chief. In no case, except an imminent danger to the health or safety of an employee or employees, is advance notice to be authorized when the investigation or inspection is to be made as a result of an employee complaint.

Any person who gives advance notice of any inspection to be conducted, without authority from the chief or his designees, is guilty of a misdemeanor and shall, upon conviction, be punished by a fine of not more than one thousand dollars ($1,000) or by imprisonment for not more than six months, or by both. *(Added by Stats.1973, c. 993, p. 1934, § 82, eff. Oct. 1, 1973.)*

§ 6322. Confidential information; trade secrets

All information reported to or otherwise obtained by the chief or his representatives in connection with any inspection or proceeding of the division which contains or which might reveal a trade secret referred to in Section 1905 of Title 18 of the United States Code, or other information that is confidential pursuant to Chapter 3.5 (commencing with Section 6250) of Division 7 of Title 1 of the Government Code, shall be considered confidential, except that such information may be disclosed to other officers or employees of the division concerned with carrying out the purposes of the division or when relevant in any proceeding of the division. The appeals board, standards board, the courts, or the director shall in any such proceeding issue such orders as may be appropriate to protect the confidentiality of trade secrets. Violation of this section is a misdemeanor. *(Added by Stats.1973, c. 993, p. 1935, § 83, eff. Oct. 1, 1973.)*

§ 6323. Injunction against use or operation of dangerous machine, apparatus or equipment

If the condition of any employment or place of employment or the operation of any machine, device, apparatus, or equipment constitutes a serious menace to the lives or safety of persons about it, the division may apply to the superior court of the county in which such place of employment, machine, device, apparatus, or equipment is situated, for an injunction restraining the use or operation thereof until such condition is corrected. *(Added by Stats.1973, c. 993, p. 1935, § 84, eff. Oct. 1, 1973.)*

§ 6324. Temporary restraining order; sufficiency of showing

The application to the superior court accompanied by affidavit showing that such place of employment, machine, device, apparatus, or equipment is being operated in violation of a safety order or standard, or in violation of Section 25910 of the Health and Safety Code, and that such use or operation constitutes a menace to the life or safety of any person employed thereabout and accompanied by a copy of the order or standard applicable thereto is a sufficient prima facie showing to warrant, in the discretion of the court, the immediate granting of a temporary restraining order. No bond shall be required from the division as a prerequisite to the granting of any restraining order. *(Added by Stats.1973, c. 993, p. 1935, § 85, eff. Oct. 1, 1973. Amended by Stats.1974, c. 1284, p. 2783, § 12; Stats.1977, c. 62, p. 461, § 6, eff. May 18, 1977; Stats.1979, c. 373, p. 1349, § 235.)*

§ 6325. Dangerous condition; notice of prohibited use

When, in the opinion of the division, a place of employment, machine, device, apparatus, or equipment or any part thereof is in a dangerous condition, is not properly guarded or is dangerously placed so as to constitute an imminent hazard to employees, entry therein, or the use thereof, as the case may be, shall be prohibited by the division, and a conspicuous notice to that effect shall be attached thereto. Such prohibition of use shall be limited to the immediate area in which the imminent hazard exists, and the division shall not prohibit any entry in or use of a place of employment, machine, device, apparatus, or equipment, or any part thereof, which is outside such area of imminent hazard. Such notice shall not be removed except by an authorized representative of the division, nor until the place of employment, machine, device, apparatus, or equipment is made safe and the required safeguards or safety appliances or devices are provided. This section shall not prevent the entry or use with the division's knowledge and permission for the sole purpose of eliminating the dangerous conditions. *(Added by Stats.1973, c. 993, p. 1935, § 86, eff. Oct. 1, 1973.)*

§ 6325.5. Friable asbestos in workplace; prohibited use

If the division has reasonable cause to believe that any workplace contains friable asbestos, and if there appears to be inadequate protection for employees at that workplace to the hazards from airborne asbestos fibers, the division may issue an order prohibiting use. *(Added by Stats.1985, c. 1587, § 7.4, eff. Oct. 2, 1985.)*

§ 6326. Violation against prohibition of use; offense

Every person who, after such notice is attached as provided in Section 6325, enters any such place of employment, or uses or operates any such place of employment, machine, device, apparatus, or equipment before it is made safe and the required safeguards or safety appliances or devices are provided, or who defaces, destroys or removes any such notice without the authority of the division, is guilty of a misdemeanor punishable by a fine of up to one thousand dollars ($1,000), or up to one year in the county jail, or both. *(Added by Stats.1973, c. 993, p. 1936, § 87, eff. Oct. 1, 1973.)*

§ 6327. Prohibited entry or use; contest by employer

Once an authorized representative of the division has prohibited entry in or use of a place of employment, machine, device, apparatus, or equipment, as specified in Section 6325, the employer may contest the order and shall be granted, upon request, a hearing by the division to review the validity of the representative's order. The hearing shall be held within 24 hours following the employer's request. *(Added by Stats.1986, c. 1178, § 2.)*

§ 6327.5. Mandamus to compel division to act

If the division arbitrarily or capriciously fails to take action to prevent or prohibit any conditions or practices in any employment or place of employment which are such that danger exists which could reasonably be expected to cause death or serious physical harm immediately or before the imminence of such danger can be eliminated through other available means, any employee who may be injured by reason of such failure, or the representatives of such employees, may bring an action against the chief of the division in any appropriate court for a writ of mandate to compel the division to prevent or prohibit the condition. Nothing contained in this section shall be deemed to prevent the bringing of a writ of mandate against any appropriate person or entity as may be provided by law. *(Added by Stats.1973, c. 993, p. 1937, § 89, eff. Oct. 1, 1973.)*

§ 6328. Notice relating to safety rules and right to report unsafe conditions, etc.; posting

The division shall prepare a notice containing pertinent information regarding safety rules and regulations. The notice shall contain the address and telephone number of the nearest division office; a clear explanation of an employee's right to report any unsafe working conditions; the right to request a safety inspection by the division for unsafe conditions; the right to refuse to work under conditions which endanger his life or health; the right to receive information under the Hazardous Substances Information and Training Act (Ch. 2.5 (commencing with Section 6360)); posting and notice requirements of employers and the division; and any other information the division deems necessary. It shall be supplied to employers as soon as practical. The division shall promulgate regulations on the content and the required location and number of notices which must be posted by employers. Sufficient posters in both English and Spanish shall be printed to supply employers in this state. *(Added by Stats.1973, c. 993, p. 1937, § 90, eff. Oct. 1, 1973. Amended by Stats.1984, c. 507, § 1.)*

§ 6329. Disposition of funds collected for violations

All money collected for violation of standards, orders, or special orders of, or for fees paid pursuant to this division shall be paid into the state treasury to the credit of the General Fund.

The Department of Industrial Relations shall account to the Department of Finance and the State Controller for all moneys so received and furnish proper vouchers therefor. *(Added by Stats.1973, c. 993, p. 1937, § 91, eff. Oct. 1, 1973.)*

§ 6330. Annual report

The director shall prepare and submit to the Legislature, not later than March 1, an annual report on the division activities. The report shall include, but need not be limited to, the following information for the previous calendar year:

(a) The amount of funds allocated and spent in enforcement, education and research, and administration by the division.

(b) Total inspections made, and citations issued by the division.

(c) The number of civil penalties assessed, total amount of fines collected and the number of appeals heard.

(d) The number of contractors referred to the Contractor's State License Board for hearing, pursuant to Section 7109.5 of the Business and Professions Code, and the total number of these cases resulting in suspension or revocation of a license.

(e) The report from the division prepared by the Bureau of Investigations for submission to the director pursuant to Section 6315.3.

(f) Recommendations for legislation which improves the ability of the division to provide safety in places of employment.

The report shall be made to the Speaker of the Assembly and the Chairman of the Rules Committee of the Senate, for assignment to the appropriate committee or committees for evaluation. *(Added by Stats.1973, c. 993, p. 1937, § 92, eff. Oct. 1, 1973. Amended by Stats.1984, c. 1317, § 8.)*

§ 6331. Tests to define safety standards for use of positive pressure, closed circuit, breathing apparatus in interior structural fires

The division shall enter into a contract for the development and execution of tests to define safety standards for the use of positive pressure, closed circuit, breathing apparatus in interior structural fires. The testing shall define numerically what constitutes positive pressure in breathing apparatus. The testing shall also address the issues of the heat of the oxygen coming into the mask, the condensation inside the mask, the possibility of, and effect of, moisture condensation in the lungs of the wearer of the mask, and the risks associated with a dislodgement of the mask in an interior structural fire situation. The development of these tests shall utilize the resources of recognized specialists in fire research to design, conduct, and execute the tests and develop the standards. The standards board shall adopt or revise safety standards based on the results of these tests.

The test parameters, the location where the testing will take place, and the level of expertise required shall be determined by the Cal-OSHA Self Contained Breathing Apparatus Advisory Committee. *(Added by Stats.1984, c. 1571, § 1.)*

§ 6332. Record of violence against community health care workers

(a) For purposes of this section, the following terms have the following meanings:

(1) "Community health care worker" means an individual who provides health care or health care related services to clients in home settings.

(2) "Employer" means a person or entity that employs a community health care worker. "Employer" does not include an individual who is a recipient of home-based services and who is responsible for hiring his or her own community health care worker.

(3) "Violence" means a physical assault or a threat of a physical assault.

(b) Every employer shall keep a record of any violence committed against a community health care worker and shall file a copy of that record with the Division of Labor Statistics and Research in the form and detail and within the time limits prescribed by the Division of Labor Statistics and Research. *(Added by Stats.2000, c. 493 (S.B.1272), § 1.)*

CHAPTER 2. EDUCATION AND RESEARCH

Section
6350. Program; purpose.
6351. Distribution of information.
6352. Safety training programs.
6353. Research.
6354. Consulting services; prevention training programs.
6354.5. Occupational safety and health loss control consultation services; standards and fees.

Section

6354.7. Workers' Occupational Safety and Health Education
         Fund; worker safety and health training and edu-
         cation program.

6354.7. Workers' Occupational Safety and Health Education
         Fund; worker safety and health training and edu-
         cation program.

6355.   Restriction on citations to and prosecution of em-
         ployer receiving consulting service.

6356.   Worker Safety Bilingual Investigative Support, En-
         forcement, and Training Account; establishment;
         funding; restrictions on funding.

6357.   Standards for workplace ergonomics.

6359.   Legislative findings and declarations; prevention of
         occupational injuries and illnesses among young
         workers.

§ 6350. Program; purpose

The division shall maintain an education and research program for the purpose of providing in-service training of division personnel, safety education for employees and employers, research and consulting safety services. *(Added by Stats.1973, c. 993, p. 1938, § 94, eff. Oct. 1, 1973.)*

§ 6351. Distribution of information

The division shall be responsible for preparation and distribution of information concerning occupational safety and health programs, methods, techniques or devices. Such information may include but is not limited to safety publications, films and audiovisual material, speeches and conferences on safety. *(Added by Stats.1973, c. 993, p. 1938, § 94, eff. Oct. 1, 1973.)*

§ 6352. Safety training programs

The division shall provide safety training programs, upon request, for employees and employers. Priority for the development of safety training programs shall be in those occupations which pose the greatest hazard to the safety and health of employees. *(Added by Stats.1973, c. 993, p. 1938, § 94, eff. Oct. 1, 1973.)*

§ 6353. Research

The division shall conduct continuing research into methods, means, operations, techniques, processes and practices necessary for improvement of occupational safety and health of employees. *(Added by Stats.1973, c. 993, p. 1938, § 94, eff. Oct. 1, 1973.)*

§ 6354. Consulting services; prevention training programs

The division shall, upon request, provide a full range of occupational safety and health consulting services to any employer or employee group. These consulting services shall include:

(a) A program for identifying categories of occupational safety and health hazards causing the greatest number and most serious preventable injuries and illnesses and workers' compensation losses and the places of employment where they are occurring. The hazards, industries, and places of employment shall be identified from the data system that is used in the targeted

inspection program pursuant to Section 6314.1. The division shall develop procedures for offering consultation services to high hazard employers who are identified pursuant to this section. The services may include the development of educational material and procedures for reducing or eliminating safety and health hazards, conducting workplace surveys to identify health and safety problems, and development of plans to improve employer health and safety loss records.

The program shall include a component for reducing the number of work-related, repetitive motion injuries, including, but not limited to, back injuries. The division may formulate recommendations for reducing repetitive motion injuries after conducting a survey of the workplace of the employer who accepts services of the division. The recommendations shall include, wherever appropriate, the application of generally accepted ergonomic and engineering principles to eliminate repetitive motions that are generally expected to result in injuries to workers. The recommendations shall also include, wherever appropriate, training programs to instruct workers in methods for performing job-related movements, such as lifting heavy objects, in a manner that minimizes strain and provides safeguards against injury.

The division shall establish model injury and illness prevention training programs to prevent repetitive motion injuries, including recommendations for the minimum qualifications of instructors. The model programs shall be made available to employers, employer associations, workers' compensation insurers, and employee organizations on request.

(b) A program for providing assistance in the development of injury prevention programs for employees and employers. The highest priority for the division's consulting services shall be given to development of these programs for businesses with fewer than 250 employees in industries identified in the regional plans developed pursuant to subdivision (b) of Section 6314.1.

(c) A program for providing employers or employees with information, advice, and recommendations on maintaining safe employment or place of employment, and on applicable occupational safety and health standards, techniques, devices, methods, practices, or programs. *(Added by Stats.1973, c. 993, p. 1938, § 94, eff. Oct. 1, 1973. Amended by Stats.1989, c. 1369, § 9, eff. Oct. 2, 1989; Stats.1993, c. 121 (A.B.110), § 69, eff. July 16, 1993; Stats.1995, c. 903 (A.B.739), § 9.)*

§ 6354.5. Occupational safety and health loss control consultation services; standards and fees

(a) Any insurer desiring to write workers' compensation insurance shall maintain or provide occupational safety and health loss control consultation services. The insurer may employ qualified personnel to provide these services or provide the services through another entity.

(b) The program of an insurer for furnishing loss control consultation services shall be adequate to meet minimum standards prescribed by this section. Required loss control consultation services shall be adequate to identify the hazards exposing the insured to, or causing the insured, significant workers' compensation losses, and to advise the insured of steps needed to mitigate the identified workers' compensation losses or exposures. The program of an insurer for furnishing loss control consultation services shall provide all of the following:

(1) A workplace survey, including discussions with management and, where appropriate, nonmanagement personnel with permission of the employer.

(2) A review of injury records with appropriate personnel.

(3) The development of a plan to improve the employer's health and safety loss control experience, which shall include, where appropriate, modifications to the employer's injury and illness prevention program established pursuant to Section 6401.7. At the time that an insurance policy is issued and annually thereafter, and again when notified by Cal–OSHA that an insured employer has been identified as a targeted employer pursuant to Section 6314.1, the insurer shall provide each insured employer with a written description of the consultation services together with a notice that the services are available at no additional charge to the employer. These notices to the employer shall appear in at least 10–point bold type.

(c) The insurer shall not charge any fee in addition to the insurance premium for safety and health loss control consultation services.

(d) Nothing in this section shall be construed to require insurers to provide loss control services to places of employment that do not pose significant preventable hazards to workers.

(e) The director shall establish an insurance loss control services coordinator position in the Department of Industrial Relations. The coordinator shall provide information to employers about the availability of loss control consultation services and respond to employers' questions and complaints about loss control consultation services provided by their insurer. The coordinator shall notify the insurer of every complaint concerning loss control consultation services. If the employer and the insurer are unable to agree on a mutually satisfactory solution to the complaint, the coordinator shall investigate the complaint. Whenever the coordinator determines that the loss control consultation services provided by the insurer are inadequate or inappropriate, he or she shall recommend to the employer and the insurer the actions required to bring the loss control program into compliance. If the employer and the insurer are unable to agree on a mutually satisfactory solution to the complaint, the coordinator shall forward his or her recommendations to the director. The cost of providing the coordinator services shall be paid out of the Workers' Occupational Safety and Health Education Fund created by subdivision (a) of Section 6354.7. However, no more than 20 percent of that fund may be expended for this

purpose each year. *(Added by Stats.1995, c. 556 (S.B. 1051), § 5. Amended by Stats.2002, c. 6 (A.B.749), § 83.)*

§ 6354.7. Workers' Occupational Safety and Health Education Fund; worker safety and health training and education program

Text of section as added by Stats.2002, c. 6 (A.B.749), § 84.

(a) The Workers' Occupational Safety and Health Education Fund is hereby created as a special account in the State Treasury. Proceeds of the fund may be expended, upon appropriation by the Legislature, by the Commission on Health and Safety and Workers' Compensation for the purpose of establishing and maintaining a worker occupational safety and health training and education program and insurance loss control services coordinator. The director shall levy and collect fees to fund these purposes from insurers subject to Section 6354.5. However, the fee assessed against any insurer shall not exceed the greater of one hundred dollars ($100) or 0.0286 percent of paid workers' compensation indemnity claims as reported for the previous calendar year to the designated rating organization for the analysis required under subdivision (b) of Section 11759.1 of the Insurance Code. All fees shall be deposited in the fund.

(b) The commission shall establish and maintain a worker safety and health training and education program. The purpose of the worker occupational safety and health training and education program shall be to promote awareness of the need for prevention education programs, to develop and provide injury and illness prevention education programs for employees and their representatives, and to deliver those awareness and training programs through a network of providers throughout the state. The commission may conduct the program directly or by means of contracts or interagency agreements.

(c) The commission shall establish an employer and worker advisory board for the program. The advisory board shall guide the development of curricula, teaching methods, and specific course material about occupational safety and health, and shall assist in providing links to the target audience and broadening the partnerships with worker-based organizations, labor studies programs, and others that are able to reach the target audience.

(d) The program shall include the development and provision of a needed core curriculum addressing competencies for effective participation in workplace injury and illness prevention programs and on joint labor-management health and safety committees. The core curriculum shall include an overview of the requirements related to injury and illness prevention programs and hazard communication.

(e) The program shall include the development and provision of additional training programs for any or all of the following categories:

(1) Industries on the high hazard list.

711

(2) Hazards that result in significant worker injuries, illnesses, or compensation costs.

(3) Industries or trades where workers are experiencing numerous or significant injuries or illnesses.

(4) Occupational groups with special needs, such as those who do not speak English as their first language, workers with limited literacy, young workers, and other traditionally underserved industries or groups of workers. Priority shall be given to training workers who are able to train other workers and workers who have significant health and safety responsibilities, such as those workers serving on a health and safety committee or serving as designated safety representatives.

(f) The program shall operate one or more libraries and distribution systems of occupational safety and health training material, which shall include, but not be limited to, all material developed by the program pursuant to this section.

(g) The advisory board shall annually prepare a written report evaluating the use and impact of programs developed.

(h) The payment of administrative costs incurred by the commission in conducting the program shall be made from the Workers' Occupational Safety and Health Education Fund. *(Added by Stats.2002, c. 6 (A.B.749), § 84.)*

> *For another section of the same number, with similar subject matter and text, added by Stats. 2002, c. 866 (A.B.486), § 15, see Labor Code § 6354.7, post.*

§ 6354.7. Workers' Occupational Safety and Health Education Fund; worker safety and health training and education program

Text of section as added by Stats.2002, c. 866 (A.B.486), § 15.

(a) The Workers' Occupational Safety and Health Education Fund is hereby created as a special account in the State Treasury. Proceeds of the fund may be expended, upon appropriation by the Legislature, by the Commission on Health and Safety and Workers' Compensation for the purpose of establishing and maintaining a worker occupational safety and health training and education program and an insurance loss control services coordinator. The director shall levy and collect fees to fund these purposes from insurers subject to Section 6354.5. However, the fee assessed against any insurer shall not exceed the greater of one hundred dollars ($100) or 0.0286 percent of paid workers' compensation indemnity amounts for claims as reported for the previous calendar year to the designated rating organization for the analysis required under subdivisions (b) and (c) of Section 11759.1 of the Insurance Code. All fees shall be deposited in the fund.

(b) The commission shall establish and maintain a worker safety and health training and education program. The purpose of the worker occupational safety and health training and education program shall be to promote awareness of the need for prevention education programs, to develop and provide injury and illness prevention education programs for employees and their representatives, and to deliver those awareness and training programs through a network of providers throughout the state. The commission may conduct the program directly or by means of contracts or interagency agreements.

(c) The commission shall establish an employer and worker advisory board for the program. The advisory board shall guide the development of curricula, teaching methods, and specific course material about occupational safety and health, and shall assist in providing links to the target audience and broadening the partnerships with worker-based organizations, labor studies programs, and others that are able to reach the target audience.

(d) The program shall include the development and provision of a needed core curriculum addressing competencies for effective participation in workplace injury and illness prevention programs and on joint labor-management health and safety committees. The core curriculum shall include an overview of the requirements related to injury and illness prevention programs and hazard communication.

(e) The program shall include the development and provision of additional training programs for any or all of the following categories:

(1) Industries on the high hazard list.

(2) Hazards that result in significant worker injuries, illnesses, or compensation costs.

(3) Industries or trades in which workers are experiencing numerous or significant injuries or illnesses.

(4) Occupational groups with special needs, such as those who do not speak English as their first language, workers with limited literacy, young workers, and other traditionally underserved industries or groups of workers. Priority shall be given to training workers who are able to train other workers and workers who have significant health and safety responsibilities, such as those workers serving on a health and safety committee or serving as designated safety representatives.

(f) The program shall operate one or more libraries and distribution systems of occupational safety and health training material, which shall include, but not be limited to, all material developed by the program pursuant to this section.

(g) The advisory board shall annually prepare a written report evaluating the use and impact of programs developed.

(h) The payment of administrative costs incurred by the commission in conducting the program shall be made from the Workers' Occupational Safety and Health Education Fund. *(Added by Stats.2002, c. 866 (A.B.486), § 15.)*

> *For another section of the same number, with similar subject matter and text, added by Stats.*

2002, c. 6 (A.B.749), § 84, see Labor Code § 6354.7, ante.

§ 6355. Restriction on citations to and prosecution of employer receiving consulting service

If the employer requests or accepts consulting services offered pursuant to Section 6354, the division in providing such services at the employer's employment or place of employment shall neither institute any prosecution under Section 6423 nor issue any citations for a violation of any standard or order adopted pursuant to Chapter 6 (commencing with Section 140) of Division 1. In any instance in which the division representative providing the consulting service finds that the conditions of employment, place of employment, any work procedure, or the operation of any machine, device, apparatus, or equipment constitutes an imminent hazard or danger, within the meaning of Section 6325, to the lives, safety, or health of employees, entry therein, or the use thereof, as the case may be, shall be prohibited by the division pursuant to Section 6325. The employer shall not, however, be liable to prosecution under Section 6423, nor shall the division issue any citations or assess any civil penalties, except in any case where the employer fails to comply with the division's prohibition of entry or use, or in any case where the provisions of Section 6326 apply. *(Added by Stats.1973, c. 993, p. 1938, § 94, eff. Oct. 1, 1973. Amended by Stats.1977, c. 460, p. 1516, § 2; Stats.1993, c. 121 (A.B.110), § 70, eff. July 16, 1993.)*

§ 6356. Worker Safety Bilingual Investigative Support, Enforcement, and Training Account; establishment; funding; restrictions on funding

(a) There is hereby created, in the General Fund, the Worker Safety Bilingual Investigative Support, Enforcement, and Training Account. The moneys in the account may be expended by the department, upon appropriation by the Legislature, for the purposes of this part.

(b) The department may receive and accept a contribution of funds from an individual or private organization, including the proceeds from a judgment in a state or federal court, if the contribution is made to carry out the purposes of this part. The department shall immediately deposit the contribution in the account established by subdivision (a).

(c) The department may not receive or accept a contribution of funds under this section made from the proceeds of a judgment in a criminal action filed pursuant to Section 6423 or 6425 of the Labor Code. *(Added by Stats.2002, c. 885 (A.B.2837), § 5.)*

§ 6357. Standards for workplace ergonomics

On or before January 1, 1995, the Occupational Safety and Health Standards Board shall adopt standards for ergonomics in the workplace designed to minimize the instances of injury from repetitive motion. *(Added by Stats.1993, c. 121 (A.B.110), § 71, eff. July 16, 1993.)*

§ 6359. Legislative findings and declarations; prevention of occupational injuries and illnesses among young workers

(a) The Legislature finds and declares the following:

(1) Every year 70 adolescents die from work injuries in the United States and 200,000 are injured, 70,000 seriously enough to require hospital treatment. Most of these injuries are preventable.

(2) A recent report by the Institute of Medicine and the National Research Council has brought national attention to the need for better education and interventions to aid injury and illness prevention efforts aimed at young workers.

(3) Since 1996, the California Study Group on Young Workers' Health and Safety, consisting of 30 representatives from key agencies and organizations involved with California youth employment and education issues, including representatives from government agencies, business, labor, parent and teacher organizations, and others, has met to develop recommendations to better protect and educate California's young workers.

(4) The study group recommended the establishment of a Resource Network on Young Workers' Health and Safety, to assist in increasing the ability of young workers and their communities to identify and address workplace hazards in order to prevent young workers from becoming injured or ill on the job.

(b) It is the intent of the Legislature that the Department of Industrial Relations, the University of California, the State Department of Education, the State Department of Health Services, and the Employment Development Department cooperatively and individually conduct activities aimed at the prevention of occupational injuries and illnesses among young workers.

(c) The Department of Industrial Relations shall contract with a coordinator to establish a statewide young worker health and safety resource network. The primary function of the resource network shall be to assist in increasing the ability of young workers and their communities statewide to identify and address workplace hazards in order to prevent young workers from becoming injured or ill on the job. The network shall coordinate and augment existing outreach and education efforts and provide technical assistance, education materials and other support to schools, job training programs, employers and other organizations working to educate students and their communities about workplace health and safety and child labor laws.

(d) The resource network shall provide, and the lead center shall coordinate, services to all key groups throughout the state involved in education and protecting young workers, including, but not limited to:

(1) Teachers.

(2) Schools.

(3) Job training programs.

(4) Employers of youth.

(5) Parent groups.

(6) Youth organizations.

(7) Work permit issuers.

(e) The resource network shall be advised by a state-wide advisory group, including, but not limited to, representatives from the Department of Industrial Relations, the Commission on Health and Safety and Worker's Compensation, the University of California, the State Department of Education, the Department of Health Services, and the Employment Development Department, as well as business, labor, parents, and others experienced in working with youth doing agricultural and nonagricultural work. The advisory group shall represent diverse geographic regions of the state.

(f) This section shall be implemented subject to the availability of funding for the purposes of this section in the 2000–01 Budget Act. *(Added by Stats.2000, c. 598 (A.B.1599), § 1.)*

CHAPTER 2.5. HAZARDOUS SUBSTANCES INFORMATION AND TRAINING

Article	Section
1. General Provisions	6360
2. Definitions	6365
3. Hazardous Substances	6380
4. Duties	6390
5. Liability and Remedies	6399.5
6. Repeal [Repealed]	

ARTICLE 1. GENERAL PROVISIONS

Section
6360. Short title.
6361. Legislative findings, declarations and intent.
6362. Applicability of chapter.
6363. No requirement for development of new information.

§ 6360. Short title

This chapter shall be known and may be cited as the Hazardous Substances Information and Training Act. *(Added by Stats.1980, c. 874, p. 2735, § 1.)*

§ 6361. Legislative findings, declarations and intent

(a) The Legislature finds and declares the following:

(1) Hazardous substances in the workplace in some forms and concentrations pose potential acute and chronic health hazards to employees who are exposed to these substances.

(2) Employers and employees have a right and a need to know the properties and potential hazards of substances to which they may be exposed, and such knowledge is essential to reducing the incidence and cost of occupational disease.

(3) Employers do not always have available adequate data on the contents and properties of specific hazardous substances necessary for the provision of a safe and healthful workplace and the provision of information and training to employees as is the responsibility of the employer under existing law.

(4) Many effective employee information and training programs now exist, and with the increased availability of basic information and with the extension of such programs to all affected employees, preventable health risks in the workplace would be further reduced.

(b) The Legislature, therefore, intends by this chapter to ensure the transmission of necessary information to employees regarding the properties and potential hazards of hazardous substances in the workplace. *(Added by Stats.1980, c. 874, p. 2735, § 1.)*

§ 6362. Applicability of chapter

The rights and duties set forth in this chapter apply to all employers who use hazardous substances in this state, to any person who sells a hazardous substance to any employer in this state, and to manufacturers who produce or sell hazardous substances in this state. The provisions of this chapter apply to hazardous substances which are present in the workplace as a result of workplace operations in such a manner that employees may be exposed under normal conditions of work or in a reasonably foreseeable emergency resulting from workplace operations. For purposes of this chapter, an emergency includes, but is not limited to, equipment failure, rupture of containers, or failure of control equipment, which may or do result in a release of a hazardous substance into the workplace. *(Added by Stats.1980, c. 874, p. 2735, § 1.)*

§ 6363. No requirement for development of new information

Nothing in this chapter shall be construed to require a manufacturer or employer to conduct studies to develop new information. *(Added by Stats.1980, c. 874, p. 2735, § 1.)*

ARTICLE 2. DEFINITIONS

Section
6365. Construction of chapter.
6366. CAS number.
6367. Chemical name.
6368. Common name.
6370. Expose, exposure.
6371. Impurity.
6372. Manufacturer.
6373. Mixture.
6374. MSDS.

§ 6365. Construction of chapter

Unless the context otherwise requires, the definitions in this article and the provisions of Article 1 shall govern the construction of provisions of this chapter. *(Added by Stats.1980, c. 874, p. 2736, § 1.)*

§ 6366. CAS number

"CAS number" means the unique identification number assigned by the Chemical Abstracts Service to specific chemical substances. *(Added by Stats.1980, c. 874, p. 2736, § 1.)*

§ 6367. Chemical name

"Chemical name" is the scientific designation of a substance in accordance with the nomenclature system developed by the International Union of Pure and Applied Chemistry or the system developed by the Chemical Abstracts Service. *(Added by Stats.1980, c. 874, p. 2736, § 1.)*

§ 6368. Common name

"Common name" means any designation or identification such as code name, code number, trade name, or brand name used to identify a substance other than by its chemical name. *(Added by Stats.1980, c. 874, p. 2736, § 1.)*

§ 6370. Expose, exposure

"Expose" or "exposure" means any situation arising from work operation where an employee may ingest, inhale, absorb through the skin or eyes, or otherwise come into contact with a hazardous substance; provided, that such contact shall not be deemed to constitute exposure if the hazardous substance present is in a physical state, volume, or concentration for which it has been determined pursuant to Sections 6382 and 6390 that there is no valid and substantial evidence that any adverse acute or chronic risk to human health may occur from such contact. *(Added by Stats.1980, c. 874, p. 2736, § 1.)*

§ 6371. Impurity

"Impurity" means a hazardous substance which is unintentionally present with another substance or mixture. *(Added by Stats.1980, c. 874, p. 2736, § 1.)*

§ 6372. Manufacturer

"Manufacturer" means a person who produces, synthesizes, extracts, or otherwise makes a hazardous substance. *(Added by Stats.1980, c. 874, p. 2736, § 1.)*

§ 6373. Mixture

"Mixture" means any solution or intimate admixture of two or more substances, at least one of which is present as a hazardous substance, as designated pursuant to Sections 6382 and 6383, which do not react chemically with each other. *(Added by Stats.1980, c. 874, p. 2736, § 1.)*

§ 6374. MSDS

"MSDS" means a material safety data sheet prepared pursuant to Section 6390. A label in 8-point or larger type, prepared pursuant to Section 6390, shall constitute an MSDS for the purposes of this chapter. *(Added by Stats.1980, c. 874, p. 2736, § 1.)*

ARTICLE 3. HAZARDOUS SUBSTANCES

Section
6380. Establishment of list of hazardous substances by director; availability of list; regulations.
6380.5. Submission of list to occupational safety and health standards board for approval; additions to list; responsibilities of board; adoption as regulation.
6381. Absence of designation as a hazardous substance in adopted list; effect.
6382. Preparation and amendment of list; procedure; review.
6383. Concentration requirement for hazardous substance.
6384. Impurities developing as intermediate materials but not present in final product; inapplicability of chapter.
6385. Inapplicability of chapter.
6386. Exemption from employer or manufacturer status; technically qualified individual.

§ 6380. Establishment of list of hazardous substances by director; availability of list; regulations

For the purposes of this chapter, the director, pursuant to Section 6382, shall establish a list of hazardous substances and shall make the list available to manufacturers, employers, and the public. Substances on the list shall be designated by their chemical and common name or names. The director shall adopt, amend, and repeal regulations for the establishment of the list of hazardous substances pursuant to the provisions of Chapter 3.5 (commencing with Section 11340) of Part 1 of Division 3 of Title 2 of the Government Code. *(Added by Stats. 1980, c. 874, p. 2736, § 1.)*

§ 6380.5. Submission of list to occupational safety and health standards board for approval; additions to list; responsibilities of board; adoption as regulation

(a) Prior to the director's adoption of the list of hazardous substances, the director shall submit the list to the Occupational Safety and Health Standards Board for its approval. Within 90 days of receiving the list from the director, the board, after holding a hearing and considering the recommendations of the employers and employees who may be affected, shall do the following:

(1) Determine whether the substances listed are properly listed as hazardous substances pursuant to the criteria of Section 6382.

(2) Modify the list as necessary to achieve compliance with Section 6382.

(3) Approve the list of hazardous substances.

Upon receipt of the list approved by the board, the director shall adopt the list as a regulation pursuant to the procedures set forth in Section 6380. The inclusion or exclusion of any individual substance on the list of hazardous substances shall not be subject to Section 11346.2 or 11346.9 of the Government Code.

(b) Prior to the director's adoption of any additions to the list of hazardous substances pursuant to subdivision (c) of Section 6382, the director shall submit the additions

715

to the board for its approval. Within 60 days of receiving the additions from the director, the board, after holding a hearing and considering the recommendations of the employers and employees who may be affected, shall do the following:

(1) Determine whether the substances listed are properly listed as hazardous substances pursuant to the criteria of Section 6382.

(2) Modify the additions as necessary to achieve compliance with Section 6382.

(3) Approve the list of hazardous substances.

Upon receipt of the additions approved by the board, the director shall adopt the additions as a regulation pursuant to the procedures set forth in Section 6380. The inclusion or exclusion of any individual substance on the list of hazardous substances shall not be subject to Section 11346.2 or 11346.9 of the Government Code. *(Added by Stats.1980, c. 874, p. 2736, § 1. Amended by Stats.1995, c. 938 (S.B.523), § 78, operative Jan. 1, 1996.)*

§ 6381. Absence of designation as a hazardous substance in adopted list; effect

Substances not present on the list of hazardous substances adopted pursuant to Section 6380 shall not be subject to the provisions of this chapter. However, the absence of designation as a hazardous substance in the list adopted pursuant to Section 6380 shall not in any way affect any other liability of an employer with regard to safeguarding the health and safety of an employee or other persons exposed to a toxic or hazardous substance; nor shall it affect any other duty or responsibility of a manufacturer, producer, or other maker to warn ultimate users of a substance pursuant to other provisions of law. *(Added by Stats.1980, c. 874, p. 2736, § 1.)*

§ 6382. Preparation and amendment of list; procedure; review

The director shall prepare and amend the list of hazardous substances according to the following procedure:

(a) Any substance designated in any of the following listings in subdivision (b) shall be presumed by the director to be potentially hazardous and shall be included on the list; provided, that the director shall not list a substance or form of the substance from the listings in subdivision (b) if he or she finds, upon a showing pursuant to the procedures set forth in Section 6380, that the substance as present occupationally is not potentially hazardous to human health; and provided further, that a substance, mixture, or product shall not be considered hazardous to the extent that the hazardous substance present is in a physical state, volume, or concentration for which there is no valid and substantial evidence that any adverse acute or chronic risk to human health may occur from exposure.

(b) The listings referred to in subdivision (a) are as follows:

(1) Substances listed as human or animal carcinogens by the International Agency for Research on Cancer (IARC).

(2) Those substances designated by the Environmental Protection Agency pursuant to Section 307 (33 U.S.C. Sec. 1317) and Section 311 (33 U.S.C. Sec. 1321) of the federal Clean Water Act of 1977 (33 U.S.C. Sec. 1251 et seq.) or as hazardous air pollutants pursuant to Section 112 of the federal Clean Air Act, as amended (42 U.S.C. Sec. 7412) which have known, adverse human health risks.

(3) Substances listed by the Occupational Safety and Health Standards Board as an airborne chemical contaminant pursuant to Section 142.3.

(4) Those substances designated by the Director of Pesticide Regulation as restricted materials pursuant to Section 14004.5 of the Food and Agricultural Code which have known, adverse human health risks.

(5) Substances for which an information alert has been issued by the repository of current data established pursuant to Section 147.2.

(c) The director shall at least every two years review the listings in subdivision (b) and shall revise the list to include new substances so listed or exclude substances no longer on the listings, pursuant to the standards set forth in subdivision (a).

(d) Notwithstanding Section 6381, in addition to those substances on the director's list of hazardous substances, any substance within the scope of the federal Hazard Communication Standard (29 C.F.R. Sec. 1910.1200) is a hazardous substance subject to this chapter. *(Added by Stats.1980, c. 874, p. 2737, § 1. Amended by Stats.1985, c. 1000, § 1; Stats.1986, c. 248, § 160; Gov.Reorg.Plan No. 1 of 1991, § 149, eff. July 17, 1991.)*

§ 6382.1. Rejected

§ 6383. Concentration requirement for hazardous substance

(a) For the purposes of this chapter, a hazardous substance is present in any mixture or product if it is present in any of the following concentrations:

(1) One percent or more of the mixture or product.

(2) Two percent of the mixture or product if the hazardous substance exists as an impurity in the mixture.

(3) One-tenth of 1 percent of the mixture or product if the hazardous substance in the mixture or product is designated as a carcinogen pursuant to the Occupational Carcinogens Control Act of 1976 (Ch. 2 (commencing with Section 24200), Div. 20, H. & S.C.) or the federal Hazard Communication Standard (29 C.F.R. Sec. 1910.1200).

The director may, by regulation, raise the concentration requirement for a hazardous substance which the director finds is not hazardous at the threshold levels; and, lower the concentration requirement for a hazardous substance for which there is valid and substantial evidence that the substance is extraordinarily hazardous.

(b) The manufacturer of a hazardous substance shall notify the director of any valid evidence which indicates that the concentration requirement for a hazardous substance established pursuant to subdivision (a) is higher than what is necessary to protect employees who work with, or may be exposed to, the substance. *(Added by Stats.1980, c. 874, p. 2738, § 1. Amended by Stats.1985, c. 1000, § 2.)*

§ 6384. Impurities developing as intermediate materials but not present in final product; inapplicability of chapter

This chapter does not apply to impurities which develop as intermediate materials during chemical processing but are not present in the final product, and to which employee exposure is unlikely. *(Added by Stats. 1980, c. 874, p. 2738, § 1.)*

§ 6385. Inapplicability of chapter

The provisions of this chapter do not apply to hazardous substances contained in either of the following:

(a) Products intended for personal consumption by employees in the workplace, or consumer products packaged for distribution to, and use by, the general public.

(b) Retail food sale establishments and all other retail trade establishments, exclusive of processing and repair work areas. *(Added by Stats.1980, c. 874, p. 2738, § 1.)*

§ 6386. Exemption from employer or manufacturer status; technically qualified individual

(a) A laboratory in which a hazardous substance is used by or under the direct supervision of a technically qualified individual is not an employer or manufacturer for the purposes of this chapter.

(b) This exemption does not excuse a laboratory from any of the following duties:

(1) A laboratory employer shall ensure that labels of incoming containers of hazardous substances are not removed or defaced.

(2) A laboratory employer shall maintain any material safety data sheets that are received with incoming shipments of hazardous substances and ensure that they are readily available to laboratory employees.

(c) This exemption does not include a laboratory that primarily provides a quality control analysis for a manufacturing process or produces hazardous substances for commercial purposes.

(d) "Technically qualified individual" means a person who, because of education, training, or experience, understands the risks associated with the use of the particular hazardous substance or mixture involved, and who conveys this knowledge to employees in terms of safe work practices. *(Added by Stats.1980, c. 874, p. 2739, § 1. Amended by Stats.1985, c. 1000, § 3.)*

ARTICLE 4. DUTIES

Section
6390. Manufacturer preparation and provision to direct purchasers of MSDS; new information.
6390.5. Labeling of containers.
6391. Information provided to purchasers.
6392. Proof of compliance.
6393. Relief from obligation to provide MSDS to purchaser.
6394. Copy of MSDS provided to department.
6395. Provision of MSDS on entire product mixture instead of on each hazardous substance in it; conditions.
6396. Protection of trade secrets; disclosure of information; prohibitions.
6397. Sale by person other than manufacturer.
6398. Adoption of standard regarding employer's duties toward its employees; guidelines.
6399. Availability of MSDS to employers upon request; employee requests; responses to inquiries.
6399.1. Employer compliance with obligations to employees.
6399.2. Operative date of article.

Operative Effect

For operation of Article 4, see Labor Code § 6399.2.

§ 6390. Manufacturer preparation and provision to direct purchasers of MSDS; new information

The manufacturer of any hazardous substance listed pursuant to the provisions of Section 6380 shall prepare and provide its direct purchasers of the hazardous substance with an MSDS containing the information specified in Section 6391 which, to the best of the manufacturer's knowledge, is current, accurate, and complete, based on information then reasonably available to the manufacturer. For purposes of this section, a substance, mixture, or product shall not be considered a hazardous substance if present in a physical state, volume, or concentration for which there is no valid and substantial evidence that any adverse acute or chronic risk to human health may occur from exposure. The manufacturer shall revise an MSDS on a timely basis as appropriate to the importance of any new information which would affect the contents of the existing MSDS, and in any event within one year of such information becoming available to the manufacturer. If the new information indicates significantly increased risks to, or measures necessary to protect, employee health, as compared to those stated on the MSDS previously provided, the manufacturer shall provide such new information to persons who have purchased the product directly from the manufacturer within the last year. *(Added by Stats. 1980, c. 874, p. 2739, § 1.)*

§ 6390.5. Labeling of containers

The manufacturer, importer, and distributor of any hazardous substance, and the employer, shall label each container of a hazardous substance in a manner consistent with the federal Hazard Communication Standard (29 C.F.R. Sec. 1910.1200) and as set forth in applicable occupational safety and health standards adopted by the standards board. *(Added by Stats.1985, c. 1000, § 4.)*

§ 6391. Information provided to purchasers

The information which manufacturers shall provide to their purchasers pursuant to the provisions of Section 6390 shall include the following, if pertinent:

(a) The chemical name, any common names, and the CAS number of the hazardous substance.

(b) The hazards or other risks in the use of the hazardous substance, including all of the following:

(1) The potential for fire, explosion, and reactivity.

(2) The acute and chronic health effects or risks from exposure.

(3) The potential routes of exposure and symptoms of overexposure.

(c) The hazards or other risks of exposure to the combustion products of the hazardous substance.

(d) The proper precautions, handling practices, necessary personal protective equipment, and other safety precautions in the use of or exposure to the hazardous substance, and its combustion products.

(e) The emergency procedures for spills, fire, disposal, and first aid.

(f) A description in lay terms, if not otherwise provided, on either a separate sheet or with the body of the information specified in this section, of the specific potential health risks posed by the hazardous substance and its combustion products intended to alert any person reading the information.

(g) The month and year that the information was compiled and, for an MSDS issued after January 1, 1981, the name and address of the manufacturer responsible for preparing the information. *(Added by Stats.1980, c. 874, p. 2739, § 1. Amended by Stats.1988, c. 423, § 1.)*

§ 6392. Proof of compliance

Provision of a federal Material Safety Data Sheet or equivalent shall constitute prima facie proof of compliance with Section 6390. *(Added by Stats.1980, c. 874, p. 2740, § 1. Amended by Stats.1992, c. 1214 (A.B.2968), § 2.)*

§ 6393. Relief from obligation to provide MSDS to purchaser

The manufacturer shall be relieved of the obligation to provide a specific purchaser of a hazardous substance with an MSDS pursuant to Section 6390 if the manufacturer has a record of having provided the specific purchaser with the most current version of the MSDS, or if the product is one sold at retail and is incidentally sold to an employer or the employer's employees, in the same form, approximate amount, concentration, and manner as it is sold to consumers, and, to the seller's knowledge, employee exposure to the product is not significantly greater than the consumer exposure occurring during the

718

principal consumer use of the product. Except for products so labeled, this section does not relieve the manufacturer of the requirement to provide direct purchasers with new, revised, or later information or an MSDS pursuant to Section 6390. *(Added by Stats.1980, c. 874, p. 2740, § 1. Amended by Stats.1991, c. 274 (A.B. 1204), § 3; Stats.1992, c. 427 (A.B.3355), § 123.)*

§ 6393.1. Rejected

§ 6394. Copy of MSDS provided to department

The preparer of an MSDS shall provide the department with a copy of the MSDS on each hazardous substance it manufactures. The preparer may transmit the MSDS to the department in either paper or electronic form. In the electronic filing of an MSDS, it is the responsibility of the preparer to protect any trade secret information contained in the MSDS during transmission to the department. Upon receipt by the department of the MSDS, it is the responsibility of the department to protect any trade secret information. *(Added by Stats. 1980, c. 874, p. 2740, § 1. Amended by Stats.1999, c. 366 (A.B.184), § 1.)*

§ 6395. Provision of MSDS on entire product mixture instead of on each hazardous substance in it; conditions

(a) The manufacturer may provide the information required by Section 6390 on an entire product mixture, instead of on each hazardous substance in it, when all of the following conditions exist:

(1) Hazard test information exists on the mixture itself, or adequate information exists to form a valid judgment of the hazardous properties of the mixture itself and the MSDS indicates that the information presented and the conclusions drawn are from some source other than direct test data on the mixture itself, and that an MSDS on each constituent hazardous substance identified on the MSDS is available upon request.

(2) Provision of information on the mixture will be as effective in protecting employee health as information on the ingredients.

(3) The hazardous substances in the mixture are identified on the MSDS unless it is either unfeasible to describe all the ingredients in the mixture or the identity of the ingredients is itself a valid trade secret, in either case the reason why the hazardous substances in the mixture are not identified shall be stated on the MSDS.

(b) A single mixture MSDS may be provided for more than one formulation of a product mixture if the information provided pursuant to Section 6390 does not vary for the formulation. *(Added by Stats.1980, c. 874, p. 2740, § 1.)*

§ 6396. Protection of trade secrets; disclosure of information; prohibitions

(a) The Director of Industrial Relations shall protect from disclosure any and all trade secrets coming into his or her possession, as defined in subdivision (d) of Section 6254.7 of the Government Code, when requested in writing or by appropriate stamping or marking of documents by the manufacturer or producer of a mixture.

(b) Any information reported to or otherwise obtained by the Director of Industrial Relations, or any of his or her representatives or employees, which is exempt from disclosure under subdivision (a), shall not be disclosed to anyone except an officer or employee of the state or of the United States of America, in connection with the official duties of that officer or employee under any law for the protection of health, or to contractors with the state and their employees if in the opinion of the director the disclosure is necessary and required for the satisfactory performance of a contract for performance of work in connection with this act.

(c) Any officer or employee of the state, or former officer or employee, who by virtue of that employment or official position has obtained possession of or has access to material the disclosure of which is prohibited by this section, and who, knowing that disclosure of the material is prohibited, knowingly and willfully discloses the material in any manner to any person not entitled to receive it, is guilty of a misdemeanor. Any contractor with the state and any employee of that contractor, who has been furnished information as authorized by this section, shall be considered to be an employee of the state for purposes of this section.

(d) Information certified to by appropriate officials of the United States, as necessarily kept secret for national defense purposes, shall be accorded the full protections against disclosure as specified by that official or in accordance with the laws of the United States.

(e)(1) The director, upon his or her own initiative, or upon receipt of a request pursuant to the California Public Records Act, (Chapter 3.5 (commencing with Section 6250) of Division 7 of Title 1 of the Government Code) for the release of data submitted and designated as a trade secret by an employer, manufacturer, or producer of a mixture, shall determine whether any or all of the data so submitted are a properly designated trade secret.

(2) If the director determines that the data is not a trade secret, the director shall notify the employer, manufacturer, or producer of a mixture by certified mail.

(3) The employer, manufacturer, or producer of a mixture shall have 15 days after receipt of notification to provide the director with a complete justification and statement of the grounds on which the trade secret privilege is claimed. This justification and statement shall be submitted by certified mail.

(4) The director shall determine whether the data are protected as a trade secret within 15 days after receipt of the justification and statement, or if no justification and statement is filed, within 30 days of the original notice, and shall notify the employer or manufacturer and any party who has requested the data pursuant to the California Public Records Act of that determination by

certified mail. If the director determines that the data are not protected as a trade secret, the final notice shall also specify a date, not sooner than 15 days after the date of mailing of the final notice, when the data shall be available to the public.

(5) Prior to the date specified in the final notice, an employer, manufacturer, or producer of a mixture may institute an action in an appropriate superior court for a declaratory judgment as to whether the data are subjected to protection under subdivision (a).

(f) This section does not authorize a manufacturer to refuse to disclose information required pursuant to this chapter to the director. *(Added by Stats.1980, c. 874, p. 2741, § 1. Amended by Stats.1983, c. 142, § 112; Stats. 1995, c. 91 (S.B.975), § 109.)*

§ 6397. Sale by person other than manufacturer

(a) Any person other than a manufacturer who sells a mixture or any hazardous substance shall provide its direct purchasers of the mixture or hazardous substance at the time of sale with a copy of the most recent MSDS or equivalent information prepared and supplied to the person pursuant to either Section 6390 or subdivision (b) whenever it is foreseeable that the provisions of this chapter may apply to the purchaser.

(b) Any person who produces a mixture may, for the purposes of this section, prepare and use a mixture MSDS, subject to the provisions of Section 6395.

(c) Any person subject to the provisions of subdivision (a) shall be relieved of the obligation to provide a specific purchaser of a hazardous substance with an MSDS if he or she has a record of having provided the specific purchaser with the most recent version of the MSDS, or if the product is one sold at retail and is incidentally sold to an employer or the employer's employees, in the same form, approximate amount, concentration, and manner as it is sold to consumers, and, to the seller's knowledge, employee exposure to the product is not significantly greater than the consumer exposure occurring during the principal consumer use of the product. *(Added by Stats.1980, c. 874, p. 2742, § 1. Amended by Stats.1991, c. 274 (A.B.1204), § 4.)*

§ 6398. Adoption of standard regarding employer's duties toward its employees; guidelines

The Occupational Safety and Health Standards Board shall adopt a standard setting forth an employer's duties toward its employees under this chapter, on or before July 1, 1981, consistent with the following guidelines:

(a) An MSDS shall be available to an employee, collective bargaining representative, or the employee's physician, on a timely and reasonable basis, on substances in the workplace.

(b) Employers shall furnish employees who may be exposed to a hazardous substance with information on the contents of the MSDS for the hazardous substances or equivalent information, either in written form or through training programs, which may be generic to the extent appropriate and related to the job.

(c) Provision shall be made for employees to be informed of their rights under this chapter and under the standard to be adopted. *(Added by Stats.1980, c. 874, p. 2742, § 1.)*

§ 6399. Availability of MSDS to employers upon request; employee requests; responses to inquiries

Upon request, the manufacturer of a hazardous substance or the producer of a mixture who has produced a mixture MSDS pursuant to the provisions of subdivision (b) of Section 6397 shall make available to any employer, whose employees may be exposed to its product in the workplace, an MSDS on its product. If the employer does not already have an MSDS and has not already made written inquiry within 12 months as to whether a substance or product is subject to the requirements of this chapter or if the employer has not already made written inquiry within 6 months as to whether any new, revised, or later information has been issued for a hazardous substance, the employer shall do so within seven working days of a request to do so by an employee or employee's collective bargaining representative or physician. The employer may adopt reasonable procedures for acting upon such employee requests to avoid interruption of normal work operations. The manufacturer or the producer of a mixture MSDS pursuant to the provisions of Section 6397 shall answer such inquiries within 15 working days of their receipt, stating that the substance or product is subject to the requirements of this chapter and furnishing the most current MSDS or a statement that the MSDS is under development and the estimated completion date, or stating that it is not subject to the requirements of this chapter, with a brief explanation of why the chapter is not applicable. If an employer has not received a response from a manufacturer within 25 working days of the date the request was made, the employer shall send a copy of the request made of the manufacturer to the director with the notation that no response has been received. *(Added by Stats.1980, c. 874, p. 2743, § 1.)*

§ 6399.1. Employer compliance with obligations to employees

Compliance with regulations of the Director of Pesticide Regulation issued pursuant to Section 12981 of the Food and Agricultural Code shall be deemed compliance with the obligations of an employer toward his or her employees under this chapter. *(Added by Stats.1980, c. 874, p. 2743, § 1. Amended by Gov.Reorg.Plan No. 1 of 1991, § 150, eff. July 17, 1991.)*

§ 6399.2. Operative date of article

This article shall become operative 180 days after adoption of the initial list of hazardous substances pursuant to Article 3 (commencing with Section 6380). *(Added by Stats.1980, c. 874, p. 2743, § 1.)*

720

ARTICLE 5. LIABILITY AND REMEDIES

Section
6399.5. Enforcement.
6399.6. Provision of information to employee; effect on employer liability and responsibility.
6399.7. Retaliation for filing complaint or instituting proceeding prohibited.

§ 6399.5. Enforcement

The provisions of this chapter regarding manufacturers, employers, and persons subject to the provisions of Section 6397, shall be enforced pursuant to the provisions of this division pertaining to enforcement of standards adopted under Section 142.3. *(Added by Stats.1980, c. 874, p. 2743, § 1.)*

§ 6399.6. Provision of information to employee; effect on employer liability and responsibility

The provision of information to an employee pursuant to the provisions of this chapter shall not in any way affect any other liability of an employer with regard to safeguarding the health and safety of an employee or other persons exposed to a toxic or hazardous substance; nor shall it affect any other duty or responsibility of a manufacturer, producer, or other maker to warn ultimate users of a substance pursuant to other provisions of law. *(Added by Stats.1980, c. 874, p. 2743, § 1.)*

§ 6399.7. Retaliation for filing complaint or instituting proceeding prohibited

No person shall discharge or in any manner discriminate against, any employee because such employee has filed any complaint or has instituted, or caused to be instituted, any proceeding under or related to the provisions of this chapter, or has testified, or is about to testify, in any such proceeding, or because of the exercise of any right afforded pursuant to the provisions of this chapter on such employee's behalf or on behalf of others, nor shall any pay, seniority, or other benefits be lost for exercise of any such right. A violation of the provisions of this section shall be a violation of the provisions of Section 6310. *(Added by Stats.1980, c. 874, p. 2744, § 1.)*

ARTICLE 6. REPEAL [REPEALED]

CHAPTER 3. RESPONSIBILITIES AND DUTIES OF EMPLOYERS AND EMPLOYEES

Section
6400. Safe and healthful employment and place of employment.
6401. Duty to furnish safety devices and adopt safe practices and procedures.
6401.5. Salvage of material prohibited; demolition in progress.
6401.7. Injury prevention programs.
6402. Preventing entry into unsafe or unhealthful place.
6403. Failure to furnish safety devices or adopt safe practices and procedures.

Section
6404. Occupancy or maintenance of unsafe or unhealthful place of employment.
6404.5. Enclosed place of employment; smoking prohibition; legislative findings, declarations, and intent; uniform statewide standard; violation; penalties.
6405. Construction of unsafe or unhealthful place of employment.
6406. Unlawful acts.
6407. Compliance with standards, regulations, etc.
6408. Information for employees.
6409. Reports of occupational injuries or occupational illness by physicians; employee's report; pesticide poisoning; filing; occupational illness defined.
6409.1. Occupational injury or illness report; penalty for violation of section.
6409.1. Occupational injury or illness report; penalty for violation of section.
6409.2. Fire or police agency at accident involving employee; notice by telephone to division of occupational safety and health.
6409.3. Treatment for pesticide poisoning to not be deemed first aid treatment.
6409.5. Garment manufacturing operations; fire or safety hazards; registration; notice.
6410. Reports; time, place of filing and contents; records and reports for federal acts; state and local government employers.
6410. Reports; time, place of filing and contents; records and reports for federal acts; state and local government employers.
6410.5. Reports under this chapter; required notice.
6411. Completion of forms by employers and insurers.
6412. Information confidential; admissibility of evidence.
6413. Report; state prisoner injured during work; person to file report.
6413.2. Reports on injured prisoners; transmittal to division of occupational safety and health; recommendations to improve safety; hearings; orders, rules or regulations.
6413.5. Failure to file report on injured employee; penalty.

§ 6400. Safe and healthful employment and place of employment

(a) Every employer shall furnish employment and a place of employment that is safe and healthful for the employees therein.

(b) On multiemployer worksites, both construction and nonconstruction, citations may be issued only to the following categories of employers when the division has evidence that an employee was exposed to a hazard in violation of any requirement enforceable by the division:

(1) The employer whose employees were exposed to the hazard (the exposing employer).

(2) The employer who actually created the hazard (the creating employer).

(3) The employer who was responsible, by contract or through actual practice, for safety and health conditions on the worksite, which is the employer who had the authority for ensuring that the hazardous condition is corrected (the controlling employer).

(4) The employer who had the responsibility for actually correcting the hazard (the correcting employer).

The employers listed in paragraphs (2) to (4), inclusive, of this subdivision may be cited regardless of whether their own employees were exposed to the hazard.

(c) It is the intent of the Legislature, in adding subdivision (b) to this section, to codify existing regulations with respect to the responsibility of employers at multiemployer worksites. Subdivision (b) of this section is declaratory of existing law and shall not be construed or interpreted as creating a new law or as modifying or changing an existing law. *(Added by Stats.1973, c. 993, p. 1939, § 96, eff. Oct. 1, 1973. Amended by Stats.1999, c. 615 (A.B.1127), § 4.)*

§ 6401. Duty to furnish safety devices and adopt safe practices and procedures

Every employer shall furnish and use safety devices and safeguards, and shall adopt and use practices, means, methods, operations, and processes which are reasonably adequate to render such employment and place of employment safe and healthful. Every employer shall do every other thing reasonably necessary to protect the life, safety, and health of employees. *(Added by Stats.1973, c. 993, p. 1939, § 96, eff. Oct. 1, 1973.)*

§ 6401.5. Salvage of material prohibited; demolition in progress

No salvage of materials shall be permitted while demolition is in progress on any building, structure, falsework, or scaffold more than three stories high or the equivalent height for which a permit is required under subdivision (c) of Section 6500.

For this purpose salvage does not include removal of material from premises solely for the purpose of clearing the area to facilitate the continuation of the demolition. *(Added by Stats.1976, c. 33, p. 59, § 1, eff. March 6, 1976.)*

§ 6401.7. Injury prevention programs

(a) Every employer shall establish, implement, and maintain an effective injury prevention program. The program shall be written, except as provided in subdivision (e), and shall include, but not be limited to, the following elements:

(1) Identification of the person or persons responsible for implementing the program.

(2) The employer's system for identifying and evaluating workplace hazards, including scheduled periodic inspections to identify unsafe conditions and work practices.

(3) The employer's methods and procedures for correcting unsafe or unhealthy conditions and work practices in a timely manner.

(4) An occupational health and safety training program designed to instruct employees in general safe and healthy work practices and to provide specific instruction

with respect to hazards specific to each employee's job assignment.

(5) The employer's system for communicating with employees on occupational health and safety matters, including provisions designed to encourage employees to inform the employer of hazards at the worksite without fear of reprisal.

(6) The employer's system for ensuring that employees comply with safe and healthy work practices, which may include disciplinary action.

(b) The employer shall correct unsafe and unhealthy conditions and work practices in a timely manner based on the severity of the hazard.

(c) The employer shall train all employees when the training program is first established, all new employees, and all employees given a new job assignment, and shall train employees whenever new substances, processes, procedures, or equipment are introduced to the work-place and represent a new hazard, and whenever the employer receives notification of a new or previously unrecognized hazard. Beginning January 1, 1994, an employer in the construction industry who is required to be licensed under Chapter 9 (commencing with Section 7000) of Division 3 of the Business and Professions Code may use employee training provided to the employer's employees under a construction industry occupational safety and health training program approved by the division to comply with the requirements of subdivision (a) relating to employee training, and shall only be required to provide training on hazards specific to an employee's job duties.

(d) The employer shall keep appropriate records of steps taken to implement and maintain the program. Beginning January 1, 1994, an employer in the construction industry who is required to be licensed under Chapter 9 (commencing with Section 7000) of Division 3 of the Business and Professions Code may use records relating to employee training provided to the employer in connection with an occupational safety and health training program approved by the division to comply with the requirements of this subdivision, and shall only be required to keep records of those steps taken to implement and maintain the program with respect to hazards specific to an employee's job duties.

(e)(1) The standards board shall adopt a standard setting forth the employer's duties under this section, on or before January 1, 1991, consistent with the require-ments specified in subdivisions (a), (b), (c), and (d). The standards board, in adopting the standard, shall include substantial compliance criteria for use in evaluating an employer's injury prevention program. The board may adopt less stringent criteria for employers with few employees and for employers in industries with insignifi-cant occupational safety or health hazards.

(2) Notwithstanding subdivision (a), for employers with fewer than 20 employees who are in industries that are not on a designated list of high hazard industries and who have a workers' compensation experience modifica-tion rate of 1.1 or less, and for any employers with fewer than 20 employees who are in industries that are on a designated list of low hazard industries, the board shall adopt a standard setting forth the employer's duties under this section consistent with the requirements specified in subdivisions (a), (b), and (c), except that the standard shall only require written documentation to the extent of documenting the person or persons responsible for implementing the program pursuant to paragraph (1) of subdivision (a), keeping a record of periodic inspec-tions pursuant to paragraph (2) of subdivision (a), and keeping a record of employee training pursuant to paragraph (4) of subdivision (a). To any extent beyond the specifications of this subdivision, the standard shall not require the employer to keep the records specified in subdivision (d).

(3) The division shall establish a list of high hazard industries using the methods prescribed in Section 6314.1 for identifying and targeting employers in high hazard industries. For purposes of this subdivision, the "desig-nated list of high hazard industries" shall be the list established pursuant to this paragraph.

For the purpose of implementing this subdivision, the Department of Industrial Relations shall periodically review, and as necessary revise, the list.

(4) For the purpose of implementing this subdivision, the Department of Industrial Relations shall also estab-lish a list of low hazard industries, and shall periodically review, and as necessary revise, that list.

(f) The standard adopted pursuant to subdivision (e) shall specifically permit employer and employee occupa-tional safety and health committees to be included in the employer's injury prevention program. The board shall establish criteria for use in evaluating employer and employee occupational safety and health committees. The criteria shall include minimum duties, including the following:

(1) Review of the employer's (A) periodic, scheduled worksite inspections, (B) investigation of causes of inci-dents resulting in injury, illness, or exposure to hazardous substances, and (C) investigation of any alleged hazard-ous condition brought to the attention of any committee member. When determined necessary by the committee, the committee may conduct its own inspections and investigations.

(2) Upon request from the division, verification of abatement action taken by the employer as specified in division citations.

If an employer's occupational safety and health com-mittee meets the criteria established by the board, it shall be presumed to be in substantial compliance with para-graph (5) of subdivision (a).

(g) The division shall adopt regulations specifying the procedures for selecting employee representatives for employer-employee occupational health and safety com-mittees when these procedures are not specified in an applicable collective bargaining agreement. No employee or employee organization shall be held liable for any act or omission in connection with a health and safety committee.

(h) The employer's injury prevention program, as required by this section, shall cover all of the employer's employees and all other workers who the employer controls or directs and directly supervises on the job to the extent these workers are exposed to worksite and job assignment specific hazards. Nothing in this subdivision shall affect the obligations of a contractor or other employer that controls or directs and directly supervises its own employees on the job.

(i) When a contractor supplies its employee to a state agency employer on a temporary basis, the state agency employer may assess a fee upon the contractor to reimburse the state agency for the additional costs, if any, of including the contract employee within the state agency's injury prevention program.

(j)(1) The division shall prepare a Model Injury and Illness Prevention Program for Non–High–Hazard Employment, and shall make copies of the model program prepared pursuant to this subdivision available to employers, upon request, for posting in the workplace. An employer who adopts and implements the model program prepared by the division pursuant to this paragraph in good faith shall not be assessed a civil penalty for the first citation for a violation of this section issued after the employer's adoption and implementation of the model program.

(2) For purposes of this subdivision, the division shall establish a list of non-high-hazard industries in California. These industries, identified by their Standard Industrial Classification Codes, as published by the United States Office of Management and Budget in the Manual of Standard Industrial Classification Codes, 1987 Edition, are apparel and accessory stores (Code 56), eating and drinking places (Code 58), miscellaneous retail (Code 59), finance, insurance, and real estate (Codes 60–67), personal services (Code 72), business services (Code 73), motion pictures (Code 78) except motion picture production and allied services (Code 781), legal services (Code 81), educational services (Code 82), social services (Code 83), museums, art galleries, and botanical and zoological gardens (Code 84), membership organizations (Code 86), engineering, accounting, research, management, and related services (Code 87), private households (Code 88), and miscellaneous services (Code 89). To further identify industries that may be included on the list, the division shall also consider data from a rating organization, as defined in Section 11750.1 of the Insurance Code, the Division of Labor Statistics and Research, and all other appropriate information. The list shall be established by June 30, 1994, and shall be reviewed, and as necessary revised, biennially.

(3) The division shall prepare a Model Injury and Illness Prevention Program for Employers in Industries with Intermittent Employment, and shall determine which industries have historically utilized seasonal or intermittent employees. An employer in an industry determined by the division to have historically utilized seasonal or intermittent employees shall be deemed to have complied with the requirements of subdivision (a) with respect to a written injury prevention program if the employer adopts the model program prepared by the division pursuant to this paragraph and complies with any instructions relating thereto.

(k) With respect to any county, city, city and county, or district, or any public or quasi-public corporation or public agency therein, including any public entity, other than a state agency, that is a member of, or created by, a joint powers agreement, subdivision (d) shall not apply.

(l) Every workers' compensation insurer shall conduct a review, including a written report as specified below, of the injury and illness prevention program (IIPP) of each of its insureds with an experience modification of 2.0 or greater within six months of the commencement of the initial insurance policy term. The review shall determine whether the insured has implemented all of the required components of the IIPP, and evaluate their effectiveness. The training component of the IIPP shall be evaluated to determine whether training is provided to line employees, supervisors, and upper level management, and effectively imparts the information and skills each of these groups needs to ensure that all of the insured's specific health and safety issues are fully addressed by the insured. The reviewer shall prepare a detailed written report specifying the findings of the review and all recommended changes deemed necessary to make the IIPP effective. The reviewer shall be or work under the direction of a licensed California professional engineer, certified safety professional, or a certified industrial hygienist. *(Added by Stats.1989, c. 1369, § 10, eff. Oct. 2, 1989. Amended by Stats.1991, c. 964 (A.B.1495), § 1; Stats.1993, c. 927 (A.B.1930), § 1; Stats.1993, c. 928 (A.B.395), § 2.5; Stats.1993, c. 929 (A.B.2380), § 4; Stats.2003, c. 639 (S.B.228), § 47; Stats.2004, c. 34 (S.B.899), § 45, eff. April 19, 2004.)*

Operative Effect

Section 47 of Stats.2004, c. 34 (S.B.899) provides that "[t]he amendment, addition, or repeal of, any provision of law made by this act shall apply prospectively from the date of enactment of this act, regardless of the date of injury, unless otherwise specified, but shall not constitute good cause to reopen or rescind, alter, or amend any existing order, decision, or award of the Workers' Compensation Appeals Board."

§ 6402. Preventing entry into unsafe or unhealthful place

No employer shall require, or permit any employee to go or to be in any employment or place of employment which is not safe and healthful. *(Added by Stats.1973, c. 993, p. 1939, § 96, eff. Oct. 1, 1973.)*

§ 6403. Failure to furnish safety devices or adopt safe practices and procedures

No employer shall fail or neglect to do any of the following:

(a) To provide and use safety devices and safeguards reasonably adequate to render the employment and place of employment safe.

(b) To adopt and use methods and processes reasonably adequate to render the employment and place of employment safe.

(c) To do every other thing reasonably necessary to protect the life, safety, and health of employees. *(Added by Stats.1973, c. 993, p. 1939, § 96, eff. Oct. 1, 1973. Amended by Stats.1983, c. 142, § 113.)*

§ 6404. Occupancy or maintenance of unsafe or unhealthful place of employment

No employer shall occupy or maintain any place of employment that is not safe and healthful. *(Added by Stats.1973, c. 993, p. 1939, § 96, eff. Oct. 1, 1973.)*

§ 6404.5. Enclosed place of employment; smoking prohibition; legislative findings, declarations, and intent; uniform statewide standard; violation; penalties

(a) The Legislature finds and declares that regulation of smoking in the workplace is a matter of statewide interest and concern. It is the intent of the Legislature in enacting this section to prohibit the smoking of tobacco products in all (100 percent of) enclosed places of employment in this state, as covered by this section, thereby eliminating the need of local governments to enact workplace smoking restrictions within their respective jurisdictions. It is further the intent of the Legislature to create a uniform statewide standard to restrict and prohibit the smoking of tobacco products in enclosed places of employment, as specified in this section, in order to reduce employee exposure to environmental tobacco smoke to a level that will prevent anything other than insignificantly harmful effects to exposed employees, and also to eliminate the confusion and hardship that can result from enactment or enforcement of disparate local workplace smoking restrictions. Notwithstanding any other provision of this section, it is the intent of the Legislature that any area not defined as a "place of employment" pursuant to subdivision (d) or in which the smoking of tobacco products is not regulated pursuant to subdivision (e) shall be subject to local regulation of smoking of tobacco products.

(b) No employer shall knowingly or intentionally permit, and no person shall engage in, the smoking of tobacco products in an enclosed space at a place of employment. "Enclosed space" includes lobbies, lounges, waiting areas, elevators, stairwells, and restrooms that are a structural part of the building and not specifically defined in subdivision (d).

(c) For purposes of this section, an employer who permits any nonemployee access to his or her place of employment on a regular basis has not acted knowingly or intentionally in violation of this section if he or she has taken the following reasonable steps to prevent smoking by a nonemployee:

(1) Posted clear and prominent signs, as follows:

(A) Where smoking is prohibited throughout the building or structure, a sign stating "No smoking" shall be posted at each entrance to the building or structure.

(B) Where smoking is permitted in designated areas of the building or structure, a sign stating "Smoking is prohibited except in designated areas" shall be posted at each entrance to the building or structure.

(2) Has requested, when appropriate, that a nonemployee who is smoking refrain from smoking in the enclosed workplace.

For purposes of this subdivision, "reasonable steps" does not include (A) the physical ejection of a nonemployee from the place of employment or (B) any requirement for making a request to a nonemployee to refrain from smoking, under circumstances involving a risk of physical harm to the employer or any employee.

(d) For purposes of this section, "place of employment" does not include any of the following:

(1) Sixty-five percent of the guestroom accommodations in a hotel, motel, or similar transient lodging establishment.

(2) Areas of the lobby in a hotel, motel, or other similar transient lodging establishment designated for smoking by the establishment. An establishment may permit smoking in a designated lobby area that does not exceed 25 percent of the total floor area of the lobby or, if the total area of the lobby is 2,000 square feet or less, that does not exceed 50 percent of the total floor area of the lobby. For purposes of this paragraph, "lobby" means the common public area of an establishment in which registration and other similar or related transactions, or both, are conducted and in which the establishment's guests and members of the public typically congregate.

(3) Meeting and banquet rooms in a hotel, motel, other transient lodging establishment similar to a hotel or motel, restaurant, or public convention center, except while food or beverage functions are taking place, including setup, service, and cleanup activities, or when the room is being used for exhibit purposes. At times when smoking is not permitted in a meeting or banquet room pursuant to this paragraph, the establishment may permit smoking in corridors and prefunction areas adjacent to and serving the meeting or banquet room if no employee is stationed in that corridor or area on other than a passing basis.

(4) Retail or wholesale tobacco shops and private smokers' lounges. For purposes of this paragraph:

(A) "Private smokers' lounge" means any enclosed area in or attached to a retail or wholesale tobacco shop that is dedicated to the use of tobacco products, including, but not limited to, cigars and pipes.

(B) "Retail or wholesale tobacco shop" means any business establishment the main purpose of which is the sale of tobacco products, including, but not limited to, cigars, pipe tobacco, and smoking accessories.

(5) Cabs of motortrucks, as defined in Section 410 of the Vehicle Code, or truck tractors, as defined in Section 655 of the Vehicle Code, if no nonsmoking employees are present.

(6) Warehouse facilities. For purposes of this paragraph, "warehouse facility" means a warehouse facility with more than 100,000 square feet of total floorspace, and 20 or fewer full-time employees working at the facility, but does not include any area within a facility that is utilized as office space.

(7) Gaming clubs, in which smoking is permitted by subdivision (f). For purposes of this paragraph, "gaming club" means any gaming club, as defined in Section 19802 of the Business and Professions Code, or bingo facility, as defined in Section 326.5 of the Penal Code, that restricts access to minors under 18 years of age.

(8) Bars and taverns, in which smoking is permitted by subdivision (f). For purposes of this paragraph, "bar" or "tavern" means a facility primarily devoted to the serving of alcoholic beverages for consumption by guests on the premises, in which the serving of food is incidental. "Bar or tavern" includes those facilities located within a hotel, motel, or other similar transient occupancy establishment. However, when located within a building in conjunction with another use, including a restaurant, "bar" or "tavern" includes only those areas used primarily for the sale and service of alcoholic beverages. "Bar" or "tavern" does not include the dining areas of a restaurant, regardless of whether alcoholic beverages are served therein.

(9) Theatrical production sites, if smoking is an integral part of the story in the theatrical production.

(10) Medical research or treatment sites, if smoking is integral to the research and treatment being conducted.

(11) Private residences, except for private residences licensed as family day care homes, during the hours of operation as family day care homes and in those areas where children are present.

(12) Patient smoking areas in long-term health care facilities, as defined in Section 1418 of the Health and Safety Code.

(13) Breakrooms designated by employers for smoking, provided that all of the following conditions are met:

(A) Air from the smoking room shall be exhausted directly to the outside by an exhaust fan. Air from the smoking room shall not be recirculated to other parts of the building.

(B) The employer shall comply with any ventilation standard or other standard utilizing appropriate technology, including, but not limited to, mechanical, electronic, and biotechnical systems, adopted by the Occupational Safety and Health Standards Board or the federal Envi-

ronmental Protection Agency. If both adopt inconsistent standards, the ventilation standards of the Occupational Safety and Health Standards Board shall be no less stringent than the standards adopted by the federal Environmental Protection Agency.

(C) The smoking room shall be located in a nonwork area where no one, as part of his or her work responsibilities, is required to enter. For purposes of this subparagraph, "work responsibilities" does not include any custodial or maintenance work carried out in the breakroom when it is unoccupied.

(D) There are sufficient nonsmoking breakrooms to accommodate nonsmokers.

(14) Employers with a total of five or fewer employees, either full time or part time, may permit smoking where all of the following conditions are met:

(A) The smoking area is not accessible to minors.

(B) All employees who enter the smoking area consent to permit smoking. No one, as part of his or her work responsibilities, shall be required to work in an area where smoking is permitted. An employer who is determined by the division to have used coercion to obtain consent or who has required an employee to work in the smoking area shall be subject to the penalty provisions of Section 6427.

(C) Air from the smoking area shall be exhausted directly to the outside by an exhaust fan. Air from the smoking area shall not be recirculated to other parts of the building.

(D) The employer shall comply with any ventilation standard or other standard utilizing appropriate technology, including, but not limited to, mechanical, electronic, and biotechnical systems, adopted by the Occupational Safety and Health Standards Board or the federal Environmental Protection Agency. If both adopt inconsistent standards, the ventilation standards of the Occupational Safety and Health Standards Board shall be no less stringent than the standards adopted by the federal Environmental Protection Agency.

This paragraph shall not be construed to (i) supersede or render inapplicable any condition or limitation on smoking areas made applicable to specific types of business establishments by any other paragraph of this subdivision or (ii) apply in lieu of any otherwise applicable paragraph of this subdivision that has become inoperative.

(e) Paragraphs (13) and (14) of subdivision (d) shall not be construed to require employers to provide reasonable accommodation to smokers, or to provide breakrooms for smokers or nonsmokers.

(f)(1) Except as otherwise provided in this subdivision, smoking may be permitted in gaming clubs, as defined in paragraph (7) of subdivision (d), and in bars and taverns, as defined in paragraph (8) of subdivision (d), until the earlier of the following:

(A) January 1, 1998.

725

(B) The date of adoption of a regulation (i) by the Occupational Safety and Health Standards Board reducing the permissible employee exposure level to environmental tobacco smoke to a level that will prevent anything other than insignificantly harmful effects to exposed employees or (ii) by the federal Environmental Protection Agency establishing a standard for reduction of permissible exposure to environmental tobacco smoke to an exposure level that will prevent anything other than insignificantly harmful effects to exposed persons.

(2) If a regulation specified in subparagraph (B) of paragraph (1) is adopted on or before January 1, 1998, smoking may thereafter be permitted in gaming clubs and in bars and taverns, subject to full compliance with, or conformity to, the standard in the regulation within two years following the date of adoption of the regulation. An employer failing to achieve compliance with, or conformity to, the regulation within this two-year period shall prohibit smoking in the gaming club, bar, or tavern until compliance or conformity is achieved. If the Occupational Safety and Health Standards Board and the federal Environmental Protection Agency both adopt regulations specified in subparagraph (B) of paragraph (1) that are inconsistent, the regulations of the Occupational Safety and Health Standards Board shall be no less stringent than the regulations of the federal Environmental Protection Agency.

(3) If a regulation specified in subparagraph (B) of paragraph (1) is not adopted on or before January 1, 1998, the exemptions specified in paragraphs (7) and (8) of subdivision (d) shall become inoperative on and after January 1, 1998, until a regulation is adopted. Upon adoption of such a regulation on or after January 1, 1998, smoking may thereafter be permitted in gaming clubs and in bars and taverns, subject to full compliance with, or conformity to, the standard in the regulation within two years following the date of adoption of the regulation. An employer failing to achieve compliance with, or conformity to, the regulation within this two-year period shall prohibit smoking in the gaming club, bar, or tavern until compliance or conformity is achieved. If the Occupational Safety and Health Standards Board and the federal Environmental Protection Agency both adopt regulations specified in subparagraph (B) of paragraph (1) that are inconsistent, the regulations of the Occupational Safety and Health Standards Board shall be no less stringent than the regulations of the federal Environmental Protection Agency.

(4) From January 1, 1997, to December 31, 1997, inclusive, smoking may be permitted in gaming clubs, as defined in paragraph (7) of subdivision (d), and in bars and taverns, as defined in paragraph (8) of subdivision (d), subject to both of the following conditions:

(A) If practicable, the gaming club or bar or tavern shall establish a designated nonsmoking area.

(B) If feasible, no employee shall be required, in the performance of ordinary work responsibilities, to enter any area in which smoking is permitted.

726

(g) The smoking prohibition set forth in this section shall constitute a uniform statewide standard for regulating the smoking of tobacco products in enclosed places of employment and shall supersede and render unnecessary the local enactment or enforcement of local ordinances regulating the smoking of tobacco products in enclosed places of employment. Insofar as the smoking prohibition set forth in this section is applicable to all (100–percent) places of employment within this state and, therefore, provides the maximum degree of coverage, the practical effect of this section is to eliminate the need of local governments to enact enclosed workplace smoking restrictions within their respective jurisdictions.

(h) Nothing in this section shall prohibit an employer from prohibiting smoking in an enclosed place of employment for any reason.

(i) The enactment of local regulation of smoking of tobacco products in enclosed places of employment by local governments shall be suspended only for as long as, and to the extent that, the (100–percent) smoking prohibition provided for in this section remains in effect. In the event this section is repealed or modified by subsequent legislative or judicial action so that the (100–percent) smoking prohibition is no longer applicable to all enclosed places of employment in California, local governments shall have the full right and authority to enforce previously enacted, and to enact and enforce new, restrictions on the smoking of tobacco products in enclosed places of employment within their jurisdictions, including a complete prohibition of smoking. Notwithstanding any other provision of this section, any area not defined as a "place of employment" or in which smoking is not regulated pursuant to subdivision (d) or (e), shall be subject to local regulation of smoking of tobacco products.

(j) Any violation of the prohibition set forth in subdivision (b) is an infraction, punishable by a fine not to exceed one hundred dollars ($100) for a first violation, two hundred dollars ($200) for a second violation within one year, and five hundred dollars ($500) for a third and for each subsequent violation within one year. This subdivision shall be enforced by local law enforcement agencies, including, but not limited to, local health departments, as determined by the local governing body.

(k) Notwithstanding Section 6309, the division shall not be required to respond to any complaint regarding the smoking of tobacco products in an enclosed space at a place of employment, unless the employer has been found guilty pursuant to subdivision (j) of a third violation of subdivision (b) within the previous year.

(l) If any provision of this act or the application thereof to any person or circumstances is held invalid, that invalidity shall not affect other provisions or applications of the act that can be given effect without the invalid provision or application, and to this end the provisions of this act are severable. *(Added by Stats.1994, c. 310 (A.B.13), § 1. Amended by Stats.1995, c. 91 (S.B.975),*

§ 110; Stats.1996, c. 989 (A.B.3037), § 1; Stats.1998, c. 606 (S.B.1880), § 5; Stats.2006, c. 736 (A.B.2067), § 2.)

§ 6405. Construction of unsafe or unhealthful place of employment

No employer, owner, or lessee of any real property shall construct or cause to be constructed any place of employment that is not safe and healthful. *(Added by Stats.1973, c. 993, p. 1939, § 96, eff. Oct. 1, 1973.)*

§ 6406. Unlawful acts

No person shall do any of the following:

(a) Remove, displace, damage, destroy or carry off any safety device, safeguard, notice, or warning, furnished for use in any employment or place of employment.

(b) Interfere in any way with the use thereof by any other person.

(c) Interfere with the use of any method or process adopted for the protection of any employee, including himself, in such employment, or place of employment.

(d) Fail or neglect to do every other thing reasonably necessary to protect the life, safety, and health of employees. *(Added by Stats.1973, c. 993, p. 1939, § 96, eff. Oct. 1, 1973.)*

§ 6407. Compliance with standards, regulations, etc.

Every employer and every employee shall comply with occupational safety and health standards, with Section 25910 of the Health and Safety Code, and with all rules, regulations, and orders pursuant to this division which are applicable to his own actions and conduct. *(Added by Stats.1973, c. 993, p. 1939, § 96, eff. Oct. 1, 1973. Amended by Stats.1977, c. 62, p. 461, § 7, eff. May 18, 1977.)*

§ 6408. Information for employees

All employers shall provide information to employees in the following ways, as prescribed by authorized regulations:

(a) Posting of information regarding protections and obligations of employees under occupational safety and health laws.

(b) Posting prominently each citation issued under Section 6317, or a copy or copies thereof, at or near each place a violation referred to in the notice of violation occurred.

(c) The opportunity for employees or their representatives to observe monitoring or measuring of employee exposure to hazards conducted pursuant to standards promulgated under Section 142.3.

(d) Allow access by employees or their representatives to accurate records of employee exposures to potentially toxic materials or harmful physical agents.

(e) Notification of any employee who has been or is being exposed to toxic materials or harmful physical agents in concentrations or at levels exceeding those prescribed by an applicable standard, order, or special order, and informing any employee so exposed of corrective action being taken. *(Added by Stats.1973, c. 993, p. 1939, § 96, eff. Oct. 1, 1973.)*

§ 6409. Reports of occupational injuries or occupational illness by physicians; employee's report; pesticide poisoning; filing; occupational illness defined

(a) Every physician as defined in Section 3209.3 who attends any injured employee shall file a complete report of every occupational injury or occupational illness to the employee with the employer, or if insured, with the employer's insurer, on forms prescribed for that purpose by the Division of Labor Statistics and Research. A portion of the form shall be completed by the injured employee, if he or she is able to do so, describing how the injury or illness occurred. The form shall be filed within five days of the initial examination. Inability or failure of an injured employee to complete his or her portion of the form shall not affect the employee's rights under this code, and shall not excuse any delay in filing the form. The employer or insurer, as the case may be, shall file the physician's report with the Department of Industrial Relations, through its Division of Labor Statistics and Research, within five days of receipt. Each report of occupational injury or occupational illness shall indicate the social security number of the injured employee. If the treatment is for pesticide poisoning or a condition suspected to be pesticide poisoning, the physician shall also file a complete report, which need not include the affidavit required pursuant to this section, with the Division of Labor Statistics and Research, and within 24 hours of the initial examination shall file a complete report with the local health officer by facsimile transmission or other means. If the treatment is for pesticide poisoning or a condition suspected to be pesticide poisoning, the physician shall not be compensated for the initial diagnosis and treatment unless the report is filed with the employer, or if insured, with the employer's insurer, and includes or is accompanied by a signed affidavit which certifies that a copy of the report is filed with the local health officer pursuant to the requirements of this section.

(b) As used in this section, "occupational illness" means any abnormal condition or disorder caused by exposure to environmental factors associated with employment, including acute and chronic illnesses or diseases which may be caused by inhalation, absorption, ingestion, or direct contact. *(Added by Stats.1973, c. 993, p. 1940, § 96, eff. Oct. 1, 1973. Amended by Stats.1977, c. 1016, p. 3050, § 3; Stats.1979, c. 889, p. 3078, § 3, eff. Sept. 22, 1979; Stats.1987, c. 1019, § 5; Stats.1994, c. 667 (S.B.555), § 1.)*

§ 6409.1. Occupational injury or illness report; penalty for violation of section

Text of section prior to amendment by Stats. 2008, c. 740 (A.B.2181), § 1, operative upon adoption of regulations as specified by § 3 of that Act. See, also, text of section as amended by

727

Stats.2008, c. 740 (A.B.2181), § 1, operative upon adoption of regulations as specified by § 3 of that Act.

(a) Every employer shall file a complete report of every occupational injury or occupational illness, as defined in subdivision (b) of Section 6409, to each employee which results in lost time beyond the date of the injury or illness, or which requires medical treatment beyond first aid, with the Department of Industrial Relations, through its Division of Labor Statistics and Research or, if an insured employer, with the insurer, on a form prescribed for that purpose by the Division of Labor Statistics and Research. A report shall be filed concerning each injury and illness which has, or is alleged to have, arisen out of and in the course of employment, within five days after the employer obtains knowledge of the injury or illness. Each report of occupational injury or occupational illness shall indicate the social security number of the injured employee. In the case of an insured employer, the insurer shall file with the division immediately upon receipt, a copy of the employer's report, which has been received from the insured employer. In the event an employer has filed a report of injury or illness pursuant to this subdivision and the employee subsequently dies as a result of the reported injury or illness, the employer shall file an amended report indicating the death with the Department of Industrial Relations, through its Division of Labor Statistics and Research or, if an insured employer, with the insurer, within five days after the employer is notified or learns of the death. A copy of any amended reports received by the insurer shall be filed with the division immediately upon receipt.

(b) In every case involving a serious injury or illness, or death, in addition to the report required by subdivision (a), a report shall be made immediately by the employer to the Division of Occupational Safety and Health by telephone or telegraph. An employer who violates this subdivision may be assessed a civil penalty of not less than five thousand dollars ($5,000). Nothing in this subdivision shall be construed to increase the maximum civil penalty, pursuant to Sections 6427 to 6430, inclusive, that may be imposed for a violation of this section. *(Added by Stats.1979, c. 889, p. 3079, § 4, eff. Sept. 22, 1979. Amended by Stats.1984, c. 1317, § 9; Stats.1987, c. 1019, § 6; Stats.1990, c. 617 (S.B.2534), § 1; Stats.1992, c. 386 (S.B.1976), § 3; Stats.2002, c. 885 (A.B.2837), § 6.)*

§ 6409.1. Occupational injury or illness report; penalty for violation of section

Text of section as amended by Stats.2008, c. 740 (A.B.2181), § 1, operative upon adoption of regulations as specified by § 3 of that Act. See, also, text of section prior to amendment by Stats.2008, c. 740 (A.B.2181), § 1, operative upon adoption of regulations as specified by § 3 of that Act.

(a) Every employer shall file a complete report of every occupational injury or occupational illness, as defined in subdivision (b) of Section 6409, to each employee which results in lost time beyond the date of the injury or illness, or which requires medical treatment beyond first aid. An insured employer shall file the report with the insurer on a form prescribed by the Administrative Director of the Division of Workers' Compensation for that purpose within five days after the employer obtains knowledge of the injury or illness that has, or is alleged to have, arisen out of and in the course of employment. A self-insured employer, the state, or the insurer of an insured employer shall file the report in the electronic form prescribed for that purpose by the administrative director pursuant to Section 138.6 within the time prescribed by the administrative director. The administrative director shall ensure that the report required by this subdivision contains necessary information to continue to be acceptable as substitute documentation for purposes of recordkeeping required under the federal Occupational Safety and Health Act of 1970 (29 U.S.C. Sec. 651 et seq.). Each report of occupational injury or occupational illness shall indicate the social security number of the injured employee. In the event an employer has filed a report of injury or illness pursuant to this subdivision and the employee subsequently dies as a result of the reported injury or illness, the employer shall file an amended report indicating the death with the Department of Industrial Relations, through its Division of Workers' Compensation or, if an insured employer, with the insurer, within five days after the employer is notified or learns of the death. A copy of any amended reports received by the insurer shall be filed with the Division of Workers' Compensation in electronic form as prescribed by the administrative director.

(b) In every case involving a serious injury or illness, or death, in addition to the report required by subdivision (a), a report shall be made immediately by the employer to the Division of Occupational Safety and Health by telephone or telegraph. An employer who violates this subdivision may be assessed a civil penalty of not less than five thousand dollars ($5,000). Nothing in this subdivision shall be construed to increase the maximum civil penalty, pursuant to Sections 6427 to 6430, inclusive, that may be imposed for a violation of this section. *(Added by Stats.1979, c. 889, p. 3079, § 4, eff. Sept. 22, 1979. Amended by Stats.1984, c. 1317, § 9; Stats.1987, c. 1019, § 6; Stats.1990, c. 617 (S.B.2534), § 1; Stats.1992, c. 386 (S.B.1976), § 3; Stats.2002, c. 885 (A.B.2837), § 6; Stats. 2008, c. 740 (A.B.2181), § 1, operative contingent.)*

§ 6409.2. Fire or police agency at accident involving employee; notice by telephone to division of occupational safety and health

Whenever a state, county, or local fire or police agency is called to an accident involving an employee covered by this part in which a serious injury or illness, or death occurs, the responding agency shall immediately notify the nearest office of the Division of Occupational Safety and Health by telephone. Thereafter, the division shall immediately notify the appropriate prosecuting authority of the accident. *(Added by Stats.1979, c. 889, p. 3079, § 5, eff. Sept. 22, 1979. Amended by Stats.2002, c. 885 (A.B.2837), § 7.)*

§ 6409.3. Treatment for pesticide poisoning to not be deemed first aid treatment

In no case shall the treatment administered for pesticide poisoning or a condition suspected as pesticide poisoning be deemed to be first aid treatment. *(Added by Stats.1979, c. 889, p. 3080, § 6, eff. Sept. 22, 1979.)*

§ 6409.5. Garment manufacturing operations; fire or safety hazards; registration; notice

(a) Whenever any local public fire agency has knowledge that a place of employment where garment manufacturing operations take place contains fire or safety hazards for which fire and injury prevention measures have not been taken in accordance with local fire and life safety ordinances, the agency may notify the Division of Occupational Safety and Health. This referral shall be made only after the garment manufacturing employer has been given a reasonable amount of time to correct violations.

(b) Whenever the Division of Occupational Safety and Health has knowledge or reasonable suspicion that a place of employment where garment manufacturing operations take place contains fire or safety hazards for which fire and injury prevention measures have not been taken in accordance with local fire and life safety ordinances, the division shall notify the appropriate local public fire agency.

(c) Whenever the Division of Occupational Safety and Health receives a referral by a local public fire agency pursuant to subdivision (a) which informs the division that a place of employment where garment manufacturing operations take place is not safe or is injurious to the welfare of any employee, it shall constitute a complaint for purposes of Section 6309 and shall be investigated.

(d) Whenever a local public fire agency receives a referral by the Division of Occupational Safety and Health pursuant to subdivision (b) which informs the local public fire agency that a place of employment where garment manufacturing operations take place is not safe or is injurious to the welfare of any employee, the local public fire agency may investigate the referral at its discretion.

(e)(1) If the Division of Occupational Safety and Health acquires knowledge that the garment manufacturing employer is not currently registered, it shall notify the Division of Labor Standards Enforcement.

(2) Local public fire agencies may make referrals of individuals not registered as garment manufacturers to the Division of Labor Standards Enforcement.

(3) Whenever the Division of Labor Standards Enforcement is informed by the Division of Occupational Safety and Health or by a local public fire agency that a garment manufacturing employer is unregistered, the Division of Labor Standards Enforcement shall take measures it deems appropriate to obtain compliance. *(Added by Stats.1991, c. 7 (A.B.42), § 2, eff. Dec. 13, 1990, operative Jan. 1, 1991.)*

§ 6410. Reports; time, place of filing and contents; records and reports for federal acts; state and local government employers

Text of section prior to amendment by Stats. 2008, c. 740 (A.B.2181), § 2, operative upon adoption of regulations as specified by § 3 of that Act. See, also, text of section as amended by Stats.2008, c. 740 (A.B.2181), § 2, operative upon adoption of regulations as specified by § 3 of that Act.

The reports required by subdivision (a) of Section 6409, subdivision (a) of Section 6409.1, and Section 6413 shall be made in the form and detail and within the time limits prescribed by reasonable rules and regulations adopted by the Division of Labor Statistics and Research in accordance with Chapter 3.5 (commencing with Section 11340) of Part 1 of Division 3 of Title 2 of the Government Code.

Nothing in this chapter requiring recordkeeping and reporting by employers shall relieve the employer of maintaining records and making reports to the assistant secretary, United States Department of Labor, as required under the Federal Occupational Safety and Health Act of 1970 (P.L. 91–596).[1] The Division of Labor Statistics and Research shall prescribe and provide the forms necessary for maintenance of the required records, and the Division of Occupational Safety and Health shall enforce by citation and penalty assessment any violation of the recordkeeping requirements of this chapter.

All state and local government employers shall maintain records and make reports in the same manner and to the same extent as required of other employers by this section. *(Added by Stats.1973, c. 993, p. 1939, § 96, eff. Oct. 1, 1973. Amended by Stats.1973, c. 1067, p. 2142, § 1; Stats.1974, c. 1284, p. 2783, § 13; Stats.1979, c. 889, p. 3080, § 7, eff. Sept. 22, 1979; Stats.1983, c. 142, § 114.)*

[1] 29 U.S.C.A. §651 et seq.

§ 6410. Reports; time, place of filing and contents; records and reports for federal acts; state and local government employers

Text of section as amended by Stats.2008, c. 740 (A.B.2181), § 2, operative upon adoption of regulations as specified by § 3 of that Act. See, also, text of section prior to amendment by Stats.2008, c. 740 (A.B.2181), § 2, operative upon adoption of regulations as specified by § 3 of that Act.

The reports required by subdivision (a) of Section 6409 and Section 6413 shall be made in the form and detail and within the time limits prescribed by reasonable rules and regulations adopted by the Division of Labor Statistics and Research in accordance with Chapter 3.5 (commencing with Section 11340) of Part 1 of Division 3 of Title 2 of the Government Code.

Nothing in this chapter requiring recordkeeping and reporting by employers shall relieve the employer of maintaining records and making reports to the assistant secretary, United States Department of Labor, as required under the Federal Occupational Safety and Health Act of 1970 (P.L. 91–596) [1]. The Division of Labor Statistics and Research shall prescribe and provide the forms necessary for maintenance of the required records, and the Division of Occupational Safety and Health shall enforce by citation and penalty assessment any violation of the recordkeeping requirements of this chapter.

All state and local government employers shall maintain records and make reports in the same manner and to the same extent as required of other employers by this section. *(Added by Stats.1973, c. 993, p. 1939, § 96, eff. Oct. 1, 1973. Amended by Stats.1973, c. 1067, p. 2142, § 1; Stats.1974, c. 1284, p. 2783, § 13; Stats.1979, c. 889, p. 3080, § 7, eff. Sept. 22, 1979; Stats.1983, c. 142, § 114; Stats.2008, c. 740 (A.B.2181), § 2, operative contingent.)*

[1] 29 U.S.C.A. §651 et seq.

§ 6410.5. Reports under this chapter; required notice

The reports required by subdivision (a) of Section 6409, subdivision (a) of Section 6409.1, and Section 6413 shall contain, prominently stated, the statement set forth in Section 5401.7. *(Added by Stats.1991, c. 116 (S.B. 1218), § 34.)*

§ 6411. Completion of forms by employers and insurers

Every employer or insurer receiving forms with directions from the Division of Labor Statistics and Research to complete them shall cause them to be properly filled out so as to answer fully and correctly each question propounded therein. In case of inability to answer any such questions, a good and sufficient reason shall be given for such failure. *(Added by Stats.1973, c. 993, p. 1941, § 96, eff. Oct. 1, 1973.)*

§ 6412. Information confidential; admissibility of evidence

No report of injury or illness required by subdivision (a) of Section 6409.1 shall be open to public inspection or made public, nor shall those reports be admissible as evidence in any adversary proceeding before the Workers' Compensation Appeals Board. However, the reports required of physicians by subdivision (a) of Section 6409 shall be admissible as evidence in the proceeding, except that no physician's report shall be admissible as evidence to bar proceedings for the collection of compensation, and the portion of any physician's report completed by an employee shall not be admissible as evidence in any proceeding before the Workers' Compensation Appeals Board. *(Added by Stats.1973, c. 993, p. 1941, § 96, eff. Oct. 1, 1973. Amended by Stats.1979, c. 889, p. 3080, § 8, eff. Sept. 22, 1979; Stats.1987, c. 1019, § 7.)*

730

§ 6413. Report; state prisoner injured during work; person to file report

(a) The Department of Corrections, and every physician or surgeon who attends any injured state prisoner, shall file with the Division of Labor Statistics and Research a complete report, on forms prescribed under Sections 6409 and 6409.1, of every injury to each state prisoner, resulting from any labor performed by the prisoner unless disability resulting from such injury does not last through the day or does not require medical service other than ordinary first aid treatment.

(b) Where the injury results in death a report, in addition to the report required by subdivision (a), shall forthwith be made by the Department of Corrections to the Division of Labor Statistics and Research by telephone or telegraph.

(c) Except as provided in Section 6304.2, nothing in this section or in this code shall be deemed to make a prisoner an employee, for any purpose, of the Department of Corrections.

(d) Notwithstanding subdivision (a), no physician or surgeon who attends any injured state prisoner outside of a Department of Corrections institution shall be required to file the report required by subdivision (a), but the Department of Corrections shall file the report. *(Added by Stats.1973, c. 1067, p. 2142, § 2. Amended by Stats. 1977, c. 1215, p. 4092, § 4; Stats.1979, c. 889, p. 3080, § 9, eff. Sept. 22, 1979; Stats.1983, c. 142, § 115; Stats.1992, c. 386 (S.B.1976), § 4.)*

§ 6413.2. Reports on injured prisoners; transmittal to division of occupational safety and health; recommendations to improve safety; hearings; orders, rules or regulations

(a) The Division of Labor Statistics and Research shall, within five working days of their receipt, transmit to the Division of Occupational Safety and Health copies of all reports received by the Division of Labor Statistics and Research pursuant to Section 6413.

(b) With regard to any report required by Section 6413, the Division of Occupational Safety and Health may make recommendations to the Department of Corrections of ways in which the department might improve the safety of the working conditions and work areas of state prisoners, and other safety matters. The Department of Corrections shall not be required to comply with these recommendations.

(c) With regard to any report required by Section 6413, the Division of Occupational Safety and Health may, in any case in which the Department of Corrections has not complied with recommendations made by the division pursuant to subdivision (b), or in any other case in which the division deems the safety of any state prisoner shall require it, conduct hearings and, after these hearings, adopt special orders, rules, or regulations or otherwise proceed as authorized in Chapter 1 (commencing with Section 6300) of this part as it deems necessary. The Department of Corrections shall comply with any order, rule, or regulation so adopted by the Division of Occupational Safety and Health. *(Added by Stats.1973, c. 1067, p. 2143, § 3. Amended by Stats.1980, c. 676, p. 1978, § 237.)*

§ 6413.5. Failure to file report on injured employee; penalty

Any employer or physician who fails to comply with any provision of subdivision (a) of Section 6409, or Section 6409.1, 6409.2, 6409.3, or 6410 may be assessed a civil penalty of not less than fifty dollars ($50) nor more than two hundred dollars ($200) by the director or his or her designee if he or she finds a pattern or practice of violations, or a willful violation of any of these provisions. Penalty assessments may be contested in the manner provided in Section 3725. Penalties assessed pursuant to this section shall be deposited in the General Fund. *(Added by Stats.1973, c. 1067, p. 2143, § 4. Amended by Stats.1979, c. 889, p. 3081, § 10, eff. Sept. 22, 1979; Stats.1983, c. 1092, § 219, eff. Sept. 27, 1983, operative Jan. 1, 1984; Stats.1987, c. 1019, § 8.)*

CHAPTER 4. PENALTIES

Section
6423.   Misdemeanors; penalties.
6425.   Violation causing death or impairment of body of employee; punishment.
6426.   False statement, representation or certification; punishment.
6427.   Minor violation; civil penalty.
6428.   Serious violation; civil penalty.
6428.5.   Injury prevention program; criteria for substantial compliance.
6429.   Willful or repeated violations; civil penalties.
6430.   Failure to correct violation in time; civil penalty.
6431.   Violation of posting requirements; civil penalty.
6432.   Serious violation; substantial probability.
6433.   Civil penalties not criminal penalties.
6434.   Educational entities and institutions; assessed civil or administrative penalties; deposit; refund; allocation of funds.
6434.5.   Public police or city, county, or special district fire department or the California Department of Forestry and Fire Protection; assessed civil or administrative penalties; deposit; refund; allocation of funds.
6435.   Civil penalties for violation of permit requirements; operability of section.
6436.   Criminal complaints for failure to check for asbestos materials; payment of penalties.

§ 6423. Misdemeanors; penalties

(a) Except where another penalty is specifically provided, every employer and every officer, management official, or supervisor having direction, management, control, or custody of any employment, place of employment, or of any other employee, who does any of the following is guilty of a misdemeanor:

(1) Knowingly or negligently violates any standard, order, or special order, or any provision of this division, or of any part thereof in, or authorized by, this part the violation of which is deemed to be a serious violation pursuant to Section 6432.

(2) Repeatedly violates any standard, order, or special order, or provision of this division, or any part thereof in, or authorized by, this part, which repeated violation creates a real and apparent hazard to employees.

(3) Knowingly fails to report to the division a death, as required by subdivision (b) of Section 6409.1.

(4) Fails or refuses to comply, after notification and expiration of any abatement period, with any such standard, order, special order, or provision of this division, or any part thereof, which failure or refusal creates a real and apparent hazard to employees.

(5) Directly or indirectly, knowingly induces another to commit any of the acts in paragraph (1), (2), (3), or (4) of subdivision (a).

(b) Any violation of paragraph (1) of subdivision (a) is punishable by imprisonment in the county jail for a period not to exceed six months, or by a fine not to exceed five thousand dollars ($5,000), or by both that imprisonment and fine.

(c) Any violation of paragraph (3) of subdivision (a) is punishable by imprisonment in county jail for up to one year, or by a fine not to exceed fifteen thousand dollars ($15,000), or by both that imprisonment and fine. If the violator is a corporation or a limited liability company, the fine prescribed by this subdivision may not exceed one hundred fifty thousand dollars ($150,000).

(d) Any violation of paragraph (2), (4), or (5) of subdivision (a) is punishable by imprisonment in a county jail for a term not exceeding one year, or by a fine not exceeding fifteen thousand dollars ($15,000), or by both that imprisonment and fine. If the defendant is a corporation or a limited liability company, the fine may not exceed one hundred fifty thousand dollars ($150,000).

(e) In determining the amount of fine to impose under this section, the court shall consider all relevant circumstances, including, but not limited to, the nature, circumstance, extent, and gravity of the violation, any prior history of violations by the defendant, the ability of the defendant to pay, and any other matters the court determines the interests of justice require. *(Added by Stats.1973, c. 993, p. 1941, § 98, eff. Oct. 1, 1973. Amended by Stats.1976, c. 1125, p. 5034, § 13.6; Stats. 1999, c. 615 (A.B.1127), § 5; Stats.2002, c. 885 (A.B. 2837), § 8.)*

§ 6425. Violation causing death or impairment of body of employee; punishment

(a) Any employer and any employee having direction, management, control, or custody of any employment, place of employment, or of any other employee, who willfully violates any occupational safety or health standard, order, or special order, or Section 25910 of the Health and Safety Code, and that violation caused death to any employee, or caused permanent or prolonged impairment of the body of any employee, is guilty of a public offense punishable by imprisonment in a county jail for a term not exceeding one year, or by a fine not exceeding one hundred thousand dollars ($100,000), or by both that imprisonment and fine; or by imprisonment in the state prison for 16 months, or two or three years, or by a fine of not more than two hundred fifty thousand dollars ($250,000), or by both that imprisonment and fine; and in either case, if the defendant is a corporation or a limited liability company, the fine may not exceed one million five hundred thousand dollars ($1,500,000).

(b) If the conviction is for a violation committed within seven years after a conviction under subdivision (b), (c), or (d) of Section 6423 or subdivision (c) of Section 6430, punishment shall be by imprisonment in state prison for a term of 16 months, two, or three years, or by a fine not exceeding two hundred fifty thousand dollars ($250,000), or by both that fine and imprisonment, but if the defendant is a corporation or limited liability company, the fine may not be less than five hundred thousand dollars ($500,000) or more than two million five hundred thousand dollars ($2,500,000).

(c) If the conviction is for a violation committed within seven years after a first conviction of the defendent for any crime involving a violation of subdivision (a), punishment shall be by imprisonment in the state prison for two, three, or four years, or by a fine not exceeding two hundred fifty thousand dollars ($250,000), or by both that fine and imprisonment, but if the defendant is a corporation or a limited liability company, the fine shall not be less than one million dollars ($1,000,000) but may not exceed three million five hundred thousand dollars ($3,500,000).

(d) In determining the amount of fine to be imposed under this section, the court shall consider all relevant circumstances, including, but not limited to, the nature, circumstance, extent, and gravity of the violation, any prior history of violations by the defendant, the ability of the defendant to pay, and any other matters the court determines the interests of justice require.

(e) As used in this section, "willfully" has the same definition as it has in Section 7 of the Penal Code. This subdivision is intended to be a codification of existing law.

(f) This section does not prohibit a prosecution under Section 192 of the Penal Code. *(Added by Stats.1973, c. 993, p. 1942, § 98, eff. Oct. 1, 1973. Amended by Stats.1977, c. 62, p. 461, § 8, eff. May 18, 1977; Stats.1990, c. 1384 (A.B.1675), § 1; Stats.1991, c. 599 (A.B.1545), § 2, eff. Oct. 7, 1991; Stats.1999, c. 615 (A.B.1127), § 6.)*

§ 6426. False statement, representation or certification; punishment

Whoever knowingly makes any false statement, representation, or certification in any application, record, report, plan, or other document filed or required to be maintained pursuant to this division shall, upon conviction, be punished by a fine of not more than seventy thousand dollars ($70,000), or by imprisonment for not more than six months, or by both. *(Added by Stats.1973,*

c. 993, p. 1942, § 98, eff. Oct. 1, 1973. Amended by Stats.1991, c. 599 (A.B.1545), § 3, eff. Oct. 7, 1991.)

§ 6427. Minor violation; civil penalty

Any employer who violates any occupational safety or health standard, order, or special order, or Section 25910 of the Health and Safety Code, and the violation is specifically determined not to be of a serious nature, may be assessed a civil penalty of up to seven thousand dollars ($7,000) for each violation. *(Added by Stats.1973, c. 993, p. 1942, § 98, eff. Oct. 1, 1973. Amended by Stats.1977, c. 62, p. 462, § 9, eff. May 18, 1977; Stats.1989, c. 1369, § 11, eff. Oct. 2, 1989; Stats.1991, c. 599 (A.B.1545), § 4, eff. Oct. 7, 1991; Stats.1993, c. 928 (A.B.395), § 3.)*

§ 6428. Serious violation; civil penalty

Any employer who violates any occupational safety or health standard, order, or special order, or Section 25910 of the Health and Safety Code, if that violation is a serious violation, shall be assessed a civil penalty of up to twenty-five thousand dollars ($25,000) for each violation. Employers who do not have an operative injury prevention program shall receive no adjustment for good faith of the employer or history of previous violations as provided in paragraphs (3) and (4) of subdivision (c) of Section 6319. *(Added by Stats.1973, c. 993, p. 1942, § 98, eff. Oct. 1, 1973. Amended by Stats.1977, c. 62, p. 462, § 10, eff. May 18, 1977; Stats.1983, c. 1088, § 1; Stats.1989, c. 1369, § 12, eff. Oct. 2, 1989; Stats.1991, c. 599 (A.B.1545), § 5, eff. Oct. 7, 1991; Stats.1999, c. 615 (A.B.1127), § 7.)*

§ 6428.5. Injury prevention program; criteria for substantial compliance

An employer's injury prevention program shall be deemed to be operative for the purposes of Sections 6427 and 6428 if it meets the criteria for substantial compliance established by the standards board pursuant to Section 6401.7. *(Added by Stats.1989, c. 1369, § 13, eff. Oct. 2, 1989.)*

§ 6429. Willful or repeated violations; civil penalties

(a) Any employer who willfully or repeatedly violates any occupational safety or health standard, order, or special order, or Section 25910 of the Health and Safety Code, may be assessed a civil penalty of not more than seventy thousand dollars ($70,000) for each violation, but in no case less than five thousand dollars ($5,000) for each willful violation.

(b) Any employer who repeatedly violates any occupational safety or health standard, order, or special order, or Section 25910 of the Health and Safety Code, shall not receive any adjustment of a penalty assessed pursuant to this section on the basis of the regulations promulgated pursuant to subdivision (c) of Section 6319 pertaining to the good faith of the employer or the history of previous violations of the employer.

(c) The division shall preserve and maintain records of its investigations and inspections and citations for a period of not less than seven years. *(Added by Stats.1973, c. 993, p. 1942, § 98, eff. Oct. 1, 1973. Amended by Stats.1977, c. 62, p. 462, § 11, eff. May 18, 1977; Stats. 1983, c. 1088, § 2; Stats.1991, c. 599 (A.B.1545), § 6, eff. Oct. 7, 1991; Stats.1999, c. 615 (A.B.1127), § 8; Stats 2000, c. 135 (A.B.2539), § 128.)*

§ 6430. Failure to correct violation in time; civil penalty

(a) Any employer who fails to correct a violation of any occupational safety or health standard, order, or special order, or Section 25910 of the Health and Safety Code, within the period permitted for its correction shall be assessed a civil penalty of not more than fifteen thousand dollars ($15,000) for each day during which the failure or violation continues.

(b) Notwithstanding subdivision (a), for any employer who submits a signed statement affirming compliance with the abatement terms pursuant to Section 6320, and is found upon a reinspection not to have abated the violation, any adjustment to the civil penalty based on abatement shall be rescinded and the additional civil penalty assessed for failure to abate shall not be adjusted for good faith of the employer or history of previous violations as provided in paragraphs (3) and (4) of subdivision (c) of Section 6319.

(c) Notwithstanding subdivision (a), any employer who submits a signed statement affirming compliance with the abatement terms pursuant to subdivision (b) of Section 6320, and is found not to have abated the violation, is guilty of a public offense punishable by imprisonment in a county jail for a term not exceeding one year, or by a fine not exceeding thirty thousand dollars ($30,000), or by both that fine and imprisonment; but if the defendant is a corporation or a limited liability company the fine shall not exceed three hundred thousand dollars ($300,000). In determining the amount of the fine to be imposed under this section, the court shall consider all relevant circumstances, including, but not limited to, the nature, circumstance, extent, and gravity of the violation, any prior history of violations by the defendant, the ability of the defendant to pay, and any other matters the court determines the interests of justice require. Nothing in this section shall be construed to prevent prosecution under any law that may apply. *(Added by Stats.1973, c. 993, p. 1942, § 98, eff. Oct. 1, 1973. Amended by Stats.1977, c. 62, p. 462, § 12, eff. May 18, 1977; Stats. 1983, c. 1088, § 3; Stats.1989, c. 1369, § 14, eff. Oct. 2, 1989; Stats.1991, c. 599 (A.B.1545), § 7, eff. Oct. 7, 1991; Stats.1999, c. 615 (A.B.1127), § 9.)*

§ 6431. Violation of posting requirements; civil penalty

Any employer who violates any of the posting or recordkeeping requirements as prescribed by regulations adopted pursuant to Sections 6408 and 6410, or who fails to post any notice required by Section 3550, shall be assessed a civil penalty of up to seven thousand dollars ($7,000) for each violation. *(Added by Stats.1973, c. 993, p. 1941, § 98, eff. Oct. 1, 1973. Amended by Stats.1974, c.*

1284, p. 2784, § 14; Stats.1987, c. 1019, § 9; Stats.1991, c. 599 (A.B.1545), § 8, eff. Oct. 7, 1991.)*

§ 6432. Serious violation; substantial probability

(a) As used in this part, a "serious violation" shall be deemed to exist in a place of employment if there is a substantial probability that death or serious physical harm could result from a violation, including, but not limited to, circumstances where there is a substantial probability that either of the following could result in death or great bodily injury:

(1) A serious exposure exceeding an established permissible exposure limit.

(2) The existence of one or more practices, means, methods, operations, or processes which have been adopted or are in use, in the place of employment.

(b) Notwithstanding subdivision (a), a serious violation shall not be deemed to exist if the employer can demonstrate that it did not, and could not with the exercise of reasonable diligence, know of the presence of the violation.

(c) As used in this section, "substantial probability" refers not to the probability that an accident or exposure will occur as a result of the violation, but rather to the probability that death or serious physical harm will result assuming an accident or exposure occurs as a result of the violation. *(Added by Stats.1973, c. 993, p. 1942, § 98, eff. Oct. 1, 1973. Amended by Stats.1984, c. 1317, § 10; Stats.1990, c. 1384 (A.B.1675), § 2; Stats.1999, c. 615 (A.B.1127), § 10.)*

§ 6433. Civil penalties not criminal penalties

The civil penalties set forth in Sections 6427 to 6431, inclusive, shall not be considered as other penalties specifically provided within the meaning of Section 6423. *(Added by Stats.1973, c. 993, p. 1943, § 98, eff. Oct. 1, 1973.)*

§ 6434. Educational entities and institutions; assessed civil or administrative penalties; deposit; refund; allocation of funds

(a) Any civil or administrative penalty assessed pursuant to this chapter against a school district, county board of education, county superintendent of schools, charter school, community college district, California State University, University of California, or joint powers agency performing education functions shall be deposited with the Workplace Health and Safety Revolving Fund established pursuant to Section 78.

(b) Any school district, county board of education, county superintendent of schools, charter school, community college district, California State University, University of California, or joint powers agency performing education functions may apply for a refund of their civil penalty, with interest, if all conditions previously cited have been abated, they have abated any other outstanding citation, and if they have not been cited by the division for a serious violation at the same school within two years of

733

the date of the original violation. Funds not applied for within two years and six months of the time of the original violation shall be expended as provided for in Section 78 to assist schools in establishing effective occupational injury and illness prevention programs. *(Added by Stats. 1973, c. 993, p. 1943, § 98, eff. Oct. 1, 1973. Amended by Stats.1978, c. 759, p. 2372, § 2; Stats.1991, c. 599 (A.B. 1545), § 9, eff. Oct. 7, 1991; Stats.1999, c. 615 (A.B.1127), § 11; Stats.2000, c. 135 (A.B.2539), § 129.)*

§ 6434.5. Public police or city, county, or special district fire department or the California Department of Forestry and Fire Protection; assessed civil or administrative penalties; deposit; refund; allocation of funds

(a) Any civil or administrative penalty assessed pursuant to this chapter against a public police or city, county, or special district fire department or the California Department of Forestry and Fire Protection shall be deposited into the Workers' Compensation Administration Revolving Fund established pursuant to Section 62.5.

(b) Any public police or city, county, or special district fire department or the California Department of Forestry and Fire Protection may apply for a refund of any civil or administrative penalty assessed pursuant to this chapter, with interest, if all conditions previously cited have been abated, the department has abated any other outstanding citation, and the department has not been cited by the division for a serious violation within two years of the date of the original violation. Funds received as a result of a penalty, for which a refund is not applied for within two years and six months of the time of the original violation, shall be expended in accordance with Section 78 as follows:

(1) Funds received as a result of a civil or administrative penalty imposed on a city, county, or special district fire department or the California Department of Forestry and Fire Protection shall be allocated to the California Firefighter Joint Apprenticeship Program for the purpose of establishing and maintaining effective occupational injury and illness prevention programs.

(2) Funds received as a result of a civil or administrative penalty imposed on a police department shall be allocated to the Office of Criminal Justice Planning, or any succeeding agency, for the purpose of establishing and maintaining effective occupational injury and illness prevention programs.

(c) This section does not apply to that portion of any civil or administrative penalty that is distributed directly to an aggrieved employee or employees pursuant to the provisions of Section 2699. *(Added by Stats.2005, c. 141 (A.B.186), § 1.)*

§ 6435. Civil penalties for violation of permit requirements; operability of section

(a) Any employer who violates any of the requirements of Chapter 6 (commencing with Section 6500) of

this part shall be assessed a civil penalty under the appropriate provisions of Sections 6427 to 6430, inclusive.

(b) This section shall become inoperative on January 1, 1987, and shall remain inoperative until January 1, 1991, at which time it shall become operative, unless a later enacted statute, which becomes effective on or before January 1, 1991, deletes or extends that date. *(Added by Stats.1973, c. 993, p. 1943, § 98, eff. Oct. 1, 1973. Amended by Stats.1986, c. 1178, § 3.)*

§ 6436. Criminal complaints for failure to check for asbestos materials; payment of penalties

The criminal complaint regarding a violation of Section 6505.5 may be brought by the Attorney General or by the district attorney or prosecuting attorney of any city, in the superior court of any county in the state with jurisdiction over the contractor or employer, by reason of the contractor's or employer's act or failure to act within that county. Any penalty assessed by the court shall be paid to the office of the prosecutor bringing the complaint, but if the case was referred to the prosecutor by the division, or some other governmental unit, one-half of the civil or criminal penalty assessed shall be paid to that governmental unit. *(Added by Stats.1985, c. 1587, § 8, eff. Oct. 2, 1985. Amended by Stats.1986, c. 1451, § 9, eff. Sept. 30, 1986; Stats.2003, c. 449 (A.B.1712), § 30.)*

CHAPTER 5. TEMPORARY VARIANCES

Section
6450. Application; grounds; order; renewal.
6451. Contents of application.
6452. Authority to grant temporary variance.
6454. Rules and regulations.
6455. Appeal to standards board.
6456. Effect of decision; judicial review.
6457. Hearings; finality of decision.

§ 6450. Application; grounds; order; renewal

(a) Any employer may apply to the division for a temporary order granting a variance from an occupational safety or health standard. Such temporary order shall be granted only if the employer files an application which meets the requirements of Section 6451, and establishes that (1) he is unable to comply with a standard by its effective date because of unavailability of professional or technical personnel or of materials and equipment needed to come into compliance with the standard or because necessary construction or alteration of facilities cannot be completed by the effective date, (2) he is taking all available steps to safeguard his employees against the hazards covered by the standard, and (3) he has an effective program for coming into compliance with the standard as quickly as practicable.

(b) Any temporary order issued under this section shall prescribe the practices, means, methods, operations, and processes which the employer must adopt and use while the order is in effect and state in detail his program for coming into compliance with the standard. Such a temporary order may be granted only after notice to employees and an opportunity for a hearing. However, the division may issue one interim order for a temporary variance upon submission of an application showing that the employment or place of employment will be safe for employees pending a hearing on the application for a temporary variance. No temporary order may be in effect for longer than the period needed by the employer to achieve compliance with the standard or one year, whichever is shorter, except that such an order may be renewed not more than twice provided that the requirements of this section are met and an application for renewal is filed prior to the expiration date of the order. No single renewal of an order may remain in effect for longer than 180 days. *(Added by Stats.1973, c. 993, p. 1943, § 99, eff. Oct. 1, 1973.)*

§ 6451. Contents of application

An application for a temporary order under Section 6450 shall contain all of the following:

(a) A specification of the standard or portion thereof from which the employer seeks a variance.

(b) A representation by the employer, supported by representations from qualified persons having firsthand knowledge of the facts represented, that he is unable to comply with the standard or portion thereof and a detailed statement of the reasons therefor.

(c) A statement of the steps he has taken and will take, with specific dates, to protect employees against the hazard covered by the standard.

(d) A statement of when he expects to be able to comply with the standard and what steps he has taken and what steps he will take, with dates specified, to come into compliance with the standard.

(e) A certification that he has informed his employees of the application by giving a copy thereof to their authorized representative, posting a statement giving a summary of the application and specifying where a copy may be examined at the place or places where notices to employees are normally posted, and by other appropriate means. A description of how employees have been informed shall be contained in the certification. The information to employees shall also inform them of their right to petition the division for a hearing. *(Added by Stats.1973, c. 993, p. 1943, § 99, eff. Oct. 1, 1973.)*

§ 6452. Authority to grant temporary variance

The division is authorized to grant a temporary variance from any standard or portion thereof whenever it determines such variance is necessary to permit an employer to participate in an experiment approved by the director designed to demonstrate or validate new and improved techniques to safeguard the health or safety of workers. *(Added by Stats.1973, c. 993, p. 1944, § 99, eff. Oct. 1, 1973.)*

§ 6454. Rules and regulations

The division may, in accordance with Chapter 3.5 (commencing with Section 11340) of Part 1 of Division 3 of Title 2 of the Government Code, make such rules and regulations as are reasonably necessary to carry out the provisions of this chapter and to establish rules and regulations relating to the granting or denial of temporary variances. *(Added by Stats.1973, c. 993, p. 1944, § 99, eff. Oct. 1, 1973. Amended by Stats.1983, c. 142, § 116.)*

§ 6455. Appeal to standards board

Any employer or other person adversely affected by the granting or denial of a temporary variance may appeal to the standards board within 15 working days from receipt of the notice granting or denying the variance. The 15-day period may be extended by the standards board for good cause. *(Added by Stats.1973, c. 993, p. 1944, § 99, eff. Oct. 1, 1973.)*

§ 6456. Effect of decision; judicial review

A decision of the standards board on a variance appeal is binding on the director and the division with respect to the parties involved in the particular appeal. The director shall have the right to seek judicial review of a standards board decision irrespective of whether he appeared or participated in the appeal to the standards board. *(Added by Stats.1973, c. 993, p. 1944, § 99, eff. Oct. 1, 1973.)*

§ 6457. Hearings; finality of decision

The standards board shall conduct hearings and render decisions on appeals of decisions of the division relating to allowance or denial of temporary variances. All board decisions on such variance appeals shall be in writing and shall be final except for any rehearing or judicial review. *(Added by Stats.1973, c. 993, p. 1945, § 99, eff. Oct. 1, 1973.)*

CHAPTER 6 PERMIT REQUIREMENTS

Section
6500.   Types of employment requiring permits.
6501.   Application.
6501.5.   Asbestos-related work; registration; application; requirements; enforcement; regulation concerning asbestos-related work.
6501.7.   Asbestos defined.
6501.8.   Definitions; asbestos-related work; asbestos containing construction material.
6501.9.   Determination of presence of asbestos.
6502.   Issuance.
6503.   Safety conference.
6503.5.   Safety conference for asbestos handling jobs.
6504.   Posting.
6505.   Revocation.
6505.5.   Revocation or suspension of asbestos-related work registration; failure to determine if asbestos is present; penalties; defense.
6506.   Denial or revocation of permit; appeal to director; stay.
6507.   Fee.

Section

6508.   Entities exempt.

6508.5. No exemption from registration; no registration fees for public agencies.

6509.   Violations of chapter; misdemeanor.

6509.5. Asbestos consultants; inspection with knowledge of report being required as condition for loan or permit concerning the property; performance of corrective work; violations; offense.

6510.   Violations of chapter; injunctions.

§ 6500. Types of employment requiring permits

(a) For those employments or places of employment that by their nature involve a substantial risk of injury, the division shall require the issuance of a permit prior to the initiation of any practices, work, method, operation, or process of employment. The permit requirement of this section is limited to employment or places of employment that are any of the following:

(1) Construction of trenches or excavations that are five feet or deeper and into which a person is required to descend.

(2) The construction of any building, structure, false-work, or scaffolding more than three stories high or the equivalent height.

(3) The demolition of any building, structure, false-work, or scaffold more than three stories high or the equivalent height.

(4) The underground use of diesel engines in work in mines and tunnels.

This subdivision does not apply to motion picture, television, or theater stages or sets, including, but not limited to, scenery, props, backdrops, flats, greenbeds, and grids.

(b) On or after January 1, 2000, this subdivision shall apply to motion picture, television, or theater stages or sets, if there has occurred within any one prior calendar year in any combination at separate locations three serious injuries, fatalities, or serious violations related to the construction or demolition of sets more than 36 feet in height for the motion picture, television, and theatrical production industry.

An annual permit shall be required for employers who construct or dismantle motion picture, television, or theater stages or sets that are more than three stories or the equivalent height. A single permit shall be required under this subdivision for each employer, regardless of the number of locations where the stages or sets are located. An employer with a currently valid annual permit issued under this subdivision shall not be required to provide notice to the division prior to commencement of any work activity authorized by the permit. The division may adopt procedures to permit employers to renew by mail the permits issued under this subdivision. For purposes of this subdivision, "motion picture, television, or theater stages or sets" include, but are not limited to, scenery, props, backdrops, flats, greenbeds, and grids. *(Added by Stats.1973, c. 993, p. 1945, § 100, eff. Oct. 1,*

736

1973.   Amended by Stats.1983, c. 142, § 117; Stats.1986, c. 1178, § 4; Stats.1996, c. 664 (S.B.987), § 1; Stats.1997, c. 17 (S.B.947), § 92.)

§ 6501. Application

Any employer subject to Section 6500 shall apply to the division for a permit pursuant to Section 6500. Such application for a permit shall contain such information as the division may deem necessary to evaluate the safety of the proposed employment or place of employment.

An application by an employer shall include a provision that the applicant has knowledge of applicable occupational safety and health standards and will comply with such standards and any other lawful order of the division. *(Added by Stats.1973, c. 993, p. 1945, § 100, eff. Oct. 1, 1973.)*

§ 6501.5. Asbestos-related work; registration; application; requirements; enforcement; regulation concerning asbestos-related work

Effective January 1, 1987, any employer or contractor who engages in asbestos-related work, as defined in Section 6501.8, and which involves 100 square feet or more of surface area of asbestos-containing material, shall register with the division.

The division may grant registration based on a determination that the employer has demonstrated evidence that the conditions, practices, means, methods, operations, or processes used, or proposed to be used, will provide a safe and healthful place of employment. This section is not intended to supersede existing laws and regulations under Title 8, California Administrative Code, Section 5208.

An application for registration shall contain such information and attachments, given under penalty of perjury, as the division may deem necessary to evaluate the safety and health of the proposed employment or place of employment. It shall include, but not be limited to, all of the following:

(a) Every employer shall meet each of the following criteria:

(1) If the employer is a contractor, the contractor shall be certified pursuant to Section 7058.5 of the Business and Professions Code.

(2) Provide health insurance coverage to cover the entire cost of medical examinations and monitoring required by law and be insured for workers' compensation, or provide a five hundred dollar ($500) trust account for each employee engaged in asbestos-related work. The health insurance coverage may be provided through a union, association, or employer.

(3) Train and certify all employees in accordance with all training required by law and Title 8 of the California Administrative Code.

(4) Be proficient and have the necessary equipment to safely do asbestos-related work.

(b) Provide written notice to the division of each separate job or phase of work, where the work process used is different or the work is performed at noncontiguous locations, noting all of the following:

(1) The address of the job.

(2) The exact physical location of the job at that address.

(3) The start and projected completion date.

(4) The name of a certified supervisor with sufficient experience and authority who shall be responsible for the asbestos-related work at that job.

(5) The name of a qualified person, who shall be responsible for scheduling any air sampling, laboratory calibration of air sampling equipment, evaluation of sampling results, and conducting respirator fit testing and evaluating the results of those tests.

(6) The type of work to be performed, the work practices that will be utilized, and the potential for exposure.

Should any change be necessary, the employer or contractor shall so inform the division at or before the time of the change. Any oral notification shall be confirmed in writing.

(c) Post the location where any asbestos-related work occurs so as to be readable at 20 feet stating, "Danger— Asbestos. Cancer and Lung Hazard. Keep Out."

(d) A copy of the registration shall be provided before the start of the job to the prime contractor or other employers on the site and shall be posted on the jobsite beside the Cal-OSHA poster.

(e) The division shall obtain the services of three industrial hygienists and one clerical employee to implement and to enforce the requirements of this section unless the director makes a finding that these services are not necessary or that the services are not obtainable due to a lack of qualified hygienists applying for available positions. Funding may, at the director's discretion, be appropriated from the Asbestos Abatement Fund.

(f) Not later than January 1, 1987, the Division of Occupational Safety and Health shall propose to the Occupational Safety and Health Standards Board for review and adoption a regulation concerning asbestos-related work, as defined in Section 6501.8, which involves 100 square feet or more of surface area of asbestos-containing material. The regulation shall protect most effectively the health and safety of employees and shall include specific requirements for certification of employees, supervisors with sufficient experience and authority to be responsible for asbestos-related work, and a qualified person who shall be responsible for scheduling any air sampling, for arranging for calibration of the air sampling equipment and for analysis of the air samples by a NIOSH approved method, for conducting respirator fit testing, and for evaluating the results of the air sampling.

The Division of Occupational Safety and Health shall also propose a regulation to the Occupational Safety and Health Standards Board for review and adoption specifying sampling methodology for use in taking air samples. *(Added by Stats.1985, c. 1587, § 9, eff. Oct. 2, 1985. Amended by Stats.1986, c. 1451, § 10, eff. Sept. 30, 1986.)*

§ 6501.7. Asbestos defined

"Asbestos" means fibrous forms of various hydrated minerals, including chrysotile (fibrous serpentine), crocidolite (fibrous riebecktite), amosite (fibrous cummingtonite—grunerite), fibrous tremolite, fibrous actinolite, and fibrous anthophyllite. *(Added by Stats.1985, c. 1587, § 11, eff. Oct. 2, 1985.)*

§ 6501.8. Definitions; asbestos-related work; asbestos containing construction material

(a) For purposes of this chapter, "asbestos-related work" means any activity which by disturbing asbestos-containing construction materials may release asbestos fibers into the air and which is not related to its manufacture, the mining or excavation of asbestos-bearing ore or materials, or the installation or repair of automotive materials containing asbestos.

(b) For purposes of this chapter, "asbestos containing construction material" means any manufactured construction material that contains more than one-tenth of 1 percent asbestos by weight.

(c) For purposes of this chapter, "asbestos-related work" does not include the installation, repair, maintenance, or nondestructive removal of asbestos cement pipe used outside of buildings, if the installation, repair, maintenance, or nondestructive removal of asbestos cement pipe does not result in asbestos exposures to employees in excess of the action level determined in accordance with Sections 1529 and 5208 of Title 8 of the California Code of Regulations, and if the employees and supervisors involved in the operation have received training through a task-specific training program, approved pursuant to Section 9021.9, with written certification of completion of that training by the training entity responsible for the training. *(Added by Stats.1985, c. 1587, § 12, eff. Oct. 2, 1985. Amended by Stats.1986, c. 1451, § 11, eff. Sept. 30, 1986; Stats.1993, c. 1075 (S.B.877), § 1.)*

§ 6501.9. Determination of presence of asbestos

The owner of a commercial or industrial building or structure, employer, or contractor who engages in, or contracts for, asbestos-related work shall make a good faith effort to determine if asbestos is present before the work is begun. The contractor or employer shall first inquire of the owner if asbestos is present in any building or structure built prior to 1978. *(Added by Stats.1985, c. 1587, § 12.5, eff. Oct. 2, 1985. Amended by Stats.1986, c. 1451, § 12, eff. Sept. 30, 1986.)*

§ 6502. Issuance

The division may issue a permit based on a determination the employer has demonstrated evidence that the conditions, practices, means, methods, operations or processes used or proposed to be used will provide a safe and healthful place of employment. The division may issue a single permit for two or more projects to be performed by a single employer if similar conditions exist on each project and the chief or his representative is satisfied an adequate safety program has been developed for all the projects. The division may, upon its motion, conduct any investigation or hearing it deems necessary for the purpose of this section, and may require a safety conference prior to the start of actual work. *(Added by Stats.1973, c. 993, p. 1945, § 100, eff. Oct. 1, 1973.)*

§ 6503. Safety conference

A safety conference shall include representatives of the owner or contracting agency, the contractor, the employer, employees and employee representatives. The safety conference shall include a discussion of the employer's safety program and such means, methods, devices, processes, practices, conditions or operations as he intends to use in providing safe employment and a safe place of employment. *(Added by Stats.1973, c. 993, p. 1945, § 100, eff. Oct. 1, 1973.)*

§ 6503.5. Safety conference for asbestos handling jobs

A safety conference shall be held for all asbestos handling jobs prior to the start of actual work. It shall include representatives of the owner or contracting agency, the contractor, the employer, employees, and employee representatives. It shall include a discussion of the employer's safety program and such means, methods, devices, processes, practices, conditions, or operations as the employer intends to use in providing a safe place of employment. *(Added by Stats.1985, c. 1587, § 13, eff. Oct. 2, 1985.)*

§ 6504. Posting

Any employer issued a permit pursuant to this chapter shall post a copy or copies of the permit pursuant to subdivision (a) of Section 6408. *(Added by Stats.1973, c. 993, p. 1946, § 100, eff. Oct. 1, 1973.)*

§ 6505. Revocation

The division may at any time, upon good cause being shown therefor, and after notice and an opportunity to be heard revoke any permit issued pursuant to this chapter. *(Added by Stats.1973, c. 993, p. 1946, § 100, eff. Oct. 1, 1973.)*

§ 6505.5. Revocation or suspension of asbestos-related work registration; failure to determine if asbestos is present; penalties; defense

(a) The division may, upon good cause shown, and after notice to the employer or contractor by the division and an opportunity to be heard, revoke or suspend any registration issued to the employer or contractor to do asbestos-related work until certain specified written conditions are met.

(b) Any person who owns a commercial or industrial building or structure, any employer who engages in or contracts for asbestos-related work, any contractor, public agency, or any employee acting for any of the foregoing, who, contracts for, or who begins, asbestos-related work in any commercial or industrial building or structure built prior to 1978 without first determining if asbestos-containing material is present, and thereby fails to comply with the applicable laws and regulations, is subject to one of the following penalties:

(1) For a knowing or negligent violation, a fine of not more than five thousand dollars ($5,000) or imprisonment in the county jail for not more than six months, or both the fine and imprisonment.

(2) For a willful violation which results in death, serious injury or illness, or serious exposure, a fine of not more than ten thousand dollars ($10,000) or imprisonment in the county jail for not more than one year, or both the fine and imprisonment. A second or subsequent conviction under this paragraph may be punishable by a fine of not more than twenty thousand dollars ($20,000) or by imprisonment in the county jail for not more than one year, or by both the fine and imprisonment.

(3) A civil penalty of not more than two thousand dollars ($2,000) for each violation, to be imposed pursuant to the procedures set forth in Sections 6317, 6318, and 6319.

(4) For a willful or repeat violation, a civil penalty of not more than twenty thousand dollars ($20,000) for each violation.

(c) It is a defense to an action for violation of this section if the owner, contractor, employer, public agency, or agent thereof, proves, by a preponderance of the evidence, that he or she made a reasonable effort to determine whether asbestos was present. *(Added by Stats.1985, c. 1587, § 14, eff. Oct. 2, 1985. Amended by Stats.1986, c. 1451, § 13, eff. Sept. 30, 1986.)*

§ 6506. Denial or revocation of permit; appeal to director; stay

(a) Any employer denied a permit upon application, or whose permit is revoked, may appeal such denial or revocation to the director.

(b) The filing of an appeal to the director from a permit revocation by the division shall not stay the revocation. Upon application by the employer with proper notice to the division, and after an opportunity for the division to respond to the application, the director may issue an order staying the revocation while the appeal is pending. *(Added by Stats.1973, c. 993, p. 1945, § 100, eff. Oct. 1, 1973. Amended by Stats.1974, c. 1284, p. 2784, § 16; Stats.1978, c. 1222, p. 3954, § 1.)*

§ 6507. Fee

The division shall set a fee to be charged for such permits in an amount reasonably necessary to cover the costs involved in investigating and issuing such permits. *(Added by Stats.1973, c. 993, p. 1946, § 100, eff. Oct. 1, 1973.)*

§ 6508. Entities exempt

No permit shall be required of the State of California, a city, city and county, county, district, or public utility subject to the jurisdiction of the Public Utilities Commission. *(Added by Stats.1973, c. 993, p. 1946, § 100, eff. Oct. 1, 1973.)*

§ 6508.5. No exemption from registration; no registration fees for public agencies

No entity shall be exempt from registration. The State of California, a city, city and county, county, district, or public utility subject to the jurisdiction of the Public Utilities Commission, shall be required to apply for a registration through the designated chief executive officer of that body. No registration fees shall be required of any public agencies. *(Added by Stats.1985, c. 1587, § 15, eff. Oct. 2, 1985.)*

§ 6509. Violations of chapter; misdemeanor

Any person, or agent or officer thereof, who violates this chapter is guilty of a misdemeanor. *(Added by Stats.1976, c. 33, p. 59, § 2, eff. March 6, 1976.)*

§ 6509.5. Asbestos consultants; inspection with knowledge of report being required as condition for loan or permit concerning the property; performance of corrective work; violations; offense

(a) If an asbestos consultant has made an inspection for the purpose of determining the presence of asbestos or the need for related remedial action with knowledge that the report has been required by a person as a condition of making a loan of money secured by the property, or is required by a public entity as a condition of issuing a permit concerning the property, the asbestos consultant or any employee, subsidiary, or any company with common ownership, shall not require, as a condition of performing the inspection, that the consultant also perform any corrective work on the property that was recommended in the report.

(b) This section does not prohibit an asbestos consultant that has contracted to perform corrective work after the report of another company has indicated the presence of asbestos or the need for related remedial action from making its own inspection prior to performing that corrective work or from making an inspection to determine whether the corrective measures were successful and, if not, thereafter performing additional corrective work.

(c) A violation of this section is grounds for disciplinary action against any asbestos consultant who engages in that work pursuant to any license from a state agency.

(d) A violation of this section is a misdemeanor punishable by a fine of not less than three thousand dollars ($3,000) and not more than five thousand dollars ($5,000), or by imprisonment in the county jail for not more than one year, or both.

(e) For the purpose of this section:

(1) "Asbestos consultant" means any person who, for compensation, inspects property to identify asbestos containing materials, determining the risks, or the need for related remedial action.

(2) "Asbestos" has the meaning set forth in Section 6501.7. *(Added by Stats.1988, c. 1491, § 2.)*

§ 6510. Violations of chapter; injunctions

(a) If, after inspection or investigation, the division finds that an employer, without a valid permit, is engaging in activity for which a permit is required, it may, through its attorneys, apply to the superior court of the county in which such activity is taking place for an injunction restraining such activity.

(b) The application to the superior court, accompanied by an affidavit showing that the employer, without a valid permit, is engaging in activity for which a permit is required, is a sufficient prima facie showing to warrant, in the discretion of the court, the immediate granting of a temporary restraining order. No bond shall be required of the division as a prerequisite to the granting of any restraining order. *(Added by Stats.1978, c. 1222, p. 3954, § 2.)*

CHAPTER 7. APPEAL PROCEEDINGS

Section
6600. Time for appeal; matters reviewable.
6600.5. Special order or action order; time for appeal; matters reviewable.
6601. Effect of failure to appeal in time; extension of time.
6601.5. Special order or action order; effect of failure to appeal in time; extension of time.
6602. Timely notice of contest; hearing; decision.
6603. Rules of practice and procedure.
6604. Hearing officer; duties.
6605. Hearing officer; appointment, powers and jurisdiction; transfer of proceedings.
6606. Objections to particular hearing officer.
6607. Oath of hearing officer.
6608. Filing findings, order or decision; summary of evidence; reasons for decision.
6609. Action by appeals board upon hearing officer's findings, order or decision.
6610. Service of notices, orders or decisions.
6611. Procedure upon employer's failure to appear; mitigation; reinstatement of appeal.
6612. Effect of informalities.
6613. Depositions.
6614. Reconsideration.
6615. Necessity of reconsideration or petition therefor.
6616. Petition for reconsideration; contents.
6617. Petition for reconsideration; grounds.
6618. Waiver of grounds not stated in petition for reconsideration.
6619. Service of petition for reconsideration; answer.
6620. Powers upon reconsideration; notice of hearing.
6621. Reconsideration without hearing.
6622. Order or decision after reconsideration.
6623. Decision to grant or deny reconsideration to be made by appeals board.

Section
6624.　Denial of petition for reconsideration by failure to act.
6625.　Suspension or stay of order or decision.
6626.　Reconsideration of order or decision made by appeals board.
6627.　Application for writ of mandate; time.
6628.　Writ of mandate; return; certification of record; hearing on record.
6629.　Scope of judicial review.
6630.　Conclusiveness of fact findings; appearance of parties; judgment; remand.
6631.　Law applicable; service of pleadings.
6632.　Jurisdiction to review.
6633.　Suspension or stay during pendency of writ of mandate.

§ 6600.　Time for appeal; matters reviewable

Any employer served with a citation or notice pursuant to Section 6317, or a notice of proposed penalty under this part, or any other person obligated to the employer as specified in subdivision (b) of Section 6319, may appeal to the appeals board within 15 working days from the receipt of such citation or such notice with respect to violations alleged by the division, abatement periods, amount of proposed penalties, and the reasonableness of the changes required by the division to abate the condition. *(Added by Stats.1973, c. 993, p. 1946, § 101, eff. Oct. 1, 1973. Amended by Stats.1974, c. 1284, p. 2784, § 17; Stats.1976, c. 1404, p. 6324, § 2.)*

§ 6600.5.　Special order or action order; time for appeal; matters reviewable

Any employer served with a special order or any action order by the division pursuant to Section 6308, or any other person obligated to the employer as specified in subdivision (b) of Section 6319, may appeal to the appeals board within 15 working days from the receipt of the order with respect to the action ordered by the division, abatement periods, the reasonableness of the changes required by the division to abate the condition. *(Added by Stats.1984, c. 1138, § 4.)*

§ 6601.　Effect of failure to appeal in time; extension of time

If within 15 working days from receipt of the citation or notice of civil penalty issued by the division, the employer fails to notify the appeals board that he intends to contest the citation or notice of proposed penalty, and no notice contesting the abatement period is filed by any employee or representative of the employee within such time, the citation or notice of proposed penalty shall be deemed a final order of the appeals board and not subject to review by any court or agency. The 15-day period may be extended by the appeals board for good cause. *(Added by Stats.1973, c. 993, p. 1946, § 101, eff. Oct. 1, 1973. Amended by Stats.1974, c. 1284, p. 2784, § 18.)*

§ 6601.5.　Special order or action order; effect of failure to appeal in time; extension of time

If, within 15 working days from receipt of a special order, or action order by the division, the employer fails to notify the appeals board that he or she intends to contest the order, and no notice contesting the abatement period is filed by any employee or representative of the employee within that time, the order shall be deemed a final order of the appeals board and not subject to review by any court or agency. The 15-day period may be extended by the appeals board for good cause. *(Added by Stats. 1984, c. 1138, § 5.)*

§ 6602.　Timely notice of contest; hearing; decision

If an employer notifies the appeals board that he or she intends to contest a citation issued under Section 6317, or notice of proposed penalty issued under Section 6319, or order issued under Section 6308, or if, within 15 working days of the issuance of a citation or order any employee or representative of an employee files a notice with the division or appeals board alleging that the period of time fixed in the citation or order for the abatement of the violation is unreasonable, the appeals board shall afford an opportunity for a hearing. The appeals board shall thereafter issue a decision, based on findings of fact, affirming, modifying or vacating the division's citation, order, or proposed penalty, or directing other appropriate relief. *(Added by Stats.1973, c. 993, p. 1946, § 101, eff. Oct. 1, 1973. Amended by Stats.1974, c. 1284, p. 2784, § 19; Stats.1984, c. 1138, § 6.)*

§ 6603.　Rules of practice and procedure

(a) The rules of practice and procedure adopted by the appeals board shall be consistent with Article 8 (commencing with Section 11435.05) of Chapter 4.5 of Part 1 of Division 3 of Title 2 of, and Sections 11507, 11507.6, 11507.7, 11513, 11514, 11515, and 11516 of, the Government Code, and shall provide affected employees or representatives of affected employees an opportunity to participate as parties to a hearing under Section 6602.

(b) The superior courts shall have jurisdiction over contempt proceedings, as provided in Article 12 (commencing with Section 11455.10) of Chapter 4.5 of Part 1 of Division 3 of Title 2 of the Government Code. *(Added by Stats.1973, c. 993, p. 1946, § 101, eff. Oct. 1, 1973. Amended by Stats.1974, c. 1284, p. 2784, § 20; Stats.1995, c. 938 (S.B.523), § 78.5, operative July 1, 1997.)*

§ 6604.　Hearing officer; duties

The appeals board may, in accordance with rules of practice and procedure which it shall adopt, direct and order a hearing officer:

(a) To try the issues in any proceeding before it, whether of fact or of law, and make and file a finding, order, or decision based thereon.

(b) To hold hearings and ascertain facts necessary to enable the appeals board to determine any proceeding or to make any order or decision that the appeals board is authorized to make, or necessary for the information of the appeals board. *(Added by Stats.1973, c. 993, p. 1947, § 101, eff. Oct. 1, 1973.)*

§ 6605. Hearing officer, appointment, powers and jurisdiction; transfer of proceedings

The appeals board may appoint one or more hearing officers in any proceeding, as it may deem necessary or advisable, and may defer, remove to itself, or transfer to a hearing officer the proceedings on any appeal. Any hearing officer appointed by the appeals board has the powers, jurisdiction, and authority granted by law, by the order of appointment, and by the rules of the appeals board. *(Added by Stats.1973, c. 993, p. 1947, § 101, eff. Oct. 1, 1973.)*

§ 6606. Objections to particular hearing officer

Any party to the proceeding may object to the reference of the proceeding to a particular hearing officer upon any one or more of the grounds specified in Section 641 of the Code of Civil Procedure and such objection shall be heard and disposed of by the appeals board. Affidavits may be read and witnesses examined as to such objections. *(Added by Stats.1973, c. 993, p. 1947, § 101, eff. Oct. 1, 1973.)*

§ 6607. Oath of hearing officer

Before entering upon his duties, the hearing officer shall be sworn, before an officer authorized to administer oaths, faithfully and fairly to hear and determine the matters and issues referred to him, to make just findings and to report according to his understanding. In any proceedings under this chapter, the hearing officer shall have the power to administer oaths and affirmations and to certify official acts. *(Added by Stats.1973, c. 993, p. 1947, § 101, eff. Oct. 1, 1973.)*

§ 6608. Filing findings, order or decision; summary of evidence; reasons for decision

The appeals board or a hearing officer shall, within 30 days after the case is submitted, make and file findings upon all facts involved in the appeal and file an order or decision. Together with the findings or the decision, there shall be served upon all the parties to the proceedings a summary of the evidence received and relied upon and the reasons or grounds upon which the decision was made. *(Added by Stats.1973, c. 993, p. 1947, § 101, eff. Oct. 1, 1973.)*

§ 6609. Action by appeals board upon hearing officer's findings, order or decision

Within 30 days after the filing of the findings, decision, or order, the appeals board may confirm, adopt, modify or set aside the findings, order, or decision of a hearing officer and may, with or without further proceedings, and with or without notice, enter its order, findings, or decision based upon the record in the case. *(Added by Stats.1973, c. 993, p. 1947, § 101, eff. Oct. 1, 1973.)*

§ 6610. Service of notices, orders or decisions

Any notice, order, or decision required by this part to be served upon any person either before, during, or after the institution of any proceeding before the appeals board, shall be served in the manner provided by Chapter 5 (commencing with Section 1010) of Title 14 of Part 2 of the Code of Civil Procedure, unless otherwise directed by the appeals board. In the latter event the document shall be served in accordance with the order or direction of the appeals board. The appeals board may, in the cases mentioned in the Code of Civil Procedure, order service to be made by publication of notice of time and place of hearing. Where service is ordered to be made by publication the date of the hearing shall be fixed at more than 30 days from the date of filing the application. *(Added by Stats.1973, c. 993, p. 1947, § 101, eff. Oct. 1, 1973.)*

§ 6611. Procedure upon employer's failure to appear; mitigation; reinstatement of appeal

(a) If the employer fails to appear, the appeals board may dismiss the appeal or may take action upon the employer's express admissions or upon other evidence, and affidavits may be used without any notice to the employer. Where the burden of proof is upon the employer to establish the appeals board action sought, the appeals board may act without taking evidence. Nothing in this section shall be construed to deprive the employer of the right to make any showing by way of mitigation.

(b) The appeal may be reinstated by the appeals board upon a showing of good cause by the employer for his failure to appear. *(Added by Stats.1973, c. 993, p. 1948, § 101, eff. Oct. 1, 1973. Amended by Stats.1974, c. 1284, p. 2785, § 21.)*

§ 6612. Effect of informalities

No informality in any proceeding or in the manner of taking testimony shall invalidate any order, decision, or finding made and filed as specified in this division. No order, decision, or finding shall be invalidated because of the admission into the record, and use as proof of any fact in dispute of any evidence not admissible under the common law or statutory rules of evidence and procedure. *(Added by Stats.1973, c. 993, p. 1948, § 101, eff. Oct. 1, 1973.)*

§ 6613. Depositions

The appeals board, a hearing officer, or any party to the action or proceeding, may, in any investigation or hearing before the appeals board, cause the deposition of witnesses residing within or without the state to be taken in the manner prescribed by law for like depositions in civil actions in the superior courts of this state under Title 4 (commencing with Section 2016.010) of Part 4 of the Code of Civil Procedure. To that end the attendance of witnesses and the production of records may be required. Depositions may be taken outside the state before any officer authorized to administer oaths. The appeals board or a hearing officer in any proceeding before the appeals board may cause evidence to be taken in other jurisdictions before the agency authorized to hear similar matters in such other jurisdictions. *(Added by Stats.1973, c. 993, p. 1948, § 101, eff. Oct. 1, 1973. Amended by Stats.1974, c. 1284, p. 2785, § 22; Stats.1998, c. 931 (S.B.2139), § 349, eff. Sept. 28, 1998; Stats.2004, c. 182 (A.B.3081), § 48, operative July 1, 2005.)*

§ 6614. Reconsideration

(a) At any time within 30 days after the service of any final order or decision made and filed by the appeals board or a hearing officer, any party aggrieved directly or indirectly by any final order or decision, made and filed by the appeals board or a hearing officer under any provision contained in this division, may petition the appeals board for reconsideration in respect to any matters determined or covered by the final order or decision and specified in the petition for reconsideration. Such petition shall be made only within the time and in the manner specified in this chapter.

(b) At any time within 30 days after the filing of an order or decision made by a hearing officer and the accompanying report, the appeals board may, on its own motion, grant reconsideration. *(Added by Stats.1973, c. 993, p. 1948, § 101, eff. Oct. 1, 1973. Amended by Stats.1974, c. 1284, p. 2785, § 23.)*

§ 6615. Necessity of reconsideration or petition therefor

No cause of action arising out of any final order or decision made and filed by the appeals board or a hearing officer shall accrue in any court to any person until and unless the appeals board on its own motion sets aside such final order or decision and removes such proceeding to itself or such person files a petition for reconsideration, and such reconsideration is granted or denied. Nothing herein contained shall prevent the enforcement of any such final order or decision, in the manner provided in this division. *(Added by Stats.1973, c. 993, p. 1948, § 101, eff. Oct. 1, 1973.)*

§ 6616. Petition for reconsideration; contents

The petition for reconsideration shall set forth specifically and in full detail the grounds upon which the petitioner considers the final order or decision made and filed by the appeals board or a hearing officer to be unjust or unlawful, and every issue to be considered by the appeals board. The petition shall be verified upon oath in the manner required for verified pleadings in courts of record and shall contain a general statement of any evidence or other matters upon which the applicant relies in support thereof. *(Added by Stats.1973, c. 993, p. 1949, § 101, eff. Oct. 1, 1973.)*

§ 6617. Petition for reconsideration; grounds

The petition for reconsideration may be based upon one or more of the following grounds and no other:

(a) That by such order or decision made and filed by the appeals board or hearing officer, the appeals board acted without or in excess of its powers.

(b) That the order or decision was procured by fraud.

(c) That the evidence does not justify the findings of fact.

(d) That the petitioner has discovered new evidence material to him, which he could not, with reasonable diligence, have discovered and produced at the hearing.

(e) That the findings of fact do not support the order or decision. *(Added by Stats.1973, c. 993, p. 1949, § 101, eff. Oct. 1, 1973. Amended by Stats.1974, c. 1284, p. 2785, § 24.)*

§ 6618. Waiver of grounds not stated in petition for reconsideration

The petitioner for reconsideration shall be deemed to have finally waived all objections, irregularities, and illegalities concerning the matter upon which the reconsideration is sought other than those set forth in the petition for reconsideration. *(Added by Stats.1973, c. 993, p. 1949, § 101, eff. Oct. 1, 1973.)*

§ 6619. Service of petition for reconsideration; answer

A copy of the petition for reconsideration shall be served forthwith upon all parties by the person petitioning for reconsideration. Any party may file an answer thereto within 30 days thereafter. Such answer shall likewise be verified. The appeals board may require the petition for reconsideration to be served on other persons designated by it. *(Added by Stats.1973, c. 993, p. 1949, § 101, eff. Oct. 1, 1973. Amended by Stats.1979, c. 344, p. 1210, § 1.)*

§ 6620. Powers upon reconsideration; notice of hearing

Upon the filing of a petition for reconsideration, or having granted reconsideration upon its own motion, the appeals board may, with or without further proceedings and with or without notice affirm, rescind, alter, or amend the order or decision made and filed by the appeals board or hearing officer on the basis of the evidence previously submitted in the case, or may grant reconsideration and direct the taking of additional evidence. Notice of the time and place of any hearing on reconsideration shall be given to the petitioner and adverse parties and to such other persons as the appeals board orders. *(Added by Stats.1973, c. 993, p. 1949, § 101, eff. Oct. 1, 1973.)*

§ 6621. Reconsideration without hearing

If at the time of granting reconsideration, it appears to the satisfaction of the appeals board that no sufficient reason exists for taking further testimony, the appeals board may affirm, rescind, alter or amend the order or decision made and filed by the appeals board or hearing officer and may, without further proceedings, without notice, and without setting a time and place for further hearing, enter its findings, order or decision based upon the record in the case. *(Added by Stats.1973, c. 993, p. 1949, § 101, eff. Oct. 1, 1973.)*

§ 6622. Order or decision after reconsideration

After the taking of additional evidence and a consideration of all of the facts the appeals board may affirm, rescind, alter, or amend the original order or decision. An order or decision made following reconsideration which affirms, rescinds, alters, or amends the original order or decision shall be made by the appeals board but shall not affect any right or the enforcement of any right arising from or by virtue of the original order or decision unless so ordered by the appeals board. *(Added by Stats.1973, c. 993, p. 1950, § 101, eff. Oct. 1, 1973.)*

§ 6623. Decision to grant or deny reconsideration to be made by appeals board

Any decision of the appeals board granting or denying a petition for reconsideration or affirming, rescinding, altering, or amending the original findings, order, or decision following reconsideration shall be made by the appeals board and not by a hearing officer and shall be in writing, signed by a majority of the appeals board members assigned thereto, and shall state the evidence relied upon and specify in detail the reasons for the decision. *(Added by Stats.1973, c. 993, p. 1950, § 101, eff. Oct. 1, 1973.)*

§ 6624. Denial of petition for reconsideration by failure to act

A petition for reconsideration is deemed to have been denied by the appeals board unless it is acted upon within 45 days from the date of filing. The appeals board may, upon good cause being shown therefor, extend the time within which it may act upon that petition for not exceeding 15 days. *(Added by Stats.1973, c. 993, p. 1950, § 101, eff. Oct. 1, 1973. Amended by Stats.1991, c. 734 (A.B.1980), § 1.)*

§ 6625. Suspension or stay of order or decision

The filing of a petition for reconsideration shall suspend for a period of 10 days the order or decision affected, insofar as it applies to the parties to the petition, unless otherwise ordered by the appeals board. The appeals board upon the terms and conditions which it by order directs, may stay, suspend, or postpone the order or decision during the pendency of the reconsideration. *(Added by Stats.1973, c. 993, p. 1950, § 101, eff. Oct. 1, 1973.)*

§ 6626. Reconsideration of order or decision made by appeals board

Nothing contained in this chapter shall be construed to prevent the appeals board, on petition of an aggrieved party or on its own motion, from granting reconsideration of an original order or decision made and filed by the appeals board within the same time specified for reconsideration of an original order or decision. *(Added by Stats.1973, c. 993, p. 1950, § 101, eff. Oct. 1, 1973.)*

§ 6627. Application for writ of mandate; time

Any person affected by an order or decision of the appeals board may, within the time limit specified in this section, apply to the superior court of the county in which he resides, for a writ of mandate, for the purpose of inquiring into and determining the lawfulness of the original order or decision or of the order or decision following reconsideration. The application for writ of mandate must be made within 30 days after a petition for reconsideration is denied, or, if a petition is granted or reconsideration is had on the appeals board's own motion, within 30 days after the filing of the order or decision following reconsideration. *(Added by Stats.1973, c. 993, p. 1950, § 101, eff. Oct. 1, 1973.)*

§ 6628. Writ of mandate; return; certification of record; hearing on record

The writ of mandate shall be made returnable at a time and place then or thereafter specified by court order and shall direct the appeals board to certify its record in the case to the court within the time therein specified. No new or additional evidence shall be introduced in such court, but the cause shall be heard on the record of the appeals board, as certified to by it. *(Added by Stats.1973, c. 993, p. 1950, § 101, eff. Oct. 1, 1973.)*

§ 6629. Scope of judicial review

The review by the court shall not be extended further than to determine, based upon the entire record which shall be certified by the appeals board, whether:

(a) The appeals board acted without or in excess of its powers.

(b) The order or decision was procured by fraud.

(c) The order or decision was unreasonable.

(d) The order or decision was not supported by substantial evidence.

(e) If findings of fact are made, such findings of fact support the order or decision under review.

Nothing in this section shall permit the court to hold a trial de novo, to take evidence, or to exercise its independent judgment on the evidence. *(Added by Stats.1973, c. 993, p. 1951, § 101, eff. Oct. 1, 1973.)*

§ 6630. Conclusiveness of fact findings; appearance of parties; judgment; remand

The findings and conclusions of the appeals board on questions of fact are conclusive and final and are not subject to review. Such questions of fact shall include ultimate facts and the findings and conclusions of the appeals board. The appeals board and each party to the action or proceeding before the appeals board shall have the right to appear in the mandate proceeding. Upon the hearing, the court shall enter judgment either affirming or annulling the order or decision, or the court may remand the case for further proceedings before the appeals board. *(Added by Stats.1973, c. 993, p. 1951, § 101, eff. Oct. 1, 1973. Amended by Stats.1974, c. 1284, p. 2786, § 25.)*

§ 6631. Law applicable; service of pleadings

The provisions of the Code of Civil Procedure relating to writs of mandate shall, so far as applicable, apply to proceedings in the courts under the provisions of this part. A copy of every pleading filed pursuant to the terms of this part shall be served on the appeals board and upon every party who entered an appearance in the action before the appeals board and whose interest therein is adverse to the party filing such pleading. *(Added by Stats.1973, c. 993, p. 1951, § 101, eff. Oct. 1, 1973.)*

§ 6632. Jurisdiction to review

No court of this state, except the Supreme Court, the courts of appeal, and the superior court to the extent herein specified, has jurisdiction to review, reverse, correct, or annul any order or rule, or decision of the appeals board, or to suspend or delay the operation or execution thereof, or to restrain, enjoin, or interfere with the appeals board in the performance of its duties. *(Added by Stats.1973, c. 993, p. 1951, § 101, eff. Oct. 1, 1973. Amended by Stats.1974, c. 1284, p. 2786, § 26.)*

§ 6633. Suspension or stay during pendency of writ of mandate

The filing of a petition for, or the pendency of, a writ of mandate shall not of itself stay or suspend the operation of any order, rule or decision of the appeals board, but the court before which the petition is filed may stay or suspend, in whole or in part, the operation of the order or decision of the appeals board subject to review, upon the terms and conditions which it by order directs. *(Added by Stats.1973, c. 993, p. 1951, § 101, eff. Oct. 1, 1973. Amended by Stats.1974, c. 1284, p. 2786, § 27.)*

CHAPTER 8. ENFORCEMENT OF CIVIL PENALTIES

Section
6650. Filing copies of notice of civil penalty and other documents; entry of judgment; service of notice; interest.
6651. Limitation of actions.
6652. Copy of notice of civil penalty to contractors' state license board.

§ 6650. Filing copies of notice of civil penalty and other documents; entry of judgment; service of notice; interest

(a) After the expiration of the period during which a penalty may be appealed, no appeal having been filed, the department may file with the clerk of the superior court in any county a certified copy of the citation and notice of civil penalty, the certification by the department that the penalty remains unpaid, and the division's proof of

service on the employer of the items filed with the clerk of the court.

(b) After the exhaustion of the review procedures provided for in Chapter 7 (commencing with Section 6600), an appeal having been filed, the department may file with the clerk of the superior court in any county a certified copy of the citation and notice of civil penalty, a certified copy of the order, findings or decision of the appeals board, the certification of the department that the penalty remains unpaid, and proof of service on the employer at the employer's address as shown on the official address record by the appeals board.

(c) The clerk, immediately upon the filing of a notice of civil penalty by the department pursuant to subdivision (a) or (b), shall enter judgment for the state against the person assessed the civil penalty in the amount of the penalty, plus interest due for each day from the date of issuance of the notice of civil penalty that the penalty remains unpaid.

(d) The department shall serve the notice of entry of judgment provided by Section 664.5 of the Code of Civil Procedure on the employer.

(e) A judgment entered pursuant to this section shall bear the same rate of interest, have the same effect as other judgments, and be given the same preference allowed by law on other judgments rendered for claims for taxes pursuant to Section 7170 of the Government Code.

(f) No fees shall be charged by the clerk of any court for the performance of any official service required by this chapter. *(Added by Stats.1974, c. 1253, p. 2712, § 1; Stats.1974, c. 1284, p. 2786, § 29. Amended by Stats.1983, c. 142, § 118; Stats.1991, c. 1210 (A.B.186), § 1; Stats. 2000, c. 135 (A.B.2539), § 130.)*

§ 6651. Limitation of actions

(a) Notwithstanding Section 340 of the Code of Civil Procedure, an action to collect any civil penalty, fee, or penalty fee under this division shall be commenced within three years from the date the penalty or fee became final.

(b) The amendments made to this section by the act adding this subdivision shall only apply to penalty assessments or fees for which the three-year period prescribed in this section for the commencement of an action to collect a civil penalty or fee has not expired on the effective date of the act adding this subdivision. *(Added by Stats.1991, c. 1210 (A.B.186), § 3. Amended by Stats.1993, c. 998 (A.B.2016), § 2.)*

§ 6652. Copy of notice of civil penalty to contractors' state license board

The division shall provide the Contractors' State License Board with a certified copy of every notice of civil penalty deemed to be a final order pursuant to Section 6601 or after the exhaustion of all other review procedures pursuant to Chapter 7 (commencing with Section 6600) when both of the following have occurred:

(a) The employer served with the notice of civil penalty is, or is thought to be, a licensee licensed by the Contractors' State License Board.

(b) The employer referred to in subdivision (a) has failed to pay the civil penalty after a period of 60 days following that employer's receipt of the notice of civil penalty.

(c) When the employer has paid the civil penalty referenced in the certified copy of notice of civil penalty that was provided to the Contractors' State License Board, including all interest owed thereon, then the division shall provide to the employer who was the subject of the certified copy of notice a written confirmation or receipt stating that the employer has paid the amount owed that was the subject of the certified notice provided to the board. *(Added by Stats.1991, c. 1210 (A.B.186), § 4.)*

CHAPTER 9. MISCELLANEOUS SAFETY PROVISIONS

Section
6700. Gas pipe lines; presumption.
6701. Emission standards for internal combustion engines used inside buildings.
6702. Exhaust purifier device for internal combustion engines used inside buildings; certification; enforcement.
6703. Application of sections relating to internal combustion engines used in buildings; exception.
6704. Crane boomstops.
6705. Trench excavation; plan for protection from caving.
6705.5. Swimming pools; application of rules on excavation.
6706. Trenches and excavations; number of permits; emergency repairs.
6707. Bids for trenching and excavation work; item for shoring, etc.
6708. Construction contractors; first aid for employees.
6710. Explosives; use; licensed person to supervise and direct.
6711. Examination of persons using explosives in avalanche blasting.
6712. Field sanitation standards; agricultural places of employment.
6716. Lead-related construction work.
6717. Standard for protection of health and safety of employees engaged in lead-related construction work; submission to standards board; adoption of standard; requirements and specifications.
6718. Gasoline cargo tanks; compliance with vapor emissions standards; employee requirements.
6719. Repetitive motion injuries in the workplace; Legislature's concern.

§ 6700. Gas pipe lines; presumption

(a) Any employer who causes or allows the use of any flammable or combustible material for the installation acceptance pressure test of any gas houseline or piping shall be conclusively presumed to be maintaining an unsafe place of employment.

(b) Any employer who causes or allows gas pipelines to be tested with gas at pressures in excess of that permitted by applicable sections of the American Society of Mechanical Engineers Code for Pressure Piping shall be conclusively presumed to be maintaining an unsafe place of employment. *(Added by Stats.1973, c. 993, p. 1952, § 103, eff. Oct. 1, 1973.)*

§ 6701. Emission standards for internal combustion engines used inside buildings

It shall be the duty of the standards board to determine by the maximum allowable standards of emissions of contaminants from portable and from mobile internal combustion engines used inside factories, manufacturing plants, warehouses, buildings and other enclosed structures, which standards are compatible with the safety and health of employees. *(Added by Stats.1973, c. 993, p. 1952, § 103, eff. Oct. 1, 1973.)*

§ 6702. Exhaust purifier device for internal combustion engines used inside buildings; certification; enforcement

All portable and all mobile internal combustion engines that are used inside factories, manufacturing plants, warehouses, buildings and other enclosed structures shall be equipped with a certified exhaust purifier device after the certification of the device by the State Air Resources Board.

The Division of Occupational Safety and Health shall be responsible for the enforcement of the provisions of this section. *(Added by Stats.1973, c. 993, p. 1952, § 103, eff. Oct. 1, 1973. Amended by Stats.1980, c. 676, p. 1978, § 238.)*

§ 6703. Application of sections relating to internal combustion engines used in buildings; exception

Sections 6701 and 6702 shall apply to all portable and all mobile internal combustion engines used inside factories, manufacturing plants, warehouses, buildings and other enclosed structures unless the operation of such an engine used inside a particular factory, plant, warehouse, building or enclosed structure does not result in harmful exposure to concentrations of dangerous gases or fumes in excess of maximum acceptable concentrations as determined by the standards board. *(Added by Stats. 1973, c. 993, p. 1953, § 103, eff. Oct. 1, 1973. Amended by Stats.1974, c. 1284, p. 2786, § 30.)*

§ 6704. Crane boomstops

All crawler and wheel cranes with cable-controlled booms and with rated lifting capacity of more than 10 tons sold or operated in this state shall be equipped with boomstops that meet standards that shall be established therefor by the standards board. *(Added by Stats.1973, c. 993, p. 1953, § 103, eff. Oct. 1, 1973.)*

§ 6705. Trench excavation; plan for protection from caving

No contract for public works involving an estimated expenditure in excess of twenty-five thousand dollars ($25,000), for the excavation of any trench or trenches five feet or more in depth, shall be awarded unless it contains a clause requiring submission by the contractor and acceptance by the awarding body or by a registered civil or structural engineer, employed by the awarding body, to whom authority to accept has been delegated, in advance of excavation, of a detailed plan showing the design of shoring, bracing, sloping, or other provisions to be made for worker protection from the hazard of caving ground during the excavation of such trench or trenches. If such plan varies from the shoring system standards, the plan shall be prepared by a registered civil or structural engineer.

Nothing in this section shall be deemed to allow the use of a shoring, sloping, or protective system less effective than that required by the Construction Safety Orders.

Nothing in this section shall be construed to impose tort liability on the awarding body or any of its employees.

The terms "public works" and "awarding body", as used in this section, shall have the same meaning as in Sections 1720 and 1722, respectively, of the Labor Code. *(Added by Stats.1973, c. 993, p. 1953, § 103, eff. Oct. 1, 1973.)*

§ 6705.5. Swimming pools; application of rules on excavation

Regulations of the department requiring the shoring, bracing, or sloping of excavations, or which contain similar requirements for excavations, shall only apply to the excavation of swimming pools where a reasonable examination by a qualified person reveals recognizable conditions which would expose employees to injury from possible moving ground. If these conditions are found to exist with respect to a swimming pool excavation, employees shall not be permitted to enter the excavation until the condition is abated or otherwise no longer exists. *(Added by Stats.1985, c. 815, § 1.)*

§ 6706. Trenches and excavations; number of permits; emergency repairs

For the purposes of subdivision (a) of Section 6500, only one permit shall be required for a project involving several trenches or excavations. The provisions of Section 6500 shall not apply to the construction of trenches or excavations for the purpose of performing emergency repair work to underground facilities, or the construction of swimming pools, or the construction of "graves" as defined in Section 7014 of the Health and Safety Code or to the construction or final use of excavations or trenches where the construction or final use does not require a person to descend into the excavations or trenches. *(Added by Stats.1973, c. 993, p. 1953, § 103, eff. Oct. 1, 1973.)*

§ 6707. Bids for trenching and excavation work; item for shoring, etc.

Whenever the state, a county, city and county, or city issues a call for bids for the construction of a pipeline, sewer, sewage disposal system, boring and jacking pits, or similar trenches or open excavations, which are five feet or deeper, such call shall specify that each bid submitted in response thereto shall contain, as a bid item, adequate sheeting, shoring, and bracing, or equivalent method, for the protection of life or limb, which shall conform to applicable safety orders. Nothing in this section shall be construed to impose tort liability on the body awarding the contract or any of its employees. This section shall not apply to contracts awarded pursuant to the provisions of Chapter 3 (commencing with Section 14250) of Part 5 of Division 3 of Title 2 of the Government Code. *(Added by Stats.1973, c. 993, p. 1953, § 103, eff. Oct. 1, 1973.)*

§ 6708. Construction contractors; first aid for employees

Every contractor on a construction project, including but not limited to any public works, shall maintain adequate emergency first aid treatment for his employees. As used in this section, "adequate" shall be construed to mean sufficient to comply with the Federal Occupational Safety and Health Act of 1970 (P.L. 91–596).[1] *(Added by Stats.1973, c. 993, p. 1954, § 103, eff. Oct. 1, 1973.)*

[1] 29 U.S.C.A. § 651 et seq.

§ 6710. Explosives; use; licensed person to supervise and direct

(a) At every place of employment where explosives are used in the course of employment, there shall be a person licensed pursuant to the provisions of Chapter 3 (commencing with Section 7990) of Part 9 of Division 5, to supervise and visually direct the blasting operation.

(b) For the purposes of this section, "explosives" shall include, but not be limited to, class A and B explosives, blasting caps, detonating cord, and charges or projectiles used in the control of avalanches. For the purposes of this section, "explosives" shall not include small arms ammunition or class C explosives such as explosive powerpacks in the form of explosive cartridges or explosive-charged construction devices, explosive rivets, bolts, and charges for driving pins and studs, and cartridges for explosive-actuated power devices.

(c) This section shall not apply to persons, firms, or corporations licensed pursuant to Part 2 (commencing with Section 12500) of Division 11 of the Health and Safety Code. *(Added by Stats.1983, c. 788, § 1. Amended by Stats.1985, c. 958, § 1.)*

§ 6711. Examination of persons using explosives in avalanche blasting

(a) The division shall develop and administer an oral and written examination for persons using explosives, as defined in Section 6710, while engaged in snow avalanche blasting. Any person engaged in snow avalanche blasting shall pass this examination prior to being licensed by the division.

(b) The division shall select an advisory committee to assist the division in preparing the data and information for the written and oral qualifying examination. The advisory committee shall consist of not less than seven members, nor more than nine members, with at least one representative from explosives manufacturers, snow avalanche blasting consultants, the recreational snow ski industry, a public recreation area, the California Department of Transportation, and the division. *(Added by Stats.1985, c. 958, § 2.)*

§ 6712. Field sanitation standards; agricultural places of employment

(a) The standards board shall, no later than December 1, 1991, adopt an occupational safety and health standard for field sanitation. The standard shall comply with all of the following:

(1) The standard shall be at least as effective as the federal field sanitation standard contained in Section 1928.110 of Title 29 of the Code of Federal Regulations.

(2) The standard shall be at least as effective as California field sanitation requirements in effect as of July 1, 1990, pursuant to Article 4 (commencing with Section 113310) of Chapter 11 of Part 6 of Division 104 of the Health and Safety Code, Article 1 (commencing with Section 118375) of Chapter 1 of Part 15 of Division 104 of the Health and Safety Code, and Section 2441 of this code.

(3) The standard shall apply to all agricultural places of employment.

(4) The standard shall require that toilets are serviced and maintained in a clean, sanitary condition and kept in good repair at all times, including written records of that service and maintenance.

(b) Consistent with its mandatory investigation and reinspection duties under Sections 6309, 6313, and 6320, the division shall develop and implement a special emphasis program for enforcement of the standard for at least two years following its adoption. Not later than March 15, 1995, the division shall also develop a written plan to coordinate its enforcement program with other state and local agencies. The division shall be the lead enforcement agency. Other state and local agencies shall cooperate with the division in the development and implementation of the plan. The division shall report to the Legislature, not later than January 1, 1994, on its enforcement program. The plan shall provide for coordination between the division and local officials in counties where the field sanitation facilities required by the standard adopted pursuant to subdivision (a) are registered by the county health officer or other appropriate official of the county where the facilities are located. The division shall establish guidelines to assist counties that choose to register sanitation facilities pursuant to this section, for developing service charges, fees, or assess-

ments to defray the costs of registering the facilities, taking into consideration the differences between small and large employers.

(c)(1) Past violations by a fixed-site or nonfixed-site employer, occurring anywhere in the state within the previous five years, of one or more field sanitation regulations established pursuant to this section, or of Section 1928.110 of Title 29 of the Code of Federal Regulations, shall be considered for purposes of establishing whether a current violation is a repeat violation under Section 6429.

(2) Past violations by a fixed-site or nonfixed-site employer, occurring anywhere in the state within the previous five years, of one or more field sanitation regulations established pursuant to this section, Article 4 (commencing with Section 113310) of Chapter 11 of Part 6 of Division 104 of the Health and Safety Code, Article 1 (commencing with Section 118375) of Part 15 of Division 104 of the Health and Safety Code, or Section 2441 of this code, or of Section 1928.110 of Title 29 of the Code of Federal Regulations, shall constitute evidence of willfulness for purposes of Section 6429.

(d)(1) Notwithstanding Sections 6317 and 6434, any employer who fails to provide the facilities required by the field sanitation standard shall be assessed a civil penalty under the appropriate provisions of Sections 6427 to 6430, inclusive, except that in no case shall the penalty be less than seven hundred fifty dollars ($750) for each violation.

(2) Abatement periods fixed by the division pursuant to Section 6317 for violations shall be limited to one working day. However, the division may, pursuant to Section 6319.5, modify the period in cases where a good faith effort to comply with the abatement requirement is shown. The filing of an appeal with the appeals board pursuant to Sections 6319 and 6600 shall not stay the abatement period.

(3) An employer cited pursuant to paragraph (1) of this subdivision shall be required to annually complete a field sanitation compliance form which shall list the estimated peak number of employees, the toilets, washing, and drinking water facilities to be provided by the employer, any rental and maintenance agreements, and any other information considered relevant by the division for a period of five years following the citation. The employer shall be required to annually submit the completed form, subscribed under penalty of perjury, to the division, or to an agency designated by the division.

(e) The division shall notify the State Department of Health Services and the appropriate local health officers whenever a violation of the standard adopted pursuant to this section may result in the adulteration of food with harmful bacteria or other deleterious substances within the meaning of Article 5 (commencing with Section 110545) of Chapter 5 of Part 5 of Division 104 of the Health and Safety Code.

(f) Pending final adoption and approval of the standard required by subdivision (a), the division may enforce the field sanitation standards prescribed by Section 1928.110 of Title 29 of the Code of Federal Regulations, except subdivision (a) of Section 1928.110, in the same manner as other standards contained in this division. *(Added by Stats.1990, c. 1541 (S.B.1341), § 3. Amended by Stats.1994, c. 1203 (S.B.1689), § 1; Stats.1996, c. 1023 (S.B.1497), § 383, eff. Sept. 29, 1996.)*

§ 6716. Lead-related construction work

For the purposes of this division, "lead-related construction work" means any of the following:

(a) Any construction, alteration, painting, demolition, salvage, renovation, repair, or maintenance of any building or structure, including preparation and cleanup, that, by using or disturbing lead-containing material or soil, may result in significant exposure of employees to lead as determined by the standard adopted pursuant to Section 6717.

(b) The transportation, disposal, storage, or containment of materials containing lead on site or at a location at which construction activities are performed. "Lead-related construction work" does not include any activity related to the manufacture or mining of lead or the installation or repair of automotive materials containing lead. *(Added by Stats.1993, c. 1122 (A.B.383), § 4.)*

§ 6717. Standard for protection of health and safety of employees engaged in lead-related construction work; submission to standards board; adoption of standard; requirements and specifications

(a) On or before February 1, 1994, the division shall propose to the standards board for its review and adoption, a standard that protects the health and safety of employees who engage in lead-related construction work and meets all requirements imposed by the federal Occupational Safety and Health Administration. The standards board shall adopt the standard on or before December 31, 1994. The standard shall at least prescribe protective measures appropriate to the work activity and the lead content of materials to be disturbed by the activity, and shall include requirements and specifications pertaining to the following:

(1) Sampling and analysis of surface coatings and other materials that may contain significant amounts of lead.

(2) Concentrations and amounts of lead in surface coatings and other materials that may constitute a health hazard to employees engaged in lead-related construction work.

(3) Engineering controls, work practices, and personal protective equipment, including respiratory protection, fit-testing requirements, and protective clothing and equipment.

(4) Washing and showering facilities.

(5) Medical surveillance and medical removal protection.

(6) Establishment of regulated areas and appropriate posting and warning requirements.

(7) Recordkeeping.

(8) Training of employees engaged in lead-related construction work and their supervisors, that shall consist of current certification as required by regulations adopted under subdivision (c) of Section 105250 of the Health and Safety Code and include training with respect to at least the following:

(A) Health effects of lead exposure, including symptoms of overexposure.

(B) The construction activities, methods, processes, and materials that can result in lead exposure.

(C) The requirements of the lead standard promulgated pursuant to this section.

(D) Appropriate engineering controls, work practices, and personal protection for lead-related work.

(E) The necessity for fit-testing for respirator use and how fit-testing is conducted. *(Added by Stats.1993, c. 1122 (A.B.383), § 5. Amended by Stats.1996, c. 1023 (S.B.1497), § 384, eff. Sept. 29, 1996.)*

§ 6718. Gasoline cargo tanks; compliance with vapor emissions standards; employee requirements

Notwithstanding any other provision of law, any test procedures adopted by a state agency to determine compliance with vapor emission standards, by vapor recovery systems of cargo tanks on tank vehicles used to transport gasoline, shall not require any person to climb upon the cargo tank during loading operations. *(Added by Stats.1997, c. 84 (A.B.292), § 1.)*

§ 6719. Repetitive motion injuries in the workplace; Legislature's concern

The Legislature reaffirms its concern over the prevalence of repetitive motion injuries in the workplace and reaffirms the Occupational Safety and Health Standards Board's continuing duty to carry out Section 6357. *(Added by Stats.1999, c. 615 (A.B.1127), § 12.)*

Part 2

SAFEGUARDS ON RAILROADS

Chapter	Section
1. Jurisdiction	6800
2. Operation Personnel	6900
3. Safety Devices	6950
4. Trains	7000

CHAPTER 1. JURISDICTION

Section
6800. Jurisdiction of division.
6801. Jurisdiction of Public Utilities Commission.

Section

6802. Power of Public Utilities Commission over division orders.

§ 6800. Jurisdiction of division

The division has jurisdiction over:

(a) The safety and health of railroad employees employed in offices and in shops devoted to the construction, maintenance or repair of railroad equipment, and all other railroad employees with respect to occupational health, including, but not limited to, air contaminants, noise, sanitation and availability of drinking water.

(b) The occupational safety and health of employees of rail rapid transit systems, electric interurban railroads, or street railroads.

(c) The safety of employees of all other public utilities as defined in the Public Utilities Act. *(Stats.1937, c. 90, p. 313, § 6800. Amended by Stats.1945, c. 1431, p. 2705, § 112; Stats.1978, c. 1248, p. 4060, § 2; Stats.1982, c. 338, p. 1641, § 2.)*

§ 6801. Jurisdiction of Public Utilities Commission

The jurisdiction vested in the division shall in no instance, except those affecting exclusively the safety of employees, impair, diminish, or in any way affect the jurisdiction of the Public Utilities Commission over the construction, reconstruction, replacement, maintenance, or operation of the properties of public utilities or over any matter affecting the relationship between public utilities and their customers or the general public. *(Stats.1937, c. 90, p. 313, § 6801. Amended by Stats.1945, c. 1431, p. 2705, § 113; Stats.1953, c. 699, p. 1968, § 4.)*

§ 6802. Power of Public Utilities Commission over division orders

If the division makes or issues any order, decision, ruling or direction under this chapter which, in the judgment of the Public Utilities Commission, unduly and prejudicially interferes with the construction or operation of any public utility affected thereby, or with the public, or with a consumer or other patron of a public utility affected thereby, the Public Utilities Commission, of its own motion, or upon application of any utility or person so affected, may suspend, modify, alter, or annul such order, decision, ruling, or direction of the commission. The action of the Public Utilities Commission shall supersede and control the order, decision, ruling, or direction of the division previously made. *(Stats.1937, c. 90, p. 313, § 6802. Amended by Stats.1945, c. 1431, p. 2705, § 114; Stats.1953, c. 699, p. 1968, § 5.)*

CHAPTER 2. OPERATION PERSONNEL

Section

6900. Enforcement of chapter by public utilities commission.
6900.1. Short title.

Section

6900.5. Elimination of featherbedding practices; public policy; applicability of award of federal arbitration board.
6901. Required employees for passenger, mail, or express trains; application; exceptions.
6902. Local agencies; contracted or provided revenue services; contractually required compliance; exemptions.
6904. Locomotive without cars.
6905. Relief and wrecking trains.
6906. Qualifications of engineers, conductors, and brakemen.
6907. Operation of locomotives at terminals, shops, and engine houses.
6908. Violations; offense.
6909. Operation during strike or lockout.
6910. Gasoline motor cars; electric trains.

§ 6900. Enforcement of chapter by public utilities commission

Notwithstanding Section 6800, the Public Utilities Commission shall enforce the provisions of this chapter. *(Added by Stats.1959, c. 2187, p. 5310, § 1.)*

§ 6900.1. Short title

This Act shall be known and cited as the Railroad Anti-Featherbedding Law of 1964. *(Initiative Measure, Stats. 1965, p. A–133, § 1.)*

§ 6900.5. Elimination of featherbedding practices; public policy; applicability of award of federal arbitration board

It is the policy of the people of the State of California that featherbedding practices in the railroad industry should be eliminated and that national settlement of labor controversies relating to the manning of trains should be made effective in California. Accordingly the award of the Federal Arbitration Board No. 282 appointed by President John F. Kennedy pursuant to Congressional Public Law 88–108 of August 28, 1963, providing for the elimination of excess firemen and brakemen on diesel powered freight trains, or awards made pursuant thereto, shall be made effective in this State. Said award was the culmination of the proceedings originating with the Presidential Railroad Commission which was appointed by President Dwight D. Eisenhower at the request of both railroad labor and management and reported to President Kennedy on February 26, 1962.

Nothing contained in the laws of this State or in any order of any regulatory agency of this State shall prevent a common carrier by railroad from manning its trains in accordance with said award, in accordance with any federal legislation or awards pursuant thereto, or in accordance with any agreement between a railroad company and its employees or their representatives. *(Initiative Measure, Stats.1965, p. A–133, § 2.)*

§ 6901. Required employees for passenger, mail, or express trains; application; exceptions

(a) No common carrier operating more than four trains each way per day of 24 hours on any main track or branch line of railroad within this state, or on any part of a main track or branch line, shall run or permit to be run, on any part of a main track or branch line, any passenger, mail, or express train on which there is not employed at least one conductor, one brakeman, and the following:

(1) One engineer and one fireman for each diesel locomotive.

(2) One electric motorman for each train propelled or run by electricity.

(3) One motor or power control man for each train propelled by motive power other than diesel or electricity.

(4) Two brakemen, where four or more cars, exclusive of railroad officers' private cars, are hauled.

(5) One baggageman, except on a train upon which baggage is not hauled, and on gasoline motorcars.

(b) This section does not apply to any diesel locomotive weighing 45 tons or less.

(c) Paragraph (4) of subdivision (a) does not apply where its application would conflict with the terms of a collective bargaining agreement.

(d) Subdivision (a) does not apply to the San Diego Metropolitan Transit Development Board or the North San Diego County Transit Development Board.

(e) With respect to commuter train service provided by the San Diego Metropolitan Transit Development Board or the North San Diego County Transit Development Board, there shall be at least one qualified crewmember inside a train car set during revenue service. For the purpose of this subdivision, "revenue service" means service during which passengers are carried or are scheduled to be carried. *(Stats.1937, c. 90, p. 314, § 6901. Amended by Stats.1937, c. 701, p. 1973; Stats. 1959, c. 2188, p. 5310, § 1; Stats.1989, c. 392, § 1; Stats.1993, c. 681 (A.B.1133), § 1.)*

§ 6902. Local agencies; contracted or provided revenue services; contractually required compliance; exemptions

(a) For purposes of this section, "revenue service" means passenger train service during which passengers are carried or are scheduled to be carried.

(b) For purposes of this section, "local agency" means any city, county, special district, or other public entity in the state, including a charter city or a charter county.

(c) Except as otherwise provided by subdivision (e) of Section 6901, during revenue service provided by a local agency, or by any entity under contract with a local agency, there shall be in addition to the train operator at least one qualified employee inside a train car set of six or fewer coaches and at least two qualified employees inside a train car set of seven or more coaches.

(d)(1) A request for proposal or request for bid to provide revenue service issued by a local agency shall require compliance with subdivision (c).

(2) A contract to provide revenue service awarded by a local agency shall require compliance with subdivision (c).

(3) If a court of competent jurisdiction determines that an entity receiving a request for proposal or request for bid from a local agency for revenue service is exempt from the requirements of this section, all other entities that received the same request for proposal or request for bid shall also be exempt from the requirements of this section in responding to that request for proposal or request for bid.

(e) This section does not apply to heavy rail transit systems that are owned or operated by a public entity, or to light rail public transit systems. *(Added by Stats.1994, c. 976 (A.B.3776), § 1.)*

§ 6904. Locomotive without cars

Nothing in this chapter shall apply to a locomotive or locomotives without cars, except that each locomotive shall have one engineer and one fireman when being moved in train under steam, unless the engine is disabled. *(Stats.1937, c. 90, p. 316, § 6904.)*

§ 6905. Relief and wrecking trains

This chapter shall not apply to any relief or wrecking train in any case where a number of employees sufficient to comply with this chapter is not available for service on such relief or wrecking train. *(Stats.1937, c. 90, p. 316, § 6905.)*

§ 6906. Qualifications of engineers, conductors, and brakemen

No common carrier shall employ any person as:

(a) A locomotive engineer who has not had at least three years' actual service as a locomotive fireman or one year's actual service as a locomotive engineer.

(b) A conductor who has not had at least two years' actual service as a railroad brakeman in road service on steam or electric railroad other than street railway, or one year's actual service as a railroad conductor in road service.

(c) A brakeman who has not passed the regular examination required by transcontinental railroads. *(Stats.1937, c. 90, p. 316, § 6906. Amended by Stats.1957, c. 180, p. 825, § 1.)*

§ 6907. Operation of locomotives at terminals, shops, and engine houses

Nothing in this chapter shall apply to the running or operating of locomotives or motor power cars to and from trains at terminals by hostlers or of steam locomotives or motive power cars to and from engine houses or to the doing of work on steam locomotives or motive power cars at shops or engine-houses. *(Stats.1937, c. 90, p. 316, § 6907.)*

§ 6908. Violations; offense

Any violation of this chapter is a misdemeanor. *(Stats. 1937, c. 90, p. 317, § 6908.)*

§ 6909. Operation during strike or lockout

Nothing in this chapter shall apply to the operation of any train by a common carrier during times of strikes or walkouts, participated in by any of the employees mentioned in this chapter. *(Stats.1937, c. 90, p. 317, § 6909.)*

§ 6910. Gasoline motor cars; electric trains

Nothing in this chapter shall apply to gasoline motor cars operated exclusively on branch lines or to trains of less than three cars propelled by electricity. *(Stats.1937, c. 90, p. 317, § 6910.)*

CHAPTER 3. SAFETY DEVICES

Section
6950. Opening in roof of engine cab.
6951. Violation; misdemeanor; penalty.
6952. Handrails and footboards on engine cabs; violation; misdemeanor; penalty.
6953. Safety glass on electric cars and locomotives.
6954. Operation of electric car without laminated safety glass.
6955. Laminated safety glass defined.
6956. Violation; misdemeanor; penalty; separate offense for each day.

§ 6950. Opening in roof of engine cab

On any railroad train where the engine is accompanied by a tender of the Vanderbilt or similar type of construction and where the clearance between the overhang of the roof of the cab of the engine and the top of the tender accompanying the engine is less than twenty-eight inches, an opening not less than twenty-four inches square shall be cut out in the overhang of the roof of the cab, for the purpose of enabling an engineman with safety to go from the cab of the engine to the top of the tender. *(Stats. 1937, c. 90, p. 317, § 6950.)*

§ 6951. Violation; misdemeanor; penalty

Any railroad company operating a line in whole or in part within this state, or any receiver of any railroad, that fails to comply with any provision of section 6950 is guilty of a misdemeanor, punishable by a fine of not less than one hundred dollars ($100) for each offense. Each day that such failure continues is a separate offense. *(Stats. 1937, c. 90, p. 317, § 6951. Amended by Stats.1983, c. 1092, § 220, eff. Sept. 27, 1983, operative Jan. 1, 1984.)*

§ 6952. Handrails and footboards on engine cabs; violation; misdemeanor; penalty

Every railroad company operating engines within any part of this state shall provide each engine cab with a substantial and safe handrail along the top on each side of the cab extending from the front to the rear of the cab. Every engine cab other than one having front windows of not less than 14 inches in width and 42 inches in height shall be provided and equipped with a substantial and safe footboard, of not less than one and one-half inches, projecting outward from each side of the cab level with the floor and extending from the front to the rear of the cab.

Any railroad company, or receiver thereof, which fails to comply with any provisions of this section is guilty of a misdemeanor, punishable by a fine of two hundred dollars ($200) for each offense.

The provisions of this section shall not apply to any railroad company which issued in writing before July 2, 1921, and maintains in force, an order forbidding the engine or train crew to go from the engine cab to that portion of the engine in front of the cab while the cab is in motion. *(Stats.1937, c. 90, p. 317, § 6952. Amended by Stats.1983, c. 1092, § 221, eff. Sept. 27, 1983, operative Jan. 1, 1984.)*

§ 6953. Safety glass on electric cars and locomotives

Any electric car operated in interurban service and any electric locomotive shall be equipped exclusively with laminated safety glass in the compartment of the motorman or engineer, or if there is no compartment, the window in front of the motorman shall be so equipped, if the following conditions concur:

(a) The car or locomotive is built after the effective date of this section.

(b) The car or locomotive is operated by an overhead wire.

(c) The car or locomotive can exceed a speed of 45 miles per hour. *(Added by Stats.1941, c. 292, p. 1435, § 1.)*

§ 6954. Operation of electric car without laminated safety glass

On and after the first day of September, 1946, it shall be unlawful to operate any electric car in interurban service or any electric locomotive which is not so equipped with laminated safety glass. *(Added by Stats. 1941, c. 292, p. 1435, § 2.)*

§ 6955. Laminated safety glass defined

Laminated safety glass is glass so treated or combined with other materials as to reduce, in comparison with ordinary sheet glass or plate glass, the likelihood of injury to persons, by objects from external sources, or by glass when the glass is cracked or broken. *(Added by Stats. 1941, c. 292, p. 1435, § 3.)*

§ 6956. Violation; misdemeanor; penalty; separate offense for each day

Any common carrier violating Sections 6953 or 6954 is guilty of a misdemeanor for each violation, punishable by a fine of not less than two hundred dollars ($200) for each offense. Each day that any electric car is operated in interurban service or that any electric locomotive is operated, is a separate offense. *(Added by Stats.1941, c. 292, p. 1436, § 4. Amended by Stats.1983, c. 1092, § 222, eff. Sept. 27, 1983, operative Jan. 1, 1984.)*

751

CHAPTER 4. TRAINS

Section

7000. Caboose defined; placement of pusher engine ahead of caboose; use of electric locomotive at rear of train; scope of section.

§ 7000. Caboose defined; placement of pusher engine ahead of caboose; use of electric locomotive at rear of train; scope of section

As used in this section "caboose" means a caboose forming a part of a train and occupied by employees or caretakers, or both.

If conditions warrant it for the safety of the occupants of a caboose the conductor, in using a pusher engine, may place it ahead of the caboose.

This section applies only to main line movements of over five miles.

This section shall not prevent the use of an electric locomotive at the rear of any train.

This section shall not apply in any case of casualty, unavoidable accident, or act of God; nor under circumstances which are the result of a cause not known to, and which could not have been foreseen by, the railroad corporation, or its officer or agent in charge of a train. This section shall not apply to the operation of wrecking, or relief trains. *(Added by Stats.1939, c. 1060, p. 2989, § 1.)*

Part 3

SAFETY ON BUILDINGS

Chapter	Section
1. **Buildings under Construction or Repair**	7100
2. **Elevators, Escalators, Platform and Stairway Chair Lifts, Dumbwaiters, Moving Walks, Automated People Movers, and Other Conveyances**	7300
3. **Safety Devices upon Buildings to Safeguard Window Cleaners**	7325
4. **Aerial Passenger Tramways**	7340
5. **Cranes**	7370

CHAPTER 1. BUILDINGS UNDER CONSTRUCTION OR REPAIR

Article	Section
1. **Floors and Walls**	7100
2. **Scaffolding**	7150
3. **Construction Elevators**	7200
4. **Structural Steel Framed Buildings**	7250

ARTICLE 1. FLOORS AND WALLS

Section

7100. Building defined.
7101. Protective flooring during work.
7102. Concrete building construction; installation of flooring or forms before work on next floor.

Section

7103. Underflooring or planking of wooden floors; installation before work on next floor.
7104. Intermediate beams to support temporary flooring.
7105. Removal of temporary flooring; replanking of building.
7106. Building constructed in sections.
7107. Planked floor construction.
7108. Safety belts and nets.
7109. Working or permitting work while planking or nets not in place; misdemeanor.
7110. Enforcement agency.

§ 7100. Building defined

As used in this article, "building" means any multifloor building, other than structural steel framed building, more than two stories high in the course of construction. *(Added by Stats.1970, c. 1498, p. 2978, § 2.)*

§ 7101. Protective flooring during work

Every building shall have the joists, beams, or girders of floors below the floor or level where any work is being done, or about to be done, covered with flooring laid close together, or with other suitable material to protect workmen engaged in such building from falling through joists or girders, and from falling substances, whereby life or safety is endangered. *(Added by Stats.1970, c. 1498, p. 2978, § 2.)*

§ 7102. Concrete building construction; installation of flooring or forms before work on next floor

Every building which is of reinforced concrete construction, with reinforced concrete floors, shall have the floor filled in, either with forms or concrete, on each floor before the commencement of work upon the walls of the second floor above or the commencement of work upon the floor of the next floor above. *(Added by Stats.1970, c. 1498, p. 2978, § 2.)*

§ 7103. Underflooring or planking of wooden floors; installation before work on next floor

Every building having wooden floors other than a steel frame building shall have the underflooring, if double flooring is to be used, laid on each floor within the time prescribed above for reinforced concrete floors. Where single wooden floors are to be used, each floor shall be planked over within the time prescribed above for reinforced concrete floors. *(Added by Stats.1970, c. 1498, p. 2978, § 2.)*

§ 7104. Intermediate beams to support temporary flooring

If a span of a floor on a building exceeds 13 feet, an intermediate beam shall be used to support the temporary flooring, but spans not to exceed 16 feet may be covered by three-inch planks without an intermediate beam. The intermediate beam shall be of a sufficient strength to sustain a live load of 50 pounds per square foot of the area supported. *(Added by Stats.1970, c. 1498, p. 2979, § 2.)*

§ 7105. Removal of temporary flooring; replanking of building

If building operations are suspended and the temporary flooring required by this article is removed, the building shall be replanked upon the resumption of work so that every man at work has a covered floor not more than two stories below. *(Added by Stats.1970, c. 1498, p. 2979, § 2.)*

§ 7106. Building constructed in sections

Where a building is being constructed in sections each section constitutes a building for the purpose of this article. *(Added by Stats.1970, c. 1498, p. 2979, § 2.)*

§ 7107. Planked floor construction

Planked floors on buildings shall be tightly laid together of proper thickness, grade and span to carry the working load; such working load to be assumed as at least 25 pounds per square foot. *(Added by Stats.1970, c. 1498, p. 2979, § 2.)*

§ 7108. Safety belts and nets

Safety belts and nets shall be required in accordance with Article 24 (commencing with Section 1669) of subchapter 4 of Chapter 4 of Part 1 of Title 8 of the California Administrative Code, Construction Safety Orders of the Division of Occupational Safety and Health. *(Added by Stats.1970, c. 1498, p. 2979, § 2. Amended by Stats.1980, c. 676, p. 1979, § 239.)*

§ 7109. Working or permitting work while planking or nets not in place; misdemeanor

No person shall proceed with any work assigned to or undertaken by him, or require or permit any other person to proceed with work assigned to or undertaken by either, unless the planking or nets required by this article are in place. Violation of this section is a misdemeanor. *(Added by Stats.1970, c. 1498, p. 2979, § 2.)*

§ 7110. Enforcement agency

The Division of Occupational Safety and Health shall enforce this article. *(Added by Stats.1970, c. 1498, p. 2979, § 2. Amended by Stats.1980, c. 676, p. 1979, § 240.)*

ARTICLE 2. SCAFFOLDING

Section
7150. Scaffolding defined.
7151. Safety rail; suspended scaffolding.
7152. Safety lines.
7153. Platforms and floors.
7154.1. Prohibition of lean-to or jack scaffolds.
7155. Violation; misdemeanor.
7156. Offenses; misdemeanor.
7157. Safety orders.
7158. Enforcement agency.

§ 7150. Scaffolding defined

As used in this article, "scaffolding" includes scaffolding and staging. *(Stats.1937, c. 90, p. 319, § 7150.)*

§ 7151. Safety rail; suspended scaffolding

If the working platform of any scaffolding swung or suspended from an overhead support is more than 10 feet above the ground, floor or area to which an employee on the scaffolding might fall, it shall have a safety rail of wood or other equally rigid material of adequate strength. The rail shall comply with the applicable orders of the Division of Occupational Safety and Health.

Suspended scaffolding shall be fastened so as to prevent the scaffolding from swaying from the building, or structure, or other object being worked on from the scaffolding. All parts of the scaffolding shall be of sufficient strength to support, bear, or withstand with safety any weight of persons, tools, appliances, or materials which might reasonably be placed on it or which are to be supported by it. *(Stats.1937, c. 90, p. 319, § 7151. Amended by Stats.1947, c. 700, p. 1757, § 1; Stats.1980, c. 676, p. 1979, § 241.)*

§ 7152. Safety lines

In addition to the duties imposed by any law regulating or relating to scaffolding, an employer who uses or permits the use of scaffolding described in Section 7151 in connection with construction, alteration, repairing, painting, cleaning or doing of any work upon any building or structure, shall:

(a) Furnish safety lines to tie all hooks and hangers back on the roof of such building or structure.

(b) Provide safety lines hanging from the roof, securely tied thereto, for all swinging scaffolds which rely upon stirrups of the single point suspension type to support the working platform. One such line shall be provided for each workman with a minimum of one line between each pair of hangers or falls.

The standards board may adopt occupational safety and health standards different from the requirements of this section or grant variances from these requirements if the standards or variances provide equivalent or superior safety for employees. *(Stats.1937, c. 90, p. 319, § 7152. Amended by Stats.1947, c. 700, p. 1757, § 2; Stats.1981, c. 905, p. 2846, § 1.)*

§ 7153. Platforms and floors

Platforms or floors of such scaffolding shall be not less than 14 inches in width and shall be free from knots or fractures impairing their strength. *(Stats.1937, c. 90, p. 320, § 7153. Amended by Stats.1947, c. 700, p. 1757, § 3.)*

§ 7154.1. Prohibition of lean-to or jack scaffolds

The use of lean-to scaffolds, sometimes known as jack scaffolds, as support for scaffolds is hereby prohibited. *(Added by Stats.1943, c. 257, p. 1171, § 1.)*

§ 7155. Violation; misdemeanor

Violation of any provision of section 7151 to 7154 inclusive is a misdemeanor. *(Stats.1937, c. 90, p. 320, § 7155.)*

§ 7156. Offenses; misdemeanor

Any person employing or directing another to do or perform any labor in the construction, alteration, repairing, painting, or cleaning of any house, building, or structure within this state is guilty of a misdemeanor who does any of the following:

(a) Knowingly or negligently furnishes or erects, or causes to be furnished or erected for the performance of that labor, unsafe or improper scaffolding, slings, hammers, blocks, pulleys, stays, braces, ladders, irons, ropes, or other mechanical contrivances.

(b) Hinders or obstructs any officer or inspector of the Division of Occupational Safety and Health attempting to inspect such equipment under the provisions of this article or any law or safety order of this state.

(c) Destroys or defaces, or removes any notice posted thereon by any division officer or inspector, or permits the use thereof, after the equipment has been declared unsafe by the officer or inspector. *(Stats.1937, c. 90, p. 320, § 7156. Amended by Stats.1945, c. 1431, p. 2706, § 116; Stats.1980, c. 676, p. 1979, § 242.)*

§ 7157. Safety orders

The division may make and enforce safety orders in the manner prescribed by law, to supplement and carry into effect the purposes and provisions of this article. *(Stats. 1937, c. 90, p. 320, § 7157. Amended by Stats.1945, c. 1431, p. 2706, § 117.)*

§ 7158. Enforcement agency

The division shall enforce the provisions of this article. *(Stats.1937, c. 90, p. 320, § 7158. Amended by Stats.1945, c. 1431, p. 2706, § 118.)*

ARTICLE 3. CONSTRUCTION ELEVATORS

Section
7200. Definitions.
7201. Signal system.
7202. Appointment of person to operate signal.
7203. Safety orders.
7204. Inspection; direction to remedy defects; use pending compliance.
7205. Violation; misdemeanor; penalty.

§ 7200. Definitions

As used in this article:

(a) "Construction elevator" includes any means used to hoist persons or material of any kind on a building under course of construction, when operated by any power other than muscular power.

(b) "Building" includes structures of all kinds during the course of construction, regardless of the purposes for which they are intended and whether such construction be below or above the level of the ground. *(Stats.1937, c. 90, p. 320, § 7200.)*

§ 7201. Signal system

Every construction elevator used in buildings shall have a system of signals for the purpose of signaling the person operating or controlling the machinery which operates or controls the construction elevator. *(Stats.1937, c. 90, p. 320, § 7201.)*

§ 7202. Appointment of person to operate signal

The person in charge of a building shall appoint one or more persons to give such signals. Such person shall be selected from those most familiar with the work for which the construction elevator is being used. The signaling devices provided shall be protected against unauthorized or accidental operation. *(Stats.1937, c. 90, p. 320, § 7202.)*

§ 7203. Safety orders

The board shall make, and may from time to time amend, general safety orders in the manner prescribed by law. Such orders shall specify and fix the nature and methods of signals and signaling devices and uniform signals to be used in this State under this article. *(Stats.1937, c. 90, p. 321, § 7203. Amended by Stats.1945, c. 1431, p. 2706, § 119.)*

§ 7204. Inspection; direction to remedy defects; use pending compliance

The division shall inspect all construction elevators. If any part of the construction or system of signals used on a construction elevator is defective or endangers the lives of the persons working in the immediate vicinity of the construction elevator, the division shall direct the person in charge thereof to remedy such defect. Such construction elevator shall not be used again until the order of the division is complied with. *(Stats.1937, c. 90, p. 321, § 7204. Amended by Stats.1945, c. 1431, p. 2706, § 120.)*

§ 7205. Violation; misdemeanor; penalty

Any person, or the agent or officer thereof, who violates any provision of this article is guilty of a misdemeanor, punishable by a fine of not less than one hundred dollars ($100) and not more than one thousand dollars ($1,000), or imprisonment in the county jail for not less than 30 days and not more than six months, or both. *(Stats.1937, c. 90, p. 321, § 7205. Amended by Stats.1983, c. 1092, § 223, eff. Sept. 27, 1983, operative Jan. 1, 1984.)*

ARTICLE 4. STRUCTURAL STEEL FRAMED BUILDINGS

Section
7250. Building defined.
7251. Application of act.
7252. Derrick or working floor.
7253. Temporary floors; safety belts.
7254. Temporary floors; requirements.
7255. Temporary floors; securing against displacement.
7256. Planks.
7257. Wire mesh or plywood covers.

Section

7258. Metal decking.
7259. Floor planks; replacement.
7260. Instructions prior to removal of temporary floor plank.
7261. Transferring planks; procedure.
7262. Safety equipment for personnel gathering and stacking planks.
7263. Sequence of construction.
7264. Building being constructed in sections.
7265. Safety belts and nets.
7266. Working or permitting work while planking or nets are not in place, misdemeanor.
7267. Enforcement agency.

§ 7250. Building defined

As used in this article "building" means any multifloor structural steel framed building more than two stories high in the course of construction. *(Added by Stats.1970, c. 1498, p. 2979, § 3.)*

§ 7251. Application of act

As defined above, these provisions shall apply to buildings erected in tiers or stories and shall not apply to steel framed buildings having large open spans or areas such as, mill buildings, gymnasiums, auditoriums, hangars, arenas, or stadiums *(Added by Stats.1970, c. 1498, p. 2979, § 3.)*

§ 7252. Derrick or working floor

The derrick or working floor of every building shall be solidly decked over its entire surface except for access openings. *(Added by Stats.1970, c. 1498, p. 2979, § 3.)*

§ 7253. Temporary floors; safety belts

There shall be a tight and substantial temporary floor within two floors below and directly under that portion of each tier of beams on which erection, riveting, bolting, welding or painting is being done. For operations of short duration of exposure to falling, safety belts shall be required as set forth in Section 7265. *(Added by Stats. 1970, c. 1498, p. 2979, § 3.)*

§ 7254. Temporary floors; requirements

Temporary floors shall be wood planking of proper thickness, grade and span to carry the working load, but shall not be less than two inches thick, full size undressed. *(Added by Stats.1970, c. 1498, p. 2980, § 3.)*

§ 7255. Temporary floors; securing against displacement

Provision shall be made to secure temporary flooring against displacement by strong winds or other forces. *(Added by Stats.1970, c. 1498, p. 2980, § 3.)*

§ 7256. Planks

Planks shall extend a minimum of 12 inches beyond centerline of their supports at each end. *(Added by Stats.1970, c. 1498, p. 2980, § 3.)*

§ 7257. Wire mesh or plywood covers

Wire mesh or plywood (exterior grade) shall be used to cover openings adjacent to columns where planks do not fit tightly. *(Added by Stats.1970, c. 1498, p. 2980, § 3.)*

§ 7258. Metal decking

Metal decking where used in lieu of wood planking shall be of equivalent strength and shall be laid tightly and secured to prevent movement. *(Added by Stats.1970, c. 1498, p. 2980, § 3.)*

§ 7259. Floor planks; replacement

Floor planks that are temporarily removed for any reason whatsoever shall be replaced as soon as work requiring their removal is completed or the open area shall be properly guarded. *(Added by Stats.1970, c. 1498, p. 2980, § 3.)*

§ 7260. Instructions prior to removal of temporary floor plank

Prior to removal of temporary floor plank, employees shall be instructed by assigned supervision the steps to be taken to perform the work safely and in proper sequence. *(Added by Stats.1970, c. 1498, p. 2980, § 3.)*

§ 7261. Transferring planks; procedure

When gathering and stacking temporary floor plank on a lower floor, in preparation for transferring such plank for use on an upper working floor, the steel erector's personnel shall remove such plank successively, working toward the last panel of such floor, so that the work is always being done from the planked floor. *(Added by Stats.1970, c. 1498, p. 2980, § 3.)*

§ 7262. Safety equipment for personnel gathering and stacking planks

When gathering and stacking temporary floor planks from the last panel, the steel erector's personnel assigned to such work shall be protected by safety belts with life lines attached to a catenary line or other substantial anchorage. *(Added by Stats.1970, c. 1498, p. 2980, § 3.)*

§ 7263. Sequence of construction

The sequence of erection, bolting, temporary guying, riveting and welding shall be such as to maintain the stability of the structural frame at all times during construction. This applies to the dead weight of the structure, plus weight and working reactions of all construction equipment placed thereon plus any external forces that may be applied. *(Added by Stats.1970, c. 1498, p. 2980, § 3.)*

§ 7264. Building being constructed in sections

Where a building is being constructed in sections, each section constitutes a building as defined in Section 7250. *(Added by Stats.1970, c. 1498, p. 2980, § 3.)*

§ 7265. Safety belts and nets

Safety belts and nets shall be required in accordance with Article 24 (commencing with Section 1669) of subchapter 4 of Chapter 4 of Part 1 of Title 8 of the California Administrative Code, Construction Safety Orders of the Division of Occupational Safety and Health. *(Added by Stats.1970, c. 1498, p. 2980, § 3. Amended by Stats.1980, c. 676, p. 1979, § 243.)*

§ 7266. Working or permitting work while planking or nets are not in place, misdemeanor

No person shall proceed with any work assigned to or undertaken by him, or require or permit any other person to proceed with work assigned to or undertaken by either, unless the planking or nets required by this article are in place. Violation of this section is a misdemeanor. *(Added by Stats.1970, c. 1498, p. 2980, § 3.)*

§ 7267. Enforcement agency

The Division of Occupational Safety and Health shall enforce this article. *(Added by Stats.1970, c. 1498, p. 2980, § 3. Amended by Stats.1980, c. 676, p. 1979, § 244.)*

CHAPTER 2. ELEVATORS, ESCALATORS, PLATFORM AND STAIRWAY CHAIR LIFTS, DUMBWAITERS, MOVING WALKS, AUTOMATED PEOPLE MOVERS, AND OTHER CONVEYANCES

Section
7300.   Legislative intent and declarations.
7300.1.   Definitions.
7300.2.   Application of chapter to specified conveyances.
7300.3.   Exclusion from application of chapter for specified equipment.
7300.4.   Exemption from application of chapter for specified work.
7301.   Requirement of permit; posting; violations; penalties.
7301.1.   Requirement of permit for conveyances erected, constructed, installed, or materially altered on or after June 30, 2003; application procedure and requirements; expiration; revocation.
7301.5.   Regulations by standards board; conveyances; certification of emergency certified competent conveyance mechanics; certification of temporary certified competent conveyance mechanics.
7302.   Operation of a conveyance without a permit; misdemeanor; separate offense for each day.
7302.1.   Persons, contractors and employers contracting for or authorizing operation of a conveyance without a permit; misdemeanor.
7302.2.   Persons, contractors and employers contracting for or authorizing operation of a conveyance without a permit; civil penalty.
7303.   Injunction; temporary restraining order; bond; civil penalty for violation of order.
7304.   Annual inspection; issuance of annual permit; conveyances subject to full maintenance service contract.
7305.   Preliminary order for repairs and alterations; use pending compliance.
7306.   Hearing on preliminary order.

Section
7307.   Final repair or alteration order; rehearing; misdemeanor punishment for violation of order.
7308.   Temporary permit pending repairs and alterations.
7309.   Inspectors.
7309.1.   Reinspections conducted on or after June 30, 2003; qualified conveyance inspectors; certification.
7310.   Inspection by municipal inspectors; issuance of permit.
7311.   Certificate of competency for inspectors; qualifications; rescission of certificate.
7311.1.   Certified qualified conveyance companies; application of section; certification procedures and requirements; proof of insurance; disclosure.
7311.2.   Persons subject to application of chapter on or after June 30, 2003; certified competent conveyance mechanics; application procedure and requirements.
7311.25. Agricultural production, processing, and handling facilities; maintenance and inspection of manlifts.
7311.3.   Duration of certificates issued by the division; fees; renewal; continuing education; waiver; falsified attendance records as grounds for suspension or revocation.
7311.4.   Fees associated with certification process; refundability.
7311.5.   Qualifying as a certified qualified conveyance company or certified competent conveyance mechanic; limited purpose of certification; definitions.
7312.   Revocation of permit.
7313.   Inspection reports.
7314.   Fees associated with inspections or field consultations performed by a division safety engineer; penalties for failure to pay fees; regulations.
7315.   Payment of fee.
7316.   Elevator safety account; disposition of fees; criteria for fee charges; annual report.
7317.   Exemption from application of chapter for certain conveyances.
7318.   Safety orders.
7319.   Failure to provide operator's seat; misdemeanor; penalty.
7320.   Operation without permit; penalty.
7321.   Operation in dangerous condition; penalty.
7321.5.   Enforcement.
7322.   Orders from division prohibiting use; hearings; misdemeanor punishment for violation of order.
7323.   Regulations adopted by the standards board; notice and hearing; final regulations.
7324.   Certification of compliance with State Fire Prevention and Building Code.
7324.1.   Defective workmanship; liability.
7324.2.   Retroactive application.

§ 7300. Legislative intent and declarations

The Legislature finds and declares all of the following:

(a) It is the purpose of this chapter to promote public safety awareness and to assure, to the extent feasible, the safety of the public and of workers with respect to conveyances covered by this chapter.

(b) The use of unsafe or defective conveyances imposes a substantial probability of serious and preventable injury to employees and the public. The prevention of these injuries and protection of employees and the public from unsafe conditions is in the best interest of the people of this state. Therefore, this chapter also establishes minimum standards for persons operating or maintaining conveyances covered by this chapter. These standards include familiarity with the operation and safety functions of the components and equipment, and documented training or experience or both, which shall include, but not be limited to, recognizing the safety hazards and performing the procedures to which they are assigned in conformance with all legal requirements.

(c) This chapter is not intended to prevent the division from implementing regulations, nor to prevent the use of systems, methods, or devices of equivalent or superior quality, strength, fire resistance, code effectiveness, durability, and safety to those required by the law, provided that there is technical documentation to demonstrate that the equivalency of the system, method, or device, is at least as effective as that prescribed in ASME A17.1, ASME A17.3, ASME A18.1, or ASCE 21. *(Added by Stats.2002, c. 1149 (S.B.1886), § 3.)*

§ 7300.1. Definitions

As used in this chapter:

(a) "ASCE 21" means the Automated People Mover Standards, as adopted by the American Society of Civil Engineers.

(b) "ASME A17.1" means the Safety Code for Elevators and Escalators, an American National Standard, as adopted by the American Society of Mechanical Engineers.

(c) "ASME A17.3" means the Safety Code for Existing Elevators and Escalators, an American National Standard, as adopted by the American Society of Mechanical Engineers.

(d) "ASME A18.1" means the Safety Standard for Platform Lifts and Stairway Chairlifts, an American National Standard, as adopted by the American Society of Mechanical Engineers.

(e) "Automated people mover" has the same meaning as defined in ASCE 21.

(f) "Board" or "standards board" means the Occupational Safety and Health Standards Board.

(g) "Certified qualified conveyance company" means any person, firm, or corporation that (1) possesses a valid contractor's license if required by Chapter 9 (commencing with Section 7000) of Division 3 of the Business and Professions Code and (2) is certified as a qualified conveyance company by the division in accordance with this chapter.

(h) "Certified competent conveyance mechanic" means any person who has been determined by the division to have the qualifications and ability of a competent journey-level conveyance mechanic and is so certified by the division in accordance with this chapter.

(i) "Conveyance" means any elevator, dumbwaiter, escalator, moving platform lift, stairway chairlift, material lift or dumbwaiter with automatic transfer device, automated people mover, or other equipment subject to this chapter.

(j) "Division" means the Division of Occupational Safety and Health.

(k) "Dormant elevator, dumbwaiter, or escalator" means an installation placed out of service as specified in ASME A17.1 and ASME A18.1.

(*l*) "Elevator" means an installation defined as an "elevator" in ASME A17.1.

(m) "Conveyance inspector" means any conveyance safety inspector of the division or other conveyance inspector determined by the division to be qualified pursuant to this chapter.

(n) "Escalator" means an installation defined as an "escalator" in ASME A17.1.

(*o*) "Existing installation" means an installation defined as an "installation, existing" in ASME A17.1.

(p) "Full maintenance service contract" means an agreement by a certified competent conveyance company and the person owning or having the custody, management, or control of the operation of the conveyance, if the agreement provides that the certified competent conveyance company is responsible for effecting repairs necessary to the safe operation of the equipment and will provide services as frequently as is necessary, but no less often than monthly.

(q) "Material alteration" means an alteration as defined in ASME A17.1 or A18.1.

(r) "Moving walk" or "moving sidewalk" means an installation defined as a "moving walk" in ASME A17.1.

(s) "Permit" means a document issued by the division that indicates that the conveyance has had the required safety inspection and tests and fees have been paid as set forth in this chapter.

(t) "Temporary permit" means a document issued by the division which permits the use of a noncompliant conveyance by the general public for a limited time while minor repairs are being completed or until permit fees are paid.

(u) "Repair" has the same meaning as defined in ASME A17.1 or A18.1. A "repair" does not require a permit.

(v) "Temporarily dormant elevator, dumbwaiter, or escalator" means a conveyance, the power supply of which has been disconnected by removing fuses and placing a padlock on the mainline disconnect switch in the "off" position. In the case of an elevator or dumbwaiter, the car shall be parked and the hoistway doors shall be in the closed and latched position. A wire seal shall be installed on the mainline disconnect switch by a conveyance inspector of the division. The wire seal and padlock shall not be removed for any purpose without permission from a conveyance inspector of the division. A temporarily dormant elevator, dumbwaiter, or escalator shall not be used again until it has been put in safe running order and is in condition for use. Annual inspections by a conveyance inspector shall continue for the duration of the temporarily dormant status. Temporarily dormant status may be renewed annually, but shall not exceed five years. After each inspection, the conveyance inspector shall file a report with the chief of the division describing the current condition of the conveyance.

(w) The meanings of building transportation terms not otherwise defined in this section shall be as defined in the latest editions of ASME A17.1 and ASME A18.1. *(Added by Stats.2002, c. 1149 (S.B.1886), § 4. Amended by Stats.2004, c. 503 (A.B.2350), § 1.)*

§ 7300.2. Application of chapter to specified conveyances

Except as provided in Section 7300.3, this chapter covers the design, erection, construction, installation, material alteration, inspection, testing, maintenance, repair, service, and operation of the following conveyances and their associated parts and hoistways:

(a) Hoisting and lowering mechanisms equipped with a car or platform which move between two or more landings. This equipment includes, but is not limited to, the following:

(1) Elevators.

(2) Platform lifts and stairway chair lifts.

(b) Power-driven stairways and walkways for carrying persons between landings. This equipment includes, but is not limited to, the following:

(1) Escalators.

(2) Moving walks.

(c) Hoisting and lowering mechanisms equipped with a car which serve two or more landings and are restricted to the carrying of material by limited size or limited access to the car. This equipment includes, but is not limited to, the following:

(1) Dumbwaiters.

(2) Material lifts and dumbwaiters with automatic transfer devices.

(d) Automatic guided transit vehicles on guideways with an exclusive right-of-way. This equipment includes, but is not limited to, automated people movers. *(Added by Stats.2002, c. 1149 (S.B.1886), § 5.)*

§ 7300.3. Exclusion from application of chapter for specified equipment

Equipment not covered by this chapter includes the following:

(a) Material hoists within the scope of standard A10.5 as adopted by the American National Standards Institute.

(b) Mobile scaffolds, towers, and platforms within the scope of standard A92 as adopted by the American National Standards Institute.

(c) Powered platforms and equipment for exterior and interior maintenance within the scope of standard 120.1 as adopted by the American National Standards Institute.

(d) Cranes, derricks, hoists, hooks, jacks, and slings within the scope of standard B30 as adopted by the American Society of Mechanical Engineers.

(e) Industrial trucks within the scope of standard B56 as adopted by the American Society of Mechanical Engineers.

(f) Portable equipment, except for portable escalators that are covered by standard A17.1 as adopted by the American National Standards Institute.

(g) Tiering or piling machines used to move materials to and from storage located and operating entirely within one story.

(h) Equipment for feeding or positioning materials, including that equipment used with machine tools or printing presses.

(i) Skip or furnace hoists.

(j) Wharf ramps.

(k) Railroad car lifts or dumpers.

(*l*) Line jacks, false cars, shafters, moving platforms, and similar equipment used for installing a conveyance by a contractor licensed in this state. *(Added by Stats.2002, c. 1149 (S.B.1886), § 6. Amended by Stats.2004, c. 503 (A.B.2350), § 2.)*

§ 7300.4. Exemption from application of chapter for specified work

This chapter does not apply to work that is not related to standards for conveyances that are (a) incorporated in codes promulgated by the American National Standards Institute or the American Society of Mechanical Engineers or (b) included in regulations of the division, in effect immediately prior to January 1, 2003, prescribing conveyance safety orders. Work exempted pursuant to this section includes, but is not limited to, routine nonmechanical maintenance, such as cleaning panels and changing light fixtures. *(Added by Stats.2002, c. 1149 (S.B.1886), § 7. Amended by Stats.2004, c. 503 (A.B. 2350), § 3.)*

§ 7301. Requirement of permit; posting; violations; penalties

No conveyance shall be operated in this state unless a permit for its operation is issued by or in behalf of the division, and unless the permit remains in effect and is kept posted conspicuously on the conveyance. Operation of a conveyance without a permit or failure to post the permit conspicuously shall constitute cause for the division to prohibit use of the conveyance, unless it can be shown that a request for issuance or renewal of a permit has been made and the request has not been acted upon by the division. *(Stats.1937, c. 90, p. 321, § 7301. Amended by Stats.1945, c. 1431, p. 2707, § 122; Stats. 1985, c. 701, § 2; Stats.1990, c. 1022 (A.B.3039), § 1;*

Stats.1991, c. 258 (A.B.1718), § 1; Stats.2002, c. 1149 (S.B.1886), § 8.)

§ 7301.1. Requirement of permit for conveyances erected, constructed, installed, or materially altered on or after June 30, 2003; application procedure and requirements; expiration; revocation

(a) On and after June 30, 2003, no conveyance may be erected, constructed, installed, or materially altered, as defined by regulation of the division, unless a permit has been obtained from the division before the work is commenced. A copy of the permit shall be kept at the construction site at all times while the work is in progress and shall be made available for inspection upon request. This section shall not apply to platform lifts and stairway chairlifts installed in a private residence as provided in paragraph (2) or (3) of subdivision (a) of Section 7317.

(b) Before March 1, 2003, the division shall establish an application procedure and all requirements for a permit under this section, which shall include the following:

(1) At a minimum, the applicant for a permit under this section shall meet all of the following requirements:

(A) The applicant shall hold a current elevator contractor's license issued pursuant to Chapter 9 (commencing with Section 7000) of Division 3 of the Business and Professions Code.

(B) The applicant shall be a certified qualified conveyance company.

(C) The applicant shall submit proof of the following types of insurance coverage, in the form of certified copies of policies or certificates of insurance:

(i) Liability insurance to provide general liability coverage of not less than one million dollars ($1,000,000) for the injury or death of any one person or persons in any one occurrence, with coverage of not less than five hundred thousand dollars ($500,000) for property damage in any one occurrence.

(ii) Workers' compensation insurance coverage.

(D) In the event of any material alteration, nonrenewal, or cancellation of any insurance required by this subparagraph, the applicant or permitholder shall submit written notice thereof to the division within five working days.

(2) At a minimum, each application for a permit under this section shall include all of the following:

(A) Copies of specifications and accurately scaled and fully dimensioned plans showing the location of the installation in relation to the plans and elevation of the building; the location of the machinery room and the equipment to be installed, relocated, or altered; and all structural supporting members thereof, including foundations. The plans and specifications shall identify all materials to be employed and all loads to be supported or conveyed. The plans and specifications shall be suffi-ciently complete to illustrate all details of construction and design.

(B) The name, residence, and business address of the applicant and each partner, or for a corporation, the principal officers and anyone who is authorized to accept service of process or official notices; the number of years the applicant has engaged in the business of constructing, erecting, installing, or altering conveyances; and the approximate number of persons to be employed on the permitted job.

(C) The permit fee.

(3) The division shall establish, and may from time to time amend, a fee for a permit under this section in an amount sufficient to defray the division's actual costs in administering the permit process, including the costs of investigation, revocation, or other associated costs. Permit fees collected by the division are nonrefundable.

(c)(1) The permit shall expire when the work authorized by that permit is not commenced within six months after the date of issuance, or within a shorter period as the division may specify at the time the permit is issued.

(2) The permit shall expire following commencement of work, if the permitholder suspends or abandons the work for a period of 60 days, or for a shorter period of time as the division may specify at the time the permit is issued.

(3) Upon application and for good cause shown, the division may extend a permit that would otherwise expire under this subdivision.

(d) The division may revoke any permit at any time, upon good cause, and after notice and an opportunity to be heard. *(Added by Stats.2002, c. 1149 (S.B.1886), § 9. Amended by Stats.2004, c. 503 (A.B.2350), § 4.)*

§ 7301.5. Regulations by standards board; conveyances; certification of emergency certified competent conveyance mechanics; certification of temporary certified competent conveyance mechanics

(a) The standards board shall adopt regulations pertaining to conveyances, including, but not limited to, conveyance emergency and signal devices, and the operation of conveyances under fire and other emergency conditions.

(b) Before January 1, 2003, the division shall establish an application procedure and all requirements for certification under this subdivision as an emergency certified competent conveyance mechanic. To ensure the safety of the public when a disaster or other emergency exists within the state and the number of certified competent conveyance mechanics in the state is insufficient to cope with the emergency, any certified qualified conveyance company may, within five business days after commencing work requiring certified competent conveyance mechanics, apply to the division, on behalf of all persons performing the work who are not certified competent conveyance mechanics, for certification as emergency certified competent conveyance mechanics. Any person

759

for whom emergency certification is sought under this subdivision shall be certified by a certified qualified conveyance company to have an acceptable combination of documented experience and education to perform work covered by this chapter without direct and immediate supervision. The certified qualified conveyance company shall furnish proof of competency as the division may require. The division shall issue an emergency certified competent conveyance mechanic certificate upon receipt of acceptable documentation and payment of the required fee. Each certificate issued pursuant to this subdivision shall recite that it is valid for a period of 30 days from the date of issuance and for those particular conveyances and geographical areas as the division may designate, and otherwise shall entitle the person being certified to the rights and privileges of a certified competent conveyance mechanic as set forth in this chapter. The division shall renew an emergency certified competent conveyance mechanic certificate during the existence of the emergency.

(c) Before January 1, 2004, the division shall establish an application procedure and all requirements for certification under this subdivision as a temporary certified competent conveyance mechanic. If there are no certified qualified conveyance mechanics available to perform elevator work, a certified qualified conveyance company may apply to the division for certification of one or more temporary certified competent conveyance mechanics. Any person seeking to work as a temporary certified competent conveyance mechanic shall, before beginning work, be approved by the division as having an acceptable combination of documented experience and education to perform work covered by this chapter without direct and immediate supervision. The certified qualified conveyance company shall furnish proof of competency as the division may require. The division may issue a temporary certified competent conveyance mechanic certificate upon acceptable documentation and payment of the required fee. Each certificate issued pursuant to this subdivision shall recite that it is valid for a period of 30 days from the date of issuance and while the certificate holder is employed by the certified qualified conveyance company that certified the individual as competent. The certificate shall be renewable as long as the shortage of certified competent conveyance mechanics continues. *(Added by Stats.1985, c. 701, § 2.5. Amended by Stats. 2002, c. 1149 (S.B.1886), § 10; Stats.2004, c. 503 (A.B. 2350), § 5.)*

§ 7302. Operation of a conveyance without a permit; misdemeanor; separate offense for each day

The operation of a conveyance without a permit by any person owning or having the custody, management, or control of the operation of the conveyance, is a misdemeanor, punishable by a fine of not more than one thousand dollars ($1,000), imprisonment in the county jail for not more than 10 days, or by both that fine and imprisonment. Each day of operation for each conveyance without a permit is a separate offense. Any person

who has requested the issuance or renewal of a permit if the request has not been acted upon by the division may not be prosecuted for a violation of this section. *(Added by Stats.2002, c. 1149 (S.B.1886), § 12.)*

§ 7302.1. Persons, contractors and employers contracting for or authorizing operation of a conveyance without a permit; misdemeanor

(a) Any person who contracts for or authorizes the erection, construction, installation, or material alteration of a conveyance without a permit in violation of Section 7301.1 is guilty of a misdemeanor punishable by a fine of not more than seventy thousand dollars ($70,000), imprisonment in the county jail for not more than one year, or by both that fine and imprisonment.

(b) Any employer or contractor who contracts for or engages in the erection, construction, installation, or material alteration of a conveyance without a permit in violation of Section 7301.1 is guilty of a misdemeanor punishable by a fine of not more than seventy thousand dollars ($70,000), imprisonment in the county jail for not more than one year, or by both that fine and imprisonment. *(Added by Stats.2002, c. 1149 (S.B.1886), § 13.)*

§ 7302.2. Persons, contractors and employers contracting for or authorizing operation of a conveyance without a permit; civil penalty

The division may assess a civil penalty of not more than seventy thousand dollars ($70,000) against any person, and against any employer or contractor, who contracts for or authorizes the erection, construction, installation, or material alteration of a conveyance without a permit issued pursuant to Section 7301.1. *(Added by Stats.2002, c. 1149 (S.B.1886), § 14.)*

§ 7303. Injunction; temporary restraining order; bond; civil penalty for violation of order

(a) Whenever any conveyance is operated without a current valid permit issued pursuant to Section 7304, and is in a condition that its use is dangerous to the life or safety of any person, the division or any affected person may apply to the superior court of the county in which the conveyance is located for an injunction restraining the operation of the conveyance until the condition is corrected. Proof by certification of the division that a permit has not been issued, has expired, or has been revoked, together with the affidavit of any safety inspector of the division or other expert that the operation of the conveyance is dangerous to the life or safety of any person, is sufficient ground, in the discretion of the court, for the immediate granting of a temporary restraining order.

(b) No bond shall be required from the division as a prerequisite for the division to seek or obtain any restraining order under subdivision (a).

(c) Any person who intentionally violates any injunction prohibiting the operation of the conveyance issued pursuant to subdivision (a) shall be liable for a civil penalty, to be assessed by the division, not to exceed seven thousand dollars ($7,000) for each violation. Each day of operation for each conveyance is a separate violation. *(Stats.1937, c. 90, p. 321, § 7303. Amended by Stats.1945, c. 1431, p. 2707, § 123; Stats.1982, c. 517, p. 2405, § 311; Stats.1985, c. 701, § 3; Stats.2002, c. 1149 (S.B.1886), § 15.)*

§ 7304. Annual inspection; issuance of annual permit; conveyances subject to full maintenance service contract

(a) Except as provided in subdivision (b), the division shall cause all conveyances to be inspected at least once each year. If a conveyance is found upon inspection to be in a safe condition for operation, a permit for operation for not longer than one year shall be issued by the division.

(b) If a conveyance is subject to a full maintenance service contract, the division may, after investigation and inspection, issue a permit for operation for not longer than two years. *(Stats.1937, c. 90, p. 322, § 7304. Amended by Stats.1945, c. 1431, p. 2707, § 124; Stats.1985, c. 701, § 4; Stats.2002, c. 1149 (S.B.1886), § 16; Stats. 2004, c. 183 (A.B.3082), § 265.)*

§ 7305. Preliminary order for repairs and alterations; use pending compliance

If inspection shows that a conveyance is in an unsafe condition, the division may issue a preliminary order requiring repairs or alterations to be made to the conveyance that are necessary to render it safe, and may prohibit its operation or use until the repairs or alterations are made or the unsafe conditions are removed. *(Stats.1937, c. 90, p. 322, § 7305. Amended by Stats.1945, c. 1431, p. 2707, § 125; Stats.2002, c. 1149 (S.B.1886), § 17.)*

§ 7306. Hearing on preliminary order

Unless the preliminary order is complied with, a hearing before the division shall be allowed, upon request, at which the owner, operator, or other person in charge of the conveyance may appear and show cause why he or she should not comply with the order. *(Stats.1937, c. 90, p. 322, § 7306. Amended by Stats.1945, c. 1431, p. 2707, § 126; Stats.2002, c. 1149 (S.B.1886), § 18.)*

§ 7307. Final repair or alteration order; rehearing; misdemeanor punishment for violation of order

(a) If it thereafter appears to the division that the conveyance is unsafe and that the requirements contained in the preliminary order should be complied with, or that other things should be done to make the conveyance safe, the division may order or confirm the withholding of the permit and may impose requirements as it deems proper for the repair or alteration of the conveyance or for the correction of the unsafe condition. The order may thereafter be reheard by the division or reviewed by the courts in the manner specified for safety orders by Part 1

(commencing with Section 6300) of this division, and not otherwise.

(b) The operation of a conveyance by any person owning or having the custody, management, or control of the operation thereof, while an order to repair is outstanding pursuant to subdivision (a), is a misdemeanor punishable by a fine of not more than seven thousand dollars ($7,000), by imprisonment in the county jail for not more than 30 days, or by both that fine and imprisonment. Each day of operation for each conveyance without a permit is a separate offense. *(Stats.1937, c. 90, p. 322, § 7307. Amended by Stats.1945, c. 1431, p. 2707, § 127; Stats.2002, c. 1149 (S.B.1886), § 19.)*

§ 7308. Temporary permit pending repairs and alterations

If the operation of a conveyance during the making of repairs or alterations is not immediately dangerous to the safety of persons, the division may issue a temporary permit for its operation for a period not to exceed 30 days during the making of repairs or alterations. *(Stats.1937, c. 90, p. 322, § 7308. Amended by Stats.1945, c. 1431, p. 2708, § 128; Stats.1985, c. 701, § 5; Stats.2002, c. 1149 (S.B.1886), § 20.)*

§ 7309. Inspectors

The division may cause the inspection herein provided for to be made either by its safety inspectors or by any qualified elevator inspector employed by an insurance company. *(Stats.1937, c. 90, p. 322, § 7309. Amended by Stats.1945, c. 1431, p. 2708, § 129.)*

§ 7309.1. Reinspections conducted on or after June 30, 2003; qualified conveyance inspectors; certification

(a) On and after June 30, 2003, no conveyance subject to this chapter shall be reinspected by any person unless the person is a conveyance inspector employed by the division or certified as qualified by the division.

(b) Before March 1, 2003, the division shall establish an application procedure and all requirements for the certification of conveyance inspectors. Each application for certification shall include information as the division may require and the applicable fee. At a minimum, the applicant shall present proof of certification as a qualified conveyance inspector by the American Society of Mechanical Engineers or proof of education and experience equivalent to what is required to obtain that certification from the American Society of Mechanical Engineers. *(Added by Stats.2002, c. 1149 (S.B.1886), § 21. Amended by Stats.2004, c. 503 (A.B.2350), § 6.)*

§ 7310. Inspection by municipal inspectors; issuance of permit

The division may also issue its permit or a permit may be issued on its behalf based upon a certificate of inspection issued by a conveyance inspector of any municipality, upon proof to the satisfaction of the division that the safety requirements of the municipality are equal to the minimum safety requirements for conveyances adopted by the board.   *(Stats.1937, c. 90, p. 322, § 7310. Amended by Stats.1945, c. 1431, p. 2708, § 130; Stats. 1991, c. 258 (A.B.1718), § 2; Stats.2002, c. 1149 (S.B. 1886), § 22; Stats.2004, c. 503 (A.B.2350), § 7.)*

§ 7311.   Certificate of competency for inspectors; qualifications; rescission of certificate

All persons inspecting conveyances shall first secure from the division a certificate of competency to make those inspections.   The division may determine the competency of any applicant for the certificate, either by examination or by other satisfactory proof of qualifications.   The division may rescind at any time, upon good cause being shown therefor, and after hearing, if requested, any certificate of competency issued by it to a conveyance inspector.   *(Stats.1937, c. 90, p. 322, § 7311. Amended by Stats.1945, c. 1431, p. 2708, § 131; Stats. 1957, c. 1347, p. 2678, § 1; Stats.2002, c. 1149 (S.B.1886), § 23; Stats.2004, c. 503 (A.B.2350), § 8.)*

§ 7311.1.   Certified qualified conveyance companies; application of section; certification procedures and requirements; proof of insurance; disclosure

(a) On and after June 30, 2003, no conveyance subject to this chapter shall be erected, constructed, installed, materially altered, tested, maintained, repaired, or serviced by any person, firm, or corporation unless the person, firm, or corporation is certified by the division as a certified qualified conveyance company.   A copy of the certificate shall be kept at the site of the conveyance at all times while any work is in progress, and shall be made available for inspection upon request.   However, certification under this section is not required for removing or dismantling conveyances that are destroyed as a result of the complete demolition of a secured building or structure or where the hoistway or wellway is demolished back to the basic support structure and no access is permitted that would endanger the safety of any person.   This section does not apply to platform lifts and stairway chairlifts installed in a private residence as provided in paragraph (2) or (3) of subdivision (a) of Section 7317.

(b) Before March 1, 2003, the division shall establish an application procedure and all requirements for certification under this section as a certified qualified conveyance company, consistent with this section.   At a minimum, the individual qualifying on behalf of a corporation, the owner on behalf of a sole ownership, or the partners on behalf of a partnership, shall meet either of the following requirements:

(1) Five years' work experience at a journeyperson level in the conveyance industry in construction, installation, alteration, testing, maintenance, and service and repair of conveyances covered by this chapter.   This experience shall be verified by current and previously licensed elevator contractors or by current and previously certified qualified conveyance companies.

(2) Satisfactory completion of a written examination administered by the division on the most recent applicable codes and standards.

(c) At a minimum, each application for certification as a certified qualified conveyance company shall include:

(1) The name, residence and business address, and telephone numbers and other means to contact the sole owner or each partner, or for a corporation of the principal officers and the individual qualifying for the corporation; the number of years the applicant business has engaged in the business of constructing, maintaining, and service and repair of conveyances; and other information as the division may require.

(2) The fee required by this chapter.

(d) Before bidding for or engaging in any work covered by this chapter, a certified qualified conveyance company shall submit proof to the division by certified copies of policies or certificates of insurance, of all of the following:

(1) Liability insurance providing general liability coverage of not less than one million dollars ($1,000,000) for injury or death of any one person or persons in any one occurrence, with coverage of not less than five hundred thousand dollars ($500,000) for property damage of any one person or persons in any one occurrence.

(2) Workers' compensation insurance coverage.

(3) In the event of any material alteration or cancellation of any policy specified in paragraph (1) or (2), the certified qualified conveyance company shall provide written notice thereof to the division within five working days.

(e) An elevator company subject to this chapter shall disclose its status as a certified qualified conveyance company prior to bidding on a project or prior to contracting for services.   The disclosure shall be in writing and located in a conspicuous place on the bid documents or contract in at least 10–point type.   *(Added by Stats.2002, c. 1149 (S.B.1886), § 24.   Amended by Stats.2004, c. 503 (A.B.2350), § 9; Stats.2009, c. 196 (S.B.478), § 1.)*

§ 7311.2.   Persons subject to application of chapter on or after June 30, 2003; certified competent conveyance mechanics; application procedure and requirements

(a) On and after June 30, 2003, except as provided in subdivisions (b) and (c) of Section 7301.5, any person who, without supervision, erects, constructs, installs, alters, tests, maintains, services or repairs, removes, or dismantles any conveyance covered by this chapter, shall be certified as a certified competent conveyance mechanic by the division.   This section does not apply to platform lifts and stairway chairlifts installed in a private residence as provided in paragraph (2) or (3) of subdivision (a) of Section 7317.

(b) Before March 1, 2003, the division shall establish an application procedure and all requirements for certification under this section as a certified competent conveyance mechanic, consistent with all of the following:

(1) At a minimum, a certified competent conveyance mechanic applicant shall meet both of the following requirements:

(A) Three years' work experience in the conveyance industry in construction, maintenance, and service and repair of conveyances covered by this chapter. This experience shall be verified by current and previously licensed elevator contractors or by current and previously certified qualified conveyance companies, as required by the division.

(B) One of the following:

(i) Satisfactory completion of a written examination administered by the division on the most recent applicable codes and standards.

(ii) A certificate of completion and successfully passing the mechanic examination of a nationally recognized training program for the conveyance industry, such as the National Elevator Industry Educational Program or its equivalent.

(iii) A certificate of completion of an apprenticeship program for elevator mechanic, having standards substantially equal to those of this chapter, and which program shall be registered with the Bureau of Apprenticeship and Training of the United States Department of Labor or a state apprenticeship council.

(iv) A certificate or license from another state having standards substantially equal to or more comprehensive than those of this chapter.

(v) The applicant applies on or before December 31, 2003, and within the three years immediately prior to January 1, 2003, has documented at least three years of actual work experience in the conveyance industry in construction, maintenance, and service and repair of conveyances covered by this chapter. This experience shall be as a journey-level mechanic working without direct and immediate supervision, and shall be verified by currently and previously licensed conveyance contractors or by current and previously certified qualified conveyance companies, as required by the division.

(2) At a minimum, each application for certification as a certified competent conveyance mechanic shall include the information required by the division and the fee required by this chapter. (Added by Stats.2002, c. 1149 (S.B.1886), § 25. Amended by Stats.2004, c. 503 (A.B. 2350), § 10.)

§ 7311.25. Agricultural production, processing, and handling facilities; maintenance and inspection of manlifts

(a) The following meanings apply for purposes of this section:

(1) "Agricultural production, processing, and handling facilities" includes grain elevators, feed mills, flour mills, rice mills, rice dryers, and other similar facilities.

(2) "Applicable Elevator Safety Orders" means the Elevator Safety Orders referenced in Subchapter 6 (commencing with Section 3000) of Chapter 4 of Division 1 of Title 8 of the California Code of Regulations, and any successors to those orders.

(b) Notwithstanding Section 7311.2 or any other provision of this chapter, an owner or operator of agricultural production, processing, and handling facilities may designate a competent person in his or her employ to maintain, repair, service, lubricate, or test manlifts installed and used at the facilities if the manlifts are maintained and inspected in accordance with applicable Elevator Safety Orders. The designated competent person need not be a certified competent conveyance mechanic. (Added by Stats.2009, c. 196 (S.B.478), § 2.)

§ 7311.3. Duration of certificates issued by the division; fees; renewal; continuing education; waiver; falsified attendance records as grounds for suspension or revocation

(a) A certificate issued by the division to the certified qualified conveyance inspector, certified qualified conveyance company, or certified competent conveyance mechanic as set forth in Sections 7309.1, 7311.1, and 7311.2, shall have a term of two years. The fee for biennial renewal shall be established by the division in an amount sufficient to defray the division's costs of administering this chapter.

(b) The renewal of all certificates issued under this chapter shall be conditioned upon the submission of a certificate of completion of a course designed to ensure the continuing education of certificate holders on new and existing provisions of the regulations of the board. This continuing education course shall consist of not less than eight hours of instruction that shall be attended and completed within one year immediately preceding any certificate renewal.

(c) The courses shall be taught by instructors through continuing education providers that may include, but not be limited to, division programs, association seminars, and joint labor-management apprenticeship and journeyman upgrade training programs. The division shall approve the continuing education providers and curriculum. All instructors shall be approved by the division and shall be exempt from the requirements of subdivision (b), provided that the applicant is qualified as an instructor at any time during the one-year period immediately preceding the scheduled date for renewal.

(d) A certificate holder who is unable to complete the continuing education course required under this section prior to the expiration of his or her certificate due to a temporary disability may apply for a waiver from the division. Waiver applications shall be submitted to the division on a form provided by the division. Waiver applications shall be signed and accompanied by a declaration signed by a competent physician attesting to the applicant's temporary disability. Upon the termination of the temporary disability, the certificate holder shall submit to the division a declaration from the same physician, if practicable, attesting to the termination of the temporary disability, and a waiver sticker, valid for 90 days, shall be issued to the certificate holder and affixed to his or her certificate.

(e) Continuing education providers approved by the division shall keep uniform records, for a period of 10 years, of attendance of certificate holders, following a format approved by the division. These records shall be available for inspection by the division at its request. Approved continuing education providers shall keep secure all attendance records and certificates of completion. Falsifying or knowingly allowing another to falsify attendance records or certificates of completion of continuing education provided pursuant to this section shall constitute grounds for suspension or revocation of the approval required under this section. *(Added by Stats. 2002, c. 1149 (S.B.1886), § 26. Amended by Stats.2004, c. 503 (A.B.2350), § 11.)*

§ 7311.4. Fees associated with certification process; refundability

(a) The division shall establish fees for initial and renewal applications for certification under this chapter as a certified qualified conveyance inspector, certified qualified conveyance company, or certified competent conveyance mechanic based upon the actual costs involved with the certification process, including the cost of developing and administering any tests as well as any costs related to continuing education, investigation, revocation, or other associated costs.

(b) Fees collected pursuant to this chapter are nonrefundable. *(Added by Stats.2002, c. 1149 (S.B.1886), § 27. Amended by Stats.2004, c. 503 (A.B.2350), § 12.)*

§ 7311.5. Qualifying as a certified qualified conveyance company or certified competent conveyance mechanic; limited purpose of certification; definitions

(a) A person, firm, or corporation that maintains and repairs solely special purpose personnel elevators on cranes that utilize a rack and pinion system in marine terminals as part of crane maintenance activities qualifies as a certified qualified conveyance company under Section 7311.1 if the individual qualifying individually or on behalf of the firm or corporation has five years' work experience at a journeyperson level in the crane maintenance industry, including experience in the maintenance and repair of crane elevators. This experience shall be verified by a person, firm, or corporation in the business of maintaining and repairing cranes in marine terminals.

(b) A person qualifies as a certified competent conveyance mechanic under Section 7311.2 if the person has three years' work experience in the crane maintenance industry, including experience in the maintenance and repair of crane elevators, as a journey-level mechanic without direct and immediate supervision. This experience shall be verified by a crane maintenance company

approved as a certified qualified conveyance company pursuant to subdivision (a).

(c) The certifications obtained pursuant to this section may only be used for the limited purposes of maintaining and repairing special purpose personnel elevators on cranes that utilize a rack and pinion system in marine terminals.

(d) A person, firm, or corporation that qualifies for certification as a certified qualified conveyance company or certified competent conveyance mechanic is not authorized to perform any of the following procedures:

(1) Any work on a conveyance other than a special purpose personnel elevator on cranes that utilize a rack and pinion system in marine terminals.

(2) Any work related to new elevator installations.

(3) Any modifications or alterations of existing elevator systems.

(4) Testing or replacing of emergency brakes, centrifugal brakes, emergency safety devices, or electrical systems.

(5) Annual certifications of any type of conveyance or elevator.

(e) The certifications authorized by this section require experience but do not require an examination because the general examination given pursuant to this chapter is inapplicable to the work described in this section. The division is not required to set up specialty examinations to certify persons pursuant to this chapter.

(f) For purposes of this section, the following terms shall have the following meanings:

(1) "Special purpose personnel elevators" shall have the same meaning as defined in Section 3085 of Title 8 of the California Code of Regulations.

(2) "Marine terminal" shall have the same meaning as used in Section 3460 of Title 8 of the California Code of Regulations.

(g) Nothing in this section exempts a person, firm, or corporation applying for certification as a certified qualified conveyance company or a certified competent conveyance mechanic under this section from paying the administration fees required under this chapter. *(Added by Stats.2006, c. 448 (S.B.727), § 1.)*

§ 7312. Revocation of permit

The division may at any time, upon good cause being shown therefor, and after notice and an opportunity to be heard, revoke any permit to operate a conveyance. *(Stats.1937, c. 90, p. 323, § 7312. Amended by Stats.1945, c. 1431, p. 2708, § 132; Stats.2002, c. 1149 (S.B.1886), § 28.)*

§ 7313. Inspection reports

Each conveyance inspector shall, within 21 days after he or she makes an inspection, forward to the division on forms provided by it, a report of the inspection. Failure to comply with this section shall be grounds for the division to cancel his or her certificate. *(Stats.1937, c. 90, p. 323, § 7313. Amended by Stats.1945, c. 1431, p. 2708, § 133; Stats.2002, c. 1149 (S.B.1886), § 29; Stats.2004, c. 503 (A.B.2350), § 13.)*

§ 7314. Fees associated with inspections or field consultations performed by a division safety engineer; penalties for failure to pay fees; regulations

(a) The division may fix and collect fees for the inspection of conveyances as it deems necessary to cover the actual costs of having the inspection performed by a division safety engineer, including administrative costs, and the costs related to regulatory development as required by Section 7323. An additional fee may, in the discretion of the division, be charged for necessary subsequent inspections to determine if applicable safety orders have been complied with. The division may fix and collect fees for field consultations regarding conveyances as it deems necessary to cover the actual costs of the time spent in the consultation by a division safety engineer, including administrative and travel expenses.

(b) Notwithstanding Section 6103 of the Government Code, the division may collect the fees authorized by subdivision (a) from the state or any county, city, district, or other political subdivision.

(c) Whenever a person owning or having the custody, management, or operation of a conveyance fails to pay the fees required under this chapter within 60 days after the date of notification, he or she shall pay, in addition to the fees required under this chapter, a penalty fee equal to 100 percent of the fee. Failure to pay fees within 60 days after the date of notification constitutes cause for the division to prohibit use of the conveyance.

(d) Any fees required pursuant to this section shall be set forth in regulations that shall be adopted as emergency regulations. These emergency regulations shall not be subject to the review and approval of the Office of Administrative Law pursuant to the provisions of the Administrative Procedure Act provided for in Chapter 3.5 (commencing with Section 11340) of Part 1 of Division 3 of Title 2 of the Government Code. These regulations shall become effective immediately upon filing with the Secretary of State.

(e) For purposes of this section, the date of the invoice assessing a fee pursuant to this section shall be considered the date of notification. *(Stats.1937, c. 90, p. 323, § 7314. Amended by Stats.1945, c. 1431, p. 2708, § 134; Stats.1949, c. 515, p. 923, § 1; Stats.1953, c. 1318, p. 2875, § 1; Stats.1965, c. 1191, p. 3008, § 2; Stats.1968, c. 352, p. 735, § 1; Stats.1972, c. 1347, p. 2679, § 1, eff. Dec. 22, 1972; Stats.1978, c. 1223, p. 3954, § 1; Stats.1980, c. 531, p. 1482, § 1; Stats.1981, c. 102, p. 725, § 67, eff. June 28, 1981; Stats.1982, c. 115, p. 356, § 36, eff. March 13, 1982; Stats.1990, c. 1022 (A.B.3039), § 2; Stats.1993, c. 998 (A.B.2016), § 3; Stats.2002, c. 1149 (S.B.1886), § 30; Stats.2007, c. 179 (S.B.86), § 30, eff. Aug. 24, 2007.)*

§ 7315. Payment of fee

Fees shall be paid before the issuance of any permit to operate a conveyance, but a temporary permit may be issued pending receipt of fee payment. No fee may be charged by the division where an inspection has been made by an inspector of an insurance company or municipality if that inspector holds a certificate as a conveyance inspector and an inspection report is filed with the division within 21 days after inspection is made. *(Stats.1937, c. 90, p. 323, § 7315. Amended by Stats.1945, c. 1431, p. 2709, § 135; Stats.2002, c. 1149 (S.B.1886), § 31; Stats.2004, c. 503 (A.B.2350), § 14.)*

§ 7316. Elevator safety account; disposition of fees; criteria for fee charges; annual report

All fees collected by the division under this chapter shall be paid into the Elevator Safety Account which is hereby created for the administration of the division's conveyance safety program. The division shall establish criteria upon which fee charges are based and prepare an annual report concerning revenues obtained and expenditures appropriated for the conveyance safety program. The division shall file the report with the Legislative Analyst, the Joint Legislative Audit Committee, and the Department of Finance. *(Stats.1937, c. 90, p. 323, § 7316. Amended by Stats.1945, c. 1431, p. 2707, § 136; Stats.1981, c. 102, p. 725, § 68, eff. June 28, 1981; Stats.2002, c. 1149 (S.B.1886), § 32; Stats.2004, c. 503 (A.B.2350), § 15.)*

§ 7317. Exemption from application of chapter for certain conveyances

(a) Except as provided in subdivision (b), the following conveyances are exempt from this chapter:

(1) Conveyances under the jurisdiction of the United States government.

(2) Conveyances located in a single-unit private home and not accessible to the public.

(3) Conveyances located in a multiunit residential building serving no more than two dwelling units and not accessible to the public.

(b) Conveyances otherwise exempted pursuant to paragraph (3) of subdivision (a) shall be inspected by the division upon completion of installation prior to being placed in service or after major alterations. The inspection shall be for safety and compliance with orders or regulations applicable to the type of conveyance installed. *(Stats.1937, c. 90, p. 323, § 7317. Amended by Stats.1945, c. 1431, p. 2709, § 137; Stats.1985, c. 701, § 6; Stats.1987, c. 204, § 1; Stats.2002, c. 1149 (S.B.1886), § 33.)*

§ 7318. Safety orders

Nothing in this chapter limits the authority of the division to prescribe or enforce general or special safety orders. *(Stats.1937, c. 90, p. 323, § 7318. Amended by Stats.1945, c. 1431, p. 2709, § 138; Stats.2002, c. 1149 (S.B.1886), § 34.)*

§ 7319. Failure to provide operator's seat; misdemeanor; penalty

All elevators used for the carriage of passengers shall be provided with a suitable seat for the operator in charge. Failure to comply with this section is a misdemeanor punishable by a fine not exceeding fifty dollars ($50) for each offense. *(Stats.1937, c. 90, p. 323, § 7319. Amended by Stats.1983, c. 1092, § 224, eff. Sept. 27, 1983, operative Jan. 1, 1984.)*

§ 7320. Operation without permit; penalty

The division may assess a civil penalty not to exceed one thousand dollars ($1,000) against any person owning or having custody, management, or control of the operation of a conveyance, who operates the conveyance without a permit or who fails to conspicuously post the permit in the conveyance. No penalty shall be assessed against any person who has requested the issuance or renewal of a permit and the request has not been acted upon by the division. *(Added by Stats.1990, c. 1022 (A.B.3039), § 3. Amended by Stats.2002, c. 1149 (S.B. 1886), § 35.)*

§ 7321. Operation in dangerous condition; penalty

(a) The division may assess a civil penalty not to exceed seventy thousand dollars ($70,000) against any person owning or having custody, management, or control of the operation of a conveyance, who operates or permits the operation of the conveyance in a condition that is dangerous to the life or safety of any person, or who operates or permits the operation of the conveyance in violation of an order prohibiting use issued pursuant to Section 7301, 7305, or 7314.

(b) The division shall issue an order prohibiting use and may assess a civil penalty not to exceed seventy thousand dollars ($70,000) against any person who constructs, installs, or materially alters a conveyance without a permit issued pursuant to Section 7301.1 that is dangerous to the life or safety of any person. *(Added by Stats.1990, c. 1022 (A.B.3039), § 4. Amended by Stats. 2002, c. 1149 (S.B.1886), § 36.)*

§ 7321.5. Enforcement

The division shall enforce Sections 7320 and 7321 by issuance of a citation and notice of civil penalty in a manner consistent with Sections 6317 and 6319. Any person owning or having custody, management, or control of the operation of a conveyance who receives a citation and notice of civil penalty may appeal to the Occupational Safety and Health Appeals Board in a manner consistent with Section 6319. *(Added by Stats. 1990, c. 1022 (A.B.3039), § 5. Amended by Stats.2002, c. 1149 (S.B.1886), § 37.)*

§ 7322. Orders from division prohibiting use; hearings; misdemeanor punishment for violation of order

(a) Once an authorized representative of the division has issued an order prohibiting the use of a conveyance as specified in Sections 7301, 7305, 7314, or subdivision (b) of Section 7321, the person owning or having custody, management, or operation of the conveyance may contest the order and shall be granted, upon request, a hearing to review the validity of the order. The hearing shall be held no later than 10 working days following receipt of the request for hearing.

(b) After a notice is attached as provided in Section 7305 or subdivision (b) of Section 7321, every person who enters or uses, or directs or causes another to enter or use, any conveyance before it is made safe, or who defaces, destroys, or removes the notice without the authority of the division, is guilty of a misdemeanor punishable by a fine of not more than seventy thousand dollars ($70,000), by imprisonment in the county jail for not more than one year, or by both that fine and imprisonment.

(c) After a notice is attached for failure to comply with the requirements of Section 7301 or 7314, every person who enters or uses, or directs or causes another to enter or use, any conveyance before it is made safe, or who defaces, destroys, or removes the notice without the authority of the division, is guilty of a misdemeanor punishable by a fine of not more than seven thousand dollars ($7,000), imprisonment in the county jail for not more than six months, or by both that fine and imprisonment. *(Added by Stats.1990, c. 1022 (A.B.3039), § 6. Amended by Stats.2002, c. 1149 (S.B.1886), § 38.)*

§ 7323. Regulations adopted by the standards board; notice and hearing; final regulations

The division shall propose to the standards board for review, and the standards board shall adopt, regulations for the equipment covered by this chapter. Not later than December 31, 2003, the division shall propose final rulemaking proposals to the standards board for review and adoption, which shall include provisions at least as effective as ASME A17.1, ASME A17. 3, ASME A18.1, and ASCE 21, as in effect prior to September 30, 2002. Not later than nine months after the effective date of any revision or any substantive revision to any addendum to these codes, the division shall propose additional final rulemaking proposals to the standards board for review and adoption at least as effective as those in the revised code or addendum. The standards board shall notice the division's final rulemaking proposals for public hearing within three months of their receipt and shall adopt the proposed regulations promptly and in accordance with subdivision (b) of Section 11346.4 of the Government Code. *(Added by Stats.2002, c. 1149 (S.B.1886), § 39.)*

§ 7324. Certification of compliance with State Fire Prevention and Building Code

Individuals, firms, or companies certified as described in this chapter shall ensure that installation, service, and maintenance of conveyances are performed in compliance with the provisions contained in the State Fire Prevention and Building Code and with generally accepted standards referenced in that code. *(Added by Stats.*

2002, c. 1149 (S.B.1886), § 40. Amended by Stats.2004, c. 503 (A.B.2350), § 16.)

§ 7324.1. Defective workmanship; liability

This chapter shall not be construed to relieve or lessen the responsibility or liability of any person, firm, or corporation owning, operating, controlling, maintaining, erecting, constructing, installing, altering, testing, or repairing any conveyance or other related mechanisms covered by this chapter for damages to any person or property caused by any defect therein. *(Added by Stats.2002, c. 1149 (S.B.1886), § 41.)*

§ 7324.2. Retroactive application

The provisions of this chapter added or amended by the act enacting this section shall not be applied retroactively. Equipment subject to this chapter shall be required to comply with the applicable standards in effect on the date of its installation or within the period determined by the board for compliance with ASME A17.3, whichever is more stringent. *(Added by Stats. 2002, c. 1149 (S.B.1886), § 42.)*

CHAPTER 3. SAFETY DEVICES UPON BUILDINGS TO SAFEGUARD WINDOW CLEANERS

Section
7325. Building defined.
7326. Devices for use of window cleaners; rules for manner of attachment, installation, and use.
7327. Other devices.
7328. Employing or permitting work without required safety devices; misdemeanor.
7329. Persons required to install devices; failure to comply with requirements; misdemeanor.
7330. Failure to provide and maintain required devices on new building; misdemeanor.
7331. Safety orders and rules; notice of violation.
7332. Enforcement agency.

§ 7325. Building defined

"Building," as used in this chapter, means any building three stories or more in height, and whether heretofore constructed or hereafter to be constructed, including commercial buildings of all types, office buildings, apartment houses, hotels and buildings used for manufacturing purposes, but excluding dwelling houses occupied by not more than three families, and excluding all buildings constructed with windows that may be, and are, entirely washed and cleaned from inside the building or from a sitting position on the window sill in the manner provided by safety orders issued, or which may be issued from time to time, by the division. *(Added by Stats.1941, c. 544, p. 1866, § 1. Amended by Stats.1945, c. 1431, p. 2709, § 139.)*

§ 7326. Devices for use of window cleaners; rules for manner of attachment, installation, and use

There shall be securely attached to the outside window sills or frames of the window of any building, rings, bolts, lugs, fittings, or other devices to which may be fastened safety belts or other devices to be used, or which may hereafter be used by persons engaged in cleaning windows. The division shall, prior to the installation of any such bolts, lugs, rings, fittings, or other devices, approve such bolts, lugs, rings, fittings, or other devices as to their design, durability, and safety. Except as provided in Section 18930 of the Health and Safety Code, the division shall by appropriate rules and orders designate the manner in which said safety devices are to be attached, installed, and used. *(Added by Stats.1941, c. 544, p. 1867, § 1. Amended by Stats.1945, c. 1431, p. 7326, § 140; Stats.1979, c. 1152, p. 4317, § 208.)*

§ 7327. Other devices

In lieu of the safety devices enumerated in Section 7326, the division may approve the installation or use of any other devices or means which will effectively safeguard persons engaged in cleaning windows. *(Added by Stats.1941, c. 544, p. 1867, § 1. Amended by Stats.1945, c. 1431, p. 2710, § 141.)*

§ 7328. Employing or permitting work without required safety devices; misdemeanor

Any person employing, directing or permitting another to do or perform any labor upon any windows which have not the safety devices as provided for in Sections 7326 and 7327 shall be guilty of a misdemeanor. *(Added by Stats.1941, c. 544, p. 1867, § 1.)*

§ 7329. Persons required to install devices; failure to comply with requirements; misdemeanor

Every person owning or entitled to possession, under any lease, sublease, or agreement for a longer period than one year, or under any renewal lease, sublease, or agreement for a period of less than one year, of any building heretofore constructed shall, within six months following the effective date of this chapter, install and provide the safety devices as provided for in this chapter, and thereafter maintain such safety devices in good condition. Any person failing to install or provide and maintain said safety devices as provided for in this chapter shall be guilty of a misdemeanor. *(Added by Stats.1941, c. 544, p. 1867, § 1.)*

§ 7330. Failure to provide and maintain required devices on new building; misdemeanor

Every person who fails to provide the safety devices as set forth in this chapter upon any building hereafter to be constructed, and who thereafter fails to maintain such devices in good condition, shall be guilty of a misdemeanor. *(Added by Stats.1941, c. 544, p. 1867, § 1.)*

§ 7331. Safety orders and rules; notice of violation

The division may make and enforce such safety orders and rules as it considers necessary and proper to carry into effect the purposes and provisions of this chapter.

The division shall give notice to the owner or person entitled to possession of any building that is existing in

767

violation of this chapter or of any rules issued under this chapter. Failure of the person so notified to comply with this chapter and rules issued under it, within 15 days, shall be authority for the division to proceed against such person as authorized in this chapter. *(Added by Stats. 1941, c. 544, p. 1867, § 1. Amended by Stats.1945, c. 1431, p. 2710, § 142.)*

§ 7332. Enforcement agency

The division shall enforce the provisions of this chapter. *(Added by Stats.1941, c. 544, p. 1868, § 1. Amended by Stats.1945, c. 1431, p. 2710, § 143.)*

CHAPTER 4. AERIAL PASSENGER TRAMWAYS

Section
7340.   Definitions.
7341.   Permit for operation; necessity; posting.
7342.   Operation without permit; misdemeanor.
7343.   Injunction restraining unlawful and dangerous operation.
7344.   Inspection; duration of permit.
7345.   Preliminary order requiring repairs or alterations; discontinuance of operation.
7346.   Noncompliance with preliminary order; hearing.
7347.   Order withholding permit and requiring repairs or alterations.
7348.   Temporary permit for operation during repairs or alterations.
7349.   Inspections by division safety engineer or certified tramway inspector; issuance of temporary permit.
7350.   Fees and charges; penalty for nonpayment.
7351.   Payment of fees before issuance of permit; exception.
7352.   Disposition of fees.
7353.   Certification of plans and design to division by qualified engineer.
7354.   Certification of completion of tramway.
7354.5. Inspection by licensed professional engineer; exception; inspection by division safety engineer; certificate of competency.
7355.   Chapter provisions not to limit authority of division to prescribe or enforce safety orders.
7356.   Reports of injuries.
7357.   Qualification standards for personnel.

§ 7340. Definitions

As used in this chapter:

(a) "Aerial passenger tramway" includes any method or device used primarily for the purpose of transporting persons by means of cables or ropes suspended between two or more points or structures.

(b) "Permit" means a permit issued by the division to operate an aerial passenger tramway in any place. *(Added by Stats.1965, c. 1047, p. 2685, § 1. Amended by Stats.1972, c. 479, p. 850, § 1.)*

§ 7341. Permit for operation; necessity; posting

No aerial passenger tramway shall be operated in any place in this state unless a permit for the operation thereof is issued by the division, and unless such permit remains in effect and is kept posted conspicuously in the main operating terminal of the tramway. *(Added by Stats.1965, c. 1047, p. 2685, § 1. Amended by Stats.1972, c. 479, p. 850, § 2.)*

§ 7342. Operation without permit; misdemeanor

The operation of an aerial passenger tramway by any person owning or having the custody, management, or operation thereof without a permit is a misdemeanor, and each day of operation without a permit is a separate offense. No prosecution shall be maintained where the issuance or renewal of a permit has been requested and remains unacted upon. *(Added by Stats.1965, c. 1047, p. 2686, § 1.)*

§ 7343. Injunction restraining unlawful and dangerous operation

Whenever an aerial passenger tramway in any place is being operated without the permit herein required, and is in such condition that its use is dangerous to the life or safety of any person, the division, or any person affected thereby, may apply to the superior court of the county in which the aerial passenger tramway is located for an injunction restraining the operation of the aerial passenger tramway until the condition is corrected. Proof by certification of the division that a permit has not been issued, together with the affidavit of any safety engineer of the division that the operation of the aerial passenger tramway is dangerous to the life or safety of any person, is sufficient ground, in the discretion of the court, for the immediate granting of a temporary restraining order. *(Added by Stats.1965, c. 1047, p. 2686, § 1. Amended by Stats.1972, c. 479, p. 850, § 3; Stats.1982, c. 517, p. 2405, § 312.)*

§ 7344. Inspection; duration of permit

(a) The division shall cause all aerial passenger tramways to be inspected at least two times each year.

(b) At least one of the inspections required by subdivision (a) shall take place between November 15 of each year and March 15 of the succeeding year.

(c) If an aerial passenger tramway is found upon inspection to be in a safe condition for operation, a permit for operation for not longer than one year shall be issued by the division. *(Added by Stats.1965, c. 1047, p. 2686, § 1. Amended by Stats.1972, c. 478, p. 849, § 1.)*

§ 7345. Preliminary order requiring repairs or alterations; discontinuance of operation

If inspection shows an aerial passenger tramway to be in an unsafe condition, the division may issue a preliminary order requiring repairs or alterations to be made to the aerial passenger tramway which are necessary to render it safe, and may order the operation or use thereof discontinued until the repairs or alterations are made or the unsafe conditions are removed. *(Added by Stats.1965, c. 1047, p. 2686, § 1.)*

§ 7346. Noncompliance with preliminary order; hearing

Unless the preliminary order is complied with, a hearing before the division shall be allowed, upon request, at which the owner, operator, or other person in charge of the aerial passenger tramway may appear and show cause why he should not comply with the order. *(Added by Stats.1965, c. 1047, p. 2686, § 1.)*

§ 7347. Order withholding permit and requiring repairs or alterations

If it thereafter appears to the division that the aerial passenger tramway is unsafe and that the requirements contained in the preliminary order should be complied with, or that other things should be done to make such aerial passenger tramway safe, the division may order or confirm the withholding of the permit and may make such requirements as it deems proper for its repair or alteration or for the correction of such unsafe condition. Such order may thereafter be reheard by the division or reviewed by the courts in the manner specified for safety orders by Part 1 of this division and not otherwise. *(Added by Stats.1965, c. 1047, p. 2686, § 1.)*

§ 7348. Temporary permit for operation during repairs or alterations

If the operation of an aerial passenger tramway during the making of repairs or alterations is not immediately dangerous to the safety of employees or others, the division may issue a temporary permit for the operation thereof for not to exceed 30 days during the making of repairs or alterations. *(Added by Stats.1965, c. 1047, p. 2686, § 1. Amended by Stats.1972, c. 479, p. 850, § 4.)*

§ 7349. Inspections by division safety engineer or certified tramway inspector; issuance of temporary permit

The inspection herein provided for shall be made by a division safety engineer or, on ski lifts, by a certified tramway inspector qualified under Section 7354.5 and employed by a licensed insurance company. A temporary permit for operation may be issued by a division engineer or by the qualified insurance inspector, on a form furnished by the division, under conditions of Sections 7348 and 7351. *(Added by Stats.1965, c. 1047, p. 2687, § 1. Amended by Stats.1974, c. 863, p. 1836, § 1.)*

§ 7350. Fees and charges; penalty for nonpayment

(a) The division may fix and collect fees for the inspection of aerial passenger tramways as it deems necessary to cover the actual cost of having the inspection performed by a division safety engineer. The division may not charge for inspections performed by certified insurance inspectors, but may charge a fee of not more than ten dollars ($10) to cover the cost of processing the permit when issued by the division as a result of the inspection. Notwithstanding Section 6103 of the Government Code, the division may collect the fees authorized by this section from the state or any county, city, district, or other political subdivision.

(b) Whenever a person owning or having custody, management, or operation of an aerial passenger tramway fails to pay any fee required under this chapter within 60 days after the date of notification by the division, the division shall assess a penalty fee equal to 100 percent of the initial fee. For purposes of this section, the date of the invoice fixing the fee shall be considered the date of notification. *(Added by Stats.1965, c. 1047, p. 2687, § 1. Amended by Stats.1972, c. 478, p. 849, § 2; Stats.1974, c. 863, p. 1836, § 2; Stats.1993, c. 998 (A.B.2016), § 4; Stats.2007, c. 179 (S.B.86), § 31, eff. Aug. 24, 2007.)*

§ 7351. Payment of fees before issuance of permit; exception

Fees shall be paid before issuance of a permit to operate an aerial passenger tramway, except that the division, at its own discretion, may issue a temporary operating permit not to exceed 30 days, pending receipt of payment of fees. *(Added by Stats.1965, c. 1047, p. 2687, § 1.)*

§ 7352. Disposition of fees

All fees collected by the division under this chapter shall be deposited into the Elevator Safety Account to support the division's aerial passenger tramway inspection program. *(Added by Stats.1965, c. 1047, p. 2687, § 1. Amended by Stats.2007, c. 179 (S.B.86), § 32, eff. Aug. 24, 2007.)*

§ 7353. Certification of plans and design to division by qualified engineer

No aerial passenger tramway shall be constructed or altered until the plans and design information have been properly certified to the division by an engineer qualified under the Civil and Professional Engineers Act (Chapter 7, commencing with Section 6700, of Division 3 of the Business and Professions Code).

Any person who owns, has custody of, manages, or operates an aerial passenger tramway shall notify the division prior to any major repair of such tramway. *(Added by Stats.1965, c. 1047, p. 2687, § 1. Amended by Stats.1971, c. 1033, p. 1980, § 1.)*

§ 7354. Certification of completion of tramway

The division shall not issue an operating permit to operate an aerial passenger tramway until it receives certification in writing by an engineer qualified under the Civil and Professional Engineers Act (Chapter 7, commencing with Section 6700, of Division 3 of the Business and Professions Code) that the erection work on such tramway has been completed in accordance with the design and erection plans for such tramway. *(Added by Stats.1965, c. 1047, p. 2687, § 1.)*

§ 7354.5. Inspection by licensed professional engineer; exception; inspection by division safety engineer; certificate of competency

Notwithstanding any other provision of this chapter, in any case in which an insurer admitted to transact insurance in this state has inspected or caused to be inspected, by a qualified, licensed professional engineer who is registered in California pursuant to Chapter 7 (commencing with Section 6700) of Division 3 of the Business and Professions Code, any aerial passenger tramway used as a ski lift, the division may, if it finds such inspections were made according to the provisions of subdivisions (a) and (b) of Section 7344, accept such inspections in lieu of any other inspections for that year, except that the initial inspection of a new ski lift or of a major alteration to an existing ski lift shall be performed by a division safety engineer. Such private inspector shall, before commencing his duties therein, secure from the division a certificate of competency to make such inspections. The division may determine the competency of any applicant for such certificate, either by examination or by other satisfactory proof of qualification.

The division may rescind at any time, upon good cause being shown therefor, and after hearing, if requested, any certificate of competency issued by it to a ski lift inspector. The inspection reports made to the division shall be in such form and content as the division may find necessary for acceptance as a proper inspection made by such private inspector. *(Added by Stats.1974, c. 61, p. 134, § 1, eff. March 12, 1974. Amended by Stats.1974, c. 863, p. 1836, § 3; Stats.1975, c. 678, p. 1490, § 54.)*

§ 7355. Chapter provisions not to limit authority of division to prescribe or enforce safety orders

Nothing in the foregoing sections of this chapter shall limit the authority of the division to prescribe or enforce general or special safety orders. *(Added by Stats.1965, c. 1047, p. 2687, § 1.)*

§ 7356. Reports of injuries

The division shall, under the authority of Section 7355, promulgate and cause to be published safety orders directing each owner or operator of an aerial passenger tramway to report to the division each known incident where the maintenance, operation, or use of such tramway results in injury to any person, unless such injury does not require medical service other than ordinary first aid treatment. *(Added by Stats.1972, c. 477, p. 849, § 1.)*

§ 7357. Qualification standards for personnel

The division shall establish standards for the qualification of persons engaged in the operation of aerial passenger tramways, whether as employees or otherwise. The standards shall be consistent with the general objective of this chapter in providing for the safety of members of the public who use aerial passenger tramways and those engaged in their operation. *(Added by Stats.1972, c. 519, p. 902, § 1.)*

770

CHAPTER 5. CRANES

Article	Section
1. Permits for Tower Cranes	7370
2. Certification	7375

ARTICLE 1. PERMITS FOR TOWER CRANES

Section
7370. Legislative findings and declarations.
7371. Definitions.
7372. Safety engineers employed to inspect tower cranes; safety inspection program; contents.
7373. Permit requirement; exception; fees; duration.
7374. Permit suspension or revocation; duration; hearing and appeal.

§ 7370. Legislative findings and declarations

(a) The Legislature finds and declares that recent statewide spot inspections of cranes have uncovered a pattern of numerous safety violations so serious and pervasive that safety inspections shall be a continuing priority with regard to all tower cranes in the state. *(Added by Stats.1990, c. 1033 (A.B.3826), § 1.)*

§ 7371. Definitions

As used in this chapter, the following definitions shall apply:

(a) "Crane" means a machine for lifting or lowering a load and moving it horizontally, in which the hoisting mechanism is an integral part of the machine. It may be driven manually or by power and may be a fixed or a mobile machine, but does not include stackers, lift trucks, power shovels, backhoes, excavators, concrete pumping equipment, or straddle type mobile boat hoists.

(b) "Straddle type mobile boat hoist" means a straddle type carrier supported by four wheels with pneumatic tires capable of straddling and carrying boats with high masts and superstructure.

(c) "Tower crane" means a crane in which a boom, swinging jib, or other structural member is mounted on a vertical mast or tower.

(d) "Mobile tower crane" means a tower crane which is mounted on a crawler, truck, or similar carrier for travel or transit.

(e) "Crane employer" means an employer who is responsible for the maintenance and operation of a tower crane.

(f) "Certificating agency" shall have the same definition as in Section 4885 of Title 8 of the California Code of Regulations. *(Added by Stats.1990, c. 1033 (A.B.3826), § 1. Amended by Stats.1992, c. 254 (A.B.3386), § 1.)*

§ 7372. Safety engineers employed to inspect tower cranes; safety inspection program; contents

(a) The division shall employ safety engineers trained to inspect tower cranes.

(b) The division shall establish a safety inspection program for all tower cranes operated in the state. This safety program shall include:

(1) Safety inspection of tower cranes twice a year.

(2) Increased penalties for the violation of tower crane safety orders and standards.

(3) Permit fees as described in Section 7373. *(Added by Stats.1990, c. 1033 (A.B.3826), § 1.)*

§ 7373. Permit requirement; exception; fees; duration

(a) No tower crane shall be operated at any worksite unless an employer obtains a permit from the division. The division shall conduct an investigation for purposes of issuing a permit in an expeditious manner. If the division does not issue a permit within 10 days after being requested to do so by a crane employer, the crane employer may operate the crane without a permit.

(b) The division shall set a fee to be charged for these permits in an amount sufficient to cover the cost of funding the issuance of the permits and the safety engineers as provided by subdivision (a) of Section 7372.

(c) The permit for a fixed tower crane shall be valid for the period of time that the tower crane is fixed to the site.

(d) The permit for a mobile tower crane shall be valid for one calendar year. *(Added by Stats.1990, c. 1033 (A.B.3826), § 1.)*

§ 7374. Permit suspension or revocation; duration; hearing and appeal

(a) The division may suspend or revoke the permit of a crane where the employer engages in gross negligence, gross incompetence, or willful or repeated disregard of any occupational safety standard or order involving the crane.

(b) The permit of the crane shall be suspended or revoked for a six-month period for first-time suspensions or revocations, and for a one-year period for each subsequent suspension or revocation. The division shall establish a suspension and revocation hearing procedure and appeal process. *(Added by Stats.1990, c. 1033 (A.B.3826), § 1.)*

ARTICLE 2. CERTIFICATION

Section
7375. Cranes and derricks; certification; procedure; exam; conflicts of interest; exceptions; duties of certificating agency.
7376. License suspension or revocation; reasons; duration; hearing and appeal.
7377. Appeal of license revocation.
7378. Fraudulent certification; misdemeanor; sentence or fine.
7379. Certification by unlicensed persons; misdemeanor; sentence or fine.
7380. Fees for examination and licensing of crane certifiers; payment to general fund.
7381. Civil penalties; serious or willful violations of standards.

Section
7382. Installing or dismantling tower cranes; "jumping or climbing a crane"; safety representative present; safety orders; time restrictions.
7383. Business identities; disclosure; forms; confidentiality; assessing penalties; purpose of section.
7384. Annual report; preparation; filing.

§ 7375. Cranes and derricks; certification; procedure; exam; conflicts of interest; exceptions; duties of certificating agency

(a) The division shall adopt regulations for the certification of all cranes and derricks used in lifting service, exceeding three tons rated capacity. Tower cranes shall be certified annually and whenever they are erected on a new site.

(b) These regulations shall specify the procedure for licensing the certificating agencies or agents to conduct certification inspections, and shall establish specific criteria for licensure as a certifier, including a written examination.

(c) No individual may certify a crane in which the individual or his or her employer has a direct or indirect financial interest, nor may an individual certify equipment that belongs to his or her employer. An individual may not certify equipment or devices that he or she has manufactured or helped to manufacture, if the equipment is owned by his or her employer. However, this subdivision shall not prohibit any of the following:

(1) The licensure of certifiers who are employed by insurance carriers that insure the specific crane.

(2) Except with respect to certification of tower cranes, the licensure of certifiers who are employed by an electrical, gas, or telephone corporation, as defined in Sections 218, 222, and 234, respectively, of the Public Utilities Code, or a municipal utility serving a city having a population of 3,000,000 or more, that is issued a certificate of self-insurance pursuant to Article 3 (commencing with Section 16050) of Chapter 1 of Division 7 of the Vehicle Code and that is a self-insured employer under Article 1 (commencing with Section 3700) of Chapter 4 of Division 4 of this code.

(d) The certificating agency shall attest that it tested or examined the device or equipment and found it to meet the requirements of the division.

(e) The certificating agency shall notify the division of any deficiencies found during the crane certification inspection. A certificate shall not be issued until all deficiencies are corrected. *(Added by Stats.1990, c. 1033 (A.B.3826), § 1. Amended by Stats.1994, c. 105 (S.B.999), § 1; Stats.1994, c. 604 (A.B.2784), § 1.)*

§ 7376. License suspension or revocation; reasons; duration; hearing and appeal

(a) The division shall suspend or revoke a license to certify for the following reasons:

(1) Gross negligence, gross incompetency, a pattern of incompetence, or fraud in the certification of a crane.

(2) Willful or deliberate disregard of any occupational safety standard while certifying a crane.

(3) Misrepresentation of a material fact in applying for, or obtaining, a license to certify under this chapter.

(4) Upon a showing of good cause.

(b) The period of suspension or revocation shall be for six months for a first suspension or revocation, and one year for each subsequent suspension or revocation. The certificating agency shall obtain a new license from the division following a suspension or revocation. The division shall establish a hearing procedure and an appeal process for license suspensions and revocations. *(Added by Stats.1990, c. 1033 (A.B.3826), § 1.)*

§ 7377. Appeal of license revocation

Revocation of a license to certify may be appealed to the Director of Industrial Relations. *(Added by Stats. 1990, c. 1033 (A.B.3826), § 1.)*

§ 7378. Fraudulent certification; misdemeanor; sentence or fine

A licensed certifier who fraudulently certifies that a crane is in compliance with the criteria established by the division under subdivision (a) of Section 7375 is guilty of a misdemeanor punishable by imprisonment in the county jail for a period not to exceed six months, or by a fine not to exceed one thousand dollars ($1,000), or both. *(Added by Stats.1990, c. 1033 (A.B.3826), § 1.)*

§ 7379. Certification by unlicensed persons; misdemeanor; sentence or fine

It shall be a misdemeanor for an individual to engage in the certification of a crane as specified in this chapter if that individual is not licensed pursuant to this chapter. Any violation of this section shall be punishable by imprisonment in the county jail for a period not to exceed six months, or by a fine not to exceed one thousand dollars ($1,000), or both. *(Added by Stats.1990, c. 1033 (A.B.3826), § 1.)*

§ 7380. Fees for examination and licensing of crane certifiers; payment to general fund

The division may collect fees for the examination and licensing of crane certifiers as necessary to cover the actual costs, including administrative costs. All fees collected by the division under this chapter shall be paid into the General Fund. *(Added by Stats.1990, c. 1033 (A.B.3826), § 1.)*

§ 7381. Civil penalties; serious or willful violations of standards

(a) Notwithstanding Sections 6319 and 6425, if serious injury or death is caused by any serious or willful repeated violation of a crane standard, order, or special order, or by any failure to correct a serious violation of a crane standard, order, or special order within the time specified for its correction, the employer shall be assessed a civil penalty in an amount equal to double the maximum penalty allowable for each violation contributing to the injury or death.

(b) Notwithstanding any provision of this division, any employer who violates any tower crane standard, order, or special order, if that violation is a serious violation, shall be assessed a civil penalty of not less than one thousand dollars ($1,000) nor more than two thousand dollars ($2,000) for each serious violation. The penalty shall not be reduced for any of the reasons listed in Section 6319. *(Added by Stats.1990, c. 1033 (A.B.3826), § 1.)*

§ 7382. Installing or dismantling tower cranes; "jumping or climbing a crane"; safety representative present; safety orders; time restrictions

No person shall install or dismantle a tower crane, or increase the height of a crane, known in the construction trade as "jumping or climbing a crane," without a safety representative of the crane manufacturer, distributor, or a representative of a licensed crane certifier being present on site for consultation during the procedure. The standards board shall adopt a regulation making failure to provide the designated safety representative a serious violation of a safety order. Local governmental entities may restrict the hours during which these procedures may be performed. *(Added by Stats.1990, c. 1033 (A.B.3826), § 1.)*

§ 7383. Business identities; disclosure; forms; confidentiality; assessing penalties; purpose of section

(a) The division shall require all crane employers to disclose all of their previous business identities within the previous 10 years. The disclosure shall be made to the division on forms provided by the division. The division shall maintain the confidentiality of this information.

(b) The division shall consider the violations of safety and health orders and standards of the previous business identities when assessing penalties against a crane employer for current violations.

(c) For purposes of this section "business identities" means current and previous business affiliations in the construction industry which involve the use of cranes. These shall include, but not be limited to, fictitious business names and corporate names.

(d) The purpose of this section is to enable the division to get a complete safety record of crane employers when assessing penalties for the violation of safety orders. *(Added by Stats.1990, c. 1033 (A.B.3826), § 1.)*

§ 7384. Annual report; preparation; filing

The division shall prepare an annual report concerning revenues obtained from all funding sources and expenditures. The division shall file the report with the Legislative Analyst, the Joint Legislative Audit Committee, the Department of Finance, and the appropriate policy committees of the Legislature. *(Added by Stats.1990, c. 1033 (A.B.3826), § 1. Amended by Stats.2006, c. 538 (S.B.1852), § 494.)*

Part 4

MINING INDUSTRIES

Chapter   Section
1. Quartz Mines [Repealed]
2. Coal Mines [Repealed]
3. Underground Telephones 7500

CHAPTER 1. QUARTZ MINES [REPEALED]

CHAPTER 2. COAL MINES [REPEALED]

CHAPTER 3. UNDERGROUND TELEPHONES

Section
7500. Requirement.
7501. Violation; misdemeanor.

§ 7500. Requirement

In all mines operated in the State where a depth of more than five hundred feet underground has been reached, a telephone system shall be established, equipped and maintained by the owners or lessees of the mine with stations at each working level below the depth aforesaid, communicating with a station on the surface of the mine. *(Stats.1937, c. 90, p. 325, § 7500.)*

§ 7501. Violation; misdemeanor

The failure or refusal of any owner or lessee to install or maintain such telephone system is a misdemeanor. *(Stats.1937, c. 90, p. 325, § 7501.)*

Part 5

SHIPS AND VESSELS

Section
7600. Employment of signalman or hatch-tender; duties.
7601. Handtrucks.
7602. Handtools.
7603. Stored material; weight limits; piles, stacks and racks.
7604. Rails.
7605. Safety inspections; correction of unsafe conditions; discarding unsafe tools, etc.
7606. Dock plates.
7607. Internal combustion engine operation.
7608. Violation; misdemeanor.
7609. Longshore and stevedore operations; applicability of sections.
7611. Safety orders.

§ 7600. Employment of signalman or hatch-tender; duties

Every person who is engaged in the business of loading or unloading ships or vessels, or who is authorized or contracts to load or unload a ship or vessel, or who is in charge of a ship or vessel while it is being loaded or unloaded, and such ship or vessel has a carrying capacity of 50 tons or greater, shall employ and supply upon every ship or vessel while being loaded or unloaded, a person over the age of 18 years to act as signalman or hatch-tender whose sole duty it shall be to observe the operations of loading or unloading of each working hatch on such ship or vessel, and to warn all persons engaged in the operation of loading or unloading of any possibility of injury to any of the articles of which the cargo is composed, or of danger to any person in or about the ship or vessel while it is being loaded or unloaded. *(Stats. 1937, c. 90, p. 325, § 7600. Amended by Stats.1971, c. 1748, p. 3760, § 50.)*

§ 7601. Handtrucks

Handtrucks shall be maintained in a safe condition by the employer. Handles shall be maintained free of hazardous burrs, splinters, cracks or splits. *(Added by Stats.1967, c. 398, p. 1622, § 2.)*

§ 7602. Handtools

Handtools shall be kept in good condition and be safely stored by the employer. Unsafe handtools shall not be used. *(Added by Stats.1967, c. 398, p. 1622, § 4.)*

§ 7603. Stored material; weight limits; piles, stacks and racks

The maximum weight of materials stored on building floors or load-carrying platforms, except those built directly on the ground, shall not exceed their safe carrying capacity.

Material, when stored, shall be piled, stacked, or racked in a manner designed to prevent it from tipping, falling, collapsing, rolling or spreading. Racks, bins, planks, sleepers, bars, strips, blocks, sheets, shall be used when necessary to make the piles stable. *(Added by Stats.1967, c. 398, p. 1622, § 6.)*

§ 7604. Rails

Adequate and substantial bull rails, stringer rails or curbs shall be installed at the waterside of all flush aprons on such wharves, docks or piers as are in active service for movement of cargo therefrom to vessels. This section shall not apply to any pier designed with depressed spur tracks on at least one side, on which cargo is worked between rail cars and ships but not in the narrow wharf area between depressed tracks and pier edge. *(Added by Stats.1967, c. 398, p. 1622, § 8.)*

§ 7605. Safety inspections; correction of unsafe conditions; discarding unsafe tools, etc.

The employer shall require that tools, machinery, gear and other equipment subject to wear be inspected at adequate intervals and unsafe conditions corrected. If tools, machinery, gear or equipment are found to be defective or otherwise unsafe, employees shall report the same to the person in charge of work who shall have it discarded, marked and so placed that it cannot be used again until made safe. *(Added by Stats.1967, c. 398, p. 1622, § 10.)*

§ 7606. Dock plates

Every dock plate shall be constructed and maintained with strength sufficient to support the load carried thereon.

Dock plates shall be secured in position when spanning the space between the dock or the unloading platform and the vehicle. The dock plate, together with its securing devices, where used over spans of different lengths, shall be of such construction as will readily obtain rigid security over such spans.

The dock plates shall be so constructed and maintained that when they are secured in position the end edges of the plate shall be in substantial contact with dock or loading platform, and with the vehicle bed in such manner as to prevent rocking or sliding. *(Added by Stats.1967, c. 398, p. 1623, § 12.)*

§ 7607. Internal combustion engine operation

Internal combustion engine-driven equipment shall be operated inside of buildings or enclosed structures only when such operation does not result in harmful exposure to concentration of dangerous gases or fumes in excess of maximum acceptable concentrations. Exhaust pipes shall be installed in such a manner that the exhaust products shall be discharged so as not to be a hazard to the operators. *(Added by Stats.1967, c. 398, p. 1623, § 14.)*

§ 7608. Violation; misdemeanor

Any person who violates any provisions of this part is guilty of a misdemeanor. *(Formerly § 7601, Stats.1937, c. 90, p. 326, § 7601. Renumbered § 7608 and amended by Stats.1963, c. 928, p. 2181, § 1.)*

§ 7609. Longshore and stevedore operations; applicability of sections

The provisions of Sections 7601 to 7607, inclusive, shall be applicable to longshore and stevedore operations. *(Added by Stats.1967, c. 398, p. 1623, § 16.)*

§ 7611. Safety orders

Nothing in the foregoing sections of this part shall limit the authority of the division to prescribe or enforce general or special safety orders. *(Added by Stats.1967, c. 398, p. 1623, § 19.)*

Part 6

TANKS AND BOILERS

Chapter		Section
1.	Scope of Chapter and General Provisions	7620
2.	Administration	7650
3.	Operation of Tanks and Boilers	7680
4.	Inspection Fees	7720
5.	Offenses	7750
6.	Mismanagement of Steam Boilers	7770

774

CHAPTER 1. SCOPE OF CHAPTER AND GENERAL PROVISIONS

Section
7620. Division defined.
7621. Boiler defined.
7622. Tank defined.
7623. Scope of part.
7624. Exempt tanks.
7625. Exempt steam boilers.
7626. Safety orders.

§ 7620. Division defined

"Division," as used in this part, means the Division of Occupational Safety and Health. *(Added by Stats.1945, c. 1142, p. 2180, § 2. Amended by Stats.1980, c. 676, p. 1980, § 245.)*

§ 7621. Boiler defined

"Boiler" as used in this part means any fired or unfired pressure vessel used to generate steam pressure by the application of heat subject to this part. *(Added by Stats.1945, c. 1142, p. 2180, § 2. Amended by Stats.1949, c. 1530, p. 2718, § 1.)*

§ 7622. Tank defined

"Tank" as used in this part, means any unfired pressure vessel, subject to this part, used for the storage of air pressure or liquefied petroleum gases; provided, however, that for the purpose of shop inspection, "tank" shall mean any unfired pressure vessel built according to the rules of any nationally recognized pressure vessel code. *(Added by Stats.1945, c. 1142, p. 2180, § 2. Amended by Stats.1949, c. 1530, p. 2718, § 2.)*

§ 7623. Scope of part

This part applies to all boilers and tanks which are not specifically exempted in this chapter, or by the general safety orders of the division now in effect or which may be hereafter adopted. *(Added by Stats.1945, c. 1142, p. 2180, § 2. Amended by Stats.1949, c. 1530, p. 2718, § 3.)*

§ 7624. Exempt tanks

The following tanks are not subject to this part:

(a) Tanks under the jurisdiction or inspection of the United States government.

(b) Air pressure tanks used in household domestic services.

(c) Tanks of 1½ cubic feet or less which are not subject to a pressure of more than 150 pounds per square inch.

(d) Air pressure tanks supplied with air by the same air compressor which supplies air for the brakes of any motor vehicle or streetcar, which units of transportation are operated by any person, firm, or corporation subject to the jurisdiction of the United States Department of Transportation or the California Highway Patrol.

(e) Tanks not subject to an internal or external pressure or more than 15 pounds per square inch, irrespective of size. *(Added by Stats.1945, c. 1142, p. 2180, § 2.*

Amended by Stats.1949, c. 1530, p. 2718, § 4; Stats.1970, c. 242, p. 502, § 3; Stats.1970, c. 518, p. 1012, § 1.)

§ 7625. Exempt steam boilers

The following steam boilers are not subject to this part:

(a) Boilers under the jurisdiction or inspection of the United States Government, and all other boilers operated by employers not subject to Division 4 of this code.

(b) Boilers on which the pressure does not exceed 15 pounds per square inch.

(c) Automobile boilers and boilers on road motor vehicles. *(Added by Stats.1945, c. 1142, p. 2181, § 2.)*

§ 7626. Safety orders

This part does not limit the authority of the division to prescribe or enforce general or special safety orders. *(Added by Stats.1945, c. 1142, p. 2181, § 2.)*

CHAPTER 2. ADMINISTRATION

Section
7650. Persons authorized to make inspections.
7651. Certificate of competency; application
7652. Examination to determine competency.
7652.5. Qualifications of inspectors.
7653. Revocation of certificate.
7654. Inspection reports.
7655. Safety regulations.

§ 7650. Persons authorized to make inspections

Inspections required by this part shall be made either by qualified safety engineers employed by the division or by certified inspectors; provided, however, that shop inspections shall be made by the division, acting through its qualified safety engineers when request therefor is made by any manufacturer of tanks or boilers.

(a) As used in this chapter a "certified inspector" is one who is qualified to make inspections or examinations of boilers or tanks according to the rules under which the vessel is constructed, who has an unrevoked certificate of competency issued pursuant to this part, and who is employed by any one of the following:

(1) A county.

(2) A city.

(3) An insurer.

(4) An employer, for the purpose of inspecting only tanks and boilers under his jurisdiction.

(b) As used in this chapter a "qualified safety engineer" is one who is qualified to make inspections or examinations of boilers or tanks according to the rules under which the vessel is constructed. Such qualification is to be determined by a written examination prescribed by the division. *(Added by Stats.1945, c. 1142, p. 2181, § 2. Amended by Stats.1949, c. 1530, p. 2718, § 5.)*

§ 7651. Certificate of competency; application

A certificate of competency may be obtained by application made to the division. *(Added by Stats.1945, c. 1142, p. 2181, § 2.)*

§ 7652. Examination to determine competency

The division may determine by examination the competency of an applicant for a certificate of competency. *(Added by Stats.1945, c. 1142, p. 2181, § 2.)*

§ 7652.5. Qualifications of inspectors

Notwithstanding any other provision of the law, a certified inspector employed by an insurer or by an employer for the purpose of inspecting only tanks and boilers under his jurisdiction need not be a citizen or an elector. *(Added by Stats.1957, c. 1347, p. 2678, § 2.)*

§ 7653. Revocation of certificate

Upon good cause being shown therefor, the division may revoke a certificate of competency. *(Added by Stats.1945, c. 1142, p. 2181, § 2.)*

§ 7654. Inspection reports

Where serious conditions are found by certified inspectors that would jeopardize the life, limb, or safety of employees, the reports of inspection shall be made forthwith to the division by telegraph or telephone within twenty-four hours.

Within twenty-one days after each routine inspection, every certified inspector shall forward a report of his inspection, on prescribed forms, to the division. His certificate of competency may be suspended or revoked by the division for failure to comply with this section. *(Added by Stats.1945, c. 1142, p. 2181, § 2. Amended by Stats.1949, c. 1530, p. 2719, § 6.)*

§ 7655. Safety regulations

The division shall prepare and adopt regulations in accordance with the Administrative Procedure Act provided for in Chapter 3.5 (commencing with Section 11340) of Part 1 of Division 3 of Title 2 of the Government Code, designed to promote safety with respect to the installation and operation of vendor facilities for the storage and pumping of compressed or liquefied natural gas and liquefied petroleum gas into vehicles. *(Added by Stats.1970, c. 1507, § 1. Amended by Stats.1983, c. 142, § 119.)*

CHAPTER 3. OPERATION OF TANKS AND BOILERS

Section
7680. Requirement of permit for operation.
7681. Inspection of tanks; dispensing unit.
7682. Inspection of boilers.
7683. Issuance of permit; duration.
7684. Posting of permit.
7685. Temporary permits.
7686. Revocation of permit.

Section
7687. Preliminary order for repairs or alterations.
7688. Hearing on preliminary order.
7689. Final order.
7690. Rehearing; judicial review.
7691. Injunction.
7692. Restraining order.

§ 7680. Requirement of permit for operation

No tank or boiler shall be operated unless a permit for its operation has been issued by or in behalf of the division. *(Added by Stats.1945, c. 1142, p. 2181, § 2. Amended by Stats.1976, c. 467, p. 1212, § 1.)*

§ 7681. Inspection of tanks; dispensing unit

(a) The division shall inspect or cause to be inspected each installed tank at least every five years, except for any tank specified in subdivision (b).

(b) Any air pressure tank which contains 25 cubic feet or less and is not subject to pressure of more than 150 pounds per square inch and any liquefied petroleum gas tank used for storage, except a tank used for dispensing purposes as part of a dispensing unit, which contains 575 gallons or less shall be inspected or caused to be inspected by the division when the tank is initially placed into service if the tank is constructed, inspected and stamped in compliance with the American Society of Mechanical Engineers (ASME) Code, or the design, material, and construction of the tank is approved by the division as equivalent to the ASME Code.

(c) "Dispensing unit," as used in this section, means a stationary liquefied petroleum gas installation, other than a bulk plant, from which a product is dispensed, for final utilization, into mobile fuel tanks or portable cylinders. *(Added by Stats.1945, c. 1142, p. 2181, § 2. Amended by Stats.1949, c. 1530, p. 2719, § 7; Stats.1955, c. 1794, p. 3310, § 1; Stats.1968, c. 353, p. 736, § 1; Stats.1980, c. 1279, p. 4324, § 1; Stats.1985, c. 413, § 1; Stats.1987, c. 1216, § 1.)*

§ 7682. Inspection of boilers

The division shall inspect or cause to be inspected each installed fired boiler internally and externally at least every year, except that the division may grant extensions to permit the interval between internal inspections to be increased to a maximum interval of 36 months where operating experience and design of the boiler has demonstrated to the satisfaction of the division that equivalent safety will be maintained.

For other classes of boilers, the division shall establish internal inspection intervals which will ensure the safety of people working in the vicinity of the boiler. In determining the intervals, the division shall consider such factors as the design and construction of the boilers and the conditions under which they operate.

External inspection shall be made of all boilers at the time of the internal inspection and at any other intervals as are deemed necessary by the division acting through qualified safety engineers and certified inspectors. *(Add-*
776

ed by Stats.1945, c. 1142, p. 2181, § 2. Amended by Stats.1949, c. 1530, p. 2719, § 8; Stats.1955, c. 1794, p. 3310, § 2; Stats.1961, c. 806, p. 2080, § 1; Stats.1965, c. 515, p. 1836, § 1; Stats.1988, c. 684, § 1.)

§ 7683. Issuance of permit; duration

(a) If a tank or boiler is found to be in a safe condition for operation, a permit shall be issued by or on behalf of the division for its operation.

(b) In the case of a tank, the permit shall continue in effect for not longer than five years, except for any tank specified in subdivision (b) of Section 7681.

(c) In the case of a tank specified in subdivision (b) of Section 7681, the permit shall remain in effect as long as the tank is in compliance with applicable provisions of this part and regulations contained in Title 8 of the California Administrative Code. A new inspection and permit for operation shall be required whenever there is a change in ownership and permanent location of the tank or there is an alteration or change in the tank which affects the tank's safety.

This subdivision applies to any permit in effect on the effective date of this subdivision as well as to any permit issued after such date. Notwithstanding any other provision of law, an insurer is not liable for any permit issued prior to the effective date of this subdivision for any tank specified in subdivision (b) of Section 7681 for any period of time exceeding the period for which the last permit was issued.

(d) In the case of a boiler, the permit shall continue in effect for a period which is not longer than one year. *(Added by Stats.1945, c. 1142, p. 2182, § 2. Amended by Stats.1955, c. 1794, p. 3310, § 3; Stats.1976, c. 467, p. 1212, § 2; Stats.1980, c. 1279, p. 4324, § 2.)*

§ 7684. Posting of permit

Each permit or a clear reproduced copy thereof shall be posted in a protective container in a conspicuous place on or near the tank or boiler covered by it. *(Added by Stats.1945, c. 1142, p. 2182, § 2. Amended by Stats.1985, c. 413, § 2.)*

§ 7685. Temporary permits

The division may issue and renew temporary permits for not to exceed 30 days each, pending the making of replacements or repairs. *(Added by Stats.1945, c. 1142, p. 2182, § 2.)*

§ 7686. Revocation of permit

Upon good cause being shown therefor, and after notice and an opportunity to be heard, the division may revoke any permit. *(Added by Stats.1945, c. 1142, p. 2182, § 2.)*

§ 7687. Preliminary order for repairs or alterations

If the inspection shows a tank or boiler to be in an unsafe or dangerous condition, the division may issue a preliminary order requiring such repairs or alterations to be made to it as are necessary to render it safe, and may order its use discontinued until the repairs or alterations are made or the dangerous or unsafe condition is remedied. *(Added by Stats.1945, c. 1142, p. 2182, § 2.)*

§ 7688. Hearing on preliminary order

Unless the preliminary order is complied with, a hearing before the division shall be allowed, upon request, at which the owner, operator, or other person in charge of the tank or boiler may appear and show cause why he should not comply with the order. *(Added by Stats.1945, c. 1142, p. 2182, § 2.)*

§ 7689. Final order

If it thereafter appears to the division that the tank or boiler is unsafe and that the requirements contained in the preliminary order should be complied with, or that other things should be done to make the tank or boiler safe, the division may order or confirm the withholding of the permit and may make such requirements as it deems proper for the repair or alteration of the tank or boiler, or the correction of the dangerous and unsafe conditions. *(Added by Stats.1945, c. 1142, p. 2182, § 2.)*

§ 7690. Rehearing; judicial review

The order may be reheard by the division, or reviewed by the courts, in the manner specified by this code for safety orders, and not otherwise. *(Added by Stats.1945, c. 1142, p. 2182, § 2.)*

§ 7691. Injunction

If the operation of a tank or boiler constitutes a serious menace to the life or safety of any person employed about it, the division or any of its safety engineers or any person affected thereby, may apply to the superior court of the county in which the tank or boiler is situated for an injunction restraining its operation until the condition has been corrected. *(Added by Stats.1945, c. 1142, p. 2182, § 2. Amended by Stats.1949, c. 1530, p. 2719, § 9.)*

§ 7692. Restraining order

The certification of the division that no valid permit exists for the operation of a tank or boiler, and the affidavit of any safety engineer of the division that its operation constitutes a menace to the life or safety of any person employed about it, is sufficient proof to warrant the immediate granting of a temporary restraining order. *(Added by Stats.1945, c. 1142, p. 2182, § 2. Amended by Stats.1949, c. 1530, p. 2719, § 10.)*

CHAPTER 4. INSPECTION FEES

Section
7720. Inspection by certified inspector.
7721. Shop, field, and resale inspection of tanks and boilers; consultations, surveys, and audits; pressure vessels; processing of permits; regulations.
7722. Pressure vessel account; disposition of fees; criteria for fee charges; annual report.
7725. Definitions.

Section
7726. Payment before issuance of permit.
7728. Penalty for failure to pay fees on time.

§ 7720. Inspection by certified inspector

No fee shall be charged by the division where an inspection is made by a certified inspector; provided, the inspection has been made and reports have been submitted within the time limits specified in this part. *(Added by Stats.1945, c. 1142, p. 2719, § 11. Amended by Stats.1949, c. 1530, p. 2719, § 11.)*

§ 7721. Shop, field, and resale inspection of tanks and boilers; consultations, surveys, and audits; pressure vessels; processing of permits; regulations

(a) The division may fix and collect fees for the shop, field, and resale inspection of tanks and boilers and for consultations, surveys, audits, and other activities required or related to national standards concerning the design or construction of boilers or pressure vessels or for evaluating fabricator's plant facilities when these services are requested of the division by entities desiring these services. The division may fix and collect the fees for the inspection of pressure vessels as it deems necessary to cover the actual costs of having the inspection performed by a division safety engineer, including administrative costs. An additional fee may, in the discretion of the division, be charged for necessary subsequent inspections to determine if applicable safety orders have been complied with.

(b) The division may charge a fee of not more than fifteen dollars ($15) to cover the cost of processing a permit.

(c) The division may fix and collect fees for field consultations regarding pressure vessels as it deems necessary to cover the actual costs of the time spent in the consultation by a division safety engineer, including administrative expenses.

(d) Whenever a person owning or having the custody, management, or operation of a pressure vessel fails to pay the fees required under this chapter within 60 days after notification, he or she shall pay, in addition to the fees required under this chapter, a penalty fee equal to 100 percent of the fee.

(e) Any fees required pursuant to this section shall be embodied in regulations which shall be adopted as emergency regulations. These emergency regulations shall not be subject to the review and approval of the Office of Administrative Law pursuant to the provisions of the Administrative Procedure Act provided for in Chapter 3.5 (commencing with Section 11340) of Part 1 of Division 3 of Title 2 of the Government Code. These regulations shall become effective immediately upon filing with the Secretary of State. *(Added by Stats.1945, c. 1142, p. 2183, § 2. Amended by Stats.1949, c. 1530, p. 2720, § 12; Stats.1965, c. 1191, p. 3008, § 3; Stats.1973, c. 617, p. 1141, § 1; Stats.1976, c. 518, p. 1271, § 1; Stats.1978, c. 1223, p. 3955, § 2; Stats.1980, c. 531, p.*

1483, § 2; Stats.1981, c. 102, p. 725, § 69, eff. June 28, 1981; Stats.1982, c. 115, p. 357, § 37, eff. March 13, 1982.)

§ 7722. Pressure vessel account; disposition of fees; criteria for fee charges; annual report

The inspection fees collected under this chapter shall be paid into the Pressure Vessel Account, which is hereby created, to be used for the administration of the division pressure vessel safety program.

The division shall establish criteria upon which fee charges are based and prepare an annual report concerning revenues obtained and expenditures appropriated for the pressure vessel safety program. The division shall file the report with the Legislative Analyst, the Joint Legislative Audit Committee, and the Department of Finance. (Added by Stats.1981, c. 102, p. 726, § 70, eff. June 28, 1981.)

§ 7725. Definitions

As used in this chapter, the following terms shall have the meaning therein given them.

(a) "Small tank" shall mean any tank 1,200 gallons water capacity or less.

(b) "Large tank" shall mean any tank of more than 1,200 gallons water capacity.

(c) "Shop inspection" shall mean the inspection and testing of tanks or boilers, manufactured, or in the process of manufacture, repair, or alteration, in the manufacturer's shops, or at the jobsite, in accordance with the applicable rules of the respective codes under which they are manufactured.

(d) "Field inspection" shall mean the inspection and testing of installed tanks or boilers or both tanks and boilers, regardless of location.

(e) "Resale inspection" shall mean the inspection of boilers or tanks in the possession of a dealer or vendor at the request of a user who contemplates the purchase thereof. (Added by Stats.1949, c. 1530, p. 2720, § 16. Amended by Stats.1976, c. 467, p. 1212, § 3.)

§ 7726. Payment before issuance of permit

All inspection fees shall be paid before the issuance of a permit. (Formerly § 7723, added by Stats.1945, c. 1142, p. 2183, § 2. Renumbered § 7726 and amended by Stats.1949, c. 1530, p. 2720, § 15.)

§ 7728. Penalty for failure to pay fees on time

Whenever an owner or user of any apparatus or equipment fails to pay the fees required under this chapter within 60 days after notification, said owner or user shall pay, in addition to the fees required under this chapter, a penalty fee equal to 100 percent of such fee. For the purposes of this section, the date of the invoice shall be considered the date of notification. (Added by Stats.1965, c. 1191, p. 3009, § 7.)

778

CHAPTER 5. OFFENSES

Section
7750. Operation of tank or boiler without permit; misdemeanor; separate offense for each day.

§ 7750. Operation of tank or boiler without permit; misdemeanor; separate offense for each day

Except during the time that a request for a permit remains unacted upon, every person owning or having the custody, management, or operation of a tank or boiler who operates it without a permit issued pursuant to this part is guilty of a misdemeanor.

The operation of a tank or boiler without a permit constitutes a separate offense for each day that it is so operated. (Added by Stats.1945, c. 1142, p. 2183, § 2.)

CHAPTER 6. MISMANAGEMENT OF STEAM BOILERS

Section
7770. Wilful or negligent operation of boiler causing accident endangering human life; felony.
7771. Criminal penalty for causing death.

§ 7770. Wilful or negligent operation of boiler causing accident endangering human life; felony

Every engineer or other person having charge of any steam-boiler, steam-engine, or other apparatus for generating or employing steam, used in any manufactory, railway, or other mechanical works, who wilfully, or from ignorance or from gross neglect, creates, or allows to be created, such an undue quantity of steam as to burst or break the boiler, engine or apparatus, or to cause any other accident whereby human life is endangered, is guilty of a felony. (Added by Stats.1945, c. 1142, p. 2183, § 2.)

§ 7771. Criminal penalty for causing death

Every person having charge of any steam boiler, steam engine, or other apparatus for generating or employing steam, used in any manufactory, railroad, vessel, or other mechanical works, who wilfully, or from ignorance or neglect, creates, or allows to be created, such an undue quantity of steam as to burst or break the boiler, engine, or apparatus, or to cause any other accident whereby the death of a human being is caused, is punishable by imprisonment in the state prison for two, three, or four years. (Added by Stats.1945, c. 1142, p. 2183, § 2. Amended by Stats.1976, c. 1139, p. 5088, § 95, operative July 1, 1977.)

Part 7

VOLATILE FLAMMABLE LIQUIDS

Section
7800. Volatile flammable liquids defined; flash points.
7801. Occupational safety and health standards board.

Section
7802.   General orders.
7803.   Extinguishers.

§ 7800.   Volatile flammable liquids defined; flash points

"Volatile flammable liquids" as used in this part means any petroleum or liquid product of petroleum or natural gas having a flash point below 100 degrees Fahrenheit, and includes any petroleum or liquid product of petroleum or natural gas while at a temperature above its flash point.   Flash points shall be as determined by means of the Tag Closed Tester, Designation D56–36 American Society for Testing Materials, or the Pensky-Martens Closed Tester, Designation D93–42 American Society for Testing Materials.   *(Added by Stats.1953, c. 922, p. 2278, § 1.)*

§ 7801.   Occupational safety and health standards board

"Occupational Safety and Health Standards Board" as used in this part means the Occupational Safety and Health Standards Board of the Division of Occupational Safety and Health, Department of Industrial Relations, State of California.   *(Added by Stats.1953, c. 922, p. 2278, § 1.   Amended by Stats.1980, c. 676, p. 1980, § 246.)*

§ 7802.   General orders

The Occupational Safety and Health Standards Board shall adopt general orders pursuant to Section 6500, to make effective the provisions of this part.   *(Added by Stats.1953, c. 922, p. 2278, § 1.   Amended by Stats.1980, c. 676, p. 1980, § 247.)*

§ 7803.   Extinguishers

Every employer who engages in any business requiring any employee to handle or use any volatile flammable liquid or to work in the close proximity of any such liquid in sufficient quantity and under conditions affording opportunity for the person or clothing becoming ignited shall provide adequate means of extinguishment whereby such employee may extinguish flames on his person or clothing.   *(Added by Stats.1953, c. 922, p. 2278, § 1.)*

Part 7.5

REFINERY AND CHEMICAL PLANTS

Chapter   Section
1.   General 7850
2.   Process Safety Management Standards 7855

CHAPTER 1.   GENERAL

Section
7850.   Short title.
7851.   Legislative findings and declarations.
7852.   Legislative intent; training and process safety management practices; work safety standards.
7853.   "Process safety management".

§ 7850.   Short title

This part shall be known and cited as the California Refinery and Chemical Plant Worker Safety Act of 1990.   *(Added by Stats.1990, c. 1632 (A.B.3672), § 1.)*

§ 7851.   Legislative findings and declarations

The Legislature finds and declares that because of the potentially hazardous nature of handling large quantities of chemicals and recent disasters involving chemical handling in other states, a greater state effort is required to assure worker safety.   The Legislature also recognizes that a key element for assuring workplace safety is adequate employee training.   The potential consequences of explosions, fires, and releases of dangerous chemicals may be catastrophic; thus immediate and comprehensive government action must be taken to ensure that workers in petroleum refineries, chemical plants, and other related facilities are thoroughly trained and that adequate process safety management practices are implemented.   *(Added by Stats.1990, c. 1632 (A.B. 3672), § 1.)*

§ 7852.   Legislative intent; training and process safety management practices; work safety standards

(a) It is the intent of the Legislature, in enacting this part, that the Occupational Safety and Health Standards Board and the Division of Occupational Health and Safety (OSHA) promote worker safety through implementation of training and process safety management practices in petroleum refineries and chemical plants and other facilities deemed appropriate.

(b) To the maximum extent practicable, the board and the division shall minimize duplications with other state statutory programs and business reporting requirements when developing standards pursuant to Chapter 2 (commencing with Section 7855).

(c) It is further the intent of the Legislature, in enacting this part, that in the interest of promoting worker safety, standards be adopted at the earliest reasonably possible date, but in no case later than July 1, 1992.   *(Added by Stats.1990, c. 1632 (A.B.3672), § 1.)*

§ 7853.   "Process safety management"

For the purposes of this part, "process safety management" means the application of management programs, which are not limited to engineering guidelines, when dealing with the risks associated with handling or working near hazardous chemicals.   Process safety management is intended to prevent or minimize the consequences of catastrophic releases of acutely hazardous, flammable, or explosive chemicals.   *(Added by Stats.1990, c. 1632 (A.B. 3672), § 1.)*

CHAPTER 2.   PROCESS SAFETY MANAGEMENT STANDARDS

Section
7855.   Purpose of chapter; intent of process safety management standards.

Section
7856.　Adoption of standards; jurisdiction; priorities.
7857.　Provisions included in standards.
7858.　Written safety information; acutely hazardous and flammable materials.
7859.　Hazard analysis; report; availability of risk management prevention program.
7860.　Written operating procedures; copies accessible to employees and others; review.
7861.　Employee training in process overview and operating procedures; certification records; testing procedures.
7862.　Employer to inform contractors of hazards, safety rules, and emergency action plan; contractors' training and supervision of employees.
7863.　Prestartup safety review; new and modified facilities.
7864.　Integrity of process equipment; inspection and testing programs; employer response.
7865.　"Hot work" permits; written procedure.
7866.　Written procedures to manage changes.
7867.　Major accidents in workplace; written procedure for investigations; reports; findings and recommendations.
7868.　Emergency action plan.
7870.　Fees; consultation, inspection, adoption of standards, etc.; expenditure of funds subject to appropriation.

§ 7855.　Purpose of chapter; intent of process safety management standards

The purpose of this chapter is to prevent or minimize the consequences of catastrophic releases of toxic, flammable, or explosive chemicals. The establishment of process safety management standards are intended to eliminate, to a substantial degree, the risks to which workers are exposed in petroleum refineries, chemical plants, and other related manufacturing facilities. *(Added by Stats.1990, c. 1632 (A.B.3672), § 1.)*

§ 7856.　Adoption of standards; jurisdiction; priorities

No later than July 1, 1992, the board shall adopt process safety management standards for refineries, chemical plants, and other manufacturing facilities, as specified in Codes 28 (Chemical and Allied Products) and 29 (Petroleum Refining and Related Industries) of the Manual of Standard Industrial Classification Codes, published by the United States Office of Management and Budget, 1987 Edition, that handle acutely hazardous material as defined in subdivision (a) of Section 25532 and subdivision (a) of Section 25536 of the Health and Safety Code and pose a significant likelihood of accident risk, as determined by the board. Alternately, upon making a finding that there is a significant likelihood of risk to employees at a facility not included in Codes 28 and 29 resulting from the presence of acutely hazardous materials or explosives as identified in Part 172 (commencing with Section 172.1) of Title 49 of the Code of Federal Regulations, the board may require that these facilities be subject to the jurisdiction of the standards provided for in this section. When adopting these standards, the board shall give priority to facilities and areas of facilities where the potential is greatest for preventing severe or catastrophic accidents because of the

size or nature of the process or business. The standards adopted pursuant to this section shall require that injury prevention programs of employers subject to this part and implemented pursuant to Section 6401.7 include the requirements of this part. *(Added by Stats.1990, c. 1632 (A.B.3672), § 1.)*

§ 7857.　Provisions included in standards

The process safety management standards shall include provisions dealing with the items prescribed by Sections 7858 to 7868, inclusive, of this chapter. *(Added by Stats.1990, c. 1632 (A.B.3672), § 1.)*

§ 7858.　Written safety information; acutely hazardous and flammable materials

The employer shall develop and maintain a compilation of written safety information to enable the employer and the employees operating the process to identify and understand the hazards posed by processes involving acutely hazardous and flammable material. The employer shall provide for employee participation in this process. This safety information shall be communicated to employees involved in the processes, and shall include information pertaining to hazards of acutely hazardous and flammable materials used in the process, information pertaining to the technology of the process, and information pertaining to the equipment in the process. A copy of this information and communication shall be accessible to all workers who perform any duties in or near the process area. *(Added by Stats.1990, c. 1632 (A.B.3672), § 1.)*

§ 7859.　Hazard analysis; report; availability of risk management prevention program

The employer shall perform a hazard analysis for identifying, evaluating, and controlling hazards involved in the process. The employer shall provide for the participation of knowledgeable operating employees in these analyses. The final report containing the results of the hazardous analysis for each process shall be available, in the respective work area, for review by any person working in that area. Upon request of any worker or any labor union representative of any worker in the area, the employer shall provide or make available a copy of any risk management prevention program prepared for that facility pursuant to Article 2 (commencing with Section 25531) of Chapter 6.95 of Division 20 of the Health and Safety Code. The board, when adopting a standard or standards pertaining to this section, may authorize employers to submit risk management prevention programs prepared pursuant to Article 2 (commencing with Section 25531) of Chapter 6.95 of Division 20 of the Health and Safety Code to satisfy related requirements in whole or in part. *(Added by Stats.1990, c. 1632 (A.B.3672), § 1.)*

§ 7860.　Written operating procedures; copies accessible to employees and others; review

(a) The employer shall develop and implement written operating procedures that provide clear instructions for safely conducting activities involved in each process consistent with the process safety information.

(b) A copy of the operating procedures shall be readily accessible to employees or to any other person who works in or near the process area.

(c) The operating procedures shall be reviewed as often as necessary to assure that they reflect current operating practice, including changes that result from changes in process chemicals, technology, and equipment, and changes to facilities. *(Added by Stats.1990, c. 1632 (A.B.3672), § 1.)*

§ 7861. Employee training in process overview and operating procedures; certification records; testing procedures

(a) Each employee whose primary duties include the operating or maintenance of a process, and each employee prior to assuming operations and maintenance duties in a newly assigned process, shall be trained in an overview of the process and in the operating procedures as specified in Section 7860. The training shall include emphasis on the specific safety and health hazards, procedures, and safe practices applicable to the employee's job tasks.

(b) Refresher and supplemental training shall be provided to each operating or maintenance employee, or both, and other worker necessary to ensure safe operation of the facility and on a recurring regular schedule as determined adequate by the board.

(c) The employer shall ensure that each worker necessary to ensure safe operation of the facility has received and successfully completed training as specified by this section. The employer, after the initial or refresher training shall prepare a certification record which contains the identity of the employee, the date of training, and the signature of the person conducting the training. Testing procedures shall be established by each employer to ensure competency in job skill levels and safe and healthy work practices. *(Added by Stats.1990, c. 1632 (A.B.3672), § 1.)*

§ 7862. Employer to inform contractors of hazards, safety rules, and emergency action plan; contractors' training and supervision of employees

(a) The employer shall inform contractors performing work on, or near, a process of the known potential fire, explosion, or toxic release hazards related to the contractor's work and the process, and require that contractors have trained their employees to a level adequate to safely perform their job. The employer shall also inform contractors of any applicable safety rules of the facility, and assure that the contractors have so informed their employees.

(b) The employer shall explain to contractors the applicable provisions of the emergency action plan required by Section 7868.

(c) Contractors shall assure that their employees have received training to safely perform their jobs and that these employees will adhere to all applicable work practices and safety rules of the facility. *(Added by Stats.1990, c. 1632 (A.B.3672), § 1.)*

§ 7863. Prestartup safety review; new and modified facilities

The employer shall perform a prestartup safety review for new facilities and for modified facilities for which the modification necessitates a change in the process safety information. These reviews shall include knowledgeable operating employees. *(Added by Stats.1990, c. 1632 (A.B.3672), § 1.)*

§ 7864. Integrity of process equipment; inspection and testing programs; employer response

The employer shall establish and implement written procedures and inspection and testing programs to maintain the ongoing integrity of process equipment. These programs shall include a process for allowing employees to identify and report potentially faulty or unsafe equipment, and to record their observations and suggestions in writing. The employer shall respond regarding the disposition of the employee's concerns contained in the reports in a timely manner. *(Added by Stats.1990, c. 1632 (A.B.3672), § 1.)*

§ 7865. "Hot work" permits; written procedure

The employer shall develop and implement a written procedure governing the issuance of "hot work" permits. "Hot work" includes electric or gas welding, cutting, brazing, or similar flame- or spark-producing operations. *(Added by Stats.1990, c. 1632 (A.B.3672), § 1.)*

§ 7866. Written procedures to manage changes

The employer shall establish and implement written procedures to manage changes, except for replacements in kind, to process chemicals, technology, and equipment, and to make changes to facilities. *(Added by Stats.1990, c. 1632 (A.B.3672), § 1.)*

§ 7867. Major accidents in workplace; written procedure for investigations; reports; findings and recommendations

The employer shall establish a written procedure for investigating every incident which results in, or, as determined by board criteria, could reasonably have resulted in, a major accident in the workplace. The procedure shall, at a minimum, require that a written report be prepared and be provided to all employees whose work assignments are within the facility where the incident occurred at the time the incident occurred and shall also include establishing a method for dealing with findings and recommendations. *(Added by Stats.1990, c. 1632 (A.B.3672), § 1.)*

§ 7868. Emergency action plan

The employer shall establish and implement an emergency action plan. The employer may use the business plan for emergency response submitted pursuant to subdivision (a) of Section 25503.5 and subdivision (b) of Section 25505 of the Health and Safety Code if it meets the standards adopted by the board. *(Added by Stats. 1990, c. 1632 (A.B.3672), § 1.)*

§ 7870. Fees; consultation, inspection, adoption of standards, etc.; expenditure of funds subject to appropriation

Notwithstanding the availability of federal funds to carry out the purposes of this part, the division may fix and collect reasonable fees for consultation, inspection, adoption of standards, and other duties conducted pursuant to this part. The expenditure of these funds shall be subject to appropriation by the Legislature in the annual Budget Act. *(Added by Stats.1990, c. 1632 (A.B.3672), § 1.)*

Part 8

AMUSEMENT RIDES SAFETY LAW

Section
7900.   Short title.
7901.   Definitions.
7902.   Rules and regulations; authority of division to prescribe or enforce general or special safety orders.
7903.   Certification by engineer.
7904.   Inspection and permit fees; annual report.
7905.   Inspectors; hiring; persons who may inspect.
7906.   Permits; application; annual inspection.
7907.   Issuance of permit.
7908.   Notice of intention to erect new ride or add to or alter existing ride.
7909.   Order for cessation of operation and permit revocation; hazardous or unsafe rides; resumption of operation.
7910.   Existing installations.
7911.   Modification of application of rules or regulations.
7912.   Insurance.
7913.   Regulation of carnivals and amusement rides by cities and counties.
7914.   Reporting of accidents; notice by agency responding to accident.
7915.   Failure to comply with part, rule, regulation or safety order; misdemeanor; failure to pay fees; penalty fee.
7916.   Amusement ride owners provide training to employees; maintaining records; demonstration of requirements met.
7917.   Amusement ride owners; violations resulting from death or reportable injury.
7918.   Amusement ride owners or operators; citations and penalties; appeals.
7919.   Rules and regulations.

§ 7900.   Short title

This part shall be known and may be cited as the Amusement Rides Safety Law. *(Added by Stats.1968, c. 1113, p. 2126, § 1.)*

§ 7901.   Definitions

As used in this part:

(a) "Amusement ride" means a mechanical device which carries or conveys passengers along, around, or over a fixed or restricted route or course for the purpose of giving its passengers amusement, pleasure, thrills, or excitement. "Amusement ride" includes the business of operating bungee jumping services or providing services to facilitate bungee jumping, but does not include slides, playground equipment, coin-operated devices or conveyances which operate directly on the ground or on the surface or pavement directly on the ground or the operation of amusement devices of a permanent nature. The division shall determine the specific devices which are amusement rides for the purposes of this part. This determination shall be made to apply equally to all operators of similar or identical rides and shall be made pursuant to a procedure promulgated by the standards board.

(b) "Operator" or "owner" means a person who owns or controls or has the duty to control the operation of an amusement ride. It includes the state and every state agency, and each county, city, district, and all public and quasi-public corporations and public agencies therein.

(c) "Permit" means a document issued by the division which indicates that an inspection of the ride has been performed pursuant to rules and regulations adopted by the division. *(Added by Stats.1968, c. 1113, p. 2126, § 1. Amended by Stats.1983, c. 705, § 1; Stats.1992, c. 520 (A.B.2778), § 1.)*

§ 7902.   Rules and regulations; authority of division to prescribe or enforce general or special safety orders

The division shall promulgate and formulate rules and regulations for adoption by the Occupational Safety and Health Standards Board for the safe installation, repair, maintenance, use, operation, and inspection of all amusement rides as the division finds necessary for the protection of the general public using amusement rides. The rules and regulations shall be in addition to the existing applicable safety orders and will be concerned with engineering force stresses, safety devices, and preventative maintenance. Nothing in this chapter shall limit the authority of the division to prescribe or enforce general or special safety orders. *(Added by Stats.1968, c. 1113, p. 2126, § 1. Amended by Stats.1980, c. 676, p. 1980, § 248; Stats.1983, c. 705, § 2.)*

§ 7903.   Certification by engineer

The division or a public entity shall not issue the original certificate of inspection for an amusement ride until it receives certification in writing by an engineer qualified under the Civil and Professional Engineers Act (Chapter 7 (commencing with Section 6700) of Division 3 of the Business and Professions Code) that such amusement ride meets the requirements established by the division for amusement rides. *(Added by Stats.1968, c. 1113, p. 2126, § 1.)*

§ 7904. Inspection and permit fees; annual report

(a) The division may fix and collect fees for the inspection of amusement rides that it deems necessary to cover the actual cost of having the inspection performed by a division safety engineer. The division may not charge for inspections performed by certified insurance inspectors or an inspector for a public entity, but may charge a fee of not more than ten dollars ($10) to cover the cost of processing the permit when issued by the division as a result of the inspection. All fees collected by the division under this section shall be deposited into the Elevator Safety Account to support the division's portable amusement ride inspection program.

(b) The division shall annually prepare and submit to the Division of Fairs and Expositions within the Department of Food and Agriculture, a report summarizing all inspections of amusement rides and accidents occurring on amusement rides. This annual report shall also contain all route location information submitted to the division by permit applicants. *(Added by Stats.1983, c. 705, § 4. Amended by Stats.2007, c. 179 (S.B.86), § 33, eff. Aug. 24, 2007.)*

§ 7905. Inspectors; hiring; persons who may inspect

The division may hire inspectors to inspect amusement rides. The division shall cause the inspection provided by this part to be made by its safety inspectors, or by a qualified inspector who is approved by the division and employed by an insurance company or a public entity. *(Added by Stats.1968, c. 1113, p. 2126, § 1. Amended by Stats.1983, c. 705, § 5.)*

§ 7906. Permits; application; annual inspection

No person shall operate an amusement ride without a permit issued by the division or a public entity. On or before March 1 of each year an operator shall apply for a permit to the division or a public entity on a form furnished by the division and containing such information as the division may require. Each application shall specifically include a route list for the ride for the permit year, which shall include the name of each town or city, street location, and dates of operation of the ride at each location. A route list may be revised at any time, but a ride may not be operated at a particular location unless notification of the revision has been given previously to the division or public entity issuing the permit.

All amusement rides shall be inspected before they are originally put into operation for the public's use and thereafter at least once every year, unless authorized to operate on a temporary permit. Amusement rides may also be inspected each time they are disassembled and reassembled. *(Added by Stats.1968, c. 1113, p. 2126, § 1. Amended by Stats.1983, c. 705, § 6.)*

§ 7907. Issuance of permit

If, after inspection, an amusement ride is found to comply with the rules and regulations of the division, the division or a public entity shall issue a permit to operate. *(Added by Stats.1968, c. 1113, p. 2126, § 1.)*

§ 7908. Notice of intention to erect new ride or add to or alter existing ride

Before a new amusement ride is erected, or whenever any additions or alterations are made which change the structure, mechanism, classification, or capacity of any amusement ride, the operator shall file with the division or a public entity a notice of his intention and any plans or diagrams requested by the division. *(Added by Stats. 1968, c. 1113, p. 2126, § 1.)*

§ 7909. Order for cessation of operation and permit revocation; hazardous or unsafe rides; resumption of operation

The division may order cessation of operation of an amusement ride and permit revocation if it has been determined after inspection to be hazardous or unsafe. Operation shall not resume until such conditions are corrected to the satisfaction of the division[1] *(Added by Stats.1968, c. 1113, p. 2126, § 1. Amended by Stats.1983, c. 705, § 7.)*

[1] So in enrolled bill.

§ 7910. Existing installations

This part shall not be construed to prevent the use of any existing installation which upon inspection is found to be in a safe condition and in conformance with the rules and regulations of the division. *(Added by Stats.1968, c. 1113, p. 2126, § 1.)*

§ 7911. Modification of application of rules or regulations

If there are practical difficulties or unnecessary hardships for an operator to comply with the rules and regulations under this part, the division may modify the application of such rules or regulations if the spirit of the rules and regulations shall be observed and the public safety is secure. Any operator may make a written request to the division stating his grounds and applying for such modification. Any authorization by the division shall be in writing and shall describe the conditions under which the modifications are permitted. A record of all modifications shall be kept in the division and open to the public. *(Added by Stats.1968, c. 1113, p. 2126, § 1.)*

§ 7912. Insurance

No person shall operate an amusement ride unless there is in existence and on file with the division a policy of insurance, issued by a company licensed by the Department of Insurance to do business in the state, or by a nonadmitted insurer employed by a surplus lines broker licensed by the Department of Insurance, in an amount of not less than five hundred thousand dollars ($500,000) until January 1, 2009, and, effective on and after January 1, 2009, one million dollars ($1,000,000) per occurrence insuring the owner or operator against liability for injury suffered by persons riding the amusement

783

ride. *(Added by Stats.1968, c. 1113, p. 2126, § 1. Amended by Stats.1982, c. 517, p. 2406, § 313; Stats.1983, c. 705, § 8; Stats.1988, c. 1274, § 1; Stats.2007, c. 478 (S.B.783), § 1.)*

§ 7913. Regulation of carnivals and amusement rides by cities and counties

Nothing contained in this part shall prevent cities, counties, and cities and counties from regulating carnivals or amusement rides, nor prevent them from enacting legislation more restrictive than this part with respect to carnivals or amusement rides. *(Added by Stats.1968, c. 1113, p. 2126, § 1.)*

§ 7914. Reporting of accidents; notice by agency responding to accident

(a) An operator of an amusement ride shall report or cause to be reported to the division immediately by telephone each known incident where the maintenance, operation, or use of the amusement ride results in any of the following:

(1) A fatality.

(2) A loss of consciousness or other injury to a person which requires medical service other than ordinary first aid treatment.

(3) Major mechanical failure. For purposes of this section, "major mechanical failure" means the stoppage of operation resulting from or in a structural failure, a mechanical or electrical failure of a drive or control system component, or a failure of a restraint system that significantly compromises ride safety. "Major mechanical failure" does not include a foreseeable malfunction that activates a safety system.

(4) A patron falling from a moving ride or from a ride that has temporarily stopped in an elevated position.

(b) If a fatality, reportable injury, or major mechanical failure, as defined in subdivision (a), is caused by the failure, malfunction, or operation of an amusement ride, the equipment or conditions that caused the accident shall be preserved for the purpose of investigation by the division.

(c) In addition to the report by telephone required under subdivision (a), an operator of an amusement ride shall submit a written accident report to the division within 24 hours of an incident on a form designated by the division.

(d) A division inspector may inspect an amusement ride upon receipt of the report of an incident.

(e) Whenever a state, county, or local fire or police agency is called to an accident involving an amusement ride covered by this part in which a serious injury or illness, or death occurs, the nearest office of the division shall be notified by telephone immediately by the responding agency. *(Added by Stats.1983, c. 705, § 9. Amended by Stats.2007, c. 478 (S.B.783), § 2.)*

§ 7915. Failure to comply with part, rule, regulation or safety order; misdemeanor; failure to pay fees; penalty fee

(a) Any owner or operator of any amusement ride who fails to comply with any provision of this part or any rule, regulation, or safety order adopted pursuant to this part shall be guilty of a misdemeanor.

(b) Whenever an owner or operator of any amusement ride fails to pay any fee required under Section 7904 within 60 days after notification, the owner or operator shall pay, in addition to the fee required, a penalty fee equal to 100 percent of the required fee. For purposes of this section, the date of the invoice shall be considered the date of notification.

(c) The division shall not issue any permit to any owner or operator of any amusement ride who fails to pay any fee until the fee is paid. *(Added by Stats.1983, c. 705, § 10. Amended by Stats.2007, c. 478 (S.B.783), § 3.)*

§ 7916. Amusement ride owners provide training to employees; maintaining records; demonstration of requirements met

(a) An owner of an amusement ride shall provide training for its employees in the safe operation and maintenance of amusement rides, as required by Sections 4, 6, 7, and 8 of ASTM F770–06, Standard Practice for Ownership and Operation of Amusement Rides and Devices, adopted by the American Society for Testing and Materials, as amended or as may be amended from time to time and as the division deems appropriate, and the injury prevention program required under Section 6401.7.

(b) The owner of an amusement ride shall maintain all of the records necessary to demonstrate that the requirements of subdivision (a) have been met, including employee training records and maintenance, repair, inspection, and injury and illness records for each amusement ride, as specified in ASTM F770–06 referenced in subdivision (a). On and after January 1, 2009, the owner of an amusement ride shall make the records available to a division inspector upon request. *(Added by Stats.2007, c. 478 (S.B.783), § 4.)*

§ 7917. Amusement ride owners; violations resulting from death or reportable injury

If the division determines that an owner or operator of an amusement ride subject to this part has willfully or intentionally violated this part or a rule or regulation promulgated under this part, and that the violation resulted in a death or reportable injury as specified in Section 7914, the division shall impose on that owner or operator a civil penalty of not less than five thousand dollars ($5,000) and not more than twenty-five thousand dollars ($25,000). *(Added by Stats.2007, c. 478 (S.B.783), § 5.)*

§ 7918. Amusement ride owners or operators; citations and penalties; appeals

The division shall enforce this part by the issuance of a citation and notice of civil penalty in a manner consistent with that specified in Section 6317 or in some other manner as deemed appropriate by the division. An owner or operator who receives a citation and penalty may appeal the citation and penalty to the Occupational Safety and Health Appeals Board in a manner consistent with that specified in Section 6319. *(Added by Stats.2007, c. 478 (S.B.783), § 6.)*

§ 7919. Rules and regulations

The division shall adopt rules and regulations necessary for the administration of this part, including, the reporting requirements established under Section 7914. *(Added by Stats.2007, c. 478 (S.B.783), § 7.)*

Part 8.1

PERMANENT AMUSEMENT RIDE SAFETY INSPECTION PROGRAM

Section
7920. Legislative intent
7921. Definitions.
7922. Applicability.
7923. Rules and regulations relating to ride safety.
7924. Amusement ride owners; submission of annual certificate of compliance; qualified safety inspectors; rides found to be unsafe; maintenance of records; annual inspections.
7925. Accident reports; inspections after accidents.
7926. Insurance and bond requirements.
7927. Training for employees.
7928. Rules and regulations for administration of this part.
7929. Fees.
7930. Violations; civil penalties.
7931. Enforcement; citation and notice of civil penalty.
7932. Exemption for rides located in counties that have adopted certain provisions of the 1994 Uniform Building Code.

§ 7920. Legislative intent

It is the intent of the Legislature in enacting this part to create a state system for the inspection of permanent amusement rides. This part shall be known and may be cited as the Permanent Amusement Ride Safety Inspection Program. *(Added by Stats.1999, c. 585 (A.B.850), § 1.)*

§ 7921. Definitions

As used in this part:

(a) "Permanent amusement ride" means a mechanical device, aquatic device, or combination of devices, of a permanent nature that carries or conveys passengers along, around, or over a fixed or restricted route or course for the purpose of giving its passengers amusement, pleasure, thrills, or excitement. "Permanent amusement ride" includes the business of operating bungee jumping services or providing services to facilitate bungee jumping, but does not include slides, playground equipment, coin-operated devices or conveyances that operate directly on the ground or on a surface or pavement directly on the ground. The division shall determine the specific devices that are permanent amusement rides for the purposes of this part. This determination shall be made to apply equally to all operators of similar or identical rides and shall be made pursuant to a procedure promulgated by the standards board.

(b) "Operator" or "owner" means a person who owns or controls or has the duty to control the operation of an amusement ride. It includes the state and every state agency, and each county, city, district, and all public and quasi-public corporations and public agencies therein.

(c) "Qualified safety inspector" means either of the following:

(1) A person who holds a valid professional engineer license issued by this state or issued by an equivalent licensing body in another state, and who has been approved by the division as a qualified safety inspector for permanent amusement rides.

(2) A person who documents to the satisfaction of the division that he or she meets all of the following requirements:

(A) The person has a minimum of five years experience in the amusement ride field, at least two years of which were involved in actual amusement ride inspection with a manufacturer, government agency, amusement park, carnival, or insurance underwriter.

(B) The person completes not less than 15 hours per year of continuing education at a school approved by the division, which education shall include inservice industry or manufacturer updates and seminars.

(C) The person has completed at least 80 hours of formal education during the past five years from a school approved by the division for amusement ride safety. Nondestructive–testing training, as determined by the division, may be substituted for up to one-half of the 80 hours of education. *(Added by Stats.1999, c. 585 (A.B. 850), § 1.)*

§ 7922. Applicability

This part does not apply to any of the following:

(a) Any playground operated by a school or local government if the playground is an incidental amenity and the operating entity is not primarily engaged in providing amusement, pleasure, thrills, or excitement.

(b) Museums or other institutions principally devoted to the exhibition of products of agriculture, industry, education, science, religion, or the arts.

(c) Skating rinks, arcades, laser or paint ball war games, indoor interactive arcade games, bowling alleys, miniature golf courses, mechanical bulls, inflatable rides, trampolines, ball crawls, exercise equipment, jet skis, paddle boats, air boats, helicopters, airplanes, parasails, hot air balloons, whether tethered or untethered, the-aters, amphitheaters, batting cages, stationary spring-mounted fixtures, rider-propelled merry-go-rounds, games, slide shows, live animal rides, or live animal shows.

(d) Permanent amusement rides operated at a private event that are not open to the general public and not subject to a separate admission charge. *(Added by Stats.1999, c. 585 (A.B.850), § 1.)*

§ 7923. Rules and regulations relating to ride safety

(a) The division shall formulate and propose rules and regulations for adoption by the Occupational Safety and Health Standards Board for the safe installation, repair, maintenance, use, operation, and inspection of all perma-nent amusement rides as the division finds necessary for the protection of the general public using permanent amusement rides. The rules and regulations shall be in addition to the existing applicable safety orders and will be concerned with engineering force stresses, safety devices, and preventative maintenance. Nothing in this part shall limit the authority of the division to prescribe or enforce general or special safety orders.

(b) It is the Legislature's intent that the rules and regulations adopted pursuant to this part be consistent with those adopted by the Occupational Safety and Health Standards Board for traveling amusement rides, to the extent that those rules and regulations are found to be appropriate. *(Added by Stats.1999, c. 585 (A.B.850), § 1.)*

§ 7924. Amusement ride owners; submission of annual certificate of compliance; qualified safety inspec-tors; rides found to be unsafe; maintenance of records; annual inspections

(a) On an annual basis, each owner of a permanent amusement ride shall submit to the division a certificate of compliance on a form prescribed by the division, which shall include the following:

(1) The legal name and address of the owner and his or her representative, if any, and the primary place of business of the owner.

(2) A description of, the name of the manufacturer of, and, if given by the manufacturer, the serial number and model number of, the permanent amusement ride.

(3) A written declaration, executed by a qualified safety inspector, stating that, within the preceding 12–month period, the permanent amusement ride was in-spected by the qualified safety inspector and that the permanent amusement ride is in material conformance with the requirements of this section and all applicable rules and regulations adopted by the division and stan-dards board.

(b) The owner of multiple permanent amusement rides at a single site may submit a single certificate of compliance that provides the information required by subdivision (a) for each permanent amusement ride at that site.

(c) A certificate of compliance shall not be required until one year following the promulgation of any rules or regulations by the division governing the submission of the certificates.

(d) No person shall operate a permanent amusement ride that has been inspected by a qualified safety inspec-tor or division inspector and found to be unsafe, unless all necessary repairs or modifications, or both, to the ride have been completed and certified as completed by a qualified safety inspector.

(e) For the purposes of satisfying this section, a qualified safety inspector shall meet the requirements in subdivision (c) of Section 7921 and shall be certified by the division. Each qualified safety inspector shall be recertified every two years following his or her initial certification. A qualified safety inspector may be an in-house, full-time safety inspector of the owner of the permanent amusement ride, an employee or agent of the insurance underwriter or insurance broker of the perma-nent amusement ride, an employee or agent of the manufacturer of the amusement ride, or an independent consultant or contractor.

(f) The owner of a permanent amusement ride shall maintain all of the records necessary to demonstrate that the requirements of this section have been met, including, but not limited to, employee training records, mainte-nance, repair, and inspection records for each permanent amusement ride, and records of accidents of which the operator has knowledge, resulting from the failure, mal-function, or operation of a permanent amusement ride, requiring medical service other than ordinary first aid, and shall make them available to a division inspector upon request. The owner shall make those records available for inspection by the division during normal business hours at the owner's permanent place of busi-ness. The owner, or representative of the owner, may be present when the division inspects the records. In conjunction with an inspection of records conducted pursuant to this subdivision, the division shall conduct an inspection of the operation of the rides at the permanent amusement park.

(g) Upon receipt of a certificate of compliance, the division shall notify the owner of the permanent amuse-ment ride or rides for which a certificate is submitted whether the certificate meets all the requirements of this section, and if not, what requirements must still be met.

(h) The division shall, in addition to the annual inspection performed by the division pursuant to subdivi-sion (f), inspect the records for a permanent amusement ride or the ride, or both, under either of the following circumstances:

(1) The division finds that the certificate of compliance submitted pursuant to this section for the ride is fraudu-lent.

(2) The division determines, pursuant to regulations it has adopted, that a permanent amusement ride has a

disproportionately high incidence of accidents required to be reported pursuant to Section 7925.

(i) The division shall conduct its inspections with the least disruption to the normal operation of the permanent park. *(Added by Stats.1999, c. 585 (A.B.850), § 1.)*

§ 7925. Accident reports; inspections after accidents

(a) Each operator of a permanent amusement ride shall report or cause to be reported to the division immediately by telephone each known accident where maintenance, operation, or use of the permanent amusement ride results in a death or serious injury to any person unless the injury does not require medical service other than ordinary first aid. If a death or serious injury results from the failure, malfunction, or operation of a permanent amusement ride, the equipment or conditions that caused the accident shall be preserved for the purpose of an investigation by the division.

(b) A division inspector may inspect any permanent amusement ride after the report of an accident to the division. The division may order a cessation of operation of a permanent amusement ride if it is determined after inspection to be hazardous or unsafe. Operation shall not resume until these conditions are corrected to the satisfaction of the division.

(c) Whenever a state, county, or local fire or police agency is called to an accident involving a permanent amusement ride covered by this part where a serious injury or death occurs, the nearest office of the division shall be notified by telephone immediately by the responding agency. *(Added by Stats.1999, c. 585 (A.B.850), § 1.)*

§ 7926. Insurance and bond requirements

(a) A person may operate a permanent amusement ride only if, at the time of operation, one of the following is in existence:

(1) The owner of the permanent amusement ride provides an insurance policy in an amount not less than one million dollars ($1,000,000) per occurrence insuring the owner or operator against liability for injury or death to persons arising out of the use of the permanent amusement ride.

(2) The owner of the permanent amusement ride provides a bond in an amount not less than one million dollars ($1,000,000), except that the aggregate liability of the surety under that bond shall not exceed the face amount of the bond.

(3) The owner of a permanent amusement ride meets a financial test of self-insurance, as prescribed by rules and regulations promulgated by the division, to demonstrate financial responsibility covering liability for injury suffered by patrons riding the permanent amusement ride.

(b) The insurance policy or bond shall be obtained from one or more insurers or sureties licensed by the Department of Insurance to do business in this state, or by a nonadmitted insurer employed by a surplus lines broker licensed by the Department of Insurance. *(Added by Stats.1999, c. 585 (A.B.850), § 1.)*

§ 7927. Training for employees

Each owner of a permanent amusement ride shall provide training for its employees in the safe operation and maintenance of amusement rides, as required by the standards adopted by the American Society for Testing Materials, Committee F770–03, Section 4.1.3, and Committee F853–93, Section 6.2, as amended or as may be amended from time to time, and the injury prevention program required under Section 6401.7. *(Added by Stats.1999, c. 585 (A.B.850), § 1.)*

§ 7928. Rules and regulations for administration of this part

The division shall adopt rules and regulations necessary for the administration of this part. The division may employ qualified safety inspectors as necessary for the purposes of this part. *(Added by Stats.1999, c. 585 (A.B.850), § 1.)*

§ 7929. Fees

(a) The division may fix and collect all fees necessary to cover the cost of administering this part. Fees shall be charged to a person or entity receiving the division's services as provided by this part or by regulations adopted pursuant to this part, including, but not limited to, approvals, determinations, certifications and recertifications, receipt and review of certificates, and inspections. In fixing the amount of these fees, the division may include a reasonable percentage attributable to the general cost of the division for administering this part. Notwithstanding Section 6103 of the Government Code, the division may collect these fees from the state or any county, city, district, or other political subdivision.

(b) Effective June 30, 2007, all fees collected pursuant to this section shall be deposited into the Elevator Safety Account to support the Permanent Amusement Ride Safety Inspection Program. All moneys in the Permanent Amusement Ride Safety Inspection Fund as of that date shall be transferred to the Elevator Safety Account to be used for the same purpose, and any outstanding liabilities and encumbrances of the fund shall become liabilities and encumbrances payable from the Elevator Safety Account. *(Added by Stats.1999, c. 585 (A.B.850), § 1. Amended by Stats.2007, c. 179 (S.B.86), § 34, eff. Aug. 24, 2007.)*

§ 7930. Violations; civil penalties

If the division determines that any owner or operator of a permanent amusement ride subject to this part has willfully or intentionally violated this part or any rule or regulation promulgated under this part, and that violation results in a death or serious injury as specified in Section 7925, the division shall impose on that owner or operator a civil penalty of not less than twenty-five thousand dollars ($25,000) and not more than seventy thousand dollars ($70,000). *(Added by Stats.1999, c. 585 (A.B.850), § 1.)*

§ 7931. Enforcement; citation and notice of civil penalty

The division shall enforce this part by the issuance of a citation and notice of civil penalty in a manner consistent with Section 6317. Any owner or operator who receives a citation and penalty may appeal the citation and penalty to the Occupational Safety and Health Appeals Board in a manner consistent with Section 6319. *(Added by Stats.1999, c. 585 (A.B.850), § 1.)*

§ 7932. Exemption for rides located in counties that have adopted certain provisions of the 1994 Uniform Building Code

(a) The provisions of this part relating to annual division inspections shall not apply to any permanent amusement ride located within a county or other political subdivision of the state that, as of April 1, 1998, has adopted the provisions of Chapter 66 (commencing with Section 6601.1) of the 1994 Uniform Building Code providing for the routine inspection of permanent amusement rides by the county or other political subdivision of the state, provided that the division determines that these inspections meet or exceed the inspection standards set forth in this part.

(b) If the county or other political subdivision suspends, revokes, or otherwise vacates its standards for permanent amusement rides, any permanent amusement ride located within the county or other political subdivision shall be subject to the inspection standards set forth in this part. *(Added by Stats.1999, c. 585 (A.B.850), § 1.)*

Part 9

TUNNEL AND MINE SAFETY

Chapter	Section
1. Tunnels and Mines	7950
2. Gassy and Extrahazardous Tunnels	7965
3. Licensing and Penalties	7990

CHAPTER 1. TUNNELS AND MINES

Section

7950. Short title.
7951. Definitions.
7952. Unit of safety engineers.
7953. Annual inspections.
7954. Industrial hygiene engineer; chemist; laboratory; contracts.
7955. Prejob safety conference; classification of tunnels and mines.
7956. Posting of classification, special orders, rules, and regulations at job site.
7957. Emergency rescue plan.
7958. Trained rescue crews.
7959. Rescue and search equipment; practice sessions.
7960. Potentially gassy tunnels or mines; gas or vapor tests prior to each shift.

Section

7961. Potentially gassy tunnels or mines; excessive gas reading; halt in operations; reclassification.
7962. Safety representative; duties.
7963. Communication systems.
7964. Access shaft; construction.
7964.5. State plan for mines under federal law; contract.

§ 7950. Short title

This part shall be known and may be cited as "The Tom Carrell Memorial Tunnel and Mine Safety Act of 1972." *(Added by Stats.1972, c. 1430, p. 3118, § 1.)*

§ 7951. Definitions

As used in this part:

(a) Tunnel shall include excavation, construction, alteration, repairing, renovating, or demolishing of any tunnel except tunnel work covered under the compressed air safety orders adopted by the Occupational Safety and Health Standards Board and manhole construction.

(b) "Tunnel" means an underground passageway, excavated by men and equipment working below the earth's surface, that provides a subterranean route along which men, equipment, or substances can move.

(c) "Mine" means any excavation or opening above or below ground used for removal of ore, minerals, gravel, sand, rock, or other materials intended for manufacturing or sale. It shall include quarries and open pit operations, other than a gravel pit or other pit where material is removed by a contractor or other person for his own use and not for sale to others. The term "mine" shall not include a mine that is operated exclusively by persons having a proprietary interest in such mine or by persons who are paid only a share of the profits from the mine, nor shall it include during any calendar year, any mine that produced less than five thousand dollars ($5,000) in ore, minerals, sand, rock, or other material during the preceding calendar year.

(d) "Access shaft" means a vertical shaft used as a regular means of worker access to underground mines and tunnels under construction, renovation, or demolition.

(e) "Lower explosive limit" means the lowest concentration at which a gas or vapor can be ignited or will explode.

(f) "Face" means the head of the tunnel where soil is being removed, or that area in a mine where digging is underway.

(g) "Muck" means excavated dirt, rock, or other material.

(h) "Permissible equipment" means equipment tested and approved by the U.S. Bureau of Mines or acceptable to other authorities recognized by the division, and acceptable by the division, which is safe for use in gassy or extrahazardous tunnels or underground mines.

(i) "Division" means the Division of Occupational Safety and Health.

(j) "Board" means the Occupational Safety and Health Standards Board.

(k) "Underground mine" means a mine that consists of a subterranean excavation. *(Added by Stats.1972, c. 1430, p. 3118, § 1. Amended by Stats.1980, c. 676, p. 1980, § 249.)*

§ 7952. Unit of safety engineers

There shall be within the division a separate unit of safety engineers trained to inspect all tunnel construction and mine operations. *(Added by Stats.1972, c. 1430, p. 3118, § 1.)*

§ 7953. Annual inspections

Sufficient manpower shall be maintained to provide for four annual inspections of underground mines, one inspection of surface mines or quarries annually, and six inspections of tunnels under construction annually. *(Added by Stats.1972, c. 1430, p. 3118, § 1.)*

§ 7954. Industrial hygiene engineer; chemist; laboratory; contracts

To assist the unit of safety engineers in determining the safety of tunnel construction and mine operation, the division shall make available at least one industrial hygiene engineer and one chemist. A laboratory for analysis of dust, gas, vapors, soil, or other materials shall be available to members of this unit. Contracts to provide for geological and other services may be signed by the division whenever it is necessary to assure safety for employees engaged in mining or tunnel work. *(Added by Stats.1972, c. 1430, p. 3118, § 1.)*

§ 7955. Prejob safety conference; classification of tunnels and mines

The division and the owner of a mine, if he is not the operator of the mine, shall be notified before any initial mining operation or construction may be started at any mines or tunnels. A prejob safety conference shall be held with an authorized representative of the division for all underground operations. Representatives of the tunnel or mine owner, the employer, and employees shall be included in the prejob safety conference.

The division shall classify all tunnels or underground mines operating on the effective date of this section, or which commence operation thereafter, as one of the classifications set forth in subdivisions (a) to (d), inclusive. Such classification shall be made prior to the request for bids on all public works projects, whenever possible. This shall not, however, prevent the division from reclassifying such mines or tunnels when conditions warrant it.

(a) Nongassy, which classification shall be applied to tunnels or underground mines where there is little likelihood of encountering gas during the construction of the tunnel or operation of an underground mine. Such tunnels shall be constructed or underground mines operated under regulations, rules, and orders developed by

the division and board and approved by the board. This subdivision shall not prohibit the division chief or his representatives from establishing any special orders that they feel are necessary for safety.

(b) Potentially gassy, which classification shall be applied to tunnels or underground mines where there exists a possibility gas will be encountered.

(c) Gassy, which classification shall be applied to tunnels or underground mines where it is likely gas will be encountered. Special safety measures, including those set forth in Sections 7965 to 7976, inclusive, those established by the division and board and adopted by the board, or special orders written by the chief or his representatives shall be observed in construction of gassy tunnels in addition to regular rules, orders, special orders, or regulations.

(d) Extrahazardous, which classification may, when the division finds that there is a serious danger to the safety of the employees, be applied to tunnels or underground mines where gas or vapors have caused an explosion or fire, where the likelihood of encountering petroleum vapors exists, or where tests show, with normal ventilation, a concentration of hydrocarbon petroleum vapors in excess of 20 percent of the lower explosive limit within three inches of the roof, face, floor, or walls of any open workings. Construction in extrahazardous tunnels or operation in extrahazardous underground mines shall conform to safety measures set forth in Sections 7977 to 7985, inclusive, any rules, regulations, orders, or special orders of the division, or any special rules, orders, or regulations adopted by the board.

The division shall not be required to reclassify any tunnel or underground mine that is shut down seasonally, when such tunnel or underground mine is put back into operation in not less than six months after date of the shutdown. *(Added by Stats.1972, c. 1430, p. 3118, § 1.)*

§ 7956. Posting of classification, special orders, rules, and regulations at job site

All personnel, including both employees working above ground and those in the tunnel or underground mine, shall be informed of the classification designated by the division for that job. A notice of the classification and any special orders, rules, or regulations to be used in construction, remodeling, demolition, or operation of the tunnel or underground mine shall be prominently posted at the site. *(Added by Stats.1972, c. 1430, p. 3118, § 1.)*

§ 7957. Emergency rescue plan

An emergency rescue plan shall be developed by the employer for every tunnel or underground mine. Such plan, including a current map of the tunnel or underground mine, shall be provided to local fire and rescue units, to the division, and to every employee at the place of employment. *(Added by Stats.1972, c. 1430, p. 3118, § 1.)*

§ 7958. Trained rescue crews

A trained rescue crew of at least five men shall be provided at underground mines with more than 25 men or tunnels with 10 or more men underground at any one time. Smaller mines shall have one man for each 10 men underground who receives annual training in the use of breathing apparatus. Two trained crews shall be provided at mines with more than 50 men underground and at tunnels with more than 25 men underground. *(Added by Stats.1972, c. 1430, p. 3118, § 1.)*

§ 7959. Rescue and search equipment; practice sessions

Rescue crews shall be familiar with all emergency equipment necessary to effect a rescue or search for missing employees in case of an accident or explosion. Such rescue crews shall hold practices with equipment and using emergency rescue plan procedures at least once monthly during construction or operation of the tunnel or underground mines. At least one rescue crew shall be maintained above ground at all times and within 30 minutes travel of the tunnel or underground mine site classified as gassy or extrahazardous. *(Added by Stats. 1972, c. 1430, p. 3118, § 1.)*

§ 7960. Potentially gassy tunnels or mines; gas or vapor tests prior to each shift

In any tunnel or underground mine classified as potentially gassy, tests for gas or vapors shall be made prior to start of work at each shift. If any concentration of gas at or above 10 percent of the lower explosive limit is recorded, the division shall be notified immediately. *(Added by Stats.1972, c. 1430, p. 3118, § 1.)*

§ 7961. Potentially gassy tunnels or mines; excessive gas reading; halt in operations; reclassification

The division shall investigate immediately any notification of a gas reading 10 percent of the lower explosive limit or higher by an employer in a tunnel or underground mine classified as potentially gassy. If the inspection determines the likelihood of encountering more gas or vapor, the division may halt operations until the tunnel or mine can be reclassified. *(Added by Stats.1972, c. 1430, p. 3118, § 1.)*

§ 7962. Safety representative; duties

A safety representative qualified to recognize hazardous conditions and certified by the division shall be designated by the employer in any tunnel or underground mine. He shall have the authority to correct unsafe conditions and unsafe practices, and shall be responsible for directing the required safety programs. *(Added by Stats.1972, c. 1430, p. 3118, § 1.)*

§ 7963. Communication systems

All underground mines and tunnels with more than five men underground at one time shall have telephone or other communication systems to the surface in operation at any time there are persons underground. Such systems shall be installed in such a manner that destruction or removal of one phone or communication device does not make other phones or communication devices inoperative. *(Added by Stats.1972, c. 1430, p. 3118, § 1.)*

§ 7964. Access shaft; construction

Whenever an access shaft is used as the normal means of entrance or exit to an underground mine or tunnel, it shall be constructed of fireproof material or fireproofed by chemical or other means. *(Added by Stats.1972, c. 1430, p. 3118, § 1.)*

§ 7964.5. State plan for mines under federal law; contract

Nothing contained in this part shall restrict the division in contracting with the Secretary of the Interior for an approved state plan for mines under P.L. 89–577 (30 U.S.C. 721 et seq.)[1]. *(Added by Stats.1972, c. 1430, p. 3118, § 1.)*

[1] Repealed; see 30 U.S.C.A. § 801 et seq.

CHAPTER 2. GASSY AND EXTRAHAZARDOUS TUNNELS

Section
7965. Gassy tunnels; operation under special procedures.
7966. Gassy tunnels; time and location of gas and vapor tests.
7967. Gassy tunnels; excess gas levels; notice to division.
7968. Gassy tunnels; shutdown for testing; notice; overruling order.
7969. Gassy tunnels; review of plans for electrical lighting and power.
7970. Gassy tunnels; smoking prohibited; collection of lighters and matches.
7971. Ignition of gas or vapor; cessation of work; removal of employees; authorized reentry.
7972. Excess gas level; removal of men; reentry upon division approval.
7973. Gassy tunnels; special orders, notice of and posting; safety meeting.
7974. Gassy tunnels; ventilation; continuous exhausting of fumes; alternative plan.
7975. Gassy tunnels; cutoff of electrical equipment power.
7976. Gassy tunnels; fire extinguishers; number and location.
7977. Extrahazardous tunnels; compliance with gassy tunnel provisions and other rules, regulations, etc.
7978. Extrahazardous tunnels; smoking and open flames prohibited; welding and cutting operations.
7979. Extrahazardous tunnels; air supply; atmospheric conditions.
7980. Extrahazardous tunnels; permissible electrical equipment and machines; use of nonpermissive equipment.
7981. Escape chamber or alternate escape route; rescue equipment.
7982. Extrahazardous tunnels; records of air flow and sample tests.
7983. Extrahazardous tunnels; main ventilation fan line; cutoff switch.
7984. Extrahazardous tunnels; automatic and continuous atmospheric testing devices.
7985. Approved testing devices; operational requirements.

§ 7965. Gassy tunnels; operation under special procedures

Any tunnel or underground mine classified by the division as gassy shall operate under special procedures adopted by the board, as well as rules, regulations, special orders, or general orders for nongassy underground mines and tunnels. *(Added by Stats.1972, c. 1430, p. 3118, § 1.)*

§ 7966. Gassy tunnels; time and location of gas and vapor tests

In any tunnel classified as gassy by the division, there shall be tests for gas or vapors taken prior to each shift and at least hourly during actual operation. If a mechanical excavator is used, gas tests shall be made prior to removal of muck or material and before any cutting or drilling in tunnels or underground mines where explosives are used. A log shall be maintained for inspection by the division showing results of each test. Whenever a tunnel excavation or underground mine operation approaches a geologic formation in which there is a likelihood of encountering gas or water, a probe hole at least 20 feet ahead of the tunnel face or area where material is being mined shall be maintained. *(Added by Stats.1972, c. 1430, p. 3118, § 1.)*

§ 7967. Gassy tunnels; excess gas levels; notice to division

Whenever gas levels in excess of 10 percent of the lower explosive limit are encountered initially in a tunnel or underground mine classified as gassy, the division shall be notified immediately by telephone or telegraph. The chief of the division or his authorized representative may waive subsequent notification for gas readings less than 20 percent of the lower explosive limits upon a finding that adequate ventilation and other safety measures are provided to assure employee safety. *(Added by Stats. 1972, c. 1430, p. 3118, § 1.)*

§ 7968. Gassy tunnels; shutdown for testing; notice; overruling order

In any gassy tunnel or underground mine, the division may order work halted until adequate testing can be completed to determine the level of hazard from gases or vapors. A notice of such shutdown shall be filed by the division inspector with his superiors as soon as practicable. Any overruling of such order must be made by the chief or his designated representative and must be in writing. An onsite inspection must be made by the person overruling an inspector's order prior to resumption of work. *(Added by Stats.1972, c. 1430, p. 3118, § 1.)*

§ 7969. Gassy tunnels; review of plans for electrical lighting and power

In any gassy tunnel or underground mine the division shall review plans for electrical lighting and power for equipment. When it is necessary for safety, the inspector may require changes in the amount and type of lighting, and may require permissive-type wiring, switches, tools,

and equipment. *(Added by Stats.1972, c. 1430, p. 3118, § 1.)*

§ 7970. Gassy tunnels; smoking prohibited; collection of lighters and matches

In any tunnel or underground mine classified gassy, smoking shall be prohibited and the employer shall be responsible for collecting all personal sources of ignition such as lighters and matches from employees entering the tunnel. *(Added by Stats.1972, c. 1430, p. 3118, § 1.)*

§ 7971. Ignition of gas or vapor; cessation of work; removal of employees; authorized reentry

Whenever there is any ignition of gas or vapor in a tunnel or underground mine, all work shall cease, employees shall be removed, and reentry except for rescue purposes shall be prohibited until the division has conducted an inspection and authorized reentry for maintenance or production in writing. *(Added by Stats.1972, c. 1430, p. 3118, § 1.)*

§ 7972. Excess gas level; removal of men; reentry upon division approval

If the level of gas in any tunnel or underground mine reaches 20 percent of its lower explosive limit at any time all men shall be removed, the division notified immediately by telephone or telegram, and no one shall reenter the tunnel or underground mine until approval is given by the division. *(Added by Stats.1972, c. 1430, p. 3118, § 1.)*

§ 7973. Gassy tunnels; special orders, notice of and posting; safety meeting

In any tunnel or underground mine classified as gassy, all employees shall be informed of any special orders made by the division following an inspection. Such notice shall be given before entering the tunnel or underground mine. A copy of any orders subsequently written by the division shall be posted and all employees shall be notified at a safety meeting called by the safety representative before they are permitted to start work. *(Added by Stats.1972, c. 1430, p. 3118, § 1.)*

§ 7974. Gassy tunnels; ventilation; continuous exhausting of fumes; alternative plan

In any tunnel classified as gassy by the division, ventilation shall include continuous exhausting of fumes and air, unless an alternative ventilation plan which is as effective or better is approved by the division. Fans for this purpose shall be located at the surface, and shall be reversible from a single switch at the portal or shaft. These requirements shall not preclude the use of auxiliary fans to supply more air or greater exhaust to a tunnel or underground mine. *(Added by Stats.1972, c. 1430, p. 3118, § 1.)*

§ 7975. Gassy tunnels; cutoff of electrical equipment power

A "kill" button capable of cutting off all electrical equipment shall be maintained in any gassy tunnel or underground mine. The safety representative or his designated representative shall cut off power at any time gas or vapor levels reach 20 percent of the lower explosive limit or more. Before work is restarted every employee underground shall be informed of the level of gas or vapor recorded, and a permanent record shall be called to the surface and retained in a special log. *(Added by Stats.1972, c. 1430, p. 3118, § 1.)*

§ 7976. Gassy tunnels; fire extinguishers; number and location

In any tunnel or underground mine classified as gassy, the division shall determine the number of fire extinguishers necessary and their locations. *(Added by Stats. 1972, c. 1430, p. 3118, § 1.)*

§ 7977. Extrahazardous tunnels; compliance with gassy tunnel provisions and other rules, regulations, etc.

Any tunnel or underground mine classified as extrahazardous by the division shall comply with the provisions for gassy tunnels in this chapter, as well as regulations, rules, special orders, and general orders of the division or board. *(Added by Stats.1972, c. 1430, p. 3118, § 1.)*

§ 7978. Extrahazardous tunnels; smoking and open flames prohibited; welding and cutting operations

In any extrahazardous tunnel or underground mine smoking by employees or open flame shall be prohibited. Welding or cutting with arc or flame underground in other than fresh air shall be done under the direct supervision of qualified persons who shall test for gas and vapors before welding or cutting starts and continuously during such an operation. No cutting or welding shall be permitted in atmospheres where any concentration of gas or vapor reaches 20 percent of the lower explosive limit or more while a probe hole is being drilled or when the tunnel face or material from a mine is being excavated. *(Added by Stats.1972, c. 1430, p. 3118, § 1.)*

§ 7979. Extrahazardous tunnels; air supply; atmospheric conditions

In tunnels or underground mines classified extrahazardous, sufficient air shall be supplied to maintain an atmosphere of all of the following conditions:

(a) Not less than 19 percent oxygen.

(b) Not more than 0.5 percent carbon dioxide.

(c) Not more than 5 parts per million nitrogen dioxide.

(d) No petroleum vapors or other toxic gases in concentrations exceeding the threshold limit values established annually by the American Conference of Governmental Industrial Hygienists. *(Added by Stats.1972, c. 1430, p. 3118, § 1.)*

§ 7980. Extrahazardous tunnels; permissible electrical equipment and machines; use of nonpermissive equipment

All electrical equipment and machines, including diesel engines, used in tunnels or underground mines classified extrahazardous shall be permissible equipment. The division may, however, permit the use of nonpermissive equipment in a tunnel or underground mine in areas where it finds there is no longer danger from gas or other hazards. *(Added by Stats.1972, c. 1430, p. 3118, § 1.)*

§ 7981. Escape chamber or alternate escape route; rescue equipment

An escape chamber or alternate escape route shall be maintained within 5,000 feet of the tunnel face or areas being used to excavate material in an underground mine classified as gassy or extrahazardous. Workers shall be provided with emergency rescue equipment and trained in its use. *(Added by Stats.1972, c. 1430, p. 3118, § 1.)*

§ 7982. Extrahazardous tunnels; records of air flow and sample tests

Records of air flow and air sample tests to assure compliance with required standards shall be maintained by the employer at the site of any tunnel or underground mine classified extrahazardous. Such records shall be made available to any division representative upon request. *(Added by Stats.1972, c. 1430, p. 3118, § 1.)*

§ 7983. Extrahazardous tunnels; main ventilation fan line; cutoff switch

The main fan line used for ventilation in any tunnel or underground mine classified extrahazardous shall contain a cutoff switch capable of halting all machinery underground automatically should the fan fail or its performance fall below minimum power needed to maintain a safe atmosphere. *(Added by Stats.1972, c. 1430, p. 3118, § 1.)*

§ 7984. Extrahazardous tunnels; automatic and continuous atmospheric testing devices

In any tunnel or underground mine classified extrahazardous a device or devices which automatically and continuously test the atmosphere for gases or vapors shall be maintained. Such device or devices shall be placed as near the face or area of operation as practical, but never more than 50 feet from such point. The division shall determine if additional monitors are necessary and where they should be located. This requirement shall apply only to tunnels or underground mines where excavation of material is by mechanical means. *(Added by Stats. 1972, c. 1430, p. 3118, § 1.)*

§ 7985. Approved testing devices; operational requirements

All such testing device or devices shall be U.S. Bureau of Mines approved or acceptable to other authorities recognized by the division and shall automatically sound an alarm and activate flashing red signals visible to employees underground whenever the concentration of gases or vapors reaches or exceeds permissible levels. Permissible levels may be established lower than the limits set in division rules, regulations, or general orders whenever a division inspector considers such action necessary to make the operation safe for employees. *(Added by Stats.1972, c. 1430, p. 3118, § 1.)*

CHAPTER 3. LICENSING AND PENALTIES

Section
7990. Use of explosives; licensed persons.
7991. Examination for license; fees.
7992. Qualifications for explosive blaster's license.
7993. Violation of safety orders; use or handling of explosives; suspension of license.
7994. Violation of safety orders; injury or death resulting from use or handling of explosives; revocation of license.
7995. Violation of safety orders subsequent to revocation; permanent revocation.
7996. Approval of safety equipment.
7997. General orders; review and updating.
7998. Development of tests to qualify gas testers and safety representatives.
7999. Necessity of certificate; passage of examination required for issuance or renewal.
8000. State preemption in certification and licensing of gas testers and safety representatives.
8001. Fees.
8002. Application fees not refundable.
8003. Violations punishable by suspension or revocations; death or injury punishable as misdemeanor.
8004. Exemption of certain public utility tunnels; exception.

§ 7990. Use of explosives; licensed persons

In any tunnel or mine under jurisdiction of the division, the use of explosives shall be limited to persons licensed by the division. *(Added by Stats.1972, c. 1430, p. 3118, § 1.)*

§ 7991. Examination for license; fees

To obtain a license under Section 7990, and to renew such a license, a person shall pass an oral and written examination given by the division. The division shall offer such examination in Spanish, or any other language, when requested by the applicant. The division shall administer such examination orally when requested by an applicant who cannot write. Application for such license shall cost fifteen dollars ($15), which is nonreturnable. Licenses shall be renewable every five years at a fee of fifteen dollars ($15). *(Added by Stats.1972, c. 1430, p. 3118, § 1. Amended by Stats.1974, c. 1284, p. 2787, § 31.)*

§ 7992. Qualifications for explosive blaster's license

The board shall determine qualifications for persons seeking an "explosive blaster's license" and rules and regulations for use of explosives in tunnels or mines. *(Added by Stats.1972, c. 1430, p. 3118, § 1.)*

§ 7993. Violation of safety orders; use or handling of explosives; suspension of license

Any person holding an "explosive blaster's license" who is convicted of violating any safety order involving the use or handling of explosives shall have his license suspended for not less than 30 days upon hearing by the division, in addition to any other penalties he may be assessed. *(Added by Stats.1972, c. 1430, p. 3118, § 1.)*

§ 7994. Violation of safety orders; injury or death resulting from use or handling of explosives; revocation of license

Any person holding an "explosive blaster's license" who is convicted of violating safety orders involving use or handling of explosives in which the violation is judged to be responsible for an accident involving serious injury or death shall have his or her license revoked for at least one year, in addition to any other penalties he or she may be assessed. Any person who has had his or her "explosive blaster's license" revoked may apply for a new license after the minimum period of revocation expires. He or she shall be required to pass all examinations before a new license is granted. *(Added by Stats.1972, c. 1430, p. 3118, § 1. Amended by Stats.2006, c. 538 (S.B.1852), § 495.)*

§ 7995. Violation of safety orders subsequent to revocation; permanent revocation

Any person who has had his "explosive blaster's license" revoked who is subsequently convicted of violations of a safety order involving the use or handling of explosives shall have his license permanently revoked in addition to other penalties he may be assessed. *(Added by Stats.1972, c. 1430, p. 3118, § 1.)*

§ 7996. Approval of safety equipment

All safety equipment required to provide safe employment in tunnels or underground mines shall be U.S. Bureau of Mines approved, or acceptable to other authorities recognized by the division, and acceptable by the division. *(Added by Stats.1972, c. 1430, p. 3118, § 1.)*

§ 7997. General orders; review and updating

The board shall review and update general orders for tunnels and mines at least every two years. Representatives of the unit inspecting tunnels and mines shall be consulted during each review and shall be permitted to submit suggested changes to the general orders at any time. *(Added by Stats.1972, c. 1430, p. 3118, § 1.)*

§ 7998. Development of tests to qualify gas testers and safety representatives

The division shall also develop tests, available in English, Spanish, or other languages where a sufficient portion of employees exists to show need, to qualify gas testers and safety representatives in tunnels and mines. *(Added by Stats.1972, c. 1430, p. 3118, § 1. Amended by Stats.1974, c. 1284, p. 2787, § 32.)*

§ 7999. Necessity of certificate; passage of examination required for issuance or renewal

No person shall be qualified to operate as a gas tester, or serve as a safety representative in a tunnel or underground mine unless he holds a certificate issued by the division. No certificate may be issued or renewed unless the applicant or licensee, as the case may be, has passed an examination given by the division. *(Added by Stats.1972, c. 1430, p. 3118, § 1. Amended by Stats.1974, c. 1284, p. 2787, § 33.)*

§ 8000. State preemption in certification and licensing of gas testers and safety representatives

Requirements established by the board shall preempt local government rules, regulations, and laws requiring certification or licensing as gas testers or safety representatives. However, local governments may contract with the division for testing applicants and issuing certifications. *(Added by Stats.1972, c. 1430, p. 3118, § 1.)*

§ 8001. Fees

A fee sufficient to cover costs of examination and certification of gas testers and safety representatives for tunnels and mines, but not more than fifteen dollars ($15) for original applications and fifteen dollars ($15) for renewals, may be charged by the division. Renewals shall be made every five years. *(Added by Stats.1972, c. 1430, p. 3118, § 1. Amended by Stats.1974, c. 1284, p. 2787, § 34.)*

§ 8002. Application fees not refundable

All fees from such applications shall be nonrefundable. Such fees shall be paid into the State Treasury by the division to the credit of the General Fund. *(Added by Stats.1972, c. 1430, p. 3118, § 1.)*

§ 8003. Violations punishable by suspension or revocations; death or injury punishable as misdemeanor

Violation of regulations, rules, orders, or special orders adopted by the board or division as a condition of certification shall be punishable by suspension or revocation of certification, unless such violation is responsible for death or injury to employees, in which case it shall be punishable as a misdemeanor. *(Added by Stats.1972, c. 1430, p. 3118, § 1.)*

§ 8004. Exemption of certain public utility tunnels; exception

The provisions of this part shall not apply to the normal operation, maintenance, or repair of any completed tunnels owned or operated by a utility as defined in Section 229 of the Public Utilities Code. However, it shall apply to the initial construction or substantial modification of such a tunnel. *(Added by Stats.1972, c. 1430, p. 3118, § 1.)*

794

Part 10

USE OF CARCINOGENS

Chapter	Section
1. General Provisions and Definitions	9000
2. Exemptions	9015
3. Standards and Administration	9020
4. Reporting	9030
5. Medical Examinations	9040
6. Inspections	9050
7. Penalties	9060

CHAPTER 1. GENERAL PROVISIONS AND DEFINITIONS

Section
9000. Short title.
9001. Purpose of part.
9002. Definitions governing construction.
9003. Affected employee defined.
9004. Carcinogen defined.
9005. Division defined.
9006. Employer defined.
9007. Standards defined.
9008. Standards board defined.
9009. Use defined.

§ 9000. Short title.

This part shall be known and may be cited as the Occupational Carcinogens Control Act of 1976. *(Added by Stats.1985, c. 947, § 2.)*

§ 9001. Purpose of part

The purpose of this part is to clarify and strengthen the provisions of state law applicable to the use of carcinogens in California. It is the intent of the Legislature to provide for effective implementation of the provisions of this part. *(Added by Stats.1985, c. 947, § 2.)*

§ 9002. Definitions governing construction

The following definitions shall govern the construction of this part. Additionally, except where the context otherwise requires, the definitions contained in Part 1 (commencing with Section 6300) shall also be applicable to this part. *(Added by Stats.1985, c. 947, § 2.)*

§ 9003. Affected employee defined

"Affected employee" means an employee who, as part of his or her employment, is involved in the use of a carcinogen, or an employee with respect to whom there is a substantial probability that he or she will become so involved as the result of his or her employer's use of a carcinogen. *(Added by Stats.1985, c. 947, § 2.)*

§ 9004. Carcinogen defined

"Carcinogen" means and includes the following recognized cancer-causing substances for which standards have been adopted pursuant to Chapter 3 (commencing with Section 9020):

(a) Any of the following substances and any compound, mixture, or product containing these substances:

(1) 2-acetylaminofluorene.

(2) 4-aminodiphenyl.

(3) Benzidine and its salts.

(4) Bis(chloromethyl) ether.

(5) 3,3'-dichlorobenzidine and its salts.

(6) 4-dimethylaminoazobenzene.

(7) Beta-naphthylamine.

(8) 4-nitrodiphenyl.

(9) N-nitrosodimethylamine.

(10) Beta-propriolactone.

(11) Methyl chloromethyl ether.

(12) Alpha-naphthylamine.

(13) 4,4'-methylene-(bis)2-chloroaniline.

(14) Ethyleneimine.

(b) Asbestos, including chrysotile, amosite, crocidolite, tremolite, anthophyllite, and actinolite.

(c) Vinyl chloride.

(d) Any other substance for which standards are adopted and in effect due to cancer-causing properties and any compound, mixture, or product containing such a substance, except as specifically exempted from the standards. *(Added by Stats.1985, c. 947, § 2.)*

§ 9005. Division defined

"Division" means the Division of Occupational Safety and Health. *(Added by Stats.1985, c. 947, § 2.)*

§ 9006. Employer defined

"Employer" means any of the following:

(a) The state and every state agency.

(b) Each county, city, district, and all public and quasi-public corporations and public agencies therein.

(c) Every person, including any public service corporation, which has any natural person in service.

(d) The legal representative of any deceased employer. *(Added by Stats.1985, c. 947, § 2.)*

§ 9007. Standards defined

"Standards" means standards and orders adopted by the standards board pursuant to Chapter 6 (commencing with Section 140) of Division 1. *(Added by Stats.1985, c. 947, § 2.)*

§ 9008. Standards board defined

"Standards board" means the Occupational Safety and Health Standards Board. *(Added by Stats.1985, c. 947, § 2.)*

§ 9009. Use defined

"Use" means any use of a carcinogen by an employer, including, but not limited to, the following:

(a) Manufacture of a carcinogen, industrial uses thereof, or formation of a carcinogen as a result of a chemical reaction.

(b) Sale or other transfer of a carcinogen.

(c) Storage or disposal of a carcinogen.

(d) Utilization of a carcinogen for research.

(e) Transport of a carcinogen. The State Department of Health Services, the Department of Toxic Substances Control, and the division shall have concurrent jurisdiction with any federal agency to protect affected employees of interstate carriers, including rail carriers, while in this state, as provided in this part or as authorized by other provisions of state law. *(Added by Stats.1985, c. 947, § 2. Amended by Gov.Reorg.Plan No. 1 of 1991, § 151, eff. July 17, 1991.)*

CHAPTER 2. EXEMPTIONS

Section
9015. Carcinogens presenting no substantial health threat; standards for implementation of section.

§ 9015. Carcinogens presenting no substantial health threat; standards for implementation of section

Except where in conflict with Section 142.3, or other applicable provisions of law, the standards board may exempt from the provisions of this part and its standards uses of carcinogens which it determines have been shown by a preponderance of the evidence to present no substantial threat to employee health and which may include, but need not be limited to, any of the following:

(a) Use of carcinogens specified in subdivision (a) of Section 9004 in operations involving the destructive distillation of carbonaceous materials, such as occurs in coke ovens.

(b) Use of asbestos, except where there is a material risk of substantial and repeated exposure of employees to this carcinogen.

Except as provided in Section 18930 of the Health and Safety Code, the standards board shall adopt regulations for the implementation of the provisions of this section. *(Added by Stats.1985, c. 947, § 2.)*

CHAPTER 3. STANDARDS AND ADMINISTRATION

Section
9020. Standards as restrictive as federal standards; legislative intent.
9021. Existing standards.
9021.5. Regulations; asbestos-related work; certification examinations; effect of section.
9021.6. Fees; applicants for certification; asbestos consultants and site surveillance technicians.
9021.7. Asbestos training and consultant certification fund; asbestos training approval and consultant certification accounts.
9021.8. Certification renewal; refresher courses.

Section

9021.9. Development of training programs; approval of
          training entities; fees.
9022.   Enforcement of standards; responsibility.

§ 9020. Standards as restrictive as federal standards; legislative intent

(a) Pursuant to Chapter 6 (commencing with Section 140) of Division 1, the standards board shall adopt standards for carcinogens at least as restrictive as the federal requirements for use of carcinogens promulgated under Section 6 of the Occupational Safety and Health Act of 1970 (P.L. 91–596), as these federal requirements may be revised from time to time. Within six months after the effective date of any change in the federal requirements, the standards board shall amend its standards as necessary to comply with this subdivision.

(b) It is the intent of the Legislature that the state shall exercise strong leadership in preventing employees, employers, and other persons from being exposed to carcinogens. In this connection, it is the further intent of the Legislature that the standards board adopt standards for substances as to which there exists a preponderance of evidence of carcinogenicity, but for which the federal government has not yet promulgated requirements specified in subdivision (a). The division shall determine the necessity for the standards and shall develop and present the proposed standards to the standards board pursuant to Section 147.1. *(Added by Stats.1985, c. 947, § 2.)*

§ 9021. Existing standards

All standards relating to the use of carcinogens which are in effect on January 1, 1986, including standards set forth in Sections 5208, 5209, and 5210 of Title 8 of the California Administrative Code, shall remain in effect until amended or repealed by the standards board. *(Added by Stats.1985, c. 947, § 2.)*

§ 9021.5. Regulations; asbestos-related work; certification examinations; effect of section

(a) Not later than January 1, 1987, the Division of Occupational Safety and Health shall propose a regulation concerning asbestos-related work, as defined in Section 6501.8, to the Occupational Safety and Health Standards Board for review and adoption so as to protect most effectively the health and safety of employees. The regulation shall also include, but not be limited to, specific work practices and specific requirements for certification of all employees engaged in asbestos-related work.

(b)(1) Not later than July 1, 1991, the Division of Occupational Safety and Health shall propose regulations for the certification of asbestos consultants and site surveillance technicians to the Occupational Safety and Health Standards Board for consideration and action. By January 1, 1992, the board shall adopt regulations regarding certification. The regulations shall address and encompass procedures to determine the requirements for the certification provided for by Article 11

796

(commencing with Section 7180) of Chapter 9 of Division 3 of the Business and Professions Code. The division shall prepare and administer an examination to determine qualifications for certification pursuant to subdivision (b) of Section 7184 and subdivision (c) of Section 7185 of the Business and Professions Code. The examination shall be administered on a periodic, regularly scheduled basis.

(2) The division may, in lieu of preparing and administering its own certification examination, approve one or more public or private institutions which offer programs in asbestos abatement training to prepare and administer the examination described in subdivision (b) of Section 7184 and subdivision (c) of Section 7185 of the Business and Professions Code. However, the division shall not approve any institution, organization, individual, or other entity for administering a certification examination if that institution, organization, individual or other entity engages, for compensation, in any aspect of asbestos abatement work. For purposes of developing or approving a certification examination pursuant to this section, the division shall consult with an advisory committee of individuals who have academic and professional experience in asbestos abatement work, including a certified industrial hygienist, representatives of asbestos abatement workers, and asbestos abatement contractors.

(c) This section does not exempt any employer from complying with the Hazardous Substances Information and Training Act (Chapter 2.5 (commencing with Section 6360) of Part 1 of Division 5 of this code) and regulations adopted thereunder, nor does it exempt any employer from complying with Section 5208 of Title 8 of the California Administrative Code. For products not requiring contractor certification pursuant to subdivision (a) of Section 7058.5 of the Business and Professions Code, training and certification of employees shall be done by the employer. *(Added by Stats.1986, c. 1451, § 14, eff. Sept. 30, 1986. Amended by Stats.1990, c. 1255 (S.B.732), § 2.)*

§ 9021.6. Fees; applicants for certification; asbestos consultants and site surveillance technicians

The division may charge a fee to each asbestos consultant and site surveillance technician who applies for certification pursuant to subdivision (b) of Section 9021.5 and Article 11 (commencing with Section 7180) of Chapter 9 of Division 3 of the Business and Professions Code. The fee shall be sufficient to cover the division's cost for administering the certification process, including preparation and administration of the examination. The fees collected shall be deposited in the Asbestos Consultant Certification Account. Establishment of any fee pursuant to this section shall be accomplished through the regulatory process required by subdivision (b) of Section 9021.5. *(Added by Stats.1990, c. 1255 (S.B.732), § 3. Amended by Stats.1993, c. 1075 (S.B.877), § 2.)*

§ 9021.7. Asbestos training and consultant certification fund; asbestos training approval and consultant certification accounts

(a) There is hereby created the Asbestos Training and Consultant Certification Fund, which shall consist of the Asbestos Training Approval Account and the Asbestos Consultant Certification Account. Moneys in the Asbestos Training Approval Account shall consist of the fees collected pursuant to Section 9021.9. Moneys in the Asbestos Consultant Certification Account shall consist of the fees collected pursuant to Section 9021.6.

(b) Moneys in the Asbestos Training Approval Account shall be available, upon appropriation by the Legislature, for expenditure only for administering the training entity approval process provided for in Section 9021.9. Moneys in the Asbestos Consultant Certification Account shall be available, upon appropriation by the Legislature, only for administering the certification process provided for in Section 9021.6. *(Added by Stats. 1993, c. 1075 (S.B.877), § 3.)*

§ 9021.8. Certification renewal; refresher courses

All asbestos consultant and site surveillance technician certifications shall be renewed annually. The division shall require asbestos consultants and site surveillance technicians to complete the annual refresher courses as required under the Asbestos Hazard Emergency Response Act (Subchapter II (commencing with Section 2641) of Chapter 53 of Title 15 of the United States Code) or the equivalent, as determined by the division. *(Added by Stats.1990, c. 1255 (S.B.732), § 5.)*

§ 9021.9. Development of training programs; approval of training entities; fees

(a) The division shall establish an advisory committee to develop and recommend by September 30, 1994, for action by the standards board in accordance with Section 142.3, specific requirements for hands-on, task-specific training programs for all craft employees who may be exposed to asbestos-containing construction materials and all employees and supervisors involved in operations pertaining to asbestos cement pipe, as specified in subdivision (c) of Section 6501.8. The training programs shall include, but not be limited to, the following information:

(1) The physical characteristics and health hazards of asbestos.

(2) The types of asbestos cement pipe or asbestos-containing construction materials an employee may encounter in his or her specific work assignments.

(3) Safe practices and procedures for minimizing asbestos exposures from operations involving asbestos cement pipe or asbestos-containing construction materials.

(4) A review of general industry and construction safety orders relating to asbestos exposure.

(5) Hands-on instruction using pipe or other construction materials and the tools and equipment employees will use in the workplace.

(b) The division shall approve training entities to conduct task-specific training programs that include the requirements prescribed by the standards board pursuant to this section for employees and supervisors involved in operations pertaining to asbestos cement pipe or asbestos-containing construction materials.

(c) The division shall charge a fee to each asbestos training entity approved by the division pursuant to subdivision (b). The fee shall be sufficient to cover the division's cost for administering the approval process provided for in subdivision (b). The fees collected shall be deposited in the Asbestos Training Approval Account. Establishment of any fee pursuant to this section shall be accomplished through the regulatory process required by subdivision (b) of Section 9021.5. *(Added by Stats.1993, c. 1075 (S.B.877), § 4. Amended by Stats.1994, c. 146 (A.B.3601), § 160.)*

§ 9022. Enforcement of standards; responsibility

The division shall have primary responsibility for enforcement of standards relating to carcinogens. However, the State Department of Health Services shall assist the division in the enforcement of the standards, in the manner prescribed by this chapter, and as shall be further defined by a written agreement between the State Department of Health Services and the department, pursuant to Section 144. *(Added by Stats.1985, c. 947, § 2.)*

CHAPTER 4. REPORTING

Section
9030. Employer report of released carcinogens.
9031. Distribution and posting of report.
9032. Education; cooperation.

§ 9030. Employer report of released carcinogens

The standards board shall adopt one or more standards requiring each employer which uses any carcinogen, including asbestos and vinyl chloride, to submit a written report regarding the use or any incident which results in the release of a potentially hazardous amount of a carcinogen into any area where employees may be exposed. The reporting requirements set forth in Sections 5209 and 5210 of Title 8 of the California Administrative Code on January 1, 1986, shall remain in effect until amended or repealed by the standards board, and any subsequent reporting requirements shall provide for reports which are at least as detailed as those required on that date. For asbestos and vinyl chloride, the standards board shall adopt a standard which requires each employer who uses vinyl chloride or asbestos to report in a manner similar to the reporting required pursuant to Section 5209 of Title 8 of the California Administrative Code. *(Added by Stats.1985, c. 947, § 2.)*

§ 9031. Distribution and posting of report

The division shall transmit a copy of each report specified in Section 9030 to any bargaining representatives, and other representatives known to the division, of affected employees of the reporting employer. A copy of each report shall be posted by the employer in the location or locations where the carcinogen is used, which shall be conspicuous to affected employees, as shall be provided in the standards. *(Added by Stats.1985, c. 947, § 2.)*

§ 9032. Education; cooperation

The division shall make every effort to ascertain the identities of existing users of carcinogens and to notify, inform, and educate them about the requirements of this part. The division shall utilize all appropriate means of communication and education, including direct mailings to employers, the use of courses, workshops, and seminars, advertising in mass media, trade and employee publications, and professional and scientific journals, contact with trade associations, employee representatives, and professional and scientific societies, and cooperation with other governmental agencies to inform affected employees, employers, and the public of the requirements of this part. *(Added by Stats.1985, c. 947, § 2.)*

CHAPTER 5. MEDICAL EXAMINATIONS

Section
9040. Requirement; standards.

§ 9040. Requirement; standards

Every employer using carcinogens shall provide for medical examinations of affected employees where required by standards adopted pursuant to subdivision (b) of Section 142.3. The standards board shall continue to require medical examinations in at least as effective a manner as provided in Sections 5208, 5209, and 5210 of Title 8 of the California Administrative Code on January 1, 1986. *(Added by Stats.1985, c. 947, § 2.)*

CHAPTER 6. INSPECTIONS

Section
9050. Priorities.
9051. Carcinogen use in violation of standards; notice.
9052. Consultation services; educational programs.

§ 9050. Priorities

The division shall establish priorities for the performance of inspections of premises for which uses have been reported pursuant to Section 9030 and shall perform as many of these inspections as possible within the limits of the resources available to it for that purpose. *(Added by Stats.1985, c. 947, § 2.)*

§ 9051. Carcinogen use in violation of standards; notice

If an authorized representative of the division determines on the basis of an inspection that an employer is using a carcinogen in violation of the standards pertaining to its use, he or she shall immediately notify the employer and affected employees. *(Added by Stats.1985, c. 947, § 2.)*

§ 9052. Consultation services; educational programs

Upon request of any employer or any employee, or upon its own initiative, the OSHA Consultation Unit of the department shall provide consultation services regarding the use of a carcinogen and may offer educational programs to inform employers and employees of the provisions of this part. *(Added by Stats.1985, c. 947, § 2.)*

CHAPTER 7. PENALTIES

Section
9060. Civil penalties.
9061. Serious violation defined.

§ 9060. Civil penalties

The civil penalties prescribed by Chapter 4 (commencing with Section 6423) of Part 1 shall be applicable to violations of standards and special orders regulating the use of carcinogens, except as modified by the following:

(a) A civil penalty assessed against an employer because of failure to report, as required by standards specified in Section 9030, shall be not less than five hundred dollars ($500).

(b) A civil penalty assessed against an employer for a serious violation, as defined in Section 9061, involving use of a carcinogen in violation of standards or special orders, except as provided by subdivision (d) and by Section 6429, shall be in the amount of two thousand dollars ($2,000).

(c) A civil penalty assessed pursuant to Section 6429 for repeated violations of standards or special orders specified in subdivision (a) shall be not less than five thousand dollars ($5,000).

(d) A civil penalty assessed pursuant to Section 6429 for repeated serious violations of standards or special orders specified in subdivision (b) shall be not less than ten thousand dollars ($10,000).

The maximum limitations on civil penalties specified in Chapter 4 (commencing with Section 6423) of Part 1 shall be applicable to civil penalties for which the minimum amount is prescribed by subdivision (a), (c), or (d). Nothing in this section shall supersede any provision of law prescribing criminal offenses or penalties. *(Added by Stats.1985, c. 947, § 2.)*

§ 9061. Serious violation defined

(a) For purposes of this part, "serious violation" shall have the meaning specified in Section 6432 and, except as provided in subdivision (b), shall additionally include any violation of a standard or special order respecting the use of a carcinogen.

(b) A violation of a standard or special order respecting the use of a carcinogen shall not, be a "serious violation" if the employer did not, and could not, with the exercise of reasonable diligence, know of the presence of the violation or if the violation is minor and resulted in no substantial health hazard, as determined by the division. *(Added by Stats.1985, c. 947, § 2.)*

Part 11

COMMERCIAL ESTABLISHMENTS

CHAPTER 1. WORKING WAREHOUSES

Section
9100. Sales floor.
9101. Working warehouse.
9102. Securing merchandise.
9103. Safety zones.
9104. Report of injuries.

§ 9100. Sales floor

For purposes of this chapter, "sales floor" means any area where the public is invited to shop, whether indoors or outdoors. *(Added by Stats.2001, c. 856 (S.B.486), § 1.)*

§ 9101. Working warehouse

For purposes of this chapter, "working warehouse" means a wholesale or retail establishment in which both of the following occur:

(a) Heavy machinery, including, but not limited to, forklifts, is used in any area where the public shops while customers are on the premises.

(b) Merchandise is stored on shelves higher than 12 feet above the sales floor. *(Added by Stats.2001, c. 856 (S.B.486), § 1.)*

§ 9102. Securing merchandise

(a) The owner, manager, or operator of a working warehouse shall secure merchandise stored on shelves higher than 12 feet above the sales floor. Methods of securing merchandise shall include rails, fencing, netting, security doors, gates, cables, or the binding of items on a pallet into one unit by shrink-wrapping, metal or plastic banding, or by tying items together with a cord.

(b) All working warehouses shall comply with the provisions of this section on or before July 1, 2002. *(Added by Stats.2001, c. 856 (S.B.486), § 1. Amended by Stats.2002, c. 664 (A.B.3034), § 166.)*

§ 9103. Safety zones

(a) When heavy machinery is used to move merchandise from a shelf, there shall be a safety zone established to temporarily block customers from entering areas where merchandise could fall during removal from a shelf.

(b) All working warehouses shall comply with the provisions of this section on or before July 1, 2002. *(Added by Stats.2001, c. 856 (S.B.486), § 1. Amended by Stats.2002, c. 664 (A.B.3034), § 167.)*

§ 9104. Report of injuries

An owner, manager, or operator of a working warehouse who employs more than 50 employees shall submit to the division, a report of all known injuries requiring hospitalization, including emergency room medical treatment, or deaths occurring to customers as the result of falling merchandise. The report shall be filed within 30 days of December 31, 2002, and within 30 days of December 31, 2003. Each year, a corporation owning, managing, or operating more than one working warehouse may submit a single report on behalf of all of the corporation's working warehouses in the state, provided that the report identifies the location of the warehouse where each reportable incident occurred. *(Added by Stats.2001, c. 856 (S.B.486), § 1.)*

Division 6

CONSTRUCTION AND REPEALS [REPEALED]

Division 10

CONSTRUCTION AND REPEALS [REPEALED]

MILITARY AND VETERANS CODE

Division 1

ADMINISTRATION OF MILITARY AND VETERANS AFFAIRS

CHAPTER 2. DEPARTMENT OF VETERANS AFFAIRS

Section
73.7. Reprisal, retaliation, threats, coercion, or similar acts against employees disclosing improper activities; disciplinary procedures; civil liability.

§ 73.7. Reprisal, retaliation, threats, coercion, or similar acts against employees disclosing improper activities; disciplinary procedures; civil liability

(a) Any state officer or employee who intentionally engages in acts of reprisal, retaliation, threats, coercion, or similar acts against an employee of any state department, board, or authority for having disclosed what the employee, in good faith, believed to be improper activities regarding veterans programs that are supported by the state shall be disciplined by adverse action as provided in Section 19572 of the Government Code. If no adverse action is instituted by the appointing power, the State Personnel Board shall take adverse action in the same manner as provided in Section 19583.5 of the Government Code.

(b) In addition to all other causes of action, penalties, or other remedies provided by law, any state officer or employee who intentionally engages in acts of reprisal, retaliation, threats, coercion, or similar acts against an employee for having disclosed what the employee, in good faith, believed to be improper activities regarding veterans programs that are supported by the state shall be liable in an action for damages brought against him or her by the injured party. Punitive damages may be awarded by the court if the acts of the offending party are proven to be malicious. If liability has been established, the injured party also shall be entitled to reasonable attorney's fees as provided by law. *(Added by Stats.1999, c. 894 (A.B.92), § 3.)*

Division 2

THE MILITARY FORCES OF THE STATE

Part 1

THE STATE MILITIA

CHAPTER 7. PRIVILEGES AND PENALTIES

Section
394. Discrimination against members of armed forces; prohibitions; penalties; additional remedies.
394.5. Temporary military leave of absence; private employees.
395. Temporary military leave of absence; public employees; conflict of section with memorandum of understanding.
395.01. Compensation of public employees on temporary military leave of absence; conflict of section with memorandum of understanding.
395.02. Salary of public employee while absent; "officer" and "employee" defined.
395.03. Maximum pay allowance under Section 395.01 or 395.02.
395.04. California National Guard member; compensation.
395.05. Public employees who are national guard members; absence from service; compensation; conflict of section with memorandum of understanding.
395.06. National guard and service members called to duty; employment rights upon return from service.

Section
395.07. Legislative, executive, or judicial officers or employees who are called into active duty; Iraq–Kuwait crisis; compensation.
395.08. Bosnia crisis; officer or employee of legislative, executive, or judicial state departments; National Guard or United States Military Reserve organization; benefits.
395.1. Public employees; return to position after termination of active service; conflict of section with memorandum of understanding.
395.2. Noncertificated school employees in active military service; return to position.
395.3. Resignation of public employee to enter military service; return to employment; "public officers and employees" defined; retroactive application; validity; conflict of section with memorandum of understanding.
395.4. Public officers and employees; leave of absence for service.
395.6. Mediators to take complaints regarding possible employment violations by state following active duty; coordination of resolution of complaints; mediation training and cooperation with other agencies.
395.8. City officers in active service; restoration to office.
395.9. State military reserve; inactive duty training; unpaid leave of absence.

Section
395.10. Ten days unpaid leave; definitions; retaliation prohibited.

§ 394. Discrimination against members of armed forces; prohibitions; penalties; additional remedies

(a) No person shall discriminate against any officer, warrant officer or enlisted member of the military or naval forces of the state or of the United States because of that membership. No member of the military forces shall be prejudiced or injured by any person, employer, or officer or agent of any corporation, company, or firm with respect to that member's employment, position or status or be denied or disqualified for employment by virtue of membership or service in the military forces of this state or of the United States.

(b) No officer or employee of the state, or of any county, city and county, municipal corporation, or district shall discriminate against any officer, warrant officer or enlisted member of the military or naval forces of the state or of the United States because of that membership. No member of the military forces shall be prejudiced or injured by any officer or employee of the state, or of any county, city and county, municipal corporation, or district with respect to that member's employment, appointment, position or status or be denied or disqualified for or discharged from that employment or position by virtue of membership or service in the military forces of this state or of the United States.

(c) No person shall prohibit or refuse entrance to any officer or enlisted member of the Army or Navy of the United States or of the military or naval forces of this state into any public entertainment or place of amusement or into any of the places described in Sections 51 and 52 of the Civil Code because that member wears the uniform of the organization to which he or she belongs.

(d) No employer or officer or agent of any corporation, company, or firm, or other person, shall discharge any person from employment because of the performance of any ordered military duty or training or by reason of being an officer, warrant officer, or enlisted member of the military or naval forces of this state, or hinder or prevent that person from performing any military service or from attending any military encampment or place of drill or instruction he or she may be called upon to perform or attend by proper authority; prejudice or harm him or her in any manner in his or her employment, position, or status by reason of performance of military service or duty or attendance at military encampments or places of drill or instruction; or dissuade, prevent, or stop any person from enlistment or accepting a warrant or commission in the California National Guard or Naval Militia by threat or injury to him or her in respect to his or her employment, position, status, trade, or business because of enlistment or acceptance of a warrant or commission.

(e)(1) No private employer or officer or agent of any corporation, company, or firm, or other person, shall

restrict or terminate any collateral benefit for employees by reason of an employee's temporary incapacitation incident to duty in the National Guard or Naval Militia. As used in this subdivision, "temporary incapacitation" means any period of incapacitation of 52 weeks or less.

(2) As used in this subdivision, "benefit" includes, but is not limited to, health care which may be continued at the employee's expense, life insurance, disability insurance, and seniority status.

(f) No person who provides lending or financing shall discriminate against any person with respect to the terms of a loan or financing, including, but not limited to, the finance charge, based on that person's membership in the military or naval forces of this state or of the United States. With respect to any loan or credit transaction covered by Section 670 of Public Law 109–364 and Section 232 of Title 32 of the Code of Federal Regulations, as published on August 31, 2007, in Volume 72 of the Federal Register, a person that does not market or extend those transactions to covered borrowers shall not be in violation of this section. For purposes of this section, a covered borrower has the same meaning as provided for in Section 232 of Title 32 of the Code of Federal Regulations, as published on August 31, 2007, in Volume 72 of the Federal Register.

(g) Any person violating this section is guilty of a misdemeanor. In addition, any person violating any of the provisions of this section shall be liable for actual damages and reasonable attorney's fees incurred by the injured party.

(h) The remedies provided for in this section are not intended to be exclusive but are in addition to the remedies provided for in other laws, including Sections 51 and 52 of the Civil Code. *(Stats.1935, c. 389, p. 1363, § 394. Amended by Stats.1947, c. 393, p. 962, § 13; Stats.1951, c. 408, p. 1377, § 13; Stats.1990, c. 1519 (A.B.3954), § 1; Stats.1991, c. 1091 (A.B.1487), § 116; Stats.1991, c. 36 (S.B.4), § 1, eff. May 28, 1991; Stats. 2001, c. 299 (A.B.120), § 1; Stats.2007, c. 358 (A.B.7), § 5, eff. Oct. 9, 2007.)*

§ 394.5. Temporary military leave of absence; private employees

Any employee of any corporation, company, or firm, or other person, who is a member of the reserve corps of the armed forces of the United States or of the National Guard or the Naval Militia shall be entitled to a temporary leave of absence without pay while engaged in military duty ordered for purposes of military training, drills, encampment, naval cruises, special exercises or like activity as such member, providing that the period of ordered duty does not exceed 17 calendar days annually including time involved in going to and returning from such duty. *(Added by Stats.1957, c. 469, p. 1506, § 1, eff. May 21, 1957.)*

§ 395. Temporary military leave of absence; public employees; conflict of section with memorandum of understanding

(a) Any public employee who is a member of the reserve corps of the Armed Forces of the United States or of the National Guard or the Naval Militia is entitled to a temporary military leave of absence as provided by federal law while engaged in military duty ordered for purposes of active military training, inactive duty training, encampment, naval cruises, special exercises or like activity, providing that the period of ordered duty does not exceed 180 calendar days, including time involved in going to and returning from that duty.

(b) Notwithstanding subdivision (a), a local public agency may, but is not required to, provide paid military leave of absence for periods of inactive duty training.

(c) The employee has an absolute right to be restored to the former office or position and status formerly had by him or her in the same locality and in the same office, board, commission, agency, or institution of the public agency upon the termination of temporary military duty. If the office or position has been abolished or otherwise has ceased to exist during his or her absence, he or she shall be reinstated to a position of like seniority, status, and pay if a position exists, or if no position exists the employee shall have the same rights and privileges that he or she would have had if he or she had occupied the position when it ceased to exist and had not taken temporary military leave of absence.

(d) Any public employee who has been in the service of the public agency from which the leave is taken for a period of not less than one year immediately prior to the date upon which a temporary military leave of absence begins, shall receive the same vacation, sick leave, and holiday privileges and the same rights and privileges to promotion, continuance in office, employment, reappointment to office, or reemployment that the employee would have enjoyed had he or she not been absent therefrom; excepting that an uncompleted probationary period, if any, in the public agency, must be completed upon reinstatement as provided by law or rule of the agency. For the purposes of this section, in determining the one year of service in a public agency all service of the employee in recognized military service shall be counted as public agency service.

(e) If this section is in conflict with a memorandum of understanding reached pursuant to Chapter 12 (commencing with Section 3560) of Division 4 of Title 1 of the Government Code, the memorandum of understanding shall be controlling without further legislative action, except that if the memorandum of understanding requires the expenditure of funds, it shall not become effective unless approved by the Legislature in the annual Budget Act. *(Stats.1935, c. 389, p. 1363, § 395. Amended by Stats.1939, c. 960, p. 2709, § 1; Stats.1947, c. 147, p. 669, § 1; Stats.1949, c. 1396, p. 2435, § 1; Stats.1951, c. 1561, p. 3555, § 1, eff. July 17, 1951; Stats.1970, c. 467, p. 926, § 1; Stats.1979, c. 1072, p. 3832, § 82, eff. Sept. 28, 1979;* *Stats.1981, c. 616, p. 2364, § 4; Stats.1994, c. 114 (A.B. 2892), § 47; Stats.2000, c. 928 (S.B.1950), § 1.)*

§ 395.01. Compensation of public employees on temporary military leave of absence; conflict of section with memorandum of understanding

(a) Any public employee who is on temporary military leave of absence for military duty ordered for purposes of active military training, inactive duty training, encampment, naval cruises, special exercises, or like activity as such member, provided that the period of ordered duty does not exceed 180 calendar days including time involved in going to and returning from the duty, and who has been in the service of the public agency from which the leave is taken for a period of not less than one year immediately prior to the day on which the absence begins, is entitled to receive his or her salary or compensation as a public employee for the first 30 calendar days of any such absence. Pay for those purposes may not exceed 30 days in any one fiscal year. For the purposes of this section, in determining the one year of public agency service, all service of a public employee in the recognized military service shall be counted as public agency service.

(b) Notwithstanding subdivision (a), a local public agency may, but is not required to, pay an employee during a period of inactive duty training.

(c) If the provisions of this section are in conflict with the provisions of a memorandum of understanding reached pursuant to Chapter 12 (commencing with Section 3560) of Division 4, of Title 1 of the Government Code, the memorandum of understanding shall be controlling without further legislative action, except that if those provisions of a memorandum of understanding require the expenditure of funds, the provisions shall not become effective unless approved by the Legislature in the annual Budget Act. *(Added by Stats.1951, c. 1561, p. 3556, § 2, eff. July 17, 1951. Amended by Stats.1979, c. 1072, p. 3833, § 83, eff. Sept. 28, 1979; Stats.1981, c. 616, p. 2365, § 5; Stats.2000, c. 928 (S.B.1950), § 2.)*

§ 395.02. Salary of public employee while absent; "officer" and "employee" defined

Every officer and employee of a public agency who is on military leave other than temporary military leave of absence who has been in the service of such public agency for a period of not less than one year immediately prior to the date on which the absence begins shall be entitled to receive his salary or compensation as such officer or employee for the first 30 calendar days while engaged in the performance of ordered military duty.

As used in this section only, the terms "officer" and "employee" mean an officer or employee who

(a) Is ordered into active military duty as a member of a reserve component of the armed forces of the United States;

(b) Is ordered into active federal military duty as a member of the National Guard or Naval Militia; or

803

(c) Is inducted, enlists, enters or is otherwise ordered or called into active duty as a member of the armed forces of the United States. *(Added by Stats.1951, c. 1561, p. 3556, § 3, eff. July 17, 1951.)*

§ 395.03.   Maximum pay allowance under Section 395.01 or 395.02

No more than the pay for a period of 30 calendar days shall be allowed under the provisions of Section 395.01 or 395.02 for any one military leave of absence or during any one fiscal year, except as otherwise authorized by resolution of the legislative body of a public agency or as provided in a memorandum of understanding reached with an employee organization pursuant to Chapter 10 (commencing with Section 3500) of Division 4 of Title 1 of the Government Code. *(Added by Stats.1951, c. 1561, p. 3556, § 4, eff. July 17, 1951. Amended by Stats.2000, c. 928 (S.B.1950), § 3.)*

§ 395.04.   California National Guard member; compensation

During the time that as an officer or enlisted man or woman of the California National Guard, who is on full-time active duty in the military service of the state, and is engaged, with the approval of the Adjutant General, in the military service of the state in attendance at drills, camps, or special exercises, sponsored by federal authority or by the United States Department of Defense, as a member of the National Guard of the United States, he or she shall receive salary, pay, and compensation as provided in Sections 320 and 321. *(Added by Stats.1951, c. 1561, p. 3556, § 5, eff. July 17, 1951. Amended by Stats.1994, c. 114 (A.B.2892), § 48; Stats.2002, c. 465 (S.B.1251), § 4.)*

§ 395.05.   Public employees who are national guard members; absence from service; compensation; conflict of section with memorandum of understanding

(a) Any public employee who is a member of the National Guard, shall be entitled to absent himself from his duties or service, without regard to the length of his public service, while engaged in the performance of ordered military or naval duty and while going to and returning from such duty, provided such duty is performed during such time as the Governor may have issued a proclamation of a state of extreme emergency or during such time as the National Guard may be on active duty in one or more of the situations described or included in Section 146 of this code provided such absence does not exceed the duration of such emergency. During the absence of such officer or employee while engaged in such military service during such emergency and while going to and returning from such duty, and for a period not to exceed 30 calendar days, he shall receive his salary or compensation as such officer or employee and shall not be subjected by any person directly or indirectly by reason of such absence to any loss or diminution of vacation or holiday privilege or be preju-

diced by reason of such absence with reference to promotion or continuance in office, employment, reappointment to office, or reemployment.

(b) If the provisions of this section are in conflict with the provisions of a memorandum of understanding reached pursuant to Chapter 12 (commencing with Section 3560) of Division 4 of Title 1 of the Government Code, the memorandum of understanding shall be controlling without further legislative action, except that if such provisions of a memorandum of understanding require the expenditure of funds, the provisions shall not become effective unless approved by the Legislature in the annual Budget Act. *(Added by Stats.1951, c. 1561, p. 3556, § 6, eff. July 17, 1951. Amended by Stats.1979, c. 1072, p. 3834, § 84, eff. Sept. 28, 1979.)*

§ 395.06.   National guard and service members called to duty; employment rights upon return from service

(a) Every officer and enlisted member of the California National Guard who, in order to undertake active military duty in the service of the state when the Governor has issued a proclamation of a state of insurrection pursuant to Section 143, or a proclamation of a state of extreme emergency or when the California National Guard is on active duty pursuant to Section 146, or a service member called to active service or duty under Chapter 7.5 (commencing with Section 400), has left a position, other than a temporary position, in private employment, receives a certificate of satisfactory service in the California National Guard or an equivalent thereof, is still qualified to perform the duties of that position, and makes application within 40 days after release from service shall be considered as on leave of absence during that period and shall be restored by the former employer to the former position or to a position of similar seniority, status, and pay without loss of retirement or other benefits, unless the employer's circumstances have so changed as to make it impossible or unreasonable to do so, and shall not be discharged from the position without cause within one year after being restored to the position.

(b) Every officer and enlisted member who has left a part-time position in private employment for purposes of service pursuant to subdivision (a), receives a certificate of satisfactory service in the California National Guard or an equivalent thereof, is still qualified to perform the duties of that position, and makes application within five days after release from service shall be considered as on leave of absence during that period and shall be restored by the former employer to the former position, or to a position of similar seniority, status, and pay, if any exists, and shall not be discharged from the position without cause within one year after being restored to the position.

(c) If any employer fails or refuses to comply with this section, the superior court of the county in which the employer maintains a place of business may, upon the filing of a motion, petition, or other appropriate pleading by the person entitled to the benefits of this section, specifically require the employer to comply with this section and compensate the person for any loss of wages or benefits suffered by reason of the employer's unlawful action. The court shall order a speedy hearing and shall advance it on the calendar. Upon application to the district attorney of the county in which the employer maintains a place of business by any person claiming to be entitled to the benefits of this section, the district attorney, if reasonably satisfied that the person is entitled to these benefits, shall appear and act as attorney for the person in the amicable adjustment of the claim or in the filing of any motion, petition, or other appropriate pleading and the prosecution thereof to specifically require the employer to comply with this section. No fees or court costs are required to be paid by the person applying for these benefits.

(d) Upon application to the city prosecutor of the city in which the employer maintains a place of business by any person claiming to be entitled to the benefits of this section, the city prosecutor, if reasonably satisfied that the person is entitled to these benefits, may appear and act as attorney for the person in the amicable adjustment of the claim or in the filing of any motion, petition, or other appropriate pleading and the prosecution thereof to specifically require the employer to comply with this section. No fees or court costs are required to be paid by the person applying for these benefits. *(Added by Stats.1951, c. 1561, p. 3557, § 7, eff. July 17, 1951. Amended by Stats.1989, c. 679, § 1; Stats.2002, c. 60 (A.B.1433), § 3, eff. June 21, 2002; Stats.2008, c. 243 (A.B.2449), § 1.)*

§ 395.07. Legislative, executive, or judicial officers or employees who are called into active duty; Iraq–Kuwait crisis; compensation

(a) In addition to the benefits provided pursuant to Sections 395.01 and 395.02, any officer or employee of the legislative, executive, or judicial department of the state, who, as a member of the California National Guard or a United States Military Reserve organization, is called into active duty as a result of the Iraq-Kuwait crisis on or after August 2, 1990, shall have the benefits provided for in subdivision (b).

(b) Any officer or employee to which subdivision (a) applies, while on active duty, shall, with respect to active duty served on or after August 2, 1990, receive from the state, for a period not to exceed 180 calendar days, as part of his or her compensation, both of the following:

(1) The difference between the amount of his or her military pay and allowances and the amount the officer or employee would have received as a state officer or employee, including any merit raises which would otherwise have been granted during the time the individual was on active duty.

(2) All benefits which he or she would have received had he or she not been called to active duty unless the benefits are prohibited or limited by vendor contracts.

(c) Any individual receiving compensation pursuant to subdivision (b) who does not return to state service within 60 days of being released from active duty shall have that compensation treated as a loan payable with interest at the rate earned on the Pooled Money Investment Account. This subdivision shall not apply to compensation received pursuant to Section 395.02.

(d) This section shall not apply to any active duty served voluntarily after the close of the Iraq-Kuwait crisis. *(Added by Stats.1990, c. 988 (S.B.1899), § 1. Amended by Stats.1991, c. 138 (S.B.91), § 2, eff. July 22, 1991.)*

§ 395.08. Bosnia crisis; officer or employee of legislative, executive, or judicial state departments; National Guard or United States Military Reserve organization; benefits

(a) In addition to the benefits provided pursuant to Sections 395.01 and 395.02, any officer or employee of the legislative, executive, or judicial department of the state, who, as a member of the California National Guard or a United States Military Reserve organization, is called into active duty as a result of the Bosnia crisis on or after November 21, 1995, shall have the benefits provided for in subdivision (b).

(b) Any officer or employee to which subdivision (a) applies, while on active duty, shall, with respect to active duty served on or after November 21, 1995, as a result of the Bosnia crisis, receive from the state, for a period not to exceed 180 calendar days, as part of his or her compensation, both of the following:

(1) The difference between the amount of his or her military pay and allowances and the amount the officer or employee would have received as a state officer or employee, including any merit raises that would otherwise have been granted during the time the individual was on active duty.

(2) All benefits that he or she would have received had he or she not been called to active duty unless the benefits are prohibited or limited by vendor contracts.

(c) Any individual receiving compensation pursuant to subdivision (b) who does not return to state service within 60 days of being released from active duty shall have that compensation treated as a loan payable with interest at the rate earned on the Pooled Money Investment Account. This subdivision shall not apply to compensation received pursuant to Section 395.02.

(d) This section shall not apply to any active duty served voluntarily after the close of the Bosnia crisis.

(e) Benefits provided under paragraph (1) of subdivision (b) shall only be provided to an employee who was not eligible to participate in the federal Ready Reserve Mobilization Income Insurance Program (10 U.S.C. Sec. 12521 et seq.) or a successor federal program that, in the determination of the Director of Personnel Administration, is substantively similar to the federal Ready Reserve Mobilization Income Insurance Program. For an employee eligible to participate in the federal Ready Re-

805

serve Mobilization Income Insurance Program or a successor program, and whose monthly salary as a state employee was higher than the sum of his or her military pay and allowances and the maximum allowable benefit under the federal Ready Reserve Mobilization Income Insurance Program or a successor program, the employee shall receive the amount payable under paragraph (1) of subdivision (b), but that amount shall be reduced by the maximum allowable benefit under the federal Ready Reserve Mobilization Income Insurance Program or a successor program. For individuals who elected the federal Ready Reserve Mobilization Income Insurance Program the state shall reimburse for the cost of the insurance premium for the period of time on active duty, not to exceed 180 calendar days. *(Added by Stats.1997, c. 780 (A.B.1606), § 2, eff. Oct. 8, 1997.)*

§ 395.1. Public employees; return to position after termination of active service; conflict of section with memorandum of understanding

(a) Notwithstanding any other provision of law to the contrary, any officer or employee of the state not subject to Chapter 11 (commencing with Section 19770) of Part 2 of Division 5 of Title 2 of the Government Code, or any public officer, deputy, assistant, or employee of any city, county, city and county, school district, water district, irrigation district, or any other district, political corporation, political subdivision, or governmental agency thereof who, in time of war or national emergency as proclaimed by the President or Congress, or when any of the armed forces of the United States are serving outside of the United States or their territories pursuant to order or request of the United Nations, or while any national conscription act is in effect, leaves or has left his or her office or position prior to the end of the war, or the termination of the national emergency or during the effective period of any order or request of this type of the United Nations or prior to the expiration of the National Conscription Act, to join the armed forces of the United States and who does or did without unreasonable and unnecessary delay join the armed forces or, being a member of any reserve force or corps of any of the armed forces of the United States or of the militia of this state, is or was ordered to duty therewith by competent military authority and served or serves in compliance with those orders, shall have a right, if released, separated or discharged under conditions other than dishonorable, to return to and reenter upon the office or position within six months after the termination of his or her active service with the armed forces, but not later than six months after the end of the war or national emergency or military or police operations under the United Nations or after the Governor finds and proclaims that, for the purposes of this section, the war, national emergency, or United Nations military or police operation no longer exists, or after the expiration of the National Conscription Act, if the term for which he or she was elected or appointed has not ended during his or her absence; provided, that the right to return to and reenter upon the

806

office or position shall not extend to or be granted to any officer or employee of the state not subject to Chapter 11 (commencing with Section 19770) of Part 2 of Division 5 of Title 2 of the Government Code, or any public officer, deputy, assistant, or employee of any city, county, city and county, school district, water district, irrigation district or any other district, political corporation, political subdivision or governmental agency thereof, who shall fail to return to and reenter upon his or her office or position within 12 months after the first date upon which he or she could terminate or could cause to have terminated his or her active service with the armed forces of the United States or of the militia of this state. He or she shall also have a right to return to and reenter upon the office or position during terminal leave from the armed forces and prior to discharge, separation or release therefrom.

(b) Upon return and reentry to the office or employment the officer or employee shall have all of the rights and privileges in, connected with, or arising out of the office or employment which he or she would have enjoyed if he or she had not been absent therefrom; provided, however, the officer or employee shall not be entitled to sick leave, vacation or salary for the period during which he or she was on leave from that governmental service and in the service of the armed forces of the United States.

If the office or position has been abolished or otherwise has ceased to exist during his or her absence, he or she shall be reinstated in a position of like seniority, status and pay if the position exists, or to a comparable vacant position for which he or she is qualified.

(c) Any officer or employee other than a probationer who is restored to his or her office or employment pursuant to this act shall not be discharged from that office or position without cause within one year after the restoration, and shall be entitled to participate in insurance or other benefits offered by the employing governmental agency pursuant to established rules and practices relating to those officers or employees on furlough or leave of absence in effect at the time the officer or employee left his or her office or position to join the armed forces of the United States.

(d) Notwithstanding any other provisions of this code, any enlisted person who was involuntarily ordered to active duty (other than for training) for a stated duration shall not lose any right or benefit conferred under this code if he or she voluntarily elects to complete the period of that duty.

(e) If the provisions of this section are in conflict with the provisions of a memorandum of understanding reached pursuant to Chapter 12 (commencing with Section 3560) of Division 4 of Title 1 of the Government Code, the memorandum of understanding shall be controlling without further legislative action, except that if such provisions of a memorandum of understanding require the expenditure of funds, the provisions shall not become effective unless approved by the Legislature in the annual Budget Act. *(Added by Stats.1946, 1st Ex.*

Sess., c. 125, p. 162, § 1, eff. March 11, 1946. Amended by Stats.1947, c. 738, p. 1793, § 1; Stats.1949, c. 422, p. 770, § 1; Stats.1950, 3rd Ex.Sess., c. 37, p. 62, § 1, eff. Oct. 16, 1950; Stats.1955, c. 393, p. 849, § 1, eff. May 5, 1955; Stats.1963, c. 566, p. 1446, § 1; Stats.1968, c. 1421, p. 2815, § 1; Stats.1971, c. 446, p. 928, § 10; Stats.1973, c. 176, p. 479, § 1; Stats.1979, c. 1072, p. 3834, § 85, eff. Sept. 28, 1979; Stats.1993, c. 381 (S.B.810), § 13; Stats. 1994, c. 146 (A.B.3601), § 161.)

§ 395.2. Noncertificated school employees in active military service; return to position

Any employee of a board of school trustees or board of education in a position not requiring certification qualifications who enters the active military service of the United States of America or of the State of California, including active service in any uniformed auxiliary of, or to, any branch of such military service created or authorized as such auxiliary by the Congress of the United States of America or by the Legislature of the State of California, or in the full time paid service of the American Red Cross, during any period of National emergency declared by the President of the United States of America or during any war in which the United States of America is engaged, shall regain all rights to his position and shall be reinstated thereto upon his application at any time within six months of the termination of that service, but in any event within one year from the date of a treaty of peace terminating the hostilities in which the United States is now engaged. The provisions of this act shall apply to service in the Merchant Marine as that phrase is now defined in any Federal statute relating to reemployment rights of persons in service in the Merchant Marine. (Added by Stats.1941, c. 74, p. 749, § 1. Amended by Stats.1943, c. 202, p. 1094, § 1, eff. April 24, 1943; Stats.1945, c. 124, p. 609, § 1; Stats.1946, 1st Ex.Sess. c. 32, p. 52, § 1.)

§ 395.3. Resignation of public employee to enter military service; return to employment; "public officers and employees" defined; retroactive application; validity; conflict of section with memorandum of understanding

In the event that any public officer or employee has resigned or resigns his or her office or employment to serve or to continue to serve in the Armed Forces of the United States or in the militia of this state, he or she shall have a right to return to and reenter the office or employment prior to the time at which his or her term of office or his or her employment would have ended if he or she had not resigned, on serving a written notice to that effect upon the authorized appointing power, or if there is no authorized appointing power, upon the officer or agency having power to fill a vacancy in the office or employment, within six months of the termination of his or her active service with the Armed Forces; provided, that the right to return and reenter upon the office or position shall not extend to or be granted to any public officer or employee, who shall fail to return to and reenter upon his or her office or position within 12 months after the first date upon which he or she could terminate or could cause to have terminated his or her active service with the Armed Forces of the United States or of the militia of this state.

As used in this section, "public officers and employees" includes all of the following:

(a) Members of the Senate and of the Assembly.

(b) Justices of the Supreme Court and the courts of appeal, judges of the superior courts, and all other judicial officers.

(c) All other state officers and employees not within Chapter 11 (commencing with Section 19770) of Part 2 of Division 5 of Title 2 of the Government Code, including all officers for whose selection and term of office provision is made in the California Constitution and laws of this state.

(d) All officers and employees of any county, city and county, city, township, district, political subdivision, authority, commission, board, or other public agency within this state.

The right of reentry into public office or employment provided for in this section shall include the right to be restored to the civil service status as the officer or employee would have if he or she had not so resigned; and no other person shall acquire civil service status in the same position so as to deprive the officer or employee of his or her right to restoration as provided for herein.

This section shall be retroactively applied to extend the right of reentry into public office or employment to public officers and employees who resigned prior to its effective date.

This section does not apply to any public officer or employee to whom the right to reenter public office or employment after service in the Armed Forces has been granted by any other provision of law.

If any provision of this section, or the application of this section to any person or circumstance, is held invalid, the remainder of this section, or the application of this section to persons or circumstances other than those as to which it is held invalid, shall not be affected thereby.

If the provisions of this section are in conflict with the provisions of a memorandum of understanding reached pursuant to Chapter 12 (commencing with Section 3560) of Division 4 of Title 1 of the Government Code, the memorandum of understanding shall be controlling without further legislative action, except that if the provisions of a memorandum of understanding require the expenditure of funds, the provisions shall not become effective unless approved by the Legislature in the annual Budget Act. (Added by Stats.1943, c. 584, p. 2160, § 1, eff. May 18, 1943. Amended by Stats.1955, c. 1534, § 1; Stats. 1965, c. 1655, p. 3757, § 1; Stats.1967, c. 17, p. 847, § 106; Stats.1971, c. 446, p. 929, § 11; Stats.1979, c. 1072, p. 3836, § 86, eff. Sept. 28, 1979; Stats.1993, c. 381 (S.B.810), § 14; Stats.1994, c. 146 (A.B.3601), § 162;

Stats.2002, c. 784 (S.B.1316), § 527; Stats.2003, c. 62 (S.B.600), § 208.)

§ 395.4. Public officers and employees; leave of absence for service

Whenever the United States is engaged in war or whenever the Governor finds and proclaims that an emergency exists in preparing for the National defense, any employee or officer, other than an elected officer, of a county, city, political subdivision, school, irrigation, public district, or other local authority or public body whatsoever who enters the armed forces of the United States shall be entitled to a leave of absence for service with such armed forces for the duration of the war or until the Governor finds and proclaims that the emergency no longer exists, and for 90 days thereafter, or until 90 days after the termination of such service. *(Added by Stats.1941, c. 82, p. 1035, § 1, eff. April 10, 1941.)*

§ 395.6. Mediators to take complaints regarding possible employment violations by state following active duty; coordination of resolution of complaints; mediation training and cooperation with other agencies

(a) The Governor may appoint a mediator in his or her office to take complaints, regarding possible violations or other issues dealing with the Uniformed Service Employment and Reemployment Rights Act (38 U.S.C. Sec. 4301 et seq.), hereafter USERRA, and Section 395.06, and to resolve and coordinate the resolution of those complaints or issues, from state employees who satisfy both of the following:

(1) Are members of either of the following:

(A) The California National Guard.

(B) A reserve component of the Armed Forces of the United States.

(2) Encounter problems regaining their state position when they return from service in the California National Guard or from service in a reserve component of the United States Armed Forces.

(b) Each state agency and department may appoint a mediator to take complaints, regarding possible violations of USERRA and other issues relating to state pay, and to resolve and coordinate the resolution of those complaints with, if necessary, the assistance of the Governor–appointed ombudsman, from employees of that department or agency who are members of either the California National Guard or a reserve component of the Armed Forces of the United States.

(c) Mediators appointed under the provisions of subdivisions (a) and (b) shall become knowledgeable about USERRA law and, to the extent possible, work with the California Committee for Employer Support of the Guard and Reserve, a Department of Defense organization, and the California National Guard. *(Added by Stats.2008, c. 642 (A.B.2641), § 1.)*

§ 395.8. City officers in active service; restoration to office

Any officer, elective or otherwise, who leaves or shall have left the service of any city in order to enter upon active service with the armed forces of the United States shall be reinstated and restored to his office upon his discharge or release from such active service with the armed forces; provided, such discharge or release is prior to the expiration of the term for which he has been elected or appointed.

The rights created by this section shall have no application to any officer who shall have been dishonorably discharged or released from such armed forces, or shall have been so mentally or physically disabled as to be incapable of performing the duties of his office or shall fail to present himself to the legislative body or other appointing authority of such city ready and willing to assume the duties of his office, within six months from the time of his discharge or release from active service with the armed forces.

The office from which such officer absents himself to enter upon active service with the armed forces shall not be considered to be vacant but the legislative body or other appointing authority, as the case may be, may appoint an officer to temporarily replace any such officer so absenting himself to enter upon active service with the armed forces. Such temporary officers shall have all of the powers and duties of the office to which he may be temporarily appointed and shall hold said office until the expiration of the term thereof or until the officer returns from service with the armed forces, whichever event first occurs. *(Added by Stats.1943, c. 314, p. 1306, § 1. Amended by Stats.1946, 1st Ex.Sess., c. 32, p. 53, § 2.)*

§ 395.9. State military reserve; inactive duty training; unpaid leave of absence

Any public employee and any employee of a corporation, company, firm, or other person who is a member of the State Military Reserve is entitled to a temporary military leave of absence without pay while engaged in military duty for purposes of military training, drills, unit training assemblies, or similar inactive duty training for not to exceed 15 calendar days annually, including time involved in going to and returning from that duty. *(Added by Stats.1987, c. 329, § 1.)*

§ 395.10. Ten days unpaid leave; definitions; retaliation prohibited

(a) Notwithstanding any other provision of law, a qualified employer shall allow a qualified employee to take up to 10 days of unpaid leave during a qualified leave period.

(b) For purposes of this section:

(1) "Period of military conflict" means either of the following:

(A) A period of war declared by the United States Congress.

(B) A period of deployment for which a member of a reserve component is ordered to active duty pursuant to either of the following:

(i) Sections 12301 and 12302 of Title 10 of the United States Code.

(ii) Title 32 of the United States Code.

(2) "Qualified employee" means a person who satisfies all of the following:

(A) Is the spouse of a qualified member.

(B) Performs service for hire for an employer for an average of 20 or more hours per week, but does not include an independent contractor.

(C) Provides the qualified employer with notice, within two business days of receiving official notice that the qualified member will be on leave from deployment, of his or her intention to take the leave provided for in subdivision (a).

(D) Submits written documentation to the qualified employer certifying that the qualified member will be on leave from deployment during the time the leave provided for in subdivision (a) is requested.

(3) "Qualified employer" includes any individual, corporation, company, firm, state, city, county, city and county, municipal corporation, district, public authority, or any other governmental subdivision, that employs 25 or more employees.

(4) "Qualified member" means a person who is any of the following:

(A) A member of the Armed Forces of the United States who has been deployed during a period of military conflict to an area designated as a combat theater or combat zone by the President of the United States.

(B) A member of the National Guard who has been deployed during a period of military conflict.

(C) A member of the Reserves who has been deployed during a period of military conflict.

(5) "Qualified leave period" means the period during which the qualified member is on leave from deployment during a period of military conflict.

(c) A qualified employer shall not retaliate against a qualified employee for requesting or taking the leave provided for in this section.

(d) The leave provided for in this section shall not affect or prevent a qualified employer from allowing a qualified employee to take a leave that the qualified employee is otherwise entitled to take.

(e) This section shall not affect a qualified employee's rights with respect to any other employee benefit provided for in other laws. *(Added by Stats.2007, c. 361 (A.B.392), § 1, eff. Oct. 9, 2007.)*

PENAL CODE

Part 1

OF CRIMES AND PUNISHMENTS

Title 10

OF CRIMES AGAINST THE PUBLIC HEALTH AND SAFETY

Section

387. Corporations; limited liability companies; managers; serious concealed dangers; disclosure; manager liability.

§ 387. Corporations; limited liability companies; managers; serious concealed dangers; disclosure; manager liability

(a) Any corporation, limited liability company, or person who is a manager with respect to a product, facility, equipment, process, place of employment, or business practice, is guilty of a public offense punishable by imprisonment in the county jail for a term not exceeding one year, or by a fine not exceeding ten thousand dollars ($10,000), or by both that fine and imprisonment; or by imprisonment in the state prison for 16 months, two, or three years, or by a fine not exceeding twenty-five thousand dollars ($25,000); or by both that fine and imprisonment, but if the defendant is a corporation or a limited liability company the fine shall not exceed one million dollars ($1,000,000), if that corporation, limited liability company, or person does all of the following:

(1) Has actual knowledge of a serious concealed danger that is subject to the regulatory authority of an appropriate agency and is associated with that product or a component of that product or business practice.

(2) Knowingly fails during the period ending 15 days after the actual knowledge is acquired, or if there is imminent risk of great bodily harm or death, immediately, to do both of the following:

(A) Inform the Division of Occupational Safety and Health in the Department of Industrial Relations in writing, unless the corporation, limited liability company, or manager has actual knowledge that the division has been so informed.

Where the concealed danger reported pursuant to this paragraph is subject to the regulatory authority of an agency other than the Division of Occupational Safety and Health in the Department of Industrial Relations, it shall be the responsibility of the Division of Occupational Safety and Health in the Department of Industrial Relations, within 24 hours of receipt of the information, to telephonically notify the appropriate government agency of the hazard, and promptly forward any written notification received.

(B) Warn its affected employees in writing, unless the corporation, limited liability company, or manager has actual knowledge that the employees have been so warned.

The requirement for disclosure is not applicable if the hazard is abated within the time prescribed for reporting, unless the appropriate regulatory agency nonetheless requires disclosure by regulation.

Where the Division of Occupational Safety and Health in the Department of Industrial Relations was not notified, but the corporation, limited liability company, or manager reasonably and in good faith believed that they were complying with the notification requirements of this section by notifying another government agency, as listed in paragraph (8) of subdivision (d), no penalties shall apply.

(b) As used in this section:

(1) "Manager" means a person having both of the following:

(A) Management authority in or as a business entity.

(B) Significant responsibility for any aspect of a business that includes actual authority for the safety of a product or business practice or for the conduct of research or testing in connection with a product or business practice.

(2) "Product" means an article of trade or commerce or other item of merchandise that is a tangible or an intangible good, and includes services.

(3) "Actual knowledge," used with respect to a serious concealed danger, means has information that would convince a reasonable person in the circumstances in which the manager is situated that the serious concealed danger exists.

(4) "Serious concealed danger," used with respect to a product or business practice, means that the normal or reasonably foreseeable use of, or the exposure of an individual to, the product or business practice creates a substantial probability of death, great bodily harm, or serious exposure to an individual, and the danger is not readily apparent to an individual who is likely to be exposed.

(5) "Great bodily harm" means a significant or substantial physical injury.

(6) "Serious exposure" means any exposure to a hazardous substance, when the exposure occurs as a result of an incident or exposure over time and to a degree or in an amount sufficient to create a substantial probability that death or great bodily harm in the future would result from the exposure.

(7) "Warn its affected employees" means give sufficient description of the serious concealed danger to all individuals working for or in the business entity who are

likely to be subject to the serious concealed danger in the course of that work to make those individuals aware of that danger.

(8) "Appropriate government agency" means an agency on the following list that has regulatory authority with respect to the product or business practice and serious concealed dangers of the sort discovered:

(A) The Division of Occupational Safety and Health in the Department of Industrial Relations.

(B) State Department of Health Services.

(C) Department of Agriculture.

(D) County departments of health.

(E) The United States Food and Drug Administration.

(F) The United States Environmental Protection Agency.

(G) The National Highway Traffic Safety Administration.

(H) The Federal Occupation Safety and Health Administration.

(I) The Nuclear Regulatory Commission.

(J) The Consumer Product Safety Commission.

(K) The Federal Aviation Administration.

(L) The Federal Mine Safety and Health Review Commission.

(c) Notification received pursuant to this section shall not be used against any manager in any criminal case, except a prosecution for perjury or for giving a false statement.

(d) No person who is a manager of a limited liability company shall be personally liable for acts or omissions for which the limited liability company is liable under subdivision (a) solely by reason of being a manager of the limited liability company. A person who is a manager of a limited liability company may be held liable under subdivision (a) if that person is also a "manager" within the meaning of paragraph (1) of subdivision (b). *(Added by Stats.1990, c. 1616 (A.B.2249), § 2. Amended by Stats.1994, c. 1200 (S.B.469), § 36, eff. Sept. 30, 1994.)*

Title 13

OF CRIMES AGAINST PROPERTY

CHAPTER 5. LARCENY [THEFT]

Section
484. Theft defined.
484b. Diversion of funds received to obtain or pay for services, labor, materials or equipment.

§ 484. Theft defined

(a) Every person who shall feloniously steal, take, carry, lead, or drive away the personal property of another, or who shall fraudulently appropriate property which has been entrusted to him or her, or who shall knowingly and designedly, by any false or fraudulent representation or pretense, defraud any other person of money, labor or real or personal property, or who causes or procures others to report falsely of his or her wealth or mercantile character and by thus imposing upon any person, obtains credit and thereby fraudulently gets or obtains possession of money, or property or obtains the labor or service of another, is guilty of theft. In determining the value of the property obtained, for the purposes of this section, the reasonable and fair market value shall be the test, and in determining the value of services received the contract price shall be the test. If there be no contract price, the reasonable and going wage for the service rendered shall govern. For the purposes of this section, any false or fraudulent representation or pretense made shall be treated as continuing, so as to cover any money, property or service received as a result thereof, and the complaint, information or indictment may charge that the crime was committed on any date during the particular period in question. The hiring of any additional employee or employees without advising each of them of every labor claim due and unpaid and every judgment that the employer has been unable to meet shall be prima facie evidence of intent to defraud.

(b)(1) Except as provided in Section 10855 of the Vehicle Code, where a person has leased or rented the personal property of another person pursuant to a written contract, and that property has a value greater than one thousand dollars ($1,000) and is not a commonly used household item, intent to commit theft by fraud shall be rebuttably presumed if the person fails to return the personal property to its owner within 10 days after the owner has made written demand by certified or registered mail following the expiration of the lease or rental agreement for return of the property so leased or rented.

(2) Except as provided in Section 10855 of the Vehicle Code, where a person has leased or rented the personal property of another person pursuant to a written contract, and where the property has a value no greater than one thousand dollars ($1,000), or where the property is a commonly used household item, intent to commit theft by fraud shall be rebuttably presumed if the person fails to return the personal property to its owner within 20 days after the owner has made written demand by certified or registered mail following the expiration of the lease or rental agreement for return of the property so leased or rented.

(c) Notwithstanding the provisions of subdivision (b), if one presents with criminal intent identification which bears a false or fictitious name or address for the purpose of obtaining the lease or rental of the personal property of another, the presumption created herein shall apply upon the failure of the lessee to return the rental property at the expiration of the lease or rental agreement, and no written demand for the return of the leased or rented property shall be required.

(d) The presumptions created by subdivisions (b) and (c) are presumptions affecting the burden of producing evidence.

(e) Within 30 days after the lease or rental agreement has expired, the owner shall make written demand for return of the property so leased or rented. Notice addressed and mailed to the lessee or renter at the address given at the time of the making of the lease or rental agreement and to any other known address shall constitute proper demand. Where the owner fails to make such written demand the presumption created by subdivision (b) shall not apply. *(Enacted 1872. Amended by Stats.1927, c. 619, p. 1046, § 1; Stats.1935, c. 802, p. 2194, § 1; Stats.1965, c. 1602, p. 3694, § 1; Stats.1967, c. 1335, p. 3167, § 1; Stats.1980, c. 1090, p. 3500, § 1; Stats.2000, c. 176 (S.B.1867), § 1.)*

§ 484b. Diversion of funds received to obtain or pay for services, labor, materials or equipment

Any person who receives money for the purpose of obtaining or paying for services, labor, materials or equipment and willfully fails to apply such money for such purpose by either willfully failing to complete the improvements for which funds were provided or willfully failing to pay for services, labor, materials or equipment provided incident to such construction, and wrongfully diverts the funds to a use other than that for which the funds were received, shall be guilty of a public offense and shall be punishable by a fine not exceeding ten thousand dollars ($10,000), or by imprisonment in the state prison, or in a county jail for a period not exceeding one year, or by both that fine and * * * imprisonment if the amount diverted is in excess of one thousand dollars ($1,000). If the amount diverted is * * * one thousand dollars ($1,000) or less, the person shall be guilty of a misdemeanor. *(Added by Stats.1965, c. 1145, p. 2890, § 1. Amended by Stats.1974, c. 910, p. 1920, § 1; Stats.1975, c. 464, p. 966, § 1; Stats.1976, c. 1139, p. 5123, § 219, operative July 1, 1977; Stats.1983, c. 1092, § 286, eff. Sept. 27, 1983, operative Jan. 1, 1984; Stats.2009, c. 35 (S.B.174), § 9.)*

Title 14

MALICIOUS MISCHIEF

Section
602. Trespasses constituting misdemeanors; enumeration.
602.8. Lands under cultivation, enclosed by fence or posted; entry without written permission; punishment; exemptions.

§ 602. Trespasses constituting misdemeanors; enumeration

Except as provided in paragraph (2) of subdivision (v), subdivision (x), and Section 602.8, every person who willfully commits a trespass by any of the following acts is guilty of a misdemeanor:

(a) Cutting down, destroying, or injuring any kind of wood or timber standing or growing upon the lands of another.

(b) Carrying away any kind of wood or timber lying on those lands.

(c) Maliciously injuring or severing from the freehold of another anything attached to it, or its produce.

(d) Digging, taking, or carrying away from any lot situated within the limits of any incorporated city, without the license of the owner or legal occupant, any earth, soil, or stone.

(e) Digging, taking, or carrying away from land in any city or town laid down on the map or plan of the city, or otherwise recognized or established as a street, alley, avenue, or park, without the license of the proper authorities, any earth, soil, or stone.

(f) Maliciously tearing down, damaging, mutilating, or destroying any sign, signboard, or notice placed upon, or affixed to, any property belonging to the state, or to any city, county, city and county, town or village, or upon any property of any person, by the state or by an automobile association, which sign, signboard or notice is intended to indicate or designate a road, or a highway, or is intended to direct travelers from one point to another, or relates to fires, fire control, or any other matter involving the protection of the property, or putting up, affixing, fastening, printing, or painting upon any property belonging to the state, or to any city, county, town, or village, or dedicated to the public, or upon any property of any person, without license from the owner, any notice, advertisement, or designation of, or any name for any commodity, whether for sale or otherwise, or any picture, sign, or device intended to call attention to it.

(g) Entering upon any lands owned by any other person whereon oysters or other shellfish are planted or growing; or injuring, gathering, or carrying away any oysters or other shellfish planted, growing, or on any of those lands, whether covered by water or not, without the license of the owner or legal occupant; or damaging, destroying, or removing, or causing to be removed, damaged, or destroyed, any stakes, marks, fences, or signs intended to designate the boundaries and limits of any of those lands.

(h)(1) Entering upon lands or buildings owned by any other person without the license of the owner or legal occupant, where signs forbidding trespass are displayed, and whereon cattle, goats, pigs, sheep, fowl, or any other animal is being raised, bred, fed, or held for the purpose of food for human consumption; or injuring, gathering, or carrying away any animal being housed on any of those lands, without the license of the owner or legal occupant; or damaging, destroying, or removing, or causing to be removed, damaged, or destroyed, any stakes, marks, fences, or signs intended to designate the boundaries and limits of any of those lands.

(2) In order for there to be a violation of this subdivision, the trespass signs under paragraph (1) must

813

be displayed at intervals not less than three per mile along all exterior boundaries and at all roads and trails entering the land.

(3) This subdivision shall not be construed to preclude prosecution or punishment under any other provision of law, including, but not limited to, grand theft or any provision that provides for a greater penalty or longer term of imprisonment.

(i) Willfully opening, tearing down, or otherwise destroying any fence on the enclosed land of another, or opening any gate, bar, or fence of another and willfully leaving it open without the written permission of the owner, or maliciously tearing down, mutilating, or destroying any sign, signboard, or other notice forbidding shooting on private property.

(j) Building fires upon any lands owned by another where signs forbidding trespass are displayed at intervals not greater than one mile along the exterior boundaries and at all roads and trails entering the lands, without first having obtained written permission from the owner of the lands or the owner's agent, or the person in lawful possession.

(k) Entering any lands, whether unenclosed or enclosed by fence, for the purpose of injuring any property or property rights or with the intention of interfering with, obstructing, or injuring any lawful business or occupation carried on by the owner of the land, the owner's agent or by the person in lawful possession.

(l) Entering any lands under cultivation or enclosed by fence, belonging to, or occupied by, another, or entering upon uncultivated or unenclosed lands where signs forbidding trespass are displayed at intervals not less than three to the mile along all exterior boundaries and at all roads and trails entering the lands without the written permission of the owner of the land, the owner's agent or of the person in lawful possession, and

(1) Refusing or failing to leave the lands immediately upon being requested by the owner of the land, the owner's agent or by the person in lawful possession to leave the lands, or

(2) Tearing down, mutilating, or destroying any sign, signboard, or notice forbidding trespass or hunting on the lands, or

(3) Removing, injuring, unlocking, or tampering with any lock on any gate on or leading into the lands, or

(4) Discharging any firearm.

(m) Entering and occupying real property or structures of any kind without the consent of the owner, the owner's agent, or the person in lawful possession.

(n) Driving any vehicle, as defined in Section 670 of the Vehicle Code, upon real property belonging to, or lawfully occupied by, another and known not to be open to the general public, without the consent of the owner, the owner's agent, or the person in lawful possession. This subdivision shall not apply to any person described in Section 22350 of the Business and Professions Code

who is making a lawful service of process, provided that upon exiting the vehicle, the person proceeds immediately to attempt the service of process, and leaves immediately upon completing the service of process or upon the request of the owner, the owner's agent, or the person in lawful possession.

(o) Refusing or failing to leave land, real property, or structures belonging to or lawfully occupied by another and not open to the general public, upon being requested to leave by (1) a peace officer at the request of the owner, the owner's agent, or the person in lawful possession, and upon being informed by the peace officer that he or she is acting at the request of the owner, the owner's agent, or the person in lawful possession, or (2) the owner, the owner's agent, or the person in lawful possession. The owner, the owner's agent, or the person in lawful possession shall make a separate request to the peace officer on each occasion when the peace officer's assistance in dealing with a trespass is requested. However, a single request for a peace officer's assistance may be made to cover a limited period of time not to exceed 30 days and identified by specific dates, during which there is a fire hazard or the owner, owner's agent or person in lawful possession is absent from the premises or property. In addition, a single request for a peace officer's assistance may be made for a period not to exceed six months when the premises or property is closed to the public and posted as being closed. However, this subdivision shall not be applicable to persons engaged in lawful labor union activities which are permitted to be carried out on the property by the California Agricultural Labor Relations Act, Part 3.5 (commencing with Section 1140) of Division 2 of the Labor Code, or by the National Labor Relations Act. For purposes of this section, land, real property, or structures owned or operated by any housing authority for tenants as defined under Section 34213.5 of the Health and Safety Code constitutes property not open to the general public; however, this subdivision shall not apply to persons on the premises who are engaging in activities protected by the California or United States Constitution, or to persons who are on the premises at the request of a resident or management and who are not loitering or otherwise suspected of violating or actually violating any law or ordinance.

(p) Entering upon any lands declared closed to entry as provided in Section 4256 of the Public Resources Code, if the closed areas shall have been posted with notices declaring the closure, at intervals not greater than one mile along the exterior boundaries or along roads and trails passing through the lands.

(q) Refusing or failing to leave a public building of a public agency during those hours of the day or night when the building is regularly closed to the public upon being requested to do so by a regularly employed guard, watchman, or custodian of the public agency owning or maintaining the building or property, if the surrounding circumstances would indicate to a reasonable person that the person has no apparent lawful business to pursue.

(r) Knowingly skiing in an area or on a ski trail which is closed to the public and which has signs posted indicating the closure.

(s) Refusing or failing to leave a hotel or motel, where he or she has obtained accommodations and has refused to pay for those accommodations, upon request of the proprietor or manager, and the occupancy is exempt, pursuant to subdivision (b) of Section 1940 of the Civil Code, from Chapter 2 (commencing with Section 1940) of Title 5 of Part 4 of Division 3 of the Civil Code. For purposes of this subdivision, occupancy at a hotel or motel for a continuous period of 30 days or less shall, in the absence of a written agreement to the contrary, or other written evidence of a periodic tenancy of indefinite duration, be exempt from Chapter 2 (commencing with Section 1940) of Title 5 of Part 4 of Division 3 of the Civil Code.

(t) Entering upon private property, including contiguous land, real property, or structures thereon belonging to the same owner, whether or not generally open to the public, after having been informed by a peace officer at the request of the owner, the owner's agent, or the person in lawful possession, and upon being informed by the peace officer that he or she is acting at the request of the owner, the owner's agent, or the person in lawful possession, that the property is not open to the particular person; or refusing or failing to leave the property upon being asked to leave the property in the manner provided in this subdivision.

This subdivision shall apply only to a person who has been convicted of a violent felony, as specified in subdivision (c) of Section 667.5, committed upon the particular private property. A single notification or request to the person as set forth above shall be valid and enforceable under this subdivision unless and until rescinded by the owner, the owner's agent, or the person in lawful possession of the property.

(u)(1) Knowingly entering, by an unauthorized person, upon any airport or passenger vessel terminal operations area if the area has been posted with notices restricting access to authorized personnel only and the postings occur not greater than every 150 feet along the exterior boundary, to the extent, in the case of a passenger vessel terminal, as defined in subparagraph (B) of paragraph (3), that the exterior boundary extends shoreside. To the extent that the exterior boundary of a passenger vessel terminal operations area extends waterside, this prohibition shall apply if notices have been posted in a manner consistent with the requirements for the shoreside exterior boundary, or in any other manner approved by the captain of the port.

(2) Any person convicted of a violation of paragraph (1) shall be punished as follows:

(A) By a fine not exceeding one hundred dollars ($100).

(B) By imprisonment in the county jail not exceeding six months, or by a fine not exceeding one thousand

dollars ($1,000), or both, if the person refuses to leave the airport or passenger vessel terminal after being requested to leave by a peace officer or authorized personnel.

(C) By imprisonment in the county jail not exceeding six months, or by a fine not exceeding one thousand dollars ($1,000), or both, for a second or subsequent offense.

(3) As used in this subdivision the following definitions shall control:

(A) "Airport operations area" means that part of the airport used by aircraft for landing, taking off, surface maneuvering, loading and unloading, refueling, parking, or maintenance, where aircraft support vehicles and facilities exist, and which is not for public use or public vehicular traffic.

(B) "Passenger vessel terminal" means only that portion of a harbor or port facility, as described in Section 105.105(a)(2) of Title 33 of the Code of Federal Regulations, with a secured area that regularly serves scheduled commuter or passenger operations. For the purposes of this section, "passenger vessel terminal" does not include any area designated a public access area pursuant to Section 105.106 of Title 33 of the Code of Federal Regulations.

(C) "Authorized personnel" means any person who has a valid airport identification card issued by the airport operator or has a valid airline identification card recognized by the airport operator, or any person not in possession of an airport or airline identification card who is being escorted for legitimate purposes by a person with an airport or airline identification card. "Authorized personnel" also means any person who has a valid port identification card issued by the harbor operator, or who has a valid company identification card issued by a commercial maritime enterprise recognized by the harbor operator, or any other person who is being escorted for legitimate purposes by a person with a valid port or qualifying company identification card.

(D) "Airport" means any facility whose function is to support commercial aviation.

(v)(1) Except as permitted by federal law, intentionally avoiding submission to the screening and inspection of one's person and accessible property in accordance with the procedures being applied to control access when entering or reentering a sterile area of an airport or passenger vessel terminal, as defined in Section 171.5.

(2) A violation of this subdivision that is responsible for the evacuation of an airport terminal or passenger vessel terminal and is responsible in any part for delays or cancellations of scheduled flights or departures is punishable by imprisonment of not more than one year in a county jail if the sterile area is posted with a statement providing reasonable notice that prosecution may result from a trespass described in this subdivision.

(w) Refusing or failing to leave a battered women's shelter at any time after being requested to leave by a managing authority of the shelter.

(1) A person who is convicted of violating this subdivision shall be punished by imprisonment in a county jail for not more than one year.

(2) The court may order a defendant who is convicted of violating this subdivision to make restitution to a battered woman in an amount equal to the relocation expenses of the battered woman and her children if those expenses are incurred as a result of trespass by the defendant at a battered women's shelter.

(x)(1) Knowingly entering or remaining in a neonatal unit, maternity ward, or birthing center located in a hospital or clinic without lawful business to pursue therein, if the area has been posted so as to give reasonable notice restricting access to those with lawful business to pursue therein and the surrounding circumstances would indicate to a reasonable person that he or she has no lawful business to pursue therein. Reasonable notice is that which would give actual notice to a reasonable person, and is posted, at a minimum, at each entrance into the area.

(2) Any person convicted of a violation of paragraph (1) shall be punished as follows:

(A) As an infraction, by a fine not exceeding one hundred dollars ($100).

(B) By imprisonment in a county jail not exceeding one year, or by a fine not exceeding one thousand dollars ($1,000), or both, if the person refuses to leave the posted area after being requested to leave by a peace officer or other authorized person.

(C) By imprisonment in a county jail not exceeding one year, or by a fine not exceeding two thousand dollars ($2,000), or both, for a second or subsequent offense.

(D) If probation is granted or the execution or imposition of sentencing is suspended for any person convicted under this subdivision, it shall be a condition of probation that the person participate in counseling, as designated by the court, unless the court finds good cause not to impose this requirement. The court shall require the person to pay for this counseling, if ordered, unless good cause not to pay is shown.

(y) Except as permitted by federal law, intentionally avoiding submission to the screening and inspection of one's person and accessible property in accordance with the procedures being applied to control access when entering or reentering a courthouse or a city, county, city and county, or state building if entrances to the courthouse or the city, county, city and county, or state building have been posted with a statement providing reasonable notice that prosecution may result from a trespass described in this subdivision. *(Enacted 1872. Amended by Code Am.1873–74, c. 614, p. 434, § 36; Code Am.1877–78, c. 467, p. 118, § 1; Stats.1905, c. 526, p. 688, § 1; Stats.1917, c. 208, p. 319, § 1; Stats.1927, c. 726, p. 1339, § 1; Stats.1929, c. 687, p. 1179, § 1; Stats.1931, c. 693, p. 1432, § 1; Stats.1941, c. 578, p. 1961, § 1; Stats.1945, c. 403, p. 864, § 1; Stats.1947, c. 647, p. 1684, § 1; Stats.1949, c. 1333, p. 2328, § 1; Stats.1957, c. 2013,*

p. 3581, § 1; Stats.1963, c. 1299, p. 2825, § 1; Stats.1967, c. 1187, p. 2896, § 4; Stats.1969, c. 43, p. 153, § 1; Stats.1970, c. 1607, p. 3375, § 1; Stats.1970, c. 1608, p. 3378, § 1; Stats.1977, c. 870, p. 2626, § 1; Stats.1978, c. 1392, p. 4605, § 1; Stats.1981, c. 349, p. 1509, § 1; Stats.1982, c. 312, p. 986, § 12, eff. June 28, 1982; Stats.1983, c. 199, § 1; Stats.1985, c. 1181, § 1, eff. Sept. 29, 1985; Stats.1988, c. 140, § 2; Stats.1988, c. 1024, § 1; Stats.1989, c. 870, § 1; Stats.1990, c. 424 (A.B.3147), § 1; Stats.1993, c. 589 (A.B.2211), § 115; Stats. 1993, c. 583 (A.B.284), § 7; Stats.1993, c. 793 (A.B.504), § 3.5; Stats. 1994, c. 680 (S.B.2088), § 2; Stats.2000, c. 149 (A.B. 1787), § 1; Stats.2002, c. 608 (S.B.510), § 2, eff. Sept. 17, 2002; Stats.2003, c. 355 (A.B.936), § 1; Stats.2003, c. 361 (A.B.1263), § 1; Stats.2003, c. 805 (S.B.993), § 1.3; Stats.2005, c. 289 (A.B.280), § 2; Stats.2005, c. 378 (S.B.584), § 3.)

§ 602.8. Lands under cultivation, enclosed by fence or posted; entry without written permission; punishment; exemptions

(a) Any person who without the written permission of the landowner, the owner's agent, or the person in lawful possession of the land, willfully enters any lands under cultivation or enclosed by fence, belonging to, or occupied by, another, or who willfully enters upon uncultivated or unenclosed lands where signs forbidding trespass are displayed at intervals not less than three to the mile along all exterior boundaries and at all roads and trails entering the lands, is guilty of a public offense.

(b) Any person convicted of a violation of subdivision (a) shall be punished as follows:

(1) A first offense is an infraction punishable by a fine of seventy-five dollars ($75).

(2) A second offense on the same land or any contiguous land of the same landowner, without the permission of the landowner, the landowner's agent, or the person in lawful possession of the land, is an infraction punishable by a fine of two hundred fifty dollars ($250).

(3) A third or subsequent offense on the same land or any contiguous land of the same landowner, without the permission of the landowner, the landowner's agent, or the person in lawful possession of the land, is a misdemeanor.

(c) Subdivision (a) shall not apply to any of the following:

(1) Any person engaged in lawful labor union activities which are permitted to be carried out on property by the California Agricultural Labor Relations Act, Part 3.5 (commencing with Section 1140) of Division 2 of the Labor Code, or by the National Labor Relations Act.

(2) Any person on the premises who is engaging in activities protected by the California or United States Constitution.

(3) Any person described in Section 22350 of the Business and Professions Code who is making a lawful service of process.

(4) Any person licensed pursuant to Chapter 15 (commencing with Section 8700) of Division 3 of the Business and Professions Code who is engaged in the lawful practice of land surveying as authorized by Section 846.5 of the Civil Code.

(d) For any infraction charged pursuant to this section, the defendant shall have the option to forfeit bail in lieu of making a court appearance. Notwithstanding subdivision (e) of Section 853.6, if the offender elects to forfeit bail pursuant to this subdivision, no further proceedings shall be had in the case. *(Added by Stats.1989, c. 870, § 2. Amended by Stats.2003, c. 101 (A.B.924), § 1.)*

Title 15

MISCELLANEOUS CRIMES

CHAPTER 2. OF OTHER AND MISCELLANEOUS OFFENSES

Section
638. Purchase, sale or procurement of telephone calling pattern record or list without consent of subscriber; penalties; use as evidence; legislative intent.

§ 638. Purchase, sale or procurement of telephone calling pattern record or list without consent of subscriber; penalties; use as evidence; legislative intent

(a) Any person who purchases, sells, offers to purchase or sell, or conspires to purchase or sell any telephone calling pattern record or list, without the written consent of the subscriber, or any person who procures or obtains through fraud or deceit, or attempts to procure or obtain through fraud or deceit any telephone calling pattern record or list shall be punished by a fine not exceeding two thousand five hundred dollars ($2,500), or by imprisonment in a county jail not exceeding one year, or by both a fine and imprisonment. If the person has previously been convicted of a violation of this section, he or she is punishable by a fine not exceeding ten thousand dollars ($10,000), or by imprisonment in a county jail not exceeding one year, or by both a fine and imprisonment.

(b) Any personal information contained in a telephone calling pattern record or list that is obtained in violation of this section shall be inadmissible as evidence in any judicial, administrative, legislative, or other proceeding except when that information is offered as proof in an action or prosecution for a violation of this section, or when otherwise authorized by law, in any criminal prosecution.

(c) For purposes of this section:

(1) "Person" includes an individual, business association, partnership, limited partnership, corporation, limited liability company, or other legal entity.

(2) "Telephone calling pattern record or list" means information retained by a telephone company that relates to the telephone number dialed by the subscriber, or other person using the subscriber's telephone with permission, or the incoming number of a call directed to the subscriber, or other data related to such calls typically contained on a subscriber telephone bill such as the time the call started and ended, the duration of the call, any charges applied, and any information described in subdivision (a) of Section 2891 of the Public Utilities Code whether the call was made from or to a telephone connected to the public switched telephone network, a cordless telephone, as defined in Section 632.6, a telephony device operating over the Internet utilizing voice over Internet protocol, a satellite telephone, or commercially available interconnected mobile phone service that provides access to the public switched telephone network via a mobile communication device employing radiowave technology to transmit calls, including cellular radiotelephone, broadband Personal Communications Services, and digital Specialized Mobile Radio.

(3) "Telephone company" means a telephone corporation as defined in Section 234 of the Public Utilities Code or any other person that provides residential or commercial telephone service to a subscriber utilizing any of the technologies or methods enumerated in paragraph (2).

(4) For purposes of this section, "purchase" and "sell" shall not include information provided to a collection agency or assignee of the debt by the telephone corporation, and used exclusively for the collection of the unpaid debt assigned by the telephone corporation, provided that the collection agency or assignee of the debt shall be liable for any disclosure of the information that is in violation of this section.

(d) An employer of, or entity contracting with, a person who violates subdivision (a) shall only be subject to prosecution pursuant to that provision if the employer or contracting entity knowingly allowed the employee or contractor to engage in conduct that violated subdivision (a).

(e) It is the intent of the Legislature to ensure that telephone companies maintain telephone calling pattern records or lists in the strictest confidence, and protect the privacy of their subscribers with all due care. While it is not the intent of the Legislature in this act to preclude the sharing of information that is currently allowed by both state and federal laws and rules governing those records, it is the Legislature's intent in this act to preclude any unauthorized purchase or sale of that information.

(f) This section shall not be construed to prevent a law enforcement or prosecutorial agency, or any officer, employee, or agent thereof from obtaining telephone records in connection with the performance of the official duties of the agency consistent with any other applicable state and federal law.

(g) Nothing in this section shall preclude prosecution under any other provision of law.

(h) The Legislature hereby finds and declares that, notwithstanding the prohibition on specific means of making available or obtaining personal calling records

817

pursuant to this section, the disclosure of personal calling records through any other means is no less harmful to the privacy and security interests of Californians. This section is not intended to limit the scope or force of Section 2891 of the Public Utilities Code in any way. *(Added by Stats.2006, c. 626 (S.B.202), § 1.)*

Part 3

OF IMPRISONMENT AND THE DEATH PENALTY

Title 1

IMPRISONMENT OF MALE PRISONERS IN STATE PRISONS

CHAPTER 7. EXECUTION OF SENTENCES OF IMPRISONMENT

ARTICLE 3. BLACKLIST OR EXTORTION OF DISCHARGED PRISONER

Section
2947. Misdemeanor.

§ 2947. Misdemeanor

Any person who knowingly and willfully communicates to another, either orally or in writing, any statement concerning any person then or theretofore convicted of a felony, and then finally discharged, and which communication is made with the purpose and intent to deprive such person so convicted of employment, or to prevent him from procuring the same, or with the purpose and intent to extort from him any money or article of value; and any person who threatens to make any such communication with the purpose and intent to extort money or any article of value from such person so convicted of a felony is guilty of a misdemeanor. *(Added by Stats.1977, c. 165, p. 664, § 41, eff. June 29, 1977, operative July 1, 1977.)*

CHAPTER 9. PRISON TO EMPLOYMENT

Section
3105. Inmate Treatment and Prison-to-Employment Plan; development.

§ 3105. Inmate Treatment and Prison-to-Employment Plan; development

The Department of Corrections and Rehabilitation shall develop an Inmate Treatment and Prison-to-Employment Plan. The plan should evaluate and recommend changes to the Governor and the Legislature regarding current inmate education, treatment, and rehabilitation programs to determine whether the programs provide sufficient skills to inmates that will likely result in their successful employment in the community, and reduce their chances of returning to prison after release to parole. The department shall report the status of the development of the plan on or before October 1, 2007, again on or before January 15, 2008, and shall submit the final plan by April 1, 2008. The department may use

resources of other state or local agencies, academic institutions, and other research organizations as necessary to develop the plan. *(Added by Stats.2007, c. 7 (A.B.900), § 13, eff. May 3, 2007.)*

Title 4

COUNTY JAILS, FARMS AND CAMPS

CHAPTER 1. COUNTY JAILS

Section
4025.5. Pilot program to assist indigent inmates with reentry process; authorization to expend money from inmate welfare fund.

§ 4025.5. Pilot program to assist indigent inmates with reentry process; authorization to expend money from inmate welfare fund

(a) There is hereby created a pilot program in the Counties of Alameda, Kern, Los Angeles, Orange, Sacramento, San Bernardino, San Francisco, San Diego, Santa Barbara, Santa Clara, and Stanislaus. In each county, the sheriff, or, in the County of Santa Clara, the chief of correction, may expend money from the inmate welfare fund to provide indigent inmates, after release from the county jail or any other adult detention facility under the jurisdiction of the sheriff, or, in the County of Santa Clara, the chief of correction, assistance with the reentry process within 14 days after the inmate's release. The assistance provided may include, but is not limited to, work placement, counseling, obtaining proper identification, education, and housing.

(b) This section shall remain in effect only until January 1, 2013, and as of that date is repealed, unless a later enacted statute, that is enacted before January 1, 2013, deletes or extends that date. *(Added by Stats.2007, c. 251 (S.B.718), § 2. Amended by Stats.2008, c. 16 (A.B.2574), § 1.)*

Repeal

For repeal of this section, see its terms.

Part 4

PREVENTION OF CRIMES AND APPREHENSION OF CRIMINALS

Title 1

INVESTIGATION AND CONTROL OF CRIMES AND CRIMINALS

CHAPTER 1. INVESTIGATION, IDENTIFICATION, AND INFORMATION RESPONSIBILITIES OF THE DEPARTMENT OF JUSTICE

ARTICLE 3. CRIMINAL IDENTIFICATION AND STATISTICS

Section
11105.3. Record of conviction involving sex crimes, drug crimes, or crimes of violence; availability to

Section

          employer or human resource agency for applicants for positions with supervisory or disciplinary power over minors.

11105.4.   Contract or proprietary security organizations; criminal history information concerning prospective employees.

11105.7.   Illegible fingerprints.

11105.75.   Criminal history information not fingerprint verified.

§ 11105.3. Record of conviction involving sex crimes, drug crimes, or crimes of violence; availability to employer or human resource agency for applicants for positions with supervisory or disciplinary power over minors

(a) Notwithstanding any other law, a human resource agency or an employer may request from the Department of Justice records of all convictions or any arrest pending adjudication involving the offenses specified in subdivision (a) of Section 15660 of the Welfare and Institutions Code of a person who applies for a license, employment, or volunteer position, in which he or she would have supervisory or disciplinary power over a minor or any person under his or her care. The department shall furnish the information to the requesting employer and shall also send a copy of the information to the applicant.

(b) Any request for records under subdivision (a) shall include the applicant's fingerprints, which may be taken by the requester, and any other data specified by the department. The request shall be on a form approved by the department, and the department may charge a fee to be paid by the employer, human resource agency, or applicant for the actual cost of processing the request. However, no fee shall be charged to a nonprofit organization. Requests received by the department for federal level criminal offender record information shall be forwarded to the Federal Bureau of Investigation by the department to be searched for any record of arrests or convictions.

(c)(1) Where a request pursuant to this section reveals that a prospective employee or volunteer has been convicted of a violation or attempted violation of Section 220, 261.5, 262, 273a, 273d, or 273.5, or any sex offense listed in Section 290, except for the offense specified in subdivision (d) of Section 243.4, and where the agency or employer hires the prospective employee or volunteer, the agency or employer shall notify the parents or guardians of any minor who will be supervised or disciplined by the employee or volunteer. A conviction for a violation or attempted violation of an offense committed outside the State of California shall be included in this notice if the offense would have been a crime specified in this subdivision if committed in California. The notice shall be given to the parents or guardians with whom the child resides, and shall be given at least 10 days prior to the day that the employee or volunteer begins his or her duties or tasks. Notwithstanding any other provision of law, any person who conveys or receives information in good faith and in conformity with this section is exempt from prosecution under Section 11142 or 11143 for that conveying or receiving of information. Notwithstanding subdivision (d), the notification requirements of this subdivision shall apply as an additional requirement of any other provision of law requiring criminal record access or dissemination of criminal history information.

(2) The notification requirement pursuant to paragraph (1) shall not apply to a misdemeanor conviction for violating Section 261.5 or to a conviction for violating Section 262 or 273.5. Nothing in this paragraph shall preclude an employer from requesting records of convictions for violating Section 261.5, 262, or 273.5 from the Department of Justice pursuant to this section.

(d) Nothing in this section supersedes any law requiring criminal record access or dissemination of criminal history information. In any conflict with another statute, dissemination of criminal history information shall be pursuant to the mandatory statute. This subdivision applies to, but is not limited to, requirements pursuant to Article 1 (commencing with Section 1500) of Chapter 3 of, and Chapter 3.2 (commencing with Section 1569) and Chapter 3.4 (commencing with Section 1596.70) of, Division 2 of, and Section 1522 of, the Health and Safety Code, and Sections 8712, 8811, and 8908 of the Family Code.

(e) The department may adopt regulations to implement the provisions of this section as necessary.

(f) As used in this section, "employer" means any nonprofit corporation or other organization specified by the Attorney General which employs or uses the services of volunteers in positions in which the volunteer or employee has supervisory or disciplinary power over a child or children.

(g) As used in this section, "human resource agency" means a public or private entity, excluding any agency responsible for licensing of facilities pursuant to the California Community Care Facilities Act (Chapter 3 (commencing with Section 1500)), the California Residential Care Facilities for the Elderly Act (Chapter 3.2 (commencing with Section 1569)), Chapter 3.01 (commencing with Section 1568.01), and the California Child Day Care Facilities Act (Chapter 3.4 (commencing with Section 1596.70)) of Division 2 of the Health and Safety Code, responsible for determining the character and fitness of a person who is:

(1) Applying for a license, employment, or as a volunteer within the human services field that involves the care and security of children, the elderly, the handicapped, or the mentally impaired.

(2) Applying to be a volunteer who transports individuals impaired by drugs or alcohol.

(3) Applying to adopt a child or to be a foster parent.

(h) Except as provided in subdivision (c), any criminal history information obtained pursuant to this section is confidential and no recipient shall disclose its contents other than for the purpose for which it was acquired.

(Formerly § 11105.2, added by Stats.1981, c. 681, p. 2481, § 2. Renumbered § 11105.3 and amended by Stats.1984, c. 144, § 163; Stats.1984, c. 714, § 1. Amended by Stats.1985, c. 1012, § 1; Stats.1985, c. 1396, § 2; Stats. 1987, c. 1418, § 8; Stats.1990, c. 1570 (A.B.2617), § 3; Stats.1991, c. 937 (A.B.1797), § 5; Stats.1992, c. 163 (A.B.2641), § 111; Stats.1992, c. 1227 (A.B.3773), § 1; Stats.1993, c. 219 (A.B.1500), § 220; Stats.1993, c. 610 (A.B.6), § 25, eff. Oct. 1, 1993; Stats.1993, c. 611 (S.B.60), § 28, eff. Oct. 1, 1993; Stats.1994, c. 1263 (A.B.1328), § 5; Stats.1994, c. 1264 (A.B.3738), § 1; Stats.1994, c. 1269 (A.B.2208), § 61.3; Stats.1997, c. 586 (S.B.1302), § 1; Stats.2000, c. 972 (A.B.2665), § 1; Stats.2002, c. 627 (S.B.900), § 4; Stats.2002, c. 990 (A.B.1855), § 1.5; Stats.2003, c. 124 (S.B.873), § 1; Stats.2004, c. 184 (S.B.1314), § 2, eff. July 23, 2004.)

§ 11105.4. Contract or proprietary security organizations; criminal history information concerning prospective employees

(a) Notwithstanding any other provision of law, a contract or proprietary security organization may request any criminal history information concerning its prospective employees that may be furnished pursuant to subdivision (n) of Section 11105.

(b) The Department of Justice shall promulgate regulations to assure that criminal record information is not released to persons or entities not authorized to receive the information under this section.

(c) Any criminal history information obtained pursuant to this section shall be subject to the same requirements and conditions that the information is subject to when obtained by a human resource agency or a bank.

(d) The Legislature finds that contract security organizations and private security organizations often provide security service for financial institutions and human resource agencies, and, consequently, they have the same need for criminal history information as do those entities. Therefore, the Legislature intends to provide authority for contract security organizations and proprietary security organizations to obtain criminal history information to the extent that financial institutions and human resource agencies have that authority concerning their own employees.

(e) As used in this section, "contract security organization" means a person, business, or organization licensed to provide services as a private patrol operator, as defined in subdivision (a) of Section 7582.1 of the Business and Professions Code.

As used in this section, "proprietary security organization" means an organization within a business entity that has the primary responsibility of protecting the employees and property of its employer, and which allocates a substantial part of its annual budget to providing security and protective services for its employer, including providing qualifying and in-service training to members of the organization.

(f) Any criminal history information obtained pursuant to this section is confidential and no recipient shall disclose its contents other than for the purpose for which it was acquired. *(Added by Stats.1990, c. 1570 (A.B.2617), § 4. Amended by Stats.2002, c. 627 (S.B.900), § 5.)*

§ 11105.7. Illegible fingerprints

(a) Notwithstanding any other provision of law, when a person is required to submit fingerprints or a fingerprint card to the Department of Justice for a criminal background investigation for purposes of employment, certification, or licensing, and the department determines either that it is impossible for the person to submit fingerprints or that the submitted fingerprints are not legible for identification purposes, the department, in its discretion, shall do either of the following:

(1) Make a determination that the person presently is unable to provide legible fingerprints, and therefore shall be deemed to have complied with the statutory requirement to submit fingerprints. The department, using available personal identifying data that the department deems appropriate, shall then conduct a search to determine if the person has a criminal history.

(2) Request that the person submit a second set of fingerprints or obtain verification from another law enforcement agency that he or she is unable to provide legible fingerprint impressions either manually or electronically. If the department requests law enforcement verification of the quality of fingerprints that the person is able to provide, it may designate the law enforcement agency that is to provide the verification and provide a form for the verification. If the second set of fingerprints is illegible or if the designated law enforcement agency verifies that the person is unable to submit legible fingerprints, the person shall be deemed to have complied with the statutory requirement to submit fingerprints, and the department, using available personal identifying data it deems appropriate, shall conduct a search to determine if the person has a criminal history.

(b) After a search of its data bases pursuant to subdivision (a), the department shall issue a certificate regarding the criminal history of the applicant to the employing, licensing, or certifying agency. This certificate shall indicate whether or not the applicant has any reportable criminal history for purposes of the employment, license, or certificate the applicant is seeking. The agency shall be entitled to receive information regarding any reportable offenses and may use this information to make a determination of eligibility.

(c) Whenever the department determines pursuant to this section that a person has a criminal record, the person shall be provided an opportunity to question the accuracy or completeness of any material matter contained in the record, under the procedures provided in Section 11126.

(d) It is the intent of the Legislature that this section shall only apply to those persons who are unable to supply legible fingerprints due to disability, illness, accident, or other circumstances beyond their control and does not apply to persons who are unable to provide fingerprints because of actions they have taken to avoid submitting their fingerprints. *(Added by Stats.1998, c. 452 (A.B.75), § 1, eff. Sept. 14, 1998.)*

§ 11105.75. Criminal history information not fingerprint verified

(a)(1) If, in the course of performing a criminal history background investigation for an agency or entity statutorily authorized to receive a criminal history, the Department of Justice determines that it appears that the applicant has criminal history record information that the requesting agency is statutorily authorized to receive, but the identity of the applicant cannot be verified with fingerprints, the department shall provide a copy of the criminal history record to the requesting agency or entity but shall note any entries as to which the identity of the subject has not been fingerprint verified.

(2) The department shall compare all available identifying characteristics of the applicant with those that appear in the criminal history information before responding to the requesting agency or entity with conviction disposition information that has not been fingerprint verified.

(b) If an agency or entity denies a license, certificate, or employment based upon information received from the department that is not fingerprint verified, the agency or entity shall notify the applicant of its decision and that he or she may challenge the identification. In that case, the applicant may appeal the decision of the agency or entity on the grounds that the applicant is not the person so identified.

(c) Neither the department nor any of its employees or any requesting agency or entity shall be liable to any applicant for misidentifications made pursuant to this section. *(Added by Stats.2000, c. 623 (A.B.2623), § 1, operative July 1, 2002.)*

CHAPTER 2. CONTROL OF CRIMES AND CRIMINALS

ARTICLE 2. REPORTS OF INJURIES

Section
11160.1. Report by health practitioner of forensic medical examination of person in custody of law enforcement from whom evidence is sought in connection with investigation of sexual assault crime.
11161.8. Injuries or condition resulting from neglect or abuse; reports.
11161.9. Immunity from liability.

§ 11160.1. Report by health practitioner of forensic medical examination of person in custody of law enforcement from whom evidence is sought in connection with investigation of sexual assault crime

(a) Any health practitioner employed in any health facility, clinic, physician's office, local or state public health department, or a clinic or other type of facility operated by a local or state public health department who, in his or her professional capacity or within the scope of his or her employment, performs a forensic medical examination on any person in the custody of law enforcement from whom evidence is sought in connection with the commission or investigation of a crime of sexual assault, as described in subdivision (d) of Section 11160, shall prepare a written report. The report shall be on a standard form developed by, or at the direction of, the Office of Emergency Services or an agency designated by the Director of Finance pursuant to Section 13820, and shall be immediately provided to the law enforcement agency who has custody of the individual examined.

(b) The examination and report is subject to the confidentiality requirements of the Confidentiality of Medical Information Act (Chapter 1 (commencing with Section 56) of Part 2.6 of Division 1 of the Civil Code), the physician-patient privilege pursuant to Article 6 (commencing with Section 990) of Chapter 4 of Division 8 of the Evidence Code, and the privilege of official information pursuant to Article 9 (commencing with Section 1040) of Chapter 4 of Division 8 of the Evidence Code.

(c) The report shall be released upon request, oral or written, to any person or agency involved in any related investigation or prosecution of a criminal case including, but not limited to, a law enforcement officer, district attorney, city attorney, crime laboratory, county licensing agency, or coroner. The report may be released to defense counsel or another third party only through discovery of documents in the possession of a prosecuting agency or following the issuance of a lawful court order authorizing the release of the report.

(d) A health practitioner who makes a report in accordance with this section shall not incur civil or criminal liability. No person, agency, or their designee required or authorized to report pursuant to this section who takes photographs of a person suspected of being a person subject to a forensic medical examination as described in this section shall incur any civil or criminal liability for taking the photographs, causing the photographs to be taken, or disseminating the photographs to a law enforcement officer, district attorney, city attorney, crime laboratory, county licensing agency, or coroner with the reports required in accordance with this section. However, this subdivision shall not be deemed to grant immunity from civil or criminal liability with respect to any other use of the photographs.

(e) Section 11162 does not apply to this section.

(f) With the exception of any health practitioner who has entered into a contractual agreement to perform forensic medical examinations, no health practitioner shall be required to perform a forensic medical examination as part of his or her duties as a health practitioner. *(Added by Stats.2005, c. 133 (A.B.998), § 1.)*

§ 11161.8. Injuries or condition resulting from neglect or abuse; reports

Every person, firm, or corporation conducting any hospital in the state, or the managing agent thereof, or the person managing or in charge of such hospital, or in charge of any ward or part of such hospital, who receives a patient transferred from a health facility, as defined in Section 1250 of the Health and Safety Code or from a community care facility, as defined in Section 1502 of the Health and Safety Code, who exhibits a physical injury or condition which, in the opinion of the admitting physician, reasonably appears to be the result of neglect or abuse, shall report such fact by telephone and in writing, within 36 hours, to both the local police authority having jurisdiction and the county health department.

Any registered nurse, licensed vocational nurse, or licensed clinical social worker employed at such hospital may also make a report under this section, if, in the opinion of such person, a patient exhibits a physical injury or condition which reasonably appears to be the result of neglect or abuse.

Every physician and surgeon who has under his charge or care any such patient who exhibits a physical injury or condition which reasonably appears to be the result of neglect or abuse shall make such report.

The report shall state the character and extent of the physical injury or condition.

No employee shall be discharged, suspended, disciplined, or harassed for making a report pursuant to this section.

No person shall incur any civil or criminal liability as a result of making any report authorized by this section. *(Added by Stats.1975, c. 719, p. 1710, § 1. Amended by Stats.1979, c. 1019, p. 3486, § 1.)*

§ 11161.9. Immunity from liability

(a) A health practitioner who makes a report in accordance with this article shall not incur civil or criminal liability as a result of any report required or authorized by this article.

(b)(1) No person required or authorized to report pursuant to this article, or designated by a person required or authorized to report pursuant to this article, who takes photographs of a person suspected of being a person described in this article about whom a report is required or authorized shall incur any civil or criminal liability for taking the photographs, causing the photographs to be taken, or disseminating the photographs to local law enforcement with the reports required by this article in accordance with this article. However, this subdivision shall not be deemed to grant immunity from civil or criminal liability with respect to any other use of the photographs.

(2) A court may award attorney's fees to a commercial film and photographic print processor when a suit is brought against the processor because of a disclosure

mandated by this article and the court finds that the suit is frivolous.

(c) A health practitioner who, pursuant to a request from an adult protective services agency or a local law enforcement agency, provides the requesting agency with access to the victim of a known or suspected instance of abuse shall not incur civil or criminal liability as a result of providing that access.

(d) No employee shall be discharged, suspended, disciplined, or harassed for making a report pursuant to this section.

(e) This section does not apply to mandated reporting of child abuse, as provided for in Article 2.5 (commencing with Section 11164). *(Added by Stats.1993, c. 992 (A.B. 1652), § 6.)*

Title 2

CONTROL OF DEADLY WEAPONS

CHAPTER 1. FIREARMS

ARTICLE 2. UNLAWFUL CARRYING AND POSSESSION OF WEAPONS

Section
12021. Specified convictions; narcotic addiction; condition of probation; restrictions on firearms possession; punishment; employment needs; relief from prohibition; justifiable violations.

§ 12021. Specified convictions; narcotic addiction; condition of probation; restrictions on firearms possession; punishment; employment needs; relief from prohibition; justifiable violations

(a)(1) Any person who has been convicted of a felony under the laws of the United States, the State of California, or any other state, government, or country or of an offense enumerated in subdivision (a), (b), or (d) of Section 12001.6, or who is addicted to the use of any narcotic drug, and who owns, purchases, receives, or has in his or her possession or under his or her custody or control any firearm is guilty of a felony.

(2) Any person who has two or more convictions for violating paragraph (2) of subdivision (a) of Section 417 and who owns, purchases, receives, or has in his or her possession or under his or her custody or control any firearm is guilty of a felony.

(b) Notwithstanding subdivision (a), any person who has been convicted of a felony or of an offense enumerated in Section 12001.6, when that conviction results from certification by the juvenile court for prosecution as an adult in an adult court under Section 707 of the Welfare and Institutions Code, and who owns or has in his or her possession or under his or her custody or control any firearm is guilty of a felony.

(c)(1) Except as provided in subdivision (a) or paragraph (2) of this subdivision, any person who has been convicted of a misdemeanor violation of Section 71, 76, 136.1, 136.5, or 140, subdivision (d) of Section 148, Section 171b, 171c, 171d, 186.28, 240, 241, 242, 243, 243.4, 244.5, 245, 245.5, 246.3, 247, 273.5, 273.6, 417, 417.6, 422, 626.9, 646.9, 12023, or 12024, subdivision (b) or (d) of Section 12034, Section 12040, subdivision (b) of Section 12072, subdivision (a) of former Section 12100, Section 12220, 12320, or 12590, or Section 8100, 8101, or 8103 of the Welfare and Institutions Code, any firearm-related offense pursuant to Sections 871.5 and 1001.5 of the Welfare and Institutions Code, or of the conduct punished in paragraph (3) of subdivision (g) of Section 12072, and who, within 10 years of the conviction, owns, purchases, receives, or has in his or her possession or under his or her custody or control, any firearm is guilty of a public offense, which shall be punishable by imprisonment in a county jail not exceeding one year or in the state prison, by a fine not exceeding one thousand dollars ($1,000), or by both that imprisonment and fine. The court, on forms prescribed by the Department of Justice, shall notify the department of persons subject to this subdivision. However, the prohibition in this paragraph may be reduced, eliminated, or conditioned as provided in paragraph (2) or (3).

(2) Any person employed as a peace officer described in Section 830.1, 830.2, 830.31, 830.32, 830.33, or 830.5 whose employment or livelihood is dependent on the ability to legally possess a firearm, who is subject to the prohibition imposed by this subdivision because of a conviction under Section 273.5, 273.6, or 646.9, may petition the court only once for relief from this prohibition. The petition shall be filed with the court in which the petitioner was sentenced. If possible, the matter shall be heard before the same judge who sentenced the petitioner. Upon filing the petition, the clerk of the court shall set the hearing date and shall notify the petitioner and the prosecuting attorney of the date of the hearing. Upon making each of the following findings, the court may reduce or eliminate the prohibition, impose conditions on reduction or elimination of the prohibition, or otherwise grant relief from the prohibition as the court deems appropriate:

(A) Finds by a preponderance of the evidence that the petitioner is likely to use a firearm in a safe and lawful manner.

(B) Finds that the petitioner is not within a prohibited class as specified in subdivision (a), (b), (d), (e), or (g) or Section 12021.1, and the court is not presented with any credible evidence that the petitioner is a person described in Section 8100 or 8103 of the Welfare and Institutions Code.

(C)(i) Finds that the petitioner does not have a previous conviction under this subdivision no matter when the prior conviction occurred.

(ii) In making its decision, the court shall consider the petitioner's continued employment, the interest of justice, any relevant evidence, and the totality of the circumstances. The court shall require, as a condition of granting relief from the prohibition under this section, that the petitioner agree to participate in counseling as deemed appropriate by the court. Relief from the prohibition shall not relieve any other person or entity from any liability that might otherwise be imposed. It is the intent of the Legislature that courts exercise broad discretion in fashioning appropriate relief under this paragraph in cases in which relief is warranted. However, nothing in this paragraph shall be construed to require courts to grant relief to any particular petitioner. It is the intent of the Legislature to permit persons who were convicted of an offense specified in Section 273.5, 273.6, or 646.9 to seek relief from the prohibition imposed by this subdivision.

(3) Any person who is subject to the prohibition imposed by this subdivision because of a conviction of an offense prior to that offense being added to paragraph (1) may petition the court only once for relief from this prohibition. The petition shall be filed with the court in which the petitioner was sentenced. If possible, the matter shall be heard before the same judge that sentenced the petitioner. Upon filing the petition, the clerk of the court shall set the hearing date and notify the petitioner and the prosecuting attorney of the date of the hearing. Upon making each of the following findings, the court may reduce or eliminate the prohibition, impose conditions on reduction or elimination of the prohibition, or otherwise grant relief from the prohibition as the court deems appropriate:

(A) Finds by a preponderance of the evidence that the petitioner is likely to use a firearm in a safe and lawful manner.

(B) Finds that the petitioner is not within a prohibited class as specified in subdivision (a), (b), (d), (e), or (g) or Section 12021.1, and the court is not presented with any credible evidence that the petitioner is a person described in Section 8100 or 8103 of the Welfare and Institutions Code.

(C)(i) Finds that the petitioner does not have a previous conviction under this subdivision, no matter when the prior conviction occurred.

(ii) In making its decision, the court may consider the interest of justice, any relevant evidence, and the totality of the circumstances. It is the intent of the Legislature that courts exercise broad discretion in fashioning appropriate relief under this paragraph in cases in which relief is warranted. However, nothing in this paragraph shall be construed to require courts to grant relief to any particular petitioner.

(4) Law enforcement officials who enforce the prohibition specified in this subdivision against a person who has been granted relief pursuant to paragraph (2) or (3) shall be immune from any liability for false arrest arising from the enforcement of this subdivision unless the person has in his or her possession a certified copy of the court order that granted the person relief from the prohibition. This immunity from liability shall not relieve any person or

entity from any other liability that might otherwise be imposed.

(d)(1) Any person who, as an express condition of probation, is prohibited or restricted from owning, possessing, controlling, receiving, or purchasing a firearm and who owns, purchases, receives, or has in his or her possession or under his or her custody or control, any firearm but who is not subject to subdivision (a) or (c) is guilty of a public offense, which shall be punishable by imprisonment in a county jail not exceeding one year or in the state prison, by a fine not exceeding one thousand dollars ($1,000), or by both that imprisonment and fine. The court, on forms provided by the Department of Justice, shall notify the department of persons subject to this subdivision. The notice shall include a copy of the order of probation and a copy of any minute order or abstract reflecting the order and conditions of probation.

(2) For any person who is subject to subdivision (a), (b), or (c), the court shall, at the time judgment is imposed, provide on a form supplied by the Department of Justice, a notice to the defendant prohibited by this section from owning, purchasing, receiving, possessing or having under his or her custody or control, any firearm. The notice shall inform the defendant of the prohibition regarding firearms and include a form to facilitate the transfer of firearms. Failure to provide the notice shall not be a defense to a violation of this section.

(e) Any person who (1) is alleged to have committed an offense listed in subdivision (b) of Section 707 of the Welfare and Institutions Code, an offense described in subdivision (b) of Section 1203.073, any offense enumerated in paragraph (1) of subdivision (c), or any offense described in subdivision (a) of Section 12025, subdivision (a) of Section 12031, or subdivision (a) of Section 12034, and (2) is subsequently adjudged a ward of the juvenile court within the meaning of Section 602 of the Welfare and Institutions Code because the person committed an offense listed in subdivision (b) of Section 707 of the Welfare and Institutions Code, an offense described in subdivision (b) of Section 1203.073, any offense enumerated in paragraph (1) of subdivision (c), or any offense described in subdivision (a) of Section 12025, subdivision (a) of Section 12031, or subdivision (a) of Section 12034, shall not own, or have in his or her possession or under his or her custody or control, any firearm until the age of 30 years. A violation of this subdivision shall be punishable by imprisonment in a county jail not exceeding one year or in the state prison, by a fine not exceeding one thousand dollars ($1,000), or by both that imprisonment and fine. The juvenile court, on forms prescribed by the Department of Justice, shall notify the department of persons subject to this subdivision. Notwithstanding any other law, the forms required to be submitted to the department pursuant to this subdivision may be used to determine eligibility to acquire a firearm.

(f) Subdivision (a) shall not apply to a person who has been convicted of a felony under the laws of the United States unless either of the following criteria is satisfied:

824

(1) Conviction of a like offense under California law can only result in imposition of felony punishment.

(2) The defendant was sentenced to a federal correctional facility for more than 30 days, or received a fine of more than one thousand dollars ($1,000), or received both punishments.

(g)(1) Every person who purchases or receives, or attempts to purchase or receive, a firearm knowing that he or she is prohibited from doing so by a temporary restraining order or injunction issued pursuant to Section 527.6 or 527.8 of the Code of Civil Procedure, a protective order as defined in Section 6218 of the Family Code, a protective order issued pursuant to Section 136.2 or 646.91 of this code, or a protective order issued pursuant to Section 15657.03 of the Welfare and Institutions Code, is guilty of a public offense, which shall be punishable by imprisonment in a county jail not exceeding one year or in the state prison, by a fine not exceeding one thousand dollars ($1,000), or by both that imprisonment and fine.

(2) Every person who owns or possesses a firearm knowing that he or she is prohibited from doing so by a temporary restraining order or injunction issued pursuant to Section 527.6 or 527.8 of the Code of Civil Procedure, a protective order as defined in Section 6218 of the Family Code, a protective order issued pursuant to Section 136.2 or 646.91 of this code, or a protective order issued pursuant to Section 15657.03 of the Welfare and Institutions Code, is guilty of a public offense, which shall be punishable by imprisonment in a county jail not exceeding one year, by a fine not exceeding one thousand dollars ($1,000), or by both that imprisonment and fine.

(3) The Judicial Council shall provide notice on all protective orders that the respondent is prohibited from owning, possessing, purchasing, receiving, or attempting to purchase or receive a firearm while the protective order is in effect. The order shall also state that the firearm shall be relinquished to the local law enforcement agency for that jurisdiction or sold to a licensed gun dealer, and that proof of surrender or sale shall be filed within a specified time of receipt of the order. The order shall state the penalties for a violation of the prohibition. The order shall also state on its face the expiration date for relinquishment.

(4) If probation is granted upon conviction of a violation of this subdivision, the court shall impose probation consistent with Section 1203.097.

(h)(1) A violation of subdivision (a), (b), (c), (d), or (e) is justifiable where all of the following conditions are met:

(A) The person found the firearm or took the firearm from a person who was committing a crime against him or her.

(B) The person possessed the firearm no longer than was necessary to deliver or transport the firearm to a law enforcement agency for that agency's disposition according to law.

(C) If the firearm was transported to a law enforcement agency, it was transported in accordance with paragraph (18) of subdivision (a) of Section 12026.2.

(D) If the firearm is being transported to a law enforcement agency, the person transporting the firearm has given prior notice to the law enforcement agency that he or she is transporting the firearm to the law enforcement agency for disposition according to law.

(2) Upon the trial for violating subdivision (a), (b), (c), (d), or (e), the trier of fact shall determine whether the defendant was acting within the provisions of the exemption created by this subdivision.

(3) The defendant has the burden of proving by a preponderance of the evidence that he or she comes within the provisions of the exemption created by this subdivision.

(i) Subject to available funding, the Attorney General, working with the Judicial Council, the California Alliance Against Domestic Violence, prosecutors, and law enforcement, probation, and parole officers, shall develop a protocol for the implementation of the provisions of this section. The protocol shall be designed to facilitate the enforcement of restrictions on firearm ownership, including provisions for giving notice to defendants who are restricted, provisions for informing those defendants of the procedures by which defendants shall dispose of firearms when required to do so, provisions explaining how defendants shall provide proof of the lawful disposition of firearms, and provisions explaining how defendants may obtain possession of seized firearms when legally permitted to do so pursuant to this section or any other provision of law. The protocol shall be completed on or before January 1, 2005. *(Added by Stats.1953, c. 36, p. 654, § 1. Amended by Stats.1965, c. 931, p. 2545, § 1; Stats.1970, c. 1345, p. 2506, § 1, eff. Sept. 17, 1970; Stats.1974, c. 1197, p. 2588, § 1; Stats.1976, c. 1139, p. 5161, § 303, operative July 1, 1977; Stats.1982, c. 136, § 6, eff. March 26, 1982, operative April 25, 1982; Stats.1983, c. 1092, § 326.5, eff. Sept. 27, 1983, operative Jan. 1, 1984; Stats.1989, c. 254, § 1; Stats.1989, c. 1044, § 3; Stats. 1990, c. 9 (A.B.497), § 2; Stats.1990, c. 1180 (A.B.1753), § 3; Stats.1991, c. 953 (A.B.108), § 4, eff. Oct. 14, 1991; Stats.1991, c. 955 (A.B.242), § 3; Stats.1992, c. 163 (A.B.2641), § 114, operative Jan. 1, 1994; Stats.1993, c. 219 (A.B.1500), § 221.3; Stats.1993, c. 297 (S.B.1184), § 1; Stats.1993, c. 600 (A.B.242), § 1; Stats.1993, c. 612 (A.B.685), § 2; Stats.1994, c. 146 (A.B.3601), § 170; Stats.1994, c. 23 (A.B.482), § 5; Stats.1994, c. 451 (A.B. 2470), § 4; Stats.1993–94, 1st Ex.Sess., c. 27 (A.B.91), § 1; Stats.1994, 1st Ex.Sess., c. 29 (A.B.68), § 4; Stats. 1993–94, 1st Ex.Sess., c. 33 (S.B.36), § 3; Stats.1993–94, 1st Ex.Sess., c. 33 (S.B.36), § 3.5; Stats.1995, c. 178 (S.B.23), § 1; Stats.1997, c. 143 (A.B.688), § 1; Stats. 1997, c. 158 (A.B.78), § 2.5; Stats.1999, c. 662 (S.B.218), § 17; Stats.2000, c. 400 (A.B.1989), § 1; Stats.2001, c. 944 (S.B.950), § 3; Stats.2002, c. 830 (A.B.2695), § 2; Stats.2003, c. 490 (A.B.319), § 1; Stats.2003, c. 495 (A.B.1290), § 3; Stats.2003, c. 498 (S.B.226), § 8; Stats. 2003, c. 499 (S.B.238), § 4.7; Stats.2004, c. 183 (A.B. 3082), § 276; Stats.2004, c. 593 (S.B.1797), § 6; Stats. 2006, c. 538 (S.B.1852), § 526; Stats.2008, c. 599 (S.B. 1302), § 4.)*

PUBLIC UTILITIES CODE

Division 2.5

THE DIGITAL INFRASTRUCTURE AND VIDEO COMPETITION ACT OF 2006

Section
5910. Background checks; persons subject to background check.
5920. Holder of state franchise employing more than 750 total employees; annual report to commission.

§ 5910. Background checks; persons subject to background check

(a) The holder of a state franchise shall perform background checks of applicants for employment, according to current business practices.

(b) A background check equivalent to that performed by the holder shall also be conducted on all of the following:

(1) Persons hired by a holder under a personal service contract.

(2) Independent contractors and their employees.

(3) Vendors and their employees.

(c) Independent contractors and vendors shall certify that they have obtained the background checks required pursuant to subdivision (b), and shall make the background checks available to the holder upon request.

(d) Except as otherwise provided by contract, the holder of a state franchise shall not be responsible for administering the background checks and shall not assume the costs of the background checks of individuals who are not applicants for employment of the holder.

(e)(1) Subdivision (a) only applies to applicants for employment for positions that would allow the applicant to have direct contact with or access to the holder's network, central office, or subscriber premises, and perform activities that involve the installation, service, or repair of the holder's network or equipment.

(2) Subdivision (b) only applies to persons that have direct contact with or access to the holder's network, central office, or subscriber premises, and perform activities that involve the installation, service, or repair of the holder's network or equipment.

(f) This section does not apply to temporary workers performing emergency functions to restore the network of a holder to its normal state in the event of a natural disaster or an emergency that threatens or results in the loss of service. *(Added by Stats.2006, c. 700 (A.B.2987), § 3. Amended by Stats.2007, c. 123 (A.B.1715), § 10.)*

§ 5920. Holder of state franchise employing more than 750 total employees; annual report to commission

(a) A holder of a state franchise employing more than 750 total employees in California shall annually report to the commission all of the following:

(1) The number of California residents employed by the holder, calculated on a full-time or full-time equivalent basis.

(2) The percentage of the holder's total domestic workforce, calculated on a full-time or full-time equivalent basis.

(3) The types and numbers of jobs by occupational classification held by residents of California employed by holders of state franchises and the average pay and benefits of those jobs and, separately, the number of out-of-state residents employed by independent contractors, companies, and consultants hired by the holder, calculated on a full-time or full-time equivalent basis, when the holder is not contractually prohibited from disclosing the information to the public. This paragraph applies only to those employees of an independent contractor, company, or consultant that are personally providing services to the holder, and does not apply to employees of an independent contractor, company, or consultant not personally performing services for the holder.

(4) The number of net new positions proposed to be created directly by the holder of a state franchise during the upcoming year by occupational classifications and by category of full-time, part-time, temporary, and contract employees.

(b) The commission shall annually report the information required to be reported by holders of state franchises pursuant to subdivision (a), to the Assembly Committee on Utilities and Commerce and the Senate Committee on Energy, Utilities and Communications, or their successor committees, and within a reasonable time thereafter, shall make the information available to the public on its Internet Web site. *(Added by Stats.2006, c. 700 (A.B. 2987), § 3.)*

Division 4

LAWS RELATING TO UTILITY CORPORATIONS AND THEIR EMPLOYEES

CHAPTER 1. RAILROAD CORPORATIONS

ARTICLE 7.3. LOCAL COMMUNITY RAIL SECURITY ACT OF 2006

Section
7666. Whistleblower protection; remedies.

§ 7666. Whistleblower protection; remedies

No rail operator or any other person covered by this article may act to punish an employee who reports a violation of this article. An employee against whom a punitive action is taken may seek civil damages of up to one million dollars ($1,000,000) from any employer that acts to punish an employee who reports a violation of this article, in addition to any other remedies the court deems appropriate. *(Added by Stats.2006, c. 867 (A.B.3023), § 3.)*

CHAPTER 3. TELEGRAPH OR TELEPHONE CORPORATIONS

Section
7910. Applicants for employment; background security checks; exceptions.

§ 7910. Applicants for employment; background security checks; exceptions

(a) Telephone corporations, holders of a state franchise pursuant to Division 2.5 (commencing with Section 5800), and a video provider, as defined in Section 53088.1 of the Government Code, shall perform background checks of applicants for employment, according to usual business practices.

(b) A background check equivalent to that performed by the contracting telephone corporation, a holder of a state franchise pursuant to Division 2.5 (commencing with Section 5800), and a video provider, as defined in Section 53088.1 of the Government Code, shall also be conducted on all of the following:

(1) Persons hired by a contracting entity under a personal services contract.

(2) Independent contractors and their employees.

(3) Vendors and their employees.

(c) Independent contractors and vendors shall certify that they have obtained the background checks required pursuant to subdivision (b), and shall make the background checks available to the contracting entity upon request.

(d) Except as otherwise provided by contract, the telephone corporation, a holder of a state franchise pursuant to Division 2.5 (commencing with Section 5800), and a video provider, as defined in Section 53088.1 of the Government Code, shall not be responsible for administering the background checks and shall not assume the cost of the background checks of individuals who are not applicants for employment of the contracting entity.

(e)(1) An individual shall not, on behalf of a telephone corporation, holder of a state franchise pursuant to Division 2.5 (commencing with Section 5800), or video provider, as defined in Section 53088.1 of the Government Code, enter upon the premises of any individual unless he or she has had the background check required by subdivisions (a) and (b).

(2) Subdivision (a) applies to applicants for employment for positions that would allow the applicant to have direct contact with or access to the company's network or central office and would require the applicant to perform activities that involve the installation, service, or repair of the company's network or equipment.

(3) Subdivision (b) applies to any person that has direct contact with or access to the company's network or central office and performs activities that involve the installation, service, or repair of the company's network or equipment.

(f) This section does not apply to temporary workers performing emergency functions to restore the network of a telephone corporation to its normal state in the event of a natural disaster or an emergency that threatens or results in the loss of service.

(g) The provisions of this section apply only to applicants for employment who apply for employment on and after January 1, 2009, and to contracts entered into on or after January 1, 2009. *(Added by Stats.2002, c. 183 (A.B.1934), § 1. Amended by Stats.2008, c. 195 (A.B. 2232), § 1.)*

REVENUE AND TAXATION CODE

Division 2

OTHER TAXES

Part 10

PERSONAL INCOME TAX

CHAPTER 2. IMPOSITION OF TAX

Section

17052.18. Credits for contributions to qualified child care plan; fees from parents; basis; indication of number of children served by plan; report to legislature.

17053.7. Credit for percentage of wages paid to certain employees; exceptions.

17053.34. Taxable years beginning on or after January 1, 1998; credit against net tax; qualified employee; qualified wages; definitions.

17053.46. Local agency military base recovery area; credit against net tax.

17053.47. Manufacturing enhancement area; employment of qualified disadvantaged individual; credit against net tax.

17053.74. Credit against net tax; taxpayers employing qualified employees in enterprise zones.

17053.75. Credit against net tax; percentage of qualified wages received by taxpayer.

17061. Unemployment insurance credit or refund.

§ 17052.18. Credits for contributions to qualified child care plan; fees from parents; basis; indication of number of children served by plan; report to legislature

(a) For each taxable year beginning on or after January 1, 1995, and before January 1, 2012, there shall be allowed as a credit against the "net tax" (as defined by Section 17039) an amount equal to the amount determined in subdivision (b).

(b)(1) The amount of the credit allowed by this section shall be 30 percent of the cost paid or incurred by the taxpayer for contributions to a qualified care plan made on behalf of any qualified dependent of the taxpayer's qualified employee.

(2) The amount of the credit allowed by this section in any taxable year shall not exceed three hundred sixty dollars ($360) for each qualified dependent.

(c) For purposes of this section:

(1) "Qualified care plan" means a plan providing qualified care.

(2) "Qualified care" includes, but is not limited to, onsite service, center-based service, in-home care or home-provider care, and a dependent care center as defined by Section 21(b)(2)(D) of the Internal Revenue Code [1] that is a specialized center with respect to short-term illnesses of an employee's dependents. "Qualified care" must be provided in this state under the authority of a license when required by California law.

(3) "Specialized center" means a facility that provides care to mildly ill children and that may do all of the following:

(A) Be staffed by pediatric nurses and day care workers.

(B) Admit children suffering from common childhood ailments (including colds, flu, and chickenpox).

(C) Make special arrangements for well children with minor problems associated with diabetes, asthma, breaks or sprains, and recuperation from surgery.

(D) Separate children according to their illness and symptoms in order to protect them from cross-infection.

(4) "Contributions" include direct payments to child care programs or providers. "Contributions" do not include amounts contributed to a qualified care plan pursuant to a salary reduction agreement to provide benefits under a dependent care assistance program within the meaning of Section 129 of the Internal Revenue Code, as applicable, for purposes of Part 11 (commencing with Section 23001) and this part.

(5) "Qualified employee" means any employee of the taxpayer who is performing services for the taxpayer in this state, within the meaning of Section 25133, during the period in which the qualified care is performed.

(6) "Employee" includes an individual who is an employee within the meaning of Section 401(c)(1) of the Internal Revenue Code (relating to self-employed individuals).

(7) "Qualified dependent" means any dependent of a qualified employee who is under the age of 12 years.

(d) If an employer makes contributions to a qualified care plan and also collects fees from parents to support a child care facility owned and operated by the employer, no credit shall be allowed under this section for contributions in the amount, if any, by which the sum of the contributions and fees exceed the total cost of providing care. The Franchise Tax Board may require information about fees collected from parents of children.

(e) If the duration of the child care received is less than 42 weeks, the employer shall claim a prorated portion of the allowable credit. The employer shall prorate the credit using the ratio of the number of weeks of care received divided by 42 weeks.

(f) If the credit allowed by this section exceeds the "net tax," the excess may be carried over to reduce the "net tax" in the following year, and succeeding years if necessary until the credit has been exhausted.

(g) The credit shall not be available to an employer if the care provided on behalf of an employee is provided by an individual who:

(1) Qualifies as a dependent of that employee or that employee's spouse under subdivision (d) of Section 17054.

(2) Is (within the meaning of Section 17056) a son, stepson, daughter, or stepdaughter of that employee and is under the age of 19 at the close of that taxable year.

(h) The contributions to a qualified care plan shall not discriminate in favor of employees who are officers, owners, or highly compensated, or their dependents.

(i) No deduction shall be allowed as otherwise provided in this part for that portion of expenses paid or incurred for the taxable year that is equal to the amount of the credit allowed under this section.

(j) If the credit is taken by an employer for contributions to a qualified care plan that is used at a facility owned by the employer, the basis of that facility shall be reduced by the amount of the credit. The basis adjustment shall be made for the taxable year for which the credit is allowed.

(k) In order to be allowed the credit authorized under this section the taxpayer shall indicate, in the form and manner prescribed by the Franchise Tax Board, the number of children of employers served by the qualified child care plan.

(*l*) On or before January 1, 2011, the Franchise Tax Board shall submit to the Legislature a report on the following:

(1) The dollar amount of credits claimed annually.

(2) The number of children of employees served by the qualified child care plan for which the taxpayer claimed a credit.

(m) This section shall remain in effect only until December 1, 2012, and as of that date is repealed. *(Added by Stats.1994, c. 748 (A.B.3144), § 3, eff. Sept. 23, 1994. Amended by Stats.1995, c. 91 (S.B.975), § 158; Stats.1998, c. 323 (A.B.2798), § 12, eff. Aug. 20, 1998; Stats.2001, c. 650 (A.B.866), § 2, eff. Oct. 10, 2001; Stats.2006, c. 712 (A.B.1282), § 2, eff. Sept. 29, 2006.)*

[1] Internal Revenue Code sections are in Title 26 of the U.S.C.A.

Repeal

For repeal of this section, see its terms.

§ 17053.7. Credit for percentage of wages paid to certain employees; exceptions

(a) There shall be allowed as a credit against the "net tax" (as defined by Section 17039) an amount equal to 10 percent of the amount of wages paid to each employee who is certified by the Employment Development Department to meet the requirements of Section 328 of the Unemployment Insurance Code.

The credit under this section shall not apply to an individual unless, on or before the day on which that individual begins work for the employer, the employer:

(1) Has received a certification from the Employment Development Department, or

(2) Has requested in writing that certification from the Employment Development Department.

For the purposes of this subdivision, if on or before the day on which the individual begins work for the employer, the individual has received from the Employment Development Department a written preliminary determination that he or she is a member of a targeted group, then the requirement of paragraph (1) or (2) shall be applicable on or before the fifth day on which the individual begins work for the employer.

(b) The credit under this section shall not apply to wages paid in excess of three thousand dollars ($3,000) during a taxable year by a taxpayer to the same individual. With respect to each qualified employee, the aggregate credit under this section shall not exceed six hundred dollars ($600).

(c) The credit under this section shall not apply to wages paid to an individual:

(1) Who bears any of the relationships described in paragraphs (1) to (8), inclusive, of Section 152(a) of the Internal Revenue Code [1] to the taxpayer; or

(2) Who, if the taxpayer is an estate or trust, is a grantor, beneficiary, or fiduciary of the estate or trust, or is an individual who bears any of the relationships described in paragraphs (1) to (8), inclusive, of Section 152(a) of the Internal Revenue Code to a grantor, beneficiary, or fiduciary of the estate or trust; or

(3) Who is a dependent (as described in Section 152(a)(9) of the Internal Revenue Code) of the taxpayer, or, if the taxpayer is an estate or trust, of a grantor, beneficiary, or a fiduciary of the estate or trust.

(d) The credit under this section shall not apply to wages paid to an individual if, prior to the hiring date of that individual, that individual has been employed by the employer at any time during which he or she was not certified by the Employment Development Department to meet the requirements of Section 328 of the Unemployment Insurance Code.

(e) If the certification of an employment has been revoked pursuant to subdivision (c) of Section 328 of the Unemployment Insurance Code, the credit under this section shall not apply to wages paid by the employer after the date on which notice of revocation is received by the employer.

(f) The credit under this section shall be in addition to any deduction under this part to which the taxpayer may be entitled, if any.

(g) The credit provided by this section shall be applied to wages paid to each qualifying employee during the 24-month period beginning on the date the employee begins working for the taxpayer.

(h)(1) A taxpayer may elect to have this section not apply for any taxable year.

(2) An election under paragraph (1) for any taxable year may be made (or revoked) at any time before the expiration of the four-year period beginning on the last date prescribed by law for filing the return for that taxable year (determined without regard to extensions).

(3) An election under paragraph (1) (or revocation thereof) shall be made in any manner which the Franchise Tax Board may prescribe.

(i)(1) In the case of a successor employer referred to in Section 3306(b)(1) of the Internal Revenue Code, the determination of the amount of the credit under this section with respect to wages paid by that successor employer shall be made in the same manner as if those wages were paid by the predecessor employer referred to in that section.

(2) No credit shall be determined under this section with respect to remuneration paid by an employer to an employee for services performed by that employee for another person, unless the amount reasonably expected to be received by the employer for those services from that other person exceeds the remuneration paid by the employer to that employee for those services.

(j) The term "wages" shall not include either of the following:

(1) Payments defined in Section 51(c)(3) of the Internal Revenue Code, relating to payments for services during labor disputes.

(2) Any amounts paid or incurred to an individual who begins work for the employer after December 31, 1993. *(Added by Stats.1986, c. 1087, § 3, eff. Sept. 24, 1986. Amended by Stats.1989, c. 1074, § 1, eff. Sept. 30, 1989; Stats.1989, c. 1352, § 13.5, eff. Oct. 2, 1989.)*

[1] Internal Revenue Code sections are in Title 26 of U.S.C.A.

§ 17053.34. Taxable years beginning on or after January 1, 1998; credit against net tax; qualified employee; qualified wages; definitions

(a) For each taxable year beginning on or after January 1, 1998, there shall be allowed a credit against the "net tax" (as defined in Section 17039) to a qualified taxpayer who employs a qualified employee in a targeted tax area during the taxable year. The credit shall be equal to the sum of each of the following:

(1) Fifty percent of qualified wages in the first year of employment.

(2) Forty percent of qualified wages in the second year of employment.

(3) Thirty percent of qualified wages in the third year of employment.

(4) Twenty percent of qualified wages in the fourth year of employment.

(5) Ten percent of qualified wages in the fifth year of employment.

(b) For purposes of this section:

(1) "Qualified wages" means:

(A) That portion of wages paid or incurred by the qualified taxpayer during the taxable year to qualified employees that does not exceed 150 percent of the minimum wage.

(B) Wages received during the 60–month period beginning with the first day the employee commences employment with the qualified taxpayer. Reemployment in connection with any increase, including a regularly occurring seasonal increase, in the trade or business operations of the qualified taxpayer does not constitute commencement of employment for purposes of this section.

(C) Qualified wages do not include any wages paid or incurred by the qualified taxpayer on or after the targeted tax area expiration date. However, wages paid or incurred with respect to qualified employees who are employed by the qualified taxpayer within the targeted tax area within the 60–month period prior to the targeted tax area expiration date shall continue to qualify for the credit under this section after the targeted tax area expiration date, in accordance with all provisions of this section applied as if the targeted tax area designation were still in existence and binding.

(2) "Minimum wage" means the wage established by the Industrial Welfare Commission as provided for in Chapter 1 (commencing with Section 1171) of Part 4 of Division 2 of the Labor Code.

(3) "Targeted tax area expiration date" means the date the targeted tax area designation expires, is revoked, is no longer binding, or becomes inoperative.

(4)(A) "Qualified employee" means an individual who meets all of the following requirements:

(i) At least 90 percent of his or her services for the qualified taxpayer during the taxable year are directly related to the conduct of the qualified taxpayer's trade or business located in a targeted tax area.

(ii) Performs at least 50 percent of his or her services for the qualified taxpayer during the taxable year in a targeted tax area.

(iii) Is hired by the qualified taxpayer after the date of original designation of the area in which services were performed as a targeted tax area.

(iv) Is any of the following:

(I) Immediately preceding the qualified employee's commencement of employment with the qualified taxpayer, was a person eligible for services under the federal Job Training Partnership Act (29 U.S.C. Sec. 1501 et seq.), or its successor, who is receiving, or is eligible to receive, subsidized employment, training, or services funded by the federal Job Training Partnership Act, or its successor.

(II) Immediately preceding the qualified employee's commencement of employment with the qualified taxpayer, was a person eligible to be a voluntary or mandatory registrant under the Greater Avenues for Independence Act of 1985 (GAIN) provided for pursuant to Article 3.2 (commencing with Section 11320) of Chapter 2 of Part 3 of Division 9 of the Welfare and Institutions Code, or its successor.

(III) Immediately preceding the qualified employee's commencement of employment with the qualified taxpayer, was an economically disadvantaged individual 14 years of age or older.

(IV) Immediately preceding the qualified employee's commencement of employment with the qualified taxpayer, was a dislocated worker who meets any of the following:

(aa) Has been terminated or laid off or who has received a notice of termination or layoff from employment, is eligible for or has exhausted entitlement to unemployment insurance benefits, and is unlikely to return to his or her previous industry or occupation.

(bb) Has been terminated or has received a notice of termination of employment as a result of any permanent closure or any substantial layoff at a plant, facility, or enterprise, including an individual who has not received written notification but whose employer has made a public announcement of the closure or layoff.

(cc) Is long-term unemployed and has limited opportunities for employment or reemployment in the same or a similar occupation in the area in which the individual resides, including an individual 55 years of age or older who may have substantial barriers to employment by reason of age.

(dd) Was self-employed (including farmers and ranchers) and is unemployed as a result of general economic conditions in the community in which he or she resides or because of natural disasters.

(ee) Was a civilian employee of the Department of Defense employed at a military installation being closed or realigned under the Defense Base Closure and Realignment Act of 1990.

(ff) Was an active member of the Armed Forces or National Guard as of September 30, 1990, and was either involuntarily separated or separated pursuant to a special benefits program.

(gg) Is a seasonal or migrant worker who experiences chronic seasonal unemployment and underemployment in the agriculture industry, aggravated by continual advancements in technology and mechanization.

(hh) Has been terminated or laid off, or has received a notice of termination or layoff, as a consequence of compliance with the Clean Air Act.

(V) Immediately preceding the qualified employee's commencement of employment with the qualified taxpayer, was a disabled individual who is eligible for or enrolled in, or has completed a state rehabilitation plan or is a service-connected disabled veteran, veteran of the Vietnam era, or veteran who is recently separated from military service.

(VI) Immediately preceding the qualified employee's commencement of employment with the qualified taxpayer, was an ex-offender. An individual shall be treated as convicted if he or she was placed on probation by a state court without a finding of guilty.

(VII) Immediately preceding the qualified employee's commencement of employment with the qualified taxpayer, was a person eligible for or a recipient of any of the following:

(aa) Federal Supplemental Security Income benefits.

(bb) Aid to Families with Dependent Children.

(cc) Food stamps.

(dd) State and local general assistance.

(VIII) Immediately preceding the qualified employee's commencement of employment with the qualified taxpayer, was a member of a federally recognized Indian tribe, band, or other group of Native American descent.

(IX) Immediately preceding the qualified employee's commencement of employment with the qualified taxpayer, was a resident of a targeted tax area.

(X) Immediately preceding the qualified employee's commencement of employment with the taxpayer, was a member of a targeted group as defined in Section 51(d) of the Internal Revenue Code, [1] or its successor.

(B) Priority for employment shall be provided to an individual who is enrolled in a qualified program under the federal Job Training Partnership Act or the Greater Avenues for Independence Act of 1985 or who is eligible as a member of a targeted group under the Work Opportunity Tax Credit (Section 51 of the Internal Revenue Code), or its successor.

(5)(A) "Qualified taxpayer" means a person or entity that meets both of the following:

(i) Is engaged in a trade or business within a targeted tax area designated pursuant to Chapter 12.93 (commencing with Section 7097) of Division 7 of Title 1 of the Government Code.

(ii) Is engaged in those lines of business described in Codes 2000 to 2099, inclusive; 2200 to 3999, inclusive; 4200 to 4299, inclusive; 4500 to 4599, inclusive; and 4700 to 5199, inclusive, of the Standard Industrial Classification (SIC) Manual published by the United States Office of Management and Budget, 1987 edition.

(B) In the case of any passthrough entity, the determination of whether a taxpayer is a qualified taxpayer under this section shall be made at the entity level and any credit under this section or Section 23634 shall be allowed to the passthrough entity and passed through to the partners or shareholders in accordance with applicable provisions of this part or Part 11 (commencing with

Section 23001). For purposes of this subdivision, the term "passthrough entity" means any partnership or S corporation.

(6) "Seasonal employment" means employment by a qualified taxpayer that has regular and predictable substantial reductions in trade or business operations.

(c) If the qualified taxpayer is allowed a credit for qualified wages pursuant to this section, only one credit shall be allowed to the taxpayer under this part with respect to those qualified wages.

(d) The qualified taxpayer shall do both of the following:

(1) Obtain from the Employment Development Department, as permitted by federal law, the local county or city Job Training Partnership Act administrative entity , [2] the local county GAIN office or social services agency, or the local government administering the targeted tax area, a certification that provides that a qualified employee meets the eligibility requirements specified in clause (iv) of subparagraph (A) of paragraph (4) of subdivision (b). The Employment Development Department may provide preliminary screening and referral to a certifying agency. The Department of Housing and Community Development shall develop regulations governing the issuance of certificates pursuant to subdivision (g) of Section 7097 of the Government Code, and shall develop forms for this purpose.

(2) Retain a copy of the certification and provide it upon request to the Franchise Tax Board.

(e)(1) For purposes of this section:

(A) All employees of trades or businesses, which are not incorporated, that are under common control shall be treated as employed by a single taxpayer.

(B) The credit, if any, allowable by this section with respect to each trade or business shall be determined by reference to its proportionate share of the expense of the qualified wages giving rise to the credit, and shall be allocated in that manner.

(C) Principles that apply in the case of controlled groups of corporations, as specified in subdivision (d) of Section 23634, shall apply with respect to determining employment.

(2) If an employer acquires the major portion of a trade or business of another employer (hereinafter in this paragraph referred to as the "predecessor") or the major portion of a separate unit of a trade or business of a predecessor, then, for purposes of applying this section (other than subdivision (f)) for any calendar year ending after that acquisition, the employment relationship between a qualified employee and an employer shall not be treated as terminated if the employee continues to be employed in that trade or business.

(f)(1)(A) If the employment, other than seasonal employment, of any qualified employee, with respect to whom qualified wages are taken into account under subdivision (a) is terminated by the qualified taxpayer at

any time during the first 270 days of that employment (whether or not consecutive) or before the close of the 270th calendar day after the day in which that employee completes 90 days of employment with the qualified taxpayer, the tax imposed by this part for the taxable year in which that employment is terminated shall be increased by an amount equal to the credit allowed under subdivision (a) for that taxable year and all prior taxable years attributable to qualified wages paid or incurred with respect to that employee.

(B) If the seasonal employment of any qualified employee, with respect to whom qualified wages are taken into account under subdivision (a) is not continued by the qualified taxpayer for a period of 270 days of employment during the 60–month period beginning with the day the qualified employee commences seasonal employment with the qualified taxpayer, the tax imposed by this part, for the taxable year that includes the 60th month following the month in which the qualified employee commences seasonal employment with the qualified taxpayer, shall be increased by an amount equal to the credit allowed under subdivision (a) for that taxable year and all prior taxable years attributable to qualified wages paid or incurred with respect to that qualified employee.

(2)(A) Subparagraph (A) of paragraph (1) shall not apply to any of the following:

(i) A termination of employment of a qualified employee who voluntarily leaves the employment of the qualified taxpayer.

(ii) A termination of employment of a qualified employee who, before the close of the period referred to in subparagraph (A) of paragraph (1), becomes disabled and unable to perform the services of that employment, unless that disability is removed before the close of that period and the qualified taxpayer fails to offer reemployment to that employee.

(iii) A termination of employment of a qualified employee, if it is determined that the termination was due to the misconduct (as defined in Sections 1256–30 to 1256–43, inclusive, of Title 22 of the California Code of Regulations) of that employee.

(iv) A termination of employment of a qualified employee due to a substantial reduction in the trade or business operations of the qualified taxpayer.

(v) A termination of employment of a qualified employee, if that employee is replaced by other qualified employees so as to create a net increase in both the number of employees and the hours of employment.

(B) Subparagraph (B) of paragraph (1) shall not apply to any of the following:

(i) A failure to continue the seasonal employment of a qualified employee who voluntarily fails to return to the seasonal employment of the qualified taxpayer.

(ii) A failure to continue the seasonal employment of a qualified employee who, before the close of the period referred to in subparagraph (B) of paragraph (1), becomes disabled and unable to perform the services of that seasonal employment, unless that disability is removed before the close of that period and the qualified taxpayer fails to offer seasonal employment to that qualified employee.

(iii) A failure to continue the seasonal employment of a qualified employee, if it is determined that the failure to continue the seasonal employment was due to the misconduct (as defined in Sections 1256–30 to 1256–43, inclusive, of Title 22 of the California Code of Regulations) of that qualified employee.

(iv) A failure to continue seasonal employment of a qualified employee due to a substantial reduction in the regular seasonal trade or business operations of the qualified taxpayer.

(v) A failure to continue the seasonal employment of a qualified employee, if that qualified employee is replaced by other qualified employees so as to create a net increase in both the number of seasonal employees and the hours of seasonal employment.

(C) For purposes of paragraph (1), the employment relationship between the qualified taxpayer and a qualified employee shall not be treated as terminated by reason of a mere change in the form of conducting the trade or business of the qualified taxpayer, if the qualified employee continues to be employed in that trade or business and the qualified taxpayer retains a substantial interest in that trade or business.

(3) Any increase in tax under paragraph (1) shall not be treated as tax imposed by this part for purposes of determining the amount of any credit allowable under this part.

(g) In the case of an estate or trust, both of the following apply:

(1) The qualified wages for any taxable year shall be apportioned between the estate or trust and the beneficiaries on the basis of the income of the estate or trust allocable to each.

(2) Any beneficiary to whom any qualified wages have been apportioned under paragraph (1) shall be treated, for purposes of this part, as the employer with respect to those wages.

(h) For purposes of this section, "targeted tax area" means an area designated pursuant to Chapter 12.93 (commencing with Section 7097) of Division 7 of Title 1 of the Government Code.

(i) In the case where the credit otherwise allowed under this section exceeds the "net tax" for the taxable year, that portion of the credit that exceeds the "net tax" may be carried over and added to the credit, if any, in succeeding taxable years, until the credit is exhausted. The credit shall be applied first to the earliest taxable years possible.

(j)(1) The amount of the credit otherwise allowed under this section and Section 17053.33, including any credit carryover from prior years, that may reduce the

"net tax" for the taxable year shall not exceed the amount of tax that would be imposed on the qualified taxpayer's business income attributable to the targeted tax area determined as if that attributable income represented all of the income of the qualified taxpayer subject to tax under this part.

(2) Attributable income shall be that portion of the taxpayer's California source business income that is apportioned to the targeted tax area. For that purpose, the taxpayer's business income attributable to sources in this state first shall be determined in accordance with Chapter 17 (commencing with Section 25101) of Part 11. That business income shall be further apportioned to the targeted tax area in accordance with Article 2 (commencing with Section 25120) of Chapter 17 of Part 11, modified for purposes of this section in accordance with paragraph (3).

(3) Business income shall be apportioned to the targeted tax area by multiplying the total California business income of the taxpayer by a fraction, the numerator of which is the property factor plus the payroll factor, and the denominator of which is two. For purposes of this paragraph:

(A) The property factor is a fraction, the numerator of which is the average value of the taxpayer's real and tangible personal property owned or rented and used in the targeted tax area during the taxable year, and the denominator of which is the average value of all the taxpayer's real and tangible personal property owned or rented and used in this state during the taxable year.

(B) The payroll factor is a fraction, the numerator of which is the total amount paid by the taxpayer in the targeted tax area during the taxable year for compensation, and the denominator of which is the total compensation paid by the taxpayer in this state during the taxable year.

(4) The portion of any credit remaining, if any, after application of this subdivision, shall be carried over to succeeding taxable years, as if it were an amount exceeding the "net tax" for the taxable year, as provided in subdivision (h).

(5) In the event that a credit carryover is allowable under subdivision (h) for any taxable year after the targeted tax area expiration date, the targeted tax area shall be deemed to remain in existence for purposes of computing the limitation specified in this subdivision. *(Added by Stats.1997, c. 602 (A.B.1217), § 4. Amended by Stats.1998, c. 323 (A.B.2798), § 14, eff. Aug. 20, 1998, operative Aug. 20, 1998; Stats.1998, c. 1039 (A.B.2809), § 1.5, eff. Sept. 30, 1998, operative Sept. 30, 1998; Stats. 2006, c. 634 (S.B.763), § 6.)*

[1] Internal Revenue Code Sections are in Title 26 of the U.S.C.A.

[2] So in enrolled bill.

Under the terms of § 23 of Stats.1998, c. 1039 (A.B.2809), eff. Sept. 30, 1998, the amendment of this section by Stats.1998, c. 1039 is operative for taxable and income years beginning on or after January 1, 1998. Section 23 also provides that the amendment made by c. 1039 to paragraph (1) of subdivision (b) of this section is consistent with the intent of the act that enacted this section and shall apply from the original effective date of that act. Further, § 23 provides that its provisions shall be construed to include changes made by other acts of the Legislature that are incorporated as provided in §§ 21 or 22 of c. 1039. Under § 21 of c. 1039, the amendment of this section by § 1.5 of c. 1039 incorporated the 1998 amendments to this section by c. 323.

§ 17053.46. Local agency military base recovery area; credit against net tax

(a) For each taxable year beginning on or after January 1, 1995, there shall be allowed as a credit against the "net tax" (as defined in Section 17039) to a qualified taxpayer for hiring a qualified disadvantaged individual or a qualified displaced employee during the taxable year for employment in the LAMBRA. The credit shall be equal to the sum of each of the following:

(1) Fifty percent of the qualified wages in the first year of employment.

(2) Forty percent of the qualified wages in the second year of employment.

(3) Thirty percent of the qualified wages in the third year of employment.

(4) Twenty percent of the qualified wages in the fourth year of employment.

(5) Ten percent of the qualified wages in the fifth year of employment.

(b) For purposes of this section:

(1) "Qualified wages" means:

(A) That portion of wages paid or incurred by the employer during the taxable year to qualified disadvantaged individuals or qualified displaced employees that does not exceed 150 percent of the minimum wage.

(B) The total amount of qualified wages which may be taken into account for purposes of claiming the credit allowed under this section shall not exceed two million dollars ($2,000,000) per taxable year.

(C) Wages received during the 60–month period beginning with the first day the individual commences employment with the taxpayer. Reemployment in connection with any increase, including a regularly occurring seasonal increase, in the trade or business operations of the qualified taxpayer does not constitute commencement of employment for purposes of this section.

(D) Qualified wages do not include any wages paid or incurred by the qualified taxpayer on or after the LAMBRA expiration date. However, wages paid or incurred with respect to qualified disadvantaged individuals or qualified displaced employees who are employed by the qualified taxpayer within the LAMBRA within the 60–month period prior to the LAMBRA expiration date shall continue to qualify for the credit under this section after the LAMBRA expiration date, in accordance with all provisions of this section applied as if the LAMBRA designation were still in existence and binding.

(2) "Minimum wage" means the wage established by the Industrial Welfare Commission as provided for in Chapter 1 (commencing with Section 1171) of Part 4 of Division 2 of the Labor Code.

(3) "LAMBRA" means a local agency military base recovery area designated in accordance with Section 7114 of the Government Code.

(4) "Qualified disadvantaged individual" means an individual who satisfies all of the following requirements:

(A)(i) At least 90 percent of whose services for the taxpayer during the taxable year are directly related to the conduct of the taxpayer's trade or business located in a LAMBRA.

(ii) Who performs at least 50 percent of his or her services for the taxpayer during the taxable year in the LAMBRA.

(B) Who is hired by the employer after the designation of the area as a LAMBRA in which the individual's services were primarily performed.

(C) Who is any of the following immediately preceding the individual's commencement of employment with the taxpayer:

(i) An individual who has been determined eligible for services under the federal Job Training Partnership Act (29 U.S.C. Sec. 1501 et seq.).

(ii) Any voluntary or mandatory registrant under the Greater Avenues for Independence Act of 1985 as provided pursuant to Article 3.2 (commencing with Section 11320) of Chapter 2 of Part 3 of Division 9 of the Welfare and Institutions Code.

(iii) An economically disadvantaged individual age 16 years or older.

(iv) A dislocated worker who meets any of the following conditions:

(I) Has been terminated or laid off or who has received a notice of termination or layoff from employment, is eligible for or has exhausted entitlement to unemployment insurance benefits, and is unlikely to return to his or her previous industry or occupation.

(II) Has been terminated or has received a notice of termination of employment as a result of any permanent closure or any substantial layoff at a plant, facility, or enterprise, including an individual who has not received written notification but whose employer has made a public announcement of the closure or layoff.

(III) Is long-term unemployed and has limited opportunities for employment or reemployment in the same or a similar occupation in the area in which the individual resides, including an individual 55 years of age or older who may have substantial barriers to employment by reason of age.

(IV) Was self-employed (including farmers and ranchers) and is unemployed as a result of general economic conditions in the community in which he or she resides or because of natural disasters.

(V) Was a civilian employee of the Department of Defense employed at a military installation being closed or realigned under the Defense Base Closure and Realignment Act of 1990.

(VI) Was an active member of the Armed Forces or National Guard as of September 30, 1990, and was either involuntarily separated or separated pursuant to a special benefits program.

(VII) Experiences chronic seasonal unemployment and underemployment in the agriculture industry, aggravated by continual advancements in technology and mechanization.

(VIII) Has been terminated or laid off or has received a notice of termination or layoff as a consequence of compliance with the Clean Air Act.

(v) An individual who is enrolled in or has completed a state rehabilitation plan or is a service-connected disabled veteran, veteran of the Vietnam era, or veteran who is recently separated from military service.

(vi) An ex-offender. An individual shall be treated as convicted if he or she was placed on probation by a state court without a finding of guilty.

(vii) A recipient of:

(I) Federal Supplemental Security Income benefits.

(II) Aid to Families with Dependent Children.

(III) Food stamps.

(IV) State and local general assistance.

(viii) Is a member of a federally recognized Indian tribe, band, or other group of Native American descent.

(5) "Qualified taxpayer" means a taxpayer or partnership that conducts a trade or business within a LAMBRA and, for the first two taxable years, has a net increase in jobs (defined as 2,000 paid hours per employee per year) of one or more employees in the LAMBRA.

(A) The net increase in the number of jobs shall be determined by subtracting the total number of full-time employees (defined as 2,000 paid hours per employee per year) the taxpayer employed in this state in the taxable year prior to commencing business operations in the LAMBRA from the total number of full-time employees the taxpayer employed in this state during the second taxable year after commencing business operations in the LAMBRA. For taxpayers who commence doing business in this state with their LAMBRA business operation, the number of employees for the taxable year prior to

commencing business operations in the LAMBRA shall be zero. If the taxpayer has a net increase in jobs in the state, the credit shall be allowed only if one or more full-time employees is employed within the LAMBRA.

(B) The total number of employees employed in the LAMBRA shall equal the sum of both of the following:

(i) The total number of hours worked in the LAMBRA for the taxpayer by employees (not to exceed 2,000 hours per employee) who are paid an hourly wage divided by 2,000.

(ii) The total number of months worked in the LAMBRA for the taxpayer by employees who are salaried employees divided by 12.

(C) In the case of a taxpayer who first commences doing business in the LAMBRA during the taxable year, for purposes of clauses (i) and (ii), respectively, of subparagraph (B), the divisors "2,000" and "12" shall be multiplied by a fraction, the numerator of which is the number of months of the taxable year that the taxpayer was doing business in the LAMBRA and the denominator of which is 12.

(6) "Qualified displaced employee" means an individual who satisfies all of the following requirements:

(A) Any civilian or military employee of a base or former base who has been displaced as a result of a federal base closure act.

(B)(i) At least 90 percent of whose services for the taxpayer during the taxable year are directly related to the conduct of the taxpayer's trade or business located in a LAMBRA.

(ii) Who performs at least 50 percent of his or her services for the taxpayer during the taxable year in a LAMBRA.

(C) Who is hired by the employer after the designation of the area in which services were performed as a LAMBRA.

(7) "Seasonal employment" means employment by a qualified taxpayer that has regular and predictable substantial reductions in trade or business operations.

(8) "LAMBRA expiration date" means the date the LAMBRA designation expires, is no longer binding, or becomes inoperative.

(c) For qualified disadvantaged individuals or qualified displaced employees hired on or after January 1, 2001, the taxpayer shall do both of the following:

(1) Obtain from the Employment Development Department, as permitted by federal law, the local county or city Job Training Partnership Act administrative entity, the local county GAIN office or social services agency, or the local government administering the LAMBRA, a certification that provides that a qualified disadvantaged individual or qualified displaced employee meets the eligibility requirements specified in subparagraph (C) of paragraph (4) of subdivision (b) or subparagraph (A) of paragraph (6) of subdivision (b). The Employment

Development Department may provide preliminary screening and referral to a certifying agency. The Department of Housing and Community Development shall develop regulations governing the issuance of certificates pursuant to Section 7114.2 of the Government Code and shall develop forms for this purpose.

(2) Retain a copy of the certification and provide it upon request to the Franchise Tax Board.

(d)(1) For purposes of this section, both of the following apply:

(A) All employees of trades or businesses that are under common control shall be treated as employed by a single employer.

(B) The credit (if any) allowable by this section with respect to each trade or business shall be determined by reference to its proportionate share of the qualified wages giving rise to the credit.

The regulations prescribed under this paragraph shall be based on principles similar to the principles that apply in the case of controlled groups of corporations as specified in subdivision (e) of Section 23622.

(2) If an employer acquires the major portion of a trade or business of another employer (hereinafter in this paragraph referred to as the "predecessor") or the major portion of a separate unit of a trade or business of a predecessor, then, for purposes of applying this section (other than subdivision (d)) for any calendar year ending after that acquisition, the employment relationship between an employee and an employer shall not be treated as terminated if the employee continues to be employed in that trade or business.

(e)(1)(A) If the employment, other than seasonal employment, of any employee, with respect to whom qualified wages are taken into account under subdivision (a) is terminated by the taxpayer at any time during the first 270 days of that employment (whether or not consecutive) or before the close of the 270th calendar day after the day in which that employee completes 90 days of employment with the taxpayer, the tax imposed by this part for the taxable year in which that employment is terminated shall be increased by an amount (determined under those regulations) equal to the credit allowed under subdivision (a) for that taxable year and all prior taxable years attributable to qualified wages paid or incurred with respect to that employee.

(B) If the seasonal employment of any qualified disadvantaged individual, with respect to whom qualified wages are taken into account under subdivision (a) is not continued by the qualified taxpayer for a period of 270 days of employment during the 60–month period beginning with the day the qualified disadvantaged individual commences seasonal employment with the qualified taxpayer, the tax imposed by this part, for the taxable year that includes the 60th month following the month in which the qualified disadvantaged individual commences seasonal employment with the qualified taxpayer, shall be increased by an amount equal to the credit allowed under

subdivision (a) for that taxable year and all prior taxable years attributable to qualified wages paid or incurred with respect to that qualified disadvantaged individual.

(2)(A) Subparagraph (A) of paragraph (1) shall not apply to any of the following:

(i) A termination of employment of an employee who voluntarily leaves the employment of the taxpayer.

(ii) A termination of employment of an individual who, before the close of the period referred to in subparagraph (A) of paragraph (1), becomes disabled to perform the services of that employment, unless that disability is removed before the close of that period and the taxpayer fails to offer reemployment to that individual.

(iii) A termination of employment of an individual, if it is determined that the termination was due to the misconduct (as defined in Sections 1256–30 to 1256–43, inclusive, of Title 22 of the California Code of Regulations) of that individual.

(iv) A termination of employment of an individual due to a substantial reduction in the trade or business operations of the taxpayer.

(v) A termination of employment of an individual, if that individual is replaced by other qualified employees so as to create a net increase in both the number of employees and the hours of employment.

(B) Subparagraph (B) of paragraph (1) shall not apply to any of the following:

(i) A failure to continue the seasonal employment of a qualified disadvantaged individual who voluntarily fails to return to the seasonal employment of the qualified taxpayer.

(ii) A failure to continue the seasonal employment of a qualified disadvantaged individual who, before the close of the period referred to in subparagraph (B) of paragraph (1), becomes disabled and unable to perform the services of that seasonal employment, unless that disability is removed before the close of that period and the qualified taxpayer fails to offer seasonal employment to that individual.

(iii) A failure to continue the seasonal employment of a qualified disadvantaged individual, if it is determined that the failure to continue the seasonal employment was due to the misconduct (as defined in Sections 1256–30 to 1256–43, inclusive, of Title 22 of the California Code of Regulations) of that qualified disadvantaged individual.

(iv) A failure to continue seasonal employment of a qualified disadvantaged individual due to a substantial reduction in the regular seasonal trade or business operations of the qualified taxpayer.

(v) A failure to continue the seasonal employment of a qualified disadvantaged individual, if that individual is replaced by other qualified displaced employees so as to create a net increase in both the number of seasonal employees and the hours of seasonal employment.

(C) For purposes of paragraph (1), the employment relationship between the taxpayer and an employee shall not be treated as terminated by reason of a mere change in the form of conducting the trade or business of the taxpayer, if the employee continues to be employed in that trade or business and the taxpayer retains a substantial interest in that trade or business.

(3) Any increase in tax under paragraph (1) shall not be treated as tax imposed by this part for purposes of determining the amount of any credit allowable under this part.

(4) At the close of the second taxable year, if the taxpayer has not increased the number of its employees as determined by paragraph (5) of subdivision (b), then the amount of the credit previously claimed shall be added to the taxpayer's net tax for the taxpayer's second taxable year.

(f) In the case of an estate or trust, both of the following apply:

(1) The qualified wages for any taxable year shall be apportioned between the estate or trust and the beneficiaries on the basis of the income of the estate or trust allocable to each.

(2) Any beneficiary to whom any qualified wages have been apportioned under paragraph (1) shall be treated (for purposes of this part) as the employer with respect to those wages.

(g) The credit shall be reduced by the credit allowed under Section 17053. 7. The credit shall also be reduced by the federal credit allowed under Section 51 of the Internal Revenue Code.

In addition, any deduction otherwise allowed under this part for the wages or salaries paid or incurred by the taxpayer upon which the credit is based shall be reduced by the amount of the credit, prior to any reduction required by subdivision (h) or (i).

(h) In the case where the credit otherwise allowed under this section exceeds the "net tax" for the taxable year, that portion of the credit that exceeds the "net tax" may be carried over and added to the credit, if any, in succeeding years, until the credit is exhausted. The credit shall be applied first to the earliest taxable years possible.

(i)(1) The amount of credit otherwise allowed under this section and Section 17053.45, including prior year credit carryovers, that may reduce the "net tax" for the taxable year shall not exceed the amount of tax that would be imposed on the taxpayer's business income attributed to a LAMBRA determined as if that attributed income represented all of the net income of the taxpayer subject to tax under this part.

(2) Attributable income shall be that portion of the taxpayer's California source business income that is apportioned to the LAMBRA. For that purpose, the taxpayer's business income that is attributable to sources in this state first shall be determined in accordance with Chapter 17 (commencing with Section 25101) of Part 11. That business income shall be further apportioned to the LAMBRA in accordance with Article 2 (commencing with Section 25120) of Chapter 17 of Part 11, modified for purposes of this section in accordance with paragraph (3).

(3) Income shall be apportioned to a LAMBRA by multiplying the total California business income of the taxpayer by a fraction, the numerator of which is the property factor plus the payroll factor, and the denominator of which is two. For purposes of this paragraph:

(A) The property factor is a fraction, the numerator of which is the average value of the taxpayer's real and tangible personal property owned or rented and used in the LAMBRA during the taxable year, and the denominator of which is the average value of all the taxpayer's real and tangible personal property owned or rented and used in this state during the taxable year.

(B) The payroll factor is a fraction, the numerator of which is the total amount paid by the taxpayer in the LAMBRA during the taxable year for compensation, and the denominator of which is the total compensation paid by the taxpayer in this state during the taxable year.

(4) The portion of any credit remaining, if any, after application of this subdivision, shall be carried over to succeeding taxable years, as if it were an amount exceeding the "net tax" for the taxable year, as provided in subdivision (h).

(j) If the taxpayer is allowed a credit pursuant to this section for qualified wages paid or incurred, only one credit shall be allowed to the taxpayer under this part with respect to any wage consisting in whole or in part of those qualified wages. *(Added by Stats.1993, c. 1216 (A.B.693), § 3, eff. Oct. 11, 1993. Amended by Stats.1994, c. 146 (A.B.3601), § 203; Stats.1996, c. 952 (S.B.715), § 12; Stats.1997, c. 605 (A.B.1040), § 5; Stats.1998, c. 49 (A.B.510), § 4; Stats.1998, c. 1012 (A.B.3), § 6; Stats. 1998, c. 1039 (A.B.2809), § 2, eff. Sept. 30, 1998, operative Sept. 30, 1998; Stats.1998, c. 1039 (A.B.2809), § 2.5, eff. Sept. 30, 1998, operative Jan. 1, 1999; Stats.2000, c. 864 (A.B.2895), § 1; Stats.2006, c. 634 (S.B.763), § 7.)*

§ 17053.47. Manufacturing enhancement area; employment of qualified disadvantaged individual; credit against net tax

(a) For each taxable year beginning on or after January 1, 1998, there shall be allowed a credit against the "net tax" (as defined in Section 17039) to a qualified taxpayer for hiring a qualified disadvantaged individual during the taxable year for employment in the manufacturing enhancement area. The credit shall be equal to the sum of each of the following:

(1) Fifty percent of the qualified wages in the first year of employment.

(2) Forty percent of the qualified wages in the second year of employment.

(3) Thirty percent of the qualified wages in the third year of employment.

(4) Twenty percent of the qualified wages in the fourth year of employment.

(5) Ten percent of the qualified wages in the fifth year of employment.

(b) For purposes of this section:

(1) "Qualified wages" means:

(A) That portion of wages paid or incurred by the qualified taxpayer during the taxable year to qualified disadvantaged individuals that does not exceed 150 percent of the minimum wage.

(B) The total amount of qualified wages which may be taken into account for purposes of claiming the credit allowed under this section shall not exceed two million dollars ($2,000,000) per taxable year.

(C) Wages received during the 60–month period beginning with the first day the qualified disadvantaged individual commences employment with the qualified taxpayer. Reemployment in connection with any increase, including a regularly occurring seasonal increase, in the trade or business operations of the taxpayer does not constitute commencement of employment for purposes of this section.

(D) Qualified wages do not include any wages paid or incurred by the qualified taxpayer on or after the manufacturing enhancement area expiration date. However, wages paid or incurred with respect to qualified employees who are employed by the qualified taxpayer within the manufacturing enhancement area within the 60–month period prior to the manufacturing enhancement area expiration date shall continue to qualify for the credit under this section after the manufacturing enhancement area expiration date, in accordance with all provisions of this section applied as if the manufacturing enhancement area designation were still in existence and binding.

(2) "Minimum wage" means the wage established by the Industrial Welfare Commission as provided for in Chapter 1 (commencing with Section 1171) of Part 4 of Division 2 of the Labor Code.

(3) "Manufacturing enhancement area" means an area designated pursuant to Section 7073.8 of the Government Code according to the procedures of Chapter 12.8 (commencing with Section 7070) of Division 7 of Title 1 of the Government Code.

(4) "Manufacturing enhancement area expiration date" means the date the manufacturing enhancement area designation expires, is no longer binding, or becomes inoperative.

(5) "Qualified disadvantaged individual" means an individual who satisfies all of the following requirements:

(A)(i) At least 90 percent of whose services for the qualified taxpayer during the taxable year are directly related to the conduct of the qualified taxpayer's trade or business located in a manufacturing enhancement area.

(ii) Who performs at least 50 percent of his or her services for the qualified taxpayer during the taxable year in the manufacturing enhancement area.

(B) Who is hired by the qualified taxpayer after the designation of the area as a manufacturing enhancement area in which the individual's services were primarily performed.

(C) Who is any of the following immediately preceding the individual's commencement of employment with the qualified taxpayer:

(i) An individual who has been determined eligible for services under the federal Job Training Partnership Act (29 U.S.C. Sec. 1501 et seq.), or its successor.

(ii) Any voluntary or mandatory registrant under the Greater Avenues for Independence Act of 1985, or its successor, as provided pursuant to Article 3.2 (commencing with Section 11320) of Chapter 2 of Part 3 of Division 9 of the Welfare and Institutions Code.

(iii) Any individual who has been certified eligible by the Employment Development Department under the federal Targeted Jobs Tax Credit Program, or its successor, whether or not this program is in effect.

(6) "Qualified taxpayer" means any taxpayer engaged in a trade or business within a manufacturing enhancement area designated pursuant to Section 7073.8 of the Government Code and who meets all of the following requirements:

(A) Is engaged in those lines of business described in Codes 0211 to 0291, inclusive, Code 0723, or in Codes 2011 to 3999, inclusive, of the Standard Industrial Classification (SIC) Manual published by the United States Office of Management and Budget, 1987 edition.

(B) At least 50 percent of the qualified taxpayer's workforce hired after the designation of the manufacturing enhancement area is composed of individuals who, at the time of hire, are residents of the county in which the manufacturing enhancement area is located.

(C) Of this percentage of local hires, at least 30 percent shall be qualified disadvantaged individuals.

(7) "Seasonal employment" means employment by a qualified taxpayer that has regular and predictable substantial reductions in trade or business operations.

(c)(1) For purposes of this section, all of the following apply:

(A) All employees of trades or businesses that are under common control shall be treated as employed by a single qualified taxpayer.

(B) The credit (if any) allowable by this section with respect to each trade or business shall be determined by reference to its proportionate share of the expense of the qualified wages giving rise to the credit and shall be allocated in that manner.

(C) Principles that apply in the case of controlled groups of corporations, as specified in subdivision (d) of Section 23622.7, shall apply with respect to determining employment.

(2) If a qualified taxpayer acquires the major portion of a trade or business of another employer (hereinafter in this paragraph referred to as the "predecessor") or the major portion of a separate unit of a trade or business of a predecessor, then, for purposes of applying this section (other than subdivision (d)) for any calendar year ending after that acquisition, the employment relationship between a qualified disadvantaged individual and a qualified taxpayer shall not be treated as terminated if the qualified disadvantaged individual continues to be employed in that trade or business.

(d)(1)(A) If the employment, other than seasonal employment, of any qualified disadvantaged individual, with respect to whom qualified wages are taken into account under subdivision (b) is terminated by the qualified taxpayer at any time during the first 270 days of that employment (whether or not consecutive) or before the close of the 270th calendar day after the day in which that qualified disadvantaged individual completes 90 days of employment with the qualified taxpayer, the tax imposed by this part for the taxable year in which that employment is terminated shall be increased by an amount equal to the credit allowed under subdivision (a) for that taxable year and all prior taxable years attributable to qualified wages paid or incurred with respect to that qualified disadvantaged individual.

(B) If the seasonal employment of any qualified disadvantaged individual, with respect to whom qualified wages are taken into account under subdivision (a) is not continued by the qualified taxpayer for a period of 270 days of employment during the 60–month period beginning with the day the qualified disadvantaged individual commences seasonal employment with the qualified taxpayer, the tax imposed by this part, for the taxable year that includes the 60th month following the month in which the qualified disadvantaged individual commences seasonal employment with the qualified taxpayer, shall be increased by an amount equal to the credit allowed under subdivision (a) for that taxable year and all prior taxable years attributable to qualified wages paid or incurred with respect to that qualified disadvantaged individual.

(2)(A) Subparagraph (A) of paragraph (1) does not apply to any of the following:

(i) A termination of employment of a qualified disadvantaged individual who voluntarily leaves the employment of the qualified taxpayer.

(ii) A termination of employment of a qualified disadvantaged individual who, before the close of the period referred to in subparagraph (A) of paragraph (1), becomes disabled to perform the services of that employment, unless that disability is removed before the close of that period and the taxpayer fails to offer reemployment to that individual.

(iii) A termination of employment of a qualified disadvantaged individual, if it is determined that the termination was due to the misconduct (as defined in Sections 1256–30 to 1256–43, inclusive, of Title 22 of the California Code of Regulations) of that individual.

(iv) A termination of employment of a qualified disadvantaged individual due to a substantial reduction in the trade or business operations of the qualified taxpayer.

(v) A termination of employment of a qualified disadvantaged individual, if that individual is replaced by other qualified disadvantaged individuals so as to create a net increase in both the number of employees and the hours of employment.

(B) Subparagraph (B) of paragraph (1) shall not apply to any of the following:

(i) A failure to continue the seasonal employment of a qualified disadvantaged individual who voluntarily fails to return to the seasonal employment of the qualified taxpayer.

(ii) A failure to continue the seasonal employment of a qualified disadvantaged individual who, before the close of the period referred to in subparagraph (B) of paragraph (1), becomes disabled and unable to perform the services of that seasonal employment, unless that disability is removed before the close of that period and the qualified taxpayer fails to offer seasonal employment to that qualified disadvantaged individual.

(iii) A failure to continue the seasonal employment of a qualified disadvantaged individual, if it is determined that the failure to continue the seasonal employment was due to the misconduct (as defined in Sections 1256–30 to 1256–43, inclusive, of Title 22 of the California Code of Regulations) of that qualified disadvantaged individual.

(iv) A failure to continue seasonal employment of a qualified disadvantaged individual due to a substantial reduction in the regular seasonal trade or business operations of the qualified taxpayer.

(v) A failure to continue the seasonal employment of a qualified disadvantaged individual, if that qualified disadvantaged individual is replaced by other qualified disadvantaged individuals so as to create a net increase in both the number of seasonal employees and the hours of seasonal employment.

(C) For purposes of paragraph (1), the employment relationship between the qualified taxpayer and a qualified disadvantaged individual shall not be treated as terminated by reason of a mere change in the form of conducting the trade or business of the qualified taxpayer, if the qualified disadvantaged individual continues to be employed in that trade or business and the qualified taxpayer retains a substantial interest in that trade or business.

(3) Any increase in tax under paragraph (1) shall not be treated as tax imposed by this part for purposes of determining the amount of any credit allowable under this part.

(e) In the case of an estate or trust, both of the following apply:

(1) The qualified wages for any taxable year shall be apportioned between the estate or trust and the beneficiaries on the basis of the income of the estate or trust allocable to each.

(2) Any beneficiary to whom any qualified wages have been apportioned under paragraph (1) shall be treated (for purposes of this part) as the employer with respect to those wages.

(f) The credit shall be reduced by the credit allowed under Section 17053. 7. The credit shall also be reduced by the federal credit allowed under Section 51 of the Internal Revenue Code.

In addition, any deduction otherwise allowed under this part for the wages or salaries paid or incurred by the qualified taxpayer upon which the credit is based shall be reduced by the amount of the credit, prior to any reduction required by subdivision (g) or (h).

(g) In the case where the credit otherwise allowed under this section exceeds the "net tax" for the taxable year, that portion of the credit that exceeds the "net tax" may be carried over and added to the credit, if any, in succeeding years, until the credit is exhausted. The credit shall be applied first to the earliest taxable years possible.

(h)(1) The amount of credit otherwise allowed under this section, including prior year credit carryovers, that may reduce the "net tax" for the taxable year shall not exceed the amount of tax that would be imposed on the qualified taxpayer's business income attributed to a manufacturing enhancement area determined as if that attributed income represented all of the net income of the qualified taxpayer subject to tax under this part.

(2) Attributable income shall be that portion of the taxpayer's California source business income that is apportioned to the manufacturing enhancement area. For that purpose, the taxpayer's business income that is attributable to sources in this state first shall be determined in accordance with Chapter 17 (commencing with Section 25101) of Part 11. That business income shall be further apportioned to the manufacturing enhancement area in accordance with Article 2 (commencing with Section 25120) of Chapter 17 of Part 11, modified for purposes of this section in accordance with paragraph (3).

(3) Income shall be apportioned to a manufacturing enhancement area by multiplying the total California business income of the taxpayer by a fraction, the numerator of which is the property factor plus the payroll factor, and the denominator of which is two. For purposes of this paragraph:

(A) The property factor is a fraction, the numerator of which is the average value of the taxpayer's real and tangible personal property owned or rented and used in the manufacturing enhancement area during the taxable year, and the denominator of which is the average value of all the taxpayer's real and tangible personal property owned or rented and used in this state during the taxable year.

(B) The payroll factor is a fraction, the numerator of which is the total amount paid by the taxpayer in the manufacturing enhancement area during the taxable year for compensation, and the denominator of which is the total compensation paid by the taxpayer in this state during the taxable year.

(4) The portion of any credit remaining, if any, after application of this subdivision, shall be carried over to succeeding taxable years, as if it were an amount exceeding the "net tax" for the taxable year, as provided in subdivision (g).

(i) If the taxpayer is allowed a credit pursuant to this section for qualified wages paid or incurred, only one credit shall be allowed to the taxpayer under this part with respect to any wage consisting in whole or in part of those qualified wages.

(j) The qualified taxpayer shall do both of the following:

(1) Obtain from the Employment Development Department, as permitted by federal law, the local county or city Job Training Partnership Act administrative entity, the local county GAIN office or social services agency, or the local government administering the manufacturing enhancement area, a certification that provides that a qualified disadvantaged individual meets the eligibility requirements specified in paragraph (5) of subdivision (b). The Employment Development Department may provide preliminary screening and referral to a certifying agency. The Department of Housing and Community Development shall develop regulations governing the issuance of certificates pursuant to subdivision (d) of Section 7086 of the Government Code and shall develop forms for this purpose.

(2) Retain a copy of the certification and provide it upon request to the Franchise Tax Board. *(Added by Stats.1997, c. 609 (S.B.200), § 2. Amended by Stats.1998, c. 7 (S.B.519), § 1.5, eff. March 14, 1998; Stats.1998, c. 323 (A.B.2798), § 15, eff. Aug. 20, 1998, operative Aug. 20, 1998; Stats.1998, c. 1039 (A.B.2809), § 3.5, eff. Sept. 30, 1998, operative Sept. 30, 1998; Stats.1999, c. 58 (S.B.113), § 1; Stats.2000, c. 864 (A.B.2895), § 2; Stats.2000, c. 865 (S.B.1445), § 2; Stats.2006, c. 634 (S.B.763), § 8.)*

§ 17053.74. Credit against net tax; taxpayers employing qualified employees in enterprise zones

(a) There shall be allowed a credit against the "net tax" (as defined in Section 17039) to a taxpayer who employs a qualified employee in an enterprise zone during the taxable year. The credit shall be equal to the sum of each of the following:

(1) Fifty percent of qualified wages in the first year of employment.

(2) Forty percent of qualified wages in the second year of employment.

841

(3) Thirty percent of qualified wages in the third year of employment.

(4) Twenty percent of qualified wages in the fourth year of employment.

(5) Ten percent of qualified wages in the fifth year of employment.

(b) For purposes of this section:

(1) "Qualified wages" means:

(A)(i) Except as provided in clause (ii), that portion of wages paid or incurred by the taxpayer during the taxable year to qualified employees that does not exceed 150 percent of the minimum wage.

(ii) For up to 1,350 qualified employees who are employed by the taxpayer in the Long Beach Enterprise Zone in aircraft manufacturing activities described in Codes 3721 to 3728, inclusive, and Code 3812 of the Standard Industrial Classification (SIC) Manual published by the United States Office of Management and Budget, 1987 edition, "qualified wages" means that portion of hourly wages that does not exceed 202 percent of the minimum wage.

(B) Wages received during the 60–month period beginning with the first day the employee commences employment with the taxpayer. Reemployment in connection with any increase, including a regularly occurring seasonal increase, in the trade or business operations of the taxpayer does not constitute commencement of employment for purposes of this section.

(C) Qualified wages do not include any wages paid or incurred by the taxpayer on or after the zone expiration date. However, wages paid or incurred with respect to qualified employees who are employed by the taxpayer within the enterprise zone within the 60–month period prior to the zone expiration date shall continue to qualify for the credit under this section after the zone expiration date, in accordance with all provisions of this section applied as if the enterprise zone designation were still in existence and binding.

(2) "Minimum wage" means the wage established by the Industrial Welfare Commission as provided for in Chapter 1 (commencing with Section 1171) of Part 4 of Division 2 of the Labor Code.

(3) "Zone expiration date" means the date the enterprise zone designation expires, is no longer binding, or becomes inoperative.

(4)(A) "Qualified employee" means an individual who meets all of the following requirements:

(i) At least 90 percent of whose services for the taxpayer during the taxable year are directly related to the conduct of the taxpayer's trade or business located in an enterprise zone.

(ii) Performs at least 50 percent of his or her services for the taxpayer during the taxable year in an enterprise zone.

(iii) Is hired by the taxpayer after the date of original designation of the area in which services were performed as an enterprise zone.

(iv) Is any of the following:

(I) Immediately preceding the qualified employee's commencement of employment with the taxpayer, was a person eligible for services under the federal Job Training Partnership Act (29 U.S.C. Sec. 1501 et seq.), or its successor, who is receiving, or is eligible to receive, subsidized employment, training, or services funded by the federal Job Training Partnership Act, or its successor.

(II) Immediately preceding the qualified employee's commencement of employment with the taxpayer, was a person eligible to be a voluntary or mandatory registrant under the Greater Avenues for Independence Act of 1985 (GAIN) provided for pursuant to Article 3.2 (commencing with Section 11320) of Chapter 2 of Part 3 of Division 9 of the Welfare and Institutions Code, or its successor.

(III) Immediately preceding the qualified employee's commencement of employment with the taxpayer, was an economically disadvantaged individual 14 years of age or older.

(IV) Immediately preceding the qualified employee's commencement of employment with the taxpayer, was a dislocated worker who meets any of the following:

(aa) Has been terminated or laid off or who has received a notice of termination or layoff from employment, is eligible for or has exhausted entitlement to unemployment insurance benefits, and is unlikely to return to his or her previous industry or occupation.

(bb) Has been terminated or has received a notice of termination of employment as a result of any permanent closure or any substantial layoff at a plant, facility, or enterprise, including an individual who has not received written notification but whose employer has made a public announcement of the closure or layoff.

(cc) Is long-term unemployed and has limited opportunities for employment or reemployment in the same or a similar occupation in the area in which the individual resides, including an individual 55 years of age or older who may have substantial barriers to employment by reason of age.

(dd) Was self-employed (including farmers and ranchers) and is unemployed as a result of general economic conditions in the community in which he or she resides or because of natural disasters.

(ee) Was a civilian employee of the Department of Defense employed at a military installation being closed or realigned under the Defense Base Closure and Realignment Act of 1990.

(ff) Was an active member of the armed forces or National Guard as of September 30, 1990, and was either involuntarily separated or separated pursuant to a special benefits program.

(gg) Is a seasonal or migrant worker who experiences chronic seasonal unemployment and underemployment in the agriculture industry, aggravated by continual advancements in technology and mechanization.

(hh) Has been terminated or laid off, or has received a notice of termination or layoff, as a consequence of compliance with the Clean Air Act.

(V) Immediately preceding the qualified employee's commencement of employment with the taxpayer, was a disabled individual who is eligible for or enrolled in, or has completed a state rehabilitation plan or is a service-connected disabled veteran, veteran of the Vietnam era, or veteran who is recently separated from military service.

(VI) Immediately preceding the qualified employee's commencement of employment with the taxpayer, was an ex-offender. An individual shall be treated as convicted if he or she was placed on probation by a state court without a finding of guilt.

(VII) Immediately preceding the qualified employee's commencement of employment with the taxpayer, was a person eligible for or a recipient of any of the following:

(aa) Federal Supplemental Security Income benefits.

(bb) Aid to Families with Dependent Children.

(cc) Food stamps.

(dd) State and local general assistance.

(VIII) Immediately preceding the qualified employee's commencement of employment with the taxpayer, was a member of a federally recognized Indian tribe, band, or other group of Native American descent.

(IX) Immediately preceding the qualified employee's commencement of employment with the taxpayer, was a resident of a targeted employment area, as defined in Section 7072 of the Government Code.

(X) An employee who qualified the taxpayer for the enterprise zone hiring credit under former Section 17053.8 or the program area hiring credit under former Section 17053.11.

(XI) Immediately preceding the qualified employee's commencement of employment with the taxpayer, was a member of a targeted group, as defined in Section 51(d) of the Internal Revenue Code, [1] or its successor.

(B) Priority for employment shall be provided to an individual who is enrolled in a qualified program under the federal Job Training Partnership Act or the Greater Avenues for Independence Act of 1985 or who is eligible as a member of a targeted group under the Work Opportunity Tax Credit (Section 51 of the Internal Revenue Code), or its successor.

(5) "Taxpayer" means a person or entity engaged in a trade or business within an enterprise zone designated pursuant to Chapter 12.8 (commencing with Section 7070) of the Government Code.

(6) "Seasonal employment" means employment by a taxpayer that has regular and predictable substantial reductions in trade or business operations.

(c) The taxpayer shall do both of the following:

(1) Obtain from the Employment Development Department, as permitted by federal law, the local county or city Job Training Partnership Act administrative entity, the local county GAIN office or social services agency, or the local government administering the enterprise zone, a certification which provides that a qualified employee meets the eligibility requirements specified in clause (iv) of subparagraph (A) of paragraph (4) of subdivision (b). The Employment Development Department may provide preliminary screening and referral to a certifying agency. The Employment Development Department shall develop a form for this purpose. The Department of Housing and Community Development shall develop regulations governing the issuance of certificates by local governments pursuant to subdivision (a) of Section 7086 of the Government Code.

(2) Retain a copy of the certification and provide it upon request to the Franchise Tax Board.

(d)(1) For purposes of this section:

(A) All employees of trades or businesses, which are not incorporated, that are under common control shall be treated as employed by a single taxpayer.

(B) The credit, if any, allowable by this section with respect to each trade or business shall be determined by reference to its proportionate share of the expense of the qualified wages giving rise to the credit, and shall be allocated in that manner.

(C) Principles that apply in the case of controlled groups of corporations, as specified in subdivision (d) of Section 23622.7, shall apply with respect to determining employment.

(2) If an employer acquires the major portion of a trade or business of another employer (hereinafter in this paragraph referred to as the "predecessor") or the major portion of a separate unit of a trade or business of a predecessor, then, for purposes of applying this section (other than subdivision (e)) for any calendar year ending after that acquisition, the employment relationship between a qualified employee and an employer shall not be treated as terminated if the employee continues to be employed in that trade or business.

(e)(1)(A) If the employment, other than seasonal employment, of any qualified employee, with respect to whom qualified wages are taken into account under subdivision (a) is terminated by the taxpayer at any time during the first 270 days of that employment (whether or not consecutive) or before the close of the 270th calendar day after the day in which that employee completes 90 days of employment with the taxpayer, the tax imposed by this part for the taxable year in which that employment is terminated shall be increased by an amount equal to the credit allowed under subdivision (a) for that taxable year and all prior taxable years attributable to qualified wages paid or incurred with respect to that employee.

(B) If the seasonal employment of any qualified employee, with respect to whom qualified wages are taken

843

into account under subdivision (a) is not continued by the taxpayer for a period of 270 days of employment during the 60–month period beginning with the day the qualified employee commences seasonal employment with the taxpayer, the tax imposed by this part, for the taxable year that includes the 60th month following the month in which the qualified employee commences seasonal employment with the taxpayer, shall be increased by an amount equal to the credit allowed under subdivision (a) for that taxable year and all prior taxable years attributable to qualified wages paid or incurred with respect to that qualified employee.

(2)(A) Subparagraph (A) of paragraph (1) shall not apply to any of the following:

(i) A termination of employment of a qualified employee who voluntarily leaves the employment of the taxpayer.

(ii) A termination of employment of a qualified employee who, before the close of the period referred to in paragraph (1), becomes disabled and unable to perform the services of that employment, unless that disability is removed before the close of that period and the taxpayer fails to offer reemployment to that employee.

(iii) A termination of employment of a qualified employee, if it is determined that the termination was due to the misconduct (as defined in Sections 1256–30 to 1256–43, inclusive, of Title 22 of the California Code of Regulations) of that employee.

(iv) A termination of employment of a qualified employee due to a substantial reduction in the trade or business operations of the taxpayer.

(v) A termination of employment of a qualified employee, if that employee is replaced by other qualified employees so as to create a net increase in both the number of employees and the hours of employment.

(B) Subparagraph (B) of paragraph (1) shall not apply to any of the following:

(i) A failure to continue the seasonal employment of a qualified employee who voluntarily fails to return to the seasonal employment of the taxpayer.

(ii) A failure to continue the seasonal employment of a qualified employee who, before the close of the period referred to in subparagraph (B) of paragraph (1), becomes disabled and unable to perform the services of that seasonal employment, unless that disability is removed before the close of that period and the taxpayer fails to offer seasonal employment to that qualified employee.

(iii) A failure to continue the seasonal employment of a qualified employee, if it is determined that the failure to continue the seasonal employment was due to the misconduct (as defined in Sections 1256–30 to 1256–43, inclusive, of Title 22 of the California Code of Regulations) of that qualified employee.

(iv) A failure to continue seasonal employment of a qualified employee due to a substantial reduction in the regular seasonal trade or business operations of the taxpayer.

(v) A failure to continue the seasonal employment of a qualified employee, if that qualified employee is replaced by other qualified employees so as to create a net increase in both the number of seasonal employees and the hours of seasonal employment.

(C) For purposes of paragraph (1), the employment relationship between the taxpayer and a qualified employee shall not be treated as terminated by reason of a mere change in the form of conducting the trade or business of the taxpayer, if the qualified employee continues to be employed in that trade or business and the taxpayer retains a substantial interest in that trade or business.

(3) Any increase in tax under paragraph (1) shall not be treated as tax imposed by this part for purposes of determining the amount of any credit allowable under this part.

(f) In the case of an estate or trust, both of the following apply:

(1) The qualified wages for any taxable year shall be apportioned between the estate or trust and the beneficiaries on the basis of the income of the estate or trust allocable to each.

(2) Any beneficiary to whom any qualified wages have been apportioned under paragraph (1) shall be treated, for purposes of this part, as the employer with respect to those wages.

(g) For purposes of this section, "enterprise zone" means an area designated as an enterprise zone pursuant to Chapter 12.8 (commencing with Section 7070) of Division 7 of Title 1 of the Government Code.

(h) The credit allowable under this section shall be reduced by the credit allowed under Sections 17053.10, 17053.17 and 17053.46 claimed for the same employee. The credit shall also be reduced by the federal credit allowed under Section 51 of the Internal Revenue Code.

In addition, any deduction otherwise allowed under this part for the wages or salaries paid or incurred by the taxpayer upon which the credit is based shall be reduced by the amount of the credit, prior to any reduction required by subdivision (i) or (j).

(i) In the case where the credit otherwise allowed under this section exceeds the "net tax" for the taxable year, that portion of the credit that exceeds the "net tax" may be carried over and added to the credit, if any, in succeeding taxable years, until the credit is exhausted. The credit shall be applied first to the earliest taxable years possible.

(j)(1) The amount of the credit otherwise allowed under this section and Section 17053.70, including any credit carryover from prior years, that may reduce the "net tax" for the taxable year shall not exceed the amount of tax which would be imposed on the taxpayer's business income attributable to the enterprise zone determined as if that attributable income represented all of the income of the taxpayer subject to tax under this part.

(2) Attributable income shall be that portion of the taxpayer's California source business income that is apportioned to the enterprise zone. For that purpose, the taxpayer's business income attributable to sources in this state first shall be determined in accordance with Chapter 17 (commencing with Section 25101) of Part 11. That business income shall be further apportioned to the enterprise zone in accordance with Article 2 (commencing with Section 25120) of Chapter 17 of Part 11, modified for purposes of this section in accordance with paragraph (3).

(3) Business income shall be apportioned to the enterprise zone by multiplying the total California business income of the taxpayer by a fraction, the numerator of which is the property factor plus the payroll factor, and the denominator of which is two. For purposes of this paragraph:

(A) The property factor is a fraction, the numerator of which is the average value of the taxpayer's real and tangible personal property owned or rented and used in the enterprise zone during the taxable year, and the denominator of which is the average value of all the taxpayer's real and tangible personal property owned or rented and used in this state during the taxable year.

(B) The payroll factor is a fraction, the numerator of which is the total amount paid by the taxpayer in the enterprise zone during the taxable year for compensation, and the denominator of which is the total compensation paid by the taxpayer in this state during the taxable year.

(4) The portion of any credit remaining, if any, after application of this subdivision, shall be carried over to succeeding taxable years, as if it were an amount exceeding the "net tax" for the taxable year, as provided in subdivision (i).

(k) The changes made to this section by the act adding this subdivision [2] shall apply to taxable years beginning on or after January 1, 1997. *(Added by Stats.1996, c. 955 (S.B.2023), § 10. Amended by Stats.1997, c. 603 (S.B. 965), § 5, eff. Oct. 3, 1997; Stats.1997, c. 609 (S.B.200), § 5.5; Stats.1998, c. 323 (A.B.2798), § 18, eff. Aug. 20, 1998, operative Aug. 20, 1998; Stats.1998, c. 1039 (A.B. 2809), § 4.5, eff. Sept. 30, 1998, operative Sept. 30, 1998; Stats.2004, c. 225 (S.B.1097), § 66, eff. Aug. 16, 2004.)*

[1] See 26 U.S.C.A. § 51.

[2] Stats.1997, c. 609 (S.B.200).

Operative Effect

Under the terms of § 23 of Stats.1998, c. 1039 (A.B.2809), eff. Sept. 30, 1998, the amendment of this section by Stats.1998, c. 1039 is operative for taxable and income years beginning on or after January 1, 1998. Section 23 also provides that the amendment made by c. 1039 to paragraph (1) of subdivision (b) of this section is consistent with the intent of the act that enacted this section and shall apply from the original effective date of that act. Further, § 23 provides that its provisions shall be construed to include changes made by other acts of the Legislature that are incorporated as provided in §§ 21 or 22 of c. 1039.

§ 17053.75. Credit against net tax; percentage of qualified wages received by taxpayer

(a) There shall be allowed as a credit against the "net tax" (as defined by Section 17039) for the taxable year an amount equal to five percent of the qualified wages received by the taxpayer during the taxable year.

(b) For purposes of this section:

(1) "Qualified employee" means a taxpayer who meets both of the following:

(A) Is described in clauses (i) and (ii) of subparagraph (A) of paragraph (4) of subdivision (b) of Section 17053.74.

(B) Is not an employee of the federal government or of this state or of any political subdivision of this state.

(2)(A) "Qualified wages" means "wages," as defined in subsection (b) of Section 3306 of the Internal Revenue Code, [1] attributable to services performed for an employer with respect to whom the taxpayer is a qualified employee in an amount that does not exceed one and one-half times the dollar limitation specified in that subsection.

(B) "Qualified wages" does not include any compensation received from the federal government or this state or any political subdivision of this state.

(C) "Qualified wages" does not include any wages received on or after the date the enterprise zone designation expires, is no longer binding, or becomes inoperative.

(3) "Enterprise zone" means any area designated as an enterprise zone pursuant to Chapter 12.8 (commencing with Section 7070) of Division 7 of Title 1 of the Government Code.

(c) For each dollar of income received by the taxpayer in excess of qualified wages, as defined in this section, the credit shall be reduced by nine cents ($0.09).

(d) The amount of the credit allowed by this section in any taxable year shall not exceed the amount of tax that would be imposed on the taxpayer's income attributable to employment within the enterprise zone as if that income represented all of the income of the taxpayer subject to tax under this part. *(Added by Stats.1996, c. 955 (S.B.2023), § 11. Amended by Stats.1997, c. 603 (S.B.965), § 7, eff. Oct. 3, 1997; Stats.1997, c. 609 (S.B.200), § 7.5.)*

[1] Internal Revenue Code sections are in Title 26 of U.S.C.A.

§ 17061. Unemployment insurance credit or refund

(a) In the case of a person entitled to a refund pursuant to Section 1176 of the Unemployment Insurance Code, there shall be a credit against the tax imposed under this part in the amount of such refund. If the tax due after deduction of any other credit under this part is less than the credit allowable pursuant to this section, the difference shall be a tax refund.

(b) If the Franchise Tax Board disallows the refund or credit provided for by this section, the Franchise Tax Board shall notify the claimant accordingly. The Franchise Tax Board's action upon the credit or refund is final unless the claimant files a protest with the Director of Employment Development pursuant to Section 1176.5 of the Unemployment Insurance Code. None of the remedies provided by this part shall be available to such claimant. *(Added by Stats.1970, c. 1356, p. 2520, § 1. Amended by Stats.1971, Ex.Sess., c. 1, p. 4900, § 15, eff. Dec. 8, 1971; Stats.1973, c. 1206, p. 2616, § 39; Stats. 1973, c. 1207, p. 2666, § 39; Stats.1973, c. 1212, p. 2756, § 68, operative July 1, 1974; Stats.1977, c. 1252, p. 4447, § 372, operative July 1, 1978.)*

CHAPTER 3. COMPUTATION OF TAXABLE INCOME

ARTICLE 6. DEDUCTIONS

Section
17276.   Net operating loss.
17276.1.   Net operating loss deductions by qualified taxpayers; carryovers.
17276.2.   Taxpayer engaged in conduct of a trade or business within a designated enterprise zone; net operating loss deduction.
17276.3.   Net operating loss deduction; taxable years 2002 and 2003; extension of carryover period.
17276.4.   Persons or entities engaged in the conduct of trade or business within the Los Angeles Revitalization Zone; net operating losses.
17276.5.   Taxpayers engaged in conduct of a trade or business within a LAMBRA; net operating loss.
17276.6.   Taxpayers engaged in a trade or business within targeted tax areas or specified lines of business; net operating loss deduction.

§ 17276. Net operating loss

Except as provided in Sections 17276.1, 17276.2, 17276.4, 17276.5, 17276.6, and 17276.7, the deduction provided by Section 172 of the Internal Revenue Code, [1] relating to a net operating loss deduction, shall be modified as follows:

(a)(1) Net operating losses attributable to taxable years beginning before January 1, 1987, shall not be allowed.

(2) A net operating loss shall not be carried forward to any taxable year beginning before January 1, 1987.

(b)(1) Except as provided in paragraphs (2) and (3), the provisions of Section 172(b)(2) of the Internal Revenue Code, relating to the amount of carryovers, shall be modified so that the applicable percentage of the entire amount of the net operating loss for any taxable year shall be eligible for carryover to any subsequent taxable year. For purposes of this subdivision, the applicable percentage shall be:

(A) Fifty–percent for any taxable year beginning before January 1, 2000.

(B) Fifty–five percent for any taxable year beginning on or after January 1, 2000, and before January 1, 2002.

(C) Sixty percent for any taxable year beginning on or after January 1, 2002, and before January 1, 2004.

(D) One hundred percent for any taxable year beginning on or after January 1, 2004.

(2) In the case of a taxpayer who has a net operating loss in any taxable year beginning on or after January 1, 1994, and who operates a new business during that taxable year, each of the following shall apply to each loss incurred during the first three taxable years of operating the new business:

(A) If the net operating loss is equal to or less than the net loss from the new business, 100 percent of the net operating loss shall be carried forward as provided in subdivision (d).

(B) If the net operating loss is greater than the net loss from the new business, the net operating loss shall be carried over as follows:

(i) With respect to an amount equal to the net loss from the new business, 100 percent of that amount shall be carried forward as provided in subdivision (d).

(ii) With respect to the portion of the net operating loss that exceeds the net loss from the new business, the applicable percentage of that amount shall be carried forward as provided in subdivision (d).

(C) For purposes of Section 172(b)(2) of the Internal Revenue Code, the amount described in clause (ii) of subparagraph (B) shall be absorbed before the amount described in clause (i) of subparagraph (B).

(3) In the case of a taxpayer who has a net operating loss in any taxable year beginning on or after January 1, 1994, and who operates an eligible small business during that taxable year, each of the following shall apply:

(A) If the net operating loss is equal to or less than the net loss from the eligible small business, 100 percent of the net operating loss shall be carried forward to the taxable years specified in subdivision (d).

(B) If the net operating loss is greater than the net loss from the eligible small business, the net operating loss shall be carried over as follows:

(i) With respect to an amount equal to the net loss from the eligible small business, 100 percent of that amount shall be carried forward as provided in subdivision (d).

(ii) With respect to that portion of the net operating loss that exceeds the net loss from the eligible small business, the applicable percentage of that amount shall be carried forward as provided in subdivision (d).

(C) For purposes of Section 172(b)(2) of the Internal Revenue Code, the amount described in clause (ii) of subparagraph (B) shall be absorbed before the amount described in clause (i) of subparagraph (B).

(4) In the case of a taxpayer who has a net operating loss in a taxable year beginning on or after January 1, 1994, and who operates a business that qualifies as both a new business and an eligible small business under this section, that business shall be treated as a new business for the first three taxable years of the new business.

(5) In the case of a taxpayer who has a net operating loss in a taxable year beginning on or after January 1, 1994, and who operates more than one business, and more than one of those businesses qualifies as either a new business or an eligible small business under this section, paragraph (2) shall be applied first, except that if there is any remaining portion of the net operating loss after application of clause (i) of subparagraph (B) of that paragraph, paragraph (3) shall be applied to the remaining portion of the net operating loss as though that remaining portion of the net operating loss constituted the entire net operating loss.

(6) For purposes of this section, the term "net loss" means the amount of net loss after application of Sections 465 and 469 of the Internal Revenue Code.

(c) Section 172(b)(1) of the Internal Revenue Code, relating to net operating loss carrybacks and carryovers and the years to which the loss may be carried, is modified as follows:

(1) Net operating loss carrybacks shall not be allowed for any net operating losses attributable to taxable years beginning before January 1, 2011.

(2) A net operating loss attributable to taxable years beginning on or after January 1, 2011, shall be a net operating loss carryback to each of the two taxable years preceding the taxable year of the loss in lieu of the number of years provided therein.

(A) For a net operating loss attributable to a taxable year beginning on or after January 1, 2011, and before January 1, 2012, the amount of carryback to any taxable year shall not exceed 50 percent of the net operating loss.

(B) For a net operating loss attributable to a taxable year beginning on or after January 1, 2012, and before January 1, 2013, the amount of carryback to any taxable year shall not exceed 75 percent of the net operating loss.

(C) For a net operating loss attributable to a taxable year beginning on or after January 1, 2013, the amount of carryback to any taxable year shall not exceed 100 percent of the net operating loss.

(3) Notwithstanding paragraph (2), Section 172(b)(1)(B) of the Internal Revenue Code, relating to special rules for REITs, and Sections 172(b)(1)(E) and 172(h) of the Internal Revenue Code, relating to corporate equity reduction interest loss, shall apply as provided.

(4) A net operating loss carryback shall not be carried back to any taxable year beginning before January 1, 2009.

(d)(1)(A) For a net operating loss for any taxable year beginning on or after January 1, 1987, and before January 1, 2000, Section 172(b)(1)(A)(ii) of the Internal Revenue Code, relating to years to which net operating losses may be carried, is modified to substitute "five taxable years" in lieu of "20 taxable years" except as otherwise provided in paragraphs (2) and (3).

(B) For a net operating loss for any taxable year beginning on or after January 1, 2000, and before January 1, 2008, Section 172(b)(1)(A)(ii) of the Internal Revenue Code, relating to years to which net operating losses may be carried, is modified to substitute "10 taxable years" in lieu of "20 taxable years."

(2) For any taxable year beginning before January 1, 2000, in the case of a "new business," the "five taxable years" in paragraph (1) shall be modified to read as follows:

(A) "Eight taxable years" for a net operating loss attributable to the first taxable year of that new business.

(B) "Seven taxable years" for a net operating loss attributable to the second taxable year of that new business.

(C) "Six taxable years" for a net operating loss attributable to the third taxable year of that new business.

(3) For any carryover of a net operating loss for which a deduction is denied by Section 17276.3, the carryover period specified in this subdivision shall be extended as follows:

(A) By one year for a net operating loss attributable to taxable years beginning in 1991.

(B) By two years for a net operating loss attributable to taxable years beginning prior to January 1, 1991.

(4) The net operating loss attributable to taxable years beginning on or after January 1, 1987, and before January 1, 1994, shall be a net operating loss carryover to each of the 10 taxable years following the year of the loss if it is incurred by a taxpayer that is under the jurisdiction of the court in a Title 11 or similar case at any time during the income year. The loss carryover provided in the preceding sentence shall not apply to any loss incurred after the date the taxpayer is no longer under the jurisdiction of the court in a Title 11 or similar case.

(e) For purposes of this section:

(1) "Eligible small business" means any trade or business that has gross receipts, less returns and allowances, of less than one million dollars ($1,000,000) during the taxable year.

(2) Except as provided in subdivision (f), "new business" means any trade or business activity that is first commenced in this state on or after January 1, 1994.

(3) "Title 11 or similar case" shall have the same meaning as in Section 368(a)(3) of the Internal Revenue Code.

(4) In the case of any trade or business activity conducted by a partnership or "S" corporation paragraphs (1) and (2) shall be applied to the partnership or "S" corporation.

(f) For purposes of this section, in determining whether a trade or business activity qualifies as a new business under paragraph (2) of subdivision (e), the following rules shall apply:

(1) In any case where a taxpayer purchases or otherwise acquires all or any portion of the assets of an existing trade or business (irrespective of the form of entity) that is doing business in this state (within the meaning of Section 23101), the trade or business thereafter conducted by the taxpayer (or any related person) shall not be treated as a new business if the aggregate fair market value of the acquired assets (including real, personal, tangible, and intangible property) used by the taxpayer (or any related person) in the conduct of its trade or business exceeds 20 percent of the aggregate fair market value of the total assets of the trade or business being conducted by the taxpayer (or any related person). For purposes of this paragraph only, the following rules shall apply:

(A) The determination of the relative fair market values of the acquired assets and the total assets shall be made as of the last day of the first taxable year in which the taxpayer (or any related person) first uses any of the acquired trade or business assets in its business activity.

(B) Any acquired assets that constituted property described in Section 1221(1) of the Internal Revenue Code in the hands of the transferor shall not be treated as assets acquired from an existing trade or business, unless those assets also constitute property described in Section 1221(1) of the Internal Revenue Code in the hands of the acquiring taxpayer (or related person).

(2) In any case where a taxpayer (or any related person) is engaged in one or more trade or business activities in this state, or has been engaged in one or more trade or business activities in this state within the preceding 36 months ("prior trade or business activity"), and thereafter commences an additional trade or business activity in this state, the additional trade or business activity shall only be treated as a new business if the additional trade or business activity is classified under a different division of the Standard Industrial Classification (SIC) Manual published by the United States Office of Management and Budget, 1987 edition, than are any of the taxpayer's (or any related person's) current or prior trade or business activities.

(3) In any case where a taxpayer, including all related persons, is engaged in trade or business activities wholly outside of this state and the taxpayer first commences doing business in this state (within the meaning of Section 23101) after December 31, 1993 (other than by purchase or other acquisition described in paragraph (1)), the trade or business activity shall be treated as a new business under paragraph (2) of subdivision (e).

(4) In any case where the legal form under which a trade or business activity is being conducted is changed, the change in form shall be disregarded and the determination of whether the trade or business activity is a new business shall be made by treating the taxpayer as having

848

purchased or otherwise acquired all or any portion of the assets of an existing trade or business under the rules of paragraph (1) of this subdivision.

(5) "Related person" shall mean any person that is related to the taxpayer under either Section 267 or 318 of the Internal Revenue Code.

(6) "Acquire" shall include any gift, inheritance, transfer incident to divorce, or any other transfer, whether or not for consideration.

(7)(A) For taxable years beginning on or after January 1, 1997, the term "new business" shall include any taxpayer that is engaged in biopharmaceutical activities or other biotechnology activities that are described in Codes 2833 to 2836, inclusive, of the Standard Industrial Classification (SIC) Manual published by the United States Office of Management and Budget, 1987 edition, and as further amended, and that has not received regulatory approval for any product from the United States Food and Drug Administration.

(B) For purposes of this paragraph:

(i) "Biopharmaceutical activities" means those activities that use organisms or materials derived from organisms, and their cellular, subcellular, or molecular components, in order to provide pharmaceutical products for human or animal therapeutics and diagnostics. Biopharmaceutical activities make use of living organisms to make commercial products, as opposed to pharmaceutical activities that make use of chemical compounds to produce commercial products.

(ii) "Other biotechnology activities" means activities consisting of the application of recombinant DNA technology to produce commercial products, as well as activities regarding pharmaceutical delivery systems designed to provide a measure of control over the rate, duration, and site of pharmaceutical delivery.

(g) In computing the modifications under Section 172(d)(2) of the Internal Revenue Code, relating to capital gains and losses of taxpayers other than corporations, the exclusion provided by Section 18152.5 shall not be allowed.

(h) Notwithstanding any provisions of this section to the contrary, a deduction shall be allowed to a "qualified taxpayer" as provided in Sections 17276.1, 17276.2, 17276.4, 17276.5, 17276.6, and 17276.7.

(i) The Franchise Tax Board may prescribe appropriate regulations to carry out the purposes of this section, including any regulations necessary to prevent the avoidance of the purposes of this section through splitups, shell corporations, partnerships, tiered ownership structures, or otherwise.

(j) The Franchise Tax Board may reclassify any net operating loss carryover determined under either paragraph (2) or (3) of subdivision (b) as a net operating loss carryover under paragraph (1) of subdivision (b) upon a showing that the reclassification is necessary to prevent evasion of the purposes of this section.

(k) Except as otherwise provided, the amendments made by Chapter 107 of the Statutes of 2000 shall apply to net operating losses for taxable years beginning on or after January 1, 2000. *(Added by Stats.1983, c. 488, § 29, eff. July 28, 1983. Amended by Stats.1984, c. 44, § 10, eff. March 20, 1984; Stats.1984, c. 938, § 12.2, eff. Sept. 7, 1984; Stats.1987, c. 1138, § 92, eff. Sept. 25, 1987; Stats.1988, c. 11, § 18, eff. Feb. 19, 1988; Stats.1988, c. 1463, § 9, eff. Sept. 28, 1988; Stats.1989, c. 581, § 2, eff. Sept. 21, 1989; Stats.1989, c. 1352, § 41, eff. Oct. 2, 1989; Stats.1991, c. 117 (S.B.169), § 26, eff. July 16, 1991; Stats.1991, c. 474 (A.B.31), § 9, eff. Oct. 2, 1991; Stats. 1993, c. 880 (A.B.34), § 1, eff. Oct. 6, 1993; Stats.1993, c. 881, (S.B.671), § 9.5, eff. Oct. 6, 1993, operative Jan. 1, 1994; Stats.1994, c. 949 (A.B.2407), § 1, eff. Sept. 28, 1994; Stats.1996, c. 954 (S.B.38), § 19, eff. Sept. 26, 1996; Stats.1998, c. 49 (A.B.510), § 8; Stats.1998, c. 322 (A.B. 2797), § 25, eff. Aug. 20, 1998; Stats.1998, c. 1039 (A.B.2809), § 5, eff. Sept. 30, 1998; Stats.2000, c. 862 (A.B.1843), § 1; Stats.2000, c. 104 (A.B.1774), § 1, eff. July 10, 2000; Stats.2000, c. 107 (A.B.511), § 7, eff. July 10, 2000; Stats.2001, c. 543 (S.B.1185), § 6; Stats.2001, c. 623 (A.B.238), § 1, eff. Oct. 9, 2001; Stats.2002, c. 488 (A.B.2065), § 1.5, eff. Sept. 12, 2002; Stats.2008, c. 763 (A.B.1452), § 3, eff. Sept. 30, 2008.)*

[1] Internal Revenue Code sections are in Title 26 of the U.S.C.A.

§ 17276.1.   Net operating loss deductions by qualified taxpayers; carryovers

(a) A qualified taxpayer, as defined in Section 17276.2, 17276.4, 17276.5, 17276.6, or 17276.7, may elect to take the deduction provided by Section 172 of the Internal Revenue Code, relating to the net operating loss deduction, as modified by Section 17276, with the following exceptions:

(1) Subdivision (a) of Section 17276, relating to years in which allowable losses are sustained, shall not be applicable.

(2) Subdivision (b) of Section 17276, relating to the 50–percent reduction of losses, shall not be applicable.

(b) The election to compute the net operating loss under this section shall be made in a statement attached to the original return, timely filed for the year in which the net operating loss is incurred and shall be irrevocable. In addition to the exceptions specified in subdivision (a), the provisions of Section 17276.2, 17276.4, 17276.5, 17276.6, or 17276.7, as appropriate, shall be applicable.

(c) Any carryover of a net operating loss sustained by a qualified taxpayer, as defined in subdivision (a) or (b) of Section 17276.2 as that section read immediately prior to January 1, 1997, shall, if previously elected, continue to be a deduction, as provided in subdivision (a), applied as if the provisions of subdivision (a) or (b) of Section 17276.2, as that section read prior to January 1, 1997, still applied. *(Added by Stats.1988, c. 32, § 3, eff. March 15, 1988. Amended by Stats.1988, c. 1463, § 10, eff. Sept. 28, 1988; Stats.1989, c. 581, § 3, eff. Sept. 21, 1989; Stats.*

1991, c. 117 (S.B.169), § 27, eff. July 16, 1991; Stats.1996, c. 953 (A.B.296), § 17; Stats.1996, c. 955 (S.B.2023), § 17; Stats.1998, c. 1039 (A.B.2809), § 6, eff. Sept. 30, 1998; Stats.2001, c. 623 (A.B.238), § 2, eff. Oct. 9, 2001.)

§ 17276.2.   Taxpayer engaged in conduct of a trade or business within a designated enterprise zone; net operating loss deduction

(a) The term "qualified taxpayer" as used in Section 17276.1 includes a person or entity engaged in the conduct of a trade or business within an enterprise zone designated pursuant to Chapter 12.8 (commencing with Section 7070) of Division 7 of Title 1 of the Government Code. For purposes of this subdivision, all of the following shall apply:

(1) A net operating loss shall not be a net operating loss carryback to any taxable year and a net operating loss for any taxable year beginning on or after the date that the area in which the taxpayer conducts a trade or business is designated as an enterprise zone shall be a net operating loss carryover to each of the 15 taxable years following the taxable year of loss.

(2) For purposes of this subdivision:

(A) "Net operating loss" means the loss determined under Section 172 of the Internal Revenue Code,[1] as modified by Section 17276.1, attributable to the taxpayer's business activities within the enterprise zone (as defined in Chapter 12.8 (commencing with Section 7070) of Division 7 of Title 1 of the Government Code) prior to the enterprise zone expiration date. That attributable loss shall be determined in accordance with Chapter 17 (commencing with Section 25101) of Part 11, modified for purposes of this subdivision, as follows:

(i) Loss shall be apportioned to the enterprise zone by multiplying total loss from the business by a fraction, the numerator of which is the property factor plus the payroll factor, and the denominator of which is two.

(ii) "The enterprise zone" shall be substituted for "this state."

(B) A net operating loss carryover shall be a deduction only with respect to the taxpayer's business income attributable to the enterprise zone as defined in Chapter 12.8 (commencing with Section 7070) of Division 7 of Title 1 of the Government Code.

(C) Attributable income is that portion of the taxpayer's California source business income that is apportioned to the enterprise zone. For that purpose, the taxpayer's business income attributable to sources in this state first shall be determined in accordance with Chapter 17 (commencing with Section 25101) of Part 11. That business income shall be further apportioned to the enterprise zone in accordance with Article 2 (commencing with Section 25120) of Chapter 17 of Part 11, modified for purposes of this subdivision as follows:

(i) Business income shall be apportioned to the enterprise zone by multiplying the total California business income of the taxpayer by a fraction, the numerator of which is the property factor plus the payroll factor, and the denominator of which is two. For purposes of this clause:

(I) The property factor is a fraction, the numerator of which is the average value of the taxpayer's real and tangible personal property owned or rented and used in the enterprise zone during the taxable year, and the denominator of which is the average value of all the taxpayer's real and tangible personal property owned or rented and used in this state during the taxable year.

(II) The payroll factor is a fraction, the numerator of which is the total amount paid by the taxpayer in the enterprise zone during the taxable year for compensation, and the denominator of which is the total compensation paid by the taxpayer in this state during the taxable year.

(ii) If a loss carryover is allowable pursuant to this section for any taxable year after the enterprise zone designation has expired, the enterprise zone shall be deemed to remain in existence for purposes of computing the limitation set forth in subparagraph (B) and allowing a net operating loss deduction.

(D) "Enterprise zone expiration date" means the date the enterprise zone designation expires, is no longer binding, or becomes inoperative.

(3) The changes made to this subdivision by the act adding this paragraph[2] shall apply to taxable years beginning on or after January 1, 1998.

(b) A taxpayer who qualifies as a "qualified taxpayer" under one or more sections shall, for the taxable year of the net operating loss and any taxable year to which that net operating loss may be carried, designate on the original return filed for each year the section which applies to that taxpayer with respect to that net operating loss. If the taxpayer is eligible to qualify under more than one section, the designation is to be made after taking into account subdivision (c).

(c) If a taxpayer is eligible to qualify under this section and either Section 17276.4, 17276.5, or 17276.6 as a "qualified taxpayer," with respect to a net operating loss in a taxable year, the taxpayer shall designate which section is to apply to the taxpayer.

(d) Notwithstanding Section 17276, the amount of the loss determined under this section or Section 17276.4, 17276.5, or 17276.6 shall be the only net operating loss allowed to be carried over from that taxable year and the designation under subdivision (b) shall be included in the election under Section 17276.1. *(Added by Stats.1988, c. 32, § 4, eff. March 15, 1988. Amended by Stats.1988, c. 1463, § 11, eff. Sept. 28, 1988; Stats.1989, c. 581, § 4, eff. Sept. 21, 1989; Stats.1990, c. 330 (A.B.379), § 5, eff. July 17, 1990; Stats.1991–92, 1st Ex.Sess., c. 17 (A.B.38), § 11, eff. Sept. 21, 1992; Stats.1993, c. 18 (A.B.18), § 8, eff. May 27, 1993; Stats.1993, c. 1216 (A.B.693), § 5, eff. Oct. 11, 1993; Stats.1994, c. 606 (A.B.3121), § 8, eff. Sept. 16, 1994; Stats.1994, c. 756 (A.B.1313), § 5, eff. Sept. 23, 1994; Stats.1995, c. 494 (S.B.712), § 10; Stats.1996, c. 953 (A.B.296), § 17.5; Stats.1996, c. 955 (S.B.2023), § 17.5;*

Stats.1997, c. 602 (A.B.1217), § 6; Stats.1997, c. 604 (S.B.1106), § 6, eff. Oct. 3, 1997; Stats.1998, c. 7 (S.B. 519), § 7, eff. March 14, 1998; Stats.1998, c. 323 (A.B. 2798), § 20, eff. Aug. 20, 1998, operative Aug. 20, 1998; Stats.1998, c. 1039 (A.B.2809), § 7.5, eff. Sept. 30, 1998, operative Sept. 30, 1998.)

[1] See 26 U.S.C.A. § 172.

[2] Stats.1998, c. 1039 (A.B.2809), eff. Sept. 30, 1998.

Application

The amendment of this section by Stats.1998, c. 1039 (A.B.2809), applies to taxable and income years beginning on or after January 1, 1998, under the terms of § 25 of that act.

§ 17276.3. Net operating loss deduction; taxable years 2002 and 2003; extension of carryover period

(a) Notwithstanding Sections 17276, 17276.1, 17276.2, 17276.4, 17276.5, 17276.6, and 17276.7 of this code and Section 172 of the Internal Revenue Code,[1] no net operating loss deduction shall be allowed for any taxable year beginning on or after January 1, 2002, and before January 1, 2004.

(b) For any carryover of a net operating loss for which a deduction is denied by subdivision (a), the carryover period under Section 172 of the Internal Revenue Code shall be extended as follows:

(1) By one year, for losses incurred in taxable years beginning on or after January 1, 2002, and before January 1, 2003.

(2) By two years, for losses incurred in taxable years beginning before January 1, 2002.

(Added by Stats.1991, c. 117 (S.B.169), § 28, eff. July 16, 1991. Amended by Stats.1991, c. 474 (A.B.31), § 10, eff. Oct. 2, 1991; Stats.1992, c. 52 (A.B.1951), § 1, eff. May 11, 1992; Stats.2002, c. 488 (A.B.2065), § 2, eff. Sept. 12, 2002.)

[1] Internal Revenue Code sections are in Title 26 of the U.S.C.A.

§ 17276.4. Persons or entities engaged in the conduct of trade or business within the Los Angeles Revitalization Zone; net operating losses

(a) The term "qualified taxpayer" as used in Section 17276.1 includes a person or entity engaged in the conduct of a trade or business within the Los Angeles Revitalization Zone designated pursuant to Section 7102 of the Government Code. For purposes of this subdivision, all of the following shall apply:

(1) A net operating loss shall not be a net operating loss carryback for any taxable year, and a net operating loss for any taxable year beginning on or after the date the area in which the taxpayer conducts a trade or business is designated the Los Angeles Revitalization Zone shall be a net operating loss carryover to each following taxable year that ends before the Los Angeles

Revitalization Zone expiration date or to each of the 15 taxable years following the taxable year of loss, if longer.

(2) "Net operating loss" means the loss determined under Section 172 of the Internal Revenue Code, [1] as modified by Section 17276.1, attributable to the taxpayer's business activities within the Los Angeles Revitalization Zone (as defined in Section 7102 of the Government Code) prior to the Los Angeles Revitalization Zone expiration date. The attributable loss shall be determined in accordance with Chapter 17 (commencing with Section 25101) of Part 11, modified as follows:

(A) Loss shall be apportioned to the Los Angeles Revitalization Zone by multiplying total loss from the business by a fraction, the numerator of which is the property factor plus the payroll factor, and the denominator of which is 2.

(B) "The Los Angeles Revitalization Zone" shall be substituted for "this state."

(3) A net operating loss carryover shall be a deduction only with respect to the taxpayer's business income attributable to the Los Angeles Revitalization Zone (as defined in Section 7102 of the Government Code) determined in accordance with subdivision (c).

(4) If a loss carryover is allowable pursuant to this section for any taxable year after the Los Angeles Revitalization Zone designation has expired, the Los Angeles Revitalization Zone shall be deemed to remain in existence for purposes of computing the limitation set forth in paragraph (2) and allowing a net operating loss deduction.

(5) Attributable income shall be that portion of the taxpayer's California source business income which is apportioned to the Los Angeles Revitalization Zone. For that purpose, the taxpayer's business income attributable to sources in this state first shall be determined in accordance with Chapter 17 (commencing with Section 25101) of Part 11. That business income shall be further apportioned to the Los Angeles Revitalization Zone in accordance with Article 2 (commencing with Section 25120) of Chapter 17 of Part 11, modified as follows:

(A) Business income shall be apportioned to the Los Angeles Revitalization Zone by multiplying total California business income of the taxpayer by a fraction, the numerator of which is the property factor plus the payroll factor, and the denominator of which is 2.

(B) The property factor is a fraction, the numerator of which is the average value of the taxpayer's real and tangible personal property owned or rented and used in the Los Angeles Revitalization Zone during the taxable year and the denominator of which is the average value of all the taxpayer's real and tangible personal property owned or rented and used in this state during the taxable year.

(C) The payroll factor is a fraction, the numerator of which is the total amount paid by the taxpayer in the Los Angeles Revitalization Zone during the taxable year for compensation, and the denominator of which is the total compensation paid by the taxpayer in this state during the taxable year.

(6) "Los Angeles Revitalization Zone expiration date" means the date the Los Angeles Revitalization Zone designation expires, is repealed, or becomes inoperative pursuant to Section 7102, 7103, or 7104 of the Government Code.

(b) This section shall be inoperative on the first day of the taxable year beginning on or after the determination date, and each taxable year thereafter, with respect to the taxpayer's business activities within a geographic area that is excluded from the map pursuant to Section 7102 of the Government Code, or an excluded area determined pursuant to Section 7104 of the Government Code. The determination date is the earlier of the first effective date of a determination under subdivision (c) of Section 7102 of the Government Code occurring after December 1, 1994, or the first effective date of an exclusion of an area from the amended Los Angeles Revitalization Zone under Section 7104 of the Government Code. However, if the taxpayer has any unused loss amount as of the date this section becomes inoperative, that unused loss amount may continue to be carried forward as provided in this section.

(c) A taxpayer who qualifies as a "qualified taxpayer" under one or more sections shall, for the taxable year of the net operating loss and any taxable year to which that net operating loss may be carried, designate on the original return filed for each year the section that applies to that taxpayer with respect to that net operating loss. If the taxpayer is eligible to qualify under more than one section, the designation is to be made after taking into account subdivision (d).

(d) If a taxpayer is eligible to qualify under this section and either Section 17276.2, 17276.5, or 17276.6 as a "qualified taxpayer," with respect to a net operating loss in a taxable year, the taxpayer shall designate which section is to apply to the taxpayer.

(e) Notwithstanding Section 17276, the amount of the loss determined under this section or Section 17276.2, 17276.5, or 17276.6 shall be the only net operating loss allowed to be carried over from that taxable year and the designation under subdivision (c) shall be included in the election under Section 17276.1.

(f) This section shall cease to be operative on December 1, 1998. However, any unused net operating loss may continue to be carried over to following years as provided in this section. *(Added by Stats.1998, c. 1039 (A.B.2809), § 8, eff. Sept. 30, 1998.)*

[1] See 26 U.S.C.A. § 172.

Operative Effect

Under the terms of § 23 of Stats.1998, c. 1039 (A.B.2809), eff. Sept. 30, 1998, this section is operative for taxable and income years ending after December 31, 1997.

§ 17276.5. Taxpayers engaged in conduct of a trade or business within a LAMBRA; net operating loss

(a) For each taxable year beginning on or after January 1, 1995, the term "qualified taxpayer" as used in Section 17276.1 includes a taxpayer engaged in the conduct of a trade or business within a LAMBRA. For purposes of this subdivision, all of the following shall apply:

(1) A net operating loss shall not be a net operating loss carryback for any taxable year, and a net operating loss for any taxable year beginning on or after the date the area in which the taxpayer conducts a trade or business is designated a LAMBRA shall be a net operating loss carryover to each following taxable year that ends before the LAMBRA expiration date or to each of the 15 taxable years following the taxable year of loss, if longer.

(2) "LAMBRA" means a local agency military base recovery area designated in accordance with Section 7114 of the Government Code.

(3) "Taxpayer" means a person or entity that conducts a trade or business within a LAMBRA and, for the first two taxable years, has a net increase in jobs (defined as 2,000 paid hours per employee per year) of one or more employees in the LAMBRA and this state. For purposes of this paragraph:

(A) The net increase in the number of jobs shall be determined by subtracting the total number of full-time employees (defined as 2,000 paid hours per employee per year) the taxpayer employed in this state in the taxable year prior to commencing business operations in the LAMBRA from the total number of full-time employees the taxpayer employed in this state during the second taxable year after commencing business operations in the LAMBRA. For taxpayers who commence doing business in this state with their LAMBRA business operation, the number of employees for the taxable year prior to commencing business operations in the LAMBRA shall be zero. The deduction shall be allowed only if the taxpayer has a net increase in jobs in the state, and if one or more full-time employees is employed within the LAMBRA.

(B) The total number of employees employed in the LAMBRA shall equal the sum of both of the following:

(i) The total number of hours worked in the LAMBRA for the taxpayer by employees (not to exceed 2,000 hours per employee) who are paid an hourly wage divided by 2,000.

(ii) The total number of months worked in the LAMBRA for the taxpayer by employees who are salaried employees divided by 12.

(C) In the case of a taxpayer who first commences doing business in the LAMBRA during the taxable year,

for purposes of clauses (i) and (ii), respectively, of subparagraph (B), the divisors "2,000" and "12" shall be multiplied by a fraction, the numerator of which is the number of months of the taxable year that the taxpayer was doing business in the LAMBRA and the denominator of which is 12.

(4) "Net operating loss" means the loss determined under Section 172 of the Internal Revenue Code, [1] as modified by Section 17276.1, attributable to the taxpayer's business activities within a LAMBRA prior to the LAMBRA expiration date. The attributable loss shall be determined in accordance with Chapter 17 (commencing with Section 25101) of Part 11, modified for purposes of this section as follows:

(A) Loss shall be apportioned to a LAMBRA by multiplying total loss from the business by a fraction, the numerator of which is the property factor plus the payroll factor, and the denominator of which is 2.

(B) "The LAMBRA" shall be substituted for "this state."

(5) A net operating loss carryover shall be a deduction only with respect to the taxpayer's business income attributable to a LAMBRA.

(6) Attributable income is that portion of the taxpayer's California source business income that is apportioned to the LAMBRA. For that purpose, the taxpayer's business income attributable to sources in this state first shall be determined in accordance with Chapter 17 (commencing with Section 25101) of Part 11. That business income shall be further apportioned to the LAMBRA in accordance with Article 2 (commencing with Section 25120) of Chapter 17 of Part 11, modified for purposes of this subdivision as follows:

(A) Business income shall be apportioned to a LAMBRA by multiplying total California business income of the taxpayer by a fraction, the numerator of which is the property factor plus the payroll factor, and the denominator of which is two. For purposes of this clause:

(i) The property factor is a fraction, the numerator of which is the average value of the taxpayer's real and tangible personal property owned or rented and used in the LAMBRA during the taxable year, and the denominator of which is the average value of all the taxpayer's real and tangible personal property owned or rented and used in this state during the taxable year.

(ii) The payroll factor is a fraction, the numerator of which is the total amount paid by the taxpayer in the LAMBRA during the taxable year for compensation, and the denominator of which is the total compensation paid by the taxpayer in this state during the taxable year.

(B) If a loss carryover is allowable pursuant to this section for any taxable year after the LAMBRA designation has expired, the LAMBRA shall be deemed to remain in existence for purposes of computing the limitation specified in paragraph (5) and allowing a net operating loss deduction.

(7) "LAMBRA expiration date" means the date the LAMBRA designation expires, is no longer binding, or becomes inoperative pursuant to Section 7110 of the Government Code.

(b) A taxpayer who qualifies as a "qualified taxpayer" under one or more sections shall, for the taxable year of the net operating loss and any taxable year to which that net operating loss may be carried, designate on the original return filed for each year the section that applies to that taxpayer with respect to that net operating loss. If the taxpayer is eligible to qualify under more than one section, the designation is to be made after taking into account subdivision (c).

(c) If a taxpayer is eligible to qualify under this section and either Section 17276.2, 17276.4, or 17276.6 as a "qualified taxpayer," with respect to a net operating loss in a taxable year, the taxpayer shall designate which section is to apply to the taxpayer.

(d) Notwithstanding Section 17276, the amount of the loss determined under this section or Section 17276.2, 17276.4, or 17276.6 shall be the only net operating loss allowed to be carried over from that taxable year and the designation under subdivision (b) shall be included in the election under Section 17276.1.

(e) This section shall apply to taxable years beginning on or after January 1, 1998. *(Added by Stats.1998, c. 1039 (A.B.2809), § 9.5, eff. Sept. 30, 1998, operative Sept. 30, 1998. Amended by Stats.1999, c. 987 (S.B.1229), § 33, eff. Oct. 10, 1999.)*

[1] See 26 U.S.C.A. § 172.

§ 17276.6. Taxpayers engaged in a trade or business within targeted tax areas or specified lines of business; net operating loss deduction

(a) For each taxable year beginning on or after January 1, 1998, the term "qualified taxpayer" as used in Section 17276.1 includes a person or entity that meets both of the following:

(1) Is engaged in a trade or business within a targeted tax area designated pursuant to Chapter 12.93 (commencing with Section 7097) of Division 7 of Title 1 of the Government Code.

(2) Is engaged in those lines of business described in Codes 2000 to 2099, inclusive; 2200 to 3999, inclusive; 4200 to 4299, inclusive; 4500 to 4599, inclusive; and 4700 to 5199, inclusive, of the Standard Industrial Classification (SIC) Manual published by the United States Office of Management and Budget, 1987 edition. In the case of any pass-through entity, the determination of whether a taxpayer is a qualified taxpayer under this section shall be made at the entity level.

(b) For purposes of subdivision (a), all of the following shall apply:

(1) A net operating loss shall not be a net operating loss carryback to any taxable year and a net operating loss for any taxable year beginning on or after the date that the area in which the qualified taxpayer conducts a trade or business is designated as a targeted tax area shall be a net operating loss carryover to each of the 15 taxable years following the taxable year of loss.

(2) "Net operating loss" means the loss determined under Section 172 of the Internal Revenue Code,[1] as modified by Section 17276.1, attributable to the qualified taxpayer's business activities within the targeted tax area (as defined in Chapter 12.93 (commencing with Section 7097) of Division 7 of Title 1 of the Government Code) prior to the targeted tax area expiration date. That attributable loss shall be determined in accordance with Chapter 17 (commencing with Section 25101) of Part 11, modified for purposes of this section as follows:

(A) Loss shall be apportioned to the targeted tax area by multiplying total loss from the business by a fraction, the numerator of which is the property factor plus the payroll factor, and the denominator of which is 2.

(B) "The targeted tax area" shall be substituted for "this state."

(3) A net operating loss carryover shall be a deduction only with respect to the qualified taxpayer's business income attributable to the targeted tax area as defined in Chapter 12.93 (commencing with Section 7097) of Division 7 of Title 1 of the Government Code.

(4) Attributable income shall be that portion of the qualified taxpayer's California source business income that is apportioned to the targeted tax area. For that purpose, the qualified taxpayer's business income attributable to sources in this state first shall be determined in accordance with Chapter 17 (commencing with Section 25101) of Part 11. That business income shall be further apportioned to the targeted tax area in accordance with Article 2 (commencing with Section 25120) of Chapter 17 of Part 11, modified for purposes of this subdivision as follows:

(A) Business income shall be apportioned to the targeted tax area by multiplying the total business income of the taxpayer by a fraction, the numerator of which is the property factor plus the payroll factor, and the denominator of which is two. For purposes of this clause:

(i) The property factor is a fraction, the numerator of which is the average value of the taxpayer's real and tangible personal property owned or rented and used in the targeted tax area during the taxable year, and the denominator of which is the average value of all the taxpayer's real and tangible personal property owned or rented and used in this state during the taxable year.

(ii) The payroll factor is a fraction, the numerator of which is the total amount paid by the taxpayer in the targeted tax area during the taxable year for compensation, and the denominator of which is the total compensation paid by the taxpayer in this state during the taxable year.

(B) If a loss carryover is allowable pursuant to this subdivision for any taxable year after the targeted tax area expiration date, the targeted tax area designation shall be deemed to remain in existence for purposes of computing the limitation specified in subparagraph (B) and allowing a net operating loss deduction.

(5) "Targeted tax area expiration date" means the date the targeted tax area designation expires, is revoked, is no longer binding, or becomes inoperative.

(b) A taxpayer who qualifies as a "qualified taxpayer" under one or more sections shall, for the taxable year of the net operating loss and any taxable year to which that net operating loss may be carried, designate on the original return filed for each year the section that applies to that taxpayer with respect to that net operating loss. If the taxpayer is eligible to qualify under more than one section, the designation is to be made after taking into account subdivision (c).

(c) If a taxpayer is eligible to qualify under this section and either Section 17276.2, 17276.4, or 17276.5 as a "qualified taxpayer," with respect to a net operating loss in a taxable year, the taxpayer shall designate which section is to apply to the taxpayer.

(d) Notwithstanding Section 17276, the amount of the loss determined under this section or Section 17276.2, 17276.4, or 17276.5 shall be the only net operating loss allowed to be carried over from that taxable year and the designation under subdivision (b) shall be included in the election under Section 17276.1.

(e) This section shall apply to taxable years beginning on or after January 1, 1998. *(Added by Stats.1998, c. 1039 (A.B.2809), § 10.5, eff. Sept. 30, 1998, operative Sept. 30, 1998.)*

[1] See 26 U.S.C.A. § 172.

Application

The addition of this section by Stats.1998, c. 1039 (A.B.2809), applies to taxable and income years beginning on or after January 1, 1998, under the terms of § 25 of that act.

Part 10.2

ADMINISTRATION OF FRANCHISE AND INCOME TAX LAWS

Continuation and restatement of law from Parts 10 and 11 into Part 10.2, see Revenue and Taxation Code § 18412 et seq.

CHAPTER 4. PAYMENTS AND ASSESSMENTS

ARTICLE 7. PENALTIES AND ADDITIONS TO TAX

Section
19176. Additional penalties; statements to employers made without reasonable basis; waiver; application of section.

§ 19176. Additional penalties; statements to employers made without reasonable basis; waiver; application of section

(a) In addition to any criminal penalty provided by law if:

(1) Any individual makes a statement under Section 13040, 13041, or 13042 of the Unemployment Insurance Code which results in a decrease in the amounts deducted and withheld under Division 6 (commencing with Section 13000) of the Unemployment Insurance Code; and

(2) As of the time the statement was made, there was no reasonable basis for the statement, the individual shall pay a penalty of five hundred dollars ($500) for the statement. Any penalty so imposed shall be paid upon notice and demand from the Franchise Tax Board and shall be collected as a tax.

(b) The Franchise Tax Board may waive (in whole or in part) the penalty imposed under subdivision (a) if the taxes imposed under Part 10 (commencing with Section 17001) with respect to the individual for the taxable year are equal to or less than the sum of both of the following:

(1) The credits against those taxes allowed by Chapter 2 (commencing with Section 17041) of Part 10 and Section 19002.

(2) The payments of estimated tax which are considered payments on account of those taxes.

(c) This section supersedes Section 13101 of the Unemployment Insurance Code and shall apply to acts and failures to act after December 31, 1981. *(Added by Stats.1993, c. 31 (S.B.3), § 26, eff. June 16, 1993, operative Jan. 1, 1994.)*

Part 10.3

EARNED INCOME TAX CREDIT INFORMATION ACT

Section
19850. Short title.
19851. Legislative findings and declarations.
19852. Definitions.
19853. Notification of EITC eligibility; acceptable methods; advance payments.
19854. Contents of notice.

§ 19850. Short title

This act shall be known and may be cited as the Earned Income Tax Credit Information Act. *(Added by Stats. 2007, c. 606 (A.B.650), § 1.)*

§ 19851. Legislative findings and declarations

The Legislature finds and declares as follows:

(a) Congress created the federal earned income tax credit (EITC) in 1975 to offset the adverse effects of the Medicare and social security payroll taxes on working poor families and to encourage low-income workers to seek employment rather than welfare.

(b) Due to a relatively low percentage of federal earned income tax credit eligible persons that participate in the federal Earned Income Tax Credit program, hundreds of millions of federal dollars go unclaimed by the working poor in California.

(c) In order to alleviate the tax burden on working poor persons and families, to enhance the wages and income of working poor persons and families, to ensure that California receives its share of the federal money available in the federal Earned Income Tax Credit program, and to inject additional federal money into the California economy, the state shall facilitate the furnishing of information to working poor persons and families regarding the availability of the federal earned income tax credit so that they may claim that credit on their federal income tax returns.

(d) It is the intent of this act to offer the most cost-effective assistance to eligible taxpayers through notices provided by their employers. *(Added by Stats.2007, c. 606 (A.B.650), § 1.)*

§ 19852. Definitions

For purposes of this part, the following terms have the following meanings:

(a) "Employer" means any California employer who is subject to, and is required to provide, unemployment insurance to his or her employees, under the Unemployment Insurance Code.

(b) "Employee" means any person who is covered by unemployment insurance by his or her employer, pursuant to the Unemployment Insurance Code.

(c) "EITC" means the federal earned income tax credit, as defined in Section 32 of the Internal Revenue Code.[1] *(Added by Stats.2007, c. 606 (A.B.650), § 1.)*

[1] Internal Revenue Code sections are in Title 26 of the U.S.C.A.

§ 19853. Notification of EITC eligibility; acceptable methods; advance payments

(a) An employer shall notify all employees that they may be eligible for the EITC within one week before or after, or at the same time, that the employer provides an annual wage summary, including, but not limited to, a Form W-2 or a Form 1099, to any employee.

(b) The employer shall provide the notification required by subdivision (a) by handing directly to the employee or mailing to the employee's last known address either of the following:

(1) Instructions on how to obtain any notices available from the Internal Revenue Service for this purpose, including, but not limited to, the IRS Notice 797 and Form W-5, or any successor notice or form.

(2) Any notice created by the employer, as long as it contains substantially the same language as the notice described in paragraph (1) or in subdivision (a) of Section 19854.

(c) The employer shall not satisfy the notification required by subdivision (a) by posting a notice on an employee bulletin board or sending it through office mail. However, these methods of notification are encouraged to help inform all employees of the EITC.

(d) Every employer shall process, in accordance with federal law, Form W-5 for advance payments of the EITC, upon the request of the employee. *(Added by Stats.2007, c. 606 (A.B.650), § 1.)*

§ 19854. Contents of notice

The notice furnished to employees regarding the availability of the EITC shall state as follows:

BASED ON YOUR ANNUAL EARNINGS, YOU MAY BE ELIGIBLE TO RECEIVE THE EARNED INCOME TAX CREDIT FROM THE FEDERAL GOVERNMENT. THE EARNED INCOME TAX CREDIT IS A REFUNDABLE FEDERAL INCOME TAX CREDIT FOR LOW-INCOME WORKING INDIVIDUALS AND FAMILIES. THE EARNED INCOME TAX CREDIT HAS NO EFFECT ON CERTAIN WELFARE BENEFITS. IN MOST CASES, EARNED INCOME TAX CREDIT PAYMENTS WILL NOT BE USED TO DETERMINE ELIGIBILITY FOR MEDICAID, SUPPLEMENTAL SECURITY INCOME, FOOD STAMPS, LOW-INCOME HOUSING OR MOST TEMPORARY ASSISTANCE FOR NEEDY FAMILIES PAYMENTS. EVEN IF YOU DO NOT OWE FEDERAL TAXES, YOU MUST FILE A TAX RETURN TO RECEIVE THE EARNED INCOME TAX CREDIT. BE SURE TO FILL OUT THE EARNED INCOME TAX CREDIT FORM IN THE FEDERAL INCOME TAX RETURN BOOKLET. FOR INFORMATION REGARDING YOUR ELIGIBILITY TO RECEIVE THE EARNED INCOME TAX CREDIT, INCLUDING INFORMATION ON HOW TO OBTAIN THE IRS NOTICE 797 OR FORM W-5, OR ANY OTHER NECESSARY FORMS AND INSTRUCTIONS, CONTACT THE INTERNAL REVENUE SERVICE BY CALLING 1-800-829-3676 OR THROUGH ITS WEB SITE AT WWW.IRS.GOV. *(Added by Stats.2007, c. 606 (A.B.650), § 1.)*

Part 11

CORPORATION TAX LAW

CHAPTER 3.5. TAX CREDITS

Section

23621. Credit for percentage of wages paid to certain employees; exception.

23622.7. Credit against tax; taxpayers employing qualified employees in enterprise zones.

23622.8. Manufacturing enhancement area; employment of qualified disadvantaged individual; credit against tax.

23623. Net increase in qualified full-time employees; credit against tax.

Section

23623.   Net increase in qualified full-time employees; credit against tax.

23624.   Wages paid prisoners employed in joint venture programs; credits against tax.

23634.   Taxable year beginning on or after January 1, 1998; qualified employees; income tax credit; qualified wages.

23645.   Local agency military base recovery area; sales tax credit.

23646.   Credit for hiring qualified disadvantaged individual or qualified displaced employee; local agency military base recovery area.

§ 23621. Credit for percentage of wages paid to certain employees; exception

(a) There shall be allowed as a credit against the "tax" (as defined by Section 23036) an amount equal to 10 percent of the amount of wages paid to each employee who is certified by the Employment Development Department to meet the requirements of Section 328 of the Unemployment Insurance Code.

The credit under this section shall not apply to an individual unless, on or before the day on which that individual begins work for the employer, the employer:

(1) Has received a certification from the Employment Development Department, or

(2) Has requested in writing that certification from the Employment Development Department.

For purposes of this subdivision, if on or before the day on which the individual begins work for the employer, the individual has received from the Employment Development Department a written preliminary determination that he or she is a member of a targeted group, then the requirement of paragraph (1) or (2) shall be applicable on or before the fifth day on which the individual begins work for the employer.

(b) The credit under this section shall not apply to wages paid in excess of three thousand dollars ($3,000) during an taxable year by a taxpayer to the same individual. With respect to each qualified employee, the aggregate credit under this section shall not exceed six hundred dollars ($600).

(c) The credit under this section shall not apply to wages paid to an individual:

(1) Who is a dependent, as described in paragraphs (1) to (8), inclusive, of Section 152(a) of the Internal Revenue Code,[1] of an individual who owns, directly or indirectly, more than 50 percent in value of the outstanding stock of the taxpayer (determined with the application of Section 267(c) of the Internal Revenue Code); or

(2) Who is a dependent (as described in paragraph (9) of Section 152(a) of the Internal Revenue Code) of an individual described in paragraph (1).

(d) The credit under this section shall not apply to wages paid to an individual if, prior to the hiring date of that individual, that individual had been employed by the employer at any time during which he or she was not certified by the Employment Development Department to meet the requirements of Section 328 of the Unemployment Insurance Code.

(e) If the certification of an employee has been revoked pursuant to subdivision (c) of Section 328 of the Unemployment Insurance Code, the credit under this section shall not apply to wages paid by the employer after the date on which notice of revocation is received by the employer.

(f) The credit under this section shall be in addition to any deduction under this part to which the taxpayer may be entitled, if any.

(g) The credit provided by this section shall be applied to wages paid to each qualifying employee during the 24–month period beginning on the date the employee begins working for the taxpayer.

(h)(1) A taxpayer may elect to have this section not apply for any taxable year.

(2) An election under paragraph (1) for any taxable year may be made (or revoked) at any time before the expiration of the four-year period beginning on the last date prescribed by law for filing the return for that taxable year (determined without regard to extensions).

(3) An election under paragraph (1)(or revocation thereof) shall be made in any manner which the Franchise Tax Board may prescribe.

(i)(1) In the case of a successor employer referred to in Section 3306(b)(1) of the Internal Revenue Code, the determination of the amount of the credit under this section with respect to wages paid by that successor employer shall be made in the same manner as if those wages were paid by the predecessor employer referred to in that section.

(2) No credit shall be determined under this section with respect to remuneration paid by an employer to an employee for services performed by that employee for another person unless the amount reasonably expected to be received by the employer for those services from that other person exceeds the remuneration paid by the employer to that employee for those services.

(j) The term "wages" shall not include either of the following:

(1) Payments defined in Section 51(c)(3) of the Internal Revenue Code, relating to payments for services during labor disputes.

(2) Any amounts paid or incurred to an individual who begins work for an employer after December 31, 1993. *(Formerly § 24330, added by Stats.1986, c. 1087, § 6, eff. Sept. 24, 1986. Amended by Stats.1987, c. 1139, § 64, eff. Sept. 25, 1987. Renumbered § 23621 and amended by Stats.1988, c. 1465, § 33, eff. Sept. 28, 1988. Amended by Stats.1989, c. 1074, § 2, eff. Sept. 30, 1989; Stats.1989, c. 1352, § 81.5, eff. Oct. 2, 1989; Stats.2000, c. 862 (A.B. 1843), § 77.)*

[1] Internal Revenue Code sections are in Title 26 of U.S.C.A.

§ 23622.7. Credit against tax; taxpayers employing qualified employees in enterprise zones

(a) There shall be allowed a credit against the "tax" (as defined by Section 23036) to a taxpayer who employs a qualified employee in an enterprise zone during the taxable year. The credit shall be equal to the sum of each of the following:

(1) Fifty percent of qualified wages in the first year of employment.

(2) Forty percent of qualified wages in the second year of employment.

(3) Thirty percent of qualified wages in the third year of employment.

(4) Twenty percent of qualified wages in the fourth year of employment.

(5) Ten percent of qualified wages in the fifth year of employment.

(b) For purposes of this section:

(1) "Qualified wages" means:

(A)(i) Except as provided in clause (ii), that portion of wages paid or incurred by the taxpayer during the taxable year to qualified employees that does not exceed 150 percent of the minimum wage.

(ii) For up to 1,350 qualified employees who are employed by the taxpayer in the Long Beach Enterprise Zone in aircraft manufacturing activities described in Codes 3721 to 3728, inclusive, and Code 3812 of the Standard Industrial Classification (SIC) Manual published by the United States Office of Management and Budget, 1987 edition, "qualified wages" means that portion of hourly wages that does not exceed 202 percent of the minimum wage.

(B) Wages received during the 60–month period beginning with the first day the employee commences employment with the taxpayer. Reemployment in connection with any increase, including a regularly occurring seasonal increase, in the trade or business operations of the taxpayer does not constitute commencement of employment for purposes of this section.

(C) Qualified wages do not include any wages paid or incurred by the taxpayer on or after the zone expiration date. However, wages paid or incurred with respect to qualified employees who are employed by the taxpayer within the enterprise zone within the 60–month period prior to the zone expiration date shall continue to qualify for the credit under this section after the zone expiration date, in accordance with all provisions of this section applied as if the enterprise zone designation were still in existence and binding.

(2) "Minimum wage" means the wage established by the Industrial Welfare Commission as provided for in Chapter 1 (commencing with Section 1171) of Part 4 of Division 2 of the Labor Code.

(3) "Zone expiration date" means the date the enterprise zone designation expires, is no longer binding, or becomes inoperative.

(4)(A) "Qualified employee" means an individual who meets all of the following requirements:

(i) At least 90 percent of whose services for the taxpayer during the taxable year are directly related to the conduct of the taxpayer's trade or business located in an enterprise zone.

(ii) Performs at least 50 percent of his or her services for the taxpayer during the taxable year in an enterprise zone.

(iii) Is hired by the taxpayer after the date of original designation of the area in which services were performed as an enterprise zone.

(iv) Is any of the following:

(I) Immediately preceding the qualified employee's commencement of employment with the taxpayer, was a person eligible for services under the federal Job Training Partnership Act (29 U.S.C. Sec. 1501 et seq.), or its successor, who is receiving, or is eligible to receive, subsidized employment, training, or services funded by the federal Job Training Partnership Act, or its successor.

(II) Immediately preceding the qualified employee's commencement of employment with the taxpayer, was a person eligible to be a voluntary or mandatory registrant under the Greater Avenues for Independence Act of 1985 (GAIN) provided for pursuant to Article 3.2 (commencing with Section 11320) of Chapter 2 of Part 3 of Division 9 of the Welfare and Institutions Code, or its successor.

(III) Immediately preceding the qualified employee's commencement of employment with the taxpayer, was an economically disadvantaged individual 14 years of age or older.

(IV) Immediately preceding the qualified employee's commencement of employment with the taxpayer, was a dislocated worker who meets any of the following:

(aa) Has been terminated or laid off or who has received a notice of termination or layoff from employment, is eligible for or has exhausted entitlement to unemployment insurance benefits, and is unlikely to return to his or her previous industry or occupation.

(bb) Has been terminated or has received a notice of termination of employment as a result of any permanent closure or any substantial layoff at a plant, facility, or enterprise, including an individual who has not received written notification but whose employer has made a public announcement of the closure or layoff.

(cc) Is long-term unemployed and has limited opportunities for employment or reemployment in the same or a similar occupation in the area in which the individual resides, including an individual 55 years of age or older who may have substantial barriers to employment by reason of age.

(dd) Was self-employed (including farmers and ranchers) and is unemployed as a result of general economic conditions in the community in which he or she resides or because of natural disasters.

(ee) Was a civilian employee of the Department of Defense employed at a military installation being closed or realigned under the Defense Base Closure and Realignment Act of 1990.

(ff) Was an active member of the armed forces or National Guard as of September 30, 1990, and was either involuntarily separated or separated pursuant to a special benefits program.

(gg) Is a seasonal or migrant worker who experiences chronic seasonal unemployment and underemployment in the agriculture industry, aggravated by continual advancements in technology and mechanization.

(hh) Has been terminated or laid off, or has received a notice of termination or layoff, as a consequence of compliance with the Clean Air Act.

(V) Immediately preceding the qualified employee's commencement of employment with the taxpayer, was a disabled individual who is eligible for or enrolled in, or has completed a state rehabilitation plan or is a service-connected disabled veteran, veteran of the Vietnam era, or veteran who is recently separated from military service.

(VI) Immediately preceding the qualified employee's commencement of employment with the taxpayer, was an ex-offender. An individual shall be treated as convicted if he or she was placed on probation by a state court without a finding of guilt.

(VII) Immediately preceding the qualified employee's commencement of employment with the taxpayer, was a person eligible for or a recipient of any of the following:

(aa) Federal Supplemental Security Income benefits.

(bb) Aid to Families with Dependent Children.

(cc) Food stamps.

(dd) State and local general assistance.

(VIII) Immediately preceding the qualified employee's commencement of employment with the taxpayer, was a member of a federally recognized Indian tribe, band, or other group of Native American descent.

(IX) Immediately preceding the qualified employee's commencement of employment with the taxpayer, was a resident of a targeted employment area (as defined in Section 7072 of the Government Code).

(X) An employee who qualified the taxpayer for the enterprise zone hiring credit under former Section 23622 or the program area hiring credit under former Section 23623.

(XI) Immediately preceding the qualified employee's commencement of employment with the taxpayer, was a member of a targeted group, as defined in Section 51(d) of the Internal Revenue Code, [1] or its successor.

(B) Priority for employment shall be provided to an individual who is enrolled in a qualified program under

the federal Job Training Partnership Act or the Greater Avenues for Independence Act of 1985 or who is eligible as a member of a targeted group under the Work Opportunity Tax Credit (Section 51 of the Internal Revenue Code), or its successor.

(5) "Taxpayer" means a corporation engaged in a trade or business within an enterprise zone designated pursuant to Chapter 12.8 (commencing with Section 7070) of Division 7 of Title 1 of the Government Code.

(6) "Seasonal employment" means employment by a taxpayer that has regular and predictable substantial reductions in trade or business operations.

(c) The taxpayer shall do both of the following:

(1) Obtain from the Employment Development Department, as permitted by federal law, the local county or city Job Training Partnership Act administrative entity, the local county GAIN office or social services agency, or the local government administering the enterprise zone, a certification that provides that a qualified employee meets the eligibility requirements specified in clause (iv) of subparagraph (A) of paragraph (4) of subdivision (b). The Employment Development Department may provide preliminary screening and referral to a certifying agency. The Employment Development Department shall develop a form for this purpose. The Department of Housing and Community Development shall develop regulations governing the issuance of certificates by local governments pursuant to subdivision (a) of Section 7086 of the Government Code.

(2) Retain a copy of the certification and provide it upon request to the Franchise Tax Board.

(d)(1) For purposes of this section:

(A) All employees of all corporations which are members of the same controlled group of corporations shall be treated as employed by a single taxpayer.

(B) The credit, if any, allowable by this section to each member shall be determined by reference to its proportionate share of the expense of the qualified wages giving rise to the credit, and shall be allocated in that manner.

(C) For purposes of this subdivision, "controlled group of corporations" means "controlled group of corporations" as defined in Section 1563(a) of the Internal Revenue Code, except that:

(i) "More than 50 percent" shall be substituted for "at least 80 percent" each place it appears in Section 1563(a)(1) of the Internal Revenue Code.

(ii) The determination shall be made without regard to subsections (a)(4) and (e)(3)(C) of Section 1563 of the Internal Revenue Code.

(2) If an employer acquires the major portion of a trade or business of another employer (hereinafter in this paragraph referred to as the "predecessor") or the major portion of a separate unit of a trade or business of a predecessor, then, for purposes of applying this section (other than subdivision (e)) for any calendar year ending after that acquisition, the employment relationship be-

tween a qualified employee and an employer shall not be treated as terminated if the employee continues to be employed in that trade or business.

(e)(1)(A) If the employment, other than seasonal employment, of any qualified employee with respect to whom qualified wages are taken into account under subdivision (a) is terminated by the taxpayer at any time during the first 270 days of that employment, whether or not consecutive, or before the close of the 270th calendar day after the day in which that employee completes 90 days of employment with the taxpayer, the tax imposed by this part for the taxable year in which that employment is terminated shall be increased by an amount equal to the credit allowed under subdivision (a) for that taxable year and all prior taxable years attributable to qualified wages paid or incurred with respect to that employee.

(B) If the seasonal employment of any qualified employee, with respect to whom qualified wages are taken into account under subdivision (a) is not continued by the taxpayer for a period of 270 days of employment during the 60–month period beginning with the day the qualified employee commences seasonal employment with the taxpayer, the tax imposed by this part, for the taxable year that includes the 60th month following the month in which the qualified employee commences seasonal employment with the taxpayer, shall be increased by an amount equal to the credit allowed under subdivision (a) for that taxable year and all prior taxable years attributable to qualified wages paid or incurred with respect to that qualified employee.

(2)(A) Subparagraph (A) of paragraph (1) shall not apply to any of the following:

(i) A termination of employment of a qualified employee who voluntarily leaves the employment of the taxpayer.

(ii) A termination of employment of a qualified employee who, before the close of the period referred to in subparagraph (A) of paragraph (1), becomes disabled and unable to perform the services of that employment, unless that disability is removed before the close of that period and the taxpayer fails to offer reemployment to that employee.

(iii) A termination of employment of a qualified employee, if it is determined that the termination was due to the misconduct (as defined in Sections 1256–30 to 1256–43, inclusive, of Title 22 of the California Code of Regulations) of that employee.

(iv) A termination of employment of a qualified employee due to a substantial reduction in the trade or business operations of the taxpayer.

(v) A termination of employment of a qualified employee, if that employee is replaced by other qualified employees so as to create a net increase in both the number of employees and the hours of employment.

(B) Subparagraph (B) of paragraph (1) shall not apply to any of the following:

(i) A failure to continue the seasonal employment of a qualified employee who voluntarily fails to return to the seasonal employment of the taxpayer.

(ii) A failure to continue the seasonal employment of a qualified employee who, before the close of the period referred to in subparagraph (B) of paragraph (1), becomes disabled and unable to perform the services of that seasonal employment, unless that disability is removed before the close of that period and the taxpayer fails to offer seasonal employment to that qualified employee.

(iii) A failure to continue the seasonal employment of a qualified employee, if it is determined that the failure to continue the seasonal employment was due to the misconduct (as defined in Sections 1256–30 to 1256–43, inclusive, of Title 22 of the California Code of Regulations) of that qualified employee.

(iv) A failure to continue seasonal employment of a qualified employee due to a substantial reduction in the regular seasonal trade or business operations of the taxpayer.

(v) A failure to continue the seasonal employment of a qualified employee, if that qualified employee is replaced by other qualified employees so as to create a net increase in both the number of seasonal employees and the hours of seasonal employment.

(C) For purposes of paragraph (1), the employment relationship between the taxpayer and a qualified employee shall not be treated as terminated by either of the following:

(i) By a transaction to which Section 381(a) of the Internal Revenue Code applies, if the qualified employee continues to be employed by the acquiring corporation.

(ii) By reason of a mere change in the form of conducting the trade or business of the taxpayer, if the qualified employee continues to be employed in that trade or business and the taxpayer retains a substantial interest in that trade or business.

(3) Any increase in tax under paragraph (1) shall not be treated as tax imposed by this part for purposes of determining the amount of any credit allowable under this part.

(f) Rules similar to the rules provided in Section 46(e) and (h) of the Internal Revenue Code shall apply to both of the following:

(1) An organization to which Section 593 of the Internal Revenue Code applies.

(2) A regulated investment company or a real estate investment trust subject to taxation under this part.

(g) For purposes of this section, "enterprise zone" means an area designated as an enterprise zone pursuant to Chapter 12.8 (commencing with Section 7070) of Division 7 of Title 1 of the Government Code.

(h) The credit allowable under this section shall be reduced by the credit allowed under Sections 23623.5, 23625, and 23646 claimed for the same employee. The credit shall also be reduced by the federal credit allowed under Section 51 of the Internal Revenue Code.

In addition, any deduction otherwise allowed under this part for the wages or salaries paid or incurred by the taxpayer upon which the credit is based shall be reduced by the amount of the credit, prior to any reduction required by subdivision (i) or (j).

(i) In the case where the credit otherwise allowed under this section exceeds the "tax" for the taxable year, that portion of the credit that exceeds the "tax" may be carried over and added to the credit, if any, in succeeding taxable years, until the credit is exhausted. The credit shall be applied first to the earliest taxable years possible.

(j)(1) The amount of the credit otherwise allowed under this section and Section 23612.2, including any credit carryover from prior years, that may reduce the "tax" for the taxable year shall not exceed the amount of tax which would be imposed on the taxpayer's business income attributable to the enterprise zone determined as if that attributable income represented all of the income of the taxpayer subject to tax under this part.

(2) Attributable income shall be that portion of the taxpayer's California source business income that is apportioned to the enterprise zone. For that purpose, the taxpayer's business attributable to sources in this state first shall be determined in accordance with Chapter 17 (commencing with Section 25101). That business income shall be further apportioned to the enterprise zone in accordance with Article 2 (commencing with Section 25120) of Chapter 17, modified for purposes of this section in accordance with paragraph (3).

(3) Business income shall be apportioned to the enterprise zone by multiplying the total California business income of the taxpayer by a fraction, the numerator of which is the property factor plus the payroll factor, and the denominator of which is two. For purposes of this paragraph:

(A) The property factor is a fraction, the numerator of which is the average value of the taxpayer's real and tangible personal property owned or rented and used in the enterprise zone during the income year, and the denominator of which is the average value of all the taxpayer's real and tangible personal property owned or rented and used in this state during the income year.

(B) The payroll factor is a fraction, the numerator of which is the total amount paid by the taxpayer in the enterprise zone during the income year for compensation, and the denominator of which is the total compensation paid by the taxpayer in this state during the income year.

(4) The portion of any credit remaining, if any, after application of this subdivision, shall be carried over to succeeding taxable years, as if it were an amount exceeding the "tax" for the taxable year, as provided in subdivision (i).

(k) The changes made to this section by the act adding this subdivision [2] shall apply to taxable years on or after January 1, 1997. *(Added by Stats.1996, c. 955 (S.B.2023),*

860

§ 22. *Amended by Stats.1997, c. 603 (S.B.965), § 17, eff. Oct. 3, 1997; Stats.1997, c. 609 (S.B.200), § 12.5; Stats. 1998, c. 323 (A.B.2798), § 27, eff. Aug. 20, 1998, operative Aug. 20, 1998; Stats.1998, c. 1039 (A.B.2809), § 11.5, eff. Sept. 30, 1998, operative Sept. 30, 1998; Stats.1999, c. 987 (S.B.1229), § 82, eff. Oct. 10, 1999; Stats.2000, c. 862 (A.B.1843), § 78; Stats.2004, c. 225 (S.B.1097), § 67, eff. Aug. 16, 2004.)*

[1] See 26 U.S.C.A. § 51.

[2] Stats.1997, c. 609 (S.B.200).

§ 23622.8. Manufacturing enhancement area; employment of qualified disadvantaged individual; credit against tax

(a) For each taxable year beginning on or after January 1, 1998, there shall be allowed a credit against the "tax" (as defined in Section 23036) to a qualified taxpayer for hiring a qualified disadvantaged individual during the taxable year for employment in the manufacturing enhancement area. The credit shall be equal to the sum of each of the following:

(1) Fifty percent of the qualified wages in the first year of employment.

(2) Forty percent of the qualified wages in the second year of employment.

(3) Thirty percent of the qualified wages in the third year of employment.

(4) Twenty percent of the qualified wages in the fourth year of employment.

(5) Ten percent of the qualified wages in the fifth year of employment.

(b) For purposes of this section:

(1) "Qualified wages" means:

(A) That portion of wages paid or incurred by the qualified taxpayer during the taxable year to qualified disadvantaged individuals that does not exceed 150 percent of the minimum wage.

(B) The total amount of qualified wages which may be taken into account for purposes of claiming the credit allowed under this section shall not exceed two million dollars ($2,000,000) per taxable year.

(C) Wages received during the 60–month period beginning with the first day the qualified disadvantaged individual commences employment with the qualified taxpayer. Reemployment in connection with any increase, including a regularly occurring seasonal increase, in the trade or business operations of the qualified taxpayer does not constitute commencement of employment for purposes of this section.

(D) Qualified wages do not include any wages paid or incurred by the qualified taxpayer on or after the manufacturing enhancement area expiration date. However, wages paid or incurred with respect to qualified employees who are employed by the qualified taxpayer within the manufacturing enhancement area within the 60–month period prior to the manufacturing enhancement area expiration date shall continue to qualify for the credit under this section after the manufacturing enhancement area expiration date, in accordance with all provisions of this section applied as if the manufacturing enhancement area designation were still in existence and binding.

(2) "Minimum wage" means the wage established by the Industrial Welfare Commission as provided for in Chapter 1 (commencing with Section 1171) of Part 4 of Division 2 of the Labor Code.

(3) "Manufacturing enhancement area" means an area designated pursuant to Section 7073.8 of the Government Code according to the procedures of Chapter 12.8 (commencing with Section 7070) of Division 7 of Title 1 of the Government Code.

(4) "Manufacturing enhancement area expiration date" means the date the manufacturing enhancement area designation expires, is no longer binding, or becomes inoperative.

(5) "Qualified disadvantaged individual" means an individual who satisfies all of the following requirements:

(A)(i) At least 90 percent of whose services for the qualified taxpayer during the taxable year are directly related to the conduct of the qualified taxpayer's trade or business located in a manufacturing enhancement area.

(ii) Who performs at least 50 percent of his or her services for the qualified taxpayer during the taxable year in the manufacturing enhancement area.

(B) Who is hired by the qualified taxpayer after the designation of the area as a manufacturing enhancement area in which the individual's services were primarily performed.

(C) Who is any of the following immediately preceding the individual's commencement of employment with the qualified taxpayer:

(i) An individual who has been determined eligible for services under the federal Job Training Partnership Act (29 U.S.C. Sec. 1501 et seq.) or its successor.

(ii) Any voluntary or mandatory registrant under the Greater Avenues for Independence Act of 1985, or its successor, as provided pursuant to Article 3.2 (commencing with Section 11320) of Chapter 2 of Part 3 of Division 9 of the Welfare and Institutions Code.

(iii) Any individual who has been certified eligible by the Employment Development Department under the federal Targeted Jobs Tax Credit Program, or its successor, whether or not this program is in effect.

(6) "Qualified taxpayer" means any corporation engaged in a trade or business within a manufacturing enhancement area designated pursuant to Section 7073.8 of the Government Code and that meets all of the following requirements:

(A) Is engaged in those lines of business described in Codes 0211 to 0291, inclusive, Code 0723, or in Codes 2011 to 3999, inclusive, of the Standard Industrial Classi-

fication (SIC) Manual published by the United States Office of Management and Budget, 1987 edition.

(B) At least 50 percent of the qualified taxpayer's workforce hired after the designation of the manufacturing enhancement area is composed of individuals who, at the time of hire, are residents of the county in which the manufacturing enhancement area is located.

(C) Of this percentage of local hires, at least 30 percent shall be qualified disadvantaged individuals.

(7) "Seasonal employment" means employment by a qualified taxpayer that has regular and predictable substantial reductions in trade or business operations.

(c)(1) For purposes of this section, all of the following apply:

(A) All employees of all corporations that are members of the same controlled group of corporations shall be treated as employed by a single qualified taxpayer.

(B) The credit (if any) allowable by this section with respect to each member shall be determined by reference to its proportionate share of the expenses of the qualified wages giving rise to the credit and shall be allocated in that manner.

(C) Principles that apply in the case of controlled groups of corporations, as specified in subdivision (d) of Section 23622.7, shall apply with respect to determining employment.

(2) If a qualified taxpayer acquires the major portion of a trade or business of another employer (hereinafter in this paragraph referred to as the "predecessor") or the major portion of a separate unit of a trade or business of a predecessor, then, for purposes of applying this section (other than subdivision (d)) for any calendar year ending after that acquisition, the employment relationship between a qualified disadvantaged individual and a qualified taxpayer shall not be treated as terminated if the qualified disadvantaged individual continues to be employed in that trade or business.

(d)(1)(A) If the employment, other than seasonal employment, of any qualified disadvantaged individual, with respect to whom qualified wages are taken into account under subdivision (b) is terminated by the qualified taxpayer at any time during the first 270 days of that employment (whether or not consecutive) or before the close of the 270th calendar day after the day in which that qualified disadvantaged individual completes 90 days of employment with the qualified taxpayer, the tax imposed by this part for the taxable year in which that employment is terminated shall be increased by an amount equal to the credit allowed under subdivision (a) for that taxable year and all prior taxable years attributable to qualified wages paid or incurred with respect to that qualified disadvantaged individual.

(B) If the seasonal employment of any qualified disadvantaged individual, with respect to whom qualified wages are taken into account under subdivision (a) is not continued by the qualified taxpayer for a period of 270 days of employment during the 60–month period beginning with the day the qualified disadvantaged individual commences seasonal employment with the qualified taxpayer, the tax imposed by this part, for the income year that includes the 60th month following the month in which the qualified disadvantaged individual commences seasonal employment with the qualified taxpayer, shall be increased by an amount equal to the credit allowed under subdivision (a) for that taxable year and all prior taxable years attributable to qualified wages paid or incurred with respect to that qualified disadvantaged individual.

(2)(A) Subparagraph (A) of paragraph (1) does not apply to any of the following:

(i) A termination of employment of a qualified disadvantaged individual who voluntarily leaves the employment of the qualified taxpayer.

(ii) A termination of employment of a qualified disadvantaged individual who, before the close of the period referred to in subparagraph (A) of paragraph (1), becomes disabled to perform the services of that employment, unless that disability is removed before the close of that period and the qualified taxpayer fails to offer reemployment to that individual.

(iii) A termination of employment of a qualified disadvantaged individual, if it is determined that the termination was due to the misconduct (as defined in Sections 1256–30 to 1256–43, inclusive, of Title 22 of the California Code of Regulations) of that individual.

(iv) A termination of employment of a qualified disadvantaged individual due to a substantial reduction in the trade or business operations of the qualified taxpayer.

(v) A termination of employment of a qualified disadvantaged individual, if that individual is replaced by other qualified disadvantaged individuals so as to create a net increase in both the number of employees and the hours of employment.

(B) Subparagraph (B) of paragraph (1) shall not apply to any of the following:

(i) A failure to continue the seasonal employment of a qualified disadvantaged individual who voluntarily fails to return to the seasonal employment of the qualified taxpayer.

(ii) A failure to continue the seasonal employment of a qualified disadvantaged individual who, before the close of the period referred to in subparagraph (B) of paragraph (1), becomes disabled and unable to perform the services of that seasonal employment, unless that disability is removed before the close of that period and the qualified taxpayer fails to offer seasonal employment to that qualified disadvantaged individual.

(iii) A failure to continue the seasonal employment of a qualified disadvantaged individual, if it is determined that the failure to continue the seasonal employment was due to the misconduct (as defined in Sections 1256–30 to 1256–43, inclusive, of Title 22 of the California Code of Regulations) of that qualified disadvantaged individual.

(iv) A failure to continue seasonal employment of a qualified disadvantaged individual due to a substantial reduction in the regular seasonal trade or business operations of the qualified taxpayer.

(v) A failure to continue the seasonal employment of a qualified disadvantaged individual, if that qualified disadvantaged individual is replaced by other qualified disadvantaged individuals so as to create a net increase in both the number of seasonal employees and the hours of seasonal employment.

(C) For purposes of paragraph (1), the employment relationship between the qualified taxpayer and a qualified disadvantaged individual shall not be treated as terminated by either of the following:

(i) By a transaction to which Section 381(a) of the Internal Revenue Code [1] applies, if the qualified disadvantaged individual continues to be employed by the acquiring corporation.

(ii) By reason of a mere change in the form of conducting the trade or business of the qualified taxpayer, if the qualified disadvantaged individual continues to be employed in that trade or business and the qualified taxpayer retains a substantial interest in that trade or business.

(3) Any increase in tax under paragraph (1) shall not be treated as tax imposed by this part for purposes of determining the amount of any credit allowable under this part.

(e) The credit shall be reduced by the credit allowed under Section 23621. The credit shall also be reduced by the federal credit allowed under Section 51 of the Internal Revenue Code.

In addition, any deduction otherwise allowed under this part for the wages or salaries paid or incurred by the qualified taxpayer upon which the credit is based shall be reduced by the amount of the credit, prior to any reduction required by subdivision (f) or (g).

(f) In the case where the credit otherwise allowed under this section exceeds the "tax" for the taxable year, that portion of the credit that exceeds the "tax" may be carried over and added to the credit, if any, in succeeding years, until the credit is exhausted. The credit shall be applied first to the earliest taxable years possible.

(g)(1) The amount of credit otherwise allowed under this section, including prior year credit carryovers, that may reduce the "tax" for the taxable year shall not exceed the amount of tax that would be imposed on the qualified taxpayer's business income attributed to a manufacturing enhancement area determined as if that attributed income represented all of the net income of the qualified taxpayer subject to tax under this part.

(2) Attributable income is that portion of the taxpayer's California source business income that is apportioned to the manufacturing enhancement area. For that purpose, the taxpayer's business income attributable to sources in this state first shall be determined in accor-

dance with Chapter 17 (commencing with Section 25101). That business income shall be further apportioned to the manufacturing enhancement area in accordance with Article 2 (commencing with Section 25120) of Chapter 17, modified for purposes of this section in accordance with paragraph (3).

(3) Income shall be apportioned to a manufacturing enhancement area by multiplying the total California business income of the taxpayer by a fraction, the numerator of which is the property factor plus the payroll factor, and the denominator of which is two. For the purposes of this paragraph:

(A) The property factor is a fraction, the numerator of which is the average value of the taxpayer's real and tangible personal property owned or rented and used in the manufacturing enhancement area during the taxable year, and the denominator of which is the average value of all the taxpayer's real and tangible personal property owned or rented and used in this state during the taxable year.

(B) The payroll factor is a fraction, the numerator of which is the total amount paid by the taxpayer in the manufacturing enhancement area during the taxable year for compensation, and the denominator of which is the total compensation paid by the taxpayer in this state during the taxable year.

(4) The portion of any credit remaining, if any, after application of this subdivision, shall be carried over to succeeding taxable years, as if it were an amount exceeding the "tax" for the taxable year, as provided in subdivision (g).

(h) If the taxpayer is allowed a credit pursuant to this section for qualified wages paid or incurred, only one credit shall be allowed to the taxpayer under this part with respect to any wage consisting in whole or in part of those qualified wages.

(i) The qualified taxpayer shall do both of the following:

(1) Obtain from the Employment Development Department, as permitted by federal law, the local county or city Job Training Partnership Act administrative entity, the local county GAIN office or social services agency, or the local government administering the manufacturing enhancement area, a certification that provides that a qualified disadvantaged individual meets the eligibility requirements specified in paragraph (5) of subdivision (b). The Employment Development Department may provide preliminary screening and referral to a certifying agency. The Department of Housing and Community Development shall develop regulations governing the issuance of certificates pursuant to subdivision (d) of Section 7086 of the Government Code and shall develop forms for this purpose.

(2) Retain a copy of the certification and provide it upon request to the Franchise Tax Board. (*Added by Stats.1997, c. 609 (S.B.200), § 13. Amended by Stats. 1998, c. 7 (S.B.519), § 27.5, eff. March 14, 1998; Stats.*

1998, c. 323 (A.B.2798), § 28, eff. Aug. 20, 1998, operative Aug. 20, 1998; Stats.1998, c. 1039 (A.B.2809), § 12.5, eff. Sept. 30, 1998, operative Sept. 30, 1998; Stats.1999, c. 58 (S.B.113), § 2; Stats.2000, c. 862 (A.B.1843), § 79; Stats. 2000, c. 864 (A.B.2895), § 3; Stats.2000, c. 865 (S.B. 1445), § 3; Stats.2001, c. 159 (S.B.662), § 183; Stats. 2001, c. 543 (S.B.1185), § 31; Stats.2006, c. 634 (S.B.763), § 9.)

[1] Internal Revenue Code Sections are in Title 26 of the U.S.C.A.

§ 23623. Net increase in qualified full-time employees; credit against tax

Section added by Stats.2009–2010, 3rd Ex.Sess., c. 10 (A.B.15), § 8, eff. Feb. 20, 2009. See, also, another section of the same number added by Stats.2009–2010, 3rd Ex.Sess., c. 17 (S.B.15), § 8, eff. Feb. 20, 2009.

(a) For each taxable year beginning on or after January 1, 2009, there shall be allowed as a credit against the "tax," as defined in Section 23036, three thousand dollars ($3,000) for each net increase in qualified full-time employees, as specified in subdivision (c), hired during the taxable year by a qualified employer.

(b) For purposes of this section:

(1) "Acquired" includes any gift, inheritance, transfer incident to divorce, or any other transfer, whether or not for consideration.

(2) "Qualified full-time employee" means:

(A) A qualified employee who was paid qualified wages during the taxable year by the qualified employer for services of not less than an average of 35 hours per week.

(B) A qualified employee who was a salaried employee and was paid compensation during the taxable year for full-time employment, within the meaning of Section 515 of the Labor Code, by the qualified employer.

(3) A "qualified employee" shall not include any of the following:

(A) An employee certified as a qualified employee in an enterprise zone designated in accordance with Chapter 12.8 (commencing with Section 7070) of Division 7 of Title 1 of the Government Code.

(B) An employee certified as a qualified disadvantaged individual in a manufacturing enhancement area designated in accordance with Section 7073.8 of the Government Code.

(C) An employee certified as a qualified employee in a targeted tax area designated in accordance with Section 7097 of the Government Code.

(D) An employee certified as a qualified disadvantaged individual or a qualified displaced employee in a local agency military base recovery area (LAMBRA) designated in accordance with Chapter 12.97 (commencing with Section 7105) of Division 7 of Title 1 of the Government Code.

(E) An employee whose wages are included in calculating any other credit allowed under this part.

(4) "Qualified employer" means a taxpayer that, as of the last day of the preceding taxable year, employed a total of 20 or fewer employees.

(5) "Qualified wages" means wages subject to Division 6 (commencing with Section 13000) of the Unemployment Insurance Code.

(6) "Annual full-time equivalent" means either of the following:

(A) In the case of a full-time employee paid hourly qualified wages, "annual full-time equivalent" means the total number of hours worked for the taxpayer by the employee (not to exceed 2,000 hours per employee) divided by 2,000.

(B) In the case of a salaried full-time employee, "annual full-time equivalent" means the total number of weeks worked for the taxpayer by the employee divided by 52.

(c) The net increase in qualified full-time employees of a qualified employer shall be determined as provided by this subdivision:

(1)(A) The net increase in qualified full-time employees shall be determined on an annual full-time equivalent basis by subtracting from the amount determined in subparagraph (C) the amount determined in subparagraph (B).

(B) The total number of qualified full-time employees employed in the preceding taxable year by the taxpayer and by any trade or business acquired by the taxpayer during the current taxable year.

(C) The total number of full-time employees employed in the current taxable year by the taxpayer and by any trade or business acquired during the current taxable year.

(2) For taxpayers who first commence doing business in this state during the taxable year, the number of full-time employees for the immediately preceding prior taxable year shall be zero.

(d) In the case where the credit allowed by this section exceeds the "tax," the excess may be carried over to reduce the "tax" in the following year, and succeeding seven years if necessary, until the credit is exhausted.

(e) Any deduction otherwise allowed under this part for qualified wages shall not be reduced by the amount of the credit allowed under this section.

(f) For purposes of this section:

(1) All employees of the trades or businesses that are treated as related under either Section 267, 318, or 707 of the Internal Revenue Code [1] shall be treated as employed by a single taxpayer.

(2) In determining whether the taxpayer has first commenced doing business in this state during the taxable year, the provisions of subdivision (f) of Section 17276,

864

without application of paragraph (7) of that subdivision, shall apply.

(g)(1)(A) Credit under this section and Section 17053.80 shall be allowed only for credits claimed on timely filed original returns received by the Franchise Tax Board on or before the cut-off date established by the Franchise Tax Board.

(B) For purposes of this paragraph, the cut-off date shall be the last day of the calendar quarter within which the Franchise Tax Board estimates it will have received timely filed original returns claiming credits under this section and Section 17053.80 that cumulatively total four hundred million dollars ($400,000,000) for all taxable years.

(2) The date a return is received shall be determined by the Franchise Tax Board.

(3)(A) The determinations of the Franchise Tax Board with respect to the cut-off date, the date a return is received, and whether a return has been timely filed for purposes of this subdivision may not be reviewed in any administrative or judicial proceeding.

(B) Any disallowance of a credit claimed due to a determination under this subdivision, including the application of the limitation specified in paragraph (1), shall be treated as a mathematical error appearing on the return. Any amount of tax resulting from such disallowance may be assessed by the Franchise Tax Board in the same manner as provided by Section 19051.

(4) The Franchise Tax Board shall periodically provide notice on its Web site with respect to the amount of credit under this section and Section 17053.80 claimed on timely filed original returns received by the Franchise Tax Board.

(h)(1) The Franchise Tax Board may prescribe rules, guidelines or procedures necessary or appropriate to carry out the purposes of this section, including any guidelines regarding the limitation on total credits allowable under this section and Section 17053.80 and guidelines necessary to avoid the application of paragraph (2) of subdivision (f) through split-ups, shell corporations, partnerships, tiered ownership structures, or otherwise.

(2) Chapter 3.5 (commencing with Section 11340) of Part 1 of Division 3 of Title 2 of the Government Code does not apply to any standard, criterion, procedure, determination, rule, notice, or guideline established or issued by the Franchise Tax Board pursuant to this section.

(i) This section shall remain in effect only until December 1 of the calendar year after the year of the cut-off date, and as of that December 1 is repealed. *(Added by Stats.2009–2010, 3rd Ex.Sess., c. 10 (A.B.15), § 8, eff. Feb. 20, 2009.)*

[1] Internal Revenue Code sections are in Title 26 of the U.S.C.A.

§ 23623. Net increase in qualified full-time employees; credit against tax

Section added by Stats.2009–2010, 3rd Ex.Sess., c. 17 (S.B.15), § 8, eff. Feb. 20, 2009. See, also, another section of the same number added by Stats.2009–2010, 3rd Ex.Sess., c. 10 (A.B.15), § 8, eff. Feb. 20, 2009.

(a) For each taxable year beginning on or after January 1, 2009, there shall be allowed as a credit against the "tax," as defined in Section 23036, three thousand dollars ($3,000) for each net increase in qualified full-time employees, as specified in subdivision (c), hired during the taxable year by a qualified employer.

(b) For purposes of this section:

(1) "Acquired" includes any gift, inheritance, transfer incident to divorce, or any other transfer, whether or not for consideration.

(2) "Qualified full-time employee" means:

(A) A qualified employee who was paid qualified wages during the taxable year by the qualified employer for services of not less than an average of 35 hours per week.

(B) A qualified employee who was a salaried employee and was paid compensation during the taxable year for full-time employment, within the meaning of Section 515 of the Labor Code, by the qualified employer.

(3) A "qualified employee" shall not include any of the following:

(A) An employee certified as a qualified employee in an enterprise zone designated in accordance with Chapter 12.8 (commencing with Section 7070) of Division 7 of Title 1 of the Government Code.

(B) An employee certified as a qualified disadvantaged individual in a manufacturing enhancement area designated in accordance with Section 7073.8 of the Government Code.

(C) An employee certified as a qualified employee in a targeted tax area designated in accordance with Section 7097 of the Government Code.

(D) An employee certified as a qualified disadvantaged individual or a qualified displaced employee in a local agency military base recovery area (LAMBRA) designated in accordance with Chapter 12.97 (commencing with Section 7105) of Division 7 of Title 1 of the Government Code.

(E) An employee whose wages are included in calculating any other credit allowed under this part.

(4) "Qualified employer" means a taxpayer that, as of the last day of the preceding taxable year, employed a total of 20 or fewer employees.

(5) "Qualified wages" means wages subject to Division 6 (commencing with Section 13000) of the Unemployment Insurance Code.

(6) "Annual full-time equivalent" means either of the following:

(A) In the case of a full-time employee paid hourly qualified wages, "annual full-time equivalent" means the total number of hours worked for the taxpayer by the employee (not to exceed 2,000 hours per employee) divided by 2,000.

(B) In the case of a salaried full-time employee, "annual full-time equivalent" means the total number of weeks worked for the taxpayer by the employee divided by 52.

(c) The net increase in qualified full-time employees of a qualified employer shall be determined as provided by this subdivision:

(1)(A) The net increase in qualified full-time employees shall be determined on an annual full-time equivalent basis by subtracting from the amount determined in subparagraph (C) the amount determined in subparagraph (B).

(B) The total number of qualified full-time employees employed in the preceding taxable year by the taxpayer and by any trade or business acquired by the taxpayer during the current taxable year.

(C) The total number of full-time employees employed in the current taxable year by the taxpayer and by any trade or business acquired during the current taxable year.

(2) For taxpayers who first commence doing business in this state during the taxable year, the number of full-time employees for the immediately preceding prior taxable year shall be zero.

(d) In the case where the credit allowed by this section exceeds the "tax," the excess may be carried over to reduce the "tax" in the following year, and succeeding seven years if necessary, until the credit is exhausted.

(e) Any deduction otherwise allowed under this part for qualified wages shall not be reduced by the amount of the credit allowed under this section.

(f) For purposes of this section:

(1) All employees of the trades or businesses that are treated as related under either Section 267, 318, or 707 of the Internal Revenue Code [1] shall be treated as employed by a single taxpayer.

(2) In determining whether the taxpayer has first commenced doing business in this state during the taxable year, the provisions of subdivision (f) of Section 17276, without application of paragraph (7) of that subdivision, shall apply.

(g)(1)(A) Credit under this section and Section 17053.80 shall be allowed only for credits claimed on timely filed original returns received by the Franchise Tax

Board on or before the cut-off date established by the Franchise Tax Board.

(B) For purposes of this paragraph, the cut-off date shall be the last day of the calendar quarter within which the Franchise Tax Board estimates it will have received timely filed original returns claiming credits under this section and Section 17053.80 that cumulatively total four hundred million dollars ($400,000,000) for all taxable years.

(2) The date a return is received shall be determined by the Franchise Tax Board.

(3)(A) The determinations of the Franchise Tax Board with respect to the cut-off date, the date a return is received, and whether a return has been timely filed for purposes of this subdivision may not be reviewed in any administrative or judicial proceeding.

(B) Any disallowance of a credit claimed due to a determination under this subdivision, including the application of the limitation specified in paragraph (1), shall be treated as a mathematical error appearing on the return. Any amount of tax resulting from such disallowance may be assessed by the Franchise Tax Board in the same manner as provided by Section 19051.

(4) The Franchise Tax Board shall periodically provide notice on its Web site with respect to the amount of credit under this section and Section 17053.80 claimed on timely filed original returns received by the Franchise Tax Board.

(h)(1) The Franchise Tax Board may prescribe rules, guidelines or procedures necessary or appropriate to carry out the purposes of this section, including any guidelines regarding the limitation on total credits allowable under this section and Section 17053.80 and guidelines necessary to avoid the application of paragraph (2) of subdivision (f) through split-ups, shell corporations, partnerships, tiered ownership structures, or otherwise.

(2) Chapter 3.5 (commencing with Section 11340) of Part 1 of Division 3 of Title 2 of the Government Code does not apply to any standard, criterion, procedure, determination, rule, notice, or guideline established or issued by the Franchise Tax Board pursuant to this section.

(i) This section shall remain in effect only until December 1 of the calendar year after the year of the cut-off date, and as of that December 1 is repealed. *(Added by Stats.2009–2010, 3rd Ex.Sess., c. 17 (S.B.15), § 8, eff. Feb. 20, 2009.)*

[1] Internal Revenue Code sections are in Title 26 of the U.S.C.A.

§ 23624. Wages paid prisoners employed in joint venture programs; credits against tax

(a) There shall be allowed as a credit against the "tax" (as defined by Section 23036) an amount equal to 10 percent of the amount of wages paid or incurred during the taxable year to each prisoner who is employed in a joint venture program established pursuant to Article 1.5

of Chapter 5 of Title 1 of Part 3 of the Penal Code, through agreement with the Director of Corrections.

(b) The Department of Corrections shall forward annually to the Franchise Tax Board a list of all employers certified by the Department of Corrections as active participants in a joint venture program pursuant to Article 1.5 (commencing with Section 2717.1) of Chapter 5 of Title 1 of Part 3 of the Penal Code. The list shall include the certified participant's federal employer identification number. *(Added by Initiative Measure (Prop. 139), approved Nov. 6, 1990. Amended by Stats.1991, c. 472 (S.B.426), § 27, eff. Oct. 2, 1991; Stats.2000, c. 862 (A.B.1843), § 80.)*

§ 23634. Taxable year beginning on or after January 1, 1998; qualified employees; income tax credit; qualified wages

(a) For each taxable year beginning on or after January 1, 1998, there shall be allowed a credit against the "tax" (as defined by Section 23036) to a qualified taxpayer who employs a qualified employee in a targeted tax area during the taxable year. The credit shall be equal to the sum of each of the following:

(1) Fifty percent of qualified wages in the first year of employment.

(2) Forty percent of qualified wages in the second year of employment.

(3) Thirty percent of qualified wages in the third year of employment.

(4) Twenty percent of qualified wages in the fourth year of employment.

(5) Ten percent of qualified wages in the fifth year of employment.

(b) For purposes of this section:

(1) "Qualified wages" means:

(A) That portion of wages paid or incurred by the qualified taxpayer during the taxable year to qualified employees that does not exceed 150 percent of the minimum wage.

(B) Wages received during the 60–month period beginning with the first day the employee commences employment with the qualified taxpayer. Reemployment in connection with any increase, including a regularly occurring seasonal increase, in the trade or business operations of the qualified taxpayer does not constitute commencement of employment for purposes of this section.

(C) Qualified wages do not include any wages paid or incurred by the qualified taxpayer on or after the targeted tax area expiration date. However, wages paid or incurred with respect to qualified employees who are employed by the qualified taxpayer within the targeted tax area within the 60–month period prior to the targeted tax area expiration date shall continue to qualify for the credit under this section after the targeted tax area expiration date, in accordance with all provisions of this section applied as if the targeted tax area designation were still in existence and binding.

(2) "Minimum wage" means the wage established by the Industrial Welfare Commission as provided for in Chapter 1 (commencing with Section 1171) of Part 4 of Division 2 of the Labor Code.

(3) "Targeted tax area expiration date" means the date the targeted tax area designation expires, is revoked, is no longer binding, or becomes inoperative.

(4)(A) "Qualified employee" means an individual who meets all of the following requirements:

(i) At least 90 percent of his or her services for the qualified taxpayer during the taxable year are directly related to the conduct of the qualified taxpayer's trade or business located in a targeted tax area.

(ii) Performs at least 50 percent of his or her services for the qualified taxpayer during the taxable year in a targeted tax area.

(iii) Is hired by the qualified taxpayer after the date of original designation of the area in which services were performed as a targeted tax area.

(iv) Is any of the following:

(I) Immediately preceding the qualified employee's commencement of employment with the qualified taxpayer, was a person eligible for services under the federal Job Training Partnership Act (29 U.S.C. Sec. 1501 et seq.), or its successor, who is receiving, or is eligible to receive, subsidized employment, training, or services funded by the federal Job Training Partnership Act, or its successor.

(II) Immediately preceding the qualified employee's commencement of employment with the qualified taxpayer, was a person eligible to be a voluntary or mandatory registrant under the Greater Avenues for Independence Act of 1985 (GAIN) provided for pursuant to Article 3.2 (commencing with Section 11320) of Chapter 2 of Part 3 of Division 9 of the Welfare and Institutions Code, or its successor.

(III) Immediately preceding the qualified employee's commencement of employment with the qualified taxpayer, was an economically disadvantaged individual 14 years of age or older.

(IV) Immediately preceding the qualified employee's commencement of employment with the qualified taxpayer, was a dislocated worker who meets any of the following:

(aa) Has been terminated or laid off or who has received a notice of termination or layoff from employment, is eligible for or has exhausted entitlement to unemployment insurance benefits, and is unlikely to return to his or her previous industry or occupation.

(bb) Has been terminated or has received a notice of termination of employment as a result of any permanent closure or any substantial layoff at a plant, facility, or enterprise, including an individual who has not received written notification but whose employer has made a public announcement of the closure or layoff.

(cc) Is long-term unemployed and has limited opportunities for employment or reemployment in the same or a similar occupation in the area in which the individual resides, including an individual 55 years of age or older who may have substantial barriers to employment by reason of age.

(dd) Was self-employed (including farmers and ranchers) and is unemployed as a result of general economic conditions in the community in which he or she resides or because of natural disasters.

(ee) Was a civilian employee of the Department of Defense employed at a military installation being closed or realigned under the Defense Base Closure and Realignment Act of 1990. [1]

(ff) Was an active member of the Armed Forces or National Guard as of September 30, 1990, and was either involuntarily separated or separated pursuant to a special benefits program.

(gg) Is a seasonal or migrant worker who experiences chronic seasonal unemployment and underemployment in the agriculture industry, aggravated by continual advancements in technology and mechanization.

(hh) Has been terminated or laid off, or has received a notice of termination or layoff, as a consequence of compliance with the Clean Air Act. [1]

(V) Immediately preceding the qualified employee's commencement of employment with the qualified taxpayer, was a disabled individual who is eligible for or enrolled in, or has completed a state rehabilitation plan or is a service-connected disabled veteran, veteran of the Vietnam era, or veteran who is recently separated from military service.

(VI) Immediately preceding the qualified employee's commencement of employment with the qualified taxpayer, was an ex-offender. An individual shall be treated as convicted if he or she was placed on probation by a state court without a finding of guilt.

(VII) Immediately preceding the qualified employee's commencement of employment with the qualified taxpayer, was a person eligible for or a recipient of any of the following:

(aa) Federal Supplemental Security Income benefits.

(bb) Aid to Families with Dependent Children.

(cc) Food stamps.

(dd) State and local general assistance.

(VIII) Immediately preceding the qualified employee's commencement of employment with the qualified taxpayer, was a member of a federally recognized Indian tribe, band, or other group of Native American descent.

(IX) Immediately preceding the qualified employee's commencement of employment with the qualified taxpayer, was a resident of a targeted tax area.

(X) Immediately preceding the qualified employee's commencement of employment with the taxpayer, was a member of a targeted group, as defined in Section 51(d) of the Internal Revenue Code, or its successor.

(B) Priority for employment shall be provided to an individual who is enrolled in a qualified program under the federal Job Training Partnership Act or the Greater Avenues for Independence Act of 1985 or who is eligible as a member of a targeted group under the Work Opportunity Tax Credit (Section 51 of the Internal Revenue Code), or its successor.

(5)(A) "Qualified taxpayer" means a person or entity that meets both of the following:

(i) Is engaged in a trade or business within a targeted tax area designated pursuant to Chapter 12.93 (commencing with Section 7097) of Division 7 of Title 1 of the Government Code.

(ii) Is engaged in those lines of business described in Codes 2000 to 2099, inclusive; 2200 to 3999, inclusive; 4200 to 4299, inclusive; 4500 to 4599, inclusive; and 4700 to 5199, inclusive, of the Standard Industrial Classification (SIC) Manual published by the United States Office of Management and Budget, 1987 edition.

(B) In the case of any passthrough entity, the determination of whether a taxpayer is a qualified taxpayer under this section shall be made at the entity level and any credit under this section or Section 17053.34 shall be allowed to the passthrough entity and passed through to the partners or shareholders in accordance with applicable provisions of this part or Part 10 (commencing with Section 17001). For purposes of this subparagraph, the term "passthrough entity" means any partnership or S corporation.

(6) "Seasonal employment" means employment by a qualified taxpayer that has regular and predictable substantial reductions in trade or business operations.

(c) If the qualified taxpayer is allowed a credit for qualified wages pursuant to this section, only one credit shall be allowed to the taxpayer under this part with respect to those qualified wages.

(d) The qualified taxpayer shall do both of the following:

(1) Obtain from the Employment Development Department, as permitted by federal law, the local county or city Job Training Partnership Act administrative entity, the local county GAIN office or social services agency, or the local government administering the targeted tax area, a certification that provides that a qualified employee meets the eligibility requirements specified in clause (iv) of subparagraph (A) of paragraph (4) of subdivision (b). The Employment Development Department may provide preliminary screening and referral to a certifying agency. The Department of Housing and Community Development shall develop regulations for the issuance of certificates pursuant to subdivision (g) of Section 7097 of the Government Code, and shall develop forms for this purpose.

868

(2) Retain a copy of the certification and provide it upon request to the Franchise Tax Board.

(e)(1) For purposes of this section:

(A) All employees of all corporations that are members of the same controlled group of corporations shall be treated as employed by a single taxpayer.

(B) The credit, if any, allowable by this section to each member shall be determined by reference to its proportionate share of the expense of the qualified wages giving rise to the credit, and shall be allocated in that manner.

(C) For purposes of this subdivision, "controlled group of corporations" means "controlled group of corporations" as defined in Section 1563(a) of the Internal Revenue Code, except that:

(i) "More than 50 percent" shall be substituted for "at least 80 percent" each place it appears in Section 1563(a)(1) of the Internal Revenue Code. [2]

(ii) The determination shall be made without regard to subsections (a)(4) and (e)(3)(C) of Section 1563 of the Internal Revenue Code.

(2) If an employer acquires the major portion of a trade or business of another employer (hereinafter in this paragraph referred to as the "predecessor") or the major portion of a separate unit of a trade or business of a predecessor, then, for purposes of applying this section (other than subdivision (f)) for any calendar year ending after that acquisition, the employment relationship between a qualified employee and an employer shall not be treated as terminated if the employee continues to be employed in that trade or business.

(f)(1)(A) If the employment, other than seasonal employment, of any qualified employee with respect to whom qualified wages are taken into account under subdivision (a) is terminated by the qualified taxpayer at any time during the first 270 days of that employment (whether or not consecutive) or before the close of the 270th calendar day after the day in which that employee completes 90 days of employment with the qualified taxpayer, the tax imposed by this part for the taxable year in which that employment is terminated shall be increased by an amount equal to the credit allowed under subdivision (a) for that taxable year and all prior taxable years attributable to qualified wages paid or incurred with respect to that employee.

(B) If the seasonal employment of any qualified employee, with respect to whom qualified wages are taken into account under subdivision (a) is not continued by the qualified taxpayer for a period of 270 days of employment during the 60–month period beginning with the day the qualified employee commences seasonal employment with the qualified taxpayer, the tax imposed by this part, for the taxable year that includes the 60th month following the month in which the qualified employee commences seasonal employment with the qualified taxpayer, shall be increased by an amount equal to the credit allowed under subdivision (a) for that taxable year and all prior taxable years attributable to qualified wages paid or incurred with respect to that qualified employee.

(2)(A) Subparagraph (A) of paragraph (1) shall not apply to any of the following:

(i) A termination of employment of a qualified employee who voluntarily leaves the employment of the qualified taxpayer.

(ii) A termination of employment of a qualified employee who, before the close of the period referred to in subparagraph (A) of paragraph (1), becomes disabled and unable to perform the services of that employment, unless that disability is removed before the close of that period and the qualified taxpayer fails to offer reemployment to that employee.

(iii) A termination of employment of a qualified employee, if it is determined that the termination was due to the misconduct (as defined in Sections 1256–30 to 1256–43, inclusive, of Title 22 of the California Code of Regulations) of that employee.

(iv) A termination of employment of a qualified employee due to a substantial reduction in the trade or business operations of the taxpayer.

(v) A termination of employment of a qualified employee, if that employee is replaced by other qualified employees so as to create a net increase in both the number of employees and the hours of employment.

(B) Subparagraph (B) of paragraph (1) shall not apply to any of the following:

(i) A failure to continue the seasonal employment of a qualified employee who voluntarily fails to return to the seasonal employment of the qualified taxpayer.

(ii) A failure to continue the seasonal employment of a qualified employee who, before the close of the period referred to in subparagraph (B) of paragraph (1), becomes disabled and unable to perform the services of that seasonal employment, unless that disability is removed before the close of that period and the qualified taxpayer fails to offer seasonal employment to that qualified employee.

(iii) A failure to continue the seasonal employment of a qualified employee, if it is determined that the failure to continue the seasonal employment was due to the misconduct (as defined in Sections 1256–30 to 1256–43, inclusive, of Title 22 of the California Code of Regulations) of that qualified employee.

(iv) A failure to continue seasonal employment of a qualified employee due to a substantial reduction in the regular seasonal trade or business operations of the qualified taxpayer.

(v) A failure to continue the seasonal employment of a qualified employee, if that qualified employee is replaced by other qualified employees so as to create a net increase in both the number of seasonal employees and the hours of seasonal employment.

(C) For purposes of paragraph (1), the employment relationship between the qualified taxpayer and a qualified employee shall not be treated as terminated by either of the following:

(i) By a transaction to which Section 381(a) of the Internal Revenue Code applies, if the qualified employee continues to be employed by the acquiring corporation.

(ii) By reason of a mere change in the form of conducting the trade or business of the qualified taxpayer, if the qualified employee continues to be employed in that trade or business and the qualified taxpayer retains a substantial interest in that trade or business.

(3) Any increase in tax under paragraph (1) shall not be treated as tax imposed by this part for purposes of determining the amount of any credit allowable under this part.

(g) Rules similar to the rules provided in Sections 46(e) and (h) of the Internal Revenue Code shall apply to both of the following:

(1) An organization to which Section 593 of the Internal Revenue Code applies.

(2) A regulated investment company or a real estate investment trust subject to taxation under this part.

(h) For purposes of this section, "targeted tax area" means an area designated pursuant to Chapter 12.93 (commencing with Section 7097) of Division 7 of Title 1 of the Government Code.

(i) In the case where the credit otherwise allowed under this section exceeds the "tax" for the taxable year, that portion of the credit that exceeds the "tax" may be carried over and added to the credit, if any, in succeeding taxable years, until the credit is exhausted. The credit shall be applied first to the earliest taxable years possible.

(j)(1) The amount of the credit otherwise allowed under this section and Section 23633, including any credit carryover from prior years, that may reduce the "tax" for the taxable year shall not exceed the amount of tax that would be imposed on the qualified taxpayer's business income attributable to the targeted tax area determined as if that attributable income represented all of the income of the qualified taxpayer subject to tax under this part.

(2) Attributable income shall be that portion of the taxpayer's California source business income that is apportioned to the targeted tax area. For that purpose, the taxpayer's business income attributable to sources in this state first shall be determined in accordance with Chapter 17 (commencing with Section 25101). That business income shall be further apportioned to the targeted tax area in accordance with Article 2 (commencing with Section 25120) of Chapter 17, modified for purposes of this section in accordance with paragraph (3).

(3) Business income shall be apportioned to the targeted tax area by multiplying the total California business income of the taxpayer by a fraction, the numerator of which is the property factor plus the payroll factor, and

the denominator of which is two. For purposes of this paragraph:

(A) The property factor is a fraction, the numerator of which is the average value of the taxpayer's real and tangible personal property owned or rented and used in the targeted tax area during the taxable year, and the denominator of which is the average value of all the taxpayer's real and tangible personal property owned or rented and used in this state during the taxable year.

(B) The payroll factor is a fraction, the numerator of which is the total amount paid by the taxpayer in the targeted tax area during the taxable year for compensation, and the denominator of which is the total compensation paid by the taxpayer in this state during the taxable year.

(4) The portion of any credit remaining, if any, after application of this subdivision, shall be carried over to succeeding taxable years, as if it were an amount exceeding the "tax" for the taxable year, as provided in subdivision (h).

(5) In the event that a credit carryover is allowable under subdivision (h) for any taxable year after the targeted tax area designation has expired or been revoked, the targeted tax area shall be deemed to remain in existence for purposes of computing the limitation specified in this subdivision. *(Added by Stats.1997, c. 602 (A.B.1217), § 9. Amended by Stats.1998, c. 323 (A.B. 2798), § 30, eff. Aug. 20, 1998, operative Aug. 20, 1998; Stats.1998, c. 1039 (A.B.2809), § 13.5, eff. Sept. 30, 1998, operative Sept. 30, 1998; Stats.2000, c. 862 (A.B.1843), § 82; Stats.2006, c. 634 (S.B.763), § 10.)*

[1] Acts of Congress, alternate or descriptive name of acts, enacting credit, and sections, if any, classified to U.S.C.A., see Popular Name Table for Acts of Congress.

[2] Internal Revenue Code Sections are in Title 26 of the U.S.C.A.

§ 23645. Local agency military base recovery area; sales tax credit

(a) For each taxable year beginning on or after January 1, 1995, there shall be allowed as a credit against the "tax" (as defined by Section 23036) for the taxable year an amount equal to the sales or use tax paid or incurred by the taxpayer in connection with the purchase of qualified property to the extent that the qualified property does not exceed a value of twenty million dollars ($20,000,000).

(b) For purposes of this section:

(1) "LAMBRA" means a local agency military base recovery area designated in accordance with Section 7114 of the Government Code.

(2) "Taxpayer" means a corporation that conducts a trade or business within a LAMBRA and, for the first two taxable years, has a net increase in jobs (defined as 2,000 paid hours per employee per year) of one or more employees in the LAMBRA.

(A) The net increase in the number of jobs shall be determined by subtracting the total number of full-time employees (defined as 2,000 paid hours per employee per year) the taxpayer employed in this state in the taxable year prior to commencing business operations in the LAMBRA from the total number of full-time employees the taxpayer employed in this state during the second taxable year after commencing business operations in the LAMBRA. For taxpayers who commence doing business in this state with their LAMBRA business operation, the number of employees for the taxable year prior to commencing business operations in the LAMBRA shall be zero. If the taxpayer has a net increase in jobs in the state, the credit shall be allowed only if one or more full-time employees is employed within the LAMBRA.

(B) The total number of employees employed in the LAMBRA shall equal the sum of both of the following:

(i) The total number of hours worked in the LAMBRA for the taxpayer by employees (not to exceed 2,000 hours per employee) who are paid an hourly wage divided by 2,000.

(ii) The total number of months worked in the LAMBRA for the taxpayer by employees that are salaried employees divided by 12.

(C) In the case of a taxpayer who first commences doing business in the LAMBRA during the taxable year, for purposes of clauses (i) and (ii), respectively, of subparagraph (B) the divisors "2,000" and "12" shall be multiplied by a fraction, the numerator of which is the number of months of the taxable year that the taxpayer was doing business in the LAMBRA and the denominator of which is 12.

(3) "Qualified property" means property that is each of the following:

(A) Purchased by the taxpayer for exclusive use in a trade or business conducted within a LAMBRA.

(B) Purchased before the date the LAMBRA designation expires, is no longer binding, or becomes inoperative.

(C) Any of the following:

(i) High technology equipment, including, but not limited to, computers and electronic processing equipment.

(ii) Aircraft maintenance equipment, including, but not limited to, engine stands, hydraulic mules, power carts, test equipment, handtools, aircraft start carts, and tugs.

(iii) Aircraft components, including, but not limited to, engines, fuel control units, hydraulic pumps, avionics, starts, wheels, and tires.

(iv) Section 1245 property, as defined in Section 1245(a)(3) of the Internal Revenue Code.[1]

(c) The credit provided under subdivision (a) shall only be allowed for qualified property manufactured in California unless qualified property of a comparable quality and price is not available for timely purchase and delivery from a California manufacturer.

(d) In the case where the credit otherwise allowed under this section exceeds the "tax" for the taxable year, that portion of the credit which exceeds the "tax" may be carried over and added to the credit, if any, in succeeding years, until the credit is exhausted. The credit shall be applied first to the earliest taxable years possible.

(e) Any taxpayer who elects to be subject to this section shall not be entitled to increase the basis of the property as otherwise required by Section 164(a) of the Internal Revenue Code with respect to sales or use tax paid or incurred in connection with the purchase of qualified property.

(f)(1) The amount of the credit otherwise allowed under this section and Section 23646, including any credit carryovers from prior years, that may reduce the "tax" for the taxable year shall not exceed the amount of tax that would be imposed on the taxpayer's business income attributed to a LAMBRA determined as if that attributable income represented all the income of the taxpayer subject to tax under this part.

(2) Attributable income shall be that portion of the taxpayer's California source business income that is apportioned to the LAMBRA. For that purpose, the taxpayer's business income that is attributable to sources in this state shall first be determined in accordance with Chapter 17 (commencing with Section 25101). That business income shall be further apportioned to the LAMBRA in accordance with Article 2 (commencing with Section 25120) of Chapter 17, modified for purposes of this section in accordance with paragraph (3).

(3) Income shall be apportioned to a LAMBRA by multiplying the total California business income of the taxpayer by a fraction, the numerator of which is the property factor, plus the payroll factor, and the denominator of which is two. For purposes of this paragraph:

(A) The property factor is a fraction, the numerator of which is the average value of the taxpayer's real and tangible personal property owned or rented and used in the LAMBRA during the taxable year, and the denominator of which is the average value of all the taxpayer's real and tangible personal property owned or rented and used in this state during the taxable year.

(B) The payroll factor is a fraction, the numerator of which is the total amount paid by the taxpayer in the LAMBRA during the taxable year for compensation, and the denominator of which is the total compensation paid by the taxpayer in this state during the taxable year.

(4) The portion of any credit remaining, if any, after application of this subdivision, shall be carried over to succeeding taxable years, as if it were an amount exceeding the "tax" for the taxable year, as provided in subdivision (d).

(g)(1) If the qualified property is disposed of or no longer used by the taxpayer in the LAMBRA, at any time before the close of the second taxable year after the property is placed in service, the amount of the credit previously claimed, with respect to that property, shall be added to the taxpayer's tax liability in the taxable year of that disposition or nonuse.

(2) At the close of the second taxable year, if the taxpayer has not increased the number of its employees as determined by paragraph (2) of subdivision (b), then the amount of the credit previously claimed shall be added to the taxpayer's tax for the taxpayer's second taxable year.

(h) If the taxpayer is allowed a credit for qualified property pursuant to this section, only one credit shall be allowed to the taxpayer under this part with respect to that qualified property.

(i) The amendments made to this section by the act adding this subdivision shall apply to taxable years beginning on or after January 1, 1998. *(Added by Stats.1993, c. 1216 (A.B.693), § 6, eff. Oct. 11, 1993. Amended by Stats.1996, c. 952 (S.B.715), § 44; Stats.1997, c. 605 (A.B.1040), § 78; Stats.1998, c. 1012 (A.B.3), § 8; Stats.1999, c. 987 (S.B.1229), § 83, eff. Oct. 10, 1999; Stats.2000, c. 862 (A.B.1843), § 86; Stats.2001, c. 543 (S.B.1185), § 33.)*

[1] Internal Revenue Code sections are in Title 26 of U.S.C.A.

§ **23646. Credit for hiring qualified disadvantaged individual or qualified displaced employee; local agency military base recovery area**

(a) For each taxable year beginning on or after January 1, 1995, there shall be allowed as a credit against the "tax" (as defined in Section 23036) to a qualified taxpayer for hiring a qualified disadvantaged individual or a qualified displaced employee during the taxable year for employment in the LAMBRA. The credit shall be equal to the sum of each of the following:

(1) Fifty percent of the qualified wages in the first year of employment.

(2) Forty percent of the qualified wages in the second year of employment.

(3) Thirty percent of the qualified wages in the third year of employment.

(4) Twenty percent of the qualified wages in the fourth year of employment.

(5) Ten percent of the qualified wages in the fifth year of employment.

(b) For purposes of this section:

(1) "Qualified wages" means:

(A) That portion of wages paid or incurred by the employer during the taxable year to qualified disadvantaged individuals or qualified displaced employees that does not exceed 150 percent of the minimum wage.

(B) The total amount of qualified wages which may be taken into account for purposes of claiming the credit allowed under this section shall not exceed two million dollars ($2,000,000) per taxable year.

(C) Wages received during the 60–month period beginning with the first day the individual commences employment with the taxpayer. Reemployment in connection with any increase, including a regularly occurring seasonal increase, in the trade or business operation of the qualified taxpayer does not constitute commencement of employment for purposes of this section.

(D) Qualified wages do not include any wages paid or incurred by the qualified taxpayer on or after the LAMBRA expiration date. However, wages paid or incurred with respect to qualified disadvantaged individuals or qualified displaced employees who are employed by the qualified taxpayer within the LAMBRA within the 60–month period prior to the LAMBRA expiration date shall continue to qualify for the credit under this section after the LAMBRA expiration date, in accordance with all provisions of this section applied as if the LAMBRA designation were still in existence and binding.

(2) "Minimum wage" means the wage established by the Industrial Welfare Commission as provided for in Chapter 1 (commencing with Section 1171) of Part 4 of Division 2 of the Labor Code.

(3) "LAMBRA" means a local agency military base recovery area designated in accordance with the provisions of Section 7114 of the Government Code.

(4) "Qualified disadvantaged individual" means an individual who satisfies all of the following requirements:

(A)(i) At least 90 percent of whose services for the taxpayer during the taxable year are directly related to the conduct of the taxpayer's trade or business located in a LAMBRA.

(ii) Who performs at least 50 percent of his or her services for the taxpayer during the taxable year in the LAMBRA.

(B) Who is hired by the employer after the designation of the area as a LAMBRA in which the individual's services were primarily performed.

(C) Who is any of the following immediately preceding the individual's commencement of employment with the taxpayer:

(i) An individual who has been determined eligible for services under the federal Job Training Partnership Act (29 U.S.C. Sec. 1501 et seq.), or its successor.

(ii) Any voluntary or mandatory registrant under the Greater Avenues for Independence Act of 1985 provided for pursuant to Article 3.2 (commencing with Section 11320) of Chapter 2 of Part 3 of Division 9 of the Welfare and Institutions Code.

(iii) An economically disadvantaged individual age 16 years or older.

(iv) A dislocated worker who meets any of the following conditions:

(I) Has been terminated or laid off or who has received a notice of termination or layoff from employment, is eligible for or has exhausted entitlement to

unemployment insurance benefits, and is unlikely to return to his or her previous industry or occupation.

(II) Has been terminated or has received a notice of termination of employment as a result of any permanent closure or any substantial layoff at a plant, facility, or enterprise, including an individual who has not received written notification but whose employer has made a public announcement of the closure or layoff.

(III) Is long-term unemployed and has limited opportunities for employment or reemployment in the same or a similar occupation in the area in which the individual resides, including an individual 55 years of age or older who may have substantial barriers to employment by reason of age.

(IV) Was self-employed (including farmers and ranchers) and is unemployed as a result of general economic conditions in the community in which he or she resides or because of natural disasters.

(V) Was a civilian employee of the Department of Defense employed at a military installation being closed or realigned under the Defense Base Closure and Realignment Act of 1990. [1]

(VI) Was an active member of the Armed Forces or National Guard as of September 30, 1990, and was either involuntarily separated or separated pursuant to a special benefits program.

(VII) Experiences chronic seasonal unemployment and underemployment in the agriculture industry, aggravated by continual advancements in technology and mechanization.

(VIII) Has been terminated or laid off or has received a notice of termination or layoff as a consequence of compliance with the Clean Air Act. [1]

(v) An individual who is enrolled in or has completed a state rehabilitation plan or is a service-connected disabled veteran, veteran of the Vietnam era, or veteran who is recently separated from military service.

(vi) An ex-offender. An individual shall be treated as convicted if he or she was placed on probation by a state court without a finding of guilty.

(vii) A recipient of:

(I) Federal Supplemental Security Income benefits.

(II) Aid to Families with Dependent Children.

(III) Food stamps.

(IV) State and local general assistance.

(viii) Is a member of a federally recognized Indian tribe, band, or other group of Native American descent.

(5) "Qualified taxpayer" means a corporation that conducts a trade or business within a LAMBRA and, for the first two taxable years, has a net increase in jobs (defined as 2,000 paid hours per employee per year) of one or more employees as determined below in the LAMBRA.

(A) The net increase in the number of jobs shall be determined by subtracting the total number of full-time employees (defined as 2,000 paid hours per employee per year) the taxpayer employed in this state in the taxable year prior to commencing business operations in the LAMBRA from the total number of full-time employees the taxpayer employed in this state during the second taxable year after commencing business operations in the LAMBRA. For taxpayers who commence doing business in this state with their LAMBRA business operation, the number of employees for the taxable year prior to commencing business operations in the LAMBRA shall be zero. If the taxpayer has a net increase in jobs in the state, the credit shall be allowed only if one or more full-time employees is employed within the LAMBRA.

(B) The total number of employees employed in the LAMBRA shall equal the sum of both of the following:

(i) The total number of hours worked in the LAMBRA for the taxpayer by employees (not to exceed 2,000 hours per employee) who are paid an hourly wage divided by 2,000.

(ii) The total number of months worked in the LAMBRA for the taxpayer by employees who are salaried employees divided by 12.

(C) In the case of a qualified taxpayer that first commences doing business in the LAMBRA during the taxable year, for purposes of clauses (i) and (ii), respectively, of subparagraph (B) the divisors "2,000" and "12" shall be multiplied by a fraction, the numerator of which is the number of months of the taxable year that the taxpayer was doing business in the LAMBRA and the denominator of which is 12.

(6) "Qualified displaced employee" means an individual who satisfies all of the following requirements:

(A) Any civilian or military employee of a base or former base that has been displaced as a result of a federal base closure act.

(B)(i) At least 90 percent of whose services for the taxpayer during the taxable year are directly related to the conduct of the taxpayer's trade or business located in a LAMBRA.

(ii) Who performs at least 50 percent of his or her services for the taxpayer during the taxable year in a LAMBRA.

(C) Who is hired by the employer after the designation of the area in which services were performed as a LAMBRA.

(7) "Seasonal employment" means employment by a qualified taxpayer that has regular and predictable substantial reductions in trade or business operations.

(8) "LAMBRA expiration date" means the date the LAMBRA designation expires, is no longer binding, or becomes inoperative.

(c) For qualified disadvantaged individuals or qualified displaced employees hired on or after January 1, 2001, the taxpayer shall do both of the following:

(1) Obtain from the Employment Development Department, as permitted by federal law, the administrative entity of the local county or city for the federal Job Training Partnership Act, or its successor, the local county GAIN office or social services agency, or the local government administering the LAMBRA, a certification that provides that a qualified disadvantaged individual or qualified displaced employee meets the eligibility requirements specified in subparagraph (C) of paragraph (4) of subdivision (b) or subparagraph (A) of paragraph (6) of subdivision (b). The Employment Development Department may provide preliminary screening and referral to a certifying agency. The Department of Housing and Community Development shall develop regulations governing the issuance of certificates pursuant to Section 7114.2 of the Government Code and shall develop forms for this purpose.

(2) Retain a copy of the certification and provide it upon request to the Franchise Tax Board.

(d)(1) For purposes of this section, both of the following apply:

(A) All employees of all corporations that are members of the same controlled group of corporations shall be treated as employed by a single employer.

(B) The credit (if any) allowable by this section to each member shall be determined by reference to its proportionate share of the qualified wages giving rise to the credit.

(2) For purposes of this subdivision, "controlled group of corporations" has the meaning given to that term by Section 1563(a) of the Internal Revenue Code, [2] except that both of the following apply:

(A) "More than 50 percent" shall be substituted for "at least 80 percent" each place it appears in Section 1563(a)(1) of the Internal Revenue Code.

(B) The determination shall be made without regard to Section 1563(a)(4) and Section 1563(e)(3)(C) of the Internal Revenue Code.

(3) If an employer acquires the major portion of a trade or business of another employer (hereinafter in this paragraph referred to as the "predecessor") or the major portion of a separate unit of a trade or business of a predecessor, then, for purposes of applying this section (other than subdivision (e)) for any calendar year ending after that acquisition, the employment relationship between an employee and an employer shall not be treated as terminated if the employee continues to be employed in that trade or business.

(e)(1)(A) If the employment of any employee, other than seasonal employment, with respect to whom qualified wages are taken into account under subdivision (a) is terminated by the taxpayer at any time during the first 270 days of that employment (whether or not consecutive) or before the close of the 270th calendar day after the day in which that employee completes 90 days of employment with the taxpayer, the tax imposed by this part for the taxable year in which that employment is

873

terminated shall be increased by an amount equal to the credit allowed under subdivision (a) for that taxable year and all prior income years attributable to qualified wages paid or incurred with respect to that employee.

(B) If the seasonal employment of any qualified disadvantaged individual, with respect to whom qualified wages are taken into account under subdivision (a) is not continued by the qualified taxpayer for a period of 270 days of employment during the 60–month period beginning with the day the qualified disadvantaged individual commences seasonal employment with the qualified taxpayer, the tax imposed by this part, for the taxable year that includes the 60th month following the month in which the qualified disadvantaged individual commences seasonal employment with the qualified taxpayer, shall be increased by an amount equal to the credit allowed under subdivision (a) for that taxable year and all prior taxable years attributable to qualified wages paid or incurred with respect to that qualified disadvantaged individual.

(2)(A) Subparagraph (A) of paragraph (1) shall not apply to any of the following:

(i) A termination of employment of an employee who voluntarily leaves the employment of the taxpayer.

(ii) A termination of employment of an individual who, before the close of the period referred to in paragraph (1), becomes disabled to perform the services of that employment, unless that disability is removed before the close of that period and the taxpayer fails to offer reemployment to that individual.

(iii) A termination of employment of an individual, if it is determined that the termination was due to the misconduct (as defined in Sections 1256–30 to 1256–43, inclusive, of Title 22 of the California Code of Regulations) of that individual.

(iv) A termination of employment of an individual due to a substantial reduction in the trade or business operations of the taxpayer.

(v) A termination of employment of an individual, if that individual is replaced by other qualified employees so as to create a net increase in both the number of employees and the hours of employment.

(B) Subparagraph (B) of paragraph (1) shall not apply to any of the following:

(i) A failure to continue the seasonal employment of a qualified disadvantaged individual who voluntarily fails to return to the seasonal employment of the qualified taxpayer.

(ii) A failure to continue the seasonal employment of a qualified disadvantaged individual who, before the close of the period referred to in subparagraph (B) of paragraph (1), becomes disabled and unable to perform the services of that seasonal employment, unless that disability is removed before the close of that period and the qualified taxpayer fails to offer seasonal employment to that qualified disadvantaged individual.

(iii) A failure to continue the seasonal employment of a qualified disadvantaged individual, if it is determined that the failure to continue the seasonal employment was due to the misconduct (as defined in Sections 1256–30 to 1256–43, inclusive, of Title 22 of the California Code of Regulations) of that individual.

(iv) A failure to continue seasonal employment of a qualified disadvantaged individual due to a substantial reduction in the regular seasonal trade or business operations of the qualified taxpayer.

(v) A failure to continue the seasonal employment of a qualified disadvantaged individual, if that individual is replaced by other qualified disadvantaged individuals so as to create a net increase in both the number of seasonal employees and the hours of seasonal employment.

(C) For purposes of paragraph (1), the employment relationship between the taxpayer and an employee shall not be treated as terminated by either of the following:

(i) A transaction to which Section 381(a) of the Internal Revenue Code applies, if the employee continues to be employed by the acquiring corporation.

(ii) A mere change in the form of conducting the trade or business of the taxpayer, if the employee continues to be employed in that trade or business and the taxpayer retains a substantial interest in that trade or business.

(3) Any increase in tax under paragraph (1) shall not be treated as tax imposed by this part for purposes of determining the amount of any credit allowable under this part.

(4) At the close of the second taxable year, if the taxpayer has not increased the number of its employees as determined by paragraph (5) of subdivision (b), then the amount of the credit previously claimed shall be added to the taxpayer's tax for the taxpayer's second taxable year.

(f) In the case of an organization to which Section 593 of the Internal Revenue Code applies, and a regulated investment company or a real estate investment trust subject to taxation under this part, rules similar to the rules provided in Section 46(e) and Section 46(h) of the Internal Revenue Code shall apply.

(g) The credit shall be reduced by the credit allowed under Section 23621. The credit shall also be reduced by the federal credit allowed under Section 51 of the Internal Revenue Code.

In addition, any deduction otherwise allowed under this part for the wages or salaries paid or incurred by the taxpayer upon which the credit is based shall be reduced by the amount of the credit, prior to any reduction required by subdivision (h) or (i).

(h) In the case where the credit otherwise allowed under this section exceeds the "tax" for the taxable year, that portion of the credit that exceeds the "tax" may be carried over and added to the credit, if any, in succeeding years, until the credit is exhausted. The credit shall be applied first to the earliest taxable years possible.

(i)(1) The amount of credit otherwise allowed under this section and Section 23645, including any prior year carryovers, that may reduce the "tax" for the taxable year shall not exceed the amount of tax that would be imposed on the taxpayer's business income attributed to a LAMBRA determined as if that attributed income represented all of the income of the taxpayer subject to tax under this part.

(2) Attributable income shall be that portion of the taxpayer's California source business income that is apportioned to the LAMBRA. For that purpose, the taxpayer's business income that is attributable to sources in this state first shall be determined in accordance with Chapter 17 (commencing with Section 25101). That business income shall be further apportioned to the LAMBRA in accordance with Article 2 (commencing with Section 25120) of Chapter 17, modified for purposes of this section in accordance with paragraph (3).

(3) Income shall be apportioned to a LAMBRA by multiplying the total California business income of the taxpayer by a fraction, the numerator of which is the property factor plus the payroll factor, and the denominator of which is two. For purposes of this paragraph:

(A) The property factor is a fraction, the numerator of which is the average value of the taxpayer's real and tangible personal property owned or rented and used in the LAMBRA during the taxable year, and the denominator of which is the average value of all the taxpayer's real and tangible personal property owned or rented and used in this state during the taxable year.

(B) The payroll factor is a fraction, the numerator of which is the total amount paid by the taxpayer in the LAMBRA during the taxable year for compensation, and the denominator of which is the total compensation paid by the taxpayer in this state during the taxable year.

(4) The portion of any credit remaining, if any, after application of this subdivision, shall be carried over to succeeding taxable years, as if it were an amount exceeding the "tax" for the taxable year, as provided in subdivision (h).

(j) If the taxpayer is allowed a credit pursuant to this section for qualified wages paid or incurred, only one credit shall be allowed to the taxpayer under this part with respect to any wage consisting in whole or in part of those qualified wages. *(Added by Stats.1993, c. 1216 (A.B.693), § 7, eff. Oct. 11, 1993. Amended by Stats.1996, c. 952 (S.B.715), § 45; Stats.1997, c. 605 (A.B.1040), § 79; Stats.1998, c. 1012 (A.B.3), § 9; Stats.1998, c. 1039 (A.B.2809), § 14, eff. Sept. 30, 1998, operative Sept. 30, 1998; Stats.1998, c. 1039 (A.B.2809), § 14.5, eff. Sept. 30, 1998, operative Jan. 1, 1999; Stats.2000, c. 862 (A.B.1843), § 87; Stats.2000, c. 864 (A.B.2895), § 4; Stats.2001, c. 159 (S.B.662), § 184; Stats.2001, c. 543 (S.B.1185), § 34; Stats.2006, c. 634 (S.B.763), § 11.)*

[1] Acts of Congress, alternate or descriptive name of acts, enacting credit, and sections, if any, classified to U.S.C.A., see Popular Name Table for Acts of Congress.

[2] Internal Revenue Code Sections are in Title 26 of the U.S.C.A.

CHAPTER 7. NET INCOME

ARTICLE 2. SPECIAL DEDUCTIONS

Section
24416.   Net operating loss deduction; carryovers and carrybacks.
24416.1. Net operating loss deduction; election; carryovers.
24416.2. Qualified taxpayer.
24416.3. Net operating loss deduction; taxable years 2002 and 2003; extension of carryover period.
24416.4. Corporations engaged in conduct of trade or business within the Los Angeles Revitalization Zone; net operating loss deductions.
24416.5. Taxpayers engaged in the conduct of a trade or business within a LAMBRA; net operating losses.
24416.6. Corporations engaged in conduct of trade or business within a targeted tax area or engaged in specified lines of business; net operating loss deductions.

§ 24416. Net operating loss deduction; carryovers and carrybacks

Except as provided in Sections 24416.1, 24416.2, 24416.4, 24416.5, 24416.6, and 24416.7, a net operating loss deduction shall be allowed in computing net income under Section 24341 and shall be determined in accordance with Section 172 of the Internal Revenue Code, [1] except as otherwise provided.

(a)(1) Net operating losses attributable to taxable years beginning before January 1, 1987, shall not be allowed.

(2) A net operating loss shall not be carried forward to any taxable year beginning before January 1, 1987.

(b)(1) Except as provided in paragraphs (2) and (3), the provisions of Section 172(b)(2) of the Internal Revenue Code, relating to the amount of carryovers, shall be modified so that the applicable percentage of the entire amount of the net operating loss for any taxable year shall be eligible for carryover to any subsequent taxable year. For purposes of this subdivision, the applicable percentage shall be:

(A) Fifty percent for any taxable year beginning before January 1, 2000.

(B) Fifty–five percent for any taxable year beginning on or after January 1, 2000, and before January 1, 2002.

(C) Sixty percent for any taxable year beginning on or after January 1, 2002, and before January 1, 2004.

(D) One hundred percent for any taxable year beginning on or after January 1, 2004.

(2) In the case of a taxpayer who has a net operating loss in any taxable year beginning on or after January 1, 1994, and who operates a new business during that taxable year, each of the following shall apply to each loss incurred during the first three taxable years of operating the new business:

(A) If the net operating loss is equal to or less than the net loss from the new business, 100 percent of the net operating loss shall be carried forward as provided in subdivision (e).

(B) If the net operating loss is greater than the net loss from the new business, the net operating loss shall be carried over as follows:

(i) With respect to an amount equal to the net loss from the new business, 100 percent of that amount shall be carried forward as provided in subdivision (e).

(ii) With respect to the portion of the net operating loss that exceeds the net loss from the new business, the applicable percentage of that amount shall be carried forward as provided in subdivision (d).

(C) For purposes of Section 172(b)(2) of the Internal Revenue Code, the amount described in clause (ii) of subparagraph (B) shall be absorbed before the amount described in clause (i) of subparagraph (B).

(3) In the case of a taxpayer who has a net operating loss in any taxable year beginning on or after January 1, 1994, and who operates an eligible small business during that taxable year, each of the following shall apply:

(A) If the net operating loss is equal to or less than the net loss from the eligible small business, 100 percent of the net operating loss shall be carried forward to the taxable years specified in paragraph (1) of subdivision (e).

(B) If the net operating loss is greater than the net loss from the eligible small business, the net operating loss shall be carried over as follows:

(i) With respect to an amount equal to the net loss from the eligible small business, 100 percent of that amount shall be carried forward as provided in subdivision (e).

(ii) With respect to that portion of the net operating loss that exceeds the net loss from the eligible small business, the applicable percentage of that amount shall be carried forward as provided in subdivision (e).

(C) For purposes of Section 172(b)(2) of the Internal Revenue Code, the amount described in clause (ii) of subparagraph (B) shall be absorbed before the amount described in clause (i) of subparagraph (B).

(4) In the case of a taxpayer who has a net operating loss in a taxable year beginning on or after January 1, 1994, and who operates a business that qualifies as both a new business and an eligible small business under this section, that business shall be treated as a new business for the first three taxable years of the new business.

(5) In the case of a taxpayer who has a net operating loss in a taxable year beginning on or after January 1, 1994, and who operates more than one business, and more than one of those businesses qualifies as either a new business or an eligible small business under this section, paragraph (2) shall be applied first, except that if there is any remaining portion of the net operating loss after application of clause (i) of subparagraph (B) of paragraph (2), paragraph (3) shall be applied to the remaining portion of the net operating loss as though that

remaining portion of the net operating loss constituted the entire net operating loss.

(6) For purposes of this section, "net loss" means the amount of net loss after application of Sections 465 and 469 of the Internal Revenue Code.

(c) For any taxable year in which the taxpayer has in effect a water's-edge election under Section 25110, the deduction of a net operating loss carryover shall be denied to the extent that the net operating loss carryover was determined by taking into account the income and factors of an affiliated corporation in a combined report whose income and apportionment factors would not have been taken into account if a water's-edge election under Section 25110 had been in effect for the taxable year in which the loss was incurred.

(d) Section 172(b)(1) of the Internal Revenue Code, relating to net operating loss carrybacks and carryovers and the years to which the loss may be carried, is modified as follows:

(1) Net operating loss carrybacks shall not be allowed for any net operating losses attributable to taxable years beginning before January 1, 2011.

(2) A net operating loss attributable to taxable years beginning on or after January 1, 2011, shall be a net operating loss carryback to each of the two taxable years preceding the taxable year of the loss in lieu of the number of years provided therein.

(A) For a net operating loss attributable to a taxable year beginning on or after January 1, 2011, and before January 1, 2012, the amount of carryback to any taxable year shall not exceed 50 percent of the net operating loss.

(B) For a net operating loss attributable to a taxable year beginning on or after January 1, 2012, and before January 1, 2013, the amount of carryback to any taxable year shall not exceed 75 percent of the net operating loss.

(C) For a net operating loss attributable to a taxable year beginning on or after January 1, 2013, the amount of carryback to any taxable year shall not exceed 100 percent of the net operating loss.

(3) Notwithstanding paragraph (2), Section 172(b)(1)(B) of the Internal Revenue Code, relating to special rules for REITs, and Sections 172(b)(1)(E) and 172(h) of the Internal Revenue Code, relating to corporate equity reduction interest loss, shall apply as provided.

(4) A net operating loss carryback shall not be carried back to any taxable year beginning before January 1, 2009.

(e)(1)(A) For a net operating loss for any taxable year beginning on or after January 1, 1987, and before January 1, 2000, Section 172(b)(1)(A)(ii) of the Internal Revenue Code, relating to years to which net operating losses may be carried, is modified to substitute "five taxable years" in lieu of "20 years" except as otherwise provided in paragraphs (2), (3), and (4).

(B) For a net operating loss for any income year beginning on or after January 1, 2000, and before January

1, 2008, Section 172(b)(1)(A)(ii) of the Internal Revenue Code, relating to years to which net operating losses may be carried, is modified to substitute "10 taxable years" in lieu of "20 taxable years."

(2) For any income year beginning before January 1, 2000, in the case of a "new business," the "five taxable years" referred to in paragraph (1) shall be modified to read as follows:

(A) "Eight taxable years" for a net operating loss attributable to the first taxable year of that new business.

(B) "Seven taxable years" for a net operating loss attributable to the second taxable year of that new business.

(C) "Six taxable years" for a net operating loss attributable to the third taxable year of that new business.

(3) For any carryover of a net operating loss for which a deduction is denied by Section 24416.3, the carryover period specified in this subdivision shall be extended as follows:

(A) By one year for a net operating loss attributable to taxable years beginning in 1991.

(B) By two years for a net operating loss attributable to taxable years beginning prior to January 1, 1991.

(4) The net operating loss attributable to taxable years beginning on or after January 1, 1987, and before January 1, 1994, shall be a net operating loss carryover to each of the 10 taxable years following the year of the loss if it is incurred by a corporation that was either of the following:

(A) Under the jurisdiction of the court in a Title 11 or similar case at any time prior to January 1, 1994. The loss carryover provided in the preceding sentence shall not apply to any loss incurred in an income year after the taxable year during which the corporation is no longer under the jurisdiction of the court in a Title 11 or similar case.

(B) In receipt of assets acquired in a transaction that qualifies as a tax-free reorganization under Section 368(a)(1)(G) of the Internal Revenue Code.

(f) For purposes of this section:

(1) "Eligible small business" means any trade or business that has gross receipts, less returns and allowances, of less than one million dollars ($1,000,000) during the income year.

(2) Except as provided in subdivision (g), "new business" means any trade or business activity that is first commenced in this state on or after January 1, 1994.

(3) "Title 11 or similar case" shall have the same meaning as in Section 368(a)(3) of the Internal Revenue Code.

(4) In the case of any trade or business activity conducted by a partnership or an "S corporation," paragraphs (1) and (2) shall be applied to the partnership or "S corporation."

(g) For purposes of this section, in determining whether a trade or business activity qualifies as a new business under paragraph (2) of subdivision (e), the following rules shall apply:

(1) In any case where a taxpayer purchases or otherwise acquires all or any portion of the assets of an existing trade or business (irrespective of the form of entity) that is doing business in this state (within the meaning of Section 23101), the trade or business thereafter conducted by the taxpayer (or any related person) shall not be treated as a new business if the aggregate fair market value of the acquired assets (including real, personal, tangible, and intangible property) used by the taxpayer (or any related person) in the conduct of its trade or business exceeds 20 percent of the aggregate fair market value of the total assets of the trade or business being conducted by the taxpayer (or any related person). For purposes of this paragraph only, the following rules shall apply:

(A) The determination of the relative fair market values of the acquired assets and the total assets shall be made as of the last day of the first taxable year in which the taxpayer (or any related person) first uses any of the acquired trade or business assets in its business activity.

(B) Any acquired assets that constituted property described in Section 1221(1) of the Internal Revenue Code in the hands of the transferor shall not be treated as assets acquired from an existing trade or business, unless those assets also constitute property described in Section 1221(1) of the Internal Revenue Code in the hands of the acquiring taxpayer (or related person).

(2) In any case where a taxpayer (or any related person) is engaged in one or more trade or business activities in this state, or has been engaged in one or more trade or business activities in this state within the preceding 36 months ("prior trade or business activity"), and thereafter commences an additional trade or business activity in this state, the additional trade or business activity shall only be treated as a new business if the additional trade or business activity is classified under a different division of the Standard Industrial Classification (SIC) Manual published by the United States Office of Management and Budget, 1987 edition, than are any of the taxpayer's (or any related person's) current or prior trade or business activities.

(3) In any case where a taxpayer, including all related persons, is engaged in trade or business activities wholly outside of this state and the taxpayer first commences doing business in this state (within the meaning of Section 23101) after December 31, 1993 (other than by purchase or other acquisition described in paragraph (1)), the trade or business activity shall be treated as a new business under paragraph (2) of subdivision (e).

(4) In any case where the legal form under which a trade or business activity is being conducted is changed, the change in form shall be disregarded and the determination of whether the trade or business activity is a new business shall be made by treating the taxpayer as having purchased or otherwise acquired all or any portion of the

assets of an existing trade or business under the rules of paragraph (1) of this subdivision.

(5) "Related person" shall mean any person that is related to the taxpayer under either Section 267 or 318 of the Internal Revenue Code.

(6) "Acquire" shall include any transfer, whether or not for consideration.

(7)(A) For taxable years beginning on or after January 1, 1997, the term "new business" shall include any taxpayer that is engaged in biopharmaceutical activities or other biotechnology activities that are described in Codes 2833 to 2836, inclusive, of the Standard Industrial Classification (SIC) Manual published by the United States Office of Management and Budget, 1987 edition, and as further amended, and that has not received regulatory approval for any product from the United States Food and Drug Administration.

(B) For purposes of this paragraph:

(i) "Biopharmaceutical activities" means those activities that use organisms or materials derived from organisms, and their cellular, subcellular, or molecular components, in order to provide pharmaceutical products for human or animal therapeutics and diagnostics. Biopharmaceutical activities make use of living organisms to make commercial products, as opposed to pharmaceutical activities that make use of chemical compounds to produce commercial products.

(ii) "Other biotechnology activities" means activities consisting of the application of recombinant DNA technology to produce commercial products, as well as activities regarding pharmaceutical delivery systems designed to provide a measure of control over the rate, duration, and site of pharmaceutical delivery.

(h) For purposes of corporations whose net income is determined under Chapter 17 (commencing with Section 25101), Section 25108 shall apply to each of the following:

(1) The amount of net operating loss incurred in any taxable year that may be carried forward to another taxable year.

(2) The amount of any loss carry forward that may be deducted in any taxable year.

(i) The provisions of Section 172(b)(1)(D) of the Internal Revenue Code, relating to bad debt losses of commercial banks, shall not be applicable.

(j) The Franchise Tax Board may prescribe appropriate regulations to carry out the purposes of this section, including any regulations necessary to prevent the avoidance of the purposes of this section through splitups, shell corporations, partnerships, tiered ownership structures, or otherwise.

(k) The Franchise Tax Board may reclassify any net operating loss carryover determined under either paragraph (2) or (3) of subdivision (b) as a net operating loss carryover under paragraph (1) of subdivision (b) upon a showing that the reclassification is necessary to prevent evasion of the purposes of this section.

(*l*) Except as otherwise provided, the amendments made by Chapter 107 of the Statutes of 2000 shall apply to net operating losses for taxable years beginning on or after January 1, 2000. *(Added by Stats.1984, c. 938, § 30, eff. Sept. 7, 1984. Amended by Stats.1985, c. 159, § 20.5, eff. July 8, 1985; Stats.1987, c. 1139, § 87, eff. Sept. 25, 1987; Stats.1988, c. 11, § 70, eff. Feb. 19, 1988; Stats. 1988, c. 1465, § 40, eff. Sept. 28, 1988; Stats.1989, c. 581, § 7.5, eff. Sept. 21, 1989; Stats.1991, c. 117 (S.B.169), § 73, eff. July 16, 1991; Stats.1991, c. 474 (A.B.31), § 12, eff. Oct. 2, 1991; Stats.1992, c. 1295 (S.B.1684), § 32; Stats.1993, c. 880 (A.B.34), § 2, eff. Oct. 6, 1993; Stats. 1994, c. 948 (S.B.707), § 7, eff. Sept. 28, 1994; Stats.1994, c. 949 (A.B.2407), § 4, eff. Sept. 28, 1994; Stats.1996, c. 954 (S.B.38), § 46, eff. Sept. 26, 1996; Stats.1997, c; 605 (A.B.1040), § 95; Stats.1998, c. 322 (A.B.2797), § 86, eff. Aug. 20, 1998; Stats.1998, c. 1039 (A.B.2809), § 15, eff. Sept. 30, 1998; Stats.2000, c. 862 (A.B.1843), § 159; Stats.2000, c. 104 (A.B.1774), § 2, eff. July 10, 2000; Stats.2000, c. 107 (A.B.511), § 9, eff. July 10, 2000; Stats.2001, c. 543 (S.B.1185), § 37; Stats.2001, c. 623 (A.B.238), § 4, eff. Oct. 9, 2001; Stats.2002, c. 488 (A.B.2065), § 10, eff. Sept. 12, 2002; Stats.2008, c. 763 (A.B.1452), § 11, eff. Sept. 30, 2008.)*

[1] Internal Revenue Code sections are in Title 26 of the U.S.C.A.

§ 24416.1. Net operating loss deduction; election; carryovers

(a) A qualified taxpayer, as defined in Section 24416.2, 24416.4, 24416.5, 24416.6, or 24416.7, may elect to take the deduction provided by Section 172 of the Internal Revenue Code, relating to the net operating loss deduction, as modified by Section 24416, in computing net income under Section 24341, with the following exceptions to Section 24416:

(1) Subdivision (a) of Section 24416, relating to years in which allowable losses are sustained, shall not be applicable.

(2) Subdivision (b) of Section 24416, relating to the 50–percent reduction of losses, shall not be applicable.

(3) The provisions of subparagraphs (B) and (C) of Section 172 (b)(1) of the Internal Revenue Code shall not apply. To the extent applicable to California law, net operating losses attributable to entities with losses described by Section 172(b)(1)(J) shall be applied in accordance with Section 172(b)(1)(A) and (B) of the Internal Revenue Code.

(b) Corporations whose income is subject to the provisions of Section 25101 or 25101.15 shall make the computations required by Section 25108.

(c) The election to compute the net operating loss under this section shall be made in a statement attached to the original return, timely filed for the year in which the net operating loss is incurred and shall be irrevocable. In addition to the exceptions specified in subdivision (a), Section 24416.2, 24416.4, 24416.5, 24416.6, or 24416.7, as appropriate, shall be applicable.

(d) Any carryover of a net operating loss sustained by a qualified taxpayer, as defined in subdivision (a) or (b) of Section 24416.2 as that section read immediately prior to January 1, 1997, shall, if previously elected, continue to be a deduction, as provided in subdivision (a), applied as if the provisions of subdivision (a) or (b) of Section 24416.2, as that section read prior to January 1, 1997, still applied. *(Added by Stats.1988, c. 32, § 5, eff. March 15, 1988. Amended by Stats.1989, c. 581, § 8, eff. Sept. 21, 1989; Stats.1991, c. 117 (S.B.169), § 74, eff. July 16, 1991; Stats.1996, c. 953 (A.B.296), § 29; Stats.1996, c. 955 (S.B.2023), § 29; Stats.1998, c. 1039 (A.B.2809), § 16, eff. Sept. 30, 1998; Stats.2001, c. 623 (A.B.238), § 5, eff. Oct. 9, 2001.)*

§ 24416.2. Qualified taxpayer

(a) The term "qualified taxpayer" as used in Section 24416.1 includes a corporation engaged in the conduct of a trade or business within an enterprise zone designated pursuant to Chapter 12.8 (commencing with Section 7070) of Division 7 of Title 1 of the Government Code. For purposes of this subdivision, all of the following shall apply:

(1) A net operating loss shall not be a net operating loss carryback for any taxable year and a net operating loss for any taxable year beginning on or after the date that the area in which the taxpayer conducts a trade or business is designated as an enterprise zone shall be a net operating loss carryover to each of the 15 taxable years following the taxable year of loss.

(2) For purposes of this subdivision:

(A) "Net operating loss" means the loss determined under Section 172 of the Internal Revenue Code, as modified by Section 24416.1, attributable to the taxpayer's business activities within the enterprise zone (as defined in Chapter 12.8 (commencing with Section 7070) of Division 7 of Title 1 of the Government Code) prior to the enterprise zone expiration date. That attributable loss shall be determined in accordance with Chapter 17 (commencing with Section 25101), modified for purposes of this subdivision as follows:

(i) Loss shall be apportioned to the enterprise zone by multiplying total loss from the business by a fraction, the numerator of which is the property factor plus the payroll factor, and the denominator of which is two.

(ii) "The enterprise zone" shall be substituted for "this state."

(B) A net operating loss carryover shall be a deduction only with respect to the taxpayer's business income attributable to the enterprise zone as defined in Chapter 12.8 (commencing with Section 7070) of Division 7 of Title 1 of the Government Code.

(C) Attributable income is that portion of the taxpayer's California source business income that is apportioned to the enterprise zone. For that purpose, the taxpayer's business income attributable to sources in this state first shall be determined in accordance with Chapter 17

(commencing with Section 25101). That business income shall be further apportioned to the enterprise zone in accordance with Article 2 (commencing with Section 25120) of Chapter 17, modified for purposes of this subdivision as follows:

(i) Business income shall be apportioned to the enterprise zone by multiplying the total California business income of the taxpayer by a fraction, the numerator of which is the property factor plus the payroll factor, and the denominator of which is two. For purposes of this clause:

(I) The property factor is a fraction, the numerator of which is the average value of the taxpayer's real and tangible personal property owned or rented and used in the enterprise zone during the taxable year, and the denominator of which is the average value of all the taxpayer's real and tangible personal property owned or rented and used in this state during the taxable year.

(II) The payroll factor is a fraction, the numerator of which is the total amount paid by the taxpayer in the enterprise zone during the taxable year for compensation, and the denominator of which is the total compensation paid by the taxpayer in this state during the taxable year.

(ii) If a loss carryover is allowable pursuant to this section for any taxable year after the enterprise zone designation has expired, the enterprise zone shall be deemed to remain in existence for purposes of computing the limitation set forth in subparagraph (B) and allowing a net operating loss deduction.

(D) "Enterprise zone expiration date" means the date the enterprise zone designation expires, is no longer binding, or becomes inoperative.

(3) The changes made to this subdivision by the act adding this paragraph shall apply to taxable years beginning on or after January 1, 1998.

(b) A taxpayer who qualifies as a "qualified taxpayer" under one or more sections shall, for the taxable year of the net operating loss and any taxable year to which that net operating loss may be carried, designate on the original return filed for each year the section which applies to that taxpayer with respect to that net operating loss. If the taxpayer is eligible to qualify under more than one section, the designation is to be made after taking into account subdivision (c).

(c) If a taxpayer is eligible to qualify under this section and either Section 24416.4, 24416.5, or 24416.6 as a "qualified taxpayer," with respect to a net operating loss in a taxable year, the taxpayer shall designate which section is to apply to the taxpayer.

(d) Notwithstanding Section 24416, the amount of the loss determined under this section, or Section 24416.4, 24416.5, or 24416.6 shall be the only net operating loss allowed to be carried over from that taxable year and the designation under subdivision (b) shall be included in the election under Section 24416.1. *(Added by Stats.1989, c. 581, § 9, eff. Sept. 21, 1989. Amended by Stats.1990, c. 330 (A.B.379), § 9, eff. July 17, 1990; Stats.1991, c. 474*

(A.B.31), § 13, eff. Oct. 2, 1991; Stats.1991–92, 1st Ex.Sess., c. 17 (A.B.38), § 17, eff. Sept. 21, 1992; Stats. 1993, c. 18 (A.B.18), § 15, eff. May 27, 1993; Stats.1993, c. 1216 (A.B.693), § 9, eff. Oct. 11, 1993; Stats.1994, c. 606 (A.B.3121), § 14, eff. Sept. 16, 1994; Stats.1994, c. 756 (A.B.1313), § 11, eff. Sept. 23, 1994; Stats.1995, c. 494 (S.B.712), § 16; Stats.1996, c. 953 (A.B.296), § 30; Stats. 1996, c. 955 (S.B.2023), § 29.5; Stats.1997, c. 602 (A.B. 1217), § 11; Stats.1997, c. 604 (S.B.1106), § 37, eff. Oct. 3, 1997; Stats.1997, c. 605 (A.B.1040), § 96.5; Stats.1998, c. 7 (S.B.519), § 33, eff. March 14, 1998; Stats.1998, c. 323 (A.B.2798), § 32, eff. Aug. 20, 1998, operative Aug. 20, 1998; Stats.1998, c. 1039 (A.B.2809), § 17.5, eff. Sept. 30, 1998, operative Sept. 30, 1998; Stats.1999, c. 83 (S.B.966), § 182; Stats.1999, c. 987 (S.B.1229), § 98, eff. Oct. 10, 1999; Stats.2000, c. 862 (A.B.1843), § 160.)

§ 24416.3.   Net operating loss deduction; taxable years 2002 and 2003; extension of carryover period

(a) Notwithstanding Sections 24416, 24416.1, 24416.2, 24416.4, 24416.5, 24416.6, and 24416.7 of this code and Section 172 of the Internal Revenue Code, no net operating loss deduction shall be allowed for any taxable year beginning on or after January 1, 2002, and before January 1, 2004.

(b) For any carryover of a net operating loss for which a deduction is denied by subdivision (a), the carryover period under Section 172 of the Internal Revenue Code shall be extended as follows:

(1) By one year, for losses incurred in taxable years beginning on or after January 1, 2002, and before January 1, 2003.

(2) By two years, for losses incurred in taxable years beginning before January 1, 2002.

(Added by Stats.1991, c. 117 (S.B.169), § 75, eff. July 16, 1991. Amended by Stats.1991, c. 474 (A.B.31), § 14, eff. Oct. 2, 1991; Stats.1992, c. 52 (A.B.1951), § 2, eff. May 8, 1992; Stats.2002, c. 488 (A.B.2065), § 11, eff. Sept. 12, 2002.)

§ 24416.4.   Corporations engaged in conduct of trade or business within the Los Angeles Revitalization Zone; net operating loss deductions

(a) The term "qualified taxpayer" as used in Section 24416.1 includes a corporation engaged in the conduct of a trade or business within the Los Angeles Revitalization Zone designated pursuant to Section 7102 of the Government Code. For purposes of this subdivision, all of the following shall apply:

(1) A net operating loss shall not be a net operating loss carryback for any taxable year and, except as provided in subparagraph (B), a net operating loss for any taxable year beginning on or after the date the area in which the taxpayer conducts a trade or business is designated the Los Angeles Revitalization Zone shall be a net operating loss carryover to each following taxable year that ends before the Los Angeles Revitalization

Zone expiration date or to each of the 15 taxable years following the taxable year of loss, if longer.

(2) In the case of a financial institution to which Section 585, 586, or 593 of the Internal Revenue Code applies, a net operating loss for any taxable year beginning on or after January 1, 1984, shall be a net operating loss carryover to each of the five years following the taxable year of the loss. Subdivision (b) of Section 24416.1 shall not apply.

(3) "Net operating loss" means the loss determined under Section 172 of the Internal Revenue Code, as modified by Section 24416.1, attributable to the taxpayer's business activities within the Los Angeles Revitalization Zone (as defined in Section 7102 of the Government Code) prior to the Los Angeles Revitalization Zone expiration date. The attributable loss shall be determined in accordance with Chapter 17 (commencing with Section 25101) of Part 11, modified as follows:

(A) The loss shall be apportioned to the Los Angeles Revitalization Zone by multiplying the loss from the business by a fraction, the numerator of which is the property factor plus the payroll factor, and the denominator of which is 2.

(B) "The Los Angeles Revitalization Zone" shall be substituted for "this state."

(4) A net operating loss carryover shall be a deduction only with respect to the taxpayer's business income attributable to the Los Angeles Revitalization Zone (as defined in Section 7102 of the Government Code) determined in accordance with subdivision (c).

(5) If a loss carryover is allowable pursuant to this section for any taxable year after the Los Angeles Revitalization Zone designation has expired, the Los Angeles Revitalization Zone shall be deemed to remain in existence for purposes of computing the limitation set forth in paragraph (2) and allowing a net operating loss deduction.

(6) Attributable income shall be that portion of the taxpayer's California source business income which is apportioned to the Los Angeles Revitalization Zone. For that purpose, the taxpayer's business income attributable to sources in this state first shall be determined in accordance with Chapter 17 (commencing with Section 25101). That business income shall be further apportioned to the Los Angeles Revitalization Zone in accordance with Article 2 (commencing with Section 25120) of Chapter 17, modified as follows:

(A) Business income shall be apportioned to the Los Angeles Revitalization Zone by multiplying total California business income of the taxpayer by a fraction, the numerator of which is the property factor plus the payroll factor, and the denominator of which is 2.

(B) The property factor is a fraction, the numerator of which is the average value of the taxpayer's real and tangible personal property owned or rented and used in the Los Angeles Revitalization Zone during the taxable year and the denominator of which is the average value of all the taxpayer's real and tangible personal property owned or rented and used in this state during the taxable year.

(C) The payroll factor is a fraction, the numerator of which is the total amount paid by the taxpayer in the Los Angeles Revitalization Zone during the taxable year for compensation, and the denominator of which is the total compensation paid by the taxpayer in this state during the taxable year.

(7) "Los Angeles Revitalization Zone expiration date" means the date the Los Angeles Revitalization Zone designation expires, is repealed, or becomes inoperative pursuant to Section 7102, 7103, or 7104 of the Government Code.

(b) This section shall be inoperative on the first day of the taxable year beginning on or after the determination date, and each taxable year thereafter, with respect to the taxpayer's business activities within a geographic area that is excluded from the map pursuant to Section 7102 of the Government Code, or an excluded area determined pursuant to Section 7104 of the Government Code. The determination date is the earlier of the first effective date of a determination under subdivision (c) of Section 7102 of the Government Code occurring after December 1, 1994, or the first effective date of an exclusion of an area from the amended Los Angeles Revitalization Zone under Section 7104 of the Government Code. However, if the taxpayer has any unused loss amount as of the date this section becomes inoperative, that unused loss amount may continue to be carried forward as provided in this section.

(c) A taxpayer who qualifies as a "qualified taxpayer" under one or more sections shall, for the taxable year of the net operating loss and any taxable year to which that net operating loss may be carried, designate on the original return filed for each year the section that applies to that taxpayer with respect to that net operating loss. If the taxpayer is eligible to qualify under more than one section, the designation is to be made after taking into account subdivision (d).

(d) If a taxpayer is eligible to qualify under this section and either Section 24416.2, 24416.5, or 24416.6 as a "qualified taxpayer," with respect to a net operating loss in a taxable year, the taxpayer shall designate which section is to apply to the taxpayer.

(e) Notwithstanding Section 24416, the amount of the loss determined under this section or Section 24416.2, 24416.5, or 24416.6 shall be the only net operating loss allowed to be carried over from that taxable year and the designation under subdivision (c) shall be included in the election under Section 24416.1.

(f) This section shall cease to be operative on December 1, 1998. However, any unused net operating loss may continue to be carried over to following years as provided in this section. *(Added by Stats.1998, c. 1039 (A.B.2809), § 18, eff. Sept. 30, 1998. Amended by Stats.2000, c. 862 (A.B.1843), § 161.)*

Inoperative Date

Inoperative date of section, see subds. (b) and (f).

§ 24416.5. Taxpayers engaged in the conduct of a trade or business within a LAMBRA; net operating losses

(a) For each taxable year beginning on or after January 1, 1995, the term "qualified taxpayer" as used in Section 24416.1 includes a taxpayer engaged in the conduct of a trade or business within a LAMBRA. For purposes of this subdivision, all of the following shall apply:

(1) A net operating loss shall not be a net operating loss carryback for any taxable year and, except as provided in subparagraph (B), a net operating loss for any taxable year beginning on or after the date the area in which the taxpayer conducts a trade or business is designated a LAMBRA shall be a net operating loss carryover to each following taxable year that ends before the LAMBRA expiration date or to each of the 15 taxable years following the taxable year of loss, if longer.

(2) In the case of a financial institution to which Section 585, 586, or 593 of the Internal Revenue Code applies, a net operating loss for any taxable year beginning on or after January 1, 1984, shall be a net operating loss carryover to each of the five years following the taxable year of the loss. Subdivision (b) of Section 24416.1 shall not apply.

(3) "LAMBRA" means a local agency military base recovery area designated in accordance with Section 7114 of the Government Code.

(4) "Taxpayer" means a bank or corporation that conducts a trade or business within a LAMBRA and, for the first two taxable years, has a net increase in jobs (defined as 2,000 paid hours per employee per year) of one or more employees in the LAMBRA and this state. For purposes of this paragraph, all of the following shall apply:

(A) The net increase in the number of jobs shall be determined by subtracting the total number of full-time employees (defined as 2,000 paid hours per employee per year) the taxpayer employed in this state in the taxable year prior to commencing business operations in the LAMBRA from the total number of full-time employees the taxpayer employed in this state during the second taxable year after commencing business operations in the LAMBRA. For taxpayers who commence doing business in this state with their LAMBRA business operation, the number of employees for the taxable year prior to commencing business operations in the LAMBRA shall be zero. The deduction shall be allowed only if the taxpayer has a net increase in jobs in the state, and if one or more full-time employees are employed within the LAMBRA.

(B) The total number of employees employed in the LAMBRA shall equal the sum of both of the following:

(i) The total number of hours worked in the LAMBRA for the taxpayer by employees (not to exceed 2,000 hours per employee) who are paid an hourly wage divided by 2,000.

(ii) The total number of months worked in the LAMBRA for the taxpayer by employees who are salaried employees divided by 12.

(C) In the case of a taxpayer that first commences doing business in the LAMBRA during the taxable year, for purposes of clauses (i) and (ii), respectively, of subparagraph (B) the divisors "2,000" and "12" shall be multiplied by a fraction, the numerator of which is the number of months of the taxable year that the taxpayer was doing business in the LAMBRA and the denominator of which is 12.

(5) "Net operating loss" means the loss determined under Section 172 of the Internal Revenue Code, as modified by Section 24416.1, attributable to the taxpayer's business activities within a LAMBRA prior to the LAMBRA expiration date. The attributable loss shall be determined in accordance with Chapter 17 (commencing with Section 25101), modified for purposes of this section as follows:

(A) Loss shall be apportioned to a LAMBRA by multiplying total loss from the business by a fraction, the numerator of which is the property factor plus the payroll factor, and the denominator of which is 2.

(B) "The LAMBRA" shall be substituted for "this state."

(6) A net operating loss carryover shall be a deduction only with respect to the taxpayer's business income attributable to a LAMBRA.

(7) Attributable income is that portion of the taxpayer's California source business income that is apportioned to the LAMBRA. For that purpose, the taxpayer's business income attributable to sources in this state first shall be determined in accordance with Chapter 17 (commencing with Section 25101). That business income shall be further apportioned to the LAMBRA in accordance with Article 2 (commencing with Section 25120) of Chapter 17, modified as follows:

(A) Business income shall be apportioned to a LAMBRA by multiplying total California business income of the taxpayer by a fraction, the numerator of which is the property factor plus the payroll factor, and the denominator of which is two. For purposes of this clause:

(i) The property factor is a fraction, the numerator of which is the average value of the taxpayer's real and tangible personal property owned or rented and used in the LAMBRA during the taxable year, and the denominator of which is the average value of all the taxpayer's real and tangible personal property owned or rented and used in this state during the taxable year.

(ii) The payroll factor is a fraction, the numerator of which is the total amount paid by the taxpayer in the LAMBRA during the taxable year for compensation, and the denominator of which is the total compensation paid by the taxpayer in this state during the taxable year.

882

(B) If a loss carryover is allowable pursuant to this section for any taxable year after the LAMBRA designation has expired, the LAMBRA shall be deemed to remain in existence for purposes of computing the limitation specified in subparagraph (D) and allowing a net operating loss deduction.

(8) "LAMBRA expiration date" means the date the LAMBRA designation expires, is no longer binding, or becomes inoperative pursuant to Section 7110 of the Government Code.

(b) A taxpayer who qualifies as a "qualified taxpayer" under one or more sections shall, for the taxable year of the net operating loss and any taxable year to which that net operating loss may be carried, designate on the original return filed for each year the section that applies to that taxpayer with respect to that net operating loss. If the taxpayer is eligible to qualify under more than one section, the designation is to be made after taking into account subdivision (c).

(c) If a taxpayer is eligible to qualify under this section and either Section 24416.2, 24416.4, or 24416.6 as a "qualified taxpayer," with respect to a net operating loss in a taxable year, the taxpayer shall designate which section is to apply to the taxpayer.

(d) Notwithstanding Section 24416, the amount of the loss determined under this section or Section 24416.2, 24416.4, or 24416.6 shall be the only net operating loss allowed to be carried over from that taxable year and the designation under subdivision (b) shall be included in the election under Section 24416.1.

(e) This section shall apply to taxable years beginning on and after January 1, 1998. *(Added by Stats.1998, c. 1039 (A.B.2809), § 19.5, eff. Sept. 30, 1998, operative Sept. 30, 1998. Amended by Stats.1999, c. 987 (S.B.1229), § 99, eff. Oct. 10, 1999; Stats.2000, c. 862 (A.B.1843), § 162.)*

§ 24416.6. Corporations engaged in conduct of trade or business within a targeted tax area or engaged in specified lines of business; net operating loss deductions

(a) For each taxable year beginning on or after January 1, 1998, the term "qualified taxpayer" as used in Section 24416.1 includes a corporation that meets both of the following:

(1) Is engaged in the conduct of a trade or business within a targeted tax area designated pursuant to Chapter 12.93 (commencing with Section 7097) of Division 7 of Title 1 of the Government Code.

(2) Is engaged in those lines of business described in Codes 2000 to 2099, inclusive; 2200 to 3999, inclusive; 4200 to 4299, inclusive; 4500 to 4599, inclusive; and 4700 to 5199, inclusive, of the Standard Industrial Classification (SIC) Manual published by the United States Office of Management and Budget, 1987 edition. In the case of any pass-through entity, the determination of whether a taxpayer is a qualified taxpayer shall be made at the entity level.

(b) For purposes of subdivision (a), all of the following shall apply:

(1) A net operating loss shall not be a net operating loss carryback for any taxable year and a net operating loss for any taxable year beginning on or after the date that the area in which the qualified taxpayer conducts a trade or business is designated as a targeted tax area shall be a net operating loss carryover to each of the 15 taxable years following the taxable year of loss.

(2) "Net operating loss" means the loss determined under Section 172 of the Internal Revenue Code, as modified by Section 24416.1, attributable to the qualified taxpayer's business activities within the targeted tax area (as defined in Chapter 12.93 (commencing with Section 7097) of Division 7 of Title 1 of the Government Code) prior to the targeted tax area expiration date. That attributable loss shall be determined in accordance with Chapter 17 (commencing with Section 25101), modified for purposes of this section as follows:

(A) Loss shall be apportioned to the targeted tax area by multiplying total loss from the business by a fraction, the numerator of which is the property factor plus the payroll factor, and the denominator of which is 2.

(B) "The targeted tax area" shall be substituted for "this state."

(3) A net operating loss carryover shall be a deduction only with respect to the qualified taxpayer's business income attributable to the targeted tax area as defined in Chapter 12.93 (commencing with Section 7097) of Division 7 of Title 1 of the Government Code.

(4) Attributable income is that portion of the taxpayer's California source business income that is apportioned to the targeted tax area. For that purpose, the taxpayer's business income attributable to sources in this state first shall be determined in accordance with Chapter 17 (commencing with Section 25101). That business income shall be further apportioned to the targeted tax area in accordance with Article 2 (commencing with Section 25120) of Chapter 17, modified for purposes of this subdivision as follows:

(A) Business income shall be apportioned to the targeted tax area by multiplying the total California business income of the taxpayer by a fraction, the numerator of which is the property factor plus the payroll factor, and the denominator of which is two. For purposes of this clause:

(i) The property factor is a fraction, the numerator of which is the average value of the taxpayer's real and tangible personal property owned or rented and used in the targeted tax area during the taxable year, and the denominator of which is the average value of all the taxpayer's real and tangible personal property owned or rented and used in this state during the taxable year.

(ii) The payroll factor is a fraction, the numerator of which is the total amount paid by the taxpayer in the targeted tax area during the taxable year for compensation, and the denominator of which is the total compensation paid by the taxpayer in this state during the taxable year.

(B) If a loss carryover is allowable pursuant to this subdivision for any taxable year after the targeted tax area expiration date, the targeted tax area designation shall be deemed to remain in existence for purposes of computing the limitation specified in subparagraph (B) and allowing a net operating loss deduction.

(5) "Targeted tax area expiration date" means the date the targeted tax area designation expires, is revoked, is no longer binding, or becomes inoperative.

(c) A taxpayer who qualifies as a "qualified taxpayer" under one or more sections shall, for the taxable year of the net operating loss and any taxable year to which that net operating loss may be carried, designate on the original return filed for each year the section that applies to that taxpayer with respect to that net operating loss. If the taxpayer is eligible to qualify under more than one section, the designation is to be made after taking into account subdivision (e).

(d) If a taxpayer is eligible to qualify under this section and either Section 24416.2, 24416.4, or 24416.5 as a "qualified taxpayer," with respect to a net operating loss in a taxable year, the taxpayer shall designate which section is to apply to the taxpayer.

(e) Notwithstanding Section 24416, the amount of the loss determined under this section or Section 24416.2, 24416.4, or 24416.5 shall be the only net operating loss allowed to be carried over from that taxable year and the designation under subdivision (c) shall be included in the election under Section 24416.1.

(f) This section shall apply to taxable years beginning on or after January 1, 1998. *(Added by Stats.1998, c. 1039 (A.B.2809), § 20.5, eff. Sept. 30, 1998, operative Sept. 30, 1998. Amended by Stats.2000, c. 862 (A.B.1843), § 163.)*

ARTICLE 3. ITEMS NOT DEDUCTIBLE

Section
24424. Insurance contracts; application of Internal Revenue Code provisions relating to deductions for amounts paid.

§ 24424. Insurance contracts; application of Internal Revenue Code provisions relating to deductions for amounts paid

Section 264 of the Internal Revenue Code,[1] relating to certain amounts paid in connection with insurance contracts, shall apply, except as otherwise provided. *(Added by Stats.2002, c. 34 (S.B.657), § 52, eff. May 8, 2002; Stats.2002, c. 35 (A.B.1122), § 52, eff. May 8, 2002.)*

[1] Internal Revenue Code sections appear in Title 26 of the U.S.C.A.

Application

Application, urgency and operative effect of Stats.2002, c. 34 (S.B.657) and Stats.2002, c. 35 (A.B.1122), see §§ 61 to 78 of those Acts.

UNEMPLOYMENT INSURANCE CODE

Division		Section
	General Provisions	1
1.	Unemployment and Disability Compensation	100
1.5.	Automation of the Employment Development Department	4900
2.	Work Incentive Programs [Repealed]	
3.	Employment Services Program	9000
4.	Career Opportunities Development [Repealed]	
5.	Leisure Sharing	12100
6.	Withholding Tax on Wages	13000
7.	California Workforce Investment Act	14000
8.	California Green Collar Jobs Act of 2008	15000
9.	CalWORKS Program: Job Creation	17000
10.	Employment Assistance for Workers with Disabilities	18000
15.	Effective Date [Repealed]	

GENERAL PROVISIONS

Section

1. Designation and citation.
2. Continuation of existing law.
3. Effect on pending proceedings.
4. Construction of code.
5. Headings.
6. Delegation of powers.
7. Amendments and additions.
8. Writing.
9. Section; subdivision.
10. Tense.
11. Gender.
12. Number.
13. City.
14. County.
15. Shall and may.
16. Oath.
17. Signature and subscription.
18. Constitutionality.
19. Tenure.
20. Reference to person, officer, board or agency; transfer of functions.
21. Workers' compensation.

§ 1. Designation and citation

This act is known and may be cited as the Unemployment Insurance Code. *(Stats.1953, c. 308, p. 1457, § 1.)*

§ 2. Continuation of existing law

The provisions of this code insofar as they are substantially the same as existing statutory provisions relating to the same subject matter shall be construed as restatements and continuations, and not as new enactments. *(Stats.1953, c. 308, p. 1457, § 2.)*

§ 3. Effect on pending proceedings

Any action or proceeding commenced before this code takes effect, or any right accrued, is not affected by this code, but all procedure taken shall conform to the provisions of this code as far as possible. *(Stats.1953, c. 308, p. 1457, § 3.)*

§ 4. Construction of code

Unless the context otherwise requires, the general provisions hereinafter set forth govern the construction of this code. *(Stats.1953, c. 308, p. 1457, § 4.)*

§ 5. Headings

Division, part, chapter, article, and section headings do not in any manner affect the scope, meaning, or intent of the provisions of this code. *(Stats.1953, c. 308, p. 1457, § 5.)*

Editorial Comment

Similar provisions appear in the existing California Codes, except the Civil Code and the Code of Civil Procedure.

The judicial construction and application of the particular sections are fully annotated under the sections to which they are pertinent.

The cases are collected in West's California Digest, Statutes ⚏211. For detailed discussion, see C.J.S. Statutes § 350.

§ 6. Delegation of powers

Whenever a power is granted to, or a duty imposed on any person or board by any provision of this code, it may be exercised or performed by any deputy or person authorized by the person or board to whom the power is granted or on whom the duty is imposed, unless it is expressly provided that the power or duty shall be exercised or performed only by the person or board to whom the power is granted or on whom the duty is imposed. *(Stats.1953, c. 308, p. 1457, § 6.)*

§ 7. Amendments and additions

Whenever any reference is made to any portion of this code or of any other law, the reference applies to all amendments and additions thereto, now or hereafter made. *(Stats.1953, c. 308, p. 1457, § 7.)*

§ 8. Writing

"Writing" includes any form of recorded message capable of comprehension by ordinary visual means. Whenever any notice, report, petition, permit, statement, or record is required by this code, it shall be made in writing in the English language. *(Stats.1953, c. 308, p. 1457, § 8.)*

§ 9. Section; subdivision

"Section" means a section of this code unless some other statute is specifically mentioned, and "subdivision" means a subdivision of the section in which the term occurs unless some other section is expressly mentioned. *(Stats.1953, c. 308, p. 1458, § 9.)*

§ 10. Tense

The present tense includes the past and future tenses; and the future, the present. *(Stats.1953, c. 308, p. 1458, § 10.)*

§ 11. Gender

The masculine gender includes the feminine and neuter. *(Stats.1953, c. 308, p. 1458, § 11.)*

§ 12. Number

The singular number includes the plural and the plural the singular. *(Stats.1953, c. 308, p. 1458, § 12.)*

§ 13. City

"City" includes incorporated city, city and county, municipal corporation, municipality, town and incorporated town. *(Stats.1953, c. 308, p. 1458, § 13.)*

§ 14. County

"County" includes city and county. *(Stats.1953, c. 308, p. 1458, § 14.)*

§ 15. Shall and may

"Shall" is mandatory and "may" is permissive. *(Stats. 1953, c. 308, p. 1458, § 15.)*

§ 16. Oath

"Oath" includes affirmation and written certification or declaration subscribed to be true under penalty of perjury. *(Stats.1953, c. 308, p. 1458, § 16. Amended by Stats.1963, c. 1548, p. 3130, § 1.)*

§ 17. Signature and subscription

"Signature" or "subscription" includes mark. The mark shall be made as required in the Civil Code. *(Stats.1953, c. 308, p. 1458, § 17.)*

§ 18. Constitutionality

If any provision of this code, or its application to any person or circumstance is held invalid, the remainder of the code, or the application of the provision to other persons or circumstances is not affected. *(Stats.1953, c. 308, p. 1458, § 18.)*

§ 19. Tenure

All persons who, at the time this code goes into effect, hold office under any of the acts repealed by this code, which offices are continued by this code, continue to hold them according to their former tenure. *(Stats.1953, c. 308, p. 1458, § 19.)*

§ 20. Reference to person, officer, board or agency; transfer of functions

Whenever any reference is made to any person, officer, board, or agency by any provision of this code, the reference applies to any other person, officer, board, or agency to whom the functions vested in the person, officer, board, or agency referred to are transferred. *(Added by Stats.1959, c. 1729, p. 4174, § 1.)*

§ 21. Workers' compensation

The Legislature hereby declares its intent that the term "workmen's compensation" shall hereafter also be known as "workers' compensation." In furtherance of this policy it is the desire of the Legislature that references to the term "workmen's compensation" in this code be changed to "workers' compensation" when such code sections are being amended for any purpose. This act is declaratory and not amendatory of existing law. *(Added by Stats.1974, c. 1454, p. 3182, § 23.)*

Division 1

UNEMPLOYMENT AND DISABILITY COMPENSATION

Part		Section
1.	Unemployment Compensation	100
2.	Disability Compensation	2601
3.	Extended Unemployment Compensation	3501
4.	Federal-State Extended Compensation	4001

Part 1

UNEMPLOYMENT COMPENSATION

Chapter		Section
1.	General Provisions	100
2.	Administration	301
3.	Scope or Coverage	601
4.	Contributions and Reports	901
5.	Unemployment Compensation Benefits	1251

Chapter		Section
5.4.	Unemployment Compensation for Employees of the Legislature [Repealed]	
5.5.	Between Terms Unemployment Compensation for Nonprofessional Employees of State Special Schools	1451
5.6.	Unemployment Compensation for County Employees [Repealed]	
5.7.	Unemployment Compensation for State Higher Education Employees [Repealed]	
5.8.	Unemployment Compensation and Disability Benefits for Former Inmates of State Prisons or Institutions [Repealed]	
6.	Financial Provisions	1501
7.	Collections	1701
8.	Hearing Procedure	1951

Chapter	Section
9. Public Employment Offices	2051
9.5. Employment for Older Workers	2070
10. Violations	2101

CHAPTER 1. GENERAL PROVISIONS

Article	Section
1. Policy and Interpretation	100
2. General Definitions	125

ARTICLE 1. POLICY AND INTERPRETATION

Section
100. Public policy.
101. Part of national plan.
102. Power of legislature.

§ 100. Public policy

As a guide to the interpretation and application of this division the public policy of this State is declared as follows:

Experience has shown that large numbers of the population of California do not enjoy permanent employment by reason of which their purchasing power is unstable. This is detrimental to the interests of the people of California as a whole.

The benefit to all persons resulting from public and private enterprise is realized in the final consumption of goods and services. It is contrary to public policy to permit the supply of consumption goods and services at prices which do not provide against that harm to the population consequent upon periods of unemployment of those who contribute to the production and distribution of such goods and services.

Experience has shown that private charity and local relief cannot alone prevent the effects of unemployment. Experience has shown that if the State awaits the coming of excessive unemployment it can neither create immediately the organization necessary to orderly, economical and effective relief nor bear the financial burden of relief without disrupting its whole system of ordinary revenues and without jeopardizing its credit.

The Legislature therefore declares that in its considered judgment the public good and the general welfare of the citizens of the State require the enactment of this measure under the police power of the State, for the compulsory setting aside of funds to be used for a system of unemployment insurance providing benefits for persons unemployed through no fault of their own, and to reduce involuntary unemployment and the suffering caused thereby to a minimum.

It is the intent of the Legislature that unemployed persons claiming unemployment insurance benefits shall be required to make all reasonable effort to secure employment on their own behalf. *(Stats.1953, c. 308, p. 1458, § 100.)*

§ 101. Part of national plan

This part is a part of a national plan of unemployment reserves and social security, and is enacted for the purpose of assisting in the stabilization of employment conditions. The imposition of the tax herein imposed upon California industry alone, without a corresponding tax being imposed upon all industry in the United States, would, by the corresponding penalty upon California industry, defeat the very purposes of this law as set forth in this article. Therefore when existing federal legislation which provides for a tax upon the payment of wages by employers in this State, against which all or any part of the employer contributions required under this part may be credited is repealed, amended, interpreted, affected or otherwise changed in such manner that no portion of such contributions may be thus credited, then upon the date of such change, the provisions of this part requiring employer contributions and providing for payment of unemployment compensation benefits shall cease to be operative and any assets in the Unemployment Fund or Unemployment Administration Fund shall in the discretion of the State Treasurer be held in the then existing depositaries or otherwise in the State Treasury. In the case of the Unemployment Administration Fund, such money may thereafter be dealt with by the State Treasurer pursuant to the conditions of the grant thereof to the State by the United States Government or agency thereof. *(Stats.1953, c. 308, p. 1459, § 101.)*

§ 102. Power of legislature

All the rights, privileges or immunities conferred by this division or by acts deemed pursuant thereto shall exist subject to the power of the Legislature to amend or repeal this division at any time. *(Added by Stats.1953, c. 449, p. 1695.)*

ARTICLE 2. GENERAL DEFINITIONS

Section
125. Construction.
125.3. American aircraft.
125.4. American employer.
125.5. American vessel.
126. Appeals board.
127. Authorized regulations.
128. Benefits.
129. Calendar quarter.
130. Contingent fund.
130.5. Benefit audit fund.
131. Contributions.
133. Department.
133.5. Department of benefit payments.
134. Director.
134.1. Director of benefit payments.
134.5. Disability fund.
135. Employing unit.
135.1. Acquisition or change in form of employing unit.
135.2. Two or more businesses constituting one employing unit.
136. Federal Unemployment Tax Act.
137. Public employment office.

Section
139.   State.
140.   Unemployment compensation benefits.
140.5. Unemployment compensation disability benefits.
141.   Unemployment insurance.
142.   Unemployment trust fund.
142.5. United States.
143.   Week.
144.   Worker contributions; contributions by workers; employee contributions; contributions by employee.

§ 125. Construction

Except where the context otherwise clearly indicates, the definitions set forth in this article shall govern the construction of the provisions of this division. *(Stats. 1953, c. 308, p. 1459, § 125.)*

§ 125.3. American aircraft

"American aircraft" means an aircraft registered under the laws of the United States. *(Added by Stats.1971, c. 1107, p. 2092, § 1, eff. Oct. 18, 1971.)*

§ 125.4. American employer

"American employer" means any of the following:

(a) An individual who is a resident of the United States.

(b) A partnership, if two-thirds or more of the partners are residents of the United States.

(c) A trust, if all of the trustees are residents of the United States.

(d) A corporation organized under the laws of the United States or of any state.

(e) A limited liability company organized under the laws of the United States or of any state.

(f) Any Indian tribe as described by subsection (u) of Section 3306 of Title 26 of the United States Code. *(Added by Stats.1971, c. 1107, p. 2092, § 2, eff. Oct. 18, 1971. Amended by Stats.1994, c. 1200 (S.B.469), § 78, eff. Sept. 30, 1994; Stats.2001, c. 255 (A.B.1537), § 1.)*

Operative Effect

Under the terms of Section 17 of Stats. 2001, c. 255 (A.B.1537), the provisions of that Act are retroactive to December 21, 2000.

§ 125.5. American vessel

"American vessel" means any vessel documented or numbered under the laws of the United States, and includes any vessel which is neither documented or numbered under the laws of the United States nor documented under the laws of any foreign country, if its crew is employed solely by one or more citizens or residents of the United States or corporations organized under the laws of the United States or of any state. *(Added by Stats.1971, c. 1107, p. 2092, § 3, eff. Oct. 18, 1971.)*

§ 126. Appeals board

"Appeals Board" means the California Unemployment Insurance Appeals Board. *(Stats.1953, c. 308, p. 1460, § 126.)*

§ 127. Authorized regulations

"Authorized regulations" means regulations promulgated pursuant to the provisions of Chapter 3.5 (commencing with Section 11340) of Part 1 of Division 3 of Title 2 of the Government Code, as modified by the provisions of this division, and "regulation" includes the amendment or repeal of a regulation. *(Stats.1953, c. 308, p. 1460, § 127. Amended by Stats.1957, c. 2035, p. 3606, § 1; Stats.1963, c. 1548, p. 3130, § 2; Stats.1984, c. 193, § 141.)*

§ 128. Benefits

"Benefits" means the money payments payable to an individual, pursuant to this division, with respect to his unemployment and includes unemployment compensation benefits, federal-state extended benefits, or extended duration benefits, or disability benefits, or all of them. *(Stats.1953, c. 308, p. 1460, § 128. Amended by Stats. 1959, c. 2035, p. 4678, § 1; Stats.1970, c. 1156, p. 2043, § 1.)*

§ 129. Calendar quarter

"Calendar quarter" means the period of three consecutive calendar months ending on March 31st, June 30th, September 30th, or December 31st, or the equivalent thereof as may be prescribed by authorized regulations. *(Stats.1953, c. 308, p. 1460, § 129.)*

§ 130. Contingent fund

"Contingent fund" means the Department of Employment Development Contingent Fund. *(Stats.1953, c. 308, p. 1460, § 130. Amended by Stats.1970, c. 350, p. 756, § 1; Stats.1973, c. 1206, p. 2616, § 41; Stats.1973, c. 1207, p. 2666, § 41; Stats.1973, c. 1212, p. 2756, § 70, operative July 1, 1974.)*

§ 130.5. Benefit audit fund

"Benefit Audit Fund" means the Employment Development Department Benefit Audit Fund.

(Added by Stats.1983, c. 1219, § 1. Amended by Stats.1986, c. 360, § 1, eff. July 16, 1986; Stats.1989, c. 1010, § 1.)

§ 131. Contributions

"Contributions" means the money payments to the Unemployment Fund, Employment Training Fund, or Unemployment Compensation Disability Fund which are required by this division. *(Stats.1953, c. 308, p. 1460, § 131. Amended by Stats.1983, c. 1169, § 1.)*

§ 133. Department

Except as otherwise provided, "department" means the Employment Development Department, which also may be referred to as the Department of Employment Development. *(Stats.1953, c. 308, p. 1460, § 133. Amended by Stats.1970, c. 350, p. 756, § 2; Stats.1973, c. 1206, p. 2616, § 42; Stats.1973, c. 1207, p. 2667, § 42; Stats.1973, c. 1212, p. 2756, § 72; Stats.1974, c. 503, p. 1177, § 1.)*

§ 133.5. Department of benefit payments

"Department of Benefit Payments" or "State Department of Benefit Payments" shall be construed to refer to and mean the Employment Development Department. *(Added by Stats.1977, c. 1252, p. 4452, § 377, operative July 1, 1978.)*

§ 134. Director

Except as otherwise provided, "director" means the Director of Employment Development. *(Stats.1953, c. 308, p. 1460, § 134. Amended by Stats.1970, c. 350, p. 757, § 3; Stats.1973, c. 1206, p. 2616, § 43; Stats.1973, c. 1207, p. 2667, § 43; Stats.1973, c. 1212, p. 2756, § 74.)*

§ 134.1. Director of benefit payments

"Director of Benefit Payments" shall be construed to refer to and mean Director of Employment Development. *(Added by Stats.1977, c. 1252, p. 4452, § 378, operative July 1, 1978.)*

§ 134.5. Disability fund

"Disability fund" means the "Unemployment Compensation Disability Fund." *(Added by Stats.1953, c. 1294, p. 2854, § 1.)*

§ 135. Employing unit

(a) "Employing unit" means any individual or type of organization that has in its employ one or more individuals performing services for it within this state, and includes but is not limited to, the following individuals and organizations:

(1) Any individual or type of organization or public entity that elects coverage pursuant to any provision of this division.

(2) Any joint venture, partnership, association, trust, estate, joint stock company, insurance company, corporation whether domestic or foreign, limited liability company, whether domestic or foreign, community chest, fund, or foundation.

(3) Any public entity. As used in this section, "public entity" means the State of California (including the Trustees of the California State University), any instrumentality of this state (including the Regents of the University of California), any political subdivision of this state or any of its instrumentalities, a county, city, district (including the governing board of any school district or community college district, any county board of education, any county superintendent of schools, or any personnel commission of a school district or community college district that has a merit system pursuant to any provision of the Education Code), entities receiving state money to conduct county fairs and agricultural fairs pursuant to Sections 25905 and 25906 of the Government Code and that perform no other functions, any public authority, public agency, or public corporation of this state, any instrumentality of more than one of the foregoing, and any instrumentality of any of the foregoing and one or more other states or political subdivisions.

(4) Any instrumentality of the United States required to make payments under this division.

(5) The receiver, trustee in bankruptcy, trustee or successor thereof, and the legal representative of a deceased person.

(6) Any Indian tribe as described by subsection (u) of Section 3306 of Title 26 of the United States Code.

(b) All individuals performing services within this state for any employing unit that maintains two or more separate establishments within this state shall be deemed to be employed by a single employing unit for all the purposes of this division. This subdivision does not apply to any Indian tribe (as described by subsection (u) of Section 3306 of Title 26 of the United States Code) and the subdivisions, subsidiaries, or other business enterprises wholly owned by the Indian tribe if the tribe chooses to treat those subdivisions, subsidiaries, or other business enterprises as separate business entities for the purposes of Section 803. *(Stats.1953, c. 308, p. 1460, § 135. Amended by Stats.1959, c. 1717, p. 4124, § 3; Stats.1961, c. 2156, p. 4460, § 1; Stats.1963, c. 2015, p. 4114, § 1; Stats.1963, c. 2016, p. 4123, § 1; Stats.1969, c. 1107, p. 2113, § 7.3; Stats.1971, c. 1107, p. 2092, § 4, eff. Oct. 18, 1971; Stats.1973, c. 77, p. 130, § 20; Stats.1978, c. 2, p. 12, § 12, eff. Jun. 30, 1978, operative Jun. 1, 1978; Stats.1978, c. 397, p. 1253, § 1, eff. July 11, 1978; Stats.1981, c. 1134, p. 4447, § 1; Stats.1983, c. 143, § 216; Stats.1994, c. 1200 (S.B.469), § 79, eff. Sept. 30, 1994; Stats.2001, c. 255 (A.B.1537), § 2.)*

Operative Effect

Under the terms of Section 17 of Stats.2001, c. 255 (A.B.1537), the provisions of that Act are retroactive to December 21, 2000.

§ 135.1. Acquisition or change in form of employing unit

(a) A new employing unit shall not be created when there is an acquisition or change in the form or organization of an existing business enterprise, or severable portion thereof, and there is a continuity of control of the business enterprise.

(b) Control of a business enterprise may occur by means of ownership of the organization conducting the business enterprise, ownership of assets necessary to conduct the business enterprise, security arrangements or lease arrangements covering assets necessary to conduct the business enterprise, or a contract when the ownership, stated arrangements or contract provide for or allow direction of the internal affairs or conduct of the business enterprise.

(c) A continuity of control will exist if one or more persons, entities, or other organizations controlling the business enterprise remains in control of the business enterprise after an acquisition or change in form. Evidence of continuity of control shall include, but not be limited to, changes of an individual proprietorship to a corporation, partnership, limited liability company, association, or estate; a partnership to an individual proprietorship, corporation, limited liability company, association, estate, or the addition, deletion, or change of partners; a limited liability company to an individual proprietorship, partnership, corporation, association, estate, or to another limited liability company; a corporation to an individual proprietorship partnership, limited liability company, association, estate, or to another corporation or from any form to another form.

(d) An employing unit described in subdivision (a) shall continue to be the same employer for the purposes of this code as before the acquisition or change in form.

(e) This section shall not modify the provisions of Article 2 (commencing with Section 1731) of Chapter 7.

(f) This section shall be subject to subdivision (e) of Section 982 and subdivision (d) of Section 1127.5. (Added by Stats.1987, c. 548, § 1. Amended by Stats.1994, c. 1200 (S.B.469), § 80, eff. Sept. 30, 1994.)

§ 135.2.   Two or more businesses constituting one employing unit

(a) If two or more business enterprises are united by factors of control, operation, and use, the director may determine that the business enterprises are one employing unit.

(1) Control of a business enterprise shall include, but not be limited to, ownership of a majority interest in an organization, ownership of the assets used to conduct the business enterprise of the organization, security arrangements or lease arrangements regarding the assets used to conduct the business enterprise of the organization, or contract when the ownership, stated arrangements, or contract provide for or allow operation of the business enterprise.

(2) Operation of the business enterprise, includes, but is not limited to, management, personnel policies, operating procedures, pricing, collections, and financing of the business enterprise.

(3) Control of two or more business enterprises shall be united if the majority interest in, or control of, each organization is in one individual, entity, association, or other organization.

(4) Unity of operation is evidenced by central financing, accounting, and management of each business enterprise which includes, but is not limited to, common management, personnel policies, operating procedures, pricing, collections, and financing.

(5) The use of two or more business enterprises shall be united if they share a general system of operation and the enterprises are organized for common purposes, and

each is coordinated with, or is a part of, the entire operation.

(b) This section shall be subject to subdivision (e) of Section 982 and subdivision (d) of Section 1127.5. (Added by Stats.1987, c. 548, § 2.)

§ 136.   Federal Unemployment Tax Act

"Federal Unemployment Tax Act" means Chapter 23 of Subtitle C of the Internal Revenue Code of 1954,[1] or the corresponding provisions of any other federal act into which such provisions may hereafter be incorporated. (Stats.1953, c. 308, p. 1460, § 136. Amended by Stats. 1957, c. 1184, p. 2474, § 1.)

[1] 26 U.S.C.A. § 3301 et seq.

§ 137.   Public employment office

"Public employment office" means a free public employment office or branch thereof operated by this State or maintained as a part of a state-controlled system of public employment offices. (Stats.1953, c. 308, p. 1460, § 137.)

§ 139.   State

"State" includes the Commonwealth of Puerto Rico, the Virgin Islands, and the District of Columbia, as well as each of the states of the United States. (Stats.1953, c. 308, p. 1460, § 139. Amended by Stats.1959, c. 2156, p. 5211, § 1; Stats.1961, c. 2156, p. 4460, § 2; Stats.1978, c. 2, p. 13, § 20, eff. Jan. 30, 1978, operative Jan. 1, 1978.)

§ 140.   Unemployment compensation benefits

"Unemployment compensation benefits" refers to benefits payable under Part 1 of this division. (Stats.1953, c. 308, p. 1461, § 140.)

§ 140.5.   Unemployment compensation disability benefits

"Unemployment compensation disability benefits" or "disability benefits" refers to money payments payable under Part 2 (commencing with Section 2601) to either of the following:

(a) An eligible unemployed individual with respect to his or her wage losses due to unemployment as a result of illness or other disability, resulting in that individual being unavailable or unable to work.

(b) An eligible individual with respect to his or her wage losses who is unable to work due to caring for a seriously ill or injured family member or bonding with a minor child within one year of the birth or placement of the child in connection with foster care or adoption. (Added by Stats.1953, c. 1294, p. 2854. Amended by Stats.2003, c. 797 (S.B.727), § 3, operative Jan. 1, 2004.)

Operative Effect

For operative effect of Stats.2003, c. 797 (S.B. 727) upon benefits payable for family temporary disability insurance claims, see section 28 of that act.

§ 141. Unemployment insurance

"Unemployment insurance" wherever it appears in this division means "unemployment compensation." *(Stats. 1953, c. 308, p. 1461, § 141.)*

§ 142. Unemployment trust fund

"Unemployment Trust Fund" means the Unemployment Trust Fund established and maintained pursuant to Section 904 of the Federal Social Security Act as amended. *(Stats.1953, c. 308, p. 1461, § 142.)*

§ 142.5. United States

"United States" includes the states, the District of Columbia, the Commonwealth of Puerto Rico, and the Virgin Islands. An individual who is a citizen of the Commonwealth of Puerto Rico or the Virgin Islands (but not otherwise a citizen of the United States) shall be considered as a citizen of the United States. *(Added by Stats.1971, c. 1107, p. 2093, § 5, eff. Oct. 18, 1971. Amended by Stats.1978, c. 2, p. 13, § 21, eff. Jan. 30, 1978, operative Jan. 1, 1978.)*

§ 143. Week

"Week" means a period of seven consecutive days as prescribed by authorized regulation. Such regulation may prescribe that a week shall be deemed to be "in," "within," or "during" that benefit year which includes the greater part of such week. *(Stats.1953, c. 308, p. 1461, § 143.)*

§ 144. Worker contributions; contributions by workers; employee contributions; contributions by employee

"Worker contributions," "contributions by workers," "employee contributions," or "contributions by employees" mean contributions to the Disability Fund. *(Stats. 1953, c. 308, p. 1461, § 144.)*

CHAPTER 2. ADMINISTRATION

Article	Section
1. **Employment Development Department**	301
2. **State Advisory Council [Repealed]**	
3. **California Unemployment Insurance Appeals Board**	401
4. **Interstate and Federal Cooperation**	451

ARTICLE 1. EMPLOYMENT DEVELOPMENT DEPARTMENT

Section

301. Establishment; administration; duties; jurisdiction.
301.6. Possession and control of records, equipment, supplies, etc.
301.7. Transfer of personnel.
302. Director.
303. Deputy directors.
304. Reference to division.
305. Administrative regulations for employment development department.

Section

305.5. Retention of regulations of director of department of human resources development.
305.6. Prior regulations; effectiveness and enforcement.
306. Regulations; adoption, amendment or repeal by director of employment development.
307. Furnishing materials; fees.
310. Rules, regulations or interpretations of director or department of employment development; retroactivity.
311. Director of employment development; assistants; appointment; powers and duties.
315. Appeals division.
316. Education and public instruction.
317. Investigating staff; creation; functions.
318. Contracts, budgets and fiscal matters; director of employment development.
320. Reports by director of employment development.
320.5. Reports by employing units; regulations.
321. Information to federal agencies; director of employment development.
322. Exchange or disclosure of information; other governmental departments and agencies.
323. Advances to unemployment fund; responsibility for repayment.
324. Administration expense.
325. Powers.
325.5. Veterans' employment and training; plan; funding.
325.6. Veterans Employment Training services; legislative intent; annual report to Legislature.
326. Unemployment hazards; investigations and reports.
327. Population survey; expansion; negotiations; report; budget request; contract; publication.
329. Joint Enforcement Strike Force on the Underground Economy; agency representatives; chairperson; duties and powers; report.
333. Benefit payment control program; automation.
334. Unemployment insurance benefit overpayments; collection.
335. Coordinated efforts with film and movie industry; department obligations.
336. Establishment of procedures to identify business transfer or acquisition to obtain lower compensation rate.

§ 301. Establishment; administration; duties; jurisdiction

There is in the Labor and Workforce Development Agency the Employment Development Department, which is vested with the duties, purposes, responsibilities, and jurisdiction heretofore exercised by the State Department of Benefit Payments or the California Health and Human Services Agency with respect to job creation activities. The Employment Development Department shall be administered by an executive officer known as the Director of Employment Development who is vested with the duties, purposes, responsibilities, and jurisdiction heretofore exercised by the Director of Benefit Payments with respect to the following functions:

(a) Job creation activities.

(b) Making manual computations and making or denying recomputations of the amount and duration of benefits.

(c) Determination of contribution rates and the administration and collection of contributions, penalties and interest, including but not limited to filing and releasing liens.

(d) Establishment, administration, and transfer of reserve accounts.

(e) Making assessments and the administration of credits and refunds.

(f) Approving elections for coverage or for financing unemployment and disability insurance coverage. *(Stats. 1953, c. 308, p. 1461, § 301. Amended by Stats.1953, c. 449, p. 1695; Stats.1968, c. 1460, p. 2903, § 2; Stats.1973, c. 1206, p. 2617, § 45; Stats.1973, c. 1207, p. 2667, § 45; Stats.1973, c. 1212, p. 2757, § 78; Stats.1974, c. 503, p. 1177, § 2; Stats.1974, c. 1159, p. 2470, § 26, eff. Sept. 23, 1974; Stats.1977, c. 1252, p. 4452, § 380, operative July 1, 1978; Stats.2002, c. 859 (S.B.1236), § 13.)*

§ 301.6. Possession and control of records, equipment, supplies, etc.

The Employment Development Department shall have the possession and control of all records, papers, offices, equipment, supplies, moneys, appropriations, land, and other property real or personal held for the benefit or use of the State Department of Benefit Payments in the performance of the duties, powers, purposes, responsibilities, and jurisdiction that are vested in the Employment Development Department by Section 301. *(Added by Stats.1973, c. 1212, p. 2759, § 81, operative July 1, 1974. Amended by Stats.1977, c. 1252, p. 4452, § 381, operative July 1, 1978.)*

§ 301.7. Transfer of personnel

All officers and employees of the State Department of Benefit Payments who, on the operative date of the statute amending this section at the 1977 portion of the 1977–78 Regular Session of the Legislature, are serving in the state civil service, other than as temporary employees, and engaged in the performance of a function vested in the Employment Development Department by Section 301 shall be transferred to the Employment Development Department. The status, positions, and rights of such persons shall not be affected by the transfer and shall be retained by them as officers and employees of the Employment Development Department pursuant to the State Civil Service Act, except as to positions exempt from civil service. *(Added by Stats.1973, c. 1212, p. 2759, § 82, operative July 1, 1974. Amended by Stats.1977, c. 1252, p. 4452, § 382, operative July 1, 1978.)*

§ 302. Director

The Director of Employment Development shall be appointed by the Governor, subject to the approval of the Senate, and shall serve as director at the pleasure of the Governor. The annual salary of the Director of Employment Development shall be as provided for by Chapter 6 of Part 1 of Division 3 of Title 2 of the Government Code.[1] *(Stats.1953, c. 308, p. 1461, 302. Amended by*

892

Stats.1953, c. 1764, p. 3521, § 4; Stats.1955, c. 1166, p. 2173, § 1; Stats.1973, c. 1212, p. 2760, § 84, operative July 1, 1974.)

[1] Government Code § 11550 et seq.

§ 303. Deputy directors

There shall be five deputy directors in the Employment Development Department who shall be appointed by the Governor subject to the approval of the Senate and shall hold office at the pleasure of the Governor. The salary of the deputy directors shall be fixed in accordance with law. *(Stats.1953, c. 308, p. 1461, § 303. Amended by Stats.1953, c. 1764, p. 3521, § 1; Stats.1955, c. 1166, p. 2173, § 2; Stats.1972, c. 618, p. 1146, § 133; Stats.1973, c. 1206, p. 2617, § 48; Stats.1973, c. 1207, p. 2668, § 48; Stats.1973, c. 1212, p. 2760, § 86, operative July 1, 1974; Stats.1977, c. 1252, p. 4453, § 382.5, operative July 1, 1978.)*

§ 304. Reference to division

Whenever a reference to this division is made in this article it shall also include all other divisions of this code. *(Added by Stats.1968, c. 1460, p. 2904, § 4. Amended by Stats.1970, c. 1000, p. 1795, § 1.)*

§ 305. Administrative regulations for employment development department

Regulations for the administration of the functions of the Employment Development Department under this code shall be adopted, amended, or repealed by the Director of Employment Development as provided in Chapter 3.5 (commencing with Section 11340) of Part 1 of Division 3 of Title 2 of the Government Code. *(Stats.1953, c. 308, p. 1462, § 305. Amended by Stats. 1957, c. 2035, p. 3606, § 2; Stats.1963, c. 1548, p. 3130, § 3; Stats.1973, c. 1212, p. 2760, § 89, operative July 1, 1974; Stats.1975, c. 1140, p. 2823, § 1; Stats.2002, c. 29 (A.B.1729), § 1.)*

§ 305.5. Retention of regulations of director of department of human resources development

All regulations heretofore adopted by the Director of the Department of Human Resources Development shall remain in effect and shall be fully enforceable unless and until readopted, amended or repealed by the Director of Employment Development. *(Added by Stats.1973, c. 1206, p. 2617, § 49; Stats.1973, c. 1207, p. 2668, § 49.)*

§ 305.6. Prior regulations; effectiveness and enforcement

All regulations heretofore adopted by the Director of Benefit Payments pursuant to this code and in effect immediately preceding the operative date of the amendment of this section enacted by the Legislature during the 1977–78 Regular Session, shall remain in effect and shall be fully enforceable unless and until readopted, amended or repealed by the Director of Employment Development. *(Added by Stats.1973, c. 1212, p. 2761, § 91, operative July 1, 1974. Amended by Stats.1977, c. 1252, p.*

4453, § 385, operative July 1, 1978; Stats.1978, c. 429, p. 1430, § 166.5, eff. July 17, 1978, operative July 1, 1978.)

§ 306. Regulations; adoption, amendment or repeal by director of employment development

The Director of Employment Development may adopt, amend, or repeal such regulations as are reasonably necessary to enforce his functions under this code. *(Stats.1953, c. 308, p. 1462, § 306. Amended by Stats. 1957, c. 2035, p. 3607, § 3; Stats.1973, c. 1212, p. 2761, § 93, operative July 1, 1974.)*

§ 307. Furnishing materials; fees

The department shall provide, upon the request of any person or entity, any or all of the department's rules, regulations, guidelines, bulletins, manuals, standards of general application, or the departmental responsibilities under any state or federal law, along with any subscription service necessary to assure prompt receipt of additional amendments to any of the above materials. The department shall charge a fee to cover (1) the costs of reproducing the materials and (2) postage associated with a subscription service; however, one free copy of the materials shall be provided to each state legislator, upon request.

Any documents properly classified as confidential shall be exempt from the requirements of this section. *(Added by Stats.1984, c. 268, § 31.7, eff. June 30, 1984.)*

§ 310. Rules, regulations or interpretations of director or department of employment development; retroactivity

The Director of Employment Development or the Department of Employment Development may prescribe the extent, if any, to which any rule, regulation or interpretation issued or promulgated in accordance with the provisions of this code shall be applied without retroactive effect. *(Stats.1953, c. 308, p. 1462, § 310. Amended by Stats.1973, c. 1212, p. 2763, § 102, operative July 1, 1974.)*

§ 311. Director of employment development; assistants; appointment; powers and duties

The Director of Employment Development shall appoint such assistants except personnel of the appeals division as he finds necessary for the administration of this division, subject to the provisions of the Government Code, and may delegate to any of the officers or employees of the department such powers and duties as he considers necessary for the proper administration of this division.

The Director of Employment Development and his authorized representatives in the enforcement of the division shall have all the powers of a head of a department as set forth in Article 2 (commencing with Section 11180) of Chapter 2, Part 1, Division 3, Title 2 of the Government Code. For the purpose of any investigation, hearing, or proceeding under this division, the Director of Employment Development may delegate his power in relation thereto to any deputy, or other person properly authorized in writing by him. *(Stats.1953, c. 308, p. 1462, § 311. Amended by Stats.1953, c. 449, p. 1695; Stats.1953, c. 1294, p. 2854; Stats.1973, c. 1212, p. 2764, § 105, operative July 1, 1974.)*

§ 315. Appeals division

The appeals division within the department includes the appeals board and its clerical staff and assistants and the administrative law judges and their supervisors and clerical staff and assistants. *(Stats.1953, c. 308, p. 1463, § 315. Amended by Stats.1973, c. 1212, p. 2766, § 115, operative July 1, 1974; Stats.1979, c. 373, p. 1372, § 284; Stats.1984, c. 537, § 1.)*

§ 316. Education and public instruction

There shall be maintained within an appropriate division of the department, a bureau, section or unit relating to education and public instruction for the purpose of informing employers and workers of their rights and responsibilities under this code, and of instructing the public generally concerning its basic purposes, provisions and operations. All standard information employee pamphlets concerning unemployment and disability insurance programs shall be printed in English and separately in Spanish, or at the discretion of the director, in English and Spanish, in such number as he may determine. *(Stats.1953, c. 308, p. 1463, § 316. Amended by Stats. 1959, c. 1446, p. 3722, § 1; Stats.1973, c. 1212, p. 2766, § 117, operative July 1, 1974; Stats.1979, c. 373, p. 1372, § 285.)*

§ 317. Investigating staff; creation; functions

The Director of Employment Development shall maintain a field investigating staff, whose function shall embrace investigation throughout the state of violations of this code, to the end that its provisions are more adequately and strictly enforced. *(Stats.1953, c. 308, p. 1464, § 317. Amended by Stats.1953, c. 1275, p. 2835; Stats.1973, c. 1212, p. 2766, § 119, operative July 1, 1974.)*

§ 318. Contracts, budgets and fiscal matters; director of employment development

The Director of Employment Development shall comply with all applicable provisions of the Government Code relating to contracts, budgets and other fiscal matters, including Sections 13320 to 13324, inclusive, of that code, in the same manner and to the same extent as other state agencies, insofar as such provisions are not inconsistent with the provisions of the Social Security Act and the rules and regulations of the Secretary of Labor. *(Stats.1953, c. 308, p. 1464, § 318. Amended by Stats. 1959, c. 1729, p. 4175, § 3; Stats.1973, c. 1212, p. 2767, § 121, operative July 1, 1974.)*

§ 320. Reports by director of employment development

The Director of Employment Development shall make such reports in such form and containing such information as the Secretary of Labor may from time to time require, and shall comply with such provisions as the secretary may from time to time find necessary to assure the correctness and verification of such reports. *(Stats. 1953, c. 308, p. 1464, § 320. Amended by Stats.1959, c. 1729, p. 4175, § 5; Stats.1973, c. 1212, p. 2767, § 124, operative July 1, 1974.)*

§ 320.5. Reports by employing units; regulations

The director may by authorized regulations prescribe the information required to be reported to the department by employing units under this division and employers subject to withholding tax under Division 6 (commencing with Section 13000) in order to make reports required by the Secretary of Labor, to provide information necessary to administer this code, to estimate unemployment rates or to make other estimates required for the purpose of dispensing or withholding money payments under the Welfare Reform Act of 1971,[1] the Employment Security Amendments of 1970,[2] the Emergency Unemployment Compensation Act of 1971,[3] or the Workforce Investment Act of 1998,[4] and to make any other reports or estimates that may be required by any other state or federal law. The authorized regulations of the director may include requirements for the reporting of employment, unemployment, hours, wages, earnings, the location and nature of the industrial, business, or other activity of each establishment for the conduct of business, performance of services, or industrial operations, and such other requirements as are necessary to comply with this section. *(Added by Stats.1973, c. 845, p. 1511, § 2. Amended by Stats.1975, c. 843, p. 1907, § 1; Stats.1980, c. 1007, p. 3226, § 58, operative July 1, 1981; Stats.2002, c. 29 (A.B.1729), § 2.)*

[1] Stats.1971, c. 578.

[2] Employment Security Amendments of 1970 (Pub.L. 91-373, Aug. 10, 1970, 84 Stat. 695). See 26 U.S.C.A. §§ 3309 and 3310, 42 U.S.C.A. § 504, and 42 U.S.C.A. §§ 1106 and 1107.

[3] Emergency Unemployment Compensation Act of 1971 (Pub.L. 92-224, Title II, Dec. 29, 1971, 85 Stat. 811). See Short Title note under 26 U.S.C.A. § 3304.

[4] Workforce Investment Act of 1998 (Pub.L. 105-220, Aug. 7, 1998, 112 Stat. 936) See Short Title note under 20 U.S.C.A. § 9201 for classification of the Act to the Code.

§ 321. Information to federal agencies; director of employment development

The Director of Employment Development shall make available, upon request, to any agency of the United States government charged with the administration of public works or assistance through public employment, the following information relating to recipients of unemployment compensation:

(a) The recipient's name.

(b) The recipient's address.

(c) The ordinary occupation and employment status of each such recipient of unemployment benefits.

(d) A statement of such recipient's rights to further compensation under this division. *(Stats.1953, c. 308, p.*

1468, § 321. Amended by Stats.1973, c. 1212, p. 2768, § 127, operative July 1, 1974.)*

§ 322. Exchange or disclosure of information; other governmental departments and agencies

The department may exchange information with other governmental departments and agencies, both federal and state, which are concerned with the administration of unemployment insurance, or the collection of taxes which may be used to finance the administration of unemployment insurance, or the relief of unemployed or destitute individuals, or legislation concerning, regulating, or in any manner affecting the obligations arising out of an employer-employee relation, and with other departments or agencies of government as the department deems necessary or desirable for the proper administration of this division in accordance with authorized regulations.

(Stats.1953, c. 308, p. 1465, § 322. Amended by Stats.1973, c. 1212, p. 2769, § 130, operative July 1, 1974; Stats.1984, c. 1127, § 3; Stats.1987, c. 855, § 1.)

§ 323. Advances to unemployment fund; responsibility for repayment

The Director of Employment Development may apply for an advance to the Unemployment Fund and accept the responsibility for the repayment of such advance in accordance with the conditions specified in Title XII of the Social Security Act, as amended,[1] to secure to this state and its citizens the advantages available under the provisions of that title. *(Stats.1953, c. 308, p. 1465, § 323. Amended by Stats.1973, c. 1212, p. 2769, § 133, operative July 1, 1974.)*

[1] 42 U.S.C.A. § 1321 et seq.

§ 324. Administration expense

The expense of the administration of this division shall be paid out of the Unemployment Administration Fund, unless otherwise provided for in this division. *(Stats. 1953, c. 308, p. 1465, § 324.)*

§ 325. Powers

(a) The department may study and make recommendations as to action which might tend to:

(1) Promote the prevention of unemployment and the stabilization of employment.

(2) Encourage and assist in the adoption of practical methods of vocational training, retraining and guidance.

(3) Promote the establishment and operation by governmental units and agencies of reserves for public work to be prosecuted in time of business depression and unemployment.

(4) Promote the reemployment of unemployed workers throughout the state in any way that may seem feasible.

(5) Reduce and prevent unemployment.

(6) Establish the most effective methods of providing economic security through all forms of social insurance.

(b) To accomplish the ends set forth in subdivision (a) of this section, the department may carry on and publish the results of investigations and research studies. *(Formerly § 352, Stats.1953, c. 308, p. 1465. Renumbered § 325, and amended by Stats.1955, c. 1166, p. 2173, § 3; Stats.1973, c. 1212, p. 2770, § 135, operative July 1, 1974; Stats.1979, c. 373, p. 1373, § 286.)*

§ 325.5. Veterans' employment and training; plan; funding

The department, in consultation and coordination with veterans' organizations and veteran service providers, shall do all of the following:

(a) Research the needs of veterans throughout the state and develop a profile of veterans' employment and training needs.

(b) Develop a statewide plan for the equitable distribution of employment funds for veterans' employment services.

(c) Seek federal funding for purposes of subdivision (a). *(Added by Stats.1990, c. 928 (A.B.3412), § 1.)*

§ 325.6. Veterans Employment Training services; legislative intent; annual report to Legislature

(a) It is the intent of the Legislature that state supported Veterans Employment Training services meet the same performance standards as those required by the federal Workforce Investment Act for services provided to veterans.

(b) Following any fiscal year in which state funds support the Veterans Employment Training services program, the Employment Development Department shall provide an annual report to the Legislature, on or before November 1, regarding the following performance measures:

(1) The number of veterans receiving individualized, case managed services.

(2) The number of veterans who receive individualized, case managed services entering employment.

(3) The retention rate for veterans who enter employment.

(4) The average earnings for veterans entering employment. *(Added by Stats.2006, c. 69 (A.B.1806), § 33, eff. July 12, 2006.)*

§ 326. Unemployment hazards; investigations and reports

The department shall investigate and report upon the degree of unemployment hazard in various industries and occupations and their cost to the Unemployment Fund. It shall recommend to employers in industries or occupations showing an excessive cost to that fund, means for stabilizing employment. It shall also, if necessary, recommend to the Legislature a higher rate of contribution for any classification of industries or occupations in which unemployment is excessive or chronic. *(Formerly § 353, Stats.1953, c. 308, p. 1465. Renumbered § 326, and*

amended by Stats.1955, c. 1166, p. 2174, § 4; Stats.1973, c. 1212, p. 2771, § 137, operative July 1, 1974; Stats.1979, c. 373, p. 1373, § 287.)*

§ 327. Population survey; expansion; negotiations; report; budget request; contract; publication

The department is authorized to enter into negotiations with the United States Bureau of the Census to expand the current population survey for a sample of up to 35,000 households in California. The department shall report its findings and the result of the negotiations to the Legislature. At such time as the Bureau of the Census is prepared to undertake the workload involved in expanding California's portion of the population survey, the department shall submit to the Legislature a budget request for funds not available from other sources to finance a contract with the Bureau of the Census. When sufficient funds are made available through the budget process or from other sources, the department is authorized to contract with the Bureau of the Census for the purpose of expanding the current population survey to a sample of up to 35,000 households in California. Based on the results of the expanded survey, the department shall compile and publish monthly information pertaining to employment and unemployment and shall provide such information to state governmental entities, including the Legislature, which are responsible for preparing state economic projections and revenue estimates. *(Added by Stats.1979, c. 997, p. 3395, § 2.)*

§ 329. Joint Enforcement Strike Force on the Underground Economy; agency representatives; chairperson; duties and powers; report

(a) The director, or his or her designee, shall serve as Chairperson of the Joint Enforcement Strike Force on the Underground Economy provided for in Executive Order W–66–93. The strike force shall include, but not be limited to, representatives of the Employment Development Department, the Department of Consumer Affairs, the Department of Industrial Relations, the Department of Insurance, and the Office of Criminal Justice Planning. Other agencies that are not part of the administration, such as the Franchise Tax Board, the State Board of Equalization, and the Department of Justice, are encouraged to participate in the strike force.

(b) The strike force shall have the following duties:

(1) To facilitate and encourage the development and sharing of information by the participating agencies necessary to combat the underground economy.

(2) To improve the coordination of activities among the participating agencies.

(3) To develop methods to pool, focus, and target the enforcement resources of the participating agencies in order to deter tax evasion and maximize recoveries from blatant tax evaders and violators of cash-pay reporting laws.

(4) To reduce enforcement costs wherever possible by eliminating duplicative audits and investigations.

(c) In addition, the strike force shall be empowered to:

(1) Form joint enforcement teams when appropriate to utilize the collective investigative and enforcement capabilities of the participating members.

(2) Establish committees and rules of procedure to carry out the activities of the strike force.

(3) To solicit the cooperation and participation of district attorneys and other state and local agencies in carrying out the objectives of the strike force.

(4) Establish procedures for soliciting referrals from the public, including, but not limited to, an advertised telephone hotline.

(5) Develop procedures for improved information sharing among the participating agencies, such as shared automated information database systems, the use of a common business identification number, and a centralized debt collection system.

(6) Develop procedures to permit the participating agencies to use more efficient and effective civil sanctions in lieu of criminal actions wherever possible.

(7) Evaluate, based on its activities, the need for any statutory change to do any of the following:

(A) Eliminate barriers to interagency information sharing.

(B) Improve the ability of the participating agencies to audit, investigate, and prosecute tax and cash-pay violations.

(C) Deter violations and improve voluntary compliance.

(D) Eliminate duplication and improve cooperation among the participating agencies.

(E) Establish shareable information databases.

(F) Establish a common business identification number for use by participating agencies.

(G) Establish centralized, automated debt collection services for the participating agencies.

(H) Strengthen civil penalty procedures to allow the strike force to emphasize civil rather than criminal penalties wherever possible.

(d) The strike force shall report to the Governor and the Legislature annually during the period of its existence, by June 30, of each year, regarding its activities.

The report shall include, but not be limited to, all of the following:

(1) The number of cases of blatant violations and noncompliance with tax and cash-pay laws identified, audited, investigated, or prosecuted through civil action or referred for criminal prosecution.

(2) Actions taken by the strike force to publicize its activities.

(3) Efforts made by the strike force to establish an advertised telephone hotline for receiving referrals from the public.

(4) Procedures for improving information sharing among the agencies represented on the strike force.

(5) Steps taken by the strike force to improve cooperation among participating agencies, reduce duplication of effort, and improve voluntary compliance.

(6) Recommendations for any statutory changes needed to accomplish the goals described in paragraph (7) of subdivision (c).

(Added by Stats.1994, c. 1117 (S.B.1490), § 5. Amended by Stats.1999, c. 306 (S.B.319), § 2; Stats.2001, c. 180 (A.B.202), § 1; Stats.2002, c. 29 (A.B.1729), § 4; Stats.2004, c. 685 (A.B.3020), § 6.)

§ 333. Benefit payment control program; automation

(a) The department shall place a high priority on the automation of the Benefit Payment Control Program, specifically including, but not limited to, automating the ledger and collection functions.

(b) An automated system for the Benefit Payment Control Program shall include a function which provides for the automatic issuance of monthly collection letters to unemployment insurance claimants who have received benefit overpayments.

(c) Personnel savings from automation of the Benefit Payment Control Program, notwithstanding any other provision of law, shall be redirected to the processing of additional willful overpayment cases. *(Added by Stats. 1983, c. 1226, § 5, eff. Sept. 30, 1983.)*

§ 334. Unemployment insurance benefit overpayments; collection

The director shall pursue the following methods to increase the collection of unemployment insurance benefit overpayments:

(a) Developing administrative or automated procedures to insure that field offices appropriately refer cases to the central office for the timely interception of a claimant's state tax refund.

(b) Modifying the automated overpayment detection system so that it will identify more overpayments.

(c) Increasing the number of potential overpayments which are reviewed by the department.

(d) Working with the Legislature and the Governor to adequately staff the Benefit Payment Control Program. *(Added by Stats.1983, c. 1226, § 6, eff. Sept. 30, 1983.)*

§ 335. Coordinated efforts with film and movie industry; department obligations

The department, in consultation and coordination with the film and movie industry, the Business, Transportation and Housing Agency, and the California Film Commission shall do all of the following, contingent upon the appropriation of funds in the annual Budget Act for these specified purposes:

(a) Research and maintain data on the employment and output of the film industry, including full-time, part-time, contract, and short duration or single event employees.

(b) Examine the ethnic diversity and representation of minorities in the entertainment industry.

(c) Determine the overall direct and indirect economic impact of the film industry.

(d) Monitor film industry employment and activity in other states and countries that compete with California for film production.

(e) Review the effect that federal and state laws and local ordinances have on the filmed entertainment industry.

(f) Prepare and release biannually a report to the chairpersons of the appropriate Senate and Assembly policy committees that details the information required by this section. *(Added by Stats.2002, c. 1042 (A.B.2410), § 2. Amended by Stats.2004, c. 225 (S.B.1097), § 68, eff. Aug. 16, 2004.)*

§ 336. Establishment of procedures to identify business transfer or acquisition to obtain lower compensation rate

The director shall establish procedures to identify the transfer or acquisition of a business that is undertaken for purposes of obtaining a lower unemployment insurance contribution rate. *(Added by Stats.2004, c. 827 (A.B.664), § 1.)*

ARTICLE 2.   STATE ADVISORY COUNCIL [REPEALED]

ARTICLE 3.   CALIFORNIA UNEMPLOYMENT INSURANCE APPEALS BOARD

Section
401.   Unemployment insurance appeals board; membership; compensation.
402.   Terms of members; vacancies.
403.   Appeals division personnel; appointment and control; budget; equipment, supplies, etc.
404.   Appointment of administrative law judges; compensation.
405.   Appointment of chief administrative law judge; qualifications.
406.   Duties of chief administrative law judge.
407.   Delegation of the taking and hearing of evidence; powers of a department head.
408.   Decisions and orders in writing.
409.   Assignment of cases; consideration and decision of cases; meetings; precedent; decisions.
409.1. Modification of precedent decision to conform to judgment of court; effect; notification to interested agencies or persons.
409.2. Validity of precedent decision; action for declaratory relief.
410.   Finality of decision; judicial review.
411.   Rules and regulations pertaining to hearing appeals.
Section
412.   Proceedings; transfer to another administrative law judge; removal to itself for review and decision; order.
413.   Action by board as a whole; authority; procedure.

§ 401.   Unemployment insurance appeals board; membership; compensation

There is in the department an Appeals Division consisting of the California Unemployment Insurance Appeals Board and its employees. The appeals board consists of seven members. Five members shall be appointed by the Governor, subject to the approval of the Senate. One member shall be appointed by the Speaker of the Assembly, and one member shall be appointed by the Senate Rules Committee. Two of the members of the appeals board shall be attorneys at law admitted to practice in the State of California. The other members need not be attorneys. Each member of the board shall devote his full time to the performance of his duties. The chairman and each member of the board shall receive the annual salary provided for by Chapter 6 (commencing with Section 11550) of Part 1 of Division 3 of Title 2 of the Government Code. The Governor shall designate the chairman of the appeals board from the membership of the appeals board. The person so designated shall hold the office of chairman at the pleasure of the Governor. The chairman shall designate a member of the appeals board to act as chairman in his absence. *(Stats.1953, c. 308, p. 1466, § 401. Amended by Stats.1967, c. 1586, p. 3797, § 1; Stats.1968, c. 280, p. 619, § 1; Stats.1970, c. 350, p. 757, § 5; Stats.1973, c. 1206, p. 2618, § 53; Stats.1973, c. 1207, p. 2668, § 53; Stats.1979, c. 373, p. 1373, § 288; Stats.1982, c. 1225, p. 4521, § 1.)*

§ 402.   Terms of members; vacancies

Each member of the appeals board shall serve for a term of four years and until his successor is appointed and qualifies. The term of office of each member of the board appointed pursuant to the 1967 amendment to this section shall also be for four years; provided, however, that of the two board members first appointed pursuant to such amendments, one shall be appointed for a term which shall expire July 1, 1970, and one for a term which shall expire July 1, 1971.

A vacancy shall be filled by the appointing power by appointment for the unexpired term. A vacancy filled by the Governor shall be subject to the approval of the Senate. *(Stats.1953, c. 308, p. 1466, § 402. Amended by Stats.1965, c. 1786, p. 4124, § 1; Stats.1967, c. 1586, p. 3797, § 2; Stats.1982, c. 1225, p. 4522, § 2.)*

§ 403.   Appeals division personnel; appointment and control; budget; equipment, supplies, etc.

All personnel of the Appeals Division shall be appointed, directed and controlled only by the appeals board or its authorized deputies or agents to whom it may delegate such powers.

The appeals board shall prepare a budget covering the necessary administrative costs of the Appeals Division. Such budget shall not be subject to change by the director except as agreed to by the appeals board. In the event that agreement cannot be reached, the final decision shall rest with the Governor. The director shall furnish the equipment, supplies, housing and nonpersonal and housekeeping services required by the Appeals Division and shall perform such other mechanics of administration as the appeals board and the director may agree upon. *(Stats.1953, c. 308, p. 1466, § 403. Amended by Stats. 1967, c. 1586, p. 3798, § 3.)*

§ 404. Appointment of administrative law judges; compensation

The appeals board, or the executive officer subject to its direction and control to whom it delegates such responsibility, shall appoint and direct the activities of one or more impartial administrative law judges who shall hear and render a decision in every matter in which a petition is filed with, or an appeal is taken to, an administrative law judge as provided in this division. The compensation of the administrative law judges shall be fixed by the State Personnel Board at a rate comparable to that of other administrative law judges or hearing officers in state service whose duties and responsibilities are comparable, without regard to whether such other positions have membership in the State Bar of California as a prerequisite to appointment. No administrative law judge shall participate in any case in which he is an interested party. *(Stats.1953, c. 308, p. 1466, § 404. Amended by Stats.1954, 1st Ex.Sess., c. 44, p. 312, § 1; Stats.1955, c. 1165, p. 2157, § 1; Stats.1984, c. 537, § 2.)*

§ 405. Appointment of chief administrative law judge; qualifications

The appeals board shall appoint a chief administrative law judge who shall be a member in good standing of the State Bar of California. *(Stats.1953, c. 308, p. 1467, § 405. Amended by Stats.1984, c. 537, § 3.)*

§ 406. Duties of chief administrative law judge

The duties of the chief administrative law judge include:

(a) Serving as the chief executive of the board in the administration of the activities of administrative law judges and their staffs.

(b) Maintaining a continuous review of the decisions of administrative law judges from which no appeal is taken to uncover decisions which appear inconsistent with the law, with established judicial decisions, with prior decisions of the board or with each other and recommending such cases to the appeals board for certification to itself for a further hearing. *(Stats.1953, c. 308, p. 1467, § 406. Amended by Stats.1984, c. 537, § 4.)*

§ 407. Delegation of the taking and hearing of evidence; powers of a department head

In any case before it, the appeals board may delegate to any one of its members or to a special examiner or administrative law judge the taking or hearing of evidence. The appeals board and its duly authorized representatives in the performance of its duties under this division shall have the powers of a head of a department as set forth in Sections 11180 to 11191, inclusive, of the Government Code. *(Stats.1953, c. 308, p. 1467, § 407. Amended by Stats.1967, c. 1586, p. 3798, § 4; Stats.1984, c. 537, § 5.)*

§ 408. Decisions and orders in writing

All decisions and orders of the Appeals Board shall be in writing. *(Stats.1953, c. 308, p. 1467, § 408. Amended by Stats.1967, c. 1656, p. 4025, § 107.)*

§ 409. Assignment of cases; consideration and decision of cases; meetings; precedent; decisions

The chairperson shall assign cases before the board to any two members of the board for consideration and decision. Assignments by the chairperson of members to the cases shall be rotated so as to equalize the workload of the members, but with the composition of the members so assigned being varied and changed to assure that there shall never be a fixed and continuous composition of members. Except as otherwise provided, the decision of the two members assigned the case shall be the decision of the appeals board. In the event that the two members do not concur in the decision, the chairperson or another member of the board designated by the chairperson shall be assigned to the panel and shall resolve the impasse. A case shall be considered and decided by the appeals board acting as a whole at the request of any member of the appeals board.

The appeals board shall meet as a whole when the chairperson may direct to consider and pass on any matters that the chairperson may bring before it, and to consider and decide cases that present issues of first impression or that will enable the appeals board to achieve uniformity of decisions by the respective members.

The appeals board, acting as a whole, may designate certain of its decisions as precedents. Precedent decisions of the appeals board are subject to Section 11425.60 of the Government Code. The appeals board, acting as a whole, may, on its own motion, reconsider a previously issued decision solely to determine whether or not the decision shall be designated as a precedent decision. Decisions of the appeals board acting as a whole shall be by a majority vote of its members. The director and the appeals board administrative law judges shall be controlled by those precedents except as modified by judicial review. If the appeals board issues decisions other than those designated as precedent decisions, anything incorporated in those decisions shall be physically attached to and be made a part of the decisions. The appeals board may make a reasonable charge as it deems necessary to defray the costs of publication and distribution of its precedent decisions and index of precedent decisions. *(Stats.1953, c. 308, p. 1467, § 409. Amended by Stats. 1961, c. 1181, p. 2917, § 1; Stats.1967, c. 1586, p. 3798, § 5; Stats.1969, c. 371, p. 906, § 47; Stats.1973, c. 1212, p. 2772, § 139, operative July 1, 1974; Stats.1975, c. 1140, p. 2824, § 7; Stats.1977, c. 1252, p. 4454, § 396, operative July 1, 1978; Stats.1982, c. 1225, p. 4522, § 3; Stats.1984, c. 537, § 6; Stats.1994, c. 967 (S.B.1584), § 1, eff. Sept. 28, 1994; Stats.1995, c. 938 (S.B.523), § 88, operative July 1, 1997.)*

§ 409.1. Modification of precedent decision to conform to judgment of court; effect; notification to interested agencies or persons

If a final judgment of a court of competent jurisdiction reverses or declares invalid a precedent decision of the appeals board issued under Section 409 or this section, the appeals board, acting as a whole, shall promptly modify the precedent decision to conform in all respects to the judgment of the court. The modified precedent decision shall supersede the prior precedent decision for all purposes. The appeals board shall promptly notify the director, the administrative law judges of the appeals board, and all other subscribers to the precedent decisions, of the modified precedent decision. *(Added by Stats.1975, c. 978, p. 2301, § 1. Amended by Stats.1977, c. 1252, p. 4454, § 397, operative July 1, 1978; Stats.1984, c. 537, § 7.)*

§ 409.2. Validity of precedent decision; action for declaratory relief

Any interested person or organization may bring an action for declaratory relief in the superior court in accordance with the provisions of the Code of Civil Procedure to obtain a judicial declaration as to the validity of any precedent decision of the appeals board issued under Section 409 or 409.1. *(Added by Stats.1975, c. 978, p. 2302, § 2.)*

§ 410. Finality of decision; judicial review

A decision of the appeals board is final, except for such action as may be taken by a judicial tribunal as permitted or required by law.

A decision of the appeals board is binding on the director with respect to the parties involved in the particular appeal.

The director shall have the right to seek judicial review from an appeals board decision irrespective of whether or not he or she appeared or participated in the appeal to the administrative law judge or to the appeals board.

Notwithstanding any other provision of law, the right of the director, or of any other party except as provided by Sections 1241, 1243, and 5313, to seek judicial review from an appeals board decision shall be exercised not later than six months after the date of the decision of the

appeals board or the date on which the decision is designated as a precedent decision, whichever is later.

The appeals board shall attach to all of its decisions where a request for review may be taken, an explanation of the party's right to seek such review. *(Stats.1953, c. 308, p. 1467, § 410. Amended by Stats.1967, c. 1586, p. 3799, § 6; Stats.1972, c. 1385, p. 2887, § 1; Stats.1973, c. 1212, p. 2773, § 141, operative July 1, 1974; Stats.1977, c. 1252, p. 4455, § 398, operative July 1, 1978; Stats.1978, c. 429, p. 1431, § 167, eff. July 17, 1978, operative July 1, 1978; Stats.1979, c. 1082, p. 3883, § 2; Stats.1984, c. 537, § 8.)*

§ 411. Rules and regulations pertaining to hearing appeals

The appeals board, acting as a whole, may promulgate rules or amend or rescind rules pertaining to hearing appeals and other matters falling within its jurisdiction. All these rules, amendments thereto, or repeals thereof, shall be made in accordance with the provisions of Chapter 3.5 (commencing with Section 11340) of Part 1 of Division 3 of Title 2 of the Government Code. *(Stats.1953, c. 308, p. 1467, § 411. Amended by Stats. 1957, c. 2035, p. 3607, § 4; Stats.1963, c. 1548, p. 3130, § 4; Stats.1967, c. 1586, p. 3799, § 7; Stats.2002, c. 29 (A.B.1729), § 5; Stats.2003, c. 62 (S.B.600), § 297.)*

§ 412. Proceedings; transfer to another administrative law judge; removal to itself for review and decision; order

(a) The appeals board acting as a whole may, by notice mailed to the director and the parties prior to the mailing of an administrative law judge's decision on an appeal or petition under this division pending before any administrative law judge, on its own motion either:

(1) Transfer the proceedings to another administrative law judge; or

(2) Remove the proceedings to itself for review and decision.

(b) If the appeals board removes any proceedings to itself for review and decision pursuant to this section, the appeals board may order the taking of additional evidence and may affirm, reverse, modify, or set aside any findings or action of the department from which the appeal or petition to the administrative law judge was taken in the proceedings. The appeals board shall promptly notify the department and the parties to the proceedings of its order or decision. *(Added by Stats. 1975, c. 538, p. 1103, § 1. Amended by Stats.1976, c. 336, p. 919, § 1, eff. July 3, 1976; Stats.1977, c. 1252, p. 4455, § 399, operative July 1, 1978; Stats.1984, c. 537, § 9.)*

§ 413. Action by board as a whole; authority; procedure

(a) The appeals board acting as a whole may, by notice mailed to the director and the parties not later than 30 days after the mailing of an administrative law judge's decision on an appeal or petition under this division to the administrative law judge, on its own motion either:

(1) Set aside the decision of the administrative law judge and remand the proceedings to another administrative law judge for review and decision; or

(2) Remove the proceedings to itself for review and decision.

(b) If the appeals board removes any proceedings to itself for review and decision pursuant to this section, the appeals board may order the taking of additional evidence and may affirm, reverse, modify or set aside the decision of the administrative law judge. The appeals board shall promptly notify the department and the parties to the proceedings of its order or decision.

(c) Notwithstanding any other provision of this division, no decision of an administrative law judge under this division shall be final if the appeals board pursuant to this section sets aside such decision or removes the proceedings to itself for review and decision. *(Added by Stats. 1975, c. 538, p. 1104, § 2. Amended by Stats.1984, c. 537, § 10.)*

ARTICLE 4. INTERSTATE AND FEDERAL COOPERATION

Section
451. Cooperation with agencies of federal government and of other states.
452. Reciprocal arrangements with foreign governments.
453. Interstate cooperation in enforcement of liabilities for contributions; authority of attorney general to commence action.
454. Reciprocal arrangements with agencies of federal government and of other states.
455. Reciprocal arrangements, payment of benefits, wages in employment.
455.5. Combining individual's wages and employment under unemployment compensation laws of other states.
455.7. Prohibition against denial or reduction of benefits for filing claim in another state.
456. Reciprocal arrangements, contributions.

§ 451. Cooperation with agencies of federal government and of other states

The administration of this division and of other state and federal unemployment compensation and public employment service laws will be promoted by cooperation between this State and such other states and the appropriate federal agencies in exchanging services, and making available facilities and information. The director may make investigations, secure and transmit information, make available services and facilities and exercise the other powers provided with respect to the administration of this division which he finds necessary or appropriate to facilitate the administration of any state or federal unemployment compensation or public employment service law, and may accept and utilize information, services and facilities made available to this State by an agency

900

charged with the administration of any such other state or federal law. *(Stats.1953, c. 308, p. 1467, § 451.)*

§ 452. Reciprocal arrangements with foreign governments

To the extent permissible under the laws and Constitution of the United States, the director may enter into or cooperate in arrangements whereby facilities and services provided under the unemployment compensation law of any foreign government, may be utilized for the taking of claims and the payment of benefits under the Unemployment Insurance Law of this State or a similar law of such government. *(Stats.1953, c. 308, p. 1468, § 452. Amended by Stats.1953, c. 449, p. 1695.)*

§ 453. Interstate cooperation in enforcement of liabilities for contributions; authority of attorney general to commence action

To encourage cooperation between this state and other states in the enforcement of the unemployment insurance law of each state and to further coordinate the nationwide system of unemployment insurance in the United States and its territories:

(a) The courts of this state shall recognize and enforce liabilities for unemployment contributions, penalties, interest, and benefit overpayments imposed by other states which extend a like comity to this state.

(b) The Attorney General may commence action in any other jurisdiction by and in the name of the department to collect unemployment contributions, penalties, interest, and benefit overpayments legally due this state. The officials of other states which extend a like comity to this state may sue for the collection of such contributions, penalties, interest, and benefit overpayments in the courts of this state. A certificate by the Secretary of State under the Great Seal of the state that the officers of the department designated by the director have authority to collect the contributions, penalties, interest, and benefit overpayments is conclusive evidence of such authority.

(c) The Attorney General may commence action in this state as agent for and on behalf of any other state to enforce judgments and liabilities for unemployment insurance contributions, penalties, interest and benefit overpayments due such state which extends a like comity to this state. The requesting state shall pay the court costs. *(Stats.1953, c. 308, p. 1468, § 453. Amended by Stats.1967, c. 1720, p. 4282, § 1.)*

§ 454. Reciprocal arrangements with agencies of federal government and of other states

The director may enter into reciprocal arrangements with authorized agencies of other states or of the Federal Government, or both, whereby:

(a) Services customarily performed in more than one state by an individual for a single employer shall be deemed to be services performed entirely within any one of the states (i) in which any part of the individual's service is performed, or (ii) in which the individual has his residence, or (iii) in which the employer maintains a place of business, if there is in effect as to such services an election by the employing unit with the acquiescence of the individual, approved by the agency charged with the administration of such state's unemployment compensation law pursuant to which all the services performed by such individual for such employer are deemed to be performed entirely within such state.

(b) Services on vessels engaged in interstate commerce wherever performed shall be deemed performed within this State or any other state on the basis of the location of the operating office of the employer from which the operations of the vessel are ordinarily and regularly supervised, managed, directed, and controlled. *(Stats. 1953, c. 308, p. 1468, § 454.)*

§ 455. Reciprocal arrangements, payment of benefits, wages in employment

The director may enter into reciprocal arrangements with authorized agencies of other states or of the Federal Government, or both, whereby:

(a) Potential rights to benefits accumulated under the unemployment compensation laws of one or more states or of the Federal Government, or both, may constitute the basis for the payment of benefits through a single appropriate agency under terms which the director finds will be fair and reasonable to all affected interests and which will not result in any substantial loss to the fund.

(b) Wages or services in employment subject to an unemployment compensation law of another state or of the Federal Government shall be deemed to be wages in employment for employers for the purpose of determining an individual's rights to unemployment compensation benefits under this part, and wages in employment for employers as defined in this part shall be deemed to be wages or services on the basis of which unemployment compensation under the law of another state or of the Federal Government is payable, but no such arrangement shall be entered into unless it contains provisions for reimbursements to the Unemployment Fund for such of the unemployment compensation benefits paid under this part upon the basis of such wages or services, and provisions for reimbursements from the Unemployment Fund for such of the compensation paid under such other law upon the basis of wages for employment as defined in this part as the director finds will be fair and reasonable to all affected interests. Reimbursements paid from the Unemployment Fund pursuant to this subdivision shall be deemed to be unemployment compensation benefits for the purposes of this part. The director may make to other state and federal agencies and receive from such other state or federal agencies reimbursements from or to the fund, in accordance with arrangements entered into pursuant to this subdivision. *(Stats.1953, c. 308, p. 1469, § 455.)*

§ 455.5. Combining individual's wages and employment under unemployment compensation laws of other states

This state shall participate in any arrangements for the payment of compensation on the basis of combining an individual's wages and employment covered under this division with his wages and employment covered under the unemployment compensation law of other states which are approved by the Secretary of Labor in consultation with the state unemployment compensation agencies as reasonably calculated to assure the prompt and full payment of compensation in such situations. Any such arrangement shall include provisions for both of the following:

(a) Applying the base period of a single state law to a claim involving the combining of an individual's wages and employment covered under two or more state laws.

(b) Avoiding duplicate use of wages and employment by reason of such combining. *(Added by Stats.1971, c. 1107, p. 2093, § 6, eff. Oct. 18, 1971, operative Jan. 1, 1972.)*

§ 455.7. Prohibition against denial or reduction of benefits for filing claim in another state

Notwithstanding any other provision of this division, benefits shall not be denied or reduced to an individual solely because he files a claim in another state, or a contiguous country with which the United States has an agreement with respect to unemployment compensation, or because he resides in another state or such a contiguous country at the time he files a claim for unemployment compensation. *(Added by Stats.1971, c. 1107, p. 2093, § 7, eff. Oct. 18, 1971, operative Jan. 1, 1972.)*

§ 456. Reciprocal arrangements, contributions

The director may enter into reciprocal arrangements with authorized agencies of other states or of the Federal Government, or both, whereby employer contributions due under this part with respect to wages for employment shall be deemed to have been paid to the Unemployment Fund of this State as of the date payment of such contributions was made under another state or federal unemployment compensation law. No arrangement shall be entered into pursuant to this section unless it contains provisions for such reimbursement to the fund of such contributions and the actual earnings thereon as the director finds will be fair and reasonable to all affected interests. The director may collect contributions in like manner for such agencies of other states and the Federal Government administering unemployment compensation laws and remit such contributions to such agencies under appropriate reciprocal arrangements. *(Stats.1953, c. 308, p. 1470, § 456.)*

CHAPTER 3. SCOPE OR COVERAGE

Article		Section
1.	Employment	601
1.5.	Employee	621

Article		Section
2.	Excluded Services	625
3.	Subject Employers	675
4.	Elective Coverage	701
5.	Elections for Financing Unemployment Insurance Coverage	801
6.	Financing Unemployment Insurance Coverage For Public School Employees	821
7.	Financing Unemployment Insurance Coverage for Local Public Entity Employees	841

ARTICLE 1.　EMPLOYMENT

Section
601.　Definitions.
601.5.　Employment defined.
602.　Services performed within, or both within and without, the state.
603.　Localized service.
603.5.　Services performed within the United States or Canada.
604.　Services performed within state by virtue of arrangement.
605.　Service for public entity or Indian tribe.
606.　Assistants to individual employed by employing unit.
606.5.　Determination of employer-employee relationship.
607.　Services performed during one-half or more of pay period; pay period defined.
608.　Service excluded from employment under Federal Unemployment Tax Act.
609.　Service performed on or in connection with American vessel operating on navigable waters or aircraft within or without United States.
610.　Service performed outside United States in employ of American employer.
611.　Inclusion of agricultural labor.

§ 601.　Definitions

"Employment" means service, including service in interstate commerce, performed by an employee for wages or under any contract of hire, written or oral, express or implied. *(Stats.1953, c. 308, p. 1470, § 601. Amended by Stats.1971, c. 1107, p. 2094, § 8, eff. Oct. 18, 1971.)*

§ 601.5.　Employment defined

For the purpose of this division only, "employment" includes any service in an artistic or literary capacity performed by an individual pursuant to a collective bargaining agreement between an employer and a labor organization in the motion picture, radio or television industry where the employer has the right to control and direct the services to be performed and the individual is defined as an employee under the terms of the collective bargaining agreement. *(Added by Stats.1965, c. 1786, p. 4124, § 2.)*

§ 602.　Services performed within, or both within and without, the state

"Employment" includes an individual's entire service, performed within, or both within and without, this State if:

(a)　The service is localized in this State; or

(b)　The service is not localized in any state but some of the service is performed in this State and (1) the base of operations, or, if there is no base of operations, then the place from which such service is directed or controlled, is in this State; or (2) the base of operations or place from which such service is directed or controlled is not in any state in which some part of the service is performed, but the individual's residence is in this State. *(Stats.1953, c. 308, p. 1470, § 602.)*

§ 603.　Localized service

Service is localized within a state if:

(a)　The service is performed entirely within the state; or

(b)　The service is performed both within and without the state, but the service performed without the state is incidental to the individual's service within the state; for example, is temporary or transitory in nature, or consists of isolated transactions. *(Stats.1953, c. 308, p. 1470, § 603.)*

§ 603.5.　Services performed within the United States or Canada

"Employment" includes an individual's entire service, wherever performed within the United States or Canada, if such service is not covered under the unemployment compensation law of any other state or Canada, and the place from which the service is directed or controlled is in this state. *(Added by Stats.1971, c. 1107, p. 2094, § 9, eff. Oct. 18, 1971. Amended by Stats.1978, c. 2, p. 13, § 22, eff. Jan. 30, 1978, operative Jan. 1, 1978.)*

§ 604.　Services performed within state by virtue of arrangement

"Employment" includes an individual's entire service, if such service is deemed performed in this State by virtue of an arrangement made pursuant to this division and does not include any service which by virtue of such an arrangement is deemed performed in another state. *(Stats.1953, c. 308, p. 1470, § 604.)*

§ 605.　Service for public entity or Indian tribe

(a)　Except as provided by Section 634.5, "employment" for the purposes of this part and Parts 3 (commencing with Section 3501) and 4 (commencing with Section 4001) includes all service performed by an individual (including blind and otherwise disabled individuals) for any public entity or Indian tribe, if the service is excluded from "employment" under the federal Unemployment Tax Act solely by reason of paragraph (7) of Section 3306(c) of that act.

(b)　For purposes of this section:

(1)　"Public entity" means the State of California (including the Trustees of the California State University and Colleges, and the California Industries for the Blind), any instrumentality of this state (including the Regents of the University of California), any political subdivision of this state or any of its instrumentalities, a county, city, district (including the governing board of any school district or community college district, any county board of education, any county superintendent of schools, or any personnel commission of a school district or community college district that has a merit system pursuant to any provision of the Education Code), entities conducting fairs as identified in Sections 19418 to 19418.3, inclusive, of the Business and Professions Code, any public authority, public agency, or public corporation of this state, any instrumentality of more than one of the foregoing, and any instrumentality of any of the foregoing and one or more other states or political subdivisions.

(2) "Indian tribe" means any Indian tribe described by subsection (u) of Section 3306 of Title 26 of the United States Code. *(Added by Stats.1978, c. 2, p. 13, § 24, eff. Jan. 30, 1978, operative Jan. 1, 1978. Amended by Stats.1978, c. 397, p. 1254, § 1.3, eff. July 11, 1978; Stats.1981, c. 1134, p. 4448, § 2; Stats.1996, c. 1110 (S.B.1397), § 32; Stats.2001, c. 255 (A.B.1537), § 3; Stats.2005, c. 152 (A.B.1577), § 2.)*

Operative Effect

Under the terms of Section 17 of Stats.2001, c. 255 (A.B.1537), the provisions of that Act are retroactive to December 21, 2000.

§ 606. Assistants to individual employed by employing unit

Each individual employed to perform or to assist in performing the work of any individual employed by an employing unit shall be deemed to be employed by that employing unit for all the purposes of this division, whether or not he was hired or paid directly by the employing unit if the employing unit had actual or constructive knowledge of the work. *(Stats.1953, c. 308, p. 1471, § 606.)*

§ 606.5. Determination of employer-employee relationship

(a) Whether an individual or entity is the employer of specific employees shall be determined under common law rules applicable in determining the employer-employee relationship, except as provided in subdivisions (b) and (c).

(b) As used in this section, a "temporary services employer" and a "leasing employer" is an employing unit that contracts with clients or customers to supply workers to perform services for the client or customer and performs all of the following functions:

(1) Negotiates with clients or customers for such matters as time, place, type of work, working conditions, quality, and price of the services.

(2) Determines assignments or reassignments of workers, even though workers retain the right to refuse specific assignments.

(3) Retains the authority to assign or reassign a worker to other clients or customers when a worker is determined unacceptable by a specific client or customer.

(4) Assigns or reassigns the worker to perform services for a client or customer.

(5) Sets the rate of pay of the worker, whether or not through negotiation.

(6) Pays the worker from its own account or accounts.

(7) Retains the right to hire and terminate workers.

(c) If an individual or entity contracts to supply an employee to perform services for a customer or client, and is a leasing employer or a temporary services employer, the individual or entity is the employer of the employee who performs the services. If an individual or entity contracts to supply an employee to perform services for a client or customer and is not a leasing employer or a temporary services employer, the client or customer is the employer of the employee who performs the services. An individual or entity that contracts to supply an employee to perform services for a customer or client and pays wages to the employee for the services, but is not a leasing employer or a temporary services employer, pays the wages as the agent of the employer.

(d) In circumstances which are in essence the loan of an employee from one employer to another employer wherein direction and control of the manner and means of performing the services changes to the employer to whom the employee is loaned, the loaning employer shall continue to be the employer of the employee if the loaning employer continues to pay remuneration to the employee, whether or not reimbursed by the other employer. If the employer to whom the employee is loaned pays remuneration to the employee for the services performed, that employer shall be considered the employer for the purposes of any remuneration paid to the employee by the employer, regardless of whether the loaning employer also pays remuneration to the employee. *(Added by Stats.1986, c. 793, § 1, eff. Sept. 15, 1986.)*

§ 607. Services performed during one-half or more of pay period; pay period defined

If the services performed during one-half or more of any pay period by an employee for the person employing him constitute employment, all the services of the employee for that period shall be deemed to be employment; but if the services performed during more than one-half of any pay period by an employee for the person employing him do not constitute employment, then none of the services of the employee for that period shall be deemed to be employment.

As used in this section "pay period" means a period of not more than 31 consecutive days for which a payment of remuneration is ordinarily made to the employee by the person employing him. *(Stats.1953, c. 308, p. 1471, § 607.)*

§ 608. Service excluded from employment under Federal Unemployment Tax Act

"Employment", except as provided by Section 634.5, includes service excluded from "employment" under the Federal Unemployment Tax Act solely by reason of paragraph (8) of Section 3306(c) [1] of that act because it is service performed in the employ of a religious, charitable, educational, or other nonprofit organization described in Section 501(c)(3) of the Internal Revenue Code of 1954 [2] which is exempt from income tax under Section 501(a) of that code. *(Added by Stats.1971, c. 1107, p. 2094, § 11, eff. Oct. 18, 1971.)*

[1] 26 U.S.C.A. § 3306(c).
[2] 26 U.S.C.A. § 501(c)(3).

§ 609. Service performed on or in connection with American vessel operating on navigable waters or aircraft within or without United States

(a) "Employment" includes service performed for an employing unit on or in connection with an American vessel operating on navigable waters within or within and without the United States or on or in connection with an American aircraft operating within or within and without the United States, if the employing unit maintains in this state an operating office from which the operations of the American vessel or American aircraft are ordinarily and regularly supervised, managed, directed, and controlled, and such services are included in "employment" under the Federal Unemployment Tax Act.[1]

(b) All of the provisions of this division shall be applicable to an employing unit and to service performed in "employment" under this section in the same manner and to the same extent as to all other employers, and the wage credits given to, and the payment of benefits to, any employee of an employing unit under this section shall be in the same amount, on the same terms, and subject to the same conditions as applied to employees of other employers under this division. *(Added by Stats.1971, c. 1107, p. 2095, § 12, eff. Oct. 18, 1971.)*

[1] 26 U.S.C.A. § 3301 et seq.

§ 610. Service performed outside United States in employ of American employer

"Employment" shall include the service of an individual who is a citizen of the United States, performed outside the United States (except in Canada), after December 31, 1971, in the employ of an American employer as defined in Section 125.4 other than service that is deemed "employment" under Section 602 or 603 or the equivalent provisions of another state's unemployment compensation law, if:

(a) The employer's principal place of business in the United States is located in this state; or

(b) The employer has no place of business in the United States, but:

(1) The employer is an individual who is a resident of this state; or

(2) The employer is a corporation or limited liability company that is organized under the laws of this state; or

(3) The employer is a partnership or a trust and the number of the partners or trustees who are residents of this state is greater than the number who are residents of any one other state; or

(c) None of the criteria of subdivisions (a) and (b) of this section is met but the employer has elected coverage in this state or, the employer having failed to elect coverage in any state, the individual has filed a claim for benefits, based on such service, under this division. *(Added by Stats.1971, c. 1107, p. 2095, § 13, eff. Oct. 18, 1971. Amended by Stats.1978, c. 2, p. 15, § 28, eff. Jan. 30, 1978, operative Jan. 1, 1978; Stats.1994, c. 1200 (S.B.469), § 81, eff. Sept. 30, 1994.)*

§ 611. Inclusion of agricultural labor

"Employment" includes agricultural labor. *(Added by Stats.1975, c. 591, p. 1304, § 1.)*

ARTICLE 1.5. EMPLOYEE

Section
621.   Definition.
621.5. Additional definition.
622.   Exclusion of director of corporation or association.

§ 621. Definition

"Employee" means all of the following:

(a) Any officer of a corporation.

(b) Any individual who, under the usual common law rules applicable in determining the employer-employee relationship, has the status of an employee.

(c)(1) Any individual, other than an individual who is an employee under subdivision (a) or (b), who performs services for remuneration for any employing unit if the contract of service contemplates that substantially all of such services are to be performed personally by such individual either:

(A) As an agent-driver or commission-driver engaged in distributing meat products, vegetable products, fruit products, bakery products, beverages (other than milk), or laundry or drycleaning services, for his or her principal.

(B) As a traveling or city salesperson, other than as an agent-driver or commission-driver, engaged upon a full-time basis in the solicitation on behalf of, and the transmission to, his or her principal (except for sideline sales activities on behalf of some other person) of orders from wholesalers, retailers, contractors, or operators of hotels, restaurants, or other similar establishments for merchandise for resale or supplies for use in their business operations.

(C) As a home worker performing work, according to specifications furnished by the person for whom the services are performed, on materials or goods furnished by such person which are required to be returned to such person or a person designated by him or her.

(2) An individual shall not be included in the term "employee" under the provisions of this subdivision if such individual has a substantial investment in facilities used in connection with the performance of such services, other than in facilities for transportation, or if the services are in the nature of a single transaction not part of a continuing relationship with the employing unit for whom the services are performed.

(d) Any individual who is an employee pursuant to Section 601.5 or 686.

(e) Any individual whose services are in subject employment pursuant to an election for coverage under any provision of Article 4 (commencing with Section 701) of this chapter. *(Added by Stats.1971, c. 1107, p. 2096, § 14, eff. Oct. 18, 1971. Amended by Stats.1972, c. 833, p. 1481, § 1; Stats.1974, c. 738, p. 1635, § 1; Stats.1977, c. 629, p. 2119, § 1; Stats.1979, c. 456, p. 1599, § 2; Stats.1982, c. 1215, p. 4501, § 1; Stats.1982, c. 1332, p. 4934, § 2.3.)*

§ 621.5. Additional definition

(a) "Employee" also means any individual who is an employee, pursuant to Section 2750.5 of the Labor Code, of a person who holds a valid state contractor's license pursuant to Chapter 9 (commencing with Section 7000) of Division 3 of the Business and Professions Code.

(b) When subdivision (a) does not apply, "employee" shall also mean any individual who is an employee, pursuant to Section 2750.5 of the Labor Code, of a person who is required to obtain a valid state contractor's license pursuant to Chapter 9 (commencing with Section 7000) of Division 3 of the Business and Professions Code. *(Added by Stats.1982, c. 1427, p. 5464, § 3. Amended by Stats.1990, c. 719 (A.B.2667), § 1.)*

§ 622. Exclusion of director of corporation or association

(a) "Employee" does not include a director of a corporation or association performing services in his or her capacity as a director. This section shall not apply to service included in "employment" pursuant to Sections 605, 608, 709, and 710.

(b) "Services in his or her capacity as a director" includes either:

(1) Presence at meetings of the board of directors, even though no further service is performed at the meeting.

(2) Services customarily performed by directors in attending meetings of the board of directors such as prescribing, regulating, and guiding the policies and administration of the corporation or association.

(c) "Services in his or her capacity as a director" does not include services performed by a director in addition to, or other than those described in subdivision (b) of this section. For example, services performed as an officer of the corporation or association, or as a member of a committee which executes the policies and administrative decisions adopted by the board of directors such as

advisory, appraisal, auditing, credit, examining, executive, loan or similar committees are not "services in his or her capacity as a director". *(Added by Stats.1971, c. 1107, p. 2096, § 14, eff. Oct. 18, 1971. Amended by Stats.1978, c. 2, p. 16, § 29, eff. Jan. 30, 1978, operative Jan. 1, 1978.)*

ARTICLE 2. EXCLUDED SERVICES

Section
629. Employment; domestic service; exception.
630. Employment; transcriber services.
631. Employment; family service.
632. Employment; service for another state or federal service.
633. Intermittent or adjunct instruction at postsecondary educational institution; inclusion as employment for disability compensation.
633.1. Employment; disability insurance coverage; ward and inmate exclusion.
634.5. Employment; services for public entities or Indian tribes.
635. Employment; service performed under unemployment compensation system.
636. Employment; political campaign worker.
637. Employment; sole shareholders of corporations; corporations engaged in agriculture.
637.1. Private corporation with sole stockholder-employee other than spouse; election to be excluded; effective date of election.
638. Contingent effect of certain sections.
639. Employment; domestic service in college club, fraternity, etc.
640. Employment; service not in course of employer's trade or business.
641. Employment; income tax exempt organization.
642. Employment; service for school by student.
642.1. Employment; students employed by camps.
643. Employment; foreign government.
644. Employment; instrumentality of foreign government.
644.5. Employment; service for international organization.
645. Employment; student nurse; intern.
646. Employment; service in educational institution which combines academic instruction with work experience.
647. Employment; service by patient for hospital.
648. Employment; service on foreign vessel or aircraft outside United States.
649. Employment; newsboy or news vendor under 18.
650. Real estate, mineral, oil and gas, or cemetery brokers, or real estate, cemetery, or direct salespersons; rebuttable presumption.
651. Employment; golf caddy.
652. Employment; official of nonprofit fraternal association.
653. Employment; baseball player.
654. Employment; free-lance jockey; exercise boy.
655. Employment; foreign professional athletes.
656. Employment; rebuttable presumption that services were performed by independent contractor; contract agreements.
657. Adoption of regulations.

§ 629. Employment; domestic service; exception

(a) "Employment" does not include domestic service in a private home, except that "employment" includes domestic service in a private home if performed for an employing unit or a person who paid in cash remuneration of one thousand dollars ($1,000) or more to individuals employed in the domestic service in any calendar quarter in the calendar year or the preceding calendar year.

(b) For purposes of subdivision (a), "employment" does not include work performed by a domestic worker for whom an employment agency, as defined in paragraph (3) of subdivision (a) or subdivision (h) of Section 1812.501 of the Civil Code, procures, offers, refers, provides, or attempts to provide domestic work in a private home, if all of the factors set forth in Section 687.2 characterize the nature of the relationship between the employment agency and the domestic worker for whom the agency procures, offers, refers, provides, or attempts to provide domestic work. *(Stats.1953, c. 308, p. 1473, § 629. Amended by Stats.1978, c. 2, p. 16, § 30, eff. Jan. 30, 1978, operative Jan. 1, 1978; Stats.1993, c. 1275 (A.B.1370), § 2.)*

§ 630. Employment; transcriber services

Notwithstanding subparagraph (C) of paragraph (1) of subdivision (c) of Section 621 or Section 13004, "employment" does not include service as a transcriber of depositions, court proceedings, and hearings performed away from the office of the person, firm, or association obligated to produce a transcript of these proceedings. *(Added by Stats.1984, c. 371, § 1.)*

§ 631. Employment; family service

"Employment" does not include service performed by a child under the age of 18 years in the employ of his father or mother, or service performed by an individual in the employ of his son, daughter, or spouse, except to the extent that the employer and the employee have, pursuant to Section 702.5, elected to make contributions to the Unemployment Compensation Disability Fund. *(Stats. 1953, c. 308, p. 1473, § 631. Amended by Stats.1971, c. 1447, p. 2858, § 1; Stats.1972, c. 579, p. 1014, § 46.)*

§ 632. Employment; service for another state or federal service

"Employment" does not include service performed in the employ of any other state or its political subdivisions or in the employ of the United States government or of any instrumentality of the United States, but if Congress permits the states to require any instrumentalities of the United States to make payments into a fund under a state unemployment compensation act, and to comply with state regulations thereunder, then, to the extent permitted by Congress, all of the provisions of this division shall be applicable to the instrumentalities and to services performed for the instrumentalities in the same manner, to the same extent, and on the same terms as to all other employers, employing units, individuals, and services.

If this state is not certified by the Secretary of Labor under Section 3304 of the Internal Revenue Code of 1986 for any year, then the payments required of the instrumentalities and their workers with respect to the year shall be refunded from the Unemployment Fund without interest. *(Stats.1953, c. 308, p. 1474, § 632. Amended by Stats.1953, c. 449, p. 1695; Stats.1957, c. 1184, p. 2474, § 2; Stats.1989, c. 1010, § 2.)*

§ 633. Intermittent or adjunct instruction at postsecondary educational institution; inclusion as employment for disability compensation

(a) For purposes of coverage under Part 2 (commencing with Section 2601) of Division 1, "employment" does not include services performed as an intermittent or adjunct instructor at a postsecondary educational institution which meets the requirements of Article 8 (commencing with Section 94900) of Chapter 7 of Part 59 of the Education Code if the intermittent or adjunct instructor and the employing unit enter a written contract with the following provisions:

(1) That any federal or state income tax liability shall be the responsibility of the party providing the services.

(2) That no disability insurance coverage is provided under the contract.

(3) That the party performing the services certifies that he or she is doing so as a secondary occupation or as a supplemental source of income.

(b) This section shall not apply to services performed under a collective bargaining agreement.

(c) This section shall become operative on January 1, 1997. *(Added by Stats.1995, c. 758 (A.B.446), § 293.5, operative Jan. 1, 1997. Amended by Stats.2002, c. 29 (A.B.1729), § 7.)*

§ 633.1. Employment; disability insurance coverage; ward and inmate exclusion

For purposes of coverage under Part 2 (commencing with Section 2601), "employment" shall not include:

(a) Services performed for any public entity, nonprofit or for profit entity, organization, or business by an inmate of a state prison under the jurisdiction of the Department of Corrections, by an individual who is otherwise in the custody of the Department of Corrections, or by an individual who is otherwise incarcerated in any of the institutions set forth in Section 2680.

(b) Services performed for any public entity, nonprofit or for profit entity, organization, or business by a ward in the custody of the Department of the Youth Authority. *(Added by Stats.1993, c. 318 (A.B.763), § 1.)*

§ 634.5. Employment; services for public entities or Indian tribes

Notwithstanding any other provision of law, no provision excluding service from "employment" shall apply to any entity defined by Section 605 or to any nonprofit organization described by Section 608, except as provided by this section. With respect to any entity defined by Section 605 or any nonprofit organization described by Section 608, "employment" does not include service excluded under Sections 629, 631, 635, and 639 to 648, inclusive, or service performed in any of the following:

(a) In the employ of either of the following:

(1) A church or convention or association of churches.

(2) An organization which is operated primarily for religious purposes and which is operated, supervised, controlled, or principally supported by a church or convention or association of churches.

(b) By a duly ordained, commissioned, or licensed minister of a church in the exercise of his or her ministry or by a member of a religious order in the exercise of duties required by the order.

(c) In the employ of any entity defined by Section 605, if the service is performed by an individual in the exercise of his or her duties as any of the following:

(1) An elected official.

(2) A member of a legislative body or a member of the judiciary of a state or a political subdivision of a state.

(3) A member of the tribal council of an Indian tribe as described by subsection (u) of Section 3306 of Title 26 of the United States Code.

(4) A member of a State National Guard or Air National Guard.

(5) An employee serving on a temporary basis in case of fire, storm, snow, earthquake, flood, or other similar emergency.

(6) An employee in a position that, under or pursuant to state or tribal law, is designated as either of the following:

(A) A major nontenured policymaking or advisory position.

(B) A policymaking or advisory position, the performance of the duties of which ordinarily does not require more than eight hours per week.

(7)(A) Except as otherwise provided in subparagraph (B), an election official or election worker if the amount of remuneration reasonably expected to be received by the individual during the calendar year for services as an election official or election worker is less than one thousand dollars ($1,000).

(B) This paragraph shall not take effect unless and until the service is excluded from service to which paragraph (1) of subdivision (a) of Section 3309 of Title 26 of the United States Code applies by reason of exemption under subdivision (b) of Section 3309 of that act.

(d) By an individual receiving rehabilitation or remunerative work in a facility conducted for the purpose of carrying out a program of either:

(1) Rehabilitation for individuals whose earning capacity is impaired by age or physical or mental deficiency or injury.

(2) Providing remunerative work for individuals who because of their impaired physical or mental capacity cannot be readily absorbed in the competitive labor market.

(e) By an individual receiving work relief or work training as part of an unemployment work relief or work training program assisted or financed in whole or in part by any of the following:

(1) A federal agency.

(2) An agency of a state or a political subdivision thereof.

(3) An Indian tribe, as described by subsection (u) of Section 3306 of Title 26 of the United States Code.

(f) By a ward or an inmate of a custodial or penal institution pursuant to Article 1 (commencing with Section 2700), Article 4 (commencing with Section 2760), and Article 5 (commencing with Section 2780) of Chapter 5 of, and Article 1 (commencing with Section 2800) of Chapter 6 of, Title 1 of Part 3 of the Penal Code, Section 4649 and Chapter 1 (commencing with Section 4951) of Part 4 of Division 4 of the Public Resources Code, and Sections 883, 884, and 1768 of the Welfare and Institutions Code.

(g) By an individual under the age of 18 years in the delivery or distribution of newspapers or shopping news, not including delivery or distribution to any point for subsequent delivery or distribution.

(h) By an individual in the sale of newspapers or magazines to ultimate consumers, under an arrangement that includes the following conditions:

(1) The newspapers or magazines are to be sold by the individual at a fixed price.

(2) The individual's compensation is based on retention of the excess of the price over the amount at which the newspapers or magazines are charged to the individual, whether or not he or she is guaranteed a minimum amount of compensation for the service or is entitled to be credited with the unsold newspapers or magazines that he or she returns.

(i)(1) Except as otherwise provided in paragraph (2), as a substitute employee whose employment does not increase the size of the employer's normal workforce, whose employment is required by law, and whose employment as a substitute employee does not occur on more than 60 days during the base period.

(2) This subdivision shall not take effect unless and until the United States Secretary of Labor, or his or her designee, finds that this subdivision is in conformity with federal requirements.

(j) As a participant in a national service program carried out using assistance provided under Section 12571 of Title 42 of the United States Code. (*Added by*

907

Stats.1978, c. 2, p. 18, § 36.5, eff. Jan. 30, 1978, operative July 1, 1978. Amended by Stats.1993, c. 318 (A.B.763), § 2; Stats.1994, c. 967 (S.B.1584), § 1.5, eff. Sept. 28, 1994; Stats.2000, c. 365 (S.B.945), § 4; Stats.2001, c. 255 (A.B.1537), § 4; Stats.2003, c. 183 (A.B.1430), § 1; Stats.2005, c. 152 (A.B.1577), § 3.)

§ 635. Employment; service performed under unemployment compensation system

"Employment" does not include service under any unemployment compensation system established by a law of the United States. *(Stats.1953, c. 308, p. 1474, § 635.)*

§ 636. Employment; political campaign worker

"Employment" does not include services performed in the employ of either a candidate for public office or a committee as defined in Section 82013 of the Government Code, where such services are performed in connection with an election campaign. *(Added by Stats.1957, c. 1352, p. 2682, § 1. Amended by Stats.1961, c. 2164, p. 4482, § 2; Stats.1976, c. 1079, p. 4887, § 85.)*

§ 637. Employment; sole shareholders of corporations; corporations engaged in agriculture

"Employment" does not include service performed by any of the following:

(a) The officers and director of a corporation who are the sole shareholders of the corporation and it is not subject to the Federal Unemployment Tax Act [1].

(b) The officers and director of a corporation engaged in agriculture who are shareholders of the corporation and it is not subject to the Federal Unemployment Tax Act.

(c) An officer of a corporation who is the sole shareholder, or the only shareholder other than his or her spouse, and the service is not subject to the Federal Unemployment Tax Act. *(Stats.1953, c. 308, p. 1475, § 637. Amended by Stats.1963, c. 1663, p. 3254, § 1; Stats.1970, c. 889, p. 1623, § 1; Stats.1971, c. 1107, p. 2099, § 22, eff. Oct. 18, 1971; Stats.1976, c. 909, p. 2083, § 1; Stats.1989, c. 798, § 1, eff. Sept. 26, 1989.)*

[1] 26 U.S.C.A. § 3301 et seq.

§ 637.1. Private corporation with sole stockholder-employee other than spouse; election to be excluded; effective date of election

In a private corporation, any individual who is included within the meaning of "employee" pursuant to subdivision (a) of Section 621 and who is the sole shareholder, or the only shareholder other than his or her spouse, may file a statement electing to be excluded from disability insurance coverage for benefits and contributions under this division. The election shall be effective on the first day of the calendar quarter in which the statement is filed. The election shall be effective during the remainder, if any, of the calendar year in which the statement is filed and not less than the two succeeding complete calendar years, and in all subsequent calendar quarters

908

while the statement is in effect. *(Added by Stats.1989, c. 798, § 2, eff. Sept. 26, 1989.)*

§ 638. Contingent effect of certain sections

Sections 639 to 648, inclusive, shall be operative only during such time as the respective type or types of service set forth in those sections are similarly excluded from the definition of "employment," in the Federal Unemployment Tax Act. *(Stats.1953, c. 308, p. 1475, § 638. Amended by Stats.1961, c. 2156, p. 4461, § 4; Stats.1971, c. 1107, p. 2099, § 24, eff. Oct. 18, 1971).*

§ 639. Employment; domestic service in college club, fraternity, etc.

"Employment" does not include domestic service in a local college club, or local chapter of a college fraternity or sorority, except that "employment" includes domestic service in a local college club, or local chapter of a college fraternity or sorority if performed for a club, chapter, or person who paid in cash remuneration of one thousand dollars ($1,000) or more to individuals employed in such domestic service in any calendar quarter in the calendar year or the preceding calendar year. *(Stats.1953, c. 308, p. 1475, § 639. Amended by Stats.1978, c. 2, p. 19, § 37, eff. Jan. 30, 1978, operative Jan. 1, 1978.)*

§ 640. Employment; service not in course of employer's trade or business

"Employment" does not include service not in the course of the employing unit's trade or business performed in any calendar quarter by an employee, unless the cash remuneration paid for such service is fifty dollars ($50) or more and such service is performed by an individual who is regularly employed by such employing unit to perform such service. For the purposes of this subdivision, an individual shall be deemed to be regularly employed by an employing unit during a calendar quarter only if on each of some 24 days during that quarter or the preceding calendar quarter such individual performs for such employing unit for some portion of the day service not in the course of the employing unit's trade or business. *(Stats.1953, c. 308, p. 1475, § 640.)*

§ 641. Employment; income tax exempt organization

"Employment" does not include service performed in any calendar quarter in the employ of any organization exempt from federal income tax under Section 501(a) of the Internal Revenue Code of 1954, as amended [1] (other than an organization described in Section 401(a) of that code), or under Section 521 of the Internal Revenue Code of 1954, as amended,[2] if the remuneration for such service is less than fifty dollars ($50). *(Stats.1953, c. 308, p. 1475, § 641. Amended by Stats.1955, c. 1165, p. 2158, § 2; Stats.1961, c. 2156, p. 4461, § 5; Stats.1971, c. 1107, p. 2099, § 24.5, eff. Oct. 18, 1971.)*

[1] 26 U.S.C.A. § 501(a).

[2] 26 U.S.C.A. § 521.

§ 642. Employment; service for school by student

"Employment" does not include service performed in the employ of a school, college, or university, if such service is performed:

(a) By a student who is enrolled and is regularly attending classes at such school, college, or university, or

(b) By the spouse of such a student, if such spouse is advised, at the time such spouse commences to perform such service, that:

(1) The employment of such spouse to perform such service is provided under a program to provide financial assistance to such student by such school, college, or university, and

(2) Such employment will not be covered by any program of unemployment insurance or disability compensation. *(Formerly § 645, Stats.1953, c. 308, p. 1476, § 645. Renumbered § 642 and amended by Stats.1961, c. 2156, p. 4461, § 9; Stats.1971, c. 1107, p. 2100, § 25, eff. Oct. 18, 1971.)*

§ 642.1. Employment; students employed by camps

(a) "Employment" does not include service performed by a full-time student employed by an organized camp, as defined in Section 18897 of the Health and Safety Code and Section 3306(c)(20) of Title 26 of the United States Code.

(b) "Full-time student" for purposes of this section means either of the following:

(1) The individual is enrolled as a full-time student of an educational institution.

(2) The individual is between academic years or terms under both of the following criteria:

(A) The individual was enrolled as a full-time student at an educational institution for the immediately preceding academic year or term.

(B) There is a reasonable assurance that the individual will be so enrolled for the immediately succeeding academic year or term after the period described in subparagraph (A).

(c) For purposes of determining whether an individual is a full-time student under this section the construction given to the corresponding definition of "full-time student" contained in Section 3306(q) of Title 26 of the United States Code shall apply. *(Added by Stats.1987, c. 545, § 1.)*

§ 643. Employment; foreign government

"Employment" does not include service performed in the employ of a foreign government (including service as a consular or other officer or employee or a nondiplomatic representative). *(Formerly § 646, Stats.1953, c. 308, p. 1476, § 646. Renumbered § 643 and amended by Stats. 1961, c. 2156, p. 4461, § 10.)*

§ 644. Employment; instrumentality of foreign government

"Employment" does not include service performed in the employ of an instrumentality wholly owned by a foreign government:

(a) If the service is of a character similar to that performed in foreign countries by employees of the United States Government or of an instrumentality thereof; and

(b) If the Secretary of State shall certify to the Secretary of the Treasury that the foreign government, with respect to whose instrumentality exemption is claimed, grants an equivalent exemption with respect to similar service performed in the foreign country by employees of the United States Government and of instrumentalities thereof. *(Formerly § 647, Stats.1953, c. 308, p. 1476, § 647. Renumbered § 644 and amended by Stats.1961, c. 2156, p. 4462, § 11.)*

§ 644.5. Employment; service for international organization

"Employment" does not include services performed in the employ of an international organization. *(Added by Stats.1973, c. 395, p. 860, § 1; Stats.1973, c. 494, p. 970, § 1.)*

§ 645. Employment; student nurse; intern

"Employment" does not include service performed as a student nurse in the employ of a hospital or a nurses' training school by an individual who is enrolled and is regularly attending classes in a nurses' training school chartered or approved pursuant to state law; and service performed as an intern in the employ of a hospital by an individual who has completed a four years' course in a medical school chartered or approved pursuant to state law. *(Formerly § 648, Stats.1953, c. 308, p. 1476, § 648. Renumbered § 645 and amended by Stats.1961, c. 2156, p. 4462, § 12.)*

§ 646. Employment; service in educational institution which combines academic instruction with work experience

"Employment" does not include service performed by an individual under the age of 22 who is enrolled at a nonprofit or public educational institution which normally maintains a regular faculty and curriculum and normally has a regularly organized body of students in attendance at the place where its educational activities are carried on as a student in a full-time program, taken for credit at such institution, which combines academic instruction with work experience, if such service is an integral part of such program, and such institution has so certified to the employer, except that this section shall not apply to service performed in a program established for or on behalf of an employer or group of employers. *(Added by Stats.1971, c. 1107, p. 2100, § 26, eff. Oct. 18, 1971.)*

§ 647. Employment; service by patient for hospital

"Employment" does not include service performed in the employ of a hospital, if such service is performed by a patient of such hospital. *(Added by Stats.1971, c. 1107, p. 2101, § 27, eff. Oct. 18, 1971.)*

§ 648. Employment; service on foreign vessel or aircraft outside United States

"Employment" does not include service performed on or in connection with a vessel or aircraft not an American vessel or an American aircraft, if the employee is employed on and in connection with such vessel or aircraft when outside the United States. *(Added by Stats.1971, c. 1107, p. 2101, § 28, eff. Oct. 18, 1971.)*

§ 649. Employment; newsboy or news vendor under 18

"Employment" does not include service performed by an individual if:

(a) Such service is performed by an individual under the age of 18 in the delivery or distribution of newspapers, shopping news, or magazines, not including delivery or distribution to any point for subsequent delivery or distribution, unless such service is performed by an individual under the age of 18 whose principal occupation is regular full-time work and whose attendance at school is incidental to full-time employment.

(b) Such service is performed by an individual in, and at the time of, the sale of newspapers or magazines to ultimate consumers, under an arrangement under which the newspapers or magazines are to be sold by him at a fixed price, his compensation being based on the retention of the excess of such price over the amount at which the newspapers or magazines are charged to him whether or not he is guaranteed a minimum amount of compensation for such service, or is entitled to be credited with the unsold newspapers or magazines turned back. *(Stats. 1953, c. 308, p. 1476, § 649. Amended by Stats.1953, c. 528, p. 1786.)*

§ 650. Real estate, mineral, oil and gas, or cemetery brokers, or real estate, cemetery, or direct salespersons; rebuttable presumption

"Employment" does not include services performed as a real estate, mineral, oil and gas, or cemetery broker or as a real estate, cemetery or direct sales salesperson, or a yacht broker or salesman, by an individual if all of the following conditions are met:

(a) The individual is licensed under the provisions of Chapter 19 (commencing with Section 9600) of Division 3 of, or Part 1 (commencing with Section 10000) of Division 4 of, the Business and Professions Code, Article 2 (commencing with Section 700) of Chapter 5 of Division 3 of the Harbors and Navigation Code, or is engaged in the trade or business of primarily inperson demonstration and sales presentation of consumer products, including services or other intangibles, in the home or sales to any buyer on a buy-sell basis, a deposit-commission basis, or any similar basis, for resale by the

buyer or any other person in the home or otherwise than from a retail or wholesale establishment.

(b) Substantially all of the remuneration (whether or not paid in cash) for the services performed by that individual is directly related to sales or other output (including the performance of services) rather than to the number of hours worked by that individual.

(c) The services performed by the individual are performed pursuant to a written contract between that individual and the person for whom the services are performed and the contract provides that the individual will not be treated as an employee with respect to those services for state tax purposes. *(Stats.1953, c. 308, p. 1477, § 650. Amended by Stats.1953, c. 1066, p. 2548; Stats.1955, c. 811, p. 1432, § 1; Stats.1967, c. 1725, p. 4297, § 2; Stats.1969, c. 216, p. 545, § 1; Stats.1983, c. 498, § 215, eff. July 28, 1983; Stats.1983, c. 1102, § 31, eff. Sept. 27, 1983; Stats.1983, c. 1104, § 4, eff. Sept. 27, 1983; Stats.1995, c. 541 (A.B.272), § 3; Stats.1998, c. 475 (A.B.2268), § 6.)*

§ 651. Employment; golf caddy

"Employment" does not include services performed by an individual as a golf caddy in caddying or carrying a golf player's clubs. *(Added by Stats.1953, c. 1751, p. 3508, § 2. Amended by Stats.1957, c. 595, p. 1691, § 1.)*

§ 652. Employment; official of nonprofit fraternal association

"Employment" does not include service performed as an elected or appointed official in any calendar quarter in the employ of any nonprofit fraternal corporation or association which is not subject to the Federal Unemployment Tax Act [1] if the remuneration for such service does not exceed one hundred dollars ($100) a month.

The provisions of this section shall be applicable with retrospective effect. *(Added by Stats.1954, 1st Ex.Sess., c. 29, p. 292, § 1. Amended by Stats.1961, c. 2164, p. 4482, § 3.)*

[1] 26 U.S.C.A. § 3301 et seq.

§ 653. Employment; baseball player

"Employment" does not include services performed in the employ of a baseball club pursuant to a contract or agreement under which the baseball player agrees to perform for expenses and a share of the profits of the club, rather than for a fixed salary. *(Added by Stats.1955, c. 1864, p. 3461, § 1.)*

§ 654. Employment; free-lance jockey; exercise boy

"Employment" does not include service performed by a free-lance jockey or exercise boy who is regularly licensed by the California Horse Racing Board. *(Added by Stats.1957, c. 620, p. 1830, § 1.)*

§ 655. Employment; foreign professional athletes

"Employment" does not include services performed by a professional athlete who is neither a citizen of nor a resident of the United States or any state when he comes to the State of California for occasional or incidental professional engagements. *(Added by Stats.1959, c. 746, p. 2736, § 1.)*

§ 656. Employment; rebuttable presumption that services were performed by independent contractor; contract agreements

"Employment" does not include professional services performed by a consultant working as an independent contractor.

For the purpose of this section, there shall be a rebuttable presumption that services provided by an individual engaged in work requiring specialized knowledge and skills attained through completion of recognized courses of instruction or experience are rendered as an independent contractor. These services shall be limited to those provided by attorneys, physicians, dentists, engineers, architects, accountants, chiropractors, and the various types of physical, chemical, natural, and biological scientists. Professional services shall not include services generally provided by persons who do not have a degree from a four-year institution of higher learning relating to the specialized knowledge and skills of the professional service being provided.

For the purposes of this section, the rebuttable presumption shall not apply to an individual who enters into a contract agreement with the recipient of the professional services which establishes an employer-employee relationship. However, the existence of a contract between a nonprofit, licensed, primary care clinic, as defined in subdivision (a) of Section 1204 of the Health and Safety Code, and a health care practitioner who is licensed as a physician and surgeon, osteopathic physician and surgeon, podiatrist, optometrist, chiropractor, or psychologist shall not constitute an employer-employee relationship if the contract stipulates that the professional services rendered to the clinic are by an independent contractor, not an employee. Independent contractors who conform to the provisions of this section or primary care clinics that contract with these individuals or organizations shall not be liable for any payments that may be required under an employer-employee relationship pursuant to this code. *(Added by Stats.1979, c. 986, p. 3365, § 1. Amended by Stats.1984, c. 773, § 1; Stats.1993, c. 226 (A.B.1987), § 14; Stats.1997, c. 39 (A.B.150), § 1.)*

§ 657. Adoption of regulations

The department shall adopt regulations by July 1, 1996, to establish clear criteria which specify under what conditions amateur athletic officials may be considered employees. *(Added by Stats.1995, c. 725 (A.B.1655), § 2.)*

ARTICLE 3. SUBJECT EMPLOYERS

Section
675. Employer.
676. Employer; performance of services included in "employment" for purposes of Part 2.
677. Employer; performance of services included in "employment" by public entity.
678. Employer; motion picture, radio or television industry.
679. Employer; motion picture payroll services company.
680. Motion picture payroll services companies; extension of voluntary plans.
682. Employer; domestic service in private home, college club, fraternity or sorority.
683. Employer; employing unit which employs individuals to perform in-home supportive services.
684. Employer; domestic service in private home, college club, fraternity or sorority.
685. Employer; employing unit which employs individuals to perform in-home supportive services.
686. Employer; contractor for specially ordered or commissioned work of authorship.
687.2. Employer; employment agency; domestic workers.

§ 675. Employer

"Employer" means any employing unit, which for some portion of a day, has within the current calendar year or had within the preceding calendar year in employment one or more employees and pays wages for employment in excess of one hundred dollars ($100) during any calendar quarter. *(Stats.1953, c. 308, p. 1477, § 675. Amended by Stats.1953, c. 1294, p. 2854, § 675; Stats. 1955, c. 1165, p. 2158, § 3; Stats.1971, c. 1107, p. 2101, § 29, eff. Oct. 18, 1971.)*

§ 676. Employer; performance of services included in "employment" for purposes of Part 2

"Employer" also means any employing unit, for which services are performed that are included in "employment" solely for the purposes of Part 2 (commencing with Section 2601) of this division, which for some portion of a day, has within the current calendar year or had within the preceding calendar year one or more employees performing such services, and pays wages for such service in excess of one hundred dollars ($100) during any calendar quarter. *(Added by Stats.1961, c. 2155, p. 4459, § 3. Amended by Stats.1971, c. 1107, p. 2101, § 30, eff. Oct. 18, 1971.)*

§ 677. Employer; performance of services included in "employment" by public entity

"Employer" also means any employing unit for which service is performed in "employment" as defined by Section 605. *(Added by Stats.1971, c. 1107, p. 2101, § 32, eff. Oct. 18, 1971. Amended by Stats.1978, c. 2, p. 20, § 39, eff. Jan. 30, 1978, operative Jan. 1, 1978.)*

§ 678. Employer; motion picture, radio or television industry

"Employer" means any employing unit which pursuant to a collective bargaining agreement between an employer and a labor organization in the motion picture, radio, or television industry, pays wages as provided in Section 926.5. *(Added by Stats.1971, c. 873, p. 1716, § 6.)*

§ 679. Employer; motion picture payroll services company

(a) Notwithstanding Sections 606.5, 621, and 678, for the purposes of this code, "employer" means any employing unit that is a motion picture payroll services company who pays and controls the payment of wages of a motion picture production worker for services either to a motion picture production company or to an allied motion picture services company. The motion picture payroll services company must also have filed a timely statement of its intent to be the employer of motion picture production workers pursuant to subdivision (b).

(b)(1) Any employing unit meeting the requirements of a motion picture payroll services company, as defined by this section, that intends to be treated as an employer of motion picture production workers pursuant to subdivision (a) shall file a statement with the department that declares its intent to be the employer of motion picture production workers, pursuant to this section, within 15 days after first paying wages to the workers. The statement shall include identification of all affiliated entities as defined by this section.

(2) Any employing unit operating as a motion picture payroll services company as of January 1, 2007, that intends to be treated as an employer of motion picture production workers pursuant to this section, shall file a statement with the department that declares its intent to be the employer of motion picture production workers, pursuant to this section, by January 15, 2007. The statement shall include identification of all affiliated entities as defined by this section.

(3) Any motion picture payroll company that quits business shall:

(A) Within 10 days of quitting business:

(i) File with the director, a final return and report of wages of its workers, as required by Section 1116.

(ii) File all statements required by this subdivision.

(B) Forty–five days in advance of quitting business, notify the motion picture production companies and allied motion picture services companies, with respect to which they have been treated as the employer of the motion picture production workers, of its intent to quit business.

(4) The director may prevent a motion picture payroll services company that fails to file a timely statement, as required by this section, from being treated as an employer of motion picture production workers, for a period not to exceed the period for which the statement is required.

(5) Any statement filed by a motion picture payroll services company pursuant to this subdivision shall be applied to all affiliated entities of the motion picture payroll services company in existence at the time the statement is filed.

(c) For each rating period beginning on or after January 1, 2007, in which an employer operating as a

motion picture payroll services company obtains or attempts to obtain a more favorable rate of contributions under this section in a manner that is due to deliberate ignorance, reckless disregard, fraud, intent to evade, misrepresentation, or willful nondisclosure, the director shall assign the maximum contribution rate plus 2 percent for each applicable rating period, the current rating period, and the subsequent rating period. Contributions paid in excess of the maximum rate under this section shall not be credited to the employing unit's reserve account.

(d)(1) On and after January 1, 2007, whenever a motion picture payroll services company creates or acquires a motion picture payroll services company, or acquires substantially all of the assets of a motion picture payroll services company, the created or acquired motion picture payroll services company shall:

(A) Constitute a separate employing unit, notwithstanding Sections 135.1 and 135.2.

(B) Have its reserve account and rate of contributions determined in accordance with subdivision (e).

(C) Notify the department of the entity being created or acquired and the nature of its affiliation to that entity.

(2) The department may promulgate regulations requiring a motion picture payroll services company, prior to the creation or acquisition of a motion picture payroll services company that will be an affiliated entity, to seek the approval of the department to apply the provisions of this section to the created or acquired entity.

(e) When a motion picture payroll services company transfers all or part of its business or payroll to another motion picture payroll services company, as defined by this section, the reserve account attributable to the transferor shall be transferred to the transferee motion picture payroll services company, and the transferee's rate of contribution shall be determined in accordance with Section 1052. The transferee shall notify the department within 15 days of the transfer of the business or payroll.

(f) For purposes of this section, the following definitions apply:

(1) "Affiliated entity" means any one or more motion picture payroll services company or companies that are united by factors of common ownership, management, or control as prescribed by Section 1061.

(2) "Allied motion picture services company" means any person engaged in an industry closely allied with, and whose work is integral to, a motion picture production company in the development, production, or postproduction of a motion picture, excluding the distribution of the completed motion picture and any activities occurring thereafter, and who hires from the same pool of craft and guild or union workers, actors, or extras as a motion picture production company.

(3) "Motion picture" means a motion picture of any type, including a theatrical motion picture, a television

production, a television commercial, a music video, or any other type of motion picture regardless of its theme or the technology used in its production or distribution.

(4)(A) "Motion picture payroll services company" means any employing unit that directly or through its affiliated entities meets all of the following criteria:

(i) Contractually provides the services of motion picture production workers to a motion picture production company or to an allied motion picture services company.

(ii) Is a signatory to a collective bargaining agreement for one or more of its clients.

(iii) Controls the payment of wages to the motion picture production workers and pays those wages from its own account or accounts.

(iv) Is contractually obligated to pay wages to the motion picture production workers without regard to payment or reimbursement by the motion picture production company or allied motion picture services company.

(v) At least 80 percent of the wages paid by the motion picture payroll services company each calendar year are paid to workers associated between contracts with motion picture production companies and motion picture payroll services companies.

(B) If the director determines that any employing unit is operating as a motion picture payroll services company but is failing to comply with any of the provisions of subparagraph (A) of paragraph (4), the employing unit is subject to determination of the employer-employee relationship pursuant to this code. When the director's ruling becomes final, the director may preclude the employing unit from being classified as a motion picture payroll services company pursuant to this section for up to three years from the date of the determination.

(5) "Motion picture production company" means any employing unit engaged in the development, production, and postproduction of a motion picture, excluding the distribution of the completed motion picture and any activities occurring thereafter.

(6) "Motion picture production worker" means an individual who provides services to a motion picture production company or allied motion picture services company and who, with regard to those services, is reported under this part as an employee by the motion picture payroll services company. An individual who has been reported as an employee by the motion picture payroll services company, without regard to the individual's status as an employee or independent contractor, shall be the employee of the motion picture payroll services company for the purposes of this code throughout the contractual period with the motion picture payroll services company.

(7) "Wages" shall have the same meaning given the term in Article 2 (commencing with Section 926) of Chapter 4 of Part 1 of Division 1, and shall include residual payments.

(g) If the director determines that an entity does not meet any of the requirements specified by this section, the director shall give notice of its determination to that entity pursuant to Section 1206. The notice shall contain a statement of the facts and circumstances upon which the determination was made. The entity so noticed shall have the right to petition for review of the director's determination within 30 days of the notice, as provided in Section 1222.

(h) The director shall prescribe the form and manner of the statements and information required to be filed or reported by this section.

(i) On or before December 31, 2010, the department may report to the Legislature regarding the impact of this section on the Unemployment Insurance Fund and the entertainment industry.

(j) This section shall remain in effect only until January 1, 2012, and as of that date is repealed, unless a later enacted statute, which is chaptered before January 1, 2012, deletes or extends that date. *(Added by Stats.2006, c. 811 (S.B.1428), § 1. Amended by Stats.2008, c. 391 (S.B.1173), § 1.)*

Repeal

For repeal of this section, see its terms.

§ 680. Motion picture payroll services companies; extension of voluntary plans

(a) Notwithstanding any other provision of law, when motion picture production workers are employed by one or more affiliated entities of a motion picture payroll services company that has elected to be treated and is being treated as the employer of those motion picture production workers pursuant to Section 679, the motion picture payroll services company may apply to the director for approval of the extension of an existing voluntary plan or plans for the payment of disability benefits to all motion picture production workers employed by all of the affiliated entities of the motion picture payroll services company. The director shall approve the extension of the voluntary plan to all of the motion picture production workers of all of the affiliated entities if he or she finds all of the following exist:

(1) The voluntary plan to be extended was in existence at the time of the election of the motion picture payroll services company to be treated as the employer of motion picture production workers pursuant to Section 679.

(2) The rights afforded to the covered employees are greater than those provided for in Chapter 2 (commencing with Section 2625) and Chapter 7 (commencing with Section 3300) of Part 2 of Division 1.

(3) The plan has been made available to all of the motion picture production workers of the employer employed in this state.

(4) If the plan provides for insurance, the form of the insurance policies to be issued has been approved by the

913

Insurance Commissioner and the policies are to be issued by an admitted disability insurer.

(5) The motion picture payroll services company has consented to the extension of the plan and has agreed to make the payroll deductions required, if any, and transmit the proceeds to the plan insurer, if any.

(6) The plan provides for the inclusion of future employees in the manner described in subparagraph (A) of paragraph (2) of subdivision (b).

(7)(A) The plan will be in effect for a period of not less than one year and, thereafter, continuously, unless the director finds that the motion picture payroll services company or a majority of motion picture production workers employed in this state covered by the plan has given notice of withdrawal from the plan. The notice shall be filed in writing with the director and shall be effective only on the anniversary of the effective date of the plan next following the filing of the notice, but in any event not less than 30 days from the date of the filing of the notice.

(B) Notwithstanding the provisions of subparagraph (A), the plan may be withdrawn on the operative date of any law increasing the benefit amounts provided by Sections 2653 and 2655 or on the operative date of any change in the rate of worker contributions as determined by Section 984, if notice of the withdrawal from the plan is transmitted to the director not less than 30 days prior to the operative date of that law or change. If the plan is not withdrawn on 30 days' notice because of the enactment of a law increasing the benefit amounts provided by Sections 2653 and 2655 or because of a change in the rate of worker contributions as determined by Section 984, the plan shall be amended to conform to that increase or change on the operative date of the increase or change.

(8) The amount of deductions from the wages of an employee in effect for any plan shall not be increased on a date other than an anniversary date of the effective date of the plan, except to the extent that any increase in the deductions from the wages of an employee allowed by Section 3260 permits that amount to exceed the amount of deductions in effect. The amount of deductions, for the purpose of providing coverage under the plan, shall not exceed that which would be required by Sections 984 and 985 if the employee were not covered by the plan.

(9) The approval of the extension of the plan will not result in a substantial selection of risks adverse to the Disability Fund.

(b) The extension of a plan approved by the director pursuant to subdivision (a) shall be deemed to have also met the consent requirements of Section 3257 if both of the following requirements are met:

(1) The plan met the consent requirements of Section 3257 when initially adopted.

(2) The plan provides for both of the following:

(A) Each employee to whom the plan is applicable shall be given written notice of his or her right to reject coverage under the plan and a written statement setting forth the essential features of the plan prior to or at the time of employment. The form of the notice and of the statement shall be approved by the director.

(B) On or before January 31 of each calendar year, each employee shall be given written notice, in a form approved by the director, of his or her right to withdraw from the plan at the beginning of any calendar quarter upon giving reasonable notice in writing directed to the motion picture payroll services company. *(Added by Stats.2008, c. 391 (S.B.1173), § 2.)*

§ 682. Employer; domestic service in private home, college club, fraternity or sorority

(a) "Employer" also means any employing unit which employs individuals to perform domestic service in a private home, local college club, or local chapter of a college fraternity or sorority and pays wages in cash of one thousand dollars ($1,000) or more for such service during any calendar quarter in the calendar year or the preceding calendar year.

(b) Any employing unit which qualifies as an employer under this section shall not be treated as an employer with respect to wages paid for any service other than domestic service specified by this section unless such employing unit also qualifies as an employer with respect to such other service under Section 675, 676, 677, or 678. *(Added by Stats.1978, c. 2, p. 20, § 40, eff. Jan. 30, 1978, operative Jan. 1, 1978. Amended by Stats.2005, c. 152 (A.B.1577), § 4.)*

§ 683. Employer; employing unit which employs individuals to perform in-home supportive services

"Employer" also means any employing unit which employs individuals to perform domestic service comprising in-home supportive services under Article 7 (commencing with Section 12300), Chapter 3, Part 3, Division 9 of the Welfare and Institutions Code and pays wages in cash of one thousand dollars ($1,000) or more for such service during any calendar quarter in the calendar year or the preceding calendar year, and is one of the following:

(a) The recipient of such services, if the state or county makes or provides for direct payment to a provider chosen by the recipient or to the recipient of such services for the purchase of services, subject to the provisions of Section 12302.2 of the Welfare and Institutions Code.

(b) The individual or entity with whom a county contracts to provide in-home supportive services.

(c) Any county which hires and directs in-home supportive personnel in accordance with established county civil service requirements or merit system requirements for those counties not having civil service systems. *(Added by Stats.1978, c. 463, p. 1571, § 3, eff. July 18, 1978.)*

§ 684. Employer; domestic service in private home, college club, fraternity or sorority

(a) Solely for the purposes of Part 2 (commencing with Section 2601) of this division, "employer" also means any employing unit which employs individuals to perform domestic service in a private home, local college club, or local chapter of a college fraternity or sorority and pays wages in cash of seven hundred fifty dollars ($750) or more to individuals employed in such service during any calendar quarter in the calendar year or the preceding calendar year.

(b) Any employing unit which qualifies as an employer under this section shall not be treated as an employer with respect to wages paid for any service other than domestic service specified by this section unless such employing unit also qualifies as an employer with respect to such other service under Section 675, 676, 677, or 678. *(Added by Stats.1981, c. 1025, p. 3939, § 1. Amended by Stats.2005, c. 152 (A.B.1577), § 5.)*

§ 685. Employer; employing unit which employs individuals to perform in-home supportive services

Solely for the purposes of Part 2 (commencing with Section 2601) of this division, "employer" also means any employing unit which employs individuals to perform domestic service comprising in-home supportive services under Article 7 (commencing with Section 12300) of Chapter 3 of Part 3 of Division 9 of the Welfare and Institutions Code and pays wages in cash of seven hundred fifty dollars ($750) or more to individuals employed in such service during any calendar quarter in the calendar year or preceding calendar year, and is one of the following:

(a) The recipient of the services, if the state or county makes or provides for direct payment to a provider chosen by the recipient or to the recipient of the services for the purchase of services, subject to the provisions of Section 12302.2 of the Welfare and Institutions Code.

(b) The individual or entity with which a county contracts to provide in-home supportive services.

(c) Any county which hires and directs in-home supportive personnel in accordance with established county civil service requirements or merit system requirements for those counties not having civil service systems. *(Added by Stats.1981, c. 1025, p. 3940, § 2.)*

§ 686. Employer; contractor for specially ordered or commissioned work of authorship

"Employer" also means any person contracting for the creation of a specially ordered or commissioned work of authorship when the parties expressly agree in a written instrument signed by them that the work shall be considered a work made for hire, as defined in Section 101 of Title 17 of the United States Code [1], and the ordering or commissioning party obtains ownership of all of the rights comprised in the copyright in the work. The ordering or commissioning party shall be the employer of the author of the work for the purposes of this part. *(Added by Stats.1982, c. 1332, p. 4937, § 3.)*

[1] 17 U.S.C.A. § 101.

§ 687.2. Employer; employment agency; domestic workers

Notwithstanding any other provision of law, an employment agency, as defined in paragraph (3) of subdivision (a) or subdivision (h) of Section 1812.501 of the Civil Code, shall not be deemed to be the employer of the domestic workers for whom it procures, offers, refers, provides, or attempts to provide work if all of the following factors exist:

(a) There is a signed contract or agreement between the employment agency and the domestic worker that contains, at a minimum, provisions that specify all of the following:

(1) That the employment agency shall assist the domestic worker in securing work.

(2) How the employment agency's referral fee shall be paid.

(3) That the domestic worker is free to sign an agreement with other employment agencies and to perform domestic work for persons not referred by the employment agency.

(b) The domestic worker informs the employment agency of any restrictions on hours, location, conditions, or type of work he or she will accept and the domestic worker is free to select or reject any work opportunity procured, offered, referred, or provided by the employment agency.

(c) The domestic worker is free to renegotiate with the person hiring him or her the amount proposed to be paid for the work.

(d) The domestic worker does not receive any training from the employment agency with respect to the performance of domestic work. However, an employment agency may provide a voluntary orientation session in which the relationship between the employment agency and the domestic worker, including the employment agency's administrative and operating procedures, and the provisions of the contract or agreement between the employment agency and the domestic worker are explained.

(e) The domestic worker performs domestic work without any direction, control, or supervision exercised by the employment agency with respect to the manner and means of performing the domestic work.

The following actions exercised by an employment agency shall not be considered to be the exercise of direction, control, or supervision:

(1) Informing the domestic worker about the services to be provided and the conditions of work specified by the person seeking to hire a domestic worker.

(2) Contacting the person who has hired the domestic worker to determine whether that person is satisfied with the agency's referral service. This contact shall not be

used to identify improvements needed in a worker's performance and to then discipline or train the worker regarding the performance of domestic work.

(3) Informing the domestic worker of the time during which new referrals are available.

(4) Requesting the domestic worker to inform the employment agency if the domestic worker is unable to perform the work accepted.

(f) The employment agency does not provide tools, supplies, or equipment necessary to perform the domestic work.

(g) The domestic worker is not obligated to pay the employment agency's referral fee, and the employment agency is not obligated to pay the domestic worker if the person for whom the services were performed fails or refuses to pay for the domestic work.

(h) Payments for domestic services are made directly to either the domestic worker or to the employment agency. Payments made directly to the employment agency shall be deposited into a trust account until payment can be made to the domestic worker. Payments made to the domestic worker by the employment agency shall not be paid from any of the employment agency's business accounts.

(i) The relationship between a domestic worker and the person for whom the domestic worker performs services may only be terminated by either of those parties and not by the employment agency that referred the domestic worker. However, an employment agency may decline to make additional referrals to a particular domestic worker, and the domestic worker may decline to accept a particular referral. *(Added by Stats.1993, c. 1275 (A.B.1370), § 3.)*

ARTICLE 4. ELECTIVE COVERAGE

Section
701.   Election to become an employer; approval.
702.   Election; services in excluded employment.
702.1.   Nonprofit organization; election for coverage.
702.5.   Employment in family service; election as covered employment.
702.6.   Disability compensation; election by employer; negotiated agreement or petition.
703.   Election; services in out-of-state employment.
704.   Approval of election.
704.1.   Termination of elective coverage; findings; notice; effect.
704.2.   Definitions.
705.   Termination of elective coverage agreement; requisite conditions.
706.   Waiver of requirement for written application for termination.
707.   Election notice; posting; objections; hearing.
708.   Employer's election to qualify for benefits; contributions; prerequisite to benefit payments.
708.5.   Self-employed persons; election; contributions; benefits.
709.   Election by public entity or Indian tribe to become an employer; filing; approval of director.
710.   Election by public entity or Indian tribe to become an employer with respect to certain services; filing; director approval; exclusions; method of financing coverage; information gathered and published by director.
710.4.   Election of public school employer.
710.5.   Election by public agency; filing; approval by director.
710.6.   Election of Indian tribe to become employer with respect to employees meeting certain conditions; filing; approval by director; Tribal–State Gaming Compact.
710.7.   Election by State of California; filing; approval by director.
710.8.   Election by California State University; filing; approval by director.
710.9.   Election by community college district; filing; approval by director.
711.   Termination of election filed by public entity or nonprofit organization.
712.   Contributions; credits; time of election.
713.   Contributions; credits.

§ 701. Election to become an employer; approval

An employing unit, not otherwise subject to this division, which files with the director its written election to become an employer for not less than two calendar years, shall, with the written approval of the election by the director, become an employer subject to this division to the same extent as other employers as of the date stated in the approval. *(Stats.1953, c. 308, p. 1478, § 701. Amended by Stats.1955, c. 9, p. 447, § 1, eff. Jan. 28, 1955; Stats.1957, c. 1183, p. 2473, § 1; Stats.1961, c. 2156, p. 4462, § 13.)*

§ 702. Election; services in excluded employment

Except as provided by Sections 702.1, 709, and 710, any employing unit for which services that do not constitute employment are performed, may file with the director a written election that all such services performed by individuals in its employ in one or more distinct establishments or places of business shall be deemed to constitute employment by an employer for all the purposes of this division for not less than two calendar years. Upon the written approval of the election by the director, such services shall be deemed to constitute employment subject to this division from and after the date stated in the approval. *(Stats.1953, c. 308, p. 1478, § 702. Amended by Stats.1965, c. 530, p. 1847, § 1; Stats.1969, c. 291, p. 647, § 1; Stats.1971, c. 1107, p. 2101, § 34, eff. Oct. 18, 1971; Stats.1978, c. 2, p. 20, § 41, eff. Jan. 30, 1978, operative Jan. 1, 1978.)*

§ 702.1. Nonprofit organization; election for coverage

(a) As used in this section, "nonprofit organization" means any corporation, community chest, fund, or foundation for which services that constitute employment under Section 608 are performed and for which other services that do not constitute employment are performed, or any nonprofit organization described in Section 608 for which all services performed do not constitute employment.

(b) No election filed by a nonprofit organization under Section 702 shall be effective for service performed after December 31, 1971. All elections for coverage filed by a nonprofit organization under Section 702 prior to January 1, 1972, shall be terminated effective December 31, 1971.

(c) Any nonprofit organization for which any services that do not constitute employment are performed may, when requested by a written petition signed by a majority of its employees to be covered by the election, file with the director a written election that the services performed in one or more distinct establishments or places of business and to be covered by the election shall be deemed to constitute employment by an employer for all the purposes of this division for not less than two calendar years. If the director finds that a majority of the employees to be covered by the election have signed the petition, a nonprofit organization shall, upon the written approval of the director, become an employer with respect to such services subject to this division to the same extent as other employers, and services performed by its employees covered by the election, shall constitute employment subject to this division. Beginning at that time it shall withhold from the wages of employees covered by the election the contributions required for unemployment compensation disability benefits.

(d) A nonprofit organization may exclude from coverage under an election pursuant to this section any service excluded under Section 634.5.

(e) Notwithstanding the provisions of subdivision (d), a nonprofit organization shall not exclude from unemployment compensation disability coverage under an election pursuant to this section any service that is included in "employment" for the purposes of Part 2 (commencing with Section 2601) of this division.

(f) In lieu of the contributions required of employers, each nonprofit organization that has elected coverage under this section may elect any method of financing coverage by an election under this section that is permitted under Section 803. Subdivision (c) of Section 801 shall apply to any such election under Section 803.

(g) Except as inconsistent with the provisions of this section, the provisions of this division and authorized regulations shall apply to any matter arising pursuant to this section. *(Added by Stats.1971, c. 1107, p. 2102, § 35, eff. Oct. 18, 1971.)*

§ 702.5. Employment in family service; election as covered employment

Any employing unit for which services that do not constitute employment under Section 631 are performed, may file with the director a written election, agreed to by both the employing unit and the individuals in its employ specified in Section 631, that all such services performed by such individuals in one or more distinct establishments or places of business shall be deemed to constitute

employment by an employer for all the purposes of Part 2 (commencing with Section 2601) of this division. Upon the written approval of the election by the director, such services shall be deemed to constitute employment subject to such part from and after the date stated in the approval. Sections 704 and 707 shall apply to elections under this section. *(Added by Stats.1971, c. 1447, p. 2858, § 2.)*

§ 702.6. Disability compensation; election by employer; negotiated agreement or petition

(a) Any employing unit who is an employer under this division may file with the director a written election to cover, for the purposes of Part 2 (commencing with Section 2601) only, services performed by any of the following:

(1) All eligible employees who are a part of a labor organization, provided the election is the result of a negotiated agreement between the employer and the recognized employee organization.

(2) All eligible employees in its employ in one or more distinct establishments or places of business who are not part of a labor organization, when the election is requested by a written petition signed by a majority of the eligible employees to be covered by the election.

(b) "Eligible employee," as used in this section, means an employee who is a California resident whose services are covered under the unemployment compensation laws of another state which does not have a disability insurance program, and who is an "employee," as defined in Section 13004, for whom the employer complies with the personal income tax withholding provisions of Division 6 (commencing with Section 13000).

(c) Upon the filing of an election, the filing entity shall, upon approval by the director, become an employer subject to Part 2 (commencing with Section 2601) to the same extent as other employers, and services performed by its employees who are subject to the election shall be deemed to constitute employment subject to that part. Sections 704, 707, 986, and 2903 shall apply to elections under this section. *(Added by Stats.1989, c. 475, § 1.)*

§ 703. Election; services in out-of-state employment

Services not included within "employment" and performed entirely without this State, with respect to no part of which contributions are required and paid under an unemployment compensation law of any other state or of the Federal Government, shall be deemed to be employment if the individual performing such services is a resident of this State and the director approves the election of the employing unit for whom the services are performed that the entire service of such individual shall be deemed to be employment subject to this division. Such election shall be for the period, made in the manner, and subject to termination as provided in this article for other elections of coverage. *(Stats.1953, c. 308, p. 1478, § 703.)*

§ 704. Approval of election

The director shall not approve an election under Section 701, 702, 702.1, 702.5, 703, 708, or 708.5 if he or she finds that any of the following conditions exist:

(a) The self-employed individual is currently unable to perform his or her regular and customary work due to injury or illness.

(b) The employing unit or self-employed individual is not normally and continuously engaged in a regular trade, business, or occupation.

(c) The employing unit or self-employed individual intends to discontinue the regular trade, business or occupation within eight calendar quarters.

(d) The regular trade, business, or occupation of the employing unit or self-employed individual is seasonal in its operations.

(e) The major portion of the self-employed individual's remuneration is not derived from his or her trade, business, or occupation.

(f) The self-employed individual is unable to provide a copy of his or her Internal Revenue Service Schedule SE as reported on or before April 15 of the preceding year showing a net profit of at least four thousand six hundred dollars ($4,600) or to certify to an average net profit of at least one thousand one hundred fifty dollars ($1,150) per quarter since becoming self-employed or for the preceding four quarters, whichever period is less.

(g) The employing unit or self-employed individual has failed to make a return or report, or to pay contributions within the time required by this division and there is an unpaid amount of contributions owing by the employing unit or self-employed individual.

(h)(1) A prior elective coverage agreement entered into pursuant to Section 708 or 708.5 has been terminated by the department under Section 704.1 or by means of a written application for termination as required by this division, and the individual has not completed a waiting period of 18 consecutive months from the date of termination.

(2) The waiting period for reinstatement to the elective coverage program may be waived for any individual who becomes eligible for coverage after being terminated under paragraph (1), (2), (4), or (5) of subdivision (a) of Section 704.1, upon receipt by the department of an application for coverage to be effective the first day of the quarter in which the application is received.

(i) The employing unit or any officer or agent of or person having charge of the affairs of the employing unit, or the self-employed individual has been convicted within the preceding eight consecutive calendar quarters of any violation under Chapter 10 (commencing with Section 2101). For the purposes of this subdivision, a plea or verdict of guilty or a conviction following a plea of nolo contendere is deemed to be a conviction irrespective of whether an order granting probation or other order is made suspending the imposition of the sentence or whether sentence is imposed but execution thereof is suspended.

(j) For purposes of this section, Internal Revenue Service Schedule SE is defined as Internal Revenue Service Form 1040 Schedule SE, or in the case of statutory employees under the Internal Revenue Code, it shall be defined as Internal Revenue Service Form 1040 Schedule C, or the California Income Tax Return, when accompanied by Internal Revenue Service Form W-2. *(Stats.1953, c. 308, p. 1479, § 704. Amended by Stats. 1955, c. 1165, p. 2158, § 4; Stats.1963, c. 1563, p. 3145, § 1; Stats.1971, c. 1107, p. 2103, § 36, eff. Oct. 18, 1971; Stats.1978, c. 2, p. 20, § 42, eff. Jan. 30, 1978, operative Jan. 1, 1978; Stats.1979, c. 661, p. 2031, § 1; Stats.1993, c. 747 (A.B.1738), § 1; Stats.1994, c. 125 (S.B.1830), § 1, eff. June 30, 1994; Stats.1994, c. 1049 (A.B.3086), § 1.)*

§ 704.1. Termination of elective coverage; findings; notice; effect

(a) Notwithstanding any other provision of this division, the director may terminate any elective coverage agreement under this article if he or she finds that any of the following conditions exist:

(1) The employing unit or self-employed individual is not normally and continuously engaged in a regular trade, business, or occupation.

(2) The employing unit or self-employed individual has discontinued the regular trade, business, or occupation.

(3) The regular trade, business, or occupation of the employing unit or self-employed individual is seasonal in its operations.

This paragraph shall not apply to any public entity.

(4) The major portion of the self-employed individual's remuneration is not derived from his or her trade, business, or occupation.

(5) The self-employed individual reports a net profit of less than four thousand six hundred dollars ($4,600) on his or her Internal Revenue Service Schedule SE for a third consecutive year.

(6) The employing unit or self-employed individual has failed to make a return or report, or to pay contributions within the time required by this division and there is an unpaid amount of contributions owing by the employing unit or self-employed individual, except when the elective coverage agreement has been in effect for less than two complete calendar years.

(7) The employing unit or self-employed individual, or a representative thereof, is found by the director to have filed a false statement in order to be considered eligible for elective coverage.

(8) The employing unit or any officer or agent of or person having charge of the affairs of the employing unit, or the self-employed individual is convicted of any violation pursuant to Chapter 10 (commencing with Section 2101). For the purposes of this paragraph, a plea or verdict of guilty or a conviction following a plea of nolo

contendere is deemed to be a conviction irrespective of whether an order granting probation or other order is made suspending the imposition of the sentence or whether sentence is imposed but execution thereof is suspended.

(b) The director shall give to the employing unit, or to the self-employed individual, a written notice pursuant to Section 1206 of the director's termination of the elective coverage agreement under this section. The date of termination may be the end of the calendar quarter immediately preceding the existence of any condition specified in subdivision (a), or the end of any subsequent calendar quarter thereafter, as determined by the director.

Any termination of elective coverage shall not affect the liability of the employing unit or self-employed individual for any contributions due, owing, and unpaid to the department.

(c) Sections 1222, 1223, and 1224 shall apply to matters arising under this section.

(d) For purposes of this section, Internal Revenue Service Schedule SE is defined as Internal Revenue Service Form 1040 Schedule SE, or in the case of statutory employees under the Internal Revenue Code, it shall be defined as Internal Revenue Service Form 1040 Schedule C, or the California Income Tax Return, when accompanied by Internal Revenue Service Form W-2. *(Added by Stats.1979, c. 661, p. 2032, § 2. Amended by Stats.1980, c. 1025, p. 3287, § 5; Stats.1988, c. 647, § 1; Stats.1993, c. 747 (A.B.1738), § 2; Stats.1994, c. 125 (S.B.1830), § 2, eff. June 30, 1994; Stats.1994, c. 1049 (A.B.3086), § 2.)*

§ 704.2. Definitions

For purposes of Sections 704 and 704.1:

(a) "Normally and continuously engaged in a regular trade, business, or occupation" means both of the following:

(1) Regularly performing services and engaging in an uninterrupted pattern of work that is customary for the individual's trade, business, or occupation.

(2) In the case of a self-employed individual or individual who is an employer is in a trade, business, or occupation that requires a valid and active license, that individual has been issued that license. An individual operating a business without a required license shall not be considered normally engaged in a trade, business, or occupation.

(b) "Seasonal in its operations" means any of the following:

(1) The trade, business, or occupation is not continuous or carried on throughout the year.

(2) The operation of the trade, business, or occupation is temporarily or intermittently suspended for regularly recurring periods of time.

(3) The performance of services in the trade, business, or occupation is regularly suspended due to weather, climate, or other conditions. *(Added by Stats.1993, c. 747 (A.B.1738), § 3.)*

§ 705. Termination of elective coverage agreement; requisite conditions

(a) An elective coverage agreement approved by the director pursuant to any section of this article may be terminated as of January 1st of any calendar year only if the agreement has been in effect for two calendar years and if the employing unit or self-employed individual, on or before the 31st day of January of that year, has filed with the director a written application for termination.

(b) An elective coverage agreement entered into prior to January 1, 1994, pursuant to Section 708 or 708.5 may be terminated on January 1, 1994, if the self-employed individual files a written application for termination with the director on or before June 30, 1994. *(Stats.1953, c. 308, p. 1479, § 705. Amended by Stats.1955, c. 1165, p. 2158, § 5; Stats.1957, c. 1183, p. 2473, § 2; Stats.1959, c. 1718, p. 4126, § 2; Stats.1978, c. 2, p. 20, § 43, eff. Jan. 30, 1978, operative Jan. 1, 1978; Stats.1993, c. 747 (A.B.1738), § 4.)*

§ 706. Waiver of requirement for written application for termination

The director may for good cause waive the requirement of Section 705 that a written application for termination shall be filed on or before the thirty-first day of January. *(Stats.1953, c. 308, p. 1479, § 706. Amended by Stats. 1955, c. 1165, p. 2158, § 6.)*

§ 707. Election notice; posting; objections; hearing

Every employing unit which files an election to become an employer pursuant to Section 701, 702, 702.1, 702.5, 703, 709, or 710, or an application for termination pursuant to Section 705, shall post and maintain printed notices of such election or application on his or her premises, as prescribed by authorized regulation. Individuals in the employ of any employing unit which files an election to become an employer shall be given a reasonable opportunity to file objections or to be heard in the matter prior to the director's approval of the election. *(Stats.1953, c. 308, p. 1479, § 707. Amended by Stats. 1957, c. 1183, p. 2473, § 3; Stats.1971, c. 1107, p. 2103, § 37, eff. Oct. 18, 1971; Stats.1978, c. 2, p. 21, § 44, eff. Jan. 30, 1978, operative Jan. 1, 1978.)*

§ 708. Employer's election to qualify for benefits; contributions; prerequisite to benefit payments

(a) Any individual who is an employer under this division or any two or more individuals who have so qualified may file with the director a written election that their services shall be deemed to be services performed by individuals in employment for an employer for all the purposes of this division. Upon the approval of the election by the director, the services of those individuals shall be deemed to constitute employment for an employer for all of the purposes of this division. Regardless of their actual earnings, for the purposes of computing benefit rights and contributions under this division, they shall be deemed to have received the following remuneration for each calendar quarter:

(1) For purposes of unemployment insurance, the highest amount of wages required to be entitled to the maximum benefit amount provided in Section 1280.

(2) For purposes of disability insurance, the highest amount of wages required to be entitled to the maximum benefit amount provided in Section 2655.

(A) For disability insurance contributions on or after July 1, 1994, the quarterly contribution shall be the product of one-fourth of the amount of net profit, but not less than one thousand one hundred fifty dollars ($1,150) except when subparagraph (B) applies, reported on or before April 15 of the preceding year as declared on the Internal Revenue Service Schedule SE filed by an individual who is an employer under this division and the contribution rate established pursuant to Section 984.5, except as provided by Section 985. On January 1, 1995, quarterly income credits for the period from July 1, 1993, to June 30, 1994, inclusive, shall be changed to one-fourth of the amount of the net profit or four thousand six hundred dollars ($4,600), whichever is greater, reported on or before April 15, 1993, as declared on the Internal Revenue Service Schedule SE for the 1992 taxable year filed by each individual having an elective coverage agreement in effect for that period or any portion thereof. If no Internal Revenue Service Schedule SE was filed, the individual shall be assigned a quarterly income credit of one thousand one hundred fifty dollars ($1,150). Quarterly income credits for this period shall not exceed seven thousand nine hundred forty-two dollars ($7,942). If any quarterly income credit for the period from July 1, 1993, to June 30, 1994, inclusive, was reduced prior to January 1, 1995, the amended income credit shall be reduced proportionately. Benefits payable for periods of disability commencing on or after January 1, 1995, shall be based on Section 2655. For purposes of this division, income credits shall be included in the term "wages."

(B) The self-employed individual shall not pay contributions for periods of any disability, including periods for which some services are performed while disabled. The self-employed individual shall file a quarterly report of wages and certify as to the period of disability in order to maintain eligibility for elective disability insurance coverage and benefits. During periods of disability, the self-employed individual shall reduce his or her quarterly contributions by dividing the quarterly contribution amount by 91 to compute the daily contribution amount, and the daily contribution amount shall be multiplied by the number of days disabled to compute the amount by which the quarterly contributions shall be reduced. The department shall reduce income credits utilizing the same calculation method.

(b) Any individual who is an employer under this division or any two or more individuals who have so

920

qualified may file with the director a written election that their services shall be deemed to be services performed by individuals in employment for an employer for the purposes of Part 2 (commencing with Section 2601) only. Upon the approval of the election by the director, the services of those individuals shall be deemed to constitute employment for an employer for the purposes of Part 2 (commencing with Section 2601) only. Regardless of their actual earnings, for the purposes of computing disability benefit rights and worker contributions, they shall be deemed to have received remuneration for each calendar quarter the highest amount of wages required to be entitled to the maximum benefit award provided in Section 2655. For contributions on or after July 1, 1994, the quarterly contribution shall be the product of one-fourth of the amount of net profit, but not less than one thousand one hundred fifty dollars ($1,150), except when subparagraph (B) of paragraph (2) of subdivision (a) applies, reported on or before April 15 of the preceding year as declared on the Internal Revenue Service Schedule SE filed by an individual who is an employer under this division and the contribution rate established pursuant to Section 984.5, except as provided by Section 985. The quarterly contribution shall be reduced as set forth in subparagraph (B) of paragraph (2) of subdivision (a) if a disability occurred during the quarter for which payment is being made. On January 1, 1995, quarterly income credits for the period from July 1, 1993, to June 30, 1994, inclusive, shall be changed to one-fourth of the amount of the net profit or four thousand six hundred dollars ($4,600), whichever is greater, reported on or before April 15, 1993, as declared on the Internal Revenue Service Schedule SE for the 1992 taxable year filed by each individual having an elective coverage agreement in effect for that period or any portion thereof. If no Internal Revenue Service Schedule SE was filed, the individual shall be assigned a quarterly income credit of one thousand one hundred fifty dollars ($1,150). Quarterly income credits for this period shall not exceed seven thousand nine hundred forty-two dollars ($7,942). If quarterly income credits were reduced prior to January 1, 1995, the amended income credits shall be reduced proportionately. Benefits payable for periods of disability commencing on or after January 1, 1995, shall be based on Section 2655. For purposes of this division, income credits shall be included in the term "wages."

(c)(1) Any individual applying for or continuing elective coverage under this section shall be requested to sign an annual statement authorizing the department to verify the net profit declared on his or her Internal Revenue Service Schedule SE. Failure of the individual to sign a statement authorizing the department to verify income shall result in the individual being assigned an annual income level of four thousand six hundred dollars ($4,600) for contribution and benefit purposes.

(2) Any individual applying for elective coverage shall submit a copy of his or her Internal Revenue Service Schedule SE filed on or before April 15 of the preceding year with his or her application for elective coverage in

order to establish first-year contributions and benefits in excess of the minimum required to qualify for elective coverage.

(d) Any self-employed individual continuing elective coverage who fails to file an Internal Revenue Service Schedule SE by April 15 of each calendar year is required to remit contributions based upon the last year the self-employed individual filed an Internal Revenue Service Schedule SE.

(e) Any self-employed individual who has not yet filed an Internal Revenue Service Schedule SE shall be assigned an annual income level of four thousand six hundred dollars ($4,600) for contribution and benefit purposes.

(f) Contributions required under this division are payable on and after the date stated in the approval of the director. The director may levy assessments under this division for any amount due when an elective coverage agreement has been in effect for less than two complete calendar years. Chapter 7 (commencing with Section 1701), relating to the collection of amount due, shall apply to this section.

(g) No benefits shall be paid to any individual based upon remuneration deemed to have been received pursuant to this section unless all contributions due with respect to all remuneration deemed to have been received by the individual pursuant to this section have been paid to the department.

(h) No benefits shall be paid to any individual based on elective coverage income credits in his or her base period if his or her elective coverage agreement has been terminated under paragraph (6) of subdivision (a) of Section 704.1.

(i) Notwithstanding subdivision (b) of Section 2627, no benefits shall be paid to any individual covered under this section, with respect to periods of disability commencing on or after January 1, 1994, until he or she has been unemployed and disabled for a waiting period of seven consecutive days during each disability benefit period.

(j) Notwithstanding Section 2653, with respect to periods of disability commencing on or after January 1, 1994, the maximum amount of benefits payable to an individual covered under this section during any one disability benefit period shall be 39 times his or her weekly benefit amount, but in no case shall the total amount of benefits payable be more than the total wages credited to the individual during his or her disability base period. If the benefit is not a multiple of one dollar ($1), it shall be computed to the next higher multiple of one dollar ($1).

(k) For purposes of this section, Internal Revenue Service Schedule SE is defined as Internal Revenue Service Form 1040 Schedule SE, or in the case of statutory employees under the Internal Revenue Code, it shall be defined as Internal Revenue Service Form 1040 Schedule C, or the California Income Tax Return, when accompanied by Internal Revenue Service Form W–2. *(Stats.1953, c. 308, p. 1479, § 708. Amended by Stats.*

1959, c. 1729, p. 4175, § 7; Stats.1961, c. 2154, p. 4449, § 1; Stats.1961, c. 2164, p. 4482, § 4; Stats.1963, c. 1563, p. 3146, § 3; Stats.1969, c. 291, p. 647, § 2; Stats.1979, c. 1053, p. 3706, § 1, operative April 1, 1981; Stats.1989, c. 1146, § 1; Stats.1989, c. 1371, § 1; Stats.1993, c. 747 (A.B.1738), § 5; Stats.1994, c. 125 (S.B.1830), § 3, eff. June 30, 1994; Stats.2005, c. 152 (A.B.1577), § 6.)

§ 708.5. Self-employed persons; election; contributions; benefits

(a) Any individual who is self-employed, who is not an employer as defined in any provision of Article 3 (commencing with Section 675), of Chapter 3 of this part, and who receives the major part of his or her remuneration from the trade, business, or occupation in which he or she is self-employed, may file with the director a written election that his or her services in connection with his or her trade, business, or occupation shall be deemed to be services performed by an individual in employment for an employer for the purposes of Part 2 (commencing with Section 2601) only. Upon the approval of the election by the director, the services of that self-employed individual in connection with his or her trade, business, or occupation shall be deemed to constitute employment for an employer for the purposes of Part 2 only of this division. Regardless of his or her actual earnings, for the purpose of computing disability benefit rights and worker contributions, he or she shall be deemed to have received remuneration for each calendar quarter the highest amount of wages required to be entitled to the maximum benefit award provided in Section 2655. For contributions on or after July 1, 1994, the quarterly contribution shall be the product of one-fourth of the amount of net profit, but not less than one thousand one hundred fifty dollars ($1,150), except when subparagraph (B) of paragraph (2) of subdivision (a) of Section 708 applies, reported on or before April 15 of the preceding year as declared on the Internal Revenue Service Schedule SE filed by an individual who is an employer under this division and the contribution rate established pursuant to Section 984.5, except as provided by Section 985. The quarterly contribution shall be reduced as set forth in subparagraph (B) of paragraph (2) of subdivision (a) of Section 708 if a disability occurred during the quarter for which payment is being made. On January 1, 1995, quarterly income credits for the period from July 1, 1993, to June 30, 1994, inclusive, shall be changed to one-fourth of the net profit or four thousand six hundred dollars ($4,600), whichever is greater, reported on or before April 15, 1993, as declared on the Internal Revenue Service Schedule SE for the 1992 taxable year filed by each individual having an elective coverage agreement in effect for that period or any portion thereof. If no Internal Revenue Service Schedule SE was filed, the individual shall be assigned a quarterly income credit of one thousand one hundred fifty dollars ($1,150). Quarterly income credits for this period shall not exceed seven thousand nine hundred forty-two dollars ($7,942). If quarterly income credits for the period from July 1, 1993, to June 30, 1994, inclusive, were reduced prior to January 1, 1995, the amended income credits shall be reduced proportionately. Benefits payable for periods of disability commencing on or after January 1, 1995, shall be based on the provisions of Section 2655. For purposes of this division, income credits shall be included in the term "wages."

(b)(1) Any individual applying for or continuing elective coverage under this section shall be requested to sign an annual statement authorizing the department to verify the net profit declared on his or her Internal Revenue Service Schedule SE. Failure of the individual to sign a statement authorizing the department to verify income shall result in the individual being assigned an annual income level of four thousand six hundred dollars ($4,600) for contribution and benefit purposes.

(2) Any individual applying for elective coverage shall submit a copy of his or her Internal Revenue Service Schedule SE filed on or before April 15 of the preceding year with his or her application for elective coverage in order to establish first-year contributions and benefits in excess of the minimum required to qualify for elective coverage.

(c) Any self-employed individual continuing elective coverage who fails to file an Internal Revenue Service Schedule SE by April 15 of each calendar year is required to remit contributions based upon the last year the self-employed individual filed an Internal Revenue Service Schedule SE.

(d) Any self-employed individual who has not yet filed an Internal Revenue Service Schedule SE shall be assigned an annual income level of four thousand six hundred dollars ($4,600) for contribution and benefit purposes.

(e) Worker contributions required under this division are payable on and after the date stated in the approval of the director. The director may levy assessments under this division for any amount due when an elective coverage agreement has been in effect for less than two complete calendar years. Chapter 7 (commencing with Section 1701), relating to the collection of amounts due, shall apply to this section.

(f) No benefits shall be paid to any individual based on elective coverage income credits in his or her base period if his or her elective coverage agreement has been terminated under paragraph (6) of subdivision (a) of Section 704.1.

(g) No benefits shall be paid to any individual based upon remuneration deemed to have been received pursuant to this section unless all contributions due with respect to all remuneration deemed to have been received by that individual pursuant to this section have been paid to the department.

(h) Notwithstanding subdivision (b) of Section 2627, no benefits shall be paid to any individual covered under this section, with respect to periods of disability commencing on or after January 1, 1994, until he or she has

922

been unemployed and disabled for a waiting period of seven consecutive days during each disability benefit period.

(i) Notwithstanding Section 2653, with respect to periods of disability commencing on or after January 1, 1994, the maximum amount of benefits payable to an individual covered under this section during any one disability benefit period shall be 39 times his or her weekly benefit amount, but in no case shall the total amount of benefits payable be more than the total wages credited to the individual during his or her disability base period. If the benefit is not a multiple of one dollar ($1), it shall be computed to the next higher multiple of one dollar ($1).

(j) For purposes of this section, Internal Revenue Service Schedule SE is defined as Internal Revenue Service Form 1040 Schedule SE, or in the case of statutory employees under the Internal Revenue Code, it shall be defined as Internal Revenue Service Form 1040 Schedule C, or the California Income Tax Return, when accompanied by Internal Revenue Service Form W–2. *(Added by Stats.1963, c. 1563, p. 3145, § 2. Amended by Stats.1965, c. 1654, p. 3755, § 3; Stats.1969, c. 291, p. 648, § 3; Stats.1993, c. 747 (A.B.1738), § 6; Stats.1994, c. 125 (S.B.1830), § 4, eff. June 30, 1994; Stats.2005, c. 152 (A.B.1577), § 7.)*

§ 709. Election by public entity or Indian tribe to become an employer; filing; approval of director

Any local public entity located in this state specified in paragraph (3) of subdivision (a) of Section 135 or Indian tribe specified in paragraph (6) of subdivision (a) of Section 135 may elect to become an employer subject to Part 2 (commencing with Section 2601) of this division with respect to all its employees, including those with civil service or tenure positions, and may file its written election with the director. That election may be made on its own motion by the appropriate governing board of the local public entity or Indian tribe making the election, or may be made by the governing board pursuant to a petition signed by a majority of the employees (including those with civil service or tenure positions) requesting the governing board to file an election with the director. Upon the filing of an election, the filing local public entity or Indian tribe shall, upon approval by the director, become an employer subject to Part 2 (commencing with Section 2601) to the same extent as other employers, and services performed by its employees, including those with civil service or tenure positions, shall constitute employment subject to that part. Beginning at that time, it shall withhold from the wages of employees the contributions required for unemployment compensation disability benefits. *(Added by Stats.1978, c. 2, p. 21, § 46, eff. Jan. 30, 1978, operative Jan. 1, 1978. Amended by Stats.2001, c. 255 (A.B.1537), § 5.)*

Operative Effect

Under the terms of Section 17 of Stats.2001, c. 255 (A.B.1537), the provisions of that Act are retroactive to December 21, 2000.

§ 710. Election by public entity or Indian tribe to become an employer with respect to certain services; filing; director approval; exclusions; method of financing coverage; information gathered and published by director

(a) Any public entity or Indian tribe for which services that do constitute employment under Section 605 are performed and for which other services that do not constitute employment are performed may elect to become an employer subject to this part and Parts 3 (commencing with Section 3501) and 4 (commencing with Section 4001) of this division for not less than two calendar years with respect to those other services and to have those other services performed by its employees constitute employment subject to this part and Parts 3 and 4 for that period. Upon the filing of an election the filing public entity or Indian tribe shall, upon approval by the director, become an employer subject to this part and Parts 3 and 4 with respect to the services covered to the same extent as other employers, and those services performed by its employees, including those with civil service or tenure positions, shall constitute employment subject to this part and Parts 3 and 4 effective on the first day of the calendar quarter following the quarter in which the election is filed.

(b) The public entity or Indian tribe may exclude from coverage under an election pursuant to this section any service excluded under Section 634.5.

(c) Any public entity or Indian tribe that has elected coverage under this section may elect any method of financing coverage otherwise permitted under Section 803 or Article 6 (commencing with Section 821), but the same method of financing coverage shall apply to all coverage by the public entity. An Indian tribe may make separate elections for itself and for each subdivision, subsidiary, or business enterprise wholly owned by that Indian tribe. Subdivision (b) of Section 802 shall apply to any election under Section 803, except that any election under Section 803 shall be terminated on the effective date of the termination of an election for coverage under this section.

(d) The director may require from the public entity or Indian tribe employment, financial, statistical, or other information and reports, properly verified, as may be deemed necessary by the director to carry out his or her duties under this division, which shall be filed with the director at the time and in the manner prescribed by him or her.

(e) The director may tabulate and publish information obtained pursuant to this section in statistical form and may divulge the name of the public entity or Indian tribe.

(f) The public entity or Indian tribe shall keep work records as prescribed by the director for the proper administration of this division.

(g) Except as inconsistent with the provisions of this section, the provisions of this division and authorized regulations shall apply to any matter arising pursuant to this section. (Added by Stats.1978, c. 2, p. 21, § 48, eff. Jan. 23, 1978, operative Jan. 1, 1978. Amended by Stats.1985, c. 1217, § 3, eff. Sept. 29, 1985; Stats.2001, c. 255 (A.B.1537), § 6.)

Operative Effect

Under the terms of Section 17 of Stats.2001, c. 255 (A.B.1537), the provisions of that Act are retroactive to December 21, 2000.

§ 710.4. Election of public school employer

Notwithstanding the provisions of Section 709, any public school employer, as defined in Section 3540.1 of the Government Code, may elect to become an employer subject to Part 2 (commencing with Section 2601) of this division, with respect to all employees who are a part of an appropriate unit established pursuant to the provisions of Chapter 10.7 (commencing with Section 3540) of Division 4 of Title 1 of the Government Code, provided such election is the result of a negotiated agreement between the public school employer and the certified employee organization, as such terms are defined in Section 3540.1 of the Government Code. The public school employer may elect to provide coverage to its management and confidential employees, as such terms are defined in Section 3540.1 of the Government Code, and to employees not a part of an appropriate unit, but such election shall not be contingent upon coverage of other employees of the public school employer.

Upon filing of such an election, the filing entity shall, upon approval by the director, become an employer subject to Part 2 (commencing with Section 2601) of this division to the same extent as other employers, and services performed by its employees, including those with civil service or tenure positions, shall constitute employment subject to such part. Beginning at that time, the public school employer shall withhold from the wages of employees the contributions required for unemployment compensation disability benefits. (Added by Stats.1976, c. 1421, p. 6351, § 1, eff. Sept. 30, 1976. Amended by Stats.1978, c. 2, p. 22, § 52, eff. Jan. 30, 1978, operative Jan. 1, 1978.)

§ 710.5. Election by public agency; filing; approval by director

Notwithstanding Section 709, any public agency, as defined in Section 3501 of the Government Code, may elect to become an employer subject to Part 2 (commencing with Section 2601) with respect to all employees who are a part of an appropriate unit established pursuant to Chapter 10 (commencing with Section 3500) of Division 4 of Title 1 of the Government Code, provided the election is the result of a negotiated agreement between the public agency and the recognized employee organization, as those terms are defined in Section 3501 of the Government Code. The public agency employer also may elect to provide coverage to its management and confidential employees and to its employees who are not a part of an appropriate unit, but the election shall not be contingent

923

upon coverage of other employees of the public agency employer.

Upon filing of such an election, the filing entity shall, upon approval by the director, become an employer subject to Part 2 (commencing with Section 2601) to the same extent as other employers, and services performed by its employees who are subject to an election under this section shall constitute employment subject to that part.

Sections 986 and 2903 shall apply to an employer making an election pursuant to this section. *(Added by Stats.1980, c. 549, p. 1532, § 1, eff. July 17, 1980. Amended by Stats.1981, c. 704, p. 2528, § 2; Stats.1982, c. 742, p. 2945, § 1; Stats.1985, c. 144, § 1, eff. July 3, 1985.)*

§ 710.6. Election of Indian tribe to become employer with respect to employees meeting certain conditions; filing; approval by director; Tribal–State Gaming Compact

(a) Notwithstanding Section 709, any Indian tribe as described by subsection (u) of Section 3306 of Title 26 of the United States Code, including those tribes not covered by the Tribal–State Gaming Compact, may elect to become an employer subject to Part 2 (commencing with Section 2601) with respect to all employees who meet either of the following conditions:

(1) Are employed in one or more distinct establishments or places of business.

(2) Are a part of an employee bargaining unit provided the election is the result of a negotiated agreement between the Indian tribe and the recognized employee organization. The Indian tribe also may elect to provide coverage to its management and confidential employees and to its employees who are not a part of an employee bargaining unit, but the election by the bargaining unit shall not be contingent upon coverage of other employees of the Indian tribe.

(b) Upon filing of an election, the filing entity shall, upon approval by the director, become an employer subject to Part 2 (commencing with Section 2601) to the same extent as other employers, and services performed by its employees who are subject to an election under this section shall constitute employment subject to that part. Sections 986 and 2903 apply to an employer making an election pursuant to this section.

(c) This section does not affect the requirement that Indian tribes covered by the Tribal–State Gaming Compact be subject to Part 2 (commencing with Section 2601). *(Added by Stats.2001, c. 255 (A.B.1537), § 7.)*

Operative Effect

Under the terms of Section 17 of Stats.2001, c. 255 (A.B.1537), the provisions of that Act are retroactive to December 21, 2000.

924

§ 710.7. Election by State of California; filing; approval by director

(a) The State of California, as defined as an employer in Section 3513 of the Government Code, may elect to become an employer subject to Part 2 (commencing with Section 2601) with respect to all employees who are part of an appropriate unit established pursuant to Chapter 10 (commencing with Section 3512) of Division 4 of Title 1 of the Government Code, provided the election is the result of a negotiated agreement between the State of California and the recognized employee organization, as those terms are defined in Section 3513 of the Government Code. The State of California may elect to provide coverage to its management and confidential employees and to its employees who are not part of an appropriate unit, provided that the election is not contingent upon coverage of other employees of the State of California.

(b) Upon filing of the election, the filing entity shall, upon approval by the director, become an employer subject to Part 2 (commencing with Section 2601) to the same extent as other employers, and services performed by its employees including those with civil service or tenure positions who are subject to an election under this section shall constitute employment subject to that part.

(c) Sections 986 and 2903 apply to an employer making an election pursuant to this section. *(Added by Stats.2002, c. 878 (A.B.2149), § 1.)*

§ 710.8. Election by California State University; filing; approval by director

(a)(1) The Trustees of the California State University, as defined as an employer in Section 3562 of the Government Code, shall elect to become an employer subject to Part 2 (commencing with Section 2601) with respect to all employees who are part of an appropriate unit established pursuant to Chapter 12 (commencing with Section 3560) of Division 4 of Title 1 of the Government Code, provided the election is the result of a negotiated agreement between the Trustees of the California State University and a recognized employee organization of the university, as those terms are defined in Section 3562 of the Government Code, or is approved through an election held by a recognized employee organization of the university in accordance with the election procedures set forth in subdivision (d) of this section.

(2) The Trustees of the California State University may also elect to provide coverage to its management and confidential employees and to its employees who are not a part of an appropriate unit, provided that the election is not contingent upon coverage of other employees of the Trustees of the California State University.

(b) Upon filing of the election, the filing entity shall, upon approval by the director, become an employer subject to Part 2 (commencing with Section 2601) to the same extent as other employers, and services performed by its employees, including those with civil service or tenure positions, who are subject to an election under this section shall constitute employment subject to that part.

(c) Sections 986 and 2903 apply to an employer making an election pursuant to this section.

(d)(1) Upon an affirmative vote of the governing body of the employee organization, that governing body shall order that an election shall be conducted by secret ballot, placing on the ballot the question of whether the employees of that appropriate bargaining unit do or do not desire that the Trustees of the California State University shall become the employer of the employees of that appropriate bargaining unit for the purposes of being subject to Part 2 (commencing with Section 2601).

(2) The recognized employee organization of the California State University shall certify the results of the election on the basis of which ballot choice receives a majority of the valid votes cast. There shall be printed on the ballot two choices, one which specifies the desire to be covered by state disability insurance and one which specifies the desire to continue to be covered by nonindustrial disability insurance.

(3) The ballot shall present the questions in a manner that stipulates that, if the election determination is in favor of the employees' desire to be covered by state disability insurance, this determination is intended to supplant the nonindustrial disability insurance program provided for in Article 1.2 (commencing with Section 89529.15) of Chapter 5 of Part 55 of the Education Code, after two calendar quarters have elapsed following the effective date of the state disability insurance coverage. *(Added by Stats.2002, c. 878 (A.B.2149), § 2. Amended by Stats.2003, c. 841 (A.B.978), § 1.)*

§ 710.9. Election by community college district; filing; approval by director

(a)(1) Notwithstanding Section 709, a community college district established pursuant to Part 43 (commencing with Section 70900) of Division 7 of the Education Code may elect to become an employer subject to Part 2 (commencing with Section 2601) with respect to all employees who are part of an appropriate unit established pursuant to Chapter 10.7 (commencing with Section 3540) of Division 4 of Title 1 of the Government Code, if the election is the result of a negotiated agreement between the community college district and the certified employee organization, as that term is defined in subdivision (b) of Section 3540.1 of the Government Code. The community college district employer may also elect to provide coverage to its management and confidential employees and to its employees who are not part of an appropriate unit, but the election shall not be contingent upon coverage of other employees of the community college district employer.

(2) Notwithstanding paragraph (1), a community college district established pursuant to Part 43 (commencing with Section 70900) of Division 7 of the Education Code that employs an academic employee, as defined in Section 87001 of the Education Code, may elect to provide coverage to permanent, part-time, or temporary academic employees, including permanent, part-time, temporary, or substitute faculty or instructors, but the election shall not be contingent upon coverage of other academic employees of the community college district employer.

(b) Upon the filing of an election pursuant to subdivision (a), the filing entity shall, upon approval by the director, become an employer subject to Part 2 (commencing with Section 2601) to the same extent as other employers, and services performed by its employees who are subject to an election under this section shall constitute employment subject to that part.

(c) Sections 986 and 2903 shall apply to an employer making an election pursuant to this section. *(Added by Stats.2009, c. 437 (A.B.381), § 1.)*

§ 711. Termination of election filed by public entity or nonprofit organization

No election filed by any public entity, as defined by Section 605, under any provision of this division shall be effective for service performed after December 31, 1977, and included in "employment" pursuant to Section 605, except that elections approved under subdivision (b) of former Section 710 as in effect prior to January 1, 1978, shall continue in effect as of such date with respect to disability insurance coverage for those employee classifications that are exempt from civil service or merit system status who perform work equivalent to those employees of the building trades crafts that are covered by collective-bargaining agreements with respect to wages, hours, fringe benefits, and other terms and conditions of employment. No election filed by any nonprofit organization under any provision of this division shall be effective for service performed after December 31, 1977, and included in "employment" pursuant to Section 608. All such elections for coverage filed prior to January 1, 1978, shall be terminated effective December 31, 1977, except as otherwise provided by this section and except that elections to reimburse benefits shall continue in effect, subject to Section 803, unless terminated by the public entity or nonprofit organization, and it shall remain liable for its proportionate share of the additional cost of benefits paid, or of the cost of benefits (including extended duration benefits and federal-state extended benefits) paid and charged to its account in the manner provided by Section 1026 which are based on wages paid for services during the period of any election for reimbursement of benefits. *(Added by Stats.1978, c. 2, p. 23, § 54, eff. Jan. 30, 1978, operative Jan. 1, 1978. Amended by Stats.1978, c. 950, p. 2932, § 1, eff. Sept. 20, 1978.)*

§ 712. Contributions; credits; time of election

To the extent permitted by federal law, no contributions shall be due from any nonprofit organization organized before 1960 which received a retroactive determination after April 1, 1981, and before April 1, 1982, that it has been a nonprofit organization from the date it was organized, which made contributions with respect to service performed in its employ prior to January 1, 1982, and which elected a method of financing and elected to use prior contributions until the additional cost of benefits reimbursable by or the cost of benefits paid and reimbursable by the nonprofit organization together with the benefits charged and chargeable to the reserve account of the nonprofit organization as the result of its prior elective coverage agreement exceed the contributions made by the nonprofit organization and credited to its reserve account pursuant to its prior elective coverage agreement.

This section shall apply only to organizations which make the elections described in this section within 120 days of the time they are legally able to do so because of a change in federal law. *(Added by Stats.1961, c. 2159, p. 4471, § 2. Amended by Stats.1970, c. 1156, p. 2046, § 3; Stats.1971, c. 883, p. 1733, § 1; Stats.1978, c. 2, p. 23, § 56, eff. Jan. 30, 1978, operative Jan. 1, 1978; Stats.1982, c. 872, p. 3233, § 1.)*

§ 713. Contributions; credits

To the extent permitted by federal law, no contributions shall be due from any nonprofit organization which first became compulsorily subject to this part on January 1, 1978, by reason of the enactment of the federal "Unemployment Compensation Amendments of 1976" (Public Law 94–566) [1] and the amendment to Section 634.5 by the 1978 portion of the 1977–78 Regular Session, which elects a method of financing under Section 803 when such election first becomes available, but not later than April 1, 1978, and which also elects to use contributions paid pursuant to an elective coverage agreement of such nonprofit organization in effect prior to January 1, 1978, until the cost of benefits paid and reimbursable by the nonprofit organization together with the benefits charged and chargeable to the reserve account of the nonprofit organization as the result of its prior elective coverage agreement exceed the contributions made by the nonprofit organization and credited to its reserve account pursuant to its prior elective coverage agreement. *(Added by Stats.1978, c. 2, p. 24, § 57, eff. Jan. 30, 1978, operative Jan. 1, 1978.)*

[1] 26 U.S.C.A. § 3304 note.

ARTICLE 5. ELECTIONS FOR FINANCING UNEMPLOYMENT INSURANCE COVERAGE

Section
801.   Authority of nonprofit organization.
801.5. Liability of nonprofit organization for reimbursement of benefits pursuant to election; limitations.
802.   Election by state, public entity or Indian tribe to finance its liability for benefits; filing; termination of election; gathering documentation; tabulation and publication; work records.
803.   Method of financing coverage.
803.1. Acquisition of or succession to another entity; liability for reimbursement; exception.

Section
803.2. Acquisition of favorable reserve account; liability for reimbursement.
804.   Notice to Internal Revenue Service and Department of Labor of failure of Indian tribe to make payment or post bond as required by § 803.
805.   Unregistered nonprofit organizations; reimbursement financing.
806.   Notice of claim to public entities electing to finance under provisions of § 803.

§ 801. Authority of nonprofit organization

(a) As used in this section, "nonprofit organization" means any corporation, community chest, fund, or foundation for which services are performed that constitute employment by compulsory coverage under Section 608.

(b) A nonprofit organization may, in lieu of the contributions required of employers, elect to finance its liability for unemployment compensation benefits, extended duration benefits, and federal-state extended benefits coverage under this division by any method of financing coverage that is permitted under Section 803.

(c) Any election under Section 803 of a method for financing coverage under this section shall, upon the written approval of the director, take effect with respect to services performed from and after the first day of the calendar quarter in which the election is filed with the director, and shall continue in effect for not less than five full calendar years. Thereafter the election under Section 803 may be terminated as of January 1 of any calendar year only if the nonprofit organization, on or before the 31st day of January of that year, has filed with the director a written application for termination. The director may for good cause waive the requirement that a written application for termination shall be filed on or before the 31st day of January. In no event shall the director approve any method of financing coverage by an election under Section 803 that would establish any different method of financing coverage for any calendar quarter where an election for coverage made by a nonprofit organization under Section 702.1 elects a method of financing coverage permitted under Section 803.

(d) To the extent permitted by federal law, a nonprofit organization which elects reimbursement financing pursuant to this section and which has a favorable reserve account on the date the election takes effect shall not be liable for the reimbursement of benefits pursuant to the election to the extent that the cost of benefits does not exceed the amount in the reserve account. Notwithstanding Section 1029, the reserve account shall not be canceled and the cost of benefits otherwise chargeable to the organization shall be charged to the reserve account until it is exhausted.

(e) Except as inconsistent with the provisions of this section, the provisions of this division and authorized regulations shall apply to any matter arising pursuant to this section. *(Added by Stats.1971, c. 1107, p. 2107, § 46, eff. Oct. 18, 1971. Amended by Stats.1984, c. 855, § 1, eff. Sept. 5, 1984.)*

§ 801.5. Liability of nonprofit organization for reimbursement of benefits pursuant to election; limitations

To the extent permitted by federal law, a nonprofit organization which before the operative date of this section elected reimbursement financing pursuant to Section 801 and which has a favorable reserve account on the operative date of this section shall not be liable for the reimbursement of benefits pursuant to the election to the extent that the cost of benefits does not exceed the amount in the reserve account. Notwithstanding Section 1029, the reserve account shall not be canceled and the cost of benefits otherwise chargeable to the organization shall be charged to the reserve account until it is exhausted. *(Added by Stats.1984, c. 855, § 2, eff. Sept. 5, 1984.)*

§ 802. Election by state, public entity or Indian tribe to finance its liability for benefits; filing; termination of election; gathering documentation; tabulation and publication; work records

(a) The State of California, any other public entity (as defined by Section 605), or any Indian tribe as described by subsection (u) of Section 3306 of Title 26 of the United States Code, or any subdivision, subsidiary, or business enterprise wholly owned by that Indian tribe, for which services are performed that do constitute employment under Section 605 may, in lieu of the contributions required of employers, elect to finance its liability for unemployment compensation benefits, extended duration benefits, and federal-state extended benefits with respect to those services by any method of financing coverage that is permitted under Section 803.

(b) Any election under Section 803 for financing coverage under this section shall take effect with respect to services performed from and after the first day of the calendar quarter in which the election is filed with the director, and shall continue in effect for not less than two full calendar years, unless the election is cancelled by the director pursuant to paragraph (2) of subdivision (g) of Section 803. Thereafter the election under Section 803 may be terminated as of January 1 of any calendar year only if the state or other public entity or Indian tribe, on or before the 31st day of January of that year, has filed with the director a written application for termination. The director may for good cause waive the requirement that a written application for termination shall be filed on or before the 31st day of January. In no event shall financing coverage by an election under Section 803 be valid that would establish any different method of financing coverage for any calendar quarter where an election for coverage has also been made by the state or other public entity or Indian tribe under any provision of Article 4 (commencing with Section 701) of this chapter.

(c) The director may require from the state and other public entity and Indian tribe, including any agent thereof, such employment, financial, statistical, or other information and reports, properly verified, as may be deemed necessary by the director to carry out his or her duties under this division, which shall be filed with the director at the time and in the manner prescribed by him or her.

(d) The director may tabulate and publish information obtained pursuant to this section in statistical form and may divulge the name of the state or other public entity or Indian tribe.

(e) The state and other public entity and Indian tribe, including any agent thereof, shall keep any work records as may be prescribed by the director for the proper administration of this division.

(f) Except as inconsistent with the provisions of this section, the provisions of this division and authorized regulations apply to any matter arising pursuant to this section. *(Added by Stats.1971, c. 1107, p. 2108, § 46, eff. Oct. 18, 1971. Amended by Stats.1971, c. 1622, p. 3489, § 7; Stats.1972, c. 319, p. 595, § 5, eff. July 10, 1972; Stats.1976, c. 909, p. 2085, § 3; Stats.1978, c. 2, p. 24, § 58, eff. Jan. 30, 1978, operative Jan. 1, 1978; Stats.2001, c. 255 (A.B.1537), § 8.)*

Operative Effect

Under the terms of Section 17 of Stats.2001, c. 255 (A.B.1537), the provisions of that Act are retroactive to December 21, 2000.

§ 803. Method of financing coverage

(a) As used in this section, "entity" means any employing unit that is authorized by any provision of Article 4 (commencing with Section 701) or by Section 801 or 802 to elect a method of financing coverage permitted by this section.

(b) In lieu of the contributions required of employers, an entity may elect any one of the following:

(1) To pay into the Unemployment Fund the cost of benefits, including extended duration benefits and federal-state extended benefits, paid based on base period wages with respect to employment for the entity and charged to its account in the manner provided by Section 1026, pursuant to authorized regulations that shall prescribe the rate or amount, time, manner, and method of payment or advance payment or providing a good and sufficient bond to guarantee payment of contributions.

(2) Two or more entities may, pursuant to authorized regulations, file an application with the director for the establishment of a joint account for the purpose of determining the rate of contributions they shall pay into the Unemployment Fund to reimburse the fund for benefits paid with respect to employment for those entities. The members of the joint account may share the cost of benefits, including extended duration benefits and federal-state extended benefits, paid based on the base period wages with respect to employment for those members and charged to the joint account in the manner

provided by Section 1026. The director shall prescribe authorized regulations for the establishment, maintenance, and dissolution of joint accounts, and for the rate or amount, time, manner, and method of payment or advance payment or providing a good and sufficient bond to guarantee payment of contributions by the members of joint accounts, on the cost of benefits charged in the manner provided by Section 1026.

(c) Sections 1030, 1031, 1032, and 1032.5, and any provision of this division for the noncharging of benefits to the account of an employer, shall not apply to an election under subdivision (b). The cost of benefits charged to an entity under this section shall include, but not be limited to, benefits or payments improperly paid in excess of a weekly benefit amount, or in excess of a maximum benefit amount, or otherwise in excess of the amount that should have been paid, due to any computational or other error of any type by the Employment Development Department or the Department of Benefit Payments, whether or not the error could be anticipated.

(d) In making the payments prescribed by subdivision (b), there shall be paid or credited to the Unemployment Fund, either in advance or by way of reimbursement, as may be determined by the director, any sums he or she estimates the Unemployment Fund will be entitled to receive from each entity for each calendar quarter, reduced or increased by any sum by which he or she finds that his or her estimates for any prior calendar quarter were greater or less than the amounts which should have been paid to the fund. The estimates may be made upon the basis of statistical sampling, or any other method as may be determined by the director.

Upon making that determination, the director shall give notice of the determination, pursuant to Section 1206, to the entity. The director may cancel any contributions or portion thereof that he or she finds has been erroneously determined.

The director shall charge to any special fund, that is responsible for the salary of any employee of an entity, the amount determined by the director for which the fund is liable pursuant to this section. The contributions due from the entity shall be paid from the liable special fund, the General Fund, or other liable fund to the Unemployment Fund by the Controller or other officer or person responsible for disbursements on behalf of the entity within 30 days of the date of mailing of the director's notice of determination to the entity. The director for good cause may extend for not to exceed 60 days the time for paying without penalty the amount determined and required to be paid. Contributions are due upon the date of mailing of the notice of determination and are delinquent if not paid on or before the 30th day following the date of mailing of the notice.

(e) Any entity that fails to pay the contributions required within the time required shall be liable for interest on the contributions at the adjusted annual rate and by the method established pursuant to Section 19521 of the Revenue and Taxation Code from and after the

date of delinquency until paid, and any entity that without good cause fails to pay any contributions required within the time required shall pay a penalty of 10 percent of the amount of the contributions. If the entity fails to pay the contributions required on or before the delinquency date, the director may assess the entity for the amount required by the notice of determination. This subdivision shall not apply to employers electing financing under Section 821, for amounts due after December 31, 1992.

(f) Article 8 (commencing with Section 1126) of Chapter 4 of Part 1 with respect to the assessment of contributions, and Chapter 7 (commencing with Section 1701) of Part 1 with respect to the collection of contributions, shall apply to the assessments provided by this section. Sections 1177 to 1184, inclusive, relating to refunds and overpayments, shall apply to amounts paid to the Unemployment Fund pursuant to this section. Sections 1222, 1223, 1224, 1241, and 1242 shall apply to matters arising under this section.

(g)(1) The director may terminate the election of any entity for financing under this section if the entity is delinquent in the payment of advances or reimbursements required by the director under this section. After any termination the entity may again make an election pursuant to this section but only if it is not delinquent in the payment of contributions and not delinquent in the payment of advances or reimbursements required by the director under this section.

(2) In the case of an Indian tribe (as described by subsection (u) of Section 3306 of Title 26 of the United States Code), the director shall terminate all elections for the tribe and all subdivisions, subsidiaries, and business enterprises wholly owned by that tribe if the tribe or any subdivision, subsidiary, or business enterprise wholly owned by that tribe is more than 90 days delinquent in the payment of contributions, bonds, advances, reimbursements, or applicable penalties or interest required under this code, after notice to the tribe. After any termination the Indian tribe may again make an election pursuant to this section but only if it is not delinquent in the payment of contributions, bonds, advances, reimbursements, or applicable penalties or interest required under this code.

(h) Notwithstanding any other provision of this section, no entity shall be liable for that portion of any extended duration benefits or federal-state extended benefits that is reimbursed or reimbursable by the federal government to the State of California.

(i) After the termination of any election under this section, the entity shall remain liable for its proportionate share of the cost of benefits paid and charged to its account in the manner provided by Section 1026, which are based on wages paid for services during the period of the election. That liability may be charged against any remaining balance of a prior reserve account used by the entity pursuant to Section 712 or 713. Any portion of the remaining balance shall be included in the reserve account of the entity following any termination of an election under this section which occurs prior to the expiration of a period of three consecutive years commencing with the effective date of the election. For purposes of Section 982, the period of an election under Section 803 shall, to the extent permitted by federal law, be included as a period during which a reserve account has been subject to benefit charges. *(Added by Stats. 1971, c. 1107, p. 2109, § 46, eff. Oct. 18, 1971. Amended by Stats.1971, c. 1622, p. 3490, § 8; Stats.1972, c. 319, p. 596, § 6, eff. July 10, 1972; Stats.1975, c. 661, p. 1444, § 69; Stats.1976, c. 909, p. 2086, § 4; Stats.1977, c. 511, p. 1645, § 1; Stats.1978, c. 2, p. 25, § 59, eff. Jan. 30, 1978, operative Jan. 1, 1978; Stats.1979, c. 1082, p. 3883, § 3; Stats.1981–82, 1st Ex.Sess., c. 5, p. 624, § 84, operative May 27, 1982; Stats.1983–84, 1st Ex.Sess., c. 10, § 31, eff. Feb. 17, 1983; Stats.1993, c. 31 (S.B.3), § 62, eff. June 16, 1993, operative Jan. 1, 1994; Stats.1993, c. 854 (A.B.1585), § 1; Stats.2001, c. 255 (A.B.1537), § 9.)*

Operative Effect

Under the terms of Section 17 of Stats.2001, c. 255 (A.B.1537), the provisions of that Act are retroactive to December 21, 2000.

§ 803.1. Acquisition of or succession to another entity; liability for reimbursement; exception

Notwithstanding any other provision of this article, if an entity acquires or succeeds to another entity in any manner, the method of reimbursement financing, in lieu of contributions required of employers, elected by the acquiring entity shall apply to all service performed in the employ of the acquiring entity. The acquiring entity shall be liable for the reimbursement of all benefits chargeable to the entity acquired under any method of reimbursement financing elected by the entity acquired, except that this provision shall not apply to the acquisition of, or succession to, less than a total entity if the remainder of the entity partially acquired or succeeded to remains in existence. "Entity" as used in this section means any entity as defined by subdivision (a) of Section 803. *(Added by Stats.1972, c. 833, p. 1482, § 2.)*

§ 803.2. Acquisition of favorable reserve account; liability for reimbursement

Notwithstanding any other provision of this article, a nonprofit organization which elected reimbursement financing under Section 803 and which has acquired a previously accumulated favorable reserve account under Section 712 or 713 shall be liable for the reimbursement of benefits pursuant to such election for any benefits chargeable to the reserve account and based upon wages paid prior to such election, to the extent that such benefits exceed the previously accumulated favorable reserve account. *(Added by Stats.1972, c. 833, p. 1482, § 3. Amended by Stats.1976, c. 909, p. 2088, § 5; Stats.1978, c. 2, p. 27, § 60, eff. Jan. 30, 1978, operative Jan. 1, 1978.)*

§ 804. Notice to Internal Revenue Service and Department of Labor of failure of Indian tribe to make payment or post bond as required by § 803

The director shall notify the United States Internal Revenue Service and the United States Department of Labor of the failure of any Indian tribe (as described by subsection (u) of Section 3306 of Title 26 of the United States Code) to make a payment or post a bond as required under subdivision (b) of Section 803 within 90 days of the delinquency date of a notice to the tribe specifying the amount due under that subdivision. If the amount due is subsequently paid by the Indian tribe, the director shall notify the United States Internal Revenue Service and the United States Department of Labor of the satisfaction of the liability. *(Added by Stats.2001, c. 255 (A.B.1537), § 10.)*

Operative Effect

Under the terms of Section 17 of Stats.2001, c. 255 (A.B.1537), the provisions of that Act are retroactive to December 21, 2000.

§ 805. Unregistered nonprofit organizations; reimbursement financing

An unregistered organization described in Section 608, and which has been determined by the Internal Revenue Service to be exempt under Section 501(a) as an organization described in Section 501(c)(3) of the Internal Revenue Code, may elect reimbursement financing under Section 801 when the director finds that it has good cause for failing to register as an employer under this division. The election under Section 801 shall be from the time the organization became an employer. The organization shall, upon election, be liable for reimbursement of the cost of benefits chargeable to the organization from the time it became an employer. Payment of the cost of benefits shall be as provided in Section 803 except that benefits paid more than 30 days prior to the date of election under Section 801 shall accrue interest as provided in Section 1113. The election under Section 801 shall be subject to all provisions of Section 803. *(Added by Stats.1987, c. 457, § 8, eff. Sept. 9, 1987.)*

§ 806. Notice of claim to public entities electing to finance under provisions of § 803

(a) The department shall give notice, as required by Section 1327, to each public entity, as defined by Section 605, which has elected a method of financing under Section 803 at a single address to be selected by the entity.

(b) The department shall implement subdivision (a) according to the following schedule:

(1) For the State of California, by July 1, 1986.

(2) For all public entities with more than 100 employees, by October 1, 1986.

(3) For all other local public entities, by January 1, 1987. *(Added by Stats.1985, c. 1217, § 4, eff. Sept. 29, 1985.)*

ARTICLE 6.   FINANCING UNEMPLOYMENT INSURANCE COVERAGE FOR PUBLIC SCHOOL EMPLOYEES

Section
821.   Payment of benefit costs in lieu of contributions.
821.3. Administrator.
821.4. Employing unit; school employer.
821.5. Filing, determination and payment of claims.
822.   Establishment of fund; deposits; appropriations.
823.   Remittance to state treasurer; determination of amount.
826.   Transfer of earnings to support management system and appeals program; amount.
827.   Unencumbered balance of interest in fund; credits to school employers; conditions.
828.   Local experience charges; calculation; formula; schedule.
829.   Amount of reimbursement; maximum percentage of wages.
831.   School employer advisory committee; members; compensation; duties.
832.   Experience calculations of school employers; annual report.

§ 821.   Payment of benefit costs in lieu of contributions

(a) Each school employer may, in lieu of the contributions required of employers, elect to pay into the Unemployment Fund the cost of benefits, including extended duration benefits and federal-state extended benefits, paid based on base period wages with respect to employment for an employing unit and charged to its account in the manner provided by Section 1026, pursuant to authorized regulations that shall prescribe the rate or amount, time, manner, and method of payment or advance payment or providing a good and sufficient bond to guarantee payment of contributions.   The provisions of this article shall apply to school employers who have elected financing under this section.

(b) Sections 1030, 1031, 1032, and 1032.5, and any provision of this division for the noncharging of benefits to the account of an employer, shall not apply to an employing unit under subdivision (a).   The cost of benefits charged to a school employer under this section shall include, but not be limited to, benefits or payments improperly paid in excess of a weekly benefit amount, or in excess of a maximum benefit amount, or otherwise in excess of the amount that should have been paid, due to any computational or other error of any type by the Employment Development Department or the Department of Benefit Payments, whether or not the error could be anticipated.

(c) In making the payments prescribed by subdivision (a), there shall be paid or credited to the Unemployment Fund, either in advance or by way of reimbursement, as may be determined by the director, any sums he or she estimates the Unemployment Fund will be entitled to receive from each employing unit for each calendar quarter, reduced or increased by any sum by which he or she finds that his or her estimates for any prior calendar quarter were greater or less than the amounts that should

have been paid to the fund.   These estimates may be made upon the basis of a statistical sampling, or other method as may be determined by the director.

Upon making the determination, the director shall mail notice of the determination, pursuant to Section 1206, to the employing unit.

The director may cancel any contributions or portion thereof that he or she finds have been erroneously determined.   The contributions due from the employing units shall be paid, transferred, or credited from the School Employees Fund established in the State Treasury by Section 822 to the Unemployment Fund by the State Treasurer, State Controller, or other officer or person responsible for disbursements on behalf of the employing unit within 30 days of the date of mailing of the director's notice of determination to the employing unit.

Each employing unit shall send a copy of any and all notices, billings, or correspondence not normally routed to the administrator and the Superintendent of Public Instruction, regarding unemployment insurance for the school employees, to the administrator, the Superintendent of Public Instruction, and the county superintendent of schools, or agent thereof, with timely documentation of charges or determination.   Article 8 (commencing with Section 1126) of Chapter 4 with respect to the assessment of contributions, and Chapter 7 (commencing with Section 1701) with respect to the collection of contributions, shall apply to the assessments provided by this article. Sections 1177 to 1184, inclusive, relating to refunds and overpayments, shall apply to amounts paid to the Unemployment Fund pursuant to this section.   Sections 1222, 1223, 1224, 1241, and 1242 shall apply to matters arising under this section.

(d) Notwithstanding any other provision of this section, no employing unit shall be liable for that portion of any extended duration benefits or federal-state extended benefits that is reimbursed or reimbursable by the federal government to the state.

(e) To the extent permitted by federal law, including Section 121(e) of Public Law 94-566,[1] any school employer that elects a method of financing under this article shall not be liable to reimburse the cost of benefits paid to any individual whose base period wages include wages for services performed prior to January 1, 1978, if the benefits are reimbursable by the federal government under Section 121 of Public Law 94-566 and to the extent that the individual would not have been eligible for the benefits had this state not provided for benefits payable based on services performed prior to January 1, 1978.

(f) The administrator and the Superintendent of Public Instruction shall adopt rules and regulations for the administration of their respective functions under this article in accordance with Chapter 3.5 (commencing with Section 11340) of Part 1 of Division 3 of Title 2 of the Government Code.   Regulations of the administrator shall be subject to Article 1 (commencing with Section 301) of Chapter 2 of Part 1 of Division 1.   Rules and regulations of the Superintendent of Public Instruction shall not be subject to the provisions of Article 1 (commencing with Section 301) of Chapter 2 of Part 1 of Division 1.

(g) Any election for financing coverage under this section shall take effect with respect to services performed from and after the first day of the calendar quarter in which the election is filed with the director, and shall continue in effect for not less than two full calendar years. Thereafter, the election under this section may be terminated as of January 1 of any calendar year only if the school employer, on or before the 31st day of January of that year, has filed with the director a written application for termination. The director may for good cause waive the requirement that a written application for termination shall be filed on or before the 31st day of January. School employers shall be prohibited from making a subsequent reelection under this section for 10 years from the date of termination of an election under this section. An election for financing coverage under this section is deemed to have been filed by every school employer effective as of January 1, 1976, is deemed to have been in effect for two calendar years prior to January 1, 1978, and may be terminated as of January 1, 1978, or as of January 1, 1980, or any later January 1 pursuant to this section. Upon the termination of any election under this section, the school employer shall be and remain liable for all benefits paid based upon wages paid by the school employer during the period of an election under this section. *(Added by Stats.1972, c. 319, p. 599, § 8, eff. July 10, 1972. Amended by Stats. 1972, c. 861, p. 1534, § 3, eff. Aug. 14, 1972; Stats.1977, c. 511, p. 1648, § 2; Stats.1978, c. 2, p. 27, § 62, eff. Jan. 30, 1978, operative Jan. 1, 1978; Stats.1979, c. 1082, p. 3886, § 4; Stats.1993, c. 854 (A.B.1585), § 2.)*

[1] Public law sections classified to U.S.C.A., see U.S.C.A. Tables.

§ 821.3. Administrator

As used in this article, "administrator" means the Director of Employment Development. *(Added by Stats. 1972, c. 319, p. 600, § 8, eff. July 10, 1972. Amended by Stats.1973, c. 1206, p. 2619, § 55; Stats.1973, c. 1207, p. 2669, § 55; Stats.1973, c. 1212, p. 2774, § 145, operative July 1, 1974; Stats.1977, c. 1252, p. 4456, § 403, operative July 1, 1978.)*

§ 821.4. Employing unit; school employer

As used in this article, "employing unit" and "school employer" means the governing board of any school district or community college district, any county board of education, any county superintendent of schools, or any personnel commission of a school district or community college district which has a merit system pursuant to any provision of the Education Code, or any instrumentality of the foregoing, or any instrumentality of more than one of the foregoing, which employs one or more employees. *(Added by Stats.1978, c. 2, p. 30, § 63, eff. Jan. 30, 1978, operative Jan. 1, 1978.)*

§ 821.5. Filing, determination and payment of claims

The provisions of Article 3 (commencing with Section 1326) of Chapter 5 of this part relating to filing, determination, and payments of unemployment compensation benefit claims, and all other provisions of this part not inconsistent with this article, shall apply to all claims and matters arising under this article. *(Added by Stats. 1972, c. 319, p. 601, § 8, eff. July 10, 1972.)*

§ 822. Establishment of fund; deposits; appropriations

(a) There is hereby established in the State Treasury the "School Employees Fund." The School Employees Fund is the successor of the "Classified School Employees Fund." Moneys received pursuant to Section 823, together with any charges, notices, fees, interest, penalties, assessments, or other revenue, shall be deposited in this fund. All moneys in the fund are hereby appropriated to the administrator without regard to fiscal year for carrying out the purposes of this article, for administrative costs, for making refunds, and for investment through the Surplus Money Investment Fund, with any interest or earnings credited to the School Employees Fund. Funds to be used for administrative costs shall be budgeted and expended in accordance with existing state law.

(b) Notwithstanding any other law, the Controller may use the moneys in the School Employees Fund for loans to the General Fund as provided in Sections 16310 and 16381 of the Government Code. However, interest shall be paid on all moneys loaned to the General Fund from the School Employees Fund. Interest payable shall be computed at a rate determined by the Pooled Money Investment Board to be the current earning rate of the fund from which loaned. This subdivision does not authorize any transfer that will interfere with the carrying out of the object for which the School Employees Fund was created. *(Added by Stats.1972, c. 319, p. 599, § 8, eff. July 10, 1972. Amended by Stats.1972, c. 864, p. 1536, § 4, eff. Aug. 14, 1972; Stats.1974, c. 382, p. 948, § 4, eff. July 5, 1974; Stats.1978, c. 2, p. 30, § 64, eff. Jan. 31, 1978, operative Jan. 1, 1978; Stats.2009–2010, 3rd Ex.Sess., c. 9 (A.B.13), § 20, eff. Feb. 20, 2009.)*

§ 823. Remittance to state treasurer; determination of amount

(a) For the purpose of payment by each school employer of all or part of the charges for unemployment compensation benefits, fees, assessments, interest, penalties, billings, notices, and other expenses of unemployment insurance for school employees pursuant to this part, moneys budgeted pursuant to subdivisions (b) and (c) of this section shall be remitted by the school employer or on the school employer's behalf by the county auditor to the Treasurer pursuant to this article, and shall be deposited in the School Employees Fund.

(b) (1) For each fiscal year, except as provided in subdivisions (c) and (d), each school employer shall budget and remit on or before the last day of the calendar

931

month following the close of each calendar quarter to the Treasurer for deposit in the School Employees Fund in the State Treasury an amount determined by multiplying the contribution rate for the fiscal year by the total wages, including taxable wages as well as wages which would be taxable except for the limitation on taxable wages provided under Section 930, but excluding, to the extent permitted by federal law, wages paid to any individual to the extent that federal law provides for reimbursement to the State of California for all benefits paid from the Unemployment Fund to the individual based on the wages.

The administrator shall, not later than March 31 each year, notify all school employers participating in the School Employees Fund of the contribution rate for the succeeding fiscal year.

(2) The contribution rate for the fiscal year beginning July 1, 1988, and for each subsequent fiscal year shall be two times the amount disbursed for claims management fees, unemployment insurance benefit charges, and School Employees Fund administrative expenditures from the School Employees Fund during the 12–month period ending December 31 and immediately preceding the fiscal year for which the rate is to be effective, less the amount in the School Employees Fund on that December 31, with the resulting figure divided by total wages as described in paragraph (1) for the 12–month period ending June 30 and immediately preceding that December 31, and then rounded to the nearest one-hundredth of 1 percent. In no event shall the contribution rate be less than five one-hundredths of 1 percent.

(c) If the administrator finds that the ability of the School Employees Fund to meet its estimated obligations promptly when due will become endangered, he or she shall increase the contribution rate otherwise provided by this section to a level estimated to be needed to protect the solvency of the fund, except that the rate shall not be increased to more than three-tenths of 1 percent. If the administrator finds that the School Employees Fund balance is in excess of an adequate reserve to meet its estimated obligations promptly when due, he or she shall, after consultation with the fund's School Advisory Committee, decrease the contribution rate otherwise provided by this section, except that the rate shall not be decreased to less than one-tenth of 1 percent. The administrator shall notify all school employers participating in the fund of any increased or decreased contribution rate under this authority. *(Added by Stats.1972, c. 319, p. 599, § 8, eff. July 10, 1972. Amended by Stats.1974, c. 382, p. 948, § 5, eff. July 5, 1974; Stats.1976, c. 906, p. 2080, § 1, eff. Sept. 13, 1976; Stats.1977, c. 1231, p. 4139, § 1, eff. Oct. 1, 1977; Stats.1978, c. 2, p. 30, § 65, eff. Jan. 30, 1978, operative Jan. 1, 1978; Stats.1978, c. 947, p. 2926, § 1; Stats.1982, c. 747, p. 2962, § 1; Stats.1986, c. 754, § 1; Stats.1987, c. 196, § 1.)*

932

§ 826. Transfer of earnings to support management system and appeals program; amount

The administrator of the School Employees Fund shall, based on the total number of covered employees reflected on reports received by March 31, 1978, and by November 30, 1978, and each year thereafter by November 30, make a transfer from available interest earnings pursuant to investments authorized by Section 822 to the Superintendent of Public Instruction or Chancellor of the California Community Colleges to support an Unemployment Insurance Management System and appeals program as set forth in Section 1330 of the Education Code. Such transfers shall be equal to two dollars ($2) per covered employee, less administrative costs of the Superintendent of Public Instruction and the Chancellor of the California Community Colleges, and shall be made by April 30, 1978, and by December 31, 1978, and each year thereafter by December 31, to the Superintendent of Public Instruction or Chancellor of the California Community Colleges, as appropriate, and expended only for the purposes set forth in Section 1330 of the Education Code. *(Added by Stats.1972, c. 319, p. 602, § 8, eff. July 10, 1972. Amended by Stats.1978, c. 2, p. 31, § 66, eff. Jan. 30, 1978, operative Jan. 1, 1978.)*

§ 827. Unencumbered balance of interest in fund; credits to school employers; conditions

Whenever the unencumbered balance of interest deposited in or earned by the School Employees Fund, after deducting administrative expenses paid or encumbered, exceeds two million dollars ($2,000,000) as of the close of each fiscal year, the unencumbered balance shall be credited as of the close of that fiscal year to the account of each school employer which has a positive balance in the fund, in the proportion that each positive account balance bears to the total of all positive account balances. *(Added by Stats.1984, c. 1018, § 1.)*

§ 828. Local experience charges; calculation; formula; schedule

Each school employer shall be responsible for a quarterly local experience charge as set forth below, together with the charges or penalties set by the administrator for administrative indiscretions, including tardiness and error, as well as all costs for benefits and administration resulting from failure to properly cover an employee. The reimbursement for charges shall be delinquent 30 days from the date of notice and if not paid within the time required, the school employer shall pay a penalty of 10 percent of the unpaid amount, plus interest at the adjusted annual rate established pursuant to Section 19521 of the Revenue and Taxation Code from and after the date of delinquency until paid. The local experience charge to be levied against each school employer shall be computed as follows:

Local Experience Charge

(a) The local experience charge rate shall be 10 percent for the first three complete fiscal years of participation in the School Employees Fund.

(b) The local experience charge rate for the fourth fiscal year, and each succeeding fiscal year, shall be determined by dividing the reserve balance at the end of the fiscal year which began 24 months prior to the fiscal year for which the rate is being calculated by the benefits paid for that same prior fiscal year.

The factor derived is the employer's reserve ratio. If, as of the computation date, the school employer's reserve ratio equals or exceeds that which appears on any line in column 1 of the following table, but is less than that which appears in column 2 of that table, the local experience charge rate shall be the figure appearing on that same line in column 3 of that table.

(Column 1) Line	(Column 2) Reserve Ratio	(Column 3) Rate
1 .... negative to	1.00	15%
2 .... 1.00 to	2.00	10%
3 .... 2.00 to	3.00	5%
4 .... 3.00 or	more	0%

(c) The rate determined in subdivision (a) or (b) shall be multiplied by the employer's quarterly benefit charges to compute the local experience charges.

The administrator shall, not later than March 31 of each year, notify each school employer participating in the School Employees Fund of their local experience charge rate for the succeeding fiscal year. (*Added by Stats.1972, c. 319, p. 603, § 8, eff. July 10, 1972. Amended by Stats.1974, c. 382, p. 948, § 8, eff. July 5, 1974; Stats.1976, c. 759, p. 1796, § 2; Stats.1978, c. 2, p. 31, § 68, eff Jan. 1, 1978, operative Jan. 1, 1978; Stats.1984, c. 1018, § 2; Stats.1993, c. 31 (S.B.3), § 63, eff. June 16, 1993, operative Jan. 1, 1994; Stats.2005, c. 152 (A.B.1577), § 8.*)

§ 829. Amount of reimbursement; maximum percentage of wages

The total amount of the local experience charge computed for each school employer pursuant to Section 828 shall be the amount that the school employer, county superintendent of schools, or empowered entity shall, on behalf of the employers under that jurisdiction, reimburse the School Employees Fund in the State Treasury. However, this amount shall not exceed 1.7 percent of the actual annual wages paid by a school employer in the immediately preceding calendar year as indicated in the four quarterly reports to the department. (*Added by Stats.1972, c. 319, p. 604, § 8, eff. July 10, 1972. Amended by Stats.1974, c. 382, p. 949, § 9, eff. July 5, 1974; Stats.1978, c. 2, p. 32, § 69, eff. Jan. 30, 1978, operative Jan. 1, 1978; Stats.1984, c. 1018, § 3; Stats.1993, c. 854 (A.B.1585), § 3.*)

§ 831. School employer advisory committee; members; compensation; duties

There is hereby created a School Employer Advisory Committee of five persons. The committee shall consist of one person appointed by each of the following: the State Superintendent of Public Instruction, Chancellor of the California Community Colleges, Association of School Administrators, California School Business Officials, and the California School Board Association.

All such members shall serve at the pleasure of the appointing power and their only compensation shall be per diem expenses for attending meetings, which shall be a cost of administration of the School Employees Fund. The advisory committee shall select a chairperson and meet at least semiannually with the administrator to consider and recommend improvements concerning the administration of this article. (*Added by Stats.1978, c. 947, p. 2928, § 3.*)

§ 832. Experience calculations of school employers; annual report

The administrator shall at least annually calculate, as of the close of and for the immediately preceding fiscal year, the experiences of school employers relative to usage of the Unemployment Fund. The calculations shall include tabulations on the experience of each school employer in relation to the expenditures from and the income to the School Employees Fund from the wages paid by the employer. All school employers shall be listed and ranked by ratio of use. The report shall contain comments and recommendations on improvements to the administration, enforcement, and financing of the provisions relative to this article. The report by the administrator on the above shall be made each year to the affected school employer and governing board thereof prior to March 31.

The administrator shall develop experience relationships on all benefits paid to employees via the School Employees Fund and on school employers' experience related to use and exposure. Data shall relate to numbers of employees and types of programs and shall be calculated as of the close of and for the immediately preceding fiscal year. A report by the administrator on the above shall be made each year to the Legislature prior to March 31 containing comments and recommendations on improvement to administration, enforcement and financing of the provisions relative thereto. (*Added by Stats.1972, c. 319, p. 604, § 8, eff. July 10, 1972. Amended by Stats.1974, c. 382, p. 950, § 11, eff. July 5, 1974; Stats.1978, c. 2, p. 33, § 71, eff. Jan. 30, 1978, operative Jan. 1, 1978; Stats.1992, c. 125 (A.B.1830), § 3; Stats. 2002, c. 29 (A.B.1729), § 8.*)

ARTICLE 7. FINANCING UNEMPLOYMENT INSURANCE COVERAGE FOR LOCAL PUBLIC ENTITY EMPLOYEES [REPEALED]

CHAPTER 4. CONTRIBUTIONS AND REPORTS

Article	Section
1. Definitions 901	

Article		Section
2.	"Wages," the Basis of the Contribution	926
3.	Contribution Rates	976
4.	Reserve Accounts	1025
5.	Transfer of Reserve Accounts	1051
6.	Records, Reports and Contribution Payments	1085
7.	Payment of Reported Contributions	1110
8.	Assessments	1126
8.5.	Employment Tax Amnesty [Repealed]	
9.	Refunds and Overpayments	1176
10.	Notice	1206
11.	Administrative Appellate Review	1221
11.5.	Taxpayer's Rights	1231
12.	Judicial Review	1241

ARTICLE 1. DEFINITIONS

Section
901. Application of definitions.
902. Computation date.
903. Rating period.
904. Net balance of reserve.
905. Average base pay roll.
906. Contributions paid on his own behalf.

§ 901. Application of definitions

The definitions set forth in this article are applicable to this chapter only. *(Stats.1953, c. 308, p. 1490, § 901.)*

§ 902. Computation date

"Computation date" means the close of business on June 30th, of each calendar year for the purpose of establishing contribution rates for the next succeeding calendar year. *(Stats.1953, c. 308, p. 1480, § 902. Amended by Stats.1957, c. 1184, p. 2475, § 3.)*

§ 903. Rating period

"Rating period" means the full calendar year next succeeding any computation date. *(Stats.1953, c. 308, p. 1480, § 903. Amended by Stats.1957, c. 1184, p. 2475, § 4.)*

§ 904. Net balance of reserve

"Net balance of reserve" means the excess, if any, of credits required to be made to any employer's account over the charges against that account as of any computation date. *(Stats.1953, c. 308, p. 1480, § 904.)*

§ 905. Average base pay roll

"Average base pay roll" means the quotient obtained by dividing by three the total amount of taxable wages paid by an employer during the most recent period of three consecutive calendar years immediately preceding the computation date. *(Stats.1953, c. 308, p. 1480, § 905.)*

§ 906. Contributions paid on his own behalf

"Contributions paid on his own behalf" means:

(a) All contributions paid under this part to the Unemployment Fund on behalf of an employer with respect to wages paid by him on or before the computation date for any rating period, which have been paid on or before the end of the calendar month next succeeding such computation date.

(b) Any additional amount of contributions paid under this part to the Unemployment Fund on behalf of an employer with respect to wages paid by him on or before the computation date for any rating period, which have been assessed pursuant to Section 1036 and have been paid before the delinquent date for the calendar quarter in which he is given notice of the assessment pursuant to Section 1036.

(c) Any additional contributions paid pursuant to Section 976.5. *(Stats.1953, c. 308, p. 1480, § 906. Amended by Stats.1961, c. 2158, p. 4465, § 1; Stats.1961, c. 2160, p. 4472, § 1; Stats.1989, c. 1146, § 2.)*

ARTICLE 2. "WAGES," THE BASIS OF THE CONTRIBUTION

Section
926. Wages defined.
926.5. Wages; assumption by employing unit.
927. Tips as wages.
928. Deferred compensation plans; definitions and qualifications.
928.5. Wages; employer contributions under certain deferred compensation plans.
929. Exclusion; business expenses.
930. Exclusion; remuneration in excess of maximum limitation.
930.1. Remuneration for services constituting employment under unemployment compensation law of another state.
930.5. Acquired business; determination of remuneration paid by acquiring employer.
931. Exclusion; employee benefits.
931.5. Third-party payer as employer; notification of last employer; sick pay; contributions; assessments; refunds.
933. Exclusion; disability benefits.
934. Exclusion; payments from or to trust, under annuity plan or contract, or under certain pension, retirement account, and deferred compensation plans.
935. Exclusion; payment of social security for domestic service employee or agricultural labor employee.
936. Exclusion; remuneration paid in medium other than cash; exception.
937. Exclusion; payments for moving expenses.
938. Exclusion; certain payments to employees or dependents.
938.1. Exclusion; payments under qualified group legal services plan.
938.3. Exclusions; payments for educational assistance, dependent care assistance programs, benefits excluded under Internal Revenue Code, and cafeteria plan benefits.
938.5. Exclusion; payments received by national guard members or armed forces reserve components.
938.7. Exclusion; payments made by employer to survivor or estate of former employee; time.
939. Contingent effect of exclusions.
940. Wages.

§ 926. Wages defined

Except as otherwise provided in this article "wages" means all remuneration payable to an employee for personal services, whether by private agreement or consent or by force of statute, including commissions and bonuses, and the reasonable cash value of all remuneration payable to an employee in any medium other than cash. *(Stats.1953, c. 308, p. 1480, § 926. Amended by Stats.1971, c. 1107, p. 2112, § 47, eff. Oct. 18, 1971.)*

§ 926.5. Wages; assumption by employing unit

"Wages" also means all remuneration payable for personal services, as specified in Section 926, when the legal obligation for the payment of such wages is assumed by an employer specified in Section 678, and the first or prior employer for whom the personal services were originally performed is relieved of the legal obligation for the payment of such remuneration. *(Added by Stats.1971, c. 873, p. 1716, § 7.)*

§ 927. Tips as wages

"Wages" also means all tips which are received while performing services which constitute employment and included in a written statement furnished to the employer pursuant to Section 6053(a) of the Internal Revenue Code.[1]

The changes in law made in this section by Chapter 1461 of the Statutes of 1985 shall apply with respect to wages earned on and after January 1, 1986, in conformity with the provisions of federal law. *(Stats.1953, c. 308, p. 1480, § 927. Amended by Stats.1985, c. 1461, § 148, eff. Oct. 1, 1985; Stats.1986, c. 4, § 1, eff. Feb. 5, 1986.)*

[1] 26 U.S.C.A. § 6053(a).

§ 928. Deferred compensation plans; definitions and qualifications

Unless otherwise specifically provided, the definitions and qualifications of deferred compensation plans shall be determined for purposes of this part in accordance with Subchapter D (commencing with Section 401) of Chapter 1 of Subtitle A of the Internal Revenue Code.[1] When applying the Internal Revenue Code for the purposes of this part, any reference to regulations of the Internal Revenue Service shall not apply if the Employment Development Department has adopted and issued regulations on this subject. In the absence of regulations issued by the Employment Development Department, regulations issued under the Internal Revenue Code shall govern the interpretation of this part. *(Added by Stats. 1986, c. 847, § 1.)*

[1] 26 U.S.C.A. § 401 et seq.

§ 928.5. Wages; employer contributions under certain deferred compensation plans

"Wages" also includes all of the following:

(a) Any employer contributions under a qualified cash or deferred arrangement, as defined by Section 401(k) of the Internal Revenue Code, to the extent the amount is excluded from the gross income of the employee under Section 402(e)(3) of the Internal Revenue Code.

(b) Any amount treated as an employer contribution under a state pickup plan as defined by Section 414(h)(2) of the Internal Revenue Code, only if the payments are made pursuant to a salary reduction arrangement.

(c) Any amount deferred under a nonqualified deferred compensation plan shall be taken into account, for purposes of this article, on the later of the following:

(1) When the services are performed.

(2) When there is no substantial risk of forfeiture of the right to the amount.

(d) Any amount taken into account as "wages" by reason of subdivision (c), and the income attributable thereto, shall be taxed only once and shall not thereafter be treated as "wages" for purposes of this article.

(e) For the purposes of this section, the term "nonqualified deferred compensation plan" means any plan or arrangement for deferral of compensation other than a plan described under Section 934. *(Added by Stats.1986, c. 847, § 2. Amended by Stats.1997, c. 611 (S.B.455), § 107, eff. Oct. 3, 1997.)*

§ 929. Exclusion; business expenses

"Wages" does not include the actual amount of any required or necessary business expense incurred by an individual in connection with his employment, or, in lieu of the actual amount of such expenses, the reasonably estimated amount allowed therefor pursuant to authorized regulations. *(Stats.1953, c. 308, p. 1481, § 929.)*

§ 930. Exclusion; remuneration in excess of maximum limitation

"Wages" does not include remuneration in excess of seven thousand dollars ($7,000) paid to an individual by an employer during any calendar year, with respect to employment. *(Stats.1953, c. 308, p. 1481, § 930. Amended by Stats.1959, c. 2154, p. 5202, § 1, Stats.1961, c. 2153, p. 4442, § 2; Stats.1961, c. 2160, p. 4473, § 2; Stats.1965, c. 1897, p. 4372, § 1; Stats.1970, c. 1468, p. 2898, § 1; Stats.1971, c. 1107, p. 2112, § 48, eff. Oct. 18, 1971, operative Jan. 1, 1972; Stats.1975, c. 1256, p. 3289, § 1; Stats.1982, c. 1075, p. 3880, § 1; Stats.1984, c. 1275, § 1, eff. Sept. 19, 1984.)*

§ 930.1. Remuneration for services constituting employment under unemployment compensation law of another state

For the purpose of determining whether an employer has paid remuneration with respect to employment in excess of the limitation prescribed by Section 930 to an individual during any calendar year, the remuneration shall be deemed to include any remuneration paid to the individual by the employer for services constituting employment under the unemployment compensation law of another state which the employer has reported to the other state as wages for contribution purposes. As used in this section, "remuneration" does not include the remuneration of the type described in Sections 931, 931.5, 933, 934, 935, 936, 937, 938, 938.1, and 938.3 when paid by the employer in another state. *(Added by Stats.1968, c. 1191, p. 2253, § 1, operative Jan. 1, 1969. Amended by Stats.1969, c. 828, p. 1656, § 2; Stats.1986, c. 847, § 2.5.)*

§ 930.5.   Acquired business; determination of remuneration paid by acquiring employer

If an employer during any calendar year acquires substantially all the property used in a trade or business of another employer, or used in a separate unit of a trade or business of the other employer, and immediately after the acquisition employs in his or her trade or business an individual who immediately prior to the acquisition was employed in the trade or business of the employer from whom the property was acquired, then, for the purpose of determining whether the acquiring employer has paid remuneration with respect to employment in excess of the limitation prescribed by Section 930, or the limitation prescribed by Section 985, to the individual during the calendar year, any remuneration with respect to employment paid to the individual by the employer from whom the property was acquired during the calendar year and prior to the acquisition shall be considered as having been paid by the acquiring employer. As used in this section, "remuneration" does not include the remuneration referred to in Sections 931, 931.5, 933, 934, 935, 936, 937, 938, 938.1, and 938.3. *(Added by Stats.1959, c. 1729, p. 4175, § 8. Amended by Stats.1961, c. 2153, p. 4442, § 3; Stats.1961, c. 2154, p. 4450, § 2; Stats.1961, c. 2160, p. 4473, § 3; Stats.1963, c. 2015, p. 4118, § 4; Stats.1963, c. 2016, p. 4127, § 3; Stats.1968, c. 1173, p. 2227, § 1; Stats.1986, c. 847, § 3.)*

§ 931.   Exclusion; employee benefits

"Wages" does not include the amount of any payment, including any amount paid by an employer for insurance or annuities, or into a fund, to provide for any payment, made to or on behalf of an employee or any of his or her dependents under a plan or system established by an employer which makes provision for his or her employees generally, or for his or her employees generally and their dependents, or for a class or classes of his or her employees, or for a class or classes of his or her employees and their dependents, on account of any of the following:

(a) Sickness or accident disability, but in the case of payments made to an employee or any of his or her dependents, this subdivision shall exclude from "wages" only those payments which are received under a workers' compensation law.

(b) Medical or hospitalization expenses in connection with sickness or accident disability.

(c) Death.

(Stats.1953, c. 308, p. 1481, § 931. Amended by Stats.1986, c. 847, § 3.5.)

§ 931.5.   Third-party payer as employer; notification of last employer; sick pay; contributions; assessments; refunds

(a) Except for Part 2 (commencing with Section 2601) of this division and Division 6 (commencing with Section 13000), any third party which makes a payment included in the term "wages" solely by reason of subdivision (a) of Section 931 shall be the employer with respect to those wages unless the third-party payer notifies the last employer, who is a member of the plan and for whom the services were performed, within 15 days of payment, and provides all of the following information to that last employer:

(1) The name and social security account number of the recipients of the wages paid pursuant to subdivision (a) of Section 931.

(2) The amount of gross wages paid pursuant to subdivision (a) of Section 931.

(b) The special rule prescribed by this subdivision applies to the payment of sick pay made by a third-party payer, such as an insurer, under a contract of insurance pursuant to a multiple employer plan that is obligated to make payments for sick pay to employees of participating employers. If the third-party payer provides the plan with the notification required by subdivision (a) within the time required, the plan, not the third-party payer, shall be treated as the employer under subdivision (a). If within six business days after receipt of the notification the plan similarly notifies the last employer for whom the services are performed, and who is a plan member, that employer, not the plan, shall be required to report and pay the contributions due with respect to the wages.

(c) The employer, as determined by subdivision (a) or (b), shall pay contributions, required by this part, except as provided in Sections 984 and 986, and shall comply with the requirements of subdivision (a) of Section 1088.

(d) When an employer receives the notification prescribed in subdivision (a) or (b), the wages described therein shall be deemed paid when the notice is received.

(e) The director shall not make an assessment pursuant to Section 1126, 1127, or 1137 to assess employee contributions required by Sections 984 and 13020 on third-party sick pay as described in subdivision (a) for the period from January 1, 1987, through the date on which this subdivision became effective.

(f) Except as provided by Section 1176 and Section 19301 of the Revenue and Taxation Code, no refunds may be made for employee contributions required by Sections 984 and 13020 paid on third-party sick pay as described in subdivision (a) for the period from January 1, 1987, through the date on which this subdivision became effective. *(Added by Stats.1986, c. 847, § 4. Amended by Stats.1987, c. 457 § 1, eff. Sept. 9, 1987; Stats.2002, c. 29 (A.B.1729), § 9.)*

§ 933. Exclusion; disability benefits

"Wages" does not include any payment on account of sickness or accident disability, or medical or hospitalization expenses in connection with sickness or accident disability made by an employer to, or on behalf of, an employee after the expiration of six calendar months following the last calendar month in which the employee worked for such employer. *(Stats.1953, c. 308, p. 1482, § 933.)*

§ 934. Exclusion; payments from or to trust, under annuity plan or contract, or under certain pension, retirement account, and deferred compensation plans

"Wages" does not include any payment made to, or on behalf of, an employee or his or her beneficiary:

(a) From or to a trust described in Section 401(a) of the Internal Revenue Code [1] which is exempt from tax under Section 501(a) of that code [2] at the time of the payment, unless the payment is made to an employee of the trust as remuneration for services rendered as an employee and not as a beneficiary of the trust.

(b) Under or to an annuity plan which, at the time of the payment, is a plan described in Section 403(a) of the Internal Revenue Code.[3]

(c) Under a simplified employee pension, as defined in Section 408(k)(1) of the Internal Revenue Code,[4] other than any contributions described in Section 408(k)(6) of the Internal Revenue Code.

(d) Under a simple retirement account, as described in Section 408(p) of the Internal Revenue Code, other than any elective contributions under Section 408(p)(2)(A)(i) of the Internal Revenue Code.

(e) Under or to an annuity contract described in Section 403(b) of the Internal Revenue Code,[5] other than a payment for the purchase of the contract which is made by reason of a salary reduction agreement, whether evidenced by a written instrument or otherwise.

(f) Under or to an exempt governmental deferred compensation plan, as defined in Section 3121(v)(3) of the Internal Revenue Code.[6]

(g) To supplement pension benefits under a plan or trust described in any of the foregoing provisions of this section to take into account some portion or all of the increase in the cost of living, as determined by the Secretary of Labor, since retirement, but only if the supplemental payments are under a plan which is treated as a welfare plan under Section 3(2)(B)(ii) of the Employee Retirement Income Security Act of 1974.[7] *(Stats.1953, c. 308, p. 1482, § 934. Amended by Stats. 1957, c. 1184, p. 2475, § 5; Stats.1963, c. 2131, p. 4429, § 1, eff. July 25, 1963; Stats.1986, c. 847, § 6; Stats.1988,*

c. 647, § 2; Stats.1997, c. 611 (S.B.455), § 108, eff. Oct. 3, 1997.)

[1] 26 U.S.C.A. § 401.
[2] 26 U.S.C.A. § 501.
[3] 26 U.S.C.A. § 403.
[4] 26 U.S.C.A. § 408.
[5] 26 U.S.C.A. § 403.
[6] 26 U.S.C.A. § 3121.
[7] 29 U.S.C.A. § 1002.

§ 935. Exclusion; payment of social security for domestic service employee or agricultural labor employee

"Wages" does not include the payment by an employer, without deduction from the remuneration of the employee, of the tax imposed upon an employee under Section 3101 of the Internal Revenue Code [1] with respect to remuneration paid to an employee for domestic service in a private home of the employer or for agricultural labor, as defined in subsection (g) of Section 3121 of the Internal Revenue Code.[2] *(Stats.1953, c. 308, p. 1482, § 935. Amended by Stats.1957, c. 1184, p. 2475, § 6; Stats.1986, c. 847, § 7.)*

[1] 26 U.S.C.A. § 3101.
[2] 26 U.S.C.A. § 3121.

§ 936. Exclusion; remuneration paid in medium other than cash; exception

"Wages" does not include remuneration paid in any medium other than cash to an employee for service not in the course of the employer's trade or business, except that this section shall not apply to remuneration paid for domestic service in a private home or in a local college club or local chapter of a college fraternity or sorority. *(Stats.1953, c. 308, p. 1482, § 936. Amended by Stats. 1978, c. 2, p. 38, § 73, eff. Jan. 30, 1978, operative Jan. 1, 1978.)*

§ 937. Exclusion; payments for moving expenses

"Wages" does not include the payment to, or on behalf of, an employee for moving expenses, if at the time of the payment it is reasonable to believe that a corresponding deduction from income is allowable to the employee under Section 217 of the Internal Revenue Code.[1] *(Added by Stats.1986, c. 847, § 9.)*

[1] 26 U.S.C.A. § 217.

§ 938. Exclusion; certain payments to employees or dependents

(a) "Wages" does not include any payment or series of payments by an employer to an employee or any of his or her dependents which is paid:

(1) Upon or after the termination of an employee's employment relationship because of death or retirement for disability, and

(2) Under a plan established by the employer which makes provision for his or her employees generally or a class or classes of his or her employees, or for the

employees or class or classes of employees and their dependents.

(b) This section shall not apply to any payment or series of payments which would have been paid if the employee's employment relationship had not been terminated as prescribed by this section. *(Added by Stats.1968, c. 1173, p. 2228, § 2. Amended by Stats.1986, c. 847, § 10.)*

§ 938.1. Exclusion; payments under qualified group legal services plan

"Wages" does not include any contribution, payment, or service provided by an employer which may be excluded from the gross income of an employee, his or her spouse, or his or her dependents, under the provisions of Section 120 of the Internal Revenue Code,[1] relating to amounts received under a qualified group legal services plan. *(Added by Stats.1986, c. 847, § 11.)*

[1] 26 U.S.C.A. § 120.

§ 938.3. Exclusions; payments for educational assistance, dependent care assistance programs, benefits excluded under Internal Revenue Code, and cafeteria plan benefits

"Wages" does not include any payment made, or benefit furnished to, or for the benefit of, an employee, for any of the following:

(a) An educational assistance program if, at the time of payment or the furnishing, it is reasonable to believe that the employee will be able to exclude the payment or benefit from income under Section 127 of the Internal Revenue Code.[1]

(b) A dependent care assistance program if, at the time of payment or the furnishing, it is reasonable to believe that the employee will be able to exclude the payment or benefit from income under Section 129 of the Internal Revenue Code.[2]

(c) Any benefit provided to or on behalf of an employee if at the time the benefit is provided it is reasonable to believe that the employee will be able to exclude the benefit from income under Section 74(c), 117, or 132 of the Internal Revenue Code.[3]

(d) Any benefit under a cafeteria plan, as described in Section 125 of the Internal Revenue Code,[4] if the benefit is excludable from wages pursuant to any other provision of this article, except Section 930. *(Added by Stats.1986, c. 847, § 12. Amended by Stats.1988, c. 647, § 3.)*

[1] 26 U.S.C.A. § 127.
[2] 26 U.S.C.A. § 129.
[3] 26 U.S.C.A. §§ 74(c), 117, or 132.
[4] 26 U.S.C.A. § 125.

§ 938.5. Exclusion; payments received by national guard members or armed forces reserve components

"Wages" does not include any payment received by a member of the National Guard or reserve component of the armed forces for inactive duty training, annual training, or emergency state active duty. *(Added by Stats.1983, c. 218, § 1.)*

§ 938.7. Exclusion; payments made by employer to survivor or estate of former employee; time

"Wages," does not include any payment made by an employer to a survivor, or the estate of a former employee, after the calendar year in which the employee died. *(Added by Stats.1985, c. 37, § 1, eff. May 7, 1985.)*

§ 939. Contingent effect of exclusions

Types of payments excluded from the definition of wages by Sections 931, 931.5, 933, 934, 935, 936, 937, 938, 938.1, 938.3, and 938.7 shall be excluded from the definition of wages only during the time that the respective type or types of payments set forth in those sections are similarly excluded from the definition of wages contained in the Federal Unemployment Tax Act.[1] *(Stats.1953, c. 308, p. 1482, § 939. Amended by Stats. 1959, c. 2156, p. 5211, § 3; Stats.1963, c. 2015, p. 4119, § 6; Stats.1963, c. 2016, p. 4128, § 5; Stats.1968, c. 1173, p. 2228, § 3; Stats.1986, c. 847, § 13.)*

[1] 26 U.S.C.A. § 3301 et seq.

§ 940. Wages

For the purposes of this section, of Sections 977 and 977.5 to the extent specified by those sections, and of Sections 1026, 1088, 1280, 1281, 1282, 2652, 2654, 2655, and 2657, "wages" means taxable wages as well as wages which would be taxable except for the limitations on taxable wages provided under Sections 930 and 985. *(Added by Stats.1959, c. 5, p. 1833, § 1, eff. Mar. 10, 1959. Amended by Stats.1961, c. 2153, p. 4442, § 4; Stats.1961, c. 2154, p. 4450, § 3; Stats.1961, c. 2164, p. 4482, § 5; Stats.1965, c. 745, p. 2153, § 1, eff. June 24, 1965; Stats.1971, Ex.Sess., c. 1, p. 5126, § 306, eff. Dec. 8, 1971, operative Jan. 1, 1972; Stats.1975, c. 1256, p. 3289, § 2; Stats.1984, c. 1275, § 2, eff. Sept. 19, 1984.)*

ARTICLE 3. CONTRIBUTION RATES

Section

976. Accrual and payment of employer contributions; not deductible from wages.
976.5. Voluntary contribution; redetermination of unemployment insurance contribution rate; reduction; application of section.
976.6. Additional contributions.
976.8. Section 976.6 inapplicable to employer having negative reserve account balance on computation date; exception.
977. Contribution rate; reserve balance.
977.5. Emergency solvency surcharge rate.
979. Statement declaring employer tax schedule to be in effect.
980. Exclusions in determining balance in unemployment fund.
980.5. Determination of fund's balance; included unreimbursed balance of paid benefits.
981. Determination of wages in employment; exclusions.

Section
982. Rate of more or less than 3.4 percent; qualifications; new employer; average base payroll; rate change because of business structural change; exception.
984. Worker contribution; amount; rate changes by director.
984.5. Contribution rates.
985. Limitations on amount of employee contributions.
986. Withholding by employer in trust; exception; pay roll records; statement to employee; transmitting contributions.
987. Liability of employer.
987.7. Payment by worker to employer or department; excess worker contributions on cash tips and cash gratuities.
988. Bankrupt or insolvent employer; priority of contribution payments.
989. Publication of annual tax rate.
990. Payments of less than one cent.
991. Erroneous payments.
992. Permissive legislation for one hundred percent offset.
993. Additional contributions; amount.
994. Contingent effect of §§ 992 and 993.
995. Unemployment Fund; Unemployment Compensation Disability Fund; status report; content.

§ 976. Accrual and payment of employer contributions; not deductible from wages

Employer contributions to the Unemployment Fund shall accrue and become payable by every employer, except an employer as defined by Section 676, for each calendar year with respect to wages paid for employment. The contributions are due and shall be paid to the department for the Unemployment Fund by each employer in accordance with this division and shall not be deducted in whole or in part from the wages of individuals in his employ. *(Stats.1953, c. 308, p. 1482, § 976. Amended by Stats.1961, c. 2155, p. 4459, § 4; Stats.1965, c. 1435, p. 3367, § 3, operative Oct. 1, 1965; Stats.1971, c. 1107, p. 2112, § 49, eff. Oct. 18, 1971; Stats.1973, c. 394, p. 858, § 2.)*

§ 976.5. Voluntary contribution; redetermination of unemployment insurance contribution rate; reduction; application of section

(a) Except as provided in subdivision (b), in addition to other contributions required by this division, every employer, except an employer to which subdivision (c) is applicable, may submit a voluntary unemployment insurance contribution for the purpose of redetermining its unemployment insurance contribution rate. No redetermination of a contribution rate shall be made unless the voluntary contribution is submitted as required in subdivision (c) of Section 1110. No redetermination shall reduce an employer's unemployment insurance contribution rate by more than three rates as provided in Section 977.

(b) This section shall not be operative in calendar years in which Contribution Rate Schedules E and F in Section 977 are in effect, or in calendar years to which the emergency solvency surcharge provided in Section 977.5 is in effect.

(c) This section does not apply to any of the following:

(1) An employer not eligible for a contribution rate other than that provided pursuant to Section 982 or subdivision (c) of Section 977.

(2) An employer with a negative reserve account balance on the computation date.

(3) An employer who was notified prior to September 1 of any unpaid amount owed to the department which is not the subject of a timely petition for reassessment pending before the appeals board on September 30 preceding the year to which a contribution rate is applicable. *(Added by Stats.1989, c. 1146, § 3. Amended by Stats.1992, c. 446 (S.B.1734), § 1; Stats.2004, c. 827 (A.B.664), § 2.)*

Operative Effect

For operative effect of this section, see its terms.

§ 976.6. Additional contributions

In addition to other contributions required by this division, every employer, except an employer defined by Section 676, 684, or 685, and except an employer that has elected an alternate method of financing its liability for unemployment compensation benefits pursuant to Article 5 (commencing with Section 801), or Article 6 (commencing with Section 821) of Chapter 3, shall pay into the Employment Training Fund contributions at the rate of 0.1 percent of wages specified in Section 930. The contributions shall be collected in the same manner and at the same time as any contributions required under Sections 977 and 977.5.

(Added by Stats.1982, c. 1075, p. 3880, § 3. Amended by Stats.1983, c. 1169, § 2; Stats.1984, c. 1275, § 3, eff. Sept. 19, 1984; Stats.1985, c. 448, § 1, eff. July 31, 1985; Stats.1986, c. 248, § 225; Stats.1989, c. 926, § 1; Stats. 1990, c. 1668 (A.B.2694), § 1, eff. Sept. 30, 1990; Stats. 1993, c. 1080 (S.B.96), § 1; Stats.1995, c. 865 (S.B.644), § 1; Stats.2001, c. 111 (A.B.429), § 18, eff. July 30, 2001.)

§ 976.8. Section 976.6 inapplicable to employer having negative reserve account balance on computation date; exception

(a) Section 976.6 does not apply to any employer who has a negative reserve account balance on the computation date.

(b) Subdivision (a) does not apply to an employer assigned the maximum rate pursuant to subdivision (c) of Section 977. *(Added by Stats.1967, c. 1725, p. 4298, § 5. Amended by Stats.1982, c. 1075, p. 3881, § 4; Stats.2004, c. 827 (A.B.664), § 3.)*

§ 977. Contribution rate; reserve balance

(a) Except as provided in subdivision (c), if, as of the computation date, the employer's net balance of reserve equals or exceeds that percentage of his or her average

939

base payroll which appears on any line in column 1 of the following table, but is less than that percentage of his or her average base payroll which appears on the same line in column 2 of that table, his or her contribution rate shall be the figure appearing on that same line in the appropriate schedule, as defined in subdivision (b), which shall be a percentage of the wages specified in Section 930.

Reserve Ratio		Contribution Rate Schedules						
Column 1	Column 2	AA	A	B	C	D	E	F
Line								
01	less than –20	5.4	5.4	5.4	5.4	5.4	5.4	5.4
02	–20 to –18	5.2	5.3	5.4	5.4	5.4	5.4	5.4
03	–18 to –16	5.1	5.2	5.4	5.4	5.4	5.4	5.4
04	–16 to –14	5.0	5.1	5.3	5.4	5.4	5.4	5.4
05	–14 to –12	4.9	5.0	5.3	5.4	5.4	5.4	5.4
06	–12 to –11	4.8	4.9	5.2	5.4	5.4	5.4	5.4
07	–11 to –10	4.7	4.8	5.1	5.3	5.4	5.4	5.4
08	–10 to –09	4.6	4.7	5.1	5.3	5.4	5.4	5.4
09	–09 to –08	4.5	4.6	4.9	5.2	5.4	5.4	5.4
10	–08 to –07	4.4	4.5	4.8	5.1	5.3	5.4	5.4
11	–07 to –06	4.3	4.4	4.7	5.0	5.3	5.4	5.4
12	–06 to –05	4.2	4.3	4.6	4.9	5.2	5.4	5.4
13	–05 to –04	4.1	4.2	4.5	4.8	5.1	5.3	5.4
14	–04 to –03	4.0	4.1	4.4	4.7	5.0	5.3	5.4
15	–03 to –02	3.9	4.0	4.3	4.6	4.9	5.2	5.4
16	–02 to –01	3.8	3.9	4.2	4.5	4.8	5.1	5.4
17	–01 to 00	3.7	3.8	4.1	4.4	4.7	5.0	5.4
18	00 to 01	3.4	3.6	3.9	4.2	4.5	4.8	5.1
19	01 to 02	3.2	3.4	3.7	4.0	4.3	4.6	4.9
20	02 to 03	3.0	3.2	3.5	3.8	4.1	4.4	4.7
21	03 to 04	2.8	3.0	3.3	3.6	3.9	4.2	4.5
22	04 to 05	2.6	2.8	3.1	3.4	3.7	4.0	4.3
23	05 to 06	2.4	2.6	2.9	3.2	3.5	3.8	4.1
24	06 to 07	2.2	2.4	2.7	3.0	3.3	3.6	3.9
25	07 to 08	2.0	2.2	2.5	2.8	3.1	3.4	3.7
26	08 to 09	1.8	2.0	2.3	2.6	2.9	3.2	3.5
27	09 to 10	1.6	1.8	2.1	2.4	2.7	3.0	3.3
28	10 to 11	1.4	1.6	1.9	2.2	2.5	2.8	3.1
29	11 to 12	1.2	1.4	1.7	2.0	2.3	2.6	2.9
30	12 to 13	1.0	1.2	1.5	1.8	2.1	2.4	2.7
31	13 to 14	0.8	1.0	1.3	1.6	1.9	2.2	2.5
32	14 to 15	0.7	0.9	1.1	1.4	1.7	2.0	2.3
33	15 to 16	0.6	0.8	1.0	1.2	1.5	1.8	2.1
34	16 to 17	0.5	0.7	0.9	1.1	1.3	1.6	1.9
35	17 to 18	0.4	0.6	0.8	1.0	1.2	1.4	1.7
36	18 to 19	0.3	0.5	0.7	0.9	1.1	1.3	1.5
37	19 to 20	0.2	0.4	0.6	0.8	1.0	1.2	1.4
38	20 or more	0.1	0.3	0.5	0.7	0.9	1.1	1.3

(b)(1) Whenever the balance in the Unemployment Fund on September 30 of any calendar year is greater than 1.8 percent of the wages (as defined by Section 940) in employment subject to this part paid during the 12–month period ending upon the computation date, employers shall pay into the Unemployment Fund contributions for the succeeding calendar year upon all wages with respect to employment at the rates specified in Schedule AA.

(2) Whenever the balance in the Unemployment Fund on September 30 of any calendar year is equal to or less than 1.8 percent and greater than 1.6 percent of the wages (as defined by Section 940) in employment subject to this part paid during the 12–month period ending upon the computation date, employers shall pay into the Unemployment Fund contributions for the succeeding

940

calendar year upon all wages with respect to employment at the rates specified in Schedule A.

(3) Whenever the balance in the Unemployment Fund on September 30 of any calendar year is equal to or less than 1.6 percent and greater than 1.4 percent of the wages (as defined by Section 940) in employment subject to this part paid during the 12–month period ending upon the computation date, employers shall pay into the Unemployment Fund contributions for the succeeding calendar year upon all wages with respect to employment at the rates specified in Schedule B.

(4) Whenever the balance in the Unemployment Fund on September 30 of any calendar year is equal to or less than 1.4 percent and greater than 1.2 percent of the wages (as defined by Section 940) in employment subject to this part paid during the 12–month period ending upon the computation date, employers shall pay into the Unemployment Fund contributions for the succeeding calendar year upon all wages with respect to employment at the rates specified in Schedule C.

(5) Whenever the balance in the Unemployment Fund on September 30 of any calendar year is equal to or less than 1.2 percent and greater than 1.0 percent of the wages (as defined by Section 940) in employment subject to this part paid during the 12–month period ending upon the computation date, employers shall pay into the Unemployment Fund contributions for the succeeding calendar year upon all wages with respect to employment at the rates specified in Schedule D.

(6) Whenever the balance in the Unemployment Fund on September 30 of any calendar year is equal to or less than 1.0 percent and greater than or equal to 0.8 percent of the wages (as defined by Section 940) in employment subject to this part paid during the 12–month period ending upon the computation date, employers shall pay into the Unemployment Fund contributions for the succeeding calendar year upon all wages with respect to employment at the rates specified in Schedule E.

(7) Whenever the balance in the Unemployment Fund on September 30 of any calendar year is less than 0.8 percent and greater than or equal to 0.6 percent of the wages (as defined by Section 940) in employment subject to this part paid during the 12–month period ending upon the computation date, employers shall pay into the Unemployment Fund contributions for the succeeding calendar year upon all wages with respect to employment at the rates specified in Schedule F.

(c) For each rating period beginning on or after January 1, 2005, in which an employer obtains or attempts to obtain a more favorable rate of contributions under this section due to deliberate ignorance, reckless disregard, fraud, intent to evade, misrepresentation, or willful nondisclosure, the director shall assign the maximum contribution rate plus 2 percent for each applicable rating period, the current rating period, and the subsequent rating period. (Added by Stats.1961, c. 2160, p. 4473, § 5; Stats.1961, c. 2161, p. 4479, § 1. Amended by Stats.1965, c. 1897, p. 4373, § 3; Stats.1970, c. 1468, p.

2898, § 2; Stats.1971, c. 1596, p. 3431, § 4; Stats.1975, c. 1256, p. 3290, § 4; Stats.1982, c. 1075, p. 3881, § 5; Stats.1984, c. 1275, § 4, eff. Sept. 19, 1984; Stats.1985, c. 784, § 1; Stats.1989, c. 1146, § 4; Stats.1992, c. 446 (S.B.1734), § 2; Stats.2004, c. 827 (A.B.664), § 4.)

§ 977.5. Emergency solvency surcharge rate

Whenever the balance in the Unemployment Fund on September 30 of any calendar year is less than 0.6 percent of the wages (as defined by Section 940) in employment, subject to this part, paid during the 12-month period ending on the computation date, employers shall pay into the Unemployment Fund contributions for the succeeding calendar year upon all wages with respect to employment at an emergency solvency surcharge rate. The emergency solvency surcharge rate shall be 1.15 times the rate the employer would have paid in Schedule F of subdivision (a) of Section 977, rounded to the nearest one-tenth of 1 percent. *(Added by Stats.1984, c. 1275, § 6, eff. Sept. 19, 1984. Amended by Stats.1989, c. 1146, § 5; Stats.1992, c. 446 (S.B.1734), § 3.)*

§ 979. Statement declaring employer tax schedule to be in effect

On or before January 10 of each calendar year, the director shall prepare a statement based on records of the department declaring which of the employer tax schedules contained in Section 977 shall be in effect for that calendar year and whether the emergency solvency surcharge pursuant to Section 977.5 shall be added. The statement shall be a public record and shall be final and binding for that calendar year. The statement shall include the official tabulation of wages in subject employment made by the department for the purpose of Sections 977 and 977.5, a summary of the data upon which that tabulation was based, and the sources from which those data were obtained, and shall further include a summary of the data upon which the computation of the balance in the Unemployment Fund was based, and their source. The director's action under Sections 977, 977.5, and this section shall not constitute an authorized regulation. *(Added by Stats.1970, c. 1468, p. 2900, § 4. Amended by Stats.1978, c. 397, p. 1255, § 1.6, eff. July 11, 1978; Stats.1982, c. 1075, p. 3884, § 9; Stats.1984, c. 1275, § 9, eff. Sept. 19, 1984.)*

§ 980. Exclusions in determining balance in unemployment fund

(a) In determining the balance in the Unemployment Fund for the purpose of Sections 977 and 977.5, there shall be excluded all of the following:

(1) Any amount credited to this state's account in the Unemployment Trust Fund pursuant to Section 903 of the federal Social Security Act, as amended, which has been appropriated for expenses of administration other than for capital assets, whether or not that amount has been withdrawn from that fund.

(2) Any unexpended advance from the federal unemployment account in the Unemployment Trust Fund received in accordance with Section 323 of this division and Title XII of the federal Social Security Act, as amended.

(3) Any amount paid in advance into the Unemployment Fund by an employer under any type of coverage pursuant to which reimbursement of benefits is permitted or required in lieu of the contributions required of employers.

(4) Any amount paid in advance into the Unemployment Fund by the federal government under any federal law that requires or permits this state to pay benefits from the Unemployment Fund and provides for advances by the federal government for reimbursement of all or part of those benefits.

(b) In determining the balance in the Unemployment Fund for the purpose of Sections 977 and 977.5, there shall also be excluded any estimated or other contributions not legally due and payable with respect to the final calendar quarter of the calendar year, except any payment of contributions made under Sections 976.5 and 1137 and except any payment of contributions by employers terminating business during any calendar quarter. *(Stats.1953, c. 308, p. 1484, § 980. Amended by Stats.1959, c. 1814, p. 4313, § 1; Stats.1961, c. 2158, p. 4465, § 2; Stats.1961, c. 2164, p. 4483, § 7; Stats.1965, c. 635, p. 1981, § 1; Stats.1965, c. 1897, p. 4375, § 6; Stats.1967, c. 1720, p. 4283, § 2; Stats.1970, c. 1156, p. 2047, § 5; Stats.1971, c. 1107, p. 2113, § 53, eff. Oct. 18, 1971; Stats.1976, c. 1009, p. 2382, § 1, eff. Sept. 17, 1976; Stats.1984, c. 1275, § 10, eff. Sept. 19, 1984; Stats.1989, c. 1146, § 6.)*

§ 980.5. Determination of fund's balance; included unreimbursed balance of paid benefits

In determining the balance in the Unemployment Fund for the purpose of Sections 977 and 977.5, there shall be included both of the following:

(a) The unreimbursed balance of all benefits paid from the Unemployment Fund to claimants when those benefits are based upon wages in employment under any type of coverage pursuant to which reimbursement of benefits is permitted or required in lieu of the contributions required of employers, whether or not the director has certified the benefits to the employer as due or payable.

(b) The unreimbursed balance of all benefits paid from the Unemployment Fund to claimants when, and to the extent that, the benefits are subject to reimbursement by the federal government under any federal law that requires or permits this state to pay benefits from the Unemployment Fund and provides for reimbursement by the federal government of all or part of those benefits. *(Added by Stats.1965, c. 1897, p. 4375, § 6.5. Amended by Stats.1970, c. 1156, p. 2047, § 6; Stats.1971, c. 1107, p. 2114, § 54, eff. Oct. 18, 1971; Stats.1976, c. 1009, p. 2383, § 2, eff. Sept. 17, 1976; Stats.1984, c. 1275, § 11, eff. Sept. 19, 1984.)*

§ 981. Determination of wages in employment; exclusions

In determining wages in employment, for the purpose of Sections 977 and 977.5, there shall be excluded all wages paid in employment under any type of coverage pursuant to which reimbursement of benefits is permitted or required in lieu of the contributions required of employers. *(Added Stats.1965, c. 1897, p. 4376, § 6.7. Amended by Stats.1976, c. 1009, p. 2383, § 3, eff. Sept. 17, 1976; Stats.1984, c. 1275, § 12, eff. Sept. 19, 1984.)*

§ 982. Rate of more or less than 3.4 percent; qualifications; new employer; average base payroll; rate change because of business structural change; exception

(a) Except as provided in subdivision (b), no employer shall be eligible for a contribution rate of more or less than 3.4 percent for any rating period unless his or her reserve account has been subject to benefit charges during the period of 12 complete consecutive calendar quarters ending on the computation date for that rating period and he or she is qualified under Sections 977 and 977.5.

(b) No new employer shall be eligible for a contribution rate of more or less than 3.4 percent unless his or her reserve account has been subject to benefit charges during the period of 12 complete consecutive calendar months ending on the computation date and the new employer is qualified under Sections 977 and 977.5.

(c) For the purposes of this section "new employer" means any of the following:

(1) An employer who first qualifies as an employer after the 1969 calendar year, and whose account is continuously subject to benefit charges from the date of first chargeability, except that a successor employer under Section 1051 is not a new employer if the successor applies for or obtains the transfer of the reserve account or part thereof of a predecessor who is not a new employer.

(2) An employer whose entire reserve account has been transferred to a successor under Article 5 (commencing with Section 1051) of Chapter 4 of this part.

(3) An employer whose reserve account has been canceled pursuant to Section 1029.

(d) Section 905 applies to a new employer, except that for the purposes of this section "average base payroll" means:

(1) The payroll in the calendar year immediately preceding the computation date for a new employer with a payroll only in that calendar year.

(2) The quotient obtained by dividing by two the total amount of taxable wages paid by a new employer during the most recent period of two consecutive calendar years immediately preceding the computation date, for a new employer with a payroll only in each of, or only in the first of, the two consecutive calendar years.

(e) The contribution rate of an employer, for any period prior to January 1, 1988, shall not be changed, other than by the provisions of Sections 977 and 977.5, when the director makes a determination, pursuant to Section 135.1 or 135.2, because of arrangements entered into or business activities conducted between January 1, 1984, and January 1, 1986.

(f) This section does not apply to an employer assigned the maximum rate pursuant to subdivision (c) of Section 977. *(Stats.1953, c. 308, p. 1484, § 982. Amended by Stats.1957, c. 1184, p. 2475, § 8; Stats.1959, c. 2154, p. 5204, § 4; Stats.1961, c. 2160, p. 4475, § 9; Stats.1961, c. 2161, p. 4479, § 2; Stats.1965, c. 1897, p. 4376, § 7; Stats.1971, c. 1596, p. 3432, § 6; Stats.1972, c. 833, p. 1483, § 4; Stats.1982, c. 1075, p. 3885, § 9.5; Stats.1984, c. 1275, § 13, eff. Sept. 19, 1984; Stats.1987, c. 548, § 3; Stats.2004, c. 827 (A.B.664), § 5.)*

§ 984. Worker contribution; amount; rate changes by director

(a)(1) Each worker shall pay worker contributions at the rate determined by the director pursuant to this section with respect to wages, as defined by Sections 926, 927, and 985. On or before October 31 of each calendar year, the director shall prepare a statement, which shall be a public record, declaring the rate of worker contributions for the calendar year and shall notify promptly all employers of employees covered for disability insurance of the rate.

(2)(A) Except as provided in paragraph (3), the rate of worker contributions for calendar year 1987 and for each subsequent calendar year shall be 1.45 times the amount disbursed from the Disability Fund during the 12–month period ending September 30 and immediately preceding the calendar year for which the rate is to be effective, less the amount in the Disability Fund on that September 30, with the resulting figure divided by total wages paid pursuant to Sections 926, 927, and 985 during the same 12–month period, and then rounded to the nearest one-tenth of 1 percent.

(B) The director shall increase the rate of worker contributions by .08 percent for the 2004 and 2005 calendar years to cover the initial cost of family temporary disability insurance benefits provided in Chapter 7 (commencing with Section 3300) of Part 2.

(3) The rate of worker contributions shall not exceed 1.5 percent or be less than 0.1 percent. The rate of worker contributions shall not decrease from the rate in the previous year by more than two-tenths of 1 percent.

(b) Worker contributions required under Sections 708 and 708.5 shall be at a rate determined by the director to reimburse the Disability Fund for unemployment compensation disability benefits paid and estimated to be paid to all employers and self-employed individuals covered by those sections. On or before November 30th of each calendar year, the director shall prepare a statement, which shall be a public record, declaring the rate of contributions for the succeeding calendar year for all employers and self-employed individuals covered under Sections 708 and 708.5 and shall notify promptly the employers and self-employed individuals of the rate. The rate shall be determined by dividing the estimated benefits and administrative costs paid in the prior year by the product of the annual remuneration deemed to have been received under Sections 708 and 708.5 and the estimated number of persons who were covered at any time in the prior year. The resulting rate shall be rounded to the next higher one-hundredth percentage point. The rate may also be reduced or increased by a factor estimated to maintain as nearly as practicable a cumulative zero balance in the funds contributed pursuant to Sections 708 and 708.5. Estimates made pursuant to this subdivision may be made on the basis of statistical sampling, or another method determined by the director.

(c) The director's action in determining a rate under this section shall not constitute an authorized regulation.

(d)(1) Notwithstanding subdivision (a), and except as provided in paragraph (2), the director may, at his or her discretion, increase or decrease, by not to exceed 0.1 percent, the rate of worker contributions determined pursuant to subdivision (a), up to a maximum worker contribution rate of 1.5 percent, if he or she determines the adjustment is necessary to reimburse the Disability Fund for disability benefits paid or estimated to be paid to individuals covered by this section or to prevent the accumulation of funds in excess of those needed to maintain an adequate fund balance.

(2) Notwithstanding paragraph (1), for the 2004, 2005, and 2006 calendar years, the director may not decrease the rate of worker contributions, regardless of whether the director determines that a decrease is necessary to prevent the accumulation of funds in excess of those needed to maintain the adequacy of the Disability Fund during program implementation. *(Stats.1953, c. 308, p. 1485, § 984. Amended by Stats.1957, c. 2107, p. 3731, § 1; Stats.1961, c. 2153, p. 4445, § 9; Stats.1961, c. 2154, p. 4450, § 4; Stats.1963, c. 1563, p. 3146, § 4; Stats.1965, c. 745, p. 2153, § 1.3, eff. June 24, 1965; Stats.1967, c. 1725, p. 4299, § 6; Stats.1977, c. 1142, p. 3668, § 2; Stats.1977, c. 1143, p. 3671, § 1; Stats.1978, c. 397, p. 1256, § 2, eff. July 11, 1978; Stats.1978, c. 950, p. 2933, § 3, eff. Sept. 20, 1978; Stats.1980, c. 1308, p. 4423, § 1; Stats.1983, c. 903, § 1; Stats.1986, c. 248, § 226; Stats. 1986, c. 1309, § 1; Stats.1987, c. 56, § 167; Stats.1991, c. 793 (A.B.2047), § 1; Stats.1993, c. 747 (A.B.1738), § 7; Stats.1993, c. 748 (S.B.4), § 2; Stats.2002, c. 901 (S.B. 1661), § 1, operative Jan. 1, 2004; Stats.2003, c. 797 (S.B.727), § 4, operative Jan. 1, 2004.)*

Operative Effect

For operative effect of Stats.2003, c. 797 (S.B. 727) upon benefits payable for family temporary disability insurance claims, see section 28 of that act.

§ 984.5. Contribution rates

(a) Effective January 1, 1994, the director shall prepare a statement on or before November 30 of each calendar year, which shall be a public record, declaring the rate of contributions of the succeeding calendar year for all employers and self-employed individuals covered under Section 708 or 708.5 and shall notify promptly the employers and self-employed individuals of the rate. For calendar years 1994 to 1996, inclusive, worker contributions required under Section 708 or 708.5 shall be at a rate determined by the director to reimburse the Disability Fund for the sum of estimated administrative costs due to those sections and unemployment compensation disability benefits estimated to be paid to all employers and self-employed individuals covered by those sections. The rate shall be determined by dividing the sum of the benefits expected to be paid in the following calendar year and the administrative costs expected to be incurred under Section 708 or 708.5 during that calendar year by earnings estimated to be reported under those sections for that same calendar year. The resulting rate shall be rounded to the next higher one-hundredth percentage point. This rate may also be reduced or increased by a factor estimated to maintain as nearly as practicable a cumulative zero balance in funds contributed pursuant to Section 708 or 708.5.

For calendar year 1997, and each calendar year thereafter, the rate established each November 30 shall be determined by multiplying the current year's rate by the ratio of 1.10 times the current year disbursements divided by contributions for the same period, under Sections 708 and 708.5. If in any calendar year the cumulative balance of contributions minus disbursements equals or exceeds 20 percent of annual disbursements, the contribution rate for the succeeding year shall be adjusted to a level necessary to maintain revenues at no more than 20 percent over annual disbursements. If legislation is enacted necessitating adjustments in the benefit levels for employers and self-employed individuals covered under Section 708 or 708.5, the rate may be adjusted by a factor estimated to provide that funds contributed pursuant to Section 708 or 708.5 cover disbursements pursuant to these sections.

For the purpose of this subdivision, disbursements are defined as the sum of unemployment compensation disability benefits paid to employers and self-employed individuals covered under Section 708 or 708.5, plus administrative costs related to those sections. Estimates made pursuant to this subdivision shall be available for public inspection.

(b) The director's action in determining a rate under this section shall not constitute an authorized regulation. *(Added by Stats.1993, c. 747 (A.B.1738), § 7.5.)*

§ 985. Limitations on amount of employee contributions

Section 984 shall not apply to that part of the remuneration which, after remuneration with respect to employment equal to four times the maximum weekly benefit for each calendar year specified in Section 2655 multiplied by 13 and divided by 55 percent has been paid to an individual by an employer, is paid to the individual by the employer. *(Stats.1953, c. 308, p. 1485, § 985. Amended by Stats.1957, c. 2107, p. 3732, § 2; Stats.1961, c. 2153, p. 4445, § 10; Stats.1961, c. 2154, p. 4450, § 5; Stats.1965, c. 745, p. 2153, § 1.5, eff. June 24, 1965; Stats.1971, c. 1747, p. 3733, § 1; Stats.1973, c. 1026, p. 2041, § 1; Stats.1973, c. 1163, p. 2421, § 1; Stats.1973, c. 1188, p. 2495, § 1; Stats.1976, c. 1182, p. 5286, § 1; Stats.1980, c. 1308, p. 4425, § 2; Stats.1989, c. 1371, § 2.)*

§ 986. Withholding by employer in trust; exception; pay roll records; statement to employee; transmitting contributions

(a) Notwithstanding any provision of law in this state to the contrary, each employer shall:

(1) Except as provided in subdivision (a)(2) of this section, withhold in trust the amount of his workers' contributions from their wages at the time the wages are paid, shall show the deduction on his payroll records, and shall furnish each worker with a statement in writing showing the amount which has been deducted, in such form and at such times as may be prescribed.

(2) Hold in trust the amount of his workers' contributions, at the time their wages are paid, where he undertakes or agrees to pay without deduction from the wages of his workers the amount of worker contributions required of his workers under this division.

(b) Each employer shall transmit all such contributions withheld or held in trust to the department for the Disability Fund, in addition to his own contributions for the Unemployment Fund, pursuant to authorized regulations. *(Stats.1953, c. 308, p. 1485, § 986. Amended by Stats.1965, c. 624, p. 1960, § 1.)*

§ 987. Liability of employer

Each employer shall be liable for any and all contributions required to be made by his workers on account of wages which he has paid to them regardless of whether or not he has deducted the contributions from the workers' wages at the time they were paid, but no employer shall be liable for worker contributions required on behalf of himself or of any of his employees with respect to wages paid while there is in effect at the time the wages were paid a rule or regulation or interpretation of the director or of the department that such wages were not subject to such contributions. *(Stats.1953, c. 308, p. 1485, § 987.)*

§ 987.7. Payment by worker to employer or department; excess worker contributions on cash tips and cash gratuities

(a) If the worker contributions required in any one month to be made because of the receipt of cash tips and cash gratuities exceed the wages of the worker under the control of the employer, the worker may furnish the employer, on or before the 10th day of the following

month, or, if the amounts are estimated, on or before the last day of the month following the calendar quarter, an amount equal to the excess.

(b) If the worker contributions required by Section 984 with respect to cash tips and cash gratuities exceed the amount of worker contributions that can be collected by the employer from the wages of the worker, the excess shall be paid by the worker, except as provided by Section 1088.6. The worker shall pay the excess to the department within 30 days from his or her receipt of the written statement furnished by his or her employer pursuant to Section 1088.6. If the worker fails to pay the excess within the time required by this subdivision, the director may make an assessment for the excess and shall give the worker a written notice of the assessment. Article 8 (commencing with Section 1126) with respect to the assessment of contributions and Chapter 7 (commencing with Section 1701) with respect to the collection of contributions shall apply to the recovery of amounts under this subdivision.

(c) The director may offset amounts assessed pursuant to subdivision (b) against any refund payable to the worker under Section 1176.5 or against any amount of disability benefits to which he or she may become entitled under Part 2 (commencing with Section 2601) within any of the following periods:

(1) The current disability benefit period.

(2) One year from the beginning date of any disability benefit period that begins during the three-year period next succeeding the service of notice of the assessment. *(Added by Stats.1977, c. 1142, p. 3669, § 5. Amended by Stats.1986, c. 248, § 229; Stats.1993, c. 402 (A.B.1668), § 1.)*

§ 988. Bankrupt or insolvent employer; priority of contribution payments

In case of the insolvency or bankruptcy of an employer, contributions by workers, payable as provided in this article, shall not be considered any part of the employer's assets and shall be paid to the director prior to the payment of any other claim against the employer. *(Stats. 1953, c. 308, p. 1486, § 988. Amended by Stats.1970, c. 1523, p. 3084, § 64; Stats.1982, c. 497, p. 2217, § 175, operative July 1, 1983.)*

§ 989. Publication of annual tax rate

The annual tax rate or contribution rate which under this division is determined to apply to any particular employee or any particular employer, or group of employees or group of employers, shall be made public and available for public inspection but in no case shall the amount of tax paid by any employee or employer, or group of employees or group of employers, be disclosed to the public. *(Stats.1953, c. 308, p. 1486, § 989.)*

§ 990. Payments of less than one cent

In the payment of any contributions, a fractional part of a cent shall be disregarded unless it amounts to one-half cent ($0.005) or more, in which case it shall be increased to one cent ($0.01). *(Stats.1953, c. 308, p. 1486, § 990.)*

§ 991. Erroneous payments

(a) Any contributions paid to the Unemployment Fund or Disability Fund either with respect to wages on which contributions previously have been paid in error and without negligence on the part of the employing unit to another state having an unemployment compensation law, or with respect to wages on which contributions computed under the Federal Unemployment Tax Act[1] previously have been paid in error and without negligence on the part of the employing unit to an agency of the federal government, shall be deemed for the purposes of this division to have been paid to the department at the time of the erroneous payment to the other state or to the federal agency, if payment is made to the department by the employing unit within 30 days after the employing unit is given notice pursuant to Section 1206 by the director of the determination that payment shall be made to the department. The 30-day period for payment may be extended by the director for good cause for a period not to exceed an additional 90 days.

(b) Any contributions paid to the Unemployment Fund or Disability Fund with respect to wages on which contributions computed under this division previously have been paid in error and without negligence on the part of the employing unit to an admitted disability insurer, to trustees administering a voluntary plan for the employing unit, to a self-insured plan of the employing unit, to another agency of this state, or to an agency of the federal government shall be deemed, solely to the extent of the amount of contributions previously paid in error and without negligence, for the purposes of this division to have been paid to the department at the time of the erroneous payment to the admitted disability insurer, to trustees administering a voluntary plan for the employing unit, to a self-insured plan of the employing unit, to another agency of this state, or to the federal agency, if payment is made to the department by the employing unit within 30 days after the employing unit is given notice pursuant to Section 1206 by the director of the determination that payment shall be made to the department. The 30-day period for payment may be extended by the director for good cause for a period not to exceed an additional 90 days. As used in this subdivision "paid" includes credits made to a self-insured plan of the employing unit. With respect to payments by an employing unit to an admitted disability insurer, to trustees administering a voluntary plan for the employing unit, or to a self-insured plan of the employing unit, this subdivision shall apply only if one or more of the following conditions are met:

(1) At the time of payment the employing unit has or prior to the time of payment had an approved voluntary plan with the recipient of the payment.

(2) Prior to the time of payment the employing unit had applied to the department for a voluntary plan which was subsequently approved by the department.

(3) At the time of payment the employing unit is a subsidiary or affiliate of an employing unit having an approved voluntary plan.

(4) At the time of payment the employing unit believed that a voluntary plan had been acquired pursuant to Section 3254.5.

(c) If payment is not made within the 30-day period or within the period for which an extension is granted, this section shall not apply and Article 7 (commencing with Section 1110), Article 8 (commencing with Section 1126), and Chapter 7 (commencing with Section 1701), with respect to the payment of reported contributions, and the assessment and collection of contributions shall apply.

(d) If the director finds that the collection of any contributions will be jeopardized by delay this section shall not apply and the director may make a jeopardy assessment and collect the contributions pursuant to Article 8 (commencing with Section 1126), and Chapter 7 (commencing with Section 1701). *(Stats.1953, c. 308, p. 1486, § 991. Amended by Stats.1955, c. 1165, p. 2159, § 8; Stats.1959, c. 1729, p. 4176, § 9; Stats.1979, c. 1082, p. 3888, § 6.)*

[1] 26 U.S.C.A. § 3301 et seq.

§ 992. Permissive legislation for one hundred percent offset

During such time as the Federal Unemployment Tax Act[1] is amended so that employers are allowed, against the tax imposed by Section 3301 of that act, credits amounting to 100 percent of such tax on account of contributions paid under this division, then the additional amount of contributions provided for by Section 993 shall be required to be paid into the Unemployment Fund. *(Stats.1953, c. 308, p. 1486, § 992. Amended by Stats. 1955, c. 1165, p. 2160, § 9; Stats.1961, c. 2153, p. 4445, § 11.)*

[1] 26 U.S.C.A. § 3301 et seq.

§ 993. Additional contributions; amount

Every employer who is subject to the tax provided for by Section 3301 of the Federal Unemployment Tax Act,[1] shall, subject to Section 992, pay into the Unemployment Fund in addition to the amounts required by other provisions of this division an amount equal to five-tenths of 1 percent, or such other percentage as applies for a calendar year pursuant to Section 6157 of the Internal Revenue Code of 1954,[2] of all wages paid by him or her in employment and included in the measure of the contributions allowed as the credit against the tax imposed by Section 3301 of the Federal Unemployment Tax Act. *(Stats.1953, c. 803, p. 1486, § 993. Amended by Stats. 1955, c. 1165, p. 2160, § 10; Stats.1961, c. 2156, p. 4462, § 14; Stats.1971, c. 1107, p. 2114, § 55, eff. Oct. 18, 1971;*

Stats.1978, c. 2, p. 39, § 74, eff. Jan. 30, 1978, operative Jan. 1, 1978.)

[1] 26 U.S.C.A. § 3301.

[2] 26 U.S.C.A. § 6157.

§ 994. Contingent effect of §§ 992 and 993

Sections 992 and 993 shall not become operative unless the Secretary of Labor certifies that they are in conformity with the provisions of Title III of the Social Security Act [1] and Sections 3302, 3303, and 3304 of the Federal Unemployment Tax Act.[2] *(Stats.1953, c. 308, p. 1486, § 994. Amended by Stats.1955, c. 1165, p. 2160, § 11.)*

[1] 42 U.S.C.A. § 501 et seq.

[2] 26 U.S.C.A. §§ 3302, 3303, 3304.

§ 995. Unemployment Fund; Unemployment Compensation Disability Fund; status report; content

The department shall submit to the Legislature in May and October of each year a report on the status of the Unemployment Fund and the Unemployment Compensation Disability Fund. Each report shall include both actual and forecasted information on the fund balances, receipts, disbursements, claim data, tax rates, and employment levels. *(Added by Stats.1994, c. 967 (S.B.1584), § 1.7, eff. Sept. 28, 1994.)*

ARTICLE 4. RESERVE ACCOUNTS

Section
1025. Keeping separate records of amounts paid into fund by each employer; pooling amount of employer contributions; availability of fund for payments.
1026. Maintaining separate reserve account for each employer; credits to and charges against accounts.
1027.1. Computation of account; cancellation of reserve account.
1027.5. Cancellation of net balance of reserve more negative than 21 percent; operation and effect of 1984 amendment by Chapter 1296.
1027.6. Cancellation of negative reserve balance for 1983.
1028. Payments chargeable to reserve account.
1029. Cancellation of inactive reserve accounts.
1030. Employer's right to notify department of cause of claimant's leaving; determination of cause of leaving; appeals and reconsiderations of department rulings.
1030.1. Conviction of offense; termination of employment; reconsideration of ruling made prior to conviction.
1031. Ruling under § 1030 not to constitute basis for disqualification of claimant.
1032. Employer's reserve account not charged; exception.
1032.5. Report of part time work; ruling on liability of employer account; appeals and reconsiderations of rulings.
1033. Furnishing statement of reserve account and contribution rate.
1034. Protest of charges to reserve account; time for protest; setting forth grounds.
1035. Protest of charges to reserve account; notice of action.
1036. Notice to employer of correction of errors; assessments; refunds.
1037. Contribution rate payable while protest pending.

§ 1025. Keeping separate records of amounts paid into fund by each employer; pooling amount of employer contributions; availability of fund for payments

The director shall keep separate records of the amounts paid into the fund by each employer in his or her own behalf, or chargeable to him or her as benefits; but nothing in this division shall be construed to grant any employer or his or her employees prior claims or rights to the amount contributed by him or her to the fund, either on his or her own account or on behalf of his or her employees. The amount of employer contributions, advances, or reimbursements under Article 5 (commencing with Section 801) of Chapter 3 of this part or Section 821, and all other amounts payable to the fund, shall be pooled and available to pay unemployment compensation benefits to any employee entitled thereto, regardless of the source of contributions or any other amounts. *(Stats. 1953, c. 308, p. 1487, § 1025. Amended by Stats.1971, c. 1107, p. 2114, § 55.5, eff. Oct. 18, 1971; Stats.1978, c. 2, p. 39, § 75, eff. Jan. 30, 1978, operative Jan. 1, 1978; Stats.2005, c. 152 (A.B.1577), § 9.)*

§ 1026. Maintaining separate reserve account for each employer; credits to and charges against accounts

(a) The director shall maintain a separate reserve account for each employer, and shall credit each reserve account with all the contributions paid on his or her behalf.

(b) Unemployment compensation benefits paid to an unemployed individual during any benefit year shall be charged against the reserve account of his or her employer during his or her base period. If the individual performed services in employment for more than one employer during his or her base period, unemployment compensation benefits paid to him or her shall be charged against the respective reserve accounts of the employers in the proportion that the total wages paid to the individual in employment for each employer bears to the total wages paid to the individual in employment for all employers during the base period.

(c) The director shall credit the interest earned by the Unemployment Fund to each positive reserve employer account in proportion to the amount the account bears to the total of all positive reserve accounts.

(d) Except as provided by Sections 803 and 821, in proportion to the amount each employer's taxable wages bears to the total of all employers' taxable wages, the director shall credit to each employer reserve account all of the following:

(1) Benefit overpayments collected in the four quarters prior to the computation date.

(2) Positive balances in reserve accounts canceled pursuant to Section 1029.

(3) Other nontax income.

(e) Except as provided by Sections 803 and 821, in the same proportion as provided in subdivision (d), the director shall charge to each employer reserve account all of the following:

(1) The increase in the total of all negative reserve account balances as computed by subtracting the total of all negative reserve account balances on July 31 of each year prior to the cancellations required by Section 1027.5 from the total of all negative reserve account balances on the prior July 31 after the cancellations required by Section 1027.5, except as provided by Section 1144.

(2) Benefit overpayments established in the four quarters prior to the computation date.

(3) Benefits not charged to employer reserve accounts pursuant to Section 1032, 1032.5, 1034, 1035, 1036, 1335, 1338, or 1380.

(4) Other items of expense and benefit charges not included in active employer reserve accounts. *(Stats. 1953, c. 308, p. 1487, § 1026. Amended by Stats.1982, c. 1075, p. 3885, § 10; Stats.1985, c. 1217, § 6, eff. Sept. 29, 1985; Stats.1987, c. 457, § 2, eff. Sept. 9, 1987; Stats.1992, c. 125 (A.B.1830), § 4; Stats.1994, c. 1050 (A.B.3122), § 1.)*

§ 1027.1. Computation of account; cancellation of reserve account

On the computation date in 1966, the portion of each negative reserve balance which has not previously been charged to the balancing account shall be transferred to that account and the employer's reserve account thereupon canceled. The computation on such date for calendar year 1967 shall be based upon the status of the employer's account prior to such transfer and cancellation subject to the requirements of Section 982. The computation for each calendar year beginning with calendar year 1968 shall be in accordance with the requirements of Section 982 and an employer whose reserve account has been canceled under this section shall be considered as first becoming a subject employer on July 1, 1966. *(Added by Stats.1965, c. 1897, p. 4377, § 10.)*

§ 1027.5. Cancellation of net balance of reserve more negative than 21 percent; operation and effect of 1984 amendment by Chapter 1296

On the computation date each year, the amount each employer's net balance of reserve is more negative than 21 percent of the employer's average base payroll shall be canceled from his or her reserve balance.

The amendment made to this section by Chapter 1296 of the Statutes of 1984 shall be deemed to have become operative on June 30, 1984, and the amendment shall be given retroactive effect to that date. *(Added by Stats. 1982, c. 1075, p. 3886, § 12. Amended by Stats.1984, c. 1275, § 14, eff. Sept. 19, 1984; Stats.1984, c. 1296, § 1, eff. Sept. 20, 1984; Stats.1985, c. 448, § 2, eff. July 31, 1985.)*

§ 1027.6. Cancellation of negative reserve balance for 1983

On the computation date of June 30, 1983, the amount each employer's net balance of reserve was more negative than 12 percent of the employer's average base payroll shall be canceled from his or her reserve balance. *(Added by Stats.1984, c. 1296, § 2, eff. Sept. 20, 1984.)*

§ 1028. Payments chargeable to reserve account

The charge of unemployment compensation benefits to an employer's account required by Section 1026 shall be made in such manner as to include as of each computation date all unemployment compensation benefit payments made on or before the computation date. In computing the charge to employers' accounts, a fractional part of a dollar shall be disregarded unless it amounts to one-half dollar ($0.50) or more, in which case it shall be increased to one dollar ($1). *(Stats.1953, c. 308, p. 1487, § 1028. Amended by Stats.1959, c. 1729, p. 4177, § 10.)*

§ 1029. Cancellation of inactive reserve accounts

(a) Whenever an employer ceases to pay wages in employment, the reserve account of the employer, unless it has been transferred under Article 5 (commencing with Section 1051), shall be canceled on the records of the department after a period of three consecutive years has elapsed following the latest calendar quarter in which the employer paid wages in employment.

(b) Whenever a period of three consecutive years has elapsed, commencing with the effective date of an election by any entity to finance benefits pursuant to Section 803, any portion of the reserve account of the entity that has not been subject to use pursuant to Section 712 or 713, unless that portion has been reacquired by the entity by termination of the election under Section 803 prior to the expiration of the three-year period, shall be canceled on the records of the department. Section 982 shall apply to that entity.

(c) Upon the termination of an election by a school employer to finance benefits pursuant to Article 6 (commencing with Section 821) of Chapter 3, any favorable balance in the account of the school employer under the election shall be canceled on the records of the department. *(Stats.1953, c. 308, p. 1487, § 1029. Amended by Stats.1971, c. 1107, p. 2115, § 57, eff. Oct. 18, 1971; Stats.1978, c. 2, p. 40, § 77, eff. Jan. 30, 1978, operative Jan. 1, 1978; Stats.1993, c. 854 (A.B.1585), § 4.)*

§ 1030. Employer's right to notify department of cause of claimant's leaving; determination of cause of leaving; appeals and reconsiderations of department rulings

(a) Any employer who is entitled under Section 1327 to receive notice of the filing of a new or additional claim may, within 10 days after mailing of the notice, submit to the department any facts within its possession disclosing whether the claimant left the employer's employ voluntarily and without good cause or left under one of the following circumstances:

(1) The claimant was discharged from the employment for misconduct connected with his or her work.

(2) The claimant's discharge or quitting from his or her most recent employer was the result of an irresistible compulsion to use or consume intoxicants including alcoholic beverages.

(3) The claimant was a student employed on a temporary basis and whose employment began within, and ended with his or her leaving to return to school at the close of, his or her vacation period.

(4) The claimant left the employer's employ to accompany his or her spouse or domestic partner to or join her or him at a place from which it is impractical to commute to the employment, to which a transfer of the claimant by the employer is not available.

(5) The claimant left the employer's employ to protect his or her children or himself or herself from domestic violence abuse.

The period during which the employer may submit these facts may be extended by the director for good cause.

(b) Any base period employer that is not entitled under Section 1327 to receive notice of the filing of a new or additional claim and is entitled under Section 1329 to receive notice of computation may, within 15 days after mailing of the notice of computation, submit to the department any facts within its possession disclosing whether the claimant left the employer's employ voluntarily and without good cause or left under one of the following circumstances:

(1) The claimant was discharged from the employment for misconduct connected with his or her work.

(2) The claimant was a student employed on a temporary basis and whose employment began within, and ended with his or her leaving to return to school at the close of, his or her vacation period.

(3) The claimant left the employer's employ to accompany his or her spouse or domestic partner to or join her or him at a place from which it is impractical to commute to the employment, to which a transfer of the claimant by the employer is not available.

(4) The claimant left the employer's employ to protect his or her children or himself or herself from domestic violence abuse.

The period during which the employer may submit these facts may be extended by the director for good cause.

(c) The department shall consider these facts together with any information in its possession. If the employer is entitled to a ruling under subdivision (b) or to a determination under Section 1328, the department shall promptly notify the employer of its ruling as to the cause of the termination of the claimant's employment. The

employer may appeal from a ruling or reconsidered ruling to an administrative law judge within 20 days after mailing or personal service of notice of the ruling or reconsidered ruling. The 20–day period may be extended for good cause, which includes, but is not limited to, mistake, inadvertence, surprise, or excusable neglect. The director is an interested party to any appeal. The department may for good cause reconsider any ruling or reconsidered ruling within either five days after the date an appeal to an administrative law judge is filed or, if no appeal is filed, within 20 days after mailing or personal service of notice of the ruling or reconsidered ruling. However, a ruling or reconsidered ruling that relates to a determination that is reconsidered pursuant to subdivision (a) of Section 1332 may also be reconsidered by the department within the time provided for reconsideration of that determination.

(d) For purposes of this section only, if the claimant voluntarily leaves the employer's employ without notification to the employer of the reasons for the leaving, and if the employer submits all of the facts within its possession concerning the leaving within the applicable time period referred to in this section, the leaving is presumed to be without good cause.

(e) An individual whose employment is terminated under the compulsory retirement provisions of a collective bargaining agreement to which the employer is a party shall not be deemed to have voluntarily left his or her employment without good cause. (Stats.1953, c. 308, p. 1487, § 1030. Amended by Stats.1955, c. 1165, p. 2161, § 12; Stats.1957, c. 1109, p. 2412, § 1; Stats.1959, c. 1402, p. 3680, § 1; Stats.1961, c. 2165, p. 4485, § 1; Stats.1961, c. 2166, p. 4487, § 1; Stats.1967, c. 1725, p. 4299, § 7; Stats.1968, c. 280, p. 619, § 2; Stats.1968, c. 1185, p. 2245, § 1; Stats.1973, c. 1212, p. 2775, § 148, operative July 1, 1974; Stats.1975, c. 751, p. 1750, § 1; Stats.1977, c. 508, p. 1636, § 1; Stats.1979, c. 456, p. 1600, § 4; Stats.1979, c. 521, p. 1711, § 2; Stats.1982, c. 1225, p. 4523, § 4; Stats.1984, c. 537, § 11; Stats.1987, c. 1108, § 1; Stats. 1988, c. 781, § 1; Stats.1998, c. 411 (S.B.165), § 2; Stats.2001, c. 893 (A.B.25), § 57.)

§ 1030.1. Conviction of offense; termination of employment; reconsideration of ruling made prior to conviction

(a) If the employment of an individual is terminated due to his absence from work for a period in excess of 24 hours because of his incarceration and he is convicted of the offense for which he was incarcerated or of any lesser included offense, he shall be deemed to have left his work voluntarily without good cause for the purposes of Sections 1030, 3701, and 4701. A plea or verdict of guilty irrespective of whether an order granting probation or other order is made suspending the imposition of the sentence or whether sentence is imposed but execution thereof is suspended, or a conviction following a plea of nolo contendere, is deemed to be a conviction within the meaning of this section.

(b) Notwithstanding any other provision of this division, any ruling made prior to a conviction or other final disposition of the criminal complaint or accusation by the court as to whether an individual who is terminated due to his absence from work because of incarceration voluntarily leaves without good cause may, if no appeal has been taken from the ruling, for good cause be reconsidered by the department during the benefit year or extended duration period or extended benefit period to which the ruling relates. Notice of any reconsidered ruling shall be given to the employer which received notice under Section 1030 or 3701 or 4701, and the employer may appeal therefrom in the manner prescribed in Section 1328 or 3655 or 4655. *(Added by Stats.1968, c. 1105, p. 2116, § 1. Amended by Stats.1975, c. 751, p. 1751, § 2.)*

§ 1031. Ruling under § 1030 not to constitute basis for disqualification of claimant

No ruling made under Section 1030 may constitute a basis for the disqualification of any claimant but a determination by the department made under the provisions of Section 1328 may constitute a ruling under Section 1030. *(Stats.1953, c. 308, p. 1488, § 1031. Amended by Stats.1973, c. 1212, p. 2777, § 152, operative July 1, 1974; Stats.1979, c. 373, p. 1374, § 289.)*

§ 1032. Employer's reserve account not charged; exception

If it is ruled under Section 1030 or 1328 that the claimant left the employer's employ voluntarily and without good cause, or left under one of the following circumstances, benefits paid to the claimant subsequent to the termination of employment that are based upon wages earned from the employer prior to the date of the termination of employment shall not be charged to the account of the employer, except as provided by Section 1026, unless the employer failed to furnish the information specified in Section 1030 within the time limit prescribed in that section or unless that ruling is reversed by a reconsidered ruling:

(a) The claimant was discharged by reason of misconduct connected with his or her work.

(b) The claimant was a student employed on a temporary basis and whose employment began within, and ended with his or her leaving to return to school at the close of, his or her vacation period.

(c) The claimant left the employer's employ to accompany his or her spouse or domestic partner to or join her or him at a place from which it is impractical to commute to the employment, to which a transfer of the claimant by the employer is not available.

(d) The claimant left the employer's employ to protect his or her children or himself or herself from domestic violence abuse.

(e) The claimant left the employer's employ to take a substantially better job.

(f) The claimant's discharge or quitting from his or her most recent employer was the result of an irresistible compulsion to use or consume intoxicants including alcoholic beverages.

For purposes of this section and Section 1030 "spouse" includes a person to whom marriage is imminent. *(Stats. 1953, c. 308, p. 1488, § 1032. Amended by Stats.1954, 1st Ex.Sess., c. 15, p. 262, § 1; Stats.1968, c. 1185, p. 2246, § 2; Stats.1975, c. 751, p. 1751, § 3; Stats.1979, c. 521, p. 1713, § 3; Stats.1983, c. 1169, § 4; Stats.1987, c. 1108, § 2; Stats.1988, c. 781, § 2; Stats.1995, c. 172 (S.B.1157), § 1; Stats.1995, c. 383 (A.B.1821), § 1; Stats.1998, c. 411 (S.B.165), § 3; Stats.2001, c. 893 (A.B.25), § 58.)*

§ 1032.5. Report of part time work; ruling on liability of employer account; appeals and reconsiderations of rulings

(a) Any base period employer may, within 15 days after mailing of a notice of computation under Section 1329, submit to the department facts within its possession disclosing that the individual claiming benefits is rendering services for that employer in less than full-time work, and that the individual has continuously, commencing in or prior to the beginning of the base period, rendered services for that employer in such less than full-time work.

(b) The department shall consider facts submitted under subdivision (a) of this section together with any information in its possession and promptly notify the employer of its ruling. If the department finds that an individual is, under Section 1252, unemployed in any week on the basis of his or her having less than full-time work, and that the employer submitting facts under this section is a base period employer for whom the individual has continuously, commencing in or prior to the beginning of the base period, rendered services in such less than full-time work, that employer's account shall not be charged, except as provided by Section 1026, for benefits paid the individual in any week in which such wages are payable by that employer to the individual. The employer may appeal from a ruling or reconsidered ruling to an administrative law judge within 20 days after mailing or personal service of notice of the ruling or reconsidered ruling. The 20-day period may be extended for good cause, which shall include, but not be limited to, mistake, inadvertence, surprise, or excusable neglect. The director shall be an interested party to any appeal. The department may for good cause reconsider any ruling or reconsidered ruling within either five days after an appeal to an administrative law judge is filed or, if no appeal is filed, within 20 days after mailing or personal service of the notice of the ruling or reconsidered ruling. *(Added by Stats.1963, c. 1640, p. 3228, § 1. Amended by Stats. 1967, c. 1720, p. 4284, § 4; Stats.1973, c. 1212, p. 2778, § 154, operative July 1, 1974; Stats.1977, c. 508, p. 1637, § 2; Stats.1979, c. 1053, p. 3707, § 2; Stats.1983, c. 1169, § 5; Stats.1984, c. 537, § 12.)*

§ 1033. Furnishing statement of reserve account and contribution rate

The director shall not less frequently than once each year furnish each employer with an itemized statement of the charges to the reserve account, and a statement of the reserve account showing the credits and charges, the net balance of the reserve account and the contribution rate for the applicable rating period. *(Stats.1953, c. 308, p. 1488, § 1033. Amended by Stats.1992, c. 446 (S.B.1734), § 4.)*

§ 1034. Protest of charges to reserve account; time for protest; setting forth grounds

(a) The employer, within 60 days after the date of mailing of any statement of charges or credits and charges to the reserve account, or within an additional period not exceeding 60 days which may for good cause be granted by the director, may file with the director a written protest on any item shown thereon. The protest shall set forth the specific grounds on which it is made. No protest may be made on the ground that a claimant was ineligible for a benefit payment where the employer was notified as required by this division and any authorized regulation of the filing of a claim for the benefits or of a determination of the claimant's eligibility therefor and the employer failed to file a timely appeal on the benefit claim, or a final decision of an administrative law judge or of the appeals board affirmed the payment of the benefits. Except as to corrections made by the director as provided in Section 1036, the contribution rate and other items shown on any such statement of charges or statement of account shall be final unless a protest is filed within the time prescribed in this section.

(b) The employer, within 30 days after the last working day of March, may file a protest on the grounds that the director did not allow voluntary unemployment insurance contributions to the reserve account in accordance with Section 976.5. *(Stats.1953, c. 308, p. 1488, § 1034. Amended by Stats.1984, c. 537, § 13; Stats.1992, c. 446 (S.B.1734), § 5.)*

§ 1035. Protest of charges to reserve account; notice of action

The director shall give notice pursuant to Section 1206 to the employer of his or her action on a protest filed under Section 1034. *(Stats.1953, c. 308, p. 1488, § 1035. Amended by Stats.1954, 1st Ex.Sess., c. 44, p. 312, § 2; Stats.1955, c. 1165, p. 2161, § 13; Stats.1965, c. 665, p. 2040, § 1; Stats.1979, c. 1082, p. 3890, § 7.)*

§ 1036. Notice to employer of correction of errors; assessments; refunds

(a) The director shall give notice, pursuant to Section 1206, to the employer of the correction of any error which the director finds in any statement of account or statement of charges. Except in the case where fraud, intent to evade, misrepresentation, or willful nondisclosure is found, the notice of correction shall be issued prior to the expiration of the rating period to which a statement relates.

(b) Any additional amount of contributions resulting from an increased contribution rate caused by the correction of any error that the director finds in any statement of reserve account or statement of charges shall be assessed within 180 days from the postmarked date of the notice of correction. These assessments shall be issued in accordance with Article 8 (commencing with Section 1126). However, these assessments shall become final on the last day of the calendar month following the calendar quarter in which the assessment is issued.

(c) Any overpaid amount of contributions resulting from a reduced rate caused by the correction of an error that the director finds on any statement of reserve account or statement of charges shall be refunded within 180 days of the postmarked date of the notice of correction. These refunds shall be issued in accordance with Article 9 (commencing with Section 1176). *(Stats. 1953, c. 308, p. 1488, § 1036. Amended by Stats.1961, c. 2158, p. 4466, § 3; Stats.1992, c. 125 (A.B.1830), § 6; Stats.2004, c. 827 (A.B.664), § 6.)*

§ 1037. Contribution rate payable while protest pending

If a protest involving the contribution rate is pending when any contribution to which such rate relates is due, the employer shall pay the contribution at the rate shown in the statement furnished by the director. Such a protest, however, shall constitute a claim for refund under Article 9 of this chapter, and if a final determination on the protest reduces the contribution rate the amount of overpayment shall be promptly credited or refunded as provided in that article. *(Stats.1953, c. 308, p. 1489, § 1037.)*

ARTICLE 5.   TRANSFER OF RESERVE ACCOUNTS

Section
1051.   Application for transfer of employer's reserve account; time for application; contents of application.
1051.5. Acquisition by nonprofit organization; transfer of reserve account.
1052.   Transfer of reserve account to successor employer; when section not applicable.
1053.   Application for transfer of reserve account after ninety-day period.
1054.   Reports in lieu of application for transfer of reserve account.
1055.   Ruling on application for transfer of reserve account; notice.
1056.   Prescribing regulations for joint reserve accounts.
1057.   Transfer of joint venture accounts upon dissolution; apportionment of actual contribution and benefit experience.
1058.   Definitions.
1060.   Effective date of change in contribution rate.
1061.   Transfer of business; combination of reserve accounts.

§ 1051. Application for transfer of employer's reserve account; time for application; contents of application

Whenever any employing unit acquires the organization, trade, or business, or substantially all of the assets thereof, or a distinct and severable portion of such organization, trade, or business, of any employer, excepting any assets retained by the employer incident to the liquidation of his obligations (whether or not the acquiring employing unit was an "employing unit" within the meaning of Section 135 prior to such acquisition), and continues such organization, trade, or business, or such distinct and severable portion thereof without substantial reduction of personnel resulting from such acquisition, an application may be made within 90 days of such acquisition for transfer of reserve account. The application shall contain the name and address of the predecessor, the date of acquisition, the name of the successor, the number of employees prior to and subsequent to the date of acquisition, and, in case of severable portions, such pay roll data as may be required by the department to determine the proper amount to be transferred. *(Stats. 1953, c. 308, p. 1489, § 1051.)*

§ 1051.5. Acquisition by nonprofit organization; transfer of reserve account

To the extent permitted by federal law, Sections 1051, 1052, and 1053 are applicable to acquisitions by a nonprofit organization which has elected reimbursement financing pursuant to Section 801 and the director shall transfer the reserve account of the predecessor employer to the successor nonprofit organization. Notwithstanding Section 1029, the reserve account shall not be canceled and the cost of benefits otherwise chargeable to the organization shall be charged to the reserve account until it is exhausted. *(Added by Stats.1984, c. 855, § 3, eff. Sept. 5, 1984.)*

§ 1052. Transfer of reserve account to successor employer; when section not applicable

Upon receipt of the application the separate account, actual contribution and benefit experience and payrolls of the predecessor or that part thereof, as determined by authorized regulations, which pertains to the organization, trade, or business, or portion thereof acquired, shall be transferred to the successor employer for the purpose of determining its rate of contribution after the acquisition with the same effect for that purpose as if the operations of the predecessor had at all times been carried on by the successor. The separate account shall be transferred by the director to the successor employer and, as of the date of the acquisition, shall become the separate account or part of the separate account, as the case may be, of the successor employer, and the benefits thereafter chargeable to the predecessor employer on account of employment relating to the transferred organization, trade, or business or transferred portion thereof prior to the date of the acquisition shall be charged to the separate account. This section shall not apply to any acquisition which is determined by the director to have been made for the purpose of obtaining a more favorable rate of contributions under Section 977. *(Stats.1953, c. 308, p. 1489, § 1052. Amended by Stats.1963, c. 2015, p. 4120, § 11; Stats.1963, c. 2016, p. 4128, § 6; Stats.1965, c. 1897, p. 4377, § 11; Stats.2004, c. 827 (A.B.664), § 7; Stats.2005, c. 22 (S.B.1108), § 193.)*

§ 1053. Application for transfer of reserve account after ninety-day period

Sections 1051 and 1052 are applicable to applications for transfer of reserve accounts made after the 90-day period beginning with the date of acquisition but prior to the cancellation of the reserve account pursuant to Section 1029 if the reserve account has not been reacquired by the predecessor on re-entering business or, in the case of distinct and severable portions, if the predecessor did not continue in business, but any amendment of the contribution rate shall be made as of the first day of the calendar quarter next succeeding the date of the application. *(Stats.1953, c. 308, p. 1490, § 1053.)*

§ 1054. Reports in lieu of application for transfer of reserve account

The provisions of this article requiring a specific application for transfer of reserve account shall not apply to any successor who through error or inadvertence continued to file contribution reports and pay contributions for the account and at the rate determined by the department to apply to the predecessor employer, but such reporting and payment shall be deemed to be in lieu of the application and shall be given the same effect as though a specific application had been filed during the 90-day period beginning with the date of acquisition. *(Stats.1953, c. 308, p. 1490, § 1054.)*

§ 1055. Ruling on application for transfer of reserve account; notice

In the event of a denial or granting of an application for transfer of reserve account, the director shall give notice pursuant to Section 1206 to the employing unit making such application, and to the predecessor employing unit to whose reserve account the application relates, if such predecessor employing unit has continued in business as an employer. *(Stats.1953, c. 308, p. 1490, § 1055. Amended by Stats.1954, 1 Ex.Sess., c. 44, p. 312, § 3; Stats.1955, c. 1165, p. 2161, § 14; Stats.1965, c. 665, p. 2040, § 2; Stats.1979, c. 1082, p. 3890, § 9.)*

§ 1056. Prescribing regulations for joint reserve accounts

The director may prescribe regulations for the establishment, maintenance, and dissolution of joint accounts by two or more employers and shall, in accordance with such regulations, upon application by two or more employers to establish such account or to merge their several individual accounts in a joint account, maintain such joint account, as if it constituted a single employer's account. *(Stats.1953, c. 308, p. 1490, § 1056.)*

§ 1057. Transfer of joint venture accounts upon dissolution; apportionment of actual contribution and benefit experience

Upon dissolution of a joint venture each participating employer may within 90 days apply for the transfer of his proportionate share of the reserve account. Upon receipt of the application the separate account, actual contribution and benefit experience and pay rolls of such joint venture shall be apportioned among the employers making such application in the same proportion that assets are distributed among the participating employers, and the portion thereof of each shall be transferred to each such employer for the purpose of determining its rate of contribution after the dissolution with the same effect for such purpose as if the applicable portion of the operations of such joint venture had at all times been carried on by such employer. Such portion of such separate account shall be transferred by the director to each such employer and as of the date of such dissolution shall become the separate account or part of the separate account, as the case may be, of such employer. The benefits thereafter chargeable to such joint venture on account of employment relating to such joint venture prior to the date of such dissolution shall be charged to the separate accounts of such employers in proportion to their participation in the joint venture. Any such joint venture shall promptly notify the director of its dissolution.

As used in this section only, "employer" includes the successor of an employer and any subsequent successor employer or employers. *(Stats.1953, c. 308, p. 1491, § 1057.)*

§ 1058. Definitions

As used in this article the term "joint venture" means a separate employing unit which has been organized by two or more employers to accomplish a contract or project or series of contracts or projects and which is wholly owned by such employers. As used in this section only, "employer" means any individual or type of organization, including any partnership, joint venture, association, trust, estate, joint stock company, insurance company, corporation whether domestic or foreign, and the receiver, trustee in bankruptcy, trustee or successor thereof, and the legal representative of a deceased person. *(Stats.1953, c. 308, p. 1491, § 1058.)*

§ 1060. Effective date of change in contribution rate

A change in contribution rate caused by a transfer under this article of all or a portion of the separate account, actual contribution and benefit experience and pay rolls shall not become effective earlier than the beginning of the calendar quarter next succeeding the effective date of the transfer. *(Stats.1953, c. 308, p. 1492, § 1060.)*

952

§ 1061. Transfer of business; combination of reserve accounts

(a) For purposes of this article, the reserve account attributable to a transferred business shall also be transferred to, and combined with, the reserve account attributable to the employer to whom that business is transferred, if both of the following are satisfied:

(1) An employer transfers all or part of its business or payroll to another employer.

(2) At the time of transfer, both employers are under common ownership, management, or control.

(b) This section shall be applied to meet the minimum requirements contained in any guidance or regulations issued by the United States Department of Labor. *(Added by Stats.2004, c. 827 (A.B.664), § 8.)*

ARTICLE 6.   RECORDS, REPORTS AND CONTRIBUTION PAYMENTS

Section
1085.   Work records required.
1086.   Registration as employer.
1087.   Board of equalization employees; authority to accept registration; reimbursement of board for additional costs.
1088.   Filing report of contributions and report of wages; annual reconciliation return; exemptions.
1088.5.   Information reported on new employees; contents; failure to report; penalty; use of information.
1088.6.   Worker contributions; excess; written statement furnished by employer.
1088.8.   Service-recipients; contracts with service-providers.
1089.   Information regarding benefits; employer's duty; noncompliance a misdemeanor.
1090.   Required notice by representative of insolvent or deceased employing unit; filing of claim by director.
1092.   Records; statement; inspection and copy; information supplied to claimants.
1093.   Presumption from absence of records; multiple employers, some with and some without records.
1094.   Information obtained in administration of code; limitations on use.
1095.   Use of information; purposes.
1096.   Appointment of agents by employers; agent's authority.
1097.   Manner of crediting employment experience; appointment of separate agents in separate places.
1098.   Agent's status.

§ 1085. Work records required

Every employing unit shall keep a true and accurate work record of:

(a) All his workers and their status, i.e., employed, on layoff or leave of absence.

(b) The wages paid by him to each worker.

(c) Such other information as the director deems necessary to proper administration of this division. *(Stats.1953, c. 308, p. 1492, § 1085. Amended by Stats.*

1961, c. 2163, p. 4480, § 1; Stats.1977, c. 1142, p. 3670, § 6; Stats.1986, c. 248, § 230.)

§ 1086. Registration as employer

(a) Each employing unit within 15 days after becoming an employer as defined in this part shall register with the department on a form prescribed by the department.

(b)(1) Notwithstanding subdivision (a), any Indian tribe (as described by subsection (u) of Section 3306 of Title 26 of the United States Code) that employed one or more workers on or after December 21, 2000, and prior to the operative date of the statute adding this subdivision at the 2001 portion of the 2001–02 Regular Session of the Legislature that has not registered with the department by the operative date of the statute, shall register with the department within 15 days of that operative date.

(2) The subject date for employers who register with the department under the provisions of paragraph (1) shall be December 21, 2000, or the date that employer first hired an employee, whichever is later. *(Stats.1953, c. 308, p. 1492, § 1086. Amended by Stats.2001, c. 255 (A.B.1537), § 11.)*

Operative Effect

Under the terms of Section 17 of Stats.2001, c. 255 (A.B.1537), the provisions of that Act are retroactive to December 21, 2000.

§ 1087. Board of equalization employees; authority to accept registration; reimbursement of board for additional costs

Any officer or employee of the Sales and Use Tax Division of the Board of Equalization who is authorized to accept an application for a seller's permit under Section 6066 of the Revenue and Taxation Code or authorized to register a retailer under Section 6226 of the Revenue and Taxation Code is a duly authorized agent of the Employment Development Department for purposes of accepting registration of employers as required in this part.

The department shall reimburse the Board of Equalization for any additional costs incurred by reason of services by any of its officers or employees to the department pursuant to this section. *(Stats.1953, c. 308, p. 1492, § 1087. Amended by Stats.1955, c. 1165, p. 2162, § 15; Stats.1970, c. 350, p. 758, § 7; Stats.1973, c. 1206, p. 2619, § 56; Stats.1973, c. 1207, p. 2669, § 56; Stats.1973, c. 1212, p. 2778, § 155, operative July 1, 1974; Stats.1977, c. 1252, p. 4456, § 405, operative July 1, 1978; Stats.2002, c. 29 (A.B.1729), § 10.)*

§ 1088. Filing report of contributions and report of wages; annual reconciliation return; exemptions

(a)(1) Each employer shall file with the director within the time required by subdivision (a) or (d) of Section 1110 for payment of employer contributions, a report of contributions and a report of wages paid to his or her workers in the form and containing any information as the director prescribes. An electronic funds transfer of contributions pursuant to subdivision (f) of Section 1110 shall satisfy the requirement for a report of contributions. The report of wages shall include individual amounts required to be withheld under Section 13020 or withheld under Section 13028.

(2)(A) In order to enhance efforts to reduce tax fraud and to reduce the personal income tax reporting burden, effective January 1, 1997, the report of wages shall also include the full first name of the employee and total wages, as defined in Section 13009, paid to each employee. This paragraph shall apply to reports of wages for all periods ending on or before December 31, 1999.

(B) For all periods beginning on or after January 1, 2000, the report of wages shall also include total wages subject to personal income tax, as defined in Section 13009.5, paid to each employee.

(b) Each employer shall file with the director within the time required by subdivision (b) or (d) of Section 1110 for payment of worker contributions, a report of contributions containing the employer's business name, address, and account number, the total amount of worker contributions due, and any other information as the director shall prescribe. The director shall prescribe the form for the report of contributions. An electronic funds transfer of contributions pursuant to subdivision (f) of Section 1110 shall satisfy the requirement for a report of contributions.

(c) In addition to the report of contributions and report of wages required by employers under subdivision (a), an individual who has elected coverage under subdivision (a) of Section 708 is also required to file a separate report of contributions, subject to Part 2 (commencing with Section 2601).

(d) Any employer making an election under subdivision (d) of Section 1110 shall submit the report of wages described in subdivision (a), within the time required for submitting employer contributions under subdivision (a) of Section 1110.

(e) In addition to the report of contributions and report of wages described in subdivision (a), each employer shall file with the director an annual reconciliation return showing the total amount of wages, employer contributions required under Sections 976 and 976.6, worker contributions required under Section 984, the amounts required to be withheld under Section 13020 or withheld under Section 13028, and any other information as the director shall prescribe. This annual reconciliation return shall be due on the first day of January following the close of the prior calendar year and shall become delinquent if not filed on or before the last day of that month.

This subdivision shall not apply to individuals electing coverage under Section 708 or 708.5 or employers electing financing under Section 821.

(f) For purposes of making a report of wages under subdivision (a), employers who are required under Sec-

UNEMPLOYMENT INSURANCE CODE

tion 6011 of the Internal Revenue Code and authorized regulations thereunder to file magnetic media returns, shall, within 90 days of becoming subject to this requirement, do one of the following:

(1) Submit a magnetic media format to the department for approval, and upon receiving approval from the department, submit any subsequent reports of wages on magnetic media.

(2) Establish to the satisfaction of the director that there is a lack of automation, a severe economic hardship, a current exemption from submitting magnetic media information returns for federal purposes, or other good cause for not complying with the provisions of this subdivision. Approved waivers shall be valid for six months or longer, at the discretion of the director.

(g) The Franchise Tax Board shall be allowed access to the information filed with the department pursuant to this section.

(h) If an employer demonstrates that an undue hardship would be imposed, the director may authorize an exemption from the requirement in subdivision (a) to report individual amounts withheld under Section 13020 and the requirement in subdivision (e) to file the annual reconciliation return for the 1995 calendar year only. Any request for exemption must be filed on or before January 15, 1995. Upon approval of a request for exemption under this subdivision, the employer shall file quarterly returns and reports of wages in the manner and method prescribed by the director for the 1995 calendar year only. *(Stats.1953, c. 308, p. 1492, § 1088. Amended by Stats.1965, c. 745, p. 2153, § 2, eff. June 24, 1965; Stats.1979, c. 1053, p. 3708, § 3, operative Jan. 1, 1980; Stats.1981–82, 1st Ex.Sess., c. 2, p. 621, § 1, operative May 1, 1982; Stats.1989, c. 1146, § 7; Stats.1993, c. 747 (A.B.1738), § 8; Stats.1994, c. 1049 (A.B.3086), § 3; Stats.1999, c. 144 (A.B.1634), § 1.)*

§ 1088.5. Information reported on new employees; contents; failure to report; penalty; use of information

(a) In addition to information reported in accordance with Section 1088, effective July 1, 1998, each employer shall file, with the department, the information provided for in subdivision (b) on new employees.

(b) Each employer shall report the hiring of any employee who works in this state and to whom the employer anticipates paying wages.

(c)(1) This section shall not apply to any department, agency, or instrumentality of the United States.

(2) State agency employers shall not be required to report employees performing intelligence or counterintelligence functions, if the head of the agency has determined that reporting pursuant to this section would endanger the safety of the employee or compromise an ongoing investigation or intelligence mission.

(d)(1) Employers shall submit a report as described in paragraph (4) within 20 days of hiring any employee

954

whom the employer is required to report pursuant to this section.

(2) Notwithstanding subdivision (a), employers transmitting reports magnetically or electronically shall submit the report by two monthly transmissions not less than 12 days no more than 16 days apart.

(3) For purposes of this section, an employer that has employees in two or more states and that transmits reports magnetically or electronically may designate one state in which the employer has employees to which the employer will transmit the report described in paragraph (4). Any employer that transmits reports pursuant to this paragraph shall notify the Secretary of Health and Human Services in writing as to which state the employer designates for the purpose of sending reports.

(4) The report shall contain the following:

(A) The name, address, and social security number of the employees.

(B) The employer's name, address, state employer identification number (if one has been issued), and identifying number assigned to the employer under Section 6109 of the Internal Revenue Code of 1986.

(C) The first date the employee worked.

(5) Employers may report pursuant to this section by submitting a copy of the employee's W–4 form, a form provided by the department, or any other hiring document transmitted by first-class mail, magnetically, or electronically.

(e) For each failure to report the hiring of an employee, as required and within the time required by this section, unless the failure is due to good cause, the department may assess a penalty of twenty-four dollars ($24), or four hundred ninety dollars ($490) if the failure is the result of conspiracy between the employer and employee not to supply the required report or to supply a false or incomplete report.

(f) Information collected pursuant to this section may be used for the following purposes:

(1) Administration of this code.

(2) Locating individuals for purposes of establishing paternity and establishing, modifying, and enforcing child support obligations.

(3) Administration of employment security and workers' compensation programs.

(4) Providing employer or employee information to the Franchise Tax Board for the purpose of tax enforcement.

(5) Verification of eligibility of applicants for, or recipients of, the public assistance programs listed in Section 1320b–7(b) of Title 42 of the United States Code.

(g) For purposes of this section, "employer" includes a labor union hiring hall.

(h) This section shall become operative on July 1, 1998. *(Added by Stats.1997, c. 606 (A.B.67), § 14, eff.*

Oct. 3, 1997, operative July 1, 1998. Amended by Stats. 1998, c. 858 (A.B.2169), § 8.)

§ 1088.6. Worker contributions; excess; written statement furnished by employer

Each employer, pursuant to authorized regulations, shall furnish a written statement to the worker showing the excess of the worker contributions required with respect to wages included in Section 927 and subdivision (n) of Section 13009 over the worker contributions withheld pursuant to Sections 984 and 13020, and shall file a copy of this statement with the director. If the employer fails to furnish the statement, as required by this section and authorized regulations, he or she shall be liable for the excess of the worker contributions. *(Added by Stats.1993, c. 402 (A.B.1668), § 2.)*

§ 1088.8. Service-recipients; contracts with service-providers

(a) Effective January 1, 2001, any service-recipient, as defined in subdivision (b), who makes or is required to make a return to the Internal Revenue Service, in accordance with subdivision (a) of Section 6041A of the Internal Revenue Code (relating to payments made to a service-provider as compensation for services) shall file with the department information as required under subdivision (c).

(b) For purposes of this section:

(1) "Service–recipient" means any individual, person, corporation, association, or partnership, or agent thereof, doing business in this state, deriving trade or business income from sources within this state, or in any manner in the course of a trade or business subject to the laws of this state. "Service-recipient" also includes the State of California or any political subdivision thereof, including the Regents of the University of California, any charter city, or any political body not a subdivision or agency of the state, and any person, employee, department, or agent thereof.

(2) "Service–provider" means an individual who is not an employee of the service-recipient for California purposes and who received compensation or executes a contract for services performed for that service-recipient within or without the state.

(c) Each service-recipient shall report all of the following information to the department, within 20 days of the earlier of first making payments that in the aggregate equal or exceed six hundred dollars ($600) in any year to a service-provider, or entering into a contract or contracts with a service-provider providing for payments that in the aggregate equal or exceed six hundred dollars ($600) in any year:

(1) The full name, address, and social security number of the service-provider.

(2) The service-recipient's name, business name, address, and telephone number.

(3) The service-recipient's federal employer identification number, California state employer account number, social security number, or other identifying number as required by the Employment Development Department in consultation with the Franchise Tax Board.

(4) The date the contract is executed, or if no contract, the date payments in the aggregate first equal or exceed six hundred dollars ($600).

(5) The total dollar amount of the contract, if any, and the contract expiration date.

(d) The department shall retain information collected pursuant to this section until November 1 following the tax year in which the contract is executed, or if no contract, the tax year in which the aggregate payments first equal or exceed six hundred dollars ($600).

(e) For each failure to fully comply with subdivision (c), unless the failure is due to good cause, the department may assess a penalty of twenty-four dollars ($24), or four hundred ninety dollars ($490) if the failure is the result of conspiracy between the service recipient and service provider not to supply the required report or to supply a false or incomplete report.

(f) Information obtained by the department pursuant to this section may be released only for purposes of establishing, modifying, or enforcing child support obligations under Section 17400 of the Family Code and for child support collection purposes authorized under Article 5 (commencing with Section 19271) of Chapter 5 of Part 10.2 of the Revenue and Taxation Code, or to the Franchise Tax Board for tax enforcement purposes or for the administration of this code.

(g) This section shall become operative on January 1, 2001. *(Added by Stats.1999, c. 478 (A.B.196), § 7, operative July 1, 2000. Amended by Stats.1999, c. 480 (S.B.542), § 28, operative Jan. 1, 2001; Stats.2000, c. 808 (A.B.1358), § 115, eff. Sept. 28, 2000, operative Jun. 1, 2001.)*

§ 1089. Information regarding benefits; employer's duty; noncompliance a misdemeanor

Each employer shall post and maintain in places readily accessible to individuals in his service such printed statements concerning benefit rights and other matters as may be prescribed by authorized regulations. Each employer shall, pursuant to authorized regulations, supply each individual at the time he becomes unemployed with copies of printed statements or materials relating to claims for benefits. Each employer shall immediately notify each employee of any change in his relationship with said employer. Failure to comply with this section by an employer shall constitute a misdemeanor. Such printed statements shall be supplied by the director to each employer without cost to him. *(Stats.1953, c. 308, p. 1492, § 1089. Amended by Stats.1961, c. 2162, p. 4480, § 1; Stats.1961, c. 2163, p. 4481, § 2; Stats.1961, c. 2164, p. 4483, § 8.)*

§ 1090. Required notice by representative of insolvent or deceased employing unit; filing of claim by director

(a) Every assignee, receiver, trustee in bankruptcy, or other representative of an insolvent employing unit, and every administrator or executor of the estate of a deceased employing unit, shall within 30 days after assuming office send notice in writing of the name and address of the employing unit, his own name and address, and such other information as may be required by the director.

(b) Within four months after the mailing of the notice required of every administrator or executor of the estate of a deceased employing unit under subdivision (a), the director shall file or present his claim for contributions, penalty, and interest based upon wages paid by the employing unit during his lifetime. The administrator or executor of the estate of a deceased employing unit shall succeed to all the rights and obligations of the deceased employing unit under this division. *(Stats.1953, c. 308, p. 1492, § 1090. Amended by Stats.1968, c. 1299, p. 2450, § 8.)*

§ 1092. Records; statement; inspection and copy; information supplied to claimants

Every employing unit shall furnish to the director, administrative law judge, or deputy, upon demand, a sworn statement of the matters contained in the records required by Section 1085. If such records are kept pursuant to contract with a financial institution as defined in Section 7465 of the Government Code, the employing unit shall also furnish to the director or the director's authorized representative an authorization for disclosure of such account or accounts. The authorization for disclosure shall be that provided for in Section 7473 of the Government Code. Such records shall be open to inspection and shall be subject to being copied by the director or his authorized representative at any time during the business hours of the employing unit. Any claimant or his authorized representative at a hearing before a deputy or administrative law judge or the appeals board shall be supplied with information from such records to the extent necessary for the proper presentation of his claim. *(Stats.1953, c. 308, p. 1493, § 1092. Amended by Stats.1979, c. 1021, p. 3490, § 3; Stats.1984, c. 537, § 14.)*

§ 1093. Presumption from absence of records; multiple employers, some with and some without records

In the event any employer shall fail to keep and furnish to the director, upon notice, any required records or reports necessary for a full determination, decision on appeal, or other proper disposition of any claim for benefits in any proceeding under this division, within such reasonable time as the director may by rule, regulation, or procedure prescribe, it shall be conclusively presumed that the claimant is entitled to the maximum total amount of benefits payable under this division unless it is established by other evidence which the director deems

956

sufficient that a lesser total amount of benefits is properly due and owing to the claimant. If so established by other evidence upon default of the employer, after notice, such lesser total amount of benefits thus determined shall be conclusive. In all cases in which such presumptions shall apply, if the claimant has earned wages in employment for more than one employer during his base period, the accounts of the employer or employers who have properly kept and furnished the required records or reports shall not be charged with benefits in an amount exceeding that which such accounts would have been charged had the claimant been entitled only to benefits determined by the total of the wages earned and the number of calendar quarters worked for them and all benefits paid in excess thereof shall be charged solely against the accounts of the employer or employers who have failed to keep or furnish the required records or reports. *(Stats.1953, c. 308, p. 1493, § 1093.)*

§ 1094. Information obtained in administration of code; limitations on use

(a) Except as otherwise specifically provided in this code, the information obtained in the administration of this code is confidential, not open to the public, and shall be for the exclusive use and information of the director in discharge of his or her duties.

(b) The information released to authorized entities pursuant to other provisions of the code shall not be admissible in evidence in any action or special proceeding, other than one arising out of the provisions of this code or one described in Section 1095.

(c) The information may be tabulated and published in statistical form for use by federal, state, and local governmental departments and agencies, and the public, except that the name of the employing unit or of any worker shall never be divulged in the course of the tabulation or publication.

(d) Wages as defined by Section 13009 and amounts required to be deducted and withheld under Section 13020 shall not be disclosed except as provided in Article 2 (commencing with Section 19542) of Chapter 7 of Part 10.2 of Division 2 of the Revenue and Taxation Code.

(e) Any employee or his or her representative may receive his or her wage information upon written request by the employee. The information shall be provided without charge.

(f) Any person who knowingly accesses, uses, or discloses any confidential information without authorization is in violation of this section and is guilty of a misdemeanor. *(Stats.1953, c. 308, p. 1493, § 1094. Amended by Stats.1971, c. 578, p. 1140, § 12, eff. Aug. 13, 1971, operative Oct. 1, 1971; Stats.1974, c. 1159, p. 2471, § 27, eff. Sept. 23, 1974; Stats.1979, c. 373, p. 1374, § 290; Stats.1979, c. 288, p. 1069, § 1; Stats.1982, c. 1080, p. 3908, § 1; Stats.1984, c. 1127, § 4; Stats.1985, c. 543, § 3; Stats.1987, c. 855, § 2; Stats.1998, c. 217 (A.B.2017), § 1; Stats.1998, c. 766 (A.B.604), § 2.)*

§ 1095. Use of information; purposes

The director shall permit the use of any information in his or her possession to the extent necessary for any of the following purposes and may require reimbursement for all direct costs incurred in providing any and all information specified in this section, except information specified in subdivisions (a) to (e), inclusive:

(a) To enable the director or his or her representative to carry out his or her responsibilities under this code.

(b) To properly present a claim for benefits.

(c) To acquaint a worker or his or her authorized agent with his or her existing or prospective right to benefits.

(d) To furnish an employer or his or her authorized agent with information to enable him or her to fully discharge his or her obligations or safeguard his or her rights under this division or Division 3 (commencing with Section 9000).

(e) To enable an employer to receive a reduction in contribution rate.

(f) To enable federal, state, or local government departments or agencies, subject to federal law, to verify or determine the eligibility or entitlement of an applicant for, or a recipient of, public social services provided pursuant to Division 9 (commencing with Section 10000) of the Welfare and Institutions Code, or Part A of Title IV of the Social Security Act, where the verification or determination is directly connected with, and limited to, the administration of public social services.

(g) To enable county administrators of general relief or assistance, or their representatives, to determine entitlement to locally provided general relief or assistance, where the determination is directly connected with, and limited to, the administration of general relief or assistance.

(h) To enable state or local governmental departments or agencies to seek criminal, civil, or administrative remedies in connection with the unlawful application for, or receipt of, relief provided under Division 9 (commencing with Section 10000) of the Welfare and Institutions Code or to enable the collection of expenditures for medical assistance services pursuant to Part 5 (commencing with Section 17000) of Division 9 of the Welfare and Institutions Code.

(i) To provide any law enforcement agency with the name, address, telephone number, birth date, social security number, physical description, and names and addresses of present and past employers, of any victim, suspect, missing person, potential witness, or person for whom a felony arrest warrant has been issued, when a request for this information is made by any investigator or peace officer as defined by Sections 830.1 and 830.2 of the Penal Code, or by any federal law enforcement officer to whom the Attorney General has delegated authority to enforce federal search warrants, as defined under Sections 60.2 and 60.3 of Title 28 of the Code of Federal Regulations, as amended, and when the requesting officer has been designated by the head of the law enforcement agency and requests this information in the course of and as a part of an investigation into the commission of a crime when there is a reasonable suspicion that the crime is a felony and that the information would lead to relevant evidence. The information provided pursuant to this subdivision shall be provided to the extent permitted by federal law and regulations, and to the extent the information is available and accessible within the constraints and configurations of existing department records. Any person who receives any information under this subdivision shall make a written report of the information to the law enforcement agency that employs him or her, for filing under the normal procedures of that agency.

(1) This subdivision shall not be construed to authorize the release to any law enforcement agency of a general list identifying individuals applying for or receiving benefits.

(2) The department shall maintain records pursuant to this subdivision only for periods required under regulations or statutes enacted for the administration of its programs.

(3) This subdivision shall not be construed as limiting the information provided to law enforcement agencies to that pertaining only to applicants for, or recipients of, benefits.

(4) The department shall notify all applicants for benefits that release of confidential information from their records will not be protected should there be a felony arrest warrant issued against the applicant or in the event of an investigation by a law enforcement agency into the commission of a felony.

(j) To provide public employee retirement systems in California with information relating to the earnings of any person who has applied for or is receiving a disability income, disability allowance, or disability retirement allowance, from a public employee retirement system. The earnings information shall be released only upon written request from the governing board specifying that the person has applied for or is receiving a disability allowance or disability retirement allowance from its retirement system. The request may be made by the chief executive officer of the system or by an employee of the system so authorized and identified by name and title by the chief executive officer in writing.

(k) To enable the Division of Labor Standards Enforcement in the Department of Industrial Relations to seek criminal, civil, or administrative remedies in connection with the failure to pay, or the unlawful payment of, wages pursuant to Chapter 1 (commencing with Section 200) of Part 1 of Division 2 of, and Chapter 1 (commencing with Section 1720) of Part 7 of Division 2 of, the Labor Code.

(*l*) To enable federal, state, or local governmental departments or agencies to administer child support enforcement programs under Title IV of the Social Security Act (42 U.S.C. Sec. 651 et seq.).

(m) To provide federal, state, or local governmental departments or agencies with wage and claim information in its possession that will assist those departments and agencies in the administration of the Victims of Crime Program or in the location of victims of crime who, by state mandate or court order, are entitled to restitution that has been or can be recovered.

(n) To provide federal, state, or local governmental departments or agencies with information concerning any individuals who are or have been:

(1) Directed by state mandate or court order to pay restitution, fines, penalties, assessments, or fees as a result of a violation of law.

(2) Delinquent or in default on guaranteed student loans or who owe repayment of funds received through other financial assistance programs administered by those agencies. The information released by the director for the purposes of this paragraph shall not include unemployment insurance benefit information.

(o) To provide an authorized governmental agency with any or all relevant information that relates to any specific workers' compensation insurance fraud investigation. The information shall be provided to the extent permitted by federal law and regulations. For the purposes of this subdivision, "authorized governmental agency" means the district attorney of any county, the office of the Attorney General, the Department of Industrial Relations, and the Department of Insurance. An authorized governmental agency may disclose this information to the State Bar, the Medical Board of California, or any other licensing board or department whose licensee is the subject of a workers' compensation insurance fraud investigation. This subdivision shall not prevent any authorized governmental agency from reporting to any board or department the suspected misconduct of any licensee of that body.

(p) To enable the Director of the Bureau for Private Postsecondary and Vocational Education, or his or her representatives, to access unemployment insurance quarterly wage data on a case-by-case basis to verify information on school administrators, school staff, and students provided by those schools who are being investigated for possible violations of Chapter 7 (commencing with Section 94700) of Part 59 of the Education Code.

(q) To provide employment tax information to the tax officials of Mexico, if a reciprocal agreement exists. For purposes of this subdivision, "reciprocal agreement" means a formal agreement to exchange information between national taxing officials of Mexico and taxing authorities of the State Board of Equalization, the Franchise Tax Board, and the Employment Development Department. Furthermore, the reciprocal agreement shall be limited to the exchange of information that is essential for tax administration purposes only. Taxing authorities of the State of California shall be granted tax information only on California residents. Taxing authorities of Mexico shall be granted tax information only on Mexican nationals.

(r) To enable city and county planning agencies to develop economic forecasts for planning purposes. The information shall be limited to businesses within the jurisdiction of the city or county whose planning agency is requesting the information, and shall not include information regarding individual employees.

(s) To provide the State Department of Developmental Services with wage and employer information that will assist in the collection of moneys owed by the recipient, parent, or any other legally liable individual for services and supports provided pursuant to Chapter 9 (commencing with Section 4775) of Division 4.5 of, and Chapter 2 (commencing with Section 7200) and Chapter 3 (commencing with Section 7500) of Division 7 of, the Welfare and Institutions Code.

(t) Nothing in this section shall be construed to authorize or permit the use of information obtained in the administration of this code by any private collection agency.

(u) The disclosure of the name and address of an individual or business entity that was issued an assessment that included penalties under Section 1128 or 1128.1 shall not be in violation of Section 1094 if the assessment is final. The disclosure may also include any of the following:

(1) The total amount of the assessment.

(2) The amount of the penalty imposed under Section 1128 or 1128.1 that is included in the assessment.

(3) The facts that resulted in the charging of the penalty under Section 1128 or 1128.1.

(v) To enable the Contractors' State License Board to verify the employment history of an individual applying for licensure pursuant to Section 7068 of the Business and Professions Code.

(w) To provide any peace officer with the Division of Investigation in the Department of Consumer Affairs information pursuant to subdivision (i) when the requesting peace officer has been designated by the Chief of the Division of Investigation and requests this information in the course of and as part of an investigation into the commission of a crime or other unlawful act when there is reasonable suspicion to believe that the crime or act may be connected to the information requested and would lead to relevant information regarding the crime or unlawful act.

(x) To enable the Labor Commissioner of the Division of Labor Standards Enforcement in the Department of Industrial Relations to identify, pursuant to Section 90.3 of the Labor Code, unlawfully uninsured employers. The information shall be provided to the extent permitted by federal law and regulations.

(y) To enable the Chancellor of the California Community Colleges, in accordance with the requirements of

Section 84754.5 of the Education Code, to obtain quarterly wage data, commencing January 1, 1993, on students who have attended one or more community colleges, to assess the impact of education on the employment and earnings of students, to conduct the annual evaluation of district-level and individual college performance in achieving priority educational outcomes, and to submit the required reports to the Legislature and the Governor. The information shall be provided to the extent permitted by federal statutes and regulations.

(z) To enable the Public Employees' Retirement System to seek criminal, civil, or administrative remedies in connection with the unlawful application for, or receipt of, benefits provided under Part 3 (commencing with Section 20000) of Division 5 of Title 2 of the Government Code. *(Stats.1953, c. 308, p. 1494, § 1095. Amended by Stats.1971, c. 578, p. 1140, § 13, eff. Aug. 13, 1971, operative Oct. 1, 1971; Stats.1973, c. 1206, p. 2619, § 57; Stats.1973, c. 1207, p. 2669, § 57; Stats.1973, c. 1212, p. 2779, § 157, operative July 1, 1974; Stats.1977, c. 1252, p. 4457, § 406, operative July 1, 1978; Stats.1979, c. 288, p. 1070, § 2; Stats.1982, c. 1080, p. 3908, § 2; Stats.1983, c. 175, § 1, eff. July 11, 1983; Stats.1984, c. 1127, § 5; Stats.1985, c. 543, § 4; Stats.1986, c. 331, § 1; Stats.1987, c. 855 § 3; Stats.1990, c. 1024 (A.B.3092), § 1; Stats. 1990, c. 1084 (S.B.2053), § 2; Stats.1991, c. 659 (A.B. 1137), § 6; Stats.1992, c. 1352 (A.B.3660), § 9, eff. Sept. 30, 1992; Stats.1993, c. 295 (S.B.774), § 8; Stats.1993, c. 891 (A.B.1881), § 3; Stats.1993, c. 1144 (S.B.857), § 19; Stats.1994, c. 146 (A.B.3601), § 216; Stats.1994, c. 1049 (A.B.3086), § 4; Stats.1995, c. 313 (A.B.817), § 16, eff. Aug. 3, 1995; Stats.1995, c. 701 (S.B.488), § 1; Stats.1996, c. 1124 (S.B.1524), § 1, eff. Sept. 30, 1996; Stats.1997, c. 78 (A.B.71), § 4; Stats.1997, c. 810 (S.B.132), § 1.4; Stats.1998, c. 217 (A.B.2017), § 2; Stats.1999, c. 83 (S.B.966), § 185; Stats.2002, c. 744 (S.B.1953), § 11; Stats.2003, c. 789 (S.B.364), § 26; Stats.2007, c. 272 (A.B.798), § 1; Stats.2007, c. 662 (S.B.869), § 3.5; Stats. 2008, c. 369 (A.B.1844), § 8.)*

§ 1096. Appointment of agents by employers; agent's authority

Where a number of workers are normally employed in employment in the course of a year by several employers, such employers, with the approval of the director, may appoint an agent. The agent may maintain records and prepare and file returns and reports required under this division with respect to such workers, including returns and reports of wages paid to the workers, and may pay the employers' and workers' contributions levied under this division with respect to wages paid to such workers and perform such other acts on behalf of such employers as the director may authorize all in the same manner as though the agent were the employer of the workers. *(Stats.1953, c. 308, p. 1494, § 1096.)*

§ 1097. Manner of crediting employment experience; appointment of separate agents in separate places

The manner of crediting to each employer the employment experience of the group of employers who have appointed an agent pursuant to Section 1096, for the purpose of any classification of employers made pursuant to this division for the determinations of future rates of employers' contributions, may be prescribed by authorized regulations. Employers who operate or do business in more than one place may, with the approval of the director, appoint a separate agent in each such place. *(Stats.1953, c. 308, p. 1494, § 1097.)*

§ 1098. Agent's status

Nothing contained in Sections 1096 or 1097 shall be construed to make the agent the employer of the workers, or relieve any employer of his obligations to comply with this division, except to the extent that his obligations are discharged by the agent. *(Stats.1953, c. 308, p. 1494, § 1098.)*

ARTICLE 7. PAYMENT OF REPORTED CONTRIBUTIONS

Section
1110. Due and delinquent date of contributions.
1110.1. Allocation of payments.
1110.6. Agreement by employer to assume liability for contributions on default by any other employer affected by contract; delinquent date.
1111. Extension of time for payment or making return or report; interest.
1111.5. Extension of time for filing and payment; declaration of state of emergency.
1112. Penalty for failure to pay; amount.
1112.5. Failure to file reports; penalty.
1113. Interest for failure to pay; amount.
1113.1. Erroneous underpayment; liability for penalty or interest.
1114. Penalty for unreported wage items; amount.
1115. Collection in jeopardy; procedure.
1116. Returns on quitting business or on commencement of proceedings to wind up and dissolve.
1117. Failure to file annual reconciliation return; penalty.
1118. Employers of domestic servants; telephonic reporting of wages.
1119. Notice to Internal Revenue Service and Department of Labor of delinquent payments by Indian tribe.

§ 1110. Due and delinquent date of contributions

(a) Employer contributions required under Sections 976 and 976.6, the amount of benefits received by any individual pursuant to this part that is deducted from an award or settlement made by the employer under the provisions of Section 1382, and, except as provided by subdivision (b) of this section, worker contributions required under Section 984 are due and payable on the first day of the calendar month following the close of each calendar quarter and shall become delinquent if not paid on or before the last day of that month.

(b) Worker contributions required under Section 984 are due and payable at the same time and by the same method as amounts required to be withheld under Section 13020 are paid to the department pursuant to

Section 13021, regardless of the amount of accumulated unpaid liability for worker contributions.

(c) Employer contributions submitted pursuant to Section 976.5 shall be paid on or before the last working day of March of the calendar year to which the reduced contribution rate would be applicable. Any employer whose eligibility for an unemployment insurance contribution rate determination is redetermined to make that employer eligible to submit voluntary unemployment insurance contributions in accordance with Section 976.5, may submit a voluntary unemployment insurance contribution within 30 days of the date of notification of the redetermination.

(d) Except as provided in subdivision (e), any employer described in Sections 682 and 684 may elect to report and pay employer contributions required under Sections 976 and 976.6, and worker contributions required under Section 984, annually. All contributions are due and payable on the first day of January following the close of the prior calendar year and shall become delinquent if not paid on or before the last day of that month. An election under this subdivision shall be effective the first day of the calendar year in which it is approved by the department. An election under this subdivision may not be approved if the employer has an outstanding return or report delinquency on the records of the department, or an unpaid amount owed to the department, that is not the subject of a timely petition for reassessment pending before the appeals board at the time the election is filed.

(e) Any employer described in Sections 682 and 684 who pays more than twenty thousand dollars ($20,000) in wages annually, shall not be entitled to the election allowed in subdivision (d). If at any time during the year the total wages paid by an employer electing to file under subdivision (d) exceeds twenty thousand dollars ($20,000), the election shall be terminated at the close of that calendar quarter. In addition to the report of wages due for that quarter, the employer shall file a return and pay any contributions due for that portion of the year during which the election was in effect, and shall pay contributions in accordance with subdivisions (a), (b), and (c) for the remainder of that year.

(f) Contributions due pursuant to this section may be submitted by electronic funds transfer, as defined in Section 13021.5. Contributions submitted by electronic funds transfer shall be deemed complete in accordance with paragraph (4) of subdivision (e) of Section 13021. *(Stats.1953, c. 308, p. 1494, § 1110. Amended by Stats. 1965, c. 745, p. 2154, § 3, eff. June 24, 1965; Stats.1971, Ex.Sess., c. 1, p. 5126, § 307, eff. Dec. 8, 1971, operative Jan. 1, 1972; Stats.1980, c. 29, p. 87, § 2; Stats.1980, c. 1007, p. 3227, § 59, operative July 1, 1981; Stats.1981–82, 1st Ex.Sess., c. 2, p. 621, § 2, operative May 1, 1982; Stats.1983, c. 1035, § 1; Stats.1983, c. 1169, § 6; Stats. 1984, c. 41, § 1, eff. March 19, 1984; Stats.1989, c. 1146, § 8; Stats.1991, c. 473 (S.B.467), § 8; Stats.1992, c. 446 (S.B.1734), § 6; Stats.1993, c. 747 (A.B.1738), § 8.7;*

Stats.1994, c. 1049 (A.B.3086), § 5; Stats.1998, c. 217 (A.B.2017), § 4; Stats.2001, c. 159 (S.B.662), § 187.)

§ 1110.1. Allocation of payments

(a) Notwithstanding any other provision of law, the director shall allocate any payment to the department relating to liability for contributions, withheld personal income tax, penalty and interest, in accordance with any designation made by the payer at or before the time the payment is made to the department.

(b) Notwithstanding any other provision of law, if a payer, at or before the time a payment is made to the department, does not designate an obligation to which the payment is to be applied, the director shall allocate the payment in the following order of priority:

(1) Employer contributions required under Sections 976 and 976.6, worker contributions, and withheld personal income tax, in proportion to the aggregate amount of such employer contributions, worker contributions, and withheld personal income tax due.

(2) Penalties and interest due under this division, and penalties and interest due based upon withheld personal income tax.

(c) The director may apply the following standards in making any allocation under this section:

(1) First priority may be given to the extinction of obligations due at the time of payment with respect to which a lien has not been recorded, in the order inverse to that in which the obligation became due.

(2) Second priority may be given to the extinction of obligations due at the time of payment with respect to which a lien has been recorded. If more than one lien has been recorded, the obligations covered by the most recent lien recorded may be extinguished in full before any payment is allocated to obligations covered by the next prior lien recorded. *(Added by Stats.1971, Ex.Sess., c. 1, p. 5126, § 308, eff. Dec. 8, 1971, operative Jan. 1, 1972. Amended by Stats.1982, c. 1075, p. 3886, § 12.3.)*

§ 1110.6. Agreement by employer to assume liability for contributions on default by any other employer affected by contract; delinquent date

Notwithstanding the provisions of Section 1110, whenever the liability of an employer for contributions under this division arises under the terms of a written contract in which such employer has agreed, for the benefit of another party to such contract, to assume ultimate liability for contributions under this division in the event of the default in payment thereof by any other employer affected by such contract, such contributions shall not become delinquent and no penalties or interest prescribed by this chapter shall commence to accrue with respect to such contracting employer, until after the 30th day following the date of mailing or service of notice upon him, by the director, of the default of any such other employer. *(Added by Stats.1965, c. 699, p. 2095, § 1.)*

§ 1111. Extension of time for payment or making return or report; interest

The director for good cause may extend for not to exceed 60 days the time for making a return or report or paying without penalty any amount required to be paid under this division. Any employer to whom an extension is granted and who pays the amount required within the period for which the extension is granted shall pay, in addition to the contributions, interest at the adjusted annual rate and by the method established pursuant to Section 19521 of the Revenue and Taxation Code from the date on which the payment would have been delinquent without the extension until the date of payment. *(Stats.1953, c. 308, p. 1495, § 1111. Amended by Stats. 1961, c. 1300, p. 3081, § 1; Stats.1975, c. 661, p. 1447, § 70; Stats.1981–82, 1st Ex.Sess., c. 5, p. 624, § 85, operative May 27, 1982; Stats.1983–84, 1st Ex.Sess., c. 10, § 32, eff. Feb. 17, 1983; Stats.1993, c. 31 (S.B.3), § 64, eff. June 16, 1993, operative Jan. 1, 1994; Stats.1994, c. 1049 (A.B.3086), § 6.)*

§ 1111.5. Extension of time for filing and payment; declaration of state of emergency

If the Governor declares a state of emergency, the director may extend the time requirements for filing returns or reports pursuant to Section 1088 and the time requirement for payment of employer and worker contributions pursuant to Section 1110. The extension granted by the director pursuant to this section shall apply only to employers prevented by the conditions giving rise to the state of emergency from timely filing their returns or reports, or from timely payment of the taxes due. *(Added by Stats.1993, c. 402 (A.B.1668), § 3. Amended by Stats.1994, c. 1049 (A.B.3086), § 7.)*

§ 1112. Penalty for failure to pay; amount

(a) Any employer who without good cause fails to pay any contributions required of him or her or of his or her workers, except amounts assessed under Article 8 of this chapter, within the time required shall pay a penalty of 10 percent of the amount of those contributions.

(b) Any employer required to remit payments by electronic funds transfer pursuant to Section 13021, who without good cause remits those amounts by means other than electronic funds transfer shall pay a penalty of 10 percent of the amount of those contributions. *(Stats. 1953, c. 308, p. 1495, § 1112. Amended by Stats.1991, c. 473 (S.B.467), § 9; Stats.1992, c. 1294 (S.B.1974), § 5; Stats.1998, c. 217 (A.B.2017), § 5.)*

§ 1112.5. Failure to file reports; penalty

(a) Any employer who without good cause fails to file the reports required by subdivision (a) of Section 1088 and subdivision (a) of Section 13021 within 60 days of the time required under subdivision (a) of Section 1110 shall pay a penalty of 10 percent of the amount of contributions and personal income tax withholding required by this report. This penalty shall be in addition to the penalties required by Sections 1112 and 1126.

(b) For purposes of subdivision (a), the amount of contributions and personal income tax required by the report of contributions shall be reduced by the amount of any contributions and personal income tax paid on or before the prescribed payment dates. *(Added by Stats. 1989, c. 1146, § 9. Amended by Stats.1994, c. 1049 (A.B.3086), § 8.)*

§ 1113. Interest for failure to pay; amount

Any employer who fails to pay any contributions required of him or of his workers, except amounts assessed under Article 8 (commencing with Section 1126), within the time required shall become liable for interest on such contributions at the adjusted annual rate and by the method established pursuant to Section 19521 of the Revenue and Taxation Code from and after the date of delinquency until paid. *(Stats.1953, c. 308, p. 1495, § 1113. Amended by Stats.1975, c. 661, p. 1447, § 71; Stats.1981–82, 1st Ex.Sess., c. 5, p. 624, § 86, operative May 27, 1982; Stats.1983–84, 1st Ex.Sess., c. 10, § 33, eff. Feb. 17, 1983; Stats.1993, c. 31 (S.B.3), § 65, eff. June 16, 1993, operative Jan. 1, 1994.)*

§ 1113.1. Erroneous underpayment; liability for penalty or interest

An employer who, through an error caused by excusable neglect, makes an underpayment of the amount due on a monthly report of contributions pursuant to subdivision (b) of Section 1088 shall not be liable for penalty or interest under Sections 1112, 1113, 1127 or 1129 if proper adjustment is made at the time of the filing of the quarterly report of contributions for the same calendar quarter under subdivision (a) of Section 1088 and an explanation of the error is attached to the report. *(Added by Stats.1965, c. 745, p. 2154, § 3.5, eff. June 24, 1965. Amended by Stats.1979, c. 1053, p. 3708, § 3.5; Stats.1989, c. 600, § 2, Stats.1989, c. 1146, § 10; Stats. 1994, c. 1049 (A.B.3086), § 9.)*

§ 1114. Penalty for unreported wage items; amount

(a) Any employer who, without good cause, fails to file within 15 days after service by the director of notice pursuant to Section 1206 of a specific written demand therefor, a report of wages of each of his or her workers required by this division, shall pay in addition to other amounts required, for each unreported wage item a penalty of ten dollars ($10).

(b) Any employer required by this division to file a report of wages of each of his or her workers on magnetic media as prescribed by subdivision (f) of Section 1088, who, without good cause, instead files a report of wages on paper or in another form, shall pay in addition to other amounts required, for each wage item a penalty of ten dollars ($10). *(Stats.1953, c. 308, p. 1495, § 1114. Amended by Stats.1961, c. 2161, p. 4479, § 3; Stats.1979, c. 1082, p. 3890, § 10; Stats.1986, c. 724, § 1; Stats.1994, c. 1049 (A.B.3086), § 10.)*

§ 1115. Collection in jeopardy; procedure

(a) If the director finds that the collection of any contributions will be jeopardized in any case where an employing unit is insolvent, or is delinquent in a substantial amount of contributions due under this division, or is about to discontinue business at any of its known places of business, or the business is of a temporary or seasonal nature, the director may, upon giving the employing unit 10 days' notice pursuant to Section 1206:

(1) Require payment of contributions with respect to wages paid from the beginning date of the calendar quarter in which notice is given to the date designated in the notice.

(2) Require payment of contributions for reporting periods less than calendar quarters.

(b) As used in this section "reporting period" means that period less than a calendar quarter which is established by the director.

(c) Contributions required under subdivision (a)(1) of this section are due and payable on the date designated in the notice and shall become delinquent if not paid within 10 days of the due date.

(d) Contributions required under subdivision (a)(2) of this section are due and payable on the first day of the reporting period following the close of each reporting period and shall become delinquent if not paid within 10 days of the due date.

(e) The employing unit shall file within the time required for payment of contributions under this section a report or return as required by Section 1088, in the form and containing the information that the director prescribes. *(Stats.1953, c. 308, p. 1495, § 1115. Amended by Stats.1955, c. 1165, p. 2162, § 16; Stats.1961, c. 2158, p. 4466, § 5; Stats.1979, c. 1082, p. 3890, § 11; Stats.1994, c. 1049 (A.B.3086), § 11.)*

§ 1116. Returns on quitting business or on commencement of proceedings to wind up and dissolve

(a)(1) Every employing unit except a domestic or foreign corporation or a domestic or foreign limited liability company shall, within 10 days of quitting business, file with the director a final return and report of wages of its workers, in such form and containing such information as the director prescribes.

(2) Every domestic corporation and domestic limited liability company shall, within 10 days of quitting business or within 10 days of the commencement of proceedings to windup its affairs and voluntarily dissolve, whichever expires the earlier, file with the director a return and a report of wages of its workers, in such form and containing such information as the director prescribes.

(3) Every foreign corporation and foreign limited liability company shall, within 10 days of quitting business or within 10 days of the surrender of its right to engage in business of this state in accordance with Section 2112 and subdivision (d) of Section 2114 of the Corporations Code for foreign corporations or Section 17455 of the Corpora-

tions Code for foreign limited liability companies, whichever expires the earlier, file with the director a final return and report of wages of its workers, in such form and containing such information as the director prescribes.

(4) As used in this section, "quitting business" does not include any change in the form or membership of an employing unit if before and after such change 50 percent or more of the control of management is held by the same individual, or is held by an individual before death and after the individual's death by the individual's estate or heirs.

(b) Contributions with respect to a return required under subdivision (a) are due and payable on the first day of the applicable 10-day period established pursuant to subdivision (a) and shall become delinquent if not paid within 10 days of the due date.

(c) The director for good cause may extend for not to exceed 30 days the time for making a return or paying without penalty or interest any amount required to be paid under this section. *(Added by Stats.1961, c. 2158, p. 4467, § 6. Amended by Stats.1975, c. 682, p. 1626, § 15, eff. Jan. 1, 1977; Stats.1978, c. 1305, p. 4291, § 42, operative Jan. 1, 1980; Stats.1994, c. 1049 (A.B.3086), § 12; Stats.1994, c. 1200 (S.B.469), § 82, eff. Sept. 30, 1994.)*

§ 1117. Failure to file annual reconciliation return; penalty

If any employer fails to file the annual reconciliation return described in subdivision (e) of Section 1088 or subdivision (j) of Section 13021 on or before 30 days after notice has been given to the employer of his or her failure to file, unless the failure is due to good cause, the employer, in addition to any other penalties imposed by this code, shall pay a penalty of one thousand dollars ($1,000), or 5 percent of the employer and worker contributions required to be reconciled by subdivision (e) of Section 1088, whichever is less. *(Added by Stats.1994, c. 1049 (A.B.3086), § 13.)*

§ 1118. Employers of domestic servants; telephonic reporting of wages

(a) This section applies only to employers who employ individuals to perform domestic service, as described in Sections 682 and 684.

(b) Effective July 1, 1997, notwithstanding Section 1088, a domestic service employer shall be authorized to file the report of wages required by Section 1088 by telephone. This does not apply to the filing of Internal Revenue Service Form W–2.

(c) The department shall notify all domestic service employers of the availability of the telephone reporting system. A domestic service employer shall be required to make an election to report by telephone or by mail. After a domestic service employer elects to report by telephone, the employer is required to report in that mode for the remainder of the calendar year. If a domestic service employer makes this election in the second or subsequent quarter of a calendar year, the employer shall be required to report by telephone for the remainder of the calendar year and for all four quarters of the subsequent calendar year. A domestic service employer who has elected to report by telephone and who is eligible under this subdivision to change the reporting mode shall provide 30 days' notice to the department in order to begin reporting by mail.

(d) A domestic service employer reporting by telephone shall be required to provide the department with the employer's account number, the social security numbers of all employees, and the wages paid to each employee for the reporting period. The department may request additional information in order to determine the amount of wages that are taxable.

(e) The department shall compute the contributions owed based upon the wage information reported by the domestic service employer.

(f) A domestic service employer reporting by telephone shall be permitted to pay the contributions owed by credit card or charge card. The payment shall be subject to the State Payment Card Act (Ch. 2.6 (commencing with Section 6160) of Div. 7, Title 1, Gov. C.).

(g) If a domestic service employer reporting by telephone does not pay by credit card or charge card, the department shall advise the employer of the due date for the payment and of any penalties and interest that will be charged if a payment is late. *(Added by Stats.1996, c. 255 (A.B.2979), § 2.)*

§ 1119. Notice to Internal Revenue Service and Department of Labor of delinquent payments by Indian tribe

The director shall notify the United States Internal Revenue Service and the United States Department of Labor of the failure of any Indian tribe (as described by subsection (u) of Section 3306 of Title 26 of the United States Code) to make a payment of any amount required to be paid under this article within 90 days of the date of a notice specifying the amount due. If the amount due is subsequently paid by the Indian tribe, the director shall notify the United States Internal Revenue Service and the United States Department of Labor of the satisfaction of the liability. *(Added by Stats.2001, c. 255 (A.B. 1537), § 12.)*

Operative Effect

Under the terms of Section 17 of Stats.2001, c. 255 (A.B.1537), the provisions of that Act are retroactive to December 21, 2000.

ARTICLE 8. ASSESSMENTS

Section
1126. Assessment and penalty for failure to make returns or reports; computation of amounts.
1126.1. Penalty for failure to register as an employer.

Section
1127. Deficiency assessment upon unsatisfactory return or report; computation of amount; penalty.
1127.5. Reporting individuals or entities not correct employers; determination of correct employer; notice.
1128. Failure to file return within required time; deficiency due to fraud or intent to evade; penalty; failure to provide information returns; additional penalty.
1128.1. Money exchanged on behalf of employers to conceal wage payments; intent; penalties.
1129. Interest.
1130. Number of assessments; offsets.
1131. Notice of assessment.
1132. Time for making notice; waiver of limitation period.
1135. When assessments become delinquent; penalty for delinquent assessments.
1136. Cancellation of erroneous assessments.
1137. Jeopardy assessment; penalties and interest; deposit of security; stay of proceedings.
1137.1. Jeopardy assessment; findings.
1141. Delinquency; notification to Labor Commissioner; evidence.
1141.1. Notice to Internal Revenue Service and Department of Labor of delinquent assessment payments by Indian tribe.
1142. False statements or representations or willful failure to report a material fact concerning either an employee's termination or reasonable assurance of claimant's reemployment; penalty provisions.
1142.1. False statements or representations or willful failure to report a material fact regarding either a claimant's performance of services for an educational institution or time granted to the claimant for professional development; penalty provisions.
1143. Disability insurance benefits; false certification of medical condition; penalties.
1144. Inducement to file false or fraudulent claim; penalty; deposit of amounts collected.
1145. Advising to violate provisions of chapter.

§ 1126. Assessment and penalty for failure to make returns or reports; computation of amounts

If any employing unit fails to make a return or report as required under this division, the director shall make an estimate based upon any information in his or her possession or that may come into his or her possession of the amount of wages paid for employment in the period or periods for which no return or report was filed and upon the basis of the estimate shall compute and assess the amounts of employer and worker contributions payable by the employing unit, adding thereto a penalty of 10 percent of the amount of contributions. *(Stats.1953, c. 308, p. 1495, § 1126. Amended by Stats.1994, c. 1049 (A.B.3086), § 14.)*

§ 1126.1. Penalty for failure to register as an employer

(a) If any employing unit fails to register with the department as required under Section 1086, and the failure is due to intentional disregard or intent to evade this division or authorized regulations, a penalty of one hundred dollars ($100) per nonreported employee shall be added to an assessment issued in accordance with Section 1126.

(b) For purposes of this section, the number of nonreported employees shall be defined as the highest number of employees determined by the department to have been engaged by the employer during any single calendar quarter included in the assessment under Section 1126. *(Added by Stats.1994, c. 1117 (S.B.1490), § 6.)*

§ 1127. Deficiency assessment upon unsatisfactory return or report; computation of amount; penalty

If the director is not satisfied with any return or report made by any employing unit of the amount of employer or worker contributions, he or she may compute the amount required to be paid upon the basis of facts contained in the return or reports or may make an estimate upon the basis of any information in his or her possession or that may come into his or her possession and make an assessment of the amount of the deficiency. If any part of the deficiency is due to negligence or intentional disregard of this division or authorized regulations, a penalty of 10 percent of the amount of the deficiency shall be added to the assessment. *(Stats.1953, c. 308, p. 1496, § 1127. Amended by Stats.1971, c. 873, p. 1717, § 8; Stats.1994, c. 1049 (A.B.3086), § 15.)*

§ 1127.5. Reporting individuals or entities not correct employers; determination of correct employer; notice

(a) If the director determines that an individual or entity that is reporting employee wages pursuant to Section 1088 or other applicable sections is not the correct employer of the employees whose wages are reported, the director shall determine the correct employer and, subject to this section, shall apply the provisions of this code to the correct employer.

(b) Upon a determination made under subdivision (a), the director shall give notice of the determination pursuant to Section 1206 to both of the following:

(1) To the individual or entity reporting employee wages of the determination that the individual or entity is not the correct employer of the reported employees.

(2) To the individual or entity determined to be the correct employer of those reported employees.

The notice shall contain a statement of the facts and circumstances upon which the determination was based. An individual or entity so noticed shall have the right to petition for review of the determination within 30 days of the notice, as provided in Section 1222.

(c) During the pendency of a petition for review pursuant to subdivision (b), the individual or entity responsible for reporting employee wages pursuant to Section 1088 or other applicable sections shall be determined as follows:

(1) When an individual or entity that has reported employee wages appeals a director's determination that it is not the correct employer of the employees whose wages were reported, that individual or entity shall continue to so report employee wages, provided the employees in question are still on its payroll, until a decision on its

964

appeal is final, whether or not the individual or entity determined to be the correct employer by the director appeals that determination.

(2) When the individual or entity determined by the director to be the correct employer appeals that determination, but the individual or entity determined not to be the correct employer does not appeal the director's determination, then the individual or entity determined to be the correct employer by the director shall report employee wages from the date it received notification pursuant to subdivision (b), and, provided the employees in question are still on its payroll, shall continue to do so at least until a decision on its appeal is final.

(d) When a director's determination that an individual or entity is the correct employer of employees whose wages have been reported by another individual becomes final:

(1) The individual or entity so determined to be the correct employer may be assessed for any underpayment of employer contributions pursuant to Article 8 (commencing with Section 1126) of Chapter 4 of Part 1 of Division 1. No assessment shall be issued for any period prior to the effective date of this section based on which individual or entity is the correct employer, unless the correct employer committed fraud in violation of this part.

(2) The individual or entity which had reported employee wages prior to the finality of the director's determination of the correct employer of the employees whose wages were so reported may file a claim for refund for any overpayment of employer contributions pursuant to Section 1178. No claim for refund may be filed for any period prior to the effective date of this section based on which individual or entity is the correct employer unless the department has issued an assessment based on fraud pursuant to paragraph (1). *(Added by Stats.1986, c. 793, § 2, eff. Sept. 15, 1986.)*

§ 1128. Failure to file return within required time; deficiency due to fraud or intent to evade; penalty; failure to provide information returns; additional penalty

(a) If the failure of the employing unit to file a return or report within the time required by this division and authorized regulations or if any part of the deficiency for which an assessment is made is due to fraud or an intent to evade this division or authorized regulations, a penalty of 50 percent of the amount of contributions assessed shall be added to the assessment. This penalty is in addition to the penalties provided pursuant to Sections 1126 and 1127.

(b) An additional penalty of 50 percent of the amount of contributions assessed shall be added to any assessment that includes a penalty under subdivision (a), if the employer paid wages and failed to provide information returns as required under Section 13050 of this code or Section 6041A of the Internal Revenue Code. This penalty shall be in addition to any penalties under Section

1126 or 1127. *(Stats.1953, c. 308, p. 1496, § 1128. Amended by Stats.1990, c. 719 (A.B.2667), § 2; Stats. 1994, c. 1049 (A.B.3086), § 16; Stats.1994, c. 1117 (S.B.1490), § 7; Stats.2002, c. 29 (A.B.1729), § 11.)*

§ 1128.1. Money exchanged on behalf of employers to conceal wage payments; intent; penalties

(a) If the director finds that an individual or business entity has exchanged money on behalf of an employer and the employer used the cash proceeds from the exchange to conceal the payment of wages with an intent to evade any provision of this code, the director shall assess a penalty against the individual or business entity in an amount equal to 100 percent of any assessed contributions that were based on the concealed wages. An employing unit subject to a penalty under Section 1128 shall not be assessed a penalty under this section for the same violation.

(b) For purposes of this section, "business entity" means a partnership, corporation, association, limited liability company, or Indian tribe (as described by subsection (u) of Section 3306 of Title 26 of the United States Code).

(c) The penalty shall apply only when there is evidence that the individual or business entity who exchanged money knew that the employer intended to use the cash proceeds from the exchange to conceal the payment of wages and thereby avoid the payment of contributions or taxes required by this code. *(Added by Stats.1996, c. 1116 (S.B.1843), § 1. Amended by Stats.2001, c. 255 (A.B. 1537), § 13.)*

Operative Effect

Under the terms of Section 17 of Stats.2001, c. 255 (A.B.1537), the provisions of that Act are retroactive to December 21, 2000.

§ 1129. Interest

The amount of each assessment shall bear interest at the adjusted annual rate and by the method established pursuant to Section 19521 of the Revenue and Taxation Code from and after the last day of the month following the close of the calendar quarter, or from and after the 15th day of the month following the close of the calendar month, for which the contributions should have been returned until the date of payment. *(Stats.1953, c. 308, p. 1496, § 1129. Amended by Stats.1965, c. 745, p. 2154, § 4, eff. June 24, 1965; Stats.1975, c. 661, p. 1447, § 72; Stats.1981–82, 1st Ex.Sess., c. 5, p. 624, § 87, operative May 27, 1982; Stats.1983–84, 1st Ex.Sess., c. 10, § 34, eff. Feb. 17, 1983; Stats.1990, c. 719 (A.B.2667), § 3; Stats.1993, c. 31 (S.B.3), § 66, eff. June 16, 1993, operative Jan. 1, 1994.)*

§ 1130. Number of assessments; offsets

One or more assessments may be made for the amount due for one or for more than one period and overpayments may be offset against underpayments. *(Stats.1953, c. 308, p. 1496, § 1130.)*

§ 1131. Notice of assessment

The director shall give to the employing unit against whom an assessment is made a written notice of the assessment pursuant to Section 1206. *(Stats.1953, c. 308, p. 1496, § 1131. Amended by Stats.1955, c. 1165, p. 2163, § 17; Stats.1979, c. 1082, p. 3891, § 12.)*

§ 1132. Time for making notice; waiver of limitation period

Except in the case of failure without good cause to file a return or report, fraud or intent to evade any provision of this division or authorized regulations, every notice of assessment shall be made within three years after the last day of the month following the close of the calendar quarter during which the contribution liability included in the assessment accrued or within three years after the deficient return or report is filed, or was due, whichever period expires the later. An employing unit may waive this limitation period or may consent to its extension.

In case of failure without good cause to file a return or report, every notice of assessment shall be made within eight years after the last day of the month following the close of the calendar quarter during which the contribution liability included in the assessment accrued. An employing unit may waive this limitation period or may consent to its extension. *(Stats.1953, c. 308, p. 1496, § 1132. Amended by Stats.1957, c. 293, p. 937, § 1; Stats.1994, c. 1049 (A.B.3086), § 17.)*

§ 1135. When assessments become delinquent; penalty for delinquent assessments

Assessments under this article become delinquent if not paid on or before the date they become final pursuant to Sections 1036, 1221, 1222, and 1224. There shall be added to the amount of each delinquent assessment a penalty of 10 percent of the amount thereof exclusive of interest and penalties. *(Stats.1953, c. 308, p. 1497, § 1135. Amended by Stats.1979, c. 1082, p. 3891, § 13; Stats.1992, c. 125 (A.B.1830), § 7.)*

§ 1136. Cancellation of erroneous assessments

If the director finds that an assessment or portion thereof has been erroneously made, he may cancel the assessment or portion thereof in the following cases:

(a) Where no petition for reassessment has been filed.

(b) Where a petition for reassessment is filed, if the cancellation is made prior to the mailing of a decision of the administrative law judge.

(c) Where a petition for reassessment has been filed and an order or decision of an administrative law judge or of the appeals board has been issued on any grounds not on the merits, if the cancellation is approved by the appeals board. *(Stats.1953, c. 308, p. 1497, § 1136. Amended by Stats.1955, c. 1165, p. 2164, § 19; Stats.1984, c. 537, § 15.)*

§ 1137. Jeopardy assessment; penalties and interest; deposit of security; stay of proceedings

(a) If the director finds, in accordance with Section 1137.1, that the collection of any contributions will be jeopardized by delay the director shall thereupon make an assessment of those contributions, served pursuant to Section 1206, noting upon the assessment that it is a jeopardy assessment levied under this section and the facts upon which the director finds that collection of contributions will be jeopardized by delay. The amount of the assessment shall be immediately delinquent, whether or not the time otherwise allowed by law or authorized regulations has expired. When applicable, the penalties provided in Sections 1126, 1127, and 1128, and interest under Section 1129, shall attach to the amount of the contributions specified in the jeopardy assessment. Penalties under Section 1135 shall apply if payment is not made, or security for payment is not provided, within 30 days of service of a jeopardy assessment.

(b) In levying the assessment, the director may demand a deposit of such security as the director deems necessary to ensure compliance with this division, including additional security from time to time, but not more frequently than monthly, in the amount of accumulating interest. The deposit of sufficient security to ensure compliance shall stay other collection action by the director while the assessment is under review. The deposit of the sufficient security shall not be a condition for the exercise of the review and appeal rights of the employer pursuant to Sections 1221, 1222, 1223, and 1224. The filing of a petition for reassessment pursuant to Section 1221 shall not stay collection action by the director while the assessment is under review, but shall stay the sale of all property other than perishable goods seized by the director pursuant to the collection action until a final decision from a preliminary hearing pursuant to subdivision (b) of Section 1221 is issued by the administrative law judge or the board. *(Stats.1953, c. 308, p. 1497, § 1137. Amended by Stats.1955, c. 1165, p. 2164, § 20; Stats.1963, c. 2015, p. 4120, § 12; Stats.1963, c. 2016, p. 4128, § 7; Stats.1979, c. 1082, p. 3891, § 16; Stats.1986, c. 89, § 1, eff. May 13, 1986.)*

§ 1137.1. Jeopardy assessment; findings

A jeopardy assessment may be made only upon a finding by the director, based upon probable cause, that any of the following conditions are met:

(a) The employing unit is insolvent.

(b) The employing unit has transferred, or is about to transfer, assets for less than fair market value, and by so doing has rendered, or is likely to render, itself insolvent.

(c) The employing unit has been dissolved.

(d) Any person liable for the employing unit's contribution, or any owner, officer, director, partner, or other person having charge of the affairs of the employing unit has departed or is about to depart the State of California

and that the departure is likely to deprive the director of a source of payment of the employing unit's contribution.

(e) Any person referred to in subdivision (d), or the employing unit, is secreting assets or is moving, placing, or depositing assets outside of the state for the purpose of interfering with the orderly collection of any contribution. The moving, placing, or depositing of assets outside of the state which constitutes a regular business practice and which does not in any way deplete the assets of the employing unit shall not be deemed to be interfering with the orderly collection of any contribution under this subdivision.

(f) The assessment to be issued against the employing unit or an individual includes a penalty under subdivision (a) of Section 1128 or Section 1128.1. *(Added by Stats.1986, c. 89, § 2, eff. May 13, 1986. Amended by Stats.1997, c. 810 (S.B.132), § 2.)*

§ 1141. Delinquency; notification to Labor Commissioner; evidence

When an assessment for worker contributions that is made pursuant to the provisions of this article becomes final against a farm labor contractor, as defined in Section 1682 of the Labor Code, which is an employing unit, as defined in Section 135 of this code, or such farm labor contractor is otherwise delinquent in the payment of worker contributions, the department shall notify the Labor Commissioner, in writing, of the amount of the delinquency of such employing unit, and shall further notify the Labor Commissioner, in writing, when such delinquency is paid. The notice of assessment and the amount of any delinquency shall be admissible in evidence in any action or special proceeding arising out of the provisions of Chapter 3 (commencing with Section 1682) of Part 6 of Division 2 of the Labor Code. *(Added by Stats.1970, c. 1216, p. 2134, § 2.)*

§ 1141.1. Notice to Internal Revenue Service and Department of Labor of delinquent assessment payments by Indian tribe

The director shall notify the United States Internal Revenue Service and the United States Department of Labor of the failure of any Indian tribe (as described by subsection (u) of Section 3306 of Title 26 of the United States Code) to pay within 90 days of the final date of an assessment any amounts assessed pursuant to the provisions of this article. If the assessment is subsequently paid by the Indian tribe, the director shall notify the United States Internal Revenue Service and the United States Department of Labor of the satisfaction of the liability. *(Added by Stats.2001, c. 255 (A.B.1537), § 14.)*

Operative Effect

Under the terms of Section 17 of Stats.2001, c. 255 (A.B.1537), the provisions of that Act are retroactive to December 21, 2000.

§ 1142. False statements or representations or willful failure to report a material fact concerning either an employee's termination or reasonable assurance of claimant's reemployment; penalty provisions

(a) If the director finds that any employer or any employee, officer, or agent of any employer, in submitting facts concerning the termination of a claimant's employment pursuant to Section 1030, 1327, 3654, 3701, 4654, or 4701, willfully makes a false statement or representation or willfully fails to report a material fact concerning that termination, the director shall assess a penalty against the employer in an amount not less than 2 nor more than 10 times the weekly benefit amount of that claimant.

(b) If the director finds that any employer or any employee, officer, or agent of any employer, in submitting a written statement concerning the reasonable assurance, as defined in subdivision (g) of Section 1253.3, of a claimant's reemployment, as required by subdivisions (b), (c), and (i) of Section 1253.3, willfully makes a false statement or representation or willfully fails to report a material fact concerning the reasonable assurance of that reemployment, the director shall assess a penalty against the employer in an amount not less than two nor more than 10 times the weekly benefit amount of that claimant.

(c) This article, Article 9 (commencing with Section 1176) of this chapter with respect to refunds, and Chapter 7 (commencing with Section 1701) of this part with respect to collections shall apply to the assessments provided by this section. Penalties collected under this section shall be deposited in the contingent fund. (Added by Stats.1977, c. 511, p. 1649, § 5. Amended by Stats.2004, c. 808 (A.B.2412), § 1.)

§ 1142.1. False statements or representations or willful failure to report a material fact regarding either a claimant's performance of services for an educational institution or time granted to the claimant for professional development; penalty provisions

(a) If the director finds that any employer or any employee, officer, or agent of any employer, in submitting facts concerning the termination of a claimant's employment, where the claimant was performing services for an educational institution, as described in Section 1253.3, willfully makes a false statement or representation or willfully fails to report a material fact regarding any week during which the services were performed, as provided in Section 1253.3, or any time granted to the claimant for professional development during his or her employment with that employer, the director shall assess a penalty against the employer of that claimant in an amount not less than two, nor more than 10, times the weekly benefit amount of that claimant.

(b) This article, Article 9 (commencing with Section 1176) of this chapter, with respect to refunds, and Chapter 7 (commencing with Section 1701) of this part, with respect to collections, shall apply to the assessments provided by this section. Penalties collected under this section shall be deposited in the Employment Development Department Contingent Fund. (Added by Stats. 2006, c. 190 (A.B.2293), § 1.)

§ 1143. Disability insurance benefits; false certification of medical condition; penalties

If the director finds that any individual falsely certifies the medical condition of any person in order to obtain disability insurance benefits, including family temporary disability insurance benefits, with the intent to defraud, whether for the maker or for any other person, the director shall assess a penalty against the individual in the amount of 25 percent of the benefits paid as a result of the false certification. The provisions of this article, the provisions of Article 9 (commencing with Section 1176) with respect to refunds, and the provisions of Chapter 7 (commencing with Section 1701) with respect to collections shall apply to the assessments provided by this section. Penalties collected under this section shall be deposited in the contingent fund. (Added by Stats.1994, c. 967 (S.B.1584), § 2, eff. Sept. 28, 1994. Amended by Stats.2003, c. 797 (S.B.727), § 5, operative Jan. 1, 2004.)

Operative Effect

For operative effect of Stats.2003, c. 797 (S.B. 727) upon benefits payable for family temporary disability insurance claims, see section 28 of that act.

§ 1144. Inducement to file false or fraudulent claim; penalty; deposit of amounts collected

(a) Any employer who induces, solicits, or coerces an employee to file a false or fraudulent claim for benefits shall be assessed a penalty in an amount equal to 100 percent of the liability established under Sections 1375 and 1375.1 against the employee. Amounts collected under this section shall be deposited in the fund from which the overpayment was made and as prescribed in Section 1375.1, in the following order of priority:

(1) First to the fund from which the overpayment was made, up to the total amount of the benefit overpayment liability assessed against the employee under Section 1375.

(2) Second to the Benefit Audit Fund, up to the total amount assessed against the employee under Section 1375.1.

(b) The reserve account of any employer who is assessed under this section shall not be relieved of the charges for benefits related to the fraudulent claim. (Added by Stats.1994, c. 1050 (A.B.3122), § 2.)

§ 1145. Advising to violate provisions of chapter

(a) If the director finds that a person or business entity knowingly advises another person or business entity to violate any provision of this chapter, the director may assess the greater of:

(1) A penalty of five thousand dollars ($5,000).

967

(2) Ten percent of the combined amount of any resulting underreporting of contribution, penalties, or interest required by law.

(b) For purposes of this section, "business entity" means a partnership, corporation, association, limited liability company, or Indian tribe, as described in subsection (u) of Section 3306 of Title 26 of the United States Code, or any other legal entity. *(Added by Stats.2004, c. 827 (A.B.664), § 9.)*

ARTICLE 8.5. EMPLOYMENT TAX AMNESTY [REPEALED]

ARTICLE 9.   REFUNDS AND OVERPAYMENTS

Section
1176.   Refunds of excess employee contributions.
1176.5.   Method of claiming refund or credit; disallowance and protest; making refunds; laws applicable.
1177.   Credit or refund of erroneous or illegal contributions; penalty or interest.
1177.5.   Overpayment by employing unit or school employees fund; federal reimbursement to state; credit to employing unit or fund; conditions.
1178.   Claim for refund or credit; time; conformity to regulations; final decision denying petition for reassessment; voluntary contributions for redetermination of contribution rate.
1179.   Claim for refund or credit; form and contents; waiver.
1179.5.   Payment before decision on petition for reassessment or on appeal; claim for refund.
1180.   Denial of claim; notice to claimant.
1180.1.   Offers in compromise; refund claims.
1180.5.   Claim erroneously denied; reversal; notice.
1181.   Interest; exception.
1184.   Recovery of erroneous refunds; assessment; interest; notice of assessment.
1185.   Overpayments; identification of taxpayers; credits.

§ 1176.   Refunds of excess employee contributions

If, by reason of an employee receiving wages from more than one employer during any calendar year, the wages received by him or her during such year exceed the remuneration upon which contributions are payable under Section 985, and the sum of the amount of tax imposed by Section 984 plus the amount of contributions under Section 3260 deducted from such wages exceeds the amount required under this division, the employee is entitled to a refund or credit of the amount of the excess. *(Stats.1953, c. 308, p. 1498, § 1176. Amended by Stats. 1957, c. 2107, p. 3732, § 3; Stats.1961, c. 2153, p. 4445, § 12; Stats.1961, c. 2154, p. 4451, § 6; Stats.1965, c. 745, p. 2154, § 5, eff. June 24, 1965; Stats.1967, c. 1484, p. 3477, § 1; Stats.1970, c. 1356, p. 2520, § 3; Stats.1971, Ex.Sess., c. 1, p. 5127, § 309, eff. Dec. 8, 1971; Stats.1971, Ex.Sess., c. 2, p. 5174, § 48, eff. Dec. 30, 1971, operative Jan. 1, 1972; Stats.1978, c. 633, p. 2089, § 1, operative Jan. 1, 1979; Stats.1996, c. 1157 (S.B.1682), § 2.)*

§ 1176.5.   Method of claiming refund or credit; disallowance and protest; making refunds; laws applicable

(a) Except as provided by subdivision (c) of this section, refunds and credits under Section 1176 shall be claimed pursuant to Section 17061 of the Revenue and Taxation Code on the personal income tax return of the claimant for the year in which the wages in excess of the applicable limitation are received. In no event shall the credit or refund be made unless the claim is made on a return filed within three years from the last day prescribed for filing the return, without regard to any extensions. The director shall transfer from the Disability Fund to the General Fund an amount equal to the amount of credits and refunds allowed by the Franchise Tax Board pursuant to Section 17061 of the Revenue and Taxation Code.

(b) If the Franchise Tax Board disallows an individual's claim filed pursuant to subdivision (a), he or she may file a protest and submit the claim to the director within 30 days of the date of mailing of the notice of disallowance by the Franchise Tax Board. An additional 30 days for the filing of the protest may for good cause be granted by the director.

(c) If any individual is not required to file a personal income tax return for a year with the Franchise Tax Board, he or she may, within three years after the calendar year in which the wages in excess of the applicable limitation are received, file a claim for refund or credit under Section 1176 with the director.

(d) The director shall make refunds from the Disability Fund if he or she allows a claim under this section. The provisions of Sections 1180, 1222, 1223, 1224, 1241, and 1242 shall apply whenever the director denies any claim for refund or credit under this section or affirms the disallowance of a claim for refund or credit by the Franchise Tax Board. *(Added by Stats.1971, Ex.Sess., c. 1, p. 5127, § 310, eff. Dec. 30, 1971. Amended by Stats.1974, c. 633, p. 1485, § 1, eff. Sept. 5, 1974; Stats.1979, c. 1055, p. 3724, § 3, eff. Sept. 27, 1979; Stats.1979, c. 1082, p. 3892, § 20.5; Stats.1989, c. 600, § 3.)*

§ 1177.   Credit or refund of erroneous or illegal contributions; penalty or interest

Except as provided by subdivision (b) of Section 1178, if the director determines that any amount of contributions, penalty or interest has been erroneously or illegally collected he shall set forth on the records of the department the amount collected in excess of the amount legally due and the name of the employing unit or other person by whom it was paid and shall refund the amount to the employing unit or other person by whom it was paid if the amount does not include refundable worker contributions. If refundable worker contributions are involved and a claim has not already been filed the director shall give notice to such employing unit or other person of such amount. The excess amount shall be credited on any amounts then due from or accrued against the employing unit and the balance shall be refunded to the employing unit or its successor, administrators or executors. *(Stats.1953, c. 308, p. 1498, § 1177. Amended by Stats.1971, c. 873, p. 1717, § 9.)*

§ 1177.5. Overpayment by employing unit or school employees fund; federal reimbursement to state; credit to employing unit or fund; conditions

(a) If the director determines that an overpayment has been made to the department by an employing unit or the School Employees Fund because of a reason specified in this subdivision, and the amount of the overpayment has been reimbursed to the state by the federal government pursuant to the federal Workforce Investment Act of 1998, [1] then the director shall credit the employing unit or the School Employees Fund with the amount of that overpayment, provided that the director determines that the overpayment was made because of one of the following:

(1) An employing unit paid unemployment insurance contributions after December 31, 1974, based on wages paid to individuals participating in a public service employment program under the federal Workforce Investment Act of 1998.

(2) An employing unit paid amounts after December 31, 1975, pursuant to Section 803 of this part, for benefits awarded based on wages paid to individuals participating in a public service employment program under the federal Workforce Investment Act of 1998.

(3) Payments were made by the School Employees Fund after December 31, 1975, to the Unemployment Fund pursuant to Section 821 of this part for benefits awarded based on wages paid to individuals participating in a public service employment program under the federal Workforce Investment Act of 1998.

(b) No overpayment described in subdivision (a) shall be refunded to an employing unit or to the School Employees Fund. *(Added by Stats.1977, c. 480, p. 1555, § 2. Amended by Stats.1978, c. 2, p. 41, § 79, eff. Jan. 30, 1978, operative Jan. 1, 1978; Stats.2002, c. 29 (A.B.1729), § 13.)*

[1] Workforce Investment Act of 1998 (Pub.L. 105-220, Aug. 7, 1998, 112 Stat. 936) See Short Title note under 20 U.S.C.A. § 9201 for classification of the Act to the Code.

§ 1178. Claim for refund or credit; time; conformity to regulations; final decision denying petition for reassessment; voluntary contributions for redetermination of contribution rate

(a) A claim for refund or credit may be filed with the director for any overpayment including, but not limited to, amounts paid subsequent to the filing for record of a certificate under Section 1703 or the entry of a judgment under Section 1815.

(b) No refund shall be made or credit allowed unless a claim therefor is filed with the director within three years from the last day of the calendar month following the close of the calendar quarter for which the overpayment was made or within six months after assessments made under Article 8 (commencing with Section 1126) of this chapter become final or within 60 days from the date of overpayment, whichever period expires the later, but prior to the expiration of such periods even though no claim is filed the director on his own initiative shall make refunds pursuant to Section 1177 or may allow credits.

(c) No refund of employer or worker contributions, penalties or interest shall be made or credit for worker contributions allowed unless the employing unit conforms, within one year after the allowance of credit or approval of the claim for refund, to authorized regulations with respect to the refund to workers entitled thereto of any money deducted by the employing unit under Section 984.

(d) Following a final decision denying a petition for reassessment pursuant to Article 11 (commencing with Section 1221), the employing unit or other person which was a party to the petition may file a claim for refund upon payment of the amount of the assessment, including interest and penalties, and thereafter may pursue all administrative and judicial review rights accorded in Article 11 (commencing with Section 1221) and Article 12 (commencing with Section 1241).

(e) No refund of employer contributions paid pursuant to Section 976.5 shall be made unless the payment is made by an employer described in subdivision (c) of Section 976.5, or the amount paid is less than or exceeds the amount needed to change the employer's contribution rate. Refunds permitted under this subdivision shall be considered an undesignated payment and allocated according to subdivision (b) of Section 1110.1. *(Stats. 1953, c. 308, p. 1499, § 1178. Amended by Stats.1955, c. 1819, p. 3357, § 1; Stats.1957, c. 1188, p. 2479, § 1; Stats.1971, c. 873, p. 1717, § 10; Stats.1986, c. 89, § 3, eff. May 13, 1986; Stats.1989, c. 1146, § 11.)*

§ 1179. Claim for refund or credit; form and contents; waiver

Every claim for refund or credit shall be in writing and shall state the specific grounds upon which the claim is founded. A waiver of any demand against the state or the director on account of overpayment shall apply when any of the following occur:

(a) Failure to file a claim with the director within the time prescribed by Section 1178.

(b) Failure, after denial of a claim by the director, to file a petition for review with an administrative law judge within the time prescribed by Section 1222.

(c) Failure to file an appeal from an adverse administrative law judge's decision to the appeals board within the time prescribed by Section 1224. *(Stats.1953, c. 308, p. 1499, § 1179. Amended by Stats.1954, 1st Ex.Sess., c. 44, p. 313, § 5; Stats.1977, c. 480, p. 1555, § 3; Stats. 1979, c. 1082, p. 3893, § 21; Stats.1984, c. 537, § 16.)*

§ 1179.5. Payment before decision on petition for reassessment or on appeal; claim for refund

If an employing unit pays the amount of contributions, penalties, and interest assessed under Article 8 (commencing with Section 1126) of Chapter 4 of Part 1 of this division:

(a) Before an administrative law judge issues his decision upon a petition for reassessment filed on such assessment, the payment shall constitute the filing of a claim for refund, the claim for refund shall be deemed denied by the director, and the petition for reassessment shall automatically become a petition to review a denial of the claim for refund.

(b) Before the appeals board issues its decision upon an appeal from the administrative law judge's decision on a petition for reassessment, the payment shall constitute the filing of a claim for refund, the claim shall be deemed denied by the director, the denial shall be deemed affirmed by the administrative law judge, and the appeal shall automatically become an appeal from an administrative law judge's decision upholding the director's denial of the claim for refund. *(Added by Stats.1959, c. 1729, p. 4178, § 11. Amended by Stats.1965, c. 664, p. 2039, § 1; Stats.1984, c. 537, § 17.)*

§ 1180. Denial of claim; notice to claimant

The director shall give notice pursuant to Section 1206 to the claimant whenever he or she denies any claim for refund or credit in whole or in part. *(Stats.1953, c. 308, p. 1499, § 1180. Amended by Stats.1954, 1st Ex.Sess., c. 44, p. 313, § 6; Stats.1955, c. 1165, p. 2165, § 24; Stats.1965, c. 665, p. 2041, § 4; Stats.1979, c. 1082, p. 3893, § 22.)*

§ 1180.1. Offers in compromise; refund claims

No claim for refund of amounts paid pursuant to Section 1870 may be filed. *(Added by Stats.1993, c. 356 (A.B.1238), § 1.)*

§ 1180.5. Claim erroneously denied; reversal; notice

(a) If the director finds that a claim for refund or credit or portion thereof, including a claim deemed made and denied pursuant to subdivision (a) of Section 1179.5, has been erroneously denied, he or she may reverse the denial of the claim or portion thereof in the following cases:

(1) Where no petition for review of denial of the claim has been filed or deemed filed, if the reversal is made prior to the expiration of the period within which a petition for review may be filed under Section 1222.

(2) Where a petition for review of denial of the claim is filed or deemed filed, if the reversal is made prior to the mailing of a decision by the administrative law judge.

(b) The director shall give notice pursuant to Section 1206 of the reversal of an erroneous denial of a claim or portion thereof under this section. With respect to that portion of any such claim which remains denied by the director, the notice of reversal shall also constitute a notice of denial of such portion and Sections 1222, 1223, 1224, 1241, and 1242 shall apply. *(Added by Stats.1961, c. 2158, p. 4467, § 7. Amended by Stats.1979, c. 1082, p. 3893, § 23; Stats.1984, c. 537, § 18.)*

§ 1181. Interest; exception

Interest shall be allowed and paid only to the extent that interest and penalties collected under this division are available therefor upon any overpayment of contributions at the adjusted rate per month, or fraction thereof, established pursuant to Section 19521 of the Revenue and Taxation Code, from the date of overpayment to the date of the allowance of the refund or credit, but no interest shall be allowed if the director determines that any overpayment was made intentionally or by reason of negligence on the part of the employing unit. *(Stats. 1953, c. 308, p. 1499, § 1181. Amended by Stats.1975, c. 661, p. 1447, § 73; Stats.1988, c. 647, § 4; Stats.1993, c. 31 (S.B.3), § 67, eff. June 16, 1993, operative Jan. 1, 1994.)*

§ 1184. Recovery of erroneous refunds; assessment; interest; notice of assessment

If any refund or portion thereof is erroneously made, the director shall assess that amount to the employing unit or other person to whom the refund was made, together with any interest paid thereon, but no assessment shall be made with respect to any amount of worker contributions which the employer has refunded to his or her employees. The amount of the assessment shall bear interest at the adjusted annual rate and by the method established pursuant to Section 19521 of the Revenue and Taxation Code commencing 30 days after the service of notice of the assessment, if not paid within that period, until the date of repayment. The director shall give the employing unit against whom the assessment is made a written notice of the assessment pursuant to Section 1206.

The notice shall be given within three years from the date the refund was made unless the employing unit waives this limitation period or consents to its extension. Sections 1135, 1136, 1222, 1223, and 1224 shall apply to assessments made under this section. The director shall collect the amount of any assessment made under this section in the same manner that other assessments are collected. *(Stats.1953, c. 308, p. 1500, § 1184. Amended by Stats.1955, c. 1165, p. 2166, § 26; Stats.1975, c. 661, p. 1448, § 75; Stats.1979, c. 1082, p. 3894, § 26; Stats.1981– 82, 1st Ex.Sess., c. 5, p. 624, § 88, operative May 27, 1982; Stats.1983–84, 1st Ex.Sess., c. 10, § 35, eff. Feb. 17, 1983; Stats.1988, c. 647, § 5; Stats.1993, c. 31 (S.B.3), § 68, eff. June 16, 1993, operative Jan. 1, 1994.)*

§ 1185. Overpayments; identification of taxpayers; credits

The director, in collaboration with the Franchise Tax Board, shall do all of the following:

(a) Identify taxpayers who have overpaid disability insurance contributions in any or all tax years from January 1, 1993, to December 31, 1995, inclusive, and have not received refunds due to them. For purposes of this subdivision, "taxpayers" means any individual who filed a FTB Form 540A or 540EZ.

(b)(1) By October 15, 1997, credit the taxpayers identified in this subdivision with the amount of any overpaid disability insurance pursuant to Section 17061 of the Revenue and Taxation Code. If the amount credited pursuant to this subdivision exceeds any amount then due from the taxpayer, the difference shall be refunded to the taxpayer. For taxable years 1993, 1994, and 1995, inclusive, interest, at the rate established pursuant to Section 19521 of the Revenue and Taxation Code, shall accrue from April 15 of the tax year following the overpayment to a date preceding the date of the refund warrant by not more than 30 days.

(2) Identify and refund overpayments, with interest, to those taxpayers who have overpaid disability insurance contributions, and who have not claimed refunds due to them.

(3) Interest on overpayments of disability insurance contributions shall be allowed and paid pursuant to Sections 19340 and 19341 of the Revenue and Taxation Code.

(4) For purposes of Section 19340 of the Revenue and Taxation Code, any overpayment of disability insurance contributions shall be deemed to have been paid on the last day prescribed for filing the return under Article 1 (commencing with Section 18501) or Article 2 (commencing with Section 18601) of Chapter 2 of Part 10.2 of the Revenue and Taxation Code without regard to any extension of time for filing the return with respect to which the overpayment is allowable as a credit under Section 17061 of the Revenue and Taxation Code. *(Added by Stats.1996, c. 1157 (S.B.1682), § 3. Amended by Stats.1999, c. 987 (S.B.1229), § 103, eff. Oct. 10, 1999.)*

ARTICLE 10. NOTICE

Section
1206. Service.

§ 1206. Service

A notice given under this chapter by the director, an administrative law judge, or the appeals board:

(a) May be served personally or by mail, except that service by mail given by the director shall be made by certified mail in the following cases:

(1) Under Sections 1137 and 1221.

(2) Under Sections 1131, 1142, 1143, 1144, 1184, 1733, and 1735 if the assessment is in excess of one thousand dollars ($1,000).

(3) Under Section 1180 if the denial of claim for refund or credit is in excess of one thousand dollars ($1,000).

(b) If served by mail, the notice shall be:

(1) Addressed to the employing unit or person at his or her address as it appears on the records of the department.

(2) Complete at the time of deposit in the United States mail.

(3) Made pursuant to Section 1013 of the Code of Civil Procedure, excepting service of notice of a hearing before or an order or a decision of an administrative law judge or of the appeals board in transfer of reserve account, reassessment and refund matters.

(c) May be served electronically or by a computerized service if service by certified mail is not required and the manner of service is agreed to by the recipient. *(Added by Stats.1979, c. 1082, p. 3894, § 27. Amended by Stats.1984, c. 537, § 19; Stats.1993, c. 402 (A.B.1668), § 4; Stats.1995, c. 541 (A.B.272), § 4.)*

ARTICLE 11. ADMINISTRATIVE APPELLATE REVIEW

Section
1221. Jeopardy assessment; petition for reassessment; procedure.
1222. Assessment, denial of refund or credit, or transfer of reserve account; petition for review or reassessment.
1223. Duty of administrative law judge to review; hearings; notice; new and additional evidence; decisions.
1224. Appeal to board; time; failure to file; consequences; power of board to decrease or increase assessment; orders; time of finality.

§ 1221. Jeopardy assessment; petition for reassessment; procedure

(a) Within 10 working days of notice of an assessment pursuant to Section 1137, the employer may file a petition for reassessment of the jeopardy assessment pursuant to Section 1222.

(b) Within five days of receiving a petition for reassessment pursuant to subdivision (a), the board shall notify the employer of the date and time of a preliminary hearing to determine the reasonableness of levying the assessment pursuant to Section 1137. The preliminary hearing shall be held before an administrative law judge and scheduled not less than 10 nor more than 20 days from the filing of the petition for reassessment. The administrative law judge shall issue a decision within 10 days of the scheduled hearing date. The date scheduled for the preliminary hearing may be continued by the administrative law judge upon the request of the employer and the director.

(c) The burden of proof on the issue of the reasonableness of levying the assessment pursuant to Section 1137 shall be on the director. In determining the reasonableness of levying the assessment pursuant to Section 1137 at the preliminary hearing, the administrative law judge shall consider and make findings on whether the director had probable cause under Section 1137.1 to levy the assessment pursuant to Section 1137. If the administrative law judge or the board, on appeal from an administrative law judge's decision, decides that the assessment should not have been levied under Section 1137, the assessment shall automatically become, and shall have the effect of, an assessment pursuant to Section 1126 or 1127, whichever is applicable. If the administrative law judge or the board decides that the assessment was properly levied under Section 1137, this decision shall be incorporated in any decision rendered following the hearing pursuant to subdivision (d). The board shall expedite any appeal from an administrative law judge's decision on a preliminary hearing.

(d) All other issues raised by a petition for reassessment filed pursuant to subdivision (a), including, but not limited to, the appropriateness of the amount assessed, shall be determined at a hearing scheduled and held pursuant to Sections 1223 and 1224. *(Added by Stats. 1986, c. 89, § 5, eff. May 13, 1986.)*

§ 1222. Assessment, denial of refund or credit, or transfer of reserve account; petition for review or reassessment

Within 30 days of service of any notice of assessment or denial of claim for refund or credit under Section 803, 821, or 991, or of any notice under Sections 704.1, 1035, 1055, 1127.5, 1131, 1142, 1143, 1144, 1180, 1184, 1733, and 1735, any employing unit or other person given the notice, or any employing unit affected by a granting or denial of a transfer of reserve account, may file a petition for review or reassessment with an administrative law judge. The administrative law judge may for good cause grant an additional 30 days for the filing of a petition. If a petition for reassessment is not filed within the 30–day period, or within the additional period granted by the administrative law judge, an assessment is final at the expiration of the period. If a petition for review of a termination of elective coverage under Section 704.1 is not filed within the 30–day period, or within the additional period granted by the administrative law judge, the termination is final at the expiration of the period. If the director fails to serve notice of his or her action within 60 days after a claim for refund or credit is filed, the person or employing unit may consider the claim denied and file a petition with an administrative law judge. *(Added by Stats.1979, c. 1082, p. 3895, § 28. Amended by Stats.1980, c. 1025, p. 3288, § 9; Stats.1984, c. 537, § 21; Stats.1986, c. 248, § 232; Stats.1986, c. 793, § 3, eff. Sept. 15, 1986; Stats.1995, c. 541 (A.B.272), § 5; Stats.2001, c. 409 (S.B.40), § 1; Stats.2002, c. 1022 (A.B.444), § 9, eff. Sept. 28, 2002; Stats.2005, c. 152 (A.B.1577), § 11; Stats.2006, c. 538 (S.B.1852), § 643.)*

§ 1223. Duty of administrative law judge to review; hearings; notice; new and additional evidence; decisions

If any petition is filed under this article within the time and meeting requirements prescribed, an administrative law judge shall review the matter and, if requested by the petitioner, shall grant a hearing. A hearing is not required on a petition if a prior hearing has been

afforded the petitioner involving the same issues, but regardless of any prior proceedings, if the petitioner files an affidavit setting forth new and additional evidence in support of his or her petition, an administrative law judge may grant an additional hearing. The administrative law judge shall give at least 20 days' notice of the time and place of the hearing on a petition by delivering or mailing the notice to the petitioner and to the director. The time of notice may be shortened with the consent of the parties. The administrative law judge shall render a decision in the matter and may decrease or increase the amount of any assessment under review. Every employing unit or person which is a party to the petition and the director shall be promptly notified of the administrative law judge's decision, together with his or her reasons therefor. *(Added by Stats.1979, c. 1082, p. 3895, § 28. Amended by Stats.1984, c. 537, § 22.)*

§ 1224. Appeal to board; time; failure to file; consequences; power of board to decrease or increase assessment; orders; time of finality

(a) The petitioner or the director may, within 30 days after the service of notice of an administrative law judge's decision under this article, file an appeal to the appeals board. The appeals board may for good cause extend the appeal period. If the administrative law judge fails to serve notice of the decision on a petition for review of denial of a claim for refund or credit within 60 days after a petition is filed, the petitioner may consider the petition denied and file an appeal with the appeals board. If an appeal is not filed within the 30-day period or within the additional period granted by the appeals board:

(1) The decision of the administrative law judge upon the petition is final in every case at the expiration of the period.

(2) Any assessment involved is final at the expiration of the period except that in cases where a decision of the administrative law judge requires an adjustment of an assessment by granting a portion of a petition or by increasing an assessment, the assessment is final 30 days after service upon the petitioner by the director of a statement of amounts due setting forth the adjusted liability pursuant to the decision.

(b) In the event of an appeal to the appeals board, it may decrease or increase the amount of any assessment involved. In cases where an order or decision of the appeals board requires an adjustment of an assessment by granting a portion of a petition or by increasing an assessment, the order or decision and the assessment become final 30 days after service upon the petitioner by the director of a statement of amounts due setting forth the adjusted liability pursuant to the order or decision of the appeals board. In all other cases, the order or decision of the appeals board and any assessment become final 30 days after service upon the petitioner of notice of the order or decision. *(Added by Stats.1979, c. 1082, p. 3895, § 28. Amended by Stats.1984, c. 537, § 23.)*

ARTICLE 11.5.   TAXPAYER'S RIGHTS

Section
1231. Taxpayer education and information program; development and implementation.
1233. Relief from taxes assessed, interest, additions to tax, or penalties for failure to make timely returns or payments due to reasonable reliance on advice from department; conditions.
1234. Authorization to grant relief under § 1233 for unemployment insurance taxes imposed pursuant to contribution rate provisions; conditions.
1236. Settlement of civil employment tax matter disputes; recommendations of settlement; procedures.
1237. Employees seeking information regarding personal rights under code; violation of rights by discharge or discrimination; remedies.

§ 1231.   Taxpayer education and information program; development and implementation

(a) The department shall develop and implement a taxpayer education and information program directed at, but not limited to, the following:

(1) Taxpayer or industry groups.

(2) Department audit and compliance staff.

(3)(A) Identifying forms, procedures, regulations, or laws that are confusing and lead to taxpayer errors.

(B) Taking appropriate action, including recommending remedial legislation to change those items identified pursuant to subparagraph (A).

(b) The education and information program described in subdivision (a) shall include all of the following:

(1) Communication with the taxpayer or industry groups which explains in simplified terms the most common errors made by taxpayers and how those errors may be avoided or corrected.

(2) Participation in small business seminars and similar programs organized by state and local agencies and may include participation in seminars organized by private organizations.

(3) In cooperation with the small business community, development of small business educational events and materials that explain, in simplified terms, the process of the department's determination of whether an individual is an employee or an independent contractor. These events and materials shall be designed to address potential tax and labor law issues that may arise when small businesses contract with microbusinesses in the production and delivery of products and services.

(4) Revision of taxpayer educational materials currently produced by the department to explain in simplified terms the most common errors made by taxpayers and how those errors may be avoided or corrected.

(5) Implementation of a continuing education program for audit personnel to include the application of new legislation to taxpayer activities and to minimize recurrent taxpayer noncompliance or inconsistency of administration. *(Added by Stats.1995, c. 541 (A.B.272), § 6.*

Amended by Stats.1998, c. 165 (A.B.632), § 1; Stats.2004, c. 828 (A.B.1643), § 2.)

§ 1233.   Relief from taxes assessed, interest, additions to tax, or penalties for failure to make timely returns or payments due to reasonable reliance on advice from department; conditions

(a) If an employing unit's failure to make a timely return or payment is due to the person's reasonable reliance on written advice from the department, the employing unit may be relieved of the taxes assessed, or any interest, additions to tax, or penalties added thereto, as follows:

(1) Taxes or any interest, additions to tax, or penalties added thereto, shall only be relieved if the employing unit's failure to make a timely return or payment was due to the employing unit's reasonable reliance on the written advice of a ruling by the director or his or her designee, and only if the department itself finds all the conditions described in subdivision (b) are satisfied.

(2) In the event that the employing unit relied on written advice of other than a ruling of the director or his or her designee, taxes shall not be relieved. Interest, additions to tax, or penalties may be waived if the department staff finds all the conditions described in subdivision (b) are satisfied.

(b) For purposes of subdivision (a), relief shall be granted if all of the following conditions are satisfied:

(1) The employing unit or the employing unit's representative requested in writing that the department advise him or her whether a particular activity or transaction is subject to tax under the tax laws administered by the department, and the specific facts and circumstances of the employment relationship, activity, or transaction were fully described in the request.

(2) The department responded in writing to the person regarding the written request for advice, stating whether or not the described employment relationship, activity, or transaction is subject to tax, or stating the conditions under which the activity or transaction is subject to tax.

(3) In reasonable reliance on the department's written advice, the person did not remit the tax due.

(4) The liability for taxes applied to a particular activity or transaction that occurred before the department rescinded or modified the advice so given, by sending written notice to the person of the rescinded or modified advice.

(5) The tax consequences expressed in the department's written advice were not subsequently changed by any of the following:

(A) A change in state or federal statutory law or case law.

(B) A change in a federal administrative ruling or regulation where the department's written advice was based on that federal administrative ruling or regulation.

(C) A change in material facts or circumstances relating to the taxpayer.

(c) Any person seeking relief under this section shall file with the department all of the following:

(1) A copy of the person's written request to the department and a copy of the department's written advice.

(2) A statement signed under penalty of perjury, setting forth the facts on which the claim is based.

(3) Any other information which the department may require.

(d) Only the person making the written request shall be entitled to rely on the department's written advice to that person.

(e) If written advice is issued pursuant to this section, it shall include a declaration that the tax consequences expressed in the advice may be subject to change for any of the reasons specified in paragraph (5) of subdivision (b) and that it is the duty of the requester to be aware of any of these possible changes.

(f) This section shall not apply if the requester's request for written advice pursuant to paragraph (1) of subdivision (b) contained a misrepresentation or omission of one or more material facts.

(g) For purposes of subdivision (a), the department shall waive only that portion of tax, penalties, interest, or additions to tax attributable to the actions taken by the employing unit after receipt of the written advice of the department which were in reasonable reliance on the written advice.

(h) When a request is made for a legal ruling, the request shall specifically so state. Director rulings shall be issued as provided in published guidelines. When a director ruling is issued, the ruling shall be signed by the director or his or her designee.

(i) This section shall not apply to an employing unit that is a nonprofit organization or a governmental agency.

(j) Notwithstanding any other provision of this section, no relief from unemployment insurance taxes imposed pursuant to Article 3 (commencing with Section 976) of Chapter 4 of Part 1, other than relief from interest and penalties, shall be granted pursuant to this section unless Section 1234, as enacted by the act enacting this section, becomes operative. *(Added by Stats.1995, c. 541 (A.B. 272), § 6.)*

§ 1234. Authorization to grant relief under § 1233 for unemployment insurance taxes imposed pursuant to contribution rate provisions; conditions

Operation of this section is contingent upon certification of the unemployment compensation law of California, see subd. (b).

(a) Relief from unemployment insurance taxes imposed pursuant to Article 3 (commencing with Section 976) of Chapter 4 of Part 1 shall be granted pursuant to Section 1233 if this section becomes operative.

(b) This section shall become operative on the January 1 immediately following a certification of the unemployment compensation law of California, including Sections 1233 and 1234, by the United States Secretary of Labor pursuant to Section 3303 of Title 26 of the United States Code.

(c) If the United States Secretary of Labor determines that the operation of this section would preclude certification of the unemployment compensation law of California pursuant to Section 3303 of Title 26 of the United States Code, this section shall remain in effect only until the director notifies the Secretary of State of that determination, and as of that date is repealed. *(Added by Stats.1995, c. 541 (A.B.272), § 6.)*

Repeal

This section is repealed by its own terms upon notification by the director to the Secretary of State that operation of this section would preclude certification of the unemployment compensation law of California, see subd. (c).

§ 1236. Settlement of civil employment tax matter disputes; recommendations of settlement; procedures

Any civil employment tax matter dispute arising under Article 8 (commencing with Section 1126), Article 9 (commencing with Section 1176), or Article 11 (commencing with Section 1221), may be settled under the following conditions:

(a)(1) The director may approve a settlement of a civil employment tax matter in dispute involving a reduction of tax in settlement of seven thousand five hundred dollars ($7,500) or less. However, once an appeal of an employment tax matter dispute has been filed with the appeals board, the appeal has been assigned to an administrative law judge, and a notice of hearing has been issued, approval of the settlement by the assigned administrative law judge shall be obtained. If the decision of the administrative law judge has been appealed, approval of the appeals board shall be obtained. A proposed settlement shall be grounds for continuance of the scheduled hearing until the Attorney General has completed a review of the proposed settlement. "Civil employment tax matters in dispute" means those matters that are the subject of protests, appeals, or refund claims.

(2) Except as provided by paragraph (3), each proposed settlement shall be submitted to the Attorney General. Within 30 days of receiving that proposed settlement, the Attorney General shall review the recommendation and advise, in writing, of his or her conclusions as to whether the recommendation is reasonable from an overall perspective. If the Attorney General determines that the settlement is reasonable from an overall perspective, the director, and the administrative law judge or the appeals board, as applicable, may then determine if a settlement will be approved.

(3) A settlement of any civil employment tax matter dispute involving a reduction of tax or penalties in settlement, the total of which reduction of tax and penalties in settlement does not exceed five thousand dollars ($5,000), may be approved by the director, and the administrative law judge or the appeals board, as applicable, without prior submission to the Attorney General.

(b) The director may recommend to the appeals board a settlement of a civil employment tax matter dispute involving a reduction in tax and exceeding seven thousand five hundred dollars ($7,500) and arising under Article 8 (commencing with Section 1126), Article 9 (commencing with Section 1176), or Article 11 (commencing with Section 1221). Each proposed settlement shall be submitted to the Attorney General in the same manner as described in subdivision (a).

(c) Whenever a reduction of tax or penalties or total tax and penalties in excess of five hundred dollars ($500) is approved pursuant to this section, there shall be placed on file in the office of the director a public record with respect to that settlement. The public record shall include, but need not be limited to, all of the following information:

(1) The name or names of the taxpayers who are parties to the settlement.

(2) The total amount involved.

(3) The amount payable or refundable pursuant to the settlement.

(4) A summary of the reasons why the settlement is in the best interests of the state.

(5) The Attorney General's conclusion as to whether the recommendation of settlement was reasonable from an overall perspective.

The public record shall not include any information that relates to any trade secret, patent, process, style of work, apparatus, business secret, or organizational structure that, if disclosed, would adversely affect the taxpayer or the national defense.

(d) All settlements entered into pursuant to this section shall be final and nonappealable, except upon a showing of fraud or misrepresentation with respect to a material fact.

(e) Any proceedings undertaken by the appeals board relating to a settlement as described in this section shall be conducted in a closed session or sessions. Except as provided in subdivision (c), any settlement entered into pursuant to this section shall constitute confidential tax information.

(f) Any settlement of a civil employment tax matter arising out of a disagreement between the department and the employing unit on the status of a worker as an employee or an independent contractor may also include an agreement on the prospective classification of that worker and any worker similarly situated for employment tax purposes, except as provided in subdivision (g).

(g) If a settlement includes a commitment on the prospective status of workers or reporting responsibilities of the employer, then the following shall apply:

(1) The settlement shall not operate to deprive workers of their eligibility for unemployment, workers' compensation, or disability insurance benefits.

(2) The commitment concerning the status of workers or reporting responsibilities of the employer will terminate if there is a change in material facts, a change in an applicable statute, or a ruling by the appeals board on the workers or employer subject to the settlement that is contrary to the commitment.

(h) For purposes of this section, settlement is defined as a compromise on the amount of the tax liability, consistent with the reasonable evaluation of the costs and risks associated with litigation of these matters.

(i) The amendments to this section made in the 1997 portion of the 1997–98 Regular Session shall become operative January 1, 1998. *(Added by Stats.1995, c. 541 (A.B.272), § 6, operative Jan. 1, 1997. Amended by Stats.1997, c. 636 (A.B.318), § 1.)*

§ 1237. Employees seeking information regarding personal rights under code; violation of rights by discharge or discrimination; remedies

(a) No business entity shall discharge or otherwise discriminate against any person because he or she has sought information from the department concerning his or her rights under this code or the Labor Code, cooperated with any investigation undertaken by the department, or has testified or is about to testify in any proceeding brought pursuant to this code or the Labor Code.

(b) Any employee who believes that his or her rights under subdivision (a) have been violated may file a complaint with the Labor Commissioner, and with respect to that complaint shall be entitled to the same rights, remedies, and procedures as are applicable for a violation of Section 98.6 of the Labor Code. *(Added by Stats.1997, c. 636 (A.B.318), § 2.)*

ARTICLE 12. JUDICIAL REVIEW

Section
1241. Actions for recovery of contributions, interest, or penalties; prerequisites; venue; time; failure to bring; waiver of claims; suit by church or religious organization to challenge exemption denial.
1242. Judgment for plaintiff; credit against contributions, interest, and penalties; interest on judgment.
1243. Decisions denying protest of charges to reserve account; transfer of account; time to bring action.

§ 1241. Actions for recovery of contributions, interest, or penalties; prerequisites; venue; time; failure to bring; waiver of claims; suit by church or religious organization to challenge exemption denial

(a) No suit or proceeding shall be maintained in any court for the recovery of any amount of contributions,

975

interest or penalties alleged to have been erroneously or illegally assessed or collected unless a claim for refund or credit has been filed pursuant to this chapter. Within 90 days after the service of the notice of the decision of the appeals board upon an appeal, the claimant may bring an action against the director on the grounds set forth in the claim in a court of competent jurisdiction in the County of Sacramento for the recovery of the whole or any part of the amount with respect to which the claim has been denied. The director may, in writing, extend for a period of not exceeding two years the time within which such action may be instituted if written request for such extension is filed with the director within the 90-day period. Failure to bring action within the time specified constitutes a waiver of any demand against the state on account of alleged overpayments. If the appeals board fails to serve notice of its decision on the appeal within 90 days after an appeal is filed, the claimant may consider the claim denied and may bring an action against the director under this section.

(b) To the extent permitted by federal law, any entity or organization which has made a bona fide claim that it is a church or convention or association of churches, or an organization which is operated primarily for religious purposes and which is operated, supervised, controlled, or principally supported by a church or convention or association of churches, may bring suit to challenge a decision of the appeals board denying an exemption as a church or religious organization by paying the amount of the last quarter assessed immediately preceding the initial appeals board decision denying the exemption and then making a claim for refund or credit pursuant to this section.

An entity or organization shall be deemed to have made a bona fide claim that it is a church or religious entity for purposes of this section if either of the following is established:

(1) That it has been recognized as a church or religious organization by any entity of state or federal government.

(2) That the appeals board found that the department has failed to show by a preponderance of the evidence admitted at the proceedings to determine tax liability that the petitioner has not made a bona fide claim of coverage under subdivision (a) as a church or religious entity.

(c) A petition for writ of mandate shall lie to challenge any decision denying eligibility under subdivision (b), and shall not be deemed an action proscribed by or within the meaning of Section 32 of Article XIII of the California Constitution or Section 1851. The time within which to file any claim or action under subdivision (a) shall be extended during the pendency of any action brought pursuant to this subdivision. *(Added by Stats.1979, c. 1082, p. 3896, § 29. Amended by Stats.1982, c. 984, p. 3570, § 2.)*

976

§ 1242. Judgment for plaintiff; credit against contributions, interest, and penalties; interest on judgment

If, in any action authorized by Section 1241, judgment is rendered for the plaintiff, the amount of the judgment shall first be credited on any contributions, interest, and penalties due from the plaintiff under this division, and the balance of the judgment shall be refunded to the plaintiff. In any such judgment, interest shall be allowed and paid only to the extent that interest and penalties collected under this division are available therefor, at the rate of 12 percent per annum upon the amount of contributions found to have been illegally collected from the date of the payment of the contributions to the date of the judgment. *(Added by Stats.1979, c. 1082, p. 3896, § 29.)*

§ 1243. Decisions denying protest of charges to reserve account; transfer of account; time to bring action

A decision of the appeals board on an appeal from a denial of a protest under Section 1034 or on an appeal from a denial or granting of an application for transfer of reserve account under Article 5 (commencing with Section 1051) shall be subject to judicial review if an appropriate proceeding is filed by the employer within 90 days of the service of notice of the decision. The director may, in writing, extend for a period of not exceeding two years the time within which such proceeding may be instituted if written request for such extension is filed with the director within the 90-day period. *(Added by Stats.1979, c. 1082, p. 3896, § 29.)*

CHAPTER 5. UNEMPLOYMENT COMPENSATION BENEFITS

Article		Section
1.	Eligibility and Disqualifications	1251
1.5.	Retraining Benefits	1266
2.	Computation (Amount and Duration)	1275
2.2.	Self–Employment Assistance Program	1300
3.	Filing, Determination, and Payment of Unemployment Compensation Benefit Claims	1326
4.	Overpayments	1375
5.	Rights of Trainees [Repealed]	

ARTICLE 1. ELIGIBILITY AND DISQUALIFICATIONS

Section
1251.	Individuals entitled to benefits.
1252.	Unemployed individual defined.
1252.1.	Totally unemployed individual; commercial fishermen.
1252.2.	Partially unemployed individuals; commercial fishermen.
1253.	Eligibility for benefits.
1253.1.	Eligibility for work; unlawful or lawful detention; reconsideration of determination.
1253.12.	Eligibility for work; death in immediate family.
1253.15.	Dischargee from United States armed services; eligibility during unexpired leave time.

Section

1253.2. Eligibility for work; days off and holidays.

1253.3. Payment of unemployment compensation benefits, extended duration benefits, and federal-state extended benefits.

1253.4. Participation in sports, athletic events or training between sport seasons or similar periods; ineligibility for benefits.

1253.5. Physical or mental illness or injury; amount of benefits.

1253.6. Jury duty or responding to subpoena.

1253.7. Jury duty or emergency hospitalization.

1253.8. Unemployed individuals only available for part-time work.

1253.9. Disqualification from unemployment compensation benefits based on student status; factors.

1254. Conditions to have week counted as week of unemployment.

1255. Benefits from other states, etc.; ineligibility.

1255.3. Reduction of benefits by retirement pay based on previous work; exceptions.

1255.5. Cash payments under certain laws; ineligibility; exception; computation.

1255.7. Claimants owing child support obligations; deductions from unemployment compensation payable; payment of amounts deducted; application of section.

1256. Disqualification; voluntary leaving without good cause; discharge for misconduct.

1256.1. Conviction of offense; termination of employment; reconsideration of determination made prior to conviction.

1256.2. Deprivation of equal employment opportunities; exceptions.

1256.3. Most recent work.

1256.4. Disqualification for intoxicants; duration; assistance.

1256.5. Sexual harassment; good cause to leave employment.

1257. Disqualification; falsification; refusal of employment.

1258. Suitable employment.

1258.5. Suitable employment.

1259. Refusal of unsuitable employment.

1260. Duration of disqualification.

1260.1. Denial of benefits; misconduct, fraud, disqualifying income; construction of section.

1261. Successive disqualifications; extension of period of ineligibility.

1262. Strike; ineligibility.

1262.5. Trade disputes; investigation; findings.

1263. Conviction for false statement or concealment.

1264. Services performed by aliens; ineligibility for benefits; exception; procedures respecting aliens who have applied for temporary resident status.

1265. Payments under plan by employer supplementing unemployment compensation not construed as wages or compensation.

1265.1. Employer's violation of federal Worker Adjustment and Retraining Notification Act (WARN).

1265.5. Vacation pay earned but not paid prior to termination of employment.

1265.6. Holiday pay.

1265.7. Sick pay not wages or compensation.

Section

1265.9. Severance or terminal pay for termination of employment due to expansion of federal redwood parks not wages or compensation.

§ 1251. Individuals entitled to benefits

Unemployment compensation benefits are payable from the Unemployment Fund to unemployed individuals who are eligible under this part. *(Stats.1953, c. 308, p. 1501, § 1251.)*

§ 1252. Unemployed individual defined

(a) An individual is "unemployed" in any week in which he or she meets any of the following conditions:

(1) Any week during which he or she performs no services and with respect to which no wages are payable to him or her.

(2) Any week of less than full-time work, if the wages payable to him or her with respect to the week, when reduced by twenty-five dollars ($25) or 25 percent of the wages payable, whichever is greater, do not equal or exceed his or her weekly benefit amount.

(3) Any week for which, except for the requirements of subdivision (d) of Section 1253, he or she would be eligible for benefits under Section 1253.5.

(4) Any week during which he or she performs full-time work for five days as a juror, or as a witness under subpoena.

(b) Authorized regulations shall be prescribed making such distinctions as may be necessary in the procedures applicable to unemployed individuals as to total unemployment, part-total employment, partial unemployment of individuals attached to their regular jobs, and other forms of short-time work.

(c) For the purpose of this section only "wages" includes any and all compensation for personal services whether performed as an employee or as an independent contractor or as a juror or as a witness, but does not include any payment received by a member of the National Guard or reserve component of the armed forces for inactive duty training, annual training, or emergency state active duty. *(Stats.1953, c. 308, p. 1501, § 1252. Amended by Stats.1973, c. 582, p. 1101, § 1; Stats.1974, c. 1185, p. 2555, § 1; Stats.1975, c. 889, p. 1968, § 1; Stats.1977, c. 473, p. 1539, § 1; Stats.1979, c. 1053, p. 3708, § 4; Stats.1983, c. 761, § 1.)*

§ 1252.1. Totally unemployed individual; commercial fishermen

With respect to individuals hired as commercial fishermen a "totally unemployed individual" means an individual who, during a particular week, while still attached to his employer from the standpoint that there did not occur any severance of the employer-employee relationship, earned no wages and performed no services because his employer's boat was tied up for one or more of the following reasons:

(a) Inclement weather.

(b) Absence of fish in fishable waters.

(c) Lack of orders for fish from buyers.

(d) Boat is laid up for repairs. *(Added by Stats.1959, c. 1721, p. 4130, § 1. Amended by Stats.1961, c. 2164, p. 4483, § 9.)*

§ 1252.2. Partially unemployed individuals; commercial fishermen

With respect to individuals hired as commercial fishermen a "partially unemployed individual" means an individual who, during a particular week meets all of the following conditions:

(a) Was employed by his or her regular employer in the act of catching or attempting to catch fish.

(b) Was during the week continuously attached to his or her employer from the standpoint that there did not occur any severance of the employer-employee relationship.

(c)(1) Worked less than normal customary full-time hours or full number of days per week for his or her regular employer because of lack of full-time work, or

(2) If normal customary full-time hours or full number of days per week are not determinable, he or she worked less than four (4) days during a payroll week for his or her regular employer because of lack of full-time work.

(d) Earned wages which, when reduced by twenty-five dollars ($25) or 25 percent of the wages, whichever is greater, do not equal or exceed his or her weekly benefit amount. *(Formerly § 145, added by Stats.1957, c. 2244, p. 3912, § 1. Amended by Stats.1959, c. 375, p. 2300, § 1. Renumbered § 1252.2 and amended by Stats.1961, c. 2164, p. 4481, § 1; Stats.1979, c. 1053, p. 3709, § 5; Stats.1983, c. 761, § 2.)*

§ 1253. Eligibility for benefits

An unemployed individual is eligible to receive unemployment compensation benefits with respect to any week only if the director finds that:

(a) A claim for benefits with respect to that week has been made in accordance with authorized regulations.

(b) He or she has registered for work, and thereafter continued to report, at a public employment office or any other place as the director may approve. Either or both of the requirements of this subdivision may be waived or altered by authorized regulation as to partially employed individuals attached to regular jobs.

(c) He or she was able to work and available for work for that week.

(d) He has been unemployed for a waiting period of one week as defined in Section 1254, unless this waiting period has been waived pursuant to Section 8571 of the Government Code.

(e) He or she conducted a search for suitable work in accordance with specific and reasonable instructions of a public employment office.

(f) He or she participated as required by the director in reemployment activities, such as orientation and assessment if the individual has been identified pursuant to an automated profiling system as likely to exhaust regular unemployment benefits unless the individual has shown good cause for failure to participate. *(Stats.1953, c. 308, p. 1501, § 1253. Amended by Stats.1953, c. 1289, p. 2842; Stats.1961, c. 2208, p. 4553, § 1; Stats.1990, c. 1474 (A.B.3977), § 2; Stats.1994, c. 967 (S.B.1584), § 3, eff. Sept. 28, 1994; Stats.1994, c. 1116 (S.B.1482), § 1.)*

§ 1253.1. Eligibility for work; unlawful or lawful detention; reconsideration of determination

An unemployed individual who is in all respects otherwise eligible for unemployment compensation benefits shall not be deemed ineligible for any week in which, for not exceeding two working days, he cannot reasonably be expected to work because:

(a) He is unlawfully detained.

(b) He is lawfully detained or arrested, but the charge against such individual is subsequently dismissed.

(c) Notwithstanding any other provision of this division, any determination made pursuant to subdivision (b) of this section may, if no appeal has been filed therefrom, be reconsidered by the department within 15 days from the date that the charge is dismissed. Notice of any reconsidered determination shall be given to the claimant and any employer or employing unit which received notice under Section 1328 or 1331, and the claimant or employer may appeal therefrom in the manner prescribed in Section 1328. *(Added by Stats.1959, c. 2153, p. 5201, § 1, eff. July 20, 1959. Amended by Stats.1967, c. 1721, p. 4292, § 6; Stats.1975, c. 768, p. 769, § 1.)*

§ 1253.12. Eligibility for work; death in immediate family

An unemployed individual who is in all respects otherwise eligible for unemployment compensation benefits, shall not be deemed ineligible for any week in which:

(a) For not exceeding two working days, he or she cannot reasonably be expected to work because there has been a death in his or her immediate family in the state in which he or she resides.

(b) For not exceeding four working days, he or she cannot reasonably be expected to work because there has been a death in his or her immediate family outside of the state in which he or she resides. *(Added by Stats.1975, c. 768, p. 769, § 2. Amended by Stats.1978, c. 397, p. 1257, § 4, eff. July 11, 1978.)*

§ 1253.15. Dischargee from United States armed services; eligibility during unexpired leave time

An unemployed individual who has been discharged from any branch of the United States armed services and who is in all respects otherwise eligible for unemployment compensation benefits shall not be deemed ineligible in any week for which he has unexpired leave time for which he has been compensated upon his discharge. *(Added by Stats.1971, c. 1306, p. 2593, § 1.)*

§ 1253.2. Eligibility for work; days off and holidays

An unemployed individual who is in all respects otherwise eligible for unemployment compensation benefits shall not be deemed ineligible for any week in which pursuant to the provisions of a collective bargaining agreement he is allowed not more than one uncompensated day off in that week or is allowed not more than one uncompensated holiday on one day in that week if:

(a) He is employed in longshoring operations;

(b) His employer regularly offers employment to individuals employed in such operations seven days a week;

(c) He is able to work and available for work for six days of the week except as provided in Section 1253.1 or 1253.12. *(Added by Stats.1965, c. 1101, p. 2747, § 1. Amended by Stats.1979, c. 373, p. 1374, § 291.)*

§ 1253.3. Payment of unemployment compensation benefits, extended duration benefits, and federal-state extended benefits

(a) Notwithstanding any other provision of this division, unemployment compensation benefits, extended duration benefits, and federal-state extended benefits are payable on the basis of service to which Section 3309(a)(1) of the Internal Revenue Code of 1954 [1] applies, in the same amount, on the same terms, and subject to the same conditions as benefits payable on the basis of other service subject to this division, except as provided by this section.

(b) Benefits specified by subdivision (a) based on service performed in the employ of a nonprofit organization, or of any entity as defined by Section 605, with respect to service in an instructional, research, or principal administrative capacity for an educational institution are not payable to any individual with respect to any week which begins during the period between two successive academic years or terms or, when an agreement provides instead for a similar period between two regular but not successive terms, during that period, or during a period of paid sabbatical leave provided for in the individual's contract, if the individual performs services in the first of the academic years or terms and if there is a contract or a reasonable assurance that the individual will perform services for any educational institution in the second of the academic years or terms.

(c) Benefits specified by subdivision (a) based on service performed in the employ of a nonprofit organization, or of any entity as defined by Section 605, with respect to service in any other capacity than specified in subdivision (b) for an educational institution shall not be payable to any individual with respect to any week which commences during a period between two successive academic years or terms if the individual performs the service in the first of the academic years or terms and there is a reasonable assurance that the individual will perform the service in the second of the academic years

or terms. However, if the individual was not offered an opportunity to perform the services for an educational institution for the second of the academic years or terms, the individual shall be entitled to a retroactive payment of benefits for each week for which the individual filed a timely claim for benefits and for which benefits were denied solely by reason of this subdivision. Retroactive benefits shall be claimed in accordance with the department's procedures which shall specify that except where the individual was entitled to benefits based on services performed for other than an educational institution, an individual who has a reasonable assurance of reemployment may satisfy the search for work requirement of subdivision (e) of Section 1253, by registering for work pursuant to subdivision (b) of Section 1253 during the period between the first and second academic terms or years. A claim for retroactive benefits may be made no later than 30 days following the commencement of the second academic year or term.

(d) Benefits specified by subdivision (a) based on service performed in the employ of a nonprofit organization, or of any entity as defined by Section 605, with respect to services specified by subdivision (b) or (c), are not payable to any individual with respect to any week that commences during an established and customary vacation period or holiday recess if the individual performs the services in the period immediately before the vacation period or holiday recess, and there is a reasonable assurance that the individual will perform the services in the period immediately following the vacation period or holiday recess.

(e) With respect to any services specified by subdivision (b) or (c), compensation payable on the basis of services in that capacity may be denied as specified in subdivision (b), (c), or (d) to any individual who performed the services in an educational institution while in the employ of an educational service agency, and for this purpose the term "educational service agency" means a governmental agency or governmental entity that is established and operated exclusively for the purpose of providing the services to one or more educational institutions.

(f) Benefits specified by subdivision (a) based on service performed in the employ of a nonprofit organization, or of any entity as defined by Section 605, are not payable during the periods of time, and subject to the same conditions, contained in subdivisions (b), (c), (d), and (h), if the services are provided to, or on behalf of, an educational institution.

(g) For purposes of this section, "reasonable assurance" includes, but is not limited to, an offer of employment or assignment made by the educational institution, provided that the offer or assignment is not contingent on enrollment, funding, or program changes. An individual who has been notified that he or she will be replaced and does not have an offer of employment or assignment to perform services for an educational institution is not considered to have reasonable assurance.

(h) For purposes of this section, if the time for service performed during the period of and pursuant to any contract for any academic year or term by an individual for any employing unit as specified in subdivision (b) or (c) constitutes one-half or more of the time in total service performed for the employing unit by the individual during that same period for remuneration, all the services of the individual for the employing unit for that period shall be deemed subject to the benefit payment restriction provisions of this section.

(i) Any entity as defined by Section 605, with respect to any individual performing a service in any other capacity other than specified in subdivision (b) for an educational institution, shall provide a written statement indicating the following to the individual no later than 30 days before the end of the first of the academic years or terms:

(1) Whether or not there is a reasonable assurance of reemployment.

(2) Whether or not it is stated that the individual has no reasonable assurance of reemployment, that the individual should file a claim for benefits at the close of the academic year or term.

(3) If it is stated that the individual has reasonable assurance of reemployment, the written statement shall also inform the employee that he or she may file a claim for benefits and that the determination for eligibility for benefits is made by the Employment Development Department and not by the employer.

(4) If it is stated that the individual has reasonable assurance of reemployment, that the individual shall be entitled to a retroactive payment of benefits if the individual is not offered an opportunity to perform the services for the educational institution for the second of the academic years or terms, if the individual is otherwise eligible and he or she filed a claim for each week benefits are claimed, and if a claim for retroactive benefits is made no later than 30 days following the commencement of the second academic year or term. *(Added by Stats.1971, c. 1107, p. 2116, § 58, eff. Oct. 18, 1971, operative Jan. 1, 1972; Amended by Stats.1978, c. 2, p. 42, § 80, eff. Jan. 30, 1978, operative Jan. 1, 1978; Stats.1978, c. 397, p. 1257, § 5, eff. July 11, 1978; Stats.1983, c. 60, § 2, eff. June 2, 1983; Stats.1984, c. 1099, § 1; Stats.1984, c. 1296, § 3, eff. Sept. 20, 1984; Stats.1984, c. 1296, § 4, eff. Sept. 20, 1984, operative Jan. 1, 1985; Stats.1984, c. 1306, § 4; Stats.1985, c. 1488, § 2. Amended by Stats.1989, c. 1146, § 12; Stats.2001, c. 255 (A.B.1537), § 15.)*

[1] 26 U.S.C.A. § 3309, subd. (a), par. (1) ("1954" should probably read "1986").

Operative Effect

Under the terms of Section 17 of Stats.2001, c. 255 (A.B.1537), the provisions of that Act are retroactive to December 21, 2000.

§ 1253.4. Participation in sports, athletic events or training between sport seasons or similar periods; ineligibility for benefits

Unemployment compensation benefits, extended duration benefits, and federal-state extended benefits shall not be payable to any individual on the basis of any services, substantially all of which consist of participating in sports or athletic events or training or preparing to so participate, for any week which commences during the period between two successive sport seasons, or similar periods, if such individual performed such services in the first of such seasons, or similar periods, and there is a reasonable assurance that such individual will perform such services in the later of such seasons, or similar periods. *(Added by Stats.1978, c. 2, p. 43, § 82, eff. Jan. 30, 1978, operative Jan. 1, 1978.)*

§ 1253.5. Physical or mental illness or injury; amount of benefits

Notwithstanding the provisions of subdivision (c) of Section 1253, if an individual is, in all other respects, eligible for benefits under this part, and such individual becomes unable to work due to a physical or mental illness or injury for one or more days during such week, he shall be paid unemployment compensation benefits at the rate of one-seventh the weekly benefit amount payable for that week for each day which he is available for work and able to work. The amount of benefits payable, if not a multiple of one dollar ($1), shall be computed to the next higher multiple of one dollar ($1). The individual shall not be entitled to unemployment compensation benefits for any day during such week which he is unable to work due to such physical or mental illness or injury. *(Added by Stats.1974, c. 1185, p. 2555, § 2.)*

§ 1253.6. Jury duty or responding to subpoena

For purposes of subdivision (c) of Section 1253, an unemployed individual who is in all respects otherwise eligible for unemployment compensation benefits, shall not be deemed to be not able to, or unavailable for, work for any week in which such person is not able to, or available for, work solely because such person is serving on a grand or petit jury, or is responding to a subpoena. *(Added by Stats.1975, c. 889, p. 1969, § 2. Amended by Stats.1977, c. 473, p. 1540, § 2.)*

§ 1253.7. Jury duty or emergency hospitalization

For the purposes of subdivision (e) of Section 1253, an individual shall not be disqualified for any week solely because of either of the following:

(a) The individual is before any court of the United States or any state pursuant to a lawfully issued summons to appear for jury duty.

(b) The individual is hospitalized for treatment of an emergency or life-threatening condition. *(Added by Stats.1985, c. 716, § 1.)*

§ 1253.8. Unemployed individuals only available for part-time work

An unemployed individual shall not be disqualified for eligibility for unemployment compensation benefits solely on the basis that he or she is only available for part-time work. If an individual restricts his or her availability to part-time work, he or she may be considered to be able to work and available for work pursuant to subdivision (c) of Section 1253 if it is determined that all of following conditions exist:

(a) The claim is based on the part-time employment.

(b) The claimant is actively seeking and is willing to accept work under essentially the same conditions as existed while the wage credits were accrued.

(c) The claimant imposes no other restrictions and is in a labor market in which a reasonable demand exists for the part-time services he or she offers. *(Added by Stats.2001, c. 409 (S.B.40), § 3.)*

§ 1253.9. Disqualification from unemployment compensation benefits based on student status; factors

An unemployed individual may not be disqualified for unemployment compensation benefits solely on the basis that he or she is a student. An unemployed individual may be considered to be able and available for work pursuant to subdivision (c) of Section 1253, if the school attendance does not eliminate a substantial portion of the individual's full-time labor market availability. If an unemployed individual restricts his or her availability to part-time work due to school attendance, he or she may be considered to be able to work and available for work if he or she meets the criteria set forth in Section 1253.8. *(Added by Stats.2002, c. 1022 (A.B.444), § 10, eff. Sept. 28, 2002.)*

§ 1254. Conditions to have week counted as week of unemployment

No week shall be counted as a week of unemployment under subdivision (d) of Section 1253:

(a) Unless it occurs within the benefit year which includes the week with respect to which he claims payment of unemployment compensation benefits, but this requirement shall not interrupt the payment of such benefits for consecutive weeks of unemployment. The week immediately preceding a benefit year, if part of one uninterrupted period of unemployment which continues into that benefit year shall be deemed, for the purposes of this section only, to be within such benefit year as well as within the preceding benefit year.

(b) If unemployment compensation benefits have been paid with respect to that week.

(c) Unless the individual was eligible for unemployment compensation benefits with respect thereto in all respects, except for the requirements of subdivision (d) of Section 1253 and Section 1281. *(Stats.1953, c. 308, p. 1502, § 1254.)*

§ 1255. Benefits from other states, etc.; ineligibility

An individual is not eligible for unemployment compensation benefits on account of unemployment for any week or part of any week with respect to which he has received or is seeking unemployment benefits under an unemployment compensation law of any other state or of the United States. If the appropriate agency of the other state or of the United States finally determines that he is not entitled to unemployment compensation benefits, this section shall not apply. *(Stats.1953, c. 308, p. 1502, § 1255.)*

§ 1255.3. Reduction of benefits by retirement pay based on previous work; exceptions

(a) Except as provided by subdivisions (c) and (d), the amount of unemployment compensation benefits, extended duration benefits, and federal-state extended benefits payable to an individual for any week which begins after March 31, 1980, and which begins in a period with respect to which that individual is receiving a governmental or other pension, retirement or retired pay, annuity, or any other similar periodic payment which is based on the previous work of the individual shall be reduced, but not below zero, by an amount equal to the amount of the pension, retirement or retired pay, annuity, or other payment, which is reasonably attributable to that week.

(b) Subdivision (a) shall be operative only during such time as Section 3304 of the Federal Unemployment Tax Act requires that state unemployment insurance laws contain those provisions as a condition of certification of state unemployment insurance laws by the Secretary of Labor.

(c) Subdivision (a) shall apply to any pension, retirement or retired pay, annuity, or other similar periodic payment only if both of the following are met.

(1) The pension, retirement or retired pay, annuity, or similar payment is under a plan maintained (or contributed to) by a base period or chargeable employer.

(2) In the case of such a payment not made under the federal Social Security Act or the federal Railroad Retirement Act of 1974 (or the corresponding provisions of prior law), services performed for the employer by the individual after the beginning of the base period (or remuneration for such services) affect eligibility for, or increase the amount of, such pension, retirement or retired pay, annuity, or similar periodic payment.

(d)(1) Subdivision (a) shall not apply to any pension, retirement or retired pay, annuity or other similar periodic payment if the individual has made any contribution to the pension, retirement or retired pay, annuity, or other similar periodic payment.

(2) The amendments made to this subdivision during the 1986 portion of the 1985–86 Regular Session shall apply to new claims filed with an effective date beginning on or after January 1, 1987.

(e) The amendments made to subdivision (c) of this section during the 1985 portion of the 1985–86 Regular

Session shall apply retroactively to all unemployment compensation benefits, extended duration benefits, and federal-state extended benefits, payable to an individual for any week which begins after November 1, 1980.

(Added by Stats.1979, c. 754, p. 2611, § 1. Amended by Stats.1980, c. 1174, p. 3944, § 1, eff. Sept. 29, 1980; Stats.1981, c. 1134, p. 4448, § 3; Stats.1985, c. 1217, § 7, eff. Sept. 29, 1985; Stats.1986, c. 1014, § 1, eff. Sept. 23, 1986; Stats.1987, c. 956, § 1, eff. Sept. 22, 1987.)

§ 1255.5. Cash payments under certain laws; ineligibility; exception; computation

(a) An individual is not eligible for unemployment compensation benefits or extended duration benefits for the same day or days of unemployment for which he is allowed by the Workmen's Compensation Appeals Board, or for which he receives, benefits in the form of cash payments for temporary total disability indemnity, under a workmen's compensation law, or employer's liability law of this state, or of any other state, or of the federal government, except that if such cash payments are less than the amount he would otherwise receive as unemployment compensation benefits or extended duration benefits under this division, he shall be entitled to receive for such day or days, if otherwise eligible, unemployment compensation benefits or extended duration benefits reduced by the amount of such cash payments.

(b) Notwithstanding any other provision of this division, an individual who is ineligible to receive unemployment compensation benefits or extended duration benefits under subdivision (a) of this section for one or more days of a week of unemployment and who is eligible to receive unemployment compensation benefits or extended duration benefits for the other days of that week is, with respect to that week, entitled to an amount of unemployment compensation benefits or extended duration benefits computed by reducing his weekly benefit amount by the amount of temporary total disability indemnity received for that week.

(c) The amount determined under subdivision (a) or (b), if not a multiple of one dollar ($1), shall be computed to the next higher multiple of one dollar ($1). *(Added by Stats.1967, c. 1721, p. 4293, § 7.)*

§ 1255.7. Claimants owing child support obligations; deductions from unemployment compensation payable; payment of amounts deducted; application of section

(a) The Department of Child Support Services shall notify the director whether an individual filing a claim for unemployment compensation after October 1, 1982, owes support obligations as defined under subdivision (h), and notify the department of any changes in the status of these individuals to ensure that the department has a current record.

(b) The department shall maintain and keep current a record of individuals who owe support obligations and

who may have claims for unemployment compensation benefits.

(c) The department shall deduct and withhold support obligations as defined under subdivision (h) from any unemployment compensation payable to an individual who owes these obligations.

(d) Any amount deducted and withheld under subdivision (c) shall be paid by the department to the appropriate county or to the Department of Child Support Services as the assigned payee, as stipulated by mutual agreement, in the interagency agreement between the department and the Department of Child Support Services.

(e) Any amount deducted and withheld under subdivision (c) shall for all purposes be treated as if it were paid to the individual as unemployment compensation and paid by the individual to the Department of Child Support Services.

(f) For purposes of subdivisions (a) to (e), inclusive, "unemployment compensation" means any compensation payable under this division, except Part 2 (commencing with Section 2601), but including amounts payable by the department pursuant to an agreement under any federal unemployment compensation law.

(g) This section applies only if appropriate arrangements have been made for reimbursement by the Department of Child Support Services for the administrative costs incurred by the Employment Development Department.

(h) For purposes of this section, "support obligations" means the child and related spousal support obligations which are being enforced pursuant to a plan described in Section 454 of the Social Security Act and as that section may hereafter be amended. However, to the extent "related spousal support obligations" may not be collected from unemployment compensation under federal law, those obligations shall not be included in the definition of support obligations under this section. *(Added by Stats. 1982, c. 1072, p. 3858, § 4, eff. Sept. 15, 1982. Amended by Stats.1988, c. 261, § 2, eff. July 5, 1988; Stats.1990, c. 1024 (A.B.3092), § 3; Stats.1991, c. 110 (S.B.101), § 17; Stats.2000, c. 808 (A.B.1358), § 116, eff. Sept. 28, 2000.)*

§ 1256. Disqualification; voluntary leaving without good cause; discharge for misconduct

An individual is disqualified for unemployment compensation benefits if the director finds that he or she left his or her most recent work voluntarily without good cause or that he or she has been discharged for misconduct connected with his or her most recent work.

An individual is presumed to have been discharged for reasons other than misconduct in connection with his or her work and not to have voluntarily left his or her work without good cause unless his or her employer has given written notice to the contrary to the department as provided in Section 1327, setting forth facts sufficient to overcome the presumption. The presumption provided by this section is rebuttable.

An individual whose employment is terminated under the compulsory retirement provisions of a collective bargaining agreement to which the employer is a party, shall not be deemed to have left his or her work without good cause.

An individual may be deemed to have left his or her most recent work with good cause if he or she leaves employment to accompany his or her spouse or domestic partner to a place from which it is impractical to commute to the employment. For purposes of this section "spouse" includes a person to whom marriage is imminent.

An individual may be deemed to have left his or her most recent work with good cause if he or she leaves employment to protect his or her children, or himself or herself, from domestic violence abuse.

An individual shall be deemed to have left his or her most recent work with good cause if he or she elects to be laid off in place of an employee with less seniority pursuant to a provision in a collective bargaining agreement that provides that an employee with more seniority may elect to be laid off in place of an employee with less seniority when the employer has decided to lay off employees. (Added by Stats.1953, c. 1294, p. 2854. Amended by Stats.1959, c. 1402, p. 3681, § 2; Stats.1973, c. 761, p. 1371, § 1; Stats.1982, c. 1073, p. 3864, § 1; Stats.1983, c. 761, § 3; Stats.1984, c. 1084, § 1; Stats. 1988, c. 781, § 3; Stats.1998, c. 411 (S.B.165), § 4; Stats.2001, c. 893 (A.B.25), § 59.)

§ 1256.1. Conviction of offense; termination of employment; reconsideration of determination made prior to conviction

(a) If the employment of an individual is terminated due to his absence from work for a period in excess of 24 hours because of his incarceration and he is convicted of the offense for which he was incarcerated or of any lesser included offense, he shall be deemed to have left his work voluntarily without good cause for the purposes of Section 1256. A plea or verdict of guilty, or a conviction following a plea of nolo contendere, is deemed to be a conviction within the meaning of this section irrespective of whether an order granting probation or other order is made suspending the imposition of the sentence or whether sentence is imposed but execution thereof is suspended.

(b) Notwithstanding any other provision of this division, any determination made prior to a conviction or other final disposition of the criminal complaint or accusation by the court as to whether an individual who is terminated due to his absence from work because of incarceration voluntarily leaves without good cause may, if no appeal has been taken from the determination, for good cause be reconsidered by the department during the benefit year or extended duration period to which the determination relates. Notice of any reconsidered deter-

mination shall be given to the claimant and any employer or employing unit which received notice under Section 1328 or 1331, and the claimant or employer may appeal therefrom in the manner prescribed in Section 1328. (Added by Stats.1968, c. 1105, p. 2117, § 2. Amended by Stats.1972, c. 833, p. 1483, § 5.)

§ 1256.2. Deprivation of equal employment opportunities; exceptions

(a) Except as otherwise provided in subdivision (b), an individual who terminates his or her employment shall not be deemed to have left his or her most recent work without good cause if his or her employer deprived the individual of equal employment opportunities on any basis listed in subdivision (a) of Section 12940 of the Government Code, as those bases are defined in Sections 12926 and 12926.1 of the Government Code.

(b) Subdivision (a) does not apply to the following:

(1) A deprivation of equal employment opportunities that is based upon a bona fide occupational qualification or applicable security regulations established by the United States or this state, specifically, as provided in Section 12940 of the Government Code.

(2) An individual who fails to make reasonable efforts to provide the employer with an opportunity to remove any unintentional deprivation of the individual's equal employment opportunities. (Added by Stats.1975, c. 715, p. 1706, § 1. Amended by Stats.2004, c. 788 (A.B.2900), § 32.)

§ 1256.3. Most recent work

For the purposes of Sections 1256, 1256.1, 1256.2, 1256.4, and 1256.5, "most recent work" is that work in which a claimant last performed compensated services:

(a) Prior to and nearest the date of filing a valid new, reopened, or additional claim for unemployment compensation benefits, a valid primary, reopened, or additional claim for extended duration benefits, or a valid application, or reopened or additional claim for federal-state extended benefits.

(b) During the calendar week for which a continued claim is filed. (Added by Stats.1979, c. 770, p. 2640, § 1, eff. Sept. 19, 1979. Amended by Stats.2005, c. 152 (A.B.1577), § 12.)

§ 1256.4. Disqualification for intoxicants; duration; assistance

(a) An individual is disqualified for unemployment compensation benefits if either of the following occur:

(1) The director finds that he or she was discharged from his or her most recent work for chronic absenteeism due to intoxication or reporting to work while intoxicated or using intoxicants on the job, or gross neglect of duty while intoxicated, when any of these incidents is caused by an irresistible compulsion to use or consume intoxicants, including alcoholic beverages.

(2) He or she otherwise left his or her most recent employment for reasons caused by an irresistible compulsion to use or consume intoxicants, including alcoholic beverages.

(b) An individual disqualified under this section, under a determination transmitted to him or her by the department, is ineligible to receive unemployment compensation benefits under this part for the week in which the separation occurs, and continuing until he or she has performed service in bona fide employment for which remuneration is received equal to or in excess of five times his or her weekly benefit amount, or until a physician or authorized treatment program administrator certifies that the individual has entered into and is continuing in, or has completed, a treatment program for his or her condition and is able to return to employment.

(c) The department shall advise each individual disqualified under this section of the benefits available under Part 2 (commencing with Section 2601), and, if assistance in locating an appropriate treatment program is requested, refer the individual to the appropriate county drug or alcohol program administrator. *(Formerly § 1256.5, added by Stats. 1983, c. 1065, § 1. Amended by Stats.1986, c. 924, § 1. Renumbered § 1256.4 and amended by Stats.2005, c. 152 (A.B.1577), § 13.)*

§ 1256.5. Sexual harassment; good cause to leave employment

(a) An individual shall be deemed to have left his or her most recent work with good cause if the director finds that he or she leaves employment because of sexual harassment if the individual has taken reasonable steps to preserve the working relationship. No steps shall be required if the director finds it would have been futile. For purposes of this subdivision, unwelcome sexual advances, requests for sexual favors, and other verbal, visual, or physical conduct of a sexual nature constitutes sexual harassment when any of the following occur:

(1) Submission to the conduct is made either explicitly or implicitly a term or condition of an individual's employment.

(2) Submission to or rejection of the conduct by an individual is used as the basis for employment decisions affecting the individual.

(3) The conduct has the purpose or effect of unreasonably interfering with an individual's work performance or creating an intimidating, hostile, or offensive working environment.

(b) Findings of fact and law by the director shall not collaterally estop adjudication of the issue of sexual harassment in another forum. *(Formerly § 1256.7, added by Stats.1984, c. 1058, § 1. Renumbered § 1256.5 and amended by Stats.2005, c. 152 (A.B.1577), § 14. Amended by Stats.2006, c. 538 (S.B.1852), § 644.)*
984

§ 1257. Disqualification; falsification; refusal of employment

An individual is also disqualified for unemployment compensation benefits if:

(a) He or she willfully, for the purpose of obtaining unemployment compensation benefits, either made a false statement or representation, including, but not limited to, using a false name, false social security number, or other false identification, with actual knowledge of the falsity thereof, or withheld a material fact in order to obtain any unemployment compensation benefits under this division.

(b) He or she, without good cause, refused to accept suitable employment when offered to him or her, or failed to apply for suitable employment when notified by a public employment office. *(Added by Stats.1953, c. 1294, p. 2854. Amended by Stats.1979, c. 890, p. 3081, § 1; Stats.1995, c. 397 (A.B.212), § 1.)*

§ 1258. Suitable employment

"Suitable employment" means work in the individual's usual occupation or for which he is reasonably fitted, regardless of whether or not it is subject to this division.

In determining whether the work is work for which the individual is reasonably fitted, the director shall consider the degree of risk involved to the individual's health, safety, and morals, his physical fitness and prior training, his experience and prior earnings, his length of unemployment and prospects for securing local work in his customary occupation, and the distance of the available work from his residence, and such other factors as would influence a reasonably prudent person in the individual's circumstances. *(Added by Stats.1953, c. 1294, p. 2854. Amended by Stats.1975, c. 715, p. 1706, § 2.)*

§ 1258.5. Suitable employment

"Suitable employment" does not include employment with an employer who does not:

(a) Possess an appropriate state license to engage in his business, trade, or profession; or

(b) Withhold or hold in trust the employee contributions required by Part 2 (commencing with Section 2601) of this division for unemployment compensation disability benefits and does not transmit all such employee contributions to the department for the Disability Fund as required by Section 986; or

(c) Carry either workers' compensation insurance or possess a certificate of self-insurance as required by Division 4 (commencing with Section 3201) of the Labor Code. *(Added by Stats.1973, c. 1210, p. 2712, § 1. Amended by Stats.1974, c. 1159, p. 2471, § 28, eff. Sept. 23, 1974; Stats.1977, c. 1252, p. 4457, § 406.5, operative July 1, 1978; Stats.1979, c. 373, p. 1374, § 292.)*

§ 1259. Refusal of unsuitable employment

Notwithstanding any other provisions of this division, no work or employment shall be deemed suitable and benefits shall not be denied to any otherwise eligible and qualified individual for refusing new work under any of the following conditions:

(a) If the position offered is vacant due directly to a strike, lockout, or other labor dispute.

(b) If the wages, hours, or other conditions of the work offered are substantially less favorable to the individual than those prevailing for similar work in the locality.

(c) If, as a condition of being employed, the individual would be required to join a company union or to resign from or refrain from joining any bona fide labor organization.

(d) If the offer of employment is from an employer who does not possess an appropriate state license to engage in his business, trade, or profession if required by state law.

(e) If the offer of employment is from an employer who does not carry either workmen's compensation insurance or possess a certificate of self-insurance as required by Division 4 (commencing with Section 3201) of the Labor Code.

(f) If the offer of employment is from an employer who does not withhold or hold in trust the employee contributions required by Part 2 (commencing with Section 2601) of this division for unemployment compensation disability benefits and does not transmit all such employee contributions to the department for the Disability Fund as required by Section 986. *(Added by Stats.1953, c. 1294, p. 2854. Amended by Stats.1973, c. 1000, p. 1988, § 1; Stats.1974, c. 1159, p. 2471, § 29, eff. Sept. 23, 1974; Stats.1977, c. 1252, p. 4457, § 406.6, operative July 1, 1978.)*

§ 1260. Duration of disqualification

(a) An individual disqualified under Section 1256, under a determination transmitted to him or her by the department, is ineligible to receive unemployment compensation benefits for the week in which the act that causes his or her disqualification occurs and continuing until he or she has, subsequent to the act that causes disqualification and his or her registration for work, performed service in bona fide employment for which remuneration is received equal to or in excess of five times his or her weekly benefit amount.

(b) An individual disqualified under subdivision (b) of Section 1257, under a determination transmitted to him or her by the department, is ineligible to receive unemployment compensation benefits for not less than 2 nor more than 10 consecutive weeks beginning with:

(1) The week in which the cause of his or her disqualification occurs, if he or she registers for work in that week.

(2) The week subsequent to the occurrence of the cause of his or her disqualification in which he or she first registers for work, if he or she does not register for work in the week in which the cause of his or her disqualification occurs.

(c) An individual disqualified under subdivision (a) of Section 1257, under a determination transmitted to him or her by the department, and who was not paid any benefit amount as a result of his or her false statement or representation, is ineligible to receive unemployment compensation benefits for two weeks commencing with the week in which the determination is mailed to or personally served upon him or her, or any subsequent week, for which he or she is first otherwise in all respects eligible for unemployment compensation benefits and for not more than 13 subsequent weeks for which he or she is otherwise in all respects eligible for unemployment compensation benefits. No disqualification under this subdivision shall be applied to any week if all or any portion of the week is beyond the three-year period next succeeding the date of the mailing or personal service of the determination. This subdivision shall not apply to an individual convicted under Section 2101.

(d) An individual disqualified under subdivision (a) of Section 1257, under a determination transmitted to him or her by the department, and who was paid any benefit amount as a result of his or her false statement or representation, is ineligible to receive unemployment compensation benefits for five weeks commencing with the week in which the determination is mailed to or personally served upon him or her, or any subsequent week, for which he or she is first otherwise in all respects eligible for unemployment compensation benefits and for not more than 10 subsequent weeks for which he or she is otherwise in all respects eligible for unemployment compensation benefits. No disqualification under this subdivision shall be applied to any week if all or any portion of the week is beyond the three-year period next succeeding the date of the mailing or personal service of the determination. This subdivision shall not apply to an individual convicted under Section 2101.

(e) Notwithstanding subdivision (c) or (d), an individual who is subject to a disqualification that is imposed under subdivision (b) of Section 1257 may, if he or she is otherwise in all respects eligible for unemployment compensation benefits, concurrently serve a disqualification imposed under subdivision (a) of Section 1257. *(Stats.1953, c. 1294, p. 2854. Amended by Stats.1955, c. 899, p. 1526, § 3; Stats.1957, c. 2257, p. 3944, § 3; Stats.1961, c. 1924, p. 4042, § 1; Stats.1965, c. 1897, p. 4377, § 12; Stats.1967, c. 1721, p. 4293, § 8; Stats.1969, c. 291, p. 649, § 6; Stats.1983, c. 761, § 4; Stats.1987, c. 929, § 1; Stats.1989, c. 1146, § 13.)*

§ 1260.1. Denial of benefits; misconduct, fraud, disqualifying income; construction of section

Notwithstanding any other provision of this division, benefits shall not be denied to any individual by reason of cancellation of wage credits or total reduction of his benefit rights for any cause other than discharge for misconduct connected with his work, fraud in connection with a claim for benefits, or receipt of disqualifying income. This section shall not be construed to authorize cancellation of wage credits or total reduction of benefit

985

rights for any cause whatsoever, nor shall it limit or affect any other section that provides for cancellation of wage credits or total reduction of benefit rights for any cause permitted under this section. *(Added by Stats.1972, c. 833, p. 1484, § 6.)*

§ 1261. Successive disqualifications; extension of period of ineligibility

When successive disqualifications under Section 1257 occur, the director may extend the period of ineligibility provided for in Section 1260 for an additional period not to exceed eight additional weeks. *(Added by Stats.1953, c. 1294. Amended by Stats.1965, c. 1897, p. 4378, § 12.5.)*

§ 1262. Strike; ineligibility

An individual is not eligible for unemployment compensation benefits, and these benefits shall not be payable to him or her, if the individual left his or her work because of a trade dispute. The individual shall remain ineligible for the period during which he or she continues out of work by reason of the fact that the trade dispute is still in active progress in the establishment in which he or she was employed. *(Added by Stats.1953, c. 1294, p. 2854. Amended by Stats.2006, c. 538 (S.B.1852), § 645.)*

§ 1262.5. Trade disputes; investigation; findings

Whenever the department learns that a trade dispute is in progress, the department shall promptly conduct an investigation and make investigation findings as to the nature, location, labor organizations and employers involved, and other relevant facts concerning the trade dispute as it deems necessary. The department shall provide its findings to its field offices in locations affected by the trade dispute, and shall, upon request, make its findings available to any employer, employers' association or labor organization involved in the trade dispute. The department's investigation findings shall be based upon the information then available to it and shall not be a determination as to the eligibility of any claimant for benefits under Section 1262. *(Added by Stats.1976, c. 1100, p. 4972, § 2.)*

§ 1263. Conviction for false statement or concealment

(a) Any individual convicted under Section 2101 by any court of competent jurisdiction of willfully making a false statement or knowingly failing to disclose a material fact to obtain or increase any benefit or payment under this division shall forfeit any rights to benefits for the week in which the criminal complaint was filed and for the 51 consecutive calendar weeks which immediately follow that week, irrespective of a subsequent order under the provisions of Section 1203.4 of the Penal Code allowing the individual to withdraw his or her plea of guilty and to enter a plea of not guilty, or setting aside the verdict of guilty or dismissing the criminal complaint, but a forfeiture of benefits under this subdivision shall extend no later than the effective date of any order under Section 1203.4 of the Penal Code, and, if the period of forfeiture has not previously expired, the forfeiture of

benefits under this subdivision shall terminate as of the effective date of any such order.

(b) Any individual convicted under Section 2101 by any court of competent jurisdiction of willfully making a false statement or knowingly failing to disclose a material fact to obtain or increase any benefit or payment under this part, Part 3 (commencing with Section 3501), or Part 4 (commencing with Section 4001) shall, irrespective of a subsequent order under the provisions of Section 1203.4 of the Penal Code allowing the individual to withdraw his or her plea of guilty and to enter a plea of not guilty, or setting aside the verdict of guilty or dismissing the criminal complaint, be ineligible to receive unemployment compensation or extended duration benefits or federal-state extended benefits for the week in which the criminal complaint was filed, or any subsequent week, for which he or she is first otherwise in all respects eligible for unemployment compensation or extended duration benefits or federal-state extended benefits and for 14 subsequent weeks for which he or she is otherwise in all respects eligible for unemployment compensation or extended duration benefits or federal-state extended benefits. No disqualification under this subdivision shall be applied to any week if all or any portion of the week is beyond the three-year period next succeeding the date of the filing of the criminal complaint.

(c) The department shall, effective upon the date of the filing of a criminal complaint against an individual prosecuted under Section 2101, suspend the payment of benefits to the individual.

(d) A plea or verdict of guilty, or a conviction following a plea of nolo contendere, is deemed to be a conviction within the meaning of this section irrespective of whether an order granting probation or other order is made suspending the imposition of the sentence or whether sentence is imposed but execution thereof is suspended.

(e) Notwithstanding the provisions of this section, an individual may during a period of forfeiture under subdivision (a) of this section meet the conditions to remove any disqualification that is imposed under Sections 1260 or 1261, or subdivision (b) of this section, but no week during the period of forfeiture shall be used to offset the amount of any overpayment. *(Formerly § 1308, added by Stats.1953, c. 1294, p. 2854. Renumbered § 1263, and amended by Stats.1955, c. 899, p. 1527, § 4. Amended by Stats.1961, c. 1924, p. 4043, § 2; Stats.1970, c. 1156, p. 2049, § 9; Stats.1972, c. 833, p. 1484, § 7; Stats.1991, c. 212 (A.B.2108), § 1.)*

§ 1264. Services performed by aliens; ineligibility for benefits; exception; procedures respecting aliens who have applied for temporary resident status

(a) Unemployment compensation benefits, extended duration benefits, and federal-state extended benefits shall not be payable on the basis of services performed by an alien unless the alien is an individual who was lawfully admitted for permanent residence at the time the services were performed, was lawfully present for purposes of performing the services, or was permanently residing in the United States under color of law at the time the services were performed, including an alien who was lawfully present in the United States as a result of the application of the provisions of Section 203(a)(7) or Section 212(d)(5) of the Immigration and Nationality Act.

(b) Any data or information required of individuals applying for benefits specified by subdivision (a) to determine whether these benefits are not payable to them because of their alien status shall be uniformly required from all applicants for these benefits.

(c) In the case of an individual whose application for benefits specified by subdivision (a) would otherwise be approved, no determination by the department, an administrative law judge, or the appeals board that these benefits to the individual are not payable because of his or her alien status shall be made except upon a preponderance of the evidence.

(d) If an alien presents evidence that the Immigration and Naturalization Service has granted the alien employment authorization as a result of the alien's application for temporary residence status under the federal Immigration Reform and Control Act of 1986 (Public Law 99-603), pending a final determination on this application the department shall not do either of the following:

(1) Commence or continue to pursue any administrative or judicial action to collect benefits where there has been a final determination that these benefits have been overpaid or chargeable to the alien, because of the alien's immigration status at the time he or she performed the services compensated by his or her base period wages.

(2) Determine that the alien was overpaid benefits in the current benefit year or in any prior benefit year, if the basis for the determination is the assumption that because the alien is an applicant for temporary resident status he or she was not, while performing the services compensated by base period wages, lawfully admitted for permanent residence, lawfully present for purposes of performing the services that were compensated by his or her base period wages, or permanently residing in the United States under color of law.

(e) If the Immigration and Naturalization Service grants the application and adjusts the alien's status to that of lawful temporary resident, the department shall not take any action described in paragraph (1) of subdivision (d) or make any determination described in paragraph (2) of subdivision (d). If an alien is not in the status of being lawfully admitted for permanent residence, lawfully present for the purpose of performing the services compensated by his or her base period wages, or permanently residing in the United States under color of law, at the time the alien's lawful temporary permanent status terminates, then compensation shall not be payable on the basis of services performed by the alien after the termination.

(f) Nothing in subdivision (d) shall be construed to require the department to do any of the following:

(1) Repay any amounts collected under any present or past action as described in paragraph (1) of subdivision (d).

(2) Redetermine the eligibility for unemployment compensation benefits of any alien who the department originally determined to be ineligible because of the alien's status at the time he or she performed the services compensated by his or her base period wages and with respect to whom the determination has become final.

(3) Apply subdivision (d) or (e) retroactively.

(g) If the United States Secretary of Labor finds that subdivisions (d) and (e) are not in conformity with the federal Unemployment Tax Act, and effective as of the date that this finding becomes final, subdivisions (d), (e), and (f) shall be inoperative and of no legal force or effect.

(h) Unless subdivisions (d), (e), and (f) have earlier become inoperative and of no legal force or effect pursuant to a finding by the Secretary of Labor under subdivision (g), subdivisions (d), (e), (f), and (g) shall remain in effect only until September 30, 1990, and as of that date shall become inoperative, unless a later enacted statute which is chaptered before September 30, 1990, deletes or extends that date. Notwithstanding this subdivision, however, the department shall not take any action to collect benefits from an individual when the collection against that individual was suspended pursuant to subdivision (e) prior to September 30, 1990. *(Added by Stats.1978, c. 2, p. 43, § 83, eff. Jun. 30, 1978, operative Jan. 1, 1978. Amended by Stats.1984, c. 537, § 24; Stats.1988, c. 1379, § 1, eff. Sept. 27, 1988; Stats.1989, c. 1360, § 151; Stats.1989, c. 1333, § 1, eff. Oct. 2, 1989; Stats.1990, c. 216 (S.B.2510), § 108.)*

Subdivisions (d), (e), (f), and (g) became inoperative Sept. 30, 1990, under the provisions of subd. (h).

§ 1265. Payments under plan by employer supplementing unemployment compensation not construed as wages or compensation

Notwithstanding any other provisions of this division, payments to an individual under a plan or system established by an employer which makes provisions for his employees generally, or for a class or group of his employees, for the purpose of supplementing unemployment compensation benefits shall not be construed to be wages or compensation for personal services under this division and benefits payable under this division shall not be denied or reduced because of the receipt of payments under such arrangements or plans.

This amendment is hereby declared to be merely a clarification of the original intention of the Legislature and is not a substantive change, and is in conformity with the existing administrative interpretation of the law. *(Added by Stats.1959, c. 1077, p. 3138, § 1.)*

§ 1265.1. Employer's violation of federal Worker Adjustment and Retraining Notification Act (WARN)

(a) Notwithstanding any other provision of this division, payments to an individual by an employer who has failed to provide the advance notice of facility closure required by the federal Worker Adjustment and Retraining Notification (WARN) Act (29 U.S.C. Sec. 2101 et seq.) or Chapter 4 (commencing with Section 1400) of Part 4 of Division 2 of the Labor Code may not be construed to be wages or compensation for personal services under this division.

(b) Benefits payable under this division may not be denied or reduced because of the receipt of payments related in any way to an employer's violation of the WARN Act or Chapter 4 (commencing with Section 1400) of Part 4 of Division 2 of the Labor Code. *(Added by Stats.2001, c. 409 (S.B.40), § 4. Amended by Stats. 2002, c. 1022 (A.B.444), § 11, eff. Sept. 28, 2002; Stats. 2004, c. 776 (A.B.2028), § 1.)*

§ 1265.5. Vacation pay earned but not paid prior to termination of employment

Notwithstanding any other provision of this division, payments to an individual for vacation pay which was earned but not paid for services performed prior to termination of employment shall not be construed to be wages or compensation for personal services under this division and benefits payable under this division shall not be denied or reduced because of the receipt of these payments. *(Added by Stats.1971, c. 1272, p. 2492, § 1. Amended by Stats.1972, c. 864, p. 1536, § 6, eff. Aug. 14, 1972; Stats.1976, c. 1054, p. 4682, § 1; Stats.1987, c. 929, § 2; Stats.1991, c. 1134 (A.B.540), § 1.)*

§ 1265.6. Holiday pay

Notwithstanding any other provision of this division, payments to an individual for holiday pay for any holiday occurring in a week during which the individual was unemployed shall be deemed wages received for the week in which the individual returns to work, if holiday pay is not paid until the individual returns to work from a definite period of layoff. Payments to an individual for holiday pay for any holiday occurring in a week during which the individual was unemployed shall be deemed wages received for the week in which the holiday falls, if holiday pay is paid prior to the individual's return to work from a definite period of layoff.

However, payments to an individual for holiday pay which was earned but not paid prior to an indefinite layoff, or termination of employment, or commencement of unemployment caused by disability, as the case may be, shall not be construed to be wages or compensation for personal services under this division and benefits payable under this division shall not be denied or reduced because of the receipt of these payments.

(Added by Stats.1982, c. 1250, p. 4590, § 1. Amended by Stats.1987, c. 929, § 3.)

§ 1265.7. Sick pay not wages or compensation

Notwithstanding any other provision of this division, payments to an individual for sick pay which was earned but not paid for services performed prior to termination of employment, shall not be construed to be wages or compensation for personal services under this division and benefits payable under this division shall not be denied or reduced because of the receipt of such payments. *(Added by Stats.1976, c. 1054, p. 4682, § 2.)*

§ 1265.9. Severance or terminal pay for termination of employment due to expansion of federal redwood parks not wages or compensation

Notwithstanding any other provision of this division, payments for severance pay or terminal pay to an individual who is terminated from his or her employment as a direct result of the expansion of a federal redwood park in northern California by reason of legislation enacted by Congress in 1977 or 1978, shall not be construed to be wages or compensation for personal services under this division, and benefits payable under this division shall not be denied or reduced because of the receipt of such payment. *(Formerly § 1265.7, added by Stats.1977, c. 1156, p. 3, § 3, eff. Sept. 30, 1977. Renumbered § 1265.9 and amended by Stats.1979, c. 373, p. 1375, § 293.)*

ARTICLE 1.5.   RETRAINING BENEFITS

Section
1266.   Legislative findings; purpose.
1267.   Effect of training or retraining on other benefits.
1268.   Application for determination of potential eligibility.
1269.   Issuance of determination; findings.
1270.   Definitions.
1271.   Training extension.
1271.5.   Notification of potential benefits.
1272.   Eligibility of unemployed individual able to work; certification.
1272.5.   Failure to submit certification; notice of termination of instruction.
1273.   Effect of right to federal benefits; conditions of approval.
1274.   Publication of list of high demand occupations.
1274.10.   Duration of article.

Repeal

For repeal of this article, see Unemployment Insurance Code § 1274.10.

§ 1266.   Legislative findings; purpose

Experience has shown that the ability of a large number of the population of California to compete for jobs in the labor market is impaired by advancement in technological improvements, the widespread effects of automation and relocation in our economy, and foreign competition as set forth in petitions certified under the federal Trade Act of 1974, as amended (Title 19, United States Code, Sections 2101 et seq.). The Legislature finds that many individuals in California are lacking in skills which would make them competitive in the labor market. They are in need of training or retraining in skills required in demand occupations. It is the policy of this state to assist these individuals by providing unemployment compensation benefits, extended duration benefits, and other federally funded unemployment compensation benefits, including those available under the federal Trade Act of 1974 (Public Law 93–618), as amended by the federal Trade Act of 2002 (Public Law 107–210), during a period of retraining to qualify them for new jobs in demand occupations and thus avoid long-term unemployment. *(Formerly § 1274, added by Stats.1980, c. 522, p. 1457, § 1. Renumbered § 1266 and amended by Stats.1984, c. 1211, § 3. Amended by Stats.2008, c. 507 (A.B.3056), § 1.)*

Repeal

For repeal of this article, see Unemployment Insurance Code § 1274.10.

§ 1267. Effect of training or retraining on other benefits

Notwithstanding any other provision of this division, with respect to an unemployed individual otherwise eligible for benefits, such benefits shall not be denied to an individual for any week because he or she is in training or retraining with the approval of the director, or because of the application to any such week in training or retraining of any law of this state relating to availability for work, active search for work, refusal to accept work, or for leaving his or her most recent work, if continuing the most recent work would require the individual to terminate his or her training or retraining course of instruction. The individual is considered to be in training or retraining during regularly scheduled vacation or recess periods, such as Christmas and Thanksgiving holidays, or semester breaks, but not during a summer vacation period. As used in this article, "individual" includes an exhaustee as defined in Section 3503, and any individual claiming federal-state extended benefits under Part 4 (commencing with Section 4001), and anyone receiving federally funded unemployment compensation benefits. *(Formerly § 1274.1, added by Stats.1980, c. 522, p. 1457, § 1. Renumbered § 1267 and amended by Stats.1984, c. 1211, § 4.)*

Repeal

For repeal of this article, see Unemployment Insurance Code § 1274.10.

§ 1268. Application for determination of potential eligibility

An unemployed individual who files a claim for unemployment compensation benefits or extended duration benefits, or an application for federal-state extended benefits or any federally funded unemployment compensation benefits, may apply to the department for a determination of potential eligibility for benefits during a period of training or retraining. *(Formerly § 1274.2,*

added by Stats.1980, c. 522, p. 1457, § 1. Renumbered § 1268 and amended by Stats.1984, c. 1211, § 5.)

Repeal

For repeal of this article, see Unemployment Insurance Code § 1274.10.

§ 1269. Issuance of determination; findings

A determination of potential eligibility for benefits under this article shall be issued to an unemployed individual if the director finds that any of the following apply:

(a) The training is authorized by the federal Workforce Investment Act or by the Employment Training Panel established pursuant to Chapter 3.5 (commencing with Section 10200) of Part 1 of Division 3.

(b) The training is authorized by the federal Trade Act of 1974, (19 U.S.C. Sec. 2101 et seq.), as amended by the federal Trade Act of 2002 (Public Law 107–210), pursuant to a certified petition.

(c) The individual is a participant in the California Work Opportunity and Responsibility to Kids (Cal-WORKs) program pursuant to Article 3.2 (commencing with Section 11320) or Article 3.3 (commencing with Section 11330) of Chapter 2 of Part 3 of Division 9 of the Welfare and Institutions Code, and has entered into a contract with the county welfare department to participate in an education or training program.

(d) That all of the following apply:

(1) The individual has been unemployed for four or more continuous weeks, or the individual is unemployed and unlikely to return to his or her most recent workplace because work opportunities in the individual's job classification are impaired by a plant closure or a substantial reduction in employment at the individual's most recent workplace, by advancement in technological improvements, by the effects of automation and relocation in the economy, or because of a mental or physical disability which prohibits the individual from utilizing existing occupational skills.

(2) One of the substantial causes of the individual's unemployment is a lack of sufficient current demand in the individual's labor market area for the occupational skills for which the individual is fitted by training and experience or current physical or mental capacity and that the lack of employment opportunities is expected to continue for an extended period of time, or, if the individual's occupation is one for which there is a seasonal variation in demand in the labor market and the individual has no other skill for which there is current demand.

(3) The training or retraining course of instruction relates to an occupation or skill for which there are, or are expected to be in the immediate future, reasonable employment opportunities in the labor market area in this state in which the individual intends to seek work and

there is not a substantial surplus of workers with requisite skills in the occupation in that area.

(4) If the individual is a journey level union member, the training or retraining course of instruction is specific job-related training necessary due to changes in technology, or necessary to retain employment or to become more competitive in obtaining employment.

(5) The training or retraining course of instruction is one approved by the director and can be completed within one year.

(6) The training or retraining course is a full-time course prescribed for the primary purpose of training the applicant in skills that will allow him or her to obtain immediate employment in a demand occupation and is not primarily intended to meet the requirements of any degree from a college, community college, or university.

(7) The individual can be reasonably expected to complete the training or retraining successfully.

(8) The beginning date of training is more than three years after the beginning date of training last approved for the individual under this subdivision. *(Formerly § 1274.3, added by Stats.1980, c. 522, p. 1457, § 1. Amended by Stats.1981, c. 1134, p. 4449, § 5; Stats.1982, c. 1374, p. 5254, § 2; Stats.1983, c. 39, § 1, eff. May 17, 1983. Renumbered § 1269 and amended by Stats.1984, c. 1231, § 2. Amended by Stats.1987, c. 956, § 2, eff. Sept. 22, 1987; Stats.1992, c. 577 (S.B.2004), § 1; Stats.1996, c. 1124 (S.B.1524), § 2, eff. Sept. 30, 1996; Stats.2000, c. 299 (A.B.2906), § 2; Stats.2008, c. 507 (A.B.3056), § 2.)*

Repeal

For repeal of this article, see Unemployment Insurance Code § 1274.10.

§ 1270. Definitions

As used in this article:

(a) "Demand occupation" means an occupation in a labor market area in which the director determines work opportunities are available and there is not a surplus of qualified applicants.

(b) "Labor market area" means a county, or aggregation of counties designated by the department that meets criteria of population, population density, commute patterns, and social and economic integration specified by the department.

(Formerly § 1274.4, added by Stats.1980, c. 522, p. 1457, § 1. Renumbered § 1270 and amended by Stats. 1984, c. 1211, § 8. Amended by Stats.1992, c. 577 (S.B.2004), § 2.)

Repeal

For repeal of this article, see Unemployment Insurance Code § 1274.10.

§ 1271. Training extension

(a) Any unemployed individual receiving unemployment compensation benefits payable under this division, who applies for a determination of potential eligibility for benefits under this article no later than the 16th week of his or her receiving these benefits, and is determined eligible for benefits under this article, is entitled to a training extension on his or her unemployment compensation claim, if necessary, to complete approved training.

(b) The training extension shall provide the claimant with a maximum of 52 times the weekly benefit amount, which shall include the maximum benefit award on the parent unemployment compensation claim.

(c) The parent unemployment compensation claim shall be the unemployment compensation claim in existence at the time the claimant is determined eligible for benefits pursuant to subdivision (a).

(d) Benefits payable under this section are subject to the following limitations:

(1) The individual shall remain eligible for benefits under this article for all weeks potentially payable under this section.

(2) The individual shall file any unemployment compensation claim to which he or she becomes entitled under state or federal law, and shall draw any unemployment compensation benefits on that claim until it has expired or has been exhausted, in order to maintain his or her eligibility under this article.

(3) To the extent permitted by federal law, benefits payable under any federal unemployment compensation law shall be included as benefits payable under this section. *(Formerly § 1274.35, added by Stats.1982, c. 546, p. 2484, § 1, eff. Aug. 23, 1982. Amended by Stats.1982, c. 1385, p. 5281, § 1, eff. Sept. 24, 1982; Stats.1983, c. 39, § 2, eff. May 17, 1983; Stats.1984, c. 41, § 2, eff. March 19, 1984. Renumbered § 1271 and amended by Stats. 1984, c. 1211, § 7. Amended by Stats.1986, c. 1197, § 1; Stats.1987, c. 956, § 3, eff. Sept. 22, 1987; Stats.2000, c. 299 (A.B.2906), § 3.)*

Repeal

For repeal of this article, see Unemployment Insurance Code § 1274.10.

§ 1271.5. Notification of potential benefits

(a) The department shall inform all individuals who claim unemployment compensation benefits in this state of the benefits potentially available under this article and Section 1271. The department may convey this information verbally or in written form. If in written form, the department may utilize publications or handbooks that inform individuals of their rights and duties in regard to unemployment compensation benefits. These publications, issued by the department pursuant to authorized regulations, may be used to satisfy the requirements of this section.

(b) Benefits paid under Section 1271 shall be charged to individual employer reserve accounts, consistent with the provisions of this code. *(Added by Stats.2000, c. 299 (A.B.2906), § 4.)*

Repeal

For repeal of this article, see Unemployment Insurance Code § 1274.10.

§ 1272. Eligibility of unemployed individual able to work; certification

Notwithstanding subdivision (c) of Section 1253, an unemployed individual who is able to work is eligible to receive benefits under this article with respect to any week during a period of training or retraining only if the director finds both of the following:

(a) He or she has been determined potentially eligible under Section 1269 or 1271.

(b) He or she submits with each claim a written certification executed by a responsible person connected with the training or retraining program certifying that he or she is enrolled in and satisfactorily pursuing the training or retraining course of instruction. *(Formerly § 1274.6, added by Stats.1980, c. 522, p. 1457, § 1. Renumbered § 1272 and amended by Stats.1984, c. 1211, § 9.)*

Repeal

For repeal of this article, see Unemployment Insurance Code § 1274.10.

§ 1272.5. Failure to submit certification; notice of termination of instruction

If an individual fails to submit for any week during a period of training or retraining the certification required by Section 1272, he or she shall be ineligible to receive any benefits for that week. This section shall not render an individual ineligible for benefits for any week during the period of training or retraining if on or before Monday of that week he or she notifies the department that his or her training or retraining course of instruction has been or is being discontinued or terminated prior to that week. *(Formerly § 1274.7, added by Stats.1980, c. 522, p. 1457, § 1. Renumbered § 1272.5 and amended by Stats.1984, c. 1211, § 10.)*

Repeal

For repeal of this article, see Unemployment Insurance Code § 1274.10.

§ 1273. Effect of right to federal benefits; conditions of approval

(a) Notwithstanding any other provision of this article, no payment of benefits during a period of training or retraining as described in this article shall be made to any individual for any week or part of any week with respect to which he or she receives training or retraining benefits, allowances, or stipends pursuant to the provisions of any state or federal law providing for the payment of such benefits, but excluding costs of training paid pursuant to the federal Trade Act of 1974 (19 U.S.C. Sec. 2101 et seq.), as amended by the federal Trade Act of 2002 (Public Law 107–210).

(b) "Training or retraining benefits, allowances, or stipends," as used in this section, means discretionary use, cash in-hand payments available to the individual to be used as he or she sees fit. Direct and indirect compensation for training costs, such as tuition, books, and supplies, is excluded as a condition of approval. *(Formerly § 1274.8, added by Stats. 1980, c. 522, p. 1457, § 1. Amended by Stats. 1981, c. 1134, p. 4450, § 6; Stats. 1983, c. 39, § 3, eff. May 17, 1983. Renumbered § 1273 and amended by Stats. 1984, c. 1211, § 11. Amended by Stats.2008, c. 507 (A.B.3056), § 3.)*

Repeal

For repeal of this article, see Unemployment Insurance Code § 1274.10.

§ 1274. Publication of list of high demand occupations

The director may publish a list of high demand occupations in each labor market area of this state. If a demand occupation is limited to a particular industry, the director may identify the industry of the demand occupation. *(Formerly § 1274.5, added by Stats.1980, c. 522, p. 1457, § 1. Renumbered § 1274 and amended by Stats. 1987, c. 956, § 5, eff. Sept. 22, 1987.)*

Repeal

For repeal of this article, see Unemployment Insurance Code § 1274.10.

§ 1274.10. Duration of article

This article shall remain in effect only until January 1, 2015, and as of that date is repealed, unless a later enacted statute, which is chaptered before that date, deletes or extends the date. *(Added by Stats.1980, c. 522, p. 1457, § 1. Amended by Stats.1984, c. 41, § 2.5, eff. March 19, 1984; Stats.1984, c. 1211, § 13; Stats.1987, c. 956, § 7, eff. Sept. 22, 1987; Stats.1992, c. 577 (S.B.2004), § 3; Stats.1996, c. 1124 (S.B.1524), § 4, eff. Sept. 30, 1996; Stats.2000, c. 299 (A.B.2906), § 5; Stats.2004, c. 800 (A.B.1845), § 1; Stats.2008, c. 507 (A.B.3056), § 4.)*

ARTICLE 2. COMPUTATION (AMOUNT AND DURATION)

Section
1275. Computation of benefit award; base period defined.
1276. Benefit year; valid claim.
1277. Wages usable in computation of new claim; applicability of section.
1277.5. Computation of wages for purpose of meeting eligibility requirements of § 1281.
1278. Wages for employment for employers.
1279. Benefits during partial employment; wages.

Section

1279.5.   Shared work unemployment benefit; approval of plans; weekly amount.

1280.   Weekly benefit amount.

1281.   Minimum earnings requirement; maximum benefits; wages.

1282.   Determination of weekly wage when payments are irregular.

§ 1275. Computation of benefit award; base period defined

Unemployment compensation benefit award computations shall be based on wages paid in the base period. "Base period" means: for benefit years beginning in October, November, or December, the four calendar quarters ended in the next preceding month of June; for benefit years beginning in January, February, or March, the four calendar quarters ended in the next preceding month of September; for benefit years beginning in April, May, or June, the four calendar quarters ended in the next preceding month of December; for benefit years beginning in July, August, or September, the four calendar quarters ended with the next preceding month of March. Wages used in the determination of benefits payable to an individual during any benefit year may not be used in determining that individual's benefits in any subsequent benefit year. *(Stats.1953, c. 308, p. 1504, § 1275. Amended by Stats.1959, c. 2156, p. 5211, § 4; Stats.1961, c. 2160, p. 4476, § 12; Stats.2001, c. 409 (S.B.40), § 5.)*

§ 1276. Benefit year; valid claim

"Benefit year", with respect to any individual, means the 52-week period beginning with the first day of the week with respect to which the individual first files a valid claim for benefits and thereafter the 52-week period beginning with the week in which such individual again files a valid claim after the termination of his or her last preceding benefit year. As used in this section, "valid claim" means any claim for benefits made in accordance with this division and authorized regulations if the individual filing the claim is unemployed and has met the requirements of subdivision (a) of Section 1281. For the purpose of determining whether a claim is a "valid claim" within the meaning of this section, an individual otherwise unemployed shall be deemed unemployed even though wages, as defined in Section 1252, which are for a period subsequent to the termination of performance of services are payable with respect to the week for which he or she files the claim. *(Stats.1953, c. 308, p. 1504, § 1276. Amended by Stats.1955, c. 1165, p. 2167, § 27; Stats.1961, c. 2165, p. 4486, § 2; Stats.1979, c. 1053, p. 3709, § 6, operative May 1, 1981.)*

§ 1277. Wages usable in computation of new claim; applicability of section

Notwithstanding Section 1281, if the base period of a new claim includes wages which were paid prior to the effective date of, and not used in the computation of the award for, a previous valid claim, the new claim shall only

be valid if, during the 52-week period beginning with the effective date of the previous valid claim, either of the following applies:

(a) The individual earned or was paid sufficient wages to meet the eligibility requirements of subdivision (a) of Section 1281 and performed some work.

(b) The individual did not receive benefits under this part, and was disabled and was entitled to receive, wage loss benefits under Part 2 (commencing with Section 2601) of this division or under Division 4 (commencing with Section 3201) of the Labor Code, or under any workers' compensation law, employer's liability law, or disability insurance law of any other state or of the federal government.

For the purpose of this section only, the term "wages" includes any and all compensation for personal services performed as an employee for the purpose of meeting the eligibility requirements under subdivision (a) of Section 1281. This section is not applicable to the computation of an award for disability benefits. *(Stats.1953, c. 308, p. 1504, § 1277. Amended by Stats.1965, c. 1897, p. 4378, § 13; Stats.1971, c. 1107, p. 2117, § 61, eff. Oct. 18, 1971, operative Jan. 1, 1972; Stats.1972, c. 833, p. 1485, § 8; Stats.1979, c. 1053, p. 3709, § 7, operative May 1, 1981; Stats.1990, c. 787 (S.B.1981), § 1.)*

§ 1277.5. Computation of wages for purpose of meeting eligibility requirements of § 1281

In determining, under Section 1277, whether a new claim is valid, twice the amount which an individual was entitled to receive under Part 2 (commencing with Section 2601) of this division or under Division 4 (commencing with Section 3201) of the Labor Code, or under any workers' compensation law, employer's liability law, or disability insurance law of any other state or of the federal government, during the 52-week period beginning with the effective date of the previous valid claim, shall be considered as wages earned or paid to the individual during that 52-week period for purposes of meeting the eligibility requirements of subdivision (a) of Section 1281. The amounts so included shall not be considered wages for the purpose of computing the weekly benefit amount of the individual under Section 1280 or the maximum amount payable to the individual under Section 1281. *(Added by Stats.1961, c. 1462, p. 3313, § 1. Amended by Stats.1971, c. 1107, p. 2117, § 62, eff. Oct. 18, 1971, operative Jan. 1, 1972; Stats.1971, c. 1112, p. 2126, § 2; Stats.1972, c. 833, p. 1485, § 9; Stats.1973, c. 86, p. 147, § 1, eff. June 12, 1973; Stats.1974, c. 277, p. 540, § 1; Stats.1979, c. 1053, p. 3710, § 8, operative May 1, 1981; Stats.1990, c. 787 (S.B.1981), § 2.)*

§ 1278. Wages for employment for employers

For the purposes of this chapter, wages shall be counted as "wages for employment for employers" for benefit purposes with respect to any benefit year only if the benefit year begins subsequent to the date on which the employer from whom the wages were earned has satisfied the conditions of this division with respect to being an employer. *(Stats.1953, c. 308, p. 1505, § 1278.)*

§ 1279. Benefits during partial employment; wages

(a) Each individual eligible under this chapter who is unemployed in any week shall be paid with respect to that week an unemployment compensation benefit in an amount equal to his or her weekly benefit amount less the smaller of the following:

(1) The amount of wages in excess of twenty-five dollars ($25) payable to him or her for services rendered during that week.

(2) The amount of wages in excess of 25 percent of the amount of wages payable to him or her for services rendered during that week.

(b) The benefit payment, if not a multiple of one dollar ($1), shall be computed to the next higher multiple of one dollar ($1).

(c) For the purpose of this section only "wages" includes any and all compensation for personal services whether performed as an employee or as an independent contractor or as a juror or as a witness, but does not include any payments, regardless of their designation, made by a city of this state to an elected official thereof as an incident to public office, nor any payment received by a member of the National Guard or reserve component of the armed forces for inactive duty training, annual training, or emergency state active duty. *(Stats.1953, c. 308, p. 1505, § 1279. Amended by Stats.1959, c. 2154, p. 5204, § 6; Stats.1971, c. 1107, p. 2117, § 63, eff. Oct. 18, 1971; Stats.1973, c. 582, p. 1101, § 2; Stats.1974, c. 1510, p. 3316, § 1; Stats.1977, c. 1128, p. 3622, § 1; Stats.1979, c. 1053, p. 3710, § 9; Stats.1983, c. 761, § 5.)*

§ 1279.5. Shared work unemployment benefit; approval of plans; weekly amount

(a) Notwithstanding Section 1252 or 1252.2 or any other provision of this part, for the purposes of this section an individual is "unemployed" in any week if the individual works less than his or her normal weekly hours of work for the individual's regular employer, and the director finds that the regular employer has reduced or restricted the individual's normal hours of work, or has rehired an individual previously laid off and reduced that individual's normal hours of work from those previously worked, as the result of a plan by the regular employer to, in lieu of layoff, reduce employment and stabilize the work force by a program of sharing the work remaining after a reduction in total hours of work and a corresponding reduction in wages of at least 10 percent. The application for approval of a plan shall require the employer to briefly describe the circumstances requiring the use of work sharing to avoid a layoff. Normal weekly hours of work means the number of hours in a week that the employee normally would work for the regular employer or 40 hours, whichever is less. The plan must involve the participation of at least two employees and include not less than 10 percent of the employer's regular permanent work force involved in the affected work unit or units in each week, or in at least one week of a two-consecutive-week period. A plan approved by the director shall expire six months after the effective date of the plan.

(b) Except as otherwise provided in this section, each individual eligible under this chapter who is "unemployed" in any week shall be paid with respect to that week a weekly shared work unemployment compensation benefit amount equal to the percentage of reduction of the individual's wages resulting from an approved plan, rounded to the nearest 5 percent, multiplied by the individual's weekly benefit amount.

(c) No individual who receives any benefits under this section during any benefit year shall receive any benefits pursuant to Section 1252 or 1252.2 as a partially unemployed individual with respect to any week during such benefit year while in employment status with the regular employer who initiated the program of sharing work under this section. No benefits under this section shall be payable on any type of extended claim.

(d) Any amount payable under this section shall be reduced by the amount of any and all compensation payable for personal services whether performed as an employee or an independent contractor or as a juror or as a witness, except compensation payable by the regular employer under a shared work plan.

For the purposes of this subdivision, "regular employer" may include, pursuant to an approved plan, a labor organization which periodically employs individuals in accordance with a collective bargaining agreement.

(e) The benefit payment under this section, if not a multiple of one dollar ($1), shall be increased to the next higher multiple of one dollar ($1).

(f) Sections 1253.5 and 1279 shall not apply to any individual eligible for any payment under this section.

(g) For the purposes of this section, an individual shall not be disqualified under subdivision (c) of Section 1253 for any week if both of the following conditions exist:

(1) The individual has not been absent from work without the approval of the regular employer.

(2) The individual accepted all work the regular employer made available to the individual during hours scheduled off due to the work-sharing plan.

(h) Except as otherwise provided by or inconsistent with this section, all provisions of this division and authorized regulations apply to benefits under this section. Authorized regulations may, to the extent permitted by federal law, make such distinctions and requirements as may be necessary in the procedures and provisions applicable to unemployed individuals to carry out the purposes of this section, including regulations defining normal hours, days, workweek, and wages.

(i) Employees shall not be eligible to receive any benefits under this section unless their employer agrees, in writing, and their bargaining agent pursuant to any

993

applicable collective bargaining agreement agrees, in writing, to voluntarily participate in the shared work unemployment insurance benefit program created by this section.

(j) Notwithstanding Section 1327, the department shall not be required to notify an employer of additional claims which result from an approved plan submitted by the employer under which benefits are not paid in each week.

(k) The director may terminate a shared work plan for good cause if the plan is not being carried out according to its terms and intent. *(Added by Stats.1986, c. 1202, § 2. Amended by Stats.1988, c. 520, § 2.)*

§ 1280. Weekly benefit amount

(a) For any new claims filed with an effective date on or after January 1, 1992, and prior to September 11, 2001, an individual's weekly benefit amount is the amount appearing in column B in the following table opposite that wage bracket in column A that contains the amount of wages paid to the individual for employment by employers during the quarter of his or her base period in which his or her wages were the highest.

A Amount of wages in highest quarter	B Weekly benefit amount
$ 900.00–948.99	40
949.00–974.99	41
975.00–1,000.99	42
1,001.00–1,026.99	43
1,027.00–1,052.99	44
1,053.00–1,078.99	45
1,079.00–1,117.99	46
1,118.00–1,143.99	47
1,144.00–1,169.99	48
1,170.00–1,195.99	49
1,196.00–1,221.99	50
1,222.00–1,247.99	51
1,248.00–1,286.99	52
1,287.00–1,312.99	53
1,313.00–1,338.99	54
1,339.00–1,364.99	55
1,365.00–1,403.99	56
1,404.00–1,429.99	57
1,430.00–1,455.99	58
1,456.00–1,494.99	59
1,495.00–1,520.99	60
1,521.00–1,546.99	61
1,547.00–1,585.99	62
1,586.00–1,611.99	63
1,612.00–1,637.99	64
1,638.00–1,676.99	65
1,677.00–1,702.99	66
1,703.00–1,741.99	67
1,742.00–1,767.99	68
1,768.00–1,806.99	69
1,807.00–1,832.99	70
1,833.00–1,871.99	71
1,872.00–1,897.99	72
1,898.00–1,936.99	73
1,937.00–1,975.99	74
1,976.00–2,001.99	75
2,002.00–2,040.99	76
2,041.00–2,066.99	77
2,067.00–2,105.99	78
2,106.00–2,144.99	79
2,145.00–2,170.99	80
2,171.00–2,209.99	81
2,210.00–2,248.99	82
2,249.00–2,287.99	83
2,288.00–2,326.99	84
2,327.00–2,352.99	85
2,353.00–2,391.99	86
2,392.00–2,430.99	87
2,431.00–2,469.99	88
2,470.00–2,508.99	89
2,509.00–2,547.99	90
2,548.00–2,586.99	91
2,587.00–2,625.99	92
2,626.00–2,664.99	93
2,665.00–2,703.99	94
2,704.00–2,742.99	95
2,743.00–2,781.99	96
2,782.00–2,820.99	97
2,821.00–2,859.99	98
2,860.00–2,898.99	99
2,899.00–2,937.99	100
2,938.00–2,989.99	101
2,990.00–3,028.99	102
3,029.00–3,067.99	103
3,068.00–3,106.99	104
3,107.00–3,158.99	105
3,159.00–3,197.99	106
3,198.00–3,236.99	107
3,237.00–3,288.99	108
3,289.00–3,327.99	109
3,328.00–3,379.99	110
3,380.00–3,418.99	111
3,419.00–3,470.99	112
3,471.00–3,509.99	113
3,510.00–3,561.99	114
3,562.00–3,600.99	115
3,601.00–3,652.99	116
3,653.00–3,704.99	117
3,705.00–3,743.99	118
3,744.00–3,795.99	119
3,796.00–3,847.99	120
3,848.00–3,899.99	121
3,900.00–3,938.99	122
3,939.00–3,990.99	123
3,991.00–4,042.99	124
4,043.00–4,079.99	125
4,080.00–4,116.99	126
4,117.00–4,153.99	127
4,154.00–4,190.99	128
4,191.00–4,227.99	129
4,228.00–4,264.99	130
4,265.00–4,301.99	131
4,302.00–4,338.99	132
4,339.00–4,375.99	133
4,376.00–4,412.99	134
4,413.00–4,449.99	135
4,450.00–4,486.99	136
4,487.00–4,523.99	137
4,524.00–4,560.99	138
4,561.00–4,597.99	139

A Amount of wages in highest quarter	B Weekly benefit amount
4,598.00–4,634.99	140
4,635.00–4,671.99	141
4,672.00–4,708.99	142
4,709.00–4,745.99	143
4,746.00–4,782.99	144
4,783.00–4,819.99	145
4,820.00–4,856.99	146
4,857.00–4,893.99	147
4,894.00–4,930.99	148
4,931.00–4,966.99	149

If the amount of wages paid an individual for employment by employers exceeds four thousand nine hundred sixty-six dollars and ninety-nine cents ($4,966.99) in the quarter of his or her base period in which these wages were highest, the individual's weekly benefit amount shall be 39 percent of these wages divided by 13, but in no case shall this amount exceed two hundred thirty dollars ($230). If the benefit payable under this subdivision is not a multiple of one dollar ($1), it shall be computed to the next higher multiple of one dollar ($1).

(b) Notwithstanding subdivision (a), for existing claims on or after September 11, 2001, provided that the unemployment benefits have not been exhausted as of September 11, 2001, and for all new claims filed with an effective date beginning on or after September 11, 2001, and prior to January 1, 2003, an individual's weekly benefit amount is the amount for weeks of unemployment beginning on or after September 11, 2001, appearing in column B in the following table opposite that wage bracket in column A that contains the amount of wages paid to the individual for employment by employers during the quarter of his or her base period in which his or her wages were the highest.

A Amount of wages in highest quarter	B Weekly benefit amount
$ 900.00–948.99	40
949.00–974.99	41
975.00–1,000.99	42
1,001.00–1,026.99	43
1,027.00–1,052.99	44
1,053.00–1,078.99	45
1,079.00–1,117.99	46
1,118.00–1,143.99	47
1,144.00–1,169.99	48
1,170.00–1,195.99	49
1,196.00–1,221.99	50
1,222.00–1,247.99	51
1,248.00–1,286.99	52
1,287.00–1,312.99	53
1,313.00–1,338.99	54
1,339.00–1,364.99	55
1,365.00–1,403.99	56
1,404.00–1,429.99	57
1,430.00–1,455.99	58
1,456.00–1,494.99	59
1,495.00–1,520.99	60
1,521.00–1,546.99	61
1,547.00–1,585.99	62

A Amount of wages in highest quarter	B Weekly benefit amount
1,586.00–1,611.99	63
1,612.00–1,637.99	64
1,638.00–1,676.99	65
1,677.00–1,702.99	66
1,703.00–1,741.99	67
1,742.00–1,767.99	68
1,768.00–1,806.99	69
1,807.00–1,832.99	70
1,833.00–1,871.99	71
1,872.00–1,897.99	72
1,898.00–1,936.99	73
1,937.00–1,975.99	74
1,976.00–2,001.99	75
2,002.00–2,040.99	76
2,041.00–2,066.99	77
2,067.00–2,105.99	78
2,106.00–2,144.99	79
2,145.00–2,170.99	80
2,171.00–2,209.99	81
2,210.00–2,248.99	82
2,249.00–2,287.99	83
2,288.00–2,326.99	84
2,327.00–2,352.99	85
2,353.00–2,391.99	86
2,392.00–2,430.99	87
2,431.00–2,469.99	88
2,470.00–2,508.99	89
2,509.00–2,547.99	90
2,548.00–2,586.99	91
2,587.00–2,625.99	92
2,626.00–2,664.99	93
2,665.00–2,703.99	94
2,704.00–2,742.99	95
2,743.00–2,781.99	96

If the amount of wages paid an individual for employment by employers exceeds two thousand seven hundred eighty-one dollars and ninety-nine cents ($2,781.99) in the quarter of his or her base period in which these wages were highest, the individual's weekly benefit amount shall be 45 percent of these wages divided by 13, but in no case may this amount exceed three hundred thirty dollars ($330).

(c) For new claims filed with an effective date beginning on or after January 1, 2003, an individual's weekly benefit amount is the amount appearing in column B in the following table opposite the wage bracket in column A that contains the wages paid to the individual for employment by employers during the quarter of his or her base period in which his or her wages were the highest.

A Amount of wages in highest quarter	B Weekly benefit amount
$ 900.00–948.99	40
949.00–974.99	41
975.00–1,000.99	42
1,001.00–1,026.99	43
1,027.00–1,052.99	44
1,053.00–1,078.99	45
1,079.00–1,117.99	46
1,118.00–1,143.99	47

A Amount of wages in highest quarter	B Weekly benefit amount
1,144.00–1,169.99	48
1,170.00–1,195.99	49
1,196.00–1,221.99	50
1,222.00–1,247.99	51
1,248,00–1,286.99	52
1,287.00–1,312.99	53
1,313.00–1,338.99	54
1,339.00–1,364.99	55
1,365.00–1,403.99	56
1,404.00–1,429.99	57
1,430.00–1,455.99	58
1,456.00–1,494.99	59
1,495.00–1,520.99	60
1,521.00–1,546.99	61
1,547.00–1,585.99	62
1,586.00–1,611.99	63
1,612.00–1,637.99	64
1,638.00–1,676.99	65
1,677.00–1,702.99	66
1,703.00–1,741.99	67
1,742.00–1,767.99	68
1,768.00–1,806.99	69
1,807.00–1,832.99	70

If the amount of wages paid an individual for employment by employers exceeds one thousand eight hundred thirty-two dollars and ninety-nine cents ($1,832.99) in the quarter of his or her base period in which these wages were highest, the individual's weekly benefit amount shall be 50 percent of these wages divided by 13, but in no case shall this amount exceed the applicable of the following:

(1) For new claims filed with an effective date beginning on or after January 1, 2003, and before January 1, 2004, three hundred seventy dollars ($370).

(2) For new claims filed with an effective date beginning on or after January 1, 2004, and before January 1, 2005, four hundred ten dollars ($410).

(3) For new claims filed with an effective date beginning on or after January 1, 2005, four hundred fifty dollars ($450).

If the benefit payable under this subdivision is not a multiple of one dollar ($1), it shall be computed to the next higher multiple of one dollar ($1). (Added by Stats.1979, c. 1053, p. 3713, § 11, operative May 1, 1981. Amended by Stats.1982, c. 1075, p. 3887, § 12.5; Stats. 1986, c. 114, § 1; Stats.1989, c. 1146, § 14; Stats.2001, c. 409 (S.B.40), § 6; Stats.2001–2002, 3rd Ex.Sess., c. 4 (S.B.2), § 1, eff. Aug. 1, 2002.)

§ 1281. Minimum earnings requirement; maximum benefits; wages

(a) An individual cannot establish a valid claim or a benefit year during which any benefits are payable unless during his or her base period, for new claims filed with an effective date beginning on or after January 1, 1992, he or she has met either of the following conditions:

(1) He or she has been paid wages for employment by employers during the quarter of his or her base period in

which his or her wages were the highest of not less than one thousand three hundred dollars ($1,300).

(2) He or she has been paid wages for employment by employers during the quarter of his or her base period in which his or her wages were the highest of not less than nine hundred dollars ($900) and been paid wages for employment by employers during his or her base period equal to 1.25 times the amount he or she was paid in this same quarter.

(b) Except as provided by subdivision (c), the maximum amount of unemployment compensation benefits payable to an individual during any one benefit year shall not exceed the lower of the following:

(1) Twenty-six times his or her weekly benefit amount.

(2) One-half the total wages paid to the individual during his or her base period.

(c) If the maximum amount computed under subdivision (b) is not a multiple of one dollar ($1) it shall be computed to the next higher multiple of one dollar ($1).

(d) For the purpose of this section and Section 1280, in determining wages paid, "wages" includes wages due to any individual but unpaid within the time limit provided by law. (Stats.1953, c. 308, p. 1505, § 1281. Amended by Stats.1954, 1st Ex.Sess., c. 14, p. 262, § 3; Stats.1955, c. 899, p. 1526, § 2; Stats.1963, c. 1565, p. 3148, § 2; Stats.1965, c. 1897, p. 4380, § 15; Stats.1971, c. 1596, p. 3435, § 10; Stats.1979, c. 1053, p. 3717, § 12, operative Jan. 1, 1980; Stats.1989, c. 1146, § 15; Stats.2007, c. 272 (A.B.798), § 2.)

§ 1282. Determination of weekly wage when payments are irregular

If the remuneration of an individual is not based upon a fixed period or duration of time or if the individual's wages are paid at irregular intervals or in such manner as not to extend regularly over the period of employment, the wages for any week or for any calendar quarter for the purpose of computing an individual's right to unemployment compensation benefits shall be determined pursuant to authorized regulations. The regulations shall, so far as possible, secure results reasonably similar to those which would prevail if the individual were paid his wages at regular intervals. (Added by Stats.1961, c. 2153, p. 4447, § 14. Amended by Stats.1973, c. 1212, p. 2780, § 158, operative July 1, 1974; Stats.1977, c. 1252, p. 4458, § 407, operative July 1, 1978.)

ARTICLE 2.2. SELF–EMPLOYMENT ASSISTANCE PROGRAM

Section
1300. Legislative findings; purpose of article.

§ 1300. Legislative findings; purpose of article

The Legislature finds that the traditional system of unemployment compensation is primarily designed to provide income support for workers who are temporarily laid off or expect to be unemployed for only a short time. However, increasing numbers of workers are losing their jobs permanently due to rapid technological change, elimination of trade barriers, and similar causes. These workers need additional tools besides the basic income maintenance provided by the unemployment compensation system in order to reenter the workforce. For some of those workers, access to a self-employment program would be the best path for them to do so. Accordingly, it is the purpose of this article to authorize the payment of unemployment compensation benefits, and to provide appropriate training and support services, for eligible dislocated workers who wish to become self-employed in their transition back into the workforce. *(Added by Stats.1994, c. 1116 (S.B.1482), § 2.)*

ARTICLE 3.   FILING, DETERMINATION, AND PAYMENT OF UNEMPLOYMENT COMPENSATION BENEFIT CLAIMS

Section
1326.   Filing benefit claims; payment or denial of claims.
1327.   Notice of claim; submission by employing unit of facts affecting eligibility.
1328.   Determination of eligibility; notice; appeal; good cause.
1329.   Computation of benefit amount; notice.
1330.   Protest of computation; extension of period; notice of determination; appeal.
1331.   Submission of facts by base period employer; notice of determination; appeal.
1332.   Notice of determination of eligibility; reconsideration of determination or computation.
1332.5. Time limiting reconsideration not applicable in case of fraud, misrepresentation or willful nondisclosure.
1333.   Regulations on notices and protests.
1334.   Hearing and decision by administrative law judge; notice; finality of decision; extension of limitation period.
1335.   Appeal precluding benefit payments; exceptions.
1336.   Proceedings by appeals board; notice of findings and decision.
1337.   Time limit on decisions of appeals board.
1338.   Payment of benefits upon appeals board decision allowing benefits; effect of further action or court proceedings.
1339.   Place of payment of benefits; contents of check or certification.
1340.   Payments to minors; receipt.
1341.   Payments or benefits due deceased or incompetent person.
1342.   Invalidity of waiver of benefits or rights; assignment, release or commutation of benefits; invalidity of agreement of employee to pay employer's contribution.
1342.1. New claims for unemployment compensation; taxation.
1345.   Redirection of voluntary plan benefits to cover cost of employee-paid benefits; conditions; request; delay of disability benefits; spousal election.

§ 1326.   Filing benefit claims;   payment or denial of claims

Claims for unemployment compensation benefits shall be made in accordance with authorized regulations of the director. Except as otherwise provided in this article, the department shall promptly pay benefits if it finds the claimant is eligible or shall promptly deny benefits if it finds the claimant is ineligible. *(Stats.1953, c. 308, p. 1507, § 1326. Amended by Stats.1973, c. 1212, p. 2780, § 160, operative July 1, 1974; Stats.1979, c. 373, p. 1375, § 294.)*

§ 1327.   Notice of claim;   submission by employing unit of facts affecting eligibility

The department shall give a notice of the filing of a new or additional claim to the employing unit by which the claimant was last employed immediately preceding the filing of the claim unless the additional claim is the result of the filing of a partial claim as defined by the department, there has not been a subsequent employing unit which is designated as the last employer, and there is no separation issue. The employing unit so notified shall submit within 10 days after the mailing of the notice any facts then known that may affect the claimant's eligibility for benefits, including, but not limited to, facts pertaining to eligibility under Section 1256. The 10–day period may be extended for good cause. If after the 10–day period the employing unit acquires knowledge of facts that may affect the eligibility of the claimant and facts could not reasonably have been known within the period, the employing unit shall, within 10 days of acquiring the knowledge, submit the facts to the department, and the 10–day period may also be extended for good cause. *(Stats.1953, c. 308, p. 1507, § 1327. Amended by Stats. 1973, c. 1212, p. 2781, § 162, operative July 1, 1974; Stats.1979, c. 373, p. 1375, § 295; Stats.1979, c. 456, p. 1602, § 5; Stats.1983, c. 761, § 6; Stats.1985, c. 716, § 2; Stats.2001, c. 409 (S.B.40), § 7.)*

§ 1328.   Determination of eligibility;   notice;   appeal;   good cause

The department shall consider the facts submitted by an employer pursuant to Section 1327 and make a determination as to the claimant's eligibility for benefits. The department shall promptly notify the claimant and any employer who prior to the determination has submitted any facts or given any notice pursuant to Section 1327 or this section and authorized regulations of the determination or reconsidered determination and the reasons therefor. If after notice of a determination or reconsidered determination the employing unit acquires knowledge of facts which may affect the eligibility of the claimant and those facts could not reasonably have been known within the 10–day period provided by Section 1327, the employing unit shall within 10 days of acquiring that knowledge submit those facts to the department, and the 10–day period may be extended for good cause. The claimant and any such employer may appeal from a determination or reconsidered determination to an administrative law judge within 20 days from mailing or personal service of notice of the determination or reconsidered determination. The 20–day period may be extended for good cause, which shall include, but not be limited to, mistake, inadvertence, surprise, or excusable neglect. The director shall be an interested party to any appeal. *(Stats.1953, c. 308, p. 1508, § 1328. Amended by Stats.1967, c. 1586, p. 3799, § 8; Stats.1973, c. 1212, p. 2781, § 164, operative July 1, 1974; Stats.1975, c. 979, p. 2302, § 1; Stats.1979, c. 456, p. 1602, § 6; Stats.1981, c. 1018, p. 3928, § 1; Stats.1984, c. 537, § 25; Stats.1998, c. 217 (A.B.2017), § 6.)*

§ 1329. Computation of benefit amount; notice

Upon the filing of a new claim for benefits, the department shall promptly make a computation on the claim which shall set forth the maximum amount of benefits potentially payable during the benefit year, and the weekly benefit amount. The department shall promptly notify the claimant of the computation. The department shall promptly notify each of the claimant's base period employers of the computation after the payment of the first weekly benefit. *(Stats.1953, c. 308, p. 1508, § 1329. Amended by Stats.1967, c. 1720, p. 4286, § 6; Stats.1973, c. 1212, p. 2781, § 165, operative July 1, 1974; Stats.1974, c. 1159, p. 2472, § 30, eff. Sept. 23, 1974; Stats.1979, c. 373, p. 1375, § 296; Stats.1979, c. 1053, p. 3718, § 13, operative May 1, 1981; Stats.1989, c. 1146, § 16.)*

§ 1330. Protest of computation; extension of period; notice of determination; appeal

The claimant and any base period employer to whom a notice of computation or recomputation is given may, within 20 days after the mailing or personal service of such notice, protest the accuracy of the computation or recomputation. The 20-day period may be extended for good cause. The department shall consider any such protest and shall promptly notify the claimant and the base period employer submitting the protest of the recomputation or denial of recomputation. An appeal may be taken from a notice of denial of recomputation in the manner prescribed in Section 1328. The director shall be an interested party to any appeal.

"Good cause," as used in this section, shall include, but not be limited to, mistake, inadvertence, surprise, or excusable neglect. *(Stats.1953, c. 308, p. 1508, § 1330. Amended by Stats.1967, c. 1720, p. 4286, § 7; Stats.1973, c. 1212, p. 2781, § 166, operative July 1, 1974; Stats.1975, c. 979, p. 2302, § 2; Stats.1977, c. 1252, p. 4458, § 408, operative July 1, 1978.)*

§ 1331. Submission of facts by base period employer; notice of determination; appeal

Any base period employer shall, within 15 days after mailing of a notice of computation, submit to the department any facts then known which he or she was not previously required to submit to the department under Section 1327 which may affect the claimant's eligibility for benefits. The 15-day period may be extended for good cause. If after such 15-day period the employing unit acquires knowledge of facts which may affect the eligibility of the claimant and such facts could not reasonably have been known within the period, the employing unit shall, within 10 days of acquiring such knowledge, submit such facts to the department. The 10-day period may be extended for good cause. The department shall make a determination or reconsidered determination thereon and shall promptly notify the claimant and the base period employer submitting the facts of the determination or reconsidered determination and the reasons therefor. An appeal may be taken in the manner prescribed in Section 1328. The director shall be an interested party to any appeal. *(Stats.1953, c. 308, p. 1508, § 1331. Amended by Stats.1973, c. 1212, p. 2782, § 168, operative July 1, 1974; Stats.1979, c. 373, p. 1375, § 297; Stats.1979, c. 456, p. 1603, § 7.)*

§ 1332. Notice of determination of eligibility; reconsideration of determination or computation

(a) The department shall promptly serve notice of any determination of eligibility for benefits under this part or Part 3 or Part 4 of this division on the claimant and on any employer or employing unit which prior to this determination has furnished the department with information regarding the claimant's eligibility pursuant to Sections 1327 and 1331. Service shall be made personally or by mail. Failure to serve this notice shall not affect the determination of eligibility.

(1) "Notice" is that notification which apprises the party of a determination of eligibility and allows that party to respond accordingly.

(2) If the department is or should be aware that the notice was not received by the party to whom it was addressed, including, but not limited to, the return to the department of the notice by the United States Post Office, the department shall reissue the notice at such time as the department can determine a corrected mailing address for the affected party or otherwise ensure receipt. The affected party shall have appeal rights pursuant to subdivisions (b) and (c), and pursuant to Section 1328.

(b) The department may for good cause reconsider any determination within 15 days after an appeal to an administrative law judge is filed. If no appeal is filed, the department may for good cause reconsider any determination within 20 days after mailing or personal service of the notice of determination. The department may, if a claimant has not filed an appeal to an administrative law judge from any determination which finds that a claimant is ineligible or disqualified, or if an appeal has been filed but is either withdrawn or dismissed, for good cause also reconsider the determination during the benefit year or extended duration period or extended benefit period to which the determination relates. The department shall give notice of any reconsidered determination to the claimant and any employer or employing unit which received notice under Sections 1328 and 1331 and the claimant or employer may appeal therefrom in the manner prescribed in Section 1328.

The director shall designate individuals to review and reconsider appealed determinations. No individual designated shall be the same individual who made the initial determination in the same matter.

(c) The department may for good cause reconsider any computation or recomputation provided for in this article during the benefit year or extended duration period to which the notice of computation or recomputation relates, except that no recomputation may be considered with respect to any issue considered or under consideration in an appeal taken from a denial of recomputation. The department shall promptly notify the claimant and each of the claimant's base period employers of the recomputation. The claimant and any base period employer may protest the accuracy of the recomputation as prescribed in Section 1330. *(Stats.1953, c. 308, p. 1508, § 1332. Amended by Stats.1961, c. 2165, p. 4486, § 3; Stats.1967, c. 1720, p. 4286, § 8; Stats.1973, c. 1212, p. 2783, § 170, operative July 1, 1974; Stats.1975, c. 751, p. 1751, § 4; Stats.1977, c. 1252, p. 4458, § 409, operative July 1, 1978; Stats.1977, c. 508, p. 1638, § 3; Stats.1978, c. 429, p. 1431, § 168, eff. July 17, 1978, operative July 1, 1978; Stats.1982, c. 1225, p. 4524, § 5; Stats.1984, c. 537, § 26; Stats.1989, c. 1146, § 17; Stats.1991, c. 212 (A.B. 2108), § 2.)*

§ 1332.5. Time limiting reconsideration not applicable in case of fraud, misrepresentation or willful nondisclosure

Notwithstanding any other provision of this division any provision that prescribes time limits within which the department may reconsider any determination, ruling, or computation or any provision that otherwise restricts or prevents such reconsideration, shall not apply in any case of fraud, misrepresentation or willful nondisclosure. *(Added by Stats.1967, c. 1720, p. 4287, § 9. Amended by Stats.1973, c. 1212, p. 2783, § 172, operative July 1, 1974; Stats.1977, c. 1252, p. 4459, § 410, operative July 1, 1978.)*

§ 1333. Regulations on notices and protests

Notices, protests, and information required under this article shall be submitted in accordance with authorized regulations. *(Stats.1953, c. 308, p. 1508, § 1333.)*

§ 1334. Hearing and decision by administrative law judge; notice; finality of decision; extension of limitation period

An administrative law judge after affording a reasonable opportunity for fair hearing, shall, unless such appeal is withdrawn, affirm, reverse, modify, or set aside any determination which is appealed under this article. The claimant, any employer becoming a party to the appeal by submitting a protest or information pursuant to Sections 1326 to 1333, inclusive, of this article, and the director shall be promptly notified in writing of the administrative law judge's decision, together with his reasons therefor.

The decision shall be final unless, within 20 days after mailing of such decision, further appeal is initiated to the appeals board pursuant to Section 1336. The 20-day limitation may be extended for good cause.

"Good cause," as used in this section, shall include, but not be limited to, mistake, inadvertence, surprise, or excusable neglect. *(Stats.1953, c. 308, p. 1508, § 1334. Amended by Stats.1967, c. 1586, p. 3800, § 9; Stats.1974, c. 503, p. 1179, § 4; Stats.1975, c. 979, p. 2303, § 3; Stats.1984, c. 537, § 27.)*

§ 1335. Appeal precluding benefit payments; exceptions

If an appeal is filed, benefits with respect to the period prior to the final decision on the appeal shall be paid only after the decision, except that:

(a) If benefits for any week are payable in accordance with a determination by the department irrespective of any decision on the issues set forth in the appeal, such benefits shall be promptly paid regardless of such appeal.

(b) If an administrative law judge affirms a determination allowing benefits, such benefits shall be promptly paid regardless of any appeal which may thereafter be taken, and regardless of any action taken under Section 1336 or otherwise by the director, appeals board, or other administrative body or by any court.

If the determination is finally reversed, no employer's account shall be charged with benefits paid because of that determination, except as provided in Section 1026.

(c) If benefits for any week are payable in accordance with a determination by the department, or an administrative law judge issues a decision allowing benefits, the benefits shall be promptly paid regardless of any appeal, and regardless of any action taken by the appeals board pursuant to Section 412 or 413. If the determination of the department or the decision of the administrative law judge is finally reversed, no employer's reserve account shall be charged with benefits paid pursuant to this subdivision, except as provided in Section 1026. *(Stats. 1953, c. 308, p. 1509, § 1335. Amended by Stats.1971, c. 1107, p. 2118, § 64, eff. Oct. 18, 1971; Stats.1975, c. 538, p. 1104, § 3; Stats.1982, c. 1075, p. 3892, § 13; Stats. 1984, c. 537, § 28.)*

§ 1336. Proceedings by appeals board; notice of findings and decision

The director or any party to a decision by an administrative law judge may appeal to the appeals board from the decision. The appeals board may order the taking of additional evidence and may affirm, reverse, modify, or set aside the decision of the administrative law judge. The appeals board shall promptly notify the director and the parties to any appeal of its order or decision. *(Stats.1953, c. 308, p. 1509, § 1336. Amended by Stats. 1967, c. 1586, p. 3800, § 10; Stats.1974, c. 503, p. 1179, § 5; Stats.1975, c. 538, p. 1105, § 4; Stats.1984, c. 537, § 29.)*

§ 1337. Time limit on decisions of appeals board

The decision of the appeals board on an appeal from the decision of an administrative law judge must be rendered within 60 days after the submission of the appeal unless the board requires the taking of further evidence. If the appeals board requires the taking of further evidence, the hearing shall be commenced within 60 days after the submission of the appeal, and the decision of the board shall be mailed within 60 days after completion of the hearing. *(Stats.1953, c. 308, p. 1509, § 1337. Amended by Stats.1963, c. 2015, p. 4121, § 14; Stats.1963, c. 2016, p. 4129, § 9; Stats.1984, c. 537, § 30; Stats.1985, c. 716, § 3.)*

§ 1338. Payment of benefits upon appeals board decision allowing benefits; effect of further action or court proceedings

If the appeals board issues a decision allowing benefits the benefits shall be paid regardless of any further action taken by the director, the appeals board, or any other administrative agency, and regardless of any appeal or mandamus, or other proceeding in the courts. If the decision of the appeals board is finally reversed or set aside, no employer's account shall be charged with the benefits paid pursuant to this section, except as provided in Section 1026. *(Stats.1953, c. 308, p. 1509, § 1338. Amended by Stats.1973, c. 1212, p. 2784, § 174, operative July 1, 1974; Stats.1977, c. 1252, p. 4459, § 411, operative July 1, 1978; Stats.1982, c. 1075, p. 3893, § 14.)*

§ 1339. Place of payment of benefits; contents of check or certification

(a) The department shall pay unemployment compensation benefits through public employment offices or such other agency as may be prescribed by authorized regulations of the director.

(b) Each check or certification (pay order) issued in payment of unemployment insurance compensation benefits shall have prominently imprinted upon it: "State unemployment insurance benefits under the California Unemployment Insurance Code are paid for by employers." *(Stats.1953, c. 308, p. 1509, § 1339. Amended by Stats.1968, c. 1121, p. 2137, § 1; Stats.1973, c. 1212, p. 2784, § 176, operative July 1, 1974; Stats.1979, c. 373, p. 1376, § 298.)*

§ 1340. Payments to minors; receipt

Minors who are eligible for benefits may be paid and receive benefits in their own right, and a receipt signed by a minor shall be valid and binding. *(Stats.1953, c. 308, p. 1509, § 1340.)*

§ 1341. Payments or benefits due deceased or incompetent person

Benefits due a deceased or legally declared incompetent person may be paid to such person or persons as appears to the Director of Employment Development to be legally entitled thereto in accordance with authorized regulations of the Director of Employment Development.

Such payment shall be made upon affidavit executed by the person or persons claiming to be entitled to the benefits and the receipt of the affidavit or affidavits shall fully discharge the Director of Employment Development from any further liability with reference to the payments, without the necessity of inquiring into the truth of any of the facts stated in the affidavit. *(Stats.1953, c. 308, p. 1509, § 1341. Amended by Stats.1973, c. 1212, p. 2785, § 178, operative July 1, 1974.)*

§ 1342. Invalidity of waiver of benefits or rights; assignment, release or commutation of benefits; invalidity of agreement of employee to pay employer's contribution

Any waiver by any person of any benefit or right under this code is invalid, except as provided by Sections 1255.7, 1342.1, 1345, and 2630. Benefits under this code, incentive payments provided by Division 2 (commencing with Section 5000), and payments to an individual under a plan or system established by an employer which makes provisions for his or her employees generally, or for a class or group of his or her employees, for the purpose of supplementing unemployment compensation benefits, are not subject to assignment, release, or commutation, except as provided by Sections 1255.7, 1342.1, 1345, and 2630. Any agreement by any individual in the employ of any person or concern to pay all or any portion of the contributions required of his or her employer under this division is void. *(Stats.1953, c. 308, p. 1510, § 1342. Amended by Stats.1961, c. 1336, p. 3114, § 1; Stats.1970, c. 1523, p. 3084, § 65; Stats.1973, c. 1206, p. 2620, § 58; Stats.1973, c. 1207, p. 2670, § 58; Stats.1982, c. 497, p. 2217, § 176, operative July 1, 1983; Stats.1982, c. 1072, p. 3859, § 5, eff. Sept. 15, 1982; Stats.1983, c. 155, § 30, eff. June 30, 1983, operative July 1, 1983; Stats.1988, c. 261, § 3, eff. July 5, 1988; Stats.1994, c. 960 (A.B.3320), § 1; Stats.1996, c. 1124 (S.B.1524), § 5, eff. Sept. 30, 1996.)*

§ 1342.1. New claims for unemployment compensation; taxation

(a) An individual filing a new claim for unemployment compensation shall, at the time of filing the claim, be advised that:

(1) Unemployment compensation and disability insurance benefits, when paid in lieu of unemployment compensation, are subject to federal income tax.

(2) Requirements exist pertaining to estimated tax payments.

(3) The individual may elect to have federal income tax deducted and withheld from the compensation at the amount specified in the Internal Revenue Code.

(4) The individual is permitted to change a previously elected withholding status.

(b) Amounts deducted and withheld from unemployment and disability compensation shall be made in accordance with procedures specified by the United States Department of Labor and Internal Revenue Service pertaining to the deducting and withholding of income tax, and in accordance with the priorities established in department regulations developed by the director. *(Added by Stats.1996, c. 1124 (S.B.1524), § 6, eff. Sept. 30, 1996.)*

§ 1345. Redirection of voluntary plan benefits to cover cost of employee-paid benefits; conditions; request; delay of disability benefits; spousal election

(a) An individual covered by a voluntary plan approved under Section 3254 may, at the time he or she applies for voluntary plan benefits or at any time while receiving voluntary plan benefits, voluntarily choose to allow his or her employer or an agent of the employer, appointed under Section 1096, to redirect a portion of the voluntary plan benefits payable under this code to cover all or part of the cost of employee-paid benefits, if both the following requirements are satisfied:

(1) The individual has given written authorization for the redirection of a weekly dollar amount of voluntary plan benefits for the payment of the employee-paid benefits.

(2) The individual may terminate or change the terms of the voluntary redirection of benefits paid at any time while receiving benefits under the voluntary plan.

(b) Any request to redirect benefits as provided in subdivision (a) shall be in writing. The form of employee authorization required under this section shall be approved by the director.

(c) In no event shall disability benefits payments be delayed because an individual elects to redirect a portion of his or her benefits payable under this division.

(d) Should an individual be legally declared incompetent, the spouse of the individual, in the absence of any other legally authorized representative, shall have the right to continue or cancel the authorization. *(Added by Stats.1994, c. 960 (A.B.3320), § 2.)*

ARTICLE 4. OVERPAYMENTS

Section
1375.   Liability for overpayment of benefits.
1375.1. False statement or representation or withholding of material fact; assessment.
1375.3. Determination of overpayment; bases.
1375.5. Discharge and satisfaction of allowable liens.
1376.   Overpayment and assessment determination; notice.
1377.   Time for appeal; hearing and decision of administrative law judge; finality; further appeal; extension of appeal period.
1378.   Determination by appeals board.
1379.   Recovery of overpayments; civil action; summary judgment; offset.
1379.5. Recordation of judgment; lien; duration; extension; execution.
1379.6. Acknowledgement of satisfaction.
1380.   Liability for benefits if determination affirmed; charging employer's experience rating account.
1381.   Enforcement of collection of judgments; deposit.
1382.   Backpay award or settlement resulting from wrongful discharge; liability for benefits received.

Section
1383.   Recovery of overpayments; assistance of franchise tax board.
1384.   Deposit of amounts collected.

§ 1375. Liability for overpayment of benefits

Any person who is overpaid any amount of benefits under this part is liable for the amount overpaid unless any of the following is applicable:

(a)(1) The overpayment was not due to fraud, misrepresentation or willful nondisclosure on the part of the recipient, and (2) the overpayment was received without fault on the part of the recipient, and its recovery would be against equity and good conscience.

(b) The person who received the overpayment cooperates with the department in an investigation that results in the assessment of a penalty under Section 1144 or the prosecution or other action taken to impose a penalty pursuant to Section 2121.

(c) The department determines that it is in the interest of justice to waive all or part of the liability established under this section because the overpayment was a direct result of inducement, solicitation, or coercion on the part of the employer. *(Stats.1953, c. 308, p. 1510, § 1375. Amended by Stats.1955, c. 1153, p. 2146, § 1; Stats.1994, c. 1050 (A.B.3122), § 3.)*

§ 1375.1. False statement or representation or withholding of material fact; assessment

If the director finds that an individual has been overpaid unemployment compensation benefits because he or she willfully, for the purpose of obtaining unemployment compensation benefits, either made a false statement or representation, with actual knowledge of the falsity thereof, or withheld a material fact, the director shall assess against the individual an amount equal to 30 percent of the overpayment amount. Assessments collected under this section shall be deposited in the Benefit Audit Fund.

(Added by Stats.1983, c. 1219, § 2. Amended by Stats.1986, c. 360, § 2, eff. July 16, 1986; Stats.1989, c. 1010, § 3.)

§ 1375.3. Determination of overpayment; bases

No determination of overpayment shall be based upon the disallowance by the Workmen's Compensation Appeals Board of a claim of lien filed under subdivision (g) of Section 4903 of the Labor Code, or the allowance of such lien for less than the amount claimed as a lien, or upon the approval by the said appeals board of a compromise and release agreement providing for the allowance of such lien in an amount less than the amount claimed as a lien. *(Added by Stats.1967, c. 1721, p. 4294, § 9.)*

§ 1375.5. Discharge and satisfaction of allowable liens

Any claim of lien filed with the Workmen's Compensation Appeals Board under the provisions of Section 4903 of the Labor Code shall be fully discharged and satisfied by payment of the amount of such lien allowed by the said appeals board under the provisions of Section 4904 of said code or the amount specified in any compromise and release agreement filed and approved by the said appeals board pursuant to Sections 5000 through 5004 of said code. *(Added by Stats.1967, c. 1721, p. 4294, § 10.)*

§ 1376. Overpayment and assessment determination; notice

The Director of Employment Development shall determine the amount of the overpayment and any assessment authorized under Section 1375.1 and shall notify the liable person of the basis of the overpayment determination. In the absence of fraud, misrepresentation, or willful nondisclosure, notice of the overpayment determination shall be mailed or personally served within the latest of the following periods:

(a) Not later than one year after the close of the benefit year in which the overpayment was made.

(b) Not later than six months after the date a backpay award was made. *(Stats.1953, c. 308, p. 1510, § 1376. Amended by Stats.1955, c. 1153, p. 2146, § 2; Stats.1973, c. 1212, p. 2785, § 180, operative July 1, 1974; Stats.1983, c. 1219, § 4; Stats.1984, c. 1348, § 1.)*

§ 1377. Time for appeal; hearing and decision of administrative law judge; finality; further appeal; extension of appeal period

Within 20 days from the date of mailing or serving of the notice of overpayment, the person affected may file an appeal to an administrative law judge. The director shall be an interested party to any such appeal. The administrative law judge, after affording reasonable opportunity for a fair hearing, shall unless the appeal is withdrawn, affirm, reverse, modify, or set aside the findings set forth in the notice of overpayment. The party and the director shall be notified of the administrative law judge's decision, together with his reasons therefor, which shall be final unless within 20 days from the date of notification or mailing of the decision a further appeal is initiated to the appeals board pursuant to Section 1336. The 20-day period for an appeal to the administrative law judge or to the appeals board may be extended for good cause.

"Good cause," as used in this section, shall include, but not be limited to, mistake, inadvertence, surprise, or excusable neglect. *(Stats.1953, c. 308, p. 1510, § 1377. Amended by Stats.1967, c. 1586, p. 3800, § 11; Stats.1974, c. 503, p. 1179, § 6; Stats.1975, c. 979, p. 2303, § 4; Stats.1984, c. 537, § 31.)*

§ 1378. Determination by appeals board

The Appeals Board shall review an appeal from an overpayment determination as provided in Sections 1336 and 1337 and determine what amount, if any, shall be recovered. *(Stats.1953, c. 308, p. 1510, § 1378. Amended by Stats.1965, c. 266, p. 1262, § 1.)*

§ 1379. Recovery of overpayments; civil action; summary judgment; offset

The director, subject to this article, may do any or all of the following in the recovery of overpayments of unemployment compensation benefits:

(a) File a civil action against the liable person for the recovery of the amount of the overpayment within one year after any of the following, or, in cases where the individual has been overpaid benefits due to fraud, misrepresentation, or nondisclosure as described in Section 1375.1, within three years of any of the following:

(1) The mailing or personal service of the notice of overpayment determination if the person affected does not file an appeal to an administrative law judge.

(2) The mailing of the decision of the administrative law judge if the person affected does not initiate a further appeal to the appeals board.

(3) The date of the decision of the appeals board.

(b) Initiate proceedings for a summary judgment against the liable person. However, this subdivision applies only where the director has found, pursuant to Section 1375, that the overpayment may not be waived because it was due to fraud, misrepresentation, or willful nondisclosure on the part of the recipient. The director may, not later than three years after the overpayment became final, file with the clerk of the proper court in the county from which the overpayment of benefits was paid or in the county in which the claimant resides, a certificate containing all of the following:

(1) The amount due, including the assessment made under Section 1375.1, plus interest from the date that the initial determination of overpayment was made pursuant to Section 1376.

(2) A statement that the director has complied with all the provisions of this article prior to the filing of the certificate.

(3) A request that judgment be entered against the liable person in the amount set forth in the certificate.

The clerk, immediately upon the filing of the certificate, shall enter a judgment for the State of California against the liable person in the amount set forth in the certificate.

For the purposes of this subdivision only, an overpayment is final and due and payable after any of the following:

(A) The liable person has not filed an appeal pursuant to Section 1377.

(B) The liable person has filed an appeal to the administrative law judge and a decision of an administrative law judge has become final.

(C) The liable person has filed an appeal to the appeals board and the decision of the appeals board has become final because the liable person has not sought judicial review within the six-month period provided by Section 410.

(c) Reduce or vacate a summary judgment by filing a certificate to that effect with the clerk of the proper court.

(d) Offset the amount of the overpayment received by the liable person against any amount of benefits to which he or she may become entitled under this division within six years of the date of the mailing or personal service of the notice of overpayment determination. *(Stats.1953, c. 308, p. 1510, § 1379. Amended by Stats.1955, c. 1153, p. 2147, § 3; Stats.1965, c. 452, p. 1763, § 1; Stats.1973, c. 1212, p. 2786, § 182, operative July 1, 1974; Stats.1975, c. 890, p. 1969, § 1; Stats.1983, c. 1226, § 7, eff. Sept. 30, 1983; Stats.1984, c. 537, § 32; Stats.1984, c. 1236, § 1; Stats.1985, c. 716, § 4; Stats.1987, c. 929, § 4; Stats.1989, c. 1010, § 4.)*

§ 1379.5. Recordation of judgment; lien; duration; extension; execution

An abstract of judgment obtained pursuant to subdivision (a) or (b) of Section 1379, or a copy thereof, may be recorded with the county recorder of any county. From the time of recording, the judgment shall constitute a lien against all real or personal property of the liable person in that county owned by the liable person at the time, or which the liable person may afterwards, but before the lien expires, acquire. The lien shall have the force, effect, and priority of a judgment lien and shall continue for 10 years from the time of recording of the abstract of judgment obtained pursuant to subdivision (a) or (b) of Section 1379, unless sooner released or otherwise discharged.

The lien may, within 10 years from the date of recording of the abstract of judgment or within 10 years from the date of the last extension of the lien in the manner provided in this section, be extended by recording a new abstract in the office of the county recorder of any county. From the date of such recording, the lien shall be extended for 10 years unless sooner released or otherwise discharged.

Execution shall issue upon such a judgment upon request of the director in the same manner as execution may issue upon other judgments. Sales shall be held under such execution as prescribed in the Code of Civil Procedure. In all proceedings under this section, the director or his or her authorized agents may act on behalf of the state. *(Added by Stats.1984, c. 1236, § 2.)*

§ 1379.6. Acknowledgement of satisfaction

(a) If an abstract has been recorded as provided in Section 1379.5, and the lien, including any interest, costs, and penalty, has been satisfied in full, the department shall, pursuant to Section 724.050 of the Code of Civil Procedure do all of the following:

(1) File an acknowledgment of satisfaction of judgment with the court.

(2) Serve an acknowledgment of satisfaction of judgment on the claimant. Service shall be made personally or by mail.

(3) Record an acknowledgment of satisfaction of judgment in the office of the county recorder where the abstract of judgment is recorded.

(b) If an acknowledgment of satisfaction of judgment is recorded, the cost of recording is an obligation of the claimant and may be collected from the claimant in any manner provided by law for the collection of benefit overpayments.

(c) If payment is made by check, any action specified in subdivision (a) shall not be required until the check has been paid by the financial institution upon which it was drawn. *(Added by Stats.1989, c. 1010, § 5.)*

§ 1380. Liability for benefits if determination affirmed; charging employer's experience rating account

No person shall be liable for the amount of benefits received where the benefits were paid pursuant to an administrative law judge's decision which affirmed an initial determination or in accordance with a final decision of the appeals board, regardless of any further appeal. An employer's experience rating account shall not be charged with any benefits erroneously or unlawfully paid, except as provided in Section 1026 or 1144. *(Stats.1953, c. 308, p. 1511, § 1380. Amended by Stats. 1982, c. 1075, p. 3893, § 15; Stats.1984, c. 537, § 33; Stats.1994, c. 1050 (A.B.3122), § 4.)*

§ 1381. Enforcement of collection of judgments; deposit

The director shall enforce collection of any judgment obtained by the director under subdivision (a) or (b) of Section 1379. Amounts collected under this section shall be deposited in the fund from which the overpayment was made, except that the amounts collected to offset the costs of collections shall be deposited in the Unemployment Administration Fund and the amounts collected pursuant to Section 1375.1 shall be deposited in the Benefit Audit Fund. *(Added by Stats.1974, c. 1159, p. 2472, § 31, eff. Sept. 23, 1974. Amended by Stats.1977, c. 1252, p. 4459, § 412, operative July 1, 1978; Stats.1984, c. 1236, § 3.)*

§ 1382. Backpay award or settlement resulting from wrongful discharge; liability for benefits received

No person shall be liable for the amount of benefits received for any period for which the person also received an award or settlement of backpay resulting from an action or grievance for wrongful discharge, if the amount of the backpay award or settlement was reduced by the amount of benefits received pursuant to this part. When the amount of the backpay award or settlement was reduced by the amount of benefits received, the employer shall pay to the Unemployment Fund an amount equal to the amount subtracted from the backpay award or settlement for benefits received by the person in order to reimburse the fund. When an individual has been awarded or receives backpay, the amount of the backpay shall constitute wages paid in the period for which it is awarded.

A mediator or arbitrator who is a party to the backpay award or settlement shall, within 30 days of the settlement, report to the department the name and address of the employer, the amount of benefits by which the award or settlement was reduced, and the name and social security number of the person who received the award or settlement. *(Added by Stats.1983, c. 1035, § 2.)*

§ 1383. Recovery of overpayments; assistance of franchise tax board

Notwithstanding any other provision of law to the contrary, the Franchise Tax Board shall aid the department in the recovery of overpayments of unemployment compensation benefits pursuant to Section 1379 for up to six years after the date of the mailing or personal service of the notice of overpayment determination. *(Added by Stats.1983, c. 1226, § 8, eff. Sept. 30, 1983.)*

§ 1384. Deposit of amounts collected

Amounts collected by the Controller for benefit overpayment accounts, pursuant to Section 12419.2 of the Government Code, shall be deposited in the fund from which the overpayment was made, except that the amounts collected to offset the costs of collections shall be deposited in the Unemployment Administration Fund. *(Added by Stats.1984, c. 1581, § 3, eff. Sept. 30, 1984.)*

ARTICLE 5. RIGHTS OF TRAINEES [REPEALED]

CHAPTER 5.4. UNEMPLOYMENT COMPENSATION FOR EMPLOYEES OF THE LEGISLATURE [REPEALED]

CHAPTER 5.5. BETWEEN TERMS UNEMPLOYMENT COMPENSATION FOR NONPROFESSIONAL EMPLOYEES OF STATE SPECIAL SCHOOLS

Section
1451. Specified schools.
1452. Payment of funds.
1453. Transfer of funds; information and reports.
1454. Multiple benefits; repayment.

§ 1451. Specified schools

Nonprofessional employees of the Fremont and Riverside campuses of the California School for the Deaf, the Fremont campus of the California School for the Blind, and the diagnostic schools for individuals with neurological disabilities located in Los Angeles, San Francisco, and Fresno, shall be eligible for benefits provided by this chapter, on the same terms and conditions as are specified by this part, Part 3 (commencing with Section 3501), and Part 4 (commencing with Section 4001), for all other individuals, except where inconsistent with the provisions of this chapter. Except where inconsistent with the provisions of this chapter, the provisions of this division and authorized regulations shall apply to any

matter arising pursuant to this chapter. *(Added by Stats.1985, c. 1488, § 4. Amended by Stats.2005, c. 152 (A.B.1577), § 23.)*

§ 1452. Payment of funds

Notwithstanding Section 1253.3, between terms unemployment compensation benefits are payable by the Controller, from funds appropriated for support of the State Department of Education and allocated to the state special schools, upon authorization by the Employment Development Department to individuals who are eligible to receive these benefits under this chapter. These benefits shall only be paid for weeks of unemployment occurring between school terms and during an established and customary vacation period or holiday recess when other benefits are denied solely by reason of Section 1253.3. *(Added by Stats.1985, c. 1488, § 4.)*

§ 1453. Transfer of funds; information and reports

(a) There shall be transferred to the Employment Development Department from funds appropriated for support of the State Department of Education and allocated to the state special schools, at the times and in the manner provided in subdivision (b), an amount equal to the additional cost to the Employment Development Department for added administrative work arising out of this chapter.

(b) The director shall determine the sums he or she estimates the department will be entitled to receive from the State Department of Education under this section for each fiscal year, reduced or increased by any sum by which he or she finds that his or her estimates for any prior fiscal year were greater or less than the amounts which were actually required. The sum of the amounts transferred or expended pursuant to Section 1452, subdivision (a), and this subdivision in any one fiscal year shall not exceed the amount appropriated in the then current fiscal year to the State Department of Education for the purposes of this chapter.

(c) The director may require from the State Department of Education such employment, wage, financial, statistical, or other information and reports, properly verified, as may be deemed necessary by the director to carry out his or her duties under this division, which shall be filed with the director at the time and in the manner prescribed by him or her.

(d) The director may tabulate and publish information obtained pursuant to this chapter in statistical form and may divulge the name of the employing unit.

(e) The State Department of Education shall provide each employee subject to this chapter, at the end of each school term, with written information advising the employee of benefit rights pursuant to this chapter. *(Added by Stats.1985, c. 1488, § 4.)*

§ 1454. Multiple benefits; repayment

An individual who receives any unemployment compensation benefits otherwise payable irrespective of this chapter, including retroactive unemployment compensation benefits paid pursuant to subdivision (c) of Section 1253.3, who has received benefits under this chapter for the same period, shall be liable for repayment to the state of the amount of benefits paid under this chapter for that period. *(Added by Stats.1985, c. 1488, § 4.)*

CHAPTER 5.6. UNEMPLOYMENT COMPENSATION FOR COUNTY EMPLOYEES [REPEALED]

CHAPTER 5.7. UNEMPLOYMENT COMPENSATION FOR STATE HIGHER EDUCATION EMPLOYEES [REPEALED]

CHAPTER 5.8. UNEMPLOYMENT COMPENSATION AND DISABILITY BENEFITS FOR FORMER INMATES OF STATE PRISONS OR INSTITUTIONS [REPEALED]

CHAPTER 6. FINANCIAL PROVISIONS

Article		Section
1.	Deposit Account	1501
2.	Unemployment Fund	1521
3.	Administration Fund	1555
4.	Contingent Fund	1585
4.1.	Building Fund	1591
4.5.	Benefit Audit Fund	1595
5.	Investments in or Expenditures for Property	1601
6.	Employment Training Fund	1610

ARTICLE 1. DEPOSIT ACCOUNT

Section
1501. Bank deposits for clearance; deposit in state treasury.

§ 1501. Bank deposits for clearance; deposit in state treasury

The director may in accordance with law deposit for the purpose of clearance by the director all money collected under this division, in a state or national bank in this state. After clearance the money so deposited shall be deposited in the State Treasury to the credit of the proper fund as prescribed in this division. *(Added by Stats.1953, c. 308, p. 1513, § 1501. Amended by Stats. 1973, c. 1212, p. 2787, § 183, operative July 1, 1974; Stats.1977, c. 1252, p. 4459, § 413, operative July 1, 1978.)*

ARTICLE 2. UNEMPLOYMENT FUND

Section
1521. Continuance of fund; composition; appropriation.
1522. Administration; purpose; state liability.
1523. Withdrawals.
1524. State treasurer custodian; duties; official bond.
1525. Accounts; clearing; unemployment trust fund; benefit.
1526. Clearing account; deposit.
1526.1. Deposits in personal income tax fund.
1526.2. Deposits in disability fund.
1526.3. Deposits in contingent fund.
1526.4. Deposits in unemployment administration fund.
1527. Deposits or investments; entry in unemployment trust fund account.
1528. Benefit account; transfer of money.
1528.5. Requisition or use of money in unemployment trust fund.
1529. Requisition of amounts for benefit account appropriation; deposit of such money; use of balances remaining unclaimed or unpaid.
1530. Duration of provisions relating to unemployment trust fund; disposition of funds upon termination; investment of money.
1531. Withdrawals from benefit account; deposit of sums after withdrawal; payment of insurance premiums for protection of money.
1532. Benefit payment account; use; refunds; procedure; unclaimed or unpaid balance.
1533. Deposit of money in clearing and benefit accounts; no commingling with other state funds; security by bank or public depositary.
1534. Payment of refunds or judgments.
1535. Contingent appropriation for administration.
1536. Unclaimed refunds.
1537. Unclaimed warrant.

§ 1521. Continuance of fund; composition; appropriation

The Unemployment Fund is continued in existence as a special fund, separate and apart from all public money or funds of this state. This fund shall consist of (1) all employer contributions collected under this division; (2) interest earned upon any money in the fund; (3) any property or securities acquired through the use of money belonging to the fund; (4) all earnings of such property or securities; (5) all money credited to this state's account in the Unemployment Trust Fund pursuant to Section 903 of the Social Security Act, as amended; and (6) all other money received for the fund from any other source. All money in the fund shall be mingled and undivided.

Notwithstanding Section 13340 of the Government Code, all money in the Unemployment Fund and in the various accounts of that fund, except any money deposited pursuant to Section 1528.5, is continuously appropriated for the purposes authorized in this article. *(Added by Stats.1953, c. 313, p. 1554. Amended by Stats.1959, c. 1814, p. 4313, § 2; Stats.1965, c. 649, p. 2004, § 1; Stats.1983, c. 203, § 1, eff. July 13, 1983; Stats.1984, c. 1642, § 1, eff. Sept. 30, 1984.)*

§ 1522. Administration; purpose; state liability

The Unemployment Fund shall be administered by the director exclusively for the purposes of this division without liability upon the part of the State beyond the amounts paid into and earned by the fund. *(Added by Stats.1953, c. 313, p. 1554.)*

§ 1523. Withdrawals

Withdrawals by the director from the Unemployment Fund are exempted from the operation of Sections 925.4 and 925.6 of the Government Code. *(Added by Stats. 1953, c. 313, p. 1554. Amended by Stats.1959, c. 2156, p. 5211, § 6; Stats.1963, c. 2015, p. 4121, § 15.)*

§ 1524. State treasurer custodian; duties; official bond

The State Treasurer is ex officio the treasurer and custodian of the Unemployment Fund. He shall administer the fund in accordance with the directions of the director. The official bond of the State Treasurer shall cover the faithful performance of his duties as treasurer of the Unemployment Fund. *(Added by Stats.1953, c. 313, p. 1554.)*

§ 1525. Accounts; clearing; unemployment trust fund; benefit

There shall be maintained within the fund three separate accounts:

(a) A clearing account.

(b) An Unemployment Trust Fund account.

(c) A benefit account. *(Added by Stats.1953, c. 313, p. 1554.)*

§ 1526. Clearing account; deposit

All contributions and amounts payable to the Unemployment Fund after proper clearance shall be forwarded to the Treasurer who shall immediately deposit them in the clearing account. *(Added by Stats.1953, c. 313, p. 1554.)*

§ 1526.1. Deposits in personal income tax fund

All withheld income taxes and amounts payable to the Personal Income Tax Fund after proper clearance shall be forwarded to the Treasurer who shall immediately deposit them in that fund. *(Added by Stats.1971, Ex.Sess., c. 1, p. 5128, § 311, eff. Dec. 8, 1971, operative Jan. 1, 1972.)*

§ 1526.2. Deposits in disability fund

All worker contributions and amounts payable to the Disability Fund after proper clearance shall be forwarded to the Treasurer who shall immediately deposit them in that fund. *(Added by Stats.1971, Ex.Sess., c. 1, p. 5128, § 312, eff. Dec. 8, 1971, operative Jan. 1, 1972.)*

§ 1526.3. Deposits in contingent fund

All amounts specified in Section 1585 payable to the Contingent Fund after proper clearance shall be forwarded to the Treasurer who shall immediately deposit them in that fund. *(Added by Stats.1971, Ex.Sess., c. 1, p. 5128, § 313, eff. Dec. 8, 1971, operative Jan. 1, 1972.)*

§ 1526.4. Deposits in unemployment administration fund

All amounts payable to the Unemployment Administration Fund after proper clearance shall be forwarded to the Treasurer who shall immediately deposit them in that fund. *(Added by Stats.1971, Ex.Sess., c. 1, p. 5129, § 314, eff. Dec. 8, 1971, operative Jan. 1, 1972.)*

§ 1527. Deposits or investments; entry in unemployment trust fund account

Immediately after clearance, all money in the clearing account except interest on contributions, and penalties collected shall be deposited in or invested in the obligations of the Unemployment Trust Fund of the United States of America or its authorized agent to the credit of this State, any provisions of law in this State relating to the deposit, administration, release, or disbursement of money in the possession or custody of this State to the contrary notwithstanding. The amounts so deposited or invested shall be entered in the Unemployment Trust Fund Account. *(Added by Stats.1953, c. 313, p. 1554. Amended by Stats.1955, c. 1165, p. 2168, § 34.)*

§ 1528. Benefit account; transfer of money

The benefit account consists of all money requisitioned from this State's account in the Unemployment Trust Fund, except money requisitioned for administration pursuant to Section 1528.5, and any money so requisitioned, except money requisitioned for administration pursuant to Section 1528.5, shall be transferred out of the Unemployment Trust Fund account into the benefit account. *(Added by Stats.1953, c. 313, p. 1554. Amended by Stats.1959, c. 1814, p. 4314, § 3.)*

§ 1528.5. Requisition or use of money in unemployment trust fund

(a) Money credited to the account of this state in the Unemployment Trust Fund by the Secretary of the Treasury of the United States of America pursuant to Section 903 of the Social Security Act, as amended,[1] may not be requisitioned from this state's account or used except for the payment of benefits and for the payment of expenses incurred for the administration of this part. Such money may be requisitioned pursuant to Section 1529 for the payment of benefits. Such money may also be requisitioned and used for the payment of expenses incurred for the administration of this part but only pursuant to a specific appropriation by the Legislature and only if the expenses are incurred and the money is requisitioned after the enactment of an appropriation law which:

(1) Specifies the purposes for which such money is appropriated and the amounts appropriated therefor.

(2) Limits the period within which such money may be obligated to a period ending not more than two years after the date of the enactment of the appropriation law.

(3) Provides that the total amount which may be obligated shall be limited to the restrictions specified by,

and charged in accordance with, Section 903(c)(2)(D) of the Social Security Act, as amended.

(b) Money appropriated pursuant to this section for the payment of expenses of administration shall be requisitioned as needed for the payment of obligations incurred under such appropriation and, upon requisition, shall be deposited in the Unemployment Administration Fund, but, until expended, shall remain a part of the Unemployment Fund. The director and the Controller shall maintain a separate record of the deposit, obligation, expenditure, and return of funds so deposited. Any money so deposited which will not be expended shall be returned promptly to the account of this state in the Unemployment Trust Fund. *(Added by Stats.1959, c. 1814, p. 4314, § 4. Amended by Stats.1965, c. 649, p. 2004, § 2; Stats.1969, c. 1250, p. 2444, § 1; Stats.1972, c. 833, p. 1486, § 10; Stats.1973, c. 394, p. 859, § 3; Stats.1977, c. 397, p. 1393, § 1, eff. Aug. 27, 1977.)*

[1] 42 U.S.C.A. § 1103.

§ 1529. Requisition of amounts for benefit account appropriation; deposit of such money; use of balances remaining unclaimed or unpaid

Except as provided in Section 1528.5, money shall be requisitioned from this State's account in the Unemployment Trust Fund solely for the payment of benefits and in accordance with authorized regulations. The director shall from time to time requisition from the Unemployment Trust Fund such amounts, not exceeding the amounts standing to this State's account therein, as he deems necessary for the payment of benefits for a reasonable future period. Upon receipt thereof the Treasurer shall deposit such money in the benefit account of the Unemployment Fund. Any balance of money requisitioned from the Unemployment Trust Fund which remains unclaimed or unpaid in the benefit account after the expiration of the period for which such sums were requisitioned shall either be considered in preparing subsequent estimates and may be utilized for the payment of benefits during succeeding periods, or, in the discretion of the director, shall be redeposited with the Secretary of the Treasury of the United States of America, to the credit of this State's account in the Unemployment Trust Fund. *(Added by Stats.1953, c. 313, p. 1554. Amended by Stats.1959, c. 1814, p. 4315, § 5.)*

§ 1530. Duration of provisions relating to unemployment trust fund; disposition of funds upon termination; investment of money

The provisions of this article to the extent that they relate to the Unemployment Trust Fund, shall be operative only so long as that fund continues to exist and so long as the Secretary of the Treasury of the United States of America continues to maintain for this State a separate book account of all funds deposited therein by this State for benefit purposes, together with this State's proportionate share of the earnings of the Unemployment Trust Fund, from which no other state nor the United States is permitted to make withdrawals. If and when such Unemployment Trust Fund ceases to exist, or such separate book account is no longer maintained, all money, properties, or securities therein, belonging to the Unemployment Fund of this State shall be transferred to the treasurer of the Unemployment Fund, who shall hold, invest, transfer, sell, deposit, and release such money, properties, or securities in a manner approved by the director in accordance with the provisions of this division. Such money shall be invested in bonds or other interest-bearing obligations of the United States of America or the State of California. Such investment shall at all times be so made that all the assets of the fund shall always be readily convertible into cash when needed for the payment of benefits. The Treasurer shall dispose of securities or other properties belonging to the Unemployment Fund only under the direction of the director. *(Added by Stats.1953, c. 313, p. 1554.)*

§ 1531. Withdrawals from benefit account; deposit of sums after withdrawal; payment of insurance premiums for protection of money

The director shall, without presenting vouchers and itemized statements therefor, withdraw from the benefit account any sums which he deems necessary for the payment of benefits for a reasonable future period. The Controller shall draw his warrant for any claim presented by the director for the payment of benefits under this account and the Treasurer shall pay the warrant. Upon the withdrawal thereof, such sums shall be deposited in a benefit payment account in such bank, savings and loan association, or public depository and under such conditions as the director determines, with the approval of the Department of Finance. Such bank, savings and loan association, or public depository shall be one in which general funds of the state may be deposited, but no public deposit insurance charge or premium shall be paid out of the benefit payment account. The director may, out of funds available for administration, pay premiums on insurance for the protection of money in his possession. *(Added by Stats.1953, c. 313, p. 1554. Amended by Stats.1965, c. 371, p. 1595, § 277; Stats.1974, c. 1221, p. 2653, § 43; Stats.1976, c. 349, p. 991, § 34, eff. July 9, 1976.)*

§ 1532. Benefit payment account; use; refunds; procedure; unclaimed or unpaid balance

Money in the benefit payment account shall be used solely to pay benefits pursuant to authorized regulations and no other disbursement shall be made therefrom, but amounts erroneously and illegally deposited in such account may be refunded therefrom, except that money credited to this State's account pursuant to Section 903 of the Social Security Act, as amended [1], shall be used exclusively as provided in Section 1528.5. The procedure prescribed by such regulations shall be deemed to satisfy and shall be in lieu of any and all statutory requirements not contained in this division of specific appropriation or other form of release by state officers of money in their custody prior to expenditure which might otherwise be

1007

applicable to withdrawals from the benefit payment account. Any balance of money withdrawn from the benefit account which remains unclaimed or unpaid in the benefit payment account after the expiration of the period for which such sums were withdrawn shall be considered in preparing subsequent estimates and may be utilized for the payment of benefits during succeeding periods or, in the discretion of the director, shall be redeposited in the benefit account. *(Added by Stats.1953, c. 313, p. 1554. Amended by Stats.1959, c. 1814, p. 4315, § 6.)*

[1] 42 U.S.C.A. § 1103.

§ 1533. Deposit of money in clearing and benefit accounts; no commingling with other state funds; security by bank or public depositary

Except as otherwise provided in this chapter, money in the clearing and benefit accounts may be deposited by the Treasurer, under the direction of the director, in any bank, savings and loan association, or public depositary in which public funds of the state may be deposited, but no public deposit insurance charge or premium shall be paid out of the fund. Money in the clearing and benefit accounts shall not be commingled with other state funds, but shall be maintained in a separate account on the books of the depositary. Such money shall be secured by the bank or public depositary to the same extent and in the same manner as required under Chapter 4, Part 2, Division 4, Title 2 of the Government Code [1] if deposited in a bank or public depositary, not a savings and loan association or to the same extent and in the same manner as required under Chapter 4.5 (commencing with Section 16600) of Part 2 of Division 4 of Title 2 of the Government Code if deposited in a savings and loan association and collateral pledged shall be maintained in a separate custody account. *(Added by Stats.1953, c. 313, p. 1554. Amended by Stats.1976, c. 349, p. 992, § 35, eff. July 9, 1976.)*

[1] See, Government Code, § 16500 et seq.

§ 1534. Payment of refunds or judgments

Refunds or judgments payable pursuant to this part, may be paid from the clearing account or from the benefit account with respect to any money erroneously deposited therein, upon warrants issued by the Controller under the direction of and in accordance with authorized regulations, except that money credited to this state's account pursuant to Section 903 of the Social Security Act, as amended [1], shall be used exclusively as provided in Section 1528.5. Refunds of interest, penalties, and fines and interest payable on refunds and judgments pursuant to this division may not be paid from the benefit account but may be paid from the clearing account to the extent that interest, penalties, and fines collected are currently on deposit in that account. *(Added by Stats.1953, c. 313, p. 1554. Amended by Stats.1959, c. 1814, p. 4316, § 7; Stats.1980, c. 1025, p. 3289, § 10.)*

[1] 42 U.S.C.A. § 1103.

1008

§ 1535. Contingent appropriation for administration

During such time as the Federal Social Security Act [1] and Federal Unemployment Tax Act [2] are amended so as to remove the requirement that all money withdrawn from the Unemployment Fund be used solely in the payment of unemployment compensation, exclusive of expenses of administration, and for refunds of sums erroneously paid into such fund and refunds paid in accordance with the provisions of Section 3305(b) of the Federal Unemployment Tax Act [3], then notwithstanding any other provisions of this division to the contrary there is hereby continuously appropriated out of the Unemployment Fund for the purpose of administering this division, including salaries and other expenses of the department and the acquisition of necessary real property, all amounts collected under Section 993. *(Added by Stats.1953, c. 313, p. 1554. Amended by Stats.1955, c. 1165, p. 2169, § 35; Stats.1970, c. 350, p. 759, § 9.)*

[1] 42 U.S.C.A. § 301 et seq.
[2] 26 U.S.C.A. §§ 3301 to 3309.
[3] 26 U.S.C.A. § 3305(b).

§ 1536. Unclaimed refunds

Any amounts determined by the director or his authorized representatives to be payable to employing units as refunds of contributions erroneously paid which are unclaimed at the end of three years from such determination shall be included in the revenue to the Unemployment Fund or in the case of interest or penalties, to the Contingent Fund. The employing unit or person entitled to such payment shall not thereafter maintain any claim, action or proceeding with respect to such amounts. *(Added by Stats.1953, c. 313, p. 1554. Amended by Stats.1970, c. 350, p. 759, § 10; Stats.1973, c. 1212, p. 2787, § 184, operative July 1, 1974; Stats.1977, c. 1252, p. 4460, § 414, operative July 1, 1978.)*

§ 1537. Unclaimed warrant

Whenever any warrant drawn on an account in the Unemployment Fund or on the Unemployment Administration Fund or the Contingent Fund by the State Controller remains unclaimed after three years the amount thereof shall revert to the account and the fund from which the amount was payable. *(Added by Stats. 1953, c. 313, p. 1554. Amended by Stats.1970, c. 350, p. 759, § 11; Stats.1973, c. 1212, p. 2787, § 185, operative July 1, 1974.)*

ARTICLE 3. ADMINISTRATION FUND

Section
1555. Continuation of fund; appropriations; availability of balances.
1556. Composition of fund.
1557. Keeping money in separate account; security by depositary.
1558. Purposes for which money may be used.
1558.5. Expenditures; deposit of advances.
1559. Manner of depositing, administering and disbursing money; creation of revolving fund; accounting.

Section
1560.   Deposit and investment of excess money.
1561.   Liability of state treasurer on official bond; disposition of funds recovered on bond.
1562.   Replacement of federal advances; report of amount required.

§ 1555. Continuation of fund; appropriations; availability of balances

The Unemployment Administration Fund is continued in existence as a special fund in the State Treasury. All money which is deposited or paid into this fund, except any money deposited pursuant to Section 1528.5, is hereby continuously appropriated and made available to the director for the purposes authorized in this article without regard to fiscal years. Any balances in this fund shall not lapse at any time, but shall be continuously available to the director for expenditure consistent with the purposes authorized. *(Added by Stats.1953, c. 311, p. 1554. Amended by Stats.1959, c. 1814, p. 4316, § 8; Stats.1965, c. 649, p. 2005, § 3.)*

§ 1556. Composition of fund

Except for money deposited pursuant to Section 1528.5, the Unemployment Administration Fund shall consist of all money appropriated by this state for the purpose of administering this part, money deposited for the purpose of expenditure pursuant to Section 1558.5, and all money received from the United States of America, or any agency thereof, including the Secretary of Labor, or from any other source for such purpose. Money requisitioned and deposited in this fund pursuant to Section 1528.5 shall remain part of the Unemployment Fund and shall be used only in accordance with the conditions specified in that section. *(Added by Stats. 1953, c. 311, p. 1554. Amended by Stats.1959, c. 1814, p. 4316, § 9; Stats.1965, c. 649, p. 2005, § 4; Stats.1980, c. 1025, p. 3289, § 11.)*

§ 1557. Keeping money in separate account; security by depositary

Money in the Unemployment Administration Fund shall not be commingled with other state funds, but shall be maintained in a separate account on the books of the depositary. Such money shall be secured by the depositary in which it is held to the same extent and in the same manner as required under Chapter 4, Part 2, Division 4, Title 2 [1] of the Government Code, if deposited in a bank, or under Chapter 4.5 (commencing with Section 16600) of Part 2 of Division 4 of Title 2 of the Government Code if deposited in a savings and loan association and collateral pledged shall be maintained in a separate custody account. *(Added by Stats.1953, c. 311, p. 1554. Amended by Stats.1976, c. 349, p. 992, § 36, eff. July 9, 1976.)*

[1] See, Government Code § 16500 et seq.

§ 1558. Purposes for which money may be used

Except as provided by Section 1558.5, all money in the Unemployment Administration Fund shall be expended solely for the purpose of defraying the cost of the administration of this division, including, but not limited to, payments authorized under Section 1786 and 1788 [1], and for no other purpose whatsoever, and all money, except money received pursuant to Section 1528.5, received from the federal government for the fund pursuant to Section 302 of the Social Security Act [2] shall be expended solely for the purposes and in the amounts found necessary by the Secretary of Labor for the proper and efficient administration of this division. *(Added by Stats.1953, c. 311, p. 1554. Amended by Stats.1955, c. 1165, p. 2169, § 36; Stats.1959, c. 1814, p. 4316, § 10; Stats.1975, c. 767, p. 1786, § 1.)*

[1] Repealed.

[2] 42 U.S.C.A. § 502.

§ 1558.5. Expenditures; deposit of advances

Money in the Unemployment Administration Fund may be expended for any cost of administration under this code, or for any expenditure by the department chargeable pursuant to state or federal law to another state or federal fund or appropriation or to a subvention, payment under a contract, or other source and expended for any purpose authorized by such state or federal law, in accordance with a plan or system of accrual cost accounting approved by the United States Department of Labor under which expenditures from the Unemployment Administration Fund are charged against advances from or subsequently reimbursed from another fund or funds or appropriation or a subvention or payment under a contract or other source to which the actual costs of such expenditures are chargeable. The director shall deposit in the Unemployment Administration Fund advances from another fund or funds or appropriation or subvention or contract payment or other source made in accordance with an approved plan or system under this section. *(Added by Stats.1975, c. 767, p. 1786, § 2. Amended by Stats.1977, c. 1252, p. 4460, § 414.5, operative July 1, 1978; Stats.1980, c. 1025, p. 3289, § 12.)*

§ 1559. Manner of depositing, administering and disbursing money; creation of revolving fund; accounting

All money in the Unemployment Administration Fund shall be deposited, administered, and disbursed in the same manner and under the same conditions and requirements as is provided by law for other special funds in the State Treasury, but the director may draw, without at the time furnishing vouchers and itemized statements, sums not to exceed in the aggregate an amount equal to 1 percent of the total disbursements made from the fund during the immediately preceding fiscal year to be used as a revolving fund where payment of compensation earned, traveling expense advances, payments under Sections 1786 and 1788 [1], the fees, commissions and expenses authorized to be charged in connection with the levy of writs of attachment or execution under Article 7 (commencing with Section 26720) of Chapter 2 of Part 3 of Division 2 of Title 3 of the Government Code, or other cash payments are necessary. At the close of each fiscal year or at any other time, upon the demand of the Department of Finance, the money so drawn shall be accounted for and substantiated by vouchers and itemized statements submitted to and audited by the Controller. *(Added by Stats.1953, c. 311, p. 1554. Amended by Stats.1955, c. 1165, p. 2169, § 37; Stats.1957, c. 2132, p. 3783, § 2; Stats.1977, c. 438, p. 1474, § 1; Stats.1980, c. 1025, p. 3290, § 13.)*

[1] Repealed.

§ 1560. Deposit and investment of excess money

All money in the Unemployment Administration Fund, in excess of current requirements, and not otherwise invested, may be deposited by the State Treasurer in banks and savings and loan associations and otherwise held and invested by him in the same manner as provided by law in the case of other special funds in the State Treasury, and under the same rules and regulations that govern the deposit of other public funds. *(Added by Stats.1953, c. 311, p. 1554. Amended by Stats.1976, c. 349, p. 992, § 37, eff. July 9, 1976.)*

§ 1561. Liability of state treasurer on official bond; disposition of funds recovered on bond

The State Treasurer is liable on his official bond for the faithful performance of his duties in connection with the Unemployment Administration Fund. This liability shall exist in addition to any liability upon any separate bond now existing or which may be given in the future. All sums recovered on the official bond for losses sustained by the Unemployment Administration Fund shall be deposited in that fund. *(Added by Stats.1953, c. 311, p. 1554.)*

§ 1562. Replacement of federal advances; report of amount required

This state recognizes its obligations to replace, and pledges the faith of this state that funds shall be provided in the future, and applied to the replacement of, any money received from the federal government under Title 3 of the Social Security Act [1], any unencumbered balances in the Unemployment Administration Fund and any money granted to this state pursuant to the provisions of the Wagner-Peyser Act, which the Secretary of Labor finds have, because of any action or contingency, been lost or expended for purposes other than, or in amounts in excess of, those found necessary by the Secretary of Labor for the proper administration of this part and Parts 3 (commencing with Section 3501) and 4 (commencing with Section 4001) of this division. Such money shall be replaced within a reasonable time by money appropriated by the Legislature from the general funds of this state to the Unemployment Administration Fund. The director shall report to the Director of Finance, in the same manner as is provided generally for the submission of financial requirements for the ensuing year, and the Governor shall include in his or her next budget report to the Legislature, the amount required for such replace-

ment. *(Added by Stats.1953, c. 311, p. 1554. Amended by Stats.1959, c. 1729, p. 4178, § 12; Stats.1970, c. 1156, p. 2050, § 10; Stats.1980, c. 1025, p. 3290, § 14.)*

[1] 42 U.S.C.A. § 501 et seq.

ARTICLE 4. CONTINGENT FUND

Section
1585.   Employment development department contingent fund; deposits and transfers.
1585.5.   Estimate and transfer of certain penalties and interest to personal income tax fund.
1586.   Appropriation.
1586.5.   Appropriations; augmentation.
1588.   Transfer of amount to be expended.
1589.   Refunds from various funds; filing single claim.
1590.   Unencumbered balance of contingent fund exceeding $1,000,000; transfer to unemployment fund and disability fund.
1590.5.   Budget act; appropriation.

§ 1585. Employment development department contingent fund; deposits and transfers

There is in the State Treasury a special fund known as the Employment Development Department Contingent Fund. The Employment Development Department Contingent Fund is the successor of the Department of Human Resources Development Contingent Fund. There shall be deposited in or transferred to this fund:

(a) All interest on contributions collected under this division, except as provided in Section 1595 and in Article 6 (commencing with Section 821) of Chapter 3.

(b) All penalties collected under this division, except as provided in Sections 1375.1, 1958, and 3654.2, and in Article 6 (commencing with Section 821) of Chapter 3.

(c) Notwithstanding any other provision of law, all penalties and interest collected by the department pursuant to Division 6 (commencing with Section 13000) relating to the withholding of personal income tax.

(d) Rental payments or proceeds attributable to property derived from amounts expended from this fund.

(e) Interest on amounts expended from this fund. *(Added by Stats.1978, c. 2, p. 46, § 92.5, eff. Jan. 30, 1978, operative July 1, 1978. Amended by Stats.1980, c. 676, p. 2020, § 303; Stats.1980, c. 1007, p. 3227, § 60, operative July 1, 1981; Stats.1983, c. 1219, § 5; Stats.1985, c. 1217, § 8, eff. Sept. 29, 1985.)*

§ 1585.5. Estimate and transfer of certain penalties and interest to personal income tax fund

The director shall estimate the amount of penalties and interest collected by the department pursuant to Division 6 (commencing with Section 13000) relating to the withholding of personal income tax and shall transfer such amount to the Personal Income Tax Fund on a quarterly basis. *(Added by Stats.1971, Ex.Sess., c. 1, p. 5129, § 314.6, eff. Dec. 8, 1971, operative Jan. 1, 1972. Amended by Stats.1973, c. 1212, p. 2788, § 189, operative July 1, 1974; Stats.1977, c. 1252, p. 4460, § 416, operative*

July 1, 1978; Stats.1980, c. 1007, p. 3228, § 61, operative July 1, 1981.)

§ 1586. Appropriation

All amounts in the Contingent Fund are hereby continuously appropriated without regard to fiscal years for refund of amounts collected and erroneously deposited therein, for interest payable under this division on refunds and judgments and for the administration of the department. *(Added by Stats.1953, c. 310, p. 1554. Amended by Stats.1970, c. 350, p. 759, § 13; Stats.1973, c. 1212, p. 2788, § 191, operative July 1, 1974; Stats.1977, c. 1252, p. 4460, § 417, operative July 1, 1978; Stats.1980, c. 1025, p. 3290, § 15.)*

§ 1586.5. Appropriations; augmentation

There is hereby appropriated from the Contingent Fund to the Employment Development Department an amount sufficient to augment an appropriation available from the Unemployment Trust Fund pursuant to Section 1528.5 for acquisition of real property, or for construction and equipment of state public works projects, in order to provide for payment of such public work projects for which an appropriation is available where such project cannot be undertaken because the estimate exceeds the amount available or bids received are in excess of the estimate, and upon such augmentation, contracts may be awarded therefor, notwithstanding the provisions of Section 14275 [1] of the Government Code.

Allocations may be made for acquisition of real property in augmentation of appropriations made for acquisition of real property and which cannot be acquired because acquisition costs are in excess of the amounts provided in the appropriation.

Allocations may be made for purchase of equipment in augmentation of appropriations made from which purchase of equipment is authorized.

Expenditures shall be pursuant to executive orders of the Director of Finance upon approval of the State Public Works Board. *(Added by Stats.1978, c. 941, p. 2917, § 1.)*

[1] Repealed. See, now, Public Contract Code § 10125.

§ 1588. Transfer of amount to be expended

Any amount authorized to be expended from the Contingent Fund for administration may be transferred to the Unemployment Administration Fund, but any amount not needed for the purpose for which authorized shall, upon order of the Director of Finance, be retransferred to the Contingent Fund. *(Added by Stats.1953, c. 310, p. 1554.)*

§ 1589. Refunds from various funds; filing single claim

In lieu of filing claims for refund and interest payable on refunds against each of the funds from which an amount has been determined to be due under this division, the director may file a single claim with the State Controller showing the amount payable from each fund for payment from the Contingent Fund, and the Control-

ler shall thereupon draw his warrant on the Contingent Fund and transfer the amounts certified by the director to be due from the Clearing Account—Unemployment Fund, the Employment Training Fund, the Unemployment Compensation Disability Fund, and the Personal Income Tax Fund, to the Contingent Fund. *(Added by Stats.1953, c. 310, p. 1554. Amended by Stats.1972, c. 333, p. 628, § 12, eff. July 11, 1972, operative Aug. 10, 1972; Stats.1973, c. 1212, p. 2789, § 194, operative July 1, 1974; Stats.1977, c. 1252, p. 4461, § 419, operative July 1, 1978; Stats.1983, c. 1169, § 7.)*

§ 1590. Unencumbered balance of contingent fund exceeding $1,000,000; transfer to unemployment fund and disability fund

Except as provided by Section 1585.5, the director shall from time to time determine, and the State Controller shall from time to time transfer, the unencumbered balance of the Contingent Fund which at any time during any calendar year exceeds one million dollars ($1,000,000) to the Unemployment Fund and the Disability Fund in the proportion that the year's estimated revenues for penalties and interest relating to employer contributions attributable to the Unemployment Fund bear to the year's estimated revenues for penalties and interest relating to worker contributions attributable to the Disability Fund. *(Added by Stats.1974, c. 1458, p. 3185, § 1.)*

§ 1590.5. Budget act; appropriation

It is the intent of the Legislature that the Budget Act for each fiscal year shall appropriate the entire amount available in the Contingent Fund during the fiscal year for the purposes of this article. *(Formerly § 1591, added by Stats.1989, c. 1146, § 18. Renumbered § 1590.5 and amended by Stats.1990, c. 216 (S.B.2510), § 109.)*

ARTICLE 4.1. BUILDING FUND

Section
1591. Employment development department building fund.
1592. Acquisition, construction or renovation of facilities; use of fund.

§ 1591. Employment development department building fund

(a) There is in the State Treasury the Employment Development Department Building Fund. There shall be deposited in, or transferred to, the fund the following:

(1) All money received from the sale or lease of real property, the purchase, acquisition, or construction of which was made by an appropriation to the Employment Development Department for that specific purpose, which was amortized with federal funds paid out of the Unemployment Administration Fund.

(2) All interest earned by the fund.

(b) Money in the fund shall only be expended pursuant to appropriations by the Legislature. *(Added by Stats. 1989, c. 1036, § 1.)*

§ 1592. Acquisition, construction or renovation of facilities; use of fund

The Employment Development Department Building Fund shall be used for the acquisition, construction, or renovation of department facilities, necessary for the director to administer this code and laws relating thereto. *(Added by Stats.1989, c. 1036, § 1.)*

ARTICLE 4.5. BENEFIT AUDIT FUND

Section
1595. Creation of fund; deposit or transfer of funds.
1596. Appropriation.

§ 1595. Creation of fund; deposit or transfer of funds

There is in the State Treasury a special fund known as the Employment Development Department Benefit Audit Fund. There shall be deposited in, or transferred to, this fund all sums collected pursuant to Section 1375.1 and all interest from these sums. *(Added by Stats.1983, c. 1219, § 6.)*

§ 1596. Appropriation

All amounts in the Benefit Audit Fund are hereby continuously appropriated without regard to fiscal years for the refund of amounts collected and erroneously deposited therein, and shall be appropriated annually in the Budget Act by the Legislature for the financing of administrative costs associated with the discovery and collection of unemployment compensation benefit overpayments. *(Added by Stats.1983, c. 1219, § 6.)*

ARTICLE 5. INVESTMENTS IN OR EXPENDITURES FOR PROPERTY

Section
1601. Protection of property; insurance.
1602. Sale of property; federal equity.

§ 1601. Protection of property; insurance

When money other than Disability Fund money is used in the purchase of property and in the construction of buildings, and appurtenant facilities, or in the purchase of property, or in the construction of buildings, and appurtenant facilities, for the use of the department, or for the use of the department and other state agencies, the director may do any and all things necessary to protect the property including purchasing insurance against the loss of or damage to the property or the loss of use and occupancy of the property. Any transaction entered into by the director under this section shall be subject to the approval of the Department of General Services. *(Added by Stats.1961, c. 1688, p. 3663, § 1. Amended by Stats. 1965, c. 371, p. 1596, § 278; Stats.1970, c. 350, p. 760, § 15; Stats.1973, c. 1212, p. 2789, § 196, operative July 1, 1974; Stats.1977, c. 1252, p. 4461, § 420, operative July 1, 1978.)*
1012

§ 1602. Sale of property; federal equity

The department shall comply with all federal regulations with regard to the sale of property in which the federal government has an equity. *(Added by Stats.1989, c. 1036, § 2.)*

ARTICLE 6. EMPLOYMENT TRAINING FUND

Section
1610. Creation; deposits and transfers; appropriations.
1611. Expenditures; purpose.
1611.5. Welfare-to-work activities under CalWORKS program; appropriation to fund local assistance portion.

§ 1610. Creation; deposits and transfers; appropriations

There is in the State Treasury a special fund known as the Employment Training Fund. There shall be deposited in or transferred to this fund all contributions collected from employers pursuant to Section 976.6. Costs incurred for the purposes specified in Section 1611 in fiscal year 1982–83 shall be reimbursed, and thereafter shall be annually appropriated by the Legislature from the Employment Training Fund. *(Added by Stats.1982, c. 1075, p. 3893, § 16.)*

§ 1611. Expenditures; purpose

Moneys in the Employment Training Fund shall be expended only for the purposes of Chapter 3.5 (commencing with Section 10200) of Part 1 of Division 3, and for the costs of administering this article and Section 976.6, except those moneys may be used for any of the following:

(a) With the approval of the Legislature, the fund or contributions to it may be used to pay interest charged on federal loans to the Unemployment Fund.

(b) Commencing with allocations made to the Employment Training Panel in the 1992–93 fiscal year, any moneys allocated to the panel in a fiscal year that are not encumbered by the panel in that fiscal year, shall revert to the Unemployment Insurance Fund.

(c) It is the intent of the Legislature that the panel shall closely monitor program performance and expenditures for employment training programs administered by the panel, and that the panel shall expeditiously disencumber funds that are not needed for employment training program completion. Commencing with the 1992–93 fiscal year, those moneys that are disencumbered during the fiscal year that are not reencumbered during the same fiscal year shall revert to the Unemployment Insurance Fund.

(d) Notwithstanding any other law, the Controller may use the moneys in the Employment Training Fund for loans to the General Fund as provided in Sections 16310 and 16381 of the Government Code. However, interest shall be paid on all moneys loaned to the General Fund from the Employment Training Fund. Interest payable shall be computed at a rate determined by the Pooled Money Investment Board to be the current earning rate of the fund from which loaned. This subdivision does not authorize any transfer that will interfere with the carrying out of the object for which the Employment Training Fund was created. *(Added by Stats.1982, c. 1075, p. 3894, § 16. Amended by Stats.1990, c. 1667 (S.B.1033), § 12.5; Stats.1990, c. 1668 (A.B.2694), § 1, eff. Sept. 30, 1990; Stats.1992, c. 727 (S.B.522), § 1, eff. Sept. 17, 1992; Stats.1993, c. 1080 (S.B.96), § 2; Stats.1994, c. 916 (S.B.1327), § 1, eff. Sept. 28, 1994; Stats.2003, c. 225 (A.B.1752), § 21.5, eff. Aug. 11, 2003; Stats.2009–2010, 3rd Ex.Sess., c. 9 (A.B.13), § 21, eff. Feb. 20, 2009.)*

§ 1611.5. Welfare-to-work activities under CalWORKS program; appropriation to fund local assistance portion

Notwithstanding Section 1611, the Legislature may appropriate from the Employment Training Fund an amount specified in the annual Budget Act to fund the local assistance portion of welfare- to-work activities under the CalWORKs program, provided for pursuant to Article 3.2 (commencing with Section 11320) of Chapter 2 of Part 3 of Division 9 of the Welfare and Institutions Code, as administered by the State Department of Social Services. *(Added by Stats.1997, c. 270 (A.B.1542), § 24, eff. Aug. 11, 1997, operative Jan. 1, 1998. Amended by Stats.1999, c. 147 (A.B.1111), § 7.5, eff. July 22, 1999; Stats.2000, c. 108 (A.B.2876), § 17, eff. July 10, 2000; Stats.2001, c. 111 (A.B.429), § 19, eff. July 30, 2001; Stats.2002, c. 1022 (A.B.444), § 13, eff. Sept. 28, 2002; Stats.2003, c. 225 (A.B.1752), § 22, eff. Aug. 11, 2003; Stats.2004, c. 229 (S.B.1104), § 15, eff. Aug. 16, 2004; Stats.2005, c. 78 (S.B.68), § 13, eff. July 19, 2005; Stats. 2006, c. 75 (A.B.1808), § 25, eff. July 12, 2006.)*

CHAPTER 7. COLLECTIONS

Article	Section
1. Priority and Lien of Tax	1701
2. Liability of Successors, Officers and Fiduciaries	1731
3. Notices of Levy	1755
4. Warrant for Collection	1785
5. Summary Judgment	1815
6. Civil Action	1851
7. Additional Remedies	1860
8. Offers in Compromise	1870

ARTICLE 1. PRIORITY AND LIEN OF TAX

Section
1701. Priority of contributions in enumerated cases.
1702. Preferences; recorded or perfected liens and security interests; claims for personal services.
1703. Perfection and enforcement of lien; amounts due and payable.

§ 1701. Priority of contributions in enumerated cases

The wage earner and employer contributions required to be paid by any employing unit under this division,

together with interest and penalties, shall be satisfied first in any of the following cases:

(a) Whenever the employing unit is insolvent.

(b) Whenever the employing unit makes a voluntary assignment of its assets.

(c) Whenever the estate of the employing unit in the hands of the executors, administrators, or heirs is insufficient to pay all the debts due from the deceased.

(d) Whenever the estate and effects of an absconding, concealed, or absent employing unit required to pay any amount under this division are levied upon by process of law. *(Stats.1953, c. 308, p. 1519, § 1701. Amended by Stats.1953, c. 449, p. 1695.)*

§ 1702. Preferences; recorded or perfected liens and security interests; claims for personal services

Section 1701 does not give the state a preference over any lien or security interest which was recorded or perfected prior to the time when the state records or files its lien as provided in Section 7171 of the Government Code. The preference given to the state by Section 1701 is subordinate to the preferences given to claims for personal services by Sections 1204 and 1206 of the Code of Civil Procedure. *(Stats.1953, c. 308, p. 1519, § 1702. Amended by Stats.1977, c. 481, p. 1595, § 69, operative July 1, 1978; Stats.1980, c. 600, p. 1648, § 63.)*

§ 1703. Perfection and enforcement of lien; amounts due and payable

(a) If any employing unit or other person fails to pay any amount imposed under this division at the time that it becomes due and payable, the amount thereof, including penalties and interest, together with any costs, shall be a perfected and enforceable state tax lien. This lien is subject to Chapter 14 (commencing with Section 7150) of Division 7 of Title 1 of the Government Code.

(b) For purposes of this section, amounts are "due and payable" on the following dates:

(1) For amounts disclosed on a return or report received by the director, the date of the notice by the director to the taxpayer of the amount due.

(2) For penalties imposed pursuant to Sections 1112.5, 1114, and 13052.5, the date of the notice by the director to the taxpayer of the amount due.

(3) For any amounts reestablished under Section 1875, the date of the written notice of rescission provided under subdivision (c) of that section.

(4) For all other amounts, the date the assessment is final.

(c) The lien provided by this section shall not arise during any period that Section 362 of the United States Bankruptcy Code [1] applies to the employing unit or other person against whom the lien would otherwise apply. *(Added by Stats.1977, c. 481, p. 1595, § 71, operative July 1, 1978. Amended by Stats.1979, c. 322, p. 1171, § 20; Stats.1979, c. 1082, p. 3897, § 30; Stats.1980, c. 600, p.*

1649, § 64; Stats.1983, c. 1102, § 31.2, eff. Sept. 27, 1983; Stats.1990, c. 719 (A.B.2667), § 4; Stats.1992, c. 125 (A.B.1830), § 8; Stats.1993, c. 356 (A.B.1238), § 2; Stats.1994, c. 1049 (A.B.3086), § 18.)

[1] 11 U.S.C.A. § 362.

ARTICLE 2.   LIABILITY OF SUCCESSORS, OFFICERS AND FIDUCIARIES

Section
1731.   Withholding by purchaser; amount; duration.
1732.   Certificate of contributions due; withholding; release.
1733.   Liability for failure to withhold; notice of assessment.
1734.   Remedies for collection; time within which obligations may be enforced.
1735.   Payment of contributions or withholdings; personal liability; assessments; collection remedies.
1735.1.   Assessments for money exchanged on behalf of employer to conceal wage payments; personal liability for amounts due from employers.
1736.   Penalty for failure to file required notice; enforcement of liability.

§ 1731.   Withholding by purchaser; amount; duration

Any person or employing unit that acquires the organization, trade or business, or substantially all the assets thereof, of an employer shall withhold in trust money or other property sufficient in amount or value to cover the amount of any contributions, interest and penalties due or unpaid from such employer until such employer produces a certificate from the department stating that no contributions, interest or penalties are due. If such employer does not produce such certificate, the acquiring person or employing unit shall pay the amount or the value of the property so withheld to the department at the time of such acquisition. (Stats.1953, c. 308, p. 1520, § 1731. Amended by Stats.1967, c. 1720, p. 4287, § 10.)

§ 1732.   Certificate of contributions due; withholding; release

(a) Upon request of either of the parties to an acquisition as described in Section 1731, the department shall within 30 days issue a certificate, or a statement showing the amount of any contributions, interest and penalties claimed to be due. The failure to issue a certificate or a statement within the period of 30 days shall be deemed equivalent to the issuance of a certificate stating that no contributions, interest or penalties are due.

(b) If the department issues a statement showing the amount of contributions, interest and penalties claimed to be due, the amount stated therein shall be withheld and paid to the department such amount, however, not to exceed the purchase price. The issuance of any certificate stating that no contributions, interest and penalties are due, or the failure to issue such certificate or statement within the period of 30 days shall not release the employer from liability on account of any contributions, interest and penalties then or thereafter deter-

mined to be due from him, but shall release the acquiring person or employing unit from any further liability on account of any such contributions, interest and penalties. (Stats.1953, c. 308, p. 1520, § 1732. Amended by Stats. 1967, c. 1720, p. 4287, § 11.)

§ 1733.   Liability for failure to withhold; notice of assessment

Any person or employing unit that fails to withhold money or other property or fails to pay the amount or value of the property withheld as provided in Sections 1731 and 1732 shall be personally liable for the payment of the contributions, interest and penalties due from the employer up to but not exceeding the purchase price. The director shall assess such amount to the acquiring person or employing unit and shall give a written notice of the assessment pursuant to Section 1206. Sections 1135, 1136, 1137, 1221, 1222, 1223, and 1224 apply to assessments under this section. (Stats.1953, c. 308, p. 1520, § 1733. Amended by Stats.1967, c. 1720, p. 4287, § 12; Stats.1979, c. 1082, p. 3900, § 31.)

§ 1734.   Remedies for collection; time within which obligations may be enforced

The director shall have all of the remedies for collection against any person or employing unit that acquires the organization, trade or business, or substantially all the assets thereof of an employer as are provided by this division against any employer liable for contributions, interest and penalties due. The time within which the obligation may be enforced against the person or employing unit acquiring the organization, trade or business, or substantially all the assets thereof of an employer shall start to run with the day the assessment against such person or employing unit becomes final. (Stats.1953, c. 308, p. 1521, § 1734. Amended by Stats.1967, c. 1720, p. 4288, § 13.)

§ 1735.   Payment of contributions or withholdings; personal liability; assessments; collection remedies

Any officer, major stockholder, or other person, having charge of the affairs of a corporate, association, registered limited liability partnership or foreign limited liability partnership, or limited liability company employing unit, who willfully fails to pay contributions required by this division or withholdings required by Division 6 (commencing with Section 13000) on the date on which they become delinquent, shall be personally liable for the amount of the contributions, withholdings, penalties, and interest due and unpaid by such employing unit. The director may assess such officer, stockholder, or other person for the amount of such contributions, withholdings, penalties, and interest. The provisions of Article 8 (commencing with Section 1126) and Article 9 (commencing with Section 1176) of Chapter 4 of Part 1 apply to assessments made pursuant to this section. Sections 1221, 1222, 1223, and 1224 shall apply to assessments made pursuant to this section. With respect to such officer, stockholder, or other person, the director shall have all the collection remedies set forth in this chapter. *(Added by Stats.1977, c. 838, p. 2513, § 2. Amended by Stats.1979, c. 1082, p. 3900, § 32; Stats.1980, c. 1007, p. 3228, § 62, operative July 1, 1981; Stats.1994, c. 1200 (S.B.469), § 83, eff. Sept. 30, 1994; Stats.1995, c. 679 (S.B.513), § 18, eff. Oct. 10, 1995.)*

§ 1735.1. Assessments for money exchanged on behalf of employer to conceal wage payments; personal liability for amounts due from employers

(a) An individual who has been assessed under the provisions of Section 1128.1, or any officer, major stockholder, or other person having charge of the affairs of a business entity that has been assessed under the provisions of that section, shall be personally liable for the amount of contributions, withholdings, penalties, and interest due and unpaid by the employer, other than those under subdivisions (a) and (b) of Section 1128, for whom money was exchanged as described in Section 1128.1. The director may assess that person for the amount of contributions, withholdings, all penalties other than those under Section 1128, and interest. The provisions of Article 8 (commencing with Section 1126) and Article 9 (commencing with Section 1176) of Chapter 4 of Part 1 shall apply to assessments made pursuant to this section. Sections 1221, 1222, 1223, and 1224 shall apply to assessments made pursuant to this section. With respect to that person, the director shall have all the collection remedies set forth in this chapter.

(b) For purposes of this section, "business entity" means a partnership, corporation, association, limited liability company, or Indian tribe (as described by subsection (u) of Section 3306 of Title 26 of the United States Code). *(Added by Stats.1996, c. 1116 (S.B.1843), § 2. Amended by Stats.2001, c. 255 (A.B.1537), § 16.)*

Operative Effect

Under the terms of Section 17 of Stats.2001, c. 255 (A.B.1537), the provisions of that Act are retroactive to December 21, 2000.

§ 1736. Penalty for failure to file required notice; enforcement of liability

In addition to other penalties prescribed in this division, failure to file the notice required by Section 1090 shall cause the assignee, receiver, trustee in bankruptcy, or other representative of an insolvent employing unit, or the administrator or executor of the estate of the deceased employing unit to be personally responsible for all loss in contributions, penalties and interest attributable to such failure. This liability may be enforced by civil action in the name of the State of California against the assignee, receiver, trustee in bankruptcy, or other representative of the insolvent employing unit, and against the administrator or executor of the deceased employing unit. *(Stats.1953, c. 308, p. 1521, § 1736.)*

ARTICLE 3. NOTICES OF LEVY

Section
1755. Service of notice of levy; duties of persons served.
1756. Notices to state; to whom given.
1757. Personal liability of persons upon whom notices of levy have been served.
1758. Person defined.

§ 1755. Service of notice of levy; duties of persons served

If any person or employing unit is delinquent in the payment of any contributions, penalties or interest provided for in this division, the director may, not later than three years after the payment became delinquent or within 10 years after the last entry of a judgment under Article 5 (commencing with Section 1815) or within 10 years after the last recording or filing of a notice of state tax lien under Section 7171 of the Government Code, collect the delinquency or enforce any liens by levy served either personally or by certified mail, to all persons having in their possession or under their control any credits or personal property belonging to the delinquent person or employing unit, or owing any debts to the person or employing unit at the time of the receipt of the notice of levy or coming into their possession or under their control for the period of one year from the time of receipt of the notice of levy. Any person upon whom a levy has been served having in his or her possession or under his or her control any credits or personal property belonging to the delinquent person or employing unit or owing any debts to the person or employing unit at the time of the receipt of the levy or coming into his or her possession or under his or her control for the period of one year from the time of receipt of the notice of levy, shall surrender the credits or personal property to the director or pay to the director the amount of any debt owing the delinquent employer within five days of service of the levy, and shall surrender the credits or personal property, or the amount of any debt owing to the delinquent employer coming into his or her possession or under his or her control within one year of receipt of the notice of levy within five days of the date of coming into possession or control of the credits or personal property, or the amount of any debt owing to the delinquent employer is incurred. Any person in possession of any credits or personal property or owing any debts to the delinquent person or employing unit who surrenders the credits or personal property or pays the debts owing the delinquent person or employing unit shall be discharged from any obligation or liability to the delinquent person or employing unit with respect to the credits or personal property surrendered or debts paid to the director. If the levy is made on a deposit or credits or personal property in the possession or under the control of a bank or savings and loan association, the notice of levy shall be delivered or mailed to the branch or office of the bank or savings and loan association at which the deposit is carried or at which credits or personal property is held. If the levy is made on a bank or savings and loan association it will apply to all credits or personal property as provided in this section, except that it will apply to credits and personal property in a deposit account, as defined in paragraph (29) of subdivision (a) of Section 9102 of the Commercial Code, only at the time the notice of levy is received by the bank or savings and loan association. *(Stats.1953, c. 308, p. 1521, § 1755. Amended by Stats.1953, c. 659, p. 1908; Stats.1955, c. 1165, p. 2169, § 38; Stats.1957, c. 1188, p. 2480, § 3; Stats.1971, c. 873, p. 1718, § 12; Stats.1977, c. 481, p. 1598, § 74, operative July 1, 1978; Stats.1980, c. 600, p. 1649, § 68; Stats.1986, c. 924, § 2; Stats.1999, c. 991 (S.B.45), § 73, operative July 1, 2001.)*

§ 1756.   Notices to state; to whom given

Notices of levy to the state, pursuant to Section 1755, shall be given to the state department, board, office or commission prior to the time it presents the claim of the person or employing unit to the State Controller. *(Stats. 1953, c. 308, p. 1522, § 1756. Amended by Stats.1971, c. 873, p. 1718, § 13.)*

§ 1757.   Personal liability of persons upon whom notices of levy have been served

Any person notified pursuant to Section 1755 who fails or refuses to surrender any credits or other personal property, or pay any debts owing to the delinquent employer, up to the amount specified in the levy, shall be liable in his own person and estate to the director in an amount equal to the value of the credits or other personal property in the amount of the debt, but not exceeding the amount specified in the notice of levy, if solely by reason of such failure or refusal, the department is unable to recover the contributions, penalties, or interest owing by the person with respect to which the notice was given. *(Stats.1953, c. 308, p. 1522, § 1757. Amended by Stats. 1953, c. 659, p. 1908; Stats.1971, c. 873, p. 1719, § 14.)*

§ 1758.   Person defined

As used in this article "person" includes this State and any county, city and county, municipality, district or other political subdivision thereof. *(Stats.1953, c. 308, p. 1523, § 1758.)*

ARTICLE 4.   WARRANT FOR COLLECTION

Section
1785. Issuance; effect; levy and sale.
1786. Fees, commissions and expenses; approval.
1787. Liability for expenses of levying and execution of warrant; manner of collecting.

§ 1785.   Issuance; effect; levy and sale

If any amount required to be paid under this division is not paid when due, the director or the director's authorized representative may, not later than three years after the payment became delinquent, or within 10 years after the last entry of a judgment under Article 5 (commencing with Section 1815) or within 10 years after the last recording or filing of a notice of state tax lien under

Section 7171 of the Government Code, issue a warrant for the enforcement of any liens and for the collection of any amount required to be paid to the state under this division. The warrant shall be directed to any sheriff, marshal, or peace officer of the Department of the California Highway Patrol and shall have the same effect as a writ of execution. The warrant shall be levied and sale made pursuant to it in the same manner and with the same effect as a levy of and a sale pursuant to a writ of execution. *(Stats.1953, c. 308, p. 1523, § 1785. Amended by Stats.1957, c. 1188, p. 2480, § 4; Stats.1977, c. 481, p. 1598, § 75, operative July 1, 1978; Stats.1980, c. 600, p. 1650, § 69; Stats.1988, c. 620, § 1; Gov.Reorg.Plan No. 1 of 1995, § 62, eff. July 12, 1995; Stats.1996, c. 872 (A.B.3472), § 175; Stats.1996, c. 305 (A.B.3103), § 63; Stats.1998, c. 931 (S.B.2139), § 451, eff. Sept. 28, 1998.)*

§ 1786.   Fees, commissions and expenses; approval

The department may pay or advance to the sheriff, marshal, or peace officer of the Department of the California Highway Patrol the same fees, commissions, and expenses for his or her services under this article as are provided by law for similar services pursuant to a writ of execution. The director, and not the court, shall approve the fees for publication in a newspaper. *(Stats. 1953, c. 308, p. 1523, § 1786. Amended by Stats.1988, c. 620, § 2; Gov.Reorg.Plan No. 1 of 1995, § 63, eff. July 12, 1995; Stats.1996, c. 872 (A.B.3472), § 176; Stats.1996, c. 305 (A.B.3103), § 64; Stats.1998, c. 931 (S.B.2139), § 452, eff. Sept. 28, 1998.)*

§ 1787.   Liability for expenses of levying and execution of warrant; manner of collecting

The fees, commissions, and expenses incurred in connection with the levying and execution of a warrant are the obligation of the person or employing unit required to pay any amount under this division and may be collected from him by virtue of the warrant or in any other manner provided in this chapter for the collection of the tax. *(Stats.1953, c. 308, p. 1523, § 1787.)*

ARTICLE 5.   SUMMARY JUDGMENT

Section
1815. Recording certificate; where to be recorded; contents; entry of judgment; filing of judgment.
1816. Recording abstract of judgment; force and effect; priority; duration; extension; authority to act for state.
1817. Release or subordination of lien; certificate as conclusive evidence.
1818. Other collection procedures.

§ 1815.   Recording certificate; where to be recorded; contents; entry of judgment; filing of judgment

If any employing unit is delinquent in the payment of any contributions, penalties or interest provided for in this division, the director may, not later than 10 years after the payment became delinquent or within 10 years after the last entry of a judgment under this article or within 10 years after the last recording or filing of a notice of state tax lien under Section 7171 of the Government Code, file in the office of the Clerk of the Superior Court of Sacramento County, or with the clerk of the superior court of the county in which the employer has its principal place of business, a certificate specifying the amount of the contributions, interest and penalty due and the name and last known address of the employer liable therefor. The certificate shall also contain a statement that the director has complied with all the provisions of this division in relation to the computation and levy of the contributions, interest and penalty, and a request that judgment be entered against the employer in the amount set forth in the certificate. The clerk immediately upon the filing of the certificate shall enter a judgment for the State of California against the employer in the amount set forth in the certificate. Such judgment may be filed by the clerk in a looseleaf book entitled "Unemployment Contributions Judgments." *(Stats.1953, c. 308, p. 1523, § 1815. Amended by Stats.1957, c. 1188, p. 2481, § 5; Stats.1977, c. 481, p. 1599, § 76, operative July 1, 1978; Stats.1980, c. 600, p. 1650, § 70; Stats.2002, c. 784 (S.B.1316), § 592.)*

§ 1816. Recording abstract of judgment; force and effect; priority; duration; extension; authority to act for state

An abstract of a judgment secured pursuant to this article or a copy thereof may be recorded with the county recorder of any county and from the time of the recording, the amount of the judgment shall constitute a lien upon all the real property of the employer in that county, owned or acquired by him during the life of the lien. The lien shall have the force, effect and priority of a judgment lien and shall continue for 10 years after the last entry of a judgment under this article unless sooner released or otherwise discharged. The lien may, within 10 years after the last entry of a judgment under this article or within 10 years from the date of the last extension of the lien, be extended by recording a new abstract in the office of the county recorder of any county and from the time of such recording, the lien shall be extended to all the real property in such county for 10 years unless sooner released or otherwise discharged. Execution shall issue upon such a judgment upon request of the director in the same manner as execution may issue upon other judgments and sales shall be held under such execution as prescribed in the Code of Civil Procedure. In all proceedings under this section the director or his authorized agents may act on behalf of the state. *(Stats. 1953, c. 308, p. 1524, § 1816. Amended by Stats.1957, c. 1632, p. 2997, § 1; Stats.1977, c. 481, p. 1599, § 77, operative July 1, 1978.)*

§ 1817. Release or subordination of lien; certificate as conclusive evidence

(a) If the director determines that the amount of any contributions, interest, and penalties are sufficiently secured by a lien on other property or that the release or subordination of the lien imposed under Section 1816 will not jeopardize the collection of the amount of the contributions, interest, and penalties, the director may at any time release all or any portion of the property subject to the lien imposed by Section 1816 from the lien or may subordinate the lien imposed by Section 1816 to other liens and encumbrances.

(b) If the director finds that the liability represented by the lien imposed under Section 1816, including any interest accrued thereon, is legally unenforceable, the director may release the lien.

(c) A certificate by the director to the effect that any property has been released from a lien or that the lien has been subordinated to other liens and encumbrances is conclusive evidence that such property has been released or that the lien has been subordinated as provided in the certificate. *(Added by Stats.1980, c. 600, p. 1650, § 70.5.)*

§ 1818. Other collection procedures

The right of the director to use the summary judgment procedure contained in this article shall be in addition to any other collection procedure contained in this division. No action taken by the director shall be construed to be an election to pursue the summary judgment procedure to the exclusion of any other collection procedure in this division. *(Stats.1953, c. 308, p. 1524, § 1818.)*

ARTICLE 6. CIVIL ACTION

Section
1851.   No injunction against collection.
1852.   Action for administration or collection; limitations.
1853.   Court calendar preference.
1854.   Certificate of delinquency as prima facie evidence.
1855.   Action to enjoin inducement of employers or employees to violate code or to evade contributions or taxes.

§ 1851. No injunction against collection

No injunction or writ of mandate or other legal or equitable process shall issue in any suit, action or proceeding, in any court against this State or against any officer thereof to prevent or enjoin the collection of any contribution sought to be collected under this division. *(Stats.1953, c. 308, p. 1524, § 1851.)*

§ 1852. Action for administration or collection; limitations

In addition to any other tax administration and collection procedures authorized in this division, the director may bring an action in the courts of this or any other state or of the United States, in the name of the State of California, to administer the provisions of, and to collect the amount of any delinquent contributions or taxes, together with penalties and interest, due under this code. No such action shall be commenced later than:

(a) Three years after the date on which any amount due on a return or report filed by an employing unit or on an assessment made by the director becomes delinquent.

(b) Ten years after:

(1) The date on which a judgment is last entered under Article 5 of this chapter.

(2) The date on which a notice of state tax lien is last recorded or filed under Section 7171 of the Government Code. *(Stats.1953, c. 308, p. 1524, § 1852. Amended by Stats.1957, c. 1188, p. 2481, § 7; Stats.1977, c. 481, p. 1600, § 78, operative July 1, 1978; Stats.1980, c. 600, p. 1651, § 71; Stats.1983, c. 1102, § 31.3, eff. Sept. 27, 1983; Stats.1994, c. 1049 (A.B.3086), § 19.)*

§ 1853. Court calendar preference

The courts of this State shall give preference on their calendar to any civil action brought by or against the director over all other civil litigation except equity cases, cases involving extraordinary writs, or summary proceedings. *(Stats.1953, c. 308, p. 1525, § 1853.)*

§ 1854. Certificate of delinquency as prima facie evidence

In any civil action brought by or against the director a certificate under oath by the director or his authorized agent showing the delinquency shall be prima facie evidence of the levy of the contributions, of the delinquency of the amounts set forth, and of the compliance by the director with all the provisions of this division relating to the computation and levy of the amounts. *(Stats.1953, c. 308, p. 1525, § 1854. Amended by Stats.1969, c. 828, p. 1656, § 3.)*

§ 1855. Action to enjoin inducement of employers or employees to violate code or to evade contributions or taxes

(a) A civil action may be commenced at the request of the director in the name of the State of California to enjoin any individual or entity from conduct that, by solicitation, sale, or advertising, is inducing or otherwise attempting to persuade employers or employees, or potential employers or employees, to violate this code or to otherwise attempt to evade contributions or taxes provided for under this code by scheme, device, or similar activity. Any action under this section shall be brought in the Superior Court of the County of Sacramento or in the superior court of the county in which that individual or entity resides, has its principal place of business, or has engaged in conduct subject to penalty under this code.

(b) In any action under subdivision (a), the court may enjoin the person from engaging in the conduct or in any other activity specified in subdivision (a), if the court finds both of the following:

(1) That the person has engaged in any conduct specified in subdivision (a).

(2) That injunctive relief is appropriate to prevent recurrence of that conduct.

(c) For purposes of the civil action referred to in subdivisions (a) and (b), the court may issue without bond, a temporary restraining order upon the filing of a statement, certified by the director, which contains both of the following:

(1) That a determination has been made that the individual or entity is engaging in conduct described in subdivision (a), accompanied by a detailed description of the reasons for the determination.

(2) That the activity of the individual or entity will result in the nonpayment of contributions or taxes required under this code and that the contributions or taxes would be otherwise payable.

(d) The director shall provide the court clerk with an exact copy of the certified statement upon filing, which copy will be endorsed or certified by the court clerk and returned to the director, along with a certified copy of the court's order. From the time of service of the endorsed or certified copy of the statement and order, that individual or entity shall be temporarily restrained from the activity set forth in the statement. That temporary restraining order will continue in effect unless dissolved after a hearing on a preliminary injunction in the Superior Court of Sacramento County or the county in which the individual or entity resides, has its place of business, or has engaged in the conduct specified in the statement. That hearing or preliminary injunction shall be held under the rules of the superior court. *(Added by Stats.1983, c. 1102, § 31.5, eff. Sept. 27, 1983. Amended by Stats.2006, c. 538 (S.B.1852), § 646.)*

ARTICLE 7. ADDITIONAL REMEDIES

Section
1860. Collection of delinquent contributions, interest, and penalties; agreements with private debt collection services outside the state.

§ 1860. Collection of delinquent contributions, interest, and penalties; agreements with private debt collection services outside the state

(a) For the purpose of collecting delinquent contributions, interest, and penalties, the director may enter into an agreement with one or more private persons, companies, associations, or corporations providing debt collection services outside this state with respect to the collection of delinquent contributions, interest, and penalties. That agreement may provide, at the discretion of the director, the rate of payment and the manner in which compensation for services shall be paid. The compensation, fees, and expenses may be added to the amount of the delinquent contributions, interest, and penalties and may be collected by the contractor from the debtor. The director shall provide the necessary information for the contractor to fulfill its obligation under the agreement.

(b) At the discretion of the director, the contractor may, as part of the collection process, refer the debt to legal representatives for litigation in the name of the director.

(c) No action taken by the director, pursuant to this section, shall be construed to be an election to forego other collection procedures in this division. *(Added by Stats.1988, c. 1097, § 1.)*

ARTICLE 8.   OFFERS IN COMPROMISE

Section
1870.   Partial payment agreement; conditions.
1871.   Negotiated agreement; board review.
1872.   Partial payment determination; administrative appeal or judicial review.
1873.   Agreement terms satisfaction; statement; duties.
1874.   Joint and several liability; partial payment effect.
1875.   Partial payment agreement; rescission; statute of limitations.

§ 1870.   Partial payment agreement; conditions

(a) When an employer or any individual assessed under Section 1735 owes delinquent contributions, withholdings, penalty, or interest to the department, the director may enter into an agreement to accept partial payment in satisfaction of the full liability under the following conditions when he or she believes that it will be in the best interest of the state.

(1) Offers in compromise shall be considered only for liabilities of inactive out-of-business accounts, and of individuals assessed under Section 1735 or partners only if the individual assessed or partner no longer has a controlling interest or association with the business that incurred the liability to which the offer in compromise applies.

(2) The employer, individual assessed under Section 1735, or partner does not have access to current income sufficient to pay more than the accumulating interest and 6.7 percent of the liability on an annual basis.

(3) The employer, individual assessed under Section 1735, or partner does not have reasonable prospects of acquiring increased income or assets that would enable him or her to liquidate the liability in a reasonable period.

(4) The employer, individual assessed under Section 1735, or partner does not have assets, whether or not subjected to lien by the department, that if sold, would satisfy the liability.

(5) The amount offered in compromise is more than the department could reasonably expect to collect through involuntary means during the four-year period beginning on the date on which a compromise agreement is tendered by the employer, individual assessed under Section 1735, or partner.

(6) The compromise offer is submitted by the taxpayer in writing and is accompanied by cash, a cashier's check, or money order equal to the amount offered in compromise.

(7) Only nondisputed, final tax liabilities shall be considered for compromise.

(8) Liabilities that arose as a result of fraud or actions that resulted in a conviction for a violation of this code shall not be compromised.

(b) When in the director's judgment it serves the best interest of the state, the director may permit the agreed upon amount to be paid in installments under a payment agreement not to exceed five years in length.

(c) The employer or individual submitting an offer shall be notified in writing when an offer in compromise is accepted or rejected.

(1) Moneys paid to the department along with an offer shall not be applied against the liability by the department until the offer has been accepted or rejected.

(2) In the event an offer is rejected, the amount will either be applied to the liability or refunded, at the discretion of the employer or individual submitting the offer.   *(Added by Stats.1993, c. 356 (A.B.1238), § 3.)*

§ 1871.   Negotiated agreement; board review

No agreement negotiated by the director under Section 1870 that reduces any liability by ten thousand dollars ($10,000) or more shall be effective until it is reviewed and approved by the Unemployment Insurance Appeals Board.   In reviewing any agreement, the Unemployment Insurance Appeals Board shall be restricted to determining, based on the case file submitted by the director, whether the director has exercised due diligence in determining whether the conditions set forth in subdivision (a) of Section 1870 have been satisfied.   *(Added by Stats.1993, c. 356 (A.B.1238), § 3.)*

§ 1872.   Partial payment determination; administrative appeal or judicial review

A determination by the director that it would not be in the best interest of the state to accept partial payment in satisfaction of a tax liability shall not be subject to administrative appeal or judicial review.   *(Added by Stats.1993, c. 356 (A.B.1238), § 3.)*

§ 1873.   Agreement   terms   satisfaction;   statement; duties

(a) Once the terms of the compromise agreement are fulfilled, including payment of the amount offered, the following shall occur:

(1) The liability shall be considered satisfied in full.

(2) All tax liens filed or recorded, or both, in accordance with Article 1 (commencing with Section 1701) shall be released.

(3) A statement shall be placed on file with the department containing the following information:

(A) The taxpayer's name and identification number.

(B) The year or years and quarter or quarters involved.

(C) The reason or reasons the liability was reduced by an offer in compromise.

(D) The total amount of unpaid tax, interest, additions to tax, and penalties at issue in the compromise.

(E) The terms of the offer in compromise.

(F) The total amount paid under the offer in compromise.

(b) All records of compromise required to be kept by the department may be reviewed as part of the annual single audit of the Employment Development Department.

(c) The department shall do all of the following:

(1) Notify the employer or individual submitting the offer in writing that the terms of the compromise agreement have been fulfilled, and that all liens filed or recorded, or both, in accordance with Article 1 (commencing with Section 1701) against the taxpayer's interests have been released.

(2) Furnish the employer or individual submitting the offer with a copy of the statement that is on file in accordance with paragraph (3) of subdivision (a).

(d) For a period of one year from the date that the statement is placed on file as required under paragraph (3) of subdivision (a), the statement shall be available for public inspection. However, no lists shall be distributed by the department in connection with these statements. *(Added by Stats.1993, c. 356 (A.B.1238), § 3.)*

§ 1874. Joint and several liability; partial payment effect

In cases of joint and several liability, and where amounts are owed under Section 1735, an agreement under Section 1870 to accept partial payment in satisfaction of the liability of one or more debtors shall neither relieve any other debtors of the obligation to liquidate the entire balance of the debt remaining unpaid, nor grant to the debtor or debtors any right to appeal or seek judicial review of the director's determination. *(Added by Stats. 1993, c. 356 (A.B.1238), § 3.)*

§ 1875. Partial payment agreement; rescission; statute of limitations

(a) If an offer under Section 1870 to accept partial payment in satisfaction of the liability has been accepted, and it is subsequently determined that any person willfully did any of the following, the acceptance shall be rescinded and all compromised liabilities shall be reestablished without regard to any statute of limitations that is applicable to this division:

(1) Concealed from any officer or employee of the state any property belonging to the estate of the employer or other person liable with respect to the tax.

(2) Received, withheld, destroyed, mutilated, or falsified any book, document, or record.

(3) Made any false statement relating to the estate or financial conditions of the employer or other person liable with respect to the tax.

(4) Failed to pay any tax liability owed the department for any subsequent, active business in which the employer or individual who previously submitted the offer in compromise has a controlling interest or association.

(b) Upon any rescission pursuant to subdivision (a), the department, at its discretion, may file a Notice of State Tax Lien against the individuals or entity responsible for the previously compromised liability.

(c) For all rescissions under subdivision (a), the department shall notify the employer or individual who previously submitted the offer in compromise in writing of both of the following:

(1) The rescission of any offer and reasons therefor.

(2) The amount of reestablished liability that is due and payable. *(Added by Stats.1993, c. 356 (A.B.1238), § 3. Amended by Stats.1994, c. 146 (A.B.3601), § 217.)*

CHAPTER 8.   HEARING PROCEDURE

Section
1951.   Disputed claims, appeals and petitions; presentation; conduct of hearings and appeals; consolidation for hearing.
1952.   Rules of evidence or procedure; recording proceedings.
1953.   Power to administer oaths, take depositions, certify official acts, and issue subpoenas.
1953.5. Hearing by electronic means.
1954.   Enforcement of subpenas.
1955.   Duty to attend, testify and produce required records before appeals board; effect of claim of privilege against self-incrimination.
1956.   Witness fees; fees and expenses as part of expense of administering division.
1957.   Right to representation by counsel; counsel fees; penalty for violation.
1957.5. Authorization for representation of claimant; form; service.
1958.   Costs; penalty.
1959.   Delegation of powers by appeals board.
1960.   Separate or subsequent actions or proceedings; use of findings of fact or law, judgment, conclusion, or final order.

§ 1951.   Disputed claims, appeals and petitions; presentation; conduct of hearings and appeals; consolidation for hearing

The manner in which disputed claims, appeals and petitions shall be presented, the reports required thereon from the claimant and from any employing unit and the conduct of hearings and appeals shall be in accordance with rules prescribed by the appeals board. The appeals board shall require administrative law judges to consolidate for hearing cases with respect to which the alleged facts and the points of law are the same. *(Stats.1953, c. 308, p. 1525, § 1951. Amended by Stats.1954, 1st Ex.Sess., c. 44, p. 315, § 9; Stats.1984, c. 537, § 34.)*

§ 1952.   Rules of evidence or procedure; recording proceedings

The appeals board and its representatives and administrative law judges are not bound by common law or statutory rules of evidence or by technical or formal rules of procedure but may conduct the hearings and appeals in such manner as to ascertain the substantial rights of the parties. A full and complete record shall be kept of all proceedings in connection with disputed claims. All testimony at any hearing held in this state upon a disputed claim arising under this division shall be recorded and, when feasible, by a reporter in shorthand or by machine writing. The testimony need not be transcribed unless the disputed claim is further appealed. *(Stats. 1953, c. 308, p. 1525, § 1952. Amended by Stats.1957, c. 1668, p. 3048, § 1; Stats.1984, c. 537, § 35.)*

§ 1953. Power to administer oaths, take depositions, certify official acts, and issue subpoenas

In any proceeding, hearing, investigation or in the discharge of any duties imposed under this division any member of the appeals board, an administrative law judge and any authorized employee designated by it may administer oaths, take depositions, certify to official acts and issue subpoenas to compel the attendance of witnesses and the production of books, papers, correspondence, memoranda and other records. *(Stats.1953, c. 308, p. 1525, § 1953. Amended by Stats.1954, 1st Ex.Sess., c. 44, p. 315, § 10; Stats.1984, c. 537, § 36.)*

§ 1953.5. Hearing by electronic means

The presiding officer may conduct all or part of a hearing by telephone, television, or other electronic means, notwithstanding a party's objection pursuant to Section 11440.30 of the Government Code, on a showing of good cause by the party requesting the hearing by telephone, television, or other electronic means. *(Added by Stats.1997, c. 220 (S.B.68), § 34, eff. Aug. 4, 1997.)*

§ 1954. Enforcement of subpenas

Obedience to subpenas issued in accordance with this chapter may be enforced by application to the superior court as set forth in Article 2, Chapter 2, Part 1 of Division 3 of Title 2 of the Government Code.[1] *(Stats. 1953, c. 308, p. 1525, § 1954.)*

[1] Government Code § 11180 et seq.

§ 1955. Duty to attend, testify and produce required records before appeals board; effect of claim of privilege against self-incrimination

No person shall be excused from attending and testifying or from producing books, papers, correspondence, memoranda and other records as required by a subpena issued pursuant to this chapter on the ground that the testimony or evidence, documentary or otherwise, required of him may tend to incriminate him or subject him to a penalty or forfeiture. No individual shall be prosecuted or subjected to any penalty or forfeiture for or on account of any transaction, matter, or thing concerning which he is compelled, after having claimed his privilege against self-incrimination, to testify or produce evidence, documentary or otherwise. Nothing in this section exempts any individual from prosecution and punishment for perjury committed in so testifying. *(Stats.1953, c. 308, p. 1526, § 1955.)*

§ 1956. Witness fees; fees and expenses as part of expense of administering division

Witnesses subpoenaed pursuant to this division shall be allowed the same fees which are prescribed in Section 68093 of the Government Code relative to proceedings in the superior court. Such fees and all expenses incurred in any proceeding, hearing, review or investigation by the director or the Appeals Board or the representative of either, except charges for services by counsel or other agent representing claimant, employer, or other interested person, shall be part of the expenses of administering this division, and no individual claiming benefits shall be charged by the Appeals Board, or its representative, fees of any kind in any procedure under this division. *(Stats. 1953, c. 308, p. 1526, § 1956. Amended by Stats.1959, c. 1729, p. 4179, § 14.)*

§ 1957. Right to representation by counsel; counsel fees; penalty for violation

Any individual claiming benefits in any proceedings before the appeals board or its authorized representative may be represented by counsel or agent but no such counsel or agent shall charge or receive for such services more than an amount approved by the appeals board. Any person who violates any provision of this section shall for each such violation be fined not less than fifty dollars ($50) nor more than one thousand dollars ($1,000) or be imprisoned not more than six months or both. *(Stats.1953, c. 308, p. 1526, § 1957. Amended by Stats.1983, c. 1092, § 378, eff. Sept. 27, 1983, operative Jan. 1, 1984.)*

§ 1957.5. Authorization for representation of claimant; form; service

The department shall make available without charge printed forms for the use of any individual claiming benefits to authorize a counsel or an agent to represent him in any proceedings before the appeals board or its administrative law judges or authorized representatives. If any claimant files an authorization for such representation with the appeals board or its administrative law judges, the appeals board or its administrative law judges shall, upon request by the claimant, serve copies of all notices and transcript pertinent to such proceedings on the claimant and his counsel or agent. *(Added by Stats.1975, c. 1038, p. 2453, § 1. Amended by Stats.1984, c. 537, § 37.)*

§ 1958. Costs; penalty

No cost shall be awarded in hearings on appeal by the Appeals Board, but if in the opinion of the Appeals Board, the claimant or an employer has acted in bad faith and without reasonable basis for appeal, a penalty not exceeding 10 percent of the amount finally awarded on the appeal may be taxed against and deducted from the award by the Appeals Board and shall be placed in the Unemployment Fund. In those cases where a penalty is assessed against an employer his account, as maintained under this act, shall be debited with the amount of the penalty so assessed. *(Stats.1953, c. 308, p. 1526, § 1958.)*

§ 1959. Delegation of powers by appeals board

For the purpose of any investigation, hearing or proceeding under this division, the appeals board may delegate its power in relation thereto to any deputy, administrative law judge, or other person properly authorized in writing by it. *(Stats.1953, c. 308, p. 1526, § 1959. Amended by Stats.1953, c. 1294, p. 2854; Stats. 1984, c. 537, § 38.)*

§ 1960. Separate or subsequent actions or proceedings; use of findings of fact or law, judgment, conclusion, or final order

Any finding of fact or law, judgment, conclusion, or final order made by a hearing officer, administrative law judge, or any person with the authority to make findings of fact or law in any action or proceeding before the appeals board, shall not be conclusive or binding in any separate or subsequent action or proceeding, and shall not be used as evidence in any separate or subsequent action or proceeding, between an individual and his or her present or prior employer brought before an arbitrator, court, or judge of this state or the United States, regardless of whether the prior action was between the same or related parties or involved the same facts. *(Added by Stats.1986, c. 283, § 1.)*

CHAPTER 9. PUBLIC EMPLOYMENT OFFICES

Section
2051. Wagner-Peyser Act accepted; department as state agency for purposes of act.
2052. Cooperation with federal authorities; authority of director.
2053. Expenditure of funds.
2054. Establishment and maintenance of public employment offices; outreach to active duty service personnel at military bases.
2055. Location of public employment offices.
2056. Creation of unemployment districts; promulgation of rules for registration of unemployed; acceptance of financial contributions.
2057. Agreements with railroad retirement board or other federal agencies for purpose of maintaining public employment offices; acceptance of contributions.
2058. Youth placement services; employment programs; cooperation by department; maintenance and distribution of information.
2059. Recipients of public assistance; training and placement.
2061. Job order sharing.

§ 2051. Wagner-Peyser Act accepted; department as state agency for purposes of act

The State of California accepts the provisions of the Wagner–Peyser Act, approved June 6, 1933, as amended by the Workforce Investment Act of 1998 (Public Law 105–220) passed by the Congress of the United States, and entitled "An act to provide for the establishment of a national employment system and for cooperation with the states in the promotion of the system, and for other purposes,"[1] in conformity with Section 4 thereof,[2] and will observe and comply with the requirements of that act.

The department is the agency of this state for the purposes of that act. *(Stats.1953, c. 308, p. 1527, § 2051. Amended by Stats.2005, c. 152 (A.B.1577), § 24.)*

[1] 29 U.S.C.A. § 49 et seq.; 39 U.S.C.A. § 4152 (repealed; see, now, 39 U.S.C.A. § 3202).

[2] 29 U.S.C.A. § 49c.

§ 2052. Cooperation with federal authorities; authority of director

The director may cooperate with any authority of the United States having powers and duties under the Wagner-Peyser Act,[1] and may do and perform all things necessary to secure to this State the benefits of that act in the promotion and maintenance of a system of public employment offices. *(Stats.1953, c. 308, p. 1527, § 2052.)*

[1] 5 U.S.C.A. § 616 (repealed; see, now, 29 U.S.C.A. § 557); 29 U.S.C.A. § 49 et seq.; 39 U.S.C.A. § 338 (repealed; see, now, 39 U.S.C.A. § 3202).

§ 2053. Expenditure of funds

All money received by the State under the Wagner-Peyser Act[1] and paid into the Unemployment Administration Fund shall be expended as provided by this division and by that act of Congress. *(Stats.1953, c. 308, p. 1527, § 2053. Amended by Stats.1959, c. 1729, p. 4179, § 15.)*

[1] 29 U.S.C.A. § 49 et seq.; 39 U.S.C.A. § 4152 (repealed; see, now, 39 U.S.C.A. § 3202).

§ 2054. Establishment and maintenance of public employment offices; outreach to active duty service personnel at military bases

(a) The director shall:

(1) Establish, maintain, and operate adequately staffed public employment offices for men, women, and youth who are legally qualified to engage in gainful occupations and shall maintain a veterans' placement service to be devoted to securing work for veterans and a farm placement service to promote the placement and clearance of agricultural labor, and a youth placement service to promote the placement of youth in suitable fields of employment. The director shall also establish and maintain a job counseling and placement service for those persons who are encountering, or may be expected to encounter difficulty in securing or keeping a job principally because of their age. The maintenance of a farm placement service shall not be required during such time as applicable federal laws provide for a system of farm labor placement financed from federal funds which is separate and apart from the general system of public employment offices. Adequate records and statistics on all the classifications specified in this subdivision shall be compiled and kept, and a report of these records, statistics, applications, and placements shall be made semiannually.

(2) Procure, by lease or otherwise, suitable offices, and incur the necessary expenses in the conduct thereof.

(b) It is the policy of this state to make every reasonable effort to assist men and women who are leaving active duty with the armed services of the United States in obtaining employment in the civilian workforce. These efforts shall include outreach to those service personnel who will be leaving active duty in the near future, including job seminars and job fairs at military bases.

(c) The director shall perform the duties required by this section within existing budgetary resources of the agency within which the department operates. *(Stats. 1953, c. 308, p. 1527, § 2054. Amended by Stats.1959, c. 1802, p. 4288, § 1; Stats.1994, c. 987 (S.B.1646), § 2, eff. Sept. 29, 1994.)*

§ 2055. Location of public employment offices

Free public employment offices shall be maintained in the Cities of San Francisco, Los Angeles, Oakland and Sacramento, and, whenever the director deems it necessary, in other cities. *(Stats.1953, c. 308, p. 1527, § 2055. Amended by Stats.1959, c. 1729, p. 4179, § 16.)*

§ 2056. Creation of unemployment districts; promulgation of rules for registration of unemployed; acceptance of financial contributions

The director may:

(a) Create unemployment districts.

(b) Promulgate such rules as he finds desirable for the registration of unemployed persons, and for placing them in available employment. To this end he may accept financial contributions from any governmental unit or agency, or private persons. *(Stats.1953, c. 308, p. 1527, § 2056.)*

§ 2057. Agreements with railroad retirement board or other federal agencies for purpose of maintaining public employment offices; acceptance of contributions

For the purpose of establishing and maintaining free public employment offices, the director may enter into agreements with the Railroad Retirement Board, or any other agency of the United States charged with the administration of an unemployment compensation law, with any political subdivision of this State, or with any private, nonprofit organization, and as a part of any such agreement, may accept money, services, quarters, or other valuable consideration as a contribution to the employment service account in the Unemployment Administration Fund. *(Stats.1953, c. 308, p. 1528, § 2057.)*

§ 2058. Youth placement services; employment programs; cooperation by department; maintenance and distribution of information

The department shall cooperate with other departments, agencies, and institutions both public and private in providing youth placement services and in the development of youth employment programs.

The department shall maintain current information on operations within the State of all types of youth employment programs such as the Youth Employment Service (Y.E.S.) and the Youth Employment Organization (Y.E.O.) plans, the work experience experimental program of the Department of Education, the Berkeley Workreation program, the effort by the Congress of Youth Coordinating Councils, and other similar programs. Upon request the department shall distribute to public and private agencies and groups information concerning any or all recognized plans for developing youth employment programs, the cooperative services offered by the various state and other public agencies in the field of youth employment, and the methods of initiating and developing such programs. *(Added by Stats.1957, c. 1490, p. 2812, § 1.)*

§ 2059. Recipients of public assistance; training and placement

For the purpose of implementing the program set forth in Chapter 2.5 (commencing with Section 10650) of Part 2 of Division 9 of the Welfare and Institutions Code, the department may utilize funds available to provide training and placement for present and potential recipients of public assistance to the extent permitted by federal law. *(Added by Stats.1967, c. 1457, p. 3399, § 2.)*

§ 2061. Job order sharing

It is the intent of the Legislature in adopting this section to ensure that job order information registered with the Job Service of the Employment Development Department and the One–Stop Career Centers System be shared as expeditiously and thoroughly as possible between the department's field offices and one-stop career centers both in the local labor market and throughout the state.

The Legislature finds that job order sharing will result in better service to employers and more efficient service to job seekers.

The provisions of this section shall be subject to the limitations of federal budgetary constraints. *(Added by Stats.1984, c. 1057, § 1. Amended by Stats.2005, c. 152 (A.B.1577), § 25.)*

CHAPTER 9.5. EMPLOYMENT FOR OLDER WORKERS

Section
2070. Statement of policy.
2071. Definitions.
2073. Co-operation of department of employment.
2074. Formulation of policies.
2075. Continuing program of education; local advisory agencies; composition.
2076. Publications and results of research; issuance.
2078. Age limitations of apprenticeship programs.

§ 2070. Statement of policy

It is the public policy of the State of California that manpower should be used to its fullest extent. This statement of policy compels the further conclusion that human beings seeking employment, or retention thereof, should be judged fairly and without resort to rigid and unsound rules that operate to disqualify significant portions of the population from gainful and useful employment. Accordingly, use by employers, employment agencies, and labor organizations of arbitrary and unreasonable rules which bar or terminate employment on the ground of age offend the public policy of this State. *(Added by Stats.1961, c. 1623, p. 3517, § 1.)*

§ 2071. Definitions

As used in this chapter:

(a) "Employee" does not include any individual employed by his parents, spouse or child or in the domestic service of any person.

(b) "Employer" does not include any employer with less than six persons in his employ. It does include any employer with six or more employees. It also includes the State of California and any political subdivision thereof.

(c) "Employment agency" includes any person undertaking to procure employees or opportunities to work.

(d) "Labor organization" includes any organization that is constituted for the purpose, in whole or in part, of collective bargaining or in dealing with employers concerning grievances, terms or conditions of employment or of other mutual aid or protection in connection with employees.

(e) "Person" includes one or more individuals, partnerships, associations, corporations, limited liability companies, legal representatives, trustees, trustees in bankruptcy or receivers. *(Added by Stats.1961, c. 1623, p. 3517, § 1. Amended by Stats.1970, c. 350, p. 760, § 16; Stats.1994, c. 1200 (S.B.469), § 84, eff. Sept. 30, 1994.)*

§ 2073. Co-operation of department of employment

The department shall co-operate with other departments, agencies, and institutions both public and private in providing job counseling and placement services and developing employment programs for older workers, including employment programs to protect and safeguard the right and opportunity of such workers to seek, obtain, and hold employment without discrimination or abridgement on account of age, unless based upon a bona fide occupational qualification or upon applicable security regulations established by the United States or the State of California. *(Added by Stats.1961, c. 1623, p. 3518, § 1.)*

§ 2074. Formulation of policies

The department shall formulate policies to effectuate the purposes of this chapter and make recommendations to agencies and officers of the State and of local governments in aid of such policies and purposes. Noth-

ing herein shall modify or supersede the authority or responsibility of the State Personnel Board to enforce the provisions of the State Civil Service Act.[1] *(Added by Stats.1961, c. 1623, p. 3519, § 1.)*

[1] Government Code § 18500 et seq.

§ 2075. Continuing program of education; local advisory agencies; composition

The department shall carry on a continuing program of education, information, research, study, and community organization concerning the problems of older workers in seeking, obtaining, and holding employment without discrimination on account of age. The department shall create such local advisory agencies as in its judgment will aid in effectuating the purposes of this section, and may empower them to study the problems of discrimination on account of age and all problems relating to employment programs for older workers, and to foster through community effort co-operation among the various groups and elements of the population of the State and to make recommendations to the department for the development of policies and procedures to carry out the purposes of this section. Such advisory agencies shall be composed of representative citizens, serving without pay. *(Added by Stats.1961, c. 1623, p. 3519, § 1.)*

§ 2076. Publications and results of research; issuance

The department shall issue such publications and such results of research and other activities as in its judgment will tend to minimize or eliminate discrimination in employment on account of age. *(Added by Stats.1961, c. 1623, p. 3519, § 1.)*

§ 2078. Age limitations of apprenticeship programs

The age limitations of the apprenticeship programs in which the State participates shall not be considered discriminatory within the meaning of this chapter. *(Added by Stats.1961, c. 1623, p. 3519, § 1.)*

CHAPTER 10. VIOLATIONS

Section
2101.   False statement, representation or concealment to obtain, increase, reduce or defeat benefit or payment.
2101.5. False statement, representation or concealment for purpose of lowering or avoiding contribution on becoming subject to division.
2101.6. Advising prohibited acts; aid or assistance in prohibited acts.
2102.   False statement or representation or concealment to obtain benefits under employment laws of another state.
2103.   Deductions from wages larger than required.
2104.   Failure to appear, testify or produce records.
2105.   Failure or neglect to make records available for inspection.
2106.   Failure or neglect to furnish reports.
2107.   Withholding information to aid individual to obtain benefits.
2108.   Nonpayment of contributions due.

Section
2109. Failure to register or report.
2110. Failure to pay deductions withheld from workers.
2110.3. Failure to pay contributions agreed to be paid for workers without deduction from remuneration.
2110.5. Failure to withhold deductions in trust.
2110.7. Failure to hold in trust contributions agreed to be paid for workers without deduction from remuneration.
2111. Disclosure of confidential information.
2112. Violation of law or authorized regulations.
2113. Restitution for overpayment of benefits.
2114. Report on registration of fictitious employer or employee and wages.
2115. False reports of wages or time period.
2116. Disability insurance benefits; unlawful acts.
2117. Failure to file return or report or to supply information; false or fraudulent return, report or statements; punishment.
2117.5. Intentional failure to file return or report or to supply information; false or fraudulent return or statement; punishment.
2118. Failure to withhold or to pay over tax withheld; punishment.
2118.5. Willful failure to collect, truthfully account for or pay over tax or amount; penalties.
2119. Willful furnishing of false or fraudulent statement or failure to furnish statement.
2120. Willfully supplying false information or failure to supply information.
2121. Preparation or presentation of false or fraudulent document.
2122. Violations of chapter; punishment.
2122.5. Fines; allocation.
2123. Prima facie evidence of failure to file return or report or that information not supplied.
2124. Venue.
2125. Limitations of actions.
2126. Costs.
2127. Penalties; compromise; cumulative effect.
2128. Undocumented workers; wage statements or documents provided for immigration legalization; employer immunity.
2129. Person defined.

§ 2101. False statement, representation or concealment to obtain, increase, reduce or defeat benefit or payment

(a) It is a violation of this chapter to willfully make a false statement or representation, to knowingly fail to disclose a material fact, or to use a false name, false social security number, or other false identification to obtain, increase, reduce, or defeat any benefit or payment, whether for the maker or for any other person, under any of the following statutes administered by the department:

(1) The provisions of this division.

(2) The provisions of any unemployment insurance law of the federal government.

(3) The provisions of any training allowance law of the federal government.

(4) The provisions of any trade readjustment allowance law of the federal government.

(5) The provisions of any other allowance law of the federal government.

(b) Nothing in this section shall be construed to preclude the applicability of Section 470 of the Penal Code to any acts or omissions which violate this section. *(Stats.1953, c. 308, p. 1528, § 2101. Amended by Stats. 1965, c. 1072, p. 2721, § 1; Stats.1977, c. 820, p. 2489, § 1; Stats.1986, c. 724, § 2; Stats.1995, c. 397 (A.B.212), § 2.)*

§ 2101.5. False statement, representation or concealment for purpose of lowering or avoiding contribution on becoming subject to division

It is a violation of this chapter to willfully make a false statement or representation or knowingly fail to disclose a material fact for the purpose of lowering or avoiding any contribution required of the maker or other person, or to avoid becoming or remaining subject to this division. *(Added by Stats.1965, c. 1072, p. 2722, § 2. Amended by Stats.1986, c. 724, § 3.)*

§ 2101.6. Advising prohibited acts; aid or assistance in prohibited acts

(a) It is a violation of this chapter for any person to procure, counsel, advise, or coerce anyone to willfully make a false statement or representation, or to knowingly fail to disclose a material fact in order to lower or avoid any contribution or to avoid being or remaining subject to this division.

(b) It is a violation of this chapter for any person to willfully aid or assist anyone in making a false statement or representation, or in knowingly failing to disclose a material fact, in order to lower or avoid any contribution, or to avoid being or remaining subject to this division. *(Added by Stats.2004, c. 827 (A.B.664), § 10.)*

§ 2102. False statement or representation or concealment to obtain benefits under employment laws of another state

(a) It is a violation of this chapter for any person residing in this state to willfully make a false statement or representation or knowingly fail to disclose a material fact to obtain or increase benefits or payments under the provisions of the unemployment insurance law of any other state.

(b) Nothing in this section shall be construed to preclude the applicability of Section 470 of the Penal Code to any acts or omissions which violate this section. *(Stats.1953, c. 308, p. 1528, § 2102. Amended by Stats. 1977, c. 820, p. 2490, § 2; Stats.1986, c. 724, § 4.)*

§ 2103. Deductions from wages larger than required

It is a violation of this chapter for any employing unit or any officer or agent of an employing unit to make a greater deduction from the wages of a worker than the contribution required of such worker under this division, for the purpose of paying any contribution required under this division. *(Stats.1953, c. 308, p. 1528, § 2103. Amended by Stats.1986, c. 724, § 5.)*

§ 2104. Failure to appear, testify or produce records

It is a violation of this chapter for any employing unit or any officer or agent of an employing unit to willfully and unlawfully fail to appear, testify, or produce books, papers, and records, required at any hearing under this division. *(Stats.1953, c. 308, p. 1528, § 2104. Amended by Stats.1986, c. 724, § 6.)*

§ 2105. Failure or neglect to make records available for inspection

It is a violation of this chapter for any employing unit or any officer or agent of an employing unit, to willfully and unlawfully fail or neglect to make available required records for the inspection of the director or his authorized representatives at any reasonable time during business hours. *(Stats.1953, c. 308, p. 1528, § 2105. Amended by Stats.1986, c. 724, § 7.)*

§ 2106. Failure or neglect to furnish reports

It is a violation of this chapter for any employing unit, or any officer or agent of an employing unit, to willfully and unlawfully fail or neglect to furnish to the director reports required by him when necessary for the enforcement of this division. *(Stats.1953, c. 308, p. 1529, § 2106. Amended by Stats.1986, c. 724, § 8.)*

§ 2107. Withholding information to aid individual to obtain benefits

It is a violation of this chapter for any employing unit, including a manager or managing member of a limited liability company, or any officer or agent of an employing unit or any individual to connive or conspire to aid such individual to obtain benefits to which he or she is not entitled by the willful withholding of information or by the willful failure to report any relevant information. *(Stats.1953, c. 308, p. 1529, § 2107. Amended by Stats. 1986, c. 724, § 9; Stats.1994, c. 1200 (S.B.469), § 85, eff. Sept. 30, 1994.)*

§ 2108. Nonpayment of contributions due

It is a violation of this chapter for any person to willfully fail or refuse to make any contributions which are due under this division. *(Stats.1953, c. 308, p. 1529, § 2108. Amended by Stats.1986, c. 724, § 10.)*

§ 2109. Failure to register or report

The executive officer, general manager, or any other person having charge of the affairs of a corporation, association, or limited liability company who willfully fails to register such corporation, association, or limited liability company as an employing unit, or willfully fails to submit contribution returns, earning reports, or other returns and reports required by this division, or by authorized regulations, is in violation of this chapter. *(Stats.1953, c. 308, p. 1529, § 2109. Amended by Stats.*

1026

1986, c. 724, § 11; Stats.1994, c. 1200 (S.B.469), § 86, eff. Sept. 30, 1994.)*

§ 2110. Failure to pay deductions withheld from workers

Any employing unit, including any individual member of a partnership employing unit, any officer of a corporate or association employing unit, any manager or managing member of a limited liability company, or any other person having charge of the affairs of a corporate, association, or limited liability company employing unit, that knowingly withholds the deductions required by this division from remuneration paid to its workers, and willfully fails or is willfully financially unable to pay such deductions to the department on the date on which they become delinquent is in violation of this chapter. *(Stats. 1953, c. 308, p. 1529, § 2110. Amended by Stats.1955, c. 1165, p. 2171, § 41; Stats.1965, c. 624, p. 1960, § 2; Stats.1973, c. 1212, p. 2790, § 198, operative July 1, 1974; Stats.1977, c. 1252, p. 4461, § 422, operative July 1, 1978; Stats.1986, c. 724, § 12; Stats.1994, c. 1200 (S.B.469), § 87, eff. Sept. 30, 1994.)*

§ 2110.3. Failure to pay contributions agreed to be paid for workers without deduction from remuneration

Any employing unit, including any individual member of a partnership employing unit, any officer of a corporate or association employing unit, any manager or managing member of a limited liability company, or any other person having charge of the affairs of a corporate, association, or limited liability company employing unit, that knowingly undertakes or agrees to pay without deduction from remuneration paid to its workers the amount of any contributions to the Disability Fund required of the workers under this division and that willfully fails or is willfully financially unable to pay the amount to the department on the date on which the contributions become delinquent is in violation of this chapter. *(Added by Stats.1965, c. 624, p. 1961, § 3. Amended by Stats.1973, c. 1212, p. 2790, § 199, operative July 1, 1974; Stats.1977, c. 1252, p. 4462, § 423, operative July 1, 1978; Stats.1986, c. 724, § 13; Stats.1994, c. 1200 (S.B.469), § 88, eff. Sept. 30, 1994.)*

§ 2110.5. Failure to withhold deductions in trust

Any employing unit, including any individual member of a partnership employing unit, any officer of a corporate or association employing unit, any manager or managing member of a limited liability company, or any other person having charge of the affairs of a corporate, association, or limited liability company employing unit, that willfully fails to withhold in trust the deductions required by this division from remuneration paid to its workers, except where such employing unit undertakes or agrees to pay without deduction from the wages of its workers the amount of worker contributions required of its workers under this division, is in violation of this chapter. *(Added by Stats.1961, c. 1183, p. 2918, § 1. Amended by Stats.1965, c. 624, p. 1961, § 4; Stats.1986, c.*

724, § 14; Stats.1994, c. 1200 (S.B.469), § 89, eff. Sept. 30, 1994.)

§ 2110.7. Failure to hold in trust contributions agreed to be paid for workers without deduction from remuneration

Any employing unit, including any individual member of a partnership employing unit, any officer of a corporate or association employing unit, any manager or managing member of a limited liability company, or any other person having charge of the affairs of a corporate, association, or limited liability company employing unit, that knowingly undertakes or agrees to pay without deduction from remuneration paid to its workers the amount of any contributions to the Disability Fund required of such workers under this division and that willfully fails to hold in trust the amount of worker contributions required of such workers under this division is in violation of this chapter. (Added by Stats.1965, c. 624, p. 1961, § 5. Amended by Stats.1986, c. 724, § 15; Stats.1994, c. 1200 (S.B.469), § 90, eff. Sept. 30, 1994.)

§ 2111. Disclosure of confidential information

Except as otherwise provided in Section 1094, and except with respect to information furnished by the department in connection with its participation as a party or as a lien claimant in a judicial or administrative proceeding, information obtained in the course of administration of this division is confidential and shall not be published or open to public inspection in any manner. Any officer or employee of the state (including its political subdivisions), or any former member, officer or employee or other individual, who in the course of his or her employment or duty has or had access to returns, reports, or documents maintained under this division, who violates this section is in violation of this chapter. (Stats.1953, c. 308, p. 1529, § 2111. Amended by Stats. 1955, c. 1166, p. 2176, § 13; Stats.1973, c. 77, p. 131, § 24; Stats.1973, c. 1206, p. 2620, § 60; Stats.1973, c. 1207, p. 2671, § 60; Stats.1973, c. 1212, p. 2791, § 201, operative July 1, 1974; Stats.1977, c. 1252, p. 4462, § 424, operative July 1, 1978; Stats.1980, c. 1025, p. 3291, § 16; Stats.1986, c. 724, § 16.)

§ 2112. Violation of law or authorized regulations

Unless otherwise specified in subdivision (b) of Section 2101 or in Section 2114, 2115, or 2116, every person who willfully violates any provision of this division or any authorized regulation promulgated or published in accordance with this division, is in violation of this chapter. (Stats.1953, c. 308, p. 1529, § 2112. Amended by Stats. 1982, c. 999, p. 3680, § 2; Stats.1983, c. 711, § 2; Stats.1986, c. 724, § 17.)

§ 2113. Restitution for overpayment of benefits

Nothing in this division shall prevent the department from accepting restitution or an acceptable arrangement for restitution, made voluntarily before the department files a criminal complaint under Section 2101 or 2102, for overpayment of benefits from any person, who has not previously claimed any right under this section, who has not been convicted of an offense under Section 2101 or 2102 within three years preceding the service under this section of a written notice of intent to file a criminal complaint and who has willfully made a false statement or representation or knowingly failed to disclose a material fact to obtain or increase any benefit under any provision of this division. The department shall by mail or personal service give the person written notice of intent to file a criminal complaint under Section 2101 or 2102 not less than 10 days prior to the filing of the criminal complaint. The department may accept restitution or an arrangement for restitution and any such acceptance shall be in lieu of any criminal action against the person, except that the department shall not be precluded from filing a criminal action against any person who defaults under an arrangement for restitution which it has accepted. For purposes of this section, no period of time during which an arrangement for restitution is in effect shall be a part of any limitation of the time for commencing a criminal action. The department shall deposit amounts received from any person under this section in the fund from which the overpayments were made. (Added by Stats. 1967, c. 1419, p. 3340, § 1. Amended by Stats.1973, c. 1212, p. 2791, § 203, operative July 1, 1974; Stats.1979, c. 373, p. 1376, § 299; Stats.1986, c. 724, § 18.)

§ 2114. Report on registration of fictitious employer or employee and wages

Any individual who, with the intent to defraud, reports or registers a fictitious employer or fictitious employee, and fictitious wages, to the department in order to obtain benefits or increase any benefit or payment, whether for the maker or for any other person, is in violation of this chapter. (Added by Stats.1982, c. 999, p. 3680, § 3. Amended by Stats.1986, c. 724, § 18.5.)

§ 2115. False reports of wages or time period

Any employing unit or any officer or agent of an employing unit who, with the intent to defraud, falsely reports the amount of wages earned by an employee or who falsely reports the time period in which wages are earned by an employee for the purpose of obtaining or increasing any benefit amount for that employee, is in violation of this chapter. (Added by Stats.1982, c. 999, p. 3680, § 4. Amended by Stats.1986, c. 724, § 19.)

§ 2116. Disability insurance benefits; unlawful acts

It is unlawful to do any of the following:

(a) Falsely certify the medical condition of any person in order to obtain disability insurance benefits, including family temporary disability insurance benefits, whether for the maker or for any other person.

(b) Knowingly present or cause to be presented any false or fraudulent written or oral material statement in support of any claim for disability insurance including family temporary disability insurance benefits.

(c) Knowingly solicit, receive, offer, pay, or accept any rebate, refund, commission, preference, patronage, dividend, discount, or other consideration, whether in the form of money or otherwise, as compensation or inducement for soliciting a claimant to apply for disability insurance including family temporary disability insurance benefits unless the payment is lawful pursuant to Section 650 of the Business and Professions Code.

(d) Knowingly assist, abet, solicit, or conspire with any person who engages in an unlawful act under this section. *(Added by Stats.1994, c. 967 (S.B.1584), § 5, eff. Sept. 28, 1994. Amended by Stats.2002, c. 901 (S.B.1661), § 1.5, operative Jan. 1, 2004.)*

Operative Effect

Stats.2002, c. 901 (S.B.1661), § 7, provides that benefits shall be payable for periods of family temporary disability leave commencing on or after July 1, 2004.

§ 2117. Failure to file return or report or to supply information; false or fraudulent return, report or statements; punishment

Any person who, with or without intent to evade any requirement of this code or any lawful requirement of the department under this code, fails to file any return or report, or to supply any information required by this code or who, with or without like intent, makes, renders, signs, or verifies any false or fraudulent return, report, or statement, or supplies any false or fraudulent information, is liable for a civil penalty of not more than one thousand dollars ($1,000), and is also guilty of a misdemeanor and shall, upon conviction, be fined an amount not to exceed one thousand dollars ($1,000), or be imprisoned for not more than one year, or both the fine and imprisonment, at the discretion of the court. *(Added by Stats.1986, c. 724, § 21. Amended by Stats.1994, c. 1049 (A.B.3086), § 20.)*

§ 2117.5. Intentional failure to file return or report or to supply information; false or fraudulent return or statement; punishment

Any person who, within the time required by this code, willfully fails to file any return or report, or to supply any information with intent to evade any tax imposed by this code, or who, willfully and with like intent, makes, renders, signs, or verifies any false or fraudulent return, report, or statement or supplies any false or fraudulent information, is punishable by imprisonment in the county jail not to exceed one year, or in the state prison, or by a fine of not more than twenty thousand dollars ($20,000), or by both the fine and imprisonment, at the discretion of the court. *(Added by Stats.1986, c. 724, § 21.5. Amended by Stats.1994, c. 1049 (A.B.3086), § 21.)*

§ 2118. Failure to withhold or to pay over tax withheld; punishment

Any person or employer who, with or without intent to evade, fails to withhold, pursuant to Section 13020, or fails to pay over any tax withheld, is guilty of a misdemeanor and, upon conviction, shall be fined an amount not to exceed one thousand dollars ($1,000), or imprisoned for not more than one year, or both the fine and imprisonment, at the discretion of the court. *(Added by Stats.1986, c. 724, § 22.)*

§ 2118.5. Willful failure to collect, truthfully account for or pay over tax or amount; penalties

Any person required by this code to collect, account for, and pay over any tax or amount required to be withheld who willfully fails to collect or truthfully account for and pay over the tax or amount shall, in addition to other penalties provided by law, be guilty of a felony and, upon conviction thereof, shall be fined an amount not more than twenty thousand dollars ($20,000), or imprisoned in the state prison, or both the fine and imprisonment, at the discretion of the court. *(Added by Stats. 1986, c. 724, § 22.5. Amended by Stats.1989, c. 1010, § 7.)*

§ 2119. Willful furnishing of false or fraudulent statement or failure to furnish statement

Any person or employer required under Section 13050 to furnish a statement who willfully furnishes a false or fraudulent statement or who willfully fails to furnish a statement in the manner, at the time, and showing the information required under Section 13050, or regulations prescribed thereunder, is in violation of this chapter. *(Added by Stats.1986, c. 724, § 23.)*

§ 2120. Willfully supplying false information or failure to supply information

Any individual required to supply information to his or her employer under Section 13040, 13041, or 13042, who willfully supplies false or fraudulent information, or who willfully fails to supply information thereunder which would require an increase in the tax to be withheld under Section 13020, is in violation of this chapter. *(Added by Stats.1986, c. 724, § 24.)*

§ 2121. Preparation or presentation of false or fraudulent document

Any person who willfully aids or assists in, or procures, counsels, advises, or coerces anyone in the preparation or presentation under, or in connection with any matter arising under, this code, of a return, report, affidavit, claim, or other document, that is fraudulent or is false as to any material matter, whether or not the falsity or fraud is with the knowledge or consent of the person authorized or required to present the return, report, affidavit, claim, or document is in violation of this chapter. *(Added by Stats.1986, c. 724, § 25. Amended by Stats.1994, c. 1049 (A.B.3086), § 22; Stats.1994, c. 1050 (A.B.3122), § 5.)*

§ 2122. Violations of chapter; punishment

Except as provided in Sections 2117, 2117.5, 2118, and 2118.5, a violation of this chapter is punishable by imprisonment in the county jail not to exceed one year, or in the state prison, or by a fine of not more than twenty thousand dollars ($20,000), or by both the fine and imprisonment, at the discretion of the court. *(Added by Stats.1986, c. 724, § 26.)*

§ 2122.5. Fines; allocation

Any fine imposed by the court pursuant to this chapter, except for fines imposed under Sections 2101 and 2102, shall be paid to the office of the prosecutor bringing the complaint, but if the case was referred to the prosecutor by the department, or some other governmental unit, one-half of the criminal fine shall be paid to that governmental unit. *(Added by Stats.1987, c. 604, § 1.)*

§ 2123. Prima facie evidence of failure to file return or report or that information not supplied

The certificate of the department to the effect that a return or report has not been filed or that information has not been supplied as required by Division 6 (commencing with Section 13000) is prima facie evidence that the return or report has not been filed or that the information has not been supplied. *(Added by Stats.1986, c. 724, § 27. Amended by Stats.1994, c. 1049 (A.B.3086), § 23.)*

§ 2124. Venue

The place of trial for offenses enumerated in this chapter shall be in the county of residence or principal place of business of the defendant or defendants, except that if the defendant has no residence or principal place of business in this state, the trial shall be held in the County of Sacramento. *(Added by Stats.1986, c. 724, § 28.)*

§ 2125. Limitations of actions

Any action or prosecution under this chapter shall be instituted within four years after the discovery of the offense. *(Added by Stats.1986, c. 724, § 29.)*

§ 2126. Costs

Any person or employing unit convicted under this chapter may be charged the costs of investigation and prosecution at the discretion of the court. *(Added by Stats.1986, c. 724, § 30.)*

§ 2127. Penalties; compromise; cumulative effect

The prosecutor may, with the consent of the department, compromise any penalty for which he or she may bring an action under this chapter. The penalties provided by this chapter are additional to all other penalties provided in this code and Part 10 (commencing with Section 17001) of Division 2 of the Revenue and Taxation Code. *(Added by Stats.1986, c. 724, § 30.5.)*

§ 2128. Undocumented workers; wage statements or documents provided for immigration legalization; employer immunity

Any employer or agent of an employer who provides a wage statement or similar document to any undocu-

mented worker or former undocumented worker at that person's request for the purpose of documenting that person's eligibility for legalization pursuant to the federal Immigration Reform and Control Act (Public Law 99–603), shall not be liable for any penalty or criminal or civil violation under this division relative to any undocumented worker or former undocumented worker based on any facts disclosed in the wage statement or similar document so provided.

Nothing in this section shall be construed to limit the liability under any provision of law of any person who engages in the procurement or production of false or fraudulent wage statements or similar documents to any person for purposes of legalization under the federal Immigration Reform and Control Act.

This section does not apply to penalties assessed or criminal actions filed prior to May 1, 1987.

This section does not apply where the Employment Development Department, through independent means, discovers that an employer has withheld personal income tax and disability insurance contributions from workers' paychecks and has not remitted those moneys to the department.

The immunity from liability pursuant to this section shall apply only to facts disclosed in the wage statement or similar document provided commencing on or after the effective date of this section and only until the date of the termination of the legalization provisions for agricultural and nonagricultural workers of the federal Immigration Reform and Control Act. However, the immunity from liability pursuant to this section shall continue until the cause of action is tolled by the applicable statute of limitations. *(Added by Stats.1987, c. 1363, § 2, eff. Sept. 29, 1987.)*

§ 2129. Person defined

For the purposes of this chapter, "person" includes, a claimant for benefits and any officer, employee, director, partner, or agent having charge of the affairs of any employer or employing unit with regard to the violation which occurred. "Person" also includes both natural persons and legal entities. More than one person may be charged with violations under this chapter, where control of the affairs of the employing unit, or employer, is shared by more than one person. *(Added by Stats.1989, c. 1010, § 8.)*

Part 2

DISABILITY COMPENSATION

Chapter		Section
1.	General Provisions	2601
2.	Disability Benefits	2625
2.4.	Nonindustrial Disability Insurance For State Employees	2781
3.	Additional Benefits [Repealed]	
3.5.	Prorated Benefits [Repealed]	
4.	Contributions	2901

Chapter	Section
5. Financial Provisions	3001
6. Voluntary Plans	3251
7. Paid Family Leave	3300

CHAPTER 1. GENERAL PROVISIONS

Section
2601. Purpose; construction.
2602. Application of provisions of first part.
2603. Employer's account not to be charged for disability benefits.
2604. Change in contribution rate or disability benefit amounts to protect solvency; recommendations; declaration of emergency.
2605. Conformity with federal laws.
2606. Employment defined.
2606.4. Employment; clerk-carrier in employ of U.S. Postal Service.
2606.5. Employment; domestic services.
2608. Disability benefit period defined.
2609. Valid claim defined.
2610. Disability base period with respect to individual not having unexpired benefit year for unemployment compensation benefits.
2611. Disability base period with respect to individual having unexpired benefit year for unemployment compensation benefits.
2612. Exclusion from disability base period of quarters during which unemployed; substitution of preceding quarters.
2613. Education program; notice of rights and benefits.
2614. Fraud deterrence and detection activities; report to Legislature.

§ 2601. Purpose; construction

The purpose of this part is to compensate in part for the wage loss sustained by any individual who is unable to work due to the employee's own sickness or injury, the sickness or injury of a family member, or the birth, adoption, or foster care placement of a new child, and to reduce to a minimum the suffering caused by unemployment resulting therefrom. This part shall be construed liberally in aid of its declared purpose to mitigate the evils and burdens that fall on the unemployed worker and his or her family. *(Stats.1953, c. 308, p. 1529, § 2601. Amended by Stats.2002, c. 901 (S.B.1661), § 2, operative Jan. 1, 2004; Stats.2003, c. 797 (S.B.727), § 6, operative Jan. 1, 2004.)*

Operative Effect

For operative effect of Stats.2003, c. 797 (S.B. 727) upon benefits payable for family temporary disability insurance claims, see section 28 of that act.

§ 2602. Application of provisions of first part

(a) Except as otherwise provided, the provisions and definitions of Part 1 (commencing with Section 100) of this division apply to this part. In case of any conflict between the provisions of Part 1 and the provisions of this part, the provisions of this part shall prevail with respect to unemployment compensation disability benefits, and the provisions of Part 1 shall prevail with respect to unemployment compensation benefits.

(b) The provisions of Chapter 6 (commencing with Section 1501) of Part 1, of this division do not apply to this part.

(c) Sections 312, 318, 1251, 1253, 1253.3, 1254, 1255, 1262, 1279, 1326 to 1333, inclusive, 1339, 1340, 1375 to 1378, inclusive, and 1380 do not apply to this part. *(Stats.1953, c. 308, p. 1529, § 2602. Amended by Stats. 1953, c. 1371, p. 2946; Stats.1955, c. 1153, p. 2147, § 4; Stats.1955, c. 1165, p. 2171, § 42; Stats.1955, c. 1167, p. 2176, § 1; Stats.1961, c. 2155, p. 4459, § 5; Stats.1965, c. 1654, p. 3756, § 5; Stats.1973, c. 1212, p. 2793, § 206, operative July 1, 1974; Stats.1975, c. 591, p. 1307, § 11; Stats.1975, c. 752, p. 1754, § 1.5; Stats.1976, c. 336, p. 919, § 2, eff. July 3, 1976; Stats.1977, c. 1252, p. 4462, § 425, operative July 1, 1978; Stats.1978, c. 397, p. 1260, § 6.5, eff. July 11, 1978; Stats.1985, c. 144, § 2, eff. July 3, 1985.)*

§ 2603. Employer's account not to be charged for disability benefits

Disability benefits paid pursuant to this part shall not be charged against an employer's account maintained pursuant to Article 4 of Chapter 4, Part 1 of this division.[1] *(Stats.1953, c. 308, p. 1530, § 2603.)*

[1] Section 1025 et seq.

§ 2604. Change in contribution rate or disability benefit amounts to protect solvency; recommendations; declaration of emergency

Whenever the Director of Employment Development believes that a change in contributions rate or disability benefit amounts may become necessary to protect the solvency of the Disability Fund, he shall at once inform the Governor and the Legislature thereof and make recommendations accordingly. In such case the Governor may declare an emergency and authorize the Director of Employment Development to announce a modified scale of benefits or increased waiting period, or other changes in regulations regarding the eligibility for payment of benefits which the Director of Employment Development may deem necessary to assure the solvency of the Disability Fund; such modified regulations to be in effect until the Governor declares the emergency at an end or until further action is taken by the Legislature. *(Stats.1953, c. 308, p. 1530, § 2604. Amended by Stats. 1955, c. 1166, p. 2175, § 8; Stats.1973, c. 1212, p. 2794, § 209, operative July 1, 1974.)*

§ 2605. Conformity with federal laws

If at any time the Secretary of Labor or other higher authority rules or determines that any section of this part is not in conformity with the provisions of Title III of the Social Security Act or Section 3302 and Section 3303 of the Federal Unemployment Tax Act by reason of any provision contained in this part, such section shall be immediately inoperative. *(Stats.1953, c. 308, p. 1530, § 2605. Amended by Stats.1957, c. 1184, p. 2476, § 10.)*

§ 2606. Employment defined

"Employment" for the purposes of this part means:

(a) Service included in "employment" as defined by Part 1 (commencing with Section 100) of this division, except that with respect to service for any public entity as defined by Section 605 "employment" for the purposes of this part includes only:

(1) Service for a hospital established, maintained and operated pursuant to Division 23 (commencing with Section 32000) of the Health and Safety Code.

(2) Service performed for a public housing administration agency whether operated by state or local governmental subdivisions.

(3) Service performed by a state employee to the extent provided by Section 2781.

(4) Service covered under this part by an elective coverage agreement.

(b) Notwithstanding any other provision of this division, all service performed in the employ of a corporation, community chest, fund, or foundation, in connection with the operation of a health facility as defined in Section 1250 of the Health and Safety Code including the institutions described in subdivision (a) of Section 1270 of the Health and Safety Code but not including county hospitals, no part of the net earnings of which inures to the benefit of any private shareholder or individual, no substantial part of the activities of which is carrying on propaganda, or otherwise attempting to influence legislation, which does not participate in, or intervene in (including the publishing or distributing of statements), any political campaign on behalf of any candidate for public office and which is exempt from income tax under Section 501(a) of the Internal Revenue Code of 1954, except service performed by an individual as a duly ordained priest, clergyman, rabbi, rector, vicar, pastor, or minister of religion, or by a practitioner who heals the sick by prayer in the practice of religion, or by a reader whose duty it is to conduct regular religious services of a religious organization, or by a member of a religious order in the exercise of duties required by the order, or by any other individual performing service in the practice of religion by designation of the governing body of a religious organization and subject to discipline by, including removal by, the governing body.

This section shall become operative on July 1, 1978. *(Added by Stats.1978, c. 2, p. 47, § 94.5, eff. Jan. 30, 1978, operative July 1, 1978. Amended by Stats.1979, c. 373, p. 1376, § 300; Stats.1993, c. 318 (A.B.763), § 3; Stats.2002, c. 29 (A.B.1729), § 14.)*

§ 2606.4. Employment; clerk-carrier in employ of U.S. Postal Service

Notwithstanding Section 632, "employment" for purposes of this part also means service performed as a clerk-carrier in the employ of the United States Postal Service, to the extent Congress permits this part to be applicable to the postal service, and if Congress permits the states to require the postal service to withhold workers' contributions and to transmit those contributions into a state fund for unemployment compensation disability benefits. *(Added by Stats.1976, c. 694, p. 1700, § 1.)*

§ 2606.5. Employment; domestic services

(a) "Employment" for purposes of this part also means domestic service in a private home, local college club, or local chapter of a college fraternity or sorority performed for an employing unit which pays wages in cash of seven hundred fifty dollars ($750) or more to individuals employed in such service during any calendar quarter in the calendar year or the preceding calendar year.

(b) "Employment" for purposes of this part also means domestic service comprising in-home supportive services under Article 7 (commencing with Section 12300) of Chapter 3 of Part 3 of Division 9 of the Welfare and Institutions Code, performed for an employing unit which pays wages in cash of seven hundred fifty dollars ($750) or more to individuals employed in such service during any calendar quarter in the calendar year or preceding calendar year, and is one of the following:

(1) The recipient of such services, if the state or county makes or provides for direct payment to a provider chosen by the recipient or to the recipient of such services for the purchase of services, subject to the provisions of Section 12302.2 of the Welfare and Institutions Code.

(2) The individual or entity with which a county contracts to provide in-home supportive services.

(3) Any county which hires and directs in-home supportive personnel in accordance with established county civil service requirements or merit system requirements for those counties not having civil service systems. *(Added by Stats.1981, c. 1025, p. 3940, § 3.)*

§ 2608. Disability benefit period defined

"Disability benefit period," with respect to any individual, means the continuous period of unemployment and disability beginning with the first day with respect to which the individual files a valid claim for unemployment compensation disability benefits. For the purposes of this part, two consecutive periods of disability due to the same or related cause or condition and separated by a period of not more than 14 days shall be considered as one disability benefit period. *(Added by Stats.1953, c. 1371, p. 2946.)*

§ 2609. Valid claim defined

"Valid claim" means any claim for unemployment compensation disability benefits made in accordance with the provisions of this code and rules and regulations adopted thereunder if the individual is unemployed and disabled and has been paid wages in employment for employers necessary to qualify for benefits under Section 2652. *(Added by Stats.1953, c. 1371, p. 2946.)*

§ 2610. Disability base period with respect to individual not having unexpired benefit year for unemployment compensation benefits

"Disability base period," with respect to an individual who does not have an unexpired benefit year for unemployment compensation benefits, means for disability benefit periods beginning in October, November, or December, the four calendar quarters ended in the next preceding month of June; the disability base period for disability benefit periods beginning in January, February, or March, shall be the four calendar quarters ended in the next preceding month of September; the disability base period for disability benefit periods beginning in April, May, or June, shall be the four calendar quarters ended in the next preceding month of December; the disability base period for disability benefit periods beginning in July, August, or September shall be the four calendar quarters ended with the next preceding month of March. *(Added by Stats.1953, c. 1371, p. 2946. Amended by Stats.2002, c. 52 (S.B.467), § 1; Stats.2004, c. 183 (A.B. 3082), § 342.)*

§ 2611. Disability base period with respect to individual having unexpired benefit year for unemployment compensation benefits

"Disability base period," with respect to an individual who has an unexpired benefit year for unemployment compensation benefits, shall be:

(a) The same as the disability base period in Section 2610 if the individual has sufficient qualifying earnings in that disability base period.

(b) The same as the base period used to establish the benefit year for unemployment compensation benefits if the individual does not have sufficient qualifying earnings in the disability base period in Section 2610. *(Added by Stats.1953, c. 1371, p. 2946. Amended by Stats.1977, c. 1143, p. 3671, § 3.)*

§ 2612. Exclusion from disability base period of quarters during which unemployed; substitution of preceding quarters

Notwithstanding any other provision of law, except as provided in subdivision (b) of Section 2611, in determining the benefit rights of any person who cannot establish a valid claim pursuant to Section 2652 because he or she is unemployed during the normal disability base period established pursuant to Section 2610, there shall be excluded from the disability base period those quarters during which the person performed no services in employment for 60 days or more and was actively seeking work. For all quarters so excluded, there shall be substituted an equal number of quarters immediately preceding the commencement of the normal disability base period. Benefit rights under this section shall terminate for any disability benefit period that begins when the substitution quarters no longer contain sufficient wages to establish a valid claim under Section 2652.

(Added by Stats.1982, c. 904, p. 3386, § 1, eff. Sept. 13, 1982.)

§ 2613. Education program; notice of rights and benefits

(a) The Director of Employment Development shall develop and maintain a program of education concerning disability insurance rights and benefits.

(b) The director shall provide to each employer of employees subject to this part a notice informing workers of their disability insurance rights and benefits due to sickness, injury, or pregnancy. The notice shall be given by every employer to each new employee hired on or after June 1, 1988, and to each employee leaving work due to pregnancy or nonoccupational sickness or injury on or after July 1, 1989.

(c) Commencing January 1, 2004, the director shall provide to each employer of employees subject to this part a notice informing workers of their disability insurance rights and benefits due to the employee's own sickness, injury, or pregnancy, or the employee's need to provide care for any sick or injured family member, or the employee's need to bond with a minor child within the first year of the child's birth or placement in connection with foster care or adoption. The notice shall also instruct the employee to provide notification of the reason for taking leave in a manner consistent with company policy. The notice shall be given by every employer to each new employee hired on or after January 1, 2004, and to each employee leaving work on or after July 1, 2004, due to pregnancy, nonoccupational sickness or injury, or the need to provide care for any sick or injured family member, or the need to bond with a minor child within the first year of the child's birth or placement in connection with foster care or adoption. *(Added by Stats.1987, c. 609, § 2. Amended by Stats.1988, c. 687, § 1; Stats.2002, c. 901 (S.B.1661), § 3, operative Jan. 1, 2004; Stats.2003, c. 797 (S.B.727), § 7, operative Jan. 1, 2004.)*

Operative Effect

For operative effect of Stats.2003, c. 797 (S.B. 727) upon benefits payable for family temporary disability insurance claims, see section 28 of that act.

§ 2614. Fraud deterrence and detection activities; report to Legislature

The director shall report to the Legislature by June 30 of each year on the department's fraud deterrence and detection activities. *(Added by Stats.1994, c. 967 (S.B. 1584), § 6, eff. Sept. 28, 1994.)*

CHAPTER 2. DISABILITY BENEFITS

Article	Section
1. Eligibility	2625
2. Computation (Amount and Duration)	2651
3. Disqualifications	2675

Article		Section
4.	**Filing, Determination and Payment of Disability Benefit Claims**	**2701**
5.	**Overpayments**	**2735**
6.	**Rights of Trainees**	**2765**
7.	**Rights of Industrially Disabled Persons**	**2775**

ARTICLE 1. ELIGIBILITY

Section

2625.   To whom disability benefits are payable.

2626.   Disability or disabled defined.

2626.1.   Alcoholic recovery home residents; certification; review expense reimbursements; residents outside the State of California.

2626.2.   Drug-free residential facility residents; certification; review expense reimbursements; residents outside the State of California.

2627.   Amount of, and eligibility for, benefits.

2628.   Ineligible if receiving unemployment insurance.

2629.   Entitlement to other benefits; effect on eligibility; reducing amount of benefits.

2629.1.   Time for payment of benefits; initial determination of entitlement to other benefits; notice; reimbursement to department.

2629.5.   Restitution and settlement payments; effect upon reduction.

2630.   Individuals with claims for unemployment disability benefits who are certified as having support obligations; notifications; deductions and withholding; periodic payments.

§ 2625. To whom disability benefits are payable

Unemployment compensation disability benefits are payable from the Disability Fund to individuals who are eligible to receive such benefit payments under this part. *(Stats.1953, c. 308, p. 1531, § 2625.)*

§ 2626. Disability or disabled defined

(a) An individual shall be deemed disabled on any day in which, because of his or her physical or mental condition, he or she is unable to perform his or her regular or customary work.

(b) For purposes of this section, "disability" or "disabled" includes:

(1) Illness or injury, whether physical or mental, including any illness or injury resulting from pregnancy, childbirth, or related medical condition.

(2) Inability to work because of a written order from a state or local health officer to an individual infected with, or suspected of being infected with, a communicable disease.

(3) Acute alcoholism being medically treated or, to the extent specified in Section 2626.1, resident status in an alcoholic recovery home.

(4) Acute drug-induced illness being medically treated or, to the extent specified in Section 2626.2, resident status in a drug-free residential facility.

(c) For purposes of this section, if an individual participates in a vocational rehabilitation plan under Article 2.6 (commencing with Section 4635) of Chapter 2 of Part 2 of Division 4 of the Labor Code, regular or customary work shall, upon completion of the plan, mean only that employment for which the individual has been retrained under the vocational rehabilitation plan. *(Stats.1953, c. 308, p. 1531, § 2626. Amended by Stats. 1973, c. 1026, p. 2042, § 2; Stats.1973, c. 1163, p. 2421, § 2; Stats.1977, c. 469, p. 1529, § 1; Stats.1978, c. 944, p. 2921, § 1; Stats.1979, c. 663, p. 2035, § 3, eff. Sept. 14, 1979; Stats.1982, c. 717, p. 2884, § 1; Stats.1993, c. 748 (S.B.4), § 3.)*

§ 2626.1. Alcoholic recovery home residents; certification; review expense reimbursements; residents outside the State of California

(a) An individual who is a resident in an alcoholic recovery home pursuant to referral or recommendation by a physician shall be eligible for disability benefits for a period not in excess of 30 days in any disability benefit period while receiving resident services, if an authorized representative of the alcoholic recovery home certifies that the individual is a resident participating in an alcoholic recovery program which has been certified by the State Department of Alcohol and Drug Programs. The individual shall be eligible for disability benefits for an additional period not in excess of 60 days if the referring physician certifies to the need of the individual for continuing resident services.

(b) The department shall reimburse the State Department of Alcohol and Drug Programs from the Disability Fund, in a reasonable amount as determined by the department, for the expense of reviewing any alcoholic recovery program, as required by the department in the administration of subdivision (a) which is not funded in the county alcohol program plan provided for in Article 3 (commencing with Section 11810) or Article 4 (commencing with Section 11830) of Part 2 of Division 10.5 of the Health and Safety Code.

(c) Outside the State of California, an individual who is a resident in an alcohol recovery home pursuant to referral or recommendation by a physician shall be eligible for disability benefits for a period not in excess of 30 days in any disability benefit period while receiving resident services, if an authorized representative of the alcoholic recovery home certifies that the individual is a resident participating in an alcoholic recovery program, licensed by or satisfying a program review by the state in which the facility is located. The individual shall be eligible for disability benefits for an additional period not in excess of 60 days if the referring physician certifies to the need of the individual for continuing resident services. *(Added by Stats.1978, c. 944, p. 2921, § 2. Amended by Stats.1982, c. 717, p. 2884, § 2; Stats.1984, c. 1328, § 85; Stats.1986, c. 788, § 1; Stats.1987, c. 255, § 1.)*

§ 2626.2. Drug-free residential facility residents; certification; review expense reimbursements; residents outside the State of California

(a) An individual who is a resident in a drug-free residential facility pursuant to referral or recommendation by a physician shall be eligible for disability benefits for a period not in excess of 45 days in any disability benefit period while receiving resident services, if an authorized representative of the drug-free residential facility certifies that the individual is a resident participating in a drug-free residential facility which has satisfied a program review by the State Department of Alcohol and Drug Programs. The individual shall be eligible for disability benefits for an additional period not in excess of 45 days if the referring physician certifies to the need of the individual for continuing resident services.

(b) The department shall reimburse the State Department of Alcohol and Drug Programs from the Disability Fund, in a reasonable amount as determined by the department, for the expense of reviewing any drug-free residential facility, as required by the department in the administration of subdivision (a), which is not funded under the federal Drug Abuse Office and Treatment Act of 1972 (Public Law 92–255) or in conformance with Chapter 4 (commencing with Section 11980) of Part 3 of Division 10.5 of the Health and Safety Code.

(c) Outside the State of California, an individual who is a resident in a drug-free residential facility pursuant to referral or recommendation by a physician shall be eligible for disability benefits for a period not in excess of 45 days in any disability benefit period while receiving resident services, if an authorized representative of the drug-free residential facility certifies that the individual is a resident participating in a drug-free residential program, licensed by or satisfying a program review by the state in which the facility is located. The individual shall be eligible for disability benefits for an additional period, but not in excess of 45 days, if the referring physician certifies to the need of the individual for continuing resident services. *(Added by Stats.1982, c. 717, p. 2885, § 3.). Amended by Stats.1986, c. 788, § 2; Stats.1987, c. 255, § 2.)*

§ 2627.   Amount of, and eligibility for, benefits

A disabled individual is eligible to receive disability benefits equal to one-seventh of his or her weekly benefit amount for each full day during which he or she is unemployed due to a disability only if the director finds that:

(a) He or she has made a claim for disability benefits as required by authorized regulations.

(b) He or she has been unemployed and disabled for a waiting period of seven consecutive days during each disability benefit period with respect to which waiting period no disability benefits are payable.

(c) Except as provided in Sections 2626.1, 2626.2, and 2709, he or she has submitted to such reasonable examinations as the director may require for the purpose of determining his or her disability.

(d) Except as provided in Section 2708.1, he or she has filed a certificate as required by Section 2708 or 2709. *(Stats.1953, c. 308, p. 1532, § 2627. Amended by Stats. 1953, c. 449, p. 1695; Stats.1953, c. 1371, p. 2946;*

Stats.1977, c. 1143, p. 3672, § 4; Stats.1978, c. 944, p. 2922, § 3; Stats.1979, c. 1049, p. 3698, § 1; Stats.1980, c. 1162, p. 3909, § 1; Stats.1982, c. 717, p. 2885, § 4; Stats.1993, c. 747 (A.B.1738), § 9; Stats.1993, c. 748 (S.B.4), § 4.)

§ 2628.   Ineligible if receiving unemployment insurance

An individual is not eligible for disability benefits with respect to any period for which the director finds that he has received or is entitled to receive unemployment compensation benefits under Part 1 of this division or under an unemployment compensation act of any other state or of the Federal Government. *(Stats.1953, c. 308, p. 1533, § 2628.)*

§ 2629.   Entitlement to other benefits; effect on eligibility; reducing amount of benefits

(a) Except as provided in this section, an individual is not eligible for disability benefits under this part for any day of unemployment and disability for which he or she has received, or is entitled to receive, "other benefits" in the form of cash payments.

(b) "Other benefits," as used in this section and Section 2629.1, means any of the following:

(1) Temporary disability indemnity under a workers' compensation law of this state or of any other state or of the federal government including, for purposes of this code and Sections 4903 and 4904 of the Labor Code, a maintenance allowance paid pursuant to Section 139.5 of the Labor Code.

(2) Temporary disability benefits under any employer's liability law of this state or of any other state or of the federal government.

(3) Permanent disability benefits for the same injury or illness under the workers' compensation law of this state, any other state, or the federal government.

(c) Except for a maintenance allowance paid pursuant to Section 139.5 of the Labor Code, if these "other benefits" are less than the amount an individual would otherwise receive as disability benefits under this part, he or she shall be entitled to receive, for that day, if otherwise eligible, disability benefits under this part reduced by the amount of these "other benefits."

(d) An individual shall be entitled to receive, for any day, if otherwise eligible, disability benefits under this part reduced by the amount of the maintenance allowance and permanent disability indemnity if both of the following conditions are met:

(1) The individual elects to receive the maximum permanent disability indemnity pursuant to paragraph (2) of subdivision (d) of Section 139.5 of the Labor Code.

(2) The sum of the maintenance allowance and permanent disability indemnity is less than the amount an individual would otherwise receive as disability benefits under this part. *(Stats.1953, c. 308, p. 1533, § 2629. Amended by Stats.1957, c. 1977, p. 3526, § 6; Stats.1972, c. 833, p. 1487, § 11; Stats.1973, c. 86, p. 147, § 2, eff.*

June 12, 1973; Stats.1980, c. 1040, p. 3320, § 2; Stats. 1989, c. 1280, § 3; Stats.1990, c. 1550 (A.B.2910), § 64; Stats.1993, c. 748 (S.B.4), § 8.)

§ 2629.1. Time for payment of benefits; initial determination of entitlement to other benefits; notice; reimbursement to department

(a) Nothing in Section 2629 shall be construed to authorize the delay of payment of unemployment compensation disability benefits except where the claimant is currently in receipt of other benefits or where the department has received notice that the claimant's employer or insurer has agreed to commence the payment of other benefits.

(b) Notwithstanding Section 2701.5, payments shall commence within 14 days after notice to the employer or insurer under this section unless the employer or insurer has either paid or has agreed to commence the payment of other benefits.

(c) Upon the filing of a claim for unemployment compensation disability benefits, the department shall make an initial determination as to the claimant's entitlement to other benefits for purposes of Section 2629.

(1) The department shall notify the claimant and the claimant's employer if it determines that the claimant is entitled to other benefits.

(2) The notice to the claimant shall inform the claimant that disability benefits will be paid pending receipt of other benefits if the employer fails to agree to pay these other benefits within 14 days of notification of industrial injury and shall advise the claimant of the provisions of Section 2629.

(3) The department shall also include with the claimant's notice a pamphlet to be provided by the Department of Industrial Relations which meets the criteria specified in subdivision (b) of Section 139.6 of the Labor Code.

(4) The notice to the employer shall constitute a claim for compensation and knowledge of an injury for purposes of Section 5402 of the Labor Code, and shall inform the employer of its potential liability for interest and penalties under this section.

(d) If the employer or the insurance carrier disputes liability for the payment of other benefits, or the extent thereof, the department's right to reimbursement shall be subject to the jurisdiction of the Workers' Compensation Appeals Board in accordance with Part 4 (commencing with Section 5300) of Division 4 of the Labor Code.

(e) An employer or insurance carrier who subsequently assumes liability or is determined to be liable for reimbursement to the department for unemployment compensation disability benefits which the department has paid in lieu of other benefits shall be assessed for this liability by the department. In addition, the employer shall pay the department interest on the disability benefits at the annual rate provided in Section 19521 of the Revenue and Taxation Code. The employer shall also pay a penalty of 10 percent of the amount reimbursed to

the department if the Workers' Compensation Appeals Board finds that the failure of the employer to pay other benefits upon notice by the department under this section was unreasonable and a penalty has not been awarded for the delay under Section 5814 of the Labor Code. All funds received by the department pursuant to this section shall be deposited in the Disability Fund.

(f) The employer shall reimburse the department in accordance with subdivision (e) within 60 days of either voluntarily accepting liability for other benefits or after a final award, order, or decision of the Workers' Compensation Appeals Board. *(Added by Stats.1989, c. 1280, § 5. Amended by Stats.1993, c. 877 (S.B.673), § 95, eff. Oct. 6, 1993, operative Jan. 1, 1994.)*

§ 2629.5. Restitution and settlement payments; effect upon reduction

To the extent permitted by federal law, excludable restitution payments, as defined in Section 17131.1 of the Revenue and Taxation Code, and excludable settlement payments, as defined in Section 17131.2 of the Revenue and Taxation Code, may not be applied to reduce the amount of disability benefits to which an individual may otherwise be entitled under law. *(Added by Stats.2002, c. 701 (A.B.989), § 3. Amended by Stats.2004, c. 402 (S.B.1689), § 3.)*

§ 2630. Individuals with claims for unemployment disability benefits who are certified as having support obligations; notifications; deductions and withholding; periodic payments

(a) The Department of Child Support Services shall periodically notify the department of individuals who are certified, as provided in Section 17518 of the Family Code, as having support obligations, as defined by subdivision (g) and notify the department of any changes in the status of these individuals to ensure that the department has a current record.

(b) Upon receipt of the notifications referred to in subdivision (a), the department shall determine whether the individuals have claims for unemployment compensation disability benefits, either with the department or under an approved voluntary plan.

(c) If the department determines that an individual referred to in subdivision (a) has a claim for unemployment compensation disability benefits with an approved voluntary plan, it shall notify the voluntary plan payer. When the Department of Child Support Services notifies the department of any changes in the individual's status as to his or her support obligations, the department shall in turn notify the voluntary plan payer. Upon notification from the department, the voluntary plan payer shall deduct and withhold the amounts specified in Section 17518 of the Family Code from the unemployment compensation disability benefits that would otherwise be payable to the individual. For each withholding, the voluntary plan payer shall deduct an amount which represents the amount withheld for support obligations and may also deduct an administrative fee representing actual costs, not to exceed two dollars ($2). In no event shall the withholding and the administrative fee exceed 25 percent or a lesser amount as specified in subdivision (e) of Section 17518 of the Family Code. The voluntary plan payer shall pay the amounts for support deducted and withheld pursuant to this section to the appropriate certifying county.

(d) The department shall maintain a current record of individuals certified as owing support obligations. If the department determines that the individual has a claim for unemployment compensation disability benefits with the department, it shall deduct and withhold the amounts specified in Section 17518 of the Family Code from the unemployment compensation disability benefits that would otherwise be payable to the individual. The department shall periodically pay the amounts deducted and withheld to the appropriate county or to the Department of Child Support Services as the assigned payee, as stipulated by mutual agreement, in the interagency agreement between the department and the Department of Child Support Services.

(e) Amounts deducted and withheld from an individual's unemployment compensation disability benefits in accordance with subdivision (c) or (d) shall for all purposes be treated as if it were paid to the individual and then paid by the individual to the Department of Child Support Services or the appropriate certifying county.

(f) This section shall apply only if appropriate arrangements are made for the Department of Child Support Services to reimburse the department for its administrative costs for performing the functions required of it by this section.

(g) For purposes of this section, "support obligations" means the child and related spousal support obligations described in the state plan approved pursuant to Section 454 of the Social Security Act and as that section may hereafter be amended. However, to the extent "related spousal support obligations" may not be collected from unemployment compensation under federal law, those obligations shall not be included in the definition of support obligations under this section. *(Added by Stats. 1988, c. 261, § 4, eff. July 5, 1988. Amended by Stats.1990, c. 1024 (A.B.3092), § 4; Stats.1991, c. 110 (S.B.101), § 18; Stats.2000, c. 808 (A.B.1358), § 117, eff. Sept. 28, 2000.)*

ARTICLE 2. COMPUTATION (AMOUNT AND DURATION)

Section
2652. Requirement for valid claim.
2653. Maximum amount payable to individual; period of applicability of section.
2654. Wages due and unpaid deemed wages paid.
2655. Weekly benefit amount; table; highest quarter.

Section
2656. Maximum benefits where individual is receiving wages; amount of wages stated by individual, presumption of accuracy.
2657. Determination of weekly wages where payments are irregular.
2658. Trade dispute; disability base period.

§ 2652. Requirement for valid claim

An individual cannot establish a valid claim unless he has during his disability base period been paid wages for employment by employers of not less than three hundred dollars ($300). *(Added by Stats.1953, c. 1371, p. 2946. Amended by Stats.1955, c. 957, p. 1854, § 2; Stats.1957, c. 2107, p. 3733, § 4.)*

§ 2653. Maximum amount payable to individual; period of applicability of section

Except as provided in Sections 708 and 708.5, the maximum amount of benefits payable to an individual during any one disability benefit period shall be 52 times his or her weekly benefit amount, but in no case shall the total amount of the benefits payable be more than the total wages paid to the individual during his or her disability base period. If the benefit is not a multiple of one dollar ($1) it shall be computed to the next higher multiple of one dollar ($1).

This section shall apply to periods of disability commencing on or after January 1, 1984. *(Added by Stats. 1953, c. 1371, p. 2946. Amended by Stats.1965, c. 745, p. 2155, § 6, eff. June 24, 1965; Stats.1979, c. 1049, p. 3699, § 3; Stats.1979, c. 1051, p. 3705, § 2; Stats.1983, c. 1266, § 1; Stats.1986, c. 1455, § 1; Stats.1989, c. 1371, § 3; Stats.1993, c. 747 (A.B.1738), § 14.)*

§ 2654. Wages due and unpaid deemed wages paid

For the purpose of this article wages due to any individual but unpaid within the time limit provided by law, shall be deemed wages paid to such individual. *(Added by Stats.1953, c. 1371, p. 2946.)*

§ 2655. Weekly benefit amount; table; highest quarter

(a) Except as provided in subdivisions (b), (c), and (d), an individual's "weekly benefit amount" shall be the amount appearing in column B in the table set forth in this subdivision on the line of which in column A of the table there appears the wage bracket containing the amount of wages paid to the individual for employment by employers during the quarter of his or her disability base period in which wages were the highest.

A Amount of wages in highest quarter	B Weekly benefit amount
$ 75–1,149.99	$50
1,150–1,174.99	51
1,175–1,199.99	52
1,200–1,224.99	53
1,225–1,249.99	54
1,250–1,274.99	55
1,275–1,299.99	56

A Amount of wages in highest quarter	B Weekly benefit amount
1,300–1,324.99	57
1,325–1,349.99	58
1,350–1,374.99	59
1,375–1,399.99	60
1,400–1,424.99	61
1,425–1,449.99	62
1,450–1,474.99	63
1,475–1,499.99	64
1,500–1,524.99	65
1,525–1,549.99	66
1,550–1,574.99	67
1,575–1,599.99	68
1,600–1,624.99	69
1,625–1,649.99	70
1,650–1,674.99	71
1,675–1,699.99	72
1,700–1,724.99	73
1,725–1,749.20	74

(b) For periods of disability commencing on or after January 1, 1990, and prior to January 1, 1991, if the amount of wages paid an individual for employment by employers during the quarter of his or her disability base period in which these wages were highest exceeds one thousand seven hundred forty-nine dollars and twenty cents ($1,749.20), the weekly benefit amount shall be 55 percent of these wages divided by 13, but not exceeding two hundred sixty-six dollars ($266) or the maximum workers' compensation temporary disability indemnity weekly benefit amount, whichever is less. If the benefit payable under this subdivision is not a multiple of one dollar ($1), it shall be computed to the next higher multiple of one dollar ($1).

(c) For periods of disability commencing on or after January 1, 1991, but before January 1, 2000, if the amount of wages paid an individual for employment by employers during the quarter of his or her disability base period in which these wages were highest exceeds one thousand seven hundred forty-nine dollars and twenty cents ($1,749.20), the weekly benefit amount shall be 55 percent of these wages divided by 13, but not exceeding three hundred thirty-six dollars ($336). If the benefit payable under this subdivision is not a multiple of one dollar ($1), it shall be computed to the next higher multiple of one dollar ($1).

(d)(1) For periods of disability commencing on or after January 1, 2000, if the amount of wages paid an individual for employment by employers during the quarter of his or her disability base period in which these wages were highest exceeds one thousand seven hundred forty-nine dollars and twenty cents ($1,749.20), the weekly benefit amount shall be equal to 55 percent of these wages divided by 13, but not exceeding the maximum workers' compensation temporary disability indemnity weekly benefit amount.

(2) Notwithstanding the maximum workers' compensation temporary disability indemnity weekly benefit amount of paragraph (1) of subdivision (d), if the benefit

under this subdivision is not a multiple of one dollar ($1), it shall be computed to the next higher multiple of one dollar ($1). (Added by Stats.1953, c. 1371, p. 2946. Amended by Stats.1955, c. 957, p. 1853, § 1; Stats.1957, c. 2107, p. 3733, § 5; Stats.1959, c. 2155, p. 5206, § 1; Stats.1961, c. 2153, p. 4447, § 16; Stats.1961, c. 2154, p. 4452, § 7; Stats.1963, c. 1864, p. 3847, § 1; Stats.1965, c. 745, p. 2155, § 7, eff. June 24, 1965; Stats.1968, 1st Ex.Sess., c. 5, p. 34, § 2; Stats.1971, c. 1747, p. 3733, § 2; Stats.1973, c. 1188, p. 2496, § 2; Stats.1977, c. 1143, p. 3674, § 6; Stats.1979, c. 1049, p. 3699, § 4; Stats.1981, c. 793, p. 3081, § 1; Stats.1983, c. 903, § 2; Stats.1989, c. 1371, § 5; Stats.1993, c. 748 (S.B.4), § 9; Stats.1999, c. 973 (S.B.656), § 1; Stats.2006, c. 519 (S.B.1690), § 1.)

§ 2656. Maximum benefits where individual is receiving wages; amount of wages stated by individual, presumption of accuracy

(a) An individual eligible to receive disability benefits who receives wages or regular wages from his or her employer during the period of his or her disability or period of family care leave shall be paid disability benefits for any seven-day week or partial week in an amount not to exceed his or her maximum weekly amount which together with the wages or regular wages does not exceed his or her weekly wage, exclusive of wages paid for overtime work, immediately prior to the commencement of his or her disability or period of family care leave.

(b) For purposes of this section, to determine the wages or regular wages received by the eligible individual, the amount as stated by the individual shall be presumed to be accurate. This presumption is one affecting the burden of producing evidence.

(c) Except as provided in subdivision (g) of Section 3303, for purposes of periods of disability commencing on or after January 1, 1992, vacation pay is not considered wages for determining eligibility for disability benefits. (Formerly § 2653, Stats.1953, c. 308, p. 1531. Renumbered § 2656 and amended Stats.1953, c. 1371, p. 2946. Amended by Stats.1955, c. 957, p. 1855, § 3; Stats.1968, c. 1090, p. 2099, § 1; Stats.1979, c. 13, p. 38, § 3, eff. March 23, 1979; Stats.1985, c. 155, § 1; Stats.1991, c. 1134 (A.B.540), § 4; Stats.2003, c. 797 (S.B.727), § 8, operative Jan. 1, 2004.)

Operative Effect

For operative effect of Stats.2003, c. 797 (S.B. 727) upon benefits payable for family temporary disability insurance claims, see section 28 of that act.

§ 2657. Determination of weekly wages where payments are irregular

If the remuneration of an individual is not based upon a fixed period or duration of time or if the individual's wages are paid at irregular intervals or in such manner as not to extend regularly over the period of employment, the wages for any week or for any calendar quarter for the purpose of computing an individual's right to disability benefits shall be determined pursuant to authorized regulations. The regulations shall, so far as possible, secure results reasonably similar to those which would prevail if the individual were paid his wages at regular intervals. *(Added by Stats.1961, c. 2153, p. 4449, § 17. Amended by Stats.1973, c. 1212, p. 2796, § 212, operative July 1, 1974; Stats.1977, c. 1252, p. 4462, § 426, operative July 1, 1978.)*

§ 2658.   Trade dispute; disability base period

Notwithstanding any inconsistent provisions in this part, except as provided in subdivision (b) of Section 2611, in determining the benefit rights of any person who was involved in a trade dispute during the disability base period, as determined pursuant to Section 2610, there shall be excluded from the disability base period those quarters during which the person performed no services in employment for 60 days or more as a result of a trade dispute. For all quarters so excluded there shall be substituted an equal number of quarters immediately preceding the commencement of the trade dispute. In the event the disability base period so determined includes wages in calendar quarters for which the records have been destroyed under proper approval, a claimant may establish the amount of wages by affidavit in accordance with authorized regulations. The quarter of commencement of the trade dispute shall be counted as a completed quarter if the director finds that the inclusion thereof would be more equitable to the claimant. *(Added by Stats.1975, c. 865, p. 1938, § 1. Amended by Stats.1985, c. 1211, § 3.)*

ARTICLE 3.   DISQUALIFICATIONS

Section
2675. Disqualification for false statements; length of ineligibility for benefits; application of assessed days of ineligibility to subsequent disability benefit period.
2676. Application of disqualifications; presumption.
2677. Trade disputes.
2678. Disqualification of individual confined as dipsomaniac, drug addict or sexual psychopath.
2679. Day of death; prohibition of disqualification.
2680. Incarcerated individual; application of section.
2681. Disability due to commission of crime; felony conviction; application of section.

§ 2675.   Disqualification for false statements; length of ineligibility for benefits; application of assessed days of ineligibility to subsequent disability benefit period

(a) An individual shall be disqualified from receiving benefits under this part if he or she has willfully, for the purpose of obtaining benefits, either made a false statement or representation, with actual knowledge of the falsity thereof, or withheld a material fact in order to obtain any benefits under this part.

(b) An individual disqualified under subdivision (a) under a determination transmitted to him or her by the department, shall be ineligible to receive benefits from

the date the disqualifying determination was issued and for not less than seven nor more than 35 subsequent days for which he or she is otherwise eligible for benefits under this part. When successive disqualifications under subdivision (a) occur, the director may extend the period of ineligibility for an additional period not to exceed 56 days.

(c) If all or any of the assessed days of ineligibility cannot be served because the individual is no longer otherwise eligible for benefits under this part, the assessed days of ineligibility shall be applied to any subsequent disability benefit period for which he or she is otherwise eligible for benefits. No disqualification under this subdivision shall be applied, however, to any day of eligibility which falls beyond the three-year period next succeeding the date upon which the determination was mailed or served by the department.

(d) The amendments made to this section by the act adding this subdivision [1] shall apply to disqualifying determinations issued on or after January 1, 1992. *(Stats.1953, c. 308, p. 1535, § 2675. Amended by Stats. 1979, c. 890, p. 3082, § 2; Stats.1985, c. 1211, § 4; Stats.1991, c. 1134 (A.B.540), § 5.)*

[1] Added by Stats.1991, c. 1134.

§ 2676.   Application of disqualifications; presumption

An individual who is disqualified from receiving unemployment compensation benefits under Sections 1256, 1257, 1260, 1261, and 1263 shall be presumed to be ineligible to receive disability benefits under this part for the same period or periods unless he or she establishes to the satisfaction of the director that he or she is suffering a bona fide illness or injury or claiming a period of family care leave and the director finds that there is good cause for paying disability benefits. *(Stats.1953, c. 308, p. 1536, § 2676. Amended by Stats.1953, c. 1294, p. 2854; Stats. 2003, c. 797 (S.B.727), § 9, operative Jan. 1, 2004.)*

Operative Effect

For operative effect of Stats.2003, c. 797 (S.B. 727) upon benefits payable for family temporary disability insurance claims, see section 28 of that act.

§ 2677.   Trade disputes

An individual who is otherwise eligible for benefits under this part shall not be disqualified from receiving such benefits because of a disqualification from receiving unemployment compensation benefits under Section 1262. *(Added by Stats.1979, c. 1052, p. 3706, § 2.)*

§ 2678.   Disqualification of individual confined as dipsomaniac, drug addict or sexual psychopath

An individual shall be disqualified from receiving benefits under this part while he is confined, pursuant to commitment or court order or certification, in an institution or other place, as a dipsomaniac, drug addict or sexual psychopath. *(Added by Stats.1953, c. 1805, p. 3589, § 1.)*

§ 2679. Day of death; prohibition of disqualification

Notwithstanding any other provision of law, an individual who is otherwise eligible shall not be disqualified for benefits under this part for the day on which he or she or a family member, as defined in Chapter 7 (commencing with Section 3300), for whom the individual is providing care, died. *(Added by Stats.1983, c. 723, § 1. Amended by Stats.2003, c. 797 (S.B.727), § 10, operative Jan. 1, 2004.)*

Operative Effect

For operative effect of Stats.2003, c. 797 (S.B. 727) upon benefits payable for family temporary disability insurance claims, see section 28 of that act.

§ 2680. Incarcerated individual; application of section

(a) An individual shall be ineligible for benefits under this part for any day during which he or she is incarcerated in any federal, state, or municipal penal institution, jail, medical facility, public or private hospital, or in any other place because of a criminal violation of a federal, state, or other municipal law or ordinance. For purposes of this section, "incarceration" includes any time spent in the custody of law enforcement authorities upon adjudication or conviction by a court of competent jurisdiction.

(b) This section shall apply only with respect to periods of incarceration commencing on or after January 1, 1994. *(Added by Stats.1993, c. 318 (A.B.763), § 4.)*

§ 2681. Disability due to commission of crime; felony conviction; application of section

(a) Any individual who commits a crime shall be ineligible for benefits under this part if the individual is disabled due to an illness or injury caused by, or arising out of the commission of, arrest, investigation, or prosecution of any crime that results in a felony conviction.

(b) For purposes of this section, a plea or verdict of guilty, or a felony conviction following a plea of nolo contendere or no contest shall be considered to be a felony conviction under this part, irrespective of whether an order granting probation or suspending the imposition or execution of any sentence is issued.

(c) This section shall apply only with respect to convictions rendered on or after January 1, 1994, regardless of the date the disability commenced, or benefits were paid. *(Added by Stats.1993, c. 318 (A.B.763), § 5.)*

ARTICLE 4. FILING, DETERMINATION AND PAYMENT OF DISABILITY BENEFIT CLAIMS

Section
2701. Manner of payment of benefits.
2701.5. Initial payment of benefits; time limit.
2702. Payment of benefits to minors; receipt.
2703. Establishment of disability benefit period; filing valid claim; effect.
2705. Benefits due person who dies before making claim.
2705.1. Eligible person mentally unable to make claim; affidavit by spouse or other person claiming entitlement to benefits.
2706. Manner of making claims; posting information by employers.
2706.1. Time for filing first claim.
2706.2. Continued medical certification; time of submission.
2707. Notice of filing of first claim.
2707.1. Employer's furnishing of information which may bear upon claimant's eligibility.
2707.2. Consideration of facts submitted by employer; determination of eligibility; notice; right of appeal.
2707.3. Computation of claim; notice to claimant; exceptions.
2707.4. Protest of computation time; determination; notice; appeal.
2707.5. Reconsideration of determination or computation; notice; appeal or protest.
2707.6. Manner of submitting notices, protests and information.
2708. Establishing medical eligibility for uninterrupted period of disability; filing first and subsequent claims for disability benefits; medical certificate and contents; development of certification form; medical evidence.
2708.1. Persons receiving temporary workers' compensation benefits; certificate of physician.
2709. Certificate of disability by authorized religious practitioners.
2712. Settlement of disputed claims liability between disability fund and voluntary plans; prescribing rules and regulations; reimbursement of fund.
2712.5. Enforcement of reimbursement.
2713. Closed hearing.
2714. Confidentiality of medical records.

§ 2701. Manner of payment of benefits

Disability benefits shall be paid by the department through public employment offices or other agencies approved by the director. *(Stats.1953, c. 308, p. 1536, § 2701. Amended by Stats.1973, c. 1212, p. 2796, § 213.5, operative July 1, 1974; Stats.1979, c. 373, p. 1377, § 301.)*

§ 2701.5. Initial payment of benefits; time limit

The department shall issue the initial payment for unemployment compensation disability benefits to a monetarily eligible claimant who is otherwise determined eligible by the department under applicable law and regulation within 14 days of receipt of his or her properly completed first disability claim. *(Added by Stats.1985, c. 1093, § 1.)*

§ 2702. Payment of benefits to minors; receipt

Minors who are eligible for disability benefits may be paid and receive such benefits in their own right and a receipt signed by a minor shall be valid and binding in all respects. *(Stats.1953, c. 308, p. 1537, § 2702.)*

§ 2703. Establishment of disability benefit period; filing valid claim; effect

The establishment of a disability benefit period for unemployment compensation disability benefits shall not establish a benefit year for unemployment compensation benefits and the filing of a valid claim for one shall not establish a valid claim for the other. Wages used to establish a valid claim for disability benefits may be used to establish a subsequent claim for disability benefits or unemployment compensation benefits provided such wages were paid in the base period applicable to the subsequent claim. *(Stats.1953, c. 308, p. 1537, § 2703. Amended by Stats.1953, c. 1371, p. 2946.)*

§ 2705. Benefits due person who dies before making claim

Where an individual who would be eligible to receive disability benefits dies before making a claim therefor, the director may in accordance with authorized regulations allow the filing of a claim for such benefits by a person legally entitled thereto under Section 1341. *(Stats.1953, c. 308, p. 1537, § 2705.)*

§ 2705.1. Eligible person mentally unable to make claim; affidavit by spouse or other person claiming entitlement to benefits

Where an individual who would be eligible to receive disability benefits is mentally unable to make a claim therefor, the director shall, in accordance with authorized regulations, allow the filing of a claim for these benefits by the spouse or domestic partner of the individual, in the absence of any other legally authorized representative of the individual. A payment shall be made upon affidavit executed by the spouse or domestic partner or person or persons claiming to be entitled to the benefits and the receipt of the affidavit or affidavits shall fully discharge the Director of Employment Development from any further liability with reference to the payments, without the necessity of inquiring into the truth of any of the facts stated in the affidavit.

For the purposes of this section "mentally unable to make a claim" shall be limited to those cases in which the individual is certified by a healing arts practitioner specified in Sections 2708 and 2709 to be mentally unable to make a claim pursuant to this part. *(Added by Stats.1977, c. 849, p. 2550, § 1. Amended by Stats.2001, c. 893 (A.B.25), § 60.)*

§ 2706. Manner of making claims; posting information by employers

Claims for disability benefits shall be made in accordance with authorized regulations of the Director of Employment Development. Each employer shall post and maintain in places readily accessible to individuals in his service printed statements concerning such regulations and shall make available to each such individual copies of such printed statements, regulations or matters relating to claims for disability benefits as the Director of Employment Development may prescribe. Such printed

statements shall be supplied to each employer by the Director of Employment Development without cost to the employer. *(Stats.1953, c. 308, p. 1537, § 2706. Amended by Stats.1973, c. 1212, p. 2797, § 215, operative July 1, 1974.)*

§ 2706.1. Time for filing first claim

A first claim, accompanied by a certificate on a form furnished by the department to the claimant, shall be filed not later than the 41st consecutive day following the first compensable day of unemployment and disability with respect to which the claim is made for benefits, which time shall be extended by the department upon a showing of good cause. If a first claim is not complete, the claim form shall be returned to the claimant for completion and it shall be completed and returned not later than the 10th consecutive day after the date it was mailed by the department to the claimant, except that such time shall be extended by the department upon a showing of good cause. *(Added by Stats.1968, 1st Ex.Sess., c. 5, p. 36, § 3. Amended by Stats.1973, c. 1212, p. 2797, § 217, operative July 1, 1974; Stats.1979, c. 373, p. 1377, § 302; Stats.1982, c. 904, p. 3336, § 2, eff. Sept. 13, 1982.)*

§ 2706.2. Continued medical certification; time of submission

Any continued medical certification shall be submitted to the department within 20 days of the date the claimant is issued a notice of final payment or departmental request for additional medical certification. The 20-day time limit shall be extended by the department upon a showing of good cause. *(Added by Stats.1991, c. 1134 (A.B.540), § 6.)*

§ 2707. Notice of filing of first claim

The department shall give a notice of the filing of a first claim for each disability benefit period to the employing unit by which the claimant was last employed immediately preceding the filing of such claim. *(Added by Stats.1953, c. 1371, p. 2946. Amended by Stats.1973, c. 1212, p. 2792, § 219, operative July 1, 1974; Stats.1979, c. 373, p. 1378, § 303.)*

§ 2707.1. Employer's furnishing of information which may bear upon claimant's eligibility

Within two working days after receipt of the notice provided for in Section 2707, or if there has been a termination of the claimant's service within five days after such termination, whichever is the later, the last employer shall notify the department of any information known to him which may bear upon the eligibility of the claimant. *(Added by Stats.1953, c. 1371, p. 2946. Amended by Stats.1973, c. 1212, p. 2798, § 221, operative July 1, 1974; Stats.1979, c. 373, p. 1378, § 304.)*

§ 2707.2. Consideration of facts submitted by employer; determination of eligibility; notice; right of appeal

The department shall consider the facts submitted by the employer pursuant to Section 2707.1 and make a determination as to the eligibility of the claimant for benefits. The department shall promptly notify the claimant of the determination and the reasons therefor. The claimant may appeal therefrom to an administrative law judge within 20 days from mailing or personal service of the notice of determination. The 20-day period may be extended for good cause. The director shall be an interested party to any appeal.

"Good cause," as used in this section, shall include, but not be limited to, mistake, inadvertence, surprise, or excusable neglect. *(Added by Stats.1953, c. 1371, p. 2946. Amended by Stats.1967, c. 1586, p. 3800, § 12; Stats.1973, c. 1212, p. 2798, § 223, operative July 1, 1974; Stats.1975, c. 979, p. 2303, § 5; Stats.1977, c. 1252, p. 4463, § 427, operative July 1, 1978; Stats.1984, c. 537, § 39.)*

§ 2707.3. Computation of claim; notice to claimant; exceptions

(a) Except as provided in subdivision (b) of this section, upon the filing of a claim for unemployment compensation disability benefits, the Employment Development Department shall promptly make a computation on the claim which shall set forth the maximum amount of benefits potentially payable during the disability benefit period and the weekly benefit amount. The Employment Development Department shall promptly notify the claimant of the computation.

(b) No computation shall be made on a claim of an employee for disability benefits under an approved self-insured plan if the uninterrupted period of disability for such claim does not exceed the waiting period prescribed for benefits from the Disability Fund under subdivision (b) of Section 2627. *(Added by Stats.1953, c. 1371, p. 2946. Amended by Stats.1961, c. 1760, p. 3765, § 1; Stats.1973, c. 1212, p. 2798, § 224, operative July 1, 1974; Stats.1974, c. 1159, p. 2472, § 32, eff. Sept. 23, 1974; Stats.1977, c. 1143, p. 3676, § 7.)*

§ 2707.4. Protest of computation time; determination; notice; appeal

The claimant may, within 20 days after the mailing or personal service of the notice of computation or recomputation, protest the accuracy of the computation or recomputation. The 20-day period may be extended for good cause. The department shall consider any such protest and shall promptly notify the claimant of the recomputation or denial of recomputation. The claimant may appeal from a notice of denial of recomputation in the manner prescribed in Section 2707.2. The director shall be an interested party to any appeal.

"Good cause," as used in this section, shall include, but not be limited to, mistake, inadvertence, surprise, or excusable neglect. *(Added by Stats.1953, c. 1371, p. 2946. Amended by Stats.1973, c. 1212, p. 2799, § 225, operative July 1, 1974; Stats.1974, c. 1159, p. 2473, § 33, eff. Sept. 23, 1974; Stats.1975, c. 843, p. 1907, § 2; Stats.1975, c. 979, p. 2304, § 6; Stats.1977, c. 1252, p. 4463, § 428, operative July 1, 1978.)*

§ 2707.5. Reconsideration of determination or computation; notice; appeal or protest

(a) The department may for good cause reconsider any determination provided for in this part prior to the filing of an appeal therefrom, or within 30 days after an appeal to an administrative law judge is filed. The department shall promptly notify the claimant of any reconsidered determination, and the claimant may appeal therefrom in the manner prescribed in Section 2707.2. The director shall be an interested party to any appeal.

(b) The department may for good cause reconsider any computation or recomputation provided for in this part within one year from the beginning date of the disability benefit period to which the notice of computation or recomputation relates, except that no recomputation may be considered with respect to any issue considered or under consideration in an appeal taken from a denial of recomputation. The department shall promptly notify the claimant of the recomputation. The claimant may protest the accuracy of the recomputation as prescribed in Section 2707.4. *(Added by Stats.1953, c. 1371, p. 2946. Amended by Stats.1973, c. 1212, p. 2799, § 227, operative July 1, 1974; Stats.1975, c. 843, p. 1908, § 4; Stats.1977, c. 1252, p. 4463, § 429, operative July 1, 1978; Stats.2002, c. 103 (A.B.1932), § 1; Stats.2003, c 797 (S.B.727), § 11, operative Jan. 1, 2004.)*

Operative Effect

For operative effect of Stats.2003, c. 797 (S.B. 727) upon benefits payable for family temporary disability insurance claims, see section 28 of that act.

§ 2707.6. Manner of submitting notices, protests and information

Notices, protests, and information required under this article shall be submitted in accordance with authorized regulations. *(Added by Stats.1953, c. 1371, p. 2946. Amended by Stats.1973, c. 1212, p. 2800, § 229, operative July 1, 1974; Stats.1974, c. 1159, p. 2473, § 34, eff. Sept. 23, 1974.)*

§ 2708. Establishing medical eligibility for uninterrupted period of disability; filing first and subsequent claims for disability benefits; medical certificate and contents; development of certification form; medical evidence

(a)(1) In accordance with the director's authorized regulations, and except as provided in subdivision (c) and Sections 2708.1 and 2709, a claimant shall establish medical eligibility for each uninterrupted period of disability by filing a first claim for disability benefits supported by the certificate of a treating physician or practitioner that establishes the sickness, injury, or pregnancy of the employee, or the condition of the family member that warrants the care of the employee. For subsequent periods of uninterrupted disability after the period covered by the initial certificate or any preceding continued claim, a claimant shall file a continued claim for those benefits supported by the certificate of a treating physician or practitioner. A certificate filed to establish medical eligibility for the employee's own sickness, injury, or pregnancy shall contain a diagnosis and diagnostic code prescribed in the International Classification of Diseases, or, where no diagnosis has yet been obtained, a detailed statement of symptoms.

(2) A certificate filed to establish medical eligibility of the employee's own sickness, injury, or pregnancy shall also contain a statement of medical facts including secondary diagnoses when applicable, within the physician's or practitioner's knowledge, based on a physical examination and a documented medical history of the claimant by the physician or practitioner, indicating the physician's or practitioner's conclusion as to the claimant's disability, and a statement of the physician's or practitioner's opinion as to the expected duration of the disability.

(b) An employee shall be required to file a certificate to establish eligibility when taking leave to care for a family member with a serious health condition. The certificate shall be developed by the department. In order to establish medical eligibility of the serious health condition of the family member that warrants the care of the employee, the information shall be within the physician's or practitioner's knowledge and shall be based on a physical examination and documented medical history of the family member and shall contain all of the following:

(1) A diagnosis and diagnostic code prescribed in the International Classification of Diseases, or, where no diagnosis has yet been obtained, a detailed statement of symptoms.

(2) The date, if known, on which the condition commenced.

(3) The probable duration of the condition.

(4) An estimate of the amount of time that the physician or practitioner believes the employee is needed to care for the child, parent, spouse, or domestic partner.

(5)(A) A statement that the serious health condition warrants the participation of the employee to provide care for his or her child, parent, spouse, or domestic partner.

(B) "Warrants the participation of the employee" includes, but is not limited to, providing psychological comfort, and arranging "third party" care for the child, parent, spouse, or domestic partner, as well as directly providing, or participating in, the medical care.

(c) The department shall develop a certification form for bonding that is separate and distinct from the certificate required in subdivision (a) for an employee taking leave to bond with a minor child within the first year of the child's birth or placement in connection with foster care or adoption.

(d) The first and any continuing claim of an individual who obtains care and treatment outside this state shall be supported by a certificate of a treating physician or practitioner duly licensed or certified by the state or foreign country in which the claimant is receiving the care and treatment. If a physician or practitioner licensed by and practicing in a foreign country is under investigation by the department for filing false claims and the department does not have legal remedies to conduct a criminal investigation or prosecution in that country, the department may suspend the processing of all further certifications until the physician or practitioner fully cooperates, and continues to cooperate with the investigation. A physician or practitioner licensed by and practicing in a foreign country who has been convicted of filing false claims with the department may not file a certificate in support of a claim for disability benefits for a period of five years.

(e) For purposes of this part:

(1) "Physician" has the same meaning as defined in Section 3209.3 of the Labor Code.

(2) "Practitioner" means a person duly licensed or certified in California acting within the scope of his or her license or certification who is a dentist, podiatrist, or as to normal pregnancy or childbirth, a midwife, nurse midwife, or nurse practitioner.

(f) For a claimant who is hospitalized in or under the authority of a county hospital in this state, a certificate of initial and continuing medical disability, if any, shall satisfy the requirements of this section if the disability is shown by the claimant's hospital chart, and the certificate is signed by the hospital's registrar. For a claimant hospitalized in or under the care of a medical facility of the United States government, a certificate of initial and continuing medical disability, if any, shall satisfy the requirements of this section if the disability is shown by the claimant's hospital chart, and the certificate is signed by a medical officer of the facility duly authorized to do so.

(g) Nothing in this section shall be construed to preclude the department from requesting additional medical evidence to supplement the first or any continued claim if the additional evidence can be procured without additional cost to the claimant. The department may require that the additional evidence include any or all of the following:

(1) Identification of diagnoses.

(2) Identification of symptoms.

(3) A statement setting forth the facts of the claimant's disability. The statement shall be completed by any of the following individuals:

(A) The physician or practitioner treating the claimant.

(B) The registrar, authorized medical officer, or other duly authorized official of the hospital or health facility treating the claimant.

(C) An examining physician or other representative of the department. *(Added by Stats.1991, c. 1134 (A.B.540), § 8. Amended by Stats.1993, c. 748 (S.B.4), § 10; Stats.*

1994, c. 967 (S.B.1584), § 7, eff. Sept. 28, 1994; Stats. 1998, c. 128 (A.B.2558), § 1; Stats.2002, c. 901 (S.B. 1661), § 4, operative Jan. 1, 2004; Stats.2003, c. 797 (S.B.727), § 12, operative Jan. 1, 2004.)

Operative Effect

For operative effect of Stats.2003, c. 797 (S.B. 727) upon benefits payable for family temporary disability insurance claims, see section 28 of that act.

§ 2708.1. Persons receiving temporary workers' compensation benefits; certificate of physician

(a) Except as provided in subdivision (b), where an individual is entitled to receive unemployment compensation disability benefits reduced by the amount of temporary workers' compensation received for any day under Section 2629, it shall not be necessary that he or she obtain a certificate of a physician as required by subdivision (a) of Section 2708 to receive the reduced amount of disability benefits for that day, provided that the claimant submits evidence to the department of receipt of temporary disability benefits under a workers' compensation law for that day.

(b) This section does not apply to Chapter 7 (commencing with Section 3300). *(Added by Stats.1959, c. 1196, p. 3285, § 1. Amended by Stats.1981, c. 714, p. 2791, § 432; Stats.2003, c. 797 (S.B.727), § 13, operative Jan. 1, 2004.)*

Operative Effect

For operative effect of Stats.2003, c. 797 (S.B. 727) upon benefits payable for family temporary disability insurance claims, see section 28 of that act.

§ 2709. Certificate of disability by authorized religious practitioners

If any individual in good faith adheres to the teachings of any bona fide church, sect, denomination or organization and in accordance with its principles depends for healing entirely upon prayer or spiritual means, no medical examination shall be required, but in lieu thereof the director may accept the certificate of a duly authorized and accredited practitioner of that bona fide church, sect, denomination or organization as to the disability of the claimant, or the serious health condition of the family member that warrants the care of the individual, for purposes of Chapter 7 (commencing with Section 3300) of Part 2, and the estimated duration of such disability, and no authorized regulation prescribing the manner of proof of illness, injury, or serious health condition shall discriminate against that individual. *(Stats.1953, c. 308, p. 1539, § 2709. Amended by Stats.2003, c. 797 (S.B.727), § 14, operative Jan. 1, 2004.)*

Operative Effect

For operative effect of Stats.2003, c. 797 (S.B. 727) upon benefits payable for family temporary

disability insurance claims, see section 28 of that act.

§ 2712. Settlement of disputed claims liability between disability fund and voluntary plans; prescribing rules and regulations; reimbursement of fund

Whenever an individual is entitled to benefits under this part but there is a dispute whether such benefits are payable from the Disability Fund or from one or another voluntary plan, benefits shall be paid to the individual, pursuant to authorized regulations, from the source against which his claim was first filed, at not less than the Disability Fund rate, pending the determination of the dispute. The appeals board may prescribe by regulation the time, manner, method, and procedure through which such disputes may be determined by administrative law judges and the appeals board. If it is finally determined that the benefits should have been paid from one of said sources other than the one which paid the benefits, reimbursement shall be promptly made from the Disability Fund or the voluntary plan, as the case may be, and the claimant shall be promptly paid the accumulated excess, if any, to which he is entitled. Reimbursement shall also be made to the extent of actual liability for benefits from one to another of the above mentioned sources when it is determined that benefits have been paid in error from one source which should have been paid from another. *(Stats.1953, c. 308, p. 1540, § 2712. Amended by Stats. 1984, c. 537, § 40.)*

§ 2712.5. Enforcement of reimbursement

(a) If, in a disputed coverage proceeding under Section 2712 a final decision of an administrative law judge or of the appeals board finds that an employer or insurer shall reimburse the Disability Fund and the employer or insurer fails to pay all or any part of the reimbursement within 15 days after the decision of an administrative law judge or of the appeals board becomes final, the director shall assess the unpaid amount against the employer or the insurer. The provisions of Article 8 (commencing with Section 1126) of Chapter 4 of Part 1 with respect to the assessment of contributions shall apply to the recovery of the unpaid amount. The provisions of Chapter 7 (commencing with Section 1701) of Part 1 with respect to the collection of contributions shall apply to the recovery of unpaid amounts under this section. Amounts so collected shall be deposited in the Disability Fund.

(b) The provisions of Article 9 (commencing with Section 1176) of Chapter 4 of Part 1 shall apply to amounts collected under this section and to amounts reimbursed to the Disability Fund after a final decision by an administrative law judge or the appeals board in a disputed coverage proceeding under Section 2712. *(Added by Stats.1969, c. 885, p. 1728, § 1. Amended by Stats.1984, c. 537, § 41; Stats.1987, c. 226, § 2.)*

§ 2713. Closed hearing

In proceedings under this part the claimant, upon a showing of good cause, may request a closed hearing except that the last employer and each base period employer of the claimant shall be entitled to participate in any such hearing. *(Stats.1953, c. 308, p. 1540, § 2713.)*

§ 2714. Confidentiality of medical records

All medical records of the department obtained under this part, except to the extent necessary for the proper administration of this part, or as provided elsewhere in law shall be confidential and shall not be published or be open to public inspection in any manner revealing the identity of the claimant or family member, or the nature or cause of his or her disability. Medical records that are disclosed shall be disclosed only pursuant to Section 1095, and shall remain confidential. *(Added by Stats.1983, c. 974, § 2, eff. Sept. 21, 1983, operative Jan. 1, 1986. Amended by Stats.1984, c. 1127, § 7; Stats.1985, c. 1331, § 2, operative Jan. 1, 1988; Stats.1987, c. 855, § 4; Stats.1992, c. 1352 (A.B.3660), § 10, eff. Sept. 30, 1992; Stats.1993, c. 120 (A.B.1300), § 10, eff. July 16, 1993; Stats.1998, c. 217 (A.B.2017), § 8; Stats.2003, c. 797 (S.B.727), § 15, operative Jan. 1, 2004.)*

Operative Effect

For operative effect of Stats.2003, c. 797 (S.B. 727) upon benefits payable for family temporary disability insurance claims, see section 28 of that act.

ARTICLE 5. OVERPAYMENTS

Section
2735.   Liability for amount overpaid.
2735.1. Overpayment due to false statement; assessment.
2735.5. Basis of claim for overpayment.
2736.   Determination of amount; notice of determination.
2737.   Appeal to administrative law judge; powers on appeal; notice of decision; appeal to appeals board.
2738.   Review by appeals board.
2739.   Recovery of overpayments.
2739.1. Abstract of judgment; recording; lien; execution.
2739.2. Acknowledgment of satisfaction of judgment.
2739.5. Franchise tax board; aid in recovery of overpayments.
2740.   Liability for benefits paid pursuant to decision on appeal.
2741.   Discharge of lien.
2742.   Enforcement of collection of judgment; deposit.

§ 2735. Liability for amount overpaid

Any person who is overpaid any amount as benefits under this part is liable for the amount overpaid unless:

(a) The overpayment was not due to fraud, misrepresentation or wilful nondisclosure on the part of the recipient, and

(b) The overpayment was received without fault on the part of the recipient, and its recovery would be against equity and good conscience. *(Added by Stats.1955, c. 1153, p. 2147, § 6.)*

§ 2735.1. Overpayment due to false statement; assessment

If the director finds that an individual has been overpaid unemployment compensation disability benefits because he or she willfully, for the purpose of obtaining unemployment compensation disability benefits, either made a false statement or representation, with actual knowledge of the falsity thereof, or withheld a material fact, the director shall assess against the individual an amount equal to 30 percent of the overpayment amount. For the purpose of collection, an assessment made pursuant to this section may be treated as an overpayment. Assessments collected under this section shall be deposited in the Unemployment Compensation Disability Fund. No penalty under this section shall be assessed with regard to any false statement or representation made prior to January 1, 1986. *(Added by Stats.1985, c. 1211, § 5.)*

§ 2735.5. Basis of claim for overpayment

No claim of overpayment shall be based upon the disallowance by the Workmen's Compensation Appeals Board of a claim of lien filed under Section 4903 of the Labor Code, or the allowance of such lien for less than the amount claimed, or upon the approval by the said appeals board of a compromise and release agreement providing for the allowance of such lien in an amount less than the claim. *(Added by Stats.1957, c. 1977, p. 3526, § 4. Amended by Stats.1961, c. 1837, p. 3916, § 1; Stats.1963, c. 310, p. 1088, § 1; Stats.1967, c. 1484, p. 3478, § 3.)*

§ 2736. Determination of amount; notice of determination

The Director of Employment Development shall determine the amount of the overpayment and shall notify the recipient of the basis of the overpayment determination. In the absence of fraud, misrepresentation or willful nondisclosure, notice of the overpayment determination shall be mailed to or personally served on the recipient within two years after the beginning of the disability benefit period for which the overpayment was made. *(Added by Stats.1955, c. 1153, p. 2148, § 6. Amended by Stats.1973, c. 1212, p. 2802, § 236, operative July 1, 1974.)*

§ 2737. Appeal to administrative law judge; powers on appeal; notice of decision; appeal to appeals board

Within 20 days from the date of mailing or serving of the notice of overpayment determination, the person affected may file an appeal to an administrative law judge. The director shall be an interested party to any such appeal. The administrative law judge, after affording reasonable opportunity for a fair hearing, shall unless the appeal is withdrawn, affirm, reverse, modify, or set aside the findings set forth in the notice of overpayment determination. The party and the director shall be notified of the administrative law judge's decision, together with his reasons therefor, which shall be final unless within 20 days from the date of notification or mailing of the decision a further appeal is initiated to the appeals board pursuant to Section 1336. The 20-day period for an appeal to the administrative law judge or to the appeals board may be extended for good cause.

"Good cause," as used in this section, shall include, but not be limited to, mistake, inadvertence, surprise, or excusable neglect. *(Added by Stats.1955, c. 1153, p. 2148, § 6. Amended by Stats.1967, c. 1586, p. 3801, § 13; Stats.1974, c. 503, p. 1179, § 7; Stats.1975, c. 979, p. 2304, § 7; Stats.1984, c. 537, § 42.)*

§ 2738.   Review by appeals board

The Appeals Board shall review an appeal from an overpayment determination as provided in Sections 1336 and 1337 and determine what amount, if any, shall be recovered. *(Added by Stats.1955, c. 1153, p. 2148, § 6. Amended by Stats.1965, c. 266, p. 1262, § 2.)*

§ 2739.   Recovery of overpayments

The Director of Employment Development, subject to this article, may do any or all of the following in the recovery of overpayments of disability benefits:

(a) File a civil action against the liable person for the recovery of the amount of the overpayment within one year after any of the following, or, in cases where the individual has been overpaid benefits due to fraud, misrepresentation, or nondisclosure as described in Section 2735.1, within three years of any of the following:

(1) The mailing or personal service of the notice of overpayment determination if the person affected does not file an appeal to an administrative law judge.

(2) The mailing of the decision of the administrative law judge if the person affected does not initiate a further appeal to the appeals board.

(3) The date of the decision of the appeals board.

(b) Initiate proceedings for a summary judgment against the liable person. However, this subdivision applies only where the director has found, pursuant to Section 2735, that the overpayment shall not be waived because it was due to fraud, misrepresentation, or willful nondisclosure on the part of the recipient. The director may, not later than three years after the overpayment became final, file with the clerk of the proper court in the county in which the claimant resides, a certificate containing all of the following:

(1) The amount due, including the assessment made under Section 2735.1, plus interest from the date that the initial determination of overpayment was made pursuant to Section 2735.

(2) A statement that the director has complied with all of the provisions of this article prior to the filing of the certificate.

(3) A request that judgment be entered against the liable person in the amount set forth in the certificate.

The clerk, immediately upon filing of the certificate, shall enter a judgment for the State of California against the liable person in the amount set forth in the certificate.

For purposes of this subdivision only, an overpayment is final and due and payable after one of the following:

(A) The liable person has not filed an appeal pursuant to Section 2737.

(B) The liable person has filed an appeal to an administrative law judge and a decision of the administrative law judge upholding the overpayment has become final.

(C) The liable person has filed an appeal to the appeals board and the decision of the appeals board upholding the overpayment has become final because the liable person has not sought judicial review within the six-month period provided by Section 410.

(c) Reduce or vacate a summary judgment by filing a certificate to that effect with the clerk of the proper court.

(d) Offset the amount of the overpayment received by the liable person against any amount of disability benefits to which he or she may become entitled under this division within six years of the date of mailing or personal service of the notice of overpayment determination. *(Added by Stats.1955, c. 1153, p. 2148, § 6. Amended by Stats.1965, c. 452, p. 1763, § 2; Stats.1973, c. 1212, p. 2803, § 237.5, operative July 1, 1974; Stats.1975, c. 890, p. 1970, § 2; Stats.1984, c. 537, § 43; Stats.1989, c. 1010, § 9; Stats.2008, c. 179 (S.B.1498), § 212.)*

§ 2739.1.   Abstract of judgment; recording; lien; execution

An abstract of judgment obtained pursuant to subdivision (a) or (b) of Section 2739, or a copy thereof, may be recorded with the county recorder of any county. From the time of recording, the judgment shall constitute a lien against all real or personal property of the liable person in that county owned by the liable person at the time, or which the liable person may afterwards, but before the lien expires, acquire. The lien shall have the force, effect, and priority of a judgment lien and shall continue for 10 years from the time of recording of the abstract of judgment obtained pursuant to subdivision (a) or (b) of Section 2739, unless sooner released or otherwise discharged.

The lien may, within 10 years from the date of recording of the abstract of judgment or within 10 years from the date of the last extension of the lien in the manner provided, be extended by recording a new abstract in the office of the county recorder of any county. From the date of the recording, the lien shall be extended for 10 years unless sooner released or otherwise discharged.

Execution shall issue upon the judgment upon request of the director in the same manner as execution may issue upon other judgments. Sales shall be held under the execution as prescribed in the Code of Civil Procedure. In all proceedings under this section, the director or his or her authorized agents may act on behalf of the state. *(Added by Stats.1989, c. 1010, § 10.)*

§ 2739.2. Acknowledgment of satisfaction of judgment

(a) If an abstract has been recorded as provided in Section 2739.1 and the lien, including any interest, costs, and penalty has been satisfied in full, the department shall, pursuant to Section 724.050 of the Code of Civil Procedure do all of the following:

(1) File an acknowledgment of satisfaction of judgment with the court.

(2) Serve an acknowledgment of satisfaction of judgment on the claimant. Service shall be made personally or by mail.

(3) Record an acknowledgment of satisfaction of judgment in the office of the county recorder where the abstract of judgment is recorded.

(b) If an acknowledgment of satisfaction of judgment is recorded, the cost of recording shall be an obligation of the claimant and may be collected from the claimant in any manner provided by law for the collection of the benefit overpayment.

(c) If payment is made by check, any action specified in subdivision (a) shall not be required until the check has been paid by the financial institution upon which it was drawn. *(Added by Stats.1989, c. 1010, § 11.)*

§ 2739.5. Franchise tax board; aid in recovery of overpayments

Notwithstanding any other provision of law to the contrary, the Franchise Tax Board shall aid the director in the recovery of overpayments of disability benefits through the exchange of information. *(Added by Stats. 1987, c. 226, § 3.)*

§ 2740. Liability for benefits paid pursuant to decision on appeal

No person shall be liable for the amount of benefits received where the benefits were paid pursuant to an administrative law judge's decision which affirmed an initial determination or in accordance with a final decision of the appeals board, regardless of any further appeal. *(Added by Stats.1955, c. 1153, p. 2148, § 6. Amended by Stats.1984, c. 537, § 44.)*

§ 2741. Discharge of lien

Any claim of lien filed with the Workmen's Compensation Appeals Board under the provisions of Section 4903 of the Labor Code shall be fully discharged and satisfied by payment of the amount of such lien allowed by the said appeals board under the provisions of Section 4904 of said code or the amount specified in any compromise and release agreement filed and approved by the said appeals board pursuant to Sections 5000 through 5004 of said code. *(Added Stats.1957, c. 1977, p. 3526, § 5. Amended by Stats.1961, c. 1837, p. 3916, § 2; Stats.1967, c. 1484, p. 3478, § 4.)*

§ 2742. Enforcement of collection of judgment; deposit

The director shall enforce collection of any judgment obtained by him or her under subdivision (a) or subdivision (b), or both, of Section 2739. Amounts collected under this section shall be deposited in the fund from which the overpayment was made. *(Added by Stats.1974, c. 1159, p. 2473, § 35, eff. Sept. 23, 1974. Amended by Stats.1977, c. 1252, p. 4464, § 431, operative July 1, 1978; Stats.1989, c. 1010, § 12.)*

ARTICLE 6. RIGHTS OF TRAINEES

Section
2765. Determination.
2766. Military service.
2767. Trainee.
2768. Unexpended balance of benefits; reestablishment; payment; lost records; claims; lapse.
2769. Establishment of benefit period.
2770. Disability base period.
2771. Disqualification for acts prior to military service.
2772. Disability suffered in military service; benefits; repayment.

§ 2765. Determination

Notwithstanding any inconsistent provisions of this part the benefit rights of trainees shall be determined in accordance with the provisions of this article for the periods and with respect to the matters specified in this article. Except as otherwise provided in this article all other provisions of this part shall continue to be applicable in connection with such benefits. *(Added by Stats. 1955, c. 1165, p. 2171, § 43.)*

§ 2766. Military service

"Military service" as used in this article means active service in the land or naval forces of the United States, but the service of an individual in any reserve component of the land or naval forces of the United States who is ordered to active duty in any such force for a period of 30 days or less shall not be deemed active service in that force during that period. *(Added by Stats.1955, c. 1165, p. 2171, § 43.)*

§ 2767. Trainee

"Trainee" as used in this article means an individual who entered military service after April 1, 1940, and who continued such service for not less than 90 consecutive days. *(Added by Stats.1955, c. 1165, p. 2172, § 43. Amended by Stats.1957, c. 1124, p. 2422, § 2; Stats.1959, c. 2156, p. 5212, § 7; Stats.1967, c. 1692, p. 4229, § 1.)*

§ 2768. Unexpended balance of benefits; reestablishment; payment; lost records; claims; lapse

When any trainee has an unexpired benefit year for disability benefits at the time of induction into the armed forces, the unexpended balance of disability benefits remaining to his account shall be reestablished beginning with the first day of the first week succeeding the date of his termination of service. The balance shall be paid at a weekly rate in accordance with Section 2655. In the event the records relating to the unexpended balance have been destroyed under proper approval, the trainee may establish the unexpended balance by affidavit as provided by authorized regulation. Whenever this balance is exhausted the trainee may file a claim and his disability base period shall be determined in accordance with Sections 2770 and 2610 or Section 2611. All reestablished balances shall lapse 65 weeks after termination of military service. *(Added by Stats.1955, c. 1165, p. 2172, § 43. Amended by Stats.1961, c. 2154, p. 4454, § 9; Stats.1969, c. 291, p. 651, § 8.)*

§ 2769. Establishment of benefit period

The filing of a valid claim for disability benefits by a trainee shall establish a disability benefit period. *(Added by Stats.1955, c. 1165, p. 2172, § 43.)*

§ 2770. Disability base period

Except when subdivision (b) of Section 2611 is applicable, in determining the benefit rights of trainees the disability base period shall exclude those quarters during which the trainee was in military service 60 days or more. For all quarters so excluded there shall be substituted an equal number of quarters immediately preceding the trainee's entry into military service. In the event the base period so determined includes wages in calendar quarters for which the records have been destroyed under proper approval, the claimant may establish the amount of the wages by affidavit in accordance with authorized regulation. The quarter of entry into military service shall be counted as a completed quarter if the director finds that the inclusion thereof would be more equitable to the trainee. *(Added by Stats.1955, c. 1165, p. 2172, § 43. Amended by Stats.1985, c. 1211, § 6.)*

§ 2771. Disqualification for acts prior to military service

No disqualification shall be applied to any trainee after the termination of his military service, by reason of any act or course of action on his part prior to the date of his entry into such service. *(Added by Stats.1955, c. 1165, p. 2172, § 43.)*

§ 2772. Disability suffered in military service; benefits; repayment

Notwithstanding any inconsistent provision of this part, any trainee who was a resident of this state at the time of his entrance into the military service, who is a resident of this state at the time he applies for disability compensation benefits under this section, and who has been disabled in the military service and is eligible to receive disability compensation from the federal government for such disability, shall be eligible, upon his discharge from the military service, to receive disability compensation benefits under Section 2655 from the time he is determined by the federal government to be eligible for disability compensation payments from the federal government until such time as he begins to receive his disability compensation payments from the federal government.

Such trainee's weekly benefit amount shall be the maximum amount specified in Section 2655 or the amount of the disability compensation which he is eligible to receive from the federal government, whichever is smaller.

Each trainee receiving any benefits pursuant to this section shall repay to the state the amount received as benefits hereunder. Each trainee, as a condition of receiving benefits hereunder, shall assign to the state the disability compensation which he is eligible to receive from the federal government to the extent that he receives benefits from the state pursuant to this section and shall enter into a contract with the director, in a form prescribed by the director, under which the trainee will be obligated to repay the state over a period of not more than one year following the date he first receives disability compensation from the federal government for his disability. Repayments made by such trainees shall be deposited by the director in the General Fund. *(Added by Stats.1968, c. 1449, p. 2859, § 1, eff. Aug. 22, 1968.)*

ARTICLE 7. RIGHTS OF INDUSTRIALLY DISABLED PERSONS

Section
2775. Application of article.
2776. Industrially disabled person and industrial disability defined.
2777. Base period computation.
2778. Disqualification for prior act or course of action.

§ 2775. Application of article

Notwithstanding any inconsistent provisions of this part, the benefit rights of industrially disabled persons shall be determined in accordance with the provisions of this article for the period and with respect to the matters specified in this article. Except as otherwise provided in this article, all of the provisions of this part shall continue to be applicable in connection with such benefits. *(Added by Stats.1973, c. 1027, p. 2043, § 1.)*

§ 2776. Industrially disabled person and industrial disability defined

As used in this article:

(a) "Industrially disabled person" means an individual who has received or is entitled to receive benefits under Division 4 (commencing with Section 3201) of the Labor Code, and who is unable to perform his regular or customary work for 60 consecutive days or more, but not to exceed two calendar years from the date of commencement of his industrial disability.

(b) "Industrial disability" means a disability compensable under Division 4 (commencing with Section 3201) of the Labor Code. *(Added by Stats.1973, c. 1027, p. 2043, § 1.)*

§ 2777. Base period computation

Except as provided in subdivision (b) of Section 2611, in determining the benefit rights of any industrially disabled person the disability base period shall exclude those quarters during which such person was industrially disabled for 60 days or more. For all quarters so excluded there shall be substituted an equal number of quarters immediately preceding the commencement of his or her industrial disability. In the event the base period so determined includes wages in calendar quarters for which the records have been destroyed under proper approval, a claimant may establish the amount of wages by affidavit in accordance with authorized regulations. The quarter of commencement of an industrial disability shall be counted as a completed quarter if the director finds that the inclusion thereof would be more equitable to the industrially disabled person. *(Added by Stats.1973, c. 1027, p. 2043, § 1. Amended by Stats.1985, c. 1211, § 7.)*

§ 2778. Disqualification for prior act or course of action

No disqualification shall be applied to any industrially disabled person after the termination of his industrial disability, by reason of any act or course of action on his part prior to the date on which his industrial disability commenced. *(Added by Stats.1973, c. 1027, p. 2043, § 1.)*

CHAPTER 2.4. NONINDUSTRIAL DISABILITY INSURANCE FOR STATE EMPLOYEES

Section
2781. Eligibility; construction of chapter.
2782. Provisions not applicable to this chapter.
2783. Payment of benefits; state payments to fund; reports from state agencies.

§ 2781. Eligibility; construction of chapter

Except as provided in this chapter and Chapter 2.5 [1] (commencing with Section 19878) of Part 2.6 of Division 5 of Title 2 of the Government Code, a state employee shall be eligible for nonindustrial disability benefits on the same terms and conditions as are specified by this part. Except as inconsistent with the provisions of this chapter and Chapter 2.6 [1] (commencing with Section 19878) of Part 2.6 of Division 5 of Title 2 of the Government Code, the provisions of this division and authorized regulations shall apply to any matter arising pursuant to this chapter. *(Added by Stats.1976, c. 341, p. 937, § 14, eff. July 7, 1976. Amended by Stats.2005, c. 152 (A.B.1577), § 26.)*

[1] So in enrolled bill. Probably should be Article 5 of Chapter 2.5.

§ 2782. Provisions not applicable to this chapter

(a) The provisions of Chapter 4 (commencing with Section 2901), Chapter 5 (commencing with Section 3001), and Chapter 6 (commencing with Section 3251) of Part 2 do not apply to this chapter.

(b) The provisions of Article 2 (commencing with Section 2652), Article 6 (commencing with Section 2765) and Article 7 (commencing with Section 2775) of Chapter 2 of Part 2 do not apply to this chapter.

(c) Sections 2609, 2610, 2611, 2625, 2712, and 2712.5 do not apply to this chapter. *(Added by Stats.1976, c. 341, p. 937, § 14, eff. July 7, 1976. Amended by Stats.1979, c. 373, p. 1378, § 305; Stats.1980, c. 1025, p. 3291, § 18.)*

§ 2783. Payment of benefits; state payments to fund; reports from state agencies

(a) Nonindustrial disability benefits are payable by the Controller upon authorization by the Employment Development Department to individuals who are eligible to receive such benefit payments under this chapter.

(b) In lieu of the contributions required of employees, the State of California shall pay into the Disability Fund in the State Treasury at the times and in the manner provided in subdivision (c), an amount equal to the additional cost to the Disability Fund for added administrative work arising out of nonindustrial disability insurance for state employees.

(c) In making the payments prescribed by subdivision (b), there shall be paid or credited to the Disability Fund, either in advance or by way of reimbursement, as may be determined by the director, such sums as he estimates the Disability Fund will be entitled to receive from the State of California under this section for each fiscal year, reduced or increased by any sum by which he finds that his estimates for any prior fiscal year were greater or less than the amounts which should have been paid to the fund. Such estimates may be made upon the basis of statistical sampling, or other method as may be determined by the director.

Upon making such determination, the director shall certify to the Controller the amount determined with respect to the State of California. The Controller shall pay to the Disability Fund the contributions due from the State of California.

(d) The director may require from each state agency such employment, wage, financial, statistical, or other information and reports, properly verified, as may be deemed necessary by the director to carry out his duties under this chapter, which shall be filed with the director at the time and in the manner prescribed by him.

(e) The director may tabulate and publish information obtained pursuant to this chapter in statistical form and may divulge the name of the employing unit.

(f) Each state agency shall keep such work records as may be prescribed by the director for the proper administration of this chapter. *(Added by Stats.1976, c. 341, p. 937, § 14, eff. July 7, 1976.)*

CHAPTER 3. ADDITIONAL BENEFITS [REPEALED]

CHAPTER 3.5. PRORATED BENEFITS [REPEALED]

CHAPTER 4. CONTRIBUTIONS

Section
2901. Worker contributions.

Section

2902. Exemption of individual on religious grounds; ineligibility for benefits.

2903. Time and method of payment.

§ 2901. Worker contributions

Each individual performing services for an employer in employment shall contribute to the Disability Fund the contributions required of such individual by Sections 984 and 985. *(Stats.1953, c. 308, p. 1542, § 2901. Amended by Stats.1961, c. 2153, p. 4449, § 18; Stats.1961, c. 2154, p. 4455, § 11.)*

§ 2902. Exemption of individual on religious grounds; ineligibility for benefits

Notwithstanding any other provision of this division, any individual who adheres to the faith or teaching of any bona fide religious sect, denomination, or organization, and in accordance with its creed, tenets, or principles, depends for healing upon prayer in the practice of religion, upon filing with the department and with each of his employers a statement declaring such adherence and dependence and disclaiming any benefits under this part, shall be exempt from contributions under this division in respect to any wages paid to him by any such employer in the calendar quarter in which such statement is filed, in all subsequent calendar quarters while such statement is in effect, and, if the individual so elects, in any prior calendar quarter for which wages are reported to the department on or after the date such statement is filed. Such individual shall be ineligible to receive benefits under this part based upon such wages. *(Stats.1953, c. 308, p. 1542, § 2902. Amended by Stats.1959, c. 1729, p. 4179, § 17; Stats.1973, c. 1212, p. 2803, § 238, operative July 1, 1974; Stats.1977, c. 1252, p. 4464, § 432, operative July 1, 1978.)*

§ 2903. Time and method of payment

The time, procedure, manner of payment and collection of contributions under this part shall be in accordance with the provisions of Part 1 of this division. *(Stats.1953, c. 308, p. 1542, § 2903.)*

CHAPTER 5. FINANCIAL PROVISIONS

Article   **Section**

1. Disability Fund 3001
2. Disability Administration Account 3051
3. Disability Benefit Payment Account 3075
4. Pregnancy Benefits [Repealed] ....
5. Investments in Buildings [Repealed] ....
6. Investments in Branch Office Buildings [Repealed] ....

ARTICLE 1. DISABILITY FUND

Section

3001. Disability fund as special fund; held in trust; administration of fund.

Section

3002. State treasurer as custodian of disability fund; bond; supervision of investments; election to come under provisions of surplus money investment fund.

3003. Investment of surplus money; interest or earnings.

3004. Content of disability fund.

3005. Deposit of receipts from federal government; money available under Title 3 of Social Security Act.

3006. Transfer of money from unemployment trust fund to disability fund.

3008. Collections to be deposited in disability fund.

3009. Payment of refunds, credits or judgments, and interest thereon.

3010. Unclaimed refunds; inclusion in account after three years; time limitation of claims or actions.

3011. Unclaimed warrants; reversion to account from which amount was payable.

3012. Continuous appropriation of money in fund; purpose; eligible person defined; unemployed disabled account.

3013. Availability of sum for administrative costs.

3014. Effect of withdrawals from fund.

3015. Occupation of space in buildings and facilities; priority; rental rates.

§ 3001. Disability fund as special fund; held in trust; administration of fund

(a) The Unemployment Compensation Disability Fund is continued in existence as a special fund in the State Treasury, separate and apart from all other public money or funds of this state. The moneys and assets of this fund shall be held in trust by the State Treasurer and administered under the direction of the director exclusively, for the purpose of this part.

(b) Notwithstanding any other law, the Controller may use the moneys in the Unemployment Compensation Disability Fund for loans to the General Fund as provided in Sections 16310 and 16381 of the Government Code. However, interest shall be paid on all moneys loaned to the General Fund from the Unemployment Compensation Disability Fund. Interest payable shall be computed at a rate determined by the Pooled Money Investment Board to be the current earning rate of the fund from which loaned. This subdivision does not authorize any transfer that will interfere with the carrying out of the object for which the Unemployment Compensation Disability Fund was created. *(Added by Stats.1953, c. 309, p. 1553. Amended by Stats.2009–2010, 3rd Ex. Sess., c. 9 (A.B.13), § 22, eff. Feb. 20, 2009.)*

§ 3002. State treasurer as custodian of disability fund; bond; supervision of investments; election to come under provisions of surplus money investment fund

The State Treasurer is the treasurer of the Disability Fund and shall have the custody of all money belonging to the Disability Fund and not otherwise held, deposited or invested under this part. The official bond of the State Treasurer shall cover the faithful performance of his or her duties as treasurer of the Disability Fund. The State Treasurer shall invest or otherwise deal with the Disability Fund under the supervision of the director.

The State Treasurer may, pursuant to Section 16470 of the Government Code, file with the Pooled Money Investment Board a notice of election that investment of surplus money in the Disability Fund shall come under the provisions of the Surplus Money Investment Fund, and may revoke such election pursuant to Section 16470 of the Government Code. As of the effective date of any election with respect to the Disability Fund filed pursuant to Section 16470 of the Government Code, the State Treasurer shall transfer the surplus money in the Disability Fund to the Surplus Money Investment Fund, and may transfer all or any portion of the investments held by the Disability Fund at the date of such election, from the Disability Fund to the Surplus Money Investment Fund. As of the effective date of the revocation of any such election, the State Treasurer shall transfer from the Surplus Money Investment Fund to the Disability Fund the surplus money and earnings attributable to the Disability Fund. *(Added by Stats.1953, c. 309, p. 1553. Amended by Stats.1969, c. 829, p. 1657, § 1; Stats.1975, c. 533, p. 1098, § 3; Stats.1980, c. 1025, p. 3291, § 19.)*

§ 3003. Investment of surplus money; interest or earnings

(a) Except as provided in subdivision (c), all surplus money in the Disability Fund may be invested solely in securities set forth in subdivision (b) of this section, and all interest or earnings therefrom shall be deposited in the Disability Fund.

(b) Eligible securities for the investment of surplus money shall be:

(1) Bonds or interest-bearing notes or obligations of the United States, or those for which the faith and credit of the United States are pledged for the payment of principal and interest.

(2) Bonds of this state, or those for which the faith and credit of this state are pledged for the payment of principal and interest.

(3) Bonds of any county, city, metropolitan water district, municipal utility district, or school district of this state.

(4) Bonds, consolidated bonds, collateral trust debentures, consolidated debentures, or other obligations issued by federal land banks or federal intermediate credit banks established under the Federal Farm Loan Act [1].

(5) Debentures and consolidated debentures issued by the Central Bank for Cooperatives and banks for cooperatives established under the Farm Credit Act of 1933 [2].

(6) Bonds or debentures of the Federal Home Loan Bank Board established under the Federal Home Loan Bank Act [3].

(7) Bonds of any federal home loan bank established under the Federal Home Loan Bank Act [4].

(8) Stock, bonds, debentures and other obligations of the Federal National Mortgage Association [5] established under the National Housing Act [6].

(9) Bonds, notes, and other obligations issued by the Tennessee Valley Authority under the Tennessee Valley Authority Act [7].

(c) This section shall not apply during the period of any election under Section 16470 of the Government Code for investment of surplus money in the Disability Fund under the provisions of the Surplus Money Investment Fund. *(Stats.1953, c. 309, p. 1553. Amended by Stats.1954, 1st Ex.Sess., c. 16, p. 264, § 2; Stats.1957, c. 60, p. 629, § 1; Stats.1961, c. 1688, p. 3663, § 2; Stats.1969, c. 829, p. 1657, § 2; Stats.1975, c. 533, p. 1099, § 4; Stats.1976, c. 1079, p. 4887, § 86; Stats.1980, c. 1025, p. 3292, § 20.)*

[1] 12 U.S.C.A. § 641 et seq. (repealed; see, now, 12 U.S.C.A. § 2001 et seq.).

[2] 12 U.S.C.A. § 1131 et seq. (repealed; see, now, 12 U.S.C.A. § 2001 et seq.).

[3] 12 U.S.C.A. § 1421 et seq.

[4] 12 U.S.C.A. § 1421 et seq.

[5] 12 U.S.C.A. § 1716 et seq.

[6] 12 U.S.C.A. § 1701 et seq.

[7] 16 U.S.C.A. §§ 831 to 831dd.

§ 3004. Content of disability fund

The Disability Fund consists of all contributions required of individuals under Section 984 with respect to wages paid by employers for employment; all money received for the purpose of disability benefits from the United States of America or any agency thereof, or from any other source; and any property or securities acquired through the use of money belonging to the Disability Fund and all earnings of such money or securities. *(Added by Stats.1953, c. 309, p. 1553. Amended by Stats.1959, c. 1729, p. 4179, § 18.)*

§ 3005. Deposit of receipts from federal government; money available under Title 3 of Social Security Act

All money received from the Federal Government for disability benefit purposes or for the administration of this part shall be deposited in the Disability Fund in accordance with the terms of the federal grant. Unless the Federal Government approves, no money made available to this State under Title 3 of the Social Security Act [1] shall be used for disability benefits or for the administration of this part. *(Added by Stats.1953, c. 309, p. 1553.)*

[1] 42 U.S.C.A. § 501 et seq.

§ 3006. Transfer of money from unemployment trust fund to disability fund

There shall be no further transfer of money from the Unemployment Trust Fund to the Disability Fund. *(Added by Stats.1953, c. 309, p. 1553. Amended by Stats.1961, c. 2154, p. 4455, § 12; Stats.1978, c. 397, p. 1260, § 8, eff. July 11, 1978.)*

§ 3008. Collections to be deposited in disability fund

All money collected under Section 984 shall be deposited in the Disability Fund. *(Added by Stats.1953, c. 309, p. 1553. Amended by Stats.1980, c. 1025, p. 3292, § 21.)*

§ 3009. Payment of refunds, credits or judgments, and interest thereon

Refunds, credits, or judgments, and interest thereon, payable for contributions erroneously collected under Sections 984 and 985 may be paid from the Disability Fund on warrants issued by the Controller under the direction of the director. *(Added by Stats.1953, c. 309, p. 1553. Amended by Stats.1970, c. 1356, p. 2521, § 4; Stats.1973, c. 1212, p. 2804, § 239, operative July 1, 1974; Stats.1977, c. 1252, p. 4464, § 433, operative July 1, 1978; Stats.1980, c. 1025, p. 3292, § 22.)*

§ 3010. Unclaimed refunds; inclusion in account after three years; time limitation of claims or actions

Any amounts determined by the director or his authorized representatives to be payable to employing units or workers as refunds of amounts deposited in the various accounts of the Disability Fund which are unclaimed at the end of three years from such determination, shall be included in the revenue to the account in the Disability Fund in which they were deposited. The employing unit or person entitled to such payment shall not thereafter maintain any claim, action or proceeding with respect to such amounts. *(Added by Stats.1953, c. 309, p. 1553. Amended by Stats.1973, c. 1212, p. 2804, § 240, operative July 1, 1974; Stats.1977, c. 1252, p. 4464, § 434, operative July 1, 1978.)*

§ 3011. Unclaimed warrants; reversion to account from which amount was payable

Whenever any warrant is drawn on an account in the Disability Fund by the State Controller, and the same remains unclaimed after three years, the amount thereof shall revert to that account in the Disability Fund from which the amount was payable. *(Added by Stats.1953, c. 309, p. 1553. Amended by Stats.1973, c. 1212, p. 2804, § 241, operative July 1, 1974.)*

§ 3012. Continuous appropriation of money in fund; purpose; eligible person defined; unemployed disabled account

(a) Notwithstanding Section 13340 of the Government Code, all money in the Disability Fund is continuously appropriated for the purpose of providing disability benefits pursuant to this part, including the payment of refunds, credits, or judgments, and interest thereon, the payment of disability benefits to all eligible persons not covered exclusively by an approved voluntary plan, and the payment of the expenses of administration of this part and Section 17061 of the Revenue and Taxation Code by the department and the Franchise Tax Board. "Eligible persons" as used in this section, means those individuals who are covered by the Disability Fund at the time his or her disability benefit period commences, or whose employment has terminated or who is in noncovered employment at the time his or her disability benefit period commences, and who is otherwise eligible for benefits under this part.

(b) For the purpose of keeping a record of the payments to and the disbursements from the Disability Fund with respect to the payment of benefits to persons whose employment has terminated or who are in noncovered employment at the time his or her disability period commences, the director shall maintain the Unemployed Disabled Account in the Disability Fund. This account shall be credited with 12 percent of the product obtained by multiplying the rate of worker contributions as determined in Section 984, by the amount of the taxable wages paid to employees covered by voluntary plans for disability benefits for each calendar year. This account shall also be credited with an amount equal to 12 percent of the product obtained by multiplying the rate of worker contributions, as determined in Section 984, by the amount of the taxable wages paid to employees covered by the Disability Fund for each calendar year. This account shall be charged each calendar year with disbursements from the Disability Fund for the payment of benefits and the additional administrative costs of the payment of benefits to persons whose employment has terminated or who are in noncovered employment at the time his or her disability benefit period commences. *(Added by Stats.1953, c. 309, p. 1553. Amended by Stats.1961, c. 2154, p. 4455, § 14; Stats.1967, c. 1484, p. 3478, § 5; Stats.1970, c. 1356, p. 2521, § 5; Stats.1973, c. 1206, p. 2621, § 63; Stats.1973, c. 1207, p. 2672, § 63; Stats.1973, c. 1212, p. 2805, § 243, operative July 1, 1974; Stats.1977, c. 1252, p. 4465, § 435, operative July 1, 1978; Stats.1978, c. 633, p. 2090, § 2, operative Jan. 1, 1979; Stats.1979, c. 1055, p. 3725, § 5, eff. Sept. 27, 1979; Stats.1980, c. 1308, p. 4425, § 2.5; Stats.1983, c. 203, § 2, eff. July 13, 1983; Stats.1984, c. 1642, § 2, eff. Sept. 30, 1984; Stats.1989, c. 600, § 5; Stats.2003, c. 797 (S.B.727), § 16, operative Jan. 1, 2004.)*

Operative Effect

For operative effect of Stats.2003, c. 797 (S.B. 727) upon benefits payable for family temporary disability insurance claims, see section 28 of that act.

§ 3013. Availability of sum for administrative costs

A sum to be determined by the Director of Finance, of amounts deposited in the disability fund, may be used for the necessary expenses of administration of this part and Sections 17061 and 17061.5 of the Revenue and Taxation Code in addition to any other fund or money available for such purpose. Such sum shall be available to the department for the payment of the expenses of administration of this part and Sections 17061 and 17061.5 of the Revenue and Taxation Code by the department and the Franchise Tax Board only to the extent that money received from the United States or any of its agencies is not available for such purposes. *(Added by Stats.1953, c.*

309, p. 1553. Amended by Stats.1973, c. 1212, p. 2806, §§ 244, 245, operative July 1, 1974; Stats.1977, c. 1252, p. 4465, § 436, operative July 1, 1978; Stats.1979, c. 1055, p. 3726, § 6, eff. Sept. 27, 1979.)

§ 3014. Effect of withdrawals from fund

Withdrawals by the director from the Disability Fund for the payment of refunds, credits, or judgments, and disability benefits are exempted from the operation of Section 925.6 of the Government Code. (Added by Stats.1953, c. 309, p. 1553. Amended by Stats.1959, c. 2156, p. 5212, § 9; Stats.1963, c. 2015, p. 4122, § 17; Stats.1970, c. 1356, p. 2521, § 6; Stats.1973, c. 1212, p. 2806, § 246, operative July 1, 1974; Stats.1977, c. 1252, p. 4465, § 437, operative July 1, 1978.)

§ 3015. Occupation of space in buildings and facilities; priority; rental rates

The department shall have priority to occupy any space in the buildings and facilities financed by the Disability Fund, which comprise any space in the department's central office building and related parking facilities in Sacramento and the department's branch office in Los Angeles, at rental rates not exceeding the cost of providing maintenance and other services. (Added by Stats.1980, c. 1025, p. 3292, § 23.)

ARTICLE 2. DISABILITY ADMINISTRATION ACCOUNT

Section
3051. Withdrawal from disability administration account to establish revolving fund; vouchers and itemized statements required.

§ 3051. Withdrawal from disability administration account to establish revolving fund; vouchers and itemized statements required

There is a Disability Administration Account within the Disability Fund. The director may, without at the time furnishing vouchers and itemized statements, withdraw from this account sums not to exceed in the aggregate an amount equal to three percent of the total disbursements made from the fund during the immediately preceding fiscal year to be used as a revolving fund where payment of compensation earned, traveling expense advances, or other cash payments are necessary. At the close of each fiscal year or at any other time, upon the demand of the Department of Finance, the money so drawn shall be accounted for and substantiated by vouchers and itemized statements submitted to and audited by the Controller. (Stats.1953, c. 308, p. 1544, § 3051. Amended by Stats.1977, c. 438, p. 4466, § 2; Stats.1980, c. 1025, p. 3293, § 24.)

ARTICLE 3. DISABILITY BENEFIT PAYMENT ACCOUNT

Section
3075. Withdrawals from disability fund; deposit of withdrawals; use of account.

§ 3075. Withdrawals from disability fund; deposit of withdrawals; use of account

The director shall, without presenting vouchers and itemized statements, withdraw from the Disability Fund any sums which he deems necessary for the payment of disability benefits for a reasonable future period. The Controller shall draw his warrant for any claim presented by the director for such payment and the Treasurer shall pay the warrant. Upon the withdrawal thereof, such sums shall be deposited in a disability benefit payment account in such bank or public depositary and under such conditions as the director determines, with the approval of the Department of Finance. Such bank or public depositary shall be one in which general funds of the state may be deposited, but no public deposit insurance charge or premium shall be paid out of such account. Money in this account shall be used solely to pay disability benefits by checks drawn on the account by the department pursuant to authorized regulations and no other disbursement shall be made from that account, except that amounts erroneously and illegally deposited in such account may be refunded. The procedure prescribed by such regulations shall satisfy and be in lieu of any and all statutory requirements of specific appropriation or other form of release by state officers of money in their custody prior to expenditure which might otherwise be applicable to withdrawals from such account. (Stats.1953, c. 308, p. 1545, § 3075. Amended by Stats.1965, c. 371, p. 1596, § 279; Stats.1974, c. 1221, p. 2653, § 44.)

ARTICLE 4. PREGNANCY BENEFITS [REPEALED]

ARTICLE 5. INVESTMENTS IN BUILDINGS [REPEALED]

ARTICLE 6. INVESTMENTS IN BRANCH OFFICE BUILDINGS [REPEALED]

CHAPTER 6. VOLUNTARY PLANS

Section
3251. Application for approval of voluntary plan; separate statement of benefits payable under voluntary plan.
3252. Exemption from contributions; payments for disability fund; return.
3253. Employee covered by approved voluntary plan not entitled to benefits of disability fund; exception; liability for payment of benefits.
3254. Requirements for approval of voluntary plans.
3254.5. Successor employing units; effect on voluntary plan.
3255. Voluntary plans for rotational workers; plan for payment of wages at central place; requirements for approval of plan.
3256. Pay roll deductions.
3257. Requirements for adoption of voluntary plan for all employees; withdrawal by employee.
3258. Security for uninsured plans; conditions and amount of bond; approval and deposit; receipt; responsibility of state treasurer.
3259. Insurer liable for voluntary plan assessments.

Section
3260. Assumption of cost of plan by employer.
3260.5. Employee contributions to plan; deduction from wages.
3261. Trust funds under approved voluntary plans; accounting.
3262. Termination of voluntary plan by Director; grounds; effective date of termination; remittance of interest to Disability Fund; notice; appeal.
3263. Eligibility for voluntary plan; rights of employer no longer covered by plan.
3264. Appeal to appeals board upon denial of liability; judicial review.
3265. Procedure upon failure of employer or insurer to pay employee.
3266. Determination by director of portion of aggregate amount of refunds to employees under § 1176 applicable to voluntary plans for which deductions made under § 3260.
3267. Reports and information to department.
3268. Furnishing of information by director of employment development.
3269. Expenditures for added administrative work; annual determination.
3270. Reinstatement of provisions dealing with selection of risks.
3271. Amendments; approval; regulations.
3272. Refunds and overpayments.

§ 3251. Application for approval of voluntary plan; separate statement of benefits payable under voluntary plan

An employer, a majority of the employees employed in this state of an employer, or both, may apply to the Director of Employment Development for approval of a voluntary plan for the payment of disability benefits to the employees so electing. The benefits payable as indemnification for loss of wages under any voluntary plan shall be separately stated and designated in the plan "unemployment compensation disability benefits" separate and distinct from other benefits, if any. *(Stats.1953, c. 308, p. 1548, § 3251. Amended by Stats.1973, c. 1212, p. 2811, § 268, operative July 1, 1974.)*

§ 3252. Exemption from contributions; payments for disability fund; return

(a) Except as provided by subdivision (b) of this section, neither an employee nor his or her employer shall be liable for the worker contributions required under this division with respect to wages paid by the employer while the employee is covered by an approved voluntary plan.

(b) Each voluntary plan shall pay to the department for the Disability Fund 14 percent of the product obtained by multiplying the rate of worker contributions, as determined in Section 984, by the amount of the taxable wages paid to employees covered by the voluntary plan for disability benefit coverage for each calendar year. Such payments shall not constitute a part of the voluntary plan premium for purposes of any tax under any provision of law. Payments under this section shall be deposited in the Disability Fund.

(c) The payments made under subdivision (b) of this section in excess of the credit to the unemployed disabled account made pursuant to Section 3012 shall reimburse the Disability Fund for the amounts paid for administrative costs arising out of voluntary plans as determined pursuant to Section 3269, and the aggregate amount paid as refunds and credits made to employees applicable to voluntary plans pursuant to Section 1176 as determined pursuant to Section 3266.

(d) Each voluntary plan shall file with the director within the time required for payments under subdivision (e) of this section, a return containing the employer's business name, address, and account number, and such other information as the director shall prescribe. The director shall prescribe the form for the return.

(e) Payments required under this section are due and payable on the first day of the calendar month following the close of each calendar quarter and shall become delinquent if not paid on or before the last day of such month.

(f) The provisions of Article 8 (commencing with Section 1126) of Chapter 4 of Part 1 of this division with respect to the assessment of contributions and the provisions of Chapter 7 (commencing with Section 1701) of Part 1 of this division with respect to the collection of contributions shall apply to payments required by this section.

(g) Whenever the director believes that a change in the percentage rate of payment specified in subdivision (b) may be necessary, he or she shall inform the Governor and the Legislature thereof and make recommendations accordingly. *(Stats.1953, c. 308, p. 1548, § 3252. Amended by Stats.1961, c. 2154, p. 4456, § 16, operative Jan. 1, 1962; Stats.1967, c. 1484, p. 3479, § 6; Stats.1973, c. 1212, p. 2811, § 269, operative July 1, 1974; Stats.1977, c. 1252, p. 4467, § 443, operative July 1, 1978; Stats.1978, c. 633, p. 2090, § 3, operative Jan. 1, 1979; Stats.1980, c. 1308, p. 4426, § 3.)*

§ 3253. Employee covered by approved voluntary plan not entitled to benefits of disability fund; exception; liability for payment of benefits

Except as provided in this part, an employee covered by an approved voluntary plan at the commencement of a disability benefit period shall not be entitled to benefits from the Disability Fund. Benefits payable to that employee shall be the liability of the approved voluntary plan under which the employee was covered at the commencement of the disability benefit period, regardless of any subsequent disabling condition which may occur during that disability benefit period. The Director of Employment Development shall prescribe authorized regulations to allow benefits to individuals simultaneously covered by one or more approved voluntary plans and the Disability Fund. *(Stats.1953, c. 308, p. 1548, § 3253. Amended by Stats.1961, c. 2153, p. 4449, § 19; Stats.1973, c. 1212, p. 2812, § 271, operative July 1, 1974; Stats.1989,*

c. 1280, § 6; Stats.2003, c. 797 (S.B.727), § 17, operative Jan. 1, 2004.)

Operative Effect

For operative effect of Stats.2003, c. 797 (S.B. 727) upon benefits payable for family temporary disability insurance claims, see section 28 of that act.

§ 3254. Requirements for approval of voluntary plans

The Director of Employment Development shall approve any voluntary plan, except one filed pursuant to Section 3255, as to which he or she finds that there is at least one employee in employment and all of the following exist:

(a) The rights afforded to the covered employees are greater than those provided for in Chapter 2 (commencing with Section 2625), including those provided for in Chapter 7 (commencing with Section 3300).

(b) The plan has been made available to all of the employees of the employer employed in this state or to all employees at any one distinct, separate establishment maintained by the employer in this state. "Employees" as used in this subdivision includes those individuals in partial or other forms of short-time employment and employees not in employment as the Director of Employment Development shall prescribe by authorized regulations.

(c) A majority of the employees of the employer employed in this state or a majority of the employees employed at any one distinct, separate establishment maintained by the employer in this state have consented to the plan.

(d) If the plan provides for insurance the form of the insurance policies to be issued have been approved by the Insurance Commissioner and are to be issued by an admitted disability insurer.

(e) The employer has consented to the plan and has agreed to make the payroll deductions required, if any, and transmit the proceeds to the plan insurer, if any.

(f) The plan provides for the inclusion of future employees.

(g) The plan will be in effect for a period of not less than one year and, thereafter, continuously unless the Director of Employment Development finds that the employer or a majority of its employees employed in this state covered by the plan have given notice of withdrawal from the plan. The notice shall be filed in writing with the Director of Employment Development and shall be effective only on the anniversary of the effective date of the plan next following the filing of the notice, but in any event not less than 30 days from the time of the filing of the notice; except that the plan may be withdrawn on the operative date of any law increasing the benefit amounts provided by Sections 2653 and 2655 or the operative date of any change in the rate of worker contributions as determined by Section 984, if notice of the withdrawal

1054

from the plan is transmitted to the Director of Employment Development not less than 30 days prior to the operative date of that law or change. If the plan is not withdrawn on the 30 days' notice because of the enactment of a law increasing benefits or because of a change in the rate of worker contributions as determined by Section 984, the plan shall be amended to conform to that increase or change on the operative date of the increase or change.

(h) The amount of deductions from the wages of an employee in effect for any plan shall not be increased on other than an anniversary of the effective date of the plan except to the extent that any increase in the deductions from the wages of an employee allowed by Section 3260 permits that amount to exceed the amount of deductions in effect.

(i) The approval of the plan or plans will not result in a substantial selection of risks adverse to the Disability Fund. *(Stats.1953, c. 308, p. 1548, § 3254. Amended by Stats.1959, c. 1729, p. 4179, § 19; Stats.1961, c. 1905, p. 4017, § 1, operative Jan. 1, 1962; Stats.1973, c. 1212, p. 2813, § 273, operative July 1, 1974; Stats.1977, c. 1143, p. 3677, § 11; Stats.1980, c. 1308, p. 4427, § 4; Stats.2002, c. 52 (S.B.467), § 2; Stats.2002, c. 901 (S.B.1661), § 5, operative Jan. 1, 2004; Stats.2003, c. 797 (S.B.727), § 18, operative Jan. 1, 2004.)*

Operative Effect

For operative effect of Stats.2003, c. 797 (S.B. 727) upon benefits payable for family temporary disability insurance claims, see section 28 of that act.

§ 3254.5. Successor employing units; effect on voluntary plan

A voluntary plan in force and effect at the time a successor employing unit acquires the organization, trade, or business, or substantially all the assets thereof, or a distinct and severable portion of the organization, trade, or business, and continues its operation without substantial reduction of personnel resulting from the acquisition, shall not withdraw without specific request for withdrawal thereof. The successor employing unit and the insurer shall be deemed to have consented to the provisions of the plan unless written request for withdrawal, effective as of the date of acquisition, is transmitted to the Director of Employment Development, by the employer or the insurer, within 30 days after the acquisition date, or within 30 days after notification from the Director of Employment Development that the plan is to continue, whichever is later. Unless the plan is withdrawn as of the date of acquisition by the successor employer or the insurer, a written request for withdrawal shall be effective only on the anniversary of the effective date of the plan next occurring on or after the date of acquisition, except that the plan may be withdrawn on the operative date of any law increasing the benefit amounts provided by Sections 2653 and 2655 or the operative date of any change in the rate of worker contributions as determined by Section 984, if notice of the withdrawal of the plan is transmitted to the Director of Employment Development not less than 30 days prior to the operative date of law or change. If the plan is not withdrawn on 30 days' notice because of the enactment of a law increasing benefits or because of a change in the rate of worker contributions as determined by Section 984, the plan shall be amended to conform to the increase or change on the operative date of the increase or change. Promptly, upon notice of change in ownership, any insurer of a plan shall prepare and issue policy forms and amendments as required, unless the plan is withdrawn. Nothing contained in this section shall prevent future withdrawal of any plans on an anniversary of the effective date of the plan upon 30 days' notice, except that the plan may be withdrawn on the operative date of any law increasing the benefit amounts provided by Sections 2653 and 2655 or the operative date of any change in the rate of worker contributions as determined by Section 984, if notice of the withdrawal of the plan is transmitted to the Director of Employment Development not less than 30 days prior to the operative date of the law or change. If the plan is not withdrawn on 30 days' notice because of the enactment of a law increasing benefits or because of a change in the rate of worker contributions as determined by Section 984, the plan shall be amended to conform to the increase or change on the operative date of the increase or change. *(Added by Stats.1957, c. 2107, p. 3735, § 9, operative Jan. 1, 1958. Amended by Stats.1961, c. 1905, p. 4018, § 2; Stats.1963, c. 1864, p. 3848, § 1.5; Stats.1973, c. 1212, p. 2815, § 275, operative July 1, 1974; Stats.1977, c. 1143, p. 3678, § 12; Stats.1980, c. 1308, p. 4428, § 5; Stats.2005, c. 152 (A.B.1577), § 27, Stats.2006, c. 538 (S.B.1852), § 647.)*

§ 3255. Voluntary plans for rotational workers; plan for payment of wages at central place; requirements for approval of plan

When workers are engaged in an employment that normally involves working for several employers in the same industry interchangeably, and several employers or some of them cooperate to establish a plan for the payment of wages at a central place or places, and have appointed an agent under Section 1096, that agent, or a majority of workers regularly paid through a central place or places, or both, may apply to the Director of Employment Development for approval of a voluntary plan for the payment of disability benefits applicable to all employees whose wages are paid at one or more central place or places. The Director of Employment Development shall approve any voluntary plan under this section as to which he or she finds that all of the following exist:

(a) The rights afforded to the covered employees are greater than those provided for in Chapter 2 (commencing with Section 2625) of this part, and are separately stated and designated "unemployment compensation disability benefits" separate and distinct from other benefits, if any.

(b) The plan applies to all employees whose wages are paid at a central place or places with respect to all employment for which wages are paid at central place or places.

(c) Seventy-five percent of the workers regularly paid at the central place or places have consented to the plan prior to the filing of the initial application for approval.

(d) If the plan provides for insurance the form of the insurance policies to be issued have been approved by the Insurance Commissioner and are to be issued by an admitted disability insurer.

(e) All employers paying wages through the central place or places have agreed to participate in the plan and the agent appointed under Section 1096 has agreed to make the payroll deductions required, if any, and transmit the proceeds to the plan insurer, if any.

(f) The plan provides for the inclusion of all future employees paid at the central place or places.

(g) The plan is to be in effect for a period of not less than one year and, thereafter, continuously unless the Director of Employment Development finds that the agent or a majority of the employees regularly paid at the central place or places has given written notice of withdrawal from the plan. The notice shall be filed in writing with the Director of Employment Development at least 30 days before it is to become effective and, upon the filing, will be effective only as to wages paid after the beginning of the calendar quarter next occurring on or after the anniversary of the effective date of the plan; except that the plan may be withdrawn on the operative date of any law increasing the benefit amounts provided by Sections 2653 and 2655 or the operative date of any change in the rate of worker contributions as determined by Section 984, if notice of the withdrawal from the plan is transmitted to the Director of Employment Development not less than 30 days prior to the operative date of that law or change. If the plan is not withdrawn on 30 days' notice because of the enactment of a law increasing benefits or because of a change in the rate of worker contributions as determined by Section 984, the plan shall be amended to conform to that increase or change on the operative date of the increase or change.

(h) The amount of deductions from the wages of an employee in effect for any plan shall not be increased on other than an anniversary of the effective date of the plan except to the extent that any increase in the deductions from the wages of an employee allowed by Section 3260 permits that amount to exceed the amount of deductions in effect.

(i) The approval of the plan or plans will not result in a substantial selection of risks adverse to the Disability Fund. *(Stats.1953, c. 308, p. 1549, § 3255. Amended by Stats.1961, c. 1905, p. 4019, § 3, operative Jan. 1, 1962; Stats.1969, c. 291, p. 651, § 10; Stats.1973, c. 1212, p. 2817, § 277, operative July 1, 1974; Stats.1977, c. 1143, p. 3678, § 13; Stats.1980, c. 1308, p. 4429, § 6; Stats.2002, c. 52 (S.B.467), § 3.)*

§ 3256. Pay roll deductions

During the effective period of a plan approved under Section 3255 the employer, or his agent appointed under Section 1096, may make the pay roll deductions provided for by the plan, with respect to all employment covered by the plan. *(Stats.1953, c. 308, p. 1550, § 3256.)*

§ 3257. Requirements for adoption of voluntary plan for all employees; withdrawal by employee

Whenever eighty-five percent (85%) of the employees to whom a plan is available have consented to the plan, the employer, or seventy-five percent (75%) of the employees who have consented to the plan, or both, may elect to make the plan applicable to all employees to whom it is available, except those who reject the plan. In such case, there shall be filed with the Director of Employment Development a notice stating that the requisite percentage of employees has consented to the plan and fixing the date upon which the plan will become applicable to all employees to whom it is available. At least 10 days before the date fixed in the notice, a notice shall be posted and circulated in a manner reasonably calculated to bring it to the attention of all employees to whom the plan is available but who have not consented thereto. The notice to such employees shall set forth the date the plan is to become applicable and the manner in which an employee may reject it.

From the time fixed in the notice filed with the Director of Employment Development all employees to whom the plan is available shall be deemed to have elected to be covered by the plan, except those who advise the employer in writing of their rejection within the time fixed.

Every person employed after the date the plan becomes applicable and to whom the plan is available, shall be deemed to have elected to be covered by the plan from the time of employment unless he rejects the plan prior to or at the time of employment. Each employee at the time of employment shall be given a written notice specifying his right to consent to or to reject such plan and a written statement setting forth the essential features of the plan.

Any employee covered by a plan may withdraw from the plan as of the beginning of any calendar quarter upon giving reasonable notice in writing directed to the employer.

The form of the statement and the forms of the notices required under this Section shall be approved by the Director of Employment Development. *(Stats.1953, c. 308, p. 1550, § 3257. Amended by Stats.1973, c. 1212, p. 2819, § 279, operative July 1, 1974.)*

§ 3258. Security for uninsured plans; conditions and amount of bond; approval and deposit; receipt; responsibility of state treasurer

If a voluntary plan does not provide for the assumption by an admitted disability insurer of the liability of the employer to pay the benefits afforded by the plan, the

director shall not approve it unless the employer files with the director the bond of an admitted surety insurer conditioned on the payment by the employer of its obligations under the plan, deposits with the director securities approved by the director to secure the payment of the obligations, or deposits with the director an irrevocable letter of credit. The penal sum of the bond or the amount of the deposit of securities or letter of credit shall be determined by the director and shall be not less than the product obtained by multiplying the rate of worker contributions in the ensuing year, as determined in Section 984, by 0.5 of the estimated taxable wages prescribed by Section 985 to be paid to the employees for the ensuing year. Upon approval, the bond, money, or securities shall upon the director's written order be deposited with the Treasurer for the purpose specified in this section. The Treasurer shall give a receipt for the deposits and the state shall be responsible for the custody and safe return of any securities so deposited. *(Stats. 1953, c. 308, p. 1550, § 3258. Amended by Stats.1971, c. 786, p. 1539, § 1; Stats.1973, c. 1212, p. 2820, § 281, operative July 1, 1974; Stats.1981, c. 793, p. 3084, § 2; Stats.1994, c. 960 (A.B.3320), § 3.)*

§ 3259. Insurer liable for voluntary plan assessments

Whenever an approved voluntary plan is insured by an admitted disability insurer, the insurer shall be substituted for the employer with respect to any assessments under this part which relate to the portion of the voluntary plan insured by such insurer. *(Stats.1953, c. 308, p. 1551, § 3259.)*

§ 3260. Assumption of cost of plan by employer

An employer may, but need not, assume all or part of the cost of the plan, and may deduct from the wages of an employee covered by the plan, for the purpose of providing the disability benefits specified in this part, an amount not in excess of that which would be required by Sections 984 and 985 if the employee were not covered by the plan. *(Stats.1953, c. 308, p. 1551, § 3260. Amended by Stats.1957, c. 2107, p. 3736, § 10; Stats.1959, c. 2156, p. 5212, § 10; Stats.1961, c. 2154, p. 4456, § 17; Stats.1965, c. 745, p. 2156, § 8, eff. June 24, 1965; Stats.1967, c. 1725, p. 4299, § 8; Stats.1971, c. 786, p. 3259, § 2; Stats.1973, c. 1212, p. 2821, § 283, operative July 1, 1974; Stats.1977, c. 1252, p. 4468, § 444, operative July 1, 1978; Stats.1980, c. 1308, p. 4430, § 7; Stats.2002, c. 52 (S.B.467), § 4.)*

§ 3260.5. Employee contributions to plan; deduction from wages

(a) All deductions from the wages of an employee remaining in the possession of the employer upon its voluntary withdrawal of the plan as a result of plan contributions being in excess of plan costs, that are not disposed of in conformity with authorized regulations of the Director of Employment Development, shall be remitted to the department and deposited in the Disability Fund. If an employer fails to remit any deductions to the Disability Fund, the Director of Employment Development shall assess the amount thereof against the employer.

(b) The provisions of Article 8 (commencing with Section 1126) of Chapter 4 of Part 1, with respect to the assessment of contributions, and the provisions of Chapter 7 (commencing with Section 1701) of Part 1, with respect to the collection of contributions, shall apply to assessments provided by this section, except that interest may not accrue until 30 days after issuance of the notice of assessment.

(c) With respect to individuals covered by a voluntary plan on January 1 of any calendar year for which the limitation on wages under Section 985 is increased or the tax rate under Section 984 is increased, the amount of the deduction on or after that date may be increased to apply to not more than the maximum limitation on taxable wages or to not more than the maximum tax rate, as applicable, without any further consent of the individual or approval of the Director of Employment Development, but only if such increase in the amount of the deductions is made effective as of January 1 of the affected calendar year. *(Added by Stats.2002, c. 52 (S.B.467), § 5.)*

§ 3261. Trust funds under approved voluntary plans; accounting

All employee contributions and income arising therefrom received or retained by an employer under an approved voluntary plan are trust funds that are not considered to be part of an employer's assets. An employer shall either maintain a separate, specifically identifiable account for voluntary plan trust funds in a financial institution, or an employer may transmit voluntary plan trust funds, including any earned interest or income, directly to the admitted disability insurer. If an employer, with prior approval from the Director of Employment Development, invests voluntary plan trust funds in securities purchased through a commercial bank under Article 4 of Chapter 10 of Division 1 of the Financial Code, the securities account shall be separately identifiable from any other securities accounts maintained by the employer. In the event of commingling of voluntary plan trust funds, or the bankruptcy or insolvency of the employer, or the appointment of a receiver for the business of the employer, those voluntary plan trust funds are entitled to the same preference as are the claims of the state under Sections 1701 and 1702. *(Stats.1953, c. 308, p. 1551, § 3261. Amended by Stats. 2002, c. 52 (S.B.467), § 6.)*

§ 3262. Termination of voluntary plan by Director; grounds; effective date of termination; remittance of interest to Disability Fund; notice; appeal

(a) The Director of Employment Development may terminate any voluntary plan if the director finds that there is danger that the benefits accrued or to accrue will not be paid, that the security for the payment is insufficient, or for other good cause shown. The Director of Employment Development shall give notice of his or her intention to terminate a plan to the employer, employee group, and insurer. The notice shall state the effective date and the reason for the withdrawal. The Director of Employment Development may change or stay the effective date of the termination.

(b) Notwithstanding Section 3260.5, on the effective date of the termination of a plan by the Director of Employment Development, all moneys in the plan, including moneys paid by the employer, moneys paid by the employee, moneys owed to the voluntary plan by the employer but not yet paid to the plan, and any interest accrued on all these moneys, shall be remitted to the department and deposited into the Disability Fund.

(c) If an employer fails to remit all moneys owed to the Disability Fund after termination of the plan, the Director of Employment Development shall make an assessment against the employer equal to the amount of the moneys owed. The Director of Employment Development shall also make an assessment against the employer for all benefits paid from the Disability Fund after the termination of the plan, less any moneys received from the employer after the termination of the plan.

(d) The provisions of Article 8 (commencing with Section 1126) of Chapter 4 of Part 1, with respect to the assessment of moneys, and the provisions of Chapter 7 (commencing with Section 1701) of Part 1, with respect to the collection of moneys owed, shall apply to assessments authorized under this section, except that interest may not accrue until 30 days after issuance of the notice of assessment.

(e) The employer, employee group or insurer may, within 10 days from mailing or personal service of the notice, appeal to the Appeals Board. The 10–day period may be extended for good cause. The Appeals Board may prescribe by regulation the time, manner, method and procedure through which it may determine appeals under this section.

(f) The payment of benefits from the Disability Fund and the transfer of moneys in the voluntary plan may not be delayed during an employer's appeal of the termination of a voluntary plan. *(Stats.1953, c. 308, p. 1551, § 3262. Amended by Stats.1957, c. 1181, p. 2472, § 1; Stats.1973, c. 1212, p. 2822, § 285, operative July 1, 1974; Stats.2002, c. 52 (S.B.467), § 7.)*

§ 3263. Eligibility for voluntary plan; rights of employer no longer covered by plan

(a) An employee is no longer covered by an approved voluntary plan if a disability arose after the employment relationship with the voluntary plan employer ends, or if the Director of Employment Development terminates a voluntary plan in accordance with Section 3262.

(b) An employee who has ceased to be covered by an approved voluntary plan shall, if otherwise eligible, thereupon immediately become entitled to benefits from the Disability Fund to the same extent as though there had been no exemption from contributions as provided in this chapter. *(Stats.1953, c. 308, p. 1551, § 3263. Amended by Stats.1953, c. 1371, p. 2946; Stats.2002, c. 52 (S.B.467), § 8.)*

§ 3264. Appeal to appeals board upon denial of liability; judicial review

If any employer or insurer wholly or partially denies liability upon the claim of an employee for disability benefits under an approved plan, the employee may appeal the denial in the manner provided by law and authorized regulations for an appeal on a claim for benefits payable out of the Disability Fund. All decisions of the Appeals Board denying benefits under this section shall be subject to review by the courts of this State by the exclusive remedy of filing a petition for writ of mandate. No such petition may be filed, however, until the employee exhausts the administrative remedies provided for in this division, nor may any other action be commenced by an employee upon a denial of his claim by his employer or insurer, as the case may be, other than that prescribed herein. *(Stats.1953, c. 308, p. 1551, § 3264.)*

§ 3265. Procedure upon failure of employer or insurer to pay employee

(a) If, on appeal, it is decided that an employee is entitled to receive disability benefits under an approved voluntary plan and the employer or insurer fails to pay the same within 15 days after notice of a decision by an administrative law judge or the appeals board, the director shall pay such benefits and shall assess the amount thereof against the employer or the insurer, and the provisions of Article 8 (commencing with Section 1126) of Chapter 4 of Part 1 of this division with respect to the assessment of contributions and the provisions of Chapter 7 (commencing with Section 1701) of Part 1 of this division with respect to the collection of contributions shall apply to the recovery of such benefit payments. Amounts so collected shall be deposited in the Disability Fund.

(b) If an approved voluntary plan is not terminated because of the enactment of any law increasing the benefit amounts provided by Sections 2653 and 2655, and the employer or insurer fails to pay such increase under the plan, the director shall pay such benefits to an employee, if otherwise eligible, and shall assess the amount thereof against the employer or the insurer and the provisions of Article 8 (commencing with Section 1126) of Chapter 4 of Part 1 of this division with respect to the assessment of contributions and the provisions of Chapter 7 (commencing with Section 1701) of Part 1 of this division with respect to the collection of contributions shall apply to the recovery of such benefit payments. Amounts so collected shall be deposited in the Disability Fund. *(Stats.1953, c. 308, p. 1552, § 3265. Amended by Stats.1961, c. 1905, p. 4020, § 4, operative Jan. 1, 1962; Stats.1967, c. 1725, p. 4300, § 9; Stats.1973, c. 1212, p. 2823, § 286.5, operative July 1, 1974; Stats.1977, c. 1252, p. 4468, § 445, operative July 1, 1978; Stats.1977, c. 1143, p. 3680, § 14; Stats.1978, c. 429, p. 1433, § 172, eff. July 17, 1978, operative Jan. 1, 1979; Stats.1984, c. 537, § 45.)*

1058

§ 3266. Determination by director of portion of aggregate amount of refunds to employees under § 1176 applicable to voluntary plans for which deductions made under § 3260

The director shall in accordance with his or her authorized regulations determine the portion of the aggregate amount of refunds and credits to employees made under Section 1176 during any calendar year which is applicable to voluntary plans for which deductions were made under Section 3260, such determination to be based upon the relation during the preceding calendar year of the amount of wages subject to contributions to the Disability Fund to the amount of wages exempt from contributions to the Disability Fund under Section 3252. *(Added by Stats.1967, c. 1484, p. 3479, § 1. Amended by Stats.1970, c. 1356, p. 2522, § 7; Stats.1973, c. 1212, p. 2824, § 287, operative July 1, 1974; Stats.1977, c. 1252, p. 4469, § 446, operative July 1, 1978; Stats.1978, c. 633, p. 2091, § 4, operative Jan. 1, 1979.)*

§ 3267. Reports and information to department

Employers whose employees are participating in an approved voluntary plan and any insurer of an approved plan shall furnish such reports and information and make available to the department such records as the director may by authorized regulations require for the proper administration of this part. *(Stats.1953, c. 308, p. 1552, § 3267. Amended by Stats.1973, c. 1212, p. 2825, § 289, operative July 1, 1974; Stats.1979, c. 373, p. 1378, § 306.)*

§ 3268. Furnishing of information by director of employment development

The Director of Employment Development shall, in accordance with his authorized regulations, promptly furnish to employers, employees, or insurers, such information as may be required for the proper administration of an approved voluntary plan. *(Stats.1953, c. 308, p. 1552, § 3268. Amended by Stats.1973, c. 1212, p. 2825, § 292, operative July 1, 1974.)*

§ 3269. Expenditures for added administrative work; annual determination

The director shall in accordance with his or her authorized regulations, determine each fiscal year the total amount expended for added administrative work arising out of voluntary plans. *(Added by Stats.1961, c. 2154, p. 4457, § 19. Amended by Stats.1967, c. 1725, p. 4301, § 10; Stats.1973, c. 1212, p. 2825, § 294, operative July 1, 1974; Stats.1977, c. 1252, p. 4469, § 449, operative July 1, 1978; Stats.1978, c. 633, p. 2091, § 5, operative Jan. 1, 1979.)*

§ 3270. Reinstatement of provisions dealing with selection of risks

The provisions of subdivision (i) of Section 3254 and subdivision (i) of Section 3255, dealing with substantial selection of risks adverse to the Disability Fund, shall be operative as of January 1, 1962. *(Stats.1953, c. 1371, p. 2946. Amended by Stats.1955, c. 957, p. 1855, § 6;*

Stats.1957, c. 2107, p. 3736, § 11; Stats.1959, c. 2155, p. 5209, § 5; Stats.1961, c. 2154, p. 4457, § 20; Stats.1967, c. 1725, p. 4301, § 11.)

§ 3271. Amendments; approval; regulations

(a) The director shall approve any amendment to a voluntary plan adjusting the provisions thereof as to periods after the effective date of the amendment as to which he or she finds that the plan, as amended, will conform to the standards set forth in Section 3254, and that any of the following exist:

(1) A majority of the employees covered by the plan have consented in writing to the amendment.

(2) All of the employees covered by the plan who are adversely affected by the amendment have consented in writing to the amendment.

(3) The insurer of such plan, if any, has certified to the director that notice of the amendment either separately or as a part of a new certificate or statement of coverage, has, at least 10 days prior to the effective date of the proposed amendment, been delivered to the employer for distribution to his or her employees within 10 days thereafter and has further certified that such notice specifically included notification to the employees covered by the plan of their right to withdraw from the plan.

(b) Nothing contained in this section is intended to deny or limit the right of the director to make regulations supplementary thereto, nor on the general subject of requirements for amendments of voluntary plans. *(Added by Stats.1955, c. 957, p. 1855, § 7. Amended by Stats.1957, c. 2107, p. 3736, § 12; Stats.1959, c. 2155, p. 5209, § 6; Stats.1961, c. 1849, p. 3941, § 1; Stats.1963, c. 1212, p. 2730, § 1; Stats.1965, c. 1335, p. 3219, § 1; Stats.1968, 1st Ex.Sess., c. 5, p. 36, § 4; Stats.1970, c. 1076, p. 1913, § 1; Stats.1971, c. 695, p. 1353, § 1; Stats.1973, c. 496, p. 971, § 1; Stats.1973, c. 1212, p. 2826, § 296, operative July 1, 1974; Stats.1978, c. 941, p. 2918, § 2.)*

§ 3272. Refunds and overpayments

The provisions of Article 9 (commencing with Section 1176) of Chapter 4 of Part 1 of this division shall apply to amounts collected under Sections 3252, 3260, and 3265, to amounts remitted to the Disability Fund under Section 3260, and to amounts paid to an employee by an employer or insurer after a final decision on appeal under Section 3264 to an administrative law judge or the appeals board that the employee is entitled to disability benefits. *(Added by Stats.1969, c. 885, p. 1685, § 2. Amended by Stats.1978, c. 633, p. 2091, § 6, operative Jan. 1, 1979; Stats.1984, c. 537, § 46.)*

CHAPTER 7. PAID FAMILY LEAVE

Section
3300. Legislative findings and declarations.
3301. Purpose of chapter; "weekly benefit amount"; maximum amount payable; time period.
3302. Definitions.
3302.1. Disability benefit period.

Section
3303. Eligibility.
3303.1. Coordination of benefits.
3304. Receipt of benefits by eligible workers.
3305. False or fraudulent claims.
3306. Additional medical evidence; examinations.

Operative Effect

For operative effect of Stats.2003, c. 797 (S.B. 727) upon benefits payable for family temporary disability insurance claims, see section 28 of that act.

§ 3300. Legislative findings and declarations

The Legislature finds and declares all of the following:

(a) It is in the public benefit to provide family temporary disability insurance benefits to workers to care for their family members. The need for family temporary disability insurance benefits has intensified as the participation of both parents in the workforce has increased, and the number of single parents in the workforce has grown. The need for partial wage replacement for workers taking family care leave will be exacerbated as the population of those needing care, both children and parents of workers, increases in relation to the number of working age adults.

(b) Family Temporary Disability Insurance shall be known as Paid Family Leave.

(c) Developing systems that help families adapt to the competing interests of work and home not only benefits workers, but also benefits employers by increasing worker productivity and reducing employee turnover.

(d) The federal Family and Medical Leave Act (FMLA) and California's Family Rights Act (CFRA) entitle eligible employees working for covered employers to take unpaid, job-protected leave for up to 12 workweeks in a 12-month period. Under the FMLA and the CFRA, unpaid leave may be taken for the birth, adoption, or foster placement of a new child; to care for a seriously ill child, parent, or spouse; or for the employee's own serious health condition.

(e) State disability insurance benefits currently provide wage replacement for workers who need time off due to their own non-work-related injuries, illnesses, or conditions, including pregnancy, that prevent them from working, but do not cover leave to care for a sick or injured child, spouse, parent, domestic partner, or leave to bond with a new child.

(f) The majority of workers in this state are unable to take family care leave because they are unable to afford leave without pay. When workers do not receive some form of wage replacement during family care leave, families suffer from the worker's loss of income, increasing the demand on the state unemployment insurance system and dependence on the state's welfare system.

(g) It is the intent of the Legislature to create a family temporary disability insurance program to help reconcile the demands of work and family. The family temporary disability insurance program shall be a component of the state's unemployment compensation disability insurance program, shall be funded through employee contributions, and shall be administered in accordance with the policies of the state disability insurance program created pursuant to this part. Initial and ongoing administrative costs associated with the family temporary disability insurance program shall be payable from the Disability Fund. *(Added by Stats.2002, c. 901 (S.B.1661), § 6, operative Jan. 1, 2004. Amended by Stats.2003, c. 797 (S.B.727), § 20, operative Jan. 1, 2004.)*

Operative Effect

For operative effect of Stats.2003, c. 797 (S.B. 727) upon benefits payable for family temporary disability insurance claims, see section 28 of that act.

§ 3301. Purpose of chapter; "weekly benefit amount"; maximum amount payable; time period

(a)(1) The purpose of this chapter is to establish, within the state disability insurance program, a family temporary disability insurance program. Family temporary disability insurance shall provide up to six weeks of wage replacement benefits to workers who take time off work to care for a seriously ill child, spouse, parent, domestic partner, or to bond with a minor child within one year of the birth or placement of the child in connection with foster care or adoption.

(2) Nothing in this chapter shall be construed to abridge the rights and responsibilities conveyed under the CFRA or pregnancy disability leave.

(b) An individual's "weekly benefit amount" shall be the amount provided in Section 2655. An individual is eligible to receive family temporary disability insurance benefits equal to one-seventh of his or her weekly benefit amount for each full day during which he or she is unable to work due to caring for a seriously ill or injured family member or bonding with a minor child within one year of the birth or placement of the child in connection with foster care or adoption.

(c) The maximum amount payable to an individual during any disability benefit period for family temporary disability insurance shall be six times his or her "weekly benefit amount," but in no case shall the total amount of benefits payable be more than the total wages paid to the individual during his or her disability base period. If the benefit is not a multiple of one dollar ($1), it shall be computed to the next higher multiple of one dollar ($1).

(d) No more than six weeks of family temporary disability insurance benefits shall be paid within any 12–month period.

(e) An individual shall file a claim for family temporary disability insurance benefits not later than the 41st consecutive day following the first compensable day with respect to which the claim is made for benefits, which time shall be extended by the department upon a showing of good cause. If a first claim is not complete, the claim

1060

form shall be returned to the claimant for completion and it shall be completed and returned not later than the 10th consecutive day after the date it was mailed by the department to the claimant, except that such time shall be extended by the department upon a showing of good cause. *(Added by Stats.2002, c. 901 (S.B.1661), § 6, operative Jan. 1, 2004. Amended by Stats.2003, c. 797 (S.B.727), § 21, operative Jan. 1, 2004.)*

Operative Effect

For operative effect of Stats.2003, c. 797 (S.B. 727) upon benefits payable for family temporary disability insurance claims, see section 28 of that act.

§ 3302. Definitions

For purposes of this part:

(a) "Care recipient" means the family member who is receiving care for a serious health condition or the new child with whom the care provider is bonding.

(b) "Care provider" means the family member who is providing the required care for a serious health condition or the family member who is bonding with the new child.

(c) "Child" means a biological, adopted, or foster son or daughter, a stepson or stepdaughter, a legal ward, a son or daughter of a domestic partner, or the person to whom the employee stands in loco parentis.

(d) "Domestic partner" has the same meaning as defined in Section 297 of the Family Code.

(e) "Family care leave" means any of the following:

(1) Leave to bond with a minor child within the first year of the child's birth or placement in connection with foster care or adoption.

(2) Leave to care for a child, parent, spouse, or domestic partner who has a serious health condition.

(f) "Family member" means child, parent, spouse, or domestic partner as defined in this section.

(g) "Parent" means a biological, foster, or adoptive parent, a stepparent, a legal guardian, or other person who stood in loco parentis to the employee when the employee was a child.

(h) "Serious health condition" means an illness, injury, impairment, or physical or mental condition that involves inpatient care in a hospital, hospice, or residential health care facility, or continuing treatment or continuing supervision by a health care provider, as defined in Section 12945.2 of the Government Code.

(i) "Spouse" means a partner to a lawful marriage.

(j) "Valid claim" means any claim for family temporary disability insurance benefits made in accordance with the provisions of this code, and any rules and regulations adopted thereunder, if the individual claiming benefits is unemployed and has been paid the necessary wages in employment for employers to qualify for benefits under Section 2652 and is caring for a seriously ill family member, or bonding with a minor child during the first year after the birth or placement of the child in connection with foster care or adoption.

(k) "Twelve-month period," with respect to any individual, means the 365 consecutive days that begin with the first day the individual first establishes a valid claim for family temporary disability benefits. *(Added by Stats.2002, c. 901 (S.B.1661), § 6, operative Jan. 1, 2004. Amended by Stats.2003, c. 797 (S.B.727), § 22, operative Jan. 1, 2004.)*

Operative Effect

For operative effect of Stats.2003, c. 797 (S.B. 727) upon benefits payable for family temporary disability insurance claims, see section 28 of that act.

§ 3302.1. Disability benefit period

For purposes of this chapter:

(a) "Disability benefit period" with respect to any individual, means the period of unemployment beginning with the first day an individual establishes a valid claim for family temporary disability insurance benefits to care for a seriously ill family member, or to bond with a minor child during the first year after the birth or placement of the child in connection with foster care or adoption.

(b) Periods of family care leave for the same care recipient within a 12–month period shall be considered one disability benefit period.

(c) Periods of disability for pregnancy, as defined in Section 2608, and periods of family care leave for bonding associated with the birth of that child shall be considered one disability benefit period. *(Added by Stats.2003, c. 797 (S.B.727), § 23, operative Jan. 1, 2004.)*

Operative Effect

For operative effect of Stats.2003, c. 797 (S.B. 727) upon benefits payable for family temporary disability insurance claims, see section 28 of that act.

§ 3303. Eligibility

An individual shall be deemed eligible for family temporary disability insurance benefits equal to one-seventh of his or her weekly benefit amount on any day in which he or she is unable to perform his or her regular or customary work because he or she is bonding with a minor child during the first year after the birth or placement of the child in connection with foster care or adoption or caring for a seriously ill child, parent, spouse, or domestic partner, only if the director finds all of the following:

(a) The individual has made a claim for temporary disability benefits as required by authorized regulations.

(b) The individual has been unable to perform his or her regular or customary work for a seven-day waiting period during each disability benefit period, with respect to which waiting period no family temporary disability insurance benefits are payable.

(c) The individual has filed a certificate, as required by Sections 2708 and 2709. *(Added by Stats.2002, c. 901 (S.B.1661), § 6, operative Jan. 1, 2004. Amended by Stats.2003, c. 797 (S.B.727), § 24, operative Jan. 1, 2004.)*

Operative Effect

For operative effect of Stats.2003, c. 797 (S.B. 727) upon benefits payable for family temporary disability insurance claims, see section 28 of that act.

§ 3303.1. Coordination of benefits

(a) An individual is not eligible for family temporary disability insurance benefits with respect to any day that any of the following apply:

(1) The individual has received, or is entitled to receive, unemployment compensation benefits under Part 1 (commencing with Section 100) or under an unemployment compensation act of any other state or of the federal government.

(2) The individual has received, or is entitled to receive, "other benefits" in the form of cash benefits as defined in Section 2629.

(3) The individual has received, or is entitled to receive, state disability insurance benefits under Part 2 (commencing with Section 2601) or under a disability insurance act of any other state.

(4) Another family member, as defined in Section 3302, is ready, willing, and able and available for the same period of time in a day that the individual is providing the required care.

(b) An individual who is entitled to leave under the FMLA and the CFRA must take Family Temporary Disability Insurance (FTDI) leave concurrent with leave taken under the FMLA and the CFRA.

(c) As a condition of an employee's initial receipt of family temporary disability insurance benefits during any 12–month period in which an employee is eligible for these benefits, an employer may require an employee to take up to two weeks of earned but unused vacation leave prior to the employee's initial receipt of these benefits. If an employer so requires an employee to take vacation leave, that portion of the vacation leave that does not exceed one week shall be applied to the waiting period required under subdivision (b) of Section 3303. This subdivision may not be construed in a manner that relieves an employer of any duty of collective bargaining the employer may have with respect to the subject matter of this subdivision. *(Added by Stats.2003, c. 797 (S.B. 727), § 25, operative Jan. 1, 2004.)*

Operative Effect

For operative effect of Stats.2003, c. 797 (S.B. 727) upon benefits payable for family temporary disability insurance claims, see section 28 of that act.

§ 3304. Receipt of benefits by eligible workers

Eligible workers shall receive benefits in accordance with provisions established under this division. *(Added by Stats.2002, c. 901 (S.B.1661), § 6, operative Jan. 1, 2004.)*

Operative Effect

Stats.2002, c. 901 (S.B.1661), § 7, provides that benefits shall be payable for periods of family temporary disability leave commencing on or after July 1, 2004.

§ 3305. False or fraudulent claims

If the director finds that any individual falsely certifies the medical condition of any person in order to obtain family temporary disability insurance benefits, with the intent to defraud, whether for the maker or for any other person, the director shall assess a penalty against the individual in the amount of 25 percent of the benefits paid as a result of the false certification. The provisions of Article 8 (commencing with Section 1126) of Chapter 4 of Part 1, with respect to assessments, the provisions of Article 9 (commencing with Section 1176) of Chapter 4 of Part 1, with respect to refunds, and the provisions of Chapter 7 (commencing with Section 1701) of Part 1, with respect to collections, shall apply to the assessments provided by this section. Penalties collected under this section shall be deposited in the contingent fund. *(Added by Stats.2002, c. 901 (S.B.1661), § 6, operative Jan. 1, 2004. Amended by Stats.2003, c. 797 (S.B.727), § 26, operative Jan. 1, 2004; Stats.2004, c. 183 (A.B.3082), § 343.)*

Operative Effect

For operative effect of Stats.2003, c. 797 (S.B. 727) upon benefits payable for family temporary disability insurance claims, see section 28 of that act.

§ 3306. Additional medical evidence; examinations

(a) The director may request additional medical evidence to supplement the first or any continued claim if the additional evidence can be procured without additional cost to the care recipient. The director may require that the additional evidence include any or all of the following information:

(1) Identification of diagnoses.

(2) Identification of symptoms.

(3) A statement setting forth the facts of the care recipient's serious health condition that warrants the participation of the employee. The statement shall be completed by any of the following people:

(A) The physician or practitioner treating the care recipient.

(B) The registrar, authorized medical officer, or other duly authorized official of the hospital or health facility treating the care recipient.

(C) An examining physician or other representative of the department.

(b) Except as provided in Section 2709, the director may require the care recipient to submit to reasonable examinations for the purpose of determining all of the following:

(1) Whether a serious health condition exists.

(2) Whether a care provider's participation is warranted.

(3) The period of time that the care provider's participation is warranted. *(Added by Stats.2003, c. 797 (S.B.727), § 27, operative Jan. 1, 2004.)*

Operative Effect

For operative effect of Stats.2003, c. 797 (S.B. 727) upon benefits payable for family temporary disability insurance claims, see section 28 of that act.

Part 3

EXTENDED UNEMPLOYMENT COMPENSATION

Chapter	Section
1. General Provisions	3501
2. Extended Duration Benefits	3551
3. Additional Contributions [Repealed]	
4. Retraining Benefits [Repealed]	

CHAPTER 1. GENERAL PROVISIONS

Section
3501. Purpose of part; short title.
3502. Applicability of Parts 1 and 2.
3503. Definitions.
3504. Weekly computation of insured unemployment rate.
3505. Persons not entitled to extended duration benefits; benefits under Federal-State Extended Unemployment Compensation Act of 1970.
3506. Suspension of extended duration benefits; emergency benefits; payment.

§ 3501. Purpose of part; short title

The purpose of this part is to compensate in part for the added wage loss sustained by individuals because of the extended duration of unemployment during prolonged periods of cyclical and technological unemployment in California. This part may be cited as the "Miller-Collier Act." *(Added by Stats.1959, c. 2035, p. 4679, § 2.)*

§ 3502. Applicability of Parts 1 and 2

(a) Except as otherwise provided, the provisions and definitions of Part 1 [1] of this division apply to this part. In case of any conflict between the provisions of Part 1 and the provisions of this part, the provisions of this part shall prevail with respect to extended unemployment compensation.

(b) Except as otherwise provided, subdivision (d) of Section 1253, and Sections 1030, 1032, 1254, 1277, 1281, 1327, 1328, 1329, 1330, and 1331 do not apply to this part.

(c) The provisions of Part 2 [2] of this division do not apply to this part. *(Added by Stats.1959, c. 2035, p. 4679, § 2.)*

[1] Section 100 et seq.
[2] Section 2601 et seq.

§ 3503. Definitions

For the purposes of this part:

(a) "Extended duration benefits" means the extended unemployment compensation benefits payable under this part.

(b) "Normal benefits" means the unemployment compensation benefits payable under Part 1 (commencing with Section 100) of this division.

(c) "Exhaustee" means an individual who is not entitled to normal benefits due to either of the following:

(1) He or she has an unexpired benefit year and has exhausted his or her normal benefits.

(2) His or her most recent benefit year expired in the week in which he or she filed a primary claim or in the immediately preceding 13 calendar weeks and he or she is not entitled to establish a benefit year.

(d) "Insured unemployment rate" for a week means the percentage arrived at by dividing:

(1) The average weekly number of individuals filing claims for regular compensation for weeks of unemployment with respect to the period consisting of the week and the immediately preceding 12 weeks, by

(2) The average monthly covered employment for the same period.

The director shall interpret this definition in accordance with regulations and guidelines prescribed by the United States Secretary of Labor which are applicable to subdivision (e) of Section 203 of the federal act.

(e) "Extended benefit period" means the period beginning with the third week after the first week for which there is an "on" indicator, and ending with the third week after the first week for which there is an "off" indicator, except no extended benefit period shall last for a period of less than 13 consecutive weeks and no extended benefit period may begin before the 14th week after the close of a prior extended benefit period. There is an "on" indicator for a week if the insured unemployment rate equals or exceeds 6 percent. There is an "off" indicator for a week if the insured unemployment rate is less than 6 percent.

(f) "Primary claim" means the first claim for extended duration benefits filed by an exhaustee with an effective date within an extended benefit period for the purpose of establishing an extended duration award and an extended duration period.

(g) "Extended duration award" means the maximum amount of extended duration benefits allowable under this part to an eligible exhaustee.

(h) "Extended duration period" means a period beginning with the first day of the week with respect to which an exhaustee filed a valid primary claim and ending with the last week which begins on or before the last day of the fifth calendar month following the calendar month which contains the extended duration week or a major portion of the extended duration week in which the valid primary claim was filed.

(i) "Parent benefit year" means the benefit year with respect to which an individual becomes an exhaustee.

(j) "Federal act" means the "Federal-State Extended Unemployment Compensation Act of 1970".[1] *(Added by Stats.1959, c. 2035, p. 4679, § 2. Amended by Stats.1961, c. 5, p. 526, § 1; Stats.1961, c. 868, p. 2278, § 1; Stats.1963, c. 1548, p. 3130, § 5; Stats.1970, c. 1156, p. 2050, § 11; Stats.1982, c. 1073, p. 3869, § 3.)*

[1] 26 U.S.C.A. § 3304 note.

§ 3504. Weekly computation of insured unemployment rate

The director shall during the week immediately preceding each calendar week compute the insured unemployment rate for that calendar week. The computation shall be a public record. *(Added by Stats.1959, c. 2035, p. 4680, § 2. Amended by Stats.1961, c. 5, p. 528, § 3, eff. Feb. 25, 1961; Stats.1961, c. 2157, p. 4463, § 1; Stats.1970, c. 1156, p. 2051, § 12; Stats.1973, c. 1212, p. 2827, § 297.5, operative July 1, 1974; Stats.1978, c. 397, p. 1260, § 9, eff. July 11, 1978; Stats.1982, c. 1073, p. 3870, § 4.)*

§ 3505. Persons not entitled to extended duration benefits; benefits under Federal-State Extended Unemployment Compensation Act of 1970

(a) Notwithstanding any other provision of this part, no payment of extended duration benefits shall be made to any individual for any week or part of any week with respect to which he is entitled to receive unemployment compensation benefits as a result of participation by this state pursuant to the provision of any federal law providing for the payment of such benefits or as a result of the application in any other manner to this state of any federal law providing for the payment of such benefits.

(b) With respect to weeks commencing on or after November 29, 1970, this subdivision shall apply and subdivision (a) of this section shall not apply to benefits under the "Federal-State Extended Unemployment Compensation Act of 1970".

(1) Notwithstanding any other provision of this part, if an individual would have rights to receive benefits under the federal act within an "extended benefit period" under the federal act, the director shall cancel such individual's

rights to extended duration benefits within that "extended benefit period".

(2) A cancellation under this section does not affect extended duration benefits paid with respect to a week preceding such cancellation.

(3) Notwithstanding a cancellation under this section, an individual otherwise qualified for extended duration benefits during an "extended benefit period" under the federal act, may, upon the expiration of his "eligibility period" specified by the federal act, establish rights to, and be paid, extended duration benefits subject to the following conditions:

(A) If the individual has filed a primary claim in the "extended benefit period", under the federal act, he may reestablish his extended duration benefit rights, if the extended duration period would not have expired.

(B) If the individual has not filed a primary claim in the "extended benefit period", under the federal act, and he has claimed benefits pursuant to the federal act during an extended duration week in such "extended benefit period", he may file a primary claim effective with that extended duration week, if the extended duration period would not have expired.

(C) If the individual has not filed a primary claim in the "extended benefit period", under the federal act, and he has claimed benefits pursuant to the federal act but not during an extended duration week in such "extended benefit period", he may file a primary claim in an extended duration week.

(D) The individual shall not be paid extended duration benefits for any week for which he receives federal benefits.

(4) An individual may be paid extended duration benefits with respect to a parent benefit year only to the extent that the total amount of such extended duration benefits and benefits paid under the federal act since the beginning of such parent benefit year does not exceed 13 times his weekly benefit amount or one-half of the maximum amount of normal benefits payable to him during that parent benefit year, whichever is the lesser. *(Added by Stats.1959, c. 2035, p. 4680, § 2. Amended by Stats.1961, c. 5, p. 528, § 4; Stats.1961, c. 868, p. 2279, § 2; Stats.1963, c. 1548, p. 3131, § 7; Stats.1970, c. 1156, p. 2052, § 13.)*

§ 3506. Suspension of extended duration benefits; emergency benefits; payment

Notwithstanding any other provision of this part, the Governor may, if permitted by federal law, suspend the payment of extended duration benefits under this part, to the extent necessary to ensure that otherwise eligible individuals are not denied, in whole or in part, the receipt of emergency unemployment compensation benefits authorized by the federal Emergency Unemployment Compensation Act of 1991 (P.L. 102-164) [1] or any extension of that act, including, but not limited to, Public Law 102-244, and that the state receives maximum reimbursement from

the federal government for the payment of those emergency benefits. *(Added by Stats.1992, c. 22 (S.B.589), § 1, eff. April 1, 1992.)*

[1] See 26 U.S.C.A. § 3304 note.

CHAPTER 2. EXTENDED DURATION BENEFITS

Article	Section
1. Eligibility and Disqualifications	3551
2. Computation (Amount and Duration)	3601
3. Filing, Determination, and Payment of Extended Duration Benefit Claims	3651
4. Reserve Accounts	3701
5. Overpayments	3751

ARTICLE 1. ELIGIBILITY AND DISQUALIFICATIONS

Section
3551. Payment from unemployment fund to eligible unemployed individuals.
3552. Unemployed individuals; eligibility to receive extended benefits.
3553. Filing valid primary claim as constituting election to claim extended benefits.

§ 3551. Payment from unemployment fund to eligible unemployed individuals

Extended duration benefits are payable from the Unemployment Fund to unemployed individuals who are eligible under this part. *(Added by Stats.1959, c. 2035, p. 4680, § 2.)*

§ 3552. Unemployed individuals; eligibility to receive extended benefits

An unemployed individual is eligible to receive extended duration benefits with respect to any week only if the director finds that:

(a) An extended duration award has been established for the individual.

(b) The week is:

(1) Within the extended duration period of the award; and

(2) Within an extended benefit period.

(c) He or she meets the eligibility requirements of Part 1 (commencing with Section 100) of this division, except those excluded under subdivision (b) of Section 3502.

(d) He or she is not subject to disqualification, and is not under disqualification for normal benefits, under any provision of Part 1 (commencing with Section 100) of this division.

(e) He or she had earnings from employment subject to the provisions of this division which exceed 40 times his or her most recent weekly benefit amount in the base period in which he or she exhausted all rights to regular compensation.

For the purpose of this section "wages" includes wages due to an individual but unpaid within the time limit provided by law.

(f) During any week within an extended benefit period under the federal act, the provisions of subdivision (d) of Section 4552 and Sections 4553, 4554, 4555, and 4556 shall apply to claims filed under this part. *(Added by Stats.1959, c. 2035, p. 4680, § 2. Amended by Stats.1965, c. 1897, p. 4380, § 17; Stats.1970, c. 1156, p. 2053, § 14; Stats.1982, c. 1073, p. 3871, § 5; Stats.1983, c. 761, § 7.)*

§ 3553. Filing valid primary claim as constituting election to claim extended benefits

The filing of a valid primary claim by an exhaustee shall constitute an election by him to claim extended duration benefits to the exclusion of filing a new claim for normal benefits for any week of unemployment subsequent to the filing of such primary claim for which extended duration benefits are payable to him. *(Added by Stats.1959, c. 2035, p. 4680, § 2.)*

ARTICLE 2. COMPUTATION (AMOUNT AND DURATION)

Section
3601. Weekly benefit amount.
3602. Duration.
3603. Number of extended duration awards.

§ 3601. Weekly benefit amount

An exhaustee's weekly benefit amount under an extended duration award shall be the same as his weekly benefit amount for the parent benefit year. *(Added by Stats.1959, c. 2035, p. 4681, § 2.)*

§ 3602. Duration

An exhaustee's extended duration award during any one extended duration period shall be 13 times his weekly benefit amount or one half of the maximum amount of normal benefits payable to him during his parent benefit year, whichever is the lesser. *(Added by Stats.1959, c. 2035, p. 4681, § 2.)*

§ 3603. Number of extended duration awards

Only one extended duration award may be established for an exhaustee based on any one parent benefit year. *(Added by Stats.1959, c. 2035, p. 4681, § 2.)*

ARTICLE 3. FILING, DETERMINATION, AND PAYMENT OF EXTENDED DURATION BENEFIT CLAIMS

Section
3651. Claims; procedure.
3652. Necessity of filing valid primary claim; effective date.
3653. Determination of effective date of valid primary claim.
3654. Notice of filing; submission of facts affecting exhaustee's eligibility.

Section
3654.1. Submission of wage and employment information for determination of eligibility.
3654.2. Noncompliance; penalties.
3654.3. Determination upon available information.
3654.4. Determination of exhaustee's eligibility for extended duration benefits; notice; appeal.
3655. Consideration of facts submitted by last employer; determination; notice; appeal to administrative law judge.
3656. Extended duration award computation; contests; notice protest; extension of protest period; appeal.

§ 3651. Claims; procedure

Claims for extended duration benefits shall be made as provided in this article. *(Added by Stats.1959, c. 2035, p. 4681, § 2.)*

§ 3652. Necessity of filing valid primary claim; effective date

An exhaustee who desires to claim extended duration benefits shall file a valid primary claim. A primary claim for extended duration benefits shall be valid only if its effective date is within an extended benefit period and the individual filing it is an unemployed exhaustee. For the purpose of determining whether a primary claim is a "valid primary claim" within the meaning of this section, an individual otherwise unemployed shall be deemed unemployed even though wages, as defined in Section 1252, which are for a period subsequent to the termination of performance of services are payable with respect to the week for which the individual files the claim. *(Added by Stats.1959, c. 2035, p. 4681, § 2. Amended by Stats.1961, c. 5, p. 528, § 5, eff. Feb. 25, 1961; Stats.1961, c. 2165, p. 4487, § 4; Stats.1970, c. 1156, p. 2054, § 15; Stats.1982, c. 1073, p. 3871, § 6.)*

§ 3653. Determination of effective date of valid primary claim

The effective date of a valid primary claim shall be determined in the same manner as the effective date of a new claim for normal benefits pursuant to Section 1326. *(Added by Stats.1959, c. 2035, p. 4681, § 2.)*

§ 3654. Notice of filing; submission of facts affecting exhaustee's eligibility

The department shall give a notice of the filing of a primary claim or an additional claim to the employing unit by which the exhaustee was last employed immediately preceding the filing of the claim unless the additional claim is the result of the filing of a partial claim as defined by the department, there has not been a subsequent employing unit which is designated as the last employer, and there is no separation issue. The employing unit so notified shall submit within 10 days after the mailing of the notice any facts then known which may affect the exhaustee's eligibility for extended duration benefits. The 10-day period may be extended for good cause. If after the 10-day period the employing unit acquires knowledge of facts which may affect the eligibility of the exhaustee and those facts could not reasonably have been known within the period, the employing unit shall within 10 days of acquiring that knowledge submit those facts to the department, and the 10-day period may also be extended for good cause. *(Added by Stats.1959, c. 2035, p. 4681, § 2. Amended by Stats.1965, c. 1897, p. 4381, § 18; Stats.1973, c. 1212, p. 2827, § 299, operative July 1, 1974; Stats.1979, c. 373, p. 1378, § 307; Stats.1979, c. 456, p. 1603, § 8; Stats.1985, c. 716, § 5.)*

§ 3654.1. Submission of wage and employment information for determination of eligibility

(a) For the purpose of determining whether an unemployed individual meets the eligibility requirements of subdivision (e) of Section 3552, the director may pursuant to his authorized regulations require that wage and employment information shall be submitted to the director, within 10 days after the mailing of a request by the director, by any or all of the following:

(1) Each employing unit subsequent to the end of the base period of the new claim and prior to the effective date of a valid primary claim for extended duration benefits.

(2) Each employing unit in the four quarters immediately preceding the beginning of the base period of the new claim.

(b) The 10-day period may be extended for good cause. *(Added by Stats.1973, c. 1212, p. 2828, § 300, operative July 1, 1974. Amended by Stats.1977, c. 1252, p. 4470, § 450, operative July 1, 1978.)*

§ 3654.2. Noncompliance; penalties

Any employing unit who fails to furnish wage information requested by the director pursuant to Section 3654.1 shall be subject to a penalty of ten dollars ($10) for each such report not submitted. The director shall assess the penalty and the provisions of Part 1 (commencing with Section 100) of this division with respect to assessments, refunds, and collections shall apply. Penalties collected under this section shall be deposited in the Unemployment Fund. *(Formerly § 3654.1, added by Stats.1965, c. 1897, p. 4382, § 19. Renumbered § 3654.2 and amended by Stats.1973, c. 1212, p. 2828, § 301, operative July 1, 1974; Stats.1977, c. 1252, p. 4470, § 451, operative July 1, 1978.)*

§ 3654.3. Determination upon available information

If any employing unit fails to respond to a request for wage information within the period prescribed by Section 3654.1, the director shall make a determination based upon available information. *(Formerly § 3654.2, added by Stats.1965, c. 1897, p. 4382, § 20. Renumbered § 3654.3 and amended by Stats.1973, c. 1212, p. 2828, § 302, operative July 1, 1974; Stats.1977, c. 1252, p. 4470, § 452, operative July 1, 1978.)*

§ 3654.4. Determination of exhaustee's eligibility for extended duration benefits; notice; appeal

The department shall consider the facts submitted by an employing unit pursuant to Section 3654.1 and make a determination as to the exhaustee's eligibility for extended duration benefits under subdivision (e) of Section 3552. The department shall promptly notify the exhaustee and any employing unit who prior to the determination has submitted any facts pursuant to Section 3654.1 of the determination and the reasons therefor. The exhaustee and any such employing unit may appeal therefrom to an administrative law judge within 20 days from mailing or personal service of notice of the determination. The 20-day period may be extended for good cause. The director shall be an interested party to any appeal.

"Good cause," as used in this section, shall include, but not be limited to, mistake, inadvertence, surprise, or excusable neglect. *(Added by Stats.1973, c. 1212, p. 2828, § 303, operative July 1, 1974. Amended by Stats.1975, c. 979, p. 2304, § 8; Stats.1977, c. 1252, p. 4470, § 453, operative July 1, 1978; Stats.1984, c. 537, § 47.)*

§ 3655. Consideration of facts submitted by last employer; determination; notice; appeal to administrative law judge

The Employment Development Department shall consider the facts submitted by an employer pursuant to Section 3654 and, if benefits are claimed subsequent to the filing of the extended duration benefits claim, make a determination as to the exhaustee's eligibility for the extended duration benefits. The Employment Development Department shall promptly notify the exhaustee and any employer who prior to the determination has submitted any facts pursuant to Section 3654 of the determination and the reasons therefor. The exhaustee and any such employer may appeal therefrom to an administrative law judge within 20 days from mailing or personal service of notice of the determination. The 20-day period may be extended for good cause. The Director of Employment Development shall be an interested party to any appeal.

"Good cause," as used in this section, shall include, but not be limited to, mistake, inadvertence, surprise, or excusable neglect. *(Added by Stats.1959, c. 2035, p. 4681, § 2. Amended by Stats.1967, c. 1586, p. 3801, § 14; Stats.1973, c. 1212, p. 2829, § 305, operative July 1, 1974; Stats.1975, c. 979, p. 2304, § 9; Stats.1981, c. 1018, p. 3929, § 2; Stats.1984, c. 537, § 48.)*

§ 3656. Extended duration award computation; contests; notice protest; extension of protest period; appeal

Upon the filing of a valid primary claim by an exhaustee, the department shall promptly make an extended duration award computation which shall set forth the maximum amount of extended duration benefits potentially payable during the extended duration period, the weekly benefit amount, and the expiration date of the extended duration period. The department shall promptly notify the exhaustee of the computation. He may, within 20 days after the mailing or personal service of the notice of computation, protest its accuracy. The 20-day period may be extended for good cause. The department shall consider any such protest and shall promptly notify the exhaustee of the recomputation or denial of recomputation. An appeal may be taken from a notice of denial of recomputation in the manner prescribed in Section 3655. The director shall be an interested party to any appeal.

"Good cause," as used in this section, shall include, but not be limited to, mistake, inadvertence, surprise, or excusable neglect. *(Added by Stats.1959, c. 2035, p. 4682, § 2. Amended by Stats.1967, c. 1720, p. 4288, § 14; Stats.1973, c. 1212, p. 2829, § 306, operative July 1, 1974; Stats.1975, c. 979, p. 2305, § 10; Stats.1977, c. 1252, p. 4471, § 454, operative July 1, 1978.)*

ARTICLE 4. RESERVE ACCOUNTS

Section
3701. Ruling as to cause of termination of exhaustee's employment; reconsideration; appeal; effect of ruling.
3702. Extended duration benefits charged against employer's reserve account; multiple employers charged.

§ 3701. Ruling as to cause of termination of exhaustee's employment; reconsideration; appeal; effect of ruling

(a) Any employer who is entitled under Section 3654 to notice of the filing of a primary claim or additional claim and who, within 10 days after mailing of the notice, submits to the department any facts within its possession disclosing whether the exhaustee left the most recent employment with the employer voluntarily and without good cause or was discharged from the employment for misconduct connected with his or her work, or whether the claimant was a student employed on a temporary basis and whose employment began within, and ended with his or her leaving to return to school at the close of, his or her vacation period, or whether the claimant left the employer's employ to accompany his or her spouse to or join her or him at a place from which it is impractical to commute to the employment, to which a transfer of the claimant by the employer is not available or whether the claimant's discharge or quit from his or her most recent employer was the result of an irresistable compulsion to use or consume intoxicants including alcoholic beverages, shall be entitled to a ruling as prescribed by this section. The period during which the employer may submit these facts may be extended by the director for good cause.

For purposes of this section, "spouse" includes a person to whom marriage is imminent.

(b) The department shall consider these facts together with any information in its possession. If the employer is entitled to a determination pursuant to Section 3655, the department shall promptly notify the employer of its ruling as to the cause of the termination of the exhaustee's most recent employment. The employer may appeal from a ruling or reconsidered ruling to an administrative law judge within 20 days after mailing or personal service of notice of the ruling or reconsidered ruling. The 20-day period may be extended for good cause, which shall include, but not be limited to, mistake, inadvertence, surprise, or excusable neglect. The director shall be an interested party to any appeal. The department may for good cause reconsider any ruling or reconsidered ruling within either five days after the date an appeal to an administrative law judge is filed or, if no appeal is filed, within 20 days after mailing or personal service of notice of the ruling or reconsidered ruling, except that any ruling or reconsidered ruling which related to a determination is reconsidered pursuant to subdivision (a) of Section 1332 may also be reconsidered by the department within the time provided for reconsideration of that determination.

(c) For purposes of this section only, if the claimant voluntarily leaves the employer's employ without notification to the employer of the reasons therefor, and if the employer submits all of the facts within its possession concerning the leaving within the applicable time period referred to in this section, the leaving shall be presumed to be without good cause.

(d) An individual whose employment is terminated under the compulsory retirement provisions of a collective-bargaining agreement to which the employer is a party shall not be deemed to have voluntarily left his or her employment without good cause.

(e) Rulings under this section shall have the effect prescribed by Section 1032. *(Added by Stats.1959, c. 2035, p. 4682, § 2. Amended by Stats.1967, c. 1725, p. 4301, § 12; Stats.1968, c. 1185, p. 2246, § 3; Stats.1973, c. 1212, p. 2830, § 308, operative July 1, 1974; Stats.1975, c. 751, p. 1752, § 5; Stats.1977, c. 508, p. 1639, § 4; Stats.1979, c. 456, p. 1604, § 9; Stats.1980, c. 676, p. 2021, § 304; Stats.1980, c. 1025, p. 3293, § 26; Stats.1982, c. 1225, p. 4525, § 6; Stats.1984, c. 537, § 49; Stats.1988, c. 781, § 4.)*

§ 3702. Extended duration benefits charged against employer's reserve account; multiple employers charged

Extended duration benefits, to the extent that such extended duration benefits are not reimbursed or reimbursable by the federal government to the State of California, shall be charged except as provided by Section 1032, 1032.5, 1034, 1036, 1335, 1338, or 1380, against the reserve account of the exhaustee's employer during his or her base period. If the individual performed services in employment for more than one employer during his or her base period, unemployment compensation benefits paid to him or her shall be charged against the respective reserve accounts of such employers in the proportion that the total wages paid to the individual in employment for each employer bears to the total wages paid to the individual in employment for all employers during the base period. *(Added by Stats.1959, c. 2035, p. 4682, § 2. Amended by Stats.1982, c. 1075, p. 3894, § 18; Stats.1983, c. 1169, § 8.)*

ARTICLE 5.　OVERPAYMENTS

Section
3751.　Notice of overpayment; limit; offsetting overpayments.

§ 3751.　Notice of overpayment; limit; offsetting overpayments

The provisions of Article 4 (commencing with Section 1375) of Chapter 5 of Part 1 of this division are modified in the following respects:

(a) In the absence of fraud, misrepresentation, or willful nondisclosure, the notice of overpayment of extended duration benefits shall be mailed or personally served by the Employment Development Department not later than one year after the close of the extended duration period in which the overpayment was made.

(b) The Director of Employment Development may offset an overpayment of extended duration benefits, or federal-state extended benefits, or unemployment compensation benefits against any of such three types of benefits or against disability benefits to which the liable person may become entitled under this division. The Director of Employment Development may offset the amount of any such overpayments within any of the periods prescribed by subdivision (b) of Section 1379, and further within the current extended duration period or current extended benefit period established under Part 4 (commencing with Section 4001) of this division or any extended benefit period or any extended duration period which begins during the three-year period next succeeding the date of the mailing or personal service of such notice of overpayment. *(Added by Stats.1959, c. 2035, p. 4682, § 2. Amended by Stats.1970, c. 1156, p. 2054, § 16; Stats.1973, c. 1212, p. 2831, § 310; Stats.1974, c. 544, p. 1260, § 44; Stats.1975, c. 890, p. 1970, § 3.)*

CHAPTER 3.　ADDITIONAL CONTRIBUTIONS [REPEALED]

CHAPTER 4.　RETRAINING BENEFITS [REPEALED]

Part 4

FEDERAL–STATE EXTENDED COMPENSATION

Chapter	Section
1.　General Provisions	4001
2.　Federal-State Extended Benefits	4551

CHAPTER 1.　GENERAL PROVISIONS

Section
4001.　Purpose of part.
4002.　Application of part.
4003.　Application of Federal–State Extended Unemployment Compensation Act of 1970 and American Recovery and Reinvestment Act of 2009; "on" or "off" indicators; determination of rate of insured unemployment; suspension of extended duration benefits.
4004.　Extended compensation account; amount of account; weekly benefit amount; high unemployment periods.

§ 4001.　Purpose of part

The purpose of this part is to provide that payment of extended compensation, in accordance with the "Federal-State Extended Unemployment Compensation Act of 1970" [1], as amended by the Omnibus Budget Reconciliation Act of 1981 (Public Law 97–35), shall be made, for any week of unemployment which begins in the individual's eligibility period, to individuals who have exhausted all rights to regular compensation under this division and who have no rights to regular compensation with respect to such week under this division or any other state unemployment compensation law or to compensation under any other federal law. For purposes of this section, an individual shall have exhausted his rights to regular compensation under any state law (A) when no payments of regular compensation can be made under such law because such individual has received all regular compensation available to him based on wage credits for his base period, or (B) when his rights to such compensation have terminated by reason of the expiration of the benefit year with respect to which such rights existed. Except where inconsistent with the provisions of the "Federal-State Extended Unemployment Compensation Act of 1970", as amended by the Omnibus Budget Reconciliation Act of 1981 (Public Law 97–35), the terms and conditions of this division which apply to claims for regular compensation and to the payment thereof shall apply to claims for extended compensation and to the payment thereof under such federal act. This part shall be operative on September 25, 1982, and extended compensation shall be payable as provided by the Federal-State Extended Unemployment Compensation Act of 1970, as amended by the Omnibus Budget Reconciliation Act of 1981 (Public Law 97–35), subject to limitations provided by that act, with respect to weeks of unemployment and extended benefit periods beginning after September 25, 1982. The provisions of this section in effect prior to the amendments by the Omnibus Budget Reconciliation Act of 1981 shall continue to apply to weeks beginning after November 28, 1970, and before September 25, 1982. *(Added by Stats.1970, c. 1156, p. 2054, § 17. Amended by Stats.1982, c. 1072, p. 3859, § 6, eff. Sept. 15, 1982.)*

[1] 26 U.S.C.A. § 3304 note.

§ 4002. Application of part

(a) Except as otherwise provided, the provisions and definitions of Part 1 (commencing with Section 100) apply to this part. In case of any conflict between the provisions of Part 1 and the provisions of this part, the provisions of this part shall prevail with respect to federal-state extended benefits.

(b) Except as otherwise provided, subdivision (d) of Section 1253, and Sections 1030, 1032, 1254, 1277, 1281, 1327, 1328, 1329, 1330, and 1331 do not apply to this part.

(c) The provisions of Part 2 (commencing with Section 2601) of, and of Part 3 (commencing with Section 3501) do not apply to this part. *(Added by Stats.1970, c. 1156, p. 2055, § 17. Amended by Stats.1983, c. 998, § 7; Stats. 1985, c. 1488, § 5.)*

§ 4003. Application of Federal–State Extended Unemployment Compensation Act of 1970 and American Recovery and Reinvestment Act of 2009; "on" or "off" indicators; determination of rate of insured unemployment; suspension of extended duration benefits

(a) The provisions and definitions of terms in the * * * Federal–State Extended Unemployment Compensation Act of 1970, * * * as amended by the federal Omnibus Budget Reconciliation Act of 1981 (Public Law 97–35) [1], apply to this part. "Federal-state extended benefits" means benefits payable under this part.

(b) To the extent that the provisions and definitions of terms in the American Recovery and Reinvestment Act of 2009 (Public Law 111–5) [1] are in conflict with, or supplement the provisions and definitions applicable pursuant to subdivision (a), the provisions and definitions of the American Recovery and Reinvestment Act of 2009 shall apply to this part.

(c) There is an "on" indicator for purposes of federal-state extended benefits for a week * * * if one of the following applies:

(1) The rate of insured unemployment * * * under this part for the period consisting of that week and the * * * 12 weeks * * * immediately preceding the week equaled or exceeded 120 percent of the average of the rates for the corresponding 13–week period ending in each of the preceding two calendar years, and * * * equaled or exceeded 5 percent.

* * *

(2) The rate of insured unemployment under this part for the period consisting of that week and the 12 weeks immediately preceding the week equaled or exceeded 6 percent, regardless of the rate of insured unemployment in the two previous years.

(3) With respect to weeks of unemployment beginning on or after February 1, 2009, and continuing until the week ending three weeks prior to the last week for which 100 percent federal sharing is authorized by subdivision (a) of Section 2005 of Public Law 111–5 for all claims, except for reimbursable entities described in Section 3306(c)(7) of the Internal Revenue Code [2], both of the following apply:

(A) The average rate of total unemployment in this state, seasonally adjusted, as determined by the United States Secretary of Labor, for the period consisting of the most recent three months for which data for all states are published before the close of that week, equals or exceeds 6.5 percent.

(B) The average rate of total unemployment in this state, seasonally adjusted, as determined by the United States Secretary of Labor, for the three-month period referred to in subparagraph (A) equals or exceeds 110 percent of that average rate of total unemployment for either or both of the corresponding three-month periods ending in the two preceding calendar years.

(d) There is an "off" indicator for a week * * * if, for the period consisting of that week, and the * * * 12 weeks * * * immediately preceding the week, none of the criteria specified in subdivision (c) results in an "on" indicator.

* * *

(e) For purposes of this section, the rate of insured unemployment for a 13–week period shall be determined by reference to the average monthly covered employment for the first four of the most recent six calendar quarters ending before the close of the period. * * *

(f) The indicators specified in subdivisions (c) and (d) shall be operative only if mandated or permitted by federal law. * * *

(g) Notwithstanding any other provision of this part, the Governor may, if permitted by federal law, suspend the payment of extended duration benefits under this part, to the extent necessary to ensure that otherwise eligible individuals are not denied, in whole or in part, the receipt of emergency unemployment compensation benefits authorized by the federal * * * Supplemental Appropriations Act of 2008 (Public Law 110–252) [1], the Unemployment Compensation * * * Extension Act of 2008 (Public Law 110–449) [1], and the American Recovery and Reinvestment Act of 2009 (Public Law 111–5) [1], and that the state receives maximum reimbursement from the federal government for the payment of those emergency benefits. *(Added by Stats.1970, c. 1156, p. 2055, § 17. Amended by Stats.1974, c. 73, p. 159, § 1, eff. March 14, 1974; Stats.1974, c. 155, p. 301, § 1, eff. April 4, 1974; Stats.1974, c. 382, p. 950, § 11.5, eff. July 5, 1974; Stats.1974, c. 1545, p. 3535, § 1, eff. Oct. 9, 1974; Stats.1975, c. 446, p. 941, § 1, eff. Aug. 30, 1975; Stats. 1976, c. 1054, p. 4682, § 2.5; Stats.1977, c. 43, p. 420, § 1, eff. May 10, 1977; Stats.1981, c. 1134, p. 4450, § 7; Stats.1982, c. 1072, p. 3860, § 7, eff. Sept. 15, 1982; Stats.1992, c. 22 (S.B.589), § 2, eff. April 1, 1992; Stats. 2009–2010, 3rd Ex.Sess., c. 22 (A.B.23), § 1, eff. March 27, 2009.)*

[1] Public law sections classified to U.S.C.A., see U.S.C.A. Tables.

[2] Internal Revenue Code sections are in Title 26 of the U.S.C.A.

§ 4004. Extended compensation account; amount of account; weekly benefit amount; high unemployment periods

(a) The department shall establish, for each eligible individual who files an application therefor, an extended compensation account with respect to such individual's benefit year. The amount established in that account, subject to subdivision (b) of this section, shall be not less than whichever of the following is the least:

(1) Fifty percent of the total amount of regular compensation payable to him or her during that benefit year under this division.

(2) Thirteen times his or her average weekly benefit amount.

(3) Thirty-nine times his or her average weekly benefit amount, reduced by the regular compensation paid to him or her during that benefit year under this division.

(b) The amount determined under subdivision (a) of this section shall be reduced by the aggregate amount of additional compensation paid to the individual under Part 3 (commencing with Section 3501) of this division for prior weeks of unemployment in such benefit year which did not begin in an extended benefit period.

(c) For purposes of subdivision (a) of this section, an individual's weekly benefit amount for a week is the amount of regular compensation under Part 1 (commencing with Section 100) of this division payable to such individual for such week of total unemployment.

(d) With respect to weeks beginning in a high unemployment period, subdivision (a) shall be applied in accordance with the following percentages:

(1) In paragraph (1) of subdivision (a), 80 percent shall be substituted for 50 percent.

(2) In paragraph (2) of subdivision (a), 20 times shall be substituted for 13 times.

(3) In paragraph (3) of subdivision (a), 46 times shall be substituted for 39 times.

(e) For purposes of subdivision (d), "high unemployment period" means a period during which an extended benefit period would be in effect if subparagraph (A) of paragraph (3) of subdivision (c) of Section 4003 were applied by substituting 8 percent for 6.5 percent. *(Added by Stats.1970, c. 1156, p. 2055, § 17. Amended by Stats.1979, c. 373, p. 1379, § 308; Stats.2009–2010, 3rd Ex.Sess., c. 22 (A.B.23), § 2, eff. March 27, 2009.)*

CHAPTER 2. FEDERAL–STATE EXTENDED BENEFITS

Article		Section
1.	Eligibility and Disqualifications	4551
2.	Computation (Amount and Duration)	4601
3.	Filing, Determination, and Payment of Federal-State Extended Benefit Claims	4651
4.	Reserve Accounts	4701
5.	Overpayments	4751

ARTICLE 1. ELIGIBILITY AND DISQUALIFICATIONS

Section
4551. Benefits payable unemployment fund.
4552. Eligibility to receive benefits.
4553. Refusal to accept or apply for suitable work; disqualification for benefits; exception.
4554. Failure to actively engage in seeking work; disqualification for benefits; exception.
4555. Determination of disqualification under §§ 4553 or 4554; ineligibility for benefits; time.
4556. Referrals to suitable work.
4557. No extended compensation payment if interstate claim payable; exception.
4558. Operative effect of 1981 legislation.

§ 4551. Benefits payable unemployment fund

Federal-state extended benefits are payable from the Unemployment Fund to unemployed individuals who are eligible under this part. *(Added by Stats.1970, c. 1156, p. 2056, § 17.)*

§ 4552. Eligibility to receive benefits

An unemployed individual is eligible to receive federal-state extended benefits with respect to any week only if the director finds that:

(a) An extended compensation claim has been established for him or her.

(b) The week is within an extended benefit period and his or her eligibility period.

(c) He or she meets the eligibility requirements of Part 1 (commencing with Section 100), except those excluded under subdivision (b) of Section 4002.

(d) He or she is not subject to disqualification for normal benefits under any provision of Part 1 (commencing with Section 100). If the individual has been subject to disqualification under subdivision (b) of Section 1257, he or she has satisfied subdivision (b) of Section 1260 and, during a week following the first week of disqualification, has done either of the following:

(1) Performed service in bona fide employment during a week on a full-time basis.

(2) Performed service in bona fide employment during a week from which service he or she earned remuneration at least equal to his or her weekly benefit amount.

(e) With respect to compensation payable to any individual for any week, he or she had earnings from employment subject to the provisions of this division which exceed 40 times his or her most recent weekly benefit amount or 1.5 times the highest quarter, in the base period in which he or she exhausted all rights to regular compensation.

(f) An individual subject to disqualification under subdivision (a) of Section 1256.4 has satisfied subdivision (a) of Section 1260.

(g) The amendments to subdivision (e) made by the act adding this subdivision shall not be implemented unless the director determines that those amendments have been approved by the United States Department of Labor. The director shall immediately seek approval of the amendments to subdivision (e) from the United States Department of Labor. *(Added by Stats.1970, c. 1156, p. 2056, § 17. Amended by Stats.1981, c. 10, p. 21, § 1, eff. March 31, 1981; Stats.1982, c. 1072, p. 3861, § 8, eff. Sept. 15, 1982; Stats.1986, c. 924, § 3; Stats.1992, c. 22 (S.B.589), § 3, eff. April 1, 1992; Stats.2009–2010, 3rd Ex.Sess., c. 22 (A.B.23), § 3, eff. March 27, 2009.)*

Implementation

Implementation of 1992 amendments to subd. (e) contingent on conditions specified in subd. (g).

§ 4553. Refusal to accept or apply for suitable work; disqualification for benefits; exception

An unemployed individual is disqualified for federal-state extended benefits if the individual, without good cause, refused to accept suitable work when offered to the individual, or failed to apply for suitable work when referred by a public employment office.

(a) For purposes of this section, the term "suitable work" means any work which is within the individual's capabilities.

(b) An individual shall not be disqualified under this section if any of the following apply:

(1) The gross average weekly remuneration payable to the individual for the position offered or to which referred, does not exceed the individual's weekly benefit amount plus the amount of any additional benefits (as defined in Section 501(c)(17)(D) of the Internal Revenue Code of 1954)[1] payable to such individual for such week.

(2) The position was not offered to such individual in writing and was not listed with a public employment office.

(3) The provisions of subdivision (a), (b), or (c) of Section 1259 or the provisions of Article 1.5 (commencing with Section 1266) or Article 1.8 (commencing with Section 1274) of Chapter 5 of Part 1 apply.

(4) The position pays less than the federal or state minimum wage, whichever is higher.

(5) The department determines that the individual's prospects for obtaining work in his or her customary occupation within a reasonably short period are good.

(c) If the department makes a determination described in paragraph (5) of subdivision (b), the determination of whether any work is "suitable work" and whether there is a disqualification from benefits with respect to the individual shall be made in accordance with subdivision (b) of Section 1257, Sections 1258, 1258.5, and 1259, and subdivision (b) of Section 1260. *(Added by Stats.1981, c. 10, p. 21, § 2, eff. March 31, 1981. Amended by Stats. 1981, c. 1134, p. 4451, § 8.)*

[1] 26 U.S.C.A. § 501(c)(17)(D).

Duration of section, see § 4558.

§ 4554. Failure to actively engage in seeking work; disqualification for benefits; exception

An individual is disqualified for federal-state extended benefits if the individual fails to actively engage in seeking work.

(a) For purposes of this section, an individual shall be treated as actively engaged in seeking work during any week if both of the following conditions are met:

(1) The individual has engaged in a systematic and sustained effort to obtain work during the week.

(2) The individual provides tangible evidence to the department that he or she has engaged in such an effort during the week.

(b) An individual shall not be disqualified under this section for any week in which the individual is in a training or retraining program under Article 1.5 (commencing with Section 1266) of Chapter 5 of Part 1.

(c) An individual shall not be disqualified under this section for any week solely because the individual is before any court of the United States or any state pursuant to a lawfully issued summons to appear for jury duty, or the individual is hospitalized for treatment of an emergency or life-threatening condition. *(Added by Stats.1981, c. 10, p. 22, § 3, eff. March 31, 1981. Amended by Stats.1985, c. 716, § 6.)*

Duration of section, see § 4558.

§ 4555. Determination of disqualification under §§ 4553 or 4554; ineligibility for benefits; time

If an individual is disqualified for federal-state extended benefits under Section 4553 or 4554 pursuant to a determination transmitted to him or her by the department, the individual shall be ineligible to receive federal-state extended benefits:

(a) Beginning with the week in which the disqualifying act occurs, and

(b) Continuing until the individual has, during at least four weeks subsequent to the week in which the disqualifying act occurred, performed services in bona fide employment for which remuneration is earned equal to or in excess of four times the individual's weekly benefit amount. *(Added by Stats.1981, c. 10, p. 22, § 4, eff. March 31, 1981. Amended by Stats.1981, c. 1134, p. 4451, § 9.)*

Duration of section, see § 4558.

§ 4556. Referrals to suitable work

When the department refers individuals who have applied for federal-state extended benefits to work, the referrals shall include suitable work, as defined by subdivision (a) of Section 4553, to which any part of subdivision (b) of Section 4553 would not apply. *(Added by Stats.1981, c. 10, p. 23, § 5, eff. March 31, 1981.)*

Duration of section, see § 4558.

§ 4557. No extended compensation payment if interstate claim payable; exception

(a) Except as provided in subdivision (b), payment of federal-state extended compensation shall not be made to any individual for any week if both of the following apply:

(1) Extended compensation would, but for this section, have been payable for such week pursuant to an interstate claim filed in any state under the interstate benefit payment plan.

(2) An extended benefit period is not in effect for such week in such state.

(b) Subdivision (a) shall not apply with respect to the first two weeks for which extended compensation is payable as determined without regard to this section, pursuant to an interstate claim filed under the interstate benefit payment plan to the individual from the extended compensation account established with respect to the benefit year. *(Added by Stats.1981, c. 10, p. 23, § 6, eff. March 31, 1981.)*

Duration of section, see § 4558.

§ 4558. Operative effect of 1981 legislation

Sections 4553 to 4557, inclusive, and the amendments made to Section 4552 by legislation enacted during the 1981 portion of the 1981–82 Regular Session of the Legislature shall be operative only during such time as Section 202 of the Federal-State Extended Unemployment Compensation Act of 1970 [1] requires that state unemployment insurance laws contain such provisions as a condition of certification of state unemployment insurance laws by the Secretary of Labor. *(Added by Stats. 1981, c. 10, p. 23, § 7, eff. March 31, 1981.)*

[1] 26 U.S.C.A. § 3304 notes.

ARTICLE 2. COMPUTATION (AMOUNT AND DURATION)

Section
4601. Computation of amount and duration of benefits.

§ 4601. Computation of amount and duration of benefits

The computation of the amount and duration of federal-state extended benefits shall be in accordance with Section 4004. *(Added by Stats.1970, c. 1156, p. 2056, § 17.)*

ARTICLE 3. FILING, DETERMINATION, AND PAYMENT OF FEDERAL–STATE EXTENDED BENEFIT CLAIMS

Section
4651. Claims to be made as provided in article.
4652. Application for benefits; valid application.
4653. Effective date of valid application.
4654. Notice of filing of application; submission of facts affecting eligibility.

Section
4655. Determination of eligibility; notification of determination; appeal.
4656. Benefit award computation; notification to individual; protest of accuracy of computation; extension of protest period; appeal.

§ 4651. Claims to be made as provided in article

Claims for federal-state extended benefits shall be made as provided in this article. *(Added by Stats.1970, c. 1156, p. 2056, § 17.)*

§ 4652. Application for benefits; valid application

(a) An individual who desires to claim federal-state extended benefits shall file a valid application. An application for federal-state extended benefits shall be valid only if its effective date is within an extended benefit period and his eligibility period and the individual filing it otherwise meets the requirements of Section 4001. For the purpose of determining whether an application is a "valid application" within the meaning of this section, an individual otherwise unemployed shall be deemed unemployed even though wages, as defined in Section 1252, which are for a period subsequent to the termination of performance of services are payable with respect to the week for which he files the application. *(Added by Stats.1970, c. 1156, p. 2056, § 17.)*

§ 4653. Effective date of valid application

The effective date of a valid application shall be determined in the same manner as the effective date of a new claim for normal benefits pursuant to Section 1326. *(Added by Stats.1970, c. 1156, p. 2057, § 17.)*

§ 4654. Notice of filing of application; submission of facts affecting eligibility

The department shall give a notice of the filing of an application or an additional claim to the employing unit by which the individual was last employed immediately preceding the filing of the application or claim unless the additional claim is the result of the filing of a partial claim as defined by the department, there has not been a subsequent employing unit which is designated as the last employer, and there is no separation issue. The employing unit so notified shall submit within 10 days after the mailing of the notice any facts then known which may affect the individual's eligibility for federal-state extended benefits. The 10-day period may be extended for good cause. If after the 10-day period the employing unit acquires knowledge of facts which may affect the eligibility of the individual and those facts could not reasonably have been known within the period, the employing unit shall within 10 days of acquiring that knowledge submit those facts to the department, and the 10-day period may also be extended for good cause. *(Added by Stats.1970, c. 1156, p. 2057, § 17. Amended by Stats.1973, c. 1212, p. 2832, § 312, operative July 1, 1974; Stats.1979, c. 373, p. 1379, § 309; Stats.1979, c. 456, p. 1604, § 10; Stats.1985, c. 716, § 7.)*

§ 4655. Determination of eligibility; notification of determination; appeal

The Employment Development Department shall consider the facts submitted by an employer pursuant to Section 4654 and, if benefits are claimed subsequent to the filing of the federal-state extended benefits claim, make a determination as to the individual's eligibility for the federal-state extended benefits. The Employment Development Department shall promptly notify the individual and any employer who prior to the determination has submitted any facts pursuant to Section 4654 of the determination and the reasons therefor. The individual and any such employer may appeal therefrom to an administrative law judge within 20 days from mailing or personal service of notice of the determination. The 20-day period may be extended for good cause. The Director of Employment Development shall be an interested party to any appeal.

"Good cause," as used in this section, shall include, but not be limited to, mistake, inadvertence, surprise, or excusable neglect. *(Added by Stats.1970, c. 1156, p. 2057, § 17. Amended by Stats.1973, c. 1212, p. 2833, § 314, operative July 1, 1974; Stats.1975, c. 979, p. 2305, § 11; Stats.1981, c. 1018, p. 3929, § 3; Stats.1984, c. 537, § 50.)*

§ 4656. Benefit award computation; notification to individual; protest of accuracy of computation; extension of protest period; appeal

Upon the filing of a valid application by an individual, the department shall promptly make a federal-state extended benefit award computation which shall set forth the maximum amount of federal-state extended benefits potentially payable during the extended benefit period, and the weekly benefit amount. The department shall promptly notify the individual of the computation. He may, within 20 days after the mailing or personal service of the notice of computation or recomputation, protest its accuracy. The 20-day period may be extended for good cause. The department shall consider any such protest and shall promptly notify the individual of the recomputation or denial of recomputation. An appeal may be taken from a notice of denial of recomputation in the manner provided in Section 4655. The director shall be an interested party to any appeal.

"Good cause," as used in this section, shall include, but not be limited to, mistake, inadvertence, surprise, or excusable neglect. *(Added by Stats.1970, c. 1156, p. 2057, § 17. Amended by Stats.1973, c. 1212, p. 2833, § 315, operative July 1, 1974; Stats.1975, c. 979, p. 2306, § 12; Stats.1977, c. 1252, p. 4471, § 455, operative July 1, 1978.)*

ARTICLE 4. RESERVE ACCOUNTS

Section
4701. Submission of facts by employer affecting eligibility; rulings; reconsideration or appeal; effect.
4702. Benefits charged to employer's reserve account; multiple employer's charged.

§ 4701. Submission of facts by employer affecting eligibility; rulings; reconsideration or appeal; effect

(a)(1) Any employer who is entitled under Section 4654 to notice of the filing of an application or additional claim and who, within 10 days after mailing of the notice, submits to the department any facts within its possession disclosing whether the individual left the most recent employment with the employer voluntarily and without good cause or was discharged from the employment for misconduct connected with his or her work, or whether the claimant was a student employed on a temporary basis and whose employment began within, and ended with his or her leaving to return to school at the close of, his or her vacation period, or whether the claimant left the employer's employ to accompany his or her spouse to or join her or him at a place from which it is impractical to commute to the employment, to which a transfer of the claimant by the employer is not available or whether the claimant's discharge or quit from his or her most recent employer was the result of an irresistible compulsion to use or consume intoxicants including alcoholic beverages, shall be entitled to a ruling as prescribed by this section. The period during which the employer may submit these facts may be extended by the director for good cause.

(2) For purposes of this section, "spouse" includes a person to whom marriage is imminent.

(b) The department shall consider the facts together with any information in its possession. If the employer is entitled to a determination pursuant to Section 4655, the department shall promptly issue to the employer its ruling as to the cause of the termination of the individual's most recent employment. The employer may appeal from a ruling or reconsidered ruling to an administrative law judge within 20 days after mailing or personal service of notice of the ruling or reconsidered ruling. The 20 day period may be extended for good cause, which shall include, but not be limited to, mistake, inadvertence, surprise, or excusable neglect. The director shall be an interested party to any appeal. The department may for good cause reconsider any ruling or reconsidered ruling within either five days after the date an appeal to an administrative law judge is filed or, if no appeal is filed, within 20 days after mailing or personal service of notice of the ruling or reconsidered ruling, except that any ruling or reconsidered ruling that relates to a determination that is reconsidered pursuant to subdivision (a) of Section 1332 may also be reconsidered by the department within the time provided for reconsideration of that determination.

(c) For purposes of this section only, if the claimant voluntarily leaves the employer's employ without notification to the employer of the reasons therefor, and if the employer submits all of the facts within its possession concerning the leaving within the applicable time period referred to in this section, the leaving shall be presumed to be without good cause.

(d) An individual whose employment is terminated under the compulsory retirement provisions of a collective-bargaining agreement to which the employer is a party shall not be deemed to have voluntarily left his or her employment without good cause.

(e) Rulings under this section shall have the effect prescribed by Section 1032. *(Added by Stats.1970, c. 1156, p. 2057, § 17. Amended by Stats.1973, c. 1212, p. 2834, § 317, operative July 1, 1974; Stats.1975, c. 751, p. 1753, § 6; Stats.1977, c. 508, p. 1639, § 5; Stats.1979, c. 456, p. 1605, § 11; Stats.1980, c. 1025, p. 3294, § 27; Stats.1982, c. 1225, p. 4526, § 7; Stats.1984, c. 537, § 51; Stats.1988, c. 781, § 5; Stats.2006, c. 538 (S.B.1852), § 648.)*

§ 4702. Benefits charged to employer's reserve account; multiple employer's charged

Federal-state extended benefits, to the extent that these extended benefits are not reimbursed or reimbursable by the federal government to the State of California, shall be charged except as provided by Section 1032, 1032.5, 1034, 1036, 1335, 1338, or 1380, against the reserve account of the individual's employer during his or her base period. If the individual performed services in employment for more than one employer during his or her base period, unemployment compensation benefits paid to him or her shall be charged against the respective reserve accounts of such employers in the proportion that the total wages paid to the individual in employment for each employer bears to the total wages paid to the individual in employment for all employers during the base period. *(Added by Stats.1970, c. 1156, p. 2058, § 17. Amended by Stats.1982, c. 1075, p. 3894, § 19; Stats.1983, c. 1169, § 9.)*

ARTICLE 5. OVERPAYMENTS

Section
4751. Overpayments; notice; offsetting amount against other types of benefits.

§ 4751. Overpayments; notice; offsetting amount against other types of benefits

The provisions of Article 4 (commencing with Section 1375) of Chapter 5 of Part 1 of this division are modified in the following respects:

(a) In the absence of fraud, misrepresentation, or willful nondisclosure, the notice of overpayment of federal-state extended benefits shall be mailed or personally served by the Employment Development Department not later than one year after the close of the extended benefit period in which the overpayment was made.

(b) The Director of Employment Development may offset an overpayment of extended duration benefits, or federal-state extended benefits, or unemployment compensation benefits against any of such three types of benefits or against disability benefits to which the liable person may become entitled under this division. The Director of Employment Development may offset the amount of any such overpayments within any of the periods prescribed by subdivision (b) of Section 1379, and further within the current extended duration period or current extended benefit period or any extended benefit period or extended duration period which begins during the three-year period next succeeding the date of the mailing or personal service of such notice of overpayment. *(Added by Stats.1970, c. 1156, p. 2058, § 17. Amended by Stats.1973, c. 1212, p. 2835, § 319, operative July 1, 1974; Stats.1975, c. 890, p. 1971, § 4.)*

Division 1.5

AUTOMATION OF THE EMPLOYMENT DEVELOPMENT DEPARTMENT

Chapter　　　　　　　　　　　　　　　　　　Section
1. Annual Reports 4900

CHAPTER 1. ANNUAL REPORTS

Section
4900. Definitions.
4901. Automation plans; recommendation on improvements.
4902. Transmission of report to legislative committees; contents of report.
4903. Comments and review of report by Office of Information Technology.

§ 4900. Definitions

As used in this division:

(a) "Department" means the Employment Development Department.

(b) "Director" means the Director of Employment Development. *(Added by Stats.1986, c. 799, § 3, eff. Sept. 15, 1986.)*

§ 4901. Automation plans; recommendation on improvements

The director shall prepare a biennial report to the Legislature, on or before February 1, 1994, and on or before February 1 of each even-numbered year thereafter, on the department's automation plans, including any recommendation on improvements for the purpose of consideration by both policy and fiscal committees of the Legislature. *(Added by Stats.1986, c. 799, § 3, eff. Sept. 15, 1986. Amended by Stats.1992, c. 713 (A.B.3564), § 28, eff. Sept. 15, 1992.)*

§ 4902. Transmission of report to legislative committees; contents of report

The report, required by Section 4901, shall be transmitted to the Legislative Analyst, the Assembly Committees on Insurance, Consumer Protection, Governmental Efficiency, and Economic Development, Labor and Employment, and Ways and Means, the Senate Committees on Industrial Relations and Budget and Fiscal Review, the Department of Finance, and the Governor, on or before February 1 of each even-numbered year. The report shall do all of the following:

(a) Provide a strategic information plan that describes the long-term goals and strategies which shall be undertaken by the department to create an information technology environment that will not only support the achievement of the department's strategic business mission and goals but set the foundation for using information technology to make substantial and sustainable improvements in how it conducts business. The plan shall cover a 10-year planning horizon and include the department's information vision, its information management principles, and long-term goals and strategies for achieving its information vision.

(b) Provide a tactical information plan of specific automation and infrastructure projects to be undertaken within three years of the date of the report. The plan shall include project description and scope, consistency with the strategic information plan, relationship to other projects, priority of development, estimated project costs and benefits, and improvements in services. For automation projects, it shall also provide reductions in personnel and operating costs, and identification of how personnel and cost savings will be used, transferred, or otherwise accounted for.

(c) Not necessarily be in addition to or replace any reports now submitted by the director to the State Office of Information Technology in the Department of Finance. *(Added by Stats.1986, c. 799, § 3, eff. Sept. 15, 1986. Amended by Stats.1992, c. 713 (A.B.3564), § 29, eff. Sept. 15, 1992.)*

§ 4903. Comments and review of report by Office of Information Technology

(a) Thirty days prior to the release of the report identified in Section 4901, the director shall submit it to the Office of Information Technology in the Department of Finance, which shall review and comment on it. These comments shall be attached to the report by the director and distributed with the report.

(b) When commenting on the report, the Office of Information Technology shall include, but not be limited to, an assessment of whether:

(1) The requirements for the report have been met.

(2) The strategic plan is consistent with the formal strategic plan submitted separately to the Office of Information Technology.

(3) The costs and benefits identified in the report are consistent with the projects previously submitted for approval or contained in the Information Management Annual Plans. *(Added by Stats.1986, c. 799, § 3, eff. Sept. 15, 1986. Amended by Stats.1992, c. 713 (A.B.3564), § 30, eff. Sept. 15, 1992.)*

Division 2

WORK INCENTIVE PROGRAMS [REPEALED]

Division 3

EMPLOYMENT SERVICES PROGRAMS

Part	Section
1. Employment and Employability Services	9000
2. Employment Opportunities Act of 1971 [Repealed]	

Part 1

EMPLOYMENT AND EMPLOYABILITY SERVICES

Chapter	Section
1. General Provisions and Definitions	9000
2. Employment Development Department	9500
2.5. Youth Employment and Development [Repealed]	

Chapter	Section
2.7. California Work-Site Education and Training Act [Repealed]	
2.8. Displaced Worker Education and Training Act of 1982 [Repealed]	
2.9. Regional Employment Assessment, Job Search Assistance, and Placement Services For Displaced Workers [Repealed]	
3. Welfare–to–Work Grant Program [Repealed]	
3.5. Employment Training Panel	10200
4. Programs	10500
4.5. California Employment and Training Planning	10510
5. Employment Services for the Deaf and Hearing Impaired	11000
6. Regional Work Force Preparation and Economic Development Act [Repealed]	

Chapter   Section
7.   Caregiver Training Initiative 11020

CHAPTER 1. GENERAL PROVISIONS AND DEFINITIONS

Article   Section
1.   General Provisions 9000
2.   Definitions 9100
3.   Training for Energy-Related Jobs [Repealed] 9120

ARTICLE 1. GENERAL PROVISIONS

Section
9000.   Declaration of legislative purpose and intent.
9001.   Additional legislative findings and declarations.
9002.   Coordination of job placement and related programs.
9003.   Individuals with disabilities; certification as potentially employable.
9004.   Conformity of state plan with federal requirements.

§ 9000. Declaration of legislative purpose and intent

The Legislature hereby makes the following declaration of purpose and intent in enacting the Employment Development Act of 1973.

It is the public policy of the State of California to provide for comprehensive statewide and local manpower planning, to improve the efficiency of, and the accountability for, delivery systems for manpower programs, to promptly place job-ready individuals in suitable jobs, to provide qualified job applicants to employers, to assist potentially employable individuals to become job ready, and to create employment opportunities. *(Added by Stats.1973, c. 1206, p. 2623, § 73; Stats.1973, c. 1207, p. 2673, § 73.)*

§ 9001. Additional legislative findings and declarations

In enacting the Employment Development Act of 1973, the Legislature further finds and declares that it is essential to the health and welfare of the people of this state that action be taken by local, state and federal governments to effectively and economically utilize public funds for job training and placement services. To achieve this, it is necessary that:

(a) Explicit priorities be established for the allocation of these funds to ensure that they are first used to assist those in greatest need for job training and placement services;

(b) Definitive goals be established for the total system of job training and placement services to maximize the effectiveness of the system in assisting individuals to find and maintain gainful, competitive employment;

(c) Efforts be made to enlist the full support of private industry in securing jobs for enrollees of training programs, and a closer, more integrated and coordinated effort be established with the federal government as well as state and local public and private agencies involved in performing job training and placement services; and

(d) New approaches involving improved services and changes in traditional organization structures be used to assist persons in economically disadvantaged areas.

It is hereby declared to be the intent of the Legislature to concentrate and account for the funds available for job training and placement services in one state agency whose functions shall be subject to periodic review by the Legislature and appropriate federal agencies, and to which is assigned the responsibility for the efficient administration of job training and placement services in this state and the allocation of these funds to the end that such funds will be more effectively utilized and will be directed primarily to those areas of the state with the largest concentrations of chronically unemployed persons.

It is the further intent of the Legislature (a) to maintain policy control over all job training and placement programs administered by the department pursuant to this part to the maximum extent feasible, consistent with effective program operations, (b) to organize existing job training and placement programs now operating in the state into a coordinated system designed to remove employable persons from dependency on public assistance, and to enlist the full support of private industry in securing jobs, (c) to use funds for job training and placement services in a flexible manner to provide needed services for individuals through contractual arrangements with public and private agencies, (d) to provide a unified system for timely delivery of improved job training placement and related services to eligible persons including individual case responsibility, an outreach effort to seek out those persons who need but do not apply for services, followup to insure that the needs of eligible persons and their families are met, dissemination of information and knowledge to residents of the economically disadvantaged area about available services, and location of services in areas readily accessible to those who need them, and (e) to involve members of each community in identifying the needs to be met and relating them to the services available in order to reduce the isolation of the disadvantaged from their government and the community as a whole and to improve their confidence in government at all levels. *(Added by Stats.1968, c. 1460, p. 2906, § 11. Amended by Stats.1973, c. 1206, p. 2623, § 74; Stats.1973, c. 1207, p. 2674, § 74.)*

§ 9002. Coordination of job placement and related programs

Subject to the provisions of Sections 9600 and 9605, the Secretary of the Health and Welfare Agency shall coordinate all job training placement, and related programs, conducted by state agencies, with the federal government and ensure that there is no duplication of the programs among state agencies and that all agreements, contracts, plans, or programs conform to the provisions of this part. Any plan proposed to be submitted by any agency to the federal government in relation to a job training, placement, or related program, shall first be submitted to the Secretary of the Health and Welfare Agency for his or her review. The Health and Welfare Agency may require state departments to contract with it for services to carry out the provisions of this part. *(Added by Stats.1968, c. 1460, p. 2907, § 11. Amended by Stats.1981, c. 714, p. 2791, § 433.)*

§ 9003. Individuals with disabilities; certification as potentially employable

Notwithstanding any other provisions of this code, individuals with disabilities who are clients of the Department of Rehabilitation shall not be barred as participants in manpower programs, including, but not limited to, retraining programs, work incentive programs, job training and placement programs, career opportunity development programs, and vocational educational programs, because of their mental or physical disability when certified by the Department of Rehabilitation as being potentially employable. *(Formerly § 10501, added by Stats.1972, c. 1146, p. 2215, § 1. Renumbered § 9003 and amended by Stats.1973, c. 1206, p. 2633, § 112; Stats.1973, c. 1207, p. 2683, § 112. Amended by Stats.2005, c. 152 (A.B.1577), § 29.)*

§ 9004. Conformity of state plan with federal requirements

Upon receipt of a formal ruling from the United States Secretary of Labor, the United States Secretary of Health and Human Services, or the head of any federal agency that any provision of Chapter 1206 of the Statutes of 1973 or Chapter 1212 of the Statutes of 1973 cannot be given effect without causing the state's plan to be out of conformity with federal requirements or would result in decertification of provisions of this code and notification of intention to withdraw federal funds from the state, that provision shall become inoperative to the extent that it is not in conformity with federal requirements. *(Added by Stats.1976, c. 504, p. 1248, § 1, eff. Aug. 20, 1976. Amended by Stats.1985, c. 106, § 159.)*

ARTICLE 2. DEFINITIONS

Section
9100. Construction.
9101. Department.
9102. Director.
9105. State agency.
9107. Job training and placement services or programs.
9108. Unemployed person.
9109. Underemployed person.
9110. Economic deprivation.
9111. Economically disadvantaged area.
9112. Eligible person.
9115. Economically displaced persons.

§ 9100. Construction

Unless the context otherwise requires, the definitions in this article govern the construction of this division. *(Added by Stats.1968, c. 1460, p. 2907, § 11. Amended by Stats.1973, c. 1206, p. 2624, § 75; Stats.1973, c. 1207, p. 2675, § 75.)*

§ 9101. Department

"Department" means the Employment Development Department, which may also be referred to as the Department of Employment Development. *(Added by Stats.1968, c. 1460, p. 2907, § 11. Amended by Stats.1973, c. 1206, p. 2625, § 76; Stats.1973, c. 1207, p. 2675, § 76; Stats.1974, c. 503, p. 1180, § 9.)*

§ 9102. Director

"Director" means the Director of Employment Development. *(Added by Stats.1968, c. 1460, p. 2907, § 11. Amended by Stats.1973, c. 1206, p. 2625, § 77; Stats.1973, c. 1207, p. 2675, § 77.)*

§ 9105. State agency

"State agency" means those agencies enumerated in section 11000 of the Government Code. *(Added by Stats.1968, c. 1460, p. 2907, § 11.)*

§ 9107. Job training and placement services or programs

"Job training and placement services" or "job training and placement programs" means any job training, placement, or related services administered or supervised by or provided under contract with the department, directly calculated to increase employability or improve the employment of the individual. *(Added by Stats.1968, c. 1460, p. 2908, § 11. Amended by Stats.1973, c. 1206, p. 2625, § 81; Stats.1973, c. 1207, p. 2675, § 81.)*

§ 9108. Unemployed person

"Unemployed person" means a person who lacks a bona fide employment, suffers economic deprivation because of lack of employment, and is employable or capable of being made employable through the services available under this part. *(Added by Stats.1968, c. 1460, p. 2908, § 11.)*

§ 9109. Underemployed person

"Underemployed person" means a person who has a bona fide employment but whose employment, be it full time, or part time, or intermittent, is insufficient to provide an income adequate to avoid economic deprivation. *(Added by Stats.1968, c. 1460, p. 2908, § 11.)*

§ 9110. Economic deprivation

"Economic deprivation" means annual income insufficient to enable the family or individual to meet a table of income criteria adopted by the director, which takes appropriate factors into account, including, but not limited to, the level indicated by multiplying by 3 the cost of the Low Cost Food Plan of the United States Department of Agriculture for the Western Region of the United States. *(Added by Stats.1968, c. 1460, p. 2908, § 11. Amended by Stats.1970, c. 1000, p. 1796, § 5.)*

§ 9111. Economically disadvantaged area

(a) "Economically disadvantaged area" means an area which meets all of the following requirements:

(1) It is composed of contiguous census tracts within or partly within an urbanized area as defined by the most recent federal census for which statistics are available.

(2) In the area 20 percent of the families report annual income less than four thousand dollars ($4,000) according to the most recent federal census for which statistics are available.

(3) The area has a population of not less than 25,000.

(b) "Economically disadvantaged area" also includes any portion of an area if:

(1) Such portion is within or partly within an urbanized area but because of technical factors such portion cannot be isolated as a census tract or tracts or cannot be isolated as a "contiguous" census tract; and

(2) The total area when such portion is included meets the requirements of paragraphs (2) and (3) of subdivision (a) of this section.

(c) The director shall periodically review the definition set forth in this section and Section 9110, and he shall recommend necessary changes to the Legislature and the Governor. *(Added by Stats.1968, c. 1460, p. 2908, § 11. Amended by Stats.1970, c. 1000, p. 1796, § 6; Stats.1973, c. 1206, p. 2625, § 82; Stats.1973, c. 1207, p. 2675, § 82.)*

§ 9112. Eligible person

"Eligible person" means an unemployed person or underemployed person who resides in an economically disadvantaged area or resides outside of an economically disadvantaged area but who resides in a county in which an economically disadvantaged area exists and qualifies under criteria established by the director. *(Added by Stats.1968, c. 1460, p. 2908, § 11. Amended by Stats.1970, c. 1243, p. 2234, § 1.)*

§ 9115. Economically displaced persons

"Economically displaced persons" means those persons who have been subjected to an involuntary layoff or separation from their employment, and who have not quit voluntarily or been dismissed for disciplinary reasons. *(Added by Stats.1971, c. 1563, p. 3129, § 1.)*

ARTICLE 3. TRAINING FOR ENERGY– RELATED JOBS [REPEALED]

CHAPTER 2. EMPLOYMENT DEVELOPMENT DEPARTMENT

Article		Section
1.	Administration	9500
2.	Powers and Duties	9600
3.	San Diego Multiuse Biotechnology Training Center	9700
4.	California YouthBuild Program	9800
5.	Jobs for California Graduates Program	9900
6.	Employer Elder Care Benefits	9910

ARTICLE 1. ADMINISTRATION

Section
9500. Duties.
9502. Establishment of offices.

§ 9500. Duties

The department shall administer all job training and placement programs and services for eligible persons as defined in this division, except as otherwise provided by federal statute or regulation. *(Added by Stats.1968, c. 1460, p. 2908, § 11. Amended by Stats.1969, c. 1068, p. 2054, § 4; Stats.1973, c. 1206, p. 2626, § 85; Stats.1973, c. 1207, p. 2676, § 85.)*

§ 9502. Establishment of offices

For purposes of administration, the director may establish such offices as are appropriate for the administration of this part. Offices administering programs under this part shall be established to the fullest extent possible in economically disadvantaged areas. *(Added by Stats.1968, c. 1460, p. 2909, § 11.)*

ARTICLE 2. POWERS AND DUTIES

Section
9600. Representation of state and local governments; development of statewide and area plans.
9600.5. Training expenditures; annual report.
9600.7. Administration of federal Workforce Investment Act of 1998; rules and regulations.
9601. Contracts with public agencies, etc.
9601.5. Public agencies or contracted private organizations; legal status or authorization to work; verification; exception.
9601.7. Availability of services to citizens or persons authorized to work; posted notice.
9602. Designation of economically disadvantaged areas; services; nondiscrimination; priorities.
9602.5. Training of women in nontraditional occupations; establishment of systemwide policy.
9604. Administrative information; annual report.
9605. Job training and placement.
9606. Referrals to employers; assistance to individuals who are potentially employable.
9607. Community employment development centers.
9608. Services.
9609. Administration of manpower service funds; provision of services.
9610. Contracts for public and private job training and placement programs.
9612. Civil service.
9613. Use of federal funds; placement and manpower information services.
9615. Priority for services; federal funding.
9616. Military personnel; civilian counterpart jobs requiring licenses; barriers impeding reentry.
9616.1. Local entities convened; plan to coordinate employer outreach activities and solicitation of job listings.
9617. Competitive grants to certain faith-based organizations; criteria for provision of services; collection and analysis of information.
9618. Solar training program.
9619. Regional nursing simulation laboratories.

§ 9600. Representation of state and local governments; development of statewide and area plans

(a) The department shall represent the state and local governments upon their request in dealing with the federal government regarding the kinds and quality of job training and placement, employability, and related programs contained in the statewide plan described in subdivision (b), which are administered by or in the State of California pursuant to this division.

(b) The department shall develop a statewide plan and area plans to coordinate all programs it administers pursuant to this division and shall present such plans annually to the Legislature. Such plans shall include, but not be limited to, the review required in Section 9604. *(Added by Stats.1968, c. 1460, p. 2909, § 11. Amended by Stats.1973, c. 1206, p. 2626, § 87; Stats.1973, c. 1207, p. 2676, § 87.)*

§ 9600.5. Training expenditures; annual report

The director of the Employment Development Department shall report annually to the Governor, the Legislature, and the California Workforce Investment Board, no later than November 30, regarding the training expenditures made by local workforce investment boards in the prior fiscal year. The department shall specify what expenditures qualify as training expenditures, including, but not limited to, the price paid for classroom instruction or other training opportunities, contracted services for customized training and on-the-job training, development of training materials, and supportive services, including case management, that enable a participant to attend and complete training. The annual report shall specify the total amount of federal funding provided to the state and to each of the local workforce investment areas for the adult and dislocated persons programs and the amount within each program expended for training services. *(Added by Stats.2008, c. 376 (S.B.302), § 1.)*

§ 9600.7. Administration of federal Workforce Investment Act of 1998; rules and regulations

(a) The department shall have the authority to administer the requirements of the federal Workforce Investment Act of 1998 including, but not limited to, establishing accounting, monitoring, auditing, and reporting procedures and criteria in order to ensure state compliance with the objectives and requirements of the federal Workforce Investment Act.

(b) The department shall adopt, amend, or repeal any rules and regulations as necessary to implement Division 7 (commencing with Section 14000). *(Added by Stats. 2008, c. 376 (S.B.302), § 2.)*

§ 9601. Contracts with public agencies, etc.

The department may enter into any contractual agreements with public agencies, community action agencies, private organizations and individuals which are necessary to carry out the purposes of this part. Priority in contracts for services to carry out the provisions of this part shall be given to community action agencies, if the director determines that the agency can effectively provide such services. *(Added by Stats.1968, c. 1460, p. 2909, § 11.)*

§ 9601.5. Public agencies or contracted private organizations; legal status or authorization to work; verification; exception

Each state or local government agency or community action agency, or any private organization contracting with a state or local government agency, that provides employment services, including, but not limited to, job training, retraining, or placement, shall verify an individual's legal status or authorization to work prior to providing services to that individual in accordance with procedures established under federal law. For purposes of this section, proof of legal status or authorization to work includes, but is not limited to, a social security card, immigration visa, birth certificate, passport, or other valid document providing evidence of legal residence or authorization to work in the United States. This section shall not apply to employment services offered by school districts under secondary school and adult education programs. *(Added by Stats.1993, c. 819 (S.B.733), § 1.)*

§ 9601.7. Availability of services to citizens or persons authorized to work; posted notice

(a) Each state or local government agency or community action agency, or any private organization contracting with a state or local government agency, that enters into an agreement with the department to provide employment services including, but not limited to, job training, retraining, or placement, shall post in a prominent location in the workplace, a notice stating that only citizens or those persons legally authorized to work in the United States will be permitted to use the agency's or organization's employment services that are funded by the federal or state government.

(b) The notice shall read:

NOTICE: Attention All Job Seekers

The Immigration and Reform Control Act of 1986 (IRCA) requires that all employers verify the identity and employment authorization of all individuals hired after November 6, 1986. An employer is required to examine documents provided by the job seeker establishing identity and authorization for employment in the United States. In addition, it is a violation of both state and federal law to discriminate against job seekers on the basis of ancestry, race, or national origin. This agency provides employment services funded by the federal or state government that are available only to individuals who are United States citizens or who are legally authorized to work in the United States. *(Added by Stats.1993, c. 819 (S.B.733), § 2. Amended by Stats.1994, c.146 (A.B.3601), § 218.)*

§ 9602. Designation of economically disadvantaged areas; services; nondiscrimination; priorities

(a) The director shall designate economically disadvantaged areas. These areas shall be priority areas for services provided under this part. To the fullest extent possible, offices shall be established within the boundaries of the disadvantaged areas designated by the director.

(b) To the extent permitted by law, the department shall serve eligible persons in such a way as to prevent discrimination by serving persons whose minority group characteristics coincide to the fullest extent possible with the minority group characteristics of the unemployed and underemployed in the economically disadvantaged areas of their community.

A minority shall be interpreted to include women to assure equality of opportunity in employment in accordance with Executive Order 11478 under the Federal Affirmative Action Program.

(c) The department shall to the extent permitted by law provide services under this part in accordance with the following priorities:

(1) Unemployed heads of households.

(2) Underemployed heads of households.

(3) Other unemployed and underemployed persons.

(4) Veterans shall be accorded priority pursuant to federal law.

(d) For purposes of this division, women as a class shall be deemed to constitute a minority group. *(Added by Stats.1968, c. 1460, p. 2909, § 11. Amended by Stats.1973, c. 1206, p. 2626, § 88; Stats.1973, c. 1207, p. 2676, § 88; Stats.1974, c. 1468, p. 3207, § 1.)*

§ 9602.5. Training of women in nontraditional occupations; establishment of systemwide policy

The department shall establish, in conjunction with the Department of Social Services, the Department of Industrial Relations, the Department of Education, and the Chancellor's office of the California Community Colleges, a systemwide policy of actively promoting the training of women in nontraditional occupations. For purposes of this section, "nontraditional occupations" means any job classification in which not more than 25 percent of the employees are women, according to the statistics of the United States Department of Labor.

This section is not intended, and shall not be construed, to require any local agency to make any expenditures to further the policy set forth in this section. *(Added by Stats.1982, c. 1114, p. 4033, § 1. Amended by Stats.1986, c. 356, § 1.)*

§ 9604. Administrative information; annual report

(a) The department shall establish necessary data systems which shall provide administrative information on persons served including, but not limited to, the following information:

(1) Pertinent data on the characteristics of persons served.

(2) The services provided.

(3) The results of services provided.

(b) The department shall also compile annually a report for the state and its principal labor market areas. The report shall contain information on the characteristics of the unemployed and analyses of current trends and projections for population, labor force, employment, and unemployment and shall be provided on a regular basis to cooperative area manpower systems councils or successors. *(Added by Stats.1968, c. 1460, p. 2910, § 11. Amended by Stats.1970, c. 1000, p. 1796, § 7; Stats.1973, c. 1206, p. 2626, § 90; Stats.1973, c. 1207, p. 2677, § 90; Stats.2002, c. 1022 (A.B.444), § 16, eff. Sept. 28, 2002; Stats.2005, c. 152 (A.B.1577), § 31.)*

§ 9605. Job training and placement

The department shall:

(a) Conduct the state manpower program, with the exception of manpower programs conducted by units of local general purpose government.

(b) Be the sole state agency to approve and coordinate publicly funded job training and placement programs, which it administers. The department shall approve programs only if consistent with the plans developed under Section 9600 and other provisions of this division.

(c) Be responsible for developing program objectives for each category of the service program it administers, establishing cost-effective results measurement, and providing accountability for results as related to the objectives set.

(d) Appoint an advisory committee of representatives of employers and employer organizations to enlist the advice and support of private industry in developing a statewide system for making jobs available to job trainees following successful completion of job training and placement programs.

(e) Develop controls to insure that job training and placement programs, it administers meet existing labor market needs as viewed by employers. The department shall study training and personnel selection methods used successfully by private industry.

(f) Encourage placement of eligible persons in public employment with the assistance of an advisory group representing state and local officials and representatives of economically disadvantaged areas appointed by the department.

(g) Evaluate the need for specific new public employment opportunities.

(h) Determine the kinds and quality of job training and placement programs, it administers necessary to provide placement in public employment for eligible persons and develop means to realign job tasks to develop greater employment opportunities for eligible persons.

(i) Cooperate with the State Personnel Board and local personnel officials in developing and upgrading employment opportunities for and in eliminating unnecessary barriers to the placement of eligible persons in public employment.

The State Personnel Board and other state and local agencies shall cooperate to the maximum extent feasible to achieve the purposes of this division.

(Added by Stats.1968, c. 1460, p. 2910, § 11. Amended by Stats.1970, c. 1000, p. 1797, § 8; Stats.1973, c. 1206, p. 2627, § 91; Stats.1973, c. 1207, p. 2677, § 91; Stats. 1981, c. 819, p. 3175, § 3; Stats.2005, c. 152 (A.B.1577), § 32.)

§ 9606. Referrals to employers; assistance to individuals who are potentially employable

The state manpower program shall serve the needs of employers by providing them with referrals of qualified job applicants. In addition the manpower program shall assist those individuals who are ready for employment, those who are employable with some direct assistance, and those individuals who are potentially employable. *(Added by Stats.1973, c. 1206, p. 2629, § 93; Stats.1973, c. 1207, p. 2679, § 93.)*

§ 9607. Community employment development centers

In the administration of the state manpower program, the director shall establish community employment development centers. Within his administrative discretion, he shall determine the number, location and management structure for community employment development centers based on identified community needs. Each center shall be responsible for identifying and meeting manpower needs within the community and for maintaining current community labor market information. This labor market information shall be the basis for more realistic direction to manpower and vocational training efforts. *(Added by Stats.1973, c. 1206, p. 2629, § 95; Stats.1973, c. 1207, p. 2679, § 95.)*

§ 9608. Services

The director shall, within each community employment development center, establish an intake system to appraise the individual needs of applicants. Each community employment development center shall provide the following services:

(a) Job referral and labor market information services to applicants who are occupationally competitive and qualified by training or experience in the labor market. These applicants shall be encouraged to utilize self-help services.

(b) Employment exploration and job development services to applicants who are employable but need some directed assistance in planning an effective job search or coping with minor barriers to employment. Employment exploration and job development services are designed as follows:

(1) To prepare groups of applicants to use job referral and information services by instructing them in job finding techniques and how to initiate their own job search.

(2) To assist applicants directly by developing job opportunities.

(3) To provide, as necessary, usually on a one-time basis, the following services:

(A) Contacting an employer to explain an applicant's qualifications or limitations, such as a disability not affecting ability to work, in relation to requirements for a particular job and arranging an interview.

(B) A more thorough appraisal of the applicant's capabilities and desires in relation to the job market than is required of an applicant seeking only job referral and labor market information.

(4) To arrange for short-term supplemental services.

(c) Individual employability development and placement services to applicants who are potentially employable but are in need of more intensive services before becoming employable because they have vocational barriers due to disability, lack of skills, obsolescence of job skills, limited education, or poor work habits and attitudes. Intensive employability services shall be provided by case-responsible persons to applicants where case-responsible persons are assigned.

(d) Through case managers or case-responsible persons, case services to applicants to the extent funds are available. Case services funds may be made available for services to the disadvantaged. "Case services" means an applicant's expenses necessary for or incident to training or employability development and includes, but is not limited to, the following:

(1) Medical and dental treatment necessary for employability.

(2) Temporary child care.

(3) Transportation costs.

(4) Wearing apparel.

(5) Books and supplies.

(6) Tools and safety equipment.

(7) Union fees.

(8) Business license fees. *(Added by Stats.1973, c. 1206, p. 2629, § 97; Stats.1973, c. 1207, p. 2679, § 97. Amended by Stats.2002, c. 1022 (A.B.444), § 17, eff. Sept. 28, 2002; Stats.2005, c. 152 (A.B.1577), § 33; Stats.2006, c. 538 (S.B.1852), § 649.)*

§ 9609. Administration of manpower service funds; provision of services

The department shall administer manpower service funds and shall provide, in a balanced and flexible manner, needed services as provided in this part. *(Added by Stats.1973, c. 1206, p. 2630, § 99; Stats.1973, c. 1207, p. 2681, § 99.)*

§ 9610. Contracts for public and private job training and placement programs

The director may enter into contracts for public and private job training and placement programs as may be required, and shall maintain quarterly projections of manpower needs in the public and private sector in each area. *(Formerly § 9606, added by Stats.1968, c. 2911, p. 2906, § 11. Renumbered § 9610 and amended by Stats. 1973, c. 1206, p. 2628, § 92; Stats.1973, c. 1207, p. 2679, § 92.)*

§ 9612. Civil service

The employees of the department shall be subject to the State Civil Service Act, except for exempt appointees. Members of the California Commission on Aging shall continue to be appointed by the Governor. *(Formerly § 9609, added by Stats.1968, c. 1460, p. 2911, § 11. Renumbered § 9612 and amended by Stats.1973, c. 1206, p. 2630, § 98; Stats.1973, c. 1207, p. 2680, § 98; Stats. 1981, c. 819, p. 3176, § 4.)*

§ 9613. Use of federal funds; placement and manpower information services

(a) The director shall make every effort to secure to the fullest extent possible federal funds available for participation under this part and shall provide that effective and comprehensive placement and manpower information services are made available to eligible persons, both youth and adults, who are served by the department, using funds available to the department under Title III and Title IX of the Social Security Act, in accordance with a plan of service developed by the department and approved by the United States Department of Labor as required by federal law and regulations.

(b) Under a plan of service developed by the department, funds under Title III and Title IX used for the administration of employment service offices and funds under the Manpower Development and Training Act shall be used to administer programs designed to find employment for economically displaced personnel toward the end of meeting the following goals:

(1) Developing a broad inventory of skills of displaced workers.

(2) Establishing labor market information systems necessary to identify the need for skills in waste disposal, power, water reclamation, sea water conversion, communications, biomedical techniques, air pollution control, and transportation systems. *(Added by Stats.1973, c. 1206, p. 2630, § 100; Stats.1973, c. 1207, p. 2681, § 100.)*

§ 9615. Priority for services; federal funding

Eligible persons who are registrants pursuant to Article 3.2 (commencing with Section 11320) of Chapter 2 of Part 3 of Division 9 of the Welfare and Institutions Code shall receive priority for services. The department shall use up to 50 percent of the funds available to it pursuant to Section 7(b) of the federal Wagner–Peyser Act (29 U.S.C. Sec. 49f) to provide for job services required

pursuant to subdivision (c) of Section 11320.3 of the Welfare and Institutions Code. *(Added by Stats.1985, c. 1025, § 3, eff. Sept. 26, 1985. Amended by Stats.2002, c. 1022 (A.B.444), § 18.5, eff. Sept. 28, 2002; Stats.2005, c. 152 (A.B.1577), § 34.)*

§ 9616. Military personnel; civilian counterpart jobs requiring licenses; barriers impeding reentry

(a) The department, in coordination with the United States Department of Defense and the various branches of the military of the United States, shall determine which military occupational specialties have civilian counterpart jobs that require licensure by state or local agencies.

(b) The department shall further determine, to the degree possible, if any procedural, financial, technological, educational, or bureaucratic barriers exist that impede military personnel reentering the civilian workforce from acquiring these licenses.

(c) The department shall implement this section only to the extent federal funds are available for the costs of implementation. *(Added by Stats.1990, c. 854 (A.B.3415), § 1. Amended by Stats.2001, c. 745 (S.B.1191), § 216, eff. Oct. 12, 2001.)*

§ 9616.1. Local entities convened; plan to coordinate employer outreach activities and solicitation of job listings

(a) The department shall convene groups that represent local department field offices, county welfare departments, local workforce investment areas, and community colleges for the purpose of developing a local plan on how these entities will regularly coordinate employer outreach activities and the solicitation of entry-level and other job listings, in order to reduce duplication of effort and to enhance the overall job development activities. Each local plan shall be signed by the local entities convened pursuant to this subdivision and submitted to the department.

(b) The entities involved in formulating each local plan and the department shall review each plan on at least an annual basis. *(Added by Stats.1997, c. 606 (A.B.67), § 15, eff. Oct. 3, 1997. Amended by Stats.2001, c. 745 (S.B. 1191), § 217, eff. Oct. 12, 2001; Stats.2005, c. 152 (A.B.1577), § 35.)*

§ 9617. Competitive grants to certain faith-based organizations; criteria for provision of services; collection and analysis of information

(a) To the extent that funds are provided in the Budget Act of 2000 for the purposes of providing competitive grants to faith-based organizations that are not owned or operated as pervasively sectarian organizations, those organizations receiving funding shall demonstrate that they are able to meet the following six criteria in the provision of services:

(1) Establishing linkages with local workforce development service delivery systems.

(2) Leveraging resources through collaboration and partnerships.

(3) Establishing intermediate and long-term outcome goals, with measurable indicators.

(4) Collecting and maintaining data that can be used for management decisionmaking.

(5) Using data to assess progress and evaluate effectiveness.

(6) Sharing information with stakeholders.

(b) The department shall provide technical assistance to organizations as needed to enable them to meet the six criteria specified in paragraphs (1) to (6), inclusive, of subdivision (a).

(c) The department shall collect and analyze the following information as it relates to the organizations funded under this section:

(1) The number of participants who experienced job placements, wage gains, increased job retention, increased educational achievement, and reduced use of public assistance programs.

(2) The cost per participant.

(3) Organizations' effectiveness in serving populations with barriers to employment who are missed by traditional service providers.

(4) The department's success in transitioning the organizations to longer-term funding sources.

(d) The department shall provide an interim report with regard to the competitive grants provided under this section to the Legislature on or before May 15, 2001, and shall provide a final report to the Legislature on or before September 1, 2001. *(Added by Stats.2000, c. 108 (A.B. 2876), § 17.5, eff. July 10, 2000.)*

§ 9618. Solar training program

(a) The department shall administer a solar training program. The department shall coordinate with the Division of Apprenticeship Standards and the State Contractors' License Board to ensure solar energy product and service providers in California possess and maintain the necessary skills, training, and certification.

(b) Elements of the training program shall include, but need not be limited to, all of the following:

(1) The science of photovoltaics and small scale solar thermal technologies.

(2) The design of solar systems.

(3) The installation of solar systems.

(4) Permitting of solar systems.

(5) Safety.

(6) System and component certification.

(7) State and federal incentive programs. *(Added by Stats.2001–2002, 2nd Ex.Sess., c. 17 (A.B.48), § 4, eff. Aug. 8, 2002.)*

§ 9619. Regional nursing simulation laboratories

(a)(1) To the extent that funds are appropriated for this purpose in the annual Budget Act, the department may award grants to regional collaboratives for the creation of regional nursing simulation laboratories that will allow additional nursing students to have access to clinical educational facilities. No single grant made under this section may exceed two hundred and fifty thousand dollars ($250,000).

(2) During the 2005–06 fiscal year, all grants made under this section shall be made for the creation of regional nursing simulation laboratories that serve rural areas.

(b) The department shall administer grants made under this section, and shall establish procedures and criteria for the awarding of those grants. *(Added by Stats.2005, c. 74 (A.B.139), § 73, eff. July 19, 2005.)*

ARTICLE 3. SAN DIEGO MULTIUSE BIOTECHNOLOGY TRAINING CENTER

Section
9700. "Center" defined.
9701. Legislative findings and declaration; biotechnology industry.
9702. Memoranda of understanding; utilization of staff and resources.

§ 9700. "Center" defined

For purposes of this article, "center" means the San Diego Multiuse Biotechnology Training Center. *(Added by Stats.2003, c. 628 (A.B.1551), § 1.)*

§ 9701. Legislative findings and declaration; biotechnology industry

(a) The Legislature finds and declares the following:

(1) Biotechnology represents one of the most promising, innovation-based growth industries of this era. California is the nation's leading state in biotechnology innovation and production.

(2) The San Diego region, as the world's third largest biotechnology industry cluster, is host to world-class generators of science and technology in biotechnology and the related life sciences.

(3) Despite the specialized nature of emerging biotechnology firms, their recent growth has been extensive, and with that growth has come an ever-increasing demand for trained biotechnology workers at all levels. The industry's workforce has grown at an annual rate of about 15 percent over the past five years, and California's biotechnology workforce could easily grow to over 250,000 by the year 2015 from its current level of 100,000.

(4) Biotechnology employers need entry-level and advanced professionals that have a background in, and familiarity with, industrylike conditions for basic, applied, and translational research, development, and production.

Based on recent studies, there is a clear and strong demand for applied bioscience training, but that demand is currently not being met by the region's universities and colleges.

(5) Companies nationally have overwhelmingly endorsed an "industry-focused" approach of providing internship training programs directly with the companies, combined with "company-like" training activities.

(6) Many firms have identified the difficulty in finding entry level biotechnology workers at both the graduate and undergraduate levels as being directly related to the students' lack of applied industry training or exposure. Many firms have had to extensively train new employees to teach them how to function in a biotechnology business environment. Additionally, nearly three-fourths of firms surveyed in San Diego and nationally have indicated that they would benefit from being able to hire workers that have been prepared to enter the workforce through advanced biotechnology internships and training of a "specific" nature.

(7) San Diego and the surrounding area is served by many well-recognized academic institutions, from community colleges to universities offering doctorate programs, that supply educated workers to the biotechnology industry. At each academic level (AA, BS/BA, MS/MA, Ph.D.) curricula are in place, but most of the curricula are only marginally related to biotechnology workforce preparation in the applied sector. Applied education in the form of internships or instruction in practical science skills that would smooth the transition from academic institutions to the commercial biotechnology environment is even less prevalent than the biotechnology curricula offered at many schools, and is only now just emerging.

(8) Many of California's firms have found that many students graduate from four-year university programs with adequate conceptual understanding of biotechnology, but with relatively little practical laboratory experience, especially in the skills and protocols that are specific to commercial ventures as opposed to academic research.

(9) In 2001, the Legislature created the Pasadena Bioscience Center to address biotechnology workforce needs in the Los Angeles region. The Pasadena Bioscience Center provides applied workforce training and includes components for research and innovation, new business incubation, and bioinformatics. In cooperation with California State University, the City of Pasadena, Pasadena City College, the California Institute of Technology, Huntington Medical Research Institutes, and local biotechnology companies and organizations, the Pasadena Bioscience Center serves as a successful model of focused education and training, tailored to specific industry needs, and that may be utilized in other areas of the state.

(b) The Legislature further finds and declares that to address workforce needs in biotechnology, a multiuse biotechnology training center is being created in San Diego to serve as an anchor and catalyst for the growth of biotechnology enterprises in San Diego. The center will

operate as a nonprofit organization under Section 501(c)(3) of the Internal Revenue Code, and will serve as a catalyst for accelerating the growth and formation of new bioscience enterprises that will create value-added jobs and high economic multipliers in the San Diego region. For this purpose:

(1) The center will provide state-of-the-art, industry-oriented bioscience training and act as a strong contributor to the growth and retention of bioscience companies in the region. As such, the center, as proposed, will help encourage biotechnology companies to remain in the region, thereby offsetting the pull of other, less expensive business environments that have been recruiting both startup and existing local area bioscience companies.

(2) The center will utilize the organization, programs, and work of the Pasadena Bioscience Center as successful models in the development of the San Diego Multiuse Biotechnology Training Center and its programs.

(3) The new center will serve as a world class technology workforce training facility offering practical, hands-on learning experiences, including short-term workshops and courses, and more extended training that will involve putting together multidisciplinary, multilevel teams of researchers, technicians, production specialists, apprentices, and students to work in a businesslike environment.

(4) The center will coordinate an extensive applied biotechnology internship program that will place students in local biotechnology companies for practical training and experience.

(5) The center will have the most relevant and advanced training possible, including an emphasis in bioinformatics, that will ensure that the center attains a position at the forefront of this rapidly expanding, cross-application specialization within biotechnology.

(6) The center will have facilities and a collection of instruments not generally available to the region's secondary schools, colleges, or universities.

(7) The center can serve as a capstone training site for regional institutions.

(8) The center will address the needs of existing as well as future industry employees.

(9) The center may appoint directors to a board of directors, and existing participants in the center may serve as the original board of directors. The center may appoint new directors, as necessary, in its discretion.

(10) The center will work with private universities, companies, associations, and various public agencies through memoranda of understanding under Section 9702, for the purpose of coordinating services and receiving assistance and support. *(Added by Stats.2003, c. 628 (A.B.1551), § 1.)*

§ 9702. Memoranda of understanding; utilization of staff and resources

The San Diego Community College District, California State University, University of California, Employment Development Department, Employment Training Panel, California Health and Human Services Agency, Labor and Workforce Development Agency, California Workforce Investment Board, and the San Diego Workforce Partnership may enter into memoranda of understanding with the center to utilize existing staff and resources to provide any of the following:

(a) Funding, if moneys are appropriated.

(b) Staff.

(c) Program development.

(d) Outreach.

(e) Coordination.

(f) Implementation.

(g) Strategy.

(h) Physical office, administration, and training space. *(Added by Stats.2003, c. 628 (A.B.1551), § 1.)*

ARTICLE 4. CALIFORNIA YOUTHBUILD PROGRAM

Section
9800. Purpose.
9801. Program grants.
9802. Program services.
9802.5. Funding proposals.
9803. Use of program grants.
9805. Eligible participants.
9806. Use of federally funded programs; eligible grant recipients.
9807. Grant applications.
9808. Use of "YouthBuild" name.
9809. Reports by grant recipients.
9809.5. Additional reports by grant recipients.

Operative Effect

Operation of Stats.1999, c. 829 (A.B.643), is contingent on funding, pursuant to § 3 of that act.

§ 9800. Purpose

The purposes of the California YouthBuild Program shall be all of the following:

(a) To enable economically disadvantaged youth, especially youth who have not finished high school, to obtain the education, job skills training, personal counseling, leadership development skills training, job placement assistance, and long-term followup services necessary for them to achieve permanent economic self-sufficiency, while at the same time providing valuable community service that addresses urgent community needs, including the demand for affordable housing and the need for young role models and mentors for younger teenagers and children.

(b) To provide communities with the opportunity to establish or rebuild neighborhood stability in economically depressed and low-income areas, as well as historic areas requiring restoration or preservation, while providing economically disadvantaged youth, and youth who have not finished high school, an opportunity for a meaningful participation in society.

(c) To allow communities to expand the supply of affordable housing for homeless and other low-income individuals by utilizing the energies and talents of economically disadvantaged youth and young people who have not graduated from school.

(d) To foster the development of leadership skills and a commitment to community development among youth. *(Added by Stats.1999, c. 829 (A.B.643), § 2.)*

Operative Effect

Operation of Stats.1999, c. 829 (A.B.643), is contingent on funding, pursuant to § 3 of that act.

§ 9801. Program grants

(a) The director, from funds appropriated for this purpose to the YouthBuild Program, may make grants to applicants for the purpose of carrying out programs as authorized by this article. For the purpose of administering and managing the grant-making process, the director may contract with a qualified nonprofit corporation designated by the United States Department of * * * Labor to provide technical assistance to YouthBuild programs. All programs shall have strong youth and community involvement.

(b) For purposes of this article, the following terms have the following meaning:

(1) "YouthBuild Program" means the overall California YouthBuild Program, as coordinated by the director.

(2) "Program" means an individual program funded by a grant made by the director to an applicant as part of the overall YouthBuild Program.

(c) "Applicant" means an entity that applies for a program grant pursuant to Section 9807.

(d) "Participant" means a person eligible to participate in a program pursuant to Section 9805. *(Added by Stats.1999, c. 829 (A.B.643), § 2. Amended by Stats.2009, c. 95 (A.B.271), § 1.)*

§ 9802. Program services

Programs shall provide, at a minimum, all of the following services:

(a)(1) Acquisition, rehabilitation, acquisition and rehabilitation, or construction of housing and related facilities to be used for the purpose of providing homeownership for disadvantaged persons, residential housing for homeless individuals and very low income families, or transitional housing for persons who are homeless, ill, deinstitutionalized, or who have disabilities or special needs.

(2) Rehabilitation or construction of community facilities owned by public agencies or nonprofit entities.

(b)(1) Integrated education and job training services and activities or an equally-divided basis, with 50 percent of participants' time spent in classroom-based instruction, counseling, and leadership development instruction, and 50 percent of participants' time spent in experiential training on the construction site.

(2) The education component described in paragraph (1) shall include basic skills instruction, secondary education services, and other activities designed to lead to the attainment of a high school diploma or its equivalent. The curriculum for this component shall include math, language arts, vocational education, life skills training, social studies related to the cultural and community history of the participants, leadership skills, and other topics at the discretion of the program. Bilingual services shall be available for individuals with limited-English proficiency. A program shall have a goal of a minimum teacher-to-participant ratio of one teacher for every 18 participants.

(3) The job training component described in paragraph (1) shall involve work experience and skills training apprenticeships related to construction and rehabilitation activities described in subdivision (a). The process of construction shall be coupled with skills training and with close onsite supervision by experienced trainers. The curriculum for this component shall contain a set of locally agreed upon skills and competencies that are systematically taught, with participants' mastery assessed individually on a regular, ongoing basis. Safety skills shall be taught at the outset. A program shall have a goal of a minimum trainer-to-participant ratio of one trainer for every seven participants. This component shall be coordinated to the maximum extent feasible with preapprenticeship and apprenticeship opportunities.

(4) Assistance in attaining postsecondary education and in obtaining financial aid shall be made available to participants prior to graduation from the program.

(c) Counseling services designed to assist participants in positively participating in society, including all of the following, as necessary: outreach, assessment, and orientation; individual and peer counseling; life skills training, drug and alcohol abuse education and prevention; and referral to appropriate drug rehabilitation, medical, mental health, legal, housing, and other community services and resources. A program shall have a goal of a minimum counselor-to-participant ratio of one counselor for every 28 participants.

(d)(1) Leadership development training that provides participants with meaningful opportunities to develop leadership skills, including decisionmaking, problemsolving, and negotiating. A program shall encourage participants to develop strong peer group ties that support their mutual pursuit of skills and values.

(2) Each program shall establish a youth council in which participants are afforded opportunities to develop

public speaking and negotiating skills, and management and policymaking participation in specific aspects of the program.

(e) Each participant shall be provided with a training subsidy, living allowance, or stipend of not less than eight dollars ($8) per hour for the time spent at the worksite in construction training. For those participants who receive public assistance, this training subsidy, living allowance, or stipend shall not affect housing benefits, medical benefits, child care benefits, or food stamp benefits, to the extent consistent with federal law. The training subsidy, living allowance, or stipend may be distributed in a manner that offers incentives for good performance.

(f) Full–time participation in a program shall be offered for a period of not less than six months and not more than 24 months.

(g) A concentrated effort shall be made to find construction, construction-related, or nonconstruction jobs for all graduates of the program who have performed well. The job training curriculum shall provide participants with basic preparation for seeking and maintaining a job. Followup counseling and assistance in job seeking shall also be provided to participants for a period of 12 months following graduation from the program.

(h) A program serving 20 or more participants is required to have a full-time director responsible for the coordination of the requirements of this article. *(Added by Stats.1999, c. 829 (A.B.643), § 2.)*

Operative Effect

Operation of Stats.1999, c. 829 (A.B.643), is contingent on funding, pursuant to § 3 of that act.

§ 9802.5.   Funding proposals

The department may accept proposals for funding from applicants who establish their eligibility for funding under this article by submitting proof that they have been funded or designated as a federal YouthBuild program by the United States Department of * * * Labor. *(Added by Stats.1999, c. 829 (A.B.643), § 2. Amended by Stats. 2009, c. 95 (A.B.271), § 2.)*

Operative Effect

Operation of Stats.1999, c. 829 (A.B.643), is contingent on funding, pursuant to § 3 of that act.

§ 9803.   Use of program grants

Program grants may be used for the activities in Section 9802 and for any of the following activities:

(a) Legal fees for housing acquisition.

(b) Administrative and technical assistance costs of the program applicant that may not exceed 15 percent of the program grant, or another amount as is determined by the director to be necessary to support capacity development of a private nonprofit community-based organization. The applicant may contract with a technical assistance provider approved by the director.

(c) Defraying costs for the ongoing training and technical assistance needs of the program applicant that are related to developing and carrying out the program. *(Added by Stats.1999, c. 829 (A.B.643), § 2.)*

Operative Effect

Operation of Stats.1999, c. 829 (A.B.643), is contingent on funding, pursuant to § 3 of that act.

§ 9805. Eligible participants

(a) Except as provided in subdivision (b), eligible participants in a program shall be youth between the ages of 17 and 24, inclusive, who are economically disadvantaged, as defined in Section 1503 of Title 29 of the United States Code, and who are in one of the following groups:

(1) Persons who are not attending any school and who have not received a secondary school diploma or its equivalent.

(2) Persons currently enrolled in a traditional or alternative school setting or a GED program and who are in danger of dropping out of school.

(3) Very low income persons whose incomes are at or less than 50 percent of the area median income area, adjusted for family size, as estimated by the United States Department of Housing and Urban Development.

(b) Not more than 25 percent of program participants may be individuals who do not meet the requirements of subdivision (a). These participants shall be persons who have educational needs despite the attainment of a high school diploma. *(Added by Stats.1999, c. 829 (A.B.643), § 2.)*

Operative Effect

Operation of Stats.1999, c. 829 (A.B.643), is contingent on funding, pursuant to § 3 of that act.

§ 9806. Use of federally funded programs; eligible grant recipients

(a) The director shall use the existing infrastructure of federally funded YouthBuild programs to the maximum extent possible. In the 1999–2000 fiscal year, the director shall give first priority in awarding grants under this article to applicants seeking to continue YouthBuild programs established with federal or other funding.

(b) Entities eligible for grants under this article shall be nonprofit private entities and public agencies with experience in operating youth construction skills training, education, job placement, personal development, leadership development, and housing rehabilitation or construction programs. *(Added by Stats.1999, c. 829 (A.B.643), § 2.)*

Operative Effect

Operation of Stats.1999, c. 829 (A.B.643), is contingent on funding, pursuant to § 3 of that act.

§ 9807. Grant applications

An application for a grant under this article shall, at a minimum, contain all of the following:

(a) The amount of the grant requested and the proposed use of the grant.

(b) A description of the applicant and a statement of the applicant's qualifications, including a description of the applicant's past experience in running a YouthBuild program, if applicable, a description of the applicant's past experience with housing rehabilitation or construction, youth and youth education, youth leadership development, and youth employment training programs, and a description of the applicant's relationship with apprenticeship programs and with community-based organizations.

(c) A description of the proposed construction site and evidence of site control, and a description of the proposed construction or rehabilitation activities to be undertaken and the anticipated schedule for carrying out those activities.

(d) A description of the educational and job training activities, work opportunities, and other services that will be provided to participants.

(e) A description of the manner in which eligible youths will be recruited and selected, including a description of the arrangements that will be made with community-based organizations, local education agencies and education agencies of Native American nations, public assistance agencies, courts of jurisdiction for status and youth offenders, shelters for homeless individuals and other agencies serving homeless youth, foster care agencies, and other appropriate public agencies and private entities.

(f) A description of the special efforts that will be undertaken to recruit eligible young women as participants, including women with dependent children, including a description of how those women can receive appropriate support, including child care.

(g) A description of how the proposed program will be coordinated with other federal, state, Native American nation, and local agency activities, including public school programs, the Americorps program, crime prevention programs, vocational, adult, and bilingual education programs, and other job training programs.

(h) Substantive assurances that there will be a sufficient number of adequately trained supervisory personnel in the program who have attained the journey level or its equivalent.

(i) A description of the applicant's relationship with any local building trades union, including a description of the union's involvement in training and the proposed relationship of the activities to be undertaken pursuant to the grant with established apprenticeship programs.

(j) A description of activities that will be undertaken to develop the leadership skills of participants, including their role in decisionmaking.

(k) A detailed budget and description of a system of fiscal controls and auditing and accountability procedures that will be used to ensure fiscal soundness.

(*l*) A description of any contracts and arrangements entered into between the applicant and other entities, including all in-kind donations and grants from both public and private sources that will augment grant funds made available pursuant to this article.

(m) Identification and description of the financing proposed for any acquisition of property, or the rehabilitation or construction of housing.

(n) Identification and description of the entity that will operate and manage the property.

(o) A certification that the applicant will comply with the requirements of applicable federal laws, including the Fair Housing Act, Title VI of the Civil Rights Act of 1964, Section 504 of the Rehabilitation Act of 1973, and the Age Discrimination Act of 1975, and that the applicant will work to further fair housing policies.

(p) A description of the qualifications and past experience of the person who will be the full-time director for the applicant's project to be funded pursuant to this article.

(q) A description of the applicant pool profile, including, but not limited to, the number of participants currently on parole or probation, the number of participants with children requiring paid supervision, and the number of participants with Department of Motor Vehicles or court-sanctioned holds on their drivers' licenses. *(Added by Stats.1999, c. 829 (A.B.643), § 2.)*

Operative Effect

Operation of Stats.1999, c. 829 (A.B.643), is contingent on funding, pursuant to § 3 of that act.

§ 9808. Use of "YouthBuild" name

The term "YouthBuild" shall only be used in connection with a program funded pursuant to this article or by the United States Department of * * * Labor, or if the program is an affiliate of YouthBuild U.S.A. *(Added by Stats.1999, c. 829 (A.B.643), § 2. Amended by Stats.2009, c. 95 (A.B.271), § 3.)*

Operative Effect

Operation of Stats.1999, c. 829 (A.B.643), is contingent on funding, pursuant to § 3 of that act.

§ 9809. Reports by grant recipients

Each grant recipient, at the beginning of the grant cycle, shall report to the director, at a minimum, regarding the number of participants who have done any of the following:

(a) Obtained a general education degree (GED).

(b) Obtained full-time, unsubsidized employment in the building trades industry.

(c) Obtained full-time, unsubsidized employment in other industries.

(d) Obtained part-time, unsubsidized employment in the building trades industry or in other industries.

(e) Gained acceptance into a trade apprenticeship program.

(f) Successfully enrolled in a vocational or two-year community college.

(g) Successfully enrolled in a state university, the University of California, or any other four-year college. *(Added by Stats.1999, c. 829 (A.B.643), § 2.)*

Operative Effect

Operation of Stats.1999, c. 829 (A.B.643), is contingent on funding, pursuant to § 3 of that act.

§ 9809.5. Additional reports by grant recipients

Each grant recipient shall report to the director on other participant outcomes as required by the Governor under Section 122(h) of the federal Workforce Investment Act of 1998. *(Added by Stats.1999, c. 829 (A.B.643), § 2.)*

Operative Effect

Operation of Stats.1999, c. 829 (A.B.643), is contingent on funding, pursuant to § 3 of that act.

ARTICLE 5. JOBS FOR CALIFORNIA GRADUATES PROGRAM

Section
9900. Legislative intent.
9901. Contribution of in-kind and financial resources.
9902. Local affiliates; required elements.
9903. Eligible entities.
9904. Eligible youths.
9905. Local grants and local programs.
9907. Annual report.
9908. State funds; use.

§ 9900. Legislative intent

(a) It is the intent of the Legislature in enacting this article to support the expansion of the Jobs for California Graduates pilot project in Merced into a regional system of local programs based on the Jobs for America's Graduates model. The Jobs for California Graduates nonprofit, public-private partnership will create a network of local programs to help California's at-risk youth complete their secondary education and acquire the basic skills necessary to successfully transition into the workforce or enroll in postsecondary education.

(b) The director of the Employment Development Department, from funds appropriated for this purpose to the Jobs for California Graduates Program, may make grants to applicants for the purpose of carrying out programs as authorized by this article. The grants shall be used to support new and existing Jobs for California Graduates Programs in the central valley region in one or more of the following counties: Sacramento, San Joaquin, Stanislaus, Merced, Fresno, Madera, and Kern. The director shall develop criteria for ranking grant applications, and performance standards and auditing procedures for evaluating the effectiveness of the grants. The director may contract with a qualified nonprofit corporation designated by the national organization, Jobs for America's Graduates, to provide technical assistance to Jobs for California Graduates local programs.

(c) The regional system of Jobs for California Graduates local programs shall be designed to accomplish all of the following goals:

(1) To decrease absenteeism rates for at-risk youth.

(2) To improve the performance of at-risk youth in school and in the workplace.

(3) To improve secondary education completion rates.

(4) To improve employability skills of at-risk youth.

(5) To improve employment placement rates for at-risk youth.

(6) To improve enrollment rates of at-risk youth in postsecondary education and training. (Added by Stats. 2000, c. 313 (A.B.2827), § 2.)

§ 9901. Contribution of in-kind and financial resources

(a) In order to encourage a regional system of long-lasting, self-sustaining model local programs, communities served pursuant to this article shall contribute in-kind and financial resources in direct support of the model local program, according to the following schedule:

(1) During its initial year of implementation, a Jobs for California Graduates local program may receive state funds in an amount equal to 100 percent of the costs of implementing each Jobs for California Graduates Program site, but not to exceed sixty thousand dollars ($60,000).

(2) During any year subsequent to the initial year of implementation, a model local program may receive state funds in the amount equal to 75 percent of the costs of implementing the model local program, but not to exceed forty-five thousand dollars ($45,000).

(b) Community partners providing matching resources to the model local programs may include private nonprofit corporations, community-based organizations, workforce investment agencies, school districts, and other public and private sources. (Added by Stats.2000, c. 313 (A.B.2827), § 2.)

§ 9902. Local affiliates; required elements

Local affiliates of the Jobs for California Graduates Program shall include all of the following elements:

(a)(1) A trained youth specialist employed year-round providing individual and group instruction to 25 to 45 eligible youth recruited and selected by a school-based advisory committee comprised of faculty, administrators, and counselors.

(2) The youth specialist shall provide individual attention to students to help them overcome barriers preventing them from receiving a high school diploma or securing employment, or both, or pursuing a postsecondary education that will lead to a career.

(3) The youth specialist shall provide informal guidance to students on academic, career, and life decisions and, based on the individual needs of students, connect them to professional counseling services to address more serious barriers, such as mental health problems or drug abuse.

(4) The youth specialist shall be actively involved in intensive, one-on-one employer marketing and job development activities to identify entry-level job opportunities for students upon graduation. Likewise, the youth specialist shall assist graduates in the exploration of postsecondary education opportunities and help them navigate the financial aid process to pursue these opportunities.

(b) Youth shall be taught a minimum of 37 employment competencies designed to prepare them to secure a quality entry-level job or pursue a postsecondary education, or both, upon completion of their secondary education.

(c) Placement services shall be provided to students during the summer months or partnerships developed with summer youth employment programs to support yearlong learning. Youth specialists shall maintain contact with youth during the summer months.

(d) A student-led organization, associated with a state and national association, shall build on the competency-based curriculum and provide the opportunity for students to develop, practice, and refine their leadership and team membership skills.

(e) It shall serve as a school-based "one-stop center" for participating at-risk youth to ensure that they receive appropriate academic and social services from available resources in the school and community.

(f) It shall provide no less than 12 months of followup and support on the job and in postsecondary education after leaving the school.

(g) It shall provide computerized tracking of youth served, services delivered and performance outcomes, such as graduation rate, positive outcome rates, aggregate employment rate, full-time jobs rate, full-time placement rate, further education rate, wages, and return to school rate, at local and state levels.

(h) It shall provide continuous improvement of results through the ongoing professional development of managers, supervisors, and specialists. (Added by Stats.2000, c. 313 (A.B.2827), § 2.)

§ 9903. Eligible entities

(a) Entities eligible to conduct a Jobs for California Graduates local program shall include, but need not be limited to, local education agencies, community colleges, and nonprofit organizations with an interest in serving at-risk youth.

(b) To maintain eligibility after the initial year of implementation, participating entities shall conduct the Jobs for California Graduates Program in accordance with Jobs for America's Graduates performance standards, receiving no less than a "Meets Standards" rating on an accreditation review. *(Added by Stats.2000, c. 313 (A.B.2827), § 2.)*

§ 9904.   Eligible youths

To be eligible to receive services through a Jobs for California Graduates local program under this article, a youth shall meet at least two of the following criteria:

(a) One or more years behind modal grade for one's age group, with particular emphasis on those two or more years behind modal grade.

(b) Below average academic grade point average relative to students in his or her class.

(c) Above average number of absences during the past school year in comparison to other students in the school.

(d) Placed on probation, suspended, or expelled from school one or more times during the past two years.

(e) Pregnant or parenting teen.

(f) Physically or mentally challenged.

(g) Involved with substance abuse or criminal activities.

(h) Member of an economically disadvantaged family.

(i) Lives with only one or neither of his or her natural parents.

(j) Receives little or no academic or social support from home or family.

(k) Mother has not graduated from high school.

(*l*) Closest friends have limited educational expectations. For example, they do not expect to graduate from high school or have already dropped out of high school. *(Added by Stats.2000, c. 313 (A.B.2827), § 2.)*

§ 9905.   Local grants and local programs

(a) For purposes of establishing and expanding these programs, the department shall, to the extent feasible, make local grants available throughout the region.

(b) Notwithstanding subdivision (a), it is the intent of the Legislature that Jobs for California Graduates local programs be conducted in a broad range of settings, including urban, suburban, and rural districts, which are representative of all California youth during the initial year of the regional program, in order to test the effectiveness of the model local programs throughout the state. *(Added by Stats.2000, c. 313 (A.B.2827), § 2.)*

§ 9907.   Annual report

(a) The department shall submit an annual report to the Legislature on the performance outcomes of the Jobs

for California Graduates local programs on an annual basis.

(b) The department shall report the following outcomes at the end of the 12–month followup period:

(1) Secondary education completion rate as compared to the Jobs for America's Graduates standard of 90 percent for senior participants.

(2) Positive outcomes rate, such as youth employed, enrolled in a postsecondary institution, or serving in the military, or all of these, as compared to the Jobs for America's Graduates standard of 80 percent positive outcomes for graduates.

(3) Full–time placement rate, such as youth engaged in full-time employment, full-time military, or combining postsecondary education with employment.

(4) All other participant outcomes as required by the Governor under Section 122(h) of the federal Workforce Investment Act of 1998. *(Added by Stats.2000, c. 313 (A.B.2827), § 2.)*

§ 9908.   State funds; use

State funds made available pursuant to this article shall be used to carry out both of the following:

(a) The Jobs for California Graduates local program elements specified in Section 9902.

(b) Regional management and technical assistance activities, including, but not limited to, all of the following:

(1) Operation of an office, including the hiring of staff, that shall be responsible for managing and monitoring model local program compliance.

(2) Conducting research and evaluation of all Jobs for California Graduates local programs, retaining a third-party provider as appropriate.

(3) Making available regional training and development opportunities for consistent, effective implementation of the model local programs.

(4) Conducting educational and outreach activities to engage private and public sector employers, secondary and postsecondary educational institutions, the military, state and local elected officials, community and social service organizations, and other interested parties.

(5) Conducting regional activities for students, including, at a minimum, a leadership development conference and a career development conference.

(6) Providing for the continuous improvement of model local program performance outcomes.

(7) Developing and maintaining state and local partnerships with private and public employers, secondary and postsecondary educational institutions, and community and social services organizations.

(8) Providing other support and oversight to promote the continuous improvement of Jobs for California Graduates local programs.

(9) Directly operating local programs as appropriate. *(Added by Stats.2000, c. 313 (A.B.2827), § 2.)*

ARTICLE 6. EMPLOYER ELDER CARE BENEFITS

Section
9910. Legislative findings, declaration and intent.
9912. Outreach program; participation by designated organizations.

§ 9910. Legislative findings, declaration and intent

(a) The Legislature finds and declares all of the following:

(1) The percentage of California employers offering pension and retirement plans to employees is substantially lower than the national average.

(2) Many employers lack an understanding of the implications of our coming "age wave," and how to best assist employees in preparing for the long-term care needs of themselves and their families.

(b) It is the intent of the Legislature, in future years, to develop and to enact legislation to institute elder care and caregiving programs as an employee benefit, holding employers to the same standard in providing benefits and leave time for employees caring for elders as those provided employees caring for children. *(Added by Stats.2002, c. 541 (S.B.953), § 12.)*

§ 9912. Outreach program; participation by designated organizations

(a) The Legislature requests that the Senior Worker Advocate Office of the Employment Development Department work with the California Commission on Aging and other interested organizations including, but not limited to, AARP, in order to conduct outreach to the business community. The Legislature encourages other state entities, including, but not limited to, the California Department of Aging, to join in this effort.

(b) The Legislature requests that this outreach effort be directed at educating employers about the implications of the impending "age wave," and at providing employers with information on matters relevant to the aging population and on related employment implications.

(c) State funds may not be appropriated for purposes of this article. The Employment Development Department is not required to undertake any new task pursuant to this article unless the department receives federal or private funds for the purposes of this article. *(Added by Stats.2002, c. 541 (S.B.953), § 12.)*

CHAPTER 2.5. YOUTH EMPLOYMENT AND DEVELOPMENT [REPEALED]

CHAPTER 2.7. CALIFORNIA WORK–SITE EDUCATION AND TRAINING ACT [REPEALED]

CHAPTER 2.8. DISPLACED WORKER EDUCATION AND TRAINING ACT OF 1982 [REPEALED]

CHAPTER 2.9. REGIONAL EMPLOYMENT ASSESSMENT, JOB SEARCH ASSISTANCE, AND PLACEMENT SERVICES FOR DISPLACED WORKERS [REPEALED]

CHAPTER 3. WELFARE–TO–WORK GRANT PROGRAM [REPEALED]

CHAPTER 3.5. EMPLOYMENT TRAINING PANEL

Section
10200. Legislative findings and declarations; development of skills of frontline workers and employment training.
10201. Definitions.
10201.5. Waiver of minimum wage requirements.
10202. Establishment of panel.
10202.5. Membership.
10203. Meetings; offices; assignment of person to develop training for small businesses.
10204. Coordination of programs.
10205. Duties.
10206. Allocation of money in fund.
10207. Decision on application; time limit; expedited procedures.
10208. Contracts with public or private training entity for services.
10209. Contracts for job training; approval; distribution of funds; delegation of authority; payments; new hire training.
10210. Contracts with training agencies; requirements.
10211. Trainee or employee participating in program considered to be in training program.
10212.2. Budget.
10213. Employment development department to cooperate with panel.
10214. Continuous employment, wage and benefit history of participants in project.
10214.5. Special employment training projects; allocation of funds; major seasonal industries.
10214.6. Partnership for Workforce Recovery Training (PWRT).
10214.7. Training programs for recipients of CalWORKs benefits; funding; panel authority and duties.
10214.9. Licensed nurse training programs; authority and conditions for funding.
10215. Funding of individual project grants; forms; credits to employer's liability for unemployment insurance contributions.
10217. Funds to be appropriated in Budget Act by legislature.

§ 10200. Legislative findings and declarations; development of skills of frontline workers and employment training

The Legislature finds and declares the following:

(a) California's economy is being challenged by competition from other states and overseas. In order to meet this challenge, California's employers, workers, labor organizations, and government need to invest in a skilled and productive workforce, and in developing the skills of frontline workers. For purposes of this section, "frontline worker" means a worker who directly produces or delivers goods or services.

The purpose of this chapter is to establish a strategically designed employment training program to promote a healthy labor market in a growing, competitive economy that shall fund only projects that meet the following criteria:

(1) Foster creation of high-wage, high-skilled jobs, or foster retention of high-wage, high-skilled jobs in manufacturing and other industries that are threatened by out-of-state and global competition, including, but not limited to, those industries in which targeted training resources for California's small and medium-sized business suppliers will increase the state's competitiveness to secure federal, private sector, and other nonstate funds. In addition, provide for retraining contracts in companies that make a monetary or in-kind contribution to the funded training enhancements.

(2) Encourage industry-based investment in human resources development that promotes the competitiveness of California industry through productivity and product quality enhancements.

(3) Result in secure jobs for those who successfully complete training. All training shall be customized to the specific requirements of one or more employers or a discrete industry and shall include general skills that trainees can use in the future.

(4) Supplement, rather than displace, funds available through existing programs conducted by employers and government-funded training programs, such as the Workforce Investment Act of 1998 (29 U.S.C. Sec. 2801 et seq.), the Carl D. Perkins Vocational Education Act (P.L. 98–524), CalWORKs (Chapter 2 (commencing with Section 11200) of Part 3 of Division 9 of the Welfare and Institutions Code), the Enterprise Zone Act (Chapter 12.8 (commencing with Section 7070) of Division 7 of Title 1 of the Government Code), and the McKinney–Vento Homeless Assistance Act (42 U.S.C. Sec. 11301 et seq.), the California Community Colleges Economic Development Program, or apportionment funds allocated to the community colleges, regional occupational centers and programs, or other local educational agencies. In addition, it is further the intention of the Legislature that programs developed pursuant to this chapter shall not replace, parallel, supplant, compete with, or duplicate in any way already existing approved apprenticeship programs.

(b) The Employment Training Panel, in funding projects that meet the requirements of subdivision (a), shall give funding priority to those projects that best meet the following goals:

(1) Result in the growth of the California economy by stimulating exports from the state and the production of goods and services that would otherwise be imported from outside the state.

(2) Train new employees of firms locating or expanding in the state that provide high-skilled, high-wage jobs and are committed to an ongoing investment in the training of frontline workers.

(3) Develop workers with skills that prepare them for the challenges of a high performance workplace of the future.

(4) Train workers who have been displaced, have received notification of impending layoff, or are subject to displacement, because of a plant closure, workforce reduction, changes in technology, or significantly increasing levels of international and out-of-state competition.

(5) Are jointly developed by business management and worker representatives.

(6) Develop career ladders for workers.

(7) Promote the retention and expansion of the state's manufacturing workforce.

(c) The program established through this chapter is to be coordinated with all existing employment training programs and economic development programs, including, but not limited to, programs such as the Workforce Investment Act of 1998 (29 U.S.C. Sec. 2801 et seq.), the California Community Colleges, the regional occupational programs, vocational education programs, joint labor-management training programs, and related programs under the Employment Development Department and the Business, Transportation and Housing Agency. *(Added by Stats.1982, c. 1074, p. 3874, § 1. Amended by Stats.1989, c. 926, § 3; Stats.1993, c. 1080 (S.B.96), § 4; Stats.2000, c. 491 (S.B.43), § 4; Stats.2003, c. 844 (A.B. 1061), § 3; Stats.2004, c. 183 (A.B.3082), § 344; Stats. 2004, c. 225 (S.B.1097), § 69, eff. Aug. 16, 2004; Stats. 2006, c. 538 (S.B.1852), § 650.)*

§ 10201. Definitions

As used in this chapter:

(a) "Department" means the Employment Development Department.

(b) "Employer" or "eligible employer" means any employer subject to Part 1 (commencing with Section 100) of Division 1, except any public entity, or any nonprofit organization which has elected an alternate method of financing its liability for unemployment insurance compensation benefits pursuant to Article 5 (commencing with Section 801), or Article 6 (commencing with Section 821) of Chapter 3.

Any public entity or nonprofit organization that has elected an alternate method of financing its liability for unemployment insurance compensation benefits pursuant to Article 5 (commencing with Section 801), or Article 6 (commencing with Section 821) of Chapter 3, shall be deemed to be an employer only for purposes of placement of new hire trainees who received training as an incidental part of a training project designed to meet the needs of one or more private sector employers.

(c) "Eligible participant" means any person who, prior to beginning training or employment pursuant to this chapter, is any of the following:

(1) Unemployed and has established an unemployment insurance claim in this state, or has exhausted eligibility for unemployment insurance benefits from this state within the previous 24 months.

(2) Employed for a minimum of 90 days by his or her employer, or if employed for less than 90 days, met the conditions of paragraph (1) at the time of hire, had received a notice of layoff from the prior employer, or was employed by an employer for a period of not less than 90 days during the 180-day period prior to the employee's current employment at the start of training with an eligible employer, as provided in subdivision (b). The panel may waive this requirement for trainees employed by a business locating or expanding operations in the state, provided it is part of a state and local economic development effort endeavoring to create or retain California jobs. The panel may also waive the requirement for up to 10 percent of the trainee population, if it determines a business meets standard funding requirements set out under subdivision (a) of Section 10200.

(d) "Executive director" means the executive director appointed pursuant to Section 10202.

(e) "Fund" means the Employment Training Fund created by Section 1610.

(f) "Job" means employment on a basis customarily considered full time for the occupation and industry. The employment shall have definite career potential and a substantial likelihood of providing long-term job security, with reportable California earnings during the employment retention period. Furthermore, the employment shall provide earnings, upon completion of the employment requirement specified in subdivision (f) of Section 10209, equal to 50 percent, in the case of new hire training, or 60 percent, in the case of retraining, of the state or regional average hourly wage. However, in no case shall the employment result in earnings of less than 45 percent of the state average hourly wage for new hire training and 55 percent of the state average hourly wage for retraining. The panel may consider the dollar value of health benefits that are voluntarily paid for by an employer when computing earnings to meet the minimum wage requirements.

(g) "New hire training" means employment training, including job-related literacy training, for persons who, at the start of training, are unemployed.

(h) "Panel" means the Employment Training Panel created by Section 10202.

(i) "Retraining" means employment-related skill and literacy training for persons who are employed and who meet the definition of paragraph (2) of subdivision (c) prior to commencement of training and will continue to be employed by the same employer for at least 90 days following completion of training.

(j) "State average hourly wage" means the average weekly wage paid by employers to employees covered by unemployment insurance, as reported to the Employment Development Department for the four calendar quarters ending June 30 of the preceding calendar year, divided by 40 hours.

(k) "Trainee" means an eligible participant.

(l) "Training agency" means any private training entity or local educational agency. *(Added by Stats.1982, c. 1074, p. 3875, § 1. Amended by Stats.1984, c. 41, § 3, eff. March 19, 1984; Stats.1984, c. 193, § 143; Stats.1984, c. 604, § 1; Stats.1985, c. 106, § 160; Stats.1986, c. 1130, § 1; Stats.1989, c. 926, § 4; Stats.1990, c. 1668 (A.B. 2694), § 3, eff. Sept. 30, 1990; Stats.1993, c. 1080 (S.B.96), § 5; Stats.1994, c. 916 (S.B.1327), § 2, eff. Sept. 28, 1994; Stats.1996, c. 1124 (S.B.1524), § 7, eff. Sept. 30, 1996; Stats.2000, c. 491 (S.B.43), § 5; Stats.2003, c. 844 (A.B. 1061), § 4; Stats.2008, c. 497 (A.B.2570), § 1.)*

§ 10201.5. Waiver of minimum wage requirements

With respect to funding appropriated in the annual Budget Act to the Employment Development Department for allocation by the Employment Training Panel and identified for training of workers in regions suffering from high unemployment and low job creation, including the working poor, the panel, notwithstanding subdivision (g) of Section 10201, may waive the minimum wage requirements included in that subdivision provided that the post-retention wage of each trainee who has completed training and the required training period exceeds his or her wage before and during training. This determination shall be made on a case-by-case basis to ensure that post-training improvements in earnings are sufficient to warrant the investment of public funds. *(Added by Stats.2000, c. 108 (A.B.2876), § 18, eff. July 10, 2000.)*

§ 10202. Establishment of panel

(a) The Employment Training Panel is established in the Employment Development Department.

(b) The executive director shall be appointed by the Governor, and shall be well qualified for the position with experience in government. The executive director may perform all duties, exercise all powers, discharge all responsibilities, and administer and enforce all laws, rules, and regulations under the jurisdiction of the panel, with the approval of the panel. The executive director shall administer this chapter, with the approval of the panel, in the manner he or she deems necessary to conduct the work of the panel properly. With the approval of the panel, the executive director may create divisions and subdivisions as necessary, and change and abolish these divisions and subdivisions from time to time.

(c) The panel may employ personnel necessary to carry out the purposes of this chapter. All personnel shall be appointed pursuant to the State Civil Service Act (Part 1 (commencing with Section 18000) of Division 5 of Title 2 of the Government Code), except for an executive director, and two assistant directors, who shall be exempt from state civil service.

(d) All personnel of the panel shall be appointed, directed, and controlled only by the panel or its authorized deputies or agents to whom it may delegate its powers.

(e) The Governor shall appoint two assistant directors, to serve at the pleasure of the Governor. The assistant directors shall have the duties as assigned by the executive director, and shall be responsible to the executive director for the performance of their duties.

(Added by Stats.2000, c. 491 (S.B.43), § 7. Amended by Stats.2008, c. 497 (A.B.2570), § 2.)

§ 10202.5. Membership

(a) The panel shall consist of eight persons, seven of whom shall be appointed as provided in subdivision (b), and shall have experience and a demonstrated interest in business management and employment relations. The Secretary of Business, Transportation and Housing, or his or her designee, shall also serve on the panel as an ex officio, voting member.

(b)(1) Two members of the panel shall be appointed by the Speaker of the Assembly. One of those members shall be a private sector labor representative and the other member shall be a business representative.

(2) Two members of the panel shall be appointed by the President pro Tempore of the Senate. One of those members shall be a private sector labor representative and the other member shall be a business representative.

(3) Three members of the panel shall be appointed by the Governor. One of those members shall be a private sector labor representative, one member shall be a business representative, and one member shall be a public member.

(4) Labor appointments shall be made from nominations from state labor federations. Business appointments shall be made from nominations from state business organizations and business trade associations.

(5) The Governor shall designate a member to chair the panel, and the person so designated shall serve as the chair of the panel at the pleasure of the Governor.

(c) The appointive members of the panel shall serve for two-year terms.

(d) Appointive members of the panel shall receive the necessary traveling and other expenses incurred by them in the performance of their official duties out of appropriations made for the support of the panel. In addition,

each appointive member of the panel shall receive one hundred dollars ($100) for each day attending meetings of the panel, and may receive one hundred dollars ($100) for each day spent conducting other official business of the panel, but not exceeding a maximum of three hundred dollars ($300) per month. *(Added by Stats.2000, c. 491 (S.B.43), § 8. Amended by Stats.2004, c. 225 (S.B.1097), § 70, eff. Aug. 16, 2004; Stats.2008, c. 497 (A.B.2570), § 3.)*

§ 10203. Meetings; offices; assignment of person to develop training for small businesses

The panel may meet as necessary at locations throughout the state. The panel shall maintain a minimum of three regional offices. The central office shall be located in Sacramento. Two regional offices shall be located in the southern part of the state, and one regional office shall be located in the northern part of the state.

The executive director will assign one person, with experience in meeting the needs of small businesses, to each of the regional offices for the purpose of developing training projects for small businesses and expediting the processing of training proposals from small businesses. *(Added by Stats.1982, c. 1074, p. 3876, § 1. Amended by Stats.1984, c. 41, § 4, eff. March 19, 1984; Stats.1989, c. 926, § 6; Stats.1993, c. 1080 (S.B.96), § 6; Stats.2000, c. 491 (S.B.43), § 9.)*

§ 10204. Coordination of programs

The panel shall coordinate its programs with local and state workforce investment boards and other partners of the federal Workforce Investment Act of 1998. This coordination shall include, but not be limited to, the adoption of a plan, including regular sharing of data, for the coordination of training authorized pursuant to this chapter with programs administered under Division 8 (commencing with Section 15000).

(Added by Stats.1989, c. 926, § 8. Amended by Stats.2000, c. 491 (S.B.43), § 10; Stats.2008, c. 497 (A.B.2570), § 4.)

§ 10205. Duties

The panel shall do all of the following:

(a) Establish a three-year plan that shall be updated annually, based on the demand of employers for trained workers, changes in the state's economy and labor markets, and continuous reviews of the effectiveness of panel training contracts. The updated plan shall be submitted to the Governor and the Legislature not later than January 1 of each year. In carrying out this section, the panel shall review information in the following areas:

(1) Labor market information, including the state-local labor market information program in the Employment Development Department, the California Economic Strategy Panel, and other relevant regional or statewide initiatives and collaboratives.

(2) Evaluations of the effectiveness of training as measured by increased security of employment for workers and benefits to the California economy.

(3) The demand for training by industry, type of training, and size of employer.

(4) Changes in skills necessary to perform jobs, including changes in basic literacy skills.

(5) Changes in the demographics of the labor force and the population entering the labor market.

(6) Proposed expenditures by other agencies of federal Workforce Investment Act funds and other state and federal training and vocational education funds on eligible participants.

(b) Maintain a system to continuously monitor economic and other data required under this plan. If this data changes significantly during the life of the plan, the plan shall be amended by the panel. Each plan shall include all of the following:

(1) The panel's objectives with respect to the criteria and priorities specified in Section 10200 and the distribution of funds between new-hire training and retraining.

(2) The identification of specific industries, production and quality control techniques, and regions of the state where employment training funds would most benefit the state's economy and plans to encourage training in these areas, including specific standards and a system for expedited review of proposals that meet the standards.

(3) A system for expedited review of proposals that are substantially similar with respect to employer needs, training curriculum, duration of training, and costs of training, in order to encourage the development of proposals that meet the needs identified in paragraph (2).

(4) The panel's goals, operational objectives, and strategies to meet the needs of small businesses, including, but not limited to, those small businesses with 100 or fewer employees. These strategies proposed by the panel may include, but not be limited to, pilot demonstration projects designed to identify potential barriers that small businesses may experience in accessing panel programs and workforce training resources, including barriers that may exist within small businesses.

(5) The research objectives of the panel that contribute to the effectiveness of this chapter in benefiting the economy of the state as a whole.

(6) A priority list of skills or occupations that are in such short supply that employers are choosing to not locate or expand their businesses in the state or are importing labor in response to these skills shortages.

(7) A review of the panel's efforts to coordinate with the California Workforce Investment Board and local boards to achieve an effective and coordinated approach in the delivery of the state's workforce resources.

(A) The panel will consider specific strategies to achieve this goal that include the development of initiatives to engage local workforce investment boards in enhancing the utilization of panel training resources by companies in priority sectors, special populations, and in geographically underserved areas of the state.

(B) Various approaches to foster greater program integration between workforce investment boards and the panel will also be considered, which may include marketing agreements, expanded technical assistance, modification of program regulations and policy, and expanded use of multiple employer contracts.

(c) Solicit proposals and write contracts on the basis of proposals made directly to it. Contracts for the purpose of providing employment training may be written with any of the following:

(1) An employer or group of employers.

(2) A training agency.

(3) A local workforce investment board with the approval of the appropriate local elected officials in the local workforce investment area.

(4) A grant recipient or administrative entity selected pursuant to the federal Workforce Investment Act of 1998, with the approval of the local workforce investment board and the appropriate local elected officials.

These contracts shall be in the form of fixed-fee performance contracts. Notwithstanding any provision of law to the contrary, contracts entered into pursuant to this chapter shall not be subject to competitive bidding procedures. Contracts for training may be written for a period not to exceed 24 months for the purpose of administration by the panel and the contracting employer or any group of employers acting jointly or any training agency for the purpose of providing employment training.

(d) Fund training projects that best meet the priorities identified annually. In doing so, the panel shall seek to facilitate the employment of the maximum number of eligible participants.

(e) Establish minimum standards for the consideration of proposals, which shall include, but not be limited to, evidence of labor market demand, the number of jobs available, the skill requirements for the identified jobs, the projected cost per person trained, hired, and retained in employment, the wages paid successful trainees upon placement, and the curriculum for the training. No proposal shall be considered or approved that proposes training for employment covered by a collective bargaining agreement unless the signatory labor organization agrees in writing.

(f) Ensure the provision of adequate fiscal and accounting controls for, monitoring and auditing of, and other appropriate technical and administrative assistance to, projects funded by this chapter.

(g) Provide for evaluation of projects funded by this chapter. The evaluations shall assess the effectiveness of training previously funded by the panel to improve job security and stability for workers, and benefit participating employers and the state's economy, and shall compare the wages of trainees in the 12–month period prior to training as well as the 12–month period subsequent to completion of training, as reflected in the department's unemployment insurance tax records. Individual project evaluations shall contain a summary description of the project, the number of persons entering training, the number of persons completing training, the number of persons employed at the end of the project, the number of persons still employed three months after the end of the project, the wages paid, the total costs of the project, and the total reimbursement received from the Employment Training Fund.

(h) Report annually to the Legislature, by November 30, on projects operating during the previous state fiscal year. These annual reports shall provide separate summaries of all of the following:

(1) Projects completed during the year, including their individual and aggregate performance and cost.

(2) Projects not completed during the year, briefly describing each project and identifying approved contract amounts by contract and for this category as a whole, and identifying any projects in which funds are expected to be disencumbered.

(3) Projects terminated prior to completion and the reasons for the termination.

(4) A description of the amount, type, and effectiveness of literacy training funded by the panel.

(5) Results of complete project evaluations.

(6) A description of pilot projects, and the strategies that were identified through these projects, to increase access by small businesses to panel training contracts.

(7) A listing of training projects that were funded in high unemployment areas and a detailed description of the policies and procedures that were used to designate geographic regions and municipalities as high unemployment areas.

In addition, based upon its experience in administering job training projects, the panel shall include in these reports policy recommendations concerning the impact of job training and the panel's program on economic development, labor-management relations, employment security, and other related issues.

(i) Conduct ongoing reviews of panel policies with the goal of developing an improved process for developing, funding, and implementing panel contracts as described in this chapter.

(j) Expedite the processing of contracts for firms considering locating or expanding businesses in the state, in accordance with the priorities for employment training programs set forth in subdivision (b) of Section 10200.

(k) Coordinate and consult regularly with business groups and labor organizations, the California Workforce Investment Board, the State Department of Education, the office of the Chancellor of the California Community Colleges, and the Employment Development Department.

1096

(*l*) Adopt by regulation procedures for the conduct of panel business, including the scheduling and conduct of meetings, the review of proposals, the disclosure of contacts between panel members and parties at interest concerning particular proposals, contracts or cases before the panel or its staff, the awarding of contracts, the administration of contracts, and the payment of amounts due to contractors. All decisions by the panel shall be made by resolution of the panel and any adverse decision shall include a statement of the reason for the decision.

(m) Adopt regulations and procedures providing reasonable confidentiality for the proprietary information of employers seeking training funds from the panel if the public disclosure of that information would result in an unfair competitive disadvantage to the employer supplying the information. The panel may not withhold information from the public regarding its operations, procedures, and decisions that would otherwise be subject to disclosure under the California Public Records Act (Chapter 3.5 (commencing with Section 6250) of Division 7 of Title 1 of the Government Code).

(n) Review and comment on the budget and performance of any program, project, or activity funded by the panel utilizing funds collected pursuant to Section 976.6. *(Added by Stats.1982, c. 1074, p. 3876, § 1. Amended by Stats.1983, c. 39, § 4, eff. May 17, 1983; Stats.1984, c. 449, § 46, eff. July 17, 1984; Stats.1986, c. 1130, § 2; Stats. 1987, c. 1051, § 1; Stats.1989, c. 926, § 9; Stats.1990, c. 1668 (A.B.2694), § 4, eff. Sept. 30, 1990; Stats.1992, c. 727 (S.B.522), § 2, eff. Sept. 17, 1992; Stats.1993, c. 589 (A.B.2211), § 184; Stats.1993, c. 1080 (S.B.96), § 7; Stats.1995, c. 865 (S.B.644), § 3; Stats.2000, c. 491 (S.B.43), § 11; Stats.2001, c. 111 (A.B.429), § 20, eff. July 30, 2001; Stats.2003, c. 844 (A.B.1061), § 5; Stats.2004, c. 225 (S.B.1097), § 71, eff. Aug. 16, 2004; Stats.2008, c. 497 (A.B.2570), § 5.)*

§ 10206. Allocation of money in fund

(a) The panel may allocate money in the fund for any of the following purposes:

(1) Reimbursement of reasonable training costs, and administrative costs incurred by contractors. In making a determination of costs to be reimbursed under this paragraph, the panel may allocate funds in accordance with any of the following methods:

(A) For purposes of providing simplified fixed-fee performance contracts, a flat rate per hour for categories of training that are substantially similar with respect to content, methodology, and duration, as determined by the panel, not to exceed the reasonable and normal costs for the training. The panel shall periodically adjust the standardized rates established pursuant to this paragraph to reflect changes in training costs.

(B) A complete review of the proposal and its costs, including a budget listing the planned costs of training, including personnel, fringe benefits, equipment, supplies, fees for consulting or administrative services, and other costs attributable to training; the services provided by subcontractors; the length and complexity of the training; the method of training; the wages and occupations following training; whether the trainees are new hires or retrainees; and the cost of similar training that the panel has funded previously. The cost of administration shall not exceed 15 percent of the training costs under this paragraph, except that for new hire training the panel may fund administrative costs of up to 25 percent of the training cost.

(C) The panel may modify the specific requirements of this paragraph as they apply to employers or contractors proposing projects that involve training for a significant number of small employers in the same project.

(D) A contractor is prohibited from utilizing any funds earned or paid as advances or progress payments for the purpose of making payments to any other individual or entity, either directly or indirectly, for costs incurred as a finder's fee or for other compensation related to the predevelopment or development phase of a training program, which is based on a percentage of the preliminary or final panel award to the contractor for the training project.

(2)(A) Costs of program administration incurred under this chapter. These costs shall be reviewed annually by the Department of Finance and the Legislature and determined through the normal budgetary process.

(B) The panel's administrative costs, exclusive of the cost of administering Section 976.6, shall not exceed 15 percent of the total amount annually appropriated for expenditure by the panel. Expenditures for marketing, research, and evaluations provided under the contract to the panel that otherwise would have been provided directly by the panel shall not be included in this limitation.

(3) Service related to the purposes of this chapter provided by the Small Business Development Centers.

(b) For all training contracts, the panel shall establish requirements for in-kind contributions by either the contractor or the employer that reflect a substantial commitment on the part of the contractor or the employer to the value of the training. In developing these requirements, the panel shall take into account the ability of the contractor or the employer, because of size or financial condition, to make any contribution, and the ability of the Employment Training Fund to meet the demand for training authorized by this chapter. In developing policies regarding in-kind contributions, the panel shall hold public hearings. *(Added by Stats.1982, c. 1074, p. 3877, § 1. Amended by Stats.1983, c. 39, § 5, eff. May 17, 1983; Stats.1984, c. 193, § 144; Stats.1984, c. 604, § 2; Stats.1985, c. 106, § 161; Stats.1986, c. 1267, § 4; Stats.1989, c. 926, § 10; Stats.1990, c. 1668 (A.B. 2694), § 5, eff. Sept. 30, 1990; Stats.1993, c. 1080 (S.B.96), § 8; Stats.1994, c. 916 (S.B.1327), § 3, eff. Sept. 28, 1994; Stats.1995, c. 865 (S.B.644), § 4; Stats.1997, c. 606 (A.B.67), § 17, eff. Oct. 3, 1997; Stats.1998, c. 329 (A.B.2779), § 12, eff. Aug. 21, 1998; Stats.2000, c. 491 (S.B.43), § 12; Stats.2001, c. 111 (A.B.429), § 21, eff. July 30, 2001; Stats.2004, c. 225 (S.B.1097), § 72, eff. Aug. 16, 2004.)*

§ 10207. Decision on application; time limit; expedited procedures

(a) The panel shall accept or reject a completed application within 60 days of the receipt by the executive director.

(b) The panel shall develop expedited procedures for reviewing proposals submitted by the state agencies which are participants in a special interagency agreement with the panel for purposes of this chapter. *(Added by Stats.1989, c. 926, § 12. Amended by Stats.2000, c. 491 (S.B.43), § 14.)*

§ 10208. Contracts with public or private training entity for services

Nothing in this chapter shall be construed to preclude any employer from contracting with any public or private training entity for services, subject to the approval of the panel. *(Added by Stats.1982, c. 1074, p. 3877, § 1.)*

§ 10209. Contracts for job training; approval; distribution of funds; delegation of authority; payments; new hire training

(a) Contracts shall only be made for training in job-related vocational skills that are necessary for participants to attain a new job or retain an existing job with definite career potential and long-term job security. The contracts for vocational skills training may include ancillary training for job-related basic and literacy skills training if the panel finds that the training is necessary to achieve the objectives of the vocational training.

(b) The panel shall not approve any training proposal which facilitates the change in ownership of a business leading to the likelihood that an existing collective bargaining agreement would be declared void.

(c) To encourage a broad and equitable distribution of funds, the panel may require an employer who has previously received funds pursuant to this chapter for retraining of workers at a facility to contribute proportionately more to the cost of training in subsequent panel contracts for training of workers at the same facility.

(d) The panel may delegate to the executive director the authority to approve training contracts of up to one hundred thousand dollars ($100,000), provided the contracts meet the requirements of this chapter and the policies established by the panel, and provided that the panel regularly reviews the actions taken by the executive director pursuant to this subdivision.

(e) Payments shall be made in accordance with a performance contract under which partial payments may be made during training, a partial payment may be made on placement or retention of each trainee, and not less than 25 percent of the negotiated fee is withheld until the trainee has been retained in employment for 90 days after the end of training with a single employer, except for those occupations in which it is not customary for a worker to be employed 90 consecutive days with a single employer. In these latter cases, the panel may substitute a period similar to the probationary period customary to the occupation. The probationary period shall not be less than 500 work hours and shall be completed within 272 days of the completion of the training. In no case shall any payment be considered to have been earned until the trainee has been retained in employment for 90 days or the equivalent probationary period for an occupation in which it is not customary for a worker to be employed 90 consecutive days with a single employer.

(f) Contracts for new hire training shall require the contractor to provide the placement services necessary to ensure the trainees are placed in jobs for which they have been trained. *(Added by Stats.1982, c. 1074, p. 3877, § 1. Amended by Stats.1984, c. 604, § 3; Stats.1987, c. 1051, § 2; Stats.1989, c. 926, § 13; Stats.1993, c. 1080 (S.B.96), § 9; Stats.2008, c. 497 (A.B.2570), § 6.)*

§ 10210. Contracts with training agencies; requirements

Contracts shall be made with training agencies only if the training agency can demonstrate all of the following:

(a) The training agency has a satisfactory record of past performance in the placement and retention of former trainees and employer satisfaction with former trainees.

(b) The training agency can demonstrate labor market demand for the proposed training. Proof shall include, but not be limited to, the documented need of specific employers for the workers proposed to be trained in the skills proposed by the training agency.

(c) The training agency can demonstrate that the training prepares trainees in a manner satisfactory to employers.

(d) The training agency can demonstrate that its accounting systems include controls adequate to check the accuracy and reliability of accounting data, promote operating efficiency, and assure compliance with government requirements and generally accepted accounting principles. The panel shall have full access at any time to these accounting systems to assure compliance with these standards. *(Added by Stats.1982, c. 1074, p. 3878, § 1.)*

§ 10211. Trainee or employee participating in program considered to be in training program

A trainee or employee participating in a training program pursuant to this chapter shall be considered to be in a training program having the approval of the director under Article 1.5 (commencing with Section 1266) of Chapter 5 of Part 1 of Division 1. *(Added by Stats.1982, c. 1074, p. 3878, § 1. Amended by Stats.1984, c. 1211, § 15.)*

§ 10212.2. Budget

The panel shall prepare a budget covering necessary administrative costs of the panel. The budget shall not be subject to change by the director except as agreed to

by the panel. In the event that agreement cannot be reached, the Secretary of the Labor and Workforce Development Agency shall attempt to reach a mutual agreement. In the event a mutual agreement cannot be reached, the final decision shall rest with the Governor.

(Added by Stats.1983, c. 39, § 7, eff. May 17, 1983. Amended by Stats.2001, c. 111 (A.B.429), § 22, eff. July 30, 2001; Stats.2005, c. 152 (A.B.1577), § 37; Stats.2008, c. 497 (A.B.2570), § 7.)

§ 10213. Employment development department to cooperate with panel

The Employment Development Department shall cooperate with the panel by offering necessary technical assistance, which may include, but is not limited to, labor market information, projections of occupational demand, and information and advice on alternative training strategies. *(Added by Stats.1982, c. 1074, p. 3878, § 1.)*

§ 10214. Continuous employment, wage and benefit history of participants in project

To assist the panel and the Legislature in assessing the impact of this chapter over an extended period of time, the Employment Development Department shall develop and maintain a continuous employment, wage, and benefit history of unemployment insurance participants. *(Added by Stats.1982, c. 1074, p. 3879, § 1. Amended by Stats.2008, c. 497 (A.B.2570), § 8.)*

§ 10214.5. Special employment training projects; allocation of funds; major seasonal industries

(a) The panel may allocate up to 15 percent of the annually available training funds for the purpose of funding special employment training projects that improve the skills and employment security of frontline workers, as defined in subdivision (a) of Section 10200. Notwithstanding any other provision of this chapter, participants in these projects are not required to meet the eligibility criteria set forth in paragraph (1) of subdivision (a) of Section 10200 or subdivision (c) of Section 10201.

(b) The panel shall, on an annual basis, identify industries and occupations that shall be priorities for funding under this section. Training shall be targeted to frontline workers who earn at least the state average hourly wage.

(c) The panel may waive the minimum wage provisions pursuant to subdivision (f) of Section 10201 for projects in regions of the state where the unemployment rate is significantly higher than the state average, and may waive the employment retentions provisions specified in subdivision (f) of Section 10209 and instead require that the trainee has been retained in employment for a minimum of 90 days out of 120 consecutive days after the end of training with no more than three employers.

(d)(1) The panel may allocate funds pursuant to subdivision (a) to increase the productivity and extended employment retention of workers in the state's major seasonal industries.

(2) In funding special employment training projects for this purpose, the panel may do all of the following:

(A) When the amount of the postretention wages of each trainee who has completed training exceeds the amount of wages that the trainee earned before and during training, waive the minimum wage requirements set forth in subdivision (f) of Section 10201.

(B) Waive the employment retention requirements set forth in subdivision (f) of Section 10209 and instead require that the trainee be retained in employment for not less than 500 hours within the 12–month period following the completion of the training.

(C) When the panel finds that the training is necessary to achieve the objectives of vocational training, waive the limitation on job-related basic and literacy skills training set forth in subdivision (a) of Section 10209.

(3) For purposes of this section, "major seasonal industries" means eligible employers who satisfy all of the following requirements:

(A) Have a workforce comprised of at least 50 percent of workers whose employment period is necessarily cyclical, including, but not limited to, businesses directly involved in the harvesting, packing, or processing of goods or products.

(B) Have retained at least 50 percent of the same seasonal employees for at least one season of not less than 500 hours for the preceding 12–month period.

(C) Pay wages and provide benefits that exceed industry averages.

(c) The panel shall adopt minimum standards for consideration of proposals to be funded pursuant to this section.

(f) The panel may select contracts funded under this section based on competitive bidding.

(g) It is the intent of the Legislature in providing the authority for these projects that the panel allocate these funds in a manner consistent with the objectives of this chapter as provided in Section 10200. *(Added by Stats. 2000, c. 491 (S.B.43), § 18. Amended by Stats.2001, c. 111 (A.B.429), § 23, eff. July 30, 2001; Stats.2006, c. 519 (S.B.1690), § 2; Stats.2008, c. 497 (A.B.2570), § 9.)*

§ 10214.6. Partnership for Workforce Recovery Training (PWRT)

(a) The panel shall establish the Partnership for Workforce Recovery Training (PWRT) for the purposes of supporting and implementing the workforce development goals set forth in the federal American Recovery and Reinvestment Act of 2009 (ARRA)(Public Law 111–5) [1]. The panel shall develop and publish guidelines for implementing of the PWRT, consistent with, and including adequate fiscal and accounting controls, as prescribed in subdivision (g) of Section 10205.

(b) The panel may allocate any funds it receives pursuant to the federal Workforce Investment Act of 1998 (29 U.S.C. Sec. 2801 et seq.) and the ARRA to support the activities of the PWRT. Any funds received by the panel pursuant to this section shall be deposited into a separate account established by the department in the State Treasury, and used for the purposes of this section.

(c) The panel may adopt any regulations necessary to implement this section, but any regulations so adopted are exempt from the requirements of Chapter 3.5 (commencing with Section 11340) of Part 1 of Division 3 of Title 2 of the Government Code.

(d) The panel may solicit proposals and enter into contracts or other agreements to secure funding for the purposes of this section, but those proposals, contracts, and agreements shall be exempt from any competitive bidding requirements otherwise prescribed in statute. *(Added by Stats.2009–2010, 4th Ex.Sess., c. 12 (A.B.12), § 32, eff. July 28, 2009.)*

[1] Public law sections classified to U.S.C.A., see U.S.C.A. Tables.

§ 10214.7. Training programs for recipients of Cal-WORKs benefits; funding; panel authority and duties

The panel shall allocate funds available in the annual Budget Act for training programs designed for individuals who are eligible to receive benefits under Chapter 2 (commencing with Section 11200) of Part 3 of Division 9 of the Welfare and Institutions Code or who have received CalWORKs benefits within one year of the commencement of the training program.

(a) It is the intent of the Legislature in providing authority for these training programs that the panel allocate these funds in a manner consistent with the objectives of this chapter as provided in Section 10200.

(b) Notwithstanding any other provisions of this chapter, the eligibility criteria for individuals trained under this section shall be employment with an eligible employer as defined in subdivision (a) of Section 10201 and:

(1) Receipt of CalWORKs benefits at the time training begins, or

(2) Receipt of CalWORKs benefits within one year of the time training commenced.

(c) For purposes of this section, the panel may waive, if necessary, any of the following:

(1) The employer eligibility criteria outlined in paragraph (1) of subdivision (a) of Section 10200.

(2) The minimum training wage requirements pursuant to subdivision (g) of Section 10201.

(3) The employment retention provisions specified in subdivision (f) of Section 10209 and instead require that the trainee has been retained in employment for a minimum of 90 days out of 120 consecutive days after the end of training with no more than three employers.

(d) Notwithstanding any other provisions of this chapter, the panel shall consider proposals that use innovative strategies and training options to enable current and prior

CalWORKs recipients and eligibles to retain employment, including, but not limited to, projects that provide basic skills training.

(e) The panel shall adopt administrative procedures for approving and administering contracts under this section to expedite contracts, minimize barriers to completion of training, and facilitate the training of single trainees and small groups of trainees from one worksite. *(Added by Stats.1997, c. 270 (A.B.1542), § 25, eff. Aug. 11, 1997, operative Jan. 1, 1998. Amended by Stats.2008, c. 497 (A.B.2570), § 10.)*

§ 10214.9. Licensed nurse training programs; authority and conditions for funding

(a)(1) The panel may fund licensed nurse training programs to train individuals who are currently working as nurse assistants or caregivers in a health facility, as defined in Section 1250 of the Health and Safety Code.

(2) It is the intent of the Legislature that the panel allocate these funds in a manner consistent with the objectives of this chapter as provided in Section 10200.

(b) Notwithstanding any other provisions of this chapter, the panel shall waive the minimum wage provisions, pursuant to subdivision (f) of Section 10201, if all of the following conditions are met:

(1) The employee is enrolled in an approved licensed nurse training program that consists of not less than 1,000 hours of training.

(2) The employer pays the employee not less than 120 percent of the state minimum wage for not less than the first 20 hours of work per week during each week the employee is enrolled in the training program.

(3) Each program results in full-time employment customary for the occupation for which the individuals are being trained.

(c) Notwithstanding any other provisions of this chapter, the panel shall waive any limitation on the hourly length of training programs to allow approval and funding for up to 750 hours of a licensed nurse training program; provided, however, that those funds be used to pay for up to 750 training hours that remain in the licensed nurse training program after the employee has completed the first 800 hours of that program.

(d) Notwithstanding any other provision of this chapter, employers that participate in the nurse training programs funded pursuant to this section, are not required to meet the eligibility criteria set forth in paragraph (1) of subdivision (a) of Section 10200. *(Added by Stats.2005, c. 593 (S.B.102), § 1. Amended by Stats.2008, c. 497 (A.B.2570), § 11.)*

§ 10215. Funding of individual project grants; forms; credits to employer's liability for unemployment insurance contributions

The funding of individual project grants by the panel may take the form of either direct grants to the employer or training agency, or credits to the employer's liability for unemployment insurance contributions or reimbursements. Credits to the employer's liability for unemployment insurance contributions or reimbursements shall be drawn from the Employment Training Fund. *(Added by Stats.1982, c. 1074, p. 3879, § 1.)*

§ 10217. Funds to be appropriated in Budget Act by legislature

Funds in the Employment Training Fund created by Section 1610 shall be appropriated annually in the Budget Act by the Legislature for allocation by the panel for the purposes of this chapter, except those funds determined by the Legislature to be necessary to administer Section 976.6 and Article 6 (commencing with Section 1610) of Chapter 6 of Part 1 of Division 1 shall be appropriated to the department. *(Added by Stats.1982, c. 1074, p. 3879, § 1. Amended by Stats.1983, c. 39, § 8, eff. May 17, 1983; Stats.1984, c. 41, § 6, eff. March 19, 1984.)*

CHAPTER 4. PROGRAMS

ARTICLE 1. ELIGIBILITY

Section
10501. Public assistance recipient completing job training program; state employment fees; exemption.

§ 10501. Public assistance recipient completing job training program; state employment fees; exemption

Any public assistance recipient who successfully completes a job training program approved under this part shall be exempted from the payment of those fees normally associated with any examination or certification required by state law if the employment opportunity is for the job for which the recipient was trained. *(Added by Stats.1972, c. 1281, p. 2547, § 1.)*

CHAPTER 4.5. CALIFORNIA EMPLOYMENT AND TRAINING PLANNING

Article   Section
1.   Policies and Purposes 10510
2.   General Provisions and Definitions 10521
2.5   California Workforce and Economic Information Program 10529
3.   Coordination of Labor Market Information 10530

ARTICLE 1. POLICIES AND PURPOSES

Section
10510. Legislative intent.

§ 10510. Legislative intent

It is the intent of the Legislature, in enacting this chapter, to establish and implement a program of comprehensive and coordinated employment and training planning in California in accordance with the federal Job Training Partnership Act, as amended. [1] The Legislature recognizes the need for a new employment and training planning structure which will provide for comprehensive analysis of alternative expenditure possibilities for the fiscal resources available in this field. The basic principles of the system are as follows:

(a) That the employment and training needs at the local, regional, and state levels, be addressed.

(b) That the expenditure of available funds meets the needs at the local level.

(c) That employment and training programs be integrated into a uniform employment and training services planning system within substate regions.

(d) That a uniform planning system shall coordinate employment and training programs and eliminate duplication of programs among state and local agencies.

(e) That decisionmaking be decentralized, insofar as is practicable, to the governmental level closest to the people. *(Added by Stats.1973, c. 1206, p. 2634, § 113; Stats.1973, c. 1207, p. 2684, § 113. Amended by Stats. 1980, c. 766, p. 2281, § 2, eff. July 28, 1980; Stats.1983, c. 1234, § 2, eff. Sept. 30, 1983; Stats.1990, c. 1667 (S.B. 1033), § 14.)*

[1] 29 U.S.C.A. § 1501 et seq.

ARTICLE 2. GENERAL PROVISIONS AND DEFINITIONS

Explanatory Note

Provisions under this heading have been repealed.

ARTICLE 2.5. CALIFORNIA WORKFORCE AND ECONOMIC INFORMATION PROGRAM

Section
10529. Inclusion of workforce and economic information in labor market information system

§ 10529. Inclusion of workforce and economic information in labor market information system

(a) The services provided by the existing labor market information system within the department shall include workforce and economic information that does all of the following:

(1) Provides data and information to the state Workforce Investment Board created pursuant to Section 2821 of Title 29 of the United States Code, to enable the board to plan, operate, and evaluate investments in the state's workforce preparation system that will make the California economy more productive and competitive.

(2) Provides data and information to the California Economic Strategy Panel for continuous strategic planning and the development of policies for the growth and competitiveness of the California economy.

(3) Identifies and combines information from various state data bases to produce useful, geographically based analysis and products, to the extent possible using existing resources.

(4) Provides technical assistance related to accessing workforce and economic information to local governments, public-sector entities, research institutes, nonprofit organizations, and community groups that have various levels of expertise, to the extent possible using existing resources.

(b) The department shall coordinate with the State Department of Education, the Chancellor of the California Community Colleges, the State Department of Social Services, the California Postsecondary Education Commission, the Department of Finance, and the Franchise Tax Board in developing economic and workforce information. The department shall also solicit input in the operation of the program from public and private agencies and individuals that make use of the labor market information provided by the department. *(Added by Stats.2000, c. 108 (A.B.2876), § 18.2, eff. July 10, 2000. Amended by Stats.2004, c. 225 (S.B.1097), § 75, eff. Aug. 16, 2004.)*

ARTICLE 3. COORDINATION OF LABOR MARKET INFORMATION

Section
10530. Legislative intent; establishment of system.
10533. State-local cooperative labor market information program; objectives; funding.

§ 10530. Legislative intent; establishment of system

It is the intent of the Legislature to establish a statewide comprehensive labor market and occupational supply and demand information system to coordinate the labor market information needs, including those specified in the statutes cited below, for the following entities:

(1) The Board of Governors of the California Community Colleges pursuant to its responsibilities under Sections 70901, 70901.5, 71050, 78015, and 78016 of the Education Code.

(2) The State Department of Education, pursuant to its responsibilities under Sections 321, 323, 332, 341, 343, 421, 422, and 423 of the federal Carl D. Perkins Vocational Education Act (20 U.S.C. Sec. 2301 et seq.), and Sections 8031, 8081, 8500, 51228, 52300, 52301.5, 52302, 52302.3, 52302.5, 52304, 52309, 52381, 52519, 52520, 52910, 52911, and 52912 of the Education Code.

(3) The Employment Development Department, pursuant to its responsibilities under Article 1 (commencing with Section 1251) and Article 1.5 (commencing with Section 1266) of Chapter 5 of Part 1 of Division 1, Chapter 9 (commencing with Section 2051) of Part 1 of Division 1, Article 2 (commencing with Section 10521) of Chapter 4.5 of Part 1 of Division 3, and Chapter 6 (commencing with Section 15050) and Chapter 7.5 (commencing with Section 15075) of Division 8.

(4) The Employment Training Panel, pursuant to its responsibilities under Chapter 3.5 (commencing with Section 10200) of Part 1 of Division 3.

(5) The Department of Rehabilitation, pursuant to its responsibilities under Section 19152 of the Welfare and Institutions Code.

(6) The State Department of Social Services, pursuant to its responsibilities under Article 3.2 (commencing with Section 11320) of Chapter 2 of Part 3 of Division 9 of the Welfare and Institutions Code.

(7) The State Job Training Coordinating Council, pursuant to its responsibilities under Chapter 4.5 (commencing with Section 10510) of Part 1 of Division 3, and Chapter 3 (commencing with Section 15020.1), Chapter 4 (commencing with Section 15030), Chapter 4.5 (commencing with Section 15035), and Chapter 7.5 (commencing with Section 15075) of Division 8. *(Added by Stats.1990, c. 1667 (S.B.1033), § 18.)*

§ 10533. State-local cooperative labor market information program; objectives; funding

(a) The Employment Development Department shall operate the State–Local Cooperative Labor Market Information Program as the primary component of the comprehensive labor market and occupational supply and demand information system described by Section 10530. The department shall consult with agencies listed in Section 10530 in the development and operation of this program.

(b) The objectives of this program shall be to produce, through extensive local participation and for distribution in effective formats to all local users, reliable occupational information, and to achieve cost-efficient production by avoiding duplication of efforts. The program shall be a primary source for local and statewide occupational information and shall be available in all labor market areas in the state.

(c) In producing this information, state and local agencies shall use state occupational forecasts and other indicators of occupational growth, combined with local employer surveys of recruitment practices, job qualifications, earnings and hours, advancement and outlook, to provide statistically valid occupational analyses for local job training and education programs.

(d) Local labor market information studies shall be conducted by the department or by a local entity and shall include the participation of local users of the information. *(Added by Stats.1990, c. 1667 (S.B.1033), § 18. Amended by Stats.2003, c. 225 (A.B.1752), § 22.5, eff. Aug. 11, 2003; Stats.2005, c. 208 (S.B.665), § 5.)*

CHAPTER 5.   EMPLOYMENT SERVICES FOR THE DEAF AND HEARING IMPAIRED

Section
11000.   Legislative findings.
11000.5.   Contractor defined.
11001.   Contracts for employment services; duration; renegotiation.
11002.   Services included.
11003.   Choosing contractors; criteria; preference.

Section
11004.   Duties of department.
11006.   Administrative costs; limitation.

§ 11000.   Legislative findings

The Legislature finds that over 1.5 million persons in California are deaf or suffer from significant hearing impairment. Private and public employment agencies are not routinely adapted to meet the communication needs of persons who are deaf and hard of hearing and, therefore, the services they receive may be less than those provided to other persons. The Legislature also finds that employment opportunities for persons who are deaf and hard of hearing are increased when specialized counseling, interpretive, job placement, and followup services supplement conventional employment services. In addition, the limited programs which provide these specialized employment services to persons who are deaf and hard of hearing have recently been subject to significant local funding reductions. Therefore, the Legislature finds that a more stable funding source, as provided by this chapter, is necessary to ensure the continuance of these programs. *(Added by Stats.1984, c. 1157, § 1, eff. Sept. 17, 1984. Amended by Stats.2005, c. 152 (A.B.1577), § 43.)*

§ 11000.5.   Contractor defined

As used in this chapter "contractor" means a public agency or a private nonprofit corporation. *(Added by Stats.1984, c. 1157, § 1, eff. Sept. 17, 1984.)*

§ 11001.   Contracts for employment services; duration; renegotiation

(a) The department shall contract with public agencies or private nonprofit corporations for a period not to exceed one year to provide employment services for persons who are deaf and hard of hearing. These employment services shall be provided onsite at the department's offices which are selected pursuant to Section 11004.

(b) At the end of each contract year, the department may renegotiate the terms of each contract in accordance with allowable increases or decreases in the contractor's costs and the contractor's demonstrated ability to provide the specified services.

(c) If a contractor is a private nonprofit corporation, it shall submit a complete financial statement audited by a certified public accountant prior to a renewal of the contract. *(Added by Stats.1984, c. 1157, § 1, eff. Sept. 17, 1984. Amended by Stats.2005, c. 152 (A.B.1577), § 44.)*

§ 11002.   Services included

Employment services for persons who are deaf and hard of hearing shall include, but not be limited to, the following:

(a) Complete communication services for all preparatory, job placement, and followup activities. The communication services shall include interpreter services by a professional interpreter for persons who are deaf and hard of hearing possessing the comprehensive skills certification of the National Registry of Interpreters for the Deaf or the equivalent, telecommunications, and, when necessary, training in communication skills.

(b) Advocacy to assure that persons who are deaf and hard of hearing receive equal access to public and private employment services.

(c) Job development and job placement.

(d) Employment counseling, including peer counseling by persons who are deaf and hard of hearing.

(e) Followup counseling and problemsolving after placement. *(Added by Stats.1984, c. 1157, § 1, eff. Sept. 17, 1984. Amended by Stats.2005, c. 152 (A.B.1577), § 45.)*

§ 11003. Choosing contractors; criteria; preference

(a) The department, with the advice of persons knowledgeable about providing employment services to persons who are deaf and hard of hearing, shall establish the criteria for choosing contractors.

(b) The criteria shall include, but not be limited to, all of the following:

(1) The ability to provide services to a person who is deaf or hard of hearing in the person's preferred mode of communication.

(2) The ability to secure community support, including written endorsements of local officials, employers, the workforce investment board of the local workforce investment area and organizations of and for persons who are deaf and hearing impaired.

(3) The existence of funding from one or more public or private sources.

(c) Preference shall be given in the selection of a contractor to those proposals which demonstrate all of the following:

(1) Participation of persons who are deaf and hard of hearing on the potential contractor's employment services staff, and in the case of a private nonprofit corporation, on the board of directors.

(2) A commitment to the development and maintenance of self-determination for persons who are deaf and hard of hearing. *(Added by Stats.1984, c. 1157, § 1, eff. Sept. 17, 1984. Amended by Stats.2005, c. 152 (A.B.1577), § 46.)*

§ 11004. Duties of department

The department shall do all of the following:

(a) Determine the number and location of its offices within the state providing employment services to individuals who are deaf and hard of hearing and shall decide which offices shall be served by contractors given the resources available under this chapter. The department shall give priority to offices where contracts are necessary in order to prevent or minimize the disruption or the discontinuance of employment services to individuals who are deaf and hard of hearing which have been provided in conjunction with the department prior to July 1, 1984.

(b) Coordinate the provision of employment services for individuals who are deaf and hard of hearing with the State Department of Social Services and the Department of Rehabilitation so that employment services provided by this chapter supplement or provide alternatives to services provided or funded by the departments.

(c) Establish uniform accounting procedures and contracts for use with regard to this chapter.

(d) Promulgate requests for proposals and conduct bidders' conferences, and evaluate proposals according to the criteria established pursuant to Section 11003.

(e) Utilize the definitions of deafness and significant hearing impairment which have been used or established by regulation by the State Department of Social Services.

(f) Conduct a management or fiscal audit of any contract whenever it is necessary for proper supervision of that contract.

(g) Annually consider incorporation of the services described in this chapter in the job service plan required by Section 8 of the federal Wagner–Peyser Act (29 U.S.C. Sec. 49g).

(h) Assist contractors in maintaining all of the following information:

(1) The number of persons receiving services.

(2) A description of the services provided.

(3) The cost of the services provided.

(4) The number of persons placed in jobs.

(5) The number of persons assisted by followup activities.

(6) The number and qualifications of staff providing the services. *(Added by Stats.1984, c. 1157, § 1, eff. Sept. 17, 1984. Amended by Stats.2005, c. 152 (A.B.1577), § 47.)*

§ 11006. Administrative costs; limitation

The Employment Development Department shall not expend over 5 percent of the sum appropriated for this chapter for its administrative costs. *(Added by Stats.1984, c. 1157, § 1, eff. Sept. 17, 1984.)*

CHAPTER 6. REGIONAL WORK FORCE PREPARATION AND ECONOMIC DEVELOPMENT ACT [REPEALED]

CHAPTER 7. CAREGIVER TRAINING INITIATIVE

Section
11020. Establishment; advisory council; duties; membership.
11022. Employment Development Department; administration of regional collaborative program selection and funding; duties and responsibilities; evaluation of programs.

Section
11024.　Program model;　topics included in funding proposals;
　　　　regional collaborative program criteria.

§ 11020. Establishment; advisory council; duties; membership

(a) There is hereby established a project known as the Caregiver Training Initiative.

(b) It is the intent of the Legislature that the Caregiver Training Initiative develop and implement proposals to recruit, train, and retain health care providers such as certified nurse assistants, certified nurses, registered nurses, licensed vocational nurses, and other types of nursing and direct-care staff.

(c)(1) An advisory council is hereby established for purposes of the Caregiver Training Initiative.

(2) The advisory council shall develop goals, policies, and a general work plan for the Caregiver Training Initiative. For purposes of this paragraph, the advisory council shall consider the program model set forth in Section 11024.

(3) The duties of the advisory council shall include all of the following:

(A) Making recommendations regarding the identification of regions of the state for purposes of the initiative.

(B) Making recommendations to the Employment Development Department and the State Department of Social Services regarding the number of regional collaborative programs that should be funded under the initiative.

(C) Based on the number and size of the regions and programs to be funded, making recommendations to the Employment Development Department and the State Department of Social Services regarding the number of staff that should be assigned to the regions to assist in developing collaborative programs consisting of partnerships and funding proposals.

(D) Making suggestions and recommendations to the Employment Development Department and the State Department of Social Services with regard to the selection of the collaborative programs to be funded in each region under the initiative and of the contracts entered into between the state and the local agencies representing regional partners.

(E) Providing oversight of the progress of the initiative and identifying any needed corrective actions.

(F) Designating a member of the advisory council to participate in the work group established by the Employment Development Department, in conjunction with the State Department of Social Services, pursuant to paragraph (2) of subdivision (a) of Section 11022.

(d) The advisory council shall consist of the following:

(1) Each director, or a designee of the director, of the following departments in the California Health and Human Services Agency:

(A) Employment Development Department.

(B) Office of Statewide Health Planning and Development.

(C) State Department of Social Services.

(D) State Department of Health Services.

(E) California Department of Aging.

(2) A representative from each of the following:

(A) County Welfare Directors Association.

(B) State Department of Education.

(C) Chancellor's Office of the California Community Colleges.

(D) California Association of Health Facilities.

(E) California Association of Homes and Services for the Aging.

(F) American Red Cross.

(G) California Nurses Association.

(H) Service Employees International Union. *(Added by Stats.2000, c. 108 (A.B.2876), § 18.4, eff. July 10, 2000.)*

§ 11022. Employment Development Department; administration of regional collaborative program selection and funding; duties and responsibilities; evaluation of programs

(a)(1) The Employment Development Department, in consultation with the State Department of Social Services, shall administer regional collaborative program selection and funding under the Caregiver Training Initiative.

(2) The Employment Development Department, in conjunction with the State Department of Social Services, shall establish and lead a work group that shall be responsible for staff support to the advisory committee established pursuant to subdivision (c) of Section 11020.

(3) The Employment Development Department, in conjunction with the State Department of Social Services, shall be responsible for all of the following:

(A) Under the direction of the California Health and Human Services Agency, developing the criteria for regional collaborative programs, the number of staff to be assigned to regions, and the process for selecting regional collaborative programs to be funded.

(B) Assigning staff to each region to assist in developing collaborative programs consisting of partnerships and proposals for funding.

(C) Determining the date by which collaborative programs from each region shall submit their proposals for consideration.

(D) Selecting the collaborative program proposal from each region that best meets the criteria established by the department.

(E) Working with representatives from the health care provider and caregiver industries and labor, negotiating contract terms that best serve the initiative's goals.

(F) Approving all contracts for participation under the initiative.

(G) Distributing funds to the appropriate local agencies to commence the regional collaborative programs.

(H) Providing staff support to the advisory council established under subdivision (c) of Section 11020.

(I) Carrying out state-level activities identified by the department that are necessary for the initiative's success.

(b) The Employment Development Department, in conjunction with the State Department of Social Services, shall evaluate or contract for the evaluation of the regional collaborative programs funded under the initiative. The evaluation of each program site funded under the initiative shall include the following elements:

(1) A thorough assessment of implementation issues faced by grantees.

(2) An analysis, using appropriate statistical techniques, of identified outcomes of interest, including employment retention, advancement, earnings, and worker well-being measures.

(3) Annual population-based surveys of current and former CalWORKs recipients as they enter training programs and make choices about employment or subsequent job change.

(4) Identification and collection of well-being data regarding health care providers and caregivers and the recipients of their care.

(5) Construction and analysis of longitudinal administrative data.

(6) In–depth interviews with workers, staff, health care providers, and caregivers.

(c) The Employment Development Department shall develop a strategy to improve understanding of the demand and supply of labor, and the labor market dynamics for low-skilled workers who choose occupations such as certified nurse assistants. To develop the strategy, the department shall develop information about and analyze all of the following:

(1) Alternative occupations competing for available labor.

(2) The effect of conditions in other occupations using similar skill sets on the supply of labor in occupations related to health care providers and caregivers.

(3) Occupational ladders for health care providers and caregivers.

(4) The efforts by county welfare departments to increase interest in the health care provider and caregiver industry.

(5) Factors that draw individuals into or push them away from entering the health care provider or caregiver industry.

(6) Ways that nursing homes, long-term care facilities, and in-home care provider communities can improve the quality of employment of health care providers and caregivers.

(7) The treatment of staff in nursing homes and long-term care facilities.

(8) Worker compensation claims and claims of workplace violence due to patients with Alzheimer's disease or dementia.

(9) Benefit packages.

(10) On–the–job training for career advancement as a health care provider or caregiver in nursing homes or long-term care facilities or advancement in fields related to an occupation as a health care provider or caregiver. *(Added by Stats.2000, c. 108 (A.B.2876), § 18.4, eff. July 10, 2000.)*

§ 11024. Program model; topics included in funding proposals; regional collaborative program criteria

(a) The program model for implementation of the Caregiver Training Initiative shall consist of a solicitation and competitive selection process to identify proposals from regional collaborative programs that offer the best solutions to removing barriers for attracting and retaining qualified health care providers, such as certified nurse assistants, certified nurses, registered nurses, licensed vocational nurses, and other types of nursing and direct care staff.

(b) Proposals for funding under the initiative submitted by regional collaborative programs shall address all of the following topics:

(1) Marketing and outreach strategies that will attract eligible participants to begin careers in the health care provider industry and promote public awareness, especially among employers, to the opportunity to hire trained health care providers.

(2) Collaboration and agreements with state and local agency partners to help identify, refer, and provide services to eligible participants.

(3) Development and use of innovative training strategies, coupled with industry cooperation, to provide matching career paths that will enable participants to advance in the health care industry, including in nursing occupations such as certified nurse assistants, certified nurses, registered nurses, and licensed vocational nurses.

(4) Strategies for providing incentives to health care employers to hire program participants, such as taking advantage of existing tax credits, and incentives for participants to remain in and graduate from the program, such as postemployment training and support components.

(5) Leveraging additional resources to support activities that are not allowable with local welfare-to-work (Article 3.2 (commencing with Section 11320) of Chapter 1 of Part 3 of Division 9 of the Welfare and Institutions Code) funds and Workforce Investment Act of 1998 (29 U.S.C. Sec. 2801, et seq.) funds and that will provide flexibility in serving participants.

(c) The regional collaborative programs that compete for contracts under the initiative may include partnerships of any combination of local governmental entities, private nonprofit entities, and employer or employee groups. In order to ensure oversight for funds used in these contracts, fiscal agents representing these collaborative programs shall demonstrate all of the following:

(1) The capacity to retain fiduciary responsibility for funds.

(2) That the fiscal agent was chosen by agreement of collaborating partners.

(3) Previous experience using public funds for similar projects.

(4) The ability to properly account for and administer funds. *(Added by Stats.2000, c. 108 (A.B.2876), § 18.4, eff. July 10, 2000.)*

Part 2

EMPLOYMENT OPPORTUNITIES ACT OF 1971 [REPEALED]

Division 4

CAREER OPPORTUNITIES DEVELOPMENT [REPEALED]

Division 5

LEISURE SHARING

Chapter	Section
1. General Provisions	12100
2. Program Grants	12110
3. Technical Assistance	12120
4. Program Evaluation	12130
5. Miscellaneous	12140
6. Funding	12150

Contingent Operation

Division 5 becomes operative upon the date that federal or other funds are received and shall remain operative for a period of three years after such date, see Stats.1979, c. 751, § 2.

Legislative Counsel, by letter dated Feb. 26, 1986, advised that the condition specified in § 2 of Stats.1979, c. 751 has not been satisfied.

CHAPTER 1.　GENERAL PROVISIONS

Section
12100.　　Legislative finding, declaration and intent.
12100.5.　Construction.
12101.　　Administration.
12102.　　Definitions.

Contingent Operation

Division 5 becomes operative upon the date that federal or other funds are received and shall remain operative for a period of three years after such date, see Stats.1979, c. 751, § 2.

Legislative Counsel, by letter dated Feb. 26, 1986, advised that the condition specified in § 2 of Stats. 1979, c. 751 has not been satisfied.

§ 12100.　Legislative finding, declaration and intent

The Legislature finds and declares that the persistence of high levels of unemployment, even during periods of

substantial economic growth, is a matter of serious concern to the people of California, and requires a continuing search for solutions.

The Legislature further finds that measures undertaken at all levels of government to stimulate employment and to abate unemployment are by and large appropriate and useful, but that the aggregate impact of such measures over the years has fallen short of achieving and maintaining full employment. The Legislature therefore finds it proper and prudent to augment existing efforts by encouraging the development of new measures intended to increase employment opportunities.

It is the intent of this legislation to promote experimentation with means of creating employment opportunities through voluntary redistribution of hours of work, permitting more time away from work for those who desire additional leisure while providing employment for those who have no work.

It is explicitly not the intent of this legislation to impose any constraints upon participating employers to modify any of their policies governing the operation of their business. *(Added by Stats.1979, c. 751, p. 2602, § 1.)*

Contingent Operation

Division 5 becomes operative upon the date that federal or other funds are received and shall remain operative for a period of three years after such date, see Stats.1979, c. 751, § 2.

Legislative Counsel, by letter dated Feb. 26, 1986, advised that the condition specified in § 2 of Stats. 1979, c. 751 has not been satisfied.

§ 12100.5.　Construction

Nothing in this division shall be construed to supersede or impair any contrary provisions contained in an existing collective bargaining agreement. *(Added by Stats.1979, c. 751, p. 2602, § 1.)*

Contingent Operation

Division 5 becomes operative upon the date that federal or other funds are received and shall remain operative for a period of three years after such date, see Stats.1979, c. 751, § 2.

Legislative Counsel, by letter dated Feb. 26, 1986, advised that the condition specified in § 2 of Stats. 1979, c. 751 has not been satisfied.

§ 12101. Administration

The Employment Development Department shall administer the provisions of this division subject to the provisions of Section 12112. The department shall develop administrative procedures and guidelines necessary to carry out the intent of this division, including, but not limited to, means to monitor and measure program effectiveness. *(Added by Stats.1979, c. 751, p. 2602, § 1.)*

Contingent Operation

Division 5 becomes operative upon the date that federal or other funds are received and shall remain operative for a period of three years after such date, see Stats.1979, c. 751, § 2.

Legislative Counsel, by letter dated Feb. 26, 1986, advised that the condition specified in § 2 of Stats. 1979, c. 751 has not been satisfied.

§ 12102. Definitions

Definitions:

(a) "Leisure sharing" means a job-creation concept in which some full-time workers voluntarily reduce worktime under such circumstances that additional employment opportunities result from the employer's desire to maintain a given level of production.

The term leisure sharing is to be distinguished from work sharing or shared work as such terms are used in Sections 978.5 and 1279.5. In the context of this code, leisure sharing refers to the creation of employment opportunities through voluntary reduced worktime conjoined with a maintenance of production, whereas work sharing or shared work refer to the preservation of existing employment opportunities to the extent possible through worktime reductions in the face of diminished production requirements.

(b) "Reduced worktime" means a period of worktime less than that established by law or usage in a given work setting to be the standard for full-time.

(c) "Reduced workday" means fewer than the standard number of hours for a full-time workday.

(d) "Reduced workweek" means fewer than the standard number of days for a full-time workweek.

(e) "Reduced workyear" means additional days or weeks off work beyond those normally granted to a full-time worker.

(f) "Extended leave" or "sabbatical leave" means a very long continuous leave of absence from work of up to one year, with return rights, when granted, coming usually after a number of years of continuous service with the same employer.

(g) "Job sharing," "job pairing," or "twinning" means a form of job structuring in which two or more persons jointly fulfill the responsibilities of one full-time position with some degree of cooperation between them. *(Added by Stats.1979, c. 751, p. 2602, § 1.)*

Contingent Operation

Division 5 becomes operative upon the date that federal or other funds are received and shall remain operative for a period of three years after such date, see Stats.1979, c. 751, § 2.

Legislative Counsel, by letter dated Feb. 26, 1986, advised that the condition specified in § 2 of Stats. 1979, c. 751 has not been satisfied.

CHAPTER 2. PROGRAM GRANTS

Section
12110. Purpose.
12111. Identification of potentially reimbursable costs.
12112. Development of procedure for applying for grants.
12113. Applications.
12114. Priorities.
12115. Time limit.
12116. Reimbursements.

Contingent Operation

Division 5 becomes operative upon the date that federal or other funds are received and shall remain operative for a period of three years after such date, see Stats.1979, c. 751, § 2.

Legislative Counsel, by letter dated Feb. 26, 1986, advised that the condition specified in § 2 of Stats.1979, c. 751 has not been satisfied.

§ 12110. Purpose

In order to encourage voluntary participation by employers in the private sector, grants shall be made to offset increases in such employers' labor costs which are directly attributable to participation in the leisure sharing program authorized by this division. *(Added by Stats. 1979, c. 751, p. 2602, § 1.)*

Contingent Operation

Division 5 becomes operative upon the date that federal or other funds are received and shall remain operative for a period of three years after such date, see Stats.1979, c. 751, § 2.

Legislative Counsel, by letter dated Feb. 26, 1986, advised that the condition specified in § 2 of Stats. 1979, c. 751 has not been satisfied.

§ 12111. Identification of potentially reimbursable costs

The director shall identify potentially reimbursable costs, which shall include, but need not be limited to:

(a) Costs of additional payroll taxes, and costs of fringe benefits that are part of the employer's regular compensation package which by law cannot be prorated to a participating employee's worktime reduction under this program.

(b) Additional costs of recruitment and training that cannot reasonably or appropriately be defrayed under another program.

(c) Administrative costs of developing and maintaining participation in the program not covered by the technical assistance provided or in other ways.

(d) Special costs such as experience rating increases consequent on layoffs resulting from modifying or dropping participation either by the employer or employees, or at the termination of the experimental period.

(e) Costs of maintaining full selected fringe benefits of participating employees where, in the judgment of the panel established pursuant to Section 12112, such costs would enhance the research objectives of the program by presenting an opportunity to study the effects of such incentives on participation in a controlled setting, and would not be unduly costly relative to the funds available to the program. *(Added by Stats.1979, c. 751, p. 2602, § 1.)*

Contingent Operation

Division 5 becomes operative upon the date that federal or other funds are received and shall remain operative for a period of three years after such date, see Stats.1979, c. 751, § 2.

Legislative Counsel, by letter dated Feb. 26, 1986, advised that the condition specified in § 2 of Stats. 1979, c. 751 has not been satisfied.

§ 12112. Development of procedure for applying for grants

A procedure for applying for grants shall be developed by a panel consisting of the Directors of the Employment Development Department, and the Department of Industrial Relations, who shall also make the final decision on the awarding of grants. *(Added by Stats.1979, c. 751, p. 2602, § 1. Amended by Stats.1984, c. 449, § 48, eff. July 17, 1984; Stats.2000, c. 1055 (A.B.2889), § 56, eff. Sept. 30, 2000; Stats.2004, c. 225 (S.B.1097), § 78, eff. Aug. 16, 2004.)*

Contingent Operation

Division 5 becomes operative upon the date that federal or other funds are received and shall remain operative for a period of three years after such date, see Stats.1979, c. 751, § 2.

Legislative Counsel, by letter dated Feb. 26, 1986, advised that the condition specified in § 2 of Stats. 1979, c. 751 has not been satisfied.

§ 12113. Applications

Applications for grants may be considered for award if the application indicates that the employer is prepared to:

(a) Permit a sufficient number of employees to elect a sufficient amount of additional leave from work, provide evidence that such employees are in fact willing and ready to reduce worktime, and that the number of employees in the subject work force will be increased to maintain output. It shall also be clear that workers understand participation is strictly voluntary and reversible under the circumstances specified in subdivisions (b) and (c).

(b) Outline a reasonable number of options as to manner and duration of reducing worktime.

(c) Specify a reasonable time period after which participating workers may revise their options or revert to their prior status, and in which nonparticipating workers may elect to participate.

(d) Present a plan for proration of items of compensation of participating workers to each worker's new worktime pattern, which plan shall include the right of a worker to reimburse the employer the pro rata cost for maintenance of full benefits where the employee wishes to maintain such benefits. *(Added by Stats.1979, c. 751, p. 2602, § 1.)*

Contingent Operation

Division 5 becomes operative upon the date that federal or other funds are received and shall remain operative for a period of three years after such date, see Stats.1979, c. 751, § 2.

Legislative Counsel, by letter dated Feb. 26, 1986, advised that the condition specified in § 2 of Stats. 1979, c. 751 has not been satisfied.

§ 12114. Priorities

The following priorities shall be considered in making grant awards:

(a) The application shows high potential for creating a substantial number of permanent employment opportunities which would not otherwise exist.

(b) The application, when considered with other applications, offers an opportunity to broaden the experimentation with reduced worktime through the variety and flexibility offered to employees in the manner and duration of reduced worktime options.

(c) The application, when considered with other applications, offers an opportunity to expand an understanding of the characteristics of employees who are likely to participate.

(d) The extent of the opportunity to study the interaction of this program with other employment opportunity programs.

(e) The application, when considered with other grant applications, provides an opportunity to compare cost issues in relatively similar settings.

(f) The application provides an appropriate opportunity to study the effect of incentives to participation such as those outlined in subdivision (e) of Section 12111. *(Added by Stats.1979, c. 751, p. 2602, § 1.)*

Contingent Operation

Division 5 becomes operative upon the date that federal or other funds are received and shall remain operative for a period of three years after such date, see Stats.1979, c. 751, § 2.

Legislative Counsel, by letter dated Feb. 26, 1986, advised that the condition specified in § 2 of Stats. 1979, c. 751 has not been satisfied.

§ 12115. Time limit

No grant applicant shall be authorized to receive reimbursement under this chapter for a period exceeding two years. *(Added by Stats.1979, c. 751, p. 2602, § 1.)*

Contingent Operation

Division 5 becomes operative upon the date that federal or other funds are received and shall remain operative for a period of three years after such date, see Stats.1979, c. 751, § 2.

Legislative Counsel, by letter dated Feb. 26, 1986, advised that the condition specified in § 2 of Stats. 1979, c. 751 has not been satisfied.

§ 12116. Reimbursements

The director shall make appropriate reimbursements to grantees for expenses designated by Section 12111 in a timely manner agreed upon by the grantee at the outset of the grantee's participation in the program. *(Added by Stats.1979, c. 751, p. 2602, § 1.)*

Contingent Operation

Division 5 becomes operative upon the date that federal or other funds are received and shall remain operative for a period of three years after such date, see Stats.1979, c. 751, § 2.

Legislative Counsel, by letter dated Feb. 26, 1986, advised that the condition specified in § 2 of Stats. 1979, c. 751 has not been satisfied.

CHAPTER 3. TECHNICAL ASSISTANCE

Section
12120. Duties of department.
12121. Legislative intent; windfalls.

Contingent Operation

Division 5 becomes operative upon the date that federal or other funds are received and shall remain operative for a period of three years after such date, see Stats.1979, c. 751, § 2.

Legislative Counsel, by letter dated Feb. 26, 1986, advised that the condition specified in § 2 of Stats. 1979, c. 751 has not been satisfied.

§ 12120. Duties of department

The department shall disseminate information to employers explaining the nature and purpose of the leisure sharing program.

The department shall also provide technical assistance:

(a) To employers who wish to apply for participation in the program and to measure the extent of interest among employees of such employer.

(b) To participating employers to set up and operate such program in order to maximize the impact on employment, minimize costs, and maximize research findings.

(c) To participating employers to make the maximum appropriate use of existing federal, state, and local government aid programs related to objectives of this program, such as the Comprehensive Employment Training Act program and other recruitment programs, and to assist an employer in qualifying for any benefits to which he may be eligible under employment incentive tax or similar programs. Such assistance shall be designed to reduce to an absolute minimum administrative efforts and expenses required of the employer; provided, however, that the department shall specifically advise each applicant that utilization of any other voluntary aid or incentive program as described in this section shall be solely at the discretion of the applicant and shall in no way be construed as a condition or precondition of an employer's participation in the demonstration program under this division. *(Added by Stats.1979, c. 751, p. 2602, § 1.)*

Contingent Operation

Division 5 becomes operative upon the date that federal or other funds are received and shall remain operative for a period of three years after such date, see Stats.1979, c. 751, § 2.

Legislative Counsel, by letter dated Feb. 26, 1986, advised that the condition specified in § 2 of Stats. 1979, c. 751 has not been satisfied.

§ 12121. Legislative intent; windfalls

In enacting this division, the Legislature specifically intends that the director shall not take into consideration as a possible offset against reimbursable labor costs under Section 12111 such windfalls to a participating employer as:

(a) A tax incentive benefit or similar benefit gained by the employer through another public program specifically designed to encourage the employment of certain individuals, when such individuals have become employed as a result of the operation of the program under this division.

(b) A decline in total wages paid as a result of prorating the wages of high seniority employees while hiring new employees at lower wage rates as a result of the operation of the program under this division.

(c) Any productivity gains which may be attributable to a positive effect of this program. *(Added by Stats.1979, c. 751, p. 2602, § 1.)*

Contingent Operation

Division 5 becomes operative upon the date that federal or other funds are received and shall remain operative for a period of three years after such date, see Stats.1979, c. 751, § 2.

Legislative Counsel, by letter dated Feb. 26, 1986, advised that the condition specified in § 2 of Stats. 1979, c. 751 has not been satisfied.

CHAPTER 4. PROGRAM EVALUATION

Section
12130. Contracts.
12131. Determinations.

Contingent Operation

Division 5 becomes operative upon the date that federal or other funds are received and shall remain operative for a period of three years after such date, see Stats.1979, c. 751, § 2.

Legislative Counsel, by letter dated Feb. 26, 1986, advised that the condition specified in § 2 of Stats. 1979, c. 751 has not been satisfied.

§ 12130. Contracts

The department shall competitively contract with organizations competent in the field or program evaluation for the evaluation of the program established by this division. Pursuant to procedures and guidelines adopted by the department, such contractors shall monitor the progress and performance of each program to determine the effectiveness of such programs pursuant to the criteria established by Section 12131. *(Added by Stats. 1979, c. 751, p. 2602, § 1.)*

Contingent Operation

Division 5 becomes operative upon the date that federal or other funds are received and shall remain operative for a period of three years after such date, see Stats.1979, c. 751, § 2.

Legislative Counsel, by letter dated Feb. 26, 1986, advised that the condition specified in § 2 of Stats. 1979, c. 751 has not been satisfied.

§ 12131. Determinations

Each program for which a grant has been awarded shall be evaluated periodically to determine:

(a) The cost to government of creating jobs in the manner prescribed by this division. Such evaluation shall determine and distinguish between costs incurred in averting an increase in the participating employers' unit labor costs, the cost of providing technical assistance, and other costs of administering the program.

(b) The comparison of such costs with the costs of creating jobs through other government assisted programs, such as the Comprehensive Employment and Training Act (29 U.S.C.A. 801 et seq.)[1] and Work Incentive Programs authorized by Division 2 (commencing with Section 5000) of this code.

(c) The comparison of such costs with the costs of providing public assistance and similar services to households in which the employable wage earner is unemployed, including, but not limited to, a comparison of tax collections from employed individuals versus direct and indirect expenditures from tax revenues on behalf of such persons.

(d) The benefits to employers such as productivity improvements attributable to the program resulting from, among other things, improved morale, reduced personnel turnover, and a larger trained reserve work force.

(e) The benefits to participating employees which shall include a survey of the employees' expectations and experience.

(f) Broad social and economic benefits, if any, that may reasonably be projected from a potential expansion of the concept to a larger segment of the labor market.

(g) To the extent possible, what kinds of employers and employees are most likely to participate, and why, including an evaluation of the effectiveness of incentives to participation as outlined in subdivision (e) of Section 12111. *(Added by Stats.1979, c. 751, p. 2602, § 1.)*

[1] Repealed.

Contingent Operation

Division 5 becomes operative upon the date that federal or other funds are received and shall remain operative for a period of three years after such date, see Stats.1979, c. 751, § 2.

Legislative Counsel, by letter dated Feb. 26, 1986, advised that the condition specified in § 2 of Stats. 1979, c. 751 has not been satisfied.

CHAPTER 5. MISCELLANEOUS

Section
12140. Construction; selection of personnel.
12141. Reports.

Contingent Operation

Division 5 becomes operative upon the date that federal or other funds are received and shall remain operative for a period of three years after such date, see Stats.1979, c. 751, § 2.

Legislative Counsel, by letter dated Feb. 26, 1986, advised that the condition specified in § 2 of Stats. 1979, c. 751 has not been satisfied.

§ 12140. Construction; selection of personnel

Nothing in this division shall be construed to impose upon any employer who is participating in a job creation experimental program under this division any requirement beyond what is contained in other provisions of law with respect to what persons shall or may be hired by such employer to fill job vacancies created by the operation of the experimental program. *(Added by Stats.1979, c. 751, p. 2602, § 1.)*

Contingent Operation

Division 5 becomes operative upon the date that federal or other funds are received and shall remain operative for a period of three years after such date, see Stats.1979, c. 751, § 2.

Legislative Counsel, by letter dated Feb. 26, 1986, advised that the condition specified in § 2 of Stats. 1979, c. 751 has not been satisfied.

§ 12141. Reports

The department shall report to the Legislature, on or before January 1 and July 1 of each year, its progress in implementing this division, including the number of persons employed as a result of the enactment of this division. *(Added by Stats.1979, c. 751, p. 2602, § 1.)*

Contingent Operation

Division 5 becomes operative upon the date that federal or other funds are received and shall remain operative for a period of three years after such date, see Stats.1979, c. 751, § 2.

Legislative Counsel, by letter dated Feb. 26, 1986, advised that the condition specified in § 2 of Stats. 1979, c. 751 has not been satisfied.

CHAPTER 6. FUNDING

Section
12150. Authority to accept federal aid.
12151. Application for funds.
12152. Compliance with conditions.

Contingent Operation

Division 5 becomes operative upon the date that federal or other funds are received and shall remain operative for a period of three years after such date, see Stats.1979, c. 751, § 2.

Legislative Counsel, by letter dated Feb. 26, 1986, advised that the condition specified in § 2 of Stats. 1979, c. 751 has not been satisfied.

§ 12150. Authority to accept federal aid

The Employment Development Department is authorized to accept any federal or other funds which are available for the purposes of this division. *(Added by Stats.1979, c. 751, p. 2602, § 1.)*

Contingent Operation

Division 5 becomes operative upon the date that federal or other funds are received and shall remain operative for a period of three years after such date, see Stats.1979, c. 751, § 2.

Legislative Counsel, by letter dated Feb. 26, 1986, advised that the condition specified in § 2 of Stats. 1979, c. 751 has not been satisfied.

§ 12151. Application for funds

It is the intent of the Legislature that the Employment Development Department, with the assistance of the Department of Industrial Relations, seek and apply for funds from the federal government and other potential sources to implement the program established under this division. *(Added by Stats.1979, c. 751, p. 2602, § 1. Amended by Stats.1984, c. 449, § 49, eff. July 17, 1984; Stats.2000, c. 1055 (A.B.2889), § 57, eff. Sept. 30, 2000; Stats.2004, c. 225 (S.B.1097), § 79, eff. Aug. 16, 2004.)*

Contingent Operation

Division 5 becomes operative upon the date that federal or other funds are received and shall remain operative for a period of three years after such date, see Stats.1979, c. 751, § 2.

Legislative Counsel, by letter dated Feb. 26, 1986, advised that the condition specified in § 2 of Stats. 1979, c. 751 has not been satisfied.

§ 12152. Compliance with conditions

If, as a condition of receiving funds for implementing the program established under this division from federal or other sources, it is required that windfalls to a participating employer such as those described in Section 12121 be taken into consideration in determining reimbursable labor costs, the provisions of Section 12121 shall be inoperative to the extent required by the conditions for receiving such implementation funds. *(Added by Stats. 1979, c. 751, p. 2602, § 1.)*

Contingent Operation

Division 5 becomes operative upon the date that federal or other funds are received and shall remain operative for a period of three years after such date, see Stats.1979, c. 751, § 2.

Legislative Counsel, by letter dated Feb. 26, 1986, advised that the condition specified in § 2 of Stats. 1979, c. 751 has not been satisfied.

Division 6

WITHHOLDING TAX ON WAGES

Chapter		Section
1.	General Provisions	13000
2.	Withholding and Payment of Tax	13020
3.	Withholding Exemptions	13040
4.	Reports, Returns, and Statements	13050
5.	Collections	13070
6.	Violations	13090

CHAPTER 1. GENERAL PROVISIONS

Section

13000. Powers and duties of department.

13001. Definitions.

13002. Applicability of certain provisions.

13003. Construction of division; incorporation of certain definitions and provisions.

13004. Employee.

13004.1. Exclusion of individuals from definition of employee; conditions.

13004.5. Employee; additional definitions.

13005. Employer.

13005.7. Employment agency; domestic workers.

13006. Gross income.

13007. Miscellaneous payroll period.

13008. Payroll period.

13009. Wages.

13009.5. Wages subject to personal income tax.

13010. Withholding agent.

13011. Possession and control of records, papers, property, etc., previously held by Franchise Tax Board.

13013. Regulations adopted by Franchise Tax Board.

13014. Payment of interest obligations; applicability of division.

13015. Authority to require information.

13016. Payor's right to require name and address of recipient.

13017. Laws affecting changes in withholdings; time of compliance.

13018. Unauthorized inspection or unwarranted disclosure or use of information; misdemeanor; notice to affected taxpayers.

13019. Tax advice; privileged communications.

§ 13000. Powers and duties of department

The department shall have the powers and duties necessary to administer the reporting, collection, refunding to the employer, and enforcement of taxes required to be withheld by employers pursuant to Section 13020, except as otherwise provided by this division. *(Added by Stats.1980, c. 1007, p. 3228, § 64, operative July 1, 1981.)*

§ 13001. Definitions

The definitions set forth in Sections 126, 127, 129, 133, 134, and 144 shall apply to this division. *(Added by Stats.1980, c. 1007, p. 3228, § 64, operative July 1, 1981.)*

§ 13002. Applicability of certain provisions

The following provisions of this code shall apply to any amount required to be deducted, reported, and paid to the department under this division:

(a) Sections 301, 305, 306, 310, 311, 312, 317, and 318, relating to general administrative powers of the department.

(b) Sections 403 to 413, inclusive, Section 1336, and Chapter 8 (commencing with Section 1951) of Part 1 of Division 1, relating to appeals and hearing procedures.

(c) Sections 1110.6, 1111, 1111.5, 1112, 1113, 1113.1, 1114, 1115, 1116, and 1117, relating to the making of returns or the payment of reported contributions.

(d) Article 8 (commencing with Section 1126) of Chapter 4 of Part 1 of Division 1, relating to assessments.

(e) Article 9 (commencing with Section 1176), except Section 1176, of Chapter 4 of Part 1 of Division 1, relating to refunds and overpayments.

(f) Article 10 (commencing with Section 1206) of Chapter 4 of Part 1 of Division 1, relating to notice.

(g) Article 11 (commencing with Section 1221) of Chapter 4 of Part 1 of Division 1, relating to administrative appellate review.

(h) Article 12 (commencing with Section 1241) of Chapter 4 of Part 1 of Division 1, relating to judicial review.

(i) Chapter 7 (commencing with Section 1701) of Part 1 of Division 1, relating to collections.

(j) Chapter 10 (commencing with Section 2101) of Part 1 of Division 1, relating to violations. *(Added by Stats.1980, c. 1007, p. 3228, § 64, operative July 1, 1981. Amended by Stats.1986, c. 724, § 31; Stats.1994, c. 1049 (A.B.3086), § 24; Stats.2005, c. 152 (A.B.1577), § 50; Stats.2006, c. 538 (S.B.1852), § 651.)*

§ 13003. Construction of division; incorporation of certain definitions and provisions

(a) Except where the context otherwise requires, the definitions set forth in this chapter, and in addition the definitions and provisions of the Personal Income Tax Law referred to and hereby incorporated by reference as set forth in the following provisions of the Revenue and Taxation Code, shall apply to and govern the construction of this division:

(1) "Corporation" as defined by Section 17009.

(2) "Fiduciary" as defined by Section 17006.

(3) "Fiscal year" as defined by Section 17011.

(4) "Foreign country" as defined by Section 17019.

(5) "Franchise Tax Board" as defined by Section 17003.

(6) "Husband" and "wife" as defined by Section 17021.

(7) "Individual" as defined by Section 17005.

(8) "Military or naval forces" as defined by Section 17022.

(9) "Nonresident" as defined by Section 17015.

(10) "Partnership" as defined by Section 17008.

(11) "Person" as defined by Section 17007.

(12) "Resident" as defined by Sections 17014 and 17016.

(13) "State" as defined by Section 17018.

(14) "Taxable year" as defined by Section 17010.

(15) "Taxpayer" as defined by Section 17004.

(16) "Trade or business" as defined by Section 17020.

(17) "United States" as defined by Section 17017.

(b) The provisions of Part 10 (commencing with Section 17001) and Part 10. 2 (commencing with Section 18401) of Division 2 of the Revenue and Taxation Code, relating to the following items, are hereby incorporated by reference and shall apply to and govern construction of this division:

(1) Trade or business expense (Article 6 (commencing with Section 17201) of Chapter 3 of Part 10).

(2) Deductions for retirement savings (Article 6 (commencing with Section 17201) of Chapter 3 of Part 10).

(3) Distributions of property by a corporation to a shareholder (Chapter 4 (commencing with Section 17321) of Part 10).

(4) Deferred compensation (Chapter 5 (commencing with Section 17501) of Part 10).

(5) Partners and partnerships (Chapter 10 (commencing with Section 17851) of Part 10).

(6) Gross income of nonresident taxpayers Chapter 11 (commencing with Section 17951) of Part 10).

(7) Postponement of the time for certain acts by individuals in or in support of the armed forces (Article 3 (commencing with Section 18621) of Chapter 2 of Part 10.2).

(8) Disclosure of information (Article 2 (commencing with Section 19542) of Chapter 7 of Part 10.2). For this purpose "Franchise Tax Board" as used therein shall mean the Employment Development Department in respect to information obtained in the administration of this division. *(Added by Stats.1980, c. 1007, p. 3228, § 64, operative July 1, 1981. Amended by Stats.1986, c. 847, § 14; Stats.1993, c. 31 (S.B.3), § 69, eff. June 16, 1993, operative Jan. 1, 1994; Stats.1993, c. 402 (A.B.1668), § 5; Stats.2002, c. 29 (A.B.1729), § 15.)*

§ 13004. Employee

"Employee" means a resident individual who receives remuneration for services performed within or without this state or a nonresident individual who receives remuneration for services performed within this state and includes an officer, employee, or elected official of the United States, a state, territory, or any political subdivision thereof, or any agency or instrumentality of any one or more of the foregoing. "Employee" also includes an officer of a corporation.

Whether an individual provides equipment in the performance of services for remuneration shall not be considered in a determination of whether that individual is an employee. *(Added by Stats.1980, c. 1007, p. 3228, § 64, operative July 1, 1981. Amended by Stats.1986, c. 847, § 15.)*

§ 13004.1. Exclusion of individuals from definition of employee; conditions

"Employee" does not include any individual if all of the following conditions exist:

(a) The individual is licensed pursuant to the provisions of Part 1 (commencing with Section 10000) of Division 4 of the Business and Professions Code and is performing services in the capacity of a licensee, or the individual is engaged in the trade or business of primarily in-person demonstration and sales presentation of consumer products, including services or other intangibles, in the home or sales to any buyer on a buy-sell basis, a deposit-commission basis, or any similar basis, for resale by the buyer or any other person in the home or otherwise than in a retail or wholesale establishment.

(b) Substantially all of the remuneration (whether or not paid in cash) for the services performed by that individual is directly related to sales or other output (including the performance of services) rather than to the number of hours worked by that individual.

(c) The services performed by the individual are performed pursuant to a written contract between that individual and the person for whom the services are performed and the contract provides that the individual will not be treated as an employee with respect to those services for state tax purposes. *(Added by Stats.1983, c. 498, § 216, eff. July 28, 1983. Amended by Stats.1995, c. 541 (A.B.272), § 8.)*

§ 13004.5. Employee; additional definitions

(a) "Employee" also means any individual who is an employee pursuant to Section 2750.5 of the Labor Code, of a person who holds a valid state contractor's license pursuant to Chapter 9 (commencing with Section 7000) of Division 3 of the Business and Professions Code.

(b) When subdivision (a) does not apply, "employee" shall also mean any individual who is an employee, pursuant to Section 2750.5 of the Labor Code, of a person who is required to obtain a valid state contractor's license pursuant to Chapter 9 (commencing with Section

7000) of Division 3 of the Business and Professions Code. *(Added by Stats.1990, c. 719 (A.B.2667), § 5.)*

§ 13005. Employer

(a) "Employer" means any individual, person, corporation, association, partnership, or limited liability company, or any agent thereof, doing business in this state, deriving income from sources within this state, or in any manner whatsoever subject to the laws of this state, the State of California or any political subdivision or agency thereof, including the Regents of the University of California, any city organized under a freeholders' charter, or any political body not a subdivision or agency of the state, and any person, officer, employee, department, or agency thereof, making payment of wages to employees for services performed within this state, except as provided in subdivision (b).

(b) If the employer, as defined in subdivision (a), for whom the employee performs or performed the service does not have control of the payment of wages for such services, "employer" (except for purposes of Section 13009) means the person having control of the payment of such wages, whether or not the person having control of the payment of such wages is subject to the jurisdiction of the laws of this state. *(Added by Stats.1980, c. 1007, p. 3228, § 64, operative July 1, 1981. Amended by Stats.1994, c. 1200 (S.B.469), § 91, eff. Sept. 30, 1994.)*

§ 13005.7. Employment agency; domestic workers

An employment agency, as defined in paragraph (3) of subdivision (a) or (h) of Section 1812.501 of the Civil Code shall not be deemed the employer of the domestic worker for whom it procures, offers, refers, provides, or attempts to provide work if all of the factors set forth in Section 687.2 exist. *(Added by Stats.1993, c. 1275 (A.B. 1370), § 4.)*

§ 13006. Gross income

"Gross income" means all compensation for services including fees, commissions, and similar items, except as otherwise provided by this division. "Gross income" shall specifically include those items relating to compensation specified by Article 2 (commencing with Section 17081) of, and shall specifically exclude those items relating to compensation specified by Article 3 (commencing with Section 17131) of, Chapter 3 of Part 10 of Division 2 of the Revenue and Taxation Code. *(Added by Stats.1980, c. 1007, p. 3228, § 64, operative July 1, 1981. Amended by Stats.1986, c. 847, § 16.)*

§ 13007. Miscellaneous payroll period

"Miscellaneous payroll period" means a payroll period other than a daily, weekly, biweekly, semimonthly, monthly, quarterly, semiannual, or annual payroll period. *(Added by Stats.1980, c. 1007, p. 3228, § 64, operative July 1, 1981.)*

§ 13008. Payroll period

"Payroll period" means a period for which a payment of wages is ordinarily made to the employee by his or her employer. *(Added by Stats.1980, c. 1007, p. 3228, § 64, operative July 1, 1981.)*

§ 13009. Wages

"Wages" means all remuneration, other than fees paid to a public official, for services performed by an employee for his or her employer, including all remuneration paid to a nonresident employee for services performed in this state, and the cash value of all remuneration paid in any medium other than cash, except as provided by this section. "Wages" includes tips received by an employee in the course of his or her employment. The wages shall be deemed to be paid at the time a written statement including tips is furnished to the employer pursuant to Section 13055 or, if no statement including those tips is so furnished, at the time received.

"Wages" shall not include remuneration paid under any of the following conditions:

(a) For agricultural labor, as defined in subdivision (g) of Section 3121 of the Internal Revenue Code.[1]

(b) For domestic service in a private home, local college club, or local chapter of a college fraternity or sorority.

(c) For service not in the course of the employer's trade or business performed in any calendar quarter by an employee, unless the cash remuneration paid for that service is fifty dollars ($50) or more and the service is performed by an individual who is regularly employed by the employer to perform the service. For purposes of this subdivision, an individual shall be deemed to be regularly employed by an employer during a calendar quarter only if either of the following conditions is met:

(1) On each of some 24 days during the quarter, the individual performs for the employer for some portion of the day service not in the course of the employer's trade or business.

(2) The individual was regularly employed, as determined under paragraph (1), by the employer in the performance of the service during the preceding calendar quarter.

(d) For services by a citizen or resident of the United States for a foreign government or an international organization.

(e) For services performed by a nonresident alien individual as designated by regulations prescribed by the department.

(f) For services performed by a duly ordained, commissioned, or licensed minister of a church in the exercise of his or her ministry or by a member of a religious order in the exercise of duties required by the order.

(g)(1) For services performed by an individual under the age of 18 in delivery or distribution of newspapers or shopping news, not including delivery or distribution to any point for subsequent delivery or distribution.

(2) For services performed by an individual in, and at the time of, the sale of newspapers or magazines to ultimate consumers, under an arrangement under which the newspapers or magazines are to be sold by him or her at a fixed price, his or her compensation being based on the retention of the excess of the price over the amount at which the newspapers or magazines are charged to him or her whether or not he or she is guaranteed a minimum amount of compensation for the services, or is entitled to be credited with the unsold newspapers or magazines turned back.

(h) For services not in the course of the employer's trade or business, to the extent paid in any medium other than cash.

(i) To, or on behalf of, an employee or his or her beneficiary under any of the following situations:

(1) From or to a trust which is exempt from tax under Section 17631 of the Revenue and Taxation Code at the time of payment, unless the payment is made to an employee of the trust as remuneration for services rendered as an employee and not as a beneficiary of the trust.

(2) Under or to an annuity plan which, at the time of payment, is a plan qualified pursuant to Chapter 5 (commencing with Section 17501) of Part 10 of Division 2 of the Revenue and Taxation Code.

(3) Under or to a bond purchase plan which, at the time of payment, is a bond purchase plan qualified pursuant to Chapter 5 (commencing with Section 17501) of Part 10 of Division 2 of the Revenue and Taxation Code.

(4) For a payment which qualifies for deduction by an employee pursuant to Section 219 of the Internal Revenue Code [2] if, at the time of payment, it is reasonable to believe that the employee will be entitled to a deduction under that section for payment.

(5) Under a cafeteria plan (within the meaning of Section 125 of the Internal Revenue Code).[3]

(j) To a master, officer, or any other seaman who is a member of a crew on a vessel engaged in foreign, coastwise, intercoastal, interstate, or noncontiguous trade.

(k) Pursuant to any provision of law other than Section 5(c) [4] or 6(l) [5] of the Peace Corps Act, for service performed as a volunteer or volunteer leader within the meaning of that act.

(l) In the form of group-term life insurance on the life of an employee.

(m) To or on behalf of an employee, and to the extent that, at the time of the payment of remuneration it is reasonable to believe that a corresponding deduction is allowable for moving expenses pursuant to Article 6 (commencing with Section 17201) of Chapter 3 of Part 10 of Division 2 of the Revenue and Taxation Code.

(n)(1) As tips in any medium other than cash.

(2) As cash tips to an employee in any calendar month in the course of his or her employment by an employer, unless the amount of the cash tips is twenty dollars ($20) or more.

(o) For service performed by an individual on a boat engaged in catching fish or other forms of aquatic animal life under an arrangement with the owner or operator of the boat pursuant to which all of the following apply:

(1) The individual does not receive any cash remuneration, other than as provided in paragraph (2).

(2) The individual receives a share of the boat's (or the boats' in the case of a fishing operation involving more than one boat) catch of fish or other forms of aquatic animal life or a share of the proceeds from the sale of the catch.

(3) The amount of the individual's share depends on the amount of the boat's (or the boats' in the case of a fishing operation involving more than one boat) catch of fish or other forms of aquatic animal life.

This subdivision shall apply only where the operating crew of the boat (or each boat from which the individual receives a share in the case of a fishing operation involving more than one boat) is normally made up of fewer than 10 individuals.

(p) For any medical care reimbursement made to, or for the benefit of, an employee under a self-insured medical reimbursement plan pursuant to Section 105(h)(6) of the Internal Revenue Code.[6]

(q) To, or on behalf of, an employee to the extent not includable in gross income pursuant to Section 13006.

(r) For services to which Section 633 applies. *(Added by Stats.1980, c. 1007, p. 3228, § 64, operative July 1, 1981. Amended by Stats.1985, c. 400, § 1; Stats.1986, c. 847, § 17; Stats.1987, c. 851, § 2; Stats.1987, c. 1138, § 185, eff. Sept. 25, 1987; Stats.1988, c. 11, § 92, eff. Feb. 19, 1988.)*

[1] 26 U.S.C.A. § 3121(g).

[2] 26 U.S.C.A. § 219.

[3] 26 U.S.C.A. § 125.

[4] 22 U.S.C.A. § 2504(c).

[5] 22 U.S.C.A. § 2505(1).

[6] 26 U.S.C.A. § 105(h)(6).

§ 13009.5. Wages subject to personal income tax

(a) For purposes of the report required by subdivision (a) of Section 1088 and the statement required by Section 13050, "wages subject to personal income tax" means all of the following:

(1) Remuneration defined as wages by Section 13009, except that in the case of tips received by an employee in the course of his or her employment, the amounts shall include only those tips included in statements furnished to the employer, pursuant to Section 13055.

(2) Remuneration described in subdivisions (a), (b), (f), and (*l*) of Section 13009, to the extent included in gross income.

(3) Payments made by a third party for sick pay as specified in Section 931.5.

(A) Any employer who receives a report of wages from a third-party payer as provided for in subdivisions (a) and (b) of Section 931.5 shall report those wages to the department as required under paragraph (2) of subdivision (a) of Section 1088.

(B) Any third-party payer described in Section 931.5 who fails to report wages to an employer as provided for in that section shall report those wages to the department as required under paragraph (2) of subdivision (a) of Section 1088.

(b)(1) A person or entity shall not be required to register with the Employment Development Department solely for the purpose of reporting wages subject to personal income tax pursuant to Section 1088 unless that registration is otherwise required by this code.

(2) A person or entity shall not be required to withhold any tax under Section 13020 for wages, as defined by this section, unless that person or entity is required to withhold tax for those wages as defined by Section 13009. *(Added by Stats.1999, c. 144 (A.B.1634), § 2.)*

§ 13010. Withholding agent

"Withholding agent" means any person required to deduct and withhold any tax under the provisions of Section 13020. *(Added by Stats.1980, c. 1007, p. 3228, § 64, operative July 1, 1981.)*

§ 13011. Possession and control of records, papers, property, etc., previously held by Franchise Tax Board

The department shall retain the possession and control of all records, papers, offices, equipment, supplies, moneys, funds, appropriations, land, and other property real or personal held for the benefit or use of the Franchise Tax Board in the performance of the duties, powers, purposes, responsibilities, and jurisdiction of the Franchise Tax Board that were previously delegated by Section 15702.1 of the Government Code and that are vested in the department by Section 13000. *(Added by Stats.1980, c. 1007, p. 3228, § 64, operative July 1, 1981.)*

§ 13013. Regulations adopted by Franchise Tax Board

All regulations heretofore adopted by the Franchise Tax Board pursuant to powers transferred to the department by this division and in effect immediately preceding the operative date of this division, shall remain in effect and shall be fully enforceable unless and until readopted, amended, or repealed by the director. *(Added by Stats. 1980, c. 1007, p. 3228, § 64, operative July 1, 1981.)*

§ 13014. Payment of interest obligations; applicability of division

This division does not apply to the payment of interest obligations not taxable under this division. *(Added by Stats.1980, c. 1007, p. 3228, § 64, operative July 1, 1981.)*

§ 13015. Authority to require information

The department is authorized to require such information with respect to persons subject to the taxes imposed by this division as is necessary or helpful in securing proper identification of such persons. *(Added by Stats. 1980, c. 1007, p. 3228, § 64, operative July 1, 1981.)*

§ 13016. Payor's right to require name and address of recipient

When necessary to make effective the provisions of this division, the name and address of the recipient of income shall be furnished upon demand of the person paying the income. *(Added by Stats.1980, c. 1007, p. 3228, § 64, operative July 1, 1981.)*

§ 13017. Laws affecting changes in withholdings; time of compliance

Unless otherwise specifically provided, the provisions of any law effecting changes in withholding under this division shall begin in the manner set forth by Section 18665 of the Revenue and Taxation Code. *(Added by Stats.1980, c. 1007, p. 3228, § 64, operative July 1, 1981. Amended by Stats.1993, c. 877 (S.B.673), § 96, eff. Oct. 6, 1993, operative Jan. 1, 1994.)*

§ 13018. Unauthorized inspection or unwarranted disclosure or use of information; misdemeanor; notice to affected taxpayers

(a) Except as otherwise provided by this division or other express provision of law, the information furnished or secured pursuant to this division shall be used solely for the purpose of administering the tax laws or other laws administered by the person or agency obtaining it. Any willful unauthorized inspection or unwarranted disclosure or use of the information by the person or agency, or the employees and officers thereof, is a misdemeanor. For purposes of this section, "inspection" means any examination of confidential information furnished or secured pursuant to this division.

(b) The department shall notify a taxpayer of any known incidents of willful unauthorized inspection or unwarranted disclosure or use of the taxpayer's confidential tax records, but only if criminal charges have been filed for the willful unauthorized inspection or unwarranted disclosure. *(Added by Stats.1998, c. 623 (S.B.1383), § 4.)*

§ 13019. Tax advice; privileged communications

(a)(1) With respect to tax advice, the protections of confidentiality that apply to a communication between a client and an attorney, as set forth in Article 3 (commencing with Section 950) of Chapter 4 of Division 8 of the Evidence Code, also shall apply to a communication between a taxpayer and any federally authorized tax practitioner to the extent the communication would be considered a privileged communication if it were between a client and an attorney.

(2) Paragraph (1) may only be asserted in any non-criminal tax matter before the Employment Development Department.

(3) For purposes of this section:

(A) "Federally authorized tax practitioner" means any individual who is authorized under federal law to practice before the Internal Revenue Service if the practice is subject to federal regulation under Section 330 of Title 31 of the United States Code, as provided by federal law as of January 1, 2000.

(B) "Tax advice" means advice given by an individual with respect to a state tax matter, which may include federal tax advice if it relates to the state tax matter. For purposes of this subparagraph, "federal tax advice" means advice given by an individual within the scope of his or her authority to practice before the federal Internal Revenue Service on noncriminal tax matters.

(C) "Tax shelter" means a partnership or other entity, any investment plan or arrangement, or any other plan or arrangement if a significant purpose of that partnership, entity, plan, or arrangement is the avoidance or evasion of federal income tax.

(b) The privilege under subdivision (a) shall not apply to any written communication between a federally authorized tax practitioner and a director, shareholder, officer, or employee, agent, or representative of a corporation in connection with the promotion of the direct or indirect participation of the corporation in any tax shelter, or in any proceeding to revoke or otherwise discipline any license or right to practice by any governmental agency.

(c) This section shall be operative for communications made on or after the effective date of the act adding this section.[1] *(Added by Stats.2009, c. 411 (A.B.129), § 3, eff. Oct. 11, 2009.)*

[1] Stats.2009, c. 411 (A.B.129), eff. Oct. 11, 2009.

CHAPTER 2. WITHHOLDING AND PAYMENT OF TAX

Section
13020. Amount; method of determination; accounting machines.
13021. Withholding report and report of wages; remittal of taxes; time; annual reconciliation return.
13021.5. Definitions.
13022. Computation of wages to nearest dollar.
13023. Authority to estimate wages.
13024. Additional withholding.
13025. Remuneration other than cash.
13026. Withholding exemption certificate.
13027. Tips.

Section
13028. Wages subject to withholding; election to include or exclude withholding; methods for determining amount.
13028.1. Nonpayment of tax; withholding; notice.
13028.5. Supplemental unemployment compensation benefits.
13028.6. Sick pay; deductions and withholding.
13029. Remuneration not constituting wages; other appropriate payments; agreements.
13030. Wages paid with respect to period not a payroll period.
13031. Status of remuneration paid during one-half or more of pay period.

§ 13020. Amount; method of determination; accounting machines

(a)(1) Every employer who pays wages to a resident employee for services performed either within or without this state, or to a nonresident employee for services performed in this state, shall deduct and withhold from those wages, except as provided in subdivision (c) and Sections 13025 and 13026, for each payroll period, a tax computed in that manner as to produce, so far as practicable, with due regard to the credits for personal exemptions allowable under Section 17054 of the Revenue and Taxation Code, a sum which is substantially equivalent to the amount of tax reasonably estimated to be due under Part 10 (commencing with Section 17001) of Division 2 of the Revenue and Taxation Code resulting from the inclusion in the gross income of the employee of the wages which were subject to withholding. The method of determining the amount to be withheld shall be prescribed by the Franchise Tax Board pursuant to Section 18663 of the Revenue and Taxation Code.

(2) For each payroll period ending on or after November 1, 2009, the sum shall comport with the changes made to Section 18663 of the Revenue and Taxation Code, by the act adding this paragraph.

(b) The department upon request may permit the use of accounting machines to calculate the proper amount to be deducted and withheld from wages, if the calculation produces an amount substantially equivalent to the amount of tax required to be withheld under subdivision (a).

(c) Withholding shall not be required by this section with respect to wages, salaries, fees, or other compensation paid by a corporation for services performed in California for that corporation to a nonresident corporate director for director services, including attendance at a board of directors' meeting. *(Added by Stats.1980, c. 1007, p. 3228, § 64, operative July 1, 1981. Amended by Stats.1981, c. 279, p. 1397, § 20, eff. Aug. 31, 1981; Stats.1993, c. 31 (S.B.3), § 70, eff. June 16, 1993, operative Jan. 1, 1994; Stats.1995, c. 475 (S.B.298), § 3; Stats.2009–2010, 4th Ex.Sess., c. 15 (A.B.17), § 5, eff. Oct. 23, 2009.)*

§ 13021. Withholding report and report of wages; remittal of taxes; time; annual reconciliation return

(a) Every employer required to withhold any tax under Section 13020 shall for each calendar quarter, whether or not wages or payments are paid in the quarter, file a withholding report and a report of wages in a form prescribed by the department, and pay over the taxes so required to be withheld. The report of wages shall include individual amounts required to be withheld under Section 13020 or withheld under Section 13028. Except as provided in subdivisions (c) and (d), the employer shall file a withholding report and remit the total amount of income taxes withheld during the calendar quarter on or before the last day of the month following the close of the calendar quarter.

(b) Every employer electing to file a single annual return under subdivision (d) of Section 1110 shall report and pay any taxes withheld under Section 13020 on an annual basis within the time specified in subdivision (d) of Section 1110.

(c)(1) Effective January 1, 1995, whenever an employer is required, for federal income tax purposes, to remit the total amount of withheld federal income tax in accordance with Section 6302 of the Internal Revenue Code and regulations thereunder, and the accumulated amount of state income tax withheld is more than five hundred dollars ($500), the employer shall remit the total amount of income tax withheld for state income tax purposes within the number of banking days as specified for withheld federal income taxes by Section 6302 of the Internal Revenue Code, and regulations thereunder.

(2) Effective January 1, 1996, the five hundred dollar ($500) amount referred to in paragraph (1) shall be adjusted annually as follows, based on the annual average rate of interest earned on the Pooled Money Investment Fund as of June 30 in the prior fiscal year:

Average Rate of Interest	
Greater than or equal to 9 percent:	$ 75
Less than 9 percent, but greater than or equal to 7 percent:	250
Less than 7 percent, but greater than or equal to 4 percent:	400
Less than 4 percent:	500

(d)(1) Notwithstanding subdivisions (a) and (c), for calendar years beginning prior to January 1, 1995, if in the 12–month period ending June 30 of the prior year the cumulative average payment made pursuant to this division or Section 1110, for eight-month periods, as defined under Section 6302 of the Internal Revenue Code and regulations thereunder, was fifty thousand dollars ($50,-000) or more, the employer shall remit the total amount of income tax withheld within three banking days following the close of each eight-month period, as defined by Section 6302 of the Internal Revenue Code and regulations thereunder. For purposes of this subdivision, payment shall be made by electronic funds transfer in accordance with Section 13021.5, for one calendar year

beginning on January 1. Payment is deemed complete on the date the electronic funds transfer is initiated if settlement to the state's demand account occurs on or before the banking day following the date the transfer is initiated. If settlement to the state's demand account does not occur on or before the banking day following the date the transfer is initiated, payment is deemed complete on the date settlement occurs. The department shall, on or before October 31 of the prior year, notify all employers required to make payment by electronic funds transfer of these requirements.

(2) Notwithstanding subdivisions (a) and (c), for calendar years beginning on or after January 1, 1995, if in the 12–month period ending June 30 of the prior year, the cumulative average payment made pursuant to this division or Section 1110 for any deposit periods, as defined under Section 6302 of the Internal Revenue Code and regulations thereunder, was twenty thousand dollars ($20,000) or more, the employer shall remit the total amount of income tax withheld within the number of banking days as specified for federal income taxes by Section 6302 of the Internal Revenue Code and regulations thereunder. For purposes of this subdivision, payment shall be made by electronic funds transfer in accordance with Section 13021.5, for one calendar year beginning on January 1. Payment is deemed complete on the date the electronic funds transfer is initiated if settlement to the state's demand account occurs on or before the banking day following the date the transfer is initiated. If settlement to the state's demand account does not occur on or before the banking day following the date the transfer is initiated, payment is deemed complete on the date settlement occurs. The department shall, on or before October 31 of the prior year, notify all employers required by this paragraph to make payments by electronic funds transfer of these requirements.

(3) Notwithstanding paragraph (2), effective January 1, 1995, electronic funds transfer payments that are subject to the one-day deposit rule, as defined by Section 6302 of the Internal Revenue Code and regulations thereunder, shall be deemed timely if the payment settles to the state's demand account within three banking days after the date the employer meets the threshold for the one-day deposit rule.

(4) Any taxpayer required to remit payments pursuant to paragraphs (1) and (2) may request from the department a waiver of those requirements. The department may grant a waiver only if it determines that the particular amounts paid in excess of fifty thousand dollars ($50,000) or twenty thousand dollars ($20,000), as stated in paragraphs (1) and (2), respectively, were the result of an unprecedented occurrence for that employer, and were not representative of the employer's cumulative average payment in prior years.

(5) Any state agency required to remit payments pursuant to paragraphs (1) and (2) may request a waiver of those requirements from the department. The department may grant a waiver if it determines that there will

not be a negative impact on the interest earnings of the General Fund. If there is a negative impact to the General Fund, the department may grant a waiver if the requesting state agency follows procedures designated by the department to mitigate the impact to the General Fund.

(e) Any employer not required to make payment pursuant to subdivision (d) of this section may elect to make payment by electronic funds transfer in accordance with Section 13021.5 under the following conditions:

(1) The election shall be made in a form, and shall contain information, as prescribed by the director, and shall be subject to approval by the department.

(2) If approved, the election shall be effective on the date specified in the notification to the employer of approval.

(3) The election shall be operative from the date specified in the notification of approval, and shall continue in effect until terminated by the employer or the department.

(4) Funds remitted by electronic funds transfer pursuant to this subdivision shall be deemed complete in accordance with subdivision (d) or as deemed appropriate by the director to encourage use of this payment method.

(f) Notwithstanding Section 1112, no interest or penalties shall be assessed against any employer who remits at least 95 percent of the amount required by subdivision (c) or (d) if the failure to remit the full amount is not willful and any remaining amount due is paid with the next payment. The director may allow any employer to submit the amounts due from multiple locations upon a showing that those submissions are necessary to comply with subdivision (c) or (d).

(g) The department may, if it believes that action is necessary, require any employer to make the report required by this section and pay to it the tax deducted and withheld at any time, or from time to time but no less frequently than provided for in subdivision (a).

(h) Any employer required to withhold any tax and who is not required to make payment under subdivision (c) shall remit the total amount of income tax withheld during each month of each calendar quarter, on or before the 15th day of the subsequent month if the income tax withheld for any of the three months or, cumulatively for two or more months, is three hundred fifty dollars ($350) or more.

(i) For purposes of subdivisions (a), (c), and (h), payment is deemed complete when it is placed in a properly addressed envelope, bearing the correct postage, and it is deposited in the United States mail.

(j) In addition to the withholding report and report of wages described in subdivision (a), each employer shall file with the director an annual reconciliation return showing the amount required to be withheld under Section 13020, and any other information the director shall prescribe. This annual reconciliation return shall be due on the first day of January following the close of the prior calendar year and shall become delinquent if not filed on or before the last day of that month. *(Added by Stats.1980, c. 1007, p. 3228, § 64, operative July 1, 1981. Amended by Stats.1981–82, 1st Ex.Sess., c. 2, p. 621, § 3, operative May 1, 1982; Stats.1983–84, 1st Ex.Sess., c. 10, § 36, eff. Feb. 17, 1983; Stats.1983, c. 323, § 93.75, eff. July 21, 1983; Stats.1986, c. 683, § 1; Stats.1991, c. 473 (S.B.467), § 10; Stats.1992, c. 1294 (S.B.1974), § 6; Stats.1993, c. 402 (A.B.1668), § 6; Stats.1993, c. 747 (A.B.1738), § 15; Stats.1994, c. 1049 (A.B.3086), § 25; Stats.1999, c. 144 (A.B.1634), § 3; Stats.2005, c. 152 (A.B.1577), § 51; Stats.2006, c. 538 (S.B.1852), § 652.)*

§ 13021.5. Definitions

(a) "Electronic funds transfer" means any transfer of funds, other than a transaction originated by check, draft, or similar paper instrument, that is initiated through an electronic terminal, telephonic instrument, or computer or magnetic tape, so as to order, instruct, or authorize a financial institution to debit or credit an account. Electronic funds transfers shall be accomplished by an automated clearinghouse debit, an automated clearinghouse credit, Fedwire, or by other specific electronic funds transfer methods approved in advance by the department.

(b) "Automated clearinghouse" means any federal reserve bank, or an organization established in agreement with the National Automated Clearing House Association, that operates as a clearinghouse for transmitting or receiving entries between banks and/or bank accounts and which authorizes an electronic transfer of funds between those banks or bank accounts.

(c) "Automated clearinghouse debit" means a transaction in which the state, through its designated depository bank, originates an automated clearinghouse transaction debiting the employer's bank account and crediting the state's bank account for the amount of tax. Banking costs incurred for the automated clearinghouse debit transaction shall be paid by the state.

(d) "Automated clearinghouse credit" means an automated clearinghouse transaction in which the employer through its own bank, originates an entry crediting the state's bank account and debiting its own bank account. Banking costs incurred for the automated clearinghouse credit transaction charged to the employer and to the state shall be paid by the employer.

(e) "Fedwire" means any transaction originated by the employer and utilizing the national electronic payment system to transfer funds through the federal reserve banks, pursuant to which the employer debits its own bank account and credits the state's bank account. Electronic funds transfer payments may be made by Fedwire only if prior approval is obtained from the department and payment cannot, for good cause, be made pursuant to subdivision (a). Banking costs incurred for the Fedwire transaction charged to the employer and to the state shall be paid by the employer.

(f) "Banking day" means any day other than a Saturday, Sunday, or banking holiday as recognized by the Internal Revenue Service.

(g) "Settlement date" means the date on which an exchange of funds with respect to an entry is reflected on the books of the Federal Reserve Bank.

(h) For the purposes of Section 13021, the "cumulative average payment" means the cumulative dollar amount of deposits divided by the number of payments submitted during a given period. For the purposes of this section, the "cumulative average payment" may also be defined as a single annual deposit, when only one payment is made during the 12–month period ending June 30. *(Added by Stats.1991, c. 473 (S.B.467), § 11. Amended by Stats. 1994, c. 1049 (A.B.3086), § 26; Stats.2002, c. 29 (A.B. 1729), § 16.)*

§ 13022. Computation of wages to nearest dollar

In determining the amount to be deducted and withheld under Section 13020, the wages may, at the election of the employer, be computed to the nearest dollar. *(Added by Stats.1980, c. 1007, p. 3228, § 64, operative July 1, 1981.)*

§ 13023. Authority to estimate wages

The department may, by regulation, permit employers to estimate the wages which will be paid to any employee in any quarter of the calendar year, to determine the amount to be deducted and withheld upon each payment of wages to such employee during such quarter as if the appropriate average of the wages so estimated constituted the actual wages paid, and to deduct and withhold upon any payment of wages to such employee, during such quarter such amount as may be necessary to adjust the amount actually deducted and withheld upon the wages of such employee during such quarter to the amount that would be required to be deducted and withheld during such quarter if the payroll period of the employee were quarterly. *(Added by Stats.1980, c. 1007, p. 3228, § 64, operative July 1, 1981.)*

§ 13024. Additional withholding

The department may provide by authorized regulation, under such conditions and to such extent as it deems proper, for withholding in addition to that otherwise required under Section 13020 in cases in which the employer and employee agree to such additional withholding. Such additional withholding shall for all purposes be considered a tax required to be deducted and withheld under this division. *(Added by Stats.1980, c. 1007, p. 3228, § 64, operative July 1, 1981.)*

§ 13025. Remuneration other than cash

In the case of remuneration paid in any medium other than cash for services performed by an individual as a retail salesperson for a person where the service performed by such individual for such person is ordinarily performed for remuneration solely by way of cash commission an employer shall not be required to deduct or withhold any tax under this division with respect to such remuneration, if such employer files with the department such information with respect to such remuneration as the department may prescribe by regulation. *(Added by Stats.1980, c. 1007, p. 3228, § 64, operative July 1, 1981.)*

§ 13026. Withholding exemption certificate

An employer shall not be required to deduct and withhold any tax under this division upon a payment of wages (except wages exempt from federal income tax but not exempt under this division) to an employee if there is in effect with respect to such payment a withholding exemption certificate, in such form and containing such other information as the department may prescribe, furnished to the employer by the employee certifying that the employee—

(a) Incurred no liability for federal income tax imposed under subtitle A of the Internal Revenue Code of 1954 for his or her preceding taxable year, and

(b) Anticipates that he or she will incur no liability for federal income tax imposed under subtitle A of the Internal Revenue Code of 1954 for his or her current taxable year. *(Added by Stats.1980, c. 1007, p. 3228, § 64, operative July 1, 1981.)*

§ 13027. Tips

In the case of tips which constitute wages, subdivision (a) of Section 13020 shall be applicable only to such tips as are included in a written statement furnished to the employer pursuant to Section 13055, and only to the extent that the tax can be deducted and withheld by the employer, at or after the time such statement is so furnished and before the close of the calendar year in which such statement is furnished, from such wages of the employee (excluding tips, but including funds turned over by the employee to the employer for the purpose of such deduction and withholding) as are under the control of the employer. An employer who is furnished by an employee a written statement of tips (received in a calendar month) pursuant to Section 13055 to which paragraph (2) of subdivision (n) of Section 13009 is applicable may deduct and withhold the tax with respect to such tips from any wages of the employee (excluding tips) under his or her control, even though at the time such statement is furnished the total amount of the tips included in statements furnished to the employer as having been received by the employee in such calendar month in the course of his or her employment by the employer is less than twenty dollars ($20). Such tax shall not at any time be deducted and withheld in any amount which exceeds the aggregate of such wages and funds. *(Added by Stats.1980, c. 1007, p. 3228, § 64, operative July 1, 1981.)*

§ 13028. Wages subject to withholding; election to include or exclude withholding; methods for determining amount

(a) For purposes of this division (and so much of Part 10 (commencing with Section 17001) and Part 10.2

(commencing with Section 18401) of Division 2 of the Revenue and Taxation Code as relates to this division) pensions, annuities, and other deferred income, as described in Section 3405 of the Internal Revenue Code, are wages and subject to withholding under this division. Amounts withheld shall be treated as if the amounts are withheld by an employer for a payroll period and only amounts withheld shall be reported to the department pursuant to Section 1088 and Section 13021.

(b) If an individual makes an election under Section 3405(a)(2) or Section 3405(b)(2) of the Internal Revenue Code not to have tax withheld, that election shall apply to withholding under this division, unless the individual elects, with the consent of the payer, to have those payments subject to withholding under this division. If an individual has not made an election under Section 3405(a)(2) or Section 3405(b)(2) of the Internal Revenue Code, that individual may elect to exclude those payments from withholding under this division. Elections provided in this subdivision shall be made pursuant to regulations of the director.

(c) Where Section 3405 of the Internal Revenue Code provides that tables or other computational procedures shall be prescribed by the Secretary of the Treasury, for the purposes of this division, any of the following amounts may be withheld, upon election of the payer:

(1) An amount determined by the method prescribed under Section 13020.

(2) A designated dollar amount as requested by the payee.

(3) Ten percent of the amount of federal withholding computed pursuant to Section 3405 of the Internal Revenue Code.

(d) Where the amount of withholding computed pursuant to subdivision (c) is less than ten dollars ($10) per month, the payer shall not be required to withhold that amount.

(e) This section shall not apply to pensions, annuities, and other deferred income of payees with addresses outside this state, as shown on the most current records of the payer.

(f) The department shall, in consultation with the affected payers and payees, issue regulations to implement this section.

Those regulations shall provide for delay (but not beyond July 1, 1987) of the application of this section with respect to any payer or class of payers until that time as the payers are able to comply without undue hardship with the requirements of this section. In that case, no retroactive compliance shall be required. *(Added by Stats.1980, c. 1007, p. 3228, § 64, operative July 1, 1981. Amended by Stats.1982, c. 195, p. 659, § 39, eff. May 5, 1982; Stats.1985, c. 159, § 22, eff. July 8, 1985, operative July 1, 1986; Stats.1986, c. 1014, § 2, eff. Sept. 23, 1986; Stats.1990, c. 216 (S.B.2510), § 111; Stats.1991, c. 475 (A.B.156), § 2, eff. Oct. 2, 1991; Stats.1993, c. 31 (S.B.3), § 71, eff. June 16, 1993, operative Jan. 1, 1994; Stats.1999,*

c. 144 (A.B.1634), § 4; Stats.2002, c. 29 (A.B.1729), § 17.)

§ 13028.1. Nonpayment of tax; withholding; notice

If the director determines that nonpayment of tax by a nonresident under the income tax laws of this state may occur, the director shall notify the payer of payments described in subdivision (a) of Section 13028 that withholding shall be made from those payments. Upon notice from the director, the payer shall withhold from those payments as if they were subject to Section 13020. The director shall also notify the payee that withholding has been ordered pursuant to this section, and the reason for his or her determination that nonpayment of tax may occur. *(Added by Stats.1985, c. 159, § 23, eff. July 8, 1985, operative July 1, 1986.)*

§ 13028.5. Supplemental unemployment compensation benefits

(a) For purposes of this division (and so much of Part 10 (commencing with Section 17001) and Part 10.2 (commencing with Section 18401) of Division 2 of the Revenue and Taxation Code as relates to this division) any supplemental unemployment compensation benefit paid to an individual shall be treated as if it were a payment of wages by an employer to an employee for a payroll period.

(b) For purposes of subdivision (a), "supplemental unemployment compensation benefits" means amounts which are paid to an employee, pursuant to a plan to which the employer is a party, because of an employee's involuntary separation from employment (whether or not that separation is temporary), resulting directly from a reduction in force, the discontinuance of a plant or operation, or other similar conditions, but only to the extent those benefits are includable in the employee's gross income. *(Added by Stats.1985, c. 159, § 24, eff. July 8, 1985, operative July 1, 1986 Amended by Stats.1993, c. 31 (S.B.3), § 72, eff. June 16, 1993, operative Jan. 1, 1994.)*

§ 13028.6. Sick pay; deductions and withholding

(a) For purposes of this division (and so much of Part 10 (commencing with Section 17001) and Part 10.2 (commencing with Section 18401) of Division 2 of the Revenue and Taxation Code as relates to this division), any payment to an individual of sick pay which does not constitute wages (determined without regard to this subdivision), if at the time the payment is made a request that such sick pay be subject to withholding under this division is in effect, shall be treated as if it were a payment of wages by an employer to an employee for a payroll period.

(b) For purposes of this subdivision, "sick pay" means any amount which satisfies both of the following:

(1) Is paid to an employee pursuant to a plan to which the employer is a party.

(2) Constitutes remuneration or a payment in lieu of remuneration for any period during which the employee

is temporarily absent from work on account of sickness or personal injuries.

(c) If a payee makes a request that any sick pay be subject to withholding under this chapter, the amount to be deducted and withheld under this chapter from any payment to which that request applies shall be an amount (not less than a minimum amount determined by the Franchise Tax Board) specified by the payee in that request. The amount deducted and withheld with respect to a payment which is greater or less than a full payment shall bear the same relation to the specified amount as that payment bears to a full payment.

(1) A request that any sick pay be subject to withholding under this chapter shall satisfy all of the following:

(A) Shall be made by the payee in writing to the person making the payments and shall contain the social security number of the payee.

(B) Shall specify the amount to be deducted and withheld from each full payment.

(C) Shall take effect with respect to payments made more than seven days after the date on which that request is furnished to the payer, or as the department shall by regulations prescribe. That request may be changed or terminated by furnishing to the person making the payments a written statement of change or termination which shall take effect in the same manner as provided in the preceding sentence. At the election of the payer, any such request (or statement of change or revocation) may take effect earlier than as provided in this subparagraph.

(2) Any sick pay paid pursuant to a collective bargaining agreement between employee representatives and one or more employers which contains a provision specifying that this paragraph is to apply to sick pay paid pursuant to that agreement and contains a provision for determining the amount to be deducted and withheld from each payment of that sick pay as follows:

(A) The requirement of paragraph (3) of subdivision (a) that a request for withholding be in effect shall not apply.

(B) Except as provided in Section 13026, the amounts to be deducted and withheld under this chapter shall be determined in accordance with that agreement.

The preceding sentence shall not apply with respect to sick pay paid pursuant to any agreement to any individual, unless the social security number of that individual is furnished to the payer and the payer is furnished with that information as is necessary to determine whether the payment is pursuant to the agreement and to determine the amount to be deducted and withheld. *(Added by Stats.1985, c. 159, § 25, eff. July 8, 1985, operative July 1, 1986. Amended by Stats.1993, c. 31 (S.B.3), § 73, eff. June 16, 1993, operative Jan. 1, 1994.)*

§ 13029. Remuneration not constituting wages; other appropriate payments; agreements

The department may by authorized regulations provide for withholding—

(a) From remuneration for services performed by an employee for his or her employer which (without regard to this section) does not constitute wages, and

(b) From any other type of payment with respect to which the department finds that withholding would be appropriate under the provisions of this division, if the employer and the employee, or in the case of any other type of payment the person making and the person receiving the payment, agree to the withholding. The agreement shall be made in the form and manner as the department may by authorized regulations provide. For purposes of this division (and so much of Part 10 (commencing with Section 17001) and Part 10.2 (commencing with Section 18401) of Division 2 of the Revenue and Taxation Code as relates to this division) remuneration or other payments with respect to which the agreement is made shall be treated as if they were wages paid by an employer to an employee to the extent that the remuneration is paid or other payments are made during the period for which the agreement is in effect.

(Added by Stats.1980, c. 1007, p. 3228, § 64, operative July 1, 1981. Amended by Stats.1993, c. 31 (S.B.3), § 74, eff. June 16, 1993, operative Jan. 1, 1994.)

§ 13030. Wages paid with respect to period not a payroll period

If wages are paid with respect to a period which is not a payroll period, the amount to be deducted and withheld shall be that applicable in the case of a miscellaneous payroll period containing a number of days, including Sundays and holidays, equal to the number of days in the period with respect to which such wages are paid. In any case in which wages are paid by an employer without regard to any payroll period or other period, the amount to be deducted and withheld shall be that applicable in the case of a miscellaneous payroll period containing a number of days equal to the number of days, including Sundays and holidays, which have elapsed since the date of the last payment of such wages by such employer during the calendar year, or the date of commencement of employment with such employer during such year, or January 1st of such year, whichever is the later. In any case in which the period of time described, or the time prescribed in the preceding sentence in respect of any wages, is less than one week, the department may by authorized regulation permit an employer, in computing the tax required to be deducted and withheld, to use the excess of the aggregate of the wages paid to the employee during the calendar week over the withholding exemption allowed by Section 13020 for a weekly payroll period. *(Added by Stats.1980, c. 1007, p. 3228, § 64, operative July 1, 1981.)*

§ 13031. Status of remuneration paid during one-half or more of pay period

If the remuneration paid by an employer to an employee for services performed during one-half or more of any payroll period of not more than 31 consecutive days constitutes wages, all the remuneration paid by such employer to such employee for such period shall be deemed to be wages, but if the remuneration paid by an employer to an employee for services performed during more than one-half of any such payroll period does not constitute wages, then none of the remuneration paid by such employer to such employee for such period shall be deemed to be wages. *(Added by Stats.1980, c. 1007, p. 3228, § 64, operative July 1, 1981.)*

CHAPTER 3. WITHHOLDING EXEMPTIONS

Section
13040. Computation of exemptions.
13041. Number and amount.
13042. Time of taking effect of new withholding exemption certificate; status determination date defined.
13043. Manner of withholding and amount to be deducted.

§ 13040. Computation of exemptions

(a) An employer shall use the exemption certificate filed by the employee with the employer in such form and containing such information as the department may prescribe, for determining the number of withholding exemptions to be allowed in computing the tax required to be deducted and withheld under Section 13020. However, if the employer cannot determine the employee's marital status from the exemption certificate the employee shall be considered unmarried.

(b) No withholding exemptions shall be allowed until the employee files a new withholding exemption certificate if the department finds that the withholding exemption certificate filed under this division does not properly reflect the number of exemptions allowable and so advises the employer in writing. *(Added by Stats.1980, c. 1007, p. 3228, § 64, operative July 1, 1981.)*

§ 13041. Number and amount

The number and amount of withholding exemptions allowed shall be based upon the persons claimed in a withholding exemption certificate in effect under Section 13040, except that if no such certificate is in effect, the number of withholding exemptions claimed shall be considered to be zero. *(Added by Stats.1980, c. 1007, p. 3228, § 64, operative July 1, 1981.)*

§ 13042. Time of taking effect of new withholding exemption certificate; status determination date defined

A new withholding exemption certificate filed under this division in cases in which a previous certificate was in effect shall take effect with respect to the first payment of wages made on or after the first status determination date which occurs at least 30 days from the date on which such certificate is so furnished, except that at the election of the employer such certificate may be made effective with respect to any payment of wages made on or after the date on which such certificate is so furnished.

For purposes of this section, "status determination date," means January 1, May 1, July 1, and October 1, of each year. *(Added by Stats.1980, c. 1007, p. 3228, § 64, operative July 1, 1981.)*

§ 13043. Manner of withholding and amount to be deducted

(a) The amount to be deducted and withheld under this division shall be prescribed pursuant to Section 18663 of the Revenue and Taxation Code when a payment of wages is made to an employee by an employer in any of the following cases:

(1) With respect to a payroll period or other period, any part of which is included in a payroll period or other period with respect to which wages are also paid to the employee by the employer.

(2) Without regard to any payroll period or other period, but on or prior to the expiration of a payroll period or other period with respect to which wages are also paid to the employee by the employer.

(3) With respect to a period beginning in one and ending in another calendar year.

(4) Through an agent, fiduciary, or other person who also has the control, receipt, custody, or disposal of, or pays, the wages payable by another employer to the employee.

(b) For purposes of this section, an employee's remuneration may consist of wages paid for a payroll period and supplemental wages.

Supplemental wages include, but are not limited to, bonus payments, overtime payments, commissions, sales awards, back pay including retroactive wage increases, and reimbursements for nondeductible moving expenses that are paid for the same or different period, or without regard to a particular period.

(c) When any supplemental wages are paid subsequent to the payment of regular wages, the employer may determine the personal income tax to be withheld from supplemental wages paid by (1) using a flat percentage rate pursuant to subdivision (b) of Section 18663 of the Revenue and Taxation Code without allowance for exemptions and credits and without reference to any regular payment of wages, or (2) adding the supplemental wages to the regular wages paid the employee and computing the personal income tax to be withheld on the whole amount (the computed tax minus the tax withheld from the regular wages shall be withheld from the supplemental wages). Where supplemental wages are paid at the same time as regular wages, the personal income tax to be withheld shall be computed on the total of the supplemental and regular wages and shall be determined as if the total of the supplemental wages and the regular wages constituted a single wage payment for the regular payroll period.

(d) For stock options and bonus payments that constitute wages paid on or after January 1, 2002, the employer may determine the personal income tax to be withheld

1123

from the stock options and bonus payments paid by either (1) using a flat percentage rate pursuant to subdivision (c) of Section 18663 of the Revenue and Taxation Code, without allowance for exemptions and credits and without reference to any regular payment of wages, or (2) adding the stock options and bonus payments to the regular wages paid the employee and computing the personal income tax to be withheld on the whole amount (the computed tax minus the tax withheld from the regular wages shall be withheld from the stock options and bonus payments). Where the stock options and bonus payments are paid at the same time as regular wages, the personal income tax to be withheld shall be computed on the total of the stock options and bonus payments and regular wages, and shall be determined as if the total of the stock options and bonus payments and the regular wages constituted a single wage payment for the regular payroll period. *(Added by Stats.1980, c. 1007, p. 3228, § 64, operative July 1, 1981. Amended by Stats.1991, c. 117 (S.B.169), § 109, eff. July 16, 1991; Stats.1991 c. 474 (A.B.31), § 16, eff. Oct. 2, 1991; Stats.1993, c. 877 (S.B.673), § 97, eff. Oct. 6, 1993, operative Jan. 1, 1994; Stats.2002, c. 488 (A.B.2065), § 13, eff. Sept. 12, 2002.)*

CHAPTER 4. REPORTS, RETURNS, AND STATEMENTS

Section

13050.   Withholding statement.
13052.   False or fraudulent statement; failure to furnish statement; penalty.
13052.5.   Failure to report remuneration paid for personal services; penalty.
13055.   Report of tips; written statement.
13056.   Identifying number; regulations; use.
13057.   Failure to furnish or include identifying number; penalty.
13058.   Verification; form; filing.
13059.   Extension of time for filing; declaration of state of emergency.

§ 13050. Withholding statement

(a) Every employer or person required to deduct and withhold from an employee a tax under Section 986, 3260, or 13020, or who would have been required to deduct and withhold a tax under Section 13020 (determined without regard to Section 13025) if the employee had claimed no more than one withholding exemption, shall furnish to each employee in respect of the remuneration paid by the person to the employee during the calendar year, on or before January 31 of the succeeding year, or, if his or her employment is terminated before the close of the calendar year, on the day on which the last payment of remuneration is made, a written statement showing all of the following:

(1) The name of the person.

(2) The name of the employee, and his or her social security or identifying number if wages have been paid.

(3) The total amount of wages subject to personal income tax, as defined by Section 13009.5.

(4) The total amount deducted and withheld as tax under Section 13020.

(5) The total amount of worker contributions paid by the employee pursuant to Section 986.

(6) The total amount of worker contributions paid by the employee pursuant to Section 3260.

(7) The total amount of elective deferrals (within the meaning of Section 402(g)(3) of the Internal Revenue Code) and compensation deferred pursuant to Section 457 of the Internal Revenue Code.

(b) The statement required to be furnished pursuant to this section in respect of any remuneration shall be furnished at other times, shall contain other information, and shall be in a form, as the department may by authorized regulations prescribe.

(c)(1) A duplicate of any statement made pursuant to this section and in accordance with authorized regulations prescribed by the department shall, when required by the regulations, be filed with the department.

(2) Effective January 1, 1995, this subdivision shall apply only to those employers exempted under subdivision (h) of Section 1088 or subdivision (k) of Section 13021 from the requirements to report individual amounts withheld on the report of wages and to file the annual reconciliation return for the 1995 calendar year only. This subdivision shall remain in effect only until March 1, 1996, and on that date is repealed, unless a later enacted statute that is enacted before March 1, 1996, deletes or extends that date.

(d) If, during any calendar year, any person makes a payment of third-party sick pay to an employee, that person shall, on or before January 15 of the succeeding year, furnish a written statement to the employer in respect of whom the payment was made showing all of the following:

(1) The name and, if there is withholding under this division, the social security number of that employee.

(2) The total amount of the third-party sick pay paid to that employee during the calendar year.

(3) The total amount, if any, deducted and withheld from that sick pay under this division. For purposes of the preceding sentence, the term "third-party sick pay" means any sick pay, as defined in subdivision (b) of Section 13028.6, which does not constitute wages for purposes of this division, determined without regard to subdivision (a) of Section 13028.6.

(A) For purposes of Chapter 10 (commencing with Section 2101) of Part 1 of Division 1, the statements required to be furnished by this subdivision shall be treated as statements required under this section to be furnished to employees.

(B) Every employer who receives a statement under this subdivision with respect to sick pay paid to any employee during any calendar year shall, on or before January 31 of the succeeding year, furnish a written statement to that employee showing all of the information shown on the statement furnished under this subdivision.

(e) The Franchise Tax Board shall be allowed access to the information filed with the department pursuant to this section. *(Added by Stats.1980, c. 1007, p. 3228, § 64, operative July 1, 1981. Amended by Stats.1982, c. 195, p. 663, § 40, eff. May 5, 1982; Stats.1986, c. 847, § 18; Stats.1987, c. 1138, § 186, eff. Sept. 25, 1987; Stats.1989, c. 600, § 6; Stats.1993, c. 877 (S.B.673), § 98, eff. Oct. 6, 1993, operative Jan. 1, 1994; Stats.1994, c. 1049 (A.B. 3086), § 27; Stats.1999, c. 144 (A.B.1634), § 5; Stats. 2002, c. 29 (A.B.1729), § 18.)*

§ 13052. False or fraudulent statement; failure to furnish statement; penalty

Any person or employer required under Section 13050 to furnish a statement to an employee who furnishes a false or fraudulent statement, or who fails to furnish a statement in the manner, at the time, and showing the information required under Section 13050, or regulations prescribed thereunder, shall for each such failure, unless due to reasonable cause, pay a penalty of fifty dollars ($50). The penalty shall be assessed and collected in the same manner as the tax. *(Added by Stats.1980, c. 1007, p. 3228, § 64, operative July 1, 1981.)*

§ 13052.5. Failure to report remuneration paid for personal services; penalty

(a) In addition to the penalty imposed by Section 19183 of the Revenue and Taxation Code (relating to failure to file information returns), if any person, or entity fails to report amounts paid as remuneration for personal services as required under Section 13050 of this code or Section 6041A of the Internal Revenue Code on the date prescribed thereof (determined with regard to any extension of time for filing), that person or entity may be liable for a penalty determined under subdivision (b).

(b) For purposes of subdivision (a), the amount determined under this subdivision is the maximum rate under Section 17041 of the Revenue and Taxation Code multiplied by the unreported amounts paid as remuneration for personal services.

(c) The penalty imposed by subdivision (a) shall be assessed against that person or entity required to file a return under Section 13050 of this code or Section 6041A of the Internal Revenue Code.

(d) Sections 1221 and 1222 of the Unemployment Insurance Code shall not apply to assessments imposed by this section.

(e) The penalty imposed under this section shall be in lieu of the penalty imposed under Section 19175 of the Revenue and Taxation Code. In the event that a penalty is imposed under both this section and Section 19175 of the Revenue and Taxation Code, only the penalty imposed under this section shall apply.

(f) The penalty imposed by this section may be assessed in lieu of, or in addition to, the penalty imposed by Section 13052 with respect to the failure to furnish a withholding statement to an employee. *(Added by Stats. 1989, c. 600, § 7. Amended by Stats.1990, c. 719 (A.B. 2667), § 6; Stats.1990, c. 766 (A.B.3582), § 6; Stats.1993, c. 31 (S.B.3), § 75, eff. June 16, 1993, operative Jan. 1, 1994; Stats.2002, c. 29 (A.B.1729), § 19.)*

§ 13055. Report of tips; written statement

Every employee who, in the course of his or her employment by an employer, receives in any calendar month tips which are wages shall report all such tips in one or more written statements furnished to his or her employer on or before the 10th day following such month. Such statements shall be furnished by the employee under such authorized regulations, at such other times before such 10th day, and in such form and manner as may be prescribed by the department. *(Added by Stats. 1980, c. 1007, p. 3228, § 64, operative July 1, 1981.)*

§ 13056. Identifying number; regulations; use

(a) When required by authorized regulations prescribed by the department:

(1) Any person or employer required under the authority of this division to make a return, report, statement, or other document shall include in the return, report, statement, or other document the identifying number as may be prescribed for securing proper identification of the person.

(2) Any person with respect to whom a return, report, statement, or other document is required under the authority of this division to be made by another person shall furnish to the other person the identifying number as may be prescribed for securing his or her proper identification.

(3) Any person or employer required under the authority of this division to make a return, report, statement, or other document with respect to another person shall request from the other person, and shall include in the return, report, statement, or other document, the identifying number as may be prescribed for securing proper identification of the other person.

(b)(1) Except as provided in paragraph (2), a return or report of any person with respect to his or her liability for tax, or any statement or other document in support thereof, shall not be considered for purposes of paragraphs (2) and (3) of subdivision (a) as a return, report, statement, or other document with respect to another person.

(2) For purposes of paragraphs (2) and (3) of subdivision (a), a return or report of an estate or trust with respect to its liability for tax, and any statement or other document in support thereof, shall be considered as a return, report, statement, or other document with respect to each beneficiary of the estate or trust.

(c) For purposes of this section, the department is authorized to require the information that may be

1125

necessary to assign an identifying number to any person. *(Added by Stats.1980, c. 1007, p. 3228, § 64, operative July 1, 1981. Amended by Stats.1994, c. 1049 (A.B.3086), § 31.)*

§ 13057. Failure to furnish or include identifying number; penalty

(a) If any person who is required by regulations prescribed under Section 13056 to provide a required identifying number fails without good cause to comply with that requirement at the time prescribed by the regulations, the person shall pay a penalty of five dollars ($5) for each failure:

(1) To include his or her identifying number in any return, report, statement, or other document.

(2) To furnish his or her identifying number to another person.

(3) To include in any return, report, statement, or other document made with respect to another person the identifying number of the other person.

(4) To furnish any other agency's taxpayer identification number.

(b) The penalty under this section shall be assessed and collected in the same manner as the tax. *(Added by Stats.1980, c. 1007, p. 3228, § 64, operative July 1, 1981. Amended by Stats.1983, c. 1102, § 32, eff. Sept. 27, 1983; Stats.1994, c. 1049 (A.B.3086), § 32.)*

§ 13058. Verification; form; filing

Except as otherwise provided by the department, any return, report, statement, or other document required to be made under any provision of this division or authorized regulations shall contain, or be verified by, a written declaration that it is made under the penalty of perjury. The returns, reports, and all other returns, reports, statements, or other documents or copies thereof required by this division, shall be in the form as the department may from time to time prescribe, and shall be filed with the department. The department shall prepare blank forms for the returns, reports, declarations, statements, or other documents and shall distribute them throughout the state and furnish them upon application. Failure to receive or secure the form does not relieve any employer or person from making any return, report, statement, or other document required. *(Added by Stats.1980, c. 1007, p. 3228, § 64, operative July 1, 1981. Amended by Stats.1994, c. 1049 (A.B.3086), § 33.)*

§ 13059. Extension of time for filing; declaration of state of emergency

If the Governor declares a state of emergency, the director may extend the time requirements for filing returns, reports, and statements required by this chapter. The extension granted by the director pursuant to this section shall only apply to employers prevented by the conditions giving rise to the state of emergency from timely filing their returns, reports, and statements of

wages or timely payment of the taxes due. *(Added by Stats.1993, c. 402 (A.B.1668), § 7.)*

CHAPTER 5. COLLECTIONS

Section
13070. Liability of employer for payment of tax; special trust fund.
13071. Failure of employer to deduct and withhold; tax not to be collected from employer.
13072. Withhold notice; service; duty of recipient.
13073. Withhold notice; liability on failure to comply.
13074. Withhold notice; compliance without resort to court; nonliability to taxpayer.
13075. Withhold notice; service on state.
13076. United States, state or political subdivision as employer; persons authorized to deduct and withhold.
13077. Payment of wages or supply of funds by lender, surety or other person.

§ 13070. Liability of employer for payment of tax; special trust fund

(a) The employer shall be liable for the payment of the tax required to be deducted and withheld under Section 13020, and shall not be liable to any person for the amount of such payment.

(b) Whenever any employer or person has withheld any amount pursuant to this division, the amount so withheld shall be held to be a special fund in trust for the State of California. *(Added by Stats.1980, c. 1007, p. 3228, § 64, operative July 1, 1981.)*

§ 13071. Failure of employer to deduct and withhold; tax not to be collected from employer

If the employer, in violation of the provisions of this division, fails to deduct and withhold the tax under this division, and thereafter the tax against which the tax may be credited is paid or the taxpayer reports to the Franchise Tax Board the wages or gross income against which the tax would have been imposed, the tax so required to be deducted and withheld shall not be collected from the employer, but this section shall in no case relieve the employer from liability for any penalties or additions to the tax otherwise applicable with respect to the failure to deduct and withhold. *(Added by Stats.1980, c. 1007, p. 3228, § 64, operative July 1, 1981. Amended by Stats.1993, c. 402 (A.B.1668), § 8.)*

§ 13072. Withhold notice; service; duty of recipient

The department may by notice, served personally or by first-class mail, require any employer, person, officer or department of the state, political subdivision or agency of the state, including the Regents of the University of California, a city organized under a freeholders' charter, or a political body not a subdivision or agency of the state, having in their possession, or under their control, any credits or other personal property or other things of value, belonging to a taxpayer or to an employer or person who has failed to withhold and transmit amounts due pursuant to Section 13070 or 13073 to withhold, from such credits or other personal property or other things of value, the amount of any tax, interest, or penalties due from the taxpayer or the amount of any liability incurred by such employer or person for failure to withhold and transmit amounts due from a taxpayer and to transmit the amount withheld to the department at such times as it may designate. *(Added by Stats.1980, c. 1007, p. 3228, § 64, operative July 1, 1981.)*

§ 13073. Withhold notice; liability on failure to comply

Any employer or person failing to withhold the amount due from any taxpayer and to transmit the same to the department after service of a notice pursuant to Section 13072 is liable for such amounts. *(Added by Stats.1980, c. 1007, p. 3228, § 64, operative July 1, 1981.)*

§ 13074. Withhold notice; compliance without resort to court; nonliability to taxpayer

Any employer or person required to withhold and transmit any amount pursuant to this division shall comply with the requirement without resort to any legal or equitable action in a court of law or equity. Any employer or person paying to the department any amount required by it to be withheld is not liable therefor to the person from whom withheld unless the amount withheld is refunded to the withholding agent. *(Added by Stats. 1980, c. 1007, p. 3228, § 64, operative July 1, 1981.)*

§ 13075. Withhold notice; service on state

Whenever, under any provision of this division, service is authorized upon the state of any notice to withhold, unless expressly exempted from the provisions of this section, such service to be effective must, in addition to any other requirements, be made on the state agency owing the obligation prior to the time such agency presents the claim for payment thereof to the State Controller. *(Added by Stats.1980, c. 1007, p. 3228, § 64, operative July 1, 1981.)*

§ 13076. United States, state or political subdivision as employer; persons authorized to deduct and withhold

If the employer is the United States, or this state, or any political subdivision thereof, including the Regents of the University of California, a city organized under a freeholders' charter, or any agency or instrumentality of any one or more of the foregoing, the return of the amount deducted and withheld upon any wages may be made by any officer or employee of the United States, or of such state, city organized under a freeholders' charter, or political subdivision, or of such agency or instrumentality, as the case may be, having control of the payment of such wages, or appropriately designated for that purpose. *(Added by Stats.1980, c. 1007, p. 3228, § 64, operative July 1, 1981.)*

§ 13077. Payment of wages or supply of funds by lender, surety or other person

(a) For purposes of Sections 13020 and 13070, if a lender, surety, or other person, who is not an employer under such sections with respect to an employee or group of employees, pays wages directly to such an employee or group of employees, employed by one or more employers, or to an agent on behalf of such employee or employees, such lender, surety, or other person shall be liable in his or her own person and estate to the State of California in a sum equal to the taxes (together with interest) required to be deducted and withheld from such wages by such employer.

(b) If a lender, surety, or other person supplies funds to or for the account of an employer for the specific purpose of paying wages of the employees of such employer, with actual notice or knowledge that such employer does not intend to or will not be able to make timely payment or deposit of the amounts of tax required by this part to be deducted and withheld by such employer from such wages, such lender, surety, or other person shall be liable in his or her own person and estate to the State of California in a sum equal to the taxes (together with interest) which are not paid over to the State of California by such employer with respect to such wages. However, the liability of such lender, surety, or other person shall be limited to an amount equal to 25 percent of the amount so supplied to or for the account of such employer for such purpose.

(c) Any amounts paid to the State of California pursuant to this section shall be credited against the liability of the employer. *(Added by Stats.1980, c. 1007, p. 3228, § 64, operative July 1, 1981.)*

CHAPTER 6. VIOLATIONS

Section
13101. Additional penalty; waiver; applicability of review provisions.

§ 13101. Additional penalty; waiver; applicability of review provisions

(a) In addition to any criminal penalty provided by law, if any individual makes a statement under Section 13040, 13041, or 13042 which results in a decrease in the amounts deducted and withheld under this division, and as of the time the statement was made, there was no reasonable basis for the statement, the individual shall pay a penalty of five hundred dollars ($500) for the statement.

(b) The department may waive, in whole or in part, the penalty imposed under subdivision (a) if the taxes imposed with respect to the individual under Part 10 (commencing with Section 17001) of Division 2 of the Revenue and Taxation Code for the taxable year are equal to or less than the sum of both of the following:

(1) The credits against those taxes allowed by Sections 17052.1 through 17053.7 and Section 19002.

(2) The payments of estimated tax which are considered payments on account of those taxes.

(c) Article 11 (commencing with Section 1221) of Chapter 4 of Part 1, relating to administrative appellate review, shall not apply to the assessment or collection of any penalty imposed by subdivision (a).

(d) This section shall apply to acts and failures to act after December 31, 1981. *(Added by Stats.1982, c. 1558,*

p. 6151, § 50, eff. Sept. 30, 1982. Amended by Stats.1986, c. 847, § 19; Stats.1993, c. 31 (S.B.3), § 77, eff. June 16, 1993, operative Jan. 1, 1994.)

Superseded

For supersession of § 13101, see Revenue and Taxation Code § 19176.

Division 7

CALIFORNIA WORKFORCE INVESTMENT ACT

CHAPTER 1. GENERAL PROVISIONS

Section
14000. Legislative findings and declarations.
14002. Screening to detect unidentified disabilities.
14003. Restrictions on awards of grants or contracts to sectarian organizations.
14004. Eligibility for funding; awards under California Community and Faith Based Initiative; requirements.

§ 14000. Legislative findings and declarations

(a) The Legislature finds and declares that, in order for California to remain prosperous and globally competitive, it needs to have a highly skilled workforce.

(b) The Legislature recognizes all of the following:

(1) California must transform its current job training, job placement, and vocational education programs into an integrated, accessible, and accountable workforce investment system that can effectively serve job seekers, students, and employers.

(2) California's workforce investment system must provide lifelong learning for all Californians, promote self-sufficiency, link education and training to economic development, and prepare California to successfully compete in the global economy.

(3) The programs described in paragraphs (1) and (2) must be accessible to all Californians, including persons with economic, physical, or other barriers to employment. *(Added by Stats.2006, c. 630 (S.B.293), § 2.)*

§ 14002. Screening to detect unidentified disabilities

(a) The Legislature finds and declares that screening designed to detect unidentified disabilities, including learning disabilities, improves workforce preparation and enhances the use of employment and training resources.

(b) Section 134(d)(2) of the federal Workforce Investment Act (29 U.S.C. Sec. 2864(d)(2)) allows for the use of funds for initial assessment of skill levels, aptitudes, abilities and support services, and Section 134(d)(3) of that act (29 U.S.C. Sec. 2864(d)(3)) allows for comprehensive and specialized assessments of skill levels and service needs, including, but not limited to, diagnostic testing and the use of other assessment tools and in-depth interviewing and evaluation to identify employment barriers and appropriate employment goals.

(c) The Legislature encourages one-stop career centers to maximize the use of Workforce Investment Act resources and other federal and state workforce development resources for screening designed to detect unidentified disabilities, and if indicated, appropriate diagnostic assessment. *(Added by Stats.2001, c. 111 (A.B.429), § 24, eff. July 30, 2001.)*

§ 14003. Restrictions on awards of grants or contracts to sectarian organizations

(a) Grants or contracts awarded under the federal Workforce Investment Act, codified in Chapter 30 (commencing with Section 2801) of Title 29 of the United States Code, or any other state or federally funded workforce development program, may not be awarded to organizations that are owned or operated as pervasively sectarian organizations.

(b) Grants or contracts awarded under the federal Workforce Investment Act, codified in Chapter 30 (commencing with Section 2801) of Title 29 of the United States Code, or any other state or federally funded workforce development program, shall comply with Section 4 of Article I and Section 5 of Article XVI of the California Constitution, state and federal civil rights laws, and the First Amendment to the United States Constitution in regard to pervasively sectarian organizations. These legal constraints include prohibitions on the discrimination against beneficiaries and staff based on protected categories and on the promoting of religious doctrine to advance sectarian beliefs. *(Added by Stats. 2003, c. 225 (A.B.1752), § 23, eff. Aug. 11, 2003.)*

§ 14004. Eligibility for funding; awards under California Community and Faith Based Initiative; requirements

To be eligible for state or federal workforce development funds awarded by the state under the California Community and Faith Based Initiative, an organization must be a separate nonprofit entity or affiliate that is a tax-exempt organization under Section 501(c)(3) of the Internal Revenue Code. *(Added by Stats.2003, c. 225 (A.B.1752), § 23.1, eff. Aug. 11, 2003.)*

CHAPTER 2. DEFINITIONS AND SEVERABILITY

Section
14005. Definitions.
14006. Severability of provisions.
14007. Construction with federal law.

§ 14005. Definitions

For purposes of this division:

(a) "Board" shall mean the California Workforce Investment Board.

(b) "Agency" means the Labor and Workforce Development Agency.

(c) "Workforce Investment Act of 1998" means the federal act enacted as Public Law 105–220. [1]

(d) "Local labor federation" means a central labor council that is an organization of local unions affiliated with the California Labor Federation or a local building and construction trades council affiliated with the State Building and Construction Trades Council. *(Added by Stats.2006, c. 630 (S.B.293), § 3. Amended by Stats.2008, c. 376 (S.B.302), § 3.)*

[1] See 29 U.S.C.A. § 2801 et seq.

§ 14006. Severability of provisions

The provisions of this division are severable. If any provision of this division or its application is held invalid, that invalidity shall not affect other provisions or applications that can be given effect without the invalid provision or application. *(Added by Stats.2006, c. 630 (S.B.293), § 3.)*

§ 14007. Construction with federal law

Each provision of this division shall remain in effect unless the United States Secretary of Labor determines that any provision of this division or its application is not in conformity with the requirements of federal law, at which time only those provisions of this division that are not in conformity with federal law shall be repealed. *(Added by Stats.2006, c. 630 (S.B.293), § 3.)*

CHAPTER 3. STATE RESPONSIBILITIES

ARTICLE 1. CALIFORNIA WORKFORCE INVESTMENT BOARD

Section
14010. Purpose of Workforce Investment Board.
14011. Reporting structure.
14012. Appointed by governor; composition of board.
14013. Board responsibilities.
14015. Compensation of members.

§ 14010. Purpose of Workforce Investment Board

The California Workforce Investment Board is the body responsible for assisting the Governor in the development, oversight, and continuous improvement of California's workforce investment system. *(Added by Stats.2006, c. 630 (S.B.293), § 4.)*

§ 14011. Reporting structure

The board shall report, through its executive director, to the Secretary of the Labor and Workforce Development Agency. *(Added by Stats.2006, c. 630 (S.B.293), § 4.)*

§ 14012. Appointed by governor; composition of board

The board shall be appointed by the Governor to assist in the development of the State Workforce Investment Plan and to carry out other functions, as described in Section 14103. The board shall be comprised of the Governor and representatives from the following categories:

(a) Two members of each house of the Legislature, appointed by the appropriate presiding officer of each house.

(b)(1) A majority of board members shall be representatives of business who:

(A) Are owners of small and large businesses, chief executives or operating officers of small and large businesses, and other small and large business executives or employers with optimum policymaking or hiring authority, including members of local workforce investment boards.

(B) Represent businesses with employment opportunities that reflect the employment opportunities of the state.

(C) Are appointed from a group of individuals nominated by state business organizations and business trade associations.

(2) At least one representative shall be a private sector member of the California Economic Strategy Panel, created pursuant to Section 15570 of the Government Code.

(c) Chief elected officials representing both cities and counties, where appropriate.

(d) Representatives of labor organizations that are appointed to the board by the Governor shall have been nominated by state labor federations. At least 15 percent of board members shall be representatives of labor organizations.

(e) Representatives of individuals and organizations that have experience with regard to youth activities.

(f) Representatives of individuals and organizations that have experience and expertise in the delivery of workforce investment activities, including the Chancellor of the California Community Colleges, representatives of school districts, and representatives of community-based organizations within the state.

(g) The lead state agency officials with responsibility for the programs, services, or activities that are mandatory participants in the one-stop system, or, where there are no lead state agency officials responsible for those programs, services, or activities, a representative with expertise relating to those programs, services, or activities.

(h) Any other representatives and state agency officials as the Governor may designate, such as the state agency officials responsible for economic development and juvenile justice programs in the state.

(i) Members of the board that represent organizations, agencies, or other entities shall be individuals with optimum policymaking authority within those organizations, agencies, or entities.

(j) In making appointments to the board, the Governor shall consider the ethnic, race, gender, and geographic distribution of the state's population, and members of the board shall represent diverse regions of the state, including urban, rural, and suburban areas.

(k) The Governor may appoint a single member to the board to represent multiple constituencies on the board.

(*l*) The Governor shall select a chairperson for the board from the business representatives. (*Added by Stats.2006, c. 630 (S.B.293), § 4.*)

§ 14013. Board responsibilities

The board shall assist the Governor in the following:

(a) Promoting the development of a well-educated and highly skilled workforce.

(b) Developing the State Workforce Investment Plan.

(c) Developing guidelines for the continuous improvement and operation of the workforce investment system, including:

(1) Developing policies to guide the one-stop system.

(2) Providing technical assistance for the continuous improvement of the one-stop system.

(3) Recommending state investments in the one-stop system.

(4) Targeting resources to high-wage industry sectors that are either high-growth sectors or critical to California's economy, or both.

(d) Developing and continuously improving the statewide workforce investment system as delivered via the one-stop delivery system, including:

(1) Developing linkages in order to assure coordination and nonduplication among workforce programs and activities.

(2) Reviewing local workforce investment plans.

(3) Providing guidance to ensure services reflect the needs of high-wage industry sectors.

(e) Commenting, at least once annually, on the measures taken pursuant to the Carl D. Perkins Vocational and Applied Technology Education Act Amendments of 1990 (Public Law 101–392; 20 U.S.C. Sec. 2301 et seq.).

(f) Designating local workforce investment areas within the state based on information derived from all of the following:

(1) Consultations with the Governor.

(2) Consultations with the chief local elected officials.

(3) Consideration of comments received through the public comment process, as described in Section 112(b)(9) of the federal Workforce Investment Act of 1998.

(g) Developing and modifying allocation formulas, as necessary, for the distribution of funds for adult employment and training activities, for youth activities to local workforce investment areas, and dislocated worker employment and training activities, as permitted by federal law.

(h) Coordinating the development and continuous improvement of comprehensive state performance measures, including state adjusted levels of performance, to assess the effectiveness of the workforce investment activities in the state.

(i) Preparing the annual report to the United States Secretary of Labor.

(j) Recommending policy for the development of the statewide employment statistics system, including workforce and economic data, as described in Section 15 of Title 29 of the United States Code, and using, to the fullest extent possible, the Employment Development Department's existing labor market information systems.

(k) Recommending strategies to the Governor for strategic training investments of the Governor's 15–percent discretionary funds.

(*l*) Developing and recommending waivers, in conjunction with local workforce investment boards, to the Governor as provided for in the federal Workforce Investment Act of 1998.

(m) Recommending policy to the Governor for the use of the 25–percent rapid response funds, as authorized under the federal Workforce Investment Act of 1998.

(n) Developing an application to the United States Department of Labor for an incentive grant under Section 9273 of Title 20 of the United States Code. (*Added by Stats.2006, c. 630 (S.B.293), § 4. Amended by Stats.2008, c. 376 (S.B.302), § 4.*)

§ 14015. Compensation of members

Members of the board may receive up to one hundred dollars ($100) for each day's actual attendance at meetings and other official business of the board, not to exceed three hundred dollars ($300) per month, and shall receive their necessary and actual expenses incurred in the performance of their official duties. (*Added by Stats.2006, c. 630 (S.B.293), § 4.*)

ARTICLE 2.   STATE PLANNING

Section
14020. Strategic workforce plan.
14022. Green Technology/Green Collar Jobs; grant allocations of funds; report.

§ 14020. Strategic workforce plan

The California Workforce Investment Board, in collaboration with state and local partners, including the Chancellor of the California Community Colleges, the State Department of Education, other appropriate state agencies, and local workforce investment boards, shall develop a strategic workforce plan to serve as a framework for the development of public policy, fiscal investment, and operation of all state labor exchange, workforce education, and training programs to address the state's economic, demographic, and workforce needs. The strategic workforce plan shall also serve as the framework for the single state plan required by the Workforce Investment Act of 1998. The plan shall be updated at least every five years. *(Added by Stats.2006, c. 630 (S.B.293), § 4. Amended by Stats.2008, c. 376 (S.B.302), § 5.)*

§ 14022. Green Technology/Green Collar Jobs; grant allocations of funds; report

(a) The California Workforce Investment Board, in coordination with the department, shall participate in the development of Request for Proposal (RFP) language and the evaluation of proposals for determining grant allocations of the funds, as identified in Item 7100–001–0869, Schedule (4) 61.60—WIA Removing Barriers for Special Needs Populations for Green Technology/Green Collar Jobs, and Schedule (2) 61.40—WIA Growth Industries for Green Technology/Green Collar Jobs, of Section 2.00 of the Budget Act of 2009 (Chapter 1 of the Statutes of the 2009 Third Extraordinary Session), and future budget acts, to ensure consistency with the green collar strategic initiative required to be developed by the Green Collar Jobs Council pursuant to Section 15002.

(b) The board shall also annually prepare and submit to the Legislature a report containing all of the following information:

(1) A list of any funds allocated, or not allocated for the purposes of subdivision (a), including a statement of the reasons for any such action.

(2) The name of each grant recipient, and the amount allocated to the recipient. *(Added by Stats.2009–2010, 4th Ex.Sess., c. 12 (A.B.12), § 33, eff. July 28, 2009.)*

CHAPTER 4. LOCAL SERVICE DELIVERY

ARTICLE 1. LOCAL WORKFORCE INVESTMENT BOARD

Section
14200. Local boards.
14201. Purpose of local boards.
14202. Membership; criteria.
14203. Other members.
14204. Majority of members to be local business representatives.
14205. Chairperson.
14206. Duties of local board.
14207. Activities of local board.

Section
14208. Youth councils.
14209. Appointment of members to youth council.
14210. Youth council activities.

§ 14200. Local boards

(a) The local chief elected officials in a local workforce development area shall form, pursuant to guidelines established by the Governor and the board, a local workforce investment board to plan and oversee the workforce investment system.

(b) The Governor shall certify one local board for each local area in the state once every two years, following the requirements of the Workforce Investment Act of 1998. *(Added by Stats.2006, c. 630 (S.B.293), § 5.)*

§ 14201. Purpose of local boards

Local workforce investment boards shall be established in each local workforce investment area of the state to assist the local chief elected official in planning, oversight, and evaluation of local workforce investment. The local board shall promote effective outcomes consistent with statewide goals, objectives, and negotiated local performance standards. *(Added by Stats.2006, c. 630 (S.B.293), § 5.)*

§ 14202. Membership; criteria

Membership of the local board shall be appointed by the local chief elected official using criteria established by the Governor and the board, and shall include:

(a) Representatives of business in the local area appointed from among individuals nominated by local business organizations and business trade associations and that reflect employment opportunities of the local area. Business representatives shall be owners of businesses, chief executives, or operating officers of businesses or other business executives, including human resources executives, or employers with optimum policy-making or hiring authority.

(b) Representatives of local educational entities, including representatives of local educational agencies, local school boards, entities providing adult education and literacy activities, public and private postsecondary educational institutions, including representatives of community colleges, selected from among individuals nominated by regional or local educational agencies, institutions, or organizations representing local educational entities.

(c) Representatives of labor organizations nominated by local labor federations, including a representative of an apprenticeship program. At least 15 percent of local board members shall be representatives of labor organizations unless the local labor federation fails to nominate enough members. If this occurs, then at least 10 percent of the local board members shall be representatives of labor organizations.

(d) Representatives of local community-based organizations, including organizations representing individuals with disabilities and veterans, and organizations that serve populations with barriers to employment, such as the economically disadvantaged, youth, farmworkers, homeless, and immigrants.

(e) Representatives of economic development agencies, including private sector economic development entities.

(f) Representatives of each of the one-stop partners.

(g) Members of the local board that represent organizations, agencies, or other entities shall be individuals with optimum policymaking authority within those organizations, agencies, or entities. *(Added by Stats.2006, c. 630 (S.B.293), § 5.)*

§ 14203. Other members

Membership of local boards may include other individuals or representatives of entities as the local elected official in the local area may determine to be appropriate. A single member of the local board may be appointed to represent multiple constituencies on the local board. *(Added by Stats.2006, c. 630 (S.B.293), § 5.)*

§ 14204. Majority of members to be local business representatives

A majority of the members of the local board shall be representatives of businesses in the local area. *(Added by Stats.2006, c. 630 (S.B.293), § 5.)*

§ 14205. Chairperson

The local board shall elect a chairperson for the local board from among the business representatives. *(Added by Stats.2006, c. 630 (S.B.293), § 5.)*

§ 14206. Duties of local board

It shall be the duty of the local board to do all of the following:

(a) Coordinate workforce investment activities in the local area with economic development strategies.

(b) Promote participation of private sector employers in the local workforce investment system.

(c) Develop and submit a local workforce investment plan to the Governor.

(d) Select one-stop operators, with the agreement of the local chief elected official, annually review their operations, and terminate for cause the eligibility of such operators.

(e) Award grants or contracts to eligible providers of youth activities in the local area on a competitive basis, consistent with the Workforce Investment Act of 1998, based upon the recommendations of the youth council.

(f) Identify, consistent with the Workforce Investment Act of 1998, eligible providers of training services.

(g) Identify eligible providers of intensive services and, when the one-stop operator does not provide intensive services to the local area, award contracts to those providers.

(h) Develop local policy on the amount and duration of individual training accounts based upon the market rate for local training programs.

(i) Conduct program oversight over workforce investment activities in the local area.

(j) Negotiate with the local chief elected official in the local area and the Governor on local performance measures for the local area.

(k) Assist in the development of a statewide employment statistics system, which shall be developed in conjunction with and shall utilize to the fullest extent possible, the Employment Development Department's labor market information system. *(Added by Stats.2006, c. 630 (S.B.293), § 5.)*

§ 14207. Activities of local board

The local board, in order to carry out its functions:

(a) Shall prepare a budget for the purpose of carrying out the duties of the local board as specified under this section, subject to the approval of the local chief elected official.

(b) Shall direct the activities of the local board's executive director.

(c) May employ additional staff to carry out the activities as described in the local board's strategic plan.

(d) May solicit and accept contributions and grant funds from other sources.

(e) Shall not provide training services unless the Governor grants a written waiver of this provision.

(f) Shall not provide other workforce investment services or be designated as a one-stop operator without the agreement of the local chief elected official and the Governor. *(Added by Stats.2006, c. 630 (S.B.293), § 5.)*

§ 14208. Youth councils

A youth council shall be established as a subgroup within each local board, appointed by the local board in cooperation with the local chief elected official. Youth council membership shall conform with the requirements of the Workforce Investment Act of 1998. *(Added by Stats.2006, c. 630 (S.B.293), § 5.)*

§ 14209. Appointment of members to youth council

It is the intent of the Legislature that when appointing members to the youth council, the local workforce investment board and the local chief elected official appoint:

(a) Representatives of youth who are enrolled in school, and out of school youth.

(b) Representatives from the private sector.

(c) Representatives of local educational agencies serving youth.

(d) Representatives of private nonprofit agencies serving youth.

(e) Representatives of apprenticeship training programs serving youth. *(Added by Stats.2006, c. 630 (S.B.293), § 5.)*

§ 14210. Youth council activities

The youth council shall do all of the following:

(a) Develop the portions of the local plan relating to youth.

(b) Make recommendations of eligible providers of youth activities for the award of grants or contracts on a competitive basis by the local board to carry out youth activities.

(c) Leverage other youth program funds in the local area for the purpose of improving the effectiveness of local youth programs through collaborative planning, funding, and service delivery.

(d) Conduct oversight of eligible youth activities in the local area.

(e) Make recommendations to the local board for connecting youth program activities, including those provided by local educational entities to the one-stop delivery system.

(f) Make recommendations to the local board for including training in nontraditional occupations for women and girls and preapprenticeship training in youth program activities. *(Added by Stats.2006, c. 630 (S.B. 293), § 5.)*

ARTICLE 2. LOCAL WORKFORCE INVESTMENT PLAN

Section
14220. Submission to Governor of local plan.
14221. Content of plan.
14222. Local unified plan.
14223. Public comment.

§ 14220. Submission to Governor of local plan

Each local board shall develop and submit to the Governor a comprehensive five-year local plan in partnership with the appropriate chief local elected official. The plan shall be consistent with the state workforce investment plan. *(Added by Stats.2006, c. 630 (S.B.293), § 5.)*

§ 14221. Content of plan

The local plan shall include all of the following:

(a) A local labor market assessment which contains an identification of local and regional workforce investment needs of key industry sectors, businesses, jobseekers, and incumbent workers in the local area, the current and projected employment opportunities and the job skills necessary to obtain that employment.

(b) A description of the local one-stop delivery system, including all of the following:

(1) A description of how the local board will achieve system integration that will improve services to employers, incumbent workers, and jobseekers, and a description of local funding sources.

(2) A copy of each memorandum of understanding between the local board and each of the one-stop partners concerning the operation of the one-stop delivery system in the local area.

(c) A description of the local levels of performance negotiated with the Governor and chief local elected official to be used to measure the performance of the local area and the performance of the local fiscal agent, eligible providers, and the one-stop delivery system in the local area. Performance standards shall not create disincentives for serving clients for whom it is more difficult to provide service.

(d) A description and assessment of the type and availability of adult and dislocated worker employment and training activities in the local area.

(e) A description of how the local board will provide services to the business community, including, but not limited to, recruitment and staffing services, training, and development, information and resources, and outplacement and business retention services.

(f) A description of how the local board will coordinate workforce investment activities carried out in the local area with statewide rapid response activities, as appropriate.

(g) A description and assessment of the type and availability of youth activities in the local area, including an identification of successful providers of those activities.

(h) A description of the process used by the local board, consistent with Section 14223, to provide an opportunity for public comment, including comment by representatives of businesses, labor organizations, and community-based organizations, and input into the development of the local plan, prior to submission of the plan.

(i) An identification of the entity, as prescribed in the Workforce Investment Act of 1998, responsible for the disbursal of funds under the Workforce Investment Act of 1998.

(j) A description of the competitive process to be used to award the grants and contracts in the local area for activities carried out under the Workforce Investment Act of 1998. *(Added by Stats.2006, c. 630 (S.B.293), § 5. Amended by Stats.2008, c. 376 (S.B.302), § 6.)*

§ 14222. Local unified plan

The local board may submit a local unified plan that includes or integrates the local workforce investment and other local workforce plans such as:

(a) An instructional and job training plan required by Section 10200 of the Education Code.

(b) A plan for community college curriculum development or redesign required pursuant to Section 79202 of the Education Code.

(c) A county plan for CalWORKs required by Section 10531 of the Welfare and Institutions Code.

(d) A local welfare-to-work plan required by Section 5063, to the extent permitted under federal law. *(Added by Stats.2006, c. 630 (S.B.293), § 5.)*

§ 14223. Public comment

The local board shall make available copies of a proposed local plan, allow members of the local board and members of the public to submit comments on the proposed local plan to the local board not later than the end of the 30–day period beginning on the date on which the proposed local plan is made available and submit the plan to the Governor along with any comments that were in disagreement with the plan. *(Added by Stats.2006, c. 630 (S.B.293), § 5.)*

ARTICLE 3.   ONE-STOP CAREER
CENTER SYSTEM

Section
14230. Legislative intent.
14231. Required partners in local one-stop system.
14232. Local board oversight of one-stop delivery system; memorandum of understanding.
14233. One-stop career center operators; compliance with applicable labor agreements affecting employees.
14234. Conflicts of interest.
14235. Employment Development Department support.

§ 14230. Legislative intent

(a) It is the intent of the Legislature that:

(1) California deliver comprehensive workforce services to jobseekers, students, and employers through a system of one-stop career centers.

(2) Services and resources target high-wage industry sectors with career advancement opportunities.

(3) Universal access to core services shall be available to adult residents regardless of income, education, employment barriers, or other eligibility requirements. Core services shall include, but not be limited to:

(A) Outreach, intake, and orientation to services available through the one-stop delivery system.

(B) Initial assessment of skill levels, aptitudes, abilities, and supportive service needs.

(C) Job search and placement assistance.

(D) Career counseling, where appropriate.

(E) Provision of labor market information.

(F) Provision of program performance and cost information on eligible providers of training services and local area performance measures.

(G) Provision of information on supportive services in the local area.

(H) Provision of information on the filing of claims for unemployment compensation benefits and unemployment compensation disability benefits.

(I) Assistance in establishing eligibility for welfare-to-work activities pursuant to Section 11325.8 of the Welfare and Institutions Code, and financial aid assistance.

(4) State and federally funded workforce education, training, and employment programs shall be integrated in the one-stop delivery system to achieve universal access to the core services described in paragraph (3).

(5) Intensive services shall be available to individuals who have completed at least one core service, have been unable to obtain employment, and who have been determined, by the one-stop operator, as being in need of more intensive services, or who are employed but in need of intensive services to obtain or retain employment to achieve self-sufficiency.   Intensive services may include comprehensive and specialized assessments of skill levels and service needs, including learning disability screening, the development of individual employment plans, counseling, career planning, and short-term prevocational services to prepare an individual for training and employment.

(6) Training services shall be made available to individuals who have met the requirements for intensive services, have been unable to obtain or retain employment through these services, and who, after an interview, evaluation, or assessment, are determined to be in need of training, and have selected a program of services directly linked to occupations in demand in the local or regional area.   Training services may include:

(A) Occupational skill training including training for nontraditional employment.

(B) On-the-job training.

(C) Programs that combine workplace training with related instruction.

(D) Training programs operated by the private sector.

(E) Skill upgrading and retraining.

(F) Entrepreneurial training.

(G) Job readiness training.

(H) Adult education and literacy activities, including vocational English as a second language, provided in combination with subparagraphs (A) through (G), inclusive.

(I) Customized training conducted by an employer or a group of employers or a labor-management training partnership with a commitment to employ an individual upon completion of the training.

(7) As prescribed in the Workforce Investment Act of 1998, when funds are limited, priority for intensive services and training services shall be given to adult recipients of public assistance and other low-income adults, such as CalWORKs participants.

(b) Each local workforce investment board shall establish at least one full service one-stop career center in the local workforce investment area.   Each full service one-stop career center shall have all entities specified in Section 14231 as partners and shall provide jobseekers with integrated employment, education, training, and job search services. Additionally, employers will be provided with access to comprehensive career and labor market information, job placement, economic development information, performance and program information on service providers, and other such services as the businesses in the community may require.

(c) Local boards may also establish affiliated and specialized centers, as defined in the Workforce Investment Act of 1998, which shall act as portals into the larger local one-stop system, but are not required to have all of the partners specified for full service one-stop centers.

(d) Each local board shall develop a policy for identifying individuals who, because of their skills or experience, should be referred immediately to training services. This policy, along with the methods for referral of individuals between the one-stop operators and the one-stop partners for appropriate services and activities, shall be contained in the memorandum of understanding between the local board and the one-stop partners.

(e) In light of California's diverse population, each one-stop career center should have the capacity to provide the appropriate services to the full range of languages and cultures represented in the community served by the one-stop career center. *(Added by Stats. 2006, c. 630 (S.B.293), § 5. Amended by Stats.2008, c. 376 (S.B.302), § 7.)*

§ 14231. Required partners in local one-stop system

(a) The local providers of the following programs or activities shall be required partners in the local one-stop system:

(1) Programs authorized under Title I of the Workforce Investment Act of 1998.

(2) Programs authorized under the Wagner–Peyser Act (29 U.S.C. Sec. 49 et seq.).

(3) Adult education and literacy activities authorized under Title II of the Workforce Investment Act of 1998.

(4) Programs authorized under Title I of the Rehabilitation Act of 1973 (29 U.S.C. Sec. 720 et seq.).

(5) Programs authorized under Section 403(a)(5) of the Social Security Act (42 U.S.C. Sec. 603(a)(5) as added by Section 5001 of the Balanced Budget Act of 1997).

(6) Activities authorized under Title V of the Older Americans Act of 1965 (42 U.S.C. Sec. 3056 et seq.).

(7) Postsecondary vocational education activities authorized under the Carl D. Perkins Vocational and Applied Technology Education Act (20 U.S.C. Sec. 2301 et seq.), including community colleges and regional occupational centers and programs.

(8) Activities authorized under Chapter 2 of Title II of the Trade Act of 1974 (19 U.S.C. Sec. 2271 et seq.).

(9) Activities authorized under Chapter 41 (commencing with Section 4100) of Title 38 of the United States Code.

(10) Employment and training activities carried out under the Community Services Block Grant Act (42 U.S.C. Sec. 9901 et seq.).

(11) Employment and training activities carried out by the Department of Housing and Urban Development.

(12) Programs authorized by this code, in accordance with applicable federal law.

(13) Small business development centers, as defined in Section 15382 of the Government Code, where they exist.

(b) Community-based organizations that provide intensive services as described in paragraph (4) of subdivision (a) of Section 14230, shall be encouraged to be one-stop partners. *(Added by Stats.2006, c. 630 (S.B.293), § 5.)*

§ 14232. Local board oversight of one-stop delivery system; memorandum of understanding

The local board, with the agreement of the chief local elected official for the local area, shall develop and enter into a memorandum of understanding with the local one-stop partners, designate or certify one-stop operators, and conduct oversight over the local one-stop delivery system. *(Added by Stats.2006, c. 630 (S.B.293), § 5.)*

§ 14233. One-stop career center operators; compliance with applicable labor agreements affecting employees

One-stop career center operators shall recognize and comply with applicable labor agreements affecting employees of one-stop career centers, including the right to access by labor representatives pursuant to the Ralph C. Dills Act (Chapter 10.3 (commencing with Section 3512) of Division 4 of Title 1 of the Government Code). *(Added by Stats.2006, c. 630 (S.B.293), § 5.)*

§ 14234. Conflicts of interest

In order to avoid a conflict of interest, operators of one-stop career centers that issue vouchers shall not be the recipient of vouchers issued by their center without the approval of the chief local elected official and the state board in instances when there are no other potential one-stop partners in the local area. *(Added by Stats.2006, c. 630 (S.B.293), § 5.)*

§ 14235. Employment Development Department support

To the full extent permitted by federal law, the Employment Development Department shall utilize its Wagner–Peyser funded activities and programs to support local one-stop career centers. *(Added by Stats.2006, c. 630 (S.B.293), § 5.)*

CHAPTER 5. EDUCATIONAL SERVICES

Section
14500. Use of Workforce Investment Act individual training account funds.

Section

14510.   Provision by local youth councils of training and skills to attain secondary school diploma.

14530.   Use of funds to improve academic skills of low-achieving youth.

§ 14500. Use of Workforce Investment Act individual training account funds

Notwithstanding any other provision of law, when a person using his or her Workforce Investment Act individual training account enrolls in an adult education program, a noncredit curricula program at a community college, or a regional occupational center or program, for which state funds are allocated, all of the following shall apply:

(a) The entities administering the program may use Workforce Investment Act individual training account funds only to increase the number of hours of services provided above their adult block entitlement pursuant to Section 52616 of the Education Code and funding limit for regional occupational center programs for the purpose of enhancing services already supported with state funds. Any state funds provided to these entities above their adult block entitlements and funding limit for regional occupational center programs shall be subject to an appropriation in the annual Budget Act.

(b) Any state funds allocated to the entity administering the program shall not be offset with the Workforce Investment Act individual training account funds.

(c) The entity administering the program shall use the Workforce Investment Act individual training account funds received for the program. *(Added by Stats.2006, c. 630 (S.B.293), § 6.)*

§ 14510. Provision by local youth councils of training and skills to attain secondary school diploma

To the extent permitted by federal law, school districts and county offices of education are eligible to apply to local youth councils to provide basic skills training and skills necessary for attaining a secondary school diploma. *(Added by Stats.2006, c. 630 (S.B.293), § 6.)*

§ 14530. Use of funds to improve academic skills of low-achieving youth

To the extent permissible under federal law, the Governor may set aside a portion of the youth funding specifically for programs to improve the academic skills of low-achieving youth, including those at risk of not passing the high school exit examination required by Section 60850 of the Education Code, and for dropout prevention activities. *(Added by Stats.2006, c. 630 (S.B.293), § 6.)*

Division 8

CALIFORNIA GREEN COLLAR JOBS ACT OF 2008

Section

15000.   Short title.

15001.   Legislative findings and declarations.

15002.   Establishment of Green Collar Job Council; duties.

15003.   Annual report to the legislature.

§ 15000. Short title

This division shall be known, and may be cited, as the California Green Collar Jobs Act of 2008. *(Added by Stats.2008, c. 312 (A.B.3018), § 1.)*

§ 15001. Legislative findings and declarations

(a) The Legislature finds and declares all of the following:

(1) The State of California has long been a national and international leader on environmental, natural resource, pollution prevention, and energy issues, as well as recent landmark laws in the areas of climate change, renewable energy, energy efficiency, and alternative transportation fuels.

(2) The passage of these laws has resulted in billions of dollars of investment capital flowing into the State of California for research, development, and commercialization of new green and clean technologies. This investment of capital is indicative of the rapidly growing clean and green technology sector of the California economy.

(3) The California Economic Strategy Panel has identified California's economy as an economy of regions. The panel also adopted a new way of looking at industry sectors and how they function and grow as industry clusters. California's green economy is about the potential of new technologies combined with innovative public policy and strategic investments to stimulate the growth of new markets for green products and services.

(4) As the green economy grows, it will be accompanied by an increased demand for a highly skilled and well-trained "green collar" workforce.

(5) California state government must act promptly to build the partnerships, expand the programs, and secure the resources necessary to meet our green workforce needs. This effort must involve both our K–12 and higher education systems, labor unions, the environmental community, workforce development programs, nongovernmental organizations, philanthropy, and private sector industries.

(6) In acknowledgment of the tremendous size of California's economy and related infrastructure, the application of sector strategies in a wide variety of industry sectors is essential to providing labor for industry and career paths for current and potential employees. The California Workforce Investment Board shall adopt a sector strategy approach in responding to industry sector

workforce and economic development needs. This strategy will ensure industry has a qualified workforce and can offer opportunities for employment, training, and career advancement for all Californians. The initial drive of this sector strategy approach will be the California Green Collar Jobs Act of 2008. *(Added by Stats.2008, c. 312 (A.B.3018), § 1.)*

§ 15002. Establishment of Green Collar Job Council; duties

(a) The California Workforce Investment Board (CWIB) shall establish a special committee known as the Green Collar Jobs Council (GCJC), comprised of the appropriate representatives from the CWIB existing membership, including the K–12 representative, the California Community Colleges representative, the Business, Transportation and Housing Agency representative, the Employment Development Department representative, and other appropriate members. The CWIB may call on other state agencies, other higher education representatives, and industry representatives as well as philanthropic, nongovernmental, and environmental groups as appropriate and necessary to serve as consultants to the GCJC in the development of this strategic initiative.

(b) As part of the strategic initiative the GCJC shall identify and develop the framework, funding, strategies, programs, policies, partnerships, and opportunities necessary to address the growing need for a highly skilled and well-trained workforce to meet the needs of California's emerging green economy. The GCJC shall do all of the following:

(1) Assist in identifying and linking green collar job opportunities with workforce development training opportunities in local workforce investment areas (LWIAs), encouraging regional collaboration among LWIAs to meet regional economic demands.

(2) Develop public, private, philanthropic, and nongovernmental partnerships to build and expand the state's workforce development programs, network, and infrastructure.

(3) Provide policy guidance for job training programs in the clean and green technology sectors to assist and prepare specific populations, such as at-risk youth, displaced workers, veterans, formerly incarcerated individuals, and others facing barriers to employment.

(4) Develop, collect, interpret, and distribute statewide and regional labor market data on California's new and emerging green industries workforce needs, trends, and job growth.

(5) Identify funding resources and make recommendations on how to expand and leverage these funds.

(6) Foster regional collaboratives in the green economic sector. *(Added by Stats.2008, c. 312 (A.B.3018), § 1.)*

§ 15003. Annual report to the legislature

On or before April 1, 2009, and each April 1 yearly thereafter, the CWIB shall report to the Legislature on the status of GCJC activities and its development of a green workforce strategic initiative. *(Added by Stats. 2008, c. 312 (A.B.3018), § 1.)*

Division 9

CALWORKS PROGRAM: JOB CREATION

Section
17000. Department.
17001. Organization of employers and community leaders to create jobs.
17002. Council of corporate executives; clearinghouse; forum for leaders.

§ 17000. Department

As used in this division "department" means the Employment Development Department. *(Added by Stats.1997, c. 270 (A.B.1542), § 29, eff. Aug. 11, 1997, operative Jan. 1, 1998.)*

§ 17001. Organization of employers and community leaders to create jobs

Consistent with the ongoing relationships that the department maintains with private sector employers, the department shall encourage and organize the involvement of private sector employers and other community leaders in creating the necessary jobs for recipients of aid under Chapter 2 (commencing with Section 11200) of Part 3 of Division 9 of the Welfare and Institutions Code to move from welfare into unsubsidized employment. *(Added by Stats.1997, c. 270 (A.B.1542), § 29, eff. Aug. 11, 1997, operative Jan. 1, 1998.)*

§ 17002. Council of corporate executives; clearinghouse; forum for leaders

In carrying out the provisions of this division, the department shall conduct activities including, but not limited to, the following:

(a) Establish a council of corporate executives consisting of 13 members drawn from the business community including, but not limited to, retired or former chief executive officers of major California corporations. Seven members shall be appointed by the Governor, three shall be appointed by the Senate Committee on Rules, and three shall be appointed by the Speaker of the Assembly. Appointments shall be made no later than January 31, 1998. This council shall provide ongoing advice and assistance to the department in recruiting private employers to hire recipients of aid.

(b) In consultation with the council described in subdivision (a), establish a clearinghouse for information on the Internet or other forms of toll-free communication for private sector employers to obtain information about assistance and resources for hiring CalWORKs recipients and to register their pledges to assist the state in finding the jobs necessary to meet the local welfare-to-work goals throughout the state.

(c) In consultation with the council described in subdivision (a), provide a forum for leaders in the faith-based communities, as well as other civic leaders, to assist the state in promoting welfare-to-work goals as part of the civic duty of their constituents.

(Added by Stats.1997, c. 270 (A.B.1542), § 29, eff. Aug. 11, 1997, operative Jan. 1, 1998. Amended by Stats.1998, c. 902 (A.B.2772), § 8; Stats.2001, c. 745 (S.B.1191), § 223, eff. Oct. 12, 2001.)

Division 10

EMPLOYMENT ASSISTANCE FOR WORKERS WITH DISABILITIES

Section
18000. Legislative intent.
18002. One-stop centers.
18004. Performance reviews.
18006. Supplemental Security Income; State Supplemental Program; Social Security Disability Insurance; Medi-Cal benefits.
18008. Evaluations.
18010. Report.
18012. California Workforce Investment Board; local workforce investment boards; inclusion of persons with disabilities.

§ 18000. Legislative intent

(a) It is the purpose of this division to ensure that workforce preparation services provided through California's one-stop centers, including information and services provided electronically, are accessible to employers and jobseekers with disabilities.

(b) It is further the intent of the Legislature that one-stop centers provide appropriate services to individuals with disabilities to enhance their employability.

(c) It is further the intent of the Legislature that, in order to achieve the goals specified in subdivisions (a) and (b), local workforce investment boards plan for and report on services to jobseekers and employers with disabilities, including the implementation of the federal Ticket to Work program for those local workforce investment boards and one-stop centers that choose to implement the Ticket to Work program in their local workforce investment areas. *(Added by Stats.2002, c. 1088 (A.B.925), § 5.)*

§ 18002. One-stop centers

Each local workforce investment board shall establish at least one comprehensive one-stop career center in each local workforce investment area. These one-stop centers shall ensure access to services pursuant to Section 134(d) of the federal Workforce Investment Act of 1998 (29 U.S.C. Sec. 2864(d)), including services for persons with disabilities, including, but not limited to, all of the following:

(a) Outreach, intake, and orientation.

(b) Initial assessments of skills, aptitudes, abilities, and need for support services.

(c) Program eligibility determinations.

(d) Information on the local, regional, and national labor market.

(e) Information on filing for unemployment insurance.

(f) Access to intensive services as needed, including, but not limited to, comprehensive and specialized assessments of skill levels and service needs, development of individual employment plans, group counseling, individual counseling and career planning, case management for participants seeking training services under subdivision (g), and short-term prevocational services, such as learning, communication, interview, and other jobseeking and work related skills to help prepare individuals for unsubsidized employment and training.

(g) Training services, including, but not limited to, occupational skills training, on-the-job training, workplace training and cooperative education programs, private sector training programs, skills upgrade and retraining, entrepreneurial training, job readiness training, adult education, and literacy activities combined with training, and customized training. *(Added by Stats.2002, c. 1088 (A.B.925), § 5.)*

§ 18004. Performance reviews

The local workforce investment boards shall schedule and conduct regular performance reviews of their one-stop centers to determine whether the centers and providers are providing effective and meaningful opportunities for persons with disabilities to participate in the programs and activities of the centers and providers. *(Added by Stats.2002, c. 1088 (A.B.925), § 5.)*

§ 18006. Supplemental Security Income; State Supplemental Program; Social Security Disability Insurance; Medi-Cal benefits

One-stop center counselor staff shall provide accurate information to beneficiaries of Supplemental Security Income and the State Supplemental Program and Social Security Disability Insurance on the implications of work for these individuals. The information shall include, but not be limited to, referrals to appropriate benefits' planners. One–stop center counselor staff shall also provide accurate information to individuals with disabilities on how they may gain access to Medi–Cal benefits pursuant to Section 14007.9 of the Welfare and Institutions Code. *(Added by Stats.2002, c. 1088 (A.B.925), § 5.)*

§ 18008. Evaluations

In order to ensure that one-stop career centers operated by local workforce investment boards meet the needs of workers and employers with disabilities, the Governor shall ensure that evaluations conducted pursuant to Sections 134 (a)(2)(B)(ii) and (v) of the federal Workforce Investment Act of 1998 (29 U.S.C. Sec. 2864(a)(2)(B)(ii) and (v)), address how local one-stop centers provide all of the following:

(a) Full access to workforce development services for their disabled community.

(b) Assistive technology to ensure access to services.

(c) Staff training on assessment and service strategies for jobseekers and employers with disabilities.

(d) Representation of the disability community in program planning and service delivery.

(e) The development of regional employment networks to participate in the federal Ticket to Work program and the role of the local board and one-stop centers in the Ticket to Work program. *(Added by Stats.2002, c. 1088 (A.B.925), § 5.)*

§ 18010. Report

The California Workforce Investment Board shall report to the Governor and the Legislature by September 30, 2004, on the status of one-stop services to individuals with disabilities and implementation of the federal Ticket to Work program in California. *(Added by Stats.2002, c. 1088 (A.B.925), § 5.)*

§ 18012. California Workforce Investment Board; local workforce investment boards; inclusion of persons with disabilities

If permitted by federal law, the California Workforce Investment Board and local workforce investment boards shall include persons with disabilities or their representatives, with a particular effort to include such persons who are not employees of state or local government. *(Added by Stats.2002, c. 1088 (A.B.925), § 5.)*

Division 15

EFFECTIVE DATE [REPEALED]

VEHICLE CODE

Division 6

DRIVERS' LICENSES

CHAPTER 7. COMMERCIAL MOTOR VEHICLE SAFETY PROGRAM

ARTICLE 7. SANCTIONS

Section
15311.1. Allowing or requiring employee to violate out-of-service order.
15312.1. Allowing or requiring employee to violate railroad crossing laws.

§ 15311.1. Allowing or requiring employee to violate out-of-service order

(a) An employer that knowingly allows or requires an employee to operate a commercial motor vehicle in violation of an out-of-service order is, upon conviction, subject to a civil penalty of not less than two thousand seven hundred fifty dollars ($2,750) nor more than eleven thousand dollars ($11,000).

(b) This section shall become operative on September 20, 2005. *(Added by Stats.2004, c. 952 (A.B.3049), § 23, operative Sept. 20, 2005.)*

§ 15312.1. Allowing or requiring employee to violate railroad crossing laws

(a) An employer that knowingly allows or requires an employee to operate a commercial motor vehicle in violation of a federal, state, or local law or regulation pertaining to railroad crossings is, upon conviction, subject to a civil penalty of not more than ten thousand dollars ($10,000).

(b) This section shall become operative on September 20, 2005. *(Added by Stats.2004, c. 952 (A.B.3049), § 25, operative Sept. 20, 2005.)*

WELFARE AND INSTITUTIONS CODE

Division 2.5

YOUTHS

CHAPTER 1. THE YOUTH AUTHORITY

ARTICLE 4. POWERS AND DUTIES OF YOUTH AUTHORITY

Section
1768.1. Prohibition of employment or limitation of hours of work for replacement of employees on strike or subject to lockout.

§ 1768.1. Prohibition of employment or limitation of hours of work for replacement of employees on strike or subject to lockout

No contract shall be executed with an employer that will initiate employment by persons committed to the authority in the same job classification as other employees of the same employer who, at the time of execution of the contract, are on strike, as defined in Section 1132.6 of the Labor Code, or who are then subject to lockout, as defined in Section 1132.8 of the Labor Code. The total daily hours worked by persons committed to the authority and employed in the same job classification as other employees of the same employer who, subsequent to the employer's hiring of persons committed to the authority, go on strike, as defined in Section 1132.6 of the Labor Code, or are subjected to a lockout, as defined in Section 1132.8 of the Labor Code, shall not exceed, for the duration of the strike or lockout, the average daily hours worked for the preceding six months, or, if the authority's contract with the employer has been in operation for less than six months, the average for the period of operation. *(Added by Stats.1991, c. 739 (A.B.1787), § 2.)*

Division 4.5

SERVICES FOR THE DEVELOPMENTALLY DISABLED

CHAPTER 13. HABILITATION SERVICES FOR PERSONS WITH DEVELOPMENTAL DISABILITIES

Section
4865.1. Regional centers; payment of rate in effect as of June 30, 2004, for supported employment placement groups; conditions.

§ 4865.1. Regional centers; payment of rate in effect as of June 30, 2004, for supported employment placement groups; conditions

(a) A regional center shall continue to pay the rate in effect as of June 30, 2004, for a supported employment placement group composed of a coach-to-client ratio of 1:3 when the provider submits to the State Department of Developmental Services and the regional center, by July 30, 2004, documentation that all of the following conditions apply:

(1) The group was established prior to July 1, 2002.

(2) The group was at the 1:3 ratio on May 1, 2004.

(3) The employer will only accommodate a group of three.

(b) In consultation with the regional center, the State Department of Developmental Services shall determine whether the requirements of this section have been met. The department's decision shall be final.

(c) Groups paid under this section shall meet the requirements of subdivision (r) of Section 4851 by July 1, 2005, or be subject to termination of funding pursuant to subdivision (b) of Section 4860. *(Added by Stats.2004, c. 228 (S.B.1103), § 9.4, eff. Aug. 16, 2004.)*

CHAPTER 14. EMPLOYMENT

Section
4868. Employment First Committee; members; duties; report.

§ 4868. Employment First Committee; members; duties; report

(a) The State Council on Developmental Disabilities shall form a standing Employment First Committee consisting of the following members:

(1) One designee of each of the members of the state council specified in subparagraphs (B), (C), (D), (F), and (H) of paragraph (2) of subdivision (b) of Section 4521.

(2) A member of the consumer advisory committee of the state council.

(b) In carrying out the requirements of this section, the committee shall meet and consult, as appropriate, with other state and local agencies and organizations, including, but not limited to, the Employment Development Department, the Association of Regional Center Agencies, one or more supported employment provider organi-

1143

zations, an organized labor organization representing service coordination staff, and one or more consumer family member organizations.

(c) The responsibilities of the committee shall include, but need not be limited to, all of the following:

(1) Identifying the respective roles and responsibilities of state and local agencies in enhancing integrated and gainful employment opportunities for people with developmental disabilities.

(2) Identifying strategies, best practices, and incentives for increasing integrated employment and gainful employment opportunities for people with developmental disabilities, including, but not limited to, ways to improve the transition planning process for students 14 years of age or older, and to develop partnerships with, and increase participation by, public and private employers and job developers.

(3) Identifying existing sources of employment data and recommending goals for, and approaches to measuring progress in, increasing integrated employment and gainful employment of people with developmental disabilities.

(4) Recommending legislative, regulatory, and policy changes for increasing the number of individuals with developmental disabilities in integrated employment, self-employment, and microenterprises, and who earn wages at or above minimum wage, including, but not limited to, recommendations for improving transition planning and services for students with developmental disabilities who are 14 years of age or older. This shall include, but shall not be limited to, the development of an Employment First Policy, the intended outcome of which is a significant increase in the number of individuals with developmental disabilities who engage in integrated employment, self-employment, and microenterprises, and in the number of individuals who earn wages at or above minimum wage. This proposed policy shall be in furtherance of the intent of this division that services and supports be available to enable persons with developmental disabilities to approximate the pattern of everyday living available to people without disabilities of the same age and that support their integration into the mainstream life of the community, and that those services and supports result in more independent, productive, and normal lives for the persons served. The proposed Employment First Policy shall not limit service and support options otherwise available to consumers, or the rights of consumers, or, where appropriate, parents, legal guardians, or conservators to make choices in their own lives.

(d) For purposes of this chapter, "integrated employment" shall have the same definition as "integrated work" as defined in subdivision (*o*) of Section 4851.

(e) The committee, by July 1, 2011, and annually thereafter, shall provide a report to the appropriate policy committees of the Legislature and to the Governor describing its work and recommendations. The report due by July 1, 2011, shall include the proposed Employment First Policy described in paragraph (4) of subdivision (c). *(Added by Stats.2009, c. 231 (A.B.287), § 2.)*

Division 9

PUBLIC SOCIAL SERVICES

Part 3

AID AND MEDICAL ASSISTANCE

CHAPTER 3.   STATE SUPPLEMENTARY PROGRAM FOR AGED, BLIND AND DISABLED

ARTICLE 7.   IN–HOME SUPPORTIVE SERVICES

Section
12301.8.   Public authority or nonprofit consortium; assistance with criminal background checks; recovery of costs; funding.

§ 12301.8.   Public authority or nonprofit consortium; assistance with criminal background checks; recovery of costs; funding

(a)(1) A public authority or nonprofit consortium established pursuant to Section 12301.6, upon the request of an aged or disabled adult or that individual's authorized representative, may assist an employer, as defined in paragraph (2), in obtaining a criminal background check conducted by the Department of Justice, as authorized pursuant to Section 15660, of a provider, as described in paragraph (3).

(2) For purposes of this section, an "employer" means an aged or disabled adult, or that individual's authorized representative, who is ineligible for benefits under this chapter and who receives care by a provider as described in paragraph (3).

(3) For purposes of this section, a "provider" means a person who is unlicensed and provides nonmedical domestic or personal care to an aged or disabled adult who is ineligible to receive benefits under this chapter, in the adult's own home.

(b) A public authority or nonprofit consortium may recover the costs of administering this section, including the cost to the Department of Justice for processing the criminal background check, from the individual making the request, as described in subdivision (a).

(c) No General Fund moneys shall be used to implement this section. *(Added by Stats.2008, c. 2 (S.B.692), § 1.)*

CHAPTER 5.5. COUNTY ADMINISTRATION OF REFUGEE SOCIAL SERVICES AND TARGETED ASSISTANCE FUNDS

Section

13283. Victims of trafficking, domestic violence, and other serious crimes; access to refugee cash assistance and employment social services; exemption from work requirements; use of state funds.

§ 13283. Victims of trafficking, domestic violence, and other serious crimes; access to refugee cash assistance and employment social services; exemption from work requirements; use of state funds

Notwithstanding any other provision of law, the department shall ensure that noncitizen victims of trafficking, domestic violence, and other serious crimes, as defined in subdivision (b) of Section 18945, have access to refugee cash assistance, and refugee employment social services set forth in this chapter, to the same extent as individuals who are admitted to the United States as refugees under Section 1157 of Title 8 of the United States Code. These individuals shall be subject to the same work requirements and exemptions as other participants, provided that compliance with these requirements is authorized by law. An exemption from these requirements shall be available if physical or psychological trauma related to or arising from the victimization impedes their ability to comply. Assistance and services under this subdivision shall be paid from state funds to the extent federal funding is unavailable. *(Added by Stats.2006, c. 672 (S.B.1569), § 1.)*

CHAPTER 7. BASIC HEALTH CARE

Operation

For operation of Chapter 7, see Welfare and Institutions Code § 14020.

ARTICLE 3. ADMINISTRATION

Section

14110.6. Payment rates; employee wages and benefits; Medi–Cal reimbursement rate.

Operative Effect

Operation of Chapter 7 is contingent upon availability of federal funds, see Welfare and Institutions Code § 14020.

§ 14110.6. Payment rates; employee wages and benefits; Medi–Cal reimbursement rate

(a) The director shall adopt regulations, establishing payment rates for nursing facilities, intermediate care facilities/developmentally disabled, and intermediate care facilities/developmentally disabled-habilitative as defined in Section 1250 of the Health and Safety Code, which are sufficient to provide an increase of one dollar and ninety-six cents ($1.96) per patient day for patients receiving skilled nursing services, one dollar and fifty-eight cents ($1.58) per patient day, for patients receiving intermediate care services, two dollars and twenty-nine cents ($2.29) per patient day for intermediate care facilities/developmentally disabled patients, to be used for wage increases and benefits to all employees, except a licensed nursing home administrator or an administrator-in-training and two dollars and thirty-five cents ($2.35) per patient day for intermediate care facilities/developmentally disabled-habilitative patients in facilities with 4 to 6 beds, and one dollar and ninety-eight cents ($1.98) per patient day for intermediate care facilities/developmentally disabled-habilitative patients in facilities with 7 to 15 beds, to be used for wage increases and benefits to all direct care staff. However, if either (1) the entry level wages of the lowest paid nonadministrative employee of a nursing facility, intermediate care facility/developmentally disabled, or intermediate care facility/developmentally disabled-habilitative, exceeds six dollars ($6) per hour as of August 1, 1984; or (2) upon the election of a county board of supervisors, for any nursing facility, intermediate care facility/developmentally disabled, or intermediate care facility/developmentally disabled-habilitative, which is operated by a county, the funds received pursuant to regulations adopted pursuant to this section shall be used solely for labor costs directly related to providing patient care services in order to meet patients' needs including the uses of funds provided for under subdivision (d) of Section 14110.7. Any increase in wages and benefits required by this section shall be in addition to any future mandatory increases required by federal or state law. The rate shall provide funding for the portion of additional costs necessary to implement the wage and benefit increase required by this section attributable to Medi–Cal patients. The portion of those additional costs shall be the same as the ratio of Medi–Cal patients to the total number of patients in the facility. These regulations shall be adopted, effective March 15, 1985, for skilled nursing facilities, intermediate care facilities, and intermediate care facilities/developmentally disabled, and by October 1, 1985, for intermediate care facilities/developmentally disabled-habilitative. Commencing October 1, 1990, these requirements shall become operative for nursing facilities.

(b) Each nursing facility or intermediate care facility/developmentally disabled, or, for the period prior to October 1, 1990, each skilled nursing facility or intermediate care facility, shall certify all of the following:

(1) All employees, except a licensed nursing home administrator or an administrator-in-training of a licensed nursing home, shall receive at least the prevailing federal or state minimum wage rate plus the average hourly wage increase established pursuant to Chapter 19 of the Statutes of 1978, and this section.

(2) All employees of the facility, except a licensed administrator or administrator-in-training, shall be paid not less than the sum of the employee's actual rate of pay as of the effective date of the Medi–Cal rate increase

provided for under Section 14110.7 plus the amount of the adjustment specified pursuant to this section, or not less than the applicable agreed to rate plus the amount of the adjustment, whichever is greater.

(3) Any wage increase required pursuant to Section 1268.5 of the Health and Safety Code, is in addition to any minimum wages provided in this section.

(4) For purposes of determining the amount of Medi–Cal funds to be distributed for employee wages and benefits, the total Medi–Cal patient days recorded by the facility in the month of December 1983 shall be multiplied by the amount per patient day specified in subdivision (a) plus the amount provided by Chapter 19 of the Statutes of 1978. The new wage levels shall be determined by dividing the Medi–Cal funds received by the nonovertime hours worked by covered employees in December 1983, plus any adjustments due to additional employees as specified in Section 14110.7 and adjustments to reflect employee benefit allowances.

(c) Each intermediate care facility/developmentally disabled-habilitative shall certify all of the following:

(1) All direct care staff, as defined in the department's regulations developed pursuant to Section 1267.7 of the Health and Safety Code, shall receive at least the prevailing federal or state minimum wage plus the average hourly wage increase pursuant to this section.

(2) For purposes of determining the amount of Medi–Cal funds to be distributed for intermediate care facilities/developmentally disabled-habilitative for employee wages and benefits, the total Medi–Cal patient days in the month of December 1984, shall be multiplied by the amount per patient day specified in subdivision (a). The new wage level shall be determined by dividing the Medi–Cal funds received by the nonovertime hours by covered direct care employees in December 1984, and adjustments to reflect employee benefit allowances.

(d) The director shall order the inspection of relevant payroll and personnel records of facilities which are reimbursed for Medi–Cal patients under the rate of reimbursement established pursuant to subdivision (a) to ensure that the wage and benefit increases provided for have been implemented.

(e) The department shall, commencing August 1, 1999, increase the Medi–Cal reimbursement for level A and level B nursing facilities solely to provide funds for salaries, wages, and benefits increases for direct care staff. For the purposes of this subdivision, "direct care staff" means registered nurses, licensed vocational nurses, and nurse assistants, who provide direct patient care. The amount of funds to be provided to each level A and level B facility pursuant to this subdivision shall be calculated on a per patient day basis, and shall be added to the per diem rate paid to each facility. The amount of funds provided under this subdivision to each nursing facility peer group shall be published in a Medi–Cal provider bulletin. Level A and level B facilities shall compensate their registered nurses, licensed vocational nurses, and

1146

nurse assistants that portion of the rate increase provided under this subdivision in the form of salaries, wages, and benefits increases for their direct care staff. The total amount to be passed through by each facility shall be the per diem amount received by the facility pursuant to this subdivision times the facility's number of Medi–Cal patient days.

(f) Subject to an appropriation for this purpose in the Budget Act of 2000, in addition to the increase specified in subdivision (e), the department shall, commencing August 1, 2000, increase the Medi–Cal reimbursement rate for nursing facilities, intermediate care facilities/developmentally disabled, intermediate care facilities/developmentally disabled-habilitative, and intermediate care facilities/developmentally disabled-nursing solely to provide funds for salaries, wages, and benefits increases for direct care staff and other staff, subject to all of the following:

(1) For purposes of this subdivision "direct care staff in nursing facilities" means the following:

(A) Registered nurses and licensed vocational nurses, when employed in the performance of direct care to patients.

(B) Employees in the nurse assistant classification employed in the performance of direct care to patients at a freestanding or distinct-part nursing facility, including job titles such as nursing aide, aide, practical nurse, orderly, nurse assistant, and certified nurse assistant.

(C) Employees performing respiratory therapy services for Medi–Cal pediatric subacute patients, including job titles such as respiratory care practitioner, respiratory technician, respiratory therapist inhalation technician, and inhalation therapist.

(2) For purposes of this subdivision, "direct care staff in intermediate care facilities/developmentally disabled, intermediate care facilities/developmentally disabled-habilitative, and intermediate care facilities/developmentally disabled-nursing" means all of the following:

(A) Qualified mental retardation professionals employed in the performance of direct care to patients.

(B) Lead personnel employed in the performance of direct care to patients. Lead personnel described in this subparagraph shall not be considered to be supervisory.

(C) Employees in the nurse assistant classification employed in the performance of direct care to patients at a freestanding or distinct-part nursing facility, including job titles such as nurse assistants and aides.

(D) Other nonsupervisory staff providing direct patient care.

(E) Registered nurses and licensed vocational nurses, if employed in the performance of direct care to patients.

(3) For purposes of paragraphs (1) and (2), "direct care staff" shall not include registered nurses or other personnel performing supervisory functions or housekeeping or maintenance staff in any facility.

(4) For purposes of this subdivision, "other staff" means all of the following personnel:

(A) Linen and laundry staff.

(B) Plant operations and maintenance staff.

(C) Housekeeping staff.

(D) Dietary staff.

(5)(A) The amount of funds to be provided to each facility pursuant to this subdivision shall be added to the per diem rate paid to each facility on a per patient day basis.

(B) The per diem amount of funds provided to each facility type and peer group pursuant to this subdivision shall be published in a Medi–Cal provider bulletin. Nursing facilities that are part of an acute care hospital and subacute facilities shall be notified of their per diem amount provided pursuant to this subdivision in a separate letter to each facility.

(6)(A) Facilities receiving funds pursuant to this subdivision shall compensate staff that portion of the rate increase provided pursuant to this subdivision in the form of salaries, wages, and benefits increases. The total amount to be passed through pursuant to this subdivision by each facility shall be the per diem amount received by the facility pursuant to this subdivision multiplied by the facility's number of Medi–Cal patient days.

(B) Each direct care and other staff employee classification shall receive a portion of the rate increase provided pursuant to this subdivision in the form of an increase in salary, wage, and benefits. The facility may allocate the amounts that each classification may receive, but the amount shall not be nominal or zero.

(C) Funds passed through pursuant to this subdivision for purposes of salary, wages, or benefits increases may not be used for any salary, wage, or benefit increase that were committed to by a facility prior to August 1, 2000, nor may these funds be used for any salaries, wages, or benefits that the facility would have paid in the absence of this subdivision.

(D) Funds passed through pursuant to this subdivision for purposes of salary, wages, or benefits increases may not be distributed to direct care and other staff in the form of bonuses. These funds may, however, be used to provide retroactive pay increases if those wage increases also increase the employee's base salary rate.

(7) The base from which direct care and other staff salaries, wages, and benefits shall be increased shall be the aggregate per hour salaries, wages, and benefits for the period of August 1, 1999, to July 31, 2000, inclusive.

(8) The department may inspect relevant payroll and personnel records of facilities receiving funds pursuant to this subdivision in order to ensure that the salary, wage, and benefit increases provided for pursuant to this subdivision have been implemented.

(9) Each facility receiving funds from the department, or from a county organized health system described in paragraph (10) pursuant to this subdivision shall certify on the form provided by the department that these funds were expended for increased direct care and other staff salary, wages, and benefits increases in accordance with this subdivision. The facility shall return the form to the department by October 1, 2001. The facility shall submit a copy of the completed form to all collective bargaining agents with whom the facility has collective bargaining agreements for direct care and other staff at the facility.

(10) County organized health systems contracting with the department pursuant to Article 2.8 (commencing with Section 14087.5) and Article 7 (commencing with Section 14490) of Chapter 8 shall certify to the department, in a manner to be specified by the department, that the August 1, 2000, wage pass-through funds, received pursuant to this section in the form of capitated rate payments, were passed through to the facilities described in this subdivision.

(g) Any facility which is paid under the rate provided for in subdivision (a), (e), or (f) which the director finds has not made the wage and benefit increases provided for shall be liable for the amount of funds paid to the facility based upon the wage and benefit requirements provided for by this section but not distributed to employees for wages and benefits, plus a penalty equal to 10 percent of the funds not so distributed. The facility shall be subject to Section 14107. *(Added by Stats.1985, c. 11, § 20, eff. March 6, 1985. Amended by Stats.1985, c. 1336, § 1, eff. Oct. 1, 1985; Stats.1989, c. 731, § 15; Stats.1990, c. 1329 (S.B.1524), § 20, eff. Sept. 26, 1990; Stats.1999, c. 146 (A.B.1107), § 62, eff. July 22, 1999; Stats.2000, c. 93 (A.B.2877), § 88, eff. July 7, 2000.)*

ARTICLE 4. THE MEDI–CAL BENEFITS PROGRAM

Section
14132.955. Personal care services at person's place of employment.

Operative Effect

Operation of Chapter 7 is contingent upon availability of federal funds, see Welfare and Institutions Code § 14020.

§ 14132.955. Personal care services at person's place of employment

Personal care services that are provided pursuant to Section 14132.95 shall include services in the recipient's place of employment if both of the following conditions are met:

(a) The personal care services are limited to those that are currently authorized for the recipient in the recipient's home and those services are to be utilized by the recipient at the recipient's place of employment to enable the recipient to obtain, retain, or return to, work. Authorized services utilized by the recipient at the recipient's place of employment shall be services that are relevant and necessary in supporting and maintaining employment. However, work place services shall not be used to supplant any reasonable accommodations required of an employer by the Americans with Disabilities Act (42 U.S.C. Sec. 12101 et seq.) or other legal entitlements or third-party obligations.

(b) The provision of personal care services at the recipient's place of employment shall be authorized only to the extent that the total hours utilized at the work place are within the total personal care services hours authorized for the recipient in the home. Additional personal care services hours may not be authorized in connection with a recipient's employment. *(Added by Stats.2002, c. 1088 (A.B.925), § 9.)*

CHAPTER 11. ELDER ABUSE AND DEPENDENT ADULT CIVIL PROTECTION ACT

ARTICLE 3. MANDATORY AND NONMANDATORY REPORTS OF ABUSE

Section
15630.1.   Mandated reporter of suspected financial abuse of
                  an elder or dependent adult; definitions and
                  reporting requirements.

§ 15630.1. Mandated reporter of suspected financial abuse of an elder or dependent adult; definitions and reporting requirements

(a) As used in this section, "mandated reporter of suspected financial abuse of an elder or dependent adult" means all officers and employees of financial institutions.

(b) As used in this section, the term "financial institution" means any of the following:

(1) A depository institution, as defined in Section 3(c) of the Federal Deposit Insurance Act (12 U.S.C. Sec. 1813(c)).

(2) An institution-affiliated party, as defined in Section 3(u) of the Federal Deposit Insurance Act (12 U.S.C. Sec. 1813(u)).

(3) A federal credit union or state credit union, as defined in Section 101 of the Federal Credit Union Act (12 U.S.C. Sec. 1752), including, but not limited to, an institution-affiliated party of a credit union, as defined in Section 206(r) of the Federal Credit Union Act (12 U.S.C. Sec. 1786(r)).

(c) As used in this section, "financial abuse" has the same meaning as in Section 15610.30.

(d)(1) Any mandated reporter of suspected financial abuse of an elder or dependent adult who has direct contact with the elder or dependent adult or who reviews or approves the elder or dependent adult's financial documents, records, or transactions, in connection with providing financial services with respect to an elder or dependent adult, and who, within the scope of his or her employment or professional practice, has observed or has

knowledge of an incident, that is directly related to the transaction or matter that is within that scope of employment or professional practice, that reasonably appears to be financial abuse, or who reasonably suspects that abuse, based solely on the information before him or her at the time of reviewing or approving the document, record, or transaction in the case of mandated reporters who do not have direct contact with the elder or dependent adult, shall report the known or suspected instance of financial abuse by telephone immediately, or as soon as practicably possible, and by written report sent within two working days to the local adult protective services agency or the local law enforcement agency.

(2) When two or more mandated reporters jointly have knowledge or reasonably suspect that financial abuse of an elder or a dependent adult for which the report is mandated has occurred, and when there is an agreement among them, the telephone report may be made by a member of the reporting team who is selected by mutual agreement. A single report may be made and signed by the selected member of the reporting team. Any member of the team who has knowledge that the member designated to report has failed to do so shall thereafter make that report.

(3) If the mandated reporter knows that the elder or dependent adult resides in a long-term care facility, as defined in Section 15610.47, the report shall be made to the local ombudsman or local law enforcement agency.

(e) An allegation by the elder or dependent adult, or any other person, that financial abuse has occurred is not sufficient to trigger the reporting requirement under this section if both of the following conditions are met:

(1) The mandated reporter of suspected financial abuse of an elder or dependent adult is aware of no other corroborating or independent evidence of the alleged financial abuse of an elder or dependent adult. The mandated reporter of suspected financial abuse of an elder or dependent adult is not required to investigate any accusations.

(2) In the exercise of his or her professional judgment, the mandated reporter of suspected financial abuse of an elder or dependent adult reasonably believes that financial abuse of an elder or dependent adult did not occur.

(f) Failure to report financial abuse under this section shall be subject to a civil penalty not exceeding one thousand dollars ($1,000) or if the failure to report is willful, a civil penalty not exceeding five thousand dollars ($5,000), which shall be paid by the financial institution that is the employer of the mandated reporter to the party bringing the action. Subdivision (h) of Section 15630 shall not apply to violations of this section.

(g)(1) The civil penalty provided for in subdivision (f) shall be recovered only in a civil action brought against the financial institution by the Attorney General, district attorney, or county counsel. No action shall be brought under this section by any person other than the Attorney General, district attorney, or county counsel. Multiple actions for the civil penalty may not be brought for the same violation.

(2) Nothing in the Financial Elder Abuse Reporting Act of 2005 shall be construed to limit, expand, or otherwise modify any civil liability or remedy that may exist under this or any other law.

(h) As used in this section, "suspected financial abuse of an elder or dependent adult" occurs when a person who is required to report under subdivision (a) observes or has knowledge of behavior or unusual circumstances or transactions, or a pattern of behavior or unusual circumstances or transactions, that would lead an individual with like training or experience, based on the same facts, to form a reasonable belief that an elder or dependent adult is the victim of financial abuse as defined in Section 15610.30.

(i) Reports of suspected financial abuse of an elder or dependent adult made by an employee or officer of a financial institution pursuant to this section are covered under subdivision (b) of Section 47 of the Civil Code.

(j) This section shall remain in effect only until January 1, 2013, and as of that date is repealed, unless a later enacted statute, that is enacted before January 1, 2013, deletes or extends that date. *(Added by Stats.2005, c. 140 (S.B.1018), § 4, operative Jan. 1, 2007.)*

Repeal

For repeal of this section, see its terms.

ARTICLE 4. CONFIDENTIALITY

Section
15633. Confidentiality of reports; disclosure.
15633. Confidentiality of reports; disclosures.
15634. Civil or criminal liability of reporter.
15634. Civil or criminal liability of reporter.

§ 15633. Confidentiality of reports; disclosure

Text of section operative until Jan. 1, 2013.

(a) The reports made pursuant to Sections 15630, 15630.1, and 15631 shall be confidential and may be disclosed only as provided in subdivision (b). Any violation of the confidentiality required by this chapter is a misdemeanor punishable by not more than six months in the county jail, by a fine of five hundred dollars ($500), or by both that fine and imprisonment.

(b) Reports of suspected abuse of an elder or dependent adult and information contained therein may be disclosed only to the following:

(1) Persons or agencies to whom disclosure of information or the identity of the reporting party is permitted under Section 15633.5.

(2)(A) Persons who are trained and qualified to serve on multidisciplinary personnel teams may disclose to one another information and records that are relevant to the prevention, identification, or treatment of abuse of elderly or dependent persons.

(B) Except as provided in subparagraph (A), any personnel of the multidisciplinary team or agency that receives information pursuant to this chapter, shall be under the same obligations and subject to the same confidentiality penalties as the person disclosing or providing that information. The information obtained shall be maintained in a manner that ensures the maximum protection of privacy and confidentiality rights.

(c) This section shall not be construed to allow disclosure of any reports or records relevant to the reports of abuse of an elder or dependent adult if the disclosure would be prohibited by any other provisions of state or federal law applicable to the reports or records relevant to the reports of the abuse, nor shall it be construed to prohibit the disclosure by a financial institution of any reports or records relevant to the reports of abuse of an elder or dependent adult if the disclosure would be required of a financial institution by otherwise applicable state or federal law or court order.

(d) This section shall remain in effect only until January 1, 2013, and as of that date is repealed, unless a later enacted statute, that is enacted before January 1, 2013, deletes or extends that date. *(Added by Stats.1994, c. 594 (S.B.1681), § 14. Amended by Stats.1998, c. 946 (S.B.2199) § 9; Stats.1998, c. 980 (A.B.1780), § 2; Stats. 2005, c. 140 (S.B.1018), § 5, operative Jan. 1, 2007.)*

Repeal

For repeal of this section, see its terms.

For text of section operative Jan. 1, 2013, see Welfare and Institutions Code § 15633, post.

§ 15633. Confidentiality of reports; disclosures

Text of section operative Jan. 1, 2013.

(a) The reports made pursuant to Sections 15630 and 15631 shall be confidential and may be disclosed only as provided in subdivision (b). Any violation of the confidentiality required by this chapter is a misdemeanor punishable by not more than six months in the county jail, by a fine of five hundred dollars ($500), or by both that fine and imprisonment.

(b) Reports of suspected elder or dependent adult abuse and information contained therein may be disclosed only to the following:

(1) Persons or agencies to whom disclosure of information or the identity of the reporting party is permitted under Section 15633.5.

(2)(A) Persons who are trained and qualified to serve on multidisciplinary personnel teams may disclose to one another information and records that are relevant to the prevention, identification, or treatment of abuse of elderly or dependent persons.

(B) Except as provided in subparagraph (A), any personnel of the multidisciplinary team or agency that receives information pursuant to this chapter, shall be under the same obligations and subject to the same confidentiality penalties as the person disclosing or providing that information. The information obtained shall be maintained in a manner that ensures the maximum protection of privacy and confidentiality rights.

(c) This section shall not be construed to allow disclosure of any reports or records relevant to the reports of elder or dependent adult abuse if the disclosure would be prohibited by any other provisions of state or federal law applicable to the reports or records relevant to the reports of the abuse.

(d) This section shall become operative on January 1, 2013. *(Added by Stats.2005, c. 140 (S.B.1018), § 6, operative Jan. 1, 2013.)*

For text of section operative until Jan. 1, 2013,
see Welfare and Institutions Code § 15633, ante.

§ 15634. Civil or criminal liability of reporter

Text of section operative until Jan. 1, 2013.

(a) No care custodian, clergy member, health practitioner, mandated reporter of suspected financial abuse of an elder or dependent adult, or employee of an adult protective services agency or a local law enforcement agency who reports a known or suspected instance of abuse of an elder or dependent adult shall be civilly or criminally liable for any report required or authorized by this article. Any other person reporting a known or suspected instance of abuse of an elder or dependent adult shall not incur civil or criminal liability as a result of any report authorized by this article, unless it can be proven that a false report was made and the person knew that the report was false. No person required to make a report pursuant to this article, or any person taking photographs at his or her discretion, shall incur any civil or criminal liability for taking photographs of a suspected victim of abuse of an elder or dependent adult or causing photographs to be taken of such a suspected victim or for disseminating the photographs with the reports required by this article. However, this section shall not be construed to grant immunity from this liability with respect to any other use of the photographs.

(b) No care custodian, clergy member, health practitioner, mandated reporter of suspected financial abuse of an elder or dependent adult, or employee of an adult protective services agency or a local law enforcement agency who, pursuant to a request from an adult protective services agency or a local law enforcement agency investigating a report of known or suspected abuse of an elder or dependent adult, provides the requesting agency with access to the victim of a known or suspected instance of abuse of an elder or dependent adult, shall incur civil or criminal liability as a result of providing that access.

(c) The Legislature finds that, even though it has provided immunity from liability to persons required to report abuse of an elder or dependent adult, immunity does not eliminate the possibility that actions may be brought against those persons based upon required reports of abuse. In order to further limit the financial hardship that those persons may incur as a result of

1150

fulfilling their legal responsibilities, it is necessary that they not be unfairly burdened by legal fees incurred in defending those actions. Therefore, a care custodian, clergy member, health practitioner, or an employee of an adult protective services agency or a local law enforcement agency may present to the State Board of Control a claim for reasonable attorneys' fees incurred in any action against that person on the basis of making a report required or authorized by this article if the court has dismissed the action upon a demurrer or motion for summary judgment made by that person, or if he or she prevails in the action. The State Board of Control shall allow that claim if the requirements of this subdivision are met, and the claim shall be paid from an appropriation to be made for that purpose. Attorneys' fees awarded pursuant to this section shall not exceed an hourly rate greater than the rate charged by the Attorney General at the time the award is made and shall not exceed an aggregate amount of fifty thousand dollars ($50,000). This subdivision shall not apply if a public entity has provided for the defense of the action pursuant to Section 995 of the Government Code.

(d) This section shall remain in effect only until January 1, 2013, and as of that date is repealed, unless a later enacted statute, that is enacted before January 1, 2013, deletes or extends that date. *(Added by Stats.1985, c. 1164, § 11, eff. Sept. 28, 1985. Amended by Stats.1986, c. 769, § 14, eff. Sept. 15, 1986; Stats.1990, c. 241 (S.B.1911), § 2; Stats.2002, c. 54 (A.B.255), § 11; Stats. 2005, c. 140 (S.B.1018), § 7, operative Jan. 1, 2007.)*

Repeal

For repeal of this section, see its terms.

For text of section operative Jan. 1, 2013, see
Welfare and Institutions Code § 15634, post.

§ 15634. Civil or criminal liability of reporter

Text of section operative Jan. 1, 2013.

(a) No care custodian, clergy member, health practitioner, or employee of an adult protective services agency or a local law enforcement agency who reports a known or suspected instance of elder or dependent adult abuse shall be civilly or criminally liable for any report required or authorized by this article. Any other person reporting a known or suspected instance of elder or dependent adult abuse shall not incur civil or criminal liability as a result of any report authorized by this article, unless it can be proven that a false report was made and the person knew that the report was false. No person required to make a report pursuant to this article, or any person taking photographs at his or her discretion, shall incur any civil or criminal liability for taking photographs of a suspected victim of elder or dependent adult abuse or causing photographs to be taken of the suspected victim or for disseminating the photographs with the reports required by this article. However, this section shall not be construed to grant immunity from this liability with respect to any other use of the photographs.

(b) No care custodian, clergy member, health practitioner, or employee of an adult protective services agency or a local law enforcement agency who, pursuant to a request from an adult protective services agency or a local law enforcement agency investigating a report of known or suspected elder or dependent adult abuse, provides the requesting agency with access to the victim of a known or suspected instance of elder or dependent adult abuse, shall incur civil or criminal liability as a result of providing that access.

(c) The Legislature finds that, even though it has provided immunity from liability to persons required to report elder or dependent adult abuse, immunity does not eliminate the possibility that actions may be brought against those persons based upon required reports of abuse. In order to further limit the financial hardship that those persons may incur as a result of fulfilling their legal responsibilities, it is necessary that they not be unfairly burdened by legal fees incurred in defending those actions. Therefore, a care custodian, clergy member, health practitioner, or employee of an adult protective services agency or a local law enforcement agency may present to the California Victim Compensation and Government Claims Board a claim for reasonable attorney's fees incurred in any action against that person on the basis of making a report required or authorized by this article if the court has dismissed the action upon a demurrer or motion for summary judgment made by that person, or if he or she prevails in the action. The California Victim Compensation and Government Claims Board shall allow that claim if the requirements of this subdivision are met, and the claim shall be paid from an appropriation to be made for that purpose. Attorney's fees awarded pursuant to this section shall not exceed an hourly rate greater than the rate charged by the Attorney General at the time the award is made and shall not exceed an aggregate amount of fifty thousand dollars ($50,000). This subdivision shall not apply if a public entity has provided for the defense of the action pursuant to Section 995 of the Government Code.

(d) This section shall become operative on January 1, 2013. *(Added by Stats.2005, c. 140 (S.B.1018), § 8, operative Jan. 1, 2013. Amended by Stats.2006, c. 538 (S.B.1852), § 711, operative Jan. 1, 2013.)*

For text of section operative until Jan. 1, 2013, see Welfare and Institutions Code § 15634, ante.

ARTICLE 10. EMPLOYEE STATEMENT

Section
15659. Written statements concerning § 15630 reporting requirements; acknowledgement as prerequisite to employment for certain agencies; statements to licensed or certificated professionals required to report.

§ 15659. Written statements concerning § 15630 reporting requirements; acknowledgement as prerequisite to employment for certain agencies; statements to licensed or certificated professionals required to report

(a) Any person who enters into employment on or after January 1, 1995, as a care custodian, clergy member, health practitioner, or with an adult protective services agency or a local law enforcement agency, prior to commencing his or her employment and as a prerequisite to that employment, shall sign a statement on a form that shall be provided by the prospective employer, to the effect that he or she has knowledge of Section 15630 and will comply with its provisions. The employer shall provide a copy of Section 15630 to the employee. The statement shall inform the employee that he or she is a mandated reporter and inform the employee of his or her reporting obligations under Section 15630. The signed statement shall be retained by the employer.

(b) Agencies or facilities that employ persons who were employed prior to January 1, 1995, and who are required to make reports pursuant to Section 15630, shall inform those persons of their responsibility to make reports by delivering to them a copy of the statement specified in subdivision (a).

(c) The cost of printing, distribution, and filing of these statements shall be borne by the employer.

(d) On and after January 1, 1995, when a person is issued a state license or certificate to engage in a profession or occupation the members of which are required to make a report pursuant to Section 15630, the state agency issuing the license or certificate shall send to the person a statement substantially similar to the one contained in subdivision (a) at the same time that it transmits to the person the document indicating licensure or certification.

(e) As an alternative to the procedure required by subdivision (d), a state agency may cause the required statement to be printed on all application forms for a license or certificate printed on or after January 1, 1995.

(f) The retention of statements required by subdivision (a), and the delivery of statements required by subdivision (b), shall be the full extent of the employer's duty pursuant to this section. The failure of any employee or other person associated with the employer to report abuse of elders or dependent adults pursuant to Section 15630 or otherwise meet the requirements of this chapter shall be the sole responsibility of that person. The employer or facility shall incur no civil or other liability for the failure of these persons to comply with the requirements of this chapter. *(Added by Stats.1994, c. 594 (S.B.1681), § 25. Amended by Stats.1998, c. 946 (S.B.2199), § 12; Stats.2002, c. 54 (A.B.255), § 12.7.)*

ARTICLE 11. CRIMINAL RECORD REPORTING

Section
15660. Criminal record information; employer request and submission of fingerprints; unlicensed persons pro-

viding nonmedical domestic or personal care to aged or disabled adult; notification; Department of Justice fee.

§ 15660. Criminal record information; employer request and submission of fingerprints; unlicensed persons providing nonmedical domestic or personal care to aged or disabled adult; notification; Department of Justice fee

(a) The Department of Justice shall secure any criminal record of a person to determine whether the person has ever been convicted of a violation or attempted violation of Section 243.4 of the Penal Code, a sex offense against a minor, or of any felony that requires registration pursuant to Section 290 of the Penal Code, or whether the person has been convicted or incarcerated within the last 10 years as the result of committing a violation or attempted violation of Section 273a or 273d, or subdivision (a) or (b) of Section 368, of the Penal Code, or as the result of committing a theft, robbery, burglary, or any felony, and shall provide a subsequent arrest notification pursuant to Section 11105.2 of the Penal Code, if both of the following conditions are met:

(1) An employer of the person requests the determination and submits fingerprints of the person to the Department of Justice. For purposes of this paragraph, "employer" includes, but is not limited to, an in-home supportive services recipient, as defined by Section 12302.2, an aged or disabled adult who is ineligible for benefits under Chapter 3 (commencing with Section 12000), who receives care by a person as described in paragraph (2), any recipient of personal care services under the Medi–Cal program pursuant to Sections 14132.95 to 14132.97, inclusive, and any public authority or nonprofit consortium, as described in subdivision (a) of Section 12301.6.

(2) The person is unlicensed and provides nonmedical domestic or personal care to an aged or disabled adult in the adult's own home.

(b)(1) If it is found that the person has ever been convicted of a violation or attempted violation of Section 243.4 of the Penal Code, a sex offense against a minor, or of any felony which requires registration pursuant to Section 290 of the Penal Code, or that the person has been convicted or incarcerated within the last 10 years as the result of committing a violation or attempted violation of Section 273a or 273d, or subdivision (a) or (b) of Section 368, of the Penal Code, or as the result of committing a theft, robbery, burglary, or any felony, the Department of Justice shall notify the employer of that fact. If no criminal record information has been recorded, the Department of Justice shall provide the employer with a statement of that fact.

(2) Any employer may deny employment to any person who is the subject of a report under paragraph (1) when the report indicates that the person has committed any of the crimes identified in paragraph (1).

(3) Nothing in this section shall be construed to require any employer to hire any person who is the subject of a report under paragraph (1) when the report indicates that the person has not committed any of the crimes indicated in paragraph (1).

(c)(1) Fingerprints shall be on a card provided by the Department of Justice for the purpose of obtaining a set of fingerprints. The employer shall submit the fingerprints to the Department of Justice. Within 30 calendar days of the receipt of the fingerprints, the Department of Justice shall notify the employer of the criminal record information, as provided in this subdivision. If no criminal record information has been recorded, the Department of Justice shall provide the employer with a statement of that fact as soon as possible, but not later than 30 calendar days from the date of receipt of the fingerprints. If new fingerprints are required for processing, the Department of Justice shall, as soon as possible, but not later than 30 calendar days from the date of receipt of the fingerprints, notify the employer that the fingerprints were illegible.

(2) Fingerprints may be taken by any local law enforcement officer or agency for purposes of paragraph (1).

(3) Counties shall notify any recipient of, or applicant for, in-home supportive services or personal care services under the Medi–Cal program, upon his or her application for in-home supportive services or personal care services or during his or her annual redetermination, or upon the recipient's changing providers, that a criminal record check is available, and that the check can be performed by the Department of Justice.

(d)(1) The Department of Justice shall charge a fee to the employer to cover the costs of administering this section.

(2)(A) If the employer is an in-home supportive services recipient, as defined in Section 123202.2, a recipient of personal care services under the Medi–Cal program pursuant to Sections 14132.95 to 14132.97, inclusive, or any public authority or nonprofit consortium as described in subdivision (a) of Section 12301.6, the fee shall be shared by the county and the state in the same ratio as described in Section 12306.

(B)(i) Notwithstanding any other provision of law, and except as provided in clause (ii), the department shall, no later than January 1, 2009, implement subparagraph (A) through an all-county letter from the director.

(ii) No later than July 1, 2009, the department shall adopt regulations to implement the provisions listed in * * * subparagraph (A).

(e) It is the intent of the Legislature that the Department of Justice charge a fee to cover its cost in providing services in accordance with this section to comply with the 30–calendar–day requirement for provision to the department of the criminal record information, as contained in subdivision (c). *(Added by Stats.1993, c. 537 (A.B.1653), § 4. Amended by Stats.1996, c. 911 (A.B.857), § 1; Stats.2000, c. 972 (A.B.2665), § 2; Stats.2001, c. 845*

(A.B.530), § 2; Stats.2002, c. 627 (S.B.900), § 6; Stats. 2007, c. 447 (S.B.868), § 2; Stats.2008, c. 179 (S.B.1498), § 250; Stats.2008, c. 2 (S.B.692), § 2; Stats.2009, c. 140 (A.B.1164), § 217.)

*

Chapter 1

GENERAL PROVISIONS

Rule
3.1100.   Application.
3.1103.   Definitions and construction.

Rule 3.1100.   Application

The rules in this division apply to proceedings in civil law and motion, as defined in rule 3.1103, and to discovery proceedings in family law and probate. *(Formerly Rule 301, adopted, eff. Jan. 1, 1984. As amended, eff. July 1, 1984; July 1, 1997; Jan. 1, 2002. Renumbered Rule 3.1100 and amended, eff. Jan. 1, 2007.)*

Rule 3.1103.   Definitions and construction

(a) Law and motion defined

"Law and motion" includes any proceedings:

(1) On application before trial for an order, except for causes arising under the Welfare and Institutions Code, the Probate Code, the Family Code, or Code of Civil Procedure sections 527.6, 527.7, and 527.8; or

(2) On application for an order regarding the enforcement of judgment, attachment of property, appointment of a receiver, obtaining or setting aside a judgment by default, writs of review, mandate and prohibition, a petition to compel arbitration, and enforcement of an award by arbitration.

(b) Application of rules on extending or shortening time

Rules 1.10(c) and 2.20 on extending or shortening time apply to proceedings under this division.

(c) Application to demurrers

Unless the context or subject matter otherwise requires, the rules in this division apply to demurrers. *(Formerly Rule 303, adopted, eff. Jan. 1, 1984. As amended, eff. July 1, 1984; July 1, 1997. Renumbered Rule 3.1103 and amended, eff. Jan. 1, 2007.)*

Chapter 3

PROVISIONAL AND INJUNCTIVE RELIEF

Article 3

INJUNCTIONS

Rule
3.1151.   Requirements for injunction in certain cases.
3.1152.   Civil harassment and workplace violence.
3.1153.   Minors may appear without counsel to seek specified restraining orders.

Rule 3.1151.   Requirements for injunction in certain cases

A petition for an injunction to limit picketing, restrain real property encroachments, or protect easements must depict by drawings, plot plans, photographs, or other appropriate means, or must describe in detail the premises involved, including, if applicable, the length and width of the frontage on a street or alley, the width of sidewalks, and the number, size, and location of entrances. *(Formerly Rule 361, adopted, eff. Jan. 1, 1984. Renumbered Rule 3.1151 and amended, eff. Jan. 1, 2007.)*

Rule 3.1152.   Civil harassment and workplace violence

(a) Scheduling of hearing

On the filing of a petition for an injunction under Code of Civil Procedure section 527.6 or 527.8, a hearing must be set in accordance with the requirements of subdivision (d) of section 527.6 or subdivision (f) of section 527.8.

(b) Temporary restraining order

A temporary restraining order may be granted in accordance with the provisions of Code of Civil Procedure section 527.6(c) or 527.8(e), but unless otherwise ordered no memorandum is required.

(c) Service of petition and orders

The petition and order to show cause, and any temporary restraining order, must be personally served on the defendant. Service must be made in the manner provided by law for personal service of summons in civil actions.

(d) Response by defendant

A response by defendant must be filed and delivered to plaintiff or plaintiff's attorney no later than 48 hours before the hearing. *(Formerly Rule 363, adopted, eff. Jan. 1, 1984. As amended, eff. Jan. 1, 1993; July 1, 1995; Jan. 1, 2000; Jan. 1, 2002. Renumbered Rule 3.1152 and amended, eff. Jan. 1, 2007.)*

Rule 3.1153. Minors may appear without counsel to seek specified restraining orders

A minor, accompanied by a duly appointed and acting guardian ad litem, may be permitted to appear in court without counsel for the limited purpose of obtaining or opposing:

(1) An injunction or temporary restraining order or both to prohibit harassment under Code of Civil Procedure section 527.6;

(2) An injunction or temporary restraining order or both against violence or a credible threat of violence in the workplace under Code of Civil Procedure section 527.8;

(3) A protective order under Family Code section 6200 et seq.; or

(4) A protective order under Family Code sections 7710 and 7720.

In making the determination concerning allowing appearance without counsel, the court should consider whether the minor and the guardian have divergent interests. *(Formerly Rule 364, adopted, eff. July 1, 1995. Renumbered Rule 3.1153 and amended, eff. Jan. 1, 2007.)*

RULES OF THE STATE BAR OF CALIFORNIA
CALIFORNIA RULES OF PROFESSIONAL CONDUCT

Chapter 2

RELATIONSHIP AMONG MEMBERS

Rule
2–100.   Communication With a Represented Party.
2–400.   Prohibited Discriminatory Conduct in a Law Practice.

Rule 2–100. Communication With a Represented Party

(A) While representing a client, a member shall not communicate directly or indirectly about the subject of the representation with a party the member knows to be represented by another lawyer in the matter, unless the member has the consent of the other lawyer.

(B) For purposes of this rule, a "party" includes:

(1) An officer, director, or managing agent of a corporation or association, and a partner or managing agent of a partnership; or

(2) An association member or an employee of an association, corporation, or partnership, if the subject of the communication is any act or omission of such person in connection with the matter which may be binding upon or imputed to the organization for purposes of civil or criminal liability or whose statement may constitute an admission on the part of the organization.

(C) This rule shall not prohibit:

(1) Communications with a public officer, board, committee, or body; or

(2) Communications initiated by a party seeking advice or representation from an independent lawyer of the party's choice; or

(3) Communications otherwise authorized by law.

DISCUSSION

Rule 2–100 is intended to control communications between a member and persons the member knows to be represented by counsel unless a statutory scheme or case law will override the rule. There are a number of express statutory schemes which authorize communications between a member and person who would otherwise be subject to this rule. These statutes protect a variety of other rights such as the right of employees to organize and to engage in collective bargaining, employee health and safety, or equal employment opportunity. Other applicable law also includes the authority of government prosecutors and investigators to conduct criminal investigations, as limited by the relevant decisional law.

Rule 2–100 is not intended to prevent the parties themselves from communicating with respect to the subject matter of the representation, and nothing in the rule prevents a member from advising the client that such communication can be made. Moreover, the rule does not prohibit a member who is also a party to a legal matter from directly or indirectly communicating on his or her own behalf with a represented party. Such a member has independent rights as a party which should not be abrogated because of his or her professional status. To prevent any possible abuse in such situations, the counsel for the opposing party may advise that party (1) about the risks and benefits of communications with a lawyer-party, and (2) not to accept or engage in communications with the lawyer-party.

Rule 2–100 also addresses the situation in which member A is contacted by an opposing party who is represented and, because of dissatisfaction with that party's counsel, seeks A's independent advice. Since A is employed by the opposition, the member cannot give independent advice.

As used in paragraph (A), "the subject of the representation," "matter," and "party" are not limited to a litigation context.

Paragraph (B) is intended to apply only to persons employed at the time of the communication. (See Triple A Machine Shop, Inc. v. State of California (1989) 213 Cal.App.3d 131 [261 Cal.Rptr. 493].)

Subparagraph (C)(2) is intended to permit a member to communicate with a party seeking to hire new counsel or to obtain a second opinion. A member contacted by such a party continues to be bound by other Rules of Professional Conduct. (See, e.g., rules 1–400 and 3–310.)

(Adopted Nov. 28, 1988, eff. May 27, 1989. As amended, eff. Sept. 14, 1992.)

Rule 2–400. Prohibited Discriminatory Conduct in a Law Practice

(A) For purposes of this rule:

(1) "law practice" includes sole practices, law partnerships, law corporations, corporate and governmental legal departments, and other entities which employ members to practice law;

(2) "knowingly permit" means a failure to advocate corrective action where the member knows of a discriminatory policy or practice which results in the unlawful discrimination prohibited in paragraph (B); and

(3) "unlawfully" and "unlawful" shall be determined by reference to applicable state or federal statutes or decisions making unlawful discrimination in employment and in offering goods and services to the public.

(B) In the management or operation of a law practice, a member shall not unlawfully discriminate or knowingly permit unlawful discrimination on the basis of race, national origin, sex, sexual orientation, religion, age or disability in:

(1) hiring, promoting, discharging, or otherwise determining the conditions of employment of any person; or

(2) accepting or terminating representation of any client.

(C) No disciplinary investigation or proceeding may be initiated by the State Bar against a member under this rule unless and until a tribunal of competent jurisdiction, other than a disciplinary tribunal, shall have first adjudicated a complaint of alleged discrimination and found that unlawful conduct occurred. Upon such adjudication, the tribunal finding or verdict shall then be admissible evidence of the occurrence or non-occurrence of the alleged discrimination in any disciplinary proceeding initiated under this rule. In order for discipline to be imposed under this rule, however, the finding of unlawfulness must be upheld and final after appeal, the time for filing an appeal must have expired, or the appeal must have been dismissed.

DISCUSSION

In order for discriminatory conduct to be actionable under this rule, it must first be found to be unlawful by an appropriate civil administrative or judicial tribunal under applicable state or federal law. Until there is a finding of civil unlawfulness, there is no basis for disciplinary action under this rule.

A complaint of misconduct based on this rule may be filed with the State Bar following a finding of unlawful-

ness in the first instance even though that finding is thereafter appealed.

A disciplinary investigation or proceeding for conduct coming within this rule may be initiated and maintained, however, if such conduct warrants discipline under California Business and Professions Code sections 6106 and 6068, the California Supreme Court's inherent authority to impose discipline, or other disciplinary standard.

(Adopted March 6, 1993, eff. March 1, 1994.)

Chapter 3

PROFESSIONAL RELATIONSHIP WITH CLIENTS

Rule

3–200.   Prohibited Objectives of Employment.

Rule 3–200.   Prohibited Objectives of Employment

A member shall not seek, accept, or continue employment if the member knows or should know that the objective of such employment is:

(A) To bring an action, conduct a defense, assert a position in litigation, or take an appeal, without probable cause and for the purpose of harassing or maliciously injuring any person; or

(B) To present a claim or defense in litigation that is not warranted under existing law, unless it can be supported by a good faith argument for an extension, modification, or reversal of such existing law. *(Adopted Nov. 28, 1988, eff. May 27, 1989.)*

CALIFORNIA CODE OF REGULATIONS

Title 2. Administration

**Division 4. Fair Employment
and Housing Commission**

Chapter 1. Administration

Subchapter 1. Administration

§ 7285.0. Generally

The authority for the rules and regulations set forth in this chapter is briefly described at the beginning of each chapter below and in some cases is set out with more particularity at the beginning of a constituent subchapter within a chapter. Special definitions or rules of construction which only apply to a particular chapter or subchapter are set forth at the beginning of the chapter or subchapter to which they pertain.

§ 7285.1. Construction

(a) These rules and regulations are to be construed liberally so as to further the policy and purposes of the statutes which they interpret and implement.

(b) Except as required by the Supremacy Clause of the United States Constitution, federal laws and their interpretations regarding discrimination in employment and housing are not determinative of the construction of these rules and regulations and the California statutes which they interpret and implement but, in the spirit of comity, shall be considered to the extent practical and appropriate.

(c) Unless the context dictates otherwise, terms used herein which are in the singular include the plural and which are in the plural include the singular.

(d) If any rule or regulation, or portion thereof, in this chapter is adjudged by a court of competent jurisdiction to be invalid, or if any such rule or regulation, or portion thereof, loses its force and effect by legislative action, that judgment or action does not affect the remainder of the rules and regulations.

(e) Pursuant to the Governor's Reorganization Plan No. 1 (1980), the Fair Employment Practice Act is to be renamed the Fair Employment and Housing Act and renumbered in Part 2.8 of Division 3 of Title 2 of the Government Code. Authorities and references cited herein to the Labor Code are parenthetically cited to sections of the Government Code which will become applicable when legislation is enacted.

§ 7285.2. Definitions

Unless a different meaning clearly applies from the context, the meaning of the words and phrases as defined in this section shall apply throughout this chapter:

(a) "Commission or FEHC" means the State Fair Employment and Housing Commission created by section 1414 of the Labor Code and Section 12903 of the Government Code pursuant to the Governor's Reorganization Plan No. 1 (1980).

(b) "Department or DFEH" means the Department of Fair Employment and Housing created by section 1413.1 of the Labor Code and Sections 12901 and 12925 of the Government Code pursuant to the Governor's Reorganization Plan No. 1 (1980).

(c) "Person" includes one or more individuals, partnerships, associations or corporations, legal representatives, trustees, trustees in bankruptcy, or receivers.

(d) "Complainant" means the person who files a timely, verified complaint with the DFEH alleging aggrievement by an unlawful practice.

(e) "Respondent" means the person who is alleged to have committed an unlawful practice in a complaint filed with the DFEH, or against whom an accusation has been issued.

(f) "Act" means the California Fair Employment and Housing Act created by section 1410 seq. of the Labor Code, sections 35700 et seq. of the Health and Safety Code and Government Code section 12900.

Subchapter 2. Powers and Duties of the Commission

§ 7285.3. Staff

(a) Responsible to the Fair Employment and Housing Commission there shall be an Executive and Legal Affairs Secretary and such legal, professional, administrative and support staff as are necessary to carry out the day-to-day responsibilities of the Commission.

§ 7285.4. Rules, Regulations and Guidelines

(a) The Commission shall adopt, promulgate, amend and rescind suitable rules, regulations and guidelines as are necessary to interpret, implement and apply laws within its jurisdiction and as are necessary to carry out all of its other functions and duties.

(b) All rules and regulations shall be adopted pursuant to Chapter 4.5 (commencing with Section 11371) of Part 1 of Division 3 of Title 2 of the Government Code.

§ 7285.5. Hearings and Precedential Opinions

(a) The Commission shall hold hearings and issue findings and orders on accusations of unlawful practices within the Commission's jurisdiction filed by the Department, including charges of discrimination in employment, housing, public accommodation, contract compliance, and licensing and testing.

(b) All hearings after accusation shall be conducted pursuant to Chapter 5 (commencing with Section 11500) of Part 1 of Division 3 of Title 2 of the Government Code (known as the California Administrative Procedure Act) and pursuant to Title 2, Division 4, Chapter 4 of the California Administrative Code ("Procedures of the Commission").

(c) The Commission shall establish and publish a system of precedential opinions to assist in interpreting the laws under its jurisdiction.

(d) The Commission shall establish a system and procedure for Declaratory Rulings regarding any rule or statute enforceable by the Commission, and shall make such rulings available to the public.

§ 7285.6. Investigative Authority

Where necessary to carry out its duties relating to any matter under investigation or in question before the Commission, the Commission may hold hearings, subpoena witnesses, compel witnesses' attendance, order production of any books and papers relating to an investigation, administer oaths, and examine any person under oath at times and places set by the Commission, and make other related written and oral inquiries.

§ 7285.7. Other Powers and Duties

The functions, powers and duties of the Commission shall also include, but are not limited to, the authority to:

(a) Make inquiries into general discrimination problems and issue informal and formal findings, including published reports;

(b) Establish such advisory agencies and councils as will assist in fostering goodwill, cooperation and conciliation among groups and elements of the population of the state through studies, conciliation, hearings, and recommendations to the Commission;

(c) Develop standards and policy for application and implementation by the Department of Fair Employment and Housing; and

(d) Advise and concur with the Secretary of Health and Welfare in establishing standards and guidelines determining unlawful practices of state contractors under Section 11135, et seq.

Chapter 2. Discrimination in Employment

Subchapter 1. General Matters

§ 7286.0. Fair Employment and Housing Commission– Conflict of Interest Code

The Political Reform Act, Government Code Sections 81000, et seq., requires state and local government agencies to adopt and promulgate Conflict of Interest Codes. The Fair Political Practices Commission has adopted a regulation, 2 Cal. Code of Regs. section 18730, which contains the terms of a standard Conflict of Interest Code, which can be incorporated by reference,

and which may be amended by the Fair Political Practices Commission to conform to amendments in the Political Reform Act after public notice and hearings. Therefore, the terms of 2 Cal. Code of Regs. section 18730 and any amendments to it duly adopted by the Fair Political Practices Commission are hereby incorporated by reference and, along with the attached appendix in which officials and employees are designated and disclosure categories are set forth, constitute the Conflict of Interest Code of the Fair Employment and Housing Commission.

Designated employees shall file statements of economic interests with their agency. Upon receipt of the statements of the Commission members, the agency shall make and retain a copy and forward the original of these statements to the Fair Political Practices Commission. The statements for all other designated positions shall be retained with the agency and made available for public inspection and reproduction upon request. (Gov. Code section 81008).

Appendix A

Designated Positions	Disclosure Category
Commission Members	1
Executive and Legal Affairs Secretary	1
Administrative Law Judge	1
FEH Counsel	1
Staff Services Manager	2
Consultants [1]	1

[1] With respect to Consultants, the Chairperson may determine in writing that a particular consultant is hired to perform a range of duties that are limited in scope and thus is not required to comply with the disclosure requirements described in these categories. Such determination shall include a description of the consultant's duties and, based upon that description, a statement of the extent of disclosure requirements. The Chairperson's determination is a public record and shall be retained for public inspection at offices of the Fair Employment and Housing Commission. Nothing herein excuses any such consultant from any other provision of this Conflict of Interest Code.

Appendix B

General Provisions

When a designated employee is required to disclose investments and sources of income, he or she need only disclose investments in business entities and sources of income which do business in the jurisdiction, plan to do business in the jurisdiction or have done business in the jurisdiction within the past two years. In addition to other activities, a business entity is doing business within the jurisdiction if it owns real property within the jurisdiction. When a designated employee is required to disclose interests in real property, he/she need only disclose real property which is located in whole or in part within or not more than two miles outside the boundaries of the jurisdiction or within two miles of any land owned or used by the Fair Employment & Housing Commission.

Designated employees shall disclose their financial interests pursuant to the appropriate disclosure category as indicated in appendix A.

Disclosure Categories

Category 1

Designated officials and employees assigned to this disclosure category must report all investments and business positions in business entities, sources of income and interests in real property.

Category 2

Designated officials and employees assigned to this disclosure category must report investments and business positions in business entities and sources of income of the type which within the past two years have contracted to provide services, supplies, materials or equipment to the Department.

§ 7286.1. Department of Fair Employment and Housing–Conflict of Interest Code

The Political Reform Act, Government Code sections 81000, et seq., requires state and local government agencies to adopt and promulgate conflict of interest codes. The Fair Political Practices Commission has adopted a regulation (2 Cal. Code of Regs., Section 18730) which contains the terms of a standard conflict of interest code, which can be incorporated by reference, and which may be amended by the Fair Political Practices Commission to conform to amendments to the Political Reform Act after public notice and hearings. Therefore, the terms of California Code of Regulations, title, 2. section 18730 and any amendments to it duly adopted by the Fair Political Practices Commission, along with the attached Appendix in which officials and employees are designated and disclosure categories are set forth, are hereby incorporated by reference and constitute the conflict of interest code of the Department of Fair Employment and Housing.

Designated employees shall file statements of economic interests with their agency which shall be retained with the agency and made available for public inspection and reproduction upon request (Gov. Code Section 81008). Upon receipt of the statement of the Director, the agency shall make and retain a copy and forward the original of these statements to the Fair Political Practices Commission.

Appendix A

Designated Positions	Disclosure Category
Accountant I (Specialist)	2
Administrator I, FEH	1
Administrator II, FEH	1
Business Service Officer I (Specialist)	2
Business Service Officer I (Supervisor)	2
CEA1	
Level 1	
Level 2	
Level 3	
Chief Counsel I, CEA	1
Chief Deputy Director, DFEH	1
Data Processing Manager II	2
Deputy Director, Legislation and Policy Development	1
Deputy Director, Public Affairs and External Communications	1
Director	1
FEH Consultant I	1
Range A	

Designated Positions	Disclosure Category
Range B	
Range C	
FEH Consultant II	1
FEH Consultant III (Specialist)	1
FEH Consultant III (Supervisor)	1
FEH Counsel	1
Range A	
Range B	
Range C	
Range D	
Graduate Student Assistant	1
Range A	
Range B	
Range C	
Range D	
Information Systems Technician	2
Legal Analyst	1
Legal Assistant	1
Programmer I	2
Senior Accounting Officer (Supervisor)	2
Senior FEH Counsel (Specialist)	1
Senior FEH Counsel (Supervisor)	1
Senior Legal Analyst	1
Senior Programmer Analyst (Specialist)	2
Staff Information Systems Analyst (Supervisor)	2
Staff Programmer Analyst (Specialist)	2
Staff Services Manager I	1
Staff Services Manager II (Managerial)	1
Staff Services Manager II (Supervisory)	1
Staff Services Manager III	1

Appendix B

General Provisions

When a designated employee is required to disclose investments and sources of income, he or she need only disclose investments in business entities and sources of income which do business in the jurisdiction, plan to do business in the jurisdiction or have done business in the jurisdiction within the past two years. In addition to other activities, a business entity is doing business within the jurisdiction if it owns real property within the jurisdiction. When a designated employee is required to disclose interests in real property, he/she need only disclose real property which is located in whole or in part within or not more than two miles outside the boundaries of the jurisdiction or within two miles of any land owned or used by the Department of Fair Employment and Housing.

Designated employees shall disclose their financial interests pursuant to the appropriate disclosure category as indicated in Appendix A.

Disclosure Categories

Category 1

Designated officials and employees assigned to this disclosure category must report all investments and business positions in business entities, sources of income, including gifts, loans, and travel payments, and interests in real property

Category 2

Designated officials and employees assigned to this disclosure category must report investments and business positions in business entities and sources of income, including gifts, loans, and travel payments, of the type which, within the past two years, have contracted to provide services, supplies, materials or equipment to the Department.

§ 7286.3.   Statement of Policy and Purpose

The public policy of the State of California is to protect and safeguard the civil rights of all individuals to seek, have access to, obtain, and hold employment without discrimination because of race, religious creed, color, national origin, ancestry, physical disability, mental disability, medical condition, marital status, or sex, and age for individuals over forty years of age. Employment practices should treat all individuals equally, evaluating each on the basis of individual skills, knowledge and abilities and not on the basis of characteristics generally attributed to a group enumerated in the Act. The objectives of the California Fair Employment and Housing Act and these regulations are to promote equal employment opportunity and to assist all persons in understanding their rights, duties and obligations, so as to facilitate achievement of voluntary compliance with the law.

§ 7286.4.   Authority

The FEHC issues these regulations under the authority vested in the Commission by the Fair Employment and Housing Act, specifically Labor Code Section 1418(a) Government Code Section 12935(a)

§ 7286.5.   Definitions

As used in this chapter, the following definitions shall apply unless the context otherwise requires:

(a) "Employer." Any person or individual engaged in any business or enterprise regularly employing five or more individuals, including individuals performing any service under any appointment, contract of hire or apprenticeship, express or implied, oral or written.

(1) "Regularly employing" means employing five or more individuals for each working day in any twenty consecutive calendar weeks in the current calendar year or preceding calendar year.

(2) For purposes of "counting" the (five or more) employees, the individuals employed need not be employees as defined below; nor must any of them be full-time employees.

(3) Any person or individual acting as an agent of an employer, directly or indirectly, is also an employer.

(4) "Employer" includes the State of California, any political or civil subdivision thereof, counties, cities, city and county, local agencies, or special districts, irrespective of whether that entity employs five or more individuals.

(5) A religious association or religious corporation not organized for private profit is not an employer under the meaning of this Act; any non-profit religious organization exempt from federal and state income tax as a non-profit religious organization is presumed not to be an employer under this Act. Notwithstanding such status, any portion of such tax exempt religious association or religious corporation subject to state or federal income taxes as an unrelated business and regularly employing five or more individuals is an employer.

(6) "Employer" includes any non-profit corporation or non-profit association other than that defined in subsection (5).

(b) "Employee." Any individual under the direction and control of an employer under any appointment or contract of hire or apprenticeship, express or implied, oral or written.

(1) Employee does not include an independent contractor as defined in Labor Code Section 3353.

(2) Employee does not include any individual employed by his or her parents, by his or her spouse, or by his or her child.

(3) Employee does not include any individual employed under special license in a non-profit sheltered workshop or rehabilitation facility.

(4) An employment agency is not an employee of the person or individual for whom it procures employees.

(5) An individual compensated by a temporary service agency for work to be performed for an employer contracting with the temporary service agency may be considered an employee of that employer for such terms, conditions and privileges of employment under the control of that employer. Such an individual is an employee of the temporary service agency with regard to such terms, conditions and privileges of employment under the control of the temporary service agency.

(c) "Employment Agency." Any person undertaking for compensation to procure job applicants, employees or opportunities to work.

(d) "Labor Organization." Any organization which exists and is constituted for the purpose, in whole or in part, of collective bargaining or of dealing with employers regarding grievances, terms or conditions of employment, or of providing other mutual aid or protection.

(e) "Employer or Other Covered Entity." Any employer, employment agency, labor organization or apprenticeship training program as defined herein and subject to the provisions of the Act.

(f) "Employment Benefit." Except as otherwise provided in the Act, any benefit of employment covered by the Act, including hiring, employment, promotion, selection for training programs leading to employment or promotions, freedom from disbarment or discharge from employment or a training program, compensation, provision of a discrimination-free workplace, and any other favorable term, condition or privilege of employment.

(1) For a labor organization, "employment benefit" includes all rights and privileges of membership, including freedom from exclusion, expulsion or restriction of membership, second class or segregated membership, discrimination in the election of officers or selection of staff, or any other action against a member or any employee or person employed by an employer.

(2) "Employment benefit" also includes the selection or training of any person in any apprenticeship training program or any other training program leading to employment or promotion.

(3) "Provision of a discrimination-free workplace" is a provision of a workplace free of harassment, as defined in Section 7287.6(b).

(g) "Employment Practice." Any act, omission, policy or decision of an employer or other covered entity affecting any of an individual's employment benefits or consideration for an employment benefit.

(h) "Applicant." Any individual who files a written application or, where an employer or other covered entity does not provide an application form, any individual who otherwise indicates a specific desire to an employer or other covered entity to be considered for employment. Except for recordkeeping purposes, "Applicant" is also an individual who can prove that he or she has been deterred from applying for a job by an employer's or other covered entity's alleged discriminatory practice. "Applicant" does not include an individual who without coercion or intimidation willingly withdraws his or her application prior to being interviewed, tested or hired.

(i) "Apprenticeship Training Program." Any apprenticeship program, including local or state joint apprenticeship committees, subject to the provision of Chapter 4 of Division 3 of the California Labor Code, Sections 3070, et seq.

§ 7286.6.　Principles of Employment Discrimination

(a) Unlawful Practices and Individual Relief. In allegations of employment discrimination, a finding that a respondent has engaged in an unlawful employment practice is not dependent upon a showing of individual back pay or other compensable liability. Upon a finding that a respondent has engaged in an unlawful employment practice and on order of appropriate relief, a severable and separate showing may be made that the complainant, complainants or class of complainants is entitled to individual or personal relief including, but not limited to, hiring, reinstatement or upgrading, back pay, restoration to membership in a respondent labor organization, or other relief in furtherance of the purpose of the Act.

(b) Liability of Employers. In view of the common law theory of respondeat superior and its codification in California Civil Code Section 2338, an employer or other covered entity shall be liable for the discriminatory actions of its supervisors, managers or agents committed within the scope of their employment or relationship with the covered entity or, as defined in Section 7287.6(b), for the discriminatory actions of its employees where it is demonstrated that, as a result of any such discriminatory action, the applicant or employee has suffered a loss of or has been denied an employment benefit.

§ 7286.7.　Affirmative Defenses to Employment Discrimination

If employment discrimination is established, this employment discrimination is nonetheless lawful where a proper, relevant affirmative defense is proved and less discriminatory alternatives are not shown to be available. Except where otherwise specifically noted, one or more of the following affirmative defenses may be appropriate in a given situation to justify the employment practice in question. The following defenses are generally referred to in the text of these regulations as "Permissible Defenses:"

(a) Bona Fide Occupational Qualification (BFOQ). Where an employer or other covered entity has a practice which on its face excludes an entire group of individuals on a basis enumerated in the Act (e.g., all women or all individuals with lower back defects), the employer or other covered entity must prove that the practice is justified because all or substantially all of the excluded individuals are unable to safely and efficiently perform the job in question and because the essence of the business operation would otherwise be undermined.

(b) Business Necessity. Where an employer or other covered entity has a facially neutral practice which has an adverse impact (i.e., is discriminatory in effect), the employer or other covered entity must prove that there exists an overriding legitimate business purpose such that the practice is necessary to the safe and efficient operation of the business and that the challenged practice effectively fulfills the business purpose it is supposed to serve. The practice may still be impermissible where it is shown that there exists an alternative practice which would accomplish the business purpose equally well with a lesser discriminatory impact.

(c) Job–Relatedness. See Section 7287.4(e) for the defense of job-relatedness which is permissible in employee selection cases.

(d) Security Regulations. Notwithstanding a showing of discrimination, an employment practice which conforms to applicable security regulations established by the United States or the State of California is lawful.

(e) Non–Discrimination Plans or Affirmative Action Plans. Notwithstanding a showing of discrimination, such an employment practice is lawful which conforms to:

(1) A bona fide voluntary affirmative action plan as discussed below in section 7286.8;

(2) A non-discrimination plan pursuant to Labor Code Section 1431 (Government Code Section 12990); or

(3) An order of a state or federal court or administrative agency of proper jurisdiction.

(f) Otherwise Required by Law. Notwithstanding a showing of discrimination, such an employment practice is lawful where required by state or federal law or where pursuant to an order of a state or federal court of proper jurisdiction.

§ 7286.8. Affirmative Action Programs

Voluntary action by employers and other covered entities is an effective means for eliminating employment discrimination. The Commission hereby adopts the Affirmative Action Guidelines of the federal Equal Employment Opportunity Commission. [(29 CFR Section 1608 (1979).)]

§ 7286.9. Remedies

Upon proof of unlawful practices under the Act, the Commission has broad statutory authority to fashion remedies which are consistent with the purposes of the Act, including, but not limited to, those described below.

(a) Retroactive Relief. Where it has been proved that an individual has been unlawfully denied an employment benefit, the most common remedy shall be to "make whole" the individual through relief which may include, but is not limited to, any or all of the following:

(1) Back Pay. Back pay remedies shall be available to both individual and class complainants.

(A) Mitigation and Other Defenses. Mitigating circumstances, including interim earnings, may be considered in determining the amount of back pay. However, unemployment compensation or other collateral benefits recompensable to the State shall not normally be utilized in considering mitigation of back pay.

(B) Fringe Benefits. Where appropriate, fringe benefits shall normally be included in calculations of back pay. Where such benefits are no longer available or appropriate, then equivalent monetary values may be awarded.

(2) Injunctive and Other Equitable Relief. The Act makes available injunctive relief including, but not limited to, cease and desist orders, hiring, reinstatement or upgrading of employees, or restoration of membership in labor organizations.

(A) Seniority. Where appropriate, "constructive seniority" or other temporal measures of service may be awarded so as to place the individual adversely affected into the position or status he or she would have enjoyed but for the unlawful practice.

(B) Goals and Timetables. Where appropriate, relief may include the setting of goals and timetables for correcting past discriminatory actions. Alternative mandatory injunctive remedies may also be ordered where the past practices of an employer or other covered entity would justify more stringent remedies.

(b) Prospective Relief. In certain circumstances, appropriate relief requires continuing remedies to correct past unlawful practices. Such relief may include, but is not limited to:

(1) "Rightful Place" and "Front Pay." Where previously closed positions or lines of progression are made available, an employee shall be restored to his or her "rightful place" and shall not be penalized for lacking prior status or position in that line. In such situations, "front pay" may be awarded to offset losses to an employee until such time as the employee takes his or her "rightful place," or until such time as an offer of the appropriate position is made to the employee.

(2) "Red Circling." Where an employee transfers to a previously closed line of progression which starts at a lower rate of compensation, the employee shall not be penalized and may be awarded the higher rate of compensation until such time as the rates of compensation are equal.

§ 7287.0. Recordkeeping

Employers and other covered entities are required to maintain certain relevant records of personnel actions. Each employer or other covered entity subject to this section shall retain at all times at each reporting unit, or at company or divisional headquarters, a copy of the most recent CEIR or appropriate substitute and applicant identification records for each such unit and shall make them available upon request to any officer, agent, or employee of the Commission or Department.

(a) California Employer Information Report. All employers regularly employing one hundred or more employees, apprenticeship programs with five or more apprentices and at least one sponsoring employer with 25 or more employees and at least one sponsoring union which operates a hiring hall or has 25 or more members, and labor organizations with 100 or more members shall prepare an annual personnel report called the "California Employer Information Report" (CEIR) in conformity with guidelines on reporting issued by the Department.

(1) Substituting Federal Reports. An employer or other covered entity may utilize an appropriate federal report in lieu of the CEIR. Appropriate federal reports include the Equal Employment Opportunity Commission's EEO–1, EEO–2, EEO–3, EEO–4, EEO–5, and EEO–6 reports and appropriate reports filed with the Office of Federal Contract Compliance Programs.

(2) Sample Forms and Guidelines. Appropriate copies of sample forms and applicable guidelines shall be available to any employer or other covered entity from the Sacramento administrative office of the Department of Fair Employment and Housing.

(3) Special Reporting. If an employer or other covered entity is engaged in activities for which the standard reporting criteria are not appropriate, special reporting procedures may be required. In such case, the employer or other covered entity should so advise the Department and submit a specific proposal for an alternative reporting system prior to the date on which the report should be prepared. If it is claimed that the preparation of the report would create undue hardship, an employer may apply to the Department for an exemption from the requirements of this section.

(4) Remedy for Failure to Prepare or Make Reports Available. Upon application by the FEHC or DFEH for judicial relief, any employer failing or refusing to prepare or to make available reports as required under this

section may be compelled to do so by a Superior Court of California.

(5) Penalties for False Statements. The willful making of false statements on a CEIR or other required record is a violation of California Labor Code Section 1430.3 (Government Code Section 12976), and is punishable by fine or imprisonment as set forth therein.

(b) Applicant Identification Records. Unless otherwise prohibited by law and for recordkeeping purposes only, every employer or other covered entity shall maintain data regarding the race, sex, and national origin of each applicant and for the job for which he or she applied. If such data is to be provided on an identification form, this form shall be separate or detachable from the application form itself. Employment decisions shall not be based on whether an applicant has provided this information, nor shall the applicant identification information be used for discriminatory purposes, except pursuant to a bona fide affirmative action or non-discrimination plan.

(1) For recordkeeping purposes only, "applicant" means any individual who files a formal application or, where an employer or other covered entity does not provide application forms, any individual who otherwise indicates to the employer or other covered entity a specific desire to be considered for employment. An individual who simply appears to make an informal inquiry or who files an unsolicited resume upon which no employment action is taken is not an applicant.

(2) An employer or other covered entity shall either retain the original documents used to identify applicants, or keep statistical summaries of the collected information.

(3) Applicant records shall be preserved for the time period set forth in Section 7286.9(c) (1) and (2).

(c) Preservation of Records. Any personnel or other employment records made or kept by any employer or other covered entity dealing with any employment practice and affecting any employment benefit of any applicant or employee (including all applications, personnel, membership or employment referral records or files) shall be preserved by the employer or other covered entity for a period of two years from the date of the making of the record or the date of the personnel action involved, whichever occurs later. However, the State Personnel Board shall maintain such records and files for a period of one year.

(1) California Employment Information Report. Every employer subject to subsection (a) above shall preserve for a period of two years from the date of preparation of the CEIR such records as were necessary for completion of the CEIR.

(2) Applicant Identification Records. Every employer subject to subsection (b) above shall preserve applicant identification information for a period of two years from the date it was received.

(3) Separate Records on Sex, Race, and National Origin. Records as to the sex, race, or national origin of any individual accepted for employment shall be kept separately from the employee's main personnel file or other records available to those responsible for personnel decisions. For example, such records could be kept as part of an automatic data processing system in the payroll department.

(4) After Filing of Complaint. Upon notice of or knowledge that a complaint has been filed against it under the Act, any respondent, including the State Personnel Board, shall maintain and preserve any and all relevant records and files until such complaint is fully and finally disposed of and all appeals from related proceedings have concluded.

(A) For purposes of this subsection, "related proceedings" shall include any action brought in Superior Court pursuant to Section 1422.2 of the Labor Code (Section 12965 of the Government Code).

(B) The term "records and files relevant to the complaint" shall include, but is not limited to, personnel or employment records relating to the complaining party and to all other employees holding similar positions to that held or sought by the complainant at the facility or other relevant subdivision where the discriminatory practice allegedly occurred. The term also includes applications, forms or test papers completed by the complainant and by all other candidates for the same position at that facility or other relevant subdivision where the employment practice occurred. All relevant records made or kept pursuant to subsections (a) and (b) above shall also be preserved.

(C) The term "fully and finally disposed of and all appeals from related proceedings have concluded" refers to the expiration of the statutory period within which a complainant or respondent may bring an action in Superior Court, or an agreement has been reached by the parties whereby no further judicial review is available to any of the parties, or a final order has been entered by the Commission or a body of judicial review for which the time for filing a notice of appeal has expired.

(d) Posting of Act. Every employer or other covered entity shall post in a conspicuous place or places on its premises a notice to be prepared and distributed by the Department which sets forth excerpts of the Act and such relevant information which the Department deems necessary to explain the Act. Such employers employing significant numbers, no less than 10% of their work force, of non-English-speaking persons (e.g., Chinese or Spanish speaking) at any facility or establishment must also post in the appropriate foreign language at each such facility or establishment. Such notices may be obtained from the Department.

Subchapter 2. Particular Employment Practices

§ 7287.1. Statement of Purpose

Certain employment practices have the effect, either directly or indirectly, of discriminating against individuals on a basis enumerated in the Act. Such practices are discussed in this subchapter and the provisions are applicable to all discriminatory actions as more specifically discussed in the following subchapters.

§ 7287.2.   Definitions

(a) "Recruitment." The practice of any employer or other covered entity that has the purpose or effect of informing any individual about an employment opportunity, or assisting an individual to apply for employment, an activity leading to employment, membership in a labor organization, acceptance in an apprenticeship training program, or referral by an employment agency.

(b) "Date of Determination to Hire." The time at which an employer or other covered entity has made an offer of employment to the individual.

(c) "Pre-employment Inquiry." Any oral or written request made by an employer or other covered entity for information concerning the qualifications of an applicant for employment or for entry into an activity leading to employment.

(d) "Application." Except for recordkeeping purposes, any writing or other device used by an employer or other covered entity to make a pre-employment inquiry or submitted to an employer or other covered entity for the purpose of seeking consideration for employment.

(e) "Placement." Any status, category, rank, level, location, department, division, program, duty or group of duties, or any other similar classification or position for which an employee can be selected or to which an employee can be assigned by any employment practice. Employment practices that can determine placement in this way include, but are not limited to: hiring, discharge, promotion, transfer, callback, or other change of classification or position; inclusion in membership in any group or organization; any referral assignment to any place, unit, division, status or type of work.

§ 7287.3.   Pre-Employment Practices

(a) Recruitment.

(1) Duty Not to Discriminate. Any employer or other covered entity engaged in recruitment activity shall recruit in a non-discriminatory manner. However, nothing in these regulations shall preclude affirmative efforts to utilize recruitment practices to attract minorities, individuals of one sex or the other, individuals with disabilities, individuals over 40 years of age, and any other individual covered by the Act.

(2) Prohibited Recruitment Practices. An employer or other covered entity shall not, unless pursuant to a permissible defense, engage in any recruitment activity which:

(A) Restricts, excludes, or classifies individuals on a basis enumerated in the Act;

(B) Expresses a preference for individuals on a basis enumerated in the Act; or

1166

(C) Communicates or uses advertising methods to communicate the availability of employment benefits in a manner intended to discriminate on a basis enumerated in the Act.

(b) Pre-Employment Inquiries.

(1) Limited Permissible Inquiries. An employer or other covered entity may make any pre-employment inquiries which do not discriminate on a basis enumerated in the Act. Inquiries which directly or indirectly identify an individual on a basis enumerated in the Act are unlawful unless pursuant to a permissible defense. Except as provided in the Americans with Disabilities Act of 1990 (Public Law 101–336) (42 U.S.C.A. s12101 et seq.) and the regulations adopted pursuant thereto, nothing in Government Code section 12940, subdivision (d), or in this subdivision, shall prohibit any employer from making, in connection with prospective employment, an inquiry as to, or a request for information regarding, the physical fitness, medical condition, physical condition, or medical history of applicants if that inquiry or request for information is directly related and pertinent to the position the applicant is applying for or directly related to a determination of whether the applicant would endanger his or her health or safety or the health or safety of others.

(2) Applicant Flow and Other Statistical Recordkeeping. Notwithstanding any prohibition in these regulations on pre-employment inquiries, it is not unlawful for an employer or other covered entity to collect applicant-flow and other recordkeeping data for statistical purposes as provided in Section 7287.0(b) of these regulations or in other provisions of state and federal law.

(c) Applications.

(1) Application Forms. When employers or other covered entities provide, accept, and consider application forms in the normal course of business, in so doing they shall not discriminate on a basis enumerated in the Act.

(2) Photographs. Photographs shall not be required as part of an application unless pursuant to a permissible defense.

(3) Separation or Coding. Application forms shall not be separated or coded or otherwise treated so as to identify individuals on a basis enumerated in the Act unless pursuant to a permissible defense or for recordkeeping or statistical purposes.

(d) Interviews. Personal interviews shall be free of discrimination. Notwithstanding any internal safeguards taken to secure a discrimination-free atmosphere in interviews, the entire interview process is subject to review for adverse impact on individuals on a basis enumerated in the Act.

§ 7287.4.   Employee Selection

(a) Selection and Testing. Any policy or practice of an employer or other covered entity which has an adverse impact on employment opportunities of individuals on a basis enumerated in the Act is unlawful unless the policy or practice is job-related, as defined in Section 7287.4(e). The Commission herein adopts the Uniform Guidelines on Employee Selection Procedures promulgated by various federal agencies, including the EEOC and Department of Labor. [29 CFR 1607 (1978)].

(b) Placement. Placements that are less desirable in terms of location, hours or other working conditions are unlawful where such assignments segregate, or otherwise discriminate against individuals on a basis enumerated in the Act, unless otherwise pursuant to a permissible defense to employment discrimination. An assignment labeled or otherwise deemed to be "protective" of a category of persons on a basis enumerated in the Act is unlawful unless pursuant to a permissible defense. (See also Section 7291.2(d)(2) regarding permissible transfers on account of pregnancy by employees not covered under Title VII of the federal Civil Rights Act of 1964.)

(c) Promotion and Transfer. An employer or other covered entity shall not restrict information on promotion and transfer opportunities to certain employees or classes of employees when the restriction has the effect of discriminating on a basis enumerated in the Act.

(1) Requests for Transfer or Promotion. An employer or other covered entity who considers bids or other requests for promotion or transfer shall do so in a manner that does not discriminate against individuals on a basis enumerated in the Act, unless pursuant to a permissible defense.

(2) Training. Where training which may make an employee eligible for promotion and/or transfer is made available, it shall be made available in a manner which does not discriminate against individuals on a basis enumerated in the Act.

(3) No–Transfer Policies. Where an employment practice has operated in the past to segregate employees on a basis enumerated in the Act, a no-transfer policy or other practice that has the effect of maintaining a continued segregated pattern is unlawful.

(d) Specific Practices.

(1) Criminal Records. Except as otherwise provided by law (e.g., 12 U.S.C. 1829; Labor Code Section 432.7), it is unlawful for an employer or other covered entity to inquire or seek information regarding any applicant concerning:

(A) Any arrest or detention which did not result in conviction;

(B) Any conviction for which the record has been judicially ordered sealed, expunged, or statutorily eradicated (e.g., juvenile offense records sealed pursuant to Welfare and Institutions Code Section 389 and Penal Code Sections 851.7 or 1203.45); any misdemeanor conviction for which probation has been successfully completed or otherwise discharged and the case has been judicially dismissed pursuant to Penal Code Section 1203.4; or

(C) Any arrest for which a pretrial diversion program has been successfully completed pursuant to Penal Code Sections 1000.5 and 1001.5.

(2) Height Standards. Height standards which discriminate on a basis enumerated in the Act shall not be used by an employer or other covered entity to deny an individual an employment benefit unless pursuant to a permissible defense.

(3) Weight Standards. Weight standards which discriminate on a basis enumerated in the Act shall not be used by an employer or other covered entity to deny an individual an employment benefit unless pursuant to a permissible defense.

(e) Permissible Selection Devices. A testing device or other means of selection which is facially neutral, but which has an adverse impact (as described in the Uniform Guidelines on Employee Selection Procedures (29 CFR 1607 (1978)) upon persons on a basis enumerated in the Act, is permissible only upon a showing that the selection practice is sufficiently related to an essential function of the job in question to warrant its use. (See Section 7287.4(a).)

§ 7287.6. Terms, Conditions and Privileges of Employment

(a) Fringe Benefits. (Reserved.)

(b) Harassment.

(1) Harassment includes but is not limited to:

(A) Verbal harassment, e.g., epithets, derogatory comments or slurs on a basis enumerated in the Act;

(B) Physical harassment, e.g., assault, impeding or blocking movement, or any physical interference with normal work or movement, when directed at an individual on a basis enumerated in the Act;

(C) Visual forms of harassment, e.g., derogatory posters, cartoons, or drawings on a basis enumerated in the Act; or

(D) Sexual favors, e.g., unwanted sexual advances which condition an employment benefit upon an exchange of sexual favors. [See also Section 7291.1 (f) (l).]

(E) In applying this subsection, the rights of free speech and association shall be accommodated consistently with the intent of this subsection.

(2) Harassment of an applicant or employee by an employer or other covered entity, its agents or supervisors is unlawful.

(3) Harassment of an applicant or employee by an employee other than those listed in subsection (b)(2) above is unlawful if the employer or other covered entity, its agents or supervisors knows of such conduct and fails to take immediate and appropriate corrective action. Proof of such knowledge may be direct or circumstantial. If the employer or other covered entity, its agents or supervisors did not know but should have known of the harassment, knowledge shall be imputed unless the employer or other covered entity can establish that it took

reasonable steps to prevent harassment from occurring. Such steps may include affirmatively raising the subject of harassment, expressing strong disapproval, developing appropriate sanctions, informing employees of their right to raise and how to raise the issue of harassment under California law, and developing methods to sensitize all concerned.

(4) An employee who has been harassed on the job by a co-employee should inform the employer or other covered entity of the aggrievement; however, an employee's failure to give such notice is not an affirmative defense.

(c) Physical Appearance, Grooming, and Dress Standards. It is lawful for an employer or other covered entity to impose upon an employee physical appearance, grooming, or dress standards. However, if such a standard discriminates on a basis enumerated in the Act and if it also significantly burdens the individual in his or her employment, it is unlawful.

(d) Reasonable Discipline. Nothing in these regulations may be construed as limiting an employer's or other covered entity's right to take reasonable disciplinary measures which do not discriminate on a basis enumerated in the Act.

(e) Seniority. (Reserved.)

§ 7287.7. Aiding and Abetting

(a) Prohibited Practices.

(1) It is unlawful to assist any person or individual in doing any act known to constitute unlawful employment discrimination.

(2) It is unlawful to solicit or encourage any person or individual to violate the Act, whether or not the Act is in fact violated.

(3) It is unlawful to coerce any person or individual to commit unlawful employment discrimination with offers of cash, other consideration, or an employment benefit, or to impose or threaten to impose any penalty, including denial of an employment benefit.

(4) It is unlawful to conceal or destroy evidence relevant to investigations initiated by the Commission or the Department or their staffs.

(5) It is unlawful to advertise for employment on a basis prohibited in the Act.

(b) Permissible Practices.

(1) It shall not be unlawful, without more, to have been present during the commission of acts amounting to unlawful discrimination or to fail to prevent or report such acts unless it is the normal business duty of the person or individual to prevent or report such acts.

(2) It shall not be unlawful to maintain good faith lawful defenses or privileges to charges of discrimination.

§ 7287.8. Retaliation

(a) Retaliation Generally. It is unlawful for an employer or other covered entity to demote, suspend, reduce, fail

to hire or consider for hire, fail to give equal consideration in making employment decisions, fail to treat impartially in the context of any recommendations for subsequent employment which the employer or other covered entity may make, adversely affect working conditions or otherwise deny any employment benefit to an individual because that individual has opposed practices prohibited by the Act or has filed a complaint, testified, assisted or participated in any manner in an investigation, proceeding, or hearing conducted by the Commission or Department or their staffs.

(1) Opposition to practices prohibited by the Act includes, but is not limited to:

(A) Seeking the advice of the Department or Commission, whether or not a complaint is filed, and if a complaint is filed, whether or not the complaint is ultimately sustained;

(B) Assisting or advising any person in seeking the advice of the Department or Commission, whether or not a complaint is filed, and if a complaint is filed, whether or not the complaint is ultimately sustained;

(C) Opposing employment practices which an individual reasonably believes to exist and believes to be a violation of the Act;

(D) Participating in an activity which is perceived by the employer or other covered entity as opposition to discrimination, whether or not so intended by the individual expressing the opposition; or

(E) Contacting, communicating with or participating in the proceeding of a local human rights or civil rights agency regarding employment discrimination on a basis enumerated in the Act.

(2) Assistance with or participation in the proceedings of the Commission or Department includes, but is not limited to:

(A) Contacting, communicating with or participating in the proceedings of the Department or Commission due to a good faith belief that the Act has been violated; or

(B) Involvement as a potential witness which an employer or other covered entity perceives as participation in an activity of the Department or the Commission.

(b) Exception for Reasonable Discipline. Nothing in these regulations shall be construed to prevent an employer or other covered entity from enforcing reasonable disciplinary policies and practices, nor from demonstrating that the actions of an applicant or employee were either disruptive or otherwise detrimental to legitimate business interests so as to justify the denial of an employment benefit.

§ 7287.9. Association

(a) It is unlawful for an employer or other covered entity to deny employment benefits to, harass, or intimidate any applicant or employee because the employer or other covered entity disapproves generally of the applicant's or employee's association with individuals because they are in a category enumerated in the Act.

(b) It shall be unlawful for an employer or other covered entity to deny equal consideration to any applicant or employee on the basis that he or she sympathizes with, encourages or participates in groups organized for the protection or assertion of rights protected under the Act.

§ 7288.0. Sexual Harassment Training and Education

(a) Definitions. For purposes of this section:

(1) "Contractor" is a person performing services pursuant to a contract to an employer, meeting the criteria specified by Government Code section 12940, subdivision (j)(5), for each working day in 20 consecutive weeks in the current calendar year or preceding calendar year.

(2) "Effective interactive training" includes any of the following:

(A) "Classroom" training is in-person, trainer-instruction, whose content is created by a trainer and provided to a supervisor by a trainer, in a setting removed from the supervisor's daily duties.

(B) "E–learning" training is individualized, interactive, computer-based training created by a trainer and an instructional designer. An e-learning training shall provide a link or directions on how to contact a trainer who shall be available to answer questions and to provide guidance and assistance about the training within a reasonable period of time after the supervisor asks the question, but no more than two business days after the question is asked.

(C) "Webinar" training is an internet-based seminar whose content is created and taught by a trainer and transmitted over the internet or intranet in real time. An employer utilizing a webinar for its supervisors must document and demonstrate that each supervisor who was not physically present in the same room as the trainer nonetheless attended the entire training and actively participated with the training's interactive content, discussion questions, hypothetical scenarios, quizzes or tests, and activities. The webinar must provide the supervisors an opportunity to ask questions, to have them answered and otherwise to seek guidance and assistance.

(D) Other "effective interactive training" and education includes the use of audio, video or computer technology in conjunction with classroom, webinar and/or e-learning training.

(E) For any of the above training methods, the instruction shall include questions that assess learning, skill-building activities that assess the supervisor's application and understanding of content learned, and numerous hypothetical scenarios about harassment, each with one or more discussion questions so that supervisors remain engaged in the training.

(3) "Employee" includes full time, part time, and temporary workers.

(4) "Employer" means any of the following:

(A) any person engaged in any business or enterprise in California, who employs 50 or more employees to perform services for a wage or salary or contractors or any person acting as an agent of an employer, directly or indirectly.

(B) the state of California, counties, and any other political or civil subdivision of the state and cities, regardless of the number of employees. For the purposes of this section, governmental and quasi-governmental entities such as boards, commissions, local agencies and special districts are considered "political subdivisions of the state."

(5) "Having 50 or more employees" means employing or engaging fifty or more employees or contractors for each working day in any twenty consecutive weeks in the current calendar year or preceding calendar year. There is no requirement that the 50 employees or contractors work at the same location or all work or reside in California.

(6) "Instructional Designer" under this section is an individual with expertise in current instructional best practices, and who develops the training content based upon material provided by a trainer.

(7) "New" supervisory employees are employees promoted or hired to a supervisory position after July 1, 2005.

(8) "Supervisory employees" or "supervisors" under this section are supervisors located in California, defined under Government Code section 12926, subdivision (r). Attending training does not create an inference that an employee is a supervisor or that a contractor is an employee or a supervisor.

(9) "Trainers" or "Trainers or educators" qualified to provide training under this section are individuals who, through a combination of training and experience have the ability to train supervisors about the following: 1) what are unlawful harassment, discrimination and retaliation under both California and federal law; 2) what steps to take when harassing behavior occurs in the workplace; 3) how to report harassment complaints; 4) how to respond to a harassment complaint; 5) the employer's obligation to conduct a workplace investigation of a harassment complaint; 6) what constitutes retaliation and how to prevent it; 7) essential components of an anti-harassment policy; and 8) the effect of harassment on harassed employees, co-workers, harassers and employers.

(A) A trainer shall be one or more of the following:

1. "Attorneys" admitted for two or more years to the bar of any state in the United States and whose practice includes employment law under the Fair Employment and Housing Act and/or Title VII of the federal Civil Rights Act of 1964, or

2. "Human resource professionals" or "harassment prevention consultants" working as employees or inde-

pendent contractors with a minimum of two or more years of practical experience in one or more of the following: a. designing or conducting discrimination, retaliation and sexual harassment prevention training; b. responding to sexual harassment complaints or other discrimination complaints; c. conducting investigations of sexual harassment complaints; or d. advising employers or employees regarding discrimination, retaliation and sexual harassment prevention, or

3. "Professors or instructors" in law schools, colleges or universities who have a post-graduate degree or California teaching credential and either 20 instruction hours or two or more years of experience in a law school, college or university teaching about employment law under the Fair Employment and Housing Act and/or Title VII of the federal Civil Rights Act of 1964.

(B) Individuals who do not meet the qualifications of a trainer as an attorney, human resource professional, harassment prevention consultant, professor or instructor because they lack the requisite years of experience may team teach with a trainer in classroom or webinar trainings provided that the trainer supervises these individuals and the trainer is available throughout the training to answer questions from training attendees.

(10) "Training" as used in this section, is effective interactive training as defined at section 7288.0, subdivision (a)(2).

(11) "Two hours" of training is two hours of classroom training or two hours of webinar training or, in the case of an e-learning training, a program that takes the supervisor no less than two hours to complete.

(b) Training.

(1) Frequency of Training. An employer shall provide two hours of training, in the content specified in section 7288.0, subdivision (c), once every two years, and may use either of the following methods or a combination of the two methods to track compliance.

(A) "Individual" Tracking. An employer may track its training requirement for each supervisory employee, measured two years from the date of completion of the last training of the individual supervisor.

(B) "Training year" tracking. An employer may designate a "training year" in which it trains some or all of its supervisory employees and thereafter must again retrain these supervisors by the end of the next "training year," two years later. Thus, supervisors trained in training year 2005 shall be retrained in 2007. For newly hired or promoted supervisors who receive training within six months of assuming their supervisory positions and that training falls in a different training year, the employer may include them in the next group training year, even if that occurs sooner than two years. An employer shall not extend the training year for the new supervisors beyond the initial two year training year. Thus, with this method, assume that an employer trained all of its supervisors in 2005 and sets 2007 as the next training year. If a new supervisor is trained in 2006 and the employer wants to

include the new supervisor in its training year, the new supervisor would need to be trained in 2007 with the employer's other supervisors.

(2) Documentation of Training. An employer shall keep documentation of the training it has provided its employees under this section to track compliance, including the name of the supervisory employee trained, the date of training, the type of training, and the name of the training provider and shall retain the records for a minimum of two years.

(3) Training at New Businesses. Businesses created after January 1, 2006, must provide training to supervisors within six months of their establishment and thereafter biennially. Businesses that expand to 50 employees and/or contractors and thus become eligible under these regulations, must provide training to supervisors within six months of their eligibility and thereafter biennially.

(4) Training for New Supervisors. New supervisors shall be trained within six months of assuming their supervisory position and thereafter shall be trained once every two years, measured either from the individual or training year tracking method.

(5) Duplicate Training. A supervisor who has received training in compliance with this section within the prior two years either from a current, a prior, an alternate or a joint employer need only be given, be required to read and to acknowledge receipt of, the employer's anti-harassment policy within six months of assuming the supervisor's new supervisory position or within six months of the employer's eligibility. That supervisor shall otherwise be put on a two year tracking schedule based on the supervisor's last training. The burden of establishing that the prior training was legally compliant with this section shall be on the current employer.

(6) Duration of Training. The training required by this section does not need to be completed in two consecutive hours. For classroom training or webinars, the minimum duration of a training segment shall be no less than half an hour. E-learning courses may include bookmarking features which allow a supervisor to pause their individual training so long as the actual e-learning program is two hours.

(c) Content.

The learning objectives of the training mandated by California Government Code section 12950.1 shall be: 1) to assist California employers in changing or modifying workplace behaviors that create or contribute to "sexual harassment" as that term is defined in California and federal law; and 2) to develop, foster and encourage a set of values in supervisory employees who complete mandated training that will assist them in preventing and effectively responding to incidents of sexual harassment.

Towards that end, the training mandated by California Government Code section 12950.1, shall include but is not limited to:

(1) A definition of unlawful sexual harassment under the Fair Employment and Housing Act and Title VII of

the federal Civil Rights Act of 1964. In addition to a definition of sexual harassment, an employer may provide a definition of and train about other forms of harassment covered by the FEHA, as specified at Government Code section 12940, subdivision (j), and discuss how harassment of an employee can cover more than one basis.

(2) FEHA and Title VII statutory provisions and case law principles concerning the prohibition against and the prevention of unlawful sexual harassment, discrimination and retaliation in employment.

(3) The types of conduct that constitutes sexual harassment.

(4) Remedies available for sexual harassment.

(5) Strategies to prevent sexual harassment in the workplace.

(6) "Practical examples," such as factual scenarios taken from case law, news and media accounts, hypotheticals based on workplace situations and other sources which illustrate sexual harassment, discrimination and retaliation using training modalities such as role plays, case studies and group discussions.

(7) The limited confidentiality of the complaint process.

(8) Resources for victims of unlawful sexual harassment, such as to whom they should report any alleged sexual harassment.

(9) The employer's obligation to conduct an effective workplace investigation of a harassment complaint.

(10) Training on what to do if the supervisor is personally accused of harassment.

(11) The essential elements of an anti-harassment policy and how to utilize it if a harassment complaint is filed. Either the employer's policy or a sample policy shall be provided to the supervisors. Regardless of whether the employer's policy is used as part of the training, the employer shall give each supervisor a copy of its anti-harassment policy and require each supervisor to read and to acknowledge receipt of that policy.

(d) Remedies.

As part of an order in an adjudicatory proceeding pursuant to California Code of Regulations, Title 2, section 7429, the Commission may issue an order finding an employer failed to comply with Government Code section 12950.1 and order such compliance within 60 days of the effective date of the Commission's order.

(e) Compliance with section 12950.1 prior to effective date of Commission regulations.

An employer who has made a substantial, good faith effort to comply with section 12950.1 by completing training of its supervisors prior to the effective date of these regulations shall be deemed to be in compliance with section 12950.1 regarding training as though it had been done under these regulations.

Subchapter 3. Race and Color Discrimination (Reserved)

Subchapter 4. National Origin and Ancestry Discrimination

§ 7289.4. Defenses

These regulations incorporate the defenses set forth in Section 7286.7.

§ 7289.5. Specific Employment Practices

(a)-(c) (Reserved)

(d) An employer may have a rule requiring that employees speak only in English at certain times if the employer can show that the rule is justified by business necessity (See Section 7286.7(b)), and if the employer has effectively notified its employees of the circumstances and time when speaking only in English is required and of the consequences of violating the rule.

(e) (Reserved)

(f) Citizenship requirements. Citizenship requirements which have the purpose or effect of discriminating against applicants or employees on the basis of national origin or ancestry are unlawful unless pursuant to a permissible defense.

Subchapter 5. Ancestry Discrimination (Reserved)

Subchapter 6. Sex Discrimination

§ 7290.6. General Prohibition Against Discrimination on the Basis of Sex

(a) Statutory Source. These regulations are adopted by the Fair Employment and Housing Commission pursuant to Sections 1420, 1420.2 and 1420.35 of the Labor Code. (Sections 12940, 12943, and 12945 of the Government Code.)

(b) Statement of Purpose. The purpose of the law against discrimination in employment because of sex is to eliminate the means by which individuals of the female sex have historically been relegated to inferior jobs and to guarantee that in the future both sexes will enjoy equal employment benefits.

(c) Incorporation of General Regulations. These regulations pertaining to discrimination on the basis of sex incorporate each of the provisions of Subchapters 1 and 2 of Chapter 2, unless a provision is specifically excluded or modified.

§ 7290.7. Definitions

(a) "Sex." An applicant's or employee's gender; however, nothing herein shall limit protections due an individual on account of pregnancy, childbirth, or related medical conditions.

(b) "Sex Stereotype." An assumption about an individual's ability or inability to perform certain kinds of work

1171

based on a myth or generalization about the individual's gender.

§ 7290.8. Defenses

Once employment discrimination on the basis of sex has been established, an employer or other covered entity may prove one or more appropriate affirmative defenses as generally set forth in Section 7286.7, including, but not limited to, the defense of Bona Fide Occupational Qualification (BFOQ).

(a) Among situations which will not justify the application of the BFOQ defense are the following:

(1) A correlation between individuals of one sex and physical agility or strength;

(2) A correlation between individuals of one sex and height;

(3) Customer preference for employees of one sex;

(4) The necessity for providing separate facilities for one sex or

(5) The fact that members of one sex have traditionally been hired to perform the particular type of job.

(b) Personal privacy considerations may justify a BFOQ only where:

(1) The job requires an employee to observe other individuals in a state of nudity or to conduct body searches, and

(2) It would be offensive to prevailing social standards to have an individual of the opposite sex present, and

(3) It is detrimental to the mental or physical welfare of individuals being observed or searched to have an individual of the opposite sex present.

(c) Employers or other covered entities shall assign job duties and make other reasonable accommodation so as to minimize the number of jobs for which sex is a BFOQ.

§ 7290.9. Pre–Employment Practices

(a) Recruitment and Advertising.

(1) Employers or other covered entities engaged in recruiting activity (see Section 7287.2(a)) shall recruit individuals of both sexes for all jobs unless pursuant to a permissible defense.

(2) It is unlawful for any publication or other media to separate listings of job openings into "male" and "female" classifications.

(b) Pre–Employment Inquiries and Applications.

(1) For all employers or other covered entities who provide, accept and consider applications, it shall be unlawful to refuse to provide, accept and consider applications from individuals of one sex unless pursuant to a permissible defense.

(2) It is unlawful for an employer or other covered entity to ask the sex of the applicant on an application form or pre-employment questionnaire unless pursuant to a permissible defense or for recordkeeping purposes. After an individual is hired, the employer or other

covered entity may record the employee's sex for non-discriminatory personnel purposes.

(3) It is unlawful for an employer or other covered entity to ask questions regarding childbearing, pregnancy, birth control, or familial responsibilities unless they are related to specific and relevant working conditions of the job in question.

§ 7291.0. Employee Selection

(a) Tests of Physical Agility or Strength. Tests of physical agility or strength shall not be used unless the test is administered pursuant to a permissible defense. No applicant or employee shall be refused the opportunity to demonstrate that he or she has the requisite strength or agility to perform the job in question.

(b) Height and Weight Standards.

(1) Use of height or weight standards which discriminate against one sex or the other is unlawful unless pursuant to a permissible defense.

(2) Use of separate height and/or separate weight standards for males and females is unlawful unless pursuant to a permissible defense.

(c) Hiring Applicants of Childbearing Age. It is unlawful to refuse to hire a female applicant because she is of childbearing age.

(d) Prior Work Experience. If an employer or other covered entity considers prior work experience in the selection or assignment of an employee, the employer or other covered entity shall also consider prior unpaid or volunteer work experience.

(e) Sex Stereotypes. Use of any criterion which is based exclusively or in part on a sex stereotype is unlawful unless pursuant to a permissible defense.

§ 7291.1. Terms, Conditions, and Privileges of Employment

(a) Compensation.

(1) Except as otherwise required or permitted by regulation, an employer or other covered entity shall not base the amount of compensation paid to an employee, in whole or in part, on the employee's sex.

(2) Equal Compensation for Comparable Work. (Reserved.)

(b) Fringe Benefits.

(1) It is unlawful for an employer to condition the availability of fringe benefits upon an employee's sex.

(2) Insofar as an employment practice discriminates against one sex, an employer or other covered entity shall not condition the availability of fringe benefits upon whether an employee is a "head of household," "principal wage earner," "secondary wage earner," or of other similar status.

(3) Except where otherwise required by state law, an employer or other covered entity shall not require unequal employee contributions by similarly situated

male and female employees to fringe benefit plans, nor shall different amounts of basic benefits be established under fringe benefit plans for similarly situated male and female employees.

(4) It shall be unlawful for an employer or other covered entity to have a pension or retirement plan which establishes different optional or compulsory retirement ages based on the sex of the employee.

(c) Lines of Progression.

(1) It is unlawful for an employer or other covered entity to classify a job as "male" or "female" or to maintain separate lines of progression or separate seniority lists based on sex unless it is justified by a permissible defense. For example, a line of progression or seniority system is unlawful which:

(A) Prohibits a female from applying for a job labelled "male" or for a job in a "male" line of progression, and vice versa; or

(B) Prohibits a male scheduled for layoff from displacing a less senior female on a "female" seniority list, and vice versa.

(2) An employer or other covered entity shall provide equal opportunities to all employees for upward mobility, promotion, and entrance into all jobs for which they are qualified. However, nothing herein shall prevent an employer or other covered entity from implementing mobility programs to accelerate the promotability of underrepresented groups.

(d) Dangers to Health, Safety, or Reproductive Functions.

(1) If working conditions pose a greater danger to the health, safety, or reproductive functions of applicants or employees of one sex than to individuals of the other sex working under the same conditions, the employer or other covered entity shall make reasonable accommodation to:

(A) Upon the request of an employee of the more endangered sex, transfer the employee to a less hazardous or strenuous position for the duration of the greater danger, unless it can be demonstrated that the transfer would impose an undue hardship on the employer; or

(B) Alter the working conditions so as to eliminate the greater danger, unless it can be demonstrated that the modification would impose an undue hardship on the employer. Alteration of working conditions includes, but is not limited to, acquisition or modification of equipment or devices and extension of training or education.

(2) An employer or other covered entity may require an applicant or employee to provide a physician's certification that he or she is endangered by the working conditions.

(3) The existence of a greater risk for employees of one sex than the other shall not justify a BFOQ defense.

(4) An employer may not discriminate against members of one sex because of the prospective application of this subsection.

(5) With regard to protections due on account of pregnancy, childbirth, or related medical conditions, see Section 7291.2.

(6) Nothing in this subsection shall be construed to limit the rights or obligations set forth in Labor Code Section 6300 et seq.

(e) Working Conditions.

(1) Where rest periods are provided, equal rest periods must be provided to employees of both sexes.

(2) Equal access to comparable and adequate toilet facilities shall be provided to employees of both sexes. This requirement shall not be used to justify any discriminatory employment decision.

(3) Support services and facilities, such as clerical assistance and office space, shall be provided to employees without regard to the employee's sex.

(4) Job duties shall not be assigned according to sex stereotypes.

(5) It is unlawful for an employer or other covered entity to refuse to hire, employ or promote, or to transfer, discharge, dismiss, reduce, suspend, or demote an individual of one sex and not the other on the grounds that the individual is not sterilized or refuses to undergo sterilization.

(6) It shall be lawful for an employer or labor organization to provide or make financial provision for child-care services of a custodial nature for its employees or members who are responsible for the care of their minor children.

(f) Interpersonal Conduct and Appearance.

(1) Sexual Harassment. Sexual harassment is unlawful as defined in Section 7287.6(b), and includes verbal, physical, and visual harassment, as well as unwanted sexual advances.

(2) Physical Appearance, Grooming, and Dress Standards. It is lawful for an employer or other covered entity to impose upon an applicant or employee physical appearance, grooming or dress standards. However, if such a standard discriminates on the basis of sex and if it also significantly burdens the individual in his or her employment, it is unlawful.

Subchapter 6A. Sex Discrimination: Pregnancy, Childbirth or Related Medical Conditions

§ 7291.2. Definitions

The following definitions apply only to this subchapter:

(a) "Accrued leave," as that term is used in Government Code section 12945, subdivision (b)(1), and section 7291.11, subdivision (a)(1)(A), is any right of an employee, accumulated over the course of his or her employ-

1173

ment, to leave work for a period of time with monetary compensation from the employer.

(b) "Affected by pregnancy," as that term is used in section 7291.6, means that a woman is pregnant or has a related medical condition and that, because of pregnancy, her health care provider has certified that it is medically advisable for her to transfer, in accordance with the provisions of section 7291.2, subdivision (d).

(c) "Because of pregnancy" includes because of pregnancy, childbirth or a related medical condition or because of an employer's or other covered entity's perception that a woman is pregnant or has a related medical condition.

(d) "Certification" means a written communication from the heal;th care provider of the employee that either the employee is disabled due to pregnancy or that it is medically advisable for the employee to be transferred to a less strenuous or hazardous position or to less strenuous or hazardous duties.

(1) The certification indicating disability necessitating a leave should contain:

(A) The date on which the woman became disabled due to pregnancy;

(B) The probable duration of the period or periods of disability, and

(C) An explanatory statement that, due to the disability, the employee is unable to work at all or is unable to perform any one or more of the essential functions of her position without undue risk to herself, the successful completion of her pregnancy, or to other persons.

(2) The certification indicating the medical advisability of the transfer should contain:

(A) The date on which the need to transfer became medically advisable;

(B) The probable duration of the period or periods of the need to transfer; and

(C) An explanatory statement that, due to the woman's pregnancy, the transfer is medically advisable.

(e) "CFRA" means the Moore–Brown–Roberti Family Rights Act of 1993. (California Family Rights Act, Gov. Code ss 12945.1 and 12945.2.) "CFRA leave" means family care or medical leave taken pursuant to CFRA.

(f) A "covered entity" is any person (as defined in Government Code section 12925, subdivision (d)), labor organization, apprenticeship training program, training program leading to employment, employment agency, governing board of a school district, licensing board or other entity to which the provisions of Government Code sections 12940, 12943, 12944 or 12945 apply.

(g) A woman is "disabled by pregnancy" if, in the opinion of her health care provider, she is unable because of pregnancy to work at all or is unable to perform any one or more of the essential functions of her job or to perform these functions without undue risk to herself, the successful completion of her pregnancy, or to other

persons. The term "essential functions" is defined in Government Code section 12926, subdivision (f). For purposes of this subdivision, a woman is also considered to be "disabled by pregnancy" if she is suffering from severe "morning sickness" or needs to take time off for prenatal care.

(h) "Employer," as used in these regulations, except for section 7291.3, is any employer with five or more full or part time employees, who is an employer within the meaning of Government Code section 12926, subdivision (d), and section 7286.5, subdivision (a), of these regulations. "Employer" includes "non-Title VII employers" and "Title VII employers," as those terms are defined below. "Employer" includes the state of California, counties, and any other political or civil subdivision of the state and cities, regardless of the number of employees. The terms "all employers" and "any employer" refer to employers covered by the FEHA.

(1) A "non-Title VII employer" is any employer with five to 14 employees who is not subject to any provision of Title VII of the federal Civil Rights Act of 1964, 42 U.S.C. section 2000e, et seq.

(2) A "Title VII employer" is any employer with 15 or more employees who is also subject to any provision of Title VII of the federal Civil Rights Act of 1964.

(i) "Employment in the same position" means employment in, or reinstatement to, the original position that an employee held before being transferred and/or taking a disability leave, or both, because of pregnancy.

(j) "Employment in a comparable position" means employment in a position which is virtually identical to the employee's original position in terms of pay, benefits, and working conditions, including privileges, perquisites, and status. It must involve the same or substantially similar duties and responsibilities, which must entail substantially equivalent skill, effort, responsibility, and authority. It must be performed at the same or geographically proximate worksite from where the employee was previously employed. It ordinarily means the same shift or the same or an equivalent work schedule.

(k) "FMLA" means the federal Family and Medical Leave Act of 1993, 29 U.S.C. s2601, et seq., and its implementing regulations, 29 CFR Part 825, issued January 6, 1995. "FMLA leave" means family care or medical leave taken pursuant to FMLA.

(l) "Four months," as that term is used in Government Code section 12945, subdivision (b)(2), means the number of days the employee would normally work within four months. (See also section 7291.7, subdivision (a)(1).)

(m) "Health Care Provider" means either:

(1) an individual holding either a physician's and surgeon's certificate issued pursuant to Article 4 (commencing with Section 2080) of Chapter 5 of Division 2 of the Business and Professions Code or an osteopathic physician's and surgeon's certificate issued pursuant to Article 4.5 (commencing with Section 2099.5) of Chapter 5 of Division 2 of the Business and Professions Code, or

any other individual duly licensed as a physician, surgeon, or osteopathic physician or surgeon in another state or jurisdiction, including another country, who directly treats or supervises the treatment of the pregnancy, childbirth or related medical condition, or

(2) any other persons, including nurse practitioners, nurse midwives, or others who meet the definition of "others capable of providing health care services" under FMLA and its implementing regulations.

(n) A "normal pregnancy, childbirth or related medical condition" is a pregnancy or childbirth that in the opinion of the woman's health care provider involves neither high risk nor complications.

(o) "Pregnancy disability leave" is any leave, whether paid or unpaid, taken by an employee, for any period(s) up to a total of four months during which she is disabled by pregnancy.

(p) A "related medical condition" is any medically recognized physical or mental condition that is related to pregnancy or childbirth. This term is not the same as the term "medical condition" defined in Government Code section 12926, subdivision (h), which means any health impairment related to or associated with a diagnosis of cancer, for which a person has been rehabilitated or cured, based on competent medical evidence.

(q) "Transfer," as that term is used throughout these regulations, refers to the transfer of an employee because of pregnancy to a less strenuous or hazardous position or to less strenuous or hazardous duties.

§ 7291.3. Prohibition Against Harassment

It is an unlawful employment practice for any employer with one or more employee or other covered entity to harass, as defined in Government Code section 12940, subdivision (h)(3)(C), an employee or applicant because of pregnancy.

§ 7291.4. Responsibilities of Covered Entities Other than Employers

Unless a permissible defense applies, discrimination because of pregnancy by any covered entity other than employers constitutes discrimination because of sex under Government Code sections 12926, subdivision (o), 12940, subdivisions (b), (c), (d), (f), (g), (h) and (i), 12943 and 12944.

§ 7291.5. Responsibilities of Employers

Discrimination by employers because of pregnancy constitutes discrimination because of sex under Government Code sections 12926, subdivision (o), and 12940, subdivisions (a), (d), (f), (g), (h), and (i).

(a) Employer Obligations

Except as excused by a permissible defense, it is unlawful for any employer, because of pregnancy of an employee or applicant, to:

(1) refuse to hire or employ the applicant;

(2) refuse to select the applicant or employee for a training program leading to employment or promotion, except for non-Title VII employers, as set forth at subdivision (c), below;

(3) refuse to promote the employee;

(4) bar or to discharge the applicant or employee from employment or from a training program leading to employment or promotion;

(5) refuse to provide health benefits for pregnancy if the employer provides such benefits for other temporary disabilities, except for non-Title VII employers, as set forth at subdivision (d), below;

(6) discriminate against the applicant or employee in terms, conditions or privileges of employment, except for non-Title VII employers, as set forth at section 7291.11, subdivision (a)(1)(A), below;

(7) harass the applicant or employee because of pregnancy, as set forth in section 7291.3;

(8) retaliate, as set forth in section 7291.14, against the employee because of pregnancy or because that employee has exercised her right to take a pregnancy disability leave or transfer; or

(9) refuse to accommodate the employee who is temporarily disabled by pregnancy to the same extent that other temporarily disabled employees are accommodated under the employer's policy, practice or collective bargaining agreement.

(10) refuse to transfer the employee affected by pregnancy, as set forth at section 7291.6, below;

(11) refuse to grant the employee disabled by pregnancy a pregnancy disability leave, as set forth at section 7291.7, below:

(12) discriminate otherwise against the applicant or employee by any practice that is prohibited by Government Code section 12940, subdivisions (a) and (c) through (*l*), on the basis of sex.

(b) Permissible defenses, as defined at section 7286.7, include a bona fide occupational qualification, business necessity or where the practice is otherwise required by law.

(c) Training Programs Leading to Promotion—Exception for non-Title VII Employers

It is lawful for a non-Title VII employer to refuse to select a pregnant employee for a formal training program leading to promotion if the employee is unable to complete the training program at least three months prior to the date, anticipated at the time she applies for the training program, on which she intends to depart on pregnancy disability leave.

(d) Provision of Medical Benefits—Exception for non-Title VII Employers

A non-Title VII employer with five to 14 employees is not required to provide its employees with health insurance coverage for the medical costs of pregnancy, childbirth, or related medical conditions even if the employer provides coverage for other temporary disabilities.

§ 7291.6.　Transfer

(a) Transfer—All Employers

It is unlawful for an employer to deny the request of an employee affected by pregnancy to transfer provided that:

(1) The employee's request is based on the certification of her health care provider that a transfer is medically advisable; and

(2) Such transfer can be reasonably accommodated by the employer. No employer is required to create additional employment that the employer would not otherwise have created, discharge another employee, violate the terms of a collective bargaining agreement, transfer another employee with more seniority, or promote or transfer any employee who is not qualified to perform the new job. Nothing in these regulations is intended to prevent an employer from accommodating a transfer request by transferring another employee, but there is no obligation to do so.

(b) Burden of Proof

The burden shall be on the employer to prove, by a preponderance of the evidence, that such transfer cannot be reasonably accommodated for one or more of the enumerated reasons listed is section 7291.6, subdivision (a)(2).

(c) Transfer to Accommodate Intermittent Leave or a Reduced Work Schedule

If it is medically advisable for an employee to take intermittent leave or leave on a reduced work schedule and it is foreseeable based on planned medical treatment because of pregnancy, the employer may require the employee to transfer temporarily to an available alternative position. This alternative position must have the equivalent rate of pay and benefits, the employee must be qualified for the position, and it must better accommodate recurring periods of leave than the employee's regular job. It does not have to have equivalent duties. Transfer to an alternative position may include altering an existing job to accommodate better the employee's need for intermittent leave or a reduced work schedule.

(d) Right to Reinstatement After Transfer

When the employee's health care provider certifies that there is no further medical advisability for the transfer, intermittent leave, or leave on a reduced work schedule, the employer must reinstate her to her same or comparable position in accordance with the requirements of section 7291.9.

(e) No Eligibility Requirement

There is no length of service requirement before an employee affected by pregnancy is eligible for a transfer.

§ 7291.7.　Pregnancy Disability Leave

The following provisions apply to leave taken for disability because of pregnancy.

(a) Four–Month Leave Requirement for all Employers

All employers must provide a leave of up to four months, as needed, for the period(s) of time a woman is actually disabled by pregnancy even if an employer has a policy or practice which provides less than four months of leave for other similarly situated temporarily disabled employees.

(1) A "four month leave," as that term is defined in section 7291.2, subdivision (l), means the number of days the employee would normally work within four months. For a full time employee who works five eight-hour days per week, "four months" means 88 working and/or paid eight-hour days of leave entitlement, based on an average of 22 working days per month for four months.

(2) For employees who work more or less than five days a week, or who work on alternative work schedules, the number of working days which constitutes "four months" is calculated on a pro rata or proportional basis.

(A) For example, for an employee who works half time, "four months" may mean 44 eight-hour days or 88 four-hour days, or four months of whatever is the employee's normal half time work schedule. For an employee who normally works six eight-hour days in a week, "four months" means 104 working and/or paid days of leave entitlement.

(B) If an employee takes leave on an intermittent leave or a reduced work schedule, only the amount of leave actually taken may be counted toward the four months of leave to which the employee is entitled. For example, if an employee misses two hours of work in a morning because of morning sickness, only two hours would be charged against her pregnancy disability leave entitlement.

(C) If a holiday falls within a week taken as a pregnancy disability leave, the week is nevertheless counted as a week of pregnancy disability leave. If, however, the employer's business activity has temporarily ceased for some reason and employees generally are not expected to report for work for one or more weeks, (e.g., a school closing for two weeks for the Christmas/New Year holiday or summer vacation or an employer closing the plant for retooling), the days the employer's activities have ceased do not count against the employee's pregnancy disability leave entitlement.

(3) Minimum Duration

Leave may be taken intermittently or on a reduced work schedule when medically advisable, as determined by the health care provider of the employee. An employer may limit leave increments to the shortest period of time that the employer's payroll system uses to account for absences or use of leave.

(b) Employers With More Generous Leave Policies

If an employer has a more generous leave policy for other temporary disabilities than is required under section 7291.7, subdivision (a), above, the employer must provide such leave to employees temporarily disabled by pregnancy.

(c) No Eligibility Requirement

There is no length of service requirement before an employee disabled by pregnancy is entitled to a pregnancy disability leave.

§ 7291.8. Denial of Leave

(a) Unlawful Employment Practice

It is an unlawful employment practice for an employer to refuse to grant a pregnancy disability leave to an eligible employee.

(b) Burden of Proof

Denial of a request for pregnancy disability leave is established if the Department or the employee proves, by a preponderance of the evidence, the following elements.

(1) The employer was an employer under the FEHA with five or more employees.

(2) The employee was disabled by pregnancy.

(3) The request was reasonable.

(4) The employer denied the request for pregnancy disability leave.

(c) Reasonable Request

A request to take a pregnancy disability leave is reasonable if it complies with any applicable notice requirements, as specified in section 7291.10, and if it is accompanied, where required, by a certification, as that term is defined in section 7291.2, subdivision (d).

§ 7291.9. Right to Reinstatement from Pregnancy Disability Leave

The following rules apply to reinstatement from any leave or transfer taken for disability because of pregnancy.

(a) Guarantee of Reinstatement

Upon granting the pregnancy disability leave or transfer, the employer shall guarantee to reinstate the employee to the same position, or, if excused by section 7291.9, subdivisions (c)(1)(A) or (c)(1)(B), to a comparable position, and shall provide the guarantee in writing upon request of the employee. It is an unlawful employment practice for any employer, after granting a requested pregnancy disability leave or transfer, to refuse to honor its guarantee of reinstatement unless the refusal is justified by the defenses below in subdivision (c)(1) and (c)(2).

(b) Refusal to Reinstate

(1) Definite Date of Reinstatement

Where a definite date of reinstatement has been agreed upon at the beginning of the leave or transfer, a refusal to reinstate is established if the Department or employee proves, by a preponderance of the evidence, that the leave or transfer was granted by the employer and that the employer failed to reinstate the employee by the date agreed upon to the same position or, where

applicable to a comparable position, as specified below in subdivisions (c)(1) and (c)(2).

(2) Change in Date of Reinstatement

If the reinstatement date differs from the employer's and the employee's original agreement, a refusal to reinstate is established if the Department or employee proves, by a preponderance of the evidence, that the employer failed to reinstate the employee within two business days, where feasible, after the employee notifies the employer of her readiness to return, to the same, or, where applicable, to a comparable position, as specified below in subdivisions (c)(1) and (c)(2).

(c) Permissible Defenses

(1) Right to Reinstatement to the Same Position

An employee has no greater right to reinstatement to the same position or to other benefits and conditions of employment than if the employee had been continuously employed in this position during the pregnancy disability leave or transfer period. A refusal to reinstate the employee to her same position or duties is justified if the employer proves, by a preponderance of the evidence, either of the following:

(A) That the employee would not otherwise have been employed in her same position at the time reinstatement is requested for legitimate business reasons unrelated to the employee taking a pregnancy disability leave or transfer (such as a layoff pursuant to a plant closure).

(B) That each means of preserving the job or duties for the employee (such as leaving it unfilled or filling it with a temporary employee) would substantially undermine the employer's ability to operate the business safely and efficiently.

(2) Right to Reinstatement to a Comparable Position

An employee has no greater right to reinstatement to a comparable position or to other benefits and conditions of employment than an employee who has been continuously employed in another position that is being eliminated. If the employer is excused from reinstating the employee to her same position, or with the same duties, a refusal to reinstate the employee to a comparable position is justified if the employer proves, by a preponderance of the evidence, either of the following:

(A) That there is no comparable position available. A position is "available" if there is a position open on the employee's scheduled date of reinstatement or within 10 working days thereafter for which the employee is qualified, or to which the employee is entitled by company policy, contract, or collective bargaining agreement.

(B) For am employer whose employee takes a pregnancy disability leave which does not qualify as a FMLA leave, that a comparable position is available, but filling the available position with the returning employee would substantially undermine the employer's ability to operate the business safely and efficiently.

(d) Right to Reinstatement to Job If Pregnancy Disability Leave Exceeds Four Months

If an employee disabled by pregnancy has taken a pregnancy disability leave for longer than four months, an employer must treat the employee the same regarding reinstatement rights as it treats any other similarly situated employee who has taken a similar length disability leave. For example, if the employer has a policy which allows reinstatement to other temporarily disabled employees who are disabled for six months, the employer must also allow reinstatement to a woman disabled by pregnancy for six months.

(e) Right to Reinstatement to Job If CFRA Leave is Taken Following Pregnancy Disability Leave

At the expiration of a pregnancy disability leave, if an employee takes a CFRA leave for reason of the birth of her child, the employee's right to reinstatement to her job is governed by CFRA and not sections 7291.9, subdivisions (c)(1) and (c)(2), above. Under CFRA, an employer may reinstate an employee either to her same or a comparable job.

§ 7291.10. Requests for Pregnancy Disability Leave or Transfer: Advance Notice; Certification; Employer Response

The following rules apply to any pregnancy disability leave or transfer.

(a) Advance Notice

(1) Verbal Notice

An employee shall provide at least verbal notice sufficient to make the employer aware that the employee needs a pregnancy disability leave or transfer, and the anticipated timing and duration of the leave or transfer.

(2) 30 Days Advance Notice

An employee must provide the employer at least 30 days advance notice before pregnancy disability leave or transfer is to begin if the need for the leave or transfer is foreseeable because of pregnancy. The employee shall consult with the employer and make a reasonable effort to schedule any planned medical treatment or supervision so as to minimize disruption to the operations of the employer. Any such scheduling, however, shall be subject to the approval of the health care provider of the employee.

(3) When 30 Days Not Practicable

If 30 days advance notice is not practicable, such as because of a lack of knowledge of approximately when leave or transfer will be required to begin, a change in circumstances, or a medical emergency, notice must be given as soon as practicable.

(4) Prohibition Against Denial of Leave or Transfer in Emergency or Unforeseeable Circumstances

An employer shall not deny a pregnancy disability leave or transfer, the need for which is an emergency or is otherwise unforeseeable, on the basis that the employee

did not provide advance notice of the need for the leave or transfer.

(5) Employer Obligation to Inform Employees of Notice Requirement

An employer shall give its employees reasonable advance notice of any notice requirements which it adopts. The employer may incorporate its notice requirements in the general notice requirements in section 7291.16 and such incorporation shall constitute "reasonable advance notice." Failure of the employer to give or post such notice(s) shall preclude the employer from taking any adverse action against the employee, including denying pregnancy disability leave, for failing to furnish the employer with advance notice of a need to take pregnancy disability leave.

(6) Employer Response to Leave or Transfer Request

The employer shall respond to the leave or transfer request as soon as practicable and in any event no later than ten calendar days after receiving the request. The employer shall attempt to respond to the leave request before the date the leave is due to begin. Once given, approval shall be deemed retroactive to the date of the first day of the leave.

(b) Medical Certification

As a condition of granting a pregnancy disability leave or transfer, the employer may require medical certification, as defined in section 7291.2, subdivision (d), if the employer requires certification of other similarly situated employees. If the certification satisfies the requirements of section 7291.2, subdivision (d), the employer must accept it as sufficient. Upon expiration of the time period which the health care provider originally estimated that the employee needed, the employer may require the employee to obtain recertification if additional time is requested if the employer has similar requirements for other similarly situated employees.

(1) The employer may not ask the employee to provide additional information beyond that allowed by these regulations.

(2) The employer is responsible for complying with all applicable law regarding the confidentiality of any medical information requested.

(c) Release to Return to Work

As a condition of an employee's return from pregnancy disability leave or transfer, the employer may require that the employee obtain a release to "return-to-work" from her health care provider stating that she is able to resume her original job duties only if the employer has a uniformly applied practice or policy of requiring such releases from other similarly situated employees returning to work after a non-pregnancy related disability leave or transfer.

§ 7291.11. Terms of Pregnancy Disability Leave

(a) Paid Leave

An employer is not required to pay an employee during a pregnancy disability leave except:

(1) If the employer pays for other temporary disability leaves.

(A) A non-Title VII employer with five to 14 employees must pay an employee disabled by pregnancy only six weeks of accrued, paid leave for a normal pregnancy regardless of its paid leave policy for other disabled employees.

1) A "six week leave," means the equivalent of six of the employee's normally scheduled workweeks. For a full time employee working five eight-hour days per week, this means 30 working and/or paid eight hour days of leave entitlement. For employees who work less than full time, or who work full time but on alternative work schedules, the number of working days which constitutes "six weeks" is calculated on a pro rata or proportional basis.

2) This exception does not apply to any employee disabled by pregnancy that is not normal as defined at section 7291.2, subdivision (n).

(b) Accrued Time Off

(1) Sick Leave

An employer may require an employee to use, or an employee may elect to use, any accrued sick leave during the otherwise unpaid portion of her pregnancy disability leave.

(2) Vacation Time and Other Accrued Time Off

An employee may elect, at her option, to use any vacation time or other accrued personal time off (including undifferentiated paid time off ("PTO")) that the employee is otherwise eligible to take during the otherwise unpaid portion of the pregnancy disability leave.

(c) Other Benefits and Seniority Accrual

During the period of pregnancy disability leave, the employee is entitled to accrual of seniority and to participate in health plans, employee benefit plans, including life, short-term and long-term disability or accident insurance, pension and retirement plans, and supplemental unemployment benefit plans to the same extent and under the same conditions as would apply to any other unpaid disability leave granted by the employer for any reason other than a pregnancy disability.

(1) If the employer's policy allows seniority to accrue when employees are on paid leave, such as paid sick or vacation leave, and/or unpaid leave, then seniority will accrue during any part of a paid and/or unpaid pregnancy disability leave, consistent with the employer's policy.

(2) The employee returning from a pregnancy disability leave shall return with no less seniority than the employee had when the leave commenced for purposes of layoff, recall, promotion, job assignment, and seniority-related benefits such as vacation.

(d) Employee Status

The employee shall retain employee status during the period of the pregnancy disability leave. The leave shall not constitute a break in service for purposes of longevity and/or seniority under any collective bargaining agreement or under any employee benefit plan. Benefits must be resumed upon the employee's reinstatement in the same manner and at the same levels as provided when the leave began, without any new qualification period, physical exam, et cetera.

§ 7291.12. Relationship Between Pregnancy Leave and FMLA Leave

(a) A Pregnancy Leave May Also Be a FMLA Leave

If the employer is a covered employer and the employee is eligible for leave under the federal Family Care and Medical Leave Act (FMLA), the employer may be able to count the employee's pregnancy disability leave under this subchapter, up to a maximum of 12 weeks, against her FMLA leave entitlement.

(b) Pregnancy a "Serious Health Condition" under FMLA

Any period of incapacity or treatment due to pregnancy, including prenatal care, is included as a "serious health condition" under FMLA.

(c) Employer Obligation under FMLA to Continue Group Health Plan Benefits

During any part of the pregnancy disability leave which is also a FMLA leave, if the employer provides health benefits under any "group health plan," the employer may have a FMLA obligation to continue providing such benefits.

(d) FMLA Coverage

In general, only employees working for employers with 50 or more employees are eligible to take a family care leave under FMLA. For more specifics on rights and obligations under FMLA, consult the FMLA regulations regarding family care and medical leave (Title 29, Part 825 of the Code of Federal Regulations, issued January 6, 1995).

§ 7291.13. Relationship Between CFRA and Pregnancy Leaves

(a) Separate and Distinct Entitlements

The right to take a pregnancy disability leave under Government Code section 12945, subdivision (b)(2), and these regulations is separate and distinct from the right to take a CFRA leave under the California Family Rights Act, Government Code sections 12945.1 and 12945.2.

(b) "Serious Health Condition"—Pregnancy

An employee's own disability due to pregnancy, childbirth or related medical conditions is not included as a "serious health condition" under CFRA.

(c) CFRA Leave after Pregnancy Disability Leave

At the end of the employee's period(s) of pregnancy disability, or at the end of four months pregnancy disability leave, whichever occurs first, a CFRA-eligible employee may request to take CFRA leave of up to 12 workweeks for reason of the birth of her child, if the child has been born by this date. There is no requirement that either the employee or child have a serious health condition in order for the employee to take CFRA leave. There is also no requirement that the employee no longer be disabled by her pregnancy before taking CFRA leave for reason of the birth of her child.

(1) As provided in section 7297.6, subdivision (c)(1), where an employee has utilized four months of pregnancy disability leave prior to the birth of her child, and her health care provider determines that a continuation of the leave is medically necessary, an employer may, but is not required to, allow an eligible employee to utilize CFRA leave prior to the birth of her child. No employer shall, however, be required to provide more CFRA leave than the amount to which the employee is otherwise entitled.

(d) Maximum Entitlement

The maximum possible combined statutory leave entitlement for CFRA/FMLA employees for both pregnancy disability leave (under FMLA and Government Code section 12945, subdivision (b)(2)) and CFRA leave for reason of the birth of the child is four months and 12 workweeks. This assumes that the employee is disabled by pregnancy for four months and then requests, and is eligible for, a 12–week CFRA leave for reason of the birth of her child.

(e) CFRA Coverage

In general, employers who are covered by CFRA and employees who are eligible to take CFRA leave are the same as under FMLA. For more specifics on rights and obligations under CFRA, consult the CFRA regulations (Cal. Code of Regs., tit. 2, s7297.0, et seq.).

§ 7291.14.　Retaliation

In addition to the retaliation prohibited by Government Code section 12940, subdivision (f), and section 7287.8 of the regulations, it shall be an unlawful employment practice for any person to discharge, fine, suspend, expel, punish, refuse to hire, or otherwise discriminate against any individual, except as otherwise permitted in this subchapter, because:

(a) of the individual's pregnancy and/or

(b) because that individual has exercised her right to take a pregnancy disability leave or transfer and/or

(c) because that individual has given information or testimony regarding her pregnancy disability leave, in any inquiry or proceeding related to any right guaranteed under this subchapter.

§ 7291.15.　Remedies

Upon determining that an employer has violated Government Code sections 12940, 12943, or 12945, the Commission may order any remedy available under Government Code section 12970, and section 7286.9 of the regulations. The remedy, however, for a violation of

1180

section 7291.16, subdivision (b), (failure to provide notice) shall be an order that the employer provide such notice.

§ 7291.16.　Notice of Right to Request Pregnancy Disability Leave or Transfer

(a) Employers to Post Notice

All employers shall provide notice to their employees of the right to request pregnancy disability leave or transfer under the Fair Employment and Housing Act as specified at section 7291.16, subdivisions (d) and (e) and as contained in "Notice A" and "Notice B". Employers shall post the appropriate notice in a conspicuous place or places where employees tend to congregate. If the employer publishes an employee handbook which describes other kinds of temporary disability leaves or transfers available to its employees, that employer shall include a description of pregnancy disability leave or transfer in the next edition of its handbook which it publishes following adoption of these regulations. If an employer qualifies as a CFRA employer, the employer may include both pregnancy disability leave and CFRA leave requirements in a single notice. An employer is also required to give an employee a copy of the appropriate notice as soon as practicable after the employee tells the employer of her pregnancy or sooner if the employee inquires about pregnancy disability leaves or transfers.

(b) Employers to Give Notice

Employers are also encouraged to give a copy of the notice to each current and new employee, ensure that copies are otherwise available to each current and new employee, and disseminate the notice in any other way.

(c) Non–English Speaking Workforce

Any CFRA-covered employer whose work force at any facility or establishment contains ten percent or more of persons who speak a language other than English as their primary language shall translate the notice into the language or languages spoken by this group or these groups of employees.

(d) "Notice A"

The text below in "Notice A" contains only the minimum requirements of the Fair Employment and Housing Act's provisions regarding pregnancy, childbirth or related medical conditions. This Notice is suitable for use by employers with less than 50 employees and who are therefore not subject to CFRA or FMLA. Nothing in this notice requirement prohibits an employer from providing a leave policy which is more generous than that required by this act if that more generous policy is provided to all similarly situated disabled employees. At employer may provide its own notice of its own policy. Employers may develop their own notice or they may choose to use the text provided below, unless it does not accurately reflect their own policy.

(e) "Notice B"

The text below in "Notice B" combines notice of both an employee's CFRA leave rights and pregnancy disability leave rights. Adoption of this notice, or a comparable notice, satisfies the employer's notice obligations under both this subchapter and section 7297.9 of the regulations. This notice is suitable for use by all employers with 50 employees or more.

"NOTICE A"
PREGNANCY DISABILITY LEAVE

Under the California Fair Employment and Housing Act (FEHA), if you are disabled by pregnancy, childbirth or related medical conditions, you are eligible to take a pregnancy disability leave (PDL). If you are affected by pregnancy or a related medical condition, you are also eligible to transfer to a less strenuous or hazardous position or to less strenuous or hazardous duties, if this transfer is medically advisable.

• The PDL is for any period(s) of actual disability caused by your pregnancy, childbirth or related medical conditions up to four months (or 88 work days for a full time employee) per pregnancy.

• The PDL does not need to be taken in one continuous period of time but can be taken on an as-needed basis.

• Time off needed for prenatal care, severe morning sickness, doctor-ordered bed rest, childbirth, and recovery from childbirth would all be covered by your PDL.

• Generally, we are required to treat your pregnancy disability the same as we treat other disabilities of similarly situated employees. This affects whether your leave will be paid or unpaid.

• You may be required to obtain a certification from your health care provider of your pregnancy disability or the medical advisability for a transfer. The certification should include:

1) the date on which you become disabled due to pregnancy or the date of the medical advisability for the transfer;

2) the probable duration of the period(s) of disability or the period(s) for the advisability of the transfer; and,

3) a statement that, due to the disability, you are unable to work at all or to perform any one or more of the essential functions of your position without undue risk to yourself, the successful completion of your pregnancy or to other persons or a statement that, due to your pregnancy, the transfer is medically advisable.

• At your option, you can use any accrued vacation or other accrued time off as part of your pregnancy disability leave before taking the remainder of your leave as an unpaid leave. We may require that you use up any available sick leave during your leave. You may also be eligible for state disability insurance for the unpaid portion of your leave.

• Taking a pregnancy disability leave may impact certain of your benefits and your seniority date. If you want more information regarding your eligibility for a leave, the impact of the leave on your seniority and benefits, and our policy for other disabilities, please contact_____.

"NOTICE B"
FAMILY CARE AND MEDICAL LEAVE (CFRA LEAVE)
AND PREGNANCY DISABILITY LEAVE

Under the California Family Rights Act of 1993 (CFRA), if you have more than 12 months of service with us and have worked at least 1,250 hours in the 12–month period before the date you want to begin your leave, you may have a right to an unpaid family care or medical leave (CFRA leave). This leave may be up to 12 workweeks in a 12–month period for the birth, adoption, or foster care placement of your child or for your own serious health condition or that of your child, parent or spouse.

Even if you are not eligible for CFRA leave, if disabled by pregnancy, childbirth or related medical conditions, you are entitled to take a pregnancy disability leave of up to four months, depending on your period(s) of actual disability. If you are CFRA-eligible, you have certain rights to take BOTH a pregnancy disability leave and a CFRA leave for reason of the birth of your child. Both leaves contain a guarantee of reinstatement to the same or to a comparable position at the end of the leave, subject to any defense allowed under the law.

If possible, you must provide at least 30 days advance notice for foreseeable events (such as the expected birth of a child or a planned medical treatment for your self or of a family member). For events which are unforeseeable, we need you to notify us, at least verbally, as soon as you learn of the need for the leave.

Failure to comply with these notice rules is grounds for, and may result in, deferral of the requested leave until you comply with this notice policy.

We may require certification from your health care provider before allowing you a leave for pregnancy or your own serious health condition or certification from the health care provider of your child, parent, or spouse who has a serious health condition before allowing you a leave to take care of that family member. When medically necessary, leave may be taken on an intermittent or a reduced work schedule.

If you are taking a leave for the birth, adoption or foster care placement of a child, the basic minimum duration of the leave is two weeks and you must conclude the leave within one year of the birth or placement for adoption or foster care.

Taking a family care or pregnancy disability leave may impact certain of your benefits and your seniority date. If you want more information regarding your eligibility for a leave and/or the impact of the leave on your seniority and benefits, please contact _____.

1181

Subchapter 7. Marital Status Discrimination

§ 7292.0. General Prohibition Against Discrimination on the Basis of Marital Status

(a) Statutory Source. These regulations are adopted by the Fair Employment and Housing Commission pursuant to Section 1420 of the Labor Code (Section 12940 of the Government Code).

(b) Statement of Purpose. The purpose of the law prohibiting marital status discrimination is to make it unlawful for an employer or other covered entity to deny or grant employment benefits for the reason that an applicant or employee is either married or unmarried.

(c) Incorporation of General Regulations. These regulations pertaining to discrimination on the basis of marital status incorporate each of the provisions of Subchapters 1 and 2 of Chapter 2, unless a provision is specifically excluded or modified.

§ 7292.1. Definitions

(a) "Marital Status." An individual's state of marriage, non-marriage, divorce or dissolution, separation, widowhood, annulment, or other marital state.

(b) "Spouse." A partner in marriage as defined in Civil Code Section 4100.

§ 7292.2. Establishing Marital Status Discrimination

Marital status discrimination may be established by showing that an applicant or employee has been denied an employment benefit by reason of:

(a) The fact that the applicant or employee is not married;

(b) An applicant's or employee's "single" or "married" status, or

(c) The employment or lack of employment of an applicant's or employee's spouse.

§ 7292.3. Defenses

Any defense permissible under Subchapter 1 is applicable to this subchapter, in addition to any other defense provided herein.

§ 7292.4. Pre–Employment Practices

(a) Impermissible Inquiries. It is unlawful to ask an applicant to disclose his or her marital status as part of a pre-employment inquiry unless pursuant to a permissible defense.

(b) Request for Names. For business reasons other than ascertaining marital status, an applicant may be asked whether he or she has ever used another name, e.g., to enable an employer or other covered entity to check the applicant's past work record.

(c) Employment of Spouse. It is lawful to ask an applicant to state whether he or she has a spouse who is presently employed by the employer, but this information may not be used as a basis for an employment decision except as stated below.

§ 7292.5. Employee Selection

(a) Employment of Spouse. An employment decision shall not be based on whether an individual has a spouse presently employed by the employer except in accordance with the following criteria:

(1) For business reasons of supervision, safety, security or morale, an employer may refuse to place one spouse under the direct supervision of the other spouse.

(2) For business reasons of supervision, security or morale, an employer may refuse to place both spouses in the same department, division or facility if the work involves potential conflicts of interest or other hazards greater for married couples than for other persons.

(b) Accommodation for Co–Employees Who Marry. If co-employees marry, an employer shall make reasonable efforts to assign job duties so as to minimize problems of supervision, safety, security, or morale.

§ 7292.6. Terms, Conditions and Privileges of Employment

(a) Fringe Benefits.

(1) The availability of benefits to any employee shall not be based on the employee's marital status. However:

(A) Bona fide fringe benefit plans or programs may provide benefits to an employee's spouse or dependents;

(B) Such bona fide fringe benefit plans or programs may decline to provide benefits to any individual who is not one of the following: an employee of the employer, a spouse of an employee of the employer, or a dependent of an employee of the employer.

(2) Insofar as an employment practice discriminates against individuals on the basis of marital status, fringe benefits shall not be conditioned upon whether an employee is "head of household," "principal wage earner," "secondary wage earner," or other similar status.

(b) Inter–Personal Conduct.

(1) An employer or other covered entity shall not use job responsibilities such as travel, entertainment, or other non-office hour duties as a justification for discriminating on the basis of marital status.

(2) It is unlawful to require a married female applicant or employee to use her husband's name.

Subchapter 8. Religious Creed Discrimination

§ 7293.0. General Prohibition Against Religious Creed Discrimination

(a) Statutory Source. These regulations concerning religious discrimination are adopted by the Commission pursuant to Section 1420 of the Labor Code. (Section 12940 of the Government Code.)

(b) Statement of Purpose. The freedom to worship as one believes is a basic human right. To that end, the accommodation to religious pluralism is an important and necessary part of our society. Questions of religious discrimination and accommodation to the varied religious practices of the people of the State of California often arise in complex and emotionally charged situations; therefore, each case must be reviewed on an individual basis to best balance often contradictory social needs.

(c) Incorporation of General Regulations. These regulations incorporate all of the provisions of Subchapters 1 and 2 of Chapter 2, unless specifically excluded or modified.

§ 7293.1. Establishing Religious Creed Discrimination

"Religious creed" includes any traditionally recognized religion as well as beliefs, observances, or practices which an individual sincerely holds and which occupy in his or her life a place of importance parallel to that of traditionally recognized religions. Religious creed discrimination may be established by showing:

(a) Employment benefits have been denied, in whole or in part, because of an applicant's or employee's religious creed or lack of religious creed.

(b) The employer or other covered entity has failed to reasonably accommodate the applicant's or employee's religious creed despite being informed by the applicant or employee or otherwise having become aware of the need for reasonable accommodation.

§ 7293.2. Defenses

Any permissible defense set forth in Subchapter 1 shall be applicable to this Subchapter.

§ 7293.3. Reasonable Accommodation

An employer or other covered entity shall make accommodation to the known religious creed of an applicant or employee unless the employer or other covered entity can demonstrate that the accommodation is unreasonable because it would impose an undue hardship.

(a) Reasonable accommodation may include, but is not limited to, job restructuring, job reassignment, modification of work practices, or allowing time off in an amount equal to the amount of non-regularly scheduled time the employee has worked in order to avoid a conflict with his or her religious observances.

(b) In determining whether a reasonable accommodation would impose an undue hardship on the operations of an employer or other covered entity, factors to be considered include, but are not limited to:

(1) The size of the relevant establishment or facility with respect to the number of employees, the size of budget, and other such matters;

(2) The overall size of the employer or other covered entity with respect to the number of employees, number and type of facilities, and size of budget;

(3) The type of the establishment's or facility's operation, including the composition and structure of the workforce or membership;

(4) The type of the employer's or other covered entity's operation, including the composition and structure of the workforce or membership;

(5) The nature and cost of the accommodation involved;

(6) Reasonable notice to the employer or other covered entity of the need for accommodation; and

(7) Any available reasonable alternative means of accommodation.

(c) Reasonable accommodation includes, but is not limited to, the following specific employment policies or practices:

(1) Interview and examination times. Scheduled times for interviews, examinations, and other functions related to employment opportunities shall reasonably accommodate religious practices.

(2) Dress Standards. Dress standards or requirements for personal appearance shall be flexible enough to take into account religious practices.

(3) Union Dues. An employer or union shall not require membership from any employee or applicant whose religious creed prohibits such membership. An applicant's or employee's religious creed shall be reasonably accommodated with respect to union dues.

§ 7293.4. Pre–Employment Practices

Pre-employment inquiries regarding an applicant's availability for work on weekends or evenings shall not be used as a pretext for ascertaining his or her religious creed, nor shall such inquiry be used to evade the requirement of reasonable accommodation. However, inquiries as to the availability for work on weekends or evenings are permissible where reasonably related to the normal business requirements of the job in question.

Subchapter 9.   Disability Discrimination

§ 7293.5. General Prohibitions Against Discrimination on the Basis of Disability

(a) Statutory Source. These regulations are adopted by the Commission pursuant to Sections 12926 and 12940 of the Government Code.

(b) Statement of Purpose. The Fair Employment and Housing Commission is committed to ensuring each individual employment opportunities commensurate with his or her abilities. These regulations are designed to assure discrimination-free access to employment opportunities notwithstanding any individual's actual or perceived disability.

(c) Incorporation of General Regulations. These regulations governing discrimination on the basis of disability incorporate each of the provisions of Subchapters 1 and 2 of Chapter 2, unless specifically excluded or modified.

§ 7293.6. Definitions

As used in this subchapter, the following definitions apply:

(a) "Disability" means and includes:

(1) "Physical disability," as defined in Government Code Section 12926, subdivision (k), and Section 7293.6, subdivision (e), herein; and

(2) "Mental disability," as defined in Government Code Section 12926, subdivision (i), and Section 7293.6, subdivision (f), herein; and

(3) "Medical condition," as defined in Government Code Section 12926, subdivision (h), and Section 7293.6, subdivision (g), herein; and

(4) "Disability," as used in the Americans with Disabilities Act of 1990 (Public Law 101–336) ("ADA"), if:

(A) the ADA definition of "disability" would result in broader protection of the civil rights of individuals with a mental disability or physical disability, as defined in subdivision (i) or (k) of Government Code Section 12926; or

(B) the ADA definition of "disability" would include any medical condition not included within subdivision (i) or (k) of Government Code Section 12926.

(b) "Disability" does not include:

(1) Transvestism, transsexualism, pedophilia, exhibitionism, voyeurism, gender identity disorders not resulting from physical impairments, or other sexual behavior disorders;

(2) Compulsive gambling, kleptomania, or pyromania; or

(3) Psychoactive substance use disorders resulting from current illegal use of drugs.

(c) Homosexuality and bisexuality are not impairments and as such are not disabilities.

(d) The unlawful use of controlled substances or other drugs shall not be deemed, in and of itself, to constitute a physical disability or a mental disability.

(e) "Physical disability"

(1) "Physical disability" includes, but is not limited to, all of the following:

(A) Having any physiological disease, disorder, condition, cosmetic disfigurement, or anatomical loss that does both of the following:

1) Affects one or more of the following body systems: neurological, immunological, musculoskeletal, special sense organs, respiratory, including speech organs, cardiovascular, reproductive, digestive, genitourinary, hemic and lymphatic, skin, and endocrine.

2) Limits an individual's ability to participate in major life activities.

a) "Major Life Activities" are functions such as caring for one's self, performing manual tasks, walking, seeing, hearing, speaking, breathing, learning, and working. Pri-

mary attention is to be given to those life activities that affect employability, or otherwise present a barrier to employment or advancement.

(B) Any other health impairment not described in paragraph (A) that requires special education or related services.

(C) Being regarded as having or having had a disease, disorder, condition, cosmetic disfigurement, anatomical loss, or health impairment described in paragraph (A) or (B).

(D) Being regarded as having, or having had, a disease, disorder, condition, cosmetic disfigurement, anatomical loss, or health impairment that has no present disabling effect but may become a physical disability as described in paragraph (A) or (B).

(2) It is the intent of the Legislature that the definition of "physical disability" in Government Code Section 12926, subdivision (k), and in this subdivision, shall have the same meaning as the term "physical handicap" formerly defined by Government Code Section 12926 and construed in American National Ins. Co. v. Fair Employment & Housing Com., (1982) 32 Cal.3d 603.

(f) "Mental disability" includes any mental or psychological disorder, such as mental retardation, organic brain syndrome, emotional or mental illness, and specific learning disabilities.

(g) "Medical condition" includes any health impairment related to or associated with a diagnosis of cancer, for which a person has been rehabilitated or cured, based on competent medical evidence.

§ 7293.7. Establishing Disability Discrimination

Disability discrimination is established by showing that an employment practice denies, in whole or in part, an employment benefit to an individual because he or she is an individual with a disability.

§ 7293.8. Defenses

(a) In addition to any other defense provided herein, any defense permissible under Subchapter 1 shall be applicable to this subchapter.

(b) Inability to Perform. It is a permissible defense for an employer or other covered entity to demonstrate that, after reasonable accommodation has been made, the applicant or employee cannot perform the essential functions of the position in question because of his or her disability.

(c) Health or Safety of an Individual With a Disability. It is a permissible defense for an employer or other covered entity to demonstrate that after reasonable accommodation the applicant or employee cannot perform the essential functions of the position in question in a manner which would not endanger his or her health or safety because the job imposes an imminent and substantial degree of risk to the applicant or employee.

(d) Health and Safety of Others. It is a permissible defense for an employer or other covered entity to demonstrate that after reasonable accommodation has been made, the applicant or employee cannot perform the essential functions of the position in question in a manner which would not endanger the health or safety of others to a greater extent than if an individual without a disability performed the job.

(e) Future Risk. However, it is no defense to assert that an individual with a disability has a condition or a disease with a future risk, so long as the condition or disease does not presently interfere with his or her ability to perform the job in a manner that will not immediately endanger the individual with a disability or others, and the individual is able to safely perform the job over a reasonable length of time. "A reasonable length of time" is to be determined on an individual basis.

(f) Factors to be considered when determining the merits of the defenses enumerated in Section 7293.8(c)-(e) include, but are not limited to:

(1) Nature of the disability;

(2) Length of the training period relative to the length of time the employee is expected to be employed;

(3) Type of time commitment, if any, routinely required of all other employees for the job in question; and

(4) Normal workforce turnover.

(g) "Essential functions" means the fundamental job duties of the employment position the individual with a disability holds or desires. "Essential functions" does not include the marginal functions of the position.

(1) A job function may be considered essential for any of several reasons, including, but not limited to, any one or more of the following:

(A) The function may be essential because the reason the position exists is to perform that function.

(B) The function may be essential because of the limited number of employees available among whom the performance of that job function can be distributed.

(C) The function may be highly specialized, so that the incumbent in the position is hired for his or her expertise or ability to perform the particular function.

(2) Evidence of whether a particular function is essential includes, but is not limited to, the following:

(A) The employer's judgment as to which functions are essential.

(B) Written job descriptions prepared before advertising or interviewing applicants for the job.

(C) The amount of time spent on the job performing the function.

(D) The consequences of not requiring the incumbent to perform the function.

(E) The terms of a collective bargaining agreement.

(F) The work experiences of past incumbents in the job.

(G) The current work experience of incumbents in similar jobs.

§ 7293.9. Reasonable Accommodation

Any employer or other covered entity shall make reasonable accommodation to the disability of any individual with a disability if the employer or other covered entity knows of the disability, unless the employer or other covered entity can demonstrate that the accommodation would impose an undue hardship.

(a) Examples of Reasonable Accommodation. Reasonable accommodation may, but does not necessarily, include, nor is it limited to, such measures as:

(1) Accessibility. Making existing facilities used by employees readily accessible to and usable by individuals with disabilities;

(2) Job Restructuring. Job restructuring, reassignment to a vacant position, part-time or modified work schedules, acquisition or modification of equipment or devices, adjustment or modification of examinations, training materials or policies, the provision of qualified readers or interpreters, and other similar actions.

(b) "Undue hardship" means an action requiring significant difficulty or expense, when considered in light of the following factors:

(1) the nature and cost of the accommodation needed;

(2) the overall financial resources of the facilities involved in the provision of the reasonable accommodations, the number of persons employed at the facility, and the effect on expenses and resources or the impact otherwise of these accommodations upon the operation of the facility;

(3) the overall financial resources of the covered entity, the overall size of the business of a covered entity with respect to the number of employees, and the number, type, and location of its facilities;

(4) the type of operations, including the composition, structure, and functions of the workforce of the entity;

(5) the geographic separateness, administrative, or fiscal relationship of the facility or facilities.

(c) Accessibility Standards. To comply with Section 7293.9(a), the design, construction or alteration of premises shall be in conformance with the standards set forth by the Division of the State Architect in the State Building Code, Title 24, pursuant to Chapter 7 (commencing with Section 4450), Division 5 of Title 1 of the Government Code and Part 5.5 (commencing with Section 19955) and Division 13 of the Health and Safety Code.

§ 7294.0. Pre–Employment Practices

(a) Recruitment and Advertising.

(1) Employers and other covered entities engaged in recruiting activities shall consider individuals with disabilities on an equal basis with individuals without disabilities for all jobs unless pursuant to a permissible defense.

(2) It is unlawful to advertise or publicize an employment benefit in any way which discourages or is designed

to discourage individuals with disabilities to a greater extent than individuals without disabilities.

(b) Applications.

(1) An employer or other covered entity must consider applications from individuals with disabilities equally with applications from individuals without disabilities. Where applications are being accepted in the normal course of business, an application from an individual with a disability must be accepted.

(2) Prohibited Inquiries. It is unlawful to ask general questions on disability in an application form or pre-employment questionnaire or in the course of the selection process. Examples of prohibited inquiries are:

(A) "Do you have any particular disabilities?"

(B) "Have you ever been treated for any of the following diseases or conditions?"

(C) "Are you now receiving or have you ever received Workers Compensation?"

(3) Permissible Job–Related Inquiry. Except as provided in the Americans with Disabilities Act of 1990 (Public Law 101–336) (42 U.S.C.A. s12101 et seq.) and the regulations adopted pursuant thereto, nothing in Government Code Section 12940, subdivision (d), or in this subdivision, shall prohibit any employer from making, in connection with prospective employment, an inquiry as to, or a request for information regarding, the physical fitness, medical condition, physical condition, or medical history of applicants if that inquiry or request for information is directly related and pertinent to the position the applicant is applying for or directly related to a determination of whether the applicant would endanger his or her health or safety or the health or safety of others.

(c) Interviews. An employer or other covered entity shall make reasonable accommodation to the needs of individuals with disabilities in interviewing situations, e.g., providing interpreters for the hearing-impaired, or scheduling the interview in a room accessible to wheelchairs.

(d) Medical Examination. An employer may condition an offer of employment on the results of a medical examination conducted prior to the employee's entrance on duty in order to determine fitness for the job in question provided that:

(1) All entering employees in similar positions are subjected to such an examination.

(2) Where the results of such medical examination would result in disqualification, an applicant or employee may submit independent medical opinions for consideration before a final determination on disqualification is made.

(3) The results are to be maintained on separate forms and shall be accorded confidentiality as medical records, except that:

(A) Supervisors and managers may be informed of restrictions on the work or duties of individuals with disabilities and necessary accommodations; and

(B) First aid and safety personnel may be informed, where appropriate, that the condition might require emergency treatment.

§ 7294.1. Employee Selection

(a) Prospective Need for Reasonable Accommodation. An employer or other covered entity shall not deny an employment benefit because of the prospective need to make reasonable accommodation to an individual with a disability.

(b) Testing.

(1) An employer or other covered entity shall not make use of any testing criterion that discriminates against individuals with disabilities, unless:

(A) The test score or other selection criterion used is shown to be job-related for the position in question; and

(B) An alternative job-related test or criterion that does not discriminate against individuals with disabilities is not available.

(2) Tests of physical agility or strength shall not be used unless the physical agility or strength measured by such test is related to job performance.

(3) An employer or other covered entity shall select and administer tests concerning employment so as to best ensure that, when administered to any individual, including an individual with a disability, the test results accurately reflect the applicant's or employee's job skills, aptitude, or whatever other factor the test purports to measure rather than reflecting the applicant's or employee's disability, except when those skills are the factors that the tests purport to measure. To accomplish this end, reasonable accommodation must be made in testing conditions. For example:

(A) The test site must be accessible to applicants with a disability.

(B) For blind persons, an employer or other covered entity might translate written tests into Braille, provide or allow the use of a reader, or provide oral presentation of the test.

(C) For quadriplegic individuals, an employer or other covered entity might provide or allow someone to write for the applicant or to allow oral responses to written test questions.

(D) For individuals with a hearing impairment, an employer or other covered entity might provide or allow the services of an interpreter.

(E) For individuals whose disabilities interfere with their ability to communicate, an employer or other covered entity might allow additional time to complete the examination.

(F) Alternate tests or individualized assessments may be necessary where test modification is inappropriate.

Competent advice should be sought before attempting such modification since the validity of the test may be affected.

(4) Where reasonable accommodation is appropriate, an employer shall permit the use of readers, interpreters, or similar supportive individuals or instruments.

§ 7294.2. Terms, Conditions and Privileges of Employment

(a) Fringe Benefits. It shall be unlawful to condition any employment decision regarding an applicant or employee with a disability upon the waiver of any fringe benefit.

Subchapter 11.   Age Discrimination

§ 7295.0.   General Prohibition Against Discrimination on the Basis of Age over the Age of Forty

(a) Statement of Purpose. The purpose of the law prohibiting age discrimination in employment is to guarantee all protected individuals 40 or over employment opportunities commensurate with their abilities. These regulations are promulgated to assure that employment opportunities for those protected persons over the age of forty are based upon their abilities and are not conditioned upon age-based stereotypes and unsupported generalizations about their qualifications or job performance. In addition, these regulations are promulgated to clarify when the use of mandatory retirement programs which are based upon age over the age of forty is unlawful.

(b) Incorporation of General Regulations. These regulations pertaining to discrimination on the basis of age incorporate each of the provisions of Subchapters 1 and 2 of Chapter 2, unless a provision is specifically excluded or modified.

§ 7295.1.   Definitions

As used in this article the following definitions of terms apply, unless the context in which they are used indicates otherwise:

(a) "Employer" refers to all employers, public and private, as defined in Government Code Section 12926, except employers mandatorily or voluntarily subject to Government Code Sections 20983.5, 20983.6, 21258.1, 31671.03 or 45346, or subject to Education Code Section 23922.

(b) "Public employer" refers to public agencies as defined in Government Code Sections 31204 and 20009.

(c) "Private employer" refers to all employers not defined in subsection (b) above.

(d) "Retirement or Pension Program" refers to any plan, program or policy of an employer which is in writing and has been communicated to eligible or affected employees, which is intended to provide an employee with income upon retirement (this may include pension plans, profit-sharing plans, money-purchase plans, tax-sheltered annuities, employer sponsored Individual Retirement Accounts, employee stock ownership plans, matching thrift plans, or stock bonus plans or other forms of defined benefit or defined contribution plans).

(e) "Collective Bargaining Agreement" refers to any collective bargaining agreement between an employer and a labor organization which is in writing.

(f) "Normal Retirement Date or NRD" refers to one of the following dates:

(1) for employees participating in a private employee pension plan regulated under the federal Employee Retirement Income Security Act of 1974, the NRD refers to the time a plan participant reaches normal retirement age under the plan or refers to the later of either the time a plan participant reaches 65 or the tenth anniversary of the time a plan participant commenced participation in the plan;

(2) for employees not described under (1) whose employers have a written retirement policy or whose employers are parties to a collective bargaining agreement which specifies retirement practices, the NRD refers to the normal retirement time or age specified in such a policy or agreement; or

(3) for employees not described under either (1) or (2) the NRD refers to the last calendar day of the month in which an employee reaches his or her seventieth, 70th, birthday.

(g) (Reserved.)

(h) "Basis of Age" or "Ground of Age" refers to age over forty.

(i) "Over Forty" refers to the chronological age of an individual who has reached his or her fortieth birthday.

(j) "Age Based Stereotype" refers to generalized opinions about matters including the qualifications, job performance, health, work habits, and productivity of individuals over forty.

(k) "Employment Benefit" refers to employment benefit as defined in Section 7286.5(f). It also includes a workplace free of harassment as defined in Section 7286.7(b) of Subchapter 2.

§ 7295.2.   Establishing Age Discrimination

(a) Employers. Discrimination on the basis of age may be established by showing that a job applicant's or employee's age over forty was considered in the denial of an employment benefit.

(b) Employment Agencies, Labor Organizations, and Apprenticeship Training Programs in Which the State Participates. Discrimination on the basis of age may be established against employment agencies, labor organizations, and apprenticeship training programs in which the state participates upon a showing that they have engaged in recruitment, screening, advertising, training, job referral, placement or similar activities which discriminate against an individual or individuals over forty.

§ 7295.3. Defenses

(a) Defenses. Generally. In addition to any other defense provided herein, once an inference of employment discrimination on the basis of age has been established, an employer or other covered entity may prove one or more appropriate defenses as generally set forth in Section 7286.7 of Subchapter 2.

(b) Specific Defenses, Exemptions, Permissible Practices. An employment practice which discriminates on the basis of age is permissible, exempted, or has a valid defense:

(1) If the practice is otherwise mandated or permitted, by federal or state law which preempts, supersedes, or otherwise takes precedence over the Act;

(2) If the practice, at the time it occurred, was deemed lawful by the terms of one or more sections of this subchapter;

(3) If the practice is declared by one or more sections of this subchapter to be permissible or lawful.

§ 7295.4. Pre–Employment Practices

(a) Recruitment and Advertising.

(1) Recruitment. The provisions of Section 7287.3 (a) are applicable and are incorporated by reference herein.

Generally, during recruitment it is unlawful for employers to refuse to consider applicants because they are over forty years of age. However, it is lawful for an employer to participate in established recruitment programs with high schools, colleges, universities and trade schools. It is also lawful for employers to utilize temporary hiring programs directed at youth, even though such programs traditionally provide disproportionately few applicants who are over forty. However, exclusive screening and hiring of applicants provided through the above recruitment or temporary programs will constitute discrimination on the basis of age if the programs are used to evade the Act's prohibition against age discrimination.

(2) Advertising. It is unlawful for an employer to either express a preference for individuals under forty or to express a limitation against individuals over forty when advertising employment opportunities by any means such as the media, employment agencies, and job announcements.

§ 7295.5. Pre–Employment Inquiries, Interviews and Applications

(a) Pre–Employment Inquiries. Pre-employment inquiries which would result in the direct or indirect identification of persons on the basis of age are unlawful. This provision applies to oral and written inquiries and interviews. (See Section 7287.3(b), which is applicable and incorporated by reference herein.)

Pre-employment inquiries which result in the identification of persons on the basis of age shall not be unlawful when made for purposes of applicable reporting requirements or to maintain applicant flow data provided that the inquiries are made in a manner consistent with

Section 7287.0 (and particularly subsection (b) of Subchapter 2.

(b) Applications. It is discrimination on the basis of age for an employer or other covered entity to reject or refuse to seriously and fairly consider the application form, preemployment questionnaire, oral application or the oral or written inquiry of an individual because such individual is over forty. (See Section 7287.3(c), which is applicable and incorporated by reference herein.)

§ 7295.6. Physical or Medical Examination of Applicants and Employees

(a) It is not a violation of this subchapter for an employer to require an applicant who is over forty to undergo physical or medical examinations to determine whether or not the applicant meets the job-related physical or medical standards for the position sought so long as such examinations are uniformly and equally required of all applicants for the position, regardless of their age.

(b) It is not a violation of this subchapter for an employer to require an employee who is over forty to undergo a physical or medical examination at reasonable times and intervals and at the expense of the employer to determine whether or not the employee continues to meet the job-related physical or medical standards for the position held so long as such examinations are uniformly and equally required of all similarly situated employees in the particular job class regardless of their age.

(c) It is discrimination based on age to require an applicant or employee over forty to meet physical or medical examination standards which are higher then those standards applied to applicants or employees who are below the age of forty and are seeking or holding the same job.

§ 7295.7. Employee Selection

(a) Selection. So long as age is not a factor, this subchapter does not preclude an employer from selecting an individual who is in fact better qualified than other applicants, and it does not preclude an employer from hiring an individual on the basis of experience and training superior to other applicants.

(b) Selection Based Upon Seniority or Prior Service. So long as age is not a factor, it is not a violation of this subchapter for an employer, during the process of selection, to give a candidate who has a record of seniority or time in prior service with that employer preference over a candidate who has no such record or who has less seniority or time in prior service with that employer. However, where candidates for hire have the same record of seniority or time in prior service, it is discrimination based on age, in selecting from among them, to refuse to select a candidate because he or she is over forty.

§ 7295.8. Promotions

(a) In selecting a candidate for promotion, it is not, itself, a violation of this subchapter, for an employer to limit the group of eligible candidates to members of the employer's existing workforce or to give a preference in selection to an incumbent employee over a candidate who is not an incumbent employee. However, in evaluating or selecting candidates for promotion from among its existing workforce, it is discrimination on the basis of age for an employer to evaluate unequally or to fail to select a candidate who is over forty because of the age of the candidate.

(b) In selecting a candidate for promotion, it is not, itself, a violation of this subchapter for an employer to promote a candidate under the age of forty in preference to a candidate over forty on the basis of the superior experience and training of the younger candidate, or on the basis of other legitimate reasons, so long as age is not a factor.

(c) It is discrimination on the basis of age for an employer to deny an employee the opportunity to gain the experience and training necessary to achieve promotion, because such employee is over forty.

§ 7296.0. Retirement Practices

(a) Mandatory Retirement–Generally. Generally, it is discrimination on the basis of age for a private employer to discharge or force the retirement of an employee because such employee has reached a certain chronological age over forty.

(b) Retirement Plans Generally. Generally, any provision in a private employer's retirement plan, pension plan, collective bargaining agreement or similar plan or agreement which requires mandatory retirement of an employee over forty years of age is unlawful.

(c) Mandatory Retirement Permitted. Mandatory retirement of the following employees is not unlawful:

(1) Prior to July 1, 1982, any employee who has attained 65 years of age, and thereafter 70 years of age, and is serving under a contract of unlimited tenure, or similar arrangement providing for unlimited tenure at an institution of higher education as defined by Section 1201(a) of the Federal Higher Education Act of 1965;

(2) Any employee who has attained 65 years of age and who for the two year period immediately prior to retirement, was employed in a bona fide executive or high policymaking position, providing that at the time of mandatory retirement, the employee is entitled to receive an immediate non-forfeitable annual retirement benefit from the current employer which equals a minimum of $27,000.00, and is either derived from one or a combination of plans such as profitsharing, pension, savings, or deferred compensation plans.

(3) Any employee who has attained 70 years of age and is a physician employed by a professional medical corporation, the articles or bylaws of which provide for compulsory retirement.

§ 7296.1. Procedures for Continuing in Employment Past the Normal Retirement Date

Where a private employer has a private pension or retirement program, the following procedures apply:

(a) Advisory Notice by the Employer. Private employers must advise their employees who are nearing their normal retirement date that if they intend to continue in employment beyond their NRD, they must file a written notice of this intention. The employer's Advisory Notice should be in writing, and should be provided to the employee no later than ninety (90) days prior to the NRD and no earlier than one hundred and eighty (180) days prior to the NRD. The Advisory Notice to the employee must clearly indicate when his or her Continuation Notice, as described in subsection (b), must be submitted.

(b) Continuation Notice by the Employee. An employee of a private employer who wishes to continue working beyond his or her NRD must provide a written notification of this intention to the employer not more than forty-five (45) days after the employee receives an Advisory Notice from the employer as described in subsection (a).

(c) Notice by Employee Following the Normal Retirement Date. An employee continuing in employment past the normal retirement date has an obligation to provide his or her private employer with written notice in advance of the date on which he or she intends to retire from employment. Such notice of retirement should be provided at a reasonable time, no later than sixty (60) days prior to the employee's anticipated date of retirement.

(d) Notice by Private Employer Following the Normal Retirement Date. Where an employee continues in employment beyond his or her NRD, a private employer does not violate this article by periodically sending a written notice to such employee seeking to determine if the employee intends to continue in employment. However, the initial notice of this kind should not be sent to the employee until at least two years following his or her normal retirement date has elapsed. Subsequent thereto, the notice should not be sent more frequently than on an annual basis.

§ 7296.2. Termination and Disciplinary Actions

(a) It is not a violation of this subchapter for an employer to terminate, discharge, dismiss, demote or otherwise discipline an employee over forty who fails to perform the normal functions of his or her position or who fails to conform to the bona fide requirements of his or her position, so long as the performance standards and job requirements do not discriminate against employees over forty.

(b) Where an employee is continuing in employment beyond his or her normal retirement date, it is not a violation of this subchapter for an employer to terminate, force the retirement of, or otherwise discipline such an employee if the employee's job performance no longer satisfies the employer's performance standards. Any such performance standards for quality of work must not be arbitrary and must not be based upon the age of the employee.

Subchapter 12.   Family Care and Medical Leave

§ 7297.0.   Definitions

The following definitions apply only to this subchapter. The definitions in the federal regulations issued January 6, 1995 (29 CFR Part 825), interpreting the Family and Medical Leave Act of 1993 (FMLA) (29 U.S.C. ss 2601 et seq.) shall also apply to this subchapter, to the extent that they are not inconsistent with the following definitions:

(a) "Certification" means a written communication from the health care provider of the child, parent, spouse, or employee with a serious health condition to the employer of the employee requesting a family care leave to care for the employee's child, parent or spouse or a medical leave for the employee's own serious health condition.

(1) For family care leave for the employee's child, parent, or spouse, this certification need not identify the serious health condition involved, but shall contain:

(A) the date, if known, on which the serious health condition commenced,

(B) the probable duration of the condition,

(C) an estimate of the amount of time which the health care provider believes the employee needs to care for the child, parent or spouse, and

(D) a statement that the serious health condition warrants the participation of the employee to provide care during a period of treatment or supervision of the child, parent or spouse.

1) "Warrants the participation of the employee" includes, but is not limited to, providing psychological comfort, and arranging "third party" care for the child, parent or spouse, as well as directly providing, or participating in, the medical care.

(2) For medical leave for the employee's own serious health condition, this certification need not, but may, at the employee's option, identify the serious health condition involved. It shall contain:

(A) The date, if known, on which the serious health condition commenced,

(B) The probable duration of the condition, and

(C) A statement that, due to the serious health condition, the employee is unable to work at all or is unable to perform any one or more of the essential functions of his or her position.

(b) "CFRA" means the Moore–Brown–Roberti California Family Rights Act of 1993. (California Family Rights Act, Gov. Code ss 12945.1 and 12945.2.) "CFRA leave" means family care or medical leave taken pursuant to CFRA.

(c) "Child" means a biological, adopted, or foster son or daughter, a stepson or stepdaughter, a legal ward, or a

child of an employee who stands in loco parentis to that child, who is either under 18 years of age or an adult dependent child. An adult dependent child is an individual who is 18 years of age or older and who is incapable of self-care because of a mental or physical disability within the meaning of Government Code section 12926, subdivisions (i) and (k).

(1) "In loco parentis" means in the place of a parent; instead of a parent; charged with a parent's rights, duties, and responsibilities. It does not require a biological or legal relationship.

(d) "Covered employer" means any person or individual engaged in any business or enterprise in California who directly employs 50 or more persons within any State of the United States, the District of Columbia or any Territory or possession of the United States to perform services for a wage or salary. It also includes the state of California, counties, and any other political or civil subdivision of the state and cities, regardless of the number of employees. There is no requirement that the 50 employees work at the same location or work full time.

(1) "Directly employs" means that the employer maintains an aggregate of at least fifty part or full time employees on its payroll(s) for each working day during each of 20 or more calendar workweeks in the current or preceding calendar year. The workweeks do not have to be consecutive. The phrase "current or preceding calendar year" refers to the calendar year in which the employee requests the leave or the calendar year preceding this request.

(2) "Perform services for a wage or salary" excludes independent contractors as defined in Labor Code section 3353 but includes persons who are compensated in whole or in part by commission.

(e) "Eligible employee" means a full or part time employee working in California with more than 12 months (52 weeks) of service with the employer at any time, and who has actually worked (within the meaning of the Fair Labor Standards Act, 29 CFR Part 785) for the employer at least 1,250 hours during the 12–month period immediately prior to the date the CFRA leave or FMLA leave is to commence.

(1) Once the employee meets these two eligibility criteria and takes a leave for a qualifying event, the employee does not have to requalify, in terms of the numbers of hours worked, in order to take additional leave for the same qualifying event during the employee's 12–month leave period.

(2) For an employee who takes a pregnancy disability leave which is also a FMLA leave, and who then wants to take CFRA leave for reason of the birth of her child immediately after her pregnancy disability leave, the 12–month period during which she must have worked 1,250 hours is that period immediately preceding her first day of FMLA leave based on her pregnancy, not the first day of the subsequent CFRA leave for reason of the birth of her child.

(3) In order to be eligible, the employee must also work for an employer who maintains on the payroll, as of the date the employee gives notice of the need for leave, at least 50 part or full time employees within 75 miles, measured in surface miles, using surface transportation, of the worksite where the employee requesting the leave is employed.

(A) Once the employee meets this eligibility criterion and takes a leave for a qualifying event, the employer may not cut short the leave or deny any subsequent leave taken for the same qualifying event during the employee's 12–month leave period, even if the number of employees within the relevant 75–mile radius falls below 50. In such cases, however, the employee would not be eligible for any subsequent leave requested for a different qualifying event.

(f) "Employment in the same position" means employment in, or reinstatement to, the original position which the employee held prior to taking a CFRA leave.

(g) "Employment in a comparable position" means employment in a position which is virtually identical to the employee's original position in terms of pay, benefits, and working conditions, including privileges, perquisites and status. It must involve the same or substantially similar duties and responsibilities, which must entail substantially equivalent skill, effort, responsibility, and authority. It must be performed at the same or geographically proximate worksite from where the employee was previously employed. It ordinarily means the same shift or the same or an equivalent work schedule. It has the same meaning as the term "equivalent position" in FMLA and its implementing regulations.

(h) "Family care leave" means either:

(1) Leave of up to a total of 12 workweeks in a 12–month period for reason of the birth of a child of the employee, the placement of a child with an employee in connection with the adoption or foster care of the child by the employee, and a guarantee of employment, made at the time the leave is granted, in the same or a comparable position upon termination of the leave; or

(2) Leave of up to a total of 12 workweeks in a 12–month period to care for a child, parent or spouse of the employee who has a serious health condition, and a guarantee of employment, made at the time the leave is granted, in the same or a comparable position upon termination of the leave.

(i) "FMLA" means the federal Family and Medical Leave Act of 1993, 29 U.S.C. ss 2601 et seq., and its implementing regulations, 29 CFR Part 825, issued January 6, 1995. "FMLA leave" means family care or medical leave taken pursuant to FMLA.

(j) "Health care provider" means either:

(1) an individual holding either a physician's and surgeon's certificate issued pursuant to Article 4 (commencing with Section 2080) of Chapter 5 of Division 2 of the Business and Professions Code or an osteopathic physician's and surgeon's certificate issued pursuant to

Article 4.5 (commencing with Section 2099.5) of Chapter 5 of Division 2 of the Business and Professions Code, or any other individual duly licensed as a physician, surgeon, or osteopathic physician or surgeon in another state or jurisdiction, including another country, who directly treats or supervises the treatment of the serious health condition, or

(2) any other person who meets the definition of others "capable of providing health care services," as set forth in FMLA and its implementing regulations.

(k) "Medical leave" means leave of up to a total of 12 workweeks in a 12–month period because of an employee's own serious health condition that makes the employee unable to work at all or unable to perform any one or more of the essential functions of the position of that employee. The term "essential functions" is defined in Government Code section 12926, subdivision (f). "Medical leave" does not include leave taken for an employee's pregnancy disability, as defined in (m) below, except as specified below in section 7297.6, subdivision (c)(1).

(l) "Parent" means a biological, foster, or adoptive parent, a stepparent, a legal guardian, or other person who stood in loco parentis to the employee when the employee was a child. A biological or legal relationship is not necessary for a person to have stood in loco parentis to the employee as a child. Parent does not include a parent-in-law.

(m) "Pregnancy disability leave" means a leave taken for disability on account of pregnancy, childbirth, or related medical conditions, pursuant to Government Code section 12945, subdivision (b)(2), and defined in section 7291.2, subdivision (o) of the regulations.

(n) "Reinstatement" means "restoration" within the meaning of FMLA and its implementing regulations.

(o) "Serious health condition" means an illness, injury (including on-the-job injuries), impairment, or physical or mental condition of the employee or a child, parent or spouse of the employee which involves either:

(1) inpatient care (i.e., an overnight stay) in a hospital, hospice, or residential health care facility, or

(2) continuing treatment or continuing supervision by a health care provider, as detailed in FMLA and its implementing regulations.

(p) "Spouse" means a partner in marriage as defined in Family Code section 300.

(q) "Twelve workweeks" means the equivalent of twelve of the employee's normally scheduled workweeks. (See also section 7297.3, subdivision (d).)

§ 7297.1. Right to CFRA Leave: Denial of Leave; Reasonable Request; Permissible Limitation

(a) It is an unlawful employment practice for a covered employer to refuse to grant, upon reasonable request, a CFRA leave to an eligible employee, unless such refusal is justified by the permissible limitation specified below in subdivision (c).

(b) Denial of leave.

(1) Burden of proof.

Denial of a request for CFRA leave is established if the Department or the employee shows, by a preponderance of the evidence, that the employer was a covered employer, the employee making the request was an eligible employee, the request was for a CFRA qualifying purpose, the request was reasonable, and the employer denied the request for CFRA leave.

(2) Reasonable request.

A request to take a CFRA leave is reasonable if it complies with any applicable notice requirements, as specified in section 7297.4, and if it is accompanied, where required, by a certification, as that term is defined in section 7297.0, subdivision (a).

(c) Limitation on Entitlement.

If both parents are eligible for CFRA leave but are employed by the same employer, that employer may limit leave for the birth, adoption or foster care placement of their child to 12 workweeks in a 12–month period between the two parents. The employer may not limit their entitlement to CFRA leave for any other qualifying purpose. If the parents are unmarried, they may have different family care leave rights under FMLA.

§ 7297.2. Right to Reinstatement: Guarantee of Reinstatement; Refusal to Reinstate; Permissible Defenses

(a) Guarantee of Reinstatement.

Upon granting the CFRA leave, the employer shall guarantee to reinstate the employee to the same or a comparable position, subject to the defenses permitted by section 7297.2, subdivisions (c)(1) and (c)(2), and shall provide the guarantee in writing upon request of the employee. It is an unlawful employment practice for an employer, after granting a requested CFRA leave, to refuse to honor its guarantee of reinstatement to the same or a comparable position at the end of the leave, unless the refusal is justified by the defenses stated in s 7297.2, subdivisions (c)(1) and (c)(2).

(b) Refusal to reinstate.

(1) Definite Date of Reinstatement.

Where a definite date of reinstatement has been agreed upon at the beginning of the leave, a refusal to reinstate is established if the Department or employee proves, by a preponderance of the evidence, that the leave was granted by the employer and that the employer failed to reinstate the employee to the same or a comparable position by the date agreed upon.

(2) Change in Date of Reinstatement.

If the reinstatement date differs from the employer's and employee's original agreement, a refusal to reinstate is established if the Department or employee proves, by a preponderance of the evidence, that the employer failed to reinstate the employee to the same or a comparable position within two business days, where feasible, after the employee notifies the employer of his or her readiness to return, as required by the FMLA regulations.

(c) Permissible defenses.

(1) Employment Would Have Ceased

An employee has no greater right to reinstatement or to other benefits and conditions of employment than if the employee had been continuously employed during the CFRA leave period. An employer has the burden of proving, by a preponderance of the evidence, that an employee would not otherwise have been employed at the time reinstatement is requested in order to deny reinstatement.

(A) If an employee is laid off during the course of taking CFRA leave and employment is terminated, the employer's responsibility to continue CFRA leave, maintain group health plan benefits and reinstate the employee ceases at the time the employee is laid off, provided the employer has no continuing obligations under a collective bargaining agreement or otherwise.

(2) "Key Employee."

A refusal to reinstate a "key employee" to his or her same position or to a comparable position is justified if the employer shows, by a preponderance of the evidence, that all of the following conditions exist:

(A) The employee requesting the CFRA leave is a salaried employee, and

(B) The employee requesting the leave is among the highest paid ten percent of the employer's employees who are employed within 75 miles of the worksite at which that employee is employed at the time of the leave request, and

(C) The refusal to reinstate the employee is necessary because the employee's reinstatement will cause substantial and grievous economic injury to the operations of the employer, and

(D) The employer notifies the employee of the intent to refuse reinstatement at the time the employer determines that the refusal is necessary under (C) above, and

(E) In any case in which the leave has already commenced, the employer shall give the employee a reasonable opportunity to return to work following the notice prescribed in (D) above.

§ 7297.3. Computation of Time Periods: Twelve Workweeks; Minimum Duration

(a) CFRA leave does not need to be taken in one continuous period of time. It cannot exceed more than 12 workweeks total for any purpose in a 12–month period.

(b) If the leave is common to both CFRA and FMLA, this 12–month period will run concurrently with the 12–month period under FMLA. An employer may choose any of the methods allowed in the FMLA regulations, issued January 6, 1995, 29 CFR Part 825, section 825.200, subdivision (b), for determining the "12–month period" in which the 12 weeks of leave entitlement occurs. The employer must, however, apply the chosen method consistently and uniformly to all employees.

(c) "Twelve workweeks" as that term is defined in section 7297.0, subdivision (q), means the equivalent of twelve of the employee's normally scheduled workweeks. For eligible employees who work more or less than five days a week, or who work on alternative work schedules, the number of working days which constitutes "twelve weeks" is calculated on a pro rata or proportional basis.

(1) For example, for a full time employee who works five eight-hour days per week, "twelve workweeks" means 60 working and/or paid eight-hour days of leave entitlement. For an employee who works half time, "twelve workweeks" may mean 30 eight-hour days or 60 four-hour days, or twelve workweeks of whatever is the employee's normal half-time work schedule. For an employee who normally works six eight-hour days, "twelve workweeks" means 72 working and/or paid eight-hour days of leave entitlement.

(2) If an employee takes leave on an intermittent or reduced work schedule, only the amount of leave actually taken may be counted toward the twelve weeks of leave to which the employee is entitled. For example, if an employee needs physical therapy which requires an absence from work of two hours a week, only those two hours can be charged against the employee's CFRA leave entitlement.

(3) If a holiday falls within a week taken as CFRA leave, the week is nevertheless counted as a week of CFRA leave. If, however, the employer's business activity has temporarily ceased for some reason and employees generally are not expected to report for work for one or more weeks, (e.g., a school closing for two weeks for the Christmas/New Year holiday or summer vacation or an employer closing the plant for retooling), the days the employer's activities have ceased do not count against the employee's CFRA entitlement.

(d) Minimum duration for CFRA leaves taken for the birth, adoption, or foster care placement of a child. CFRA leave taken for reason of the birth, adoption, or foster care placement of a child of the employee does not have to be taken in one continuous period of time. Any leave(s) taken shall be concluded within one year of the birth or placement of the child with the employee in connection with the adoption or foster care of the child by the employee. The basic minimum duration of the leave shall be two weeks. However, an employer shall grant a request for a CFRA leave of less than two weeks' duration on any two occasions.

(e) Minimum duration for CFRA leaves taken for the serious health condition of a parent, child, or spouse or for the serious health condition of the employee. Where CFRA leave is taken for a serious health condition of the employee's child, parent or spouse or of the employee, leave may be taken intermittently or on a reduced work schedule when medically necessary, as determined by the health care provider of the person with the serious health condition. An employer may limit leave increments to the shortest period of time that the employer's payroll system uses to account for absences or use of leave.

(1) If an employee needs intermittent leave or leave on a reduced work schedule that is foreseeable based on planned medical treatment for the employee or a family member, the employer may require the employee to transfer temporarily to an available alternative position. This alternative position must have the equivalent rate of pay and benefits, the employee must be qualified for the position, and it must better accommodate recurring periods of leave than the employee's regular job. It does not have to have equivalent duties. Transfer to an alternative position may include altering an existing job to accommodate better the employee's need for intermittent leave or a reduced work schedule.

(2) CFRA leave, including intermittent leave and/or reduced work schedules, is available to instructional employees of educational establishments and institutions under the same conditions as apply to all other eligible employees.

§ 7297.4. Requests for CFRA Leave: Advance Notice; Certification; Employer Response

(a) Advance Notice.

(1) Verbal Notice.

An employee shall provide at least verbal notice sufficient to make the employer aware that the employee needs CFRA-qualifying leave, and the anticipated timing and duration of the leave. The employee need not expressly assert rights under CFRA or FMLA, or even mention CFRA or FMLA, to meet the notice requirement; however, the employee must state the reason the leave is needed, such as, for example, the expected birth of a child or for medical treatment. The employer should inquire further of the employee if it is necessary to have more information about whether CFRA leave is being sought by the employee and obtain the necessary details of the leave to be taken.

(A) Under all circumstances, it is the employer's responsibility to designate leave, paid or unpaid, as CFRA or CFRA/FMLA qualifying, based on information provided by the employee or the employee's spokesperson, and to give notice of the designation to the employee.

(B) Employers may not retroactively designate leave as "CFRA leave" after the employee has returned to work, except under those same circumstances provided for in FMLA and its implementing regulations for retroactively counting leave as "FMLA leave."

(2) 30 Days Advance Notice.

An employer may require that employees provide at least 30 days advance notice before CFRA leave is to begin if the need for the leave is foreseeable based on an expected birth, placement for adoption or foster care, or planned medical treatment for a serious health condition of the employee or a family member. The employee shall consult with the employer and make a reasonable effort to schedule any planned medical treatment or supervision so as to minimize disruption to the operations of the employer. Any such scheduling, however, shall be subject to the approval of the health care provider of the employee or the employee's child, parent or spouse.

(3) When 30 Days Not Practicable.

If 30 days notice is not practicable, such as because of a lack of knowledge of approximately when leave will be required to begin, a change in circumstances, or a medical emergency, notice must be given as soon as practicable.

(4) Prohibition Against Denial of Leave in Emergency or Unforeseeable Circumstances.

An employer shall not deny a CFRA leave, the need for which is an emergency or is otherwise unforeseeable, on the basis that the employee did not provide advance notice of the need for the leave.

(5) Employer Obligation to Inform Employees of Notice Requirement.

An employer shall give its employees reasonable advance notice of any notice requirements which it adopts. The employer may incorporate its notice requirements in the general notice requirements in section 7297.9 and such incorporation shall constitute "reasonable advance notice." Failure of the employer to give or post such notice shall preclude the employer from taking any adverse action against the employee, including denying CFRA leave, for failing to furnish the employer with advance notice of a need to take CFRA leave.

(6) Employer Response to Leave Request.

The employer shall respond to the leave request as soon as practicable and in any event no later than ten calendar days after receiving the request. The employer shall attempt to respond to the leave request before the date the leave is due to begin. Once given, approval shall be deemed retroactive to the date of the first day of the leave.

(b) Medical Certification.

(1) Serious Health Condition of Child, Parent, or Spouse.

As a condition of granting a leave for the serious health condition of the employee's child, parent or spouse, the employer may require certification of the serious health condition, as defined in section 7297.0, subdivision (a)(1). If the certification satisfies the requirements of section 7297.0, subdivision (a)(1), the employer must accept it as sufficient. Upon expiration of the time period which the health care provider originally estimated that the employee needed to take care of the employee's child, parent or spouse, the employer may require the employee to obtain recertification if additional leave is requested.

(2) Serious Health Condition of Employee.

As a condition of granting a leave for the serious health condition of the employee, the employer may require certification of the serious health condition, as defined in section 7297.0, subdivision (a)(2). Upon expiration of the

time period which the health care provider originally estimated that the employee needed for his/her own serious health condition, the employer may require the employee to obtain recertification if additional leave is requested.

(A) If the employer has reason to doubt the validity of the certification provided by the employee for his/her own serious health condition, the employer may require, at the employer's own expense, that the employee obtain the opinion of a second health care provider, designated or approved by the employer, concerning any information in the certification. The health care provider designated or approved by the employer shall not be employed on a regular basis by the employer.

1) The employer may not ask the employee to provide additional information beyond that allowed by these regulations.

2) The employer is responsible for complying with all applicable law regarding the confidentiality of any medical information received.

(B) In any case in which the second opinion described in (b)(2)(A) differs from the opinion in the original certification, the employer may require, at the employer's expense, that the employee obtain the opinion of a third health care provider, designated or approved jointly by both the employer and the employee, concerning any information in the certification.

(C) The opinion of the third health care provider concerning the information in the certification shall be considered to be final and shall be binding on the employer and the employee.

(D) The employer is required to provide the employee with a copy of the second and third medical opinions, where applicable, without cost, upon the request of the employee.

(E) As a condition of an employee's return from medical leave, the employer may require that the employee obtain a release to "return-to-work" from his/her health care provider stating that he/she is able to resume work only if the employer has a uniformly applied practice or policy of requiring such releases from other employees returning to work after illness, injury or disability.

(3) Providing Certification.

The employer may require that the employee provide any certification within fifteen calendar days of the employer's request for such certification, unless it is not practicable for the employee to do so despite the employee's good faith efforts. This means that, in some cases, the leave may begin before the employer receives the certification.

§ 7297.5. Terms of CFRA Leave

(a) The following rules apply to the permissible terms of a CFRA leave, to the extent that they are consistent with the requirements of the Employee Retirement Income Security Act (ERISA), 29 U.S.C. s 1001 et seq.

Nothing in these regulations infringes on the employer's obligations, if any, under the Consolidated Omnibus Budget Reconciliation Act of 1985 (COBRA) (29 U.S.C. s1161 et seq.) or prohibits an employer from granting CFRA leave on terms more favorable to the employee than those listed below.

(b) Paid Leave.

An employer is not required to pay an employee during a CFRA leave except:

(1) An employee may elect to use any accrued vacation time or other paid accrued time off (including undifferentiated paid time off ("PTO")), other than accrued sick leave, that the employee is otherwise eligible to take during the otherwise unpaid portion of the CFRA leave.

(2) Only if the employee asks for leave for what would be a CFRA-qualifying event may an employer require the employee to use any accrued vacation time or other paid accrued time off (including "PTO" time), other than accrued sick leave, that the employee is otherwise eligible to take during the otherwise unpaid portion of the CFRA leave.

(A) If an employee requests to utilize accrued vacation time or other paid accrued time off without reference to a CFRA-qualifying purpose, an employer may not ask whether the employee is taking the time off for a CFRA-qualifying purpose.

1) If the employer denies the employee's request and the employee then provides information that the requested time off is or may be for a CFRA-qualifying purpose, the employer may inquire further into the reasons for the absence. If the absence is CFRA-qualifying, then the rules in section 7297.5, subdivision (b)(1) and (2), above, apply.

(3) An employer may require the employee to use, or an employee may elect to use, any accrued sick leave that the employee is otherwise eligible to take during the otherwise unpaid portion of a CFRA leave for:

(A) the employee's own serious health condition, or

(B) any other reason if mutually agreed to between the employer and the employee.

(4) An employer and employee may negotiate for the employee's use of any additional paid or unpaid time off to substitute for the CFRA leave provided by this section.

(c) Provision of Health Benefits.

If the employer provides health benefits under any "group health plan," the employer has an obligation to continue providing such benefits during an employee's CFRA leave, FMLA leave, or both. The following rules apply:

(1) The employer shall maintain and pay for the employee's health coverage at the same level and under the same conditions as coverage would have been provided if the employee had been continuously employed during the entire leave period.

(2) This obligation commences on the date leave first begins under FMLA (i.e., for pregnancy disability leaves) or under FMLA/CFRA (i.e., for all other family care and medical leaves). The obligation continues for the duration of the leave(s), up to a maximum of 12 workweeks in a 12–month period.

(3) A "group health plan" is as defined in section 5000, subdivision (b)(1), of the Internal Revenue Code of 1986. If the employer's group health plan includes dental care, eye care, mental health counselling, et cetera, or if it includes coverage for the employee's dependents as well as for the employee, the employer shall also continue this coverage.

(4) Although the employer's obligation to continue group health benefits under either FMLA or CFRA, or both, does not exceed 12 workweeks in a 12–month period, nothing shall preclude the employer from maintaining and paying for health care coverage for longer than 12 workweeks.

(5) An employer may recover the premium that the employer paid for maintaining group health care coverage during any unpaid part of the CFRA leave if both of the following conditions occur:

(A) The employee fails to return from leave after the period of leave to which the employee is entitled has expired. An employee is deemed to have "failed to return from leave" if he/she works less than 30 days after returning from CFRA leave.

(B) The employee's failure to return from leave is for a reason other than the continuation, recurrence, or onset of a serious health condition that entitles the employee to CFRA leave, or other circumstances beyond the control of the employee.

(d) Other Benefits and Seniority Accrual

During the period of CFRA leave, the employee is entitled to accrual of seniority and to participate in health plans for any additional period of leave not covered by (c) above, and also in any employee benefit plans, including life, short-term or long-term disability or accident insurance, pension and retirement plans, and supplemental unemployment benefit plans to the same extent and under the same conditions as would apply to any other leave granted by the employer for any reason other than CFRA leave.

(1) Unpaid CFRA leave for the serious health condition of the employee shall be compared to other unpaid disability leaves whereas unpaid CFRA leaves for all other purposes shall be compared to other unpaid personal leaves offered by the employer.

(2) If the employer's policy allows seniority to accrue when employees are out on paid leave, such as paid sick or vacation leave, then seniority will accrue during any part of a paid CFRA leave.

(3) The employee returning from CFRA leave shall return with no less seniority than the employee had when the leave commenced for purposes of layoff, recall,

promotion, job assignment, and seniority-related benefits such as vacation.

(e) Continuation of Other Benefits.

If the employer has no policy, practice or collective bargaining agreement which requires or authorizes any other type of unpaid personal or disability leave or if the employer's other unpaid personal or disability leaves do not allow for the continuation of benefits during these leaves, an employee taking a CFRA leave shall be entitled to continue to participate in the employer's health plans, pension and retirement plans, supplemental unemployment benefit plans or any other health and welfare employee benefit plan, in accordance with the terms of those plans, during the period of the CFRA leave.

(1) As a condition of continued coverage of group medical benefits (beyond the employer's obligation during the 12–week period described above in (c)), life insurance, short-or long-term disability plans or insurance, accident insurance, or other similar health and welfare employee benefit plans during any unpaid portion of the leave, the employer may require the employee to pay premiums at the group rate.

(A) If the employee elects not to pay premiums to continue these benefits, this nonpayment of premiums shall not constitute a break in service for purposes of longevity, seniority under any collective bargaining agreement or any employee benefit plan requiring the payment of premiums.

(2) An employer is not required to make plan payments to any pension and/or retirement plan or to count the leave period for purposes of "time accrued" under any such plan during any unpaid portion of the CFRA leave. The employer shall allow an employee covered by a pension and/or retirement plan to continue to make contributions, in accordance with the terms of these plans, during the unpaid portion of the leave period.

(f) Employee Status.

The employee shall retain employee status during the period of the CFRA leave. The leave shall not constitute a break in service for purposes of longevity and/or seniority under any collective bargaining agreement or under any employee benefit plan. Benefits must be resumed upon the employee's reinstatement in the same manner and at the same levels as provided when the leave began, without any new qualification period, physical exam, et cetera.

§ 7297.6. Relationship Between CFRA Leave and Pregnancy Disability Leave

(a) Separate and Distinct Entitlements.

The right to take a CFRA leave under Government Code section 12945.2 is separate and distinct from the right to take a pregnancy disability leave under Government Code section 12945, subdivision (b)(2), and section 7291.2 et seq. of the regulations.

(b) Serious Health Condition—Pregnancy.

An employee's own disability due to pregnancy, childbirth or related medical conditions is not included as a "serious health condition" under CFRA. Any period of incapacity or treatment due to pregnancy, including prenatal care, is included as a "serious health condition" under FMLA.

(c) CFRA Leave after Pregnancy Disability Leave.

At the end of the employee's period(s) of pregnancy disability, or at the end of four months pregnancy disability leave, whichever occurs first, a CFRA-eligible employee may request to take CFRA leave of up to 12 workweeks for reason of the birth of her child, if the child has been born by this date. There is no requirement that either the employee or child have a serious health condition in order for the employee to take CFRA leave. There is also no requirement that the employee no longer be disabled by her pregnancy, childbirth or related medical conditions before taking CFRA leave for reason of the birth of her child.

(1) Where an employee has utilized four months of pregnancy disability leave prior to the birth of her child, and her health care provider determines that a continuation of the leave is medically necessary, an employer may, but is not required to, allow an eligible employee to utilize CFRA leave prior to the birth of her child. No employer shall, however, be required to provide more CFRA leave than the amount to which the employee is otherwise entitled.

(d) Maximum Entitlement.

The maximum possible combined leave entitlement for both pregnancy disability leave (under FMLA and Government Code section 12945, subdivision (b)(2)) and CFRA leave for reason of the birth of the child (under this subchapter) is four months and 12 workweeks. This assumes that the employee is disabled by pregnancy, childbirth or related medical conditions for four months and then requests, and is eligible for, a 12–week CFRA leave for reason of the birth of her child.

§ 7297.7. Retaliation

In addition to the retaliation prohibited by Government Code section 12940, subdivision (f), and section 7287.8 of the regulations, it shall be an unlawful employment practice for any person to discharge, fine, suspend, expel, punish, refuse to hire, or otherwise discriminate against any individual, except as otherwise permitted in this subchapter, because that individual has:

(a) exercised his or her right to CFRA leave, and/or

(b) given information or testimony regarding his or her CFRA leave, or another person's CFRA leave, in any inquiry or proceeding related to any right guaranteed under this subchapter.

§ 7297.8. Remedies

Upon determining that an employer has violated Government Code section 12945.2, the Commission may order any remedy available under Government Code section 12970, and section 7286.9 of the regulations. The remedy, however, for a violation of section 7297.9 (failure to provide notice) shall be an order that the employer provide such notice.

§ 7297.9. Notice of Right to Request CFRA Leave

(a) Employers to Post Notice.

Covered employers shall provide notice to their employees of the right to request CFRA leave under the California Family Rights Act. Employers shall post the notice in a conspicuous place or places where employees tend to congregate. If the employer publishes an employee handbook which describes other kinds of personal or disability leaves available to its employees, that employer shall include a description of CFRA leave in the next edition of its handbook which it publishes following adoption of these regulations. The employer may include both pregnancy disability leave and CFRA leave requirements in a single notice.

(b) Employers to Give Notice.

Employers are also encouraged to give a copy of the notice to each current and new employee, ensure that copies are otherwise available to each current and new employee, and disseminate the notice in any other way.

(c) Non–English Speaking Workforce.

Any employer whose workforce at any facility or establishment contains ten percent or more of persons who speak a language other than English as their primary language shall translate the notice into the language or languages spoken by this group or these groups of employees.

(d) Text of Notice.

The text below contains only the minimum requirements of the California Family Rights Act of 1993 and of the employer's obligation to provide pregnancy disability leave. Nothing in this notice requirement prohibits an employer from providing a leave policy which is more generous than that required by this act and providing its own notice of its own policy. Covered employers may develop their own notice or they may choose to use the text provided below, unless it does not accurately reflect their own policy.

FAMILY CARE AND MEDICAL LEAVE (CFRA LEAVE) AND PREGNANCY DISABILITY LEAVE

Under the California Family Rights Act of 1993 (CFRA), if you have more than 12 months of service with us and have worked at least 1,250 hours in the 12–month period before the date you want to begin your leave, you may have a right to an unpaid family care or medical leave (CFRA leave). This leave may be up to 12 workweeks in a 12–month period for the birth, adoption, or foster care placement of your child or for your own serious health condition or that of your child, parent or spouse.

Even if you are not eligible for CFRA leave, if you are disabled by pregnancy, childbirth or related medical conditions, you are entitled to take a pregnancy disability leave of up to four months, depending on your period(s) of actual disability. If you are CFRA-eligible, you have certain rights to take BOTH a pregnancy disability leave and a CFRA leave for reason of the birth of your child. Both leaves contain a guarantee of reinstatement to the same or to a comparable position at the end of the leave, subject to any defense allowed under the law.

If possible, you must provide at least 30 days advance notice for foreseeable events (such as the expected birth of a child or a planned medical treatment for yourself or of a family member). For events which are unforeseeable, we need you to notify us, at least verbally, as soon as you learn of the need for the leave. Failure to comply with these notice rules is grounds for, and may result in, deferral of the requested leave until you comply with this notice policy.

We may require certification from your health care provider before allowing you a leave for pregnancy or your own serious health condition or certification from the health care provider of your child, parent or spouse who has a serious health condition before allowing you a leave to take care of that family member. When medically necessary, leave may be taken on an intermittent or reduced work schedule.

If you are taking a leave for the birth, adoption or foster care placement of a child, the basic minimum duration of the leave is two weeks and you must conclude the leave within one year of the birth or placement for adoption or foster care.

Taking a family care or pregnancy disability leave may impact certain of your benefits and your seniority date. If you want more information regarding your eligibility for a leave and/or the impact of the leave on your seniority and benefits, please contact _____.

§ 7297.10. Relationship with FMLA Regulations

To the extent that they are not inconsistent with this subchapter, other state law or the California Constitution, the Commission incorporates by reference the federal regulations interpreting FMLA issued January 6, 1995 (29 CFR Part 825), which govern any FMLA leave which is also a leave under this subchapter.

§ 7297.11. Certification Form

For leaves involving serious health conditions, the employer may utilize the following "Certification of Health Care Provider" form or its equivalent. Employers may also utilize any other certification form, such as the United States Department of Labor Form WH–380, revised December 1994 ("Certification of Health Care Provider/Family and Medical Leave Act of 1993"), provided that the health care provider does not disclose the underlying diagnosis of the serious health condition involved without the consent of the patient.

FAIR EMPLOYMENT & HOUSING COMMISSION
CERTIFICATION OF HEALTH CARE PROVIDER
(California Family Rights Act of 1993 (CFRA))

1. Employee's Name:

2. Patient's Name (If other than employee): _____
_____

3. Date medical condition or need for treatment commenced [NOTE: THE HEALTH CARE PROVIDER IS NOT TO DISCLOSE THE UNDERLYING DIAGNOSIS WITHOUT THE CONSENT OF THE PATIENT]:
_____

4. Probable duration of medical condition or need for treatment:
_____

5. The attached sheet describes what is meant by a "serious health condition" under both the federal Family and Medical Leave Act (FMLA) and the California Family Rights Act (CFRA). Does the patient's condition qualify under any of the categories described? If so, please check the appropriate category.

    (1)　(2)　(3)　(4)　(5)　(6)

6. If the certification is for the serious health condition of the employee, please answer the following:

   Yes　No

   ☐　☐　Is employee able to perform work of any kind? (If "No", skip next question.)

   ☐　☐　Is employee unable to perform any one or more of the essential functions of employee's position? (Answer after reviewing statement from employer of essential functions of employee's position, or, if none provided, after discussing with employee.)

7. If the certification is for the care of the employee's family member, please answer the following:

   Yes　No

   ☐　☐　Does (or will) the patient require assistance for basic medical, hygiene, nutritional needs, safety or transportation?

   ☐　☐　After review of the employee's signed statement (See Item tO below), does the condition warrant the participation of the employee? (This participation may include psychological comfort and/or arranging for third-party care for the family member.)

8. Estimate the period of time cam needed or during which the employee's presence would be beneficial:

9. Please answer the following question only if the employee is asking for intermittent leave or a reduced work schedule.

   Yes　No

   ☐　☐　Is it medically necessary for the employee to be off work on an intermittent basis or to work less than the employee's normal work schedule in order to deal with the serious health condition of the employee or family member?

   ☐　☐　If the answer to 9. is yes, please indicate the estimated number of doctor's visits, and/or estimated duration of medical treatment, either by the health care practitioner or another provider of health services, upon referral from the health care provider. _____

ITEM 10 IS TO BE COMPLETED BY THE EMPLOYEE NEEDING FAMILY LEAVE.
* * **TO BE PROVIDED TO THE HEALTH CARE PROVIDER UNDER SEPARATE COVER.

10. When family care leave is needed to care for a seriously-ill family member, the employee shall state the care he or she will provide and an estimate of the time period during which this care will be provided, including a schedule if leave is to be taken intermittently or on a reduced work schedule:
_____
_____
_____

11. Signature of health care provider.
_____

    Date: _____

12. Signature of Employee:
_____

    Date: _____

A "Serious Health Condition" means an illness, injury, impairment, or physical or mental condition that involves one of the following:

1. Hospital Care
   Inpatient care (i.e., an overnight stay) in a hospital, hospice, or residential medical care facility, including any period of incapacity or subsequent treatment in connection with or consequent to such inpatient care.

2. Absence Plus Treatment
   (a) A period of incapacity of more than three consecutive calendar days (including any subsequent treatment or period of incapacity relating to the same condition), that also involves:

      (1) Treatment (two or more times by a health care provider, by a nurse or physician's assistant under direct supervision of a health care provider, or by a provider of health care services (e.g., physical therapist) under orders of, or on referral by, a health care provider, or

      (2) Treatment by a health care provider on at least one occasion which results in a regimen of continuing treatment under the supervision of the health care provider.

3. Pregnancy [NOTE: An employee's own incapacity due to pregnancy is covered as a serious health condition under FMLA but not under CFRA.]

   Any period of incapacity due to pregnancy, or for prenatal care.
4. Chronic Conditions Requiring Treatment
   A chronic condition which:

      (1) Requires periodic visits for treatment by a health care provider, or by a nurse or physician's assistant under direct supervision of a health cam provider,

      (2) Continues over an extended period of time (including recurring episodes of a single underlying condition); and

      (3) May cause episodic rather than a continuing period of incapacity (e.g., asthma, diabetes, epilepsy, etc.).

5. Permanent/Long—term Conditions Requiring Supervision
   A period of incapacity which is permanent or long-term due to a condition for which treatment may not be effective. The employee or family member must be under the continuing supervision of, but need not be receiving active treatment by, a health care provider. Examples include Alzheimer's, a severe stroke, or the terminal stages of a disease.

6. Multiple Treatments (Non—Chronic Conditions)

Any period of absence to receive multiple treatments (including any period of recovery therefrom) by a health care provider or by a provider of health care services under orders of, or on referral by, a health care provider, either for restorative surgery after an accident or other injury, or for a condition that would likely result in a period of incapacity of more than three consecutive calendar days in the absence of medical intervention or treatment. such as cancer (chemotherapy, radiation, etc.) severe arthritis (physical therapy), kidney disease (dialysis).

A "Serious Health Condition" means an illness, injury, impairment, or physical or mental condition that involves one of the following:

1. Hospital Care Inpatient care (i.e., an overnight stay) in a hospital, hospice, or residential medical care facility, including any period of incapacity or subsequent treatment in connection with or consequent to such inpatient care.

2. Absence Plus Treatment

(a) A period of incapacity of more than three consecutive calendar days (including any subsequent treatment or period of incapacity relating to the same condition), that also involves:

(1) Treatment two or more times by a health care provider, by a nurse or physician's assistant under direct supervision of a health care provider, or by a provider of health care services (e.g., physical therapist) under orders of, or on referral by, a health care provider; or

(2) Treatment by a health care provider on at least one occasion which results in a regimen of continuing treatment under the supervision of the health care provider.

3. Pregnancy [NOTE: An employee's own incapacity due to pregnancy is covered as a serious health condition under FMLA but not under CFRA.]

Any period of incapacity due to pregnancy, or for prenatal care.

4. Chronic Conditions Requiring Treatment A chronic condition which:

(1) Requires periodic visits for treatment by a health care provider, or by a nurse or physician's assistant under direct supervision of a health care provider;

(2) Continues over an extended period of time (including recurring episodes of a single underlying condition); and

(3) May cause episodic rather than a continuing period of incapacity (e.g., asthma, diabetes, epilepsy, etc.).

5. Permanent/Long-term Conditions Requiring Supervision A period of incapacity which is permanent or long-term due to a condition for which treatment may not be effective. The employee or family member must be under the continuing supervision of, but need not be receiving active treatment by, a health care provider. Examples include Alzheimer's, a severe stroke, or the terminal stages of a disease.

6. Multiple Treatments (Non–Chronic Conditions) Any period of absence to receive multiple treatments (including any period of recovery therefrom) by a health

care provider or by a provider of health care services under orders of, or on referral by, a health care provider, either for restorative surgery after an accident or other injury, or for a condition that would likely result in a period of incapacity of more than three consecutive calendar days in the absence of medical intervention or treatment, such as cancer (chemotherapy, radiation, etc.) severe arthritis (physical therapy), kidney disease (dialysis).

Chapter 3. Discrimination In Housing (Reserved)

Chapter 4. Procedures of the Commission

Subchapter 1. General Matters

§ 7400. Statement of Purpose

These regulations interpret, implement, and supplement the procedures set forth in Articles 1 (employment, Unruh Act and Ralph Act, discrimination) (Gov. Code, s12960 et seq.) and 2 (housing discrimination) of the Fair Employment and Housing Act (FEHA) (Gov. Code, s12980 et seq.). These regulations and provisions of the FEHA shall govern the practice and procedure in all matters before the Fair Employment and Housing Commission (Commission). They incorporate the requirements of the Administrative Adjudication Bill of Rights, Government Code sections 11425.10 et seq., and incorporate by reference certain sections of the Administrative Procedure Act, Government Code sections 11370 et seq., as specified.

§ 7401. Delegation of Powers

Except where otherwise prohibited by law or by these regulations, the Commission may delegate any of the powers and duties of the Commission to the Chairperson, the Hearing Officers, or other members of the staff of the Commission. When a regulation requires something to be delivered or mailed to the "Commission," it may be delivered or mailed, unless otherwise specified, to the Executive and Legal Affairs Secretary (ELAS) or Hearing Officer if there is a Hearing Officer assigned to the case.

§ 7402. Definitions

(a) "Accusation" means the charging document issued by the Department pursuant to Government Code sections 12965 and 12981.

(b) "Administrative adjudication" means any stage of any proceeding, including but not limited to, the hearing of the Commission following the issuance of an accusation by the Department of Fair Employment and Housing (Department) and enforcement of any judgment entered.

(c) "Amicus brief" means a written submission to the Commission by a non-party who has an interest in the subject matter of a particular adjudicative proceeding.

(d) "Chairperson" means the Chairman or Chairwoman of the Commission.

(e) "Clerk of the Commission" means any individual assigned administrative responsibilities by the ELAS.

(f) "Commission" means the Fair Employment and Housing Commission and includes any Commissioner, officer, employee, or other individual delegated any function, power, or duty of the Commission.

(g) "Commissioner" means any member of the Fair Employment and Housing Commission, including the Chairperson.

(h) "Complainant" means a person claiming to be aggrieved by a practice which is unlawful under the FEHA and who files a complaint with the Department, pursuant to Government Code section 12960 or 12980.

(i) "Complaint" means a complaint filed with the Department, pursuant to Government Code section 12960 or 12980, by a person alleging a practice which is unlawful under the FEHA. It also means a complaint of housing discrimination filed by the California Attorney General, pursuant to Government Code section 12980, subdivision (b).

(j) "Deliver" or "mail" includes, but is not limited to, sending something by facsimile (fax) or other means of electronic transmission, as allowed by the rules set forth in sections 7406 and 7407.

(k) "Department" means the Department of Fair Employment and Housing and includes any officer, employee, or other individual delegated any function, power, or duty of the Department.

(l) "Director" means the Director of the Department who is the executive officer of the Department and includes any officer, employee, or other individual delegated any function, power, or duty of the Director.

(m) "ELAS" means the Executive and Legal Affairs Secretary and chief executive officer of the Commission and includes any officer, employee or other individual delegated any function, power, or duty of the ELAS.

(n) "Hearing" means the evidentiary hearing of the Commission held pursuant to the issuance of an accusation by the Department.

(o) "Hearing Officer" means an administrative law judge of the Commission.

(p) "Motion in limine" means a written request to the Hearing Officer brought prior to the taking of evidence at hearing to exclude irrelevant or prejudicial matters at hearing.

(q) "Party" includes the Department, the respondent(s), and any person who has been allowed by the Commission to intervene in the proceeding.

(r) "Person" includes one or more individuals, limited liability companies, partnerships, associations, governmental entity, corporations, legal representatives, trustees, trustees in bankruptcy, and receivers or other fiduciaries.

(s) "Respondent" means any person who is alleged to have committed an unlawful practice in a complaint filed

with the Department pursuant to Government Code section 12960 or 12980 and/or a person against whom an accusation is filed pursuant to Government Code section 12965 or 12981.

(t) "Section 12948 discrimination" means allegations of a denial of public accommodation rights or a denial of rights because of hate violence pursuant to Civil Code section 51, 51.7, 54, 54.1, or 54.2, as incorporated in Government Code section 12948.

(u) "Vice chairperson" is a person elected by the Commission as a whole to assume the duties of the chair when the chairperson is absent. Whenever the word "chairperson" appears in these regulations, it shall include "vice chairperson."

§ 7403. Department to Maintain Current Addresses and Telephone Numbers of Complainants and Respondents

All complainants and respondents shall keep the Department advised of their current telephone number and mailing address.

(a) Complainants shall file with the Department their telephone numbers, mailing addresses and addresses at which they can be personally served with documents at the time they sign the complaint and shall notify the Department of any changes of addresses and telephone numbers during the investigation and administrative adjudication of the complaint and until payment of any judgment is complete.

(b) When serving the complaint on respondents, the Department shall notify respondents in writing that a complaint has been filed against them, that they are required to file their telephone numbers and mailing addresses and addresses at which they can be personally served documents with the Department, and that they must notify the Department of any changes of addresses or telephone number during the investigation and administrative adjudication of the complaint and until payment of any judgment is complete.

§ 7404. Public Hearing Records

The official record of the Commission in every case which is to proceed to hearing shall be available for public inspection upon making appropriate arrangements with the Clerk of the Commission.

§ 7405. Representation in Matters Before the Commission

(a) At all stages of the investigation and administrative adjudication, a respondent may represent himself or herself, may have representation by legal counsel, or may have non-legal representation.

(b) When a party is unrepresented or chooses representation other than by legal counsel, the Commission shall make reasonable efforts to ensure that the rights of the party are protected. Where not otherwise prohibited by law, these efforts may include interpreting papers as motions before hearings or requests for discovery, granting extensions of time to file papers, and waiving procedural requirements when in the interests of justice.

(c) Nothing in this section shall be interpreted to permit a party to engage in dilatory or delaying tactics, such as choosing not to respond to an accusation, or delaying choice of representation.

§ 7406. Filing of Papers with the Commission

(a) To file a document with the Commission, a party shall submit two copies of the document to the Clerk of the Commission at its office in San Francisco, California.

(b) Filing of a document is effective if the document is mailed to the Commission by first class, overnight or express mail, registered, or certified mail, postmarked no later than the last day of the time limit. Where mail is metered and bears a later postmark, the date of the postmark shall control for timeliness purposes.

(c) Filing of a document is also effective if it is delivered or sent by facsimile transmission (fax) or other electronic delivery, such as electronic mail (e-mail), when approved by the Commission, on or before the last day of the time limit. If a document is filed by facsimile or other approved electronic means of delivery, the sender shall also place two hard copies of the document in the mail to the Commission, postmarked no later than the last day of the time limit. The copy of any document filed by facsimile or other approved electronic means of delivery shall bear a notation of the date and place of transmission and the facsimile telephone number or e-mail address, where appropriate, to which it is being transmitted.

§ 7407. Service of Parties and Complainants

Whenever a party files any papers with the Commission, the party shall serve copies of the same on all other parties and on the complainant, or on their attorneys or representatives of record. Service may be by first class mail, registered or certified mail, overnight or express mail, or any other form of mail delivery. Service may also be by facsimile transmission or other approved electronic means of delivery. If a document is served by facsimile or other approved electronic means of delivery, the person serving the document shall also place a hard copy in the mail within any applicable time limit. Service may also be by personal service.

(a) Proof of Service. Service shall be made simultaneously with filing and proof of such service, by means of a written declaration under penalty of perjury, shall be attached to the papers. Any proof of service which meets the requirements of Code of Civil Procedure section 1013a is acceptable. A sample proof of service, which assumes service by facsimile, followed by placing a hard copy of the document in the mail, is the following:

Declaration of Service by [insert means of service]

I, the undersigned, hereby declare:

I am over eighteen years of age and not a party to the within cause. My address is [insert address]. On [insert date], I served a copy of the [list all documents by title or description] on each of the following, by [insert means of service], facsimile transmission and by placing the same in an envelope (or envelopes) addressed respectively as follows:

[insert names and addresses of all persons served with the documents and, if applicable, which party each person represents]

Each said envelope was then on said date sealed and deposited in the United States mail at [insert location], the county in which I am employed, with the postage thereon fully prepaid.

I declare under penalty of perjury that the foregoing is true and correct. Executed on [insert date] at [insert location].

[Signed by the person executing the service]

(b) Date of Service. The date of service of papers served on parties and on complainants, and papers served by the Commission, shall be when the paper is deposited in the United States mail, including overnight mail, delivered in person, or sent by facsimile transmission or other approved means of electronic delivery (assuming that a hard copy was also sent by mail, as required by this section). Where mail is metered and bears a later postmark, the date of the postmark shall control for timeliness purposes.

(c) Computation of Time Periods.

(1) Beginning and end of time period. In computing time periods prescribed by these rules, the day of the event which starts the time period running is not counted, but the last day of the period is included. If the last day of the period falls on a Saturday, Sunday, or a state legal holiday, the time period expires at the corresponding time on the next business day.

(2) Extension for service by mail. Whenever a time period is triggered by service of papers on a party or on a complainant and such service is made by regular mail, five days shall be added to the prescribed period for response. When service is made by overnight or other express mail, or by facsimile transmission, two state business days shall be added to the prescribed period for response. No days will be added to any time period when an extension of time has been granted.

(d) The rules contained in this regulation shall also govern all notices, Commission decisions, and other papers sent out by the Commission pertaining to administrative adjudication.

(e) Service and orders adverse to respondents. If the respondent has not filed a Notice of Defense or appeared at the hearing, the Commission may issue an order adversely affecting the respondent only if the Department proves that it has served the respondent with the accusation, accusation package, and Notice of Hearing, either personally or by registered or certified mail addressed to the last known mailing address on file with the Department, as required by section 7403(b).

§ 7408. Accusations

(a) Only the Director or individual within the Department delegated such authority may, in his or her discretion, issue an accusation.

(b) An accusation shall be deemed issued on the date it is filed with the Commission. An accusation shall be filed with the Commission in the manner set forth in section 7406.

(c) All accusations issued pursuant to Government Code section 12965, subdivision (a), alleging employment or Section 12948 discrimination, shall be issued by the Department and filed with the Commission on or before the one-year anniversary date of the filing of the complaint.

(d) All accusations issued pursuant to Government Code section 12981, subdivision (a), alleging unlawful housing practices, shall be issued by the Department and filed with the Commission on or before the 100th day after the date of the filing of the complaint, unless impracticable for the Department to do so. If the Department determines that it is impracticable to meet this deadline, it shall file in the Pleading File a copy of the notification provided to the complainant and respondent explaining the Department's reason(s) for the delay.

(e) Contents of accusation. The form and contents of an accusation may be determined by the Department but, at a minimum, shall meet all of the following:

(1) be written;

(2) be in the name of the Department;

(3) contain the name of each respondent and, if applicable, the capacity in which each respondent is being named;

(4) set forth the nature of the charges in ordinary and concise language with appropriate references to specific sections of the FEHA or other applicable statutes and regulations sufficient to allow the respondent(s) to prepare a defense; and

(5) set forth the relief sought by the Department.

(f) Accusations need not be verified.

(g) The Commission may ignore or correct any error or defect in the accusation which does not substantially affect the rights of any party.

(h) Contents of accusation package. Upon the filing of an accusation, the Department shall serve on the respondent and the complainant, in accordance with the rules in section 7406, an "accusation package." The accusation package shall include, but is not limited to, the following documents:

(1) a copy of the accusation;

(2) a copy of the underlying complaint(s) which is the subject of the accusation;

(3) a copy of the Commission's procedural regulations accompanied by a statement that these regulations are the governing procedure for administrative adjudication before the Commission;

1202

(4) a copy of a subpoena and a subpoena duces tecum form with instructions for their use;

(5) a copy of the Statement to Respondents;

(6) a Notice of Defense form;

(7) a notice of the right to request, as needed, an interpreter or reasonable accommodation;

(8) if applicable under Government Code section 12965(c) for allegations of employment or Section 12948 discrimination, a statement regarding respondent's right to elect to transfer the proceedings to court in lieu of administrative adjudication, and a form notice to transfer proceedings to court;

(9) for accusations issued pursuant to Government Code section 12981(a), regarding allegations of housing discrimination, a statement regarding respondent's, complainant's, or other aggrieved person's right to elect to have the claims adjudicated in a civil action in lieu of administrative adjudication, and a form notice to transfer proceedings to court;

(10) if applicable under Government Code section 12981(g), for housing discrimination cases, a statement to the complainant that she or he may only be able to recover damages for emotional distress or other intangible injuries through a civil action;

(11) a notice asking the respondent to consent to electronic, rather than stenographic, reporting of the proceedings at hearing;

(12) a copy of the Department's notice informing respondents and complainants of their obligation to keep the Department informed of any change of mailing address or telephone number;

(13) a Notice of Hearing or Notice of Impending Hearing;

(14) a proof of service specifying that all of the above documents have been served.

(i) Service of accusation and accompanying materials. The accusation and accusation package shall be served on each respondent in accordance with the rules in section 7407. The complainant will be provided with a copy of the accusation and related papers pertinent to complainant.

§ 7409. Amended Accusations

(a) The Department may amend an accusation, issued pursuant to Government Code section 12965 regarding allegations of employment or Section 12948 discrimination, to pray either for damages for emotional injury or for administrative fines, or both, only within the first thirty days after the issuance of the original accusation.

(b) The Department may amend an accusation with new charges (other than those in subdivision (a)) any time up to 30 calendar days prior to the original or continued date the hearing is scheduled to commence. After that time, the Department may amend an accusation which contains new charges only upon such terms as the Hearing Officer approves, including, but not limited to, granting a continuance to the respondent. "New charges" include any amendment which may affect the liability of respondents, such as, but not limited to, the addition of a new respondent or the naming of an existing respondent in a new capacity; the charging of a violation of new sections of the FEHA; the pleading of substantive new facts; and the prayer for new or significantly modified relief.

(c) Any new charges shall be deemed controverted and the respondent does not need to file a new Notice of Defense. Any objections to the amended accusation may be made orally and shall be noted on the record.

(d) At any time before the matter is submitted to the Hearing Officer for decision, the Department may amend an accusation to make nonsubstantive changes.

(e) The first amended accusation shall be clearly labeled "First Amended Accusation," and any subsequent amended accusations shall be labeled consecutively. The Department shall clearly identify the changes made to each amended accusation either by highlighting the changes or identifying them in a separate written statement.

(f) Any amended accusations shall be filed with the Commission and served on all parties and the complainant in accordance with sections 7406 and 7407.

§ 7410. Election to Transfer Proceedings to Court in Lieu of Administrative Adjudication

(a) Accusations Issued Pursuant to Government Code Section 12965(a) Regarding Allegations of Employment or Section 12948 Discrimination. If the accusation (or amended accusation if the purpose of the amendment is to add a prayer for damages for emotional injuries and/or administrative fines) includes a prayer for damages for emotional injury or for administrative fines, or both, any respondent may elect to transfer the proceedings to a court instead of having the matter heard by the Commission. In order to do this, the respondent must serve written notice to this effect. The respondent may use the form provided for this purpose in the Statement to Respondents or available from the Department, or any comparable form. The respondent must serve this notice on the Department, the Commission, and the complainant within 30 days after service of the accusation (or an accusation which has been amended to add a prayer for damages for emotional injuries and/or administrative fines) on the respondent. Where not all of the named respondents exercise election to transfer proceedings to court, the case may be bifurcated and proceed with administrative adjudication as to those non-electing respondents.

(b) Accusations Issued Pursuant to Government Code Section 12981 Regarding Allegations of Housing Discrimination. Any respondent or complainant may elect to have the charges asserted in the accusation adjudicated in a civil action rather than before the Commission. In order to do this, the person seeking election must serve written notice to this effect. The person may use the form provided for this purpose in the Statement to Respon-

dents or available from the Department, or any comparable form. The person must serve the notice on the Department, the Commission, and all other parties, and the complainant, within 20 days after service of the accusation.

§ 7411. Statement to Respondent

The Statement to Respondent shall be substantially in the following form:

You may make a request for a hearing by delivering or mailing the enclosed form, called a Notice of Defense, to the Fair Employment and Housing Commission, [fill in address of the Commission] within 15 days after the accusation is served on you or you receive it by mail. You may also fax the Notice of Defense to the Commission at [fill in facsimile number], as long as you also place two hard copies of the Notice of Defense in the mail within the 15–day time limit. Either you or your representative must sign the Notice of Defense. If you do not file a Notice of Defense, the Department may proceed to hearing without you. You have a right to be represented by a lawyer or other person in these proceedings. The Department will always be represented by a lawyer. Whether or not you hire an attorney to represent you at the hearing, you may want to seek legal advice to better understand your rights and obligations.

The potential monetary damages that may be assessed by the Commission against you in an administrative adjudication may include, among other things, actual damages, compensatory damages for emotional distress, and administrative fines or civil penalties. In an employment case brought pursuant to Government Code section 12965, the maximum monetary recovery per complainant for the emotional distress and administrative fines combined shall not exceed $50,000 against each respondent. These damages are in addition to any actual damages, such as back pay, front pay, medical expenses and other out-of-pocket costs. In a housing case brought pursuant to Government Code section 12981, there is no upper limit on the emotional distress damages that may be awarded against you.

You are entitled to receive the names and addresses of Department witnesses and to inspect and copy the items mentioned in section 7417 which are held by the Department. You may contact: (here insert name and address of appropriate Department attorney) to obtain these items.

Once the hearing is set, it may be postponed only for good cause. If you have good cause, you must notify the Commission within 10 working days after you discover the good cause. Failure to give notice within 10 days may mean that the hearing will not be postponed.

You must at all times keep the Department notified of your current address, telephone number, and, if applicable, fax number.

[Add appropriate "election to transfer" language from section 7410, subdivision (a) or (b), and state that the appropriate "election to transfer" notice is included in the Statement to Respondent.]

§ 7412. Notice of Defense

(a) Within 15 days after service of the accusation, the respondent may file with the Commission a Notice of Defense, using the form provided by the Department in the accusation package or any substantially equivalent form. In the Notice of Defense, the respondent may request a hearing and state any objections the respondent may have to the form or substance of the accusation.

(b) The Notice of Defense shall be in writing and signed by, or on behalf of, the respondent and shall state the respondent's mailing address, address at which the respondent can be personally served with documents, and telephone number. If the respondent is represented by an attorney or non-attorney representative, or is a corporation, the Notice of Defense shall state the name, mailing address and telephone number of respondent's representative. It need not be verified, or follow any particular form.

(c) The respondent shall be entitled to a hearing on the merits if the respondent files a Notice of Defense.

§ 7413. Subpoenas

(a) Subpoenas and subpoenas duces tecum may be issued for attendance at the hearing and for production of documents at any reasonable time and place in advance of the hearing or at the hearing.

(b) The Department and each party represented by legal counsel shall issue and sign its own subpoenas and subpoenas duces tecum, using the form in the Appendix to these regulations. Parties who are not represented by legal counsel may request the Commission to issue and sign subpoena and subpoena duces tecum forms.

(c) The process extends to all parts of the state and shall be served in accordance with Code of Civil Procedure sections 1987 and 1988. A subpoena or subpoena duces tecum may also be delivered by certified mail, return receipt requested, or by personal service.

(d) No witness is obliged to attend unless the witness is a resident of the state at the time of service.

(e) A person served with a subpoena or subpoena duces tecum may object to its terms by a motion which shall be resolved by the ELAS or a Hearing Officer in an appropriate order.

(f) A witness appearing pursuant to a subpoena or subpoena duces tecum, other than a party, shall receive for the appearance the same mileage and fees allowed by law to a witness in a civil case (see Government Code sections 68092.5–68093), to be paid by the party at whose request the witness is subpoenaed. Fees for witnesses who are officers and employees of the state or political subdivision of the state shall be governed by Government Code sections 68096.1–68097.10).

(g) Subpoenas and subpoenas duces tecum shall be served on the opposing party in the manner provided in section 7407 and shall comply with consumer notice requirements, Code of Civil Procedure sections 1985.3 and 1985.6, where applicable.

1204

§ 7414. Setting of Hearing

(a) Requests for hearing. Where respondent has not stipulated in writing to waive the 90–day hearing requirement pursuant to regulation section 7429(c), the Department shall request the Commission to set the hearing within 90 days of issuance of the accusation. Where respondent has stipulated in writing to waive the 90–day hearing requirement, the Department shall make an effort to consult with the respondent and the complainant regarding hearing dates, and shall then request the Commission to set the hearing.

(b) Notice of hearing. The Department shall deliver or mail a Notice of Hearing to all parties and the complainant at least 30 days prior to the date the hearing is scheduled to commence. If the hearing is continued, advance notice as short as 10 days may be given. The Notice of Hearing shall be substantially in the following form but may include other information:

You are hereby notified that a hearing will be held before the Fair Employment and Housing Commission at [place of hearing] on the [date and time of hearing] upon the charges made in the accusation served upon you. If you do not attend the hearing, the case will be decided without you and an order may be entered which directs you to pay money or take other action.

You have the right to be represented by a lawyer or other representative at your own expense.

You are not entitled to the appointment of a lawyer to represent you at public expense. The Department will be represented by a lawyer. You are entitled to represent yourself without legal counsel. You may present any relevant evidence, and will be given full opportunity to cross-examine all witnesses testifying against you.

You are entitled to the issuance of subpoenas to compel the attendance of witnesses at the hearing and the production of books, documents or other things, either before the hearing at a reasonable time and place or at the hearing. If you are represented by a lawyer, your lawyer may use the subpoena forms attached to this Notice. If you are unrepresented or represented by someone other than a lawyer, you may obtain signed subpoena forms from the Fair Employment and Housing Commission at [here, insert the Commission's address and telephone number]. You are responsible for serving the subpoenaed person or entity with the subpoena, as well as serving a copy of the subpoena on the opposing party, in the manner set forth in section 7407. You must also comply with any consumer notice requirements (Code of Civil Procedure sections 1985.3 and 1985.6) where applicable.

If you or any of your witnesses will need language assistance, including sign language, or other accommodation, you must notify the Commission of this need as soon as possible, but no later than fifteen (15) days before the hearing is to start. The Commission will secure the appropriate interpreter.

Attached is the Commission's regulation on Pre–Hearing Statements and a form for you to use. Please make sure that you comply with its requirements.

(c) Requests for continuance of the hearing. A request for a continuance of a hearing date shall be made in writing, filed with the ELAS, and served on all of the parties and the complainant. Before making a request, the moving party shall contact all other parties to determine if there is any opposition and shall state whether there is any opposition in its papers to the ELAS.

(1) Requests for continuance will be granted only for good cause.

(2) A continuance beyond the 90–day time limitation after issuance of an accusation provided by Government Code section 12968 will only be granted by written stipulation of the parties, written waiver of the time limit by all respondents, and upon approval of the ELAS. If approved, the order of the Commission shall specify new hearing dates or shall order the parties to set new dates.

§ 7415. Withdrawal of Accusation

(a) Accusations issued pursuant to Government Code section 12965 regarding allegations of employment or section 12948 discrimination. The Department may at any time withdraw the accusation. If a complainant's right-to-sue notice has expired and that complainant objects to the withdrawal, however, the Commission shall decide whether to let the Department withdraw the accusation and whether to allow the administrative adjudication to proceed without the Department, and, if so, on what terms.

(b) Accusations issued pursuant to Government Code section 12981 regarding allegations of housing discrimination. The Department shall not withdraw the accusation unless the complainant withdraws the underlying complaint or the Department determines, after a thorough investigation, that, based on the facts, no reasonable cause exists to believe that an unlawful housing practice, as prohibited by the Act, has occurred or is about to occur or the Department determines that respondent has eliminated the violation which has occurred or is about to occur.

§ 7416. Notification of Settlement or Withdrawal of Accusation

The Department shall promptly notify the Clerk of the Commission of all settlements and withdrawals of accusations or any other action terminating a matter before the Commission. When properly notified, the Commission will vacate any hearing date and close its file on the matter on receipt of the withdrawal of the accusation.

§ 7417. Discovery

(a) Once an accusation is issued, a party is entitled to discovery. The party may make a written request to another party prior to the hearing and within 30 days after service by the Department of the initial accusation or within 15 days after service of an amended accusation or additional pleading. Unless otherwise agreed to by the parties, all responses to written requests for discovery are due 30 days after the request has been made. The following discovery is allowable:

(1) obtain the names and addresses of witnesses who have knowledge of the matters raised in the accusation, to the extent known to the other party, including, but not limited to, those intended to be called to testify at the hearing, and

(2) inspect and make a copy of any of the following in the possession or custody or under the control of the other party or the complainant:

(A) A statement pertinent to the subject matter of the accusation, made by the complainant or any party or any person employed by or related to a party.

(B) Statements of witnesses proposed to be called by the party and of other persons having personal knowledge of the acts, omissions or events which are the basis for the proceeding, not included in (A) above;

(C) All writings, including, but not limited to, reports of mental, physical and blood examinations and things which the party proposes to offer in evidence;

(D) Any writing or thing which is relevant and which would be admissible in evidence and which is in the possession or control of a party or the complainant;

(E) Investigative or progress reports made by or on behalf of the Department or other party pertaining to the subject matter of the proceeding, to the extent that these reports 1. contain the names and addresses of witnesses or of persons having personal knowledge of the acts, omissions or events which are the basis for the proceeding, or 2. reflect matters perceived by the Department in the course of its investigation, or 3. contain or include by attachment any statement or writing described in (A) to (E), inclusive, or summary thereof.

(3) For the purpose of this section, "statements" include written statements by the person signed or otherwise authenticated by him or her, stenographic, mechanical, electrical or other recordings, or transcripts thereof, of oral statements by the person, and written reports or summaries of these oral statements.

(4) Nothing in this section shall authorize the inspection or copying of any writing or thing which is privileged from disclosure by law or otherwise made confidential or protected as the attorney's work product.

(5) If the Department alleges conduct which constitutes sexual harassment, sexual assault, or sexual battery, the following rule shall apply: Evidence of specific instances of a complainant's sexual conduct with individuals other than the alleged perpetrator is not discoverable unless it is to be offered at hearing to attack the credibility of the complainant as provided for in section 7429(f)(7).

(b) In addition to the above, the Department and each respondent or other party may each take a single deposition, which shall continue day to day until completed. If an accusation charges multiple respondents, the Department may take a single deposition per respondent. A notice of deposition may also include a notice for production at the deposition of papers, books, accounts and documents. Unless agreed to otherwise by the parties or upon approval of the ELAS or Hearing Officer assigned to the case, depositions shall be scheduled for a date at least ten days after service of the deposition notice and shall be completed on or before the 30th day before the date initially set for hearing or the date of any continued hearing. However, the 30–day cut-off shall not apply where respondent has not stipulated in writing to waive the 90–day hearing requirement pursuant to regulation section 7429(c). In those cases, the deposition shall be completed on or before the 10th day before the hearing date.

Depositions are to be taken in the manner prescribed by Code of Civil Procedure section 2025, except that any application for a protective order, an order to stay the taking of the deposition and quash the deposition notice, or an order to compel the taking of the deposition shall be made to the Commission rather than to the courts. The rules and time limits for enforcement of discovery set forth below in subdivision (c) shall apply to depositions as well.

(c) Procedures for enforcement

(1) Any party claiming that its discovery, including subpoenas and subpoenas duces tecum, has not been complied with (the Moving Party) may serve on the Opposing Party and file with the ELAS, or Hearing Officer, if one has been assigned to hear the discovery matter, a motion to compel discovery, against the party refusing or failing to comply with this section (the Opposing Party). The motion shall state facts showing that the Opposing Party failed or refused to comply with this section, a description of the matters sought to be discovered, the reason or reasons why the matter is discoverable under this section, that a reasonable and good faith attempt to reach an informal resolution of the issue with the Opposing Party has been made, and the ground or grounds of the Opposing Party's refusal so far as known to the Moving Party.

(2) The Moving Party shall serve the motion upon the Opposing Party and file the motion with the Commission within thirty (30) days after the Opposing Party has failed or refused to respond to the written request for discovery or to testify pursuant to a deposition notice. The Opposing Party shall have seven (7) days from the date of service of the motion to file and serve a response. The ELAS or assigned Hearing Officer, in his or her discretion, may allow a greater or lesser time in which to file a motion or response.

(3) A party's "failure or refusal to respond" to discovery includes when that party has stated or indicated that it will not provide any response to the discovery or where, on the Moving Party's notification to the party that the response provided is incomplete or inadequate, that the party will not supplement the response, or where the

Moving Party has advised that party in writing that its lack of meaningful, good faith response shall be considered a failure or refusal to respond for the purposes of section 7417(c)(2).

(4) The ELAS or assigned Hearing Officer has the discretion to decide the matter without hearing. If the ELAS or Hearing Officer decides that a hearing is necessary, s/he has the discretion to conduct it by telephone or with the parties present.

(5) Where the matter sought to be discovered is under the custody or control of the Opposing Party and the Opposing Party asserts that the matter is not a discoverable matter under the provisions of this section, or is privileged against disclosure under these provisions, the ELAS or Hearing Officer may order matters provided in subdivision (b) of section 915 of the Evidence Code to be lodged with the Commission and may examine the matters in accordance with its provisions.

(6) Unless otherwise stipulated by the parties, the ELAS or Hearing Officer shall, no later than 15 days after the hearing (or, if no hearing has been held, within 15 days after receipt of the moving papers), make an order denying or granting the motion. The order shall be in writing setting forth the matters which the Moving Party is entitled to discover under this section. The ELAS or Hearing Officer shall serve by mail upon the parties a copy of the order. Where the order grants the motion in whole or in part, the order shall not become effective until 10 days after the date the order is served. Where the order denies relief to the Moving Party, the order shall be effective on the date it is served.

(7) Unless the ELAS or Hearing Officer rules otherwise, any discovery enforcement proceedings shall stay the 90–day requirement under Government Code section 12968 for the commencement of the hearing.

§ 7418.　Interpreters and Accommodation

(a) In proceedings where a party, a party's representative, or a party's expected witness requires an interpreter for any language, including sign language, that party shall be responsible for notifying the Commission, following the pre-hearing motion procedure in section 7419. The Commission shall be responsible for securing the interpreter and shall assess the costs of the interpreter as an ordinary cost of the hearing.

(b) In proceedings where a party, a party's representative, or a party's expected witness has a disability requiring accommodation either at the hearing or at any other stage of the administrative adjudication, that party shall be responsible for complying with Judicial Rule 989.3 and/or Evidence Code section 754, set forth in the Appendix to these regulations.

§ 7419.　Pre–Hearing Motions

Pre-hearing motions before the Commission shall not decide substantive matters. Substantive matters, including jurisdictional or legal challenges, are to be presented at the hearing on the merits and, except as expressly provided below, shall not be the subject of proceedings before hearing.

(a) If all parties stipulate in writing that there is a jurisdictional or other threshold dispositive issue which should, in the interests of judicial economy, be decided before proceeding to the merits of the case, the Hearing Officer assigned to hear the case may take evidence solely on the jurisdictional or other threshold issue and issue a written ruling on this issue alone. If the Hearing Officer rules for the Department, the parties shall set the case for the hearing on the merits. If the Hearing Officer rules against the Department, the procedure in section 7434 shall be followed and the issue will be placed before the Commission for decision in the matter. If the Commission decides for the Department, the case will then be remanded to the Hearing Officer for a hearing on the merits.

(b) Allowable pre-hearing (non-discovery) motions.

(1) Intervention.

(2) Amicus briefs.

(3) Motion compelling deposition of an unavailable witness.

(4) Consolidation or severance of matters for hearing.

(5) Request for Interpreter, in compliance with the rules set forth in section 7418 and Government Code sections 11435.05 through 11435.65.

(6) Motion for disqualification of the hearing officer, in compliance with the rules set forth in Government Code section 11425.40, subdivisions (a) through (c).

(7) Motion to Amend Accusation.

(8) Motion to Withdraw Accusation.

(9) Motion to Change Venue.

(10) Other motions, on prior approval of the ELAS.

(c) Pre-hearing motions: procedure.

(1) Pre-hearing motions shall be filed with the ELAS, or assigned Hearing Officer, be in writing, and include a proof of service indicating service on all parties and the complainant.

(2) No special form of motion is required.

(3) Unless these regulations set forth a different time for filing a particular motion (see, e.g., section 7409 for Amended Accusation; section 7415 for Withdrawal of Accusation; and section 7429(c), for Motion to Change Venue), pre-hearing motions shall be filed and served at least 15 calendar days before the date set for commencement of the hearing. Such motions may be heard on shorter notice on written application to, and approval of, the ELAS, for good cause, on such terms as determined by the ELAS. The non-moving party shall have seven (7) days from the date of service of the motion to file and serve a response. The ELAS, or Hearing Officer assigned to hear the case, in his or her discretion, may allow a lesser or greater time in which to file a motion or response.

(4) An order granting or denying a motion shall be made by the ELAS or Hearing Officer assigned to hear the case. The order shall be in writing and served by mail on all parties of record.

§ 7420. Ex Parte Communications

Except as otherwise allowed under the Administrative Procedure Act, Government Code sections 11430.10–11430.80, or as authorized by Judicial Rule 989.3 or under these regulations, there shall be no communication, direct or indirect, regarding any issue in a pending proceeding, to the Hearing Officer, ELAS, or Commission from an employee or representative of the Department or from an interested person outside of the Department, or from the respondent or complainant, without notice and opportunity for all parties to participate in the communication.

§ 7421. Consolidation and Severance

(a) A Hearing Officer, on his or her own motion, may order consolidation of two or more cases or severance of any consolidated cases or of issues in a single case. The Hearing Officer shall provide notice to all parties and allow a reasonable time for the parties to file and serve any objections in writing. Failure to assert objections within the time allowed shall constitute a waiver of objection to the order of consolidation or severance.

(b) A party who brings a motion for consolidation or severance shall comply with section 7419.

§ 7422. Pre–Hearing Statements

(a) Prior to hearing, the parties shall make best efforts to confer in person or by telephone to resolve or define any issues relating to the hearing. Thereafter, each party shall prepare a pre-hearing statement.

(b) No later than five (5) state business days prior to the scheduled date of hearing, each party shall file with the Commission a pre-hearing statement signed by the party or his/her representative of record. This statement shall include, if relevant, but need not be limited to, the following:

(1) A brief summary of any stipulated facts.

(2) Identification of all operative pleadings by their title and date signed.

(3) A current estimate from each party of the time necessary to try its case.

(4) The name of each witness each party may call at hearing, along with a brief statement of the content of each witness's expected testimony.

(5) The name and address of each expert witness each party intends to call at hearing, along with a brief statement of the opinion each expert is expected to give and a copy of the current resume or curriculum vitae of each expert witness.

(6) A list of documentary exhibits each party intends to present at hearing and a description of any physical or demonstrative evidence.

(7) The identity of any witness whose testimony will be presented by affidavit pursuant to section 7428 or by deposition pursuant to section 7427.

(8) A concise statement of any significant evidentiary issues.

(9) A copy of any pre-hearing motion filed by either party, any response filed thereto, and, if applicable, any order from the ELAS or Hearing Officer.

(10) Any anticipated motions in limine.

(c) The pre-hearing statement may be prepared in the format provided in the Appendix to these regulations.

(d) Failure to disclose fully all required items in the pre-hearing statement without good cause will, at the discretion of the Hearing Officer, result in the exclusion or restriction of evidence at hearing.

(e) The parties are not required to disclose any witnesses or exhibits which may be presented for rebuttal or impeachment purposes.

§ 7423. Pre–Hearing Conferences

(a) The Hearing Officer assigned to hear the case may order a pre-hearing conference, which ordinarily will be held by telephone, unless the Hearing Officer determines otherwise.

(b) The pre-hearing statements and any pre-hearing motions and responsive papers shall provide the basis for discussion of issues and rulings at the pre-hearing conference.

(c) At or after the pre-hearing conference, the Hearing Officer may issue a prehearing order, or dictate into the record, the matters determined at the conference.

(d) Pre-hearing conferences need not be open to public observation.

§ 7424. Settlement Conferences

(a) At any time after the Department issues an accusation, any party may file with the ELAS and serve upon all parties and the complainant a request for a settlement conference. Nothing in these regulations precludes the parties from discussing settlement whether or not a settlement conference is convened.

(b) Upon receipt of a request for a settlement conference, the ELAS shall ascertain if the other party agrees and shall assess whether a settlement conference is feasible, and, if so, shall assign a settlement conference Hearing Officer to convene a settlement conference. The conference may be conducted by telephone or with the parties and complainant present, within the discretion of the settlement conference Hearing Officer.

(c) The discussions at the settlement conference shall remain confidential and shall not be disclosed to the Hearing Officer assigned to hear the case. All settlement materials received by the settlement conference Hearing Officer shall be maintained in a separate settlement file. If efforts at settlement are unsuccessful or if the matter goes to hearing, a different Hearing Officer, who shall have no access to the settlement file, shall be assigned to hear the case.

(d) No evidence of an offer of compromise or settlement made in settlement negotiations shall be admissible in any administrative adjudication before the Commission, whether as affirmative evidence, by way of impeachment, or for any other purpose.

(e) The respondent and his/her representative, the Department's representative, and any other party to the action shall attend the settlement conference, or otherwise be available. Each party shall send, or have available, someone who has the authority to discuss and give tentative approval of a settlement. The complainant may be present, but in all events shall be available by telephone for consultation during the conference.

(f) If a settlement is reached at, or as a result of, a settlement conference, the terms of the settlement shall be set forth in a written stipulation, settlement agreement or consent order, or orally placed on the record.

(g) Settlement conferences are not open to public observation.

§ 7425. Intervention

(a) The complainant may intervene as a matter of right in any administrative adjudication before the Commission. In order to intervene, the complainant shall notify the Commission and the parties in writing of his/her intent to intervene.

(b) Any other person who wishes to intervene in the administrative adjudication of a case which is before the Commission shall file a motion so requesting with the Commission in accordance with section 7419(b).

§ 7426. Amicus Briefs

Before the hearing has commenced, any person wishing to file an amicus curiae brief in a matter which is before the Commission shall file a motion so requesting with the Commission in accordance with section 7419(b). After the hearing has commenced, the Commission may, in its discretion, permit any person to file an amicus brief at any time before the Commission decides the case.

§ 7427. Depositions of Unavailable Witnesses

Where a witness will be unable to attend or cannot be compelled to attend the hearing, any party may move the Commission for an order that the witness be deposed in the manner prescribed by law for depositions in Code of Civil Procedure section 2025. The motion shall be governed by the procedure set forth for pre-hearing motions in section 7419(b). The motion shall set forth the nature of the pending proceeding; the name and address of the witness whose testimony is desired; a showing of the materiality of the testimony; a showing that the witness will be unable, as defined in Evidence Code section 240, or cannot be compelled to attend, and shall request an order requiring the witness to appear and testify before an officer named in the petition for that purpose. Where the witness resides outside the state and where the

Commission has ordered the taking of the testimony by deposition, the Moving Party shall obtain an order of the court to that effect by filing a petition therefor in the superior court in Sacramento County. The proceedings thereon shall be in accordance with the provisions of Government Code section 11189. At the hearing, the deposition may be used in accordance with the rules in Code of Civil Procedure section 2025, subdivision (u). This section is in addition to the deposition authorized by section 7417(b).

§ 7428. Evidence by Affidavit

(a) At any time 10 or more days prior to a hearing or a continued hearing, any party may serve on the opposing party a copy of any affidavit which he or she proposes to introduce into evidence, together with a notice as provided in subdivision (b). Unless the opposing party, within seven days after such receipt of the affidavit, serves on the proponent a request to cross-examine the affiant, the opposing party's right to cross-examine the affiant is waived and the affidavit, if introduced in evidence, shall be given the same effect as if the affiant had testified orally. If an opportunity to cross-examine the affiant is not afforded after a timely request to do so is made as provided herein, the affidavit may be introduced in evidence, but shall be given only the same effect as other hearsay evidence.

(b) The notice referred to in subdivision (a) shall be substantially in the following form: The enclosed affidavit of [name of affiant] will be introduced as evidence at the hearing in [title of proceeding]. [Name of affiant] will not be called to testify orally and you will not be entitled to question [him/her] unless you notify [name of person offering the testimony or his/her attorney] at [address] that you wish to cross-examine this person. To be effective, your request must be mailed, sent by facsimile machine (faxed) or delivered to [name of person offering the testimony or his/her attorney] on or before [date which is at least seven days after the date of mailing or delivering the affidavit to the opposing party], together with a proof of service.

§ 7429. Hearings

(a) Every hearing in a contested case shall be presided over by a Hearing Officer appointed by the Commission. The Hearing Officer shall hear the case alone, unless a quorum of the Commission decides to hear the case along with the Hearing Officer. If the Commission itself decides to hear the case, the rules in the Administrative Procedure Act, Government Code sections 11512 and 11517(a), shall govern the proceeding.

(b) The hearing shall be open to public observation, unless the Hearing Officer orders closure of a hearing for one of the reasons set forth in Government Code section 11425.20, subdivision (a) (1)-(3).

(1) The Hearing Officer may exclude persons whose conduct impedes the orderly conduct of the hearing; restrict or regulate attendance because of the physical limitations of the hearing room; or take other action to promote due process or the orderly conduct of the hearing.

(2) The Hearing Officer may grant a motion to exclude witnesses under Evidence Code section 777.

(c) Time and place of hearing.

(1) The hearing shall commence within 90 days of the filing of the accusation unless the parties waive the 90–day hearing requirement contained in Government Code section 12968, or a continuance has been granted, subject to the rule in section 7414, subdivision (c).

(2) The Department shall make arrangements for the place of hearing, unless otherwise ordered by the Commission. The hearing shall be held in the county in which the alleged violation of the Fair Employment and Housing Act occurred or where the respondent does business, unless the parties agree, or the Commission orders, that the hearing take place in some other place. A party may move for a change in the place in hearing by written motion to the Commission in compliance with regulation sections 7406, 7407 and 7419, no later than 10 days after service of the Notice of Hearing, because of economic hardship, convenience of witnesses, or other good cause.

(3) The hearing shall ordinarily be conducted with the parties present before the Hearing Officer, unless the Hearing Officer, with the approval of the parties, permits the hearing to be conducted by telephone, television, or other electronic means.

(4) The Department shall attempt to consult with the respondent or respondent's representative prior to sending out the Notice of Hearing, in order to select mutually agreeable dates of hearing.

(d) Conduct of hearings

(1) The proceedings at the hearing shall be reported by a stenographic reporter. Upon the consent of all the parties, however, the proceedings may be reported electronically.

(2) If the Hearing Officer determines to order a transcript, the Commission shall receive an original and one copy. The Commission retains the original and the copy goes to the Department. Respondents and complainants, if they desire a copy of the transcript, are responsible for ordering their own copy of the transcript.

(e) Motions during hearing

(1) Motions during the hearing, including motions in limine, shall be directed to the Hearing Officer, and may be made orally on the record or in writing with copies served on all parties and the complainant. The Hearing Officer shall rule on all motions, except as provided below in 2., orally on the record, unless s/he reserves ruling until after the close of the hearing, in which case the ruling shall be made a part of the proposed decision.

(2) The Hearing Officer shall not entertain motions in the nature of motions for non-suit, dismissal, or for judgment, but must proceed with the taking of evidence

until all of the testimony to be offered by all the parties has been received.

(f) Evidence rules

(1) Oral evidence shall be taken only on oath or affirmation.

(2) Each party shall have these rights: to call and examine witnesses, to introduce exhibits; to cross-examine opposing witnesses on any matter relevant to the issues, even though that matter was not covered in the direct examination; to impeach any witness, regardless of which party first called him or her to testify; and to rebut the evidence against him or her. Any party may call any other party during its case in chief, pursuant to Evidence Code section 776.

(3) The hearing need not be conducted according to technical rules relating to evidence and witnesses, except as hereinafter provided. Any relevant evidence shall be admitted if it is the sort of evidence on which responsible persons are accustomed to rely in the conduct of serious affairs, regardless of the existence of any common law or statutory rule which might make improper the admission of the evidence over objection in civil actions.

(4) Hearsay evidence may be used for the purpose of supplementing or explaining other evidence. If an appropriate objection is made at hearing, hearsay evidence shall not be sufficient in itself to support a finding unless it would be admissible over objection in civil actions.

(5) The rules of privilege shall apply in administrative adjudications before the Commission to the extent that they are recognized under the Evidence Code.

(6) The Hearing Officer has discretion to exclude evidence if its probative value is substantially outweighed by the probability that its admission will necessitate undue consumption of time because of its collateral or cumulative nature, or create substantial danger of undue prejudice or of confusing the issues.

(7) In any proceeding under subdivisions (a), (h) or (i) of Government Code section 12940, or section 12955, alleging conduct that constitutes sexual harassment, sexual assault, or sexual battery, evidence of specific instances of a complainant's sexual conduct with individuals other than the alleged perpetrator is subject to all of the following limitations:

(A) The evidence is not discoverable unless it is to be offered at a hearing to attack the credibility of the complainant as provided for under (C) below. This paragraph is intended only to limit the scope of discovery; it is not intended to affect the methods of discovery allowed by statute.

(B) The evidence is not admissible at the hearing unless offered to attack the credibility of the complainant as provided for under (C) below. Reputation or opinion evidence regarding the sexual behavior of the complainant is not admissible for any purpose.

(C) Evidence of specific instances of a complainant's sexual conduct with individuals other than the alleged

perpetrator is presumed inadmissible absent an offer of proof establishing its relevance and reliability and that its probative value is not substantially outweighed by the probability that its admission will create substantial danger of undue prejudice or confuse the issue.

(8) At the beginning of the hearing, the Department shall introduce into the record, for jurisdictional purposes only, the Pleading File in the case. The Pleading File shall contain, at a minimum, the complaint(s) and accusations(s), any Notice(s) of Defense or other responsive papers filed by the respondent(s) and the proofs of service for each document. If applicable under Government Code section 12980(f), 12981(a), or 12981(c), the pleading file shall also contain a copy of any notifications provided to the complainant and respondent explaining the Department's reason(s) for failing to complete the investigation or issue the accusation within 100 days, or make a final administrative disposition of the complaint within one year.

§ 7430. Default Hearings

(a) At a default hearing, the Hearing Officer may take action based upon the respondent's express admission or upon other evidence introduced at the hearing by the Department. Affidavits or declarations under penalty of perjury may be used as evidence without notice to respondent as allowed by section 7428.

(b) The Hearing Officer and/or Commission may issue an order adversely affecting the respondent in a default hearing if the Department has complied with the rules set forth in section 7407(e).

§ 7431. Official Notice

In reaching a decision, official notice may be taken, either before or after submission of the case for decision, of any generally accepted technical or scientific matter within the Commission's special field, and of any fact which may be judicially noticed by the courts of this state, pursuant to Evidence Code sections 451 and 452. Parties present at the hearing shall be informed by the Hearing Officer or Commission of the matters to be noticed, and those matters shall be noted in the record, referred to therein, or appended thereto. All parties shall be given a reasonable opportunity to refute the officially noticed matters by evidence or by written or, if requested, oral presentation of authority to the Commission.

§ 7432. Post–Hearing Matters

(a) Post-hearing briefs. The parties shall be given the opportunity to file post-hearing briefs, as directed at the hearing. Copies shall be served on the parties and on the complainants as provided in section 7407.

(b) Date of submission of matter for decision. The matter will be deemed submitted to the Hearing Officer for decision on the date the Hearing Officer receives the transcripts of the hearing, hears oral argument, or receives the last timely post-hearing brief, whichever event occurs last.

§ 7433. Proposed Decisions

(a) Form of decision.

(1) The decision shall be in writing, be based on the record, and include a statement of the factual and legal basis of the decision.

(2) If the factual basis for the decision includes a determination based substantially on the credibility of a witness, the statement shall identify specific evidence of the observed demeanor, manner, or attitude of the witness that supports the determination, and on judicial review the court shall give great weight to the determination, to the extent that the determination identifies the observed demeanor, manner, or attitude of the witness that supports it.

(3) The statement of the factual basis for the decision shall be based exclusively on the evidence of record in the proceeding and on matters officially noticed in the proceeding. The Hearing Officer's experience, technical competence, and specialized knowledge may be used in evaluating evidence.

(b) Preparation of proposed decision. Within 60 days after the case is submitted, the Hearing Officer shall prepare and serve on the Commission, all parties and the complainant, or their representatives of record, a proposed decision in such a form that it may be adopted by the Commission as the Commission's decision in the case. Failure of the Hearing Officer to deliver a proposed decision within the time required does not prejudice the rights of the Commission in the case.

§ 7434. Commission Decisions

(a) Adoption or modification of proposed decision. Upon receipt of a proposed decision, the Commission may do any of the following:

(1) Adopt the proposed decision in its entirety.

(2) Reduce or otherwise mitigate the proposed remedy and adopt the balance of the proposed decision.

(3) Make technical or other minor changes in the proposed decision and adopt it as the decision. Action by the Commission under this paragraph is limited to clarifying changes or changes of a similar nature that do not affect the factual or legal basis of the proposed decision.

(b) Non-adoption of proposed decision. If the proposed decision is not adopted as provided in subdivision (a), the Commission may decide the case upon the record, including the transcript, or may refer the case to the same Hearing Officer, if available, to take additional evidence. The parties shall be notified of their ability to order a transcript in the case. If the case is assigned to a Hearing Officer for the taking of additional evidence, he or she shall prepare a proposed decision as provided in section 7433, subdivision (a) upon the receipt of the additional evidence and the transcript and other papers which are part of the record of the prior hearing. A copy of the proposed decision shall be served on the Commis-

sion and all parties and complainant, as prescribed below in subdivision (e).

(1) Before deciding any case on the record, the Commission shall give the parties the opportunity to present further written argument and/or, if the Commission so chooses, to present further oral argument before the Commission.

(2) If the analysis of the further argument reveals the need for additional evidence, the Commission may order the taking of additional evidence, either by the Commission or by the Hearing Officer. Following receipt of the additional evidence, the Commission may require further written or oral argument before deeming the case submitted to it for decision. If additional oral evidence is taken by the Commission, no Commissioner may vote unless the member heard the additional oral evidence.

(c) The proposed decision shall be deemed adopted by the Commission 100 days after service to the Commission by the Hearing Officer, unless within that time: (1) the Commission notifies the parties that the proposed decision is not adopted and commences proceedings to decide the case itself upon the record, or (2) the Commission refers the case to the Hearing Officer to take additional evidence.

(d) The decision of the Commission shall be a public record.

(e) Copies of the Commission decision shall be served by the Commission by first class, certified or registered mail on all parties and the complainant or their representatives of record. Proof of service shall be as set forth in section 7407.

(f) Within 15 days after service of a copy of the decision on a party, but not later than the effective date of the decision, the party may apply to the Commission for correction of a mistake or clerical error in the decision, stating the specific ground on which the application is made. Notice of the application shall be given to the other parties to the proceeding. The application is not a prerequisite for seeking judicial review.

(1) The Commission may refer the application to the Hearing Officer who wrote the proposed decision or may delegate its authority under this section to one or more persons.

(2) The Commission may deny the application, grant the application and modify the decision, or grant the application and set the matter for further proceedings. The application is considered denied if the Commission does not dispose of it within 30 days after it is made.

(3) Nothing in this section precludes the Commission on its own motion, or on motion of the Hearing Officer, from modifying the decision to correct a mistake or clerical error. A modification under this subdivision shall be made within 30 days after issuance of the decision.

(4) The Commission shall, within 15 days after correction of a mistake or clerical error in the decision, serve a

copy of the correction on each party and complainant on which a copy of the decision was previously served.

(g) The decision shall become effective 30 days after it is mailed to the parties and the complainant, unless a reconsideration of the decision is ordered within that time, or the Commission orders that the decision shall become effective sooner, or a stay of execution is granted by the Commission.

§ 7435. Precedential Decisions

(a) The Commission may designate, as a precedential decision, any decision or part of any decision that contains a significant legal or policy determination of general application that is likely to recur. Once the Commission designates a decision or part of a decision as precedential, the Commission may rely on it or that part of it as precedent and the parties may cite to such decisions in their argument to the Commission and courts.

(b) The Commission shall publish, on an annual basis, an index of significant legal and policy determinations made in its precedential decisions and shall publish annually the availability of this index in the California Regulatory Notice Register. The Commission shall also make the index and precedential decisions available for inspection in its office and shall make the index available to the public by subscription or other on-line means.

§ 7436. Reconsideration

(a) The Commission may order a reconsideration of all or part of a Commission decision on its own motion or by petition of any party. A party may petition the Commission for reconsideration within 20 days of the date a decision is mailed to the party. The power to order reconsideration shall expire 30 days after the delivery or mailing of a Commission decision to all parties and the complainant or upon the termination of a stay of not to exceed 30 days which the Commission may grant for the purpose of filing a petition for reconsideration. If the Commission needs additional time to evaluate a timely petition for reconsideration, the Commission may grant a stay of the expiration for no more than 10 days, for the sole purpose of considering the petition.

(b) The decision may be reconsidered by the Commission on all the pertinent parts of the record and such additional evidence and argument as the Commission permits, or the Commission may assign the case back to the Hearing Officer for the taking of additional evidence, pursuant to the rules set forth in section 7435, subdivision (b). If oral evidence is introduced before the Commission, no Commissioner may vote unless he or she heard the evidence.

§ 7437. Judicial Review

The Commission incorporates by reference the rules for judicial review which are found in the Administrative Procedure Act, Government Code section 11523, and, for housing discrimination cases, Government Code section 12987.1.

§ 7438. Appendices

A. Subpoena and subpoena duces tecum form.

B. Judicial Council Rule 989.3 and Evidence Code section 754.

C. Pre-hearing statement form.

Appendix A

Attorney (Name and Address):

_____
_____

Attorney for (Name):_____

_____

Telephone Number: _____

In the Matter of the Accusation   )
   of the   )
DEPARTMENT OF FAIR EMPLOYMENT)   Case No. _____
AND HOUSING   )
     v.   )
_____,)   [ ] SUBPOENA
           Respondent(s).)   [ ] SUBPOENA DUCES TECUM
. . . .)
_____,)
        Complainant(s).)

TO (Name): _____

1. YOU ARE ORDERED TO APPEAR AS A WITNESS in this action at the date, time and place shown in the box below UNLESS you make a special agreement with the person named in item 3:

    a. Date: Time:

    b. Address:

2. AND YOU ARE
    a. ☐ ordered to appear in person.
    b. ☐ ordered to appear in person and to produce the records described in the accompanying affidavit. The personal attendance of the custodian or other qualified witness and the production of the original records are required by this subpoena. The procedure authorized by subdivision (b) of section 1560, and sections 1561 and 1562, of the Evidence Code will not be deemed sufficient compliance with this subpoena.
    c. ☐ **You are not required to appear in person if you comply with Evidence Code sections 1560 and 1561.**

3. IF YOU HAVE ANY QUESTIONS ABOUT THE TIME OR DATE FOR YOU TO APPEAR, OR IF YOU WANT TO BE CERTAIN THAT YOUR PRESENCE IS REQUIRED, CONTACT THE FOLLOWING PERSON BEFORE THE DATE ON WHICH YOU ARE TO APPEAR:
    a. Name: _____
    b. Telephone Number: _____

4. Witness Fees: You are entitled to witness fees and mileage actually traveled both ways, as provided by law, if you request them before your scheduled appearance from the person named in item 3.

           DISOBEDIENCE OF THIS SUBPOENA MAY BE PUNISHED AS CONTEMPT.

Date Issued:

_____   _____
(Type or Print Name)   (Signature of Person issuing Subpoena)

                                  _____
                                        (Title)

THE SUBPOENAING PARTY IS REQUIRED TO SERVE A COPY OF THIS SUBPOENA ON THE OPPOSING PARTY (DEPARTMENT OF FAIR EMPLOYMENT AND HOUSING OR RESPONDENT), AS WELL AS ON THE WITNESS WHO IS BEING SUBPOENAED, AND MUST COMPLY WITH ANY APPLICABLE CONSUMER NOTICE REQUIREMENTS (Code of Civil Procedure §§ 1985.3 and 1985.6).

Appendix B

RULE 989.3 REQUESTS FOR ACCOMMODATIONS BY PERSONS WITH DISABILITIES

  (a) [Policy] It shall be the policy of the courts of this state to assure that qualified individuals with disabilities have equal and full access to the judicial system. Nothing in this rule shall be construed to impose limitations or to invalidate the remedies, rights, and procedures accorded to any qualified individuals with disabilities under state or federal law.

  (b) [Definitions] The following definitions shall apply under this rule:

  (1) "Qualified individuals with disabilities" means persons covered by the Americans with Disabilities Act of 1990 (42 U.S.C. s12101 et seq.); Civil Code section 51 et seq.; and other related state and federal laws; and includes individuals who have a physical or mental impairment that substantially limits one or more of the major life activities; have a record of such an impairment; or are regarded as having such an impairment.

  (2) "Applicant" means any lawyer, party, witness, juror, or any other individual with an interest in attending any proceeding before any court of this state.

  (3) "Accommodation(s)" may include, but are not limited to, making reasonable modifications in policies, practices, and procedures; furnishing, at no charge, to the qualified individuals with disabilities, auxiliary aids and services, which are not limited to equipment, devices, materials in alternative formats, and qualified interpreters or readers; and making each service, program, or activity, when viewed in its entirety, readily accessible to and usable by qualified individuals with disabilities requesting accommodations. While not requiring that each existing facility be accessible, this standard, known as "program accessibility," must be provided by methods

including alteration of existing facilities, acquisition or construction of additional facilities, relocation of a service or program to an accessible facility, or provision of services at alternate sites.

(4) The "rule" means this rule regarding requests for accommodations in state courts by qualified individuals with disabilities.

(5) "Confidentiality" applies to the identity of the applicant in all oral or written communications, including all files and documents submitted by an applicant as part of the application process.

(c) [Process] The following process for requesting accommodations is established:

(1) Applications requesting accommodation(s) pursuant to this rule may be presented ex parte in writing, on a form approved by the Judicial Council and provided by the court, or orally as the court may allow. Applications should be made at the designated Office of the Clerk, or to the courtroom clerk or judicial assistant where the proceeding will take place, or to the judicial officer who will preside over the proceeding.

(2) All applications for accommodations shall include a description of the accommodation sought, along with a statement of the impairment that necessitates such accommodation. The court, in its discretion, may require the applicant to provide additional information about the qualifying impairment.

(3) Applications should be made as far in advance of the requested accommodations implementation date as possible, and in any event should be made no less than five court days prior to the requested implementation date. The court may, in its discretion, waive this requirement.

(4) Upon request, the court shall place under seal the identity of the applicant as designated on the application form and all other identifying information provided to the court pursuant to the application.

(d) [Permitted communication] An applicant may make ex parte communications with the court; such communications shall deal only with the accommodation(s) the applicant's disability requires and shall not deal in any manner with the subject matter or merits of the proceedings before the court.

(e) [Grant of accommodation] A court shall grant an accommodation as follows:

(1) In determining whether to grant an accommodation and what accommodation to grant, the court shall consider, but is not limited by, the provisions of the Americans with Disabilities Act of 1990 and related state and federal laws.

(2) The court shall inform the applicant in writing of findings of fact and orders, as may be appropriate, that the request for accommodations is granted or denied, in whole or in part, and the nature of the accommodation(s) to be provided, if any.

(f) [Denial of accommodation] An application may be denied only if the court finds that:

(1) The applicant has failed to satisfy the requirements of this rule; or

(2) The requested accommodation(s) would create an undue financial or administrative burden on the court; or

(3) The requested accommodation(s) would fundamentally alter the nature of the service, program, or activity.

(g) [Review procedure]

(1) An applicant or any participant in the proceeding in which an accommodation has been denied or granted may seek review of a determination made by nonjudicial court personnel within 10 days of the date of the notice of denial or grant by submitting a request for review to the judicial officer who will preside over the proceeding or to the presiding judge if the matter has not been assigned.

(2) An applicant or any participant in the proceeding in which an accommodation has been denied or granted may seek review of a determination made by a presiding judge or any other judicial officer of a court within 10 days of the date of the notice of denial or grant by filing a petition for extraordinary relief in a court of superior jurisdiction.

(h) [Duration of accommodations] The accommodations by the court shall commence on the date indicated in the notice of accommodation and shall remain in effect for the period specified in the notice of accommodation. The court may grant accommodations for indefinite periods of time or for a particular matter or appearance.

Adopted, eff. Jan. 1, 1996.

EVIDENCE CODE

§ 754. Deaf or Hearing Impaired Persons; Interpreters; Qualifications; Guidelines; Compensation; Questioning; Use of Statements

(a) As used in this section, "individual who is deaf or hearing impaired" means an individual with a hearing loss so great as to prevent his or her understanding language spoken in a normal tone, but does not include an individual who is hearing impaired provided with, and able to fully participate in the proceedings through the use of, an assistive listening system or computer-aided transcription equipment provided pursuant to Section 54.8 of the Civil Code.

(b) In any civil or criminal action, including, but not limited to, any action involving a traffic or other infraction, any small claims court proceeding, any juvenile court proceeding, any family court proceeding or service, or any proceeding to determine the mental competency of a person, in any court-ordered or court-provided alternative dispute resolution, including mediation and arbitration, or any administrative hearing, where a party or witness is an individual who is deaf or hearing impaired and the individual who is deaf or hearing impaired is present and participating, the proceedings shall be interpreted in a language that the individual who is deaf or hearing impaired understands by a qualified interpreter appointed by the court or other appointing authority, or as agreed upon.

(c) For purposes of this section, "appointing authority" means a court, department, board, commission, agency licensing or legislative body, or other body for proceedings requiring a qualified interpreter.

(d) For the purposes of this section, "interpreter" includes, but is not limited to, an oral interpreter, a sign language interpreter, or a deaf-blind interpreter, depending upon the needs of the individual who is deaf or hearing impaired.

(e) For purposes of this section, "intermediary interpreter" means an individual who is deaf or hearing impaired, or a hearing individual who is able to assist in providing an accurate interpretation between spoken English and sign language or between variants of sign language or between American Sign Language and other foreign languages by acting as an intermediary between the individual who is deaf or hearing impaired and the qualified interpreter.

(f) For purposes of this section, "qualified interpreter" means an interpreter who has been certified as competent to interpret court proceedings by a testing organization, agency, or educational institution approved by the Judicial Council as qualified to administer tests to court interpreters for individuals who are deaf or hearing impaired.

(g) In the event that the appointed interpreter is not familiar with the use of particular signs by the individual who is deaf or hearing impaired or his or her particular variant of sign language, the court or other appointing authority shall, in consultation with the individual who is deaf or hearing impaired or his or her representative, appoint an intermediary interpreter.

(h) Prior to July 1, 1992, the Judicial Council shall conduct a study to establish the guidelines pursuant to which it shall determine which testing organizations, agencies, or educational institutions will be approved to administer tests for certification of court interpreters for individuals who are deaf or hearing impaired. It is the intent of the Legislature that the study obtain the widest possible input from the public, including, but not limited to, educational institutions, the judiciary, linguists, members of the State Bar, court interpreters, members of professional interpreting organizations, and members of the deaf and hearing-impaired communities. After obtaining public comment and completing its study, the Judicial Council shall publish these guidelines. By January 1, 1997, the Judicial Council shall approve one or more entities to administer testing for court interpreters for individuals who are deaf or hearing impaired. Testing entities may include educational institutions, testing organizations, joint powers agencies, or public agencies.

Commencing July 1, 1997, court interpreters for individuals who are deaf or hearing impaired shall meet the qualifications specified in subdivision (f).

(i) Persons appointed to serve as interpreters under this section shall be paid, in addition to actual travel costs, the prevailing rate paid to persons employed by the court to provide other interpreter services unless such service is considered to be a part of the person's regular duties as an employee of the state, county, or other political subdivision of the state. Payment of the interpreter's fee shall be a charge against the county, or other political subdivision of the state, in which that action is pending. Payment of the interpreter's fee in administrative proceedings shall be a charge against the appointing board or authority.

(j) Whenever a peace officer or any other person having a law enforcement or prosecutorial function in any criminal or quasi-criminal investigation or proceeding questions or otherwise interviews an alleged victim or witness who demonstrates or alleges deafness or hearing impairment, a good faith effort to secure the services of an interpreter shall be made, without any unnecessary delay unless either the individual who is deaf or hearing impaired affirmatively indicates that he or she does not need or cannot use an interpreter, or an interpreter is not otherwise required by Title II of the Americans with Disabilities Act of 1990 (Public Law 101–336) and federal regulations adopted thereunder.

(k) No statement, written or oral, made by an individual who the court finds is deaf or hearing impaired in reply to a question of a peace officer, or any other person having a law enforcement or prosecutorial function in any criminal or quasi-criminal investigation or proceeding, may be used against that individual who is deaf or hearing impaired unless the question was accurately interpreted and the statement was made knowingly, voluntarily, and intelligently and was accurately interpreted, or the court makes special findings that either the individual could not have used an interpreter or an interpreter was not otherwise required by Title II of the Americans with Disabilities Act of 1990 (Public Law 101–336) and federal regulations adopted thereunder and that the statement was made knowingly, voluntarily, and intelligently.

(*l*) In obtaining services of an interpreter for purposes of subdivision (j) or (k), priority shall be given to first obtaining a qualified interpreter.

(m) Nothing in subdivision (j) or (k) shall be deemed to supersede the requirement of subdivision (b) for use of a qualified interpreter for individuals who are deaf or hearing impaired participating as parties or witnesses in a trial or hearing.

(n) In any action or proceeding in which an individual who is deaf or hearing impaired is a participant, the appointing authority shall not commence proceedings until the appointed interpreter is in full view of and spatially situated to assure proper communication with the participating individual who is deaf or hearing impaired.

(*o*) Each superior court shall maintain a current roster of qualified interpreters certified pursuant to subdivision (f).

(Amended by Stats. 1995, c. 143 (A.B. 1833), s1. eff. July 18, 1995.)

Appendix C

PRE–HEARING STATEMENT

You may, but do not have to, use this form to prepare your Pre–Hearing Statement which must be filed with the Commission no later than five working days before the scheduled date of hearing. Failure to fully disclose all required items in the Pre–Hearing Statement may result in the exclusion or restriction of evidence at the hearing. Please see the Commission's procedural regulations, at California Code of Regulations, Title 2, sections 7400 et seq., for more details.

In the Matter of the Accusation of the	)))
DEPARTMENT OF FAIR EMPLOYMENT AND HOUSING	) **PRE–HEARING STATEMENT**) (Cal. Code Regs. s7422)))
v.	)) Case No.:) Hearing Date:
(RESPONDENT'S NAME),	)
.... Respondent(s).	))
.... (COMPLAINANT'S NAME), Complainant(s).	))))

1. Brief summary of any stipulated facts:
2. Pleadings in the case: Date of accusation: Date(s) of any amended accusation(s): Date of Notice of Defense: Title and date of any other pleading filed in the case:
3. Estimated time necessary to try your case:
4. List of all witnesses as follows:
   Name of witnesses/brief statement of anticipated testimony.
5. List of all expert witnesses as follows: Name of expert witness/brief statement of anticipated testimony.
6. Exhibits Each exhibit shall be separately listed and shall include a description that is sufficient for identification.
7.   Evidence by Affidavit or Deposition (must comply with California Code of Regulations, Title 2, ss 7427 and 7428.)

Name of Witness	Reason that witness is unavailable
_____	_____
_____	_____

8. Major evidentiary issues, if any, in the case:
9. Attach copy of any pre-hearing motion, any response to the motion, and any order.
10 Attach any anticipated motions in limine.
11. Other issues or matters.

Date: _____

Signature: _____

Typed Name: _____

Attorney for: _____

Subchapter 3.   Investigative Hearing (Reserved)

Subchapter 4.   Advisory Agencies and Councils (Reserved)

Chapter 5.   Contractor Nondiscrimination and Compliance

Subchapter 1.   General Matters

§ 8101.   Office of Compliance Programs

(a) Creation and Authority. The Department of Fair Employment and Housing (DFEH) is responsible for the

administration of policies, the implementation of standards, and the enforcement of the rules and regulations set forth in this chapter. The DFEH has created the Office of Compliance Programs (OCP) to carry out these responsibilities. The OCP will operate under the procedures established in this chapter as well as under other procedures of the Commission as set out in this division.

COMMENT As of the date these regulations were adopted, DFEH headquarters and OCP were located at 1201 I Street, Suite 211, Sacramento, CA 95814, telephone (916) 323–4547.

(b) Administrator. The OCP will operate under the direction of an Administrator of Compliance Programs who shall be appointed by and be responsible to the Director of the Department. The Administrator will have direct responsibility for the appointment of staff and the organization and operation of the OCP consistent with the terms of the Act and the provisions of this chapter.

§ 8102.   Definitions

The words defined in this section shall have the meanings set forth below whenever they appear in this chapter, unless:

(1) the context in which they are used clearly requires a different meaning; or

(2) a different definition is prescribed for a particular subchapter or provision.

The definitions set forth previously in this division in Sections 7285.2, 7286.5, 7287.2, 7290.7, 7291.2(b), 7292.1, 7293.6, and 7295.1 are also applicable to this chapter.

(a) Bid means any proposal or other request by an employer to a contract awarding agency wherein the employer seeks to be awarded a state contract.

(b) Business means any corporation, partnership, individual, sole proprietorship, joint stock company, joint venture, or any other legal entity.

(c) Construction means the process of building, altering, repairing, improving, or demolishing any public structure or building, or other public improvements of any kind to any State of California real property. It does not include the routine operation, routine repair, or routine maintenance of existing structures, buildings, or real property.

(d) Contract or state contract means all types of agreements, regardless of what they may be called, for the purchase or disposal of supplies, services, or construction to which a contract awarding agency is a party. It includes awards and notices of award; contracts of a fixed-price, cost, cost-plus-a-fixed-fee, or incentive type; contracts providing for the issuance of job or task orders. It also includes supplemental agreements or contract modifications with respect to any of the foregoing.

(e) Contract awarding agency or awarding agency means any department, agency, board, commission, division or other unit of the State of California which is authorized to enter into state contracts.

(f) Contractor means any person having a contract with a contract awarding agency or a subcontract for the performance of a contract with such an agency.

(g) Data means recorded information, regardless of form or characteristic.

(h) (Reserved)

(i) Decertification means the decision by OCP that an employer's nondiscrimination program fails to comply with the requirements of the Fair Employment and Housing Act and/or its implementing regulations either because it is poorly designed or because it has not been properly implemented or because of the person's failure to cooperate with OCP it cannot be determined whether the nondiscrimination program meets the requirements of this chapter. Decertification of a program shall continue until OCP certifies that the contractor is in compliance with the requirements of this chapter.

(j) Decision means the decision of the hearing officer regarding the allegations of a show cause notice issued pursuant to Section 8503 of this chapter. A decision shall dismiss, modify, or sustain the allegations of the show cause notice; provide the factual basis for the decision; and include any sanctions to be recommended to the awarding agency together with a statement of the reasons in support thereof.

(k) Employee means an individual under the direction and control of a contractor under any appointment or contract of hire or apprenticeship, express or implied, oral or written.

(l) (Reserved)

(m) May denotes the permissive.

(n) Minority refers to an individual who is ethnically or racially classifiable in one of four major groups: Black, Hispanic. Asian or Pacific Islander; or American Indian or Alaskan Native.

(1) Black includes persons having their primary origins in any of the black racial groups of Africa, but not of Hispanic origin;

(2) Hispanic includes persons of primary culture or origin in Mexico, Puerto Rico, Cuba, Central or South America, or other Spanish derived culture or origin regardless of race;

(3) Asian/Pacific Islander includes persons having primary origins in any of the original peoples of the Far East, Southeast Asia, the Indian Subcontinent, or the Pacific Islands. This area includes, for example, China, Japan, Korea, the Philippine Islands, and Samoa; and

(4) American Indian/Alaskan Native includes persons having primary origins in any of the original peoples of North America, and who maintain culture identification through tribal affiliation or community recognition.

(o) Nondiscrimination Clause means the clause to be included in each state contract or subcontract pursuant to these regulations.

(p) Person means any business, individual, union, committee, club, or other organization or group of individuals.

(q) Prime contractor means any individual or organization who directly contracts with the State of California.

(r) Service and supply contract includes any contract except a construction contract.

(s) Services means the furnishing of labor, time, or effort by a contractor, not involving the delivery of a specific end product other than reports which are merely incidental to the required performance. This term shall not include collective bargaining agreements or arrangements between parties which constitute that of employer and employee.

(t) Shall denotes the imperative.

(u) Subcontract means any agreement or arrangement executed by a contractor with a third party in which the latter agrees to provide all or specified part of the supplies, services or construction required in the original state contract. This does not include arrangements between parties which constitute that of employer and employee.

(v) Subcontractor means any individual or organization holding a subcontract for the performance of all or any part of a state contract.

§ 8102.5. Nondiscrimination Agreement

State contracts exempt from the requirements of Section 8107 shall include, as an express or implied term, the term set out in either Section 8107 Clause (a) or Clause (b). Breach of this term of contract may constitute a material breach of the contract, and may result in the imposition of sanctions by the awarding agency and may result in decertification from future opportunities to contract with the state.

§ 8103. Requirement of Nondiscrimination Program

All employers who are, or wish to become, contractors with the state must develop and implement a nondiscrimination program as defined in Section 8104 of this chapter unless specifically exempted pursuant to Section 8115 of this chapter.

§ 8104. Nondiscrimination Program

(a) Definition and Purpose. A nondiscrimination program (hereinafter referred to as "the Program") is a set of specific and result-oriented procedures to which a contractor or subcontractor commits itself for the purpose of insuring equal employment opportunity for all employees or applicants for employment. It may include an affirmative action component which establishes goals and timetables to remedy any underutilization of minorities and/or women which is identified. The Program shall contain the following elements:

(1) Development or reaffirmation of the contractor's equal employment opportunity policy in all personnel actions.

(2) Formal internal and external dissemination of the contractor's policy.

(3) Establishment of responsibilities for implementation of the contractor's program.

(4) Annual identification of any existing practices which have resulted in disproportionately inhibiting the employment, promotion or retention of those protected by the Act.

(A) Analysis of Employment Selection Procedures. The Program shall include an identification and analysis of contractor promotional and entry-level selection procedures and shall identify any such procedures which have resulted in disproportionately inhibiting the employment, promotion or retention of minorities or women. The retention of such practices so identified can only be justified according to the principles of "business necessity" upon a demonstration that no reasonable alternatives to such practices exist. The prospective contractor shall eliminate any practices which cannot be so justified.

(B) Workforce Analysis. The Program will contain a workforce analysis which shall consist of a listing of each job title which appears in applicable collective bargaining agreements of payroll records ranked from the lowest paid to the highest paid within each department or other similar organizational unit, including departmental or unit supervisory personnel. For each job title, the total number of incumbents, and the total number of male and female incumbents, and the total number of male and female incumbents in each of the following groups must be given: Blacks, Hispanics, Asian/Pacific Islanders, and American Indian/Native Alaskans. The wage rate or salary range for each job title must be given. All job titles, including all managerial job titles, must be listed. If there are separate work units or lines of progression within a department, a separate list must be provided for each such work unit, or line, including unit supervisors. For lines of progression there must be indicated the order of jobs in the line through which an employee could move to the top of the line. Where there are no formal progression lines or usual promotional sequences, job titles should be listed by department, job families, or disciplines, in order of wage rates or salary ranges.

(C) Utilization Analysis. Employers with 250 or more employees must perform a utilization analysis which shall consist of an analysis of the major job groups at the facility in order to determine whether women and minorities are being underutilized when compared to their availability. A job group for this purpose shall consist of one or more jobs which have similar content, wage rates and opportunities. Underutilization is defined as having a statistically significant lower utilization of minorities or women in a particular job group than their availability. Availability is defined as the availability in the labor force. The labor force for this purpose may vary depending upon the type of job in question, and the contractor's past practice, and could encompass the contractor's existing employees, the area immediately surrounding the facility where the vacancy exists for low-skill jobs or it could encompass the entire nation for highly-skilled managerial positions. The employer shall conduct a separate utilization analysis for each minority group and women.

(5) Development and execution of action oriented programs designed to correct problems and attain equal employment opportunities for all applicants and employees.

(6) Design and implementation of internal audit and reporting systems to measure the effectiveness of the total program.

(b) Employers who have identified a practice or practices which have an adverse impact on one or more groups protected by the Act and which may unlawfully discriminate against members of such groups may wish to include an affirmative action component in their nondiscrimination programs to minimize liability for discrimination, and correct past injustices; such affirmative action may be required of employers who are found to have discriminated in violation of the Act. Such a voluntary affirmative action component might contain, but need not be limited to, the following:

(1) Active support of local and national community action programs and community service programs designed to improve the employment opportunities of minorities and women;

(2) Providing training opportunities to minorities and women within the employer's organization which will qualify them for promotion when openings become available;

(3) Encouraging qualified women and minorities within the employer's organization to seek and accept transfers and promotions which increase their future opportunities;

(4) Actively recruit qualified minorities and women, even those not currently seeking such employment;

(5) Establishing and/or supporting training programs for entry level positions; and

(6) Establishing goals and objectives by organizational units and job groups, including timetables for completion. Establishment and implementation of a nondiscrimination program which contains an effective affirmative action component will create a rebuttable presumption that a contractor is in compliance with the requirements of Government Code, Section 12990 and its implementing regulations.

(c) An employer with multiple facilities may establish a single nondiscrimination program for its organization, but must perform separate analyses pursuant to subsections (a)(4)(A), (B), and (C) above for each establishment.

§ 8106. Prima Facie Compliance

Compliance with a nondiscrimination or affirmative action program subject to review and approval by a federal compliance agency shall constitute prima facie evidence that a contractor has complied with the requirements of Sections 8103 and 8104, unless the federal agency has found that the program is not in compliance with federal law, in which case compliance with a current federal commitment letter or conciliation agreement shall constitute prima facie evidence that a contractor has complied with the requirements of Sections 8103 and 8104. Such prima facie evidence can be rebutted by a preponderance of the evidence to the contrary.

§ 8107. Nondiscrimination Clause

Each state contract shall contain a Nondiscrimination Clause unless specifically exempted pursuant to Section 8115. The governmental body awarding the contract may use either clause (a) or clause (b) below. Clause (a) will satisfy the requirements of Section 12990 of the Government Code only; clause (b) contains language which will satisfy the requirements of both the Fair Employment and Housing Act and Article 9.5, Chapter 1, Part 1, Division 3, Title 2 of the Government Code (adopted pursuant to Government Code, Sections11135–11139.5). Standardized state form OCP–1, containing clause (a), and OCP–2, containing clause (b), will be available through the OCP. These forms may be incorporated into a contract by reference and will fulfill the requirement of this section. The contracting parties may, in lieu of incorporating form OCP–1 or OCP–2, include the required clause in the written contract directly.

Clause (a)

1. During the performance of this contract, contractor and its subcontractors shall not unlawfully discriminate against any employee or applicant for employment because of race, religion, color, national origin, ancestry, physical handicap, medical condition, marital status, age (over 40) or sex. Contractors and subcontractors shall insure that the evaluation and treatment of their employees and applicants for employment are free of such discrimination. Contractors and subcontractors shall comply with the provisions of the Fair Employment and Housing Act (Gov. Code, Section 12900 et seq.) and the applicable regulations promulgated thereunder (Cal. Admin. Code, Tit. 2, Section 7285.0 et seq.). The applicable regulations of the Fair Employment and Housing Commission implementing Government Cod, Section 12990, set forth in Chapter 5 of Division 4 of Title 2 of the California Administrative Code are incorporated into this contract by reference and made a part hereof as if set forth in full. Contractor and its subcontractors shall give written notice of their obligations under this clause to labor organizations with which they have a collective bargaining or other agreement.

2. This Contractor shall include the nondiscrimination and compliance provisions of this clause in all subcontracts to perform work under the contract.

Clause (b)

1. During the performance of this contract, the recipient, contractor and its subcontractors shall not deny the contract's benefits to any person on the basis of religion, color, ethnic group identification, sex, age, physical or mental disability, nor shall they discriminate unlawfully against any employee or applicant for employment because of race, religion, color, national origin, ancestry, physical handicap, mental disability, medical condition, marital status, age (over 40) or sex. Contractor shall insure that the evaluation and treatment of employees and applicants for employment are free of such discrimination.

2. Contractor shall comply with the provisions of the Fair Employment and Housing Act (Gov. Code, Section 12900 et seq.), the regulations promulgated thereunder (Cal. Admin. Code, Tit. 2, Sections 7285.0 et seq.), the provisions of Article 9.5, Chapter 1, Part 1, Division 3, Title 2 of the Government Code (Gov. Code, Sections 11135–11139.5), and the regulations or standards adopted by the awarding state agency to implement such article.

3. Contractor or recipient shall permit access by representatives of the Department of Fair Employment and Housing and the awarding state agency upon reasonable notice at any time during the normal business hours, but in no case less than 24 hours notice, to such of its books, records, accounts, other sources of information and its facilities as said Department or Agency shall require to ascertain compliance with this clause.

4. Recipient, contractor and its subcontractors shall give written notice of their obligations under this clause to labor organizations with which they have a collective bargaining or other agreement.

5. The contractor shall include the nondiscrimination and compliance provisions of this clause in all subcontracts to perform work under the contract.

§ 8108. Subcontracts

The contractor shall include the nondiscrimination clause in its contract in all subcontracts to perform work under the contract, either directly or by incorporation by reference. Any such incorporation by reference shall be specific and prominent.

§ 8109. Enforcement of Clause

The "Nondiscrimination Clause" in state contracts and subcontracts shall be fully and effectively enforced. Any breach of its terms may constitute a material breach of the contract and may result in the imposition of sanctions against the contractor, including but not limited to cancellation, termination, or suspension of the contract in whole or in part, by the contract awarding agency or decertification from future opportunities to contract with the State of California by DFEH.

§ 8112. Contract Awarding Agency, Unresponsive Bids

(a) A contract awarding agency shall refuse to accept a bid or proposal on a state contract subject to this chapter when the bid is unaccompanied by a "Statement of Compliance" pursuant to Section 8113, and shall declare any such bid or proposal unresponsive.

(b) A contract awarding agency shall declare unresponsive any bid or proposal on a state contract that is submitted by a contractor on OCP's list of decertified contractors.

§ 8113. Statement of Compliance

(a) As a part of its bid an eligible prospective contractor which bids on a state contract must submit a statement under penalty of perjury to the awarding agency that it has complied with the requirement of Section 8103 of this chapter.

(b) No state contract, unless otherwise exempted pursuant to Section 8115, shall be awarded by any contract awarding agency unless the prospective contractor has filed with the agency as a part of its bid a statement, made under penalty of perjury, that the prospective contractor has complied with the requirements of Section 8103 of this chapter.

§ 8114. Subcontracting Prohibited with Ineligible Entities

(a) OCP shall establish and maintain a list of decertified contractors, which shall be updated monthly and published in the first California Notice Register published each month.

(b) No contractor with the State of California shall, during the performance of any contract with the State, enter into any subcontract with any person listed on OCP's list of decertified contractors during the month in which the bid is submitted.

(c) Subcontracting with a decertified contractor in violation of the provisions of this section may constitute a material breach of the contract and may result in the imposition of sanctions against the contractor, including but not limited to cancellation, termination, or suspension of the contract, in whole or in part by the awarding agency, or decertification by DFEH. Specific knowledge of the unlawfulness of the subcontract is not required to establish a breach, but will be considered by OCP and the contract awarding agency in their determination of the appropriate sanctions.

§ 8115. Exemptions

(a) Licensed rehabilitation workshops which are contractors of state contracting agencies are exempted from the requirements of this chapter.

(b) Contracts of less than $5,000 are automatically exempt from the requirements of Section 8107; contractors holding only such contracts are automatically exempt from the requirements of Section 8103, but are subject to Section 8102.5.

(c) A contractor with fewer than fifty (50) employees in its entire workforce may receive an automatic exemption from the Program requirements of Section 8104, subdivisions (a)(4)(B)-(C) pertaining to workforce and utilization analyses by filing a current "California Employer Information Report" annually with OCP. The OCP may remove any exemption granted under this subsection, in connection with any detailed review or any investigation instituted pursuant to Section 8401 or 8402,

or whenever the contractor is found to be in substantial noncompliance with the requirements of this chapter.

(d) Contracts and subcontracts which are awarded pursuant to a declaration of public emergency, a declaration or determination of emergency pursuant to Government Code, Section 14809 or Government Code, Section 14272, subdivision (a), (b), or (c), or a declared threat to the health, welfare or safety of the public are fully exempted from the requirements of Section 8107, and contractors holding only such contracts are exempt from the requirements of Section 8103, but remain subject to Section 8102.5.

(e) A construction contractor with fewer than 50 permanent employees may obtain an exemption from the requirements of Section 8104, subdivision (a)(4)(B)-(C) pertaining to workforce and utilization analyses by filing a CEIR annually with OCP. The OCP may remove any exemption granted under this subsection, in connection with any detailed review or any investigation instituted pursuant to Section 8401 or 8402, or whenever the contractor is found to be in substantial noncompliance with the requirements of this chapter.

(f) Exemptions of subsections (a) and (d) of this section shall be granted only upon application to the state contract awarding agency prior to the date the contract is awarded. The contract awarding agency shall, prior to the grant of any exemption under this section, require proof of satisfaction of the exemption conditions of this section. The OCP may issue opinion letters and guidelines from time to time to assist contact awarding agencies in making determinations under this section.

§ 8116. Advertisements for New Employees

In all written advertisements or recruitment efforts for new employees during the performance of a regulated contract, a contractor is required to prominently identify itself with the phrase "State Equal Opportunity Employer" or similar wording.

§ 8117. Recruitment

In the event that any labor organization from which employees are normally recruited and/or with which the contractor has a collective bargaining agreement is unable or unwilling to refer minorities or women the contractor or subcontractor shall take the following steps and, for a period of two years, keep a record thereof:

(a) Notify the California Employment Development Department and at least two minority or female referral organizations of the personnel needs and request appropriate referrals, and

(b) Notify any minority or female persons who have personally listed themselves with the contractor or subcontractor as seeking employment of any existing vacancies for which they may qualify;

(c) Notify minority, women's and community organizations that employment opportunities are available.

(d) Immediately notify OCP of the existence of the historical and present relationship between the contractor and labor organizations and detail the efforts of the contractor to secure adequate referrals through the labor organizations.

Neither the provisions of any collective bargaining agreement, nor the failure by a union with which the contractor has a collective bargaining agreement, to refer either minorities or women shall excuse the contractor's obligations under Government Code, Section 12990, or the regulations in this chapter.

§ 8117.5.   Notice of Contract

Contract awarding agencies shall give written notice to the Administrator within 10 working days of award of all contracts over $5,000. The notice shall include name, address and telephone number of the contractor; federal employer identification number; state contract identification number; date of contract award; contract amount; project location; name of contractor's agent who signed the contract; name of contract awarding agency and contract awarding officer; and brief description of the purpose or subject of the contract.

§ 8118.   Contract Forms

The State Department of General Services will have printed copies of the forms referred to in this chapter and shall make them available upon request.

§ 8119.   Access to Records and Employment Site

(a) Each contractor shall provide OCP with any relevant information requested and shall permit OCP access to its premises, upon reasonable notice, during normal business hours for the purpose of conducting on-site compliance reviews, employee interviews, and inspecting and copying such books, records, accounts and other material as may be relevant to a matter under investigation for the purpose of determining and enforcing compliance with this chapter.

(b) All information provided to DFEH in response to a request from OCP which contains or might reveal a trade secret referred to in Section 1905 of Title 18 of the United States Code, or other information that is confidential pursuant to Chapter 3.5 (commencing with Section 6250) of Division 7 of Title 1 of the Government Code, shall be considered confidential, except that such information may be disclosed to other officers or employees of DFEH and may be introduced as evidence in any hearing conducted pursuant to Section 8503 of this Chapter or Section 12967 of the Government Code. The hearing officer or the director shall issue such orders as may be appropriate to protect the confidentiality of such information.

§ 8120.   Complaints of Discrimination or Noncompliance

(a) Any interested person may lodge a written complaint of noncompliance with either DFEH or the contract awarding agency. The complaint shall state the name and address of the contractor, and shall set forth a description of the alleged noncompliance. Complaints lodged with the awarding agency shall be immediately referred to the Administrator of OCP. No complaint may be lodged after the expiration of one year from the date upon which the alleged noncompliance occurred.

OCP shall cause any written complaint lodged under the provisions of this section on which it intends to take action to be served, either personally or by ordinary first class mail, upon the respondent contractor and the awarding agency within 45 days. At the discretion of the Administrator, the complaint may not contain the name of the complaining party.

(b) OCP shall notify the contract awarding agency of any action pursuant to Section 8501 instituted against a contractor of the agency, and permit the agency to become a party to the action, except that the agency shall be fully responsive to any request for information made by OCP in connection with the action.

Subchapter 2. Regulations Applicable to Construction Contracts

§ 8200.   Scope

This subchapter applies to all nonexempt businesses which seek or hold any state construction contract or subcontract. The regulations in this subchapter are applicable to all of a construction contractor's employees who are engaged in on-site construction including those employees who work on a construction site where no state work is being performed.

§ 8201.   Notice of Requirements

The following notice shall be included in, and shall be a part of, all solicitations for offers and bids on all nonexempt state construction contracts and subcontracts, except that newspaper or trade publication advertisements need only state that the contract is subject to state contractor nondiscrimination and compliance requirements pursuant to Government Code, Section 12990:

NOTICE OF REQUIREMENT FOR NONDISCRIMINATION PROGRAM (GOV. CODE, SECTION 12990)

Your attention is called to the "Nondiscrimination Clause" set forth or referred to herein, which is applicable to all nonexempt state construction contracts and subcontracts and to the "Standard California Nondiscrimination Construction Contract Specifications" set forth herein. The Specifications are applicable to all nonexempt state construction contracts and subcontracts of $5,000 or more.

§ 8202.   Application to Permanent and Temporary Workforce

A construction contractor's nondiscrimination program established pursuant to Sections 8103 and 8104 of this chapter must ensure nondiscrimination within both its

1221

permanent workforce and its temporary on-site work-force. The Section 8104 requirements of workforce and utilization analyses, however, must be prepared only for permanent employees.

§ 8202.5. Transfers Prohibited

It is a violation of the contract, of Government Code Section 12990 and the regulations in Chapter 5 of Division 4 of Title 2 of the California Administrative Code to transfer women and minority employees or trainees from contractor to contractor or from project to project for the sole purpose of meeting the contractor's nondiscrimination obligations.

§ 8203. Standard California Nondiscrimination Construction Contract Specifications. (Gov. Code, Section 12990.)

In addition to the nondiscrimination clause set forth in Section 8107, all non-exempt state construction contracts and subcontracts of $5,000 or more shall include the specifications set forth in this section.

STANDARD CALIFORNIA NONDISCRIMINATION CONSTRUCTION CONTRACT SPECIFICATIONS

(GOV. CODE, SECTION 12990)

These specifications are applicable to all state contractors and subcontractors having a construction contract or subcontract of $5,000 or more.

1. As used in the specifications:

a. "Administrator" means Administrator, Office of Compliance Programs, California Department of Fair Employment and Housing, or any person to whom the Administrator delegates authority;

b. "Minority" includes:

(i) Black (all persons having primary origins in any of the black racial groups of Africa, but not of Hispanic origin);

(ii) Hispanic (all persons of primary culture or origin in Mexico, Puerto Rico, Cuba, Central or South America or other Spanish derived culture or origin regardless of race);

(iii) Asian/Pacific Islander (all persons having primary origins in any of the original peoples of the Far East, Southeast Asia, the Indian Subcontinent or the Pacific Islands); and

(iv) American Indian/Alaskan Native (all persons having primary origins in any of the original peoples of North America and who maintain culture identification through tribal affiliation or community recognition).

2. Whenever the contractor or any subcontractor subcontracts a portion of the work, it shall physically include in each subcontract of $5,000 or more the nondiscrimination clause in this contract directly or through incorporation by reference. Any subcontract for work involving a construction trade shall also include the

Standard California Construction Contract Specifications, either directly or through incorporation by reference.

3. The contractor shall implement the specific nondiscrimination standards provided in paragraphs 6(a) through (e) of these specifications.

4. Neither the provisions of any collective bargaining agreement, nor the failure by a union with whom the contractor has a collective bargaining agreement, to refer either minorities or women shall excuse the contractor's obligations under these specifications, Government Code, Section 12990, or the regulations promulgated pursuant thereto.

5. In order for the nonworking training hours of apprentices and trainees to be counted, such apprentices and trainees must be employed by the contractor during the training period, and the contractor must have made a commitment to employ the apprentices and trainees at the completion of their training, subject to the availability of employment opportunities. Trainees must be trained pursuant to training programs approved by the U.S. Department of Labor or the California Department of Industrial Relations.

6. The contractor shall take specific actions to implement its nondiscrimination program. The evaluation of the contractor's compliance with these specifications shall be based upon its effort to achieve maximum results from its actions. The contractor must be able to demonstrate fully its efforts under Steps a. through e. below:

a. Ensure and maintain a working environment free of harassment, intimidation, and coercion at all sites, and at all facilities at which the contractor's employees are assigned to work. The contractor, where possible, will assign two or more women to each construction project. The contractor shall specifically ensure that all foremen, superintendents, and other on-site supervisory personnel are aware of and carry out the contractor's obligations to maintain such a working environment, with specific attention to minority or female individuals working at such sites or in such facilities.

b. Provide written notification within seven days to the director of DFEH when the union or unions with which the Contractor has a collective bargaining agreement has not referred to the Contractor a minority person or woman sent by the Contractor, or when the Contractor has other information that the union referral process has impeded the Contractor's efforts to meet its obligations.

c. Disseminate the Contractor's equal employment opportunity policy by providing notice of the policy to unions and training, recruitment and outreach programs and requesting their cooperation in assisting the Contractor to meet its obligations; and by posting the company policy on bulletin boards accessible to all employees at each location where construction work is performed.

d. Ensure all personnel making management and employment decisions regarding hiring, assignment, layoff, termination, conditions of work, training, rates of pay or other employment decisions, including all supervisory personnel, superintendents, general foremen, on-site foremen, etc., are aware of the Contractor's equal employment opportunity policy and obligations, and discharge their responsibilities accordingly.

e. Ensure that seniority practices, job classifications, work assignments and other personnel practices, do not have a discriminatory effect by continually monitoring all personnel and employment related activities to ensure that the equal employment opportunity policy and the Contractor's obligations under these specifications are being carried out.

7. Contractors are encouraged to participate in voluntary associations which assist in fulfilling their equal employment opportunity obligations. The efforts of a contractor association, joint contractor-union, contractor-community, or other similar group of which the contractor is a member and participant, may be asserted as fulfilling any one or more of its obligations under these specifications provided that the contractor actively participates in the group, makes every effort to assure that the group has a positive impact on the employment of minorities and women in the industry, ensures that the concrete benefits of the program are reflected in the Contractor's minority and female workforce participation, and can provide access to documentation which demonstrates the effectiveness of actions taken on behalf of the Contractor. The obligation to comply, however, is the Contractor's.

8. The Contractor is required to provide equal employment opportunity for all minority groups, both male and female, and all women, both minority and non-minority. Consequently, the Contractor may be in violation of the Fair Employment and Housing Act (Gov. Code, Section 12990 et seq.) if a particular group is employed in a substantially disparate manner.

9. Establishment and implementation of a bona fide affirmative action plan pursuant to Section 8104 (b) of this Chapter shall create a rebuttable presumption that a contractor is in compliance with the requirements of Section 12990 of the Government Code and its implementing regulations.

10. The Contractor shall not use the nondiscrimination standards to discriminate against any person because of race, color, religion, sex, national origin, ancestry, physical handicap, medical condition, marital status or age over 40.

11. The Contractor shall not enter into any subcontract with any person or firm decertified from state contracts pursuant to Government Code Section 12990.

12. The Contractor shall carry out such sanctions and penalties for violation of these specifications and the nondiscrimination clause, including suspension, termination and cancellation of existing subcontracts as may be imposed or ordered pursuant to Government Code Section 12990 and its implementing regulations by the awarding agency. Any Contractor who fails to carry out such sanctions and penalties shall be in violation of these specifications and Government Code Section 12990.

13. The Contractor shall designate a responsible official to monitor all employment related activity to ensure that the company equal employment opportunity policy is being carried out, to submit reports relating to the provisions hereof as may be required by OCP and to keep records. Records shall at least include for each employee the name, address, telephone numbers, construction trade, union affiliation if any, employee identification number when assigned, social security number, race, sex, status, (e.g., mechanic, apprentice trainee, helper, or laborer), dates of changes in status, hours worked per week in the indicated trade, rate of pay, and locations at which the work was performed. Records shall be maintained in any easily understandable and retrievable form; however, to the degree that existing records satisfy this requirement, contractors shall not be required to maintain separate records.

§ 8204. Reporting Requirement

Contractors holding construction contracts of $50,000 or more must submit quarterly utilization reports to OCP on forms to be provided by OCP. In such reports the contractor must provide identifying information and report the number and percentage of journey worker, apprentice, and trainee hours worked in each job classification by sex and ethnic group, together with the total number of employees and total number of minority employees in each classification by sex. The quarterly utilization reports must cover each calendar quarter and must be received by OCP no later than the 15th day of the month following the end of the quarter (April 15, July 15, October 15, and January 15). Contractors who are required to submit utilization reports to the federal government may submit a copy of the federal report to the OCP at the same time they submit the report to the federal government in lieu of the state quarterly utilization report.

§ 8205. Effect on Other Regulations

The Regulations in this subchapter are in addition to the regulations contained in this division which apply to contractors and subcontractors generally. See particularly, California Administrative Code, Title 2, Division 4, Chapter 1 through 5, Sections 7285.0 through 7285.7, 7286.3 through 7296.4, 7400 through 7469.1, 8100 through 8120, and 8400 through 8407.

Subchapter 3. Regulations Applicable to Service and Supply Contracts

Article 1. Small Contracts

§ 8300. Scope

This subchapter applies to all contractors which seek or hold any nonexempt state service and supply contract or subcontract.

§ 8301. Definition of Small Contract

All state contracts with a dollar value of twenty-five thousand dollars ($25,000) or less are for purposes of this subchapter defined as "small" contracts.

§ 8302. Post Award Filing

Contractors awarded small contracts need not file any information with OCP after execution of the contract, but must provide OCP access to records required under Section 8303 upon request.

§ 8303. Post Award Compliance

(a) Each contractor of a "small" contract shall compile and shall maintain for inspection for two years after award:

(1) Information regarding the contractor: Federal Employer Identification number; state contract identification number; legal name of the business organization, parent corporation or other outside ownership interest, if applicable, business telephone number, street address, city, state and zip code; mailing address, if different; total number of employees, identified by sex, race and national origin; name, business phone and mailing address of contractor's EEO/AA officer, if there is one, and name of the person responsible for the maintenance of information required pursuant to subsection (b) below.

(2) Information regarding the contract: Dollar value of contract; time for performance of the contract; date of contract award; name of contract awarding agency, and contract awarding officer; brief description of the purpose or subject of the contract.

(3) A copy, if one was required to be prepared of the prime contractor's current California Employer Identification Report (CEIR), or equivalent federal form (See Section 7287.0(a) of this division regarding the preparation of CEIR's.)

(b) Failure to comply with the requirements of this section may result in a determination that the contractor has materially breached the state contract and the decertification of the contractor from future state contracts.

§ 8304. Verification

A contract awarding agency shall, upon request by OCP, verify information provided to OCP by an agency contractor performing a small contract. Such requests for verification shall be limited to that information required by OCP on any standardized state forms or other form where such information is specifically required by these regulations, and such information is also contained in the awarding agency's files.

Article 2. Regulated Contracts

§ 8310. Regulated Contracts, Dollar Value

All State contracts with a dollar value of more than twenty-five thousand dollars ($25,000) are for the pur-

poses of this subchapter classified as "regulated" contracts.

§ 8311. Post Award Informational Filing

(a) The prime contractor of a "regulated" contract shall file with OCP within twenty-eight (28) days from the date of execution of a "regulated" contract or the effective date of these regulations, whichever occurs later:

(1) Information Regarding the Contractor: Federal Employer Identification Number; state contract identification number; legal name of the business organization; business telephone number, street address, city, state and zip code; mailing address, if different; name, business phone and mailing address of contractor's EEO/AA Officer.

(2) Information Regarding the Contract: Dollar value of contract; date of contract award; name of contract awarding agency, and contract awarding officer; brief description of the purpose or subject of the contract.

(3) (Reserved)

(4) A copy of the prime contractor's current California Employer Identification Report (CEIR) or equivalent federal form (EEO–1). If the prime contractor is not otherwise required to prepare a CEIR, it must do so in order to comply with the requirements of this section. (See Section 7287.0 (a) of this division regarding the preparation of CEIR's.)

This information shall be updated annually thereafter, so long as the contractor remains subject to these regulations.

(b) Contractors awarded more than one state contract in one year may file only the information required in subdivision (a)(2) and (a)(4) above for the second and all subsequent contracts awarded during the year.

(c) The OCP and the contract awarding agency shall make forms available for providing the information required under this section.

(d) Failure to comply with the requirements of this section may result in a determination that the contractor has materially breached the state contract and the decertification of the contractor from future state contracts.

§ 8312. Designating EEO/Affirmative Action Officer

All contractors of regulated contracts shall designate an individual responsible for the implementation of the contractor's Nondiscrimination Program.

Subchapter 4. OCP Review Procedures

§ 8400. Scope

This subchapter sets forth the review procedures to be followed by OCP in implementing this chapter.

§ 8401. OCP Review Procedures

In order to monitor the equal employment practices of contractors and their compliance with the requirements of this chapter, contractors shall be subject to review. Contractors may be selected for review on the basis of any specific neutral criteria contained in a general administrative plan for the enforcement of this chapter.

(a) Desk Review. All contracts shall be subject to desk reviews conducted by and at the discretion of OCP. A desk review will involve a review of the applicable contract(s), the information required of the contractor pursuant to Section 8303 or 8311 of these regulations, the compliance with and implementation of the Program required by this Chapter, and any additional related information required by OCP. In addition, OCP may review the current and past personnel procedures and practices of a contractor whenever such a review is, within the discretion of OCP, considered appropriate.

(b) Field Review. OCP may conduct a field review of a contractor's workplace. Field reviews will be made during contractor's regular business hours. OCP shall notify the contractor of its intent to conduct a field review under this section and shall arrange a mutually convenient time to conduct it.

(c) A contractor will not be selected for a routine desk or field review if it has been the subject of such a review within the preceding 24 months and was found to be in compliance. Prior review will not exempt a contractor from compliance investigations conducted pursuant to Section 8402, or follow-up desk or field reviews.

§ 8402. Compliance Investigations

(a) OCP may conduct a compliance investigation of a contractor's employment practices for the purpose of determining whether the contractor holding a state contract is acting or has acted in violation of the nondiscrimination and compliance requirements imposed by this chapter. Investigations under this section shall involve a detailed review of the contractor's entire employment practices and procedures. Investigations under this section may be conducted when the Administrator determines a pattern of unlawful discrimination in employment may have occurred within the past twelve months or be ongoing. Such a determination shall be in writing and shall be based upon:

(1) A complaint by a contract awarding agency; or

(2) The results of the regular compliance review activities of the OCP; or

(3) A notice of any complaint of employment discrimination filed pursuant to Section 8120 of this Chapter or Government Code, Section 12960; or

(4) The failure of the contractor to provide compliance information required by this chapter or reasonably requested by OCP.

(b) Whenever a contractor which is the subject of a compliance investigation pursuant to this section is also the subject of a complaint pursuant to Government Code, Section 12960, if possible, OCP and any other unit of DFEH investigating the contractor's employment practices shall coordinate their investigations.

§ 8403. Letters of Commitment

If, in the course of a compliance investigation, OCP concludes that a contractor may be in violation of the provisions of this chapter, OCP and the contractor may informally agree to resolve the identified deficiencies through the mechanism of a written letter of commitment. The letter of commitment shall set forth the deficiencies identified by OCP, the action the contractor shall take to correct the deficiencies, and the time by which the corrective action shall be taken and the deficiencies resolved.

Subchapter 5. OCP Enforcement Proceedings

§ 8500. Scope

This subchapter sets forth the enforcement procedures to be followed by OCP in implementing this chapter.

§ 8501. Show Cause Notice

(a) When the Administrator has reasonable cause to believe that a contractor performing under a state contract is in violation of the nondiscrimination and compliance requirements imposed by this chapter or is in violation of a letter of commitment or conciliation agreement, he or she may issue a notice requiring the contractor to show cause before a hearing officer, why appropriate action to ensure compliance should not be instituted. The show cause notice shall specifically state the contractor's noncompliance and any recommended sanctions. The show cause notice shall be dated and served on the contractor personally or by registered mail, and such service shall constitute notice to the contractor of the deficiencies. In addition, the show cause notice shall be served by ordinary first class mail on the contract awarding agency. A hearing on the show cause notice shall be held no sooner than the thirtieth day after the issuance of the show cause notice but shall be at the earliest date OCP can reasonably schedule the hearing.

(b) During the thirty (30) day "show cause" period, OCP and the contractor shall make every effort to resolve the deficiencies which led to the issuance of the show cause notice through conciliation, mediation, and persuasion.

§ 8502. Conciliation Agreements

At the discretion of the Administrator, deficiencies contained in a show cause notice may be resolved through the use of written conciliation agreements. A conciliation agreement shall provide for such remedial action as may be necessary to correct the violations and/or deficiencies noted. In addition, the Administrator may require periodic compliance reports detailing the actions taken by the contractor to correct the deficiencies, and identifying statistical results of such actions.

§ 8503. Hearing

If the deficiencies listed in the show cause notice are not resolved during the thirty (30) day period, a hearing shall be held before a hearing officer appointed by the Director of the Department of Fair Employment and Housing.

A notice of hearing will be dated and served upon the contractor personally or by registered mail. The hearing may be postponed by OCP for good cause. If the contractor has good cause, the contractor shall contact the OCP within 10 days of receiving notice of hearing.

The procedures of hearing shall include: testimony under oath, the right to cross-examination and to confront adversary witnesses, the right to representation, and the issuance of a formal decision.

In addition to the above requirements of this section, the hearing shall be conducted in accordance with Government Code Sections 11507.6, 11507.7, 11508 (with the exception that the Office of Compliance Programs shall be substituted for the Office of Administrative Hearings), 11510, 11511, 11512(c) and (d), 11513, 11514, 11520, 11523; the sections cited above are incorporated herein by reference.

The hearing officer shall decide whether to dismiss, modify or sustain the allegations of the show cause notice.

The form and content of the decision will be in accordance with the requirements of Government Code Section 11518 herein incorporated by reference.

§ 8504. Potential Remedies

If a violation of this chapter is found at the hearing, the hearing officer may decertify the contractor's nondiscrimination program and may recommend to the contract awarding agency that the existing contract be terminated. Decertification shall continue until the deficiency is corrected and satisfactory evidence thereof is presented to OCP. Other potential remedies include, but are not limited to the imposition of periodic reporting requirements and the withdrawal of exemptions.

Title 8. Industrial Relations

Division 1. Department of Industrial Relations

Chapter 3.2. California Occupational Safety and Health Regulations (CAL/OSHA)

Subchapter 1. Regulations of the Director of Industrial Relations

Article 1. Definitions Under California Occupational Safety and Health Act of 1973

§ 330. Definitions

In this chapter unless otherwise specifically indicated:

(a) "Chief" means the Chief Administrative Officer of the Division of Occupational Safety and Health.

(b) "Working days" means Mondays through Fridays but shall not include Saturday, Sunday or State Holidays. In computing 15 working days, the day of receipt of any notice shall not be included, and the last day of the 15 working days shall be included.

(c) "Inspection" means any inspection of an employer's factory, plant, establishment, construction site, or other area, workplace or environment where work is performed by an employee of an employer and includes any inspection conducted pursuant to a complaint, any reinspection, or follow-up inspection.

(d) "Code" means the California Labor Code.

(e) "Order" included within the term "order" are the General Orders adopted by the Industrial Safety Board or the Industrial Accident Commission, Rules and Regulations promulgated by the Director of the Department of Industrial Relations and the Division of Occupational Safety and Health, decisions, requirements and orders made by the Division of Occupational Safety and Health.

(f) "Carcinogen" includes the following recognized cancer causing substances for which standards have been adopted:

(1) Any of the following substances and any compound, mixture, or product containing such substances:

(A) 2–acetylaminofluorene.

(B) 4–aminodiphenyl.

(C) Benzidine (and its salts).

(D) Bis (chloromethyl) ether.

(E) 3,3 '–dichlorobenzidine (and its salts).

(F) 4–dimethylaminoazobenzene.

(G) Beta-naphthylamine.

(H) 4–Nitrobiphenyl.

(I) N-nitrosodimethylamine.

(J) Beta-propriolactone.

(K) Methyl chloromethyl ether.

(L) Alpha-naphthylamine.

(M) 4,4 '-Methylenebis (2–Chloroaniline.)

(N) Ethyleneimine.

(2) Asbestos, including chrysotile, amosite, crocidolite, tremolite, anthophyllite, and actinolite.

(3) Vinyl chloride.

(4) 1,2–dibromo–3 chloropropane (DBCP).

(5) Coke oven emissions

(6) Acrylonitrile.

(7) Inorganic Arsenic.

(8) Ethylene Dibromide (EDB)

(9) Ethylene Oxide

(10) Any other substance for which standards are adopted and in effect due to cancer causing properties and any compound, mixture, or product containing such a substance, except as specifically exempted from such standards.

(g) "Order To Take Special Action" means any order written by the Chief or his or her authorized representative which requires the employer to comply with applicable provisions of Division 5 of the California Labor Code, or with specific standards, orders or regulations of the Standards Board whose enforcement upon the employer are at the discretion of the Division

(h) "Serious injury or illness" means any injury or illness occurring in a place of employment or in connection with any employment which requires inpatient hospitalization for a period in excess of 24 hours for other than medical observation or in which an employee suffers a loss of any member of the body or suffers any serious degree of permanent disfigurement, but does not include any injury or illness or death caused by the commission of a Penal Code violation, except the violation of Section 385 of the Penal Code, or an accident on a public street or highway.

Article 2. Advance Notice of Inspections

§ 331. Advance Notice

The intent of these regulations is the complete avoidance of the advance notice to employers of pending inspections or investigations unless there are important advantages in performance of inspections to be gained by the Division of Occupational Safety and Health. Any advance notification not allowed under these rules may constitute a violation of Labor Code Section 6321, punishable by a fine of not more than $1,000 or by imprisonment for not more than six months, or by both.

§ 331.1. When Advance Notice Justified

(a) Except when the investigation or inspection is to be made as the result of an employee complaint, situations justifying advance notice include the following:

(1) Situations of apparent imminent danger where prompt abatement is essential;

1227

(2) Situations when, to be effective, the inspection must be arranged to assure availability of essential personnel or access to the site, equipment, or process;

(3) Other situations where, in the judgment of the Chief or his designee, the giving of advance notice is advantageous for achieving a thorough inspection.

(b) When the investigation or inspection is to be made as the result of an employee complaint, advance notice is to be authorized only if the situation appears to present imminent danger to the health or safety of an employee or employees.

§ 331.2.   Time of Advance Notice

The lapse of time between advance notice and the inspection shall not exceed a minimum that is consistent with the reason for such notice. In no instance will advance notice be given more than 24 hours prior to the scheduled inspection or investigation except in unusual circumstances, where imminent danger exists or where practical considerations mandate a longer period.

§ 331.3.   Notification to Employee Representative

Any employer receiving advance notice shall promptly inform the employee representative of this fact, if there is one.

§ 331.4.   Arrangement for Inspection

The employer receiving advance notice shall make any necessary arrangements at his place of business so that the inspection can proceed on schedule as planned.

Article 3.   Citation, Notice, Special Order, Order to Take Special Action, Notice of No Violations After Investigation: Procedures

§ 332.   Form of Citation

The citation form shall set forth:

(a) The name of the employer, the employer's address and the workplace inspected;

(b) The nature of the violation, in specific terms with reference to the provision of the code, standard, regulation or order alleged to have been violated;

(c) Time allowed for correction of alleged violation;

(d) Rights of employees respecting the time fixed for correction of violations;

(e) Posting requirements

(f) Time within which an employer may contest a citation; and

(g) Such other information as the Division of Occupational Safety and Health deems appropriate for clear understanding of the form issued.

§ 332.1.   Issuance of Notice

(a) If, after an inspection or investigation, the Division determines that a violation exists which is not classified as willful, serious, repeated, or related to a failure to abate,

the Division may issue a Notice in lieu of citation if either of the following requirements are met:

(1) The violation does not bear a direct relationship upon employee safety or health, or;

(2) The violation bears a direct, but not immediate relationship upon employee safety or health, and is general or regulatory in nature.

(b) The Notice may be issued only if the criteria set forth in subdivision (a) hereof are satisfied, and in addition thereto, the employer agrees to abate the violative condition within a reasonable time as determined by the Division and agrees that the Notice will not be appealed. The agreement shall be indicated by the signature of the employer, or authorized employer representative, on the Notice itself.

(c) A Notice shall not be issued if the number of first instance violations, either general or regulatory, is 10 or more.

§ 332.2.   Issuance of Special Order

If upon inspection or investigation the Division determines that an unsafe condition, device, or place of employment poses a threat to the health and safety of an employee which cannot be made safe under existing standards or orders of the Standards Board the Division may issue a special order.

§ 332.3.   Issuance of Order to Take Special Action

After inspection or investigation the Division may require the employer to comply with applicable provisions of Division 5 of the California Labor Code or with specific standards or orders of the Standards Board whose enforcement upon the employer are at the discretion of the Division.

§ 332.4.   Posting of Citation, Special Order, Order to Take Special Action, and Notice of No Violation After Investigation

Citations issued pursuant to Labor Code Section 6317, Special Orders or Orders to Take Special Action issued pursuant to Labor Code Section 6308, and Notices of No Violation After Investigation issued pursuant to Labor Code Section 6318, or copies thereof, shall be posted at or near the referenced site of the violation or condition giving rise to the citation or order. The posted Citation, Special Order, Order to Take Special Action, or Notice of No Violation After Investigation shall be positioned so as to be easily read by employees working nearby. All postings shall be maintained for a period of three working days or until the unsafe condition is abated, whichever is longer.

Article 4.   Proposed Penalty Procedure

§ 333.   Notice of Proposed Assessment of Civil Penalties

Where a civil penalty is indicated, the Division shall after, or concurrent with the issuance of a citation, and within a reasonable time after the date the violation occurred, notify the employer by certified mail of the civil penalty proposed by the Division respecting the item(s) set forth as violation(s) in the citation. Any citation and/or Notice of Proposed Civil Penalty shall be deemed to be the final order of the Appeals Board, not subject to review by or appeal to any court or agency, unless within 15 working days from the date of the receipt of such citation or such notice of proposed civil penalty, the employer notifies the Appeals Board in writing of his intention to contest the citation and/or the civil penalty, with respect to violations alleged by the division, abatement periods, amount of proposed penalties, and the reasonableness of the changes required by the division to abate the condition.

§ 334. Classification of Violations and Definitions

For purposes of penalty assessments, violations of occupational safety and health standards, violations of California Health and Safety Code Sections 2950 and 25910, orders, special orders and regulations are classified as follows:

(a) Regulatory Violation—is a violation, other than one defined as Serious or General that pertains to permit, posting, recordkeeping, and reporting requirements as established by regulation or statute. For example, failure to obtain permit; failure to post citation, poster; failure to keep required records; failure to report industrial accidents, etc.

(b) General Violation—is a violation which is specifically determined not to be of a serious nature, but has a relationship to occupational safety and health of employees.

(c) Serious Violation.

(1) A "serious violation" shall be deemed to exist in a place of employment if there is a substantial probability that death or serious physical harm could result from a violation, including, but not limited to, circumstances where there is a substantial probability that either of the following could result in death or great bodily injury:

(A) A serious exposure exceeding an established permissible exposure limit or

(B) A condition which exists, or from one or more practices, means, methods, operations, or processes which have been adopted or are in use, in the place of employment.

(2) Notwithstanding subsection (c)(1), a serious violation shall not be deemed to exist if the employer can demonstrate that it did not, and could not with the exercise of reasonable diligence, know of the presence of the violation.

(3) As used in subsection (c)(1), "substantial probability" refers not to the probability that an accident or exposure will occur as a result of the violation, but rather to the probability that death or serious physical harm will result assuming an accident or exposure occurs as a result of the violation.

(4) For Carcinogens—is a violation of any standard, order, or special order respecting the use of a carcinogen, as defined in 8 California Code of Regulations 330(f). However, the violation shall not be considered serious if the employer can demonstrate that he did not, and could not with the exercise of reasonable diligence, know of the presence of the violation or he can demonstrate that the Division should have determined that the violation was minor and resulted in no substantial health hazard.

(d) Repeat Violation

(1) General—is a violation where the employer has corrected, or indicated correction of an earlier violation, for which a citation was issued, and upon a later inspection is found to have committed the same violation again within a period of three years immediately preceding the latter violation. For the purpose of considering whether a violation is repeated, a repeat citation issued to employers having fixed establishments (e.g., factories, terminals, stores . . .) will be limited to the cited establishment; for employers engaged in businesses having no fixed establishments (e.g., construction, painting, excavation . . .) a repeat violation will be based on prior violations cited within the same Region of the Division.

(2) Field Sanitation Violations Is a violation of the State Field Sanitation Standard, currently set forth in 8 CCR 3457, or of the Federal Field Sanitation Standard, currently set forth in 29 CFR 1928.110, where the employer has corrected, or indicated correction of an earlier violation, for which a citation was issued, and upon a later inspection is found to have committed the same violation within a period of five years immediately preceding the latter violation.

For the purpose of considering whether a violation is repeated, a repeat violation will be based on prior violations cited within the State.

(e) Willful Violation—is a violation where evidence shows that the employer committed an intentional and knowing, as contrasted with inadvertent, violation, and the employer is conscious of the fact that what he is doing constitutes a violation of a safety law; or, even though the employer was not consciously violating a safety law, he was aware that an unsafe or hazardous condition existed and made no reasonable effort to eliminate the condition.

(f) Abatement Date—is the date by which the employer is allowed and required to correct the condition constituting the violation.

§ 335. Factors Considered in Assessing Civil Penalties

In the assessment of civil penalties, the following factors shall be considered:

(a) The Gravity of the Violation-the Division establishes the degree of gravity of General and Serious violations from its findings and evidence obtained during the inspection/investigation, from its files and records, and other records of governmental agencies pertaining to occupational injury, illness or disease. The degree of gravity of General and Serious violations is determined by assessing and evaluating the following criteria:

(1) Severity.

(A) General Violation.

i. When the safety order violated pertains to employee illness or disease, Severity shall be based upon the degree of discomfort, temporary disability and time loss from normal activity (including work) which an employee is likely to suffer as a result of occupational illness or disease which could result from the violation. Depending on the foregoing, Severity shall be rated as follows:

LOW— No time loss from work or normal activity; or minimum discomfort.

MEDIUM—Loss of part or all of a day from work or normal activity including time for medical attention; or moderate temporary discomfort.

HIGH— Loss of more than one day from regular work or normal activity including time for medical attention; or considerable temporary discomfort.

ii. When the safety order violated does not pertain to employee illness or disease, Severity shall be based upon the type and amount of medical treatment likely to be required or which would be appropriate for the type of injury that would most likely result from the violation. Depending on such treatment, Severity shall be rated as follows:

LOW— Requiring first-aid only.

MEDIUM—Requiring medical attention but not more than 24–hour hospitalization.

HIGH— Requiring more than 24–hour hospitalization.

(B) Serious Violation.

The Severity of a Serious violation is considered to be HIGH.

(2) Extent.

i. When the safety order violated pertains to employee illness or disease, Extent shall be based upon the number of employees exposed:

LOW— 1 to 5 employees.

MEDIUM—6 to 25 employees.

HIGH— 26 or more employees.

ii. When the safety order violated does not pertain to employee illness or disease, Extent shall be based upon the degree to which a safety order is violated. It is related to the ratio of the number of violations of a certain order to the number of possibilities for a violation on the premises or site. It is an indication of how widespread the violation is. Depending on the foregoing, Extent is rated as:

LOW— When an isolated violation of the standard occurs, or less than 15% of the units are in violation.

MEDIUM—When occasional violation of the standard occurs or 15–50% of the units are in violation.

HIGH— When numerous violations of the standard occur, or more than 50% of the units are in violation.

(3) Likelihood.

Likelihood is the probability that injury, illness or disease will occur as a result of the violation. Thus, Likelihood is based on (i) the number of employees exposed to the hazard created by the violation, and (ii) the extent to which the violation has in the past resulted in injury, illness or disease to the employees of the firm and/or industry in general, as shown by experience, available statistics or records. Depending on the above two criteria, Likelihood is rated as:

LOW, MODERATE OR HIGH

(b) The Size of the Business of the Employer-is based upon the number of individuals employed at the time of the inspection/investigation. Size of the Business is evaluated based upon the following classifications of the number of persons employed: 10 or fewer employees.

> 10 or fewer employees.
> 11 to 25 employees.
> 26 to 60 employees.
> 61 to 100 employees.
> More than 100 employees.

(c) The Good Faith of the Employer-is based upon the quality and extent of the safety program the employer has in effect and operating. It includes the employer's awareness of CAL/OSHA, and any indications of the employer's desire to comply with the Act, by specific displays of accomplishments. Depending on such safety programs and the efforts of the employer to comply with the Act, Good Faith is rated as:

GOOD—Effective safety program.

FAIR— Average safety program.

POOR— No effective safety program.

(d) The History of Previous Violations-is the employer's history of compliance, determined by examining and evaluating the employer's records in the Division's files. Depending on such records, the History of Previous Violations is rated as:

GOOD—Within the last three years, no Serious, Repeat, or Willful violations and less than one General or Regulatory violation per 100 employees at the establishment.

FAIR— Within the last three years, no Serious, Repeat, or Willful violations and less than 20 General or Regulatory violations per 100 employees at the establishment.

POOR— Within the last three years, a Serious, Repeat, or Willful violation or more than 20 General or Regulatory violations per 100 employees at the establishment.

For the purpose of this subsection, establishment and the three-year computation, shall have the same meaning as in Section 334(d) of this Article.

§ 336. Assessment of Civil Penalties

Civil penalties for Regulatory, General, Serious, Repeat, Willful, and Failure to Abate violations shall be assessed in the following manner:

(a) Regulatory Violation—

(1) In General—Any employer who commits any Regulatory violation (as provided in Section 334(a) of this article) shall be assessed a civil penalty of up to $7000 for each such violation. Except as set forth in parts (2) through (4) of this subsection, a minimum proposed penalty of $500, representing the gravity of the violation, shall be assessed against employers who commit Regulatory violations. The proposed penalty shall be adjusted for Size, Good Faith, and History; however, an abatement credit shall not be granted.

(2) For Carcinogens—A minimum proposed penalty of $1,000 for all carcinogen standard regulatory violations, other than reporting use violations, representing the gravity of the violation, shall be assessed against the employers who commit such violations. The proposed penalty shall be adjusted for Size, Good Faith and History; however, an abatement credit shall not be granted.

(3) For Carcinogens Failure to Report Use. Any employer who violates a reporting requirement respecting the use of a carcinogen as defined in Title 8 of the California Code of Regulations section 330(f), shall be assessed a minimum proposed civil penalty of $2,500. The proposed penalty shall be adjusted for Size, Good Faith, and History; however, an abatement credit shall not be granted.

(4) For Violation of Permit or Registration Requirements. Any employer who violates the permit requirements of article 2, Permits-Excavations, Trenches, Construction and Demolition, and The Underground Use of Diesel Engines in Work in Mines and Tunnels, commencing with section 341 of Title 8 of the California Code of Regulations, or the Registration requirements of article 2.5, Registration-Asbestos-Related Work commencing with section 341.6 of Title 8 of the California Code of Regulations, shall be assessed a minimum proposed civil penalty of $1,250. The proposed penalty shall be adjusted for Size, Good Faith, and History; however, an abatement credit shall not be granted.

(5) For Violation of Elevator Permit and Posting Requirements. Any person owning or having custody, management, or operation of an elevator who operates any such elevator without a valid permit, or who fails to post the permit as required, may be assessed a civil penalty pursuant to the provisions of this article of up to $1000.

(b) General Violation—Any employer who violates any occupational safety and health standard, order or special order and such violation is determined to be a General violation (as provided in section 334(b) of this article) may be assessed a civil penalty of up to $7000 for each such violation.

Gravity of a General Violation—The Base Penalty of a General violation is determined by evaluating Severity (as provided in section 335(a)(1)(A) of this article). If the Severity is:

LOW— The Base Penalty shall be $1,000.
MEDIUM—The Base Penalty shall be $1,500.
HIGH— The Base Penalty shall be $2,000.

The Base Penalty for the General violation determined under this subsection is then subjected to an adjustment for Extent (as provided in section 335(a)(2) of this article). If the Extent is:

LOW— 25% of the Base Penalty shall be subtracted.
MEDIUM—No adjustment shall be made.
HIGH— 25% of the Base Penalty shall be added.

The Base Penalty for the General violation thus far determined is further subjected to an adjustment for Likelihood (as provided in section 335(a)(3) of this article). If Likelihood is:

LOW— 25% of the Base Penalty shall be subtracted.
MEDIUM—No adjustment shall be made.
HIGH— 25% of the Base Penalty shall be added.

The resulting figure is called the Gravity-based penalty.

(c) Serious Violation

(1) In General—Any employer who violates any occupational safety and health standard, order, or special order, and such violation is determined to be a Serious violation (as provided in section 334(c)(1) of this article) shall be assessed a civil penalty of up to $25,000 for each such violation. Because of the extreme gravity of a Serious violation an initial base penalty of $18,000 shall be assessed.

The Base Penalty for the Serious violation determined under this subsection is then subjected to an adjustment for Extent (as provided in section 335(a)(2) of this article). If the Extent is:

LOW— 25% of the Base Penalty shall be subtracted.
MEDIUM—No adjustment shall be made.
HIGH— 25% of the Base Penalty shall be added.

The Base Penalty for the Serious violation thus far determined is further subjected to an adjustment for Likelihood (as provided in section 335(a)(3) of this article). If Likelihood is:

LOW— 25% of the Base Penalty shall be subtracted.
MEDIUM—No adjustment shall be made.
HIGH— 25% of the Base Penalty shall be added.

The resulting figure is called the Gravity-based penalty.

(2) For Carcinogens—Any employer who violates any occupational safety and health standard, order, or special order respecting the use of a carcinogen, and such violation is determined to be a Serious violation (as provided in section 334(c)(4) of this article) shall be assessed a total civil penalty of $2000 for each such violation. This penalty is not subject to adjustment.

(3) Serious Violation Causing Death or Serious Injury, Illness or Exposure — If the employer commits a Serious violation and the Division has determined that the

violation caused death or serious injury, illness or exposure as defined pursuant to Labor Code section 6302, the penalty shall not be reduced pursuant to this subsection, except the penalty may be reduced for Size as set forth in subsection (d)(1) of this section. The penalty shall not exceed $25,000.

(4) Operation of an Elevator in an Unsafe Condition or in Violation of an Order Prohibiting Use.

Any person owning or having custody, management or operation of an elevator who operates or permits the operation of the elevator in a condition which is dangerous to life or the safety of any person, or who operates or permits the operation of the elevator in violation of any Order Prohibiting Use issued by the Division, may be assessed a civil penalty pursuant to the provisions of this article of up to $2000.

(5) For Tower Cranes—Any employer who violates any tower crane standard, order or special order and such violation is determined to be a serious violation (as provided in section 334(c)(1) of this article) shall be assessed a penalty of $2,000. The penalty shall not be subject to adjustment as set forth in subsections (d) and (e) of this section.

(d) Further Adjustment of Regulatory, General, and Serious Violations — Subject to the provisions of parts (5) through (9) of this subsection, the Gravity-based Penalty established under either subsection (a), (b) or (c) of this section, shall be appropriately adjusted by giving due consideration to the following factors:

(1) The Size of the Business If the Size of the Business (as provided under section 335(b) of this article) is:

10 or fewer employees	—40% of the Gravity-based Penalty shall be subtracted.
11–25 employees	—30% of the Gravity-based Penalty shall be subtracted.
26–60 employees	—20% of the Gravity-based Penalty shall be subtracted.
61–100 employees	—10% of the Gravity-based Penalty shall be subtracted.

More than 100 employees—No adjustment shall be made.

(2) The Good Faith of the Employer—If the Good Faith of the Employer (as provided under section 335(c) of this article) is:

GOOD—30% of the Gravity-based Penalty shall be subtracted.
FAIR— 15% of the Gravity-based Penalty shall be subtracted.
POOR— No adjustment shall be made.

(3) The History of Previous Violations—If the employer's History of Compliance (as provided under section 335(d) of this article) is:

GOOD—10% of the Gravity-based Penalty shall be subtracted.
FAIR— 5% of the Gravity-based Penalty shall be subtracted.
POOR— No adjustment shall be made.

Following the preceding adjustments of the Gravity-based Penalty, the resultant penalty is termed Adjusted Penalty.

1232

(4) If an employer cited for a violation of a safety and health provision within title 8 of the California Code of Regulations was, at the time of citation, making a good faith effort to abate the alleged violation, pursuant to written recommendations of a Consultant of the CAL/OSHA Consultation Service, the following penalty adjustments may apply:

(A) General Violation. All penalties assessed for such General violations may be waived by the Division.

(B) Serious Violation. All penalties for such Serious violations may be subject to an additional adjustment reducing the proposed penalty 50%.

(5) Serious Violations Respecting the Use of a Carcinogen—The penalty for any Serious violation respecting the use of a carcinogen as set forth in subsection (c)(2) of this section is not subject to adjustment pursuant to this subsection and shall not be otherwise reduced.

(6) Regulatory Violations of the Permit and Registration Requirements—The minimum penalty for any Regulatory violation of the permit or registration requirements as set forth in subsection (a)(4) of this section is $250.

(7) Serious Violations Causing Death or Serious Injury, Illness or Exposure— Subject to the provisions of subsection (c)(3) of this section, the penalty for any Serious violation determined by the Division to have caused death or serious injury, illness or exposure as defined pursuant to Labor Code section 6302, shall not be adjusted pursuant to this subsection, except for Size set forth in part (1) of this subsection.

(8) Injury Prevention Program—The penalty for any Serious violation shall not be subject to adjustment pursuant to this subsection other than for Size as set forth in part (1) of this subsection where the employer does not have an operative injury prevention program as set forth in Labor Code section 6401.7 and applicable regulations of the California Occupational Safety and Health Standards Board.

(9) False Declarations of Abatement—Subject to the provisions of subsection (e) of this section, where it is determined after reinspection that the employer has not complied with the abatement requirements of the Division and employer has previously submitted a statement affirming compliance therewith, the recomputed penalty shall not be adjusted pursuant to this subsection, except for Size as set forth in part (1) of this subsection.

(10) No civil penalty shall be assessed against any new employer for a period of one year after the date the new employer establishes a business in the state for a regulatory or general violation of the Injury and Illness Prevention Program Standard adopted pursuant to Labor Code section 6401.7 and applicable regulations of the California Occupational Safety and Health Standards Board, if the employer has made a good faith effort to comply with the requirement set forth therein.

(11) No civil penalty shall be assessed against an employer who adopts, posts, and implements in good faith the Model Injury and Illness Prevention Program for

Non-High-Hazard Employment prepared by the Division for a first violation of the Injury and Illness Prevention Program standard adopted pursuant to Labor Code section 6401.7 and applicable regulations of the California Occupational Safety and Health Standards Board.

(12) For an employer who commits a repeat violation (as provided under section 334(d) of this article), the penalty shall not be subject to adjustment pursuant to this subsection, other than for Size as set forth in part (1) of this subsection.

(e) Abatement Credit for General and Serious Violations—The Adjusted Penalty for General and Serious violations is reduced by 50% on the presumption that the employer will correct the violations by the abatement date. The resultant penalty is termed Proposed Penalty. The following types of violations are not subject to an abatement credit:

(1) Violations designated as Repeat or Willful;

(2) Serious violations for which extent and likelihood are rated high;

(3) Serious violations respecting the use of a carcinogen; and

(4) Serious violation causing death or serious injury, illness or exposure as defined pursuant to Labor Code section 6302.

(f) Penalty for Failure to Abate Regulatory, General or Serious Violations— If the employer fails to abate the violation by the date permitted for its correction or fails to submit to the Division a signed statement of abatement of a violation within ten working days of the date set by the Division for correction of the violative condition, any abatement credit extended pursuant to subsection (e) of this Section shall be rescinded and this amount assessed as part of the failure to abate penalty. In addition, a penalty shall be assessed that is based upon the initial Gravity-based penalty for each calendar day that the previously cited violation continues unabated after expiration of the abatement period. Subject to the provisions of part (1) hereof, the Gravity-based penalty is reduced by the reevaluated adjustment factors. The adjustment factors of Size, Good Faith, and History shall be determined by evaluation of the circumstances at the time of the subsequent inspection when the failure to abate is discovered. The daily additional penalty for failure to abate a violation shall not exceed $15,000.

Limitations:

(1) Except (A) where the gravity of the violation is high and exposure to employees is continuous, or (B) the employer has exhibited a high degree of negligence in failing to correct the violation, the daily penalty for failure to abate a Regulatory or General violation may be further reduced up to 90% for the first 120 days the violation continues to exist and up to 50% thereafter where the violation does not bear a direct relationship on employee health and safety. The daily penalty for a Serious violation may be reduced up to 50% where the adjustment factors calculated pursuant to subsection (c) of this section are Low and the History and Good Faith calculated pursuant to subsection (d) of this section are Good.

(2) When a violation consisted of a number of instances and upon subsequent inspection some instances are found to have been abated and others have not, the daily penalty shall be calculated in proportion to the extent that the violation has been abated.

(3) Failure to Abate a Serious Violation Causing Death or Serious Injury, Illness or Exposure—If the employer fails to abate a Serious violation and the Division has determined that the failure to abate caused death or serious injury, illness, or exposure as defined pursuant to Labor Code section 6302, the penalty shall not be adjusted pursuant to this subsection, except for Size as set forth in subsection (d)(1) of this section.

(4) Failure to Abate a Serious Violation of Crane Standard, Order, or Special Order Causing Death or Serious Injury—If the employer fails to abate a serious violation of a crane standard, order, or special order and the Division has determined that the failure to abate caused death or serious injury as defined pursuant to Labor Code 6302, the penalty shall be $14,000 for each calendar day. The penalty is not subject to adjustment.

(5) False Declaration of Abatement—If it is determined after reinspection that the employer has not complied with the abatement requirements of the Division, and the employer has previously submitted a statement affirming compliance therewith, the recomputed penalty shall not be adjusted pursuant to this subsection, except for Size pursuant to part (1) of subsection (d) of this section.

(g) Repeat Violation—

(1) In General If a Regulatory, General, or Serious violation is repeated (as provided under section 334(d) of this article) the Proposed Penalty is adjusted upward as follows:

> 1st repeat—the Proposed Penalty is multiplied by two.
> 2nd repeat—the Proposed Penalty is multiplied by four.
> 3rd repeat—the Proposed Penalty is multiplied by ten.
> The resultant penalty shall not exceed $70,000.

(2) For Carcinogens—If a Serious violation respecting the use of a carcinogen or a Regulatory violation concerning a reporting requirement respecting the use of a carcinogen is repeated (as provided in section 334(d) of this article), the total civil penalty shall be as follows:

(A) For repeated Regulatory violations concerning a reporting requirement.

> 1st repeat—$5,000
> 2nd repeat—$10,000
> 3rd repeat—$20,000

(B) For repeated Serious violations respecting the use of a carcinogen.

1st repeat—$10,000
2nd repeat—$20,000
3rd repeat—$40,000

These penalties are not subject to adjustment.

(3) Repeated Violation Causing Death or Serious Injury, Illness or Exposure— The computation of the Proposed Penalty for a repeated violation shall not be subject to reduction, other than the Size pursuant to part (1) of subsection (d) of this section, where the violation is determined by the Division to have caused death or serious injury, illness or exposure within the meaning of Labor Code section 6302.

(h) Willful Violation—If a Regulatory, General, or Serious violation is determined to be willful (as provided under section 334(e) of this article) the Proposed Penalty is adjusted upward as follows:

Regulatory, General and Serious—the Proposed Penalty is multiplied by five. However, the penalty for any willful violation shall not be less than $5,000 and shall not exceed $70,000.

(1) Willful Violation Causing Death or Serious Injury, Illness or Exposure— The computation of the Proposed Penalty for a willful violation shall not be subject to reduction, other than the Size pursuant to part (1) of subsection (d) of this section, where the violation is determined by the Division to have caused death or serious injury, illness or exposure within the meaning of Labor Code section 6302.

(i) Serious Repeated or Willful Repeated Violation of Crane Standard, Order, or Special Order Causing Death or Serious Injury—If the employer commits a serious repeated or willful repeated violation of a crane standard, order, or special order, and the Division has determined that the violation caused death or serious injury as defined pursuant to Labor Code 6302, the penalty shall be $140,000. This penalty is not subject to adjustment.

(j) Rounding of the Fractions Amounts of the civil penalties are rounded down to the next whole dollar during the calculation stages, and final figures are adjusted downward to the next lower five dollar ($5) value.

(k) Multiple Violations Pertaining To A Single Hazard. When a single hazard is the subject matter of multiple violations resulting in civil penalties, the Division may, in its discretion, depart from the preceding criteria to mitigate the cumulative effect of such penalties.

(1) This subsection does not apply to any penalty assessed for a Serious, Willful or Repeated violation or a failure to abate a Serious violation where such violation or violations have been determined by the Division to have caused death or serious injury, illness or exposure pursuant to Labor Code section 6302. This subsection does not apply to any Regulatory, General or Serious violation where the employer does not have an operative injury prevention program as set forth in subsection (d) of this section.

1234

Article 4.5.   Multi–Employer Worksites

§ 336.10.   Determination of Citable Employer

On multi-employer worksites, both construction and non-construction, citations may be issued only to the following categories of employers when the Division has evidence that an employee was exposed to a hazard in violation of any requirement enforceable by the Division:

(a) The employer whose employees were exposed to the hazard (the exposing employer);

(b) The employer who actually created the hazard (the creating employer);

(c) The employer who was responsible, by contract or through actual practice, for safety and health conditions on the worksite; i.e., the employer who had the authority for ensuring that the hazardous condition is corrected (the controlling employer); or

(d) The employer who had the responsibility for actually correcting the hazard (the correcting employer).

§ 336.11.   Determination of Applicability of Defenses

Prior to issuing any citation to an exposing employer, the Division shall first determine whether available information indicates that the employer meets each of the defenses listed below. If the Division concludes that all five defenses have been met, the citation shall not be issued. These defenses are:

(a) The employer did not create the hazard.

(b) The employer did not have the responsibility or the authority to have the hazard corrected.

(c) The employer did not have the ability to correct or remove the hazard.

(d) The employer can demonstrate that the creating, the controlling and/or the correction employers, as appropriate, were specifically notified or were aware of the hazards to which his/her employees were exposed.

(e) The employer took appropriate feasible steps to protect his/her employees from the hazard, instructed them to recognize the hazard and, where necessary, informed them how to avoid the dangers associated with it. For the purposes of this section, where an extreme hazard is involved, appropriate feasible steps include removing the employer's employees from the job, if there is no other way to protect them from the hazard.

Article 5.   Hazardous Substances Information and Training

§ 337.   Development and Maintenance of List

(a) Establishment of Initial List. Substances designated in the sources specified in Labor Code section 6382(b) shall be considered in formulating the initial list.

The Director shall presume all such substances to be potentially hazardous to human health when present occupationally except those which the Director determines do not pose any adverse acute or chronic risk to human health as present occupationally. Those substances which do not pose any risk shall be removed from the list. Evidence of risk shall include any immediate or long-term adverse effect which causes impairment of function, alteration of structure, or increased susceptibility to disease or contributes to adverse effects of other substances. In making a determination of risk, the Director shall consider available scientific data including, but not limited to, data from human epidemiological studies, data from short-term in vitro studies, and data from animal bioassay tests.

Animal bioassay data is admissible and generally indicative of potential effects in humans.

For purposes of this regulation, substances are present occupationally when there is a possibility of exposure either as a result of normal work operations or a reasonably foreseeable emergency resulting from workplace operations. A reasonably foreseeable emergency is one which a reasonable person should anticipate based on usual work conditions, a substance's particular chemical properties (e.g., potential for explosion, fire, reactivity), and the potential for human health hazards. A reasonably foreseeable emergency includes, but is not limited to, spills, fires, explosions, equipment failure, rupture of containers, or failure of control equipment which may or do result in a release of a hazardous substance into the workplace.

(b) Administrative Procedure Followed by the Director for the Development of the Initial List. The Director shall hold a public hearing concerning the initial list. The record will remain open 30 days after the public hearing for additional written comment. Requests to exempt a substance in a particular physical state, volume, or concentration from the provisions of Labor Code sections 6390 to 6399.2 may be made at this time. If no comments in opposition to such a request are made at the public hearing or received during the comment period, or if the Director can find no valid reason why the request should not be considered, it will be incorporated during the Director's preparation of the list.

After the public comment period the Director shall formulate the initial list and send it to the Standards Board for approval. After receipt of the list or a modified list from the Standards Board, the Director will adopt the list and file it with the Office of Administrative Law.

(c) Concentration Requirement. In determining whether the concentration requirement of a substance should be changed pursuant to Labor Code section 6383, the Director shall consider valid and substantial evidence. Valid and substantial evidence shall consist of clinical evidence or toxicological studies including, but not limited to, animal bioassay tests, short-term in vitro tests, and human epidemiological studies. Upon adoption, a regulation indicating the concentration requirement for a substance shall consist of a footnote on the list.

(d) Procedures for Modifying the List. The Director will consider petitions from any member of the public to modify the list or the concentration requirements, pursu-

ant to the procedures specified in Government Code section 11347.1. With petitions to modify the list, the Director shall make any necessary deletions or additions in accordance with the procedures herein set forth for establishing the list. The Director will review the existing list at least every two years and shall make any necessary additions or deletions in accordance with the procedures herein set forth for establishing the list.

(e) Criteria for Modifying the List. Petitions to add or remove a substance on the list, modify the concentration level of a substance, or reference when a particular substance is present in a physical state which does not pose any human health risk must be accompanied with relevant and sufficient scientific data which may include, but is not limited to, short-term tests, animal studies, human epidemiological studies, and clinical data. If the applicant does not include the complete content of a referenced study or other document, there must be sufficient information to permit the Director to identify and obtain the referenced material. The petitioner bears the burden of justifying any proposed modification of the list.

The Director shall consider all evidence submitted, including negative and positive evidence. All evidence must be based on properly designed studies for toxicological endpoints indicating adverse health effects in humans, e.g., carcinogenicity, mutagenicity, neurotoxicity, organ damage/effects.

For purposes of this regulation, animal data is admissible and generally indicative of potential effects in humans.

The absence of a particular category of studies shall not be used to prove the absence of risk.

Negative results generally indicate the absence of statistically positive results in appropriate studies. As all tests for toxicological effects have inherent insensitivities, negative results must be reevaluated in light of the limits of sensitivity of each study, its test design, and the protocol followed.

In evaluating different results among proper tests, as a general rule, positive results shall be given more weight than negative results for purposes of including a substance on the list or modifying the list in reference to concentration, physical state or volume, so that appropriate information may be provided regarding those positive results. In each case, the relative sensitivity of each test shall be a factor in resolving such conflicts.

§ 338. Special Procedures for Supplementary Enforcement of State Plan Requirements Concerning Proposition 65.

(a) This section sets forth special procedures necessary to comply with the terms of the approval by the United States Department of Labor of the California Hazard Communication Standard, pertaining to the incorporation of the occupational applications of the California Safe Drinking and Toxic Enforcement Act (hereinafter Proposition 65), as set forth in 62 Federal Register 31159

(June 6, 1997). This approval specifically placed certain conditions on the enforcement of Proposition 65 with regard to occupational exposures, including that it does not apply to the conduct of manufacturers occurring outside the State of California. Any person proceeding 'in the public interest' pursuant to Health and Safety Code s 25249.7(d) (hereinafter 'Supplemental Enforcer') or any district attorney or city attorney or prosecutor pursuant to Health and Safety Code s 25249.7(c) (hereinafter 'Public Prosecutor'), who alleges the existence of violations of Proposition 65, with respect to occupational exposures as incorporated into the California Hazard Communication Standard (hereinafter 'Supplemental Enforcement Matter'), shall comply with the requirements of this section. No Supplemental Enforcement Matter shall proceed except in compliance with the requirements of this section.

(b) 22 CCR s 12903, setting forth specific requirements for the content and manner of service of sixty-day notices under Proposition 65, in effect on April 22, 1997, is adopted and incorporated by reference. In addition, any sixty-day notice concerning a Supplemental Enforcement Matter shall include the following statement:

'This notice alleges the violation of Proposition 65 with respect to occupational exposures governed by the California State Plan for Occupational Safety and Health. The State Plan incorporates the provisions of Proposition 65, as approved by Federal OSHA on June 6, 1997. This approval specifically placed certain conditions with regard to occupational exposures on Proposition 65, including that it does not apply to the conduct of manufacturers occurring outside the State of California. The approval also provides that an employer may use the means of compliance in the general hazard communication requirements to comply with Proposition 65. It also requires that supplemental enforcement is subject to the supervision of the California Occupational Safety and Health Administration. Accordingly, any settlement, civil complaint, or substantive court orders in this matter must be submitted to the Attorney General.'

(c) A Supplemental Enforcer or Public Prosecutor who commences a Supplemental Enforcement Matter shall serve a file-endorsed copy of the complaint upon the Attorney General within ten days after filing with the Court.

(d) A Supplemental Enforcer or Public Prosecutor shall serve upon the Attorney General a copy of any motion, or opposition to a motion for summary judgment or summary adjudication of issues, a demurrer, motion for preliminary or injunctive relief, or other dispositive motion, and all memoranda of points and authorities in support of or opposing such motions. These materials shall be served upon the Attorney General on the same day which they are served on the opposing party. A Supplemental Enforcer or Public Prosecutor shall serve upon the Attorney General any decision or order of a court granting or denying summary adjudication, a demurrer, preliminary or final injunctive relief, penalties, or

damages relating to a Supplemental Enforcement Matter within five working days after receipt.

(e) A Supplemental Enforcer or Public Prosecutor who agrees to a settlement of a Supplemental Enforcement Matter shall serve the settlement upon the Attorney General within two working days after the agreement is signed by the parties. Where the settlement is submitted to a court for its approval, the Supplemental Enforcer or Public Prosecutor shall notify the court in writing upon presentation of the settlement of its submission to the Attorney General pursuant to this regulation. The submission to the Attorney General shall contain the entire agreement between the parties.

(f) When this section requires that any document or information be provided to the Attorney General, service shall be in a manner prescribed by Code of Civil Procedure s 1010 et seq. The envelope in which the document is transmitted shall state prominently 'Hazard Communication Standard/Proposition 65 Supplemental Enforcement Matter.' The Attorney General may then specify that further documents be served upon a particular office and deputy.

(g) The special procedures set forth in subsections (a) through (f) shall be followed for motions or other applications for judicial enforcement of any existing or future settlement agreements pertaining to Proposition 65, with reference to occupational exposures.

(h) Where, in the judgment of the Director and the Attorney General, a Supplemental Enforcer or Public Prosecutor has not complied with the provisions of this section, or the provisions of the OSHA approval decision of June 6, 1997, the Attorney General may seek to intervene in the action, or take such actions within his authority as he deems appropriate to assure compliance.

§ 339. The Hazardous Substances List

(a) Purpose. The following is the List of Hazardous Substances prepared by the Director pursuant to Labor Code Section 6380. The substances on this list are subject to the provisions of Labor Code Sections 6360 through 6399.7 and Section 5194 in Title 8 of the California Code.

(b) Definitions.

(1) CAS number means the unique identification number assigned by the Chemical Abstracts Service to specific chemical substances.

(2) Source means the sublists which the Director used in preparing the Hazardous Substances List pursuant to Labor Code 6382. The source(s) of each hazardous substance on the list is designated by a number in the middle column of the list. The numbers represent the following sources: (1) International Agency for Research on Cancer (IARC); (2) Environmental Protection Agency lists pursuant to the Clean Air and Clean Water Acts; (3) General Industry Safety Order Section 5155; (4) California Department of Pesticide Regulation's list of Restricted Materials; (5) Information Alerts put out by the

Hazard Evaluation and Information Service pursuant to Labor Code Section 147.2.

(3) Synonym means an entry in the list which refers to another entry. This type of entry may identify alternate names for a given substance or associate a particular substance with a class of substances. Synonyms appear in the list as entries of the form: Substance x; see Substance y. The synonym entries included in this list are not all inclusive.

HAZARDOUS SUBSTANCES LIST *

* An MSDS is not required for tapes, films, or extruded, molded or coated products containing listed hazardous substances in bound form except when these substances can be released in the workplace under normal conditions of work or in reasonably foreseeable emergencies resulting from workplace operations.

CAS No.	Source	Substance	Footnotes
26148685	1	A-alpha-C (2–Amino–9H–pyrido[2,3–b]indole)	
3688537	1	AF–2 ([2–(2–Furyl)–3 (5–nitro–2–furyl)] acrylamide)	
86884	3	ANTU; see 1–(1–Naphthyl) –2thiourea	
83329	2	Acenaphthene	
75070	1,2,3	Acetaldehyde	
60355	1	Acetamide	
64197	2,3	Acetic acid	1
108247	2,3	Acetic anhydride	
67641	3	Acetone	
75865	2	Acetone cyanohydrin	
75058	3	Acetonitrile	
81812	3	3–(alpha- Acetonylbenzyl) –4hydroxycoumarin; see Warfarin	
53963	3	2–Acetylaminofluorene	
506967	2	Acetyl bromide	
79367	2	Acetyl chloride	
74862	3	Acetylene	
540590	2,3	Acetylene dichloride	
79276	3	Acetylene tetrabromide	
79345	1,3	Acetylene tetrachloride	
50782	3	Acetylsalicylic acid	37
107028	2,3,4	Acrolein	
79061	1,3	Acrylamide	
79107	3	Acrylic acid	
107131	1,2,3,4	Acrylonitrile	
50760	1	Actinomycin D	
124049	2	Adipic acid	
23214928	1	Adriamycin	
	1	Aflatoxins	
116063	4	Aldicarb	
51285	2	Aldifen; see Dinitrophenols	
309002	1,2,3,4	Aldrin	
107186	2,3,4	Allyl alcohol	
107051	2,3	Allyl chloride	
106923	3	Allyl glycidyl ether	12
57067	1	Allyl isothiocyanate	
2835394	1	Allyl isovalerate	
2179591	3	Allyl propyl disulfide	
	3	Aluminum	3
	3	Aluminum, alkyls	
7429905	3	Aluminum metal and oxide	
20859738	4	Aluminum phosphide	
	3	Aluminum pyro powders	
	3	Aluminum, soluble salts	2
10043013	2	Aluminum sulfate; see Aluminum, soluble salts	
117793	1	2–Aminoanthraquinone	

CAS No.	Source	Substance	Footnotes
60093	1	para-Aminoazobenzene	
97563	1	o-Aminoazotoluene	
1300738	3	Aminodimethylbenzene; see Xylidine	
92671	1,3	4–Aminodiphenyl	31
75047	2	Aminoethane; see Ethylamine	
141435	3	2–Aminoethanol; see Ethanolamine	
82280	1	1–Amino–2–methylanthraquinone	
91598	3	2–Aminonaphthalene; see beta-Naphthylamine	
712685	1	2–Amino–5– (5–nitro– 2furyl) –1,3,4– thiadiazole	
121664	1	2–Amino–5– nitrothiazole	
504290	3	2–Aminopyridine	
504245	4	4–Aminopyridine	
1918021	4	4–Amino–3,5,6– trichloropicolinic acid; see Picloram	
2432997	1	11–Aminoundecanoic acid	
61825	1,3	Amitrole	
7773060	2	Ammate; see Ammonium sulfamate	
7664417	2,3	Ammonia	
631618	2	Ammonium acetate	
1863634	2	Ammonium benzoate	
1066337	2	Ammonium bicarbonate	
7789095	2	Ammonium bichromate; see Chromium compounds	
1341497	2	Ammonium bifluoride; see Flouride and inorganic fluoride compounds	
10192300	2	Ammonium bisulfite	
1111780	2	Ammonium carbamate	
506876	2	Ammonium carbonate	
3012655	2	Ammonium citrate dibasic	
12125029	2,3	Ammonium chloride fume	
7788989	2	Ammonium chromate; see Chromium compounds	
13826830	2	Ammonium fluoborate	
12125018	2	Ammonium fluoride; see Fluoride, and inorganic fluoride compounds	
1336216	2	Ammonium hydroxide	29
6009707	2	Ammonium oxalate	
16919190	2	Ammonium silicofluoride	
7773060	2,3	Ammonium sulfamate	
12135761	2	Ammonium sulfide	
10196040	2	Ammonium sulfite	
3164292	2	Ammonium tartrate	
1762954	2	Ammonium thiocyanate	
628637, 123922,	2,3	Amyl acetate, all isomers	
626380, 625161	1	Anabolic steroids (Androgenic steroids)	
62533	1,2,3	Aniline	
90040	1,3	o-Anisidine	
104949	3	p-Anisidine	
191264	1	Anthanthrene	
120127	2	Anthracene	
7440360	2,3	Antimony	3
	2,3	Antimony compounds	4
7647189	2	Antimony pentachloride; see Antimony compounds	
28300745	2	Antimony potassium tartrate; see Antimony compounds	
7789619	2	Antimony tribromide; see Antimony compounds	
10025919	2	Antimony trichloride; see Antimony compounds	
77883564	2	Antimony trifluoride; see Antimony compounds	

CAS No.	Source	Substance	Footnotes	CAS No.	Source	Substance	Footnotes
1309644	2	Antimony trioxide		108463	2	1,3–Benzenediol; see Resor-cinol	
140578	1	Aramite [; see 2–(p-tert Bu-typhenoxy) isopropyl–2 chloroethyl sulfite)		118741	1,4	Benzene hexachloride; see Chlorinated benzenes	
7440382	1,2,3,4	Arsenic and arsenic com-pounds	32	531851, 531862, 92875	1,2,3 1	Benzidine (and its salts) Benzidine-based dyes	31
1303328	2	Arsenic disulfide; see Ar-senic and arsenic com-pounds		205992 205823 207089	1,2 1 1,2	Benzo [b]fluoranthene Benzo[i[fluoranthene Benzo[k] fluoranthene	
1303282	1,2	Arsenic pentoxide; see Ar-senic and arsenic com-pounds		207089	2	11,12 Benzo fluoranthene; see Benzo[k] fluoran-thene	
1327533	1,2	Arsenic trioxide; see Arsen-ic and arsenic compounds		205992	2	3,4 Benzo fluoranthene; see Benzo[b] fluoranthene	
1303339	1,2	Arsenic trisulfide; see Ar-senic and arsenic com-pounds		65850 71432 100470	2 3 2	Benzoic Acid Benzol; see Benzene Benzonitrile	7
784421	3	Arsine		191242	2	1,12–Benzoperylene	
1332214	1,2,3	Asbestos	5	191242	2	Benzo(ghi) perylene; see 1,12– Benzoperylene	
8052424	3	Asphalt (petroleum) fumes	6				
50782	3	Aspirin; see Acetylsalicylic acid		50328	1,2	Benzo [a]pyrene	
1912249	1,3,4	Atrazine		91225	2	Benzo(b)pyridine; see Qui-noline	
12174117	1	Attapulgite		105113	1	para-Benzoquinone dioxime	
492808	1	Auramine		106514	3	p-Benzoquinone; see Qui-none	
12192573	1	Aurothioglucose					
320672	1	5–Azacytidine		98077	1	Benzotrichloride	
115026	1	Azaserine		98884	2	Benzoyl chloride	
446866	1	Azathioprine		94360	3	Benzoyl peroxide	
86500	2,3,4	Azinphos methyl; see O,O–Dimethyl S-(4–oxo ben-zotri- azino–3– methyl) phosphorodithioate		140114 100447 1694093 7440417	1 1,2,3 1 1,2,3	Benzyl acetate Benzyl chloride Benzyl violet 4B Beryllium	34
151564	1	Aziridine; see Ethylenei-mine 1072522 1 2–(1–Aziridinyl) ethanol		7787475	1,2 1,2,3	Berryllium chloride; see Be-ryllium compounds Beryllium compounds	
800248	1	Aziridyl benzoquinone		7787497	1,2	Beryllium fluoride; see Be-ryllium compounds	
103333	1	Azobenzene		7787555	2	Beryllium nitrate; see Beryl-lium compounds	
3333526	3	2,2 '-Azobisisobu tyronitrile decomposition product; see Tetramethyl succi-nonitrile		141662	4	Bidrin; see 3–Hydroxy N,N-dimethyl- cis- crotonam-ide dimethyl phosphate	
6923224	4	Azodrin; see 3–(Dimethoxy phosphinyloxy)-N methyl-cis- crotonamide		92524 2168685	3 1	Biphenyl Bis(1–aziridinyl) morpholi-no phosphine sulphide	
154938	1	BCNU; see 1,3–bis (2–Chlo-roethyl) –1–nitrosourea		111911	2	Bis(2–chloroethoxy) meth-ane	
2426086	3	BGE; see n-Butyl glycidyl ether		111444	2,3	Bis (2–chloroethyl) ether; see Chloroalkyl ethers	
58899	2	BHC; see Hexachlorocy clo-hexanes		494031	1	N,N–Bis (2–chloroethyl) –2-naphthylamine	
319846	2	alpha-BHC		154938	1	1,3–Bis (2–chloroethyl)– 1-nitrosourea	
319857	2	beta-BHC					
319869	2	delta-BHC		154938	1	Bischloroethyl nitrosourea; see 1,3–Bis (2– chloroe-thyl) 1–nitrosourea	
58899	2	gamma-BHC; see Lindane					
86884	3	Bantu; see 1– (1–Na-phthyl) –2–thiourea		13483186	1	1,2–Bis (chloromethoxy) ethane	
101279	2	Barban		56894981	1	1,4–Bis (chloromethoxy me-thyl) benzene	
	2,3	Barium, soluble compounds	2				
542621		Barium cyanide; see Cya-nides, inorganic salts		542881 108601	1,3 1	Bis (chloromethyl) ether Bis(2–chloro– 1–methyle-thyl) ether	
17804352	3	Benomyl					
25057890	4	Bentazon		108601	2	Bis(2– chloroisopropyl) ether	
225514	1	Benz[c]acridine					
56553	1,2	Benz [a]anthracene		115322	1,2	1,1–Bis- (p-chlorophenyl) –2,2,2– trichloroethanol (dicofol)	
56553	2	1,2–Benzanthracene; see Benz[a]anthracene					
71432	1,2,3	Benzene		137268	3	Bis- (dimethylthio carba-moyl) disulfide	
108907	2,3	Benzene chloride; see Chlo-rinated benzenes					
123319	3	1,4–Benzenediol; see Hy-droquinone		2238075	3	Bis(2,3– epoxypropyl) ether; see Diglycidyl ether	

CAS No.	Source	Substance	Footnotes	CAS No.	Source	Substance	Footnotes
117817	2	Bis(2– ethylhexyl) phthalate; see Phthalate esters		13010474	1	CCNU; see 1–(2– Chloroethyl) –3 cyclohexyl– 1–nitrosourea	
1304821	3	Bismuth telluride; see Tellurium compounds		543908	1,2	Cadmium acetate; see Cadmium compounds	
11056067	1	Bleomycins		7440439, 1306190	1,2,3,4	Cadmium and cadmium oxide	3
129179	1	Blue VRS					
	3	Borates, tetra, sodium salts	8	7789426	2	Cadmium bromide; see Cadmium compounds	
1303862	3	Boron oxide	8	10108642	1,2	Cadmium chloride; see Cadmium compunds	
10294334	3	Boron tribromide			1,2,3,4	Cadmium compounds	
7637072	3	Boron trifluoride		7440702	2	Calcium	
3844459	1	Brilliant Blue FCF		7778441	1,2,3	Calcium arsenate; see Arsenic and arsenic compounds	
314409	3	Bromacil					
7726956	3	Bromine		52740166	2	Calcium arsenite; see Arsenic and arsenic compounds	
7789302	3	Bromine pentafluoride					
74975	3	Bromochloro methane		75207	2	Calcium carbide	
75274	2	Bromodichloro methane		13765190	1,2	Calcium chromate; see Chromium compounds	
74964	3	Bromoethane; see Ethyl bromide		156627	3	Calcium cyanamide	
593602	3	Bromoethylene; see Vinyl bromide		592018	2,4	Calcium cyanide; see Cyanides, inorganic salts	
75252	2,3	Bromoform		13765190	1,2	Calcium chromate; see Chromium compounds	
74839	3	Bromomethane; see Methyl bromide		26264062	2	Calcium dodecylbenzene-sulfonate	9
101553	2	4– Bromophenyl phenyl ether		1305620	3	Calcium hydroxide	
75638	3	Bromotri fluoromethane		7778543	2	Calcium hypochlorite	
1689845	4	Bromoxynil		1305788	3	Calcium oxide	
106990	1,2,3	1,3–Butadiene		76222	3	Camphor	
106978	3	Butane		56257	1	Cantharidin	
55981	1	1,4–Butanediol dimethanesulfonate (Busulfan)		105602	3	Caprolactam	
109795	3	Butanethiol; see n-Butyl mercaptan		2425061	1,3	Captafol	
71363	3	Butanol; see Butyl alcohol		133062	1,2,3	Captan	
78933	3	2–Butanone		63252	2,3,4	Carbaryl	
123739	2	2–Butenal propylene aldehyde; see Crotonaldehyde		86748	1	Carbazole	
2426086	3	1–Butoxy–2, 3–epoxypropane; see n-Butyl glycidyl ether		7786347	2,3,4	alpha–2– Carbomethoxy– 1–methylvinyl dimethyl phosphate (mevinphos)	
111762	3	2–Butoxyethanol; see Ethylene glycol monobutyl ether		7786347	3	2–Carbomethoxy-l- propen–2–yl dimethyl phosphate; see alpha–2 Carbomethoxy- l-methylvinyl dimethyl phosphate	
123864, 105564 540885, 510190	2,3	Butyl acetate, all isomers					
141322	3	Butyl acrylate		75150	2,4	Carbon bisulfide; see Carbon disulfide	
71363, 78922, 75650	3	Butyl alcohol		1333864	1,3	Carbon black-Extracts	10
109739, 78819, 513495, 13952846, 75649	2,3	Butylamine, all isomers		124389	3	Carbon dioxide	
				75150	2,3,4	Carbon disulfide	
				630080	3	Carbon monoxide	
25013165	1	Butylated hydroxyanisole		558134	3	Carbon tetrabromide	
128370	1	Butylated hydroxytoluene; see 2,6–Ditert- butyl- p-cresol		56235	1,2,3,4	Carbon tetrachloride	
				75445	2,3	Carbonyl chloride; see Phosgene	
85687	2	Butyl benzyl phthalate		353504	3	Carbonyl Fluoride	
299865	3	4-tert-Butyl– 2–chlorophenyl methyl methylphospho ramidate		786196	4	Carbophenothion	
				154938	1	Carmoisine; see 1,3–Bis (2–chloro ethyl)–1– nitrosourea	
1189851	3	tert-Butyl chromate; see Chromium compounds		120809	3	Catechol	
2426086	3	n-Butyl glycidyl ether	12	1310732	3	Caustic soda; see Sodium hydroxide	
138227	3	n-Butyl lactate					
109795	3	n-Butyl mercaptan		110805	5	Cellosolve; see Ethylene glycol mono ethyl ether	
89725	3	o-sec-Butylphenol					
140578	1	2–(p-tert- Butylphenoxy) isopropyl 2–chloroethyl sulfite		21351791	3	Cesium hydroxide	
				305033	1	Chlorambucil	
				56757	1	Chloramphenicol	
84742	2	n-Butyl phthalate; see Phthalate esters		57749	1,2,3,4	Chlordane	
				143500	1,2	Chlordecone	
98511	3	p-tert- Butyltoluene		6164983	4	Chlordimeform	
107926	2	Butyric acid		115286	1	Chlorendic acid	
3068880	1	beta-Butyrolactone		470906	4	Chlorfenvinphos	

CAS No.	Source	Substance	Footnotes
	1,2,3	Chlorinated benzenes	
8001352	3	Chlorinated camphene; see Toxaphene	
	2	Chlorinated cresols	
55720995	3	Chlorinated diphenyl oxide	
	2	Chlorinated ethanes	
	2	Chlorinated naphthalenes, (other than those listed elsewhere)	
108171262	1	Chlorinated paraffins	
	2	Chlorinated phenols; see Chlorinated cresols	
	1	a-Chlorinated toluenes	
7782505	2,3	Chlorine	
10049044	3	Chlorine dioxide	
7790912	3	Chlorine trifluoride	
494031	1	Chlornaphazine; see N,N-bis(2 Chloroethyl)- 2-naph thylamine	
107200	3	Chloroacetal dehyde	
532274	3	alpha- Chloroacetophenone	
79049	3	Chloroacetyl chloride	
	1,2,3	Chloroalkyl ethers	
108907	2,3	Chlorobenzene; see Chlorinated benzenes	
510156	1	Chlorobenzilate	
2698411	3	o-Chlorobenzylidene- malononitrile	
74975	3	Chlorobromo methane; see Bromochloro methane	
126998	3	2-Chloro-1, 3-butadiene; see Chloroprene	
124481	2	Chlorodibromo methane	
75456	1,3	Chlorodifluoro methane (FC-22)	
53449219	3	Chlorodiphenyl; see Polychloro biphenyls	
106898	3	1-Chloro-2,3, -epoxypropane; see Epichlorohydrin	
75003	2,3	Chloroethane; see Ethyl chloride	
107073	3	2-Chloroethanol; see Ethylene chlorohydrin	
13010474	1	1-(2-Chloroethyl) -3-cyclohexyl -1nitrosourea	
75014	3	Chloroethylene; see Vinyl chloride	
13909096	1	1-(2-Chloroethyl) -3-(4-methycyclo hexyl)- 1-nitrosourea (Methyl-CCNU)	
110758	2	2-Chloroethyl vinyl ether	
593704	1	Chlorofluoromethane	
67663	1,2,3	Chloroform	
75445	2	Chloroformyl chloride; see Phosgene	
59507	2	para-Chloro- meta-cresol	
74873	3	Chloromethane; see Methyl chloride	
107302	3	Chloromethyl methyl ether; see Methyl chloromethyl ether	
91587	2	2-Chloronaphthalene	
100005	3	1-Chloro- 4-nitrobenzene; see p Nitrochloro benzene	
600259	3	1-Chloro- 1-nitropropane	
76153	3	Chloropenta fluoroethane	
95578	2	2-Chlorophenol; see Chlorophenols	
	1	Chlorophenols	
	1	Chlorophenoxy herbicides	
95830	1	4-Chloro-o- phenylenediamine	
7005723	2	4-Chlorophenyl phenyl ether	
76062	3,4	Chloropicrin	
126998	2,3	Chloroprene	
1331288	3	o-Chlorostyrene	
7790945	2	Chlorosulfonic acid	
1897456	1	Chlorothalonil	
95498	3	o-Chlorotoluene	
100447	3	alpha-Chlorotoluene; see Benzyl chloride	
95692	1	p-Chloro- o-toluidine	
7745893	4	3-Chloro-p- toluidine hydrochloride	
1929824	3	2-Chloro-6- (trichloromethyl) pyridine	
75887	1	2-Chloro-1,1, 1-trifluoroethane	
2921882	2,3	Chlorpyrifos	
1066304	2	Chromic acetate; see Chromium compounds	
11115745	2	Chromic acid; see Chromium compounds	
10101538	2	Chromic sulfate; see Chromium compounds	
7440473	2,3	Chromium	3
	1,2,3	Chromium compounds	
7440473	3	Chromium metal; see Chromium	
11115745	2	Chromium troixide; see Chromium compounds	
10049055	2	Chromous chloride; see Chromium compounds	
14977618	3	Chromyl chloride;	
218019	1,2	Chrysenes; see Polynuclear aromatic hydrocarbons	
532821	1	Chrysoidine	
87296	1	Cinnamyl anthranilate	
108316	2,3	Cis-butenedioic anhydride; see Maleic anhydride	
15663271	1	Cisplatin	
51875	1	Citrinin	
6358538	1	Citrus Red no. 2	
637070	1	Clofibrate	
1420048	4	Clonitralid	
2971906	3	Clopidol	
	3	Coal (Bituminous) dust	
65996932	1	Coal-tar pitches	
8007452	1,3	Coal tar pitch volatiles	11
7440484	2,3	Cobalt	3, 34
10210681	3	Cobalt carbonyl	
16842038	3	Cobalt hydrocarbonyl	
7789437	2	Cobaltous bromide	
544183	2	Cobaltous formate	
14017415	2	Cobaltous sulfamate	
62748	4	Compound 1080; see Sodium fluoroacetate	
7440508	2,3	Copper	3
	2,3	Copper compounds	39
	3	Cotton dust	27
56724	2	Coumaphos	
91645	1	Coumarin	
8001589	1	Creosotes	
120718	1	p-Cresidine	
95487, 106445, 108394, 1319773	2,3	Cresol (all isomers)	
123739	2,3	Crotonaldehyde	
299865	3	Crufomate; see 4-tert-Butyl (-2-chlor ophenylmethyl) methylphos phoramidate	
98828	3	Cumene	

CAS No.	Source	Substance	Footnotes	CAS No.	Source	Substance	Footnotes
142712	2	Cupric acetate; see Copper compounds		57147	3	DMH; see Dimethylhydrazine (all isomers)	
12002038	2	Cupric acetoarsenite; see Copper compounds		81889	1	D & C Red No. 19; see Rhodamine B	
7447394	2	Cupric chloride; see Copper compounds		432034	1	Dacarbazine	
				80080	1	Dapsone	
3251238	2	Cupric nitrate; see Copper compounds		115902	4	Dasanit; see O,O–Diethyl O-[4 (methylsulfinyl) phenyl] phospho rothioate	
5893663	2	Cupric oxalate; see Copper compounds					
10380297	2	Cupric sulfate, ammoniated; see Copper compounds		20830813	1	Daunomycin	
				17702419	3	Decaborane	
7758987	2	Cupric sulfate; see Copper compounds		8065483	3,4	Demeton	
				298033	2	Demeton–O	
				126750	2	Demeton–S	
815827	2	Cupric tartrate; see Copper compounds		123422	3	Diacetone alcohol; see 4–Hydroxy 4–methyl– 2–pentanone	
420042	3	Cyanamide					
	2,3,4	Cyanides, inorganic salts		613354	1	N,N '-Diacetyl benzidine	
100470	2	Cyanobenzene; see Benzonitrile		10311849	4	Dialifor	
				2303164	1	Diallate	
460195	3	Cyanogen		615054	1	2,4– Diaminoanisofle	
506774	2,3	Cyanogen chloride		39156417	1	2,4–Diaminoanisole sulfate	
14901087	1	Cycasin		92875	3	4,4 '-Diaminobiphenyl; see Benzidine (and its salts)	
	1	Cyclamates					
110827	2,3	Cyclohexane		91941	3	4,4 'Diamino–3,3 '-dichloro-biphenyl; see Dichloro-benzidine and its salts	
108930	3	Cyclohexanol					
108941	3	Cyclohexanone					
110838	3	Cyclohexene		101814	1	4,4 '-Diaminodiphenyl ether	
66819	4,5	Cycloheximide		107153	2,3	1,2–Diaminoethane; see Ethylenediamine	
108918	3	Cyclohexylamine					
121824	3	Cyclonite; see Cyclotri methylenetri nitramine		95807	1	2,4–Diaminotoluene	
				119904	1	ortho- Dianisidine; see 3,3–Dimethoxy benzidine	
542927	3	Cyclopentadiene					
12079651	3	Cyclopentadienyl triocarbonyl manganese; see Manganese compounds		333415	2,3	Diazinon	
				334883	1,3	Diazomethane	
				226368	1	Dibenz [a,h]acridine	
287923	3	Cyclopentane		224420	1	Dibenz [a,j]acridine	
27208373	1	Cyclopenta[c,d]pyrene		53703	1,2	Dibenz [a,h]anthracene	
50180	1	Cyclophosphamide		215587	1	Dibenz [a,c]anthracene	
6055192				224419	1	Dibenz[a,j] anthracene	
121824	3	Cyclotrimethylene- trinitramine		53703	2	1,2,5,6– Dibenzanthracene; see Dibenz[a,h] anthracene	
13121705	3	Cyhexatin; see Tin compounds			1,2	Dibenzanthracenes; see Polynuclear aromatic hydrocarbons	
94757	2,3,4	2,4–D					
94111,	2	2,4–D esters (2,4–dichloro		194592	1	7H–Dibenzo [c,g]carbazole	
94791, 94804,				5385751	1	Dibenzo[a,e] fluoranthene	
1320189,		phenoxyacetic acid esters)		192472	1	Dibenzo[h,rst] pentaphene	
1928387,1928616,				192654	1	Dibenzo [a,e]pyrene	
1929733,271382,				189640	1	Dibenzo [a,h]pyrene	
25168267,53467111				189559	1	Dibenzo [a,i]pyrene	
94826	4	2,4–DB (2,4–dichloro- phenoxybutyric acid)		191300	1	Dibenzo[a,l] pyrene	
				92842	3	Dibenzothiazine; see Phenothiazine	
72548		2,4DDD; see TDE					
72548	2	4,4–DDD; see TDE					
72559	2	DDE; see 1,1–Dichloro–2,2–bis(p chlorophenyl) -ethylene		94360	3	Dibenzoyl Perozide; see Benzoyl peroxide	
				19287457	3	Diborane	
72559	2	4,4–DDE; see 1,1–Dichloro –2,2–bis (p chlorophenyl) -ethylene		300765	2	Dibrom; see O,O–Dimethyl O (1,2–dibromo –2,2– dichloroethyl) phosphate	
120365	4	2,4–DP (2,4–dichloro phenoxy- propionic acid)		96128	1,3	1,2–Dibromo– 3–chloropropane	
50293	1,2,3,4	DDT-(1,1,1– trichloro– 2,2–bis (p-chlorophenyl) ethane)		75616	3	Dibromodi fluoromethane	
				106934	2,3	1,2–Dibromoethane; see Ethylene dibromide	
50293	2	4,4–DDT; see DDT		102818	3	2-(Dibutylamino) ethanol	
62737	3	DDVP; see Dichlorvos		128370	1,3	2,6–Di-tert- butyl-p-cresol	7
78488	4	DEF; see S,S,S Tributyl phosphoro trithioate		107664	3	Dibutyl phosphate	
				84742	3	Dibutyl phthalate; see Phthalate esters	
2238075	3	DGE; see Diglycidyl ether					
68122	3	DMF; see N,N–Dimethyl formamide		84742	2	Di-n-butyl phthalate; see Phthaltate esters	

CAS No.	Source	Substance	Footnotes
1918009	2,4	Dicamba	
1194656	2	Dichlobenil	
117806	2	Dichlone	
7572294	1,3	Dichloroacetylene	
541731	2	m-Dichlorobenzene	
106467	1,2,3	p-Dichlorobenzene	
95501	2,3	o-Dichlorobenzene	
95501	2	1,2– Dichlorobenzene; see o Dichlorobenzene	
541731	2	1,3–Dichlorobenzene; see m Dichlorobenzene	
106467	2	1,4–Dichlorobenzene; see p Dichlorobenzene	
225321226	1,2,3	Dichlorobenzenes; see Chlorinated benzenes	
	1,2,3	Dichlorobenzidine (and its salts)	
91941	1,2,3	3,3 '-Dichlorobenzidine; see Dichlorobenzidene (and its salts)	
72548	2	1,1–Dichloro–2, 2-bis(p-chlorophenyl) ethane; see TDE	
72559	2,4	1,1–Dichloro–2, 2-bis (p-chlorophenyl) ethylene	
75274	2	Dichlorobromo methane; see Bromodichloro methane	
28434868	1	3,3 '-Dichloro–4,4 '-diaminodiphenyl ether	
75718	3	Dichlorodi fluoromethane (FC–12)	
118525	3	1,3–Dichloro–5, 5-dimethyl-hydantoin	
107062	1,2	1,2–Dichloroethane; see Ethylene dichloride	
75343	2,3	1,1–Dichloroethane; see Ethylidene chloride	
156605	2	1,2-trans- Dichloroethylene	
540590	2,3	1,2–Dichloroethylene; see Acetylene dichloride	
75354	2,3	1,1 Dichloroethylene; see Vinylidene chloride	
111444	1,3	Dichloroethyl ether; see Chloroaikyl ethers	
75092	3	Dichloromethane; see Methylene chloride	
75434	3	Dichloromonofluoromethane (FC–21)	
117806	2	Dichloronaph thoquinone; see Dichlone	
594729	3	1,1–Dichloro– 1–nitroethane	
120832	2	2,4–Dichlorophenol	
94757	2,3,4	2,4–Dichlorophen oxyacetic acid; see 2,4–D	
609201	1	2,6–Dichloro- para-phenylene diamine	
1836755	1,4	2,4–Dichlorophenyl p-nitrophenyl ether	
26638197, 78875,142289, 78999	1,2,3	Dichloropropanes	
78875	1,2	1,2–Dichloropropane; see Dichloropropanes	
8003198	2	Dichloropropene- dichloropropane (mixture)	
26952238, 542756,78886	1,2,3,4	Dichloropropenes	
709988	4	3,4–Dichloropro pionanilide; see Propanil	
75990	2,3	2,2–Dichloropro pionic acid	
8003198	2	1,2–Dichloropropylene	

CAS No.	Source	Substance	Footnotes
76142	3	1,2–Dichloro– 1,1,2,2– tetrafluoro- ethane (FC–114)	
62737	2	2,2–Dichlorovinyl dimethyl phosphate; see Dichlorvos	
62737	1,2,3	Dichlorvos	
102307,99309	2	Dicloran	
115322	1,2	Dicofol; see 1,1–Bis (p-chlorophenyl) –2,2,2– trichloro ethanol	
5124301	3	Dicyclohexyl methane–4,4 '-diisocyanate	
77736	3	Dicyclopentadiene	
102545	3	Dicyclopentadienyl iron	
60571	1,2,3,4	Dieldrin	
84173	1	Dienestrol	
1464535	1	Diepoxybutane	
111422	3	Diethanolamine	
109897	2,3	Diethylamine	
100378	3	2-(Diethylamino) ethanol	
12391	3	1,4–Diethylene dioxide; see p-Dioxane	
111400	3	Diethylenetriamine	
60297	3	Diethyl ether; see Ethyl ether	
298044	3	O,O–Diethyl S–2–(ethylthio) ethyl phosphoro dithioate; see Disulfoton	
298022	3	O,O–Diethyl S-(ethylthio) methyl phosphoro dithioate; see Phorate	
103231	1	Di(2–ethylehexyl) adipate	
117817	1	Di- (2–ethylhexyl) phthalate; see Phthalate esters	
1615801	1	1,2–Diethyl hydrazine	
333415	3	O,O–Diethyl O-(2–isopropyl –6–methy 4–pyrimidinyl phosphoro thioate; see Diazinon	
96220	3	Diethyl ketone	
115902, 115913	3,4	O,O–diethyl O-[4– (methylsufiny) phenyl] phosphoro thioate (fensulfothion)	
56382	3	O,O–Diethyl O-(p-nitrophenyl) phosphorothioate; see Parathion	
84662	2,3	Diethyl phthalate; see Phthalate esters	
56531	1	Diethylstilbestrol	
64675	1	Diethyl sulfate	
75616	3	Difluorodibromo methane; see Dibromodi fluoromethane	
2238075	3	Diglycidyl ether	
101906	1	Diglycidyl resorcinol ether	
1563662	2,3,4	2,3–Dihydro –2,2–dimethyl –7–benzofuranyl methylcarbamate (carbofuran)	
94586	1	Dihydrosafrole	
123319	3	p-Dihydroxybenzene; see Hydroquinone	
108463	2	meta-Dihydroxybenzene; see Resorcinol	
794934	1	Dihydroxymethyl furatrizine	
108838	3	Diisobutyl ketone	
108189	3	Diisopropylamine	
108203	3	Diisopropyl ether; See Isopropyl ether	
828002	1	Dimethoxane	
119904	1	3,3 '-Dimethoxybenzidine	

CAS No.	Source	Substance	Footnotes	CAS No.	Source	Substance	Footnotes
91930	1	3,3 '-Dimethoxy benzidine–4,4'		105679	2	2,4–Dimethylphenol	
109875	3	3,3 '-Dimethoxy benzidine–4,4'		1300716	2	Dimethylphenol; see Xylenol	
6923224	3,4	diisocyanate		121697	3	Dimethyl phenylamine; see N,N Dimethy laniline	
127195	3	Dimethoxy methane; see Methylal		10265926	4	0,S–Dimethyl phospho ram-idothioate	
124403	2,3	3-(Dimethoxy phosphiny-loxy) -Nmethyl- cis- cro-tonamide (Monocrotophos)		950378	4	0,0–Dimethyl phosphoro-dithioate, Sester with 4–(mercapto methyl) 2–me-thoxy–0 super2–1,3,4 thia-diazolin –5–one	
60117	1,3	N,N–Dimethy lacetamide		77781	2,3	Dimethyl phthaltate; see Phthalate esters	
1300738	3	Dimethylamine		77781	1,3	Dimethyl sulfate	
55738540	1	4–Dimethylaminoa zoben-zene		299843	2,3	O,O–Dimethyl O-(2,4,5–trichlorophenyl) phos-phoro thioate; see Ronnel	
121697	3	Dimethylamino benzene; see Xylidine		148016	3	Dinitrolmide; see 3,5–Dini-tro-o toluamide	
108383	2,3	trans–2– [(Dimethylamino)		25154545, 99650,100254, 528290	2,3	Dinitrobenzenes, all isomers	
119937	1	methylimino] –5–[2–(5– ni-tro–2–furyl) vinyl]1,3, 4– oxadiazole		25154545	2	Dinitrobenzol; see Dinitro-benzenes, all isomers	
108849	3	N,N– Dimethylaniline		534521	2,3,4	4,6–Dinitro- o-cresol	
79447	1	Dimethylbenzene; see Xy-lene, all isomers		534521	2	Dinitrocresol; see Nitrophe-nols, all isomers	
300765	2,3	3,3 '-Dimethylbenzidine		51285	2,4	2,4–Dinitrophenol; see Din-itrophenols	
121755	3	1,3–Dimethylbutyl acetate; see sec		51285, 329715,573568	2,4	Dinitrophenols	
8022002	3	Hexyl acetate		42397648	1	1,6–Dinitropyrene	
68122	3	Dimethylcarbamoyl chlo-ride		43977659	1	1,8–Dinitropyrene	
108838	3	0,0–Dimethyl 0–(1,2–dibro-mo–2, 2–dichloroethyl) phosphate (Naled)		148016	3	3,5–Dinitro- o-toluamide	
				606202	2	2,6–Dinitrotoluene	
540738	1	O,O–Dimethyl S-(1,2 dicar-boethoxyethyl)		121142	2	2,4–Dinitrotoluene	
57147, 540738	1,3	Phosphorodithioate; see Malathion		25321146, 121142,121142, 606202,610399, 602017,619518	2,3	Dinitrotoluenes, all isomers	
67641	3	O,O–Dimethyl O-(2-(ethyl-thio)-ethyl)		88857	4	Dinoseb	
		phosphorothioate and O,O–Dimethyl		117840	2	Di-n-octyl phthalate	
		S-(2–(ethylthio) -ethyl) phosphoro		117817	3	Di-sec-octyl phthalate; see Phthalate esters	
		thioate mixture; see Methyl demeton		123911	3	1,4–Dioxacy clohexane; see p Dioxane	
		N,N Dimethyl formamide 2,6–Dimethyl– 4–hepta-none; see Diisobutyl ke-tone		123911	1,3	p-Dioxane	
				123911	1	1,4–Dioxane; see p-Dioxane	
		1,2–Dimethylhydrazine Dimethylhydrazine (all iso-mers)		78342	3,4	2,3–p–Dioxanedithiol S,S-bis (0,0diethyl phosphoro dithioate) (dioxathion)	
		Dimethyl ketone; see Ace-tone		78342	3,4	Dioxathion; see 2,3–p– Di-oxanedithiol S,S-bis (O,O-diethyl phosphoro dithioate)	
115902,	3,4	0,0–Dimethyl 0–[p- (methyl-sulfinyl)					
115913		phenyl] phosphoro thioate (fensulfothion)		92524	3	Diphenyl; see Biphenyl	
				122394	3	Diphenylamine	
55389	3	O,O-dimethyl O-[3–methyl–4 (methylthio) phenyl] phospho rothioate; see Fenthion		57410	1	Diphenyl hydantoin (Pheny-toin)	
				630933	1	Diphenyl hydantoin (Pheny-toin), sodium salt	
298000	3	O,O–Dimethyl O-(p-nitro-phenyl) phospho roth-ioate; see Methyl para-thion		38622183	2	Diphenyl hydrazine	
				122667	2	1,2–Diphenyl hydrazine; see Hydrazobenzene	
62759	1,3	N,N–Dimethyl nitrosamine; see N–Nitrosodi methyla-mine		101688	3	Diphenylmethane diisocya-nate; see Methylene bis(4– phenylisocyanate)	
86500	2,3,4	0,0–Dimethyl S-(4–oxo-benzotriazino –3–methyl)		34590948	3	Dipropylene glycol mono-methyl ether	
		phosphoro dithioate (Az-inphos methyl)		123193	3	Dipropyl ketone	
				85007, 2764729	2,3	Diquat	

CAS No.	Source	Substance	Footnotes
1937377	1	Direct Black 38 (technical grade)	
2602462	1	Direct Blue 6 (technical grade)	
16071866	1	Direct Brown 95	
2475458	1	Disperse Blue 1	
97778	3	Disulfiram	
298044	2,3,4	Disulfoton	
298044	2,4	Disyston; see Disulfoton	
1189851	3	Di-tert-butyl chromate; see Chromium compounds	
330541	2,3	Diuron	
108576	3	Divinyl benzene	
27176870	2	Dodecylbenzene sulfonic acid	9
23214928	1	Doxorubicin hydrochloride; see Adriamycin	
60004	2	EDTA	
115297	2,3,4	Endosulfan	
959988	2	alpha- Endosulfan	
33213659	2	beta-Endosulfan	
1031078	2	Endosulfan-sulfate	
72208	2,3,4	Endrin	
7421934	2	Endrin aldehyde	
106898	1,2,3	Epichlorohydrin	12
2104645	3,4	EPN	
106876	1	1–Epoxyethyl –3,4–epixycy clohexane; see Vinyl cyclohexene dioxide	
4016142	3	1,2–Epoxy–3– isopropoxypropane; see Isopropyl glycidyl ether	
141377	1	3,4–Epoxy–6– methylcyclo hexyimethyl 3,4–epoxy–6–methylcyclohexane carboxylate	
122601	3	1,2–Epoxy–3– phenoxypropane; see Phenyl glycidyl ether	
75569	3	1,2–Epoxypropane; see Propylene oxide	
556525	3	2,3–Epoxypropanol; see Glycidol	
12510428	1	Erionite	
75058	3	Ethanenitrile; see Acetonitrile	
75081	3	Ethanethiol; see Ethyl mercaptan	
64175	1,3	Ethanol; see Ethyl alcohol	
141435	3	Ethanolamine	
463514	3	Ethenone; see Ketene	
57636	1	Ethinyloestradiol	
563122	2,3,4	Ethion	
536334	1	Ethionamide	
110805	3	2-Ethoxyethanol; see Ethylene glycol monoethyl ether	
111159	3	2–Ethoxyethanol acetate; see Ethylene glycol monoethyl ether acetate	
141786	3	Ethyl acetate	
140885	1,3	Ethyl acrylate	
64175	1,3	Ethyl alcohol	13
75047	2,3	Ethylamine	
541855	3	Ethyl sec-amyl ketone	
100414	2,3	Ethylbenzene	
74964	3	Ethyl bromide	
106354	3	Ethyl butyl ketone	
75003	3	Ethyl chloride	
510156	1	Ethyl–4,4 '-dichlorobenzilate; see Chlorobenzilate	

CAS No.	Source	Substance	Footnotes
13194484	4	0–Ethyl S,S-dipropyl phosphorodithioate (ethoprop)	
85007	3	1,1 '-Ethylene–2,2 '-bipyridinium dibromide; see Diquat	
107073	3	Ethylene chlorohydrin	
107153	2,3	Ethylenediamine	
106934	1,2,3,4,5	Ethylene dibromide	33
107062	1,2,3,4	Ethylene dichloride	
107211	3	Ethylene glycol	14
628966	3	Ethylene glycol dinitrate	
111762	2,3	Ethylene glycol monobutyl ether	
110805	3,5	Ethylene glycol monoethyl ether	
111159	3,5	Ethylene glycol monoethyl ether acetate	
109864	3,5	Ethylene glycol monomethyl ether	
110496	3,5	Ethylene glycol monomethyl ether acetate	
151564	1,3	Ethyleneimine	
75218	1,2,3,5	Ethylene oxide	12
420122	1	Ethylene sulphide	
96457	1	Ethylenethiourea	
79016	2	Ethylene trichloride; see Trichlorethylene	
60297	3	Ethyl ether	
109944	3	Ethyl formate	
75343	3	Ethylidene chloride	
16219753	3	Ethylidene norbornene	
75081	3	Ethyl mercaptan	
62500	1	Ethyl methanesulphonate	
563122	2	Ethyl methylene; see Ethion	
78933	3	Ethyl methyl ketone; see 2–Butanone	
22224926	3,4	Ethyl 3–methyl–4– (methylthio) -phenyl (1–methylethyl) phosphoramidate	
100743	3	N–Ethylmorpholine	
2104645	3	O–Ethyl O-(p-nitrophenyl) phenyl phospho nothioate; see EPN	
759739	1	N–Ethyl–N –Nitrosourea; see N–Nitroso N-ethylurea	
56382	2,4	Ethyl parathion; see Parathion	
78104	3	Ethyl silicate	
100743	3	4–Ethyl–1, 4–tetrahydrooxazine; see N–Ethylmorpholine	
110805	3	2–Ethyoxyethanol; see Ethylene glycol monoethyl ether	
97530	1	Eugenol	
314136	1	Evans blue	
2353459	1	Fast Green FCF	
22224926	3,4	Fenamiphos; see Ethyl– 3–methyl–4 (methylthio) phenyl (1–methylethyl) phosphoramidate	
115902	3	Fensulfothion; see O,O–Diethyl O [4–(methyl sulfinyl) phenyl] phospho rothioate	
55389	3	Fenthion	
101428	2	Fenuron	
4482557	2	Fenuron–TCA	
14484641	3,4	Ferbam	

CAS No.	Source	Substance	Footnotes	CAS No.	Source	Substance	Footnotes
1185575	2	Ferric ammonium citrate; see Iron salts, soluble		765344	1	Glycidaldehyde	
				556525	3	Glycidol	
2944674	2	Ferric ammonium oxalate; see Iron salts, soluble		7782425	3	Graphite	
				126078	1	Griseofulvin	
7705080	2	Ferric chloride; see Iron salts, soluble		4680788	1	Guinea Green B	
14484641	3	Ferric N,N-dimethyl thiocarbamate; see Ferbam		86500	2	Guthion; see O,O–Dimethyl S-(4 phobenzotriazino – 3–methyl) phosphoro dithioate	
7783508	2	Ferric fluoride; see Iron salts, soluble					
10421484	2	Ferric nitrate; see Iron salts, soluble		16568028	1	Gyromitrin (Acetaldehyde methylformyl hydrazone)	
10028225	2	Ferric sulfate; see Iron salts, soluble		822060	3	HDI; see Hexamethylene diisocyanate	
10045893	2	Ferrous ammonium sulfate; see Iron salts, soluble		7440586	3	Hafnium	
				2784943			
7758943	2	Ferrous chloride; see Iron salts, soluble		76448	1,2,3,4	Haloethers (other than those listed elsewhere, includes chloro- phenyl-phenyl ethers, bromophenylphenyl ether, bis (dichloroisopropyl) ether, bis (chloroethoxy) methane and polychlorinated diphenyl ethers)	
7720787	2	Ferrous sulfate; see Iron salts, soluble					
12604589	3	Ferrovanadium dust	3				
206440	2	Fluoranthene					
53963	3	n-Fluoren–2– yl-acetamide; see 2 Acetylamino- fluorene					
	2,3	Fluoride, and inorganic fluoride compounds		1024573	2	Halomethanes	
				76448	3	HC Blue	1
7782414	2,3	Fluorine		142845	3	Heptachlor	
640197	4	Fluoroacetamide/1081		106354	3	Heptachlor epoxide	
75694	3	Fluorocarbon 11; see Fluorotri chlormethane		110430	3	1,4,5,6,7,8,8, -Heptachloro– 3a, 4,7,7a- tetrahydro –4,7 methanoindene; see Heptachlor	
75718	3	Fluorocarbon 12; see Dichlorodi fluoromethane					
75434	3	Fluorocarbon 21; see Dichloromono fluoromethane		118741	1,2	n-Heptane	
				87683	1,2,3	3 Heptanone; see Ethyl butyl ketone	
75456	3	Fluorocarbon 22; see Chlorodi fluoromethane		608731	2	2–Heptanone; see Methyl n-amyl ketone	1
76120	3	Fluorocarbon 112; see 1,1,2,2 Tetrachloro–1,2– difluoroethane		77474	2,3	Hexachlorobenzene; see Benzene hexachloride	
				72208	3	Hexachlorobutadiene	
				60571	3	Hexachlorocy clohexane	
76131	3	Fluorocarbon 113; see 1,1,2 Trichloro– 1,2,2– trifluoroethane		67721	1,2,3	Hexachlorocyclohexanes	
				115297	3	Hexachlorocy clopentadiene	
76142	3	Fluorocarbon 114; see 1,2– Dichloro –1,1,2,2 tetrafluoroethane		309002	3	1,2,3,4,10, 10–Hexachloro– 6, 7–epoxy-, 1,4,4a,5,6, 7,8,8a octahydro 1,4, endo endo 5, 8 dimethano naphthalene and methabolites; see Endrin	
75694	3	Fluorotri chloromethane					
150505	4	Folex; see s,s,s-Tributyl phosphoro tritthioite					
133073	4	Folpet		1335871	2,3	1,2,3,4,10, 10–Hexachloro – 6,7–epoxy 1,4,4a,5, 6,7,8,8a- octahydro–1,4, endo-exo–5,8– dimethanonaphtha lene; see Dieldrin	
944229	3,4	Fonofos					
50000	1,2,3	Formaldehyde					
75127	3	Formamide					
64186	2,3	Formic acid		70304	2	Hexachloroethane	
3570750	1	2–(2– Formylhydrazino) –4– (5nitro–2–furyl) thiazole		684162	3	6,7,8,9,10, 10–Hexachloro	
110178	2	Fumaric acid	15	684162	3	1,5,5a,6,9, 9a-hexahydro – 6,9 methano–2,4, 3–benzodioxa thiepin 6–oxide; see Endosulfan	
6164983	4	Fundal; see Chlordimeform					
98011	2	2–Furaldehyde; see Furfural					
98011	2,3	Furfural					
98000	3	Furfuryl alcohol					
6164983	4	Galecron; see Chlordimeform		822060	3	1,2,3,4,10, 10–Hexachloro – 1,4,4a,5, 8ahexahydro- endo–1,2– exo–5, 8–di methanonaph thalene; see Aldrin	
8006619	3	Gasoline	16				
7782652	3	Germanium tetrahydride					
	3	Glass, fibrous or dust	38	680319	1	Hexachloronaph thalene	3
67730114	1	Glu–P–1 (2–Amino–6 methyldipyrido [1,2–a:3 ',2 ' d]imidazole)		591761	3	Hexachlorophene (HCP)	
				108101	3	Hexafluoroacetone	
67730103	1	Glu–P–2 (2–Aminodipyrido [1,2–a:3 ',2-d] imidazole)		108849	3	1,1,1,3,3,3, -Hexafluoro –2– propanone; see Hexafluoroacetone	
111308	3	Glutaraldehyde					

CAS No.	Source	Substance	Footnotes	CAS No.	Source	Substance	Footnotes
107415	3	Hexamethylene diisocyanate		54853	1	Isonicotinic acid hydrazide (Isoniazid)	
86544	1	Hexamethyl phosphoramide		26952216	3	Isooctyl alcohol	
302012	1,3	Hexane (all isomers)		78591	2,3	Isophorone	
10035106	3	2–Hexanone; see Methyl n-butyl ketone		4098719	3	Isophorone diisocyanate	
				3778732	1	Isophosphamide	
7647010	2,3	Hexone; see Methyl isobutyl ketone sec-Hexyl acetate		78795	2	Isoprene	
74908	2,3,4	Hexylene glycol		42504461	2	Isopropano lamine dodecyl benzenesul fonate	9
7664393	2,3	Hydralazine		109591	3	Isopropoxyethanol	
1333740	3	Hydrazine		114261	3	2–Isopropoxyphenyl N-methylcarbamate (propoxur)	
5124301	3	Hydrobromic acid; see Hydrogen bromide	3	108214	3	Isopropyl acetate	
10035106	3	Hydrochloric acid; see Hydrogen chloride		67630	1,3	Isopropyl alcohol	
				75310	3	Isopropylamine	
7647010	2,3	Hydrocyanic acid; see Hydrogen cyanide		643287	3	N–Isopropylaniline	
74908	2,3,4	Hydrofluoric acid; see Hydrogen fluoride		98828	3	Isopropylbenzene; see Cumene	
7664393	2,3	Hydrogen		108203	3	Isopropyl ether	
7722841	1,3	Hydrogenated MDI; see Dicyclohexyl methane–4,4' diisocyanate		4016142	3	Isopropyl glycidyl ether	12
				120581	1	Isosafrole	
		Hydrogenated terphenyls		115322	2	Kelthane; see 1,1–Bis (p-chlorophenyl) 2,2,2– trichloro ethanol	
		Hydrogen bromide					
		Hydrogen chloride		143500	1,2	Kepone; see Chlordecone	
		Hydrogen cyanide		463514	3	Ketene	
		Hydrogen fluoride		16752775	4	Lannate; see S–Methyl N-((methyl carbamoyl) oxy)-thioacetimidate	
		Hydrogen peroxide					
7783075	2	Hydrogen selenide; see Selenium and selenium compounds		303344	1	Lasiocarpine	
				7439921	1,2,3	Lead	3
7783064	2,3	Hydrogen sulfide		301042	2	Lead acetate; see Lead compounds	
123319	3	Hydroquinone		7784409,	2,3	Lead arsenate; see Lead compounds	
141662	3,4	3–Hydroxy –N,N-dimethyl -cis- crotonamide dimethyl phosphate (dicrotophos)		7645252, 10102480			
6923224	3	3–Hydroxy– N-methyl-cis-crotonamide dimethyl phosphate; see 3 (Dimethoxy phosphinyloxy) -N methyl- ciscrotonamide		7758954	2	Lead chloride; see Lead compounds	
				7758976	3	Lead chromate; see Chromium compounds	
					1,2,3	Lead compounds	
123422	3	4–Hydroxy– 4–methyl– 2–pentanone		13814965	2	Lead fluoborate; see Lead compounds	
999611	3	Hydroxypropyl acrylate		7783462	2	Lead fluoride; see Lead compounds	
4016142	3	IGE; see Isopropyl glycidyl ether		10101630	2	Lead iodide; see Lead compounds	
4098719	3	IPDI; see Isophorone diisocyanate		10099748	2	Lead nitrate; see Lead compounds	
76180966	1	IQ; (2–Amino–3 methylimidazo [4,5–f] quinoline)		7446277	1	Lead phosphate; see Lead compounds	
95316	3	Indene		7428480,	2	Lead stearate; see Lead compounds	
193395	1,2	Indeno (1,2,3–cd) pyrene					
	2,3	Indium and indium compounds		1072351, 52652592			
7553562	3	Iodine		1335326	1	Lead subacetate; see Lead compounds	
75478	3	Iodoform					
7439896	2	Iron		7446142	2	Lead sulfate; see Lead compounds	
9004664	1	Iron dextran					
8050939	1	Iron-dextrin complex		1314870	2	Lead sulfide; see Lead compounds	
1309371	3	Iron oxide fume					
13463406	3	Iron pentacarbonyl		78002	2,3	Lead tetraethyl; see Lead compounds	
	2,3	Iron salts, soluble	18				
15503863	1	Isatidine		75741	3	Lead tetramethyl; see Lead compounds	
12392	3	Isoamyl acetate; see Amyl acetate					
				592870	2	Lead thiocyanate; see Lead compounds	
123513	3	Isoamyl alcohol					
110190	3	Isobutyl acetate (2–methyl propyl acetate)		5141208	1	Light Green SF	
				58899	2,3,4	Lindane and other Hexachlorocy clohexane isomers	
78831	3	Isobutyl alcohol					
78819	2	Isobutylamine; see Butylamine, all isomers		330552	2	Linuron	

CAS No.	Source	Substance	Footnotes	CAS No.	Source	Substance	Footnotes
14307358	2	Lithium chromate; see Chromate compounds		109864	3	2–Methoxyethanol; see Ethylene glycol monomethyl ether	
7580678	3	Lithium hydride					
21884446	1	Luteoskyrin		110496	3	2–Methoxyethyl acetate; see Ethylene glycol monomethyl ether acetate	
101144	3	MBOCA; see 4,4'-Methylene bis(2 chloroaniline)					
94746	4	MCPA (2–methyl– 4–chloro phenoxyacetic acid)		150765	3	4–Methoxyphenol	
				484208		5–Methoxypsoralen	
101779	3	MDA; see 4,4'-Methylene dianiline		298817	1	8–Methoxypsoralen; see Methoxsalen	
101688	3	MDI; see Methylene bis(4–phenyliso cyanate)		79209	3	Methyl acetate	
				74997	3	Methyl acetylene	
68006837	1	MeA-a-C (2–Amino– 3–methyl–9H pyrido [2,3 –b]indole)			3	Methyl acetylene- propadiene mixture	
				123739	3	beta- Methylacrolein; see Crotonaldehyde	
78933	3	MEK; see 2–Butanone					
101144	1	MOCA; see 4,4'-Methylene bis(2– chloroaniline)		96333	3	Methyl acrylate	
				126987	3	alpha- Methylacrylo nitrile	
	1	MOPP		109875	3	Methylal	
7439954	2	Magnesium		67561	3	Methyl alcohol	30
1309484	3	Magnesium oxide	3	74895	2,3	Methylamine	
121755	2,3	Malathion		108112	3	Methyl amyl alcohol; see Methyl isobutyl carbinol	
110167	2	Maleic acid					
108316	2,3	Maleic anhydride		110430	3	Methyl n-amyl ketone	
7439965	2,3	Manganese	3		1	5–Methylangelicin	
	3	Manganese compounds		100618	3	N–Methylaniline	
12079651	3	Manganese, cyclopentadienyl tricarbonyl		95534	1,3	o-Methylaniline	
				75558	1,3	2–Methylaziridine	
1317537		Manganese tetroxide; see Manganese compounds		590965	1	Methylazoxymethanol	
				592621	1	Methylazoxymethyl acetate	
551746	1	Mannomustine		74839	1,2,3,4	Methyl bromide	
71589	1	Medroxy progesterone acetate		78795	2	2–Methyl–1, 3–butadiene; see Isoprene	
148823	1	Melphalan		123513	3	3–Methylbutanol; see Isoamyl alcohol	
2032657	2	Mercaptodimethur					
592041	2	Mercuric cyanide; see Mercury and mercury compounds		123922	3	3–Methylbutyl acetate; see Amyl acetate, all isomers	
				591786	3	Methyl n-butyl ketone	
10045940	2	Mercuric nitrate; see Mercury and mercury compounds		13909096	1	Methyl–CCNU; see 1–(2–Chloroethyl) –3–(4 methylcy clohexyl)– 1–nitrosourea	
7783359	2	Mercuric sulfate; see Mercury and mercury compounds					
592858	2	Mercuric thiocyanate; see Mercury and mercury compounds		109864	5	Methyl Cellosolve [; see Ethylene glycol monomethyl ether	
				74873	2,3	Methyl chloride	
7782867	2	Mercurous nitrate; see Mercury and mercury compounds		71556	2,3	Methyl chloroform	
				107302	1,3	Methyl chloromethyl ether	31
				3351324	1	2–Methylchrysene	
	2,3,4	Mercury and mercury compounds		3351313	1	3–Methylchrysene	
				3351302	1	4–Methylchrysene	
531760	1	Merphalan		3697243	1	5–Methylchrysene	
108678	3	Mesitylene; see Trimethylbenzene (all isomers)		1705857	1	6–Methylchrysene	
				75058	3	Methyl cyanide; see Acetonitrile	
141797	3	Mesityl oxide		137053	3	Methyl 2–cyanoacrylate	
72333	1	Mestranol		108872	3	Methylcyclohexane	
2032657	2	Mesurol; see Mercap todimethur		1331233,	3	Methylcyclo hexanol, all isomers	
79414	3	Methacrylic acid		591231,			
74931	2,3	Methanethiol; see Methyl mercaptan		583595, 25639423			
67561	3	Methanol; see Methyl alcohol		583608	3	o-Methylcyclo hexanone	
2032657	2	Methiocarb; see Mercaptodimethur		12108133	3	2–Methylcy clopentadienyl manganese tricarbonyl	
				8022002	3	Methyl demeton	
16752775	3,4	Methomyl; see 5–Methyl N–[(methyl carbamoyl) oxy] thioace tanide		534521	2,3	2–Methyl–4, 6–dinitrophenol; see 4,6–Dinitro –O–cresol	
298817	1	Methoxsalen (with ultraviolet therapy)		99809	1	N–Methyl–N, 4–Dinitrosoaniline	
72435	2,3	Methoxychlor		75092	1,2,3,5	Methylene chloride	

CAS No.	Source	Substance	Footnotes	CAS No.	Source	Substance	Footnotes
101144	1,3	4,4 '-Methylene bis(2– chloroaniline)		443481	1	Metronidazole	
5124301	3	Methylene bis(4– cyclohexylisocyanate); see Dicyclohexyl methane 4,4'- diisocyanate		7786347	2,3,4	Mevinphos; see alpha–2–Carbomethoxy–1 methyl-vinyl dimethyl phosphate	
				315184	2	Mexacarbate	
101611	1	4,4 '-Methylene bis(N,N- dimethyl) benzenamine		12001262	3	Mica	19
					3	Mineral wool fiber	
838880	1	4,4 '-Methylene bis(2– methylaniline)		2385855	1,2	Mirex	
				50077	1	Mitomycin C	
101688	3	Methylenebis (4–phenyl isocyanate)		13194484	4	Mocap; see O–Ethyl S,S dipropyl phospho rodithioate	
101779	1,3	4,4' Methylene dianiline		2212671	4	Molinate	
13552448		4,4' -Methylene dianiline dihydro chloride		7439987	2,3	Molybdenum	3
					3	Molybdenum compounds	20
78933	3	Methyl ethyl ketone; see 2–Butanone		10265926	4	Monitor; see O,S–Dimethyl phosphorami dothioate	
1338234	3	Methyl ethyl ketone peroxide		108907	2,3	Monochloro benzene; see Chlorinated benzenes	
33543316	1	2-Methyl fluoranthene		315220	1	Monocrotaline	
107313	3	Methyl formate		6923224	3,4	Monocrotophos; see 3 (Dimethoxy phosphinyloxy) - N methyl- cis- crotonamide	
541855	3	5–Methyl– 3–heptanone; see Ethyl sec-amyl ketone					
60344	3	Methyl hydrazine		75047	2	Monoethylamine; see Ethylamine	
74884	1,3	Methyl iodide					
110123	3	Methyl isoamyl ketone		74895	2	Monomethylamine; see Methylamine	
108112	3	Methyl isobutyl carbinol					
108101	3	Methyl isobutyl ketone		100618	3	Monomethylaniline; see N–Methylaniline	
624839	3	Methyl isocyanate					
563804	3	Methyl isopropyl ketone		60344	3	Monomethyl hydrazine; see Methyl hydrazine	
74931	2,3	Methyl mercaptan					
80626	2,3	Methyl methacrylate		150685	1,2	Monuron	
66273	1	Methyl methane sulfonate		140410	2	Monuron–TCA	
16752775	3,4	S–Methyl N-[(methylcarbamoyl) oxy]thio acetamida– te (Methomyl)		110918	3	Morpholine	
				139913	1	5–(Morpholino methyl)–3 [(5–nitro furfurylidene) - amino] –2– oxazolidinone	
80626	2,3	Methyl 2–methyl– 2–propenoate; see Methyl methacrylate					
				7647010	2	Muriatic acid; see Hydrogen chloride	
129157	1	2–Methyl– 1–nitro anthraquinone		505602	1	Mustard Gas	
70257	1	N–Methyl–N '-nitro-N- nitroso guanidine		25551284	3	NDI; see Naphthalene diisocyanate	
684935	1	N–Methyl– N–Nitrosourea; see N–Nitroso– N-methylurea		139139	2	NTA; see Nitrilo triacetic acid	
				3771195	1	Nafenopin	
615532	1	N–Methyl– N–Nitrosourethane; see N–Nitroso–N-methylurethane		300765	3	Naled; see O,O–Dimethyl O (1,2–dibromo –2,2 dichloroethyl) phosphate	
298000	2,3,4	Methyl parathion		8030317	3	Naphtha, coal tar	
108112	3	4–Methyl– 2–pentanol; see Methyl isobutyl carbinol		91203	2,3	Naphthalene	
				2243621	1	1,5–Naphtha lenediamine	
141797	3	4–Methyl– 3–pentene–2– one; see Mesityl oxide		25551284	3	Napthalene diisocyanate	
				1338245	2	Naphthenic acid	
108849	3	4–Methyl– 2–pentyl acetate; see sec-Hexyl acetate		134327	3	1–Naphthylamine; see alpha- Naphthylamine	
98839	3	1–Methyl-l- phenylethene; see alpha Methylstyrene		91598	1	2–Naphthylamine; see beta- Naphthylamine	
78831	3	2–Methylpropanol; see Isobutyl alcohol		134327	3	alpha- Naphthylamine	
				91598	1,3	beta- Naphthylamine	31
110190	3	2–Methylpropyl acetate; see Isobutyl acetate		63252	3	1–Naphthyl N-methyl carbamate; see Carbaryl	
107879	3	Methyl propyl ketone; see 2–Pentanone		86884	3	1–(1–Naphthyl) –2–thiourea	
54115	3	1–Methyl–2– (3–pyridyl) pyrrolidine; see Nicotine		22224926	4	Nemacur; see Ethyl 3–methyl 4–(methylthio) phenyl (1–methyl ethyl) phospho ramidate	
681845	3	Methyl silicate					
98839	3	alpha- Methylstyrene		563122	2	Nialate; see Ethion	
77781	3	Methyl sulfate; see Dimethyl sulfate		7440020	1,2,3	Nickel	3
				15699180	2	Nickel ammonium sulfate; see Nickel compounds	
58184	1	Methyl testosterone					
56042	1	Methyl thiouracil		13463393	3	Nickel carbonyl; see Nickel compounds	
484208	1	5–Methy oxypsoralen					

CAS No.	Source	Substance	Footnotes	CAS No.	Source	Substance	Footnotes
37211055	2	Nickel chloride; see Nickel compounds		10595956	1	N–Nitrosome thylethyla- mine	
7718549	1,2,3	Nickel compounds		684935	1	N–Nitroso– N-methylurea	
12054487	2	Nickel hydroxide; see Nickel compounds		615532	1	N–Nitroso– N-methylure- thane	
14216752	2	Nickel nitrate; see Nickel compounds		4549400	1	N–Nitrosome thylvinyla- mine	
12035722	1	Nickel subsulphide; see Nickel compounds		59892	1	N–Nitrosomorpholine	
				16543558	1	N–Nitrosonor nicotine	
778614	2	Nickel sulfate; see Nickel compounds		100754	1	N–Nitroso piperidine	
				930552	1	N–Nitrosopyr rolidine	
54115	3,4	Nicotine		13256229	1	N–Nitrososarcosine	
56382	2	Niran; see Parathion		1321126, 88722, 99081, 99990	2,3	Nitrotoluenes	
61574	1	Niridazole					
139946	1	Nithiazide					
1929824	3	Nitrapyrin; see 2–Chloro 6– (trichloro methyl) pyri- dine		76062	3	Nitrotri chloromethane; see Chloropicrin	
				10024972	3	Nitrous oxide	
7697372	2,3	Nitric acid		111842	3	Nonane	
10102439	3	Nitric oxide		68224	1	Norethisterone	
139139	2	Nitrilotriacetic acid		51989	1	Norethisterone acetate	
602879	1	5-Nitroace naphthene		2698411	3	OCBM; see O–Chloroben- zylidine malonitrile	
100016	3	p-Nitroaniline					
99592	1	5-Nitro-o- anisidine		152169	4	OMPA; see Schradan	
98953	2,3	Nitrobenzene		303479	1	Ochratoxin A	
100005	3	p-Nitro chlorobenzene		2234131	2,3	Octachloro naphthalene	
7496028	1	6-Nitrochrysene		57749	3	1,2,4,5,6,7,8,8 –Octachloro 3a,4,7,7a, -tetrahydro–4,7 methanoindane; see Chlordane	
92933	3	4-Nitrodiphenyl	31				
79243	3	Nitroethane					
1836755	1	Nitrofen (technical grade); see 2,4– Dichlorphenyl p- nitrophenyl ether		111659	3	Octane	
				50282	1	Oestradiol–17B	
				22966796	1	Oestradiol mustard	
607578	1	2-Nitrofluorene			1	Oestrogens, steroidal	
59870	1	Nitrofurazone			1	Oestrogens, nonsteroidal	
555840	1	1–[(5–Nitrofur furylidene) - amino] –2imidazoli- di- none		53167	1	Oestrone	
					1,2,3	Oil mist, particulate	21
				2646175	1	Oil orange SS	
531828	1	N–4–[(5– Nitro–2–furyl) -2– thiazolyl] acetamide			1	Oral contraceptives, certain Oestrogen-progestin combinations	
10102440	2,3	Nitrogen dioxide					
51752, 55867	1	Nitrogen mustard and its hydrochloride		20816120	3	Osmium tetroxide	
				144627	3	Oxalic acid	
302705, 126852	1	Nitrogen mustard N-oxide and its hydrochloride		604751	1	Oxazepam	
				301122	4	Oxydemetonmethyl	
10102440	2,3	Nitrogen tetroxide; see Ni trogen dioxide		7783417	3	Oxygen difluoride	
				10028156	3	Ozone	22
7783542	3	Nitrogen trifluoride			1,2,3	PCB; see Polychloro biphe- nyls	
55630	3	Ntroglycerin					
75525	3	Nitromethane		12674112	2	PCB–1016; see Polychloro biphenyls	
25154556, 554847, 88755, 100027	2	Nitrophenols, all isomers		11104282	2	PCB–1221; see Polychloro biphenyls	
				11141165	2	PCB–1232; see Polychloro biphenyls	
79469	1,3	2–Nitropropane; see Nitro- propanes		53469219	2	PCB–1242; see Polychloro biphenyls	
108032, 794691	3	Nitropropanes		12672296	2	PCB–1248; see Polychloro biphenyls	
57835924	1	4-Nitropyrene					
5522430	1	1-Nitropyrene		11097691	2	PCB–1254; see Polychloro biphenyls	
	2	Nitrosamines					
1133648	1	N´-Nitrosoanabasine		11096825	2	PCB–1260; see Polychloro biphenyls	
924163	1	N–Nitroso-di- n-butylamine					
1116547	1	N–Nitroso diethanolamine		82688	2	PCNB; see Quintozene (Pentachloro nitroben- zene)	
55185	1	N–Nitroso diethylamine					
62759	1,2,3	N–Nitroso dimethylamine					
86306	1,2	N–Nitrosodi phenylamine		87865	2,3	PCP; see Penta chlorophe- nol	
621647	1,2	N–Nitroso-di- n-propyla- mine					
759739	1	N–Nitroso– N-ethylurea		6423434	3	PGDN; see Propylene gly- col dinitrate	
60153493	1	3–(N–Nitrosome thylamino) propionitrile		122601	3	PGE; see Phenyl glycidyl ether	
64091914	1	4–(N–Nitrosome thylami- no)–1 (3–pyridyl)–1 –bu- tanone (NNK)		7440053	2	Palladium	

CAS No.	Source	Substance	Footnotes
794394	1	Panfuran S; see Dihydroxy methylfura trizine	
8002742	3	Paraffin wax fume	
30525894	2	Paraformaldehyde	
2074502, 1910425	3,4	Paraquat	
10048325	1	Parasorbic acid	
56382	2,3,4	Parathion	
90653	1	Penicillic acid	
19624227	3	Pentaborane	
76017	1	Penta chloroethane	
1321648	2,3	Pentachloro naphthalene	
87865	2,3	Pentachlorophenol	
109660	3	Pentane	
107879	3	2–Pentanone	
77474	2	Perchloro cyclopentadiene; see Hexachlorocyclo - pentadiene	
67721	3	Perchloroethane; see Hexa- chloroethane	
127184	1,2,3,5	Perchloroethylene	
594423	3	Perchloromethyl mercaptan	
7616946	3	Perchloryl fluoride	
72560	2	Perthane	
60102376	1	Petasitenine	
62442	1	Phenacetin	
532274	3	Phenacyl chloride; see al- pha- Chloroace tophe- none	
85018	2	Phenanthrene	
136403, 94780	1	Phenazopyridine and its hy- drochloride	
156514	1	Phenelzine sulphate	
103037	1	Phenicarbazide	
50066	1	Phenobarbital	
108952	2,3	Phenol	
	2	Phenolic compounds (4AAP)	
	2	Phenols	
92842	3	Phenothiazine	
59861, 63923	1	Phenoxybenzamine and its hydrochloride	
122394	3	n-Phenylaniline; see Diphe- nylamine	
92524	3	Phenylbenzene; see Biphe- nyl	
100470	2	Phenyl cyanide; see Benzon- itrile	
106503	3	p-Phenylenediamine	
100414	2	Phenylethane; see Ethylben- zene	
101848	3	Phenyl ether, vapor	14
100425	2,3	Phenylethylene; see Styr- ene, monomer	
122601	1,3	Phenyl glycidyl ether	12
100630	3	Phenylhydrazine	
108985	3	Phenyl mercaptan	
135886	1	N–Phenyl–2– naphthyla- mine	
132274	1	o-Phenylphenate, sodium; see Sodium ortho- phe- nylphenate	
638211	3	Phenylphosphine	
57410	1	Phenytoin; see Diphenyl hy- dantoin	
298022	3,4	Phorate	
4104144	4	Phosacetim	
7786347	2,4	Phosdrin; see alpha–2 Car- bomethoxy– 1–methylvi- nyl dimethyl phosphate	
75445	2,3	Phosgene	
13171216	4	Phosphamidon	
7803512	3	Phosphine	
7664382	2,3	Phosphoric acid	

CAS No.	Source	Substance	Footnotes
563122	2	Phosphorodithioate; see Ethion	
7723140	2,3	Phosphorus	
10025873	2,3	Phosphorus oxychloride	
10026138	3	Phosphorus pentachloride	
1314803	2,3	Phosphorus pentasulfide	
7719122	2,3	Phosphorus trichloride	
121755	2	Phosphothion; see Mala- thion	
	1,2,3	Phthalate esters	36
85449	3	Phthalic anhydride	
626175	3	m-Phthalodinitrile	
1918021	1,3,4	Picloram	
88891	3	Picric acid	
83261	3	Pindone; see 2–Pivalyl–1, 3– indandione	
142643	3	Piperazine dihydrochloride	
83261	3	2–Pivalyl–1, 3–indandione (pindone)	
744064	2,3	Platinum, metal	
	3	Platinum, soluble salts	
	1	Polybrominated biphenyls	
1336363, 53449219, 11097691	1,2,3	Polyhloro biphenyls	
	2	Polychlorinated biphenyls; see Polychloro biphenyls	
	2	Polycyclic Organic Matter; see Polynuclear aromatic hydrocarbons	
	1,2	Polynuclear aromatic hydro- carbons	23
	3	Polytetra fluoroethylene, decomposition products	
9003398	1	Polyvinyl pyrrolidone	
3761533	1	Ponceau MX	
3564098	1	Ponceau 3R	
7440097	2	Potassium	
7784410	2	Potassium arsenate; see Ar- senic and arsenic com- pounds	
10124502	2	Potassium arsenite; see Ar- senic and arsenic com- pounds	
7778509	2	Potassium bichromate; see Chromuim compounds	
23746341	1	Potassium bis(2– hydroxye- thyl) dithiocarbamate	
7758012	1	Potassium bromate	
7789006	2	Potassium chromate; see Chromium compounds	
151508	2	Potassium cyanide; see Cya- nides, inorganic salts	
1310583	2,3	Potassium hydroxide	
7722647	2	Potassium permanganate	
366701	1	Procarbazine hydrochloride	
57830	1	Progesterone	
	1	Progestins	
51025	1	Pronetalol hydrochloride	
120714	1	1,3–Propane sultone	
709988	4	Propanil	
2312358	2,4	Propargite	
107197	3	Propargyl alcohol	
122429	2	Propham	
57578	1,3	beta- Propiolactone	
79094	2,3	Propionic acid	
123626	2	Propionic anhydride	
114261	2,3	Propoxur; see 2–Isopropo xyphenyl N-methyl carba- mate	
109604	3	n-Propyl acetate	
71238	3	n-Propyl alcohol	
627123	1	n-Propyl carbamate	
115071	3	Propylene	

CAS No.	Source	Substance	Footnotes	CAS No.	Source	Substance	Footnotes
78875	2,3	Propylene dichloride; see Dichloro propanes		7803625	3	Silicon tetrahydride; see Silane	
6423434	3	Propylene glycol dinitrate		7440224	2,3	Silver	3
107982	3	Propylene glycol monomethyl ether			2,3	Silver compounds	26
75558	3	Propyleneimine; see 2-Methy laziridine		7761888	2	Silver nitrate; see Silver compounds	
75569	1,2,3	Propylene oxide	12	93721	2,4	Silvex; see 2,4,5 TP acid	
627134	3	n-Propyl nitrate			3	Soapstone	19
51525	1	Propylthiouracil		7440235	2	Sodium	
74997	3	Propyne; see Methylacetylene		7631892	2	Sodium arsenate; see Arsenic and arsenic compounds	
107197	3	2-Propyn-l-ol; see Propargyl alcohol		7784465	2	Sodium arsenite; see Arsenic and arsenic compounds	
87625625	1	Ptaquiloside		26628228	3	Sodium azide	
129000	2	Pyrene		10588019	2	Sodium bichromate; see Chromium compounds	
121299, 121211	2	Pyrethrins		1333831	2	Sodium bifluoride; see Fluoride and fluoride compounds	
8003347	3	Pyrethrum		7631905	2,3	Sodium bisulfite	
110861	3	Pyridine		7775113	2	Sodium chromate; see Chromium compounds	
58140	1	Pyrimethamine					
120809	3	Pyrocatechol; see Catechol		143339	2,4	Sodium cyanide; see Cyanides, inorganic salts	
98011	2	Pyromucic aldehyde; see Furfural		136787	3	Sodium 2-(2,4- dichloro phenoxy)- ethyl sulfate	
117359	1	Quercetin		25155300	2	Sodium dodecylbenzene-sulfonate	9
91225	2	Quinoline					
106514	3	Quinone		7681494	2	Sodium fluoride; see Fluoride and fluoride compounds	
82688	1	Quintozene (Pentachloro nitrobenzene)					
121824	3	RDX; see Cyclotri methylene trinitramine		62748	3,4	Sodium fluoroacetate	
	2	Radionuclides		16721805	2	Sodium hydrosulfide	
13982633	2	Radium 226		1310732	2,3	Sodium hydroxide	
10043922	1	Radon		7681529	2	Sodium hypochlorite	
86884	3	Ratrack; see l-(1-Naphthyl) -2-thiourea		7681574	3	Sodium metabisulfite	
50555	1	Reserpine		124414	2	Sodium methylate	
108463	2,3	Resorcinol		7632000	2	Sodium nitrite	
480546	1	Retrorsine		132274	1	Sodium ortho- phenylphenate	
989388	1	Rhodamine 6G					
81889	1	Rhodamine B		7558794, 10039324, 10140655	2	Sodium phosphate, dibasic	
7440166	3	Rhodium	3				
	3	Rhodium compounds		778544, 7601549, 10101890, 10361894, 7758294, 10124568	2	Sodium phosphate, tribasic	
36791045	5	Ribavirin					
13292461	1	Rifampicin					
299843	2,3	Ronnel					
	3	Rosin core solder, pyrolysis products	24	10102188	2	Sodium selenite; see Selenium and selenium compounds	
83794	3	Rotenone, commercial					
	3	Rubber solvent (naphtha)			1	Soots, tars, and certain mineral oils	
8047674	1	Saccharated iron oxide		52017	1	Spironolactone	
94597	1	Safrole		7745893	4	Starlicide; see 3-Chloro-p toluidine hydrochloride	
152169	4	Schradan					
	2,3	Selenium and selenium compounds		10048132	1	Sterigmatocystin	
7783791	3	Selenium hexafluoride; see Selenium and selenium compounds		7803523	3	Stibine; see Antimony compounds	
				8052413	3	Stoddard solvent	
7446084	2	Selenium oxide; see Selenium and selenium compounds		18883664	1	Streptozotocin	
				7440246	2	Strontium	
563417	1	Semicarbazide hydrochloride		7789062	2	Strontium chromate; see Chromium compounds	
2318185	1	Senkirkine		57249	2,3,4	Strychnine	
136787	3	Sesone; see Sodium 2 (2,4-dichloro phenoxy) ethyl sulfate		100425	1,2,3	Styrene, monomer	
				96093	1	Styrene oxide	
63252	2,4	Sevin; see Carbaryl		1395217,	3	Subtilisins (proteolytic enzymes)	
68308349	1	Shale-oils		9014011			
1982496	2	Siduron		108305	1	Succinic anhydride	
7803625	3	Silane		842079	1	Sudan I	
7631869	1,3	Silica	25, 35	3118976	1	Sudan II	
				95067	1	Sulfallate	

CAS No.	Source	Substance	Footnotes	CAS No.	Source	Substance	Footnotes
723466	1	Sulfamethoxazole		58220	1	Testosterone (and its esters)	
3689245	3,4	Sulfotepp; see Tetraethyl di-thiopyro phosphate		315377	1	Testosterone enanthate	
7704349	2	Sulfur		79276	3	1,1,2,2– Tetrabromoethane; see Acetylene tetrabrom-ide	
10025679	2	Sulfur chloride; see Sulfur monochloride		1746016	1,2	2,3,7, 8–Tetrachloro diben-zo- p-dioxin	
7446095	3	Sulfur dioxide					
2551624	3	Sulfur hexafluoride		76119	3	1,1,1, 2–Tetrachloro–2, 2–difluoroethane	
7664939	2,3	Sulfuric acid					
7790945	2	Sulfuric chlorohydrin; see Chlorosulfonic acid		72548	2	Tetrachloro diphenyleth-ane; see TDE	
10025679	2,3	Sulfur monochloride		603206	1	1,1,1, 2–Tetrachloroethane	
5714227	3	Sulfur pentafluoride		76120	3	1,1,2, 2–Tetrachloro– 1,2–difluoroethane (FC–112)	
7783600	3	Sulfur tetrafluoride					
2699798	3	Sulfuryl fluoride		79345	1,2,3	1,1,2, 2–Tetrachloro ethane; see Acetylene tetrachlo-ride	
35400432	3	Sulprofos					
950378	4	Surpracide; see O,O–Di-methyl phosphoro dith-ioate, S-ether with 4–(mercaptomethyl) –2–me-thoxy O super2 –1,3,4–thiadiazolin –5–one		127184	2,3,5	Tetrachloro ethylene; see Perchloroethylene	
				56235	2,3	Tetrachloro methane; see Carbon tetrachloride	
				1335882	2,3	Tetrachloron aphthalene	
1918189	2	Swep		961115	1	Tetrachlor vinphos	
8065483	4	Systox; see Demeton		3689245	3,4	Tetraethyl dithiopyro phos-phate (Sulfotepp)	
93765	2,3,4	2,4,5–T; 2,4,5– Trichloro-phenoxyacetic acid		78002	2	Tetraethyl lead; see Lead compounds	
6369966, 6369977, 1319728, 3813147	2	2,4,5–T amines		107493	2,3,4	Tetraethyl pyrophosphate	
				78104	3	Tetraethyl silicate; see Ethyl silicate	
2545597, 93798, 61792072,	2	2,4,5–T esters; 2,4, 5–trichloro phenoxya-cetic acid		109999	3	Tetrahydrofuran	
				110918	3	Tetrahydro –4H–1–4– oxa-zine; see Morpholine	
1928478, 25168154		esters		75741	3	Tetramethyl lead; see Lead compounds	
13560991	2	2,4,5–T salt; acetic acid, 2,4,5– trichloro phenoxy-sodium salt		681845	3	Tetramethyl silicate; see Methyl silicate	
93721	2,4	2,4,5–TP acid; propanoic acid, 2–(2,4,5– trichloro-phenoxy)		3383968	3	Tetramethyl 0,0 '-thio-di-p-phenylene phospho roth-ioate (temephos)	
32534955	2	2,4,5–TP ester; propanoic acid, 2–(2,4,5– trichloro phenoxy)-, isooctyl ester)		3333526	3	Tetramethyl succinonitrile (decomposition product of 2,2' azobisiso butyroni-trile)	
1746016	1,2	TCDD; see 2,3,7,8 Tetra-chloro dibenzo- p-dioxin		137268	3	Tetramethyl thiuran disul-fide; see Bis(dimethyl thiocarbamoyl) disulfide	
78308	3	TCP; see Tri-o-creysl phos-phate					
72548	2,4	TDE		509148	3	Tetranitromethane	
584849	3	TDI; see Tolulene–2, 4-dii-socyanate		7722885	3	Tetra sodium pyrophosp-hate	
3689245	3	TEDP; see Tetraethyl di-thionopyro phosphate		479458	3	Tetryl	
				7440280	2	Thallium	3
107493	2,3,4	TEPP; see Tetraethyl pyro-phosphate			2,3	Thallium compounds	
				10031591, 446186	2	Thallium sulfate; see Thallium compounds	
109999	3	THF; see Tetrahydrofuran		298022	4	Thimet; see Phorate	
118967	3	TNT; see 2,4,6– Trinitroto-luene		62555	2	Thioacetamide	
				28249776	4	Thiobencarb	
115866	3	TPP; see Triphenyl phos-phate		96695	3	4,4 '-Thiobis (6–tert-butyl-m-cresol)	
14807966	1,3	Talc	19	115297	2	Thiodan; see Endosulfan	
	1	Tannic acid and tannins		139651	1	4,4 '-Thiodianiline	
7440257	2,3	Tantalum	3	68111	3	Thioglycolic acid	
1314610	3	Tantalum oxide		7719097	3	Thionyl chloride	
10028167	3	Tellurium	3	52244	1	Thiotepa; see Tris (1–aziri-dinyl) phosphine sulphide	
	3	Tellurium compounds					
7783804	3	Tellurium hexafluoride; see Tellurium compounds		141902	1	Thiouracil	
				62566	1	Thiourea	
3383968	3	Temephos; see Tetramethyl O, O'-thio-di- p-pheny-lene phospho rothiate		137268	3	Thiram; see Bis(dimethyl thiocarbamyl) disulfide	
				7440315	2,3	Tin	3
8001501	1	Terpene polychlorinates (Strobane6 [3 Terphenyls			3	Tin compounds	
				7440326	2	Titanium	

CAS No.	Source	Substance	Footnotes	CAS No.	Source	Substance	Footnotes
1836755	4	Tok; see 2,4– Dichlorophenyl -p nitrophenyl ether		76131	2,3	1,1,2–Trichloro –1,2, 2–trifluoroethane (FC–113)	
119937	1	o-Tolidine; see 3,3 ' Dimethyl benzidine		78308	3	Tri-o-cresyl phosphate	
108883	2,3	Toluene		13121705	3	Tricyclohexyltin hydroxide; see Tin compounds	
584849	1,3	Toluene–2, 4–diisocyanate		27323417	2	Triethanolamine dodecyl-benzene sulfonate	9
26471625, 91087, 26471625, 584849	1	Toluene diisocyanates		121448	2,3	Triethylamine	
				1954285	1	Triethylene glycol diglycidyl ether	
108441	3	m-Toluidine		75638	3	Triflorobromo methane; see Bromotrifluoro methane	
106490	3	p-Toluidine					
95534	3	o-Toluidine; see o-Methylaniline		1582098	1,2	Trifuralin	
				552307	3	Trimellitic anhydride	
636215	1	ortho- Toluidine; hydrochloride		75503	2,3	Trimethylamine	
				137177	1	2,4,5– Trimethylaniline	
108883	2,3	Toluol; see Toluene			3	Trimethylbenzene (all isomers)	
10311849	4	Torak; see Dialifor					
8001352	1,2,3,4	Toxaphene		78591	3	3,5,5– Trimethyl– 2–cyclohexene 1–one; see Isophorone	
14567738	3	Tremolite					
299752	1	Treosulfan		121459	3	Trimethyl phosphite	
299752	1	Treosulphan; see Treosulfan		88891	3	2,4,6 Trinitrophenol; see Picric acid	
75252	3	Tribomomethane; see Bromoform		479458	3	2,4,6– Trinitrophenyl methylnitramine; see Tetryl	
126738	3	Tributyl phosphate		118967	3	2,4, 6–Trinitrotoluene	
78488	4	S,S,S–Tributyl phosphorotrithioate		78308	3	Tri-ortho- cresyl phosphate; Tri-o-cresyl phosphate	
150505	4	S,S,S– Tributyl phosphoro trithioite		603349	3	Triphenylamine	
	4	Tributyltin, coatings containing		115866	3	Triphenyl phosphate	
				68768	1	Tris (aziridinyl)- para- benzoquinone; (Triaziquone)	
52686	2	Trichlorfon		52244	1	Tris (1–aziridinyl) phosphine sulfide	
76039	3	Trichloroacetic acid					
120821	2,3	1,2,4– Trichlorobenzene; see Chlorinated benzenes		51183	1	2,4,6– Tris (1–aziridinyl)- s-triazine	
50293	3	1,1,1–Trichloro –2–2,bis (p-chlorophenyl) ethane; see DDT		38571732	1	1,2,3– Tris (chloromethoxy) propane	
72435	3	1,1,1 Trichloro –2,2–bis (p-methoxphenyl) -ethane; see Methoxychlor		126727	1	Tris (2,3– dibromopropyl) phosphate	
				786196	4	Trithion; see Carbophenothion	
79005	1,2,3	1,1,2– Trichloroethane		62450060	1	Trp–P–1 (Tryptophan –P–1)	
71556	2,3	1,1,1– Trichloroethane; see Methyl chloroform		62450071	1	Trp-P2 (Tryptophan –P–2)	
79016	3	Trichloroethene; see Trichloroethylene		72571	1	Trypan blue (commercial grade)	
79016	1,2,3	Trichloroethylene		7440337	2,3	Tungsten, Tungsten compounds	3, 34
75694	3	Trichloro fluoromethane; see Fluorotri chloromethane		8006642	3	Turpentine	
				66751	1	Uracil mustard	
67663	2,3	Trichloromethane; see Chloroform		7440611	2,3	Uranium	3, 34
					2,3	Uranium compounds	
594423	3	Trichloro methanethiol; see Perchloromethyl mercaptan		541093	2	Uranyl acetate; see Uranium compounds	
1321659	2,3	Trichloronaph thalene		10102064	2	Uranyl nitrate; see Uranium compounds	
76062	3	Trichloronitro methane; see Chloropicrin		51796	1	Urethane	
88062	2	2,4, 6–Trichlorophenol; see Trichlorophenols		8030306	3	VM & P (Varnish Makers & Painters) naphtha	
25167822, 15950660, 933788, 933755, 95954, 609198, 88062	1,2	Trichlorophenols		110623	3	Valeraldehyde	
				7440622	2	Vanadium	
				1314621	2,3	Vanadium pentoxide	3
				27774136	2	Vanadyl sulfate	
				62737	2	Vapona; see Dichlorvos	
				108054	2,3	Vinyl acetate	
136254	2	2–(2,4,5– Trichloro phenoxy) ethyl 2,2–dichloro propionate (Erbon)		100425	2	Vinylbenzene; see Styrene, monomer	
				593602	1,3	Vinyl bromide	
				75014	1,2,3	Vinyl chloride	
				107131	2,3	Vinyl cyanide; see Acrylonitrile	
96184	3	1,2, 3–Trichloro propane		100403	1	4–Vinylcy clohexene	

CAS No.	Source	Substance	Footnotes
106876	1,3	Vinyl cyclohexene dioxide	
106876	1	4–Vinyl– 1–cyclohexene diepoxide; see Vinyl cyclohexene dioxide	
75354	1,2,3	Vinylidene chloride	
25013154	3	Vinyltoluene	
79005	1	Vinyl trichloride; see 1,1,2 Trichloroethane	
81812	3	Warfarin	
13983170	1	Wollastonite	
1330207,95476, 106423, 108383	2,3	Xylene, all isomers	
1477550	3	m-Xylene-a ',a '-diamine	
1300716	2	Xylenol	
1300738	3	Xylidine	
95476	2,3	Xylol; see Xylene, all isomers	
131793	1	Yellow OB	
	3	Yttrium compounds	
17924924	1	Zearalenone	
7440666	2	Zinc	3
557346	2	Zinc acetate; see Zinc compounds	
14639975, 14639986, 52628258	2	Zinc ammonium chloride; see Zinc compounds	
1332076	2	Zinc borate; see Zinc compounds	
7699458	2	Zinc bromide; see Zinc compounds	
3486359	2	Zinc carbonate; see Zinc compounds	
7646857	2,3	Zinc chloride; see Zinc compounds	
1350659	3	Zinc chromate; see Chromium compounds	
	2,3,4	Zinc compounds	28
557211	2	Zinc cyanide; see Cyanides, inorganic salts	
7783495	2	Zinc fluoride; see Zinc compounds	
557415	2	Zinc formate; see Zinc compounds	
7779864	2	Zinc hydrosulfite; see Zinc compounds	
7779886	2	Zinc Nitrate; see Zinc compounds	
1314132	3	Zinc oxide fume; see Zinc compounds	
127822	2	Zinc phenolsulfonate; see Zinc compounds	
1314847	2,4	Zinc phosphide; see Zinc compounds	
16871719	2	Zinc silicofluoride; see Zinc compounds	
7733020	2	Zinc sulfate; see Zinc compounds	
12122677		Zineb	
7440677	2	Zirconium	
7440677	2,3	Zirconium compounds, as Zr	
13746899	2	Zirconium nitrate; see Zirconium compounds	
16923958	2	Zirconium potassium fluoride; see Zirconium compounds	
14644612	2	Zirconium sulfate; see Zirconium compounds	
10026116	2	Zirconium tetrachloride	

FOOTNOTES FOR HAZARDOUS SUBSTANCE LIST

[1] Refers to solutions greater than or equal to 10%. Exempt when present in food or beverages, such as vinegar, apple cider, and wine, regardless of concentration.

[2] Refers to water-soluble salts only; all other salts are exempt.

[3] An MSDS must be provided under the following circumstances:

a) The metal is supplied as a fine powder.

b) The metal is in welding or brazing rods.

c) The metal may be melted with the generation of toxic fume.

d) Under normal use, toxic dust or fume is likely to be generated by any manufacturing process.

[4] Exempt when in bonded form or when antimony compounds cannot be released due to cutting, grinding, heating, etc.

[5] Except:

a) Exterior and interior coatings and laminating resins containing encapsulated asbestos fibers within such products.

b) Cold process asphalt roof coatings.

c) Non-friable encapsulated products such as floor tiles.

[6] Any liquids; and products that could give rise to asphalt fume under normal conditions are included. Mechanical breakup of hardened asphalt surfaces is exempt.

[7] Exempt when used in foods and feeds as a preservative.

[8] Exempt except when present as free crystal/powder.

[9] Exempt when in solution.

[10] Exempt when in form where exposure to dust cannot occur.

[11] Products that could give rise to coal tar pitch volatiles during normal use are included.

[12] Exempt when part of a cured epoxy or rubber.

[13] Refers to solutions greater than or equal to 25%. Beverage alcohol (as defined by Sections 23004 and 23005 of the California Alcoholic Beverage Control Act) in any concentration is exempt.

[14] Exempt except when vapors or particulates are or can be formed due to work practices or procedures.

[15] Exempt except when present as a dust.

[16] Exempt when used as fuel.

[17] Exempt except when inhalable dust and/or particulates are present or are generated through use of the product.

[18] Refers to the water-soluble salts only; exempt when mixed in food or animal feed.

[19] Exempt except when inhalable dust is present or can be generated through use.

[20] Exempt when in mixture, suspension, or where inhalable dust or particles are not present or cannot be formed.

[21] Exempt except where mineral oil mists can be generated in the ordinary use of the products, e.g. cutting oils

[22] Occupational sources of ozone include, but are not limited to:

a) during oxidizing process of fine organic chemicals production (primarily ozolaic acid);

b) during operations involving high-intensity UV light (plasma torch operations, glass blowing, hot metal operations, photoengraving operations, use of mercury vapor lamps, direct copying machines, projecting equipment);

c) during operations involving high voltage electrical equipment (spectrographic and fluorometric apparatus, electroplating operations, high-volt linear accelerators, and electrostatic precipitators);

d) during operations involving ozonizing process in treatment of water, industrial waste, and sewage; during air purification;

e) during drilling, cutting, and welding operations utilizing laser radiation;

f) during bleaching operations (textiles, pulp, paper, waxes, starch, sugar, Teflon, and synthetic fibers), refining of mineral oils and their derivatives, processing of perfumes, vanillin, and camphor, aging and drying operations (wood, wines, whiskeys, varnishes, and printing inks);

g) during food preserving operations for mold and bacteria control;

h) during welding operations using inert gas shielded arc welding devices, bare wire arc welding; and

i) during manufacturing production of ozone.

[23] Includes benzanthracenes, benzopyrenes, benzofluoranthrene, chrysenes, dibenzanthracenes, and indenopyrenes.

[24] Refers to smoke and fume products given off during soldering.

[25] Exempt except when inhalable particulates are present or can be generated.

26 Silver compounds existing in stable emulsions or suspensions, as in photographic film, are exempt.

27 Applicable to cotton fiber for use in industries or operations covered by General Industry Safety Order 5219, Cotton Dust.

28 Exempt when present in motor oils at 2.5% or below. Zinc oxide is exempt except when present as dust or when generated as a fume. Zinc stearate is exempt except when present as dust.

29 Refers to solutions greater than or equal to 4%.

30 Refers to solutions greater than or equal to 3%.

31 Refers to any mixture containing 0.1% or greater of this substance.

32 Refers to any mixture containing 0.02% or greater inorganic arsenic.

33 Refers to any mixture containing 0.1% or greater EDB.

34 Exempt when encapsulated in a capsule which meets the definition of "Special Form Materials" prescribed in 49 CFR 173.403(z).

35 Applies to silica sand and silica flour, but naturally occurring dirt and sand which has not been increased in silica concentration by beneficiation are exempt.

36 Except butyl benzyl phthalate.

37 Exempt except when crystalline powder is being manufactured or being used.

38 Fibrous glass is a mechanical irritant. There is no present scientific evidence as to the existence of any other adverse health effect.

39 Except Copper phthalocyanine crudes and pigments.

Article 6. Workers' Compensation Loss Control Consultation Services, Annual Health and Safety Loss Control Plan–Requirements and Procedures

§ 339.1. Scope and Application

This Article applies to all insurers and insureds as defined in section 339.3.

§ 339.2. Effective Dates and Start–Up Procedures

(a) This article shall take effect immediately, except for section 339.4 which shall take effect on April 1, 1994.

(b) Provisional Certification Periods.

(1) Provisional certification shall be granted by the Division for a period of 120 days upon receipt by the Loss Control Consultation Certification Unit of an application which complies, at a minimum, with the requirements of 339.7(b) and (c)(1) through (3).

(2) The Division may extend an insurer's provisional certification for an additional period of up to 120 days if the volume of applications received results in the Division's inability to process the insurer's application within the initial 120 day period.

(c) Certification Periods.

(1) The first period of certification shall include the period of provisional certification and shall last for one year unless extended by the Division for purposes of evenly distributing the workload associated with the ongoing processing of applications for recertification.

(2) All subsequent certifications shall last for a period of one year.

§ 339.3. Definitions

(a) "Annual Plan" means the insurer's annual health and safety loss control plan.

(b) "Budget" means a description of anticipated expenditures to be incurred in providing loss control consultation services to targeted employers as described by the insurer's annual plan, including the amount of funds allocated, the categories of services to be funded, and the amount of funding budgeted for each category.

(c) "Director" means the Director of the Department of Industrial Relations or an authorized representative.

(d) "Division" means the Division of Occupational Safety and Health.

(e) "Employer" means any insured.

(f) "Insured" means any person or entity other than a person or entity which has received a certificate of consent to self-insure pursuant to Labor Code Section 3700(b), which has secured workers' compensation insurance from an insurer.

(g) "Insurer" means any entity licensed by the California Department of Insurance to write workers' compensation insurance coverage.

(h) "Loss control" means reduction of exposure to workers' compensation losses and control of significant preventable health and safety hazards to workers.

(i) "Loss control consultation services" means assistance in recognizing, evaluating, and controlling significant preventable health and safety hazards and other potential sources of workers' compensation losses. Loss control consultation services consist of services provided by an insurer only to those employers to which the insurer has extended workers' compensation coverage.

(j) "On site consultation" means observation of an insured's work operations to determine the existence of significant preventable health and safety hazards, including, where appropriate, monitoring of hazardous physical, chemical, and biological agents.

(k) "Significant preventable health and safety hazards" means those hazards which are capable of being controlled by the employer and which have the potential to substantially affect the frequency and severity of workplace injuries and illnesses and workers' compensation losses.

(l) "Targeted employer" means an employer selected by the insurer to receive loss control consultation services, based on the criteria set forth in section 339.11. This term does not include any part of the employer's operations which is outside of California.

NOTE: Where the employer has more than one worksite, "targeted employer" means only those worksites selected by the insurer to receive loss control consultation services based on the criteria set forth in section 339.11

(m) "Workers' compensation insurance" means only that workers' compensation insurance provided under the laws and regulations of the State of California. This term does not include excess reinsurance or any form of homeowner's insurance.

(n) "Workplace survey" means an evaluation of an insured's work operations which can consist of a comprehensive on-site consultation or any other procedure which effectively identifies significant preventable health and safety hazards to workers.

§ 339.4.　Provision of Loss Control Consultation Services

(a) Every insurer issuing or maintaining a workers' compensation insurance policy covering an employer's current or future operations shall maintain or provide loss control consultation services certified by the Division in accordance with this Article.

NOTE: Insurers may elect to provide all or part of their loss control consultation services through another entity, e.g., consultants, insurance groups or health care organizations, to the extent that the services to be provided meet the requirements of this section. However, such an election shall not alter the insurer's responsibility to maintain certification and to direct and control the provision of all loss control consultation services required by this Article.

(b) At the time the insurance policy is issued, and annually thereafter, the insurer shall provide to each of its insureds a written description of the insurer's loss control consultation services, including a notice stating that the services are available at no additional charge to the insured. The following statement shall be included with the notice: "Workers' compensation insurance policyholders may register comments about the insurer's loss control consultation services by writing to: State of California, Department of Industrial Relations, Division of Occupational Safety and Health, P.O. Box 420603, San Francisco, CA 94142."

(c) The insurer shall not charge the employer any fee in addition to the insurance premium for the provision of loss control consultation services.

(d) Targeted Employers.

(1) The insurer shall provide loss control consultation services to all targeted employers, which, at a minimum, shall include the following:

(A) Effective evaluation of the employer's operations, including:

1. Comprehensive on-site consultation for each targeted employer identified by the insurer's annual plan;

2. Discussions with management and, with permission of the employer, non-management personnel; and

3. Review with appropriate personnel of relevant records, including, but not limited to, the employer's log and summary of injuries and illnesses maintained pursuant to section 14301 and the employer's section 3203 injury and illness prevention program;

(B) Identification of the factors most related to the losses experienced by the employer, including:

1. First aid and other emergency or post-injury response procedures;

2. Workplace health and safety hazards;

3. Management policy and practices related to loss control;

4. The effectiveness with which company loss control policy is communicated among management personnel and between management and non-management personnel;

5. The effectiveness of training;

6. The extent and nature of worker participation in health and safety promotion efforts;

7. The adequacy of recordkeeping; and

8. The adequacy of the employer's section 3203 injury and illness prevention program.

(C) Formulation of recommended loss control measures, including specification of those critical to reduction of the employer's losses or potential for losses;

(D) A written report detailing the consultation provided, the findings of the consultation, and all loss control measures formulated pursuant to subsection (d)(1)(C); and

(E) Ongoing evaluation of the targeted employer to determine the impact of the consultation on the employer's loss control experience.

(2) The insurer shall maintain records of all loss control consultation services provided to targeted employers for 4 years and shall make those records available to the Division upon request.

(e) Non-targeted Employers. Loss control consultation services available upon request to non-targeted employers shall, at a minimum, include the following:

(1) A workplace survey, including discussions with management, and, where appropriate, nonmanagement personnel with permission of the employer;

(2) Review of injury records with appropriate personnel; and

(3) Development of a plan to improve the employer's health and safety loss control experience, which shall include, where appropriate, modifications to the employer's section 3203 injury and illness prevention program.

Exception: An insurer may, but is not required, to provide loss control consultation services to any insured whose place of employment does not pose significant preventable health and safety hazards to workers. Criteria for determining that a place of employment does not pose significant preventable health and safety hazards must be clearly identified in the annual plan.

§ 339.5.　Requirements for Certification and Recertification of Loss Control Consultation Services

(a) Certification lasts for a period of one year, except as specified by section 339.2. To apply for certification or recertification, an insurer must submit a completed application and all supporting documentation as required by section 339.7.

(b) To qualify for certification and recertification the insurer shall demonstrate that:

(1) The insurer has developed and is prepared to implement an annual plan which meets the requirements of section 339.6; and

(2) The insurer has the capability to deliver effective loss control consultation services meeting the requirements of section 339.4. Such a demonstration shall include, but not be limited to, each of the following:

(A) Identification of each entity supplying loss control consultation personnel, if consultation services are to be provided by personnel other than employees of the insurer.

(B) A description of the categories, the number in each category, and the individual qualifications, including professional licenses and certification, of the personnel who will be providing loss control consultation services.

(C) A detailed description of the services to be provided by each of the personnel and the types of industrial activities and settings with which their services will be associated, together with an explanation of how these personnel are qualified to address these activities and settings.

(D) An estimate of:

1. The number of on-site consultations the insurer's loss control consultation personnel will provide for the coming certification year, specifying what portion will consist of consultations to targeted employers;

2. The average number of hours to be spent on each on site consultation, not including preparation and travel time; and

3. The number of workplace surveys not consisting of on-site consultation to be provided for the coming certification year, including the average amount of time to be spent per survey.

(c) To maintain certification, the insurer shall notify the Division of any substantial change in the information provided to obtain certification from the Division and shall cooperate with any audit or request for information by the Division to determine the effectiveness of the loss control consultation services provided by the insurer.

(d) The Division shall provide written notice to the insurer of any finding of deficiency related to the loss control consultation services audited by the Division, and any corrective actions deemed necessary to retention of the insurer's certification by the Division.

§ 339.6. Annual Health and Safety Loss Control Plan

(a) Every insurer seeking certification or recertification shall submit an annual plan as required by section 339.7(c)(5).

(b) The annual plan shall detail the insurer's program objectives for delivering loss control consultation services to those insureds selected as targeted employers, and shall include, at a minimum, the following:

(1) A budget;

(2) The methodology used by the insurer to select targeted employers;

NOTE: Section 339.11 contains guidelines for selecting targeted employers.

(3) One-year and three-year loss reduction goals for targeted employers;

(4) Size, type, and identity of each targeted employer for the coming year; and

(5) A description of the loss control consultation services provided to targeted employers during the previous year, including:

(A) Identity of targeted employers served and a summary of the services provided to each;

(B) Total expenditures for all targeted employers served;

(C) Evaluation of the effectiveness of the consultations provided, including the extent to which the previous year's loss reduction goals were met for targeted employers and an analysis of any failure to meet such goals; and

(D) A list of all employers to whom loss control consultation services have been provided through an entity other than the insurer or the insurance group to which the insurer belongs. The list shall include the identities and qualifications of the personnel who provided the consultation services.

(c) The plan shall demonstrate that the insurer has reliably identified as targeted employers those of its insureds who have the greatest worker's compensation losses and most significant preventable health and safety hazards, and that the insurer's loss control consultation services will effectively serve the needs of targeted employers.

(d) The Division shall maintain the confidentiality of all information provided by the plan, except for aggregate statistical data.

§ 339.7. Application for Certification or Recertification of Loss Control Consultation Services

(a) Applications may be obtained from the Loss Control Consultation Services Certification Unit of the Division.

(b) The application (Form LCC–1; 10–94) shall be lodged with the Loss Control Consultation Services Certification Unit and shall be accompanied by the required application fee.

(c) The application shall provide, be accompanied by, or be supplemented with the following items:

(1) Names under which the applicant is authorized to write workers' compensation insurance;

(2) Name and address of the insurer's employee directly responsible for administering the insurer's loss control consultation services;

1257

(3) Proof of authorization from the California Department of Insurance to write workers' compensation insurance within the State of California;

(4) Documentation demonstrating the insurer's capability to deliver loss control consultation services as described by section 339.5(b)(2);

(5) A copy of the insurer's annual plan; and

(6) Any additional information requested by the Division, if reasonably necessary to evaluate the insurer's suitability for certification consistent with the requirements of this Article.

(d) Within 30 business days of receipt of an application for certification, the Division shall inform the applicant in writing either that the application is either complete and accepted for filing, or that the application is deficient and requires supplementation with additional information or documentation.

(1) An application shall be deemed complete if it is in compliance with the requirements of this section.

(2) A notice that the application is deficient shall explain what specific information or documentation is required to complete the application.

NOTE: If the volume of applications received results in the Division's inability to process the insurer's start-up application for certification in compliance within the 30–business-day period, the Division may extend the period for up to 120 days. Where such an extension is made by the Division, the insurer's period of provisional certification shall be deemed extended by an equal amount of time pursuant to section 339.2(b).

(e) Within 30 business days of the date of acceptance for filing of a completed application, the Division shall issue to the applicant:

(1) A Notice of Certification which includes the date of expiration of the certification and specifies any conditions which attach to retention of the certification; or

(2) A Notice of Denial of Certification, accompanied by a written explanation of the reasons for the denial.

§ 339.8. Annual Collection of the Workers' Occupational Safety and Health Fund Fees

(a) The Director designates the Commission on Health and Safety and Workers' Compensation to collect the fee required by Labor Code Section 6354.7 for the purpose of establishing and maintaining a workers' occupational safety and health training and education program and insurance loss control services coordinator.

(b) On or before April 1 of each year, each insurer subject to Labor Code Section 6354.5 shall pay to the Commission on Health and Safety and Workers' Compensation the workers' occupational safety and health training and education program fee required by Labor Code Section 6354.7. All fees collected pursuant to this section shall be deposited in the Workers' Occupational Safety and Health Education Fund, as provided in Section 6354.7 of the Labor Code.

(c) The annual fee required under this section shall be the greater of one hundred dollars ($100) or 0.0286 percent of paid workers' compensation indemnity as reported for the previous calendar year to the designated rating organization for the analysis required under subdivisions (b) and (c) of Section 11759.1 of the Insurance Code.

(d) Along with the payment required by this section, each insurer shall submit:

(1) A copy of the insurer's response to the annual 'Call for California Workers' Compensation Experience' for the preceding calendar year.

(2) A summary report, on form CHSWC-1 'Workers' Occupational Safety and Health Fund Fee Report Form. (Rev.1/03)' The Commission shall provide a copy of the form CHSWC-1 to each insurer subject to Labor Code Section 6354.5 not later than February 1 of the year in which the fee is collected. The form CHSWC-1 shall include the following information:

(A) the name of the insurer submitting the report, including a list of all insurer names used to write workers' compensation insurance in California. For each insurer listed, a copy of each insurer's Certificate of Authority, issued by the California Department of Insurance, to write workers' compensation insurance shall be submitted with the report as an attachment;

(B) the name and contact information for a company officer to be contacted concerning the insurer's loss control services or the workers' occupational safety and health training and education program;

(C) the amount of paid indemnity as reported by the insurer for the previous calendar year to the Workers' Compensation Insurance Rating Bureau in response to the annual 'Call for California Workers' Compensation Experience;' and,

(D) the amount of the fee being paid by the insurer.

Note: Copies of the form CHSWC-1 may be obtained upon request from the Commission or downloaded from the Commission's web site at: http://www.dir.ca.gov/CHSWC/.

(e) A group of insurers under the same management, direction and control may elect to submit a single consolidated payment so long as the information required by the Commission is separately provided for each insurer.

§ 339.8.1. Workers' Occupational Safety and Health Fund Fee Report Form

State of California
Department of Industrial Relations
Commission on Health and Safety and Workers' Compensation
WORKERS' OCCUPATIONAL SAFETY AND HEALTH
FUND FEE REPORT FORM

- Labor Code Section 6354.7 requires all Workers' Compensation Insurers to fund the "Workers' Occupational Safety and Health Education Fund" by paying an annual fee of the greater of $100 or a percentage of their paid workers' compensation indemnity as reported for the prior calendar year on the "Call for California workers' compensation experience" filed with the workers' compensation insurance rating bureau of California.
- Please complete and submit this report form with the required fees and attachments to the address listed below. Payment is due on or before April 1 of this year.

1. NAME OF INSURER(S):	List all insurer names used to write workers' compensation insurance in California. For each insurer listed, attach a copy of each insurer's Certificate of Authority, issued by the California Department of Insurance, to write workers' compensation insurance. (Attach additional pages if needed.)
	_____
	_____
	_____
	_____

2. COMPANY OFFICER:	Name of the person with the authority to establish the program to provide loss control consultation services in California, and authorize the payment of fees into the Fund.
Signature of Company Officer:	Date:
Printed Name of Officer:	Title:
(The address given below will be only address used for all future correspondence from this office.)	
Name of Company	
Address:	
Phone Number:	Fax Number: E-Mail Address:

3. FEE CALCULATION:	Indicate the total amount of Paid Indemnity as reported for the prior calendar year on the "Call for California Workers' Compensation Experience" filed with the Workers' Compensation Insurance Rating Bureau of California for each insurer listed above, and calculate the fees due.
	Include a copy of the prior year's Calendar Year "Call" for each insurer listed on this application.
Calendar Year Paid Indemnity $_____ × 0.0286% =	Enter Total Fee Here: --> $*

> * Attach a check payable to *Workers' Occupational Safety and Health Education Fund* for the greater of $100.00 or .0286 percent of the amount listed above. [Example: $43,060,531.00 (PI) − 0.000286 = $12,315.31 (Fee)]

4. SUBMISSION:	Please mail this completed report with the "Call(s)", the Certificate(s) of Authority, and fees to the following **address before April 1:**

Commission on Health and Safety and Workers' Compensation
Attention: WOSHEF
P. O. Box 420603
San Francisco, CA 94102

If you have questions regarding this fee or report process, call (415) 703-4220 or e-mail us at chswc@hq.dir.ca.gov.
CHSWC-1 (Rev. 1/03)

§ 339.9. Denial of Certification or Recertification

(a) The Division shall deny certification or recertification if the insurer does not satisfy the requirements of this article.

(b) An applicant denied certification may:

(1) Reapply by submitting a new application together with a new application fee; or

(2) Appeal for reconsideration to the Director.

(c) Any applicant who wishes to appeal a denial of certification shall lodge with the Division, within 10 working days of receipt of the Notice of Denial, a written notice of the applicant's intent to appeal.

(1) The Director shall hold a hearing, at the Division's headquarters offices or such other location as the Director may designate, within five working days of the appeal.

(2) At the hearing, the insurer shall have the burden of establishing qualification for certification.

(d) The Director shall issue a decision within 10 days of the hearing. The Director's decision shall be final. A final decision by the Director may not be appealed except as provided for by law.

(e) The Insurance Commissioner shall be notified of every final decision by the Director to deny certification.

§ 339.10. Revocation, Suspension or Attachment of Conditions to Certification

(a) The Division may at any time, upon a showing of good cause and after notice and an opportunity to be heard, revoke, suspend, or attach conditions to the retention of, any certification issued pursuant to this article. Good cause shall be deemed to exist if the Division establishes that the insurer has substantially failed to meet or comply with the requirements of this article.

(b) Notice of the Division's intent to take any adverse action with respect to a certification shall be in writing and served at least fifteen days in advance of the hearing. Service shall be deemed complete if notice of the hearing is sent by certified mail or hand delivered to the address shown on the application form. The notice shall specify the action intended to be taken by the Division and the reasons for the action in sufficient detail to allow the insurer to prepare for the hearing.

(c) The hearing shall be held at the Division's Headquarters offices, or at such other location as may be designated by the Director, and shall be conducted by the Chief or Deputy Chief of the Division.

(d) The insurer may appeal any adverse action to the Director in the same manner as provided for appeal of denial of certification by section 339.9(c) and (d) and the filing of an appeal shall stay the adverse action until the issuance of a final decision by the Director.

(e) The Insurance Commissioner shall be notified of every final decision by the Director to suspend or revoke certification.

§ 339.11. Guidelines for Selecting Targeted Employers

(a) Section 339.6(b)(2) requires the insurer's annual plan to include a methodology for selecting targeted employers and section 339.6(c) requires the annual plan to demonstrate that the insurer has reliably identified as targeted employers those of its insureds who have the greatest workers' compensation losses and most significant preventable health and safety hazards, and that the

insurer's loss control consultation services will effectively serve the needs of targeted employers.

(b) The Division will review the annual plan to determine the effectiveness of the insurer's targeting methodology. Targeting methodologies may be different depending on the insurer and the type of insureds served, but shall utilize an effective combination of any of the following factors, or similar factors:

(1) Type, number, and rate of occupational injuries and illnesses;

(2) Number of workers' compensation claims, or injuries and illnesses, per payroll or premium dollar;

(3) Severity of workers' compensation claims, or injuries and illnesses, per payroll or premium dollar;

(4) Experience modification rating, or other ways of comparing the employer's loss experience to similar employers;

(5) Data from the insurers' previous evaluations of the employer; and

(6) Cal/OSHA citation history.

Exception: Other information, e.g., direct written premium per employer or the number of employees per employer, may be used as additional factors to be considered in selecting targeted employers. However, such information shall not be used in a manner which results in exclusion of those insureds who have the greatest workers' compensation losses and most significant preventable health and safety hazards.

Subchapter 2. Regulations of the Division of Occupational Safety and Health

Article 1. Employers' Obligation to Provide Information to Employees

§ 340. Contents and Posting Requirements of CAL/OSHA Notice

Every employer shall be required to post immediately upon receipt and to keep posted the CAL/OSHA Notice of Employee Protections and Obligations entitled "Safety and Health Protection on the Job," which is furnished pursuant to Labor Code Section 6328 by the Division of Occupational Safety and Health, Department of Industrial Relations, State of California, containing information on pertinent safety laws, regulations and certain rights of employees under the California Labor Code.

Each employer must post at least one Notice (CAL/OSHA Notice) in each establishment in a conspicuous place where notices to employees are customarily posted. "Establishment" as used in this regulation means a single physical location where business is conducted or where services or industrial operations are performed. Where employers are engaged in activities which are physically dispersed such as construction or transportation, the notice required by this section shall be posted at each location to which employees report each day. Where employees do not usually work at, or report to, a single establishment, such notice or notices shall be posted at the location or locations from which the employees operate to carry out their activities.

Each employer shall take steps to insure that such notices are not altered, defaced or covered by other material.

This notice shall contain the address and telephone number of the nearest Division of Occupational Safety and Health office, and shall inform the employees of their right to report any unsafe working conditions in their place of employment to the Division of Occupational Safety and Health and their right to request a safety inspection by the Division of Occupational Safety and Health for unsafe conditions.

The Notice shall also inform the employees that no employee shall be laid off or discharged for refusing to perform work in the performance of which the provisions of the California Labor Code, any occupational safety or health standard or any safety order of the Division will be violated, where such violation would create a real and apparent hazard to the employee or his fellow employees.

The Notice shall contain the information that each citation issued under Section 6317 of the California Labor Code, Special Order or Order to Take Special Action issued under Section 6308 or a copy or copies thereof shall be prominently displayed at or near each place a violation referred to in the citation or order occurred.

The Notice shall inform employees that employers who use any substance listed as a hazardous substance in Section 339 of Title 8 of the California Administrative Code must provide employees with information on the contents of material safety data sheets (MSDS) or equivalent information about the substance which trains employees to use the substance safely. That the employer is required to make available on a timely and reasonable basis a MSDS on each hazardous substance in the workplace upon request of an employee, collective bargaining representative, or an employee's physician. Further, that employees have the right to see and copy the medical record and other records of employee exposure to potentially toxic materials or harmful physical agents.

The Notice shall inform the employees that the employer shall provide an opportunity for employees or their representatives to observe monitoring or measuring of employee exposure to hazards conducted pursuant to standards promulgated under California Labor Code Section 142.3, and shall allow the employee or his representative access to accurate records of employee exposures to potentially toxic materials or harmful physical agents.

The Notice shall contain a statement that every employer and every employee shall comply with occupational safety and health standards and all rules, regulations and orders pursuant to Division 5 of the California Labor Code which are applicable to his or her own actions and conduct.

Failure of any employer to post the CAL/OSHA Notice entitled "Safety and Health Protection on the Job" as required by this regulation may result in imposition of a fine of up to $1,000 upon the employer for each violation as set forth in Labor Code Section 6431.

§ 340.1. Rights of Employees to Observe Monitoring or Measuring

(a) Whenever an employer is required to conduct tests or to engage in monitoring or measuring, to determine employee exposure to hazards by specific standards promulgated under Labor Code Section 142.3, the employer shall notify the affected employee or employees or their representative, prior to commencement of the date, time and place of the testing, monitoring or measuring of employee exposure. The employer shall provide the affected employee or employees, or their representatives with the opportunity to observe the testing, sampling, monitoring or measuring undertaken pursuant to such standards.

(b) The affected employee, employees or their representatives shall be allowed access to the records and reports of the results of the testing monitoring or measuring when carried out under the requirements of a standard promulgated under Labor Code Section 142.3.

§ 340.2. Notification to Employee of Exposure Required

Whenever any employee has been or is being exposed to toxic materials or harmful physical agents in concentrations or at levels exceeding those prescribed by applicable standard, order, or special order, the employer of the affected employee must promptly notify any employee so affected in writing of the fact that the employee has been exposed, and of the corrective action being taken by the employer.

Article 1.5. Employer's Declaration of Abatement and Other Documentation of Abatement—Employee Notification—Posting Requirements

§ 340.4. Declaration of Abatement, Other Documentation, Employee Notification and Posting Requirements

(a) Scope and application. This section applies to employers who receive a citation for a violation of Title 8 of the California Code of Regulations.

(b) Definitions.

(1) Abatement means action by an employer to comply with a cited standard or regulation or to eliminate a recognized hazard identified by the Division during an inspection.

(2) Abatement date means:

(i) For an uncontested citation item, the later of:

(A) The date in the citation for abatement of the violation;

(B) The date otherwise approved by the Division as the result of an informal conference; or

(C) The date established in a citation by an informal settlement agreement.

(ii) For a contested citation item for which the Occupational Safety and Health Appeals Board (OSHAB) has issued a final order affirming the violation, the later of:

(A) The date identified in the final order for abatement; or

(B) The date computed by adding the period allowed in the citation for abatement to the final order date; or

(C) The date established by a formal settlement agreement.

(3) Affected employees means those employees who are exposed to the hazard(s) identified as violation(s) in a citation.

(4) Final order date means:

(i) For an uncontested citation item, the fifteenth working day after the employer's receipt of the citation;

(ii) For a contested citation item:

(A) The thirty-fifth day after the date on which a decision or order of an administrative law judge has been issued, unless a Petition for Reconsideration or Order of Reconsideration has been filed with or by OSHAB; or

(B) Where a Petition for Reconsideration or Order of Reconsideration has been filed, the thirty-fifth day after the date on which OSHAB issues its decision or order disposing of the matter; or

(C) The date on which the superior court issues a decision affirming the violation in a case in which a final order of OSHAB has been stayed.

(5) Movable equipment means a hand-held or non-hand-held machine or device, powered or unpowered, that is used to do work and is moved within or between worksites.

(c) Abatement certification.

(1) Within 10 calendar days after the abatement date, the employer must certify to the Division that each cited violation has been abated, except as provided in paragraph (c)(2) of this section.

(2) The employer is not required to certify abatement if the OSHA Compliance Officer, during the on-site portion of the inspection:

(i) Observes, within 24 hours after a violation is identified, that abatement has occurred; and

(ii) Notes in the citation that abatement has occurred.

(3) The employer's certification that abatement is complete must include, for each cited violation, in addition to the information required by paragraph (h) of this section, the date and method of abatement and a

statement that affected employees and their representatives have been informed of the abatement.

(4) For serious violations the certification of abatement must be submitted under penalty of perjury as required pursuant to Labor Code section 6320(b). Note: See Appendix A for sample content and form of Abatement Certification Letter.

(d) Abatement documentation.

(1) The employer must submit to the Division, along with the information on abatement certification required by paragraph (c)(3) of this section, documents demonstrating that abatement is complete for each willful or repeat violation and for any serious violation for which the Division indicates in the citation that such abatement documentation is required.

(2) Documents demonstrating that abatement is complete may include, but are not limited to, evidence of the purchase or repair of equipment, photographic or video evidence of abatement, or other written records.

(e) Abatement plans.

(1) The Division may require an employer to submit an abatement plan for each cited violation (except non-serious violations) when the time permitted for abatement is more than 90 calendar days. If an abatement plan is required, the citation must so dictate.

(2) The employer must submit an abatement plan for each cited violation within 25 calendar days from the final order date when the citation indicates that such a plan is required. The abatement plan must identify the violation and the steps to be taken to achieve abatement, including a schedule for completing abatement and, where necessary, how employees will be protected from exposure to the violative condition in the interim until abatement is complete. Note: See Appendix B for sample content and form of Abatement Plan.

(f) Progress reports.

(1) An employer who is required to submit an abatement plan may also be required to submit periodic progress reports for each cited violation. The citation must indicate:

(i) That periodic progress reports are required and the citation items for which they are required;

(ii) The date on which an initial progress report must be submitted, which may be no sooner than 30 calendar days after submission of an abatement plan;

(iii) Whether additional progress reports are required; and

(iv) The date(s) on which additional progress reports must be submitted.

(2) For each violation, the progress report must identify, as briefly as possible, the action taken to achieve abatement and the date the action was taken. Note: See Appendix B for sample content and form of Progress Report.

(g) Employee notification.

(1) The employer must inform affected employees and their representative(s) about abatement activities covered by this section by posting a copy of each document

submitted to the Division, or a summary of the document(s), near the place where the violation occurred.

(2) Where such posting does not effectively inform employees and their representatives about abatement activities (for example, for employers who have mobile work operations), the employer must:

(i) Post each document or a summary of the document(s) in a location where it will be readily observable by affected employees and their representatives; or

(ii) Take other steps to communicate fully to affected employees and their representatives about abatement activities.

(3) The employer must inform employees and their representatives of their right to examine and copy all abatement documents submitted to the Division.

(i) An employee or an employee representative must submit a request to examine and copy abatement documents within 3 working days of receiving notice that the documents have been submitted.

(ii) The employer must comply with an employee's or employee representative's request to examine and copy abatement documents within 5 working days of receiving the request.

(4) The employer must ensure that notice to employees and employee representatives is provided at the same time or before the information is provided to the Division and that abatement documents are:

(i) Not altered, defaced, or covered by other material; and

(ii) Remain posted for three working days after submission to the Division.

(h) Transmitting abatement documents.

(1) The employer must include, in each submission required by this section, the following information:

(i) The employer's name and address;

(ii) The inspection number to which the submission relates;

(iii) The citation and item numbers to which the submission relates;

(iv) A statement that the information submitted is accurate; and

(v) The signature of the employer and the employer's authorized representative.

(vi) For serious violations the documentation must be submitted under penalty of perjury as required pursuant to Labor Code section 6320(b).

(2) The date of postmark is the date of submission for mailed documents. For documents transmitted by other means, the date the Division receives the document is date of submission.

(i) Moveable equipment.

(1) For serious, repeat, and willful violations involving movable equipment, the employer must attach a warning tag or a copy of the citation to the operating controls or to the cited component of equipment that is moved within the worksite or between worksites. Note: Attaching a copy of the citation to the equipment will satisfy the tagging requirement of paragraph (i)(1) of this section as well as the posting requirements of section 332.4 of Title 8 of the California Code of Regulations.

(2) If the employer attaches a warning tag, in lieu of the citation, it must warn employees about the nature of the violation involving the equipment and identify the location of the citation issued. Note: See Appendix C for sample form and content of a Warning Tag.

(3) If the violation has not already been abated, a warning tag or copy of the citation must be attached to the equipment:

(i) For hand-held equipment, immediately after the employer receives the citation; or

(ii) For non-hand-held equipment, prior to moving the equipment within or between worksites.

(4) The employer must assure that the tag or copy of the citation attached to movable equipment is not altered, defaced, or covered by other material.

(5) The employer must assure that the tag or copy of the citation attached to movable equipment remains attached until:

(i) The violation has been abated and all abatement verification documents required by this regulation have been submitted to the Division;

(ii) The cited equipment has been permanently removed from service or is no longer within the employer's control; or

(iii) OSHAB issues a final order vacating the citation; or

(iv) As otherwise directed by the Division. Note: Appendices A through C provide information and non-mandatory guidelines to assist employers and employees in complying with the appropriate requirements of this section.

Appendix A to Section 340.4–Sample Abatement–Certification Letter (Non-Mandatory)

(Name), District Manager

Division of Occupational Safety and Health

Address of the District Office (on the citation)

[Company's Name]

[Company's Address]

The hazard referenced in Inspection Number [insert 9–digit #] for violation identified as:

Citation [insert #] and item [insert #] was corrected on [insert date] by: _____.

Citation [insert #] and item [insert #] was corrected on [insert date] by: _____.

(NOTE: Follow sample format for each citation or item) I attest that the information contained in this document is accurate.

_____
Signature

_____
Typed or Printed Name

Note: For serious violations the submittal must be made under penalty of perjury. For Example:

"I declare under penalty of perjury the foregoing is true and correct. Executed this _____ day of (month) in the city of _____, California. _____"

_____
(Signature)

Appendix B to Section 1903.19–Sample Abatement Plan or Progress Report (Non-Mandatory)

(Name), District Manager
Division of Occupational Safety and Health
Address of the District Office (on the citation)
[Company's Name]
[Company's Address]

Check one:
   Abatement Plan [ ]
   Progress Report [ ]
Inspection Number
Page _____ of _____
Citation Number(s) [*] _____
Item Numbers _____

Action	Proposed Completion Date (for abatement plans only)	Completion Date (for progress reports only)
1.	_____	
2.	_____	

Date required for final abatement:
I attest that the information contained in this document is accurate.
(NOTE: For serious violations the document must be submitted under penalty of perjury. See Appendix A, above)

_____
Signature

Typed or Printed Name
Name of primary point of contact for questions: _____
                            [optional]
Telephone Number _____

  *Abatement plans or progress reports for more than one citation item may be combined in a single abatement plan or progress report if the abatement actions, proposed completion dates, and actual completion dates (for progress reports only) are the same for each of the citation items.

Appendix C to Section 340.4–Sample Warning Tag (Non–Mandatory)

WARNING:

EQUIPMENT HAZARD
CITED BY CAL/OSHA

EQUIPMENT CITED:

_____

HAZARD CITED:

_____

FOR DETAILED INFORMATION
SEE CAL/OSHA CITATION
POSTED AT:

_____

Article 1.6. Adjudicative Hearings—General Rules of Practice and Procedure—Denial, Suspension or Revocation of Permits, Licenses, Certifications, Registrations or Other Authorizations and Orders Prohibiting Use, Issued by the Division of Occupational Safety and Health

§ 340.40. Scope and Application

(a) These general rules of practice and procedure of the Division of Occupational Safety and Health (hereinafter "the Division") are applicable to proceedings involving the denial, suspension or revocation of any license, permit, certification, registration or other authorization issued by the Division, and proceedings involving an Order Prohibiting Use (for purposes of this article, hereinafter referred to as "OPU") issued pursuant to Labor Code section 6325.

(b) These general rules of practice and procedure may supplement, but shall not replace, other codified administrative notice and appeal procedures. In case of conflict with codified notice and appeal procedures, the more-specific procedures shall apply.

§ 340.41. Notification of Division Proceedings for Denial, Suspension or Revocation

(a) When, after review, examination, investigation or inspection, the Division determines that good cause exists to deny, suspend or revoke any permit, license, certification, registration, or other authorization issued by the Division, written notification shall be provided to the person or entity against whom the Division intends to take such action.

(b) The notification shall cite the statute or regulation authorizing the action taken by the Division, and shall state the grounds constituting good cause for the denial, suspension, revocation or other action proposed by the Division.

(c) The notification may be served personally, by facsimile, by overnight delivery, or by certified mail. The provisions of this article are subject to Section 1013 of the California Code of Civil Procedure.

(d) The Director of the Department of Industrial Relations (for purposes of this article, the Director of the Department of Industrial Relations shall hereinafter be referred to as "the Director") or the Division shall make a copy of these regulations available to appellants, and shall advise appellants that the appeal proceedings shall not be subject to the provisions of Chapter 5 (commencing with Section 11500) of Part 1, Division 3, of Title 2 of the California Government Code.

§ 340.42. Request for Hearing

(a) Within five working days after receipt of the Division's denial of an application for any license, permit, certification, registration or other authorization, or the suspension or revocation of a permit, license, certification, registration or other authorization, or the issuance of an Order Prohibiting Use, the affected applicant or employer may request a hearing to review the validity of the Division's action.

(b) The request for hearing must be in writing and must set forth specific reasons why the Division's action was improper. An appellant's failure to mail or otherwise deliver a request for hearing within five working days of receipt of notification of the action will result in the Division's action being considered final and not subject to review, except where review is otherwise provided by law.

(1) For the denial of an application for a permit, license, certification, registration or other authorization, the written request for hearing shall be mailed or otherwise delivered to the headquarters office of the Director.

(2) For the suspension or revocation of a permit, license, certification, registration, or other authorization, the written request for hearing shall be mailed or otherwise delivered to the headquarters of the Division.

(3) For the issuance of an Order Prohibiting Use, the request for hearing shall be mailed or otherwise delivered to the District Manager of the district office which issued the Order Prohibiting Use.

§ 340.43. Designation of Presiding Officer and Notification of Hearing

(a) Upon receipt of a request for an appeal hearing regarding the Division's denial of an application for a permit, license, certification, registration, or other authorization, the Director or the Director's Chief Counsel shall designate a Presiding Officer to conduct the hearing. Upon receipt of a request for hearing regarding the suspension or revocation of a permit, license, certification, registration, or other authorization, the Chief of the Division shall designate a Presiding Officer to conduct the hearing. The Presiding Officer may be a Deputy Chief, Regional Manager, or other designated representative. For hearings regarding the issuance of Orders Prohibiting Use, the District Manager shall serve as Presiding Officer.

(b) The Department or Division shall notify the appellant of the date, time and location of the hearing, and of the name of the Presiding Officer. The date and time of the hearing shall be subject to the specific provisions of the statute or regulation, if any, authorizing the action. Where no statute or regulation imposes specific time limitations, a hearing shall be set so as to provide sufficient time for preparation and attendance at the hearing, but in no event less than five working days following the receipt of a request for hearing, unless appellant agrees to or requests an earlier hearing. Hearings regarding the issuance of an OPU shall be held within 24 hours following receipt of the appellant's request for a hearing, unless appellant agrees to or requests a later hearing.

(c) The Presiding Officer may change the date, time and location of the hearing for good cause upon his or her own motion or upon the written motion of either party at any time prior to the hearing.

(d) The appellant must immediately notify all affected employees, former employees, and employee representatives, if any, of the date, time and location of the hearing along with a description of the purpose for the hearing, by posting the notification of hearing or otherwise providing written notice. The notification of hearing must remain posted in a conspicuous place for at least three working days or until the date of the hearing, whichever is less.

(e) The Division or Department may serve the notification of hearing, as required under subsection (b), personally, by facsimile or by overnight delivery.

§ 340.44. Conduct of Hearing

(a) The Presiding Officer shall be responsible for receiving evidence both from Division representatives and the appellant and shall issue a decision as set forth in this article. Parties shall have the opportunity to present relevant documentary or other evidence through the presentation of direct testimony, the cross-examination of witnesses, and the rebuttal of any evidence presented during hearing. The Presiding Officer may also examine witnesses or request the presentation of additional relevant evidence.

(1) Upon motion, the Presiding Officer may exclude witnesses from the hearing room. Each party may designate one representative who may stay in the hearing room, even if the representative will also serve as a witness.

(2) A party may appear in person or through a representative who is not required to be an attorney.

(3) Designated employee representatives may make written request to participate in the hearing if it is established that such participation will be relevant to any issues presented at the hearing.

(4) The Presiding Officer shall receive evidence under oath or affirmation under penalty of perjury. The hearing shall be tape-recorded, unless the parties agree to some other method of recording the hearing. If the parties do not agree to an alternative method of recording, the Presiding Officer shall make the official record of the hearing by tape recording, and may allow each party to make and pay for an additional record if, in the Presiding Officer's opinion, the making of the additional record or records would not unduly disrupt the proceedings.

(b) The hearing shall not be subject to the technical rules relating to evidence or witnesses. However, only relevant evidence of the sort responsible persons are accustomed to rely upon in conducting serious affairs shall be admitted and relied upon in rendering a decision. Hearsay evidence is admissible but, if objected to, may not be solely relied upon without other supporting evidence unless the hearsay would be admissible over objection in a civil proceeding.

(c) Any hearing conducted pursuant to this article shall be open to the public as required pursuant to Government Code section 11425.20.

(d) During all stages of a hearing, the Presiding Officer and all parties to the hearing shall be subject to the provisions of Article 7 (commencing with section 11430.10), of Chapter 4.5 of Part 1, Division 3, Title 2 of the Government Code regarding ex parte communication.

(e) The matter shall be deemed submitted at the conclusion of the hearing unless some other submission date is agreed to between the parties or otherwise designated by the Presiding Officer.

(f) The Presiding Officer shall, on behalf of the Director or Division, issue and serve a written decision on the parties no later than thirty (30) calendar days after submission of the matter for decision, except as follows.

(1) The time for issuance and service of the decision may be extended by the Presiding Officer for good cause.

(2) For an Order Prohibiting Use, a decision concerning the validity of the order shall be made as soon as possible, but not more than two working days, after the conclusion of the hearing.

(g) Decisions shall be in writing and shall include findings of fact and conclusions supporting the decision. However, at his or her discretion, a Presiding Office may issue a preliminary decision without setting forth findings of fact and conclusions supporting the decision, as long as a complete decision is issued within the time period provided in this section.

(h) Any right to request review of the decision shall be governed by the specific regulation or statute authorizing the action taken by the Division.

§ 340.45. Presiding Officer—Grounds for Disqualification

Any Presiding Officer may be disqualified for any ground set forth in Government Code sections 11425.30 and 11425.40. A request for disqualification must be in writing to the Director and shall specifically detail the grounds upon which disqualification is sought and the factual basis for the request. The request shall be filed with the Director pursuant to the provisions of section 340.46 of this Article.

§ 340.46. Service of Process

(a) Unless otherwise required, service may be made by personal delivery or by depositing the documents in a post office, mailbox or mail chute, or other like facility regularly maintained by the United States Postal Service, sealed, properly addressed, with first-class postage prepaid.

(b) Service is complete at the time of the personal delivery or mailing.

(c) Proof of service shall be filed with the document and may be made by any of the following means:

(1) Affidavit or declaration of service by personal delivery or mail;

(2) Written statement endorsed upon the document served and signed by the party making the statement; or

(3) Letter of transmittal.

(d) Facsimile (fax) machines may be used to serve and file documents under the following conditions:

(1) The length of the document to be filed and/or served shall be no more than twelve (12) pages including cover page and attachments.

(2) A copy sheet shall be attached containing the number of pages transmitted, the fax number of the sender, the sender's telephone number, and the name of the contact person.

(3) If a document is filed by fax, all parties shall be served in the same manner or by guaranteed overnight delivery. The fax transmission shall include a proof of service indicating the method of service on each party, and

(4) No later than 24 hours after transmission, the sending party shall file and serve on all parties the original of any faxed document as set forth in this section.

(e) For facsimile service and filing of documents, a document is considered received on the following working day if transmission begins later than 5:00 p.m. Pacific Time.

§ 340.47. Discovery

(a) Upon written request made to the other party prior to hearing, a party to the proceeding is entitled to obtain the names and addresses of witnesses to the extent known to the other party, including, but not limited to, those intended to be called to testify at the hearing. Nothing in this section requires the disclosure of the identity of a person who submitted a complaint regarding the unsafe nature of an employment or place of employment unless the complainant requests otherwise.

(b) A party is entitled upon written request to inspect and make copies of any of the following materials in the possession or custody or under the control of the other party:

(1) Any statements of parties or witnesses relating to the subject matter of the proceeding;

(2) All writings or things which the party then proposes to offer in evidence;

(3) Any other writing or thing which is relevant and which would be admissible in evidence;

(4) Inspection and investigative reports made by, or on behalf of, the Division or other party pertaining to the subject matter of the proceeding, to the extent that such reports: contain the names and addresses of witnesses or persons having personal knowledge of the acts, omissions or events which are the basis of the proceeding; reflect matters perceived by the Division or other party in the course of its inspection, investigation or survey; or contain or include by attachment any statement or writing described in this section.

(c) The parties shall arrange for a mutually-agreeable time for exchange of requested materials and information but in no event later than 24 hours prior to the time set for hearing.

(d) The Presiding Officer may, upon written request by either party, make provision for timely completion of discovery.

§ 340.48. Subpoenas and Subpoenas Duces Tecum— Witness Fees

(a) Before the hearing has commenced, the Division or any party may issue a subpoena or subpoena duces tecum requiring the attendance of a person or the production of documents or things at the hearing.

(b) Any subpoena or subpoena duces tecum issued pursuant to subsection (a) of this section extends to all parts of the state and shall be served in accordance with the provisions of sections 1985.3, 1987, 1987.5 and 1988 of the Code of Civil Procedure, except for the provisions governing the time for issuance of subpoenas and subpoenas duces tecum. Service of a subpoena or subpoena duces tecum is made by delivering a copy to the witness.

(c) All witnesses appearing pursuant to subpoena, other than the parties, or their representatives directly associated with the action, shall be entitled to receive the following fees and mileage, payable in advance:

(1) Witness fee for each day's actual attendance of thirty-five dollars ($35.00);

(2) Mileage actually traveled, both ways, of twenty cents ($.20) a mile;

(3) Per diem compensation of three dollars ($3.00) for expenses of subsistence for each day of actual attendance and for each day necessarily occupied in traveling to and from the hearing, if the hearing is at a point so far removed from a residence as to reasonably preclude return thereto from day to day;

(d) Fees, mileage and expenses of subsistence shall be paid by the party at whose request the witness is subpoenaed.

(e) A party who subpoenas a peace officer as listed at Government Code section 68097.1 or individuals designated by Government Code 68097.2 shall reimburse the public entity for the full cost of the public entity incurred in paying the officer his or her salary or other compensation and traveling expenses for each day that such officer is required to remain in attendance.

§ 340.49. Official Notice

(a) In reaching a decision, a Presiding Officer may take official notice either before or after submission of the proceeding for a decision, of any generally accepted technical or scientific matter within the field of occupational safety and health, and determinations, rulings, orders, findings and decisions, required by law to be made by the Division, Occupational Safety and Health Appeals Board or Occupational Safety and Health Standards Board.

(b) The Presiding Officer shall take official notice of those matters set forth in section 451 of the Evidence Code and may take official notice of those matters set forth in section 452 of the Evidence Code.

(c) Each party shall be given reasonable opportunity on request to present information relevant to (1) the propriety of taking official notice, and (2) the tenor of the matter to be noticed.

§ 340.50. Confidential Evidence

(a) A Presiding Officer shall consider confidential any exhibit which might reveal a trade secret referred to in section 1905 of Title 18 of the United States Code, information that is confidential pursuant to Chapter 3.5 (commencing with section 6250) of Division 7 of Title 1 of the Government Code, or photographs taken by the Division during the course of any inspection or investigation.

(1) The Presiding Officer shall issue necessary orders to protect the confidentiality of such information, including the exclusion of witnesses during the course of the hearing if testimony might tend to reveal the substance of the confidential information.

(2) Parties shall request confidentiality at the time the evidence is submitted.

§ 340.51. Prehearing Motions

(a) No later than 24 hours prior to a hearing, a party may make a written motion for continuance or for clarification of issues related to discovery or other matters deemed important to the issues to be addressed during the course of the hearing.

(b) Such written motion shall be filed with the Presiding Officer and served upon the other party in conformance with section 340.46 of this article.

(c) The Presiding Officer may issue such orders as it deems necessary to address the issues referenced in such written motion.

(d) Prehearing motions in connection with the appeal of an OPU may be made up until and including the day of the appeal hearing.

§ 340.52. Interpreters

(a) All hearings shall be conducted in the English language. The Division shall notify each party of the right to an interpreter at the time it serves notification of a proceeding pursuant to Section 340.41, or at the time it issues an OPU.

(b) A party who does not proficiently speak or understand the English language, who calls a witness who does not proficiently speak or understand the English language, or who requests an interpreter, shall be provided with an approved interpreter during the hearing. A request for an interpreter shall be made at the same time as the request for appeal. The party requesting the interpreter shall pay the cost of the interpreter, unless the

Division elects to pay the interpreter based on the financial hardship of the requesting party.

(c) For purposes of this section, an approved interpreter is a person whose name appears on the list of interpreters approved by the Occupational Safety and Health Appeals Board, the State Personnel Board, or the Superior Court for the County in which the hearing is conducted.

Article 2.　Permits–Excavations, Trenches, Construction and Demolition and the Underground Use of Diesel Engines in Work in Mines and Tunnels

§ 341.　Permit Requirements

(a) Scope and Application.

(1) This article specifies:

(A) Work activities that require permits;

(B) What permit holders must do to comply with permit requirements;

(C) What types of permits can be obtained; and

(D) How to apply for a permit.

(2) The purpose of a permit is to provide notice to the Division that an employer will undertake permit-required activity and to allow the Division an effective means of ensuring that the proposed permit-required activity will be performed safely.

(3) There are two types of permits: Project Permits and Annual Permits. Both types are defined below in subsection (b) and explained in subsections (c), (d), and (e).

(4) The Permit application process is explained in section 341.1.

(b) Definitions. The following definitions apply to this article:

(1) "Annual permit" means a permit issued pursuant to section 341.1(a)(2) that allows a qualifying employer to conduct specified permit-required activity at any jobsite for a period of one year.

(2) "Climbing a fixed tower crane" means altering the height of the revolving section of the crane by adding or removing tower sections with the use of a climbing frame.

(3) "Conduct permit-required activity" means either:

(A) Engage in permit-required activity by having employees who actually perform the activity; or

(B) Act in the role of a projet administrator at a site where permit-required activity is taking place, regardless of whether this role involves having employees who actually perform the activity.

NOTE: See definition of "permit required activity" below.

(4) "Emergency repair work to underground facilities" means the unscheduled repair or replacement of pipes or othr underground structures for the purposes of protecting life or property.

1268

(5) "Height" when used to describe a structure means the distance from the top of the structure, including any parapet walls, mechanical rooms or other penthouse structures, to the lowest point of the surrounding grade or ground level below. Mechanical screens, antennas, chimneys, flag poles, and similar attachments are not to be considered in determining the height of a structure.

(6) "Hold a project permit" or "Hold an annual permit" means to have a valid applicable permit which was obtained prior to the start of work. In the case of underground use of a diesel engine in a mine or tunnel the permit shall be obtained prior to placing the engine in the mine or tunnel.

(7) "Permit-required activity" means activity for which a permit is required by this Article.

NOTE: See section 341(d) below for a description of these activities.

(8) "Project Administrator" means a person or entity that has overall onsite responsibility for the planning, quality, management, or completion of a project involving the erection or demolition of a structure. Examples of Project Administrators include, without limitation, general contractors, prime contractors, owner/builders, joint ventures, and construction managers.

(9) "Project permit" means a permit issued pursuant to section 341.1(a)(1) that authorizes an employer to conduct permit-required activity at the specific location(s) named in the permit.

(10) "Structure" means any creation by human activity of a piece of work, formation, or series of parts joined together, including but not necessarily limited to the following:

Billboards.

Bridges.

Buildings.

Chimneys.

Dams.

Elevated highways.

Falsework.

Outdoor signs.

Powerhouses.

Scaffolding.

Silos.

Smokestacks.

Tanks or tank towers.

Transmission or communication towers.

(c) Basic permit requirement.

(1) Project Permits.

(A) Work on permit-required activities on a project subject to Project Permit requirements shall not begin until a Project Permit has been issued for the project.

(B) Only one Project Permit is required per project as long as the Project Permit holder continues to act in the role of Project Administrator, even though the project may have more than one employer fitting the description of a Project Administrator. If the holder of the current Project Permit no longer continues to act in the role of Project Administrator, that Project Permit is no longer valid, and no project work shall continue until a new Project Permit has been issued.

NOTE: See Sections 341.1(f) and 341.1(g) of this article for additional details regarding the scope of coverage of a Project Permit.

(2) Annual Permits.

(A) Any employer other than a Project Permit holder who conducts permit-required activity shall hold a current Annual Permit before engaging in the activity.

(B) An employer who conducts activity subject to Annual Permit requirements shall obtain an Annual Permit once per year and shall notify the Division each time the permit holder begins permit-required activity at a new site.

(d) Work Activities Subject to Permit Requirements and the Types of Permits Required to Conduct the Activities.

(1) To erect, raise or lower, or dismantle a fixed tower crane, the fixed tower crane erector, climber, or dismantler shall hold a Project Permit.

NOTE No. 1: See Section 341.1 of this article for additional details on Project Permit requirements for fixed tower cranes.

NOTE No. 2: See Sections 344.70 et seq. of Title 8 of the California Code of Regulations for additional requirements applicable to permits to operate a fixed tower crane.

(2) To engage in the underground use of a diesel engine in any mine or tunnel, each employer or entity who is to operate the diesel engine shall hold a Project Permit. The permit shall be obtained prior to placing the engine in the mine or tunnel.

(3) To conduct the demolition or dismantling of any building or structure more than 36 feet in height, the Project Administrator shall hold a Project Permit and all other employers directly engaging in demolition or dismantling activity shall hold an Annual Permit.

(4) To conduct any of the following activities on a structure intended to be more than 36 feet high when completed, the Project Administrator shall hold a Project Permit and all other employers directly engaging in these activities shall hold an Annual Permit:

(A) Erection and placement of structural steel or erection and placement of structural members made of materials other than steel.

NOTE: No permit is required for work limited to the erection or placement of reinforcing bars used in reinforced concrete construction.

(B) Installation of metal decking or decking made of substitute materials.

(C) Installation of curtain walls, precast panels, or fascia.

(D) Forming or placement of concrete structures or concrete decks on steel structures.

(E) Installation of structural framing, including roof framing, or the installation of panelized roof systems.

NOTE: No permit is required for work limited to the installation of interior partitions.

(5) To conduct the following activities, the employer shall hold an Annual or a Project Permit, and may apply for either:

(A) Construction of trenches or excavations 5 feet or deeper into which any person is required to descend.

NOTE: For purposes of this subsection, "descend" means to enter any part of the trench or excavation once the excavation has attained a depth of 5 feet or more.

(B) Erection and placement of scaffolding, vertical shoring, or falsework intended to be more than 36 feet high when completed.

(e) Exceptions to Permit Requirements. The provisions of this section shall not apply to the following:

(1) Government Bodies—United States of America, its officers or agencies, State of California, county, city and county, city, or district.

(2) Any public utility subject to the jurisdiction of the Public Utilities Commission.

(3) Construction of trenches or excavations for the purpose of performing emergency repair work to underground facilities.

(4) Construction or final use of excavations or trenches where the construction or final use does not require a person to descend into the excavation or trench.

(5) Excavation for the construction of graves as defined in Section 7014 of the Health and Safety Code.

(6) Excavation for the construction of swimming pools.

NOTE: The construction of motion picture, television, or theater stages and sets does not require a permit unless the conditions specified in Section 6500(b) of the California Labor Code have occurred. For purposes of this requirement, stages and sets include, without limitation, scenery, props, backdrops, flats, greenbeds, and grids.

§ 341.1. Issuance of Permits

(a) Where to Submit Permit Applications.

(1) Project Permits. A Project Permit application shall be submitted to the Division district office that has jurisdiction over the site of the project to be covered by the Project Permit.

(2) Annual Permits. An Annual Permit application shall be submitted to the Division district office where the employer's California headquarters is located. If the

employer has no California headquarters, the application shall be submitted to the Division's headquarters.

NOTE: Project and Annual Permit application forms are available at all Division offices. Generally, the addresses and telephone numbers of Division district offices may be found on the Cal/OSHA Notice poster required pursuant to Section 340 of Title 8 of the California Code of Regulations.

(3) Permits for Use of Diesel Engines in Mines and Tunnels. Permit applications for the use of diesel engines in mines and tunnels shall be submitted to the nearest office of the Division's Mining and Tunneling Unit.

NOTE: Permit application forms for the underground use of diesel engines are available at all offices of the Division's Mining and Tunneling Unit.

(b) General Requirements for Permit Applications.

(1) All Permit applications shall include the following:

(A) The applicant's business name, business address, telephone number, fax number and, if applicable, the applicant's email address.

(B) The name of the applicant's representative; and that representative's contact telephone number(s).

(C) A valid and applicable license number issued by the California Contractors State License Board, if applicable.

(D) An attached copy of a current policy, binder or other proof of workers' compensation insurance, if applicable.

(E) An attached check or money order for the permit fee as provided in section 341.3 of this article.

(F) A certification from the applicant's representative that he or she has knowledge of the applicable occupational safety and health standards and will comply with such standards and any other lawful order of the Division.

(G) A description of the conditions, practices, means, methods, operations or processes used or proposed to be used by the applicant to provide a safe and healthful place of employment.

NOTE: No cash or credit card payments will be accepted by the Division.

(2) In addition, an application for a project permit shall include the following information:

(A) A jobsite telephone number.

(B) The specific jobsite location(s), including street address(es) or cross streets.

(C) The anticipated start date and date of completion.

(D) The permit-required activity to be covered by the permit and a description of the activity for which the permit is sought in sufficient detail to allow an effective evaluation of the safety of the proposed project.

(c) Additional application Requirements for Permits for Underground Use of Diesel Engines in Mines and Tunnels and Permits for Fixed Tower Cranes.

1270

(1) Permits for Underground Use of Diesel Engines in Mines and Tunnels. A permit application for the underground use of diesel engines in mines and tunnels, in addition to the information set forth in this section, shall provide the following:

(A) Complete details and specifications of each diesel engine and exhaust purifying device.

(B) Location of the mine or tunnel and details of how the diesel equipment is to be used.

(C) Length, cross-section, and layout of the underground haulage ways.

(D) Maximum number and brake horsepower of diesels to be operated in any aircourse.

(E) Ventilation plans, including direction of airflow, fan capacity, duct sizes, and auxiliary ventilation.

(F) Date when proposed diesel use is to begin and dates and locations where a representative of the Division may conduct tests of the diesel exhaust gases and mechanical conditions affecting exhaust gas emission.

(2) Permits for Erecting, Climbing, and Dismantling of Fixed Tower Cranes.

Each application for a permit to erect, climb, or dismantle a fixed tower crane shall, in addition to providing the information required by this article, certify that:

(A) A Division-licensed tower crane certifier or surveyor or safety representative for the distributor or manufacturer of the fixed tower crane will be present during erection, climbing, and dismantling operations to assure that such processes and operations are performed in accordance with manufacturer recommendations and applicable standards or orders; and

NOTE: See Sections 344.70 et seq. of Title 8 of the California Code of Regulations for additional requirements applicable for permits to operate a fixed tower crane.

(B) The applicant will notify the Division of the following dates and times:

(i) Initial erection at this site;

(ii) Completion of erection and commencement of operation;

(iii) Climbing of the tower crane; and

(iv) Dismantling of the tower crane.

NOTE: The notification must be received by the Division at least 24 hours prior to the activity which is the subject of the notification and may be in writing or by telephone followed by written notification. The notification shall be made to the district office of the Division from which the permit was obtained and must include the date and time of the intended activity.

(d) Safety Conference for Project Permits and Annual Permits.

(1) The Division may conduct any investigation and/or hearing it deems necessary for the purpose of this article,

and may require a safety conference to discuss the permit applicant's safety program and the means, methods, devices, processes, practices, conditions or operations the permit applicant intends to use to provide employment and a place of employment that are safe and healthful.

(2) When scheduling a safety conference, the Division shall make a reasonable effort to accommodate the scheduling needs of the applicant, shall furnish the applicant with a recommended checklist of information and documentation to bring to the safety conference, and shall clearly inform the applicant which parties are required to attend.

(3) The safety conference shall be held at a district office or at a designated place convenient for the attending parties, and shall be open to the permit applicant, representatives of the owner, contracting agencies, and employees and their representatives. The permit applicant shall notify all attending parties of the safety conference a reasonable time prior to the holding of the safety conference. Proof of such notification shall be made at the safety conference.

(e) General Requirements Applicable to Issuance of All Permits.

(1) A permit may be issued to an applicant following the filing of a completed Permit Application form, compliance with all the requisites therein, payment of the permit fee as provided in Section 341.3 of this article, and a determination by the Division that all qualifications for receipt of a permit have been met by the applicant. Except as provided in Section 8470(*l*), the Division shall issue a Project Permit within five working days of the initial project permit safety conference, if the application materials presented by the applicant at the safety conference are complete. If the application materials are not complete, the applicant shall be given a written list before leaving the safety conference of the materials or information needed to complete the application. The Division shall issue the Project Permit within five working days of receiving complete application materials or deny the permit in writing pursuant to the requirements of Section 341.2.

NOTE: Where Project Permits are required for structures subject to the requirements of Section 341(d)(4), the Division may issue conditional permits when specific information is not yet available.

(2) Each permit issued by the Division shall include the following information:

(A) The person or entity to whom the permit has been issued.

(B) The permit number.

(C) The type of permit issued.

(D) The date through which the permit will remain valid.

(E) The fee amount collected; the check or money order number; and the name of the person collecting the fee.

(F) The name of the person who investigated the permit application and held the permit conference, and the name of the person approving the issuance of the permit.

(G) The specific activities and/or projects covered by the permit.

(f) Issuance of Project Permits for All Projects Other Than Erection of Tower Cranes. The permit applicant shall be required to obtain only one Project Permit for the following work activities:

(1) The construction or demolition of a building or structure over 36 feet high, and the associated excavation of trenches and excavations at the same site.

(2) Any project of construction of a building, structure, vertical shoring, or falsework and/or erection of scaffolding at the same site.

(3) Any project or demolition of a building, structure, or dismantling of scaffolding, vertical shoring or falsework at the same site.

(4) For all or any combination of activities listed in subsection (f)(1), (2), and (3) above at the same jobsite.

(5) Two or more projects when the work is part of the same contract but is located in different Division districts, and the work to be performed is the installation or erection of essentially identical structures.

(A) Such essentially identical structures may include structures such as silos, outdoor signs, tanks or tank towers, and transmission or communication towers.

(B) Such essentially identical structures shall not include bridges, dams, elevated highways, buildings, or tower cranes.

(C) The Project Permit for work on such essentially identical structures shall be issued by the Division district office where the first project scheduled to be commenced is located.

(D) For each subsequent project covered by the Project Permit, the permit holder shall notify the Division district office that has jurisdiction over the site of the project at least 24 hours prior to the activity which is the subject of the notification. Notification shall be given by mail, personal delivery, fax transmission or electronic mail, and shall provide the location of the project and the date and time the work activity is to commence.

(g) Issuance of Project Permits for Fixed Tower Cranes.

Only one permit is required to erect, alter the height of, and dismantle a single fixed tower crane, provided all of this work is done by the same entity. If another entity engages in any of these activities, that entity shall also obtain a Project Permit. If a fixed tower crane is relocated to a new position on the same project a new Project Permit is required.

(h) Issuance of Annual Permits.

(1) An Annual Permit may be issued upon the applicant's demonstration that it has an adequate safety

program that has been developed for the work activity to be covered by the permit, subject to the conditions specified below and any additional conditions specified by the Division. Except as provided in the Note below, the permit shall expire one year later at the close of business on the day prior to the anniversary date of issuance. The permit shall display the expiration date.

NOTE: During the first year following the effective date of this article, the Division may issue Annual Permits for longer than one year in order to stagger the expiration dates.

(2) Annual Permits shall be issued subject to all of the following conditions:

(A) The work shall be performed by the entity named in the permit.

(B) The permit holder shall notify the Division district office that has juris-diction over the site of the project at least 24 hours prior to the activity which is the subject of the notification. Notification shall be given by mail, personal delivery, fax transmission or electronic mail, and shall provide the location of the project and the date and time the work activity is to commence.

(3) Annual Permits may be renewed by mail.

§ 341.2.   Denial of Permit

(a) The Division shall deny issuance of a permit if in its opinion, based on available facts, the employer has failed to show that the conditions, practices, means, methods, operations or processes used or proposed to be used will provide a safe and healthful place of employment. A relevant factor in the Division's determination will be the employer's prior occupational safety and health history. In denying a permit to an applicant employer, the district or field office shall immediately notify the employer, in writing, specifying the reasons for such denial and shall send a copy thereof to the Director.

(b) Any employer denied a permit by the Division may appeal such denial to the Director. The Director shall hold a hearing at such place designated by the Director or his authorized designee for the convenience of the attending parties within two working days of the employer's appeal. The employer has the burden of establishing that it qualifies for a permit.

The hearing shall be presided by the Director or his authorized designee and shall also be open to employees or employees' representative. The employer shall notify the employees or employees' representative of such hearing a reasonable time prior to the holding of such hearing. Proof of such notification by the employer shall be made at the hearing.

(c) Following the hearing, the Director shall issue his decision. The Director's decision shall be final except for any rehearing or judicial review provided for by law. All requests for rehearing shall be filed with the Director within ten days from the date of the Director's decision.

1272

§ 341.3.   Permit Fees

To cover the costs involved in investigating the permit application, and issuing permits, the following schedule of fees are deemed reasonable and necessary. Such applicable fees shall be paid by the employer to the Division of Occupational Safety and health before the issuance of the permit:

(a) Construction of excavations and/or trenches—$50.00.

(b) Construction of building, structure, or dismantling of falsework or scaffolding—$50.00.

(1) For the erection, including climbing and dismantling of the tower structure of a fixed tower crane—$350.00.

(c) Demolition of building or structure, or dismantling of scaffolding or falsework—$50.00.

(d) The underground use of diesel engines in work in mines and tunnels—$50.00.

(e) Annual permits as specified in section 341.1(e) of this article, for period January 1 to December 31—$100.00.

(f) All fees collected by the Division under this section shall be paid into the General Fund of the State Treasury.

§ 341.4.   Posting of Permit

Any employer issued a permit pursuant to this Article shall post a copy or copies of the permit at or near each place of employment. If such posting is impracticable at the site of an excavation, the permit shall be made available at such site at all times, or, in the case of a mobile unit, the permit shall be made available at all times at the employer's head office in the district.

§ 341.5.   Revocation or Suspension of Permit

(a) The Division may at any time, upon a showing of good cause and after notice and an opportunity to be heard, revoke or suspend any permit issued pursuant to this Article.

(b) Notice shall be in writing and served upon the employer at least 24 hours in advance of the hearing. Service shall be by personal service or certified mail to the employer's address as shown on the Permit Application Form. The notice shall specify the reasons for the action taken by the Division in order that the employer may prepare for the hearing.

(c) The hearing shall be held as soon as possible at the district or field office, shall be presided by the district manager or his authorized designee and shall also be open to the affected employees or their representative.

The employer shall notify the employees or employees' representative a reasonable time prior to such hearing. Proof of such notification by the employer shall be made at the hearing.

(d) At the hearing the Division shall establish good cause for the action taken by it. Good cause is established after the Division establishes that the employer has failed to comply with the requirements of the issuance of the permit, and that to permit the continuance of the project under the circumstances would constitute a hazard to the employees.

The employer may appeal such revocation or suspension to the Director in the same manner specified in Section 341.2 of this Article. The filing of an appeal shall not stay the revocation or suspension, except as provided for in Labor Code Section 6506. The employer has the burden of establishing that the Division did not have good cause for the action taken.

Article 2.5.   Registration–Asbestos-Related Work

§ 341.6.   Registration Requirements

(a) An employer who will be engaging in asbestos-related work, as defined, in subsection (b), involving 100 square feet or more of surface area of asbestos-containing material, computed in accordance with subsection (e) of this section, shall apply for and obtain a registration from the division prior to the commencement of any such work.

The registration shall be valid for one year after issuance by the division.

(b) "Asbestos-related work" means any activity which by disturbing asbestos-containing construction materials may release asbestos fibers into the air and which is not related to its manufacture, the mining or excavation of asbestos-bearing ore or materials, or the installation or repair of automotive materials containing asbestos.

(c) "Asbestos containing construction materials" means any manufactured construction material which contains more than 1/10 th of 1% asbestos by weight.

(d) "Asbestos" means fibrous forms of various hydrated minerals including chrysotile (fibrous serpentine), crocidolite (fibrous riebeckite), amosite (fibrous cummingtonite-grunerite), fibrous tremolite, fibrous actinolite, and fibrous anthophyllite.

(e) The square footage of asbestos containing construction material, as defined in subsection (c) of this section, shall be determined by computing the surface area of any such material which will be handled during the course of the work being performed by the employer at a single worksite. If the asbestos containing construction material is situated in noncontiguous locations at a single worksite, the total square footage of such asbestos containing construction material shall be included in the computation, unless the work is performed as part of a routine and continuing maintenance and repair plan of existing fixtures or machinery where each component of such work involves less than 100 square feet.

"A single worksite," as used in this subsection, shall include all buildings, structures, premises, fixtures, machinery or other areas containing asbestos containing construction material which will be handled during the course of the work for which the employer has contracted

whether pursuant to single or multiple contracts with the same hirer.

This article is not intended to apply to asbestos-related work involving less than 100 square feet of asbestos containing construction material performed at separate unrelated worksites by the same employer even though the aggregate total of all such work equals or exceeds one hundred square feet annually.

Note: The requirements of this section apply only to asbestos-related work involving 100 square feet or more of surface area of asbestos-containing construction material. Compliance with this section shall constitute compliance with the reporting requirements of section 5208 of title 8 of the California Code of Regulations. For asbestos-related work involving less than 100 square feet of surface area of asbestos-containing construction material, and for other work involving the use or handling of asbestos, employers shall comply with the reporting requirements of section 5208 of title 8 of the California Code of Regulations.

§ 341.7.   Application for Registration and Renewal of Registration

(a) An employer subject to the provisions of Section 341.6 of this Article shall register with the Division by applying for and obtaining a registration from the Division. Registration application forms may be obtained by writing or calling the headquarter offices of the Division located at 525 Golden Gate Avenue, San Francisco, CA 94102.

(b) Registration application form. A registration may be issued to any employer subject to the provisions of this article following the filing of a completed registration application form and full compliance with all the requirements thereof. All information and attachments given with the application for registration shall be given under penalty of perjury.

The registration application form shall contain the following:

(1) If a contractor, proof of certification if required pursuant to Section 7058.5 of the Business and Professions Code.

(2) Proof that sufficient health insurance coverage has been obtained to cover the entire cost of medical examinations and monitoring required by law or present proof that a $500 trust account has been provided for each employee engaged in such asbestos related work. In addition the employer must provide proof of coverage for worker's compensation insurance.

(3) Proof that all training and certification requirements for employees engaged in asbestos-related work have been completed in accordance with all requirements of law and section 5208, Title 8, California Code of Regulations.

(4) Proof that the employer has knowledge of the applicable occupational safety and health standards, and will comply with such standards and any other such lawful

orders of the Division. In addition, that the conditions, practices, means, methods, operations or processes used or proposed to be used will provide a safe and healthful place of employment and that the employer is proficient in and has the necessary equipment to safely perform asbestos-related work.

(c) An employer may renew the registration by filing an application for renewal meeting the criteria of subsection (b) hereof, and paying a renewal fee as set forth in section 341.12(b) of this article. The application for renewal must be filed with the Division no later than thirty (30) days prior to the expiration date of the current registration.

§ 341.8. Registration Application–Processing Time

(a) Within 15 business days of receipt of an application for registration pursuant to this subsection, the Division shall inform the applicant in writing that it is either complete and accepted for filing or that it is deficient and what specific information or documentation is required to complete the application. An application is considered complete if it is in compliance with the requirements of Section 6501.5, Labor Code and the provisions of this subsection.

(b) Within 30 business days from date of filing of a completed application, the Division shall inform the applicant in writing of its decision regarding the application.

§ 341.9. Notification to the Division–Asbestos–Related Work

(a) When an employer will be conducting separate jobs or phases of work which are the subject of the registration required under this article, or where the work process may differ or is performed at noncontiguous locations, written notice shall be provided to the nearest District Office of the Division prior to commencement of any such work activity, except where the circumstances require immediate abatement action in which case, the employer shall immediately notify the nearest district office by telephone or otherwise orally of the start of work, to be confirmed in writing no later than 24 hours thereafter.

The written notice shall contain the following:

(1) The address of the job.

(2) The precise physical location of the job at the given address.

(3) The projected starting and completion date.

(4) The name of the certified supervisor who has sufficient experience and authority and who will be responsible for the asbestos-related work activity.

(5) The name of the qualified person who will be responsible for conducting air sampling, calibration of air sampling equipment, evaluation of sampling results, and respiratory fit testing as well as the evaluation of those tests.

(6) A description of the type of work to be performed, work practices that will be utilized, and an evaluation of the potential for exposure.

Any change in the information provided the Division by the written notice shall be reported to the Division at or before the time of the change. If notification of any change is made by telephone, or otherwise orally, such notification shall be confirmed immediately in writing but in any event no later than 24 hours after the change.

§ 341.10. Posting and Notification–Asbestos–Related Work

(a) The employer shall post a sign readable at 20 feet at the location where any asbestos-related work subject to the registration and notification requirements of this article is to take place stating "Danger–Asbestos. Cancer and Lung Hazard. Keep Out."

(b) The employer shall provide a copy of the registration before the commencement of any asbestos-related work to the prime contractor and other employers at the site. A copy of the registration shall be posted at the jobsite beside the Cal/OSHA poster.

§ 341.11. Safety Conference

The Employer shall conduct a safety conference prior to the commencement of any asbestos-related work subject to the registration and notification requirements of this article. The safety conference shall include representatives of the owner or contracting agency, the contractor, the employer, employees, and employee representatives. The safety conference shall include a discussion of employer's safety program and such means, methods, devices, processes, practices, conditions, or operations as the employer intends to utilize in providing a safe and healthful place of employment. The requirement of this section shall apply to all asbestos-handling jobs regardless of the amount of asbestos to be handled.

§ 341.12. Registration Fees and Renewal Fees

(a) To cover the costs involved in investigating the registration application, and issuing the registration, an application fee of $350.00 is deemed reasonable and necessary.

(b) To cover the costs involved in investigating the application for renewal of registration, and issuing the renewed registration, a fee of $150.00 is deemed reasonable and necessary.

(c) Such application or renewal fee shall be paid by the employer to the Division of Occupational Safety and Health before the issuance of the registration or renewal.

§ 341.13. Denial of Registration

(a) The Division shall deny the issuance of a registration if in its opinion, based on available facts, including the information provided by employer in the application for registration, the employer has failed to show that the conditions, practices, means, methods, operations or processes used or proposed to be used will provide a safe and healthful place of employment. A relevant factor in the Division's determination will be the employer's compliance history with the Division. In denying the registration to an applicant employer, the Division shall immediately notify the employer, in writing, specifying the reasons for such denial and shall send a copy thereof to the Director.

(b) Any employer denied a registration by the Division may appeal such denial to the Director. The Director shall hold a hearing at such place designated by the Director or his authorized designee for the convenience of the attending parties within two working days of the employer's appeal. Employer shall have the burden of establishing that it qualifies for the registration.

The hearing shall be presided by the director or his authorized designee and shall also be open to employees or employees' representative. The employer shall notify the employees or employees' representatives of such hearing a reasonable time prior to the holding of such hearing. Proof of such notification by the employer shall be made at the hearing.

(c) Following the hearing, the Director shall issue a decision. The Director's decision shall be final except for any rehearing or judicial review provided for by law. All requests for rehearings shall be filed with the Director within 10 days from the date of the Director's decision.

§ 341.14. Revocation or Suspension of Registration

(a) The Division may at any time, upon a showing of good cause and after notice and an opportunity to be heard, revoke or suspend any registration issued pursuant to this article.

(b) Notice shall be in writing and served upon the employer at least 24 hours in advance of the hearing. Service shall be by personal service or certified mail to the employer's address as shown on the registration application form. The notice shall specify the reasons for the action taken by the Division in order that the employer may prepare for the hearing. The Division shall also include within the notice of revocation or suspension specific conditions which must be met before the employer will be entitled to apply for a new registration or continue asbestos-related work under an existing registration.

(c) The hearing shall be held as soon as possible at the Division's headquarter offices or at such other location as may be designated by the Director and shall be presided by the Chief of the Division or his authorized designee and shall also be open to any affected employees or their representatives.

The employer shall notify the employees or employees' representative, a reasonable time prior to such hearing. Proof of such notification by the employer shall be made at the hearing.

(d) At the hearing the Division shall establish good cause for the action taken by it. Good cause is deemed to exist if the Division establishes that the employer has failed to comply with the requirements of the issuance of the registration, and that to permit the continuance of the asbestos-related work activity under the circumstances could cause serious injury or illness to employees.

The employer may appeal such revocation or suspension to the Director in the same manner specified in Section 341.13 of this article. The filing of an appeal shall not stay the revocation or suspension, and such action shall remain in effect until such time as the employer presents proof that the specified written conditions required by the Division are met or until otherwise ordered after resolution of the appeal.

Article 2.6. Asbestos Consultants and
Site Surveillance Technicians

§ 341.15. Certification of Asbestos Consultants and Site Surveillance Technicians

(a) Scope and Application.

Any individual performing services as an asbestos consultant or site surveillance technician as referenced and defined in section 1529(b) of Title 8 of the California Code of Regulations must apply for and obtain a certification pursuant to this article.

Note: This does not apply to individuals who perform preliminary site assessments or other such building inspection activities which may identify asbestos-containing construction materials but which are not for the primary purpose of finding asbestos-containing construction materials in buildings and evaluating the materials for the need of asbestos abatement.

(b) Application for Examination and Certification.

(1) Any individual desiring to be certified as set forth in subsection (a) of this section must submit an application for examination and certification as set forth herein. The application and all information and attachments shall be submitted under penalty of perjury, and accompanied by all applicable fees as set forth herein. No application will be accepted for processing by the Division unless accompanied by all required fees as set forth in subsection (c) herein.

Applications may be obtained from any District Office for the Division and shall be filed by mailing the completed application to the following address:

DIVISION OF OCCUPATIONAL SAFETY AND HEALTH

P.O. BOX 420603

SAN FRANCISCO, CA 94142

ATTENTION: ASBESTOS CONSULTANT CERTIFICATION

The application shall include:

(A) Type of certification desired: Asbestos Consultant or Site Surveillance Technician.

(B) Full name of the applicant including the name under which the individual will be conducting business under the certification, and any other names the applicant has used to conduct business as an asbestos consultant within five years previous to the date of the application.

(C) Birthdate and Social Security Number.

(D) Address (Employment and Home).

(E) Telephone Number (Work and Home).

(F) 2 copies of 1 1/2″ x 1 1/2″ current color photograph of applicant (passport type taken within the past 30 days).

(G) Copies of valid certificates from AHERA training providers approved by the Division.

Note: The Division will publish a list of approved AHERA training providers.

(1) Asbestos consultant applicants shall submit copies of AHERA training certificates for management planner, abatement project designer, abatement contractor and supervisor, and all subsequent annual refresher courses. The complete abatement project designer course certificate will be required only for applications submitted after July 1, 1994.

Note: The project designer refresher course will be sufficient for applications submitted prior to July 1, 1994.

(2) Site surveillance technician applicants shall submit copies of AHERA training completion certificates for inspector, and abatement contractor and supervisor, and all subsequent annual refresher courses. Certificates for abatement worker and abatement project designer may be submitted in lieu of the abatement contractor and supervisor certificate.

(H) Required fee(s).

(I) Description of qualifications as required pursuant to section 1529(*o*) of Title 8 of the California Code of Regulations outlining the applicant's educational qualifications, (attach copy of diploma, official transcript, or other proof), and description of qualifying work experience as specified in Business and Professions Code sections 7184 and 7185. Qualifying work experience includes technical work associated with asbestos consulting activities. Written references attesting to the applicant's qualifying work experience which are certified under the penalty of perjury are required.

(c) Examination Requirements for Certification.

(1) All applicants must pass a written examination as set forth herein.

(2) The examination shall be a closed book written examination pertaining to the subjects described in (*o*)(6)(A) and (*o*)(7)(A) of section 1529 of Title 8 of the California Code of Regulations. The minimum passing score shall be correctly answering 70% of all the questions in the written examination.

(3) The examination shall be conducted at various locations as determined by the Division and administered at least annually or at other intervals when necessary.

1276

(d) Fees for Certification and Renewal.

(1) Fees for asbestos consultant:

Application and Examination Fee	$500
Annual Renewal Fee	$325

(2) Fees for site surveillance technician:

Application and Examination Fee	$400
Annual Renewal Fee	$270

(3) All fees must be paid at the time the application is filed with the Division. Except as set forth in Part (5) of this subsection, all fees are non-refundable.

(4) All required fees shall be made payable to the Asbestos Consultant Certification Fund.

(5) The Division may refund 75% of the fee when an application is withdrawn by the applicant within 15 business days of the initial submission of the application. The Division may refund 50% of the fee when the Division determines that the applicant is not qualified to take the examination. The Division shall make no refund of the fee when a qualified applicant fails the written examination.

(e) Processing of Application.

(1) Within 15 business days of receipt of an application for certification, the Division shall inform the applicant in writing of its determination either that the application is complete or that it is deficient. The notice shall specify what additional information or documentation is necessary.

(2) Within 45 business days from the date the Division has determined an application is complete the Division shall:

(A) Inform the applicant that the application for certification is denied, specifying the reasons for the denial; or

(B) Inform the applicant that the qualification requirements of this article have been satisfied and that the applicant may take the required written examination; and,

(C) Inform the applicant of the date, time, and location of the examination.

(f) Provisional Certification.

(1) The Division may issue a provisional certification to an applicant when:

(A) The applicant has submitted a completed application and is qualified to take the written examination.

(B) The Division is not able to schedule an examination and issue the certification within 45 business days after the Division has found the application to be complete as set forth in subsection (c) above.

(2) The provisional certification card will authorize the applicant to perform services as an asbestos consultant or site surveillance technician. The provisional certification

shall expire 15 days after the scheduled examination date of the applicant who receives the provisional certification.

(3) Only one provisional certification may be issued to an applicant.

(g) Re-examinations.

Within 30 days of notification, any applicant who fails the examination may take the next scheduled examination. The request shall be made to the Division in writing and accompanied by a re-examination fee in the amount of 50% of the application and examination fee specified in subsection (d) above. Any applicant who fails is entitled to retake the examination one time. If an applicant fails the examination twice the request for certification will be denied and the applicant must submit a new application.

(h) Renewal or Replacement of Certification.

(1) A certification issued pursuant to this article shall be valid for one year from the date of issuance as designated on the certification. Any individual certified under this article may renew the certification by filing a request for renewal with the Division at least 60 days prior to the expiration date of the certification. Any individual who fails to renew as required herein must submit a new application for certification.

(2) All requests for renewal must be submitted with a current photograph, copies of required AHERA refresher training certificates, and the required renewal fee specified in subsection (d) above.

(3) Any person whose certification card has been lost or mutilated may request a replacement card from the Division. Such request shall be in writing and accompanied with a current photograph and replacement fee in the amount of 30% of the annual renewal fee specified in (d) of this section.

(i) Denial, Suspension, or Revocation of Certification.

(1) The Division may for good cause deny certification to an applicant. Good cause shall be deemed to exist when the applicant does not satisfy the qualification requirements of this article or has failed the written examination.

(2) The Division may for good cause and after notice and hearing suspend or revoke the certification of a person certified pursuant to this section. Good cause shall be deemed to exist if the person certified has committed gross negligence or fraud, or engaged in repeated acts of negligence during the performance of activities subject to the certification.

Note: Revocation proceedings shall comply with the procedural requirements of Chapter 5 (commencing with section 11500) of Division 3 of Part 1 of Title 2 of the Government Code applicable to administrative adjudication.

(3) For denial or suspension of a certification, notice shall be given in writing and served upon the person certified at least 24 hours in advance of the hearing to suspend or revoke the certification. Service shall be by personal service or certified mail to the person's address as shown on the certification application or other address known to the Division. The notice shall specify the reasons for the action taken by the Division in order that the person may prepare for the hearing.

(4) Any applicant may appeal the denial, suspension or revocation to the Director. The appeal shall be in writing and made within 5 business days of receipt of the notification of the decision regarding the certification.

(5) The Director or authorized representative shall schedule a hearing within 5 business days of receipt of an appeal. The applicant shall have the burden of establishing that he/she qualifies for the certification at the hearing.

(6) Following the hearing the Director shall issue a decision. The Director's decision shall be final except for any rehearing or judicial review provided for by law. Requests for rehearings shall be filed with the Director within 5 business days of the Director's decision.

Article 2.7.   Approval of Courses and Course Providers

§ 341.16. Approval of Asbestos Training and Course Providers for Training Requirements Relating to Asbestos–Related Work and AHERA

(a) Scope and Application.

(1) Any course provider (individual or business entity) providing asbestos training for the purpose of satisfying Division approved training requirements of 1529(k)(9)(B) for employees engaged in asbestos-related work or providing asbestos training for the purpose of satisfying the accreditation requirements of AHERA must submit the training program to the Division for approval in accordance with the provisions of this article.

(2) The Division will approve initial and annual refresher training courses for Construction Craft Worker, and for each of the following AHERA crafts or disciplines: Inspector, Management Planner, Abatement Project Designer, Abatement Contractor/Supervisor, and Asbestos Abatement Worker. Construction Craft Worker means any employee engaged in asbestos-related work (other than asbestos-related work included under the above named AHERA disciplines) requiring employer registration under Section 341.6 and Section 1529.

(3) AHERA as used in this Article means the Asbestos Hazard Emergency Response Act which is codified in 15 U.S.C. Section 2641, et seq.

(b) Requirements for Asbestos Course Approval.

(1) General Requirements.

(A) The course provider shall inform the Division in writing of the starting date, time and location for each training course scheduled at least 15 days prior to each starting date. In cases where the 15–day notice cannot be provided, FAX or telephone with written follow-up notification may be made as soon as possible before commencement of the training, but in no case later than 24 hours prior to commencement.

(B) The Asbestos Abatement Worker courses, including the course materials and examinations, shall be given in a language that is understood by both the course instructor and trainees.

(C) The instructor directing each course shall have at least one year of experience in teaching courses of a similar nature or other professional teaching qualifications in areas related to occupational safety and health issues. The instructor for the hands-on portion of the course shall have at least one year of relevant work experience in asbestos-related work.

(D) The course provider shall update the information submitted to the Division whenever a substantive change is made to information previously submitted for Division approval. Such notification shall be made in writing to the Division at the address given in (d)(1) of this Section no later than 24 hours after the change is instituted.

(E) Only individuals who have successfully completed an initial training course shall be allowed to take the corresponding refresher training course. Only holders of a certificate which is less than one year past the expiration date shown on the certificate shall be permitted to take the refresher training course.

(F) Training attendance is required for at least the duration specified for each course as set forth below. Breaks, including a lunch break, may be included in each eight hours of training.

(2) Specific Course Requirements

(A) Initial Course for Construction Craft Worker: the initial Construction Craft Worker course shall include the following:

1. The course curriculum and the course length in hours shall meet the requirements in Section 1529 for Class I, II, or III work or other federal requirements.

2. Hands-on training that is specific to the asbestos-related work for the construction craft of each employee attending the course.

Note: Except for AHERA courses, a course provider may combine trainees of various crafts for training on the common parts of the curricula involved when appropriate, and separate the trainees after the common training for the specific training peculiar to each craft involved.

(B) Refresher Course for Construction Craft Worker: the annual refresher shall include at least two hours of review of the important elements covered in the corresponding initial course, any changes in federal and state asbestos regulations, and the latest developments in the state of the art practices for asbestos-related work involving the specific construction craft.

(C) Initial AHERA Course: The initial course for each AHERA craft or discipline shall include and conform with the AHERA training course curriculum and required hours of instruction specified in the USEPA Model Accreditation Plan found in 40 CFR Part 763,

Subpart E, Appendix C. The Model Accreditation Plan is included as Appendix A of this section.

1. When hands-on training is specified, the hands-on training must allow contractors, supervisors and workers to have actual experience performing tasks associated with asbestos abatement. Simulated asbestos materials shall be used instead of actual asbestos during the hands-on training.

2. The training course shall include a review of applicable federal and state regulations, including but not limited to, Sections 341.6, et seq. and Sections 1529 and 5208 of Title 8 of the California Code of Regulations.

(D) Annual AHERA Refresher Course: The refresher AHERA course shall include and conform with the AHERA training course curriculum described in the USEPA Model Accreditation Plan found in 40 CFR Part 763, Subpart E, Appendix C and shall be specific to each AHERA discipline.

1. The refresher training course shall include a review of the important elements covered in the initial course, any changes in federal, state, and local regulations, and the latest developments in state of the art practices.

2. A minimum of eight (8) hours training shall be given for the refresher training course for Asbestos Abatement Worker, Abatement Contractor/Supervisor and Abatement Project Designer. A minimum of four (4) hours training shall be given for the refresher training course for Inspector. Only the rightful holder of a valid current AHERA Inspector certificate shall be allowed to take the Management Planner refresher accreditation training.

(E) Course Examinations.

1. As indicated in the table of examination requirements below an initial training course shall include an examination administered as a final part of the training course. The examination shall adequately cover the topics of the training course. Demonstration testing may be included as a part of the examination. The minimum number of multiple choice questions, each question having at least 4 choices for an answer, and the minimum passing score required for each type of training course are shown in Table 1.

Table 1
Course Examination Specifications

Craft/Discipline	Number of Questions	Passing Score
Construction Craft Worker: (closed book exam)	20	70%
Inspector (closed book exam):	50	70%
Management Planner (closed book exam)	50	70%
Asbestos Project Designer: (closed book exam)	100	70%
Asbestos Contractor/Supervisor: (closed book exam)	100	70%
Asbestos Abatement Worker: (closed book exam)	50	70%

2. Any trainee failing the examination may retake an equivalent but different examination one time; the course

provider shall allow the trainee to retake the examination as soon as practicable after notifying the trainee of the exam results but no later than thirty (30) days after such date. If the trainee fails the second examination, the trainee must retake the course in order to take the examination again.

(F) Course Certificates.

1. The training provider shall issue certificates to trainees who complete a training course and pass the examination.

2. The certificate shall be issued within 15 business days after the course completion date. Compliance with this requirement may be delayed until the course provider receives payment for the course. The certificate shall be valid for one year after the successful completion of the examination.

3. Each certificate shall contain the following information:

A. The name, address and telephone number of the training provider that issued the certificate. The name of the training course with an indication that it is approved by the Division.

B. The Course Approval Number issued by the Division and a unique certificate number issued by the training course provider. If the certificate is for a Construction Craft Worker, also include on the certificate a designation of the type of craft and the class of asbestos work as described in Section 1529; e.g., Roofer—Class II, General Building Maintenance Worker—Class III, etc.

C. The name of the trainee.

D. The dates when the training course started and ended, and the date of the examination if applicable.

E. The certificate expiration date.

F. The name and signature of an authorized officer of the training course provider with a written statement that the person receiving the certificate has completed the required training and passed the examination (if one is required). In the case of training for AHERA disciplines (but not for Construction Craft Workers), the written statement shall also indicate that the training completed is that required for asbestos accreditation under Toxic Substances Control Act, Title II.

(c) Division Roster of Certificate Holders.

(1) The course provider shall provide the following information to the Division on forms provided by the Division with the appropriate fee specified in subsection (e) for each certificated trainee within 15 business days after each course examination.

(A) The name of the training course and its State of California course approval number.

(B) Full name of certificated trainee.

(C) The unique certificate number issued by the training course provider. If the certificate is for a Construction Craft Worker, also include a designation of the type of craft and the class of asbestos work.

(D) Home address of trainee.

(E) The expiration date of the certificate.

(2) The Division will utilize this information to develop a roster of individuals who have received a certificate of training from an approved course provider. Only those individuals who appear on the roster will be considered in compliance with the training requirements of AHERA or subsections 1529(k)(9) for employees engaged in asbestos-related work requiring employer registration.

Note: To provide an orderly transition individuals who possess valid and current AHERA certificates issued by USEPA approved or USEPA state approved course providers will be considered in compliance with this provision until December 31, 1999. After December 31, 1999, these individuals must appear on the Division roster showing initial or refresher AHERA certificates issued by Division approved AHERA course providers.

(d) Application for Course Approval.

(1) Any individual or organization that desires to become a course provider and satisfies the requirements of this article may apply to the Division for approval of an asbestos training course. The course provider shall complete a separate application for each training course for which approval is being sought using the following forms which are hereby incorporated by reference: Worker initial course, Form W–I 8/28/98; Contractor/Supervisor initial course, Form CS–I 8/28/98; Building Inspector initial course, Form BI–I 8/28/98; Project Designer initial course, Form PD–I 8/28/98; Management Planner initial course, Form MP–I 8/28/98; Construction Craft Worker initial course, Form CCW–I 8/28/98; Worker refresher course, Form W–R 8/28/98; Contractor/Supervisor refresher course, Form CS–R 8/28/98; Building Inspector refresher course, Form BI–R 8/28/98; Project Designer refresher course, Form PD–R 8/28/98; Management Planner refresher course, Form MP–R 8/28/98; Construction Craft Worker refresher course, Form CCW–R 8/28/98. Requests for application information and completed applications shall be sent to:

Division of Occupational Safety and Health P.O. Box 420603 San Francisco, CA 94142

(2) The application shall include:

(A) The name of the training course.

(B) The name of the course provider, the name and title of the person whom the Division will contact regarding course approval matters, address, phone number, and the name and title of the person completing the application with his or her signature and a statement certifying that the information in the application is correct.

(C) The appropriate fee specified in subsection (e).

(D) Evidence of any previous approval from USEPA or another state for the training course.

(E) Materials describing the contents and parameters of the training course.

(F) Copies of all training documents and visual training aids (projection transparencies, etc.) used in the training course.

(G) A sample copy of the examination to be administered for the training course, including the test key.

(H) A sample copy of the certificate issued for the training course.

(I) The name(s) and qualifications of the instructor(s) of the training course.

(J) A list of the equipment which is used in the training course with a description of each type of equipment and the quantity of each type available on site for training.

(e) Fees for Course Approval.

(1) The application fee is $200 for the initial Construction Craft Worker course approval and $100 for the refresher course approval.

(2) The application fee is $600 for any initial AHERA course approval and $400 for any refresher AHERA course approval.

(3) Submitted application fees are not refundable. An appropriate application fee is required for each application.

(4) Fees are required to defray the cost of administering the approval process for assuring that approved providers continue to provide effective training as required. The continuing approval process includes course audits and the auditing activity for an approved provider will be related to the number of trainees trained by the provider and other information available to the Division. A roster fee shall be paid by the approved provider to fund this continuing approval process and to fund the maintenance of the roster specified in subsection (c). The course provider shall remit a roster fee of $5 for each certificated trainee of a Construction Craft Worker Course, and $10 for each certificated trainee of each AHERA training course as specified in Section 341.16(c)(1). The annual cumulative roster fees must total a minimum of $150 for each approved course. If the annual cumulative roster fees is less than $150 for an approved course and the course provider wants to maintain the approval for the course, the course provider must remit a supplemental amount needed to make the $150 minimum annual total by the end of the annual interval. The annual interval commences from the anniversary date of the issuance of approval for the approved course.

(5) Fees required by this subsection shall be payable to the Asbestos Training Approval Account.

(f) Processing of Application.

(1) Within 15 business days of receipt of an application for approval, the Division shall inform the applicant in writing whether the submitted application information required by (d)(2) is complete or additional information needs to be submitted.

(2) Within 45 business days from the date the Division has determined an application is complete, the Division shall inform the applicant that the training course is approved and issue a State of California Course Approval Number to the applicant or inform the applicant that the application for approval is denied, specifying the reason for denial. After an application is denied, a new application with another fee must be submitted if the applicant wishes to continue to seek course approval.

(g) Audit of Training Course.

(1) Each course provider, as a condition of approval, shall permit the Division to attend and audit any training course in part or in its entirety without prior notification to the course provider.

(2) The Division may administer a questionnaire to the trainees at the conclusion of an approved training course to evaluate training effectiveness.

(h) Suspension and Revocation of Course Approval and of Training Certificates.

(1) The Division may at any time, upon a showing of good cause and after notice and an opportunity to be heard, suspend or revoke any course approval or training certificate issued pursuant to this section.

(2) Notice shall be in writing and served upon the party receiving adverse action from the Division at least 24 hours in advance of the hearing. Service shall be by personal service or certified mail to the course provider's address as shown on the course approval application. The notice shall specify the reasons for the action proposed by the Division in order that the notified party may prepare for the hearing.

(3) The hearing shall be held as soon as possible at the Division's headquarters offices or at such other location as may be designated by the Division and shall be presided over by the Chief of the Division or his authorized designee.

(4) At the hearing the Division shall establish good cause for the action proposed by it. Good cause is deemed to exist if the Division establishes that the course provider issued a certificate, but did not provide the corresponding required training.

(5) The adversely affected party receiving a suspension or revocation from the Division may appeal such action to the Director. The Director shall hold a hearing at such place designated by the Director or his authorized designee for the convenience of the attending parties within two working days of the receipt of the course provider's appeal. The course provider shall have the burden of establishing that the suspension or revocation is not justified. The hearing shall be presided over by the Director or his authorized designee.

(6) Following the hearing, the Director shall issue a decision. The Director's decision shall be final except for any rehearing or judicial review provided for by law. All requests for rehearing shall be filed with the Director within 10 business days from the date of the Director's

Decision by mailing or personally serving a request for rehearing to the Director.

Appendix A

40 CFR Part 763, Appendix C to Subpart E, Asbestos Model Accreditation Plan.

I. Asbestos Model Accreditation Plan for States

The Asbestos Model Accreditation Plan (MAP) for States has eight components:

(A) Definitions

(B) Initial Training

(C) Examinations

(D) Continuing Education

(E) Qualifications

(F) Recordkeeping Requirements for Training Providers

(G) Deaccreditation

(H) Reciprocity

A. Definitions

For purposes of Appendix C:

1. "Friable asbestos-containing material (ACM)" means any material containing more than one percent asbestos which has been applied on ceilings, walls, structural members, piping, duct work, or any other part of a building, which when dry, may be crumbled, pulverized, or reduced to powder by hand pressure. The term includes non-friable asbestos-containing material after such previously non-friable material becomes damaged to the extent that when dry it may be crumbled, pulverized, or reduced to powder by hand pressure.

2. "Friable asbestos-containing building material (ACBM)" means any friable ACM that is in or on interior structural members or other parts of a school or public and commercial building.

3. "Inspection" means an activity undertaken in a school building, or a public and commercial building, to determine the presence or location, or to assess the condition of, friable or non-friable asbestos-containing building material (ACBM) or suspected ACBM, whether by visual or physical examination, or by collecting samples of such material. This term includes reinspections of friable and non-friable known or assumed ACBM which has been previously identified. The term does not include the following:

a. Periodic surveillance of the type described in 40 CFR 763.92(b) solely for the purpose of recording or reporting a change in the condition of known or assumed ACBM;

b. Inspections performed by employees or agents of Federal, State, or local government solely for the purpose of determining compliance with applicable statutes or regulations; or

c. visual inspections of the type described in 40 CFR 763.90(i) solely for the purpose of determining completion of response actions.

4. "Major fiber release episode" means any uncontrolled or unintentional disturbance of ACBM, resulting in a visible emission, which involves the falling or dislodging of more than 3 square or linear feet of friable ACBM.

5. "Minor fiber release episode" means any uncontrolled or unintentional disturbance of ACBM, resulting in a visible emission, which involves the falling or dislodging of 3 square or linear feet or less of friable ACBM.

6. "Public and commercial building" means the interior space of any building which is not a school building, except that the term does not include any residential apartment building of fewer than 10 units or detached single-family homes. The term includes, but is not limited to: industrial and office buildings, residential apartment buildings and condominiums of 10 or more dwelling units, government-owned buildings, colleges, museums, airports, hospitals, churches, preschools, stores, warehouses and factories. Interior space includes exterior hallways connecting buildings, porticos, and mechanical systems used to condition interior space.

7. "Response action" means a method, including removal, encapsulation, enclosure, repair, and operation and maintenance, that protects human health and the environment from friable ACBM.

8. "Small-scale, short-duration activities (SSSD)" are tasks such as, but not limited to:

a. Removal of asbestos-containing insulation on pipes.

b. Removal of small quantities of asbestos-containing insulation on beams or above ceilings.

c. Replacement of an asbestos-containing gasket on a valve.

d. Installation or removal of a small section of drywall.

e. Installation of electrical conduits through or proximate to asbestos-containing materials.

SSSD can be further defined by the following considerations:

f. Removal of small quantities of ACM only if required in the performance of another maintenance activity not intended as asbestos abatement.

g. Removal of asbestos-containing thermal system insulation not to exceed amounts greater than those which can be contained in a single glove bag.

h. Minor repairs to damaged thermal system insulation which do not require removal.

i. Repairs to a piece of asbestos-containing wallboard.

j. Repairs, involving encapsulation, enclosure, or removal, to small amounts of friable ACM only if required in the performance of emergency or routine maintenance

1281

activity and not intended solely as asbestos abatement. Such work may not exceed amounts greater than those which can be contained in a single prefabricated mini-enclosure. Such an enclosure shall conform spatially and geometrically to the localized work area, in order to perform its intended containment function.

B.   Initial Training

Training requirements for purposes of accreditation are specified both in terms of required subjects of instruction and in terms of length of training. Each initial training course has a prescribed curriculum and number of days of training. One day of training equals 8 hours, including breaks and lunch. Course instruction must be provided by EPA or State-approved instructors. EPA or State instructor approval shall be based upon a review of the instructor's academic credentials and/or field experience in asbestos abatement.

Beyond the initial training requirements, individual States may wish to consider requiring additional days of training for purposes of supplementing hands-on activities or for reviewing relevant state regulations. States also may wish to consider the relative merits of a worker apprenticeship program. Further, they might consider more stringent minimum qualification standards for the approval of training instructors. EPA recommends that the enrollment in any given course be limited to 25 students so that adequate opportunities exist for individual hands-on experience.

States have the option to provide initial training directly or approve other entities to offer training. The following requirements are for the initial training of persons required to have accreditation under TSCA Title II.

Training requirements for each of the five accredited disciplines are outlined below. Persons in each discipline perform a different job function and distinct role. Inspectors identify and assess the condition of ACBM, or suspect ACBM. Management planners use data gathered by inspectors to assess the degree of hazard posed by ACBM in schools to determine the scope and timing of appropriate response actions needed for schools. Project designers determine how asbestos abatement work should be conducted. Lastly, workers and contractor/supervisors carry out and oversee abatement work. In addition, a recommended training curriculum is also presented for a sixth discipline, which is not federally-accredited, that of "Project Monitor." Each accredited discipline and training curriculum is separate and distinct from the others. A person seeking accreditation in any of the five accredited MAP disciplines cannot attend two or more courses concurrently, but may attend such courses sequentially.

In several instances, initial training courses for a specific discipline (e.g., workers, inspectors) require hands-on training. For asbestos abatement contractor/supervisors and workers, hands-on training should include working with asbestos-substitute materials, fitting and using respirators, use of glovebags, donning protective

1282

clothing, and constructing a decontamination unit as well as other abatement work activities.

1.   Workers

A person must be accredited as a worker to carry out any of the following activities with respect to friable ACBM in a school or public and commercial building: (1) A response action other than a SSSD activity, (2) a maintenance activity that disturbs friable ACBM other than a SSSD activity, or (3) a response action for a major fiber release episode. All persons seeking accreditation as asbestos abatement workers shall complete at least a 4-day training course as outlined below. The 4-day worker training course shall include lectures, demonstrations, at least 14 hours of hands-on training, individual respirator fit testing, course review, and an examination. Hands-on training must permit workers to have actual experience performing tasks associated with asbestos abatement. A person who is otherwise accredited as a contractor/supervisor may perform in the role of a worker without possessing separate accreditation as a worker.

Because of cultural diversity associated with the asbestos workforce, EPA recommends that States adopt specific standards for the approval of foreign language courses for abatement workers. EPA further recommends the use of audio-visual materials to complement lectures, where appropriate.

The training course shall adequately address the following topics:

(a) Physical characteristics of asbestos. Identification of asbestos, aerodynamic characteristics, typical uses, and physical appearance, and a summary of abatement control options.

(b) Potential health effects related to asbestos exposure. The nature of asbestos-related diseases; routes of exposure; dose-response relationships and the lack of a safe exposure level; the synergistic effect between cigarette smoking and asbestos exposure; the latency periods for asbestos-related diseases; a discussion of the relationship of asbestos exposure to asbestosis, lung cancer, mesothelioma, and cancers of other organs.

(c) Employee personal protective equipment. Classes and characteristics of respirator types; limitations of respirators; proper selection, inspection; donning, use, maintenance, and storage procedures for respirators; methods for field testing of the facepiece-to-face seal (positive and negative-pressure fit checks); qualitative and quantitative fit testing procedures; variability between field and laboratory protection factors that alter respiratory fit (e.g., facial hair); the components of a proper respiratory protection program; selection and use of personal protective clothing; use, storage, and handling of non-disposable clothing; and regulations covering personal protective equipment.

(d) State-of-the-art work practices. Proper work practices for asbestos abatement activities, including descriptions of proper construction; maintenance of barriers and decontamination enclosure systems; positioning of warning signs; lock-out of electrical and ventilation systems; proper working techniques for minimizing fiber release; use of wet methods; use of negative pressure exhaust ventilation equipment; use of high-efficiency particulate air (HEPA) vacuums; proper clean-up and disposal procedures; work practices for removal, encapsulation, enclosure, and repair of ACM; emergency procedures for sudden releases; potential exposure situations; transport and disposal procedures; and recommended and prohibited work practices.

(e) Personal hygiene. Entry and exit procedures for the work area; use of showers; avoidance of eating, drinking, smoking, and chewing (gum or tobacco) in the work area; and potential exposures, such as family exposure.

(f) Additional safety hazards. Hazards encountered during abatement activities and how to deal with them, including electrical hazards, heat stress, air contaminants other than asbestos, fire and explosion hazards, scaffold and ladder hazards, slips, trips, and falls, and confined spaces.

(g) Medical monitoring. OSHA and EPA Worker Protection Rule requirements for physical examinations, including a pulmonary function test, chest X-rays, and a medical history for each employee.

(h) Air monitoring. Procedures to determine airborne concentrations of asbestos fibers, focusing on how personal air sampling is performed and the reasons for it.

(i) Relevant Federal, State, and local regulatory requirements, procedures, and standards. With particular attention directed at relevant EPA, OSHA, and State regulations concerning asbestos abatement workers.

(j) Establishment of respiratory protection programs.

(k) Course review. A review of key aspects of the training course.

2. Contractor/Supervisors

A person must be accredited as a contractor/supervisor to supervise any of the following activities with respect to friable ACBM in a school or public and commercial building: (1) A response action other than a SSSD activity, (2) a maintenance activity that disturbs friable ACBM other than a SSSD activity, or (3) a response action for a major fiber release episode. All persons seeking accreditation as asbestos abatement contractor/supervisors shall complete at least a 5–day training course as outlined below. The training course must include lectures, demonstrations, at least 14 hours of hands-on training, individual respirator fit testing, course review, and a written examination. Hands-on training must permit supervisors to have actual experience performing tasks associated with asbestos abatement.

EPA recommends the use of audiovisual materials to complement lectures, where appropriate.

Asbestos abatement supervisors include those persons who provide supervision and direction to workers performing response actions. Supervisors may include those individuals with the position title of foreman, working foreman, or leadman pursuant to collective bargaining agreements. At least one supervisor is required to be at the worksite at all times while response actions are being conducted. Asbestos workers must have access to accredited supervisors throughout the duration of the project.

The contractor/supervisor training course shall adequately address the following topics:

(a) The physical characteristics of asbestos and asbestos-containing materials. Identification of asbestos, aerodynamic characteristics, typical uses, physical appearance, a review of hazard assessment considerations, and a summary of abatement control options.

(b) Potential health effects related to asbestos exposure. The nature of asbestos-related diseases; routes of exposure; dose-response relationships and the lack of a safe exposure level; synergism between cigarette smoking and asbestos exposure; and latency period for diseases.

(c) Employee personal protective equipment. Classes and characteristics of respirator types; limitations of respirators; proper selection, inspection, donning, use, maintenance, and storage procedures for respirators; methods for field testing of the facepiece-to-face seal (positive and negative-pressure fit checks); qualitative and quantitative fit testing procedures; variability between field and laboratory protection factors that alter respiratory fit (e.g., facial hair); the components of a proper respiratory protection program; selection and use of personal protective clothing; and use, storage, and handling of non-disposable clothing; and regulations covering personal protective equipment.

(d) State-of-the-art work practices. Proper work practices for asbestos abatement activities, including descriptions of proper construction and maintenance of barriers and decontamination enclosure systems; positioning of warning signs; lock out of electrical and ventilation systems; proper working techniques for minimizing fiber release; use of wet methods; use of negative pressure exhaust ventilation equipment; use of HEPA vacuums; and proper clean-up and disposal procedures. Work practices for removal, encapsulation, enclosure, and repair of ACM; emergency procedures for unplanned releases; potential exposure situations; transport and disposal procedures; and recommended and prohibited work practices. New abatement-related techniques and methodologies may be discussed.

(e) Personal hygiene. Entry and exit procedures for the work area; use of showers; and avoidance of eating, drinking, smoking, and chewing (gum or tobacco) in the work area. Potential exposures, such as family exposure, shall also be included.

(f) Additional safety hazards. Hazards encountered during abatement activities and how to deal with them, including electrical hazards, heat stress, air contaminants other than asbestos, fire and explosion hazards, scaffold and ladder hazards, slips, trips, and falls, and confined spaces.

(g) Medical monitoring. OSHA and EPA Worker Protection Rule requirements for physical examinations, including a pulmonary function test, chest X-rays and a medical history for each employee.

(h) Air monitoring. Procedures to determine airborne concentrations of asbestos fibers, including descriptions of aggressive air sampling, sampling equipment and methods, reasons for air monitoring, types of samples and interpretation of results.

EPA recommends that transmission electron microscopy (TEM) be used for analysis of final air clearance samples, and that sample analyses be performed by laboratories accredited by the National Institute of Standards and Technology's (NIST) National Voluntary Laboratory Accreditation Program (NVLAP).

(i) Relevant Federal, State, and local regulatory requirements, procedures, and standards, including:

(i) Requirements of TSCA Title II.

(ii) National Emission Standards for Hazardous Air Pollutants (40 CFR part 61), Subparts A (General Provisions) and M (National Emission Standard for Asbestos).

(iii) OSHA standards for permissible exposure to airborne concentrations of asbestos fibers and respiratory protection (29 CFR 1910.134).

(iv) OSHA Asbestos Construction Standard (29 CFR 1926.58).

(v) EPA Worker Protection Rule (40 CFR part 763, Subpart G).

(j) Respiratory Protection Programs and Medical Monitoring Programs.

(k) Insurance and liability issues. Contractor issues; worker's compensation coverage and exclusions; third-party liabilities and defenses; insurance coverage and exclusions.

(*l*) Recordkeeping for asbestos abatement projects. Records required by Federal, State, and local regulations; records recommended for legal and insurance purposes.

(m) Supervisory techniques for asbestos abatement activities. Supervisory practices to enforce and reinforce the required work practices and discourage unsafe work practices.

(n) Contract specifications. Discussions of key elements that are included in contract specifications.

(*o*) Course review. A review of key aspects of the training course.

3. Inspector

All persons who inspect for ACBM in schools or public and commercial buildings must be accredited. All persons seeking accreditation as an inspector shall complete at least a 3–day training course as outlined below. The course shall include lectures, demonstrations, 4 hours of hands-on training, individual respirator fit-testing, course review, and a written examination.

EPA recommends the use of audiovisual materials to complement lectures, where appropriate. Hands-on training should include conducting a simulated building walk-through inspection and respirator fit testing. The inspector training course shall adequately address the following topics:

(a) Background information on asbestos. Identification of asbestos, and examples and discussion of the uses and locations of asbestos in buildings; physical appearance of asbestos.

(b) Potential health effects related to asbestos exposure. The nature of asbestos-related diseases; routes of exposure; dose-response relationships and the lack of a safe exposure level; the synergistic effect between cigarette smoking and asbestos exposure; the latency periods for asbestos-related diseases; a discussion of the relationship of asbestos exposure to asbestosis, lung cancer, mesothelioma, and cancers of other organs.

(c) Functions/qualifications and role of inspectors. Discussions of prior experience and qualifications for inspectors and management planners; discussions of the functions of an accredited inspector as compared to those of an accredited management planner; discussion of inspection process including inventory of ACM and physical assessment.

(d) Legal liabilities and defenses. Responsibilities of the inspector and management planner; a discussion of comprehensive general liability policies, claims-made, and occurrence policies, environmental and pollution liability policy clauses; state liability insurance requirements; bonding and the relationship of insurance availability to bond availability.

(e) Understanding building systems. The interrelationship between building systems, including: an overview of common building physical plan layout; heat, ventilation, and air conditioning (HVAC) system types, physical organization, and where asbestos is found on HVAC components; building mechanical systems, their types and organization, and where to look for asbestos on such systems; inspecting electrical systems, including appropriate safety precautions; reading blueprints and as-built drawings.

(f) Public/employee/building occupant relations. Notifying employee organizations about the inspection; signs to warn building occupants; tact in dealing with occupants and the press; scheduling of inspections to minimize disruptions; and education of building occupants about actions being taken.

(g) Pre-inspection planning and review of previous inspection records. Scheduling the inspection and obtaining access; building record review; identification of probable homogeneous areas from blueprints or as-built drawings; consultation with maintenance or building personnel; review of previous inspection, sampling, and abatement records of a building; the role of the inspector in exclusions for previously performed inspections.

(h) Inspecting for friable and non-friable ACM and assessing the condition of friable ACM. Procedures to follow in conducting visual inspections for friable and non-friable ACM; types of building materials that may contain asbestos; touching materials to determine friability; open return air plenums and their importance in HVAC systems; assessing damage, significant damage, potential damage, and potential significant damage; amount of suspected ACM, both in total quantity and as a percentage of the total area; type of damage; accessibility; material's potential for disturbance; known or suspected causes of damage or significant damage; and deterioration as assessment factors.

(i) Bulk sampling/documentation of asbestos. Detailed discussion of the "Simplified Sampling Scheme for Friable Surfacing Materials (EPA 560/5–85–030a October 1985)"; techniques to ensure sampling in a randomly distributed manner for other than friable surfacing materials; sampling of non-friable materials, techniques for bulk sampling; inspector's sampling and repair equipment; patching or repair of damage from sampling; discussion of polarized light microscopy; choosing an accredited laboratory to analyze bulk samples; quality control and quality assurance procedures. EPA's recommendation that all bulk samples collected from school or public and commercial buildings be analyzed by a laboratory accredited under the NVLAP administered by NIST.

(j) Inspector respiratory protection and personal protective equipment. Classes and characteristics of respirator types; limitations of respirators; proper selection, inspection; donning, use, maintenance, and storage procedures for respirators; methods for field testing of the facepiece-to-face seal (positive and negative-pressure fit checks); qualitative and quantitative fit testing procedures; variability between field and laboratory protection factors that alter respiratory fit (e.g., facial hair); the components of a proper respiratory protection program; selection and use of personal protective clothing, use, storage, and handling of non-disposable clothing.

(k) Recordkeeping and writing the inspection report. Labeling of samples and keying sample identification to sampling location; recommendations on sample labeling; detailing of ACM inventory; photographs of selected sampling areas and examples of ACM condition; information required for inclusion in the management plan required for school buildings under TSCA Title II, section 203(i)(1). EPA recommends that States develop and require the use of standardized forms for recording the results of inspections in schools or public or commercial buildings, and that the use of these forms be incorporated into the curriculum of training conducted for accreditation.

(l) Regulatory review. The following topics should be covered: National Emission Standards for Hazardous Air Pollutants (NESHAP; 40 CFR part 61, Subparts A and M); EPA Worker Protection Rule (40 CFR part 763, Subpart G); OSHA Asbestos Construction Standard (29 CFR 1926.58); OSHA respirator requirements (29 CFR 1910.134); the Asbestos–Containing Materials in Schools Rule (40 CFR Part 763, Subpart E); applicable State and local regulations, and differences between Federal and State requirements where they apply, and the effects, if any, on public and nonpublic schools or commercial or public buildings.

(m) Field trip. This includes a field exercise, including a walk-through inspection; on-site discussion about information gathering and the determination of sampling locations; on-site practice in phsical[1] assessment; classroom discussion of field exercise.

(n) Course review. A review of key aspects of the training course.

4. Management Planner

All persons who prepare management plans for schools must be accredited. All persons seeking accreditation as management planners shall complete a 3–day inspector training course as outlined above and a 2–day management planner training course. Possession of current and valid inspector accreditation shall be a prerequisite for admission to the management planner training course. The management planner course shall include lectures, demonstrations, course review, and a written examination.

EPA recommends the use of audiovisual materials to complement lectures, where appropriate.

TSCA Title II does not require accreditation for persons performing the management planner role in public and commercial buildings. Nevertheless, such persons may find this training and accreditation helpful in preparing them to design or administer asbestos operations and maintenance programs for public and commercial buildings.

The management planner training course shall adequately address the following topics:

(a) Course overview. The role and responsibilities of the management planner; operations and maintenance programs; setting work priorities; protection of building occupants.

(b) Evaluation/interpretation of survey results. Review of TSCA Title II requirements for inspection and management plans for school buildings as given in section 203(i)(1) of TSCA Title II; interpretation of field data and laboratory results; comparison of field inspector's data sheet with laboratory results and site survey.

(c) Hazard assessment. Amplification of the difference between physical assessment and hazard assessment; the role of the management planner in hazard assessment; explanation of significant damage, damage, potential damage, and potential significant damage; use of a description (or decision tree) code for assessment of ACM; assessment of friable ACM; relationship of accessibility, vibration sources, use of adjoining space, and air plenums and other factors to hazard assessment.

(d) Legal implications. Liability; insurance issues specific to planners; liabilities associated with interim control

1285

measures, in-house maintenance, repair, and removal; use of results from previously performed inspections.

(e) Evaluation and selection of control options. Overview of encapsulation, enclosure, interim operations and maintenance, and removal; advantages and disadvantages of each method; response actions described via a decision tree or other appropriate method; work practices for each response action; staging and prioritizing of work in both vacant and occupied buildings; the need for containment barriers and decontamination in response actions.

(f) Role of other professionals. Use of industrial hygienists, engineers, and architects in developing technical specifications for response actions; any requirements that may exist for architect sign-off of plans; team approach to design of high-quality job specifications.

(g) Developing an operations and maintenance (O & M) plan. Purpose of the plan; discussion of applicable EPA guidance documents; what actions should be taken by custodial staff; proper cleaning procedures; steam cleaning and HEPA vacuuming; reducing disturbance of ACM; scheduling O & M for off-hours; rescheduling or canceling renovation in areas with ACM; boiler room maintenance; disposal of ACM; in-house procedures for ACM-bridging and penetrating encapsulants; pipe fittings; metal sleeves; polyvinyl chloride (PVC), canvas, and wet wraps; muslin with straps, fiber mesh cloth; mineral wool, and insulating cement; discussion of employee protection programs and staff training; case study in developing an O & M plan (development, implementation process, and problems that have been experienced).

(h) Regulatory review. Focusing on the OSHA Asbestos Construction Standard found at 29 CFR 1926.58; the National Emission Standard for Hazardous Air Pollutants (NESHAP) found at 40 CFR part 61, Subparts A (General Provisions) and M (National Emission Standard for Asbestos), EPA Worker Protection Rule found at 40 CFR part 763, Subpart G; TSCA Title II; applicable State regulations.

(i) Recordkeeping for the management planner. Use of field inspector's data sheet along with laboratory results; on-going recordkeeping as a means to track asbestos disturbance; procedures for recordkeeping. EPA recommends that States require the use of standardized forms for purposes of management plans and incorporate the use of such forms into the initial training course for management planners.

(j) Assembling and submitting the management plan. Plan requirements for schools in TSCA Title II section 203(i)(1); the management plan as a planning tool.

(k) Financing abatement actions. Economic analysis and cost estimates; development of cost estimates; present costs of abatement versus future operation and maintenance costs; Asbestos School Hazard Abatement Act grants and loans.

(*l*) Course review. A review of key aspects of the training course.

5.   Project Designer

A person must be accredited as a project designer to design any of the following activities with respect to friable ACBM in a school or public and commercial building: (1) A response action other than a SSSD maintenance activity, (2) a maintenance activity that disturbs friable ACBM other than a SSSD maintenance activity, or (3) a response action for a major fiber release episode. All persons seeking accreditation as a project designer shall complete at least a minimum 3–day training course as outlined below. The project designer course shall include lectures, demonstrations, a field trip, course review and a written examination.

EPA recommends the use of audiovisual materials to complement lectures, where appropriate.

The abatement project designer training course shall adequately address the following topics:

(a) Background information on asbestos. Identification of asbestos; examples and discussion of the uses and locations of asbestos in buildings; physical appearance of asbestos.

(b) Potential health effects related to asbestos exposure. Nature of asbestos-related diseases; routes of exposure; dose-response relationships and the lack of a safe exposure level; the synergistic effect between cigarette smoking and asbestos exposure; the latency period of asbestos-related diseases; a discussion of the relationship between asbestos exposure and asbestosis, lung cancer, mesothelioma, and cancers of other organs.

(c) Overview of abatement construction projects. Abatement as a portion of a renovation project; OSHA requirements for notification of other contractors on a multi-employer site (29 CFR 1926.58).

(d) Safety system design specifications. Design, construction, and maintenance of containment barriers and decontamination enclosure systems; positioning of warning signs; electrical and ventilation system lock-out; proper working techniques for minimizing fiber release; entry and exit procedures for the work area; use of wet methods; proper techniques for initial cleaning; use of negative-pressure exhaust ventilation equipment; use of HEPA vacuums; proper clean-up and disposal of asbestos; work practices as they apply to encapsulation, enclosure, and repair; use of glove bags and a demonstration of glove bag use.

(e) Field trip. A visit to an abatement site or other suitable building site, including on-site discussions of abatement design and building walk-through inspection. Include discussion of rationale for the concept of functional spaces during the walk-through.

(f) Employee personal protective equipment. Classes and characteristics of respirator types; limitations of respirators; proper selection, inspection; donning, use, maintenance, and storage procedures for respirators; methods for field testing of the facepiece-to-face seal (positive and negative-pressure fit checks); qualitative and quantitative fit testing procedures; variability between field and laboratory protection factors that alter respiratory fit (e.g., facial hair); the components of a proper respiratory protection program; selection and use of personal protective clothing; use, storage, and handling of non-disposable clothing.

(g) Additional safety hazards. Hazards encountered during abatement activities and how to deal with them, including electrical hazards, heat stress, air contaminants other than asbestos, fire, and explosion hazards.

(h) Fiber aerodynamics and control. Aerodynamic characteristics of asbestos fibers; importance of proper containment barriers; settling time for asbestos fibers; wet methods in abatement; aggressive air monitoring following abatement; aggressive air movement and negative-pressure exhaust ventilation as a clean-up method.

(i) Designing abatement solutions. Discussions of removal, enclosure, and encapsulation methods; asbestos waste disposal.

(j) Final clearance process. Discussion of the need for a written sampling rationale for aggressive final air clearance; requirements of a complete visual inspection; and the relationship of the visual inspection to final air clearance. EPA recommends the use of TEM for analysis of final air clearance samples. These samples should be analyzed by laboratories accredited under the NIST NVLAP.

(k) Budgeting/cost estimating. Development of cost estimates; present costs of abatement versus future operation and maintenance costs; setting priorities for abatement jobs to reduce costs.

(l) Writing abatement specifications. Preparation of and need for a written project design; means and methods specifications versus performance specifications; design of abatement in occupied buildings; modification of guide specifications for a particular building; worker and building occupant health/medical considerations; replacement of ACM with non-asbestos substitutes.

(m) Preparing abatement drawings. Significance and need for drawings, use of as-built drawings as base drawings; use of inspection photographs and on-site reports; methods of preparing abatement drawings; diagramming containment barriers; relationship of drawings to design specifications; particular problems related to abatement drawings.

(n) Contract preparation and administration.

(o) Legal/liabilities/defenses. Insurance considerations; bonding; hold-harmless clauses; use of abatement contractor's liability insurance; claims made versus occurrence policies.

(p) Replacement. Replacement of asbestos with asbestos-free substitutes.

(q) Role of other consultants. Development of technical specification sections by industrial hygienists or engineers; the multi-disciplinary team approach to abatement design.

(r) Occupied buildings. Special design procedures required in occupied buildings; education of occupants;

extra monitoring recommendations; staging of work to minimize occupant exposure; scheduling of renovation to minimize exposure.

(s) Relevant Federal, State, and local regulatory requirements, procedures and standards, including, but not limited to:

(i) Requirements of TSCA Title II.

(ii) National Emission Standards for Hazardous Air Pollutants, (40 CFR part 61) subparts A (General Provisions) and M (National Emission Standard for Asbestos).

(iii) OSHA Respirator Standard found at 29 CFR 1910.134.

(iv) EPA Worker Protection Rule found at 40 CFR part 763, subpart G.

(v) OSHA Asbestos Construction Standard found at 29 CFR 1926.58.

(vi) OSHA Hazard Communication Standard found at 29 CFR 1926.59.

(t) Course review. A review of key aspects of the training course.

6. Project Monitor

EPA recommends that States adopt training and accreditation requirements for persons seeking to perform work as project monitors. Project monitors observe abatement activities performed by contractors and generally serve as a building owner's representative to ensure that abatement work is completed according to specification and in compliance with all relevant statutes and regulations. They may also perform the vital role of air monitoring for purposes of determining final clearance. EPA recommends that a State seeking to accredit individuals as project monitors consider adopting a minimum 5–day training course covering the topics outlined below. The course outlined below consists of lectures and demonstrations, at least 6 hours of hands-on training, course review, and a written examination. The hands-on training component might be satisfied by having the student simulate participation in or performance of any of the relevant job functions or activities (or by incorporation of the workshop component described in item "n" below of this unit).

EPA recommends that the project monitor training course adequately address the following topics:

(a) Roles and responsibilities of the project monitor. Definition and responsibilities of the project monitor, including regulatory/specification compliance monitoring, air monitoring, conducting visual inspections, and final clearance monitoring.

(b) Characteristics of asbestos and asbestos-containing materials. Typical uses of asbestos; physical appearance of asbestos; review of asbestos abatement and control techniques; presentation of the health effects of asbestos exposure, including routes of exposure, dose-response relationships, and latency periods for asbestos-related diseases.

(c) Federal asbestos regulations. Overview of pertinent EPA regulations, including: NESHAP, 40 CFR part 61, subparts A and M; AHERA, 40 CFR part 763, subpart E; and the EPA Worker Protection Rule, 40 CFR part 763, subpart G. Overview of pertinent OSHA regulations, including: Construction Industry Standard for Asbestos, 29 CFR 1926.58; Respirator Standard, 29 CFR 1910.134; and the Hazard Communication Standard, 29 CFR 1926.59. Applicable State and local asbestos regulations; regulatory interrelationships.

(d) Understanding building construction and building systems. Building construction basics, building physical plan layout; understanding building systems (HVAC, electrical, etc.); layout and organization, where asbestos is likely to be found on building systems; renovations and the effect of asbestos abatement on building systems.

(e) Asbestos abatement contracts, specifications, and drawings. Basic provisions of the contract; relationships between principle parties, establishing chain of command; types of specifications, including means and methods, performance, and proprietary and nonproprietary; reading and interpreting records and abatement drawings; discussion of change orders; common enforcement responsibilities and authority of project monitor.

(f) Response actions and abatement practices. Pre-work inspections; pre-work considerations, precleaning of the work area, removal of furniture, fixtures, and equipment; shutdown/modification of building systems; construction and maintenance of containment barriers, proper demarcation of work areas; work area entry/exit, hygiene practices; determining the effectiveness of air filtration equipment; techniques for minimizing fiber release, wet methods, continuous cleaning; abatement methods other than removal; abatement area clean-up procedures; waste transport and disposal procedures; contingency planning for emergency response.

(g) Asbestos abatement equipment. Typical equipment found on an abatement project; air filtration devices, vacuum systems, negative pressure differential monitoring; HEPA filtration units, theory of filtration, design/construction of HEPA filtration units, qualitative and quantitative performance of HEPA filtration units, sizing the ventilation requirements, location of HEPA filtration units, qualitative and quantitative tests of containment barrier integrity; best available technology.

(h) Personal protective equipment. Proper selection of respiratory protection; classes and characteristics of respirator types, limitations of respirators; proper use of other safety equipment, protective clothing selection, use, and proper handling, hard/bump hats, safety shoes; breathing air systems, high pressure v. low pressure, testing for Grade D air, determining proper backup air volumes.

(i) Air monitoring strategies. Sampling equipment, sampling pumps (low v. high volume), flow regulating devices (critical and limiting orifices), use of fibrous aerosol monitors on abatement projects; sampling media, types of filters, types of cassettes, filter orientation, storage and shipment of filters; calibration techniques,

1288

primary calibration standards, secondary calibration standards, temperature/pressure effects, frequency of calibration, recordkeeping and field work documentation, calculations; air sample analysis, techniques available and limitations of AHERA on their use, transmission electron microscopy (background to sample preparation and analysis, air sample conditions which prohibit analysis, EPA's recommended technique for analysis of final air clearance samples), phase contrast microscopy (background to sample preparation, and AHERA's limits on the use of phase contrast micrscopy [2]), what each technique measures; analytical methodologies, AHERA TEM protocol, NIOSH 7400, OSHA reference method (non clearance), EPA recommendation for clearance (TEM); sampling strategies for clearance monitoring, types of air samples (personal breathing zone v. fixed-station area) sampling location and objectives (pre-abatement, during abatement, and clearance monitoring), number of samples to be collected, minimum and maximum air volumes, clearance monitoring (post-visual-inspection) (number of samples required, selection of sampling locations, period of sampling, aggressive sampling, interpretations of sampling results, calculations), quality assurance; special sampling problems, crawl spaces, acceptable samples for laboratory analysis, sampling in occupied buildings (barrier monitoring).

(j) Safety and health issues other than asbestos. Confined-space entry, electrical hazards, fire and explosion concerns, ladders and scaffolding, heat stress, air contaminants other than asbestos, fall hazards, hazardous materials on abatement projects.

(k) Conducting visual inspections. Inspections during abatement, visual inspections using the ASTM E1368 document; conducting inspections for completeness of removal; discussion of "how clean is clean?"

(l) Legal responsibilities and liabilities of project monitors. Specification enforcement capabilities; regulatory enforcement; licensing; powers delegated to project monitors through contract documents.

(m) Recordkeeping and report writing. Developing project logs/daily logs (what should be included, who sees them); final report preparation; recordkeeping under Federal regulations.

(n) Workshops (6 hours spread over 3 days). Contracts, specifications, and drawings: This workshop could consist of each participant being issued a set of contracts, specifications, and drawings and then being asked to answer questions and make recommendations to a project architect, engineer or to the building owner based on given conditions and these documents.

Air monitoring strategies/asbestos abatement equipment: This workshop could consist of simulated abatement sites for which sampling strategies would have to be developed (i.e., occupied buildings, industrial situations). Through demonstrations and exhibition, the project monitor may also be able to gain a better understanding of the function of various pieces of equipment used on abatement projects (air filtration units, water filtration units, negative pressure monitoring devices, sampling pump calibration devices, etc.).

Conducting visual inspections: This workshop could consist, ideally, of an interactive video in which a participant is "taken through" a work area and asked to make notes of what is seen. A series of questions will be asked which are designed to stimulate a person's recall of the area. This workshop could consist of a series of two or three videos with different site conditions and different degrees of cleanliness.

C. Examinations

1. Each State shall administer a closed book examination or designate other entities such as State-approved providers of training courses to administer the closed-book examination to persons seeking accreditation who have completed an initial training course. Demonstration testing may also be included as part of the examination. A person seeking initial accreditation in a specific discipline must pass the examination for that discipline in order to receive accreditation. For example, a person seeking accreditation as an abatement project designer must pass the State's examination for abatement project designer.

States may develop their own examinations, have providers of training courses develop examinations, or use standardized examinations developed for purposes of accreditation under TSCA Title II. In addition, States may supplement standardized examinations with questions about State regulations. States may obtain commercially developed standardized examinations, develop standardized examinations independently, or do so in cooperation with other States, or with commercial or non-profit providers on a regional or national basis. EPA recommends the use of standardized, scientifically-validated testing instruments, which may be beneficial in terms of both promoting competency and in fostering accreditation reciprocity between States.

Each examination shall adequately cover the topics included in the training course for that discipline. Each person who completes a training course, passes the required examination, and fulfills whatever other requirements the State imposes must receive an accreditation certificate in a specific discipline. Whether a State directly issues accreditation certificates, or authorizes training providers to issue accreditation certificates, each certificate issued to an accredited person must contain the following minimum information:

a. A unique certificate number

b. Name of accredited person

c. Discipline of the training course completed.

d. Dates of the training course.

e. Date of the examination.

f. An expiration date of 1 year after the date upon which the person successfully completed the course and examination.

g. The name, address, and telephone number of the training provider that issued the certificate.

h. A statement that the person receiving the certificate has completed the requisite training for asbestos accreditation under TSCA Title II.

States or training providers who reaccredit persons based upon completion of required refresher training must also provide accreditation certificates with all of the above information, except the examination date may be omitted if a State does not require a refresher examination for reaccreditation.

Where a State licenses accredited persons but has authorized training providers to issue accreditation certificates, the State may issue licenses in the form of photo-identification cards. Where this applies, EPA recommends that the State licenses should include all of the same information required for the accreditation certificates. A State may also choose to issue photo-identification cards in addition to the required accreditation certificates.

Accredited persons must have their initial and current accreditation certificates at the location where they are conducting work.

2. The following are the requirements for examination in each discipline:

a. Worker:

i. 50 multiple-choice questions

ii. Passing score: 70 percent correct

b. Contractor/Supervisor:

i. 100 multiple-choice questions

ii. Passing score: 70 percent correct

c. Inspector:

i. 50 Multiple-choice questions

ii. Passing score: 70 percent correct

d. Management Planner:

i. 50 Multiple-choice questions

ii. Passing score: 70 percent correct

e. Project Designer:

i. 100 multiple-choice questions

ii. Passing score: 70 percent correct

D. Continuing Education

For all disciplines, a State's accreditation program shall include annual refresher training as a requirement for reaccreditation as indicated below:

1. Workers: One full day of refresher training.

2. Contractor/Supervisors: One full day of refresher training.

3. Inspectors: One half-day of refresher training.

4. Management Planners: One half-day of inspector refresher training and one half-day of refresher training for management planners.

5. Project Designers: One full day of refresher training.

The refresher courses shall be specific to each discipline. Refresher courses shall be conducted as separate and distinct courses and not combined with any other training during the period of the refresher course. For each discipline, the refresher course shall review and discuss changes in Federal, State, and local regulations, developments in state-of-the-art procedures, and a review of key aspects of the initial training course as determined by the State. After completing the annual refresher course, persons shall have their accreditation extended for an additional year from the date of the refresher course. A State may consider requiring persons to pass reaccreditation examinations at specific intervals (for example, every 3 years).

EPA recommends that States formally establish a 12–month grace period to enable formerly accredited persons with expired certificates to complete refresher training and have their accreditation status reinstated without having to re-take the initial training course.

E.   Qualifications

In addition to requiring training and an examination, a State may require candidates for accreditation to meet other qualification and/or experience standards that the State considers appropriate for some or all disciplines. States may choose to consider requiring qualifications similar to the examples outlined below for inspectors, management planners and project designers. States may modify these examples as appropriate. In addition, States may want to include some requirements based on experience in performing a task directly as a part of a job or in an apprenticeship role. They may also wish to consider additional criteria for the approval of training course instructors beyond those prescribed by EPA.

1. Inspectors: Qualifications—possess a high school diploma. States may want to require an Associate's Degree in specific fields (e.g., environmental or physical sciences).

2. Management Planners: Qualifications—Registered architect, engineer, or certified industrial hygienist or related scientific field.

3. Project Designers: Qualifications—registered architect, engineer, or certified industrial hygienist.

4. Asbestos Training Course Instructor: Qualifications—academic credentials and/or field experience in asbestos abatement.

EPA recommends that States prescribe minimum qualification standards for training instructors employed by training providers.

F.   Recordkeeping Requirements for Training Providers

All approved providers of accredited asbestos training courses must comply with the following minimum record-keeping requirements.

1. Training course materials. A training provider must retain copies of all instructional materials used in

the delivery of the classroom training such as student manuals, instructor notebooks and handouts.

2. Instructor qualifications. A training provider must retain copies of all instructors' resumes, and the documents approving each instructor issued by either EPA or a State. Instructors must be approved by either EPA or a State before teaching courses for accreditation purposes. A training provider must notify EPA or the State, as appropriate, in advance whenever it changes course instructors. Records must accurately identify the instructors that taught each particular course for each date that a course is offered.

3. Examinations. A training provider must document that each person who receives an accreditation certificate for an initial training course has achieved a passing score on the examination. These records must clearly indicate the date upon which the exam was administered, the training course and discipline for which the exam was given, the name of the person who proctored the exam, a copy of the exam, and the name and test score of each person taking the exam. The topic and dates of the training course must correspond to those listed on that person's accreditation certificate. States may choose to apply these same requirements to examinations for refresher training courses.

4. Accreditation certificates. The training providers or States, whichever issues the accreditation certificate, shall maintain records that document the names of all persons who have been awarded certificates, their certificate numbers, the disciplines for which accreditation was conferred, training and expiration dates, and the training location. The training provider or State shall maintain the records in a manner that allows verification by telephone of the required information.

5. Verification of certificate information. EPA recommends that training providers of refresher training courses confirm that their students possess valid accreditation before granting course admission. EPA further recommends that training providers offering the initial management planner training course verify that students have met the prerequisite of possessing valid inspector accreditation at the time of course admission.

6. Records retention and access.

(a) The training provider shall maintain all required records for a minimum of 3 years. The training provider, however, may find it advantageous to retain these records for a longer period of time.

(b) The training provider must allow reasonable access to all of the records required by the MAP, and to any other records which may be required by States for the approval of asbestos training providers or the accreditation of asbestos training courses, to both EPA and to State Agencies, on request. EPA encourages training providers to make this information equally accessible to the general public.

(c) If a training provider ceases to conduct training, the training provider shall notify the approving government body (EPA or the State) and give it the opportunity to take possession of that providers asbestos training records.

G. Deaccreditation

1. States must establish criteria and procedures for deaccrediting persons accredited as workers, contractor/supervisors, inspectors, management planners, and project designers. States must follow their own administrative procedures in pursuing deaccreditation actions. At a minimum, the criteria shall include:

(a) Performing work requiring accreditation at a job site without being in physical possession of initial and current accreditation certificates;

(b) Permitting the duplication or use of one's own accreditation certificate by another;

(c) Performing work for which accreditation has not been received; or

(d) Obtaining accreditation from a training provider that does not have approval to offer training for the particular discipline from either EPA or from a State that has a contractor accreditation plan at least as stringent as the EPA MAP. EPA may directly pursue deaccreditation actions without reliance on State deaccreditation or enforcement authority or actions. In addition to the above-listed situations, the Administrator may suspend or revoke the accreditation of persons who have been subject to a final order imposing a civil penalty or convicted under section 16 of TSCA, 15 U.S.C. 2615 or 2647, for violations of 40 CFR part 763, or section 113 of the Clean Air Act, 42 U.S.C. 7413, for violations of 40 CFR part 61, subpart M.

2. Any person who performs asbestos work requiring accreditation under section 206(a) of TSCA, 15 U.S.C. 2646(a), without such accreditation is in violation of TSCA. The following persons are not accredited for purposes of section 206(a) of TSCA:

(a) Any person who obtains accreditation through fraudulent representation of training or examination documents;

(b) Any person who obtains training documentation through fraudulent means;

(c) Any person who gains admission to and completes refresher training through fraudulent representation of initial or previous refresher training documentation; or

(d) Any person who obtains accreditation through fraudulent representation of accreditation requirements such as education, training, professional registration, or experience.

H. Reciprocity

EPA recommends that each State establish reciprocal arrangements with other States that have established accreditation programs that meet or exceed the requirements of the MAP. Such arrangements might address cooperation in licensing determinations, the review and approval of training programs and/or instructors, candi-

date testing and exam administration, curriculum development, policy formulation, compliance monitoring, and the exchange of information and data. The benefits to be derived from these arrangements include a potential cost-savings from the reduction of duplicative activity and the attainment of a more professional accredited workforce as States are able to refine and improve the effectiveness of their programs based upon the experience and methods of other States.

II. EPA Approval Process for State Accreditation Programs

A. States may seek approval for a single discipline or all disciplines as specified in the MAP. For example, a State that currently only requires worker accreditation may receive EPA approval for that discipline alone. EPA encourages States that currently do not have accreditation requirements for all disciplines required under section 206(b)(2) of TSCA, 15 U.S.C. 2646(b)(2), to seek EPA approval for those disciplines the State does accredit. As States establish accreditation requirements for the remaining disciplines, the requested information outlined below should be submitted to EPA as soon as possible. Any State that had an accreditation program approved by EPA under an earlier version of the MAP may follow the same procedures to obtain EPA approval of their accreditation program under this MAP.

B. Partial approval of a State Program for the accreditation of one or more disciplines does not mean that the State is in full compliance with TSCA where the deadline for that State to have adopted a State Plan no less stringent than the MAP has already passed. State Programs which are at least as stringent as the MAP for one or more of the accredited disciplines may, however, accredit persons in those disciplines only.

C. States seeking EPA approval or reapproval of accreditation programs shall submit the following information to the Regional Asbestos Coordinator at their EPA Regional office:

1. A copy of the legislation establishing or upgrading the State's accreditation program (if applicable).

2. A copy of the State's accreditation regulations or revised regulations.

3. A letter to the Regional Asbestos Coordinator that clearly indicates how the State meets the program requirements of this MAP. Addresses for each of the Regional Asbestos Coordinators are shown below:

EPA, Region I, (ATC–111) Asbestos Coordinator, JFK Federal Bldg., Boston, MA 02203–2211, (617) 565–3836.

EPA, Region II, (MS–500), Asbestos Coordinator, 2890 Woodbridge Ave., Edison, NJ 08837–3679, (908) 321–6671.

EPA, Region III, (3AT–33), Asbestos Coordinator, 841 Chestnut Bldg., Philadelphia, PA 19107, (215) 597–3160.

EPA, Region IV, Asbestos Coordinator, 345 Courtland St., N.E., Atlanta, GA 30365, (404) 347–5014.

EPA, Region V, (SP–14J), Asbestos Coordinator, 77 W. Jackson Blvd., Chicago, IL 60604–3590, (312) 886–6003.

EPA, Region VI, (6T–PT), Asbestos Coordinator, 1445 Ross Ave., Dallas, TX 75202–2744, (214) 655–7244.

EPA, Region VII, (ARTX/ASBS), Asbestos Coordinator, 726 Minnesota Ave., Kansas City, KS 66101, (913) 551–7020.

EPA, Region VIII, (8AT–TS), Asbestos Coordinator, 1 Denver Place, Suite 500, 999—18th St., Denver, CO 80202–2405, (303) 293–1442.

EPA, Region IX, (A–4–4), Asbestos Coordinator, 75 Hawthorne St., San Francisco, CA 94105, (415) 744–1128.

EPA, Region X, (AT–083), Asbestos Coordinator, 1200 Sixth Ave., Seattle, WA 98101, (206) 553–4762.

EPA maintains a listing of all those States that have applied for and received EPA approval for having accreditation requirements that are at least as stringent as the MAP for one or more disciplines. Any training courses approved by an EPA-approved State Program are considered to be EPA-approved for purposes of accreditation.

III.   Approval of Training Courses

Individuals or groups wishing to sponsor training courses for disciplines required to be accredited under section 206(b)(1)(A) of TSCA, 15 U.S.C. 2646(b)(1)(A), may apply for approval from States that have accreditation program requirements that are at least as stringent as this MAP. For a course to receive approval, it must meet the requirements for the course as outlined in this MAP, and any other requirements imposed by the State from which approval is being sought. Courses that have been approved by a State with an accreditation program at least as stringent as this MAP are approved under section 206(a) of TSCA, 15 U.S.C. 2646(a), for that particular State, and also for any other State that does not have an accreditation program as stringent as this MAP.

A.   Initial Training Course Approval

A training provider must submit the following minimum information to a State as part of its application for the approval of each training course:

1.   The course provider's name, address, and telephone number.

2.   A list of any other States that currently approve the training course.

3.   The course curriculum.

4.   A letter from the provider of the training course that clearly indicates how the course meets the MAP requirements for:

a.   Length of training in days.

b.   Amount and type of hands-on training.

c.   Examination (length, format, and passing score).

d.   Topics covered in the course.

5.   A copy of all course materials (student manuals, instructor notebooks, handouts, etc.).

6.   A detailed statement about the development of the examination used in the course.

7.   Names and qualifications of all course instructors. Instructors must have academic and/or field experience in asbestos abatement.

8.   A description of and an example of the numbered certificates issued to students who attend the course and pass the examination.

B.   Refresher Training Course Approval

The following minimum information is required for approval of refresher training courses by States:

1.   The length of training in half-days or days.

2.   The topics covered in the course.

3.   A copy of all course materials (student manuals, instructor notebooks, handouts, etc.).

4.   The names and qualifications of all course instructors. Instructors must have academic and/or field experience in asbestos abatement.

5.   A description of and an example of the numbered certificates issued to students who complete the refresher course and pass the examination, if required.

C.   Withdrawal of Training Course Approval

States must establish criteria and procedures for suspending or withdrawing approval from accredited training programs. States should follow their own administrative procedures in pursuing actions for suspension or withdrawal of approval of training programs. At a minimum, the criteria shall include:

(1) Misrepresentation of the extent of a training course's approval by a State or EPA;

(2) Failure to submit required information or notifications in a timely manner;

(3) Failure to maintain requisite records;

(4) Falsification of accreditation records, instructor qualifications, or other accreditation information; or

(5) Failure to adhere to the training standards and requirements of the EPA MAP or State Accreditation Program, as appropriate.

In addition to the criteria listed above, EPA may also suspend or withdraw a training course's approval where an approved training course instructor, or other person with supervisory authority over the delivery of training has been found in violation of other asbestos regulations administered by EPA. An administrative or judicial finding of violation, or execution of a consent agreement and order under 40 CFR 22.18, constitutes evidence of a failure to comply with relevant statutes or regulations. States may wish to adopt this criterion modified to include their own asbestos statutes or regulations. EPA may also suspend or withdraw approval of training programs where a training provider has submitted false information as a part of the self-certification required under Unit V.B. of the revised MAP.

Training course providers shall permit representatives of EPA or the State which approved their training courses to attend, evaluate, and monitor any training course without charge. EPA or State compliance inspection staff are not required to give advance notice of their inspections. EPA may suspend or withdraw State or EPA approval of a training course based upon the criteria specified in this Unit III.C.

IV. EPA Procedures for Suspension or Revocation of Accreditation or Training Course Approval

A. If the Administrator decides to suspend or revoke the accreditation of any person or suspend or withdraw the approval of a training course, the Administrator will notify the affected entity of the following:

1. The grounds upon which the suspension, revocation, or withdrawal is based.

2. The time period during which the suspension, revocation, or withdrawal is effective, whether permanent or otherwise.

3. The conditions, if any, under which the affected entity may receive accreditation or approval in the future.

4. Any additional conditions which the Administrator may impose.

5. The opportunity to request a hearing prior to final Agency action to suspend or revoke accreditation or suspend or withdraw approval.

B. If a hearing is requested by the accredited person or training course provider pursuant to the preceding paragraph, the Administrator will:

1. Notify the affected entity of those assertions of law and fact upon which the action to suspend, revoke, or withdraw is based.

2. Provide the affected entity an opportunity to offer written statements of facts, explanations, comments, and arguments relevant to the proposed action.

3. Provide the affected entity such other procedural opportunities as the Administrator may deem appropriate to ensure a fair and impartial hearing.

4. Appoint an EPA attorney as Presiding Officer to conduct the hearing. No person shall serve as Presiding Officer if he or she has had any prior connection with the specific case.

C. The Presiding Officer appointed pursuant to the preceding paragraph shall:

1. Conduct a fair, orderly, and impartial hearing, without unnecessary delay.

2. Consider all relevant evidence, explanation, comment, and argument submitted pursuant to the preceding paragraph.

3. Promptly notify the affected entity of his or her decision and order. Such an order is a final Agency action.

D. If the Administrator determines that the public health, interest, or welfare warrants immediate action to suspend the accreditation of any person or the approval of any training course provider, the Administrator will:

1. Notify the affected entity of the grounds upon which the emergency suspension is based;

2. Notify the affected entity of the time period during which the emergency suspension is effective.

3. Notify the affected entity of the Administrator's intent to suspend or revoke accreditation or suspend or withdraw training course approval, as appropriate, in accordance with Unit IV.A. above. If such suspension, revocation, or withdrawal notice has not previously been issued, it will be issued at the same time the emergency suspension notice is issued.

E. Any notice, decision, or order issued by the Administrator under this section, and any documents filed by an accredited person or approved training course provider in a hearing under this section, shall be available to the public except as otherwise provided by section 14 of TSCA or by 40 CFR part 2. Any such hearing at which oral testimony is presented shall be open to the public, except that the Presiding Officer may exclude the public to the extent necessary to allow presentation of information which may be entitled to confidential treatment under section 14 of TSCA or 40 CFR part 2.

V. Implementation Schedule

The various requirements of this MAP become effective in accordance with the following schedules:

A. Requirements applicable to State Programs

1. Each State shall adopt an accreditation plan that is at least as stringent as this MAP within 180 days after the commencement of the first regular session of the legislature of the State that is convened on or after April 4, 1994.

2. If a State has adopted an accreditation plan at least as stringent as this MAP as of April 4, 1994, the State may continue to:

a. Conduct TSCA training pursuant to this MAP.

b. Approve training course providers to conduct training and to issue accreditation that satisfies the requirements for TSCA accreditation under this MAP.

c. Issue accreditation that satisfies the requirements for TSCA accreditation under this MAP.

3. A State that had complied with an earlier version of the MAP, but has not adopted an accreditation plan at least as stringent as this MAP by April 4, 1994, may:

a. Conduct TSCA training which remains in compliance with the requirements of Unit V.B. of this MAP. After such training has been self-certified in accordance with Unit V.B. of this MAP, the State may issue accreditation that satisfies the requirement for TSCA accreditation under this MAP.

b. Sustain its approval for any training course providers to conduct training and issue TSCA accreditation that the State had approved before April 4, 1994, and that remain in compliance with Unit V.B. of this MAP.

c. Issue accreditation pursuant to an earlier version of the MAP that provisionally satisfies the requirement for TSCA accreditation until October 4, 1994. Such a State may not approve new TSCA training course providers to conduct training or to issue TSCA accreditation that satisfies the requirements of this MAP until the State adopts an accreditation plan that is at least as stringent as this MAP.

4. A State that had complied with an earlier version of the MAP, but fails to adopt a plan as stringent as this MAP by the deadline established in Unit V.A.1., is subject to the following after that deadline date:

a. The State loses any status it may have held as an EPA-approved State for accreditation purposes under section 206 of TSCA, 15 U.S.C. 2646.

b. All training course providers approved by the State lose State approval to conduct training and issue accreditation that satisfies the requirements for TSCA accreditation under this MAP.

c. The State may not:

i. Conduct training for accreditation purposes under section 206 of TSCA, 15 U.S.C. 2646.

ii. Approve training course providers to conduct training or issue accreditation that satisfies the requirements for TSCA accreditation; or

iii. Issue accreditation that satisfies the requirement for TSCA accreditation. EPA will extend EPA-approval to any training course provider that loses State approval because the State does not comply with the deadline, so long as the provider is in compliance with Unit V.B. of this MAP, and the provider is approved by a State that had complied with an earlier version of the MAP as of the day before the State loses its EPA approval.

5. A State that does not have an accreditation program that satisfies the requirements for TSCA accreditation under either an earlier version of the MAP or this MAP, may not:

a. Conduct training for accreditation purposes under section 206 of TSCA, 15 U.S.C. 2646;

b. Approve training course providers to conduct training or issue accreditation that satisfies the requirements for TSCA accreditation; or

c. Issue accreditation that satisfies the requirement for TSCA accreditation.

B. Requirements applicable to Training Courses and Providers

As of October 4, 1994, an approved training provider must certify to EPA and to any State that has approved the provider for TSCA accreditation, that each of the provider's training courses complies with the requirements of this MAP. The written submission must document in specific detail the changes made to each training course in order to comply with the requirements of this

MAP and clearly state that the provider is also in compliance with all other requirements of this MAP, including the new recordkeeping and certificate provisions. Each submission must include the following statement signed by an authorized representative of the training provider: "Under civil and criminal penalties of law for the making or submission of false or fraudulent statements or representations (18 U.S.C. 1001 and 15 U.S.C. 2615), I certify that the training described in this submission complies with all applicable requirements of Title II of TSCA, 40 CFR part 763, Appendix C to Subpart E, as revised, and any other applicable Federal, state or local requirements." A consolidated self-certification submission from each training provider that addresses all of its approved training courses is permissible and encouraged.

The self-certification must be sent via registered mail, to EPA Headquarters at the following address: Attn. Self–Certification Program, Field Programs Branch, Chemical Management Division (7404), Office of Pollution Prevention and Toxics, Environmental Protection Agency, 401 M St., SW., Washington, DC 20460. A duplicate copy of the complete submission must also be sent to any States from which approval had been obtained.

The timely receipt of a complete self-certification by EPA and all approving States shall have the effect of extending approval under this MAP to the training courses offered by the submitting provider. If a self-certification is not received by the approving government bodies on or before the due date, the affected training course is not approved under this MAP. Such training providers must then reapply for approval of these training courses pursuant to the procedures outlined in Unit III.

C. Requirements applicable to Accredited Persons.

Persons accredited by a State with an accreditation program no less stringent than an earlier version of the MAP or by an EPA-approved training provider as of April 3, 1994, are accredited in accordance with the requirements of this MAP, and are not required to retake initial training. They must continue to comply with the requirements for annual refresher training in Unit I.D. of the revised MAP.

D. Requirements applicable to Non–Accredited Persons.

In order to perform work requiring accreditation under TSCA Title II, persons who are not accredited by a State with an accreditation program no less stringent than an earlier version of the MAP or by an EPA-approved training provider as of April 3, 1994, must comply with the upgraded training requirements of this MAP by no later than October 4, 1994. Non-accredited persons may obtain initial accreditation on a provisional basis by successfully completing any of the training programs approved under an earlier version of the MAP, and thereby perform work during the first 6 months after this MAP takes effect. However, by October 4, 1994, these persons must have successfully completed an upgraded training program that fully complies with the requirements of this MAP in order to continue to perform work requiring accreditation under section 206 of TSCA, 15 U.S.C. 2646.

[52 FR 15876, Apr. 30, 1987; 59 FR 5236, Feb. 3, 1994; 60 FR 31917, June 19, 1995]

¹ So in official copy, probably should be "physical".

² So in official copy, probably should be "microscopy".

§ 341.17. Approval of Asbestos Cement Pipe Training and Asbestos Cement Pipe Course Providers for the Purpose of Employer Exemption from Registration Requirements.

(a) Scope and Application.

Any course provider (individual or business entity) desiring to provide asbestos cement pipe training for the purpose of employer exemption from requirements for "asbestos-related work" as provided by Section 1529(r) and Labor Code Section 6501.8(c) shall apply for and obtain approval pursuant to this section.

(b) Criteria for Asbestos Cement Pipe Course Approval.

(1) Initial course. The course shall consist of a minimum of four (4) hours training for workers and for supervisors, and shall include, but is not limited to the following topics:

(A) The physical characteristics and health hazards of asbestos.

(B) The types of asbestos cement pipe an employee may encounter in his or her specific work assignments.

(C) Safe practices and procedures for minimizing asbestos exposures from operations involving asbestos cement pipe.

(D) A review of general industry and construction safety orders relating to asbestos exposure.

(E) Hands-on instruction using pipe and the tools and equipment employees will use in the work place.

(2) Refresher course. Annual re-training must be provided in accordance with Section 1529(k)(9)(B). The annual refresher shall include at least two hours of review of the important elements covered in the initial course, any changes in federal and state asbestos regulations, and the latest developments in state of the art practices for work involving asbestos cement pipe.

(c) Applying for Course Approval.

Any individual or entity that desires to provide Division approved asbestos cement pipe training may apply to the Division at this address:

Division of Occupational Safety and Health AC Pipe Training Approval, P.O. Box 420603, San Francisco, CA 94142

The following information shall be provided:

(1) The name and address of the individual or entity providing the training, the name and title of the person submitting the application with his or her signature and a statement certifying that the information and material submitted will be used in the course for which approval is being sought, and the name, title, and telephone number of the person whom the Division should contact regarding course approval matters.

(2) A written description of the training topics and hands-on practices that will be taught, and a copy of any training documents and visual training aids that will be used.

(d) Application Fee.

(1) The application fee is $200 for the initial course and $100 for the annual refresher course.

(2) Remittance for the application fee shall be made payable to Asbestos Training Approval Account.

(3) The fee is not refundable.

(e) Process of Application.

(1) Within 25 business days of receipt of an application, the Division shall notify the applicant in writing that the application is approved and issue a Division Course Approval Number, or that the application is deficient. The notice shall specify what additional information or documentation is necessary when the application is found to be deficient.

(2) Within 15 business days of receipt of the requested additional information or documentation, the Division shall notify the applicant in writing that the application is approved and issue a Division Approval Number, or that the application is still deficient and denied.

(3) An applicant whose application is denied may submit a new application with another application fee.

(f) Training Records.

(1) To maintain the course approval, the course provider shall maintain records which give the names of the trainees, the dates that the training was provided, the name(s) of the instructor(s) giving the training, and the Division issued Course Approval Number. This applies whether or not the course provider is also the employer.

(2) The course provider shall provide a copy of the training records to the Division when requested.

(3) Training records shall be maintained for a minimum of three years.

(g) Revocation of Course Approval.

(1) The Division may at any time, upon showing of good cause and after notice and an opportunity to be heard, revoke any course approval issued pursuant to this section.

(2) Notice shall be writing and served upon the course provider at least 24 hours in advance of the hearing. Service shall be by personal service or certified mail to the course provider address as shown on the course approval application. The notice shall specify the reasons for the action taken by the Division in order that the course provider may prepare for the hearing.

(3) The hearing shall be held as soon as possible at the Division's headquarters office or at such other location as may be designated by the Division and shall be presided over by the Chief of the Division or authorized designee.

(4) At the hearing the Division shall establish good cause for the action taken by it. Good cause is deemed to exist if the Division establishes that the course provider did not provide the required training.

(5) The course provider receiving a revocation from the Division may appeal such revocation to the Director. The Director shall hold a hearing at such place designated by the Director or authorized designee for the convenience of the attending parties within two working days of the course provider's appeal. The course provider shall have the burden of establishing that the revocation is not justified. The hearing shall be presided over by the Director or authorized designee.

(6) Following the hearing, the Director shall issue a decision. The Director's decision shall be final except for any rehearing or judicial review provided for by law. All requests for hearing shall be filed with the Director within 10 days from the date of the Director's decision.

Article 3.   Reporting Work–Connected Injuries

§ 342.   Reporting Work–Connected Fatalities and Serious Injuries

(a) Every employer shall report immediately by telephone or telegraph to the nearest District Office of the Division of Occupational Safety and Health any serious injury or illness, or death, of an employee occurring in a place of employment or in connection with any employment.

Immediately means as soon as practically possible but not longer than 8 hours after the employer knows or with diligent inquiry would have known of the death or serious injury or illness. If the employer can demonstrate that exigent circumstances exist, the time frame for the report may be made no longer than 24 hours after the incident.

Serious injury or illness is defined in section 330(h), Title 8, California Administrative Code.

(b) Whenever a state, county, or local fire or police agency is called to an accident involving an employee covered by this part in which a serious injury, or illness, or death occurs, the nearest office of the Division of Occupational Safety and Health shall be notified by telephone immediately by the responding agency.

(c) When making such report, whether by telephone or telegraph, the reporting party shall include the following information, if available:

(1) Time and date of accident.

(2) Employer's name, address and telephone number.

(3) Name and job title, or badge number of person reporting the accident.

(4) Address of site of accident or event.

(5) Name of person to contact at site of accident.

(6) Name and address of injured employee(s).

(7) Nature of injury.

(8) Location where injured employee(s) was (were) moved to.

(9) List and identity of other law enforcement agencies present at the site of accident.

(10) Description of accident and whether the accident scene or instrumentality has been altered.

(d) The reporting in (a) and (b) above, is in addition to any other reports required by law and may be made by any person authorized by the employers, state, county, or local agencies to make such reports.

Article 4.   Aerial Passenger Tramway Inspection Fee Schedule

§ 343.   Aerial Passenger Tramway Inspection Fee Schedule

(a) Inspection Fees. Pursuant to Section 7350 of the Labor Code the Division hereby fixes inspection fees as follows:

(1) A fee of $125.00 per hour or fraction thereof shall be charged for new inspections, major alterations, operational inspections, and consultations performed by a Division engineer.

(2) Fees shall be charged for actual inspection time. Actual inspection time begins from the time the Division engineer arrives, by appointment, in the area and continues until the engineer has completed the Division's report and is ready to leave the area.

(3) Permit of an existing installation shall be:

Rope Toe	$ 125.00 per unit
Surface Lift	$ 250.00 per unit
Fixed Grip Lift	
-up to 1000 feet	$ 250.00 per unit
-up to 4000 feet	$ 375.00 per unit
-over 4000 feet	$ 625.00 per unit
Detachable Grip Lift	
Chair-up to 1000 feet	$ 750.00 per unit
Chair-up to 4000 feet	$1,000.00 per unit
Chair-over 4000 feet	$1,250.00 per unit
Gondola-up to 2000 feet	$ 750.00 per unit
Gondola-over 2000 feet	$1,250.00 per unit
Aerial Tramway	$1,500.00 per unit

(b) No charge shall be made in any one permit year for more than two inspections except where safety orders have not been complied with and subsequent inspections are necessary. Then, an additional fee not to exceed $125.00 per hour or fraction thereof may, at the discretion of the Division, be charged.

(c) The Division will charge no fee for an inspection performed by a certified insurance inspector except a charge of $10.00 to cover the cost of processing the permit to operate.

(d) Aerial passenger tramways shall be inspected at least two times each year.

(e) At least one of the inspections required by subdivision (d) shall take place between November 15 of each year and March 15 of the succeeding year.

Article 5.   Boiler and Tank Permit and Inspection Fee Schedule

§ 344.   Shop and Resale Inspection Fees, Consultation and Audit Fees, Boilers and Tanks

(a) A fee of $110.00 per hour, or part thereof, including travel time as set forth in part (1) of this subsection, based on quarter hour intervals, with a minimum of one-half hour, shall be charged for all shop, field erection and resale inspections of all tanks, boilers, parts of tanks and boilers, nuclear components and for consultation, surveys, audits, manual review and other activities required or related to the ASME code or other national standards concerning the design or construction of boilers or pressure vessels or for evaluating fabricator's plant facilities when these services are requested of the division by entities desiring these services.

(1) Travel time shall include the travel time from the Division's local office or the site of previous inspection, whichever is less, to the inspection site and travel time from the inspection site to the Division's local office or the site of a following inspection, whichever is less. The Division shall not charge more than one employer for the same period of travel time.

(b) Whenever a person using qualified engineers of the division to perform services stated in Section 344(a) fails to pay the fees required under this section within 60 days after notification, said person shall pay, in addition to the fees required under this section, a penalty fee equal to 100 percent of the fee. For the purpose of this section, the date of the invoice shall be considered the date of notification.

(c) Expenses.

(1) When the mileage from the division's office of the authorized inspector or authorized inspector-supervisor is in excess of 50 miles round trip to the inspection site a charge of 31 cents per mile will be added to the hourly rate charges.

(2) When overnight expenses are incurred by the authorized inspector or the authorized inspector-supervisor, the actual cost of meals and lodging, up to a maximum per day of $150.00 when lodging is obtained in the counties of Alameda, San Francisco, San Mateo and Santa Clara, and Central and Western Los Angeles, and up to a maximum per day of $124.00 when lodging is obtained in any other location in the state, will be added to the hourly rate charges.

(3) The division shall not charge more than one employer for the same amount of expenses incurred the same day except as follows: When more than one employer incurs these expenses the division may, at its discretion, equitably allocate the expenses among the parties inspected.

§ 344.1.   Air Tank, Liquefied Petroleum Gas (L.P.G.), and Boiler Inspection Fees

(a) A fee of $135.00 per hour or any part thereof, including travel time as set forth in part (1) of this subsection, based on quarter hour intervals with a minimum of one-half hour, shall be charged for field permit inspection of air tanks, L.P.G. tanks, and boilers by qualified safety engineers employed by the division. Such fees may also, in the division's discretion, be charged for subsequent consultation or inspections to determine if applicable safety orders have been complied with. No additional fees shall be assessed for follow-up inspections when Safety Order requirements have been complied with, and the division notified, within 15 days of the compliance date shown on the Preliminary Order.

(1) Travel time shall include the travel time from the Division's local office or the site of previous inspection, whichever is less, to the inspection site and travel time from the inspection site to the Division's local office or the site of a following inspection, whichever is less. The Division shall not charge more than one employer for the same period of travel time.

(b) Whenever a person owning or having the custody, management or operation of an air tank, L.P.G. tank, or boiler fails to pay the fees required under this section within 60 days after notification, said person shall pay, in addition to the fees required under this section, a penalty fee equal to 100 percent of the fee. For the purpose of this section, the date of the invoice shall be considered the date of notification.

§ 344.2.   Boiler, Tank and Resale Inspection Reports and Permits to Operate

(a) Permits to operate and Resale Permits shall be issued by the Division, a qualified city or county, or an insurance company, or a corporation or company that inspects only boilers and tanks to be used by such company and not for resale. A qualified city or county or insurance company or a corporation or company that inspects only boilers and tanks to be used by such company and not for resale, is one that employs certified inspectors, as provided for in Section 779 of the Boiler and Fired Pressure Vessel Safety Orders.

(b) The Division shall issue a permit to operate upon receipt of the inspection reports required by Labor Code section 7654 and a fee of $15.00 to cover the costs of processing the Permit to Operate. If a Permit to Operate is issued on the Division's behalf by a certified inspector employed by an insurance company or by an employer who inspects boilers and tanks for the employer's own use and not for resale, the Division shall assess a fee of $15.00 to cover the cost of processing the Permit to Operate.

(c) Whenever a person owning or having the custody, management or operation of an air tank, L.P.G. tank, or boiler fails to pay the fees required under this section within 60 days after notification, said person shall pay, in addition to the fees required under this section, a penalty fee equal to 100 percent of the fee. For the purpose of this section, the date of the invoice shall be considered the date of notification.

Article 6. Permanent Amusement Rides

§ 344.5. Application.

(a) This Article governs permanent amusement rides operated anywhere in the State of California.

(b) This Article does not apply to any of the following:

(1) Any playground operated by a school or local government if the playground is an incidental amenity and the operating entity is not primarily engaged in providing amusement, pleasure, thrills or excitement;

(2) Museums or other institutions principally devoted to the exhibition of products of agriculture, industry, education, science, religion or the arts;

(3) Skating rinks, arcades, laser or paint ball war games, indoor interactive arcade games, bowling alleys, miniature golf courses, mechanical bulls, inflatable rides, trampolines, ball crawls, exercise equipment, jet skis, paddle boats, air boats, helicopters, airplanes, parasails, hot air balloons (tethered or untethered,) theaters, amphitheaters, batting cages, stationary spring-mounted fixtures, rider-propelled merry-go-rounds, games, slide shows, live-animal rides, or live-animal shows; or

(4) Permanent amusement rides operated at a private event that is not open to the general public and not subject to a separate admission fee.

(5) Amusement rides that are not permanent amusement rides.

§ 344.6. Definitions.

For purposes of this Article, the following terms are defined as set forth herein:

(a) An "as-built document" is a document signed by a licensed engineer responsible for the construction of the permanent amusement ride stating that the ride has been constructed according to its final plans.

(b) A "California-licensed engineer" is a professional engineer with a certificate of registration issued by the California Board of Professional Engineers and Land Surveyors.

(c) A "licensed engineer" is a California-licensed engineer or a professional engineer with equivalent licensing by another state.

(d) A "major modification" is any change in the structure or operation of a permanent amusement ride that materially alters either the performance of the ride or any safety-related system of the ride. For the purposes of this definition, the disassembly and relocation of a ride is considered to be a major modification of the ride.

(e) A "new permanent amusement ride" is a permanent amusement ride that is placed in operation and opened to the public for the first time on or after November 5, 2001.

(f) An "operational inspection" is an inspection that consists of inspecting the operation of the permanent amusement ride, including its safety-related systems and procedures, and reviewing any other specific information that is substantially related to the safe operation of the ride.

(g) An "owner" or "operator" is a person or entity who owns or controls or has the duty to control the operation of a permanent amusement ride. The terms include the State and every political subdivision of the State, including every state agency, and each county, city, district, and all the public and quasi-public corporations and public agencies therein.

(h) A "permanent amusement ride" is a mechanical device, aquatic device, or combination of devices of a permanent nature that carries or conveys passengers along, around, or over a fixed or restricted course for the purpose of giving its passengers amusement, pleasure, thrills, or excitement. "Permanent amusement ride" includes bungee-jumping services, but does not include dry slides, playground equipment, coin-operated devices, conveyances that operate directly on the ground or on pavement or a surface directly on the ground, or aerial passenger tramways as defined by *Labor Code section 7340(a)*. For the purposes of this definition, the phrase "of a permanent nature" means remaining at a single location for longer than 180 days.

(i) A "qualified safety inspector," or "QSI," is an individual certified by the Division pursuant to section 344.10. A QSI may be a safety inspector employed by the owner or operator of a permanent amusement ride, an employee or agent of the insurance underwriter or insurance broker of a permanent amusement ride, an employee or agent of the manufacturer of a permanent amusement ride, an employee of the Division of Occupational Safety and Health, or an independent consultant or contractor.

(j) "Safety–Related Systems and Procedures" are systems and procedures that materially affect safety or are designed or intended to increase the safety of a permanent amusement ride, including, but not limited to:

(1) Ride-control devices, including safety devices;

(2) Speed-limiting devices;

(3) Brakes;

(4) Passenger-carrying devices, including restraint systems;

(5) Mechanical systems that materially affect the safe operation of the ride;

(6) Ride electrical or electronic systems, including process-control equipment that are designed or intended to ensure safe operation of the ride;

(7) Daily pre-operational safety-related tests;

(8) Owner or operator safety-related maintenance, inspection and operational activities;

(9) Emergency procedures related to the operation of the ride, including, but not limited to, cessation of operation, evacuation procedures, ingress and egress controls, location of communication devices, and summoning of medical or emergency assistance; and

(10) Signage.

(k) A "structural inspection" is an inspection of a permanent amusement ride, which includes examination of the following structural attributes:

(1) Structural supports and foundations including wind and seismic integrity;

(2) Structural bracing; and

(3) Ride track elements, if any.

§ 344.7. Certificate of Compliance.

(a) On or before November 5, 2002, the owner or operator of a permanent amusement ride who does not elect to have a Division QSI perform the annual inspection required by section 344.8(c) shall submit to the Division a Certificate of Compliance together with the fee required by section 344.16(c). A new Certificate of Compliance shall be submitted annually and shall become due on each anniversary date of the first submission, unless the owner or operator elects in compliance with section 344.8(c)(2) to have a Division QSI conduct the annual inspection.

(b) The Certificate of Compliance shall include each of the following items:

(1) The legal name and address of the owner and his, her or its representative, if any, and the primary place of business of the owner;

(2) The legal name and address of the operator, if different from those of the owner;

(3) The name and a description of the permanent amusement ride, the address at which it is located, the name(s) of the manufacturer(s) of the ride, and if provided by the manufacturer(s), the serial number and model number of the permanent amusement ride; and

(4) A written declaration stating that, within the preceding 12–month period, the permanent amusement ride was inspected by a QSI, together with all of the individuals necessary to competently review the ride's safety-related systems and structural attributes, and that the permanent amusement ride is in conformance with the requirements of Subchapter 6.2 of Chapter 4 of Division 1 (starting at section 3195.1) of this Title. The written declaration shall be executed by a QSI under penalty of perjury.

Note : The requirement that the written declaration state that the permanent amusement ride is in conformance with the requirements of Subchapter 6.2 of Chapter 4 of Division 1 (starting at section 3195.1) of this Title shall not take effect until November 5, 2002, or 180 days after the date that Subchapter 6.2 has been adopted and takes effect, whichever is later.

(c) The owner or operator of multiple permanent amusement rides at one address may submit a single Certificate of Compliance that provides the information required in section 344.7(b) for all of the permanent amusement rides located at that address.

(d) Upon receipt of the Certificate of Compliance, the Division shall notify the owner or operator in writing within five (5) business days, that the Certificate of Compliance has been received and whether it meets the requirements of this Article. If a Certificate of Compliance is determined to be deficient, the Division's written notification shall enumerate the deficiencies and the information required to correct such deficiencies.

(e) All current written notifications issued by the Division pursuant to subsection (d) shall be available for public inspection during normal business hours at a readily accessible location at the site where the permanent amusement ride is located. Such documents may either be posted at the entrance to each permanent amusement ride, or at the election of the owner or operator, located at a readily accessible central location. If the owner or operator chooses not to maintain the documents at the entrance to a ride, a sign shall be posted at the entrance to the ride notifying the public of the location where the documents can be viewed.

(f) No person shall operate a permanent amusement ride unless the permanent amusement ride complies with all applicable requirements of this Article and Subchapter 6.2 of Chapter 4 of Division 1 (starting at section 3195.1) of this Title.

Note: The requirement that the amusement ride comply with all applicable requirements of Subchapter 2 shall not take effect unless and until Subchapter 2 is adopted and takes effect.

(g) Starting on November 5, 2002, an owner or operator who has not elected in compliance with sections 344.8(c)(1) and (c)(2) to have the Division conduct the annual inspection required by section 344.8(c) shall not operate an amusement ride with passengers unless a valid Certificate of Compliance applicable to the ride has been submitted to, and accepted by, the Division as required by section 344.7.

Exception No. 1: If the Division fails to notify the owner or operator within 5 business days of receipt of a Certificate of Compliance that the Certificate has been received and whether it meets the requirements of this Article as required by subsection (d), the owner or operator may continue to operate the ride, unless and until the Division notifies the owner or operator that the Certificate is deficient.

Exception No. 2: If a tardy request for a Division-conducted annual inspection is made, and the Division can accommodate the request, the ride may be operated after the inspection has been initiated and the Division

1299

informs the owner or operator that the ride may be operated.

§ 344.8. Inspections.

(a) Initial Division Inspection of New Permanent Amusement Rides. A Division QSI shall conduct an operational inspection of each new permanent amusement ride before the ride is placed in operation and opened to the public to evaluate the safety of the ride.

(1) The owner or operator of the ride shall notify the Division, in writing, at least 30 days prior to opening the ride to the public.

(2) The notification shall state the location of the ride, the date the owner or operator intends to commence public operation, and the earliest date the ride will be ready for inspection by the Division.

(3) If the Division receives notification in compliance with section 344.8(a)(1), the Division shall initiate the inspection before the date indicated by the operator for commencement of public operation of the ride, and shall make a reasonable effort to complete the inspection prior to that date. If the Division is unable to complete the inspection within 30 days of receiving notification by the owner or operator, and the lack of completion of the inspection is not attributable to the action or inaction of the owner or operator, the ride may by opened to the public until the inspection is completed, unless there is a substantial reason to question the safety of the ride.

(4) The ride owner or operator shall ensure that a representative is present to operate the ride and perform the tests requested by the Division QSI as necessary to complete the operational inspection.

(5) In conjunction with the inspection, the owner or operator of the ride shall make available to the Division each of the following:

(A) A written certification from a licensed engineer that the ride meets the all applicable design requirements set forth in Subchapter 6.2 of Chapter 4 of Division 1 (starting at section 3195.1) of this Title.

Note : This requirement shall not take effect unless and until Subchapter 6.2 has been adopted and takes effect.

(B) An as-built document.

(C) A copy of the certificate of occupancy issued by the local building authority, if the local building authority has such a requirement.

(b) Division Inspection of Major Modifications. After any major modification has been made to a permanent amusement ride, a Division QSI shall conduct an operational inspection of the ride before the ride is reopened to the public.

(1) The owner or operator of the ride shall provide the Division with at least 30 days advance written notice of the anticipated date of reopening the ride to the public following the major modification.

(2) The advance written notice shall state the date the owner or operator intends to resume public operation,

and the earliest date the ride will be ready for Division inspection.

(3) If the Division receives notification in compliance with section 344.8(b)(1), the Division shall initiate the inspection before the date indicated by the operator for reopening of the ride to the public, and shall make a reasonable effort to complete the inspection prior to that date. If the Division is unable to complete the inspection within 30 days of receiving notification by the owner or operator, and the lack of completion of the inspection is not attributable to the action or inaction of the owner or operator, the ride may by opened to the public until the inspection is completed, unless there is a substantial reason to question the safety of the ride.

(4) In conjunction with the Division's major modification inspection, the owner or operator of a permanent amusement ride shall make available to the Division each of the following:

(A) A written certification from a licensed engineer that the ride as modified meets all applicable design requirements set forth in Subchapter 6.2 of Chapter 4 of Division 1 (starting at section 3195.1) of this Title.

Note : This requirement shall not take effect unless and until Subchapter 6.2 has been adopted and takes effect.

(B) An as-built document.

(C) A copy of the certificate of occupancy issued by the local building authority, if the local building authority has such a requirement.

(c) Annual QSI Inspection. An annual QSI inspection shall be conducted of each permanent amusement ride at least once each year by either a QSI selected by the owner/operator or by a Division QSI, at the election of the owner or operator.

(1) If the owner or operator elects to have a Division QSI conduct the Annual QSI Inspection, the owner or operator shall submit a written request that the Division conduct the inspection. The request shall be submitted to the Division no later than 60 days prior to the date the Certificate of Compliance becomes due.

(2) Whenever an owner or operator elects to have a Division QSI conduct an annual inspection, the date of completion of the Division's inspection shall become the anniversary date by which the owner or operator's Certificate of Compliance becomes due the following year if a request for a Division-conducted QSI inspection is not made pursuant to subsection (c)(1).

(3) The annual QSI inspection shall include both a structural inspection and an operational inspection.

(4) A permanent amusement ride found on inspection to be unsafe shall be closed to the public and shall not be reopened to the public until all necessary repairs and modifications have been completed and certified as completed by a QSI.

(d) Annual Division Records Audit and Inspection.

(1) Starting on December 4, 2002, a Division QSI shall annually audit the records pertaining to each permanent amusement ride, including, but not limited to, records of accidents, records of employee training, and records of maintenance, repair, and inspection of the ride.

(2) A Division QSI shall conduct an operational inspection in conjunction with the annual records audit. The operational inspection shall be conducted in two phases, as follows:

(A) One phase shall consist of an unannounced inspection conducted during business hours to observe the normal operation of the ride with passengers.

(B) The other phase, consisting of all other aspects of the operational inspection, shall be pre-announced and conducted without passengers present.

(e) Exception to subsections (a), (b), (c), and (d): The following provisions shall apply to each permanent amusement ride that is located within a county or other political subdivision of the State that, as of April 1, 1998, has adopted the provisions of Chapter 66 (commencing with section 6601.1) of the 1994 Uniform Building Code providing for the routine inspection of permanent amusement rides by counties and other political subdivisions of the State, provided that the Division determines that these inspections meet or exceed the inspection standards set forth in this Article:

(1) The ride shall not be subject to the inspection or records audit requirements of subsections (a), (b), or (d), to the extent that the county or other political subdivision provides inspections according to the same criteria as those specified in each of these subsections.

(2) The ride shall be subject to the requirements of subsection (c). However, the employer may elect to have the county or other political subdivision conduct the Annual QSI Inspection on the same basis that it may elect to have the Division conduct the Annual QSI Inspection, provided that the county or other political subdivision provides inspections according to the same criteria as those specified in subsection (c) and the owner or operator complies with all applicable deadlines for making written requests.

(f) Discretionary Division Inspections. A Division QSI may conduct an inspection to determine the safety of a permanent amusement ride, in a manner consistent with any reasonable safety concern raised by the information available to the Division, whenever the Division:

(1) Receives notification, or otherwise learns, of an accident involving the permanent amusement ride required to be reported pursuant to section 344.15;

(2) Determines that a fraudulent Certificate of Compliance for the permanent amusement ride was submitted;

(3) Determines, based on factors such as ride cycles or number of riders, that a permanent amusement ride has a disproportionately-high incidence of accidents when compared to other rides of similar type and design in the State of California; or

(4) Receives a complaint or otherwise becomes aware of information, when the complaint or information reasonably appears to be reliable and credible, that one of the safety-related systems or structural components of a ride is unsafe, or that a particular practice associated with a ride is unsafe.

(g) The Division shall cause the least possible disruption to the normal operation of a permanent amusement ride consistent with the effective completion of an inspection.

§ 344.9. Order Prohibiting Operation.

(a) If, after inspection by a Division QSI, the Division determines that a permanent amusement ride, or any part thereof, presents an imminent hazard or is otherwise unsafe for patrons, the Division may prohibit the operation of the ride, or any affected part thereof. The Division shall frame the scope of the prohibition with the narrowest scope reasonably necessary to ensure the protection of the public.

Exception No. 1: The Division shall not issue an Order Prohibiting Operation if the hazardous or unsafe condition can be corrected immediately and the operator, after being informed of the condition by the Division, immediately abates the hazardous or unsafe condition.

Exception No. 2: If an unsafe condition does not constitute an imminent hazard to patrons, the Division shall, prior to issuing an Order Prohibiting Operation, engage in an informal consultation with the owner or operator in an effort to resolve any factual questions or gather information relevant to determining whether the public operation of the amusement ride should be prohibited.

(b) The Division shall notify the owner or operator in writing of the grounds for prohibition of operation and of the conditions in need of correction at the time it issues the Order Prohibiting Operation.

(c) Operation of the permanent amusement ride shall not be reopened to the public until the conditions cited in the Order Prohibiting Operation have been corrected and approved by an authorized Division representative.

(d) The owner or operator may appeal any Order Prohibiting Operation. The Division shall conduct appeal proceedings in accordance with *Labor Code Section 6327.*

§ 344.10. Certification of a QSI.

(a) No person shall perform the services of a QSI for permanent amusement rides unless he or she possesses a current, valid QSI Certificate issued by the Division.

(b) An application for certification as a QSI shall be made to the Division on a form prescribed by the Division, which shall require the applicant to provide information limited to his or her name, social security number, mailing address, daytime telephone number, two passport photographs, and information required to satisfy subsection (c).

(1) All statements on the application shall be made under penalty of perjury.

(2) Within 20 business days of receipt of an application for certification as a QSI, the division shall notify the applicant in writing that the application is complete and accepted for filing or incomplete and what additional evidence, documentation, or information is necessary to complete the application. An application shall be considered to be complete once all evidence, documentation, and information required by subsection (c)(1) or (c)(2) have been submitted.

(3) Within 20 business days of receipt of a completed application, the Division shall notify the applicant in writing of its decision to approve or disapprove the application. If the application is made pursuant to subsection (c)(2), the Division shall, upon approval of the application, allow the applicant to sit for an examination pursuant to subsection (c)(2)(D).

(4) If the applicant has qualified for certification under subsection (c)(1), the Division shall issue a QSI Certificate to the applicant upon approval of the application. If the applicant has qualified for certification under subsection (c)(2), the Division shall issue a QSI Certificate to the applicant upon completion of the QSI Examination with a score of at least 80% as required by subsection (c)(2)(D).

(c) To be eligible for certification as a QSI, an applicant shall qualify as either a licensed engineer or as a non-engineer.

(1) To qualify as a licensed engineer, the applicant shall do all of the following:

(A) Provide satisfactory evidence that the applicant is a licensed engineer and has completed at least two years of experience in the amusement ride field, consisting of at least one year of actual inspection of amusement rides for a manufacturer, government agency, amusement park, carnival or insurance underwriter, and an additional year of practicing any combination of amusement ride inspection, design, fabrication, installation, maintenance, testing, repair, or operation.

(B) Provide any other information reasonably requested by the Division.

(2) To qualify as a non-engineer, the applicant shall do all of the following:

(A) Provide satisfactory evidence of completing a minimum of five years of experience in the amusement ride field, at least two years of which consisted of actual inspection of amusement rides for a manufacturer, government agency, amusement park, carnival or insurance underwriter. The remaining experience may consist of any combination of amusement ride inspection, design, fabrication, installation, maintenance, testing, repair, or operation.

(B) Provide any other information reasonably requested by the Division.

(C) Produce a valid certificate from a QSI Training Program approved by the Division pursuant to section 344.11, evidencing the applicant's successful completion of 80–hour QSI certification training. For the purposes of this subsection, the training must have been completed within the past five years as of the time the application is made, but must not have been received earlier than January 1, 1999.

Note : A certificate of completion from an approved QSI Training Program which is based on training received prior to the date this Article takes effect is acceptable if the course work has been retroactively approved pursuant to section 344.11(f).

Exception: An applicant may apply up to 40 hours of successfully completed nondestructive testing (NDT) training toward completion of the requirement for 80 hours of QSI certification training from an approved QSI Training Program. For the purposes of this exception, an acceptable NDT training course is one offered by an instructor certified by the American Society for Nondestructive Testing, Inc. ("ASNT") Nondestructive Training Level III, and covering the test method body of knowledge as described in the ASNT Recommended Practice No. SNT–TC–1A, 1996. The applicant shall provide all documentation or evidence reasonably necessary to demonstrate that the NDT training sought to be applied toward the 80–hour requirement meets these criteria. Other NDT courses shall be considered to be acceptable if the QSI applicant can demonstrate that the course instructor and content are equally effective in imparting skills and subject matter to attendees that are necessary for competent inspection of permanent amusement rides. No course shall be considered acceptable if the Division reasonably determines that the subject matter is insufficiently related to the inspection of permanent amusement rides to qualify as substitutable NDT training, or if the Division reasonably determines that the manner of instruction is insufficiently managed or monitored to be considered bona fide training.

(D) Achieve a score of at least 80% on a written examination (QSI Examination) pertaining to the subjects addressed in this Article and Subchapter 6.2 of Chapter 4 of Division 1 (starting at section 3195.1) of this Title and subject matter applicable to the safe operation of permanent amusement rides. The examination shall be given during the Division's normal business hours in Sacramento or Anaheim at a time convenient to the applicant.

Note: The examination shall not require knowledge of any requirements in Subchapter 6.2 unless and until Subchapter 6.2 has been adopted and takes effect.

(d) A QSI Certificate shall be valid for a period of two years from the date of issuance.

(e) Application for renewal of a QSI Certificate shall be made to the Division on a form prescribed by the

Division, which shall require the certificate holder to provide his or her name and daytime telephone number.

(1) All statements on the renewal application shall be made under penalty of perjury.

(2) Each application shall be accompanied by the application fee fixed by section 344.16(b).

(3) The applicant shall provide evidence of having completed, during the previous biennial renewal cycle, at least 30 hours of training from the continuing education component of a QSI Training Program approved pursuant to section 344.11(c). This training shall include inservice industry or manufacturer updates and seminars.

(4) The applicant shall provide any additional information reasonably requested by the Division.

(5) Within 10 business days of receipt of an application for renewal of a QSI certificate, the Division shall notify the applicant in writing either that the application is complete and accepted for filing or deficient and what specific information is required to complete the application. Within 10 business days of receipt of a completed application for certification as a QSI or an application for renewal of a QSI certificate, the Division shall notify the applicant of its decision to approve or disapprove the application.

(f) The Division shall determine whether the applicant meets the criteria necessary for certification or renewal of certification pursuant to this Article and Part 8.1 of Division 5 of the Labor Code, and shall approve or disapprove the application for certification or renewal of certification accordingly.

(g) The Division may revoke or suspend the certification of a QSI, upon determining that the holder:

(1) Has submitted a fraudulent inspection report to the Division or to the owner or operator of a permanent amusement ride; or

(2) Has not performed competently as a QSI.

§ 344.11. Approval of QSI Training Programs.

(a) A school or training provider may apply to the Division for approval of a QSI Training Program (referred to in this section as "Program") by submitting the following information:

(1) The name(s) of the training courses offered by the Program.

(2) The name, title, business address, and phone number of the person whom the Division will contact regarding Program approval matters, a statement certifying that the information provided with the application is true and correct to the best of the applicant's knowledge, and the name title, business address, and phone number of the person signing the declaration if different from the person who will be the Division's contact.

(3) Materials describing the subject matter and hours of instruction of each course required by the Program, with an explanation as to which courses are to apply toward:

(A) The QSI certification training requirements of section 344.10(c)(2)(C);

(B) QSI certification training requirements based on completion of up to 40 hours of NDT training as allowed by the exception to section 344.10(c)(2)(C); and

(C) The QSI continuing education requirements of section 344.10(e)(3).

Note : A school or training provider may offer any or all of the above three options.

(4) The name(s) and qualifications of the instructor(s) of the Program.

(5) Any other information reasonably requested by the Division.

(b) Processing of Application.

(1) Within 20 business days of receipt of an application for approval, the Division shall inform the applicant in writing whether the submitted application information is complete or additional information needs to be submitted.

(2) Within 45 business days of receipt of a completed application for approval, the Division shall inform the applicant that the Program is approved or inform the applicant that the application for approval is denied, specifying the reasons for denial.

(c) Criteria for Approval. Upon receiving complete application materials from the provider, the Division shall determine whether the applicant meets the criteria necessary for approval pursuant to this Article and the Permanent Amusement Ride Safety Inspection Program, *Labor Code section 7920* et seq., and shall approve or disapprove the application accordingly. The approval shall specify each component of QSI Training, as described in section 344.11(a)(3), to which the approval applies. To qualify for approval, the applicant shall demonstrate that its Program will meet all of the following requirements:

(1) Ensure that the instructor for each course required by the Program is experienced in the subject matter of the course.

(2) Ensure that the course content is current and will be kept current.

(3) Require Program participants to attend each course required by the Program for its full duration so that the applicable requirements for hours of instruction as described by sections 344.10(c)(2)(C) and 344.10(e)(3) are met.

(4) Utilize a reliable testing method to determine whether the course participants have learned the subject matter presented by the course.

(5) Provide a certificate of completion to all successful participants at the completion of the Program.

(6) Ensure that the courses required by the Program provide classroom training related to the inspection, design, maintenance, testing, and operation of permanent amusement rides and applicable provisions of Title 8 of

this Code, ensure that the subject matter of the training is current and will be kept current, and ensure that the overall content of courses required by the Program meets the intent of the Permanent Amusement Ride Safety Inspection Program, *Labor Code section 7920*, et seq., that QSIs receive training allowing them to perform competent and effective inspections of permanent amusement rides for the purpose of ensuring the safety of patrons.

(d) To maintain QSI Training Program approval, a school or training provider shall promptly notify the Division in writing each time the provider makes a substantive change to any of the information required pursuant to subsection (a).

(e) The Division may suspend or revoke the approval of a QSI Training Program upon determining that the Program has substantially failed to comply with approval requirements.

(f) The Division may grant retroactive approval of training provided after January 1, 1999 but before this Article takes effect, if the provider demonstrates that the training met the QSI Training Program approval criteria of this section.

§ 344.12. Suspension and Revocation Procedures.

All suspension and revocation proceedings conducted by the Division shall be initiated by the provision of written notice of the Division's intent to conduct a hearing to determine whether a certification or approval will be suspended or revoked.

(a) The written notice shall be served at least 48 hours in advance of the scheduled hearing date.

(b) Service shall be by personal service or certified mail to the address shown on the application for certification or approval, or to any other address known to the Division and reasonably believed to be the current address of the certificate holder or course provider.

(c) The written notice shall specify the time, date, and location of the hearing, and the reasons for the action proposed by the Division.

(d) At the hearing the Division shall have the burden of establishing good cause for the action taken by it. Good cause shall be deemed to exist if the Division establishes that the holder of a certification has substantially failed to comply with the requirements for certification pursuant to section 344.10(g), or that the holder of an approval has substantially failed to comply with the requirements of approval pursuant to section 344.11(e).

§ 344.13. Appeals to the Director.

(a) The following may be appealed to the Director:

(1) Suspensions and revocations by the Division.

(2) Denials of applications for QSI certification or QSI Training Program approval.

(3) Any final decision after hearing by the Division to uphold an Order Prohibiting Operation.

(b) All appeals to the Director shall be in writing and shall be served within 5 business days of receipt of the notification of the Division's decision resulting in a denial, suspension, or revocation.

(c) The Director or authorized representative shall schedule a hearing to be held within 5 business days of receipt of an appeal. At the hearing, the appellant shall have the burden of establishing that the Division's decision is in error.

(d) Within 3 business days of completing the hearing, the Director shall issue a decision. The Director's decision shall be final except for any rehearing or judicial review provided for by law.

§ 344.14. Insurance Requirements.

A person or entity may operate a permanent amusement ride only if, at the time of operation, he, she, or it:

(a) Has obtained a valid insurance policy in an amount not less than one million dollars ($1,000,000) per occurrence, and;

(1) Has submitted to the Division a copy of the policy;

(2) Has clearly identified in the policy the permanent amusement rides included and excluded; and

(3) Does not operate permanent amusement rides for which coverage is not provided; or

(b) Has obtained a bond in an amount not less than one million dollars ($1,000,000), except that the aggregate liability of the surety under that bond shall not exceed the face amount of the bond. A copy of the bond shall be submitted to the Division; or

(c) Qualifies as self-insured. Qualification as self-insured shall be demonstrated by providing a letter to the Division attesting that the owner has total assets of at least ten million dollars ($10,000,000), and that the owner's total assets exceed the owner's total liabilities by either a minimum of two million dollars or a ratio of at least ten to one. All statements in the attestation letter to the Division shall be made under penalty of perjury.

Exception: State and local governmental entities shall be deemed to qualify as self-insured.

§ 344.15. Accident Response and Notification.

(a) Reporting of Accidents.

Each operator of a permanent amusement ride shall report or cause to be reported to the Division's Anaheim or Sacramento Amusement Ride Section Office immediately by telephone each known accident where maintenance, operation, or use of the permanent amusement ride results in a death or serious injury to any person unless the injury does not require medical service other than ordinary first aid.

(b) Preservation of Accident Scene.

(1) If a death or serious injury results from the failure, malfunction, or operation of a permanent amusement ride, the equipment or conditions that caused the acci-

dent shall be preserved for the purpose of an investigation by the division.

(2) Upon receiving a report of an accident from an owner or operator, the Division shall make a determination as to whether preservation is necessary and inform the owner or operator of its determination.

(A) If the Division determines that preservation is necessary, the Division shall make a reasonable effort to initiate the inspection within 24 hours of receipt of the report from the owner or operator.

(B) Upon initiating the inspection, the Division shall provide the owner or operator with an instruction as to how long the equipment or conditions shall continue to be preserved.

(c) Notification of the Division by Emergency Responders.

Whenever a state, county, or local fire or police agency is called to an accident involving a permanent amusement ride covered by this Article where the death of a patron or a patron injury requiring medical service other than first aid has occurred, the Anaheim or Sacramento Amusement Ride Section Office of the Division shall be notified by telephone immediately by the responding agency.

§ 344.16. Fee Schedule.

(a) The application fee for a QSI Certificate shall be five hundred dollars ($500.00).

(b) The fee for the biennial renewal of a QSI Certificate shall be one hundred and twenty five dollars ($125.00).

(c) The fee for review of Certificates of Compliance and provision of related notifications shall be two hundred and fifty dollars ($250.00).

(d) A fee of one hundred and twenty-five dollars ($125.00) per hour, or fraction thereof, shall be charged for all work performed in connection with audits, inspections and investigations conducted pursuant to section 344.8.

§ 344.17. Confidentiality.

The Division shall maintain the confidentiality of all documentation received pursuant to this Article to the extent that such documentation is protected by *Labor Code Section 6322* or any other applicable provision of law.

Article 6.1 Amusement Ride Inspection Fee Schedule

§ 344.18. Amusement Ride Fee Schedule

(a) Inspection Fees.

(1) A fee of $125.00 per hour or fraction thereof shall be charged for all inspections, reinspections, and accident investigations pertaining to amusement rides. A minimum fee of $125.00 will be charged per amusement ride.

(2) Fees shall be charged for actual inspection time. Actual inspection time begins from the time the Division engineer arrives, generally by appointment, in the area and continues until the engineer has completed the Division's report and is ready to leave the area.

(b) The Division will charge no fee for an inspection performed by a certified insurance inspector except a charge of $10.00 to cover the cost of processing the permit to operate.

Article 7. Blaster's License

§ 344.20. Blaster's License–Application and Examination

(a) Every person requesting a Blaster's License shall submit a completed application form to the Division.

(b) The Division shall evaluate every applicant for a Blaster's License. This evaluation will be conducted of the person's training and experience as shown on the application.

(c) In order to obtain a Blaster's License, the applicant shall pass a written or an oral qualifying examination given at such times and places as determined by the Division. The examination shall include questions related to the license classification requested. Field tests may also be required as deemed necessary to determine the candidate's qualifications to perform the duties of a blaster.

(d) License classification.

Class	Category	Description
A	Unlimited	All types of blasting.
B	General Above Ground	All phases of blasting operations in quarries, open pit mines, and above ground construction.
C	General Underground	All phases of blasting operations in underground mines, shafts, tunnels, and drifts.
D	Demolition	All phases of demolition.
E	Limited	Specific blasting operations indicated on the License.

(e) The Blaster's License may be endorsed by any limitation or classification the Division may determine.

(f) The Blaster's License is not transferable.

§ 344.21. Expiration and Renewal

(a) Each Blaster's License issued under this Article shall be valid for a period of five years with renewal privileges.

(b) Application for, and granting of a renewal, shall be administered in the same manner as an original Blaster's License. The Blaster's License examination will be required each five years.

§ 344.22. Suspension or Revocation–Blaster's License

(a) The Division may suspend or revoke a blaster's license when in the opinion of the Division;

(1) There is a question or doubt as to the competency of the blaster, or

(2) The blaster has not complied with requirements, safety orders, or rules of the Division.

(b) The blaster shall be given notice and a hearing before suspending or revoking a blaster's license.

(c) In the event of suspension or revocation of a blaster's license, the person may not apply for a new license for a period of 6 months and the application shall be handled in the same manner as an original blaster's license.

Article 8.   Elevator Inspection Fee Schedule

§ 344.30.   Conveyance Inspection Program Fees

Pursuant to the provisions of Section 7314 of the Labor Code, the Division has fixed a schedule of inspection fees as follows:

(a) Reinspection (periodic inspection) and witnessing of periodic tests of an existing installation shall be:

(1) Hand dumbwaiters	$ 70.00 per unit
(2) Power dumbwaiters and material lifts	$105.00 per unit
(3) Hand elevators	$ 70.00 per unit
(4) Material lifts with automatic transfer devices	$140.00 per unit
(5) Power sidewalk elevators	$140.00 per unit
(6) Hand-powered man platforms	$140.00 per unit
(7) Escalators and moving walks	$280.00 per unit
(8) Manlifts	$140.00 per unit
(9) Hydraulic elevator -direct plunger and roped hydraulic up to three stories	$105.00 per unit
(10) Hydraulic elevator -direct plunger and roped hydraulic 4 stories or more	$ 140.00 per unit
(11) Cabled elevator -up to 3 stories	$ 140.00 per unit
(12) Cabled elevator -4 to 10 stories	$ 210.00 per unit
(13) Cabled elevator -11 to 20 stories	$ 280.00 per unit
(14) Cabled elevator -21 or more stories	$ 350.00 per unit
(15) Special access elevators	$ 140.00 per unit
(16) Screw type elevator	$ 140.00 per unit
(17) Wheel chair lift, vertical or incline	$ 105.00 per unit
(18) Stairway chair lift	$ 70.00 per unit
(19) Elevator installed by variance	$ 140.00 per hour
(20) Elevators or dumbwaiters with automatic transfer devices	$ 140.00 per unit
(21) Incline elevators	$ 210.00 per unit
(22) Construction personnel hoist	$ 140.00 per hour
(23) Special purpose personnel elevator	$ 140.00 per unit
(24) Rack & Pinon elevator	$ 140.00 per unit
(25) Vertical and inclined reciprocating conveyors	$ 140.00 per unit
(26) Witnessing of periodic tests	$ 140.00 per hour
(27) Automatic guided vehicles on guideways	$1120.00 per unit

(b) The fee for the inspection of a new installation of any type of conveyance will be $210.00 per hour or any fraction thereof.

(c) The fee for the inspection of any alteration to a conveyance will be $210.00 per hour or any fraction thereof.

(d) The fee for replacement inspections required under Section 3001(b)(3) will be $140.00 per hour, or any fraction thereof.

(e) The fee for field consultations will be $280.00 per hour or any fraction thereof. If the distance to the job site is more than 50 miles from the District Elevator Unit

Office, the actual travel time will be added to the inspection time in order to obtain the total charge.

(f) No charge shall be made in any one permit year for more than one inspection except where safety orders have not been complied with and subsequent inspections are necessary or where an alteration has been made to a conveyance. A fee of $140.00 per hour or any fraction thereof shall be charged to determine if applicable safety orders have been complied with.

(g) A fee will be charged for processing and mailing a permit. The fee shall reflect the actual cost of processing and mailing up to a maximum of $15.00.

(h) The fees to cover the cost of various certifications are as follows:

(1) Certified Qualified Conveyance Company (CQCC)	$ 700.00
(2) Certified Qualified Conveyance Inspection Company (CQCIC)	$ 700.00
(3) Certified Competent Conveyance Mechanic (CCCM)	$ 210.00
(4) Temporary Certified Competent Conveyance Mechanic (TCCCM)	$ 35.00/application
(5) Emergency Certified Competent Elevator Mechanic (ECCEM)	$ 35.00/application
(6) Certified Qualified Conveyance Inspector (CQCI)	$ 210.00
(7) Renewal of a CQCC, CCCM, CQCIC or a CQCI certification	$ 140.00
(8) Replacement of a CQCC, CCCM, CQCIC, or a CQCI certification	$ 35.00
(9) Administration of Exam	$ 100/exam

(i) The fee for an erection, construction, or installation permit, including the plan approval, is as follows:

(1) First hydraulic elevator, including direct plunger elevator and roped hydraulic elevator in a building	$ 140.00 per story
(2) Additional similar conveyances in the same building	$ 140.00 per unit
(3) First cable-, screw- and rack and pinion type-elevators in a building	$ 210.00 per story
(4) Additional similar conveyances in the same building	$ 210.00 per unit
(5) Dumbwaiters, material lifts, vertical reciprocating conveyors and sidewalk elevators	$ 350.00 per unit
(6) Wheelchair lifts, stairway lifts, hand-powered elevators and dumbwaiters	$ 280.00 per unit
(7) First Escalator or moving walk in a building	$ 560.00 per unit
(8) Additional similar conveyances in the same building	$ 140.00 per unit
(9) Automatic guided vehicles on guideways	$1120.00 per unit
(10) All other conveyances	$ 140.00 per hour

(j) The fee for an alteration permit, including plan review, is as follows:

(1) Permit for one or two alterations to a single unit	$280.00
(2) Permit for same alterations to similar conveyances in the same building	$140.00 per unit
(3) Permit for three or more alterations to a single conveyance	$560.00
(4) Permit for same alterations to similar conveyances in the same building	$140.00 per unit

(k) The fee for any change order review of plans shall be $140.00 per hour with a minimum charge of $280.00.

(l) Whenever a person owning or having the custody, management or operation of an elevator fails to pay the fees required under this section within 60 days after notification, he or she shall pay in addition to the fees required by this section, a penalty fee equal to 100 percent of the fee.

Article 9. Correctional Industries

§ 344.40. Definitions

(a) Complaint. As used in this article, the term complaint shall refer to any written allegation of unsafe or unhealthful working conditions at the place of employment of a state prisoner working in a correctional industry. The Cal/OSHA form 7 may be used as a complaint form, but shall not be required.

(b) Committee. As used in this article, the term committee shall refer to the correctional industry safety committee established in accordance with Department of Corrections administrative procedures at each Department of Corrections facility maintaining a correctional industry.

(c) Committee Notice. A committee notice is a written notice suggesting the institution take specific corrective measures and setting forth an appropriate abatement date. The notice shall be served upon the Department of Corrections employee having supervisory responsibility over the unsafe or unhealthful condition. Copies of the notice shall be served upon the warden or superintendent of the institution and upon the complainant. Further, a copy of the notice shall be posted by the committee at a location where employees exposed to the unsafe or unhealthful condition will be likely to see it. Such posting shall be for a period of 15 days or until the unsafe condition is corrected, whichever is longer.

(d) Filing a complaint. A complaint is deemed filed for purposes of this article upon either being deposited in a readily accessible complaint box or being personally presented to any member of the committee.

§ 344.41. Complaint Procedure

(a) Any state prisoner working in a correctional industry may file with the committee, a complaint alleging unsafe or unhealthful working conditions at her/his place of employment.

(b) The committee shall provide correctional industry employees with an expedient means of transmitting complaints to the committee. All correctional industry employees shall be informed by posted notice of the manner available to them for filing a complaint.

§ 344.42. Operation of the Committee

(a) The committee shall meet as often as necessary but at least every 60 days to discuss health and safety issues relating to employees of correctional industries and to hear and act upon health and safety complaints filed by correctional industry employees.

(b) The committee shall review and take appropriate action on every complaint within 15 calendar days of its filing.

(c) The committee shall take one of the following actions on each complaint:

(1) Issue a notice recommending specific corrective measures in the manner set forth in Section 344.40 above. In addition, the committee shall inform the complainant in writing of his/her right to have the committee forward the original complaint and the notice for correction to the Division of Occupational Safety and Health for review if the complainant believes that the notice is insufficient to make the conditions safe or healthful or if the Department of Corrections refuses or fails to comply with the notice.

(2) Refer the complaint to the appropriate district office of the Division of Occupational Safety and Health for review. Such referral shall be made whenever the committee is unable, for any reason, to resolve the issues raised by the complaint within 15 days from the date of filing. Such referral shall be in writing and shall be made by the 15th calendar day from the day of filing. The complainant, if known to the committee, shall immediately be informed in writing of the referral.

(3) Dismiss the complaint for lack of merit. Unless the complainant is anonymous the committee shall set forth its reasons for dismissal in writing to the complainant. Said writing shall also inform the complainant of his/her right to require the committee to have the initial complaint and the committee finding reviewed by the Division in the event that the complainant finds the conclusions of the committee to be unsatisfactory for any reason.

§ 344.43. Duties of the Department of Corrections and the Committee

(a) Neither the Department of Corrections nor the correctional industry safety committee shall in any way abridge the right of correctional industry employees to file complaints pursuant to this article or to require referral of the complaints to the Division of Occupational Safety and Health.

§ 344.44. Division Participation

(a) Upon receipt of a complaint from the committee, which it determines to constitute a bona fide allegation of a safety or health violation, the Division shall investigate within 3 working days after receipt if the complaint alleges a serious violation, and not later than 14 calendar days after receipt if the complaint alleges a general violation. The Division may give advance notice of an inspection or investigation and may postpone the same if such action is necessary for the maintenance of security at the facility where the inspection or investigation is to be held, or for ensuring the safety and health of the Division's representative who will be conducting the inspection or investigation.

(b) In addition to the investigations required under subsection (a) above, the Division shall investigate every fatality and every employment accident involving serious injury to five or more correctional industry employees. The Division may in its discretion investigate any other accident or report of a safety or health violation involving correctional industry employees which are reported to it.

§ 344.45. Other Duties of the Correctional Industry Safety Committee

(a) The committee shall retain each complaint or a copy thereof and a record of all action taken pursuant to that complaint for a period of 3 years from the date that all issues with respect to the complaint have been resolved. Such records shall be made available to the Division.

§ 344.46. Other Division Jurisdiction over Unsafe Conditions Pertaining to State Prisoners

(a) When the Division receives information, pursuant to Labor Code Section 6314, about injury or death of a state prisoner resulting from labor performed by the prisoner, the Division may make recommendations to the Department of Corrections, with or without conducting an inspection, of ways in which corrections might improve the safety of the working conditions and work areas of state prisoners and other safety matters.

(b) If the Department of Corrections fails to comply with the recommendations described in subsection (a) above, or in any other case in which the Division deems the safety of any state prisoner shall require it, the Division may conduct hearings and after such hearings may adopt such special orders, rules, or regulations, or otherwise proceed as authorized in Chapter 1 (commencing with Section 6300 of Division 5 Part 1 of the Labor Code) as it deems necessary. The Department of Corrections shall comply with any such order, rule, or regulations so adopted by the Division.

Article 10. Civil and Criminal Enforcement Policy of the Division of Occupational Safety and Health

§ 344.50. Civil Inspections and Investigations

Compliance personnel of the Division are responsible for conducting inspections and investigations under the California Occupational Safety and Health Act for the purpose of invoking civil enforcement remedies only. If hazardous or violative conditions are found, the civil enforcement remedies which can be utilized include, but are not limited to, the issuance of citations and civil penalties, special orders, orders to take special action, the initiation of injunction proceedings, issuance of orders prohibiting use, and the revocation or suspension of permits. Division compliance personnel have no authority to initiate criminal proceedings.

§ 344.51. Criminal Investigations

The central function of the Bureau of Investigations, within the Division of Occupational Safety and Health, is to conduct criminal investigations. The Bureau must investigate accidents involving violations of a standard, order, or special order, or section 25910 of the Health and Safety Code in which there is a serious injury to five or more employees, death, or request for prosecution by a Division representative. The Bureau of Investigations is the only entity within the Division which is empowered to conduct criminal investigations and to refer the results of such investigations when appropriate to a city attorney or district attorney for necessary action. The Bureau must analyze the circumstances surrounding the violation to determine whether the conduct is sufficiently aggravated to fall within the scope of Labor Code sections 6423, 6425 and other penal statutes.

§ 344.52. Referral of Cases Other Than Accident Cases by Compliance Personnel to the Bureau of Investigations

If Division compliance personnel become aware that there are conditions which may constitute criminal violations, the case must be referred through the Regional Manager/Supervising Industrial Hygienist, with a copy to the appropriate Deputy, to the respective Northern or Southern Office of the Bureau of Investigations. In cases referred for investigation the Supervising Special Investigator will assign the case to a Special investigator for investigation. The investigator will review the facts of the case, interview witnesses, and otherwise, conduct a thorough investigation. The assigned investigator shall prepare a report to the Supervising Special Investigator which shall include a summary of evidence, findings, and recommendations for appropriate action.

§ 344.53. Nonreferral of Other Than Willful or Repeated Violations in the Context of Scheduled Inspections by Compliance Personnel to the Bureau of Investigations

Whenever the Division conducts a scheduled inspection according to a general administrative plan in contrast to an accident, complaint, or follow-up investigation, Division compliance personnel shall invoke only the civil enforcement remedies as set forth in Section 344.50 unless the violation is characterized as willful or repeated. This section shall not limit he Division's prerogative to enforce Labor Code Section 6326.

Article 11. License Requirements–Crane and Derrick Certification

§ 344.60. Licensing of Certifiers of Cranes and Derricks–Requirements

(a) Any person engaging in the testing, examination and/or certification of cranes, including but not limited to tower cranes, or derricks, used in lifting service exceeding three tons rated capacity, as defined in section 4885 of title 8 of the California Code of Regulations, as required pursuant to Labor Code section 7375 and sections 5020 through 5025 of title 8 of the California Code of Regulations shall apply for and obtain a license from the Division pursuant to this article or be approved by the Division to work as a surveyor under a license issued pursuant to this article prior to engaging in such activities.

(1) For the purposes of this article a "licensed certifier" refers to any individual or agency holding a license pursuant to this article.

(2) For the purposes of this article "approval", "approved surveyor" or "surveyor" refers to an individual who has been approved to certify cranes only under the authority and supervision of a licensed certifier.

(b) Any person authorized by the Division to certify cranes and/or derricks prior to the effective date of this article may continue to perform services under such authority. Any such authority shall expire, however, in the year 1992. For purposes of the month of expiration in the year 1992, the Division will use the first day of the month in which the authorization was regularly scheduled to expire regardless of year. Any certificating agency or person desiring to continue to provide services pursuant to this article must have applied for and obtained a license from the Division prior to expiration of the existing authorization.

(c) All persons or agencies licensed or approved pursuant to this Article shall comply with the provisions of Labor Code section 7375(c).

§ 344.61. License and Approval–Application Form and Applicant Qualifications

(a) A license to certify cranes pursuant to this article may be obtained by submitting a completed application to the Division and successfully completing a written examination as set forth herein. Application forms may be obtained by calling the Headquarters offices of the Division or by written request to Post Office Box 603, San Francisco, California 94101.

(1) An applicant seeking a license must satisfy one of the following criteria:

(A) Be an agency or person satisfying the definition of "certificating agency" as set forth in section 4885 of title 8 of the California Code of Regulations, or,

(B) Be an agency or person qualified to certify cranes pursuant to section 5021(a)(1) of title 8 of the California Code of Regulations who is not a certificating agency as defined but who will be operating under the direct technical supervision of a certificating agency as defined.

(2) All applicants must possess knowledge of sections 4884, et. seq. of Title 8 of the California Code of Regulations, as well as ANSI (American National Standards Institute) and SAE (Society of Automotive Engineers) standards, relating to the design and operation of cranes and derricks, including those specifically applicable to the types of cranes for which a license will be issued. In addition, all applicants must demonstrate at least five years related experience with cranes or derricks. This five years of experience must include not less than two years of crane related field duties such as crane inspection as a crane operator, heavy equipment mechanic, shop foreman, operations supervision, rigging specialist, or mechanical or civil engineer. Related education may be substituted for experience at a ratio of two years of education for one year of experience up to three years.

(A) Individuals who have been approved by the Division pursuant to section 5021(a) of Title 8 of the California Code of Regulations and engaging in the certification of cranes prior to the effective date of this Article may use such periods of time to satisfy the experience requirements of this Part.

(b) Any applicant for a license desiring to employ persons as surveyors to conduct inspections and examinations under the authority and supervision of the license must request that such individuals be approved by the Division in the application for license. Any surveyor desiring to work under the authority and supervision of a licensed certifier must meet the requirements of this subsection and successfully complete a written examination as set forth herein.

(1) To be approved the surveyor must possess knowledge and experience with the specific equipment subject to the license and demonstrate at least five years of related experience as set forth in subsection (a)(2) above. Such surveyors will be approved by the Division to perform certification services only under the authority and supervision of the person issued a license pursuant to this article. Approval of a surveyor pursuant to this subsection does not constitute authorization to engage in certification activities outside the authority of the license.

Note: A person may be considered approved as a surveyor by the Division if the person has been previously approved by the Division as a surveyor under another license issued pursuant to this article and the surveyor will be engaging in the certification of the same type(s) of equipment authorized under the previous license.

(c) In the case of a business entity, such as a corporation, or a business association, a license will be issued only where a designated responsible managing agent of the entity or association has been licensed pursuant to this article. In such cases the license will be valid only so long as the responsible managing agent remains with the entity or association. If the qualifying managing agent should leave the entity or association a new managing agent must meet the requirements of this article and be licensed pursuant thereto.

(d) Application Form. Any application for license and approval will be accepted by the Division upon the filing of a completed application, payment of the application fee and full compliance with all other requirements thereof. All information and attachments shall be given under penalty of perjury. In the case of an entity or agency, all submissions shall be made by a person expressly authorized in writing to act on behalf of the

1309

applicant. The application shall include, but not be limited to, the following:

(1) A statement of the types of cranes and/or derricks, including their capacities, the applicant desires to certify pursuant to the license.

(2) A statement of qualifications and experience satisfying at a minimum the criteria set forth in this section as well as any and all other qualifications the applicant wishes the Division to consider.

(3) A list of surveyors, if any, to be approved under the license, including their respective qualifications, whether any have been previously approved by the Division, and the license under which the prior approval was issued.

(4) Any other relevant information the applicant desires to be considered by the Division.

(e) Written examination.

Any qualified applicant and surveyor to be approved under a license must successfully complete a written examination administered by the Division or its authorized representative, as set forth in this section. The Division will evaluate the applicant's qualifications based on the application and the applicant's training, knowledge and experience before allowing participation in the written examination.

Note: An applicant will be considered "qualified" if the qualification and experience requirements of this article are satisfied.

The written examination will address the following, among other things:

(1) Applicable provisions of title 8 of the California Code of Regulations, including operation, testing, inspection and maintenance requirements, and the duties and recordkeeping responsibilities as set forth in this article.

(2) Safe operating and engineering principles and practices with respect to the specific types cranes or derricks subject to the license, including inspection and proof loading requirements.

§ 344.62.　Issuance of License and Approvals

(a) If the applicant and the surveyor(s) the applicant is seeking to be approved under the license satisfy the requirements of this article, the Division shall issue a license and approval(s).

(b) The Division may impose restrictions on the scope and use of the license or approval(s), such as limiting it to specific types of cranes or derricks based upon the qualifications of the applicant, the desired license, and the qualifications of any surveyor approved under the license.

§ 344.63.　License Application–Processing Time

(a) Within 30 business days of receipt of a completed application for license the Division shall inform the applicant in writing that it is either complete and accepted for filing or that it is deficient and what specific information or documentation is required to complete

the application. An application is considered complete if it is in compliance with the requirements of this article.

(b) Within 30 business days of the date of the filing of a Completed application the Division shall inform the applicant if the minimum requirements of this article are satisfied and of the applicants eligibility to take the written examination.

(c) Within 60 business days from the date of completion of the written examination the Division shall inform the applicant in writing of its decision regarding the issuance of the license or approval(s).

§ 344.64.　Duration and Renewal of License

(a) The license shall be valid for three years.

(b) Application for renewal shall be filed with the Division not less than 60 days prior to expiration. A renewal may be obtained by filing a completed application for renewal meeting the requirements of section 344.61 hereof.

(c) All applicants for renewal and approved surveyors shall successfully complete a written examination every six years.

§ 344.65.　License Application, Renewal and Examination Fees

(a) To cover the costs associated with investigating and evaluating the application for a license and administering the required written examination, a fee of $250.00 for the application, plus $190.00 for the written examination shall be paid.

(b) Where the applicant is seeking the approval of surveyors to work under the authority and supervision of the license either in the application for license or subsequent to the issuance of the license, a fee of $190.00 for each surveyor to be approved shall be paid to cover the costs associated with investigating the request for approval and administering the written examination.

(c) To cover the costs associated with investigating and evaluating an application for renewal of a license a fee of $75.00 shall be paid.

(d) To cover the costs associated with investigating and evaluating a request to transfer a person approved under an existing license to another license a fee of $50.00 shall be paid.

§ 344.66.　Denial of License

(a) The Division shall deny issuance of a license if the applicant does not satisfy the requirements of this article. In denying a license, the Division shall notify the applicant, in writing, as set forth in this article, specifying the reasons for such denial and shall send a copy thereof to the Director.

(b) Any applicant denied a license by the Division may appeal such denial to the Director. The Director shall hold a hearing at such place designated by the Director or his authorized representative within five working days of the appeal. The applicant has the burden of establishing qualification for a license. The hearing shall be presided over by the Director or authorized representative.

(c) The Director shall issue a decision within 10 days of the hearing. The Director's decision shall be final except for any rehearing or judicial review provided for by law. All requests for rehearing shall be filed with the Director within ten days from the date of the Director's denial.

§ 344.67. Revocation or Suspension of License

(a) The Division may at any time, upon a showing of good cause and after notice and an opportunity to be heard, revoke or suspend any license issued pursuant to this article.

(b) Notice shall be in writing and served at least two days in advance of the hearing. Service shall be by personal service or certified mail to the address as shown on the application form. The notice shall specify the reasons for the action taken by the Division in order that the applicant may prepare for the hearing. The Division shall also include within the notice of revocation or suspension specific conditions which must be met before the applicant will be entitled to apply for a new certification.

(c) The hearing shall be held at the Division's Headquarters offices or at such other location as may be designated by the Director and shall be presided over by the Chief of the Division or authorized representative.

(d) During the hearing, the Division shall establish good cause for the action taken. Good cause is deemed to exist if the Division establishes any of the criteria set forth in Labor Code section 7376(a) or that the licensed certifier has committed any of the following acts:

(1) Failure to meet or comply with the requirements of this article or the limitations imposed on the license;

(2) Performance of work not in compliance with applicable laws and regulations.

(e) The period of suspension or revocation for the commission of any act referenced in Labor Code section 7376(a) shall be six months for the first such suspension and one year for each subsequent suspension or revocation.

(1) The commission of any other act referenced in subsection (d) may result in suspension or revocation of up to one year.

(f) Following the period of suspension or revocation, an application for license may be filed with the Division.

(g) The certifying agency or person may appeal such suspension or revocation to the Director. The Director shall hold a hearing at such place designated by the Director or authorized representative within five working days of the appeal. The certifying agency shall have the burden of establishing qualification for licensure.(h) Following the hearing, the Director shall issue a decision. The Director's decision shall be final except for any rehearing or judicial review provided for by law. All requests for rehearings shall be filed with the Director within 10 days from the date of the Director's decision.(i) The filing of an appeal shall not stay the revocation or suspension, and such action shall remain in effect until such time as the applicant presents proof that the specified written conditions required by the Division are met or until otherwise ordered after resolution of the appeal.

Article 12. Tower Cranes–Operating Permit and Certification Requirements

§ 344.70. Tower Cranes–Operating Permit–Scope and Requirements

(a) The permit requirements of this article apply to two types of tower cranes referred to in these orders as:

(1) "Fixed Tower Crane", which includes free standing and climber type tower cranes where the vertical mast or tower is attached to a fixed anchorage, foundation or undercarriage attached to rails, as defined in Labor Code section 7371(a) and (b) and section 4885 of title 8 of the California Code of Regulations, and,

(2) "Mobile Tower Crane", which includes mobile and self erecting type tower cranes, as defined in Labor Code section 7371(a) and (c) and section 4885 of title 8 of the California Code of Regulations.

(b) Any employer operating a fixed or mobile tower crane as described in this section shall obtain a permit from the District Office of the Division pursuant to this article prior to operating the tower crane.

Note: The requirements of this article are in addition to the permit requirements of section 341 et seq. of title 8 of the California Code of Regulations applicable to the erection of the vertical mast or tower for a fixed tower crane.

(c) For the purposes of this article an operating permit is required when the fixed or mobile tower crane is ready for operation, which means the crane has been erected (in the case of a fixed tower crane) and certified for operation by a Division-licensed crane certifier.

§ 344.71. Application for and Issuance of Operating Permit

(a) Fixed and Mobile Tower Cranes—Application for Permit—Location.

(1) In the case of a fixed tower crane the application must be filed at he District Office nearest the location where the tower crane will be operated.

(2) In the case of a mobile tower crane the application may be filed at the District Office nearest the location where the mobile tower crane will be operated or nearest the principal business offices of the applicant.

(b) If the responsibility for operation of the fixed or mobile tower crane changes during the effective period of an existing permit the new employer shall apply for and obtain a separate permit from the Division as set forth in this article prior to continuing operation of the crane.

(c) Blank application forms and fee schedules may be obtained from any district Office of the Division.

(d) A permit may be issued by the Division following the filing of a completed application form and full compliance with all the requirements thereof. Application fees must be paid to the Division upon filing of the application. All inspection fees must be paid by the applicant before the permit will be issued by the Division, unless a temporary permit has been issued pursuant to section 344.72(d) of this article.

(1) In the case of a fixed tower crane the operating permit shall be valid only for the period it is located and operated at the specific site referenced in the permit.

(A) If a fixed tower crane is relocated to a new position on the same project a new operating permit is required.

(2) In the case of a mobile tower crane the permit shall be valid for one year.

(e) The information and attachments submitted with the application for an operating permit shall comply with this section and be given under penalty of perjury by a person duly authorized in writing to act on the behalf of the applicant with respect to the matters referenced in the application. The application shall contain the following:

(1) Employer/Applicant name, address, phone number, project safety contact person, employer's representative at the site including title and phone number and employer/applicant Contractor's Licence No.

(2) Designation of type of contractor and description of crane being operated.

(3) Location and phone number of crane jobsite including nearest cross street, city and county.

(4) Number of employees and anticipated starting date.

(5) Designation of existence of high voltage lines.

(6) Certification that the applicant possesses knowledge of the applicable occupational safety and health standards and manufacturer's operating instructions for the subject crane, as well as a statement of the applicants related training, education and/or experience within the last five years.

(7) Certification that the applicant will comply with all applicable standards and other lawful orders of the Division, and, that the conditions, practices, means, methods, operations or processes used or proposed to be used will be safe, and healthful and that the permit to operate will be posted at the site of operation.

(A) In addition, in the case of a fixed tower crane, the employer shall provide a written job plan which describes the intended operation of the subject crane including the specific uses of the crane and the nature and weight of anticipated loads.

(8) In the case of a fixed tower crane, certification that a Division-licensed certifier or surveyor, or safety repre-

sentative for the distributor or manufacturer, will be present during erection, climbing and dismantling operations to ensure that such processes and operations are performed in accordance with manufacturer recommendations and applicable standards or orders.

(9) A statement of all previous business identities of the applicant within 10 years prior to the date of application.

(A) 'Business identities' include, but shall not be limited to, fictitious business names, corporate names, and/or joint venture partnerships and any other business affiliations in the construction industry involving the use of cranes.

(10) A certification issued by a Division-licensed certifier for subject crane.

(f) The applicant issued a permit pursuant to this article shall have the fixed or mobile tower crane subject to the permit inspected by the Division twice a year. One of these required inspections must be completed prior to the issuance of a permit pursuant to this article.

Note: The initial permit inspection shall be considered as one of the two mandatory yearly inspections.

(g) The holder of a permit issued pursuant to this article shall notify the Division of the following:

(1) In the case of a fixed tower crane the date and time:

(A) The crane will commence operation;

(B) The climbing of the crane; and,

(C) The dismantling of the crane.

(2) In the case of a mobile tower crane the date, time and location of for each new site of operation. This notification is required only in instances where the mobile tower crane will be located at any given site in excess of one day. Where the crane will be operated at any site, or multiple sites, for less then one da notification is not required.

Note: The notification must be provided to the Division at least 24 hours prior to the activity which is the subject of the notification, and may be made in writing or by telephone followed by written notification. The notification shall be made to the District Office of the Division from which the permit was obtained and must include the date and time of the intended activity.

§ 344.72. Tower Crane Operating Permit Application–
        Issuance and Processing Time

(a) Within 5 business days of receipt of an application the Division shall inform the applicant in writing of whether it is accepted for filing and if not what deficiencies exist with reference to the application.

(b) The Division shall issue a permit within 10 days of the receipt of a completed application.

(c) The Division may issue a temporary permit pending the payment of any inspection fees where such fees are not paid in advance. All inspection fees must be paid within 30 business days of the date of the invoice indicating such fees are due. If the inspection fees are not paid within thirty business days as set forth herein, the temporary permit shall immediately expire.

§ 344.73. Tower Crane Operating Permit and Inspection Fee Schedule

(a) To cover the costs associated with investigating and issuing an operating permit for a fixed or mobile tower crane, the fee of $200.00 shall be paid.

Note: The permit to operate and the associated application fee is separate from, and in addition to, the permit and fee requirements of section 341 of title 8 of the California Code of Regulations for the erection of a fixed tower crane.

(b) In addition to the fees set forth in subsection (a) of this section, the hourly fee of $75.00 or fraction thereof, including travel time as set forth in part (1) of this subsection, based on quarter hour intervals, with a minimum of one-half hour, shall be paid to cover the costs associated with inspecting any fixed or mobile tower crane pursuant to the permit requirements of this article and Labor Code section 7373.

(1) Travel time shall include the time from the District Office of the Division processing the request for a permit to the inspection site, and from the inspection site back to the District Office. In the event the travel encompasses multiple permit inspections of different cranes operated by different employers the Division shall allocate the travel time equitably among the permit applicants.

§ 344.74. Denial of Permit

(a) The Division shall deny issuance of an operating permit if the provisions of this article are not satisfied. Upon denying an operating permit to an applicant employer, the Division shall promptly notify the employer, in writing, specifying the reasons for such denial and shall send a copy thereof to the Director.

(b) Any employer denied a permit by the Division may appeal such denial to the Director. The Director shall hold a hearing at such place designated by the Director or authorized representative for the convenience of the attending parties within two working days of the employer's appeal. The employer has the burden of establishing that it qualifies for a permit. The hearing shall be presided by the Director or authorized representative and shall also be open to employees or employees' representative. The employer shall notify the employees or employees' representative of such hearing a reasonable time prior to the such hearing, but in no case later than 24 hours prior to the hearing. Proof of such notification by the employer shall be made at the hearing.

(c) The Director shall issue a decision within ten business days of the hearing. The Director's decision shall be final except for any rehearing or judicial review provided for by law. All requests for rehearing shall be filed with the Director within ten days from the date of the Director's decision.

§ 344.75. Revocation or Suspension of Permit

(a) The Division may at any time, upon a showing of good cause and after notice and an opportunity to be heard, revoke or suspend any permit issued pursuant to this article.

(b) Notice shall be in writing and served upon the applicant at least 24 hours in advance of the hearing. Service shall be by personal service or certified mail to the project address as shown on the application form. The notice shall specify the reasons for the action taken by the Division. The Division shall also include within the notice of revocation or suspension specific conditions which must be met before the applicant will be entitled to resume operation of the tower crane.

(c) The hearing shall be held as soon as possible at the Division's headquarters offices or at such other location as may be designated by the Director and shall be presided by the Chief of the Division or authorized representative.

(d) During the hearing, the Division shall establish good cause for the action taken. Good cause is deemed to exist if the Division establishes any of the criteria set forth in Labor Code section 7374(a).

(e) The period of suspension or revocation for the commission of any act referenced in Labor Code section 7374(a) shall be six months for the first such suspension and one year for each subsequent suspension or revocation.

(1) The commission of any other act referenced in subsection (d) may result in suspension or revocation of up to one year.

(f) The crane employer may appeal such suspension or revocation to the Director. The Director shall hold a hearing at such place designated by the Director or authorized representative for the convenience of the attending parties within five working days of the appeal. The crane employer shall notify employees and employees' representatives of such hearing in a reasonable time prior to the hearing.

The crane employer shall have the burden of establishing qualification for crane operation.

(g) Following the hearing, the Director shall issue a decision within ten business days. The Director's decision shall be final except for any rehearing or judicial review provided for by law. All requests for rehearings shall be filed with the Director within ten days from the date of the Director's decision.

(h) The filing of an appeal shall not stay the revocation or suspension, and such action shall remain in effect until such time as the applicant presents proof that the specified written conditions required by the Division are met or until otherwise ordered after resolution of the appeal.

Article 13.   Certification Requirements

§ 344.80.   License–Duties and Recordkeeping Requirements

Every crane or derrick certifier, licensed pursuant to article 11 of these orders shall comply with the following requirements:

(a) All tests and examinations shall be performed in accordance with the requirements of title 8 of the California Code of Regulations commencing with section 4884.

(1) No certification shall be issued without first performing all necessary tests and examinations as required by applicable standards or orders, including but not limited to the examination of items 1 through 14 referenced in Plate V of section 4885 of title 8 of the California Code of Regulations.

(2) All certifications shall be issued in a form consistent with that set forth in Plate V of section 4885 of title 8 of the California Code of Regulations.

(b) All testing, examinations, inspections, heat treatments, and recordkeeping procedures shall be carried out by or under the direct supervision of the licensed certifier or surveyor.

(1) Certificates issued pursuant to the license shall be completed and personally signed by the licensed certifier or surveyor performing the test and/or examination.

(c) The District Office of the Division nearest the site of inspection shall be notified of any deficiencies affecting the safe operation of the crane found during the course of any certification inspection. This notification shall be made within five working days following the test/examination date and shall be submitted on a form equivalent to Division form No. IS–162 containing the information set forth in subsection (j) of this section.

Note: Blank IS–162 forms may be obtained from any District Office of the Division: or, see Plate 1 appended to these orders.

(d) Deficiencies for the purposes of this article include any and all conditions found during the course of the certification examination or testing which do not comply with applicable safety orders or manufacturer's specifications.

(e) Correction of all deficiencies affecting the safe operation of the crane shall be verified by the licensed certifier or surveyor prior to issuance of a certification. A signed and dated verification of correction shall be submitted to the Division location where notification was given pursuant to subsection (d) of this section and on the IS–162 form or equivalent along with the certificate issued.

(f) Complete and accurate records of all inspections, tests, and other work performed shall be maintained. At a minimum the licensed certifier shall maintain an inspection record for each crane or derrick inspected and/or tested for certification indicating all items inspected or tested during the course of the certification inspection, as well as copies of any Certifier's Notice of Crane Safety Deficiencies issued and records pertaining to the verification of corrections of any such deficiencies, and all certificates issued. All records shall be maintained for a period of at least five years and shall be made available to the Division upon request.

(g) The following records of the operating history of each crane being examined and/or tested for certification shall be reviewed, if available:

(1) Records of previous certifications and Notices of Crane Safety Deficiencies.

(2) Records of tests performed by others, and,

(3) Records of any modifications, downgrading, upgrading, accidents, and damage relating to the crane or derrick.

(h) Any inspection and/or testing, including proof load tests, being performed shall be limited to those machines authorized by the License.

(i) The Division shall be notified, within 24 hours, in writing if any approved surveyor ceases to be employed by the licensed certifier.

(j) The Notice of Crane Safety deficiencies shall contain at least the following:

(1) Name, address, license number and signature of the licensed certifier or surveyor conducting the inspection.

(2) Name, address and phone number of crane owner and location of crane.

(3) Description and rated capacity of equipment or device, including manufacturer, model No., serial No., and owners identification No., if any.

(4) Date of inspection and notification to the owner and description of deficiencies found during the course of the inspection.

(5) A statement that a certification will not be issued until all deficiencies affecting the safe operation of the crane or derrick have been corrected.

(6) Verification and dates of correction of noted deficiencies.

Note: See Plate 1 appended hereto for a sample form IS–162.

PLATE 1

NOTICE OF CRANE SAFETY DEFICIENCIES

(Sample format-IS 162)

Equipment Operator: _____   Owner: _____

Address: _____   Address: _____

Description and location of equipment inspected: _____
_____

Manufacturer: _____ Model No.: _____ Serial No.: _____

Owner I.D.: _____ Rated Capacity: _____

The following deficiencies were found to exist during the inspection, testing and/or examination of the above-referenced equipment on _____.

Description of Condition to be Corrected	Verification Date and Signature
1.	
2.	
3.	
4.	
6.	
7.	
8.	
9.	

(See attached sheet for additional items or descriptions, if any.)

A certificate to operate the above-referenced equipment will not be issued until the items noted herein are corrected and verified as such by the undersigned.

A copy of this Notice, as well as any subsequent verification of corrections, shall be sent, as required, to the Division of Occupational Safety and Health. Labor Code 7375 and Sections 344.6, et. seq. and 4884, et. seq. of Title 8 of the California Code of Regulations prohibit the operation of any crane or derrick subject to the certification requirements thereof to be operated without a valid certification issued by a Division-licensed certifier or approved surveyor.

Licensed Certifier, Name: _____ License No.: _____

Address: _____

Approved Surveyor, Name: _____ Title: _____

Date: _____ Signature: _____

§ 344.81. Fixed and Mobile Tower Crane Certification

(a) Fixed tower cranes and mobile tower cranes subject to this article shall be examined, tested and certified pursuant to article 99 annually and in the case of a fixed tower crane whenever it is erected at a new site.

(b) If a fixed tower crane is relocated to a new position on the same project a new certification is required. This requirement does not apply to the climbing of the tower crane.

(c) Each annual certification of a fixed or mobile tower crane shall include examination and testing of the crane structure and its parts as required pursuant to sections 4884 et seq. of title 8 of the California Code of Regulations and manufacturer recommendations. In the case of any fixed tower crane the annual certification must include detailed non-destructive tests of the load hook, slewing ring, tower section and slewing ring bolts, as well as all structural welds in the crane's tower section, mast and the jibs shall be performed where applicable. All deficiencies shall be corrected prior to use.

Note: Written records of the tests and test procedures performed shall be maintained and made available to the Division upon request for a period of five years.

Article 14. Limitations on Division Eligibility for Certifications, Licenses, and Registrations for Aliens

§ 344.85. Limitations on Division Eligibility for Certifications, Licenses, and Registrations for Aliens

(a) All eligibility requirements contained herein shall be applied without regard to the race, creed, color, gender, religion, or national origin of the applicant.

(b) Pursuant to Section 411 of the Personal Responsibility and Work Opportunity Reconciliation Act of 1996, [Pub. L. No. 104–193 (PRWORA)], (8 U.S.C. section 1621), and notwithstanding any other provision of this division, an alien who is not a qualified alien, a nonimmigrant alien under the Immigration and Nationality Act (INA) (8 U.S.C. section 1101 et seq.), or an alien paroled into the United States under Section 212(d)(5) of the INA [(8 U.S.C. 1182(d)(5)], for less than one year, is not eligible for any of the following benefits, except as provided in 8 U.S.C. 1621(c)(2):

(1) A certification as an asbestos consultant or site surveillance technician pursuant to 8 CCR sections 341.15 and Business and Professions Code Section 7180,

(2) A blaster's license pursuant to 8 CCR sections 344.20 through 344.22 and Labor Code Section 7990,

(3) A license to certify cranes or derricks pursuant to 8 CCR section 344.60 through 344.67 and Labor Code Section 7375,

(4) A registration for asbestos-related work pursuant to 8 CCR sections 341.6 through 341.14 and Labor code Section 6501.5,

(5) A certification as a gas tester pursuant to 8 CCR sections 7104, 8406 and 8424 and Labor Code Section 7999.

(6) A certification as a safety representative pursuant to 8 CCR section 8406 and Labor Code Section 7999.

(c) A qualified alien is an alien who, at the time he or she applies for, receives, or attempts to receive a public benefit, is, under Section 431(b) and (c) of the PRWORA [8 U.S.C. section 1641(b) and (c)], any of the following:

(1) An alien lawfully admitted for permanent residence under the INA (8 U.S.C. section 1101 et seq.).

(2) An alien who is granted asylum under Section 208 of the INA (8 U.S.C. section 1158).

(3) A refugee who is admitted to the United States under Section 207 of the INA (8 U.S.C. section 1157).

(4) An alien who is paroled into the United States under Section 212(d)(5) of the INA [8 U.S.C. section 1182(d)(5)] for a period of at least one year.

(5) An alien whose deportation is being withheld under Section 243(h) of the INA [8 U.S.C. section

1253(h)], as in effect immediately before the effective date of Section 307 of division C of Public Law 104–208), or Section 241(b)(3) of such Act [8 U.S.C. Section 1251(b)(3)], (as amended by Section 305(a) of division C of Public Law 104–208).

(6) An alien who is granted conditional entry pursuant to Section 203(a)(7) of the INA as in effect prior to April 1, 1980. [8 U.S.C. s 1153(a)(7)] (See editorial note under 8 U.S.C. Section 1101, "Effective Date of 1980 Amendment.")

(7) An alien who is a Cuban or Haitian entrant (as defined in Section 501(e) of the Refugee Education Assistance Act of 1980 [8 U.S.C. s 1522 note)].

(8) An alien who meets all of the conditions of subparagraphs (A), (B), (C), and (D) below:

(A) The alien has been battered or subjected to extreme cruelty in the United States by a spouse or a parent, or by a member of the spouse's or parent's family residing in the same household as the alien, and the spouse or parent of the alien consented to, or acquiesced in, such battery or cruelty. For purposes of this subsection, the term "battered or subjected to extreme cruelty" includes, but is not limited to being the victim of any act or threatened act of violence including any forceful detention, which results or threatens to result in physical or mental injury. Rape, molestation, incest (if the victim is a minor), or forced prostitution shall be considered to be acts of violence.

(B) There is a substantial connection between such battery or cruelty and the need for the benefits to be provided in the opinion of Division. For purposes of this subsection, the following circumstances demonstrate a substantial connection between the battery or cruelty and the need for the benefits to be provided:

1. The benefits are needed to enable the alien to become self-sufficient following separation from the abuser.

2. The benefits are needed to enable the alien to escape the abuser and/or the community in which the abuser lives, or to ensure the safety of the alien from the abuser.

3. The benefits are needed due to a loss of financial support resulting from the alien's separation from the abuser.

4. The benefits are needed because the battery or cruelty, separation from the abuser, or work absences or lower job performance resulting from the battery or extreme cruelty or from legal proceedings relating thereto (including resulting child support, child custody, and divorce actions), cause the alien to lose his or her job or to earn less or to require the alien to leave his or her job for safety reasons.

5. The benefits are needed because the alien requires medical attention or mental health counseling, or has become disabled, as a result of the battery or extreme cruelty.

6. The benefits are needed because the loss of a dwelling or source of income or fear of the abuser following separation from the abuser jeopardizes the alien's ability to care for his or her children (e.g., inability to house, feed, or clothe children or to put children into day care for fear of being found by the abuser).

7. The benefits are needed to alleviate nutritional risk or need resulting from the abuse or following separation from the abuser.

8. The benefits are needed to provide medical care during a pregnancy resulting from the abuser's sexual assault or abuse of, or relationship with, the alien and/or to care for any resulting children.

9. Where medical coverage and/or health care services are needed to replace medical coverage or health care services the alien had when living with the abuser.

(C) The alien has a petition that has been approved or has a petition pending which sets forth a prima facie case for:

1. Status as a spouse or child of a United States citizen pursuant to clause (ii), (iii), or (iv) of Section 204(a)(1)(A) of the INA [8 U.S.C. section 1154(a)(1)(A)(ii), (iii) or (iv)].

2. Classification pursuant to clause (ii) or (iii) of Section 204(a)(1)(B) of the INA [8 U.S.C. section 1154(a)(1)(B)(ii) or (iii)].

3. Suspension of deportation and adjustment of status pursuant to Section 244(a)(3) of the INA [8 U.S.C. section 1254(a)(3)], as in effect prior to April 1, 1997 [Pub.L. 104–208, sec. 501 (effective Sept. 30, 1996, pursuant to sec. 591); Pub.L. 104–208, sec. 304 (effective April 1, 1997, pursuant to sec. 309) Pub.L. 105–33, sec. 5581 (effective pursuant to sec. 5582)] (incorrectly codified as "cancellation of removal under Section 240A of such act (8 U.S.C. Section 1229b) as in effect prior to April 1, 1997").

4. Status as a spouse or child of a United States citizen pursuant to clause (i) of Section 204(a)(1)(A) of the INA [(8 U.S.C. section 1154(a)(1)(A)] or classification pursuant to clause (i) of Section 204(a)(1)(B) of the INA [8 U.S.C. section 1154(a)(1)(B)(i)].

5. Cancellation of removal pursuant to Section 240A(b)(2) of the INA (8 U.S.C. Section 1229(b)(2)).

(D) For the period for which benefits are sought, the individual responsible for the battery or cruelty does not reside in the same household or family eligibility unit as the individual subjected to the battery or cruelty.

(9) An alien who meets all of the conditions of subparagraphs (A), (B), (C), (D) and (E) below:

(A) The alien has a child who has been battered or subjected to extreme cruelty in the United States by a spouse or a parent of the alien (without the active participation of the alien in the battery or cruelty), or by a member of the spouse's or parent's family residing in the same household as the alien, and the spouse or parent consented or acquiesced to such battery or cruelty. For purposes of this subsection, the term "battered or subjected to extreme cruelty" includes, but is not limited to being the victim of any act or threatened act of violence including any forceful detention, which results or threatens to result in physical or mental injury. Rape, molestation, incest (if the victim is a minor), or forced prostitution shall be considered as acts of violence.

(B) The alien did not actively participate in such battery or cruelty.

(C) There is a substantial connection between such battery or cruelty and the need for benefits to be provided in the opinion of the Division. For purposes of this subsection, the following circumstances demonstrate a substantial connection between the battery or cruelty and the need for the benefits to be provided:

1. The benefits are needed to enable the alien's child to become self-sufficient following separation from the abuser.

2. The benefits are needed to enable the alien's child to escape the abuser and/or the community in which the abuser lives, or to ensure the safety of the alien's child from the abuser.

3. The benefits are needed due to a loss of financial support resulting from the alien's child's separation from the abuser.

4. The benefits are needed because the battery or cruelty, separation from the abuser, or work absences or lower job performance resulting from the battery or extreme cruelty or from legal proceedings relating thereto (including resulting child support, child custody, and divorce actions) cause the alien's child to lose his or her job or to earn less or to require the alien's child to leave his or her job for safety reasons.

5. The benefits are needed because the alien's child requires medical attention or mental health counseling, or has become disabled, as a result of the battery or extreme cruelty.

6. The benefits are needed because the loss of a dwelling or source of income or fear of the abuser following separation from the abuser jeopardizes the alien's child's ability to care for his or her children (e.g., inability to house, feed, or clothe children or to put children into day care for fear of being found by the abuser).

7. The benefits are needed to alleviate nutritional risk or need resulting from the abuse or following separation from the abuser.

8. The benefits are needed to provide medical care during a pregnancy resulting from the abuser's sexual assault or abuse of, or relationship with, the alien's child and/or to care for any resulting children.

9. Where medical coverage and/or health care services are needed to replace medical coverage or health care services the alien's child had when living with the abuser.

(D) The alien meets the requirements of subsection (c)(8)(C) above.

(E) For the period for which benefits are sought, the individual responsible for the battery or cruelty does not reside in the same household or family eligibility unit as the individual subjected to the battery or cruelty.

(10) An alien child who meets all of the conditions of subparagraphs (A), (B), and (C) below:

(A) The alien child resides in the same household as a parent who has been battered or subjected to extreme cruelty in the United States by that parent's spouse or by a member of the spouse's family residing in the same household as the parent and the spouse consented or acquiesced to such battery or cruelty. For purposes of this subsection, the term "battered or subjected to extreme cruelty" includes, but is not limited to being the victim of any act or threatened act of violence including any forceful detention, which results or threatens to result in physical or mental injury. Rape, molestation, incest (if the victim is a minor), or forced prostitution shall be considered acts of violence.

(B) There is a substantial connection between such battery or cruelty and the need for the benefits to be provided in the opinion of the Division. For purposes of this subsection, the following circumstances demonstrate a substantial connection between the battery or cruelty and the need for the benefits to be provided:

1. The benefits are needed to enable the alien child's parent to become self-sufficient following separation from the abuser.

2. The benefits are needed to enable the alien child's parent to escape the abuser and/or the community in which the abuser lives, or to ensure the safety of the alien child's parent from the abuser.

3. The benefits are needed due to a loss of financial support resulting from the alien child's parent's separation from the abuser.

4. The benefits are needed because the battery or cruelty, separation from the abuser, or work absences or lower job performance resulting from the battery or extreme cruelty or from legal proceedings relating thereto (including resulting child support, child custody, and divorce actions) cause the alien child's parent to lose his or her job or to earn less or to require the alien child's parent to leave his or her job for safety reasons.

5. The benefits are needed because the alien child's parent requires medical attention or mental health counseling, or has become disabled, as a result of the battery or extreme cruelty.

6. The benefits are needed because the loss of a dwelling or source of income or fear of the abuser following separation from the abuser jeopardizes the alien child's parent's ability to care for his or her children (e.g., inability to house, feed, or clothe children or to put children into a day care for fear of being found by the abuser).

7. The benefits are needed to alleviate nutritional risk or need resulting from the abuse or following separation from the abuser.

8. The benefits are needed to provide medical care during a pregnancy resulting from the abuser's sexual assault or abuse of, or relationship with the alien child's parent and/or to care for any resulting children.

9. Where medical coverage and/or health care services are needed to replace medical coverage or health care services the alien child's parent had when living with the abuser.

(c) The alien child meets the requirements of Subsection (c)(8)(C).

(d) For purposes of this section, "nonimmigrant" is defined the same as in Section 101(a)(15) of the INA [8 U.S.C. section 1101(a)(15)].

(e) For purposes of establishing eligibility for benefits, as described in subsection (b)(1)-(b)(6), all of the following must be met:

(1) The applicant shall declare himself or herself to be a citizen of the United States or a qualified alien under subsection (c), a nonimmigrant alien under subsection (d), or an alien paroled into the United States for less than one year under Section 212(d)(5) of the INA [8 U.S.C. section 1182(d)(5)]. The applicant shall declare that status through use of the "Statement of Citizenship, Alienage, and Immigration Status for State Public Benefits," Cal/OSHA–W–1 issued on April 30, 1998, incorporated herein by reference.

(2) The applicant shall present documents of a type acceptable to the Immigration and Naturalization Service (INS) which serve as reasonable evidence of the applicant's declared status.

(3) The applicant shall complete and sign a Cal/OSHA–W–1 issued on April 30, 1998, incorporated herein by reference.

(4) Where authorized by the INS, the documentation presented by an alien as reasonable evidence of the alien's declared immigration status must be submitted to the INS for verification through the Systematic Alien Verification for Entitlements (SAVE) system procedures as follows:

(A) Unless the primary SAVE system is unavailable for use, the primary SAVE system verification shall be used to access the biographical/immigration status computer record contained in the Alien Status Verification Index maintained by the INS. Except as provided in the next paragraph (subparagraph (B), this procedure shall be used to verify the status of all aliens who claim to be qualified aliens and who present an INS-issued document that contains an alien registration or alien admission number.

(B) In any of the following cases, the secondary SAVE system verification procedure shall be used to forward copies of original INS documents evidencing an alien's status as a qualified alien, as a nonimmigrant alien under

1318

the INA, or as an alien paroled into the United States under Section 212(d)(5) of the INS [8 U.S.C. section 1182(d)(5)], for less than one year:

1. The primary SAVE system is unavailable for verification.

2. A primary check of the Alien Status Verification Index instructs the Division to institute secondary verification.

3. The document presented indicates immigration status but does not include an alien registration or alien admission number.

4. The Alien Status Verification Index record includes the alien registration or admission number on the document presented by the alien but does not match other information contained in the document.

5. The document is suspected to be counterfeit or to have been altered.

6. The document includes an alien registration number in the "not yet issued" or "illegal border crossing" series, as defined by the INS.

Note: The numbers used by the INS for each series are A60 000 000 and A80 000 000 respectively, as of the date of adoption of this regulation.

7. The document is a fee receipt from INS for replacement of a lost, stolen, or unreadable INS document.

8. The document is one of the following: an INS Form I–181b notification letter issued in connection with an INS Form I–181 Memorandum of Creation of Record of Permanent Residence; an Arrival–Departure Record (INS Form I–94); or a foreign passport stamped "PROCESSED FOR I–551, TEMPORARY EVIDENCE OF LAWFUL PERMANENT RESIDENCE" that INS issued more than one year before the date of application for a benefit described in subsection (b)(1)-(b)(6.

(5) Where verification through the SAVE system is not available, if the documents presented do not on their face reasonably appear to be genuine or to relate to the individual presenting them, the government entity that originally issued the document shall be contacted for verification. With regard to naturalized citizens and derivative citizens presenting certificates of citizenship and aliens, the INS is the appropriate government entity to contact for verification. The Division shall request verification by the INS by filing INS Form G–845 with copies of the pertinent documents provided by the applicant with the local INS office. If the applicant has lost his or her original documents, or presents expired documents or is unable to present any documentation evidencing his or her immigration status, the applicant should be referred to the local INS office to obtain documentation.

(6) If the INS advises that the applicant has citizenship status or immigration status which makes him or her a qualified alien, a nonimmigrant or alien paroled for less than one year under section 212(d)(5) of the INA, the

INS verification shall be accepted. If the INS advises that it cannot verify that the applicant has citizenship status or an immigration status that makes him or her a qualified alien, or a nonimmigrant or an alien paroled for less than one year under section 212(d)(5) of the INA, benefits shall be denied and the applicant notified pursuant to subsection (h) or (i) of his or her rights to appeal the denial of benefits.

(7) Provided that the alien has completed and signed form Cal/OSHA–W–1 issued on April 30, 1998, incorporated herein by reference, under penalty of perjury, eligibility for benefits for certification, license or registration, as found in subsection (b)(1)-(b)(6), shall not be delayed, denied, reduced or terminated while the status of the alien is verified.

(f) Pursuant to Section 432(d) of the PRWORA (8 U.S.C. section 1642(d)), a nonprofit charitable organization that provides federal, state, or local public benefits shall not be required to determine, verify, or otherwise require proof of eligibility of any applicant or beneficiary with respect to his or her immigration status or alienage.

(g) Pursuant to Section 434 of the PRWORA (8 U.S.C. section 1644), where the Division reasonably believes that an alien is unlawfully in the State based on the failure of the alien to provide reasonable evidence of the alien's declared status, after an opportunity to do so, said alien shall be reported to the Immigration and Naturalization Service.

(h) Denial of Application.

(1) The Division shall deny issuance of the benefit applied for if the applicant does not meet the requirements of this section. Upon denial of the benefit the Division shall promptly notify the applicant specifying the reason for the denial.

(2) Any applicant denied certification, license or registration by the Division may appeal such denial to the Director. The Director shall hold a hearing at such place designated by the Director or his authorized designee for the convenience of the applicant within two working days of the applicant's appeal. The hearing shall be presided by the Director or his authorized designee.

(3) Following the hearing, the Director shall issue a decision. The Director's decision shall be final except for any rehearing or judicial review provided for by law. All requests for rehearing shall be filed with the Director within 10 days from the date of the Director's decision.

(i) Revocation or Suspension of Certification, License or Registration.

(1) The Division may at any time, upon a showing of good cause and after notice and an opportunity to be heard, revoke or suspend any benefit issued pursuant to this section.

(2) Notice shall be in writing and served upon the recipient of the benefit at least 24 hours in advance of the hearing. Service shall be by personal service or certified mail to the recipient of the benefit to the address as shown on the application form. The notice shall specify the reasons for the action taken by the Division in order that the recipient may prepare for the hearing. The Division shall also include within the notice of revocation or suspension specific conditions which must be met before the recipient of the benefit will be entitled to reapply for the benefit of this section.

(3) The hearing shall be held as soon as possible at the Division's headquarters offices or at such other location as may be designated by the Director and shall be presided by the Chief of the Division or his authorized representative.

(4) At the hearing the Division shall establish good cause for the action taken by it. Good cause is deemed to exist if the Division establishes that the recipient of the benefit has failed to comply with the requirements of this section.

The recipient of the benefit may appeal such revocation or suspension to the Director in the same manner specified in subsection (h). The filing of an appeal shall not stay the revocation or suspension, and such action shall remain in effect until the benefit recipient provides proof that the requirements of this section have been met.

344.90. Impalement Protection. Specifications and Testing Criteria (See Construction Safety Orders, Title 8, CCR § 1712).

(a) Scope: This section governs the testing of manufactured protective covers designed to prevent accidental impalement from exposed reinforcing steel (rebar) or other similar projections.

(b) Effective Date: This section applies to all protective covers manufactured on or after October 1, 2000.

(c) All manufactured protective covers used as protection against impalement for workers at grade or the same level as the projection shall:

(1) Pass the drop test described in subsection (e) of this section, except that the drop height may be reduced to 7 1/2 '.

(2) Meet all other applicable requirements of section 1712 of this Code.

(d) All manufactured protective covers used as protection against impalement for work performed at levels not to exceed 7 1/2 ' above grade shall:

(1) Have a minimum of 4" by 4" square surface area, or if round, a minimum diameter of 4 1/2". Troughs shall be at least 4" wide.

(2) Pass the drop test specified in subsection (e) of this section.

(3) Meet all other applicable requirements of section 1712 of this Code.

(e) Manufactured protective covers shall be able to pass the following penetration tests, as verified by a person, firm, or entity with appropriate registered-engineering competence, or by a person, firm, or entity, independent of the manufacturer of the subject protective covers, with demonstrated competence in the field of such evaluation.

(1) Protective covers for rebar shall be tested for penetration by dropping a 250-lb. bag of dry sand (less than 10% moisture by weight) onto the subject protective cover from a height of 10 ' . The 10 ' shall be measured from the bottom of the bag to the top of the protective cover.

(A) The sandbag shall be generally round, and shall have a circumference of 36" to 42" . When filled with 250 lbs. of sand, the bag shall be tightly closed by use of crimping, drawstring, or twisting at the top level of the sand so that there is little extra room in the bag to allow the sand to shift. The bag shall be constructed and reinforced (as necessary) with material, which will not rupture or be penetrated by the protective cover for rebar.

(B) The protective cover for rebar shall be installed over the sheared end of a piece of #4 rebar. The rebar shall be mounted on a support with 6" of the rebar projecting vertically above the surface of the support. The support shall be of such height and width that it shall not interfere with the falling sandbag, and shall allow the full initial impact of the sandbag to be borne by the protective cover.

(C) The drop test shall be repeated three times, using a new protective cover for each test. One drop test shall be performed with the protective cover sitting squarely on top of the rebar; the other two drop tests shall be performed with the protective cover sitting at the maximum angle out of square (out of level) that the protective cover will permit with its stabilizer vanes/fins removed.

(2) Protective covers for projections or equipment other than rebar, (such as lighting rods,) shall be tested in the same manner as protective covers for rebar, except that protruding equipment which is normally installed with a protective cover as a single unit may be tested as a unit, using the equipment in lieu of the rebar.

(3) Rebar troughs shall be tested for penetration by dropping a 250-lb bag of dry sand (less than 10% moisture by weight) onto the subject trough from a height of 10 ' . The 10 ' shall be measured from the bottom of the bag to the top of the protective cover.

(A) The sandbag shall be generally round, and shall have a circumference of 36" to 42" . When filled with 250 lbs. of sand, the bag shall be tightly closed by use of crimping, drawstring, or twisting at the top level of the sand so that there is little extra room in the bag to allow the sand to shift. The bag shall be constructed and reinforced (as necessary) with material, which will not rupture or be penetrated by the protective cover for rebar.

(B) The trough shall be installed over the sheared ends of three pieces of #4 rebar. The three pieces rebar shall be mounted in a straight line, 24" apart, on a support with 6" of each piece of rebar projecting vertically above the

1320

surface of the support. The trough shall be 72" in length, and shall be centered over the three pieces of rebar so that 12" of the trough extends beyond each of the outside pieces of rebar.

(C) The drop test shall be repeated four times, using a new trough for each test. The sandbag shall be dropped: (i) once with the trough level and the sandbag centered over the middle piece of rebar; (ii) once with the trough level and the sandbag centered over one of the end pieces of rebar; (iii) once with the trough tilted (at the maximum angle allowed by the design) with the sandbag centered over the middle piece of rebar; (iv) once with the trough tilted (at the maximum angle allowed by the design) with the sandbag centered over one of the end pieces of rebar.

(4) Other methods for penetration testing may be substituted for those set forth in this section where acceptable to the Division as being equally effective.

(f) Each manufacturer, or other person or entity reselling or distributing manufactured protective covers, shall furnish the ultimate user of the protective cover with instructions regarding appropriate use of the protective covers. The instructions, written in English, shall include at least the following:

(1) Instructions as to whether the protective cover is designed for use at grade or above grade.

(2) A statement indicating the maximum height of fall that the cover is designed to protect against impalement, but not to exceed 7 1/2 '.

(3) Installation instructions.

(4) Instructions regarding the inspection and/or use of damaged or defective protective covers. The effects, if any, of damaged stabilizer vanes/fins shall be included in this instruction.

(5) Any other instructions deemed necessary by the manufacturer regarding the use of the protective covers.

(g) Each employer whose employees use or work around or above protective covers shall inform its employees of the content of the manufacturer's instructions. Such information shall be provided to employees in a manner that allows them to understand the appropriate use of protective covers and the hazards associated with impalement.

(h) Marking -Each protective cover shall be marked with the following information:

(1) Model Number or Trademark.

(2) California Approval Number as issued pursuant to Sections 1712 and 1505 of this Code.

(3) Size(s) designation.

Chapter 5.   Industrial Welfare Commission

Group 1.   General Minimum Wage Order

Article 1.   Minimum Wage Order

§ 11000.   Order Regulating the Minimum Wage

1. Applicability—The provisions of this Order shall not apply to outside salespersons and individuals who are the

parent, spouse, or children of the employer previously contained in this Order and the IWC's industry and occupation orders. The IWC has eliminated other exemptions from the minimum wage previously contained in this Order and in sections of the IWC's industry and occupation orders. (See Section 5, Amended Provisions, below.) Exceptions and modifications provided by statute or in Section 1, Applicability, and other sections of the IWC's industry and occupation orders may be used where any such provisions are enforceable and applicable to the employer.

2. Minimum Wages—Every employer shall pay to each employee wages not less than six dollars and twenty-five cents ($6.25) per hour for all hours worked, effective January 1, 2001, and not less than six dollars and seventy-five cents ($6.75) per hour for all hours worked, effective January 1, 2002.

3. Meals and Lodging—Meals or lodging may not be credited against the minimum wage without a voluntary written agreement between the employer and the employee. When credit for meals or lodging is used to meet part of the employer's minimum wage obligation, the amounts so credited may not be more than the following:

Lodging—	Effective January 1, 2001	Effective January 1, 2002
Room occupied alone	$29.40 per week	$31.75 per week
Room shared	$24.25 per week	$26.20 per week
Apartment—two-thirds (2/3) of the ordinary rental value, and in no event more than:	$352.95 per month	$381.20 per month
Where a couple are both employed by the employer, two-thirds (2/3) of the ordinary rental value, and in no event more than:	$522.10 per month	$563.90 per month
Meals—		
Breakfast	$2.25	$2.45
Lunch	$3.10	$3.35
Dinner	$4.15	$4.50

4. Separability—If the application of any provision of this Order, or any section, subsection, subdivision, sentence, clause, phrase, word or portion of this Order should be held invalid, unconstitutional, unauthorized, or prohibited by statute, the remaining provisions thereof shall not be affected thereby, but shall continue to be given full force and effect as if the part so held invalid or unconstitutional had not been included herein.

5. Amended Provisions—This order amends the minimum wage and meals and lodging credits in MW-98, as well as in the IWC's industry and occupation orders. (See Orders 1-15, Secs. 4 and 10; and Order 16, Secs. 4 and 9.) This Order also amends the following other provisions of the IWC's industry and occupations orders to be consistent with the IWC's actions regarding the elimination of certain exemptions from the minimum wage: Order 1, Secs. 1(B) and 4(A)(1) and (2); Order 2, Secs. 1(B) and 4(A)(1) and (2); Order 3, Secs. 1(B) and 4(A)(1) and (2); Order 4, Secs. 1(B) and 4(A)(1) and (2); Order 5, Secs. 1(A) and (C), and 4(A)(1) and (2); Order 6, Secs. 1(B)

and 4(A)(1) and (2); Order 7, Secs. 1(B) and 4(A)(1) and (2); Order 8, Secs. 1(B) and 4(A)(1) and (2); Order 9, Secs. 1(B) and 4(A)(1) and (2); Order 10, Secs. 1(B) and (D), and 4(A)(1) and (2); Order 11, Secs. 1(B) and (C) and 4(A)(1) and (2); Order 12, Secs. 1(B) and (C) and 4(A)(1) and (2); Order 13, Secs. 1(B) and 4(A)(1) and (2); Order 14, Secs. 1(B) and 4(A)(1) and (2); Order 15, Secs. 1(B) and 4(A)(1) and (2); and, Order 16, Sec. 1(B). These amendments were adopted on October 23, 2000 in Sacramento.

These Amendments to the Wage Orders shall be in effect as of January 1, 2001

Group 2. Industry and Occupation Orders

See Appendices for text of Wage Orders.

Article 4. Professional, Technical, Clerical, Mechanical, and Similar

§ 11040. Order Regulating Wages, Hours, and Working Conditions in Professional, Technical, Clerical, Mechanical, and Similar Occupations.

1. Applicability of Order This order shall apply to all persons employed in professional, technical, clerical, mechanical, and similar occupations whether paid on a time, piece rate, commission, or other basis, except that:

(A) Provisions of sections 3 through 12 shall not apply to persons employed in administrative, executive, or professional capacities. The following requirements shall apply in determining whether an employee's duties meet the test to qualify for an exemption from those sections:

(1) Executive Exemption A person employed in an executive capacity means any employee:

(a) Whose duties and responsibilities involve the management of the enterprise in which he/she is employed or of a customarily recognized department or subdivision thereof; and

(b) Who customarily and regularly directs the work of two or more other employees therein; and

(c) Who has the authority to hire or fire other employees or whose suggestions and recommendations as to the hiring or firing and as to the advancement and promotion or any other change of status of other employees will be given particular weight; and

(d) Who customarily and regularly exercises discretion and independent judgment; and

(e) Who is primarily engaged in duties which meet the test of the exemption. The activities constituting exempt work and non-exempt work shall be construed in the same manner as such items are construed in the following regulations under the Fair Labor Standards Act effective as of the date of this order: 29 C.F.R. Sections 541.102, 541.104–111, and 541.115–16. Exempt work shall include, for example, all work that is directly and closely related to exempt work and work which is properly viewed as a means for carrying out exempt functions. The work actually performed by the employee during the course of the workweek must, first and foremost, be examined and the amount of time the employee spends on such work, together with the employer's realistic expectations and the realistic requirements of the job, shall be considered in determining whether the employee satisfies this requirement.

(f) Such an employee must also earn a monthly salary equivalent to no less than two (2) times the state minimum wage for full-time employment. Full-time employment is defined in Labor Code Section 515(c) as 40 hours per week.

(2) Administrative Exemption A person employed in an administrative capacity means any employee:

(a) Whose duties and responsibilities involve either:

(I) The performance of office or non-manual work directly related to management policies or general business operations of his/her employer or his employer's customers; or

(II) The performance of functions in the administration of a school system, or educational establishment or institution, or of a department or subdivision thereof, in work directly related to the academic instruction or training carried on therein; and

(b) Who customarily and regularly exercises discretion and independent judgment; and

(c) Who regularly and directly assists a proprietor, or an employee employed in a bona fide executive or administrative capacity (as such terms are defined for purposes of this section); or

(d) Who performs under only general supervision work along specialized or technical lines requiring special training, experience, or knowledge; or

(e) Who executes under only general supervision special assignments and tasks; and

(f) Who is primarily engaged in duties that meet the test of the exemption. The activities constituting exempt work and non-exempt work shall be construed in the same manner as such terms are construed in the following regulations under the Fair Labor Standards Act effective as of the date of this order: 29 C.F.R. Sections 541.201–205, 541.207–208, 541.210, and 541.215. Exempt work shall include, for example, all work that is directly and closely related to exempt work and work which is properly viewed as a means for carrying out exempt functions. The work actually performed by the employee during the course of the workweek must, first and foremost, be examined and the amount of time the employee spends on such work, together with the employer's realistic expectations and the realistic requirements of the job, shall be considered in determining whether the employee satisfies this requirement.

(g) Such employee must also earn a monthly salary equivalent to no less than two (2) times the state minimum wage for full-time employment. Full-time employment is defined in California Labor Code Section 515(c) as 40 hours per week.

(3) Professional Exemption A person employed in a professional capacity means any employee who meets all of the following requirements:

(a) Who is licensed or certified by the State of California and is primarily engaged in the practice of one of the following recognized professions: law, medicine, dentistry, optometry, architecture, engineering, teaching, or accounting; or

(b) Who is primarily engaged in an occupation commonly recognized as a learned or artistic profession. For the purposes of this subsection, "learned or artistic profession" means an employee who is primarily engaged in the performance of:

(i) Work requiring knowledge of an advanced type in a field or science or learning customarily acquired by a prolonged course of specialized intellectual instruction and study, as distinguished from a general academic education and from an apprenticeship, and from training in the performance of routine mental, manual, or physical processes, or work that is an essential part of or necessarily incident to any of the above work; or

(ii) Work that is original and creative in character in a recognized field of artistic endeavor (as opposed to work which can be produced by a person endowed with general manual or intellectual ability and training), and the result of which depends primarily on the invention, imagination, or talent of the employee or work that is an essential part of or necessarily incident to any of the above work; and

(iii) Whose work is predominantly intellectual and varied in character (as opposed to routine mental, manual, mechanical, or physical work) and is of such character that the output produced or the result accomplished cannot be standardized in relation to a given period of time.

(c) Who customarily and regularly exercises discretion and independent judgment in the performance of duties set forth in subparagraphs (a) and (b).

(d) Who earns a monthly salary equivalent to no less than two (2) times the state minimum wage for full-time employment. Full-time employment is defined in Labor Code Section 515(c) as 40 hours per week.

(e) Subparagraph (b) above is intended to be construed in accordance with the following provisions of federal law as they existed as of the date of this wage order: 29 C.F.R. Sections 541.207, 541.301(a)-(d), 541.302, 541.306, 541.307, 541.308, and 541.310.

(f) Notwithstanding the provisions of this subparagraph, pharmacists employed to engage in the practice of pharmacy, and registered nurses employed to engage in the practice of nursing, shall not be considered exempt professional employees, nor shall they be considered exempt from coverage for the purposes of this subparagraph unless they individually meet the criteria established for exemption as executive or administrative employees.

(g) Subparagraph (f) above shall not apply to the following advanced practice nurses:

(i) Certified nurse midwives who are primarily engaged in performing duties for which certification is required pursuant to Article 2.5 (commencing with Section 2746) of Chapter 6 of Division 2 of the Business and Professions Code.

(ii) Certified nurse anesthetists who are primarily engaged in performing duties for which certification is required pursuant to Article 7 (commencing with Section 2825) of Chapter 6 of Division 2 of the Business and Professions Code.

(iii) Certified nurse practitioners who are primarily engaged in performing duties for which certification is required pursuant to Article 8 (commencing with Section 2834) of Chapter 6 of Division 2 of the Business and Professions Code.

(iv) Nothing in this subparagraph shall exempt the occupations set forth in clauses (i), (ii), and (iii) from meeting the requirements of subsection 1(A)(3)(a)-(d) above.

(h) Except, as provided in subparagraph (i), an employee in the computer software field who is paid on an hourly basis shall be exempt, if all of the following apply:

(i) The employee is primarily engaged in work that is intellectual or creative and that requires the exercise of discretion and independent judgment.

(ii) The employee is primarily engaged in duties that consist of one or more of the following:

-The application of systems analysis techniques and procedures, including consulting with users, to determine hardware, software, or system functional specifications.

-The design, development, documentation, analysis, creation, testing, or modification of computer systems or programs, including prototypes, based on and related to user or system design specifications.

-The documentation, testing, creation, or modification of computer programs related to the design of software or hardware for computer operating systems.

(iii) The employee is highly skilled and is proficient in the theoretical and practical application of highly specialized information to computer systems analysis, programming, and software engineering. A job title shall not be determinative of the applicability of this exemption.

(iv) The employee's hourly rate of pay is not less than forty-two dollars and sixty four cents ($42.64). The Division of Labor Statistics and Research shall adjust this pay rate on October 1 of each year to be effective on January 1 of the following year by an amount equal to the percentage increase in the California Consumer Price Index for Urban Wage Earners and Clerical Workers.

(i) The exemption provided in subparagraph (h) does not apply to an employee if any of the following apply:

(i) The employee is a trainee or employee in an entry-level position who is learning to become proficient in the theoretical and practical application of highly specialized information to computer systems analysis, programming, and software engineering.

(ii) The employee is in a computer-related occupation but has not attained the level of skill and expertise necessary to work independently and without close supervision.

(iii) The employee is engaged in the operation of computers or in the manufacture, repair, or maintenance of computer hardware and related equipment.

(iv) The employee is an engineer, drafter, machinist, or other professional whose work is highly dependent upon or facilitated by the use of computers and computer software programs and who is skilled in computer-aided design software, including CAD/CAM, but who is not in a computer systems analysis or programming occupation.

(v) The employee is a writer engaged in writing material, including box labels, product descriptions, documentation, promotional material, setup and installation instructions, and other similar written information, either for print or for on screen media or who writes or provides content material intended to be read by customers, subscribers, or visitors to computer-related media such as the World Wide Web or CD–ROMs.

(vi) The employee is engaged in any of the activities set forth in subparagraph (h) for the purpose of creating imagery for effects used in the motion picture, television, or theatrical industry.

(B) Except as provided in Sections 1, 2, 4, 10, and 20, the provisions of this order shall not apply to any employees directly employed by the State or any political subdivision thereof, including any city, county, or special district.

(C) The provisions of this order shall not apply to outside salespersons.

(D) The provisions of this order shall not apply to any individual who is the parent, spouse, child, or legally adopted child of the employer.

(E) The provisions of this order shall not apply to any individual participating in a national service program, such as AmeriCorps, carried out using assistance provided under Section 12571 of Title 42 of the United States Code. (See Stats. 2000, ch. 365, amending Labor Code Section 1171.)

2. Definitions

(A) An "alternative workweek schedule" means any regularly scheduled workweek requiring an employee to work more than eight (8) hours in a 24–hour period.

(B) "Commission" means the Industrial Welfare Commission of the State of California.

(C) "Division" means the Division of Labor Standards Enforcement of the State of California.

(D) "Emergency" means an unpredictable or unavoidable occurrence at unscheduled intervals requiring immediate action.

(E) "Employ" means to engage, suffer, or permit to work.

(F) "Employee" means any person employed by an employer.

(G) "Employees in the health care industry" means any of the following:

(1) Employees in the health care industry providing patient care; or

(2) Employees in the health care industry working in a clinical or medical department, including pharmacists dispensing prescriptions in any practice setting; or

(3) Employees in the health care industry working primarily or regularly as a member of a patient care delivery team; or

(4) Licensed veterinarians, registered veterinary technicians and unregistered animal health technicians providing patient care.

(H) "Employer" means any person as defined in Section 18 of the Labor Code, who directly or indirectly, or through an agent or any other person, employs or exercises control over the wages, hours, or working conditions of any person.

(I) "Health care emergency" consists of an unpredictable or unavoidable occurrence at unscheduled intervals relating to healthcare delivery, requiring immediate action.

(J) "Health care industry" is defined as hospitals, skilled nursing facilities, intermediate care and residential care facilities, convalescent care institutions, home health agencies, clinics operating 24 hours per day, and clinics performing surgery, urgent care, radiology, anesthesiology, pathology, neurology or dialysis.

(K) "Hours worked" means the time during which an employee is subject to the control of an employer, and includes all the time the employee is suffered or permitted to work, whether or not required to do so. Within the health care industry, the term "hours worked" means the time during which an employee is suffered or permitted to work for the employer, whether or not required to do so, as interpreted in accordance with the provisions of the Fair Labor Standards Act.

(L) "Minor" means, for the purpose of this order, any person under the age of 18 years.

(M) "Outside salesperson" means any person, 18 years of age or over, who customarily and regularly works more than half the working time away from the employer's place of business selling tangible or intangible items or obtaining orders or contracts for products, services or use of facilities.

(N) "Primarily" as used in Section 1, Applicability, means more than one-half the employee's work time.

(O) "Professional, Technical, Clerical, Mechanical, and Similar Occupations" includes professional, semiprofessional, managerial, supervisorial, laboratory, research, technical, clerical, office work, and mechanical occupations. Said occupations shall include, but not be limited to, the following: accountants; agents; appraisers; artists; attendants; audio-visual technicians; bookkeepers; bundlers; billposters; canvassers; carriers; cashiers; checkers; clerks; collectors; communications and sound technicians; compilers; copy holders; copy readers; copy writers; computer programmers and operators; demonstrators and display representatives; dispatchers; distributors; door-keepers; drafters; elevator operators; estimators; editors; graphic arts technicians; guards; guides; hosts; inspectors; installers; instructors; interviewers; investigators; librarians; laboratory workers; machine operators; mechanics; mailers; messengers; medical and dental technicians and technologists; models; nurses; packagers; photographers; porters and cleaners; process servers; printers; proof readers; salespersons and sales agents; secretaries; sign erectors; sign painters; social workers; solicitors; statisticians; stenographers; teachers; telephone, radio-telephone, telegraph and call-out operators; tellers; ticket agents; tracers; typists; vehicle operators; x-ray technicians; their assistants and other related occupations listed as professional, semiprofessional, technical, clerical, mechanical, and kindred occupations.

(P) "Shift" means designated hours of work by an employee, with a designated beginning time and quitting time.

(Q) "Split shift" means a work schedule, which is interrupted by non-paid non-working periods established by the employer, other than bona fide rest or meal periods.

(R) "Teaching" means, for the purpose of Section 1 of this order, the profession of teaching under a certificate from the Commission for Teacher Preparation and Licensing or teaching in an accredited college or university.

(S) "Wages" includes all amounts for labor performed by employees of every description, whether the amount is fixed or ascertained by the standard of time, task, piece, commission basis, or other method of calculation.

(T) "Workday" and "day" mean any consecutive 24–hour period beginning at the same time each calendar day.

(U) "Workweek" and "week" mean any seven (7) consecutive days, starting with the same calendar day each week. "Workweek" is a fixed and regularly recurring period of 168 hours, seven (7) consecutive 24–hour periods.

3. Hours and Days of Work

(A) Daily Overtime–General Provisions

(1) The following overtime provisions are applicable to employees 18 years of age or over and to employees 16 or 17 years of age who are not required by law to attend school and are not otherwise prohibited by law from

engaging in the subject work. Such employees shall not be employed more than eight (8) hours in any workday or more than 40 hours in any workweek unless the employee receives one and one-half (1 1/2) times such employee's regular rate of pay for all hours worked over 40 hours in the workweek. Eight (8) hours of labor constitutes a day's work. Employment beyond eight (8) hours in any workday or more than six (6) days in any workweek is permissible provided the employee is compensated for such overtime at not less than:

(a) One and one-half (1 1/2) times the employee's regular rate of pay for all hours worked in excess of eight (8) hours up to and including 12 hours in any workday, and for the first eight (8) hours worked on the seventh (7th) consecutive day of work in a workweek; and

(b) Double the employee's regular rate of pay for all hours worked in excess of 12 hours in any workday and for all hours worked in excess of eight (8) hours on the seventh (7th) consecutive day of work in a workweek.

(c) The overtime rate of compensation required to be paid to a nonexempt full-time salaried employee shall be computed by using the employee's regular hourly salary as one-fortieth (1/40) of the employee's weekly salary.

(B) Alternative Workweek Schedules

(1) No employer shall be deemed to have violated the daily overtime provisions by instituting, pursuant to the election procedures set forth in this wage order, a regularly scheduled alternative workweek schedule of not more than ten (10) hours per day within a 40 hour workweek without the payment of an overtime rate of compensation. All work performed in any workday beyond the schedule established by the agreement up to 12 hours a day or beyond 40 hours per week shall be paid at one and one-half (1 1/2) times the employee's regular rate of pay. All work performed in excess of 12 hours per day and any work in excess of eight (8) hours on those days worked beyond the regularly scheduled number of workdays established by the alternative workweek agreement shall be paid at double the employee's regular rate of pay. Any alternative workweek agreement adopted pursuant to this section shall provide for not less than four (4) hours of work in any shift. Nothing in this section shall prohibit an employer, at the request of the employee, to substitute one day of work for another day of the same length in the shift provided by the alternative workweek agreement on an occasional basis to meet the personal needs of the employee without the payment of overtime. No hours paid at either one and one-half (1 1/2) or double the regular rate of pay shall be included in determining when 40 hours have been worked for the purpose of computing overtime compensation.

(2) If an employer, whose employees have adopted an alternative workweek agreement permitted by this order requires an employee to work fewer hours than those that are regularly scheduled by the agreement, the employer shall pay the employee overtime compensation at a rate of one and one-half (1 1/2) times the employee's regular rate of pay for all hours worked in excess of eight (8) hours, and double the employee's regular rate of pay for all hours worked in excess of 12 hours for the day the employee is required to work the reduced hours.

(3) An employer shall not reduce an employee's regular rate of hourly pay as a result of the adoption, repeal or nullification of an alternative workweek schedule.

(4) An employer shall explore any available reasonable alternative means of accommodating the religious belief or observance of an affected employee that conflicts with an adopted alternative workweek schedule, in the manner provided by subdivision (j) of Section 12940 of the Government Code.

(5) An employer shall make a reasonable effort to find a work schedule not to exceed eight (8) hours in a workday, in order to accommodate any affected employee who was eligible to vote in an election authorized by this section and who is unable to work the alternative workweek schedule established as the result of that election.

(6) An employer shall be permitted, but not required, to provide a work schedule not to exceed eight (8) hours in a workday to accommodate any employee who is hired after the date of the election and who is unable to work the alternative workweek schedule established by the election.

(7) Arrangements adopted in a secret ballot election held pursuant to this order prior to 1998, or under the rules in effect prior to 1998, and before the performance of the work, shall remain valid after July 1, 2000 provided that the results of the election are reported by the employer to the Division of Labor Statistics and Research by January 1, 2001, in accordance with the requirements of section (C) below (Election Procedures). If an employee was voluntarily working an alternative workweek schedule of not more than ten (10) hours a day as of July 1, 1999, that alternative workweek schedule was based on an individual agreement made after January 1, 1998 between the employee and employer, and the employee submitted, and the employer approved, a written request on or before May 30, 2000 to continue the agreement, the employee may continue to work that alternative workweek schedule without payment of an overtime rate of compensation for the hours provided in the agreement. The employee may revoke his/her voluntary authorization to continue such a schedule with 30 days written notice to the employer. New arrangements can only be entered into pursuant to the provisions of this section. Notwithstanding the foregoing, if a health care industry employer implemented a reduced rate for 12–hour shift employees in the last quarter of 1999 and desires to re-implement a flexible work arrangement that includes 12–hour shifts at straight time for the same work unit, the employer must pay a base rate to each affected employee in the work unit that is no less than that employee's base rate in 1999 immediately prior to the date of the rate reduction.

(8) Notwithstanding the above provisions regarding alternative workweek schedules, no employer of employees in the health care industry shall be deemed to have

violated the daily overtime provisions by instituting, pursuant to the election procedures set forth in this wage order a regularly scheduled alternative workweek schedule that includes work days exceeding ten (10) hours but not more than 12 hours within a 40 hour workweek without the payment of overtime compensation, provided that:

(a) An employee who works beyond 12 hours in a workday shall be compensated at double the employee's regular rate of pay for all hours in excess of 12;

(b) An employee who works in excess of 40 hours in a workweek shall be compensated at one and one-half (1 1/2) times the employee's regular rate of pay for all hours over 40 hours in the workweek;

(c) Any alternative workweek agreement adopted pursuant to this section shall provide for not less than four (4) hours of work in any shift;

(d) The same overtime standards shall apply to employees who are temporarily assigned to a work unit covered by this subsection;

(e) Any employer who instituted an alternative workweek schedule pursuant to this subsection shall make a reasonable effort to find another work assignment for any employee who participated in a valid election prior to 1998 pursuant to the provisions of Wage Orders 4 and 5 and who is unable to work the alternative workweek schedule established;

(f) An employer engaged in the operation of a licensed hospital or in providing personnel for the operation of a licensed hospital who institutes, pursuant to a valid order of the Commission, a regularly scheduled alternative workweek that includes no more than three (3) 12–hour workdays, shall make a reasonable effort to find another work assignment for any employee who participated in the vote which authorized the schedule and is unable to work the 12–hour shifts. An employer shall not be required to offer a different work assignment to an employee if such a work assignment is not available or if the employee was hired after the adoption of the 12 hour, three (3) day alternative workweek schedule.

(9) No employee assigned to work a 12–hour shift established pursuant to this order shall be required to work more than 12–hours in any 24–hour period unless the Chief Nursing Officer or authorized executive declares that:

(a) A "health care emergency", as defined above, exists in this order; and

(b) All reasonable steps have been taken to provide required staffing; and

(c) Considering overall operational status needs, continued overtime is necessary to provide required staffing.

(10) Provided further that no employee shall be required to work more than 16 hours in a 24 hour period unless by voluntary mutual agreement of the employee and the employer, and no employee shall work more than 24 consecutive hours until said employee receives not less

than eight (8) consecutive hours off duty immediately following the twenty-four consecutive hours of work.

(11) Notwithstanding subsection (B)(9) above, an employee may be required to work up to 13 hours in any 24 hour period if the employee scheduled to relieve the subject employee does not report for duty as scheduled and does not inform the employer more than two (2) hours in advance of that scheduled shift that he/she will not be appearing for duty as scheduled.

(C) Election Procedures

Election procedures for the adoption and repeal of alternative workweek schedules require the following:

(1) Each proposal for an alternative workweek schedule shall be in the form of a written agreement proposed by the employer. The proposed agreement must designate a regularly scheduled alternative workweek in which the specified number of work days and work hours are regularly recurring. The actual days worked within that alternative workweek schedule need not be specified. The employer may propose a single work schedule that would become the standard schedule for workers in the work unit, or a menu of work schedule options, from which each employee in the unit would be entitled to choose. If the employer proposes a menu of work schedule options, the employee may, with the approval of the employer, move from one menu option to another.

(2) In order to be valid, the proposed alternative workweek schedule must be adopted in a secret ballot election, before the performance of work, by at least a two-thirds (2/3) vote of the affected employees in the work unit. The election shall be held during regular working hours at the employees' work site. For purposes of this subsection, "affected employees in the work unit" may include all employees in a readily identifiable work unit, such as a division, a department, a job classification, a shift, a separate physical location, or a recognized subdivision of any such work unit. A work unit may consist of an individual employee as long as the criteria for an identifiable work unit in this subsection are met.

(3) Prior to the secret ballot vote, any employer who proposed to institute an alternative workweek schedule shall have made a disclosure in writing to the affected employees, including the effects of the proposed arrangement on the employees' wages, hours, and benefits. Such a disclosure shall include meeting(s), duly noticed, held at least 14 days prior to voting, for the specific purpose of discussing the effects of the alternative workweek schedule. An employer shall provide that disclosure in a non-English language, as well as in English, if at least five (5) percent of the affected employees primarily speak that non-English language. The employer shall mail the written disclosure to employees who do not attend the meeting. Failure to comply with this paragraph shall make the election null and void.

(4) Any election to establish or repeal an alternative workweek schedule shall be held at the work site of the affected employees. The employer shall bear the costs of

conducting any election held pursuant to this section. Upon a complaint by an affected employee, and after an investigation by the labor commissioner, the labor commissioner may require the employer to select a neutral third party to conduct the election.

(5) Any type of alternative workweek schedule that is authorized by the Labor Code may be repealed by the affected employees. Upon a petition of one-third (1/3) of the affected employees, a new secret ballot election shall be held and a two-thirds (2/3) vote of the affected employees shall be required to reverse the alternative workweek schedule. The election to repeal the alternative workweek schedule shall be held not more than 30 days after the petition is submitted to the employer, except that the election shall be held not less than 12 months after the date that the same group of employees voted in an election held to adopt or repeal an alternative workweek schedule. However, where an alternative workweek schedule was adopted between October 1, 1999 and October 1, 2000, a new secret ballot election to repeal the alternative workweek schedule shall not be subject to the 12 month interval between elections. The election shall take place during regular working hours at the employees' work site. If the alternative workweek schedule is revoked, the employer shall comply within 60 days. Upon proper showing of undue hardship, the Division of Labor Standards Enforcement may grant an extension of time for compliance.

(6) Only secret ballots may be cast by affected employees in the work unit at any election held pursuant to this section. The results of any election conducted pursuant to this section shall be reported by the employer to the Division of Labor Statistics and Research within 30 days after the results are final, and the report of election results shall be a public document. The report shall include the final tally of the vote, the size of the unit, and the nature of the business of the employer.

(7) Employees affected by a change in the work hours resulting from the adoption of an alternative workweek schedule may not be required to work those new work hours for at least 30 days after the announcement of the final results of the election.

(8) Employers shall not intimidate or coerce employees to vote either in support of or in opposition to a proposed alternative workweek. No employees shall be discharged or discriminated against for expressing opinions concerning the alternative workweek election or for opposing or supporting its adoption or repeal. However, nothing in this section shall prohibit an employer from expressing his/her position concerning that alternative workweek to the affected employees. A violation of this paragraph shall be subject to Labor Code Section 98 et seq.

(D) The provisions of subsections (A), (B) and (C) above shall not apply to any employee whose earnings exceed one and one-half (1 1/2) times the minimum wage if more than half of that employee's compensation represents commissions.

(E) One and one-half (1 1/2) times a minor's regular rate of pay shall be paid for all work over 40 hours in any workweek except minors 16 or 17 years old who are not required by law to attend school and may therefore be employed for the same hours as an adult are subject to subsection (A) or (B) and (C) above.

(VIOLATIONS OF CHILD LABOR LAWS are subject to civil penalties of from $500 to $10,000 as well as to criminal penalties. Refer to California Labor Code Sections 1285 to 1312 and 1390 to 1399 for additional restrictions on the employment of minors and for descriptions of criminal and civil penalties for violation of the child labor laws. Employers should ask school districts about any required work permits.)

(F) An employee may be employed on seven (7) workdays in one workweek when the total hours of employment during such workweek do not exceed 30 and the total hours of employment in any one workday thereof do not exceed six (6).

(G) If a meal period occurs on a shift beginning or ending at or between the hours of 10 p.m. and 6 a.m., facilities shall be available for securing hot food and drink or for heating food or drink, and a suitable sheltered place shall be provided in which to consume such food or drink.

(H) The provisions of Labor Code Sections 551 and 552 regarding one (1) day's rest in seven (7) shall not be construed to prevent an accumulation of days of rest when the nature of the employment reasonably requires the employee to work seven (7) or more consecutive days; provided, however, that in each calendar month, the employee shall receive the equivalent of one (1) day's rest in seven (7).

(I) Except as provided in subsections (E), (H) and (L), this section shall not apply to any employee covered by a valid collective bargaining agreement if the agreement expressly provides for the wages, hours of work, and working conditions of the employees, and if the agreement provides premium wage rates for all overtime hours worked and a regular hourly rate of pay for those employees of not less than 30 percent more than the state minimum wage.

(J) Notwithstanding subsection (I) above, where the employer and a labor organization representing employees of the employer have entered into a valid collective bargaining agreement pertaining to the hours of work of the employees, the requirement regarding the equivalent of one (1) day's rest in seven (7) (see subsection (H) above) shall apply, unless the agreement expressly provides otherwise.

(K) The provisions of this section are not applicable to employees whose hours of service are regulated by:

(1) The United States Department of Transportation Code of Federal Regulations, Title 49, Sections 395.1 to 395.13, Hours of Service of Drivers; or

(2) Title 13 of the California Code of Regulations, subchapter 6.5, Section 1200 and following sections, regulating hours of drivers.

(L) No employee shall be terminated or otherwise disciplined for refusing to work more than 72 hours in any workweek, except in an emergency as defined in Section 2(D).

(M) If an employer approves a written request of an employee to make up work time that is or would be lost as a result of a personal obligation of the employee, the hours of that makeup work time, if performed in the same workweek in which the work time was lost, may not be counted toward computing the total number of hours worked in a day for purposes of the overtime requirements, except for hours in excess of 11 hours of work in one (1) day or 40 hours of work in one (1) workweek. If an employee knows in advance that he/she will be requesting makeup time for a personal obligation that will recur at a fixed time over a succession of weeks, the employee may request to make up work time for up to four (4) weeks in advance; provided, however, that the makeup work must be performed in the same week that the work time was lost. An employee shall provide a signed written request for each occasion that the employee makes a request to make up work time pursuant to this subsection. While an employer may inform an employee of this makeup time option, the employer is prohibited from encouraging or otherwise soliciting an employee to request the employer's approval to take personal time off and make up the work hours within the same workweek pursuant to this subsection.

4.   Minimum Wages

(A) Every employer shall pay to each employee wages not less than six dollars and twenty-five cents ($6.25) per hour for all hours worked, effective January 1, 2001, and not less than six dollars and seventy-five cents ($6.75) per hour for all hours worked, effective January 1, 2002, except:

LEARNERS: Employees during their first one 160 hours of employment in occupations in which they have no previous similar or related experience, may be paid not less than 85 percent of the minimum wage rounded to the nearest nickel.

(B) Every employer shall pay to each employee, on the established payday for the period involved, not less than the applicable minimum wage for all hours worked in the payroll period, whether the remuneration is measured by time, piece, commission, or otherwise.

(C) When an employee works a split shift, one (1) hour's pay at the minimum wage shall be paid in addition to the minimum wage for that workday, except when the employee resides at the place of employment.

(D) The provisions of this section shall not apply to apprentices regularly indentured under the State Division of Apprenticeship Standards.

5.   Reporting Time Pay

(A) Each workday an employee is required to report for work and does report, but is not put to work or is furnished less than half said employee's usual or scheduled day's work, the employee shall be paid for half the usual or scheduled day's work, but in no event for less than two (2) hours nor more than four (4) hours, at the employee's regular rate of pay, which shall not be less than the minimum wage.

(B) If an employee is required to report for work a second time in any one workday and is furnished less than two (2) hours of work on the second reporting, said employee shall be paid for two (2) hours at the employee's regular rate of pay, which shall not be less than the minimum wage.

(C) The foregoing reporting time pay provisions are not applicable when:

(1) Operations cannot commence or continue due to threats to employees or property; or when recommended by civil authorities; or

(2) Public utilities fail to supply electricity, water, or gas, or there is a failure in the public utilities, or sewer system; or

(3) The interruption of work is caused by an Act of God or other cause not within the employer's control.

(D) This section shall not apply to an employee on paid standby status who is called to perform assigned work at a time other than the employee's scheduled reporting time.

6.   Licenses for Disabled Workers

(A) A license may be issued by the Division authorizing employment of a person whose earning capacity is impaired by physical disability or mental deficiency at less than the minimum wage. Such licenses shall be granted only upon joint application of employer and employee and employee's representative if any.

(B) A special license may be issued to a nonprofit organization such as a sheltered workshop or rehabilitation facility fixing special minimum rates to enable the employment of such persons without requiring individual licenses of such employees.

(C) All such licenses and special licenses shall be renewed on a yearly basis or more frequently at the discretion of the Division. (See California Labor Code, Sections 1191 and 1191.5)

7.   Records

(A) Every employer shall keep accurate information with respect to each employee including the following:

(1) Full name, home address, occupation and social security number.

(2) Birth date, if under 18 years, and designation as a minor.

(3) Time records showing when the employee begins and ends each work period. Meal periods, split shift intervals and total daily hours worked shall also be

recorded. Meal periods during which operations cease and authorized rest periods need not be recorded.

(4) Total wages paid each payroll period, including value of board, lodging, or other compensation actually furnished to the employee.

(5) Total hours worked in the payroll period and applicable rates of pay. This information shall be made readily available to the employee upon reasonable request.

(6) When a piece rate or incentive plan is in operation, piece rates or an explanation of the incentive plan formula shall be provided to employees. An accurate production record shall be maintained by the employer.

(B) Every employer shall semimonthly or at the time of each payment of wages furnish each employee, either as a detachable part of the check, draft, or voucher paying the employee's wages, or separately, an itemized statement in writing showing: (1) all deductions; (2) the inclusive dates of the period for which the employee is paid; (3) the name of the employee or the employee's social security number; and (4) the name of the employer, provided all deductions made on written orders of the employee may be aggregated and shown as one item.

(C) All required records shall be in the English language and in ink or other indelible form, properly dated, showing month, day and year, and shall be kept on file by the employer for at least three years at the place of employment or at a central location within the State of California. An employee's records shall be available for inspection by the employee upon reasonable request.

(D) Clocks shall be provided in all major work areas or within reasonable distance thereto insofar as practicable.

8. Cash Shortage and Breakage

No employer shall make any deduction from the wage or require any reimbursement from an employee for any cash shortage, breakage, or loss of equipment, unless it can be shown that the shortage, breakage, or loss is caused by a dishonest or willful act, or by the gross negligence of the employee.

9. Uniforms and Equipment

(A) When uniforms are required by the employer to be worn by the employee as a condition of employment, such uniforms shall be provided and maintained by the employer. The term "uniform" includes wearing apparel and accessories of distinctive design or color. NOTE': This section shall not apply to protective apparel regulated by the Occupational Safety and Health Standards Board.

(B) When tools or equipment are required by the employer or are necessary to the performance of a job, such tools and equipment shall be provided and maintained by the employer, except that an employee whose wages are at least two (2) times the minimum wage provided herein may be required to provide and maintain hand tools and equipment customarily required by the trade or craft. This subsection (B) shall not apply to

apprentices regularly indentured under the State Division of Apprenticeship Standards. NOTE': This section shall not apply to protective equipment and safety devices on tools regulated by the Occupational Safety and Health Standards Board.

(C) A reasonable deposit may be required as security for the return of the items furnished by the employer under provisions of subsections (A) and (B) of this section upon issuance of a receipt to the employee for such deposit. Such deposits shall be made pursuant to Section 400 and following of the Labor Code or an employer with the prior written authorization of the employee may deduct from the employee's last check the cost of an item furnished pursuant to (A) and (B) above in the event said item is not returned. No deduction shall be made at any time for normal wear and tear. All items furnished by the employer shall be returned by the employee upon completion of the job.

10. Meals and Lodging

(A) "Meal" means an adequate, well-balanced serving of a variety of wholesome, nutritious foods.

(B) "Lodging" means living accommodations available to the employee for full-time occupancy which are adequate, decent, and sanitary according to usual and customary standards. Employees shall not be required to share a bed.

(C) Meals or lodging may not be credited against the minimum wage without a voluntary written agreement between the employer and the employee. When credit for meals or lodging is used to meet part of the employer's minimum wage obligation, the amounts so credited may not be more than the following:

Effective Dates.	January 1, 2001	January 1, 2002
Lodging:		
Room occupied alone	$29.10 per week	$31.75 per week
Room shared	$24.25 per week	$26.20 per week
Apartment-two thirds (2/3) of the ordinary rental value, and in no event more than	$352.90 per month	$381.20 per month
Where a couple are both employed by the employer, two-thirds (2/3) of the ordinary rental value, and in no event more than	$522.10 per month	$563.90 per month
Meals:		
Breakfast	$2.25	$2.45
Lunch	$3.10	$3.35
Dinner	$4.15	$4.50

(D) Meals evaluated as part of the minimum wage must be bona fide meals consistent with the employee's work shift. Deductions shall not be made for meals not received or lodging not used.

(E) If, as a condition of employment, the employee must live at the place of employment or occupy quarters owned or under the control of the employer, then the employer may not charge rent in excess of the values listed herein.

11. Meal Periods

(A) No employer shall employ any person for a work period of more than five (5) hours without a meal period of not less than 30 minutes, except that when a work period of not more than six (6) hours will complete the day's work the meal period may be waived by mutual consent of the employer and the employee. Unless the employee is relieved of all duty during a 30 minute meal period, the meal period shall be considered an "on duty" meal period and counted as time worked. An "on duty" meal period shall be permitted only when the nature of the work prevents an employee from being relieved of all duty and when by written agreement between the parties an on-the-job paid meal period is agreed to. The written agreement shall state that the employee may, in writing, revoke the agreement at any time.

(B) If an employer fails to provide an employee a meal period in accordance with the applicable provisions of this order, the employer shall pay the employee one (1) hour of pay at the employee's regular rate of compensation for each workday that the meal period is not provided.

(C) In all places of employment where employees are required to eat on the premises, a suitable place for that purpose shall be designated.

(D) Notwithstanding any other provision of this order, employees in the health care industry who work shifts in excess of eight (8) total hours in a workday may voluntarily waive their right to one of their two meal periods. In order to be valid, any such waiver must be documented in a written agreement that is voluntarily signed by both the employee and the employer. The employee may revoke the waiver at any time by providing the employer at least one (1) day's written notice. The employee shall be fully compensated for all working time, including any on-the-job meal period, while such a waiver is in effect.

12. Rest Periods

(A) Every employer shall authorize and permit all employees to take rest periods, which insofar as practicable shall be in the middle of each work period. The authorized rest period time shall be based on the total hours worked daily at the rate of ten (10) minutes net rest time per four (4) hours or major fraction thereof. However, a rest period need not be authorized for employees whose total daily work time is less than three and one-half (3 1/2) hours. Authorized rest period time shall be counted as hours worked for which there shall be no deduction from wages.

(B) If an employer fails to provide an employee a rest period in accordance with the applicable provisions of this order, the employer shall pay the employee one (1) hour of pay at the employee's regular rate of compensation for each workday that the rest period is not provided.

13. Change Rooms and Resting Facilities

(A) Employers shall provide suitable lockers, closets, or equivalent for the safekeeping of employees' outer clothing during working hours, and when required, for

their work clothing during non-working hours. When the occupation requires a change of clothing, change rooms or equivalent space shall be provided in order that employees may change their clothing in reasonable privacy and comfort. These rooms or spaces may be adjacent to but shall be separate from toilet rooms and shall be kept clean. NOTE': This section shall not apply to change rooms and storage facilities regulated by the Occupational Safety and Health Standards Board.

(B) Suitable resting facilities shall be provided in an area separate from the toilet rooms and shall be available to employees during work hours.

14. Seats

(A) All working employees shall be provided with suitable seats when the nature of the work reasonably permits the use of seats.

(B) When employees are not engaged in the active duties of their employment and the nature of the work requires standing, an adequate number of suitable seats shall be placed in reasonable proximity to the work area and employees shall be permitted to use such seats when it does not interfere with the performance of their duties.

15. Temperature

(A) The temperature maintained in each work area shall provide reasonable comfort consistent with industry-wide standards for the nature of the process and the work performed.

(B) If excessive heat or humidity is created by the work process, the employer shall take all feasible means to reduce such excessive heat or humidity to a degree providing reasonable comfort. Where the nature of the employment requires a temperature of less than 60 ||degreesŒŒ F., a heated room shall be provided to which employees may retire for warmth, and such room shall be maintained at not less than 68 ||degreesŒŒ.

(C) A temperature of not less than 68 ||degreesŒŒ shall be maintained in the toilet rooms, resting rooms, and change rooms during hours of use.

(D) Federal and State energy guidelines shall prevail over any conflicting provision of this section.

16. Elevators

Adequate elevator, escalator or similar service consistent with industry-wide standards for the nature of the process and the work performed shall be provided when employees are employed four floors or more above or below ground level.

17. Exemptions

If, in the opinion of the Division after due investigation, it is found that the enforcement of any provision contained in Section 7, Records; Section 12, Rest Periods; Section 13, Change Rooms and Resting Facilities; Section 14, Seats; Section 15, Temperature; or Section 16, Elevators, would not materially affect the welfare or comfort of employees and would work an undue hardship on the employer, exemption may be made at the discretion of the Division. Such exemptions shall be in writing to be effective and may be revoked after reasonable notice is given in writing. Application for exemption shall be made by the employer or by the employee and/or the employee's representative to the Division in writing. A copy of the application shall be posted at the place of employment at the time the application is filed with the Division.

18. Filing Reports (See California Labor Code, Section 1174(a))

19. Inspection (See California Labor Code, Section 1174)

20. Penalties (See California Labor Code, Section 1199)

(A) In addition to any other civil penalties provided by law, any employer or any other person acting on behalf of the employer who violates, or causes to be violated, the provisions of this order, shall be subject to the civil penalty of:

(1) Initial Violation—$50. 00 for each underpaid employee for each pay period during which the employee was underpaid in addition to the amount which is sufficient to recover unpaid wages.

(2) Subsequent Violations—$100.00 for each underpaid employee for each pay period during which the employee was underpaid in addition to an amount which is sufficient to recover unpaid wages.

(3) The affected employee shall receive payment of all wages recovered.

(B) The labor commissioner may also issue citations pursuant to California Labor Code Section 1197.1 for non-payment of wages for overtime work in violation of this order.

21. Separability

If the application of any provision of this order, or any section, subsection, subdivision, sentence, clause, phrase, word, or portion of this order should be held invalid or unconstitutional or unauthorized or prohibited by statute, the remaining provisions thereof shall not be affected thereby, but shall continue to be given full force and effect as if the part so held invalid or unconstitutional had not been included herein.

22. Posting of Order

Every employer shall keep a copy of this order posted in an area frequented by employees where it may be easily read during the workday. Where the location of work or other conditions make this impractical, every employer shall keep a copy of this order and make it available to every employee upon request.

Chapter 6. Division of Labor Standards Enforcement

Subchapter 1. Child Labor Orders– Prohibited Occupations

Article 1. Prohibited Occupations

§ 11701. Prohibited Occupations

The following occupations are sufficiently dangerous to the lives and limbs and injurious to the health and morals of children under 16 years of age to justify their exclusion therefrom:

(a) All occupations where such children come in close proximity to moving machinery.

(b) All building or construction work of any kind.

(c) Delivering goods, merchandise, commodities, papers or packages from motor vehicles.

§ 11702. No Child Under 16 Years of Age Shall Work in Prohibited Occupations

No child under 16 years of age shall be employed, permitted or suffered to work in any of said occupations.

§ 11703. Further Prohibited Occupations

The following occupations are sufficiently dangerous to the lives or limbs or injurious to the health or morals of minors under 16 years of age to justify their exclusion therefrom:

All occupations in or about any plant manufacturing explosives or articles containing explosive components, and all occupations in the transportation and sale of explosives or articles containing explosive components.

§ 11704. No Child Under 16 Years of Age Shall Work in Prohibited Occupations

No child under 16 years of age shall be employed, permitted or suffered to work in any of said occupations.

§ 11705. Scope of Regulations and Definitions

For the purpose of these regulations the term "minors" shall be defined in accordance with Section 1286(c) of the Labor Code; except that, with respect to the number of hours a minor may be allowed to work, "minor" shall include those minors under six (6) years of age.

§ 11706. Dangerous Activities and Occupations for Minors Under the Age of Sixteen (16) Years

Dangerous activities and occupations for minors under the age of sixteen (16) years are determined to be as follows:

(a) Door-to-door selling of newspaper or magazine subscriptions, or of candy, cookies, flowers or other merchandise or commodities, unless the following conditions are met:

(1) Minors so engaged work in pairs, as a team, on the same or opposite side of the street;

(2) Minors so engaged shall be supervised by an adult supervisor for each crew of ten (10) or fewer minors;

(3) Such minors shall be within the sight or sound of the adult supervisor at least once every fifteen (15) minutes;

(4) Such minors shall be returned to their respective homes or places of rendezvous daily after each day's work.

(b) Selling to passing motorists of newspapers, candy, flowers, or other merchandise or commodities from a fixed location on a street, highway or freeway island or divider, or freeway on or off ramp, or the side of a freeway or highway entrance or exit shoulder.

§ 11706.1. Definition of "Door-to-Door" Selling

"Door-to-door" selling within the meaning of Section 11706 shall include selling by such minors, either alone or in pairs or teams, in parking lots, or malls.

§ 11706.2. Non–Abridgement of Rights of Regular News Carrier of Newspapers

Nothing in Section 11706 shall prohibit or abridge the right of a minor to solicit subscriptions to, or to sell newspapers door-to-door, or prohibit or abridge the right of any person to so engage or employ a minor when such minor is a regular news carrier of such newspaper and delivers such newspaper on a regular basis to an established readership for a requested consideration.

§ 11707. Further Dangerous Activities for Minors Under the Age of 16

Further dangerous activities for minors under the age of 16 are determined to be as follows:

Working in close proximity to explosives or the functioning parts of unguarded and dangerous moving equipment, aircraft or vessels, or of functioning blades or propellers.

Subchapter 2. Employment of Minors in the Entertainment Industry

Article 1. Motion Picture Industries

§ 11750. Scope of Regulations and Definitions

(a) For the purpose of these regulations the term "minors" shall be defined in accordance with Section 1286(c) of the Labor Code; except that, with respect to the number of hours a minor may be allowed to work, "minor" shall include those minors under six (6) years of age.

§ 11751. Entertainment Industry Defined; Employment of Minors in the Entertainment Industry

(a) The Entertainment Industry, hereinafter referred to as the employer, shall be defined as any organization, or individual, using the services of any minor in: Motion pictures of any type (e.g. film, videotape, etc.), using any format (theatrical film, commercial, documentary, television program, etc.) by any medium (e.g. theater, television, videocassette, etc.); photography; recording; modeling; theatrical productions; publicity; rodeos; circuses; musical performances; and any other performances where minors perform to entertain the public.

(b) Any employer in the Entertainment Industry desiring to employ minors in any such work or activity which is not hazardous or detrimental to the health, safety, morals or education of such minors shall make an application to the Division for a Permit to Employ Minors in such work

or activity. In determining what is hazardous or detrimental to "morals" within the meaning of these regulations, due regard shall be given to the acts proscribed by Sections 311 through 314 of the California Penal Code.

§ 11752. Issuance of Permit to Employ Minor

The Division of Labor Standards Enforcement (hereinafter called "Division") shall issue a "Permit to Employ Minors" if the conditions as to permissible work or activity, as prescribed by Sections 11701, 11703, 11705, and 11707 of this Article, are satisfied.

§ 11753. Procedure for Obtaining Entertainment Work Permit by Minor

(a) A minor desiring to be employed in the entertainment industry must obtain an Entertainment Work Permit. The application for permit can be obtained at any of the Division's District offices. The minor must provide the information called for on the application, to-wit: his/her name, age, birth date, address, sex, height, weight and color of hair and eyes. In addition, such minor must obtain verification in writing from the appropriate school district of the minor's school record and attendance, and must satisfactorily meet the requirements of that school district with respect to age, school record, attendance and health. Such verification of school record and attendance and proof that the school district's requirements with respect to age, school record, attendance and health have been met must be filed with the Division, concurrently with the filing of the application. Such verification and proof may be in any form as provided by the school district if reasonably demonstrative of the information required to be furnished by this subsection. The Division may require in appropriate cases a physical examination of the minor to ensure that the minor's physical condition permits the minor to perform the work or activity called for by the Permit to Employ Minor and Entertainment Work Permit.

(b) Upon the filing by a minor with the Division of a completed Application for Entertainment Work Permit satisfying the requirements of this Section, the Division shall issue an Entertainment Work Permit to such minor. Such permit shall permit the minor to work only under the conditions prescribed by these regulations and in conformity with all provisions of law governing the working hours, health, safety, morals and other conditions of employment of minors. The permit shall be for a period not to exceed six (6) months, and application for renewal must be made in the same manner and under the same conditions as the original permit.

§ 11754. Blanket Permits

Blanket permits may be secured by the employer under the following conditions and/or limitations:

(a) Groups and organizations of minors may be granted blanket rather than individual permits.

(b) Blanket permits shall be valid only for the particular production for which issued and only for the periods of time limited therein.

(c) Application for a blanket permit must be supported by satisfactory evidence that appropriate services of studio teachers will be provided. Special arrangements may be made for the number of studio teachers required with groups of minors numbering one hundred (100) or more.

(d) An application for a blanket permit must be supported by proof that the minors covered by such permits are covered by workers' compensation insurance.

(e) There must be a parent or guardian for every twenty (20) minors, or fraction thereof.

§ 11755. Studio Teacher; Definition and Certification

(a) A studio teacher within the meaning of these regulations must be a certificated teacher who holds one California teaching credential listed in paragraphs (1) through (4) of subsection (d) of this section and one California teaching credential listed in paragraphs (5) through (7) of subsection (d) of this section which are valid and current, and who has been certified by the Labor Commissioner. The teaching credential listed in (5) or (6) of subsection (d) of this section must be in one of the following subject areas: English, Math, Social Science, Science or Foreign Language.

(b) Certification by the Labor Commissioner shall be for a maximum three-year period, not to exceed the earliest expiration date of any one of the qualifying teaching credentials submitted in support of certification. A written examination will be required of the studio teacher by the Labor Commissioner at the time of certification or renewal. Such examination shall be designed to ascertain the studio teacher's knowledge of the labor laws and regulations of the State of California as they apply to the employment of minors in the entertainment industry. In addition, each studio teacher applicant will be required to successfully complete a twelve-hour course of instruction designed by the Labor Commissioner to instruct the applicant in the duties and responsibilities of the studio teacher. Every studio teacher, as a condition of renewal of certification by the Labor Commissioner, must complete three hours of instruction in a class designed by the Labor Commissioner to ensure that the studio teacher remains abreast of any changes in the laws and regulations and duties and responsibilities of the studio teacher.

(c) For the purpose of this section:

(1) "English" means composition, creative writing, debate, forensics, humanities, journalism, language arts, literature, public speaking, speech (oral communication), writing, and other subjects with content related to English.

(2) "Math" means algebra, calculus, geometry, mathematical analysis, number systems, probability and statistics, trigonometry, and other subjects with content related to mathematics.

(3) "Social Science" means American government and politics, anthropology, comparative government, economics, ethnic studies, European history, geography, government, history, humanities/cultural studies, international politics, psychology, sociology, United States history, world history, and other subjects with content related to social science.

(4) "Science" means astronomy, biology, botany, chemistry, conservation, general science, geology, physics, physiology, zoology and other subjects with content related to science.

(5) "Foreign Language" means any language other than English.

(d) The California teaching credentials which satisfy subsection (a) are as follows:

(1) A Multiple Subject credential issued under the provisions of the Teacher Credentialing Law of 1988, Education Code Sections 44200, et seq., as amended (commonly known as the Bergeson Act), or issued under the provisions of the Teacher Preparation and Licensing Act of 1970, Education Code Sections 44200 et seq., (commonly known as the Ryan Act) as amended;

(2) An Elementary credential issued under the provisions of the Education Code in effect prior to the enactment of the Ryan Act, (former Education Code Sections 13101 et seq., commonly known as the Fisher Act; a so-called "Standard Credential");

(3) An Early Childhood Education credential issued under the provisions of the Education Code in effect prior to the enactment of the Ryan Act, (former Education Code Sections 13101 et seq., commonly known as the Fisher Act; a so-called "Standard Credential");

(4) An Elementary credential issued under the provisions of the Education Code in effect prior to the enactment of the Fisher Act (former Education Code Sections 12025 et seq., as amended; a so-called "General Credential");

(5) A Single Subject credential issued under the provisions of the Teacher Credentialing Law of 1988, Education Code Section 44200, et seq., as amended (commonly known as the Bergeson Act), or issued under the provisions of the Teacher Preparation and Licensing Act of 1970, Education Code Sections 44200 et seq., (commonly known as the Ryan Act) as amended, in one of the following subject areas: English, Math, Social Science, Science or Foreign Language;

(6) A Secondary credential issued under the provisions of the Education Code in effect prior to the enactment of the Ryan Act, (former Education Code Sections 13101 et seq., commonly known as the Fisher Act; a so-called "Standard Credential"), in one of the following subject areas: English, Math, Social Science, Science or Foreign Language;

(7) A General Secondary Teaching credential or a Special Secondary Teaching credential in Speech Arts issued under the provisions of the Education Code in effect prior to the enactment of the Fisher Act (former Education Code Sections 12025 et seq., as amended; a so-called "General Credential").

(e) A studio teacher who already possesses a certification by the Labor Commissioner and who possesses only one of the credentials listed in subsections (1) through (7) of subsection (d) above may continue to be certified by the Labor Commissioner, provided that the applicant provides sufficient evidence to the Labor Commissioner that the applicant is currently in the process of obtaining a second credential to meet the requirements of subsection (a) above and such credential is obtained by the applicant no later than December 31, 2000. After December 31, 2000, no person shall be permitted to continue to be certified as a studio teacher who has not obtained two credentials of a type provided for in subsections (d)(1), (2), (3), or (4) and subsection (d)(5), (6), or (7) of this section.

(f) The Labor Commissioner may issue a special certificate as a studio teacher for a limited purpose where is it shown that a particular child actor may benefit from a particular applicant who may hold credentials of a special nature in order to meet the particular needs of that child actor. Studio teachers holding special certificates do not count toward satisfying the studio teacher to minor ratios specified in Section 11755.2.

§ 11755.1.   Filing Schedule

(a) Within sixty (60) calendar days of receiving an application, the Labor Commissioner shall inform the applicant in writing that either:

(1) the application is complete and accepted for filing, or

(2) the application is incomplete, specifying the information required to correct the deficiency.

(b) Within forty-five (45) calendar days of accepting a complete application, the Labor Commissioner shall inform the applicant in writing of the decision on the application.

(c) The following information is provided pursuant to Government Code Section 15376. During the past two years, the Division's time periods for processing an application from the receipt of the initial application to the final issuance or denial of certification were as follows:

(1) The median time was fifty (50) calendar days;

(2) The minimum time was thirty (30) calendar days;

(3) The maximum time was one hundred thirty-five (135) calendar days.

§ 11755.2.   Use of Studio Teachers

Employers shall provide a studio teacher on each call for minors from age fifteen (15) days to their sixteenth (16th) birthday (age sixteen (16)), and for minors from age sixteen (16) to age eighteen (18) when required for the education of the minor. One (1) studio teacher must be provided for each group of ten (10) minors or fraction thereof. With respect to minors age fifteen (15) days to age sixteen (16), one (1) studio teacher must be provided for each group of twenty (20) minors or fraction thereof on Saturdays, Sundays, holidays, or during school vacation periods.

§ 11755.3.   Studio Teacher's Authority

The studio teacher, in addition to teaching, shall also have responsibility for caring and attending to the health, safety and morals of minors under sixteen (16) years of age for whom they have been provided by the employer, while such minors are engaged or employed in any activity pertaining to the entertainment industry and subject to these regulations. In the discharge of these responsibilities, the studio teacher shall take cognizance of such factors as working conditions, physical surroundings, signs of the minor's mental and physical fatigue, and the demands placed upon the minor in relation to the minor's age, agility, strength and stamina. The studio teacher may refuse to allow the engagement of a minor on a set or location and may remove the minor therefrom, if in the judgment of the studio teacher, conditions are such as to present a danger to the health, safety or morals of the minor. Any such action by the studio teacher may be immediately appealed to the Labor Commissioner who may affirm or countermand such action.

§ 11755.4.   Studio Teacher's Remuneration

The remuneration of the studio teacher shall be paid by the employer.

§ 11756.   Employers Taking Minors of Compulsory School Age from California to Work on Location in Another State

When minors resident in the State of California and employed by an employer in the entertainment industry located in the State of California, are taken from the State of California to work on location in another state, as part of, and pursuant to, contractual arrangements made in the State of California for their employment in the entertainment industry, the child labor laws of California and the regulations based thereon shall be applicable, including, but not limited to, the requirement that a studio teacher must be provided for such minor in accordance with Section 11755.1.

§ 11757.   Presence of Parents or Guardians of Minors Under Sixteen (16) Years of Age

A parent or guardian of a minor under sixteen (16) years of age must be present with, and accompany, such minor on the set or location and be within sight or sound of said minor at all times.

§ 11758. Sanctions for Violation of the Labor Code or Regulations

Any misdemeanor violation of any Labor Code provision respecting child labor, or any violation of these regulations may constitute grounds for denying a Permit to Employ Minors in the entertainment industry, or for suspending or revoking any such permit.

§ 11758.1. Other Grounds for Denial, Suspension or Revocation of Permit

(a) It shall also constitute grounds for denial of the issuance or renewal, or suspension or revocation of a Permit to Employ Minors in the Entertainment Industry for any permit holder or authorized agent or representative of such holder to discharge or in any manner discriminate against any studio teacher because such studio teacher either:

(1) made any oral or written complaint to the Division or the permit holder, its agents, representatives or employees, that conditions on the set or location were dangerous to the health, safety or morals of minors employed on said set or location; or

(2) took any action to preclude, suspend or terminate the employment of minors on a set or location for reasons of health, safety, or morals of the minors.

§ 11758.2. Appeal Rights of Permit Holder or Applicant upon Denial, Suspension or Revocation of Permit

(a) Any applicant for the issuance or renewal of a Permit to Employ Minors in the Entertainment Industry who has been denied the issuance or renewal thereof, or any permit holder whose permit has been suspended or revoked by a duly authorized representative of the Labor Commissioner may appeal any such action directly to the Labor Commissioner.

(b) Before denying, suspending or revoking any such permit hereunder, the Labor Commissioner shall afford the applicant or holder thereof an opportunity to request a hearing. Any such hearing on appeal of a denial of permit or on the proposed suspension or revocation of such permit, shall be conducted in accordance with Chapter 5 of Part 1 of Division 3 of Title 2 of the Government Code (Sections 11500 et seq.) and the Labor Commissioner shall have all the powers granted therein.

§ 11759. Travel Time for Minors Employed in the Entertainment Industry

(a) Except as provided in subsection (b) of this section, all time spent in traveling from a studio to a location or from a location to a studio shall count as part of the working day of a minor.

(b) When a minor with a company on a location which is sufficiently distant to require an overnight stay is required to travel daily between living quarters and the place where the company is actually working, the time spent by the minor in such traveling will not count as work time, provided the company does not spend more

than forty-five (45) minutes traveling each way and furnishes the necessary transportation. This is a general rule and subject to reasonable changes by the studio teacher. Factors such as working and transportation conditions, and ages of minors shall be considered by the studio teacher in making any such decision.

§ 11760. Working Hours of Minors

The amount of time minors are permitted at the place of employment within a twenty-four (24) hour period is limited according to age, as follows:

(a) Babies who have reached the age of fifteen (15) days but have not reached the age of six (6) months may be permitted to remain at the place of employment for a maximum of two (2) hours.

(1) The day's work shall not exceed twenty (20) minutes and under no conditions shall the baby be exposed to light of greater than one hundred (100) foot candlelight intensity for more than thirty (30) seconds at a time.

(2) When babies between the age of fifteen (15) days and six (6) weeks of age are employed, a nurse and a studio teacher must be provided for each three (3) or fewer babies. When infants from age six (6) weeks to six (6) months are employed, one (1) nurse and one (1) studio teacher must be provided for each ten (10) or fewer infants.

(b) Minors who have reached the age of six (6) months but who have not attained the age of two (2) years may be permitted at the place of employment for a maximum of four (4) hours. Such four (4)-hour period shall consist of not more than two (2) hours of work; the balance of the four (4)-hour period shall be rest and recreation.

(c) Minors who have reached the age of two (2) years but who have not attained the age of six (6) years may be permitted at the place of employment for a maximum of six (6) hours. Such six (6)-hour period shall consist of not more than three (3) hours of work; the balance of the six (6)-hour period shall be rest and recreation and/or education.

(d) Minors who have reached the age of six (6) years but have not attained the age of nine (9) years may be permitted at the place of employment for a maximum of eight (8) hours. Such eight (8)-hour period shall consist of not more than four (4) hours of work and at least three (3) hours of schooling when the minor's school is in session. The studio teacher shall assure that the minor receives up to one (1) hour of rest and recreation. On days when the minor's school is not in session, working hours may be increased to six (6) hours, with one (1) hour of rest and recreation.

(e) Minors who have reached the age of nine (9) years but who have not attained the age of sixteen (16) years may be permitted at the place of employment for a maximum of nine (9) hours. Such nine (9)-hour period shall consist of not more than five (5) hours of work and at least three (3) hours of schooling when the minor's school is in session. The studio teacher shall assure that the minor receives at least one (1) hour of rest and recreation. On days when the minor's school is not in session, working hours may be increased to seven (7) hours, with one (1) hour of rest and recreation.

(f) Minors who have reached the age of sixteen (16) years but who have not attained the age of eighteen (18) years may be permitted at the place of employment for a maximum of ten (10) hours. Such ten (10)-hour period shall consist of not more than six (6) hours of work and at least three (3) hours of schooling when the minor's school is in session, and one (1) hour of rest and recreation. On days when school is not in session, working hours may be increased to not more than eight (8) hours, with one (1) hour of rest and recreation.

(g) If emergency situations arise, for example, early morning or night exteriors shot as exteriors, live television or theatrical productions presented after the hours beyond which a minor may not work as prescribed by law, a request may be made to the Labor Commissioner for permission for the minor to work earlier or later than such hours. Each request shall be considered individually by the Division and must be submitted in writing at least forty-eight (48) hours prior to the time needed.

(h) When any minor between ages fourteen (14) and eighteen (18) obtains permission from school authorities to work during school hours for a period not to exceed two (2) consecutive days, the working hours for such minor during either or both of such days may be extended to but shall not exceed eight (8) hours in twenty-four (24) hours.

(i) Twelve (12) hours must elapse between the minor's time of dismissal and time of call on the following day. If the minor's regular school starts less than twelve (12) hours after his or her dismissal time, the minor must be schooled the following day at the employer's place of business.

§ 11761. Meal Period for Minors

All hours for the minor at the place of employment are exclusive of the meal period. The working day may not be extended by a meal period longer than one half (1/2) hour.

§ 11762. Minor's General Supervision by Studio Teacher; Minor's Accompaniment by Parent or Guardian Required for Certain Purposes Under Specified Conditions

No minor under the age of sixteen (16) may be sent to wardrobe, make-up, hairdressing or employed in any manner unless under the general supervision of a studio teacher. If any such minor is not called to the set but is called for a period up to one (1) hour into wardrobe, make-up, hairdressing, promotional publicity, personal appearances, or for audio recording, when such minor's school is not in session, a studio teacher need not be present but the minor must be accompanied by a parent or guardian.

§ 11763. Work Time

All time spent in make-up or hairdressing in the homes of minors with the assistance of other persons employed in connection therewith, shall be counted as work time. No make-up person or hairdresser shall be permitted to work on minors at home before 8:30 a.m. In every case, 12 hours must elapse between the time the minor is dismissed on one day and the time make-up or hairdressing begins on the following day.

§ 11764. Work Time for Infants–Medical Examination

Infants under six months of age shall not be given medical examinations except between the hours of 9:30 a.m. and 11:30 a.m. or between 2:30 p.m. and 4:30 p.m. Work time for said infants shall be limited to one period of two consecutive hours in any one day, and such period must be either between 9:30 a.m. and 11:30 a.m. or between 2:30 p.m. and 4:30 p.m.

§ 11765. Care of Children

If children are dismissed early and are not to be picked up for several hours, they shall be under the supervision of a teacher-welfare worker until picked up or until such time as they may be placed under the care of some other responsible adult.

Subchapter 2.5.   Child Labor Law Violations

Article 1.   Regulations Regarding Citation and Penalty Procedure for Violation of Child Labor Provisions

§ 11775. Designation of Labor Commissioner

The Labor Commissioner is the designee of the Director of Industrial Relations for the purpose of issuing citations, assessing penalties, determining types of violations after public hearing, other than those enumerated in Labor Code Sections 1288, 1293.1, and to determine, after public hearing, other hazards that constitute an agricultural zone of danger.

§ 11776. Applicability to Previously Determined Findings

Citation and penalty provisions are applicable to previously determined findings of prohibited occupations, as set forth in Sections 11701 through 11705, of Group 1, of this Chapter 6.

§ 11777. Form of Citation, Method of Payment of Penalty and Service

The Labor Commissioner, for use of his deputies and agents, shall provide citation forms designed to include:

(a) The name and title of the alleged violator, whether sole proprietor, corporate entity or partnership, with space for listing partners;

(b) Designated space for indicating the nature of the violation and reference to statutory provisions, rule, or regulation, alleged to have been violated;

(c) Designated space for indication of proposed penalty assessment, indicating thereon whether assessment is for original, repeated or willful violation;

(d) Bold face type advising the alleged violator of rights to an informal hearing, time of application therefor, place where request may be filed and also where amount of penalty may be paid.

(1) Payment shall be made by cash, certified check, or money order payable to the Labor Commissioner.

(e) Service of a citation and proposed assessment may be made personally, or, by registered mail if the respondent (alleged violator) is otherwise required by the Labor Commissioner to file his address with the Labor Commissioner, and to notify the Labor Commissioner of any change, and such registered mail is sent to the latest address on file with the Labor Commissioner.

§ 11778. Labor Commissioner Records of Violations

The Labor Commission shall keep on file, by name of employer, or responsible entity, records of violations of child labor laws, for use of deputies and agents in determining the range of proposed penalty assessments to be made.

§ 11779. Penalties for Class "A" Violations

An original violation of a child labor law, rule or regulation designated as a class "A" violation shall subject the employer, or responsible entity, to a penalty assessment of $1,000.00. The second citation for a class "A" violation shall subject the employer, or responsible entity, to a penalty assessment of $2,000.00. The third, and each succeeding violation, shall subject the employer, or responsible entity, to a penalty assessment of $5,000.00 for the latter violation. Prior violations are such that have not been contested, or that have been upheld on proceedings thereon. In determining penalty assessments, a citation will be considered as referring to a single violation in the class affected at the time the violation cited, regardless of the number of minors in said group at such time.

§ 11779.1. Definition and Penalty for Willful Violation of Class "A" Type

A willful violation cited, of the class "A" type shall be subject to a penalty assessment of $5,000.00. "Willful," as defined therein, implies a purpose or willingness to engage, employ, or assign minors to activities proscribed by Labor Code Section 1228(a) and regulations relating thereto.

§ 11780. Definition of Class "A" Violation

A class "A" violation is a violation of Section 1292, or 1293, or 1294, or 1308, or 1391, or 1392 of the Labor Code, or, such other violations which the director, by his designee the Labor Commissioner, determines to present an imminent danger to minor employees or substantial probability that death or serious physical harm would result from exposure of a minor to particular working environments.

§ 11780.1. Agricultural Zone of Danger Violations

A violation of Labor Code Section 1293.1 shall be considered and acted upon consistent with provisions respecting class "A" violations.

§ 11781. Penalties for Class "B" Violations

An original violation of a child labor law, rule or regulation, designated as a class "B" violation, shall subject the employer, or responsible entity, to a penalty assessment of $100.00. The second citation for a class "B" violation shall subject the employer, or responsible entity, to a penalty assessment of $200.00. The third, or more instances of citations for class "B" violations shall subject the employer, or responsible entity, to a penalty assessment of $500.00 for such further violations. Prior violations are such that have not been contested, or that have been upheld on proceedings thereon. In determining penalty assessments a citation will be considered as referring to a single violation in the class affected at the time the violation is cited, regardless of the number of minors in the group at such time.

§ 11781.1. Definition and Penalty for Willful Violation of Class "B" Type

A willful violation, cited, of the class "B" type, shall be subject to a penalty assessment of $500.00. "Willful," as defined herein, implies a purpose or willingness to engage, employ, or assign minors to activities proscribed by Labor Code Section 1288(b) and regulations related thereto.

§ 11782. Definition of Class "B" Violation

A class "B" violation is a violation of Section 1299 or 1308.5 of the Labor Code, or such other violations which the director, by his designee the Labor Commissioner, determines have a direct or immediate relationship to the health, safety, or security of minor employees, other than class "A" violations.

§ 11782.1. Violations for Minor Employment in Manufacturing Establishments or Other Places Not Excepted

A violation of Labor Code Section 1290 shall be considered and acted upon consistent with provisions respecting class "B" violations.

Section 30.5 of Chapter 144, 1975 Laws, to which chaptered law these regulations apply, states:

Notwithstanding Section 2231 of the Revenue and Taxation Code, there shall be no reimbursement pursuant to this section nor shall there be an appropriation made by this act because the Legislature recognizes that during any legislative session a variety of changes to laws relating to crimes and infractions may cause increased and decreased costs to local government entities and school districts which in the aggregate, do not result in significant identifiable cost changes.

§ 11783. Request, Notice, and Time of Hearing

When a person requests an informal hearing by oral or written communication, on a citation, said person should be given, at least, 3 days notice of the time and place of hearing. Such notice may be given by oral communication, with confirming letter, or, by mail to the address set forth in the citation or by the address designated by the person requesting the hearing.

§ 11784. Conduct of Hearing

Testimony shall be given under oath.

Subchapter 3. Employment Agencies

Article 1. General Rules and Regulations for Artists' Managers

§ 12000. Application

Application for the original license shall be made upon the form prescribed by the Labor Commissioner and shall contain the following information:

(a) The proposed business name of the talent agency, which may not be identical or similar to that of another licensed talent agency.

(b) The proposed places of business and the main office address of the talent agency in California, which address shall also be its mailing address for purposes of notice required by these regulations and provisions of the Labor Code or any other applicable statute.

(c) If applicant is not a corporation, names and addresses of all persons who are financially interested either as partners, associates, profit sharers, or employees or other persons receiving as compensation a share of the net profits from the operation of the talent agency; said application shall also show the share of said net profit each person is to receive.

(d) If the applicant is a corporation, the following information must be shown: name, address and title of the persons acting as executive officers of the corporation who have managing responsibility in California.

(e) If applicant is not a corporation, questions must be answered as to each person or profit sharer listed in the application as having a financial interest in or the right to share in the net profits of the talent agency (1) regarding his business or occupation for the preceding five (5) years; (2) whether or not such person or profit sharer has ever been associated in any capacity in the operation or business of a talent agency; (3) whether or not such person has had a talent agency license or any license or permit issued by any agency of the State of California revoked, suspended, or refused, or any disciplinary action taken with respect to any such license or permit; (4) whether or not such person has been convicted of a crime except for minor traffic violations.

(f) In the case of an application by a corporation, the foregoing information must be submitted by the executive

1338

officers acting in a managerial capacity for or on behalf of the corporation within the State of California.

(g) Application, if by an individual, must be signed, giving full name; if by partnership, must be signed by all partners; if by a corporation, must be signed by an officer of the corporation, affixing the seal of the corporation thereto.

§ 12000.1. Required Documents

The following documents, in addition to those required by Labor Code Section 1700.6, must be filed with the application for license:

(a) Surety bond as required by Labor Code Section 1700.15, issued by a corporate surety company authorized to write surety bonds in California, and on the form prescribed by the Labor Commissioner. The name of the talent agency and principal on the bond must correspond to the name of the talent agency and principal on the application.

(b) Contract forms in triplicate which are proposed to be used in the conduct of the business of the talent agency in accordance with the requirements of Labor Code Section 1700.23. If any of said proposed contract forms is a standard form of union contract previously approved by, and on file with the Labor Commissioner, that form need not be submitted by the applicant if it is identified on the application.

(c) Fee schedules in triplicate in the form required by Labor Code Section 1700.24, and California Code of Regulations, Title 8, Section 12003.4.

§ 12000.2. Application and Documents in Proper Form

If the application and/or the required documents are not in proper form or contain any provisions contrary to law when submitted and are not corrected and resubmitted in proper form within 30 days after written notice from the Labor Commissioner, the license applied for will be denied without prejudice to either the submission of a new application or the required documents in proper form.

§ 12000.3. Renewal Applications

Renewal applications shall be filed with the Labor Commissioner by each licensee at least 30 days before the commencement of the new license year. If mailed, the postmark will be considered the date of filing. If the renewal application is not filed on or before the expiration date of the license as set forth in Labor Code Section 1700.10, the license expires and cannot be renewed. Such licensee, having failed to renew his, her, its license, must submit a new application and comply with the provisions of Labor Code Section 1700.12 in the same manner as a new applicant.

§ 12000.4. Fees for License

The license fee, together with the filing fee as required by Labor Code Section 1700.12, shall be submitted in the form of cashier's check, certified check, or money order and must accompany the application for a license or for a renewal thereof.

§ 12000.5. Transfer of License

Consent for the transfer of a license, as required by Labor Code Section 1700.20, shall be given only after the filing of a transfer application executed by the licensee and the proposed transferee in the form prescribed by the Labor Commissioner, which must be accompanied by the required filing fee, a surety bond as required in the case of a new application, together with the information required by Labor Code Section 1700.6(d) and California Code of Regulations, Title 8, Section 12000(e) regarding the proposed transferee. The proposed transferee must also submit, for approval or certification, any contract forms, or fee schedules in their proposed new form should changes in substance from previously approved or certified forms be intended.

§ 12000.6. Transfer of Interest in the Business or Right to Participate in Profits

Before the issuance of written consent for the transfer of interest in the talent agency or in the right to participate in the profits as required by Labor Code Section 1700.30, notification shall be made to the Labor Commissioner in writing within 10 days of the transfer. The Labor Commissioner may require, pursuant to his or her discretion, that the person or persons to whom such interest in the business of the talent agency or right to share in the profits thereof is to be sold, transferred or given, complete the transfer application required by California Code of Regulations, Title 8, Section 12000.5 and supply the information required by Labor Code Section 1700.6(d) and California Code of Regulations, Title 8, Section 12000(e).

§ 12000.7. Change in Location of Main or Branch Office

A talent agency shall notify the Labor Commissioner of a proposed change of address of its main or branch office at least 20 days before such change.

§ 12001. Form of Talent Agency Contracts–General Provisions

Any contract in writing to be entered into between a talent agency and an artist wherein the talent agency agrees to act or function as such for, or on behalf of the artist, shall contain in words or substance in addition to any other provisions set forth therein, each of the following provisions:

(a) A provision stating the term of employment of the talent agency by the artist or a blank space for the insertion of said term.

(b) A provision containing a blank space for the insertion of the compensation or rate of compensation to be paid by the artist to the talent agency which compensation shall not exceed the maximum compensation or maximum rate of compensation set forth in the schedule of fees filed with the Labor Commissioner by the talent agency. Said talent agency contract may provide for the payment of compensation after the termination thereof with respect to any employment contracts entered into or negotiated for or to any employment accepted by the artist during the term of the talent agency contract, or any extensions, options or renewals of said employment contracts or employment.

To be entitled to the payment of compensation after termination of the contract between the artist and the talent agency, the talent agency shall be obligated to serve the artist and perform obligations with respect to any employment contract or to extensions or renewals of said employment contract or to any employment requiring the services of the artist on which such compensation is based.

(c) A provision that the talent agency may advise, counsel or direct the artist in the development or advancement of his professional career.

(d) A provision that the talent agency shall, subject to the availability of the artist, use all reasonable efforts to procure employment for the artist in the field or fields of endeavor specified in the contract in which the talent agency is representing the artist.

(e) A provision that, in the event of the failure of the artist to obtain employment or a bona fide offer therefor from a responsible employer, in the field or fields of endeavor specified in the contract in which the talent agency is representing the artist, for a period of time in excess of four consecutive months, such failure shall be deemed cause for the termination of the contract by either party; provided, however, that the artist shall at all times during such period of four consecutive months be ready, willing, able and available to accept employment and to render the services required in connection therewith. Notices of intention of either party to such a contract to terminate same must be given in writing to the other party to such a contract directed to the last known address of said party. In the event the artist accepts employment prior to any written notice of termination, said right of termination is deemed waived as to all past periods of unemployment but not as to future four consecutive months of employment.

(f) A provision that in all cases of controversy between a talent agency and an artist arising under the Labor Code, or under these Rules and Regulations, relating to the terms of the contract, the parties involved therein shall refer the matters in dispute to the Labor Commissioner or one of his duly authorized agents to be determined, as provided in Section 1700.44 of the Labor Code. However, such a provision need not be inserted in contracts governed by the provisions of Section 1700.45 of the Labor Code.

§ 12001.1. Copy of Contract to Artist

The talent agency shall deliver to the artist a copy of the contract required by California Code of Regulations, Title 8, Section 12001 which has been executed by the talent agency and the artist.

§ 12002.   Oral Contracts

A talent agency shall be entitled to recover a fee, commission or compensation under an oral contract between a talent agency and an artist as long as the particular employment for which such fee, commission or compensation is sought to be charged shall have been procured directly through the efforts or services of such talent agency and shall have been confirmed in writing within 72 hours thereafter. Said confirmation may be denied within a reasonable time by the other party. However, the fact that no written confirmation was ever sent shall not be, in and of itself, sufficient to invalidate the oral contract.

§ 12003.   Form of Contracts Must Be Approved

Approval of the form of contract as required by Labor Code Section 1700.23 will be indicated by an endorsement thereon by the Labor Commissioner which must be retained by the talent agency, or by a letter from the Labor Commissioner that the contract adopted by the talent agency has been endorsed by the Labor Commissioner.

§ 12003.1.   Required Statements on Contract Forms Indicating Approval of Labor Commissioner

After approval of the form of contract by the Labor Commissioner, the same may be legibly reproduced, which reproduction must bear thereon the following statement:

"THIS TALENT AGENCY IS LICENSED BY
THE LABOR COMMISSIONER OF
THE STATE OF CALIFORNIA

The form of this contract has been approved by the State Labor Commissioner on the _____ day of _____ 19____."

§ 12003.2.   Approval of the Labor Commissioner for Reproduction of Approved Contract Forms

No form of contract which incorporates substantial changes in the form of contract previously approved shall be reproduced again unless the same shall be submitted to the Labor Commissioner for approval and shall not be reproduced again prior to the granting of approval and written consent by the Labor Commissioner.

§ 12003.3.   Modifications of Contract Forms Which Do Not Require Approval of the Labor Commissioner

Modifications of contract forms previously approved by the Labor Commissioner which do not substantially change the substance and which, therefore, do not require further approval by the Labor Commissioner pursuant to California Code of Regulations, Title 8, Section 12003.2 include, but are not limited to the following:

1.   A provision for the commencement of the term of the contract at some specified date in the future, which

date may be fixed by the occurrence of an event or contingency.

2.   The deletion of certain fields of endeavor, such as motion pictures, television, etc., from the scope of the talent agency's representation, or a designation of specific engagements.

3.   A reduction in the compensation to be paid by the artist to the talent agency.

4.   Any waiver by the talent agency of commission or compensation to be received from the artist.

5.   A reduction in the four month termination period required by California Code of Regulations, Title 8, Section 12001(e).

6.   Any provision for additional or special services, facilities or benefits to be rendered by the talent agency on behalf of the artist.

7.   Any other modification which operates to the advantage of the artist.

§ 12003.4.   Fee Schedule

Fee schedules posted, as required by Labor Code Section 1700.24, shall be printed or lettered in a size no less than Twelve–Point Cheltenham Roman Type or its equivalent. The printing or lettering shall be in a legible style and there shall be adequate separation between the various classifications. Each fee schedule, when submitted to the Labor Commissioner, must have a clear space of at least 2 1/2 inches at the bottom to permit certification.

§ 12003.5.   Contents–Fee Schedule

(a)   Each fee schedule shall be headed by the words, SCHEDULE OF FEES.

(b)   Additionally, in each fee schedule the following paragraphs shall appear at the end of said fee schedule:

1.   "If any controversy arises between the parties, including one as to liability for the payment of fees, the parties involved shall refer the matter in dispute to the Labor Commissioner for hearing and determination as provided in Labor Code Section 1700.44, unless such controversy can be handled in accordance with the provisions of Labor Code Section 1700.45."

2.   "In the event that a talent agency shall collect from an artist a fee or expenses for obtaining employment for the artist, and the artist shall fail to procure such employment, or the artist shall fail to be paid for such employment, such talent agency shall, upon demand therefor, repay to the artist the fee and expenses so collected. Unless repayment thereof is made within forty-eight (48) hours after demand therefor, the talent agency shall pay to the artist an additional sum equal to the amount of the fee." (Section 1700.40, California Labor Code).

§ 12003.6.   Regulations Do Not Affect Prior Contracts

These rules and regulations shall not apply to contracts heretofore entered into between talent agencies and artists, if the same have been approved by the Labor

Commissioner and said contracts do not contain any provisions contrary to law.

§ 12004. Termination of Contract

Any incapacity which shall prevent a talent agency from performing the services to be rendered by such talent agency to an artist for a period of three consecutive months or the failure of the talent agency to maintain a regular office for the transaction of business in the State of California for a period of one month shall be sufficient grounds for cancellation or termination of the contract by the artist.

§ 12005. Revocation or Suspension of License

The failure of any talent agency to comply with these Rules and Regulations or with any order made by the Labor Commissioner in pursuance thereof shall be cause for the suspension or revocation of the license of such talent agency pursuant to Labor Code Section 1700.21.

Article 2.   Controversies Submitted Under
Section 1700.44, Labor Code

§ 12022. Filing of Application for Hearing to Determine Controversy

Proceedings shall be commenced by filing at the office of the Labor Commissioner, Licensing Division, P.O. Box 420603, San Francisco, CA 94142–0603, a petition to determine controversy between the artist and talent agency, which shall set forth the claim or demand of the petitioner and shall be signed by the petitioner or a person duly authorized to act for him and shall set forth:

(a) A statement as to the nature of the controversy, including submission of such pertinent information as is within the knowledge of the petitioner.

(b) The claim or demand of the petitioner.

(c) A copy of any contract pertaining to the controversy.

§ 12022.1. Form of Petition

The following form represents the minimum requirements for Petition to Determine Controversy.

NAME:
ADDRESS:
CITY & STATE:

Telephone:

In Propria Persona

BEFORE THE LABOR COMMISSIONER

OF THE STATE OF CALIFORNIA

_____   No. _____
          Petitioner,   )
)
)

)
)   **PETITION TO DETERMINE**
)   **CONTROVERSY**
    vs.   )
)
_____.)   (Labor Code Section 1700.44)
     Respondents.   )
_____   )

Petitioner alleges as follows:

I

This petition is filed pursuant to the authority of Section 1700.44 of the Labor Code of the State of California.

II

At the time mentioned herein _____ was and is now a resident of the county of _____ State of California, and an artist (Talent Agency) as that term is defined in Section 1700.44 of the Labor Code.

III

At all times mentioned herein petitioner (respondent acted in the capacity of the Talent Agency and was (was not) duly licensed by the laws of the State of California.

IV

On or about _____, 19 ___, the parties hereto entered into a written contract. A copy of said contract is attached hereto marked Exhibit "A".

V

A controversy has arisen between petitioner and respondent under said contract in that petitioner contends, and respondent denies as follows:

WHEREFORE, petitioner seeks the following determination:

DATED: _____   SIGNED: _____
                                    In Propria Persona

§ 12023. Requirements As to Documents for Filing

All pleadings, petitions and papers, before being filed or served, shall be printed or written on white paper of standard quality not less than 13–pound weight, 8 1/2 by 11 inches in size with numbered lines, connected at the top and paged at the bottom, and shall be written or printed upon only one side of the paper. All copies served shall be true and legible copies of the original. The office address and telephone number of the representative appearing for a party filing any petition, answer or notice, or the office or residence address and telephone number of a party appearing in his own behalf must be endorsed upon such petition, answer or notice, in the upper left hand corner of the first page.

§ 12024. Service of Copy of Petition on Other Party to the Controversy

An exact copy of the petition to determine controversy shall be served upon the opposing party after filing of the original petition, and declaration of service thereof shall be filed with the Labor Commissioner within 10 days of the date service is made. Service of the petition shall be made in the manner prescribed by the Code of Civil Procedure for service of summons in a civil action.

§ 12024.1. Dismissal of Petition

No petition to determine controversy heretofore or hereafter commenced shall be further prosecuted, and no further proceedings shall be had therein, and all petitions to determine controversies heretofore or hereafter commenced must be dismissed by the Labor Commissioner on his own motion, or on the motion of any party interested therein, whether named in the petition as party or not, unless petition be served and return thereon made within one year after the filing of said petition. But all such petitions may be prosecuted if general appearance has been made in said proceedings by the respondent within said one year in the same manner as if said petition had been served; provided that no dismissal shall be had under this section as to any respondent because of the failure to serve the petition on him during his absence from the State, or while he has secreted himself within the State to prevent the service of said petition on him.

§ 12025. Answer to Petition

Written notice to the respondent, requiring him to answer said petition within 20 days from service thereof, shall be served upon the respondent at the time of service of said petition to determine controversy.

Within 20 days from, and after service of the petition to determine controversy, the respondent in said proceeding shall serve and file an answer thereto, setting forth the defense and any claims of said respondent. Said answer shall be signed by the respondent or a person duly authorized to act for said respondent.

§ 12025.1. Forms for Notice to Answer

Notice to Answer as set forth in Section 12025 above, shall be in the following form:

TO THE ABOVE NAMED _____, respondent.

YOU ARE DIRECTED to file at the office of the State Labor Commissioner, _____, insert address a written pleading in response to the Petition to Determine Controversy within 20 days after the service on you of this notice. You are notified that unless you so file a written responsive pleading, the petitioner may apply to the Labor Commissioner for any relief demanded in the petition.

§ 12026. Setting and Notice of Hearing

In a proceeding for the determination of a controversy, either party, after service of petition and filing of the answer, or, if no answer has been filed after the 20 day period set forth in California Code of Regulations, Title 8, Section 12025, may file with the Labor Commissioner a Request for Setting of Hearing; said request for hearing shall include a certificate of service by mail on the opposing party. Thereafter, the Labor Commissioner shall give notice of the time and place of hearing to each of the parties, using first-class mail.

§ 12027. Right to Subpoena

(a) Subpoena. Upon request of either party to the controversy, the Labor Commissioner may issue a subpoena for the attendance of witnesses before the Labor Commissioner at the time and place of the hearing of the controversy. Said subpoena shall be served in the manner provided for serving subpoenas in civil actions.

(b) Subpoena Duces Tecum. Upon request of either party to the controversy, accompanied by a declaration showing good cause for the production thereof and showing the relevance thereof, and upon the determination of the Labor Commissioner, he or she may issue a subpoena duces tecum requiring the production of books, documents or other things under the control of the party subpoenaed, which the party is bound to produce at the time and place of the hearing. Said subpoena duces tecum shall be served in the manner provided for serving subpoenas in civil actions.

§ 12028. Depositions

On application of a party to the controversy, the Labor Commissioner may order the deposition of a witness to be taken for use as evidence, and not for discovery, if the witness cannot be compelled to attend the hearing or if such exceptional circumstances exist as to make it desirable, in the interest of justice and with due regard to the importance of presenting the testimony of witnesses orally at the hearing, to allow the deposition to be taken . The deposition shall be taken in the manner prescribed by law for the taking of depositions in civil actions.

§ 12029. Proceedings to Be Had Under Oath

All testimony adduced at the hearing of the controversy shall be under oath.

§ 12030. Proceedings May Be Reported

Any proceedings held before the Labor Commissioner may be reported. The person desiring the reporting shall bear the expense thereof, and if the testimony is transcribed, a copy of this transcript shall be furnished without cost to the Labor Commissioner.

§ 12031. Conduct of Hearing

The hearing may be reported or phonographically recorded. The parties to the controversy are entitled to be heard, to present evidence and to cross-examine witnesses appearing at the hearing, but the Labor Commissioner is not bound by the rules of evidence or judicial procedure.

§ 12032. Decision of Labor Commissioner

The decision of the Labor Commissioner shall be in writing and shall be served upon the parties to the controversy by first-class mail. Either party to the controversy, at the commencement of the hearing, may request that findings of fact be made by the Labor Commissioner, but the making of such findings of fact shall be discretionary with the Labor Commissioner.

§ 12033. Custody of Papers Filed with the Labor Commissioner

All papers on file in the office of the Labor Commissioner shall remain in his or her custody, and no paper on file therein shall be taken from the Labor Commissioner's office, unless the same is subpoenaed in an action pending before a court of competent jurisdiction; except that documents introduced by the parties into evidence may be withdrawn upon stipulation of the parties or by their respective representatives.

Subchapter 5. Registration of Persons Who Unload Farm Products

Article 1. Registration of Unloaders

§ 13200. Registration of Unloaders

Unloaders of farm produce who unload in markets in which five or more dealers operate shall register in person at the nearest office of the Labor Commissioner. Unloaders shall present the following at time of registration:

(a) Social Security Card

(b) Union Card, if a member

§ 13201. Contents of Registration

Registration shall show:

(a) Name and address of registrant.

(b) Social Security number.

(c) Union affiliation, if any.

(d) Age.

(e) Height.

(f) Weight.

(g) Color hair.

(h) Color eyes.

§ 13202. Period of Registration

Registration shall be valid for a period of 12 months.

§ 13203. Change of Address

Registrants shall report any change of address in person to the nearest office of the Labor Commissioner within 10 days of such change.

Article 2. Registration of Producers

§ 13220. Registration of Producers

Producers who transport and unload their own farm products, in markets in which five or more dealers operate, shall register in person at the nearest office of the Labor Commissioner.

§ 13221. Contents of Registration

Registration shall show:

(a) Name and address of producer.

(b) Age.

(c) Height.

(d) Weight.

(e) Color hair.

(f) Color eyes.

(g) Vehicle or vehicles used by producer to transport his (her) produce to market.

§ 13222. Period of Registration

Registration shall be valid for a period of 12 months.

§ 13223. Change of Address

Registrant shall report any change of address in person to the nearest office of the Labor Commissioner within 10 days of such change.

Article 3. Registration of Producer's Unloaders

§ 13230. Registration of Producer's Unloaders

Any registered producer who desires to use the services of his (her) father, mother, son(s), daughter(s) or regular employee(s) in unloading his (her) produce shall register the following information with respect to each such person:

(a) Name

(b) Relationship to producer-i.e., father, mother, son, daughter or regular employee.

(c) If an employee, capacity in which employed.

§ 13231. Registration in Person

Each person so registered by a producer shall complete his (her) registration in person.

§ 13232. Contents of Registration

Registration shall show:

(a) Name and address.

(b) Age.

(c) Height.

(d) Weight.

(e) Color hair.

(f) Color eyes.

(g) Relationship to producer-i.e., father, mother, son, daughter, or regular employee.

(h) If an employee:

(1) Capacity in which employed; and

(2) Date employment commenced.

§ 13233. Period of Registration

Registration shall be valid for a period of 12 months.

§ 13234. Registration Void, When

Registration of any employee shall become void upon termination of his (her) employment with the producer to whom he (she) is registered, and shall be surrendered to the Labor Commissioner.

§ 13235. Change of Address

Registrant shall report any change of address in person to the nearest office of the Labor Commissioner within 10 days of such change.

§ 13236. Change of Vehicle or License Number

Registrant shall report any change of vehicle or vehicle license number to the nearest office of the Labor Commissioner within 10 days of such change.

Subchapter 5.5. Unloading of Farm Products in the Markets of San Mateo, Alameda, and San Francisco

Article 1.   Unloading of Farm Products in the Markets of San Mateo, Alameda, and San Francisco

§ 13260. Commissioner

Whenever used herein, "Commissioner" shall be defined as stated in California Food and Agricultural Code section 57004.

§ 13261. Drivers Unloading

Drivers of a vehicle transporting produce to a particular market subject to these regulations, and co-drivers of the same vehicle accompanying such driver, where the distance of transport to market involves out-of-state travel, or travel involving such distance as would ordinarily require two drivers, shall not be prohibited from unloading said trucks and shall be exempt from the registration provisions of these regulations; and such drivers shall not be subject to charge or fee for unloading their truck nor shall such drivers be required to employ any person for unloading said vehicle.

§ 13262. Limitation of Registrations

Upon application, the Commissioner shall issue registrations up to the time at which the produce dealers of a particular market subject to these regulations shall certify in writing that no further unloaders are needed, at which time, the Commissioner may after investigation (which shall include consultation with interested labor and employer organizations) cease to issue further registrations, all in the interest of the orderly marketing of farm products, and such a cessation of issuance shall continue

until such time as the particular market, subject to these regulations, certifies in writing, or until truckers or unloaders file a petition certifying, that there is again need for registered unloaders; and after investigation, the Commissioner determines that there is such a need.

§ 13263. Receipt Required

(a) The produce dealer shall have on hand at his place of business a responsible person to distribute a form receipt to drivers for each drop and to execute a receipt for any farm product which is unloaded at his place of business during posted receiving hours.

(b) A registered unloader who is paid an unloading fee is required to sign A form receipt which shall include at least the following information:

(1) name of the market;

(2) date;

(3) name of the hauler;

(4) quantity, unit price and amount of charges for each type of farm product unload;

(5) number of pallets, unit price and amount of charges for pallets unloaded;

(6) miscellaneous charges;

(7) total charges for load;

(8) the following acknowledgement, "undersigned registered unloader acknowledges receipt of above charges"; and

(9) badge number and signature of registered unloader.

§ 13264. Dealers' Association

Produce dealers who operate in a market may organize an association to facilitate the carrying out of responsibilities under these regulations.

§ 13265. Registration, Revocation or Denial

The Commissioner may deny or revoke a registration issued to any unloader on the following grounds for the following time periods:

(a) conviction of any criminal offense or adverse judgment for activity involving the market shall be grounds for revocation or denial for a period of three (3) years;

(b) conviction of any felony shall be grounds for revocation or denial for a period of two (2) years;

(c) Failure of a registered unloader to report such conviction or adverse judgments shall be grounds for an additional denial or revocation period of two (2) years.

§ 13266. Inspection

All books and records of produce dealers shall be open for investigation and audit by duly authorized agents and representatives of the Department of Industrial Relations and the Division of Labor Standards Enforcement during normal business hours.

§ 13267. Fee

The fee is set by the Director of the Department of Industrial Relations pursuant to Section 57042 of the Food and Agricultural Code at $400; and the fee is payable by produce dealers and shall be for the exclusive use in administering the provisions of Chapter 8.5 of Division 20 of the Food and Agricultural Code.

(a) Fees shall be due and payable on or before January 1 of each year, to the Fiscal Officer, Division of Labor Standards Enforcement, P.O. Box 420603, San Francisco, California 94142–0603.

(b) Checks should be made payable as follows: PRODUCE UNLOADING FUND.

Subchapter 6.   Security for Wages

Article 1.   Logging and Sawmill Industry

§ 13300.   Amount of Bond to Be Deposited with Labor Commissioner

The bond to be deposited with the Labor Commissioner pursuant to the provisions of Labor Code Section 270.5(a)(2) shall be in an amount equal to the highest contemplated payroll of the employer for any period for which a single payment of wages is made, or for four calendar weeks, whichever is the longer.

§ 13301.   Application for Determination of Amount

Every employer seeking determination of the amount of the bond required by Labor Code Section 270.5(a)(2) shall file a written application with the Labor Commissioner under oath upon a form prescribed by the Labor Commissioner, setting forth his (her) contemplated payroll as specified in Section 13300.

§ 13302.   Period for Which Determination Effective

Any determination of the amount of the bond made by the Labor Commissioner shall remain effective only so long as no payroll of the employer exceeds the amount of the highest contemplated payroll reported in the application made pursuant to Section 13301, and when any payroll exceeds such amount, the determination shall become void two weeks thereafter unless a new application is made by the employer during said period. This section shall not operate to affect the validity of or liability under any bond then outstanding.

Subchapter 6.5.   Hearings on Actions to Recover Wages, Penalties, and Other Demands for Compensation and on Claims from Holders of Dishonored Payroll Checks or Drafts

Article 1.   Rules of Practice and Procedure

§ 13500.   Definition of "DIVISION"

As used herein, the term "DIVISION" shall mean the DIVISION OF LABOR STANDARDS ENFORCEMENT of the Department of Industrial Relations of the State of California, formerly called DIVISION OF LABOR LAW ENFORCEMENT.

§ 13501.   Filing of Complaint

An employee complaint or claim for wages, penalties or other demand for compensation properly before the DIVISION or the Labor Commissioner, including Orders of the Industrial Welfare Commission, under Labor Code Section 98(a) shall be initiated by the filing of a complaint on the form prescribed herein in any District Office of the DIVISION. If the District Office is not the proper office serving the county in which compensation claimed was earned or in which any of the acts complained of was performed, the complaint shall be referred to the proper office of the DIVISION serving said county, for investigation and hearing.

§ 13501.5.   Form of Complaint

The complaint contemplated by Labor Code Section 98 and filed with the DIVISION shall be in writing and substantially in the following form:

LABOR COMMISSIONER, STATE OF CALIFORNIA Department of Industrial Relations DIVISION OF LABOR STANDARDS ENFORCEMENT	DATE FILED
	DISTRICT OFFICE
PLAINTIFF	TAKEN BY
DEFENDANT	
	DOES I THROUGH V, Defendant(s)
STATE CASE NUMBER	COMPLAINT

PLAINTIFF ALLEGES:

1.   He/She was employed by the defendant named above to perform personal services as: _____

2. for the period _____ to _____

3. in the County of _____, California; under the terms of the (written) (oral) agreement at the promised rate of compensation of _____
_____

4. that there is due, owing and payable from the defendant to the plaintiff an amount as and for wages, penalties and/or other demands for compensation:

   ☐ a. as shown in attached Exhibit A, incorporated herein;
   ☐ b. as set out below:

   ☐ c. plus additional wages accrued pursuant to Labor Code Section 203 as a penalty at the rate of $_____ per day for an indeterminate number of days not to exceed thirty (30) days.

   Plaintiff certifies that the foregoing is true and correct to the best of his/her knowledge and belief.

Executed at _____, County of _____, California
on _____, 19____. _____
                                              Signature of Plaintiff

COMPLAINT

§ 13501.6. Form of Complaint on Claim from Holder of Dishonored Payroll Check or Draft

A complaint on a claim from a holder of a dishonored payroll check or draft, contemplated by Labor Code Section 98 and filed with the DIVISION shall be in writing and substantially in the following form:

LABOR COMMISSIONER, STATE OF CALIFORNIA **Department of Industrial Relations** DIVISION OF LABOR STANDARDS ENFORCEMENT	DATE FILED
	DISTRICT OFFICE
COMPLAINANT	**TAKEN BY**
DEFENDANT	
STATE CASE NUMBER	**COMPLAINT** **PAYROLL CHECK OR DRAFT–PAYMENT REJECTED**

Claimant and Complainant named above complains of and makes claim against Defendant named above as follows:

1. That the claimant and complainant furnished goods and/or services and/or Cash to those employee-payees listed on the attached Schedule "A", and received from the employee-payee: in exchange *and/or* in payment of same, the payroll check or draft issued by the Defendant named above, in the amount set forth opposite the name of the employee-payee; and that each employee-payee properly endorsed his/her payroll check or draft to claimant and complainant, who thereby became a holder in due course thereof.

2. That the check or draft is simultaneously being deposited by claimant and complainant with the office of the Labor Commissioner of the *State of California*, for payment and prosecution of claimant-complainant's rights thereunder, and a copy of the check is attached as Schedule "B", and incorporated for all purposes as though set forth in full;

3. That each check or draft totaling $_____ was presented by claimant and complainant to (name of bank) _____ the bank upon which it was drawn and was returned to claimant and complainant, unpaid and dishonored;

4. That claimant and complainant has made diligent search for the employee-payee but is still unable to return the dishonored check or draft to the employee-payee for the recovery from the employee-payee of the respective sum of the check or draft as shown on Schedule "A", paid out by claimant and complainant, and that the dishonored check or draft in the total sum of $_____ remains fully unpaid and unsatisfied;

5. That claimant and complainant requests the Labor Commissioner of the State of California to set the matter of this complaint for hearing; and

6. That claimant and complainant asks for Order, Decision or Award determining the claim in his favor, and more particularly, as follows:

   a. Defendant pay to claimant—complainant the sum of $_____, the amount of the dishonored payroll check or draft.

Claimant and complainant certifies under penalty of perjury that the foregoing is true and correct to the best of his/her knowledge and belief.

Executed at _____, California, on _____, 19_____.

_____
Signature of Claimant—Complainant

COMPLAINT
PAYROLL CHECK OR DRAFT–PAYMENT REJECTED

§ 13501.7. Form of Answer

The answer which may be filed by the defendant or defendants pursuant to Labor Code Section 98(c) shall be in writing and substantially in the following form:

LABOR COMMISSIONER, STATE OF CALIFORNIA Department of Industrial Relations DIVISION OF LABOR STANDARDS ENFORCEMENT	
PLAINTIFF	
DEFENDANT	
STATE CASE NUMBER	ANSWER

Defendant answers the complaint on the file as follows:

AGREES:

DENIES
(Set forth any particulars in which the complaint is inaccurate or incomplete and the facts upon which you intend to rely. Use additional sheet if necessary.)

Defendant certified that the foregoing, including attachments, is true and correct to the best of his/her knowledge and belief.

Executed at _____, California, on _____, 19 ___.

_____
(Signature of person answering, with title if answer is made on behalf of another person or entity.)

_____
(Type or print your name and name of person or entity, if any, on whose behalf this form is signed.)

§ 13502. Conduct of Hearings

Hearings by the Labor Commissioner under Sections 98 et seq., of the Labor Code shall be presided over by a Deputy Labor Commissioner. The hearing shall be reported or phonographically recorded. Either party may request a copy of the transcript or recording, and shall bear all costs incidental to the preparation of same. If the record of the hearing is transcribed by any party, a copy thereof shall be provided to the Labor Commissioner free of any charge or cost within five (5) days of such transcription. Proceedings need not be conducted according to technical rules relating to evidence and witnesses. Any relevant evidence shall be admitted if it is the sort of evidence on which responsible persons are accustomed to rely in the conduct of serious affairs, regardless of the existence of any common law or statutory rule which might make improper the admission of such evidence over objection in civil actions.

§ 13505. Taking of Evidence

Oral evidence shall be taken only on oath or affirmation. Each party shall have the right to call and examine witnesses; to introduce exhibits; to cross-examine opposing witnesses on any matter relevant to the issues even though that matter was not covered in the direct examination; to impeach any witness regardless of which party first called him (her) to testify; and to rebut the evidence against him (her).

§ 13506. Deputy Labor Commissioner's Authority

In presiding over a hearing conducted hereunder, the Deputy Labor Commissioner shall control the order of presentation of evidence at the hearing, and direct and rule on matters concerning the conduct of the hearing and of the parties appearing. Prior to a hearing, upon the application of any party to the proceedings, the Deputy Labor Commissioner may issue subpoenas to compel the attendance of necessary witnesses and the production of books and documents. In the exercise of his (her) sound discretion, the Deputy Labor Commissioner may limit the number of witnesses subpoenaed either for the purpose of corroboration or establishing a single material fact in issue, or where the party requesting the subpoena has not furnished satisfactory evidence that the witness will be able to give necessary and competent testimony, material to the issues, at the hearing.

§ 13507. Right to Counsel

Any party to a proceedings conducted hereunder may, but need not, be represented by counsel.

§ 13508. Continuances

Continuance of hearing ordinarily will not be granted. The Deputy Labor Commissioner, in the exercise of his (her) sound discretion, may grant a continuance of hearing upon a showing of extraordinary circumstances and good cause for continuance by the party requesting same.

§ 13520. Definition of "Willful."

A willful failure to pay wages within the meaning of Labor Code Section 203 occurs when an employer intentionally fails to pay wages to an employee when those wages are due. However, a good faith dispute that any wages are due will preclude imposition of waiting time penalties under Section 203.

(a) Good Faith Dispute. A "good faith dispute" that any wages are due occurs when an employer presents a defense, based in law or fact which, if successful, would preclude any recover on the part of the employee. The fact that a defense is ultimately unsuccessful will not preclude a finding that a good faith dispute did exist. Defenses presented which, under all the circumstances, are unsupported by any evidence, are unreasonable, or are presented in bad faith, will preclude a finding of a "good faith dispute."

Subchapter 7. Industrial Homework

Article 1. Enforcement of Industrial Homework Act

§ 13600. Definitions

Employee means anyone engaged, suffered, or permitted to do industrial homework. It shall be the presumption that persons working in their homes for remuneration on articles to be delivered to another person not for his (her) personal or his (her) family's use are employees and not independent contractors.

§ 13601. Records

(a) Industrial homeworkers shall keep an accurate count of the hours they work daily, and shall record said hours required in the handbook furnished by the Division of Labor Standards Enforcement. The homeworker shall submit regularly to the employer all information regarding hours worked which are required for his (her) records.

(b) The record keeping required of an employer of industrial homeworkers shall include an accurate recording of the hours worked during the pay roll period as reported by each industrial homeworker, and these hours shall be posted to the same record as wages. Industrial homeworkers shall be designated as such on the pay roll records.

§ 13602. Preliminary Information Required by Employer

Prior to obtaining an industrial homework license, the employer shall submit an application in accordance with Labor Code Section 2665, to the Division of Labor Standards Enforcement on a form supplied by the Division of Labor Standards Enforcement (see Exhibit A).

(b) Within 30 calendar days of receipt of an application for a license to employ industrial homeworkers the Division of Labor Standards Enforcement shall inform the applicant in writing that it is either complete and accepted for filing or that it is deficient and what specific information or documentation is required to complete the application.

(c) Within 60 calendar days from the date of filing of a completed application, the Division of Labor Standards Enforcement shall inform the applicant in writing of its decision regarding the application.

§ 13603. Inspections

(a) Every employer possessing an industrial homework license shall allow any duly authorized representative of the Division of Labor Standards Enforcement free access to his (her) place of business for the purpose of making inspections of, or excerpts from, all books, reports, contracts, pay rolls, documents or papers relating to the employment of homeworkers; or for the purpose of inspecting any articles sent out for industrial homework or samples thereof; or in order to make time studies of work performed in a factory to determine whether the piece rates paid for industrial homework are sufficient to yield the legal minimum wage.

(b) Industrial homeworkers shall permit entry into their homes by duly authorized representatives of the Division of Labor Standards Enforcement possessing a search warrant as defined in Labor Code Section 2656, for the purpose of making investigations as to the homeworker's compliance with Sections 2651 and 2661 of the State Labor Code; to inspect articles on which industrial homework is being performed; to check homeworker's observance of record keeping requirements; or to make on the homeworker's premises, or elsewhere, such time studies of work performance as may be required to determine compliance with legal wage requirements.

§ 13604. Revocations of Licenses or Permits

If, after investigation the Division of Labor Standards Enforcement, believes that an employer possessing an industrial homework license, or an industrial homeworker possessing an industrial homework permit has failed to comply with provisions of the Industrial Homework Act or its rules and regulations, a hearing may be held by the Division of Labor Standards Enforcement to determine whether there has been a violation. Before denying, suspending or revoking any license or permit, the Labor Commissioner shall afford the applicant or holder an opportunity to request a hearing in accordance with Chapter 5 Part I of Division 3 of Title 2 of the Government Code Sections 11500 et. seq. Any such hearing on appeal of a denial of a license or permit or on the proposed suspension or revocation of such license or permit, shall be conducted in accordance with Chapter 5 of Part I of Division 3 of Title 2 of the Government Code (Section 11500 et seq.) and the Labor Commissioner shall have all the powers granted therein. Written notices of such hearing will be sent to the employer or industrial homeworker in question and the license or permit may be revoked upon a finding that there has been such violation.

Article 2. Prohibiting Industrial Homework in the Garment Manufacturing Industry

§ 13620. Prohibiting Industrial Homework in the Garment Manufacturing Industry

Industrial homework and the distribution of articles for industrial homework by any employer in the garment manufacturing industry is prohibited.

§ 13621. Definitions

The garment manufacturing industry is defined as follows: All persons engaged in the business of manufacturing garments for wear upon the human body.

For the purpose of this order the term garment manufacturing means and includes every process, either hand or machine, involved in the manufacture of any or all garments for wear upon the human body, whether such process be applied to fabric, textile, fur, leather, or leather substitute, or other material of a similar nature, and also means to prepare, alter, repair, or finish in whole or in part.

Hand knitting is hereby specifically excepted from the operation of this order.

"Employer" means any person who, directly or indirectly or through an employee, agent, independent contractor, or any other person, delivers to another person any materials or articles to be manufactured in a home and thereafter to be returned to him, not for the personal use of himself or of a member of his family.

"Industrial homework" means any manufacture in a home of materials or articles for an employer.

"Industrial homeworker" means any person who does industrial homework.

All outstanding permits to employers and all outstanding certificates to industrial homeworkers in the garment manufacturing industry, as defined above, shall be null and void after September 1, 1941, and no permits shall hereafter be issued to employers for the distribution of articles for industrial homework and no certificates shall hereafter be issued to homeworkers on such articles, except in accordance with the provisions of Sections 11022 and 11023.

§ 13622. Special Authorization for Aged and Disabled Homeworkers

(a) Terms of Issuance. If not inconsistent with the purposes of Part 10, Labor Code, employers and homeworkers in the garment manufacturing industry may be granted special homework permits and certificates on condition that the Chief of the Division of Industrial Welfare, after investigation, finds:

(1) That the industrial homeworker was working for an employer as an industrial homeworker in the garment manufacturing industry on or prior to September 1, 1941, and is:

(A) Unable to adjust to factory work because of advanced age; or

(B) Physically or mentally disabled or suffering from an injury and an examination by a physician, designated by the Chief of the Division of Industrial Welfare, reveals that such disability would prevent the worker from adjusting to factory employment; or

(C) Unable to leave home because such worker's services are essential to care for an invalid in the home.

(2) That the industrial homeworker is covered by workmen's compensation insurance;

(3) That the employer maintains a factory in which one or more employees are employed on operations which are similar to the homework operations.

§ 13623. Conditions of Employment

(a) Work for One Employer Only. An industrial homeworker shall be permitted to work for one employer only.

(b) Factory Work Prohibited to Homeworker. The industrial homeworker shall not be employed as a factory worker while he or she holds a homework certificate.

(c) Work Distributed Directly to the Homeworker. The employer shall distribute and collect all materials and articles free of charge to the homeworker.

(d) Labels. The employer shall conspicuously affix to each article or material or, if this is impossible, to the package or other container in which such goods are delivered or are to be kept, a label or other mark of identification bearing the employer's name and address, printed or written legibly in English.

(e) Limitation of Work. The maximum amount of work which may be given to any industrial homeworker in any week shall not exceed the average weekly amount produced by workers working legal hours on similar operations in the shop.

(f) Rates Paid to Homeworkers. On any operation, a female or minor homeworker shall be paid a piece-rate sufficient to yield to workers on similar operations in the factory the legally established minimum wage established by the Industrial Welfare Commission.

(g) Employer's Record:

(1) The employer shall keep a record of the name and address of the industrial homeworker, of all articles or materials which such homeworker has manufactured, the date on which articles or materials are issued to the homeworker, a list of articles or materials given out, the kind of work performed on such articles or materials, and the operations to be performed, the piece rates per dozen or per unit paid to the homeworker, the date and amount of finished articles or materials returned, the wages paid for each lot of articles or materials returned, and the total weekly payment made to the homeworker.

Each employer shall, on demand, submit to the Chief of the Division of Industrial Welfare or to her representative a sworn copy of such records, together with such information as the Chief of the Division of Industrial Welfare may in her discretion deem necessary.

(2) Any person who does not deliver articles or materials directly to an industrial homeworker shall keep the name and address of each agent, distributor, or contractor through whom industrial homework is distributed and of all persons from whom he has received materials or articles to be so manufactured.

(h) Homeworker's Record. The homeworker shall keep a record on a form issued by the Division of Industrial Welfare on which the homeworker shall enter the date on which articles or materials are received by the homeworker; a list of all articles or materials received; the kind of work performed on such articles or materials; the piece rates paid per dozen or per unit; the date and amount of finished articles or materials returned; an accurate record of the number of hours worked per day and the total hours worked per week; the total amount received for the work performed during each week; and the date payment was received. All of the above required information shall be certified to by the homeworker. Such records shall be the property of the Division of Industrial Welfare and shall be returned to the division not later than the 10th of the month succeeding the month in which the work was performed; or at any time upon demand by the division.

(i) Revocation of Certificates and Permits. Industrial homework certificates and permits may be revoked or suspended at any time after the holder has been given reasonable notice and an opportunity to be heard, if, upon investigation, the Chief of the Division of Industrial Welfare finds that the industrial homeworker is performing industrial homework contrary to the above conditions or has permitted any person not holding a valid homeworker's certificate to assist him or her in performing industrial homework, or that the employer has not complied with the above regulations or any applicable provision of the Labor Code or the orders or regulations of the Industrial Welfare Division.

§ 13624. Effect of Invalid Sections

Every section or part of this order is declared to be separate and independent of every other section or part and if any section or part of this order is declared invalid, said construction shall not invalidate any of the remaining sections or parts of said order, but the same shall remain in full force and effect as if the invalid portion had never been enacted.

Subchapter 8. Garment Manufacturers

§ 13630. Registration of Manufacturers and Contractors

All persons, within the meaning of Labor Code Section 2671(a), engaged in "garment manufacturing," as defined in Labor Code Section 2671(b), must register with the Labor Commissioner as either a "contractor"(defined at Labor Code Section 2671(d)), or a "manufacturer," according to that person's bona fide business practices. A person's designation on a registration as a "contractor" or "manufacturer" shall not preclude the introduction of evidence in any proceeding before the Labor Commissioner on the actual business practices of such person.

§ 13631. Recordkeeping

Every employer engaged in the business of garment manufacturing shall keep accurate records as required by Labor Code Sections 226 and 2673, any applicable order of the Industrial Welfare Commission, and section 13659 of this subchapter. These records shall be maintained for a period of no less than four years, unless otherwise specified, at the place of employment or at a central location within the State of California, and shall be made available to the Labor Commissioner, or his or her

agents, upon request for inspection and/or copying. Failure to provide these records to the Labor Commissioner within ten days of the date of request, or providing records that have been falsified, shall constitute grounds for revocation of registration or denial of an application for registration.

§ 13632. Advisory Committee

The Labor Commissioner shall appoint a 15–member advisory committee on issues related to employment and the enforcement of wage and hour laws in the garment industry, which shall meet, at least semi-annually, alternately in Los Angeles and San Francisco. Members shall serve without compensation or reimbursement for expenses. At each meeting the Committee may authorize distribution of a publication to be prepared by the Division of Labor Standards Enforcement, focusing on industry practices and patterns of violations.

§ 13633. Registration of Employee Leasing Companies and Temporary Agencies

(a) Every employee leasing company or temporary agency that leases or otherwise provides garment manufacturers or contractors with the services of employees engaged in sewing, cutting, making, processing, repairing, finishing, assembling, or otherwise preparing any garment or article of wearing apparel or accessories designed or intended to be worn by any individual is itself engaged in garment manufacturing, and must register with and obtain a valid registration certificate from the Labor Commissioner as a contractor.

(b) Every employee leasing company or temporary agency shall provide the Labor Commissioner with written notice whenever it enters into, or terminates, an arrangement to lease or otherwise provide employees engaged in any of the above enumerated garment manufacturing operations to a garment manufacturer or contractor. This notice shall include the name and address of the garment manufacturer or contractor that was or will be a party to the arrangement, the dates from beginning to end that employees were or will be leased or otherwise provided under the arrangement, the address(es) where the employees performed or will perform the garment manufacturing operations, and the number of employees that have been or will be leased or otherwise provided to the garment manufacturer or contractor under the arrangement. This notice shall be mailed to: Division of Labor Standards Enforcement, Licensing & Registration Unit, PO Box 420603, San Francisco, CA 94142. Failure to provide this notice within ten days of the date of entering into or terminating the arrangement will constitute grounds for revocation of registration or denial of an application for registration.

§ 13634. Requirements for Registration

(a) Applicants for registration shall complete the application form provided by the Labor Commission entitled "Application for Registration Garment Manufacturing Industry" [DLSE 810 (REV. 03/02)], which is hereby

1351

incorporated by reference. The form includes the following information which the applicant shall certify under penalty of perjury:

(1) Name and business address of applicant, and the address of each location where employees will be engaged in garment manufacturing;

(2) Form of business entity;

(3) Name, social security number, California driver's license number, and residence address of owner, if sole proprietorship;

(4) Name(s), social security number(s), California driver's license number(s), and residence address(es) of co-owners, if any;

(5) Fictitious name, if any, under which the business is operated;

(6) Names, social security number(s), California driver's license number(s), and residence addresses of all partners, if a partnership;

(7) Names, social security numbers, California driver's license numbers, and residence addresses of all officers and directors, and their respective titles, if a corporation;

(8) Number of employees, and a copy of the most recently filed quarterly report to the Employment Development Department reflecting the number of employees employed;

(9) Type of business, and whether the business primarily operates as a garment manufacturer or a garment contractor;

(10) Proof of current workers' compensation insurance coverage;

(11) The name(s), address(es), and form(s) of business entities of persons and entities engaged in the business of garment manufacturing with whom the applicant has entered into contracts for the performance of garment manufacturing services during the past three years;

(12) The applicant's employer tax identification number;

(13) Name(s), social security number(s), California driver's license number(s), and residence address(es) of all managers and supervisors who directly or indirectly control the wages, hours, or working conditions of the applicant's employees.

(14) Name(s), social security number(s), California driver's license number(s), and residence addresses of all substantial shareholders, and the percentage of their ownership in the business, if a corporation. For the purpose of this section, the term "substantial shareholder" shall mean any shareholder who owns at least 20% of the total value of all classes of stock, or, if no stock has been issued, who owns at least 20% of the beneficial interests in the corporation.

(15) Names, social security number(s), California driver's license number(s), and residence addresses of all members, if a limited liability corporation.

(16) Name and business address of the agent for service of process, if a corporation or limited liability company.

(17) The amount of gross sales receipts, as defined in section 13635(d), for the 12-month period immediately preceding the filing of the application.

(18) A list of all assessments of wages due and all penalty citations for violations of provisions of the Fair Labor Standards Act or the California Labor Code that were issued by the United States Department of Labor or the California Department of Industrial Relations within the past three years to the applicant or the applicant's owner(s), partners (if the applicant is a partnership), corporate officers, directors and substantial shareholders (if the applicant is a corporation), members (if the applicant is a limited liability company), or managers and supervisors; the names of the persons and businesses that were cited or assessed; the date and amount of each citation or assessment; the disposition of any appeal on the citation or assessment; and whether or not the citation or assessment has been paid, and if so, the date it was paid.

(19) A list of all judgments and settlement agreements for unpaid wages that were entered within the past five years against the applicant or the applicant's owner(s), partners (if the applicant is a partnership), corporate officers, directors and substantial shareholders (if the applicant is a corporation), members (if the applicant is a limited liability company), or managers and supervisors; the names of the persons and businesses against whom judgments or settlement agreements for unpaid wages were entered; the date of entry of judgment or the date of execution of the settlement agreement; the court that entered the judgment, the case number, and the amount found due in each judgment or settlement agreement; and whether or not the judgment or settlement agreement has been paid, and if so, the date it was paid.

(20) Whether the applicant or the applicant's owner(s), partners (if the applicant is a partnership), corporate officers, directors and substantial shareholders (if the applicant is a corporation), members (if the applicant is a limited liability company), or managers and supervisors have had a garment registration certificate revoked or an application for registration denied, and if so, the name and address of the business whose registration or application for registration was revoked or denied, the period of revocation or date of denial, and the reasons for the revocation or denial.

(21) For any applicant that had an application for registration denied, or a registration revoked or suspended, pursuant to proceedings under section 13646 at any time during the past three years, whether the applicant has had any gross sales receipts, as defined in section 13635(d), at any time during the three years prior to the filing of the application.

(22) For new applicants, whether the applicant or the applicant's owner(s), partners (if the applicant is a partnership), corporate officers, directors and substantial

shareholders (if the applicant is a corporation), members (if the applicant is a limited liability company), managers and supervisors, or immediate family members of any of the above persons have ever previously operated as a garment manufacturer, contractor, or in any other capacity in garment manufacturing, including but not limited to exercising direct or indirect control over garment workers' wages, hours and working conditions, and if so, the name(s) and address(es) of the business(es), dates of operation, garment registration number(s), and dates of registration.

(b) Every person applying for registration as a manufacturer shall certify in writing that he or she is aware of the wage guarantee provision of Labor Code Section 2673.1, under which every garment manufacturer guarantees payment of his or her proportionate share of any unpaid minimum wages and overtime wages owing to any employees of the contractors with whom the manufacturer contracts, for work performed by the contractor's employees on behalf of the manufacturer.

(c) The residence addresses, social security numbers, and California driver's license numbers listed in the application for registration pursuant to subsections (a)(3),(4), (6), (7), (13), (14) and (15), above, are for the Labor Commissioner's use for licensing and law enforcement purposes, and are confidential and shall not be disclosed to any person other than an employee of a law enforcement agency, except if required by court order or if necessary for the prosecution, by the Labor Commissioner, of any judicial or administrative proceeding.

§ 13635. Registration and Examination Fees

(a) The Labor Commissioner shall collect the following amounts in fees for initial registration and annual renewal of registration from contractors who have not had an application for registration denied or a registration revoked or suspended pursuant to proceedings under section 13646 during any portion of the three year period prior to the submission of the application for registration:

(1) A $250 fee for contractors with gross sales receipts of $100,000 or less during the 12-month period prior to application.

(2) A $350 fee for contractors with gross sales receipts from $100,001 to $500,000 during the 12-month period prior to application.

(3) A $500 fee for contractors with gross sales receipts from $500,001 to $1,000,000 during the 12-month period prior to application.

(4) A $1,000 fee for contractors with gross sales receipts of $1,000,001 or more during the 12-month period prior to application.

(b) The Labor Commissioner shall collect the following amounts in fees for initial registration and annual renewal of registration from manufacturers who have not had an application for registration denied or a registration revoked or suspended pursuant to proceedings under

section 13646 during any portion of the three year period prior to the submission of the application for registration:

(1) A $750 fee for manufacturers with gross sales receipts of $500,000 or less during the 12-month period prior to application.

(2) A $1,000 fee for manufacturers with gross sales receipts from $500,001 to $3,000,000 during the 12-month period prior to application.

(3) A $1,500 fee for manufacturers with gross sales receipts from $3,000,001 to $7,000,000 during the 12-month period prior to application.

(4) A $2,500 fee for manufacturers with gross sales receipts of $7,000,001 or more during the 12-month period prior to application.

(c) The Labor Commissioner shall collect the following amounts in fees for initial registration and annual renewal of registration from any manufacturer or contractor who has had an application for registration denied or a registration revoked or suspended, pursuant to proceedings under section 13646, at any time during the three year period prior to the submission of the application for registration:

(1) A $500 fee for contractors with no gross sales receipts during the three-year period prior to application.

(2) A $1,000 fee for contractors with any gross sales receipts during the three-year period prior to application.

(3) A $1,500 fee for manufacturers with no gross sales receipts during the three-year period prior to application.

(4) A $2,500 fee for manufacturers with any gross sales receipts during the three-year period prior to application.

(d) For the purpose of this section, gross sales receipts means all amounts received by the applicant, in the form of money, promissory notes, credit, or any other items of value, for the sale or transfer of goods, or for services provided by the applicant or its employees. In determining gross sales receipts, the applicant shall not deduct from sales receipts or adjust sales receipts for any expenses, including but not limited to the cost of material, labor, services, storage, transportation, rent, utilities, interest on loans, insurance, taxes, and any business losses.

(e) An applicant or registrant shall, within a reasonable time and in no event more than 15 days from the date of a request, provide the Labor Commissioner any documents deemed necessary by the Labor Commissioner for verifying gross receipts. Failure to provide the requested documentation or providing any false and misleading information concerning gross receipts shall constitute grounds for denial of the application or revocation of registration.

(f) Every applicant required to take the examination(s) provided by Labor Code Section 2675(c) or (f) shall pay an examination fee of $25 to the Labor Commissioner prior to taking the examination(s). An individual will not be permitted to take the examination(s) on behalf of an applicant unless the individual has at least a 20%

ownership interest in the applicant's business, or will function as the applicant's director of labor relations, and in that capacity will exercise direct or indirect control over employees' wages, hours and working conditions.

§ 13635.1. Filing Schedule for Applications

(a) Within 30 calendar days of receiving an application, the Labor Commissioner shall inform the applicant in writing that either:

(1) the application is complete and has been accepted for processing, or

(2) the application is incomplete, and specify the information or items needed to correct the deficiency.

(b) Within 60 days from the date on the written notice of an incomplete application, the applicant must correct the application by providing the required information or items, and return the application to the Labor Commissioner. If the applicant fails to meet this deadline, the application will be rejected, and the applicant shall forfeit the application fee. Following a rejection pursuant to this subsection, the applicant may submit a subsequent application which must be accompanied by the required fee.

(c) Within 60 calendar days after accepting a completed application, the Labor Commissioner shall inform the applicant in writing of the decision on the application.

(d) In the event that the Labor Commissioner fails to reach an application decision within 60 days of accepting a completed application, the applicant may appeal to the Secretary of the Labor and Workforce Development Agency in accordance with the following procedure:

(1) The appeal shall be in writing and shall be delivered in person or postmarked within 15 calendar days after the maximum time period specified in subsection (c) has elapsed.

(2) After receiving the appeal, the Secretary of the Labor and Workforce Development Agency shall determine whether or not the maximum time period of subsection (c) was exceeded, and if so, whether there was good cause for the failure to comply. Good cause as set forth in this section means, in accordance with Government Code Section 15376, that either:

(A) the Labor Commissioner processed 15% more applications than in the same calendar quarter of the proceeding year, or;

(B) the Labor Commissioner was required to rely on another public or private entity to process any part of the application, and that other entity was responsible for the delay, or;

(C) the delay was caused by a natural disaster or other catastrophe that substantially impeded the Labor Commissioner's ability to process the application in a timely manner.

(3) If the Secretary of the Labor and Workforce Development Agency finds no good cause for the failure to reach a decision on the completed application within the time set forth in subsection(c), the Labor Commis-

sioner shall refund any applicable filing fee in full, and shall ensure that the application is expeditiously processed without any additional fee.

(4) If the Secretary of the Labor and Workforce Development Agency finds good cause for the failure to reach a decision on the completed application within the time set forth in subsection (c), the Labor Commissioner shall not refund the applicable filing fee or any portion thereof.

(5) A finding of untimely processing by the Labor Commissioner shall have no bearing on the merits of the application or the decision on whether to issue a Registration Certificate. Any such application shall be subject to denial under the criteria set out at Labor Code Section 2675, and in accordance with the procedures set out under section 13646, below.

(e) The following information is provided pursuant to Government Code Section 15376: During the past two years, the Labor Commissioner's time periods for processing an application for registration from receipt of the application to the final issuance or denial of registration were as follows:

(1) The median time was 45 calendar days.

(2) The minimum time was 7 calendar days.

(3) The maximum time was 365 calendar days.

§ 13636. Registration Certificate

The Registration Certificate shall be valid for a period of one year from the date of issuance, unless revoked. The Certificate is non-transferrable and is valid only for the address(es) shown on its face.

§ 13637. Amended Certificate

The registrant shall notify the Labor Commissioner in writing at least two weeks prior to any change(s) of address. Such notification is required as to each location not already listed on the Registration Certificate where employees will be engaged in garment manufacturing. Following receipt of written notice from a garment contractor or manufacturer in possession of a current Registration Certificate, the Labor Commissioner shall, without additional cost, issue an amended certificate listing the new address(es), unless the business of garment manufacturing cannot legally or safely be carried on at the proposed address(es).

§ 13638. Duplicate Certificate

If the original certificate is lost, the Labor Commissioner shall, on written request and without additional cost, issue a duplicate certificate.

§ 13639. Penalty Assessment

Penalties assessed under Labor Code Section 2678(a) shall be computed by using any of the following:

(a) The number of affected employees present at the time of inspection;

(b) The number of affected employees present when the violations occurred, as determined from the employers' records;

(c) The number of affected employees present when the violations occurred, as established from other information available to the Division of Labor Standards Enforcement.

§ 13640. Notice of Penalty Assessment and Right to Hearing

If penalties are assessed under Labor Code Section 2678(a), the Division of Labor Standards Enforcement shall serve written notice as required by Labor Code Section 2678(b) on all persons liable as well as those who may assume liability for the violations. Notice shall include information on hearing and appeal rights under Labor Code Section 2681.

§ 13641. Bonds for Continued Registration

(a) The amount of the registration bond to be deposited with the Labor Commissioner under the provisions of Labor Code Sections 2675(a)(3), 2679(a) and 2679(b) shall be sufficient to insure payment of wages and benefits to all employees up to a maximum of four calendar weeks. In no event shall the number of employees used for such computations be less than the highest number of employees employed during any one pay period during the preceding 12-month period. The registration bond shall be issued by a surety licensed to do business in the State of California.

(b) An undertaking in the form of a cashier's check or money order made payable to the Labor Commissioner may be provided to the Labor Commissioner in lieu of depositing a surety bond as a condition for continued registration under Labor Code Sections 2675(a)(3), 2679(a) and 2679(b). The Labor Commissioner shall deposit the undertaking in a bank account in which the Labor Commissioner is named as a trustee. Any earned interest, along with the principal, shall be used to satisfy claims against the undertaking. Upon return of the undertaking, any remaining amount, including interest, shall be transmitted to the employer.

§ 13642. Return of Registration Bond

If an employer that has posted a bond or undertaking pursuant to section 13641 of this subchapter does not commit additional violations as set forth in Labor Code Sections 2673, 2675 and 2678 within any three-year period, the bond or undertaking shall be returned to the employer.

§ 13643. Action Against Registration Bond

If an employer that has posted a bond or undertaking pursuant to section 13641 of this subchapter fails to pay wages and benefits to employees, as set forth in Labor Code Section 2675, the Labor Commissioner may proceed against the bond or undertaking by written notice to the employer and the surety; and shall take appropriate action to recover the unpaid wages and benefits from the bond or undertaking.

§ 13644. Bonds for Filing an Appeal from an Order, Decision or Award

(a) The bond that is required pursuant to Labor Code Section 2673.1(g), as a condition precedent to filing an appeal from an order, decision or award of the Labor Commissioner, shall be issued by a surety licensed to do business in the State of California, in an amount equal to one and one-half times the award, and shall be made payable to and posted with the Labor Commissioner. An undertaking in the form of a cashier's check or money order made payable to the Labor Commissioner may be provided to the Labor Commissioner in lieu of posting this surety bond. The surety bond or undertaking shall be delivered to the office of the Labor Commissioner where the hearing that resulted in the order, decision or award was held. The bond or undertaking shall be conditioned that if any judgment is entered in favor of the employee, the contractor or guarantor shall pay the amount owed pursuant to the judgment, and if the appeal is withdrawn or dismissed without entry of judgment, the contractor or guarantor shall pay the amount owed pursuant to the order, decision or award of the Labor Commissioner unless the parties have executed a settlement agreement for payment of some other amount, in which case the contractor or guarantor shall pay the amount that it is obligated to pay under the terms of the settlement agreement. If the contractor or guarantor fails to pay the amount owed within 10 days of the entry of judgment, dismissal or withdrawal of the appeal, or the execution of a settlement agreement, a portion of the bond or undertaking equal to the amount owed, or the entire bond or undertaking if the amount owed exceeds the bond or undertaking, shall be forfeited to the employee.

(b) Upon receipt of this appeal bond or undertaking, the Labor Commissioner shall provide the contractor or guarantor posting the bond or undertaking with a notice of posting of the bond with the Labor Commissioner pursuant to Labor Code Section 2673.1, stating the name and case number of the order, decision or award, the amount posted with the Labor Commissioner, the date this amount was posted, and that no additional appeal bond need be posted with the court because this case involves minimum wages or overtime compensation owed to garment workers, and thus, the appeal bond provisions of Labor Code Section 2673.1(g), rather than the appeal bond provisions of Labor Code Section 98.2(b), apply to the filing of a de novo appeal from the Labor Commissioner's order, decision or award. The contractor or guarantor filing an appeal from the order, decision or award shall advise the court with which it is filing this appeal that it has posted the required bond with the Labor Commissioner by attaching to its notice of appeal a copy of the notice of posting of the bond with the Labor Commissioner.

§ 13645.　Periods of Revocation

(a) Revocation periods under Labor Code Section 2679(b) shall be 30-90 days if one of the violations relates to minimum wage, overtime, or child labor; 3-6 months if two of the violations relate to minimum wage, overtime, or child labor; and 6 months-1 year if three or more of the violations relate to minimum wage, overtime, or child labor.

(b) A garment manufacturer or contractor whose registration is revoked under this section may apply for a new registration upon expiration of the revocation. An application for new registration will be denied unless all judgments and settlement agreements for the payment of wages have been satisfied.

§ 13646.　Hearings to Deny an Application and to Revoke or Suspend Registration

(a) Denial of an application for registration and revocation or suspension of registration shall be upon proper notice and upon hearing, if appealed. The appeal shall be directed to the Labor Commissioner who shall assign the matter to a hearing officer for hearing. The hearing shall be conducted according to the rules set forth below, and except as specifically provided herein, the provisions of Title 2, Division 3, Part 1, Chapter 5 of the Government Code (commencing with Government Code Section 11500) shall not apply to these proceedings.

(b) Proceedings to determine whether a registration shall be revoked, suspended or conditioned shall be initiated by filing an accusation. The accusation shall be a written statement of charges which set forth in ordinary and concise language the acts or omissions with which the registrant is charged, and shall specify the statutes or rules which the registrant is alleged to have violated. The accusation shall be verified unless made by a public officer acting in his or her official capacity or by an employee of the Division of Labor Standards Enforcement.

(c) Proceedings to determine whether a registration certificate shall be issued or renewed shall be initiated by filing a statement of issues. The statement of issues shall be a written statement specifying the statutes and rules with which the applicant must show compliance by producing proof at the hearing and, in addition, any particular matters that have come to the attention of the initiating party that would authorize a denial of the application for registration. The statement of issues shall be verified unless made by a public officer acting in his or her official capacity or by an employee of the Division of Labor Standards Enforcement.

(d) Upon the filing of an accusation or statement of issues, the Division of Labor Standards Enforcement shall serve a copy thereof on the registrant or applicant in a manner provided by Government Code Section 11505(c). The copy of the accusation or statement of issues shall include or be accompanied by:

(1) a statement that the respondent may request a hearing by filing a notice of defense within 15 days after

service upon the respondent of the accusation or statement of issues, and that failure to do so will constitute a waiver of the respondent's right to a hearing, and

(2) a form entitled notice of defense which, when signed by or on behalf of the respondent and returned to the Division, will constitute a request for a hearing.

(e) Within 15 days after service of the accusation or statement of issues, the respondent may file with the Division a notice of defense in which the respondent may:

(1) Request a hearing;

(2) Object to the accusation or statement of issues on the ground that it does not state acts or omissions upon which the Division may proceed;

(3) Object to the form of the accusation or statement of issues on the ground that it is so indefinite or uncertain that the respondent cannot prepare a defense;

(4) Admit the accusation or statement of issues in whole or in part; or

(5) Present new matter by way of a defense.

The respondent shall be entitled to a hearing on the merits if the respondent files a timely notice of defense, and the notice shall be deemed a specific denial of all parts of the accusation or statement of issues not expressly admitted. Failure to file a notice of defense shall constitute a waiver of respondent's right to a hearing, but the Division, in its discretion, may nevertheless grant a hearing.

(f) If the respondent either fails to file a notice of defense or to appear at the hearing, the Division may take action based upon the respondent's express admissions or upon other evidence, and declarations may be used as evidence without any notice to respondent; and where the burden of proof is on the respondent to establish that the respondent is entitled to the issuance or renewal of a registration, the Division may proceed by default without scheduling a hearing or taking evidence.

(g) Declarations may be admitted into evidence at a contested hearing in accordance with the procedure for admitting affidavits set forth at Government Code Section 11514.

(h) At any time before the matter is submitted for decision, the Division may file or permit the filing of an amended or supplemental accusation or statement of issues. If the amended or supplemental accusation or statement of issues presents new charges, the Division shall afford the respondent a reasonable opportunity to prepare a defense thereto. Any new charges shall be deemed controverted, and any objections to the amended or supplemental accusation or statement of issues may be made orally during the hearing.

(i) The provisions of Government Code Section 11507.6 provide the exclusive right to and method of discovery as to any proceeding to deny an application for registration or to revoke or suspend a registration. A party shall have 20 days from the date of the mailing of the request for discovery to provide the requested discovery to the requesting party. Any party claiming non-compliance with a discovery request made under this section may file with the hearing officer a motion to compel discovery. Any such motion shall be served upon the party from whom discovery is sought within 15 days of that party's failure or refusal to provide the discovery. The party against whom discovery is sought may file a written response to the motion by filing such response within 10 days of service of the motion. The motion may be decided with or without a hearing, at the discretion of the hearing officer. The order denying the motion, or granting the motion in whole or in part, shall be in writing.

(j) The Division shall deliver or mail a notice of hearing to all parties at least 10 days prior to the hearing. The notice of hearing shall be in substantially the same form as set forth at Government Code Section 11509, and shall include notice of the right to request an interpreter for a party or witness who cannot proficiently speak or understand English.

(k) The hearing shall be presided over by a hearing officer appointed by the Labor Commissioner. A contested hearing shall be conducted in accordance with the procedures set forth at sections 13651 to 13654 of this subchapter.

(*l*) The hearing officer's proposed decision shall be in writing, be based on the record, and include a statement of the factual and legal basis of the decision, as provided in Government Code Section 11425.50. Within 45 days of the conclusion of the hearing, the hearing officer shall transmit the proposed decision to the Labor Commissioner, who may either:

(1) Adopt the proposed decision in its entirety, or

(2) Modify any part of the proposed decision, including the order, or

(3) Remand the case to the hearing officer for further proceedings. Within 60 days of the conclusion of the hearing, copies of the Labor Commissioner's decision, and the hearing officer's proposed decision which shall be attached thereto, shall be delivered to the parties personally or sent to them by certified mail. The decision shall become effective 30 days after it is delivered or mailed to the respondent, unless the decision provides for an earlier date, or a stay of execution has been granted by the Division. A stay of execution may be included in the decision or granted by the Division at any time before the decision becomes effective, and may be accompanied by an express condition that the respondent comply with specified conditions or terms of probation.

§ 13647. Registration After Revocation

After the revocation period expires, and liabilities as set forth in Labor Code Sections 2673.1, 2677, 2678, and 2679(b) have been assumed and satisfied, the garment manufacturer or contractor may file a new application for registration with the Labor Commissioner.

§ 13648. Confiscation

(a) If garments are confiscated pursuant to Labor Code Section 2679(b), or 2680(a), a notice of confiscation and hearing and appeal rights, as provided by Labor Code Section 2681, shall be served on all persons liable or who may assume liability for violations.

(b) If the contractor's means of production, including manufacturing equipment or property, are confiscated pursuant to Labor Code Section 2680(b), notice of confiscation and hearing and appeal rights shall be served on the contractor and on any other person or entity known to have an ownership interest in the equipment or property. Hearing and appeal rights shall be according to the same provisions for the appeal and hearing of garment confiscations, as set forth in Labor Code Section 2681, and section 13650 of this subchapter.

§ 13649. Disposition of Confiscated Goods

(a) Garments or wearing apparel confiscated pursuant to Labor Code Section 2658.7, 2664, 2679(b), or 2680(a), and not otherwise returned, shall be disposed of as follows:

(1) The confiscated goods may be released to nonprofit organizations whose articles of association or incorporation include religious, charitable, social, and educational purposes, provided that the organizations agree, in writing, that these goods will be made available at no cost to impoverished or needy persons, that these goods will not be offered for sale to any person, and that these goods will not be given to any for-profit business; or

(2) The confiscated goods may be released to public agencies, including, but not limited to, State agencies, political subdivisions, municipal corporations, or school districts, which conduct power machine sewing classes, for instructional use in such classes; or

(3) The confiscated goods may be destroyed by shredding, by burning, or by otherwise rendering them useless as items of wearing apparel.

(b) Confiscated manufacturing equipment or property (other than garments or wearing apparel) may be disposed of by destruction, donation to a non-profit charitable organization or educational institution, or by sale to any purchaser. If such equipment or property is sold by the Labor Commissioner, the proceeds of the sale shall be deposited as provided by Labor Code Section 2680(c).

§ 13650. Hearings on Appeals of Penalty Assessments or Confiscations

A hearing held pursuant to Labor Code Section 2681 on an appeal of a garment penalty assessment or a confiscation of garments, wearing apparel or other property shall be conducted in accordance with the procedures set forth at sections 13651 to 13654 of this subchapter.

§ 13651. Conduct of Hearing; Rules of Evidence

(a) The hearing need not be conducted according to the technical rules of evidence relating to evidence and witnesses. Any relevant evidence shall be admitted if it is the sort of evidence on which responsible persons are accustomed to rely in the conduct of serious affairs, regardless of the existence of any common law or statutory rule which might make improper the admission of such evidence over objection in civil actions, except that the rules of privilege shall be effective to the extent that they are otherwise required by statute to be recognized at the hearing.

(b) Hearsay evidence may be used to supplement or explain other evidence, but shall not of itself be sufficient to support a finding. An objection is timely if made before submission of the case.

§ 13652. Rights of Parties at Hearing; Taking of Evidence; and Rules of Procedure

(a) Each party to a hearing shall have the right to appear in person and by counsel; to call and examine witnesses and cross-examine opposing witnesses on any matter relevant to the issues even though that matter was not covered in the direct examination; to impeach any witness regardless of which party first called the witness to testify; to rebut evidence; and to introduce documentary exhibits and other evidence.

(b) Oral evidence shall be taken only on oath or affirmation.

(c) The hearing proceedings shall be electronically recorded. In lieu of or supplemental to an electronic recording, the hearing officer shall allow a party to have the proceedings transcribed by a court reporter, provided that the court reporter furnish the Labor Commissioner with a certified copy of the transcript as soon as it is prepared, and that the party requesting that the proceedings be transcribed pay the cost of all transcripts.

§ 13653. Role of Hearing Officer

The hearing officer who presides over the hearing, in exercising sound discretion, may control the order of presentation of evidence at the hearing; keep out repetitive and cumulative evidence; and otherwise rule on the evidence.

§ 13654. Issuance of Subpoenas

Subpoenas and subpoenas duces tecum may be issued for the attendance of witnesses at the hearing, and for the production of documents at any reasonable place and time or at a hearing, in accordance with the procedures set forth at Government Code Sections 11450.05 to 11450.50.

§ 13655. Determination of Guarantor's Proportionate Share of Liability

The Labor Commissioner may determine the proportionate share of liability of a wage guarantor under Labor Code Section 2673.1 by using any one of the following methods, at the discretion of the Labor Commissioner. Records maintained by the contractor and guarantor(s) may be used to establish proportionate share, but in the event that any necessary records are not produced,

incomplete, or inaccurate, the Labor Commissioner may rely on any other available evidence, including the testimony of claimants, with respect to these issues:

(a) Contractor's Gross Sales—The amount earned by the contractor as a result of work performed by the contractor's employees on behalf of the wage guarantor during a pay period as a percentage of the total amount earned by the contractor as a result of work performed by its employees during that pay period.

(b) Employees' Hours Worked—The amount of time that the contractor's employees spent performing work on behalf of the wage guarantor during a pay period as a percentage of the total hours worked by the contractor's employees during that pay period.

(c) Garments Produced—The number of garments or articles of wearing apparel finished, assembled, produced or otherwise prepared by the contractor's employees on behalf of the wage guarantor during a pay period as a percentage of the total number of garments or articles of wearing apparel finished, assembled, produced or otherwise prepared by the contractor's employees during that pay period.

(d) Presumption in the Absence of Records—In the absence of records, the Labor Commissioner will make just and reasonable inferences about a guarantor's proportionate share based on the competent testimony of the claimant(s). If such testimony is insufficient to allow the Labor Commissioner to determine proportionality based on subsections (a), (b), or (c) above, the full amount of the claim for unpaid minimum wages and overtime will be apportioned equally amongst the known guarantors.

§ 13656. Amounts Included in Assessment of Wages Owed and Order, Decision or Award

The Labor Commissioner's assessment of wages owed issued pursuant to Labor Code Section 2673.1, and any subsequently issued order, decision or award, shall set out the amounts owed by the contractor and wage guarantor(s) as follows:

(a) The amounts owed by the contractor for:

(1) Unpaid minimum wages;

(2) Unpaid overtime wages;

(3) Other unpaid wages;

(4) Other compensation owed, including unreimbursed business expenses, pursuant to the Labor Code or applicable Industrial Welfare Commission order;

(5) Liquidated damages in an amount equal to the unpaid minimum wages;

(6) Liquidated damages in an amount equal to the unpaid overtime wages,

(7) Interest on all unpaid wages and on the liquidated damages from the date such wages became due, pursuant to Labor Code Section 98.1(c);

(8) Penalties pursuant to Labor Code Section 203; and,

(9) Any other penalties or damages arising under the Labor Code or applicable Industrial Welfare Commission order.

(b) The amounts owed by each wage guarantor for the guarantor's proportionate share of liability for:

(1) Unpaid minimum wages;

(2) Unpaid overtime wages;

(3) Interest on all unpaid minimum wages and overtime wages from the date such wages became due, pursuant to Labor Code Section 98.1(c); and,

(4) If it is found that the guarantor acted in bad faith within the meaning of Labor Code Section 2673.1(e), liquidated damages in an amount equal to the unpaid minimum wages and overtime wages, plus interest thereon.

§ 13657. Attorney's Fees and Costs

(a) For the purpose of Labor Code Section 2673.1(f), the failure by the contractor or guarantor to pay the full amount of the assessment at the meet- and-confer conference shall be deemed to constitute a refusal to pay the full amount of the assessment, and the employee will subsequently be deemed to have prevailed at the hearing held pursuant to Labor Code Section 2673.1(d)(4), if the Labor Commissioner issues an order, decision or award in any amount in favor of the employee.

(b) For the purpose of Labor Code Section 2673.1(f), if the employee rejects the assessment at the meet-and-confer conference, the employee will subsequently be deemed to have prevailed at the hearing held pursuant to Labor Code Section 2673.1(d)(4), if the Labor Commissioner issues an order, decision or award in favor of the employee for a total amount (excluding attorney's fees and costs) greater than the amount deposited with the Labor Commissioner by the contractor or guarantor for payment to the employee of the amount assessed against the contractor or guarantor. To be considered for this purpose, the full amount of the assessment must be deposited with the Labor Commissioner at the meet-and-confer conference held pursuant to Labor Code Section 2673.1(f), for immediate and unconditional payment to the employee, regardless of the outcome of the hearing. Any such amounts deposited with the Labor Commissioner shall be transmitted to the employee forthwith, and a form shall be transmitted by a deputy labor commissioner to the hearing officer stating (without specifying the amount) that prior to the conclusion of the meet-and-confer conference, the contractor and/or guarantors unconditionally paid the full amount of the assessment to the employee. In the event that the full amount of the assessment is not so paid, attorney's fees shall be awarded to the claimant on the basis of any net recovery at the adjudicative hearing.

(c) Attorney's fees recoverable under Labor Code Section 2673.1(f) shall be based on the reasonable hours expended on the case multiplied by a reasonable hourly rate for the legal work performed. A reasonable hourly rate is the prevailing hourly rate charged by private attorneys in the geographic area with similar experience to that of the attorney(s) making the application for fees.

(d) Costs recoverable under Labor Code Section 2673.1(f) shall mean the costs of preparing for and proceeding with the hearing, including but not limited to witness fees, mileage fees, and cost of service of process.

(e) At the hearing held pursuant to Labor Code Section 2673.1(d)(4), the employee, or his or her attorney(s), shall submit evidence of reasonable attorneys' fees and costs sought to be recovered under Labor Code Section 2673.1(f). Such evidence may be in the form of a declaration signed by the attorney(s) under penalty of perjury, setting forth an itemization of hours worked on the case, the basis of the hourly rate(s) claimed, and costs incurred. The other parties at the hearing shall have the right to present any contrary evidence, and to cross-examine the employee, or his or her attorney(s), on these matters.

(f) Reasonable attorneys' fees and costs, if any, shall be included in the order, decision or award of the Labor Commissioner as follows:

(1) Reasonable fees and costs are awarded against the contractor if the contractor refused to pay the assessment and the claimant prevails at the hearing, as provided in subsection (a) herein;

(2) Reasonable fees and costs are awarded against the contractor if the claimant rejects the assessment and prevails at the hearing, as provided in subsection (b) herein;

(3) Reasonable fees and costs are awarded against the guarantor(s) if the guarantor(s) refuse(s) to pay the assessment, and the claimant prevails at the hearing, as provided in subsection (a) herein;

(4) Reasonable fees and costs are awarded jointly and severally against the guarantor(s) for the contractor's share of the attorney's fees and costs if the guarantor(s) acted in bad faith, within the meaning of Labor Code Section 2673.1(f).

§ 13658. Labor Commissioner's Enforcement of Wage Guarantee

(a) The Labor Commissioner may, during the course of an investigation pursuant to Labor Code Section 2673.1(j), serve a subpoena duces tecum on any contractor or manufacturer subject to the investigation in order to examine any books and records as may be necessary to determine the amount of wages or other compensation that may be owed to any employees and the identity of any potential guarantors for payment of the unpaid wages. The failure to comply with such a request for books and records, within 10 days of service of the notice, shall constitute grounds for revocation of registration or denial of an application for registration.

(b) The Labor Commissioner may perform a payroll audit based on the relevant documentation and information received during the course of the investigation. If the

Labor Commissioner decides to proceed against any wage guarantors, he or she shall issue findings and an assessment of the amount of wages due, which shall include a determination of each wage guarantor's proportionate share of liability. The Labor Commissioner shall schedule a meet-and-confer conference with the guarantors, contractors, and affected employees to attempt to resolve the matter, and shall provide written notice to each contractor, wage guarantor and affected employee, to the extent that the identities and whereabouts of such persons are known, of the assessment and the date, time, location and purpose of the meet-and-confer conference.

(c) During the meet-and-confer conference, the Labor Commissioner's investigator shall present his or her findings and assessment of wages owed and each guarantor's proportionate share, and shall make a demand for payment of the amount of the assessment. In the event that the amounts found due are not paid within 10 days of the conclusion of the meet-and-confer conference, the Labor Commissioner shall set the matter for an investigative hearing. The contractor, wage guarantors and affected employees, to the extent that the identities and whereabouts of such persons are known, shall be provided with written notice of the date, time, location, and purpose of the investigative hearing.

(d) The hearing conducted under this section shall be investigative in nature, and the purpose of the hearing is to assist the Labor Commissioner in deciding whether to initiate a civil action pursuant to Labor Code Section 2673.1(j). The provisions of Government Code Sections 11400,et seq.are not applicable to this hearing. The Labor Commissioner may subpoena the attendance of witnesses and the production of records to the hearing as provided by Labor Code Section 92. The hearing officer shall inquire fully into all matters at issue. The hearing may be electronically recorded, and testimony shall be given under oath or affirmation. In the hearing officer's discretion, the parties may be permitted to call, examine, and cross-examine witnesses, and to introduce documentary evidence. The hearing shall be informal, and shall not be conducted in accordance with technical and formal rules of evidence. Evidence shall be admitted if it is the sort of evidence upon which responsible persons are accustomed to rely upon in the conduct of serious affairs. The investigator's findings and assessment shall be admitted into evidence, provided the investigator is available to testify thereto. Within thirty days after the close of the hearing, the hearing officer shall issue a written recommended disposition of the case, stating the amounts, if any, that the hearing officer believes are owed by the contractor and wage guarantors. The hearing officer's recommended disposition shall have no res judicata or collateral estoppel effect, and shall be entitled to no weight in any subsequently filed civil action.

(e) If the matter is not resolved to the Labor Commissioner's satisfaction within 10 days of the issuance of the hearing officer's recommended disposition, the Labor Commissioner may thereupon file a civil action to enforce

the wage guarantee, and for any other appropriate relief. Any guarantors whose identity or existence was unknown at the time of the investigative hearing may be sued in the civil action without the necessity of further administrative proceedings.

(f) The time limits set forth in Labor Code Section 2673.1(d) shall not apply to any proceedings under this section.

(g) All notices under this section may be served by regular first class mail to the last known address of the affected employees, and to the last address of record for the contractor and wage guarantors, as set forth on the most recent application for registration as required under this subchapter.

§ 13659. Information To Be Contained in Contracts Between Manufacturers and Contractors, and on Itemized Wage Statements Provided to Employees

(a) Every applicant for registration shall certify, in writing and under oath, that the applicant will maintain for inspection and copying, and will make available upon request to the Labor Commissioner or any agent thereof, for a period of no less than four years from the date of execution, a written contract with each party with whom it contracts for the manufacture, sewing, cutting, making, processing, repairing, finishing, assembling, or otherwise preparing any garment or any article of wearing apparel or accessories. Each such contract shall contain the following:

(1) The garment manufacturer's correct legal entity, any fictitious business names, and if a corporation or limited liability company, the name and address of the designated agent for service of process;

(2) The garment manufacturer's business address, telephone and facsimile numbers;

(3) The garment manufacturer's garment registration certificate number, and its date of expiration;

(4) The garment manufacturer's workers' compensation carrier, policy number, and its date of expiration;

(5) The contractor's correct legal entity, any fictitious business names, and if a corporation or limited liability company, the name and address of the designated agent for service of process;

(6) The contractor's business address, telephone and facsimile numbers;

(7) The contractor's garment registration certificate number, and its date of expiration;

(8) The contractor's workers' compensation carrier, policy number, and its date of expiration;

(9) The date the contract was entered into;

(10) The date the contracted garments or articles of wearing apparel are due for completion;

(11) The unit price, number of garments or articles of wearing apparel covered by the contract, and a description of the garment or apparel type, style, and color;

(12) The style numbers, cut or lot numbers;

(13) The total price of the contract; and,

(14) The date that payment is due from the manufacturer.

(15) Any changes from the original contract, including but not limited to changes in completion dates, unit price, number of units, and total price.

(b) Every contract between persons engaged in garment manufacturing for the manufacture, sewing, cutting, making, processing, repairing, finishing, assembling, or preparation of any garment or article of wearing apparel or accessories for sale or resale shall be in writing, shall be maintained for no less than four years from the date of its execution, shall be made available upon request to the Labor Commissioner or any agent thereof for inspection and copying, and shall contain the information set out in subsection (a)(1) (15), above. The failure to maintain such written contracts, or to make them available to the Labor Commissioner for inspection and copying, shall constitute grounds for revocation of registration or denial of an application for registration.

(c) Every garment contractor shall include, in the written itemized wage earnings and deduction statements it is required, pursuant to Labor Code Section 226, to provide to its employees whenever wages are paid, the name(s) of any manufacturer(s) for whom the contractor performed any garment manufacturing operations at the location at which such employees were employed during the pay period covered by the itemized wage statements. The failure to include this information on employees' itemized wage statements shall constitute grounds for revocation of registration or denial of an application for registration.

Subchapter 9. Labor Commissioner's Farm Labor Contractor Fund

§ 13660. Definition of "Damages."

Damages under Section 1684(c) and (d) of the Labor Code are defined as the following:

(a) Wages including interest;

(b) Damages including interest according to proof of actual damages incurred by an employee of a farm labor contractor, by a person who has been recruited, solicited, supplied, hired, furnished or transported by the contractor on behalf of an employer engaged in the growing or producing of farm products or pursuant to a loss suffered by an employee of a farm labor contractor, or person described above, for any violation of Division 2, Part 6, Chapter 3 of the Labor Code;

(c) Damages shall not include penalties assessed pursuant to Section 203 of the Labor Code or penalties assessed pursuant to any other provision of law.

§ 13661. Procedure for Obtaining Damages from the Fund

A claim for recovery from the fund must be made in writing by an employee(s), or other claimant(s), or his or her (their) representative. The claim need not be in any particular form but must contain the following:

(a) A list naming each employee or claimant for whom recovery is sought. The list shall include the name and address of each employee or claimant, the amount of the recovery sought under each of the items listed in Section 13660 above, including the particular provision of Division 2, Part 6, Chapter 3 of the Labor Code allegedly violated, and the name and address of the farm labor contractor(s) whose conduct has allegedly damaged the employee(s) or claimant(s).

(b) A copy of the written assignment of the claim(s) to the representative, if applicable.

(c) A declaration or affidavit under penalty of perjury which complies with the provisions of Code of Civil Procedure Section 2015 .5 containing information regarding attempts made to satisfy the claim by demand against the surety bond provided in Labor Code Section 1684(c) and the results of that demand. The declaration or affidavit must also disclose what attempts, if any, were made to collect the recovery sought directly from the farm labor contractor and the results of those attempts. If no attempts have been made to collect either from the surety bond or the farm labor contractor, the declaration must explain the reasons for such inaction. The fact that no attempts have been made will not of itself defeat recovery from the fund, if the failure to make any attempts is reasonable. The declaration or affidavit required herein may be signed by the representative of the employee(s) or claimant(s), if the information submitted does not require the personal knowledge of the employee(s) or claimant(s).

(d) A copy of any judgment or award issued by a court or the Labor Commissioner, which relates to or supports the recovery sought by the employee(s) or claimant(s). If the judgment was uncontested or obtained by default or other summary procedure, the employee(s), claimant(s) or representative seeking recovery shall submit declarations under penalty of perjury signed by each employee or claimant seeking recovery setting forth the actual losses that were suffered by the employee(s) or claimant(s) including the information set forth below in subsections (1)-(6). If the judgment or award was contested, it must contain the information set forth below in subdivisions (1) to (6); if the judgment or award does not contain such information, additional declarations under penalty of perjury signed by the employee or claimant providing the missing information must be submitted. The representative of the employee(s) or claimant(s) may sign declarations submitting information to comply with this subsection, if the information submitted does not require the personal knowledge of the employee(s) or claimant(s).

(1) The name and address (if known) of the contractor;

(2) The period of time during which the wages were earned;

(3) The number of hours worked or the pieces picked or completed;

(4) The promised rate of pay;

(5) The total amount of wages owed less any amount recovered from the farm labor contractor or the surety bond and/or employer of the farm labor contractor;

(6) Proof of any actual damages suffered pursuant to the particular provision of Division 2, Part 6, Chapter 3 of the Labor Code allegedly violated.

(e) If no judgment or award has been obtained from a court or the Labor Commissioner, the employee(s), claimant(s) or his or her (their) representative seeking recovery shall submit declarations under penalty of perjury signed by each employee or claimant providing the information set forth in subdivisions (1)-(6) in (d), above. The representative of the employee(s) or claimant(s) may sign declarations submitting information to comply with subsection (d), if the information submitted does not require the personal knowledge of the employee(s) or claimant(s).

(f) If the declarations are insufficient to sustain a recovery from the fund, either due to lack of information or due to a belief that the information submitted is potentially inaccurate, the Labor Commissioner may order an investigatory hearing pursuant to the provisions of Section 13662.

(g) A claimant who contracts with a farm labor contractor may also seek recovery from the fund if he or she has been damaged by a farm labor contractor within the meaning of Section 13660. When such a claim is submitted, besides documenting the claimant's own loss, the claimant must also satisfy the requirements of subsections 13661(a)-(e) regarding the loss of the employees or other claimants.

§ 13662. Hearing

The Labor Commissioner shall have the authority to order an investigatory hearing to determine the amount of damages, if any, actually suffered by the employee(s) or other claimant(s) seeking recovery from the fund. Notice of the hearing shall be served on the defendant farm labor contractor and the employee(s) or other claimant(s) seeking recovery from the fund either personally or by registered mail in accordance with the provisions of subdivision (c) of Section 11505 of the Government Code. The hearing shall be conducted by a Deputy Labor Commissioner and shall be held in the District Office having jurisdiction over the area where the non-payment of wages allegedly occurred or any other appropriate venue.

Subchapter 10. Registration of Employers, Transporters, and Supervisors of Minors Engaged in Door-to-Door Sales

§ 13670. Definitions

For the purposes of this Subchapter:

1362

(a) Any location more than ten miles from the minor's residence, means any point beyond a straight-line radius of ten miles in any direction from the minor's residence. The radius shall be drawn upon a commonly available city or regional road map by placing the point of a compass on the approximate site of the minor's residence and adjusting the compass according to the scale of miles provided on the map. In the event of a dispute over which commonly available city or regional road map should be used for the measurement, the Labor Commissioner shall select the map that will be used as the basis for the measurement.

(b) "Applicant" is a person who applies for a new registration or renewal of a registration pursuant to this Subchapter.

(c) "Division" and "Labor Commissioner" mean the Division of Labor Standards Enforcement. "Labor Commissioner" also means the chief of the Division of Labor Standards Enforcement and his or her agents.

(d) "Door-to-door sales" is defined in accordance with Labor Code Section 1286(e) and Section 11706.1 of this Chapter 6.

(e) "Door-to-door sales operation" is broadly construed to mean any activity directly or indirectly associated with the door-to-door sales activity including, but not limited to, the person's business activities, recruitment, or any activity directly or indirectly involving a minor employed or used in door-to-door sales.

(f) "Employer" means a person subject to Labor Code Section 1308.3 and this Subchapter who exercises control, direction or supervision, either directly or indirectly, of minors engaged in door-to-door sales operations.

(g) "Person" means an individual, corporation, partnership, limited liability company, association, or other legal entity.

(h) "Registrant" is a person who has a valid and current registration issued pursuant to this Subchapter.

(i) "Registration" means a registration issued pursuant to Labor Code Section 1308.2 or 1308.3, and/or this Subchapter.

(j) "Transporter" and/or "Supervisor" means an individual subject to Labor Code Section 1308.2 and this Subchapter. A "Transporter" and/or "Supervisor" must be at least eighteen (18) years of age. A "Transporter" and/or "Supervisor" includes a person who: (1) recruits, (2) solicits, (3) hires, (4) directs, or (5) controls, directly or indirectly, any activity that facilitates the minor's participation in door-to-door sales operations. A "Transporter" and/or "Supervisor" also includes any employer who: (1) recruits, (2) solicits, (3) hires, (4) directs, or (5) controls, directly or indirectly, any activity that facilitates the minor's participation in door-to-door sales operations.

§ 13670.1. Applicability of Subchapter 10

(a) This Subchapter requires any person who employs, transports, or supervises a minor under sixteen (16) years of age in door-to-door sales more than ten (10) miles from the minor's residence to register as either an employer and/or a transporter and/or supervisor with the Labor Commissioner pursuant to Section 1308.2 or 1308.3 of the Labor Code or this Subchapter.

(b) Any employer who plans to be a transporter and/or supervisor must have a transporter/supervisor registration in addition to the employer registration.

(c) Registration is not required by those exempted by Labor Code Sections 1308.2(f) and 1308.3(g):

(1) a person, group of individuals, corporation, or other legal entity acting on behalf of a bona fide trustee of charitable assets or on behalf of a charitable organization;

(2) a government agency (including a public school);

(3) a bona fide cemetery corporation;

(4) a bona fide political committee;

(5) or a bona fide charitable corporation organized and operated primarily as a religious organization, educational institution, hospital, or a licensed health care service plan.

(d) Labor Code Section 1308.2 excludes from registration a minor's parent or guardian or any person who provides only transportation for hire and is not otherwise involved in the door-to-door sales operation.

§ 13671. Form of Application

The following form shall be submitted to the Division of Labor Standards Enforcement, Licensing Unit by each employer and/or transporter/supervisor of minors engaged in any door-to-door sales operation:

State of California
Department of Industrial Relations

DIVISION OF LABOR STANDARDS ENFORCEMENT

MINORS' DOOR–TO–DOOR SALES
EMPLOYER, TRANSPORTER & SUPERVISOR APPLICATION FOR REGISTRATION
(LC 1308.2) (LC 1308.3)

IMPORTANT INSTRUCTIONS: Read the questions carefully and follow the enclosed instructions. Submit this application with the required fees to Division of Labor Standards Enforcement, Licensing Unit, P.O. Box 420603, San Francisco, CA 94142. Fees shall be payable to the Division of Labor Standards Enforcement by certified check, cashier's check or money order.

*Please type or print clearly, in ink, all requested information. If additional space is needed to answer any question on the application, continue the answer on a separate sheet and indicate the item #.

I am completing this application as: Employer ☐　　Transporter/Supervisor ☐　　Both ☐

1. (a) Name(s) of individual or of legal entity applying for registration	2. Doing Business As (DBA) Name(s)
1. (b) State Employment Tax (SEIN) No. _____	3. This application is . . . . . ___ New ___ Renewal
1. (c) Internal Revenue Service (EIN) No. _____	If renewal, give previous Registration No. _____
4. Main Office Address (Number, Street, City, State, Zip Code) (Do not use a P.O. Box Address)	5. (a) Area Code & Telephone No. _____
	5. (b) E-mail Address:
	5. (c) Fax No. _____
6. Branch Location Address(es) (Number, Street, City, State, Zip Code) (Do not use a P.O. Box Address)	7. Area Code(s) & Telephone No(s).
8. If applying as transporter/supervisor, name and address of your employer (Do not use a P.O. Box Address)	
9. The applicant business will be operated as (Check One): ___ Individual ___ Partnership Corporation ___ Limited Liability Co. ___ Other _____ (Specify)	10. Birthdate (See instructions).
11. **Enclose** a copy of the filed Statement by Domestic Stock Corporation, and, if a foreign corporation, a copy of the filed Certificate of Qualification.	
12. (a) Name and address of organization from which the items to be sold are purchased (Do not use a P.O. Box Address)	12. (b) Area Code & Telephone No.
	12. (c) State Employment Tax (SEIN) No.
	12. (d) Internal Revenue Service (EIN) No.

SHADED AREA FOR OFFICE USE ONLY

___ VI	___ F/C	___ A/C	Date Received	Date Approved	Approved by
___ P/S	___ WCI	___ CON			
			Reviewed by	Effective Date	Expiration Date
___ REGS	___ ENTITY	___ BRO			

Amount Received $_____   Registration No. _____

DLSE 453 (New 12/96)   Minors' Door-to-Door Sales: Application for Registration   Page 1 of 5

13. In the space below, provide the following information:

Full Name	Residence Address & Telephone No. (Do not use a P.O.Box Address)	Social Security #	Percentage of Interest	Driver's License No. & Issuing State
(a). Individual				( )
(b). Partnership (List each partner)				
			___%	( )
			___%	( )
			___%	( )
(c). Limited Liability Company (List each member. Include only those having financial interest of 25% or more.)				
			___%	( )
			___%	( )
			___%	( )
(d). Corporation (List each officer and corporate title. Include only those having financial interest of 25% or more.)				
			___%	( )
			___%	( )
			___%	( )
(e). Persons with profit sharing interest in the business (Exclude bona fide employees on slated salaries. Include only those having financial interest of 25% or more.)				
			___%	( )
			___%	( )
			___%	( )
(f). Persons with responsibility and authority to manage the business (List title)				

14. Name, Social Security number and residence address of each person who will be engaged by you to accompany, supervise, recruit, solicit, hire, furnish, transport, or otherwise direct the activity of the minor. Include the name of each person listed in Item #13 whom you wish to have authorized to perform these activities.

Name and Social Security No. _____   Name and Social Security No. _____

Residence Address (Number, Street—Do not use P.O. Box Address)   Residence Address (Number, Street—Do not use P.O. Box Address)

(City, State, Zip Code)   (City, State, Zip Code)

Name and Social Security No. _____   Name and Social Security No. _____

Residence Address (Number, Street—Do not use P.O. Box Address)   Residence Address (Number, Street—Do not use P.O. Box Address)

(City, State, Zip Code)   (City, State, Zip Code)

15. Include two (2) original fingerprint cards, [form BID–7 (5/90)] for each person listed in Items #13 and #14. (Not required for renewals if previously submitted.)

16. Include a copy of a valid and current Certificate of Workers' Compensation Insurance.

17. Include a copy of any written contract or other written agreement to be offered by the applicant to the minor employed or used by the applicant in door-to-door sales.

DLSE 453 (New 12/96)   Minors' Door-to-Door Sales: Application for Registration   Page 2 of 5

18. Include a copy of door-to-door sales regulations in Subchapter I of Chapter 6 of Title 8 of the California Code of Regulations, signed by the applicant and each person listed in Items #13 or #14 (who does not already hold a valid and current Transporter or Supervisor registration), indicating that such person has read and understood these regulations. These regulations are included in the information packet accompanying the registration materials, and this shall satisfy the statutory requirement that the applicant describe the methods and levels of adult supervision to be provided in the door-to-door sales operation.

19. Describe the merchandise (including brand names) to be sold or distributed, and how it will be represented to the public. **Include** each promotional brochure and circular if used as part of presentation.

20. Describe how your door-to-door sales operation(s) will be represented to the public and to minors you plan to recruit. **Include** each brochure and circular to be used, including those used for worker recruitment.

21. **Enclose** a copy of the promotional statement(s) you expect the minor to deliver.

22. If applicant business does not have a permanent and fixed place of business or residence in California, post security for wages with the Division as required by Labor Code § 270.6, which is included in the information packet.

23. How will the minor be paid? ___ Daily ___ Weekly ___ Other (Explain)

24. Do you intend to transport or provide transportation for the minor(s)? .... ___ Yes ___ No

25. State the largest number of minors you plan to transport in one vehicle on any one trip.

26. If yes to Item #24, provide the information requested below for each vehicle.

Veh   Name and address of owner   Make, Model, Year   Vehicle License No.

v e h i c l e #1		Passenger Capacity	
v e h i c l e #2	Name and address of owner	Make, Model, Year	Vehicle License No.
		Passenger Capacity	
V e h i c l e #3	Name and address of owner	Make, Model, Year	Vehicle License No.
		Passenger Capacity	

27. **Enclose** a copy of the Certificate of Vehicle Liability Insurance for each vehicle.

28. Have you conducted the door-to-door sales operation under any other name? . . . . __ Yes __ No

29. If yes to Item #28, describe the type of business and provide the name and address of the business and dates of operation.

30. Do you, or any person named in Item #13 presently
(a) Owe any unpaid wages? . . . . __ Yes __ No
(b) Have any judgments outstanding? . . . . __ Yes __ No
(c) Have any liens or suits pending in court against them? . . . . __ Yes __ No
(d) Owe any delinquent payroll taxes, personal or business taxes, Social Security taxes, or disability insurance? __ Yes __ No

31. If yes to any question in Item #30, indicate details below. Include the name of the person, the type of debt, and the amount owed.

32. Have you or has any person in Items #13 or #14 ever plead guilty or nolo contendere to or been convicted* of a crime, either a misdemeanor or felony? . . . . __ Yes __ No

(*The term convicted includes suspended sentences, grants of probation, and expungements of proceeding under California Penal Code Sections 1203.4, et seq.)

DLSE 453 (New 12/96)   Minors' Door-to-Door Sales: Application for Registration   Page 3 of 5

33. If yes to Item #32, indicate the date, place, and circumstances below. **Include** disposition for each conviction and proof of completion of any program required by the court. Continue on a separate sheet if necessary

34. Have you or person(s) listed in Items #13 or #14 ever had any license or permit issued by any agency of the state of California suspended, revoked, denied, or have you (they) received any disciplinary action of any nature in connection with the holding of any such license or permit? . . . . __ Yes __ No

35. If yes, to Item #34, indicate the type of license or permit, date, place and circumstances below.

36. List two references for each applicant named in Items #13 or #14. (A person listed as a reference must be a resident of California, at least eighteen years of age, who has known the applicant for at least one year and is not a relative of the applicant.) Use additional paper if necessary.

Name of Reference _____ Reference for (Applicant's Name) _____

Address (Number, Street, City, State, Zip Code. Do not use a P.O. Box address) _____

Area Code and Telephone Number _____

Name of Reference _____ Reference for (Applicant's Name) _____

Address (Number, Street, City, State, Zip Code. Do not use a P.O. Box address) _____

Area Code and Telephone Number _____

I am /We are aware of and agree to comply with Labor Code Section 3700 which requires every employer to have workers' compensation coverage.

I/We agree to employ or use minors engaged in door-to-door sales in compliance with the provisions of the California Labor Code and the California Code of Regulations.

I/We agree that if transportation is provided, each vehicle is safe and carries liability coverage as required by law.

I understand that I must carry the proof of Registration issued by the Labor Commissioner with me at all times and that failure to do so is a misdemeanor.

I certify that all information contained in this application and all accompanying documents is true and correct.

I hereby certify under penalty of perjury under the laws of California that the foregoing is true and correct. I am aware that **ANY MATERIAL MISREPRESENTATION IS GROUNDS FOR DENIAL OR SUBSEQUENT REVOCATION OF REGISTRATION.**

Executed at*_____, California, this _____ day of _____ 19____

SIGNATURES (The individual owner or a partner MUST SIGN. If business is a corporation, any authorized corporate officer may sign. He or she must also indicate his or her corporate title. If business is a limited liability company, a member MUST SIGN. Any person listed in Item #13 whom you wish to have authorized to perform duties as a transporter or supervisor MUST SIGN.)

*If place of execution is outside California, the foregoing statements must be sworn to before a notary public or other officer authorized to take oaths and affirmations.

DLSE 453 (New 12/96)   Minors' Door-to-Door Sales: Application for Registration   Page 4 of 5

IMPORTANT NOTICE

Your application will be rejected and returned to you if you fail to comply with all the requirements contained in this application. **MAKE CERTAIN that you have:**

_____ **Included** each document required in Items #11, 15, 16, 17, 18, 19, 20, 21, 22, 27, and 33 of this application, properly executed.

_____ **Included** all necessary supplemental information for which there was insufficient space on the application and indicated the Item # to which each piece of supplemental information applies.

_____ **Completed** each and every question on the application.

_____ **Signed** the application, **including** the signature of each person listed in Item #14 whom you wish to have authorized to perform the duties of a transporter or supervisor.

PRIVACY ACT NOTICE

We ask for the information on the "Minors' Door-to-Door Sales: Employer, Transporter & Supervisor Application for Registration" [form DLSE 453 (New 12/96)] for the review of licensing qualifications and to determine fitness for licensing. The disclosure of your social security number (SSN) is mandated by Labor Code Sections 1308.2 and 1308.3. The only purpose of this disclosure is to enable us to properly identify individual applicants when accessing law enforcement records.

DLSE 453 (New 12/96)   Minors' Door-to-Door Sales: Application for Registration   Page 5 of 5

§ 13671.1. Application for Registration

(a) A person who employs or uses, transports or supervises a minor under sixteen (16) years of age at any location more than ten (10) miles from the minor's residence in door-to-door sales shall complete the application form provided by the Labor Commissioner entitled "Minors' Door-to-Door Sales: Employer, Transporter and Supervisor Application for Registration" [form DLSE 453 (New 12/96)]. The applicant shall comply with each applicable requirement contained in the application. The application shall be returned with the Department of Justice fingerprint card form BID–7 (5/90), all required accompanying documents and an indication that the applicant has authorized the release of required tax information.

(b) The applicant shall sign and submit to the Labor Commissioner a complete application in the original

accompanied by the required fee and each additional document required in the application, duly executed.

(c) If an applicant fails to comply with any requirement of this Section, the Labor Commissioner shall refuse the application and return it to the applicant in accordance with Section 13672 of this Subchapter.

(d) A new application is required if the form of the legal entity changes.

§ 13672. Filing Schedule for Applications

(a) Within sixty (60) calendar days of receiving an application, the Labor Commissioner shall inform the applicant in writing that either:

(1) The application is complete and accepted for filing, or

(2) The application is incomplete, specifying the information required to correct the deficiency.

(A) Within thirty (30) calendar days from the date on the written notice of an incomplete application, the applicant must correct and return the application to the Labor Commissioner.

(B) If the applicant fails to meet this deadline, the application will be rejected, and the applicant shall forfeit the application fee. Following a rejection pursuant to this subdivision, the applicant may submit a subsequent application, which must be accompanied by the required fee.

(b) Within forty-five (45) calendar days after accepting a complete application, the Labor Commissioner shall inform the applicant in writing of the decision on the application.

(c) In the event that the Labor Commissioner fails to reach a permit decision within forty-five (45) calendar days of accepting a complete application, the applicant may appeal to the Labor Commissioner as the chief of the Division of Labor Standards Enforcement in accordance with the following procedure:

(1) The appeal shall be in writing and shall be delivered in person or postmarked within fifteen (15) calendar days after the maximum time period specified in subdivision (b) has elapsed.

(2) After receiving the appeal, the Labor Commissioner shall determine whether or not the Division exceeded the maximum time limit provided in subdivision (c) with good cause. "Good cause" pursuant to subdivision (h) of Government Code Section 15376 means that:

(A) The Division processed 15% more registrations than in the same calendar quarter of the preceding year, or

(B) The Division was required to reply on another public or private entity to process any part of the application and that entity was responsible for the delay.

(3) If the Labor Commissioner finds no good cause for the Division's failure to reach a permit decision after no more than forty-five (45) calendar days of accepting a complete application, the Labor Commissioner shall refund the appellant's application fee in full and the Commissioner shall ensure that the appellant's application is expedited without additional delay or any additional fee.

(4) If the Labor Commissioner finds good cause for the untimely processing, the Labor Commissioner shall not refund the appellant's application fee or any portion of the fee.

(5) A finding on timely processing by the Labor Commissioner shall have no bearing on the sufficiency or the validity of the application, which shall be determined in the same manner as any other application.

(d) The following information is provided pursuant to Government Code Section 15376. During the past two years, the Division's time periods for processing an application from the receipt of the initial application to the final issuance or denial of certification were as follows:

(1) The median time was fifty (50) calendar days;

(2) The minimum time was thirty (30) calendar days;

(3) The maximum time was one hundred thirty-five (135) calendar days.

§ 13673. Registration Renewal Dates

(a) The registration of an employer is valid for a period of one year from the date of issuance unless revoked or suspended. Registration must be renewed annually. An application for renewal of a registration must be submitted at least thirty (30) calendar days prior to expiration of the current registration.

(b) The registration of a transporter or supervisor is valid for a period of one year from the date of issuance unless revoked or suspended. Registration must be renewed annually. An application for renewal of a registration must be submitted at least thirty (30) calendar days prior to expiration of the current registration.

(c) The registration of an employer with a Transporter/Supervisor authorization is valid for a period of one year from the date of issuance unless revoked or suspended. An application for renewal of a registration must be submitted at least thirty (30) calendar days prior to expiration of the current registration.

§ 13673.1. Change of Address or Doing Business as ("DBA") Name, Vehicle, or Vehicle License Number

(a) Registrants shall report any proposed change of address at least twenty (20) days before such change to the Division of Labor Standards Enforcement, Licensing Unit. Failure to notify the Division of an address change voids the registration.

(b) Registrants shall report any proposed change of a doing business as ("dba") name at least twenty (20) days before such change to the Division of Labor Standards Enforcement, Licensing Unit. Failure to notify the Division of a doing business as ("dba") name change voids the registration.

(c) Registrants shall report any change of vehicle or vehicle license number within twenty (20) days of such change to the Division of Labor Standards Enforcement, Licensing Unit. Failure to notify the Division of a change of vehicle or vehicle license number voids the registration.

§ 13673.2. Registration Void, When

(a) Registration of any transporter/supervisor shall become void upon termination of his (her) employment with the employer to whom he (she) is registered, and shall be surrendered to the Labor Commissioner.

(b) Registration of any employer shall become void when there is a change of the form of the legal entity or when the employer ceases operations, and shall be surrendered to the Labor Commissioner.

§ 13674. Fees

(a) The Labor Commissioner shall collect:

(1) A $350 fee for an initial application for an employer's registration.

(2) A $200 fee for an application for renewal of an employer's registration.

(3) A $100 fee for an initial application for a transporter's or supervisor's registration.

(4) A $50 fee for an application for renewal of a transporter's or supervisor's registration.

(b) An employer registering as a transporter/supervisor shall pay the applicable initial or renewal fees required for both the employer and the transporter/supervisor registrations.

(c) A fee paid pursuant to this subdivision may not be prorated.

(d) A fee or portion of a fee may not be refunded except in the event of demonstrable error by the Labor Commissioner or pursuant to Section 13672 of this Subchapter.

(e) If an applicant attempts to renew his or her registration after the expiration date for filing, the Labor Commissioner shall charge the initial application fee.

§ 13675. Transfer of a Registration

A registrant may not transfer his or her registration to any other person.

§ 13676. Suspension and Revocation of Registration and Denial of an Application

(a) The Labor Commissioner may revoke or suspend a registration or deny an application for a registration if the registrant or applicant has:

(1) Falsified or directed the falsification of any statement in an application or in any document that accompanies the application.

(2) Misrepresented or directed another person to misrepresent a significant fact orally or in writing to the minor, the minor's parent or guardian, a member of the public, a school official, a labor investigator, or a law enforcement officer related to:

(A) The minor's activity or prospective activity in the door-to-door sales operation, including, but not limited to, the nature of the minor's work activity, its purpose, location, or duration; or

(B) The nature or purpose of the door-to-door sales operation. The misrepresentation may be contained in, but not limited to, an advertisement, brochure, circular, or written or oral agreement, or written or oral statement; or

(C) Any other significant fact concerning the door-to-door sales operation.

(3) Violated or willfully aided or abetted a person in the violation of any law or regulation related to door-to-door sales, employment, the payment of wages, health

and safety, or the health and morals of a minor, including any law or regulation that prohibits contributing to the delinquency of a minor.

(4) Failed to comply with any provision of this Subchapter.

(5) Failed to notify the Labor Commissioner in writing of any change in the promotional materials or any work agreement with the minor.

(b) If after investigation, the Labor Commissioner determines that the applicant does not possess the requisite character, competency, or responsibility, a registration may be suspended, revoked, or the application denied.

§ 13676.1. Hearings to Revoke or Suspend a Registration or Deny an Application

Before revoking or suspending a registration or denying an application for registration, the Labor Commissioner shall notify the registrant in writing and shall provide an opportunity for hearing in accordance with the following procedures:

(a) Revocation or suspension proceedings shall be initiated by the Labor Commissioner by filing an accusation. Denial proceedings shall be initiated by the Labor Commissioner by filing a statement of issues. The accusation or statement of issues, along with a blank notice of request for hearing and a copy of this Section 13676.1, shall be served on the registrant or applicant either personally or by certified mail.

(b) The registrant or applicant may request a hearing by filing a notice of request for hearing with the Labor Commissioner within fifteen (15) calendar days after service of the accusation or statement of issues. If service of the accusation or statement of issues was by certified mail, the period for filing a notice of request for hearing shall be extended in accordance with the provision of Section 1013 of the Code of Civil Procedure. Failure to file a notice of request for hearing within said time shall constitute a waiver of the right to a hearing.

(c) A hearing shall be held within sixty (60) calendar days of the filing of a timely notice of request for hearing. The Labor Commissioner shall assign a hearing officer to conduct the hearing and shall deliver or mail to all parties a notice of hearing at least ten (10) calendar days prior to the hearing.

(d) Prior to a hearing, upon the application of any party to the proceedings, the hearing officer may issue subpoenas to compel the attendance of necessary witnesses and the production of books, papers, and documents. In the exercise of sound discretion, the hearing officer may decline to issue a subpoena absent satisfactory evidence that the witness will be able to give necessary and competent testimony that is material to the issues or in order to limit the introduction of unduly repetitive evidence.

(e) Each party to a hearing shall have the right to appear in person or by counsel; to call and examine witnesses and cross-examine opposing witnesses on any matter relevant to the issues, even though that matter was not covered in the direct examination; to impeach any witness regardless of which party first called the witness to testify; to rebut the evidence against him or her; and to introduce documentary exhibits and other evidence. Oral evidence shall be taken only on oath or affirmation.

(f) The Labor Commissioner shall record the hearing on audio tape. A party may have the hearing transcribed by a court reporter if a copy of the transcription is provided to the Labor Commissioner at no charge.

(g) The hearing need not be conducted according to the technical rules of evidence. Any relevant evidence shall be admitted if it is the sort of evidence on which a responsible person is accustomed to rely in the conduct of serious affairs, regardless of the existence of any common law or statutory rule which might make improper the admission of such evidence over objection in a civil action. Hearsay evidence may be used to supplement or explain other evidence, but shall not of itself be sufficient to support a finding.

(h) The hearing officer in exercising sound discretion, may control the order of presentation of evidence at the hearing, keep out repetitive and cumulative evidence, and otherwise rule on the evidence.

(i) Within forty-five (45) calendar days of closing the hearing record, the hearing officer shall issue a written proposed decision and transmit that proposed decision to the Labor Commissioner for review. The proposed decision shall set forth the findings of fact and legal grounds upon which the proposed decision is based. Within fifteen (15) calendar days of the issuance of the proposed decision, the Labor Commissioner shall issue, and serve upon all parties along with a copy of the proposed decision, a final decision, either adopting, modifying or rejecting the hearing officer's proposed decision. A final decision modifying or rejecting the proposed decision shall set forth the grounds therefor.

(j) A registrant or applicant may seek review of the Labor Commissioner's final decision by filing a petition for a writ of mandate with the appropriate court pursuant to Section 1094.5 of the Code of Civil Procedure.

§ 13677. Inspections

(a) Every employer, transporter, or supervisor applying for or possessing an Employer or Transporter/Supervisor registration shall allow the Labor Commissioner free access to his or her place of business, vehicle, or place of operation for the purpose of making an inspection of all books, records, and other papers pertaining to the door-to-door sales operation, including:

(1) Informing the Labor Commissioner, upon his or her request, of any sales, planning, organizational, motivational, or similar meeting involving a minor and permitting the Labor Commissioner to attend any such meeting in order to ascertain the character, competency, and responsibility of an applicant or registrant; or

(2) Providing proof that the applicant or registrant has filed all applicable state and federal income and employment tax forms and owes no outstanding taxes upon the request of the Labor Commissioner in order to ascertain the character, competency, and responsibility of an applicant or registrant; or

(3) Providing any other information deemed relevant by the Labor Commissioner upon his or her request in order to ascertain the character, competency, and responsibility of an applicant or registrant.

Subchapter 11. Car Washing and Polishing

§ 13680. Definitions.

The following definitions shall apply to the provisions contained in this subchapter 11:

(a) Business days has the same meaning as defined in Section 9 of the California Civil Code.

(b) Branch means a separate location of the employer's business where employees carry out car washing and polishing operations as specified in subdivision (a) of Labor Code Section 2051, including the employer's main or central location.

(c) Damaged means the suffering of a loss or diminution of what is the employee's own by reason of the employer's failure to pay wages and penalties.

(d) Other related damages means a loss suffered by an employee or diminution of what is the employee's own by reason of some action or inaction on the part of the employer other than the employer's failure to pay wages and penalties, and includes interest on wages, fringe benefits, gratuities, reporting time pay, reimbursable business expenses, and the one hour of pay an employer is required to pay an employee if the employer fails to provide the employee with a meal period or rest period in accordance with an applicable order of the Industrial Welfare Commission. Other related damages includes only those damages or losses for which recovery can be sought pursuant to laws enforced by the Labor Commissioner, and excludes all others.

(e) Registration packet means the Car Washing and Polishing Registration Application [DLSE 666 (9/05)] which is hereby incorporated by reference and the group of documents and items listed below in (e)(1) through (14) as applicable. The registration packet shall be delivered to the Labor Commissioner in order for the application to be processed by the Labor Commissioner.

(1) A surety bond as specified in subdivisions (b)(1), (2) and (3) of section 13682 of this subchapter 11;

(2) Proof of compliance with the local government's business licensing or regional regulatory requirements;

(3) Annual registration fee as set forth in subdivision (a) of section 13683 of this subchapter 11;

(4) Annual assessment as set forth in subdivision (c) of section 13683 of this subchapter 11;

(5) A valid workers' compensation insurance certificate or a copy of the certificate from the Director of the Department of Industrial Relations consenting to the applicant being self insured;

(6) A copy of the signed contract between applicant and the employee leasing company, if the applicant intends to contract with an employee leasing company as the employer;

(7) A current workers' compensation insurance certificate provided by the employee leasing company, if the applicant intends to contract with an employee leasing company as the employer;

(8) A copy of the fictitious business name statement(s) applicant uses or intends to use;

(9) A copy of applicant's state employer identification number (SEIN) or a copy of applicant's application for a SEIN;

(10) A copy of applicant's federal employer identification number (FEIN) or a copy of applicant's application for a FEIN;

(11) A copy of the articles of incorporation, if a corporation;

(12) A copy of the statement of information by a domestic stock corporation, if a corporation;

(13) A copy of the articles of organization, if a limited liability company; and

(14) A sample form of the contract and the 24–hour cancellation notice applicant uses or intends to use, if an employee leasing company.

§ 13681. Recordkeeping.

(a) An employer engaged in the business of car washing and polishing shall keep accurate records as required by Labor Code Sections 226, 1174, and 2052, and any applicable order of the Industrial Welfare Commission. These records shall be maintained for at least three years, except for the records required under Section 1174 which must be kept for not less than two years, at the place of employment or at a central location within the State of California, and upon written or oral request from the Labor Commissioner, or his or her agents, shall be made available for inspection or copying, or both.

(b) Failure to provide the Labor Commissioner with all of the requested records within ten calendar days after the date of a request, or providing records that are falsified, constitutes grounds for suspension or revocation of an employer's registration, or denial of an employer's application for registration.

§ 13682. Conditions for Registration, Initial and Renewal.

The Labor Commissioner may not register an employer, either initially or as a renewal, until the employer fully satisfies all conditions of registration, including the following:

(a) The employer completes, signs, and submits the application form provided by the Labor Commissioner, Car Washing and Polishing Registration Application [DLSE 666 (09/05)], which is hereby incorporated by reference. The employer shall sign the application and certify, under penalty of perjury, that the information he, she, or it has provided on the application form and in any supplementary documents or information submitted by the employer in support of the application is true and correct. Information required on the application includes the following:

(1) Whether the applicant is permissively self-insured against liability to pay workers' compensation insurance claims as described in subdivision (d)(1) of this section;

(2) An indication as to whether the employer's form of legal entity is one of the following:

(A) Sole proprietorship;

(B) General partnership;

(C) Limited partnership;

(D) Limited liability company; or,

(E) Corporation;

(3) The residential address and home telephone number of every person listed on the form, Car Washing and Polishing Registration Application [DLSE 666 (09/05)] as having any one of the following positions, titles, responsibilities, or interests:

(A) Sole proprietor;

(B) General partner;

(C) Limited partner;

(D) Limited liability company member;

(E) Corporate officer;

(F) A person who exercises management responsibility in the employer's business, regardless of the form of legal entity; or,

(G) A person, except bona fide employees, who has a financial interest of 10 percent or more in the employer's business, regardless of the form of legal entity.

(4) If a corporation or limited liability company, the name and business address of the agent for service of process;

(5) Whether the employer or any person having a position, title, responsibility, or interest identified in subparagraphs (A) through (G) of paragraph (3) of subdivision (a) of this section and who is so identified on the form Car Washing and Polishing Registration Application [DLSE 666 (09/05)] owes an employee any unpaid wages, and if so, the employee's name, residential address, residential telephone number, amount of wages owed, and a description of any existing payment arrangements;

(6) Whether the employer or any person having a position, title, responsibility, or interest identified in subparagraphs (A) through (G) of paragraph (3) of subdivision (a) of this section and who is so identified on

the form Car Washing and Polishing Registration Application [DLSE 666 (09/05)] has any unpaid judgments outstanding, and if so, the name, address and telephone number of the judgment creditor, the amount owed, and a description of any existing payment arrangements;

(7) Whether the employer or any person having a position, title, responsibility, or interest identified in subparagraphs (A) through (G) of paragraph (3) of subdivision (a) of this section and who is so identified on the form Car Washing and Polishing Registration Application [DLSE 666 (09/05)] has an outstanding lien or lawsuit pending in court against him, her, or it, and if so, the name, address and telephone number of the lienholder or opposing party, the type of lien or nature of the lawsuit, the location of the court where the case is pending, and the current status of the lien or lawsuit;

(8) Whether the employer or any person having a position, title, responsibility, or interest identified in subparagraphs (A) through (G) of paragraph (3) of subdivision (a) of this section and who is so identified on the form Car Washing and Polishing Registration Application [DLSE 666 (09/05)] owes any payroll taxes, personal, partnership, or corporate income taxes, social security taxes, or disability insurance contributions, and if so, the type of tax or contribution owed, the agency to whom the tax or contribution is owed, the amount owed, and a description of any payment arrangements;

(9) Whether the employer or any person having a position, title, responsibility or interest identified in subparagraphs (A) through (G) of paragraph (3) of subdivision (a) of this section and who is so identified on the form Car Washing and Polishing Registration Application [DLSE 666 (09/05)] has ever been cited or assessed a penalty for violating any provision of the California Labor Code or an order of the Industrial Welfare Commission regulating wages, hours and working conditions, and if so, the name of the person or business, or both, that was cited or assessed, the date, nature, and amount of the citation or assessment, the disposition of the citation or assessment, if any, whether or not an appeal challenging the citation or assessment was filed, and if so, whether the citation or assessment was upheld on appeal, and if upheld, whether the citation or assessment has been paid, and if paid, the date on which it was paid;

(b) The employer obtains a surety bond ensuring the payment of wages, interest on wages, gratuities, and fringe benefits of its employees.

(1) Except as provided in paragraph (3) of subdivision (b) of this section, the bond shall be in the principal sum equal to fifteen thousand dollars ($15,000.00).

(2) The bond must be issued by a surety company licensed to do business in the State of California, and the original bond must be filed with the Labor Commissioner along with the application for registration. The bond must be in favor of, and payable to the People of the State of California, and be for the benefit of any employee damaged by his or her employer's failure to pay wages, interest on wages, or fringe benefits, or damaged by a violation of Labor Code Section 351(gratuities) or 353 (accurate record keeping of gratuities), or both. The bond shall be on a form provided by the Labor Commissioner, Car Wash Bond [DLSE 668 (09/05)], which is hereby incorporated by reference.

(3) The Labor Commissioner may determine that the principal sum of the surety bond be an amount greater than that described in paragraph (1) of subdivision (b) of this section. If the Labor Commissioner makes such a determination, he or she will serve written notice of the increased amount on the employer at least 30 calendar days prior to the date. Service of the notice may be by regular first-class mail. Factors the Labor Commissioner may consider in determining that a surety bond be in an amount greater than that described in paragraph (1) of subdivision (b) of this section include, history of violations including matters such as wage claims, orders, decisions, or awards of the Labor Commissioner, final determinations of the Labor Commissioner in retaliation or discrimination complaints, and final judgments of any type against the employer, and the size of the employer's business, including number of employees and/or branch locations.

(c) The employer presents the Labor Commissioner, along with the application for registration, with proof of compliance with the local government's business licensing or regional regulatory requirements. For purposes of this subdivision, proof of compliance with the local government's business licensing or regional regulatory requirements includes a copy of the employer's business license issued by the local government's business licensing or regional regulatory authority, or both, and such other licenses or permits required by those authorities in order for the employer to operate a car washing and polishing business in that jurisdiction.

(d) The employer presents the Labor Commissioner along with the application for registration with either of the following:

(1) A copy of the certificate from the Director of the Department of Industrial Relations consenting to the employer being self-insured against liability to pay compensation under the State's workers' compensation laws either as an individual employer, or as one employer in a group of employers; or,

(2) A certificate of insurance evidencing that a current workers' compensation insurance policy issued by an insurance company licensed to do business in the State of California is in effect for its employees.

(e) The employer completes and submits to the Internal Revenue Service, the form entitled, Tax Information Authorization. Form 8821 (4/04), Department of Treasury, Internal Revenue Service. The applicant must submit the completed form to the address of the Internal Revenue Service specified on that form. The Labor Commissioner will provide this form to all persons who are sent the Car Washing and Polishing Registration Application [DLSE 666 (09/05)] or to any person who makes a written or oral request to the office of the Labor Commissioner for a copy of Form 8821 (4/04).

(f) The employer presents the Labor Commissioner, along with the application for registration, with payment of the annual registration fee and annual assessment established pursuant to Labor Code subsections 2059(a) and (b), respectively.

(g) The employer has fully complied with any citation issued by the Labor Commissioner after the citation is final and has been served on the employer.

(h) The employer presents the Labor Commissioner, along with the application for registration, with a complete registration packet.

§ 13683. Annual Registration Fee and Assessment; Proof of Registration.

(a) An employer shall pay to the Labor Commissioner an annual registration fee of two hundred and fifty ($250.00) for each branch the employer operates.

(b) The Labor Commissioner may periodically adjust the registration fee, pursuant to the Administrative Procedure Act, for inflation to ensure that the fee is sufficient to fund all costs to administer and enforce the provisions of part 8.5 of Division 2 of the Labor Code, Section 2050, et seq.

(c) In addition to the annual registration fee specified in subdivision (a) of this section, the employer shall pay to the Labor Commissioner an annual assessment of fifty dollars ($50.00) for each branch the employer operates.

(d) For employers who operate multiple branches, the Labor Commissioner will issue an official Division of Labor Standards Enforcement certificate of registration for each branch registered.

§ 13684. Registration, Initial and Renewal.

(a) Except as may be provided in subsection (d) of this section with respect to the first renewal of a registration, an employer shall register with the Labor Commissioner annually.

(b) To register, an employer must submit a completed and signed application and registration packet (one application and packet for all branches) to the Labor Commissioner. Commencing with the effective date of this subchapter 11 and including the 209 calendar days that follow that date (for a total of 210 days), applications for registration shall be submitted according to the following schedule:

(1) For a branch located in the County of Los Angeles, the employer shall submit its application and registration packet to the Labor Commissioner no later than 30 calendar days after the effective date of this section.

(2) Except as provided in subdivision (c) of this section, for a branch located in the County of Orange, the employer shall submit its application and registration packet to the Labor Commissioner no earlier than 61 calendar days, and no later than 90 calendar days after the effective date of this section.

(3) Except as provided in subdivision (c) of this section, for a branch located in the County of San Diego, the employer shall submit its application and registration packet to the Labor Commissioner no earlier than 91 calendar days, and no later than 120 calendar days after the effective date of this section.

(4) Except as provided in subdivision (c) of this section, for a branch located in the County of Riverside or San Bernardino, the employer shall submit its application and registration packet to the Labor Commissioner no earlier than 121 calendar days, and no later than 150 calendar days after the effective date of this section.

(5) Except as provided in subdivision (c) of this section, for a branch located in the County of Santa Clara, Alameda, Sacramento, Ventura, Fresno, or Contra Costa, the employer shall submit its application and registration packet to the Labor Commissioner no earlier than 151 calendar days, and no later than 180 calendar days after the effective date of this section.

(6) Except as provided in subdivision (c) of this section, for a branch located in a county other than those specified in (1) through (5) above of this subdivision (b), the employer shall submit its application and registration packet to the Labor Commissioner no earlier than 181 calendar days, and no later than 210 calendar days after the effective date of this section.

(c) If an employer operates multiple branches and any of them are located in different counties, the employer shall submit its application and registration packet to the Labor Commissioner during the time period specified for the branch requiring the earliest submission as set forth in paragraphs (1) through (6) of subdivision (b) of this section.

(d) Except as otherwise provided by paragraph (1) of this subdivision (d), the registration issued by the Labor Commissioner will be valid for a period of one year.

(1) In order to distribute registration dates evenly over the year, the Labor Commissioner may, with respect to the time period for the first renewal of a registration only, shorten to less than 12 months or lengthen to not more than 18 months the period of the registration, and prorate the annual fees accordingly.

(2) If the period of the registration for the first renewal is either shortened or lengthened, the Labor Commissioner shall set subsequent renewals at yearly intervals.

§ 13685. Transfer of a Registration Prohibited.

(a) An employer may not transfer its registration to any other person.

(b) For purposes of this section, person includes an individual, association, organization, partnership, joint venture, business trust, limited liability company, corporation, or private entity of any character.

§ 13686. Registration Void, When.

(a) An employer's registration is void when:

(1) The employer ceases engaging in the business of car washing and polishing.

(2) The employer changes its form of legal entity.

(3) The employer transfers its registration.

(4) The Labor Commissioner revokes an employer's registration.

(b) Upon the voidance of a registration, the employer shall immediately surrender and return to the Labor Commissioner the certificate of registration for each branch location.

(c) If voidance of an employer's registration is due to a change of legal entity, the new legal entity (employer) must submit a complete registration packet to the Labor Commissioner and meet all of the conditions of registration set forth in Section 13682 of this subchapter 11, including payment of the annual registration fee and assessment, in order for a new certificate of registration to be issued.

§ 13687. Failure to Obtain Tax Clearance.

An employer's failure to obtain a tax clearance from the Internal Revenue Service constitutes a ground for the Labor Commissioner to deny an application for registration, including a renewal.

§ 13688. Temporary Registration.

(a) If in submitting an application for registration, including a renewal, the Labor Commissioner determines that the Internal Revenue Service has issued the employer a temporary tax clearance instead of a full tax clearance, the Labor Commissioner may issue the employer a temporary registration that runs concurrently with the temporary tax clearance. The temporary registration shall expire at the same time the temporary tax clearance expires.

(b) If, following the issuance of a temporary registration the Labor Commissioner issues the employer a regular registration, the period of time during which the temporary registration was in effect shall be applied to and counted against the time period for the regular registration.

§ 13689. Citation for Failure to Register.

The Labor Commissioner may cite an employer and impose a civil fine if, upon inspection or investigation he or she determines that the employer has failed to register pursuant to Labor Code Section 2054. The citation may be served personally or by registered mail in accordance with subdivision (c) of Government Code Section 11505. A citation must be in writing and describe the nature of the violation, including reference to the statutory provision allegedly violated.

§ 13690. Failure to Comply with Citation for Failure to Register.

An employer's failure to comply with a citation containing an assessment issued pursuant to Labor Code Section 2064 after the citation is final and has been served on the employer, constitutes a ground for the Labor Commissioner to deny an application for registration, including a renewal.

§ 13691. Appeal of Citation for Failure to Register.

(a) If an employer served with a citation pursuant to Labor Code Section 2064 desires to contest the citation or the proposed assessment of the civil fine therefore, he, she, or it must, within 15 business days after issuance of the citation, notify in writing the office of the Labor Commissioner that appears on the citation of his, her, or its request for an informal hearing. The proceeding under this section is an informal hearing conducted in accordance with the adjudication provisions of the Administrative Procedure Act, Chapters 4.5 and 5 (commencing with Section 11400) of Part 1 of Division 3 of Title 2 of the Government Code. Except as provided in subdivision (b) of this section, the Labor Commissioner, or the deputy or agent he or she appoints as the presiding officer, shall, within 30 calendar days after the Labor Commissioner's receipt of the employer's request for an informal hearing, hold a hearing at the conclusion of which a decision is made and the citation or proposed assessment of a civil fine is either affirmed, modified, or dismissed. The decision of the Labor Commissioner consists of a notice of findings, findings, and order, which shall be served on all parties to the hearing within 15 calendar days after the hearing by regular first-class mail at the last known address of the party on file with the Labor Commissioner. Service shall be completed pursuant to Section 1013 of the California Code of Civil Procedure. Any amount found due by the Labor Commissioner as a result of a hearing is due and payable 45 calendar days after notice of the findings and written findings and order have been mailed to the party assessed. A party who is assessed a fine may take a writ of mandate from the findings to the appropriate superior court, as long as he, she, or it agrees to pay any judgment and costs ultimately rendered by the court against him, her, or it for the assessment. To take a writ of mandate, an aggrieved party shall file the writ within 45 calendar days after service of the notice of findings, findings, and order thereon.

(b) The Labor Commissioner or presiding officer for good cause may extend the 30–calendar day period for holding a hearing described in subdivision (a) of this section. Good cause is determined by the Labor Commissioner or presiding deputy.

(c) If findings and the order thereon affirm or modify a citation or the proposed assessment of a civil fine after hearing, a certified copy of the findings and the order may be entered by the Labor Commissioner in the office of the clerk of the superior court in any county in which the employer has property, or in which he, she, or it has or had a place of business. The clerk, immediately upon the filing, shall enter judgment for the state against the employer in the amount shown on the certified order.

(d) A judgment entered pursuant to the procedure described in either subdivision (c) or (i) of this section bears the same rate of interest and has the same effect as other judgments, and is given the same preference allowed by the law on other judgments rendered for claims for taxes.

(e) A cited employer who appeals his, her, or its citation to the Labor Commissioner and fails to appear at the time and place of the hearing is deemed to have withdrawn his, her, or its appeal, and the citation constitutes a final order of the Labor Commissioner and is not subject to administrative review.

(f) Submittal of a written request by an employer for an informal hearing as provided in subdivision (a) of this section stays the time period in which to pay the fine.

(g) If the written request for an informal hearing as provided in subdivision (a) of this section is not submitted in writing to the Labor Commissioner within 15 business days after issuance of a citation, the cited employer is deemed to have waived his, her, or its right to a hearing.

(h) In lieu of contesting a citation, a cited employer may, within 15 business days after issuance of a citation, transmit to the office of the Labor Commissioner designated on the citation, the amount specified for the violation.

(i) If a cited employer does not request a hearing in accordance with subdivision (a) of this section, the Labor Commissioner may file a certified copy of the citation or proposed assessment of civil fine in the office of the clerk of the superior court in any county in which the employer has property, or in which he, she, or it has or had a place of business. The clerk, immediately upon the filing shall enter judgment for the state against the employer in the amount shown on the citation or proposed assessment of civil fine.

§ 13692. Immediate Family Member Defined.

For purposes of subdivision (d) of Labor Code Section 2066, immediate family member means spouse, domestic partner, cohabitant, child, stepchild, grandchild, parent, stepparent, mother-in-law, father-in-law, son-in-law, daughter-in-law, grandparent, great grandparent, brother, sister, half-brother, half-sister, stepsibling, brother-in-law, sister-in-law, aunt, uncle, niece, nephew, or first cousin (that is, a child of an aunt or uncle).

§ 13693. Action Against Bond, Inadequacy of Bond, Cancellation of Bond.

(a) If an employer fails to pay wages, interest on wages, fringe benefits, or violates Section 351 or 353 of the Labor Code and an employee is damaged thereby, the Labor Commissioner or the employee, who is damaged because of the employer's failure to pay wages, interest on wages, gratuities or fringe benefits, may proceed against the employer's surety bond by taking whatever action he or she deems appropriate to obtain the unpaid wages, interest on wages, fringe benefits, or gratuities from the bond.

(b) If the Labor Commissioner or an employee who is damaged because of the employer's failure to pay wages,

interest on wages, gratuities, or fringe benefits proceeds against the surety bond and payment is made therefrom to the Labor Commissioner or the employee, the employer shall take all steps and actions necessary to ensure that a surety bond which meets all of the requirements set forth in paragraphs (1) and (2) of subdivision (b) of Section 13682) of this subchapter 11, including the required principal sum, is continuously in place so that there is not a break at anytime in the continuity of the protection afforded by the bond. If the employer at any time fails to provide a surety bond that meets all of the requirements of paragraphs (1) and (2) of subdivision (b) of Section 13682 of this subchapter 11, the Labor Commissioner may suspend or revoke the employer's registration, or deny his, her or its application for a registration.

(c) If the surety bond required by Labor Code Section 2055 is cancelled or terminated, the employer may not conduct any business until he, she, or it obtains a new surety bond that meets all of the requirements of paragraphs (1) and (2) of subdivision (b) of Section 13682 of this subchapter 11, and files a copy with the Labor Commissioner.

§ 13694. Procedure for Obtaining Damages from the Car Wash Worker Restitution Fund, Disbursement of Moneys from the Car Wash Worker Restitution Fund, Hearing.

The Labor Commissioner shall determine which claims are accepted, and the amount of money, if any, to be disbursed from the Car Wash Worker Restitution Fund on an accepted claim. The Commissioner shall make these determinations based on a consideration of the information requested in subsection (b) of this section.

(a) An employee who has been damaged by an employer's failure to pay wages, penalties, or other related damages, or a combination of them, must, before making a claim for payment from the Car Wash Worker Restitution Fund, attempt to collect the wages, penalties, or other related damages directly from the employer and the employer's surety bond.

(b) An employee or his or her authorized representative seeking recovery of unpaid wages, penalties or other related damages, or a combination of them, from the Car Wash Worker Restitution Fund must submit a claim in writing to the Labor Commissioner. The claim itself need not be in any particular form, but must include the following information and documents:

(1) Name, street mailing address, and home telephone number of employee for whom recovery is sought;

(2) Employee's social security number or individual taxpayer identification number;

(3) Name, street address, and telephone number (if known) of the employer that failed to pay the employee his or her wages, penalties, or other related damages;

(4) The period of time during which the wages were earned, giving both the beginning and ending dates specified as month, day, year;

(5) The number of hours worked or other basis for being paid wages;

(6) The promised rate of pay;

(7) The actual rate of pay;

(8) Amount of wages sought;

(9) Amount of penalty sought, if any, and Labor Code section pursuant to which the penalty is imposed;

(10) Amount of other related damages sought, if any, described and itemized;

(11) Amount of recovery sought less any amount recovered from the employer or the employer's surety bond, or both;

(12) Net amount of total recovery sought, if different from the amount in subsection (11);

(13) Proof of actual damages suffered;

(14) A copy of the employee's written assignment of the claim to the representative, if applicable;

(15) A declaration or affidavit under penalty of perjury that complies with the provisions of Section 2015.5 of the California Code of Civil Procedure containing information regarding attempts made by the employee or his or her representative to satisfy the claim by demand against the surety bond required by Labor Code Section 2055(b), and the results of the demand. The declaration or affidavit must also disclose the attempt(s) made to collect the recovery sought directly from the employer, and the results of the attempt(s). The employee's representative may sign the declaration or affidavit required by this subdivision if the information submitted does not require the personal knowledge of the employee.

(c) The Information required in paragraphs (3) through (13) must be provided in one of the following ways:

(1) Submission of a copy of a judgment obtained from a court or an award from the Labor Commissioner which was issued after a contested proceeding which contains all of the information required in paragraphs (3) through (13) inclusive. If the judgment or award omits any of the required information, it shall be supplemented by a declaration under penalty of perjury which provides the missing information. The declaration must be signed by the employee or the employee's authorized representative, if the information submitted does not require the personal knowledge of the employee.

(2) Submission of a copy of a judgment obtained from the court or an award from the Labor Commissioner which was issued after an uncontested or default proceeding and a declaration under penalty of perjury that provides the information required by paragraphs (3) through (13) inclusive. The declaration must be signed by the employee or the employee's authorized representative, if the information submitted does not require the personal knowledge of the employee.

(3) If no judgment has been obtained from a court or an award from the Labor Commissioner, submission of a declaration under penalty of perjury which contains all of the information required in paragraphs (3) through (13), inclusive. The declaration must be signed by the employee or the employee's authorized representative, if the information submitted does not require the personal knowledge of the employee.

(d) If the Labor Commissioner determines that a declaration required under this section is insufficient to sustain a recovery from the Car Wash Worker Restitution Fund because of lack of information, or reason to believe that the information submitted is inaccurate, incomplete or false, the Labor Commissioner may order an investigatory hearing pursuant to subdivision (d) of this section.

(e) The Labor Commissioner shall have the authority to order an investigatory hearing to determine the validity of a claim seeking recovery from the Car Wash Worker Restitution Fund, including the amount of any damages actually suffered by the employee, if any. Notice of a hearing shall be served on the employer and employee either personally or by registered mail in accordance with the provisions of subdivision (c) of Section 11505 of the Government Code. The hearing shall be conducted by a Deputy Labor Commissioner, and may be held in the Division of Labor Standards Enforcement's district office having jurisdiction over the geographical location of where the nonpayment of wages allegedly occurred, or the Labor Commissioner may designate any other venue he or she deems appropriate. In the hearing, the employer and the employee shall have the opportunity to present evidence. The Labor Commissioner shall issue, serve, and enforce any necessary subpoenas.

Subchapter 12. Collections

§ 13800. Collection Cost Fees: Referrals to the Franchise Tax Board.

For cases referred by the Department of Industrial Relations and its component divisions to the Franchise Tax Board (FTB) for collection of judgments and delinquent debts pursuant to Section 19290 of the Revenue and Taxation Code, a fee shall be imposed and collected from the judgment debtor to cover collection costs incurred as a result of the referral to FTB for collection. The collection cost fee for each referred case shall be one-hundred and fifteen dollars ($115). This fee of $115 is the reasonable fee for actual collection costs, and is exclusive of court costs and attorney's fees which may be collected upon FTB becoming a judgment creditor under Labor Code section 98.2(j).

SAN FRANCISCO ADMINISTRATIVE CODE

Chapter 12B

Nondiscrimination in Contracts[1]

[1] For preemption challenges to this provision, see *Alioto's Fish Co. v. Human Rights Com. of San Francisco*, 120 Cal.App.3d 594, 174 Cal.Rptr. 763 (Cal.App., 1 Dist, 1981), *cert denied*, 455 U.S. 944, 102 S.Ct. 1441, 71 L.Ed.2d 657 (1982) (state law); *Delaney v. Superior Fast Freight*, 14 Cal.App.4th 590, 18 Cal. Rptr.2d 33 (Cal.App., 2 Dist, 1993) (same). On September 11, 2001, the Ninth Circuit Court of Appeals in *Air Transport Association v. City and County of San Francisco*, 2001 WL 1042113, held that San Francisco Administrative Code Chapter 12B was not preempted by the federal Airline Deregulation Act (49 USCA § 41713(b)(1)) or the Railway Labor Act (45 USCA § 151 et seq.) and remanded to the District court to determine whether the ordinance was preempted by California Family Code § 299.6.

Section 12B.1. All contracts and property contracts to include nondiscrimination provisions; Definitions

(a) All contracting agencies of the City, or any department thereof, acting for or on behalf of the City and County, shall include in all contracts and property contracts hereinafter executed or amended in any manner or as to any portion thereof, a provision obligating the contractor not to discriminate on the basis of the fact or perception of a person's race, color, creed, religion, national origin, ancestry, age, sex, sexual orientation, gender identity, domestic partner status, marital status, disability or Acquired Immune Deficiency Syndrome, HIV status (AIDS/HIV status), weight, height, association with members of classes protected under this chapter or in retaliation for opposition to any practices forbidden under this chapter against any employee of, any City employee working with, or applicant for employment with such contractor and shall require such contractor to include a similar provision in all subcontracts executed or amended thereunder.

(b) No contracting agency of the City, or any department thereof, acting for or on behalf of the City and County, shall execute or amend any contract or property contract with any contractor that discriminates in the provision of bereavement leave, family medical leave, health benefits, membership or membership discounts, moving expenses, pension and retirement benefits or travel benefits as well as any benefits other than bereavement leave, family medical leave, health benefits, membership or membership discounts, moving expenses, pension and retirement benefits or travel benefits between employees with domestic partners and employees with spouses, and/or between the domestic partners and spouses of such employees, where the domestic partnership has been registered with a governmental entity pursuant to State or local law authorizing such registration, subject to the following conditions. In the event that the contractor's actual cost of providing a certain benefit for the domestic partner of an employee exceeds that of providing it for the spouse of an employee, or the contractor's actual cost of providing a certain benefit for the spouse of an employee exceeds that of providing it for the domestic partner of an employee, the contractor shall not be deemed to discriminate in the provision of benefits if the contractor conditions providing such benefit upon the employee agreeing to pay the excess costs. In addition, in the event a contractor is unable to provide a certain benefit, despite taking reasonable measures to do so, the contractor shall not be deemed to discriminate in the provision of benefits if the contractor provides the employee with a cash equivalent.

(c) Definitions. As used in this Chapter the following words and phrases shall have the meanings indicated herein:

"Age" shall mean the age of any employee or applicant for employment who has attained the age of 40 years and has not attained the age of 65 years. For the purposes of this Chapter, discrimination because of age shall mean dismissal from employment of, or refusal to employ or rehire any person because of his or her age, if such person has attained the age of 40 years and has not attained the age of 65 years, if the person is physically able and mentally competent to perform the services required. Age limitations of apprenticeship programs in which the State or its political subdivisions participate shall not be considered discriminatory within the meaning of this Chapter.

"Amend" shall mean to substantively change the terms of a pre-existing contract, and shall not include amendments to decrease the scope of work or the amount to be paid under a contract. Construction change orders shall not be construed as contract amendments for the purposes of this Chapter.

"City" shall mean the City and County of San Francisco.

"Commission" shall mean the Human Rights Commission of the City and County of San Francisco.

"Contract" shall mean an agreement for public works or improvements to be performed, or for goods or services to be purchased or grants to be provided, at the expense of the City and County or to be paid out of moneys deposited in the treasury or out of trust moneys under the control or collected by the City and County, and does not include property contracts, agreements entered into after June 1, 1997 pursuant to settlement of legal proceedings, contracts for urgent litigation expenses, or contracts for a cumulative amount of $5,000 or less per vendor in each fiscal year.

"Contractor" means any person or persons, firm, partnership, corporation, or combination thereof, who enters into a contract or property contract with a department head or officer empowered by law to enter

1377

into contracts or property contracts on the part of the City and County.

"Director" shall mean the Director of the Human Rights Commission.

"Disability" shall mean a physical or mental impairment which substantially limits one or more major life activities, or a record of such an impairment.

"Domestic partner" shall mean any person who has a currently registered domestic partnership with a governmental body pursuant to State or local law authorizing such registration.

"Gender identity" shall mean a person's various individual attributes as they are understood to be masculine and/or feminine.

"Property contract" shall mean a written agreement for the exclusive use or occupancy of real property for a term exceeding 29 days in any calendar year, whether by singular or cumulative instrument, (i) for the operation or use by others of real property owned or controlled by the City for the operation of a business, social, or other establishment or organization, including leases, concessions, franchises and easements, or (ii) for the City's use or occupancy of real property owned by others, including leases, concessions, franchises and easements. For the purposes of this Chapter, "exclusive use" means the right to use or occupy real property to the exclusion of others, other than the rights reserved by the fee owner. "Property contract" shall not include a revocable at-will use or encroachment permit for the use of or encroachment on City property regardless of the ultimate duration of such permit, except that "property contract" shall include such permits granted to a private entity for the use of City property for the purpose of a for-profit activity. "Property contract" shall also not include street excavation, street construction or street use permits, agreements for the use of City right-of-way where a contracting utility has the power of eminent domain, or agreements governing the use of City property which constitutes a public forum for activities that are primarily for the purpose of espousing or advocating causes or ideas and that are generally recognized as protected by the First Amendment to the U.S. Constitution, or which are primarily recreational in nature.

"Qualified disabled employee" shall mean a person able to perform the essential functions of a job with reasonable accommodation.

"Sex" shall mean the character of being male or female.

"Sexual orientation" shall mean the status of being lesbian, gay, bisexual or heterosexual.

"Subcontract" shall mean an agreement to (i) provide goods and/or services, including construction labor, materials or equipment, to a contractor, if such goods or services are procured or used in the fulfillment of the contractor's obligations arising from a contract with the City, or (ii) to transfer the right to occupy or use all or a portion of a real property interest subject to a property

contract to a subcontractor and pursuant to which the contractor remains obligated under the property contract.

"Subcontractor" means any person or persons, firm, partnership, corporation or any combination thereof, who enters into a subcontract with a contractor. Such term shall include any person or entity who enters into an agreement with any subcontractor for the performance of 10 percent or more of any subcontract.

(d) The requirements of this Chapter shall apply to (i) any of a contractor's operations within San Francisco; (ii) a contractor's operations on real property outside of San Francisco owned by the City or which the City has a right to occupy if the contractor's presence at that location is connected to a contract or property contract with the City; (iii) where the work is being performed by a contractor for the City within the United States; and (iv) any of a contractor's operations elsewhere within the United States.

Section 12B.2. Nondiscrimination provisions

Every contract and property contract for or on behalf of the City shall incorporate by reference and require the contractor to comply with the provisions of Section 12B.2. In addition, all contractors must incorporate by reference in all subcontracts and require subcontractors to comply with the requirements set forth in Sections 12B.2(a) and 12B.2(c) through 12B.2(k), and failure to do so shall constitute a material breach of contract.

In the performance of a contract the contractor agrees as follows:

(a) The contractor or subcontractor will not discriminate against any employee, City and County employee working with such contractor or subcontractor, or applicant for employment with such contractor or subcontractor on the basis of the fact or perception of that person's race, color, religion, ancestry, national origin, age, sex, sexual orientation, gender identity, domestic partner status, marital status, disability, weight, height, AIDS/HIV status, or association with members of classes protected under this chapter or in retaliation for opposition to any practices forbidden under this chapter. Discrimination on the basis of sex includes sexual harassment as defined in Section 16.9–25(b) of this Code. The contractor or subcontractor will take action to ensure that applicants are employed, and that employees are treated equally during employment, without regard to the fact or perception of their race, color, creed, religion, ancestry, national origin, age, sex, sexual orientation, gender identity, domestic partner status, marital status, disability or AIDS/HIV status. Such action shall include, but not be limited to, the following: Employment, upgrading, demotion or transfer; recruitment or recruitment advertising; layoff or termination; rate of pay or other forms of compensation; and selection for training, including apprenticeship. Nothing in this Chapter shall require or prohibit the establishment of new classifications of employees in any given craft. The provisions of this Section with respect to age shall not apply to (1) termination of employment because of the terms or conditions of any bona fide retirement or pension plan, (2) operation of the terms or conditions of any bona fide retirement or pension plan which has the effect of a minimum service requirement, and (3) operation of the terms or conditions of any bona fide group or insurance plan. The contractor or subcontractor agrees to post in conspicuous places, available to employees and applicants for employment, notices in such form and content as shall be furnished or approved by the awarding authority setting forth the provisions of this Section.

(b) The prime contractor shall state that the prime contractor does not, and will not during the term of the contract discriminate in the provision of bereavement leave, family medical leave, health benefits, membership or membership discounts, moving expenses, pension and retirement benefits or travel benefits as well as any benefits other than bereavement leave, family medical leave, health benefits, membership or membership discounts, moving expenses, pension and retirement benefits or travel benefits between employees with domestic partners and employees with spouses, and/or between the domestic partners and spouses of such employees, where the domestic partnership has been registered with a governmental entity pursuant to State or local law authorizing such registration, subject to the following conditions. In the event that the contractor's actual cost of providing a certain benefit for the domestic partner of an employee exceeds that of providing it for the spouse of an employee, or the contractor's actual cost of providing a certain benefit for the spouse of an employee exceeds that of providing it for the domestic partner of an employee, the contractor shall not be deemed to discriminate in the provision of benefits if the contractor conditions providing such benefit upon the employee agreeing to pay the excess costs. In addition, in the event a contractor is unable to provide a certain benefit, despite taking reasonable measures to do so, the contractor shall not be deemed to discriminate in the provision of benefits if the contractor provides the employee with a cash equivalent. The Director shall be the final arbiter of a contractor's or property contractor's compliance or substantial compliance with this Chapter and the Director's determination shall not be appealable to the Commission. Contractors shall treat as confidential to the maximum extent allowed by law or the requirements of contractor's insurance provider any request by an employee or applicant for employment for domestic partner or spousal benefits or any documentation of eligibility for domestic partner or spousal benefits submitted by an employee or applicant for employment.

In adopting this Section 12B.2(b), the intent of the Board of Supervisors is to equalize to the maximum extent legally permitted the total compensation between similarly situated employees with spouses and employees with domestic partners.

In particular, consistent with the severability clause set forth in Section 12B.6 below, the Board of Supervisors intends that if a court or agency of competent jurisdiction finds that a State or federal law, rule or regulation invalidates (1) the application of this Section to any business, person, type of compensation or benefit, or location; or (2) any other requirement of this Section, then the court or agency should sever the invalid clause and leave in effect the remainder of this Section.

(c) The contractor or subcontractor shall provide reasonable accommodation for qualified disabled applicants for employment and for qualified disabled employees. Said contractor or subcontractor need not provide reasonable accommodation if such would present an undue hardship. An undue hardship may include but not be limited to more than a de minimus cost, violation of the seniority rights of other co-workers as established by a bona fide seniority system, or a health or safety risk to the employee or co-employees. The burden of establishing an undue hardship rests on the employer.

(d) The contractor or subcontractor will in all solicitations or advertisements for employees placed by or on his or her behalf, state that qualified applicants will receive consideration for employment without regard to the fact or perception of their race, creed, religion, color, ancestry, national origin, age, sex, sexual orientation, gender identity, domestic partner status, marital status, disability, weight, height or AIDS/HIV status.

(e) The contractor or subcontractor will send to each labor union or representative of workers with which he or she has a collective bargaining agreement or other agreement or understanding, a notice, in such form and content as shall be furnished or approved by the awarding authority, advising the said labor union or workers' representative of the contractor's or subcontractor's commitments under this Section, and shall post copies of the notice in conspicuous places available to employees and applicants for employment.

(f) The contractor or subcontractor will permit access to its records of employment, employment advertisements, application forms, and other pertinent data and records by the Commission, the City's awarding authority or the Fair Employment and Housing Commission, for the purposes of investigation to ascertain compliance with the nondiscrimination provisions of this Chapter, and upon request shall provide evidence that the contractor has complied or will comply with the nondiscrimination provisions of this Chapter.

(g) A contractor or subcontractor shall be deemed to have breached the nondiscrimination provisions of this Chapter upon:

(1) A finding by the Director or such other official who may be designated by the Commission, that the contractor or subcontractor has wilfully violated such nondiscrimination provisions; or

(2) A finding by the California Fair Employment and Housing Commission that a contractor or subcontractor has violated any provision of the California Fair Employment and Housing Act or the nondiscrimination provi-

sions of this Chapter, provided that the California Fair Employment and Housing Commission has issued a final order pursuant to Section 12970 of the Government Code, or has obtained a judgment and order enforcing the final order pursuant to Section 12973 of the Government Code; provided further, that for the purposes of these provisions, an order or injunction shall not be considered final during the period within which (1) appeal may be taken, or (2) the same has been stayed by order of court, or (3) further proceedings for vacation, reversal or modification are in progress before a competent administrative or judicial tribunal.

(3) Upon such finding by the Director or other official designated by the Commission, or the California Fair Employment and Housing Commission, the awarding authority shall notify the contractor or subcontractor that unless the contractor or subcontractor demonstrates to the satisfaction of the Director or other official designated by the Commission, within such reasonable period as the Commission shall determine, that the violation has been corrected, action will be taken as set forth in Subparagraphs (h) and (i) hereof.

(4) The Commission shall, within 10 days of the date of issuance of any finding by the Director or other official designated by the Commission for the enforcement of this Chapter, mail to any person or persons affected by said finding, a copy of said finding, together with written notice of the right to appeal such finding. Notice of appeal must be filed in writing with the Chairperson of the Commission within 20 days of the date of mailing said copy and notice.

(5) For purpose of appeal proceedings under this Section, a quorum shall consist of eight members of the Commission. The vote of the majority of the full Commission shall be necessary to affirm, reverse or modify such decisions, order or other action rendered hereunder. Should a member of the Commission be designated under Section 12B.2(g)(1) of this Chapter, that Commissioner may not participate in an appeal under this Section except as a witness.

(6) The presiding officer of the Commission shall have the power to administer oaths to witnesses in appeals before the Commission under this Section. In the event that any person shall fail or refuse to appear as a witness in any such proceeding after being requested to do so, and if it shall appear to the Commission that his or her testimony, or books, records, documents or other things under his or her control are material and relevant as evidence in the matter under consideration by the Commission in the proceeding, the presiding officer of the Commission may subpoena such person, requiring his or her presence at the proceeding, and requiring him or her to bring such books, records, documents or other things under his or her control.

(7) All appeals to the Commission shall be open to the public. Records and minutes shall be kept of such proceedings and shall be open to public inspection. Upon reaching a decision in any appeal, the Commission shall

give written notice thereof to the Director or other official designated by the Commission, and the appellant or appellants. The decision of the Commission shall be final unless within 15 days of the filing and service of written notice thereof appropriate legal proceedings are filed in a court of competent jurisdiction by any party to the contract, property contract or subcontract.

(8) If any contractor or subcontractor shall fail to appear at an appeal proceeding of the Commission after having been given written notice to appear, such failure to appear shall be grounds for termination of the contract, property contract or subcontract and such contractor or subcontractor shall be deemed to have forfeited all rights, benefits and privileges thereunder.

(9) The Commission shall promulgate rules and regulations for the implementation of the nondiscrimination provisions of this Chapter.

(h) The awarding authority may deduct from the amount payable to the contractor or subcontractor by the City under any contract or property contract subject to this Chapter, or may impose upon the contractor or subcontractor, a penalty of $50 for each person for each calendar day during which such person was discriminated against in violation of the provisions of this Chapter. In addition to any other penalties provided for the violation of the nondiscrimination provisions of this Chapter or for the failure of any contractor or subcontractor to abide by the rules and regulations of the Commission, the contract, property contract or subcontract may be terminated or suspended, in whole or in part, by the awarding authority upon the basis of a finding as set forth in Section 12B.2(g) that the contractor has discriminated contrary to the provisions of this Chapter, and all moneys due or to become due hereunder may be forfeited to, and retained by, the City.

(i) A breach of the nondiscrimination provisions in the performance of a contract, property contract or subcontract shall be deemed by the City to be material breach of contract and the basis for determination by the awarding authority that the contractor or subcontractor is an irresponsible bidder as to all future contracts or property contracts for which such contractor or subcontractor may submit bids. Such contractor or subcontractor shall not for a period of up to two years thereafter, or until it shall establish and carry out a program in conformity with the nondiscrimination provisions of this Chapter, be allowed to act as a contractor or subcontractor under any contract or property contract.

(j) Nothing contained in this Chapter shall be construed in any manner so as to prevent the City from pursuing any other remedies that may be available at law, equity or under any contract or property contract.

(k) The contractor or subcontractor will meet the following standards for compliance:

(1) If the contractor or subcontractor has been held to be an irresponsible bidder under Section 12B.2(i) hereof, the contractor or subcontractor shall furnish evidence

that it has established and is carrying out a program in conformity with the nondiscrimination provisions of this Chapter.

(2) The contractor or subcontractor may be required to file with the Commission a basic compliance report, which may be a copy of the federal EEO–1, or a more detailed report as determined by the Commission. Wilful false statements made in such reports shall be punishable as provided by law. No contractor or subcontractor shall be held in noncompliance for not filing such a report with the Commission unless it has been specifically required to do so in writing by the Commission.

(3) Personally, or through its representatives, the contractor or subcontractor shall, through negotiations with the unions with whom it has collective bargaining or other agreements requiring the contractor or subcontractor to obtain or clear its employees through the union, or when the contractor or subcontractor otherwise uses a union as an employment resource, attempt to develop an agreement which will:

(A) Define and outline responsibilities for nondiscrimination in hiring, referral, upgrading and training;

(B) Otherwise implement a nondiscrimination program in terms of the unions' specific areas of skill and geography, such as an apprenticeship program, to the end that minority workers will be available and given an equal opportunity for employment.

(4) The contractor or subcontractor shall notify the awarding authority of opposition to the nondiscrimination provisions of a contract by individuals, firms or organizations during the term of the contract.

Section 12B.3. Human Rights Commission Empowered

The San Francisco Human Rights Commission, its presiding officer and its director are hereby granted the power to do all acts and exercise all powers referred to in Section 12B.2 hereof.

Section 12B.4. Nondiscrimination Guidelines

The following nondiscrimination guidelines shall apply to all contracts and property contracts subject to this Chapter.

In order to be eligible to submit a bid or proposal or to have a bid or proposal considered by the awarding authority, the prospective contractor shall agree to abide by a nondiscrimination program which conforms to the requirements of the Commission.

The Commission may also require contractors and subcontractors to take part in a pre-bid or pre-award conference in order to develop, improve or implement a qualifying nondiscrimination program.

(a) Nondiscrimination programs developed pursuant to this Section shall be effective for a period of 12 months from the date of approval by the Commission. Contractors or subcontractors who are members in good standing of a trade association which has negotiated a nondiscrimination program with the Commission may make this

association program their commitment for the specific contract or property contract upon approval of the Commission without the process of a separate pre-bid or pre-award conference. Such an association agreement shall be effective for a period of 12 months from the date of approval by the Commission. Trade associations shall more provide the Commission with a list of members in good standing in such association. The Commission shall annually supply contracting agencies of the City and County with a list of contractors and subcontractors who have developed approved nondiscrimination programs.

(b) The awarding authority shall be responsible for notifying all prospective bidders or proposers of the requirements of this Section and, when requested by the Commission, for notifying the Commission of each contract or property contract which is being proposed to be put to public bid.

(c) The proposed nondiscrimination program described by this Section, and the pre-bid or pre-award conference which may be required by the Commission, shall, without limitation as to the subject or nature of employment activity, be concerned with such employment practices as:

(1) Apprenticeship where approved programs are functioning, and other on-the-job training for nonapprenticeable occupations;

(2) Classroom preparation for the job when not apprenticeable;

(3) Pre-apprenticeship education and preparation;

(4) Upgrading training and opportunities;

(5) Encouraging the use of contractors and subcontractors of all ethnic groups, provided, however, that any contract or property contract subject to this Chapter shall require the contractor or subcontractor to provide not less than the prevailing wage, working conditions, and practices generally observed in private industries in the City for such work; and

(6) The entry of qualified minority journeypersons into the industry.

(d) Nondiscrimination agreements resulting from the proposed nondiscrimination programs or the pre-bid or pre-award conferences shall not be confidential and may be publicized by the Commission at its discretion. In addition, the Commission may report to the Board of Supervisors, either on request of the Board or on its own initiative, on the progress or the problems which attend the implementation of these agreements or any other aspect of enforcement of this Chapter.

(e) Any job training or education program using the funds, facilities, or staff of the City which, in the judgment of the Board of Supervisors or the Commission, can make a contribution to the implementation of this Chapter shall submit reports to the Commission as requested and shall be required to cooperate with the contractors, subcontractors and unions and with the Commission for the effectuation of the nondiscrimination programs developed under this Chapter.

Section 12B.5.   Chapter Applies Only to Discriminatory Employment Practices

(a) This Chapter shall not confer upon the City and County of San Francisco or any agency, board or commission thereof any power not otherwise provided by law to determine the legality of any existing collective bargaining agreement and shall have application only to discriminatory employment practices by contractors or subcontractors engaged in the performance of City and County contracts or property contracts.

(b) The Board of Supervisors shall appropriate such funds from the General Fund of the City, subject to budgetary and fiscal provisions of the Charter, as it may deem necessary for the enforcement of this Chapter.

Section 12B.5–1.   Non-applicability, Exceptions and Waivers

(a) The Director shall waive the requirements of this Chapter under the following circumstances:

1.   Whenever the Director finds, upon the advice of the awarding authority, that there is only one prospective contractor willing to enter into a property contract with the City for use of City property on the terms and conditions established by the City, or that the needed goods, services, construction services for a public work or improvement, or interest in or right to use real property are available only from a sole source and the prospective contractor is not currently disqualified from doing business with the City, or from doing business with any governmental agency based on any contract compliance requirements;

2.   If the contracting department, board or commission certifies in writing to the Director that pursuant to Administrative Code Sections 6.30 or 21.25 the contract or property contract is necessary to respond to an emergency which endangers the public health or safety and no entity which complies with the requirements of this Chapter capable of responding to the emergency is immediately available; provided that such certification must be made prior to the Controller's contract certification;

3.   Where the City Attorney certifies in writing to the Director that the contract involves specialized litigation requirements such that it would be in the best interests of the City to waive the requirements of this Chapter.

(b) This Chapter shall not apply where the prospective contractor is a public entity and the Director finds that goods, services, construction services for a public work or improvement or interest in or right to use real property of comparable quality or accessibility as are available under the proposed contract or property contract are not available from another source, or that the proposed contract or property contract is necessary to serve a substantial public interest.

(c) This Chapter shall not apply where the contracting officer finds that the requirements of this Chapter will violate or are inconsistent with the terms or conditions of a grant, subvention or agreement with a public agency or the instructions of an authorized representative of any such agency with respect to any such grant, subvention or agreement, provided that the contracting officer has made a good faith attempt to change the terms or conditions of any such grant, subvention or agreement to authorize application of this Chapter.

(d) Upon the request of a potential contractor or upon the contracting officer's own initiative, after taking all reasonable measures to find an entity that complies with the law, the contracting officer may waive any or all of the requirements of this Chapter for any contract, property contract or bid package advertised and made available to the public, or any competitive or sealed bids received by the City as of the date of the enactment of this ordinance under the following circumstances:

(1) Where the contracting officer determines that there are no qualified responsive bidders or prospective contractors who could be certified by the Commission as being in compliance with the requirements of this Chapter and that the contract or property contract is for goods, a service or a project that is essential to the City or City residents; or

(2) Where the contracting officer determines that transactions entered into pursuant to bulk purchasing arrangements through federal, State or regional entities which actually reduce the City's purchasing costs would be in the best interests of the City; or

(3) Where the contracting officer determines that the requirements of this Chapter would result in the City's entering into a contract with an entity that was set up, or is being used, for the purpose of evading the intent of this Chapter, which is to prohibit the City from entering into contracts with entities that discriminate based on the criteria set forth in this Chapter;

(4) The waiver authority granted to contracting officers in this Section 12B.5–1(d) shall be subject to the requirements that:

(i) All proposed waivers must be submitted to the Director and the Clerk of the Board of Supervisors. All proposed waivers must set forth the reasons the contracting officer is requesting the waiver, what steps were taken to find an entity that complies with this Chapter and why the waiver does not defeat the intent of this Chapter, which is to prohibit the City from entering into contracts with entities that discriminate based on the criteria set forth in this Chapter. Such waivers shall be subject to the prior approval of the Director, who shall take action approving or denying a proposed waiver within 30 days of receiving a notification of a proposed waiver from a contracting officer. If after 30 days the Director has taken no action on the proposed waiver, the waiver shall be deemed approved. The Clerk of the Board of Supervisors shall list the notice of the proposed waiver at the rear of the next available Board agenda, and

(ii) Contracting officers report to the Director whenever such a waiver is granted within five days of granting the waiver, and

(iii) For any contract subject to approval by the Board, the contracting officer shall state in the approving resolution whether any waiver under this Section 12B.5–1(d) has been or is proposed to be granted for that contract, and

(iv) The Director shall conduct quarterly comprehensive reviews of the use of the waiver authority by departments and shall make a report to the Board of Supervisors. Contracting officers who have exercised waiver authority under this Section 12B.5–1(d) in the previous quarter must appear before a Board of Supervisors committee and report on their use of such waiver authority. If the Board finds abuse of waiver authority by a department under this Section 12B.5–1(d), either as a result of a report of the Director or upon its own initiative, the Board may by resolution transfer that waiver authority for that department to the Director, to be exercised by the Director upon recommendation of the contracting officer under any or all of the circumstances enumerated in this Section 12B.5–1(d):

(5) Nothing in this Section 12B.5–1(d) shall limit the right of the Board of Supervisors to waive the provisions of this Chapter.

(e) This Chapter shall not apply to (i) the investment of trust moneys or agreements relating to the management of trust assets, (ii) City moneys invested in U.S. government securities or under pre-existing investment agreements, or (iii) the investment of City moneys where the Treasurer finds that:

(1) No person, entity or financial institution doing business in the City and County which is in compliance with this Chapter is capable of performing the desired transactions(s); or

(2) The City will incur a financial loss which in the opinion of the Treasurer would violate his or her fiduciary duties.

This subparagraph (e) shall be subject to the requirement that City moneys shall be withdrawn or divested at the earliest possible maturity date if deposited or invested with a person, entity or financial institution other than the U.S. government which does not comply with this Chapter.

(f) The General Manager of the Public Utilities Commission may waive the requirements of this Chapter where the contractor is providing wholesale or bulk water, power or natural gas, the conveyance or transmission of same, or ancillary services such as spinning reserve, voltage control, or loading scheduling, as required for assuring reliable services in accordance with good utility practice, to or on behalf of the San Francisco Public Utilities Commission; provided that the purchase of same may not practically be accomplished through the City's standard competitive bidding procedures; and further provided that this exemption shall not apply to contractors or franchisees providing direct, retail services to end users within the City and County of San Francisco.

(g) Sections 12B.1(b) and 12B.2(b) shall not apply to any contracts or property contracts executed or amended prior to June 1, 1997, or to bid packages advertised and made available to the public, or any competitive or sealed bids received by the City, prior to June 1, 1997, unless and until such contracts or property contracts are amended after June 1, 1997, and would otherwise be subject to this Chapter.

Section 12B.6. Severability

This Chapter shall be construed so as not to conflict with applicable federal or State laws, rules or regulations. Nothing in this Chapter shall authorize any City agency to impose any duties or obligations in conflict with limitations on municipal authority established by federal law at the time such agency action is taken.

In the event that a court or agency of competent jurisdiction holds that the State or federal law, rule or regulation invalidates any clause, sentence, paragraph or section of this Chapter or the application thereof to any person or circumstances, it is the intent of the Board of Supervisors that the court or agency sever such clause, sentence, paragraph or section so that the remainder of this Chapter shall remain in effect.

APPENDICES

[Industrial Welfare Commission Wage Orders; California and Federal
Jury Instructions; Federal Labor and Employment Laws]

INDUSTRIAL WELFARE COMMISSION WAGE ORDERS

Order MW–2007 California Minimum Wage

Order No. 1–2001 Regulating Wages, Hours and Working Conditions in the Manufacturing Industry

Order No. 2–2001 Regulating Wages, Hours and Working Conditions in the Personal Service Industry

Order No. 3–2001 Regulating Wages, Hours and Working Conditions in the Canning, Freezing, and Preserving Industry

Order No. 4–2001 Regulating Wages, Hours and Working Conditions in the Professional, Technical, Clerical, Mechanical and Similar Occupations

Order No. 5–2001 Regulating Wages, Hours and Working Conditions in the Public Housekeeping Industry

Order No. 6–2001 Regulating Wages, Hours and Working Conditions in the Laundry, Linen Supply, Dry Cleaning and Dyeing Industry

Order No. 7–2001 Regulating Wages, Hours and Working Conditions in the Mercantile Industry

Order No. 8–2001 Regulating Wages, Hours and Working Conditions in the Industries Handling Products After Harvest

Order No. 9–2001 Regulating Wages, Hours and Working Conditions in the Transportation Industry

Order No. 10–2001 Regulating Wages, Hours and Working Conditions in the Amusement and Recreation Industry

Order No. 11–2001 Regulating Wages, Hours and Working Conditions in the Broadcasting Industry

Order No. 12–2001 Regulating Wages, Hours and Working Conditions in the Motion Picture Industry

Order No.13–2001 Regulating Wages, Hours and Working Conditions in the Industries Preparing Agricultural Products for Market, on the Farm

Order No. 14–2001 Regulating Wages, Hours and Working Conditions in the Agricultural Occupations

Order No. 15–2001 Regulating Wages, Hours and Working Conditions in the Household Occupations

Order No.16–2001 Regulating Wages, Hours and Working Conditions in the Certain On–Site Occupations in the Construction, Drilling, Logging and Mining Industries

Order No. 17–2001 Regulating Wages, Hours and Working Conditions in the Miscellaneous Employees

Publisher's Notes

The Industrial Welfare Commission acts as a quasi-legislative body in promulgating minimum wage orders. *Rivera v. Division of Industrial Welfare (19??) 265 Cal. App.2d 576, 586, 71 Cal.Rptr. 739. See also Bell v. Farmers Ins. Exchange (2001) 87 Cal.App.4th 805, 809–810* (wage orders are quasi-legislative enactments involving a " . . . 'considerable degree of policy-making judgment and discretion.' ").

Although often patterned after federal regulations, the Industrial Welfare Commission's wage orders sometimes provide greater protection than is provided under federal law in the Fair Labor Standards Act (FLSA) and accompanying federal regulations. *Ramirez v. Yosemite Water Co., Inc. (1999) 20 Cal.4th 785, 978 P.2d 2, 85 Cal.Rptr.2d 844.*

Since California's wage laws are patterned on federal statutes, federal cases construing those federal statutes provide persuasive guidance to state courts. *Alcala v. Western Ag Enterprises (1986) 182 Cal.App.3d 546, 550, 227 Cal.Rptr. 453,* citing *Brennan v. Elmer's Disposal Service, Inc., 510 F.2d 84, 86 (9th Cir. 1975). See also* research references below.

In determining whether wage orders apply, where state and federal law do not conflict, California's territorial boundaries are determined by state law. *Tidewater Marine Western, Inc. v. Bradshaw (1996) 14 Cal.4th 557, 927 P.2d 296, 59 Cal.Rptr.2d 186*

As to limitation of actions generally, see *Aubry v. Goldhor (1988) 201 Cal.App.3d 399, 247 Cal.Rptr. 205* (CCP § 338 limitation period governed claims based upon violations of wage orders).

Research References

Who is employed in "executive capacity" within exemption, under 29 U.S.C.A. § 213(a), from minimum wage and maximum hours provisions of Fair Labor Standards Act (29 U.S.C.A. §§ 201 et seq.), *131 ALR Fed 1.*

Who is employed in "administrative capacity" within exemption, under 29 U.S.C.A. § 213(a)(1), from minimum wage and maximum hours provisions of Fair Labor Standards Act, *124 ALR Fed. 1.*

Who is employed in "professional capacity," within exemption, under 29 U.S.C.A. § 213(a)(1), from minimum wage and maximum hours provisions of Fair Labor Standards Act, *77 ALR Fed 681*.

Who is employed in "capacity of outside salesman" within meaning of § 13(a)(1) of Fair Labor Standards Act (29 U.S.C.A. § 213(a)(1)), as amended, exempting such employees from minimum wage and overtime requirements of Act, *26 ALR Fed. 941*.

Construction of § 7(f) of the Fair Labor Standards Act (29 U.S.C.A. § 207(f)) exempting from overtime provisions employees whose duties necessitate irregular hours of work, *5 ALR Fed. 793*.

Call or waiting time as working time within the minimum wage and overtime provisions of the Fair Labor Standards Act (29 U.S.C.A. §§ 206, 207), *3 ALR Fed 675*.

Who is executive, administrator, supervisor, or the like, under exemption for such employees from state minimum wage and overtime pay statutes, *85 ALR4th 519*.

CALIFORNIA MINIMUM WAGE

ORDER MW–2007

(Effective January 1, 2007)

Minimum Wage—Every employer shall pay to each employee wages not less than the following:

$7.50	**$8.00**
per hour beginning January 1, 2007	*per hour beginning January 1, 2008*

To employers and representatives of persons working in industries and occupations in the State of California:

Summary of Actions

TAKE NOTICE that on September 12, 2006, the California Legislature enacted legislation signed by the Governor of California, raising the minimum wage for all industries. (AB 1835, Ch. 230, Stats of 2006, adding sections 1182.12 and 1182.13 to the California Labor Code.) Pursuant to its authority under Labor Code section 1182.13, the Department of Industrial Relations amends and republishes Sections 1, 2, 3, and 5 of the General Minimum Wage Order. MW–2001, Section 4, Separability, has not been changed. Consistent with this enactment, amendments are made to the minimum wage, and the meals and lodging credits sections of all of the IWC's industry and occupation orders.

This summary must be made available to employees in accordance with the IWC's wage orders. Copies of the full text of the amended wage orders may be obtained by ordering on-line at www.dir.ca.gov/WP.asp, or by contacting your local Division of Labor Standards Enforcement office.

1. Applicability

The provisions of this Order shall not apply to outside salespersons and individuals who are the parent, spouse, or children of the employer previously contained in this Order and the IWC's industry and occupation orders. Exceptions and modifications provided by statute or in Section 1, Applicability, and in other sections of the IWC's industry and occupation orders may be used where any such provisions are enforceable and applicable to the employer.

2. Minimum Wages

Every employer shall pay to each employee wages not less than seven dollars and fifty cents ($7.50) per hour for all hours worked, effective January 1, 2007, and not less than eight dollars ($8.00) per hour for all hours worked, effective January 1, 2008.

3. Meals and Lodging

Meals or lodging may not be credited against the minimum wage without a voluntary written agreement between the employer and the employee. When credit for meals or lodging is used to meet part of the employer's minimum wage obligation, the amounts so credited may not be more than the following:

Effective	January 1, 2007	January 1, 2008
LODGING		
Room occupied alone	$35.27 per week	$37.63 per week
Room shared	$29.11 per week	$31.06 per week
Apartment—two-thirds (⅔) of the ordinary rental value, and in no event more than:	$423.51 per month	$451.89 per month
Where a couple are both employed by the employer, two-thirds (⅔) of the ordinary rental value, and in no event more than:	$626.49 per month	$668.46 per month
MEALS		
Breakfast	$2.72	$2.90
Lunch	$3.72	$3.97
Dinner	$5.00	$5.34

4. Separability

If the application of any provision of this Order, or any section, subsection, subdivision, sentence, clause, phrase, word or portion of this Order should be held invalid, unconstitutional, unauthorized, or prohibited by statute, the remaining provisions thereof shall not be affected thereby, but shall continue to be given full force and effect as if the part so held invalid or unconstitutional had not been included herein.

5. Amended Provisions

This Order amends the minimum wage and meals and lodging credits in MW–2001, as well as in the IWC's industry and occupation orders. (See Orders 1–15, Secs. 4 and 10; and Order 16, Secs. 4 and 9.) This Order makes no other changes to the IWC's industry and occupation orders.

Please Post With This Side Showing
OFFICIAL NOTICE
Effective July 1, 2002 as amended
Sections 4(A) and 10(C) amended and republished by the Department of Industrial Relations, effective January 1, 2007, pursuant to AB 1835, Chapter 230, Statutes of 2006
INDUSTRIAL WELFARE COMMISSION
ORDER NO. 1–2001
REGULATING
WAGES, HOURS AND WORKING CONDITIONS IN THE
MANUFACTURING INDUSTRY

TAKE NOTICE: To employers and representatives of persons working in industries and occupations in the State of California:

The Department of Industrial Relations amends and republishes the minimum wage and meals and lodging credits in the Industrial Welfare Commission's Orders as a result of legislation enacted (AB 1835, Ch. 230, Stats of 2006, adding sections 1182.12 and 1182.13 to the California Labor Code.) The amendments and republishing make no other changes to the IWC's Orders.

1. Applicability of Order. This order shall apply to all persons employed in the manufacturing industry whether paid on a time, piece rate, commission, or other basis, except that:

(A) Provisions of Sections 3 through 12 of this order shall not apply to persons employed in administrative, executive, or professional capacities. The following requirements shall apply in determining whether an employee's duties meet the test to qualify for an exemption from those sections:

(1) Executive Exemption. A person employed in an executive capacity means any employee:

(a) Whose duties and responsibilities involve the management of the enterprise in which he/she is employed or of a customarily recognized department or subdivision thereof; and

(b) Who customarily and regularly directs the work of two or more other employees herein; and

(c) Who has the authority to hire or fire other employees or whose suggestions and recommendations as to the hiring or firing and as to the advancement and promotion or any other change of status of other employees will be given particular weight; and

(d) Who customarily and regularly exercises discretion and independent judgment; and

(e) Who is primarily engaged in duties which meet the test of the exemption. The activities constituting exempt work and non-exempt work shall be construed in the same manner as such items are construed in the following regulations under the Fair Labor Standards Act effective as of the date of this order: 29 C.F.R. Sections 541.102, 541.104–111, and 541.115–116. Exempt work shall include, for example, all work that is directly and closely related to exempt work and work which is properly viewed as a means for carrying out exempt functions. The work actually performed by the employee during the course of the work week must, first and foremost, be examined and the amount of time the employee spends on such work, together with the employer's realistic expectations and the realistic requirements of the job, shall be considered in determining whether the employee satisfies this requirement.

(f) Such an employee must also earn a monthly salary equivalent to no less than two (2) times the state minimum wage for full-time employment. Full–time employment is defined in Labor Code Section 515(c) as 40 hours per week.

(2) Administrative Exemption. A person employed in an administrative capacity means any employee:

(a) Whose duties and responsibilities involve either:

(i) The performance of office or non-manual work directly related to management policies or general business operations of his employer or his employer's customers, or

(ii) The performance of functions in the administration of a school system, or educational establishment or institution, or of a department or subdivision thereof, in work directly related to the academic instruction or training carried on therein; and

(b) Who customarily and regularly exercises discretion and independent judgment; and

(c) Who regularly and directly assists a proprietor, or an employee employed in a bona fide executive or administrative capacity (as such terms are defined for purposes of this section); or

(d) Who performs under only general supervision work along specialized or technical lines requiring special training, experience, or knowledge; or

(e) Who executes under only general supervision special assignments and tasks; and

1387

(f) Who are primarily engaged in duties that meet the test of the exemption. The activities constituting exempt work and non-exempt work shall be construed in the same manner as such terms are construed in the following regulations under the Fair Labor Standards Act effective as of the date of this order: 29 C.F.R. Sections 541.201–205, 541.207–208, and 541.210, 541.215. Exempt work shall include, for example, all work that is directly and closely related to exempt work and work which is properly viewed as a means for carrying out exempt functions. The work actually performed by the employee during the course of the work week must, first and foremost, be examined and the amount of time the employee spends on such work, together with the employer's realistic expectations and the realistic requirements of the job, shall be considered in determining whether the employee satisfies this requirement.

(g) Such employee must also earn a monthly salary equivalent to no less than two times the state minimum wage for full-time employment. Full–time employment is defined in Labor Code Section 515(c) as 40 hours per week.

(3) Professional Exemption. A person employed in a professional capacity means any employee who meets *all* of the following requirements:

(a) Who is licensed or certified by the State of California and is primarily engaged in the practice of one of the following recognized professions: law, medicine, dentistry, optometry, architecture, engineering, teaching, or accounting; or

(b) Who is primarily engaged in an occupation commonly recognized as a learned or artistic profession. For the purposes of this subsection, "learned or artistic profession" means an employee who is primarily engaged in the performance of:

(i) Work requiring knowledge of an advanced type in a field or science or learning customarily acquired by a prolonged course of specialized intellectual instruction and study, as distinguished from a general academic education and from an apprenticeship, and from training in the performance of routine mental, manual, or physical processes, or work that is an essential part of or necessarily incident to any of the above work; or

(ii) Work that is original and creative in character in a recognized field of artistic endeavor (as opposed to work which can be produced by a person endowed with general manual or intellectual ability and training), and the result of which depends primarily on the invention, imagination, or talent of the employee or work that is an essential part of or necessarily incident to any of the above work; and

(iii) Whose work is predominantly intellectual and varied in character (as opposed to routine mental, manual, mechanical, or physical work) and is of such character that the output produced or the result accomplished cannot be standardized in relation to a given period of time.

(c) Who customarily and regularly exercises discretion and independent judgment in the performance of duties set forth in paragraphs (a) and (b).

(d) Who earns a monthly salary equivalent to no less than two (2) times the state minimum wage for full-time employment. Full–time employment is defined in Labor Code Section 515(c) as 40 hours per week.

(e) Subparagraph (b) above is intended to be construed in accordance with the following provisions of federal law as they existed as of the date of this wage order: 29 C.F.R. Sections 541.207, 541.301(a)–(d), 541.302, 541.306, 541.307, 541.308, and 541.310.

(f) Notwithstanding the provisions of this subparagraph, pharmacists employed to engage in the practice of pharmacy, and registered nurses employed to engage in the practice of nursing, shall not be considered exempt professional employees, nor shall they be considered exempt from coverage for the purposes of this subparagraph unless they individually meet the criteria established for exemption as executive or administrative employees.

(g) Subparagraph (f) above, shall not apply to the following advanced practice nurses:

(i) Certified nurse midwives who are primarily engaged in performing duties for which certification is required pursuant to Article 2.5 (commencing with Section 2746) of Chapter 6 of Division 2 of the Business and Professions Code.

(ii) Certified nurse anesthetists who are primarily engaged in performing duties for which certification is required pursuant to Article 7 (commencing with Section 2825) of Chapter 6 of Division 2 of the Business and Professions Code.

(iii) Certified nurse practitioners who are primarily engaged in performing duties for which certification is required pursuant to Article 8 (commencing with Section 2834) of Chapter 6 of Division 2 of the Business and Professions Code.

(iv) Nothing in this subparagraph shall exempt the occupations set forth in clauses (i), (ii), and (iii) from meeting the requirements of subsection 1(A)(3)(a)–(d) above.

(h) Except, as provided in subparagraph (i), an employee in the computer software field who is paid on an hourly basis shall be exempt, if *all* of the following apply:

(i) The employee is primarily engaged in work that is intellectual or creative and requires the exercise of discretion and independent judgment.

(ii) The employee is primarily engaged in duties that consist of one or more of the following:

-The application of systems analysis techniques and procedures, including consulting with users, to determine hardware, software, or system functional specifications.

-The design, development, documentation, analysis, creation, testing, or modification of computer systems or programs, including prototypes, based on and related to user or system design specifications.

-The documentation, testing, creation, or modification of computer programs related to the design of software or hardware for computer operating systems.

(iii) The employee is highly skilled and is proficient in the theoretical and practical application of highly specialized information to computer systems analysis, programming, and software engineering. A job title shall not be determinative of the applicability of this exemption.

(iv) The employee's hourly rate of pay is not less than forty-one dollars ($41.00). The Division of Labor Statistics and Research shall adjust this pay rate on October 1 of each year to be effective on January 1 of the following year by an amount equal to the percentage increase in the California Consumer Price Index for Urban Wage Earners and Clerical Workers.[1]

(i) The exemption provided in subparagraph (h) does not apply to an employee if *any* of the following apply:

(i) The employee is a trainee or employee in an entry-level position who is learning to become proficient in the theoretical and practical application of highly specialized information to computer systems analysis, programming, and software engineering.

(ii) The employee is in a computer-related occupation but has not attained the level of skill and expertise necessary to work independently and without close supervision.

(iii) The employee is engaged in the operation of computers or in the manufacture, repair, or maintenance of computer hardware and related equipment.

(iv) The employee is an engineer, drafter, machinist, or other professional whose work is highly dependent upon or facilitated by the use of computers and computer software programs and who is skilled in computer-aided design software, including CAD/CAM, but who is not in a computer systems analysis or programming occupation.

(v) The employee is a writer engaged in writing material, including box labels, product descriptions, documentation, promotional material, setup and installation instructions, and other similar written information, either for print or for on screen media or who writes or provides content material intended to be read by customers, subscribers, or visitors to computer-related media such as the World Wide Web or CD–ROMs.

(vi) The employee is engaged in any of the activities set forth in subparagraph (h) for the purpose of creating imagery for effects used in the motion picture, television, or theatrical industry.

(B) Except as provided in Sections 1, 2, 4, 10, and 20, the provisions of this order shall not apply to any employees directly employed by the State or any political subdivision thereof, including any city, county, or special district.

(C) The provisions of this order shall not apply to outside salespersons.

(D) Provisions of this order shall not apply to any individual who is the parent, spouse, child, or legally adopted child of the employer.

(E) The provisions of this order shall not apply to any individual participating in a national service program, such as AmeriCorps, carried out using assistance provided under Section 12571 of Title 42 of the United States Code. (See Stats. 2000, ch. 365, amending California Labor Code Section 1171.)

2. Definitions

(A) An "alternative workweek schedule" means any regularly scheduled workweek requiring an employee to work more than eight (8) hours in a 24–hour period.

(B) "Commission" means the Industrial Welfare Commission of the State of California.

(C) "Division" means the Division of Labor Standards Enforcement of the State of California.

(D) "Employ" means to engage, suffer, or permit to work.

(E) "Employee" means any person employed by an employer.

(F) "Employer" means any person as defined in Section 18 of the Labor Code, who directly or indirectly, or through an agent or any other person, employs or exercises control over the wages, hours, or working conditions of any person.

(G) "Hours worked" means the time during which an employee is subject to the control of an employer, and includes all the time the employee is suffered or permitted to work, whether or not required to do so.

(H) "Manufacturing Industry" means any industry, business, or establishment operated for the purpose of preparing, producing, making, altering, repairing, finishing, processing, inspecting, handling, assembling, wrapping, bottling, or packaging goods, articles, or commodities, in whole or in part; EXCEPT when such activities are covered by Orders in the: Canning, Preserving, and Freezing Industry; Industries Handling Products After Harvest; Industries Preparing Agricultural Products for Market, on the Farm; or Motion Picture Industry.

(I) "Minor" means, for the purpose of this Order, any person under the age of 18 years.

(J) "Outside salesperson" means any person, 18 years of age or over, who customarily and regularly works more than half the working time away from the employer's place of business selling tangible or intangible items or obtaining orders or contracts for products, services or use of facilities.

(K) "Primarily" as used in Section 1, Applicability, means more than one-half the employee's work time.

(L) "Shift" means designated hours of work by an employee, with a designated beginning time and quitting time.

(M) "Split shift" means a work schedule, which is interrupted by non-paid non-working periods established by the employer, other than bona fide rest or meal periods.

(N) "Teaching" means, for the purpose of Section 1 of this order, the profession of teaching under a certificate from the Commission for Teacher Preparation and Licensing or teaching in an accredited college or university.

(O) "Wages" includes all amounts for labor performed by employees of every description, whether the amount is fixed or ascertained by the standard of time, task, piece, commission basis, or other method of calculation.

(P) "Workday" and "day" means any consecutive 24–hour period beginning at the same time each calendar day.

(Q) "Workweek" and "week" means any seven (7) consecutive days, starting with the same calendar day each week. "Workweek" is a fixed and regularly recurring period of 168 hours, seven (7) consecutive 24–hour periods.

3. Hours and Days of Work

(A) *Daily Overtime–General Provisions*

(1) The following overtime provisions are applicable to employees 18 years of age or over and to employees 16 or 17 years of age who are not required by law to attend school and are not otherwise prohibited by law from engaging in the subject work. Such employees shall not be employed more than eight (8) hours in any workday or more than 40 in a workweek unless the employee receives one and one half (1 ½) times such employee's regular rate of pay for all hours worked over 40 hours in the workweek. Eight (8) hours of labor constitutes a day's work. Employment beyond eight (8) hours in any workday or more than six (6) days in any workweek is permissible provided the employee is compensated for such overtime at not less than:

(a) One and one-half (1 ½) times the employee's regular rate of pay for all hours worked in excess of eight (8) hours up to and including twelve (12) hours in any workday, and for the first eight (8) hours worked on the seventh (7th) consecutive day of work in a workweek; and

(b) Double the employee's regular rate of pay for all hours worked in excess of 12 hours in any workday and for all hours worked in excess of eight (8) hours on the seventh (7th) consecutive day of work in a workweek.

(c) The overtime rate of compensation required to be paid to a nonexempt full-time salaried employee shall be computed by using the employee's regular hourly salary as one fortieth (1/40) of the employee's weekly salary.

(2) The provisions of this section are not applicable to employees whose hours of service:

(a) The United States Department of Transportation Code of Federal Regulations, Title 49, Sections 395.1 to 395.13, Hours of Service of Drivers; or

(b) Title 13 of the California Code of Regulations, subchapter 6.5, Section 1200 and the following sections, regulating hours of drivers.

(B) *Alternative Workweeks*

(1) No employer shall be deemed to have violated the daily overtime provisions by instituting, pursuant to the election procedures set forth in this wage order, a regularly scheduled alternative workweek schedule of not more than ten (10) hours per day within a 40 hour workweek without the payment of an overtime rate of compensation. All work performed in any workday beyond the schedule established by the agreement up to 12 hours a day or beyond 40 hours per week shall be paid at one and one-half (1 ½) times the employee's regular rate of pay. All work performed in excess of 12 hours per day and any work in excess of eight (8) hours on those days worked beyond the regularly scheduled number of workdays established by the alternative workweek agreement shall be paid at double the employee's regular rate of pay. Any alternative workweek agreement adopted pursuant to this section shall provide for not less than four (4) hours of work in any shift. Nothing in this section shall prohibit an employer, at the request of the employee, to substitute one day of work for another day of the same length in the shift provided by the alternative workweek agreement on an occasional basis to meet the personal needs of the employee without the payment of overtime. No hours paid at either one and one-half (1 ½) or double the regular rate of pay shall be included in determining when 40 hours have been worked for the purpose of computing overtime compensation.

(2) Any agreement adopted pursuant to this section shall provide not less than two (2) consecutive days off within a workweek.

(3) If an employer, whose employees have adopted an alternative workweek agreement permitted by this order requires an employee to work fewer hours than those that are regularly scheduled by the agreement, the employer shall pay the employee overtime compensation at a rate of one and one-half (1 ½) times the employee's regular rate of pay for all hours worked in excess of eight (8) hours, and double the employee's regular rate of pay for all hours worked in excess of 12 hours for the day the employee is required to work the reduced hours.

(4) An employer shall not reduce an employee's regular rate of hourly pay as a result of the adoption, repeal or nullification of an alternative workweek schedule.

(5) An employer shall explore any available reasonable alternative means of accommodating the religious belief or observance of an affected employee that conflicts with an adopted alternative workweek schedule, in the manner provided by subdivision (j) of Section 12940 of the Government Code.

(6) An employer shall make a reasonable effort to find a work schedule not to exceed eight (8) hours in a workday, in order to accommodate any affected employee who was eligible to vote in an election authorized by this

section and who is unable to work the alternative workweek schedule established as the result of that election.

(7) An employer shall be permitted, but not required, to provide a work schedule not to exceed eight (8) hours in a workday to accommodate any employee who is hired after the date of the election and who is unable to work the alternative workweek schedule established by the election.

(8) Arrangements adopted in a secret ballot election held pursuant to this order prior to 1998, or under the rules in effect prior to 1998, and before the performance of the work, shall remain valid after July 1, 2000 provided that the results of the election are reported by the employer to the Division of Labor Statistics and Research by January 1, 2001, in accordance with the requirements of subsection (C) below (Election Procedures). If an employee was voluntarily working an alternative work-week schedule of not more than ten (10) hours a day as of July 1, 2000, that alternative workweek schedule was based on an individual agreement made after January 1, 1998 between the employee and employer, and the employee submitted, and the employer approved, a written request on or before May 30, 2000 to continue the agreement, the employee may continue to work that alternative workweek schedule without payment of an overtime rate of compensation for the hours provided in the agreement. The employee may revoke his or her voluntary authorization to continue such a schedule with 30 days written notice to the employer. New arrange ments can only be entered into pursuant to the provisions of this section.

(C) *Election Procedures*

Election procedures for the adoption and repeal of alternative workweek schedules require the following:

(1) Each proposal for an alternative workweek sched ule shall be in the form of a written agreement proposed by the employer. The proposed agreement must desig-nate a regularly scheduled alternative workweek in which the specified number of work days and work hours are regularly recurring. The actual days worked within that alternative workweek schedule need not be specified. The employer may propose a single work schedule that would become the standard schedule for workers in the work unit, or a menu of work schedule options, from which each employee in the unit would be entitled to choose. If the employer proposes a menu of work schedule options, the employee may, with the approval of the employer, move from one menu option to another.

(2) In order to be valid, the proposed alternative workweek schedule must be adopted in a secret ballot election, before the performance of work, by at least a two-thirds (2/03) vote of the affected employees in the work unit. The election shall be held during regular working hours at the employees' work site. For purposes of this subsection, "affected employees in the work unit" may include all employees in a readily identifiable work unit, such as a division, a department, a job classification,

a shift, a separate physical location, or a recognized subdivision of any such work unit. A work unit may consist of an individual employee as long as the criteria for an identifiable work unit in this subsection is met.

(3) Prior to the secret ballot vote, any employer who proposed to institute an alternative workweek schedule shall have made a disclosure in writing to the affected employees, including the effects of the proposed arrange-ment on the employees' wages, hours, and benefits. Such a disclosure shall include meeting(s), duly noticed, held at least 14 days prior to voting, for the specific purpose of discussing the effects of the alternative workweek sched-ule. An employer shall provide that disclosure in a non–English language, as well as in English, if at least five (5) percent of the affected employees primarily speak that non–English language. The employer shall mail the written disclosure to employees who do not attend the meeting. Failure to comply with this paragraph shall make the election null and void.

(4) Any election to establish or repeal an alternative workweek schedule shall be held at the work site of the affected employees. The employer shall bear the costs of conducting any election held pursuant to this section. Upon a complaint by an affected employee, and after an investigation by the Labor Commissioner, the Labor Commissioner may require the employer to select a neutral third party to conduct the election.

(5) Any type of alternative workweek schedule that is authorized by the Labor Code may be repealed by the affected employees. Upon a petition of one-third (1/03) of the affected employees, a new secret ballot election shall be held and a two-thirds (2/03) vote of the affected employees shall be required to reverse the alternative workweek schedule. The election to repeal the alterna-tive workweek schedule shall be held not more than 30 days after the petition is submitted to the employer, except that the election shall be held not less than 12 months after the date that the same group of employees voted in an election held to adopt or repeal an alternative workweek schedule. The election shall take place during regular working hours at the employees' work site. If the alternative workweek schedule is revoked, the employer shall comply within 60 days. Upon proper showing of undue hardship, the Division of Labor Standards En-forcement may grant an extension of time for compliance.

(6) Only secret ballots may be cast by affected employ-ees in the work unit at any election held pursuant to this section. The results of any election conducted pursuant to this section shall be reported by the employer to the Division of Labor Statistics and Research within 30 days after the results are final, and the report of election results shall be a public document. The report shall include the final tally of the vote, the size of the unit, and the nature of the business of the employer.

(7) Employees affected by a change in the work hours resulting from the adoption of an alternative workweek schedule may not be required to work those new work

hours for at least 30 days after the announcement of the final results of the election.

(8) Employers shall not intimidate or coerce employees to vote either in support of or in opposition to a proposed alternative workweek. No employees shall be discharged or discriminated against for expressing opinions concerning the alternative workweek election or for opposing or supporting its adoption or repeal. However, nothing in this section shall prohibit an employer from expressing his/her position concerning that alternative workweek to the affected employees. A violation of this paragraph shall be subject to Labor Code Section 98 et seq.

(D) One and one-half (1 ½) times a minor's regular rate of pay shall be paid for all work over 40 hours in any workweek except minors 16 or 17 years old who are not required by law to attend school and may therefore be employed for the same hours as an adult are subject to subsection (A) or (B) and (C) above.

(Violations of Child Labor Laws are subject to civil penalties of from $500 to $10,000 as well as to criminal penalties. Refer to California Labor Code sections 1285 to 1312 and 1390 to 1399 for additional restrictions on the employment of minors and for descriptions of criminal and civil penalties for violation of the child labor laws. Employers should ask school districts about any required work permits.)

(E) An employee may be employed on seven (7) workdays in one workweek when the total hours of employment during such workweek do not exceed 30 and the total hours of employment in any one workday thereof do not exceed six (6).

(F) The provisions of Labor Code Sections 551 and 552 regarding one (1) day's rest in seven (7) shall not be construed to prevent an accumulation of days of rest when the nature of the employment reasonably requires the employee to work seven (7) or more consecutive days; provided, however, that in each calendar month, the employee shall receive the equivalent of one (1) day's rest in seven (7).

(G) If a meal period occurs on a shift beginning or ending at or between the hours of 10 p.m. and 6 a.m., facilities shall be available for securing hot food and drink or for heating food or drink, and a suitable sheltered place shall be provided in which to consume such food or drink.

(H) Except as provided in subsections (D) and (F), this section shall not apply to any employee covered by a valid collective bargaining agreement if the agreement expressly provides for the wages, hours of work, and working conditions of the employees, and if the agreement provides premium wage rates for all overtime hours worked and a regular hourly rate of pay for those employees of not less than 30 percent more than the state minimum wage.

(I) Notwithstanding subsection (H) above, where the employer and a labor organization representing employ-

ees of the employer have entered into a valid collective bargaining agreement pertaining to the hours of work of the employees, the requirement regarding the equivalent of one (1) day's rest in seven (7) (see section (F) above) shall apply, unless the agreement expressly provides otherwise.

(J) If an employer approves a written request of an employee to make up work time that is or would be lost as a result of a personal obligation of the employee, the hours of that makeup work time, if performed in the same workweek in which the work time was lost, may not be counted toward computing the total number of hours worked in a day for purposes of the overtime requirements, except for hours in excess of 11 hours of work in one (1) day or 40 hours of work in one (1) workweek. If an employee knows in advance that he or she will be requesting makeup time for a personal obligation that will recur at a fixed time over a succession of weeks, the employee may request to make up work time for up to four (4) weeks in advance; provided, however, that the make up work must be performed in the same week that the work time was lost. An employee shall provide a signed written request for each occasion that the employee makes a request to make up work time pursuant to this subsection. While an employer may inform an employee of this makeup time option, the employer is prohibited from encouraging or otherwise soliciting an employee to request the employer's approval to take personal time off and make up the work hours within the same workweek pursuant to this subsection.

4. Minimum Wages

(A) Every employer shall pay to each employee wages not less than seven dollars and fifty cents ($7.50) per hour for all hours worked, effective January 1, 2007, and not less than eight dollars ($8.00) per hour for all hours worked, effective January 1, 2008, except:

Learners: Employees during their first 160 hours of employment in occupations in which they have no previous similar or related experience, may be paid not less than 85 percent of the minimum wage rounded to the nearest nickel.

(B) Every employer shall pay to each employee, on the established payday for the period involved, not less than the applicable minimum wage for all hours worked in the payroll period, whether the remuneration is measured by time, piece, commission, or otherwise.

(C) When an employee works a split shift, one hour's pay at the minimum wage shall be paid in addition to the minimum wage for that workday, except when the employee resides at the place of employment.

(D) The provisions of this section shall not apply to apprentices regularly indentured under the State Division of Apprenticeship Standards.

5. Reporting Time Pay

(A) Each workday an employee is required to report for work and does report, but is not put to work or is furnished less than half said employee's usual or scheduled day's work, the employee shall be paid for half the usual or scheduled day's work, but in no event for less than two (2) hours nor more than four (4) hours, at the employee's regular rate of pay, which shall not be less than the minimum wage.

(B) If an employee is required to report for work a second time in any one workday and is furnished less than two hours of work on the second reporting, said employee shall be paid for two (2) hours at the employee's regular rate of pay, which shall not be less than the minimum wage.

(C) The foregoing reporting time pay provisions are not applicable when:

(1) Operations cannot commence or continue due to threats to employees or property; or when recommended by civil authorities; or

(2) Public utilities fail to supply electricity, water, or gas, or there is a failure in the public utilities, or sewer system; or

(3) The interruption of work is caused by an Act of God or other cause not within the employer's control.

(D) This section shall not apply to an employee on paid standby status who is called to perform assigned work at a time other than the employee's scheduled reporting time.

6. Licenses for Disabled Workers

(A) A license may be issued by the Division authorizing employment of a person whose earning capacity is impaired by physical disability or mental deficiency at less than the minimum wage. Such licenses shall be granted only upon joint application of employer and employee and employee's representative if any.

(B) A special license may be issued to a nonprofit organization such as a sheltered workshop or rehabilitation facility fixing special minimum rates to enable the employment of such persons without requiring individual licenses of such employees.

(C) All such licenses and special licenses shall be renewed on a yearly basis or more frequently at the discretion of the Division.

(See California Labor Code, Sections 1191 and 1191.5)

7. Records

(A) Every employer shall keep accurate information with respect to each employee including the following:

(1) Full name, home address, occupation and social security number.

(2) Birth date, if under 18 years, and designation as a minor.

(3) Time records showing when the employee begins and ends each work period. Meal periods, split shift intervals and total daily hours worked shall also be recorded. Meal periods during which operations cease and authorized rest periods need not be recorded.

(4) Total wages paid each payroll period, including value of board, lodging, or other compensation actually furnished to the employee.

(5) Total hours worked in the payroll period and applicable rates of pay. This information shall be made readily available to the employee upon reasonable request.

(6) When a piece rate or incentive plan is in operation, piece rates or an explanation of the incentive plan formula shall be provided to employees. An accurate production record shall be maintained by the employer.

(B) Every employer shall semimonthly or at the time of each payment of wages furnish each employee, either as a detachable part of the check, draft, or voucher paying the employee's wages, or separately, an itemized statement in writing showing: (1) all deductions; (2) the inclusive dates of the period for which the employee is paid; (3) the name of the employee or the employee's social security number; and (4) the name of the employer, provided all deductions made on written orders of the employee may be aggregated and shown as one item.

(C) All required records shall be in the English language and in ink or other indelible form, properly dated, showing month, day, and year and shall be kept on file by the employer for at least three (3) years at the place of employment or at a central location within the State of California. An employee's records shall be available for inspection by the employee upon reasonable request.

(D) Clocks shall be provided in all major work areas or within reasonable distance thereto insofar as practicable.

8. Cash Shortage and Breakage. No employer shall make any deduction from the wage or require any reimbursement from an employee for any cash shortage, breakage, or loss of equipment, unless it can be shown that the shortage, breakage, or loss is caused by a dishonest or willful act, or by the gross negligence of the employee.

9. Uniforms and Equipment

(A) When uniforms are required by the employer to be worn by the employee as a condition of employment, such uniforms shall be provided and maintained by the employer. The term "uniform" includes wearing apparel and accessories of distinctive design or color.

Note: This section shall not apply to protective apparel regulated by the Occupational Safety and Health Standards Board.

(B) When tools or equipment are required by the employer or are necessary to the performance of a job, such tools and equipment shall be provided and maintained by the employer, except that an employee whose wages are at least two (2) times the minimum wage provided herein may be required to provide and maintain hand tools and equipment customarily required by the trade or craft. This subsection (B) shall not apply to apprentices regularly indentured under the State Division of Apprenticeship Standards.

Note: This section shall not apply to protective equipment and safety devices on tools regulated by the Occupational Safety and Health Standards Board.

(C) A reasonable deposit may be required as security for the return of the items furnished by the employer under provisions of subsection (A) and (B) of this section upon issuance of a receipt to the employee for such deposit. Such deposits shall be made pursuant to Section 400 and following of the Labor Code or an employer with the prior written authorization of the employee may deduct from the employee's last check the cost of an item furnished pursuant to subsections (A) and (B) above in the event said item is not returned. No deduction shall be made at any time for normal wear and tear. The employee upon completion of the job shall return all items furnished by the employer.

10. Meals and Lodging

(A) "Meal" means an adequate, well-balanced serving of a variety of wholesome, nutritious foods.

(B) "Lodging" means living accommodations available to the employee for full-time occupancy, which are adequate, decent, and sanitary according to usual and customary standards. Employees shall not be required to share a bed.

(C) Meals or lodging may not be credited against the minimum wage without a voluntary written agreement between the employer and the employee. When credit for meals or lodging is used to meet part of the employer's minimum wage obligation, the amounts so credited may not be more than the following:

Effective	January 1, 2007	January 1, 2008
Lodging:		
Room occupied alone	$35.27 per week	$37.63 per week
Room shared	$29.11 per week	$31.06 per week
Apartment—two–thirds (2/03) of the ordinary rental value, and in no event more than	$423.51 per month	$451.89 per month
Where a couple are both employed by the employer, two-thirds (2/03) of the ordinary rental value, and in no event more than	$626.49 per month	$668.46 per month
Meals:		
Breakfast	$2.72	$2.90
Lunch	$3.72	$3.97
Dinner	$5.00	$5.34

(D) Meals evaluated, as part of the minimum wage must be bona fide meals consistent with the employee's work shift. Deductions shall not be made for meals not received or lodging not used.

(E) If, as a condition of employment, the employee must live at the place of employment or occupy quarters owned or under the control of the employer, then the

employer may not charge rent in excess of the values listed herein.

11. Meal Periods

(A) No employer shall employ any person for a work period of more than five (5) hours without a meal period of not less than 30 minutes, except that when a work period of not more than six (6) hours will complete the day's work the meal period may be waived by mutual consent of the employer and employee. In the case of employees covered by a valid collective bargaining agreement, the parties to the collective bargaining agreement may agree to a meal period that commences after no more than six (6) hours of work.

(B) An employer may not employ an employee for a work period of more than ten (10) hours per day without providing the employee with a second meal period of not less than 30 minutes, except that if the total hours worked is no more than 12 hours, the second meal period may be waived by mutual consent of the employer and the employee only if the first meal period was not waived.

(C) Unless the employee is relieved of all duty during a 30 minute meal period, the meal period shall be considered an "on duty" meal period and counted as time worked. An "on duty" meal period shall be permitted only when the nature of the work prevents an employee from being relieved of all duty and when by written agreement between the parties an on-the-job paid meal period is agreed to. The written agreement shall state that the employee may, in writing, revoke the agreement at any time.

(D) If an employer fails to provide an employee a meal period in accordance with the applicable provisions of this order, the employer shall pay the employee one (1) hour of pay at the employee's regular rate of compensation for each work day that the meal period is not provided.

(E) In all places of employment where employees are required to eat on the premises, a suitable place for that purpose shall be designated.

12. Rest Periods

(A) Every employer shall authorize and permit all employees to take rest periods, which insofar as practicable shall be in the middle of each work period. The authorized rest period time shall be based on the total hours worked daily at the rate of ten (10) minutes net rest time per four (4) hours or major fraction thereof.

However, a rest period need not be authorized for employees whose total daily work time is less than three and one-half (3 $\frac{1}{2}$) hours. Authorized rest period time shall be counted as hours worked for which there shall be no deduction from wages.

(B) If an employer fails to provide an employee a rest period in accordance with the applicable provisions of this order, the employer shall pay the employee one (1) hour of pay at the employee's regular rate of compensation for each work day that the rest period is not provided.

13. Change Rooms and Resting Facilities

(A) Employers shall provide suitable lockers, closets, or equivalent for the safekeeping of employees' outer clothing during working hours, and when required, for their work clothing during non-working hours. When the occupation requires a change of clothing, change rooms or equivalent space shall be provided in order that employees may change their clothing in reasonable privacy and comfort. These rooms or spaces may be adjacent to but shall be separate from toilet rooms and shall be kept clean.

Note: This section shall not apply to change rooms and storage facilities regulated by the Occupational Safety and Health Standards Board.

(B) Suitable resting facilities shall be provided in an area separate from the toilet rooms and shall be available to employees during work hours.

14. Seats

(A) All working employees shall be provided with suitable seats when the nature of the work reasonably permits the use of seats.

(B) When employees are not engaged in the active duties of their employment and the nature of the work requires standing, an adequate number of suitable seats shall be placed in reasonable proximity to the work area and employees shall be permitted to use such seats when it does not interfere with the performance of their duties.

15. Temperature

(A) The temperature maintained in each work area shall provide reasonable comfort consistent with industry-wide standards for the nature of the process and the work performed.

(B) If excessive heat or humidity is created by the work process, the employer shall take all feasible means to reduce such excessive heat or humidity to a degree providing reasonable comfort. Where the nature of the employment requires a temperature of less than 60° F., a heated room shall be provided to which employees may retire for warmth, and such room shall be maintained at not less than 68°.

(C) A temperature of not less than 68° shall be maintained in the toilet rooms, resting rooms, and change rooms during hours of use.

(D) Federal and State energy guidelines shall prevail over any conflicting provision of this section.

16. Elevators.
Adequate elevator, escalator or similar service consistent with industry-wide standards for the nature of the process and the work performed shall be provided when employees are employed four floors or more above or below ground level.

17. Exemptions.
If, in the opinion of the Division after due investigation, it is found that the enforcement of any provision contained in Section 7, Records; Section 12, Rest Periods; Section 13, Change Rooms and Resting Facilities; Section 14, Seats; Section 15, Temperature; or Section 16, Elevators, would not materially affect the welfare or comfort of employees and would work an undue hardship on the employer, exemption may be made at the discretion of the Division. Such exemptions shall be in writing to be effective and may be revoked after reasonable notice is given in writing. Application for exemption shall be made by the employer or by the employee and/or the employee's representative to the Division in writing. A copy of the application shall be posted at the place of employment at the time the application is filed with the Division.

18. Filing Reports.
(See California Labor Code, Section 1174(a))

19. Inspection.
(See California Labor Code, Section 1174)

20. Penalties.
(See California Labor Code, Section 1199)

(A) In addition to any other civil penalties provided by law, any employer or any other person acting on behalf of the employer who violates, or causes to be violated, the provisions of this order, shall be subject to the civil penalty of:

(1) Initial Violation—$50.00 for each underpaid employee for each pay period during which the employee was underpaid in addition to the amount which is sufficient to recover unpaid wages.

(2) Subsequent Violations—$100.00 for each underpaid employee for each pay period during which the employee was underpaid in addition to an amount which is sufficient to recover unpaid wages.

(3) The affected employee shall receive payment of all wages recovered.

(B) The Labor Commissioner may also issue citations pursuant to California Labor Code Section 1197.1 for non-payment of wages for overtime work in violation of this order.

21. Separability.
If the application of any provision of this order, or any section, subsection, subdivision, sentence, clause, phrase, word, or portion of this order should be held invalid or unconstitutional or unauthorized or prohibited by statute, the remaining provisions thereof shall not be affected thereby, but shall continue to be given full force and effect as if the part so held invalid or unconstitutional had not been included herein.

22. Posting of Order.
Every employer shall keep a copy of this order posted in an area frequented by employees where it may be easily read during the workday. Where the location of work or other conditions make this impractical, every employer shall keep a copy of this order and make it available to every employee upon request.

¹ Pursuant to Labor Code section 515.5, subdivision (a)(4), the Division of Labor Statistics and Research, Department of Industrial Relations, has adjusted the minimum hourly rate of pay specified in this subdivision to be $49.77, effective January 1, 2007. This hourly rate of pay is adjusted on October 1 of each year to be effective on January 1, of the following year, and may be obtained at www.dir.ca.gov/IWC or by mail from the Department of Industrial Relations.

Publisher's Notes

See Rawson v. Tosco Refining Co. (1991) 57 Cal.App.4th 1520, 67 Cal.Rptr.2d 790 (regulation permitting reduced overtime wage if collectively bargained for did not constitute impermissible intrusion into collective bargaining process so as to be preempted by National Labor Relations Act (29 U.S.C.A. §§ 151 et seq.).

See Skyline Homes, Inc. v. Department of Industrial Relations (1985) 165 Cal.App.3d 239, 246, 211 Cal.Rptr. 792, 795, disapproved on other grounds by Tidewater

Marine Western, Inc. v. Bradshaw (1996) 14 Cal.4th 557, 927 P.2d 296, 59 Cal.Rptr.2d 186 (validity of interpretation of wage order adopted by the DLSE which prohibits the use of the fluctuating workweek method of computing overtime compensation).

See Industrial Welfare Com. v. Superior Court (1980) 27 Cal.3d 690, 613 P.2d 579, 166 Cal.Rptr. 331 (validity of 1980 order).

Research References

See notes following listing of Wage Orders.

Please Post With This Side Showing
OFFICIAL NOTICE
Effective January 1, 2001 as amended
Sections 4(A) and 10(C) amended and republished by the Department of Industrial Relations, effective January 1, 2007, pursuant to AB 1835, Chapter 230, Statutes of 2006
INDUSTRIAL WELFARE COMMISSION
ORDER NO. 2–2001
REGULATING
WAGES, HOURS AND WORKING CONDITIONS IN THE
PERSONAL SERVICE INDUSTRY

TAKE NOTICE: To employers and representatives of persons working in industries and occupations in the State of California:

The Department of Industrial Relations amends and republishes the minimum wage and meals and lodging credits in the Industrial Welfare Commission's Orders as a result of legislation enacted (AB 1835, Ch. 230, Stats of 2006, adding sections 1182.12 and 1182.13 to the California Labor Code.) The amendments and republishing make no other changes to the IWC's Orders.

1. Applicability of Order. This order shall apply to all persons employed in the personal service industry whether paid on a time, piece rate, commission, or other basis, except that:

(A) Provisions of Sections 3 through 12 of this order shall not apply to persons employed in administrative, executive, or professional capacities. The following requirements shall apply in determining whether an employee's duties meet the test to qualify for an exemption from those sections:

(1) <u>Executive Exemption</u>. A person employed in an executive capacity means any employee:

(a) Whose duties and responsibilities involve the management of the enterprise in which he/she is employed or of a customarily recognized department or subdivision thereof; and

(b) Who customarily and regularly directs the work of two or more other employees therein; and

(c) Who has the authority to hire or fire other employees or whose suggestions and recommendations as to the hiring or firing and as to the advancement and promotion or any other change of status of other employees will be given particular weight; and

(d) Who customarily and regularly exercises discretion and independent judgment; and

(e) Who is primarily engaged in duties which meet the test of the exemption. The activities constituting exempt work and non-exempt work shall be construed in the same manner as such items are construed in the following regulations under the Fair Labor Standards Act effective as of the date of this order: 29 C.F.R. Sections 541.102, 541.104–111, and 541.115–116. Exempt work shall include, for example, all work that is directly and closely related to exempt work and work which is properly viewed as a means for carrying out exempt functions. The work actually performed by the employee during the course of the workweek must, first and foremost, be examined and the amount of time the employee spends on such work, together with the employer's realistic expectations and the realistic requirements of the job, shall be considered in determining whether the employee satisfies this requirement.

(f) Such an employee must also earn a monthly salary equivalent to no less than two (2) times the state minimum wage for full-time employment. Full–time employment is defined in Labor Code Section 515(c) as 40 hours per week.

(2) <u>Administrative Exemption</u>. A person employed in an administrative capacity means any employee:

(a) Whose duties and responsibilities involve either:

(i) The performance of office or non-manual work directly related to management policies or general business operations of his/her employer or his/her employer's customers; or

(ii) The performance of functions in the administration of a school system, or educational establishment or institution, or of a department or subdivision thereof, in work directly related to the academic instruction or training carried on therein; and

(b) Who customarily and regularly exercises discretion and independent judgment; and

(c) Who regularly and directly assists a proprietor, or an employee employed in a bona fide executive or administrative capacity (as such terms are defined for purposes of this section); or

(d) Who performs under only general supervision work along specialized or technical lines requiring special training, experience, or knowledge; or

(e) Who executes under only general supervision special assignments and tasks; and

(f) Who is primarily engaged in duties that meet the test of the exemption. The activities constituting exempt work and non-exempt work shall be construed in the same manner as such terms are construed in the following regulations under the Fair Labor Standards Act effective as of the date of this order: 29 C.F.R. Sections 541.201–205, 541.207–208, 541.210, and 541.215. Exempt work shall include, for example, all work that is directly and closely related to exempt work and work which is properly viewed as a means for carrying out exempt functions. The work actually performed by the employee during the course of the workweek must, first and foremost, be examined and the amount of time the employee spends on such work, together with the employer's realistic expectations and the realistic requirements of the job, shall be considered in determining whether the employee satisfies this requirement.

(g) Such employee must also earn a monthly salary equivalent to no less than two (2) times the state minimum wage for full-time employment. Full-time employment is defined in Labor Code Section 515(c) as 40 hours per week.

(3) Professional Exemption. A person employed in a professional capacity means any employee who meets *all* of the following requirements:

(a) Who is licensed or certified by the State of California and is primarily engaged in the practice of one of the following recognized professions: law, medicine, dentistry, optometry, architecture, engineering, teaching, or accounting; or

(b) Who is primarily engaged in an occupation commonly recognized as a learned or artistic profession. For the purposes of this subsection, "learned or artistic profession" means an employee who is primarily engaged in the performance of:

(i) Work requiring knowledge of an advanced type in a field or science or learning customarily acquired by a prolonged course of specialized intellectual instruction and study, as distinguished from a general academic education and from an apprenticeship, and from training in the performance of routine mental, manual, or physical

processes, or work that is an essential part of or necessarily incident to any of the above work; or

(ii) Work that is original and creative in character in a recognized field of artistic endeavor (as opposed to work which can be produced by a person endowed with general manual or intellectual ability and training), and the result of which depends primarily on the invention, imagination, or talent of the employee or work that is an essential part of or necessarily incident to any of the above work; and

(iii) Whose work is predominantly intellectual and varied in character (as opposed to routine mental, manual, mechanical, or physical work) and is of such character that the output produced or the result accomplished cannot be standardized in relation to a given period of time.

(c) Who customarily and regularly exercises discretion and independent judgment in the performance of duties set forth in subparagraphs (a) and (b).

(d) Who earns a monthly salary equivalent to no less than two (2) times the state minimum wage for full-time employment. Full-time employment is defined in Labor Code Section 515 (c) as 40 hours per week.

(e) Subparagraph (b) above is intended to be construed in accordance with the following provisions of federal law as they existed as of the date of this wage order: 29 C.F.R. Sections 541.207, 541.301(a)–(d), 541.302, 541.306, 541.307, 541.308, and 541.310.

(f) Notwithstanding the provisions of this subparagraph, pharmacists employed to engage in the practice of pharmacy, and registered nurses employed to engage in the practice of nursing, shall not be considered exempt professional employees, nor shall they be considered exempt from coverage for the purposes of this subparagraph unless they individually meet the criteria established for exemption as executive or administrative employees.

(g) Subparagraph (f) above shall not apply to the following advanced practice nurses:

(i) Certified nurse midwives who are primarily engaged in performing duties for which certification is required pursuant to Article 2.5 (commencing with Section 2746) of Chapter 6 of Division 2 of the Business and Professions Code.

(ii) Certified nurse anesthetists who are primarily engaged in performing duties for which certification is required pursuant to Article 7 (commencing with Section 2825) of Chapter 6 of Division 2 of the Business and Professions Code.

(iii) Certified nurse practitioners who are primarily engaged in performing duties for which certification is required pursuant to Article 8 (commencing with Section 2834) of Chapter 6 of Division 2 of the Business and Professions Code.

(iv) Nothing in this subparagraph shall exempt the occupations set forth in clauses (i), (ii), and (iii) from meeting the requirements of subsection 1(A)(3)(a)–(d) above.

(h) Except, as provided in subparagraph (i), an employee in the computer software field who is paid on an hourly basis shall be exempt, if *all* of the following apply:

(i) The employee is primarily engaged in work that is intellectual or creative and requires the exercise of discretion and independent judgment.

(ii) The employee is primarily engaged in duties that consist of one or more of the following:

-The application of systems analysis techniques and procedures, including consulting with users, to determine hardware, software, or system functional specifications.

-The design, development, documentation, analysis, creation, testing, or modification of computer systems or programs, including prototypes, based on and related to user or system design specifications.

-The documentation, testing, creation, or modification of computer programs related to the design of software or hardware for computer operating systems.

(iii) The employee is highly skilled and is proficient in the theoretical and practical application of highly specialized information to computer systems analysis, programming, and software engineering. A job title shall not be determinative of the applicability of this exemption.

(iv) The employee's hourly rate of pay is not less than forty-one dollars ($41.00). The Division of Labor Statistics and Research shall adjust this pay rate on October 1 of each year to be effective on January 1 of the following year by an amount equal to the percentage increase in the California Consumer Price Index for Urban Wage Earners and Clerical Workers.[1]

(i) The exemption provided in subparagraph (h) does not apply to an employee if any of the following apply:

(i) The employee is a trainee or employee in an entry-level position who is learning to become proficient in the theoretical and practical application of highly specialized information to computer systems analysis, programming, and software engineering.

(ii) The employee is in a computer-related occupation but has not attained the level of skill and expertise necessary to work independently and without close supervision.

(iii) The employee is engaged in the operation of computers or in the manufacture, repair, or maintenance of computer hardware and related equipment.

(iv) The employee is an engineer, drafter, machinist, or other professional whose work is highly dependent upon or facilitated by the use of computers and computer software programs and who is skilled in computer-aided design software, including CAD/CAM, but who is not in a computer systems analysis or programming occupation.

(v) The employee is a writer engaged in writing material, including box labels, product descriptions, documentation, promotional material, setup and installation instructions, and other similar written information, either for print or for on screen media or who writes or provides content material intended to be read by customers, subscribers, or visitors to computer-related media such as the World Wide Web or CD–ROMs.

(vi) The employee is engaged in *any* of the activities set forth in subparagraph (h) for the purpose of creating imagery for effects used in the motion picture, television, or theatrical industry.

(B) Except as provided in Sections 1, 2, 4, 10, and 20, the provisions of this order shall not apply to any employees directly employed by the State or any political subdivision thereof, including any city, county, or special district.

(C) The provisions of this order shall not apply to outside salespersons.

(D) The provisions of this order shall not apply to any individual who is the parent, spouse, child, or legally adopted child of the employer.

(E) The provisions of this order shall not apply to any individual participating in a national service program, such as Ameri–Corps, carried out using assistance provided under Section 12571 of Title 42 of the United States Code. (See Stats. 2000, ch. 365, amending Labor Code Section 1171.)

2. Definitions

(A) An "alternative workweek schedule" means any regularly scheduled workweek requiring an employee to work more than eight (8) hours in a 24–hour period.

(B) "Commission" means the Industrial Welfare Commission of the State of California.

(C) "Division" means the Division of Labor Standards Enforcement of the State of California.

(D) "Employ" means to engage, suffer, or permit to work.

(E) "Employee" means any person employed by an employer, and includes any lessee who is charged rent, or who pays rent for a chair, booth, or space; and

(1) Who does not use his/her own funds to purchase requisite supplies; and

(2) Who does not maintain an appointment book separate and distinct from that of the establishment in which the space is located; and

(3) Who does not have a business license where applicable.

(F) "Employer" means any person as defined in Section 18 of the Labor Code, who directly or indirectly, or through an agent or any other person, employs or exercises control over the wages, hours, or working conditions of any person.

(G) "Hours worked" means the time during which an employee is subject to the control of an employer, and includes all the time the employee is suffered or permitted to work, whether or not required to do so.

(H) "Minor" means, for the purpose of this order, any person under the age of 18 years.

(I) "Outside salesperson" means any person, 18 years of age or over, who customarily and regularly works more than half the working time away from the employer's place of business selling tangible or intangible items or obtaining orders or contracts for products, services or use of facilities.

(J) "Personal Service Industry" means any industry, business, or establishment operated for the purpose of rendering, directly or indirectly, any service, operation, or process used or useful in the care, cleansing, or beautification of the body, skin, nails, or hair, or in the enhancement of personal appearance or health, including but not limited to beauty salons, schools of beauty culture offering beauty care to the public for a fee, barber shops, bath and massage parlors, physical conditioning, weight control salons, health clubs, and mortuaries.

(K) "Primarily" as used in Section 1, Applicability, means more than one-half the employee's work time.

(L) "Shift" means designated hours of work by an employee, with a designated beginning time and ending time.

(M) "Split shift" means a work schedule, which is interrupted by non-paid non-working periods established by the employer, other than bona fide rest or meal periods.

(N) "Teaching" means, for the purpose of Section 1 of this order, the profession of teaching under a certificate from the Commission for Teacher Preparation and Licensing or teaching in an accredited college or university.

(O) "Wages" includes all amounts for labor performed by employees of every description, whether the amount is fixed or ascertained by the standard of time, task, piece, commission basis, or other method of calculation.

(P) "Workday" and "day" mean any consecutive 24–hour period beginning at the same time each calendar day.

(Q) "Workweek" and "week" mean any seven (7) consecutive days, starting with the same calendar day each week. "Workweek" is a fixed and regularly recurring period of 168 hours, seven (7) consecutive 24–hour periods.

3. Hours and Days of Work

(A) *Daily Overtime—General Provisions*

(1) The following overtime provisions are applicable to employees 18 years of age or over and to employees 16 or 17 years of age who are not required by law to attend school and are not otherwise prohibited by law from engaging in the subject work. Such employees shall not be employed more than eight (8) hours in any workday or more than 40 hours in any workweek unless the employee receives one and one-half (1 ½) times such employee's regular rate of pay for all hours worked over 40 hours in the workweek. Eight (8) hours of labor constitutes a day's work. Employment beyond eight (8) hours in any workday or more than six (6) days in any workweek is permissible provided the employee is compensated for such overtime at not less than:

(a) One and one-half (1 ½) times the employee's regular rate of pay for all hours worked in excess of eight (8) hours up to and including 12 hours in any workday, and for the first eight (8) hours worked on the seventh (7th) consecutive day of work in a workweek; and

(b) Double the employee's regular rate of pay for all hours worked in excess of 12 hours in any workday and for all hours worked in excess of eight (8) hours on the seventh (7th) consecutive day of work in a workweek.

(2) The overtime rate of compensation required to be paid to a nonexempt full-time salaried employee shall be computed by using the employee's regular hourly salary as one-fortieth (1/40) of the employee's weekly salary.

(B) *Alternative Workweek*

(1) No employer shall be deemed to have violated the daily overtime provisions by instituting, pursuant to the election procedures set forth in this wage order, a regularly scheduled alternative workweek schedule of not more than ten (10) hours per day within a 40 hour workweek without the payment of an overtime rate of compensation. All work performed in any workday beyond the schedule established by the agreement up to 12 hours a day or beyond 40 hours per week shall be paid at one and one-half (1 ½) times the employee's regular rate of pay. All work performed in excess of 12 hours per day and any work in excess of eight (8) hours on those days worked beyond the regularly scheduled number of workdays established by the alternative workweek agreement shall be paid at double the employee's regular rate of pay. Any alternative workweek agreement adopted pursuant to this section shall provide for not less than four (4) hours of work in any shift. Nothing in this section shall prohibit an employer, at the request of the employee, to substitute one day of work for another day of the same length in the shift provided by the alternative workweek agreement on an occasional basis to meet the personal needs of the employee without the payment of overtime. No hours paid at either one and one-half (1 ½) or double the regular rate of pay shall be included in determining when 40 hours have been worked for the purpose of computing overtime compensation.

(2) Any agreement adopted pursuant to this section shall provide not less than two consecutive days off within a workweek.

(3) If an employer whose employees have adopted an alternative workweek agreement permitted by this order requires an employee to work fewer hours than those that are regularly scheduled by the agreement, the employer shall pay the employee overtime compensation at a rate of one and one-half (1 ½) times the employee's regular rate of pay for all hours worked in excess of eight (8) hours, and double the employee's regular rate of pay for

1399

all hours worked in excess of 12 hours for the day the employee is required to work the reduced hours.

(4) An employer shall not reduce an employee's regular rate of hourly pay as a result of the adoption, repeal or nullification of an alternative workweek schedule.

(5) An employer shall explore any available reasonable alternative means of accommodating the religious belief or observance of an affected employee that conflicts with an adopted alternative workweek schedule, in the manner provided by subdivision (j) of Section 12940 of the Government Code.

(6) An employer shall make a reasonable effort to find a work schedule not to exceed eight (8) hours in a workday, in order to accommodate any affected employee who was eligible to vote in an election authorized by this section and who is unable to work the alternative workweek schedule established as the result of that election.

(7) An employer shall be permitted, but not required, to provide a work schedule not to exceed eight (8) hours in a workday to accommodate any employee who is hired after the date of the election and who is unable to work the alternative workweek schedule established by the election.

(8) Arrangements adopted in a secret ballot election held pursuant to this order prior to 1998, or under the rules in effect prior to 1998, and before the performance of the work, shall remain valid after July 1, 2000 provided that the results of the election are reported by the employer to the Division of Labor Statistics and Research by January 1, 2001, in accordance with the requirements of subsection (C) below (Election Procedures). If an employee was voluntarily working an alternative workweek schedule of not more than ten (10) hours a day as of July 1, 1999, that alternative workweek schedule was based on an individual agreement made after January 1, 1998 between the employee and employer, and the employee submitted, and the employer approved, a written request on or before May 30, 2000 to continue the agreement, the employee may continue to work that alternative workweek schedule without payment of an overtime rate of compensation for the hours provided in the agreement. The employee may revoke his/her voluntary authorization to continue such a schedule with 30 days written notice to the employer. New arrangements can only be entered into pursuant to the provisions of this section.

(C) *Election Procedures*

Election procedures for the adoption and repeal of alternative workweek schedules require the following:

(1) Each proposal for an alternative workweek schedule shall be in the form of a written agreement proposed by the employer. The proposed agreement must designate a regularly scheduled alternative workweek in which the specified number of work days and work hours are regularly recurring. The actual days worked within that alternative workweek schedule need not be specified.

The employer may propose a single work schedule that would become the standard schedule for workers in the work unit, or a menu of work schedule options, from which each employee in the unit would be entitled to choose. If the employer proposes a menu of work schedule options, the employee may, with the approval of the employer, move from one menu option to another.

(2) In order to be valid, the proposed alternative workweek schedule must be adopted in a secret ballot election, before the performance of work, by at least a two-thirds (2/03) vote of the affected employees in the work unit. The election shall be held during regular working hours at the employees' work site. For purposes of this subsection, "affected employees in the work unit" may include all employees in a readily identifiable work unit, such as a division, a department, a job classification, a shift, a separate physical location, or a recognized subdivision of any such work unit. A work unit may consist of an individual employee as long as the criteria for an identifiable work unit in this subsection are met.

(3) Prior to the secret ballot vote, any employer who proposed to institute an alternative workweek schedule shall have made a disclosure in writing to the affected employees, including the effects of the proposed arrangement on the employees' wages, hours, and benefits. Such a disclosure shall include meeting(s), duly noticed, held at least 14 days prior to voting, for the specific purpose of discussing the effects of the alternative workweek schedule. An employer shall provide that disclosure in a non–English language, as well as in English, if at least five (5) percent of the affected employees primarily speak that non–English language. The employer shall mail the written disclosure to employees who do not attend the meeting. Failure to comply with this paragraph shall make the election null and void.

(4) Any election to establish or repeal an alternative workweek schedule shall be held at the work site of the affected employees. The employer shall bear the costs of conducting any election held pursuant to this section. Upon a complaint by an affected employee, and after an investigation by the labor commissioner, the labor commissioner may require the employer to select a neutral third party to conduct the election.

(5) Any type of alternative workweek schedule that is authorized by the Labor Code may be repealed by the affected employees. Upon a petition of one-third (1/03) of the affected employees, a new secret ballot election shall be held and a two-thirds (2/03) vote of the affected employees shall be required to reverse the alternative workweek schedule. The election to repeal the alternative workweek schedule shall be held not more than 30 days after the petition is submitted to the employer, except that the election shall be held not less than 12 months after the date that the same group of employees voted in an election held to adopt or repeal an alternative workweek schedule. The election shall take place during regular working hours at the employees' work site. If the alternative workweek schedule is revoked, the employer

shall comply within 60 days. Upon proper showing of undue hardship, the Division of Labor Standards Enforcement may grant an extension of time for compliance.

(6) Only secret ballots may be cast by affected employees in the work unit at any election held pursuant to this section. The results of any election conducted pursuant to this section shall be reported by the employer to the Division of Labor Statistics and Research within 30 days after the results are final, and the report of election results shall be a public document. The report shall include the final tally of the vote, the size of the unit, and the nature of the business of the employer.

(7) Employees affected by a change in the work hours resulting from the adoption of an alternative workweek schedule may not be required to work those new work hours for at least 30 days after the announcement of the final results of the election.

(8) Employers shall not intimidate or coerce employees to vote either in support of or in opposition to a proposed alternative workweek. No employees shall be discharged or discriminated against for expressing opinions concerning the alternative workweek election or for opposing or supporting its adoption or repeal. However, nothing in this section shall prohibit an employer from expressing his/her position concerning that alternative workweek to the affected employees. A violation of this paragraph shall be subject to Labor Code Section 98 *et seq*.

(D) One and one-half (1 ½) times a minor's regular rate of pay shall be paid for all work over 40 hours in any workweek except minors 16 or 17 years old who are not required by law to attend school and may therefore be employed for the same hours as an adult are subject to subsection (A) or (B) and (C) above.

(**Violations of Child Labor Laws** are subject to civil penalties of from $500 to $10,000 as well as to criminal penalties. Refer to California Labor Code Sections 1285 to 1312 and 1390 to 1399 for additional restrictions on the employment of minors and for descriptions of criminal and civil penalties for violation of the child labor laws. Employers should ask school districts about any required work permits.)

(E) An employee may be employed on seven (7) workdays in one workweek when the total hours of employment during such workweek do not exceed 30 and the total hours of employment in any one workday thereof do not exceed six (6).

(F) The provisions of Labor Code Sections 551 and 552 regarding one (1) day's rest in seven (7) shall not be construed to prevent an accumulation of days of rest when the nature of the employment reasonably requires the employee to work seven (7) or more consecutive days; provided, however, that in each calendar month, the employee shall receive the equivalent of one (1) day's rest in seven (7).

(G) If a meal period occurs on a shift beginning or ending at or between the hours of 10 p.m. and 6 a.m., facilities shall be available for securing hot food and drink or for heating food or drink, and a suitable sheltered place shall be provided in which to consume such food or drink.

(H) Except as provided in subsections (D) and (F), this section shall not apply to any employee covered by a valid collective bargaining agreement if the agreement expressly provides for the wages, hours of work, and working conditions of the employees, and if the agreement provides premium wage rates for all overtime hours worked and a regular hourly rate of pay for those employees of not less than 30 percent more than the state minimum wage.

(I) Notwithstanding subsection (H) above, where the employer and a labor organization representing employees of the employer have entered into a valid collective bargaining agreement pertaining to the hours of work of the employees, the requirement regarding the equivalent of one (1) day's rest in seven (7) (see subsection (F) above) shall apply, unless the agreement expressly provides otherwise.

(J) The provisions of this section are not applicable to employees whose hours of service are regulated by:

(1) The United States Department of Transportation Code of Federal Regulations, Title 49, Sections 395.1 to 395.13, Hours of Service of Drivers; or

(2) Title 13 of the California Code of Regulations, subchapter 6.5, Section 1200 and the following sections, regulating hours of drivers.

(K) If an employer approves a written request of an employee to make up work time that is or would be lost as a result of a personal obligation of the employee, the hours of that makeup work time, if performed in the same workweek in which the work time was lost, may not be counted toward computing the total number of hours worked in a day for purposes of the overtime requirements, except for hours in excess of 11 hours of work in one (1) day or 40 hours of work in one (1) workweek. If an employee knows in advance that he/she will be requesting makeup time for a personal obligation that will recur at a fixed time over a succession of weeks, the employee may request to make up work time for up to four (4) weeks in advance; provided, however, that the makeup work must be performed in the same week that the work time was lost. An employee shall provide a signed written request for each occasion that the employee makes a request to make up work time pursuant to this subsection. While an employer may inform an employee of this makeup time option, the employer is prohibited from encouraging or otherwise soliciting an employee to request the employer's approval to take personal time off and make up the work hours within the same workweek pursuant to this subsection.

4. Minimum Wages

(A) Every employer shall pay to each employee wages not less than seven dollars and fifty cents ($7.50) per hour for all hours worked, effective January 1, 2007, and not less than eight dollars ($8.00) per hour for all hours worked, effective January 1, 2008, except:

Learners. Employees during their first 160 hours of employment in occupations in which they have no previous similar or related experience, may be paid not less than 85 percent of the minimum wage rounded to the nearest nickel.

(B) Every employer shall pay to each employee, on the established payday for the period involved, not less than the applicable minimum wage for all hours worked in the payroll period, whether the remuneration is measured by time, piece, commission, or otherwise.

(C) When an employee works a split shift, one (1) hour's pay at the minimum wage shall be paid in addition to the minimum wage for that workday, except when the employee resides at the place of employment.

(D) The provisions of this section shall not apply to apprentices regularly indentured under the State Division of Apprenticeship Standards.

5. Reporting Time Pay

(A) Each workday an employee is required to report for work and does report, but is not put to work or is furnished less than half said employee's usual or scheduled day's work, the employee shall be paid for half the usual or scheduled day's work, but in no event for less than two (2) hours nor more than four (4) hours, at the employee's regular rate of pay, which shall not be less than the minimum wage.

(B) If an employee is required to report for work a second time in any one workday and is furnished less than two (2) hours of work on the second reporting, said employee shall be paid for two (2) hours at the employee's regular rate of pay, which shall not be less than the minimum wage.

(C) The foregoing reporting time pay provisions are not applicable when:

(1) Operations cannot commence or continue due to threats to employees or property; or when recommended by civil authorities; or

(2) Public utilities fail to supply electricity, water, or gas, or there is a failure in the public utilities, or sewer system; or

(3) An Act of God or other cause not within the employer's control causes the interruption of work.

(D) This section shall not apply to an employee on paid standby status who is called to perform assigned work at a time other than the employee's scheduled reporting time.

6. Licenses for Disabled Workers

(A) A license may be issued by the Division authorizing employment of a person whose earning capacity is impaired by physical disability or mental deficiency at less than the minimum wage. Such licenses shall be granted only upon joint application of employer and employee and employee's representative if any.

(B) A special license may be issued to a nonprofit organization such as a sheltered workshop or rehabilitation facility fixing special minimum rates to enable the employment of such persons without requiring individual licenses of such employees.

(C) All such licenses and special licenses shall be renewed on a yearly basis or more frequently at the discretion of the Division.

(See California Labor Code, Sections 1191 and 1191.5)

7. Records

(A) Every employer shall keep accurate information with respect to each employee including the following:

(1) Full name, home address, occupation and social security number.

(2) Birth date, if under 18 years, and designation as a minor.

(3) Time records showing when the employee begins and ends each work period. Meal periods, split shift intervals and total daily hours worked shall also be recorded. Meal periods during which operations cease and authorized rest periods need not be recorded.

(4) Total wages paid each payroll period, including value of board, lodging, or other compensation actually furnished to the employee.

(5) Total hours worked in the payroll period and applicable rates of pay. This information shall be made readily available to the employee upon reasonable request.

(6) When a piece rate or incentive plan is in operation, piece rates or an explanation of the incentive plan formula shall be provided to employees. The employer shall maintain an accurate production record.

(B) Every employer shall semimonthly or at the time of each payment of wages furnish each employee, either as a detachable part of the check, draft, or voucher paying the employee's wages, or separately, an itemized statement in writing showing: (1) all deductions; (2) the inclusive dates of the period for which the employee is paid; (3) the name of the employee or the employee's social security number; and (4) the name of the employer, provided all deductions made on written orders of the employee may be aggregated and shown as one item.

(C) All required records shall be in the English language and in ink or other indelible form, properly dated, showing month, day and year, and shall be kept on file by the employer for at least three years at the place of employment or at a central location within the State of California. An employee's records shall be available for inspection by the employee upon reasonable request.

(D) Clocks shall be provided in all major work areas or within reasonable distance thereto insofar as practicable.

8. Cash Shortage and Breakage.
No employer shall make any deduction from the wage or require any reimbursement from an employee for any cash shortage, breakage, or loss of equipment, unless it can be shown

that the shortage, breakage, or loss is caused by a dishonest or willful act, or by the gross negligence of the employee.

9. Uniforms and Equipment

(A) When uniforms are required by the employer to be worn by the employee as a condition of employment, such uniforms shall be provided and maintained by the employer. The term "uniform" includes wearing apparel and accessories of distinctive design or color.

Note: This section shall not apply to protective apparel regulated by the Occupational Safety and Health Standards Board.

(B) When tools or equipment are required by the employer or are necessary to the performance of a job, such tools and equipment shall be provided and maintained by the employer, except that an employee whose wages are at least two (2) times the minimum wage provided herein may be required to provide and maintain hand tools and equipment customarily required by the trade or craft. Notwithstanding any other provision of this section, employees in beauty salons, schools of beauty culture offering beauty care to the public for a fee, and barber shops may be required to furnish their own manicure implements, curling irons, rollers, clips, haircutting scissors, combs, blowers, razors, and eyebrow tweezers. This subsection (B) shall not apply to apprentices regularly indentured under the State Division of Apprenticeship Standards.

Note: This section shall not apply to protective equipment and safety devices on tools regulated by the Occupational Safety and Health Standards Board.

(C) A reasonable deposit may be required as security for the return of the items furnished by the employer under provisions of subsections (A) and (B) of this section upon issuance of a receipt to the employee for such deposit. Such deposits shall be made pursuant to Section 400 and following of the Labor Code or an employer with the prior written authorization of the employee may deduct from the employee's last check the cost of an item furnished pursuant to (A) and (B) above in the event said item is not returned. No deduction shall be made at any time for normal wear and tear. The employee upon completion of the job shall return all items furnished by the employer.

10. Meals and Lodging

(A) "Meal" means an adequate, well-balanced serving of a variety of wholesome, nutritious foods.

(B) "Lodging" means living accommodations available to the employee for full-time occupancy which are adequate, decent, and sanitary according to usual and customary standards. Employees shall not be required to share a bed.

(C) Meals or lodging may not be credited against the minimum wage without a voluntary written agreement between the employer and the employee. When credit for meals or lodging is used to meet part of the employer's minimum wage obligation, the amounts so credited may not be more than the following:

Effective	January 1, 2007	January 1, 2008
Lodging:		
Room occupied alone	$35.27 per week	$37.63 per week
Room shared	$29.11 per week	$31.06 per week
Apartment—two–thirds (2/03) of the ordinary rental value, and in no event more than	$423.51 per month	$451.89 per month
Where a couple are both employed by the employer, two-thirds (2/03) of the ordinary rental value, and in no event more than	$626.49 per month	$668.46 per month
Meals:		
Breakfast	$2.72	$2.90
Lunch	$3.72	$3.97
Dinner	$5.00	$5.34

(D) Meals evaluated as part of the minimum wage must be bona fide meals consistent with the employee's work shift. Deductions shall not be made for meals not received or lodging not used.

(E) If, as a condition of employment, the employee must live at the place of employment or occupy quarters owned or under the control of the employer, then the employer may not charge rent in excess of the values listed herein.

11. Meal Periods

(A) No employer shall employ any person for a work period of more than five (5) hours without a meal period of not less than 30 minutes, except that when a work period of not more than six (6) hours will complete the day's work the meal period may be waived by mutual consent of the employer and the employee.

(B) An employer may not employ an employee for a work period of more than ten (10) hours per day without providing the employee with a second meal period of not less than 30 minutes, except that if the total hours worked is no more than 12 hours, the second meal period may be waived by mutual consent of the employer and the employee only if the first meal period was not waived.

(C) Unless the employee is relieved of all duty during a 30 minute meal period, the meal period shall be considered an "on duty" meal period and counted as time worked. An "on duty" meal period shall be permitted only when the nature of the work prevents an employee from being relieved of all duty and when by written agreement between the parties an on-the-job paid meal period is agreed to. The written agreement shall state that the employee may, in writing, revoke the agreement at any time.

(D) If an employer fails to provide an employee a meal period in accordance with the applicable provisions of this order, the employer shall pay the employee one (1) hour of pay at the employee's regular rate of compensation for each workday that the meal period is not provided.

(E) In all places of employment where employees are required to eat on the premises, a suitable place for that purpose shall be designated.

12. Rest Periods

(A) Every employer shall authorize and permit all employees to take rest periods, which insofar as practicable shall be in the middle of each work period. The authorized rest period time shall be based on the total hours worked daily at the rate of ten (10) minutes net rest time per four (4) hours or major fraction thereof. However, a rest period need not be authorized for employees whose total daily work time is less than three and one-half (3 ½) hours. Authorized rest period time shall be counted as hours worked for which there shall be no deduction from wages.

(B) If an employer fails to provide an employee a rest period in accordance with the applicable provisions of this order, the employer shall pay the employee one (1) hour of pay at the employee's regular rate of compensation for each workday that the rest period is not provided.

13. Change Rooms and Resting Facilities

(A) Employers shall provide suitable lockers, closets, or equivalent for the safekeeping of employees' outer clothing during working hours, and when required, for their work clothing during non-working hours. When the occupation requires a change of clothing, change rooms or equivalent space shall be provided in order that employees may change their clothing in reasonable privacy and comfort. These rooms or spaces may be adjacent to but shall be separate from toilet rooms and shall be kept clean.

Note: This section shall not apply to change rooms and storage facilities regulated by the Occupational Safety and Health Standards Board.

(B) Suitable resting facilities shall be provided in an area separate from the toilet rooms and shall be available to employees during work hours.

14. Seats

(A) All working employees shall be provided with suitable seats when the nature of the work reasonably permits the use of seats.

(B) When employees are not engaged in the active duties of their employment and the nature of the work requires standing, an adequate number of suitable seats shall be placed in reasonable proximity to the work area and employees shall be permitted to use such seats when it does not interfere with the performance of their duties.

15. Temperature

(A) The temperature maintained in each work area shall provide reasonable comfort consistent with industry-wide standards for the nature of the process and the work performed.

(B) If excessive heat or humidity is created by the work process, the employer shall take all feasible means to reduce such excessive heat or humidity to a degree providing reasonable comfort. Where the nature of the employment requires a temperature of less than 60° F, a heated room shall be provided to which employees may retire for warmth, and such room shall be maintained at not less than 68°.

(C) A temperature of not less than 68° shall be maintained in the toilet rooms, resting rooms, and change rooms during hours of use.

(D) Federal and State energy guidelines shall prevail over any conflicting provision of this section.

16. Elevators. Adequate elevator, escalator or similar service consistent with industry-wide standards for the nature of the process and the work performed shall be provided when employees are employed four floors or more above or below ground level.

17. Exemptions. If, in the opinion of the Division after due investigation, it is found that the enforcement of any provision contained in Section 7, Records; Section 12, Rest Periods; Section 13, Change Rooms and Resting Facilities; Section 14, Seats; Section 15, Temperature; or Section 16, Elevators, would not materially affect the welfare or comfort of employees and would work an undue hardship on the employer, exemption may be made at the discretion of the Division. Such exemptions shall be in writing to be effective and may be revoked after reasonable notice is given in writing. Application for exemption shall be made by the employer or by the employee and/or the employee's representative to the Division in writing. A copy of the application shall be posted at the place of employment at the time the application is filed with the Division.

18. Filing Reports. (See California Labor Code, Section 1174(a))

19. Inspection. (See California Labor Code, Section 1174)

20. Penalties. (See California Labor Code, Section 1199)

(A) In addition to any other civil penalties provided by law, any employer or any other person acting on behalf of the employer who violates, or causes to be violated, the provisions of this order, shall be subject to the civil penalty of:

(1) Initial Violation—$50.00 for each underpaid employee for each pay period during which the employee was underpaid in addition to the amount which is sufficient to recover unpaid wages.

(2) Subsequent Violations—$100.00 for each underpaid employee for each pay period during which the employee was underpaid in addition to an amount which is sufficient to recover unpaid wages.

(3) The affected employee shall receive payment of all wages recovered.

(B) The labor commissioner may also issue citations pursuant to California Labor Code Section 1197.1 for non-payment of wages for overtime work in violation of this order.

21. Separability. If the application of any provision of this order, or any section, subsection, subdivision, sentence, clause, phrase, word, or portion of this order should be held invalid or unconstitutional or unauthorized or prohibited by statute, the remaining provisions thereof shall not be affected thereby, but shall continue to be given full force and effect as if the part so held invalid or unconstitutional had not been included herein.

22. Posting of Order. Every employer shall keep a copy of this order posted in an area frequented by employees where it may be easily read during the workday. Where the location of work or other conditions make this impractical, every employer shall keep a copy of this order and make it available to every employee upon request.

¹ Pursuant to Labor Code section 515.5, subdivision (a)(4), the Division of Labor Statistics and Research, Department of Industrial Relations, has adjusted the minimum hourly rate of pay specified in this subdivision to be $49.77, effective January 1, 2007. This hourly rate of pay is adjusted on October 1 of each year to be effective on January 1, of the following year, and may be obtained at www.dir.ca.gov/IWC or by mail from the Department of Industrial Relations.

Publisher's Notes

Research References

See notes following listing of Wage Orders.

Please Post With This Side Showing
OFFICIAL NOTICE
Effective January 1, 2001 as amended
Sections 4(A) and 10(C) amended and republished by the Department of Industrial Relations, effective January 1, 2007, pursuant to AB 1835, Chapter 230, Statutes of 2006
INDUSTRIAL WELFARE COMMISSION
ORDER NO. 3–2001
REGULATING
WAGES, HOURS AND WORKING CONDITIONS IN THE
CANNING, FREEZING, AND PRESERVING
INDUSTRY

TAKE NOTICE: To employers and representatives of persons working in industries and occupations in the State of California:

The Department of Industrial Relations amends and republishes the minimum wage and meals and lodging credits in the Industrial Welfare Commission's Orders as a result of legislation enacted (AB 1835, Ch. 230, Stats of 2006, adding sections 1182.12 and 1182.13 to the California Labor Code.) The amendments and republishing make no other changes to the IWC's Orders.

1. Applicability of Order. This order shall apply to all persons employed in the canning, freezing, and preserving industry whether paid on a time, piece rate, commission, or other basis, except that:

(A) Provisions of Sections 3 through 12 of this order shall not apply to persons employed in administrative, executive, or professional capacities. The following requirements shall apply in determining whether an employee's duties meet the test to qualify for an exemption from those sections:

(1) Executive Exemption. A person employed in an executive capacity means any employee:

(a) Whose duties and responsibilities involve the management of the enterprise in which he/she is employed or of a customarily recognized department or subdivision thereof; and

(b) Who customarily and regularly directs the work of two or more other employees therein; and

(c) Who has the authority to hire or fire other employees or whose suggestions and recommendations as to the hiring or firing and as to the advancement and promotion or any other change of status of other employees will be given particular weight; and

(d) Who customarily and regularly exercises discretion and independent judgment; and

(e) Who is primarily engaged in duties which meet the test of the exemption. The activities constituting exempt work and non-exempt work shall be construed in the same manner as such items are construed in the following regulations under the Fair Labor Standards Act effective as of the date of this order: 29 C.F.R. Sections 541.102, 541.104–111, and 541.115–116. Exempt work shall include, for example, all work that is directly and closely related to exempt work and work which is properly viewed as a means for carrying out exempt functions. The work actually performed by the employee during the course of the workweek must, first and foremost, be examined and the amount of time the employee spends on such work, together with the employer's realistic expectations and the realistic requirements of the job, shall be considered in determining whether the employee satisfies this requirement.

(f) Such an employee must also earn a monthly salary equivalent to no less than two (2) times the state minimum wage for full-time employment. Full–time employment is defined in Labor Code Section 515(c) as 40 hours per week.

(2) Administrative Exemption. A person employed in an administrative capacity means any employee:

(a) Whose duties and responsibilities involve either:

1405

(i) The performance of office or non-manual work directly related to management policies or general business operations of his/her employer or his/her employer's customers; or

(ii) The performance of functions in the administration of a school system, or educational establishment or institution, or of a department or subdivision thereof, in work directly related to the academic instruction or training carried on therein; and

(b) Who customarily and regularly exercises discretion and independent judgment; and

(c) Who regularly and directly assists a proprietor, or an employee employed in a bona fide executive or administrative capacity (as such terms are defined for purposes of this section); or

(d) Who performs under only general supervision work along specialized or technical lines requiring special training, experience, or knowledge; or

(e) Who executes under only general supervision special assignments and tasks; and

(f) Who is primarily engaged in duties that meet the test of the exemption. The activities constituting exempt work and non-exempt work shall be construed in the same manner as such terms are construed in the following regulations under the Fair Labor Standards Act effective as of the date of this order: 29 C.F.R. Sections 541.201–205, 541.207–208, 541.210, and 541.215. Exempt work shall include, for example, all work that is directly and closely related to exempt work and work which is properly viewed as a means for carrying out exempt functions. The work actually performed by the employee during the course of the workweek must, first and foremost, be examined and the amount of time the employee spends on such work, together with the employer's realistic expectations and the realistic requirements of the job, shall be considered in determining whether the employee satisfies this requirement.

(g) Such employee must also earn a monthly salary equivalent to no less than two (2) times the state minimum wage for full-time employment. Full–time employment is defined in Labor Code Section 515(c) as 40 hours per week.

(3) Professional Exemption. A person employed in a professional capacity means any employee who meets all of the following requirements:

(a) Who is licensed or certified by the State of California and is primarily engaged in the practice of one of the following recognized professions: law, medicine, dentistry, optometry, architecture, engineering, teaching, or accounting; or

(b) Who is primarily engaged in an occupation commonly recognized as a learned or artistic profession. For the purposes of this subsection, "learned or artistic profession" means an employee who is primarily engaged in the performance of:

(i) Work requiring knowledge of an advanced type in a field or science or learning customarily acquired by a prolonged course of specialized intellectual instruction and study, as distinguished from a general academic education and from an apprenticeship, and from training in the performance of routine mental, manual, or physical processes, or work that is an essential part of or necessarily incident to any of the above work; or

(ii) Work that is original and creative in character in a recognized field of artistic endeavor (as opposed to work which can be produced by a person endowed with general manual or intellectual ability and training), and the result of which depends primarily on the invention, imagination, or talent of the employee or work that is an essential part of or necessarily incident to any of the above work; and

(iii) Whose work is predominantly intellectual and varied in character (as opposed to routine mental, manual, mechanical, or physical work) and is of such character that the output produced or the result accomplished cannot be standardized in relation to a given period of time.

(c) Who customarily and regularly exercises discretion and independent judgment in the performance of duties set forth in subparagraphs (a) and (b).

(d) Who earns a monthly salary equivalent to no less than two (2) times the state minimum wage for full-time employment. Full–time employment is defined in Labor Code Section 515 (c) as 40 hours per week.

(e) Subparagraph (b) above is intended to be construed in accordance with the following provisions of federal law as they existed as of the date of this wage order: 29 C.F.R. Sections 541.207, 541.301(a)–(d), 541.302, 541.306, 541.307, 541.308, and 541.310.

(f) Notwithstanding the provisions of this subparagraph, pharmacists employed to engage in the practice of pharmacy, and registered nurses employed to engage in the practice of nursing, shall not be considered exempt professional employees, nor shall they be considered exempt from coverage for the purposes of this subparagraph unless they individually meet the criteria established for exemption as executive or administrative employees.

(g) Subparagraph (f) above shall not apply to the following advanced practice nurses:

(i) Certified nurse midwives who are primarily engaged in performing duties for which certification is required pursuant to Article 2.5 (commencing with Section 2746) of Chapter 6 of Division 2 of the Business and Professions Code.

(ii) Certified nurse anesthetists who are primarily engaged in performing duties for which certification is required pursuant to Article 7 (commencing with Section 2825) of Chapter 6 of Division 2 of the Business and Professions Code.

(iii) Certified nurse practitioners who are primarily engaged in performing duties for which certification is required pursuant to Article 8 (commencing with Section 2834) of Chapter 6 of Division 2 of the Business and Professions Code.

(iv) Nothing in this subparagraph shall exempt the occupations set forth in clauses (i), (ii), and (iii) from meeting the requirements of subsection 1(A)(3)(a)–(d) above.

(h) Except, as provided in subparagraph (i), an employee in the computer software field who is paid on an hourly basis shall be exempt, if *all* of the following apply:

(i) The employee is primarily engaged in work that is intellectual or creative and requires the exercise of discretion and independent judgment.

(ii) The employee is primarily engaged in duties that consist of one or more of the following:

-The application of systems analysis techniques and procedures, including consulting with users, to determine hardware, software, or system functional specifications.

-The design, development, documentation, analysis, creation, testing, or modification of computer systems or programs, including prototypes, based on and related to user or system design specifications.

-The documentation, testing, creation, or modification of computer programs related to the design of software or hardware for computer operating systems.

(iii) The employee is highly skilled and is proficient in the theoretical and practical application of highly specialized information to computer systems analysis, programming, and software engineering. A job title shall not be determinative of the applicability of this exemption.

(iv) The employee's hourly rate of pay is not less than forty-one dollars ($41.00). The Division of Labor Statistics and Research shall adjust this pay rate on October 1 of each year to be effective on January 1 of the following year by an amount equal to the percentage increase in the California Consumer Price Index for Urban Wage Earners and Clerical Workers.[1]

(i) The exemption provided in subparagraph (h) does not apply to an employee if *any* of the following apply:

(i) The employee is a trainee or employee in an entry-level position who is learning to become proficient in the theoretical and practical application of highly specialized information to computer systems analysis, programming, and software engineering.

(ii) The employee is in a computer-related occupation but has not attained the level of skill and expertise necessary to work independently and without close supervision.

(iii) The employee is engaged in the operation of computers or in the manufacture, repair, or maintenance of computer hardware and related equipment.

(iv) The employee is an engineer, drafter, machinist, or other professional whose work is highly dependent upon or facilitated by the use of computers and computer software programs and who is skilled in computer-aided design software, including CAD/CAM, but who is not in a computer systems analysis or programming occupation.

(v) The employee is a writer engaged in writing material, including box labels, product descriptions, documentation, promotional material, setup and installation instructions, and other similar written information, either for print or for on screen media or who writes or provides content material intended to be read by customers, subscribers, or visitors to computer-related media such as the World Wide Web or CD–ROMs.

(vi) The employee is engaged in *any* of the activities set forth in subparagraph (h) for the purpose of creating imagery for effects used in the motion picture, television, or theatrical industry.

(B) Except as provided in Sections 1, 2, 4, 10, and 20, the provisions of this order shall not apply to any employees directly employed by the State or any political subdivision thereof, including any city, county, or special district.

(C) The provisions of this order shall not apply to outside salespersons.

(D) The provisions of this order shall not apply to *any* individual who is the parent, spouse, child, or legally adopted child of the employer.

(E) The provisions of this order shall not apply to any individual participating in a national service program, such as Ameri–Corps, carried out using assistance provided under Section 12571 of Title 42 of the United States Code. (See Stats. 2000, ch. 365, amending Labor Code Section 1171.)

2. Definitions.

(A) An "alternative workweek schedule" means any regularly scheduled workweek requiring an employee to work more than eight (8) hours in a 24–hour period.

(B) "Canning, Freezing, and Preserving Industry" means any industry, business, or establishment operated for the purpose of canning soups, or of cooking, canning, curing, freezing, pickling, salting, bottling, preserving, or otherwise processing any fruits or vegetables, seafood, meat, poultry or rabbit product, when the purpose of such processing is the preservation of the product and includes all operations incidental thereto.

(C) "Commission" means the Industrial Welfare Commission of the State of California.

(D) "Division" means the Division of Labor Standards Enforcement of the State of California.

(E) "Employ" means to engage, suffer, or permit to work.

(F) "Employee" means any person employed by an employer.

(G) "Employer" means any person as defined in Section 18 of the Labor Code, who directly or indirectly, or through an agent or any other person, employs or exercises control over the wages, hours, or working conditions of any person.

(H) "Hours worked" means the time during which an employee is subject to the control of an employer, and includes all the time the employee is suffered or permitted to work, whether or not required to do so.

(I) "Minor" means, for the purpose of this order, any person under the age of 18 years.

(J) "Outside salesperson" means any person, 18 years of age or over, who customarily and regularly works more than half the working time away from the employer's place of business selling tangible or intangible items or obtaining orders or contracts for products, services or use of facilities.

(K) "Primarily" as used in Section 1, Applicability, means more than one-half the employee's work time.

(L) "Shift" means designated hours of work by an employee, with a designated beginning time and ending time.

(M) "Split shift" means a work schedule, which is interrupted by non-paid non-working periods established by the employer, other than bona fide rest or meal periods.

(N) "Teaching" means, for the purpose of Section 1 of this order, the profession of teaching under a certificate from the Commission for Teacher Preparation and Licensing or teaching in an accredited college or university.

(O) "Wages" includes all amounts for labor performed by employees of every description, whether the amount is fixed or ascertained by the standard of time, task, piece, commission basis, or other method of calculation.

(P) "Workday" and "day" mean any consecutive 24–hour period beginning at the same time each calendar day.

(Q) "Workweek" and "week" mean any seven (7) consecutive days, starting with the same calendar day each week. "Workweek" is a fixed and regularly recurring period of 168 hours, seven (7) consecutive 24–hour periods.

3. Hours and Days of Work

(A) *Daily Overtime—General Provisions*

(1) The following overtime provisions are applicable to employees 18 years of age or over and to employees 16 or 17 years of age who are not required by law to attend school and are not otherwise prohibited by law from engaging in the subject work. Such employees shall not be employed more than eight (8) hours in any workday or more than 40 hours in any workweek unless the employee receives one and one-half (1 $\frac{1}{2}$) times such employee's regular rate of pay for all hours worked over 40 hours in the workweek. Eight (8) hours of labor constitutes a day's work. Employment beyond eight (8) hours in any workday or more than six (6) days in any workweek is permissible under the following conditions:

(2) An employee may work up to a maximum of 72 hours in seven (7) consecutive days after which the

employee shall have a 24–hour period off duty. Overtime hours shall be compensated at:

(a) One and one-half (1 $\frac{1}{2}$) times the employee's regular rate of pay for all hours worked in excess of eight (8) hours up to and including 12 hours in any workday, and for the first eight (8) hours worked on the seventh (7th) consecutive day of work in a workweek; and

(b) Double the employee's regular rate of pay for all hours worked in excess of 12 hours in any workday and for all hours worked in excess of eight (8) hours on the seventh (7th) consecutive day of work in a workweek.

(3) The overtime rate of compensation required to be paid to a nonexempt full-time salaried employee shall be computed by using the employee's regular hourly salary as one-fortieth (1/40) of the employee's weekly salary.

(B) *Alternative Workweek*

(1) No employer shall be deemed to have violated the daily overtime provisions by instituting, pursuant to the election procedures set forth in this wage order, a regularly scheduled alternative workweek schedule of not more than ten (10) hours per day within a 40 hour workweek without the payment of an overtime rate of compensation. All work performed in any workday beyond the schedule established by the agreement up to 12 hours a day or beyond 40 hours per week shall be paid at one and one-half (1 $\frac{1}{2}$) times the employee's regular rate of pay. All work performed in excess of 12 hours per day and any work in excess of eight (8) hours on those days worked beyond the regularly scheduled number of workdays established by the alternative workweek agreement shall be paid at double the employee's regular rate of pay. Any alternative workweek agreement adopted pursuant to this section shall provide for not less than four (4) hours of work in any shift. Nothing in this section shall prohibit an employer, at the request of the employee, to substitute one day of work for another day of the same length in the shift provided by the alternative workweek agreement on an occasional basis to meet the personal needs of the employee without the payment of overtime. No hours paid at either one and one-half (1 $\frac{1}{2}$) or double the regular rate of pay shall be included in determining when 40 hours have been worked for the purpose of computing overtime compensation.

(2) Any agreement adopted pursuant to this section shall provide not less than two consecutive days off within a workweek.

(3) If an employer whose employees have adopted an alternative workweek agreement permitted by this order requires an employee to work fewer hours than those that are regularly scheduled by the agreement, the employer shall pay the employee overtime compensation at a rate of one and one-half (1 $\frac{1}{2}$) times the employee's regular rate of pay for all hours worked in excess of eight (8) hours, and double the employee's regular rate of pay for all hours worked in excess of 12 hours for the day the employee is required to work the reduced hours.

(4) An employer shall not reduce an employee's regular rate of hourly pay as a result of the adoption, repeal or nullification of an alternative workweek schedule.

(5) An employer shall explore any available reasonable alternative means of accommodating the religious belief or observance of an affected employee that conflicts with an adopted alternative workweek schedule, in the manner provided by subdivision (j) of Section 12940 of the Government Code.

(6) An employer shall make a reasonable effort to find a work schedule not to exceed eight (8) hours in a workday, in order to accommodate any affected employee who was eligible to vote in an election authorized by this section and who is unable to work the alternative workweek schedule established as the result of that election.

(7) An employer shall be permitted, but not required, to provide a work schedule not to exceed eight (8) hours in a work-day to accommodate any employee who is hired after the date of the election and who is unable to work the alternative workweek schedule established by the election.

(8) Arrangements adopted in a secret ballot election held pursuant to this order prior to 1998, or under the rules in effect prior to 1998, and before the performance of the work, shall remain valid after July 1, 2000 provided that the results of the election are reported by the employer to the Division of Labor Statistics and Research by January 1, 2001, in accordance with the requirements of subsection (C) below (Election Procedures). If an employee was voluntarily working an alternative workweek schedule of not more than ten (10) hours a day as of July 1, 1999, that alternative workweek schedule was based on an individual agreement made after January 1, 1998 between the employee and employer, and the employee submitted, and the employer approved, a written request on or before May 30, 2000 to continue the agreement, the employee may continue to work that alternative workweek schedule without payment of an overtime rate of compensation for the hours provided in the agreement. The employee may revoke his/her voluntary authorization to continue such a schedule with 30 days written notice to the employer. New arrangements can only be entered into pursuant to the provisions of this section.

(C) *Election Procedures*

Election procedures for the adoption and repeal of alternative workweek schedules require the following:

(1) Each proposal for an alternative workweek schedule shall be in the form of a written agreement proposed by the employer. The proposed agreement must designate a regularly scheduled alternative workweek in which the specified number of work days and work hours are regularly recurring. The actual days worked within that alternative workweek schedule need not be specified. The employer may propose a single work schedule that would become the standard schedule for workers in the work unit, or a menu of work schedule options, from which each employee in the unit would be entitled to choose. If the employer proposes a menu of work schedule options, the employee may, with the approval of the employer, move from one menu option to another.

(2) In order to be valid, the proposed alternative workweek schedule must be adopted in a secret ballot election, before the performance of work, by at least a two-thirds (2/03) vote of the affected employees in the work unit. The election shall be held during regular working hours at the employees' work site. For purposes of this subsection, "affected employees in the work unit" may include all employees in a readily identifiable work unit, such as a division, a department, a job classification, a shift, a separate physical location, or a recognized subdivision of any such work unit. A work unit may consist of an individual employee as long as the criteria for an identifiable work unit in this subsection are met.

(3) Prior to the secret ballot vote, any employer who proposed to institute an alternative workweek schedule shall have made a disclosure in writing to the affected employees, including the effects of the proposed arrangement on the employees' wages, hours, and benefits. Such a disclosure shall include meeting(s), duly noticed, held at least 14 days prior to voting, for the specific purpose of discussing the effects of the alternative workweek schedule. An employer shall provide that disclosure in a non–English language, as well as in English, if at least five (5) percent of the affected employees primarily speak that non–English language. The employer shall mail the written disclosure to employees who do not attend the meeting. Failure to comply with this paragraph shall make the election null and void.

(4) Any election to establish or repeal an alternative workweek schedule shall be held at the work site of the affected employees. The employer shall bear the costs of conducting any election held pursuant to this section. Upon a complaint by an affected employee, and after an investigation by the labor commissioner, the labor commissioner may require the employer to select a neutral third party to conduct the election.

(5) Any type of alternative workweek schedule that is authorized by the Labor Code may be repealed by the affected employees. Upon a petition of one-third (1/03) of the affected employees, a new secret ballot election shall be held and a two-thirds (2/03) vote of the affected employees shall be required to reverse the alternative workweek schedule. The election to repeal the alternative workweek schedule shall be held not more than 30 days after the petition is submitted to the employer, except that the election shall be held not less than 12 months after the date that the same group of employees voted in an election held to adopt or repeal an alternative workweek schedule. The election shall take place during regular working hours at the employees' work site. If the alternative workweek schedule is revoked, the employer shall comply within 60 days. Upon proper showing of

undue hardship, the Division of Labor Standards Enforcement may grant an extension of time for compliance.

(6) Only secret ballots may be cast by affected employees in the work unit at any election held pursuant to this section. The results of any election conducted pursuant to this section shall be reported by the employer to the Division of Labor Statistics and Research within 30 days after the results are final, and the report of election results shall be a public document. The report shall include the final tally of the vote, the size of the unit, and the nature of the business of the employer.

(7) Employees affected by a change in the work hours resulting from the adoption of an alternative workweek schedule may not be required to work those new work hours for at least 30 days after the announcement of the final results of the election.

(8) Employers shall not intimidate or coerce employees to vote either in support of or in opposition to a proposed alternative workweek. No employees shall be discharged or discriminated against for expressing opinions concerning the alternative workweek election or for opposing or supporting its adoption or repeal. However, nothing in this section shall prohibit an employer from expressing his/her position concerning that alternative workweek to the affected employees. A violation of this paragraph shall be subject to Labor Code Section 98 *et seq*.

(D) One and one-half (1 ½) times a minor's regular rate of pay shall be paid for all work over 40 hours in any workweek except minors 16 or 17 years old who are not required by law to attend school and may therefore be employed for the same hours as an adult are subject to subsection (A) or (B) and (C) above.

(**Violations of Child Labor Laws** are subject to civil penalties of from $500 to $10,000 as well as to criminal penalties. Refer to California Labor Code Sections 1285 to 1312 and 1390 to 1399 for additional restrictions on the employment of minors and for descriptions of criminal and civil penalties for violation of the child labor laws. Employers should ask school districts about any required work permits.)

(E) An employee may be employed on seven (7) workdays in one workweek when the total hours of employment during such workweek do not exceed 30 and the total hours of employment in any one workday thereof do not exceed six (6).

(F) If during any workday an employer declares a work recess of one-half (1/02) hour or more, other than a meal period, and the employer notifies the employees of the time to report back for work and permits them to leave the premises, such recess need not be treated as hours worked provided that there shall not be more than two (2) such recess periods within one shift and the total duration does not exceed two (2) hours. Work stoppages of less than one-half (1/02) hour may not be deducted from hours worked.

(G) If a meal period occurs on a shift beginning or ending at or between the hours of 10 p.m. and 6 a.m., facilities shall be available for securing hot food and drink or for heating food or drink, and a suitable sheltered place shall be provided in which to consume such food or drink.

(H) The provisions of Labor Code Sections 551 and 552 regarding one (1) day's rest in seven (7) shall not be construed to prevent an accumulation of days of rest when the nature of the employment reasonably requires the employee to work seven (7) or more consecutive days; provided, however, that in each calendar month, the employee shall receive the equivalent of one (1) day's rest in seven (7).

(I) The provisions of this section are not applicable to employees whose hours of service are regulated by:

(1) The United States Department of Transportation Code of Federal Regulations, Title 49, Sections 395.1 to 395.13, Hours of Service of Drivers; or

(2) Title 13 of the California Code of Regulations, subchapter 6.5, Section 1200 and the following sections, regulating hours of drivers.

(J) Except as provided in subsections (D) and (H), this section shall not apply to any employee covered by a valid collective bargaining agreement if the agreement expressly provides for the wages, hours of work, and working conditions of the employees, and if the agreement provides premium wage rates for all overtime hours worked and a regular hourly rate of pay for those employees of not less than 30 percent more than the state minimum wage.

(K) Notwithstanding subsection (J) above, where the employer and a labor organization representing employees of the employer have entered into a valid collective bargaining agreement pertaining to the hours of work of the employees, the requirement regarding the equivalent of one (1) day's rest in seven (7) (see subsection (H) above) shall apply, unless the agreement expressly provides otherwise.

(L) If an employer approves a written request of an employee to make up work time that is or would be lost as a result of a personal obligation of the employee, the hours of that makeup work time, if performed in the same workweek in which the work time was lost, may not be counted toward computing the total number of hours worked in a day for purposes of the overtime requirements, except for hours in excess of 11 hours of work in one (1) day or 40 hours of work in one (1) workweek. If an employee knows in advance that he/she will be requesting makeup time for a personal obligation that will recur at a fixed time over a succession of weeks, the employee may request to make up work time for up to four (4) weeks in advance; provided, however, that the makeup work must be performed in the same week that the work time was lost. An employee shall provide a signed written request for each occasion that the employee makes a request to make up work time pursuant to this subsection. While an employer may inform an employee of this makeup time option, the employer is prohibited from encouraging or otherwise soliciting an employee to request the employer's approval to take personal time off and make up the work hours within the same workweek pursuant to this subsection.

4. Minimum Wages

(A) Every employer shall pay to each employee wages not less than seven dollars and fifty cents ($7.50) per hour for all hours worked, effective January 1, 2007, and not less than eight dollars ($8.00) per hour for all hours worked, effective January 1, 2008, except:

Learners. Employees during their first 160 hours of employment in occupations in which they have no previous similar or related experience, may be paid not less than 85 percent of the minimum wage rounded to the nearest nickel.

(B) Every employer shall pay to each employee, on the established payday for the period involved, not less than the applicable minimum wage for all hours worked in the payroll period, whether the remuneration is measured by time, piece, commission, or otherwise.

(C) When an employee works a split shift, one (1) hour's pay at the minimum wage shall be paid in addition to the minimum wage for that workday, except when the employee resides at the place of employment.

(D) The provisions of this section shall not apply to apprentices regularly indentured under the State Division of Apprenticeship Standards.

5. Reporting Time Pay

(A) Each workday an employee is required to report for work and does report, but is not put to work or is furnished less than half said employee's usual or scheduled day's work, the employee shall be paid for half the usual or scheduled day's work, but in no event for less than two (2) hours nor more than four (4) hours, at the employee's regular rate of pay, which shall not be less than the minimum wage.

(B) If an employee is required to report for work a second time in any one workday and is furnished less than two (2) hours of work on the second reporting, said employee shall be paid for two (2) hours at the employee's regular rate of pay, which shall not be less than the minimum wage.

(C) The foregoing reporting time pay provisions are not applicable when:

(1) Operations cannot commence or continue due to threats to employees or property; or when recommended by civil authorities; or

(2) Public utilities fail to supply electricity, water, or gas, or there is a failure in the public utilities, or sewer system; or

(3) The interruption of work is caused by an Act of God or other cause not within the employer's control.

(D) This section shall not apply to an employee on paid standby status who is called to perform assigned work at a time other than the employee's scheduled reporting time.

6. Licenses for Disabled Workers

(A) A license may be issued by the Division authorizing employment of a person whose earning capacity is impaired by physical disability or mental deficiency at less than the minimum wage. Such licenses shall be granted only upon joint application of employer and employee and employee's representative if any.

(B) A special license may be issued to a nonprofit organization such as a sheltered workshop or rehabilitation facility fixing special minimum rates to enable the employment of such persons without requiring individual licenses of such employees.

(C) All such licenses and special licenses shall be renewed on a yearly basis or more frequently at the discretion of the Division.

(See California Labor Code, Sections 1191 and 1191.5)

7. Records

(A) Every employer shall keep accurate information with respect to each employee including the following:

(1) Full name, home address, occupation and social security number.

(2) Birth date, if under 18 years, and designation as a minor.

(3) Time records showing when the employee begins and ends each work period. Meal periods, split shift intervals and total daily hours worked shall also be recorded. Meal periods during which operations cease and authorized rest periods need not be recorded.

(4) Total wages paid each payroll period, including value of board, lodging, or other compensation actually furnished to the employee.

(5) Total hours worked in the payroll period and applicable rates of pay. This information shall be made readily available to the employee upon reasonable request.

(6) When a piece rate or incentive plan is in operation, piece rates or an explanation of the incentive plan formula shall be provided to employees. An accurate production record shall be maintained by the employer.

(B) Every employer shall semimonthly or at the time of each payment of wages furnish each employee, either as a detachable part of the check, draft, or voucher paying the employee's wages, or separately, an itemized statement in writing showing: (1) all deductions; (2) the inclusive dates of the period for which the employee is paid; (3) the name of the employee or the employee's social security number; and (4) the name of the employer, provided all deductions made on written orders of the employee may be aggregated and shown as one item.

(C) All required records shall be in the English language and in ink or other indelible form, properly dated, showing month, day and year, and shall be kept on file by the employer for at least three years at the place of employment or at a central location within the State of California. An employee's records shall be available for inspection by the employee upon reasonable request.

(D) Clocks shall be provided in all major work areas or within reasonable distance thereto insofar as practicable.

8. Cash Shortage and Breakage. No employer shall make any deduction from the wage or require any reimbursement from an employee for any cash shortage, breakage, or loss of equipment, unless it can be shown that the shortage, breakage, or loss is caused by a dishonest or willful act, or by the gross negligence of the employee.

9. Uniforms and Equipment

(A) When uniforms are required by the employer to be worn by the employee as a condition of employment, such uniforms shall be provided and maintained by the employer. The term "uniform" includes wearing apparel and accessories of distinctive design or color.

Note: This section shall not apply to protective apparel regulated by the Occupational Safety and Health Standards Board.

(B) When tools or equipment are required by the employer or are necessary to the performance of a job, such tools and equipment shall be provided and maintained by the employer, except that an employee whose wages are at least two (2) times the minimum wage provided herein may be required to provide and maintain hand tools and equipment customarily required by the trade or craft. This subsection (B) shall not apply to apprentices regularly indentured under the State Division of Apprenticeship Standards.

Note: This section shall not apply to protective equipment and safety devices on tools regulated by the Occupational Safety and Health Standards Board.

(C) A reasonable deposit may be required as security for the return of the items furnished by the employer under provisions of subsections (A) and (B) of this section upon issuance of a receipt to the employee for such deposit. Such deposits shall be made pursuant to Section 400 and following of the Labor Code or an employer with the prior written authorization of the employee may deduct from the employee's last check the cost of an item furnished pursuant to (A) and (B) above in the event said item is not returned. No deduction shall be made at any time for normal wear and tear. All items furnished by the employer shall be returned by the employee upon completion of the job.

10. Meals and Lodging

(A) "Meal" means an adequate, well-balanced serving of a variety of wholesome, nutritious foods.

(B) "Lodging" means living accommodations available to the employee for full-time occupancy which are adequate, decent, and sanitary according to usual and customary standards. Employees shall not be required to share a bed.

(C) Meals or lodging may not be credited against the minimum wage without a voluntary written agreement between the employer and the employee. When credit for meals or lodging is used to meet part of the employer's minimum wage obligation, the amounts so credited may not be more than the following:

Effective	January 1, 2007	January 1, 2008
Lodging:		
Room occupied alone	$35.27 per week	$37.63 per week
Room shared	$29.11 per week	$31.06 per week
Apartment—two–thirds (2/03) of the ordinary rental value, and in no event more than	$423.51 per month	$451.89 per month
Where a couple are both employed by the employer, two-thirds (2/03) of the ordinary rental value, and in no event more than	$626.49 per month	$668.46 per month
Meals:		
Breakfast	$2.72	$2.90
Lunch	$3.72	$3.97
Dinner	$5.00	$5.34

(D) Meals evaluated as part of the minimum wage must be bona fide meals consistent with the employee's work shift. Deductions shall not be made for meals not received or lodging not used.

(E) If, as a condition of employment, the employee must live at the place of employment or occupy quarters owned or under the control of the employer, then the employer may not charge rent in excess of the values listed herein.

11. Meal Periods

(A) No employer shall employ any person for a work period of more than five (5) hours without a meal period of not less than 30 minutes, except that when a work period of not more than six (6) hours will complete the day's work the meal period may be waived by mutual consent of the employer and the employee.

(B) An employer may not employ an employee for a work period of more than ten (10) hours per day without providing the employee with a second meal period of not less than 30 minutes, except that if the total hours worked is no more than 12 hours, the second meal period may be waived by mutual consent of the employer and the employee only if the first meal period was not waived.

(C) Unless the employee is relieved of all duty during a 30 minute meal period, the meal period shall be considered an "on duty" meal period and counted as time worked. An "on duty" meal period shall be permitted only when the nature of the work prevents an employee from being relieved of all duty and when by written agreement between the parties an on-the-job paid meal period is agreed to. The written agreement shall state that the employee may, in writing, revoke the agreement at any time.

(D) If an employer fails to provide an employee a meal period in accordance with the applicable provisions of this order, the employer shall pay the employee one (1) hour of pay at the employee's regular rate of compensation for each workday that the meal period is not provided.

(E) In all places of employment where employees are required to eat on the premises, a suitable place for that purpose shall be designated.

12. Rest Periods

(A) Every employer shall authorize and permit all employees to take rest periods, which insofar as practicable shall be in the middle of each work period. The authorized rest period time shall be based on the total hours worked daily at the rate of ten (10) minutes net rest time per four (4) hours or major fraction thereof. However, a rest period need not be authorized for employees whose total daily work time is less than three and one-half (3 1/2) hours. Authorized rest period time shall be counted as hours worked for which there shall be no deduction from wages.

(B) If an employer fails to provide an employee a rest period in accordance with the applicable provisions of this order, the employer shall pay the employee one (1) hour of pay at the employee's regular rate of compensation for each workday that the rest period is not provided.

13. Change Rooms and Resting Facilities

(A) Employers shall provide suitable lockers, closets, or equivalent for the safekeeping of employees' outer clothing during working hours, and when required, for their work clothing during non-working hours. When the occupation requires a change of clothing, change rooms or equivalent space shall be provided in order that employees may change their clothing in reasonable privacy and comfort. These rooms or spaces may be adjacent to but shall be separate from toilet rooms and shall be kept clean.

Note: This section shall not apply to change rooms and storage facilities regulated by the Occupational Safety and Health Standards Board.

(B) Suitable resting facilities shall be provided in an area separate from the toilet rooms and shall be available to employees during work hours.

14. Seats

(A) All working employees shall be provided with suitable seats when the nature of the work reasonably permits the use of seats.

(B) When employees are not engaged in the active duties of their employment and the nature of the work requires standing, an adequate number of suitable seats shall be placed in reasonable proximity to the work area and employees shall be permitted to use such seats when it does not interfere with the performance of their duties.

15. Temperature

(A) The temperature maintained in each work area shall provide reasonable comfort consistent with industry-wide standards for the nature of the process and the work performed.

(B) If excessive heat or humidity is created by the work process, the employer shall take all feasible means to reduce such excessive heat or humidity to a degree providing reasonable comfort. Where the nature of the employment requires a temperature of less than 60° F., a heated room shall be provided to which employees may retire for warmth, and such room shall be maintained at not less than 68°.

(C) A temperature of not less than 68° shall be maintained in the toilet rooms, resting rooms, and change rooms during hours of use.

(D) Federal and State energy guidelines shall prevail over any conflicting provision of this section.

16. Elevators. Adequate elevator, escalator or similar service consistent with industry-wide standards for the nature of the process and the work performed shall be provided when employees are employed four floors or more above or below ground level.

17. Exemptions. If, in the opinion of the Division after due investigation, it is found that the enforcement of any provision contained in Section 7, Records; Section 12, Rest Periods; Section 13, Change Rooms and Resting Facilities; Section 14, Seats; Section 15, Temperature; or Section 16, Elevators, would not materially affect the welfare or comfort of employees and would work an undue hardship on the employer, exemption may be made at the discretion of the Division. Such exemptions shall be in writing to be effective and may be revoked after reasonable notice is given in writing. Application for exemption shall be made by the employer or by the employee and/or the employee's representative to the Division in writing. A copy of the application shall be posted at the place of employment at the time the application is filed with the Division.

18. Filing Reports. (See California Labor Code, Section 1174(a))

19. Inspection. (See California Labor Code, Section 1174)

20. Penalties. (See California Labor Code, Section 1199)

(A) In addition to any other civil penalties provided by law, any employer or any other person acting on behalf of the employer who violates, or causes to be violated, the provisions of this order, shall be subject to the civil penalty of:

(1) Initial Violation—$50.00 for each underpaid employee for each pay period during which the employee was underpaid in addition to the amount which is sufficient to recover unpaid wages.

(2) Subsequent Violations—$100.00 for each underpaid employee for each pay period during which the

1413

employee was underpaid in addition to an amount which is sufficient to recover unpaid wages.

(3) The affected employee shall receive payment of all wages recovered.

(B) The labor commissioner may also issue citations pursuant to California Labor Code Section 1197.1 for non-payment of wages for overtime work in violation of this order.

21. Separability. If the application of any provision of this order, or any section, subsection, subdivision, sentence, clause, phrase, word, or portion of this order should be held invalid or unconstitutional or unauthorized or prohibited by statute, the remaining provisions thereof shall not be affected thereby, but shall continue to be given full force and effect as if the part so held invalid or unconstitutional had not been included herein.

22. Posting of Order. Every employer shall keep a copy of this order posted in an area frequented by employees where it may be easily read during the workday. Where the location of work or other condi-

tions make this impractical, every employer shall keep a copy of this order and make it available to every employee upon request.

[1] Pursuant to Labor Code section 515.5, subdivision (a)(4), the Division of Labor Statistics and Research, Department of Industrial Relations, has adjusted the minimum hourly rate of pay specified in this subdivision to be $49.77, effective January 1, 2007. This hourly rate of pay is adjusted on October 1 of each year to be effective on January 1, of the following year, and may be obtained at www.dir.ca.gov/IWC or by mail from the Department of Industrial Relations.

Publisher's Notes

See Industrial Welfare Com. v. Superior Court (1980) 27 Cal.3d 690, 613 P.2d 579, 166 Cal.Rptr. 331 (validity of 1980 order).

Research References

See notes following listing of Wage Orders.

Please Post With This Side Showing
OFFICIAL NOTICE
Effective January 1, 2001 as amended
Sections 4(A) and 10(C) amended and republished by the Department of Industrial Relations, effective January 1, 2007, pursuant to AB 1835, Chapter 230, Statutes of 2006
INDUSTRIAL WELFARE COMMISSION
ORDER NO. 4–2001
REGULATING
WAGES, HOURS AND WORKING CONDITIONS IN THE
PROFESSIONAL, TECHNICAL, CLERICAL,
MECHANICAL AND SIMILAR
OCCUPATIONS

TAKE NOTICE: To employers and representatives of persons working in industries and occupations in the State of California:

The Department of Industrial Relations amends and republishes the minimum wage and meals and lodging credits in the Industrial Welfare Commission's Orders as a result of legislation enacted (AB 1835, Ch. 230, Stats of 2006, adding sections 1182.12 and 1182.13 to the California Labor Code.) The amendments and republishing make no other changes to the IWC's Orders.

1. Applicability of Order. This order shall apply to all persons employed in professional, technical, clerical, mechanical, and similar occupations whether paid on a time, piece rate, commission, or other basis, except that:

(A) Provisions of Sections 3 through 12 shall not apply to persons employed in administrative, executive, or professional capacities. The following requirements shall apply in determining whether an employee's duties meet the test to qualify for an exemption from those sections:

(1) Executive Exemption. A person employed in an executive capacity means any employee:

(a) Whose duties and responsibilities involve the management of the enterprise in which he/she is employed or

of a customarily recognized department or subdivision thereof; and

(b) Who customarily and regularly directs the work of two or more other employees therein; and

(c) Who has the authority to hire or fire other employees or whose suggestions and recommendations as to the hiring or firing and as to the advancement and promotion or any other change of status of other employees will be given particular weight; and

(d) Who customarily and regularly exercises discretion and independent judgment; and

(e) Who is primarily engaged in duties which meet the test of the exemption. The activities constituting exempt work and non-exempt work shall be construed in the same manner as such items are construed in the following regulations under the Fair Labor Standards Act effective as of the date of this order: 29 C.F.R. Sections 541.102, 541.104–111, and 541.115–116. Exempt work shall include, for example, all work that is directly and closely related to exempt work and work which is properly viewed as a means for carrying out exempt functions. The work actually performed by the employee during the course of the workweek must, first and foremost, be examined and the amount of time the employee spends on such work, together with the employer's realistic expectations and the realistic requirements of the job, shall be considered in determining whether the employee satisfies this requirement.

(f) Such an employee must also earn a monthly salary equivalent to no less than two (2) times the state minimum wage for full-time employment. Full–time employment is defined in Labor Code Section 515(c) as 40 hours per week.

(2) <u>Administrative Exemption.</u> A person employed in an administrative capacity means any employee:

(a) Whose duties and responsibilities involve either:

(i) The performance of office or non-manual work directly related to management policies or general business operations of his/her employer or his/her employer's customers; or

(ii) The performance of functions in the administration of a school system, or educational establishment or institution, or of a department or subdivision thereof, in work directly related to the academic instruction or training carried on therein; and

(b) Who customarily and regularly exercises discretion and independent judgment; and

(c) Who regularly and directly assists a proprietor, or an employee employed in a bona fide executive or administrative capacity (as such terms are defined for purposes of this section); or

(d) Who performs under only general supervision work along specialized or technical lines requiring special training, experience, or knowledge; or

(e) Who executes under only general supervision special assignments and tasks; and

(f) Who is primarily engaged in duties that meet the test of the exemption. The activities constituting exempt work and non-exempt work shall be construed in the same manner as such terms are construed in the following regulations under the Fair Labor Standards Act effective as of the date of this order: 29 C.F.R. Sections 541.201–205, 541.207–208, 541.210, and 541.215. Exempt work shall include, for example, all work that is directly and closely related to exempt work and work which is properly viewed as a means for carrying out exempt functions. The work actually performed by the employee during the course of the workweek must, first and foremost, be examined and the amount of time the employee spends on such work, together with the employer's realistic expectations and the realistic requirements of the job, shall be considered in determining whether the employee satisfies this requirement.

(g) Such employee must also earn a monthly salary equivalent to no less than two (2) times the state minimum wage for full-time employment. Full–time employment is defined in Labor Code Section 515(c) as 40 hours per week.

(3) <u>Professional Exemption.</u> A person employed in a professional capacity means any employee who meets all of the following requirements:

(a) Who is licensed or certified by the State of California and is primarily engaged in the practice of one of the following recognized professions: law, medicine, dentistry, optometry, architecture, engineering, teaching, or accounting; or

(b) Who is primarily engaged in an occupation commonly recognized as a learned or artistic profession. For the purposes of this subsection, "learned or artistic profession" means an employee who is primarily engaged in the performance of:

(i) Work requiring knowledge of an advanced type in a field or science or learning customarily acquired by a prolonged course of specialized intellectual instruction and study, as distinguished from a general academic education and from an apprenticeship, and from training in the performance of routine mental, manual, or physical processes, or work that is an essential part of or necessarily incident to any of the above work; or

(ii) Work that is original and creative in character in a recognized field of artistic endeavor (as opposed to work which can be produced by a person endowed with general manual or intellectual ability and training), and the result of which depends primarily on the invention, imagination, or talent of the employee or work that is an essential part of or necessarily incident to any of the above work; and

(iii) Whose work is predominantly intellectual and varied in character (as opposed to routine mental, manual, mechanical, or physical work) and is of such character that the output produced or the result accomplished cannot be standardized in relation to a given period of time.

(c) Who customarily and regularly exercises discretion and independent judgment in the performance of duties set forth in subparagraphs (a) and (b).

(d) Who earns a monthly salary equivalent to no less than two (2) times the state minimum wage for full-time employment. Full–time employment is defined in Labor Code Section 515 (c) as 40 hours per week.

(e) Subparagraph (b) above is intended to be construed in accordance with the following provisions of federal law as they existed as of the date of this wage order: 29 C.F.R. Sections 541.207, 541.301(a)–(d), 541.302, 541.306, 541.307, 541.308, and 541.310.

(f) Notwithstanding the provisions of this subparagraph, pharmacists employed to engage in the practice of pharmacy, and registered nurses employed to engage in the practice of nursing, shall not be considered exempt professional employees, nor shall they be considered exempt from coverage for the purposes of this subparagraph unless they individually meet the criteria established for exemption as executive or administrative employees.

(g) Subparagraph (f) above shall not apply to the following advanced practice nurses:

(i) Certified nurse midwives who are primarily engaged in performing duties for which certification is required pursuant to Article 2.5 (commencing with Section 2746) of Chapter 6 of Division 2 of the Business and Professions Code.

(ii) Certified nurse anesthetists who are primarily engaged in performing duties for which certification is required pursuant to Article 7 (commencing with Section 2825) of Chapter 6 of Division 2 of the Business and Professions Code.

(iii) Certified nurse practitioners who are primarily engaged in performing duties for which certification is required pursuant to Article 8 (commencing with Section 2834) of Chapter 6 of Division 2 of the Business and Professions Code.

(iv) Nothing in this subparagraph shall exempt the occupations set forth in clauses (i), (ii), and (iii) from meeting the requirements of subsection 1(A)(3)(a)–(d) above.

(h) Except, as provided in subparagraph (i), an employee in the computer software field who is paid on an hourly basis shall be exempt, if *all* of the following apply:

(i) The employee is primarily engaged in work that is intellectual or creative and that requires the exercise of discretion and independent judgment.

(ii) The employee is primarily engaged in duties that consist of one or more of the following:

-The application of systems analysis techniques and procedures, including consulting with users, to determine hardware, software, or system functional specifications.

-The design, development, documentation, analysis, creation, testing, or modification of computer systems or programs, including prototypes, based on and related to user or system design specifications.

-The documentation, testing, creation, or modification of computer programs related to the design of software or hardware for computer operating systems.

(iii) The employee is highly skilled and is proficient in the theoretical and practical application of highly specialized information to computer systems analysis, programming, and software engineering. A job title shall not be determinative of the applicability of this exemption.

(iv) The employee's hourly rate of pay is not less than forty-one dollars ($41.00). The Division of Labor Statistics and Research shall adjust this pay rate on October 1 of each year to be effective on January 1 of the following year by an amount equal to the percentage increase in the California Consumer Price Index for Urban Wage Earners and Clerical Workers.[1]

(i) The exemption provided in subparagraph (h) does not apply to an employee if *any* of the following apply:

(i) The employee is a trainee or employee in an entry-level position who is learning to become proficient in the

theoretical and practical application of highly specialized information to computer systems analysis, programming, and software engineering.

(ii) The employee is in a computer-related occupation but has not attained the level of skill and expertise necessary to work independently and without close supervision.

(iii) The employee is engaged in the operation of computers or in the manufacture, repair, or maintenance of computer hardware and related equipment.

(iv) The employee is an engineer, drafter, machinist, or other professional whose work is highly dependent upon or facilitated by the use of computers and computer software programs and who is skilled in computer-aided design software, including CAD/CAM, but who is not in a computer systems analysis or programming occupation.

(v) The employee is a writer engaged in writing material, including box labels, product descriptions, documentation, promotional material, setup and installation instructions, and other similar written information, either for print or for on screen media or who writes or provides content material intended to be read by customers, subscribers, or visitors to computer-related media such as the World Wide Web or CD–ROMs.

(vi) The employee is engaged in *any* of the activities set forth in subparagraph (h) for the purpose of creating imagery for effects used in the motion picture, television, or theatrical industry.

(B) Except as provided in Sections 1, 2, 4, 10, and 20, the provisions of this order shall not apply to any employees directly employed by the State or any political subdivision thereof, including any city, county, or special district.

(C) The provisions of this order shall not apply to outside salespersons.

(D) The provisions of this order shall not apply to any individual who is the parent, spouse, child, or legally adopted child of the employer.

(E) The provisions of this order shall not apply to any individual participating in a national service program, such as AmeriCorps, carried out using assistance provided under Section 12571 of Title 42 of the United States Code. (See Stats. 2000, ch. 365, amending Labor Code Section 1171.)

2. Definitions

(A) An "alternative workweek schedule" means any regularly scheduled workweek requiring an employee to work more than eight (8) hours in a 24–hour period.

(B) "Commission" means the Industrial Welfare Commission of the State of California.

(C) "Division" means the Division of Labor Standards Enforcement of the State of California.

(D) "Emergency" means an unpredictable or unavoidable occurrence at unscheduled intervals requiring immediate action.

(E) "Employ" means to engage, suffer, or permit to work.

(F) "Employee" means any person employed by an employer.

(G) "Employees in the health care industry" means any of the following:

(1) Employees in the health care industry providing patient care; or

(2) Employees in the health care industry working in a clinical or medical department, including pharmacists dispensing prescriptions in any practice setting; or

(3) Employees in the health care industry working primarily or regularly as a member of a patient care delivery team; or

(4) Licensed veterinarians, registered veterinary technicians and unregistered animal health technicians providing patient care.

(H) "Employer" means any person as defined in Section 18 of the Labor Code, who directly or indirectly, or through an agent or any other person, employs or exercises control over the wages, hours, or working conditions of any person.

(I) "Health care emergency" consists of an unpredictable or unavoidable occurrence at unscheduled intervals relating to health care delivery, requiring immediate action.

(J) "Health care industry" is defined as hospitals, skilled nursing facilities, intermediate care and residential care facilities, convalescent care institutions, home health agencies, clinics operating 24 hours per day, and clinics performing surgery, urgent care, radiology, anesthesiology, pathology, neurology or dialysis.

(K) "Hours worked" means the time during which an employee is subject to the control of an employer, and includes all the time the employee is suffered or permitted to work, whether or not required to do so. Within the health care industry, the term "hours worked" means the time during which an employee is suffered or permitted to work for the employer, whether or not required to do so, as interpreted in accordance with the provisions of the Fair Labor Standards Act.

(L) "Minor" means, for the purpose of this order, any person under the age of 18 years.

(M) "Outside salesperson" means any person, 18 years of age or over, who customarily and regularly works more than half the working time away from the employer's place of business selling tangible or intangible items or obtaining orders or contracts for products, services or use of facilities.

(N) "Primarily" as used in Section 1, Applicability, means more than one-half the employee's work time.

(O) "Professional, Technical, Clerical, Mechanical, and Similar Occupations" includes professional, semiprofessional, managerial, supervisorial, laboratory, research, technical, clerical, office work, and mechanical occupations. Said occupations shall include, but not be limited to, the following: accountants; agents; appraisers; artists; attendants; audio–visual technicians; bookkeepers; bundlers; billposters; canvassers; carriers; cashiers; checkers; clerks; collectors; communications and sound technicians; compilers; copy holders; copy readers; copy writers; computer programmers and operators; demonstrators and display representatives; dispatchers; distributors; door–keepers; drafters; elevator operators; estimators; editors; graphic arts technicians; guards; guides; hosts; inspectors; installers; instructors; interviewers; investigators; librarians; laboratory workers; machine operators; mechanics; mailers; messengers; medical and dental technicians and technologists; models; nurses; packagers; photographers; porters and cleaners; process servers; printers; proof readers; salespersons and sales agents; secretaries; sign erectors; sign painters; social workers; solicitors; statisticians; stenographers; teachers; telephone, radiotelephone, telegraph and call-out operators; tellers; ticket agents; tracers; typists; vehicle operators; x–ray technicians; their assistants and other related occupations listed as professional, semiprofessional, technical, clerical, mechanical, and kindred occupations.

(P) "Shift" means designated hours of work by an employee, with a designated beginning time and quitting time.

(Q) "Split shift" means a work schedule, which is interrupted by non-paid non-working periods established by the employer, other than bona fide rest or meal periods.

(R) "Teaching" means, for the purpose of Section 1 of this order, the profession of teaching under a certificate from the Commission for Teacher Preparation and Licensing or teaching in an accredited college or university.

(S) "Wages" includes all amounts for labor performed by employees of every description, whether the amount is fixed or ascertained by the standard of time, task, piece, commission basis, or other method of calculation.

(T) "Workday" and "day" mean any consecutive 24–hour period beginning at the same time each calendar day.

(U) "Workweek" and "week" mean any seven (7) consecutive days, starting with the same calendar day each week. "Workweek" is a fixed and regularly recurring period of 168 hours, seven (7) consecutive 24–hour periods.

3. Hours and Days of Work

(A) *Daily Overtime—General Provisions*

(1) The following overtime provisions are applicable to employees 18 years of age or over and to employees 16 or 17 years of age who are not required by law to attend school and are not otherwise prohibited by law from engaging in the subject work. Such employees shall not be employed more than eight (8) hours in any workday or more than 40 hours in any workweek unless the employee

receives one and one-half (1 ½) times such employee's regular rate of pay for all hours worked over 40 hours in the workweek. Eight (8) hours of labor constitutes a day's work. Employment beyond eight (8) hours in any workday or more than six (6) days in any workweek is permissible provided the employee is compensated for such overtime at not less than:

(a) One and one-half (1 ½) times the employee's regular rate of pay for all hours worked in excess of eight (8) hours up to and including 12 hours in any workday, and for the first eight (8) hours worked on the seventh (7th) consecutive day of work in a workweek; and

(b) Double the employee's regular rate of pay for all hours worked in excess of 12 hours in any workday and for all hours worked in excess of eight (8) hours on the seventh (7th) consecutive day of work in a workweek.

(c) The overtime rate of compensation required to be paid to a nonexempt full-time salaried employee shall be computed by using the employee's regular hourly salary as one-fortieth (1/40) of the employee's weekly salary.

(B) *Alternative Workweek Schedules*

(1) No employer shall be deemed to have violated the daily overtime provisions by instituting, pursuant to the election procedures set forth in this wage order, a regularly scheduled alternative workweek schedule of not more than ten (10) hours per day within a 40 hour workweek without the payment of an overtime rate of compensation. All work performed in any workday beyond the schedule established by the agreement up to 12 hours a day or beyond 40 hours per week shall be paid at one and one-half (1 ½) times the employee's regular rate of pay. All work performed in excess of 12 hours per day and any work in excess of eight (8) hours on those days worked beyond the regularly scheduled number of workdays established by the alternative workweek agreement shall be paid at double the employee's regular rate of pay. Any alternative workweek agreement adopted pursuant to this section shall provide for not less than four (4) hours of work in any shift. Nothing in this section shall prohibit an employer, at the request of the employee, to substitute one day of work for another day of the same length in the shift provided by the alternative workweek agreement on an occasional basis to meet the personal needs of the employee without the payment of overtime. No hours paid at either one and one-half (1 ½) or double the regular rate of pay shall be included in determining when 40 hours have been worked for the purpose of computing overtime compensation.

(2) If an employer whose employees have adopted an alternative workweek agreement permitted by this order requires an employee to work fewer hours than those that are regularly scheduled by the agreement, the employer shall pay the employee overtime compensation at a rate of one and one-half (1 ½) times the employee's regular rate of pay for all hours worked in excess of eight (8) hours, and double the employee's regular rate of pay for all hours worked in excess of 12 hours for the day the employee is required to work the reduced hours.

1418

(3) An employer shall not reduce an employee's regular rate of hourly pay as a result of the adoption, repeal or nullification of an alternative workweek schedule.

(4) An employer shall explore any available reasonable alternative means of accommodating the religious belief or observance of an affected employee that conflicts with an adopted alternative workweek schedule, in the manner provided by subdivision (j) of Section 12940 of the Government Code.

(5) An employer shall make a reasonable effort to find a work schedule not to exceed eight (8) hours in a workday, in order to accommodate any affected employee who was eligible to vote in an election authorized by this section and who is unable to work the alternative workweek schedule established as the result of that election.

(6) An employer shall be permitted, but not required, to provide a work schedule not to exceed eight (8) hours in a workday to accommodate any employee who is hired after the date of the election and who is unable to work the alternative workweek schedule established by the election.

(7) Arrangements adopted in a secret ballot election held pursuant to this order prior to 1998, or under the rules in effect prior to 1998, and before the performance of the work, shall remain valid after July 1, 2000 provided that the results of the election are reported by the employer to the Division of Labor Statistics and Research by January 1, 2001, in accordance with the requirements of subsection (C) below (Election Procedures). If an employee was voluntarily working an alternative workweek schedule of not more than ten (10) hours a day as of July 1, 1999, that alternative workweek schedule was based on an individual agreement made after January 1, 1998 between the employee and employer, and the employee submitted, and the employer approved, a written request on or before May 30, 2000 to continue the agreement, the employee may continue to work that alternative workweek schedule without payment of an overtime rate of compensation for the hours provided in the agreement. The employee may revoke his/her voluntary authorization to continue such a schedule with 30 days written notice to the employer. New arrangements can only be entered into pursuant to the provisions of this section. Notwithstanding the foregoing, if a health care industry employer implemented a reduced rate for 12–hour shift employees in the last quarter of 1999 and desires to reimplement a flexible work arrangement that includes 12–hour shifts at straight time for the same work unit, the employer must pay a base rate to each affected employee in the work unit that is no less than that employee's base rate in 1999 immediately prior to the date of the rate reduction.

(8) Notwithstanding the above provisions regarding alternative workweek schedules, no employer of employees in the health care industry shall be deemed to have violated the daily overtime provisions by instituting, pursuant to the election procedures set forth in this wage

order a regularly scheduled alternative workweek schedule that includes workdays exceeding ten (10) hours but not more than 12 hours within a 40 hour workweek without the payment of overtime compensation, provided that:

(a) An employee who works beyond 12 hours in a workday shall be compensated at double the employee's regular rate of pay for all hours in excess of 12;

(b) An employee who works in excess of 40 hours in a workweek shall be compensated at one and one-half (1 $\frac{1}{2}$) times the employee's regular rate of pay for all hours over 40 hours in the workweek;

(c) Any alternative workweek agreement adopted pursuant to this section shall provide for not less than four (4) hours of work in any shift;

(d) The same overtime standards shall apply to employees who are temporarily assigned to a work unit covered by this subsection;

(e) Any employer who instituted an alternative workweek schedule pursuant to this subsection shall make a reasonable effort to find another work assignment for any employee who participated in a valid election prior to 1998 pursuant to the provisions of Wage Orders 4 and 5 and who is unable to work the alternative workweek schedule established;

(f) An employer engaged in the operation of a licensed hospital or in providing personnel for the operation of a licensed hospital who institutes, pursuant to a valid order of the Commission, a regularly scheduled alternative workweek that includes no more than three (3) 12–hour workdays, shall make a reasonable effort to find another work assignment for any employee who participated in the vote which authorized the schedule and is unable to work the 12–hour shifts. An employer shall not be required to offer a different work assignment to an employee if such a work assignment is not available or if the employee was hired after the adoption of the 12 hour, three (3) day alternative workweek schedule.

(9) No employee assigned to work a 12–hour shift established pursuant to this order shall be required to work more than 12 hours in any 24–hour period unless the chief nursing officer or authorized executive declares that:

(a) A "health care emergency", as defined above, exists in this order; and

(b) All reasonable steps have been taken to provide required staffing; and

(c) Considering overall operational status needs, continued overtime is necessary to provide required staffing.

(10) Provided further that no employee shall be required to work more than 16 hours in a 24–hour period unless by voluntary mutual agreement of the employee and the employer, and no employee shall work more than 24 consecutive hours until said employee receives not less than eight (8) consecutive hours off duty immediately following the 24 consecutive hours of work.

(11) Notwithstanding subsection (B)(9) above, an employee may be required to work up to 13 hours in any 24–hour period if the employee scheduled to relieve the subject employee does not report for duty as scheduled and does not inform the employer more than two (2) hours in advance of that scheduled shift that he/she will not be appearing for duty as scheduled.

(C) *Election Procedures*

Election procedures for the adoption and repeal of alternative workweek schedules require the following:

(1) Each proposal for an alternative workweek schedule shall be in the form of a written agreement proposed by the employer. The proposed agreement must designate a regularly scheduled alternative workweek in which the specified number of work days and work hours are regularly recurring. The actual days worked within that alternative workweek schedule need not be specified. The employer may propose a single work schedule that would become the standard schedule for workers in the work unit, or a menu of work schedule options, from which each employee in the unit would be entitled to choose. If the employer proposes a menu of work schedule options, the employee may, with the approval of the employer, move from one menu option to another.

(2) In order to be valid, the proposed alternative workweek schedule must be adopted in a secret ballot election, before the performance of work, by at least a two-thirds (2/03) vote of the affected employees in the work unit. The election shall be held during regular working hours at the employees' work site. For purposes of this subsection, "affected employees in the work unit" may include all employees in a readily identifiable work unit, such as a division, a department, a job classification, a shift, a separate physical location, or a recognized subdivision of any such work unit. A work unit may consist of an individual employee as long as the criteria for an identifiable work unit in this subsection are met.

(3) Prior to the secret ballot vote, any employer who proposed to institute an alternative workweek schedule shall have made a disclosure in writing to the affected employees, including the effects of the proposed arrangement on the employees' wages, hours, and benefits. Such a disclosure shall include meeting(s), duly noticed, held at least 14 days prior to voting, for the specific purpose of discussing the effects of the alternative workweek schedule. An employer shall provide that disclosure in a non-English language, as well as in English, if at least five (5) percent of the affected employees primarily speak that non-English language. The employer shall mail the written disclosure to employees who do not attend the meeting. Failure to comply with this paragraph shall make the election null and void.

(4) Any election to establish or repeal an alternative workweek schedule shall be held at the work site of the affected employees. The employer shall bear the costs of conducting any election held pursuant to this section. Upon a complaint by an affected employee, and after an investigation by the labor commissioner, the labor com-

missioner may require the employer to select a neutral third party to conduct the election.

(5) Any type of alternative workweek schedule that is authorized by the Labor Code may be repealed by the affected employees. Upon a petition of one-third (1/03) of the affected employees, a new secret ballot election shall be held and a two-thirds (2/03) vote of the affected employees shall be required to reverse the alternative workweek schedule. The election to repeal the alternative workweek schedule shall be held not more than 30 days after the petition is submitted to the employer, except that the election shall be held not less than 12 months after the date that the same group of employees voted in an election held to adopt or repeal an alternative workweek schedule. However, where an alternative workweek schedule was adopted between October 1, 1999 and October 1, 2000, a new secret ballot election to repeal the alternative workweek schedule shall not be subject to the 12–month interval between elections. The election shall take place during regular working hours at the employees' work site. If the alternative workweek schedule is revoked, the employer shall comply within 60 days. Upon proper showing of undue hardship, the Division of Labor Standards Enforcement may grant an extension of time for compliance.

(6) Only secret ballots may be cast by affected employees in the work unit at any election held pursuant to this section. The results of any election conducted pursuant to this section shall be reported by the employer to the Division of Labor Statistics and Research within 30 days after the results are final, and the report of election results shall be a public document. The report shall include the final tally of the vote, the size of the unit, and the nature of the business of the employer.

(7) Employees affected by a change in the work hours resulting from the adoption of an alternative workweek schedule may not be required to work those new work hours for at least 30 days after the announcement of the final results of the election.

(8) Employers shall not intimidate or coerce employees to vote either in support of or in opposition to a proposed alternative workweek. No employees shall be discharged or discriminated against for expressing opinions concerning the alternative workweek election or for opposing or supporting its adoption or repeal. However, nothing in this section shall prohibit an employer from expressing his/her position concerning that alternative workweek to the affected employees. A violation of this paragraph shall be subject to Labor Code Section 98 *et seq.*

(D) The provisions of subsections (A), (B) and (C) above shall not apply to any employee whose earnings exceed one and one-half (1 ½) times the minimum wage if more than half of that employee's compensation represents commissions.

(E) One and one-half (1 ½) times a minor's regular rate of pay shall be paid for all work over 40 hours in any workweek except minors 16 or 17 years old who are not required by law to attend school and may therefore be employed for the same hours as an adult are subject to subsection (A) or (B) and (C) above.

(**Violations of Child Labor Laws** are subject to civil penalties of from $500 to $10,000 as well as to criminal penalties. Refer to California Labor Code Sections 1285 to 1312 and 1390 to 1399 for additional restrictions on the employment of minors and for descriptions of criminal and civil penalties for violation of the child labor laws. Employers should ask school districts about any required work permits.)

(F) An employee may be employed on seven (7) workdays in one workweek when the total hours of employment during such workweek do not exceed 30 and the total hours of employment in any one workday thereof do not exceed six (6).

(G) If a meal period occurs on a shift beginning or ending at or between the hours of 10 p.m. and 6 a.m., facilities shall be available for securing hot food and drink or for heating food or drink, and a suitable sheltered place shall be provided in which to consume such food or drink.

(H) The provisions of Labor Code Sections 551 and 552 regarding one (1) day's rest in seven (7) shall not be construed to prevent an accumulation of days of rest when the nature of the employment reasonably requires the employee to work seven (7) or more consecutive days; provided, however, that in each calendar month, the employee shall receive the equivalent of one (1) day's rest in seven (7).

(I) Except as provided in subsections (E), (H) and (L), this section shall not apply to any employee covered by a valid collective bargaining agreement if the agreement expressly provides for the wages, hours of work, and working conditions of the employees, and if the agreement provides premium wage rates for all overtime hours worked and a regular hourly rate of pay for those employees of not less than 30 percent more than the state minimum wage.

(J) Notwithstanding subsection (I) above, where the employer and a labor organization representing employees of the employer have entered into a valid collective bargaining agreement pertaining to the hours of work of the employees, the requirement regarding the equivalent of one (1) day's rest in seven (7) (see subsection (H) above) shall apply, unless the agreement expressly provides otherwise.

(K) The provisions of this section are not applicable to employees whose hours of service are regulated by:

(1) The United States Department of Transportation Code of Federal Regulations, Title 49, Sections 395.1 to 395.13, Hours of Service of Drivers; or

(2) Title 13 of the California Code of Regulations, subchapter 6.5, Section 1200 and following sections, regulating hours of drivers.

(L) No employee shall be terminated or otherwise disciplined for refusing to work more than 72 hours in any workweek, except in an emergency as defined in Section 2(D).

(M) If an employer approves a written request of an employee to make up work time that is or would be lost as a result of a personal obligation of the employee, the hours of that makeup work time, if performed in the same workweek in which the work time was lost, may not be counted toward computing the total number of hours worked in a day for purposes of the overtime requirements, except for hours in excess of 11 hours of work in one (1) day or 40 hours of work in one (1) workweek. If an employee knows in advance that he/she will be requesting makeup time for a personal obligation that will recur at a fixed time over a succession of weeks, the employee may request to make up work time for up to four (4) weeks in advance; provided, however, that the makeup work must be performed in the same week that the work time was lost. An employee shall provide a signed written request for each occasion that the employee makes a request to make up work time pursuant to this subsection. While an employer may inform an employee of this makeup time option, the employer is prohibited from encouraging or otherwise soliciting an employee to request the employer's approval to take personal time off and make up the work hours within the same workweek pursuant to this subsection.

4. Minimum Wages

(A) Every employer shall pay to each employee wages not less than seven dollars and fifty cents ($7.50) per hour for all hours worked, effective January 1, 2007, and not less than eight dollars ($8.00) per hour for all hours worked, effective January 1, 2008, except:

Learners. Employees during their first 160 hours of employment in occupations in which they have no previous similar or related experience, may be paid not less than 85 percent of the minimum wage rounded to the nearest nickel.

(B) Every employer shall pay to each employee, on the established payday for the period involved, not less than the applicable minimum wage for all hours worked in the payroll period, whether the remuneration is measured by time, piece, commission, or otherwise.

(C) When an employee works a split shift, one (1) hour's pay at the minimum wage shall be paid in addition to the minimum wage for that workday, except when the employee resides at the place of employment.

(D) The provisions of this section shall not apply to apprentices regularly indentured under the State Division of Apprenticeship Standards.

5. Reporting Time Pay

(A) Each workday an employee is required to report for work and does report, but is not put to work or is furnished less than half said employee's usual or scheduled day's work, the employee shall be paid for half the usual or scheduled day's work, but in no event for less than two (2) hours nor more than four (4) hours, at the employee's regular rate of pay, which shall not be less than the minimum wage.

(B) If an employee is required to report for work a second time in any one workday and is furnished less than two (2) hours of work on the second reporting, said employee shall be paid for two (2) hours at the employee's regular rate of pay, which shall not be less than the minimum wage.

(C) The foregoing reporting time pay provisions are not applicable when:

(1) Operations cannot commence or continue due to threats to employees or property; or when recommended by civil authorities; or

(2) Public utilities fail to supply electricity, water, or gas, or there is a failure in the public utilities, or sewer system; or

(3) The interruption of work is caused by an Act of God or other cause not within the employer's control.

(D) This section shall not apply to an employee on paid standby status who is called to perform assigned work at a time other than the employee's scheduled reporting time.

6. Licenses for Disabled Workers

(A) A license may be issued by the Division authorizing employment of a person whose earning capacity is impaired by physical disability or mental deficiency at less than the minimum wage. Such licenses shall be granted only upon joint application of employer and employee and employee's representative if any.

(B) A special license may be issued to a nonprofit organization such as a sheltered workshop or rehabilitation facility fixing special minimum rates to enable the employment of such persons without requiring individual licenses of such employees.

(C) All such licenses and special licenses shall be renewed on a yearly basis or more frequently at the discretion of the Division. (See California Labor Code, Sections 1191 and 1191.5)

7. Records

(A) Every employer shall keep accurate information with respect to each employee including the following:

(1) Full name, home address, occupation and social security number.

(2) Birth date, if under 18 years, and designation as a minor.

(3) Time records showing when the employee begins and ends each work period. Meal periods, split shift intervals and total daily hours worked shall also be recorded. Meal periods during which operations cease and authorized rest periods need not be recorded.

(4) Total wages paid each payroll period, including value of board, lodging, or other compensation actually furnished to the employee.

(5) Total hours worked in the payroll period and applicable rates of pay. This information shall be made readily available to the employee upon reasonable request.

(6) When a piece rate or incentive plan is in operation, piece rates or an explanation of the incentive plan formula shall be provided to employees. An accurate production record shall be maintained by the employer.

(B) Every employer shall semimonthly or at the time of each payment of wages furnish each employee, either as a detachable part of the check, draft, or voucher paying the employee's wages, or separately, an itemized statement in writing showing: (1) all deductions; (2) the inclusive dates of the period for which the employee is paid; (3) the name of the employee or the employee's social security number; and (4) the name of the employer, provided all deductions made on written orders of the employee may be aggregated and shown as one item.

(C) All required records shall be in the English language and in ink or other indelible form, properly dated, showing month, day and year, and shall be kept on file by the employer for at least three years at the place of employment or at a central location within the State of California. An employee's records shall be available for inspection by the employee upon reasonable request.

(D) Clocks shall be provided in all major work areas or within reasonable distance thereto insofar as practicable.

8. Cash Shortage and Breakage. No employer shall make any deduction from the wage or require any reimbursement from an employee for any cash shortage, breakage, or loss of equipment, unless it can be shown that the shortage, breakage, or loss is caused by a dishonest or willful act, or by the gross negligence of the employee.

9. Uniforms and Equipment

(A) When uniforms are required by the employer to be worn by the employee as a condition of employment, such uniforms shall be provided and maintained by the employer. The term "uniform" includes wearing apparel and accessories of distinctive design or color.

Note: This section shall not apply to protective apparel regulated by the Occupational Safety and Health Standards Board.

(B) When tools or equipment are required by the employer or are necessary to the performance of a job, such tools and equipment shall be provided and maintained by the employer, except that an employee whose wages are at least two (2) times the minimum wage provided herein may be required to provide and maintain hand tools and equipment customarily required by the trade or craft. This subsection (B) shall not apply to apprentices regularly indentured under the State Division of Apprenticeship Standards.

Note: This section shall not apply to protective equipment and safety devices on tools regulated by the Occupational Safety and Health Standards Board.

(C) A reasonable deposit may be required as security for the return of the items furnished by the employer under provisions of subsections (A) and (B) of this section upon issuance of a receipt to the employee for such deposit. Such deposits shall be made pursuant to Section 400 and following of the Labor Code or an employer with the prior written authorization of the employee may deduct from the employee's last check the cost of an item furnished pursuant to (A) and (B) above in the event said item is not returned. No deduction shall be made at any time for normal wear and tear. All items furnished by the employer shall be returned by the employee upon completion of the job.

10. Meals and Lodging

(A) "Meal" means an adequate, well-balanced serving of a variety of wholesome, nutritious foods.

(B) "Lodging" means living accommodations available to the employee for full-time occupancy which are adequate, decent, and sanitary according to usual and customary standards. Employees shall not be required to share a bed.

(C) Meals or lodging may not be credited against the minimum wage without a voluntary written agreement between the employer and the employee. When credit for meals or lodging is used to meet part of the employer's minimum wage obligation, the amounts so credited may not be more than the following:

Effective	January 1, 2007	January 1, 2008
Lodging:		
Room occupied alone	$35.27 per week	$37.63 per week
Room shared	$29.11 per week	$31.06 per week
Apartment—two–thirds (2/03) of the ordinary rental value, and in no event more than	$423.51 per month	$451.89 per month
Where a couple are both employed by the employer, two-thirds (2/03) of the ordinary rental value, and in no event more than	$626.49 per month	$668.46 per month
Meals:		
Breakfast	$2.72	$2.90
Lunch	$3.72	$3.97
Dinner	$5.00	$5.34

(D) Meals evaluated as part of the minimum wage must be bona fide meals consistent with the employee's work shift. Deductions shall not be made for meals not received or lodging not used.

(E) If, as a condition of employment, the employee must live at the place of employment or occupy quarters owned or under the control of the employer, then the employer may not charge rent in excess of the values listed herein.

11. Meal Periods

(A) No employer shall employ any person for a work period of more than five (5) hours without a meal period of not less than 30 minutes, except that when a work period of not more than six (6) hours will complete the day's work the meal period may be waived by mutual consent of the employer and the employee. Unless the employee is relieved of all duty during a 30 minute meal period, the meal period shall be considered an "on duty" meal period and counted as time worked. An "on duty" meal period shall be permitted only when the nature of the work prevents an employee from being relieved of all duty and when by written agreement between the parties an on-the-job paid meal period is agreed to. The written agreement shall state that the employee may, in writing, revoke the agreement at any time.

(B) If an employer fails to provide an employee a meal period in accordance with the applicable provisions of this order, the employer shall pay the employee one (1) hour of pay at the employee's regular rate of compensation for each workday that the meal period is not provided.

(C) In all places of employment where employees are required to eat on the premises, a suitable place for that purpose shall be designated.

(D) Notwithstanding any other provision of this order, employees in the health care industry who work shifts in excess of eight (8) total hours in a workday may voluntarily waive their right to one of their two meal periods. In order to be valid, any such waiver must be documented in a written agreement that is voluntarily signed by both the employee and the employer. The employee may revoke the waiver at any time by providing the employer at least one (1) day's written notice. The employee shall be fully compensated for all working time, including any on-the-job meal period, while such a waiver is in effect.

12. Rest Periods

(A) Every employer shall authorize and permit all employees to take rest periods, which insofar as practicable shall be in the middle of each work period. The authorized rest period time shall be based on the total hours worked daily at the rate of ten (10) minutes net rest time per four (4) hours or major fraction thereof. However, a rest period need not be authorized for employees whose total daily work time is less than three and one-half (3 $\frac{1}{02}$) hours. Authorized rest period time shall be counted as hours worked for which there shall be no deduction from wages.

(B) If an employer fails to provide an employee a rest period in accordance with the applicable provisions of this order, the employer shall pay the employee one (1) hour of pay at the employee's regular rate of compensation for each workday that the rest period is not provided.

13. Change Rooms and Resting Facilities

(A) Employers shall provide suitable lockers, closets, or equivalent for the safekeeping of employees' outer clothing during working hours, and when required, for their work clothing during non-working hours. When the occupation requires a change of clothing, change rooms or equivalent space shall be provided in order that employees may change their clothing in reasonable privacy and comfort. These rooms or spaces may be adjacent to but shall be separate from toilet rooms and shall be kept clean.

Note: This section shall not apply to change rooms and storage facilities regulated by the Occupational Safety and Health Standards Board.

(B) Suitable resting facilities shall be provided in an area separate from the toilet rooms and shall be available to employees during work hours.

14. Seats

(A) All working employees shall be provided with suitable seats when the nature of the work reasonably permits the use of seats.

(B) When employees are not engaged in the active duties of their employment and the nature of the work requires standing, an adequate number of suitable seats shall be placed in reasonable proximity to the work area and employees shall be permitted to use such seats when it does not interfere with the performance of their duties.

15. Temperature

(A) The temperature maintained in each work area shall provide reasonable comfort consistent with industry-wide standards for the nature of the process and the work performed.

(B) If excessive heat or humidity is created by the work process, the employer shall take all feasible means to reduce such excessive heat or humidity to a degree providing reasonable comfort. Where the nature of the employment requires a temperature of less than 60° F., a heated room shall be provided to which employees may retire for warmth, and such room shall be maintained at not less than 68°.

(C) A temperature of not less than 68° shall be maintained in the toilet rooms, resting rooms, and change rooms during hours of use.

(D) Federal and State energy guidelines shall prevail over any conflicting provision of this section.

16. Elevators. Adequate elevator, escalator or similar service consistent with industry-wide standards for the nature of the process and the work performed shall be provided when employees are employed four floors or more above or below ground level.

17. Exemptions. If, in the opinion of the Division after due investigation, it is found that the enforcement of any provision contained in Section 7, Records; Section 12, Rest Periods; Section 13, Change Rooms and Resting Facilities; Section 14, Seats; Section 15, Temperature; or Section 16, Elevators, would not materially affect the welfare or comfort of employees and would work an undue hardship on the employer, exemption may be made at the discretion of the Division. Such exemptions shall be in writing to be effective and may be revoked after reasonable notice is given in writing. Application for exemption shall be made by the employer or by the employee and/or the employee's representative to the

Division in writing. A copy of the application shall be posted at the place of employment at the time the application is filed with the Division.

18. Filing Reports. (See California Labor Code, Section 1174(a))

19. Inspection. (See California Labor Code, Section 1174)

20. Penalties. (See California Labor Code, Section 1199)

(A) In addition to any other civil penalties provided by law, any employer or any other person acting on behalf of the employer who violates, or causes to be violated, the provisions of this order, shall be subject to the civil penalty of:

(1) Initial Violation—$50.00 for each underpaid employee for each pay period during which the employee was underpaid in addition to the amount which is sufficient to recover unpaid wages.

(2) Subsequent Violations—$100.00 for each underpaid employee for each pay period during which the employee was underpaid in addition to an amount which is sufficient to recover unpaid wages.

(3) The affected employee shall receive payment of all wages recovered.

(B) The labor commissioner may also issue citations pursuant to California Labor Code Section 1197.1 for non-payment of wages for overtime work in violation of this order.

21. Separability. If the application of any provision of this order, or any section, subsection, subdivision, sentence, clause, phrase, word, or portion of this order should be held invalid or unconstitutional or unauthorized or prohibited by statute, the remaining provisions thereof shall not be affected thereby, but shall continue to be given full force and effect as if the part so held invalid or unconstitutional had not been included herein.

22. Posting of Order. Every employer shall keep a copy of this order posted in an area frequented by employees where it may be easily read during the workday. Where the location of work or other conditions make this impractical, every employer shall keep a copy of this order and make it available to every employee upon request.

[1] Pursuant to Labor Code section 515.5, subdivision (a)(4), the Division of Labor Statistics and Research, Department of Industrial Relations, has adjusted the minimum hourly rate of pay specified in this subdivision to be $49.77, effective January 1, 2007. This hourly rate of pay is adjusted on October 1 of each year to be effective on January 1, of the following year, and may be obtained at www.dir.ca.gov/IWC or by mail from the Department of Industrial Relations.

Publisher's Notes

See Lujan v. Southern California Gas Co. (2002) 2002 WL 407888 (preemption by Labor Management Relations Act (29 U.S.C.A. § 185(a)) of State Labor Commissioner's state-law claims against an employer for violations of overtime standards).

See Tidewater Marine Western, Inc. v. Bradshaw (1996) 14 Cal.4th 557, 927 P.2d 296, 59 Cal.Rptr.2d 186 (in determining whether wage orders apply, where state and federal law do not conflict, California's territorial boundaries as determined by state law).

See Pacific Merchant Shipping Ass'n v. Aubry, 918 F.2d 1409 (9th Cir. 1990) (application of order to seamen working on territorial waters and on the high seas off the California coast and to maritime employees working primarily on the high seas off the California coast, when the vessels on which the employees work do not engage in foreign, intercoastal, or coastwise voyages).

See Industrial Welfare Com. v. Superior Court (1980) 27 Cal.3d 690, 613 P.2d 579, 166 Cal.Rptr. 331 (validity of 1980 order).

Research References

See notes following listing of Wage Orders.

Please Post With This Side Showing
OFFICIAL NOTICE
Effective July 1, 2003 as amended
Sections 4(A) and 10(C) amended and republished by the Department of Industrial Relations, effective January 1, 2007, pursuant to AB 1835, Chapter 230, Statutes of 2006
INDUSTRIAL WELFARE COMMISSION
ORDER NO. 5–2001
REGULATING
WAGES, HOURS AND WORKING CONDITIONS IN THE
PUBLIC HOUSEKEEPING INDUSTRY

TAKE NOTICE: To employers and representatives of persons working in industries and occupations in the State of California:

The Department of Industrial Relations amends and republishes the minimum wage and meals and lodging credits in the Industrial Welfare Commission's Orders as a result of legislation enacted (AB 1835, Ch. 230, Stats of 2006, adding sections 1182.12 and 1182.13 to the California Labor Code.) The amendments and republishing make no other changes to the IWC's Orders.

1. Applicability of Order. This order shall apply to all persons employed in the public housekeeping industry whether paid on a time, piece rate, commission, or other basis, except that:

(A) Except as provided in Sections 1,2,4,10, and 20, the provisions of this order shall not apply to student nurses in a school accredited by the California Board of Registered Nursing or by the Board of Vocational Nurse and Psychiatric Technician Examiners are exempted by the provisions of sections 2789 or 2884 of the Business and Professions Code;

(B) Provisions of sections 3 through 12 shall not apply to persons employed in administrative, executive, or professional capacities. The following requirements shall apply in determining whether an employee's duties meet the test to qualify for an exemption to those sections:

(1) Executive Exemption. A person employed in an executive capacity means any employee:

(a) Whose duties and responsibilities involve the management of the enterprise in which he or she is employed or of a customarily recognized department or subdivision thereof; and

(b) Who customarily and regularly directs the work of two or more other employees therein; and

(c) Who has the authority to hire or fire other employees or whose suggestions and recommendations as to the hiring or firing and as to the advancement and promotion or any other change of status of other employees will be given particular weight; and

(d) Who customarily and regularly exercises discretion and independent judgment; and

(e) Who is primarily engaged in duties which meet the test of the exemption. The activities constituting exempt work and nonexempt work shall be construed in the same manner as such items are construed in the following regulations under the Fair Labor Standards Act effective as of the date of this order: 29 C.F.R. Sections 541.102, 541.104–111, and 541.115–116. Exempt work shall include, for example, all work that is directly and closely related to exempt work and work which is properly viewed as a means for carrying out exempt functions. The work actually performed by the employee during the course of the work week must, first and foremost, be examined and the amount of time the employee spends on such work, together with the employer's realistic expectations and the realistic requirements of the job, shall be considered in determining whether the employee satisfies this requirement.

(f) Such an employee must also earn a monthly salary equivalent to no less than two (2) times the state minimum wage for full-time employment. Full–time employment is defined in Labor Code Section 515(c) as 40 hours per week.

(2) Administrative Exemption. A person employed in an administrative capacity means any employee:

(a) Whose duties and responsibilities involve either:

(i) The performance of office or non-manual work directly related to management policies or general business operations of his employer or his employer's customers; or

(ii) The performance of functions in the administration of a school system, or educational establishment or institution, or of a department of subdivision thereof, in work directly related to the academic instruction or training carried on therein; and

(b) Who customarily and regularly exercises discretion and independent judgment; and

(c) Who regularly and directly assists a proprietor, or an employee employed in a bona fide executive or administrative capacity (as such terms are defined for purposes of this section); or

(d) Who performs under only general supervision work along specialized or technical lines requiring special training, experience, or knowledge; or

(e) Who executes under only general supervision special assignments and tasks; and

(f) Who is primarily engaged in duties which meet the test of the exemption. The activities constituting exempt work and non-exempt work shall be construed in the same manner as such terms are construed in the following regulations under the Fair Labor Standards Act effective as of the date of this order. 29 C.F.R. Sections 541.201–205, 541.207–208, 541.210, and 541.215. Exempt work shall include, for example, all work that is directly and closely related to exempt work and work which is properly viewed as a means for carrying out exempt functions. The work actually performed by the employee during the course of the work week must, first and foremost, be examined and the amount of time the employee spends on such work, together with the employer's realistic expectations and the realistic requirements of the job, shall be considered in determining whether the employee satisfies this requirement.

(g) Such employee must also earn a monthly salary equivalent to no less than two (2) times the state minimum wage for full-time employment. Full–time employment is defined in Labor Code Section 515(c) as 40 hours per week.

(3) Professional Exemption. A person employed in a professional capacity means any employee who meets *all* of the following requirements:

(a) Who is licensed or certified by the State of California and is primarily engaged in the practice of one of the following recognized professions: law, medicine, dentistry, optometry, architecture, engineering, teaching, or accounting; or

(b) Who is primarily engaged in an occupation commonly recognized as a learned or artistic profession. For the purposes of this subsection, "learned or artistic profession" means an employee who is primarily engaged in the performance of:

(i) Work requiring knowledge of an advanced type in a field or science or learning customarily acquired by a prolonged course of specialized intellectual instruction

1425

and study, as distinguished from a general academic education and from an apprenticeship, and from training in the performance of routine mental, manual, or physical processes, or work that is an essential part of or necessarily incident to any of the above work; or

(ii) Work that is original and creative in character in a recognized field of artistic endeavor (as opposed to work which can be produced by a person endowed with general manual or intellectual ability and training), and the result of which depends primarily on the invention, imagination, or talent of the employee or work that is an essential part of or necessarily incident to any of the above work; and

(iii) Whose work is predominantly intellectual and varied in character (as opposed to routine mental, manual, mechanical, or physical work) and is of such character that the output produced or the result accomplished cannot be standardized in relation to a given period of time.

(c) Who customarily and regularly exercises discretion and independent judgment in the performance of duties set forth in paragraph (a).

(d) Who earns a monthly salary equivalent to no less than two (2) times the state minimum wage for full-time employment. Full–time employment is defined in Labor Code Section 515 (c) as 40 hours per week.

(e) Subparagraph (b) above is intended to be construed in accordance with the following provisions of federal law as they existed as of the date of this Wage Order: 29 C.F.R. Sections 541.207, 541.301(a)–(d), 541.302, 541.306, 541.307, 541.308, and 541.310.

(f) Notwithstanding the provisions of this subparagraph, pharmacists employed to engage in the practice of pharmacy, and registered nurses employed to engage in the practice of nursing, shall not be considered exempt professional employees, nor shall they be considered exempt from coverage for the purposes of this subsection unless they individually meet the criteria established for exemption as executive or administrative employees.

(g) Subparagraph (f) above, shall not apply to the following advanced practice nurses:

(i) Certified nurse midwives who are primarily engaged in performing duties for which certification is required pursuant to Article 2.5 (commencing with Section 2746) of Chapter 6 of Division 2 of the Business and Professions Code.

(ii) Certified nurse anesthetists who are primarily engaged in performing duties for which certification is required pursuant to Article 7 (commencing with Section 2825) of Chapter 6 of Division 2 of the Business and Professions Code.

(iii) Certified nurse practitioners who are primarily engaged in performing duties for which certification is required pursuant to Article 8 (commencing with Section 2834) of Chapter 6 of Division 2 of the Business and Professions Code.

1426

(iv) Nothing in this subparagraph shall exempt the occupations set forth in clauses (i), (ii), and (iii) from meeting the requirements of subsection 1(B)(3)(a)–(d), above.

(h) Except as provided in subparagraph (i), an employee in the computer software field who is paid on an hourly basis shall be exempt, if *all* of the following apply:

(i) The employee is primarily engaged in work that is intellectual or creative and requires the exercise of discretion and independent judgment.

(ii) The employee is primarily engaged in duties that consist of one or more of the following:

-The application of systems analysis techniques and procedures, including consulting with users, to determine hardware, software, or system functional specifications.

-The design, development, documentation, analysis, creation, testing, or modification of computer systems or programs, including prototypes, based on and related to, user or system design specifications.

-The documentation, testing, creation, or modification of computer programs related to the design of software or hardware for computer operating systems.

(iii) The employee is highly skilled and is proficient in the theoretical and practical application of highly specialized information to computer systems analysis, programming, and software engineering. A job title shall not be determinative of the applicability of this exemption.

(iv) The employee's hourly rate of pay is not less than forty-one dollars ($41.00). The Division of Labor Statistics and Research shall adjust this pay rate on October 1 of each year to be effective on January 1 of the following year by an amount equal to the percentage increase in the California Consumer Price Index for Urban Wage Earners and Clerical Workers.[1]

(i) The exemption provided in subparagraph (h) does not apply to an employee if *any* of the following apply:

(i) The employee is a trainee or employee in an entry-level position who is learning to become proficient in the theoretical and practical application of highly specialized information to computer systems analysis, programming, and software engineering.

(ii) The employee is in a computer-related occupation but has not attained the level of skill and expertise necessary to work independently and without close supervision.

(iii) The employee is engaged in the operation of computers or in the manufacture, repair, or maintenance of computer hardware and related equipment.

(iv) The employee is an engineer, drafter, machinist, or other professional whose work is highly dependent upon or facilitated by the use of computers and computer software programs and who is skilled in computer-aided design software, including CAD/CAM, but who is not in a computer systems analysis or programming occupation.

(v) The employee is a writer engaged in writing material, including box labels, product descriptions, documentation, promotional material, setup and installation instructions, and other similar written information, either for print or for onscreen media or who writes or provides content material intended to be read by customers, subscribers, or visitors to computer-related media such as the World Wide Web or CD–ROMs.

(vi) The employee is engaged in *any* of the activities set forth in subparagraph (h) for the purpose of creating imagery for effects used in the motion picture, television, or theatrical industry.

(C) Except as provided in Sections 1, 2, 4, 10, and 20, the provisions of this order shall not apply to any employees directly employed by the State or any political subdivision thereof, including any city, county, or special district.

(D) The provisions of this order shall not apply to outside salespersons.

(E) Provisions of this order shall not apply to any individual who is the parent, spouse, child, or legally adopted child of the employer.

(F) The provisions of this order shall not apply to any individual participating in a national service program, such as AmeriCorps, carried out using assistance provided under Section 12571 of Title 42 of the United States Code. (See Stats. 2000, ch. 365, amending Labor Code § 1171.)

2. Definitions

(A) An "alternative workweek schedule" means any regularly scheduled workweek requiring an employee to work more than eight (8) hours in a 24–hour period.

(B) "Commission" means the Industrial Welfare Commission of the State of California.

(C) "Division" means the Division of Labor Standards Enforcement of the State of California.

(D) "Emergency" means an unpredictable or unavoidable occurrence at unscheduled intervals requiring immediate action.

(E) "Employ" means to engage, suffer, or permit to work.

(F) "Employee" means any person employed by an employer, and includes any lessee who is charged rent, or who pays rent for a chair, booth, or space and

(1) who does not use his or her own funds to purchase requisite supplies, and

(2) who does not maintain an appointment book separate and distinct from that of the establishment in which the space is located, and

(3) who does not have a business license where applicable.

(G) "Employees in the Healthcare Industry" means any of the following:

(1) Employees in the healthcare industry providing patient care; or

(2) Employees in the healthcare industry working in a clinical or medical department, including pharmacists dispensing prescriptions in any practice setting; or

(3) Employees in the healthcare industry working primarily or regularly as a member of a patient care delivery team

(4) Licensed veterinarians, registered veterinary technicians and unregistered animal health technicians providing patient care.

(H) "Employer" means any person as defined in Section 18 of the Labor Code, who directly or indirectly, or through an agent or any other person, employs or exercises control over the wages, hours, or working conditions of any person.

(I) "Healthcare Emergency" consists of an unpredictable or unavoidable occurrence at unscheduled intervals relating to healthcare delivery, requiring immediate action.

(J) "Healthcare Industry" is defined as hospitals, skilled nursing facilities, intermediate care and residential care facilities, convalescent care institutions, home health agencies, clinics operating twenty-four (24) hours per day, and clinics performing surgery, urgent care, radiology, anesthesiology, pathology, neurology or dialysis.

(K) "Hours worked" means the time during which an employee is subject to the control of an employer, and includes all the time the employee is suffered or permitted to work, whether or not required to do so, and in the case of an employee who is required to reside on the employment premises, that time spent carrying out assigned duties shall be counted as hours worked. Within the health care industry, the term "hours worked" means the time during which an employee is suffered or permitted to work for the employer, whether or not required to do so, as interpreted in accordance with the provisions of the Fair Labor Standards Act.

(L) "Minor" means, for the purpose of this Order, any person under the age of 18 years.

(M) "Outside Salesperson" means any person, 18 years of age or over, who customarily and regularly works more than half the working time away from the employer's place of business selling tangible or intangible items or obtaining orders or contracts for products, services or use of facilities.

(N) "Personal attendant" includes baby sitters and means any person employed by a non-profit organization covered by this order to supervise, feed or dress a child or person who by reason of advanced age, physical disability or mental deficiency needs supervision. The status of "personal attendant" shall apply when no significant amount of work other than the foregoing is required.

(O) "Primarily" as used in Section 1, Applicability, means more than one-half the employee's work time.

(P) "Public Housekeeping Industry" means any industry, business, or establishment which provides meals, housing, or maintenance services whether operated as a primary business or when incidental to other operations in an establishment not covered by an industry order of the Commission, and includes, but is not limited to the following:

(1) Restaurants, night clubs, taverns, bars, cocktail lounges, lunch counters, cafeterias, boarding houses, clubs, and all similar establishments where food in either solid or liquid form is prepared and served to be consumed on the premises;

(2) Catering, banquet, box lunch service, and similar establishments which prepare food for consumption on or off the premises;

(3) Hotels, motels, apartment houses, rooming houses, camps, clubs, trailer parks, office or loft buildings, and similar establishments offering rental of living, business, or commercial quarters;

(4) Hospitals, sanitariums, rest homes, child nurseries, child care institutions, homes for the aged, and similar establishments offering board or lodging in addition to medical, surgical, nursing, convalescent, aged, or child care;

(5) Private schools, colleges, or universities, and similar establishments which provide board or lodging in addition to educational facilities;

(6) Establishments contracting for development, maintenance or cleaning of grounds; maintenance or cleaning of facilities and/or quarters of commercial units and living units; and

(7) Establishments providing veterinary or other animal care services.

(Q) "Shift" means designated hours of work by an employee, with a designated beginning time and quitting time.

(R) "Split shift" means a work schedule which is interrupted by non-paid non-working periods established by the employer, other than bona fide rest or meal periods.

(S) "Teaching" means, for the purpose of section 1 of this Order, the profession of teaching under a certificate from the Commission for Teacher Preparation and Licensing or teaching in an accredited college or university.

(T) "Wages" include all amounts of labor performed by employees of every description, whether the amount is fixed or ascertained by the standard of time, task, piece, commission basis, or other method of calculation.

(U) "Workday" and "day" mean any consecutive 24–hour period beginning at the same time each calendar day.

(V) "Workweek" and "week" mean any seven (7) consecutive days, starting with the same calendar day each week. "Workweek" is a fixed and regularly recur-

ring period of 168 hours, seven (7) consecutive 24–hour periods.

3. Hours and Days of Work

(A) *Daily Overtime—General Provisions*

(1) The following overtime provisions are applicable to employees 18 years of age or over and to employees 16 or 17 years of age who are not required by law to attend school and are not otherwise prohibited by law from engaging in the subject work. Such employees shall not be employed more than eight (8) hours in any workday or more than 40 hours in any workweek unless the employee receives one and one-half (1 $\frac{1}{2}$) times such employee's regular rate of pay for all hours worked over 40 hours in the workweek. Eight (8) hours of labor constitutes a day's work. Employment beyond eight (8) hours in any workday or more than six (6) days in any workweek is permissible provided the employee is compensated for such overtime at not less than:

(a) One and one-half (1 $\frac{1}{2}$) times the employee's regular rate of pay for all hours worked in excess of eight (8) hours up to and including twelve (12) hours in any workday, and for the first eight (8) hours worked on the seventh (7th) consecutive day of work in a workweek; and

(b) Double the employee's regular rate of pay for all hours worked in excess of 12 hours in any workday and for all hours worked in excess of eight (8) hours on the seventh (7th) consecutive day of work in a workweek.

(c) The overtime rate of compensation required to be paid to a nonexempt full-time salaried employee shall be computed by using the employee's regular hourly salary as one fortieth (1/40) of the employee's weekly salary.

(2) Employees with direct responsibility for children who are under 18 years of age or who are not emancipated from the foster care system and who, in either case, are receiving 24 hour residential care, may, without violating any provision of this section, be compensated as follows:

(a) An employee who works in excess of 40 hours in a workweek shall be compensated at one and one-half (1 $\frac{1}{2}$) times the employee's regular rate of pay for all hours over 40 hours in the workweek.

(b) An employee shall be compensated at two (2) times the employee's regular rate of pay for all hours in excess of 48 hours in the workweek.

(c) An employee shall be compensated at two (2) times the employee's regular rate of pay for all hours in excess of 16 in a workday.

(d) No employee shall work more than 24 consecutive hours until said employee receives not less than eight (8) consecutive hours off-duty immediately following the 24 consecutive hours of work. Time spent sleeping shall not be included as hours worked.

(e) Section (A)(2) above shall apply to employees of 24 hour non-medical out of home licensed residential facilities of 15 beds or fewer for the developmentally disabled, elderly, and mentally ill adults.

This section, (3)(A)(2)(e), shall sunset on July 1, 2005.

(B) *Alternative Workweek Schedules*

(1) No employer shall be deemed to have violated the daily overtime provisions by instituting, pursuant to the election procedures set forth in this wage order, a regularly scheduled alternative workweek schedule of not more than ten (10) hours per day within a 40 hour workweek without the payment of an overtime rate of compensation. All work performed in any workday beyond the schedule established by the agreement up to twelve (12) hours a day or beyond 40 hours per week shall be paid at one and one-half (1 ½) times the employee's regular rate of pay. All work performed in excess of twelve (12) hours per day and any work in excess of eight (8) hours on those days worked beyond the regularly scheduled number of workdays established by the alternative workweek agreement shall be paid at double the employee's regular rate of pay. Any alternative workweek agreement adopted pursuant to this section shall provide for not less than four (4) hours of work in any shift. Nothing in this section shall prohibit an employer, at the request of the employee, to substitute one day of work for another day of the same length in the shift provided by the alternative workweek agreement on an occasional basis to meet the personal needs of the employee without the payment of overtime. No hours paid at either one and one-half (1 ½) or double the regular rate of pay shall be included in determining when 40 hours have been worked for the purpose of computing overtime compensation.

(2) If an employer, whose employees have adopted an alternative workweek agreement permitted by this order requires an employee to work fewer hours than those that are regularly scheduled by the agreement, the employer shall pay the employee overtime compensation at a rate of one and one-half (1 ½) times the employee's regular rate of pay for all hours worked in excess of eight (8) hours, and double the employee's regular rate of pay for all hours worked in excess of 12 hours for the day the employee is required to work the reduced hours.

(3) An employer shall not reduce an employee's regular rate of hourly pay as a result of the adoption, repeal or nullification of an alternative workweek schedule.

(4) An employer shall explore any available reasonable alternative means of accommodating the religious belief or observance of an affected employee that conflicts with an adopted alternative workweek schedule, in the manner provided by subdivision (j) of Section 12940 of the Government Code.

(5) An employer shall make a reasonable effort to find a work schedule not to exceed eight (8) hours in a workday, in order to accommodate any affected employee who was eligible to vote in an election authorized by this Section and who is unable to work the alternative workweek schedule established as the result of that election.

(6) An employer shall be permitted, but not required, to provide a work schedule not to exceed eight (8) hours in a workday to accommodate any employee who is hired after the date of the election and who is unable to work the alternative workweek schedule established by the election.

(7) Arrangements adopted in a secret ballot election held pursuant to this order prior to 1998, or under the rules in effect prior to 1998, and before the performance of the work, shall remain valid after July 1, 2000 provided that the results of the election are reported by the employer to the Division of Labor Statistics and Research by January 1, 2001, in accordance with the requirements of Section C below (Election Procedures). If an employee was voluntarily working an alternative workweek schedule of not more than ten (10) hours a day as of July 1, 1999, that alternative workweek was based on an individual agreement made after January 1, 1998 between the employee and employer, and the employee submitted, and the employer approved, a written request on or before May 30, 2000 to continue the agreement, the employee may continue to work that alternative workweek schedule without payment of an overtime rate of compensation for the hours provided in the agreement. An employee may revoke his or her voluntary authorization to continue such a schedule with 30 days written notice to the employer. New arrangements can only be entered into pursuant to the provisions of this section. Notwithstanding the foregoing, if a health care industry employer implemented a reduced rate for 12 hour shift employees in the last quarter of 1999 and desires to re-implement a flexible work arrangement that includes 12 hour shifts at straight time for the same work unit, the employer must pay a base rate to each affected employee in the work unit that is no less than that employee's base rate in 1999 immediately prior to the date of the rate reduction.

(8) Notwithstanding the above provisions regarding alternative workweek schedules, no employer of employees in the healthcare industry shall be deemed to have violated the daily overtime provisions by instituting, pursuant to the election procedures set forth in this wage order a regularly scheduled alternative workweek schedule that includes work days exceeding ten (10) hours but not more than 12 hours within a 40–hour workweek without the payment of overtime compensation, provided that:

(a) An employee who works beyond 12 hours in a workday shall be compensated at double the employee's regular rate of pay for all hours in excess of (12);

(b) An employee who works in excess of 40 hours in a workweek shall be compensated at one and one-half (1 ½) times the employee's regular rate of pay for all hours over 40 hours in the workweek;

(c) Any alternative workweek agreement adopted pursuant to this section shall provide for not less than four (4) hours of work in any shift.

(d) The same overtime standards shall apply to employees who are temporarily assigned to a work unit covered by this subsection;

(e) Any employer who instituted an alternative workweek schedule pursuant to this subsection shall make a reasonable effort to find another work assignment for any employee who participated in a valid election prior to 1998 pursuant to the provisions of Wage Orders 4 and 5 and who is unable to work the alternative workweek schedule established.

(f) An employer engaged in the operation of a licensed hospital or in providing personnel for the operation of a licensed hospital who institutes, pursuant to a valid order of the Commission, a regularly scheduled alternative workweek that includes no more than three (3) 12–hour workdays, shall make a reasonable effort to find another work assignment for any employee who participated in the vote which authorized the schedule and is unable to work the 12–hour shifts. An employer shall not be required to offer a different work assignment to an employee if such a work assignment is not available or if the employee was hired after the adoption of the 12 hour, three (3) day alternative workweek schedule.

(9) No employee assigned to work a 12 hour shift established pursuant to this Order shall be required to work more than 12 hours in any 24 hour period unless the Chief Nursing Officer or authorized executive declares that:

(a) A "healthcare emergency", as defined, exists in this Order, and

(b) All reasonable steps have been taken to provide required staffing, and

(c) Considering overall operational status needs, continued overtime is necessary to provide required staffing.

(10) Provided further that no employee shall be required to work more than 16 hours in a 24–hour period unless by voluntary mutual agreement of the employee and employer, and no employee shall work more than 24 consecutive hours until said employee receives not less than eight (8) consecutive hours off-duty immediately following the 24 consecutive hours of work.

(11) Notwithstanding subsection (B)(9) above, an employee may be required to work up to 13 hours in any 24–hour period if the employee scheduled to relieve the subject employee does not report for duty as scheduled and does not inform the employer more than two (2) hours in advance of that scheduled shift that he/she will not be appearing for duty as scheduled.

(C) *Election Procedures*

Election procedures for the adoption and repeal of alternative workweek schedules require the following:

(1) Each proposal for an alternative workweek schedule shall be in the form of a written agreement proposed by the employer. The proposed agreement must designate a regularly scheduled alternative workweek in which the specified number of work days and work hours are regularly recurring. The actual days worked within that alternative workweek schedule need not be specified. The employer may propose a single work schedule that would become the standard schedule for workers in the work unit, or a menu of work schedule options, from which each employee in the unit would be entitled to choose. If the employer proposes a menu of work schedule options, the employee may, with the approval of the employer, move from one menu option to another.

(2) In order to be valid, the proposed alternative workweek schedule must be adopted in a secret ballot election, before the performance of work, by at least a two-thirds (2/03) vote of the affected employees in the work unit. The election shall be held during regular working hours at the employees' work site. For purposes of this subsection, "affected employees in the work unit" may include all employees in a readily identifiable work unit, such as a division, a department, a job classification, a shift, a separate physical location, or a recognized subdivision of any such work unit. A work unit may consist of an individual employee as long as the criteria for an identifiable work unit in this subsection is met.

(3) Prior to the secret ballot vote, any employer who proposed to institute an alternative workweek schedule shall have made a disclosure in writing to the affected employees, including the effects of the proposed arrangement on the employees' wages, hours, and benefits. Such a disclosure shall include meeting(s), duly noticed, held at least fourteen (14) days prior to voting, for the specific purpose of discussing the effects of the alternative workweek schedule. An employer shall provide that disclosure in a non–English language, as well as in English, if at least five (5) percent of the affected employees primarily speak that non–English language. The employer shall mail the written disclosure to employees who do not attend the meeting. Failure to comply with this paragraph shall make the election null and void.

(4) Any election to establish or repeal an alternative workweek schedule shall be held at the work site of the affected employees. The employer shall bear the costs of conducting any election held pursuant to this section. Upon a complaint by an affected employee, and after an investigation by the Labor Commissioner, the Labor Commissioner may require the employer to select a neutral third party to conduct the election.

(5) Any type of alternative workweek schedule that is authorized by the Labor Code may be repealed by the affected employees. Upon a petition of one-third (1/03) of the affected employees, a new secret ballot election shall be held and a two-thirds (2/03) vote of the affected employees shall be required to reverse the alternative workweek schedule. The election to repeal the alternative workweek schedule shall be held not more than 30 days after the petition is submitted to the employer, except that the election shall be held not less than 12

months after the date that the same group of employees voted in an election held to adopt or repeal an alternative workweek schedule. However, where an alternative workweek schedule was adopted between October 1, 1999 and October 1, 2000, a new secret ballot election to repeal that alternative workweek schedule shall not be subject to the 12–month interval between elections. The election shall take place during regular working hours at the employees' work site. If the alternative workweek schedule is revoked, the employer shall comply within 60 days. Upon proper showing of undue hardship, the Division of Labor Standards Enforcement may grant an extension of time for compliance.

(6) Only secret ballots may be cast by affected employees in the work unit at any election held pursuant to this section. The results of any election conducted pursuant to this section shall be reported by the employer to the Division of Labor Statistics and Research within 30 days after the results are final, and the report of election results shall be a public document. The report shall include the final tally of the vote, the size of the unit, and the nature of the business of the employer.

(7) Employees affected by a change in the work hours resulting from the adoption of an alternative workweek schedule may not be required to work those new work hours for at least 30 days after the announcement of the final results of the election.

(8) Employers shall not intimidate or coerce employees to vote either in support of or in opposition to a proposed alternative workweek. No employees shall be discharged or discriminated against for expressing opinions concerning the alternative workweek election or for opposing or supporting its adoption or repeal. However, nothing in this section shall prohibit an employer from expressing his/her position concerning that alternative workweek to the affected employees. A violation of this subsection shall be subject to Labor Code section 98 et seq.

(D) No employer engaged in the operation of a hospital or an establishment which is an institution primarily engaged in the care of the sick, the aged, or the mentally ill or defective who reside on the premises shall be deemed to have violated any provision of this section if, pursuant to an agreement or understanding arrived at between the employer and employee before performance of work, a work period of 14 consecutive days is accepted in lieu of the workweek of seven (7) consecutive days for purposes of overtime computation and if, for any employment in excess of 80 hours in such 14 day period, the employee receives compensation at a rate not less than one and one-half (1 ½) times the regular rate at which the employee is employed.

(E) This section does not apply to organized camp counselors who are not employed more than 54 hours and not more than six (6) days in any workweek except under the conditions set forth below. This section shall also not apply to personal attendants as defined in Section 2 (N), nor to resident managers of homes for the aged having

less than eight (8) beds; provided that persons employed in such occupations shall not be employed more than 40 hours nor more than six (6) days in any workweek, except under the following conditions:

In the case of emergency, employees may be employed in excess of forty (40) hours or six (6) days in any workweek provided the employee is compensated for all hours in excess of 40 hours and days in excess of six (6) days in the workweek at not less than one and one-half (1 ½) times the employee's regular rate of pay. However, regarding organized camp counselors, in case of emergency they may be employed in excess of 54 hours or six (6) days, provided that they are compensated at not less than one and one-half (1 ½) times the employee's regular rate of pay for all hours worked in excess of 54 hours and six (6) days in the workweek.

(F) One and one-half (1 ½) times a minor's regular rate of pay shall be paid for all work over 40 hours in any workweek except minors 16 or 17 years old who are not required by law to attend school and may therefore be employed for the same hours as an adult are subject to subsection (A), (B), (C), or (D) above.

(**Violations of Child Labor Laws** are subject to civil penalties of from $500 to $10,000 as well as to criminal penalties. Refer to California Labor Code sections 1285 to 1312 and 1390 to 1399 for additional restrictions on the employment of minors and for descriptions of criminal and civil penalties for violation of the child labor laws. Employers should ask school districts about any required work permits.)

(G) An employee may be employed on seven (7) workdays in a workweek when the total hours of employment during such workweek do not exceed 30 and the total hours of employment in any one workday thereof do not exceed six (6).

(H) If a meal period occurs on a shift beginning or ending at or between the hours of 10 p.m. and 6 a.m., facilities shall be available for securing hot food and drink or for heating food or drink, and a suitable sheltered place shall be provided in which to consume such food or drink.

(I) The provisions of this section are not applicable to employees whose hours of service are regulated by:

(1) The United States Department of Transportation Code of Federal Regulations, title 49, sections 395.1 to 395.13, Hours of Service of Drivers, or

(2) Title 13 of the California Code of Regulations, subchapter 6.5, section 1200 and following sections, regulating hours or drivers.

(J) The daily overtime provisions of subsection (A) above shall not apply to ambulance drivers and attendants scheduled for 24 hours shifts of duty who have agreed in writing to exclude from daily time worked not more than three (3) meal periods of not more than one hour each and a regularly scheduled uninterrupted sleeping period of not more than eight (8) hours. The employer shall provide adequate dormitory and kitchen facilities for employees on such a schedule.

(K) The provisions of Labor Code Sections 551 and 552 regarding one (1) day's rest in seven (7) shall not be construed to prevent an accumulation of days of rest when the nature of the employment reasonably requires the employee to work seven (7) or more consecutive days; provided, however, that in each calendar month, the employee shall receive the equivalent of one (1) day's rest in seven (7).

(L) Except as provided in subsections (F) and (K), this section shall not apply to any employee covered by a valid collective bargaining agreement if the agreement expressly provides for the wages, hours of work, and working conditions of the employees, and if the agreement provides premium wage rates for all overtime hours worked and a regular hourly rate of pay for those employees of not less than 30 percent more than the state minimum wage.

(M) Notwithstanding subsection (L) above, where the employer and a labor organization representing employees of the employer have entered into a valid collective bargaining agreement pertaining to the hours of work of the employees, the requirement regarding the equivalent of one (1) day's rest in seven (7) (see subsection (K) above) shall apply, unless the agreement expressly provides otherwise.

(N) If an employer approves a written request of an employee to make up work time that is or would be lost as a result of a personal obligation of the employee, the hours of that make up work time, if performed in the same workweek in which the work time was lost, may not be counted toward computing the total number of hours worked in a day for purposes of the overtime requirements, except for hours in excess of 11 hours of work in one (1) day or 40 hours of work in one (1) workweek. If an employee knows in advance that he or she will be requesting make up time for a personal obligation that will recur at a fixed time over a succession of weeks, the employee may request to make up work time for up to four (4) weeks in advance; provided, however, that the make up work must be performed in the same week that the work time was lost. An employee shall provide a signed written request for each occasion that the employee makes a request to make up work time pursuant to this Section. While an employer may inform an employee of this make up time option, the employer is prohibited from encouraging or otherwise soliciting an employee to request the employer's approval to take personal time off and make up the work hours within the same workweek pursuant to this Section.

4. Minimum Wages

(A) Every employer shall pay to each employee wages not less than seven dollars and fifty cents ($7.50) per hour for all hours worked, effective January 1, 2007, and not less than eight dollars ($8.00) per hour for all hours worked, effective January 1, 2008, except:

Learners. Employees during their first one hundred and sixty (160) hours of employment in occupations in which they have no previous similar or related experience, may be paid not less than 85 percent of the minimum wage rounded to the nearest nickel.

(B) Every employer shall pay to each employee, on the established payday for the period involved, not less than the applicable minimum wage for all hours worked in the payroll period, whether the remuneration is measured by time, piece, commission, or otherwise.

(C) When an employee works a split shift, one hour's pay at the minimum wage shall be paid in addition to the minimum wage for that workday, except when the employee resides at the place of employment.

(D) The provisions of this section shall not apply to apprentices regularly indentured under the State Division of Apprenticeship Standards.

5. Reporting Time Pay

(A) Each workday an employee is required to report for work and does report, but is not put to work or is furnished less than half said employee's usual or scheduled day's work, the employee shall be paid for half the usual or scheduled day's work, but in no event for less than two (2) hours nor more than four (4) hours, at the employee's regular rate of pay, which shall not be less than the minimum wage.

(B) If an employee is required to report for work a second time in any one workday and is furnished less than two hours of work on the second reporting, said employee shall be paid for two hours at the employee's regular rate of pay, which shall not be less than the minimum wage.

(C) The foregoing reporting time pay provisions are not applicable when:

(1) Operations cannot commence or continue due to threats to employees or property; or when recommended by civil authorities; or

(2) Public utilities fail to supply electricity, water, or gas, or there is a failure in the public utilities, or sewer system; or

(3) The interruption of work is caused by an Act of God or other cause not within the employer's control.

(D) This section shall not apply to an employee on paid standby status who is called to perform assigned work at a time other than the employee's scheduled reporting time.

6. Licenses for Disabled Workers

(A) A license may be issued by the Division authorizing employment of a person whose earning capacity is impaired by physical disability or mental deficiency at less than the minimum wage. Such licenses shall be granted only upon joint application of employer and employee and employee's representative if any.

(B) A special license may be issued to a nonprofit organization such as a sheltered workshop or rehabilitation facility fixing special minimum rates to enable the employment of such persons without requiring individual licenses of such employees.

(C) All such licenses and special licenses shall be renewed on a yearly basis or more frequently at the discretion of the Division. (See California Labor Code, Sections 1191 and 1191.5.)

7. Records

(A) Every employer shall keep accurate information with respect to each employee including the following:

(1) Full name, home address, occupation and social security number.

(2) Birth date, if under 18 years, and designation as a minor.

(3) Time records showing when the employee begins and ends each work period. Meal periods, split shift intervals and total daily hours worked shall also be recorded. Meal periods during which operations cease and authorized rest periods need not be recorded.

(4) Total wages paid each payroll period, including value of board, lodging, or other compensation actually furnished to the employee.

(5) Total hours worked in the payroll period and applicable rates of pay. This information shall be made readily available to the employee upon reasonable request.

(6) When a piece rate or incentive plan is in operation, piece rates or an explanation of the incentive plan formula shall be provided to employees. An accurate production record shall be maintained by the employer.

(B) Every employer shall semimonthly or at the time of each payment of wages furnish each employee, either as a detachable part of the check, draft, or voucher paying the employee's wages, or separately, an itemized statement in writing showing: (1) all deductions; (2) the inclusive dates of the period for which the employee is paid; (3) the name of the employee or the employee's social security number; and (4) the name of the employer, provided all deductions made on written orders of the employee may be aggregated and shown as one item.

(C) All required records shall be in the English language and in ink or other indelible form, properly dated, showing month, day and year, and shall be kept on file by the employer for at least three years at the place of employment or at a central location within the State of California. An employee's records shall be available for inspection by the employee upon reasonable request.

(D) Clocks shall be provided in all major work areas or within reasonable distance thereto insofar as practicable.

8. Cash Shortage and Breakage. No employer shall make any deduction from the wage or require any reimbursement from an employee for any cash shortage, breakage, or loss of equipment, unless it can be shown that the shortage, breakage, or loss is caused by a dishonest or willful act, or by the gross negligence of the employee.

9. Uniforms and Equipment

(A) When uniforms are required by the employer to be worn by the employee as a condition of employment, such uniforms shall be provided and maintained by the employer. The term "uniform" includes wearing apparel and accessories of distinctive design or color.

Note: This section shall not apply to protective apparel regulated by the Occupational Safety and Health Standards Board.

(B) When tools or equipment are required by the employer or are necessary to the performance of a job, such tools and equipment shall be provided and maintained by the employer, except that an employee whose wages are at least two (2) times the minimum wage provided herein may be required to provide and maintain hand tools and equipment customarily required by the trade or craft. Notwithstanding any other provision of this section, employees in beauty salons, schools of beauty culture offering beauty care to the public for a fee, and barber shops may be required to furnish their own manicure implements, curling irons, rollers, clips, haircutting scissors, combs, blowers, razors, and eyebrow tweezers. This subsection (B) shall not apply to apprentices regularly indentured under the State Division of Apprenticeship Standards.

Note: This section shall not apply to protective equipment and safety devices on tools regulated by the Occupational Safety and Health Standards Board.

(C) A reasonable deposit may be required as security for the return of the items furnished by the employer under provisions of subsections (A) and (B) of this section upon issuance of a receipt to the employee for such deposit. Such deposits shall be made pursuant to Section 400 and following of the Labor Code or an employer with the prior written authorization of the employee may deduct from the employee's last check the cost of an item furnished pursuant to (A) and (B) above in the event said item is not returned. No deduction shall be made at any time for normal wear and tear. All items furnished by the employer shall be returned by the employee upon completion of the job.

10. Meals and Lodging

(A) "Meal" means an adequate, well-balanced serving of a variety of wholesome, nutritious foods.

(B) "Lodging" means living accommodations available to the employee for full-time occupancy which are adequate, decent, and sanitary according to usual and customary standards. Employees shall not be required to share a bed.

(C) Meals or lodging may not be credited against the minimum wage without a voluntary written agreement between the employer and the employee. When credit for meals or lodging is used to meet part of the employer's minimum wage obligation, the amounts so credited may not be more than the following:

Effective	January 1, 2007	January 1, 2008
Lodging:		
Room occupied alone	$35.27 per week	$37.63 per week
Room shared	$29.11 per week	$31.06 per week
Apartment—two–thirds (2/03) of the ordinary rental value, and in no event more than	$423.51 per month	$451.89 per month
Where a couple are both employed by the employer, two-thirds (2/03) of the ordinary rental value, and in no event more than	$626.49 per month	$668.46 per month
Meals:		
Breakfast	$2.72	$2.90
Lunch	$3.72	$3.97
Dinner	$5.00	$5.34

(D) Meals evaluated, as part of the minimum wage, must be bona fide meals consistent with the employee's work shift. Deductions shall not be made for meals not received nor lodging not used.

(E) If, as a condition of employment, the employee must live at the place of employment or occupy quarters owned or under the control of the employer, then the employer may not charge rent in excess of the values listed herein.

11. Meal Periods

(A) No employer shall employ any person for a work period of more than five (5) hours without a meal period of not less than 30 minutes, except that when a work period of not more than six (6) hours will complete the day's work the meal period may be waived by mutual consent of the employer and employee. Unless the employee is relieved of all duty during a 30 minute meal period, the meal period shall be considered an "on duty" meal period and counted as time worked. An "on duty" meal period shall be permitted only when the nature of the work prevents an employee from being relieved of all duty and when by written agreement between the parties an on-the-job paid meal period is agreed to. The written agreement shall state that the employee may, in writing, revoke the agreement at any time.

(B) If an employer fails to provide an employee a meal period in accordance with the applicable provisions of this Order, the employer shall pay the employee one (1) hour of pay at the employee's regular rate of compensation for each work day that the meal period is not provided.

(C) In all places of employment where employees are required to eat on the premises, a suitable place for that purpose shall be designated.

(D) Notwithstanding any other provision of this order, employees in the health care industry who work shifts in excess of eight (8) total hours in a workday may voluntarily waive their right to one of their two meal periods. In order to be valid, any such waiver must be documented in a written agreement that is voluntarily signed by both the employee and the employer. The

employee may revoke the waiver at any time by providing the employer at least one day's written notice. The employee shall be fully compensated for all working time, including any on-the-job meal period, while such a waiver is in effect.

(E) Employees with direct responsibility for children who are under 18 years of age or who are not emancipated from the foster care system and who, in either case, are receiving 24 hour residential care, and employees of 24 hour residential care facilities for the elderly, blind or developmentally disabled individuals may be required to work on-duty meal periods without penalty when necessary to meet regulatory or approved program standards and one of the following two conditions is met:

(1) (a) The residential care employees eats with residents during residents' meals and the employer provides the same meal at no charge to the employee; or

(b) The employee is in sole charge of the resident(s) and, on the day shift, the employer provides a meal at no charge to the employee.

(2) An employee, except for the night shift, may exercise the right to have an off-duty meal period upon 30 days' notice to the employer for each instance where an off-duty meal is desired, provided that, there shall be no more than one off-duty meal period every two weeks.

12. Rest Periods

(A) Every employer shall authorize and permit all employees to take rest periods, which insofar as practicable shall be in the middle of each work period. The authorized rest period time shall be based on the total hours worked daily at the rate of ten (10) minutes net rest time per four (4) hours or major fraction thereof. However, a rest period need not be authorized for employees whose total daily work time is less than three and one-half (3 $\frac{1}{2}$) hours. Authorized rest period time shall be counted, as hours worked, for which there shall be no deduction from wages.

(B) If an employer fails to provide an employee a rest period in accordance with the applicable provisions of this Order, the employer shall pay the employee one (1) hour of pay at the employee's regular rate of compensation for each work day that the rest period is not provided.

(C) However, employees with direct responsibility for children who are under 18 years of age or who are not emancipated from the foster care system and who, in either case, are receiving 24 hour residential care and employees of 24 hour residential care facilities for elderly, blind or developmentally disabled individuals may, without penalty, require an employee to remain on the premises and maintain general supervision of residents during rest periods if the employee is in sole charge of residents. Another rest period shall be authorized and permitted by the employer when an employee is affirmatively required to interrupt his/her break to respond to the needs of residents.

13. Change Rooms and Resting Facilities

(A) Employers shall provide suitable lockers, closets, or equivalent for the safekeeping of employees' outer clothing during working hours, and when required, for their work clothing during non-working hours. When the occupation requires a change of clothing, change rooms or equivalent space shall be provided in order that employees may change their clothing in reasonable privacy and comfort. These rooms or spaces may be adjacent to but shall be separate from toilet rooms and shall be kept clean.

Note: This section shall not apply to change rooms and storage facilities regulated by the Occupational Safety and Health Standards Board.

(B) Suitable resting facilities shall be provided in an area separate from the toilet rooms and shall be available to employees during work hours.

14. Seats

(A) All working employees shall be provided with suitable seats when the nature of the work reasonably permits the use of seats.

(B) When employees are not engaged in the active duties of their employment and the nature of the work requires standing, an adequate number of suitable seats shall be placed in reasonable proximity to the work area and employees shall be permitted to use such seats when it does not interfere with the performance of their duties.

15. Temperature

(A) The temperature maintained in each work area shall provide reasonable comfort consistent with industry-wide standards for the nature of the process and the work performed.

(B) If excessive heat or humidity is created by the work process, the employer shall take all feasible means to reduce such excessive heat or humidity to a degree providing reasonable comfort. Where the nature of the employment requires a temperature of less than 60° F., a heated room shall be provided to which employees may retire for warmth, and such room shall be maintained at not less than 68°.

(C) A temperature of not less than 68° shall be maintained in the toilet rooms, resting rooms, and change rooms during hours of use.

(D) Federal and State energy guidelines shall prevail over any conflicting provision of this section.

16. Elevators. Adequate elevator, escalator or similar service consistent with industry-wide standards for the nature of the process and the work performed shall be provided when employees are employed four floors or more above or below ground level.

17. Exemptions. If, in the opinion of the Division after due investigation, it is found that the enforcement of any provision contained in Section 7, Records; Section 12, Rest Periods; Section 13, Change Rooms and Resting Facilities; Section 14, Seats; Section 15, Temperature; or Section 16, Elevators, would not materially affect the welfare or comfort of employees and would work an undue hardship on the employer, exemption may be made at the discretion of the Division. Such exemptions shall be in writing to be effective and may be revoked after reasonable notice is given in writing. Application for exemption shall be made by the employer or by the employee and/or the employee's representative to the Division in writing. A copy of the application shall be posted at the place of employment at the time the application is filed with the Division.

18. Filing Reports. (See California Labor Code, Section 1174(a))

19. Inspection. (See California Labor Code, Section 1174)

20. Penalties. (See Labor Code, Section 1199)

(A) In addition to any other civil penalties provided by law, any employer or any other person acting on behalf of the employer who violates, or causes to be violated, the provisions of this order, shall be subject to the civil penalty of:

(1) Initial Violation—$50.00 for each underpaid employee for each pay period during which the employee was underpaid in addition to the amount which is sufficient to recover unpaid wages.

(2) Subsequent Violations—$100.00 for each underpaid employee for each pay period during which the employee was underpaid in addition to an amount which is sufficient to recover unpaid wages.

(3) The affected employee shall receive payment of all wages recovered.

(B) The Labor Commissioner may also issue citations pursuant to Labor Code § 1197.1 for non-payment of wages for overtime work in violation of this order.

21. Separability. If the application of any provision of this Order, or any section, subsection, subdivision, sentence, clause, phrase, word, or portion of this Order should be held invalid or unconstitutional or unauthorized or prohibited by statute, the remaining provisions thereof shall not be affected thereby, but shall continue to be given full force and effect as if the part so held invalid or unconstitutional had not been included herein.

22. Posting of Order. Every employer shall keep a copy of this Order posted in an area frequented by employees where it may be easily read during the workday. Where the location of work or other conditions make this impractical, every employer shall keep a copy of this Order and make it available to every employee upon request.

Publisher's Notes

See Henning v. Industrial Welfare Com. (1998) 46 Cal.3d 1262, 762 P.2d 442, 252 Cal.Rptr. 278 (history and interpretation of Wage Order No. 5).

See Aguilar v. Association for Retarded Citizens (1991) 234 Cal.App.3d 21, 285 Cal.Rptr. 515 (meaning of "hours worked").

See Brewer v. Patel (1991) 20 Cal.App.4th 1017, 25 Cal.Rptr.2d 65 (meaning of "hours worked"—compensation of resident managers of apartment houses and motels).

See Industrial Welfare Com. v. Superior Court (1980) 27 Cal.3d 690, 613 P.2d 579, 166 Cal.Rptr. 331 (validity of 1980 order).

[1] Pursuant to Labor Code section 515.5, subdivision (a)(4), the Division of Labor Statistics and Research, Department of Industrial Relations, has adjusted the minimum hourly rate of pay specified in this subdivision to be $49.77, effective January 1, 2007. This hourly rate of pay is adjusted on October 1 of each year to be effective on January 1, of the following year, and may be obtained at www.dir.ca.gov/IWC or by mail from the Department of Industrial Relations.

Research References

See notes following listing of Wage Orders.

Please Post With This Side Showing
OFFICIAL NOTICE
Effective January 1, 2001 as amended
Sections 4(A) and 10(C) amended and republished by the Department of Industrial Relations, effective January 1, 2007, pursuant to AB 1835, Chapter 230, Statutes of 2006

INDUSTRIAL WELFARE COMMISSION
ORDER NO. 6–2001
REGULATING
WAGES, HOURS AND WORKING CONDITIONS IN THE
LAUNDRY, LINEN SUPPLY, DRY
CLEANING AND DYEING INDUSTRY

TAKE NOTICE: To employers and representatives of persons working in industries and occupations in the State of California:

The Department of Industrial Relations amends and republishes the minimum wage and meals and lodging credits in the Industrial Welfare Commission's Orders as a result of legislation enacted (AB 1835, Ch. 230, Stats of 2006, adding sections 1182.12 and 1182.13 to the California Labor Code.) The amendments and republishing make no other changes to the IWC's Orders.

1. Applicability of Order. This order shall apply to all persons employed in the laundry, linen supply, dry cleaning and dyeing industry whether paid on a time, piece rate, commission, or other basis, except that:

(A) Provisions of Sections 3 through 12 of this order shall not apply to persons employed in administrative, executive, or professional capacities. The following requirements shall apply in determining whether an employee's duties meet the test to qualify for an exemption from those sections:

(1) Executive Exemption. A person employed in an executive capacity means any employee:

(a) Whose duties and responsibilities involve the management of the enterprise in which he/she is employed or of a customarily recognized department or subdivision thereof; and

(b) Who customarily and regularly directs the work of two or more other employees therein; and

(c) Who has the authority to hire or fire other employees or whose suggestions and recommendations as to the hiring or firing and as to the advancement and promotion or any other change of status of other employees will be given particular weight; and

(d) Who customarily and regularly exercises discretion and independent judgment; and

(e) Who is primarily engaged in duties which meet the test of the exemption. The activities constituting exempt work and non-exempt work shall be construed in the same manner as such items are construed in the following regulations under the Fair Labor Standards Act effective as of the date of this order: 29 C.F.R. Sections 541.102, 541.104–111, and 541.115–116. Exempt work shall include, for example, all work that is directly and closely related to exempt work and work which is properly viewed as a means for carrying out exempt functions. The work actually performed by the employee during the course of the workweek must, first and foremost, be examined and the amount of time the employee spends on such work, together with the employer's realistic expectations and the realistic requirements of the job, shall be considered in determining whether the employee satisfies this requirement.

(f) Such an employee must also earn a monthly salary equivalent to no less than two (2) times the state minimum wage for full-time employment. Full–time employment is defined in Labor Code Section 515(c) as 40 hours per week.

(2) Administrative Exemption. A person employed in an administrative capacity means any employee:

(a) Whose duties and responsibilities involve either:

(i) The performance of office or non-manual work directly related to management policies or general business operations of his/her employer or his/her employer's customers; or

(ii) The performance of functions in the administration of a school system, or educational establishment or institution, or of a department or subdivision thereof, in work directly related to the academic instruction or training carried on therein; and

(b) Who customarily and regularly exercises discretion and independent judgment; and

(c) Who regularly and directly assists a proprietor, or an employee employed in a bona fide executive or administrative capacity (as such terms are defined for purposes of this section); or

(d) Who performs under only general supervision work along specialized or technical lines requiring special training, experience, or knowledge; or

(e) Who executes under only general supervision special assignments and tasks; and

(f) Who is primarily engaged in duties which meet the test of the exemption. The activities constituting exempt work and non-exempt work shall be construed in the same manner as such terms are construed in the following regulations under the Fair Labor Standards Act effective as of the date of this order: 29 C.F.R. Sections 541.201–205, 541.207–208, 541.210, and 541.215. Exempt work shall include, for example, all work that is directly and closely related to exempt work and work which is properly viewed as a means for carrying out exempt functions. The work actually performed by the employee during the course of the workweek must, first and foremost, be examined and the amount of time the employee spends on such work, together with the employer's realistic expectations and the realistic requirements of the job, shall be considered in determining whether the employee satisfies this requirement.

(g) Such employee must also earn a monthly salary equivalent to no less than two (2) times the state minimum wage for full-time employment. Full–time employment is defined in Labor Code Section 515(c) as 40 hours per week.

(3) Professional Exemption. A person employed in a professional capacity means any employee who meets *all* of the following requirements:

(a) Who is licensed or certified by the State of California and is primarily engaged in the practice of one of the following recognized professions: law, medicine, dentistry, optometry, architecture, engineering, teaching, or accounting; or

(b) Who is primarily engaged in an occupation commonly recognized as a learned or artistic profession. For the purposes of this subsection, "learned or artistic profession" means an employee who is primarily engaged in the performance of:

(i) Work requiring knowledge of an advanced type in a field or science or learning customarily acquired by a prolonged course of specialized intellectual instruction and study, as distinguished from a general academic education and from an apprenticeship, and from training in the performance of routine mental, manual, or physical

processes, or work that is an essential part of or necessarily incident to any of the above work; or

(ii) Work that is original and creative in character in a recognized field of artistic endeavor (as opposed to work which can be produced by a person endowed with general manual or intellectual ability and training), and the result of which depends primarily on the invention, imagination, or talent of the employee or work that is an essential part of or necessarily incident to any of the above work; and

(iii) Whose work is predominantly intellectual and varied in character (as opposed to routine mental, manual, mechanical, or physical work) and is of such character that the output produced or the result accomplished cannot be standardized in relation to a given period of time.

(c) Who customarily and regularly exercises discretion and independent judgment in the performance of duties set forth in subparagraphs (a) and (b).

(d) Who earns a monthly salary equivalent to no less than two (2) times the state minimum wage for full-time employment. Full–time employment is defined in Labor Code Section 515 (c) as 40 hours per week.

(e) Subparagraph (b) above is intended to be construed in accordance with the following provisions of federal law as they existed as of the date of this wage order: 29 C.F.R. Sections 541.207, 541.301(a)–(d), 541.302, 541.306, 541.307, 541.308, and 541.310.

(f) Notwithstanding the provisions of this subparagraph, pharmacists employed to engage in the practice of pharmacy, and registered nurses employed to engage in the practice of nursing, shall not be considered exempt professional employees, nor shall they be considered exempt from coverage for the purposes of this subparagraph unless they individually meet the criteria established for exemption as executive or administrative employees.

(g) Subparagraph (f) above shall not apply to the following advanced practice nurses:

(i) Certified nurse midwives who are primarily engaged in performing duties for which certification is required pursuant to Article 2.5 (commencing with Section 2746) of Chapter 6 of Division 2 of the Business and Professions Code.

(ii) Certified nurse anesthetists who are primarily engaged in performing duties for which certification is required pursuant to Article 7 (commencing with Section 2825) of Chapter 6 of Division 2 of the Business and Professions Code.

(iii) Certified nurse practitioners who are primarily engaged in performing duties for which certification is required pursuant to Article 8 (commencing with Section 2834) of Chapter 6 of Division 2 of the Business and Professions Code.

(iv) Nothing in this subparagraph shall exempt the occupations set forth in clauses (i), (ii), and (iii) from meeting the requirements of subsection 1(A)(3)(a)–(d) above.

(h) Except, as provided in subparagraph (i), an employee in the computer software field who is paid on an hourly basis shall be exempt, if *all* of the following apply:

(i) The employee is primarily engaged in work that is intellectual or creative and requires the exercise of discretion and independent judgment.

(ii) The employee is primarily engaged in duties that consist of one or more of the following:

-The application of systems analysis techniques and procedures, including consulting with users, to determine hardware, software, or system functional specifications.

-The design, development, documentation, analysis, creation, testing, or modification of computer systems or programs, including prototypes, based on and related to user or system design specifications.

-The documentation, testing, creation, or modification of computer programs related to the design of software or hardware for computer operating systems.

(iii) The employee is highly skilled and is proficient in the theoretical and practical application of highly specialized information to computer systems analysis, programming, and software engineering. A job title shall not be determinative of the applicability of this exemption.

(iv) The employee's hourly rate of pay is not less than forty-one dollars ($41.00). The Division of Labor Statistics and Research shall adjust this pay rate on October 1 of each year to be effective on January 1 of the following year by an amount equal to the percentage increase in the California Consumer Price Index for Urban Wage Earners and Clerical Workers.[1]

(i) The exemption provided in subparagraph (h) does not apply to an employee if *any* of the following apply:

(i) The employee is a trainee or employee in an entry-level position who is learning to become proficient in the theoretical and practical application of highly specialized information to computer systems analysis, programming, and software engineering.

(ii) The employee is in a computer-related occupation but has not attained the level of skill and expertise necessary to work independently and without close supervision.

(iii) The employee is engaged in the operation of computers or in the manufacture, repair, or maintenance of computer hardware and related equipment.

(iv) The employee is an engineer, drafter, machinist, or other professional whose work is highly dependent upon or facilitated by the use of computers and computer software programs and who is skilled in computer-aided design software, including CAD/CAM, but who is not in a computer systems analysis or programming occupation.

(v) The employee is a writer engaged in writing material, including box labels, product descriptions, documentation, promotional material, setup and installation instructions, and other similar written information, either for print or for on screen media or who writes or provides content material intended to be read by customers, subscribers, or visitors to computer-related media such as the World Wide Web or CD–ROMs.

(vi) The employee is engaged in *any* of the activities set forth in subparagraph (h) for the purpose of creating imagery for effects used in the motion picture, television, or theatrical industry.

(B) Except as provided in Sections 1, 2, 4, 10, and 20, the provisions of this order shall not apply to any employees directly employed by the State or any political subdivision thereof, including any city, county, or special district.

(C) The provisions of this order shall not apply to outside salespersons.

(D) The provisions of this order shall not apply to any individual who is the parent, spouse, child, or legally adopted child of the employer.

(E) The provisions of this order shall not apply to any individual participating in a national service program, such as Ameri–Corps, carried out using assistance provided under Section 12571 of Title 42 of the United States Code. (See Stats. 2000, ch. 365, amending Labor Code Section 1171.)

2. Definitions

(A) An "alternative workweek schedule" means any regularly scheduled workweek requiring an employee to work more than eight (8) hours in a 24–hour period.

(B) "Commission" means the Industrial Welfare Commission of the State of California.

(C) "Division" means the Division of Labor Standards Enforcement of the State of California.

(D) "Employ" means to engage, suffer, or permit to work.

(E) "Employee" means any person employed by an employer.

(F) "Employer" means any person as defined in Section 18 of the Labor Code, who directly or indirectly, or through an agent or any other person, employs or exercises control over the wages, hours, or working conditions of any person.

(G) "Hours worked" means the time during which an employee is subject to the control of an employer, and includes all the time the employee is suffered or permitted to work, whether or not required to do so.

(H) "Laundry, Linen Supply, Dry Cleaning and Dyeing Industry" means any industry, business, or establishment operated for the purpose of washing, ironing, cleaning, refreshing, restoring, pressing, dyeing, storing, fumigating, mothproofing, waterproofing, or other processes incidental thereto, on articles or fabrics of any kind, including but not limited to clothing, hats, drapery, rugs, curtains, linens, household furnishings, textiles, furs, or leather goods; and includes self-service laundries, self-service dry cleaning establishments, and the collection, distribution, storage, sale, or resale at retail or wholesale of the foregoing services.

(I) "Minor" means, for the purpose of this order, any person under the age of 18 years.

(J) "Outside salesperson" means any person, 18 years of age or over, who customarily and regularly works more than half the working time away from the employer's place of business selling tangible or intangible items or obtaining orders or contracts for products, services or use of facilities.

(K) "Primarily" as used in Section 1, Applicability, means more than one-half the employee's work time.

(L) "Shift" means designated hours of work by an employee, with a designated beginning time and quitting time.

(M) "Split shift" means a work schedule, which is interrupted by non-paid non-working periods established by the employer, other than bona fide rest or meal periods.

(N) "Teaching" means, for the purpose of Section 1 of this order, the profession of teaching under a certificate from the Commission for Teacher Preparation and Licensing.

(O) "Wages" includes all amounts for labor performed by employees of every description, whether the amount is fixed or ascertained by the standard of time, task, piece, commission basis, or other method of calculation.

(P) "Workday" and "day" mean any consecutive 24–hour period beginning at the same time each calendar day.

(Q) "Workweek" and "week" mean any seven (7) consecutive days, starting with the same calendar day each week. "Workweek" is a fixed and regularly recurring period of 168 hours, seven (7) consecutive 24–hour periods.

3. Hours and Days of Work

(A) *Daily Overtime—General Provisions*

(1) The following overtime provisions are applicable to employees 18 years of age or over and to employees 16 or 17 years of age who are not required by law to attend school and are not otherwise prohibited by law from engaging in the subject work. Such employees shall not be employed more than eight (8) hours in any workday or more than 40 hours in any workweek unless the employee receives one and one-half (1 ½) times such employee's regular rate of pay for all hours worked over 40 hours in the workweek. Eight (8) hours of labor constitutes a day's work. Employment beyond eight (8) hours in any workday or more than six (6) days in any workweek is permissible provided the employee is compensated for such overtime at not less than:

(a) One and one-half (1 ½) times the employee's regular rate of pay for all hours worked in excess of eight (8) hours up to and including 12 hours in any workday,

and for the first eight (8) hours worked on the seventh (7th) consecutive day of work in a workweek; and

(b) Double the employee's regular rate of pay for all hours worked in excess of 12 hours in any workday and for all hours worked in excess of eight (8) hours on the seventh (7th) consecutive day of work in a workweek.

(c) The overtime rate of compensation required to be paid to a nonexempt full-time salaried employee shall be computed by using the employee's regular hourly salary as one-fortieth (1/40) of the employee's weekly salary.

(B) *Alternative Workweek*

(1) No employer shall be deemed to have violated the daily overtime provisions by instituting, pursuant to the election procedures set forth in this wage order, a regularly scheduled alternative workweek schedule of not more than ten (10) hours per day within a 40 hour workweek without the payment of an overtime rate of compensation. All work performed in any workday beyond the schedule established by the agreement up to 12 hours a day or beyond 40 hours per week shall be paid at one and one-half (1 ½) times the employee's regular rate of pay. All work performed in excess of 12 hours per day and any work in excess of eight (8) hours on those days worked beyond the regularly scheduled number of workdays established by the alternative workweek agreement shall be paid at double the employee's regular rate of pay. Any alternative workweek agreement adopted pursuant to this section shall provide for not less than four (4) hours of work in any shift. Nothing in this section shall prohibit an employer, at the request of the employee, to substitute one day of work for another day of the same length in the shift provided by the alternative workweek agreement on an occasional basis to meet the personal needs of the employee without the payment of overtime. No hours paid at either one and one-half (1 ½) or double the regular rate of pay shall be included in determining when 40 hours have been worked for the purpose of computing overtime compensation.

(2) Any agreement adopted pursuant to this section shall provide not less than two consecutive days off within a workweek.

(3) If an employer whose employees have adopted an alternative workweek agreement permitted by this order requires an employee to work fewer hours than those that are regularly scheduled by the agreement, the employer shall pay the employee overtime compensation at a rate of one and one-half (1 ½) times the employee's regular rate of pay for all hours worked in excess of eight (8) hours, and double the employee's regular rate of pay for all hours worked in excess of 12 hours for the day the employee is required to work the reduced hours.

(4) An employer shall not reduce an employee's regular rate of hourly pay as a result of the adoption, repeal or nullification of an alternative workweek schedule.

(5) An employer shall explore any available reasonable alternative means of accommodating the religious belief or observance of an affected employee that conflicts with

1439

an adopted alternative workweek schedule, in the manner provided by subdivision (j) of Section 12940 of the Government Code.

(6) An employer shall make a reasonable effort to find a work schedule not to exceed eight (8) hours in a workday, in order to accommodate any affected employee who was eligible to vote in an election authorized by this section and who is unable to work the alternative workweek schedule established as the result of that election.

(7) An employer shall be permitted, but not required, to provide a work schedule not to exceed eight (8) hours in a workday to accommodate any employee who is hired after the date of the election and who is unable to work the alternative workweek schedule established by the election.

(8) Arrangements adopted in a secret ballot election held pursuant to this order prior to 1998, or under the rules in effect prior to 1998, and before the performance of the work, shall remain valid after July 1, 2000 provided that the results of the election are reported by the employer to the Division of Labor Statistics and Research by January 1, 2001, in accordance with the requirements of subsection (C) below (Election Procedures). If an employee was voluntarily working an alternative work-week schedule of not more than ten (10) hours a day as of July 1, 1999, that alternative workweek schedule was based on an individual agreement made after January 1, 1998 between the employee and employer, and the employee submitted, and the employer approved, a written request on or before May 30, 2000 to continue the agreement, the employee may continue to work that alternative workweek schedule without payment of an overtime rate of compensation for the hours provided in the agreement. The employee may revoke his/her voluntary authorization to continue such a schedule with 30 days written notice to the employer. New arrangements can only be entered into pursuant to the provisions of this section.

(C) *Election Procedures*

Election procedures for the adoption and repeal of alternative workweek schedules require the following:

(1) Each proposal for an alternative workweek schedule shall be in the form of a written agreement proposed by the employer. The proposed agreement must designate a regularly scheduled alternative workweek in which the specified number of work days and work hours are regularly recurring. The actual days worked within that alternative workweek schedule need not be specified. The employer may propose a single work schedule that would become the standard schedule for workers in the work unit, or a menu of work schedule options, from which each employee in the unit would be entitled to choose. If the employer proposes a menu of work schedule options, the employee may, with the approval of the employer, move from one menu option to another.

(2) In order to be valid, the proposed alternative workweek schedule must be adopted in a secret ballot election, before the performance of work, by at least a two-thirds (2/03) vote of the affected employees in the work unit. The election shall be held during regular working hours at the employees' work site. For purposes of this subsection, "affected employees in the work unit" may include all employees in a readily identifiable work unit, such as a division, a department, a job classification, a shift, a separate physical location, or a recognized subdivision of any such work unit. A work unit may consist of an individual employee as long as the criteria for an identifiable work unit in this subsection are met.

(3) Prior to the secret ballot vote, any employer who proposed to institute an alternative workweek schedule shall have made a disclosure in writing to the affected employees, including the effects of the proposed arrangement on the employees' wages, hours, and benefits. Such a disclosure shall include meeting(s), duly noticed, held at least 14 days prior to voting, for the specific purpose of discussing the effects of the alternative workweek schedule. An employer shall provide that disclosure in a non–English language, as well as in English, if at least five (5) percent of the affected employees primarily speak that non–English language. The employer shall mail the written disclosure to employees who do not attend the meeting. Failure to comply with this paragraph shall make the election null and void.

(4) Any election to establish or repeal an alternative workweek schedule shall be held at the work site of the affected employees. The employer shall bear the costs of conducting any election held pursuant to this section. Upon a complaint by an affected employee, and after an investigation by the labor commissioner, the labor commissioner may require the employer to select a neutral third party to conduct the election.

(5) Any type of alternative workweek schedule that is authorized by the Labor Code may be repealed by the affected employees. Upon a petition of one-third (1/03) of the affected employees, a new secret ballot election shall be held and a two-thirds (2/03) vote of the affected employees shall be required to reverse the alternative workweek schedule. The election to repeal the alternative workweek schedule shall be held not more than 30 days after the petition is submitted to the employer, except that the election shall be held not less than 12 months after the date that the same group of employees voted in an election held to adopt or repeal an alternative workweek schedule. The election shall take place during regular working hours at the employees' work site. If the alternative workweek schedule is revoked, the employer shall comply within 60 days. Upon proper showing of undue hardship, the Division of Labor Standards Enforcement may grant an extension of time for compliance.

(6) Only secret ballots may be cast by affected employees in the work unit at any election held pursuant to this section. The results of any election conducted pursuant to this section shall be reported by the employer to the

Division of Labor Statistics and Research within 30 days after the results are final, and the report of election results shall be a public document. The report shall include the final tally of the vote, the size of the unit, and the nature of the business of the employer.

(7) Employees affected by a change in the work hours resulting from the adoption of an alternative workweek schedule may not be required to work those new work hours for at least 30 days after the announcement of the final results of the election.

(8) Employers shall not intimidate or coerce employees to vote either in support of or in opposition to a proposed alternative workweek. No employees shall be discharged or discriminated against for expressing opinions concerning the alternative workweek election or for opposing or supporting its adoption or repeal. However, nothing in this section shall prohibit an employer from expressing his/her position concerning that alternative workweek to the affected employees. A violation of this paragraph shall be subject to Labor Code Section 98 *et seq.*

(D) One and one-half (1 ½) times a minor's regular rate of pay shall be paid for all work over 40 hours in any workweek except minors 16 or 17 years old who are not required by law to attend school and may therefore be employed for the same hours as an adult are subject to subsection (A) or (B) and (C) above.

(**Violations of Child Labor Laws** are subject to civil penalties of from $500 to $10,000 as well as to criminal penalties. Refer to California Labor Code Sections 1285 to 1312 and 1390 to 1399 for additional restrictions on the employment of minors and for descriptions of criminal and civil penalties for violation of the child labor laws. Employers should ask school districts about any required work permits.)

(E) An employee may be employed on seven (7) workdays in one workweek when the total hours of employment during such workweek do not exceed 30 and the total hours of employment in any one workday thereof do not exceed six (6).

(F) The provisions of Labor Code Sections 551 and 552 regarding one (1) day's rest in seven (7) shall not be construed to prevent an accumulation of days of rest when the nature of the employment reasonably requires the employee to work seven (7) or more consecutive days; provided, however, that in each calendar month, the employee shall receive the equivalent of one (1) day's rest in seven (7).

(G) If a meal period occurs on a shift beginning or ending at or between the hours of 10 p.m. and 6 a.m., facilities shall be available for securing hot food and drink or for heating food or drink, and a suitable sheltered place shall be provided in which to consume such food or drink.

(H) Except as provided in subsections (D) and (F), this section shall not apply to any employee covered by a valid collective bargaining agreement if the agreement expressly provides for the wages, hours of work, and working conditions of the employees, and if the agreement provides premium wage rates for all overtime hours worked and a regular hourly rate of pay for those employees of not less than 30 percent more than the state minimum wage.

(I) Notwithstanding subsection (H) above, where the employer and a labor organization representing employees of the employer have entered into a valid collective bargaining agreement pertaining to the hours of work of the employees, the requirement regarding the equivalent of one (1) day's rest in seven (7) (see subsection (F) above) shall apply, unless the agreement expressly provides otherwise.

(J) The provisions of this section are not applicable to employees whose hours of service are regulated by:

(1) The United States Department of Transportation Code of Federal Regulations, Title 49, Sections 395.1 to 395.13, Hours of Service of Drivers; or

(2) Title 13 of the California Code of Regulations, subchapter 6.5, Section 1200 and the following sections, regulating hours of drivers.

(K) If an employer approves a written request of an employee to make up work time that is or would be lost as a result of a personal obligation of the employee, the hours of that makeup work time, if performed in the same workweek in which the work time was lost, may not be counted toward computing the total number of hours worked in a day for purposes of the overtime requirements, except for hours in excess of 11 hours of work in one (1) day or 40 hours of work in one (1) workweek. If an employee knows in advance that he/she will be requesting makeup time for a personal obligation that will recur at a fixed time over a succession of weeks, the employee may request to make up work time for up to four (4) weeks in advance; provided, however, that the makeup work must be performed in the same week that the work time was lost. An employee shall provide a signed written request for each occasion that the employee makes a request to make up work time pursuant to this subsection. While an employer may inform an employee of this makeup time option, the employer is prohibited from encouraging or otherwise soliciting an employee to request the employer's approval to take personal time off and make up the work hours within the same workweek pursuant to this subsection.

4. Minimum Wages

(A) Every employer shall pay to each employee wages not less than seven dollars and fifty cents ($7.50) per hour for all hours worked, effective January 1, 2007, and not less than eight dollars ($8.00) per hour for all hours worked, effective January 1, 2008, except:

Learners. Employees during their first 160 hours of employment in occupations in which they have no previous similar or related experience, may be paid not less than 85 percent of the minimum wage rounded to the nearest nickel.

(B) Every employer shall pay to each employee, on the established payday for the period involved, not less than the applicable minimum wage for all hours worked in the payroll period, whether the remuneration is measured by time, piece, commission, or otherwise.

(C) When an employee works a split shift, one (1) hour's pay at the minimum wage shall be paid in addition to the minimum wage for that workday, except when the employee resides at the place of employment.

(D) The provisions of this section shall not apply to apprentices regularly indentured under the State Division of Apprenticeship Standards.

5.   Reporting Time Pay

(A) Each workday an employee is required to report for work and does report, but is not put to work or is furnished less than half said employee's usual or scheduled day's work, the employee shall be paid for half the usual or scheduled day's work, but in no event for less than two (2) hours nor more than four (4) hours, at the employee's regular rate of pay, which shall not be less than the minimum wage.

(B) If an employee is required to report for work a second time in any one workday and is furnished less than two (2) hours of work on the second reporting, said employee shall be paid for two (2) hours at the employee's regular rate of pay, which shall not be less than the minimum wage.

(C) The foregoing reporting time pay provisions are not applicable when:

(1) Operations cannot commence or continue due to threats to employees or property; or when recommended by civil authorities; or

(2) Public utilities fail to supply electricity, water, or gas, or there is a failure in the public utilities, or sewer system; or

(3) The interruption of work is caused by an Act of God or other cause not within the employer's control.

(D) This section shall not apply to an employee on paid standby status who is called to perform assigned work at a time other than the employee's scheduled reporting time.

6.   Licenses for Disabled Workers

(A) A license may be issued by the Division authorizing employment of a person whose earning capacity is impaired by physical disability or mental deficiency at less than the minimum wage. Such licenses shall be granted only upon joint application of employer and employee and employee's representative if any.

(B) A special license may be issued to a nonprofit organization such as a sheltered workshop or rehabilitation facility fixing special minimum rates to enable the employment of such persons without requiring individual licenses of such employees.

(C) All such licenses and special licenses shall be renewed on a yearly basis or more frequently at the discretion of the Division.

(See California Labor Code, Sections 1191 and 1191.5)

7.   Records

(A) Every employer shall keep accurate information with respect to each employee including the following:

(1) Full name, home address, occupation and social security number.

(2) Birth date, if under 18 years, and designation as a minor.

(3) Time records showing when the employee begins and ends each work period. Meal periods, split shift intervals and total daily hours worked shall also be recorded. Meal periods during which operations cease and authorized rest periods need not be recorded.

(4) Total wages paid each payroll period, including value of board, lodging, or other compensation actually furnished to the employee.

(5) Total hours worked in the payroll period and applicable rates of pay. This information shall be made readily available to the employee upon reasonable request.

(6) When a piece rate or incentive plan is in operation, piece rates or an explanation of the incentive plan formula shall be provided to employees. An accurate production record shall be maintained by the employer.

(B) Every employer shall semimonthly or at the time of each payment of wages furnish each employee, either as a detachable part of the check, draft, or voucher paying the employee's wages, or separately, an itemized statement in writing showing: (1) all deductions; (2) the inclusive dates of the period for which the employee is paid; (3) the name of the employee or the employee's social security number; and (4) the name of the employer, provided all deductions made on written orders of the employee may be aggregated and shown as one item.

(C) All required records shall be in the English language and in ink or other indelible form, properly dated, showing month, day and year, and shall be kept on file by the employer for at least three years at the place of employment or at a central location within the State of California. An employee's records shall be available for inspection by the employee upon reasonable request.

(D) Clocks shall be provided in all major work areas or within reasonable distance thereto insofar as practicable.

8.   Cash Shortage and Breakage. No employer shall make any deduction from the wage or require any reimbursement from an employee for any cash shortage, breakage, or loss of equipment, unless it can be shown that the shortage, breakage, or loss is caused by a dishonest or willful act, or by the gross negligence of the employee.

9.   Uniforms and Equipment

(A) When uniforms are required by the employer to be worn by the employee as a condition of employment, such uniforms shall be provided and maintained by the employer. The term "uniform" includes wearing apparel and accessories of distinctive design or color.

Note: This section shall not apply to protective apparel regulated by the Occupational Safety and Health Standards Board.

(B) When tools or equipment are required by the employer or are necessary to the performance of a job, such tools and equipment shall be provided and maintained by the employer, except that an employee whose wages are at least two (2) times the minimum wage provided herein may be required to provide and maintain hand tools and equipment customarily required by the trade or craft. This subsection (B) shall not apply to apprentices regularly indentured under the State Division of Apprenticeship Standards.

Note: This section shall not apply to protective equipment and safety devices on tools regulated by the Occupational Safety and Health Standards Board.

(C) A reasonable deposit may be required as security for the return of the items furnished by the employer under provisions of subsections (A) and (B) of this section upon issuance of a receipt to the employee for such deposit. Such deposits shall be made pursuant to Section 400 and following of the Labor Code or an employer with the prior written authorization of the employee may deduct from the employee's last check the cost of an item furnished pursuant to (A) and (B) above in the event said item is not returned. No deduction shall be made at any time for normal wear and tear. All items furnished by the employer shall be returned by the employee upon completion of the job.

10. Meals and Lodging

(A) "Meal" means an adequate, well-balanced serving of a variety of wholesome, nutritious foods.

(B) "Lodging" means living accommodations available to the employee for full-time occupancy which are adequate, decent, and sanitary according to usual and customary standards. Employees shall not be required to share a bed.

(C) Meals or lodging may not be credited against the minimum wage without a voluntary written agreement between the employer and the employee. When credit for meals or lodging is used to meet part of the employer's minimum wage obligation, the amounts so credited may not be more than the following:

Effective	January 1, 2007	January 1, 2008
Lodging:		
Room occupied alone	$35.27 per week	$37.63 per week
Room shared	$29.11 per week	$31.06 per week
Apartment—two–thirds (2/03) of the ordinary rental value, and in no event more than	$423.51 per month	$451.89 per month

Effective	January 1, 2007	January 1, 2008
Where a couple are both employed by the employer, two-thirds (2/03) of the ordinary rental value, and in no event more than	$626.49 per month	$668.46 per month
Meals:		
Breakfast	$2.72	$2.90
Lunch	$3.72	$3.97
Dinner	$5.00	$5.34

(D) Meals evaluated as part of the minimum wage must be bona fide meals consistent with the employee's work shift. Deductions shall not be made for meals not received or lodging not used.

(E) If, as a condition of employment, the employee must live at the place of employment or occupy quarters owned or under the control of the employer, then the employer may not charge rent in excess of the values listed herein.

11. Meal Periods

(A) No employer shall employ any person for a work period of more than five (5) hours without a meal period of not less than 30 minutes, except that when a work period of not more than six (6) hours will complete the day's work the meal period may be waived by mutual consent of the employer and the employee.

(B) An employer may not employ an employee for a work period of more than ten (10) hours per day without providing the employee with a second meal period of not less than 30 minutes, except that if the total hours worked is no more than 12 hours, the second meal period may be waived by mutual consent of the employer and the employee only if the first meal period was not waived.

(C) Unless the employee is relieved of all duty during a 30 minute meal period, the meal period shall be considered an "on duty" meal period and counted as time worked. An "on duty" meal period shall be permitted only when the nature of the work prevents an employee from being relieved of all duty and when by written agreement between the parties an on-the-job paid meal period is agreed to. The written agreement shall state that the employee may, in writing, revoke the agreement at any time.

(D) If an employer fails to provide an employee a meal period in accordance with the applicable provisions of this order, the employer shall pay the employee one (1) hour of pay at the employee's regular rate of compensation for each workday that the meal period is not provided.

(E) In all places of employment where employees are required to eat on the premises, a suitable place for that purpose shall be designated.

12. Rest Periods

(A) Every employer shall authorize and permit all employees to take rest periods, which insofar as practicable shall be in the middle of each work period. The authorized rest period time shall be based on the total

1443

hours worked daily at the rate of ten (10) minutes net rest time per four (4) hours or major fraction thereof. However, a rest period need not be authorized for employees whose total daily work time is less than three and one-half (3 ½) hours. Authorized rest period time shall be counted as hours worked for which there shall be no deduction from wages.

(B) If an employer fails to provide an employee a rest period in accordance with the applicable provisions of this order, the employer shall pay the employee one (1) hour of pay at the employee's regular rate of compensation for each workday that the rest period is not provided.

13. Change Rooms and Resting Facilities

(A) Employers shall provide suitable lockers, closets, or equivalent for the safekeeping of employees' outer clothing during working hours, and when required, for their work clothing during non-working hours. When the occupation requires a change of clothing, change rooms or equivalent space shall be provided in order that employees may change their clothing in reasonable privacy and comfort. These rooms or spaces may be adjacent to but shall be separate from toilet rooms and shall be kept clean.

Note: This section shall not apply to change rooms and storage facilities regulated by the Occupational Safety and Health Standards Board.

(B) Suitable resting facilities shall be provided in an area separate from the toilet rooms and shall be available to employees during work hours.

14. Seats

(A) All working employees shall be provided with suitable seats when the nature of the work reasonably permits the use of seats.

(B) When employees are not engaged in the active duties of their employment and the nature of the work requires standing, an adequate number of suitable seats shall be placed in reasonable proximity to the work area and employees shall be permitted to use such seats when it does not interfere with the performance of their duties.

15. Temperature

(A) The temperature maintained in each work area shall provide reasonable comfort consistent with industry-wide standards for the nature of the process and the work performed.

(B) If excessive heat or humidity is created by the work process, the employer shall take all feasible means to reduce such excessive heat or humidity to a degree providing reasonable comfort. Where the nature of the employment requires a temperature of less than 60° F., a heated room shall be provided to which employees may retire for warmth, and such room shall be maintained at not less than 68°.

(C) A temperature of not less than 68° shall be maintained in the toilet rooms, resting rooms, and change rooms during hours of use.

(D) Federal and State energy guidelines shall prevail over any conflicting provision of this section.

1444

16. Elevators.

Adequate elevator, escalator or similar service consistent with industry-wide standards for the nature of the process and the work performed shall be provided when employees are employed four floors or more above or below ground level.

17. Exemptions.

If, in the opinion of the Division after due investigation, it is found that the enforcement of any provision contained in Section 7, Records; Section 12, Rest Periods; Section 13, Change Rooms and Resting Facilities; Section 14, Seats; Section 15, Temperature; or Section 16, Elevators, would not materially affect the welfare or comfort of employees and would work an undue hardship on the employer, exemption may be made at the discretion of the Division. Such exemptions shall be in writing to be effective and may be revoked after reasonable notice is given in writing. Application for exemption shall be made by the employer or by the employee and/or the employee's representative to the Division in writing. A copy of the application shall be posted at the place of employment at the time the application is filed with the Division.

18. Filing Reports.

(See California Labor Code, Section 1174(a))

19. Inspection.

(See California Labor Code, Section 1174)

20. Penalties.

(See California Labor Code, Section 1199)

(A) In addition to any other civil penalties provided by law, any employer or any other person acting on behalf of the employer who violates, or causes to be violated, the provisions of this order, shall be subject to the civil penalty of:

(1) Initial Violation—$50.00 for each underpaid employee for each pay period during which the employee was underpaid in addition to the amount which is sufficient to recover unpaid wages.

(2) Subsequent Violations—$100.00 for each underpaid employee for each pay period during which the employee was underpaid in addition to an amount which is sufficient to recover unpaid wages.

(3) The affected employee shall receive payment of all wages recovered.

(B) The labor commissioner may also issue citations pursuant to California Labor Code Section 1197.1 for non-payment of wages for overtime work in violation of this order.

21. Separability.

If the application of any provision of this order, or any section, subsection, subdivision, sentence, clause, phrase, word, or portion of this order should be held invalid or unconstitutional or unauthorized or prohibited by statute, the remaining provisions thereof shall not be affected thereby, but shall continue to be given full force and effect as if the part so held invalid or unconstitutional had not been included herein.

22. Posting of Order.

Every employer shall keep a copy of this order posted in an area frequented by employees where it may be easily read during the workday. Where the location of work or other conditions make this impractical, every employer shall keep a copy of this order and make it available to every employee upon request.

[1] Pursuant to Labor Code section 515.5, subdivision (a)(4), the Division of Labor Statistics and Research, Department of Industrial Relations, has adjusted the minimum hourly rate of pay specified in this subdivision to be $49.77, effective January 1, 2007. This hourly rate of pay is adjusted on October 1 of each year to be effective on January 1, of the following year, and may be obtained at www.dir.ca.gov/IWC or by mail from the Department of Industrial Relations.

Publisher's Notes

Research References

See notes following listing of Wage Orders.

Please Post With This Side Showing
OFFICIAL NOTICE
Effective January 1, 2001 as amended

Sections 4(A) and 10(C) amended and republished by the Department of Industrial Relations, effective January 1, 2007, pursuant to AB 1835, Chapter 230, Statutes of 2006

INDUSTRIAL WELFARE COMMISSION
ORDER NO. 7–2001
REGULATING
WAGES, HOURS AND WORKING CONDITIONS IN THE
MERCANTILE INDUSTRY

TAKE NOTICE: To employers and representatives of persons working in industries and occupations in the State of California:

The Department of Industrial Relations amends and republishes the minimum wage and meals and lodging credits in the Industrial Welfare Commission's Orders as a result of legislation enacted (AB 1835, Ch. 230, Stats of 2006, adding sections 1182.12 and 1182.13 to the California Labor Code.) The amendments and republishing make no other changes to the IWC's Orders.

1. Applicability of Order. This order shall apply to all persons employed in the mercantile industry whether paid on a time, piece rate, commission, or other basis, except that:

(A) Provisions of Sections 3 through 12 of this order shall not apply to persons employed in administrative, executive, or professional capacities. The following requirements shall apply in determining whether an employee's duties meet the test to qualify for an exemption from those sections:

(1) Executive Exemption. A person employed in an executive capacity means any employee:

(a) Whose duties and responsibilities involve the management of the enterprise in which he/she is employed or of a customarily recognized department or subdivision thereof; and

(b) Who customarily and regularly directs the work of two or more other employees therein; and

(c) Who has the authority to hire or fire other employees or whose suggestions and recommendations as to the hiring or firing and as to the advancement and promotion or any other change of status of other employees will be given particular weight; and

(d) Who customarily and regularly exercises discretion and independent judgment; and

(e) Who is primarily engaged in duties which meet the test of the exemption. The activities constituting exempt work and non exempt work shall be construed in the same manner as such items are construed in the following regulations under the Fair Labor Standards Act effective as of the date of this order: 29 C.F.R. Sections 541.102, 541.104–111, and 541.115 116. Exempt work shall include, for example, all work that is directly and closely related to exempt work and work which is properly viewed as a means for carrying out exempt functions. The work actually performed by the employee during the course of the workweek must, first and foremost, be examined and the amount of time the employee spends on such work, together with the employer's realistic expectations and the realistic requirements of the job, shall be considered in determining whether the employee satisfies this requirement.

(f) Such an employee must also earn a monthly salary equivalent to no less than two (2) times the state minimum wage for full-time employment. Full–time employment is defined in Labor Code Section 515(c) as 40 hours per week.

(2) Administrative Exemption. A person employed in an administrative capacity means any employee:

(a) Whose duties and responsibilities involve either:

(i) The performance of office or non-manual work directly related to management policies or general business operations of his/her employer or his/her employer's customers; or

(ii) The performance of functions in the administration of a school system, or educational establishment or institution, or of a department or subdivision thereof, in work directly related to the academic instruction or training carried on therein; and

(b) Who customarily and regularly exercises discretion and independent judgment; and

(c) Who regularly and directly assists a proprietor, or an employee employed in a bona fide executive or administrative capacity (as such terms are defined for purposes of this section); or

(d) Who performs under only general supervision work along specialized or technical lines requiring special training, experience, or knowledge; or

(e) Who executes under only general supervision special assignments and tasks; and

(f) Who is primarily engaged in duties that meet the test of the exemption. The activities constituting exempt work and non-exempt work shall be construed in the same manner as such terms are construed in the following regulations under the Fair Labor Standards Act effective as of the date of this order: 29 C.F.R. Sections 541.201–205, 541.207–208, and 541.210, and 541.215. Exempt work shall include, for example, all work that is directly and closely related to exempt work and work which is properly viewed as a means for carrying out exempt functions. The work actually performed by the employee during the course of the workweek must, first and foremost, be examined and the amount of time the employee spends on such work, together with the employer's realistic expectations and the realistic requirements of the job, shall be considered in determining whether the employee satisfies this requirement.

(g) Such employee must also earn a monthly salary equivalent to no less than two (2) times the state minimum wage for full-time employment. Full–time employment is defined in Labor Code Section 515(c) as 40 hours per week.

(3) Professional Exemption. A person employed in a professional capacity means any employee who meets *all* of the following requirements:

(a) Who is licensed or certified by the State of California and is primarily engaged in the practice of one of the following recognized professions: law, medicine, dentistry, optometry, architecture, engineering, teaching, or accounting; or

(b) Who is primarily engaged in an occupation commonly recognized as a learned or artistic profession. For the purposes of this subsection, "learned or artistic profession" means an employee who is primarily engaged in the performance of:

(i) Work requiring knowledge of an advanced type in a field or science or learning customarily acquired by a prolonged course of specialized intellectual instruction and study, as distinguished from a general academic education and from an apprenticeship, and from training in the performance of routine mental, manual, or physical processes, or work that is an essential part of or necessarily incident to any of the above work; or

(ii) Work that is original and creative in character in a recognized field of artistic endeavor (as opposed to work

1446

which can be produced by a person endowed with general manual or intellectual ability and training), and the result of which depends primarily on the invention, imagination, or talent of the employee or work that is an essential part of or necessarily incident to any of the above work; and

(iii) Whose work is predominantly intellectual and varied in character (as opposed to routine mental, manual, mechanical, or physical work) and is of such character that the output produced or the result accomplished cannot be standardized in relation to a given period of time.

(c) Who customarily and regularly exercises discretion and independent judgment in the performance of duties set forth in subparagraphs (a) and (b).

(d) Who earns a monthly salary equivalent to no less than two (2) times the state minimum wage for full-time employment. Full-time employment as defined in Labor Code Section 515(c) as 40 hours per week.

(e) Subparagraph (b) above is intended to be construed in accordance with the following provisions of federal law as they existed as of the date of this wage order: 29 C.F.R. Sections 541.207, 541.301(a)–(d), 541.302, 541.306, 541.307, 541.308, and 541.310.

(f) Notwithstanding the provisions of this subparagraph, pharmacists employed to engage in the practice of pharmacy, and registered nurses employed to engage in the practice of nursing, shall not be considered exempt professional employees, nor shall they be considered exempt from coverage for the purposes of this subparagraph unless they individually meet the criteria established for exemption as executive or administrative employees.

(g) Subparagraph (f) above shall not apply to the following advanced practice nurses:

(i) Certified nurse midwives who are primarily engaged in performing duties for which certification is required pursuant to Article 2.5 (commencing with Section 2746) of Chapter 6 of Division 2 of the Business and Professions Code.

(ii) Certified nurse anesthetists who are primarily engaged in performing duties for which certification is required pursuant to Article 7 (commencing with Section 2825) of Chapter 6 of Division 2 of the Business and Professions Code.

(iii) Certified nurse practitioners who are primarily engaged in performing duties for which certification is required pursuant to Article 8 (commencing with Section 2834) of Chapter 6 of Division 2 of the Business and Professions Code.

(iv) Nothing in this subparagraph shall exempt the occupations set forth in clauses (i), (ii), and (iii) from meeting the requirements of subsection 1(A)(3)(a)–(d) above.

(h) Except, as provided in subparagraph (i), an employee in the computer software field who is paid on an hourly basis shall be exempt, if *all* of the following apply:

(i) The employee is primarily engaged in work that is intellectual or creative and that requires the exercise of discretion and independent judgment.

(ii) The employee is primarily engaged in duties that consist of one or more of the following:

-The application of systems analysis techniques and procedures, including consulting with users, to determine hardware, software, or system functional specifications.

-The design, development, documentation, analysis, creation, testing, or modification of computer systems or programs, including prototypes, based on and related to user or system design specifications.

-The documentation, testing, creation, or modification of computer programs related to the design of software or hardware for computer operating systems.

(iii) The employee is highly skilled and is proficient in the theoretical and practical application of highly specialized information to computer systems analysis, programming, and software engineering. A job title shall not be determinative of the applicability of this exemption.

(iv) The employee's hourly rate of pay is not less than forty-one dollars ($41.00). The Division of Labor Statistics and Research shall adjust this pay rate on October 1 of each year to be effective on January 1 of the following year by an amount equal to the percentage increase in the California Consumer Price Index for Urban Wage Earners and Clerical Workers.[1]

(i) The exemption provided in subparagraph (h) does not apply to an employee if *any* of the following apply:

(i) The employee is a trainee or employee in an entry-level position who is learning to become proficient in the theoretical and practical application of highly specialized information to computer systems analysis, programming, and software engineering. MP32(ii) The employee is in a computer-related occupation but has not attained the level of skill and expertise necessary to work independently and without close supervision.

(iii) The employee is engaged in the operation of computers or in the manufacture, repair, or maintenance of computer hardware and related equipment.

(iv) The employee is an engineer, drafter, machinist, or other professional whose work is highly dependent upon or facilitated by the use of computers and computer software programs and who is skilled in computer-aided design software, including CAD/CAM, but who is not in a computer systems analysis or programming occupation.

(v) The employee is a writer engaged in writing material, including box labels, product descriptions, documentation, promotional material, setup and installation instructions, and other similar written information, either for print or for on screen media or who writes or provides content material intended to be read by customers, subscribers, or visitors to computer-related media such as the World Wide Web or CD–ROMs.

(vi) The employee is engaged in *any* of the activities set forth in subparagraph (h) for the purpose of creating imagery for effects used in the motion picture, television, or theatrical industry.

(B) Except as provided in Sections 1, 2, 4, 10, and 20, the provisions of this order shall not apply to any employees directly employed by the State or any political subdivision thereof, including any city, county, or special district.

(C) The provisions of this order shall not apply to outside salespersons.

(D) The provisions of this order shall not apply to any individual who is the parent, spouse, child, or legally adopted child or the employer.

(E) The provisions of this order shall not apply to any individual participating in a national service program, such as Ameri–Corps, carried out using assistance provided under Section 12571 of Title 42 of the United States Code. (See Stats. 200 amending Labor Code Section 1171.)

2. Definitions

(A) An "alternative workweek schedule" means any regularly scheduled workweek requiring an employee to work more than eight (8) hours in a 24–hour period.

(B) "Commission" means the Industrial Welfare Commission of the State of California.

(C) "Division" means the Division of Labor Standards Enforcement of the State of California.

(D) "Employ" means to engage, suffer, or permit to work.

(E) "Employee" means any person employed by an employer, and includes any lessee who is charged rent, or who pays rent for a chair, booth, or space; and

(1) Who does not use his/her own funds to purchase requisite supplies; and

(2) Who does not maintain an appointment book separate and distinct from that of the establishment in which the space is located; and

(3) Who does not have a business license where applicable.

(F) "Employer" means any person as defined in Section 18 of the Labor Code, who directly or indirectly, or through an agent or any other person, employs or exercises control over the wages, hours, or working conditions of any person.

(G) "Hours worked" means the time during which an employee is subject to the control of an employer, and includes all the time the employee is suffered or permitted to work, whether or not required to do so.

(H) "Mercantile Industry" means any industry, business, or establishment operated for the purpose of purchasing, selling, or distributing goods or commodities at wholesale or retail; or for the purpose of renting goods or commodities.

(I) "Minor" means, for the purpose of this order, any person under the age of 18 years.

(J) "Outside salesperson" means any person, 18 years of age or over, who customarily and regularly works more than half the working time away from the employer's place of business selling tangible or intangible items or obtaining orders or contracts for products, services or use of facilities.

(K) "Primarily" as used in Section 1, Applicability, means more than one-half the employee's work time.

(L) "Shift" means designated hours of work by an employee, with a designated beginning time and quitting time.

(M) "Split shift" means a work schedule, which is interrupted by non-paid non-working periods established by the employer, other than bona fide rest or meal periods.

(N) "Teaching" means, for the purpose of Section 1 of this order, the profession of teaching under a certificate from the Commission for Teacher Preparation and Licensing or teaching in an accredited college or university.

(O) "Wages" includes all amounts for labor performed by employees of every description, whether the amount is fixed or ascertained by the standard of time, task, piece, commission basis, or other method of calculation.

(P) "Workday" and "day" mean any consecutive 24–hour period beginning at the same time each calendar day.

(Q) "Workweek" and "week" mean any seven (7) consecutive days, starting with the same calendar day each week. "Workweek" is a fixed and regularly recurring period of 168 hours, seven (7) consecutive 24–hour periods.

3. Hours and Days of Work

(A) *Daily Overtime—General Provisions*

(1) The following overtime provisions are applicable to employees 18 years of age or over and to employees 16 or 17 years of age who are not required by law to attend school and are not otherwise prohibited by law from engaging in the subject work. Such employees shall not be employed more than eight (8) hours in any workday or more than 40 hours in any workweek unless the employee receives one and one-half (1 ½) times such employee's regular rate of pay for all hours worked over 40 hours in the workweek. Eight (8) hours of labor constitutes a day's work. Employment beyond eight (8) hours in any workday or more than six (6) days in any workweek is permissible provided the employee is compensated for such overtime at not less than:

(a) One and one-half (1 ½) times the employee's regular rate of pay for all hours worked in excess of eight (8) hours up to and including 12 hours in any workday, and for the first eight (8) hours worked on the seventh (7th) consecutive day of work in a workweek; and

(b) Double the employee's regular rate of pay for all hours worked in excess of 12 hours in any workday and for all hours worked in excess of eight (8) hours on the seventh (7th) consecutive day of work in a workweek.

(c) The overtime rate of compensation required to be paid to a nonexempt full-time salaried employee shall be computed by using the employee's regular hourly salary as one-fortieth (1/40) of the employee's weekly salary.

(B) *Alternative Workweek*

(1) No employer shall be deemed to have violated the daily overtime provisions by instituting, pursuant to the election procedures set forth in this wage order, a regularly scheduled alternative workweek schedule of not more than ten (10) hours per day within a 40 hour workweek without the payment of an overtime rate of compensation. All work performed in any workday beyond the schedule established by the agreement up to 12 hours a day or beyond 40 hours per week shall be paid at one and one-half (1 ½) times the employee's regular rate of pay. All work performed in excess of 12 hours per day and any work in excess of eight (8) hours on those days worked beyond the regularly scheduled number of workdays established by the alternative workweek agreement shall be paid at double the employee's regular rate of pay. Any alternative workweek agreement adopted pursuant to this section shall provide for not less than four (4) hours of work in any shift. Nothing in this section shall prohibit an employer, at the request of the employee, to substitute one day of work for another day of the same length in the shift provided by the alternative workweek agreement on an occasional basis to meet the personal needs of the employee without the payment of overtime. No hours paid at either one and one-half (1 ½) or double the regular rate of pay shall be included in determining when 40 hours have been worked for the purpose of computing overtime compensation.

(2) Any agreement adopted pursuant to this section shall provide not less than two consecutive days off within a workweek.

(3) If an employer whose employees have adopted an alternative workweek agreement permitted by this order requires an employee to work fewer hours than those that are regularly scheduled by the agreement, the employer shall pay the employee overtime compensation at a rate of one and one-half (1 ½) times the employee's regular rate of pay for all hours worked in excess of eight (8) hours, and double the employee's regular rate of pay for all hours worked in excess of 12 hours for the day the employee is required to work the reduced hours.

(4) An employer shall not reduce an employee's regular rate of hourly pay as a result of the adoption, repeal or nullification of an alternative workweek schedule.

(5) An employer shall explore any available reasonable alternative means of accommodating the religious belief or observance of an affected employee that conflicts with an adopted alternative workweek schedule, in the manner provided by subdivision (j) of Section 12940 of the Government Code.

(6) An employer shall make a reasonable effort to find a work schedule not to exceed eight (8) hours in a workday, in order to accommodate any affected employee who was eligible to vote in an election authorized by this section and who is unable to work the alternative workweek schedule established as the result of that election.

(7) An employer shall be permitted, but not required, to provide a work schedule not to exceed eight (8) hours in a workday to accommodate any employee who is hired after the date of the election and who is unable to work the alternative workweek schedule established by the election.

(8) Arrangements adopted in a secret ballot election held pursuant to this order prior to 1998, or under the rules in effect prior to 1998, and before the performance of the work, shall remain valid after July 1, 2000 provided that the results of the election are reported by the employer to the Division of Labor Statistics and Research by January 1, 2001, in accordance with the requirements of subsection (C) below (Election Procedures). If an employee was voluntarily working an alternative workweek schedule of not more than ten (10) hours a day as of July 1, 1999, that alternative workweek schedule was based on an individual agreement made after January 1, 1998 between the employee and employer, and the employee submitted, and the employer approved, a written request on or before May 30, 2000 to continue the agreement, the employee may continue to work that alternative workweek schedule without payment of an overtime rate of compensation for the hours provided in the agreement. The employee may revoke his/her voluntary authorization to continue such a schedule with 30 days written notice to the employer. New arrangements can only be entered into pursuant to the provisions of this section.

(C) *Election Procedures*

Election procedures for the adoption and repeal of alternative workweek schedules require the following:

(1) Each proposal for an alternative workweek schedule shall be in the form of a written agreement proposed by the employer. The proposed agreement must designate a regularly scheduled alternative workweek in which the specified number of work days and work hours are regularly recurring. The actual days worked within that alternative workweek schedule need not be specified. The employer may propose a single work schedule that would become the standard schedule for workers in the work unit, or a menu of work schedule options, from which each employee in the unit would be entitled to choose. If the employer proposes a menu of work schedule options, the employee may, with the approval of the employer, move from one menu option to another.

(2) In order to be valid, the proposed alternative workweek schedule must be adopted in a secret ballot election, before the performance of work, by at least a two-thirds (2/03) vote of the affected employees in the work unit. The election shall be held during regular working hours at the employees' work site. For purposes of this subsection, "affected employees in the work unit" may include all employees in a readily identifiable work unit, such as a division, a department, a job classification, a shift, a separate physical location, or a recognized subdivision of any such work unit. A work unit may consist of an individual employee as long as the criteria for an identifiable work unit in this subsection are met.

(3) Prior to the secret ballot vote, any employer who proposed to institute an alternative workweek schedule shall have made a disclosure in writing to the affected employees, including the effects of the proposed arrangement on the employees' wages, hours, and benefits. Such a disclosure shall include meeting(s), duly noticed, held at least 14 days prior to voting, for the specific purpose of discussing the effects of the alternative workweek schedule. An employer shall provide that disclosure in a non–English language, as well as in English, if at least five (5) percent of the affected employees primarily speak that non–English language. The employer shall mail the written disclosure to employees who do not attend the meeting. Failure to comply with this paragraph shall make the election null and void.

(4) Any election to establish or repeal an alternative workweek schedule shall be held at the work site of the affected employees. The employer shall bear the costs of conducting any election held pursuant to this section. Upon a complaint by an affected employee, and after an investigation by the labor commissioner, the labor commissioner may require the employer to select a neutral third party to conduct the election.

(5) Any type of alternative workweek schedule that is authorized by the Labor Code may be repealed by the affected employees. Upon a petition of one-third (1/03) of the affected employees, a new secret ballot election shall be held and a two-thirds (2/03) vote of the affected employees shall be required to reverse the alternative workweek schedule. The election to repeal the alternative workweek schedule shall be held not more than 30 days after the petition is submitted to the employer, except that the election shall be held not less than 12 months after the date that the same group of employees voted in an election held to adopt or repeal an alternative workweek schedule. The election shall take place during regular working hours at the employees' work site. If the alternative workweek schedule is revoked, the employer shall comply within 60 days. Upon proper showing of undue hardship, the Division of Labor Standards Enforcement may grant an extension of time for compliance.

(6) Only secret ballots may be cast by affected employees in the work unit at any election held pursuant to this section. The results of any election conducted pursuant to this section shall be reported by the employer to the Division of Labor Statistics and Research within 30 days after the results are final, and the report of election results shall be a public document. The report shall include the final tally of the vote, the size of the unit, and the nature of the business of the employer.

(7) Employees affected by a change in the work hours resulting from the adoption of an alternative workweek schedule may not be required to work those new work hours for at least 30 days after the announcement of the final results of the election.

(8) Employers shall not intimidate or coerce employees to vote either in support of or in opposition to a proposed alternative workweek. No employees shall be discharged or discriminated against for expressing opinions concerning the alternative workweek election or for opposing or supporting its adoption or repeal. However, nothing in this section shall prohibit an employer from expressing his/her position concerning that alternative workweek to the affected employees. A violation of this paragraph shall be subject to Labor Code Section 98 *et seq.*

(D) Provisions of subsections (A), (B), and (C) above shall not apply to any employee whose earnings exceed one and one-half (1 ½) times the minimum wage if more than half of that employee's compensation represents commissions.

(E) One and one-half (1 ½) times a minor's regular rate of pay shall be paid for all work over 40 hours in any workweek except minors 16 or 17 years old who are not required by law to attend school and may therefore be employed for the same hours as an adult are subject to subsection (A) or (B) and (C) above.

(**Violations of Child Labor Laws** are subject to civil penalties of from $500 to $10,000 as well as to criminal penalties. Refer to California Labor Code Sections 1285 to 1312 and 1390 to 1399 for additional restrictions on the employment of minors and for descriptions of criminal and civil penalties for violation of the child labor laws. Employers should ask school districts about any required work permits.)

(F) An employee may be employed on seven (7) workdays in one workweek when the total hours of employment during such workweek do not exceed 30 and the total hours of employment in any one workday thereof do not exceed six (6).

(G) If a meal period occurs on a shift beginning or ending at or between the hours of 10 p.m. and 6 a.m., facilities shall be available for securing hot food and drink or for heating food or drink, and a suitable sheltered place shall be provided in which to consume such food or drink.

(H) The provisions of Labor Code Sections 551 and 552 regarding one (1) day's rest in seven (7) shall not be construed to prevent an accumulation of days of rest when the nature of the employment reasonably requires the employee to work seven (7) or more consecutive days; provided, however, that in each calendar month, the employee shall receive the equivalent of one (1) day's rest in seven (7).

(I) Except as provided in subsections (E) and (H), this section shall not apply to any employee covered by a valid collective bargaining agreement if the agreement express-

ly provides for the wages, hours of work, and working conditions of the employees, and if the agreement provides premium wage rates for all overtime hours worked and a regular hourly rate of pay for those employees of not less than 30 percent more than the state minimum wage.

(J) Notwithstanding subsection (I) above, where the employer and a labor organization representing employees of the employer have entered into a valid collective bargaining agreement pertaining to the hours of work of the employees, the requirement regarding the equivalent of one (1) day's rest in seven (7) (see subsection (H) above) shall apply, unless the agreement expressly provides otherwise.

(K) The provisions of this section are not applicable to employees whose hours of service are regulated by:

(1) The United States Department of Transportation Code of Federal Regulations, Title 49, Sections 395.1 to 395.13, Hours of Service of Drivers; or

(2) Title 13 of the California Code of Regulations, subchapter 6.5, Section 1200 and the following sections, regulating hours of drivers.

(L) If an employer approves a written request of an employee to make up work time that is or would be lost as a result of a personal obligation of the employee, the hours of that makeup work time, if performed in the same workweek in which the work time was lost, may not be counted toward computing the total number of hours worked in a day for purposes of the overtime requirements, except for hours in excess of 11 hours of work in one (1) day or 40 hours of work in one (1) workweek. If an employee knows in advance that he/she will be requesting makeup time for a personal obligation that will recur at a fixed time over a succession of weeks, the employee may request to make up work time for up to four (4) weeks in advance; provided, however, that the makeup work must be performed in the same week that the work time was lost. An employee shall provide a signed written request for each occasion that the employee makes a request to make up work time pursuant to this subsection. While an employer may inform an employee of this makeup time option, the employer is prohibited from encouraging or otherwise soliciting an employee to request the employer's approval to take personal time off and make up the work hours within the same workweek pursuant to this subsection.

4. Minimum Wages

(A) Every employer shall pay to each employee wages not less than seven dollars and fifty cents ($7.50) per hour for all hours worked, effective January 1, 2007, and not less than eight dollars ($8.00) per hour for all hours worked, effective January 1, 2008, except:

Learners. Employees during their first 160 hours of employment in occupations in which they have no previous similar or related experience, may be paid not less than 85 percent of the minimum wage rounded to the nearest nickel.

(B) Every employer shall pay to each employee, on the established payday for the period involved, not less than the applicable minimum wage for all hours worked in the payroll period, whether the remuneration is measured by time, piece, commission, or otherwise.

(C) When an employee works a split shift, one (1) hour's pay at the minimum wage shall be paid in addition to the minimum wage for that workday, except when the employee resides at the place of employment.

(D) The provisions of this section shall not apply to apprentices regularly indentured under the State Division of Apprenticeship Standards.

5. Reporting Time Pay

(A) Each workday an employee is required to report for work and does report, but is not put to work or is furnished less than half said employee's usual or scheduled day's work, the employee shall be paid for half the usual or scheduled day's work, but in no event for less than two (2) hours nor more than four (4) hours, at the employee's regular rate of pay, which shall not be less than the minimum wage.

(B) If an employee is required to report for work a second time in any one workday and is furnished less than two (2) hours of work on the second reporting, said employee shall be paid for two (2) hours at the employee's regular rate of pay, which shall not be less than the minimum wage.

(C) The foregoing reporting time pay provisions are not applicable when:

(1) Operations cannot commence or continue due to threats to employees or property; or when recommended by civil authorities; or

(2) Public utilities fail to supply electricity, water, or gas, or there is a failure in the public utilities, or sewer system; or

(3) The interruption of work is caused by an Act of God or other cause not within the employer's control.

(D) This section shall not apply to an employee on paid standby status who is called to perform assigned work at a time other than the employee's scheduled reporting time.

6. Licenses for Disabled Workers

(A) A license may be issued by the Division authorizing employment of a person whose earning capacity is impaired by physical disability or mental deficiency at less than the minimum wage. Such licenses shall be granted only upon joint application of employer and employee and employee's representative if any.

(B) A special license may be issued to a nonprofit organization such as a sheltered workshop or rehabilitation facility fixing special minimum rates to enable the employment of such persons without requiring individual licenses of such employees.

(C) All such licenses and special licenses shall be renewed on a yearly basis or more frequently at the discretion of the Division.

(See California Labor Code, Sections 1191 and 1191.5)

7. Records

(A) Every employer shall keep accurate information with respect to each employee including the following:

(1) Full name, home address, occupation and social security number.

(2) Birth date, if under 18 years, and designation as a minor.

(3) Time records showing when the employee begins and ends each work period. Meal periods, split shift intervals and total daily hours worked shall also be recorded. Meal periods during which operations cease and authorized rest periods need not be recorded.

(4) Total wages paid each payroll period, including value of board, lodging, or other compensation actually furnished to the employee.

(5) Total hours worked in the payroll period and applicable rates of pay. This information shall be made readily available to the employee upon reasonable request.

(6) When a piece rate or incentive plan is in operation, piece rates or an explanation of the incentive plan formula shall be provided to employees. An accurate production record shall be maintained by the employer.

(B) Every employer shall semimonthly or at the time of each payment of wages furnish each employee, either as a detachable part of the check, draft, or voucher paying the employee's wages, or separately, an itemized statement in writing showing: (1) all deductions; (2) the inclusive dates of the period for which the employee is paid; (3) the name of the employee or the employee's social security number; and (4) the name of the employer, provided all deductions made on written orders of the employee may be aggregated and shown as one item.

(C) All required records shall be in the English language and in ink or other indelible form, properly dated, showing month, day and year, and shall be kept on file by the employer for at least three years at the place of employment or at a central location within the State of California. An employee's records shall be available for inspection by the employee upon reasonable request.

(D) Clocks shall be provided in all major work areas or within reasonable distance thereto insofar as practicable.

8. Cash Shortage and Breakage.
No employer shall make any deduction from the wage or require any reimbursement from an employee for any cash shortage, breakage, or loss of equipment, unless it can be shown that the shortage, breakage, or loss is caused by a dishonest or willful act, or by the gross negligence of the employee.

9. Uniforms and Equipment

(A) When uniforms are required by the employer to be worn by the employee as a condition of employment, such uniforms shall be provided and maintained by the employer. The term "uniform" includes wearing apparel and accessories of distinctive design or color.

Note: This section shall not apply to protective apparel regulated by the Occupational Safety and Health Standards Board.

(B) When tools or equipment are required by the employer or are necessary to the performance of a job, such tools and equipment shall be provided and maintained by the employer, except that an employee whose wages are at least two (2) times the minimum wage provided herein may be required to provide and maintain hand tools and equipment customarily required by the trade or craft. Notwithstanding any other provision of this section, employees in beauty salons, schools of beauty culture offering beauty care to the public for a fee, and barber shops may be required to furnish their own manicure implements, curling irons, rollers, clips, haircutting scissors, combs, blowers, razors, and eyebrow tweezers. This subsection (B) shall not apply to apprentices regularly indentured under the State Division of Apprenticeship Standards.

Note: This section shall not apply to protective equipment and safety devices on tools regulated by the Occupational Safety and Health Standards Board.

(C) A reasonable deposit may be required as security for the return of the items furnished by the employer under provisions of subsections (A) and (B) of this section upon issuance of a receipt to the employee for such deposit. Such deposits shall be made pursuant to Section 400 and following of the Labor Code or an employer with the prior written authorization of the employee may deduct from the employee's last check the cost of an item furnished pursuant to (A) and (B) above in the event said item is not returned. No deduction shall be made at any time for normal wear and tear. All items furnished by the employer shall be returned by the employee upon completion of the job.

10. Meals and Lodging

(A) "Meal" means an adequate, well-balanced serving of a variety of wholesome, nutritious foods.

(B) "Lodging" means living accommodations available to the employee for full-time occupancy which are adequate, decent, and sanitary according to usual and customary standards. Employees shall not be required to share a bed.

(C) Meals or lodging may not be credited against the minimum wage without a voluntary written agreement between the employer and the employee. When credit for meals or lodging is used to meet part of the employer's minimum wage obligation, the amounts so credited may not be more than the following:

Effective	January 1, 2007	January 1, 2008
Lodging:		
Room occupied alone	$35.27 per week	$37.63 per week
Room shared	$29.11 per week	$31.06 per week
Apartment—two–thirds (2/03) of the ordinary rental value, and in no event more than	$423.51 per month	$451.89 per month
Where a couple are both employed by the employer, two-thirds (2/03) of the ordinary rental value, and in no event more than	$626.49 per month	$668.46 per month
Meals:		
Breakfast	$2.72	$2.90
Lunch	$3.72	$3.97
Dinner	$5.00	$5.34

(D) Meals evaluated as part of the minimum wage must be bona fide meals consistent with the employee's work shift. Deductions shall not be made for meals not received or lodging not used.

(E) If, as a condition of employment, the employee must live at the place of employment or occupy quarters owned or under the control of the employer, then the employer may not charge rent in excess of the values listed herein.

11. Meal Periods

(A) No employer shall employ any person for a work period of more than five (5) hours without a meal period of not less than 30 minutes, except that when a work period of not more than six (6) hours will complete the day's work the meal period may be waived by mutual consent of the employer and the employee.

(B) An employer may not employ an employee for a work period of more than ten (10) hours per day without providing the employee with a second meal period of not less than 30 minutes, except that if the total hours worked is no more than 12 hours, the second meal period may be waived by mutual consent of the employer and the employee only if the first meal period was not waived.

(C) Unless the employee is relieved of all duty during a 30 minute meal period, the meal period shall be considered an "on duty" meal period and counted as time worked. An "on duty" meal period shall be permitted only when the nature of the work prevents an employee from being relieved of all duty and when by written agreement between the parties an on-the-job paid meal period is agreed to. The written agreement shall state that the employee may, in writing, revoke the agreement at any time.

(D) If an employer fails to provide an employee a meal period in accordance with the applicable provisions of this order, the employer shall pay the employee one (1) hour of pay at the employee's regular rate of compensation for each workday that the meal period is not provided.

(E) In all places of employment where employees are required to eat on the premises, a suitable place for that purpose shall be designated.

12. Rest Periods

(A) Every employer shall authorize and permit all employees to take rest periods, which insofar as practicable shall be in the middle of each work period. The authorized rest period time shall be based on the total hours worked daily at the rate of ten (10) minutes net rest time per four (4) hours or major fraction thereof. However, a rest period need not be authorized for employees whose total daily work time is less than three and one-half (3 ½) hours. Authorized rest period time shall be counted as hours worked for which there shall be no deduction from wages.

(B) If an employer fails to provide an employee a rest period in accordance with the applicable provisions of this order, the employer shall pay the employee one (1) hour of pay at the employee's regular rate of compensation for each workday that the rest period is not provided.

13. Change Rooms and Resting Facilities

(A) Employers shall provide suitable lockers, closets, or equivalent for the safekeeping of employees' outer clothing during working hours, and when required, for their work clothing during non-working hours. When the occupation requires a change of clothing, change rooms or equivalent space shall be provided in order that employees may change their clothing in reasonable privacy and comfort. These rooms or spaces may be adjacent to but shall be separate from toilet rooms and shall be kept clean.

Note: This section shall not apply to change rooms and storage facilities regulated by the Occupational Safety and Health Standards Board.

(B) Suitable resting facilities shall be provided in an area separate from the toilet rooms and shall be available to employees during work hours.

14. Seats

(A) All working employees shall be provided with suitable seats when the nature of the work reasonably permits the use of seats.

(B) When employees are not engaged in the active duties of their employment and the nature of the work requires standing, an adequate number of suitable seats shall be placed in reasonable proximity to the work area and employees shall be permitted to use such seats when it does not interfere with the performance of their duties.

15. Temperature

(A) The temperature maintained in each work area shall provide reasonable comfort consistent with industry-wide standards for the nature of the process and the work performed.

(B) If excessive heat or humidity is created by the work process, the employer shall take all feasible means to reduce such excessive heat or humidity to a degree providing reasonable comfort. Where the nature of the employment requires a temperature of less than 60° F., a heated room shall be provided to which employees may retire for warmth, and such room shall be maintained at not less than 68°.

(C) A temperature of not less than 68° shall be maintained in the toilet rooms, resting rooms, and change rooms during hours of use.

(D) Federal and State energy guidelines shall prevail over any conflicting provision of this section.

16. Elevators. Adequate elevator, escalator or similar service consistent with industry-wide standards for the nature of the process and the work performed shall be provided when employees are employed four floors or more above or below ground level.

17. Exemptions. If, in the opinion of the Division after due investigation, it is found that the enforcement of any provision contained in Section 7, Records; Section 12, Rest Periods; Section 13, Change Rooms and Resting Facilities; Section 14, Seats; Section 15, Temperature; or Section 16, Elevators, would not materially affect the welfare or comfort of employees and would work an undue hardship on the employer, exemption may be made at the discretion of the Division. Such exemptions shall be in writing to be effective and may be revoked after reasonable notice is given in writing. Application for exemption shall be made by the employer or by the employee and/or the employee's representative to the Division in writing. A copy of the application shall be posted at the place of employment at the time the application is filed with the Division.

18. Filing Reports. (See California Labor Code, Section 1174(a))

19. Inspection. (See California Labor Code, Section 1174)

20. Penalties. (See California Labor Code, Section 1199)

(A) In addition to any other civil penalties provided by law, any employer or any other person acting on behalf of the employer who violates, or causes to be violated, the provisions of this order, shall be subject to the civil penalty of:

(1) Initial Violation—$50.00 for each underpaid employee for each pay period during which the employee was underpaid in addition to the amount which is sufficient to recover unpaid wages.

(2) Subsequent Violations—$100.00 for each underpaid employee for each pay period during which the employee was underpaid in addition to an amount which is sufficient to recover unpaid wages.

(3) The affected employee shall receive payment of all wages recovered.

(B) The labor commissioner may also issue citations pursuant to California Labor Code Section 1197.1 for non-payment of wages for overtime work in violation of this order.

21. Separability. If the application of any provision of this order, or any section, subsection, subdivision,

1453

sentence, clause, phrase, word, or portion of this order should be held invalid or unconstitutional or unauthorized or prohibited by statute, the remaining provisions thereof shall not be affected thereby, but shall continue to be given full force and effect as if the part so held invalid or unconstitutional had not been included herein.

22. Posting of Order. Every employer shall keep a copy of this order posted in an area frequented by employees where it may be easily read during the workday. Where the location of work or other conditions make this impractical, every employer shall keep a copy of this order and make it available to every employee upon request.

[1] Pursuant to Labor Code section 515.5, subdivision (a)(4), the Division of Labor Statistics and Research, Department of Industrial Relations, has adjusted the minimum hourly rate of pay specified in this subdivision to be $49.77, effective January 1, 2007. This hourly rate of pay is adjusted on October 1 of each year to be effective on January 1, of the following year, and may be obtained at www.dir.ca.gov/IWC or by mail from the Department of Industrial Relations.

Publisher's Notes

See Erichs v. Venator Group, Inc., 128 F.Supp.2d 1255, 1264 (N.D.Cal. 2001) (meaning of "earnings" in paragraph 3(D)).

See Ramirez v. Yosemite Water Co., Inc. (1998) 73 Cal.Rptr.2d 125 (meaning of "outside salesperson").

See Hernandez v. Mendoza (1988) 199 Cal.App.3d 721, 245 Cal.Rptr. 36) Ghory v. Al–Lahham (1989) 209 Cal. App.3d 1487, 257 Cal.Rptr. 924 (the appropriate method of calculating overtime wages is contained in *Skyline Homes, Inc. v. Department of Industrial Relations (1985) 165 Cal.App.3d 239, 211 Cal.Rptr. 792*).

Research References

See notes following listing of Wage Orders.

Please Post With This Side Showing
OFFICIAL NOTICE
Effective January 1, 2001 as amended
Sections 4(A) and 10(C) amended and republished by the Department of Industrial Relations, effective January 1, 2007, pursuant to AB 1835, Chapter 230, Statutes of 2006
**INDUSTRIAL WELFARE COMMISSION
ORDER NO. 8–2001
REGULATING
WAGES, HOURS AND WORKING CONDITIONS IN THE
INDUSTRIES HANDLING PRODUCTS
AFTER HARVEST**

TAKE NOTICE: To employers and representatives of persons working in industries and occupations in the State of California:

The Department of Industrial Relations amends and republishes the minimum wage and meals and lodging credits in the Industrial Welfare Commission's Orders as a result of legislation enacted (AB 1835, Ch. 230, Stats of 2006, adding sections 1182.12 and 1182.13 to the California Labor Code.) The amendments and republishing make no other changes to the IWC's Orders.

1. Applicability of Order. This order shall apply to all persons employed in the industries handling products after harvest whether paid on a time, piece rate, commission, or other basis, except that:

(A) Provisions of Sections 3 through 12 of this order shall not apply to persons employed in administrative, executive, or professional capacities. The following requirements shall apply in determining whether an employee's duties meet the test to qualify for an exemption from those sections:

(1) <u>Executive Exemption.</u> A person employed in an executive capacity means any employee:

(a) Whose duties and responsibilities involve the management of the enterprise in which he/she is employed or of a customarily recognized department or subdivision thereof; and

(b) Who customarily and regularly directs the work of two or more other employees therein; and

(c) Who has the authority to hire or fire other employees or whose suggestions and recommendations as to the hiring or firing and as to the advancement and promotion or any other change of status of other employees will be given particular weight; and

(d) Who customarily and regularly exercises discretion and independent judgment; and

(e) Who is primarily engaged in duties which meet the test of the exemption. The activities constituting exempt work and non-exempt work shall be construed in the same manner as such items are construed in the following regulations under the Fair Labor Standards Act effective as of the date of this order: 29 C.F.R. Sections 541.102, 541.104–111, and 541.115–116. Exempt work shall include, for example, all work that is directly and closely related to exempt work and work which is properly viewed as a means for carrying out exempt functions. The work actually performed by the employee during the course of the workweek must, first and foremost, be examined and the amount of time the employee spends on such work, together with the employer's realistic expectations and the realistic requirements of the job, shall be considered in determining whether the employee satisfies this requirement.

(f) Such an employee must also earn a monthly salary equivalent to no less than two (2) times the state minimum wage for full-time employment. Full–time employment is defined in Labor Code Section 515(c) as 40 hours per week.

(2) <u>Administrative Exemption.</u> A person employed in an administrative capacity means any employee:

(a) Whose duties and responsibilities involve either:

(i) The performance of office or non-manual work directly related to management policies or general business operations of his/her employer or his/her employer's customers; or

(ii) The performance of functions in the administration of a school system, or educational establishment or institution, or of a department or subdivision thereof, in work directly related to the academic instruction or training carried on therein; and

(b) Who customarily and regularly exercises discretion and independent judgment; and

(c) Who regularly and directly assists a proprietor, or an employee employed in a bona fide executive or administrative capacity (as such terms are defined for purposes of this section); or

(d) Who performs under only general supervision work along specialized or technical lines requiring special training, experience, or knowledge; or

(e) Who executes under only general supervision special assignments and tasks; and

(f) Who is primarily engaged in duties which meet the test of the exemption. The activities constituting exempt work and non-exempt work shall be construed in the same manner as such terms are construed in the following regulations under the Fair Labor Standards Act effective as of the date of this order: 29 C.F.R. Sections 541.201–205, 541.207–208, 541.210, and 541.215. Exempt work shall include, for example, all work that is directly and closely related to exempt work and work which is properly viewed as a means for carrying out exempt functions. The work actually performed by the employee during the course of the workweek must, first and foremost, be examined and the amount of time the employee spends on such work, together with the employer's realistic expectations and the realistic requirements of the job, shall be considered in determining whether the employee satisfies this requirement.

(g) Such employee must also earn a monthly salary equivalent to no less than two (2) times the state minimum wage for full-time employment. Full–time employment is defined in Labor Code Section 515(c) as 40 hours per week.

(3) <u>Professional Exemption.</u> A person employed in a professional capacity means any employee who meets *all* of the following requirements:

(a) Who is licensed or certified by the State of California and is primarily engaged in the practice of one of the following recognized professions: law, medicine, dentistry, optometry, architecture, engineering, teaching, or accounting; or

(b) Who is primarily engaged in an occupation commonly recognized as a learned or artistic profession. For the purposes of this subsection, "learned or artistic profession" means an employee who is primarily engaged in the performance of:

(i) Work requiring knowledge of an advanced type in a field or science or learning customarily acquired by a prolonged course of specialized intellectual instruction and study, as distinguished from a general academic education and from an apprenticeship, and from training in the performance of routine mental, manual, or physical processes, or work that is an essential part of or necessarily incident to any of the above work; or

(ii) Work that is original and creative in character in a recognized field of artistic endeavor (as opposed to work which can be produced by a person endowed with general manual or intellectual ability and training), and the result of which depends primarily on the invention, imagination, or talent of the employee or work that is an essential part of or necessarily incident to any of the above work; and

(iii) Whose work is predominantly intellectual and varied in character (as opposed to routine mental, manual, mechanical, or physical work) and is of such character that the output produced or the result accomplished cannot be standardized in relation to a given period of time.

(c) Who customarily and regularly exercises discretion and independent judgment in the performance of duties set forth in subparagraphs (a) and (b).

(d) Who earns a monthly salary equivalent to no less than two (2) times the state minimum wage for full-time employment. Full–time employment is defined in Labor Code Section 515 (c) as 40 hours per week.

(e) Subparagraph (b) above is intended to be construed in accordance with the following provisions of federal law as they existed as of the date of this wage order: 29 C.F.R. Sections 541.207, 541.301(a)–(d), 541.302, 541.306, 541.307, 541.308, and 541.310.

(f) Notwithstanding the provisions of this subparagraph, pharmacists employed to engage in the practice of pharmacy, and registered nurses employed to engage in the practice of nursing, shall not be considered exempt professional employees, nor shall they be considered exempt from coverage for the purposes of this subparagraph unless they individually meet the criteria established for exemption as executive or administrative employees.

(g) Subparagraph (f) above shall not apply to the following advanced practice nurses:

(i) Certified nurse midwives who are primarily engaged in performing duties for which certification is required pursuant to Article 2.5 (commencing with Section 2746) of Chapter 6 of Division 2 of the Business and Professions Code.

(ii) Certified nurse anesthetists who are primarily engaged in performing duties for which certification is required pursuant to Article 7 (commencing with Section 2825) of Chapter 6 of Division 2 of the Business and Professions Code.

(iii) Certified nurse practitioners who are primarily engaged in performing duties for which certification is required pursuant to Article 8 (commencing with Section 2834) of Chapter 6 of Division 2 of the Business and Professions Code.

(iv) Nothing in this subparagraph shall exempt the occupations set forth in clauses (i), (ii), and (iii) from meeting the requirements of subsection 1(A)(3)(a)–(d) above.

(h) Except, as provided in subparagraph (i), an employee in the computer software field who is paid on an hourly basis shall be exempt from the daily overtime pay provisions of Labor Code Section 510, if *all* of the following apply:

(i) The employee is primarily engaged in work that is intellectual or creative and requires the exercise of discretion and independent judgment.

(ii) The employee is primarily engaged in duties that consist of one or more of the following:

-The application of systems analysis techniques and procedures, including consulting with users, to determine hardware, software, or system functional specifications.

-The design, development, documentation, analysis, creation, testing, or modification of computer systems or programs, including prototypes, based on and related to user or system design specifications.

-The documentation, testing, creation, or modification of computer programs related to the design of software or hardware for computer operating systems.

(iii) The employee is highly skilled and is proficient in the theoretical and practical application of highly specialized information to computer systems analysis, programming, and software engineering. A job title shall not be determinative of the applicability of this exemption.

(iv) The employee's hourly rate of pay is not less than forty-one dollars ($41.00). The Division of Labor Statistics and Research shall adjust this pay rate on October 1 of each year to be effective on January 1 of the following year by an amount equal to the percentage increase in the California Consumer Price Index for Urban Wage Earners and Clerical Workers.[1]

(i) The exemption provided in subparagraph (h) does not apply to an employee if *any* of the following apply:

(i) The employee is a trainee or employee in an entry-level position who is learning to become proficient in the theoretical and practical application of highly specialized

information to computer systems analysis, programming, and software engineering.

(ii) The employee is in a computer-related occupation but has not attained the level of skill and expertise necessary to work independently and without close supervision.

(iii) The employee is engaged in the operation of computers or in the manufacture, repair, or maintenance of computer hardware and related equipment.

(iv) The employee is an engineer, drafter, machinist, or other professional whose work is highly dependent upon or facilitated by the use of computers and computer software programs and who is skilled in computer-aided design software, including CAD/CAM, but who is not in a computer systems analysis or programming occupation.

(v) The employee is a writer engaged in writing material, including box labels, product descriptions, documentation, promotional material, setup and installation instructions, and other similar written information, either for print or for on screen media or who writes or provides content material intended to be read by customers, subscribers, or visitors to computer-related media such as the World Wide Web or CD–ROMs.

(vi) The employee is engaged in *any* of the activities set forth in subparagraph (h) for the purpose of creating imagery for effects used in the motion picture, television, or theatrical industry.

(B) Except as provided in Sections 1, 2, 4, 10, and 20, the provisions of this order shall not apply to any employees directly employed by the State or any political subdivision thereof, including any city, county, or special district.

(C) The provisions of this order shall not apply to outside salespersons.

(D) The provisions of this order shall not apply to any individual who is the parent, spouse, child, or legally adopted child or the employer.

(E) The provisions of this order shall not apply to any individual participating in a national service program, such as AmeriCorps, carried out using assistance provided under Section 12571 of Title 42 of the United States Code. (See Stats. 2000, ch. 365, amending Labor Code Section 1171.)

2. Definitions

(A) An "alternative workweek schedule" means any regularly scheduled workweek requiring an employee to work more than eight (8) hours in a 24–hour period.

(B) "Commission" means the Industrial Welfare Commission of the State of California.

(C) "Division" means the Division of Labor Standards Enforcement of the State of California.

(D) "Employ" means to engage, suffer, or permit to work.

(E) "Employee" means any person employed by an employer.

(F) "Employer" means any person as defined in Section 18 of the Labor Code, who directly or indirectly, or through an agent or any other person, employs or exercises control over the wages, hours, or working conditions of any person.

(G) "Hours worked" means the time during which an employee is subject to the control of an employer, and includes all the time the employee is suffered or permitted to work, whether or not required to do so.

(H) "Industries Handling Products After Harvest" means any industry, business, or establishment operated for the purpose of grading, sorting, cleaning, drying, cooling, icing, packing, dehydrating, cracking, shelling, candling, separating, slaughtering, picking, plucking, shucking, pasteurizing, fermenting, ripening, molding, or otherwise preparing any agricultural, horticultural, egg, poultry, meat, seafood, rabbit, or dairy product for distribution, and includes all the operations incidental thereto.

(I) "Minor" means, for the purpose of this order, any person under the age of 18 years.

(J) "Outside salesperson" means any person, 18 years of age or over, who customarily and regularly works more than half the working time away from the employer's place of business selling tangible or intangible items or obtaining orders or contracts for products, services or use of facilities.

(K) "Primarily" as used in Section 1, Applicability, means more than one-half the employee's work time.

(L) "Shift" means designated hours of work by an employee, with a designated beginning time and quitting time.

(M) "Split shift" means a work schedule, which is interrupted by non-paid non-working periods established by the employer, other than bona fide rest or meal periods.

(N) "Teaching" means, for the purpose of Section 1 of this order, the profession of teaching under a certificate from the Commission for Teacher Preparation and Licensing or teaching in an accredited college or university.

(O) "Wages" includes all amounts for labor performed by employees of every description, whether the amount is fixed or ascertained by the standard of time, task, piece, commission basis, or other method of calculation.

(P) "Workday" and "day" mean any consecutive 24-hour period beginning at the same time each calendar day.

(Q) "Workweek" and "week" mean any seven (7) consecutive days, starting with the same calendar day each week. "Workweek" is a fixed and regularly recurring period of 168 hours, seven (7) consecutive 24-hour periods.

3. Hours and Days of Work.

(A) *Daily Overtime—General Provisions*

(1) The following overtime provisions are applicable to employees 18 years of age or over and to employees 16 or 17 years of age who are not required by law to attend school and are not otherwise prohibited by law from engaging in the subject work. Such employees shall not be employed more than eight (8) hours in any workday or more than 40 hours in any workweek unless the employee receives one and one-half (1 ½) times such employee's regular rate of pay for all hours worked over 40 hours in the workweek. Eight (8) hours of labor constitutes a day's work. Employment beyond eight (8) hours in any workday or more than six (6) days in any workweek is permissible under the following conditions:

(2) Mandatory Day Off Requirement: An employee may work up to a maximum of 72 hours in any workweek after which the employee shall have a 24-hour period off duty, except that:

(a) In the grape and tree fruit industry the following key personnel: receivers, loaders, fork lift operators, shipping clerks, and maintenance workers, may be exempt from the mandatory day off requirement; and

(b) In the cotton ginning industry and in the tree nut hulling and shelling industry, all employees shall have the voluntary right to be exempt from the mandatory day off provision in this order. Any employee desiring to exempt himself/herself from the mandatory day off provision may exercise that exemption by notifying the employee's employer in writing. Any employee who wishes to withdraw that exemption may do so by notifying the employer in writing at least five (5) days in advance of the desired day off. (This notice provision is not intended to be applicable to instances of illness or emergencies); and

(c) In the exercise of any exemption from the mandatory day off provided above or by action of the state labor commissioner, (administrative exemptions from the mandatory day off are permitted by Labor Code Section 1198.3 under certain conditions) no employer shall discriminate against any employee who desires to take 24 hours off after 72 hours worked in a workweek; and

(d) All employers who permit any employees to work more than 72 hours in a workweek must give each employee a copy of the applicable provision for exemption, including subparagraph (c) above in English and in Spanish, and post it at all times in a prominently visible place; and

(3) Overtime hours shall be compensated at:

(a) One and one-half (1 ½) times the employee's regular rate of pay for all hours worked in excess of eight (8) hours up to and including 12 hours in any workday, and for the first eight (8) hours worked on the seventh (7th) consecutive day of work in a workweek; and

(b) Double the employee's regular rate of pay for all hours worked in excess of 12 hours in any workday and for all hours worked in excess of eight (8) hours on the seventh (7th) consecutive day of work in a workweek.

(c) The overtime rate of compensation required to be paid to a nonexempt full-time salaried employee shall be computed by using the employee's regular hourly salary as one-fortieth (1/40) of the employee's weekly salary.

(B) *Alternative Workweek Schedules*

(1) No employer shall be deemed to have violated the daily overtime provisions by instituting, pursuant to the election procedures set forth in this wage order, a regularly scheduled alternative workweek schedule of not more than ten (10) hours per day within a 40 hour workweek without the payment of an overtime rate of compensation. All work performed in any workday beyond the schedule established by the agreement up to 12 hours a day or beyond 40 hours per week shall be paid at one and one-half (1 ½) times the employee's regular rate of pay. All work performed in excess of 12 hours per day and any work in excess of eight (8) hours on those days worked beyond the regularly scheduled number of workdays established by the alternative workweek agreement shall be paid at double the employee's regular rate of pay. Any alternative workweek agreement adopted pursuant to this section shall provide for not less than four (4) hours of work in any shift. Nothing in this section shall prohibit an employer, at the request of the employee, to substitute one day of work for another day of the same length in the shift provided by the alternative workweek agreement on an occasional basis to meet the personal needs of the employee without the payment of overtime. No hours paid at either one and one-half (1 ½) or double the regular rate of pay shall be included in determining when 40 hours have been worked for the purpose of computing overtime compensation.

(2) Any agreement adopted pursuant to this section shall provide not less than two consecutive days off within a workweek.

(3) If an employer whose employees have adopted an alternative workweek agreement permitted by this order requires an employee to work fewer hours than those that are regularly scheduled by the agreement, the employer shall pay the employee overtime compensation at a rate of one and one-half (1 ½) times the employee's regular rate of pay for all hours worked in excess of eight (8) hours, and double the employee's regular rate of pay for all hours worked in excess of 12 hours for the day the employee is required to work the reduced hours.

(4) An employer shall not reduce an employee's regular rate of hourly pay as a result of the adoption, repeal or nullification of an alternative workweek schedule.

(5) An employer shall explore any available reasonable alternative means of accommodating the religious belief or observance of an affected employee that conflicts with an adopted alternative workweek schedule, in the manner provided by subdivision (j) of Section 12940 of the Government Code.

(6) An employer shall make a reasonable effort to find a work schedule not to exceed eight (8) hours in a workday, in order to accommodate any affected employee who was eligible to vote in an election authorized by this section and who is unable to work the alternative

workweek schedule established as the result of that election.

(7) An employer shall be permitted, but not required, to provide a work schedule not to exceed eight (8) hours in a workday to accommodate any employee who is hired after the date of the election and who is unable to work the alternative workweek schedule established by the election.

(8) Arrangements adopted in a secret ballot election held pursuant to this order prior to 1998, or under the rules in effect prior to 1998, and before the performance of the work, shall remain valid after July 1, 2000 provided that the results of the election are reported by the employer to the Division of Labor Statistics and Research by January 1, 2001, in accordance with the requirements of subsection (C) below (Election Procedures). If an employee was voluntarily working an alternative workweek schedule of not more than ten (10) hours a day as of July 1, 1999, that alternative workweek schedule was based on an individual agreement made after January 1, 1998 between the employee and employer, and the employee submitted, and the employer approved, a written request on or before May 30, 2000 to continue the agreement, the employee may continue to work that alternative workweek schedule without payment of an overtime rate of compensation for the hours provided in the agreement. The employee may revoke his/her voluntary authorization to continue such a schedule with 30 days written notice to the employer. New arrangements can only be entered into pursuant to the provisions of this section.

(C) *Election Procedures*

Election procedures for the adoption and repeal of alternative workweek schedules require the following:

(1) Each proposal for an alternative workweek schedule shall be in the form of a written agreement proposed by the employer. The proposed agreement must designate a regularly scheduled alternative workweek in which the specified number of work days and work hours are regularly recurring. The actual days worked within that alternative workweek schedule need not be specified. The employer may propose a single work schedule that would become the standard schedule for workers in the work unit, or a menu of work schedule options, from which each employee in the unit would be entitled to choose. If the employer proposes a menu of work schedule options, the employee may, with the approval of the employer, move from one menu option to another.

(2) In order to be valid, the proposed alternative workweek schedule must be adopted in a secret ballot election, before the performance of work, by at least a two-thirds (2/03) vote of the affected employees in the work unit. The election shall be held during regular working hours at the employees' work site. For purposes of this subsection, "affected employees in the work unit" may include all employees in a readily identifiable work unit, such as a division, a department, a job classification, a shift, a separate physical location, or a recognized

subdivision of any such work unit. A work unit may consist of an individual employee as long as the criteria for an identifiable work unit in this subsection are met.

(3) Prior to the secret ballot vote, any employer who proposed to institute an alternative workweek schedule shall have made a disclosure in writing to the affected employees, including the effects of the proposed arrangement on the employees' wages, hours, and benefits. Such a disclosure shall include meeting(s), duly noticed, held at least 14 days prior to voting, for the specific purpose of discussing the effects of the alternative workweek schedule. An employer shall provide that disclosure in a non–English language, as well as in English, if at least five (5) percent of the affected employees primarily speak that non–English language. The employer shall mail the written disclosure to employees who do not attend the meeting. Failure to comply with this paragraph shall make the election null and void.

(4) Any election to establish or repeal an alternative workweek schedule shall be held at the work site of the affected employees. The employer shall bear the costs of conducting any election held pursuant to this section. Upon a complaint by an affected employee, and after an investigation by the labor commissioner, the labor commissioner may require the employer to select a neutral third party to conduct the election.

(5) Any type of alternative workweek schedule that is authorized by the Labor Code may be repealed by the affected employees. Upon a petition of one-third (1/03) of the affected employees, a new secret ballot election shall be held and a two thirds (2/03) vote of the affected employees shall be required to reverse the alternative workweek schedule. The election to repeal the alternative workweek schedule shall be held not more than 30 days after the petition is submitted to the employer, except that the election shall be held not less than 12 months after the date that the same group of employees voted in an election held to adopt or repeal an alternative workweek schedule. The election shall take place during regular working hours at the employees' work site. If the alternative workweek schedule is revoked, the employer shall comply within 60 days. Upon proper showing of undue hardship, the Division of Labor Standards Enforcement may grant an extension of time for compliance.

(6) Only secret ballots may be cast by affected employees in the work unit at any election held pursuant to this section. The results of any election conducted pursuant to this section shall be reported by the employer to the Division of Labor Statistics and Research within 30 days after the results are final, and the report of election results shall be a public document. The report shall include the final tally of the vote, the size of the unit, and the nature of the business of the employer.

(7) Employees affected by a change in the work hours resulting from the adoption of an alternative workweek schedule may not be required to work those new work hours for at least 30 days after the announcement of the final results of the election.

(8) Employers shall not intimidate or coerce employees to vote either in support of or in opposition to a proposed alternative workweek. No employees shall be discharged or discriminated against for expressing opinions concerning the alternative workweek election or for opposing or supporting its adoption or repeal. However, nothing in this paragraph shall prohibit an employer from expressing his/her position concerning that alternative workweek to the affected employees. A violation of this paragraph shall be subject to Labor Code Section 98 *et seq*.

(D) One and one-half (1 1/02) times a minor's regular rate of pay shall be paid for all work over 40 hours in any workweek except minors 16 or 17 years old who are not required by law to attend school and may therefore be employed for the same hours as an adult are subject to subsection (A) or (B) and (C) above.

(**Violations of Child Labor Laws** are subject to civil penalties of from $500 to $10,000 as well as to criminal penalties. Refer to California Labor Code Sections 1285 to 1312 and 1390 to 1399 for additional restrictions on the employment of minors and for descriptions of criminal and civil penalties for violation of the child labor laws. Employers should ask school districts about any required work permits.)

(E) An employee may be employed on seven (7) workdays in one workweek when the total hours of employment during such workweek do not exceed 30 and the total hours of employment in any one workday thereof do not exceed six (6).

(F) If during any workday an employer declares a work recess of one-half (1/02) hour or more, other than a meal period, and the employer notifies the employees of the time to report back for work and permits them to leave the premises, such recess need not be treated as hours worked provided that there shall not be more than two (2) such recess periods within one shift and the total duration does not exceed two (2) hours. Work stoppages of less than one-half (1/02) hour may not be deducted from hours worked.

(G) If a meal period occurs on a shift beginning or ending at or between the hours of 10 p.m. and 6 a.m., facilities shall be available for securing hot food and drink or for heating food or drink, and a suitable sheltered place shall be provided in which to consume such food or drink.

(H) The provisions of Labor Code Sections 551 and 552 regarding one (1) day's rest in seven (7) shall not be construed to prevent an accumulation of days of rest when the nature of the employment reasonably requires the employee to work seven (7) or more consecutive days; provided, however, that in each calendar month, the employee shall receive the equivalent of one (1) day's rest in seven (7).

(I) Except as provided in subsection (A)(1) and subsections (D) and (H), this section shall not apply to any employee covered by a valid collective bargaining agreement if the agreement expressly provides for the wages, hours of work, and working conditions of the employees, and if the agreement provides premium wage rates for all overtime hours worked and a regular hourly rate of pay for those employees of not less than 30 percent more than the state minimum wage.

(J) Notwithstanding subsection (I) above, where the employer and a labor organization representing employees of the employer have entered into a valid collective bargaining agreement pertaining to the hours of work of the employees, the requirement regarding the equivalent of one (1) day's rest in seven (7) (see subsection (H) above) shall apply, unless the agreement expressly provides otherwise.

(K) The provisions of this section are not applicable to employees whose hours of service are regulated by:

(1) The United States Department of Transportation Code of Federal Regulations, Title 49, Sections 395.1 to 395.13, Hours of Service of Drivers; or

(2) Title 13 of the California Code of Regulations, subchapter 6.5, Section 1200 and the following sections, regulating hours of drivers.

(L) If an employer approves a written request of an employee to make up work time that is or would be lost as a result of a personal obligation of the employee, the hours of that makeup work time, if performed in the same workweek in which the work time was lost, may not be counted toward computing the total number of hours worked in a day for purposes of the overtime requirements, except for hours in excess of 11 hours of work in one (1) day or 40 hours of work in one (1) workweek. If an employee knows in advance that he/she will be requesting makeup time for a personal obligation that will recur at a fixed time over a succession of weeks, the employee may request to make up work time for up to four (4) weeks in advance; provided, however, that the makeup work must be performed in the same week that the work time was lost. An employee shall provide a signed written request for each occasion that the employee makes a request to make up work time pursuant to this subsection. While an employer may inform an employee of this makeup time option, the employer is prohibited from encouraging or otherwise soliciting an employee to request the employer's approval to take personal time off and make up the work hours within the same workweek pursuant to this subsection.

4. Minimum Wages

(A) Every employer shall pay to each employee wages not less than seven dollars and fifty cents ($7.50) per hour for all hours worked, effective January 1, 2007, and not less than eight dollars ($8.00) per hour for all hours worked, effective January 1, 2008, except:

Learners. Employees during their first 160 hours of employment in occupations in which they have no previous similar or related experience, may be paid not less than 85 percent of the minimum wage rounded to the nearest nickel.

(B) Every employer shall pay to each employee, on the established payday for the period involved, not less than the applicable minimum wage for all hours worked in the payroll period, whether the remuneration is measured by time, piece, commission, or otherwise.

(C) When an employee works a split shift, one (1) hour's pay at the minimum wage shall be paid in addition to the minimum wage for that workday, except when the employee resides at the place of employment.

(D) The provisions of this section shall not apply to apprentices regularly indentured under the State Division of Apprenticeship Standards.

5. Reporting Time Pay

(A) Each workday an employee is required to report for work and does report, but is not put to work or is furnished less than half said employee's usual or scheduled day's work, the employee shall be paid for half the usual or scheduled day's work, but in no event for less than two (2) hours nor more than four (4) hours, at the employee's regular rate of pay, which shall not be less than the minimum wage.

(B) If an employee is required to report for work a second time in any one workday and is furnished less than two (2) hours of work on the second reporting, said employee shall be paid for two (2) hours at the employee's regular rate of pay, which shall not be less than the minimum wage.

(C) The foregoing reporting time pay provisions are not applicable when:

(1) Operations cannot commence or continue due to threats to employees or property; or when recommended by civil authorities; or

(2) Public utilities fail to supply electricity, water, or gas, or there is a failure in the public utilities, or sewer system; or

(3) The interruption of work is caused by an Act of God or other cause not within the employer's control.

(D) This section shall not apply to an employee on paid standby status who is called to perform assigned work at a time other than the employee's scheduled reporting time.

6. Licenses for Disabled Workers

(A) A license may be issued by the Division authorizing employment of a person whose earning capacity is impaired by physical disability or mental deficiency at less than the minimum wage. Such licenses shall be granted only upon joint application of employer and employee and employee's representative if any.

(B) A special license may be issued to a nonprofit organization such as a sheltered workshop or rehabilitation facility fixing special minimum rates to enable the employment of such persons without requiring individual licenses of such employees.

(C) All such licenses and special licenses shall be renewed on a yearly basis or more frequently at the discretion of the Division.

(See California Labor Code, Sections 1191 and 1191.5)

7. Records

(A) Every employer shall keep accurate information with respect to each employee including the following:

(1) Full name, home address, occupation and social security number.

(2) Birth date, if under 18 years, and designation as a minor.

(3) Time records showing when the employee begins and ends each work period. Meal periods, split shift intervals and total daily hours worked shall also be recorded. Meal periods during which operations cease and authorized rest periods need not be recorded.

(4) Total wages paid each payroll period, including value of board, lodging, or other compensation actually furnished to the employee.

(5) Total hours worked in the payroll period and applicable rates of pay. This information shall be made readily available to the employee upon reasonable request.

(6) When a piece rate or incentive plan is in operation, piece rates or an explanation of the incentive plan formula shall be provided to employees. An accurate production record shall be maintained by the employer.

(B) Every employer shall semimonthly or at the time of each payment of wages furnish each employee, either as a detachable part of the check, draft, or voucher paying the employee's wages, or separately, an itemized statement in writing showing: (1) all deductions; (2) the inclusive dates of the period for which the employee is paid; (3) the name of the employee or the employee's social security number; and (4) the name of the employer, provided all deductions made on written orders of the employee may be aggregated and shown as one item.

(C) All required records shall be in the English language and in ink or other indelible form, properly dated, showing month, day and year, and shall be kept on file by the employer for at least three years at the place of employment or at a central location within the State of California. An employee's records shall be available for inspection by the employee upon reasonable request.

(D) Clocks shall be provided in all major work areas or within reasonable distance thereto insofar as practicable.

8. Cash Shortage and Breakage. No employer shall make any deduction from the wage or require any reimbursement from an employee for any cash shortage, breakage, or loss of equipment, unless it can be shown that the shortage, breakage, or loss is caused by a dishonest or willful act, or by the gross negligence of the employee.

9. Uniforms and Equipment

(A) When uniforms are required by the employer to be worn by the employee as a condition of employment, such uniforms shall be provided and maintained by the employer. The term "uniform" includes wearing apparel and accessories of distinctive design or color.

Note: This section shall not apply to protective apparel regulated by the Occupational Safety and Health Standards Board.

(B) When tools or equipment are required by the employer or are necessary to the performance of a job, such tools and equipment shall be provided and maintained by the employer, except that an employee whose wages are at least two (2) times the minimum wage provided herein may be required to provide and maintain hand tools and equipment customarily required by the trade or craft. This subsection (B) shall not apply to apprentices regularly indentured under the State Division of Apprenticeship Standards.

Note: This section shall not apply to protective equipment and safety devices on tools regulated by the Occupational Safety and Health Standards Board.

(C) A reasonable deposit may be required as security for the return of the items furnished by the employer under provisions of subsections (A) and (B) of this section upon issuance of a receipt to the employee for such deposit. Such deposits shall be made pursuant to Section 400 and following of the Labor Code or an employer with the prior written authorization of the employee may deduct from the employee's last check the cost of an item furnished pursuant to (A) and (B) above in the event said item is not returned. No deduction shall be made at any time for normal wear and tear. All items furnished by the employer shall be returned by the employee upon completion of the job.

10. Meals and Lodging.

(A) "Meal" means an adequate, well-balanced serving of a variety of wholesome, nutritious foods.

(B) "Lodging" means living accommodations available to the employee for full-time occupancy which are adequate, decent, and sanitary according to usual and customary standards. Employees shall not be required to share a bed.

(C) Meals or lodging may not be credited against the minimum wage without a voluntary written agreement between the employer and the employee. When credit for meals or lodging is used to meet part of the employer's minimum wage obligation, the amounts so credited may not be more than the following:

Effective	January 1, 2007	January 1, 2008
Lodging:		
Room occupied alone	$35.27 per week	$37.63 per week
Room shared	$29.11 per week	$31.06 per week
Apartment—two–thirds (2/03) of the ordinary rental value, and in no event more than	$423.51 per month	$451.89 per month

Effective	January 1, 2007	January 1, 2008
Where a couple are both employed by the employer, two-thirds (2/03) of the ordinary rental value, and in no event more than	$626.49 per month	$668.46 per month
Meals:		
Breakfast	$2.72	$2.90
Lunch	$3.72	$3.97
Dinner	$5.00	$5.34

(D) Meals evaluated as part of the minimum wage must be bona fide meals consistent with the employee's work shift. Deductions shall not be made for meals not received or lodging not used.

(E) If, as a condition of employment, the employee must live at the place of employment or occupy quarters owned or under the control of the employer, then the employer may not charge rent in excess of the values listed herein.

11. Meal Periods

(A) No employer shall employ any person for a work period of more than five (5) hours without a meal period of not less than 30 minutes, except that when a work period of not more than six (6) hours will complete the day's work the meal period may be waived by mutual consent of the employer and the employee.

(B) An employer may not employ an employee for a work period of more than ten (10) hours per day without providing the employee with a second meal period of not less than 30 minutes, except that if the total hours worked is no more than 12 hours, the second meal period may be waived by mutual consent of the employer and the employee only if the first meal period was not waived.

(C) Unless the employee is relieved of all duty during a 30 minute meal period, the meal period shall be considered an "on duty" meal period and counted as time worked. An "on duty" meal period shall be permitted only when the nature of the work prevents an employee from being relieved of all duty and when by written agreement between the parties an on-the-job paid meal period is agreed to. The written agreement shall state that the employee may, in writing, revoke the agreement at any time.

(D) If an employer fails to provide an employee a meal period in accordance with the applicable provisions of this order, the employer shall pay the employee one (1) hour of pay at the employee's regular rate of compensation for each workday that the meal period is not provided.

(E) In all places of employment where employees are required to eat on the premises, a suitable place for that purpose shall be designated.

12. Rest Periods

(A) Every employer shall authorize and permit all employees to take rest periods, which insofar as practicable shall be in the middle of each work period. The authorized rest period time shall be based on the total hours worked daily at the rate of ten (10) minutes net rest time per four (4) hours or major fraction thereof. However, a rest period need not be authorized for employees whose total daily work time is less than three and one-half (3 ½) hours. Authorized rest period time shall be counted as hours worked for which there shall be no deduction from wages.

(B) If an employer fails to provide an employee a rest period in accordance with the applicable provisions of this order, the employer shall pay the employee one (1) hour of pay at the employee's regular rate of compensation for each workday that the rest period is not provided.

13. Change Rooms and Resting Facilities

(A) Employers shall provide suitable lockers, closets, or equivalent for the safekeeping of employees' outer clothing during working hours, and when required, for their work clothing during non-working hours. When the occupation requires a change of clothing, change rooms or equivalent space shall be provided in order that employees may change their clothing in reasonable privacy and comfort. These rooms or spaces may be adjacent to but shall be separate from toilet rooms and shall be kept clean.

Note: This section shall not apply to change rooms and storage facilities regulated by the Occupational Safety and Health Standards Board.

(B) Suitable resting facilities shall be provided in an area separate from the toilet rooms and shall be available to employees during work hours.

14. Seats

(A) All working employees shall be provided with suitable seats when the nature of the work reasonably permits the use of seats.

(B) When employees are not engaged in the active duties of their employment and the nature of the work requires standing, an adequate number of suitable seats shall be placed in reasonable proximity to the work area and employees shall be permitted to use such seats when it does not interfere with the performance of their duties.

15. Temperature

(A) The temperature maintained in each work area shall provide reasonable comfort consistent with industry-wide standards for the nature of the process and the work performed.

(B) If excessive heat or humidity is created by the work process, the employer shall take all feasible means to reduce such excessive heat or humidity to a degree providing reasonable comfort. Where the nature of the employment requires a temperature of less than 60° F., a heated room shall be provided to which employees may retire for warmth, and such room shall be maintained at not less than 68°.

(C) A temperature of not less than 68° shall be maintained in the toilet rooms, resting rooms, and change rooms during hours of use.

(D) Federal and State energy guidelines shall prevail over any conflicting provision of this section.

16. Elevators. Adequate elevator, escalator or similar service consistent with industry-wide standards for the nature of the process and the work performed shall be provided when employees are employed four floors or more above or below ground level.

17. Exemptions. If, in the opinion of the Division after due investigation, it is found that the enforcement of any provision contained in Section 7, Records; Section 12, Rest Periods; Section 13, Change Rooms and Resting Facilities; Section 14, Seats; Section 15, Temperature; or Section 16, Elevators, would not materially affect the welfare or comfort of employees and would work an undue hardship on the employer, exemption may be made at the discretion of the Division. Such exemptions shall be in writing to be effective and may be revoked after reasonable notice is given in writing. Application for exemption shall be made by the employer or by the employee and/or the employee's representative to the Division in writing. A copy of the application shall be posted at the place of employment at the time the application is filed with the Division.

18. Filing Reports. (See California Labor Code, Section 1174(a))

19. Inspection. (See California Labor Code, Section 1174)

20. Penalties. (See California Labor Code, Section 1199)

(A) In addition to any other civil penalties provided by law, any employer or any other person acting on behalf of the employer who violates, or causes to be violated, the provisions of this order, shall be subject to the civil penalty of:

(1) Initial Violation—$50.00 for each underpaid employee for each pay period during which the employee was underpaid in addition to the amount which is sufficient to recover unpaid wages.

(2) Subsequent Violations—$100.00 for each underpaid employee for each pay period during which the employee was underpaid in addition to an amount which is sufficient to recover unpaid wages.

(3) The affected employee shall receive payment of all wages recovered.

(B) The labor commissioner may also issue citations pursuant to California Labor Code Section 1197.1 for non-payment of wages for overtime work in violation of this order.

21. Separability. If the application of any provision of this order, or any section, subsection, subdivision, sentence, clause, phrase, word, or portion of this order should be held invalid or unconstitutional or unauthorized or prohibited by statute, the remaining provisions thereof shall not be affected thereby, but shall continue to be given full force and effect as if the part so held invalid or unconstitutional had not been included herein.

22. Posting of Order. Every employer shall keep a copy of this order posted in an area frequented by employees where it may be easily read during the workday. Where the location of work or other conditions make this impractical, every employer shall keep a copy of this order and make it available to every employee upon request.

[1] Pursuant to Labor Code section 515.5, subdivision (a)(4), the Division of Labor Statistics and Research, Department of Industrial Relations, has adjusted the minimum hourly rate of pay specified in this subdivision to be $49.77, effective January 1, 2007. This hourly rate of pay is adjusted on October 1 of each year to be effective on January 1, of the following year, and may be obtained at www.dir.ca.gov/IWC or by mail from the Department of Industrial Relations.

Publisher's Notes

See Industrial Welfare Com. v. Superior Court (1980) 27 Cal.3d 690, 613 P.2d 579, 166 Cal.Rptr. 331 (validity of 1980 order).

Research References

See notes following listing of Wage Orders.

Please Post With This Side Showing
OFFICIAL NOTICE
Effective July 1, 2004 as amended
Sections 4(A) and 10(C) amended and republished by the Department of Industrial Relations,
effective January 1, 2007, pursuant to AB 1835, Chapter 230, Statutes of 2006
**INDUSTRIAL WELFARE COMMISSION
ORDER NO. 9–2001
REGULATING
WAGES, HOURS AND WORKING CONDITIONS IN THE
TRANSPORTATION INDUSTRY**

TAKE NOTICE: To employers and representatives of persons working in industries and occupations in the State of California:

The Department of Industrial Relations amends and republishes the minimum wage and meals and lodging credits in the Industrial Welfare Commission's Orders as a result of legislation enacted (AB 1835, Ch. 230, Stats of

1463

2006, adding sections 1182.12 and 1182.13 to the California Labor Code.) The amendments and republishing make no other changes to the IWC's Orders.

1. Applicability of Order. This order shall apply to all persons employed in the transportation industry whether paid on a time, piece rate, commission, or other basis, except that:

(A) Provisions of Sections 3 through 12 of this order shall not apply to persons employed in administrative, executive, or professional capacities. The following requirements shall apply in determining whether an employee's duties meet the test to qualify for an exemption from those sections:

(1) Executive Exemption. A person employed in an executive capacity means any employee:

(a) Whose duties and responsibilities involve the management of the enterprise in which he/she is employed or of a customarily recognized department or subdivision thereof; and

(b) Who customarily and regularly directs the work of two or more other employees therein; and

(c) Who has the authority to hire or fire other employees or whose suggestions and recommendations as to the hiring or firing and as to the advancement and promotion or any other change of status of other employees will be given particular weight; and

(d) Who customarily and regularly exercises discretion and independent judgment; and

(e) Who is primarily engaged in duties which meet the test of the exemption. The activities constituting exempt work and non-exempt work shall be construed in the same manner as such items are construed in the following regulations under the Fair Labor Standards Act effective as of the date of this order: 29 C.F.R. Sections 541.102, 541.104–111, and 541.115–116. Exempt work shall include, for example, all work that is directly and closely related to exempt work and work which is properly viewed as a means for carrying out exempt functions. The work actually performed by the employee during the course of the workweek must, first and foremost, be examined and the amount of time the employee spends on such work, together with the employer's realistic expectations and the realistic requirements of the job, shall be considered in determining whether the employee satisfies this requirement.

(f) Such an employee must also earn a monthly salary equivalent to no less than two (2) times the state minimum wage for full-time employment. Full–time employment is defined in Labor Code Section 515(c) as 40 hours per week.

(2) Administrative Exemption. A person employed in an administrative capacity means any employee:

(a) Whose duties and responsibilities involve either:

(i) The performance of office or non-manual work directly related to management policies or general business operations of his employer or his/her employer's customers; or

(ii) The performance of functions in the administration of a school system, or educational establishment or institution, or of a department or subdivision thereof, in work directly related to the academic instruction or training carried on therein; and

(b) Who customarily and regularly exercises discretion and independent judgment; and

(c) Who regularly and directly assists a proprietor, or an employee employed in a bona fide executive or administrative capacity (as such terms are defined for purposes of this section); or

(d) Who performs under only general supervision work along specialized or technical lines requiring special training, experience, or knowledge; or

(e) Who executes under only general supervision special assignments and tasks; and

(f) Who is primarily engaged in duties that meet the test of the exemption. The activities constituting exempt work and non-exempt work shall be construed in the same manner as such terms are construed in the following regulations under the Fair Labor Standards Act effective as of the date of this order: 29 C.F.R. Sections 541.201–205, 541.207–208, 541.210, and 541.215. Exempt work shall include, for example, all work that is directly and closely related to exempt work and work which is properly viewed as a means for carrying out exempt functions. The work actually performed by the employee during the course of the workweek must, first and foremost, be examined and the amount of time the employee spends on such work, together with the employer's realistic expectations and the realistic requirements of the job, shall be considered in determining whether the employee satisfies this requirement.

(g) Such employee must also earn a monthly salary equivalent to no less than two (2) times the state minimum wage for full-time employment. Full–time employment is defined in Labor Code Section 515(c) as 40 hours per week.

(3) Professional Exemption. A person employed in a professional capacity means any employee who meets *all* of the following requirements:

(a) Who is licensed or certified by the State of California and is primarily engaged in the practice of one of the following recognized professions: law, medicine, dentistry, optometry, architecture, engineering, teaching, or accounting; or

(b) Who is primarily engaged in an occupation commonly recognized as a learned or artistic profession. For the purposes of this subsection, "learned or artistic profession" means an employee who is primarily engaged in the performance of:

(i) Work requiring knowledge of an advanced type in a field or science or learning customarily acquired by a prolonged course of specialized intellectual instruction and study, as distinguished from a general academic education and from an apprenticeship, and from training in the performance of routine mental, manual, or physical processes, or work that is an essential part of or necessarily incident to any of the above work; or

(ii) Work that is original and creative in character in a recognized field of artistic endeavor (as opposed to work which can be produced by a person endowed with general manual or intellectual ability and training), and the result of which depends primarily on the invention, imagination, or talent of the employee or work that is an essential part of or necessarily incident to any of the above work; and

(iii) Whose work is predominantly intellectual and varied in character (as opposed to routine mental, manual, mechanical, or physical work) and is of such character that the output produced or the result accomplished cannot be standardized in relation to a given period of time.

(c) Who customarily and regularly exercises discretion and independent judgment in the performance of duties set forth in subparagraphs (a) and (b).

(d) Who earns a monthly salary equivalent to no less than two (2) times the state minimum wage for full-time employment. Full–time employment is defined in Labor Code Section 515 (c) as 40 hours per week.

(e) Subparagraph (b) above is intended to be construed in accordance with the following provisions of federal law as they existed as of the date of this wage order: 29 C.F.R. Sections 541.207, 541.301(a)–(d), 541.302, 541.306, 541.307, 541.308, and 541.310.

(f) Notwithstanding the provisions of this subparagraph, pharmacists employed to engage in the practice of pharmacy, and registered nurses employed to engage in the practice of nursing, shall not be considered exempt professional employees, nor shall they be considered exempt from coverage for the purposes of this subparagraph unless they individually meet the criteria established for exemption as executive or administrative employees.

(g) Subparagraph (f) above shall not apply to the following advanced practice nurses:

(i) Certified nurse midwives who are primarily engaged in performing duties for which certification is required pursuant to Article 2.5 (commencing with Section 2746) of Chapter 6 of Division 2 of the Business and Professions Code.

(ii) Certified nurse anesthetists who are primarily engaged in performing duties for which certification is required pursuant to Article 7 (commencing with Section 2825) of Chapter 6 of Division 2 of the Business and Professions Code.

(iii) Certified nurse practitioners who are primarily engaged in performing duties for which certification is required pursuant to Article 8 (commencing with Section 2834) of Chapter 6 of Division 2 of the Business and Professions Code.

(iv) Nothing in this subparagraph shall exempt the occupations set forth in clauses (i), (ii), and (iii) from meeting the requirements of subsection 1(A)(3)(a)–(d) above.

(h) Except, as provided in subparagraph (i), an employee in the computer software field who is paid on an hourly basis shall be exempt, if *all* of the following apply:

(i) The employee is primarily engaged in work that is intellectual or creative and that requires the exercise of discretion and independent judgment.

(ii) The employee is primarily engaged in duties that consist of one or more of the following:

-The application of systems analysis techniques and procedures, including consulting with users, to determine hardware, software, or system functional specifications.

-The design, development, documentation, analysis, creation, testing, or modification of computer systems or programs, including prototypes, based on and related to user or system design specifications.

-The documentation, testing, creation, or modification of computer programs related to the design of software or hardware for computer operating systems.

(iii) The employee is highly skilled and is proficient in the theoretical and practical application of highly specialized information to computer systems analysis, programming, and software engineering. A job title shall not be determinative of the applicability of this exemption.

(iv) The employee's hourly rate of pay is not less than forty-one dollars ($41.00). The Division of Labor Statistics and Research shall adjust this pay rate on October 1 of each year to be effective on January 1 of the following year by an amount equal to the percentage increase in the California Consumer Price Index for Urban Wage Earners and Clerical Workers.[1]

(i) The exemption provided in subparagraph (h) does not apply to an employee if *any* of the following apply:

(i) The employee is a trainee or employee in an entry-level position who is learning to become proficient in the theoretical and practical application of highly specialized information to computer systems analysis, programming, and software engineering.

(ii) The employee is in a computer-related occupation but has not attained the level of skill and expertise necessary to work independently and without close supervision.

(iii) The employee is engaged in the operation of computers or in the manufacture, repair, or maintenance of computer hardware and related equipment.

(iv) The employee is an engineer, drafter, machinist, or other professional whose work is highly dependent upon or facilitated by the use of computers and computer software programs and who is skilled in computer-aided design software, including CAD/CAM, but who is not in a computer systems analysis or programming occupation.

(v) The employee is a writer engaged in writing material, including box labels, product descriptions, documentation, promotional material, setup and installation instructions, and other similar written information, either for print or for on screen media or who writes or provides content material intended to be read by customers, subscribers, or visitors to computer-related media such as the World Wide Web or CD–ROMs.

(vi) The employee is engaged in any of the activities set forth in subparagraph (h) for the purpose of creating imagery for effects used in the motion picture, television, or theatrical industry.

(B) Except as provided in Sections 1, 2, 4, 10, and 20, and with regard to commercial drivers, Sections 11 and 12, the provisions of this order shall not apply to any employees directly employed by the State or any political subdivision thereof, including any city, county, or special district. The application of Sections 11 and 12 for commercial drivers employed by governmental entities shall become effective July 1, 2004 or following the expiration date of any valid collective bargaining agreement applicable to such commercial drivers then in effect but, in any event, no later than August 1, 2005. Notwithstanding Section 21, the application of Sections 11 or 12 to public transit bus drivers shall be null and void in the event the IWC or any court of competent jurisdiction invalidates the collective bargaining exemption established by Sections 11 or 12 for those drivers.

(C) The provisions of this order shall not apply to outside salespersons.

(D) The provisions of this order shall not apply to any individual who is the parent, spouse, child, or legally adopted child of the employer.

(E) Except as provided in Sections 4, 10, 11, 12, and 20 through 22, this order shall not be deemed to cover those employees who have entered into a collective bargaining agreement under and in accordance with the provisions of the Railway Labor Act, 45 U.S.C. Sections 151 et seq.

(F) The provisions of this Order shall not apply to any individual participating in a national service program, such as AmeriCorps, carried out using assistance provided under Section 12571 of Title 42 of the United States Code. (See Stats. 2000, ch. 365, amending Labor Code § 1171.)

2. Definitions

(A) An "alternative workweek schedule" means any regularly scheduled workweek requiring an employee to work more than eight (8) hours in a 24–hour period.

(B) "Commission" means the Industrial Welfare Commission of the State of California.

(C) "Commercial driver" means an employee who operates a vehicle described in subdivision (b) of Section 15210 of the Vehicle Code.

(D) "Division" means the Division of Labor Standards Enforcement of the State of California.

(E) "Employ" means to engage, suffer, or permit to work.

(F) "Employee" means any person employed by an employer.

(G) "Employer" means any person as defined in Section 18 of the Labor Code, who directly or indirectly, or through an agent or any other person, employs or exercises control over the wages, hours, or working conditions of any person.

(H) "Hours worked" means the time during which an employee is subject to the control of an employer, and includes all the time the employee is suffered or permitted to work, whether or not required to do so.

(I) "Minor" means, for the purpose of this order, any person under the age of 18 years.

(J) "Outside salesperson" means any person, 18 years of age or over, who customarily and regularly works more than half the working time away from the employer's place of business selling tangible or intangible items or obtaining orders or contracts for products, services or use of facilities.

(K) "Primarily" as used in Section 1, Applicability, means more than one-half the employee's work time.

(L) "Public Transit Bus Driver" means a commercial driver who operates a transit bus and is employed by a governmental entity.

(M) "Shift" means designated hours of work by an employee, with a designated beginning time and quitting time.

(N) "Split shift" means a work schedule, which is interrupted by non-paid non-working periods established by the employer, other than bona fide rest or meal periods.

(O) "Teaching" means, for the purpose of Section 1 of this order, the profession of teaching under a certificate from the Commission for Teacher Preparation and Licensing or teaching in an accredited college or university.

(P) "Transportation Industry" means any industry, business, or establishment operated for the purpose of conveying persons or property from one place to another whether by rail, highway, air, or water, and all operations and services in connection therewith; and also includes storing or warehousing of goods or property, and the repairing, parking, rental, maintenance, or cleaning of vehicles.

(Q) "Wages" includes all amounts for labor performed by employees of every description, whether the amount is fixed or ascertained by the standard of time, task, piece, commission basis, or other method of calculation.

(R) "Workday" and "day" mean any consecutive 24–hour period beginning at the same time each calendar day.

(S) "Workweek" and "week" mean any seven (7) consecutive days, starting with the same calendar day each week. "Workweek" is a fixed and regularly recurring period of 168 hours, seven (7) consecutive 24–hour periods.

3. Hours and Days of Work

(A) *Daily Overtime–General Provisions*

(1) The following overtime provisions are applicable to employees 18 years of age or over and to employees 16 or 17 years of age who are not required by law to attend school and are not otherwise prohibited by law from engaging in the subject work. Such employees shall not be employed more than eight (8) hours in any workday or more than 40 hours in any workweek unless the employee receives one and one-half (1 $\frac{1}{2}$) times such employee's regular rate of pay for all hours worked over 40 hours in the workweek. Eight (8) hours of labor constitutes a day's work. Employment beyond eight (8) hours in any workday or more than six (6) days in any workweek is permissible provided the employee is compensated for such overtime at not less than:

(a) One and one-half (1 $\frac{1}{2}$) times the employee's regular rate of pay for all hours worked in excess of eight (8) hours up to and including 12 hours in any workday, and for the first eight (8) hours worked on the seventh (7th) consecutive day of work in a workweek; and

(b) Double the employee's regular rate of pay for all hours worked in excess of 12 hours in any workday and for all hours worked in excess of eight (8) hours on the seventh (7th) consecutive day of work in a workweek.

(c) The overtime rate of compensation required to be paid to a nonexempt full-time salaried employee shall be computed by using the employee's regular hourly salary as one-fortieth (1/40) of the employee's weekly salary.

(B) *Alternative Workweek Schedules*

(1) No employer shall be deemed to have violated the daily overtime provisions by instituting, pursuant to the election procedures set forth in this wage order, a regularly scheduled alternative workweek schedule of not more than ten (10) hours per day within a 40 hour workweek without the payment of an overtime rate of compensation. All work performed in any workday beyond the schedule established by the agreement up to 12 hours a day or beyond 40 hours per week shall be paid at one and one-half (1 $\frac{1}{2}$) times the employee's regular rate of pay. All work performed in excess of 12 hours per day and any work in excess of eight (8) hours on those days worked beyond the regularly scheduled number of workdays established by the alternative workweek agreement shall be paid at double the employee's regular rate of pay. Any alternative workweek agreement adopted pursuant to this section shall provide for not less than four (4) hours of work in any shift. Nothing in this section shall prohibit an employer, at the request of the employee, to substitute one day of work for another day of the same length in the shift provided by the alternative workweek agreement on an occasional basis to meet the personal needs of the employee without the payment of overtime. No hours paid at either one and one-half (1 $\frac{1}{2}$) or double the regular rate of pay shall be included in determining when 40 hours have been worked for the purpose of computing overtime compensation.

(2) If an employer whose employees have adopted an alternative workweek agreement permitted by this order requires an employee to work fewer hours than those that are regularly scheduled by the agreement, the employer shall pay the employee overtime compensation at a rate of one and one-half (1 $\frac{1}{2}$) times the employee's regular rate of pay for all hours worked in excess of eight (8) hours, and double the employee's regular rate of pay for all hours worked in excess of 12 hours for the day the employee is required to work the reduced hours.

(3) An employer shall not reduce an employee's regular rate of hourly pay as a result of the adoption, repeal or nullification of an alternative workweek schedule.

(4) An employer shall explore any available reasonable alternative means of accommodating the religious belief or observance of an affected employee that conflicts with an adopted alternative workweek schedule, in the manner provided by subdivision (j) of Section 12940 of the Government Code.

(5) An employer shall make a reasonable effort to find a work schedule not to exceed eight (8) hours in a workday, in order to accommodate any affected employee who was eligible to vote in an election authorized by this section and who is unable to work the alternative workweek schedule established as the result of that election.

(6) An employer shall be permitted, but not required, to provide a work schedule not to exceed eight (8) hours in a workday to accommodate any employee who is hired after the date of the election and who is unable to work the alternative workweek schedule established by the election.

(7) Arrangements adopted in a secret ballot election held pursuant to this order prior to 1998, or under the rules in effect prior to 1998, and before the performance of the work, shall remain valid after July 1, 2000 provided that the results of the election are reported by the employer to the Division of Labor Statistics and Research by January 1, 2001, in accordance with the requirements of subsection (C) below (Election Procedures). If an employee was voluntarily working an alternative workweek schedule of not more than ten (10) hours a day as of July 1, 1999, that alternative workweek schedule was based on an individual agreement made after January 1, 1998 between the employee and employer, and the employee submitted, and the employer approved, a written request on or before May 30, 2000 to continue the agreement, the employee may continue to work that alternative workweek schedule without payment of an overtime rate of compensation for the hours provided in the agreement. The employee may revoke his/her voluntary authorization to continue such a schedule with 30 days written notice to the employer. New arrangements can only be entered into pursuant to the provisions of this section.

(C) *Election Procedures*

Election procedures for the adoption and repeal of alternative workweek schedules require the following:

(1) Each proposal for an alternative workweek schedule shall be in the form of a written agreement proposed by the employer. The proposed agreement must designate a regularly scheduled alternative workweek in which the specified number of work days and work hours are regularly recurring. The actual days worked within that alternative workweek schedule need not be specified. The employer may propose a single work schedule that would become the standard schedule for workers in the work unit, or a menu of work schedule options, from which each employee in the unit would be entitled to choose. If the employer proposes a menu of work schedule options, the employee may, with the approval of the employer, move from one menu option to another.

(2) In order to be valid, the proposed alternative workweek schedule must be adopted in a secret ballot election, before the performance of work, by at least a two-thirds (2/03) vote of the affected employees in the work unit. The election shall be held during regular working hours at the employees' work site. For purposes of this subsection, "affected employees in the work unit" may include all employees in a readily identifiable work unit, such as a division, a department, a job classification, a shift, a separate physical location, or a recognized subdivision of any such work unit. A work unit may consist of an individual employee as long as the criteria for an identifiable work unit in this subsection are met.

(3) Prior to the secret ballot vote, any employer who proposed to institute an alternative workweek schedule shall have made a disclosure in writing to the affected employees, including the effects of the proposed arrangement on the employees' wages, hours, and benefits. Such a disclosure shall include meeting(s), duly noticed, held at least 14 days prior to voting, for the specific purpose of discussing the effects of the alternative workweek schedule. An employer shall provide that disclosure in a non–English language, as well as in English, if at least five (5) percent of the affected employees primarily speak that non–English language. The employer shall mail the written disclosure to employees who do not attend the meeting. Failure to comply with this paragraph shall make the election null and void.

(4) Any election to establish or repeal an alternative workweek schedule shall be held at the work site of the affected employees. The employer shall bear the costs of conducting any election held pursuant to this section. Upon a complaint by an affected employee, and after an investigation by the labor commissioner, the labor commissioner may require the employer to select a neutral third party to conduct the election.

(5) Any type of alternative workweek schedule that is authorized by the California Labor Code may be repealed by the affected employees. Upon a petition of one-third (1/03) of the affected employees, a new secret ballot election shall be held and a two-thirds (2/03) vote of the affected employees shall be required to reverse the alternative workweek schedule. The election to repeal the alternative workweek schedule shall be held not more than 30 days after the petition is submitted to the employer, except that the election shall be held not less than 12 months after the date that the same group of employees voted in an election held to adopt or repeal an alternative workweek schedule. The election shall take place during regular working hours at the employees' work site. If the alternative workweek schedule is revoked, the employer shall comply within 60 days. Upon proper showing of undue hardship, the Division of Labor Standards Enforcement may grant an extension of time for compliance.

(6) Only secret ballots may be cast by affected employees in the work unit at any election held pursuant to this section. The results of any election conducted pursuant to this section shall be reported by the employer to the Division of Labor Statistics and Research within 30 days after the results are final, and the report of election results shall be a public document. The report shall include the final tally of the vote, the size of the unit, and the nature of the business of the employer.

(7) Employees affected by a change in the work hours resulting from the adoption of an alternative workweek schedule may not be required to work those new work hours for at least 30 days after the announcement of the final results of the election.

(8) Employers shall not intimidate or coerce employees to vote either in support of or in opposition to a proposed alternative workweek. No employees shall be discharged or discriminated against for expressing opinions concerning the alternative workweek election or for opposing or supporting its adoption or repeal. However, nothing in this section shall prohibit an employer from expressing his/her position concerning that alternative workweek to the affected employees. A violation of this paragraph shall be subject to California Labor Code Section 98 et seq.

(D) One and one-half (1 $\frac{1}{2}$) times a minor's regular rate of pay shall be paid for all work over 40 hours in any workweek except minors 16 or 17 years old who are not required by law to attend school and may therefore by employed for the same hours as an adult are subject to subsection (A) or (B) and (C) above.

(**Violations of Child Labor Laws** are subject to civil penalties of from $500 to $10,000 as well as to criminal penalties. Refer to California Labor Code Sections 1285 to 1312 and 1390 to 1399 for additional restrictions on the employment of minors and for descriptions of criminal and civil penalties for violation of the child labor laws. Employers should ask school districts about any required work permits.)

(E) An employee may be employed on seven (7) workdays in one workweek when the total hours of employment during such workweek do not exceed 30 and the total hours of employment in any one workday thereof do not exceed six (6).

(F) If a meal period occurs on a shift beginning or ending at or between the hours of 10 p.m. and 6 a.m., facilities shall be available for securing hot food and drink or for heating food or drink, and a suitable sheltered place shall be provided in which to consume such food or drink.

(G) The provisions of Labor Code Sections 551 and 552 regarding one (1) day's rest in seven (7) shall not be construed to prevent an accumulation of days of rest when the nature of the employment reasonably requires the employee to work seven (7) or more consecutive days; provided, however, that in each calendar month, the employee shall receive the equivalent of one (1) day's rest in seven (7).

(H) Except as provided in subsections (E) and (G), this section shall not apply to any employee covered by a valid collective bargaining agreement if the agreement expressly provides for the wages, hours of work, and working conditions of the employees, and if the agreement provides premium wage rates for all overtime hours worked and a regular hourly rate of pay for those employees of not less than 30 percent more than the state minimum wage.

(I) Notwithstanding subsection (H) above, where the employer and a labor organization representing employees of the employer have entered into a valid collective bargaining agreement pertaining to the hours of work of the employees, the requirement regarding the equivalent of one (1) day's rest in seven (7) (see subsection (G) above) shall apply, unless the agreement expressly provides otherwise.

(J) If an employer approves a written request of an employee to make up work time that is or would be lost as a result of a personal obligation of the employee, the hours of that makeup work time, if performed in the same workweek in which the work time was lost, may not be counted toward computing the total number of hours worked in a day for purposes of the overtime requirements, except for hours in excess of 11 hours of work in one (1) day or 40 hours of work in one (1) workweek. If an employee knows in advance that he/she will be requesting makeup time for a personal obligation that will recur at a fixed time over a succession of weeks, the employee may request to make up work time for up to four (4) weeks in advance; provided, however, that the makeup work must be performed in the same week that the work time was lost. An employee shall provide a signed written request for each occasion that the employee makes a request to make up work time pursuant to this subsection. While an employer may inform an employee of this makeup time option, the employer is prohibited from encouraging or otherwise soliciting an employee to request the employer's approval to take personal time off and make up the work hours within the same workweek pursuant to this subsection.

(K) The daily overtime provision of subsection (A) above shall not apply to ambulance drivers and attendants scheduled for 24–hour shifts of duty who have agreed

in writing to exclude from daily time worked not more than three (3) meal periods of not more than one (1) hour each and a regularly scheduled uninterrupted sleeping period of not more than eight (8) hours. The employer shall provide adequate dormitory and kitchen facilities for employees on such a schedule.

(L) The provisions of this section are not applicable to employees whose hours of service are regulated by:

(1) The United States Department of Transportation Code of Federal Regulations, Title 49, Sections 395.1 to 395.13, Hours of Service of Drivers, or;

(2) Title 13 of the California Code of Regulations, subchapter 6.5, Section 1200 and the following sections, regulating hours of drivers.

(M) The provisions of this section shall not apply to taxicab drivers.

(N) The provisions of this section shall not apply where any employee of an airline certified by the federal or state government works over 40 hours but not more than 60 hours in a workweek due to a temporary modification in the employee's normal work schedule not required by the employer but arranged at the request of the employee, including but not limited to situations where the employee requests a change in days off or trades days off with another employee.

4. Minimum Wages

(A) Every employer shall pay to each employee wages not less than seven dollars and fifty cents ($7.50) per hour for all hours worked, effective January 1, 2007, and not less than eight dollars ($8.00) per hour for all hours worked, effective January 1, 2008, except:

Learners: Employees during their first 160 hours of employment in occupations in which they have no previous similar or related experience, may be paid not less than 85 percent of the minimum wage rounded to the nearest nickel.

(B) Every employer shall pay to each employee, on the established payday for the period involved, not less than the applicable minimum wage for all hours worked in the payroll period, whether the remuneration is measured by time, piece, commission, or otherwise.

(C) When an employee works a split shift, one (1) hour's pay at the minimum wage shall be paid in addition to the minimum wage for that workday, except when the employee resides at the place of employment.

(D) The provisions of this section shall not apply to apprentices regularly indentured under the State Division of Apprenticeship Standards.

5. Reporting Time Pay

(A) Each workday an employee is required to report for work and does report, but is not put to work or is furnished less than half said employee's usual or scheduled day's work, the employee shall be paid for half the usual or scheduled day's work, but in no event for less than two (2) hours nor more than four (4) hours, at the employee's regular rate of pay, which shall not be less than the minimum wage.

(B) If an employee is required to report for work a second time in any one workday and is furnished less than two (2) hours of work on the second reporting, said employee shall be paid for two (2) hours at the employee's regular rate of pay, which shall not be less than the minimum wage.

(C) The foregoing reporting time pay provisions are not applicable when:

(1) Operations cannot commence or continue due to threats to employees or property; or when recommended by civil authorities; or

(2) Public utilities fail to supply electricity, water, or gas, or there is a failure in the public utilities, or sewer system; or

(3) The interruption of work is caused by an Act of God or other cause not within the employer's control.

(D) This section shall not apply to an employee on paid standby status who is called to perform assigned work at a time other than the employee's scheduled reporting time.

6. Licenses for Disabled Workers

(A) A license may be issued by the Division authorizing employment of a person whose earning capacity is impaired by physical disability or mental deficiency at less than the minimum wage. Such licenses shall be granted only upon joint application of employer and employee and employee's representative if any.

(B) A special license may be issued to a nonprofit organization such as a sheltered workshop or rehabilitation facility fixing special minimum rates to enable the employment of such persons without requiring individual licenses of such employees.

(C) All such licenses and special licenses shall be renewed on a yearly basis or more frequently at the discretion of the Division.

(See California Labor Code, Sections 1191 and 1191.5)

7. Records

(A) Every employer shall keep accurate information with respect to each employee including the following:

(1) Full name, home address, occupation and social security number.

(2) Birth date, if under 18 years, and designation as a minor.

(3) Time records showing when the employee begins and ends each work period. Meal periods, split shift intervals and total daily hours worked shall also be recorded. Meal periods during which operations cease and authorized rest periods need not be recorded.

(4) Total wages paid each payroll period, including value of board, lodging, or other compensation actually furnished to the employee.

(5) Total hours worked in the payroll period and applicable rates of pay. This information shall be made readily available to the employee upon reasonable request.

(6) When a piece rate or incentive plan is in operation, piece rates or an explanation of the incentive plan formula shall be provided to employees. An accurate production record shall be maintained by the employer.

(B) Every employer shall semimonthly or at the time of each payment of wages furnish each employee, either as a detachable part of the check, draft, or voucher paying the employee's wages, or separately, an itemized statement in writing showing: (1) all deductions; (2) the inclusive dates of the period for which the employee is paid; (3) the name of the employee or the employee's social security number; and (4) the name of the employer, provided all deductions made on written orders of the employee may be aggregated and shown as one item.

(C) All required records shall be in the English language and in ink or other indelible form, properly dated, showing month, day and year, and shall be kept on file by the employer for at least three years at the place of employment or at a central location within the State of California. An employee's records shall be available for inspection by the employee upon reasonable request.

(D) Clocks shall be provided in all major work areas or within a reasonable distance thereto insofar as practicable.

8. Cash Shortage and Breakage. No employer shall make any deduction from the wage or require any reimbursement from an employee for any cash shortage, breakage, or loss of equipment, unless it can be shown that the shortage, breakage, or loss is caused by a dishonest or willful act, or by the gross negligence of the employee.

9. Uniforms and Equipment

(A) When uniforms are required by the employer to be worn by the employee as a condition of employment, such uniforms shall be provided and maintained by the employer. The term "uniform" includes wearing apparel and accessories of distinctive design or color.

Note: This section shall not apply to protective apparel regulated by the Occupational Safety and Health Standards Board.

(B) When tools or equipment are required by the employer or are necessary to the performance of a job, such tools and equipment shall be provided and maintained by the employer, except that an employee whose wages are at least two (2) times the minimum wage provided herein may be required to provide and maintain hand tools and equipment customarily required by the trade or craft. This subsection (B) shall not apply to apprentices regularly indentured under the State Division of Apprenticeship Standards.

Note: This section shall not apply to protective equipment and safety devices on tools regulated by the Occupational Safety and Health Standards Board.

(C) A reasonable deposit may be required as security for the return of the items furnished by the employer under provisions of subsections (A) and (B) of this section upon issuance of a receipt to the employee for such deposit. Such deposits shall be made pursuant to Section 400 and following of the Labor Code or an employer with the prior written authorization of the employee may deduct from the employee's last check the cost of an item furnished pursuant to (A) and (B) above in the event said item is not returned. No deduction shall be made at any time for normal wear and tear. All items furnished by the employer shall be returned by the employee upon completion of the job.

10. Meals and Lodging

(A) "Meal" means an adequate, well-balanced serving of a variety of wholesome, nutritious foods.

(B) "Lodging" means living accommodations available to the employee for full-time occupancy which are adequate, decent, and sanitary according to usual and customary standards. Employees shall not be required to share a bed.

(C) Meals or lodging may not be credited against the minimum wage without a voluntary written agreement between the employer and the employee. When credit for meals or lodging is used to meet part of the employer's minimum wage obligation, the amounts so credited may not be more than the following:

Effective	January 1, 2007	January 1, 2008
Lodging:		
Room occupied alone	$35.27 per week	$37.63 per week
Room shared	$29.11 per week	$31.06 per week
Apartment—two-thirds (2/03) of the ordinary rental value, and in no event more than	$423.51 per month	$451.89 per month
Where a couple are both employed by the employer, two-thirds (2/03) of the ordinary rental value, and in no event more than	$626.49 per month	$668.46 per month
Meals:		
Breakfast	$2.72	$2.90
Lunch	$3.72	$3.97
Dinner	$5.00	$5.34

(D) Meals evaluated as part of the minimum wage must be bona fide meals consistent with the employee's work shift. Deductions shall not be made for meals not received or lodging not used.

(E) If, as a condition of employment, the employee must live at the place of employment or occupy quarters owned or under the control of the employer, then the employer may not charge rent in excess of the values listed herein.

11. Meal Periods

(A) No employer shall employ any person for a work period of more than five (5) hours without a meal period of not less than 30 minutes, except that when a work period of not more than six (6) hours will complete the day's work the meal period may be waived by mutual consent of the employer and the employee.

(B) An employer may not employ an employee for a work period of more than ten (10) hours per day without providing the employee with a second meal period of not less than 30 minutes, except that if the total hours worked is no more than 12 hours, the second meal period may be waived by mutual consent of the employer and the employee only if the first meal period was not waived.

(C) Unless the employee is relieved of all duty during a 30 minute meal period, the meal period shall be considered an "on duty" meal period and counted as time worked. An "on duty" meal period shall be permitted only when the nature of the work prevents an employee from being relieved of all duty and when by written agreement between the parties an on-the-job paid meal period is agreed to. The written agreement shall state that the employee may, in writing, revoke the agreement at any time.

(D) If an employer fails to provide an employee a meal period in accordance with the applicable provisions of this order, the employer shall pay the employee one (1) hour of pay at the employee's regular rate of compensation for each workday that the meal period is not provided.

(E) In all places of employment where employees are required to eat on the premises, a suitable place for that purpose shall be designated.

(F) The section shall not apply to any public transit bus driver covered by a valid collective bargaining agreement if the agreement expressly provides for meal periods for those employees, final and binding arbitration of disputes concerning application of its meal period provisions, premium wage rates for all overtime hours worked, and regular hourly rate of pay of not less than 30 percent more than the State minimum wage rate.

12. Rest Periods

(A) Every employer shall authorize and permit all employees to take rest periods, which insofar as practicable shall be in the middle of each work period. The authorized rest period time shall be based on the total hours worked daily at the rate of ten (10) minutes net rest time per four (4) hours or major fraction thereof. However, a rest period need not be authorized for employees whose total daily work time is less than three and one-half (3 1/02) hours. Authorized rest period time shall be counted as hours worked for which there shall be no deduction from wages.

(B) If an employer fails to provide an employee a rest period in accordance with the applicable provisions of this order, the employer shall pay the employee one (1) hour of pay at the employee's regular rate of compensation for each workday that the rest period is not provided.

(C) This section shall not apply to any public transit bus driver covered by a valid collective bargaining agreement if the agreement expressly provides for rest periods for those employees, final and binding arbitration of disputes concerning application of its rest period provisions, premium wage rates for all overtime hours worked, and regular hourly rate of pay of not less than 30 percent more than the State minimum wage rate.

13. Change Rooms and Resting Facilities

(A) Employers shall provide suitable lockers, closets, or equivalent for the safekeeping of employees' outer clothing during working hours, and when required, for their work clothing during non-working hours. When the occupation requires a change of clothing, change rooms or equivalent space shall be provided in order that employees may change their clothing in reasonable privacy and comfort. These rooms or spaces may be adjacent to but shall be separate from toilet rooms and shall be kept clean.

Note: This section shall not apply to change rooms and storage facilities regulated by the Occupational Safety and Health Standards Board.

(B) Suitable resting facilities shall be provided in an area separate from the toilet rooms and shall be available to employees during work hours.

14. Seats

(A) All working employees shall be provided with suitable seats when the nature of the work reasonably permits the use of seats.

(B) When employees are not engaged in the active duties of their employment and the nature of the work requires standing, an adequate number of suitable seats shall be placed in reasonable proximity to the work area and employees shall be permitted to use such seats when it does not interfere with the performance of their duties.

15. Temperature

(A) The temperature maintained in each work area shall provide reasonable comfort consistent with industry-wide standards for the nature of the process and the work performed.

(B) If excessive heat or humidity is created by the work process, the employer shall take all feasible means to reduce such excessive heat or humidity to a degree providing reasonable comfort. Where the nature of the employment requires a temperature of less than 60° F., a heated room shall be provided to which employees may retire for warmth, and such room shall be maintained at not less than 68°.

(C) A temperature of not less than 68° shall be maintained in the toilet rooms, resting rooms, and change rooms during hours of use.

(D) Federal and State energy guidelines shall prevail over any conflicting provision of this section.

16. Elevators.
Adequate elevator, escalator or similar service consistent with industry-wide standards for the nature of the process and the work performed shall be provided when employees are employed four floors or more above or below ground level.

17. Exemptions.
If, in the opinion of the Division after due investigation, it is found that the enforcement of any provision contained in Section 7, Records; Section 12, Rest Periods; Section 13, Change Rooms and Resting Facilities; Section 14, Seats; Section 15, Temperature; or Section 16, Elevators, would not materially affect the welfare or comfort of employees and would work an undue hardship on the employer, exemption may be made at the discretion of the Division. Such exemptions shall be in writing to be effective and may be revoked after reasonable notice is given in writing. Application for exemption shall be made by the employer or by the employee and/or the employee's representative to the Division in writing. A copy of the application shall be posted at the place of employment at the time the application is filed with the Division.

18. Filing Reports.
(See California Labor Code, Section 1174(a))

19. Inspection.
(See California Labor Code, Section 1174)

20. Penalties.
(See California Labor Code, Section 1199)

(A) In addition to any other civil penalties provided by law, any employer or any other person acting on behalf of the employer who violates, or causes to be violated, the provisions of this order, shall be subject to the civil penalty of:

(1) Initial Violation—$50.00 for each underpaid employee for each pay period during which the employee was underpaid in addition to the amount which is sufficient to recover unpaid wages.

(2) Subsequent Violations—$100.00 for each underpaid employee for each pay period during which the employee was underpaid in addition to an amount which is sufficient to recover unpaid wages.

(3) The affected employee shall receive payment of all wages recovered.

(B) The labor commissioner may also issue citations pursuant to California Labor Code Section 1197.1 for non-payment of wages for overtime work in violation of this order.

21. Separability.
If the application of any provision of this order, or any section, subsection, subdivision, sentence, clause, phrase, word, or portion of this order should be held invalid or unconstitutional or unauthorized or prohibited by statute, the remaining provisions thereof shall not be affected thereby, but shall continue to be given full force and effect as if the part so held invalid or unconstitutional had not been included herein.

22. Posting of Order.
Every employer shall keep a copy of this order posted in an area frequented by employees where it may be easily read during the workday. Where the location of work or other condi-

tions make this impractical, every employer shall keep a copy of this order and make it available to every employee upon request.

[1] Pursuant to Labor Code section 515.5, subdivision (a)(4), the Division of Labor Statistics and Research, Department of Industrial Relations, has adjusted the minimum hourly rate of pay specified in this subdivision to be $49.77, effective January 1, 2007. This hourly rate of pay is adjusted on October 1 of each year to be effective on January 1, of the following year, and may be obtained at www.dir.ca.gov/IWC or by mail from the Department of Industrial Relations.

Publisher's Notes

See Tidewater Marine Western, Inc. v. Bradshaw (1996) 14 Cal.4th 557, 927 P.2d 296, 59 Cal.Rptr.2d 186 (in determining whether wage orders apply, where state and federal law do not conflict, California's territorial boundaries as determined by state law).

See Auchmoody v. 911 Emergency Services (1989) 214 Cal.App.3d 1510, 263 Cal.Rptr. 278 ("24–hour agreements" signed by employees conformed to Wage Order 9–80, Subsection 3(G)).

See United Air Lines, Inc. v. Industrial Welfare Com. (1963) 211 Cal.App.2d 729, 744, 28 Cal.Rptr. 238 (uniforms; preemption of wage order by the National Labor Relations Act (29 U.S.C.A. §§ 151 et seq.), the Railway Labor Act (45 U.S.C.A. §§ 151 et seq.), and the Fair Labor Standards Act (29 U.S.C.A. §§ 201 et seq)).

Research References

See notes following listing of Wage Orders.

Please Post With This Side Showing
OFFICIAL NOTICE
Effective January 1, 2001 as amended
Sections 4(A) and 10(C) amended and republished by the Department of Industrial Relations, effective January 1, 2007, pursuant to AB 1835, Chapter 230, Statutes of 2006
INDUSTRIAL WELFARE COMMISSION
ORDER NO. 10–2001
REGULATING
WAGES, HOURS AND WORKING CONDITIONS IN THE
AMUSEMENT AND RECREATION
INDUSTRY

TAKE NOTICE: To employers and representatives of persons working in industries and occupations in the State of California:

The Department of Industrial Relations amends and republishes the minimum wage and meals and lodging credits in the Industrial Welfare Commission's Orders as a result of legislation enacted (AB 1835, Ch. 230, Stats of 2006, adding sections 1182.12 and 1182.13 to the California Labor Code.) The amendments and republishing make no other changes to the IWC's Orders.

1. Applicability of Order. This order shall apply to all persons employed in the amusement and recreation industry whether paid on a time, piece rate, commission, or other basis, except that:

(A) Provisions of Sections 3 through 12 of this order shall not apply to persons employed in administrative, executive, or professional capacities. The following requirements shall apply in determining whether an employee's duties meet the test to qualify for an exemption from those sections:

(1) Executive Exemption. A person employed in an executive capacity means any employee:

(a) Whose duties and responsibilities involve the management of the enterprise in which he/she is employed or of a customarily recognized department or subdivision thereof; and

(b) Who customarily and regularly directs the work of two or more other employees therein; and

(c) Who has the authority to hire or fire other employees or whose suggestions and recommendations as to the hiring or firing and as to the advancement and promotion or any other change of status of other employees will be given particular weight; and

(d) Who customarily and regularly exercises discretion and independent judgment; and

(e) Who is primarily engaged in duties which meet the test of the exemption. The activities constituting exempt work and non-exempt work shall be construed in the same manner as such items are construed in the following regulations under the Fair Labor Standards Act effective as of the date of this order: 29 C.F.R. Sections 541.102, 541.104–111, and 541.15–116. Exempt work shall include, for example, all work that is directly and closely related to exempt work and work which is properly viewed as a means for carrying out exempt functions. The work actually performed by the employee during the course of the workweek must, first and foremost, be examined and the amount of time the employee spends on such work, together with the employer's realistic expectations and the realistic requirements of the job, shall be considered in determining whether the employee satisfies this requirement.

(f) Such an employee must also earn a monthly salary equivalent to no less than two (2) times the state minimum wage for full-time employment. Full–time employment is defined in Labor Code Section 515(c) as 40 hours per week.

(2) <u>Administrative Exemption.</u> A person employed in an administrative capacity means any employee:

(a) Whose duties and responsibilities involve either:

(i) The performance of office or non-manual work directly related to management policies or general business operations of his/her employer or his/her employer's customers; or

(ii) The performance of functions in the administration of a school system, or educational establishment or institution, or of a department or subdivision thereof, in work directly related to the academic instruction or training carried on therein; and

(b) Who customarily and regularly exercises discretion and independent judgment; and

(c) Who regularly and directly assists a proprietor, or an employee employed in a bona fide executive or administrative capacity (as such terms are defined for purposes of this section); or

(d) Who performs under only general supervision work along specialized or technical lines requiring special training, experience, or knowledge; or

(e) Who executes under only general supervision special assignments and tasks; and

(f) Who is primarily engaged in duties which meet the test of the exemption. The activities constituting exempt work and non-exempt work shall be construed in the same manner as such terms are construed in the following regulations under the Fair Labor Standards Act effective as of the date of this order: 29 C.F.R. Sections 541.201–205, 541.207–208, 541.210, and 541.215. Exempt work shall include, for example, all work that is directly and closely related to exempt work and work which is properly viewed as a means for carrying out exempt functions. The work actually performed by the employee during the course of the workweek must, first and foremost, be examined and the amount of time the employee spends on such work, together with the employer's realistic expectations and the realistic requirements of the job, shall be considered in determining whether the employee satisfies this requirement.

(g) Such employee must also earn a monthly salary equivalent to no less than two (2) times the state minimum wage for full-time employment. Full–time employment is defined in Labor Code Section 515(c) as 40 hours per week.

(3) <u>Professional Exemption.</u> A person employed in a professional capacity means any employee who meets *all* of the following requirements:

(a) Who is licensed or certified by the State of California and is primarily engaged in the practice of one of the following recognized professions: law, medicine, dentistry, optometry, architecture, engineering, teaching, or accounting; or

(b) Who is primarily engaged in an occupation commonly recognized as a learned or artistic profession. For the purposes of this subsection, "learned or artistic

profession" means an employee who is primarily engaged in the performance of:

(i) Work requiring knowledge of an advanced type in a field or science or learning customarily acquired by a prolonged course of specialized intellectual instruction and study, as distinguished from a general academic education and from an apprenticeship, and from training in the performance of routine mental, manual, or physical processes, or work that is an essential part of or necessarily incident to any of the above work; or

(ii) Work that is original and creative in character in a recognized field of artistic endeavor (as opposed to work which can be produced by a person endowed with general manual or intellectual ability and training), and the result of which depends primarily on the invention, imagination, or talent of the employee or work that is an essential part of or necessarily incident to any of the above work; and

(iii) Whose work is predominantly intellectual and varied in character (as opposed to routine mental, manual, mechanical, or physical work) and is of such character that the output produced or the result accomplished cannot be standardized in relation to a given period of time.

(c) Who customarily and regularly exercises discretion and independent judgment in the performance of duties set forth in subparagraphs (a) and (b).

(d) Who earns a monthly salary equivalent to no less than two (2) times the state minimum wage for full-time employment. Full–time employment is defined in Labor Code Section 515 (c) as 40 hours per week.

(e) Subparagraph (b) above is intended to be construed in accordance with the following provisions of federal law as they existed as of the date of this wage order: 29 C.F.R. Sections 541.207, 541.301(a)–(d), 541.302, 541.306, 541.307, 541.308, and 541.310.

(f) Notwithstanding the provisions of this subparagraph, pharmacists employed to engage in the practice of pharmacy, and registered nurses employed to engage in the practice of nursing, shall not be considered exempt professional employees, nor shall they be considered exempt from coverage for the purposes of this subparagraph unless they individually meet the criteria established for exemption as executive or administrative employees.

(g) Subparagraph (f) above shall not apply to the following advanced practice nurses:

(i) Certified nurse midwives who are primarily engaged in performing duties for which certification is required pursuant to Article 2.5 (commencing with Section 2746) of Chapter 6 of Division 2 of the Business and Professions Code.

(ii) Certified nurse anesthetists who are primarily engaged in performing duties for which certification is required pursuant to Article 7 (commencing with Section 2825) of Chapter 6 of Division 2 of the Business and Professions Code.

(iii) Certified nurse practitioners who are primarily engaged in performing duties for which certification is required pursuant to Article 8 (commencing with Section 2834) of Chapter 6 of Division 2 of the Business and Professions Code.

(iv) Nothing in this subparagraph shall exempt the occupations set forth in clauses (i), (ii), and (iii) from meeting the requirements of subsection 1(A)(3)(a)–(d) above.

(h) Except, as provided in subparagraph (i), an employee in the computer software field who is paid on an hourly basis shall be exempt, if *all* of the following apply:

(i) The employee is primarily engaged in work that is intellectual or creative and requires the exercise of discretion and independent judgment.

(ii) The employee is primarily engaged in duties that consist of one or more of the following:

-The application of systems analysis techniques and procedures, including consulting with users, to determine hardware, software, or system functional specifications.

-The design, development, documentation, analysis, creation, testing, or modification of computer systems or programs, including prototypes, based on and related to user or system design specifications.

-The documentation, testing, creation, or modification of computer programs related to the design of software or hardware for computer operating systems.

(iii) The employee is highly skilled and is proficient in the theoretical and practical application of highly specialized information to computer systems analysis, programming, and software engineering. A job title shall not be determinative of the applicability of this exemption.

(iv) The employee's hourly rate of pay is not less than forty-one dollars ($41.00). The Division of Labor Statistics and Research shall adjust this pay rate on October 1 of each year to be effective on January 1 of the following year by an amount equal to the percentage increase in the California Consumer Price Index for Urban Wage Earners and Clerical Workers.[1]

(i) The exemption provided in subparagraph (h) does not apply to an employee if *any* of the following apply:

(i) The employee is a trainee or employee in an entry-level position who is learning to become proficient in the theoretical and practical application of highly specialized information to computer systems analysis, programming, and software engineering.

(ii) The employee is in a computer-related occupation but has not attained the level of skill and expertise necessary to work independently and without close supervision.

(iii) The employee is engaged in the operation of computers or in the manufacture, repair, or maintenance of computer hardware and related equipment.

(iv) The employee is an engineer, drafter, machinist, or other professional whose work is highly dependent upon or facilitated by the use of computers and computer software programs and who is skilled in computer-aided design software, including CAD/CAM, but who is not in a computer systems analysis or programming occupation.

(v) The employee is a writer engaged in writing material, including box labels, product descriptions, documentation, promotional material, setup and installation instructions, and other similar written information, either for print or for on screen media or who writes or provides content material intended to be read by customers, subscribers, or visitors to computer-related media such as the World Wide Web or CD–ROMs.

(vi) The employee is engaged in *any* of the activities set forth in subparagraph (h) for the purpose of creating imagery for effects used in the motion picture, television, or theatrical industry.

(B) The provisions of this order shall apply to all employees employed by any employer operating a business at a horse racing facility, including stable employees. Stable employees include but are not limited to grooms, hot walkers, exercise workers, and any other employees engaged in the raising, feeding, or management of racehorses, employed by a trainer at a racetrack or other nonfarm training facility.

(C) Except as provided in Sections 1, 2, 4, 10, and 20, the provisions of this order shall not apply to any employees directly employed by the State or any political subdivision thereof, including any city, county, or special district.

(D) The provisions of this order shall not apply to outside salespersons.

(E) The provisions of this order shall not apply to any individual who is the parent, spouse, child, or legally adopted child of the employer.

(F) Except as provided in Sections 1, 2, 4, 10, and 20, the provisions of this order shall not apply to full-time carnival ride operators employed by traveling carnivals.

(G) The provisions of this order shall not apply to any individual participating in a national service program, such as AmeriCorps, carried out using assistance provided under Section 12571 of Title 42 of the United States Code. (See Stats. 2000, ch. 365, amending Labor Code Section 1171.)

(H) The provisions of this section are not applicable to any crew member employed on a commercial passenger fishing boat licensed pursuant to Article 5 (commencing with Section 7920) of Chapter 1 of Part 3 of Division 6 of the Fish and Game Code.

(I) Except as provided in Sections 1, 2, 4, 10, and 20, the provisions of this order shall not apply to professional actors.

2. **Definitions**

(A) "Amusement and Recreation Industry" means any industry, business, or establishment operated for the purpose of furnishing entertainment or recreation to the public, including but not limited to theaters, dance halls,

1475

bowling alleys, billiard parlors, skating rinks, riding academies, racetracks, amusement parks, athletic fields, swimming pools, gymnasiums, golf courses, tennis courts, carnivals, and wired music studios.

(B) An "alternative workweek schedule" means any regularly scheduled workweek requiring an employee to work more than eight (8) hours in a 24–hour period.

(C) "Commission" means the Industrial Welfare Commission of the State of California.

(D) "Division" means the Division of Labor Standards Enforcement of the State of California.

(E) "Employ" means to engage, suffer, or permit to work.

(F) "Employee" means any person employed by an employer.

(G) "Employer" means any person as defined in Section 18 of the Labor Code, who directly or indirectly, or through an agent or any other person, employs or exercises control over the wages, hours, or working conditions of any person.

(H) "Hours worked" means the time during which an employee is subject to the control of an employer, and includes all the time the employee is suffered or permitted to work, whether or not required to do so.

(I) "Minor" means, for the purpose of this order, any person under the age of 18 years.

(J) "Outside salesperson" means any person, 18 years of age or over, who customarily and regularly works more than half the working time away from the employer's place of business selling tangible or intangible items or obtaining orders or contracts for products, services or use of facilities.

(K) "Primarily" as used in Section 1, Applicability, means more than one-half the employee's work time.

(L) "Shift" means designated hours of work by an employee, with a designated beginning time and quitting time.

(M) "Split shift" means a work schedule, which is interrupted by non-paid non-working periods established by the employer, other than bona fide rest or meal periods.

(N) "Teaching" means, for the purpose of Section 1 of this order, the profession of teaching under a certificate from the Commission for Teacher Preparation and Licensing or teaching in an accredited college or university.

(O) "Wages" includes all amounts for labor performed by employees of every description, whether the amount is fixed or ascertained by the standard of time, task, piece, commission basis, or other method of calculation.

(P) "Workday" and "day" mean any consecutive 24–hour period beginning at the same time each calendar day.

(Q) "Workweek" and "week" mean any seven (7) consecutive days, starting with the same calendar day

each week. "Workweek" is a fixed and regularly recurring period of 168 hours, seven (7) consecutive 24–hour periods.

3. Hours and Days of Work

(A) *Daily Overtime—General Provisions*

(1) The following overtime provisions are applicable to employees 18 years of age or over and to employees 16 or 17 years of age who are not required by law to attend school and are not otherwise prohibited by law from engaging in the subject work. Such employees shall not be employed more than eight (8) hours in any workday or more than 40 hours in any workweek unless the employee receives one and one-half (1 ½) times such employee's regular rate of pay for all hours worked over 40 hours in the workweek. Eight (8) hours of labor constitutes a day's work. Employment beyond eight (8) hours in any workday or more than six (6) days in any workweek is permissible provided the employee is compensated for such overtime at not less than:

(a) One and one-half (1 ½) times the employee's regular rate of pay for all hours worked in excess of eight (8) hours up to and including 12 hours in any workday, and for the first eight (8) hours worked on the seventh (7th) consecutive day of work in a workweek; and

(b) Double the employee's regular rate of pay for all hours worked in excess of 12 hours in any workday and for all hours worked in excess of eight (8) hours on the seventh (7th) consecutive day of work in a workweek.

(c) The overtime rate of compensation required to be paid to a nonexempt full-time salaried employee shall be computed by using the employee's regular hourly salary as one-fortieth (1/40) of the employee's weekly salary.

(B) *Alternative Workweek Schedules*

(1) No employer shall be deemed to have violated the daily overtime provisions by instituting, pursuant to the election procedures set forth in this wage order, a regularly scheduled alternative workweek schedule of not more than ten (10) hours per day within a 40 hour workweek without the payment of an overtime rate of compensation. All work performed in any workday beyond the schedule established by the agreement up to 12 hours a day or beyond 40 hours per week shall be paid at one and one-half (1 ½) times the employee's regular rate of pay. All work performed in excess of 12 hours per day and any work in excess of eight (8) hours on those days worked beyond the regularly scheduled number of workdays established by the alternative workweek agreement shall be paid at double the employee's regular rate of pay. Any alternative workweek agreement adopted pursuant to this section shall provide for not less than four (4) hours of work in any shift. Nothing in this section shall prohibit an employer, at the request of the employee, to substitute one day of work for another day of the same length in the shift provided by the alternative workweek agreement on an occasional basis to meet the personal needs of the employee without the payment of overtime. No hours paid at either one and one-half (1

$\frac{1}{2}$) or double the regular rate of pay shall be included in determining when 40 hours have been worked for the purpose of computing overtime compensation.

(2) If an employer whose employees have adopted an alternative workweek agreement permitted by this order requires an employee to work fewer hours than those that are regularly scheduled by the agreement, the employer shall pay the employee overtime compensation at a rate of one and one-half (1 $\frac{1}{2}$) times the employee's regular rate of pay for all hours worked in excess of eight (8) hours, and double the employee's regular rate of pay for all hours worked in excess of 12 hours for the day the employee is required to work the reduced hours.

(3) An employer shall not reduce an employee's regular rate of hourly pay as a result of the adoption, repeal or nullification of an alternative workweek schedule.

(4) An employer shall explore any available reasonable alternative means of accommodating the religious belief or observance of an affected employee that conflicts with an adopted alternative workweek schedule, in the manner provided by subdivision (j) of Section 12940 of the Government Code.

(5) An employer shall make a reasonable effort to find a work schedule not to exceed eight (8) hours in a workday, in order to accommodate any affected employee who was eligible to vote in an election authorized by this section and who is unable to work the alternative workweek schedule established as the result of that election.

(6) An employer shall be permitted, but not required, to provide a work schedule not to exceed eight (8) hours in a workday to accommodate any employee who is hired after the date of the election and who is unable to work the alternative workweek schedule established by the election.

(7) Arrangements adopted in a secret ballot election held pursuant to this order prior to 1998, or under the rules in effect prior to 1998, and before the performance of the work, shall remain valid after July 1, 2000 provided that the results of the election are reported by the employer to the Division of Labor Statistics and Research by January 1, 2001, in accordance with the requirements of subsection (C) below (Election Procedures). If an employee was voluntarily working an alternative workweek schedule of not more than ten (10) hours a day as of July 1, 1999, that alternative workweek schedule was based on an individual agreement made after January 1, 1998 between the employee and employer, and the employee submitted, and the employer approved, a written request on or before May 30, 2000 to continue the agreement, the employee may continue to work that alternative workweek schedule without payment of an overtime rate of compensation for the hours provided in the agreement. The employee may revoke his/her voluntary authorization to continue such a schedule with 30 days written notice to the employer. New arrangements can only be entered into pursuant to the provisions of this section.

(C) *Election Procedures*

Election procedures for the adoption and repeal of alternative workweek schedules require the following:

(1) Each proposal for an alternative workweek schedule shall be in the form of a written agreement proposed by the employer. The proposed agreement must designate a regularly scheduled alternative workweek in which the specified number of work days and work hours are regularly recurring. The actual days worked within that alternative workweek schedule need not be specified. The employer may propose a single work schedule that would become the standard schedule for workers in the work unit, or a menu of work schedule options, from which each employee in the unit would be entitled to choose. If the employer proposes a menu of work schedule options, the employee may, with the approval of the employer, move from one menu option to another.

(2) In order to be valid, the proposed alternative workweek schedule must be adopted in a secret ballot election, before the performance of work, by at least a two-thirds (2/03) vote of the affected employees in the work unit. The election shall be held during regular working hours at the employees' work site. For purposes of this subsection, "affected employees in the work unit" may include all employees in a readily identifiable work unit, such as a division, a department, a job classification, a shift, a separate physical location, or a recognized subdivision of any such work unit. A work unit may consist of an individual employee as long as the criteria for an identifiable work unit in this subsection are met.

(3) Prior to the secret ballot vote, any employer who proposed to institute an alternative workweek schedule shall have made a disclosure in writing to the affected employees, including the effects of the proposed arrangement on the employees' wages, hours, and benefits. Such a disclosure shall include meeting(s), duly noticed, held at least 14 days prior to voting, for the specific purpose of discussing the effects of the alternative workweek schedule. An employer shall provide that disclosure in a non–English language, as well as in English, if at least five (5) percent of the affected employees primarily speak that non–English language. The employer shall mail the written disclosure to employees who do not attend the meeting. Failure to comply with this paragraph shall make the election null and void.

(4) Any election to establish or repeal an alternative workweek schedule shall be held at the work site of the affected employees. The employer shall bear the costs of conducting any election held pursuant to this section. Upon a complaint by an affected employee, and after an investigation by the labor commissioner, the labor commissioner may require the employer to select a neutral third party to conduct the election.

(5) Any type of alternative workweek schedule that is authorized by the Labor Code may be repealed by the affected employees. Upon a petition of one-third (1/03) of the affected employees, a new secret ballot election shall be held and a two-thirds (2/03) vote of the affected

employees shall be required to reverse the alternative workweek schedule. The election to repeal the alternative workweek schedule shall be held not more than 30 days after the petition is submitted to the employer, except that the election shall be held not less than 12 months after the date that the same group of employees voted in an election held to adopt or repeal an alternative workweek schedule. The election shall take place during regular working hours at the employees' work site. If the alternative workweek schedule is revoked, the employer shall comply within 60 days. Upon proper showing of undue hardship, the Division of Labor Standards Enforcement may grant an extension of time for compliance.

(6) Only secret ballots may be cast by affected employees in the work unit at any election held pursuant to this section. The results of any election conducted pursuant to this section shall be reported by the employer to the Division of Labor Statistics and Research within 30 days after the results are final, and the report of election results shall be a public document. The report shall include the final tally of the vote, the size of the unit, and the nature of the business of the employer.

(7) Employees affected by a change in the work hours resulting from the adoption of an alternative workweek schedule may not be required to work those new work hours for at least 30 days after the announcement of the final results of the election.

(8) Employers shall not intimidate or coerce employees to vote either in support of or in opposition to a proposed alternative workweek. No employees shall be discharged or discriminated against for expressing opinions concerning the alternative workweek election or for opposing or supporting its adoption or repeal. However, nothing in this section shall prohibit an employer from expressing his/her position concerning that alternative workweek to the affected employees. A violation of this paragraph shall be subject to Labor Code Section 98 *et seq*.

(D) One and one-half (1 ½) times a minor's regular rate of pay shall be paid for all work over 40 hours in any workweek except minors 16 or 17 years old who are not required by law to attend school and may therefore be employed for the same hours as an adult are subject to subsection (A) or (B) and (C) above.

(**Violations of Child Labor Laws** are subject to civil penalties of from $500 to $10,000 as well as to criminal penalties. Refer to California Labor Code Sections 1285 to 1312 and 1390 to 1399 for additional restrictions on the employment of minors and for descriptions of criminal and civil penalties for violation of the child labor laws. Employers should ask school districts about any required work permits.)

(E) An employee may be employed on seven (7) workdays in one workweek when the total hours of employment during such workweek do not exceed 30 and the total hours of employment in any one workday thereof do not exceed six (6).

(F) If a meal period occurs on a shift beginning or ending at or between the hours of 10 p.m. and 6 a.m., facilities shall be available for securing hot food and drink or for heating food or drink, and a suitable sheltered place shall be provided in which to consume such food or drink.

(G) The provisions of this section shall not apply to employees whose duties are exclusively those of a motion picture projectionist.

(H) The provisions of Labor Code Sections 551 and 552 regarding one (1) day's rest in seven (7) shall not be construed to prevent an accumulation of days of rest when the nature of the employment reasonably requires the employee to work seven (7) or more consecutive days; provided, however, that in each calendar month, the employee shall receive the equivalent of one (1) day's rest in seven (7).

(I) Except as provided in subsections (D) and (H), this section shall not apply to any employee covered by a valid collective bargaining agreement if the agreement expressly provides for the wages, hours of work, and working conditions of the employees, and if the agreement provides premium wage rates for all overtime hours worked and a regular hourly rate of pay for those employees of not less than 30 percent more than the state minimum wage.

(J) Notwithstanding subsection (I) above, where the employer and a labor organization representing employees of the employer have entered into a valid collective bargaining agreement pertaining to the hours of work of the employees, the requirement regarding the equivalent of one (1) day's rest in seven (7) (see subsection (H) above) shall apply, unless the agreement expressly provides otherwise.

(K) No employer who operates a ski establishment shall be in violation of this order by instituting a regularly scheduled workweek of not more than 48 hours during any month of the year when Alpine or Nordic skiing activities, including snowmaking and grooming activities, are actually being conducted by the ski establishment; provided, however, that any employee shall be compensated at a rate of not less than one and one-half (1 ½) times the employee's regular rate of pay for any hours worked in excess of ten (10) hours work in a day or 48 hours in a workweek. For purposes of this section, "ski establishment" means an integrated, geographically limited recreational industry which is comprised of basic skiing facilities, together with all operations and facilities related thereto.

(L) The provisions of this section are not applicable to employees whose hours of service are regulated by:

(1) The United States Department of Transportation Code of Federal Regulations, Title 49, Sections 395.1 to 395.13, Hours of Service of Drivers; or

(2) Title 13 of the California Code of Regulations, subchapter 6.5, Section 1200 and the following sections, regulating hours of drivers.

(M) If an employer approves a written request of an employee to make up work time that is or would be lost as a result of a personal obligation of the employee, the hours of that makeup work time, if performed in the same workweek in which the work time was lost, may not be counted toward computing the total number of hours worked in a day for purposes of the overtime requirements, except for hours in excess of 11 hours of work in one (1) day or 40 hours of work in one (1) workweek. If an employee knows in advance that he/she will be requesting makeup time for a personal obligation that will recur at a fixed time over a succession of weeks, the employee may request to make up work time for up to four (4) weeks in advance; provided, however, that the makeup work must be performed in the same week that the work time was lost. An employee shall provide a signed written request for each occasion that the employee makes a request to make up work time pursuant to this subsection. While an employer may inform an employee of this makeup time option, the employer is prohibited from encouraging or otherwise soliciting an employee to request the employer's approval to take personal time off and make up the work hours within the same workweek pursuant to this subsection.

(N) The provisions of this section are not applicable to any crew member employed on a commercial passenger fishing boat licensed pursuant to Article 5 (commencing with Section 7920) of Chapter 1 of Part 3 of Division 6 of the Fish and Game Code.

4. Minimum Wages

(A) Every employer shall pay to each employee wages not less than seven dollars and fifty cents ($7.50) per hour for all hours worked, effective January 1, 2007, and not less than eight dollars ($8.00) per hour for all hours worked, effective January 1, 2008, except:

Learners. Employees during their first 160 hours of employment in occupations in which they have no previous similar or related experience, may be paid not less than 85 percent of the minimum wage rounded to the nearest nickel.

(B) Every employer shall pay to each employee, on the established payday for the period involved, not less than the applicable minimum wage for all hours worked in the payroll period, whether the remuneration is measured by time, piece, commission, or otherwise.

(C) When an employee works a split shift, one (1) hour's pay at the minimum wage shall be paid in addition to the minimum wage for that workday, except when the employee resides at the place of employment.

(D) The provisions of this section shall not apply to apprentices regularly indentured under the State Division of Apprenticeship Standards.

(E) If the employee is a crew member employed on a commercial passenger fishing boat licensed pursuant to Article 5 (commencing with Section 7920) of Chapter 1 of Part 3 of Division 6 of the Fish and Game Code, the minimum wage obligation of this section may, at the employer's option, be satisfied by paying employees according to the following formula:

(1) A "one-half day trip" shall be comprised of a maximum of six (6) hours of work compensated at a rate of no less than six (6) times the hourly minimum wage.

(2) A "three-quarter day trip" shall be comprised of a maximum of ten (10) hours of work compensated at a rate of no less than ten (10) times the hourly minimum wage.

(3) A "full-day trip" shall be comprised of a maximum of 12 hours of work compensated at a rate of no less than 12 times the hourly minimum wage.

(4) An "overnight trip" shall be comprised of a maximum of 12 hours worked within a period of no less than 24 hours compensated at a rate of no less than 12 times the hourly minimum wage.

Nothing in this subsection relieves the employer of the obligation to pay employees no less than the minimum wage for all hours worked.

5. Reporting Time Pay

(A) Each workday an employee is required to report for work and does report, but is not put to work or is furnished less than half said employee's usual or scheduled day's work, the employee shall be paid for half the usual or scheduled day's work, but in no event for less than two (2) hours nor more than four (4) hours, at the employee's regular rate of pay, which shall not be less than the minimum wage.

(B) If an employee is required to report for work a second time in any one workday and is furnished less than two (2) hours of work on the second reporting, said employee shall be paid for two (2) hours at the employee's regular rate of pay, which shall not be less than the minimum wage.

(C) The foregoing reporting time pay provisions are not applicable when:

(1) Operations cannot commence or continue due to threats to employees or property; or when recommended by civil authorities; or

(2) Public utilities fail to supply electricity, water, or gas, or there is a failure in the public utilities, or sewer system; or

(3) The interruption of work is caused by an Act of God or other cause not within the employer's control.

(D) This section shall not apply to an employee on paid standby status who is called to perform assigned work at a time other than the employee's scheduled reporting time.

6. Licenses for Disabled Workers

(A) A license may be issued by the Division authorizing employment of a person whose earning capacity is impaired by physical disability or mental deficiency at less than the minimum wage. Such licenses shall be granted only upon joint application of employer and employee and employee's representative if any.

(B) A special license may be issued to a nonprofit organization such as a sheltered workshop or rehabilitation facility fixing special minimum rates to enable the employment of such persons without requiring individual licenses of such employees.

(C) All such licenses and special licenses shall be renewed on a yearly basis or more frequently at the discretion of the Division.

(See California Labor Code, Sections 1191 and 1191.5)

7. Records

(A) Every employer shall keep accurate information with respect to each employee including the following:

(1) Full name, home address, occupation and social security number.

(2) Birth date, if under 18 years, and designation as a minor.

(3) Time records showing when the employee begins and ends each work period. Meal periods, split shift intervals and total daily hours worked shall also be recorded. Meal periods during which operations cease and authorized rest periods need not be recorded.

(4) Total wages paid each payroll period, including value of board, lodging, or other compensation actually furnished to the employee.

(5) Total hours worked in the payroll period and applicable rates of pay. This information shall be made readily available to the employee upon reasonable request.

(6) When a piece rate or incentive plan is in operation, piece rates or an explanation of the incentive plan formula shall be provided to employees. An accurate production record shall be maintained by the employer.

(B) Every employer shall semimonthly or at the time of each payment of wages furnish each employee, either as a detachable part of the check, draft, or voucher paying the employees wages, or separately, an itemized statement in writing showing: (1) all deductions; (2) the inclusive dates of the period for which the employee is paid; (3) the name of the employee or the employees social security number; and (4) the name of the employer, provided all deductions made on written orders of the employee may be aggregated and shown as one item.

(C) All required records shall be in the English language and in ink or other indelible form, properly dated, showing month, day and year, and shall be kept on file by the employer for at least three years at the place of employment or at a central location within the State of California. An employee's records shall be available for inspection by the employee upon reasonable request.

(D) Clocks shall be provided in all major work areas or within reasonable distance thereto insofar as practicable.

(E) If the employee is a crew member employed on a commercial passenger fishing boat licensed pursuant to Article 5 (commencing with Section 7920) of Chapter 1 of Part 3 of Division 6 of the Fish and Game Code, the

provisions of Sections 3, Hours and Days of Work, and 5, Reporting Time Pay may, at the employer's option, be satisfied by expressing the hours worked in terms of the formula established pursuant to Section 4(E). Hours worked in excess of the formula in Section 4(E) shall be recorded on the employee's pay record as additional hours worked.

8. Cash Shortage and Breakage. No employer shall make any deduction from the wage or require any reimbursement from an employee for any cash shortage, breakage, or loss of equipment, unless it can be shown that the shortage, breakage, or loss is caused by a dishonest or willful act, or by the gross negligence of the employee.

9. Uniforms and Equipment

(A) When uniforms are required by the employer to be worn by the employee as a condition of employment, such uniforms shall be provided and maintained by the employer. The term "uniform" includes wearing apparel and accessories of distinctive design or color.

Note: This section shall not apply to protective apparel regulated by the Occupational Safety and Health Standards Board.

(B) When tools or equipment are required by the employer or are necessary to the performance of a job, such tools and equipment shall be provided and maintained by the employer, except that an employee whose wages are at least two (2) times the minimum wage provided herein may be required to provide and maintain hand tools and equipment customarily required by the trade or craft. This subsection (B) shall not apply to apprentices regularly indentured under the State Division of Apprenticeship Standards.

Note: This section shall not apply to protective equipment and safety devices on tools regulated by the Occupational Safety and Health Standards Board.

(C) A reasonable deposit may be required as security for the return of the items furnished by the employer under provisions of subsections (A) and (B) of this section upon issuance of a receipt to the employee for such deposit. Such deposits shall be made pursuant to Section 400 and following of the Labor Code or an employer with the prior written authorization of the employee may deduct from the employee's last check the cost of an item furnished pursuant to (A) and (B) above in the event said item is not returned. No deduction shall be made at any time for normal wear and tear. All items furnished by the employer shall be returned by the employee upon completion of the job.

10. Meals and Lodging

(A) "Meal" means an adequate, well-balanced serving of a variety of wholesome, nutritious foods.

(B) "Lodging" means living accommodations available to the employee for full-time occupancy which are adequate, decent, and sanitary according to usual and customary standards. Employees shall not be required to share a bed.

(C) Meals or lodging may not be credited against the minimum wage without a voluntary written agreement between the employer and the employee. When credit for meals or lodging is used to meet part of the employer's minimum wage obligation, the amounts so credited may not be more than the following:

Effective	January 1, 2007	January 1, 2008
Lodging:		
Room occupied alone	$35.27 per week	$37.63 per week
Room shared	$29.11 per week	$31.06 per week
Apartment—two–thirds (2/03) of the ordinary rental value, and in no event more than	$423.51 per month	$451.89 per month
Where a couple are both employed by the employer, two-thirds (2/03) of the ordinary rental value, and in no event more than	$626.49 per month	$668.46 per month
Meals:		
Breakfast	$2.72	$2.90
Lunch	$3.72	$3.97
Dinner	$5.00	$5.34

(D) Meals evaluated as part of the minimum wage must be bona fide meals consistent with the employee's work shift. Deductions shall not be made for meals not received or lodging not used.

(E) If, as a condition of employment, the employee must live at the place of employment or occupy quarters owned or under the control of the employer, then the employer may not charge rent in excess of the values listed herein.

11. Meal Periods

(A) No employer shall employ any person for a work period of more than five (5) hours without a meal period of not less than 30 minutes, except that when a work period of not more than six (6) hours will complete the day's work the meal period may be waived by mutual consent of the employer and the employee.

(B) An employer may not employ an employee for a work period of more than ten (10) hours per day without providing the employee with a second meal period of not less than 30 minutes, except that if the total hours worked is no more than 12 hours, the second meal period may be waived by mutual consent of the employer and the employee only if the first meal period was not waived.

(C) Unless the employee is relieved of all duty during a 30 minute meal period, the meal period shall be considered an "on duty" meal period and counted as time worked. An "on duty" meal period shall be permitted only when the nature of the work prevents an employee from being relieved of all duty and when by written agreement between the parties an on-the-job paid meal period is agreed to. The written agreement shall state that the employee may, in writing, revoke the agreement at any time.

(D) If an employer fails to provide an employee a meal period in accordance with the applicable provisions of this order, the employer shall pay the employee one (1) hour of pay at the employee's regular rate of compensation for each workday that the meal period is not provided.

(E) In all places of employment where employees are required to eat on the premises, a suitable place for that purpose shall be designated.

12. Rest Periods

(A) Every employer shall authorize and permit all employees to take rest periods, which insofar as practicable shall be in the middle of each work period. The authorized rest period time shall be based on the total hours worked daily at the rate of ten (10) minutes net rest time per four (4) hours or major fraction thereof. However, a rest period need not be authorized for employees whose total daily work time is less than three and one-half (3 $\frac{1}{2}$) hours. Authorized rest period time shall be counted as hours worked for which there shall be no deduction from wages.

(B) If an employer fails to provide an employee a rest period in accordance with the applicable provisions of this order, the employer shall pay the employee one (1) hour of pay at the employee's regular rate of compensation for each workday that the rest period is not provided.

(C) A crew member employed on a commercial passenger fishing boat who is on an overnight trip within the meaning of Section 4(E) shall receive no less than eight (8) hours off-duty time during each 24–hour period.

13. Change Rooms and Resting Facilities

(A) Employers shall provide suitable lockers, closets, or equivalent for the safekeeping of employees' outer clothing during working hours, and when required, for their work clothing during non-working hours. When the occupation requires a change of clothing, change rooms or equivalent space shall be provided in order that employees may change their clothing in reasonable privacy and comfort. These rooms or spaces may be adjacent to but shall be separate from toilet rooms and shall be kept clean.

Note: This section shall not apply to change rooms and storage facilities regulated by the Occupational Safety and Health Standards Board.

(B) Suitable resting facilities shall be provided in an area separate from the toilet rooms and shall be available to employees during work hours.

14. Seats

(A) All working employees shall be provided with suitable seats when the nature of the work reasonably permits the use of seats.

(B) When employees are not engaged in the active duties of their employment and the nature of the work requires standing, an adequate number of suitable seats shall be placed in reasonable proximity to the work area and employees shall be permitted to use such seats when it does not interfere with the performance of their duties.

15. Temperature

(A) The temperature maintained in each work area shall provide reasonable comfort consistent with industry-wide standards for the nature of the process and the work performed.

(B) If excessive heat or humidity is created by the work process, the employer shall take all feasible means to reduce such excessive heat or humidity to a degree providing reasonable comfort. Where the nature of the employment requires a temperature of less than 60° F., a heated room shall be provided to which employees may retire for warmth, and such room shall be maintained at not less than 68°.

(C) A temperature of not less than 68° shall be maintained in the toilet rooms, resting rooms, and change rooms during hours of use.

(D) Federal and State energy guidelines shall prevail over any conflicting provision of this section.

16. Elevators.
Adequate elevator, escalator or similar service consistent with industry-wide standards for the nature of the process and the work performed shall be provided when employees are employed four floors or more above or below ground level.

17. Exemptions.
If, in the opinion of the Division after due investigation, it is found that the enforcement of any provision contained in Section 7, Records; Section 12, Rest Periods; Section 13, Change Rooms and Resting Facilities; Section 14, Seats; Section 15, Temperature; or Section 16, Elevators, would not materially affect the welfare or comfort of employees and would work an undue hardship on the employer, exemption may be made at the discretion of the Division. Such exemptions shall be in writing to be effective and may be revoked after reasonable notice is given in writing. Application for exemption shall be made by the employer or by the employee and/or the employee's representative to the Division in writing. A copy of the application shall be posted at the place of employment at the time the application is filed with the Division.

18. Filing Reports.
(See California Labor Code, Section 1174(a))

19. Inspection.
(See California Labor Code, Section 1174)

20. Penalties.
(See California Labor Code, Section 1199)

(A) In addition to any other civil penalties provided by law, any employer or any other person acting on behalf of the employer who violates, or causes to be violated, the provisions of this order, shall be subject to the civil penalty of:

(1) Initial Violation—$50.00 for each underpaid employee for each pay period during which the employee was underpaid in addition to the amount which is sufficient to recover unpaid wages.

(2) Subsequent Violations—$100.00 for each underpaid employee for each pay period during which the employee was underpaid in addition to an amount which is sufficient to recover unpaid wages.

(3) The affected employee shall receive payment of all wages recovered.

(B) The labor commissioner may also issue citations pursuant to California Labor Code Section 1197.1 for non-payment of wages for overtime work in violation of this order.

21. Separability.
If the application of any provision of this order, or any section, subsection, subdivision, sentence, clause, phrase, word, or portion of this order should be held invalid or unconstitutional or unauthorized or prohibited by statute, the remaining provisions thereof shall not be affected thereby, but shall continue to be given full force and effect as if the part so held invalid or unconstitutional had not been included herein.

22. Posting of Order.
Every employer shall keep a copy of this order posted in an area frequented by employees where it may be easily read during the workday. Where the location of work or other conditions make this impractical, every employer shall keep a copy of this order and make it available to every employee upon request.

[1] Pursuant to Labor Code section 515.5, subdivision (a)(4), the Division of Labor Statistics and Research, Department of Industrial Relations, has adjusted the minimum hourly rate of pay specified in this subdivision to be $49.77, effective January 1, 2007. This hourly rate of pay is adjusted on October 1 of each year to be effective on January 1, of the following year, and may be obtained at www.dir.ca.gov/IWC or by mail from the Department of Industrial Relations.

Publisher's Notes

See Industrial Welfare Com. v. Superior Court (1980) 27 Cal.3d 690, 613 P.2d 579, 166 Cal.Rptr. 331 (validity of 1980 order).

Research References

See notes following listing of Wage Orders.

INDUSTRIAL WELFARE COMMISSION
ORDER NO. 11–2001
REGULATING
WAGES, HOURS AND WORKING CONDITIONS IN THE
BROADCASTING INDUSTRY

TAKE NOTICE: To employers and representatives of persons working in industries and occupations in the State of California:

The Department of Industrial Relations amends and republishes the minimum wage and meals and lodging credits in the Industrial Welfare Commission's Orders as a result of legislation enacted (AB 1835, Ch. 230, Stats of 2006, adding sections 1182.12 and 1182.13 to the California Labor Code.) The amendments and republishing make no other changes to the IWC's Orders.

1. Applicability of Order. This order shall apply to all persons employed in the broadcasting industry whether paid on a time, piece rate, commission, or other basis, except that:

(A) Provisions of sections 3 through 12 of this shall not apply to persons employed in administrative, executive, or professional capacities. The following requirements shall apply in determining whether an employee's duties meet the test to qualify for an exemption from those sections:

(1) Executive Exemption. A person employed in an executive capacity means any employee:

(a) Whose duties and responsibilities involve the management of the enterprise in which he or she is employed or of a customarily recognized department or subdivision thereof, and

(b) Who customarily and regularly directs the work of two or more other employees therein; and

(c) Who has the authority to hire or fire other employees or whose suggestions and recommendations as to the hiring or firing and as to the advancement and promotion or any other change of status of other employees will be given particular weight; and

(d) Who customarily and regularly exercises discretion and independent judgment; and

(e) Who is primarily engaged in duties which meet the test of the exemption. The activities constituting exempt work and non-exempt work shall be construed in the same manner as such items are construed in the following regulations under the Fair Labor Standards Act effective as of the date of this order: 29 C.F.R. §§ 541.102, 541.104–111, 541.115–116. Exempt work shall include, for example, all work that is directly and closely related to exempt work and work which is properly viewed as a means for carrying out exempt functions. The work actually performed by the employee during the course of the work week must, first and foremost, be examined and the amount of time the employee spends on such work, together with the employer's realistic expectations and the realistic requirements of the job, shall be considered in determining whether the employee satisfies this requirement.

(f) Such an employee must also earn a monthly salary equivalent to no less than two (2) times the state minimum wage for full-time employment. Full–time employment is defined in Labor Code § 515(c) as 40 hours per week.

(2) Administrative Exemption. A person employed in an administrative capacity means any employee:

(a) Whose duties and responsibilities involve either:

(i) The performance of office or non-manual work directly related to management policies or general business operations of his employer or his employer's customers, or

(ii) The performance of functions in the administration of a school system, or educational establishment or institution, or of a department of subdivision thereof; in work directly related to the academic instruction or training carried on therein; and

(b) Who customarily and regularly exercises discretion and independent judgment; and

(c) Who regularly and directly assists a proprietor, or an employee employed in a bona fide executive or administrative capacity (as such terms are defined for purposes of this section), or

(d) Who performs under only general supervision work along specialized or technical lines requiring special training, experience, or knowledge, or

(e) Who executes under only general supervision special assignments and tasks, and

(f) Who is primarily engaged in duties which meet the test of the exemption. The activities constituting exempt work and non-exempt work shall be construed in the same manner as such terms are construed in the following regulations under the Fair Labor Standards Act effective as of the date of this order: 29 C.F.R. §§ 541.201–205, 541.207–208, 541.210, 541.215. Exempt work shall include, for example, all work that is directly and closely related to exempt work and work which is properly viewed as a means for carrying out exempt functions. The work actually performed by the employee during the course of the work week must, first and foremost, be examined and the amount of time the employee spends on such work, together with the employer's realistic expectations and the realistic requirements of the job, shall be considered in determining whether the employee satisfies this requirement.

(g) Such employee must also earn a monthly salary equivalent to no less than two (2) times the state minimum wage for full-time employment. Full–time employment is defined in Labor Code § 515(c) as 40 hours per week.

(3) <u>Professional Exemption.</u> A person employed in a professional capacity means any employee who meets all of the following requirements:

(a) Who is licensed or certified by the State of California and is primarily engaged in the practice of one of the following recognized professions: law, medicine, dentistry, optometry, architecture, engineering, teaching, or accounting; or

(b) Who is primarily engaged in an occupation commonly recognized as a learned or artistic profession. For the purposes of this subsection, "learned or artistic profession" means an employee who is primarily engaged in the performance of:

(i) Work requiring knowledge of an advanced type in a field or science or learning customarily acquired by a prolonged course of specialized intellectual instruction and study, as distinguished from a general academic education and from an apprenticeship, and from training in the performance of routine mental, manual, or physical processes or work that is an essential part of or necessarily incident to any of the above work; or

(ii) Work that is original and creative in character in a recognized field of artistic endeavor (as opposed to work which can be produced by a person endowed with general manual or intellectual ability and training), and the result of which depends primarily on the invention, imagination, or talent of the employee or work that is an essential part of or necessarily incident to any of the above work; and

(iii) Whose work is predominantly intellectual and varied in character (as opposed to routine mental, manual, mechanical, or physical work) and is of such character that the output produced or the result accomplished cannot be standardized in relation to a given period of time.

(c) Who customarily and regularly exercises discretion and independent judgment in the performance of duties set forth in subparagraph (a) and (b).

(d) Who earns a monthly salary equivalent to no less than two (2) times the state minimum wage for full-time employment. Full–time employment is defined in Labor Code § 515 (c) as 40 hours per week.

(e) Subparagraph (b) above is intended to be construed in accordance with the following provisions of federal law as they existed as of the date of this Order: 29 C.F.R. §§ 541.207, 541.301(a)–(d), 541.302, 541.306, 541.307, 541.308, and 541.310.

(f) Notwithstanding the provisions of this subparagraph, pharmacists employed to engage in the practice of pharmacy, and registered nurses employed to engage in the practice of nursing, shall not be considered exempt professional employees, nor shall they be considered exempt from coverage for the purposes of this subparagraph unless they individually meet the criteria established for exemption as executive or administrative employees.

(g) Subparagraph (f) above, shall not apply to the following advanced practice nurses:

(i) Certified nurse midwives who are primarily engaged in performing duties for which certification is required pursuant to Article 2.5 (commencing with Section 2746) of Chapter 6 of Division 2 of the Business and Professions Code.

(ii) Certified nurse anesthetists who are primarily engaged in performing duties for which certification is required pursuant to Article 7 (commencing with Section 2825) of Chapter 6 of Division 2 of the Business and Professions Code.

(iii) Certified nurse practitioners who are primarily engaged in performing duties for which certification is required pursuant to Article 8 (commencing with Section 2834) of Chapter 6 of Division 2 of the Business and Professions Code.

(iv) Nothing in this subparagraph shall exempt the occupations set forth in clauses (i), (ii) and (iii) from meeting the requirements of subsection 1(A)(3)(a)—(d), above.

(h) Except as provided in subparagraph (i), an employee in the computer software field who is paid on an hourly basis shall be exempt, if all of the following apply:

(i) The employee is primarily engaged in work that is intellectual or creative and that requires the exercise of discretion and independent judgment.

(ii) The employee is primarily engaged in duties that consist of one or more of the following:

-The application of systems analysis techniques and procedures, including consulting with users, to determine hardware, software, or system functional specifications.

-The design, development, documentation, analysis, creation, testing, or modification of computer systems or programs, including prototypes, based on and related to, user or system design specifications.

-The documentation, testing, creation, or modification of computer programs related to the design of software or hardware for computer operating systems.

(iii) The employee is highly skilled and is proficient in the theoretical and practical application of highly specialized information to computer systems analysis, programming, and software engineering. A job title shall not be determinative of the applicability of this exemption.

(iv) The employee's hourly rate of pay is not less than forty-one dollars ($41.00). The Division of Labor Statistics and Research shall adjust this pay rate on October 1 of each year to be effective on January 1 of the following year by an amount equal to the percentage increase in the California Consumer Price Index for Urban Wage Earners and Clerical Workers.[1]

(i) The exemption provided in subparagraph (h) does not apply to an employee if any of the following apply:

1484

(i) The employee is a trainee or employee in an entry-level position who is learning to become proficient in the theoretical and practical application of highly specialized information to computer systems analysis, programming, and software engineering.

(ii) The employee is in a computer-related occupation but has not attained the level of skill and expertise necessary to work independently and without close supervision.

(iii) The employee is engaged in the operation of computers or in the manufacture, repair, or maintenance of computer hardware and related equipment.

(iv) The employee is an engineer, drafter, machinist, or other professional whose work is highly dependent upon or facilitated by the use of computers and computer software programs and who is skilled in computer-aided design software, including CAD/CAM, but who is not in a computer systems analysis or programming occupation.

(v) The employee is a writer engaged in writing material, including box labels, product descriptions, documentation, promotional material, setup and installation instructions, and other similar written information, either for print or for on screen media or who writes or provides content material intended to be read by customers, subscribers, or visitors to computer-related media such as the World Wide Web or CD–ROMs.

(vi) The employee is engaged in any of the activities set forth in subparagraph (h) for the purpose of creating imagery for effects used in the motion picture, television, or theatrical industry.

(B) Except as provided in sections 1, 2, 4, 10, and 20, the provisions of this order shall not apply to any employees directly employed by the State or any political subdivision thereof, including any city, county, or special district.

(C) Except as provided in sections 1, 2, 4, 10, and 20, the provisions of this order shall not apply to professional actors.

(D) The provisions of this order shall not apply to outside salespersons.

(E) Provisions of this order shall not apply to any individual who is the parent, spouse, child, or legally adopted child of the employer.

(F) The provisions of this order shall not apply to any individual participating in a national service program, such as Ameri–Corps, carried out using assistance provided under Section 12571 of Title 42 of the United States Code. (See Stats. 2000, ch. 365, amending Labor Code § 1171.)

2. Definitions

(A) An "alternative workweek schedule" means any regularly scheduled workweek requiring an employee to work more than eight (8) hours in a 24–hour period.

(B) "Broadcasting Industry" means any industry, business, or establishment operated for the purpose of broadcasting or taping and broadcasting programs through the medium of radio or television.

(C) "Commission" means the Industrial Welfare Commission of the State of California.

(D) "Division" means the Division of Labor Standards Enforcement of the State of California.

(E) "Employ" means to engage, suffer, or permit to work.

(F) "Employee" means any person employed by an employer.

(G) "Employer" means any person as defined in Section 18 of the Labor Code, who directly or indirectly, or through an agent or any other person, employs or exercises control over the wages, hours, or working conditions of any person.

(H) "Hours worked" means the time during which an employee is subject to the control of an employer, and includes all the time the employee is suffered or permitted to work, whether or not required to do so.

(I) "Location" means any place other than the studio premises of the employer, at which the employer broadcasts or tapes for broadcast all or a portion of a radio or television program.

(J) "Minor" means, for the purpose of this Order, any person under the age of 18 years.

(K) "Outside Salesperson" means any person, 18 years if age or over, who customarily and regularly works more than half the working time away from the employer's place of business selling tangible or intangible items or obtaining orders or contracts for products, services or use of facilities.

(L) "Primarily" as used in section 1, Applicability, means more than one-half the employee's work time.

(M) "Shift" means designated hours of work by an employee, with a designated beginning time and ending time.

(N) "Split shift" means a work schedule which is interrupted by non-paid non-working periods established by the employer, other than bona fide rest or meal periods.

(O) "Teaching" means, for the purpose of section 1 of this Order, the profession of teaching under a certificate from the Commission for Teacher Preparation and Licensing or teaching in an accredited college or university.

(P) "Wages" includes all amounts for labor performed by employees of every description, whether the amount is fixed or ascertained by the standard of time, task, piece, commission basis, or other method of calculation.

(Q) "Workday" and "day" mean any consecutive 24–hour period beginning at the same time each calendar day.

(R) "Workweek" and "week" mean any seven (7) consecutive days, starting with the same calendar day each week. "Workweek" is a fixed and regularly recurring period of 168 hours, seven (7) consecutive 24–hour periods.

3. Hours and Days of Work.

(A) *Daily Overtime—General Provisions*

(1) The following overtime provisions are applicable to employees 18 years of age or over and to employees 16 or 17 years of age who are not required by law to attend school and are not otherwise prohibited by law from engaging in the subject work. Such employees shall not be employed more than eight (8) hours in any workday or more than 40 hours in any workweek unless the employee receives one and one-half (1 ½) times such employee's regular rate of pay for all hours worked over 40 hours in the workweek. Eight (8) hours of labor constitutes a day's work. Employment beyond eight (8) hours in any workday or more than six (6) days in any workweek is permissible provided the employee is compensated for such overtime not less than:

(a) One and one-half (1 ½) times the employee's regular rate of pay for all hours worked in excess of eight (8) hours up to and including 12 hours in any workday, and for the first eight (8) hours worked on the seventh (7th) consecutive day of work in a workweek; and

(b) Double the employee's regular rate of pay for all hours worked in excess of 12 hours in any workday and for all hours worked in excess of eight (8) hours on the seventh (7th) consecutive day of work in a workweek.

(c) The overtime rate of compensation required to be paid to a nonexempt full-time salaried employee shall be computed by using the employee's regular hourly salary as one fortieth (1/40) of the employee's weekly salary.

(B) *Alternative Workweek Schedules*

(1) No employer shall be deemed to have violated the daily overtime provisions by instituting, pursuant to the election procedures set forth in this wage order, a regularly scheduled alternative workweek schedule of not more than ten (10) hours per day within a 40 hour workweek without the payment of an overtime rate of compensation. All work performed in any workday beyond the schedule established by the agreement up to 12 hours a day or beyond 40 hours per week shall be paid at one and one-half (1 ½) times the employee's regular rate of pay. All work performed in excess of 12 hours per day and any work in excess of eight (8) hours on those days worked beyond the regularly scheduled number of workdays established by the alternative workweek agreement shall be paid at double the employee's regular rate of pay. Any alternative workweek agreement adopted pursuant to this section shall provide for not less than four (4) hours of work in any shift. Nothing in this section shall prohibit an employer, at the request of the employee, to substitute one day of work for another day of the same length in the shift provided by the alternative workweek agreement on an occasional basis to meet the personal needs of the employee without the payment of overtime. No hours paid at either one and one-half (1 ½) or double the regular rate of pay shall be included in

determining when 40 hours have been worked for the purpose of computing overtime compensation.

(2) Any agreement adopted pursuant to this section shall provide not less than two consecutive days off within a workweek.

(3) If an employer, whose employees have adopted an alternative workweek agreement permitted by this order requires an employee to work fewer hours than those that are regularly scheduled by the agreement, the employer shall pay the employee overtime compensation at a rate of one and one-half (1 ½) times the employee's regular rate of pay for all hours worked in excess of eight (8) hours, and double the employee's regular rate of pay for all hours worked in excess of 12 hours for the day the employee is required to work the reduced hours.

(4) An employer shall not reduce an employee's regular rate of hourly pay as a result of the adoption, repeal or nullification of an alternative workweek schedule.

(5) An employer shall explore any available reasonable alternative means of accommodating the religious belief or observance of an affected employee that conflicts with an adopted alternative workweek schedule, in the manner provided by subdivision (j) of Section 12940 of the Government Code.

(6) An employer shall make a reasonable effort to find a work schedule not to exceed eight (8) hours in a workday, in order to accommodate any affected employee who was eligible to vote in an election authorized by this Section and who is unable to work the alternative workweek schedule established as the result of that election.

(7) An employer shall be permitted, but not required, to provide a work schedule not to exceed eight (8) hours in a workday to accommodate any employee who is hired after the date of the election and who is unable to work the alternative workweek schedule established by the election.

(8) Arrangements adopted in a secret ballot election held pursuant to this order prior to 1998, or under the rules in effect prior to 1998, and before the performance of the work, shall remain valid after July 1, 2000 provided that the results of the election are reported by the employer to the Division of Labor Statistics and Research by January 1, 2001, in accordance with the requirements of Section C below (Election Procedures). If an employee was voluntarily working an alternative workweek schedule of not more than ten (10) hours a day as of July 1, 1999, that alternative workweek schedule was based on an individual agreement made after January 1, 1998 between the employee and employer, and the employee submitted, and the employer approved, a written request on or before May 30, 2000 to continue the agreement, the employee may continue to work that alternative workweek schedule without payment of an overtime rate of compensation for the hours provided in the agreement. An employee may revoke his or her voluntary authorization to continue such a schedule with 30 days written

notice to the employer. New arrangements can only be entered into pursuant to the provisions of this section.

(C) *Election Procedures*

Election procedures for the adoption and repeal of alternative workweek schedules require the following:

(1) Each proposal for an alternative workweek schedule shall be in the form of a written agreement proposed by the employer. The proposed agreement must designate a regularly scheduled alternative workweek in which the specified number of work days and work hours are regularly recurring. The actual days worked within that alternative workweek schedule need not be specified. The employer may propose a single work schedule that would become the standard schedule for workers in the work unit, or a menu of work schedule options, from which each employee in the unit would be entitled to choose. If the employer proposes a menu of work schedule options, the employee may, with the approval of the employer, move from one menu option to another.

(2) In order to be valid, the proposed alternative workweek schedule must be adopted in a secret ballot election, before the performance of work, by at least a two-thirds (2/03) vote of the affected employees in the work unit. The election shall be held during regular working hours at the employees' work site. For purposes of this subsection, "affected employees in the work unit" may include all employees in a readily identifiable work unit, such as a division, a department, a job classification, a shift, a separate physical location, or a recognized subdivision of any such work unit. A work unit may consist of an individual employee as long as the criteria for an identifiable work unit in this subsection is met.

(3) Prior to the secret ballot vote, any employer who proposed to institute an alternative workweek schedule shall have made a disclosure in writing to the affected employees, including the effects of the proposed arrangement on the employees' wages, hours, and benefits. Such a disclosure shall include meeting(s), duly noticed, held at least 14 days prior to voting, for the specific purpose of discussing the effects of the alternative workweek schedule. An employer shall provide that disclosure in a non–English language, as well as in English, if at least five (5) percent of the affected employees primarily speak that non–English language. The employer shall mail the written disclosure to employees who do not attend the meeting. Failure to comply with this paragraph shall make the election null and void.

(4) Any election to establish or repeal an alternative workweek schedule shall be held at the work site of the affected employees. The employer shall bear the costs of conducting any election held pursuant to this section. Upon a complaint by an affected employee, and after an investigation by the Labor Commissioner, the Labor Commissioner may require the employer to select a neutral third party to conduct the election.

(5) Any type of alternative workweek schedule that is authorized by the Labor Code may be repealed by the affected employees. Upon a petition of one-third (1/03) of the affected employees, a new secret ballot election shall be held and a two-thirds (2/03) vote of the affected employees shall be required to reverse the alternative workweek schedule. The election to repeal the alternative workweek schedule shall be held not more than 30 days after the petition is submitted to the employer, except that the election shall be held not less than 12 months after the date that the same group of employees voted in an election held to adopt or repeal an alternative workweek schedule. The election shall take place during regular working hours at the employees' work site. If the alternative workweek schedule is revoked, the employer shall comply within 60 days. Upon proper showing of undue hardship, the Division of Labor Standards Enforcement may grant an extension of time for compliance.

(6) Only secret ballots may be cast by affected employees in the work unit at any election held pursuant to this Section. The results of any election conducted pursuant to this Section shall be reported by the employer to the Division of Labor Statistics and Research within 30 days after the results are final, and the report of election results shall be a public document. The report shall include the final tally of the vote, the size of the unit, and the nature of the business of the employer.

(7) Employees affected by a change in the work hours resulting from the adoption of an alternative workweek schedule may not be required to work those new work hours for at least 30 days after the announcement of the final results of the election.

(8) Employers shall not intimidate or coerce employees to vote either in support of or in opposition to a proposed alternative workweek. No employees shall be discharged or discriminated against for expressing opinions concerning the alternative workweek election or for opposing or supporting its adoption or repeal. However, nothing in this section shall prohibit an employer from expressing his/her position concerning that alternative workweek to the affected employees. A violation of this paragraph shall be subject to Labor Code section 98 *et seq*.

(D) One and one-half (1 $\frac{1}{2}$) times a minor's regular rate of pay shall be paid for all work over 40 hours in any workweek except that minors 16 and 17 years old who are not required by law to attend school and may therefore be employed for the same hours as an adult are subject to subsection (A) or (B), and (C) above.

(**Violations of Child Labor Laws** are subject to civil penalties of from $500 to $10,000 as well as to criminal penalties. Refer to California Labor Code sections 1285 to 1312 and 1390 to 1399 for additional restrictions on the employment of minors and for descriptions of criminal and civil penalties for violation of the child labor laws. Employers should ask school districts about any required work permits.)

(E) An employee may be employed for seven (7) days in one workweek when the total hours of employment during such workweek do not exceed 30 and the total hours of employment in any one workday thereof do not exceed six (6).

(F) If a meal period occurs on a shift beginning or ending at or between the hours of 10 p.m. and 6 a.m., facilities shall be available for securing hot food and drink or for heating food or drink, and a suitable sheltered place shall be provided in which to consume such food or drink.

(G) The provisions of Labor Code §§ 551 and 552 regarding one (1) day's rest in seven (7) shall not be construed to prevent an accumulation of days of rest when the nature of the employment reasonably requires the employee to work seven (7) or more consecutive days; provided, however, that in each calendar month, the employee shall receive the equivalent of one (1) day's rest in seven (7).

(H) Except as provided in subsections (D) and (G), this section shall not apply to any employee covered by a valid collective bargaining agreement if the agreement expressly provides for the wages, hours of work, and working conditions of the employees, and if the agreement provides premium wage rates for all overtime hours worked and a regular hourly rate of pay for those employees of not less than 30 percent more than the state minimum wage.

(I) Notwithstanding subsection (H) above, where the employer and a labor organization representing employees of the employer have entered into a valid collective bargaining agreement pertaining to the hours of work of the employees, the requirement regarding the equivalent of one (1) day's rest in seven (7) (see subsection (G) above) shall apply, unless the agreement expressly provides otherwise.

(J) If an employer approves a written request of an employee to make-up work time that is or would be lost as a result of a personal obligation of the employee, the hours of that make-up work time, if performed in the same workweek in which the work time was lost, may not be counted toward computing the total number of hours worked in a day for purposes of the overtime requirements, except for hours in excess of 11 hours of work in one (1) day or 40 hours of work in one (1) workweek. If an employee knows in advance that he or she will be requesting make-up time for a personal obligation that will recur at a fixed time over a succession of weeks, the employee may request to make-up work time for up to four (4) weeks in advance; provided, however, that the make-up work must be performed in the same week that the work time was lost. An employee shall provide a signed written request for each occasion that the employee makes a request to make-up work time pursuant to this subsection. While an employer may inform an employee of this make-up time option, the employer is prohibited from encouraging or otherwise soliciting an employee to request the employer's approval to take personal time off and make-up the work hours within the same workweek pursuant to this subsection.

(K) The provisions of this section shall not apply to any person employed as an announcer, news editor, or chief engineer, by a radio or television station in a city or town which has a population of 25,000 or less.

4. Minimum Wages

(A) Every employer shall pay to each employee wages not less than seven dollars and fifty cents ($7.50) per hour for all hours worked, effective January 1, 2007, and not less than eight dollars ($8.00) per hour for all hours worked, effective January 1, 2008, except:

Learners. Employees during their first 160 hours of employment in occupations in which they have no previous similar or related experience, may be paid not less than 85 percent of the minimum wage rounded to the nearest nickel.

(B) Every employer shall pay to each employee, on the established payday for the period involved, not less than the applicable minimum wage for all hours worked in the payroll period, whether the remuneration is measured by time, piece, commission, or otherwise.

(C) When an employee works a split shift, one (1) hour's pay at the minimum wage shall be paid in addition to the minimum wage for that workday, except when the employee resides at the place of employment.

(D) The provisions of this Section shall not apply to apprentices regularly indentured under the State Division of Apprenticeship Standards.

5. Reporting Time Pay

(A) Each workday an employee is required to report for work and does report, but is not put to work or is furnished less than half said employee's usual or scheduled day's work, the employee shall be paid for half the usual or scheduled day's work, but in no event for less than two (2) hours nor more than four (4) hours, at the employee's regular rate of pay, which shall not be less than the minimum wage.

(B) If an employee is required to report for work a second time in any one workday and is furnished less than two (2) hours of work on the second reporting, said employee shall be paid for two (2) hours at the employee's regular rate of pay, which shall not be less than the minimum wage.

(C) The foregoing reporting time pay provisions are not applicable when:

(1) Operations cannot commence or continue due to threats to employees or property; or when recommended by civil authorities; or

(2) Public utilities fail to supply electricity, water, or gas, or there is a failure in the public utilities, or sewer system; or

(3) The interruption of work is caused by an Act of God or other cause not within the employer's control.

(D) This section shall not apply to an employee on paid standby status who is called to perform assigned work at a time other than the employee's scheduled reporting time.

6. Licenses for Disabled Workers

(A) A license may be issued by the Division authorizing employment of a person whose earning capacity is impaired by physical disability or mental deficiency at less than the minimum wage. Such licenses shall be granted only upon joint application of employer and employee and employee's representative if any.

(B) A special license may be issued to a nonprofit organization such as a sheltered workshop or rehabilitation facility fixing special minimum rates to enable the employment of such persons without requiring individual licenses of such employees.

(C) All such licenses and special licenses shall be renewed on a yearly basis or more frequently at the discretion of the Division. (See California Labor Code, Sections 1191 and 1191.5.)

7. Records

(A) Every employer shall keep accurate information with respect to each employee including the following:

(1) Full name, home address, occupation and social security number.

(2) Birth date, if under 18 years, and designation as a minor.

(3) Time records showing when the employee begins and ends each work period. Meal periods, split shift intervals and total daily hours worked shall also be recorded. Meal periods during which operations cease and authorized rest periods need not be recorded.

(4) Total wages paid each payroll period, including value of board, lodging, or other compensation actually furnished to the employee.

(5) Total hours worked in the payroll period and applicable rates of pay. This information shall be made readily available to the employee upon reasonable request.

(6) When a piece rate or incentive plan is in operation, piece rates or an explanation of the incentive plan formula shall be provided to employees. An accurate production record shall be maintained by the employer.

(B) Every employer shall semimonthly or at the time of each payment of wages furnish each employee, either as a detachable part of the check, draft, or voucher paying the employee's wages, or separately, an itemized statement in writing showing: (1) all deductions; (2) the inclusive dates of the period for which the employee is paid; (3) the name of the employee or the employee's social security number; and (4) the name of the employer, provided all deductions made on written orders of the employee may be aggregated and shown as one item.

(C) All required records shall be in the English language and in ink or other indelible form, properly dated, showing month, day and year, and shall be kept on file by the employer for at least three years at the place of employment or at a central location within the State of California. An employee's records shall be available for inspection by the employee upon reasonable request.

(D) Clocks shall be provided in all major work areas or within reasonable distance thereto insofar as practicable.

8. Cash Shortage and Breakage. No employer shall make any deduction from the wage or require any reimbursement from an employee for any cash shortage, breakage, or loss of equipment, unless it can be shown that the shortage, breakage, or loss is caused by a dishonest or willful act, or by the gross negligence of the employee.

9. Uniforms and Equipment

(A) When uniforms are required by the employer to be worn by the employee as a condition of employment, such uniforms shall be provided and maintained by the employer. The term "uniform" includes wearing apparel and accessories of distinctive design or color.

Note: This section shall not apply to protective apparel regulated by the Occupational Safety and Health Standards Board.

(B) When tools or equipment are required by the employer or are necessary to the performance of a job, such tools and equipment shall be provided and maintained by the employer, except that an employee whose wages are at least two (2) times the minimum wage provided herein may be required to provide and maintain hand tools and equipment customarily required by the trade or craft. This subsection (B) shall not apply to apprentices regularly indentured under the State Division of Apprenticeship Standards.

Note: This section shall not apply to protective equipment and safety devices on tools regulated by the Occupational Safety and Health Standards Board.

(C) A reasonable deposit may be required as security for the return of the items furnished by the employer under provisions of subsections (A) and (B) of this section upon issuance of a receipt to the employee for such deposit. Such deposits shall be made pursuant to Section 400 and following of the Labor Code or an employer with the prior written authorization of the employee may deduct from the employee's last check the cost of an item furnished pursuant to (A) and (B) above in the event said item is not returned. No deduction shall be made at any time for normal wear and tear. All items furnished by the employer shall be returned by the employee upon completion of the job.

10. Meals and Lodging

(A) "Meal" means an adequate, well-balanced serving of a variety of wholesome, nutritious foods.

(B) "Lodging" means living accommodations available to the employee for full-time occupancy which are adequate, decent, and sanitary according to usual and customary standards. Employees shall not be required to share a bed.

(C) Meals or lodging may not be credited against the minimum wage without a voluntary written agreement between the employer and the employee. When credit for meals or lodging is used to meet part of the employer's minimum wage obligation, the amounts so credited may not be more than the following:

Effective	January 1, 2007	January 1, 2008
Lodging:		
Room occupied alone	$35.27 per week	$37.63 per week
Room shared	$29.11 per week	$31.06 per week
Apartment–two-thirds (2/03) of the ordinary rental value, and in no event more than	$423.51 per month	$451.89 per month
Where a couple are both employed by the employer, two-thirds (2/03) of the ordinary rental value, and in no event more than	$626.49 per month	$668.46 per month
Meals:		
Breakfast	$2.72	$2.90
Lunch	$3.72	$3.97
Dinner	$5.00	$5.34

(D) Meals evaluated as part of the minimum wage must be bona fide meals consistent with the employee's work shift. Deductions shall not be made for meals not received nor lodging not used.

(E) If, as a condition of employment, the employee must live at the place of employment or occupy quarters owned or under the control of the employer, then the employer may not charge rent in excess of the values listed herein.

11. Meal Periods

(A) No employer shall employ any person for a work period of more than five (5) hours without a meal period of not less than 30 minutes except that when a work period of not more than six (6) hours will complete the day's work the meal period may be waived by mutual consent of the employer and employee.

(B) An employer may not employ an employee for a work period of more than ten (10) hours per day without providing the employee with a second meal period of not less than 30 minutes, except that if the total hours worked is no more than 12 hours, the second meal period may be waived by mutual consent of the employer and the employee only if the first meal period was not waived.

(C) Unless the employee is relieved of all duty during a 30 minute meal period, the meal period shall be considered an "on duty" meal period and counted as time worked. An "on duty" meal period shall be permitted only when the nature of the work prevents an employee from being relieved of all duty and when by written agreement between the parties an on-the-job paid meal period is agreed to. The written agreement shall state that the employee may, in writing, revoke the agreement at any time.

(D) If an employer fails to provide an employee a meal period in accordance with the applicable provisions of this Order, the employer shall pay the employee one (1) hour of pay at the employee's regular rate of compensation for each work day that the meal period is not provided.

(E) In all places of employment where employees are required to eat on the premises, a suitable place for that purpose shall be designated.

12. Rest Periods

(A) Every employer shall authorize and permit all employees to take rest periods, which insofar as practicable shall be in the middle of each work period. The authorized rest period time shall be based on the total hours worked daily at the rate of ten (10) minutes net rest time per four (4) hours or major fraction thereof. However, a rest period need not be authorized for employees whose total daily work time is less than three and one-half (3 $\frac{1}{2}$) hours. Authorized rest period time shall be counted as hours worked for which there shall be no deduction from wages.

(B) If an employer fails to provide an employee a rest period in accordance with the applicable provisions of this Order, the employer shall pay the employee one (1) hour of pay at the employee's regular rate of compensation for each work day that the rest period is not provided.

13. Change Rooms and Resting Facilities

(A) Employers shall provide suitable lockers, closets, or equivalent for the safekeeping of employees' outer clothing during working hours, and when required, for their work clothing during non-working hours. When the occupation requires a change of clothing, change rooms or equivalent space shall be provided in order that employees may change their clothing in reasonable privacy and comfort. These rooms or spaces may be adjacent to but shall be separate from toilet rooms and shall be kept clean.

Note: This section shall not apply to change rooms and storage facilities regulated by the Occupational Safety and Health Standards Board.

(B) Suitable resting facilities shall be provided in an area separate from the toilet rooms and shall be available to employees during work hours.

14. Seats

(A) All working employees shall be provided with suitable seats when the nature of the work reasonably permits the use of seats.

(B) When employees are not engaged in the active duties of their employment and the nature of the work requires standing, an adequate number of suitable seats shall be placed in reasonable proximity to the work area and employees shall be permitted to use such seats when it does not interfere with the performance of their duties.

15. Temperature

(A) The temperature maintained in each work area shall provide reasonable comfort consistent with industry-wide standards for the nature of the process and the work performed.

(B) If excessive heat or humidity is created by the work process, the employer shall take all feasible means to reduce such excessive heat or humidity to a degree providing reasonable comfort. Where the nature of the employment requires a temperature of less than 60° F., a heated room shall be provided to which employees may retire for warmth, and such room shall be maintained at not less than 68°.

(C) A temperature of not less than 68° shall be maintained in the toilet rooms, resting rooms, and change rooms during hours of use.

(D) Federal and State energy guidelines shall prevail over any conflicting provision of this section.

16. Elevators. Adequate elevator, escalator or similar service consistent with industry-wide standards for the nature of the process and the work performed shall be provided when employees are employed four floors or more above or below ground level.

17. Exemptions. If, in the opinion of the Division after due investigation, it is found that the enforcement of any provision contained in Section 7, Records; Section 12, Rest Periods; Section 13, Change Rooms and Resting Facilities; Section 14, Seats; Section 15, Temperature; or Section 16, Elevators, would not materially affect the welfare or comfort of employees and would work an undue hardship on the employer, exemption may be made at the discretion of the Division. Such exemptions shall be in writing to be effective and may be revoked after reasonable notice is given in writing. Application for exemption shall be made by the employer or by the employee and/or the employee's representative to the Division in writing. A copy of the application shall be posted at the place of employment at the time the application is filed with the Division.

18. Filing Reports. (See California Labor Code, Section 1174(a))

19. Inspection. (See California Labor Code, Section 1174)

20. Penalties. (See Labor Code, Section 1199)

(A) In addition to any other civil penalties provided by law, any employer or any other person acting on behalf of the employer who violates, or causes to be violated, the provisions of this order, shall be subject to the civil penalty of:

(1) Initial Violation—$50.00 for each underpaid employee for each pay period during which the employee was underpaid in addition to the amount which is sufficient to recover unpaid wages.

(2) Subsequent Violations—$100.00 for each underpaid employee for each pay period during which the employee was underpaid in addition to an amount which is sufficient to recover unpaid wages.

(3) The affected employee shall receive payment of all wages recovered.

(B) The Labor Commissioner may also issue citations pursuant to Labor Code § 1197.1 for non-payment of wages for overtime work in violation of this order.

21. Separability. If the application of any provision of this Order, or any section, subsection, subdivision, sentence, clause, phrase, word, or portion of this Order should be held invalid or unconstitutional or unauthorized or prohibited by statute, the remaining provisions thereof shall not be affected thereby, but shall continue to be given full force and effect as if the part so held invalid or unconstitutional had not been included herein.

22. Posting of Order. Every employer shall keep a copy of this Order posted in an area frequented by employees where it may be easily read during the work day. Where the location of work or other conditions make this impractical, every employer shall keep a copy of this Order and make it available to every employee upon request.

[1] Pursuant to Labor Code section 515.5, subdivision (a)(4), the Division of Labor Statistics and Research, Department of Industrial Relations, has adjusted the minimum hourly rate of pay specified in this subdivision to be $49.77, effective January 1, 2007. This hourly rate of pay is adjusted on October 1 of each year to be effective on January 1, of the following year, and may be obtained at www.dir.ca.gov/IWC or by mail from the Department of Industrial Relations.

Publisher's Notes

See Nordquist v. McGraw–Hill Broadcasting Co. (1995) 32 Cal.App.4th 555, 38 Cal.Rptr.2d 221 (administrative employee exemption).

Research References

See notes following listing of Wage Orders.

Please Post With This Side Showing
OFFICIAL NOTICE
Effective January 1, 2001 as amended
Sections 4(A) and 10(C) amended and republished by the Department of Industrial Relations,
effective January 1, 2007, pursuant to AB 1835, Chapter 230, Statutes of 2006
INDUSTRIAL WELFARE COMMISSION
ORDER NO. 12–2001
REGULATING
WAGES, HOURS AND WORKING CONDITIONS IN THE
MOTION PICTURE INDUSTRY

TAKE NOTICE: To employers and representatives of persons working in industries and occupations in the State of California:

The Department of Industrial Relations amends and republishes the minimum wage and meals and lodging credits in the Industrial Welfare Commission's Orders as a result of legislation enacted (AB 1835, Ch. 230, Stats of 2006, adding sections 1182.12 and 1182.13 to the California Labor Code.) The amendments and republishing make no other changes to the IWC's Orders.

1. Applicability of Order. This order shall apply to all persons employed in the motion picture industry, including extra players, teachers, and welfare workers, whether paid on a time, piece rate, commission, or other basis, except that:

(A) Provisions of Sections 3 through 12 of this Order shall not apply to persons employed in administrative, executive, or professional capacities. The following requirements shall apply in determining whether an employee's duties meet the test to qualify for an exemption from those sections:

(1) Executive Exemption. A person employed in an executive capacity means any employee:

(a) Whose duties and responsibilities involve the management of the enterprise in which he is employed or of a customarily recognized department or subdivision thereof; and

(b) Who customarily and regularly directs the work of two or more other employees therein; and

(c) Who has the authority to hire or fire other employees or whose suggestions and recommendations as to the hiring or firing and as to the advancement and promotion or any other change of status of other employees will be given particular weight; and

(d) Who customarily and regularly exercises discretion and independent judgment; and

(e) Who is primarily engaged in duties which meet the test of the exemption. The activities constituting exempt work and non-exempt work shall be construed in the same manner as such items are construed in the following regulations under the Fair Labor Standards Act effective as of the date of this order: (29 C.F.R. §§ 541.102, 541.104–111, 541.115–116). Exempt work shall include, for example, all work that is directly and closely related to exempt work and work which is properly viewed as a means for carrying out exempt functions. The work actually performed by the employee during the course of the work week must, first and foremost, be examined and the amount of time the employee spends on such work, together with the employer's realistic expectations and the realistic requirements of the job, shall be considered in determining whether the employee satisfies this requirement.

(f) Such an employee must also earn a monthly salary equivalent to no less than two (2) times the state minimum wage for full-time employment. Full–time employment is defined in Labor Code § 515(c) as 40 hours per week.

(2) Administrative Exemption. A person employed in an administrative capacity means any employee:

(a) Whose duties and responsibilities involve either:

(i) The performance of office or non-manual work directly related to management policies or general business operations of his employer or his employer's customers, or

(ii) The performance of functions in the administration of a school system, or educational establishment or institution, or of a department of subdivision thereof, in work directly related to the academic instruction or training carried on therein; and

(b) Who customarily and regularly exercises discretion and independent judgment; and

(c) Who regularly and directly assists a proprietor, or an employee employed in a bona fide executive or administrative capacity (as such terms are defined for purposes of this section), or

(d) Who performs under only general supervision work along specialized or technical lines requiring special training, experience, or knowledge, or

(e) Who executes under only general supervision special assignments and tasks, and

(f) Who is primarily engaged in duties which meet the test of the exemption. The activities constituting exempt work and non-exempt work shall be construed in the same manner as such terms are construed in the following regulations under the Fair Labor Standards Act effective as of the date of this order: (29 C.F.R. §§ 541.201–205, 541.207–208, 541.210, 541.215). Exempt work shall include, for example, all work that is directly and closely related to exempt work and work which is properly viewed as a means for carrying out exempt functions. The work actually performed by the employee during the course of the work week must, first and foremost, be examined and the amount of time the employee spends on such work, together with the employer's realistic expectations and the realistic requirements of the job, shall be considered in determining whether the employee satisfies this requirement.

(g) Such employee must also earn a monthly salary equivalent to no less than two (2) times the state minimum wage for full-time employment. Full–time employment is defined in Labor Code § 515(c) as 40 hours per week.

(3) Professional Exemption. A person employed in a professional capacity means any employee who meets all of the following requirements:

(a) Who is licensed or certified by the State of California and is primarily engaged in the practice of one of the following recognized professions: law, medicine, dentistry, optometry, architecture, engineering, teaching, or accounting; or

(b) Who is primarily engaged in an occupation commonly recognized as a learned or artistic profession. For the purposes of this subsection, "learned or artistic profession" means an employee who is primarily engaged in the performance of:

(i) Work requiring knowledge of an advanced type in a field or science or learning customarily acquired by a prolonged course of specialized intellectual instruction and study, as distinguished from a general academic education and from an apprenticeship, and from training in the performance of routine mental, manual, or physical processes, or work that is an essential part of or necessarily incident to any of the above work; or

(ii) Work that is original and creative in character in a recognized field of artistic endeavor (as opposed to work which can be produced by a person endowed with general manual or intellectual ability and training), and the result of which depends primarily on the invention, imagination, or talent of the employee or work that is an essential part of or necessarily incident to any of the above work; and

(iii) whose work is predominantly intellectual and varied in character (as opposed to routine mental, manual, mechanical, or physical work) and is of such character that the output produced or the result accomplished cannot be standardized in relation to a given period of time.

(c) Who customarily and regularly exercises discretion and independent judgment in the performance of duties set forth in subparagraphs (a) and (b).

(d) Who earns a monthly salary equivalent to no less than two (2) times the state minimum wage for full-time employment. Full-time employment is defined in Labor Code § 515(c) as 40 hours per week.

(e) Subparagraph (b) above is intended to be construed in accordance with the following provisions of federal law as they existed as of the date of this Wage Order: 29 C.F.R. §§ 541.207, 541.301(a)–(d), 541.302, 541.306, 541.307, 541.308, and 541.310.

(f) Notwithstanding the provisions of this subparagraph, pharmacists employed to engage in the practice of pharmacy, and registered nurses employed to engage in the practice of nursing, shall not be considered exempt professional employees, nor shall they be considered exempt from coverage for the purposes of this subparagraph unless they individually meet the criteria established for exemption as executive or administrative employees.

(g) Notwithstanding subparagraph (f), the following advanced practice nurses shall be exempt from provisions of this subsection:

(i) Certified nurse midwives who are primarily engaged in performing duties for which certification is required pursuant to Article 2.5 (commencing with Section 2746) of Chapter 6 of Division 2 of the Business and Professions Code.

(ii) Certified nurse anesthetists who are primarily engaged in performing duties for which certification is required pursuant to Article 7 (commencing with Section 2825) of Chapter 6 of Division 2 of the Business and Professions Code.

(iii) Certified nurse practitioners who are primarily engaged in performing duties for which certification is required pursuant to Article 8 (commencing with Section 2834) of Chapter 6 of Division 2 of the Business and Professions Code.

(iv) Nothing in this subparagraph shall exempt the occupations set forth in clauses (i), (ii), and (iii) from meeting the requirements of subsection 1(A)(3)(a)–(d), above.

(h) Except as provided in subparagraph (i), an employee in the computer software field who is paid on an hourly basis shall be exempt, if all of the following apply:

(i) The employee is primarily engaged in work that is intellectual or creative and that requires the exercise of discretion and independent judgment.

(ii) The employee is primarily engaged in duties that consist of one or more of the following:

-The application of systems analysis techniques and procedures, including consulting with users, to determine hardware, software, or system functional specifications.

-The design, development, documentation, analysis, creation, testing, or modification of computer systems or programs, including prototypes, based on and related to, user or system design specifications.

-The documentation, testing, creation, or modification of computer programs related to the design of software or hardware for computer operating systems.

(iii) The employee is highly skilled and is proficient in the theoretical and practical application of highly specialized information to computer systems analysis, programming, and software engineering. A job title shall not be determinative of the applicability of this exemption.

(iv) The employee's hourly rate of pay is not less than forty-one dollars ($41.00). The Division of Labor Statistics and Research shall adjust this pay rate on October 1 of each year to be effective on January 1 of the following year by an amount equal to the percentage increase in the California Consumer Price Index for Urban Wage Earners and Clerical Workers.[1]

(i) The exemption provided in subparagraph (h) does not apply to an employee if any of the following apply:

(i) The employee is a trainee or employee in an entry-level position who is learning to become proficient in the theoretical and practical application of highly specialized information to computer systems analysis, programming, and software engineering.

(ii) The employee is in a computer-related occupation but has not attained the level of skill and expertise necessary to work independently and without close supervision.

(iii) The employee is engaged in the operation of computers or in the manufacture, repair, or maintenance of computer hardware and related equipment.

(iv) The employee is an engineer, drafter, machinist, or other professional whose work is highly dependent upon or facilitated by the use of computers and computer software programs and who is skilled in computer-aided design software, including CAD/CAM, but who is not in a computer systems analysis or programming occupation.

(v) The employee is a writer engaged in writing material, including box labels, product descriptions, documentation, promotional material, setup and installation instructions, and other similar written information, either for print or for on screen media or who writes or provides content material intended to be read by customers, subscribers, or visitors to computer-related media such as the World Wide Web or CD–ROMs.

(vi) The employee is engaged in any of the activities set forth in subparagraph (h) for the purpose of creating imagery for effects used in the motion picture, television, or theatrical industry.

(B) Except as provided in sections 1, 2, 4, 10, and 20, the provisions of this Order shall not apply to any employees directly employed by the State or any political subdivision thereof, including any city, county, or special district.

(C) Except as provided in sections 1, 2, 4, 10, and 20, the provisions of this Order shall not apply to professional actors.

(D) The provisions of this Order shall not apply to outside salespersons.

(E) Provisions of this Order shall not apply to any individual who is the parent, spouse, child, or legally adopted child of the employer.

(F) The provisions of this Order shall not apply to any individual participating in a national service program, such as Ameri–Corps, carried out using assistance provided under Section 12571 of Title 42 of the United States Code. (See Stats. 2000, ch. 365, amending Labor Code § 1171.)

2. **Definitions**

(A) An "alternative workweek schedule" means any regularly scheduled workweek requiring an employee to work more than eight (8) hours in a 24–hour period.

(B) "Commission" means the Industrial Welfare Commission of the State of California.

(C) "Division" means the Division of Labor Standards Enforcement of the State of California.

(D) "Employ" means to engage, suffer, or permit to work.

(E) "Employee" means any person employed by an employer.

(F) "Employer" means any person as defined in Section 18 of the Labor Code, who directly or indirectly, or through an agent or any other person, employs or exercises control over the wages, hours, or working conditions of any person.

(G) "Extra Player" means any person employed by an employer in the production of motion pictures to perform any work, including but not limited to that of a general extra, stand-in, photographic double, sports player, silent bit, or dress extra; or as extras employed in dancing, skating, swimming, diving, riding, driving, or singing; or as extras employed to perform any other actions, gestures, facial expressions, or pantomime.

(H) "Hours worked" means the time during which an employee is subject to the control of an employer, and includes all the time the employee is suffered or permitted to work, whether or not required to do so.

(I) "Location" means any place other than the studio premises of the employer, at which the employer shoots all or a portion of a motion picture.

(J) "Minor" means, for the purpose of this Order, any person under the age of 18 years.

(K) "Motion Picture Industry" means any industry, business or establishment operated for the purpose of motion picture or television film production, or primarily allied with theatrical or television, motion picture productions, including but not limited to motion pictures for entertainment, commercial, religious, or educational purposes, whether made by film, tape, or otherwise.

(L) "Outside Salesperson" means any person, 18 years of age or over, who customarily and regularly works more than half the working time away from the employer's place of business selling tangible or intangible items or obtaining orders or contracts for products, services or use of facilities.

(M) "Primarily" as used in Section 1, Applicability, means more than one-half the employee's work time.

(N) "Shift" means designated hours of work by an employee, with a designated beginning time and ending time.

(O) "Split shift" means a work schedule which is interrupted by non-paid non-working periods established by the employer, other than bona fide rest or meal periods.

(P) "Wages" includes all amounts for labor performed by employees of every description, whether the amount is fixed or ascertained by the standard of time, task, piece, commission basis, or other method of calculation.

(Q) "Workday" and "day" mean any consecutive 24–hour period beginning at the same time each calendar day.

(R) "Workweek" and "week" mean any seven (7) consecutive days, starting with the same calendar day each week. "Workweek" is a fixed and regularly recurring period of 168 hours, seven (7) consecutive 24–hour periods.

3. Hours and Days of Work

(A) *Daily Overtime—General Provisions*

(1) The following overtime provisions are applicable to employees 18 years of age or over and to employees 16 or 17 years of age who are not required by law to attend school and are not otherwise prohibited by law from engaging in the subject work. Such employees shall not be employed more than eight (8) hours in any workday or more than 40 hours in any workweek unless the employee receives one and one-half (1 ½) times such employee's regular rate of pay for all hours worked over 40 hours in the workweek. Eight (8) hours of labor constitutes a day's work. Employment beyond eight (8) hours in any workday or more than six (6) days in any workweek is permissible provided the employee is compensated for such overtime as follows:

(a) Employees may be employed up to a maximum of 16 hours including meal periods in any one day from the time they are required and do report until dismissed, provided the employee is compensated for such overtime at not less than:

(i) For daily employees and weekly employees, excluding weekly employees guaranteed more than 40 hours a workweek and "on call" employees, one and one-half (1 ½) times the employee's regular rate of pay for all hours worked in excess of eight (8) hours up to and including 12 hours in any one workday, and for the first eight (8) hours worked on the seventh (7th) consecutive day of work in a workweek; and

(ii) Double the employee's regular rate of pay for all hours worked in excess of 12 hours in any workday, and for all hours worked in excess of eight (8) hours on the seventh (7th) consecutive day of work in a workweek.

(iii) Overtime payments shall not be compounded and all payments made by the employer for daily overtime on the basis herein above specified shall be applied toward any sum for weekly overtime.

(iv) The overtime rate of compensation required to be paid to a nonexempt full-time salaried employee shall be computed by using the employee's regular hourly salary as one fortieth (1/40) of the employee's weekly salary.

(B) *Alternative Workweek Schedules*

(1) No employer shall be deemed to have violated the daily overtime provisions by instituting, pursuant to the election procedures set forth in this wage order, a regularly scheduled alternative workweek schedule of not more than ten (10) hours per day within a 40 hour workweek without the payment of an overtime rate of compensation. All work performed in any workday beyond the schedule established by the agreement up to 12 hours a day or beyond 40 hours per week shall be paid at one and one-half (1 ½) times the employee's regular rate of pay. All work performed in excess of 12 hours per day and any work in excess of eight (8) hours on those days worked beyond the regularly scheduled number of workdays established by the alternative workweek agreement shall be paid at double the employee's regular rate of pay. Any alternative workweek agreement adopted pursuant to this section shall provide for not less than four (4) hours of work in any shift. Nothing in this section shall prohibit an employer, at the request of the employee, to substitute one day of work for another day of the same length in the shift provided by the alternative workweek agreement on an occasional basis to meet the personal needs of the employee without the payment of overtime. No hours paid at either one and one-half (1 ½) or double the regular rate of pay shall be included in determining when 40 hours have been worked for the purpose of computing overtime compensation.

(2) Any agreement adopted pursuant to this section shall provide not less than two consecutive days off within a workweek.

(3) If an employer, whose employees have adopted an alternative workweek agreement permitted by this order requires an employee to work fewer hours than those that are regularly scheduled by the agreement, the employer shall pay the employee overtime compensation at a rate of one and one-half (1 ½) times the employee's regular rate of pay for all hours worked in excess of eight (8) hours, and double the employee's regular rate of pay for all hours worked in excess of 12 hours for the day the employee is required to work the reduced hours.

(4) An employer shall not reduce an employee's regular rate of hourly pay as a result of the adoption, repeal or nullification of an alternative workweek schedule.

(5) An employer shall explore any available reasonable alternative means of accommodating the religious belief or observance of an affected employee that conflicts with an adopted alternative workweek schedule, in the manner provided by subdivision (j) of Section 12940 of the Government Code.

(6) An employer shall make a reasonable effort to find a work schedule not to exceed eight (8) hours in a workday, in order to accommodate any affected employee who was eligible to vote in an election authorized by this Section and who is unable to work the alternative workweek schedule established as the result of that election.

(7) An employer shall be permitted, but not required, to provide a work schedule not to exceed eight (8) hours in a workday to accommodate any employee who is hired after the date of the election and who is unable to work the alternative workweek schedule established by the election.

(8) Arrangements adopted in a secret ballot election held pursuant to this order prior to 1998, or under the rules in effect prior to 1998, and before the performance of the work, shall remain valid after July 1, 2000 provided that the results of the election are reported by the employer to the Division of Labor Statistics and Research by January 1, 2001, in accordance with the requirements of Section C below (Election Procedures). If an employee was voluntarily working an alternative workweek schedule of not more than ten (10) hours a day as of July

1, 1999, that alternative workweek schedule was based on an individual agreement made after January 1, 1998 between the employee and employer, and the employee submitted, and the employer approved, a written request on or before May 30, 2000 to continue the agreement, the employee may continue to work that alternative work-week schedule without payment of an overtime rate of compensation for the hours provided in the agreement. An employee may revoke his or her voluntary authoriza-tion to continue such a schedule with 30 days written notice to the employer. New arrangements can only be entered into pursuant to the provisions of this section.

(C) *Election Procedures*

Election procedures for the adoption and repeal of alternative workweek schedules require the following:

(1) Each proposal for an alternative workweek sched-ule shall be in the form of a written agreement proposed by the employer. The proposed agreement must desig-nate a regularly scheduled alternative workweek in which the specified number of work days and work hours are regularly recurring. The actual days worked within that alternative workweek schedule need not be specified. The employer may propose a single work schedule that would become the standard schedule for workers in the work unit, or a menu of work schedule options, from which each employee in the unit would be entitled to choose. If the employer proposes a menu of work schedule options, the employee may, with the approval of the employer, move from one menu option to another.

(2) In order to be valid, the proposed alternative workweek schedule must be adopted in a secret ballot election, before the performance of work, by at least a two-thirds (2/03) vote of the affected employees in the work unit. The election shall be held during regular working hours at the employees' work site. For purposes of this subsection, "affected employees in the work unit" may include all employees in a readily identifiable work unit, such as a division, a department, a job classification, a shift, a separate physical location, or a recognized subdivision of any such work unit. A work unit may consist of an individual employee as long as the criteria for an identifiable work unit in this subsection is met.

(3) Prior to the secret ballot vote, any employer who proposed to institute an alternative workweek schedule shall have made a disclosure in writing to the affected employees, including the effects of the proposed arrange-ment on the employees' wages, hours, and benefits. Such a disclosure shall include meeting(s), duly noticed, held at least 14 days prior to voting, for the specific purpose of discussing the effects of the alternative workweek sched-ule. An employer shall provide that disclosure in a non–English language, as well as in English, if at least five (5) percent of the affected employees primarily speak that non–English language. The employer shall mail the written disclosure to employees who do not attend the meeting. Failure to comply with this paragraph shall make the election null and void.

(4) Any election to establish or repeal an alternative workweek schedule shall be held at the work site of the affected employees. The employer shall bear the costs of conducting any election held pursuant to this section. Upon a complaint by an affected employee, and after an investigation by the Labor Commissioner, the Labor Commissioner may require the employer to select a neutral third party to conduct the election.

(5) Any type of alternative workweek schedule that is authorized by the Labor Code may be repealed by the affected employees. Upon a petition of one-third (1/03) of the affected employees, a new secret ballot election shall be held and a two-thirds (2/03) vote of the affected employees shall be required to reverse the alternative workweek schedule. The election to repeal the alterna-tive workweek schedule shall be held not more than 30 days after the petition is submitted to the employer, except that the election shall be held not less than 12 months after the date that the same group of employees voted in an election held to adopt or repeal an alternative workweek schedule. The election shall take place during regular working hours at the employees' work site. If the alternative workweek schedule is revoked, the employer shall comply within 60 days. Upon proper showing of undue hardship, the Division of Labor Standards En-forcement may grant an extension of time for compliance.

(6) Only secret ballots may be cast by affected employ-ees in the work unit at any election held pursuant to this Section. The results of any election conducted pursuant to this Section shall be reported by the employer to the Division of Labor Statistics and Research within 30 days after the results are final, and the report of election results shall be a public document. The report shall include the final tally of the vote, the size of the unit, and the nature of the business of the employer.

(7) Employees affected by a change in the work hours resulting from the adoption of an alternative workweek schedule may not be required to work those new work hours for at least 30 days after the announcement of the final results of the election.

(8) Employers shall not intimidate or coerce employ-ees to vote either in support of or in opposition to a proposed alternative workweek. No employees shall be discharged or discriminated against for expressing opin-ions concerning the alternative workweek election or for opposing or supporting its adoption or repeal. However, nothing in this section shall prohibit an employer from expressing his/her position concerning that alternative workweek to the affected employees. A violation of this paragraph shall be subject to Labor Code section 98 *et seq.*

(D) Extra players employed in excess of eight (8) hours in any workday from the time the extra player is required and does report until dismissed, shall be paid daily overtime compensation as follows:

(1) One and one-half (1 $\frac{1}{02}$) times the extra player's rate of pay for the ninth (9th) and tenth (10th) work hours of employment and not less than double the extra

player's rate of pay for all hours worked thereafter, computed in units of one-tenth (1/10) hours.

(2) Weekly overtime. The total sum paid to an extra player who works more than 40 hours in such workweek for a particular employer shall be the extra player's regular hourly rate of pay times 40, plus one and one-half (1 ½) times such regular hourly rate of pay for all hours worked in excess of 40 during such workweek. The regular hourly rate shall be determined by dividing the amount of the weekly salary by the number of regular hours in a workweek.

(3) An extra player employed by the week shall receive payment of daily overtime for all hours or fractions thereof worked beyond eight (8) hours in any workday on which such daily overtime occurs as provided above, provided that overtime payments shall not be compounded and all payments made by the employer for daily overtime on the basis herein above specified shall be applied toward any sum due for weekly overtime.

(E) One and one-half (1 ½) times a minor's regular rate of pay shall be paid for all hours worked on the sixth (6th) consecutive workday except that minors 16 and 17 years old who are not required by law to attend school and may therefore be employed for the same hours as an adult are subject to subsections (A), (B), (C) or (D) above.

(**Violations of Child Labor Laws** are subject to civil penalties of from $500 to $10,000 as well as to criminal penalties. Refer to California Labor Code Sections 1285 to 1312 and 1390 to 1399 for additional restrictions on the employment of minors and for descriptions of criminal and civil penalties for violation of the child labor laws. Employers should ask school districts about any required work permits.)

(F) No employee shall be required to report to work unless ten (10) hours have elapsed since the termination of the previous day's employment.

(G) Hot meals and hot drinks shall be provided for employees who are required to work after 12 o'clock midnight, except off-production employees regularly scheduled to work after midnight.

(H) When employees are required to work at night and are not dismissed in time to permit their return to their homes by public service transportation, transportation shall be provided by the employer.

(I) The provisions of Labor Code §§ 551 and 552 regarding one (1) day's rest in seven (7) shall not be construed to prevent an accumulation of days of rest when the nature of the employment reasonably requires the employee to work seven (7) or more consecutive days; provided, however, that in each calendar month, the employee shall receive the equivalent of one (1) day's rest in seven (7).

(J) Except as provided in subsections (E) and (I), this section shall not apply to any employee covered by a valid collective bargaining agreement if the agreement expressly provides for the wages, hours of work, and working conditions of the employees, and if the agreement provides premium wage rates for all overtime hours worked and a regular hourly rate of pay for those employees of not less than 30 percent more than the state minimum wage.

(K) Notwithstanding subsection (J) above, where the employer and a labor organization representing employees of the employer have entered into a valid collective bargaining agreement pertaining to the hours of work of the employees, the requirement regarding the equivalent of one (1) day's rest in seven (7) (see subsection (I) above) shall apply, unless the agreement expressly provides otherwise.

(L) If an employer approves a written request of an employee to make-up work time that is or would be lost as a result of a personal obligation of the employee, the hours of that make-up work time, if performed in the same workweek in which the work time was lost, may not be counted toward computing the total number of hours worked in a day for purposes of the overtime requirements, except for hours in excess of 11 hours of work in one (1) day or 40 hours of work in one (1) workweek. If an employee knows in advance that he or she will be requesting make-up time for a personal obligation that will recur at a fixed time over a succession of weeks, the employee may request to make-up work time for up to four (4) weeks in advance; provided, however, that the make-up work must be performed in the same week that the work time was lost. An employee shall provide a signed written request for each occasion that the employee makes a request to make-up work time pursuant to this subsection. While an employer may inform an employee of this make-up time option, the employer is prohibited from encouraging or otherwise soliciting an employee to request the employer's approval to take personal time off and make-up the work hours within the same workweek pursuant to this subsection.

4. Minimum Wages

(A) Every employer shall pay to each employee wages not less than seven dollars and fifty cents ($7.50) per hour for all hours worked, effective January 1, 2007, and not less than eight dollars ($8.00) per hour for all hours worked, effective January 1, 2008, except:

Learners. Employees during their first 160 hours of employment in occupations in which they have no previous similar or related experience, may be paid not less than 85 percent of the minimum wage rounded to the nearest nickel.

(B) Every employer shall pay to each employee, on the established payday for the period involved, not less than the applicable minimum wage for all hours worked in the payroll period, whether the remuneration is measured by time, piece, commission, or otherwise.

(C) When an employee works a split shift, one (1) hour's pay at the minimum wage shall be paid in addition to the minimum wage for that workday, except when the employee resides at the place of employment.

(D) The provisions of this section shall not apply to apprentices regularly indentured under the State Division of Apprenticeship Standards.

5. Reporting Time Pay

(A) Each workday an employee is required to report for work and does report, but is not put to work or is furnished less than half said employee's usual or scheduled day's work, the employee shall be paid for half the usual or scheduled day's work, but in no event for less than two (2) hours nor more than four (4) hours, at the employee's regular rate of pay, which shall not be less than the minimum wage.

(B) If an employee is required to report for work a second time in any one workday and is furnished less than two (2) hours of work on the second reporting, said employee shall be paid for two (2) hours at the employee's regular rate of pay, which shall not be less than the minimum wage.

(C) The foregoing reporting time pay provisions are not applicable when:

(1) Operations cannot commence or continue due to threats to employees or property; or when recommended by civil authorities; or

(2) Public utilities fail to supply electricity, water, or gas, or there is a failure in the public utilities, or sewer system; or

(3) The interruption of work is caused by an Act of God or other cause not within the employer's control.

(D) This section shall not apply to an employee on paid standby status who is called to perform assigned work at a time other than the employee's scheduled reporting time.

6. Licenses for Disabled Workers

(A) A license may be issued by the Division authorizing employment of a person whose earning capacity is impaired by physical disability or mental deficiency at less than the minimum wage. Such licenses shall be granted only upon joint application of employer and employee and employee's representative if any.

(B) A special license may be issued to a nonprofit organization such as a sheltered workshop or rehabilitation facility fixing special minimum rates to enable the employment of such persons without requiring individual licenses of such employees.

(C) All such licenses and special licenses shall be renewed on a yearly basis or more frequently at the discretion of the Division.

(See California Labor Code, Sections 1191 and 1191.5.)

7. Records

(A) Every employer shall keep accurate information with respect to each employee including the following:

(1) Full name, home address, occupation and social security number.

(2) Birth date, if under 18 years, and designation as a minor.

(3) Time records showing when the employee begins and ends each work period. Meal periods, split shift intervals and total daily hours worked shall also be recorded. Meal periods during which operations cease and authorized rest periods need not be recorded.

(4) Total wages paid each payroll period, including value of board, lodging, or other compensation actually furnished to the employee.

(5) Total hours worked in the payroll period and applicable rates of pay. This information shall be made readily available to the employee upon reasonable request.

(6) When a piece rate or incentive plan is in operation, piece rates or an explanation of the incentive plan formula shall be provided to employees. An accurate production record shall be maintained by the employer.

(B) Every employer shall semimonthly or at the time of each payment of wages furnish each employee, either as a detachable part of the check, draft, or voucher paying the employee's wages, or separately, an itemized statement in writing showing: (1) all deductions; (2) the inclusive dates of the period for which the employee is paid; (3) the name of the employee or the employee's social security number; and (4) the name of the employer, provided all deductions made on written orders of the employee may be aggregated and shown as one item.

(C) All required records shall be in the English language and in ink or other indelible form, properly dated, showing month, day and year, and shall be kept on file by the employer for at least three years at the place of employment or at a central location within the State of California. An employee's records shall be available for inspection by the employee upon reasonable request.

(D) Clocks shall be provided in all major work areas or within reasonable distance thereto insofar as practicable.

8. Cash Shortage and Breakage.
No employer shall make any deduction from the wage or require any reimbursement from an employee for any cash shortage, breakage, or loss of equipment, unless it can be shown that the shortage, breakage, or loss is caused by a dishonest or willful act, or by the gross negligence of the employee.

9. Uniforms and Equipment

(A) When uniforms are required by the employer to be worn by the employee as a condition of employment, such uniforms shall be provided and maintained by the employer. The term "uniform" includes wearing apparel and accessories of distinctive design or color.

Note: This section shall not apply to protective apparel regulated by the Occupational Safety and Health Standards Board.

(B) When tools or equipment are required by the employer or are necessary to the performance of a job, such tools and equipment shall be provided and maintained by the employer, except that an employee whose wages are at least two (2) times the minimum wage provided herein may be required to provide and maintain hand tools and equipment customarily required by the trade or craft. This subsection (B) shall not apply to apprentices regularly indentured under the State Division of Apprenticeship Standards.

Note: This section shall not apply to protective equipment and safety devices on tools regulated by the Occupational Safety and Health Standards Board.

A reasonable deposit may be required as security for the return of the items furnished by the employer under provisions of subsections (A) and (B) of this section upon issuance of a receipt to the employee for such deposit. Such deposits shall be made pursuant to Section 400 and following of the Labor Code or an employer with the prior written authorization of the employee may deduct from the employee's last check the cost of an item furnished pursuant to (A) and (B) above in the event said item is not returned. No deduction shall be made at any time for normal wear and tear. All items furnished by the employer shall be returned by the employee upon completion of the job.

10. Meals and Lodging

(A) "Meal" means an adequate, well-balanced serving of a variety of wholesome, nutritious foods.

(B) "Lodging" means living accommodations available to the employee for full-time occupancy which are adequate, decent, and sanitary according to usual and customary standards. Employees shall not be required to share a bed.

(C) Meals or lodging may not be credited against the minimum wage without a voluntary written agreement between the employer and the employee. When credit for meals or lodging is used to meet part of the employer's minimum wage obligation, the amounts so credited may not be more than the following:

Effective	January 1, 2007	January 1, 2008
Lodging:		
Room occupied alone	$35.27 per week	$37.63 per week
Room shared	$29.11 per week	$31.06 per week
Apartment—two–thirds (2/03) of the ordinary rental value, and in no event more than	$423.51 per month	$451.89 per month
Where a couple are both employed by the employer, two-thirds (2/03) of the ordinary rental value, and in no event more than	$626.49 per month	$668.46 per month
Meals:		
Breakfast	$2.72	$2.90
Lunch	$3.72	$3.97
Dinner	$5.00	$5.34

(D) Meals evaluated as part of the minimum wage must be bona fide meals consistent with the employee's work shift. Deductions shall not be made for meals not received nor lodging not used.

(E) If, as a condition of employment, the employee must live at the place of employment or occupy quarters owned or under the control of the employer, then the employer may not charge rent in excess of the values listed herein.

11. Meal Periods

(A) No employer shall employ any person for a work period of more than six (6) hours without a meal period of not less than 30 minutes, nor more than one (1) hour. Subsequent meal period for all employees shall be called not later than six (6) hours after the termination of the preceding meal period.

(B) Unless the employee is relieved of all duty during a 30 minute meal period, the meal period shall be considered an "on duty" meal period and counted as time worked. An "on duty" meal period shall be permitted only when the nature of the work prevents an employee from being relieved of all duty and when by written agreement between the parties an on-the-job paid meal period is agreed to. The written agreement shall state that the employee may, in writing, revoke the agreement at any time.

(C) If an employer fails to provide an employee a meal period in accordance with the applicable provisions of this Order, the employer shall pay the employee one (1) hour of pay at the employee's regular rate of compensation for each work day that the meal period is not provided.

(D) In all places of employment where employees are required to eat on the premises, a suitable place for that purpose shall be designated.

12. Rest Periods

(A) Every employer shall authorize and permit all employees to take rest periods, which insofar as practicable shall be in the middle of each work period. The authorized rest period time shall be based on the total hours worked daily at the rate of ten (10) minutes net rest time per four (4) hours or major fraction thereof. However, a rest period need not be authorized for employees whose total daily work time is less than three and one-half (3 1/2) hours. Authorized rest period time shall be counted as hours worked for which there shall be no deduction from wages.

(B) If an employer fails to provide an employee a rest period in accordance with the applicable provisions of this Order, the employer shall pay the employee one (1) hour of pay at the employee's regular rate of compensation for each work day that the rest period is not provided.

(C) Swimmers, dancers, skaters, and other performers engaged in strenuous physical activities shall have additional interim rest periods during periods of actual rehearsal or shooting.

13. Change Rooms and Resting Facilities

(A) Employers shall provide suitable lockers, closets, or equivalent for the safekeeping of employees' outer clothing during working hours, and when required, for their work clothing during non-working hours. When the occupation requires a change of clothing, change rooms or equivalent space shall be provided in order that employees may change their clothing in reasonable privacy and comfort. These rooms or spaces may be adjacent to but shall be separate from toilet rooms and shall be kept clean.

Note: This section shall not apply to change rooms and storage facilities regulated by the Occupational Safety and Health Standards Board.

(B) Suitable resting facilities shall be provided in an area separate from the toilet rooms and shall be available to employees during work hours.

14. Seats

(A) All working employees shall be provided with suitable seats when the nature of the work reasonably permits the use of seats.

(B) When employees are not engaged in the active duties of their employment and the nature of the work requires standing, an adequate number of suitable seats shall be placed in reasonable proximity to the work area and employees shall be permitted to use such seats when it does not interfere with the performance of their duties.

15. Temperature

(A) The temperature maintained in each work area shall provide reasonable comfort consistent with industry-wide standards for the nature of the process and the work performed.

(B) If excessive heat or humidity is created by the work process, the employer shall take all feasible means to reduce such excessive heat or humidity to a degree providing reasonable comfort. Where the nature of the employment requires a temperature of less than 60° F., a heated room shall be provided to which employees may retire for warmth, and such room shall be maintained at not less than 68°.

(C) A temperature of not less than 68° shall be maintained in the toilet rooms, resting rooms, and change rooms during hours of use.

(D) Federal and State energy guidelines shall prevail over any conflicting provision of this section.

16. Elevators. Adequate elevator, escalator or similar service consistent with industry-wide standards for the nature of the process and the work performed shall be provided when employees are employed four floors or more above or below ground level.

17. Exemptions. If, in the opinion of the Division after due investigation, it is found that the enforcement of any provision contained in Section 7, Records; section 12, Rest Periods; Section 13, Change Rooms and Resting Facilities; Section 14, Seats; Section 15, Temperature; or Section 16, Elevators, would not materially affect the welfare or comfort of employees and would work an undue hardship on the employer, exemption may be made at the discretion of the Division. Such exemptions

shall be in writing to be effective and may be revoked after reasonable notice is given in writing. Application for exemption shall be made by the employer or by the employee and/or the employee's representative to the Division in writing. A copy of the application shall be posted at the place of employment at the time the application is filed with the Division.

18. Filing Reports. (See California Labor Code, Section 1174(a))

19. Inspection. (See California Labor Code, Section 1174)

20. Penalties. (See Labor Code, Section 1199)

(A) In addition to any other civil penalties provided by law, any employer or any other person acting on behalf of the employer who violates, or causes to be violated, the provisions of this order, shall be subject to the civil penalty of:

(1) Initial Violation—$50.00 for each underpaid employee for each pay period during which the employee was underpaid in addition to the amount which is sufficient to recover unpaid wages.

(2) Subsequent Violations—$100.00 for each underpaid employee for each pay period during which the employee was underpaid in addition to an amount which is sufficient to recover unpaid wages.

(3) The affected employee shall receive payment of all wages recovered.

(B) The Labor Commissioner may also issue citations pursuant to Labor Code § 1197.1 for non-payment of wages for overtime work in violation of this order.

21. Separability. If the application of any provision of this Order, or any section, subsection, subdivision, sentence, clause, phrase, word, or portion of this Order should be held invalid or unconstitutional or unauthorized or prohibited by statute, the remaining provisions thereof shall not be affected thereby, but shall continue to be given full force and effect as if the part so held invalid or unconstitutional had not been included herein.

22. Posting of Order. Every employer shall keep a copy of this Order posted in an area frequented by employees where it may be easily read during the work day. Where the location of work or other conditions make this impractical, every employer shall keep a copy of this Order and make it available to every employee upon request.

1 Pursuant to Labor Code section 515.5, subdivision (a)(4), the Division of Labor Statistics and Research, Department of Industrial Relations, has adjusted the minimum hourly rate of pay specified in this subdivision to be $49.77, effective January 1, 2007. This hourly rate of pay is adjusted on October 1 of each year to be effective on January 1, of the following year, and may be obtained at www.dir.ca.gov/IWC or by mail from the Department of Industrial Relations.

Publisher's Notes

Research References

See notes following listing of Wage Orders.

Please Post With This Side Showing
OFFICIAL NOTICE
Effective January 1, 2001 as amended
Sections 4(A) and 10(C) amended and republished by the Department of Industrial Relations,
effective January 1, 2007, pursuant to AB 1835, Chapter 230, Statutes of 2006
**INDUSTRIAL WELFARE COMMISSION
ORDER NO.13–2001
REGULATING
WAGES, HOURS AND WORKING CONDITIONS IN THE
INDUSTRIES PREPARING AGRICULTURAL
PRODUCTS
FOR MARKET, ON THE FARM**

TAKE NOTICE: To employers and representatives of persons working in industries and occupations in the State of California:

The Department of Industrial Relations amends and republishes the minimum wage and meals and lodging credits in the Industrial Welfare Commission's Orders as a result of legislation enacted (AB 1835, Ch. 230, Stats of 2006, adding sections 1182.12 and 1182.13 to the California Labor Code.) The amendments and republishing make no other changes to the IWC's Orders.

1. Applicability of Order. This order shall apply to all persons employed in industries preparing agricultural products for market, on the farm, whether paid on a time, piece rate, commission, or other basis, except that:

(A) Provisions of Sections 3 through 12 of this Order shall not apply to persons employed in administrative, executive, or professional capacities. The following requirements shall apply in determining whether an employee's duties meet the test to qualify for an exemption from those sections:

(1) Executive Exemption. A person employed in an executive capacity means any employee:

(a) Whose duties and responsibilities involve the management of the enterprise in which he or she is employed or of a customarily recognized department or subdivision thereof; and

(b) Who customarily and regularly directs the work of two or more other employees therein; and

(c) Who has the authority to hire or fire other employees or whose suggestions and recommendations as to the hiring or firing and as to the advancement and promotion or any other change of status of other employees will be given particular weight; and

(d) Who customarily and regularly exercises discretion and independent judgment; and

(e) Who is primarily engaged in duties which meet the test of the exemption. The activities constituting exempt work and non-exempt work shall be construed in the same manner as such items are construed in the following regulations under the Fair Labor Standards Act effective as of the date of this order: 29 C.F.R. §§ 541.102, 541.104–111, 541.115–116. Exempt work shall include, for example, all work that is directly and closely related to exempt work and work which is properly viewed as a means for carrying out exempt functions. The work actually performed by the employee during the course of the work week must, first and foremost, be examined and the amount of time the employee spends on such work, together with the employer's realistic expectations and the realistic requirements of the job, shall be considered in determining whether the employee satisfies this requirement.

(f) Such an employee must also earn a monthly salary equivalent to no less than two (2) times the state minimum wage for full-time employment. Full–time employment is defined in Labor Code § 515(c) as 40 hours per week.

(2) Administrative Exemption. A person employed in an administrative capacity means any employee:

(a) Whose duties and responsibilities involve either:

(i) The performance of office or non-manual work directly related to management policies or general business operations of his employer or his employer's customers, or

(ii) The performance of functions in the administration of a school system, or educational establishment or institution, or of a department of subdivision thereof, in work directly related to the academic instruction or training carried on therein; and

(b) Who customarily and regularly exercises discretion and independent judgment; and

(c) Who regularly and directly assists a proprietor, or an employee employed in a bona fide executive or administrative capacity (as such terms are defined for purposes of this section), or

(d) Who performs under only general supervision work along specialized or technical lines requiring special training, experience, or knowledge, or

(e) Who executes under only general supervision special assignments and tasks, and

(f) Who is primarily engaged in duties which meet the test of the exemption. The activities constituting exempt work and non-exempt work shall be construed in the same manner as such terms are construed in the following regulations under the Fair Labor Standards Act effective as of the date of this order: 29 C.F.R. §§ 541.201–205, 541.207–208, 541.210, 541.215. Exempt work shall include, for example, all work that is directly and closely related to exempt work and work which is properly viewed as a means for carrying out exempt functions. The work actually performed by the employee during the course of the work week must, first and foremost, be examined and the amount of time the employee spends on such work, together with the employer's realistic expectations and the realistic requirements of the job, shall be considered in determining whether the employee satisfies this requirement.

(g) Such employee must also earn a monthly salary equivalent to no less than two (2) times the state minimum wage for full-time employment. Full–time is defined in Labor Code § 515(c) as 40 hours per week.

(3) _Professional Exemption._ A person employed in a professional capacity means any employee who meets all of the following requirements:

(a) Who is licensed or certified by the State of California and is primarily engaged in the practice of one of the following recognized professions: law, medicine, dentistry, optometry, architecture, engineering, teaching, or accounting; or

(b) Who is primarily engaged in an occupation commonly recognized as a learned or artistic profession. For the purposes of this subsection, "learned or artistic profession" means an employee who is primarily engaged in the performance of:

(i) Work requiring knowledge of an advanced type in a field or science or learning customarily acquired by a prolonged course of specialized intellectual instruction and study, as distinguished from a general academic education and from an apprenticeship, and from training in the performance of routine mental, manual, or physical processes or work that is an essential part of or necessarily incident to any of the above work; or

(ii) Work that is original and creative in character in a recognized field of artistic endeavor (as opposed to work which can be produced by a person endowed with general manual or intellectual ability and training), and the result of which depends primarily on the invention, imagination,

1502

or talent of the employee or work that is an essential part of or necessarily incident to any of the above work; and

(iii) Whose work is predominantly intellectual and varied in character (as opposed to routine mental, manual, mechanical, or physical work) and is of such character that the output produced or the result accomplished cannot be standardized in relation to a given period of time.

(c) Who customarily and regularly exercises discretion and independent judgment in the performance of duties set forth in subparagraphs (a) and (b).

(d) Who earns a monthly salary equivalent to no less than two (2) times the state minimum wage for full-time employment. Full–time employment is defined in Labor Code § 515 (c) as 40 hours per week.

(e) Subparagraph (b) above is intended to be construed in accordance with the following provisions of federal law as they existed as of the date of this Wage Order: 29 C.F.R. §§ 541.207, 541.301(a)–(d), 541.302, 541.306, 541.307, 541.308, and 541.310.

(f) Notwithstanding the provisions of this subparagraph, pharmacists employed to engage in the practice of pharmacy, and registered nurses employed to engage in the practice of nursing, shall not be considered exempt professional employees, nor shall they be considered exempt from coverage for the purposes of this subparagraph unless they individually meet the criteria established for exemption as executive or administrative employees.

(g) Subparagraph (f) above, shall not apply to the following advanced practice nurses shall:

(i) Certified nurse midwives who are primarily engaged in performing duties for which certification is required pursuant to Article 2.5 (commencing with Section 2746) of Chapter 6 of Division 2 of the Business and Professions Code.

(ii) Certified nurse anesthetists who are primarily engaged in performing duties for which certification is required pursuant to Article 7 (commencing with Section 2825) of Chapter 6 of Division 2 of the Business and Professions Code.

(iii) Certified nurse practitioners who are primarily engaged in performing duties for which certification is required pursuant to Article 8 (commencing with Section 2834) of Chapter 6 of Division 2 of the Business and Professions Code.

(iv) Nothing in this subparagraph shall exempt the occupations set forth in clauses (i), (ii), and (iii) from meeting the requirements of subsection 1(A)(3)(a)–(d), above.

(h) Except as provided in subparagraph (i), an employee in the computer software field who is paid on an hourly basis shall be exempt, if all of the following apply:

(i) The employee is primarily engaged in work that is intellectual or creative and that requires the exercise of discretion and independent judgment.

(ii) The employee is primarily engaged in duties that consist of one or more of the following:

-The application of systems analysis techniques and procedures, including consulting with users, to determine hardware, software, or system functional specifications.

-The design, development, documentation, analysis, creation, testing, or modification of computer systems or programs, including prototypes, based on and related to, user or system design specifications.

-The documentation, testing, creation, or modification of computer programs related to the design of software or hardware for computer operating systems.

(iii) The employee is highly skilled and is proficient in the theoretical and practical application of highly specialized information to computer systems analysis, programming, and software engineering. A job title shall not be determinative of the applicability of this exemption.

(iv) The employee's hourly rate of pay is not less than forty-one dollars ($41.00). The Division of Labor Statistics and Research shall adjust this pay rate on October 1 of each year to be effective on January 1 of the following year by an amount equal to the percentage increase in the California Consumer Price Index for Urban Wage Earners and Clerical Workers.[1]

(i) The exemption provided in subparagraph (h) does not apply to an employee if any of the following apply:

(i) The employee is a trainee or employee in an entry-level position who is learning to become proficient in the theoretical and practical application of highly specialized information to computer systems analysis, programming, and software engineering.

(ii) The employee is in a computer-related occupation but has not attained the level of skill and expertise necessary to work independently and without close supervision.

(iii) The employee is engaged in the operation of computers or in the manufacture, repair, or maintenance of computer hardware and related equipment.

(iv) The employee is an engineer, drafter, machinist, or other professional whose work is highly dependent upon or facilitated by the use of computers and computer software programs and who is skilled in computer-aided design software, including CAD/CAM, but who is not in a computer systems analysis or programming occupation.

(v) The employee is a writer engaged in writing material, including box labels, product descriptions, documentation, promotional material, setup and installation instructions, and other similar written information, either for print or for on screen media or who writes or provides content material intended to be read by customers, subscribers, or visitors to computer-related media such as the World Wide Web or CD–ROMs.

(vi) The employee is engaged in any of the activities set forth in subparagraph (h) for the purpose of creating imagery for effects used in the motion picture, television, or theatrical industry.

(B) Except as provided in sections 1, 2, 4, 10, and 20, the provisions of this Order shall not apply to any employees directly employed by the State or any political subdivision thereof, including any city, county, or special district.

(C) The provisions of this Order shall not apply to outside salespersons.

(D) Provisions of this Order shall not apply to any individual who is the parent, spouse, child, or legally adopted child of the employer.

(E) The provisions of this Order shall not apply to any individual participating in a national service program, such as Ameri–Corps, carried out using assistance provided under Section 12571 of Title 42 of the United States Code. (See Stats. 2000, ch. 365, amending Labor Code § 1171.)

2. Definitions

(A) An "alternative workweek schedule" means any regularly scheduled workweek requiring an employee to work more than eight (8) hours in a 24–hour period.

(B) "Commission" means the Industrial Welfare Commission of the State of California.

(C) "Division" means the Division of Labor Standards Enforcement of the State of California.

(D) "Employ" means to engage, suffer, or permit to work.

(E) "Employee" means any person employed by an employer.

(F) "Employer" means any person as defined in Section 18 of the Labor Code, who directly or indirectly, or through an agent or any other person, employs or exercises control over the wages, hours, or working conditions of any person.

(G) "Hours worked" means the time during which an employee is subject to the control of an employer, and includes all the time the employee is suffered or permitted to work, whether or not required to do so.

(H) "Industries Preparing Agricultural Products for Market, on the Farm" means any operation performed in a permanently fixed structure or establishment on the farm or on a moving packing plant on the farm for the purpose of preparing agricultural, horticultural, egg, poultry, meat, seafood, rabbit, or dairy products for market when such operations are done on the premises owned or operated by the same employer who produced the products referred to herein and includes all operations incidental thereto.

(I) "Minors" means, for the purpose of this Order, any person under the age of 18 years.

(J) "Outside Salesperson" means any person, 18 years of age or over, who customarily and regularly works more than half the working time away from the employer's place of business selling tangible or intangible items or obtaining orders or contracts for products, services or use of facilities.

(K) "Primarily" as used in Section 1, Applicability, means more than one-half the employee's work time.

(L) "Shift" means designated hours of work by an employee, with a designated beginning time and ending time.

(M) "Split shift" means a work schedule which is interrupted by non-paid non-working periods established by the employer, other than bona fide rest or meal periods.

(N) "Teaching" means, for the purpose of Section 1 of this Order, the profession of teaching under a certificate from the Commission for Teacher Preparation and Licensing or teaching in an accredited college or university.

(O) "Wages" includes all amounts for labor performed by employees of every description, whether the amount is fixed or ascertained by the standard of time, task, piece, commission basis, or other method of calculation.

(P) "Workday" and "day" mean any consecutive 24–hour period beginning at the same time each calendar day.

(Q) "Workweek" and "week" mean any seven (7) consecutive days, starting with the same calendar day each week. "Workweek" is a fixed and regularly recurring period of 168 hours, seven (7) consecutive 24–hour periods.

3. Hours and Days of Work

(A) *Daily Overtime—General Provisions*

(1) The following overtime provisions are applicable to employees 18 years of age or over and to employees 16 or 17 years of age who are not required by law to attend school and are not otherwise prohibited by law from engaging in the subject work. Such employees shall not be employed more than eight (8) hours in any workday or more than 40 hours in any workweek unless the employee receives one and one-half (1 ½) times such employee's regular rate of pay for all hours worked over 40 hours in the workweek. Eight (8) hours of labor constitutes a day's work. Employment beyond eight (8) hours in any workday or more than six (6) days in any workweek is permissible under the following conditions:

(a) Any work by an employee in excess of 72 hours in any one workweek shall be on a voluntary basis. No employee shall be discharged or in any other manner discriminated against or refusing to work in excess of 72 hours in any one workweek; and

(2) Overtime hours shall be compensated at:

(a) One and one-half (1 ½) times the employee's regular rate of pay for all hours worked in excess of eight (8) hours up to and including 12 hours in any workday, and for the first eight (8) hours worked on the seventh (7th) consecutive day of work in a workweek; and

(b) Double the employee's regular rate of pay for all hours worked in excess of 12 hours in any workday and

for all hours worked in excess of eight (8) hours on the seventh (7th) consecutive day of work in a workweek.

(c) The overtime rate of compensation required to be paid to a nonexempt full-time salaried employee shall be computed by using the employee's regular hourly salary as one fortieth (1/40) of the employee's weekly salary.

(B) *Alternative Workweek Schedules*

(1) No employer shall be deemed to have violated the daily overtime provisions by instituting, pursuant to the election procedures set forth in this wage order, a regularly scheduled alternative workweek schedule of not more than ten (10) hours per day within a 40 hour workweek without the payment of an overtime rate of compensation. All work performed in any workday beyond the schedule established by the agreement up to 12 hours a day or beyond 40 hours per week shall be paid at one and one-half (1 ½) times the employee's regular rate of pay. All work performed in excess of 12 hours per day and any work in excess of eight (8) hours on those days worked beyond the regularly scheduled number of workdays established by the alternative workweek agreement shall be paid at double the employee's regular rate of pay. Any alternative workweek agreement adopted pursuant to this section shall provide for not less than four (4) hours of work in any shift. Nothing in this section shall prohibit an employer, at the request of the employee, to substitute one day of work for another day of the same length in the shift provided by the alternative workweek agreement on an occasional basis to meet the personal needs of the employee without the payment of overtime. No hours paid at either one and one-half (1 ½) or double the regular rate of pay shall be included in determining when 40 hours have been worked for the purpose of computing overtime compensation.

(2) Any agreement adopted pursuant to this section shall provide not less than two consecutive days off within each workweek.

(3) If an employer, whose employees have adopted an alternative workweek agreement permitted by this order requires an employee to work fewer hours than those that are regularly scheduled by the agreement, the employer shall pay the employee overtime compensation at a rate of one and one-half (1 ½) times the employee's regular rate of pay for all hours worked in excess of eight (8) hours, and double the employee's regular rate of pay for all hours worked in excess of 12 hours for the day the employee is required to work the reduced hours.

(4) An employer shall not reduce an employee's regular rate of hourly pay as a result of the adoption, repeal or nullification of an alternative workweek schedule.

(5) An employer shall explore any available reasonable alternative means of accommodating the religious belief or observance of an affected employee that conflicts with an adopted alternative workweek schedule, in the manner provided by subdivision (j) of Section 12940 of the Government Code.

(6) An employer shall make a reasonable effort to find a work schedule not to exceed eight (8) hours in a workday, in order to accommodate any affected employee who was eligible to vote in an election authorized by this Section and who is unable to work the alternative workweek schedule established as the result of that election.

(7) An employer shall be permitted, but not required, to provide a work schedule not to exceed eight (8) hours in a workday to accommodate any employee who is hired after the date of the election and who is unable to work the alternative workweek schedule established by the election.

(8) Arrangements adopted in a secret ballot election held pursuant to this order prior to 1998, or under the rules in effect prior to 1998, and before the performance of the work, shall remain valid after July 1, 2000 provided that the results of the election are reported by the employer to the Division of Labor Statistics and Research by January 1, 2001, in accordance with the requirements of Section C below (Election Procedures). If an employee was voluntarily working an alternative workweek schedule of not more than ten (10) hours a day as of July 1, 1999 that alternative workweek schedule was based on an individual agreement made after January 1, 1998 between the employee and employer, and the employee submitted, and the employer approved, a written request on or before May 30, 2000 to continue the agreement, the employee may continue to work that alternative workweek schedule without payment of an overtime rate of compensation for the hours provided in the agreement. The employee may revoke his or her voluntary authorization to continue such a schedule with 30 days written notice to the employer. New arrangements can only be entered into pursuant to the provisions of this section.

(C) *Election Procedures*

Election procedures for the adoption and repeal of alternative workweek schedules require the following:

(1) Each proposal for an alternative workweek schedule shall be in the form of a written agreement proposed by the employer. The proposed agreement must designate a regularly scheduled alternative workweek in which the specified number of work days and work hours are regularly recurring. The actual days worked within that alternative workweek schedule need not be specified. The employer may propose a single work schedule that would become the standard schedule for workers in the work unit, or a menu of work schedule options, from which each employee in the unit would be entitled to choose. If the employer proposes a menu of work schedule options, the employee may, with the approval of the employer, move from one menu option to another.

(2) In order to be valid, the proposed alternative workweek schedule must be adopted in a secret ballot election, before the performance of work, by at least a two-thirds (2/03) vote of the affected employees in the work unit. The election shall be held during regular working hours at the employees' work site. For purposes of this subsection, "affected employees in the work unit" may include all employees in a readily identifiable work unit, such as a division, a department, a job classification, a shift, a separate physical location, or a recognized subdivision of any such work unit. A work unit may consist of an individual employee as long as the criteria for an identifiable work unit in this subsection is met.

(3) Prior to the secret ballot vote, any employer who proposed to institute an alternative workweek schedule shall have made a disclosure in writing to the affected employees, including the effects of the proposed arrangement on the employees' wages, hours, and benefits. Such a disclosure shall include meeting(s), duly noticed, held at least 14 days prior to voting, for the specific purpose of discussing the effects of the alternative workweek schedule. An employer shall provide that disclosure in a non–English language, as well as in English, if at least five (5) percent of the affected employees primarily speak that non–English language. The employer shall mail the written disclosure to employees who do not attend the meeting. Failure to comply with this paragraph shall make the election null and void.

(4) Any election to establish or repeal an alternative workweek schedule shall be held at the work site of the affected employees. The employer shall bear the costs of conducting any election held pursuant to this section. Upon a complaint by an affected employee, and after an investigation by the Labor Commissioner, the Labor Commissioner may require the employer to select a neutral third party to conduct the election.

(5) Any type of alternative workweek schedule that is authorized by the Labor Code may be repealed by the affected employees. Upon a petition of one-third (1/03) of the affected employees, a new secret ballot election shall be held and a two-thirds (2/03) vote of the affected employees shall be required to reverse the alternative workweek schedule. The election to repeal the alternative workweek schedule shall be held not more than 30 days after the petition is submitted to the employer, except that the election shall be held not less than 12 months after the date that the same group of employees voted in an election held to adopt or repeal an alternative workweek schedule. The election shall take place during regular working hours at the employees' work site. If the alternative workweek schedule is revoked, the employer shall comply within 60 days. Upon proper showing of undue hardship, the Division of Labor Standards Enforcement may grant an extension of time for compliance.

(6) Only secret ballots may be cast by affected employees in the work unit at any election held pursuant to this Section. The results of any election conducted pursuant to this Section shall be reported by the employer to the Division of Labor Statistics and Research within 30 days after the results are final, and the report of election results shall be a public document. The report shall include the final tally of the vote, the size of the unit, and the nature of the business of the employer.

(7) Employees affected by a change in the work hours resulting from the adoption of an alternative workweek schedule may not be required to work those new work hours for at least 30 days after the announcement of the final results of the election.

(8) Employers shall not intimidate or coerce employees to vote either in support of or in opposition to a proposed alternative workweek. No employees shall be discharged or discriminated against for expressing opinions concerning the alternative workweek election or for opposing or supporting its adoption or repeal. However, nothing in this section shall prohibit an employer from expressing his/her position concerning that alternative workweek to the affected employees. A violation of this paragraph shall be subject to Labor Code section 98 *et seq.*

(D) One and one-half (1 ½) times a minor's regular rate of pay shall be paid for all work over 40 hours in any workweek except that minors 16 and 17 years old who are not required by law to attend school and may therefore be employed for the same hours as an adult are subject to subsection (A) or (B), and (C) above.

(**Violations of Child Labor Laws** are subject to civil penalties of from $500 to $10,000 as well as to criminal penalties. Refer to California Labor Code Sections 1285 to 1312 and 1390 to 1399 for additional restrictions on the employment of minors and for descriptions of criminal and civil penalties for violation of the child labor laws. Employers should ask school districts about any required work permits.)

(E) An employee may be employed on seven (7) workdays in one workweek when the total hours of employment during such workweek do not exceed 30 and the total hours of employment in any one workday thereof do not exceed six (6).

(F) If, during any workday an employer declares a work recess of one-half (1/02) hour or more, other than a meal period, and the employer notifies the employees of the time to report back for work and permits them to leave the premises, such recess need not be treated as hours worked provided that there shall not be more than two (2) such recess periods within one shift and the total duration does not exceed two (2) hours. Work stoppages of less than one-half (1/02) hour may not be deducted from hours worked.

(G) If a meal period occurs on a shift beginning or ending at or between the hours of 10 p.m. and 6 a.m., facilities shall be available for securing hot food and drink or for heating food or drink, and a suitable sheltered place shall be provided in which to consume such food or drink.

(H) The provisions of Labor Code §§ 551 and 552 regarding one (1) day's rest in seven (7) shall not be construed to prevent an accumulation of days of rest when the nature of the employment reasonably requires the employee to work seven (7) or more consecutive days; provided, however, that in each calendar month, the

employee shall receive the equivalent of one (1) day's rest in seven (7).

(I) The provisions of this subsection are not applicable to employees whose hours of service are regulated by:

(1) The United States Department of Transportation Code of Federal Regulations, title 49, sections 395.1 to 395.13, Hours of Service of Drivers, or

(2) Title 13 of the California Code of Regulations, subchapter 6.5, section 1200 and the following sections, regulating hours of drivers.

(J) Except as provided in subsection (A)(1) and subsections (D) and (H), this section shall not apply to any employee covered by a valid collective bargaining agreement if the agreement expressly provides for the wages, hours of work, and working conditions of the employees, and if the agreement provides premium wage rates for all overtime hours worked and a regular hourly rate of pay for those employees of not less than 30 percent more than the state minimum wage.

(K) Notwithstanding subsection (J) above, where the employer and a labor organization representing employees of the employer have entered into a valid collective bargaining agreement pertaining to the hours of work of the employees, the requirement regarding the equivalent of one (1) day's rest in seven (7) (see section (H) above) shall apply, unless the agreement expressly provides otherwise.

(L) If an employer approves a written request of an employee to make-up work time that is or would be lost as a result of a personal obligation of the employee, the hours of that make-up work time, if performed in the same workweek in which the work time was lost, may not be counted toward computing the total number of hours worked in a day for purposes of the overtime requirements, except for hours in excess of 11 hours of work in one (1) day or 40 hours of work in one (1) workweek. If an employee knows in advance that he or she will be requesting make-up time for a personal obligation that will recur at a fixed time over a succession of weeks, the employee may request to make-up work time for up to four (4) weeks in advance; provided, however, that the make-up work must be performed in the same week that the work time was lost. An employee shall provide a signed written request for each occasion that the employee makes a request to make-up work time pursuant to this subsection. While an employer may inform an employee of this make-up time option, the employer is prohibited from encouraging or otherwise soliciting an employee to request the employer's approval to take personal time off and make-up the work hours within the same workweek pursuant to this subsection.

4. Minimum Wages

(A) Every employer shall pay to each employee wages not less than seven dollars and fifty cents ($7.50) per hour for all hours worked, effective January 1, 2007, and not less than eight dollars ($8.00) per hour for all hours worked, effective January 1, 2008, except:

Learners. Employees during their first 160 hours of employment in occupations in which they have no previous similar or related experience, may be paid not less than 85 percent of the minimum wage rounded to the nearest nickel.

(B) Every employer shall pay to each employee, on the established payday for the period involved, not less than the applicable minimum wage for all hours worked in the payroll period, whether the remuneration is measured by time, piece, commission, or otherwise.

(C) When an employee works a split shift, one (1) hour's pay at the minimum wage shall be paid in addition to the minimum wage for that workday, except when the employee resides at the place of employment.

(D) The provisions of this section shall not apply to apprentices regularly indentured under the State Division of Apprenticeship Standards.

5. Reporting Time Pay

(A) Each workday an employee is required to report for work and does report, but is not put to work or is furnished less than half said employee's usual or scheduled day's work, the employee shall be paid for half the usual or scheduled day's work, but in no event for less than two (2) hours nor more than four (4) hours, at the employee's regular rate of pay, which shall not be less than the minimum wage.

(B) If an employee is required to report for work a second time in any one workday and is furnished less than two (2) hours of work on the second reporting, said employee shall be paid for two (2) hours at the employee's regular rate of pay, which shall not be less than the minimum wage.

(C) The foregoing reporting time pay provisions are not applicable when:

(1) Operations cannot commence or continue due to threats to employees or property; or when recommended by civil authorities; or

(2) Public utilities fail to supply electricity, water, or gas, or there is a failure in the public utilities, or sewer system; or

(3) The interruption of work is caused by an Act of God or other cause not within the employer's control.

(D) This section shall not apply to an employee on paid standby status who is called to perform assigned work at a time other than the employee's scheduled reporting time.

6. Licenses for Disabled Workers

(A) A license may be issued by the Division authorizing employment of a person whose earning capacity is impaired by physical disability or mental deficiency at less than the minimum wage. Such licenses shall be granted only upon joint application of employer and employee and employee's representative if any.

(B) A special license may be issued to a nonprofit organization such as a sheltered workshop or rehabilitation facility fixing special minimum rates to enable the employment of such persons without requiring individual licenses of such employees.

(C) All such licenses and special licenses shall be renewed on a yearly basis or more frequently at the discretion of the Division.

(See California Labor Code, Sections 1191 and 1191.5.)

7. Records

(A) Every employer shall keep accurate information with respect to each employee including the following:

(1) Full name, home address, occupation and social security number.

(2) Birth date, if under 18 years, and designation as a minor.

(3) Time records showing when the employee begins and ends each work period. Meal periods, split shift intervals and total daily hours worked shall also be recorded. Meal periods during which operations cease and authorized rest periods need not be recorded.

(4) Total wages paid each payroll period, including value of board, lodging, or other compensation actually furnished to the employee.

(5) Total hours worked in the payroll period and applicable rates of pay. This information shall be made readily available to the employee upon reasonable request.

(6) When a piece rate or incentive plan is in operation, piece rates or an explanation of the incentive plan formula shall be provided to employees. An accurate production record shall be maintained by the employer.

(B) Every employer shall semimonthly or at the time of each payment of wages furnish each employee, either as a detachable part of the check, draft, or voucher paying the employee's wages, or separately, an itemized statement in writing showing: (1) all deductions; (2) the inclusive dates of the period for which the employee is paid; (3) the name of the employee or the employee's social security number; and (4) the name of the employer, provided all deductions made on written orders of the employee may be aggregated and shown as one item.

(C) All required records shall be in the English language and in ink or other indelible form, properly dated, showing month, day and year, and shall be kept on file by the employer for at least three years at the place of employment or at a central location within the State of California. An employee's records shall be available for inspection by the employee upon reasonable request.

(D) Clocks shall be provided in all major work areas or within reasonable distance thereto insofar as practicable

8. Cash Shortage and Breakage.
No employer shall make any deduction from the wage or require any reimbursement from an employee for any cash shortage, breakage, or loss of equipment, unless it can be shown that the shortage, breakage, or loss is caused by a

dishonest or willful act, or by the gross negligence of the employee.

9. Uniforms and Equipment

(A) When uniforms are required by the employer to be worn by the employee as a condition of employment, such uniforms shall be provided and maintained by the employer. The term "uniform" includes wearing apparel and accessories of distinctive design or color.

Note: This section shall not apply to protective apparel regulated by the Occupational Safety and Health Standards Board.

(B) When tools or equipment are required by the employer or are necessary to the performance of a job, such tools and equipment shall be provided and maintained by the employer, except that an employee whose wages are at least two (2) times the minimum wage provided herein may be required to provide and maintain hand tools and equipment customarily required by the trade or craft. This subsection (B) shall not apply to apprentices regularly indentured under the State Division of Apprenticeship Standards.

Note: This section shall not apply to protective equipment and safety devices on tools regulated by the Occupational Safety and Health Standards Board.

(C) A reasonable deposit may be required as security for the return of the items furnished by the employer under provisions of subsections (A) and (B) of this section upon issuance of a receipt to the employee for such deposit. Such deposits shall be made pursuant to Section 400 and following of the Labor Code or an employer with the prior written authorization of the employee may deduct from the employee's last check the cost of an item furnished pursuant to (A) and (B) above in the event said item is not returned. No deduction shall be made at any time for normal wear and tear. All items furnished by the employer shall be returned by the employee upon completion of the job.

10. Meals and Lodging

(A) "Meal" means an adequate, well-balanced serving of a variety of wholesome, nutritious foods.

(B) "Lodging" means living accommodations available to the employee for full-time occupancy which are adequate, decent, and sanitary according to usual and customary standards. Employees shall not be required to share a bed.

(C) Meals or lodging may not be credited against the minimum wage without a voluntary written agreement between the employer and the employee. When credit for meals or lodging is used to meet part of the employer's minimum wage obligation, the amounts so credited may not be more than the following:

Effective	January 1, 2007	January 1, 2008
Lodging:		
Room occupied alone	$35.27 per week	$37.63 per week
Room shared	$29.11 per week	$31.06 per week

Effective	January 1, 2007	January 1, 2008
Apartment—two–thirds (2/03) of the ordinary rental value, and in no event more than	$423.51 per month	$451.89 per month
Where a couple are both employed by the employer, two-thirds (2/03) of the ordinary rental value, and in no event more than	$626.49 per month	$668.46 per month
Meals:		
Breakfast	$2.72	$2.90
Lunch	$3.72	$3.97
Dinner	$5.00	$5.34

(D) Meals evaluated as part of the minimum wage must be bona fide meals consistent with the employee's work shift. Deductions shall not be made for meals not received nor lodging not used.

(E) If, as a condition of employment, the employee must live at the place of employment or occupy quarters owned or under the control of the employer, then the employer may not charge rent in excess of the values listed herein.

11. Meal Periods

(A) No employer shall employ any person for a work period of more than five (5) hours without a meal period of not less than 30 minutes, except that when a work period of not more than six (6) hours will complete the day's work the meal period may be waived by mutual consent of the employer and employee.

(B) An employer may not employ an employee for a work period of more than ten (10) hours per day without providing the employee with a second meal period of not less than 30 minutes, except that if the total hours worked is no more than 12 hours, the second meal period may be waived by mutual consent of the employer and the employee only if the first meal period was not waived.

(C) Unless the employee is relieved of all duty during a 30 minute meal period, the meal period shall be considered an "on duty" meal period and counted as time worked. An "on duty" meal period shall be permitted only when the nature of the work prevents an employee from being relieved of all duty and when by written agreement between the parties an on-the-job paid meal period is agreed to. The written agreement shall state that the employee may, in writing, revoke the agreement at any time.

(D) If an employer fails to provide an employee a meal period in accordance with the applicable provisions of this Order, the employer shall pay the employee one (1) hour of pay at the employee's regular rate of compensation for each work day that the meal period was not provided.

(E) In all places of employment where employees are required to eat on the premises, a suitable place for that purpose shall be designated.

12. Rest Periods

(A) Every employer shall authorize and permit all employees to take rest periods, which insofar as practicable shall be in the middle of each work period. The authorized rest period time shall be based on the total hours worked daily at the rate of ten (10) minutes net rest time per four (4) hours or major fraction thereof. However, a rest period need not be authorized for employees whose total daily work time is less than three and one-half (3 ½) hours. Authorized rest period time shall be counted as hours worked for which there shall be no deduction from wages.

(B) If an employer fails to provide an employee a rest period in accordance with the applicable provisions of this Order, the employer shall pay the employee one (1) hour of pay at the employee's regular rate of compensation for each work day that the rest period is not provided.

13. Change Rooms and Resting Facilities

(A) Employers shall provide suitable lockers, closets, or equivalent for the safekeeping of employees' outer clothing during working hours, and when required, for their work clothing during non-working hours. When the occupation requires a change of clothing, change rooms or equivalent space shall be provided in order that employees may change their clothing in reasonable privacy and comfort. These rooms or spaces may be adjacent to but shall be separate from toilet rooms and shall be kept clean.

Note: This section shall not apply to change rooms and storage facilities regulated by the Occupational Safety and Health Standards Board.

(B) Suitable resting facilities shall be provided in an area separate from the toilet rooms and shall be available to employees during work hours.

14. Seats

(A) All working employees shall be provided with suitable seats when the nature of the work reasonably permits the use of seats.

(B) When employees are not engaged in the active duties of their employment and the nature of the work requires standing, an adequate number of suitable seats shall be placed in reasonable proximity to the work area and employees shall be permitted to use such seats when it does not interfere with the performance of their duties.

15. Temperature

(A) The temperature maintained in each work area shall provide reasonable comfort consistent with industry-wide standards for the nature of the process and the work performed.

(B) If excessive heat or humidity is created by the work process, the employer shall take all feasible means to reduce such excessive heat or humidity to a degree providing reasonable comfort. Where the nature of the employment requires a temperature of less than 60° F., a heated room shall be provided to which employees may retire for warmth, and such room shall be maintained at not less than 68°.

(C) A temperature of not less than 68° shall be maintained in the toilet rooms, resting rooms, and change rooms during hours of use.

(D) Federal and State energy guidelines shall prevail over any conflicting provision of this section.

16. Elevators.
Adequate elevator, escalator or similar service consistent with industry-wide standards for the nature of the process and the work performed shall be provided when employees are employed four floors or more above or below ground level.

17. Exemptions.
If, in the opinion of the Division after due investigation, it is found that the enforcement of any provision contained in Section 7, Records; Section 12, Rest Periods; Section 13, Change Rooms and Resting Facilities; Section 14, Seats; Section 15, Temperature; or Section 16, Elevators, would not materially affect the welfare or comfort of employees and would work an undue hardship on the employer, exemption may be made at the discretion of the Division. Such exemptions shall be in writing to be effective and may be revoked after reasonable notice is given in writing. Application for exemption shall be made by the employer or by the employee and/or the employee's representative to the Division in writing. A copy of the application shall be posted at the place of employment at the time the application is filed with the Division.

18. Filing Reports.
(See California Labor Code, Section 1174(a))

19. Inspections.
(See California Labor Code, Section 1174)

20. Penalties.
(See Labor Code, Section 1199)

(A) In addition to any other civil penalties provided by law, any employer or any other person acting on behalf of the employer who violates, or causes to be violated, the provisions of this order, shall be subject to the civil penalty of:

(1) Initial Violation $50.00 for each underpaid employee for each pay period during which the employee was underpaid in addition to the amount which is sufficient to recover unpaid wages.

(2) Subsequent Violations $100.00 for each underpaid employee for each pay period during which the employee was underpaid in addition to an amount which is sufficient to recover unpaid wages.

(3) The affected employee shall receive payment of all wages recovered.

(B) The Labor Commissioner may also issue citations pursuant to California Labor Code § 1197.1 for non-payment of wages for overtime work in violation of this order.

21. Separability.
If the application of any provision of this Order, or any section, subsection, subdivision, sentence, clause, phrase, word, or portion of this Order should be held invalid or unconstitutional or unauthorized or prohibited by statute, the remaining provisions thereof shall not be affected thereby, but shall continue to be given full force and effect as if the part so held invalid or unconstitutional had not been included herein.

22. Posting of Order. Every employer shall keep a copy of this Order posted in an area frequented by employees where it may be easily read during the work day. Where the location of work or other conditions make this impractical, every employer shall keep a copy of this Order and make it available to every employee upon request.

[1] Pursuant to Labor Code section 515.5, subdivision (a)(4), the Division of Labor Statistics and Research, Department of Industrial Relations, has adjusted the minimum hourly rate of pay specified in this subdivision to be $49.77, effective January 1, 2007. This hourly rate of pay is adjusted on October 1 of each year to be effective on January 1, of the following year, and may be obtained at www.dir.ca.gov/IWC or by mail from the Department of Industrial Relations.

Publisher's Notes

See Industrial Welfare Com. v. Superior Court (1980) 27 Cal.3d 690, 613 P.2d 579, 166 Cal.Rptr. 331 (validity of 1980 order).

Research References

See notes following listing of Wage Orders.

Please Post With This Side Showing
OFFICIAL NOTICE
Effective January 1, 2001 as amended
Sections 4(A) and 10(C) amended and republished by the Department of Industrial Relations, effective January 1, 2007, pursuant to AB 1835, Chapter 230, Statutes of 2006
INDUSTRIAL WELFARE COMMISSION
ORDER NO. 14–2001
REGULATING
WAGES, HOURS AND WORKING CONDITIONS IN THE
AGRICULTURAL OCCUPATIONS

TAKE NOTICE: To employers and representatives of persons working in industries and occupations in the State of California:

The Department of Industrial Relations amends and republishes the minimum wage and meals and lodging credits in the Industrial Welfare Commission's Orders as a result of legislation enacted (AB 1835, Ch. 230, Stats of 2006, adding sections 1182.12 and 1182.13 to the California Labor Code.) The amendments and republishing make no other changes to the IWC's Orders.

1. Applicability of Order. This order shall apply to all persons employed in an agricultural occupation whether paid on a time, piece rate, commission, or other basis, except that:

(A) No provision of this order shall apply to any employee who is engaged in work which is primarily intellectual, managerial, or creative, and which requires exercise of discretion and independent judgment, and for which the remuneration is not less than two (2) times the monthly state minimum wage for full-time employment.

(B) No provision of this order shall apply to any individual who is the parent, spouse, child, or legally adopted child of the employer.

(C) Section 5 of this order shall not apply to any employer who employs fewer than five (5) persons covered by this order. If at any one time during a calendar year an employer has five (5) or more employees covered by this order, every provision of this order, including Section 5, Reporting Time Pay, shall apply to that employer throughout that calendar year.

(D) No provision of this order shall apply to any employee covered by Order No. 8 or Order No. 13, relating to industries handling products after harvest.

(E) The provisions of this order shall not apply to any individual participating in a national service program, such as Ameri–Corps, carried out using assistance provided under Section 12571 of Title 42 of the United States Code. (See Stats. 2000, ch. 365, amending Labor Code Section 1171.)

(F) Sections 3, 4(A)–(D), 5, 6, 9, 11, 12, and 13 of this order shall not apply to an employee engaged to work as a "sheepherder," as that occupation is defined in Section 2 (N). Otherwise, this order, including Section 4 (A), shall apply to any workweek during which a sheepherder employee is engaged in any non-sheepherding agricultural or other work.

(G) Section 3 of this order shall not apply to an employee licensed pursuant to Article 3 (commencing with Section 7850) of Chapter 1 of Part 3 of Division 6 of the Fish and Game Code who serves as a crew member on a commercial fishing vessel.

2. Definitions

(A) "Commission" means the Industrial Welfare Commission of the State of California.

(B) "Division" means the Division of Labor Standards Enforcement of the State of California.

(C) "Employ" means to engage, suffer, or permit to work.

(D) "Employed in an agricultural occupation" means any of the following described occupations:

(1) The preparation, care, and treatment of farm land, pipeline, or ditches, including leveling for agricultural purposes, plowing, discing, and fertilizing the soil;

(2) The sowing and planting of any agricultural or horticultural commodity;

(3) The care of any agricultural or horticultural commodity; as used in this subdivision, "care" includes but is not limited to cultivation, irrigation, weed control, thinning, heating, pruning, or tying, fumigating, spraying, and dusting;

(4) The harvesting of any agricultural or horticultural commodity, including but not limited to picking, cutting, threshing, mowing, knocking off, field chopping, bunching, baling, balling, field packing, and placing in field containers or in the vehicle in which the commodity will be hauled, and transportation on the farm or to a place of first processing or distribution;

(5) The assembly and storage of any agricultural or horticultural commodity, including but not limited to, loading, road siding, banking, stacking, binding, and piling;

(6) The raising, feeding and management of livestock, fur bearing animals, poultry, fish, mollusks, and insects, including but not limited to herding, housing, hatching, milking, shearing, handling eggs, and extracting honey;

(7) The harvesting of fish, as defined by Section 45 of the Fish and Game Code, for commercial sale;

(8) The conservation, improvement or maintenance of such farm and its tools and equipment.

(E) "Employee" means any person employed by an employer.

(F) "Employer" means any person as defined in Section 18 of the Labor Code, who directly or indirectly, or through an agent or any other person, employs or exercises control over the wages, hours, or working conditions of any person.

(G) "Hours worked" means the time during which an employee is subject to the control of an employer, and includes all the time the employee is suffered or permitted to work, whether or not required to do so.

(H) "Minor" means, for the purpose of this order, any person under the age of 18 years.

(I) "Non–sheepherding work" means any work except the work defined in Section 2(N) below.

(J) "Open range sheepherding" means, generally, sheepherding on land that is not cultivated, but produces native forage ("browse" or herbaceous food that is available to livestock or game animals) for animal consumption, and includes land that is re-vegetated naturally or artificially to provide forage cover that is managed like range vegetation. The range may be on private, federal, or state land. Typically, the land is not only non-cultivated, but not suitable for cultivation because it is rocky, thin, semiarid, or otherwise poor. Also, many acres of range land are required to graze one animal unit

(five sheep) for one month. By its very nature, open range sheepherding is conducted over wide expanses of land, such as thousands of acres.

(K) "Outside salesperson" means any person, 18 years of age or over, who customarily and regularly works more than half the working time away from the employer's place of business selling tangible or intangible items or obtaining orders or contracts for products, services or use of facilities.

(L) "Piece rate basis" is a method of payment based on units of production or a fraction thereof.

(M) "Primarily" as used in Section 1, Applicability, means more than one-half the employee's work time.

(N) "Sheepherder" means any individual who is employed to do any of the following: tend flocks of sheep grazing on range or pasture; move sheep to and about an area assigned for grazing; prevent sheep from wandering or becoming lost, or using trained dogs to round up strays and protect sheep against predators and the eating of poisonous plants; assist in the lambing, docking, and shearing of sheep; provide water or feed supplementary rations to sheep; or perform the work of a sheepherder pursuant to an approved job order filed under the provisions of Section 101(a)(15)(H)(ii)(a) of the federal Immigration and Nationality Act (commonly referred to as the "H–2A" program (see 8 U.S.C. Section 1101 et seq.), or any successor provisions.

(O) "Shift" means designated hours of work by an employee, with a designated beginning time and quitting time.

(P) "Split shift" means a work schedule which, is interrupted by non-paid non-working periods established by the employer, other than bona fide rest or meal periods.

(Q) "Wages" includes all amounts for labor performed by employees of every description, whether the amount is fixed or ascertained by the standard of time, task, piece, commission basis, or other method of calculation.

(R) "Workday" means any consecutive 24 hours beginning at the same time each calendar day.

(S) "Workweek" means any seven (7) consecutive days, starting with the same calendar day each week. "Workweek" is a fixed and regularly recurring period of 168 hours, seven (7) consecutive 24–hour periods.

3. Hours and Days of Work

(A) The following overtime provisions are applicable to employees 18 years of age or over and to employees 16 or 17 years of age who are not required by law to attend school: such employees shall not be employed more than ten (10) hours in any one workday or more than six (6) days in any workweek unless the employee receives one and one-half (1 ½) times such employee's regular rate of pay for all hours worked over ten (10) hours in any workday and for the first eight (8) hours on the seventh (7th) day of work and double the employee's regular rate of pay for all hours worked over eight (8) on the seventh (7th) day of work in the workweek.

(See California Labor Code, Sections 1391 and 1394)

(**Violations of Child Labor Laws** are subject to civil penalties of from $500 to $10,000 as well as to criminal penalties provided herein. Refer to California Labor Code Sections 1285 to 1312 and 1390 to 1399 for additional restrictions on the employment of minors. Employers should ask school districts about required work permits.)

(B) An employee may be employed on seven (7) workdays in one workweek with no overtime pay required when the total hours of employment during such work-week do not exceed 30 and the total hours of employment in any one workday thereof do not exceed six (6).

(C) The provisions of subsection (A) above shall not apply to an employee covered by this order during any week in which more than half of such employee's working time is devoted to performing the duties of an irrigator.

(D) The provisions of this section are not applicable to employees whose hours of service are regulated by:

(1) The United States Department of Transportation Code of Federal Regulations, Title 49, Sections 395.1 to 395.13, Hours of Service of Drivers; or

(2) Title 13 of the California Code of Regulations, subchapter 6.5, Section 1200 and following sections, regulating hours of drivers.

(E) This section shall not apply to any employee covered by a collective bargaining agreement if said agreement provides premium wage rates for overtime work and a cash wage rate for such employee of not less than one dollar ($1.00) per hour more than the minimum wage.

4. Minimum Wages

(A) Every employer shall pay to each employee wages not less than seven dollars and fifty cents ($7.50) per hour for all hours worked, effective January 1, 2007, and not less than eight dollars ($8.00) per hour for all hours worked, effective January 1, 2008, except:

Learners: Employees during their first 160 hours of employment in occupations in which they have no previous similar or related experience, may be paid not less than 85 percent of the minimum wage rounded to the nearest nickel.

(B) Every employer shall pay to each employee, on the established payday for the period involved, not less than the applicable minimum wage for all hours worked in the payroll period, whether the remuneration is measured by time, piece, commission, or otherwise.

(C) When an employee works a split shift, one (1) hour's pay at the minimum wage shall be paid in addition to the minimum wage for that workday, except when the employee resides at the place of employment.

(D) The provisions of this section shall not apply to apprentices regularly indentured under the State Division of Apprenticeship Standards.

(E) Effective July 1, 2001, the minimum wage for all sheepherders shall be $1,050.00 per month; effective July 1, 2002 the minimum wage for all sheepherders shall be $1,200.00 per month. Wages paid to sheepherders shall not be offset by meals or lodging provided by the employer.

5. Reporting Time Pay

(A) Each workday an employee is required to report for work and does report, but is not put to work or is furnished less than half said employee's usual or scheduled day's work, the employee shall be paid for half the usual or scheduled day's work, but in no event for less than two (2) hours nor more than four (4) hours, at the employee's regular rate of pay, which shall not be less than the minimum wage.

(B) If an employee is required to report for work a second time in any one workday and is furnished less than two (2) hours of work on the second reporting, said employee shall be paid for two (2) hours at the employee's regular rate of pay, which shall not be less than the minimum wage.

(C) The foregoing reporting time pay provisions are not applicable when:

(1) Operations cannot commence or continue due to threats to employees or property; or when recommended by civil authorities; or

(2) Public utilities fail to supply electricity, water, or gas, or there is a failure in the public utilities, or sewer system; or

(3) The interruption of work is caused by an Act of God or other cause not within the employer's control.

(D) This section shall not apply to an employee on paid standby status who is called to perform assigned work at a time other than the employee's scheduled reporting time.

6. Licenses for Disabled Workers

(A) A license may be issued by the Division authorizing employment of a person whose earning capacity is impaired by physical disability or mental deficiency at less than the minimum wage. Such licenses shall be granted only upon joint application of employer and employee and employee's representative if any.

(B) A special license may be issued to a nonprofit organization such as a sheltered workshop or rehabilitation facility fixing special minimum rates to enable the employment of such persons without requiring individual licenses of such employees.

(C) All such licenses and special licenses shall be renewed on a yearly basis or more frequently at the discretion of the Division.

(See California Labor Code, Sections 1191 and 1191.5)

7. Records

(A) Every employer shall keep accurate information with respect to each employee including the following:

(1) Full name, home address, occupation and social security number.

(2) Birth date, if under 18 years, and designation as a minor.

(3) Time records showing when the employee begins and ends each work period. Meal periods, split shift intervals and total daily hours worked shall also be recorded. Meal periods during which, operations cease and authorized rest periods need not be recorded.

(4) Total wages paid each payroll period, including value of board, lodging, or other compensation actually furnished to the employee.

(5) Total hours worked in the payroll period and applicable rates of pay. This information shall be made readily available to the employee upon reasonable request.

(6) When a piece rate or incentive plan is in operation, piece rates or an explanation of the incentive plan formula shall be provided to employees. An accurate production record shall be maintained by the employer.

(B) Employers of sheepherders shall keep accurate information with respect to sheepherder employees, including an itemized statement showing applicable rates of pay for sheepherding and any applicable non-sheepherding agricultural or other work, all deductions, dates of period for which paid, name and social security number (if any) of employee, and name of employer.

(C) Every employer shall semimonthly or at the time of each payment of wages furnish each employee, either as a detachable part of the check, draft, or voucher paying the employee's wages, or separately, an itemized statement in writing showing: (1) all deductions; (2) the inclusive dates of the period for which the employee is paid; (3) the name of the employee or the employee's social security number; and (4) the name of the employer, provided all deductions made on written orders of the employee may be aggregated and shown as one item.

(D) Every employer of a sheepherder shall annually notify the sheepherder of his or hers rights and obligations under state and federal law.

(E) All required records shall be in the English language and in ink or other indelible form, properly dated, showing month, day and year, and shall be kept on file by the employer for at least three years at the place of employment or at a central location within the State of California. An employee's records shall be available for inspection by the employee upon reasonable request.

8. Cash Shortage and Breakage. No employer shall make any deduction from the wage or require any reimbursement from an employee for any cash shortage, breakage, or loss of equipment, unless it can be shown that the shortage, breakage, or loss is caused by a dishonest or willful act, or by the gross negligence of the employee.

9. Uniforms and Equipment

(A) When uniforms are required by the employer to be worn by the employee as a condition of employment, such uniforms shall be provided and maintained by the employer. The term "uniform" includes wearing apparel and accessories of distinctive design or color.

Note: This section shall not apply to protective apparel regulated by the Occupational Safety and Health Standards Board.

(B) When tools or equipment are required by the employer or are necessary to the performance of a job, such tools and equipment shall be provided and maintained by the employer, except that an employee whose wages are at least two (2) times the minimum wage provided herein may be required to provide and maintain hand tools and equipment customarily required by the trade or craft. This subsection (B) shall not apply to apprentices regularly indentured under the State Division of Apprenticeship Standards.

Note: This section shall not apply to protective equipment and safety devices on tools regulated by the Occupational Safety and Health Standards Board.

(C) A reasonable deposit may be required as security for the return of the items furnished by the employer under provisions of subsections (A) and (B) of this section upon issuance of a receipt to the employee for such deposit. Such deposits shall be made pursuant to Section 400 and following of the Labor Code or an employer with the prior written authorization of the employee may deduct from the employee's last check the cost of an item furnished pursuant to (A) and (B) above in the event said item is not returned. No deduction shall be made at any time for normal wear and tear. All items furnished by the employer shall be returned by the employee upon completion of the job.

10. Meals and Lodging

(A) "Meal" means an adequate, well-balanced serving of a variety of wholesome, nutritious foods.

(B) "Lodging" means living accommodations available to the employee for full-time occupancy which are adequate, decent, and sanitary according to usual and customary standards. Employees shall not be required to share a bed.

(C) Meals or lodging may not be credited against the minimum wage without a voluntary written agreement between the employer and the employee. When credit for meals or lodging is used to meet part of the employer's minimum wage obligation, the amounts so credited may not be more than the following:

Effective	January 1, 2007	January 1, 2008
Lodging:		
Room occupied alone	$35.27 per week	$37.63 per week
Room shared	$29.11 per week	$31.06 per week

Apartment—two–thirds
(2/03) of the ordinary rental

Effective	January 1, 2007	January 1, 2008
value, and in no event more than	$423.51 per month	$451.89 per month
Where a couple are both employed by the employer, two-thirds (2/03) of the ordinary rental value, and in no event more than	$626.49 per month	$668.46 per month
Meals:		
Breakfast	$2.72	$2.90
Lunch	$3.72	$3.97
Dinner	$5.00	$5.34

(D) Meals evaluated as part of the minimum wage must be bona fide meals consistent with the employee's work shift. Deductions shall not be made for meals not received or lodging not used.

(E) If, as a condition of employment, the employee must live at the place of employment or occupy quarters owned or under the control of the employer, then the employer may not charge rent in excess of the values listed herein.

(F) Paragraphs (C), (D), and (E) above shall not apply to sheepherders. Every employer shall provide to each sheepherder not less than the minimum monthly meal and lodging benefits required to be provided by employers of sheepherders employed under the provisions of the H–2A program of the Immigration and Nationality Act [8 U.S.C Section 1101 et seq], or any successor provisions.

(G) Fixed Site Housing: A sheepherder not engaged in open range sheepherding, shall be provided with fixed site housing that complies with all the following standards and requirements:

(1) Toilets (which may include portable toilets) and bathing facilities (which may include a portable facility).

(2) Heating (which may include a camp stove or other sources of heat).

(3) Indoor Lighting.

(4) Potable hot and cold water.

(5) Cooking facilities and utensils.

(6) Refrigeration for perishable foodstuffs (which may include ice chests, provided that ice is delivered to the sheepherder, as needed, to maintain a continuous temperature required to retard spoilage and assure food safety).

(7) Fixed Site Housing Inspections: housing that is erected for sheepherders at fixed locations shall be annually inspected by the State of California Employment Development Department for compliance with Paragraph (F) of this section, unless the employer receives a statement in writing from the Employment Development Department that there are no such inspectors available.

(H) Mobile Housing: When a sheepherder is engaged in open range sheepherding, the employer shall provide mobile housing that complies with all standards and inspection requirements prescribed for mobile sheepherder housing by the United States Department of Labor then in effect. Such housing shall be inspected and approved annually by an inspector from the Employment Development Department unless the employer receives a statement in writing from the Employment Development Department that there are no such inspectors available.

11. Meal Periods. Every employer shall authorize and permit all employees after a work period of not more than five (5) hours to take a meal period of not less than 30 minutes, except that when a work period of not more than six (6) hours will complete the day's work the meal period may be waived by mutual consent of employer and employee. Unless the employee is relieved of all duty during a 30 minute meal period, the meal period shall be considered an "on duty" meal period and counted as time worked. An "on duty" meal period shall be permitted only when the nature of the work prevents an employee from being relieved of all duty and when by written agreement between the parties an on-the-job paid meal period is agreed to.

12. Rest Periods. Every employer shall authorize and permit all employees to take rest periods, which insofar as practicable shall be in the middle of each work period. The authorized rest period time shall be based on the total hours worked daily at the rate of ten (10) minutes net rest time per four (4) hours or major fraction thereof. However, a rest period need not be authorized for employees whose total daily work time is less than three and one-half (3 ½) hours. Authorized rest period time shall be counted as hours worked for which there shall be no deduction from wages.

13. Seats. When the nature of the work reasonably permits the use of seats, suitable seats shall be provided for employees working on or at a machine.

14. Other Working Conditions Applicable to Sheepherders. Sheepherders shall be provided with all of the following at each work site:

(A) Regular mail service, which, in the case of open range locations, shall mean mail delivery not less frequently than once every seven days.

(B) An appropriate form of communication, including but not limited to a radio and/or telephone, which will allow sheepherders to communicate with employers, health care providers, and government regulators. Employers may charge sheepherders for all others uses.

(C) Visitor access to fixed site housing and, when practicable to mobile housing.

15. Exemptions. If, in the opinion of the Division after due investigation, it is found that the enforcement of any provisions in Section 7, Records; Section 11, Meal Periods; Section 12, Rest Periods; or Section 13, Seats, would not materially affect the welfare or comfort of employees and would work an undue hardship on the employer, exemption may be made at the discretion of the Division. Such exemptions shall be in writing to be effective any may be revoked after reasonable notice is given in writing. Application for exemption shall be made by the employer or by the employee and/or the employee's representative to the Division in writing. A copy of the application is filed with the Division.

16. Filing Reports. (See California Labor Code, Section 1174(a))

17. Inspection. (See California Labor Code, Section 1174)

18. Penalties. (See California Labor Code, Section 1199)

(A) In addition to any other civil penalties provided by law, any employer or any other person acting on behalf of the employer who violates, or causes to be violated, the provisions of this order, shall be subject to the civil penalty of:

(1) Initial Violation—$50.00 for each underpaid employee for each pay period during which the employee was underpaid in addition to an amount which is sufficient to recover unpaid wages.

(2) Subsequent Violations—$100.00 for each underpaid employee for each pay period during which the employee was underpaid in addition to an amount which is sufficient to recover unpaid wages.

(B) Any employer or any other person acting on behalf of the employer who employs sheepherders and who requires them to engage in non-sheepherding duties shall be subject to the following penalties:

(1) Initial violations—a civil penalty of one week's pay computed on a basis of a 60 hour workweek and a wage of n less than the current minimum wage in effect.

(2) Second violation—a civil penalty of one month's pay computed on a basis of a 252 hour month and a wage of no less than the current minimum wage in effect.

(3) Third and subsequent violation—a civil penalty equal to the cost of the contract of the approved "112A" job order.

(C) The affected employee shall receive payment of all wages recovered.

(D) The Labor Commissioner may also issue citations pursuant to Labor Code Section 1197.1 for non-payment of wages for overtime work in violation of this order.

19. SEPARABILITY. If the application of any provision of this Order, or any section, subsection, subdivision, sentence, clause, phrase, word, or portion of this Order should be held invalid or unconstitutional or unauthorized or prohibited by statute, the remaining provisions thereof shall not be affected thereby, but shall continue to be given full force and effect as if the part so held invalid or unconstitutional had not been included herein.

20. Posting of Order. Every employer shall keep a copy of this Order posted in an area frequented by employees where it may be easily read during the workday. Where the location of work or other conditions make this impractical, every employer shall keep a copy of this Order and make it available to every employee upon request.

Publisher's Notes

See Morillion v. Royal Packing Co. (1998) 77 Cal.Rptr.2d 616 (meaning of "hours worked").

See Alcala v. Western Ag Enterprises (1986) 182 Cal. App.3d 546, 227 Cal.Rptr. 453 (entitlement to and method of calculating overtime pay).

See Industrial Welfare Com. v. Superior Court (1980) 27 Cal.3d 690, 731–733, 166 Cal.Rptr. 331, 613 P.2d 579 (validity of 1980 order).

Research References

See notes following listing of Wage Orders.

Please Post With This Side Showing
OFFICIAL NOTICE
Effective January 1, 2001 as amended
Sections 4(A) and 10(C) amended and republished by the Department of Industrial Relations, effective January 1, 2007, pursuant to AB 1835, Chapter 230, Statutes of 2006
**INDUSTRIAL WELFARE COMMISSION
ORDER NO. 15–2001
REGULATING
WAGES, HOURS AND WORKING CONDITIONS IN THE
HOUSEHOLD OCCUPATIONS**

TAKE NOTICE: To employers and representatives of persons working in industries and occupations in the State of California:

The Department of Industrial Relations amends and republishes the minimum wage and meals and lodging credits in the Industrial Welfare Commission's Orders as a result of legislation enacted (AB 1835, Ch. 230, Stats of 2006, adding sections 1182.12 and 1182.13 to the California Labor Code.) The amendments and republishing make no other changes to the IWC's Orders.

1. Applicability of Order. This order shall apply to all persons employed in household occupations whether paid on a time, piece rate, commission, or other basis, unless such occupation is performed for an industry covered by an industry order of this Commission, except that:

(A) Provisions of Sections 3 through 12 of this order shall not apply to persons employed in administrative, executive, or professional capacities. The following requirements shall apply in determining whether an employee's duties meet the test to qualify for an exemption from those sections:

(1) Executive Exemption A person employed in an executive capacity means any employee:

(a) Whose duties and responsibilities involve the management of the enterprise in which he/she is employed or of a customarily recognized department or subdivision thereof; and

(b) Who customarily and regularly directs the work of two or more other employees therein; and

(c) Who has the authority to hire or fire other employees or whose suggestions and recommendations as to the hiring or firing and as to the advancement and promotion or any other change of status of other employees will be given particular weight; and

(d) Who customarily and regularly exercises discretion and independent judgment; and

(e) Who is primarily engaged in duties which meet the test of the exemption. The activities constituting exempt work and non-exempt work shall be construed in the same manner as such items are construed in the following regulations under the Fair Labor Standards Act effective as of the date of this order: 29 C.F.R. Sections 541.102, 541.104–111, and 541.115–116. Exempt work shall include, for example, all work that is directly and closely related to exempt work and work which is properly viewed as a means for carrying out exempt functions. The work actually performed by the employee during the course of the workweek must, first and foremost, be examined and the amount of time the employee spends on such work, together with the employer's realistic expectations and the realistic requirements of the job, shall be considered in determining whether the employee satisfies this requirement.

(f) Such an employee must also earn a monthly salary equivalent to no less than two (2) times the state minimum wage for full-time employment. Full–time employment is defined in Labor Code Section 515(c) as 40 hours per week.

(2) Administrative Exemption. A person employed in an administrative capacity means any employee:

(a) Whose duties and responsibilities involve either:

(i) The performance of office or non-manual work directly related to management policies or general business operations of his employer or his/hers employer's customers; or

(ii) The performance of functions in the administration of a school system, or educational establishment or institution, or of a department or subdivision thereof, in work directly related to the academic instruction or training carried on therein; and

1516

(b) Who customarily and regularly exercises discretion and independent judgment; and

(c) Who regularly and directly assists a proprietor, or an employee employed in a bona fide executive or administrative capacity (as such terms are defined for purposes of this section); or

(d) Who performs under only general supervision work along specialized or technical lines requiring special training, experience, or knowledge; or

(e) Who executes under only general supervision special assignments and tasks; and

(f) Who is primarily engaged in duties which meet the test of the exemption. The activities constituting exempt work and non-exempt work shall be construed in the same manner as such terms are construed in the following regulations under the Fair Labor Standards Act effective as of the date of this order 29 C.F.R. Sections 541.201–205, 541.207–208, 541.210, and 541.215. Exempt work shall include, for example, all work that is directly and closely related to exempt work and work which is properly viewed as a means for carrying out exempt functions. The work actually performed by the employee during the course of the workweek must, first and foremost, be examined and the amount of time the employee spends on such work, together with the employer's realistic expectations and the realistic requirements of the job, shall be considered in determining whether the employee satisfies this requirement.

(g) Such employee must also earn a monthly salary equivalent to no less than two (2) times the state minimum wage for full-time employment. Full–time employment is defined in Labor Code Section 515(c) as 40 hours per week.

(3) Professional Exemption A person employed in a professional capacity means any employee who meets all of the following requirements:

(a) Who is licensed or certified by the State of California and is primarily engaged in the practice of one of the following recognized professions: law, medicine, dentistry, optometry, architecture, engineering, teaching, or accounting; or

(b) Who is primarily engaged in an occupation commonly recognized as a learned or artistic profession. For the purposes of this subsection, "learned or artistic profession" means an employee who is primarily engaged in the performance of:

(i) Work requiring knowledge of an advanced type in a field or science or learning customarily acquired by a prolonged course of specialized intellectual instruction and study, as distinguished from a general academic education and from an apprenticeship, and from training in the performance of routine mental, manual, or physical processes, or work that is an essential part of or necessarily incident to any of the above work; or

(ii) Work that is original and creative in character in a recognized field of artistic endeavor (as opposed to work which can be produced by a person endowed with general manual or intellectual ability and training), and the result of which depends primarily on the invention, imagination, or talent of the employee or work that is an essential part of or necessarily incident to any of the above work; and

(iii) Whose work is predominantly intellectual and varied in character (as opposed to routine mental, manual, mechanical, or physical work) and is of such character that the output produced or the result accomplished cannot be standardized in relation to a given period of time.

(c) Who customarily and regularly exercises discretion and independent judgment in the performance of duties set forth in subparagraphs (a) and (b).

(d) Who earns a monthly salary equivalent to no less than two (2) times the state minimum wage for full-time employment.

(e) Subparagraph (b) above is intended to be construed in accordance with the following provisions of federal law as they existed as of the date of this order: 29 C.F.R. Sections 541.207, 541.301(a)–(d), 541.302, 541.306, 541.307, 541.308, and 541.310.

(f) Notwithstanding the provisions of this subparagraph, pharmacists employed to engage in the practice of pharmacy, and registered nurses employed to engage in the practice of nursing, shall not be considered exempt professional employees, nor shall they be considered exempt from coverage for the purposes of this subparagraph unless they individually meet the criteria established for exemption as executive or administrative employees.

(g) Subparagraph (f) above shall not apply to the following advanced practice nurses:

(i) Certified nurse midwives who are primarily engaged in performing duties for which certification is required pursuant to Article 2.5 (commencing with Section 2746) of Chapter 6 of Division 2 of the Business and Professions Code.

(ii) Certified nurse anesthetists who are primarily engaged in performing duties for which certification is required pursuant to Article 7 (commencing with Section 2825) of Chapter 6 of Division 2 of the Business and Professions Code.

(iii) Certified nurse practitioners who are primarily engaged in performing duties for which certification is required pursuant to Article 8 (commencing with Section 2834) of Chapter 6 of Division 2 of the Business and Professions Code.

(iv) Nothing in this subparagraph shall exempt the occupations set forth in clauses (i), (ii), and (iii) from meeting the requirements of subsection 1(A)(3)(a)–(d) above.

(h) Except, as provided in subparagraph (i), an employee in the computer software field who is paid on an hourly basis shall be exempt, if all of the following apply:

(i) The employee is primarily engaged in work that is intellectual or creative and requires the exercise of discretion and independent judgment.

(ii) The employee is primarily engaged in duties that consist of one or more of the following:

-The application of systems analysis techniques and procedures, including consulting with users, to determine hardware, software, or system functional specifications.

-The design, development, documentation, analysis, creation, testing, or modification of computer systems or programs, including prototypes, based on and related to user or system design specifications.

-The documentation, testing, creation, or modification of computer programs related to the design of software or hardware for computer operating systems.

(iii) The employee is highly skilled and is proficient in the theoretical and practical application of highly specialized information to computer systems analysis, programming, and software engineering. A job title shall not be determinative of the applicability of this exemption.

(iv) The employee's hourly rate of pay is not less than forty-one dollars ($41.00). The Division of Labor Statistics and Research shall adjust this pay rate on October 1 of each year to be effective on January 1 of the following year by an amount equal to the percentage increase in the California Consumer Price Index for Urban Wage Earners and Clerical Workers.[1]

(i) The exemption provided in subparagraph (h) does not apply to an employee if any of the following apply:

(i) The employee is a trainee or employee in an entry-level position who is learning to become proficient in the theoretical and practical application of highly specialized information to computer systems analysis, programming, and software engineering.

(ii) The employee is in a computer-related occupation but has not attained the level of skill and expertise necessary to work independently and without close supervision.

(iii) The employee is engaged in the operation of computers or in the manufacture, repair, or maintenance of computer hardware and related equipment.

(iv) The employee is an engineer, drafter, machinist, or other professional whose work is highly dependent upon or facilitated by the use of computers and computer software programs and who is skilled in computer-aided design software, including CAD/CAM, but who is not in a computer systems analysis or programming occupation.

(v) The employee is a writer engaged in writing material, including box labels, product descriptions, documentation, promotional material, setup and installation instructions, and other similar written information, either for print or for on screen media or who writes or provides content material intended to be read by customers, subscribers, or visitors to computer-related media such as the World Wide Web or CD–ROMs.

(vi) The employee is engaged in any of the activities set forth in subparagraph (h) for the purpose of creating imagery for effects used in the motion picture, television, or theatrical industry.

(B) Except as provided in Sections 1, 2, 4, 10, and 15, the provisions of this order shall not apply to personal attendants. The provisions of this order shall not apply to any person under the age of 18 who is employed as a baby sitter for a minor child of the employer in the employer's home.

(C) The provisions of this order shall not apply to any individual who is the parent, spouse, child, or legally adopted child of the employer.

(D) The provisions of this order shall not apply to any individual participating in a national service program, such as Ameri–Corps, carried out using assistance provided under Section 12571 of Title 42 of the United States Code. (See Stats. 2000, amending Labor Code Section 1171.)

2. Definitions

(A) An "alternative workweek schedule" means any regularly scheduled workweek requiring an employee to work more than eight (8) hours in a 24–hour period.

(B) "Commission" means the Industrial Welfare Commission of the State of California.

(C) "Division" means the Division of Labor Standards Enforcement of the State of California.

(D) "Emergency" means an unpredictable or unavoidable occurrence at unscheduled intervals requiring immediate action.

(E) "Employ" means to engage, suffer, or permit to work.

(F) "Employee" means any person employed by an employer.

(G) "Employer" means any person as defined in Section 18 of the Labor Code, who directly or indirectly, or through an agent or any other person, employs or exercises control over the wages, hours, or working conditions of any person.

(H) "Hours worked" means the time during which an employee is subject to the control of an employer, and includes all the time the employee is suffered or permitted to work, whether or not required to do so.

(I) "Household Occupations" means all services related to the care of persons or maintenance of a private household or its premises by an employee of a private householder. Said occupations shall include but not be limited to the following: butlers, chauffeurs, companions, cooks, day workers, gardeners, graduate nurses, grooms, house cleaners, housekeepers, maids, practical nurses, tutors, valets, and other similar occupations.

(J) "Personal attendant" includes baby sitters and means any person employed by a private householder or by any third party employer recognized in the health care industry to work in a private household, to supervise, feed, or dress a child or person who by reason of advanced age, physical disability, or mental deficiency needs supervision. The status of "personal attendant" shall apply when no significant amount of work other than the foregoing is required.

(K) "Minor" means, for the purpose of this order, any person under the age of 18 years.

(L) "Primarily" as used in Section 1, Applicability, means more than one-half the employee's work time.

(M) "Shift" means designated hours of work by an employee, with a designated beginning time and quitting time.

(N) "Split shift" means a work schedule, which is interrupted by non-paid non-working periods established by the employer, other than bona fide rest or meal periods.

(O) "Teaching" means, for the purpose of Section 1 of this Order, the profession of teaching under a certificate from the Commission for Teacher Preparation and Licensing or teaching in an accredited college or university.

(P) "Wages" includes all amounts for labor performed by employees of every description, whether the amount is fixed or ascertained by the standard of time, task, piece, commission basis, or other method of calculation.

(Q) "Workday" and "day" mean any consecutive 24–hour period beginning at the same time each calendar day.

(R) "Workweek" and "week" mean any seven (7) consecutive days, starting with the same calendar day each week. "Workweek" is a fixed and regularly recurring period of 168 hours, seven (7) consecutive 24–hour periods.

3. Hours and Days of Work

(A) A LIVE–IN employee shall have at least 12 consecutive hours free of duty during each workday of 24 hours, and the total span of hours for a day of work shall be no more than 12 hours, except under the following conditions:

(1) The employee shall have at least three (3) hours free of duty during the 12 hours span of work. Such off-duty hours need not be consecutive, and the schedule for same shall be set by mutual agreement of employer and employee, provided that

(2) An employee who is required or permitted to work during scheduled off-duty hours or during the 12 consecutive off-duty hours shall be compensated at the rate of one and one-half (1 ½) times the employee's regular rate of pay for all such ho worked.

(B) No LIVE–IN employee shall be required to work more than five (5) days in any one workweek without a day off of not less than 24 consecutive hours except in an emergency as defined in subsection 2(D), provided that the employee is compensated for time worked in excess of five (5) workdays in any workweek at one and one-half (1

½₂) times the employee's regular rate of pay for hours worked up to and including nine (9) hours. Time worked in excess of nine (9) hours on the sixth (6th) and seventh (7th) workdays shall be compensated at double the employee's regular rate of pay.

(C) The following overtime provisions are applicable to non–LIVE–IN employees 18 years of age or over and to employees 16 or 17 years of age who are not required by law to attend school and are not otherwise prohibited by law from engaging in the subject work. Such employees shall not be employed more than eight (8) hours in any workday or more than 40 hours in any workweek unless the employee receives one and one-half (1 ½₂) times such employee's regular rate of pay for all hours worked over 40 hours in the workweek. Eight (8) hours of labor constitutes a day's work. Employment beyond eight (8) hours in any workday or more than six (6) days in any workweek is permissible provided the employee is compensated for such overtime at not less than:

(1) One and one-half (1 ½₂) times the employee's regular rate of pay for all hours worked in excess of eight (8) hours up to and including 12 hours in any workday, and for the first eight (8) hours worked on the seventh (7th) consecutive day of work in a workweek; and

(2) Double the employee's regular rate of pay for all hours worked in excess of 12 hours in any workday and for all hours worked in excess of eight (8) hours on the seventh (7th) consecutive day of work in a workweek.

(3) The overtime rate of compensation required to be paid to a nonexempt full-time salaried employee shall be computed by using the employee's regular hourly salary as one-fortieth (1/40) of the employee's weekly salary.

(D) One and one-half (1 ½₂) times a minor's regular rate of pay shall be paid for all work over 40 hours in any workweek except minors 16 and 17 years old who are not required by law to attend school and may therefore be employed for the same hours as an adult are subject to subsections (A) and (B) or (C) above.

(**Violations of Child Labor Laws** are subject to civil penalties of from $500 to $10,000 as well as to criminal penalties. Refer to California Labor Code Sections 1285 to 1312 and 1390 to 1399 for additional restrictions on the employment of minors and for descriptions of criminal and civil penalties for violation of the child labor laws. Employers should ask school districts about any required work permits.)

(E) An employee may be employed on seven (7) workdays in one workweek with no overtime pay required when the total hours of employment during such workweek do not exceed 30 and the total hours of employment in any one workday thereof do not exceed six (6).

(F) The provisions of Labor Code Sections 551 and 552 regarding one (1) day's rest in seven (7) shall not be construed to prevent an accumulation of days of rest when the nature of the employment reasonably requires the employee to work seven (7) or more consecutive days; provided, however, that in each calendar month, the employee shall receive the equivalent of one (1) day's rest in seven (7).

(G) Except as provided in subsections (D) and (F), this section shall not apply to any employee covered by a valid collective bargaining agreement if the agreement expressly provides for the wages, hours of work, and working conditions of the employees, and if the agreement provides premium wage rates for all overtime hours worked and a regular hourly rate of pay for those employees of not less than 30 percent more than the state minimum wage.

(H) Notwithstanding subsection (G) above, where the employer and a labor organization representing employees of the employer have entered into a valid collective bargaining agreement pertaining to the hours of work of the employees, the requirement regarding the equivalent of one (1) day's rest in seven (7) (see subsection (F) above) shall apply, unless the agreement expressly provides otherwise.

(I) If an employer approves a written request of an employee to make up work time that is or would be lost as a result of a personal obligation of the employee, the hours of that makeup work time, if performed in the same workweek in which the work time was lost, may not be counted toward computing the total number of hours worked in a day for purposes of the overtime requirements, except for hours in excess of 11 hours of work in one (1) day or 40 hours of work in one (1) workweek. If an employee knows in advance that he/she will be requesting makeup time for a personal obligation that will recur at a fixed time over a succession of weeks, the employee may request to make up work time for up to four (4) weeks in advance; provided, however, that the makeup work must be performed in the same week that the work time was lost. An employee shall provide a signed written request for each occasion that the employee makes a request to make up work time pursuant to this subsection. While an employer may inform an employee of this makeup time option, the employer is prohibited from encouraging or otherwise soliciting an employee to request the employer's approval to take personal time off and make up the work hours within the same workweek pursuant to this subsection.

4. Minimum Wages

(A) Every employer shall pay to each employee wages not less than seven dollars and fifty cents ($7.50) per hour for all hours worked, effective January 1, 2007, and not less than eight dollars ($8.00) per hour for all hours worked, effective January 1, 2008, except:

Learners: Employees during their 160 hours of employment in occupations in which they have no previous similar or related experience, may be paid not less than 85 percent of the minimum wage rounded to the nearest nickel.

(B) Every employer shall pay to each employee, on the established payday for the period involved, not less than the applicable minimum wage for all hours worked in the payroll period, whether the remuneration is measured by time, piece, commission, or otherwise.

(C) When an employee works a split shift, one (1) hour's pay at the minimum wage shall be paid in addition to the minimum wage for that workday, except when the employee resides at the place of employment.

(D) The provisions of this section shall not apply to apprentices regularly indentured under the State Division of Apprenticeship Standards.

5. Reporting Time Pay

(A) Each workday an employee is required to report for work and does report, but is not put to work or is furnished less than half said employee's usual or scheduled day's work, the employee shall be paid for half the usual or scheduled day's work, but in no event for less than two (2) hours nor more than four (4) hours, at the employee's regular rate of pay, which shall not be less than the minimum wage.

(B) If an employee is required to report for work a second time in any one workday and is furnished less than two (2) hours of work on the second reporting, said employee shall be paid for two (2) hours at the employee's regular rate of pay, which shall not be less than the minimum wage.

(C) The foregoing reporting time pay provisions are not applicable when:

(1) Operations cannot commence or continue due to threats to employees or property; or when recommended by civil authorities; or

(2) Public utilities fail to supply electricity, water, or gas, or there is a failure in the public utilities, or sewer system; or

(3) The interruption of work is caused by an Act of God or other cause not within the employer's control.

(D) This section shall not apply to an employee on paid standby status who is called to perform assigned work at a time other than the employee's scheduled reporting time.

6. Licenses for Disabled Workers

(A) A license may be issued by the Division authorizing employment of a person whose earning capacity is impaired by physical disability or mental deficiency at less than the minimum wage. Such licenses shall be granted only upon joint application of employer and employee and employee's representative if any.

(B) A special license may be issued to a nonprofit organization such as a sheltered workshop or rehabilitation facility fixing special minimum rates to enable the employment of such persons without requiring individual licenses of such employees.

(C) All such licenses and special licenses shall be renewed on a yearly basis or more frequently at the discretion of the Division.

(See California Labor Code, Sections 1191 and 1191.5)

7. Records

(A) Every employer shall keep accurate information with respect to each employee including the following:

(1) Full name, home address, occupation and social security number.

(2) Birth date, if under 18 years, and designation as a minor.

(3) Time records showing when the employee begins and ends each work period. Meal periods, split shift intervals and total daily hours worked shall also be recorded. Meal periods during which operations cease and authorized rest periods need not be recorded.

(4) Total wages paid each payroll period, including value of board, lodging, or other compensation actually furnished to the employee.

(5) Total hours worked in the payroll period and applicable rates of pay. This information shall be made readily available to the employee upon reasonable request.

(6) When a piece rate or incentive plan is in operation, piece rates or an explanation of the incentive plan formula shall be provided to employees. An accurate production record shall be maintained by the employer.

(B) Every employer shall semimonthly or at the time of each payment of wages furnish each employee, either as a detachable part of the check, draft, or voucher paying the employee's wages, or separately, an itemized statement in writing showing: (1) all deductions; (2) the inclusive dates of the period for which the employee is paid; (3) the name of the employee or the employee's social security number; and (4) the name of the employer, provided all deductions made on written orders of the employee may be aggregated and shown as one item.

(C) All required records shall be in the English language and in ink or other indelible form, properly dated, showing month, day and year, and shall be kept on file by the employer for at least three years at the place of employment or at a central location within the State of California. An employee's records shall be available for inspection by the employee upon reasonable request.

(D) Clocks shall be provided in all major work areas or within reasonable distance thereto insofar as practicable.

8. Cash Shortage and Breakage.
No employer shall make any deduction from the wage or require any reimbursement from an employee for any cash shortage, breakage, or loss of equipment, unless it can be shown that the shortage, breakage, or loss is caused by a dishonest or willful act, or by the gross negligence of the employee.

9. Uniforms and Equipment

(A) When uniforms are required by the employer to be worn by the employee as a condition of employment, such uniforms shall be provided and maintained by the employer. The term "uniform" includes wearing apparel and accessories of distinctive design or color.

Note: This section shall not apply to protective apparel regulated by the Occupational Safety and Health Standards Board.

(B) When tools or equipment are required by the employer or are necessary to the performance of a job, such tools and equipment shall be provided and maintained by the employer, except that an employee whose wages are at least two (2) times the minimum wage provided herein may be required to provide and maintain hand tools and equipment customarily required by the trade or craft. This subsection (B) shall not apply to apprentices regularly indentured under the State Division of Apprenticeship Standards.

Note: This section shall not apply to protective equipment and safety devices on tools regulated by the Occupational Safety and Health Standards Board.

(C) A reasonable deposit may be required as security for the return of the items furnished by the employer under provisions of subsections (A) and (B) of this section upon issuance of a receipt to the employee for such deposit. Such deposits shall be made pursuant to Section 400 and following of the Labor Code or an employer with the prior written authorization of the employee may deduct from the employee's last check the cost of an item furnished pursuant to (A) and (B) above in the event said item is not returned. No deduction shall be made at any time for normal wear and tear. All items furnished by the employer shall be returned by the employee upon completion of the job.

10. Meals and Lodging

(A) "Meal" means an adequate, well-balanced serving of a variety of wholesome, nutritious foods.

(B) "Lodging" means living accommodations available to the employee for full-time occupancy which are adequate, decent, and sanitary according to usual and customary standards. Employees shall not be required to share a bed.

(C) Meals or lodging may not be credited against the minimum wage without a voluntary written agreement between the employer and the employee. When credit for meals or lodging is used to meet part of the employer's minimum wage obligation, the amounts so credited may not be more than the following:

Effective	January 1, 2007	January 1, 2008
Lodging:		
Room occupied alone	$35.27 per week	$37.63 per week
Room shared	$29.11 per week	$31.06 per week
Apartment—two—thirds (2/03) of the ordinary rental value, and in no event more than	$423.51 per month	$451.89 per month
Where a couple are both employed by the employer, two-thirds (2/03) of the ordinary rental value, and in no event more than	$626.49 per month	$668.46 per month
Meals:		

Effective	January 1, 2007	January 1, 2008
Breakfast	$2.72	$2.90
Lunch	$3.72	$3.97
Dinner	$5.00	$5.34

(D) Meals evaluated as part of the minimum wage must be bona fide meals consistent with the employee's work shift. Deductions shall not be made for meals not received or lodging not used.

(E) If, as a condition of employment, the employee must live at the place of employment or occupy quarters owned or under the control of the employer, then the employer may not charge rent in excess of the values listed herein.

11. Meal Periods

(A) No employer shall employ any person for a work period of more than five (5) hours without a meal period of not less than 30 minutes, except that when a work period of not more than six (6) hours will complete the day's work the meal period may be waived by mutual consent of the employer and the employee.

(B) An employer may not employ an employee for a work period of more than ten (10) hours per day without providing the employee with a second meal period of not less than 30 minutes, except that if the total hours worked is no more than 12 hours, the second meal period may be waived by mutual consent of the employer and the employee only if the first meal period was not waived.

(C) Unless the employee is relieved of all duty during a 30 minute meal period, the meal period shall be considered an "on duty" meal period and counted as time worked. An "on duty" meal period shall be permitted only when the nature of the work prevents an employee from being relieved of all duty and when by written agreement between the parties an on-the-job paid meal period is agreed to. The written agreement shall state that the employee may, in writing, revoke the agreement at any time.

(D) If an employer fails to provide an employee a meal period in accordance with the applicable provisions of this order, the employer shall pay the employee one (1) hour of pay at the employee's regular rate of compensation for each workday that the meal period is not provided.

12. Rest Periods

(A) Every employer shall authorize and permit all employees to take rest periods, which insofar as practicable shall be in the middle of each work period. The authorized rest period time shall be based on the total hours worked daily at the rate of ten (10) minutes net rest time per four (4) hours or major fraction thereof. However, a rest period need not be authorized for employees whose total daily work time is less than three and one-half (3 $\frac{1}{2}$) hours. Authorized rest period time shall be counted as hours worked for which there shall be no deduction from wages.

(B) If an employer fails to provide an employee a rest period in accordance with the applicable provisions of this order, the employer shall pay the employee one (1) hour of pay at the employee's regular rate of compensation for each workday that the rest period is not provided.

13. Change Rooms and Resting Facilities

(A) Employers shall provide suitable lockers, closets, or equivalent for the safekeeping of employees' outer clothing during working hours, and when required, for their work clothing during non-working hours. When the occupation requires a change of clothing, change rooms or equivalent space shall be provided in order that employees may change their clothing in reasonable privacy and comfort. These rooms or spaces may be adjacent to but shall be separate from toilet rooms and shall be kept clean.

Note: This section shall not apply to change rooms and storage facilities regulated by the Occupational Safety and Health Standards Board.

(B) Suitable resting facilities shall be provided in an area separate from the toilet rooms and shall be available to employees during work hours.

14. Seats

(A) All working employees shall be provided with suitable seats when the nature of the work reasonably permits the use of seats.

(B) When employees are not engaged in the active duties of their employment and the nature of the work requires standing, an adequate number of suitable seats shall be placed in reasonable proximity to the work area and employees shall be permitted to use such seats when it does not interfere with the performance of their duties.

15. Penalties. (See California Labor Code, Section 1199)

(A) In addition to any other civil penalties provided by law, any employer or any other person acting on behalf of the employer who violates, or causes to be violated, the provisions of this order, shall be subject to the civil penalty of:

(1) Initial Violation—$50.00 for each underpaid employee for each pay period during which the employee was underpaid in addition to the amount which is sufficient to recover unpaid wages.

(2) Subsequent Violations—$100.00 for each underpaid employee for each pay period during which the employee was underpaid in addition to an amount which is sufficient to recover unpaid wages.

(3) The affected employee shall receive payment of all wages recovered.

(B) The labor commissioner may also issue citations pursuant to California Labor Code Section 1197.1 for non-payment of wages for overtime work in violation of this order.

16. Elevators.
Adequate elevator, escalator or similar service consistent with industry-wide standards for the nature of the process and the work performed shall be provided when employees are employed four floors or more above or below ground level.

17. Exemptions.
If, in the opinion of the Division after due investigation, it is found that the enforcement of any provision contained in Section 7, Records; Section 12, Rest Periods; Section 13, Change Rooms and Resting Facilities; Section 14, Seats; or Section 16, Elevators, would not materially affect the welfare or comfort of employees and would work an undue hardship on the employer, exemption may be made at the discretion of the Division. Such exemptions shall be in writing to be effective and may be revoked after reasonable notice is given in writing. Application for exemption shall be made by the employer or by the employee and/or the employee's representative to the Division in writing. A copy of the application shall be posted at the place of employment at the time the application is filed with the Division.

18. Filing Reports.
(See California Labor Code, Section 1174(a))

19. Inspection.
(See California Labor Code, Section 1174)

20. Separability.
If the application of any provision of this order, or any section, subsection, subdivision, sentence, clause, phrase, word, or portion of this order should be held invalid or unconstitutional or unauthorized or prohibited by statute, the remaining provisions thereof shall not be affected thereby, but shall continue to be given full force and effect as if the part so held invalid or unconstitutional had not been included herein.

21. Posting of Order.
Every employer shall keep a copy of this order posted in an area frequented by employees where it may be easily read during the workday. Where the location of work or other conditions make this impractical, every employer shall keep a copy of this order and make it available to every employee upon request.

[1] Pursuant to Labor Code section 515.5, subdivision (a)(4), the Division of Labor Statistics and Research, Department of Industrial Relations, has adjusted the minimum hourly rate of pay specified in this subdivision to be $49.77, effective January 1, 2007. This hourly rate of pay is adjusted on October 1 of each year to be effective on January 1, of the following year, and may be obtained at www.dir.ca.gov/IWC or by mail from the Department of Industrial Relations.

***

Publisher's Notes

See Cardenas v. Mission Industries (1991) 226 Cal. App.3d 952, 277 Cal.Rptr. 247 (meaning of "personal attendants").

Research References

See notes following listing of Wage Orders.

Effective January 1, 2001 as amended
Sections 4(A) and 10(C) amended and republished by the Department of Industrial Relations,
effective January 1, 2007, pursuant to AB 1835, Chapter 230, Statutes of 2006
INDUSTRIAL WELFARE COMMISSION
ORDER NO. 16–2001
REGULATING
WAGES, HOURS AND WORKING CONDITIONS IN THE
CERTAIN ON–SITE OCCUPATIONS IN THE
CONSTRUCTION, DRILLING, LOGGING
AND MINING INDUSTRIES

TAKE NOTICE: To employers and representatives of persons working in industries and occupations in the State of California:

The Department of Industrial Relations amends and republishes the minimum wage and meals and lodging credits in the Industrial Welfare Commission's Orders as a result of legislation enacted (AB 1835, Ch. 230, Stats of 2006, adding sections 1182.12 and 1182.13 to the California Labor Code.) The amendments and republishing make no other changes to the IWC's Orders.

1. Applicability of Order. This order shall apply to all persons employed in the on-site occupations of construction, including but not limited to work involving alteration, demolition, building, excavating, renovation, remodeling, maintenance, improvement, and repair work, and work for which a contractor's license is required by the California Business and Professions Code, Division 3, Chapter 9, Sections 7025 *et seq.*; drilling, including but not limited to all work required to drill, establish, repair, and rework wells for the exploration or extraction of oil, gas, or water resources; logging work for which a timber operator's license is required pursuant to California Public Resources Code Sections 4571 through 4586; and mining (not covered by Labor Code Section 750 *et seq.*), including all work required to mine and/or establish pits, quarries, and surface or underground mines for the purposes of exploration or extraction of nonmetallic minerals and ores, coal, and building materials such as stone and gravel, whether paid on a time, piece rate, commission, or other basis, except that:

(A) The provisions of Sections 3 through 11 shall not apply to persons employed in administrative, executive, or professional capacities. No person shall be considered to be employed in an administrative, executive, or professional capacity unless the person is primarily engaged in the duties which meet the test of the exemption, and earns a monthly salary equivalent to not less than (2) two times the state minimum wage for full-time employment. The duties that meet the test of the exemption are one of the following set of conditions:

(1) The employee is engaged in work which is primarily intellectual, managerial, or creative, and which requires exercise of discretion and independent judgment; or

(2) The employee is licensed or certified by the State of California, and is engaged in the practice of one of the following recognized professions: law, medicine, dentist-ry, optometry, architecture, engineering, teaching, or accounting, or the employee is engaged in an occupation that is commonly recognized as a learned or artistic profession; provided, however, that pharmacists employed to engage in the practice of pharmacy, and registered nurses employed to engage in the practice of nursing, shall not be considered exempt professional employees, nor shall they be considered exempt from coverage for the purposes of this section unless they individually meet the criteria established for exemption as executive or administrative employees.

(3) To the extent that there is no conflict with California law (Labor Code Section 515(e) requires than an employee be "primarily" engaged in exempt work, which means more than one-half of the employee's work time. Thus the "primary duty" test set forth in federal regulations does not apply.), the duties that meet the test of the administrative and executive exemptions are defined as set forth in the following sections of the Code of Federal Regulations as they existed as of the date of this wage order: 29 C.F.R. Sections 541.1 (a)–(c), 541.102, 541.104, 541.105, 541.106, 541.108, 541.109, 541.111, 541.115, and 541.116 (defining executive duties); 29 C.F.R. Sections 541.2 (a)–(c), 541.201, 541.205, 541.208, and 541.210 (defining administrative duties).

(4) For the purposes of this section, "full-time employment" means employment in which an employee is employed for 40 hours per week.

(B) Except as provided in Sections 1, Applicability; 2, Definitions; 4, Minimum Wages; 9, Meals and Lodging; and 18, Penalties, the provisions of this order shall not apply to any employees directly employed by the State or any political subdivision thereof, including any city, county, or special district.

(C) The provisions of this order shall not apply to outside salespersons.

(D) The provisions of this order shall not apply to any individual who is the parent, spouse, child, or legally adopted child of the employer.

(E) The provisions of this order shall not apply to any individual participating in a national service program, such as Ameri–Corps, carried out using assistance provided under Section 12571 of Title 42 of the United States Code. (See Stats. 2000, ch. 365, amending Labor Code Section 1171.)

(F) This order supersedes any industry or occupational order for those employees employed in occupations covered by this order.

2. Definitions

(A) "Alternative workweek schedule" means any regularly scheduled workweek proposed by an employer who has control over the wages, hours, and working conditions of the employees, and ratified by an employee work unit in a neutral secret ballot election, that requires an employee to work more than eight (8) hours in a 24–hour period.

(B) "Commission" means the Industrial Welfare Commission of the State of California.

(C) "Construction occupations" mean all job classifications associated with construction, including but not limited to work involving alteration, demolition, building, excavation, renovation, remodeling, maintenance, improvement, and repair work, by the California Business and Professions Code, Division 3, Chapter 9, Sections 7025 et seq., and any other similar or related occupations or trades.

(D) "Division" means the Division of Labor Standards Enforcement of the State of California.

(E) "Drilling occupations" mean all job classifications associated with the exploration or extraction of oil, gas, or water resources work, including but not limited to the installation, establishment, reworking, maintenance or repair of wells and pumps by boring, drilling, excavating, casting, cementing and cleaning for the extraction or conveyance of fluids such as water, steam, gases, or petroleum.

(F) "Emergency" means an unpredictable or unavoidable occurrence at unscheduled intervals requiring immediate action.

(G) "Employ" means to engage, suffer, or permit to work.

(H) "Employee" means any person employed by an employer.

(I) "Employer" means any person as defined in Section 18 of the Labor Code, who directly or indirectly, or through an agent or any other person, employs or exercises control over the wages, hours, or working conditions of any person.

(J) "Hours worked" means the time during which an employee is subject to the control of an employer, and includes all the time the employee is suffered or permitted to work, whether or not required to do so.

(K) "Logging occupations" mean any work for which a timber operator's license is required pursuant to California Public Resources Code Sections 4571–4586, including the cutting or removal or both of timber or other solid wood forest products, including Christmas trees, from timberlands for commercial purposes, together with all the work that is incidental thereto, including but not limited to construction and maintenance of roads, fuel

breaks, fire breaks, stream crossings, landings, skid trails, beds for the falling of trees, and fire hazard abatement.

(L) "Mining occupations" mean miners and other associated and related occupations (not covered by Labor Code Sections 750 et seq.) required to engage in excavation or operations above or below ground including work in mines, quarries, or open pits, used for the purposes of exploration or extraction of nonmetallic minerals and ores, coal, and building materials such as stone, gravel, and rock, or other materials intended for manufacture or sale, whether paid on a time, piece rate, commission, or other basis.

(M) "Minor" means, for the purpose of this order, any person under the age of 18 years as defined by Labor Code Sections 1285–1312 and 1390–1399.

(N) "Outside salesperson" means any person, 18 years of age or over, who customarily and regularly works more than half the working time away from the employer's place of business selling tangible or intangible items or obtaining orders or contracts for products, services or use of facilities. An "outside salesperson" does not include an employee who makes deliveries or service calls for the purpose of installing, replacing, repairing, removing, or servicing a product.

(O) "Primarily" means more than one-half the employee's work time.

(P) "Regularly scheduled workweek" means a schedule where the length of the shift and the number of days of work are pre-designated pursuant to an alternative workweek schedule.

(Q) "Split shift" means a work schedule, which is interrupted by non-paid non-working periods established by the employer, other than bona fide rest or meal periods.

(R) "Wages" are as defined by California Labor Code Section 200.

(S) "Workday" and "day" mean any consecutive 24–hour period beginning at the same time each calendar day.

(T) "Workweek" and "week" mean any seven (7) consecutive days, starting with the same calendar day each week. "Workweek" is a fixed and regularly recurring period of 168 hours, seven (7) consecutive 24–hour periods.

(U) "Work unit" means all nonexempt employees of a single employer within a given craft who share a common work site. A work unit may consist of an individual employee as long as the criteria for an identifiable work unit in this subsection are met.

3. Hours and Days of Work

(A) *Daily Overtime—General Provisions*

(1) The following overtime provisions are applicable to employees 18 years of age or over and to employees 16 or 17 years of age who are not required by law to attend school and are not otherwise prohibited by law from

engaging in the subject work. Such employees shall not be employed more than eight (8) hours in any workday or more than 40 hours in any workweek unless the employee receives one and one-half (1 ½) times such employee's regular rate of pay for all hours worked over 40 hours in the workweek. Employment beyond eight (8) hours in any workday or more than six (6) days in any workweek is permissible provided the employee is compensated for such overtime at not less than:

(a) One and one-half (1 ½) times the employee's regular rate of pay for all hours worked in excess of eight (8) hours up to and including 12 hours in any workday, and for the first eight (8) hours worked on the seventh (7th) consecutive day of work in a workweek; and

(b) Double the employee's regular rate of pay for all hours worked in excess of 12 hours in any workday and for all hours worked in excess of eight (8) hours on the seventh (7th) consecutive day of work in a workweek.

(c) The overtime rate of compensation to be paid to a nonexempt full-time salaried employee shall be computed by using one-fortieth (1/40) of the employee's weekly salary as the employee's regular hourly rate of pay.

(B) *Alternative Workweek Schedules*

(1) No employer, who has control over the wages, hours, and working conditions of employees, shall be deemed to have violated the provisions of Section 3, Hours and Days of Work, by instituting, pursuant to the election procedures set forth in this order, a regularly scheduled alternative workweek pursuant to the following conditions:

(a) The alternative workweek schedule shall provide for work by the affected employees of no longer than ten (10) hours per day within a 40 hour workweek without the payment to the affected employees of an overtime rate of compensation pursuant to this section.

(b) An affected employee working longer than eight (8) hours but no more than ten (10) hours in a day pursuant to an alternative workweek schedule adopted pursuant to this section shall be paid an overtime rate of compensation of not less than one and one-half (1 ½) times the regular rate of pay of the employee for any work in excess of the regularly scheduled hours established by the alternative workweek agreement and for any work in excess of 40 hours per week.

(c) An overtime rate of compensation of not less than double the employee's regular rate of pay shall be paid for any work in excess of 12 hours per day and for any work in excess of eight (8) hours on those days worked beyond the regularly scheduled workdays established by the alternative workweek agreement.

(d) An employer shall not reduce an employee's regular rate of hourly pay as a result of the adoption, repeal or nullification of an alternative workweek schedule.

(e) An employer shall make a reasonable effort to find a work schedule not to exceed eight (8) hours in a workday to accommodate any affected employee who was eligible to vote in an election authorized by this section and who is unable to work the alternative schedule established as the result of that election. Employees affected by a change in work hours resulting from the adoption of an alternative workweek schedule shall not be required to work those new work hours for at least 30 days after the announcement of the final results of the election.

(f) An employer shall be permitted, but not required, to provide a work schedule not to exceed eight (8) hours in a workday to accommodate any employee who was hired after the date of the election and who is unable to work the alternative schedule established as the result of that election.

(g) An employer shall explore any available reasonable alternative means of accommodating the religious belief or observance of an affected employee that conflicts with an adopted alternative workweek schedule, in the manner provided by Government Code Section 12940(j).

(h) Notwithstanding paragraph (B)(1), subparagraphs (a)–(c), for employees working in offshore oil and gas production, drilling, and servicing occupations, as well as for employees working in onshore oil and gas separation occupations directly servicing offshore operations, an alternative workweek schedule may authorize work by the affected employees of no longer than 12 hours per day within a 40 hour workweek without the payment to the affected employees of an overtime rate of compensation. Employees working pursuant to an alternative workweek schedule adopted pursuant to this section shall be paid an overtime rate of compensation of no less than two (2) times their regular rate of pay in excess of the regularly scheduled hours established by the alternative workweek agreement, and for one and one-half (1 ½) times their regular rate of pay for any work in excess of 40 hours per week. The other provisions of this section, including those governing elections, shall apply to these occupations.

(i) In no case shall an alternative workweek requiring more than eight (8) hours of work in a day be utilized on a public works contract in violation of Labor Code Sections 1810–1815.

(C) *Election Procedures*

Election procedures for the adoption and repeal of alternative workweek schedules require the following:

(1) Each proposal for an alternative workweek schedule shall be in the form of a written agreement proposed by the employer who has control over wages, hours, and working conditions of the affected employees, and adopted in a secret ballot election, held before the performance of work, by at least a two-thirds (2/03) vote of the affected employees in the work unit. The proposed agreement must designate a regularly scheduled alternative workweek in which the specified number of work days and work hours are regularly recurring. The employer may propose a single work schedule that would

become the standard schedule for workers in the unit, or a menu of work schedule options, from which each employee in the unit would be entitled to choose. If the employer proposes a menu of work schedule options, the employee may, with the approval of the employer, move from one menu option to another.

(2) The election shall be held during regular working hours at the employees' work site. Ballots shall be mailed to the last known address of all employees in the work unit who are not present at the work site on the day of the election but have been employed by the employer within the last 30 calendar days immediately preceding the day of the election.

(3) Prior to the secret ballot vote, any employer who proposes to institute an alternative workweek schedule shall make a disclosure in writing to the affected employees, including the effects of the proposed arrangement on the employees' wages, hours, and benefits. Such a disclosure shall include meeting(s), duly noticed, held at least 14 days prior to voting, for the specific purpose of discussing the effects of the alternative workweek schedule. An employer shall provide the disclosure in a non–English language, as well as in English, if at least five (5) percent of the affected employees primarily speak that non–English language. Notices shall be mailed to the last known address of all employees in the work unit in accordance with provision (2) above. Failure to comply with this paragraph shall make the election null and void.

(4) Any election to establish or repeal an alternative workweek schedule shall be held during regular working hours at the work site of the affected employees. The employer shall bear the costs of conducting any election held pursuant to this section. Upon a complaint by an affected employee, and after an investigation by the labor commissioner, the labor commissioner may require the employer to select a neutral third party to conduct the election.

(5) Any type of alternative workweek schedule that is authorized by the Labor Code may be repealed by the affected employees. Upon a petition of one-third (1/03) of the affected employees, a new secret ballot election shall be held, provided six (6) months have passed since the election authorizing the alternative workweek. A two-thirds (2/03) vote of the affected employees shall be required to reverse the alternative workweek schedule. The election to repeal the alternative workweek schedule shall be held not more than 30 days after the petition is submitted to the employer.

(6) If the number of employees who are employed for at least 30 days in the work unit that adopted an alternative workweek schedule increases by 50 percent above the number who voted to ratify the employer-proposed alternative workweek schedule, the employer must conduct a new ratification election pursuant to the rules contained in subsection (C).

(7) The results of any election conducted pursuant to this order shall be a public document and shall be reported by the employer to the Division of Labor

Statistics and Research within 30 days after the results are final. The report of the election results shall also be posted at the job site in an area frequented by employees where it may easily be read during the workday. The report shall include the final tally of the vote, the size of the unit, and the nature of the business of the employer. Employees participating in the election shall be free from intimidation and coercion. However, nothing in this section shall prohibit an employer from expressing its position concerning that alternative workweek to the affected employees. No employees shall be discharged or discriminated against for expressing opinions concerning the alternative workweek election or for opposing or supporting its adoption or repeal. The labor commissioner shall investigate any alleged violation of this section and shall upon finding a serious violation render the alternative workweek schedule null and void.

(D) Combination of Overtime Rates. Nothing in this section requires an employer to combine more than one rate of overtime compensation in order to calculate the amount to be paid to an employee for any hour of overtime work.

(E) Nondiscrimination. No employee shall be terminated, disciplined or otherwise discriminated against for refusing to work more than 72 hours in any workweek, except in an emergency as defined in Section 2 (F) above.

(F) Makeup Time. If an employer approves a written request of an employee to make up work time that is or would be lost as a result of a personal obligation of the employee, the hours of that makeup work time, if performed in the same workweek in which the work time was lost, may not be counted toward computing the total number of hours worked in a day for purposes of the overtime requirements, except for hours in excess of 11 hours of work in one (1) day or 40 hours of work in one (1) workweek. If an employee knows in advance that he/she will be requesting makeup time for a personal obligation that will recur at a fixed time over a succession of weeks, the employee may request to make up work time for up to four (4) weeks in advance; provided, however, that the makeup work must be performed in the same week that the work time was lost. An employee shall provide a signed written request for each occasion that the employee makes a request to make up work time pursuant to this subsection. While an employer may inform an employee of this makeup time option, the employer is prohibited from encouraging or otherwise soliciting an employee to request the employer's approval to take personal time off and make up the work hours within the same workweek pursuant to this subsection. (See Labor Code Section 513.)

(G) One Day's Rest in Seven. The provisions of Labor Code Sections 551 and 552 regarding one (1) day's rest in seven (7) shall not be construed to prevent an accumulation of days of rest when the nature of the employment reasonably requires the employee to work seven (7) or more consecutive days; provided, however, that in each calendar month, the employee shall receive the equivalent of one (1) day's rest in seven (7).

(H) Collective Bargaining Agreements

(1) Subsections (A), (B), (C), (D), and (E) of Section 3, Hours and Days of Work, shall not apply to any employee covered by a valid collective bargaining agreement if the agreement expressly provides for the wages, hours of work, and working conditions of the employees, and if the agreement provides premium wage rates for all overtime hours worked and a regular hourly rate of pay for those employees of not less than 30 percent more than the state minimum wage. (See Labor Code Section 514).

(2) Subsection (F) of Section 3, Hours and Days of Work, shall apply to any employee covered by a valid collective bargaining agreement unless the collective bargaining agreement expressly provides otherwise.

4. Minimum Wages

(A) Every employer shall pay to each employee wages not less than seven dollars and fifty cents ($7.50) per hour for all hours worked, effective January 1, 2007, and not less than eight dollars ($8.00) per hour for all hours worked, effective January 1, 2008.

(B) Every employer shall pay to each employee, on the established payday for the period involved, not less than the applicable minimum wage for all hours worked in the payroll period, whether the remuneration is measured by time, piece, commission, or otherwise.

5. Reporting Time Pay

(A) All employer-mandated travel that occurs after the first location where the employee's presence is required by the employer shall be compensated at the employee's regular rate of pay or, if applicable, the premium rate that may be required by the provisions of Labor Code Section 510 and Section 3, Hours and Days of Work, above.

(B) Each workday that an employee is required to report to the work site and does report, but is not put to work or is furnished less than half of his/her usual or scheduled day's work, the employer shall pay him/her for half the usual or scheduled day's work, but in no event for less than two (2) hours nor more than four (4) hours at the employee's regular rate of pay, which shall not be less than the minimum wage.

(C) The foregoing reporting time pay provisions are not applicable when:

(1) Operations cannot commence or continue due to threats to employees or property; or when recommended by civil authorities; or

(2) Public utilities fail to supply electricity, water, or gas, or there is a failure in the public utilities, or sewer system; or

(3) The interruption of work is caused by an Act of God or other cause not within the employer's control.

(D) Collective Bargaining Agreements. This section shall apply to any employees covered by a valid collective bargaining agreement unless the collective bargaining agreement expressly provides otherwise.

6. Records

(A) Every employer who has control over wages, hours, or working conditions shall keep accurate information with respect to each employee, including the following:

(1) The employee's full name, home address, occupation, and social security number. The employee's date of birth, if under 18 years of age, and designation as a minor. Time records showing when the employee begins and ends each work period. Meal periods, split shift intervals, and total daily hours worked shall also be recorded. Meal periods during which operations cease and authorized rest periods need not be recorded.

(2) Total wages paid each payroll period, including value of board, lodging, or other compensation actually furnished to the employee.

(3) Total hours worked during the payroll period and applicable rates of pay. This information shall be made readily available to the employee upon reasonable request. When a piece rate or incentive plan is in operation, piece rates or an explanation of the incentive plan formula shall be provided to employees. An accurate production record shall be maintained by the employer.

(B) Every employer who has control over wages, hours, or working conditions shall semimonthly or at the time of each payment of wages furnish each employee an itemized statement in writing showing: (1) all deductions; (2) the inclusive dates of the period for which the employee is paid; (3) the name of the employee or the employee's social security number; and (4) the name of the employer, provided all deductions made on written orders of the employee may be aggregated and shown as one item. (See Labor Code Section 226.) This information shall be furnished either separately or as a detachable part of the check, draft, or voucher paying the employee's wages.

(C) All required records shall be in the English language and in ink or other indelible form, dated properly, showing month, day and year. The employer who has control over wages, hours, or working conditions shall also keep said records on file at the place of employment or at a central location for at least three years. An employee's records shall be available for inspection by the employee upon reasonable request.

(D) Employers performing work on public works projects should refer to Labor Code Section 1776 for additional payroll reporting requirements.

7. Deductions from Pay.
No employer shall collect or deduct from any employee any part of the wages that are paid unless such deductions are allowed by law. (See Labor Code Sections 220–226.) No fee shall be charged by the employer or agent of the employer for cashing a payroll check.

8. Uniforms and Equipment

(A) When the employer requires uniforms to be worn by the employee as a condition of employment, such uniforms shall be provided and maintained by the employer. The term "uniform" includes wearing apparel and accessories of distinctive design or color.

(B) When the employer requires the use of tools or equipment or they are necessary for the performance of a job, such tools and equipment shall be provided and maintained by the employer, except that an employee whose wages are at least two (2) times the minimum wage may provide and maintain hand tools and equipment customarily required by the particular trade or craft in conformity with Labor Code Section 2802.

9. Meals and Lodging

(A) "Meal" means an adequate, well-balanced serving of a variety of wholesome, nutritious foods.

(B) "Lodging" means living accommodations available to the employee for full-time occupancy which are adequate, decent, and sanitary according to usual and customary standards. Employees shall not be required to share a bed.

(C) Meals or lodging may not be credited against the minimum wage without a voluntary written agreement between the employer and the employee. When credit for meals or lodging is used to meet part of the employer's minimum wage obligation, the amounts so credited may not be more than the following:

(D) Meals evaluated as part of the minimum wage must be bona fide meals consistent with the employee's work shift. Deductions shall not be made for meals not received or lodging not used.

(E) If, as a condition of employment, the employee must live at the place of employment or occupy quarters owned or under

Effective	January 1, 2007	January 1, 2008
Lodging:		
Room occupied alone	$35.27 per week	$37.63 per week
Room shared	$29.11 per week	$31.06 per week
Apartment—two–thirds (2/03) of the ordinary rental value, and in no event more than	$423.51 per month	$451.89 per month
Where a couple are both employed by the employer, two-thirds (2/03) of the ordinary rental value, and in no event more than	$626.49 per month	$668.46 per month
Meals:		
Breakfast	$2.72	$2.90
Lunch	$3.72	$3.97
Dinner	$5.00	$5.34

the control of the employer, then the employer may not charge rent in excess of the values listed herein.

10. Meal Periods

(A) No employer shall employ any person for a work period of more than five (5) hours without a meal period of not less than 30 minutes, except that when a work period of not more than six (6) hours will complete the day's work the meal period may be waived by mutual consent of employer and employee. (See Labor Code Section 512.)

(B) An employer may not employ an employee for a work period of more than ten (10) hours per day without providing the employee with a second meal period of not less than 30 minutes, except that if the total hours worked is no more than 12 hours, the second meal period may be waived by mutual consent of employer and employee only if the first meal period was not waived. (See Labor Code Section 512.)

(C) In all places of employment the employer shall provide an adequate supply of potable water, soap, or other suitable cleansing agent and single use towels for hand washing.

(D) Unless the employee is relieved of all duty during a 30 minute meal period, the meal period shall be considered an "on duty" meal period and counted as time worked. An "on duty" meal period shall be permitted only when the nature of the work prevents employee from being relieved of all duty and when by written agreement between the parties an on-the-job paid meal period is agreed to and complies with Labor Code Section 512.

(E) Collective Bargaining Agreements. Subsections (A), (B), and (D) of Section 10, Meal Periods, shall not apply to any employee covered by a valid collective bargaining agreement if the agreement expressly provides for the wages, hours of work, and working conditions of the employees, and if the agreement provides premium wage rates for all overtime hours worked and a regular hourly rate of pay for those employees of not less than 30 percent more than the state minimum wage.

(F) If an employer fails to provide an employee a meal period in accordance with the applicable provisions of this order, the employer shall pay the employee one (1) hour of pay at the employee's regular rate of compensation for each workday that the meal period is not provided. In cases where a valid collective bargaining agreement provides final and binding mechanism for resolving disputes regarding enforcement of the meal period provisions, the collective bargaining agreement will prevail.

11. Rest Periods

(A) Every employer shall authorize and permit all employees to take rest periods, which insofar as practicable shall be in the middle of each work period. Nothing in this provision shall prevent an employer from staggering rest periods to avoid interruption in the flow of work and to maintain continuous operations, or from scheduling rest periods to coincide with breaks in the flow of work that occur in the course of the workday. The authorized rest period time shall be based on the total hours worked daily at the rate of ten (10) minutes net rest time for every four (4) hours worked, or major fraction thereof. Rest periods shall take place at employer designated areas, which may include or be limited to the employees' immediate work area.

(B) Rest periods need not be authorized in limited circumstances when the disruption of continuous operations would jeopardize the product or process of the work. However, the employer shall make up the missed rest period within the same workday or compensate the employee for the missed ten (10) minutes of rest time at his/her regular rate of pay within the same pay period.

(C) A rest period need not be authorized for employees whose total daily work time is less than three and one-half (3 ½) hours. Authorized rest period time shall be counted as hours worked for which there shall be no deduction from wages.

(D) If an employer fails to provide an employee a rest period in accordance with the applicable provisions of this order, the employer shall pay the employee one (1) hour of pay at the employee's regular rate of compensation for each workday that the rest period is not provided. In cases where a valid collective bargaining agreement provides final and binding mechanism for resolving disputes regarding enforcement of the rest period provisions, the collective bargaining agreement will prevail.

(E) This section shall not apply to any employee covered by a valid collective bargaining agreement if the collective bargaining agreement provides equivalent protection.

12. Seats. Where practicable and consistent with applicable industry wide standards, all working employees shall be provided with suitable seats when the nature of the process and the work performed reasonably permits the use of seats. This section shall not exceed regulations promulgated by the Occupational Safety and Health Standards Board.

13. Temperature. The temperature maintained in each interior work area shall provide reasonable comfort consistent with industry-wide standards for the nature of the process and the work performed. This section shall not exceed regulations promulgated by the Occupational Safety and Health Standards Board.

14. Elevators. Where practicable and consistent with applicable industry-wide standards, adequate elevators, escalators, or similar service consistent with industry-wide standards for the nature of the process and the work performed, shall be provided when employees are employed 60 feet or more above or below ground level. This section shall not exceed regulations promulgated by the Occupational Safety and Health Standards Board.

15. Exemptions. If, in the opinion of the Division after due investigation, it is found that the enforcement of any provision contained in Section 6, Records; Section 11, Rest Periods; Section 12, Seats; Section 13, Temperature; or Section 14, Elevators, would not materially affect the welfare or comfort of employees and would work an undue hardship on the employer, exemption may be made at the discretion of the Division. Such exemptions shall be in writing to be effective and may be revoked after reasonable notice is given in writing. Application for exemption shall be made by the employer or by the employee and/or the employee's representative to the Division in writing. A copy of the application shall be posted at the place of employment at the time the application is filed with the Division.

16. Filing Reports. (See California Labor Code, Section 1174(a))

17. Inspection. (See California Labor Code, Section 1174)

18. Penalties

(A) Penalties for Violations of the Provisions of this Order. Any employer or any other person acting on behalf of the employer who violates, or causes to be violated, the provisions of this order, shall be subject to civil and criminal penalties as provided by law. In addition, violation of any provision of this order shall be subject to a civil penalty as follows:

(1) Initial Violation—$50.00 for each underpaid employee for each pay period during which the employee was underpaid in addition to the amount which is sufficient to recover unpaid wages.

(2) Subsequent Violations—$100.00 for each underpaid employee for each pay period during which the employee was underpaid in addition to an amount which is sufficient to recover unpaid wages.

(3) The affected employee shall receive payment of all wages recovered. The labor commissioner may also issue citations pursuant to California Labor Code Section 1197.1 for non-payment of wages for overtime work in violation of this order.

(B) Penalties for Violations of Child Labor Laws. Any employer or other person acting on behalf of the employer is subject to civil penalties of from $500 to $10,000 as well as to criminal penalties for violation of child labor laws. (See Labor Code Sections 1285 to 1312 and 1390 to 1399 for additional restrictions on the employment of minors and for descriptions of criminal and civil penalties for violation of the child labor laws.) Employers should inquire at local school districts about any required work permits required for minors attending school.

(In addition, see California Labor Code, Section 1199)

19. SEPARABILITY. If the application of any provision of this order, or any section, subsection, subdivision, sentence, clause, phase, word, or portion of this order should be held invalid or unconstitutional or unauthorized or prohibited by statute, the remaining provisions thereof shall not be affected thereby, but shall continue to be given full force and effect as if the part is held to be invalid or unconstitutional had not been included herein.

20. Posting of Order. Every employer shall keep a copy of this order posted in an area frequented by employees where it may be easily read during the workday. Where the location of work or other conditions make this impractical, every employer shall keep a copy of this order, and make it available to every employee upon request.

Publisher's Notes

Interpretation of Wage Order 16 Rest Period Provisions

A letter from Arthur S. Lujan, State Labor Commissioner to Robert L. Balgenorth, President, State Building & Construction Trades Council, dated September 17, 2001, provided in pertinent part as follows:

This in response to questions that you and other members of the Building Trades have asked, seeking our interpretation as to the extent of employer flexibility in providing and scheduling rest periods that are required under Industrial Welfare Commission ("IWC") Order 16–2001. This wage order went into effect on January 1, 2001, and applies to all persons employed in the on-site occupations of construction, drilling, logging, and mining.

Although rest period requirements are found in all of the IWC industry or occupational wage orders, these requirements are new to construction employers (at least as to those employees covered by Order 16), in that prior to January 1, 2001, on-site construction employees, though covered by the general minimum wage order, were not covered by any IWC industry or occupational wage order. Thus, the past few months have been difficult as employers, employees and labor organizations in the construction industry have grappled with the day-to-day issues of implementing the wage order's rest period requirements.

Adding to the difficulty is the fact that, in recognition of some of the unique operational requirements of on-site construction, drilling, logging, and mining, the IWC fashioned rest period provisions in Order 16–2001 that markedly differ from those found in the other wage orders. We must therefore strongly caution all employers who employ workers covered by wage orders other than Order 16 that the following responses—which are founded upon the far greater flexibility regarding rest period scheduling under Order 16 than is found under any other wage order—do not apply to any workers other than those covered by Order 16. For example, a construction employer should not rely on these responses in implementing rest period requirements for its office clerical workers, as those employees have always been, and still are, covered by IWC Order 4, and its stricter provisions governing rest period scheduling.

The rest period requirements are found at section 11 of Order 16–2001. As is the case with the other industry and occupational wage orders, "authorized rest period time shall be counted as hours worked for which there shall be no deduction from wages." (Order 16–2001, sect. 11(C)) Also, "authorized rest period time shall be based on the total hours worked daily at the rate of ten minutes net

rest time for every four hours worked, or major fraction thereof." (Order 16–2001, sect. 11(A)) However, "a rest period need not be authorized for employees whose total daily work time is less than three and one-half hours." (Order 16–2001, sect. 11(C)) And as is the case with all other industry and occupational wage orders, section 11, subsection (A) starts as follows: "Every employer shall authorize and permit all employees to take rest periods, which insofar as practicable, shall be in the middle of each work period." The language that follows this sentence distinguishes Order 16's rest period requirements from those founded upon the other wage orders. Specifically, Order 16 goes on to provide:

"Nothing in this provision shall prevent an employer from staggering rest periods to avoid interruption in the flow of work and to maintain continuous operations, or from scheduling rest periods to coincide with breaks in the flow of work that occur in the course of the workday. . . . " (Sect. 11, subd. (A))

"Rest periods need not be authorized in limited circumstances when the disruption of continuous operations would jeopardize the product or process of the work. However, the employer shall make-up the missed rest period within the same workday or compensate the employee for the missed ten minutes of rest time at his or her regular rate of pay within the same pay period." (Sect. 11, subd. (B))

Order 16 then goes on to set out the premium pay provision for rest period violations that is was contained in all of the 2000 industry and occupational wage orders except for Order 14, and that is now contained in all of 2001 wage orders (including Order 14): "If an employer fails to provide an employee a rest period in accordance with the applicable provisions of this Order, the employer shall pay the employee one hour of pay at the employee's regular rate of compensation for each work day that the rest period was not provided." (Sect. 11, subd. (D))

Finally, Order 16 differs from the other wage orders with respect to rest period provisions in two other ways. First, most of the other wage orders require that "suitable resting facilities shall be provided in an area separate from the toilet rooms and shall be available to employees during work hours." (Order 4–2001, sect. 13) Order 16 contains no such requirement, but rather, provides that "rest periods shall take place at employer designated areas, which may include or be limited to the employees' immediate work area." Second, none of the other wage orders contain a collective bargaining agreement opt-out from rest period requirements. In contrast, Order 16–2001 provides for a very restrictive collective bargaining agreement opt-out, under which section 11 of the order "shall not apply to any employee covered by a valid collective bargaining agreement if the collective bargaining agreement provides equivalent protection." Of course, in order to provide "equivalent protection," the collective bargaining agreement would have to provide the same substantive requirements, both as to the right to rest periods and the right to premium pay for rest period violations.

With this background out of the way, we will now respond to the specific questions that have been asked:

1. An employer typically begins the day at 7:00 a.m., working five hours before the 12:00 noon thirty minute lunch break. Can that employer comply by providing a ten minute rest period sometime during the morning and then add 10 minutes to lunch in order to comply with the afternoon break requirement? Yes, as long as the first rest period is within the first four hours worked. The combined meal period and afternoon rest period would run from 12 noon to 12:40 p.m., of which ten minutes would constitute paid rest time. The afternoon portion of the regular workday would run until 3:30 p.m.

2. Can an employer who begins work at 7 a.m., working five hours before the 12 p.m. lunch, combine the 10–minute morning break with lunch at the end of the five hour period, and then provide a 10–minute break in the afternoon and be in compliance? No. In order to comply with the wage order, the first rest period would have to start no later than 10:50 a.m. (so that it is taken within four hours after the start of the workday), and the morning rest period would have to precede the meal period. In other words, the morning break would run from 10:50 a.m. to 11:00 a.m., the meal period would commence at 11:00 a.m., and the workers would be entitled to their 10 minute afternoon break during the afternoon.

3. Can an employer provide the ten minute rest period at the end of the day by having the employees leave work ten minutes early? No. A rest period must be preceded and followed by some work period during the workday. Otherwise, it is not a rest period, but rather, merely a means of shortening the workday. The purpose of the rest period is to refresh workers during the workday, and this purpose would be subverted by essentially eliminating the rest period in exchange for a shorter workday.

4. The wage order requires the employer to "authorize and permit" rest periods. Does this imply that employees can opt not to take a rest period or waive a rest period? Unlike meal periods, during which the employer has an affirmative obligation to ensure that workers are actually relieved of all duty, not performing any work, and free to leave the worksite; the employer is merely required to "authorize and permit all employees to take rest periods." An employer is not subject to any sort of penalty or premium pay obligation if an employee, who was truly authorized and allowed to take a rest break, *freely chooses without any coercion or encouragement* to forego or waive a rest period.

5. If an employer regularly requires employees to work five hours prior to their 30 minute lunch break, could that employer provide a ten minute rest period after two hours, followed by a second ten minute rest break upon the fourth hour, and then work a fifth hour, break for lunch and then work the final three hours of the eight hour day without another break? As a general matter, the first rest period should come sometime before the meal break and the second rest period should come sometime after the meal break. Unless the nature of the work after lunch is such that any rest break would jeopardize the product or process of work, so as to permit an employer to shift the afternoon rest period to the morning, the scenario described in this question appears not to comport with the requirement that rest periods "insofar as practicable, shall be in the middle of each work period." While it is true that Order 16 offers employers far more flexibility than is found in any other wage order as to the scheduling of rest periods, this scenario goes beyond what would be permitted absent truly unusual circumstances.

6. Can an employer comply by providing one 20 minute break in the morning or afternoon? A combined 20 minute rest period is never allowed under ordinary circumstances. Rather, the first break must precede the meal period and the second break must follow the meal period. A combined 20 minute break may be allowed only "in limited circumstances where the disruption of continuous operations would jeopardize the product or process of work." These "limited circumstances" are intended to be exceptional, not routine.

7. If an employee does have the right to waive a rest period, is there any prohibition on an employer paying an employee for a full day's work if the employee voluntarily waives the afternoon rest period and then leaves the worksite ten minutes early? The problem with this scenario is that it appears to cross the line into encouragement and solicitation of a waiver of the rest period. The IWC intended that as a normal practice, employees ought to have two 10 minute rest period during an eight hour day, one in the first four hours of the day, and the other in the second four hours of the day. As noted above, a "ten minute break" followed by quitting time is not a rest break at all, and having the employer pay for that fictitious break seems like a subterfuge.

8. Does the wage order allow employers to change the schedule of rest periods from one workday to the next, or does the schedule need to be fixed? There is no requirement that the scheduling of rest periods be fixed. Quite the opposite, as Order 16–2001 permits flexibility in scheduling rest periods on a day-to-day basis based on the employer's operational needs, so as to "avoid interruption in the flow of work and to maintain continuous operations," and to permit the "scheduling [of] rest periods to coincide with breaks in the flow of work that occur in the course of the workday."

9. Under the wage order, rest periods need not be authorized in limited circumstances when the disruption of work would "jeopardize the product or process of work." Does this provision give discretion to the employer to determine when the product or process of work is jeopardized? Does DLSE have any established standards to be used? Although it is initially the employer that gets to decide whether "the disruption of continuous opera-

tions would jeopardize the product or process of the work," so as to permit the employer to prohibit employees from taking an otherwise required and scheduled rest period, the employer must exercise this discretion in a manner consistent with the legal standard set out in Order 16. And ultimately, it is the Division of Labor Standards Enforcement ("DLSE") or the courts that will rule on any claim that may be filed challenging the employer's decision to prohibit employees from taking a rest period. Other than the language of the wage order itself, DLSE does not have any established regulation or standard that would be used in determining whether circumstances exist under which a disruption of work for purposes of a ten minute rest period would "jeopardize the product or process of work." In view of the multitude of variables, this would be a fact intensive inquiry, with determinations made as cases arise.

10. Would this exception apply to processes, such as cement pours, plaster applications, or certain types of welds that might be compromised if work is disrupted? These sorts of work processes would appear to be of the type where a disruption of work *might* "jeopardize the product or process of work." Of course, certain cement pours may be less critical than others with respect to the sort of cement used, the purpose for which the cement is being poured, the precise weather conditions, the number of workers on the job, the amount of time that it is safe to halt operations, etc. These are the sorts of factors that would be considered in determining whether an employer can refuse to permit a rest period.

11. Under this provision, can an employer determine that for safety concerns, such as limiting an employee's exposure to potentially dangerous conditions such as conditions on many highway projects, to not provide breaks and instead make it up later or pay straight time for the missed break? Certainly, bona fide safety considerations would be a factor in determining whether a disruption of work for a ten minute rest period would "jeopardize the product or process of work. Toward that end, however, it would appear that as a general rule, safety considerations would militate in favor of permitting a rest break, so as to refresh workers and provide them with a period of respite from potentially hazardous work.

Research References

See notes following listing of Wage Orders.

Please Post With This Side Showing
OFFICIAL NOTICE
Effective January 1, 2001 as amended
Sections 4(A) and 10(C) amended and republished by the Department of Industrial Relations, effective January 1, 2007, pursuant to AB 1835, Chapter 230, Statutes of 200

6

INDUSTRIAL WELFARE COMMISSION
ORDER NO. 17–2001
REGULATING
WAGES, HOURS AND WORKING CONDITIONS IN THE
MISCELLANEOUS EMPLOYEES

TAKE NOTICE: To employers and representatives of persons working in industries and occupations in the State of California:

The Department of Industrial Relations amends and republishes the minimum wage and meals and lodging credits in the Industrial Welfare Commission's Orders as a result of legislation enacted (AB 1835, Ch. 230, Stats of 2006, adding sections 1182.12 and 1182.13 to the California Labor Code.) The amendments and republishing make no other changes to the IWC's Orders.

1. Applicability of Order. This wage order implements changes in the law as a result of the Legislature's enactment of the "Eight–Hour–Day Restoration and Workplace Flexibility Act," Stats. 1999, ch. 134 (commonly referred to as AB 60).

(A) Any industry or occupation not previously covered by, and all employees not specifically exempted in, the Commission's wage orders in effect in 1997, or otherwise exempted by law, are covered by this order.

(B) Except as provided in subsection (C), an employee in the computer software field who is paid on an hourly basis shall be exempt from the daily overtime pay provisions of California Labor Code Section 510, if all of the following apply:

(1) The employee is primarily engaged in work that is intellectual or creative and requires the exercise of discretion and independent judgment, and the employee is primarily engaged in duties that consist of one or more of the following:

(a) The application of systems analysis techniques and procedures, including consulting with users, to determine hardware, software, or system functional specifications.

(b) The design, development, documentation, analysis, creation, testing, or modification of computer systems or programs, including prototypes, based on and related to user or system design specifications.

(c) The documentation, testing, creation, or modification of computer programs related to the design of software or hardware for computer operating systems.

(2) The employee is highly skilled and is proficient in the theoretical and practical application of highly specialized information to computer systems analysis, program-

ming, and software engineering. A job title shall not be determinative of the applicability of this exemption.

(3) The employee's hourly rate of pay is not less than forty-one dollars ($41.00). The Division of Labor Statistics and Research shall adjust this pay rate on October 1 of each year to be effective on January 1 of the following year by an amount equal to the percentage increase in the California Consumer Price Index for Urban Wage Earners and Clerical Workers.[1]

(C) The exemption provided in subsection (B) does not apply to an employee if any of the following apply:

(1) The employee is a trainee or employee in an entry-level position who is learning to become proficient in the theoretical and practical application of highly specialized information to computer systems analysis, programming, and software engineering.

(2) The employee is in a computer-related occupation but has not attained the level of skill and expertise necessary to work independently and without close supervision.

(3) The employee is engaged in the operation of computers or in the manufacture, repair, or maintenance of computer hardware and related equipment.

(4) The employee is an engineer, drafter, machinist, or other professional whose work is highly dependent upon or facilitated by the use of computers and computer software programs and who is skilled in computer-aided design software, including CAD/CAM, but who is not in a computer systems analysis or programming occupation.

(5) The employee is a writer engaged in writing material, including box labels, product descriptions, documentation, promotional material, setup and installation instructions, and other similar written information, either for print or for on screen media or who writes or provides content material intended to be read by customers, subscribers, or visitors to computer-related media such as the World Wide Web or CD–ROMs.

(6) The employee is engaged in any of the activities set forth in subsection (B) for the purpose of creating imagery for effects used in the motion picture, television, or theatrical industry.

(D) The provisions of this order shall not apply to any individual participating in a national service program, such as Ameri–Corps, carried out using assistance provided under Section 12571 of Title 42 of the United States Code. (See Stats. 2000, ch. 365, amending Labor Code Section 1171.)

2. Definitions

(A) An "alternative workweek schedule" means any regularly scheduled workweek requiring an employee to work more than eight (8) hours in a 24–hour period.

(B) "Shift" means designated hours of work by an employee, with a designated beginning time and quitting time.

(C) "Workday" and "day" mean any consecutive 24–hour period beginning at the same time each calendar day.

(D) "Workweek" and "week" mean any seven (7) consecutive days, starting with the same calendar day each week. "Workweek" is a fixed and regularly recurring period of 168 hours, seven (7) consecutive 24–hour periods.

3. Administrative, Executive, and Professional Employees. The following provisions shall not apply to persons employed in administrative, executive, or professional capacities. No person shall be considered to be employed in an administrative, executive, or professional capacity unless the person is primarily engaged in the duties which meet the test of the exemption and earns a monthly salary equivalent to no less than two (2) times the state minimum wage for full-time employment. The duties that meet the tests of the exemption are one of the following set of conditions:

(A) The employee is engaged in work which is primarily intellectual, managerial, or creative, and which requires exercise of discretion and independent judgment; or

(B) The employee is licensed or certified by the State of California and is engaged in the practice of one of the following recognized professions: law, medicine, dentistry, optometry, architecture, engineering, teaching, or accounting, or is engaged in an occupation commonly recognized as a learned or artistic profession; provided, however, that pharmacists employed to engage in the practice of pharmacy, and registered nurses employed to engage in the practice of nursing, shall not be considered exempt professional employees, nor shall they be considered exempt from coverage for the purposes of this subsection unless they individually meet the criteria established for exemption as executive or administrative employees.

(C) For the purposes of this section, "full-time employment" means employment in which an employee is employed for 40 hours per week.

(D) For the purposes of this section, "primarily" means more than one-half of the employee's work time.

4. Daily Overtime—General Provisions. The following overtime provisions are applicable to employees 18 years of age or over and to employees 16 or 17 years of age who are not required by law to attend school and are not otherwise prohibited by law from engaging in the subject work. Such employees shall not be employed more than eight (8) hours in any workday or more than 40 hours in any workweek unless the employee receives one and one-half (1 $\frac{1}{2}$) times such employee's regular rate of pay for all hours worked over 40 hours in the workweek. Eight (8) hours of labor constitutes a day's work. Employment beyond eight (8) hours in any workday or more than six (6) days in any workweek is permissible provided the employee is compensated for such overtime at not less than:

(A) One and one-half (1 ½) times the employee's regular rate of pay for all hours worked in excess of eight (8) hours up to and including 12 hours in any workday, and for the first eight (8) hours worked on the seventh (7th) consecutive day of work in a workweek; and

(B) Double the employee's regular rate of pay for all hours worked in excess of 12 hours in any workday and for all hours worked in excess of eight (8) hours on the seventh (7th) consecutive day of work in a workweek.

(C) The overtime rate of compensation required to be paid to a nonexempt full-time salaried employee shall be computed by using the employee's regular hourly salary as one-fortieth (1/40) of the employee's weekly salary.

5. Alternative Workweek

(A) No employer shall be deemed to have violated the daily overtime provisions by instituting, pursuant to the election procedures set forth in this wage order, a regularly scheduled alternative workweek schedule of not more than ten (10) hours per day within a 40 hour workweek without the payment of an overtime rate of compensation. All work performed in any workday beyond the schedule established by the agreement up to 12 hours a day or beyond 40 hours per week shall be paid at one and one-half (1 ½) times the employee's regular rate of pay. All work performed in excess of 12 hours per day and any work in excess of eight (8) hours on those days worked beyond the regularly scheduled number of workdays established by the alternative workweek agreement shall be paid at double the employee's regular rate of pay. Any alternative workweek agreement adopted pursuant to this section shall provide for not less than four (4) hours of work in any shift. Nothing in this section shall prohibit an employer, at the request of the employee, to substitute one (1) day of work for another day of the same length in the shift provided by the alternative workweek agreement on an occasional basis to meet the personal needs of the employee without the payment of overtime. No hours paid at either one and one-half (1 ½) or double the regular rate of pay shall be included in determining when 40 hours have been worked for the purpose of computing overtime compensation.

(B) If an employer whose employees have adopted an alternative workweek agreement permitted by this order requires an employee to work fewer hours than those that are regularly scheduled by the agreement, the employer shall pay the employee overtime compensation at a rate of one and one-half (1 ½) times the employee's regular rate of pay for all hours worked in excess of eight (8) hours, and double the employee's regular rate of pay for all hours worked in excess of 12 hours for the day the employee is required to work the reduced hours.

(C) An employer shall not reduce an employee's regular rate of hourly pay as a result of the adoption, repeal or nullification of an alternative workweek schedule.

(D) An employer shall explore any available reasonable alternative means of accommodating the religious belief or observance of an affected employee that conflicts with an adopted alternative workweek schedule, in the manner provided by subdivision (j) of Section 12940 of the Government Code.

(E) An employer shall make a reasonable effort to find a work schedule not to exceed eight (8) hours in a workday, in order to accommodate any affected employee who was eligible to vote in an election authorized by this section and who is unable to work the alternative workweek schedule established as the result of that election.

(F) An employer shall be permitted, but not required, to provide a work schedule not to exceed eight (8) hours in a workday to accommodate any employee who is hired after the date of the election and who is unable to work the alternative workweek schedule established by the election.

(G) The provisions of Labor Code Sections 551 and 552 regarding one (1) day's rest in seven (7) shall not be construed to prevent an accumulation of days of rest when the nature of the employment reasonably requires the employee to work seven (7) or more consecutive days; provided, however, that in each calendar month, the employee shall receive the equivalent of one (1) day's rest in seven (7).

(H) Arrangements adopted in a secret ballot election held pursuant to this order prior to 1998, or under the rules in effect prior to 1998, and before the performance of the work, shall remain valid after July 1, 2000 provided that the results of the election are reported by the employer to the Division of Labor Statistics and Research by January 1, 2001, in accordance with the requirements of Election Procedures subsection F. New arrangements can only be entered into pursuant to the provisions of this section.

Election Procedures

(A) Each proposal for an alternative workweek schedule shall be in the form of a written agreement proposed by the employer. The proposed agreement must designate a regularly scheduled alternative workweek in which the specified number of work days and work hours are regularly recurring. The actual days worked within that alternative workweek schedule need not be specified. The employer may propose a single work schedule that would become the standard schedule for workers in the work unit, or a menu of work schedule options, from which each employee in the unit would be entitled to choose. If the employer proposes a menu of work schedule options, the employee may, with the approval of the employer, move from one menu option to another.

(B) In order to be valid, the proposed alternative workweek schedule must be adopted in a secret ballot election, before the performance of work, by at least a two-thirds (2/03) vote of the affected employees in the work unit. The election shall be held during regular working hours at the employees' work site. For purposes of this subsection, "affected employees in the work unit" may include all employees in a readily identifiable work unit, such as a division, a department, a job classification, a shift, a separate physical location, or a recognized subdivision of any such work unit. A work unit may consist of an individual employee as long as the criteria for an identifiable work unit in this subsection are met.

(C) Prior to the secret ballot vote, any employer who proposed to institute an alternative workweek schedule shall have made a disclosure in writing to the affected employees, including the effects of the proposed arrangement on the employees' wages, hours, and benefits. Such a disclosure shall include meeting(s), duly noticed, held at least 14 days prior to voting, for the specific purpose of discussing the effects of the alternative workweek schedule. An employer shall provide that disclosure in a non–English language, as well as in English, if at least five (5) percent of the affected employees primarily speak that non–English language. The employer shall mail the written disclosure to employees who do not attend the meeting. Failure to comply with this section shall make the election null and void.

(D) Any election to establish or repeal an alternative workweek schedule shall be held during regular working hours at the work site of the affected employees. The employer shall bear the costs of conducting any election held pursuant to this section. Upon a complaint by an affected employee, and after an investigation by the labor commissioner, the labor commissioner may require the employer to select a neutral third party to conduct the election.

(E) Any type of alternative workweek schedule that is authorized by the Labor Code may be repealed by the affected employees. Upon a petition of one-third (1/03) of the affected employees, a new secret ballot election shall be held and a two-thirds (2/03) vote of the affected employees shall be required to reverse the alternative workweek schedule. The election to repeal the alternative workweek schedule shall be held not more than 30 days after the petition is submitted to the employer, except that the election shall be held not less that 12 months after the date that the same group of employees voted in an election held to adopt or repeal an alternative workweek schedule. The election shall take place during regular working hours at the employees' work site. If the alternative workweek schedule is revoked, the employer shall comply within 60 days. Upon proper showing of undue hardship, the Division of Labor Standards Enforcement may grant an extension of time for compliance.

(F) Only secret ballots may be cast by affected employees in the work unit at any election held pursuant to this section. The results of any election conducted pursuant to this section shall be reported by the employer to the Division of Labor Statistics and Research within 30 days after the results are final, and the report of election results shall be a public document. The report shall include the final tally of the vote, the size of the unit, and the nature of the business of the employer.

(G) Employees affected by a change in the work hours resulting from the adoption of an alternative workweek schedule may not be required to work those new work hours for at least 30 days after the announcement of the final results of the election.

(H) Employers shall not intimidate or coerce employees to vote either in support of or in opposition to a proposed alternative workweek. No employees shall be discharged or discriminated against for expressing opinions concerning the alternative workweek election or for opposing or supporting its adoption or repeal. However, nothing in this section shall prohibit an employer from expressing his/her position concerning that alternative workweek to the affected employees. A violation of this subsection shall be subject to Labor Code Section 98 *et seq*.

6. Minors. Violations of Child Labor Laws are subject to civil penalties of from $500 to $10,000 as well as to criminal penalties. Refer to California Labor Code Sections 1285 to 1312 and 1390 to 1399 for additional restrictions on the employment of minors and for descriptions of criminal and civil penalties for violation of the child labor laws. Employers should ask school districts about any required work permits.

7. Collective Bargaining Agreements

(A) Sections 4 and 5 of this order shall not apply to any employee covered by a valid collective bargaining agreement if the agreement expressly provides for the wages, hours of work, and working conditions of the employees, and if the agreement provides premium wage rates for all overtime hours worked and a regular hourly rate of pay for those employees of not less than 30 percent more than the state minimum wage.

(B) Notwithstanding Section 7(A), where the employer and a labor organization representing employees of the employer have entered into a valid collective bargaining agreement pertaining to the hours of work of the employees, the requirement regarding the equivalent of one (1) day's rest in seven (7) (see Section 5(G) above) shall apply, unless the agreement expressly provides otherwise.

8. Makeup Time. If an employer approves a written request of an employee to make up work time that is or would be lost as a result of a personal obligation of the employee, the hours of that makeup work time, if performed in the same workweek in which the work time was lost, may not be counted toward computing the total number of hours worked in a day for purposes of the overtime requirements, except for hours in excess of 11 hours of work in one (1) day or 40 hours of work in one workweek. If an employee knows in advance that he/she will be requesting makeup time for a personal obligation that will recur at a fixed time over a succession of weeks, the employee may request to make up work time for up to four (4) weeks in advance; provided, however, that the makeup work must be performed in the same week that the work time was lost. An employee shall provide a signed written request for each occasion that the employee makes a request to make up work time pursuant to this section. While an employer may inform an employee of this makeup time option, the employer is prohibited from encouraging or otherwise soliciting an employee to request the employer's approval to take personal time off and make up the work hours within the same workweek pursuant to this section.

9. Meal Periods

(A) No employer shall employ any person for a work period of more than five (5) hours without a meal period of not less than 30 minutes, except that when a work period of not more than six (6) hours will complete the day's work the meal period may be waived by mutual consent of the employer and the employee.

(B) An employer may not employ an employee for a work period of more than ten (10) hours per day without providing the employee with a second meal period of not less than 30 minutes, except that if the total hours worked is no more than 12 hours, the second meal period may be waived by mutual consent of the employer and the employee only if the first meal period was not waived.

(C) If an employer fails to provide an employee a meal period in accordance with the applicable provisions of this order, the employer shall pay the employee one (1) hour of pay at the employee's regular rate of compensation for each workday that the meal period is not provided.

10. Penalties. In addition to any other civil or criminal penalty provided by law, any employer or any other person acting on behalf of the employer who violates, or causes to be violated, the provisions of this order, shall be subject to the civil penalty of:

(A) Initial Violation—$50.00 for each underpaid employee for each pay period during which the employee was underpaid in addition to the amount which is sufficient to recover unpaid wages.

(B) Subsequent Violations—$100.00 for each underpaid employee for each pay period during which the employee was underpaid in addition to an amount which is sufficient to recover unpaid wages.

(C) The affected employee shall receive payment of all wages recovered.

(D) The labor commissioner may also issue citations pursuant to California Labor Code Section 1197.1 for non-payment of wages for overtime work in violation of this order.

11. Separability. If the application of any provision of this order, or any section, subsection, subdivision, sentence, clause, phrase, word, or portion of this order should be held invalid or unconstitutional or unauthorized or prohibited by statute, the remaining provisions thereof shall not be affected thereby, but shall continue to be given full force and effect as if the part so held invalid or unconstitutional had not been included herein.

12. Posting of Order. Every employer shall keep a copy of this order posted in an area frequented by employees where it may be easily read during the workday. Where the location of work or other conditions make this impractical, every employer shall keep a copy of this order and make it available to every employee upon request.

[1] Pursuant to Labor Code section 515.5, subdivision (a)(4), the Division of Labor Statistics and Research, Department of Industrial Relations, has adjusted the minimum hourly rate of pay specified in this subdivision to be $49.77, effective January 1, 2007. This hourly rate of pay is adjusted on October 1 of each year to be effective on January 1, of the following year, and may be obtained at www.dir.ca.gov/IWC or by mail from the Department of Industrial Relations.

———

Publisher's Notes

Research References

See notes following listing of Wage Orders.

CALIFORNIA JURY INSTRUCTIONS

This table indicates where sections of the California Codes appearing in this pamphlet are referenced in the California Jury Instructions—Civil, 9th (BAJI), the California Jury Instructions–Criminal, 6th Edition (CALJIC), and the Judicial Council of California Civil Jury Instructions (CACI)

CIVIL CODE

44	CACI 1700
45	CACI 1700, 1702, 1704
45a	CACI 1701, 1703, 1705
46	CACI 1700
47	BAJI 7.05, 7.05.1, 7.36, 7.86, 7.86.1, CACI 1501
48a	CACI 1701, 1703, 1705
49	BAJI 7.97
51	BAJI 7.92, 7.92.1, 7.94; CACI 3020, 3026, VF-3010
51.1	BAJI 7.92.1
51.7	BAJI 7.92.1, 7.93, 7.94; CACI 3023, 3020, VF-3013; CALJIC 16.501
51.9	CACI 3024
52	BAJI 7.92, 7.92.1, 7.93, 7.94; CACI 3020, VF-3010
846	BAJI 8.01
1714	BAJI 8.01
1714.2	CACI 425
1929	CACI 4326
1941	CACI 4326
1941.1	BAJI 8.01
1941.2	CACI 4326
1942	CACI 4326
2079	BAJI 6.38.1, CACI 4107
2079.2	BAJI 6.38
3283	CACI 1700, 1702, 1704
3294	BAJI 2.62, 7.10.1, 7.12, 7.12.1, 10.43, 12.25, 14.61, 14.71, 14.72.1, 14.72.2, 14.73, 14.73.1, 14.75, 16.81; CACI 2500, 3102A, 3102B, 3942, 3943, 3945, 3947, 3949
3334	CACI 3903F, 3903G
3346	CACI 2030
3426.1	CACI 4402, 4412
3490	CACI 2030

CODE OF CIVIL PROCEDURE

338	CACI 1925, 2030
425.13	BAJI 6.00.1
527.6	BAJI 7.20, 7.58
1161.1	CACI 4324
1174	CACI 3903F, 3903G

GOVERNMENT CODE

821.6	CACI 1500, 1501, 1502
835.4	BAJI 11.61; CACI VF-1101
12900	BAJI 10.41
12926	BAJI 7.92, 12.01, 12.05, 12.06, 12.08, 12.12, 12.12.5, 12.13, 12.14, 12.15, 12.20; CACI 2541, 2542, 2500
12926.1	BAJI 12.15, CACI 2541, 2542, 2546
12940(a)	BAJI 12.01, 12.12, 12.14, 12.16; CACI 2500, VF-2500, VF-2501, VF-2502, VF-2503, VF-2508
12940(b)	CACI 2500
12940(c)	CACI 2500
12940(d)	CACI 2500

12940(g)	BAJI 12.10
12940(h)	BAJI 12.10; CACI 2527, VF-2504
12940(j)	BAJI 12.05, 12.06, 12.08, 12.20; CACI VF-2506, VF-2507
12940(k)	CACI 2527
12940(l)	CACI VF-2511, VF-2512
12940(m)	BAJI 12.12.5, 12.15; CACI 2541, 2542, VF-2509, VF-2510, VF-2513
12940(n)	BAJI 12.12.6; CACI 2546, VF-2513
12941	BAJI 10.42
12941.1	BAJI 12.22
12945.2	CACI 2600, VF-2600, VF-2601, VF-2602

LABOR CODE

201	CACI VF-2700
202	CACI VF-2700
203	CACI 2704, VF-2703
218	CACI 2704, VF-2700, VF-2703
970	CACI 2710, VF-2704
1050	CACI 2711, VF-2705
1102.5	BAJI 10.42
1194	CACI 2701, 2702, VF-2701, VF-2702
2750	BAJI 10.00
2750.6	BAJI 6.20, 6.21
2922	BAJI 10.10, 10.11, 10.31, 10.33; CACI 2403
2924	BAJI 10.10, 10.11, 10.31, 10.32, 10.33
3600	BAJI 15.12; CACI 3726
3601	BAJI 15.12; CACI 2811, 2812, VF-2804, VF-2805
3602	BAJI 15.13; CACI 2801, 2802, 2803, VF-2800, VF-2801, VF-2802
3706	BAJI 15.13
3854	BAJI 14.02
3855	BAJI 16.75
4558	BAJI 15.13; CACI 2804, VF-2803
6304.5	BAJI 3.45

PENAL CODE

25	CALJIC 4.00
26	CALJIC 4.47
25.5	CALJIC 4.00
186.9	CALJIC 12.99
186.10	CALJIC 12.99
189	CALJIC 8.20, 8.25, 8.67, 8.81.15.1
190.2	CALJIC 8.81.15.1
197	CALJIC 5.56
211	CALJIC 9.40
241	CALJIC 16.100
245.1	CALJIC 16.100
459	CALJIC 14.50
597	CALJIC 14.96
597a	CALJIC 16.325
599b	CALJIC 14.96, 16.325
599c	CALJIC 14.96
602	CACI VF-2000, VF-2001, VF-2002

647	CALJIC 16.400
664	CALJIC 8.67
830	CALJIC 16.100
1127f	CACI 224
4573.8	CALJIC 7.34.04
4573.9	CALJIC 7.34.05
12020	CALJIC 12.42
12022	CALJIC 14.96

REVENUE AND TAXATION CODE

17282	CALJIC 7.78

UNEMPLOYMENT INSURANCE CODE

2101	CALJIC 7.22

FEDERAL JURY INSTRUCTIONS

This table indicates where sections of federal laws relevant to the subject matter of this pamphlet are referenced in the Ninth Circuit Manual of Model Jury Instructions—Civil (Civ) (2007)

TITLE 29

185	Civ 13.2
216	Civ 11.7A, 11.7B
623	Civ 11.3, 11.6, 11.6A, 11.6B, 11.6D, 11.6E
626	Civ 11.7A, 11.7B, 11.7D
630	Civ 11.2
631	Civ 11.2, 11.4

TITLE 42

8–9	Civ 12.1B
1981	Civ 5.5
1981a	Civ 5.2, 5.5, 12.13
1983	Civ 5.6, 9.1–9.26
2000e–2	Civ 10.3, 10.5A, 10.5B
2000e–3	Civ 10.1A, 10.3, 11.3
2000e–4–6	Civ 12.1B
2000e–5	Civ 10.1A, 10.3, 12.13
12102	Civ 12.2
12111	Civ 12.1B, 12.6, 12.7, 12.8, 12.9, 12.12
12112	Civ 12.1B, 12.13
12113	Civ 12.11, 12.12
12114	Civ 12.6
12117	Civ 12.1B, 12.13
12203	Civ 12.10

TITLE 45

51 et seq.	Civ 6.1, 7.2
53	Civ 6.1, 6.7, 7.9

FEDERAL LABOR AND EMPLOYMENT LAWS

For the text of the provisions listed below, accompanied by Commentary, notes to Leading Cases, and Research References, consult *Carlson's Federal Employment Laws Annotated*, a single volume pamphlet published by West.

WAGES AND HOURS; CHILD LABOR

1. The Consumer Credit Protection Act (excerpts) [15 USCA §§ 1671—1677]

2. The Anti–Kickback Act (excerpt) [18 USCA § 874]

3. Fair Labor Standards Act [29 USCA §§ 201—219]

4. The Portal-to-Portal Act [29 USCA §§ 251—262]

5. The Migrant and Seasonal Agricultural Worker Protection Act (excerpts) [29 USCA §§ 1801—1803, 1821—1872]

6. The Miller Act (Public Works) [40 USCA §§ 3131—3134]

7. The Davis–Bacon Act and Related Provisions (Public Works) [40 USCA §§ 3141—3148]

8. The Contract Work Hours and Safety Standards Act [40 USCA §§ 3701—3708]

9. The Walsh–Healey Act (Public Contracts) [41 USCA §§ 35—45]

10. The Anti–Kickback Act of 1986 [41 USCA §§ 51—58]

11. The Service Contract Act [41 USCA §§ 351—358]

12. The Contract Disputes Act [41 USCA §§ 601—613]

13. Statutes Relating to Shipping Personnel [46 USCA Chapters 103, 105, 106, 107, 109, 111]

EMPLOYEE BENEFITS; FAMILY AND MEDICAL LEAVE ACT

1. The Employee Retirement Income Security Act [29 USCA §§ 1001—1461]

2. The Family and Medical Leave Act [29 USCA §§ 2601—2654]

3. Public Health Services Act (excerpts) [42 USCA §§ 300bb–1—300bb–8]

HIRING AND INVESTIGATION OF EMPLOYEES

1. The Immigration Reform and Control Act (excerpts) [8 USCA §§ 1324a—1324d]

2. The Consumer Credit Protection Act (excerpts) [15 USCA §§ 1681—1681x]

3. The Electronic Communications Privacy Act (excerpts) [18 USCA §§ 2510—2515, 2517—2518, 2520, 2701—2702, 2707, 2708]

4. Migrant and Seasonal Agricultural Worker Protection Act (excerpts) [29 USCA §§ 1811—1816]

5. The Employee Polygraph Protection Act [29 USCA §§ 2001—2009]

6. State Directory of New Hires [42 USCA § 653a]

7. Mass Transit Employees Drug and Alcohol Testing [49 USCA § 5331]

8. Railroad Employees Drug and Alcohol Testing [49 USCA § 20140]

9. Drug and Alcohol Testing for Operators of Commercial Motor Vehicles [49 USCA § 31306]

10. Drug and Alcohol Testing for Employees of Air Carriers [49 USCA §§ 45101—45107]

EMPLOYMENT DISCRIMINATION

1. Discriminatory Treatment in Bankruptcy [11 USCA § 525]

2. The Equal Pay Act (excerpt) [29 USCA § 206(d)]

3. The Age Discrimination in Employment Act [29 USCA §§ 621—634]

4. The Rehabilitation Act (excerpts) [29 USCA §§ 705(9), (20), 791, 793, 794, 794a]

5. The Civil Rights Acts of 1866 and 1871 (as amended by the Civil Rights Act of 1991) (excerpts) [42 USCA §§ 1981, 1981a, 1983, 1985, 1988]

6. The Civil Rights Act of 1964, Title VII [42 USCA §§ 2000e—2000e–17]

7. The Glass Ceiling Act [P. L. 102–166, Title II]

8. Genetic Information Nondiscrimination Act [42 USCA §§ 2000ff–2000ff–4]

9. The Americans with Disabilities Act (excerpts) [42 USCA §§ 12101, 12102, 12111—12117, 12201—12213]

PROTECTION FOR WHISTLEBLOWING, MILITARY SERVICE AND OTHER PUBLIC SERVICE

1. Federal Contractors [10 USCA § 2409]

2. Financial Institutions Reform, Recovery and Enforcement Act (excerpt) [12 USCA § 1831j]

3. The Toxic Substances Control Act (excerpt) [15 USCA § 2622]

4. The Sarbanes-Oxley Act (excerpt) [18 USCA §§ 1513, 1514A]

5. The Jury System Improvement Act of 1978 (excerpt) [28 USCA § 1875]

6. The False Claims Act [31 USCA §§ 3729—3733]

7. The Water Pollution Control Act (excerpt) [33 USCA § 1367]

8. The Vietnam Era Veterans' Readjustment Assistance Act [38 USCA §§ 4211—4215]

9. The Uniformed Services Employment and Reemployment Rights Act of 1994 [38 USCA §§ 4301—4335]

10. Federal Acquisition Streamlining Act of 1994 (excerpt) [41 USCA § 265]

11. The Safe Drinking Water Act (excerpt) [42 USCA § 300j–9]

12. The Energy Reorganization Act (excerpt) [42 USCA § 5851]

13. The Solid Waste Disposal Act (excerpt) [42 USCA § 6971]

14. The Clean Air Act (excerpt) [42 USCA § 7622]

15. The Comprehensive Environmental Response, Compensation and Liability Act (excerpt) [42 USCA § 9610]

16. Railroad Safety—Employee Protections [49 USCA § 20109]

17. Commercial Motor Vehicle Safety–Employee Protections [49 USCA § 31105, 42121, 60129]

18. Whistleblower Protection Program [50 USCA § 2702]

19. American Recovery and Reinvestment Act of 2009 (excerpt) [Public Law No. 111–5, Section 1553, 123 Stat. 296–297]

COLLECTIVE BARGAINING

1. Federal Employees—Labor–Management Relations [5 USCA §§ 7101—7135]

2. Bankruptcy Code (excerpts) (Rejection of Collective Bargaining Agreements) [11 USCA §§ 1113–1116]

3. Sherman Act (excerpts) [15 USCA §§ 1, 2, 17]

4. Transportation of Strikebreakers [18 USCA § 1231]

5. The Clayton Act (excerpts) [29 USCA §§ 52, 53]

6. The Norris–La Guardia Act [29 USCA §§ 101—115]

7. The Labor Management Relations Act and National Labor Relations Act [29 USCA §§ 141—187]

8. The Labor–Management Reporting and Disclosure Act [29 USCA §§ 401—531]

9. Postal Service Employees [39 USCA §§ 1004, 1201—1209]

10. The Railway Labor Act [45 USCA §§ 151—188]

11. Mass Transportation—Labor Standards [49 USCA § 5333]

ARBITRATION

1. The Federal Arbitration Act [9 USCA §§ 1—16]

OCCUPATIONAL SAFETY AND HEALTH

1. The Occupational Safety and Health Act [29 USCA §§ 651—678]

2. The Federal Mine Safety and Health Act [30 USCA §§ 801—965]

3. The Drug–Free Workplace Act [41 USCA §§ 701—707]

WORKERS' COMPENSATION

1. Longshore and Harbor Workers' Compensation Act [33 USCA §§ 901—950]

2. The Federal Employers' Liability Act [45 USCA §§ 51—60]

UNEMPLOYMENT, MASS LAYOFFS AND PLANT CLOSINGS

1. The Toxic Substances Control Act (excerpt) [15 USCA § 2623]

2. Adjustment Assistance for Workers [19 USCA §§ 2271—2395]

3. The Worker Adjustment and Retraining Notification Act (WARN) [29 USCA §§ 2101—2109]

4. The Clean Air Act (excerpt) [42 USCA § 7621]

CIVIL SERVICE AND OTHER PUBLIC EMPLOYMENT PROTECTIONS

1. Government Employee Rights [2 USCA §§ 1301—1438]

2. Merit Systems Protection Board (Special Counsel; Right of Action) [5 USCA §§ 1201—1308, 2301—2305, 5596]

3. Employee Relations—Adverse Actions and Appeals [5 USCA §§ 7501—7703]

4. Disloyalty and Asserting Right to Strike [18 USCA § 1918]

INDEX

Abbreviations

Const	Constitution of California
Bus & P	Business and Professions Code
CC	Civil Code
CCP	Code of Civil Procedure
Corp	Corporations Code
Educ	Education Code
Elec	Elections Code
Evid	Evidence Code
Fam	Family Code
Fin	Financial Code
Food & A	Food and Agricultural Code
Gov	Government Code
Health & S	Health and Safety Code
Ins	Insurance Code
Labor	Labor Code
Mil & V	Military and Veterans Code
Pen	Penal Code
Pub U	Public Utilities Code
Rev & T	Revenue and Taxation Code
Un Ins	Unemployment Insurance Code
Veh	Vehicle Code
Welf & I	Welfare and Institutions Code

ABANDONED OR UNCLAIMED PROPERTY

Address, intangibles, **CCP 1510**

Apparent owner, definitions, **CCP 1501**

Banking organization, definitions, **CCP 1501**

Business associations, definitions, **CCP 1501**

Definitions, **CCP 1501**
New Act, **CCP 1501**

Disability compensation fund, unclaimed warrants, **Un Ins 3011**

Employee benefit plan distribution, definitions, **CCP 1501**

Employee benefit trust distribution, definitions, **CCP 1501**

Escheat, generally, this index

Financial organization, definitions, **CCP 1501**

Government or governmental subdivision or agency, definitions, **CCP 1501**

Holder, definitions, **CCP 1501**

Intangible personalty, **CCP 1510**

Life insurance, corporation, definitions, **CCP 1501**

Owner, definitions, **CCP 1501**

Person, definitions, **CCP 1501**

Residuals, definitions, **CCP 1501**

Sale, lease or other disposition. Escheat, generally, this index

Utilities, definitions, **CCP 1501**

ABANDONMENT

Compensation, plan for central place of payment, several employers, **Labor 204a**

ABATEMENT

Agricultural labor and employment, field sanitation standards violations, **Labor 6712**

Field sanitation standards violations, **Labor 6712**

Nuisance, this index

Occupational safety and health standard violations, commencement of abatement period, **Labor 6317**

ABATEMENT OF ACTIONS OR PROCEEDINGS

Workers Compensation, this index

ABDUCTION

Children and Minors, this index

ABETTORS

Accomplices and Accessories, generally, this index

ABODE

Domicile and Residence, generally, this index

ABSCONDERS

Unemployment compensation, priority and lien of tax, **Un Ins 1701 et seq.**

ABSENCE AND ABSENTEES

Armed forces. Military Forces, this index

Compensation, discharged or resigned employee avoiding payment, penalties, **Labor 203**

Hazardous substances lists, health and safety safeguarding duty, **Labor 6381**

Labor and Employment, this index

Leaves of absence,
District attorneys, investigators, inspectors, disability benefits, **Labor 4850**
Firefighters and Fire Departments, this index
Labor and Employment, this index
Law enforcement officers, disability benefits, **Labor 4850**
Military Forces, this index
Police, disability benefits, **Labor 4850**
Public Officers and Employees, this index
San Francisco Harbor police, lieu of disability payments, **Labor 4800 et seq.**
School Officers and Employees, this index
Sheriffs, disability benefits, **Labor 4850**
Sick Leave, generally, this index
State Officers and Employees, this index

Military Forces, this index

Unemployment compensation, alcoholics and alcoholism, disqualifications, **Un Ins 1256.4**

ABSENTEES
Absence and Absentees, generally, this index

ABUSE
Aged Persons, this index
Community Care Facilities, this index
Dependent Adults, this index
Domestic Violence, generally, this index
Nurses, this index
Nursing Homes, this index
Psychiatric technicians, long term health care facilities, temporary employment, **CC 1812.543**
Social Services, this index
Spousal abuse. Domestic Violence, generally, this index
Vocational nursing, long term health care facilities, temporary employment, **CC 1812.543**

ACADEMIES
Private Schools, generally, this index

ACCESS SHAFT
Definitions, tunnel and mine safety, **Labor 7951**

ACCESSORIES
Accomplices and Accessories, generally, this index

ACCIDENT AND HEALTH INSURANCE
Disability insurance. Insurance, this index

ACCIDENTS
Amusements,
  Permanent amusement rides, reports, **Labor 7925**
  Rides, reports, **Labor 7904, 7914**
Boiler operation, **Labor 7770, 7771**
Crew members, hours of labor, **Labor 607**
Disability compensation. Unemployment Compensation, this index
Disability insurance. Insurance, this index
Druggists, hours of labor, **Labor 854**
Health insurance, disability insurance. Insurance, this index
Hours of labor, druggists, **Labor 854**
Insurance, generally, this index
Motor Vehicles, this index
Permanent amusement rides, reports, **Labor 7925**
Personal Injuries, generally, this index
Railroads, this index
Reports,
  Injuries and fatalities, **Labor 6409 et seq.**
  Motor Vehicles, this index
Steam boiler operation, **Labor 7770, 7771**
Unemployment compensation, exclusion from wages, benefits paid, **Un Ins 931, 933**
Warehouses and warehousemen, working warehouses, **Labor 9100 et seq.**
Workers Compensation, generally, this index
Working warehouses, **Labor 9100 et seq.**

ACCOMPLICES AND ACCESSORIES
Discrimination, **CC 52**
Support, arrearages, evasion, treble damages, **CC 1714.41**
Unemployment compensation, fraudulent claims, **Un Ins 2121**

ACCORD AND SATISFACTION
Compensation and salaries, judgments and decrees, farm labor contractors, wearing apparel, manufacturers and manufacturing, **Labor 273**
Earnings withholding orders, amounts required to satisfy, determination, **CCP 706.024**
Final earnings withholding orders, **CCP 706.028**

ACCOUNTANTS
Industrial accidents division, employment, **Labor 123**
Partnership, registered limited liability partnerships. Partnership, this index
Registered limited liability partnerships. Partnership, this index
Unemployment compensation, independent contractor status, presumption, **Un Ins 656**

ACCOUNTS AND ACCOUNTING
Agricultural labor relations board, **Labor 1143**
Asbestos consultant certification account, **Labor 9021.6**
Asbestos training approval account, deposits, **Labor 9021.9**
Cash bond of employee, **Labor 404**
Children and minors, Coogan trust account, entertainment contracts, **Labor 1308.9**
Coogan trust account, children and minors, entertainment contracts, **Labor 1308.9**
Disability compensation. Unemployment Compensation, this index
Elevator safety account, **Labor 7316**
Employment. Labor and Employment, this index
Garnishment, **CCP 706.026**
Incidental expense accounts, labor commissioner, assignments, **Labor 96**
Labor and Employment, this index
Pressure vessel account, **Labor 7722**
Talent agencies, trust funds, **Labor 1700.25**
Unemployment Compensation, this index
Workers Compensation, this index

ACCREDITED DISASTER COUNCIL
Definitions, workers compensation, **Labor 3211.91**

ACCUSATION
Fair employment and housing, **Gov 12930, 12980**
Indictment and Information, generally, this index

ACKNOWLEDGMENTS
Labor commissioner, deputies and assistants, **Labor 92**
Notaries Public, generally, this index
Workers compensation, release or compromise agreement, **Labor 5003**

ACQUIRE
Definitions, corporation taxes, **Rev & T 24416**

ACQUIRED IMMUNE DEFICIENCY SYNDROME (AIDS)
AIDS, generally, this index

ACROBATS
Children and minors, vocation, occupation, encouraging, **Labor 1308**

ACTINOLITE
Occupational Carcinogens Control Act, **Labor 9000 et seq.**

ACTIONS AND PROCEEDINGS
Administrative Law and Procedure, generally, this index
Agricultural Labor and Employment, this index
Appeal and Review, generally, this index
Apprentice agreements, **Labor 3084, 3085**
Arbitration and Award, generally, this index
Armenians, genocide, **CCP 354.45**
Attachment, generally, this index
Attorney Fees, this index
Bonds (Officers and Fiduciaries), this index
Buses, displaced workers, **Labor 1073**
Civil air patrol, labor and employment, **Labor 1507**
Collective bargaining agreements, enforcement, **Labor 1126**
Commencement of actions. Limitation of Actions, generally, this index
Community colleges and districts. Colleges and Universities, this index
Compensation and Salaries, this index
Compromise and Settlement, generally, this index
Construction, this index
Consumer Credit Reporting Agencies, this index
Contempt, generally, this index
Costs, generally, this index
Counterclaim. Setoff and Counterclaim, generally, this index
Damages, generally, this index
Decrees. Judgments and Decrees, generally, this index
Depositions, generally, this index
Disability compensation, overpayment, recovery, **Un Ins 2739**
Discrimination, this index
Dissolution of marriage. Marriage, this index
Diversion programs referrals or participation, disclosure, **Labor 432.7**

ACTIONS AND PROCEEDINGS—Cont'd

Employment. Labor and Employment, this index

Employment Security Law, collection of unpaid contributions, **Un Ins 1734**

Evidence, generally, this index

Executions, generally, this index

Fair Employment and Housing, this index

Farm labor contractors, employees, civil action, attorneys fees, **Labor 1697**

Foreign labor contractors,
Liability, **Bus & P 9998.8**
Rights of workers, **Bus & P 9998.6**

Forfeitures, generally, this index

Freedom from violence, **CC 52**

Garnishment, generally, this index

Gender violence, **CC 52.4**

Health Care Providers, this index

Health Care Service Plans, this index

Health Facilities, this index

Housing, this index

Injunction, generally, this index

Insurance, this index

Interpreters and Translators, generally, this index

Interurban railroads, displaced workers, **Labor 1073**

Intervention, generally, this index

Janitors,
Contracts, labor and employment, **Labor 2810**
Discharge, **Labor 1062**

Joinder of causes of action, workers compensation, **Labor 5303**

Joinder of parties. Parties, this index

Judgments and Decrees, generally, this index

Jurisdictional strike, persons injured, **Labor 1116**

Labor and Employment, this index

Labor Camps, this index

Labor disputes, freedom from violence, **CC 52**

Labor standards enforcement division, joinder of claimants, **Labor 100**

Lewdness and obscenity, records and recordation, identity of suppliers, failure to maintain, civil penalties, enforcement, **Labor 1309.6**

Libel and Slander, generally, this index

Limitation of Actions, generally, this index

Mandamus, generally, this index

Mass transit, displaced workers, **Labor 1073**

Mechanics Liens, generally, this index

Mediation, generally, this index

Medical Records, this index

Migrant and seasonal farmworker labor camps, overcrowded housing, **Health & S 17043**

Misrepresentation, solicitation of employees, **Labor 972**

Municipal Courts, generally, this index

Negligence, generally, this index

New Trial, generally, this index

ACTIONS AND PROCEEDINGS—Cont'd

Nonpayment of wages, second and subsequent offenses, **Labor 243**

Paratransit vehicles, displaced workers, **Labor 1073**

Parties, generally, this index

Pornography, records and recordation, identity of suppliers, failure to maintain, civil penalties, enforcement, disposition of recovery, **Labor 1309.6**

Preferred claims, joinder of claimant, **Labor 100**

Priorities and preferences, farm labor violations, **Labor 1697.2**

Private patrol operators, retaliation, officers and employees, disclosure, **Bus & P 7583.46**

Private Security Services, this index

Privileges and Immunities, generally, this index

Probate Proceedings, generally, this index

Process, generally, this index

Production of Books and Papers, generally, this index

Public Buildings and Works, this index

Railroads, this index

Receivers and Receivership, generally, this index

Religious Organizations and Societies, this index

Service of process. Process, this index

Setoff and Counterclaim, generally, this index

Sex, force and violence, **CC 52.4**

Sexual Harassment, this index

Slander. Libel and Slander, generally, this index

Small Claims Courts, generally, this index

Social Services, this index

Solicitation of employees by misrepresentation, **Labor 972**

Specific Performance, generally, this index

State Agencies, this index

State Contracts, this index

State Officers and Employees, this index

Statute of limitations. Limitation of Actions, generally, this index

Stay of proceedings. Supersedeas or Stay, generally, this index

Subpoena duces tecum. Production of Books and Papers, generally, this index

Subpoenas, generally, this index

Summons. Process, this index

Superior Courts, generally, this index

Supersedeas or Stay, generally, this index

Talent agencies, fees, **Labor 1703.3, 1704.1 et seq.**

Third Parties, generally, this index

Time. Limitation of Actions, generally, this index

Translators. Interpreters and Translators, generally, this index

Transportation, this index

Trespass, generally, this index

Unemployment Compensation, this index

ACTIONS AND PROCEEDINGS—Cont'd

Unsafe conditions, **Labor 6327.5**

Venue, generally, this index

Wearing Apparel, this index

Whistle Blowing, this index

Witnesses, generally, this index

Workers Compensation, this index

Workers compensation division, duties of attorney, **Labor 119**

Wrongful discharge, unemployment compensation benefits, setoff, **Un Ins 1382**

ACTORS AND ACTRESSES

Children and Minors, this index

Compensation and salaries, talent services, **Labor 1701 et seq.**

Contracts, talent services, fees, **Labor 1701 et seq.**

Talent Agencies, generally, this index

Unemployment compensation, **Un Ins 601.5**

ACTS

Statutes, generally, this index

ACTS OF GOD

Railroads,
Hours of labor, application of law, **Labor 607**
Location of caboose, application of law, **Labor 7000**

ACTS OF LEGISLATURE

Statutes, generally, this index

ACTUAL DAMAGES

Definitions,
Fair employment and housing, **Gov 12970**
Hate crimes, **CC 52**

ACTUAL KNOWLEDGE

Definitions, dangerous business practices, **Pen 387**

ACTUARIES

Industrial accidents division, employment, **Labor 123**

ACUPUNCTURE

Definitions, workers compensation, **Labor 3209.3**

Health Care Service Plans, this index

Workers Compensation, this index

AD VALOREM TAXES

Taxation, generally, this index

ADDICTS

Drug Addicts, generally, this index

ADDRESS

Abandoned or Unclaimed Property, this index

Consumer Credit Reporting Agencies, this index

Earnings withholding orders, applications, **CCP 706.121**

ADDRESS—Cont'd

Employment agencies, contracts, employment agency and jobseeker, inclusion, **CC 1812.504**

Farm labor contractors,
Licenses, **Labor 1684, 1687, 1689**
Service of process on licensee departing state, **Labor 1694**

Garnishment, applications, **CCP 706.121 et seq.**

Income Tax—State, this index

Labor and employment, records, **Labor 1174**

Unclaimed property. Abandoned or Unclaimed Property, this index

Withholding tax on wages, **Un Ins 13016**

ADJOURNMENT

Workers compensation hearing, **Labor 5700**

ADMINISTRATIVE DIRECTORS

Definitions, workers compensation, **Labor 3206**

ADMINISTRATIVE LAW AND PROCEDURE

Adverse economic impact, assessment, **Gov 11346.3**

Assessments, adverse economic impact, **Gov 11346.3**

Building Standards, generally, this index

Business application, finding, **Gov 11346.3**

Compensation and salaries, judges, unemployment compensation, **Un Ins 404**

Cost impact, adverse economic impact, consideration, **Gov 11346.3**

Findings, business application, proposed regulations, **Gov 11346.3**

Hearings, housing discrimination, **Gov 12981**

Industrial homework, searches and seizures, appeal and review, **Labor 2664**

Judges, adverse or pecuniary interest, unemployment compensation, **Un Ins 404**

Labor and employment, assessment, job creation, elimination, proposed regulations, **Gov 11346.3**

Medical information, disclosure, **CC 56.10**

State officers and employees, whistle blowing, **Gov 8547.8**

Whistle blowing, state officers and employees, **Gov 8547.8**

ADMINISTRATIVE LAW JUDGES

Judges. Administrative Law and Procedure, this index

Unemployment Compensation, this index

ADMINISTRATIVE PROCEDURE ACT

Administrative Law and Procedure, generally, this index

ADMISSIBILITY OF EVIDENCE

Evidence, generally, this index

ADMISSIONS

Labor claims, **CCP 1207**

Preferred labor claims, **CCP 1207**

ADMISSIONS—Cont'd

Workers compensation, receipt of benefits, **Labor 4909**

ADOPTION OF CHILDREN

Agency adoption, crimes and offenses, disclosure, **Pen 11105.3**

Confidential or privileged information, crimes and offenses, employment, **Pen 11105.3**

Crimes and offenses, officers and employees, records, disclosure, **Pen 11105.3**

Family care leave, **Un Ins 3300 et seq.**

Independent adoption, crimes and offenses, disclosure, **Pen 11105.3**

Intercountry adoption, crimes and offenses, disclosure, **Pen 11105.3**

Labor and employment, crimes and offenses, disclosure, **Pen 11105.3**

Notice, criminal history, disclosure, employment, **Pen 11105.3**

Officers and employees, crimes and offenses, records, disclosure, **Pen 11105.3**

Paid family care leave, **Un Ins 3300 et seq.**

Unemployment compensation, family care leave, **Un Ins 3300 et seq.**

ADULT OR SEXUALLY ORIENTED BUSINESSES

Lewdness and Obscenity, generally, this index

ADULTS

Aged Persons, generally, this index

Dependent Adults, generally, this index

Domestic Partnership, generally, this index

ADVANCE FEES

Talent services, **Labor 1702 et seq.**

ADVANCES AND ADVANCEMENTS

Actors and actresses, talent services, **Labor 1702 et seq.**

Art and artists, talent services, **Labor 1702 et seq.**

Directors, talent services, **Labor 1702 et seq.**

Models, talent services, **Labor 1702 et seq.**

Music and musicians, talent services, **Labor 1702 et seq.**

Talent services, **Labor 1702 et seq.**

Television and radio, talent services, **Labor 1702 et seq.**

Theaters and shows, talent services, **Labor 1702 et seq.**

Unemployment compensation fund, balances, exclusion, **Un Ins 980**

Workers compensation, asbestosis, temporary disability and medical benefits, **Labor 4401 et seq.**

ADVERSE ACTION

Definitions, consumer credit reporting agencies, **CC 1785.3**

ADVERSE OR PECUNIARY INTEREST

One stop career centers, **Un Ins 14234**

Physicians and Surgeons, this index

ADVERSE OR PECUNIARY INTEREST —Cont'd

Savings Associations, this index

Talent Agencies, this index

Tax assessors or employees, **Labor 1700.6**

Unemployment compensation, administrative law judges, **Un Ins 404**

Workers Compensation, this index

ADVERTISEMENTS

Attorneys, this index

Children and minors, employment in advertising departments, **Labor 1294.3**

Compensation and salaries, misrepresentations, **Labor 976**

Crimes and offenses, industrial homework, **Labor 2658.5**

Definitions, workers compensation, attorneys and others, **Labor 5433**

Employment Agencies, this index

Employment counseling services, false advertisements, **CC 1812.513**

False advertisements. Fraud, generally, post

Fines and penalties, industrial homework, **Labor 2658.5**

Foreign labor contractors, **Bus & P 9998.3**

Fraud,
Employment counseling services, **CC 1812.513**
Job listing services, **CC 1812.520**
Nurse registries, **CC 1812.533**

Home health agencies, employment agencies distinguished, **CC 1812.508**

Housing, this index

Industrial homework, **Labor 2658.5**

Job listing services, false advertisements, **CC 1812.520**

Labor and Employment, this index

Labor disputes, injunction, **CCP 527.3**

Labor organizations, unauthorized use of labels, trademarks or insignia, **Labor 1016**

Nurses registries, **CC 1812.533**

Physicians and Surgeons, this index

Public buildings and works, contractors, debarment, **Labor 1777.1**

Salesmen, compensation or commissions, **Labor 976**

Strikes, solicitation of employees during, representation, **Labor 973**

Talent Agencies, this index

Trademarks, generally, this index

Workers Compensation, this index

ADVISORY BOARDS AND COMMISSIONS

Job training and development services, **Un Ins 9605**

Toxic materials and harmful physical agents, data repository, **Labor 147.2**

Worker safety and health training and education program, **Labor 6354.7**

ADVISORY COMMITTEES

Asbestos advisory committee, **Labor 9021.9**

ADVISORY COMMITTEES—Cont'd
Cal OSHA self contained breathing apparatus advisory committee, determination of test procedures, positive pressure closed circuit breathing apparatus for use in fires, **Labor 6331**
Electricity, this index
Explosives, examinations of supervisors, **Labor 6710**
School employer advisory committee, unemployment compensation, **Un Ins 831**
Wearing apparel, manufacturing industry, **Labor 2674.1**

ADVISORY COUNCILS
Caregiver training initiative, unemployment compensation, **Un Ins 11020**
Unemployment compensation, caregiver training initiative, **Un Ins 11020**

AERIAL PASSENGER TRAMWAYS
Generally, **Labor 7340 et seq.**
Fines and penalties, inspection fees, failure to pay, **Labor 7350**
Inspection and inspectors, **Labor 7340 et seq.**
Fees, **Labor 7350**
Inspection in lieu of state inspection, **Labor 7354.5**
Temporary permit, **Labor 7349**
Reports, injuries, **Labor 7356**

AERONAUTICS
Aircraft, generally, this index

AEROPLANES
Aircraft, generally, this index

AFFIDAVITS
Aerial passenger tramways, unlawful and dangerous operation, injunction, **Labor 7343**
Air pressure tanks, temporarily restraining use, **Labor 7692**
Boilers, temporarily restraining use, **Labor 7692**
Colleges and Universities, this index
Disability compensation, military service trainees, reestablishment of unexpended balance of disability benefits, **Un Ins 2768**
Divorce action, privileged publication, **CC 47**
Fair employment and housing department, **Gov 12930**
Injunction, this index
Labor and Employment, this index
Labor commissioner, deputies and assistants, taking, **Labor 92**
Labor statistics and research division, chief and employees, taking, **Labor 152**
Liquefied petroleum gas storage tanks, temporarily restraining use, **Labor 7692**
Occupational safety and health, **Labor 6314**

AFFIDAVITS—Cont'd
Steam boilers, temporarily restraining use, **Labor 7692**
Talent agencies, licenses and permits, **Labor 1700.6**
Unemployment compensation benefits, Disability compensation, claims, filing by spouse, mentally deficient claimant, **Un Ins 2705.1**
Payment, **Un Ins 1341**
Workers compensation proceedings, objections to reference, **Labor 5311**

AFFIRMATIONS
Oaths and Affirmations, generally, this index

AFFIRMATIVE ACTION
Generally, **Const. Art. 1, § 31**
Actions and proceedings, challenges, **Gov 8315**
Apprentices, this index
Definitions, fair employment and housing department, **Gov 12927**
State Agencies, this index

AFFIRMATIVE DEFENSES
Subpoenas, consumers, records and recordation, **CCP 1985.6**
Workers compensation, burden of proof, **Labor 5705**

AGE
Aged Persons, generally, this index
Apprentices, this index
Compulsory retirement, **Gov 12942**
Definitions, fair employment and housing department, **Gov 12926**
Discrimination, generally, this index
Domestic partnership, **Fam 297**
Fair Employment and Housing, this index
Labor and Employment, this index
Retirement and Pensions, this index

AGED PERSONS
Abuse,
Confidential or privileged information, reports, **Welf & I 15633 et seq.**
Privileges and immunities, reports, **Welf & I 15634**
Assisted living. Residential Care Facilities for the Elderly, generally, this index
Banks and banking, financial abuse, reports, **Welf & I 15630.1**
Benefits, elder care, labor and employment, **Un Ins 9910, 9912**
Caregivers, officers and employees, abuse, reports, **Welf & I 15659**
Confidential or privileged information, abuse, reports, **Welf & I 15633 et seq.**
Credit unions, financial abuse, reports, **Welf & I 15630.1**
Dependent Adults, generally, this index
Discrimination, generally, this index
Elder care, benefits, labor and employment, **Un Ins 9910, 9912**

AGED PERSONS—Cont'd
Fair Employment and Housing, generally, this index
Financial institutions, financial abuse, reports, **Welf & I 15630.1**
Fines and penalties, abuse, reports, confidentiality, **Welf & I 15633 et seq.**
Forms, caretaker employees, abuse reporting statutory knowledge statements, **Welf & I 15659**
Guardian and Ward, generally, this index
Housing,
Fair Employment and Housing, generally, this index
Residential Care Facilities for the Elderly, generally, this index
Labor and employment,
Elder care, benefits, **Un Ins 9910, 9912**
Fair Employment and Housing, generally, this index
Nursing Homes, generally, this index
Paratransit Vehicles, generally, this index
Residential Care Facilities for the Elderly, generally, this index
Savings and loan associations, financial abuse, reports, **Welf & I 15630.1**
Savings associations, financial abuse, reports, **Welf & I 15630.1**

AGENCY
Definitions,
Information practices, **CC 1798.3**
Labor and workforce development agency, **Labor 18.5**
Workforce investment, **Un Ins 14005**
Local child support agencies. Child Support Services Department, this index
Public Agencies, generally, this index

AGENCY ADOPTION
Adoption of Children, this index

AGENT FOR SERVICE OF PROCESS
Process, this index

AGENTS
Attorney in fact. Power of Attorney, generally, this index
Compensation and salaries, nonpayment, **Labor 243**
Credit ratings. Consumer Credit Reporting Agencies, generally, this index
Definitions, employment agency regulation, **CC 1812.501**
Employment Agencies, generally, this index
Government agencies. Public Agencies, generally, this index
Job training and placement services, **Un Ins 9000 et seq.**
Local Agencies, generally, this index
Nonpayment of wages, second and subsequent offenses, **Labor 243**
Power of Attorney, generally, this index
Process, this index
Public Agencies, generally, this index
Real property. Real Estate Brokers and Salespersons, generally, this index

AGENTS—Cont'd

Security Agents and Broker Dealers, generally, this index

State Agencies, generally, this index

Talent Agencies, generally, this index

Unemployment Compensation, this index

United States Agencies and Institutions, generally, this index

Workers compensation, payment, **Labor 4902**

AGGRIEVED PERSON

Definitions, fair employment and housing department, **Gov 12927**

AGREEMENTS

Contracts, generally, this index

Definitions, arbitration, **CCP 1280**

AGRICULTURAL ASSOCIATIONS AND SOCIETIES

Fairs and Expositions, generally, this index

AGRICULTURAL COMMODITIES

Agricultural Products, generally, this index

AGRICULTURAL EMPLOYEE

Definitions, labor relations, **Labor 1140.4**

AGRICULTURAL EMPLOYER

Definitions, labor relations, **Labor 1140.4**

AGRICULTURAL FAIRS

Fairs and Expositions, generally, this index

AGRICULTURAL LABOR AND EMPLOYMENT

Abatement, field sanitation standards violations, **Labor 6712**

Accounts and accounting, farm worker remedial account, payments, **Labor 1698**

Actions and proceedings,
Agricultural employers and labor organizations, **Labor 1165 et seq.**
Contracts, **Labor 2810**
Farm labor contractors, **Labor 1697**
Labor organizations, **Labor 1165 et seq.**
Transportation fees, **Labor 1697.1**

Adverse or pecuniary interest, employer payments to employees or representatives, **Labor 1155.4 et seq.**

Agent for service of process, designation for license application, **Labor 1684**

Agreements, unlicensed farm labor contractors, prohibition, **Labor 1695.6**

Alatorre Zenovich Dunlap Berman Agricultural Labor Relations Act, **Labor 1140 et seq.**

Appeal and review,
Agricultural labor relations board, final orders, **Labor 1160.8**
Mediation, orders, **Labor 1164.3 et seq.**

Applications, child labor laws, hours of labor exemption, **Labor 1393**

Assignment of work, disputes, **Labor 1160.5**

Attorney fees,
Contracts, **Labor 2810**

AGRICULTURAL LABOR AND EMPLOYMENT—Cont'd

Attorney fees—Cont'd
Farm labor contractors, **Labor 1684**
Licenses and permits, **Labor 1695.7**
Transportation fees, **Labor 1697.1**

Bargaining units, **Labor 1156.2**

Bonds (officers and fiduciaries), farm labor contractors, **Labor 1684**
Injunctive relief, **Labor 1697**

Boycotts, secondary boycotts, regulations, **Labor 1153 et seq.**

Braceros, funds, limitation of actions, **CCP 354.7**

Bribery, employer payments to employees or representatives, **Labor 1155.4 et seq.**

Buses, registration, farm labor contractors, **Labor 1696.4**

Certificates and certification,
Mediation, **Labor 1164**
Representatives, **Labor 1156.3**

Children and minors,
Hours of labor, **Labor 1394**
Exemptions, **Labor 1393, 1393.5**
Lake County, hours of labor, exemption, **Labor 1393.5**
Zone of dangers, minors under 12, **Labor 1293.1**

Collective bargaining,
Elections, **Labor 1156 et seq.**
Mediation, **Labor 1164 et seq.**

Compensation and salaries,
Crimes and offenses, **Labor 1695.7, 1697.3**
Deductions, itemized statement accompanying pay, **Labor 1696.5**
Discharge or resignation, **Labor 203**
Farm labor contractors, post
Fines and penalties, **Labor 1695.7**
Resignation or discharge, **Labor 203**
Judgments for failure to pay, revocation or suspension of license, **Labor 1691**
Payroll records, farm labor contractors, **Labor 1695.5, 1695.55**
Resignation or discharge, **Labor 203**
Time due and payable, **Labor 205, 205.5**

Complaints,
Farm labor contractors, offices, **Labor 1682.7**
Unfair labor practices, **Labor 1160.2 et seq.**

Contractors. Farm labor contractors, generally, post

Contracts, **Labor 2810**

Corporation taxes, credits, migratory workers, **Rev & T 23622.7**

Costs,
Contracts, **Labor 2810**
Farm labor contractors, licenses, **Labor 1695.7**
Transportation fees, actions to recover, **Labor 1697.1**

AGRICULTURAL LABOR AND EMPLOYMENT—Cont'd

Crimes and offenses,
Compensation and salaries, **Labor 1695.7, 1697.3**
Farm labor contractors, post

Damages, contracts, **Labor 2810**

Decertification of representatives, **Labor 1156.7**

Definitions,
Agricultural Labor Relations Act of 1975, **Labor 1140.4**
Mediation, **Labor 1164**

Deposits in lieu of bond, farm labor contractors, **Labor 1684**

Disability compensation, **Un Ins 2606**

Drinking water facilities, field sanitation standards, **Labor 6712**

Economic strikers, **Labor 1157**

Education, farm labor contractors, **Labor 1682.8**

Elections, labor organizations, **Labor 1156 et seq.**

Eligibility to vote, **Labor 1157**

Employee housing. Labor Camps, generally, this index

Employment for voting purposes only, unfair labor practice, **Labor 1154.6**

Enumeration of rights of employees, **Labor 1152**

Exclusive representatives of employees, **Labor 1156**

Fair Employment and Housing, generally, this index

Farm labor contractors, **Labor 1682 et seq.**
Attorney fees, licenses, **Labor 1695.7**
Compensation and salaries, **Labor 205, 1695, 1697.3**
Crimes and offenses, **Labor 1695.7**
Enforcement unit, **Labor 1696.8**
Judgments and decrees, satisfaction, **Labor 273**
Payroll records, **Labor 1695.55**
Wage deductions, statements, **Labor 1696.5**
Crimes and offenses, **Labor 1697 et seq.**
Compensation and salaries, **Labor 1695.7, 1697.3**
Enforcement unit, **Labor 1696.8**
Licenses, **Labor 1695.7**
Education, **Labor 1682.8**
Enforcement unit, **Labor 1696.8**
Fees, licenses and permits, **Labor 1698**
Fines and penalties, **Labor 1697 et seq.**
Compensation and salaries, **Labor 1695.7**
Farmworker remedial account, **Labor 1698**
Injunction, **Labor 1697**
Licenses, **Labor 1695.7**
Transportation fees, **Labor 1697.1**
Inspection and inspectors, licenses and permits, **Labor 1695.7**
Judgments and decrees, compensation and salaries, satisfaction, **Labor 273**

AGRICULTURAL LABOR AND EMPLOY-
MENT—Cont'd
Farm labor contractors—Cont'd
Licenses and permits, **Labor 1684, 1687,
1695.7, 1695.9**
Fees, **Labor 1698**
Lists, highway patrol, **Labor 1684.5**
Offices, **Labor 1682.7**
Revocation or suspension, **Labor
1690 et seq., 1695.7, 1695.8**
Special enforcement unit, **Labor
1682.8**
Verification unit, **Labor 1695.7**
Payroll records, **Labor 1695.5, 1695.55**
Special enforcement unit, **Labor 1682.8**
Verification unit, licenses and permits,
Labor 1695.7
Farm labor vehicles. Motor vehicles, gen-
erally, post
Farm worker remedial account, payments,
Labor 1698
Field sanitation, standards, **Labor 6712**
Findings and orders, unfair labor prac-
tices, **Labor 1160.3**
Fines and penalties,
Compensation and salaries, ante
Discharge or resignation, compensation
and salaries, **Labor 203**
Farm labor contractors, ante
Farmworker remedial account, **Labor
1698**
Sheepherders, **Labor 2695.2**
Fixed site employers, field sanitation viola-
tions, **Labor 6712**
Forms, field sanitation compliance forms,
Labor 6712
Fraud, farm labor contractors, **Labor 1696**
Transportation fees, **Labor 1697.1**
Freedom of speech, **Labor 1155**
Funds, agricultural employee relief fund,
Labor 1161
Good faith bargaining, **Labor 1155.2**
Grievances of employees, exclusive repre
sentatives, **Labor 1156**
Hours of labor, **Labor 554**
Children and minors, ante
Sheepherders, **Labor 2695.2**
Housing,
Grants, funds, **Health & S 17062.5**
Labor Camps, generally, this index
Migratory workers. Seasonal labor,
post
Mobilehomes, **Health & S 17021.7**
Sheepherders, **Labor 2695.2**
Seasonal labor, post
Informational picketing, rights of labor or-
ganization, **Labor 1155**
Injunction,
Contracts, **Labor 2810**
Farm labor contractors, ante
Unfair labor practices, **Labor 1160.4,
1160.6**
Inspection and inspectors,
Children and minors, hours of labor,
exemptions, **Labor 1393.5**

AGRICULTURAL LABOR AND EMPLOY-
MENT—Cont'd
Inspection and inspectors—Cont'd
Farm labor contractors, licenses and
permits, **Labor 1695.7**
Judgments and decrees, compensation and
salaries,
Failure to pay, license revocation, **Labor
1691**
Farm labor contractors, satisfaction, **La-
bor 273**
Jurisdiction, Agricultural Labor Relations
Act, **Labor 1165.2**
Labor Camps, generally, this index
Labor disputes, farm labor contractors,
Labor 1696
Labor organizations, elections, **Labor 1156
et seq.**
Labor Relations Act, **Labor 1140 et seq.**
Lake County, children and minors, hours
of labor, exemption, **Labor 1393.5**
Licensee list, highway patrol, farm labor
contractors, **Labor 1684.5**
Licenses and permits, **Labor 1684**
Farm labor contractors, ante
Revocation or suspension, contractors,
Labor 1690 et seq.
Limitation of actions, braceros, funds,
CCP 354.7
Limitations, Agricultural Labor Relations
Act, **Labor 1166 et seq.**
Lists of payroll, maintenance and avail-
ability, **Labor 1157.3**
Mail and mailing, sheepherders, **Labor
2695.2**
Mediation, **Labor 1164 et seq.**
Migratory workers. Seasonal labor, gen-
erally, post
Mobilehomes and mobilehome parks,
Health & S 17021.7
Sheepherders, **Labor 2695.2**
Modification, existing contract, **Labor
1155.3**
Motor vehicle insurance, farm labor con-
tractors, **Labor 1695**
Motor vehicles,
Farm labor contractors, **Labor 1682 et
seq.**
Licenses and permits, **Labor 1696.2**
Registration, farm labor contractors,
Labor 1696.4
Nonfixed site employers, field sanitation
violations, **Labor 6712**
Notice,
Child labor laws, hours of labor exemp-
tion revocation, **Labor 1393**
Field sanitation standards violations,
Labor 6712
Orders, mediation, reports, **Labor 1164.3**
Payment,
Compensation and salaries, time, **Labor
205.5**
Farm worker remedial account, **Labor
1698**

AGRICULTURAL LABOR AND EMPLOY-
MENT—Cont'd
Payroll records,
Farm labor contractors, **Labor 1695.5,
1695.55**
Maintenance and availability, **Labor
1157.3**
Pesticides, farm labor contractors, **Labor
1684**
Petitions,
Elections, **Labor 1156.3 et seq.**
Mediation, reports, **Labor 1164.3**
Placement service, operation by state, **Un
Ins 2054**
Posting, sheepherders, **Labor 2695.2**
Prevention of unfair labor practices, **Labor
1160 et seq.**
Priorities and preferences,
Actions for labor violations, **Labor
1697.2**
Unfair labor practice cases, **Labor
1160.6, 1160.7**
Process. Service of process, generally,
post
Publicity, rights of labor organization, **La-
bor 1154**
Registration,
Farm labor contractors, **Labor 1695**
Motor vehicles, ante
Reimbursement fund, damages not cov-
ered by farm labor contractors bond
or time certificate, **Labor 1684**
Relief fund, agricultural employee relief
fund, **Labor 1161**
Reports, **Labor 1143**
Children and minors, hours of labor,
exemptions, **Labor 1393.5**
Mediation, **Labor 1164**
Representatives, designation, **Labor 1156
et seq.**
Restrooms, field sanitation standards, **La-
bor 6712**
Rights of employees, enumeration, **Labor
1152**
Run off elections, representation, **Labor
1157.2**
Salaries. Compensation and salaries, gen-
erally, ante
Seasonal labor,
Bank and corporation tax credits, **Rev &
T 23622.7**
Braceros, funds, limitation of actions,
CCP 354.7
Housing,
Labor Camps, generally, this index
Overcrowded housing, actions and
proceedings, **Health & S 17043**
Labor Camps, generally, this index
Limitation of actions, braceros, funds,
CCP 354.7
Secondary boycotts, regulations, **Labor
1153 et seq.**
Security deposits, sheepherders, **Labor
2695.2**

AGRICULTURAL

AGRICULTURAL LABOR AND EMPLOY-MENT—Cont'd

Service of process, **Labor 1165.3**
Farm labor contractors, **Labor 1694, 1695**
Mediation, appeal and review, **Labor 1164.5**
Sheepherders, **Labor 2695.1 et seq.**
Standards,
Field sanitation, **Labor 6712**
Sheepherders, **Labor 2695.2**
Statute of limitations, braceros, funds, **CCP 354.7**
Students, hours of labor, **Labor 1394**
Telecommunications, sheepherders, **Labor 2695.2**
Temporary injunctions, unfair labor practices, **Labor 1160.4**
Termination, existing contract, **Labor 1155.3**
Time, elections, time between, **Labor 1156.5**
Toilets, field sanitation standards, **Labor 6712**
Tools, sheepherders, **Labor 2695.2**
Training, farm labor contractors, **Labor 1695**
Transportation,
Fees, fraud, crimes and offenses, **Labor 1697.1**
Motor vehicles, generally, ante
Unemployment Compensation, this index
Unfair labor practices, **Labor 1153 et seq.**
Venue, labor organizations, **Labor 1165**
Verification, farm labor contractors, licenses and permits, **Labor 1695.7**
Verification unit, farm labor contractors, licenses and permits, **Labor 1695.7**
Voting purposes, primary employment purpose, unfair labor practice, **Labor 1154.6**
Washing facilities, field sanitation standards, **Labor 6712**

AGRICULTURAL LABOR RELATIONS ACT

Generally, **Labor 1140 et seq.**

AGRICULTURAL LABOR RELATIONS BOARD

Generally, **Labor 1141 et seq.**
Accounts and accounting, **Labor 1143**
Applicability of National Labor Relations Act precedents, **Labor 1148**
Application of law, administrative adjudications, **Labor 1144.5**
Appointment and removal of members, **Labor 1141**
Attorneys, appointment, **Labor 1145**
Compensation and salaries, members, **Labor 1147**
Contempt, investigations, noncompliance with subpoenas, **Labor 1151**
Crimes and offenses, resisting or interfering with investigations, **Labor 1151.6**
Delegation of powers, **Labor 1142, 1146**
Evidence, investigations and investigators, **Labor 1151 et seq.**

AGRICULTURAL LABOR RELATIONS BOARD—Cont'd

Executive secretary, **Labor 1145**
Exemptions, administrative adjudications, **Labor 1144.5**
Fees, witnesses, investigations, **Labor 1151.4**
Fines and penalties, resisting or interfering with investigations, **Labor 1151.6**
General counsel, appointment, terms, duties, **Labor 1149**
Hearing officers, appointment, **Labor 1145**
Impartiality, officers and employees, **Labor 1145, 1149**
Information and counseling, telephone service, 24 hours, **Labor 1142.5**
Investigatory powers, **Labor 1151 et seq.**
Labor and workforce development agency, **Labor 1141**
Mileage, witnesses, investigations, **Labor 1151.4**
Oaths and affirmations, witnesses, investigations, **Labor 1151 et seq.**
Officers and employees, appointment, **Labor 1145**
Offices, **Labor 1142**
Outside employment, members and general counsel, **Labor 1150**
Quorum, **Labor 1146**
Reappointment, members and general counsel, **Labor 1150**
Reports, **Labor 1143**
Rules and regulations, **Labor 1144**
Self incrimination, investigations, **Labor 1151.2**
Service of process, investigations, **Labor 1151.4**
State agencies and departments, cooperation with board investigations, **Labor 1151.5**
Subpoenas, investigations, **Labor 1151 et seq.**
Telephone service, 24 hours, information and counseling, **Labor 1142.5**
Terms of office, **Labor 1141**
Witnesses, investigations, **Labor 1151 et seq.**

AGRICULTURAL LAND

Brands, marks and labels, trespass, **Pen 602**
Fences, trespass, **Pen 602**
Irrigation and Irrigation Districts, generally, this index
Signs and signals, trespass, **Pen 602**
Trespass, **Pen 602, 602.8**

AGRICULTURAL MACHINERY AND EQUIPMENT

Children and minors, tractor operation programs, certificates of completion, Child Labor Law applicability, **Labor 1295**
Motor vehicles. Agricultural Labor and Employment, this index

AGRICULTURAL PRODUCTS

Children and minors, processors, hours of labor, exemptions, **Labor 1393.5**
Fairs and Expositions, generally, this index
Fruits, generally, this index
Lake County, processors, children and minors, hours of labor, exemptions, **Labor 1393.5**
Processors,
Children and minors, hours of labor, exemptions, **Labor 1393.5**
Hours of labor, children and minors, exemptions, **Labor 1393.5**
Inspection and inspectors, children and minors, hours of labor, exemptions, **Labor 1393.5**
Lake County, children and minors, hours of labor, exemptions, **Labor 1393.5**
Reports, children and minors, hours of labor, exemptions, **Labor 1393.5**
Vegetables, generally, this index
Warehouses and Warehousemen, generally, this index

AGRICULTURAL WAREHOUSES

Warehouses and Warehousemen, generally, this index

AGRICULTURAL ZONE OF DANGER

Definitions, employment of minors, **Labor 1293.1**

AGRICULTURE

Accounts and accounting, farm worker remedial account, payments, **Labor 1698**
Animals, generally, this index
Children and minors, vocational agriculture programs, students, child labor laws applicability, **Labor 1295**
Definitions, labor relations, **Labor 1140.4**
Elevators, dumbwaiters and escalators, mechanics, **Labor 7311.25**
Employment. Agricultural Labor and Employment, generally, this index
Fairs and Expositions, generally, this index
Farm labor contractors special enforcement unit, licenses and permits, **Labor 1682.8**
Farm worker remedial account, payments, **Labor 1698**
Irrigation and Irrigation Districts, generally, this index
Labor and employment. Agricultural Labor and Employment, generally, this index
Land. Agricultural Land, generally, this index
Licenses and permits, farm labor contractors special enforcement unit, **Labor 1682.8**
Livestock. Animals, generally, this index
Payment, farm worker remedial account, **Labor 1698**
Products. Agricultural Products, generally, this index

AGRICULTURE—Cont'd
Real estate. Agricultural Land, generally, this index
Vocational agriculture programs, students, child labor laws, applicability, **Labor 1295**
Zoning and Planning, generally, this index

AIDERS AND ABETTORS
Accomplices and Accessories, generally, this index

AIDS
Blood tests,
  Health care service plans, coverage, **Health & S 1367.46**
  Labor and employment, discrimination, **Health & S 120980**
Damages, blood tests, disclosure, **Health & S 120980**
Definitions, disclosure, blood tests, **Health & S 120980**
Disclosure, blood tests, **Health & S 120980**
Discrimination,
  Jurisdiction, complaints, **Gov 12965**
  Labor and employment, **Health & S 120980**
Fines and penalties,
  Blood tests, results disclosure, **Health & S 120980**
  Confidential or privileged information, **Health & S 120980**
Health care providers, positive blood tests, disclosure, **Health & S 120980 et seq.**
Health care service plans, blood tests, coverage, **Health & S 1367.46**
Health facilities, blood tests, disclosure, **Health & S 120980 et seq.**
Insurance, this index
Labor and Employment, this index
Workers compensation,
  Death benefits, limitation of actions, **Labor 5406.6**
  Medical records, disclosure, **CC 56.31**

AIR
Ventilation, generally, this index

AIR FORCE
Military Forces, generally, this index

AIR PRESSURE TANKS
Inspection, **Labor 7681**
  Permits and safety regulations, **Labor 7620 et seq.**
Operation permits, **Labor 7683**

AIRCRAFT
Airports and Landing Fields, generally, this index
Fire suppression, workers compensation, pilot, **Labor 3365**
Hazardous substances and waste, occupational lead poisoning, **Health & S 105185 et seq.**
Landing fields. Airports and Landing Fields, generally, this index

AIRCRAFT—Cont'd
Lead poisoning, occupational health and safety, **Health & S 105185 et seq.**
Unemployment compensation, **Un Ins 609**
  Excluded services, **Un Ins 648**
Workers compensation, fire suppression, pilots, **Labor 3365**

AIRPORTS AND LANDING FIELDS
Definitions, trespass, **Pen 602**
Police, leaves of absence, workers compensation, disability benefits, **Labor 4850**
Security, trespass, sterile areas, **Pen 602**
Sterile areas, trespass, **Pen 602**
Trespass, **Pen 602**

ALATORRE ZENOVICH DUNLAP BERMAN AGRICULTURAL LABOR RELATIONS ACT
Generally, **Labor 1140 et seq.**

ALCOHOLIC BEVERAGE CONTROL DEPARTMENT
Alcoholic Beverages, generally, this index

ALCOHOLIC BEVERAGES
Alcoholics and Alcoholism, generally, this index
Children and minors, employment agencies, farm labor contractors, **Labor 1698.5**
Saloons. Taverns and Saloons, generally, this index
Seasonal labor, liquor debts, deduction from wages, **Labor 253**
Talent agencies, **Labor 1700.34**
Taverns and Saloons, generally, this index

ALCOHOLICS AND ALCOHOLISM
Confidential or privileged information, voluntary rehabilitation program enrollment, employers safeguarding of privacy, **Labor 1026**
Criminal history information, transportation, volunteers, **Pen 11105.3**
Disability compensation, **Un Ins 2678**
Foreign states, recovery home residents, unemployment compensation benefits, **Un Ins 2626.1**
Labor and employment, voluntary rehabilitation program enrollment, employer accommodation, **Labor 1025 et seq.**
Medical care and treatment, recovery home residents, unemployment compensation benefits, **Un Ins 2626.1**
Rehabilitation programs, employer accommodation, voluntary enrollment, **Labor 1025 et seq.**
Taverns and Saloons, generally, this index
Transportation, volunteers, criminal history information, **Pen 11105.3**
Treatment, unemployment compensation, disqualifications, **Un Ins 1256.4**
Unemployment Compensation, this index
Volunteers, transportation, criminal history information, **Pen 11105.3**
Workers Compensation, this index

ALIENATION
Deeds and Conveyances, generally, this index

ALIENS
Definition, public works, **Labor 1725**
Employment services, illegal aliens, ineligibility, **Un Ins 9601.5, 9601.7**
Social Services, this index
Unemployment Compensation, this index
Workers compensation, employee defined, **Labor 3351**

ALPHA NAPHTHYLAMINE
Occupational Carcinogens Control Act, **Labor 9000 et seq.**

ALTERNATIVE DISPUTE RESOLUTION
Arbitration and Award, generally, this index
Mediation, generally, this index

ALTERNATIVE WORKWEEK SCHEDULE
Generally, **Labor 500 et seq.**

AMATEUR CONTESTS
Children and minors, participation, **Labor 1308**

AMERICAN AIRCRAFT
Definitions, unemployment compensation, **Un Ins 125.3**

AMERICANS WITH DISABILITIES ACT
Unruh Civil Rights Act, violations, **CC 51**

AMERICORPS: VOLUNTEERS IN SERVICE TO AMERICA
Compensation and salaries, minimum wages, exemptions, **Labor 1171**
Unemployment compensation, excluded services, **Un Ins 634.5**

AMIDONE
Drug Addicts, generally, this index

AMOSITE
Occupational Carcinogens Control Act, **Labor 9000 et seq.**

AMUSEMENTS
Accidents, permanent amusement rides, reports, **Labor 7925**
Appeal and review, permanent amusement rides, safety, inspection and inspectors, **Labor 7931**
Bonds (officers and fiduciaries), permanent amusement rides, **Labor 7926**
Bungee jumping, licenses and permits, **Labor 7901**
Certificates and certification, permanent amusement rides, safety, inspection and inspectors, **Labor 7924**
Citations, permanent amusement rides, safety, inspection and inspectors, **Labor 7931**
Fees, permanent amusement rides, safety, inspection and inspectors, **Labor 7929**
Financial responsibility, permanent amusement rides, **Labor 7926**

AMUSEMENTS—Cont'd

Fines and penalties,
Permanent amusement rides, safety, inspection and inspectors, **Labor 7930, 7931**
Rides, safety, **Labor 7917, 7918**
Inspection and inspectors, permanent amusement rides, safety, **Labor 7920 et seq.**
Insurance, permanent amusement rides, **Labor 7926**
Liability insurance, permanent amusement rides, **Labor 7926**
Military personnel, discrimination, **Mil & V 394**
Penalties. Fines and penalties, generally, ante
Permanent amusement rides, safety, inspection and inspectors, **Labor 7920 et seq.**
Records and recordation, permanent amusement rides, safety, inspection and inspectors, **Labor 7924**
Reports, permanent amusement rides, accidents, **Labor 7925**
Rides,
Crimes and offenses, noncompliance, **Labor 7915**
Fees, inspection and inspectors, **Labor 7904**
Safety, **Labor 7900 et seq., 7920 et seq.**
Rules and regulations, permanent amusement rides, safety, inspection and inspectors, **Labor 7923, 7928**
Safety, permanent amusement rides, inspection and inspectors, **Labor 7920 et seq.**
Self insurance, permanent amusement rides, **Labor 7926**
Theaters and Shows, generally, this index
Training, permanent amusement rides, safety, **Labor 7927**

ANALYSIS AND ANALYSTS

Blood related construction work, samples analysis, employee protection, **Labor 6717**
Oil and gas, used oil, **Health & S 25250.29**

ANATOMICAL GIFTS

Tissue Banks, generally, this index

ANCESTRY

Discrimination, generally, this index

ANIMALS

Exhibitions, employment of minor, **Labor 1308**
Fish and Game, generally, this index
Game. Fish and Game, generally, this index
Labor, stock raising, compensation, time due and payable, **Labor 205**
Trespass, **Pen 602**
Wild animals and birds. Fish and Game, generally, this index

ANNUITIES

Income Tax—State, this index
Insurance, this index
Unemployment Compensation, this index

ANNULMENT

Domestic partnership, **Fam 298.5, 299**
Jurisdiction, **Fam 298**
Marriage, this index

ANSWER

Witnesses, generally, this index

ANTHOPHYLLITE

Occupational Carcinogens Control Act, **Labor 9000 et seq.**

ANTIBLACKLISTING ACT

Generally, **Labor 1050 et seq.**

ANTIDISCRIMINATION LAWS

Discrimination, generally, this index

ANTIYELLOW DOG ACT

Generally, **Labor 921**

APARTMENT HOUSES

Condominiums, generally, this index
Employee housing, **Health & S 17000 et seq.**
Exemptions, workplace smoking regulation, **Labor 6404.5**
Handicapped Persons, this index
Low and moderate income housing. Housing, this index
Managers, resident managers, rental credit, **Labor 1182.8**
Multistory dwelling units, handicapped persons, discrimination, **Gov 12955 et seq.**
Place of employment, smoking regulation, exemption, **Labor 6404.5**
Rent, resident managers, credit, **Labor 1182.8**
Resident managers, rental credit, **Labor 1182.8**
Rules and regulations, workplace smoking regulation, exemptions, **Labor 6404.5**
Workplace smoking regulation, exemption, **Labor 6404.5**

APOTHECARIES

Pharmacists, generally, this index

APPARATUS

Machinery and Equipment, generally, this index

APPAREL

Wearing Apparel, generally, this index

APPARENT OWNER

Definitions, Unclaimed Property Law, **CCP 1501**

APPEAL AND REVIEW

Aerial passenger tramways, order withholding permit and requiring repairs or alterations, **Labor 7347**

APPEAL AND REVIEW—Cont'd

Agricultural labor and employment, mediation, orders, **Labor 1164.3 et seq.**
Agricultural labor relations board, final orders, **Labor 1160.8**
Air pressure tanks, orders for repairs or alterations, **Labor 7690**
Amusements,
Permanent amusement rides, safety, inspection and inspectors, **Labor 7931**
Rides, safety, citations, **Labor 7918**
Apprentices, orders, **Labor 3082, 3084**
Attachment, this index
Boilers, orders for repairs or alterations, **Labor 7690**
Civil Rights, this index
Community colleges and districts. Colleges and Universities, this index
Compensation and salaries, seasonal wage disputes, **Labor 255**
Complaints, decisions, **Labor 98.2**
Correctional Institutions, this index
Elevators, orders for repairs or alterations, **Labor 7307**
Employment. Labor and Employment, this index
Executions, this index
Extended unemployment compensation. Unemployment Compensation, this index
Fair employment and housing, **Gov 12987.1**
Garnishment, this index
Health Care Service Plans, this index
Industrial homework, searches and seizures, **Labor 2664**
Joint enforcement strike force on the underground economy, citations or penalty assessment orders, **Labor 106**
Labor and Employment, this index
Labor commissioner, investigation of employee complaints, decision, **Labor 98.2**
Liquefied petroleum gas storage tanks, orders for repairs or alterations, **Labor 7690**
New Trial, generally, this index
Occupational safety and health. Labor and Employment, this index
Occupational safety and health appeals board. Industrial Relations Department, this index
Permanent amusement rides, safety, inspection and inspectors, **Labor 7931**
Priorities and preferences, labor claims, **CCP 1206**
Public Buildings and Works, this index
Seasonal wage disputes, **Labor 255**
Stay. Supersedeas or Stay, generally, this index
Steam boilers, orders for repairs or alterations, **Labor 7690**
Supersedeas or Stay, generally, this index
Support, this index
Talent agencies, **Labor 1700.44**

APPEAL AND REVIEW—Cont'd

Unemployment Compensation, this index

Volunteer firemen and fire departments, removal of firemen, **Labor 1964**

Workers Compensation, this index

APPEALS BOARDS

Definitions,

Occupational safety and health, **Labor 6302**

State employees, workers compensation and insurance, **Labor 6101**

Workers compensation, **Labor 3205.5**

Unemployment Compensation, this index

Workers Compensation, this index

APPEALS IN CRIMINAL PROSECUTIONS

New Trial, generally, this index

APPEARANCE

Fair employment and housing department, witnesses, **Gov 12930**

Unemployment compensation proceedings, failure to appear, **Un Ins 2104**

Workers Compensation, this index

APPELLATE COURTS

Supreme Court, generally, this index

APPLIANCES

Mechanics Liens, generally, this index

APPLICABLE CURRENT GROUP RATE

Definitions, group disability insurance, continuation benefits, **Ins 10116.5**

APPLICANT

Definitions, youthbuild program, **Un Ins 9801**

APPRENTICES

Generally, **Labor 3070 et seq.**

Actions and proceedings, agreements, **Labor 3084, 3085**

Administrators, **Labor 3072**

Investigations and investigators, joint apprenticeship committee, **Labor 1777.5**

Affirmative action, **Labor 3071, 3074.1, 3076.3**

Joint apprenticeship committee, **Labor 3076**

Age,

Discrimination, **Labor 1777.6; Un Ins 2078**

Maximum age, **Labor 3077.5**

Agreements, curriculum development and instruction classes, **Labor 3074**

Ancestry, discrimination, **Labor 3095**

Appeals, orders, **Labor 3082, 3085**

Applications, **Labor 3090**

Approval of agreement, **Labor 3079**

Audits and auditors, **Labor 3073.1**

Certificates and certification, contractors and subcontractors, public works, **Labor 1777.5**

Child Labor Law, applicability, **Labor 1295**

APPRENTICES—Cont'd

Collective bargaining agreements,

Establishing standards, **Labor 3086**

Maximum age, **Labor 3077.5**

Committees, **Labor 3075, 3076**

Community colleges and districts. Colleges and Universities, this index

Compensation and salaries, **Labor 1192**

Minimum wages, **Labor 1192**

Per diem wages, public works employees, **Labor 1773.1**

Public works, **Labor 1777.5**

Scale of wages, **Labor 3078**

Standards, **Labor 3071**

Complaints,

Instruction classes, **Labor 3074**

Violation of agreements, **Labor 3081**

Contractors, certification for public works, responsibility, **Labor 1777.5**

Contracts,

Equal opportunity, affirmative action, **Labor 3073**

Execution, **Labor 3079, 3080**

Form, **Labor 3078**

Contributions, contractors to administer apprenticeship program, public works, **Labor 1777.5**

Council. Apprenticeship Council, generally, this index

Credit, term of apprenticeship, regional occupational centers, **Labor 3092**

Curriculum development and instruction classes, agreements, **Labor 3074**

Definitions, **Labor 3077**

Disciplinary proceedings, notice, **Labor 3076**

Discrimination, **Labor 1777.6, 3095**

Affirmative action, programs, regulations, **Labor 3071**

Public works, **Labor 1777.5, 1777.6**

Disputes, adjustments, joint apprenticeship committee functions, **Labor 3076**

Electricity, **Labor 3099 et seq.**

Encouragement and utilization, public policy, state and local public agencies, **Labor 3075.1**

Ethnic derivation, surveys, **Labor 151**

Evidence, presumptions, orders, **Labor 3083**

Examinations and examiners, electricity, certificates and certification, **Labor 3099.4**

Exemptions, contractors of public works, small contracts, **Labor 1777.5**

Expenses, training program, **Labor 3091**

Explanation, selection procedure, **Labor 3076.3**

Fair employment and housing, training, **Gov 12940**

Federal funds, employment development department clients, **Labor 3097**

Federal Job Training Partnership Act, **Labor 3097**

Fees,

Electricity, registration, **Labor 3099.4**

Postgraduate courses, **Labor 3074.7**

APPRENTICES—Cont'd

Fees—Cont'd

Training program, **Labor 3091**

Fines and penalties, discrimination, **Labor 3095**

Firefighters and Fire Departments, this index

Foreign languages, electricity, certificates and certification, **Labor 3099.3**

Forms, contracts, **Labor 3078**

Funds,

Payment by contractor to apprenticeship program or apprenticeship council, **Labor 1777.5**

Payments by employer to apprenticeship funds, **Labor 228**

Training contribution fund, **Labor 1777.5**

Grants, training, **Labor 1777.5**

Hearings, violations of agreements, **Labor 3081**

High Schools or Secondary Schools, this index

Hours of labor, **Labor 3077, 3078**

Children and minors, **Labor 1392**

Standards, **Labor 3071**

Information dissemination, **Labor 3073**

Injunction, offenses involving apprentices, **Labor 3084.5**

Injuries sustained, liability, **Labor 3078**

Instruction classes,

Agreements, costs, **Labor 3074**

Prerequisites, registration, **Labor 3074.3**

Instructional materials, special deposit fund account, **Labor 3091.5**

Investigations and investigators,

Agreements, violations, **Labor 3081**

Standards division, **Labor 3090**

Isolated apprentices, related and supplemental instruction, **Labor 3074**

Joint apprenticeship committees, **Labor 3075, 3076**

Public works, apprenticeship standards, **Labor 1777.5**

Labor unilateral apprenticeship committee, **Labor 3075**

Licenses and permits, compensation, **Labor 1192**

Management unilateral apprenticeship committee, **Labor 3075**

Minimum requirements, specification, **Labor 3076**

Minority groups, **Labor 3071, 3073.3**

National origin, discrimination, **Labor 3095**

Notice, disciplinary proceedings, **Labor 3076**

Offenses, enjoining, **Labor 3084.5**

On the job training, programs for journeymen, new workers and displaced workers, **Labor 3093**

Orders and decisions of council, **Labor 3082 et seq.**

Personal injuries, **Labor 3078**

Prerequisites, registration and programs, **Labor 3074.3**

APPRENTICES—Cont'd
Presumptions, orders, **Labor 3083**
Probation period, **Labor 3078**
Programs,
    Registration, prerequisites, **Labor 3074.3**
    Sponsors, **Labor 3075**
Public Buildings and Works, this index
Public policy, encouragement and utilization, state and local public agencies, **Labor 3075.1**
Qualifications, **Labor 3076**
Records and recordation, selection procedures, explanation, **Labor 3076.3**
Regional occupational centers, credit, term of apprenticeship, **Labor 3092**
Registration, electricity, **Labor 3099.4**
Religion, discrimination, **Labor 3095**
Reports, electricity, certificates and certification, **Labor 3099.3**
Salaries. Compensation and salaries, generally, ante
Schools and School Districts, this index
Selection procedures, qualifications, **Labor 3076.3**
Service delivery areas, job training partnerships, providing services, **Labor 3097**
Severability of Act, **Labor 3088**
Sex discrimination, **Labor 1777.6, 3095**
Signatures, contracts, **Labor 3079**
Special deposit fund account, instructional material sales, **Labor 3091.5**
Standards, **Labor 3071**
    Collective bargaining agreements establishing, **Labor 3086**
Statements, selection procedure, **Labor 3076.3**
Survey of ethnic derivation, **Labor 151**
Teachers and coordinators, selection and training, **Labor 3074**
Time, electricity, certificates and certification, **Labor 3099.2**
Trade analyses and outlines of instruction, preparation, **Labor 3074**
Unilateral management, labor apprenticeship committee, **Labor 3075**
Veterans, selection standards, **Labor 3076.5**
Vocational education, credit towards term of apprenticeship, **Labor 3092**
Women, **Labor 3071, 3073.3**
Workers compensation, students, **Labor 3368**
Working conditions improvement, **Labor 3073**

APPRENTICESHIP COUNCIL
    Generally, **Labor 3070 et seq.**
Affirmative action programs, **Labor 3071**
    Equal opportunity, joint agreements, **Labor 3073**
Appointment, **Labor 3070**
Audits and auditors, training criteria, **Labor 3073.2**
Compensation and salaries, **Labor 3070**

APPRENTICESHIP COUNCIL—Cont'd
Investigations, decisions, joint apprenticeship committee, **Labor 1777.5**
Joint agreements, affirmative action programs, equal opportunity, **Labor 3073**
Notice, training criteria, **Labor 3073.2**
Powers and duties, **Labor 3071**
Reports, **Labor 3071, 3073.5**
Rules and regulations, issuance, **Labor 3071**
Training criteria, **Labor 3073.2**
Traveling expenses, **Labor 3070**

APPRENTICESHIP STANDARDS DIVISION
Industrial Relations Department, this index

APPROPRIATE GOVERNMENT AGENCY
Definitions, dangerous business practices, **Pen 387**

APPROPRIATIONS
Disability compensation fund, **Un Ins 3012**
Employment development department benefit fund, **Un Ins 1596**
Employment training fund, **Un Ins 10217**
Industrial relations department, **Labor 58, 62**
Social Services, this index
Unemployment compensation, **Un Ins 1521, 1535, 1586**

AQUACULTURE
Definitions, occupational safety and health, **Labor 6302**

AQUATIC ORGANISMS
Fish and Game, generally, this index

ARBITRATION AND AWARD
    Generally, **CCP 1280 et seq.**
Agreements,
    Definitions, **CCP 1280**
    Enforcement of arbitration agreements, **CCP 1281 et seq.**
Compensation and salaries, actions to recover, application of arbitration agreements, **Labor 229**
Consolidation of separate proceedings, **CCP 1281.3**
Controversy, definitions, **CCP 1280**
Definitions, **CCP 1280**
Delay, order of court, **CCP 1281.2**
Enforcement, agreements, **CCP 1281 et seq.**
Grounds, consolidation of separate arbitration proceedings, **CCP 1281.3**
Intervention, pending court proceedings, enforcement of agreement, **CCP 1281.2**
Irrevocability, arbitration agreements, **CCP 1281**
Joinder, pending court proceedings, enforcement of agreements, **CCP 1281.2**
Labor and employment, actions to compel arbitration, attorneys fees, **Labor 1128**
Labor Disputes, this index

ARBITRATION AND AWARD—Cont'd
Medical records, disclosure, **CC 56.10**
Neutral arbitrator, definitions, **CCP 1280**
Party to the arbitration defined, **CCP 1280**
Pending court actions, enforcement of agreements, **CCP 1281.2**
Petitions,
    Consolidation of separate arbitration proceedings, **CCP 1281.3**
    Enforcement of agreement, **CCP 1281.2**
Reference to law applying to amendments and additions, **CCP 1280.2**
Separate agreements or proceedings, consolidation, **CCP 1281.3**
Special proceedings, enforcement of agreements, **CCP 1281.2**
State mediation and conciliation service, **Labor 66**
Supersedeas or stay, **CCP 1281.4**
Talent agencies, **Labor 1700.45**
Transit Districts, this index
Workers Compensation, this index
Written agreement, definitions, **CCP 1280**

ARCHITECTS
Liens and incumbrances. Mechanics Liens, generally, this index
Mechanics Liens, generally, this index
Partnership, registered limited liability partnerships. Partnership, this index
Registered limited liability partnerships. Partnership, this index
Unemployment compensation, independent contractors, presumptions, **Un Ins 656**

ARM
Workers compensation, subsequent injuries, **Labor 4751**

ARMED FORCES
Military Forces, generally, this index

ARMENIANS
Actions and proceedings, genocide, **CCP 354.45**
Banks and banking, genocide, limitation of actions, **CCP 354.45**
Genocide,
    Actions and proceedings, **CCP 354.45**
    Banks and banking, limitation of actions, **CCP 354.45**
    Disability compensation, **Un Ins 2629.5**
    Limitation of actions, **CCP 354.45**
Limitation of actions, genocide, **CCP 354.45**
Statute of limitations, genocide, **CCP 354.45**

ARMS
Weapons, generally, this index

ARMY
Military Forces, generally, this index

ARREARAGES
Support, this index

ARREST

Colleges and Universities, this index

Confidential or Privileged Information, this index

Consumer credit reporting agencies, **CC 1786.18**

Contempt, generally, this index

Fines and penalties, labor and employment, applicants,
  Disclosure, **Labor 432.7**
  Marijuana, **Labor 432.8**

Fingerprints and Fingerprinting, generally, this index

Industrial relations department, public officers, **Labor 95**

Labor and employment,
  Records and recordation,
    Copies, **CC 1786.53**
    Disclosure, **Labor 432.7; Pen 11105.3**
      Marijuana, **Labor 432.8**
    Violation of laws, **Labor 95**

Labor standards enforcement division, officers and employees, **Labor 95**

Records and recordation, disclosure, employment, **Pen 11105.3**

Searches and Seizures, generally, this index

Unemployment compensation, eligibility for benefits, **Un Ins 1253.1**

Warrants,
  Industrial relations department, **Labor 95**
  Workers compensation appeals, board, power to issue, **Labor 134**

ART AND ARTISTS

Advance fees, talent services, **Labor 1702 et seq.**

Children and minors, employment, **Labor 1294.3**

Compensation and salaries, talent services, **Labor 1701 et seq.**

Contracts, talent services, fees, **Labor 1701 et seq.**

Definitions, talent agencies, **Labor 1700.4**
  Fees, **Labor 1701**

Fees, talent services, **Labor 1701 et seq.**

Limitation of actions, talent agencies, fee disputes, **Labor 1700.44**

Talent services, fees, **Labor 1701 et seq.**

Unemployment compensation, motion picture, radio or television industry, **Un Ins 601.5**

Workers compensation, employment on commissioned works, **Labor 3351.5**

ARTERY BANKS

Tissue Banks, generally, this index

ARTIFICIAL LIMBS

Workers compensation, **Labor 3208**

ARTISANS

Mechanics Liens, generally, this index

ARTISTS

Art and Artists, generally, this index

ASBESTOS

Accounts and accounting,
  Asbestos consultant certification, **Labor 9021.6**
  Asbestos training approval account, deposits, **Labor 9021.9**

Advisory committee, **Labor 9021.9**

Certificates and certification, consultants or site surveillance technicians, **Labor 9021.5**
  Renewal, **Labor 9021.8**

Common interest developments, notice, **Health & S 25915.2**

Consultation,
  Certificates and certification, **Labor 9021.5**
    Renewal, **Labor 9021.8**
  Inspections, requirement that consultant also perform corrective work, **Labor 6509.5**

Contractors,
  Certification,
    Good faith effort to determine presence, **Labor 6501.9**
    Registration, **Labor 6501.5**
  Notice to employees, **Health & S 25915.2**

Contracts, notice, privity of contract, **Health & S 25915.5**

Crimes and offenses,
  Asbestos related work, **Labor 6505.5**
  Building owners disclosure, failure to disclose or misleading disclosure, **Health & S 25919.7**
  Inspections, financial relationship with business performing corrective work, **Labor 6509.5**

Death benefits, limitation of actions, **Labor 5406.5**

Definitions,
  Building owners disclosure, **Health & S 25918**
  Registration, **Labor 6501.8**

Disclosure, building owners to employees, **Health & S 25915 et seq.**

Examinations and examiners, consultants and site surveillance technicians, fees, **Labor 9021.6**

Fines and penalties,
  Inspections, financial relationship with business performing corrective work, **Labor 6509.5**
  Labor and employment, **Labor 6505.5**

Firefighters and fire departments, limitation of actions, death benefits, **Labor 5406.5**

Fund, training and consultant certification, **Labor 9021.7**

Health risks, disclosure by building owners, **Health & S 25915 et seq.**

Inspection and inspectors, asbestos consultants, requirement that consultant also perform corrective work, **Labor 6509.5**

Labor and Employment, this index

ASBESTOS—Cont'd

Limitation of actions, death benefits, **Labor 5406.5**

Management plans, buildings, **Health & S 25915.1**

Notice,
  Building owners to employees, **Health & S 25915 et seq.**
  Workplace, **Labor 6501.5, 6505.5**

Occupational Carcinogens Control Act, **Labor 9000 et seq.**

Plans and specifications, management plans, buildings, **Health & S 25915.1**

Privity of contract, notice, **Health & S 25915.5**

Registration, employers, contractors, asbestos related work, **Labor 6501.5, 6505.5**

Reports, labor and employment, use, **Labor 9030 et seq.**

Residential common interest development, notice, **Health & S 25915.2**

Rules and regulations, labor and employment, **Labor 6501.5**
  Asbestos related work, **Labor 9021.5**

Second and subsequent offenses, asbestos related work, **Labor 6505.5**

Site surveillance technicians, certificates and certification, **Labor 9021.5**
  Renewal, **Labor 9021.8**

Spraying, **Labor 6307.1, 6308**
  Compliance, occupational safety and health, **Labor 6407**
  Death of employees, **Labor 6425**
  Enforcement, **Labor 6307.1, 6308**
  Fines and penalties, **Labor 6427 et seq.**
  Injunction, unsafe working conditions, **Labor 6324**
  Occupational safety and health, **Labor 6317, 6407**
  Violations, occupational safety and health, **Labor 6317**

Statute of limitations, death benefits, **Labor 5406.5**

Warnings, posting, construction or maintenance areas, **Health & S 25916**

Work related, safety conference, **Labor 6503.5**

Workplace,
  Good faith effort to determine presence, **Labor 6501.9**
  Orders prohibiting use, **Labor 6325.5**

ASBESTOS ADVISORY COMMITTEE

Generally, **Labor 9021.9**

ASBESTOS CONSULTANT CERTIFICATION ACCOUNT

Generally, **Labor 9021.6**

ASBESTOS CONTAINING CONSTRUCTION MATERIAL

Definitions, building owners disclosure, **Health & S 25919**

ASBESTOS RELATED WORK

Definitions, registration, **Labor 6501.8**

ASBESTOS TRAINING AND CONSULTANT CERTIFICATION FUND
Generally, **Labor 9021.7**

ASBESTOS TRAINING APPROVAL ACCOUNT
Deposits, **Labor 9021.9**

ASBESTOS WORKERS
Definitions, workers compensation, **Labor 4402**

ASBESTOS WORKERS ACCOUNT
State treasury, uninsured employers fund, **Labor 4401 et seq.**

ASBESTOS WORKERS BENEFITS
Definitions, workers compensation, **Labor 4402**

ASBESTOSIS
Definitions, workers compensation, **Labor 4402**

ASPHALT
Workers compensation, alternative dispute resolution system, **Labor 3201.5**

ASSASSINATION
Elected public officials, death benefits, **Labor 4720 et seq.**

ASSAULT AND BATTERY
Colleges and Universities, this index
Community health care workers, records and recordation, **Labor 6332**
Domestic Violence, generally, this index
Labor and employment, workplace violence safety, **CCP 527.8**
Medical care and treatment, community health care workers, records and recordation, **Labor 6332**
Sexual Assault, generally, this index
Workers compensation,
    Employers injury of employee, **Labor 3602**
    Fellow employee, **Labor 3600**
    Workplace violence safety, **CCP 527.8**

ASSEMBLY
Legislature, this index

ASSESSMENTS
Income Tax—State, this index
Labor Camps, this index
Unemployment Compensation, this index
Workers Compensation, this index

ASSIGNMENT FOR BENEFIT OF CREDITORS
Compensation and salaries, liens and incumbrances, priorities and preferences, **CCP 1204**
Employee benefit plans, liens and incumbrances, priorities and preferences, **CCP 1204**
Liens and incumbrances, compensation and salaries, priorities and preferences, **CCP 1204**

ASSIGNMENT FOR BENEFIT OF CREDITORS—Cont'd
Priorities and preferences, compensation and salaries, liens and incumbrances, **CCP 1204**

ASSIGNMENTS
Claims, stop orders for wages or on labor bonds, **Labor 96**
Collective bargaining, representatives, claims for wages, **Labor 96.3**
Compensation and Salaries, this index
Employees, preventing reemployment, right to bring action, **Labor 1054**
Guardian and Ward, this index
Labor and employment, preventing reemployment, right to sue, **Labor 1054**
Labor Commissioner, this index
Labor disputes, collective bargaining, representative, claims for wages, **Labor 96.3**
Mechanics Liens, this index
Salaries. Compensation and Salaries, this index
Solicitation of employees by misrepresentation, civil action, **Labor 972**
Stop orders for wages or on labor bonds, assignment of claim, **Labor 96**
Support, this index
Unemployment Compensation, this index
Wages. Compensation and Salaries, this index
Workers Compensation, this index

ASSISTANCE
Social Services, generally, this index

ASSISTED LIVING
Residential Care Facilities for the Elderly, generally, this index

ASSOCIATIONS AND SOCIETIES
Cemetery associations. Cemeteries and Dead Bodies, generally, this index
Charities, generally, this index
Committees, unemployment compensation, directors, **Un Ins 637.1**
Corporation Taxes, generally, this index
Definitions, asbestos, notice, **Health & S 25915.2, 25915.5**
Directors, unemployment compensation, **Un Ins 637, 637.1**
Income tax—state, withholdings on employee wages, failure to withhold, personal liability of officers, shareholders and others, **Un Ins 1735**
Limited Liability Companies, generally, this index
Nonprofit Associations, generally, this index
Officers and employees,
    Income tax—state, employee wages, failure to withhold, personal liability, **Un Ins 1735**
    Unemployment compensation, contributions, personal liability, **Un Ins 1735**
Partnership, generally, this index

ASSOCIATIONS AND SOCIETIES—Cont'd
Religious Organizations and Societies, generally, this index
Restaurants, generally, this index
Savings and Loan Associations, generally, this index
Savings Associations, generally, this index
Shares and shareholders,
    Income tax—state, employee wages, failure to withhold, personal liability, **Un Ins 1735**
    Unemployment compensation, contributions, personal liability, **Un Ins 1735**
Small Businesses, generally, this index
Unemployment compensation,
    Contributions, nonpayment, personal liability of officers, shareholders and others, **Un Ins 1735**
    Directors, **Un Ins 637, 637.1**
    Employing unit, **Un Ins 135**
Withholdings,
    Income tax—state, failure to withhold, personal liability of officers, shareholders and others, **Un Ins 1735**
    Unemployment compensation, contributions, nonpayment, personal liability of officers, shareholders and others, **Un Ins 1735**

ASSUMED OR FICTITIOUS NAMES
Leases, theft by fraud, **Pen 484**
Personal property, lease or rental, **Pen 484**

ASSUMPTION OF RISK
Defenses, action for death or personal injury of employee, **Labor 2801**
Workers compensation, defense abolished, **Labor 3708**

ASYLUMS
Mentally Ill Persons, generally, this index

AT RISK STUDENTS
High Schools or Secondary Schools, this index
Schools and School Districts, this index

ATHLETICS
Baseball, generally, this index
Colleges and Universities, this index
Exclusion. Workers compensation, post
Foreign professionals, unemployment compensation, **Un Ins 655**
Nonprofit organizations, amateur athletic officiating services, workers compensation coverage, **Labor 3352, 3706.5**
Public agencies, amateur athletic officiating services, workers compensation coverage, **Labor 3352, 3706.5**
Unemployment compensation,
    Amateur athletic officials, **Un Ins 657**
    Baseball players, **Un Ins 653**
    Exclusion from benefits, **Un Ins 1253.4**
    Foreign professional athletes, **Un Ins 655**

ATHLETICS—Cont'd

Workers compensation, **Labor 3600**
  Amateur athletic services, public agencies and nonprofit organizations providing, **Labor 3352, 3706.5**
  Exclusion,
    Benefits, **Un Ins 1253.4**
    Officials, **Labor 3352**
    Participants, **Labor 3352**
    Sports officials, **Labor 3352**
  Scorekeepers, exemption, **Labor 3352**
  Sports officials, exemption, **Labor 3352**
  Student athletes, public agencies, nonprofit organizations and colleges and universities, **Labor 3352**
  Timekeepers, exemption, **Labor 3352**
  Voluntary participation, liability for injuries, **Labor 3600**

ATOMIC WAR

War and Civil Defense, generally, this index

ATTACHMENT

Admission, preferred labor claims, **CCP 1207**
Appeal and review, preferred labor claims, **CCP 1206**
Assignment of wages, **Labor 300**
Bonds (officers and fiduciaries), cash bond of employee, **Labor 404**
Bonuses, exemption, **CCP 487.020**
Cash bond of employee, **Labor 404**
Claims. Exemptions, generally, post
Commissions, exemption, **CCP 487.020**
Costs,
  Labor claims, disputed claims, **CCP 1207**
  Labor standards enforcement division, **Labor 101**
County Officers and Employees Retirement Systems, this index
Door to door salesmen, money deposited as security for wages, **Labor 270.6**
Exemptions, **CCP 487.020**
  Bonuses, **CCP 487.020**
  Commissions, **CCP 487.020**
  Compensation and salaries, **CCP 487.020**
  Earnings, **CCP 487.020**
  Money judgments, **CCP 487.020**
  Support, post
  Wages, **CCP 487.020**
Itinerant merchants, money deposited as security for wages, **Labor 270.6**
Labor claims, **CCP 1206 et seq.**
Labor standards enforcement division, actions, costs, **Labor 101**
Liens and incumbrances, **CCP 1206 et seq.**
Logs and logging, cash and securities on deposit to insure wage payments, **Labor 270.5**
Money judgments, exemptions, **CCP 487.020**
Notice,
  Labor claimant of request to release original attachment, **CCP 1208**

ATTACHMENT—Cont'd

Notice—Cont'd
  Liens and incumbrances, ante
Priorities and preferences, labor claims, **CCP 1206 et seq.**
Release, labor claims, **CCP 1208**
Sawmill operations, deposits to insure wage payment, **Labor 270.5**
Support, exemptions, **CCP 487.020**
Telephone solicitors, money deposited as security for wages, **Labor 270.6**
Unemployment administration fund, fees, levy of writs, **Un Ins 1559**
Unemployment Compensation, this index
Wages, exemption, **CCP 487.020**
Warrants, workers compensation appeals board, **Labor 134**
Workers Compensation, this index

ATTEMPTS

Purchases, weapons, crimes and offenses, **Pen 12021**

ATTORNEY FEES

Actions and proceedings,
  Discrimination, **Labor 1197.5**
  Diversion program referrals or participation, disclosure, **Labor 432.7**
Agricultural Labor and Employment, this Index
Appeal and review, **Labor 98.2**
Buses, displaced workers, actions and proceedings, **Labor 1073**
Business and commerce, discrimination, **CC 52**
Civil rights, **CC 52**
Community colleges and districts. Colleges and Universities, this index
Construction, contracts, labor and employment, **Labor 2810**
Consumer Credit Reporting Agencies, this index
Disclosure,
  Arrest record, **Labor 432.7**
  Personal or confidential information, Information Practices Act, **CC 1798.46, 1798.48, 1798.53**
Discrimination, this index
Employment. Labor and Employment, this index
Fair Employment and Housing, this index
Farm labor contractors,
  Employees, civil actions, **Labor 1697**
  Time certificate for handling claims, **Labor 1684**
Gender violence, actions and proceedings, **CC 52.4**
Harassment, **CCP 527.6**
Health care providers, whistle blowing, **Health & S 1278.5**
Health Facilities, this index
Housing, this index
Indemnity, labor and employment, discharge of duties, **Labor 2802**
Information Practices Act, **CC 1798.46, 1798.48, 1798.53**
Injunction, harassment, **CCP 527.6**

ATTORNEY FEES—Cont'd

Interurban railroads, displaced workers, actions and proceedings, **Labor 1073**
Invasion of privacy, Information Practices Act, **CC 1798.53**
Janitors,
  Contracts, labor and employment, **Labor 2810**
  Discharge, **Labor 1062**
Job listing services, **CC 1812.523**
Labor and Employment, this index
Labor Camps, this index
Labor disputes, injunction, **Labor 1138.1**
Mass transit, displaced workers, actions and proceedings, **Labor 1073**
Military Forces, this index
Minimum wage violations, **Labor 1193.6**
Nonpayment actions, labor and employment, **Labor 218.5**
Occupational safety and health appeals board, award to employers, **Labor 149.5**
Paratransit vehicles, displaced workers, actions and proceedings, **Labor 1073**
Payroll, records and recordation, **Labor 226**
Photography and pictures, criminally related personal injury reports, frivolous actions, **Pen 11161.9**
Private security services, contracts, labor and employment, **Labor 2810**
Public Buildings and Works, this index
Railroads, displaced workers, actions and proceedings, **Labor 1073**
Sex, force and violence, actions and proceedings, **CC 52.4**
Sexual harassment, **CC 52**
State Agencies, this index
State Contracts, this index
State Officers and Employees, this index
Talent Agencies, this index
Transportation, displaced workers, actions and proceedings, **Labor 1073**
Unemployment compensation, appeals boards, hearings, **Un Ins 1957**
University of California. Colleges and Universities, this index
Wearing Apparel, this index
Whistle blowing,
  Health facilities, **Health & S 1278.5**
  State officers and employees, **Gov 8547.8**
Workers Compensation, this index
Youthbuild program, grants, **Un Ins 9802**

ATTORNEY GENERAL

Children and minors, enforcement of law, **Labor 1312, 1399**
Civil Rights, this index
Escheat, generally, this index
Fair employment and housing, housing discrimination actions, **Gov 12989.3**
Housing discrimination, actions and proceedings, **Gov 12989.3**
Labor and employment, children and minors, enforcement of law, **Labor 1312, 1399**

ATTORNEY GENERAL—Cont'd

Labor camps, investigations, **Health & S 17054**

Medical records, negligence, release, **CC 56.36**

Narcotics enforcement division. Justice Department, this index

Unemployment compensation, enforcement of liabilities, interstate cooperation, **Un Ins 453**

Whistle blowing, hotlines, **Labor 1102.7**

Workers Compensation, this index

ATTORNEY IN FACT

Power of Attorney, generally, this index

ATTORNEYS

Advertisements, labor and employment, disability benefits and services, **Labor 139.4 et seq.**

Affidavits, generally, this index

Attorney General, generally, this index

Chief administrative law judge, unemployment compensation, qualifications, **Un Ins 405**

Compensation and salaries. Attorney Fees, generally, this index

Confidential or privileged information, whistle blowing, application of law, **Labor 1102.5**

Correctional Institutions, this index

Counties, this index

Depositions, generally, this index

Discovery, generally, this index

District Attorneys, generally, this index

Employment Security Law, appeals board,
  Appearance, **Un Ins 1957**
  Members, **Un Ins 401**

Fair employment and housing, complaints, service of process, **Gov 12962**

Fair employment and housing department, powers and duties, **Gov 12930**

Fees. Attorney Fees, generally, this index

Income. Attorney Fees, generally, this index

Industrial Relations Department, this index

Labor and Employment, this index

Municipal Attorneys, generally, this index

Partners, registered limited liability partnerships. Partnership, this index

Pneumonia, workers compensation, **Labor 3212**

Power of Attorney, generally, this index

Prisons and prisoners. Correctional Institutions, this index

Production of Books and Papers, generally, this index

Registered limited liability partnerships. Partnership, this index

Right to counsel, agricultural labor relations board investigations, **Labor 1151.3**

Solicitation, workers compensation, exemptions, **Labor 3217**

Unemployment Compensation, this index

Witnesses, generally, this index

ATTORNEYS—Cont'd

Workers Compensation, this index

ATTRIBUTABLE INCOME

Definitions,
  Corporation taxes,
    Enterprise zones,
      Credits, **Rev & T 23622.7, 23622.8, 23634**
      Deductions, **Rev & T 24416.2**
    Military base recovery areas, **Rev & T 23645, 24416.5**
  Income tax—state, enterprise zones,
    Credits, **Rev & T 17053.34, 17053.47, 17053.74**
    Deductions, **Rev & T 17276.2**

AUDIOTAPES

Comfort stations and rest rooms, labor and employment, **Labor 435**

Labor and employment, comfort stations and rest rooms, **Labor 435**

Performers, personal service contracts, **Labor 2855**

AUDITIONS

Talent services, fees, **Labor 1701 et seq.**

AUDITS AND AUDITORS

Apprentices, **Labor 3073.1**

Apprenticeship council, training criteria, **Labor 3073.2**

California State University. Colleges and Universities, this index

Self insurers, fees, workers compensation, **Labor 3702.5**

Unemployment Compensation, this index

Workers Compensation, this index

AUTHORITIES

Cemetery authority. Cemeteries and Dead Bodies, generally, this index

Juvenile Facilities Division, generally, this index

AUTO COURTS AND RESORTS

Motels and Motor Courts, generally, this index

AUTOMATED CLEARINGHOUSE

Definitions, unemployment compensation, electronic funds transfers, withholding tax on wages, **Un Ins 13021.5**

AUTOMATED CLEARINGHOUSE CREDIT

Definitions, unemployment compensation, electronic funds transfers, withholding tax on wages, **Un Ins 13021.5**

AUTOMATED CLEARINGHOUSE DEBIT

Definitions, unemployment compensation, electronic funds transfers, withholding tax on wages, **Un Ins 13021.5**

AUTOMATED PEOPLE MOVERS

Elevators, Dumbwaiters and Escalators, generally, this index

AUTOMOBILE INSURANCE

Motor Vehicle Insurance, generally, this index

AUTOMOBILE WRECKERS

Motor Vehicles, generally, this index

AUTOMOBILES

Motor Vehicles, generally, this index

AUTOPSY

Workers compensation proceedings, **Labor 5706, 5707**

AVERAGE BASE PAY ROLL

Definitions, unemployment compensation, **Un Ins 905**

AVIATION

Aircraft, generally, this index

AWARDING BODY

Definitions, public works, **Labor 1722**

AWARDS

Arbitration and Award, generally, this index

Workers Compensation, this index

BABIES

Children and Minors, generally, this index

BACKGROUND CHECKS

Criminal History Information, generally, this index

BAD CHECKS

Negotiable Instruments, this index

BAD DEBTS

Corporation Taxes, this index

BADGES, EMBLEMS AND INSIGNIA

Labor union insignia, articles of merchandise, **Labor 1010 et seq.**

Union buttons, unlawful wearing, **Labor 1018**

BAGGAGE

Railroads, this index

BAGGERS

Children and minors, employment, **Labor 1294.3**

BAGS

Containers, generally, this index

BAILMENT

Fraud, **Pen 484**

Larceny by fraud, bailed property, **Pen 484**

Warehouses and Warehousemen, generally, this index

BALLOTS

Elections, this index

BANDAGES

Industrial homework, manufacturer, **Labor 2651**

BANK AND CORPORATION TAXES

Corporation Taxes, generally, this index

BANK DEPOSITS AND COLLECTIONS
Abandoned or Unclaimed Property, generally, this index
Bonds (officers and fiduciaries), cash bond of employee, savings deposit, **Labor 403**
Cash bond of employee, **Labor 403**
Certificates of deposit,
　Farm labor contractors, filing in lieu of bond, **Labor 1684 et seq.**
　Time certificates, filing in lieu of bond, farm labor contractors, **Labor 1684**
Compensation and salaries, deposit of wages by employer in employees bank, savings and loan association or credit union account, **Labor 213**
Garnishment, generally, this index
Logging contractor, security for payment of wages, **Labor 270.5**
Sawmill operations contractor, security for payment of wages, **Labor 270.5**
Signatures, cash bond of employee, withdrawal from bank savings account, **Labor 403**
Unclaimed property. Abandoned or Unclaimed Property, generally, this index
Unemployment compensation, **Un Ins 1501**
Workers compensation, employer deposits, disability payments, **Labor 4651**

BANKERS
Banks and Banking, generally, this index

BANKRUPTCY
Consumer credit reports, contents of records, **CC 1785.13**
　Investigative reports, employment or insurance investigations, **CC 1786.18**
Disability compensation voluntary plans, **Un Ins 3261**
Insolvency, generally, this index
Labor disputes, collective bargaining, successor clause, **Labor 1127**
Unemployment compensation,
　Contributions, exemption, **Un Ins 988**
　Duty of trustee or other representative, **Un Ins 1090**
　Employing unit, **Un Ins 135**
　Personal liability of trustee, **Un Ins 1736**
　Priority of lien for unpaid contributions, interest and penalties, **Un Ins 1701**

BANKS AND BANKING
Abandoned or Unclaimed Property, generally, this index
Aged persons, financial abuse, reports, **Welf & I 15630.1**
Armenians, genocide, limitation of actions, **CCP 354.45**
Associations and societies. Savings Associations, generally, this index
Bills and notes. Negotiable Instruments, generally, this index
Certificates of deposit. Bank Deposits and Collections, this index

BANKS AND BANKING—Cont'd
Collections. Bank Deposits and Collections, generally, this index
Compensation and salaries, deposit of wages by employer in employees account, **Labor 213**
Corporation Taxes, generally, this index
Credit Cards, generally, this index
Credit Unions, generally, this index
Definitions,
　Armenians, genocide, limitation of actions, **CCP 354.45**
　Unclaimed Property Law, **CCP 1501**
Dependent adults, financial abuse, reports, **Welf & I 15630.1**
Deposits. Bank Deposits and Collections, generally, this index
Fines and penalties,
　Aged persons, financial abuse, reports, **Welf & I 15630.1**
　Dependent adults, financial abuse, reports, **Welf & I 15630.1**
Negotiable Instruments, generally, this index
Officers and employees,
　Aged persons, financial abuse, reports, **Welf & I 15630.1**
　Dependent adults, financial abuse, reports, **Welf & I 15630.1**
Privileges and immunities,
　Aged persons, financial abuse, reports, **Welf & I 15634**
　Dependent adults, financial abuse, reports, **Welf & I 15634**
Residential mortgage lenders. Mortgages, this index
Savings and Loan Associations, generally, this index
Savings Associations, generally, this index
Small Businesses, generally, this index
Talent agencies, trust funds, **Labor 1700.25**
Taxation. Corporation Taxes, generally, this index
Unclaimed property. Abandoned or Unclaimed Property, generally, this index

BARRELS
Containers, generally, this index

BARROOMS
Taverns and Saloons, generally, this index

BASE PERIODS
Definitions, unemployment compensation, **Un Ins 1275**

BASEBALL
Children and minors, professional sports, hours of labor, **Labor 1295.5**
Professional sports, children and minors, hours of labor, **Labor 1295.5**
Unemployment compensation, players, **Un Ins 653, 1253.4**

BASKETS
Containers, generally, this index

BATHROOMS
Comfort Stations and Rest Rooms, generally, this index

BATON TRAINING FACILITIES AND INSTRUCTORS
Private Security Services, generally, this index

BATTERY
Assault and Battery, generally, this index

BEACHES
Zoning and Planning, generally, this index

BEATING
Assault and Battery, generally, this index

BEGGING
Children and minors, encouraging, **Labor 1308**

BELTS
Window cleaners, safety belts, **Labor 7325 et seq.**

BENEFIT AUDIT FUND
Definitions, unemployment compensation, **Un Ins 130.5**

BENEFIT COST RATIO
Definitions, unemployment insurance, school employees, **Un Ins 823**

BENEFIT PAYMENTS DEPARTMENT
Administration expenses, **Un Ins 3012**
Civil service, personnel transfers, employment development department, **Un Ins 301.7**
Creation of department, **Un Ins 301**
Definitions, **Un Ins 133.5**
　Director, **Un Ins 134.1**
Delegation of powers and duties to department of employment development, **Un Ins 301**
Directors,
　Administrator, definitions, financing unemployment insurance for public school employees, **Un Ins 821.3**
　Delegation of powers and duties to department of employment development, **Un Ins 301**
Transfer of powers and duties, employment development department, **Un Ins 301 et seq.**
Transfer of records and property, employment development department, **Un Ins 301.6**

BENEFIT YEAR
Definitions, unemployment compensation, **Un Ins 1276**

BENEVOLENT ASSOCIATIONS OR CORPORATIONS
Insurance, generally, this index

BENZIDINE
Occupational Carcinogens Control Act, **Labor 9000 et seq.**

BETA NAPHTHYLAMINE
Occupational Carcinogens Control Act, **Labor 9000 et seq.**

BETA PROPRIOLACTONE
Occupational Carcinogens Control Act, **Labor 9000 et seq.**

BETTING
Gambling, generally, this index

BEVERAGES
Alcoholic Beverages, generally, this index
Industrial homework, manufacturer, **Labor 2651**
Restaurants, generally, this index

BEVERLY KILLEAN LIMITED LIABILITY COMPANY ACT
Limited Liability Companies, generally, this index

BIAS AND PREJUDICE
Generally, **Const. Art. 1, § 8**
Discrimination, generally, this index

BIAS CRIMES
Hate Crimes, generally, this index

BIDS AND BIDDING
Elevators, dumbwaiters and escalators, disclosure, certificates and certification, **Labor 7311.1**
Public Buildings and Works, this index
Public Contracts, this index
Unemployment compensation, training contracts, **Un Ins 10205**

BILLS
Negotiable Instruments, generally, this index

BILLS OF EXCHANGE
Negotiable Instruments, generally, this index

BILLY
Weapons, generally, this index

BIOLOGY AND BIOLOGISTS
Unemployment compensation, independent contractor status, presumption, **Un Ins 656**

BIOPHARMACEUTICAL ACTIVITIES
Definitions,
Corporation taxes, net operating losses, **Rev & T 24416**
Income tax—state, net operating losses, **Rev & T 17276**

BIOTECHNOLOGY
Definitions, centers, training, **Un Ins 9700**
Training, **Un Ins 9700 et seq.**

BIRTH
Fair employment and housing, unlawful practices, **Gov 12945**
Family care leave, **Un Ins 3300 et seq.**
Labor and employment, unlawful practices, **Gov 12945**

BIRTH—Cont'd
Maternity wards, trespass, **Pen 602**
Neonatal units, trespass, **Pen 602**
Paid family care leave, **Un Ins 3300 et seq.**
Unemployment compensation,
Disability, **Un Ins 2626**
Family care leave, **Un Ins 3300 et seq.**

BIRTH CONTROL
Disability insurance, coverage, **Ins 10123.196**
Health Care Service Plans, this index
Insurance, disability insurance, coverage, **Ins 10123.196**
Sterilization of persons, labor and employment, condition of employment, unlawful practice, **Gov 12945.5**

BIS (CHLOROMETHYL) ETHER
Occupational Carcinogens Control Act, **Labor 9000 et seq.**

BLACK LIST
Business establishments, discrimination, **CC 52**
Labor camps, tenants or employees, exercise of rights by tenant or employee, **Health & S 17031.5**

BLACK POWDER
Explosives, generally, this index

BLACKJACKS
Weapons, generally, this index

BLACKLISTING ACT
Generally, **Labor 1050 et seq.**

BLANK FORMS
Forms, generally, this index

BLASTING CAPS
Explosives, generally, this index

BLIND PERSONS
California Industries for the Blind,
Employing unit, unemployment compensation, **Un Ins 135**
Unemployment compensation, elections for financing, **Un Ins 802, 803**
Civil rights, **CC 51**
Discrimination, generally, this index
Employment compensation, employer, definitions, **Un Ins 677**
School for the Blind, generally, this index
Unemployment compensation,
California Industries for the Blind, elections for financing, **Un Ins 802, 803**
Disability benefits, **Un Ins 2606**
Qualifications, **Un Ins 605**

BLOOD
Tissue Banks, generally, this index

BLOOD BANKS
Reports, AIDS, **Health & S 120980**

BLOOD TESTS
AIDS, this index
Crimes and Offenses, this index

BLOOD TESTS—Cont'd
Disclosure. AIDS, this index

BLOODBORNE INFECTIOUS DISEASES
Diseases, this index

BLUE SKY LAW
Securities, generally, this index

BLUEPRINTS
Plans and Specifications, generally, this index

BOARD AND ROOM
Employer furnishing, time of payment of wages to employee, **Labor 205**
Workers compensation, lodging expenses, medical examinations, **Labor 4600**
Medical legal expenses, contested cases, **Labor 4621**

BOARD OF DIRECTORS
Directors, generally, this index

BOARDS AND COMMISSIONS
Administrative Law and Procedure, generally, this index
Advisory Boards and Commissions, generally, this index
Agricultural Labor Relations Board, generally, this index
Buildings. Public Buildings and Works, generally, this index
Contracts. State Contracts, generally, this index
Definitions,
Agricultural labor relations, **Labor 1140.4**
Car washes, **Labor 2051**
Elevators, dumbwaiters and escalators, **Labor 7300.1**
Employee housing and labor camps, **Health & S 17003**
Fair employment and housing department, **Gov 12925**
Occupational safety and health standards board, **Labor 140**
Tunnel and mine safety, **Labor 7951**
Wearing apparel, manufacturing, **Labor 2671**
Workforce investment, **Un Ins 14005**
Disclosure, personal information, Information Practices Act, **CC 1798 et seq.**
Education, county boards. Schools and School Districts, generally, this index
Election Precincts, this index
Equalization state board. Taxation, this index
Fair employment and housing commission, **Gov 12903 et seq., 12935**
Franchise Tax Board, generally, this index
Industrial Welfare Commission, generally, this index
Information Practices Act, **CC 1798 et seq.**
Labor and Employment, this index
Labor Commissioner, generally, this index
Local workforce investment boards, **Un Ins 14200 et seq.**

BOARDS AND COMMISSIONS—Cont'd

Medical information, disclosure, **CC 56.10**

Minimum wages, conferring enforcement authority on commission, **Const. Art. 14, § 1**

Occupational safety and health appeals board. Industrial Relations Department, this index

Occupational safety and health standards board. Industrial Relations Department, this index

Pooled money investment board. State Treasury, this index

Privacy, Information Practices Act, **CC 1798 et seq.**

Public Agencies, generally, this index

Public Utilities Commission, generally, this index

Records and recordation,
Disclosure, Information Practices Act, **CC 1798 et seq.**
Information Practices Act, **CC 1798 et seq.**

Reports,
Disclosure, Information Practices Act, **CC 1798 et seq.**
Information Practices Act, **CC 1798 et seq.**

Resignation, military service entry, reentry into office or employment on discharge, **Mil & V 395.3**

Right to privacy, Information Practices Act, **CC 1798 et seq.**

Transit Development Boards, generally, this index

Transit Districts, this index

Workforce investment board, **Un Ins 14010 et seq.**

BOATS AND BOATING

Passengers, terminals, trespass, **Pen 602**

Ships and Shipping, generally, this index

Terminals, passengers, trespass, **Pen 602**

Trespass, passengers, terminals, **Pen 602**

BODILY INJURY

Personal Injuries, generally, this index

BODY AWARDING THE CONTRACT

Definitions, public works, **Labor 1722**

BOILERS

Generally, **Labor 7620 et seq.**

Accidents endangering human life, **Labor 7770**

Appeals, orders for repairs or alterations, **Labor 7690**

Certification of inspectors, **Labor 7650 et seq.**

Crimes and offenses, **Labor 7750 et seq.**

Death, penalty for causing death, negligent operation, **Labor 7771**

Definitions, **Labor 7620 et seq., 7725**
Inspectors, **Labor 7650**

Examinations and examiners, competency certificates, **Labor 7652**

Exemptions, **Labor 7624, 7625**

Fees, inspection, **Labor 7720 et seq.**

BOILERS—Cont'd

Field consultations, fees, **Labor 7721**

Fines and penalties,
Inspection fees, failure to pay, **Labor 7728**
Negligent operation, causing death, **Labor 7771**

Injunctions, unsafe operation, **Labor 7691**
Temporary injunctions, **Labor 7692**

Inspection, **Labor 7650 et seq.**
Fees, **Labor 7721 et seq.**

Negligence, **Labor 7770, 7771**

Operation without permit, **Labor 7750**

Orders for repairs or alterations, **Labor 7687 et seq.**

Penalty fees, **Labor 7721**

Permit processing, fees, **Labor 7721**

Permits for operation, **Labor 7680 et seq.**

Posting of permit, **Labor 7684**

Preliminary orders for repairs or alterations, **Labor 7687 et seq.**

Pressure vessel account, **Labor 7722**

Processing of permits, fees, **Labor 7721**

Rehearings, orders for repairs or alterations, **Labor 7690**

Reports,
Inspection, **Labor 7654**
Safety, **Labor 7722**

Revocation of permit, **Labor 7686**

Safety,
Orders, **Labor 7626**
Reports, **Labor 7722**

Ships and Shipping, generally, this index

Temporary permits, **Labor 7685**

Temporary restraining orders, unsafe operation, **Labor 7692**

BOMBS

Demolition, voluntary technical assistance to public entity, **Labor 3367**

BONDS

Compensation and salaries,
Bonding company, failure to pay verified claims for wages, **Labor 203.5**
Employer deposits, **Labor 240**
Payment bonds, verified claims for wages, **Labor 203.5**
State contracts, verified claims for wages, **Labor 203.5**

Employees. Bonds (Officers and Fiduciaries), generally, this index

Fiduciaries. Bonds (Officers and Fiduciaries), generally, this index

Injunction, unsafe working conditions, **Labor 6324**

Investments, generally, this index

Legal investments. Investments, generally, this index

Official bonds. Bonds (Officers and Fiduciaries), generally, this index

Unemployment compensation, payments under or to purchase plans, not included as wages, **Un Ins 934**

Unemployment insurance disability funds, investment, **Un Ins 3003**

United States, this index

BONDS—Cont'd

Unsafe working conditions, injunctions, **Labor 6324**

Workers Compensation, this index

BONDS (OFFICERS AND FIDUCIARIES)

Accounts and accounting, bond of employee, **Labor 405**

Actions and proceedings, farm labor contractors, **Labor 1693**

Agricultural employment, farm labor contractors, **Labor 1684**

Amusement rides, **Labor 7926**

Applicants for employment, **Labor 400 et seq.**

Attachment, this index

Bank Deposits and Collections, this index

Car washes, registration, **Labor 2055**

Cash bond of employee, **Labor 400 et seq.**

Commingling of property by employer, bond put up by employee, **Labor 405**

Compensation and Salaries, this index

Contractors, this index

Crimes and offenses, bonds of employees, **Labor 400 et seq.**

Disability compensation, voluntary plan, **Un Ins 3258**

Disability compensation fund, **Un Ins 3002**
Custodian, **Un Ins 3002**

Door to door salesmen, security for payment of wages, **Labor 270.6**

Employer, deposits, payment bonds, **Labor 240**

Employment Agencies, this index

Executions, this index

Farm labor contractors, **Labor 1684**
Injunctive relief, **Labor 1697**

Fines and penalties, bonds of employees, **Labor 400 et seq.**

Garnishment, cash bond of employee, **Labor 404**

Injunction, this index

Interest, cash bond of employee, **Labor 404**

Itinerant merchants, security for payment of wages, **Labor 270.6**

Job listing services, **CC 1812.515**

Labor and Employment, this index

Labor commissioner, taking assignments of claims, **Labor 96**

Labor disputes,
Deposits, return, **Labor 209**
Injunction, **Labor 1138.1**

Logging contractors, deposits, security for payment of wages, **Labor 270.5**

Misappropriation of property put up as employees bond, **Labor 405**

Nonpayment of wages, second and subsequent offenses, **Labor 243**

Nurses registries, **CC 1812.525**

Payment bonds, failure of bonding company to pay verified claim for wages, **Labor 203.5**

Permanent amusement rides, **Labor 7926**

Property put by employee as bond, use by employer, **Labor 405**

BONDS (OFFICERS AND FIDUCIARIES)
—Cont'd

Savings and Loan Associations, generally, this index

Sawmill operations contractor, deposits, security for payment of wages, **Labor 270.5**

State Contracts, this index

State Treasurer, this index

Stay. Supersedeas or Stay, this index

Striking employees, return of deposit, for faithful performance of duties, **Labor 209**

Supersedeas or Stay, this index

Talent Agencies, this index

Unemployment compensation, custodian of fund, **Un Ins 1524**

Unpaid wages, deposits, payment bonds, **Labor 240**

Wearing apparel, manufacturers,
 Persons penalized within prior three years, **Labor 2675**
 Wage and benefit payments, **Labor 2679**

Workers Compensation, this index

BONES

Tissue Banks, generally, this index

BONUSES

Compensation and Salaries, this index

BOOKS AND PAPERS

Discovery, generally, this index

Employment. Labor and Employment, this index

Evidence, generally, this index

Fair employment and housing department, inspection, **Gov 12930**

Income Tax—State, this index

Industrial relations department, **Labor 58**

Labor and Employment, this index

Labor statistics and research division, **Labor 152**

Letters and Other Correspondence, generally, this index

Lewdness and Obscenity, generally, this index

Libel and Slander, generally, this index

Obscenity. Lewdness and Obscenity, generally, this index

Occupational safety and health division, **Labor 60.7**

Production of Books and Papers, generally, this index

Subpoena duces tecum. Production of Books and Papers, generally, this index

Talent agencies, **Labor 1700.26 et seq., 1703.1**

Unemployment Compensation, this index

Withholding tax on wages, **Un Ins 13011**

BOOTBLACKS

Children and minors, occupation, **Labor 1298**

BORING PITS

Labor and employment, occupational safety and health, bids for construction of boring pits, **Labor 6707**

BOSNIA CRISIS

State officers and employees, compensation and benefits, **Mil & V 395.08**

BOTTLES

Containers, generally, this index

BOURBON

Alcoholic Beverages, generally, this index

BOWLING ALLEYS

Children and minors, employment, **Labor 1294**

Workers compensation, sponsor of bowling team, exclusion, **Labor 3301**

BOXES

Containers, generally, this index

BOYCOTTS

Business establishments, discrimination, **CC 52**

Secondary boycotts, regulation, Agricultural Labor Relations Act of 1975, **Labor 1153 et seq.**

BOYS

Children and Minors, generally, this index

BRACEROS

Limitation of actions, labor and employment, funds, **CCP 354.7**

BRACES

Workers compensation, **Labor 3208**

BRAIN

Workers compensation, injury resulting in mental illness, **Labor 4662**

BRAKEMEN

Railroads, this index

BRANCH OFFICES

Garnishment, service of process, **CCP 706.101**

Labor standards enforcement division, **Labor 81**

BRANDS, MARKS AND LABELS

Agricultural land, trespass, **Pen 602**

Class of labor employed, **Labor 1010 et seq.**

Forgery, labor organization labels, **Labor 1015**

Hazardous Substances and Waste, this index

Industrial homework, **Labor 2663**

Labor union insignia, articles of merchandise, **Labor 1010 et seq.**

Registration, labor organization labels, **Labor 1014**

Service marks. Trademarks, generally, this index

Trademarks, generally, this index

Trespass, agricultural land, **Pen 602**

BRASS KNUCKLES

Weapons, generally, this index

BREACH OF DUTY

Termination of employment, **Labor 2924**

BREASTFEEDING

Children and Minors, this index

BRIBERY AND CORRUPTION

Whistle blowing,
 Community colleges and districts, **Educ 87160 et seq.**
 School officers and employees, **Educ 44110 et seq.**

BRIEFS

Civil Rights, this index

BROADCASTS

Television and Radio, generally, this index

BROKERS

Employment agencies, misrepresentations as to earnings, **Labor 976**

Real Estate Brokers and Salespersons, generally, this index

Security Agents and Broker Dealers, generally, this index

Unemployment compensation, **Un Ins 650**

BUDGETS

Appeals division, unemployment compensation, **Un Ins 403**

Wearing apparel, manufacturers and manufacturing, budgets submitted to legislature, **Labor 2674.2**

BUILDERS

Mechanics Liens, generally, this index

BUILDING AND LOAN ASSOCIATIONS

Savings Associations, generally, this index

BUILDING CODES

Building Standards, generally, this index

BUILDING PERMITS

Workers compensation, certificates and certification, filing, **Labor 3800**

Zoning and Planning, generally, this index

BUILDING STANDARDS

Apartment houses, handicapped persons, **Gov 12955.1**

Contractors, generally, this index

Elevators, dumbwaiters and escalators, **Labor 7324**

Employee Housing Act, **Health & S 17000 et seq.**

Handicapped persons, multifamily dwellings, **Gov 12955.1**

Housing, this index

Multifamily housing, handicapped persons, **Gov 12955.1**

Occupational safety and health, **Labor 142 et seq.**

BUILDINGS

Apartment Houses, generally, this index

BUILDINGS—Cont'd

Asbestos,
    Notice, employees, **Health & S 25915 et seq.**
    Related work, **Labor 6501.9**
Codes. Building Standards, generally, this index
Comfort Stations and Rest Rooms, generally, this index
Community colleges and districts. Colleges and Universities, this index
Construction,
    Cranes, tower cranes, regulation, **Labor 7370 et seq.**
    Diversion of funds, **Pen 484b**
    Tower cranes, regulation, **Labor 7370 et seq.**
Construction sites, asbestos hazard, posted warning, **Health & S 25916**
Contractors, generally, this index
Copying, asbestos information by employees or tenants, **Health & S 25917**
Correctional Institutions, generally, this index
Cranes, tower cranes, regulation, **Labor 7370 et seq.**
Definitions,
    Construction elevators, safety, **Labor 7200**
    Safety in employment, building construction or repair, **Labor 7100**
    Window cleaners, safety devices, **Labor 7325**
Demolition of Buildings, generally, this index
Disclosure, asbestos conditions, **Health & S 25915 et seq.**
Dumbwaiters. Elevators, Dumbwaiters and Escalators, generally, this index
Elevators, Dumbwaiters and Escalators, generally, this index
Employee Housing Act, **Health & S 17000 et seq.**
Escalators. Elevators, Dumbwaiters and Escalators, generally, this index
Exemptions, workplace smoking regulation, **Labor 6404.5**
Fires and Fire Protection, generally, this index
Hospitals, generally, this index
Housing, generally, this index
Janitors, generally, this index
Labor camps, building standards, **Health & S 17000 et seq.**
Maintenance,
    Asbestos hazards, posted warnings, **Health & S 25916**
    Janitors, generally, this index
Malicious mischief, refusal to leave private property upon request, **Pen 602**
Mechanics Liens, generally, this index
Motels and Motor Courts, generally, this index
Notice, asbestos conditions, **Health & S 25915 et seq.**

BUILDINGS—Cont'd

Occupational safety and health, building standards, **Labor 142 et seq.**
Place of employment, smoking regulation, exemption, **Labor 6404.5**
Prisons. Correctional Institutions, generally, this index
Public Buildings and Works, generally, this index
Remodeling site, asbestos hazard, posted warning, **Health & S 25916**
Rules and regulations, workplace smoking regulation, exemptions, **Labor 6404.5**
Scaffolds, generally, this index
School Buildings and Grounds, generally, this index
Standards. Building Standards, generally, this index
State Contracts, generally, this index
State standards. Building Standards, generally, this index
Tower cranes, regulation, **Labor 7370 et seq.**
Trespass, private property, **Pen 602**
Warnings, asbestos hazard, construction, maintenance or remodeling site, **Health & S 25916**
Window cleaners, safety devices on buildings, **Labor 7325 et seq.**
Workers compensation declaration, perjury, **Labor 3800**
Workplace smoking regulation, exemption, **Labor 6404.5**
Zoning and Planning, generally, this index

BULL RAILS

Wharves, docks and piers, **Labor 7604**

BULLS

Animals, generally, this index

BUNGEE JUMPING

Licenses and permits, **Labor 7901**
Safety, inspection and inspectors, **Labor 7920 et seq.**

BURDEN OF PROOF

Evidence, this index

BUREAUS

Contracts. State Contracts, generally, this index
Investigations and investigators, assisting criminal prosecutions, reports, **Labor 6315.3**
Investigations bureau, department of industrial relations, division of occupational safety and health, **Labor 6315**

BURIAL

Cemeteries and Dead Bodies, generally, this index

BURIAL PARK

Cemeteries and Dead Bodies, generally, this index

BURNING

Fires and Fire Protection, generally, this index

BURNS

Workers compensation, medical care and treatment, fees, **Labor 5307.1**

BURTON STULL VIETNAM VETERANS EMPLOYMENT ACT

Generally, **Gov 7280 et seq.**

BUSES

Actions and proceedings, displaced workers, **Labor 1073**
Agricultural Labor and Employment, this index
Air pressure tanks, inspection and safety regulation, **Labor 7624**
Attorney fees, displaced workers, actions and proceedings, **Labor 1073**
Boilers, inspection and safety regulation, **Labor 7624**
Contracts, displaced workers, **Labor 1070 et seq.**
Costs, displaced workers, actions and proceedings, **Labor 1073**
Displaced workers, **Labor 1070 et seq.**
Injunction, displaced workers, **Labor 1073**
Officers and employees, displaced workers, **Labor 1070 et seq.**
Paratransit Vehicles, generally, this index
Transit Districts, generally, this index

BUSINESS AND COMMERCE

Business license taxes. Taxation, this index
Consumer Protection, generally, this index
Corporations, generally, this index
Correctional institutions, inmate labor, contract, **Const. Art. 14, § 5**
Counties, this index
Crimes and offenses, dangerous business practices, **Pen 387**
Dangerous business practices, crimes and offenses, **Pen 387**
Definitions,
    Licenses and permits, political subdivisions, **Bus & P 16300**
    Withholding tax on wages, **Un Ins 13003**
Disclosure, dangers, serious concealed dangers, failure to disclose, **Pen 387**
Discrimination, **Const. Art. 1, § 8; CC 51 et seq.**
Enterprise Zones, generally, this index
Exemptions, licenses and permits, political subdivisions, **Bus & P 16300**
Licenses and permits,
    Business license taxes. Taxation, this index
    Exemptions, political subdivisions, **Bus & P 16300**
Limited Liability Companies, generally, this index
Motion pictures, reports, **Un Ins 335**
Municipalities, this index
Partnership, generally, this index

BUSINESS

BUSINESS AND COMMERCE—Cont'd
Self employment assistance program, unemployment compensation, **Un Ins 1300 et seq.**
Small Businesses, generally, this index
Trademarks, generally, this index

BUSINESS AND PROFESSIONS CODE
Consumer Affairs Department, generally, this index

BUSINESS ASSOCIATIONS
Abandoned or Unclaimed Property, this index
Definitions, Unclaimed Property Law, **CCP 1501**

BUSINESS CORPORATIONS
Corporations, generally, this index

BUSINESS DAY
Definitions, farm labor contractors, licenses and permits, **Labor 1695.7**

BUSINESS LICENSE TAXES
Taxation, this index

BUSINESS TAXES
Corporation Taxes, generally, this index
Income Tax—State, generally, this index
Taxation, generally, this index

BUSINESS TRUSTS
Corporation Taxes, generally, this index

CABLE TELEVISION
Criminal history information,
Franchises, **Pub U 5910**
Officers and employees, **Pub U 7910**
Employees, criminal history information, **Pub U 7910**
Independent contractors, criminal history information, **Pub U 7910**
Officers and employees, criminal history information, **Pub U 7910**
Open Video Systems, generally, this index
Reports, franchises, **Pub U 5920**
Vendor and purchaser, criminal history information, **Pub U 7910**
Video Programming Services, generally, this index

CABLES
Telecommunications, generally, this index

CABOOSE
Railroads, this index

CABS
Locomotives, overhang, opening, **Labor 6950, 6951**

CADAVERS
Cemeteries and Dead Bodies, generally, this index

CADDIES
Unemployment compensation, **Un Ins 651**

CAFETERIAS
Restaurants, generally, this index

CAL COBRA
Generally, **Health & S 1366.20 et seq.; Ins 10128.50 et seq.**

CAL GRANT PROGRAM
Colleges and Universities, this index

CAL OSHA SELF CONTAINED BREATHING APPARATUS ADVISORY COMMITTEE
Determination of test procedures, positive pressure closed circuit breathing apparatus for use in fires, **Labor 6331**

CALIFORNIA INDUSTRIES FOR THE BLIND
Blind Persons, this index

CALIFORNIA SCHOOL FOR THE BLIND
School for the Blind, generally, this index

CALIFORNIA SCHOOL FOR THE DEAF
Schools for the Deaf, generally, this index

CALIFORNIA STATE UNIVERSITY
Colleges and Universities, this index

CALIFORNIA STATE UNIVERSITY INVESTIGATION OF REPORTED IMPROPER GOVERNMENTAL ACTIVITIES ACT
Generally, **Educ 89570 et seq.**

CALPERS
Public Employees Retirement System, generally, this index

CALWORKS
Social Services, this index

CAMERAS
Photography and Pictures, generally, this index

CAMPAIGNS
Elections, this index

CAMPS AND CAMPING
Compensation and salaries,
Meals and lodging, deductible from wages, **Labor 1182.4**
Student employees, **Labor 1182.4**
Counselors, hours and wages, **Labor 1182.4**
Exemptions, Wage and Hour Law, student employees, **Labor 1182.4**
Hours of labor, student employees, **Labor 1182.4**
Labor Camps, generally, this index
Lodging, student employees, deductible from wages, **Labor 1182.4**
Meals, student employees, deductible from wages, **Labor 1182.4**
Mobilehomes and Mobilehome Parks, generally, this index
Program counselors, hours and wages, **Labor 1182.4**
Students, employees, hours and wages, **Labor 1182.4**
Volunteers, workers compensation, **Labor 3352**
Workers compensation, volunteers, **Labor 3352**

CAMPUS
Definitions, workers compensation, University of California police, **Labor 3213**

CAMPUS DEPARTMENT
Definitions, workers compensation, University of California police, **Labor 3213**

CANADA
Unemployment compensation, performance of services, **Un Ins 603.5**

CANCER
Firefighters, workers compensation, **Labor 3212.1**
Labor and employment, Occupational Carcinogens Control Act, **Labor 9000 et seq.**
Lifeguards, skin cancer, workers compensation, injury, **Labor 3212.11**
Occupational Carcinogens Control Act, **Labor 9000 et seq.**
Workers compensation, firefighters, **Labor 3212.1**

CANE GUNS
Weapons, generally, this index

CANS
Containers, generally, this index

CAPITAL IMPROVEMENTS
Improvements, generally, this index

CAPITAL STOCK
Shares and shareholders. Corporations, this index

CAR COMPANIES
Railroads, generally, this index

CAR INSURANCE
Motor Vehicle Insurance, generally, this index

CAR WASH WORKER FUND
Generally, **Labor 2065**

CAR WASH WORKER RESTITUTION FUND
Generally, **Labor 2065**

CAR WASHES
Generally, **Labor 2050 et seq.**
Application of law, **Labor 2067**
Applications, registration, **Labor 2061**
Bonds (officers and fiduciaries), registration, **Labor 2055, 2060**
Certificates and certification, registration, **Labor 2056**
Children and minors, employment, **Labor 1294.5**
Compensation and salaries,
Judgments and decrees, registration, **Labor 2062**
Liabilities, successors, **Labor 2066**
Registration, disclosure, **Labor 2061**
Definitions, **Labor 2051**
Delinquencies, registration, **Labor 2062**

CAR WASHES—Cont'd

Disbursements, labor and employment, restitution, funds, **Labor 2065**

Disclosure, registration, fines and penalties, **Labor 2061**

Fees, registration, **Labor 2059**

Fines and penalties, registration, **Labor 2064**
   Disclosure, **Labor 2061**

Funds, labor and employment, **Labor 2065**

Internet, registration, posting, **Labor 2063**

Labor and employment,
   Compensation and salaries, generally, ante
   Delinquencies, registration, **Labor 2062**
   Records and recordation, **Labor 2052**
   Restitution, funds, **Labor 2065**

Liabilities, compensation and salaries, successors, **Labor 2066**

Licenses and permits, registration, **Labor 2055**

Lists, registration, Internet, **Labor 2063**

Posting, registration,
   Certificates and certification, **Labor 2057**
   Internet, **Labor 2063**

Records and recordation, labor and employment, **Labor 2052**

Registration, **Labor 2054 et seq.**
   Applications, **Labor 2061**
   Bonds (officers and fiduciaries), **Labor 2055**
   Certificates and certification, **Labor 2056**
   Compensation and salaries,
      Disclosure, **Labor 2061**
      Judgments and decrees, **Labor 2062**
   Delinquencies, **Labor 2062**
   Disclosure, fines and penalties, **Labor 2061**
   Fees, **Labor 2059**
   Fines and penalties, **Labor 2064**
      Disclosure, **Labor 2061**
   Internet, posting, **Labor 2063**
   Licenses and permits, **Labor 2055**
   Lists, Internet, **Labor 2063**
   Posting,
      Certificates and certification, **Labor 2057**
      Internet, **Labor 2063**
   Renewal, **Labor 2058**
   Workers compensation, insurance, **Labor 2055**

Renewal, registration, **Labor 2058**

Reports, **Labor 2068**

Restitution, funds, labor and employment, **Labor 2065**

Rules and regulations, **Labor 2053**

Successors, compensation and salaries, liabilities, **Labor 2066**

Workers compensation, registration, **Labor 2055**

CARCINOGENS

Definitions, Occupational Carcinogens Control Act, **Labor 9004**

CARCINOGENS—Cont'd

Occupational Carcinogens Control Act, **Labor 9000 et seq.**

CARD GAMES

Gambling, generally, this index

CARDS

Credit Cards, generally, this index

Gambling, generally, this index

Labor, compensation, issuance in payment, **Labor 212**

Labor organization, card, unlawful use to obtain aid, assistance or employment, **Labor 1017**

CAREER COUNSELING

One stop career centers, **Un Ins 14230 et seq.**

CAREER EDUCATION

Vocational Education, generally, this index

CAREER OPPORTUNITY DEVELOPMENT PROGRAMS

Handicapped clients of department of rehabilitation, **Un Ins 9003**

CAREER RESOURCE NETWORK

Generally, **Educ 53086**

CAREER TECHNICAL EDUCATION

Vocational Education, generally, this index

CAREGIVERS

Aged Persons, this index

Dependent Adults, this index

Handicapped Persons, this index

CARGO TANKS

Motor Carriers, this index

CARNIVALS

Amusement rides, safety, **Labor 7900 et seq.**

Compensation and salaries, deposits for security of payment, **Labor 271**

CARPAL TUNNEL SYNDROME

Labor and employment, occupational safety and health, **Labor 6719**

CARRIERS

Aerial passenger tramways, **Labor 7340 et seq.**

Boats and Boating, generally, this index

Buses, generally, this index

Highway carriers. Motor Carriers, generally, this index

Marine carriers. Ships and Shipping, generally, this index

Motor Carriers, generally, this index

Railroads, generally, this index

Ships and Shipping, generally, this index

Water carriers. Ships and Shipping, generally, this index

CARRYBACKS

Income tax—state, net operating losses, deductions, **Rev & T 17276**

CARRYOUTS

Children and minors, employment, **Labor 1294.3**

CARRYOVERS

Corporation Taxes, this index

CARS

Motor Vehicles, generally, this index

CARTONS

Containers, generally, this index

CAS NUMBER

Definitions, hazardous substance information and training, **Labor 6366**

CASES

Containers, generally, this index

CASHIERS

Children and minors, employment, **Labor 1294.3**

CASSETTES

Videotape, generally, this index

CATTLE

Animals, generally, this index

CAUSES OF ACTION

Actions and Proceedings, generally, this index

CEASE AND DESIST ORDERS

Fair employment and housing, **Gov 12987**

Housing discrimination, **Gov 12987**

CEMENT

Workers compensation, alternative dispute resolution system, **Labor 3201.5**

CEMETERIES AND DEAD BODIES

Coroners, generally, this index

Disinterment, workers compensation proceedings, **Labor 5707**

Tissue Banks, generally, this index

Unemployment compensation, cemetery broker or salesman, **Un Ins 650**

Workers compensation proceedings, exhumation of bodies, **Labor 5707**

CEMETERY ASSOCIATIONS

Cemeteries and Dead Bodies, generally, this index

CEMETERY AUTHORITY

Cemeteries and Dead Bodies, generally, this index

CEMETERY BROKERS AND SALESPERSONS

Unemployment compensation, **Un Ins 650**

CEMETERY CORPORATIONS

Cemeteries and Dead Bodies, generally, this index

CEMETERY

CEMETERY DISTRICTS
Cemeteries and Dead Bodies, generally, this index

CENSUS
Employment development department, United States census bureau contract, population survey sample, **Un Ins 327**

CERAMICS
Lead poisoning, occupational safety, programs, **Health & S 105185 et seq.**

CERTIFICATES AND CERTIFICATION
Aerial passenger tramways, construction, plans and design information, **Labor 7353, 7354**
Agricultural Labor and Employment, this index
Air pressure tanks, inspectors, **Labor 7650 et seq.**
Amusement rides, safety, **Labor 7900 et seq.**
Apprentices,
  Contractors and subcontractors, public works, **Labor 1777.5**
  Standards, public works, **Labor 1777.5**
Car washes, registration, **Labor 2056**
Civil air patrol, labor and employment, leaves of absence, **Labor 1503**
Corporation Taxes, this index
Cranes, tower cranes, certificating agencies and license certifiers, **Labor 7370 et seq.**
Domestic partnership, **Fam 298.5**
Electricity, this index
Elevators, Dumbwaiters and Escalators, this index
Exemptions, withholding tax on wages, **Un Ins 13040 et seq.**
Family care leave, **Un Ins 2708**
Fingerprints and fingerprinting, criminal history information, **Pen 11105.7**
Geologists and geophysicists, training, **Bus & P 7843**
Handicapped persons, manpower programs, **Un Ins 9003**
Income Tax—State, this index
Labor and Employment, this index
Labor Organizations, this index
Liquefied petroleum gas storage tanks, inspectors, **Labor 7650 et seq.**
Public Buildings and Works, this index
State Contracts, this index
Unemployment Compensation, this index
Vietnam veterans, employment trainees, **Gov 7280.8 et seq.**
Wearing apparel, manufacturers, registration, **Labor 2675**
Workers Compensation, this index

CERTIFICATES OF CONVENIENCE
Talent agencies, death or incompetency of licensee, **Labor 1700.20a, 1700.20b**

CERTIFICATES OF DEPOSIT
Bank Deposits and Collections, this index

CERTIFICATION
Certificates and Certification, generally, this index

CERTIFIED MAIL
Mail and Mailing, this index

CERTIFIED NURSE ASSISTANTS
Nurses, this index

CERTIFIED OR REGISTERED MAIL
Mail and Mailing, this index

CERTIFIED TRAINEE
Definitions, Vietnam veteran, **Gov 7280.9**

CHAIR LIFTS
Elevators, Dumbwaiters and Escalators, generally, this index

CHANCELLORS
Community colleges and districts. Colleges and Universities, this index

CHANGING ROOMS
Labor and employment, audio or video recordings, **Labor 435**

CHAPLAINS
Clergy, generally, this index

CHARACTER AND REPUTATION
Consumer Credit Reporting Agencies, generally, this index
Libel and Slander, generally, this index
Mercantile character, false reports, procurement, theft, **Pen 484**
Slander. Libel and Slander, generally, this index

CHARGE CARDS
Credit Cards, generally, this index

CHARITIES
Children and minors, appearance on entertainment, hours of labor, **Labor 1310**
Community Chest, generally, this index
Conservators and Conservatorships, generally, this index
Insurance, this index
Unemployment compensation, **Un Ins 608, 641**
  Excludable services, **Un Ins 711**
Volunteer employees, workers compensation exclusion, **Labor 3352**
Workers compensation, exclusion, charitable workers, **Labor 3352**

CHARTERED CITIES
Municipalities, this index

CHAUFFEURS LICENSE
Drivers licenses. Motor Vehicles, this index

CHECKS
Negotiable Instruments, this index

CHEMICAL ENGINEERS
Engineers, generally, this index

CHEMICAL NAMES
Definitions, hazardous substances information and training, **Labor 6367**

CHEMICALLY DEPENDENT PERSONS
Alcoholics and Alcoholism, generally, this index
Drug Addicts, generally, this index

CHEMICALS, CHEMISTRY AND CHEMISTS
Hazardous Substances and Waste, generally, this index
Lead poisoning, occupational safety, programs, **Health & S 105185 et seq.**
Unemployment compensation, independent contractor status, presumption, **Un Ins 656**

CHICO STATE COLLEGE
Colleges and Universities, generally, this index

CHILD CARE
Day Care and Nursery Schools, generally, this index

CHILD LABOR
Labor and Employment, this index

CHILD PORNOGRAPHY
Children and Minors, this index

CHILD SUPPORT
Support, generally, this index

CHILD SUPPORT OBLIGATIONS
Definitions, unemployment compensation deductions and withholding, **Un Ins 1255.7**

CHILD SUPPORT SERVICES DEPARTMENT
Local child support agencies, financial assets, liquidation, instructions, **Fam 17522.5**
State disbursement unit. Support, this index

CHILDBIRTH
Birth, generally, this index

CHILDREN AND MINORS
Abduction, **CC 49**
Accounts and accounting, Coogan trust account, entertainment contracts, **Labor 1308.9**
Actors and actresses, age, **Labor 1308**
Adoption of Children, generally, this index
Advertising departments, working in, employment, **Labor 1294.3**
Agricultural Labor and Employment, this index
Agricultural products, processors, hours of labor, exemptions, **Labor 1393.5**
Alcoholic Beverages, this index
Apprentices, generally, this index
Art and Artists, this index
Assignment of wages, written consent of parent or guardian, **Labor 300**
Baggers, employment, **Labor 1294.3**

CHILDREN AND MINORS—Cont'd

Baseball, professional sports, hours of labor, **Labor 1295.5**

Birth, generally, this index

Breastfeeding, labor and employment, **Labor 1030 et seq.**

CalWORKs. Social Services, this index

Care and development services. Day Care and Nursery Schools, generally, this index

Carryouts, employment, **Labor 1294.3**

Cashiering work, employment, **Labor 1294.3**

Cigarettes and cigars, sorting, manufacturing or packing, **Labor 1294**

Clerical work, employment, **Labor 1294.3**

Comparative shopping work, employment, **Labor 1294.3**

Compensation and Salaries, this index

Coogan trust account, entertainment contracts, **Labor 1308.9**

Corporations, this index

Crimes and offenses,
  Employment, **Labor 1308**
  Juvenile Delinquents and Dependents, generally, this index
  Lewdness and Obscenity, this index

Dancers, employment contracts, **Labor 1700.37**

Day Care and Nursery Schools, generally, this index

Deaf and Mute Persons, generally, this index

Death, benefits, elected public officials, assassination, **Labor 4720 et seq.**

Definitions,
  Employment, **Labor 1286**
  Family care and medical leave, **Gov 12945.2**
  Family care leave, **Un Ins 3302**
  Sick leave, **Labor 233**

Delivery persons, employment, **Labor 1294.3**

Dependent children. Juvenile Delinquents and Dependents, generally, this index

Disability compensation, payment of benefits, **Un Ins 2702**

Diseases,
  Family care leave, **Un Ins 3300 et seq.**
  Paid family care leave, **Un Ins 3300 et seq.**

Domestic Partnership, this index

Elected public officials, death benefits, assassination, **Labor 4720 et seq.**

Employment,
  Agricultural Labor and Employment, this index
  Labor and Employment, this index

Employment Agencies, this index

Entertainment,
  Employment contracts, **Labor 1700.37**
  Labor and employment, **Labor 1308**

Enticement, **CC 49**

Errand persons, employment, **Labor 1294.3**

CHILDREN AND MINORS—Cont'd

Exhibitions and exhibitors,
  Entertainment, hours of labor, **Labor 1310**
  Participation, **Labor 1308**

Family care leave, serious health conditions, **Un Ins 3300 et seq.**

Films. Motion Pictures, this index

Floor waxers, employment, **Labor 1294.3**

Foreign labor contractors, **Bus & P 9998.4**

Foster homes. Social Services, this index

Guardian and Ward, generally, this index

Handicapped persons. Social Services, this index

Hawkers and Peddlers, this index

Horse racing, employment, **Labor 1308**

Illness,
  Family care leave, **Un Ins 3300 et seq.**
  Paid family care leave, **Un Ins 3300 et seq.**

Income Tax—State, this index

Injuries, family care leave, **Un Ins 3300 et seq.**

Job listing services, child labor laws, **CC 1812.521**

Juvenile Delinquents and Dependents, generally, this index

Kitchen work, employment, **Labor 1294.3**

Labor and Employment, this index

Lewdness and Obscenity, this index

Limitation of actions, fair employment and housing, tolling, **Gov 12960**

Medical records,
  Disclosure, employers, **CC 56.21**
  Release authorization, **CC 56.10**

Miscreant child. Juvenile Delinquents and Dependents, generally, this index

Modeling work, employment, **Labor 1294.3**

Motion Pictures, this index

Motor vehicle service stations, employment, **Labor 1294.5**

Motor Vehicles, this index

Municipal officers and employees, sick leave, **Labor 233**
  Violations, **Labor 234**

Mute persons. Deaf and Mute Persons, generally, this index

Neglected child. Juvenile Delinquents and Dependents, generally, this index

Newspaper delivery persons, employment, **Labor 1294.4**

Notice, criminal history, disclosure, employment, **Pen 11105.3**

Nursery schools. Day Care and Nursery Schools, generally, this index

Office work, employment, **Labor 1294.3**

Paid family care leave, serious health conditions, **Un Ins 3300 et seq.**

Personal Injuries, this index

Pornography, criminal history, disclosure, employment, **Pen 11105.3**

Produce stockers, employment, **Labor 1294.3**

Producers, entertainment employment contracts, **Labor 1700.37**

CHILDREN AND MINORS—Cont'd

Public officers and employees,
  Death benefits, assassination, **Labor 4720 et seq.**
  Sick leave, **Labor 233**
    Violations, **Labor 234**

Radio. Television and Radio, this index

Salaries. Compensation and Salaries, this index

Sales, labor and employment, **Labor 1294.3**

Saleswork, employment, **Labor 1294.3**

Schools and School Districts, generally, this index

Seduction, **CC 49**

Sex Offenders, this index

Sexual assault, criminal history, disclosure, employment, **Pen 11105.3**

Sexual exploitation, criminal record, disclosure, employment, **Pen 11105.3**

Social Services, generally, this index

State Officers and Employees, this index

Stock persons, employment, **Labor 1294.3**

Support, generally, this index

Talent Agencies, this index

Telecommunications, this index

Television and Radio, this index

Theaters and Shows, this index

Unemployment Compensation, this index

Vacuum cleaner operators, employment, **Labor 1294.3**

Wages. Compensation and Salaries, this index

Window trimming work, employment, **Labor 1294.3**

Workers Compensation, this index

CHIROPODY

Podiatrists (Chiropody), generally, this index

CHIROPRACTORS

Contracts, preferred reimbursement rates, **Labor 4609**

Disclosure, preferred reimbursement rates, **Labor 4609**

Health Care Service Plans, this index

Preferred reimbursement rates, **Labor 4609**

Privileges and immunities, criminally related personal injuries, reports, **Pen 11161.9**

Rates and charges, preferred reimbursement rates, **Labor 4609**

Reimbursement, preferred reimbursement rates, **Labor 4609**

Unemployment compensation, independent contractors, **Un Ins 656**

Workers Compensation, this index

CHOICE OF LAW

Conflict of Laws, generally, this index

CHRYSOTILE

Occupational Carcinogens Control Act, **Labor 9000 et seq.**

CHURCHES
Religious Organizations and Societies, generally, this index

CHUTES
Wharves, Docks and Piers, generally, this index

CIGARETTES AND CIGARS
Children and Minors, this index
Labor and employment, workplace smoking, **Labor 6404.5**

CINEMA
Motion Pictures, generally, this index

CIRCULARS
Advertisements, generally, this index

CIRCUS
Amusement rides, safety, **Labor 7900 et seq.**
Children and minors, horseback riding, employment, **Labor 1308**
Compensation and salaries, deposits for security of payment, **Labor 271**

CITATIONS
Amusements, rides, safety, **Labor 7918**
Contractors, this index
Joint enforcement strike force on the underground economy, issuance, authority, **Labor 106**
Labor and Employment, this index
Process, generally, this index
Unemployment compensation, joint enforcement strike force on the underground economy, **Labor 106**

CITIES AND COUNTIES
Consolidated Cities and Counties, generally, this index

CITIES AND TOWNS
Municipalities, generally, this index

CITIZENS AND CITIZENSHIP
Aliens, generally, this index
Foreign labor contractors, inducements, **Bus & P 9998.7**
Unemployment relief, preference for employment on public works, **Labor 2015**

CITY
Municipalities, generally, this index

CITY ATTORNEYS
Municipal Attorneys, generally, this index

CITY COURTS
Municipal Courts, generally, this index

CITY JAILS
Jails, generally, this index

CITY OFFICERS AND EMPLOYEES
Municipal Officers and Employees, generally, this index

CIVIL ACTIONS
Actions and Proceedings, generally, this index

CIVIL AIR PATROL
Labor and employment, **Labor 1500 et seq.**

CIVIL AIR PATROL EMPLOYMENT PROTECTION ACT
Generally, **Labor 1500 et seq.**

CIVIL DEFENSE
War and Civil Defense, generally, this index

CIVIL ENGINEERS
Engineers, generally, this index

CIVIL PENALTIES
Fines and Penalties, generally, this index

CIVIL PROCESS
Process, generally, this index

CIVIL RIGHTS
Generally, **CC 51 et seq.**
Appeal and review, attorney general, briefs, service, **CC 51.1**
Attorney fees, **CC 52**
Attorney general, **CC 52**
Appeal and review, briefs, service, **CC 51.1**
Briefs, appeal and review, attorney general, service, **CC 51.1**
Discrimination, generally, this index
Fair Employment and Housing, generally, this index
Force and violence, **CC 52**
Freedom from violence, **CC 51.7**
Actions and proceedings, **CC 52**
Housing. Fair Employment and Housing, generally, this index
Immigration, labor and employment, **CC 3339; Gov 7285; Health & S 24000**
Jurisdiction, actions and proceedings, **CC 52.2**
Labor and employment. Fair Employment and Housing, generally, this index
Limitation of actions, fines and penalties, **CC 52**
Marital status, **CC 51**
Military personnel, **Mil & V 394**
Protection, immigration, labor and employment, **CC 3339**
Sexual orientation, **CC 51**
Freedom from violence, intimidation, **CC 51.7**
Small claims courts, jurisdiction, **CC 52.2**
Statute of limitations, fines and penalties, **CC 52**
Unruh Civil Rights Act, **CC 51**
Violence, freedom from, **CC 51.7**
Actions and proceedings, **CC 52**
Women. Fair Employment and Housing, generally, this index

CIVIL SERVICE
Benefit payments department, officers and employees, transfer to employment development department, **Un Ins 301.7**
Bosnia crisis, compensation and benefits, **Mil & V 395.08**
Crimes and offenses, injuries, workers compensation, waiting period, **Labor 4650.5**
Employment Development Department, this index
Exemptions, occupational safety and health division, deputy chiefs, **Labor 57.1**
Health care services department, occupational health branch employees, transfer to industrial relations department, occupational safety and health division, **Labor 60.6**
Industrial safety division, transfer of service to occupational safety and health division, retention of rights, **Labor 60.6**
Military forces, Bosnia crisis, compensation and benefits, **Mil & V 395.08**
National guard, Bosnia crisis, compensation and benefits, **Mil & V 395.08**
Personnel board, cooperation, job training and placement programs, **Un Ins 9605**
Reports,
Disclosure, Information Practices Act, **CC 1798 et seq.**
Information Practices Act, **CC 1798 et seq.**
Unemployment insurance, elective coverage, **Un Ins 711**
Workers compensation,
Public employment in violation of law, **Labor 3604**
Waiting period, **Labor 4650.5**

CLAIMS AGAINST ESTATE
Probate Proceedings, this index

CLASS ACTIONS
Labor and employment, fines and penalties, aggrieved employees, **Labor 2699**

CLASSIFIED EMPLOYEES
School Officers and Employees, this index

CLEARINGHOUSE
CalWORKs, job creation, **Un Ins 17002**

CLEMENCY
Executive clemency, Information Practices Act, **CC 1798 et seq.**

CLERGY
Definitions, employment, disability compensation, **Un Ins 2606**
Employment, definitions, disability compensation, **Un Ins 2606**
Privileges and immunities, adult abuse, reports, **Welf & I 15634**
Unemployment compensation,
Excluded service, **Un Ins 634.5**

CLERGY—Cont'd
Unemployment compensation—Cont'd
Optional exclusion, **Un Ins 711**

CLERICAL WORK
Children and minors, employment, **Labor 1294.3**

CLERKS OF COURTS
Workers compensation proceedings, fees, **Labor 5811**

CLIENTS
Definitions, temporary employment, compensation and salaries, **Labor 201.3**

CLINICAL SOCIAL WORKERS
Social Workers, this index

CLINICS
Birthing centers, trespass, **Pen 602**
Confidential or privileged information, forensic medical examinations, sexual assault, reports, **Pen 11160.1**
Contracts, preferred reimbursement rates, **Labor 4609**
Disclosure, preferred reimbursement rates, **Labor 4609**
Forensic medical examinations, sexual assault, reports, **Pen 11160.1**
Licenses and permits, primary care clinics, presumptions, physicians as independent contractors, **Labor 2750.6**
Maternity wards, trespass, **Pen 602**
Neonatal units, trespass, **Pen 602**
Outpatient settings, workers compensation, fees, **Labor 5307.1**
Preferred reimbursement rates, **Labor 4609**
Primary care clinics,
  Physicians and surgeons, presumptions, independent contractors, **Labor 2750.6**
  Unemployment compensation, health care practitioners, **Un Ins 656**
Privileges and immunities, forensic medical examinations, sexual assault, reports, **Pen 11160.1**
Rates and charges, preferred reimbursement rates, **Labor 4609**
Reimbursement, preferred reimbursement rates, **Labor 4609**
Sexual assault, forensic medical examinations, reports, **Pen 11160.1**
Unemployment compensation, primary care clinics, health care practitioners, **Un Ins 656**
Workers compensation, advertisements, **Labor 5430 et seq.**

CLOSING
Military Bases, Reservations and Areas, this index

CLOTHING
Wearing Apparel, generally, this index

CLUBS
Gambling, this index

CLUBS—Cont'd
Restaurants, generally, this index
Weapons, generally, this index

COAL AND COAL MINES
Crimes and offenses, underground telephones, installation or maintenance, **Labor 7501**
Telephones, underground telephones, **Labor 7500, 7501**

COASTING VESSELS
Ships and Shipping, generally, this index

COBRAS
Definitions, group disability insurance, continuation benefits, **Ins 10116.5**

COCKTAIL LOUNGES
Alcoholic Beverages, generally, this index

CODE OF REGULATIONS
See text preceding index

COERCION
Duress or Coercion, generally, this index

COFFEE SHOPS
Restaurants, generally, this index

COLLATERAL BENEFIT
Definitions, military forces, temporary incapacitation, restriction or termination, **Mil & V 394**

COLLATERAL ESTOPPEL
Workers compensation, criminal prosecutions, **Labor 5006, 5413, 5816**

COLLECTIVE BARGAINING
Labor Disputes, this index

COLLEGES AND UNIVERSITIES
Actions and proceedings. Community colleges and districts, post
Affidavits, force and violence, injunction, **CCP 527.85**
Appeal and review. Community colleges and districts, post
Apprentices. Community colleges and districts, post
Arrest, force and violence, injunction, **CCP 527.85**
Assault and battery, injunction, **CCP 527.85**
Athletics, workers compensation, **Labor 3352**
Attorney fees,
  Community colleges and districts, post
  University of California, post
Audits and auditors. California State University, post
Boards and commissions, board of governors. Community colleges and districts, post
Buildings and grounds,
  Community colleges and districts, post
  Construction, generally, post
Burden of proof, University of California, whistle blowing, **Gov 8547.10, 8547.12**

COLLEGES AND UNIVERSITIES—Cont'd
Cal grant program,
  Law enforcement officers and others, dependents, eligibility, **Labor 4709**
  Public officials killed in office, dependents, eligibility, **Labor 4728**
California State University,
  Audits and auditors, whistle blowing, **Educ 89570 et seq.**
  Compensation and salaries, construction, prevailing wage rate, **Labor 1771.7, 1771.75**
  Complaints, whistle blowing, **Educ 89570 et seq.**
  Confidential or privileged information, whistle blowing, **Educ 89574**
  Construction,
    Compensation and salaries, prevailing wage rate, **Labor 1771.7**
    Fees, compliance, **Labor 1771.75**
    Prevailing wage rate, **Labor 1771.7**
    Fees, compliance, **Labor 1771.75**
  Disability indemnity, police, **Labor 4819, 4820**
  Disclosure, whistle blowing, **Educ 89570 et seq.**
  Enhanced industrial disability leave, police, **Labor 4816, 4817**
  Firefighters and fire departments, workers compensation,
    Biochemical substances, presumptions, **Labor 3212.85**
    Cancer, **Labor 3212.1**
  Health and sanitation, whistle blowing, **Educ 89570 et seq.**
  Investigations and investigators, whistle blowing, **Educ 89570 et seq.**
  Officers and employees, whistle blowing, **Educ 89570 et seq.**
  Police,
    Disability,
      Enhanced industrial disability leave, **Labor 4816, 4817**
      Indemnity, disability indemnity, **Labor 4819, 4820**
    Disability indemnity, **Labor 4819, 4820**
    Enhanced industrial disability leave, **Labor 4816, 4817**
  Prevailing wage rate, construction, **Labor 1771.7, 1771.75**
  Safety, whistle blowing, **Educ 89570 et seq.**
  Trusts and trustees, unemployment compensation, disability compensation, elective coverage, **Un Ins 710.8**
  Unemployment compensation,
    Disability compensation, elective coverage, **Un Ins 710.8**
    Public entity, **Un Ins 135**
  Whistle blowing, **Educ 89570 et seq.**
Chancellors. Community colleges and districts, post

COLLEGES AND UNIVERSITIES—Cont'd

College clubs, unemployment compensation, domestic service, wages, **Un Ins 639**

Community colleges and districts,
Actions and proceedings, whistle blowing, retaliation, **Educ 87164**
Appeal and review, whistle blowing, retaliation, **Educ 87164**
Apprentices, affirmative action requirements, providing program information, **Labor 3074.1**
Attorney fees, whistle blowing, retaliation, **Educ 87164**
Board of governors, apprenticeship training, **Labor 3074, 3093**
Buildings and grounds, construction, prevailing wage rate, **Labor 1771.7**
Career resource network, **Educ 53086**
Chancellors, apprenticeship council member, **Labor 3070**
Compensation and salaries, construction, prevailing wage rate, **Labor 1771.7**
Complaints, whistle blowing, retaliation, **Educ 87164**
Construction,
Compensation and salaries, prevailing wage rate, **Labor 1771.7**
Prevailing wage rate, **Labor 1771.7**
Costs, whistleblowing, retaliation, hearings, **Educ 87164**
Crimes and offenses, whistle blowing, **Educ 87160 et seq.**
Damages, whistle blowing, retaliation, **Educ 87164**
Discipline, whistle blowing, retaliation, **Educ 87164**
Disclosure, whistle blowing, **Educ 87160 et seq.**
Duress or coercion, whistle blowing, **Educ 87160 et seq.**
Fines and penalties, whistle blowing, retaliation, **Educ 87164**
Governing boards,
Elective coverage, unemployment compensation, **Un Ins 709**
Public entity, definitions, unemployment compensation, **Un Ins 135, 605**
Unemployment compensation,
Elective coverage, **Un Ins 709**
Public entity, definitions, **Un Ins 135, 605**
Hearings, whistle blowing, retaliation, **Educ 87164**
Improper activity, whistle blowing, **Educ 87160 et seq.**
Investigations and investigators, whistle blowing, retaliation, **Educ 87164**
Labor apprentices, instruction, **Labor 3074**
Labor market information, **Un Ins 10530 et seq.**

COLLEGES AND UNIVERSITIES—Cont'd

Community colleges and districts—Cont'd
Personnel commission, unemployment compensation, public entity, definitions, **Un Ins 135, 605**
Police, death or disability in line of duty, dependents, scholarships, **Labor 4709**
Prevailing wage rate, construction, **Labor 1771.7**
Regional occupational centers. Vocational Education, this index
Remedies, whistle blowing, retaliation, **Educ 87164**
Reports, whistle blowing, retaliation, **Educ 87164**
Reprisal action, whistle blowing, **Educ 87160 et seq.**
Retaliation, whistle blowing, **Educ 87160 et seq.**
Retirement and pensions. Schoolteachers Retirement System, generally, this index
Schoolteachers Retirement System, generally, this index
Threats, whistle blowing, **Educ 87160 et seq.**
Undistributed reserve, transfer to expenditure classification, governing boards, elective coverage, **Un Ins 709**
Unemployment Compensation, this index
Whistle blowing, **Educ 87160 et seq.**
Compensation and salaries,
California State University, ante
Community colleges and districts, ante
Construction, prevailing wage rate, **Labor 1771.7, 1771.75**
University of California, post
Complaints,
California State University, whistle blowing, **Educ 89570 et seq.**
Community colleges and districts, whistle blowing, retaliation, **Educ 87164**
University of California, whistle blowing, **Gov 8547.10**
Computers, force and violence, injunction, **CCP 527.85**
Confidential or privileged information. California State University, ante
Construction,
California State University, ante
Community colleges and districts, ante
Compensation and salaries, prevailing wage rate, **Labor 1771.7, 1771.75**
Prevailing wage rate, **Labor 1771.7, 1771.75**
University of California, post
Costs,
Community colleges and districts, ante
Force and violence, injunction, **CCP 527.85**
Crimes and offenses,
Community colleges and districts, ante

COLLEGES AND UNIVERSITIES—Cont'd

Crimes and offenses—Cont'd
Injuries from criminal violence, workers compensation, waiting period, **Labor 4650.5**
University of California, post
Damages,
Community colleges and districts, ante
University of California, post
Default. Student loans, post
Definitions, force and violence, injunction, **CCP 527.85**
Discipline. Community colleges and districts, ante
Disclosure,
California State University, ante
Community colleges and districts, ante
Employee records, **Labor 1198.7**
Discrimination, housing accommodations, **Gov 12995**
Domestic violence, injunction, **CCP 527.85**
Electricity, educational curriculum, standards, **Labor 3099**
Electronic mail, force and violence, injunction, **CCP 527.85**
Employment security, **Un Ins 100 et seq.**
Auxiliary organizations, **Un Ins 711**
Domestic service in college club, **Un Ins 639**
Elections for financing, **Un Ins 802, 803**
Employer, definitions, **Un Ins 677**
Excluded services, option, **Un Ins 711**
Spouses of students, services, **Un Ins 642**
Student services, **Un Ins 642**
Evidence, University of California, whistle blowing, **Gov 8547.10, 8547.12**
Fax machines, force and violence, injunction, **CCP 527.85**
Fines and penalties,
Community colleges and districts, ante
Occupational safety and health, refunds, **Labor 6434**
Firefighters and fire departments,
California State University, ante
University of California, post
Workers compensation, cancer, **Labor 3212.1**
Force and violence, injunction, **CCP 527.85**
Fraternities, unemployment compensation, domestic service, **Un Ins 639**
Employer, definitions, **Un Ins 682**
Wages, **Un Ins 639**
Governing boards. Community colleges and districts, ante
Harassment, injunction, **CCP 527.85**
Health and sanitation, California State University, whistle blowing, **Educ 89570 et seq.**
Hearings,
Community colleges and districts, ante
Force and violence, injunction, **CCP 527.85**
Housing, discrimination, **Gov 12995**
Injunction, force and violence, **CCP 527.85**

COLLEGES AND UNIVERSITIES—Cont'd

Investigations and investigators. Community colleges and districts, ante

Junior colleges. Community colleges and districts, generally, ante

Labor camps, application of law, college operated facilities, **Health & S 17024**

Limitation of actions. University of California, post

Mail and mailing, force and violence, injunction, **CCP 527.85**

Occupational safety and health, fines and penalties, refunds, **Labor 6434**

Offenses. Crimes and offenses, generally, ante

Officers and employees,
  California State University, ante
  Memoranda of understanding, labor agreements, conflict with statutes, military duty, **Mil & V 395 et seq.**
  Peer review, records and recordation, disclosure, **Labor 1198.7**

Orders of court, force and violence, protective orders, **CCP 527.85**

Peace officers, death or disability in line of duty, dependents, scholarships, **Labor 4709**

Peer review, records and recordation, disclosure, **Labor 1198.7**

Penalties. Fines and penalties, generally, ante

Perjury, University of California, whistle blowing, **Gov 8547.10, 8547.12**

Petitions, force and violence, injunction, **CCP 527.85**

Police,
  California State University, ante
  Community colleges and districts, ante
  University of California, post

Prevailing wage rate, construction, **Labor 1771.7, 1771.75**

Protective orders, force and violence, **CCP 527.85**

Records and recordation, disclosure, **Labor 1198.7**

Regents. University of California, post

Regional occupational centers. Vocational Education, this index

Reports. Community colleges and districts, ante

Safety, California State University, whistle blowing, **Educ 89570 et seq.**

Salaries. Compensation and salaries, generally, ante

Scholarships,
  Dependents of peace officers, **Labor 4709**
  Peace officers, dependents, **Labor 4709**

Sentence and punishment. Crimes and offenses, generally, ante

Service of process, force and violence, injunction, **CCP 527.85**

Sororities, unemployment compensation, domestic service,
  Employer, definitions, **Un Ins 682**
  Wages, **Un Ins 639**

COLLEGES AND UNIVERSITIES—Cont'd

Stalking, injunction, **CCP 527.85**

State college auxiliary organizations, unemployment compensation, exclusion from coverage, **Un Ins 711**

State university. California State University, generally, ante

Stipends. Compensation and salaries, generally, ante

Student loans, default, unemployment compensation, applicant information, **Un Ins 1095**

Telecommunications, force and violence, injunction, **CCP 527.85**

Tenure, compulsory retirement policy, **Gov 12942**

Threats, force and violence, injunction, **CCP 527.85**

Trusts and trustees,
  California State University, ante
  Unemployment compensation, elective coverage, **Un Ins 709**

Unemployment Compensation, this index

University of California,
  Attorney fees, whistle blowing, **Gov 8547.10, 8547.12**
  Burden of proof, whistle blowing, **Gov 8547.10, 8547.12**
  Compensation and salaries, construction, prevailing wage rate, **Labor 1771.7**
    Fees, compliance, **Labor 1771.75**
  Complaints, whistle blowing, **Gov 8547.10**
  Construction,
    Compensation and salaries, prevailing wage rate, **Labor 1771.7, 1771.75**
    Prevailing wage rate, **Labor 1771.7**
    Fees, compliance, **Labor 1771.75**
  Crimes and offenses, whistle blowing, **Gov 8547.10**
  Damages, whistle blowing, **Gov 8547.10 et seq.**
  Employment security, **Un Ins 100 et seq.**
  Evidence, whistle blowing, **Gov 8547.10, 8547.12**
  Fines and penalties, whistle blowing, **Gov 8547.10**
  Firefighters and fire departments, workers compensation, **Labor 4804.1 et seq.**
    Biochemical substances, presumptions, **Labor 3212.85**
    Cancer, **Labor 3212.1**
  Limitation of actions, whistle blowing, **Gov 8547.10, 8547.12**
  Occupational health and medicine, program development, **Labor 50.8**
  Perjury, whistle blowing, **Gov 8547.10, 8547.12**
  Police,
    Disability payments, **Labor 4806 et seq.**
    Heart trouble, workers compensation, **Labor 3213**

COLLEGES AND UNIVERSITIES—Cont'd

University of California—Cont'd
  Police—Cont'd
    Lower back impairment, workers compensation, **Labor 3213.2**
    Pneumonia, workers compensation, **Labor 3213**
    Workers compensation, **Labor 3213, 4806 et seq.**
      Lower back impairment, **Labor 3213.2**
  Prevailing wage rate, construction, **Labor 1771.7, 1771.75**
  Regents, unemployment compensation, elective coverage, **Un Ins 709**
  Unemployment compensation, public entity, **Un Ins 135**
  Workers compensation,
    Firemen, **Labor 4804.1 et seq.**
    Police, **Labor 4806 et seq.**
      Lower back impairment, **Labor 3213.2**

Weapons, force and violence, injunction, **CCP 527.85**

Whistle blowing,
  California State University, **Educ 89570 et seq.**
  Community colleges and districts, **Educ 87160 et seq.**

Workers compensation,
  Student athletes, coverage, **Labor 3352**
  University of California, ante
  Waiting period, **Labor 4650.5**

COLLIER MILLER ACT

Extended unemployment compensation, **Un Ins 3501 et seq.**

COLLISIONS

Accidents, generally, this index

COLLUSION

Fraud, generally, this index

COMBAT

War and Civil Defense, generally, this index

COMBUSTIBLES

Explosives, generally, this index

Installation acceptance, pressure test of gas house line or piping, **Labor 6700**

Labor and employment, occupational safety and health, flammable or combustible material for installation acceptance pressure test of gas houseline or piping, **Labor 6700**

Safety in employment, volatile flammable liquids, **Labor 7800 et seq.**

COMFORT STATIONS AND REST ROOMS

Audio recordings, labor and employment, **Labor 435**

Factories and business establishments, sanitary conditions, **Labor 2350**

Foundries and metal shops, **Labor 2331**

Labor and employment, audio or video recordings, **Labor 435**

COMFORT STATIONS AND REST ROOMS
—Cont'd
Metal shops, **Labor 2331**
Videotape, labor and employment, **Labor 435**

COMITY
Reciprocity, generally, this index

COMMERCE
Business and Commerce, generally, this index

COMMERCIAL BANKS
Banks and Banking, generally, this index

COMMERCIAL BUILDINGS
Buildings, generally, this index

COMMERCIAL COACHES
Mobilehomes and Mobilehome Parks, generally, this index

COMMERCIAL FARMING ENTERPRISES
Agriculture, generally, this index

COMMERCIAL FINANCE LENDERS
Finance Lenders, generally, this index

COMMERCIAL FISHING
Fish and Game, this index

COMMERCIAL PAPER
Negotiable Instruments, generally, this index

COMMERCIAL PURPOSE
Definitions, Information Practices Act, **CC 1798.3**

COMMERCIAL VEHICLES
Motor Vehicles, this index

COMMERCIAL VESSELS
Ships and Shipping, generally, this index

COMMERCIALS
Advertisements, generally, this index

COMMINGLING FUNDS
Labor and employment, bonds, property put up by employee or applicant, **Labor 405**

COMMISSARIES
Stores, generally, this index

COMMISSIONS AND COMMISSIONERS
Boards and Commissions, generally, this index

COMMISSIONS (COMPENSATION)
Compensation and Salaries, this index

COMMITTEES
Advisory Boards and Commissions, generally, this index
Advisory Committees, generally, this index
Apprentices, joint apprenticeship committees, **Labor 3075, 3076**

COMMITTEES—Cont'd
Cal OSHA self contained breathing apparatus advisory committee, determination of test procedures, positive pressure closed circuit breathing apparatus for use in fires, **Labor 6331**
Career resource network, state agency partners committee, **Educ 53086**
Labor and employment, mentally retarded and developmentally disabled persons, **Welf & I 4868**
Mentally retarded and developmentally disabled persons, labor and employment, **Welf & I 4868**
Social Security, generally, this index
State agency partners committee, career resource network, **Educ 53086**
Toxic materials and harmful physical agents, data repository, **Labor 147.2**

COMMON CARRIERS
Marine carriers. Ships and Shipping, generally, this index
Motor Carriers, generally, this index
Railroads, generally, this index

COMMON INTEREST ASSOCIATIONS OR DEVELOPMENTS
Condominiums, generally, this index

COMMON INTEREST DEVELOPMENTS
Condominiums, generally, this index

COMMON NAMES
Definitions, hazardous substances information and training, **Labor 6368**

COMMON SCHOOL DISTRICTS
Schools and School Districts, generally, this index

COMMUNICABLE DISEASES
Diseases, generally, this index

COMMUNICATIONS
Employment agencies, misrepresentations, earnings of salesmen, brokers or agents, **Labor 976**
Letters and Other Correspondence, generally, this index
Solicitation of employees, representation, **Labor 973**
Telecommunications, generally, this index
Television and Radio, generally, this index

COMMUNITY ACTION PROGRAMS
Contracts, job training and placement, Human Resources Development Act of 1968, **Un Ins 9601**

COMMUNITY ANTENNA TELEVISION
Cable Television, generally, this index

COMMUNITY BASED ORGANIZATIONS
Nonprofit Organizations, generally, this index

COMMUNITY CARE FACILITIES
Abuse, patients, reports, **Pen 11161.8**
Foster homes. Social Services, this index

COMMUNITY CARE FACILITIES—Cont'd
Residential Care Facilities for the Elderly, generally, this index

COMMUNITY CHEST
Employment, disability compensation, **Un Ins 2606**
Unemployment compensation, elections for financing, **Un Ins 801, 803**

COMMUNITY COLLEGES AND DISTRICTS
Colleges and Universities, this index

COMMUNITY CONSERVATION CORPS
Conservation Corps, generally, this index

COMMUNITY DEVELOPMENT AND HOUSING
Limitation of actions, discrimination, **Gov 12989.1**

COMMUNITY EMPLOYMENT DEVELOPMENT CENTERS
Generally, **Un Ins 9607**
Services, **Un Ins 9608**

COMMUNITY FUNDS
Unemployment compensation, employing unit, **Un Ins 135**

COMMUNITY HEALTH SERVICES
Assault and battery, records and recordation, **Labor 6332**

COMMUNITY HOUSING
Labor and Employment, this index

COMMUNITY PROPERTY
Domestic Partnership, this index
Weapons, passing to exconvict, restraining orders, **Pen 12021**

COMMUNITY SERVICE
Compensation and salaries, minimum wages, exemptions, national service programs, **Labor 1171**
National service programs,
Compensation and salaries, minimum wages, exemptions, **Labor 1171**
Unemployment compensation, excluded services, **Un Ins 634.5**
Unemployment compensation, national service programs, excluded services, **Un Ins 634.5**

COMMUNITY WORK EXPERIENCE PROGRAMS
Social Services, generally, this index

COMPARATIVE SHOPPING
Children and minors, employment, **Labor 1294.3**

COMPENSATING TIME
Definitions, labor and employment, **Labor 204.3**

COMPENSATING TIME OFF
Definitions, labor and employment, **Labor 204.3**

COMPENSATION AND SALARIES

Generally, **Labor 200 et seq.**

Accord and satisfaction, judgments and decrees, farm labor contractors, wearing apparel, manufacturers and manufacturing, **Labor 273**

Actions and proceedings,
Deposit by employer, bonds, **Labor 240**
Employees right to sue, **Labor 218**
Failure to pay to employees, recovery of penalties, **Labor 210, 211, 225.5**
Nonpayment, **Labor 243**
Prosecuting attorneys, **Labor 218**
Recovery actions, costs, **CCP 1031**
Recovery of minimum or overtime wages, **Labor 1193.6, 1194**
Recovery of penalties,
Failure to pay compensation to employees, **Labor 210, 211, 225.5**
Violations of law, **Labor 217**
Recovery of wages, application of arbitration agreements, **Labor 229**
Unpaid wages, **Labor 98, 98.5**
Wage discrimination, **Labor 1197.5**

Actors and actresses, talent services, **Labor 1701 et seq.**

Address of employer, itemized statement, **Labor 226**

Administrative employees, payment, **Labor 204**

Administrative Law and Procedure, this index

Advertisements, this index

Agreements, intervals of payment, **Labor 219**

Agricultural Labor and Employment, this index

Agricultural Labor Relations Board, this index

Alternative workweek schedule, **Labor 500 et seq.**

AmeriCorps, minimum wages, exemptions, **Labor 1171**

Appeal and review, seasonal wage disputes, **Labor 255**

Application of law,
Arbitration agreements to action for unpaid wages, **Labor 229**
Public employment, **Labor 220**

Apprentices, this index

Apprenticeship council members, **Labor 3070**

Apprenticeship standards division, chief of division, **Labor 57**

Arbitration and Award, this index

Art and Artists, this index

Assignment for Benefit of Creditors, this index

Assignments, **Labor 300**
Collection, deposit, payment, escheat, unpaid wages, **Labor 96.7**
Collective bargaining representatives, **Labor 96.3**
Consent, **Labor 300**
Definitions, **Labor 300**

COMPENSATION AND SALARIES—Cont'd

Assignments—Cont'd
Discharge from employment for garnishment, **Labor 2929**
Earnings withholding order, suspension, **Labor 300**
Revocation, **Labor 300**
Unpaid wages, collection, deposit, payment, escheat, **Labor 96.7**

Athletics, officials, workers compensation, **Labor 3352**

Attachment, generally, this index

Attorney Fees, generally, this index

Bad checks, building and construction industry, **Labor 203.1**

Banks and Banking, this index

Benefit plan for employees, employers statement of payments made, **Labor 227.5**

Benefits, unpaid wages or benefits, collection, deposit, payment, escheat, **Labor 96.7**

Biweekly payment, **Labor 205**

Board and lodging by employer, time when wages due and payable, **Labor 205**

Bonds, this index

Bonds (officers and fiduciaries),
Judgments and decrees, satisfaction, farm labor contractors, wearing apparel, manufacturers and manufacturing, **Labor 273**
Nonpayment of wages, second and subsequent offenses, **Labor 243**

Bonuses, attachment, exemption, **CCP 487.020**

Books and papers, minimum wages, **Labor 1195.5**

Brokers, misrepresenting compensation or commissions, **Labor 976**

Building and construction industry, payment by bad check, **Labor 203.1**

Burden of proof, actions to compel deposit of bonds by employer, **Labor 240**

Camp counselors, Minimum Wage Law, **Labor 1182.4**

Car Washes, this index

Carnivals, payment, **Labor 271**

Central place for payment, several employers, **Labor 204a**

Checks,
Deposits by employer directly into employee bank, savings and loan association or credit union account, **Labor 213**
Issuance in payment, **Labor 212**

Children and minors,
Administration and enforcement of law, **Labor 61**
Adult employment, under exceptions to hours of labor restrictions, **Labor 1391.2**
Assignment of wages, written consent of parent or guardian, **Labor 300**

COMPENSATION AND SALARIES—Cont'd

Children and minors—Cont'd
Employed as adults under exceptions to hours of labor restrictions, **Labor 1391.2**
Exceptions to hours of labor restrictions, adult employment, **Labor 1391.2**
Minimum wages, crimes and offenses, payment of less than, **Labor 1197**

Circuses, payment, **Labor 271**

Cities and counties. Consolidated Cities and Counties, this index

Claims, enforcement, **Labor 98 et seq.**

Collections,
Disputes, prosecution of actions, **Labor 98 et seq.**
Labor law enforcement division, **Labor 98**
Unpaid wages or benefits, **Labor 96.7**

Collective bargaining agreements,
Covered employees, payment, **Labor 204**
Deductions, **Labor 224**

Collective bargaining representatives, assignment of claims, **Labor 96.3**

Colleges and Universities, this index

Commissions (compensation),
Amount fixed or ascertained by, **Labor 200**
Attachment, exemption, **CCP 487.020**
Garnishment, generally, this index
Misrepresentation as to, **Labor 976**
Unemployment compensation, commissions as wages, **Un Ins 926**

Community colleges and districts. Colleges and Universities, this index

Compensating time off, in lieu of overtime pay, **Labor 204.3**

Complaints,
Investigations, **Labor 98 et seq.**
Minimum wages, **Labor 1195**

Conditions of employment,
Illegal conditions, **Labor 432.5**
Nondisclosure of wages, **Labor 232**

Consolidated Cities and Counties, this index

Contractors, this index

Contracts,
Human trafficking, deductions, illegal contracts, **CC 1670.7**
Illegal terms, **Labor 432.5**

Convictions, nonpayment of wages, deposit of bonds as security for payment, **Labor 240**

Corrections, payment, **Labor 204**

Costs,
Recovery actions, **CCP 1031; Labor 1197.1**
Recovery of penalties, failure to pay to employees, **Labor 211**

County Officers and Employees, this index

County Officers and Employees Retirement Systems, this index

Coupons redeemable, issuance in payment, **Labor 212**

COMPENSATION

COMPENSATION AND SALARIES—Cont'd
Credit cards, tips, **Labor 351**
Credit Unions, this index
Crimes and Offenses, this index
Damages,
  Employers failure to provide itemized statement, **Labor 226**
  Itemized statement, employer's failure to provide, **Labor 226**
  Treble damages, wage disputes, nonpayment valid wage claims, **Labor 206**
Death benefits, economic opportunity program enrollees, **Labor 4214**
Decrees. Judgments and decrees, generally, post
Deductions, **Labor 224**
  Application of statute as to assignment, **Labor 300**
  Contributions to welfare plans, **Labor 224**
  Itemized statement, **Labor 226**
  Preemployment medical or physical examination, cost, **Labor 222.5, 225**
  Seasonal labor, **Labor 253**
Deferred compensation, employer managed plans, **Labor 2809**
Definitions,
  Commission wages, employees, motor vehicle dealers, **Labor 204.1**
  Corporation taxes, job incentive program, **Rev & T 23621 et seq.**
  Foreign labor contractors, **Bus & P 9998.1**
  Garnishment, **CCP 706.011; Labor 2929**
  Gratuities or tips, **Labor 350**
  Minimum wages, post
  Payment, **Labor 200**
  Seasonal labor, **Labor 250**
  State income tax, credit, qualified employees, **Rev & T 17053.7**
  Theatrical enterprise, deposits, security for payment of wages, **Labor 271**
  Withholding tax, **Un Ins 13009**
  Workers compensation, **Labor 3207**
Demand for payment, prerequisite to bringing action to recover penalties for failure to pay, **Labor 211**
Deposit or security for payment, **Labor 270 et seq.**
Deposits, unpaid wages or benefits, **Labor 96.7**
Deputy director, employment development department, **Un Ins 303**
Direct deposit, **Labor 213**
Director of employment development, **Un Ins 302**
  Deputy directors, **Un Ins 303**
Disability compensation. Unemployment Compensation, this index
Discharge of employee,
  Failure of employer to make payment within required time, **Labor 203**
  Garnishment of wages, **Labor 2929**
  Payment, **Labor 201, 208**
Disciplinary action, disclosure of wages, **Labor 232**

COMPENSATION AND SALARIES—Cont'd
Disclosure, condition of employment or disciplinary action, **Labor 232**
Discount, wrongfully attempting to secure, **Labor 216**
Discrimination, **Labor 1197.5**
  Fines and penalties, **Labor 1199.5**
Disputes over wages, nonpayment by employer, treble damages, **Labor 206**
District officers and employees, itemized statement, deductions, application of law, **Labor 226**
Districts, this index
Domestic servants, time due and payable, **Labor 205**
Double recovery, discrimination, repayment of smaller amount, **Labor 1197.5**
Drafts, issuance in payment, **Labor 212**
Dramas, payment, **Labor 271**
Economic opportunity programs, injury or death of enrollees, **Labor 4212**
Employee quitting, payment, **Labor 202**
Employer managed deferred compensation plans, **Labor 2809**
Employing unit registration, **Un Ins 1126.1**
Employment Agencies, this index
Employment contracts, work or service rendered or performed under, **Labor 200**
Employment Development Department, this index
Endurance contest, payment, **Labor 271**
Enforcement of laws relating to payment, **Labor 217**
Escheat, unpaid wages or benefits, **Labor 96.7**
Evidence,
  Actions to compel bond deposit, **Labor 240**
  Deposit of funds sufficient to pay employees, failure to post notice, **Labor 272**
  Equal Pay Act, discrimination, **Labor 1197.5**
  Failure to post notices, **Labor 215**
  Memorandum of protest or dishonor of instrument issued in payment, **Labor 212**
  Minimum wages, **Labor 1200**
  Security deposited for payment of wages, failure to post notice of place, **Labor 272**
  Wage discrimination, **Labor 1197.5**
Examination, books and papers, minimum wages, **Labor 1195.5**
Executive employees, payment, **Labor 204**
Exemptions,
  Layoffs, fines and penalties, **Labor 1407**
  Minimum wages, post
  Payment, **Labor 213**
  Students, camp employees, Minimum Wage Law, **Labor 1182.4**
Failure of employer to pay discharged or resigned employee within required time, **Labor 203**

COMPENSATION AND SALARIES—Cont'd
Failure to pay to employees, **Labor 210, 211, 225.5**
Fair employment and housing commission, **Gov 12905**
Fair Labor Standards Act, employers covered, payment, **Labor 204**
False advertisements, offers of employment, **Labor 976, 977**
False denial of amount or validity of compensation due, **Labor 216**
Family care and medical leave, **Gov 12945.2**
Farm labor. Agricultural Labor and Employment, this index
Federal law, deductions required, **Labor 224**
Fines and penalties, **Labor 1199, 1199.5**
  Actions to recover penalties, **Labor 217**
  Bonding company failure to pay verified claim for wages, **Labor 203.5**
  Building and construction industry, payment of wages with bad checks, **Labor 203.1**
  Deductions, itemized statement, **Labor 226**
  Failure of employer to pay discharged or resigned employee within required time, **Labor 203**
  Failure to pay to employees, **Labor 210, 211, 225.5**
  Judgments and decrees, satisfaction, farm labor contractors, wearing apparel, manufacturers and manufacturing, **Labor 273**
  Layoffs, exemptions, **Labor 1407**
  Minimum wages, violation, **Labor 1197.1**
  Nonpayment, claims, assignment to labor commissioner, **Labor 96**
  Records and recordation, inspection and inspectors, time, **Labor 226**
  Seasonal labor, civil penalty, waiting time, **Labor 256**
  State contracts, failure of bonding company to pay verified claim for wages, **Labor 203.5**
  Temporary employment, **Labor 201.3**
  Tips, disposition of fines collected, **Labor 355**
  Uninsured employers fund, liability, **Labor 3716.2**
  Violations by employers, **Labor 354**
  Wage disputes, nonpayment of valid wage claims, **Labor 206**
Foreign labor contractors, payment, **Bus & P 9998.5**
Forfeitures, this index
Fraud, farm labor contractors, wearing apparel, manufacturers and manufacturing, **Labor 273**
Fringe Benefits, generally, this index
Game. Fish and Game, this index
Garnishment, generally, this index
General occupations, payment, **Labor 200 et seq.**

COMPENSATION AND SALARIES—Cont'd

Gratuities, **Labor 350 et seq.**
  Tips, generally, post
Hazardous Substances and Waste, this index
Health and welfare or pension plan contributions, deductions, **Labor 224**
Hearings,
  Cash wages, itemized statements, deductions, **Labor 226.5**
  Itemized statements, deductions, cash wages, **Labor 226.5**
  Rehearings, minimum wages, **Labor 1188**
High speed passenger trains, prevailing wage rates, **Labor 1771.9**
Horticultural pursuits, time due and payable, **Labor 205**
Hospitalization insurance, deductions, **Labor 224**
Hours worked, itemized statement, **Labor 226**
Housing division, chief of division, **Labor 57**
Identity and identification, numbers and numbering, itemized statement, **Labor 226**
Inclusive date of pay period, itemized statement, **Labor 226**
Income Tax—State, generally, this index
Industrial homework, investigation, **Labor 2652**
Industrial Relations Department, this index
Industrial welfare commission,
  Members, **Labor 72**
  Wage board, **Labor 1179**
Infractions, records and recordation, inspection and inspectors, time, **Labor 226**
Injunction,
  Actions to compel bond deposits, **Labor 240**
  Minimum wages, **Labor 1194.5**
  Nonpayment of wages, **Labor 243**
    Second and subsequent offenses, **Labor 243**
  Records and recordation, **Labor 226**
Inspection and inspectors,
  Records and recordation, **Labor 226**
  Tips, records maintained by employers, **Labor 353**
  Wage discrimination, **Labor 1197.5**
Insufficient funds, building and construction industry, payment of wages with checks, **Labor 203.1**
Insurance, this index
Intent to annoy, harass, by denying amount or validity falsely, **Labor 216**
Interest,
  Minimum wages, **Labor 1197.1**
  Nonpayment, **Labor 218.6**
  Unpaid wages awards, **Labor 98.1**
Intervals, payment, limitations or prohibitions, **Labor 219**

COMPENSATION AND SALARIES—Cont'd

Investigations and investigators, minimum wages, **Labor 1195**
Itemized statement, **Labor 226 et seq.**
Itinerant merchants, security for wages, **Labor 270.6**
Judgments and decrees,
  Failure to pay compensation to employees, recovery of penalties, **Labor 211**
    Second and subsequent offenses, **Labor 243**
  Minimum wages, **Labor 1197.1**
  Satisfaction, farm labor contractors, wearing apparel, manufacturers and manufacturing, **Labor 273**
Jury, this index
Kick backs, **Labor 221, 225**
Labor, definitions, **Labor 200**
Labor Disputes, this index
Labor law enforcement division, chief of division, **Labor 57**
Labor standards enforcement division, chief, **Labor 79**
Labor statistics and research division,
  Chief of division, **Labor 57**
  Collection and compilation of information, **Labor 150**
Law enforcement division, chief of division, **Labor 57**
Laying off employees, payment, **Labor 201, 201.7**
Layoffs, **Labor 1402**
Licenses and permits,
  Mentally deficient or handicapped persons, minimum wages, **Labor 1191**
  Minimum wages, mentally deficient or physically handicapped persons, **Labor 1191**
Liens and incumbrances, **CCP 1204 et seq.**
Limitation of actions,
  Discharged or resigned employee not timely paid, **Labor 203**
  Discrimination, **Labor 1197**
  Sex discrimination, **Labor 1197.5**
Logging contractors, deposits, security for payment of wages, **Labor 270.5**
Mail and Mailing, this index
Mandamus, minimum wages, **Labor 1197.1**
Meals, **Labor 226.7**
Medical dues, deductions, **Labor 224**
Medical leave, **Gov 12945.2**
Memorandum, issuance in payment, **Labor 212**
Mentally Ill Persons, this index
Mentally Retarded and Developmentally Disabled Persons, this index
Method of calculation, amount fixed or ascertained, **Labor 200**
Minimum wages, **Const. Art. 14, § 1; Labor 1171 et seq., 1182, 1182.11, 1182.12**
  Actions and proceedings, **Labor 1197.1**
    Recovery, **Labor 1193.6, 1194**
  AmeriCorps, exemptions, **Labor 1171**

COMPENSATION AND SALARIES—Cont'd

Minimum wages—Cont'd
  Apartment house resident managers, **Labor 1182.8**
  Application of law, **Labor 1171**
  Apprentices, **Labor 1192**
  Attorney fees, violations, **Labor 1193.6**
  Camp counselors, **Labor 1182.4**
  Camps and camping, student employees, **Labor 1182.4**
  Children and minors, ante
  Complaints, **Labor 1195**
  Costs, **Labor 1197.1**
  County officers and employees, **Labor 1205**
  Crimes and offenses, **Labor 1197, 1197.1**
  Damages, liquidated damages, **Labor 1194.2**
  Definitions,
    Corporation taxes, credits, enterprise zones, **Rev & T 23622.8**
    Enterprise zones, **Rev & T 23622.7**
    Income tax credits, **Rev & T 17053.74**
  Districts, officers and employees, **Labor 1205**
  Evidence, **Labor 1200**
  Examination, books and papers, **Labor 1195.5**
  Exemptions,
    National service programs, **Labor 1171**
    Outside salesmen, **Labor 1171**
    Students, camp employees, **Labor 1182.4**
  Federal minimum wage, standard, **Labor 1182**
  Fines and penalties, **Labor 1197.1**
  Handicapped persons, **Labor 1191**
  Hearings, **Labor 1182**
  Injunctions, **Labor 1194.5**
  Interest, **Labor 1193.6**
    Judgments, **Labor 1197.1**
  Investigations, **Labor 1195**
  Judgments and decrees, **Labor 1197.1**
  Liquidated damages, **Labor 1194.2**
  Local agencies, officers and employees, **Labor 1205**
  Mandamus, **Labor 1197.1**
  Mentally deficient or mentally ill persons, **Labor 1191**
  Municipal officers and employees, **Labor 1205**
  National service programs, exemptions, **Labor 1171**
  Orders, **Labor 1182 et seq.**
  Records, **Labor 1195.5**
  Rehearings, **Labor 1188**
  Resident managers, apartment houses, **Labor 1182.8**
  Salesmen, outside salesmen, exemption, **Labor 1171**
  Sheepherders, **Labor 2695.2**
  Sheltered workshops or rehabilitation facilities, **Labor 1191.5**

COMPENSATION

COMPENSATION AND SALARIES—Cont'd
Minimum wages—Cont'd
  Unemployment Compensation, this index
  Unpaid, recovery by industrial welfare division, deposit, **Labor 1193.5**
  Violations, fines and penalties, **Labor 1197.1**
  Wage board, **Labor 1182**
  Wearing apparel, manufacturers and manufacturing, contractors, suretyship and guarantee, **Labor 2673.1**
Mining industries, payment, **Labor 270, 272**
Minors. Children and minors, generally, ante
Misrepresentation, solicitation of employees, **Labor 970**
Monthly payment, **Labor 205**
  Commission wages, motor vehicle dealers, **Labor 204.1**
Motion Pictures, this index
Motor vehicle dealers, commission wages, payment, **Labor 204.1**
Municipal Officers and Employees, this index
Music and musicians,
  Comedies, payment, **Labor 271**
  Talent services, **Labor 1701 et seq.**
Name of employee and employer, itemized statement, **Labor 226**
National service programs, minimum wages, exemptions, **Labor 1171**
Necessities of life,
  Assignment of wages, **Labor 300**
  Employer guaranteeing payment of employees bills, **Labor 213**
Negotiable Instruments, this index
Nonpayment,
  Claims for penalties, assignment to labor commissioner, **Labor 96**
  Second and subsequent offenses, **Labor 243**
Notes, issuance in payment, **Labor 212**
Notice,
  Deferred compensation plans, employer managed, financial risks, **Labor 2809**
  Employee quitting, payment of compensation, **Labor 202**
  Failure to post notices, evidence, **Labor 215**
  Insufficient funds or credit to cover instrument issued in payment, **Labor 212**
  Intention to quit, payment of wages, **Labor 202**
  Judgments and decrees, satisfaction, farm labor contractors, wearing apparel, manufacturers and manufacturing, **Labor 273**
  Pay days and time and place of payment, posting information, **Labor 207**
  Place of deposit, security deposited for payment of wages, **Labor 272**

COMPENSATION AND SALARIES—Cont'd
Notice—Cont'd
  Several employers, unified schedule of pay days, intention to establish plan, **Labor 204a**
  Tips, disposition, posting in employers establishment, **Labor 351**
  Unified schedule of pay days, several employers, intention to establish plan, **Labor 204a**
Nurses, this index
Occupational safety and health appeals board, **Labor 148**
Occupational safety and health division, industrial relations department, **Labor 57.1**
Occupational safety and health standards board, **Labor 141**
Offenses. Crimes and Offenses, this index
Oil and Gas, this index
Operas, payment, **Labor 271**
Overtime, generally, this index
Partial payment, undisputed amounts, disputes over compensation, **Labor 206**
Partnership, this index
Paycheck stubs, employers, failure to provide, fines and penalties, **Labor 226.3**
Payment, **Labor 200 et seq.**
  Acknowledgment of indebtedness, issuance in payment, **Labor 212**
  Administrative employees, **Labor 204c**
  Advance on wages to be earned, **Labor 212**
  Application of law, public employment, **Labor 220**
  Biweekly, **Labor 205**
  Bonding companies, failure to pay verified claim for wages, payment bonds, **Labor 203.5**
  Building and construction industry, bad checks, **Labor 203.1**
  Cards redeemable, issuance in payment, **Labor 212**
  Checks, **Labor 212**
  Concerts, discharge or layoff, collective bargaining, **Labor 201.9**
  Corrections, **Labor 204**
  Coupons redeemable, issuance in payment, **Labor 212**
  Deductions, itemization, **Labor 226**
  Demand for payment, prerequisite to action to recover penalties for failure to pay, **Labor 211**
  Deposit of security for payment, **Labor 270 et seq.**
  Direct deposit, **Labor 213**
  Discharged employees, **Labor 201, 208**
    Failure of employer to make payment within required time, **Labor 203**
  Discount, instrument issued, payable without, **Labor 212**
  Dishonor of instrument issued in payment, **Labor 212**
  Domestic servants, **Labor 205**
  Drafts, issuance in payment, **Labor 212**
  Employee quitting, **Labor 202**

COMPENSATION AND SALARIES—Cont'd
Payment—Cont'd
  Enforcement of laws relating to payment, **Labor 217**
  Evidence, memorandum of protests or dishonor of instrument issued in payment, **Labor 212**
  Executive employees, **Labor 204c**
  Exemptions, **Labor 213**
  Funds to cover instruments issued, **Labor 212**
  General occupations, **Labor 200 et seq.**
  Hours worked, itemized statement, **Labor 226**
  Intervals, limitations or prohibitions, **Labor 219**
  Itinerant merchants, security for payment, **Labor 270.6**
  Knowledge, insufficient funds or credit to cover instrument issued in payment, **Labor 212**
  Labor disputes, payment of unpaid wages, **Labor 209**
  Laying off employees, **Labor 201**
    Immediate payment, reasonable time for computing payment, oil drilling industry, **Labor 201.7**
  Logging contractors, deposits, security for payment, **Labor 270.5**
  Memorandum, issuance in payment, **Labor 212**
  Mining industries, **Labor 270, 272**
  Monthly, **Labor 205**
  Motor vehicle dealers, commission wages, **Labor 204.1**
  Negotiability of instrument issued in payment, necessity, **Labor 212**
  Notes, issuance in payment, **Labor 212**
  Orders, issuance in payment, **Labor 212**
  Partial payments, undisputed amounts, disputes over compensation, **Labor 206**
  Place, discharged or quitting employees, **Labor 208**
  Presumptions,
    Insufficient funds, knowledge, **Labor 212**
    Memorandum of protest or dishonor of instrument issued in payment, **Labor 212**
  Private agreements, intervals of payment, **Labor 219**
  Professional employees, **Labor 204c**
  Prohibited forms of payment, **Labor 212**
  Prosecution for payment by illegal means, venue, **Labor 214**
  Protest of instrument issued, **Labor 212**
  Public employment, **Labor 220**
  Quitting employment,
    Failure of employer to make payment within required time, **Labor 203**
    Place, **Labor 208**
  Redeemable script, coupons or cards, issuance in payment, **Labor 212**
  Refusal to make payment, **Labor 216**

COMPENSATION AND SALARIES—Cont'd
Payment—Cont'd
Release of compensation due, employer requiring without payment, **Labor 206.5**
Resignation of employee, **Labor 202, 208**
Failure of employer to make payment within required time, **Labor 203**
Sawmill operations contractor, deposits, security for payment, **Labor 270.5**
Script redeemable, issuance in payment, **Labor 212**
Seasonal labor, **Labor 250 et seq.**
Termination, **Labor 201**
Secretly paying lower wage than designated by statute or contract, **Labor 223, 225**
Semimonthly, **Labor 204**
Several employees, unified schedule, **Labor 204a**
Special occupations, **Labor 270 et seq.**
Statement, information required on stub of check, **Labor 226**
Striking employees, **Labor 209**
Telephone solicitors, security for payment, **Labor 270.6**
Theaters and shows, discharge or layoff, collective bargaining, **Labor 201.9**
Theatrical enterprises, **Labor 271**
Unpaid wages or benefits, **Labor 96.7**
Deposit of bonds by employers, **Labor 240**
Wage disputes, nonpayment of valid claims by employer, treble damages, **Labor 206**
Weekly payment, **Labor 204b, 205**
Withholding wages of employees, **Labor 222, 225**
Payment bonds, failure of bonding company to pay verified claim for wages, **Labor 203.5**
Payroll, generally, this index
Penalties. Fines and penalties, generally, ante
Per Diem, generally, this index
Perishable products, seasonal employment, computation and payment of wages on termination, **Labor 201**
Permanent wages, payment, **Labor 200 et seq.**
Personal service,
Contracts, **Labor 2855**
Preferred claims, **Labor 100.5**
Pharmacists, exemptions, **Labor 1186**
Piece work, fixed or ascertained by, **Labor 200**
Place of payment, employee discharged or quitting employment, **Labor 208**
Posting notice,
Failure to post notices, evidence, **Labor 215**
Regular pay days, **Labor 207**
Poultry raising, time due and payable, **Labor 205**

COMPENSATION AND SALARIES—Cont'd
Power of attorney, assignment of wages, revocability, **Labor 300**
Preemployment physical examination, deducting costs, **Labor 222.5, 225**
Preferred claims,
Personal services rendered, **Labor 100.5**
Work performed, **Labor 100.5**
Presumptions, minimum wages, **Labor 1200**
Prevailing wage rate, **Labor 1770 et seq.**
Priorities and preferences,
Assignment of wages, **Labor 300**
Liens and incumbrances, **CCP 1204**
Private agreements, intervals of payment, **Labor 219**
Privileges and perquisites, **Labor 350 et seq.**
Process, recovery of penalties, failure to pay to employees, **Labor 211**
Professional employees, payment, **Labor 204**
Program counselors, camps, Minimum Wage Law, **Labor 1182.4**
Protest of instrument issued in payment, **Labor 212**
Public aid payments. Social Services, generally, this index
Public Buildings and Works, this index
Public Employees Retirement System, this index
Public employment, payment, **Labor 220**
Quitting employment,
Failure of employer to make payment within required time, **Labor 203**
Payment of compensation, **Labor 202, 208**
Radio. Television and Radio, this index
Reasonable time, computation and payment of wages for seasonal employment, **Labor 201**
Rebates, **Labor 224**
Receivers and receivership, priorities and preferences, **CCP 1204**
Reciprocal agreements,
Actions to collect wages, judgments and demands for other states, **Labor 103, 104**
Collection in other states of claims or judgments for wages or other demands, **Labor 64**
Records and recordation,
Discrimination, wages, inspection, **Labor 1197.5**
Inspection and inspectors, **Labor 226**
Minimum wages, **Labor 1195.5**
Tips, employers, inspection, **Labor 353**
Registration, complaints, minimum wages, **Labor 1195**
Rehabilitation, facilities, minimum wage, **Labor 1191.5**
Rehearings, minimum wages, **Labor 1188**
Release of wages due, employer requiring without payment, **Labor 206.5**
Repayment of wages to employer, **Labor 221, 225**

COMPENSATION AND SALARIES—Cont'd
Reports, employer managed deferred compensation plans, **Labor 2809**
Resignation of employee,
Failure of employer to make payment within required time, **Labor 203**
Payment, **Labor 202, 208**
Rest periods, **Labor 226.7**
Retirement and Pensions, this index
Revocation or suspension, judgments and decrees, satisfaction, farm labor contractors, wearing apparel, manufacturers and manufacturing, **Labor 273**
Salesmen, misrepresenting compensation or commissions, **Labor 976**
Savings and Loan Associations, this index
Sawmill operations contractor, deposits, security for payment of wages, **Labor 270.5**
School for the Blind, this index
School Officers and Employees, this index
Schools for the Deaf, this index
Script redeemable, issuance in payment, **Labor 212**
Seamen, this index
Seasonal labor, **Labor 250 et seq.**
Appeal from amount of award, **Labor 255**
Application of law, **Labor 251, 257**
Civil penalties, waiting time, **Labor 256**
Computation and payment, **Labor 201**
Decisions, wage disputes, **Labor 253**
Definitions, **Labor 250**
Findings and award, wage disputes, **Labor 254, 255**
Gambling debts, deductions from wages, **Labor 253**
Hearing of wage disputes, **Labor 253**
Liquor debts, deductions from wages, **Labor 253**
Payment in presence of labor commissioner, **Labor 252**
Presumptions, award of wages by labor commissioner, **Labor 255**
Termination, payment, **Labor 201**
Second and subsequent offenses, nonpayment of wages, **Labor 243**
Secretly paying lower wage than designated by statute or contract, **Labor 223, 225**
Semimonthly payment, **Labor 204**
Several employers,
Assignment of wages, **Labor 300**
Central place for payment, unified schedule, **Labor 204a**
Severance,
Claims, assignment to labor commissioner, **Labor 96**
Trust funds, employee benefit plan distribution,
Definitions, Unclaimed Property Law, **CCP 1501**
Escheat to state, **CCP 1521**
Sex discrimination, **Labor 1197.5**
Fines and penalties, **Labor 1199.5**

COMPENSATION

COMPENSATION AND SALARIES—Cont'd

Sheepherders, minimum wages, **Labor 2695.2**

Sheltered workshops, minimum wage, **Labor 1191.5**

Signatures, assignment of wages, **Labor 300**

Social security, numbers and numbering, itemized statement, **Labor 226**

Social Services, this index

Solicitation of employees by misrepresentation, **Labor 970**

Special occupations, payment, **Labor 270 et seq.**

Standard of time, fixed or ascertained by, **Labor 200**

State compensation insurance fund, chief of division, **Labor 57**

State contracts, failure of bonding company to pay verified claim for wages, **Labor 203.5**

State Officers and Employees, this index

State or federal law, deductions, **Labor 224**

Statements,
  Deductions, **Labor 226**
  Farm labor contractors, wearing apparel, manufacturers and manufacturing, **Labor 273**
  Fines and penalties, **Labor 226.3**

Station plan, work or service rendered or performed under, **Labor 200**

Statute of limitations. Limitation of actions, generally, ante

Statutory wage scale, secretly paying lower wage, **Labor 223, 225**

Stock raising, time due and payable, **Labor 205**

Stop orders, assignment of claim to labor commissioner, **Labor 96**

Strikes, payment of unpaid wages, **Labor 209**

Students, camp employees, **Labor 1182.4**

Subcontracts,
  Nonpayment of wages, second and subsequent offenses, **Labor 243**
  Work or service rendered or performed under, **Labor 200**

Supplemental to wage agreement, claims, assignment to labor commissioner, **Labor 96**

Support, this index

Talent agencies, **Labor 1701 et seq.**

Tardiness deductions, **Labor 2928**

Task, amount fixed or ascertained by, **Labor 200**

Telephone solicitors, security for wages, **Labor 270.6**

Television and Radio, this index

Temporary employment, **Labor 201.3**

Temporary restraining orders. Injunction, generally, ante

Termination of employment, vacation time, payment, **Labor 227.3**

Terms of employment, illegal terms, **Labor 432.5**

COMPENSATION AND SALARIES—Cont'd

Theaters and Shows, this index

Time,
  Hours worked, itemized statement, **Labor 226**
  Nonpayment of wages, second and subsequent offenses, **Labor 243**
  Payment, generally, ante
  Records and recordation, inspection and inspectors, **Labor 226**

Time off in lieu of overtime pay, **Labor 204.3**

Tips, **Labor 350 et seq.**
  Collection by employer, **Labor 351**
  Credit cards, **Labor 351**
  Crimes and offenses, **Labor 354**
  Definitions, **Labor 350**
  Enforcement of laws, **Labor 355**
  Fines and penalties, **Labor 354**
  Fraud, **Labor 356**
  Income tax—state, withholding, **Un Ins 13027, 13055**
  Inspection, records of receipts by employers, **Labor 353**
  Notice, disposition, posting in establishment, **Labor 351**
  Private agreements contravening laws, **Labor 356**
  Public policy, **Labor 356**
  Records, receipt by employers, **Labor 353**
  Shares, employers and employees, notice, posting, **Labor 351**
  Unemployment Compensation, this index

Tools and implements used by employees, employer guaranteeing payment, **Labor 213**

Traveling Expenses, generally, this index

Treble damages, wage disputes, nonpayment of valid wage claims, **Labor 206**

Trusts and Trustees, this index

Unemployment Compensation, generally, this index

Unified schedule of pay days, several employers, **Labor 204a**

Universities. Colleges and Universities, this index

Unpaid wages,
  Actions, **Labor 98.5**
  Collection, deposits, payments, escheat, **Labor 96.7**
  Deposit of bonds by employer, **Labor 240**
  Industrial relations unpaid wage fund, deposit of excess amounts, **Labor 96.7**
  Interest, awards, **Labor 98.1**

Vacation pay, claims, assignment to labor commissioner, **Labor 96**

Vacation time,
  Payment, termination of employment, **Labor 227.3**
  Unpaid wages or benefits, collections, deposits, payment, escheat, **Labor 96.7**

COMPENSATION AND SALARIES—Cont'd

Validity of wage claim, falsely denying, **Labor 216**

Vaudeville, payment, **Labor 271**

Vegetables, seasonal employment termination, payment, **Labor 201**

Venue, prosecution for payment by illegal means, **Labor 214**

Vietnam Veterans Employment Act, **Gov 7280 et seq.**

Viticultural pursuits, time due and payable, **Labor 205**

Wage board, industrial welfare commission, **Labor 1179**

Wage claims,
  Actions, labor standards enforcement division, **Labor 98**
  Labor disputes, collective bargaining, representatives, assignment, **Labor 96.3**
  Penalties, labor commissioner taking assignments, **Labor 96**
  Unpaid wages, collections, deposits, payment, escheat, **Labor 96.7**

Wage disputes, treble damages, nonpayment of valid wage claims, **Labor 206**

Waiver, right to disclose wages, **Labor 232**

Walkathon, payment, **Labor 271**

Weekly payment, **Labor 204b, 205**

Withholding tax on wages, **Un Ins 13000 et seq.**

Withholding wages or part of wage agreed upon, **Labor 222, 225**

Work stoppage, stop order against employer not securing workers compensation payments, employees affected, **Labor 3710.1**

Workers authorization, deductions, **Labor 224**

Workers Compensation, generally, this index

Youthbuild program, **Un Ins 9802**

COMPLAINTS

Agricultural labor and employment, farm labor contractors, offices, **Labor 1682.7**

Agricultural Labor Relations Act, unfair labor practices, **Labor 1160.2 et seq.**

Apprentices, this index

California State University, whistle blowing, **Educ 89570 et seq.**

Colleges and Universities, this index

Community colleges and districts, whistle blowing, retaliation, **Educ 87164**

Correctional Institutions, this index

Costs, settling, **Labor 102**

Fair Employment and Housing, this index

Health Facilities, this index

Indigent persons, appointment of counsel, **Labor 98.4**

Labor and Employment, this index

Labor disputes, injunction, **Labor 1138.1**

Occupational safety and health. Labor and Employment, this index

Prosecution, **Labor 98.3**

COMPLAINTS—Cont'd
Rules and regulations, settling complaints, **Labor 98.8**
Wages, investigation, **Labor 98 et seq.**
Workers Compensation, this index

COMPOSERS
Music and Musicians, generally, this index

COMPROMISE AND SETTLEMENT
Arbitration and Award, generally, this index
Definitions, unemployment compensation, tax disputes, **Un Ins 1236**
Fair employment and housing, housing discrimination, **Gov 12980**
Housing, discrimination, **Gov 12980**
Labor and employment, aggrieved employees, actions and proceedings, **Labor 2699.3**
Labor disputes, injunction, **Labor 1138.2**
Mediation, generally, this index
Public buildings and works, contractors, compensation and salaries, assessments, **Labor 1742.1**
Unemployment Compensation, this index
Workers Compensation, this index

COMPUTATION
Workers Compensation, this index

COMPUTERS
Colleges and Universities, this index
Confidential or privileged information, Information Practices Act, **CC 1798 et seq.**
Information Practices Act, **CC 1798 et seq.**
Labor and Employment, this index
Privacy, rights, Information Practices Act, **CC 1798 et seq.**
Public buildings and works, compensation and salaries, records and recordation, **Labor 1776**
Software, officers and employees, overtime, **Labor 515.5**
Workplace violence safety, **CCP 527.8**

CONCEALMENT
Explosive type weapons. Weapons, generally, this index

CONCERTS
Children and minors, employment as musician, **Labor 1308**
Compensation and salaries, discharge or layoff, payment, collective bargaining, **Labor 201.9**

CONCESSIONS
Criminal history information, disclosure, concessionaire application purposes, **Labor 432.7**

CONCILIATION
Arbitration and Award, generally, this index

CONCILIATION COUNCIL
Definitions, fair employment and housing department, **Gov 12927**

CONDEMNATION
Manufacturing establishment, use of facility, **Labor 2352**

CONDOMINIUMS
Asbestos, notice, **Health & S 25915.2**
Definitions, asbestos, notice, **Health & S 25915.2, 25915.5**
Handicapped Persons, this index
Multistory dwelling units, handicapped persons, discrimination, **Gov 12955 et seq.**

CONDUCTORS
Railroads, this index

CONFIDENTIAL OR PRIVILEGED INFORMATION
Adoption of Children, this index
Adult abuse reports, **Welf & I 15633 et seq.**
Aged Persons, this index
Alcoholics and Alcoholism, this index
Arrest,
    Marijuana arrest record, **Labor 432.8**
    Record, **Labor 432.7**
Attorneys, this index
California State University,
    Colleges and Universities, this index
    Whistle blowing, **Educ 89574**
Clinics, this index
Colleges and Universities, this index
Compensation and salaries, discrimination, complaints, **Labor 1197.5**
Computers, this index
Consumer Credit Reporting Agencies, this index
Credit ratings. Consumer Credit Reporting Agencies, this index
Dependent adults, abuse, **Welf & I 15633 et seq.**
Disability compensation, medical records, **Un Ins 2714**
Disclosure, generally, this index
Discrimination, compensation and salaries, complaints, **Labor 1197.5**
Diversion programs, referrals or participation, **Labor 432.7**
Doctors. Physicians and Surgeons, this index
Fair employment and housing, discrimination, **Gov 12984**
Hazardous Substances and Waste, this index
Health Care Providers, this index
Health Care Service Plans, this index
Health care services department, forensic medical examinations, sexual assault, reports, **Pen 11160.1**
Health Facilities, this index
Hospitals, this index
Housing discrimination, **Gov 12984**
Industrial safety complaints, **Labor 6309**
Information Practices Act, **CC 1798 et seq.**

CONFIDENTIAL OR PRIVILEGED INFORMATION—Cont'd
Labor and Employment, this index
Labor disputes, **Labor 65**
Lawyers. Attorneys, this index
Lewdness and obscenity, identity of suppliers, **Labor 1309.5**
Local health departments, forensic medical examinations, sexual assault, reports, **Pen 11160.1**
Medical Records, this index
Mentally Ill Persons, this index
Occupational safety and health, trade secrets, **Labor 6322**
Peace Officers, this index
Physicians and Surgeons, this index
Police, this index
Privacy, right to, Information Practices Act, **CC 1798 et seq.**
Psychotherapists, medical records, **CC 56.104**
Public Employees Retirement System, this index
Right to privacy, Information Practices Act, **CC 1798 et seq.**
Schoolteachers Retirement System, this index
Sex discrimination, compensation and salaries, complaints, **Labor 1197.5**
Sheriffs, this index
Social Services, this index
State Agencies, this index
State Departments, this index
Tax Preparers, this index
Unemployment Compensation, this index
Workers Compensation, this index

CONFISCATION
Searches and Seizures, generally, this index

CONFLAGRATION
Fires and Fire Protection, generally, this index

CONFLICT OF INTEREST
Adverse or Pecuniary Interest, generally, this index

CONFLICT OF LAWS
Civil air patrol, labor and employment, leaves of absence, benefits, **Labor 1505**
Fair employment and housing, **Gov 12993.5**
Handicapped persons, accessibility standards, **Gov 12955.1**
Labor and employment, civil air patrol, leaves of absence, benefits, **Labor 1505**

CONSERVATION
Fish and Game, generally, this index
Zoning and Planning, generally, this index

CONSERVATION CORPS
Lyme disease, workers compensation, presumptions, **Labor 3212.12**

CONSERVATION

CONSERVATION CORPS—Cont'd

Public buildings and works, application of law, **Labor 1720.4**

Workers compensation, Lyme disease, presumptions, **Labor 3212.12**

CONSERVATION DEPARTMENT

Forestry division, fire fighting members, workers compensation, **Labor 3212**

Workers compensation, forestry division, peace officers, **Labor 3600.3**

CONSERVATORS AND CONSERVATOR-SHIPS

Artists manager licensee, certificate of convenience, **Labor 1700.20b**

Medical records, disclosure, **CC 56.10**

Talent agencies, certificate of convenience, **Labor 1700.20a et seq.**

Workers compensation, minor employee injured, **Labor 5408**

CONSERVATORS OF THE PEACE

Peace Officers, generally, this index

CONSOLIDATED CITIES AND COUNTIES

Airports and Landing Fields, generally, this index

Business license tax, exemptions, **Bus & P 16300**

Comfort Stations and Rest Rooms, generally, this index

Commercial vehicles, officers and employees, meals, collective bargaining, **Labor 512.5**

Compensation and salaries, itemized statements, deductions, application of law, **Labor 226**

Employees. Officers and employees, generally, post

Enterprise Zones, generally, this index

Exemptions, business license tax, **Bus & P 16300**

Fees, business and commerce, registration, exemptions, **Bus & P 16300**

Firefighters and Fire Departments, generally, this index

Health Facilities, generally, this index

Hours of labor, application of law, **Labor 555**

Housing, generally, this index

Jails, generally, this index

Labor and employment, hours of labor, application of law, **Labor 555**

Labor camps,
  Application of law, **Health & S 17024**
  Rules and regulations, enforcement, **Health & S 17050**

Landing fields. Airports and Landing Fields, generally, this index

Licenses and permits, business and commerce, exemptions, **Bus & P 16300**

Low and moderate income housing. Housing, this index

Motor carriers, officers and employees, meals, collective bargaining, **Labor 512.5**

CONSOLIDATED CITIES AND COUNTIES —Cont'd

Officers and employees,
  Commercial vehicles, meals, collective bargaining, **Labor 512.5**
  Compensation and salaries,
    Application of law, **Labor 220**
    Itemized statements, deductions, application of law, **Labor 226**
  Hours of labor, application of law, **Labor 555**
  Meals, motor carriers, collective bargaining, **Labor 512.5**
  Motor carriers, meals, collective bargaining, **Labor 512.5**
  Rest periods, motor carriers, collective bargaining, **Labor 512.5**

Planning and zoning. Zoning and Planning, generally, this index

Registration, business and commerce, fees, exemptions, **Bus & P 16300**

Screening, prospective concessionaires, application of law, **Labor 432.7**

Sewers and Sewer Systems, generally, this index

Unemployment compensation, elective coverage, **Un Ins 709**

Water Supply, generally, this index

Zoning and Planning, generally, this index

CONSPIRACY

Unemployment compensation, conspiracy to obtain benefits, **Un Ins 2107**

CONSTABLES

Arrest, generally, this index

County Officers and Employees Retirement Systems, generally, this index

Executions, generally, this index

Process, generally, this index

Service of process. Process, this index

Sheriffs, generally, this index

CONSTITUTION OF CALIFORNIA

Affirmative action, state, proposed amendment, **Const. Art. 1, § 31**

Appeal and review, workers compensation, **Const. Art. 14, § 4**

Arbitration and award, workers compensation, **Const. Art. 14, § 4**

Artisans, mechanics liens, **Const. Art. 14, § 3**

Awards, workers compensation, **Const. Art. 14, § 4**

Boards and commissions,
  General welfare of employees, conferring enforcement powers to commission, **Const. Art. 14, § 1**
  Minimum wages, conferring enforcement authority to commission, **Const. Art. 14, § 1**

Business and commerce, discrimination, sex, race, creed, **Const. Art. 1, § 8**

Compensation and salaries,
  Minimum wages, **Const. Art. 14, § 1**
  Workers compensation, **Const. Art. 14, § 4**

CONSTITUTION OF CALIFORNIA—Cont'd

Compromise and settlement, workers compensation, **Const. Art. 14, § 4**

Convicts, labor contracts, **Const. Art. 14, § 5**

Corporations, convict labor, **Const. Art. 14, § 5**

Correctional institutions,
  Convict labor, **Const. Art. 14, § 5**
  Inmate labor, contracts, **Const. Art. 14, § 5**

Death, workers compensation, **Const. Art. 14, § 4**

Disability benefits, workers compensation, **Const. Art. 14, § 4**

Discrimination,
  Business, profession or employment, **Const. Art. 1, § 8**
  State, proposed amendment, **Const. Art. 1, § 31**

Emergencies, public works, hours of labor, **Const. Art. 14, § 2**

Employment. Labor and employment, generally, post

Ethnic origin, discrimination, businesses, professions or employment, **Const. Art. 1, § 8**

Fair employment practices, **Const. Art. 1, § 8**

General welfare of employees, providing, **Const. Art. 14, § 1**

Hours of labor, public works, **Const. Art. 14, § 2**

Industrial accident commission, workers compensation, **Const. Art. 14, § 4**

Insurance, workers compensation, **Const. Art. 14, § 4**

Labor and employment,
  Convicts, **Const. Art. 14, § 5**
  Discrimination, sex, race, creed, **Const. Art. 1, § 8**
  General welfare of employees, **Const. Art. 14, § 1**
  Minimum wages, **Const. Art. 14, § 1**
  Workers compensation, **Const. Art. 14, § 4**

Labor relations, **Const. Art. 14, § 1 et seq.**

Laborers, mechanics liens, **Const. Art. 14, § 3**

Liens and incumbrances, mechanics liens, **Const. Art. 14, § 3**

Materialmen, mechanics lien, **Const. Art. 14, § 3**

Mechanics liens, **Const. Art. 14, § 3**

Minimum wages, **Const. Art. 14, § 1**

Municipalities. Taxation, generally, this index

National origin, discrimination, businesses, professions or employment, **Const. Art. 1, § 8**

Overtime labor, public works, **Const. Art. 14, § 2**

Partnerships, convict labor, **Const. Art. 14, § 5**

Professions, discrimination, sex, race, creed, **Const. Art. 1, § 8**

CONSTITUTION OF CALIFORNIA—Cont'd

Public buildings and works, hours of labor, **Const. Art. 14, § 2**

Race, discrimination, business, professions or employment, **Const. Art. 1, § 8**

Religion, discrimination, businesses, professions or employment, **Const. Art. 1, § 8**

Sex, discrimination,
　Business professions or employment, **Const. Art. 1, § 8**
　Qualification for business, vocation or profession, **Const. Art. 1, § 8**

State, convicts, working for benefit of state, **Const. Art. 14, § 5**

State compensation insurance fund, workers compensation, **Const. Art. 14, § 4**

War and civil defense, public buildings and works, hours of labor, **Const. Art. 14, § 2**

Workers compensation, **Const. Art. 14, § 4**

CONSTRUCTION

Actions and proceedings, contracts, labor and employment, **Labor 2810**

Attorney fees, contracts, labor and employment, **Labor 2810**

Buildings, this index

Colleges and Universities, this index

Community colleges and districts. Colleges and Universities, this index

Contractors, generally, this index

Contracts, this index

Costs, contracts, labor and employment, **Labor 2810**

Cranes, tower cranes, regulation, **Labor 7370 et seq.**

Damages, contracts, labor and employment, **Labor 2810**

Definitions, public works, **Labor 1720**

Fines and penalties,
　Elevators, safety, **Labor 7205**
　Funds, diversion, **Pen 484b**

Housing, this index

Injunction, contracts, labor and employment, **Labor 2810**

Inspection and inspectors,
　Construction elevators, **Labor 7204**
　Workers compensation, alternative dispute resolution system, **Labor 3201.5**

Labor and Employment, this index

Labor camps,
　Alternative designs, materials or methods, approval, **Health & S 17002**
　Application of regulations to existing structures, **Health & S 17023**

Lead poisoning, occupational safety, programs, **Health & S 105185 et seq.**

Machinery and Equipment, this index

Occupational safety and health. Labor and Employment, this index

School Buildings and Grounds, this index

Statutes, this index

Theft, funds, **Pen 484b**

CONSTRUCTION—Cont'd

Tower cranes, regulation, **Labor 7370 et seq.**

Workers compensation, alternative dispute resolution system, **Labor 3201.5**

Youthbuild program, **Un Ins 9800 et seq.**

CONSTRUCTION OF STATUTES

Statutes, this index

CONSTRUCTIVE NOTICE

Notice, this index

CONSULTATION

Asbestos, this index

Asbestos training and consultant certification fund, **Labor 9021.7**

Fees, occupational safety and health appeals board, award to employers, **Labor 149.5**

Labor and employment, occupational safety and health, education and research programs, **Labor 6350 et seq.**

Occupational health, local health departments promotion, **Health & S 105150**

Occupational safety and health, education and research programs, **Labor 6350 et seq.**

Unemployment compensation, qualifications, **Un Ins 656**

Workers Compensation, this index

CONSUMER AFFAIRS DEPARTMENT

Intergovernmental cooperation, joint enforcement strike force on the underground economy, **Un Ins 329**

Joint enforcement strike force on the underground economy, representative, **Un Ins 329**

Strike force on the underground economy, **Un Ins 329**

CONSUMER CREDIT

Credit Cards, generally, this index

Reports. Consumer Credit Reporting Agencies, generally, this index

CONSUMER CREDIT PROTECTION ACT

Earnings garnishment provisions, state exemption, **CCP 706.151**

Employee subjected to garnishment of earnings, discharge from employment, **Labor 2929**

CONSUMER CREDIT REPORTING AGENCIES

Generally, **CC 1785.1 et seq., 1786 et seq.**

Access to files by consumer, **CC 1785.10, 1785.15**
　Investigative consumer reporting agencies, **CC 1786.10, 1786.11, 1786.22 et seq.**

Actions and proceedings, **CC 1786.18**

Address, disclosure, **CC 1785.10**

Application of law, **CC 1785.4, 1785.5**

Arrest, **CC 1786.18**

Attorney fees, investigations and investigators, **CC 1786.50**

CONSUMER CREDIT REPORTING AGENCIES—Cont'd

Certificates and certification, disclosure, **CC 1786.16**

Confidential or privileged information,
　Furnishing reports, authorization, **CC 1785.11**
　Procedures to restrict access, **CC 1785.14**

Contents of reports, **CC 1785.13**
　Investigative consumer credit reporting agencies, **CC 1786.18**

Correction of reports, investigative consumer credit reports, **CC 1786.24**

Costs, investigations and investigators, **CC 1786.50**

Credit scores, notice, **CC 1785.15.1, 1785.15.2**

Criminal history information, **CC 1786.18**

Damages, investigations and investigators, **CC 1786.50 et seq.**

Deletions, reinvestigations, **CC 1786.24**

Disclosure, **CC 1785.10 et seq., 1786.11**
　Investigative consumer reporting agencies, **CC 1786.10 et seq.**
　Required disclosures, scope, **CC 1785.6**

Disputed information, reinvestigations, **CC 1786.24**

Dwelling houses, use of report in determining eligibility to hire, **CC 1785.3, 1785.11, 1785.13**

Fair Credit Reporting Act, application of law, **CC 1786.24**

Fair employment and housing, **CC 1786.20**

Fees,
　Credit scores, notice, **CC 1785.15.2**
　Disclosure of information, **CC 1786.26**

Forms, consumer notice, **CC 1785.15**

Fraud, discovery, **CC 1786.52**

Furnishing report,
　Authorization, **CC 1785.11**
　Credit transaction not initiated by consumer, **CC 1785.11**
　Investigative consumer credit reporting agencies, **CC 1786.12**

Governmental agencies, furnishing information, **CC 1785.12**
　Investigative consumer credit reporting agencies, **CC 1786.14**

Identity and identification, **CC 1785.14**
　Theft, post

Indictment and information, **CC 1786.18**

Information contained in report, restrictions, **CC 1785.13**

Inquiries, disclosure, **CC 1785.10**

Inspection of records, **CC 1785.10, 1785.15**

Item of information, definitions, **CC 1785.3**

Judgments and decrees, **CC 1786.18**

Labor and employment,
　Requesting report for employment purposes, notice to applicant, **CC 1785.20.5**
　Requirements, **CC 1785.18**

Landlord and Tenant, this index

I–39

CONSUMER

CONSUMER CREDIT REPORTING AGEN-CIES—Cont'd

Liens and incumbrances, release, **CC 1785.135**

Medical information, **CC 1785.13**

Notice,
Credit scores, **CC 1785.15.1, 1785.15.2**
Denial, rates and rating organizations, **CC 1786.40**
Forms, **CC 1785.15**
Identity and identification, theft, **CC 1785.15**
Information suppliers, obligations, **CC 1785.14**
Investigations and investigators, **CC 1786.29**
Prequalifying reports, transactions not initiated by consumer, **CC 1785.11**
Prohibiting user from disclosing to, **CC 1785.14**
Reinvestigations, **CC 1786.24**
Required notices, scope, **CC 1785.6**
Risk scores, **CC 1785.15.1, 1785.15.2**
Security alerts, reports, **CC 1785.15**
Security freeze, reports, **CC 1785.15**
Solicitation, lists, removal, **CC 1785.11.8**
Transaction not initiated by consumer, exclusion from list, **CC 1785.11**
Use of report to deny credit, **CC 1785.20.5**

Open end credit account, closed by consumer, notice, **CC 1785.13**

Powers and duties, **CC 1785.10 et seq.**

Privileges and immunities, user disclosing to consumer, **CC 1785.14**

Procedures, **CC 1785.14, 1786.20**

Public policy, **CC 1785.1**

Public records, disclosure of source, **CC 1785.18**

Rates and charges, disclosure of information, **CC 1786.26**

Records and recordation, **CC 1785.14, 1785.18, 1786.20**
Inspection and inspectors, **CC 1785.15**

Reinvestigation, **CC 1786.24**

Remedies, investigations and investigators, **CC 1786.50 et seq.**

Restrictions on information in report, **CC 1785.13**

Risk scores, notice, **CC 1785.15.1, 1785.15.2**

Security alerts, reports, notice, **CC 1785.15**

Security freeze, reports, notice, **CC 1785.15**

Solicitation, lists, removal, notice, **CC 1785.11.8**

State agencies,
Furnishing information, investigative consumer credit reporting agencies, **CC 1786.14**
Furnishing reports to, **CC 1785.12**

Subpoenas, inspection of records, **CC 1785.11**

Tax liens, **CC 1786.18**

Telecommunications,
Applications, disclosure, **CC 1785.3**

CONSUMER CREDIT REPORTING AGEN-CIES—Cont'd

Telecommunications—Cont'd
Numbers and numbering, disclosure, **CC 1785.10**

Theft, identity and identification, **CC 1785.15**

Time, information prohibited, **CC 1785.13**

Title of Act, **CC 1785.2**

Transactions not initiated by consumer, reports, **CC 1785.11**

Warnings, investigations and investigators, **CC 1786.29**

CONSUMER FINANCE LENDERS

Finance Lenders, generally, this index

CONSUMER PROTECTION

Employment or insurance information, investigative consumer reporting agencies, **CC 1786 et seq.**

Finance Lenders, generally, this index

Investigative consumer reporting agencies, **CC 1786 et seq.**

Reports, investigative consumer reporting agencies, **CC 1786 et seq.**

CONSUMERS

Definitions, credit reporting, **CC 1785.3**

Employment or insurance investigation, reporting agencies, **CC 1786 et seq.**

Protection. Consumer Protection, generally, this index

CONTAGIOUS DISEASES

Diseases, generally, this index

CONTAINERS

Brands, Marks and Labels, generally, this index

Hazardous substances and waste, occupational lead poisoning, **Health & S 105185 et seq.**

Labels. Brands, Marks and Labels, generally, this index

Labor union insignia, articles of merchandise, **Labor 1010 et seq.**

Occupational lead poisoning hazardous substances and waste, **Health & S 105185 et seq.**

Tanks, generally, this index

CONTEMPT

Agricultural labor relations board investigations, noncompliance with subpoenas, **Labor 1151**

Garnishment,
Employers failure to comply, **CCP 706.104**
Income tax—state levy, **CCP 706.075**

Labor and Employment, this index

Support, this index

Workers Compensation, this index

CONTINGENT FUNDS

State Treasury, this index

CONTINUANCE

Workers compensation hearing, **Labor 5700**

CONTINUATION BENEFITS REPLACEMENT ACT

Generally, **Health & S 1366.20 et seq.; Ins 10128.50 et seq.**

CONTINUATION COVERAGE

Definitions, Cal COBRA, accident and health insurance, **Health & S 1366.21; Ins 10128.51**

CONTINUING EDUCATION

Electricity, apprentices, **Labor 3099.2**

Elevators, dumbwaiters and escalators, certificates and certification, **Labor 7311.3**

Vocational Education, generally, this index

CONTORTIONISTS

Children and minors, vocation, occupation, **Labor 1308**

CONTRABAND

Weapons, generally, this index

CONTRACEPTIVES

Birth Control, generally, this index

CONTRACT ACT (PUBLIC WORKS)

State Contracts, generally, this index

CONTRACTORS

Asbestos, this index

Bonds (officers and fiduciaries),
Actions on bonds, certification of claim and amount, **Labor 96.5**
Certification of claim and amount, action on bond, **Labor 96.5**

Chemical plant workers, safety, notice of hazardous, **Labor 7862**

Citations, **Labor 1020 et seq.**
Civil sanctions, **Labor 1020 et seq.**

Civil sanctions, citations, **Labor 1020 et seq.**

Compensation and salaries, nonpayment, **Labor 243**
Second and subsequent offenses, **Labor 243**

Crimes and offenses, construction funds, diversion, **Pen 484b**

Definitions,
Apprentices, public buildings and works, **Labor 1777.5**
Deaf, mute persons, **Un Ins 11000.5**
Drug free workplaces, state contracts, **Gov 8351**
Foreign labor contractors, **Bus & P 9998.1**
Public buildings and works, **Labor 1722.1**
Public transit, displaced workers, **Labor 1071**
Wearing apparel, manufacturers and manufacturing, **Labor 2671**

CONTRACTORS—Cont'd

Deposits, unlicensed contractor penalties, industrial relations construction industry enforcement fund, **Labor 1024**

Discipline,
Certified copies, findings, **Labor 98.9**
Electricity, apprentices, **Labor 3099.2**

Division of funds or property, **Pen 484b**

Electricity, apprentices, **Labor 3099 et seq.**

Farm labor contractors. Agricultural Labor and Employment, this index

Fines and penalties,
Citation system, **Labor 1020 et seq.**
Industrial relations construction industry enforcement fund, deposit, unlicensed contractors, **Labor 1024**
Licenses and permits, post
Unlicensed contractors, **Labor 1020, 1021.5**

Foreign labor contractors, **Bus & P 9998 et seq.**

Funds, industrial relations construction industry enforcement fund, deposit of fines, unlicensed contractors, **Labor 1024**

Hearings, challenging citation, **Labor 1023**

Independent Contractors, generally, this index

Industrial relations construction industry enforcement fund, fines from unlicensed contractors, deposit, **Labor 1024**

Janitors, discharge, **Labor 1060 et seq.**

Labor and employment, foreign labor contractors, **Bus & P 9998 et seq.**

Licenses and permits,
Fines and penalties, unlicensed contractors, **Labor 1021 et seq.**
Occupational safety and health, violations, fines, notice, **Labor 6652**
Unlicensed contractors, generally, post
Workers compensation, insurance, certificates and certification, **Labor 3800**

Liens. Mechanics Liens, generally, this index

Logging, deposits, security for payment of wages, **Labor 270.5**

Mechanics Liens, generally, this index

Nonpayment of wages, second and subsequent offenses, **Labor 243**

Notice,
Challenging citations, **Labor 1023**
Employment agencies, workers compensation, **Labor 3302**

Penalties. Fines and penalties, generally, ante

Permits. Licenses and permits, generally, ante

Process, **Labor 1020 et seq.**

Public Buildings and Works, this index

Registration, asbestos related work, **Labor 6501.5**

Rules and regulations, asbestos related work, **Labor 6501.5**

CONTRACTORS—Cont'd

Sawmill operations contractor, deposits, security to pay wages, **Labor 270.5**

Unlicensed contractors, **Labor 1020, 1021.5**
Civil sanctions, **Labor 1021, 1022**

Violations, civil sanctions, citations, **Labor 1020 et seq.**

Wearing apparel, manufacturers and manufacturing, compensation and salaries, suretyship and guarantee, **Labor 2673.1**

Workers compensation,
Employment agencies, **Labor 3302**
Insurance certificate, exhibiting, building permit issuance prerequisite, **Labor 3800**

CONTRACTS

Accord and Satisfaction, generally, this index

Actors and actresses, talent services, fees, **Labor 1701 et seq.**

Adverse or Pecuniary Interest, generally, this index

Affirmative action, equal opportunity, apprentices, **Labor 3073**

Agricultural Labor and Employment, this index

Apprentices, this index

Arbitration and Award, generally, this index

Art and Artists, this index

Asbestos, notice, privity of contract, **Health & S 25915.5**

Bonds (officers and fiduciaries), use of property put up as, abrogation of law, **Labor 405**

Breach of contract. Specific Performance, generally, this index

Buses, displaced workers, **Labor 1070 et seq.**

Clinics, this index

Commission contracts, **Labor 2751, 2752**

Compensation and salaries, human trafficking, deductions, illegal contracts, **CC 1670.7**

Conflict of interest. Adverse or Pecuniary Interest, generally, this index

Construction, labor and employment, **Labor 2810**

Construction funds, diversion, **Pen 484b**

Convict labor, **Const. Art. 14, § 5**

Definitions, employment contracts, **Labor 2750**

Employment. Labor and Employment, this index

Employment Agencies, this index

Foreign labor contractors, **Bus & P 9998.2**

Fraud, generally, this index

Health Care Providers, this index

Health Facilities, this index

Human trafficking, compensation and salaries, deductions, illegal contracts, **CC 1670.7**

CONTRACTS—Cont'd

Immigration, compensation and salaries, deductions, illegal contracts, **CC 1670.7**

Independent contractors status, rebuttable presumption, **Labor 2750.5**

Interurban railroads, displaced workers, **Labor 1070 et seq.**

Inventions, ownership rights, **Labor 2871**

Janitors,
Discharge, **Labor 1060 et seq.**
Labor and employment, **Labor 2810**

Job listing services, written contracts, **CC 1812.516**

Job training and placement, Human Resources Development Act of 1968, **Un Ins 9601**

Labor and Employment, this index

Labor disputes, agreements in connection with, **Labor 1110**

Larceny by fraud, **Pen 484**

Leases, generally, this index

Mass transit, displaced workers, **Labor 1070 et seq.**

Minority, Women, or Disabled Veteran Businesses, this index

Mortgages, generally, this index

Motion pictures, talent services, fees, **Labor 1701 et seq.**

Music and musicians, talent services, fees, **Labor 1701 et seq.**

Nurses, this index

Occupational safety and health division, development of tests, breathing apparatus for use in fires, **Labor 6331**

Oil and Gas, this index

Paratransit vehicles, displaced workers, **Labor 1070 et seq.**

Performance of. Specific Performance, generally, this index

Personal interest. Adverse or Pecuniary Interest, generally, this index

Personal Services, this index

Physicians and Surgeons, this index

Private security services, labor and employment, **Labor 2810**

Public Buildings and Works, this index

Railroads, this index

Religious Organizations and Societies, this index

Salaries, human trafficking, deductions, illegal contracts, **CC 1670.7**

Satisfaction. Accord and Satisfaction, generally, this index

Specific Performance, generally, this index

State Contracts, generally, this index

Talent Agencies, this index

Television and radio, talent services, fees, **Labor 1701 et seq.**

Theaters and shows, talent services, fees, **Labor 1701 et seq.**

Tips, contravening, laws, **Labor 356**

Transit Districts, this index

Transportation, this index

Wearing Apparel, this index

CONTRACTS—Cont'd

Women and minority businesses. Minority, Women, or Disabled Veteran Businesses, this index

Workers Compensation, this index

CONTRIBUTIONS

County Officers and Employees, this index

Definitions, child care, tax credit, **Rev & T 17052.18**

Limited Liability Companies, this index

Public Employees Retirement System, this index

Retirement and Pensions, this index

CONTRIBUTORY NEGLIGENCE

Negligence, this index

CONTROLLED GROUP OF CORPORATIONS

Definitions, bank and corporation tax credits, **Rev & T 23622.7**

CONTROLLED SUBSTANCES

Definitions, drug free workplaces, state contractors and grantees, **Gov 8351**

Drugs and Medicine, generally, this index

CONTROVERSY

Definitions, arbitration, **CCP 1280**

CONVALESCENT NURSING HOMES

Nursing Homes, generally, this index

CONVERSION

Insurance, this index

CONVEYANCES

Deeds and Conveyances, generally, this index

CONVICTION OF CRIME

Crimes and Offenses, this index

CONVICTS

Correctional Institutions, generally, this index

Jails, generally, this index

COOPERATIVE CORPORATIONS

Credit Unions, generally, this index

COPARTNERSHIP

Partnership, generally, this index

CORE COVERAGE

Definitions, Cal COBRA, accident and health insurance, **Health & S 1366.21; Ins 10128.51**

CORN

Agricultural Products, generally, this index

CORNEAL EYE TISSUE

Tissue Banks, generally, this index

CORONARY DISEASE

Heart Disease, generally, this index

CORONERS

Medical records, disclosure, **CC 56.10**

CORONERS—Cont'd

Privileges and immunities, criminally related personal injuries, reports, **Pen 11161.9**

Workers compensation, autopsies, **Labor 5706, 5707**

CORPORATE CRIMINAL LIABILITY ACT

Generally, **Pen 387**

CORPORATE SECURITIES LAW

Securities, generally, this index

CORPORATION TAXES

Bad debts, commercial banks, losses, application of law, **Rev & T 24416**

Carrybacks, net operating losses, **Rev & T 24416**

Local agency military base recovery areas, credits, **Rev & T 24416.5**

Carryovers,

Enterprise zones, **Rev & T 24416.1**

Net operating loss, targeted tax areas, **Rev & T 24416.6**

Los Angeles revitalization zone, losses, net operating losses, carrybacks, **Rev & T 24416.4**

Net operating losses,

Deductions, **Rev & T 24416 et seq.**

Local agency military base recovery areas, credits, **Rev & T 24416.5**

Time, extension, **Rev & T 24416.3**

Certificates and certification,

Local agency military base recovery areas, credits, **Rev & T 23646**

Manufacturing enhancement areas, credits, **Rev & T 23622.8**

Qualified employees, credits, **Rev & T 23622.7**

Credits,

Enterprise Zones, this index

Inmate labor wages, correctional institution joint venture programs, **Rev & T 23624**

Jobs Tax Credit Act, **Rev & T 23621 et seq.**

Labor and employment,

Disadvantaged and disabled employees, Jobs Tax Credit Act, **Rev & T 23621 et seq.**

Hiring, **Rev & T 23623**

Local agency military base recovery areas, **Rev & T 23645, 23646**

Qualified wages, enterprise zones, **Rev & T 23634**

Small businesses, hiring, **Rev & T 23623**

Deductions,

Carryovers, enterprise zones, **Rev & T 24416.1**

Enterprise Zones, this index

Gains and losses, net operating losses, **Rev & T 24416**

Insurance, post

Los Angeles revitalization zone, net operating loss, **Rev & T 24416.2**

Carrybacks, **Rev & T 24416.4**

CORPORATION TAXES—Cont'd

Deductions—Cont'd

Military base recovery areas, **Rev & T 24416.2**

Net operating losses, **Rev & T 24416 et seq.**

Qualified taxpayers, net operating losses, **Rev & T 24416**

Targeted tax areas, **Rev & T 24416.2**

Definitions,

Eligible small business, **Rev & T 24416**

Net operating losses, **Rev & T 24416**

New business, **Rev & T 24416**

Title 11 or similar case, **Rev & T 24416**

Withholding tax on wages, **Un Ins 13003**

Disadvantaged persons, hiring, credit, **Rev & T 23622.7, 23622.8**

Employer, Jobs Tax Credit Act, **Rev & T 23621 et seq.**

Enterprise Zones, this index

Franchise Tax Board, generally, this index

Gains and losses,

Carryovers, generally, ante

Deductions, ante

Qualified taxpayers, net operating losses, deductions, **Rev & T 24416**

Handicapped persons, credit, hiring, **Rev & T 23622.7**

Indians, hiring, credit, **Rev & T 23622.7**

Inmate labor, correctional institutions, joint venture programs, wage payments tax credit, **Rev & T 23624**

Insurance, deductions, premiums, **Rev & T 24424**

Jobs Tax Credit Act, **Rev & T 23621 et seq.**

Labor and employment,

Credits, hiring, **Rev & T 23623**

Disadvantaged and disabled employees, Jobs Tax Credit Act, **Rev & T 23621 et seq.**

Local agency military base recovery areas, credits, **Rev & T 23645, 23646**

Net operating losses, carrybacks, **Rev & T 24416.5**

Los Angeles Revitalization Zone, this index

Military Bases, Reservations and Areas, this index

Native Americans, hiring, credit, **Rev & T 23622.7**

Net operating losses,

Carryovers, ante

Deductions, ante

Officers and employees, personal liability, withholdings on employee wages, **Un Ins 1735**

Passthrough of credits. Credits, ante

Qualified summer youth employees, jobs tax credit, **Rev & T 23621**

Small businesses, credits, hiring, **Rev & T 23623**

Targeted tax areas, deductions, **Rev & T 24416.2**

Unemployed persons, hiring, credit, **Rev & T 23622.7, 23622.8**

CORPORATIONS
Agents,
Directors, generally, post
Officers and employees, generally, post
Bankruptcy, generally, this index
Banks and Banking, generally, this index
Board of directors. Directors, generally, post
Business activities, dangerous business practices, **Pen 387**
Capital stock. Shares and shareholders, generally, post
Cemetery corporations. Cemeteries and Dead Bodies, generally, this index
Charities, generally, this index
Children and minors, unemployment compensation, disclaimer of rights, **Un Ins 637.1**
Colleges and Universities, generally, this index
Commercial banks. Banks and Banking, generally, this index
Committees, unemployment compensation, directors, **Un Ins 637.1**
Convict labor, **Const. Art. 14, § 5**
Corporate Criminal Liability Act, **Pen 387**
Corporation Taxes, generally, this index
Credit Unions, generally, this index
Crimes and offenses,
Criminal Liability Act, **Pen 387**
Dangerous business practices, **Pen 387**
Dangerous business practices, **Pen 387**
Definitions,
Unemployment insurance, withholding tax on wages, **Un Ins 13003**
Withholding tax on wages, **Un Ins 13003**
Workers compensation, **Labor 3717**
Directors,
Compensation and salaries, income tax—state, withholding, nonresidents, **Un Ins 13020**
Fees, income tax—state, withholding, nonresidents, **Un Ins 13020**
Income tax—state, withholding, nonresidents, **Un Ins 13020**
Unemployment compensation, **Un Ins 637, 637.1**
Dissolution, unemployment compensation final report and return, **Un Ins 1116, 1735**
Elections. Shares and shareholders, post
Employee owned corporations, unemployment compensation, **Un Ins 1253.3**
Employees. Officers and employees, generally, post
Expatriate corporations. Foreign Corporations, generally, this index
Fairs and Expositions, generally, this index
Financial Statements and Reports, generally, this index
Foreign Corporations, generally, this index
Franchise taxes. Corporation Taxes, generally, this index
Husband and wife, unemployment compensation, disclaimer of rights, **Un Ins 637.1**

CORPORATIONS—Cont'd
Income tax. Corporation Taxes, generally, this index
Insurance companies. Insurance, generally, this index
Limited Liability Companies, generally, this index
Merger and consolidation, unemployment insurance, employing unit, **Un Ins 135.1, 135.2**
Nonprofit Corporations, generally, this index
Officers and employees,
Leave of absence for military duty, **Mil & V 394.5**
Liabilities, unemployment compensation, contributions, **Un Ins 1735**
Purchase of stock, consideration for securing position of employment, **Labor 407**
Workers compensation, **Labor 3351**
Personal income tax. Income Tax—State, generally, this index
Personal liability of officers, shareholders and others,
Officers and employees, generally, ante
Shares and shareholders, generally, post
Practices, dangerous business practices, **Pen 387**
Public Corporations, generally, this index
Public Utilities, generally, this index
Railroads, generally, this index
Receivers and Receivership, generally, this index
Religious Organizations and Societies, generally, this index
Reverse stock split. Shares and shareholders, post
Savings and Loan Associations, generally, this index
Securities, generally, this index
Shares and shareholders,
Elections, purchase to secure position, **Labor 407**
Escheat, this index
Income Tax—State, this index
Liabilities,
Income tax—state, withholdings on employee wages, **Un Ins 1735**
Unemployment compensation, contributions, nonpayment by employer, **Un Ins 1735**
Withholdings on employee wages, employers failure to withhold, **Un Ins 1735**
Sole stockholder, unemployment compensation rights disclaimer, **Un Ins 637.1**
Unemployment compensation, contributions, nonpayment by employer, major shareholders liability, **Un Ins 1735**
Workers compensation, parties, uninsured employer actions, **Labor 3717.1**
Small Businesses, generally, this index

CORPORATIONS—Cont'd
Sole corporations. Religious Organizations and Societies, generally, this index
Stock and stockholders. Shares and shareholders, generally, ante
Taxation,
Corporation Taxes, generally, this index
Franchise taxes. Corporation Taxes, generally, this index
Unemployment Compensation, this index
Universities. Colleges and Universities, generally, this index
Utilities. Public Utilities, generally, this index

CORPSE
Cemeteries and Dead Bodies, generally, this index

CORRECTIONAL INSTITUTIONS
Appeal and review,
Complaints, occupational safety and health, **Labor 6304.3, 6304.4**
Workers compensation, **Labor 3371**
Attorneys, workers compensation, appeals board, **Labor 3371**
Committees, occupational safety and health, establishment, powers and duties, **Labor 6304.3**
Compensation and salaries,
Unemployment compensation, generally, post
Workers compensation, generally, post
Complaints, occupational safety and health, **Labor 6304.3**
Convict labor. Labor and employment, generally, post
Death, reports, **Labor 6413 et seq.**
Definitions,
Employee, state prisoners, occupational safety and health, **Labor 6304.2**
Employer, state prisoners, occupational safety and health, **Labor 6304.2**
Direct placement services, vocational rehabilitation, **Labor 3370**
Discharge. Unemployment compensation, generally, post
Employment. Labor and employment, generally, post
Fines and penalties, injuries to prisoners, reports, **Labor 6413.5**
Fires and fire protection, inmates, workers compensation, **Labor 4458**
Health and sanitation. Occupational safety and health, generally, post
Heart disease, workers compensation, presumptions, **Labor 3212.10**
Hernias, workers compensation, presumptions, **Labor 3212.10**
Industry safety. Occupational safety and health, generally, post
Inmate employment. Labor and employment, generally, post
Inmate treatment and prison to employment plan, **Pen 3105**

CORRECTIONAL

CORRECTIONAL INSTITUTIONS—Cont'd
Inspection and inspectors, occupational safety and health, **Labor 6304.3**
Jails, generally, this index
Juvenile Delinquents and Dependents, generally, this index
Juvenile Facilities Division, generally, this index
Labor and employment, **Const. Art. 14, § 5**
Benefit of state, convict labor, **Const. Art. 14, § 5**
Collection and compilation of information, **Labor 150**
Contracts, public entities or corporations, **Const. Art. 14, § 5**
Interference with employment after discharge, **Pen 2947**
Occupational safety and health, generally, post
Prison labor, information, collection and compilation, **Labor 150**
State highways, workers compensation exclusion, **Labor 3352**
Unemployment compensation, generally, post
Workers compensation, generally, post
Libel and slander, ex convict seeking employment, **Pen 2947**
Meningitis, workers compensation, presumptions, **Labor 3212.10**
Occupational safety and health,
Appeal and review, **Labor 6304.3, 6304.4**
Committee, establishment, powers and duties, **Labor 6304.3**
Complaints, **Labor 6304.3**
Injuries, reports, **Labor 6413**
Inspection and inspectors, **Labor 6304.3**
Reports, injuries, **Labor 6413**
Officers and employees,
Tuberculosis, workers compensation, **Labor 3212.6**
Workers compensation, generally, post
Parole and Probation, generally, this index
Personal injuries, prisoners, reports, **Labor 6413 et seq.**
Plans and specifications, inmate treatment and prison to employment plan, **Pen 3105**
Pneumonia, workers compensation, presumptions, **Labor 3212.10**
Psychiatrists and psychiatry, workers compensation, **Labor 3208.3**
Reports,
Forms, injuries to prisoners, **Labor 6410**
Injuries to prisoners, **Labor 6410, 6413 et seq.**
Occupational safety and health, injuries, **Labor 6413**
Review. Appeal and review, generally, ante
Rules and regulations, safety, hearings, **Labor 6413.2**

CORRECTIONAL INSTITUTIONS—Cont'd
Safety,
Occupational safety and health, generally, ante
Reports, **Labor 6413.2**
State highways, convict labor, workers compensation exclusion, **Labor 3352**
Tuberculosis,
Guards, workers compensation, **Labor 3212.6**
Workers compensation, presumptions, **Labor 3212.10**
Unemployment compensation,
Disability benefits, inmate eligibility, **Un Ins 2680, 2681**
Inmates,
Employment, definition, **Un Ins 633.1**
Excluded services, **Un Ins 633.1, 634.5**
United States, fire suppress, workers compensation, **Labor 3365**
Vocational rehabilitation, injured inmates, direct placement services, **Labor 3370**
Workers compensation,
Appeal and review, **Labor 3371**
Attorneys, appeals board, **Labor 3371**
Death benefits, limitation of actions, AIDS, **Labor 5406.6**
Employee, definitions, **Labor 3351**
Heart disease, presumptions, **Labor 3212.10**
Hernias, presumptions, **Labor 3212.10**
Injury sustained prior to incarceration, eligibility, **Labor 3370**
Meningitis, presumptions, **Labor 3212.10**
Occupational safety and health, generally, ante
Pneumonia, presumptions, **Labor 3212.10**
Prisoners engaged in fire fighting, **Labor 3365**
Psychiatric injuries, **Labor 3208.3**
Qualifications, **Labor 3370**
State highways, **Labor 3352**
Suppressing fires, **Labor 4458**
Tuberculosis,
Guards, **Labor 3212.6**
Presumptions, **Labor 3212.10**

CORRECTIONS AND REHABILITATION DEPARTMENT
Death in line of duty, dependents, scholarships, **Labor 4709**
Dependents, scholarships, **Labor 4709**
Fire suppressing in service of United States or agency thereof, workers compensation, **Labor 3365**
Handicapped persons, disability in line of duty, dependents, scholarships, **Labor 4709**
Heart trouble, workers compensation, **Labor 3212.2**
Juvenile Facilities Division, generally, this index
Occupational safety and health, state prisoners, **Labor 6304.2 et seq., 6413**

CORRECTIONS AND REHABILITATION DEPARTMENT—Cont'd
Officers and employees, workers compensation, heart trouble, **Labor 3212.2**
Scholarships, dependents, **Labor 4709**
Workers compensation,
Early intervention programs, rehabilitation, **Labor 3214**
Fire suppressing, United States service, **Labor 3365**
Heart trouble, **Labor 3212, 3212.2**
Requesting benefits, **Labor 4909.1**
Scholarships, dependents, **Labor 4709**

CORRESPONDENCE
Letters and Other Correspondence, generally, this index

COST OF LIVING
Income Tax—State, this index
Information, collection and compilation, **Labor 150**

COSTS
Acquired immune deficiency syndrome, blood tests, results disclosure action, **Health & S 120980**
Agricultural Labor and Employment, this index
AIDS, blood tests, disclosure, **Health & S 120980**
Attachment, this index
Blood tests, AIDS testing, disclosure, **Health & S 120980**
Buses, displaced workers, actions and proceedings, **Labor 1073**
Colleges and Universities, this index
Community colleges and districts. Colleges and Universities, this index
Compensation and Salaries, this index
Complaints, appeals, **Labor 98.2**
Construction, contracts, labor and employment, **Labor 2810**
Consumer Credit Reporting Agencies, this index
Damage actions, disclosure of arrest record, **Labor 432.7**
Diversion program, actions, **Labor 432.7**
Earnings withholding orders, service, registered process server fees, **CCP 706.108**
Executions, this index
Fair employment and housing, **Gov 12989.2**
Cease and desist orders, **Gov 12987**
Garnishment, this index
Gender violence, actions and proceedings, **CC 52.4**
Harassment, **CCP 527.6**
Health care providers, whistle blowing, **Health & S 1278.5**
Health Facilities, this index
Housing, this index
Indemnity, this index
Injunction, this index
Interurban railroads, displaced workers, actions and proceedings, **Labor 1073**

COSTS—Cont'd

Janitors,
Contracts, labor and employment, **Labor 2810**
Discharge, **Labor 1062**
Judgment Creditors, this index
Labor and Employment, this index
Labor Camps, this index
Labor commissioner, settling employees complaints, **Labor 101, 102**
Labor disputes, injunction, **Labor 1138.1**
Labor standards enforcement division, **Labor 101, 102**
Mass transit, displaced workers, actions and proceedings, **Labor 1073**
Nonpayment actions, labor and employment, **Labor 218.5**
Paratransit vehicles, displaced workers, actions and proceedings, **Labor 1073**
Police, this index
Private security services, contracts, labor and employment, **Labor 2810**
Public Buildings and Works, this index
Railroads, displaced workers, actions and proceedings, **Labor 1073**
Sex, force and violence, actions and proceedings, **CC 52.4**
State Agencies, this index
State Contracts, this index
Talent agencies, fees, **Labor 1704.2**
Transportation, displaced workers, actions and proceedings, **Labor 1073**
Unemployment Compensation, this index
Wearing apparel,
Contracts, labor and employment, **Labor 2810**
Manufacturers, arbitration, **Labor 2688, 2692**
Whistle blowing, health facilities, **Health & S 1278.5**
Workers Compensation, this index

COUNCILS

Apprenticeship Council, generally, this index
CalWORKs, job creation, **Un Ins 17002**
Disaster council. War and Civil Defense, this index
Green collar jobs, **Un Ins 15002**
Labor and employment, youth councils, workforce investment, **Un Ins 14208 et seq.**
Youth councils, workforce investment, **Un Ins 14208 et seq.**

COUNSEL

Attorneys, generally, this index

COUNSELORS AND COUNSELING

Employment Counseling Services, generally, this index
High Schools or Secondary Schools, this index
Parole and Probation, this index
Talent services, fees, **Labor 1701 et seq.**

COUNSELORS AND COUNSELING—Cont'd

Trespass, neonatal units, maternity wards, birthing centers, parole and probation, **Pen 602**
Youthbuild program, **Un Ins 9800 et seq.**

COUNTERCLAIM

Setoff and Counterclaim, generally, this index

COUNTIES

Agents. County Officers and Employees, generally, this index
Aid to indigent persons. Social Services, generally, this index
Attorneys,
District Attorneys, generally, this index
Medical records, negligence, release, **CC 56.36**
Business and commerce, licenses and permits, exemptions, **Bus & P 16300**
Cable Television, generally, this index
Cities and counties. Consolidated Cities and Counties, generally, this index
Civil defense. War and Civil Defense, generally, this index
Comfort Stations and Rest Rooms, generally, this index
Consolidated Cities and Counties, generally, this index
Convicts. Jails, generally, this index
Coroners, generally, this index
Correctional institutions. Jails, generally, this index
Definitions,
Labor Code, **Labor 14**
Unemployment insurance, **Un Ins 14**
District Attorneys, generally, this index
Elections, generally, this index
Employees. County Officers and Employees, generally, this index
Enterprise Zones, generally, this index
Exemptions, business and commerce, licenses and permits, **Bus & P 16300**
Fair employment and housing department, liaison, powers and duties, **Gov 12933**
Fairs and Expositions, generally, this index
Family economic security, job preparation and training services. Unemployment Compensation, this index
Firefighters and Fire Departments, generally, this index
Health Facilities, generally, this index
Housing, generally, this index
In home supportive services program,
Domestic employees, unemployment compensation coverage, **Un Ins 683**
Workers compensation coverage, **Labor 3351.5**
Indigent Persons, generally, this index
Jails, generally, this index
Job preparation and training services. Unemployment Compensation, this index
Labor and employment. County Officers and Employees, generally, this index

COUNTIES—Cont'd

Labor camps,
Application of law, **Health & S 17024**
Enforcement of laws and regulations, **Health & S 17050**
Licenses and permits, business and commerce, exemptions, **Bus & P 16300**
Local Agencies, generally, this index
Local child support agencies. Child Support Services Department, this index
National defense. War and Civil Defense, generally, this index
Officers and employees. County Officers and Employees, generally, this index
Piers. Wharves, Docks and Piers, generally, this index
Planning. Zoning and Planning, generally, this index
Prisoners. Jails, generally, this index
Public assistance. Social Services, generally, this index
Public entity, unemployment compensation, **Un Ins 135, 605**
Recreation and Park Districts, generally, this index
Regional occupational centers. Vocational Education, this index
Regional youth education facilities. Juvenile Institutions and Schools, this index
Registration, business and commerce, fees, exemptions, **Bus & P 16300**
Residential Care Facilities for the Elderly, generally, this index
Retirement and pensions. County Officers and Employees Retirement Systems, generally, this index
Screening, application of law, **Labor 432.7**
Sewers and Sewer Systems, generally, this index
Sheriffs, generally, this index
Supportive services program, domestic employees,
Unemployment compensation coverage, **Un Ins 683**
Workers compensation coverage, **Labor 3351.5**
Taxation, generally, this index
Unemployment Compensation, this index
War and Civil Defense, generally, this index
Wharves, Docks and Piers, generally, this index
Workers Compensation, this index
Zoning and Planning, generally, this index

COUNTY AGENCIES

Comatose patients, medical information disclosure, **CC 56.10**
Medical records, comatose patients, information disclosure, **CC 56.10**

COUNTY BONDS

Investments, unemployment insurance disability fund, **Un Ins 3003**
Unemployment insurance disability fund, investment, **Un Ins 3003**

COUNTY

COUNTY CLERKS
Deputies, workers compensation exclusion, holding appointment for own convenience, **Labor 3352**
Workers compensation, deputies, exclusion, **Labor 3352**

COUNTY CORONERS
Coroners, generally, this index

COUNTY EMPLOYEES
County Officers and Employees, generally, this index

COUNTY FIRE PROTECTION DISTRICTS
Fires and Fire Protection, generally, this index

COUNTY HEALTH FACILITIES
Health Facilities, generally, this index

COUNTY JAILS
Jails, generally, this index

COUNTY OFFICERS AND EMPLOYEES
Attorneys. District Attorneys, generally, this index
Commercial vehicles, meals, collective bargaining, **Labor 512.5**
Compensation and salaries,
  Application of law, **Labor 220**
  Itemized statement, deductions, application of law, **Labor 226**
  Leave of absence for military duty, **Mil & V 395.01 et seq.**
  Minimum wages, **Labor 1205**
  Unemployment compensation, generally, post
  Workers compensation, generally, post
Contributions,
  Health and welfare benefits, **Labor 220.2**
  Pension or retirement funds, **Labor 220.2**
  Vacation allowances, sick leave and retirement funds, **Labor 220.2**
District Attorneys, generally, this index
Fees. Compensation and salaries, generally, ante
Hours of labor, **Labor 1205**
Leave of absence for military duty, **Mil & V 395 et seq.**
Lie detector tests, condition of employment, **Labor 432.2**
Meals, motor carriers, collective bargaining, **Labor 512.5**
Military personnel, discrimination, **Mil & V 394**
Minimum wages, **Labor 1205**
Motor carriers, meals, collective bargaining, **Labor 512.5**
Polygraph tests, condition of employment, **Labor 432.2**
Resignation, military service entry, reentry into office or employment on discharge, **Mil & V 395.3**
Rest periods, motor carriers, collective bargaining, **Labor 512.5**

COUNTY OFFICERS AND EMPLOYEES
  —Cont'd
Retirement and pensions. County Officers and Employees Retirement Systems, generally, this index
Salaries. Compensation and salaries, generally, ante
Sheriffs, generally, this index
Soldiers and Sailors Relief Act, **Mil & V 395.1**
Standards, labor and employment, **Labor 1205**
Unemployment compensation,
  Elective coverage, **Un Ins 709**
  Voluntary plans, **Un Ins 709, 710**
Wages. Compensation and salaries, generally, ante
Workers compensation,
  Juvenile traffic offenders or probationers, rehabilitative work on public work projects, **Labor 3364.6**
  Leaves of absence, disability benefits, **Labor 4850**
  Rehabilitation plans, voluntary, **Labor 6208**
  Self insurers, medical and related treatment and supplies, former employees, **Labor 4606**
  Service of notices, orders, **Labor 5317**

COUNTY OFFICERS AND EMPLOYEES RETIREMENT SYSTEMS
Advance payments, disability payments, **Labor 4850.3, 4850.4**
Attachment, exemptions, fund, basis, **Labor 220.2**
Compensation and salaries, advanced disability payments, **Labor 4850.3, 4850.4**
Disability retirement, advanced payments, **Labor 4850.3, 4850.4**

COUNTY SUPERINTENDENTS OF SCHOOLS
School Superintendents, this index

COUNTY WARRANTS
Social Services, generally, this index

COUPONS
Labor, compensation, issuance in payment, **Labor 212**

COURSE OF TRADE, BUSINESS, PROFESSION OR OCCUPATION
Definitions, workers compensation, **Labor 3355**

COURT OFFICERS AND EMPLOYEES
Interpreters and Translators, generally, this index
Iraq Kuwait Crisis, active duty, benefits, **Mil & V 395.07**

COURT ORDERS
Orders of Court, generally, this index

COURT REPORTERS
Unemployment compensation, transcription performed away from office, **Un Ins 630**
Workers compensation proceedings, **Labor 5708**

COURTS
Appeal and Review, generally, this index
City courts. Municipal Courts, generally, this index
Contempt, generally, this index
Costs, generally, this index
Depositions, generally, this index
Guardian and Ward, generally, this index
Interpreters and Translators, generally, this index
Judgments and Decrees, generally, this index
Municipal Courts, generally, this index
Orders of Court, generally, this index
Small Claims Courts, generally, this index
Subpoenas, generally, this index
Superior Courts, generally, this index
Supreme Court, generally, this index
Translators. Interpreters and Translators, generally, this index
Venue, generally, this index
Witnesses, generally, this index

COURTS OF APPEAL
Appeal and Review, generally, this index
Judges, military service, veterans, reentry to office, **Mil & V 395.3**
Occupational safety and health orders, rules, review of, **Labor 6308**

COVENANTS
Deeds and Conveyances, this index
Housing, this index
Workers compensation proceedings, jurisdiction to review, **Labor 5955**

COVERED MULTIFAMILY DWELLINGS
Definitions, discrimination, disabled persons, **Gov 12955.1**

COWS
Animals, generally, this index

CRANE EMPLOYER
Definitions, tower crane regulation, **Labor 7371**

CRANES
Certificates and certification, tower cranes, **Labor 7375**
Crawler and wheel cranes, labor and employment, occupational safety and health, **Labor 6704**
Definitions, tower crane regulation, **Labor 7371**
Tower cranes, regulation, **Labor 7370 et seq.**

CRATES
Containers, generally, this index

CREDIBLE THREAT OF VIOLENCE
Definitions, harassment, **CCP 527.6**

CREDIT
Corporation Taxes, this index
Credit ratings. Consumer Credit Reporting Agencies, generally, this index
Definitions, denial, **CC 1785.1**
Finance Lenders, generally, this index
Income Tax—State, this index
Public policy, **CC 1785.1**
Unemployment Compensation, this index

CREDIT CARDS
Compensation and salaries, tips, **Labor 351**
Consumer Credit Reporting Agencies, generally, this index
Reports. Consumer Credit Reporting Agencies, generally, this index
Solicitation, lists, removal, notice, consumer credit reporting agencies, **CC 1785.11.8**
Tips, **Labor 351**
Unemployment compensation, domestic service employers, contributions, payment, **Un Ins 1118**

CREDIT RATINGS
Consumer Credit Reporting Agencies, generally, this index

CREDIT REPORTING AGENCIES
Consumer Credit Reporting Agencies, generally, this index

CREDIT UNIONS
Aged persons, financial abuse, reports, **Welf & I 15630.1**
Compensation and salaries, deposit of wages by employer in employees account, **Labor 213**
Dependent adults, financial abuse, reports, **Welf & I 15630.1**
Fines and penalties,
Aged persons, financial abuse, reports, **Welf & I 15630.1**
Dependent adults, financial abuse, reports, **Welf & I 15630.1**
Officers and employees,
Aged persons, financial abuse, reports, **Welf & I 15630.1**
Dependent adults, financial abuse, reports, **Welf & I 15630.1**
Privileges and immunities,
Aged persons, financial abuse, reports, **Welf & I 15634**
Dependent adults, financial abuse, reports, **Welf & I 15634**
Workers compensation, deposits by employer of disability payments in employees account, **Labor 4651**

CREDITORS
Debtors and Creditors, generally, this index

CREED
Definitions, fair employment and housing, **Gov 12926**
Discrimination, generally, this index

CRIME VICTIMS
Victims of crime. Crimes and Offenses, this index

CRIMES AND OFFENSES
Generally, **Labor 1199**
Abettors. Accomplices and Accessories, generally, this index
Accomplices and Accessories, generally, this index
Acquired immune deficiency syndrome (AIDS), blood tests, results disclosure, **Health & S 120980**
Adoption of Children, this index
Adult abuse report confidentiality violation, **Welf & I 15633 et seq.**
Advertisements, this index
Aerial passenger tramways, operation without permit, **Labor 7342**
Agricultural Labor and Employment, this index
Agricultural labor relations board, resisting or interfering with, **Labor 1151.6**
Aiders and abettors. Accomplices and Accessories, generally, this index
Air pressure tanks, operation without permit, **Labor 7750**
Amusement rides, noncompliance, **Labor 7915**
Appeals board, unemployment insurance, divulging confidential information, **Un Ins 2111**
Apprentices, discrimination, **Labor 3095**
Arrest, generally, this index
Asbestos, this index
Assassination of elected public officials, death benefits, **Labor 4727**
Assault and Battery, generally, this index
Background checks. Criminal History Information, generally, this index
Bad checks. Negotiable Instruments, this index
Battery. Assault and Battery, generally, this index
Bias and prejudice. Hate Crimes, generally, this index
Blackballing former employees, **Labor 1050 et seq.**
Blood tests, AIDS, causative agent testing, disclosure of results, **Health & S 120980**
Boilers, **Labor 7750 et seq.**
Business and Commerce, this index
Children and Minors, this index
Civil Service, this index
Class of labor employed, misrepresentation, **Labor 1010 et seq.**
Coal mines, underground telephones, installation or maintenance, **Labor 7501**
Coercing witnesses, **Gov 9414**
Colleges and Universities, this index

CRIMES AND OFFENSES—Cont'd
Community colleges and districts. Colleges and Universities, this index
Compensation and salaries, **Labor 215, 225, 1199, 1199.5**
Door to door salesmen, security for wages, **Labor 270.6**
Evidence, failure to post notices, **Labor 215**
False denial of amount or validity of wages, **Labor 216**
Itinerant merchants, security for wages, **Labor 270.6**
Logging or sawmill contractors, deposits, security for payment of wages, **Labor 270.5**
Minimum wages, **Labor 1197, 1197.1**
Refusal to make payments, **Labor 216**
Release of wages due, employer requiring without payment, **Labor 206.5**
Repayment of wages to employer, **Labor 221, 225**
Secretly paying lower wage than designated by statute or contract, **Labor 223, 225**
Special occupations, availability of funds for payment, **Labor 270 et seq.**
Theatrical enterprises, deposits, security for payment of wages, **Labor 271**
Tips, violations by employers, **Labor 354**
Withholding wages, **Labor 222, 225**
Construction elevators, safety, **Labor 7205**
Construction funds, diversion, **Pen 484b**
Consumer Credit Protection Act, discharge of employee prosecuted for violation, **Labor 2929**
Consumer credit reports, contents of records, **CC 1785.13**
Contempt, generally, this index
Contractors, this index
Conviction of crime, unemployment compensation, **Un Ins 1030.1**
Corporate Criminal Liability Act, **Pen 387**
Corporations, this index
Correctional Institutions, generally, this index
Dangerous business practices, serious concealed danger, failure to disclose, **Pen 387**
Death, this index
Death benefits, assassination of elected public officials, **Labor 4727**
Destruction or damaging of property. Malicious Mischief, generally, this index
Disclosure,
Dangerous business practices, failure to disclose, **Pen 387**
Identity of suppliers, lewdness and obscenity, **Labor 1309.5**
District Attorneys, generally, this index
Diversion programs, referrals, job applicants, disclosure, **Labor 432.7**
Domestic partnership, forms, **Fam 298**
Domestic Violence, generally, this index

CRIMES

CRIMES AND OFFENSES—Cont'd

Door to door salesmen, security for wages, **Labor 270.6**

Drug Addicts, this index

Duress or Coercion, generally, this index

Electric railroads, laminated safety glass, cars and locomotives, **Labor 6956**

Elevators, Dumbwaiters and Escalators, this index

Employee Housing Act, labor camp violations, **Health & S 17061**

Employers, requiring job applicants to disclose arrest record or diversion program referrals or participation, **Labor 432.7**

Employment Agencies, this index

Employment applications, **Labor 432.7, 432.8**

Employment counseling, **CC 1812.523**

Employment development department, divulging confidential information, **Un Ins 2111**

Employment services board, divulging confidential information, **Un Ins 2111**

Ex convicts, seeking employment, interference, **Pen 2947**

Explosives, this index

False representation. Fraud, generally, this index

Farm labor contractors, **Labor 1697, 1698.1 et seq.**

Fines and Penalties, generally, this index

Fingerprints and Fingerprinting, generally, this index

Firearms. Weapons, this index

Firefighters and Fire Departments, this index

Force and Violence, generally, this index

Foreign labor contractors, **Bus & P 9998.8**

Forfeitures, generally, this index

Foster homes. Social Services, this index

Fraud, generally, this index

Gambling, generally, this index

Garnishment, **CCP 706.152**

Gender violence, actions and proceedings, **CC 52.4**

Habitual criminals. Second and subsequent offenses, generally, post

Handicapped Persons, this index

Harassment, generally, this index

Hatch tenders, employment on ships and vessels, loading and unloading operations, **Labor 7600, 7608**

Hate Crimes, generally, this index

Health Care Service Plans, this index

Health Facilities, this index

Homicide, generally, this index

Horse Racing, this index

Hours of labor, **Labor 553**

Income Tax—State, this index

Indictment and Information, generally, this index

Industrial Homework, this index

Infants,

   Children and Minors, this index

CRIMES AND OFFENSES—Cont'd

Infants—Cont'd

   Juvenile Delinquents and Dependents, generally, this index

Information. Indictment and Information, generally, this index

Information Practices Act, **CC 1798 et seq.**

Injunction, acquisition of firearms by restrainees, **Pen 12021**

Itinerant merchants, security for wages, **Labor 270.6**

Jails, generally, this index

Job listing services, **CC 1812.523**

Jurisdictional strike, **Labor 1115**

Juvenile Delinquents and Dependents, generally, this index

Juvenile Institutions and Schools, generally, this index

Labor and Employment, this index

Labor camps, **Health & S 17061**

   House confinement, **Health & S 17061.7**

Labor commissioner, deputies and assistants,

   Neglect or refusal of employer to furnish statistics, information or access, **Labor 90**

   Wilfully impeding or preventing performance of duties, **Labor 91**

Labor Disputes, this index

Labor organizations,

   Coercion, membership, **Labor 922**

   Insignia, use on articles of merchandise, **Labor 1010 et seq.**

Laboratories, this index

Larceny. Theft, generally, this index

Legislature, this index

Lewdness and Obscenity, generally, this index

Libel and Slander, generally, this index

Liquefied petroleum gas storage tanks, operation without permit, **Labor 7750**

Local detention facilities. Jails, generally, this index

Logging contractors, deposits, security for payment of wages, **Labor 270.5**

Longshoremen, safety violations, **Labor 7608**

Malicious Mischief, generally, this index

Manufacturers and Manufacturing, this index

Medical Records, this index

Military Forces, this index

Mines and Minerals, this index

Minors. Children and Minors, this index

Motion Pictures, this index

Municipal Officers and Employees, this index

Murder. Homicide, generally, this index

New Trial, generally, this index

Notice. Victims of crime, post

Nursing Homes, this index

Obscenity. Lewdness and Obscenity, generally, this index

Parole and Probation, generally, this index

Peace Officers, this index

CRIMES AND OFFENSES—Cont'd

Penalties. Fines and Penalties, generally, this index

Perjury, generally, this index

Pharmacists, this index

Photography and pictures, attorney fees, criminally related injury reports, frivolous actions, **Pen 11161.9**

Police, this index

Political affiliations of employees, coercing or influencing, **Labor 1101 et seq.**

Pornography. Lewdness and Obscenity, generally, this index

Principal and accessory. Accomplices and Accessories, generally, this index

Prisoners. Jails, generally, this index

Private Security Services, this index

Probation. Parole and Probation, generally, this index

Professional strikebreakers, **Labor 1134 et seq.**

Protective orders, **Pen 12021**

Public Buildings and Works, this index

Public offenses, acquisition of firearms by restrainees, **Pen 12021**

Public Utilities, this index

Railroads, this index

Recidivists. Second and subsequent offenses, generally, post

Records and recordation,

   Criminal History Information, generally, this index

   Disclosure, identity of suppliers, lewdness and obscenity, **Labor 1309.5**

Reemployment privileges, **Labor 1050 et seq.**

Residential Care Facilities for the Elderly, this index

Restitution, generally, this index

Right to privacy, violation of injunctions restraining harassment, **CCP 527.6**

Safety in employment. Labor and Employment, this index

Savings Associations, this index

Sawmill operations contractors, deposits, security for payment of wages, **Labor 270.5**

Scaffolds, **Labor 7155, 7156**

School Officers and Employees, this index

Searches and Seizures, generally, this index

Second and subsequent offenses,

   Aerial passenger tramways, operation without permits, **Labor 7342**

   Asbestos related work, **Labor 6505.5**

   Labor camps, **Health & S 17061.5**

   Sex discrimination, **CC 52**

   Workplace smoking regulation violations, **Labor 6404.5**

Security Agents and Broker Dealers, this index

Sex, force and violence, actions and proceedings, **CC 52.4**

Sex Offenders, generally, this index

Sexual Assault, generally, this index

Sheriffs, this index

CRIMES AND OFFENSES—Cont'd
Ships and Shipping, this index
Slander. Libel and Slander, generally, this index
Smelters and underground workings, hours of labor, violations, **Labor 752**
Social Services, this index
Stalking, generally, this index
State civil service. Civil Service, this index
State Hospitals, this index
State Officers and Employees, this index
Steam boilers, **Labor 7750 et seq.**
Stevedore operations, safety violations, **Labor 7608**
Supersedeas or Stay, generally, this index
Talent Agencies, this index
Taxation, this index
Telecommunications, this index
Theatrical enterprises, deposits, security for payment of wages, **Labor 271**
Theft, generally, this index
Tips, violations of law by employers, **Labor 354**
Trademarks, this index
Trespass, generally, this index
Unemployment Compensation, this index
Union buttons, unlawful wearing, **Labor 1018**
Union card, unlawful use, **Labor 1017**
Universities. Colleges and Universities, this index
University of California. Colleges and Universities, this index
Venue, generally, this index
Vessels. Ships and Shipping, this index
Victims of crime,
  Compensation and salaries. Restitution, generally, this index
  Discharge, labor and employment, absence and absentees, judicial proceedings, **Labor 230.2**
  Discrimination, labor and employment, absence and absentees, judicial proceedings, **Labor 230.2**
  Labor and employment, absence and absentees, judicial proceedings, **Labor 230.2**
  Limitation of actions, labor and employment, absence and absentees, judicial proceedings, **Labor 230.2**
  Notice, labor and employment, absence and absentees, judicial proceedings, **Labor 230.2**
  Restitution, generally, this index
  Retaliation, labor and employment, absence and absentees, judicial proceedings, **Labor 230.2**
  Workers compensation, notice, eligibility, **Labor 3553**
Violent felonies,
  Foreign states, employment records, **Pen 11105.3**
  Labor and employment, records, disclosure, **Pen 11105.3**
  Records and recordation, disclosure, employment, **Pen 11105.3**

CRIMES AND OFFENSES—Cont'd
Weapons, this index
Wearing apparel, manufacturers, engaging in business without registering, **Labor 2676**
Wharves, docks and piers, safety violations, **Labor 7608**
Whistle Blowing, this index
Window cleaners, safety devices on buildings, **Labor 7328 et seq.**
Witnesses, generally, this index
Workers Compensation, this index

CRIMES OF VIOLENCE
Violent felonies. Crimes and Offenses, this index

CRIMINAL HISTORY INFORMATION
Alcoholics and alcoholism, transportation, volunteers, **Pen 11105.3**
Cable television,
  Franchises, **Pub U 5910**
  Officers and employees, **Pub U 7910**
Care facilities, fees, **Welf & I 15660**
Certificates and certification, **Pen 11105.7**
Consumer credit reporting agencies, **CC 1786.18**
Day Care and Nursery Schools, this index
Drug addicts, transportation, volunteers, **Pen 11105.3**
Federal bureau of investigation, **Pen 11105.3**
Fees, care facilities, **Welf & I 15660**
Fingerprints and Fingerprinting, this index
In home supportive services, **Welf & I 12301.8, 15660**
Labor and Employment, this index
Long term health care facilities, nurses, temporary employment, **CC 1812.542**
Nurses, this index
Nursing Homes, this index
Open video systems,
  Franchises, **Pub U 5910**
  Officers and employees, **Pub U 7910**
Peace Officers, this index
Police, this index
Psychiatric technicians, long term health care facilities, temporary employment, **CC 1812.542**
Sheriffs, this index
Social Services, this index
Telecommunications, officers and employees, **Pub U 7910**
United States, **Pen 11105.3**
Video programming services,
  Franchises, **Pub U 5910**
  Officers and employees, **Pub U 7910**
Vocational nursing, long term health care facilities, temporary employment, **CC 1812.542**

CRIMINAL JUSTICE PLANNING OFFICE
Intergovernmental cooperation, joint enforcement strike force on the underground economy, **Un Ins 329**

CRIMINAL JUSTICE PLANNING OFFICE —Cont'd
Joint enforcement strike force on the underground economy, representative, **Un Ins 329**
Strike force on the underground economy, **Un Ins 329**

CRIMINAL PROCEDURE
Crimes and Offenses, generally, this index

CRIMINAL TRESPASS ACT
Generally, **Pen 602**

CRIMINALISTIC LABORATORIES
Crimes and offenses. Laboratories, this index

CRIPPLED PERSONS
Handicapped Persons, generally, this index

CROCIDOLITE
Occupational Carcinogens Control Act, **Labor 9000 et seq.**

CROPS
Agricultural Products, generally, this index

CRUDE OIL
Oil and Gas, generally, this index

CUMULATIVE INJURIES
Workers Compensation, this index

CURBS AND GUTTERS
Wharves, docks and piers, waterside curbs, **Labor 7604**

CUSTODIANS
Janitors, generally, this index

CUSTOM AND USAGE
Labor and employment, performance in accordance with, **Labor 2857**

CUSTOMERS
Consumer Protection, generally, this index
Definitions, temporary employment, compensation and salaries, **Labor 201.3**

DAGGERS
Weapons, generally, this index

DAIRIES AND DAIRY PRODUCTS
Unemployment compensation, qualifications, **Un Ins 611 et seq.**

DAMAGES
Agricultural labor and employment, contracts, **Labor 2810**
AIDS, this index
Arrest, record, disclosure, marijuana arrest record, **Labor 432.7, 432.8**
Asbestos workers, claims or actions against persons other than employer, asbestosis, **Labor 4417**
Blood tests, AIDS causative agent testing, results disclosure, **Health & S 120980**
Business and commerce, discrimination, treble damages, **CC 52**

DAMAGES

DAMAGES—Cont'd

Community colleges and districts. Colleges and Universities, this index
Compensation and Salaries, this index
Construction, contracts, labor and employment, **Labor 2810**
Consumer Credit Reporting Agencies, this index
Definitions, workers compensation, **Labor 3209**
Discrimination, this index
Diversion program, referrals or participation, disclosure, **Labor 432.7**
Double damages, solicitation of employees by misrepresentation, **Labor 972**
Economic opportunity programs, injury or death of enrollees, **Labor 4212**
Elevators, dumbwaiters and escalators, **Labor 7324.1**
Employment. Labor and Employment, this index
Exemplary damages, **CC 3294**
    Gender violence, **CC 52.4**
    Homicide, **CC 3294**
    Sex, force and violence, **CC 52.4**
    Sexual harassment, **CC 52**
    State officers and employees, veterans, disclosure, improper activities, **Mil & V 73.7**
    Talent agencies, fees, **Labor 1704.2**
Fair Employment and Housing, this index
Firefighters and Fire Departments, this index
Foreign labor contractors, liability, **Bus & P 9998.8**
Fraud, this index
Gender violence, **CC 52.4**
Hate crimes, **CC 52**
Health Care Service Plans, this index
Homicide, exemplary damages, **CC 3294**
Housing, this index
Indemnity, generally, this index
Information Practices Act, **CC 1798.53**
Investigative consumer reporting agencies, **CC 1786.50 et seq.**
Janitors, contracts, labor and employment, **Labor 2810**
Labor and Employment, this index
Labor camps, residents, **Health & S 17055**
Labor Disputes, this index
Limited Liability Companies, this index
Liquidated damages,
    Discrimination, **Labor 1197.5**
    Minimum wages, **Labor 1194.2**
    Pay discrimination, **Labor 1197.5**
Medical Records, this index
Military Forces, this index
Minimum wages, liquidated damages, **Labor 1194.2**
Nominal damages, medical records, negligence, release, **CC 56.36**
Peace Officers, this index
Penalties. Exemplary damages, generally, ante

DAMAGES—Cont'd

Political affiliations of employees, coercion or attempted influencing by employer, **Labor 1105**
Private patrol operators, retaliation, officers and employees, disclosure, **Bus & P 7583.46**
Private security services, contracts, labor and employment, **Labor 2810**
Public Buildings and Works, this index
Punitive damages. Exemplary damages, generally, ante
Railroads, this index
Sex, force and violence, **CC 52.4**
Sex discrimination, **CC 52**
Sexual harassment, **CC 52**
Solicitation, employees by misrepresentation, **Labor 972**
Specific Performance, generally, this index
State, this index
State Contracts, this index
State Officers and Employees, this index
Support, arrearages, evasion, accomplices and accessories, **CC 1714.41**
Talent Agencies, this index
Treble damages,
    Agricultural labor, transportation fees, recovery, **Labor 1697.1**
    Business establishments, discrimination, **CC 52**
    Diversion program, referrals or participation, disclosure, **Labor 432.7**
    Employment contract with employer without permanent and fixed place of business in state, **Labor 2752**
    Former employees, preventing reemployment, **Labor 1054**
    Support, arrearages, evasion, accomplices and accessories, **CC 1714.41**
    Wage disputes, nonpayment of valid wage claims, **Labor 206**
Violence, freedom from, **CC 52**
Wearing Apparel, this index
Workers Compensation, this index
Wrongful Death, generally, this index

DAMS AND RESERVOIRS

Labor and employment,
    Obligations of employer, **Labor 2801**
    Wrongful death, personal representatives right of action, **Labor 2803**

DANCES AND DANCE HALLS

Children and minors, encouraging vocation, occupation, **Labor 1308**

DANGEROUS WEAPONS

Weapons, generally, this index

DANGERS

Businesses practices, crimes and offenses, **Pen 387**
Corporate Criminal Liability Act, **Pen 387**

DATA

Computers, generally, this index
Statistics, generally, this index

DATA PROCESSING

Computers, generally, this index

DATA REPOSITORIES

Toxic materials and harmful physical agents, **Labor 147.2**

DAY CARE AND NURSERY SCHOOLS

Criminal history information,
    Disclosure, **Pen 11105.3**
    Notice, disclosure, employment, **Pen 11105.3**
Disclosure, criminal history, labor and employment, **Pen 11105.3**
Employment agencies, referrals, trustline, **CC 1812.5093**
Income Tax—State, this index
Labor and employment, employee visits, **Labor 230.8**
Officers and employees, **Educ 8264.7**
    Disclosure, criminal history, **Pen 11105.3**
Reports, income tax—state, credits, **Rev & T 17052.18**

DAY HAULERS

Definitions, farm labor contractors, **Labor 1682.3**

DAY OF REST LAW

Generally, **Labor 550 et seq.**

DEAD BODIES

Cemeteries and Dead Bodies, generally, this index

DEADLY WEAPONS

Weapons, generally, this index

DEAF AND MUTE PERSONS

Communications, employment services, **Un Ins 11002**
Employment services, **Un Ins 11000 et seq.**
Interpreters and translators, employment services, **Un Ins 11002**
Labor and employment, deaf, hearing impaired, employment services, **Un Ins 11000 et seq.**
Schools for the Deaf, generally, this index
Social Services, generally, this index

DEATH

Amusement rides, reports, **Labor 7904, 7914**
Asbestos spraying, **Labor 6425**
Boilers, negligent operation causing death, **Labor 7771**
Children and Minors, this index
Coroners, generally, this index
Correctional Institutions, this index
Corrections and rehabilitation department, line of duty, dependents, scholarships, **Labor 4709**
Crimes and offenses, **Labor 6425**
Damages, homicide, exemplary damages, **CC 3294**
Disability compensation, death before making claim for benefits, **Un Ins 2705**

DEATH—Cont'd

Domestic partnership, powers and duties, **Fam 297.5**

Economic opportunity programs, enrollees, **Labor 4201 et seq.**

Employee benefit plan distribution, escheat to state, **CCP 1521**

Employee benefit trust distribution, escheat to state, **CCP 1510**

Employment. Labor and Employment, this index

Exemplary damages, homicide, **CC 3294**

Fines and penalties, **Labor 6425**

Firefighters and Fire Departments, this index

Highway Patrol, this index

Homicide, generally, this index

Insurance, generally, this index

Investigation. Coroners, generally, this index

Juvenile facilities division, line of duty, dependents, scholarships, **Labor 4709**

Labor and Employment, this index

Murder. Homicide, generally, this index

Peace Officers, this index

Police, this index

Priorities and preferences, proceeds of claim, **Labor 2803**

Prisons and prisoners. Correctional Institutions, this index

Probate Proceedings, generally, this index

Public Officers and Employees, this index

Sheriffs, this index

Steam boilers, negligent operation causing death, **Labor 7771**

Talent agencies, certificate of convenience to conduct business, **Labor 1700.20a, 1700.20b**

Unemployment compensation,
  Death in immediate family, eligibility for benefits, **Un Ins 1253.1, 1253.12**
  Wages, exclusion of death benefits, **Un Ins 938**

Workers Compensation, this index

Wrongful Death, generally, this index

DEBARMENT

Public buildings and works, contractors and subcontractors, **Labor 1777.1**

DEBENTURES

Bonds, generally, this index

DEBTORS AND CREDITORS

Accord and Satisfaction, generally, this index

Assignment for Benefit of Creditors, generally, this index

Attachment, generally, this index

Bankruptcy, generally, this index

Compensation and salaries, liens and incumbrances, priorities and preferences, **CCP 1204**

Consumer Credit Reporting Agencies, generally, this index

Credit Cards, generally, this index

Domestic Partnership, this index

DEBTORS AND CREDITORS—Cont'd

Employee benefit plans, liens and incumbrances, priorities and preferences, **CCP 1204**

Garnishment, generally, this index

Judgment Creditors, generally, this index

Liens and incumbrances, compensation and salaries, priorities and preferences, **CCP 1204**

Reports. Consumer Credit Reporting Agencies, generally, this index

Satisfaction. Accord and Satisfaction, generally, this index

Unemployment compensation, supplemental plans established by employer, exemption of benefits from claims, **Un Ins 1342**

DECEDENTS ESTATES

Probate Proceedings, generally, this index

DECEIT

Fraud, generally, this index

DECEPTION

Fraud, generally, this index

DECEPTIVE TRADE PRACTICES

Consumer Protection, generally, this index

DECLARATORY JUDGMENTS AND DECREES

Unemployment compensation, decisions of appeals board, **Un Ins 409.1, 409.2**

DECREES

Judgments and Decrees, generally, this index

DEEDS AND CONVEYANCES

Covenants, discrimination, **Gov 12955**

Discrimination, **Gov 12955 et seq.**

Good faith purchase, discriminatory clauses or covenants, **Gov 12995**

DEFAMATION

Libel and Slander, generally, this index

DEFAULT

Student loans. Colleges and Universities, this index

Support, this index

DEFENDANTS

Definitions, fair employment and housing, **Gov 12926**

Parties, generally, this index

DEFENSE INSTALLATIONS

Military Bases, Reservations and Areas, generally, this index

DEFENSE OF MARRIAGE ACT

Generally, **Fam 308.5**

DEFERRED COMPENSATION

Compensation and Salaries, this index

DEFINITIONS

Words and Phrases, generally, this index

DELEGATION OF AUTHORITY

Unemployment compensation appeals board, **Un Ins 1959**

DELINQUENT CHILDREN

Juvenile Delinquents and Dependents, generally, this index

DEMAND OCCUPATIONS

Definitions, unemployment compensation, training or retraining, **Un Ins 1270**

DEMEROL

Drug Addicts, generally, this index

DEMIJOHNS

Containers, generally, this index

DEMOLITION EXPERTS

Workers compensation, voluntary technical assistance to public entity, **Labor 3367**

DEMOLITION OF BUILDINGS

Lead poisoning, occupational safety, programs, **Health & S 105185 et seq.**

Licenses and permits, **Labor 6500 et seq.**

Salvaging materials, safety in employment, **Labor 6401.5**

DEMONSTRATION REELS

Talent services, **Labor 1703.4**

DENTAL HYGIENISTS

Workers compensation, **Labor 3208.05**

DENTISTS AND DENTISTRY

Disability, compensation, certificate of disability, **Un Ins 2708 et seq.**

Hypodermic Syringes and Needles, generally, this index

Outpatient settings. Clinics, this index

Privileges and immunities, criminally related personal injuries, reports, **Pen 11161.9**

Unemployment compensation, independent contractors, presumption as, **Un Ins 656**

DENTURES

Workers compensation, **Labor 3208**

DEPARTMENTAL BANKING

Banks and Banking, generally, this index

DEPARTMENTS

Administrative Law and Procedure, generally, this index

Definitions,
  CalWORKs, job creation, **Un Ins 17000**
  Children and minors, employment, **Labor 1286**
  Employee housing and labor camps, **Health & S 17004**
  Employment development department, automation reports, **Un Ins 4900**
  Employment training panel, **Un Ins 10201**
  Fair employment and housing department, **Gov 12925**

DEPARTMENTS

DEPARTMENTS—Cont'd
Definitions—Cont'd
Labor Code, **Labor 19**
Occupational safety and health, **Labor 6302**
State Departments, generally, this index

DEPENDENT ADULTS
Abuse,
Confidential or privileged information, reports, **Welf & I 15633 et seq.**
Privileges and immunities, reports, **Welf & I 15634**
Banks and banking, financial abuse, reports, **Welf & I 15630.1**
Caregivers, employees, statements, abuse reporting, statutory knowledge, **Welf & I 15659**
Confidential or privileged information, abuse, reports, **Welf & I 15633 et seq.**
Credit unions, financial abuse, reports, **Welf & I 15630.1**
Financial institutions, financial abuse, reports, **Welf & I 15630.1**
Forms, reports, abuse, **Welf & I 15659**
Savings and loan associations, financial abuse, reports, **Welf & I 15630.1**

DEPENDENT CHILDREN
Juvenile Delinquents and Dependents, generally, this index

DEPENDENTS
Definitions,
Elected public officials killed in office, college scholarships, **Labor 4728**
Public employees retirement system, scholarships, **Labor 4709**
Workers compensation, asbestos workers, **Labor 4402**
Elected public officials killed in office, scholarships, **Labor 4728**
Health Care Service Plans, this index
Juvenile Delinquents and Dependents, generally, this index
Workers Compensation, this index

DEPOSITION OFFICER
Definitions, employment records, subpoena duces tecum, **CCP 1985.6**

DEPOSITIONS
Attorney fees, workers compensation, **Labor 5710**
Fair employment and housing, **Gov 12972**
Fair employment and housing department, **Gov 12930, 12963.3**
Labor and employment, occupational safety and health, hearing officers, witnesses, **Labor 6613**
Labor commissioner, deputies and assistants, **Labor 92**
Labor statistics and research division, chief and employees, **Labor 152**
Occupational safety and health, **Labor 6314**
Unemployment compensation, appeals board, power to take, **Un Ins 1953**

DEPOSITIONS—Cont'd
Workers compensation proceedings, **Labor 5710**

DEPOSITS
Asbestos training approval account, **Labor 9021.9**
Bank Deposits and Collections, generally, this index
Cash bond of employee, **Labor 402 et seq.**
Contractors, this index
Definitions, employment agency regulation, **CC 1812.501**
Employees, cash bond, **Labor 402 et seq.**
Industrial relations unpaid wage fund, **Labor 96.7**
Excess amounts, **Labor 96.7**
Self insurance plans fund, workers compensation, **Labor 3702.5**
Special occupations, security for payment of wages, **Labor 270.5 et seq.**
State Treasury, this index
Talent agencies, bonds (officers and fiduciaries), **Labor 1703.3**
Unpaid wages or benefits, **Labor 96.7**
Wages,
Security for payment, special occupations, **Labor 270.5 et seq.**
Unpaid wages or benefits, **Labor 96.7**
Workers Compensation, this index

DEPOSITS IN BANKS
Bank Deposits and Collections, generally, this index

DESCENT AND DISTRIBUTION
Probate Proceedings, generally, this index

DESERTION
Juvenile Delinquents and Dependents, generally, this index
Support, generally, this index

DESTITUTE PERSONS
Indigent Persons, generally, this index

DESTRUCTIVE DEVICES
Explosives, generally, this index

DETECTIVES
Private Investigators, generally, this index

DETENTION FACILITIES
Juvenile Institutions and Schools, generally, this index

DEVELOPMENTAL DISABILITIES
Mentally Retarded and Developmentally Disabled Persons, generally, this index

DEVELOPMENTAL SERVICES DEPARTMENT
Disclosure, unemployment compensation information, **Un Ins 1095**
Unemployment compensation information, disclosure, **Un Ins 1095**

DEVELOPMENTALLY DISABLED PERSONS
Mentally Retarded and Developmentally Disabled Persons, generally, this index

DIAGNOSTIC LABORATORIES
Laboratories, generally, this index

DIAL A RIDE
Paratransit Vehicles, generally, this index

DIALYSIS
Workers compensation, fees, **Labor 5307.1**

DIESEL ENGINES
Mines and mining, underground use, labor permits, **Labor 6500**

DILAUDID
Drug Addicts, generally, this index

DIRECTORS
Associations and Societies, this index
Benefit Payments Department, this index
Corporations, this index
Definitions,
Children and minors, appointment, **Labor 1286**
Employment development department, automation reports, **Un Ins 4900**
Fair employment and housing department, **Gov 12925**
Labor Code, **Labor 20**
Occupational safety and health, **Labor 6302**
Workers compensation, **Labor 3700.1**
Self insurance, **Labor 3741**
Employment Development Department, this index
Fair Employment and Housing Department, this index
Industrial Relations Department, this index
Occupational safety and health, annual reports, **Labor 6330**
State compensation insurance fund, **Labor 57.5**
Television and radio, talent services, fees, **Labor 1701 et seq.**
Theaters and shows, talent services, fees, **Labor 1701 et seq.**
Unemployment Compensation, this index

DIRKS
Weapons, generally, this index

DISABILITY BENEFITS
Workers Compensation, this index

DISABILITY COMPENSATION
Social Security, this index
Unemployment Compensation, this index

DISABILITY FUND
Definitions, unemployment compensation, **Un Ins 134.5**

DISABILITY INSURANCE
Insurance, this index

DISABILITY RETIREMENT
County Officers and Employees Retirement Systems, this index
Public Employees Retirement System, this index
Schoolteachers Retirement System, this index

DISABLED
Definitions, housing discrimination, **Gov 12955.3**

DISABLED PERSONS
Handicapped Persons, generally, this index

DISASTER COUNCIL
Definitions, workers compensation, **Labor 3211.9**

DISASTER RELIEF
Medical records, disclosure, **CC 56.10**

DISASTER SERVICE
Definitions, workers compensation, **Labor 3211.93, 3211.93a**

DISASTER SERVICE WORKERS
Benefits, **Labor 3600.6**
Definitions, **Labor 3211.92**
    Workers compensation, **Labor 3211.92**
War and Civil Defense, this index
Workers Compensation, this index

DISASTERS
Disaster council. War and Civil Defense, this index
Medical records, disaster relief organizations, disclosure, **CC 56.10**
Temporary employees, unemployment compensation, **Un Ins 634.5**
War and Civil Defense, generally, this index

DISCHARGE
Firefighters and Fire Departments, this index
Janitors, **Labor 1060 et seq.**
Labor and Employment, this index
Military Forces, this index

DISCHARGING
Weapons, this index

DISCIPLINE
Abuse of patient reports, protection, **Pen 11161.8**
Contractors, this index
Electricity, apprentices, **Labor 3099.2**
Health Care Providers, this index
Hospitals, this index
Labor and Employment, this index
Nurses, this index
Physicians and Surgeons, this index
State Officers and Employees, this index

DISCLOSURE
Adult abuse report information, **Welf & I 15633 et seq.**
AIDS, this index
Attorney Fees, this index

DISCLOSURE—Cont'd
Boards and Commissions, this index
Business and Commerce, this index
California State University. Colleges and Universities, this index
Car washes, registration, fines and penalties, **Labor 2061**
Chiropractors, this index
Clinics, this index
Colleges and Universities, this index
Community colleges and districts. Colleges and Universities, this index
Consumer Credit Reporting Agencies, this index
Corporate Criminal Liability Act, **Pen 387**
Crimes and Offenses, this index
Dangerous business practices, failure to disclose, crimes and offenses, **Pen 387**
Dangers, business practices, failure to disclose, crimes and offenses, **Pen 387**
Day Care and Nursery Schools, this index
Definitions, Information Practices Act, **CC 1798.3**
Dependent adult abuse report information, **Welf & I 15633 et seq.**
Diversion programs, referrals or participation, job applicants, **Labor 432.7**
Elevators, dumbwaiters and escalators, certificates and certification, bids and bidding, **Labor 7311.1**
Hazardous Substances and Waste, this index
Health Care Providers, this index
Health Care Service Plans, this index
Health Facilities, this index
Information practices, **CC 1798 et seq.**
Injunction, this index
Insurance, this index
Invasion of privacy, Information Practices Act, **CC 1798.53**
Labor and Employment, this index
Medical Records, this index
Nursing Homes, this index
Occupational safety and health. Labor and Employment, this index
Osteopaths, this index
Peace Officers, this index
Personal information, **CC 1798 et seq.**
Physicians and Surgeons, this index
Residential Care Facilities for the Elderly, this index
School Officers and Employees, this index
Sex Offenders, this index
State Agencies, this index
State Departments, this index
State Hospitals, this index
State Officers and Employees, this index
Support, this index
Talent agencies, contracts, **Labor 1703**
Unemployment Compensation, this index
Veterans, inspector general for veterans affairs, **Mil & V 73.7**
Whistle Blowing, this index
Workers Compensation, this index

DISCOUNTS
Labor, payment, **Labor 212**

DISCOVERY
Admissions, generally, this index
Depositions, generally, this index
Employment records, **CCP 1985.6**
Fair Employment and Housing, this index
Fines and penalties, sexual conduct, motions, **CCP 2017.220**
Immigration, this index
Labor and employment, records, **CCP 1985.6**
Motions, sexual conduct, **CCP 2017.220**
Officers and employees, records, **CCP 1985.6**
Production of Books and Papers, generally, this index
Requests for admissions. Admissions, generally, this index
Sexual conduct, scope of discovery, **CCP 2017.220**
Workers compensation, medical evaluations, **Labor 4062.3**

DISCRIMINATION
Generally, **Const. Art. 1, §§ 8, 31; CC 51 et seq.**
Accomplices and accessories, **CC 52**
Actions and proceedings, **CC 52**
    Affirmative action, challenges, **Gov 8315**
    Employee rights, **Labor 98.6, 98.7**
Affirmative Action, generally, this index
Aiders and abettors, **CC 52**
AIDS, this index
AmeriCorps, overtime, **Labor 1171**
Apprentices, this index
Attorney fees, **CC 52**
    Compensation and salaries, actions, **Labor 1197.5**
Business and Commerce, this index
Businesses, professions or employment, **Const. Art. 1, § 8**
Civil air patrol, labor and employment, **Labor 1502, 1506**
Clothing, labor and employment, **Gov 12947.5**
Colleges and Universities, this index
Damages, **CC 52**
    Compensation and salaries, **Labor 1197.5**
    Occupational safety and health, employees filing complaints, **Labor 6312**
Deeds and Conveyances, this index
Definitions, **CC 51; Gov 8315**
    Fair employment and housing department, **Gov 12927**
    Health facilities, whistleblowers, **Health & S 1278.5**
    Housing, disabled persons, **Gov 12955.1**
    Race, **Gov 8315**
Domestic Partnership, this index
Electricity, apprentices, standards, labor organizations, **Labor 3099**
Employment. Labor and Employment, this index
Evidence,
    Affirmative action, **Gov 8315**
    Handicapped persons, housing practices, **Gov 12955.8**

DISCRIMINATION

DISCRIMINATION—Cont'd

Fair Employment and Housing, generally, this index

Fair Employment and Housing Department, generally, this index

Fines and penalties, **CC 52**
  Apprenticeship programs, **Labor 3095**

Firefighters and Fire Departments, this index

Force and violence,
  Fines and penalties, **CC 52**
  Freedom from discrimination, **CC 51.7**

Gender violence, actions and proceedings, **CC 52.4**

Group disability insurance, domestic partnership, **Ins 10121.7**

Handicapped Persons, this index

Health Care Service Plans, this index

Health Facilities, this index

Housing, this index

Insurance, this index

Investigation and investigators, occupational safety and health, employees filing complaints, **Labor 6312**

Jurisdiction, actions and proceedings, **CC 52.2**

Labor and Employment, this index

Labor Organizations, this index

Licenses and permits, **Gov 12944**

Limitation of actions, fines and penalties, **CC 52**

Marital status, civil rights, **CC 51**

Military Forces, this index

Mortgages, this index

Multiple listing service, **Gov 12955 et seq.**

National service programs, overtime, **Labor 1171**

Notice, occupational safety and health, employees filing complaints, **Labor 6312**

Nurses, this index

Occupational safety and health, **Labor 6310 et seq.**
  Discrimination against employees for filing complaints, **Labor 6312**

Overtime, national service programs, **Labor 1171**

Pants, labor and employment, **Gov 12947.5**

Peace Officers, this index

Police, this index

Professions and Occupations, this index

Public policy, employment, **Gov 12920.5**

Real Estate, this index

School Officers and Employees, this index

Sexual Orientation, this index

Small claims courts, jurisdiction, **CC 52.2**

State, proposed amendment, **Const. Art. 1, § 31**

State Contracts, this index

Statute of limitations, fines and penalties, **CC 52**

Talent agencies, **Labor 1700.47**

Unemployment compensation, termination of employment, eligibility for benefits, **Un Ins 1256.2**

DISCRIMINATION—Cont'd

Universities. Colleges and Universities, this index

Unruh Civil Rights Act, **CC 51**

Veterans, fair employment housing, **Gov 12940**

Violence, freedom from, **CC 51.7**
  Fines and penalties, **CC 52**

Wage rates, **Labor 1197.5**

Wearing apparel, labor and employment, **Gov 12947.5**

Workers Compensation, this index

DISEASE MANAGEMENT ORGANIZATIONS
Medical records, disclosure, **CC 56.10**

DISEASES
Acquired immune deficiency syndrome (AIDS). AIDS, generally, this index

AIDS, generally, this index

Alcoholism, recovery home residents, unemployment compensation benefits, **Un Ins 2626.1**

Bloodborne infectious diseases, workers compensation, presumptions, **Labor 3212.8**

Cancer, generally, this index

Children and Minors, this index

Epidemics, druggists, hours of labor, **Labor 854**

Genetic characteristics,
  Definitions, fair employment and housing, **Gov 12926**
  Fair employment and housing, testing, **Gov 12940**

Heart Disease, generally, this index

Industrial homework, illness of homeworker, **Labor 2661**

Managers and management, medical records, disclosure, **CC 56.10**

Medical records, disclosure, managers and management, **CC 56.10**

Occupational Diseases, generally, this index

Pneumonia, generally, this index

Tuberculosis, generally, this index

DISHONOR
Negotiable Instruments, this index

DISINTERMENT
Cemeteries and Dead Bodies, this index

DISMISSAL AND NONSUIT
Fair employment and housing, complaints, **Gov 12981.1**

Workers Compensation, this index

DISPENSARIES
Clinics, generally, this index

DISPENSING UNIT
Definitions, liquified petroleum gas installation, inspections, **Labor 7681**

DISPLACED JANITOR OPPORTUNITY ACT
Generally, **Labor 1060 et seq.**

DISPLACED WORKERS
Janitors, **Labor 1060 et seq.**

On the job training programs, **Labor 3093**

Public transit, **Labor 1070 et seq.**

DISPUTE RESOLUTION
Arbitration and Award, generally, this index

Mediation, generally, this index

DISSOLUTION
Corporations, this index

Limited Liability Companies, this index

Marriage, this index

DISSOLUTION OF MARRIAGE
Marriage, this index

DISTILLED SPIRITS
Alcoholic Beverages, generally, this index

DISTRESSED PERSONS
Social Services, generally, this index

DISTRICT ATTORNEYS
Civil rights actions, **CC 52**

Heart trouble, workers compensation, **Labor 3212**

Hernias, workers compensation, **Labor 3212**

Indictment and Information, generally, this index

Investigations and investigators, workers compensation, meningitis, presumptions, **Labor 3212.9**

Labor and employment,
  Children and minors, enforcement of law, **Labor 1312, 1399**
  Compensation, authority to prosecute actions for failure to pay, **Labor 218**

Leaves of absence, inspectors, investigators, workers compensation, disability benefits, **Labor 4850**

Medical records, negligence, release, **CC 56.36**

Public utilities, fines for failure to furnish letter to employee leaving service, collection, **Labor 1056**

Railroads, hours of labor, violations, recovery of penalties, **Labor 605**

Social Services, this index

Workers compensation,
  Action against employer for failure to secure full payment of compensation, **Labor 3712**
  Hernia, heart trouble and pneumonia, **Labor 3212**
  Investigators and inspectors, leaves of absence, disability benefits, **Labor 4850**

DISTRICT OF COLUMBIA
State, definitions, unemployment compensation, **Un Ins 139**

DISTRICTS
Community colleges and districts. Colleges and Universities, this index

DISTRICTS—Cont'd
Compensation and salaries,
Itemized statement, deductions, **Labor 226**
Officers and employees, itemized statements, deductions, application of law, **Labor 226**
Employees. Officers and employees, generally, post
Employment compensation, employer, definitions, **Un Ins 677**
Irrigation and Irrigation Districts, generally, this index
Labor and employment. Officers and employees, generally, post
Local Agencies, generally, this index
Officers and employees,
Compensation and salaries,
Itemized statement, deductions, application of law, **Labor 226**
Leave of absence for military duty, **Mil & V 395.01 et seq.**
Minimum wages, **Labor 1205**
Hours of labor, **Labor 1205**
Leave of absence for military duty, **Mil & V 395 et seq.**
Lie detector tests as condition of employment, **Labor 432.2**
Minimum wages, **Labor 1205**
Resignation, military service entry, reentry into office or employment on discharge, **Mil & V 395.3**
Social Security, generally, this index
Soldiers and Sailors Relief Act, **Mil & V 395.1**
Special districts, post
Standards, labor and employment, **Labor 1205**
Public entity, unemployment compensation, **Un Ins 135, 605**
Public officers and employees. Officers and employees, generally, ante
Recreation and Park Districts, generally, this index
Schools and School Districts, generally, this index
Screening, prospective concessionaires, criminal history information, students summary, **Labor 432.7**
Special districts,
Commercial vehicles, officers and employees, meals, collective bargaining, **Labor 512.5**
Meals, officers and employees, motor carriers, collective bargaining, **Labor 512.5**
Motor carriers, officers and employees, meals, collective bargaining, **Labor 512.5**
Officers and employees,
Commercial vehicles, meals, collective bargaining, **Labor 512.5**
Meals, motor carriers, collective bargaining, **Labor 512.5**
Motor carriers, meals, collective bargaining, **Labor 512.5**

DISTRICTS—Cont'd
Special districts—Cont'd
Officers and employees—Cont'd
Rest periods, motor carriers, collective bargaining, **Labor 512.5**
Rest periods, officers and employees, motor carriers, collective bargaining, **Labor 512.5**
Transit Districts, generally, this index
Unemployment compensation,
Elective coverage, **Un Ins 709**
Employing unit, **Un Ins 135**
Qualifications, **Un Ins 605**
Water Districts, generally, this index

DIVERSION PROGRAMS
Crimes and Offenses, this index
Definitions, labor and employment, job applicants, referrals, disclosure, **Labor 432.7**
Records and recordation, job applicants, disclosure, **Labor 432.7**

DIVIDENDS
Workers Compensation, this index

DIVISIONS
Contracts. State Contracts, generally, this index
Definitions,
Elevators, dumbwaiters and escalators, **Labor 7300.1**
Industrial homework, **Labor 2650**
Occupational Carcinogens Control Act, **Labor 9005**
Occupational safety and health, **Labor 6302**
Tunnel and mine safety, **Labor 7951**
Industrial relations department, **Labor 56 et seq.**
Juvenile Facilities Division, generally, this index
Workers Compensation, this index

DIVORCE
Dissolution of marriage. Marriage, this index

DOCKETS
Workers compensation, awards of judgment, fees and costs, **Labor 5811**

DOCKS
Wharves, Docks and Piers, generally, this index

DOCTORS
Physicians and Surgeons, generally, this index

DOLLS
Industrial homework, manufacturer, **Labor 2651**

DOMESTIC ABUSE
Domestic Violence, generally, this index

DOMESTIC AGENCIES
Definitions, employment agency regulation, **CC 1812.501**

DOMESTIC ANIMALS
Animals, generally, this index

DOMESTIC CORPORATIONS
Corporations, generally, this index

DOMESTIC INSURERS
Insurance, generally, this index

DOMESTIC LABOR
Domestic Service or Work, generally, this index

DOMESTIC LIMITED LIABILITY COMPANY
Limited Liability Companies, generally, this index

DOMESTIC PARTNERSHIP
Generally, **Fam 297 et seq.**
Abuse. Domestic Violence, generally, this index
Age, **Fam 297**
Annulment, **Fam 298.5, 299**
Jurisdiction, **Fam 298**
Application of law, **Fam 297**
Certificates and certification, **Fam 298.5**
Change of name. Names, post
Children and minors,
Powers and duties, **Fam 297.5**
Termination, **Fam 299**
Community property, **Fam 299**
Consent, **Fam 297**
Crimes and offenses, forms, **Fam 298**
Death, powers and duties, **Fam 297.5**
Debtors and creditors, termination, **Fam 299**
Declarations, **Fam 297, 298, 298.5**
Definitions, **Fam 297**
Disability compensation, filing, claims, **Un Ins 2705.1**
Discrimination, **Fam 297.5**
Group disability insurance, **Ins 10121.7**
Health care service plans, **Health & S 1374.58**
Dissolution. Termination, generally, post
Domicile and residence, **Fam 297**
Termination, **Fam 299**
Drivers licenses, identity and identification, **Fam 298.6**
Duress or coercion, termination, vacating or setting aside, **Fam 299**
Employment, sick leave, **Labor 233, 234**
Family care leave, serious health conditions, **Un Ins 3300 et seq.**
Fees, registration, **Fam 298**
Filing, declarations, **Fam 297**
Foreign states, full faith and credit, **Fam 299.2**
Former partners, powers and duties, **Fam 297.5**
Forms, **Fam 298, 298.5**
Fraud, termination, vacating or setting aside, **Fam 299**
Full faith and credit, **Fam 299.2**
Group disability insurance, discrimination, **Ins 10121.7**
Health care service plans, **Health & S 1374.58**

DOMESTIC

DOMESTIC PARTNERSHIP—Cont'd
Illness, family care leave, **Un Ins 3300 et seq.**
Injuries, family care leave, **Un Ins 3300 et seq.**
Insurance, discrimination, group disability insurance, **Ins 10121.7**
Jurisdiction, **Fam 298**
  Termination, **Fam 299**
Labor and employment, sick leave, **Labor 233, 234**
Legal separation, **Fam 299**
  Jurisdiction, **Fam 298**
Mail and mailing, termination, **Fam 299**
Mistake, termination, vacating or setting aside, **Fam 299**
Names,
  Certificates and certification, **Fam 298.5**
  Change of name, **Fam 298.6**
    Forms, **Fam 298**
Notaries public, forms, **Fam 298**
Notice,
  Secretary of state, registration, **Fam 299.3**
  Termination, **Fam 298 et seq.**
Paid family care leave, serious health conditions, **Un Ins 3300 et seq.**
Powers and duties, **Fam 297.5**
Preemption, **Fam 299.6**
Real estate, termination, **Fam 299**
Registration, **Fam 297 et seq., 298, 298.5**
Relatives, **Fam 297**
Secretary of state,
  Declarations, filing, **Fam 297**
  Forms, **Fam 298, 298.5**
  Notice, registration, **Fam 299.3**
  Termination, filing, **Fam 299**
Sick leave, **Labor 233**
  Violations, **Labor 234**
Support, termination, waiver, **Fam 299**
Survivors, powers and duties, **Fam 297.5**
Termination, **Fam 298.5, 299**
  Forms, **Fam 298, 298.5**
  Jurisdiction, **Fam 298**
Time, termination, **Fam 299**
Unemployment compensation,
  Disability compensation, filing, claims, **Un Ins 2705.1**
  Family care leave, serious health conditions, **Un Ins 3300 et seq.**
Vacating or setting aside, termination, **Fam 299**

DOMESTIC SERVICE OR WORK
Children and minors, hours of labor, **Labor 1392, 1394**
Compensation, time due and payable, **Labor 205**
Employment agencies, domestic worker employer status, conditions, **CC 1812.5095; Un Ins 687.2, 13005.7**
Unemployment compensation, **Un Ins 629, 639, 682, 935**
  Application of law, **Un Ins 684, 685**
  County in home supportive services program, coverage, **Un Ins 683**
  Homes, **Un Ins 682**

DOMESTIC SERVICE OR WORK—Cont'd
Unemployment compensation—Cont'd
  In home supportive services program, coverage, **Un Ins 683**
  Local college clubs, **Un Ins 682**
  Private homes, **Un Ins 682**
  Service in local college club, **Un Ins 639**
  Wage reports, telephone filing, **Un Ins 1118**
Workers compensation, **Labor 3352**
  County in home supportive services programs, **Labor 3351.5**

DOMESTIC VIOLENCE
Colleges and universities, injunction, **CCP 527.85**
Corporal injuries, weapons, prior convictions, possession, **Pen 12021**
Definitions, labor and employment, time off, **Labor 230, 230.1**
Discrimination, labor and employment, **Labor 230**
Emotional and mental support, support person accompanying party in court, **CCP 527.6**
Firearms.   Weapons, generally, post
Forms, injunctions, temporary restraining orders, **CCP 527.6, 527.8**
Labor and employment, time off, **Labor 230.1**
  Courts, appearances, **Labor 230**
Limitation of actions, labor and employment,
  Discrimination, **Labor 230**
  Time off, **Labor 230.1**
Moral support, support person accompanying party in court, **CCP 527.6**
Notice.   Protective orders, post
Orders of court.   Protective orders, generally, post
Protective orders,
  Fines and penalties, weapons, **Pen 12021**
  Notice, weapons, **Pen 12021**
  Weapons, **CCP 527.6**
    Acquisition of firearms by restrainees, **Pen 12021**
    Fines and penalties, **Pen 12021**
Support persons, accompanying party in court, **CCP 527.6**
Unemployment compensation, reasons for leaving employment, **Un Ins 1030, 1032, 1256**
Weapons,
  Crimes and offenses, **Pen 12021**
  Protective orders, ante

DOMESTIC WATER SUPPLIERS
Water Supply, generally, this index

DOMESTIC WORKERS
Employment Agencies, this index

DOMICILE AND RESIDENCE
Abandoned or unclaimed property, owner, intangibles, **CCP 1510**
Definitions, withholding tax on wages, **Un Ins 13003**

DOMICILE AND RESIDENCE—Cont'd
Domestic partnership, **Fam 297**
  Termination, **Fam 299**
Unemployment compensation, foreign, states, effect upon eligibility, **Un Ins 455.7**
Withholding tax on wages, **Un Ins 13020**

DOOR TO DOOR SALES
Definitions,
  Employment of children, **Labor 1286**
  Unemployment compensation, **Un Ins 13004.1**

DOUBLE DAMAGES
Damages, this index

DRAFTS
Building and construction industry, payment of wages or fringe benefits, insufficient funds, **Labor 203.1**

DRAINS AND DRAINAGE
Zoning and Planning, generally, this index

DRAMA
Compensation and salaries, deposits for security of payment, **Labor 271**
Definitions, child labor, **Labor 1390**

DRAWINGS
Gambling, generally, this index

DRAYMEN
Mechanics Liens, generally, this index

DRILL INSTRUCTION
Military Forces, this index

DRILLS AND DRILLING
Oil and Gas, this index

DRINKING WATER
Water Supply, generally, this index

DRINKS
Alcoholic Beverages, generally, this index

DRIVERS LICENSES
Motor Vehicles, this index

DROPOUTS
High Schools or Secondary Schools, this index

DROUGHT
Water Supply, generally, this index

DRUG ABUSE
Drug Addicts, generally, this index

DRUG ADDICTS
Crimes and offenses, weapons, **Pen 12021**
Criminal history information, transportation, volunteers, **Pen 11105.3**
Disability compensation, disqualification, **Un Ins 2678**
Purchases, weapons, crimes and offenses, **Pen 12021**
Transportation, volunteers, criminal history information, **Pen 11105.3**

DRUG ADDICTS—Cont'd
Volunteers, transportation, criminal history information, **Pen 11105.3**
Weapons, possession, **Pen 12021**

DRUG FREE WORKPLACE ACT
Generally, **Gov 8350 et seq.**

DRUGGISTS
Pharmacists, generally, this index

DRUGS AND MEDICINE
Abuse,
Addicts. Drug Addicts, generally, this index
Drug Addicts, generally, this index
Addicts. Drug Addicts, generally, this index
Dangerous drugs or devices. Hypodermic Syringes and Needles, generally, this index
Generic drugs, workers compensation, **Labor 4600.1**
Grants, state grantees, drug free workplaces, **Gov 8350 et seq.**
Hazardous Substances and Waste, generally, this index
Health Care Service Plans, this index
Hours of labor, **Labor 850 et seq.**
Hypodermic Syringes and Needles, generally, this index
Industrial homework, manufacturer, **Labor 2651**
Labor and Employment, this index
Needles. Hypodermic Syringes and Needles, generally, this index
Pharmacists, generally, this index
Rehabilitation, labor and employment, voluntary enrollment, **Labor 1025 et seq.**
State contracts, drug free workplaces, **Gov 8350 et seq.**
Syringes. Hypodermic Syringes and Needles, generally, this index
Unemployment Compensation, this index
Weapons, this index
Workers Compensation, this index

DRUGSTORES
Pharmacists, generally, this index

DUMBWAITERS
Elevators, Dumbwaiters and Escalators, generally, this index

DURESS OR COERCION
Domestic partnership, termination, vacating or setting aside, **Fam 299**
Employment. Labor and Employment, this index
Fair employment and housing, fines and penalties, **Gov 12987**
Handicapped persons, housing rights, **Gov 12955.7**
Labor and Employment, this index
Labor organizations, agreement not to join, **Labor 922**

DURESS OR COERCION—Cont'd
Officers and employees, particular course or line of political action or activity, **Labor 1101 et seq.**
Purchases by employees, **Labor 450 et seq.**
School Officers and Employees, this index
State Officers and Employees, this index
Whistle Blowing, this index

DWELLINGS
Housing, generally, this index

DYNAMITE
Explosives, generally, this index

EARNED INCOME TAX CREDIT INFORMATION ACT
Generally, **Rev & T 19850 et seq.**

EARNINGS
Compensation and Salaries, generally, this index

EARNINGS ASSIGNMENT ORDER FOR SUPPORT
Definitions,
Garnishment, **CCP 706.011**
Support enforcement, **Fam 5208**

EARNINGS WITHHOLDING ORDERS
Garnishment, this index

EARS
Deaf and Mute Persons, generally, this index

EARTHQUAKES
Temporary public employees, unemployment compensation, excluded service, **Un Ins 634.5**
Unemployment compensation, temporary public officers and employees, excluded service, **Un Ins 634.5**

EASEMENTS
Zoning and Planning, generally, this index

EATING PLACES
Restaurants, generally, this index

ECONOMIC DEVELOPMENT
Enterprise Zones, generally, this index
Los Angeles Revitalization Zone, generally, this index
Self employment assistance program, unemployment compensation, **Un Ins 1300 et seq.**

ECONOMIC DEVELOPMENT DEPARTMENT
Contracts, deaf, hearing impaired persons, employment services, **Un Ins 11000 et seq.**

ECONOMIC OPPORTUNITY
Workers compensation, **Labor 4201 et seq.**

ECONOMICS
Family economics security, job preparation and training services. Unemployment Compensation, this index

ECONOMICS—Cont'd
Job preparation and training services. Unemployment Compensation, this index

EDUCATION
Generally, **Labor 6350 et seq.**
Agricultural labor and employment, farm labor contractors, **Labor 1682.8**
Apprentices, generally, this index
Career preparation. Vocational Education, generally, this index
Career resource network, **Educ 53086**
Colleges and Universities, generally, this index
Day Care and Nursery Schools, generally, this index
Electricity, this index
Employee literacy education assistance, **Labor 1040 et seq.**
Farm labor contractors, **Labor 1682.8**
Labor and Employment, this index
Literacy, employee literacy education assistance, **Labor 1040 et seq.**
Nurses, this index
Occupational health, local health departments promoting, **Health & S 105150**
Public benefit corporations, religious organizations and societies, labor and employment, **Gov 12926.2**
Regional occupational centers. Vocational Education, this index
Regional youth education facilities. Juvenile Institutions and Schools, this index
Retraining benefits, unemployment insurance, **Un Ins 1266 et seq.**
Schools and School Districts, generally, this index
Small businesses, unemployment compensation, **Un Ins 1231**
Talent agencies, exemptions,
Advance fees, **Labor 1702.4**
Fees, **Labor 1703.6**
Training, generally, this index
Unemployment Compensation, this index
Vocational Education, generally, this index
Worker safety and health training and education program, **Labor 6354.7**
Workers Compensation, this index
Workforce investment, **Un Ins 14500 et seq.**

EDUCATION DEPARTMENT
Labor market information, **Un Ins 10530 et seq.**

EDUCATIONAL INSTITUTIONS
Education, generally, this index

EDUCATIONAL PERSONNEL
School Officers and Employees, generally, this index

EFFLUENT
Sewers and Sewer Systems, generally, this index

EIGHT

EIGHT HOUR ACT
Generally, **Labor 500 et seq.**

EIGHT HOUR LAW (MINORS)
Generally, **Labor 1390 et seq.**

EJECTMENT
Labor camps, tenant or employee exercising rights, **Health & S 17031.5**

ELDERLY PERSONS
Aged Persons, generally, this index

ELECTED OFFICERS
Unemployment compensation, excluded service, **Un Ins 634.5**

ELECTED PUBLIC OFFICIALS
Definitions, death benefits, **Labor 4720**

ELECTION PRECINCTS
Boards and commissions,
    Absence, members, employment, suspension or discharge, **Elec 12312**
    Discharge or suspension from regular employment, **Elec 12312**
    Suspension or discharge from regular employment, **Elec 12312**

ELECTIONS
Agricultural Labor Relations Act of 1975, **Labor 1156 et seq.**
Ballots,
    Emergencies, provisional ballots, **Elec 14313**
    Provisional ballots, emergencies, **Elec 14313**
Campaigns,
    Employment, disability compensation, **Un Ins 2606**
    Unemployment compensation coverage, **Un Ins 636**
    Workers, unemployment compensation, **Un Ins 636**
Candidates. Campaigns, generally, ante
Corporations, this index
Disability insurance, Cal COBRA, **Ins 10128.55**
Election Precincts, generally, this index
Emergencies, provisional ballots, **Elec 14313**
Employment. Labor and employment, generally, post
Health Care Service Plans, this index
Instructions. Ballots, ante
Insurance, this index
Labor and employment,
    Hours of labor, smelters and underground workers, **Labor 750.5**
    Political activities of employees, **Labor 1101 et seq.**
    Time off, voting, **Elec 14000 et seq.**
Labor organizations, employment for voting purposes only, **Labor 1154.6**
Notice,
    Posting by employer, free time for voting, **Elec 14001**
    Presidential primary, post
    Primary elections, post

ELECTIONS—Cont'd
Officers of election,
    Discharge, absent from work, **Elec 12312**
    Election Precincts, generally, this index
    Unemployment compensation, excluded service, **Un Ins 634.5**
Political campaigns. Campaigns, generally, ante
Posting, free time for voting, notice, **Elec 14001**
Precincts. Election Precincts, generally, this index
Presidential primary,
    Employees, time off, voting, **Elec 14000 et seq.**
    Notice, free time for voting, posting by employer, **Elec 14001**
Primary elections,
    Employees, time off, voting, **Elec 14000 et seq.**
    Notice, labor and employment, time for voting, **Elec 14001**
Privileges and immunities, **Elec 14000 et seq.**
Procedures, election day procedures, **Elec 14000 et seq.**
Provisional ballots. Ballots, ante
State Officers and Employees, this index
Time, employees, time off, voting, **Elec 14000 et seq.**
Unemployment compensation, political campaign workers, **Un Ins 636**
Voting privileges, **Elec 14000 et seq.**

ELECTORS
Elections, generally, this index

ELECTRIC RAILROADS
Cars, laminated safety glass, **Labor 6953 et seq.**
Motorman, necessity of presence, **Labor 6901**
Safeguards, **Labor 6800**
    Exemptions, **Labor 6910**
Use of electric locomotive at rear of train, **Labor 7000**

ELECTRICITY
Advisory committees, apprentices, standards, **Labor 3099**
Apprentices, **Labor 3099 et seq.**
Certificates and certification,
    Apprentices, **Labor 3099 et seq.**
    Educational curriculum standards, **Labor 3099**
Certification curriculum committee, **Labor 3099**
Colleges and Universities, this index
Committees, electrical certification curriculum committee, **Labor 3099**
Continuing education, apprentices, **Labor 3099.2**
Contractors, apprentices, **Labor 3099 et seq.**
Deadlines, certificates and certification, **Labor 3099.2**

ELECTRICITY—Cont'd
Discipline, apprentices, **Labor 3099.2**
Discrimination, apprentices, standards, labor organizations, **Labor 3099**
Education, apprentices, standards, **Labor 3099**
Educational curriculum standards, **Labor 3099**
Equipment, occupational lead poisoning, **Health & S 105185 et seq.**
Examinations and examiners, apprentices, certificates and certification, **Labor 3099.4**
Fees, apprentices,
    Registration, **Labor 3099.4**
    Standards, **Labor 3099**
Foreign languages, apprentices, certificates and certification, **Labor 3099.3**
Funds, electrician certification fund, **Labor 3099.5**
Labor organizations, apprentices, standards, discrimination, **Labor 3099**
Lead poisoning, occupational safety, programs, **Health & S 105185 et seq.**
Liens and incumbrances, power furnished for improvement. Mechanics Liens, generally, this index
Mechanics Liens, generally, this index
Notice, educational curriculum, continuation, **Labor 3099**
Registration, apprentices, **Labor 3099.4**
Reports, apprentices, certificates and certification, **Labor 3099.3**
Rules and regulations, apprentices, standards, **Labor 3099**
Standards, educational curriculum standards, **Labor 3099**
Tests, apprentices, standards, **Labor 3099**
Time, apprentices, certificates and certification, **Labor 3099.2**
Training, apprentices, standards, **Labor 3099**
Universities. Colleges and Universities, this index

ELECTRONIC DATA PROCESSING
Computers, generally, this index

ELECTRONIC DEVICES AND EQUIPMENT
Computers, generally, this index

ELECTRONIC MAIL
Colleges and Universities, this index
Workplace violation safety, **CCP 527.8**

ELEEMOSYNARY INSTITUTIONS
Charities, generally, this index

ELEMENTARY SCHOOLS
Schools and School Districts, generally, this index

ELEVATED RAILROADS
Transit Districts, generally, this index

ELEVATOR SAFETY ACCOUNT
Generally, **Labor 7316**

ELEVATORS, DUMBWAITERS AND ESCALATORS

Generally, **Labor 7200 et seq., 7300 et seq.**

Agriculture, mechanics, **Labor 7311.25**

Alterations, **Labor 7305 et seq.**

Appeal and review,
   Civil penalties, **Labor 7321.5**
   Orders for elevator repairs or alterations, **Labor 7307**

Application of law, **Labor 7300.2 et seq.**

Applications, licenses and permits, **Labor 7301**

Bids and bidding, disclosure, certificates and certification, **Labor 7311.1**

Bonds, injunction, operation of elevator, **Labor 7303**

Building standards, **Labor 7324**

Certificates and certification,
   Continuing education, **Labor 7311.3**
   Disclosure, bids and bidding, **Labor 7311.1**
   Fees, **Labor 7311.4**
   Inspection and inspectors, post
   Mechanics, post

Civil penalties. Fines and penalties, generally, post

Competency of inspectors, certificate, **Labor 7311**

Construction elevators, **Labor 7200 et seq.**

Continuing education, certificates and certification, **Labor 7311.3**

Crimes and offenses,
   Construction elevators, safety, **Labor 7205**
   Licenses and permits, **Labor 7302, 7302.1**
   Repairs, operation, **Labor 7307**
   Seat for operator, **Labor 7319**
   Unsafe conditions, **Labor 7322**

Damages, **Labor 7324.1**

Definitions, **Labor 7300.1**
   Multistory dwelling units, handicapped persons, discrimination, **Gov 12955.1**

Disclosure, certificates and certification, bids and bidding, **Labor 7311.1**

Elevator safety account, **Labor 7316**

Emergencies, **Labor 7301.5**

Examinations, elevator inspectors, **Labor 7311**

Exemptions, **Labor 7317**

Expiration, licenses and permits, **Labor 7301**

Fees,
   Certificates and certification, **Labor 7311.4**
   Field consultations, **Labor 7314**
   Inspection, **Labor 7314 et seq.**
   Licenses and permits, **Labor 7301**
   Penalty fees, **Labor 7314**
   Permit processing, **Labor 7314**

Field consultations, fees, **Labor 7314**

Final orders, repairs or alterations to elevators, **Labor 7307**

ELEVATORS, DUMBWAITERS AND ESCALATORS—Cont'd

Fines and penalties,
   Appeal and review, **Labor 7321.5**
   Injunction, operation, **Labor 7303**
   Licenses and permits, **Labor 7302 et seq., 7320**
   Repairs, operation, **Labor 7307**
   Seat for operator, **Labor 7319**
   Unsafe conditions, **Labor 7321, 7322**

Fires and fire protection, **Labor 7301.5**

Hearings,
   Orders, contests, **Labor 7322**
   Repairs or alterations to elevators, preliminary orders, **Labor 7306**
   Revocation of permit, **Labor 7312**

Injunction, operation of elevators, **Labor 7303**

Inspection and inspectors, **Labor 7304 et seq.**
   Appropriation, **Labor 7314**
   Certificates and certification, **Labor 7309.1, 7311, 7311.3**
      Certificate of competency, **Labor 7310**
      Fees, **Labor 7311.4**
   Construction elevators, **Labor 7204**
   Fees, **Labor 7314 et seq.**
   Insurance companies, **Labor 7309**
   Municipalities, **Labor 7310**
   Reports, **Labor 7313**

Insurance,
   Inspection by insurance companies, **Labor 7309**
   Licenses and permits, **Labor 7301**
   Qualified elevator company, **Labor 7311.1**

Insurance companies, inspection, **Labor 7309**

Liability insurance,
   Licenses and permits, **Labor 7301**
   Qualified elevator company, **Labor 7311.1**

Licenses and permits, **Labor 7301 et seq.**
   Fees, **Labor 7314**
   Fines and penalties, **Labor 7320**
   Revocation or suspension, **Labor 7312**

Manlifts, mechanics, **Labor 7311.25**

Marine terminals, mechanics, certificates and certification, **Labor 7311.5**

Mechanics,
   Agriculture, **Labor 7311.25**
   Certificates and certification, **Labor 7311.2, 7311.3**
   Emergencies, **Labor 7301.5**
   Fees, **Labor 7311.4**
   Marine terminals, **Labor 7311.5**
   Emergencies, **Labor 7301.5**

Municipal inspection, **Labor 7310**

Notice, revocation of permit to operate, **Labor 7312**

Offenses. Crimes and offenses, generally, ante

Penalties. Fines and penalties, generally, post

Penalty fees, **Labor 7314**

ELEVATORS, DUMBWAITERS AND ESCALATORS—Cont'd

Permits. Licenses and permits, generally, ante

Posting permits for elevator operation, **Labor 7301**

Preliminary order requiring repairs or alterations, use of elevator pending compliance, **Labor 7305**

Qualifications, elevator inspectors, **Labor 7311**

Qualified elevator company, **Labor 7311.1, 7311.3**
   Fees, **Labor 7311.4**

Records and recordation, continuing education, **Labor 7311.3**

Rehearing, orders for elevator repairs or alterations, **Labor 7307**

Repairs, **Labor 7305 et seq.**
   Preliminary order requiring, use of elevator pending compliance, **Labor 7305**

Reports, safety, **Labor 7316**

Reports of inspection, **Labor 7313**

Rescission, elevator inspectors certificate of competency, **Labor 7311**

Revocation of elevator permit, **Labor 7312**

Rules and regulations, **Labor 7323**

Safety,
   Orders, **Labor 7318**
   Reports, **Labor 7316**

Seat for operator, **Labor 7319**

Signals and signalling devices, construction elevators, **Labor 7201 et seq.**

Temporary permits, repairs, **Labor 7308**

Temporary restraining order, operation of elevators, **Labor 7303**

Time, licenses and permits, **Labor 7301**

Unsafe conditions,
   Crimes and offenses, **Labor 7322**
   Fines and penalties, **Labor 7321**

Withholding of elevator permit because of unsafe conditions, **Labor 7307**

Workers compensation,
   Licenses and permits, **Labor 7301**
   Qualified elevator company, **Labor 7311.1**

ELIGIBLE PARTICIPANTS

Definitions, employment training panel, **Un Ins 10201**

ELIGIBLE SMALL BUSINESS

Definitions, corporation taxes, net operating losses, **Rev & T 24416**

EMBEZZLEMENT

Employment, bond of employee, property put up as, misappropriation by employer, **Labor 405**

EMBLEMENTS

Agricultural Products, generally, this index

EMERGENCIES

Civil air patrol, labor and employment, **Labor 1500 et seq.**

EMERGENCIES—Cont'd
Definitions, hazardous substances information and training, **Labor 6362**
Disaster Service Workers, generally, this index
Druggists, hours of labor, **Labor 854**
Elections, this index
Elevators, dumbwaiters and escalators, **Labor 7301.5**
Firefighters and Fire Departments, this index
First Aid, this index
Hours of labor, **Labor 554**
  Druggists, **Labor 854**
  Smelters, mines, **Labor 751, 751.5**
Labor and Employment, this index
Occupational safety and health standards board, emergency regulations, **Labor 142.4**
Peace Officers, this index
Pharmacists, this index
Police, this index
Public Buildings and Works, this index
Temporary public employees, unemployment compensation, excluded service, **Un Ins 634.5**
Unemployment Compensation, this index

EMERGENCY ENGAGEMENT
Definitions, talent agencies, **Labor 1700.1**

EMERGENCY MEDICAL TECHNICIANS
Privileges and immunities, criminally related personal injuries, reports, **Pen 11161.9**

EMERGENCY SERVICES ACT
Disaster service workers, definitions, workers compensation, **Labor 3211.92**

EMERGENCY VEHICLES
Medical records, disclosure, radio transmissions, **CC 56.10**

EMOLUMENTS
Compensation and Salaries, generally, this index

EMOTIONAL DISTRESS
Fair employment and housing, damages, **Gov 12980**

EMPLOYEE BENEFIT PLAN DISTRIBUTION
Definitions, Unclaimed Property Law, **CCP 1501**

EMPLOYEE HOUSING
  Generally, **Health & S 17000 et seq.**
Labor Camps, generally, this index

EMPLOYEE ILLITERACY ASSISTANCE
Generally, **Labor 1040 et seq.**

EMPLOYEE OWNED CORPORATIONS
Corporations, this index

EMPLOYEE WELFARE BENEFIT PLANS
Medical records, disclosure, **CC 56.10**

EMPLOYEES
Definitions,
  California State University, whistle blowing, **Educ 89572**
  Child care, tax credit, **Rev & T 17052.18**
  Drug free workplaces, state contractors and grantees, **Gov 8351**
  Earned income tax credit, notice, **Rev & T 19852**
  Fair employment and housing department, **Gov 12926**
  Fire departments, **Labor 1961**
  Labor camps and housing, **Health & S 17005**
  Military forces, leave of absence, compensation, **Mil & V 395.02**
  Professional strikebreakers, **Labor 1132.4**
  Public transit, displaced workers, **Labor 1071**
  Unemployment compensation, contractor, **Un Ins 621.5**
  Whistle blowing, **Gov 8547.2**
  Withholding tax on wages, **Un Ins 13004**
  Workers compensation, **Labor 3351, 3352.94**
    Return to work program, **Labor 139.48**
  Workplace violence safety, **CCP 527.8**
Labor and Employment, generally, this index
Officers and Employees, generally, this index
Public Officers and Employees, generally, this index

EMPLOYERS
Definitions,
  Cal COBRA, accident and health insurance, **Health & S 1366.21; Ins 10128.51**
  Care facilities, criminal history information, **Welf & I 15660**
  Community health care workers, assault and battery, records and recordation, **Labor 6332**
  Earned income tax credit, notice, **Rev & T 19852**
  Employment agency regulation, **CC 1812.501**
  Employment training panel, **Un Ins 10201**
  Fair employment and housing department, **Gov 12926**
  Family care and medical leave, **Gov 12945.2**
  In home supportive services, criminal history information, **Welf & I 12301.8**
  Industrial homework, **Labor 2650**
  New hirees, reports, **Un Ins 1088.5**
  Occupational Carcinogens Control Act, **Labor 9006**
  Professional strikebreakers, **Labor 1132.2**

EMPLOYERS—Cont'd
Definitions—Cont'd
  Religious organizations and societies, labor and employment, **Gov 12926.2**
  Sex crimes, records, **Pen 11105.3**
  Sexual harassment, training, **Gov 12950.1**
  Sick leave, **Labor 233**
  State contracts, labor organizations, promotion or deterrence, state funds, **Gov 16645**
  Support enforcement, **Fam 5210**
  Unemployment compensation, **Un Ins 682**
    Motion picture payroll services company, **Un Ins 679**
  Unemployment insurance,
    Artist, **Un Ins 686**
    Domestic service, **Un Ins 684**
    Employment training panel, **Un Ins 10201**
    In home supportive services, **Un Ins 685**
  Withholding tax on wages, **Un Ins 13005**
  Workers compensation,
    Medical provider networks, **Labor 4616.5**
    Power press workers, **Labor 4558**
  Workplace violence safety, **CCP 527.8**
Labor and Employment, generally, this index

EMPLOYERS LIABILITY ACT
Defenses, **Labor 2801**

EMPLOYING UNIT
Definitions, unemployment compensation, **Un Ins 135, 821.4**

EMPLOYMENT
Definitions,
  Family care and medical leave, **Gov 12945.2**
  Unemployment compensation, **Un Ins 632, 642.1, 656**
    Domestic service, **Un Ins 2606.5**
Labor and Employment, generally, this index

EMPLOYMENT AGENCIES
  Generally, **CC 1812.500 et seq.**
Abandonment, job, lack of just cause, fees due, **CC 1812.506**
Actions and proceedings, **CC 1812.523**
Address, contracts, employment agency and jobseeker, inclusion, **CC 1812.504**
Advertisements, **CC 1812.506 et seq.**
  Bonds(officers and fiduciaries), licenses and permits, **CC 1812.5095**
Job orders, **CC 1812.507**
Misrepresentations,
  Earnings of salesmen, brokers or agents, **Labor 976**
  Home health agencies, **CC 1812.508**
  Job listing services, **CC 1812.520**
  Unfair competition, **CC 1812.5095**
Aged persons, **Un Ins 2070 et seq.**

EMPLOYMENT AGENCIES—Cont'd
Agricultural employment, farm labor contractors, **Labor 1682 et seq.**
Application of law, **CC 1812.502**
Assignment of claims against to labor commissioner, **Labor 96**
Attorney fees, **CC 1812.523**
Baby sitters, personal interview and verification of experience prior to placing, **CC 1812.509**
Bonds (officers and fiduciaries), **CC 1812.503**
  Advertising, **CC 1812.5095**
Bondsmen, claims against, assignment to labor commissioner, **Labor 96**
Books and papers. Records and recordation, generally, post
Business schools, application of law, **CC 1812.502**
Cessation of business, cancellation or termination of fiduciary bond, **CC 1812.503**
Child care providers, referrals, trustline registry, **CC 1812.5093**
Children and minors,
  Farm labor contractors, working conditions, **Labor 1698.7**
  Placement, child labor laws, application, **CC 1812.509**
Commissions (compensation), fees, calculation, **CC 1812.505**
Compensation and salaries,
  Advertised salary, starting salary, **CC 1812.508**
  Calculation of fees, **CC 1812.505**
  Less than agreed upon, fees due upon termination of employment, **CC 1812.506**
  Misrepresentations, salesmen, brokers or agents earnings, **Labor 976**
  Written contract, inclusion in, **CC 1812.504**
Continuing contracts, domestic help, registry, **CC 1812.504**
Contracts,
  Domestic workers, **CC 1812.5095**
  Job listing services, written contracts, **CC 1812.516**
  Jobseekers, written contracts, **CC 1812.504**
  Registration fees, fee splitting, farm labor contractors, **Labor 1698.8**
Copies,
  Bonds (officers and fiduciaries), filing, **CC 1812.503**
  Fee schedules, job seekers, **CC 1812.505**
Costs, actions and proceedings, **CC 1812.523**
Crimes and offenses, **CC 1812.523**
  Conviction, discharge from job, fees due, **CC 1812.506**
  Farm labor contractors, **Labor 1698.1 et seq.**
  Fraud, generally, post
  Misrepresentation, earnings of salesmen, brokers or agents, **Labor 977**

EMPLOYMENT AGENCIES—Cont'd
Daily hours of labor, written contract, inclusion, **CC 1812.504**
Day care and nursery schools, referrals, trustline, **CC 1812.5093**
Death, jobseeker, refund of fees, **CC 1812.506**
Definitions, **CC 1812.501**
  Domestic service, **CC 1812.5095**
  Employment agency regulation, **CC 1812.501**
  Fair employment and housing department, **Gov 12926**
  Unemployment compensation, **Un Ins 2071**
Deposits,
  Bonds (officers and fiduciaries), in lieu of, **CC 1812.503**
  Fee deposits, failure to accept employment, return, **CC 1812.506**
Discharge for misconduct, fees due, **CC 1812.506**
Discharge for reasons other than misconduct, jobseekers, fees, **CC 1812.506**
Discrimination, older workers, **Un Ins 2070 et seq.**
Domestic workers,
  Employer status, conditions, **CC 1812.5095; Un Ins 687.2, 13005.7**
  Personal interviews and verification of experience, prior to placement, **CC 1812.509**
  Registry, continuing contracts, **CC 1812.504**
Employer status,
  Domestic worker referrals, conditions, **CC 1812.5095**
  Domestic workers, conditions, **Un Ins 687.2, 13005.7**
Employment Counseling Services, generally, this index
Enforcement, regulations, **CC 1812.523**
Exemptions, **CC 1812.502**
Expiration date, written contracts, inclusion, **CC 1812.504**
Fair Employment and Housing, generally, this index
False advertisements or solicitations, **CC 1812.506 et seq.; Labor 976, 977**
  Job listing services, **CC 1812.520**
Farm labor contractors, **Labor 1682 et seq.**
Fee splitting, farm labor contractors, **Labor 1698.8**
Fees,
  Contracts, inclusion of fee and written contract, **CC 1812.504**
  Domestic workers, **CC 1812.5095**
  Failure to accept employment, refunds, **CC 1812.506**
  Job orders for employment, bona fide and in writing, prerequisite to acceptance of fees, **CC 1812.507**
  Registration fees, fee splitting, farm labor contractors, **Labor 1698.8**
  Schedules, copies to customers, **CC 1812.505**

EMPLOYMENT AGENCIES—Cont'd
Fees—Cont'd
  Splitting, prohibition, **CC 1812.505**
Fines and penalties,
  Farm labor contractors, **Labor 1698.1 et seq.**
  Unfair competition, **CC 1812.5095**
Fraud, **CC 1812.506 et seq.**
  False advertising, **CC 1812.507, 1812.508**
  Job listing services, **CC 1812.520**
  Job seekers, qualifications to perform job, discharge, fees due, **CC 1812.506**
  Salesmen, brokers or agents, earnings, **Labor 976**
  Unfair competition, misleading advertising, **CC 1812.5095**
Gamblers and gambling, farm labor contractors, frequenting premises, **Labor 1698.6**
Group job advertisements, **CC 1812.508**
Home health agencies, distinguished, advertisements, **CC 1812.508**
Illegal employment, **CC 1812.509**
  Job listing services, **CC 1812.521**
Job listing services, **CC 1812.515 et seq.**
  Actions and proceedings, **CC 1812.523**
  Advertisements, false advertisements, **CC 1812.520**
  Application of law, **CC 1812.502**
  Attorney fees, **CC 1812.523**
  Bonds (officers and fiduciaries), **CC 1812.515**
  Cancellation, right to cancel contracts, notice, **CC 1812.516**
  Children and minors, child labor laws, **CC 1812.521**
  Compensation and salaries, advertisements, agreements, **CC 1812.520**
  Contracts, written contracts, **CC 1812.516**
  Costs, actions and proceedings, **CC 1812.523**
  Crimes and offenses, **CC 1812.523**
  Enforcement, regulations, **CC 1812.523**
  False advertisements, **CC 1812.520**
  Fees, **CC 1812.517**
    Schedules, customers, copies, **CC 1812.505**
  Illegal employment, **CC 1812.521**
  Job orders, prerequisite to collecting fee, **CC 1812.519**
  Labor organizations, strikes, notice to job seeker, **CC 1812.521**
  Notice, contracts, cancellation rights, **CC 1812.516**
  Records and recordation, **CC 1812.522**
  Refunds, **CC 1812.518**
    Fees, right to, **CC 1812.516**
  Remedies, violations, **CC 1812.523**
  Schedules, fee schedules, **CC 1812.517**
Job orders, job listing services, prerequisite to collecting fees, **CC 1812.519**
Jobseekers,
  Fee schedule, copy, **CC 1812.505**

EMPLOYMENT AGENCIES—Cont'd

Jobseekers—Cont'd

Written contracts, requirements, **CC 1812.504**

Labor disputes, notice to jobseekers, **CC 1812.509**

Labor organizations,

Application of law, **CC 1812.502**

Membership requirements, notice to jobseekers, **CC 1812.509**

Labor strikes or problems, discharge, fees due, **CC 1812.506**

Licenses and permits, advertisements, referring, **CC 1812.5095**

Local agencies, employment services, illegal aliens, ineligibility, **Un Ins 9601.5, 9601.7**

Long term health care facilities, nurses, temporary employment, **CC 1812.509, 1812.540 et seq.**

Monopolies and unfair trade, fines and penalties, **CC 1812.5095**

Names,

Agency names, limitations, **CC 1812.508**

Contracts, employment agency and jobseeker name, inclusion, **CC 1812.504**

Nonprofit corporations, application of law, **CC 1812.502**

Notice,

Advertisements, special requirements, inclusion, **CC 1812.508**

Domestic help, registry, continuing contracts, termination, **CC 1812.504**

Fee schedules, failure to accept employment, right to return of fees, **CC 1812.506**

Labor contracts, union membership requirements, **CC 1812.509**

Nurses, long term health care facilities, temporary employment, **CC 1812.509, 1812.540 et seq.**

Nurses Registries, generally, this index

Nursing schools, application of law, **CC 1812.502**

Offenses. Crimes and offenses, generally, ante

Older workers, discrimination, **Un Ins 2070 et seq.**

Physical ability, inability to perform job, fees due after discharge, **CC 1812.506**

Professional associations, placement services, exemption, **CC 1812.502**

Prostitution, farm labor contractors, **Labor 1698.4**

Frequenting premises, **Labor 1698.6**

Psychiatric technicians, long term health care facilities, temporary employment, **CC 1812.540 et seq.**

Public employment offices, **Un Ins 2051 et seq.**

Records and recordation, **CC 1812.522**

Advertised jobs, **CC 1812.508, 1812.509**

Referrals,

Contracts, written contracts, **CC 1812.504**

EMPLOYMENT AGENCIES—Cont'd

Referrals—Cont'd

Domestic workers, **CC 1812.5095**

Fraud, **CC 1812.507**

Refunds,

Fees,

Cessation of employment, **CC 1812.506**

Failure to accept employment, **CC 1812.506**

Right to, written contract, inclusion in, **CC 1812.504**

Registration fees, fee splitting, farm labor contractors, **Labor 1698.8**

Registry, domestic help, continuing contracts, **CC 1812.504**

Remedies, violations, **CC 1812.523**

Reports, workers compensation, contractors, **Labor 3302**

Right to refund, notice, inclusion in written contract, **CC 1812.504**

Schedules. Fees, ante

Special requirements, advertisements, notice, **CC 1812.508**

State, employment services, illegal aliens, ineligibility, **Un Ins 9601.5, 9601.7**

Sureties and suretyship, requirements, **CC 1812.503**

Talent Agencies, generally, this index

Temporary employment,

Fees, **CC 1812.505**

Losing job within 90 days, reduction of fee, **CC 1812.504**

Type of employment, inclusion in employment contract, **CC 1812.504**

Unfair competition, fines and penalties, **CC 1812.5095**

Vocational nursing, long term health care facilities, temporary employment, **CC 1812.540 et seq.**

Vocational schools, application of law, **CC 1812.502**

Workers compensation, contractors, **Labor 3302**

EMPLOYMENT AGENCY, EMPLOYMENT COUNSELING AND JOB LISTING SERVICES ACT

Generally, **CC 1812.500 et seq.**

EMPLOYMENT CONTRACTS LAW

Generally, **Labor 430 et seq.**

EMPLOYMENT COUNSELING SERVICES

Generally, **CC 1812.510 et seq.**

Actions and proceedings, **CC 1812.523**

Advertisements, false advertisements, **CC 1812.513**

Attorney fees, **CC 1812.523**

Bonds (officers and fiduciaries), **CC 1812.510**

Business, prohibition of conduct without bond, **CC 1812.510**

Cancellation, contracts, right to cancel, notice, **CC 1812.511**

Contracts, written contracts, **CC 1812.511**

EMPLOYMENT COUNSELING SERVICES—Cont'd

Costs, actions and proceedings, **CC 1812.523**

Crimes and offenses, **CC 1812.523**

Definitions, employment agency regulation, **CC 1812.501**

Deposits, bonds (officers and fiduciaries), in lieu of, **CC 1812.510**

Enforcement, regulations, **CC 1812.523**

False advertisements, **CC 1812.513**

Fees, **CC 1812.512**

Notice, bonds (officers and fiduciaries), cancellation, **CC 1812.510**

Records and recordation, **CC 1812.522**

Advertisements, **CC 1812.513**

Remedies, violations, **CC 1812.523**

Right to cancel, contracts, **CC 1812.511**

Schedules, fees schedules, **CC 1812.512**

Sureties and suretyship, fiduciary bonds, **CC 1812.510**

EMPLOYMENT DEPARTMENT

Employment Development Department, generally, this index

EMPLOYMENT DEVELOPMENT

Generally, **Un Ins 9000 et seq.**

Agreements, conformance, **Un Ins 9002**

Allocation of funds, **Un Ins 9001**

Conformity with federal regulations, **Un Ins 9004**

Contracts, conformance, **Un Ins 9002**

Coordination of job placement and related programs, **Un Ins 9002**

Definitions, **Un Ins 9100 et seq.**

Department, definitions, **Un Ins 9101**

Director, definitions, **Un Ins 9102**

Discrimination, **Un Ins 9602**

Duplication of programs to be avoided, **Un Ins 9002**

Economic deprivation, definitions, **Un Ins 9110**

Economically disadvantaged area, definitions, **Un Ins 9111**

Economically displaced persons, definitions, **Un Ins 9115**

Eligible persons, definitions, **Un Ins 9112**

Federal aid, **Un Ins 9001**

Conformity with federal regulations, inconsistent provisions, **Un Ins 9004**

Funds,

Allocation, **Un Ins 9001**

Benefit audit fund, **Un Ins 1595 et seq.**

Contingent fund, **Un Ins 1585**

Augmentation of appropriations, **Un Ins 1586.5**

Goals, system of job training and placement, **Un Ins 9001**

Plans, conformance, **Un Ins 9002**

Priorities and preferences, **Un Ins 9602**

Public funds, job training and placement services, **Un Ins 9001**

Public policy, **Un Ins 9000**

Purpose of law, **Un Ins 9000**

Review of plans, **Un Ins 9002**

State agency, definitions, **Un Ins 9105**

EMPLOYMENT DEVELOPMENT—Cont'd

State aid, **Un Ins 9001**

Underemployed person, definitions, **Un Ins 9109**

Unemployed person, definitions, **Un Ins 9108**

Vietnam Veterans Employment Act, **Gov 7280 et seq.**

Work Incentive Programs, generally, this index

EMPLOYMENT DEVELOPMENT DEPARTMENT

Generally, **Un Ins 301 et seq., 9500 et seq.**

Administration expenses, **Un Ins 3012, 3013**

Administration of department, regulations, **Un Ins 305**

Administrative cost limitations, employment training panel, **Un Ins 10206**

Agents, board of equalization officers and employees, **Un Ins 1087**

Appeals division, **Un Ins 315, 401**

Apprenticeship standards division, services, **Labor 3097**

Assignment of division of apprenticeship standards consultant, **Labor 3097**

Assistants, **Un Ins 311**

Equalization officers and employees, agents, **Un Ins 1087**

Automation, report on progress, **Un Ins 4900 et seq.**

Benefit payment control program, automation, **Un Ins 333**

Boards and commissions, equalization officers and employees, agents, **Un Ins 1087**

Budget,

Compliance with government code, **Un Ins 318**

Employment training panel, **Un Ins 10212.2**

Buildings, construction, **Un Ins 1601**

Bureau, informing employers and workers of rights and responsibilities, **Un Ins 316**

Census bureau, contract, population survey, **Un Ins 327**

Civil service, **Un Ins 9612**

Compensation and salaries,

Deputy directors, **Un Ins 303**

Director, **Un Ins 302**

Compliance with government code, **Un Ins 318**

Confidential information, **Un Ins 2111**

Contingency fund, **Un Ins 1585**

Augmentation of appropriations, **Un Ins 1586.5**

Contracts, compliance with government code, **Un Ins 318**

Crimes and offenses, divulging confidential information, **Un Ins 2111**

Data systems, **Un Ins 9604**

Deaf, hearing impaired persons, employment services, **Un Ins 11000 et seq.**

EMPLOYMENT DEVELOPMENT DEPARTMENT—Cont'd

Definitions, employment development, **Un Ins 133, 9101**

Delegation of authority, **Un Ins 301.6, 311**

Officers and employees, **Un Ins 301.7**

Deputy directors, **Un Ins 303**

Directors, **Un Ins 301**

Administrator, definitions, financing unemployment insurance for public school employees, **Un Ins 821.3**

Appointment, **Un Ins 302**

Deputy directors, **Un Ins 303**

Assistants, **Un Ins 311**

Benefit payments, delegation of powers and duties, **Un Ins 301**

Comment, proposed public projects, employment opportunities, **Labor 50.9**

Compensation and salaries, **Un Ins 302**

Deputy directors, **Un Ins 303**

Compliance with government code, **Un Ins 318**

Crimes and offenses, divulging confidential information, **Un Ins 2111**

Definitions, employment development, **Un Ins 9102**

Deputy directors, **Un Ins 303**

Divulging confidential information, **Un Ins 2111**

Divulging confidential information, **Un Ins 2111**

Field investigating staff, **Un Ins 317**

Government Code, compliance, **Un Ins 318**

Head of department, **Un Ins 311**

Information available to United States, **Un Ins 1094**

Information to carry out responsibilities, **Un Ins 1094, 1095**

Judicial review, appeals board decision, **Un Ins 410**

Regulations adopted, **Un Ins 306**

Reports, **Un Ins 320**

Term of office, **Un Ins 302**

Deputy directors, **Un Ins 303**

Divulging confidential information, **Un Ins 2111**

Economically disadvantaged areas, designation, **Un Ins 9602**

Employment training panel, **Un Ins 10200 et seq.**

Appointment, **Un Ins 10202.5**

Budget, **Un Ins 10212.2**

Compensation and salaries, members, **Un Ins 10202.5**

Coordination with job training partnership, **Un Ins 10204**

Costs of program administration, **Un Ins 10206**

Directors, **Un Ins 10202**

Expenses and expenditures, members, **Un Ins 10202.5**

Meetings, **Un Ins 10203**

Numbers and numbering, members, **Un Ins 10202.5**

EMPLOYMENT DEVELOPMENT DEPARTMENT—Cont'd

Employment training panel—Cont'd

Officers and employees, **Un Ins 10202**

Offices, **Un Ins 10203**

Per diem, members, **Un Ins 10202.5**

Plan, **Un Ins 10205**

Powers and duties, **Un Ins 10204 et seq.**

Reports, projects operating, **Un Ins 10205**

Review of program, funding, **Un Ins 10206**

Technical assistance by department, **Un Ins 10213**

Term of office, members, **Un Ins 10202.5**

Exchange of information with other governmental departments and agencies, **Un Ins 322**

Federal agencies, exchange of information, **Un Ins 322**

Field investigating staff, **Un Ins 317**

Fiscal matters, compliance with government code, **Un Ins 318**

Funds, contingent fund, **Un Ins 1585**

Government Code, compliance, **Un Ins 318**

Insurance on property, **Un Ins 1601**

Intergovernmental cooperation, joint enforcement strike force on the underground economy, **Un Ins 329**

Investigators and investigators, unemployment hazards, **Un Ins 326**

Joint enforcement strike force on the underground economy, **Un Ins 329**

Labor analysis, **Un Ins 9604**

Labor and workforce development agency, **Un Ins 301**

Labor market information, **Un Ins 10530 et seq.**

Manpower service funds, **Un Ins 9609**

Meetings, employment training panel, **Un Ins 10203**

Officers and employees, **Un Ins 9502**

Confidential or privileged information, **Un Ins 2111**

Transfers, **Un Ins 301.7**

Panels. Employment training panel, generally, ante

Plans and specifications, automation, **Un Ins 4900 et seq.**

Population survey, census bureau, contract, **Un Ins 327**

Powers and duties, **Un Ins 9605**

Priorities and preferences, automation, benefit payment control program, **Un Ins 333**

Property purchased, **Un Ins 1601**

Recommendations on unemployment, **Un Ins 325**

Records and recordation, possession and control, **Un Ins 301.6**

Regulations adopted, **Un Ins 306**

Regulations for administration, **Un Ins 305**

Renting, space, priority, **Un Ins 3015**

EMPLOYMENT

EMPLOYMENT DEVELOPMENT DEPART-MENT—Cont'd

Reports,
Automation progress, **Un Ins 4900 et seq.**
Degree of unemployment hazard, **Un Ins 326**
Director, **Un Ins 320**
Employment training panel, projects operating, **Un Ins 10205**
Leisure sharing program, **Un Ins 12141**
Sample, population survey, census bureau, **Un Ins 327**
Secretary of Labor, inconsistency with rules and regulations, **Un Ins 318**
Social Security Act, inconsistent provisions, **Un Ins 318**
Social services, information for administration, **Un Ins 1094**
Space, priority, **Un Ins 3015**
State agencies, exchange of information, **Un Ins 322**
State local cooperative labor market information program, **Un Ins 10533**
Strike force on the underground economy, **Un Ins 329**
Studies on unemployment, **Un Ins 325**
Surveys, population survey, census bureau contract, **Un Ins 327**
Technical assistance, employment training panel, **Un Ins 10213**
Training panels. Employment training panel, generally, ante
Transfer of powers and duties from department of benefit payments, **Un Ins 301 et seq.**
Vietnam Veterans Employment Act, **Gov 7280 et seq.**
Workers and employers, rights and responsibilities, information, **Un Ins 316**

EMPLOYMENT DEVELOPMENT DEPARTMENT BENEFIT AUDIT FUND
Generally, **Un Ins 1595 et seq.**

EMPLOYMENT IN THE SAME OR A COMPARABLE POSITION
Definitions, family care and medical leave, **Gov 12945.2**

EMPLOYMENT PURPOSES
Definitions,
Consumer credit reporting, **CC 1785.3**
Investigative consumer reporting agencies, **CC 1786.2**

EMPLOYMENT RECORDS
Definitions, discovery, **CCP 1985.6**

EMPLOYMENT SERVICES
Deaf, hearing impaired persons, **Un Ins 11000 et seq.**
State or local governments, illegal aliens, ineligibility, **Un Ins 9601.5, 9601.7**

EMPLOYMENT TAXPAYERS BILL OF RIGHTS ACT
Generally, **Un Ins 1231 et seq.**

EMPLOYMENT TRAINING FUND
Generally, **Un Ins 1610 et seq.**
Allocations, **Un Ins 10205, 10206**
Appropriations, **Un Ins 10217**
CalWORKs, appropriations, **Un Ins 1611.5**
Contributions, **Un Ins 976.6**

EMPLOYMENT TRAINING PANEL
Employment Development Department, this index

ENCAMPMENTS
Military Forces, this index

ENCUMBRANCES
Liens and Incumbrances, generally, this index

ENDURANCE CONTESTS
Compensation and salaries, deposits for security of payment, **Labor 271**

ENEMY ATTACK
War and Civil Defense, generally, this index

ENERGY
Electricity, generally, this index

ENFORCEMENT AGENCY
Definitions, employee housing and labor camps, **Health & S 17007**

ENFORCEMENT OF FAIR LABOR STANDARDS ACT
Generally, **Labor 50.6**

ENGINE CAB HANDRAIL LAW
Railroads, **Labor 6952**

ENGINE TENDER CLEARANCE LAW
Railroads, **Labor 6950, 6951**

ENGINEERS
Aerial passenger tramways,
Construction plans and design information, certification, **Labor 7353, 7354**
Inspection and inspectors, **Labor 7349**
Air pressure tanks, inspection, **Labor 7650**
Definitions, qualified safety engineer, inspection of boilers and tanks, **Labor 7650**
Land surveyors. Surveys and Surveyors, generally, this index
Liens and incumbrances. Mechanics Liens, generally, this index
Liquefied petroleum gas storage tanks, inspection, **Labor 7650**
Mechanics Liens, generally, this index
Qualified safety engineer defined, inspection of boilers or tanks, **Labor 7650**
Railroads, this index
Surveys and Surveyors, generally, this index
Unemployment compensation, independent contractors, presumption as, **Un Ins 656**

ENGINES
Exhaust purifier device, internal combustion engines, use inside buildings, **Labor 6702**
Mobile internal combustion engines, occupational safety and health, **Labor 6701 et seq.**
Portable and mobile internal combustion engines, labor and employment, occupational safety and health, **Labor 6701 et seq.**

ENGLISH LANGUAGE
Interpreters and Translators, generally, this index
Labor and employment, services, **Labor 105**
Records and Recordation, this index
Unemployment compensation, publication of information, **Un Ins 316**
Unemployment insurance code, notices, **Un Ins 8**

ENTERPRISE ZONE ACT
Enterprise Zones, generally, this index

ENTERPRISE ZONE EXPIRATION DATE
Definitions, **Rev & T 24416.2**
Operating loss carryovers, **Rev & T 17276.2**

ENTERPRISE ZONES
Corporation taxes,
Certificates and certification, manufacturing enhancement areas, credits, **Rev & T 23622.8**
Credits, **Rev & T 23622.7, 23622.8**
Qualified wages, credits, **Rev & T 23634**
Single targeted tax area, **Rev & T 23634**
Deductions, net operating losses, **Rev & T 24416.1, 24416.2**
Targeted tax areas, **Rev & T 24416.6**
Qualified wages, credits, **Rev & T 23634**
Single targeted tax area, credits, **Rev & T 23634**
Credits,
Corporation taxes, ante
Income tax—state, post
Deductions,
Corporation taxes, ante
Income tax—state, post
Definitions,
Corporation taxes, credits, **Rev & T 23622.7, 23622.8**
Income tax—state, credits, **Rev & T 17053.74**
Income tax—state,
Certificates and certification, manufacturing enhancement areas, credits, **Rev & T 17053.47**
Credits,
Manufacturing enhancement areas, **Rev & T 17053.47**
Qualified wages, **Rev & T 17053.74**
Seasonal employment, **Rev & T 17053.74**

ENTERPRISE ZONES—Cont'd
Income tax—state—Cont'd
Credits—Cont'd
Seasonal employment—Cont'd
Manufacturing enhancement areas, **Rev & T 17053.47**
Single targeted tax area, **Rev & T 17053.34**
Single targeted tax area, **Rev & T 17053.34**
Deductions,
Local agency military base recovery areas, **Rev & T 17276.2**
Net operating loss carrybacks, **Rev & T 17276.2**
Operating loss carryovers, **Rev & T 17276.2**
Qualified employees, wages, **Rev & T 17053.74**
Qualified wages, income tax—state, credits, **Rev & T 17053.74**
Single targeted tax area,
Credits, **Rev & T 17053.34**
Net operating losses, carrybacks, **Rev & T 17276.6**
Local agency military base recovery areas. Military Forces, this index
Manufacturing enhancement areas, income tax—state, credits, **Rev & T 17053.47**
Single targeted tax area,
Corporation taxes, credits, **Rev & T 23634**
Income tax—state, credits, **Rev & T 17053.34**
Targeted tax area,
Corporation taxes, credits, **Rev & T 23634**
Income tax—state,
Credits, **Rev & T 17053.34**
Net operating losses, carrybacks, **Rev & T 17276.6**

ENTICEMENT
Child from parent or guardian, **CC 49**

ENTITY
Definitions,
Public buildings and works, contractors, debarment, **Labor 1777.1**
Unemployment compensation, **Un Ins 803**

ENTOMBMENT
Cemeteries and Dead Bodies, generally, this index

ENTRY ON PROPERTY
Labor and employment, safety in employment, investigations, **Labor 6314**
Labor camps, inspections, **Health & S 17050, 17052**
Labor commissioner, deputies, **Labor 90, 91**
Occupational safety and health, **Labor 6314**
Trespass, generally, this index

ENVIRONMENT
Hazardous Substances and Waste, generally, this index

EPIDEMICS
Diseases, this index

EQUAL OPPORTUNITY
Affirmative Action, generally, this index
Discrimination, generally, this index
Fair Employment and Housing, generally, this index

EQUAL PAY ACT
Generally, **Labor 1197.5**

EQUAL RIGHTS LAW
Generally, **CC 51, 52**

EQUALIZATION STATE BOARD
Taxation, this index

EQUIPMENT
Machinery and Equipment, generally, this index

EQUITY
Collective bargaining contracts, enforcement, **Labor 1126**

ERRAND PERSONS
Children and minors, employment, **Labor 1294.3**

ESCALATORS
Elevators, Dumbwaiters and Escalators, generally, this index

ESCHEAT
Benefits, unpaid wages or benefits, **Labor 96.7**
Compensation and salaries, unpaid wages or benefits, **Labor 96.7**
Employee benefit plan distribution, **CCP 1521**
Intangibles, **CCP 1510, 1521**
Residuals, employee benefit plan distributions, **CCP 1521**
Retirement and Pensions, this index
Shares and shareholders, employee stock purchase trust funds, **CCP 1510, 1521**
Trusts and Trustees, this index
Wages, unpaid wages or benefits, **Labor 96.7**

ESSENTIAL FUNCTIONS
Definitions, fair employment and housing, **Gov 12926**

ESTATES
Income Tax—State, this index
Probate Proceedings, generally, this index
Unemployment compensation, employing unit, **Un Ins 135**

ESTATES OF DECEDENTS
Probate Proceedings, generally, this index

ETHNIC GROUPS
Discrimination, generally, this index
Race, generally, this index

ETHYLENEIMINE
Occupational Carcinogens Control Act, **Labor 9000 et seq.**

EVICTION
Labor Camps, this index

EVIDENCE
Admissions, generally, this index
Aerial passenger tramways, injunction restraining unlawful and dangerous operation, **Labor 7343**
Affidavits, generally, this index
Agricultural labor relations board investigations, **Labor 1151 et seq.**
Apprentices, survey of ethnic derivation, **Labor 151**
Blackballing former employee, **Labor 1053**
Burden of proof,
Compensation and salaries, discrimination, **Labor 1197.5**
Labor and employment, whistle blowing, retaliation, **Labor 1102.6**
Volunteer firemen, removal, **Labor 1964**
Whistle blowing, labor and employment, **Labor 1102.6**
Colleges and Universities, this index
Compensation and Salaries, this index
Confiscation of goods, industrial homework, **Labor 2658.7**
Cumulative injuries, determination of liability for injury, **Labor 5500.6**
Depositions, generally, this index
Discovery, generally, this index
Discrimination, this index
Employment. Labor and Employment, this index
Fair Employment and Housing, this index
Family care leave, claims, **Un Ins 3306**
Health Facilities, this index
Immigration, status, **CC 3339**
Independent contractors, rebuttable presumption of status, **Labor 2750.5**
Industrial homework, confiscation of goods, **Labor 2658.7**
Interpreters and Translators, generally, this index
Labor and Employment, this index
Leases, this index
Libel and Slander, this index
Medical Records, this index
Motor Vehicles, this index
New Trial, this index
Occupational diseases, determination or limitation of liability, **Labor 5500.6**
Opinion and expert testimony. Witnesses, this index
Peace Officers, this index
Perjury, generally, this index
Physicians and Surgeons, this index
Presumptions,
Apprentices, orders and decisions of counsel, **Labor 3083**
Disability compensation, disqualifications, **Un Ins 2676, 2677**
Fair employment and housing, employers, **Gov 12928**

EVIDENCE—Cont'd

Presumptions—Cont'd

Health facilities, whistle blowing, **Health & S 1278.5**

Highway patrol, heart disease and pneumonia, workers compensation, **Labor 3212.3**

Independent contractors, status, **Labor 2750.5**

Industrial welfare commission, wages, hours and conditions of labor, reasonableness and lawfulness of order, **Labor 1200**

Injury, employee, **Labor 2801**

Labor and Employment, this index

Physicians and surgeons, primary care clinics, independent contractors, **Labor 2750.6**

Rebuttable presumptions,

Labor and employment, retaliation, **Labor 98.6**

Workers compensation, medical legal charges, reasonableness, **Labor 4625**

Seasonal labor, amount of wage award by labor commissioner, **Labor 255**

Theft by fraud, rented property, **Pen 484**

Unemployment Compensation, this index

Workers Compensation, this index

Privileges and Immunities, generally, this index

Production of Books and Papers, generally, this index

Rebuttable presumptions. Presumptions, ante

Social Services, this index

Solicitation of employees, responsible person, **Labor 973**

State officers and employees, whistle blowing, **Gov 8547.8**

Support, this index

Talent agencies, fees, **Labor 1703.4**

Translators. Interpreters and Translators, generally, this index

Unemployment Compensation, this index

Unpaid wages, actions to compel deposit of payment bonds, **Labor 240**

Whistle blowing, state officers and employees, **Gov 8547.8**

Witnesses, generally, this index

Workers Compensation, this index

EXCAVATIONS

Children and minors, employment, **Labor 1294**

Construction, licenses and permits, **Labor 6500 et seq.**

Labor and employment,

Occupational safety and health, public works contracts, **Labor 6705 et seq.**

Safety, **Labor 6705.5**

Licenses and permits, **Labor 6500 et seq.**

Occupational safety and health, public works contracts, **Labor 6705 et seq.**

Safety regulations, **Labor 7950 et seq.**

EXCHANGE, BILLS OF

Negotiable Instruments, generally, this index

EXCLUSIONS

Workers Compensation, this index

EXCONVICTS

Labor and employment, interference, **Pen 2947**

EXECUTIONS

Admission, preferred labor claims, **CCP 1207**

Appeal and review, preferred labor claims, **CCP 1206**

Assignments, wages, **Labor 300**

Bonds (officers and fiduciaries), employees cash bond, **Labor 404**

Cash bond of employee, **Labor 404**

Costs,

Labor claims, **CCP 1207**

Labor standards enforcement division, **Labor 101**

Door to door salesmen, money deposited as security for wages, **Labor 270.6**

Employees cash bond, **Labor 404**

Exemptions,

Cash bond of employees, **Labor 404**

Door to door salesmen, money deposited as security for wages, **Labor 270.6**

Employees cash bond, **Labor 404**

Logging or sawmill contractors, deposits, security for payment of wages, **Labor 270.5**

Hawkers and peddlers, money deposited as security for wages, exemptions, **Labor 270.6**

Itinerant merchants, money deposited as security for wages, **Labor 270.6**

Labor and employment, claims, **CCP 1206 et seq.**

Labor standards enforcement division, costs, **Labor 101**

Logs and logging, cash and securities on deposit to insure wage payments, **Labor 270.5**

Lumber. Timber and Lumber, this index

Money,

Door to door salesmen, security for wages, exemption, **Labor 270.6**

Employees cash bond, **Labor 404**

Logging or sawmill contractors, deposits, security for wages, **Labor 270.5**

Notice, labor claimant of request to release original execution, **CCP 1208**

Priorities and preferences, labor claims, **CCP 1206 et seq.**

Release, labor claims, **CCP 1208**

Sawmill operations, deposits, to insure wage payments, **Labor 270.5**

Telephone solicitors, money deposited as security for wages, **Labor 270.6**

Timber and Lumber, this index

Unemployment administration fund, fees, levy of writs, **Un Ins 1559**

EXECUTIONS—Cont'd

Unemployment Compensation, this index

Workers Compensation, this index

EXECUTIVE CLEMENCY

Information Practices Act, **CC 1798 et seq.**

EXECUTIVE DEPARTMENT

Attorney General, generally, this index

Franchise Tax Board, generally, this index

Governor, generally, this index

Justice Department, generally, this index

State Agencies, generally, this index

State Treasurer, generally, this index

EXECUTIVE DIRECTOR

Definitions, employment training panel, **Un Ins 10201**

EXEMPLARY DAMAGES

Damages, this index

EXEMPTIONS

Air pressure tanks, inspection and safety regulation, **Labor 7624**

Apprentices, contracts of public works, small contracts, **Labor 1777.5**

Attachment, this index

Boilers, inspection or safety regulation, **Labor 7625**

Buildings, this index

Business and Commerce, this index

Carcinogens, Occupational Carcinogens Control Act, **Labor 9015**

Certificates and Certification, this index

Civil Service, this index

Compensation and Salaries, this index

Consolidated Cities and Counties, this index

Counties, this index

Days off, mandatory orders, **Labor 1198.3**

Executions, this index

Garnishment, this index

Hazardous Substances and Waste, this index

Health Care Service Plans, this index

Health Facilities, this index

Hours of labor, **Labor 554**

Thirty hour week and six hour day, **Labor 556**

Housing, this index

Income Tax—State, this index

Labor and Employment, this index

Labor disputes, injunction, **Labor 1138.5**

Liquefied petroleum gas storage tanks, inspection and safety regulation, **Labor 7624**

Logs and logging, deposits to insure wage payments, **Labor 270.5**

Motion Pictures, this index

Municipalities, this index

Occupational Carcinogens Control Act, **Labor 9015**

Pharmacists, this index

Places of employment, smoking regulation, **Labor 6404.5**

Process, this index

Records and Recordation, this index

EXEMPTIONS—Cont'd
Sawmill operations, deposits to insure wage payments, **Labor 270.5**
Steam boilers, exemption from inspection or safety regulation, **Labor 7625**
Talent agencies,
  Advance fees, **Labor 1702.4**
  Fees, **Labor 1703.6**
Tanks, air pressure or liquefied petroleum gas, inspection and safety regulation, **Labor 7624**
Television and Radio, this index
Timber and Lumber, this index
Unemployment Compensation, this index
Weapons, this index
Whistleblowers, health facilities, **Health & S 1278.5**
Withholding tax on wages, **Un Ins 13040 et seq.**
Workers Compensation, this index
Workplace smoking regulations, **Labor 6404.5**

EXERCISE BOYS
Horse racing, unemployment compensation, **Un Ins 654**

EXHIBITION
Weapons, this index

EXHIBITIONS AND EXHIBITORS
Children and Minors, this index
Fairs and Expositions, generally, this index

EXHUMATION
Workers compensation, **Labor 5707**

EXPATRIATE CORPORATIONS
Foreign Corporations, generally, this index

EXPLOSIVES
Advisory committee, examinations of supervisors, **Labor 6710**
Avalanche blasting, examination of supervisors, **Labor 6711**
Chemical plant workers, safety, **Labor 7850 et seq.**
Crimes and offenses, safety violations, **Labor 8003**
Definitions, labor and employment, **Labor 6710**
Demolition experts, voluntary technical assistance to public entity, workers compensation, **Labor 3367**
Industrial homework, manufacturer, **Labor 2651**
Labor and employment, licensed supervisors, **Labor 6710**
  Avalanche blasters, **Labor 6711**
Lead poisoning, occupational safety, programs, **Health & S 105185 et seq.**
Licenses and permits,
  Avalanche blasters, **Labor 6711**
  Blasters, tunnels and mines, **Labor 7990 et seq.**
  Supervisors, **Labor 6710**
    Avalanche blasters, **Labor 6711**

EXPLOSIVES—Cont'd
Mines and tunnels, licenses and permits, **Labor 7990 et seq.**
Permits. Licenses and permits, generally, ante
Public utilities, exemption, **Labor 8004**
Supervisors, licensed supervisors, labor and employment, **Labor 6710**
  Avalanche blasters, **Labor 6711**
Technical assistance to public entity, workers compensation, **Labor 3367**
Tunnels, this index
Voluntary technical assistance to public entity, workers compensation, **Labor 3367**
Workers compensation, voluntary technical assistance to public entity, **Labor 3367**

EXPOSE OR EXPOSURE
Definitions, hazardous substance information and training, **Labor 6370**

EXPOSITIONS
Fairs and Expositions, generally, this index

EXSERVICEMEN
Veterans, generally, this index

EXTENDED CARE FACILITIES
Nursing Homes, generally, this index

EXTENDED LEAVE
Definitions, employment opportunities creation, **Un Ins 12102**

EXTENDED UNEMPLOYMENT COMPENSATION
Unemployment Compensation, this index

EXTINGUISHERS
Fire Extinguishers, generally, this index

EXTORTION
Discharged prisoners seeking employment, **Pen 2947**
Labor and employment, exconvict, **Pen 2947**

EXTRADITION
Information Practices Act, **CC 1798 et seq.**

EXTRAHAZARDOUS TUNNELS
Safety regulations, **Labor 7977 et seq.**

EYEGLASSES
Workers compensation, **Labor 3208**

EYES AND EYESIGHT
Blind Persons, generally, this index
Corneal eye tissue. Tissue Banks, generally, this index
Optometrists, generally, this index
Tissue Banks, generally, this index
Workers compensation,
  Loss of both eyes or sight, **Labor 4662**
  Subsequent injuries, **Labor 4751**

EYEWITNESSES
Witnesses, generally, this index

FABRICS
Fires and Fire Protection, generally, this index

FACE
Definitions, tunnel and mine safety, **Labor 7951**

FACTORIES
Manufacturers and Manufacturing, generally, this index

FAILURE TO INSTALL
Definitions, workers compensation, power press workers, **Labor 4558**

FAIR EMPLOYMENT AND HOUSING
Generally, **Const. Art. 1, § 8; Gov 12900 et seq., 12940 et seq.**
Accommodation, handicapped persons, discrimination, unlawful practices, **Gov 12940**
Accusation, housing discrimination, **Gov 12981**
Actions and proceedings,
  Housing discrimination, **Gov 12989 et seq.**
  Jurisdiction, **Gov 12989**
  Orders,
    Compelling discovery, **Gov 12963.5**
    Enforcement, **Gov 12964, 12981**
Actual damages, **Gov 12970**
Administrative law and procedure, hearings, housing discrimination, **Gov 12981**
Affidavits, **Gov 12930**
Affirmative actions, definitions, **Gov 12927**
Age,
  Civil rights, **Gov 12921**
  Definitions, **Gov 12926**
  Discrimination, **Gov 12940 et seq.; Un Ins 2070 et seq.**
Agricultural Labor Relations Act of 1975, **Labor 1153**
Ancestry, discrimination, unlawful practices, **Gov 12940 et seq.**
Answers, interrogatories, **Gov 12963.2**
Appeal and review, **Gov 12987.1**
  Superior court, order compelling discovery, **Gov 12963.5**
Appearance, gender identity, **Gov 12949**
Application of law, **Gov 12926.1, 12993 et seq.**
Apprentices, **Labor 1777.6, 3095**
Attorney fees, **Gov 12973, 12989.2, 12989.3**
  Cease and desist orders, **Gov 12987**
Attorney general, housing discrimination, actions and proceedings, **Gov 12989.3**
Attorneys, complaints, service of process, **Gov 12962**
Birth, unlawful practices, **Gov 12945**
Boards and commissions, **Gov 12903 et seq., 12935**
Books and papers, inspection and inspectors, **Gov 12930**
Cease and desist orders, **Gov 12987**
Class action, **Gov 12961**
Color, civil rights, **Gov 12921**

FAIR EMPLOYMENT AND HOUSING
—Cont'd
Complaints, **Gov 12980**
  Discrimination, **CC 52**
  Jurisdiction, **Gov 12965**
  Service of process, **Gov 12962, 12986**
Compliance employment programs, **Gov 12990**
Compromise and settlement, housing discrimination, **Gov 12980**
Conciliation agreements, enforcement actions, **Gov 12981**
Confidential or privileged information, discrimination, **Gov 12984**
Conflict of laws, **Gov 12993.5**
Construction of law, **Gov 12926.1**
Consumer credit reporting agencies, **CC 1786.20**
Costs, **Gov 12989.2**
  Cease and desist orders, **Gov 12987**
Creed, civil rights, **Gov 12921**
Crimes and offenses, **Gov 12975, 12976**
Damages, **Gov 12987, 12989.2, 12989.3**
  Actual damages, **Gov 12970**
  Emotional distress, **Gov 12980**
  Emotional injury, **Gov 12965**
  Offsets, **Gov 12973, 12987**
Decrees, **Gov 12973**
Definitions,
  Construction of law, **Gov 12926.1**
  Employment agencies, **Gov 12926**
Department, definitions, **Gov 12925**
Depositions, **Gov 12930, 12963.3, 12972**
Discovery, **Gov 12980**
  Depositions, **Gov 12963.3**
  Requests for production of documents and things, **Gov 12963.4**
  Subpoenas, **Gov 12963.1**
  Written interrogatories, **Gov 12963.2**
Dismissal and nonsuit, **Gov 12981.1**
Documents and things, **Gov 12963.4**
  Subpoenas, **Gov 12963.1**
Duress or coercion, fines and penalties, **Gov 12987**
Economically disadvantaged areas, minority designations, **Un Ins 9602**
Elections, actions and proceedings, **Gov 12989**
Emotional distress, damages, **Gov 12980**
Emotional injury, damages, **Gov 12965**
Employee, definitions, **Gov 12926**
Employer, definitions, **Gov 12926**
Enforcement and hearing procedures, unlawful practices, **Gov 12960 et seq.**
Evidence, **Gov 12955.8, 12970**
  Presumptions, employers, **Gov 12928**
  Subpoenas, **Gov 12963.1**
Fees, opinion and expert testimony, **Gov 12989.2, 12989.3**
Findings of fact, **Gov 12970**
Fines and penalties, **Gov 12970, 12987**
  Administrative, **Gov 12965**
  Housing discrimination, **Gov 12989.3**
  Offsets, **Gov 12973, 12987**
Fraud, fines and penalties, **Gov 12987**

FAIR EMPLOYMENT AND HOUSING
—Cont'd
Gender identity, wearing apparel, labor and employment, **Gov 12949**
Genetic characteristics,
  Definitions, **Gov 12926**
  Testing, **Gov 12940**
Grooming, gender identity, **Gov 12949**
Harassment,
  Definitions, **Gov 12940**
  Discrimination, **Gov 12955**
  Personal liability, discrimination, unlawful practices, **Gov 12940**
  Unlawful practices, **Gov 12940**
Hearings,
  Boards and commissions, **Gov 12935**
  Unlawful practices, **Gov 12960 et seq.**
Hostile work environment sexual harassment, **Gov 12940**
  Unlawful practices, **Gov 12940**
Hours of labor, exceeding mandatory orders, discharge for refusal to work, **Labor 1198.3**
Housing accommodation, definitions, **Gov 12927**
Immigration, **Health & S 24000**
Injunction, **Gov 12964, 12987, 12989.2, 12989.3**
Interrogatories, **Gov 12963.2**
Intervention, discrimination actions, **Gov 12989, 12989.1, 12989.3**
Investigations and investigators, **Gov 12963**
  Complaints, **Gov 12963.7**
  Housing discrimination, **Gov 12980**
  Powers and duties, **Gov 12930**
Job placement, **Gov 12932**
Judgments and decrees, **Gov 12973**
Jurisdiction,
  Complaints, **Gov 12965**
  Discrimination actions, **Gov 12989**
Jury, discharge of employee for service, **Labor 230**
Labor organization,
  Definitions, **Gov 12926**
  Reports of neglect or abuse, discrimination against reporter, unlawful practices, **Gov 12940**
Land use laws or ordinances, referral of case to attorney general, **Gov 12981**
Limitation of actions, **Gov 12960, 12989.1**
  Tolling, **Gov 12965**
Limits, definitions, **Gov 12926, 12926.1**
Major life activities, definitions, **Gov 12926, 12926.1**
Malice, fines and penalties, **Gov 12987**
Marital status,
  Civil rights, **Gov 12921**
  Discrimination, unlawful practices, **Gov 12940 et seq.**
Mediation, boards and commissions, **Gov 12935**
Medical condition,
  Definitions, **Gov 12926**
  Discrimination, unlawful practices, **Gov 12940 et seq.**

FAIR EMPLOYMENT AND HOUSING
—Cont'd
Minority designation, economically disadvantaged areas, **Un Ins 9602**
Nondiscrimination and compliance employment programs, **Gov 12990**
Notice,
  Actions and proceedings, elections, **Gov 12989**
  Housing discrimination, **Gov 12980**
  Transfer of proceedings to court, **Gov 12965**
Oaths and affirmations, **Gov 12930**
Occupational qualifications, unlawful practices, **Gov 12940 et seq.**
Occupational safety and health, **Labor 6310 et seq.**
On the bases enumerated in this part, definitions, **Gov 12926**
Opinion and expert testimony, fees, cease and desist orders, **Gov 12987**
Orders of court, **Gov 12973**
Owner, definitions, **Gov 12927**
Parties, complaints, **Gov 12965**
Penalties. Fines and penalties, generally, ante
Person, definitions, **Gov 12925**
Personal liability, harassment, discrimination, unlawful practices, **Gov 12940**
Personal service, subpoena, **Gov 12963.1**
Petitions, superior court, compelling discovery, **Gov 12963.5**
Physical examinations, discrimination, unlawful practices, **Gov 12940**
Physical materials, subpoenas, **Gov 12963.1**
Powers and duties, discrimination, unlawful practices, **Gov 12940 et seq.**
Pregnancy, unlawful practices, **Gov 12945**
Presumptions, employers, **Gov 12928**
Priorities and preferences, veterans, sex discrimination, **Gov 12940 et seq.**
Process, service of process, housing discrimination, complaints, **Gov 12986**
Production of books and papers, **Gov 12930, 12963.1**
  Boards and commissions, **Gov 12935**
  Department, **Gov 12930, 12963.4**
Psychological examinations, discrimination, unlawful practices, **Gov 12940**
Public policy, **Gov 12920, 12921**
Publications,
  Boards and commissions, **Gov 12935**
  Powers and duties, **Gov 12930**
Reasonable accommodation, physical or mental disabilities, unlawful practices, **Gov 12940**
Records and recordation,
  Instruction, **Gov 12930**
  Preservation, housing, **Gov 12956**
  Rental records, **Gov 12956**
  Subpoenas, **Gov 12963.1**
Reports,
  Housing discrimination, investigations, **Gov 12980**

FAIR EMPLOYMENT AND HOUSING
—Cont'd
Reports—Cont'd
Neglect or abuse, discrimination against reporter, unlawful practices, **Gov 12940**
Restrictive covenants, **Gov 12955**
Service of process,
Complaints, **Gov 12986**
Subpoena, **Gov 12963.1**
Settlement and compromise, housing discrimination, **Gov 12980**
Sexual harassment, **Gov 12940**
Sexual orientation, **Gov 12920, 12921, 12926, 12940 et seq., 12955, 12955.8**
State contractor or supplier of goods and services to state, **Gov 12966**
State contracts, nondiscrimination in compliance employment programs, **Gov 12990**
Statute of limitations. Limitation of actions, generally, ante
Studies, **Gov 12940.3**
Subcontracts, state contracts, nondiscrimination and compliance employment programs, **Gov 12990**
Subpoenas, **Gov 12930, 12963.1**
Boards and commission, **Gov 12935**
Powers and duties, **Gov 12930**
Surveys, **Gov 12940.3**
Time, accusation, **Gov 12965**
Tolling, limitation of actions, **Gov 12965**
Children and minors, **Gov 12960**
Training, **Gov 12940**
Unemployment compensation, economically disadvantaged areas, minority designation, **Un Ins 9602**
Unlawful practices, **Gov 12940 et seq.**
Venue, actions, **Gov 12965**
Veterans, preference, sex discrimination, **Gov 12940 et seq.**
Vocational rehabilitation and job placement, **Gov 12932**
Wearing apparel, gender identity, labor and employment, **Gov 12949**
Witnesses, **Gov 12930, 12963.1**
Work records, women, **Labor 1178.5**
Working days, exceeding mandatory orders, discharge for refusal to work, **Labor 1198.3**
Written interrogatories, **Gov 12963.2**
Zoning laws or ordinances, referral of case to attorney general, **Gov 12981**

FAIR EMPLOYMENT AND HOUSING COMMISSION
Generally, **Gov 12903 et seq., 12935**

FAIR EMPLOYMENT AND HOUSING DEPARTMENT
Generally, **Gov 12900 et seq.**
Accusations, powers and duties, **Gov 12930**
Affidavits, **Gov 12930**
Appearance, witnesses, **Gov 12930**
Attorneys, powers and duties, **Gov 12930**

FAIR EMPLOYMENT AND HOUSING DEPARTMENT—Cont'd
Boards and commissions, definitions, **Gov 12925**
Books and papers, inspection and inspectors, **Gov 12930**
Compensation and salaries,
Boards and commissions, **Gov 12905**
Powers and duties, **Gov 12930**
Conciliation council, definitions, **Gov 12927**
Department, definitions, **Gov 12925**
Directors, **Gov 12901**
Definitions, **Gov 12925**
Disclosure, investigations of complaints, **Gov 12963.7**
Forum, boards and commissions, **Gov 12904**
Inspection and inspectors, books and records, **Gov 12930**
Investigations and investigators,
Complaints, **Gov 12963.7**
Powers and duties, **Gov 12930**
Jurisdiction, **Gov 12963.5**
Meetings, powers and duties, **Gov 12930**
Oaths and affirmations, **Gov 12930**
Office, powers and duties, **Gov 12930**
Powers and duties, **Gov 12930 et seq.**
Records and recordation,
Inspection, **Gov 12930**
Subpoenas, **Gov 12963.1**
Removal from office, boards and commissions, **Gov 12906**
Reports, **Gov 12930**
Rules and regulations, powers and duties, **Gov 12930**
Vacancy, boards and commissions, **Gov 12904**
Witnesses, **Gov 12930**
Attendance, subpoena, **Gov 12963.1**

FAIR LABOR STANDARDS ACT
Compensation and salaries, payment by covered employers, **Labor 204**
Industrial relations department, enforcement, **Labor 50.6**

FAIRS AND EXPOSITIONS
Amusement rides, safety, **Labor 7900 et seq.**
Unemployment compensation,
Employer, definitions, **Un Ins 677**
Qualifications, **Un Ins 605**

FAITH HEALING
Disability compensation, belief in healing by prayer, **Un Ins 2902**
Health care service plans, medically necessary health care, application of law, **CC 3428**
Unemployment compensation, **Un Ins 2709**

FALSE ADVERTISING
Advertisements, generally, this index

FALSE CLAIMS ACT
Generally, **Gov 12650 et seq.**

FALSE EVIDENCE
Perjury, generally, this index

FALSE PRETENSES
Generally, **Pen 484**
Theft, **Pen 484**

FALSE REPRESENTATIONS
Fraud, generally, this index

FALSE STATEMENTS
Fraud, generally, this index

FALSE SWEARING
Perjury, generally, this index

FAMILIAL STATUS
Definitions, housing discrimination, **Gov 12955.2**

FAMILY
Acquisition of firearms by restrainees, **Pen 12021**
Children and Minors, generally, this index
Domestic Partnership, generally, this index
Domestic Violence, generally, this index
Job preparation and training services.
Unemployment Compensation, this index
Marriage, generally, this index
Moore Brown Roberti Family Rights Act, **Gov 12945.1, 12945.2**
Public Officers and Employees, this index
Support, generally, this index

FAMILY CARE AND MEDICAL LEAVE
Definitions, **Gov 12945.2**

FAMILY CARE LEAVE
Generally, **Un Ins 3300 et seq.**

FAMILY MEMBERS
Definitions, family care leave, **Un Ins 3302**

FAMILY OF THE JUDGMENT DEBTOR
Definitions, garnishment, **CCP 706.051**

FANS
Manufacturing establishment, **Labor 2353**

FARM LABOR
Agricultural Labor and Employment, generally, this index

FARM LABOR CONTRACTOR
Definitions, **Labor 1682, 1682.3**
Commercial packing house, **Labor 1682.4**

FARM LABOR CONTRACTORS SPECIAL ENFORCEMENT UNIT
Licenses and permits, **Labor 1682.8**

FARM PRODUCTS
Agricultural Products, generally, this index

FARMLAND
Agricultural Land, generally, this index

FARMS AND FARMERS
Agriculture, generally, this index

FAST FOOD OUTLETS
Children and minors, employment, **Labor 1294.3**

FATHER AND CHILD
Children and Minors, generally, this index

FAX MACHINES
Colleges and universities, force and violence, injunction, **CCP 527.85**
Labor and employment, workplace violence safety, **CCP 527.8**
Workplace violence safety, **CCP 527.8**

FEAR
Duress or Coercion, generally, this index
Threats, generally, this index

FEATHERBEDDING
Railroad Antifeatherbedding Law, **Labor 6900.1, 6900.5**

FEDERAL ACT
Definitions, unemployment compensation, **Un Ins 3503**

FEDERAL AGENCIES
United States Agencies and Institutions, generally, this index

FEDERAL AID
Employment development, **Un Ins 9001**
Job training and placement services, **Un Ins 9001**
Public Buildings and Works, this index
Unemployment compensation, workforce recovery training, **Un Ins 10214.6**

FEDERAL BUREAU OF INVESTIGATION
Criminal history information, **Pen 11105.3**

FEDERAL ECONOMIC OPPORTUNITY ACT
Director of human resources development department to advise governor of responsibilities, **Un Ins 327**

FEDERAL EMPLOYERS LIABILITY ACTS
Unemployment compensation, reduction of benefits, **Un Ins 2629**

FEDERAL GOVERNMENT
United States, generally, this index

FEDERAL JOB TRAINING PARTNERSHIP ACT
Apprentices, **Labor 3097**
Employment and training, **Un Ins 10510 et seq.**

FEDERAL OLD AGE AND SURVIVORS INSURANCE
Social Security, generally, this index

FEDERAL SOCIAL SECURITY
Social Security, generally, this index

FEDERAL STATE EXTENDED COMPENSATION
Generally, **Un Ins 4001 et seq.**

FEDERAL UNEMPLOYMENT TAX ACT
Administration fund, contributions, **Un Ins 1556**
Contributions, **Un Ins 991 et seq.**
Definitions, **Un Ins 136**
Disability compensation, nonconformity with provisions of Act, **Un Ins 2605**
Investment of funds, **Un Ins 1527, 1530**
Limitation of actions, contributions, **Un Ins 1852**
Moneys received, **Un Ins 1562**
National plan, **Un Ins 101**
Reciprocal state agreements, **Un Ins 454 et seq.**
Service of process, **Un Ins 635**
Statute of limitations, contributions, **Un Ins 1852**
Wages, effect of operation of federal act, **Un Ins 939**

FEDWIRE
Definitions, unemployment compensation, electronic funds transfers, withholding tax on wages, **Un Ins 13021.5**

FEET
Podiatrists (Chiropody), generally, this index
Workers compensation, subsequent injuries, **Labor 4751**

FELLOW SERVANT DOCTRINE
Defense, action for death or personal injury of employee, **Labor 2801**
Workers compensation, defense abolished, **Labor 3708**

FELONIES
Crimes and Offenses, generally, this index

FEMALES
Women, generally, this index

FENCES
Agricultural land, trespass, **Pen 602**
Trespass, this index

FERMENTED LIQUIDS
Alcoholic Beverages, generally, this index

FIDELITY BONDS
Bonds (Officers and Fiduciaries), generally, this index

FIDUCIARIES
Bonds (Officers and Fiduciaries), generally, this index
Conservators and Conservatorships, generally, this index
Definitions, withholding tax on wages, **Un Ins 13003**
Guardian and Ward, generally, this index
Income Tax—State, this index
Receivers and Receivership, generally, this index
Trusts and Trustees, generally, this index

FIELD CROPS
Agricultural Products, generally, this index

FIERI FACIAS
Executions, generally, this index

FILE
Definitions,
Consumer credit reporting, **CC 1785.3**
Investigative consumer reporting agencies, **CC 1786.2**

FILLING STATIONS
Motor Vehicle Service Stations, generally, this index

FILMS
Motion Pictures, generally, this index

FILMSTRIPS
Talent services, **Labor 1703.4**

FINAL JUDGMENTS, DECREES AND ORDERS
Judgments and Decrees, generally, this index

FINANCE
Military forces, discrimination, **Mil & V 394**
School Funds, generally, this index
Unemployment Compensation, this index

FINANCE DEPARTMENT
Disability compensation fund, investment, **Un Ins 3002**
Industrial accidents division, approval of arrangements with United States, **Labor 128**
Unemployment compensation, administration fund, accounting for, **Un Ins 1559**
Workers compensation,
Files, destruction or disposal, approval, **Labor 135**
State employees, adjustment and disposition of claims, **Labor 6111 et seq.**

FINANCE LENDERS
Fraud,
Licenses and permits, revocation or suspension, **Fin 22168**
Revocation or suspension, **Fin 22168**
Licenses and permits, revocation or suspension, fraud, **Fin 22168**

FINANCIAL ASSETS
Definitions, support, liquidation, instructions, **Fam 17522.5**

FINANCIAL INTEREST
Adverse or Pecuniary Interest, generally, this index

FINANCIAL ORGANIZATIONS
Definitions, Unclaimed Property Law, **CCP 1501**

FINANCIAL STATEMENTS AND REPORTS
Agricultural labor relations board, **Labor 1143**
Garnishment, **CCP 706.124**

FINANCIAL STATEMENTS AND REPORTS —Cont'd

Withholding tax on wages, **Un Ins 13050 et seq.**

Workers Compensation, this index

FINDINGS OF FACT

Agricultural labor relations board, unfair labor practice proceedings, **Labor 1160.3**

Fair employment and housing, **Gov 12970**

Garnishment, **CCP 706.106**

Industrial homework, searches and seizures, appeal and review, **Labor 2664**

Labor and employment, working conditions, **Labor 1187**

Labor disputes, injunction, **Labor 1138.3**

Seasonal labor, wage disputes, **Labor 254**

Workers Compensation, this index

FINE ARTS

Art and Artists, generally, this index

FINES AND PENALTIES

Adult abuse reports, confidentiality violations, **Welf & I 15633 et seq.**

Advertisements, this index

Aged Persons, this index

Agricultural Labor and Employment, this index

Agricultural labor relations board, resisting or interfering with, **Labor 1151.6**

AIDS, this index

Amusements, this index

Apprenticeship programs, discrimination, **Labor 3095**

Arrest, this index

Asbestos, this index

Banks and Banking, this index

Battered womens shelters, trespass, **Pen 602**

Blood tests, AIDS, **Health & S 120980**

Boilers, negligent operation, causing death, **Labor 7771**

Building and construction industry, payment of wages or fringe benefits with bad checks, **Labor 203.1**

Car washes, registration, **Labor 2064**

Disclosure, **Labor 2061**

Carcinogens, use in place of employment, **Labor 9060**

Class of labor employed, misrepresentation, **Labor 1010 et seq.**

Colleges and Universities, this index

Community colleges and districts. Colleges and Universities, this index

Compensation and Salaries, this index

Construction, this index

Contractors, this index

Corporate Criminal Liability Act, **Pen 387**

Correctional Institutions, this index

Credit Unions, this index

Dangerous business practices, serious concealed danger, failure to disclose, **Pen 387**

Discovery, this index

Discrimination, this index

FINES AND PENALTIES—Cont'd

Diversion programs, referrals or participation, employers requiring job applicant to disclose, **Labor 432.7**

Drinking water, provision for employees, **Labor 2441**

Elevators, Dumbwaiters and Escalators, this index

Employers,
Failure to make agreed payment to employee benefit plan, **Labor 227**

Requiring job applicants to disclose arrest record or diversion program referrals or participation, **Labor 432.7**

Employment Agencies, this index

Exemplary damages. Damages, this index

Explosives, generally, this index

Extended unemployment compensation, failure of employer to furnish information, **Un Ins 3654.1**

Fair Employment and Housing, this index

Farm labor contractors, **Labor 1697, 1698.1 et seq.**

Force and violence, discrimination, **CC 52**

Foreign labor contractors, **Bus & P 9998.8**

Forfeitures, generally, this index

Fraud, this index

Freedom from violence, **CC 52**

Grants, labor organizations, promotion or deterrence, **Gov 16645.2**

Hate crimes, **CC 52**

Health Care Service Plans, this index

Health Facilities, this index

Housing, this index

Income Tax—State, this index

Industrial Homework, this index

Injunction, acquisition of firearms by restrainees, **Pen 12021**

Jails, generally, this index

Joint enforcement strike force on the underground economy, assessment orders, authority, **Labor 106**

Labor and Employment, this index

Labor Camps, this index

Labor commissioner, deputies and assistants, impeding or preventing performance of duties, **Labor 91**

Neglect or refusal of employer to furnish statistics, information or access, **Labor 90**

Labor disputes, professional strikebreakers, **Labor 1136**

Labor union insignia, use on articles of merchandise, **Labor 1010 et seq.**

Laboratories, this index

Lewdness and Obscenity, this index

Manufacturers and Manufacturing, this index

Medical Records, this index

Mines and Minerals, this index

Motion Pictures, this index

Occupational Carcinogens Control Act, **Labor 9060**

Occupational safety and health, **Labor 6314, 6319**

FINES AND PENALTIES—Cont'd

Place of employment, smoking regulation violations, **Labor 6404.5**

Political affiliations of employees, coercing or influencing, **Labor 1101 et seq.**

Professional strikebreakers, **Labor 1136**

Public Buildings and Works, this index

Public Lands, this index

Railroad Crossings, this index

Railroads, this index

Savings and Loan Associations, this index

Savings Associations, this index

Schools and School Districts, this index

Second and subsequent offenses. Crimes and Offenses, this index

Sex discrimination, **CC 52**

Sexual harassment, **CC 52**

Smelters and underground workings, hours of labor, violations, **Labor 752**

Solicitation, this index

State Contracts, this index

State Officers and Employees, this index

Steam boilers, negligent operation, causing death, **Labor 7771**

Support, this index

Talent agencies, fees, **Labor 1704**

Taxation, this index

Telecommunications, this index

Temporary employment, compensation and salaries, **Labor 201.3**

Tips,
Fines paid into state treasury and credited to general fund, **Labor 355**

Violations by employers, **Labor 354**

Trespass, this index

Unemployment Compensation, this index

Union buttons, unlawful wearing, **Labor 1018**

Universities. Colleges and Universities, this index

Violence, freedom from, **CC 52**

Weapons, this index

Whistle Blowing, this index

Workers Compensation, this index

Workplace smoking regulation violations, **Labor 6404.5**

FINGERPRINTS AND FINGERPRINTING

Certificates and certification, criminal history information, **Pen 11105.7**

Criminal history information,
Care facilities, **Welf & I 15660**

Certificates and certification, **Pen 11105.7**

Legibility, **Pen 11105.7**

Labor and employment,
Improper use of employees fingerprints by employer, **Labor 1051**

Management companies, use of employees fingerprints by employer, **Labor 1057**

Live scan technology, security agents and broker dealers, **Corp 25221**

Managed health care department, officers and employees, **Gov 1041**

Management companies, employees, **Labor 1057**

FINGERPRINTS AND FINGERPRINTING —Cont'd

Savings associations, officers and employees, criminal history information, **Fin 6525**

Security agents and broker dealers, **Corp 25221**

Talent agencies, licenses and permits, applications, **Labor 1700.6**

FIRE DEPARTMENTS

Firefighters and Fire Departments, generally, this index

FIRE EXTINGUISHERS

Flammable liquids, safety in employment, **Labor 7803**

Safety in employment, volatile flammable liquids, **Labor 7803**

Volatile flammable liquids, safety in employment, **Labor 7803**

FIRE NUISANCE

Fires and Fire Protection, generally, this index

FIREARMS

Weapons, generally, this index

FIREFIGHTERS AND FIRE DEPARTMENTS

Absence and absentees. Leaves of absence, generally, post

Accident and health insurance, death in line of duty, survivors, health benefits, **Labor 4856**

Apprentices, workers compensation, biochemical substances, presumptions, **Labor 3212.85**

Asbestosis, death benefits, limitation of actions, **Labor 5406.5**

Biochemical substances, workers compensation, presumptions, **Labor 3212.85**

Blood borne infectious diseases, workers compensation, presumptions, **Labor 3212.8**

Breathing apparatus, development of safety standards, positive pressure closed circuit apparatus, **Labor 6331**

Cancer, workers compensation, **Labor 3212.1**

Colleges and Universities, this index

Complaints, volunteer firemen and fire departments, discrimination, **Labor 230.4**

Crimes and offenses,
Reserves or auxiliaries, absence and absentees, labor and employment, emergency duties, **Labor 230.3**
Volunteers taking time off to perform duties, discharge or discrimination, **Labor 230.3**

Damages, workers compensation, third parties, **Labor 3852**

Death,
Scholarships, dependents, death in line of duty, **Labor 4709**
Workers compensation, survivors, health benefits, **Labor 4856**

FIREFIGHTERS AND FIRE DEPARTMENTS —Cont'd

Death benefits, asbestosis, limitation of actions, **Labor 5406.5**

Definitions, workers compensation, **Labor 3211.5**

Dependents, scholarships, **Labor 4709**

Discharge,
Reserves or auxiliaries, absence and absentees, labor and employment, emergency duties, **Labor 230.3**
Volunteer firefighters and fire departments,
Leaves of absence, training, **Labor 230.4**
Taking time off to perform duties, **Labor 230.3**

Discrimination,
Heart trouble, **Gov 12940.1**
Employment, presumption, **Gov 12940.1**
Reserves or auxiliaries, absence and absentees,
Emergencies, **Labor 230.3**
Labor and employment, emergency duties, **Labor 230.3**
Volunteers,
Emergency duties as, **Labor 230.3**
Leaves of absence, **Labor 230.4**

Emergencies, reserves or auxiliaries, absence and absentees, labor and employment, **Labor 230.3**

Employment, heart trouble, discrimination, presumption, **Gov 12940.1**

Handicapped persons, scholarships, dependents, disability in line of duty, **Labor 4709**

Heart trouble,
Employment, discrimination, presumption, **Gov 12940.1**
Workers compensation, **Labor 3212**

Hernias, workers compensation, **Labor 3212**

Labor organizations, **Labor 1960 et seq.**

Leaves of absence,
In lieu of temporary disability payments, University of California firemen, **Labor 4804.1**
Training, volunteers, **Labor 230.4**
Workers compensation, disability benefits, **Labor 4850**

Limitation of actions, asbestosis, death benefits, **Labor 5406.5**

Meningitis, workers compensation, presumptions, **Labor 3212.9**

Methicillin resistant staphylococcus aureus (MRSA) skin infections, workers compensation, presumptions, **Labor 3212.8**

Military bases, reservations and areas, workers compensation, cancer, **Labor 3212.1**

Occupational safety and health, fines and penalties, **Labor 6434.5**

FIREFIGHTERS AND FIRE DEPARTMENTS —Cont'd

Off duty suppression activities, injuries, workers compensation, **Labor 3600.1, 3600.4**

Pneumonia, workers compensation, **Labor 3212**

Presumptions, heart trouble, employment, discrimination, **Gov 12940.1**

Private fire departments, workers compensation, death or injury, **Labor 3600.4**

Railroads, this index

Reserves or auxiliaries, discrimination, absence and absentees, labor and employment, emergency duties, **Labor 230.3**

San Luis Obispo County, leave of absence, salary in lieu of temporary disability benefits, **Labor 4850.5**

Scholarships, dependents, death or disability in line of duty, **Labor 4709**

State firemen, workers compensation, **Labor 3600.1**

Statute of limitations, asbestosis, death benefits, **Labor 5406.5**

Third parties, actions against, workers compensation, **Labor 3852 et seq.**

Training, volunteers, leaves of absence, **Labor 230.4**

Tuberculosis, workers compensation, **Labor 3212.6**

Unemployment compensation, temporary employees, excluded services, **Un Ins 634.5**

University of California. Colleges and Universities, this index

Volunteer firefighters and fire departments,
Biochemical substances, workers compensation, presumptions, **Labor 3212.85**
Cancer, workers compensation, **Labor 3212.1**
Discharge, leaves of absence, training, **Labor 230.4**
Discrimination,
Employees taking time off to perform duties as, **Labor 230.3**
Leaves of absence, training, **Labor 230.4**
Labor and employment, leaves of absence, training, **Labor 230.4**
Leaves of absence, training, **Labor 230.4**
Probationary period, **Labor 1964**
Removal, **Labor 1964**
Suspension, **Labor 1964**
Training, leaves of absence, **Labor 230.4**
Workers compensation, **Labor 3361**
Average weekly and annual earnings, **Labor 4458**
Biochemical substances, presumptions, **Labor 3212.85**
Cancer, **Labor 3212.1**

Workers compensation,
Apprentices, biochemical substances, presumptions, **Labor 3212.85**

FIREFIGHTERS AND FIRE DEPARTMENTS
—Cont'd
Workers compensation—Cont'd
Biochemical substances, presumptions, **Labor 3212.85**
Blood borne infectious diseases, presumptions, **Labor 3212.8**
Cancer, **Labor 3212.1**
Death in line of duty, survivors, health benefits, **Labor 4856**
Hepatitis, presumptions, **Labor 3212.8**
Hernia, heart trouble and pneumonia, **Labor 3212**
University of California firemen, **Labor 3212.4**
Leaves of absence, disability benefits, **Labor 4850**
Meningitis, presumptions, **Labor 3212.9**
Off duty injuries, **Labor 3600.1 et seq.**
San Luis Obispo County, leave of absence, salary in lieu of temporary disability benefits, **Labor 4850.5**
Scholarships, dependents, **Labor 4709**
Suppression of fires, **Labor 3365**
Temporary employees, excluded service, **Un Ins 634.5**
Third parties, actions against, **Labor 3852 et seq.**
Tuberculosis, **Labor 3212.6**
University of California firemen, **Labor 4804.1 et seq.**
Hernia, heart trouble and pneumonia, **Labor 3212.4**
Volunteer firefighters and fire departments, ante

FIRES AND FIRE PROTECTION
Breathing apparatus, development of safety standards, positive pressure closed circuit breathing apparatus, **Labor 6331**
Chemical plant workers, safety, **Labor 7850 et seq.**
Combustibles, generally, this index
Correctional Institutions, this index
Elevators, dumbwaiters and escalators, **Labor 7301.5**
Explosives, generally, this index
Extinguishers. Fire Extinguishers, generally, this index
Fire Extinguishers, generally, this index
Forestry and Fire Protection Department, generally, this index
Hazardous fire areas, trespass, **Pen 602**
Labor camps, local fire zones, reserved to local jurisdictions, **Health & S 17021**
Machinery and equipment. Fire Extinguishers, generally, this index
Prisons and prisoners. Correctional Institutions, this index
Private Investigators, generally, this index
Standards, breathing apparatus, positive pressure closed circuit apparatus, **Labor 6331**
Technical assistance, voluntarily rendered to public entity, workers compensation, **Labor 3367**

FIRES AND FIRE PROTECTION—Cont'd
Temporary public employees, unemployment compensation, excluded service, **Un Ins 634.5**
Trespass, hazardous fire area, **Pen 602**
Voluntary technical assistance to public entity, workers compensation, **Labor 3367**
Workers compensation,
Average weekly earnings, **Labor 4458**
Cancer, **Labor 3212.1**
Suppressing fires, **Labor 3365**
Temporary public employees, excluded service, **Un Ins 634.5**
Voluntary technical assistance to public entity, **Labor 3367**
Zoning and Planning, generally, this index

FIRM OFFER OF CREDIT
Definitions, consumer credit reporting agencies, **CC 1785.3**

FIRST AID
Emergencies, **Labor 6708**
Manufacturers and manufacturing, **Labor 2440**
Pesticide poisoning, exclusion, **Labor 6409**

FISCAL YEAR
Definitions, withholding tax on wages, **Un Ins 13003**
Income Tax—State, this index

FISH AND GAME
Commercial fishing, unemployment compensation, **Un Ins 1252.1, 1252.2**
Compensation and salaries, seasonal employment termination, payment, **Labor 201**
Conservation Corps, generally, this index
Labor and employment, termination of seasonal employment, payment of wages, **Labor 201**
Livestock. Animals, generally, this index
Oysters. Shellfish, this index
Posting, trespass, **Pen 602**
Reserve wardens, workers compensation, **Labor 3363**
Trespass, **Pen 602**
Wardens,
Heart trouble, workers compensation, **Labor 3212**
Hernias, workers compensation, **Labor 3212**
Pneumonia, workers compensation, **Labor 3212**
Reserve warden program, workers compensation, **Labor 3363**
Workers compensation, **Labor 3212**
Workers Compensation, this index

FISHING
Fish and Game, generally, this index

FLAMMABLES
Combustibles, generally, this index

FLOODS AND FLOODING
Temporary public employees, unemployment compensation, excluded service, **Un Ins 634.5**
Workers compensation, temporary public employees, excluded service, **Un Ins 634.5**

FLOOR WAXERS
Children and minors, employment, **Labor 1294.3**

FLOORS
Safety in employment, building construction or repair, **Labor 7100 et seq.**

FOOD
Agricultural Products, generally, this index
Employment, municipalities, time off to procure meals, **Labor 1900, 1901**
Fish and Game, generally, this index
Fruits, generally, this index
Grocery Stores, generally, this index
Industrial homework, manufacturer, **Labor 2651**
Labor and employment, municipalities, time off to procure meals, **Labor 1900**
Manufacturers and manufacturing, industrial homework, **Labor 2651**
Meals, generally, this index
Municipal officers and employees, time off duty to procure meals, **Labor 1900, 1901**
Restaurants, generally, this index
Support, generally, this index
Vegetables, generally, this index

FOOD AND AGRICULTURE DEPARTMENT
Officers and employees, **Food & A 221.1**
Reports, officers and employees, **Food & A 221.1**

FOOD ESTABLISHMENTS
Food, generally, this index
Grocery Stores, generally, this index
Restaurants, generally, this index

FOOD FACILITIES
Food, generally, this index
Grocery Stores, generally, this index
Restaurants, generally, this index

FOOD STAMPS
Social Services, this index

FORCE AND VIOLENCE
Actions and proceedings, injunction, **CC 52**
Assault and Battery, generally, this index
Civil Rights, this index
Colleges and Universities, this index
Community health care workers, records and recordation, **Labor 6332**
Damages, civil rights, **CC 52**
Definitions, community health care workers, records and recordation, **Labor 6332**
Discrimination, this index
Domestic Violence, generally, this index

FORCE AND VIOLENCE—Cont'd

Fines and penalties, discrimination, **CC 52**

Freedom from force and violence, **CC 51.7**

Gender violence, actions and proceedings, **CC 52.4**

Hate crimes, **CC 51.7, 52**

Injunction, **CC 52**

Intimidation, freedom from intimidation, **CC 51.7**

Labor and employment, records and recordation, disclosure, **Pen 11105.3**

Limitation of actions, fines and penalties, **CC 52**

Medical care and treatment, community health care workers, records and recordation, **Labor 6332**

Sex, actions and proceedings, **CC 52.4**

Statute of limitations, fines and penalties, **CC 52**

FORCIBLE ENTRY AND DETAINER

Consumer credit reporting agencies, use of information, **CC 1785.13**

Investigative consumer reporting agencies, use of information, **CC 1786.18**

FOREIGN BORN PERSONS

Aliens, generally, this index

FOREIGN CORPORATIONS

Dissolution and winding up, unemployment compensation final report and return, **Un Ins 1735**

Officers and employees, unemployment compensation final return, liability for failure to file, **Un Ins 1735**

Unemployment compensation,
  Employing unit, **Un Ins 135**
  Failure to file final return, liability of officers, **Un Ins 1735**
  Withdrawal from state, final report, **Un Ins 1116**

FOREIGN COUNTRIES

Choice of law. Conflict of Laws, generally, this index

Conflict of Laws, generally, this index

Contractors, foreign labor contractors, **Bus & P 9998 et seq.**

Definitions, withholding tax on wages, **Un Ins 13003**

Labor contractors, **Bus & P 9998 et seq.**

Unemployment compensation, **Un Ins 643, 644**
  Foreign professional athletes, **Un Ins 655**
  Performance of services, **Un Ins 603.5**
  Services performed outside country for American employer, **Un Ins 610**

FOREIGN LANGUAGES

Apprentices, electricity, certificates and certification, **Labor 3099.3**

Electricity, apprentices, certificates and certification, **Labor 3099.3**

Interpreters and Translators, generally, this index

FOREIGN LIMITED LIABILITY PARTNERSHIPS

Partnership, this index

FOREIGN NATION

Foreign Countries, generally, this index

FOREIGN NATIONALS

Aliens, generally, this index

FOREIGN STATES

Choice of law. Conflict of Laws, generally, this index

Conflict of Laws, generally, this index

Domestic partnership, full faith and credit, **Fam 299.2**

Interstate Commerce, generally, this index

Oil and gas, used oil, recycling, contracts, tests, reports, **Health & S 25250.30**

Reciprocity, generally, this index

Sex Offenders, this index

Support, this index

Unemployment Compensation, this index

Workers Compensation, this index

FOREIGNERS

Aliens, generally, this index

FORENSIC LABORATORIES

Crimes and offenses. Laboratories, this index

FOREST FIRES

Hazardous fire areas, trespass, **Pen 602**

FOREST PRODUCTS

Timber and Lumber, generally, this index

FORESTERS

Blood borne infectious diseases, workers compensation, presumptions, **Labor 3212.8**

Meningitis, workers compensation, presumptions, **Labor 3212.9**

Methicillin resistant staphylococcus aureus (MRSA) skin infections, workers compensation, presumptions, **Labor 3212.8**

Workers compensation,
  Blood borne infectious diseases, presumptions, **Labor 3212.8**
  Cancer, **Labor 3212.1**
  Hepatitis, presumptions, **Labor 3212.8**
  Meningitis, presumptions, **Labor 3212.9**

FORESTRY AND FIRE PROTECTION DEPARTMENT

Cancer, workers compensation, **Labor 3212.1**

Workers compensation,
  Cancer, **Labor 3212.1**
  Peace officers, **Labor 3600.3**

FORESTRY DIVISION

Forestry and Fire Protection Department, generally, this index

FORESTS AND FORESTRY

Department. Forestry and Fire Protection Department, generally, this index

FORESTS AND FORESTRY—Cont'd

Foresters, generally, this index

Forestry and Fire Protection Department, generally, this index

Lumber. Timber and Lumber, generally, this index

Professional foresters. Foresters, generally, this index

State department. Forestry and Fire Protection Department, generally, this index

Timber and Lumber, generally, this index

Zoning and Planning, generally, this index

FORFEITURES

Compensation and salaries, failure to pay employees, **Labor 211**

Industrial homework, goods confiscated as evidence, **Labor 2658.7**

Public Buildings and Works, this index

Vested vacation time, termination of employment, **Labor 227.3**

FORGERY

Definitions, labor union insignia, use on articles of merchandise, **Labor 1013**

Labor organization label or trademark, **Labor 1015**

FORMER SPOUSE

Definitions, group disability insurance, continuation of benefits, **Ins 10116.5**

FORMS

Aged Persons, this index

Agricultural labor and employment, field sanitation compliance forms, **Labor 6712**

Apprentices, contracts, **Labor 3078**

Apprenticeship council reports, **Labor 3073.5**

Apprenticeship standards division, reports, **Labor 3073.5**

Dependent Adults, this index

Domestic Partnership, this index

Domestic Violence, this index

Earnings withholding order, **CCP 706.125**

Garnishment, this index

Harassment,
  Injunction, **CCP 527.6**
  Judicial council legal forms, **CCP 527.6**

Injunction, harassment, **CCP 527.6**

Labor camps, permit applications, **Health & S 17032**

Medical records, release, employers, **CC 56.21**

Public works contracts, workers compensation, certificate, **Labor 1861**

Support, this index

Talent agencies, contracts, **Labor 1703**

Workers Compensation, this index

Workplace violence safety, petitions, **CCP 527.8**

FOSTER HOMES

Social Services, this index

FOUNDATIONS
Charities, generally, this index
Disability compensation, employees, **Un Ins 2606**
Unemployment insurance, elections for financing, **Un Ins 801, 803**

FOUNDRIES
Manufacturers and Manufacturing, generally, this index

FOUNTAIN PEN GUNS
Weapons, generally, this index

FOUR AMINODIPHENYL
Occupational Carcinogens Control Act, **Labor 9000 et seq.**

FOUR DIMETHYLAMINOAZOBENZENE
Occupational Carcinogens Control Act, **Labor 9000 et seq.**

FOUR, FOUR METHYLENE (BIS) TWO CHLOROANILINE
Occupational Carcinogens Control Act, **Labor 9000 et seq.**

FOUR NITRODIPHENYL
Occupational Carcinogens Control Act, **Labor 9000 et seq.**

FRANCHISE TAX BOARD
Definitions, withholding tax on wages, **Un Ins 13003**
Income tax—state, definitions, withholding tax on wages, **Un Ins 13003**
Joint enforcement strike force on the underground economy, representative, **Un Ins 329**
Labor camp owners, tax returns, examination, **Health & S 17061.5**
Wage withholding, **Un Ins 13000 et seq.**

FRANCHISE TAXES
Corporation Taxes, generally, this index

FRATERNAL ASSOCIATIONS AND SOCIETIES
Officers, unemployment compensation, **Un Ins 652**
Unemployment compensation, officials, **Un Ins 652**

FRATERNAL BENEFIT SOCIETIES
Insurance, this index

FRATERNITIES
Colleges and Universities, this index

FRAUD
Generally, **Labor 6426**
Advertisements, this index
Agricultural labor and employment,
Farm labor contractors, **Labor 1696**
Transportation fees, **Labor 1697.1**
Bailment, this index
Claims against state, false claims, **Gov 12650 et seq.**
Class of labor employed, misrepresentation, **Labor 1010 et seq.**

FRAUD—Cont'd
Compensation and salaries, farm labor contractors, wearing apparel, manufacturers and manufacturing, **Labor 273**
Construction funds, larceny, **Pen 484b**
Consumer Credit Reporting Agencies, this index
Damages,
Exemplary damages, **CC 3294**
Labor and employment, **CC 3294**
Solicitation of employees, **Labor 972**
Definitions, damages, **CC 3294**
Disability compensation. Unemployment Compensation, this index
Domestic partnership, termination, vacating or setting aside, **Fam 299**
Employment. Labor and Employment, this index
Employment counseling services, **CC 1812.513**
Exemplary damages, **CC 3294**
Fair employment and housing, fines and penalties, **Gov 12987**
Farm labor contractors, **Labor 1696**
Finance Lenders, this index
Fines and penalties, exemplary damages, **CC 3294**
Garnishment, **CCP 706.152, 706.154**
Income Tax—State, this index
Job listing services, **CC 1812.520**
Labor and Employment, this index
Labor organization insignia, use on articles of merchandise, **Labor 1010 et seq.**
Leases, this index
Nurse registries, **CC 1812.533**
Public Buildings and Works, this index
Residential mortgage lenders. Mortgages, this index
Solicitation, employees, **Labor 970 et seq.**
Talent Agencies, this index
Telecommunications, this index
Theft, **Pen 484**
Tips, public policy, **Labor 356**
Unemployment Compensation, this index
Workers Compensation, this index

FREEDOM OF EMPLOYMENT
Public policy, **Labor 923**

FRINGE BENEFITS
Building and construction industry, payment with bad checks, **Labor 203.1**
Mechanics Liens, this index
Trusts and Trustees, this index
Unpaid wages or benefits, collections, deposits, payment, escheat, **Labor 96.7**
Workers compensation, exclusion, average weekly earnings, **Labor 4454**

FRIVOLOUS ACTIONS
Workers compensation, **Labor 5813**

FRUIT TREES
Unemployment compensation, qualifications, **Un Ins 611 et seq.**

FRUITS
Children and minors, permissible employment, **Labor 1294.3**
Farm labor contractor, definitions, **Labor 1682.4**
Handlers, children and minors, employment, **Labor 1294.3**
Labor and employment, termination of seasonal employment, payment of wages, **Labor 201**

FULL CREW LAW
Railroads, **Labor 6901 et seq.**

FULL FAITH AND CREDIT
Domestic partnership, **Fam 299.2**

FULL TIME EMPLOYMENT
Definitions, hours of labor, exemptions, **Labor 515**

FULL TIME QUALIFIED CARE PLAN
Definitions, child care, tax credit, **Rev & T 17052.18**

FULL TIME STUDENT
Definitions, unemployment insurance, **Un Ins 642.1**

FULMINATE OF MERCURY
Explosives, generally, this index

FUNDS
Agricultural labor and employment, agricultural employees relief fund, **Labor 1161**
Apprentices, this index
Asbestos training and consultant certification, **Labor 9021.7**
Cal OSHA targeted inspection and consultation fund, **Labor 62.7, 62.9**
Car wash worker fund, **Labor 2065**
Car wash worker restitution fund, **Labor 2065**
Definitions,
Employment training fund, **Un Ins 10201**
Workers compensation, **Labor 3700.1**
Self insurance, **Labor 3741**
Department of employment development contingent fund, **Un Ins 1585**
Augmentation of appropriations, **Un Ins 1586.5**
Electricity, this index
Employment Development, this index
Employment Training Fund, generally, this index
Health and Welfare Fund, generally, this index
Improvements, this index
Income Tax—State, this index
Industrial promotion funds, negotiated, employees failure to make payments, **Labor 227**
Industrial relations construction industry enforcement funds, unlicensed contractors, deposit of funds, **Labor 1024**
Industrial relations department, **Labor 58**

FUNDS

FUNDS—Cont'd

Industrial relations unpaid wage fund. State Treasury, this index

Investments, generally, this index

Labor and Employment, this index

Manpower service funds, employment development department, **Un Ins 9609**

Public Buildings and Works, this index

Real Estate, this index

Return to work fund, workers compensation, **Labor 139.48**

School employees fund, contribution rates, **Un Ins 823**

School Funds, generally, this index

Self insurance plans funds, workers compensation, **Labor 3702.5**

Self insurers security fund, workers compensation, **Labor 3740 et seq.**

State public works enforcement fund, **Labor 1771.3**

State Treasury, generally, this index

Talent agencies, artists, trusts and trustees, **Labor 1700.25**

Trust Funds, generally, this index

Unemployment Compensation, this index

Uninsured employers benefits trust fund. Workers Compensation, this index

Withholding tax on wages, **Un Ins 13011**

Workers Compensation, this index

Workers compensation administration revolving fund, **Labor 78**

Workers occupational safety and health education fund, **Labor 6354.7**

FUNDS TRANSFERS

Public Employees Retirement System, this index

Support, this index

Unemployment Compensation, this index

FUNERAL EXPENSES

Workers Compensation, this index

FURLOUGHS

Superior courts, officers and employees, public employees retirement system, service credits, **Gov 20969.1**

GAINS AND LOSSES

Corporation Taxes, this index

Income Tax—State, this index

GAMBLING

Clubs, smoking, **Labor 6404.5**

Farm labor contractors, persons frequenting, **Labor 1698.6**

Labor and employment, seasonal labor, gambling debts, wage deductions, **Labor 253**

Seasonal labor, gambling debts, deduction from wages, **Labor 253**

GAME

Fish and Game, generally, this index

GAME BIRDS

Fish and Game, generally, this index

GAMES

Athletics, generally, this index

Gambling, generally, this index

GARDENERS AND GARDENING

Workers compensation, part time gardeners, exclusion, **Labor 3352**

GARMENT MANUFACTURING

Definitions, **Labor 2670**

GARMENTS

Wearing Apparel, generally, this index

GARNISHMENT

Generally, **CCP 706.010 et seq., 1206 et seq.**

Accelerated payments, **CCP 706.153**

Accounts and accounting, **CCP 706.026**

Addresses, application, **CCP 706.121 et seq.**

Administration, **CCP 706.151 et seq.**

Administrative law and procedure, income tax—state levy, **CCP 706.072**

Admission, preferred labor claims, **CCP 1207**

Agents and agencies, service, **CCP 706.101**

Appeal and review,
Exemption claim, **CCP 706.105**
Income tax—state, **CCP 706.082**
Support, withholding orders, **CCP 706.030**

Application of law, **CCP 706.020**
Wage assignments for support, **CCP 706.031**

Applications,
Filing, **CCP 706.102**
Forms, **CCP 706.120 et seq.**
Income tax—state levy, **CCP 706.076**

Bonds (officers and fiduciaries), **Labor 404**

Branch offices, service of process, **CCP 706.101**

Claims, loss of wages as result of discharge from employment, labor commissioner taking assignments, **Labor 2924, 2929**

Consumer Credit Protection Act (federal), exemption, **CCP 706.151**

Contempt,
Employers failure to comply, **CCP 706.104**
Income tax—state levies, **CCP 706.075**

Contest, exemption claim, **CCP 706.105**

Copies, **CCP 706.129**
Instructions, **CCP 706.103**

Costs, **CCP 706.028**
Labor claims, **CCP 1207**
Labor standards enforcement division, **Labor 101**
Registered process server, **CCP 706.101**

Crimes and offenses, **CCP 706.152**

Deferred payments, **CCP 706.153**

Definitions, **CCP 706.011**

Delivery, earnings withholding orders, **CCP 706.101**

GARNISHMENT—Cont'd

Disability compensation, unemployment compensation, refunds and overpayments, service of process, **CCP 706.101**

Discharge of employee, **Labor 2924, 2929**

Division of earnings by court, **CCP 706.052**

Door to door salesmen, money deposited as security, wages, **Labor 270.6**

Earnings withholding orders, **CCP 706.022**
Additional orders, costs and interest payment, **CCP 706.028**
Application of law, **CCP 706.031**
Applications, issuance and service, **CCP 706.108, 706.121**
Deduction per payment, employers, **CCP 706.034**
Forms, **CCP 706.125**
Income tax—state, **CCP 706.070 et seq.**
Multiple orders, **CCP 706.023**
Procedures, **CCP 706.100 et seq.**
Satisfaction, amount required, determination, **CCP 706.024**
Service, **CCP 706.108**
Spouses, issuance, **CCP 706.109**
Support enforcement, **CCP 706.030**
Foreign states, binding employer, **Fam 5230.1**
Taxes, **CCP 706.070 et seq.**
Termination, **CCP 706.032**

Enforcement, **CCP 706.151 et seq.**

Equity, exempt amount, **CCP 706.052**

Executions, generally, this index

Exemptions, **CCP 706.050 et seq.**
Amount, **CCP 706.052**
Consumer Credit Protection Act (federal), **CCP 706.151**
Family support, **CCP 706.051**
Oaths and affirmations, **CCP 706.123**

Family support, exemption, **CCP 706.051**

Filing,
Application, **CCP 706.102**
Exemptions, **CCP 706.105**

Financial statements and reports, **CCP 706.124**

Findings of fact, **CCP 706.106**

Fines and penalties, support, employers, withholding orders for support, **CCP 706.030**

Forms, **CCP 706.120 et seq.**
Earnings withholding order applications, **CCP 706.121**
Income tax—state, **CCP 706.081, 706.084**

Fraud, **CCP 706.152, 706.154**

Hearings,
Exemption claim, **CCP 706.105**
Income tax—state levy, **CCP 706.075**

Husband and wife, earnings withholding order issued against spouse, **CCP 706.109**

Immunities. Privileges and immunities, generally, post

GARNISHMENT—Cont'd
Income tax—state, **CCP 706.070 et seq.**
  Administrative law and procedure, **CCP 706.072**
  Amount, **CCP 706.074**
  Appeal and review, **CCP 706.082**
  Application, **CCP 706.076**
  Application of law, **CCP 706.071**
  Definitions, **CCP 706.070, 706.072**
  Earnings withholding orders, ante
  Forms, **CCP 706.081, 706.084**
  Hearings, **CCP 706.075**
  Jeopardy withholding order, **CCP 706.078**
  Mail and mailing, **CCP 706.072, 706.080**
  Multiple orders, priorities, **CCP 706.077**
  Notice, **CCP 706.072, 706.075**
    Application, **CCP 706.076**
  Priorities and preferences, **CCP 706.077**
  Privileges and immunities, **CCP 706.075**
  Service of process, **CCP 706.075, 706.080**
  Temporary orders, **CCP 706.076**
  Termination, jeopardy withholding order, **CCP 706.078**
  Time,
    Hearing, **CCP 706.075**
    Temporary orders, **CCP 706.076**
Instructions, **CCP 706.127**
  Copies, **CCP 706.103**
Interest, **CCP 706.028**
Itinerant merchants, moneys deposited as security for wages, **Labor 270.6**
Jeopardy withholding order, taxes, **CCP 706.078**
Labor standards enforcement division, court costs, **Labor 101**
Liability. Privileges and immunities, generally, post
Liens and incumbrances, **CCP 706.029**
Logs and logging, cash and securities on deposit to insure wage payments, **Labor 270.5**
Mail and mailing,
  Exemption, **CCP 706.105**
  Income tax—state, **CCP 706.072, 706.080**
  Service of process, **CCP 706.101**
Managing agent, service of process, **CCP 706.101**
Modification, **CCP 706.105**
Motion,
  Equitable division, **CCP 706.052**
  Spouses, earnings withholding orders against, **CCP 706.109**
Multiple orders, **CCP 706.023**
  Income tax—state, priority, **CCP 706.077**
Names, application, **CCP 706.121 et seq.**
Notice,
  Exemption claim, **CCP 706.105**
  Form, **CCP 706.122**
  Income tax—state, **CCP 706.072, 706.075**
    Application, **CCP 706.076**

GARNISHMENT—Cont'd
Notice—Cont'd
  Judgment creditors opposition to claim of exemption, **CCP 706.128**
  Spouses, earnings withholding orders, issuance, motion, **CCP 706.109**
  Support, employers, withholding orders, appeal and review, **CCP 706.030**
  Support order, **CCP 706.031**
  Termination, **CCP 706.027**
Oaths and affirmations, **CCP 706.121 et seq.**
Payment,
  Accelerated or deferred, **CCP 706.153**
  Deduction per payment, employers, earnings withholding orders, **CCP 706.034**
  Time, **CCP 706.025, 706.026**
Personal service, **CCP 706.101**
Priorities and preferences,
  Income tax—state, **CCP 706.077**
  Multiple orders, **CCP 706.023**
  Support order, **CCP 706.030, 706.031**
Privileges and immunities, **CCP 706.104**
  Employer, **CCP 706.022**
  Fraud, **CCP 706.154**
  Income tax—state, **CCP 706.075**
Procedure, **CCP 706.100 et seq.**
Publication, instructions, **CCP 706.127**
Registered process server, **CCP 706.101**
Release or discharge, **CCP 1208**
Restrictions, **CCP 706.050 et seq.**
Return,
  Form, **CCP 706.126**
  Supplemental return, earnings withholding order termination, **CCP 706.033**
Satisfaction of judgment, termination, **CCP 706.027**
Sawmill operations, deposits to insure wage payments, **Labor 270.5**
Service of process, **CCP 706.021, 706.101 et seq.**
  Income tax—state, **CCP 706.075, 706.080**
Social security number, application, **CCP 706.121 et seq.**
Spouses, earnings withholding orders, motions, **CCP 706.109**
State officers and employees, service of process, **CCP 706.101**
State taxes. Income tax—state, generally, ante
Support, **CCP 706.030, 706.031**
  Foreign states, earnings assignments, income withholding orders, binding employer, **Fam 5230.1**
Taxation. Income tax—state, generally, ante
Telephone solicitors, money deposited as security for wages, **Labor 270.6**
Temporary order, income tax—state, **CCP 706.076**
Termination, **CCP 706.022**
  Earnings withholding orders, **CCP 706.032**

GARNISHMENT—Cont'd
Termination—Cont'd
  Earnings withholding orders—Cont'd
    Supplemental return, filing, **CCP 706.033**
  Exemption claim, **CCP 706.105**
  Income tax—state, jeopardy withholding order, **CCP 706.078**
  Satisfaction of judgment, **CCP 706.027**
Time, **CCP 706.022**
  Exemption claim, contest, **CCP 706.105**
  Income tax—state,
    Hearing, **CCP 706.075**
    Temporary orders, **CCP 706.076**
  Liens and incumbrances, **CCP 706.029**
  Payment, **CCP 706.025, 706.026**
  Support order, **CCP 706.030**
Unemployment compensation,
  Contributions, exemption, **Un Ins 988**
  Delinquent contributions, **Un Ins 1755 et seq.**
  Refunds and overpayments, service of process, **CCP 706.101**

GAS
Oil and Gas, generally, this index

GAS COMPANIES
Oil and Gas, generally, this index

GAS STATIONS
Motor Vehicle Service Stations, generally, this index

GASOLINE
Liquefied Petroleum Gas, generally, this index

GASOLINE STATIONS
Motor Vehicle Service Stations, generally, this index

GATES
Trespasses, acts constituting, **Pen 602, 602.8**

GENDER
Sex, generally, this index

GENDER IDENTITY
Labor and employment, wearing apparel, **Gov 12949**

GENDER VIOLENCE
Actions and proceedings, **CC 52.4**

GENERAL ASSEMBLY
Legislature, generally, this index

GENERAL ASSISTANCE
County aid and relief. Social Services, this index

GENERAL CORPORATION LAW
Corporations, generally, this index

GENERAL ELECTIONS
Elections, generally, this index

GENERAL FUND
State Treasury, this index

GENERAL

GENERAL LAWS
Statutes, generally, this index

GENERAL NONPROFIT CORPORATION LAW
Nonprofit Corporations, generally, this index

GENERAL OBLIGATION BONDS
Bonds, generally, this index

GENERAL PUBLIC PARATRANSIT VEHICLES
Paratransit Vehicles, generally, this index

GENERAL SERVICES DEPARTMENT
Contracts. State Contracts, generally, this index
Human resources development department, purchase of insurance, approval, **Un Ins 1601**
State Contracts, generally, this index

GENERAL SESSIONS
Legislature, generally, this index

GENERAL STORES
Stores, generally, this index

GENERIC DRUGS
Drugs and Medicine, this index

GENETIC CHARACTERISTICS
Diseases, this index

GENOCIDE
Armenians, this index

GEOLOGISTS AND GEOPHYSICISTS
Certificates and certification, geologists in training, **Bus & P 7843**
Geologists in training, certificates and certification, **Bus & P 7843**
Title, geologists in training, **Bus & P 7843**
Training, certificates and certification, **Bus & P 7843**

GEOLOGY
Mines and Minerals, generally, this index

GEOPHYSICISTS
Geologists and Geophysicists, generally, this index

GIANT POWDERS
Explosives, generally, this index

GIFTS, DEVISES AND BEQUESTS
Charities, generally, this index
Labor and employment gratuitous, **Labor 2850 et seq.**
Probate Proceedings, generally, this index

GIN
Alcoholic Beverages, generally, this index

GIRLS
Children and Minors, generally, this index

GOATS
Trespass, **Pen 602**

I–78

GOLDEN GATE BRIDGE, HIGHWAY AND TRANSPORTATION DISTRICT
Labor disputes, **Labor 1137 et seq.**
Officers and employees, labor disputes, **Labor 1137 et seq.**

GOLF COURSES
Unemployment compensation, caddies, **Un Ins 651**

GOOD CAUSE
Definitions,
Unemployment compensation,
Extension of time, appeals, decision, **Un Ins 1334**
Leaving employment, **Un Ins 1256**
Workers compensation, medical evaluations, time, **Labor 139.2**

GOOD FAITH
Labor and employment, layoffs, fines and penalties, **Labor 1405**

GOODS, WARES AND MERCHANDISE
Cash bond of employee, exaction or acceptance, **Labor 402 et seq.**
Class of labor employed, labels, **Labor 1010 et seq.**
Crimes and offenses, dangerous conditions, failure to disclose, **Pen 387**
Dangerous conditions, failure to disclose, **Pen 387**
Fines and penalties, dangerous conditions, failure to disclose, **Pen 387**
Labor, compensation, script, coupon, cards, redeemable in as payment, **Labor 212**
Labor union insignia, **Labor 1010 et seq.**

GOVERNING BOARDS
Community colleges and districts. Colleges and Universities, this index
Schools and School Districts, this index

GOVERNING LAW
Conflict of Laws, generally, this index

GOVERNMENT EMPLOYEES RETIREMENT SYSTEM
Public Employees Retirement System, generally, this index

GOVERNMENTAL AGENCIES
Public Agencies, generally, this index

GOVERNMENTAL ENTITY
Definitions,
Information Practices Act, **CC 1798.3**
Unemployment compensation, **Un Ins 710**
Workers compensation, vanpooling, **Labor 3600.8**

GOVERNOR
Appointments,
Aging commission, **Un Ins 9612**
Agricultural labor relations board, **Labor 1141**
General counsel, **Labor 1149**

GOVERNOR—Cont'd
Appointments—Cont'd
Chairman,
Occupational safety and health appeals board, **Labor 148**
Occupational safety and health standards board, **Labor 140**
Directors, employment development, **Un Ins 302**
Deputy directors, **Un Ins 303**
Fair employment and housing commission, members, **Gov 12903**
Fair employment and housing department, director, **Gov 12901**
Health and safety and workers compensation board, **Labor 75**
Industrial accidents division, administrative director, **Labor 138.1**
Industrial relations director, **Labor 51**
Industrial welfare commission, **Labor 70**
Occupational safety and health appeals board,
Appointment of members, **Labor 148**
Vacancies, **Labor 148.1**
Occupational safety and health standards board members, **Labor 140**
Unemployment insurance appeals board, **Un Ins 402**
Apprenticeship council, appointment of representative, **Labor 3070**
Clemency, executive clemency, Information Practices Act, **CC 1798 et seq.**
Economic Opportunity Act, responsibilities under, **Un Ins 327**
Executive clemency, Information Practices Act, **CC 1798 et seq.**
Industrial accidents division, administrative director, appointment, **Labor 138.1**
Industrial relations department, organization, approval, **Labor 55**
Industrial relations director, appointment and removal from office, **Labor 51**
Industrial welfare commission, appointment of members, **Labor 70**
Occupational safety and health standard boards, members, appointment, **Labor 140**
Removal from office,
Industrial accidents division, administrative director, **Labor 138.1**
Industrial relations director, **Labor 51**
Unemployment insurance appeals board, appointments to fill vacancies in office, **Un Ins 402**

GRADUATION
High Schools or Secondary Schools, this index

GRAIN
Agricultural Products, generally, this index

GRAIN WAREHOUSES
Warehouses and Warehousemen, generally, this index

GRAND JURY
Accusation. Indictment and Information, generally, this index
Indictment and Information, generally, this index
Unemployment compensation, eligibility, **Un Ins 1253.6**

GRANTEES
Definitions, drug free workplaces, state grants, **Gov 8351**

GRANTS
Cal grant program. Colleges and Universities, this index
Deeds and Conveyances, generally, this index
Drug free workplaces, state grantees, **Gov 8350 et seq.**
Fines and penalties, labor organizations, promotion or deterrence, **Gov 16645.2**
Green collar jobs, **Un Ins 14022**
High Schools or Secondary Schools, this index
Housing, this index
Labor and Employment, this index
Labor organizations, promotion or deterrence, **Gov 16645.2**
Leisure sharing programs, employment opportunities creation, **Un Ins 12110 et seq.**
Nurses, this index
Records and recordation, labor organizations, promotion or deterrence, **Gov 16645.2**
Religious organizations and societies, unemployment compensation, job training and placement services, **Un Ins 9617**
Schools and School Districts, this index
State, drug free workplaces, state grantees, **Gov 8350 et seq.**
Unemployment Compensation, this index
Youthbuild program, **Un Ins 9800 et seq.**

GRATUITIES
Generally, **Labor 350 et seq.**
Income tax—state, withholding, **Un Ins 13027, 13055**

GRAVEL PITS
Safety regulations, **Labor 7950 et seq.**

GRAVES
Cemeteries and Dead Bodies, generally, this index

GRAVEYARDS
Cemeteries and Dead Bodies, generally, this index

GREAT BODILY INJURY
Definitions, dangerous business practices, **Pen 387**

GREATER AVENUES FOR INDEPENDENCE (GAIN)
Social Services, this index

GREEN COLLAR JOBS
Generally, **Un Ins 15000 et seq.**

GRENADES
Explosives, generally, this index

GRIEVANCES
Workers Compensation, this index

GROCERIES
Food, generally, this index

GROCERY STORES
Baggers, children and minors, employment, **Labor 1294.3**
Carryouts, children and minors, employment, **Labor 1294.3**
Children and minors, employment, **Labor 1294.3**
Price marking and tagging, minors, employment, **Labor 1294.3**
Produce stockers, children and minors, employment, **Labor 1294.3**
Stockers, children and minors, employment, **Labor 1294.3**

GROSS INCOME
Definitions, withholding tax on wages, **Un Ins 13006**
Income Tax State, this index

GROSS NEGLIGENCE
Negligence, this index

GROUP BENEFIT PLAN
Definitions, Cal COBRA, accident and health insurance, **Health & S 1366.21; Ins 10128.51**

GROUP DISABILITY INSURANCE
Insurance, this index

GROUP HEALTH COVERAGE
Definitions, access for infants and mothers program, unfair competition and labor practices, **Ins 12698.56**

GROUP INSURANCE
Insurance, this index

GROUP LIFE INSURANCE
Insurance, this index

GROWER
Definitions, farm labor contractors, licenses and permits, **Labor 1695.7**

GROWING CROPS
Agricultural Products, generally, this index

GUARANTY ASSOCIATIONS
Health Care Service Plans, this index

GUARDIAN AD LITEM
Workers compensation, appointment, **Labor 5307.5, 5408**

GUARDIAN AND WARD
Abduction, child, **CC 49**
Apprentices, employing, exhibiting, minor, **Labor 1308**

GUARDIAN AND WARD—Cont'd
Assignments, wages by minor, written consent, **Labor 300**
Consent, assignment of wages by minor, **Labor 300**
Enticement of child, **CC 49**
Hours of labor, children and minors, **Labor 1392**
Medical records, disclosure to investigators, determination of need for guardianship, **CC 56.10**
Talent agencies, certificate of convenience to conduct business, **Labor 1700.20a, 1700.20b**
Workers compensation, **Labor 5307.5, 5408**
Payment, children and minors, **Labor 3605**

GUARDS
Jails, this index
Private Investigators, generally, this index

GUEST HOUSES
Restaurants, generally, this index

GUN POWDER
Explosives, generally, this index

GUNS
Weapons, generally, this index

HABIT FORMING DRUGS
Drug Addicts, generally, this index
Drugs and Medicine, generally, this index

HABITUAL CRIMINALS
Second and subsequent offenses. Crimes and Offenses, this index

HABITUAL NEGLECT
Termination of employment, **Labor 2924**

HAMMERS
Building construction, repair, furnishing unsafe hammers, **Labor 7156**

HAND TOOLS
Ships and vessels, loading or unloading, safety, **Labor 7602**

HAND TRUCKS
Safety, **Labor 7601**

HANDGUNS
Weapons, generally, this index

HANDICAPPED PERSONS
Accessibility, standards, conflict of laws, **Gov 12955.1**
Apartment houses,
Discrimination, **Gov 12955 et seq.**
Multistory dwelling units, discrimination, **Gov 12955 et seq.**
Blind Persons, generally, this index
Building standards, multifamily dwellings, **Gov 12955.1**
Caregivers, crimes and offenses, disclosure, employment, **Pen 11105.3**
Civil rights, **CC 51 et seq.**

HANDICAPPED PERSONS—Cont'd

Compensation and salaries, minimum wages, **Labor 1191**

Condominiums, multistory dwelling units, discrimination, **Gov 12955 et seq.**

Conflict of laws, accessibility standards, **Gov 12955.1**

Corporation Taxes, this index

Corrections and rehabilitation department, disability in line of duty, dependents, scholarships, **Labor 4709**

Crimes and offenses, caretakers, disclosure, **Pen 11105.3**

Deaf and Mute Persons, generally, this index

Disability compensation. Unemployment Compensation, this index

Discrimination, **CC 51 et seq.**
Multifamily housing, **Gov 12955 et seq.**

Duress or coercion, housing rights, **Gov 12955.7**

Employment. Labor and employment, generally, post

Evidence, discriminatory housing practices, **Gov 12955.8**

Fair Employment and Housing, generally, this index

Guardian and Ward, generally, this index

Housing,
Discrimination, **Gov 12955 et seq.**
Fair Employment and Housing, generally, this index
Youthbuild program, **Un Ins 9800 et seq.**

Interference, housing rights, **Gov 12955.7**

Intimidation, housing rights, **Gov 12955.7**

Job training programs, **Un Ins 9003**

Juvenile facilities division, disability in line of duty, dependents, scholarships, **Labor 4709**

Labor and employment, **Un Ins 18000 et seq.**
Discrimination, **Labor 1735**
Fair Employment and Housing, generally, this index
Licenses and permits, minimum wages, **Labor 1191**
Personal care services, **Welf & I 14132.955**

Licenses and permits, labor and employment, minimum wages, **Labor 1191**

Manpower programs, **Un Ins 9003**

Minimum wages, **Labor 1191**

Multifamily housing, discrimination, **Gov 12955 et seq.**

Mute persons. Deaf and Mute Persons, generally, this index

Notice, criminal history, disclosure, employment, **Pen 11105.3**

Paratransit Vehicles, generally, this index

Peace officers, disability in lien of duty, dependents, scholarships, **Labor 4709**

Personal care services, labor and employment, **Welf & I 14132.955**

Physicians and Surgeons, this index

HANDICAPPED PERSONS—Cont'd

Public officers and employees, retraining and rehabilitation, **Labor 6200 et seq.**

Small Businesses, generally, this index

Social Services, this index

Threats, housing rights, **Gov 12955.7**

Training, **Un Ins 9003**

Unemployment Compensation, this index

Vocational Education, this index

Vocational Rehabilitation, generally, this index

HANDS

Workers compensation,
Loss of both hands or use, **Labor 4662**
Subsequent injuries, **Labor 4751**

HARASSMENT

Attorney fees, **CCP 527.6**

Colleges and universities, injunction, **CCP 527.85**

Costs, **CCP 527.6**

Definitions, fair employment and housing, **Gov 12940**

Fair Employment and Housing, this index

Forms, injunctions, temporary restraining orders, **CCP 527.6, 527.8**

Injunction, **CCP 527.6**

Judicial council legal forms, **CCP 527.6**

Labor and employment, personal liability, discrimination, unlawful practices, **Gov 12940**

Process, service of process, protective orders, **CCP 527.6**

Protective orders,
Service of process, **CCP 527.6**
Weapons,
Fines and penalties, **Pen 12021**
Surrender, **CCP 527.6 et seq.**

Right to privacy, injunctions, **CCP 527.6**

Service of process, protective orders, **CCP 527.6**

Sexual Harassment, generally, this index

Temporary restraining orders, **CCP 527.6**

Weapons, protective orders,
Fines and penalties, **Pen 12021**
Surrender, **CCP 527.6 et seq.**

HARBORS AND PORTS

Marine Terminals, generally, this index

Police,
Leaves of absence, workers compensation, disability benefits, **Labor 4850**
Workers compensation, leaves of absence, disability benefits, **Labor 4850**

San Francisco Harbor, generally, this index

Terminals. Marine Terminals, generally, this index

Wharves, Docks and Piers, generally, this index

HARRISON NARCOTIC ACT

Drugs and Medicine, generally, this index

HATCH TENDERS

Ships and vessels, loading and unloading operations, **Labor 7600, 7608**

HATE CRIMES

Generally, **CC 51.7, 52**

Limitation of actions, fines and penalties, **CC 52**

Statute of limitations, fines and penalties, **CC 52**

HAWKERS AND PEDDLERS

Children and minors,
Distance from home, **Labor 1308.1**
Door to door sales, children under age 6, **Labor 1308.1**
Employers of door to door sellers, registration, **Labor 1308.3**
Encouraging vocation, occupation, **Labor 1308**
Occupations, **Labor 1298**
Registration,
Employers and supervisors of door to door sellers, **Labor 1308.2 et seq.**
Supervisors of door to door sales, **Labor 1308.2**

Deposits, security for wages, **Labor 270.6**

Executions, exemptions, money deposited as security for wages, **Labor 270.6**

HAZARDOUS FIRE AREAS

Forest Fires, this index

HAZARDOUS MATERIALS

Hazardous Substances and Waste, generally, this index

HAZARDOUS SUBSTANCES AND WASTE

Asbestos, generally, this index

Brands, marks and labels, **Labor 6390.5**
Containers, **Labor 6390.5**

Chemical plant workers, safety, **Labor 7850 et seq.**

Compensation and salaries, discrimination, **Labor 6399.7**

Confidential or privileged information, MSDS, **Labor 6396**

Containers, this index

Disclosure, MSDS, **Labor 6398**

Exemptions, MSDS, allocation to provide, **Labor 6393**

Fees. Occupational lead poisoning, post

Labor and Employment, this index

Lists,
Information and training, **Labor 6380 et seq.**
Preparation and amendment, **Labor 6382**

Notice,
Employees, right to receive information under Hazardous Substances Information and Training Act, **Labor 6328**
Evidence, concentration of higher than necessary, **Labor 6383**

Occupational lead poisoning, fees, **Health & S 105190**

Exemption, **Health & S 105191**

HAZARDOUS SUBSTANCES AND WASTE
—Cont'd

Packages.   Containers, this index

Pesticides, generally, this index

Records and recordation, labor and employment, **Labor 147.2**

Standards, container labels, **Labor 6390.5**

Used oil.   Oil and Gas, this index

HAZARDOUS SUBSTANCES INFORMATION AND TRAINING ACT
Generally, **Labor 6360 et seq.**

HAZARDOUS WASTE
Hazardous Substances and Waste, generally, this index

HEALTH AND HUMAN SERVICES AGENCY
Secretary, coordination of job training placement programs, **Un Ins 9002**

HEALTH AND SAFETY AND WORKERS COMPENSATION BOARD
Generally, **Labor 75 et seq.**

HEALTH AND SANITATION
Asbestos, generally, this index

Business establishments, sanitary conditions, **Labor 2350 et seq.**

Cancer, generally, this index

Cemeteries and Dead Bodies, generally, this index

Clinics, generally, this index

Colleges and Universities, this index

Comfort Stations and Rest Rooms, generally, this index

Dead bodies.   Cemeteries and Dead Bodies, generally, this index

Definitions, occupational safety and health, **Labor 6306**

Diseases, generally, this index

Drugs and Medicine, generally, this index

Employment.   Labor and Employment, this index

Fees, double fees, operating camp without permit, **Health & S 17037**

Foundries and metal shops, **Labor 2330, 2331**

Hazardous Substances and Waste, generally, this index

Home Health Agencies, generally, this index

Hospitals, generally, this index

Industrial homework, prohibited materials and articles, **Labor 2651**

Labor and Employment, this index

Labor Camps, generally, this index

Lead, poisoning, occupational safety, prevention program, **Health & S 105185 et seq.**

Local health departments,
 Confidential or privileged information, forensic medical examinations, sexual assault, reports, **Pen 11160.1**
 Forensic medical examinations, sexual assault, reports, **Pen 11160.1**
 Occupational health services, **Health & S 105150**

HEALTH AND SANITATION—Cont'd
Local health departments—Cont'd
 Privileges and immunities, forensic medical examinations, sexual assault, reports, **Pen 11160.1**
 Sexual assault, forensic medical examinations, reports, **Pen 11160.1**

Manufacturing establishments, sanitary conditions, **Labor 2350 et seq.**
 Foundries and metal shops, **Labor 2330, 2331**

Medicine.   Drugs and Medicine, generally, this index

Metal shops, **Labor 2330, 2331**

Motion pictures, theaters, sanitary standards, **Labor 2260**

Municipal ordinances, **Labor 2260**

Occupational health programs, development, **Labor 50.8**

Occupational lead poisoning, prevention, **Health & S 105185 et seq.**

Occupational safety and health.   Labor and Employment, this index

Occupational safety and health appeals board, **Labor 148 et seq.**

Occupational safety and health standards board.   Industrial Relations Department, this index

Pregnancy, generally, this index

Residential Care Facilities for the Elderly, generally, this index

Sewers and Sewer Systems, generally, this index

Solicitation of employees by misrepresentation, **Labor 970**

Talent agencies, sending artist to unhealthy environment, **Labor 1700.33**

Theaters and shows, sanitary standards, **Labor 2260**

Tuberculosis, generally, this index

Universities.   Colleges and Universities, this index

Water Supply, generally, this index

HEALTH AND WELFARE BENEFITS
Social Services, generally, this index

HEALTH AND WELFARE FUND
Employee benefit plan distribution,
 Definitions, Unclaimed Property Law, **CCP 1501**
 Escheat to state, **CCP 1510, 1521**
Employee benefit trust distribution, escheat to state, **CCP 1510**

HEALTH CARE FACILITIES
Health Facilities, generally, this index

HEALTH CARE PROVIDERS
Actions and proceedings, whistle blowing, **Health & S 1278.5**

AIDS, this index

Attorney fees, whistle blowing, **Health & S 1278.5**

Caregiver training initiative, **Un Ins 11020 et seq.**

HEALTH CARE PROVIDERS—Cont'd
Confidential or privileged information, forensic medical examinations, sexual assault, reports, **Pen 11160.1**

Contracts, preferred reimbursement rates, **Labor 4609**

Costs, whistle blowing, **Health & S 1278.5**

Definitions, family care and medical leave, **Gov 12945.2**

Dentists and Dentistry, generally, this index

Disability insurance.   Insurance, this index

Discipline, whistle blowing, **Health & S 1278.5**

Disclosure, preferred reimbursement rates, **Labor 4609**

Forensic medical examinations, sexual assault, reports, **Pen 11160.1**

Health Care Service Plans, generally, this index

Health insurance, disability insurance.   Insurance, this index

Notice, safety, whistleblowers, **Health & S 1278.5**

Nurses, generally, this index

Preferred reimbursement rates, **Labor 4609**

Privileges and immunities,
 Adult abuse reports, **Welf & I 15634**
 Forensic medical examinations, sexual assault, reports, **Pen 11160.1**
 Rates and charges, preferred reimbursement rates, **Labor 4609**

Reimbursement, preferred reimbursement rates, **Labor 4609**

Retaliation, whistle blowing, **Health & S 1278.5**

Sexual assault, forensic medical examinations, reports, **Pen 11160.1**

Training, caregiver training initiative, **Un Ins 11020 et seq.**

Unemployment compensation, caregiver training initiative, **Un Ins 11020 et seq.**

Whistle blowing, **Health & S 1278.5**

Workers Compensation, this index

HEALTH CARE SERVICE PLANS
Actions and proceedings,
 Medical records, negligence, release, **CC 56.36**
 Medically necessary health care, powers and duties, **CC 3428**

Acupuncture, lists, **Health & S 1367.26**

AIDS, this index

Appeal and review, medically necessary health care, powers and duties, **CC 3428**

Benefits and coverage,
 Birth control, **Health & S 1367.25**
 Contraceptives, **Health & S 1367.25**
 Drugs and medicine, contraceptives, **Health & S 1367.25**
 Group contracts, post

Birth control, benefits and coverage, **Health & S 1367.25**

HEALTH CARE SERVICE PLANS—Cont'd

Cal COBRA, **Health & S 1366.20 et seq.; Ins 10128.50 et seq.**

Charges. Rates and charges, generally, post

Chiropractors, lists, **Health & S 1367.26**

Clinical social workers, lists, **Health & S 1367.26**

Confidential or privileged information, outpatient psychotherapy, records and recordation, **CC 56.104**

Continuation, Cal COBRA, **Health & S 1366.20 et seq.; Ins 10128.50 et seq.**

Contraceptives, benefits and coverage, **Health & S 1367.25**

Contracts. Group contracts, generally, post

Coverage. Benefits and coverage, generally, ante

Crimes and offenses, medical records, negligence, release, **CC 56.36**

Damages,
Medical records, negligence, release, **CC 56.36**
Medically necessary health care, powers and duties, **CC 3428**

Definitions, Cal COBRA, **Health & S 1366.21; Ins 10128.51**

Dependents, Cal COBRA, **Health & S 1366.23; Ins 10128.53**

Destruction, medical records, **CC 56.101**

Disclosure,
Cal COBRA, **Health & S 1366.24; Ins 10128.54**
Medical records, **CC 56.10**

Discrimination, domestic partnership, **Health & S 1374.58**

Domestic partnership, **Health & S 1374.58**

Drugs and medicine,
Benefits and coverage, ante
Birth control, benefits and coverage, **Health & S 1367.25**
Contraceptives, benefits and coverage, **Health & S 1367.25**

Elections, Cal COBRA, **Health & S 1366.23, 1366.25; Ins 10128.53**

Exemptions, Cal COBRA, **Health & S 1366.22; Ins 10128.52**

Faith healing, medically necessary health care, application of law, **CC 3428**

Fines and penalties, medical records, negligence, release, **CC 56.36**

Group contracts,
Benefits and coverage,
Birth control, **Health & S 1367.25**
Contraceptives, **Health & S 1367.25**
Birth control, benefits and coverage, **Health & S 1367.25**
Cal COBRA, **Health & S 1366.20 et seq.; Ins 10128.50 et seq.**
Continuation benefits, Cal COBRA, **Health & S 1366.20 et seq.; Ins 10128.50 et seq.**
Contraceptives, benefits and coverage, **Health & S 1367.25**

HEALTH CARE SERVICE PLANS—Cont'd

Group contracts—Cont'd
Domestic partnership, **Health & S 1374.58**

Guaranty associations, domestic partnership, **Health & S 1374.58**

HIV. AIDS, this index

Hospitals, lists, **Health & S 1367.26**

Indemnity, medically necessary health care, **CC 3428**

Information, providers, **Health & S 1367.26**

Lists, providers, **Health & S 1367.26**

Marriage and family therapists, lists, **Health & S 1367.26**

Medical records,
Disclosure, **CC 56.10**
Outpatient psychotherapy, **CC 56.104**

Medically necessary health care, powers and duties, **CC 3428**

Mentally Ill Persons, this index

Negligence,
Medical records, **CC 56.36, 56.101**
Medically necessary health care, powers and duties, **CC 3428**

Nominal damages, medical records, negligence, release, **CC 56.36**

Notice, continuation benefits, qualifying events, Cal COBRA, **Health & S 1366.24, 1366.25; Ins 10128.54**

Nurse midwives, lists, **Health & S 1367.26**

Optometrists, lists, **Health & S 1367.26**

Ordinary care standard, medically necessary health care, powers and duties, **CC 3428**

Outpatients, psychotherapy, records and recordation, **CC 56.104**

Physicians and surgeons, lists, **Health & S 1367.26**

Podiatrists (chiropody), lists, **Health & S 1367.26**

Premiums, Cal COBRA, **Health & S 1366.26, 1366.27; Ins 10128.56, 10128.57**

Providers, lists, **Health & S 1367.26**

Psychologists and psychology, lists, **Health & S 1367.26**

Qualifying events, Cal COBRA, **Health & S 1366.23; Ins 10128.53**
Notice, **Health & S 1366.24, 1366.25; Ins 10128.54**

Rates and charges, Cal COBRA, **Health & S 1366.26, 1366.27; Ins 10128.56, 10128.57**

Records and recordation,
Mentally ill persons, outpatient psychotherapy, **CC 56.104**
Outpatient psychotherapy, **CC 56.104**

Release, medical records, negligence, **CC 56.36**

Substantial harm,
Definitions, medically necessary health care, powers and duties, **CC 3428**
Medically necessary health care, powers and duties, **CC 3428**

HEALTH CARE SERVICE PLANS—Cont'd

Termination, Cal COBRA, **Health & S 1366.27; Ins 10128.57**

Time, Cal COBRA, continuation, termination, **Health & S 1366.27; Ins 10128.57**

Workers Compensation, this index

HEALTH CARE SERVICES DEPARTMENT

Confidential or privileged information, forensic medical examinations, sexual assault, reports, **Pen 11160.1**

Forensic medical examinations, sexual assault, reports, **Pen 11160.1**

Interagency agreements, occupational safety and health division, **Labor 60.9**

Occupational health branch, **Labor 60.6, 60.7**

Officers and employees, occupational health branch, transfer to occupational health and safety division, retention of rights, **Labor 60.6**

Plans and specifications, lead related construction work, employee protection, **Labor 6717**

Privileges and immunities, forensic medical examinations, sexual assault, reports, **Pen 11160.1**

Residential lead based paint hazard reduction program, **Health & S 105197**

Sexual assault, forensic medical examinations, reports, **Pen 11160.1**

Social Services, generally, this index

HEALTH DEPARTMENT

Health Care Services Department, generally, this index

HEALTH FACILITIES

Abuse, patients, reports, **Pen 11161.8**

Actions and proceedings, whistle blowing, **Health & S 1278.5**

AIDS, this index

Attorney fees, whistle blowing, **Health & S 1278.5**

Clinics, generally, this index

Complaints, whistle blowing, **Health & S 1278.5**

Confidential or privileged information, forensic medical examinations, sexual assault, reports, **Pen 11160.1**

Contracts, preferred reimbursement rates, **Labor 4609**

Costs, whistle blowing, **Health & S 1278.5**

Crimes and offenses, whistle blowing, **Health & S 1278.5**

Definitions, whistle blowing, **Health & S 1278.5**

Disclosure, preferred reimbursement rates, **Labor 4609**

Discrimination, whistle blowing, **Health & S 1278.5**

Evidence, whistle blowing, **Health & S 1278.5**

Exemptions, whistleblowers, **Health & S 1278.5**

HEALTH FACILITIES—Cont'd
Family care leave, claims, statements, **Un Ins 3306**
Fines and penalties, whistle blowing, **Health & S 1278.5**
Forensic medical examinations, sexual assault, reports, **Pen 11160.1**
Grievances, whistle blowing, **Health & S 1278.5**
Hospitals, generally, this index
Injunction, whistle blowing, peer review, **Health & S 1278.5**
Intermediate care facilities/developmentally disabled nursing facilities. Nursing Homes, this index
Labor and employment, whistle blowing, **Health & S 1278.5**
Medical Records, generally, this index
Neglect, reports, **Pen 11161.8**
Notice, safety, whistleblowers, **Health & S 1278.5**
Nurses, generally, this index
Nursing Homes, generally, this index
Outpatient settings. Clinics, this index
Patients,
    Safety, whistle blowing, **Health & S 1278.5**
    Whistle blowing, safety, **Health & S 1278.5**
Peer review, whistle blowing, injunction, **Health & S 1278.5**
Preferred reimbursement rates, **Labor 4609**
Presumptions, whistle blowing, **Health & S 1278.5**
Privileges and immunities, forensic medical examinations, sexual assault, reports, **Pen 11160.1**
Public policy, whistleblowers, **Health & S 1278.5**
Rates and charges, preferred reimbursement rates, **Labor 4609**
Records and recordation,
    Emergency personnel, disclosure, **CC 56.10**
    Medical Records, generally, this index
Reimbursement, preferred reimbursement rates, **Labor 4609**
Reports,
    Abuse of patients, **Pen 11161.8**
    Neglect of patients, **Pen 11161.8**
Retaliation, whistle blowing, **Health & S 1278.5**
Safety,
    Patients, ante
    Whistle blowing, **Health & S 1278.5**
Sexual assault, forensic medical examinations, reports, **Pen 11160.1**
Skilled nursing facilities. Nursing Homes, this index
Sterilization of persons. Birth Control, this index
Unemployment compensation, family care leave, claims, statements, **Un Ins 3306**
Whistle blowing, **Health & S 1278.5**

HEALTH FACILITIES WHISTLEBLOWERS LAW
Generally, **Health & S 1278.5**

HEALTH INSURANCE
Disability insurance. Insurance, this index

HEALTH MAINTENANCE ORGANIZATIONS
Health Care Service Plans, generally, this index

HEALTH SERVICES
Health and Sanitation, generally, this index

HEALTH SERVICES DEPARTMENT
Health Care Services Department, generally, this index

HEARING AIDS
Workers compensation, **Labor 3208**

HEARING IMPAIRED PERSONS
Deaf and Mute Persons, generally, this index

HEART DISEASE
Atascadero Hospital, officers and employees, workers compensation, **Labor 3212.2**
Criminal identification and investigation bureau, workers compensation, **Labor 3212.7**
District attorneys, workers compensation, **Labor 3212**
Firefighters, law enforcement officers, employment, discrimination, **Gov 12940.1**
Firemen, workers compensation, **Labor 3212**
    University of California, **Labor 3212.4**
Fish and game wardens, workers compensation, **Labor 3212**
Highway patrol, workers compensation, **Labor 3212.5**
Juvenile facilities division, officers and employees, workers compensation, **Labor 3212.2**
Narcotic enforcement bureau, workers compensation, **Labor 3212.7**
Police,
    University of California, workers compensation, **Labor 3213**
    Workers compensation, **Labor 3212, 3212.5**
Sheriffs, workers compensation, **Labor 3212, 3212.5**
State police, workers compensation, **Labor 3212.3**
University of California, police, workers compensation, **Labor 3213**
Workers Compensation, this index

HEPATITIS
Workers compensation, law enforcement personnel, presumptions, **Labor 3212.8**

HERNIAS
Criminal identification and investigation bureau, workers compensation, **Labor 3212.7**
District attorneys, workers compensation, **Labor 3212**
Firemen, workers compensation, **Labor 3212**
    University of California, **Labor 3212.4**
Fish and game wardens, workers compensation, **Labor 3212**
Highway patrol, workers compensation, **Labor 3212.5**
Narcotic enforcement bureau, workers compensation, **Labor 3212.7**
Police, workers compensation, **Labor 3212, 3212.5**
Sheriffs, workers compensation, **Labor 3212, 3212.5**
Workers Compensation, this index

HIGH EXPLOSIVES
Explosives, generally, this index

HIGH SCHOOLS OR SECONDARY SCHOOLS
Apprentices,
    Affirmative action requirements, providing program information, **Labor 3074.1**
    Information, public files, **Labor 3073**
At risk students, labor and employment, jobs for California graduates program, **Un Ins 9900 et seq.**
Buildings and grounds. School Buildings and Grounds, generally, this index
Career resource network, **Educ 53086**
Career technical education. Vocational Education, generally, this index
Counselors and counseling, youthbuild program, **Un Ins 9800 et seq.**
Courses of instruction or study, youthbuild program, **Un Ins 9800 et seq.**
Dropouts, youthbuild program, **Un Ins 9800 et seq.**
Graduation, youthbuild program, **Un Ins 9800 et seq.**
Grants, labor and employment, at risk youth, jobs for California graduates program, **Un Ins 9905**
Grounds. School Buildings and Grounds, generally, this index
Housing, youthbuild program, **Un Ins 9800 et seq.**
Indigent persons, youthbuild program, **Un Ins 9801 et seq.**
Information, apprenticeship information, public files, **Labor 3073**
Jobs for California graduates program, **Un Ins 9900 et seq.**
Labor and employment, at risk youth, jobs for California graduates program, **Un Ins 9900 et seq.**
Occupational training, workers compensation, **Labor 3368**
Regional occupational centers. Vocational Education, this index

HIGH SCHOOLS OR SECONDARY SCHOOLS—Cont'd

Regional youth education facilities. Juvenile Institutions and Schools, this index

Reports, labor and employment, at risk youth, jobs for California graduates program, **Un Ins 9907**

School Buildings and Grounds, generally, this index

Schoolteachers Retirement System, generally, this index

Technical schools. Vocational Education, generally, this index

Training, youthbuild program, **Un Ins 9800 et seq.**

Vocational Education, generally, this index

Work experience education,
  Child labor laws, applicability, **Labor 1295**
  Hours of labor, **Labor 1391.1**
  Workers compensation, **Labor 3368**

Youthbuild program, **Un Ins 9800 et seq.**

HIGH SPEED RAIL

Railroads, this index

HIGHER EDUCATION

Colleges and Universities, generally, this index

HIGHWAY CARRIERS

Motor Carriers, generally, this index

HIGHWAY PATROL

Death, in line of duty, dependents, scholarships, **Labor 4709**

Dependents, scholarships, **Labor 4709**

Farm labor contractors, licensee list, **Labor 1684.5**

Handicapped persons, disability in line of duty, dependents, scholarships, **Labor 4709**

Heart disease, workers compensation, **Labor 3212, 3212.3, 3212.5**

Hernias, workers compensation, **Labor 3212, 3212.5**

In line of duty. Death, ante

Leave of absence with pay in lieu of disability payments, **Labor 4800.5 et seq.**

Medical care and treatment, workers compensation, **Labor 4802**

Meningitis, workers compensation, **Labor 3212.9**

Pneumonia, workers compensation, **Labor 3212, 3212.3, 3212.5**

Presumptions, heart disease and pneumonia, workers compensation, **Labor 3212.3**

Scholarships, dependents, **Labor 4709**

Tuberculosis, workers compensation, **Labor 3212.6**

Workers compensation, **Labor 3212**
  Heart trouble and pneumonia, **Labor 3212.3**
  Medical care and treatment, **Labor 4802**
  Meningitis, **Labor 3212.9**

HIGHWAY PATROL—Cont'd

Workers compensation—Cont'd
  Scholarships, dependents, **Labor 4709**
  Special payments, **Labor 4800.5 et seq.**
  Tuberculosis, **Labor 3212.6**

HIGHWAYS AND ROADS

Convict labor, state highways, workers compensation exclusion, **Labor 3352**

Lead poisoning, occupational safety, programs, **Health & S 105185 et seq.**

Railroads, generally, this index

Sewers and Sewer Systems, generally, this index

State highways,
  Convict labor, workers compensation exclusion, **Labor 3352**
  Prison labor, workers compensation exclusion, **Labor 3352**
  Railroads, generally, this index
  Workers compensation, exclusion, convict labor, **Labor 3352**

Trespass, acts constituting, **Pen 602, 602.8**

HIRING PROPERTY

Landlord and Tenant, generally, this index

Leases, generally, this index

HIV

AIDS, generally, this index

HMO

Health Care Service Plans, generally, this index

HOGS

Trespass, **Pen 602**

HOLDER

Definitions, Unclaimed Property Law, **CCP 1501**

HOLIDAYS

Public works, wage rate, **Labor 1771**

State Officers and Employees, this index

Unemployment compensation, **Un Ins 1265.5, 1265.6**

Withholding tax on wages, **Un Ins 13030**

Workers compensation, stop orders, process, **Labor 3731**

HOLOCAUST

Unemployment compensation, disability compensation, restitution, **Un Ins 2629.5**

Victims, unemployment compensation, disability compensation, restitution, **Un Ins 2629.5**

HOME HEALTH AGENCIES

Advertisements, employment agencies, **CC 1812.508**

Employment agencies, advertisements, **CC 1812.508**

Workers compensation, fees, **Labor 5307.1**

HOMELAND SECURITY

War and Civil Defense, generally, this index

HOMELESS PERSONS

Shelters, public buildings and works, prevailing wage rate, **Labor 1720**

HOMES

Housing, generally, this index

HOMICIDE

Elected public officials, dependents, college scholarships, **Labor 4728**

Exemplary damages, wrongful death, **CC 3294**

Wrongful death, actions and proceedings, exemplary damages, **CC 3294**

HOMOSEXUALITY

Domestic Partnership, generally, this index

Freedom from violence or intimidation, **CC 51.7**

Marriage, **Fam 308.5**

HORIZONTAL PROPERTY REGIME

Condominiums, generally, this index

HORSE RACING

Children and minors, employment, **Labor 1308**

Collective bargaining, jockeys, **Labor 3201.81**

Crimes and offenses, children and minors, employment, **Labor 1308**

Jockeys, generally, this index

Labor disputes, collective bargaining, jockeys, **Labor 3201.81**

Minors, employment, **Labor 1308**

Thoroughbred racing. Jockeys, generally, this index

Unemployment compensation, **Un Ins 654**

HORTICULTURE

Compensation, time due and payable for labor, **Labor 205**

Definitions, child labor, **Labor 1390**

HOSPITAL SERVICE PLANS

Health Care Service Plans, generally, this index

HOSPITALS

Accident and health insurance, disability insurance. Insurance, this index

Birthing centers, trespass, **Pen 602**

Confidential or privileged information, forensic medical examinations, sexual assault, reports, **Pen 11160.1**

Disability insurance. Insurance, this index

Discipline, physicians and surgeons, actions against, application of law, **Bus & P 2056**

Drugs and Medicine, generally, this index

Family care leave, claims, statements, **Un Ins 3306**

Forensic medical examinations, sexual assault, reports, **Pen 11160.1**

Health Care Service Plans, this index

Health insurance, disability insurance. Insurance, this index

Labor and employment, disability compensation, **Un Ins 2606**

HOSPITALS—Cont'd

Maternity wards, trespass, **Pen 602**

Medi Cal Program, this index

Medical Records, generally, this index

Medically appropriate health care, determination, **Bus & P 2056**

Medicine. Drugs and Medicine, generally, this index

Neonatal units, trespass, **Pen 602**

Nurses, generally, this index

Outpatients, workers compensation, fees, **Labor 5307.1**

Pediatric subacute units, Medi Cal program, supplemental reimbursement, enforcement, **Labor 107**

Privileges and immunities, forensic medical examinations, sexual assault, reports, **Pen 11160.1**

Records and recordation. Medical Records, generally, this index

Reports, abuse of persons by other health facilities, **Pen 11161.8**

Sexual assault, forensic medical examinations, reports, **Pen 11160.1**

State Hospitals, generally, this index

Sterilization of persons. Birth Control, this index

Tort liability, reports of physical abuse from patients received from other health facilities, **Pen 11161.8**

Unemployment compensation,

Elections for financing, **Un Ins 802, 803**

Eligibility, **Un Ins 1253.3**

Employer defined, **Un Ins 677**

Exclusion from wages, expenses paid, **Un Ins 931, 933**

Expenses and expenditures, **Un Ins 931, 933**

Family care leave, claims, statements, **Un Ins 3306**

Interns, excluded service, **Un Ins 645**

Patients, excluded services, **Un Ins 647**

Workers Compensation, this index

HOTELS

Civil Rights Act, **CC 51 et seq.**

Employee housing, **Health & S 17000 et seq.**

Exemptions, workplace smoking regulation, **Labor 6404.5**

Rules and regulations, workplace smoking regulation, exemptions, **Labor 6404.5**

Sex discrimination, **CC 51 et seq.**

Smoking in workplace regulation, exemptions, **Labor 6404.5**

Trespass, **Pen 602**

Workplace smoking regulation, exemptions, **Labor 6404.5**

HOTLINES

Telecommunications, this index

HOURS

Labor and Employment, this index

Labor law enforcement division, office hours, **Labor 94**

HOURS OF LABOR

Apprentices, this index

Labor and Employment, this index

Public Buildings and Works, this index

HOUSE TRAILERS

Mobilehomes and Mobilehome Parks, generally, this index

HOUSING

Actions and proceedings, overcrowding, migrant labor, **Health & S 17043**

Advertisements, discrimination, **Gov 12955 et seq.**

Agricultural Labor and Employment, this index

Air pressure tanks, safety regulation, exemption, **Labor 7624**

Ancestry. Discrimination, generally, post

Apartment Houses, generally, this index

Attorney fees,

Cease and desist orders, **Gov 12987**

Discrimination, **Gov 12989.2, 12989.3**

Youthbuild program, grants, **Un Ins 9802**

Building standards, **Health & S 17000 et seq.**

Colleges and Universities, this index

Condominiums, generally, this index

Construction, youthbuild program, **Un Ins 9800 et seq.**

Contractors, generally, this index

Costs, cease and desist orders, **Gov 12987**

County low rent housing. Discrimination, generally, post

Covenants, discrimination, **Gov 12955 et seq.**

Damages, discrimination, **Gov 12987, 12989.2, 12989.3**

Definitions, industrial homework, **Labor 2650**

Disabled persons. Handicapped Persons, this index

Discrimination, **Gov 12955 et seq., 12980 et seq.**

Fair Employment and Housing, generally, this index

Good faith purchasers, discriminatory clauses or covenants, **Gov 12995**

Employee housing, **Health & S 17000 et seq.**

Immigration, status, **Gov 7285**

Exemptions, workplace smoking regulation, **Labor 6404.5**

Fair Employment and Housing, generally, this index

Familial status. Discrimination, generally, ante

Farm labor. Agricultural Labor and Employment, this index

Fees. Attorney fees, generally, ante

Financial assistance, discrimination, **Gov 12955 et seq.**

Fines and penalties, discrimination, **Gov 12987, 12989.3**

Grants, youthbuild program, **Un Ins 9800 et seq.**

HOUSING—Cont'd

Handicapped Persons, this index

Harassment, discrimination, **Gov 12955**

High Schools or Secondary Schools, this index

Hotels, generally, this index

Indigent persons,

Public buildings and works, prevailing wage rate, **Labor 1720**

Shelters. Homeless Persons, this index

Youthbuild program, **Un Ins 9800 et seq.**

Information, discrimination, **Gov 12955.5**

Injunction, discrimination, **Gov 12987, 12989.2**

Juvenile Delinquents and Dependents, this index

Labor and Employment, this index

Labor Camps, generally, this index

Lead based paint hazard reduction program, **Health & S 105197**

Limitation of actions. Community Development and Housing, this index

Loans. Mortgages, generally, this index

Low and moderate income housing,

Public buildings and works, prevailing wage rate, **Labor 1720**

Youthbuild program, **Un Ins 9800 et seq.**

Manufactured housing. Mobilehomes and Mobilehome Parks, generally, this index

Marital status. Discrimination, generally, ante

Military Forces, this index

Mobilehomes and Mobilehome Parks, generally, this index

Mortgages, generally, this index

Motels and Motor Courts, generally, this index

Multifamily housing, handicapped persons, discrimination, **Gov 12955.1**

Multiple listing service, discrimination, **Gov 12955 et seq.**

National origin. Discrimination, generally, ante

Opinion and expert testimony, fees, cease and desist orders, **Gov 12987**

Overcrowding, actions and proceedings, migrant labor, **Health & S 17043**

Paint and painting, residential lead based paint hazard reduction program, **Health & S 105197**

Place of employment, smoking regulation, exemption, **Labor 6404.5**

Race. Discrimination, generally, ante

Records and recordation, discrimination, preservation of records, **Gov 12956**

Rehabilitation, youthbuild program, **Un Ins 9800 et seq.**

Religion. Discrimination, generally, ante

Rent, discrimination, **Gov 12955 et seq.**

Rental housing. Apartment Houses, generally, this index

Reports, youthbuild program, **Un Ins 9809, 9809.5**

HOUSING—Cont'd
Restrictive covenants, discrimination, **Gov 12955 et seq.**
Rules and regulations, workplace smoking regulation, exemptions, **Labor 6404.5**
Sales, discrimination, **Gov 12955 et seq.**
Schools and School Districts, this index
Seasonal labor. Agricultural Labor and Employment, this index
Sex. Discrimination, generally, ante
Source of income. Discrimination, generally, ante
Students. Discrimination, generally, ante
Training, youthbuild program, **Un Ins 9800 et seq.**
Urban Renewal, this index
Veterans, this index
Workers compensation, mutual self help housing, exemptions, **Labor 3352**
Workplace smoking regulation, exemption, **Labor 6404.5**
Youthbuild program, **Un Ins 9800 et seq.**
Zoning and planning, discrimination, referral of case to attorney general, **Gov 12981**

HOUSING ACCOMMODATION
Definitions, fair employment and housing department, **Gov 12927**

HOUSING AND COMMUNITY DEVELOPMENT DEPARTMENT
Employee Housing Act, enforcement, delegation to cities or counties, **Health & S 17050**
Labor camps, Employee Housing Act enforcement, delegation to cities or counties, **Health & S 17050**
Mobilehomes and Mobilehome Parks, generally, this index

HOUSING DIVISION
Industrial Relations Department, this index

HOUSING FINANCE AGENCY
Low and moderate income housing. Housing, this index

HUCKSTERS
Hawkers and Peddlers, generally, this index

HUMAN IMMUNODEFICIENCY VIRUS
AIDS, generally, this index

HUMAN REMAINS
Cemeteries and Dead Bodies, generally, this index

HUMAN RESOURCE AGENCY
Definitions, criminal history, disclosure, **Pen 11105.3**

HUMAN RIGHTS
Civil Rights, generally, this index

HUMAN TRAFFICKING
Contracts, compensation and salaries, deductions, illegal contracts, **CC 1670.7**

HUMBOLDT STATE COLLEGE
Colleges and Universities, generally, this index

HUNTERS AND HUNTING
Fish and Game, generally, this index

HUSBAND AND WIFE
Marriage, generally, this index

HYBRID CONTEMPT
Definitions, workers compensation hearings, **Labor 5309**

HYDROCARBON SUBSTANCES
Oil and Gas, generally, this index

HYGIENE
Health and Sanitation, generally, this index

HYPODERMIC SYRINGES AND NEEDLES
Bloodborne pathogens, labor and employment, **Labor 144.7**
Labor and employment,
    Bloodborne pathogens, occupational safety and health, **Labor 144.7**
    Occupational safety and health, bloodborne pathogens, **Labor 144.7**

ICE AND SNOW
Temporary public employees, unemployment compensation, excluded service, **Un Ins 634.5**
Unemployment compensation, temporary public employees, excluded service, **Un Ins 634.5**

IDENTITY AND IDENTIFICATION
Consumer Credit Reporting Agencies, this index
Employment. Labor and Employment, this index
Fingerprints and Fingerprinting, generally, this index
Income Tax—State, this index
Labor and Employment, this index
Theft. Consumer Credit Reporting Agencies, this index
Withholding tax on wages, **Un Ins 13015, 13057**
Workers compensation, employer responsible, asbestosis, **Labor 4405**

ILLEGAL ALIENS
Aliens, generally, this index

ILLEGAL ORDER
Definitions, whistle blowing, **Gov 8547.2**

ILLNESS
Children and Minors, this index
Disability compensation. Unemployment Compensation, this index
Disability insurance. Insurance, this index
Domestic partnership, family care leave, **Un Ins 3300 et seq.**
Health insurance, disability insurance. Insurance, this index
Industrial homeworker, **Labor 2661**

ILLNESS—Cont'd
Marriage, family care leave, **Un Ins 3300 et seq.**
Pneumonia, generally, this index
Sick Leave, generally, this index
Unemployment compensation,
    Exclusion from wages, benefits paid, **Un Ins 931, 933**
    Sick pay, wages for personal services, **Un Ins 1265.7**

IMMIGRATION
Civil rights, labor and employment, **CC 3339; Gov 7285; Health & S 24000; Labor 1171.5**
Contracts, compensation and salaries, deductions, illegal contracts, **CC 1670.7**
Discovery, **CC 3339**
    Labor and employment, **Labor 1171.5**
    Status, **Health & S 24000**
Employee housing, **Gov 7285**
Evidence, status, **Health & S 24000**
Housing, employee housing, **Gov 7285**
Labor and employment, **CC 3339**
    Occupational safety and health, limited English proficient persons, state agencies, access, **Labor 176**
    Rights, **Gov 7285**
Liability, discovery, **Gov 7285; Health & S 24000**
Protection, labor and employment, **CC 3339; Gov 7285; Health & S 24000; Labor 1171.5**
Remedies, labor and employment, **CC 3339; Gov 7285; Labor 1171.5**
Rights, civil rights, labor and employment, **CC 3339; Gov 7285; Health & S 24000; Labor 1171.5**
Wage statements, undocumented workers, unemployment insurance, **Un Ins 2128**

IMMORAL CONDUCT
Lewdness and Obscenity, generally, this index

IMMORALITY
Lewdness and Obscenity, generally, this index

IMMUNITIES
Privileges and Immunities, generally, this index

IMPLANTS
Workers compensation, costs, reimbursement, **Labor 5318**

IMPLEMENTS
Machinery and Equipment, generally, this index
Tools, generally, this index

IMPRINTS
Labor union insignia, **Labor 1010 et seq.**

IMPRISONMENT
Correctional Institutions, generally, this index

IMPRISONMENT—Cont'd
Crimes and Offenses, generally, this index
Fines and Penalties, generally, this index

IMPROPER GOVERNMENTAL ACTIVITY
Definitions, whistle blowing, **Gov 8547.2**

IMPROVEMENT DISTRICTS
Local Agencies, generally, this index

IMPROVEMENTS
Certificates and certification,
    Apprentices, **Labor 1777.5**
    Contracts, contractors securing workers
        compensation, **Labor 1861**
Funds, theft, **Pen 484b**
Labor camps, applications, **Health & S
    17021**
Mechanics Liens, generally, this index
Sewers and Sewer Systems, generally, this
    index
Theft, construction funds, **Pen 484b**

IMPURITIES
Definitions, hazardous substance informa-
    tion and training, **Labor 6371**

IN HOME SUPPORTIVE SERVICES
Social Services, this index

INCARCERATION
Definitions, unemployment compensation
    disability, **Un Ins 2680**

INCOME
Support, this index

INCOME TAX—FEDERAL
Earned income tax credit, notice, **Rev & T
    19850 et seq.**
Indigent persons, earned income tax cred-
    it, notice, **Rev & T 19850 et seq.**
Notice, earned income tax credit, **Rev & T
    19850 et seq.**
Unemployment compensation, income tax
    exempt organizations, **Un Ins 641**

INCOME TAX—STATE
Additional withholding, withholding tax on
    wages, **Un Ins 13024**
Address, withholding tax, **Un Ins 13016**
Annuities,
    Definitions, withholding tax on wages,
        Un Ins 13028
    Withholding tax on wages, **Un Ins 13028**
Approximation of deductions, withholding
    tax on wages, **Un Ins 13022**
Assessments,
    Associations and societies, shareholders,
        officers and others, personal liabili-
        ty for failure to withhold, **Un Ins
        1735**
    Corporations, shareholders, officers and
        others, personal liability for failure
        to withhold, **Un Ins 1735**
Associations and Societies, this index
Average of wages, withholding tax on
    wages, **Un Ins 13023**

INCOME TAX—STATE—Cont'd
Biopharmaceutical activities, net operating
    losses, **Rev & T 17276**
Books and papers, withholding tax on
    wages, **Un Ins 13011**
Carrybacks, net operating losses, deduc-
    tions, **Rev & T 17276**
    Election, **Rev & T 17276.1**
Cash, withholding tax on wages, **Un Ins
    13025**
Certificates and certification,
    Exemptions, withholding tax on wages,
        Un Ins 13040 et seq.
    Local agency military base recovery ar-
        eas, credits, **Rev & T 17053.46**
    Manufacturing enhancement areas,
        credits, **Rev & T 17053.47**
Child care, credit, **Rev & T 17052.18**
Children and minors, care for children
    during workday, credit, **Rev & T
    17052.18**
Collections. Withholding, generally, post
Computation, withholding tax on wages,
    Un Ins 13020
Corporation Taxes, generally, this index
Cost of living, **Un Ins 13011**
Credits,
    Enterprise Zones, this index
    Jobs Tax Credit Act, **Rev & T 17053.7**
    Labor and employment, disadvantaged
        and disabled employees, Jobs Tax
        Credit Act, **Rev & T 17053.7**
    Local agency military base recovery ar-
        eas, **Rev & T 17053.46**
    Qualified wages, enterprise zones, **Rev
        & T 17053.74**
    Unemployment compensation, excess
        employee contributions, **Rev & T
        17061; Un Ins 1176, 1176.5, 1185**
Crimes and offenses,
    Employers statements, tax deductions,
        Labor 226.6
    Fines and penalties, generally, post
Day care and nursery schools, credits, **Rev
    & T 17052.18**
Deductions,
    Enterprise Zones, this index
    Los Angeles revitalization zone, net op-
        erating loss, **Rev & T 17276.2**
    Losses, net operating loss carrybacks,
        Rev & T 17276
        Election, **Rev & T 17276.1**
    Net operating loss carrybacks, **Rev & T
        17276 et seq.**
    Nonresidents, post
    Qualified taxpayers, net operating loss-
        es, **Rev & T 17276**
        Election, **Rev & T 17276.1**
    Targeted tax areas, **Rev & T 17276.2**
    Withholding tax, **Un Ins 13021**
Definitions,
    Net operating losses, deductions and
        carryovers, **Rev & T 17276**
    Withholding tax on wages, **Un Ins 13003**
Disposition of property. Gains and losses,
    generally, post

INCOME TAX—STATE—Cont'd
Earnings withholding orders. Garnish-
    ment, this index
Employers,
    Definitions, withholding tax on wages,
        Un Ins 13005
    Jobs Tax Credit Act, **Rev & T 17053.7**
    Statements, tax deductions, crimes and
        offenses, **Labor 226.6**
Enterprise Zones, this index
Equipment, withholding tax on wages, **Un
    Ins 13011**
Estates and trusts, **Un Ins 13011**
Estimate of wages, withholding tax on
    wages, **Un Ins 13023**
Exemptions, withholding tax on wages, **Un
    Ins 13040 et seq.**
Extension of time. Time, post
Fiduciaries, definitions, withholding tax on
    wages, **Un Ins 13003**
Financial statements and reports, with-
    holding tax on wages, **Un Ins 13050 et
    seq.**
Fines and penalties,
    Employers statements, tax deductions,
        Labor 226.6
    Fraud, **Labor 226.6**
        Statement, withholding tax on wages,
            Un Ins 13052
    Withholding, post
Fiscal year, definitions, withholding tax on
    wages, **Un Ins 13003**
Franchise tax board, definitions, withhold-
    ing tax on wages, **Un Ins 13003**
Franchise taxes. Corporation Taxes, gen-
    erally, this index
Fraud, statement, withholding tax on
    wages, **Un Ins 13052**
Funds, withholding tax on wages, **Un Ins
    13011**
Gains and losses,
    Net operating losses,
        Carryovers, **Rev & T 17276 et seq.**
        Deductions, **Rev & T 17276 et seq.**
    New businesses, deductions and carry-
        overs, **Rev & T 17276**
Garnishment, this index
Gross income,
    Annuities, ante
    Definitions, withholding tax on wages,
        Un Ins 13006
Husband and wife, definitions, withholding
    tax on wages, **Un Ins 13003**
Identity and identification, persons, with-
    holding tax on wages, **Un Ins 13015**
Imprisonment. Fines and penalties, gen-
    erally, ante
Interest, obligations, withholding tax on
    wages, **Un Ins 13014**
IRA. Pensions, profit sharing and stock
    bonus plans, post
Itemized deductions. Deductions, gener-
    ally, ante
Jobs tax credit, **Rev & T 17053.7**

I–87

INCOME

INCOME TAX—STATE—Cont'd

Labor and employment,
 Disadvantaged and disabled employees, Jobs Tax Credit Act, **Rev & T 17053.7**
 Jobs credit, **Rev & T 17053.7**
Liability. Withholding, post
Life insurance, gross income, living benefits contracts, **Un Ins 13028**
Local agency military base recovery areas, credits, **Rev & T 17053.46**
 Net operating losses, carrybacks, **Rev & T 17276.5**
Los Angeles Revitalization Zone, this index
Losses. Gains and losses, generally, ante
Military Forces, this index
Miscellaneous payroll period, definitions, withholding tax on wages, **Un Ins 13007**
Moneys of department, withholding tax on wages, **Un Ins 13011**
Net operating losses. Gains and losses, ante
New businesses, net operating losses, deductions and carryovers, **Rev & T 17276**
Nonresidents,
 Annuities and pensions related to unemployment compensation, withholding, **Un Ins 13028.1**
 Deductions, net operating losses, **Rev & T 17276**
 Definitions, **Un Ins 13028.1**
  Withholding tax on wages, **Un Ins 13003**
 Net operating losses, deductions, **Rev & T 17276**
 Unemployment compensation related to annuities, pensions or deferred income, withholding, **Un Ins 13028.1**
Notice,
 Collections, withholding tax on wages, **Un Ins 13072**
 Unemployment insurance refund or credit disallowed, **Rev & T 17061**
Oaths and affirmations, statements, withholding tax on wages, **Un Ins 13058**
Officers and employees, definitions, withholding tax on wages, **Un Ins 13004**
Options. Shares and shareholders, post
Overpayments. Refunds, generally, post
Partnership, definitions, withholding tax on wages, **Un Ins 13003**
Payroll deductions, withholding tax on wages, **Un Ins 13021**
Payroll period,
 Definitions, withholding tax on wages, **Un Ins 13008**
 Withholding tax on wages, **Un Ins 13020**
Penalties. Fines and penalties, generally, ante
Pensions, profit sharing and stock bonus plans, withholding, unemployment compensation, **Un Ins 13043**

INCOME TAX—STATE—Cont'd

Personal property of department, withholding tax on wages, **Un Ins 13011**
Persons, definitions, **Un Ins 13011**
 Withholding tax on wages, **Un Ins 13003**
Punishment. Fines and penalties, generally, ante
Qualified summer youth employee, job tax credit, **Rev & T 17053.7**
Qualified taxpayers, net operating loss deductions, **Rev & T 17276**
 Election, **Rev & T 17276.1**
Real estate of department, withholding tax on wages, **Un Ins 13011**
Records and recordation, **Un Ins 13011**
 Withholding tax on wages, **Un Ins 13011**
Refunds, unemployment compensation, excess employee contributions, **Rev & T 17061; Un Ins 1176, 1176.5**
Remuneration other than cash, withholding tax on wages, **Un Ins 13025**
Reports, withholding tax on wages, **Un Ins 13050 et seq.**
Returns,
 Examination, labor camp owner returns, **Health & S 17061.5**
 Labor camp owners, examination, **Health & S 17061.5**
 Withholding tax, **Un Ins 13050 et seq.**
Rules and regulations, withholding tax on wages, **Un Ins 13013**
Sales or exchanges,
 Gains and losses, generally, ante
 Shares and shareholders, generally, post
Shares and shareholders,
 Assessments, withholdings on employee wages, employers failure to withhold, **Un Ins 1735**
 Liabilities, withholdings on employee wages, employers failure to withhold, **Un Ins 1735**
 Options, withholding, unemployment compensation, **Un Ins 13043**
 Personal liability, withholdings on employee wages, employers failure to withhold, **Un Ins 1735**
 Withholding, options, unemployment compensation, **Un Ins 13043**
Sick pay,
 Unemployment compensation, **Un Ins 13028.6**
 Withholding tax, **Un Ins 13050**
Stock and stockholders. Shares and shareholders, generally, ante
Supplies, withholding tax on wages, **Un Ins 13011**
Targeted tax areas, deductions, **Rev & T 17276.2**
Tax certificates. Certificates and certification, generally, ante
Tax returns and reports. Returns, generally, ante
Taxable year, withholding, **Un Ins 13003**
Taxpayer, definitions, withholding tax on wages, **Un Ins 13003**

INCOME TAX—STATE—Cont'd

Time,
 Extension of time, net operating loss deduction, carryover period extension, **Rev & T 17276.3**
 Net operating loss deduction, carryover period extension, **Rev & T 17276.3**
Tips, withholding, **Un Ins 13027, 13055**
Trade or business, definitions, withholding tax on wages, **Un Ins 13003**
Unemployment compensation,
 Assessments, shareholders, personal liability for failure to withhold, **Un Ins 1735**
 Contributions, credit or refund, **Rev & T 17061**
 Disability compensation, credits, overpayments, **Un Ins 1185**
 Pensions, profit sharing and stock bonus plans, withholding, **Un Ins 13043**
 Shares and shareholders, options, withholding, **Un Ins 13043**
 Stock options, withholding, **Un Ins 13043**
 Withholding, **Un Ins 13021, 13028, 13043**
  Annuity and pension payments, **Un Ins 13028.1**
  Collection, **Un Ins 13070 et seq.**
United States, definitions, withholding tax on wages, **Un Ins 13003**
Wages, definitions,
 Credits, qualified employees, **Rev & T 17053.7**
 Withholding tax on wages, **Un Ins 13009**
Withholding, **Un Ins 13000 et seq.**
 Assessments, officers, shareholders and others, employers failure to withhold, **Un Ins 1735**
 Collection of tax, **Un Ins 13070 et seq.**
 Corporate directors, nonresidents, **Un Ins 13020**
 Exemption certificates, **Un Ins 13026**
 Failure to withhold or remit, subsequent payments, liability, **Un Ins 1735**
 Fines and penalties, deposit, **Un Ins 1585, 1585.5**
 Liability,
  Associations and societies, officers and employees, **Un Ins 1735**
  Corporations, officers and employees, **Un Ins 1735**
  Shares and shareholders, **Un Ins 1735**
 Nonresident corporate directors, **Un Ins 13020**
 Pensions, profit sharing and stock bonus plans, unemployment compensation, **Un Ins 13043**
 Persons other than employers, liability, **Un Ins 1735**
 Returns, **Un Ins 13021**
 Shares and shareholders, options, unemployment compensation, **Un Ins 13043**
 Statements, **Un Ins 13050 et seq.**

INCOME TAX—STATE—Cont'd
Withholding—Cont'd
  Stock options, unemployment compensation, **Un Ins 13043**
  Unemployment compensation, ante
Withholding agent, definition, withholding tax on wages, **Un Ins 13010**

INCOMPETENT PERSONS
Alcoholics and Alcoholism, generally, this index
Drug Addicts, generally, this index
Guardian and Ward, generally, this index
Mentally Ill Persons, generally, this index
Mentally Retarded and Developmentally Disabled Persons, generally, this index

INCORPORATED TOWNS
Municipalities, generally, this index

INCORRIGIBLE CHILDREN
Juvenile Delinquents and Dependents, generally, this index

INCUMBRANCES
Liens and Incumbrances, generally, this index

INCURRED LIABILITIES FOR THE PAYMENT OF COMPENSATION
Definitions, workers compensation, **Labor 3700.1**

INDEBTEDNESS
Assignment for Benefit of Creditors, generally, this index
Bankruptcy, generally, this index
Bonds, generally, this index
Insolvency, generally, this index
Workers compensation, exemption from debts of claimant, **Labor 4901**

INDECENCY
Lewdness and Obscenity, generally, this index

INDEMNITY
Asbestos workers, claims or actions against persons other than employer, asbestosis, **Labor 4417**
Attorney Fees, this index
Costs, labor and employment, discharge of duties, **Labor 2802**
Employees expenses and losses in discharging duties, **Labor 2802**
Health Care Service Plans, this index
Interest, labor and employment, discharge of duties, **Labor 2802**
Labor and employment, employees expenses and losses in discharging duties, **Labor 2802**

INDEPENDENT ADOPTION
Adoption of Children, this index

INDEPENDENT CONTRACTORS
Cable television, criminal history information, **Pub U 7910**

INDEPENDENT CONTRACTORS—Cont'd
Definitions, workers compensation, **Labor 3353**
Open video systems, criminal history information, **Pub U 7910**
Physicians and surgeons, primary care clinics, presumptions, **Labor 2750.6**
Rebuttable presumption, status, **Labor 2750.5**
Status, rebuttable presumption, **Labor 2750.5**
Telecommunications, criminal history information, **Pub U 7910**
Unemployment Compensation, this index
Video programming services, criminal history information, **Pub U 7910**
Workers compensation,
  Burden of proof, **Labor 5705**
  Newspapers or magazines, elective coverage, **Labor 4157**

INDIANS
Bank and corporation tax credits, hiring, **Rev & T 23622.7**
Tribal councils, unemployment compensation, exclusions, **Un Ins 634.5**
Unemployment Compensation, this index

INDICTMENT AND INFORMATION
Consumer credit reporting agencies, **CC 1786.18**
  Contents of records, **CC 1785.13**
Labor and employment, records and recordation, copies, **CC 1786.53**
Larceny. Theft, this index
Theft, this index

INDIGENT PERSONS
Assistance. Social Services, generally, this index
County health facilities. Health Facilities, generally, this index
Earned income tax credit, notice, **Rev & T 19850 et seq.**
Economic opportunity, workers compensation, **Labor 4201 et seq.**
Family economic security, job preparation and training services. Unemployment Compensation, this index
Health Facilities, generally, this index
High Schools or Secondary Schools, this index
Housing, this index
Income tax—federal, earned income tax credit, notice, **Rev & T 19850 et seq.**
Job preparation and training services. Unemployment Compensation, this index
Labor and employment, earned income tax credit, notice, **Rev & T 19850 et seq.**
Medi Cal Program, generally, this index
Schools and School Districts, this index
Shelters. Homeless Persons, this index
Social Services, generally, this index

INDIVIDUALLY IDENTIFIABLE INFORMATION
Definitions, workers compensation, **Labor 138.7**

INDIVIDUALS
Definitions,
  Information Practices Act, **CC 1798.3**
  Unemployment compensation, training or retraining, demand occupations, **Un Ins 1267**
  Withholding tax on wages, **Un Ins 13003**

INDUSTRIAL COMPENSATION LAW
Generally, **Labor 3201 et seq.**
Workers Compensation, generally, this index

INDUSTRIAL DISABILITY
Definitions, **Un Ins 2776**

INDUSTRIAL HOMEWORK
Generally, **Labor 2650 et seq.**
Access to employers place of business, **Labor 2666**
Administrative law and procedure, searches and seizures, appeal and review, **Labor 2664**
Advertisements, **Labor 2658.5**
Appeal and review, searches and seizures, **Labor 2664**
Application, homeworkers permit, **Labor 2660**
Children and minors, **Labor 2661**
Compensation and salaries, investigations, **Labor 2652**
Conditions of labor, investigations, **Labor 2652**
Confiscation, goods as evidence, **Labor 2658.7**
Crimes and offenses, **Labor 2667**
  Advertising, **Labor 2658.5**
  Failure to prevent taking articles and materials home, **Labor 2658.1**
  Home manufacturer without permit, **Labor 2660.5**
  Permitting home manufacturer, **Labor 2658.5**
  Person lacking license, **Labor 2659**
  Searches and seizures, generally, post
Defenses, crimes and offenses, **Labor 2667**
Definitions, **Labor 2650**
Destruction,
  Goods confiscated as evidence, **Labor 2658.7**
  Removed articles or materials, **Labor 2664**
Disclosure of information by homeworker, **Labor 2660.1**
Diseases, illness of homeworker, **Labor 2661**
Evidence, confiscation of goods, **Labor 2658.7**
Fees,
  Homeworkers permit, **Labor 2660**
  License, **Labor 2658**
Fines and penalties,
  Advertising, **Labor 2658.5**

INDUSTRIAL HOMEWORK—Cont'd
Fines and penalties—Cont'd
Home manufacturer without permit, **Labor 2660.5**
Permitting home manufacturer, **Labor 2658.5**
Forfeitures, goods confiscated as evidence, **Labor 2658.7**
Goods, confiscation as evidence, forfeiture destruction, **Labor 2658.7**
Hearings, orders, **Labor 2655**
Illness of homeworker, **Labor 2661**
Injunctions, **Labor 2667**
Inspection and inspectors,
Records, **Labor 2666**
Search warrants, **Labor 2656**
Investigations and investigators, **Labor 2666**
Conditions of employment, **Labor 2652**
Industry compliance, **Labor 2658.7**
Labels, **Labor 2663**
Law enforcement, state and local officials, investigative powers, **Labor 2666**
Licenses and permits, **Labor 2650 et seq.**
Homeworkers permit, fee, **Labor 2660**
Mail and mailing, removal of article or material for violation, notice, **Labor 2664**
Notice,
Hearings, **Labor 2655**
Removal of article or material for violation, **Labor 2664**
Offenses. Crimes and offenses, generally, ante
Orders to discontinue, **Labor 2654, 2655**
Penalties. Fines and penalties, generally, ante
Police, investigative powers, **Labor 2666**
Prohibited materials and articles, **Labor 2651**
Records and recordation, **Labor 2665**
Inspection and inspectors, **Labor 2666**
Removal of article or material for violation, **Labor 2664**
Reports, duties of employers, **Labor 2665**
Rules and regulations, **Labor 2666**
Crimes and offenses, **Labor 2667**
Searches and seizures, **Labor 2664**
Goods as evidence, **Labor 2658.7**
Warrants, **Labor 2656**
Second and subsequent offenses,
Home manufacturer without permit, **Labor 2660.5**
Permitting or advertising for industrial homework, **Labor 2658.5**
Service of process, searches and seizures, appeal and review, **Labor 2664**
Sickness of homeworker, **Labor 2661**
Standards of labor, compliance, **Labor 2665**
State treasury, license fees, **Labor 2658**
Suspension or revocation, license, **Labor 2658**
Transfer of license, **Labor 2658**

INDUSTRIAL HYGIENISTS
Occupational health and medicine, program development, **Labor 50.8**

INDUSTRIAL PLANTS
Manufacturers and Manufacturing, generally, this index

INDUSTRIAL PROMOTION FUNDS
Negotiated funds, employers failure to make payments, **Labor 227**

INDUSTRIAL RELATIONS CONSTRUCTION INDUSTRY AND ENFORCEMENT FUND
Unlicensed contractors, deposit of fines, **Labor 1024**

INDUSTRIAL RELATIONS DEPARTMENT
Generally, **Labor 50 et seq.**
Administrative director. Workers compensation division, post
Agencies, references to, statute of reconstruction, **Labor 1200**
Apprenticeship standards division, **Labor 56**
Chief of division, **Labor 57**
Powers and duties, **Labor 3073**
Public works contracts, notice, **Labor 1773.3**
Services to, employment development department, **Labor 3097**
Appropriations, **Labor 58, 62**
Arrests, without warrant, authority as public officers, **Labor 95**
Attorneys,
Director, appointment, **Labor 54.5**
Workers compensation division, post
Bilingual employees, occupational safety and health division, **Labor 176**
Boards and commissions. Occupational safety and health appeals board, generally, post
Books, **Labor 58**
Chiefs of divisions, **Labor 57**
Childrens Bureau, assistance and cooperation, **Labor 50.6**
Compensation and salaries,
Chiefs of divisions, **Labor 57**
Director, **Labor 51**
Industrial safety division, chief of division, **Labor 145**
Industrial welfare division, chief of division, **Labor 57**
Workers compensation division, post
Confidential records, **Labor 65**
Correctional institutions, industrial safety committee, rules and regulations, **Labor 6304.3**
Court administrator. Workers compensation division, ante
Creation, **Labor 50**
Crimes and offenses, occupational safety and health, referral, **Labor 6315**
Directors,
Appointment, **Labor 51**
Attorneys and assistants, **Labor 54.5**
Comment, proposed projects, employment opportunities, **Labor 50.9**

INDUSTRIAL RELATIONS DEPARTMENT
—Cont'd
Directors—Cont'd
Compensation, **Labor 51**
Deputies and assistants, immunity from civil liability, **Labor 95**
Executive officer, **Labor 51**
Head of department, **Labor 53**
Industrial safety board member, **Labor 141**
Powers and duties, **Labor 54**
Tenure of office, **Labor 51**
Divisions, **Labor 56 et seq.**
Employer employee agreements, workers compensation, treatment of injury, **Labor 3209.7**
Equipment, **Labor 58**
Executive officer, **Labor 51**
Expenditures, **Labor 62**
Assistance and cooperation with federal agency, reimbursement, **Labor 50.6**
Funds, possession and control, **Labor 58**
Housing, generally, this index
Housing division, chief of division, **Labor 57**
Industrial accidents division. Workers compensation division, generally, post
Industrial safety division,
Occupational safety and health division, generally, post
Transfer of powers and duties to occupational safety and health division, **Labor 60.5**
Industrial Welfare Commission, generally, this index
Industrial welfare division,
Abolition, **Labor 83**
Chief of division, **Labor 57**
Salary, **Labor 57**
Compensation and salaries, chief of division, **Labor 57**
Industrial Homework, generally, this index
Transfer of powers and duties to labor standards enforcement division, **Labor 83**
Insurance loss control services coordinator, workers compensation, **Labor 6354.5**
Intergovernmental cooperation, joint enforcement strike force on the underground economy, **Un Ins 329**
Investigations and investigators bureau, division of occupational safety and health, **Labor 6315**
Reports, **Labor 6315.3**
Joint enforcement strike force on the underground economy, representative, **Un Ins 329**
Labor and Employment, generally, this index
Labor and workforce development agency, **Labor 50**
Labor law enforcement division, abolition, **Labor 82**

INDUSTRIAL RELATIONS DEPARTMENT
—Cont'd

Labor standards enforcement division, **Labor 79 et seq.**

Access to information, **Labor 1174**

Actions and proceedings, **Labor 98, 101 et seq.**

Administration, **Labor 61**

Appointments, chief, **Labor 72**

Appropriations, **Labor 89.5**

Arrest authority, officers, **Labor 95**

Attachment, costs, **Labor 101**

Books and papers, **Labor 89**

Branch offices, **Labor 81**

Business hours, **Labor 94**

Chief, **Labor 21, 57**

Appointment, **Labor 72**

Compensation, **Labor 72, 79**

Member of industrial welfare commission, **Labor 72**

Claims, filing, **Labor 99**

Compensation and salaries, **Labor 79**

Costs, **Labor 101**

Creation, **Labor 56, 79**

Executions, costs, **Labor 101**

Fees, filing or recording documents, **Labor 101.5**

Foreign state claims or judgments, collection, **Labor 64**

Garnishment, costs, **Labor 101**

Headquarters, **Labor 80**

Hours of business, **Labor 94**

Investigations, **Labor 74, 1174**

Liens, filing, **Labor 99**

Oaths and affirmations, **Labor 74**

Officers and employees,

Hours, **Labor 94**

Process, service, **Labor 95**

Records, **Labor 88**

Status of transferred employees, **Labor 87**

Traveling expenses, **Labor 81**

Orders of industrial welfare commission, enforcement, **Labor 74**

Powers and duties, **Labor 61, 81**

Production of books and papers, **Labor 74**

Records, **Labor 89**

Rules and regulations, **Labor 82**

Subpoenas, **Labor 74**

Transfer of powers and duties from division of labor law enforcement, **Labor 82**

Transfer of powers and duties from industrial welfare division, **Labor 83**

Traveling expenses, **Labor 101**

Witnesses, **Labor 74**

Labor statistics and research division, **Labor 56**

Chief of division, **Labor 57**

Investigations, **Labor 152**

Powers and duties, **Labor 150, 152**

Principal labor statistician, chief of division, **Labor 57**

Reports, **Labor 150**

INDUSTRIAL RELATIONS DEPARTMENT
—Cont'd

Labor statistics and research division
—Cont'd

Reports—Cont'd

Omission of names of persons supplying information, **Labor 153**

Laboratory services and personnel, **Labor 60.9**

Loss control services coordinator, workers compensation, **Labor 6354.5**

Management and control of department, **Labor 51**

Mobilehomes and Mobilehome Parks, generally, this index

Occupational safety and health appeals board, **Labor 148 et seq.**

Appointment of members, **Labor 148**

Chairman, **Labor 148**

Authority and duties, delegation of, **Labor 149**

Compensation and salaries, **Labor 141, 148**

Decisions and orders, **Labor 148.4 et seq.**

Employees, appointment of personnel, **Labor 148.2**

Governor, appointment of members, **Labor 148**

Judicial review, decisions and orders of board, **Labor 148.6**

Powers and duties, **Labor 148.8**

Term of office, **Labor 148.1**

Vacancies, appointments by governor, **Labor 148.1**

Writing, decisions and orders of board, **Labor 148.4**

Occupational safety and health division, **Labor 56**

Administration, **Labor 60.5**

Agreements, health problem inspection and evaluation services, **Labor 144.5**

Bilingual employees, **Labor 176**

Carcinogen control unit, **Labor 60.9**

Chief of division, **Labor 57**

Compensation, **Labor 57.1**

Civil service employees, transfer to industrial relations department, **Labor 60.6**

Civil service police, **Labor 57.1**

Compensation and salaries, **Labor 57.1**

Constituent units, **Labor 60.9**

Contracts, development of tests, breathing apparatus for use in fires, **Labor 6331**

Creation, **Labor 56**

Definitions, **Labor 6302**

Deputy chiefs, **Labor 57.1**

Employment safety, administration and enforcement, **Labor 60.5**

Enforcement, **Labor 60.5**

Agreements, **Labor 144**

Powers, **Labor 144.5**

Standards, **Labor 142**

INDUSTRIAL RELATIONS DEPARTMENT
—Cont'd

Occupational safety and health division
—Cont'd

Expenditures or appropriations, **Labor 60.8**

Industrial safety and occupational health branch of department of health services, possession and control of records, books, **Labor 60.7**

Interagency agreements, laboratory services and personnel, **Labor 60.9**

Interpreters and translators, **Labor 176**

Investigations bureau, **Labor 6315**

Reports, **Labor 6315.3**

Jurisdiction, **Labor 6800**

Laboratory services and personnel, **Labor 60.9**

Limited English proficient persons, bilingual employees, **Labor 176**

Occupational health unit, **Labor 60.9**

Occupational safety unit, **Labor 60.9**

Officers and employees, **Labor 57.1**

Bilingual employees, **Labor 176**

Transfer from industrial safety division or occupational health branch of health services department, **Labor 60.6**

Transfer to industrial relations department, **Labor 60.6**

Powers and duties, enforcement of standards, **Labor 144.5**

Reports, evaluation of proposed variances and standards, **Labor 147**

Safety engineers, tunnels and mines, **Labor 7950 et seq.**

Standards, development and promulgation, functions, **Labor 147.1**

Transfer of powers and duties from industrial safety division, **Labor 60.5 et seq.**

Tunnels and mines, **Labor 7950 et seq.**

Units, **Labor 60.9**

Occupational safety and health standards board, **Labor 140 et seq.**

Administration of occupational safety or health standards, orders, or rules, **Labor 144**

Agreements, administration or enforcement of occupational safety or health standards, orders, or rules, **Labor 144**

Appointment of members, **Labor 140**

Chairman, **Labor 140**

Compensation and salaries, **Labor 141**

Development and enforcement, **Labor 50.7**

Emergency regulations, **Labor 142.4**

Employees, appointment of personnel, **Labor 145**

Enforcement, **Labor 50.7**

Occupational safety or health standards, orders, or rules, **Labor 144**

Safety orders, **Labor 142**

Governor, appointment of members, **Labor 140**

INDUSTRIAL

INDUSTRIAL RELATIONS DEPARTMENT
—Cont'd
Occupational safety and health standards board—Cont'd
Harmful physical agents, promulgating standards, **Labor 144.6**
Hearings, permanent variances, **Labor 143.1, 146**
Medical examinations, **Labor 142.3**
Meetings, **Labor 142.1**
Notice, meetings, **Labor 142.1**
Permanent variance from standards, orders or special orders, **Labor 143 et seq.**
Powers and duties, **Labor 145.1**
Standards and orders, adopting, amending or repealing, **Labor 142.3 et seq.**
Terms of office, **Labor 140, 141**
Toxic materials or harmful physical agents, promulgating standards, **Labor 144.6**
Traveling expenses of members, **Labor 141**
Vacancies in office, **Labor 141**
Officers and employees,
Immunity from civil liability, **Labor 95**
Labor standards enforcement division, ante
Occupational safety and health division, ante
Offices, **Labor 58**
Organization of department, **Labor 55**
Powers and duties, **Labor 54**
Apprenticeship standards division, chief, **Labor 3073**
Process, service, **Labor 95**
Property, possession and control, **Labor 58**
Reciprocal agreements, collection of claims or judgment for wages, **Labor 64**
Records and recordation, **Labor 58**
Refund of moneys paid for license fees or other services, **Labor 63**
Rules and regulations, adoption and enforcement, **Labor 55**
Sales and use taxes, licenses and permits, compliance, information, **Labor 64.5**
Service of process, **Labor 95**
State compensation insurance fund, **Labor 55 et seq.**
Statutory construction, department officers or agencies, references to, **Labor 1200**
Strike force on the underground economy, **Un Ins 329**
Supplies, **Labor 58**
Taxation, licenses and permits, compliance, information, **Labor 64.5**
Term of office, chiefs of divisions, **Labor 57**
Tips, enforcement of laws, **Labor 355**
Title to property held for use and benefit of state transferred to state, **Labor 58**
United States department of labor, assistance and cooperation, **Labor 50.6**

INDUSTRIAL RELATIONS DEPARTMENT
—Cont'd
Vacancies in office, occupational safety and health standards board, **Labor 141**
Wage and hour division, United States department of labor, assistance and cooperation, **Labor 50.6**
Worker safety bilingual investigative support, enforcement and training account, **Labor 6356**
Workers compensation division, **Labor 56, 60, 110 et seq.**
Accountants, employment, **Labor 123**
Actions, powers and duties of attorney, **Labor 119**
Actuaries, employment, **Labor 123**
Administrative assistance to workers compensation claimants, **Labor 5450 et seq.**
Administrative director, **Labor 111 et seq.**
Appointment, **Labor 138.1**
Compensation and salaries, **Labor 138.1**
Definition, **Labor 3206**
Deputies, **Labor 138**
Fees, **Labor 127**
Officers and employees, employment, **Labor 123**
Powers and duties, **Labor 124, 129, 129.5**
Application of law, **Labor 55**
Attorneys, **Labor 54.5**
Duties, **Labor 119**
Pro tempore workers compensation judges, **Labor 123.7**
Blank forms, printing and furnishing, **Labor 125**
Case files, fees, **Labor 127**
Chief of division, **Labor 57**
Child support enforcement, cooperation, **Labor 138.5**
Compensation and salaries,
Administrative director, **Labor 138.1**
Chief of division, **Labor 57**
Workers compensation judges, **Labor 123**
Continuing information program, **Labor 139.6**
Copies, papers and records, fees, **Labor 127**
Court administrator,
Appointment, **Labor 138.1**
Compensation and salaries, **Labor 138.1**
Deputies, **Labor 138**
Powers and duties, **Labor 133**
Definitions, division, **Labor 3205**
Evidence taken on proceedings, fees, transcripts, **Labor 127**
Fees, **Labor 127**
Payment into state treasury, **Labor 127**
Forms, blank forms, **Labor 125**
Headquarters, **Labor 138.2**

INDUSTRIAL RELATIONS DEPARTMENT
—Cont'd
Workers compensation division—Cont'd
Information and assistance officer, consultation, **Labor 5451**
Insurance loss control services coordinator, **Labor 6354.5**
Judges, **Labor 123 et seq.**
Jurisdiction, **Labor 133, 5305**
Loss control services coordinator, **Labor 6354.5**
Meetings open to public, **Labor 138.2**
Officers and employees, employment, **Labor 123**
Transfer to industrial safety division, **Labor 144**
Offices, **Labor 138.2**
Official reporters, **Labor 123.3**
Powers and duties, **Labor 133**
Records and recordation, **Labor 126**
Copies, fees, **Labor 127**
Reporters, **Labor 123.3**
Reports, **Labor 127**
Rules and regulations, adoption, **Labor 4726**
Secretary, administrative director, **Labor 120**
Transcripts, testimony, fees, **Labor 127**

INDUSTRIAL RELATIONS UNPAID FUND
Deposits, excess amounts, **Labor 96.7**

INDUSTRIAL RELATIONS UNPAID WAGE FUND
State Treasury, this index

INDUSTRIAL SAFETY ACT
Safety in employment. Labor and Employment, this index

INDUSTRIAL SAFETY BOARD
Volatile flammable liquids, safety orders, **Labor 7802**

INDUSTRIAL SAFETY DIVISION
Industrial Relations Department, this index

INDUSTRIAL WELFARE COMMISSION
Generally, **Labor 70 et seq.**
Appeal and review, rules and regulations, **Labor 1173**
Appointment of members, **Labor 70**
Bulletins, **Labor 1203**
Chief of division of industrial welfare, member acting as chief, **Labor 72**
Compensation, **Labor 72**
Resident apartment manager, rent, **Labor 1182.8**
Wage board, **Labor 1179**
Director, occupational safety and health standards board, member, **Labor 140, 141**
Establishment, **Labor 70**
Expenses, **Labor 72**
Head of department, definitions, **Labor 53**
Health care industries, petitions, rulings, **Labor 1182.7**

INDUSTRIAL WELFARE COMMISSION
—Cont'd
Hearings, **Labor 1173**
Investigations, hours and conditions of labor, **Labor 1173**
Jurisdiction, **Labor 1173**
Membership, additional members, **Labor 70.1**
Occupational safety and health appeals board,
Attorneys fees, **Labor 149.5**
Costs, **Labor 149.5**
Officers and employees, **Labor 73**
Orders,
Concurrence by majority of commissioners, **Labor 1177**
Enforcement, **Labor 74**
Powers and duties, **Labor 1173**
Reports, **Labor 1203**
Rules and regulations, copies, **Labor 1198.4**
Statements, orders, **Labor 1177**
Term of office, **Labor 71**
Traveling expenses, wage board, **Labor 1179**
Vacancies, **Labor 71**
Wage board,
Circumventing wage board to expedite hearing on petitions, **Labor 1182.7**
Traveling expenses, **Labor 1179**
Wage order amendments, rulings, **Labor 1182.7**

INDUSTRIAL WELFARE DIVISION
Industrial Relations Department, this index

INDUSTRY
Manufacturers and Manufacturing, generally, this index

INFANTS
Children and Minors, generally, this index

INFECTIOUS DISEASES
Diseases, generally, this index

INFORMATION
Computers, generally, this index
Health Care Service Plans, this index
Housing, this index
Indictment and Information, generally, this index
Insurance, this index
Labor and Employment, this index
Medical Care and Treatment, this index
Physicians and Surgeons, this index
Sexual harassment, workplace, **Gov 12950**
Social Services, this index
State Officers and Employees, this index
Support, this index
Unemployment Compensation, this index
Workers Compensation, this index

INFORMATION PRACTICES ACT
Generally, **CC 1798 et seq.**

INFORMATION TECHNOLOGY
Computers, generally, this index

INFORMATION TECHNOLOGY—Cont'd
Telecommunications, generally, this index

INFRACTIONS
Compensation and salaries, records and recordation, inspection and inspectors, time, **Labor 226**
Smoking, this index
Trespass, **Pen 602.8**

INJUNCTION
Aerial passenger tramways, unlawful and dangerous operation, **Labor 7343**
Affidavits,
Tanks and boilers, temporarily restraining unsafe use, **Labor 7692**
Unsafe working conditions, **Labor 6324**
Agricultural Labor and Employment, this index
Agricultural Labor Relations Act, unfair labor practices, **Labor 1160.4, 1160.6**
Air pressure tanks, unsafe operation, **Labor 7691**
Apprentices, offenses involving, **Labor 3084.5**
Attorney fees, harassment prohibiting injunctions, **CCP 527.6**
Boilers, unsafe operation, **Labor 7691**
Bonds, this index
Bonds (officers and fiduciaries), elevator operation, enjoining, **Labor 7303**
Buses, this index
Civil air patrol, labor and employment, **Labor 1507**
Civil rights, violations, **CC 52**
Collective bargaining, **CCP 527.3**
Collective bargaining agreements, **Labor 1126**
Colleges and Universities, this index
Compensation and Salaries, this index
Construction, contracts, labor and employment, **Labor 2810**
Costs, harassment, **CCP 527.6**
Crimes and offenses, acquisition of firearms by restrainees, **Pen 12021**
Disclosure, personal information held by governmental agencies, Information Practices Act, **CC 1798.46, 1798.47**
Elevators, restraining operation, **Labor 7303**
Employment. Labor and Employment, this index
Fair Employment and Housing, this index
Farm labor contractors, employees, violations, attorneys fees, **Labor 1697**
Fines and penalties, acquisition of firearms by restrainees, **Pen 12021**
Firearms. Weapons, this index
Foreign labor contractors, **Bus & P 9998.8**
Forms, harassment, **CCP 527.6**
Freedom from violence, **CC 52**
Gender violence, **CC 52.4**
Harassment, this index
Health Facilities, this index
Housing, this index
Housing discrimination, **Gov 12989.2, 12989.3**

INJUNCTION—Cont'd
Industrial homework, **Labor 2667**
Interurban railroads, displaced workers, **Labor 1073**
Janitors,
Contracts, labor and employment, **Labor 2810**
Discharge, **Labor 1062**
Jurisdictional strikes, **Labor 1116**
Labor and Employment, this index
Labor Camps, this index
Labor Disputes, this index
Liquefied petroleum gas storage tanks, unsafe operation, **Labor 7691**
Mass transit, displaced workers, **Labor 1073**
Nonpayment of wages, second and subsequent offenses, **Labor 243**
Paratransit vehicles, displaced workers, **Labor 1073**
Peace Officers, this index
Petitions, workplace violence safety, **CCP 527.8**
Picketing, **CCP 527.3**
Preliminary injunctions. Temporary injunctions, generally, post
Private security services, contracts, labor and employment, **Labor 2810**
Railroads, this index
Right to privacy, enjoining harassment of individuals, **CCP 527.6**
Sex, force and violence, **CC 52.4**
State Agencies, this index
State Contracts, this index
Steam boilers, unsafe operation, **Labor 7691**
Talent agencies, fees, **Labor 1704.1, 1704.2**
Temporary injunctions,
Agricultural Labor Relations Act, unfair labor practices, **Labor 1160.4**
Air pressure tanks, **Labor 7692**
Boilers, **Labor 7692**
Elevators, **Labor 7303**
Harassment, right to privacy, **CCP 527.6**
Liquefied petroleum gas storage tanks, **Labor 7692**
Right to privacy, harassment, **CCP 527.6**
Steam boilers, **Labor 7692**
Temporary restraining orders, harassment, **CCP 527.6**
Threats, violation of civil rights, **CC 52**
Transportation, displaced workers, **Labor 1073**
Unemployment compensation, issuance to prevent collection of contributions, **Un Ins 1851**
Unpaid wages, actions to compel deposit of payment bonds, **Labor 240**
Unsafe working conditions, **Labor 6323 et seq.**
Violence, freedom from, **CC 52**
Weapons, this index
Wearing apparel, contracts, labor and employment, **Labor 2810**
Workplace violence safety, **CCP 527.8**

INJURIES
Personal Injuries, generally, this index

INMATES
Correctional Institutions, generally, this index
Jails, generally, this index

INNKEEPERS
Hotels, generally, this index
Motels and Motor Courts, generally, this index

INORGANIC PIGMENTS
Lead poisoning, occupational safety, programs, **Health & S 105185 et seq.**

INSANE PERSONS
Mentally Ill Persons, generally, this index

INSOLVENCY
Compensation and salaries, priorities and preferences, **CCP 1204**
Disability compensation, voluntary plans, **Un Ins 3261**
Employee benefit plans, priorities and preferences, **CCP 1204**
Priorities and preferences, compensation and salaries, **CCP 1204**
Unemployment Compensation, this index

INSPECTION AND INSPECTORS
Aerial Passenger Tramways, this index
Agricultural labor and employment, children and minors, hours of labor, exemptions, **Labor 1393.5**
Air pressure tanks, **Labor 7620 et seq.**
Amusements,
    Permanent amusement rides, safety, **Labor 7920 et seq.**
    Safety, **Labor 7900 et seq.**
Boilers, **Labor 7650 et seq.**
Bungee jumping, safety, **Labor 7920 et seq.**
Carcinogens, use in place of employment, **Labor 9050 et seq.**
Compensation and Salaries, this index
Construction, this index
Correctional Institutions, this index
Cranes, tower cranes, **Labor 7370 et seq.**
Definitions,
    Farm labor contractors, licenses and permits, **Labor 1695.7**
    Unemployment compensation, confidential or privileged information, browsing, **Un Ins 13018**
Disability compensation, medical records, **Un Ins 2714**
Dumbwaiters. Elevators, Dumbwaiters and Escalators, this index
Elevators, Dumbwaiters and Escalators, this index
Employee records, **Labor 1198.5**
Employment. Labor and Employment, this index
Entry On Property, generally, this index
Escalators. Elevators, Dumbwaiters and Escalators, this index

INSPECTION AND INSPECTORS—Cont'd
Fair employment and housing department, books and records, **Gov 12930**
Industrial homework, industrial relations department, **Labor 2666**
Insurance, this index
Labor and Employment, this index
Labor camps, **Health & S 17050**
Liquefied petroleum gas, storage tanks, **Labor 7620 et seq.**
Municipalities, this index
Occupational Carcinogens Control Act, **Labor 9050 et seq.**
Occupational safety and health. Labor and Employment, this index
Oil and Gas, this index
Payroll, records and recordation, **Labor 226**
Payroll records, contractors and subcontractors, public works projects, **Labor 1776**
Permanent amusement rides, safety, **Labor 7920 et seq.**
Prisons and prisoners. Correctional Institutions, this index
Public Buildings and Works, this index
Records and Recordation, this index
Scaffolds, **Labor 7156**
Ski lifts, **Labor 7349**
Steam boilers, **Labor 7650 et seq.**
Tanks, storage of air pressure or liquefied petroleum gas, **Labor 7620 et seq.**
Tips, records maintained by employers, **Labor 353**
Tower cranes, **Labor 7370 et seq.**
Wharves, docks and piers, inspection of machinery and equipment, **Labor 7605**
Workers Compensation, this index

INSTALLMENT PAYMENTS
Unemployment compensation, offers in compromise, **Un Ins 1870**

INSTALLMENTS
Workers Compensation, this index

INSTITUTION OF HIGHER EDUCATION
Definitions, unemployment compensation, **Un Ins 1253.3**

INSTRUCTIONS
Garnishment, **CCP 706.127**

INSTRUMENTS
Books and Papers, generally, this index
Negotiable Instruments, generally, this index

INSURANCE
Accident and health insurance. Disability insurance, generally, post
Actions and proceedings, concealing policy, privileged communications, **CC 47**
Aerial tramways, inspection in lieu of state inspection, **Labor 7354.5**

INSURANCE—Cont'd
AIDS,
    Blood test results, use in determining insurability, **Health & S 120980**
    Tests, insurability, **Health & S 120980**
Air pressure tanks, inspectors, **Labor 7652.5**
Amusements, rides, **Labor 7912, 7926**
Annuities,
    Income Tax—State, this index
    Unemployment compensation, payments made under annuity plans to employee, exclusion from wages, **Un Ins 931, 934**
Automobiles. Motor Vehicle Insurance, generally, this index
Birth Control, this index
Blood, AIDS, tests, **Health & S 120980**
Boilers, inspectors, **Labor 7652.5**
Cal COBRA, accident and health insurance, **Health & S 1366.20 et seq.; Ins 10128.50 et seq.**
Charities, insurable interest, life or disability, **Ins 10110.1**
Claims. Disability insurance, post
Compensation and salaries,
    Disability insurance, post
    Employees deductions, premiums, **Labor 224**
    Premiums, deductions, **Labor 224**
Consumer credit reporting agencies, notice, denial, rates and rating organizations, **CC 1786.40**
Continuation. Disability insurance, post
Conversion, coverage, group insurance, **Labor 2800.3**
Corporation Taxes, this index
Coverage,
    Disability insurance, post
    Group disability insurance, post
Credit ratings. Consumer Credit Reporting Agencies, generally, this index
Denial,
    Consumer credit reporting agencies, notice, **CC 1786.40**
    Information, disclosure, **CC 1786.40**
Disability insurance,
    Birth control, coverage, **Ins 10123.196**
    Cal COBRA, **Health & S 1366.20 et seq.; Ins 10128.50 et seq.**
    Charities, insurable interest, **Ins 10110.1**
    Claims, children and minors, submission, **Fam 3767**
    Compensation and salaries,
        Employees deductions, payments, **Labor 224**
        Policies, rescission, **Ins 10385**
    Continuation, **Health & S 1366.20 et seq.; Ins 10128.50 et seq.**
    Contraceptives, coverage, **Ins 10123.196**
    Coverage,
        Birth control, **Ins 10123.196**
        Compensation and salaries, rescission, **Ins 10385**
    Contraceptives, **Ins 10123.196**

INSURANCE—Cont'd
Disability insurance—Cont'd
Coverage—Cont'd
Rescission, compensation and salaries, **Ins 10385**
Definitions, Cal COBRA, **Health & S 1366.21; Ins 10128.51**
Disclosure, employers, release of information to, **Ins 791.27**
Elections, Cal COBRA, **Ins 10128.55**
Family care and medical leave, coverage, **Gov 12945.2**
Firefighters and fire departments, death in line of duty, **Labor 4856**
Group disability insurance, generally, post
Health Care Service Plans, generally, this index
Labor and Employment, this index
Medical records, disclosure, **CC 56.10**
Notice, continuation benefits, qualifying events, Cal COBRA, **Ins 10128.55**
Peace officers, death in line of duty, survivors benefits, **Labor 4856**
Policies,
Compensation and salaries, rescission, **Ins 10385**
Rescission, compensation and salaries, **Ins 10385**
Premiums, unemployment, waiver, **Ins 10110.5**
Qualifying events, Cal COBRA, notice, **Ins 10128.55**
School Officers and Employees, this index
Support, this index
Time, Cal COBRA, continuation, termination, **Health & S 1366.27**
Unemployment, premiums, waiver, **Ins 10110.5**
Unemployment compensation, exclusion from wages, benefits paid, **Un Ins 931, 933**
Voluntary plans for employee disability compensation, **Un Ins 3251 et seq.**
Disclosure,
Disability insurance, ante
Group disability insurance, post
Information, denial, rates and rating organizations, **CC 1786.40**
Medical records, post
Discrimination,
Domestic partnership, group disability insurance, **Ins 10121.7**
Group disability insurance, domestic partnership, **Ins 10121.7**
Domestic Partnership, this index
Elections,
Disability insurance, Cal COBRA, **Ins 10128.55**
Group disability insurance, Cal COBRA, **Health & S 1366.23; Ins 10128.53**
Elevators, Dumbwaiters and Escalators, this index

INSURANCE—Cont'd
Employment development department, property, **Un Ins 1601**
Firefighters and fire departments, death in line of duty, survivors health benefits, **Labor 4856**
Forms. Policies, post
Fraternal benefit societies, unemployment compensation, officials, **Un Ins 652**
Group disability insurance,
Birth control, coverage, **Ins 10123.196**
Cal COBRA, **Health & S 1366.20 et seq.; Ins 10128.50 et seq.**
Continuation benefits, **Ins 10116.5**
Cal COBRA, **Health & S 1366.20 et seq.; Ins 10128.50 et seq.**
Contraceptives, coverage, **Ins 10123.196**
Conversion coverage, **Labor 2800.3**
Coverage,
Birth control, **Ins 10123.196**
Contraceptives, **Ins 10123.196**
Definitions, Cal COBRA, **Health & S 1366.21; Ins 10128.51**
Dependent child, Cal COBRA, **Health & S 1366.23; Ins 10128.53**
Disclosure, Cal COBRA, **Health & S 1366.24; Ins 10128.54**
Discrimination, domestic partnership, **Ins 10121.7**
Domestic partnership, **Ins 10121.7**
Elections, Cal COBRA, **Health & S 1366.23; Ins 10128.53**
Exemptions, Cal COBRA, **Health & S 1366.22; Ins 10128.52**
Husband and wife, continuation of benefits, **Ins 10116.5**
Individual contributions, continuance of policies during labor disputes, **Ins 10116**
Notice,
Cal COBRA, qualifying events, **Health & S 1366.24, 1366.25; Ins 10128.54, 10128.55**
Conversion coverage, **Labor 2800.2**
Policies, conversion policies, **Labor 2800.3**
Premiums, Cal COBRA, **Health & S 1366.26, 1366.27; Ins 10128.56, 10128.57**
Rates and rating organizations, Cal COBRA, **Health & S 1366.26, 1366.27; Ins 10128.56, 10128.57**
Termination of coverage, Cal COBRA, **Health & S 1366.27; Ins 10128.57**
Time, Cal COBRA, continuation, termination, **Ins 10128.57**
Work cessation, continuance of coverage, **Ins 10116**
Group insurance,
Conversion coverage, **Labor 2800.3**
Health care coverage,
Cal COBRA, **Health & S 1366.20 et seq.; Ins 10128.50 et seq.**
Continuation benefits replacement, **Health & S 1366.20 et seq.; Ins 10128.50 et seq.**

INSURANCE—Cont'd
Group insurance—Cont'd
Labor and Employment, this index
Labor disputes, continuance of policies, individual contributions, **Ins 10116**
Notice, conversion coverage, **Labor 2800.2**
Group life insurance,
Individual contributions, continuance of policies during labor disputes, **Ins 10116**
Work cessation, continuance of coverage, **Ins 10116**
Health Care Service Plans, generally, this index
Health insurance. Disability insurance, generally, ante
Hospitals. Disability insurance, generally, ante
Husband and wife. Marriage, this index
Information,
Disclosure, denial, rates and rating organizations, **CC 1786.40**
Rates and rating organizations, post
Inspection and inspectors,
Consumer reporting agencies, files, **CC 1786 et seq.**
Tanks and boilers, **Labor 7652.5**
Insurable interest,
Charities, **Ins 10110.1**
Employer, **Ins 10110.1**
Individual in oneself, **Ins 10110.1**
Time of existence, **Ins 10110.1**
Investigations and investigators, consumer investigations, **CC 1786 et seq.**
Labor and Employment, this index
Liability insurance,
Amusements, rides, **Labor 7912, 7926**
Elevators, dumbwaiters and escalators,
Licenses and permits, **Labor 7301**
Qualified elevator company, **Labor 7311.1**
Motor Vehicle Insurance, generally, this index
Permanent amusement rides, **Labor 7926**
Life insurance,
Abandoned or Unclaimed Property, this index
Charitable organizations, insurable interest, **Ins 10110.1**
Credit reports, application of law, **CC 1785.1 et seq.**
Income Tax—State, this index
Living benefits contracts, unemployment compensation withholding, **Un Ins 13028**
Medical records, disclosure, **CC 56.10**
Premiums, unemployment, waiver, **Ins 10110.5**
Unclaimed property. Abandoned or Unclaimed Property, this index
Unemployment, premiums, waiver, **Ins 10110.5**
Life insurance corporation, definitions, Unclaimed Property Law, **CCP 1501**

INSURANCE

INSURANCE—Cont'd
Liquefied petroleum gas storage tanks, inspectors, **Labor 7652.5**
Marriage, this index
Medical care and treatment,
  Disability insurance, generally, ante
  Health Care Service Plans, generally, this index
Medical insurance. Disability insurance, generally, ante
Medical records,
  Disability insurance, ante
  Disclosure, **CC 56.10**
Monopolies and unfair trade, access for infants and mothers program, health services, **Ins 12698.50 et seq.**
Motor Vehicle Insurance, generally, this index
No fault vehicle insurance. Motor Vehicle Insurance, generally, this index
Nonindustrial disability insurance, state employees, **Un Ins 2781 et seq.**
Notice,
  Consumer credit reporting agencies, denial, rates and rating organizations, **CC 1786.40**
  Consumer investigation reports, **CC 1786 et seq.**
  Conversion coverage, group insurance, **Labor 2800.2**
  Disability insurance, ante
  Group disability insurance, ante
  Investigations, consumer reporting agencies, **CC 1786.16**
  Rates and rating organizations, post
Old age and survivors insurance. Social Security, generally, this index
Orders, relieving employer from liability, insurer joined as party, **Labor 3759**
Peace Officers, this index
Permanent amusement rides, **Labor 7926**
Policies,
  Concealing existence, privileged communications, **CC 47**
  Conversion policies, group insurance, **Labor 2800.3**
  Disability compensation for employees, voluntary plans, **Un Ins 3254, 3255**
  Disability insurance, ante
  Forms, voluntary plans for employee disability compensation, **Un Ins 3254, 3255**
  Group disability insurance, ante
  Voluntary plans for employee disability compensation, **Un Ins 3255**
Premiums,
  Disability insurance, ante
  Family care and medical leave, benefit contributions, **Gov 12945.2**
  Group disability insurance, ante
  Life insurance, ante
Privileges and immunities, concealing existence of policy, communications, **CC 47**

INSURANCE—Cont'd
Rates and rating organizations,
  Consumer credit reporting agencies, notice, **CC 1786.40**
  Disclosure, information, **CC 1786.40**
  Group disability insurance, ante
  Information, disclosure, **CC 1786.40**
  Notice, consumer credit reporting agencies, **CC 1786.40**
Records and recordation, investigations, consumer reporting agencies, **CC 1786 et seq.**
Self insurance,
  Amusements, permanent amusement rides, **Labor 7926**
  Permanent amusement rides, **Labor 7926**
  Workers Compensation, this index
State Officers and Employees, this index
Steam boilers, inspectors, **Labor 7652.5**
Termination of coverage. Group disability insurance, ante
Time,
  Cal COBRA, continuation, termination, **Health & S 1366.27**
  Disability insurance, ante
Unemployment Compensation, generally, this index
Vehicles. Motor Vehicle Insurance, generally, this index
Voluntary plans for employee disability compensation, **Un Ins 3251 et seq.**
Voting. Elections, generally, ante
Workers Compensation, this index

INSURANCE COMMISSIONER
Insurance, generally, this index

INSURANCE COMPANIES
Insurance, generally, this index

INSURANCE DEPARTMENT
Insurance, generally, this index

INSURANCE TAXATION
Annuities. Income Tax—State, this index
Life insurance. Income Tax—State, this index

INSURERS
Definitions, occupational safety and health, **Labor 6302**

INTANGIBLES
Escheat, this index

INTEMPERANCE
Alcoholics and Alcoholism, generally, this index

INTERCITY RAIL TRANSPORTATION
Railroads, generally, this index

INTERCOUNTRY ADOPTION
Adoption of Children, this index

INTEREST
Compensation and Salaries, this index
Garnishment, **CCP 706.028**
Income Tax—State, this index

INTEREST—Cont'd
Indemnity, labor and employment, discharge of duties, **Labor 2802**
Judgment debtors, final earnings withholding order for interest, obtaining, **CCP 706.028**
Labor and Employment, this index
Minimum wage violations, **Labor 1193.6**
Public Buildings and Works, this index
Support, this index
Talent agencies, retention of artist funds, **Labor 1700.25**
Unemployment Compensation, this index
Unpaid wages awards, **Labor 98.1**
Withholding tax on wages, **Un Ins 13014**
Workers Compensation, this index

INTERFERENCE
Handicapped persons, housing rights, **Gov 12955.7**

INTERIOR DESIGNERS
Lead poisoning, occupational safety, programs, **Health & S 105185 et seq.**

INTERNAL COMBUSTION ENGINES
Engines, generally, this index

INTERNAL REVENUE
Income Tax—Federal, generally, this index

INTERNAL REVENUE SERVICE SCHEDULE SE
Definitions, unemployment compensation, elective coverage, **Un Ins 704, 704.1, 708, 708.5**

INTERNET
Talent agencies,
  Contracts, **Labor 1703**
  Fees, **Labor 1703.4**

INTERNS
Unemployment compensation,
  Coverage of hospital interns, **Un Ins 645**
  Optional exclusion, **Un Ins 711**

INTERPRETERS AND TRANSLATORS
Deaf and Mute Persons, this index
Fees, workers compensation, contested cases, medical legal expenses, **Labor 4620 et seq.**
Industrial relations division, occupational safety and health division, **Labor 176**
Labor and employment,
  Complaints, **Labor 105**
  Occupational safety and health, **Labor 176**
Occupational safety and health division, **Labor 176**
Workers Compensation, this index

INTERROGATORIES
Fair employment and housing department, discovery, **Gov 12963.2**

INTERSTATE COMMERCE

Air pressure tanks, exemption from inspection and safety regulation, **Labor 7624**

Liquefied petroleum gas storage tanks, exemption from inspection and safety regulation, **Labor 7624**

Workers compensation, application of law, **Labor 3203**

INTERURBAN RAILROADS

Actions and proceedings, displaced workers, **Labor 1073**

Attorney fees, displaced workers, actions and proceedings, **Labor 1073**

Contracts, displaced workers, **Labor 1070 et seq.**

Costs, displaced workers, actions and proceedings, **Labor 1073**

Displaced workers, **Labor 1070 et seq.**

Injunction, displaced workers, **Labor 1073**

Officers and employees, displaced workers, **Labor 1070 et seq.**

Safeguards, **Labor 6800**

INTERVENTION

Fair Employment and Housing, this index

Housing discrimination actions, **Gov 12989, 12989.1, 12989.3**

Labor and employment, employee complaints, **Labor 98.5**

INTIMIDATION

Duress or Coercion, generally, this index

Threats, generally, this index

INTOXICATING LIQUORS

Alcoholic Beverages, generally, this index

INTOXICATION

Alcoholics and Alcoholism, generally, this index

INVALIDS

Handicapped Persons, generally, this index

INVASION

War and Civil Defense, generally, this index

INVASION OF PRIVACY

Privacy, this index

INVENTIONS

Employees, ownership rights, **Labor 2870 et seq.**

Ownership, rights, employers and employees, **Labor 2870 et seq.**

INVENTORIES

Ownership rights, employers and employees, **Labor 2870 et seq.**

INVESTIGATIONS BUREAU

Industrial relations department, division of occupational safety and health, **Labor 6315**

Reports, **Labor 6315.3**

INVESTIGATIVE CONSUMER REPORTING AGENCIES

Consumer Credit Reporting Agencies, generally, this index

INVESTMENTS

County Bonds, this index

Disability, compensation fund, **Un Ins 3002, 3003**

Employee or applicant, investment in business, **Labor 406, 407**

Municipal Bonds, this index

Pooled money investment board. State Treasury, this index

School Bonds, this index

State Bonds, this index

Unemployment Compensation, this index

IRAQ KUWAIT CRISIS

Legislature, benefits, **Mil & V 395.07**

State officers and employees, benefits, **Mil & V 395.07**

IRRIGATION AND IRRIGATION DISTRICTS

Officers and employees,

Compensation and salaries, leave of absence for military duty, **Mil & V 395.01 et seq.**

Leave of absence for military duty, **Mil & V 395 et seq.**

Military personnel, discrimination, **Mil & V 394**

Soldiers and Sailors Relief Act, **Mil & V 395.1**

ISONIPECAINE

Drug Addicts, generally, this index

ISSUE

Children and Minors, generally, this index

ISSUES, PROOF AND VARIANCE

Evidence, generally, this index

ITINERANT VENDORS AND MERCHANTS

Hawkers and Peddlers, generally, this index

JACK SCAFFOLDS

Use as support for scaffolds, **Labor 7154.1**

JACKING PITS

Labor and employment, occupational safety and health, bids for construction, **Labor 6707**

JAILS

Guards, tuberculosis, workers compensation, **Labor 3212.6**

Officers and employees, tuberculosis, workers compensation, **Labor 3212.6**

Pilot programs, reentry, assistance, indigent persons, inmate welfare fund, **Pen 4025.5**

Reentry, assistance, indigent persons, inmate welfare fund, pilot programs, **Pen 4025.5**

Release, reentry, assistance, indigent persons, inmate welfare fund, pilot programs, **Pen 4025.5**

JAILS—Cont'd

Tuberculosis, guards, workers compensation, **Labor 3212.6**

Workers compensation, guards, tuberculosis, **Labor 3212.6**

JANITORS

Children and minors, **Labor 1294.3**

Contracts, **Labor 2810**

Discharge, **Labor 1060 et seq.**

JARS

Containers, generally, this index

JEOPARDY ASSESSMENTS

Unemployment compensation, **Un Ins 991, 1115, 1137 et seq.**

JET THRUST UNIT

Explosives, generally, this index

JETTIES

Wharves, Docks and Piers, generally, this index

JOB

Definitions, employment training panel, **Un Ins 10201**

JOB LISTING SERVICES

Employment Agencies, this index

JOB ORDERS

Definitions, employment agency regulation, **CC 1812.501**

JOB PAIRING

Definitions, employment opportunities creation, **Un Ins 12102**

JOB PREPARATION AND TRAINING SERVICES

Unemployment Compensation, this index

JOB SHARING

Definitions, employment opportunities creation, **Un Ins 12102**

JOB TRAINING COORDINATING COUNCIL

Labor market information, **Un Ins 10530 et seq.**

JOB TRAINING PROGRAMS

CalWORKs. Social Services, this index

Corporation taxes, credits, enterprise zones, **Rev & T 23622.7**

Employment Development, generally, this index

Federal Job Training Partnership Act, corporation taxes, credits, enterprise zones, **Rev & T 23622.7**

Fees, **Un Ins 10501**

Green collar jobs, **Un Ins 15000 et seq.**

Handicapped clients of department of rehabilitation, **Un Ins 9003**

Journeymen, new workers and displaced workers, **Labor 3093**

Social Services, this index

Vietnam Veterans Employment Act, **Gov 7280 et seq.**

JOBS

**JOBS FOR CALIFORNIA GRADUATES PRO-
GRAM**
Generally, **Un Ins 9900 et seq.**

JOBS TAX CREDIT
Generally, **Rev & T 23621 et seq.**

JOBSEEKER
Definitions, employment agency regulation, **CC 1812.501**

JOCKEYS
Collective bargaining, labor disputes, **Labor 3201.81**
Labor disputes, collective bargaining, **Labor 3201.81**
Unemployment compensation, services by
free lance jockey, **Un Ins 654**

JOINDER OF CAUSES OF ACTION
Actions and Proceedings, this index

JOINDER OF PARTIES
Parties, this index

JOINT ADVENTURE
Joint Ventures, generally, this index

JOINT AND SEVERAL LIABILITY
Public buildings and works, contractors,
compensation and salaries, assessments, **Labor 1743**
Wearing apparel, manufacturers, contracts
with unregistered or unbonded manufacturers, **Labor 2677**

JOINT APPRENTICESHIP COMMITTEE
Decisions, investigation, administrator of
apprenticeship, **Labor 1777.5**
Public works, apprenticeship standards,
certificate, **Labor 1777.5**

**JOINT ENFORCEMENT STRIKE FORCE ON
THE UNDERGROUND ECONOMY**
Generally, **Un Ins 329**
Citation issuance, authority, **Labor 106**
Penalty assessment orders, issuance, au-
thority, **Labor 106**

**JOINT STOCK ASSOCIATIONS AND COM-
PANIES**
Unemployment compensation, employing
unit, **Un Ins 135**

JOINT VENTURES
Definitions, unemployment compensation,
Un Ins 1058
Unemployment compensation, **Un Ins
1057, 1058**
Employing unit, **Un Ins 135**

JOURNEYMEN
On the job training programs, **Labor 3093**

JUDGES
Administrative Law and Procedure, this
index
Courts of Appeal, this index
Judgments and Decrees, generally, this in-
dex

JUDGES—Cont'd
Military forces, reentry of office after dis-
charge, **Mil & V 395.3**
Unemployment compensation, excluded
service, **Un Ins 634.5**
Workers Compensation, this index

JUDGMENT CREDITORS
Assignment for Benefit of Creditors, gen-
erally, this index
Costs, final earnings withholding order for
costs, obtaining, **CCP 706.028**
Definitions, garnishment, **CCP 706.011**
Earnings withholding orders, issuance,
CCP 706.108
Executions, generally, this index
Final earnings withholding orders, obtain-
ing, **CCP 706.028**
Garnishment, generally, this index
Interest, final earnings withholding order
for interest, obtaining, **CCP 706.028**

JUDGMENT DEBTORS
Assignment for Benefit of Creditors, gen-
erally, this index
Definitions, garnishment, **CCP 706.011**
Executions, generally, this index
Garnishment, generally, this index

JUDGMENT LIENS
Unemployment insurance,
Contributions, failure to pay, **Un Ins
1815, 1816**
Overpayments, **Un Ins 1379.5**

JUDGMENTS AND DECREES
Appeal and Review, generally, this index
Attachment, generally, this index
Collection, labor commissioner, foreign
courts, **Labor 103**
Compensation and Salaries, this index
Compromise and Settlement, generally,
this index
Consumer credit,
Reporting agencies, **CC 1786.18**
Reports, contents of records, **CC
1785.13**
Disability compensation, payment, **Un Ins
3009, 3012**
Enforcement, wearing apparel manufac-
turers, penalties or confiscation, pri-
orities, **Labor 2681**
Fair employment and housing, **Gov 12973**
Garnishment, generally, this index
Judgment Liens, generally, this index
Labor and Employment, this index
Labor camps, residents, **Health & S 17055**
Labor commissioner,
Fees, filing, **Labor 101.5**
Foreign courts, **Labor 103**
Labor standards enforcement division,
fees, filing or recording, **Labor 101.5**
Liens and incumbrances. Judgment
Liens, generally, this index
Mortgages, generally, this index
Nonpayment of wages, second and subse-
quent offenses, **Labor 243**

JUDGMENTS AND DECREES—Cont'd
Offer of judgment. Compromise and Set-
tlement, generally, this index
Reconsideration, final orders, **Labor 6614
et seq.**
Satisfaction, compensation and salaries,
farm labor contractors, wearing ap-
parel, manufacturers and manufactur-
ing, **Labor 273**
State Agencies, this index
Supersedeas or Stay, generally, this index
Unemployment Compensation, this index
Wearing Apparel, this index
Workers Compensation, this index

JUDICIAL COUNCIL
Health insurance coverage assignment
forms, adoption, **Fam 3772**

JUDICIAL REVIEW
Appeal and Review, generally, this index

JUDICIAL SALES
Executions, generally, this index

JUMPERS AND JUMPING
Bungee jumping, licenses and permits, **Labor 7901**

JUNIOR COLLEGES
Community colleges and districts. Colleges and Universities, this index

JURISDICTIONAL STRIKES
Generally, **Labor 1115 et seq.**
Labor Disputes, this index

JURY
Compensation and salaries, unemploy-
ment compensation, **Un Ins 1252**
Contempt, generally, this index
Discrimination, time off from employ-
ment, **Labor 230**
Employee rights, time off to serve as juror,
Labor 230
Fees, wages, unemployment compensa-
tion, **Un Ins 1252**
Labor and Employment, this index
Unemployment Compensation, this index

JURY TRIAL
Jury, generally, this index

JUSTICE COURTS
Claims courts. Small Claims Courts, gen-
erally, this index
Jurisdiction,
Fair employment and housing, unlawful
practices complaints, **Gov 12965**
Housing discrimination actions, **Gov
12980**
Small Claims Courts, generally, this index

JUSTICE DEPARTMENT
Attorney General, generally, this index
Joint enforcement strike force on the un-
derground economy, representative,
Un Ins 329
Juvenile Delinquents and Dependents,
generally, this index

I–98

JUSTICE DEPARTMENT—Cont'd

Leave of absence, injury, course of duty, **Labor 4800 et seq.**

Medical care and treatment, workers compensation, **Labor 4802**

Narcotics enforcement division, workers compensation, **Labor 3212.7**

State safety class employees, workers compensation, **Labor 3212.7, 4800 et seq.**

Workers compensation, **Labor 3212.7, 4800 et seq.**

JUVENILE COURTS

Juvenile Delinquents and Dependents, generally, this index

JUVENILE DELINQUENTS AND DEPENDENTS

Detention facilities. Juvenile Institutions and Schools, generally, this index

Family economic security, job preparation and training services. Unemployment Compensation, this index

Foster homes. Social Services, this index

Housing, youthbuild program, **Un Ins 9800 et seq.**

Job preparation and training services. Unemployment Compensation, this index

Juvenile Institutions and Schools, generally, this index

Labor and employment, youthbuild program, **Un Ins 9800 et seq.**

Parole and probation, workers compensation, rehabilitative work on public work projects, **Labor 3364.6**

Regional youth education facilities. Juvenile Institutions and Schools, this index

Rehabilitation,
Public work projects, **Labor 3364.6**
Workers compensation, **Labor 3364.55**

Small Businesses, generally, this index

Traffic Rules and Regulations, this index

Training, youthbuild program, **Un Ins 9800 et seq.**

Vocational education, youthbuild program, **Un Ins 9800 et seq.**

Weapons, possession, **Pen 12021**

Workers compensation,
Rehabilitative work on public work projects, **Labor 3364.6, 3364.55**
Ward performing rehabilitative work, **Labor 3364.55**

Youthbuild program, **Un Ins 9800 et seq.**

JUVENILE FACILITIES DIVISION

Death in line of duty, dependents, scholarships, **Labor 4709**

Dependents, scholarships, **Labor 4709**

Detention facilities. Juvenile Institutions and Schools, generally, this index

Handicapped persons, scholarships, dependents, **Labor 4709**

Heart disease, workers compensation, **Labor 3212.2**
Presumptions, **Labor 3212.10**

JUVENILE FACILITIES DIVISION—Cont'd

Hernias, workers compensation, presumptions, **Labor 3212.10**

Juvenile Delinquents and Dependents, generally, this index

Juvenile Institutions and Schools, generally, this index

Labor contracts, inmates replacing striking or locked out workers, **Welf & I 1768.1**

Meningitis, workers compensation, presumptions, **Labor 3212.10**

Officers and employees, heart trouble, workers compensation, **Labor 3212**

Pneumonia, workers compensation, presumptions, **Labor 3212.10**

Scholarships, dependents, **Labor 4709**

Tuberculosis, workers compensation, presumptions, **Labor 3212.10**

Unemployment compensation, wards, excluded services, **Un Ins 633.1, 634.5**

Wards, unemployment compensation, excluded services, **Un Ins 633.1, 634.5**

Workers compensation,
Early intervention programs, rehabilitation, **Labor 3214**
Heart disease, **Labor 3212**
Presumptions, **Labor 3212.10**
Requesting benefits, **Labor 4909.1**
Scholarships, dependents, **Labor 4709**

JUVENILE INSTITUTIONS AND SCHOOLS

Labor contracts, replacing striking or locked out workers, **Welf & I 1768.1**

Locked out workers, contract inmates replacing, **Welf & I 1768.1**

Regional youth education facilities, workers compensation, **Labor 3364.7**

Striking workers, contract inmates replacing, **Welf & I 1768.1**

Workers compensation, regional youth education facilities, **Labor 3364.7**

KERN COUNTY STATE COLLEGE

Colleges and Universities, generally, this index

KICKBACKS

Generally, **Labor 221, 225**

KILLING

Homicide, generally, this index

KNIVES

Weapons, generally, this index

KNOWLEDGE

Notice, generally, this index

KNUCKLES

Metal knuckles. Weapons, generally, this index

LABELS

Brands, Marks and Labels, generally, this index

LABOR AND EMPLOYMENT

Generally, **Labor 1 et seq.**

LABOR AND EMPLOYMENT—Cont'd

Absence and absentees,
Hazardous substances, lists, **Labor 6381**
Leaves of absence, generally, post
Schools and school districts, parents of expelled or suspended children, attendance in classrooms, **Labor 230.7**
Victims of crime, judicial proceedings, **Labor 230.2**

Access, labor commissioner, deputies and agents to places of labor, **Labor 90**

Accident and health insurance. Disability insurance, generally, post

Accidents. Occupational safety and health, generally, post

Accommodations, handicapped persons, discrimination, unlawful practices, **Gov 12940**

Accounts and accounting,
Bond of employee, **Labor 404, 405**
Obligations of employee, **Labor 2861 et seq.**

Acknowledgment of written instruments, **Labor 92**

Actions and proceedings,
Aggrieved employees, **Labor 2699.3**
Fines and penalties, **Labor 2699**
Appeal and review, generally, post
Arrest record, disclosure, **Labor 432.7**
Attorneys fees, **Labor 218.5**
Carcinogens, use, **Labor 9060**
Civil air patrol, **Labor 1507**
Compelling arbitration, attorneys fees, **Labor 1128**
Costs,
Labor commissioner as party, **Labor 101, 102**
Labor standards enforcement division, **Labor 101, 102**
Damages, generally, post
Discrimination, employee rights, **Labor 98.6, 98.7**
Diversion programs, referrals or participation, disclosure, **Labor 432.7**
Effect of enactment of labor code, **Labor 4**
Employees, preventing reemployment, **Labor 1054**
Fines and penalties, aggrieved employees, **Labor 2699**
Layoffs, **Labor 1404**
Migrant labor camps, overcrowded housing, **Health & S 17043**
Occupational safety and health, post
Records and recordation, copies, **CC 1786.53**
Recovery actions, **CCP 1031**
Subpoenas, generally, post
Unsafe conditions, **Labor 6327.5**

Acts repealed, effect on tenure of office, **Labor 3**

Addresses, records, **Labor 1174**

Administrative law and procedure, assessment, proposed regulations, **Gov 11346.3**

LABOR

LABOR AND EMPLOYMENT—Cont'd

Adult literacy education programs, employee assistance, **Labor 1041 et seq.**

Advances, claims for, assignment to commissioner, **Labor 96**

Advertisements,
Foreign labor contractors, **Bus & P 9998.3**
Investments as part of consideration, **Labor 407**
Personal injuries, benefits and services, **Labor 139.4 et seq.**
Solicitation of employees, misrepresentation, **Labor 970 et seq.**

Aerial passenger tramways, **Labor 7340 et seq.**

Affidavits, **Labor 92**
Execution, **Labor 17**
Injunctions, unsafe working conditions, **Labor 6324**
Layoffs, notice, **Labor 1402.5**
Workplace violence safety, **CCP 527.8**

Affirmative Action, generally, this index

Age,
Compulsory retirement, **Gov 12942**
Discrimination, generally, post
Minors,
Records and recordation, **Labor 1174**
Restrictions on employment, **Labor 1290**

Aged Persons, this index

Agencies. Employment Agencies, generally, this index

Aggrieved employees, **Labor 2699.3**
Fines and penalties, actions and proceedings, **Labor 2699**

Agricultural Labor and Employment, generally, this index

AIDS,
Blood tests, **Health & S 120980**
Discrimination, **Health & S 120980**

Alcoholics and alcoholism, voluntary enrollment and treatment program, employer accommodations, **Labor 1025 et seq.**

Alternative workweek schedule, **Labor 500 et seq.**

Amendment, orders, working conditions, **Labor 1184**

Analysis, samples, lead related construction work, employee protection, **Labor 6717**

Ancestry, discrimination, **Labor 1735**

Appeal and review,
Actions to compel arbitration, attorneys fees, **Labor 1128**
Children and minors, determination of employment dangerous to minors, **Labor 1296**
Claims, priority, **CCP 1206**
Labor camps, overcrowding, **Health & S 17043**
Occupational safety and health, post
Personnel records, inspection and inspectors, **Labor 1198.5**
Working conditions, **Labor 1190**

LABOR AND EMPLOYMENT—Cont'd

Appeals board, definitions, **Labor 6302**

Appearance, gender identity, **Gov 12949**

Application of law,
Aggrieved employees, **Labor 2699.5**
Family care and medical leave, **Gov 12945.2**
Layoffs, **Labor 1400**
Workforce investment, **Un Ins 14006, 14007**

Applications, **Labor 430 et seq.**
Bonds, **Labor 400 et seq.**
Discrimination, **Labor 98.6**
Failure to maintain and preserve, **Gov 12946**
Instruments relating to, copy to applicant upon request, **Labor 432**
Libel and slander, privileged communications, **CC 47**
Notice, investigative consumer reports, **CC 1786.16**
Purchases, coercion, **Labor 450 et seq.**
Temporary variances, **Labor 6451**

Appointments,
Local workforce investment boards, **Un Ins 14202, 14203**
Workforce investment board, **Un Ins 14012**

Apprentices, generally, this index

Arrest, this index

Asbestos, **Labor 6325.5**
Airborne fibers, prohibiting use, **Labor 6325.5**
Conference, safety, **Labor 6503.5**
Contractors, inspection and inspectors, financial relationship with business performing corrective work, **Labor 6509.5**
Crimes and offenses, related work, **Labor 6505.5**
Fines and penalties, related work, **Labor 6505.5**
Good faith effort to determine presence, **Labor 6501.9**
Inspection and inspectors, financial relationship with business performing corrective work, **Labor 6509.5**
Occupational Carcinogens Control Act, **Labor 9000 et seq.**
Registration, **Labor 6501.5, 6505.5**
Related work, **Labor 6501.5, 6505.5**
Rules and regulations, **Labor 6501.5**
Safety conference, **Labor 6503.5**
Second and subsequent offenses, related work, **Labor 6505.5**
Spraying, **Labor 6307.1, 6308, 6317, 6324**

Assault and battery, workplace violence safety, **CCP 527.8**

Assets, judgment debtor, employee complaints, enforcement, **Labor 98.2**

Assumption of risk, **Labor 2801**

Attachment by employer, employees cash bond, **Labor 404**

LABOR AND EMPLOYMENT—Cont'd

Attorney fees,
Actions to compel arbitration, **Labor 1128**
Appeals, **Labor 98.2**
Counseling services, **CC 1812.523**
Damages actions, disclosure, **Labor 432.7**
Discrimination actions, **Labor 98.7**
Enforcement of judgment, **Labor 98.2**
Fines and penalties, actions and proceedings, aggrieved employees, **Labor 2699**
Indemnity, discharge of duties, **Labor 2802**
Itemized statements, compensation and salaries, **Labor 226**
Layoffs, **Labor 1404**
Nonpayment actions, **Labor 218.5**
Recovery actions, **CCP 1031**

Attorneys, confidential or privileged information, whistle blowing, application of law, **Labor 1102.5**

Audio recordings, comfort stations and rest rooms, **Labor 435**

Awards of workmens compensation, unpaid, assignments, **Labor 96**

Benefits,
Civil air patrol, leaves of absence, **Labor 1504, 1505**
Elder care, **Un Ins 9910, 9912**
Family care and medical leave, **Gov 12945.2**
Health benefits, generally, post

Bilingual services, occupational safety and health,
State agencies, **Labor 176**
Worker safety bilingual investigative support, enforcement and training account, **Labor 6356**

Birth, unlawful practices, **Gov 12945**

Blackballing former employee, **Labor 1050 et seq.**

Blood tests, AIDS, **Health & S 120980**

Bloodborne pathogens, safety in employment, **Labor 144.7**

Boards and commissions,
Local workforce investment boards, **Un Ins 14200 et seq.**
Workforce investment board, **Un Ins 14010 et seq.**

Bonds (officers and fiduciaries),
Appeal and review, employees complaints, **Labor 98.2**
Claims, assignment to commissioner, **Labor 96**
Employees Bond Law, **Labor 400 et seq.**

Books and papers,
Compelling production, **Labor 92**
Inspection, records of employment, **Labor 1174**
Layoffs, **Labor 1406**

Braceros, funds, limitation of actions, **CCP 354.7**

Breach of duty, termination of employment, **Labor 2924**

LABOR AND EMPLOYMENT—Cont'd

Breastfeeding, **Labor 1030 et seq.**

Brokers, advertising employment opportunities, misrepresentation as to commission, **Labor 976**

Building construction or repair. Safety in employment, post

Building standards, occupational safety and health, **Labor 142 et seq.**

Burden of proof, whistle blowing, retaliation, **Labor 1102.6**

Burton Stull Vietnam Veterans Employment Act, **Gov 7280 et seq.**

CalWORKs. Social Services, this index

Camps. Labor Camps, generally, this index

Cancer causing substances, Occupational Carcinogens Control Act, **Labor 9000 et seq.**

Car Washes, this index

Carcinogens, Occupational Carcinogens Control Act, **Labor 9000 et seq.**

Career resource network, **Educ 53086**

Carpal tunnel syndrome, occupational safety and health, **Labor 6719**

CAS number, definitions, hazardous substances information and training, **Labor 6366**

Cash bond of employee, **Labor 400 et seq.**

Certificates and certification,
  Civil air patrol, leaves of absence, **Labor 1503**
  Domestic abuse, time off, **Labor 230**
  Family care and medical leave, necessity, **Gov 12945.2**
  Preexisting workweek arrangement, **Labor 1182.5**

Certified mail, notices, **Labor 8**

Changing rooms, audio or video recordings, **Labor 435**

Chemical names, definitions, hazardous substances information and training, **Labor 6367**

Chemical plant workers, safety, **Labor 7850 et seq.**

Chemical substances, carcinogens, Occupational Carcinogens Control Act, **Labor 9000 et seq.**

Child care services, failure to provide, **Gov 12947**

Children and minors, **Labor 1285 et seq.**
  Actions and proceedings, attorney general and district attorneys, **Labor 1312, 1399**
  Actors, hours of employment, **Labor 1308.5**
  Administration and enforcement of laws, **Labor 61**
  Adoption, family care and medical leave, **Gov 12945.2**
  Age,
    Limitation, **Labor 1290**
    Records, **Labor 1174**
  Agricultural zone of danger, minors under 12, **Labor 1293.1**

LABOR AND EMPLOYMENT—Cont'd

Children and minors—Cont'd
  Appeals, determination of employment dangerous to minors, **Labor 1296**
  Application to real property owners, **Labor 1301**
  Apprenticeship programs, application of law, **Labor 1295**
  Attendance supervisors, investigations, **Labor 1302**
  Baseball, professional sports, hours of labor, **Labor 1295.5**
  Bootblacking, **Labor 1298**
  Citations, **Labor 1285 et seq.**
  Classification of citations, **Labor 1288**
  Compensation and Salaries, this index
  Concerts, minors under 16, consent, **Labor 1308.5**
  Consent to employment, **Labor 1308.6**
  Coogan trust account, entertainment, **Labor 1308.9**
  Crimes and offenses,
    Class A and B violations, **Labor 1288**
    Door to door sales supervision registration violations, **Labor 1308.2**
    Employers of door to door sellers, registration violations, **Labor 1308.3**
    Entertainment industry, **Labor 1308.7**
    Failure to obtain written consent, **Labor 1308.5**
    Hours of labor, **Labor 1391 et seq.**
    Prohibited employment, **Labor 1294, 1303, 1308, 1309**
  Custody, children illegally at work, **Labor 1307**
  Death benefits, elected public officials, assassination, **Labor 4720 et seq.**
  Definitions, **Labor 1286, 1390**
  Distance from home, **Labor 1308.1**
  Domestic service or work, hours of labor, **Labor 1394**
  Door to door sales, children under age 6, **Labor 1308.1**
  Elected public officials, death benefits, assassination, **Labor 4720**
  Employers of door to door sellers, registration, **Labor 1308.3**
  Enforcement of law, **Labor 1311**
    Attorney general and district attorneys, **Labor 1312, 1399**
  Entertainment, **Labor 1308**
    Coogan trust account, **Labor 1308.9**
    Hours of labor, **Labor 1308.7**
    Minors under 16, consent, **Labor 1308.5**
  Equipment, prohibited operation, **Labor 1292 et seq.**
  Evidence, licenses to work, **Labor 1304**
  Family care and medical leave, **Gov 12945.2**
  Fines and penalties,
    Class A and B violations, **Labor 1288**
    Disposition, **Labor 1305**
    Door to door sales supervisor registration violations, **Labor 1308.2**

LABOR AND EMPLOYMENT—Cont'd

Children and minors—Cont'd
  Fines and penalties—Cont'd
    Employers of door to door sellers, registration violations, **Labor 1308.3**
    Failure to obtain written consent, **Labor 1308.5**
    Hours of labor, **Labor 1391 et seq.**
    Prohibited employment, **Labor 1294, 1303, 1308, 1309**
  Foreign labor contractors, **Bus & P 9998.4**
  Foster care, family care and medical leave, **Gov 12945.2**
  Hawkers and peddlers, **Labor 1298**
  Hazardous occupations for minors under 16, **Labor 1293.1**
  Hazardous occupations for minors 16 to 18, **Labor 1294.1**
  Hearings, citations, contests, **Labor 1289**
  Hours of labor, **Labor 1390 et seq., 1391.2, 1394**
    Actors, actresses and other performers, **Labor 1308.5**
    Baseball, professional sports, **Labor 1295.5**
    Crimes and offenses, **Labor 1391 et seq.**
    Domestic service or work, **Labor 1394**
    Enforcement of law, **Labor 1398**
    Entertainment industry, **Labor 1308.7**
    Exceptions, **Labor 1391.2**
      Restrictions on hours, **Labor 1310, 1394**
    Notice, posting, **Labor 1299**
    Work experience education, **Labor 1391.1**
  Illness, family care and medical leave, **Gov 12945.2**
  Licenses and permits,
    Cancellation, **Labor 1300**
    Evidence, **Labor 1304**
    Examinations of permits, attendance supervisors and probation officers, **Labor 1302**
    Records, **Labor 1299**
    Return of permits, cancellation, grounds, **Labor 1300**
  Limitation of age, **Labor 1290**
  Machine operation programs, certificates of completion, application of law, **Labor 1295**
  Magazines, sale or distribution, **Labor 1298**
  Mail and mailing, citation, **Labor 1287**
  Manufacturing establishment, restrictions, **Labor 1291**
  Messengers, **Labor 1297**
  Models, minors under 16, consent, **Labor 1308.5**
  Motion pictures, **Labor 1308.8**
  Motor vehicle service stations, **Labor 1294.5**
  Musicians, minors under 16, consent, **Labor 1308.5**

LABOR AND EMPLOYMENT—Cont'd
Children and minors—Cont'd
Newspapers, sale or distribution, **Labor 1297, 1298**
Notice, hours of labor, posting, **Labor 1299**
Occupational safety and health, statewide young worker health and safety resource network, **Labor 6359**
Orders, penalties, **Labor 1289**
Payment of penalties, **Labor 1289**
Penalty for misdemeanors, **Labor 23**
Permissible jobs for minors 14 and 15, **Labor 1294.3**
Petitions, orders, alteration or amendment, working conditions, **Labor 1184**
Privileges and restrictions, **Labor 1290 et seq.**
Probationary officers, investigations, **Labor 1302**
Prohibited types of employment, **Labor 1288, 1292 et seq., 1294**
Crimes and offenses, **Labor 1294, 1308, 1309**
Property, employed upon, liabilities of property owners, **Labor 1301**
Public officials, death benefits, assassination, **Labor 4720 et seq.**
Radio, minors under 16, consent, **Labor 1308.5**
Real property owners, application, **Labor 1301**
Records and recordation,
Age, **Labor 1174**
Employers, inspection, **Labor 1299**
Registration, supervisors of door to door sales, **Labor 1308.2**
Reports,
Employers, **Labor 1174**
Violations, **Labor 1302**
Request for hearing, contents of citations, **Labor 1289**
Restrictions on employment, **Labor 1290 et seq.**
Exceptions, **Labor 1394**
Safety in employment, statewide young worker health and safety resource network, **Labor 6359**
Service, citation, **Labor 1287**
Sick leave, **Labor 233**
Violations, **Labor 234**
Statewide young worker health and safety resource network, **Labor 6359**
Students, hours of labor, **Labor 1394**
Survey work, hours of labor, **Labor 1394**
Talent Agencies, this index
Telegraph and telephone companies, age limit, **Labor 1297**
Television, minors under 16, consent, **Labor 1308.5**
Tractor operation program, certificates of completion, application of law, **Labor 1295**

LABOR AND EMPLOYMENT—Cont'd
Children and minors—Cont'd
Types of employment prohibited to minors under age 16, **Labor 1292 et seq.**
Under age 16, **Labor 1292 et seq.**
Vocational education courses, exceptions to employment of minors, **Labor 1295**
Work experience, education, **Labor 1295, 1391.1**
Workforce investment, youth councils, **Un Ins 14208 et seq.**
Youth employment programs, **Un Ins 2058**
Youth placement service, operation by state, **Un Ins 2054, 2058**
Youthbuild program, **Un Ins 9800 et seq.**
Cigarettes and cigars, workplace smoking, **Labor 6404.5**
Citations,
Employment of minors, **Labor 1287 et seq.**
Lactation, **Labor 1033**
Occupational safety and health, post
Cities and counties. Consolidated Cities and Counties, this index
Civil air patrol, **Labor 1500 et seq.**
Civil rights. Fair Employment and Housing, generally, this index
Civil Service, generally, this index
Claims,
Collection, foreign courts, reciprocity, **Labor 103**
Enforcement, **Labor 98 et seq.**
Joinder of claimants, **Labor 100**
Preferred claims, **Labor 97.5**
Class actions,
Aggrieved employees, actions and proceedings, **Labor 2699.3**
Fines and penalties, aggrieved employees, **Labor 2699**
Clothing. Wearing Apparel, this index
Coercion. Duress or coercion, generally, post
Collective bargaining. Labor Disputes, this index
Combustible liquids, **Labor 7800 et seq.**
Combustible material, installation acceptance pressure tests, gas houseline or piping, unsafe place of employment, **Labor 6700**
Comfort, investigations and investigators, **Labor 1173**
Comfort stations and restrooms, audio or video recordings, **Labor 435**
Commercial paper, property put by employee as part of employment contract, **Labor 406**
Commercial vehicles, meals, time, collective bargaining, **Labor 512.5**
Commissioner. Labor Commissioner, generally, this index

LABOR AND EMPLOYMENT—Cont'd
Committees, mentally retarded and developmentally disabled persons, **Welf & I 4868**
Common names, definitions, hazardous substances information and training, **Labor 6368**
Community employment development centers, **Un Ins 9607**
Services, **Un Ins 9608**
Community housing,
Complaints by tenants, retaliatory measures, **Health & S 17031.7**
Exemptions, labor camp regulations, **Health & S 17031.3 et seq.**
Licenses and permits, operation as labor camp, **Health & S 17031.3**
Rules and regulations, **Health & S 17031.4**
Compensating time off, replacement for overtime pay, **Labor 204.3**
Compensation and Salaries, generally, this index
Complaints,
Alcoholic voluntary rehabilitation program enrollment, lack of employer accommodation, **Labor 1028**
Employees, indigent persons, appointment of counsel, **Labor 98.4**
Occupational safety and health, post
Volunteer firefighters and fire departments, discrimination, **Labor 230.4**
Wages, investigation, **Labor 98 et seq.**
Compliance with employers directions, obedience of employee, **Labor 2856**
Compromise and settlement, aggrieved employees, actions and proceedings, **Labor 2699.3**
Compulsory retirement, age, **Gov 12942**
Computers,
Electronic mail, force and violence, **CCP 527.8**
Software, compensation and salaries, overtime, **Labor 515.5**
Conditions of employment,
Hours of labor, generally, post
Investigations and investigators, **Labor 1193.5**
Nondisclosure of wages, **Labor 232**
Sterilization, unlawful practice, **Gov 12945.5**
Wage board, **Labor 1178.5, 1182**
Working conditions, generally, post
Conferences, asbestos, **Labor 6503.5**
Confidential or privileged information,
Arrest record, **Labor 432.7, 432.8**
Diversion program, referrals or participation, **Labor 432.7**
Employee privacy, alcoholic rehabilitation program enrollment, **Labor 1026**
Hazardous substances, MSDS, **Labor 6396**
Industrial safety complaints, **Labor 6309**
Medical reports, injuries to employees, **Labor 6412**

LABOR AND EMPLOYMENT—Cont'd
Confidential or privileged information
—Cont'd
Occupational safety, **Labor 6322**
Peace officer applicants, background investigations, disclosure by other employers, **Gov 1031.1**
Whistle blowing, application of law, **Labor 1102.5**
Conflict of laws, civil air patrol, leaves of absence, benefits, **Labor 1505**
Consent, termination of employment, **Labor 2922**
Consolidated Cities and Counties, this index
Construction,
Buildings, willful diversion of funds, **Pen 484b**
Contracts, **Labor 2810**
Elevators, safety in employment, **Labor 7200 et seq.**
Occupational safety and health, post
Youthbuild program, **Un Ins 9800 et seq.**
Construction of law, **Labor 5 et seq.**
Consumer Credit Protection Act of 1968, discharge of employee prosecuted for violation, **Labor 2929**
Consumer Credit Reporting Agencies, this index
Contempt, subpoenas, **Labor 93**
Continuation of existing provisions, **Labor 2**
Continuation of service, death or incapacity of employer, compensation, **Labor 2923**
Continuously operating manufacturing facility, days and hours of labor, **Labor 1182.6**
Contractors, this index
Contracts, **Labor 430 et seq., 2750**
Collective bargaining contracts, leisure sharing, **Un Ins 12100.5**
Commissions, contract with employer without permanent and fixed place of business in state, **Labor 2751, 2752**
Employer with no permanent and fixed place of business in state, **Labor 2751, 2752**
Foreign labor contractors, **Bus & P 9998.2**
Independent contractor status, rebuttable presumption, **Labor 2750.5**
Inspection and inspectors, **Labor 1174**
Inventions, ownership rights, **Labor 2871**
Janitors, discharge, **Labor 1060 et seq.**
Leisure sharing, **Un Ins 12100.5**
Property put up by employee as part of employment contract, **Labor 406**
Public policy, **Labor 920 et seq.**
Requiring employees agreement to illegal terms or conditions, **Labor 432.5**

LABOR AND EMPLOYMENT—Cont'd
Contracts—Cont'd
Vacation time, forfeiture, termination of employment, **Labor 227.3**
Convicts, **Const. Art. 14, § 5**
Coogan trust account, children and minors, entertainment, **Labor 1308.9**
Copies,
Hazardous substances, MSDS, **Labor 6394**
Industrial welfare commission, rules and regulations, **Labor 1198.4**
Instrument to employee, relating to obtaining or holding of employment, **Labor 432**
Corporation Taxes, this index
Correctional Institutions, this index
Correspondence, workplace violence safety, **CCP 527.8**
Costs,
Aggrieved employees, actions and proceedings, **Labor 2699.3**
Appeals, **Labor 98.2**
Complaints, appeals, **Labor 98.2**
Disclosure, arrest record, damage actions, **Labor 432.7**
Fines and penalties, actions and proceedings, aggrieved employees, **Labor 2699**
Indemnity, discharge of duties, **Labor 2802**
Judgments, enforcement, **Labor 98.2**
Layoffs, **Labor 1404**
Nonpayment actions, **Labor 218.5**
Peace officer applicants, background investigations, disclosure by other employers, **Gov 1031.1**
Recovery actions, **CCP 1031**
Councils, youth councils, workforce investment, **Un Ins 14208 et seq.**
Counseling. Employment Counseling Services, generally, this index
Course of conduct, definitions, workplace violence safety, **CCP 527.8**
Cranes, tower cranes, regulation, **Labor 7370 et seq.**
Crawler and wheel cranes, **Labor 6704**
Credible threat of violence, definitions, workplace violence safety, **CCP 527.8**
Credit ratings. Consumer Credit Reporting Agencies, this index
Crimes and offenses, **Labor 1199, 1199.5**
Access to information, **Labor 1175**
Arrest record, job application requirements, **Labor 432.7**
Asbestos related work, **Labor 6505.5**
Blackballing former employees, **Labor 1050 et seq.**
Bonds and photographs of employees, **Labor 400 et seq.**
Children and minors, ante
Comfort stations and rest rooms, audio or video recordings, **Labor 435**
Construction elevators, safety, **Labor 7205**

LABOR AND EMPLOYMENT—Cont'd
Crimes and offenses—Cont'd
Consumer Credit Protection Act, discharge of employee prosecuted for violation, **Labor 2929**
Dangerous conditions, failure to disclose, **Pen 387**
Death, **Labor 6425**
Diversion programs, referrals or participation, job application requirements, **Labor 432.7**
Employer failure to make agreed payments to employee benefit plans, **Labor 227**
Employment applications,
Arrest record requirements, **Labor 432.7**
Diversion programs, referrals or participation, disclosure, **Labor 432.7**
Marijuana, **Labor 432.8**
Employment contracts and applications for employment, **Labor 430 et seq.**
False advertisements or solicitations, **Labor 977**
Fines and penalties, generally, post
Firefighters and fire departments, reserves or auxiliaries, absence and absentees, emergencies, **Labor 230.3**
Foreign labor contractors, **Bus & P 9998.8**
Fraud, generally, post
Hours of labor, post
Impeding or preventing performance of duties by labor commissioner, **Labor 91**
Information, access, **Labor 1175**
Interference with exconvicts seeking employment, **Pen 2947**
Misrepresentation,
Former employee prevention from obtaining, employment, **Labor 1050 et seq.**
Solicitation of employees, **Labor 971**
Neglect or refusal to furnish information or statistics, **Labor 90**
Occupational safety and health, post
Peace officers, reserves or auxiliaries, absence and absentees, emergencies, **Labor 230.3**
Photographs or fingerprints of employees, improper use by employer, **Labor 1051**
Police, reserves or auxiliaries, absence and absentees, emergencies, **Labor 230.3**
Political activities of employees, **Labor 1101 et seq.**
Prosecution for payment of compensation by illegal means, **Labor 214**
Purchases by employees, coercion or compelling, **Labor 450 et seq.**
Records and recordation, **Labor 1175**
Disclosure, **Pen 11105.3**

LABOR AND EMPLOYMENT—Cont'd

Crimes and offenses—Cont'd

Refusing admittance to labor commissioner, deputies or agents, **Labor 90**

Safety in employment, post

Sheriffs, reserves or auxiliaries, absence and absentees, emergencies, **Labor 230.3**

Solicitation of employees, **Labor 970 et seq.**

Statements, tax deductions, **Labor 226.6**

Victims of crime, absence and absentees, judicial proceedings, **Labor 230.2**

Volunteer firefighters taking time off to perform duties, discharge or discrimination, **Labor 230.3**

Willfully ignoring subpoena calling for appearance, **Labor 93**

Window cleaners, safety devices on buildings, **Labor 7328 et seq.**

Criminal history information,

Appeal and review, **Pen 11105.75**

Copies, **CC 1786.53**

Verification, **Pen 11105.75**

Custom and usage, performance of employment, **Labor 2857**

Damages,

Arrest record, disclosure, **Labor 432.7**

Marijuana arrest record, **Labor 432.8**

Diversion program, referrals or participation, disclosure, **Labor 432.7**

Foreign labor contractors, **Bus & P 9998.8**

Fraud or malice, **CC 3294**

Layoffs, notice, **Labor 1402**

Negligence of employee, **Labor 2865**

Negligence of employer, **Labor 2800**

Political activities of employees, coercing or influencing, **Labor 1105**

Preventing reemployment, **Labor 1054**

Triple damages,

Arrest record disclosure, **Labor 432.7**

Diversion program referrals or participation, disclosure, **Labor 432.7**

Day Care and Nursery Schools, this index

Days of labor, continuously operating manufacturing facility, **Labor 1182.6**

Days off, mandatory orders, exemptions, **Labor 1198.3**

Deaf, hearing impaired persons, employment services, **Un Ins 11000 et seq.**

Death,

Asbestos spraying, **Labor 6425**

Crimes and offenses, **Labor 6425**

Fines and penalties, **Labor 6425**

Joint services, performance by survivor, **Labor 2866**

Termination of employment, **Labor 2921**

Wrongful death, right of action, **Labor 2803**

Death benefits,

Employee benefit plan distributions, escheat to state, **CCP 1521**

LABOR AND EMPLOYMENT—Cont'd

Death benefits—Cont'd

Employee benefit trust distributions, escheat to state, **CCP 1510**

Deceit. Fraud, generally, ante

Definitions, **Labor 10 et seq., 6303**

Applicant, **Labor 400, 430**

Car washes, **Labor 2051**

Construction elevators, safety, **Labor 7200**

Days rest, **Labor 550**

Emergencies, hazardous substances information and training, **Labor 6362**

Employee benefit plan distribution, Unclaimed Property Law, **CCP 1501**

Employees,

Disability compensation, voluntary plans, **Un Ins 3254**

Occupational safety and health, **Labor 6304.1**

Unemployment compensation, **Un Ins 621, 622**

Employers,

Hazardous substances, laboratories, **Labor 6386**

Occupational safety and health, **Labor 6304**

Unemployment compensation, **Un Ins 675 et seq., 678**

Joint ventures, **Un Ins 1057, 1058**

Workers compensation, **Labor 3300**

Foreign labor contractors, **Bus & P 9998.1**

Garnishment, **CCP 706.011**

Hazardous substances information and training, **Labor 6366 et seq.**

Hours of labor, **Labor 500, 515**

Language, unlawful employment practices, **Gov 12951**

Layoffs, **Labor 1400**

Licenses and permits, political subdivisions, **Bus & P 16300**

Manufacturers, hazardous substances, laboratories, **Labor 6386**

Occupational safety and health, **Labor 6301 et seq.**

Payment of wages, **Labor 200**

Pretrial or posttrial diversion program, **Labor 432.7**

Professional strike breakers, **Labor 1133**

Promise, contracts, public policy, **Labor 920**

Sheriffs, **Labor 25**

Technically qualified individuals, hazardous substances, laboratories, **Labor 6386**

Unemployment compensation, **Un Ins 633, 633.1, 2071**

Volatile flammable liquids, **Labor 7800, 7801**

Workplace violence safety, **CCP 527.8**

Delivery to employee, copy of instrument relating to obtaining or holding of employment, **Labor 432**

Demotions, jury service or witnesses, **Labor 230**

LABOR AND EMPLOYMENT—Cont'd

Denial of civil rights, **Gov 12948**

Department, definitions, **Labor 19, 6302**

Deposit,

Cash bond of employee, **Labor 402 et seq.**

Return to striking employee, **Labor 209**

Depositions, **Labor 92**

Deputies of administrative officers, exercise of power or performance of duty, **Labor 7**

Designation of representatives to negotiate terms and conditions of employment, public policy, **Labor 923**

Direct deposit, compensation and salaries, **Labor 213**

Director,

Annual reports, **Labor 6330**

Definitions, **Labor 20, 6302**

Disability insurance,

Continued coverage rights, notice, **Labor 2807**

Conversion policies, **Labor 2800.2, 2800.3**

Discontinuance, notice, **Labor 2806**

Domestic partnership, **Ins 10121.7**

Family care and medical leave, application, **Gov 12945.2**

Group disability insurance, conversion policies, **Labor 2800.2, 2800.3**

Medi Cal program, coverage, **Labor 2803.4**

Release of information to employers, **Ins 791.27**

Discharge, **Labor 20 et seq., 1400 et seq.**

Compensation, time off, **Labor 204.3**

Consumer Credit Protection Act of 1968, employees subjected to criminal prosecution, **Labor 2929**

Court witnesses, **Labor 230**

Crimes and offenses, victims of crime, absence and absentees, judicial proceedings, **Labor 230.2**

Day care and nursery schools, **Labor 230.8**

Days off, mandatory orders, refusal to work, **Labor 1198.3**

Direct deposit, compensation and salaries, **Labor 213**

Displaced Workers, generally, this index

Domestic violence, time off, **Labor 230.1**

Employee rights, complaint, **Labor 98.6, 98.7**

Filing complaints, discharge for, **Labor 6312**

Firefighters and fire departments, reserves or auxiliaries, absence and absentees, emergencies, **Labor 230.3**

For filing complaints, **Labor 6312**

Garnishment of earnings, employees subjected to, **Labor 96, 2929**

Hours of labor, exceeding mandatory orders, refusal to work, **Labor 1198.3**

LABOR AND EMPLOYMENT—Cont'd
Discharge—Cont'd
Janitors, **Labor 1060 et seq.**
Jury service, **Labor 230**
Mandatory days off, refusal to work, **Labor 1198.3**
Military personnel discrimination, **Mil & V 394**
Occupational safety and health, **Labor 6310 et seq.**
Peace officers, reserves or auxiliaries, absence and absentees, emergencies, **Labor 230.3**
Police, reserves or auxiliaries, absence and absentees, emergencies, **Labor 230.3**
Preventing employment by another, **Labor 1050 et seq.**
Reasons, stating, **Labor 1053**
School visits, discharge for, **Labor 230.8**
Sexual assault, time off, **Labor 230, 230.1**
Sheriffs, reserves or auxiliaries, absence and absentees, emergencies, **Labor 230.3**
Shopping investigators report, **Labor 2930 et seq.**
Stating reasons for discharge, **Labor 1053**
Support, earnings assignment orders, **Fam 5290**
Trucks, political affiliations, **Labor 1101 et seq.**
Unemployment compensation, **Un Ins 1237**
Vacation time, payment, **Labor 227.3**
Victims of crime, absence and absentees, judicial proceedings, **Labor 230.2**
Volunteer firefighters and fire departments,
    Emergencies, **Labor 230.3**
    Leaves of absence, training, **Labor 230.4**
Working conditions, disclosure, **Labor 232.5**
Working days, exceeding mandatory orders, refusal to work, **Labor 1198.3**
Discipline,
Child support enforcement, assignment of medical insurance benefits, **Fam 3769**
Support, earnings assignment orders, **Fam 5290**
Working conditions, disclosure, **Labor 232.5**
Disclosure,
Compensation and salaries, **Labor 232**
Employee records, **Labor 1198.5**
Hazardous substances and waste, post
Occupational safety and health, post
Working conditions, **Labor 232.5**
Discovery, employment records, **CCP 1985.6**

LABOR AND EMPLOYMENT—Cont'd
Discrimination, **Const. Art. 1, § 8; Gov 12940 et seq.; Labor 230; Un Ins 2070 et seq.**
Applications, **Labor 98.6**
Apprentices, public works, **Labor 1777.6**
Civil air patrol, **Labor 1502, 1506**
Clothing, **Gov 12947.5**
Compensation and salaries, **Labor 1197.5**
    Age discrimination, **Gov 12941**
Complaint, employee rights, **Labor 98.6, 98.7**
Court witnesses or jury duty, **Labor 230**
Crimes and offenses, victims of crime, absence and absentees, judicial proceedings, **Labor 230.2**
Day care and nursery schools, visits, **Labor 230.8**
Discharge, military service, **Mil & V 394**
Disparate impact, age discrimination, **Gov 12941**
Domestic violence, **Labor 230**
    Time off, **Labor 230.1**
Employee rights, complaint, **Labor 98.6, 98.7**
Evidence, disparate impact, age discrimination, **Gov 12941**
Fair Employment and Housing, generally, this index
Family care and medical leave, **Gov 12945.2**
Gender identity, **Gov 12949**
Handicapped persons, **Labor 1735**
Hazardous substances, **Labor 6399.7**
Health facilities, whistle blowing, **Health & S 1278.5**
Hearings, employee rights, complaint, **Labor 98.7**
Heart trouble, firefighters, law enforcement officers, **Gov 12940.1**
Jury duty or court witness, **Labor 230**
Law enforcement officers, heart trouble, **Gov 12940.1**
Leaves of absence, volunteer firefighters and fire departments, training, **Labor 230.4**
Medical information, disclosure, use, **CC 56.20 et seq.**
Military personnel, **Mil & V 394**
Notice, complaints, **Labor 98.7**
Occupational safety and health, **Labor 6310 et seq.**
Pants, **Gov 12947.5**
Pay discrimination, actions, **Labor 1197.5**
Peace officers, reserves or auxiliaries, absence and absentees, emergencies, **Labor 230.3**
Police, reserves or auxiliaries, absence and absentees, emergencies, **Labor 230.3**
Public works, **Labor 1735**
Reports, legislature, **Labor 98.75**
Retaliation, generally, post

LABOR AND EMPLOYMENT—Cont'd
Discrimination—Cont'd
Schools and school districts, visits, **Labor 230.8**
Sex discrimination, generally, post
Sexual assault, time off, **Labor 230, 230.1**
Sheriffs, reserves or auxiliaries, absence and absentees, emergencies, **Labor 230.3**
Supersedeas or stay, complaints, **Labor 98.7**
Unemployment compensation, employee enforcing rights, **Un Ins 1237**
Victims of crime, absence and absentees, judicial proceedings, **Labor 230.2**
Volunteer firefighters and fire departments,
    Emergencies, **Labor 230.3**
    Leaves of absence, training, **Labor 230.4**
Wearing apparel, **Gov 12947.5**
Working conditions, disclosure, **Labor 232.5**
Disparate impact, age discrimination, **Gov 12941**
Displaced Workers, generally, this index
Disputes. Labor Disputes, generally, this index
District Attorneys, this index
Diversion program, referral or participation, disclosure in seeking employment, **Labor 432.7**
Division, definitions, **Labor 6302**
Documents, inspection, **Labor 1174**
Domestic partnership, sick leave, **Labor 233, 234**
Domestic Service or Work, generally, this index
Domestic violence, time off, **Labor 230, 230.1**
Drinking water, **Labor 2441**
Drugs and medicine,
    Crimes and offenses, records, disclosure, **Pen 11105.3**
    Voluntary rehabilitation program enrollment, **Labor 1025 et seq.**
Duress or coercion,
    Committees, witnesses before, **Gov 9414**
    Freedom of individual worker, public policy, **Labor 923**
    Political activities of employees, **Labor 1101 et seq.**
    Purchases by employees, compelling, **Labor 450 et seq.**
    Witness before committee, misdemeanor to coerce, **Gov 9414**
E mail, workplace violence safety, **CCP 527.8**
Earned income tax credit, indigent persons, notice, **Rev & T 19850 et seq.**
Education, **Labor 6350 et seq.**
    Literacy assistance, **Labor 1040 et seq.**

LABOR AND EMPLOYMENT—Cont'd
Education—Cont'd
   Statewide young worker health and safety resource network, **Labor 6359**
   Workforce investment, **Un Ins 14500 et seq.**
Education fund, occupational safety and health, **Labor 6354.7**
Effective date, rules and regulations, industrial welfare commission, **Labor 1184**
Elections, this index
Electronic mail, force and violence, **CCP 527.8**
Elevators, Dumbwaiters and Escalators, generally, this index
Emergencies, **CCP 527.8**
   Bloodborne pathogens, safety in employment, **Labor 144.7**
   Civil air patrol, **Labor 1500 et seq.**
   Definitions, hazardous substances information and training, **Labor 6362**
   Firefighters and fire departments, reserves or auxiliaries, absence and absentees, **Labor 230.3**
   First aid, **Labor 6708**
   Hours of labor, post
   Peace officers, reserves or auxiliaries, absence and absentees, **Labor 230.3**
   Police, reserves or auxiliaries, absence and absentees, **Labor 230.3**
   Sheriffs, reserves or auxiliaries, absence and absentees, **Labor 230.3**
   Volunteer firefighters, duties as, discharge or discrimination, **Labor 230.3**
Employee benefit funds or plans, statement of employer, payments, **Labor 227.5**
Employee benefit plan distribution,
   Definitions, Unclaimed Property Law, **CCP 1501**
   Escheat to state, **CCP 1521**
Employee benefit trust distribution, escheat to state, **CCP 1510**
Employee complaints. Labor Commissioner, this index
Employee owned corporations. Corporations, this index
Employment Agencies, generally, this index
Employment and training planning, **Un Ins 10510 et seq.**
Employment contracts. Contracts, generally, ante
Encumbrances. Liens and incumbrances, generally, post
Enforcement, **Labor 55, 95**
   Bonds and photographs of employees, **Labor 410**
   Immigration, **Health & S 24000**
Engineered needle stick protection, bloodborne pathogens, **Labor 144.7**
English language, services, **Labor 105**
Enterprise Zones, generally, this index

LABOR AND EMPLOYMENT—Cont'd
Entertainment. Children and minors, ante
Escheat, trust funds for employees benefits, **CCP 1510, 1521**
Evidence,
   Age discrimination, disparate impact, **Gov 12941**
   Burden of proof, whistle blowing, retaliation, **Labor 1102.6**
   Children and minors, ante
   Independent contractors status, rebuttable presumption, **Labor 2750.5**
   Occupational safety and health, post
   Presumptions,
      Independent contractors status, **Labor 2750.5**
      Injury to employee, **Labor 2801**
   Wage board proceedings, **Labor 1180**
   Working conditions, **Labor 1200**
   Workplace violence safety, **CCP 527.8**
Ex convicts, interference, **Pen 2947**
Executions, claims, **CCP 1206 et seq.**
Exemptions,
   Hazardous substances, MSDS, obligation to provide, **Labor 6393**
   Hours of labor, post
   Layoffs, **Labor 1400**
      Notice, **Labor 1402.5**
   Licenses and permits, political subdivisions, **Bus & P 16300**
   Occupational Carcinogens Control Act, **Labor 9015**
Existing provisions, **Labor 2**
Expenses and expenditures, indemnification of employee in discharging duties, **Labor 2802**
Explosives, licensed supervisors, **Labor 6710**
   Avalanche blasting, **Labor 6711**
Expose or exposure, definitions, hazardous substances information and training, **Labor 6370**
Fair Employment and Housing, generally, this index
False advertisements, **Labor 976, 977**
False representations. Fraud, generally, post
Family care and medical leave, **Gov 12945.2**
Family economic security, job preparation and training services. Unemployment Compensation, this index
Family members, sick leave, **Labor 233**
   Violations, **Labor 234**
Fax machines, workplace violence safety, **CCP 527.8**
Federal law, family care and medical leave, application, running concurrently, **Gov 12945.2**
Fees,
   Applications, coercion, **Labor 450 et seq.**
   Peace officer applicants, background investigations, disclosure by other employers, **Gov 1031.1**

LABOR AND EMPLOYMENT—Cont'd
Fees—Cont'd
   Support enforcement, assignment of earnings, deduction by employer, **Fam 5235**
   Witnesses, investigation of working conditions, **Labor 1176**
   Workplace violence safety, **CCP 527.8**
Fellow servant, want of ordinary or reasonable care, **Labor 2801**
Felonies. Crimes and offenses, generally, ante
Females. Women, generally, post
Final orders, reconsideration, **Labor 6614 et seq.**
Findings of fact, working conditions, **Labor 1187**
Fines and penalties, **Labor 1199**
   Actions and proceedings, aggrieved employees, **Labor 2699**
   Aggrieved employees, actions and proceedings, **Labor 2699**
   Arrest records, job application requirements, **Labor 432.7**
      Marijuana conviction and arrest records, **Labor 432.8**
   Asbestos related work, **Labor 6505.5**
   Benefit plans, agreed payments by employer, **Labor 227**
   Bonds and photographs of employees, **Labor 400 et seq.**
   Carcinogens, use, **Labor 9060 et seq.**
   Children and minors, ante
   Dangerous conditions, failure to disclose, **Pen 387**
   Death, **Labor 6425**
   Diversion programs, job application requirements, **Labor 432.7**
   Employees, coercing purchases, **Labor 451**
   Employment contracts and applications for employment, **Labor 430 et seq.**
   Foreign labor contractors, **Bus & P 9998.8**
   Hours of labor, post
   Impeding or preventing performance of duties by labor commissioner, **Labor 91**
   Lactation, **Labor 1033**
   Layoffs,
      Good faith, **Labor 1405**
      Notice, **Labor 1403**
   Misdemeanors, **Labor 23**
   Neglect or refusal to supply statistics or information, **Labor 90**
   Occupational Carcinogens Control Act, **Labor 9060 et seq.**
   Occupational safety and health, post
   Political activities of employees, **Labor 1101 et seq.**
   Refusing access to place of labor to labor commissioner, deputies or agents, **Labor 90**
   Retaliation, whistle blowing, **Labor 1102.5**
   Safety in employment, post

LABOR AND EMPLOYMENT—Cont'd
Fines and penalties—Cont'd
Statements, tax deductions, **Labor 226.6**
Support, earnings assignment orders, **Fam 5290**
Wage statements, failure to provide, **Labor 226.3**
Whistle blowing, retaliation, **Labor 1102.5**
Fingerprints and fingerprinting,
Improper use, **Labor 1051**
Management companies, **Labor 1057**
Firefighters and Fire Departments, generally, this index
Firing. Discharge, generally, ante
First aid, pesticide poisoning, exclusion, **Labor 6409**
Fish and Game, this index
Flammable liquids, **Labor 7800 et seq.**
Flammable or combustible material, installation acceptance pressure tests, gas houseline or piping, unsafe place of employment, **Labor 6700**
FMLA, definitions, **Gov 12945.2**
Food, municipalities, time off to procure meals, **Labor 1900, 1901**
Force and violence, **CCP 527.8**
Foreign labor contractors, **Bus & P 9998 et seq.**
Foreign states, employees claims, prosecution, **Labor 103 et seq.**
Former employees, preventing employment by another, **Labor 1050 et seq.**
Forms, workplace violence safety, petitions, **CCP 527.8**
Fraud, **Labor 6426**
Blackballing former employees, **Labor 1050 et seq.**
Damages, **CC 3294**
Employee benefits plans, employer failure to make agreed payments, **Labor 227**
Employment conditions to commissioner, claims for damages, assignment, **Labor 96**
Fines and penalties, **Labor 6426**
Preventing employment of former employees by another employer, **Labor 1050 et seq.**
Solicitation of employees, **Labor 970 et seq.**
Freedom of association, public policy, **Labor 923**
Fringe Benefits, generally, this index
Funds, occupational safety and health, education fund, **Labor 6354.7**
Garment manufacturers, fire or safety hazards, **Labor 6409.5**
Garnishment, generally, this index
Gas pipeline tests, unsafe place of employment, **Labor 6700**
Gender identity, wearing apparel, **Gov 12949**
General welfare of employees, **Const. Art. 14, § 1**

LABOR AND EMPLOYMENT—Cont'd
Good faith, layoffs, fines and penalties, **Labor 1405**
Grants, green collar jobs, **Un Ins 14022**
Gratuitous service, **Labor 2850 et seq.**
Green collar jobs,
Grants, **Un Ins 14022**
Training, **Un Ins 15000 et seq.**
Grooming, gender identity, **Gov 12949**
Group insurance, disability insurance, conversion coverage, **Labor 2800.2, 2800.3**
Habitual neglect, termination of employment, **Labor 2924**
Handicapped Persons, this index
Harassment,
Personal liability, discrimination, unlawful practices, **Gov 12940**
Sexual, **Gov 12950**
Hardship exception, family care and medical leave, **Gov 12945.2**
Hazardous occupations,
Minors under 16, **Labor 1293.1**
Minors 16 to 18, **Labor 1294.1**
Hazardous substances and waste, **Labor 6360 et seq.**
Absence, lists, **Labor 6381**
Application of law, **Labor 6384, 6385**
Confidential or privileged information, MSDS, **Labor 6396**
Copies, MSDS, **Labor 6394**
Definitions, **Labor 6362, 6366 et seq.**
Employers or manufacturers, laboratories, **Labor 6386**
Technically qualified individuals, laboratories, **Labor 6386**
Disclosure, MSDS, **Labor 6396**
Sex crimes, **Pen 11105.3**
Violations of statutes or regulations, employee giving information, **Labor 1102.5**
Discrimination, **Labor 6399.7**
Emergencies, definitions, **Labor 6362**
Exemption, MSDS obligation to provide, **Labor 6393**
Harmful physical agent standards, **Labor 144.6**
Laboratories, status as employers or manufacturers, **Labor 6386**
Lists, **Labor 6380 et seq.**
Material safety data sheets, **Labor 6390 et seq.**
Mixtures, concentration of impurities, **Labor 6383**
MSDS, **Labor 6390 et seq.**
Confidential or privileged information, **Labor 6396**
Contents, **Labor 6394**
Copies, **Labor 6394**
Disclosure, **Labor 6396**
Electronic filing, **Labor 6394**
Entire product mixture, **Labor 6395**
Exemption from providing, **Labor 6393**
Federal form, prima facie evidence of statutory compliance, **Labor 6392**

LABOR AND EMPLOYMENT—Cont'd
Hazardous substances and waste—Cont'd
MSDS—Cont'd
Filing, **Labor 6394**
Nonmanufacturers, **Labor 6397**
Standards, duties toward employees, **Labor 6398**
Trade secrets, **Labor 6396**
Electronic filing, **Labor 6394**
New hazards, information and training, **Labor 6399.6**
Nonmanufacturers, MSDS, **Labor 6397**
Notice,
Right of employees to receive information, **Labor 6328**
Valid evidence indicating concentration higher than necessary, **Labor 6383**
Standards,
Duties toward employees, **Labor 6398**
Removal work, **Labor 142.7**
Toxic material standards, **Labor 144.6**
Trade secrets, MSDS, **Labor 6396**
Electronic filing, **Labor 6394**
Training and information, **Labor 6399.6**
Hazardous Substances Information and Training Act. Hazardous substances and waste, generally, ante
Health and sanitation,
Definitions, **Labor 6306**
Investigations, **Labor 1173**
Working conditions, **Labor 1178**
Local health services, **Health & S 105150**
Occupational safety and health, generally, post
Wages, hours and working conditions, **Labor 1178**
Whistle blowing, **Health & S 1278.5**
Working conditions, hearings, **Labor 1178**
Health and welfare plans,
Employers failure to make payments as agreed, **Labor 227**
Trust funds, escheat to state, **CCP 1510, 1521**
Health benefits,
Discontinuance, notice, **Labor 2806**
Layoffs, **Labor 1402**
Medi Cal recipients, coverage, **Labor 2803.4**
Notice, **Labor 2807**
Health funds, statement of employer payments, **Labor 227.5**
Health insurance. Disability insurance, generally, ante
Hearing impaired persons, employment services, **Un Ins 11000 et seq.**
Hearings, **Labor 1178**
Children and minors, ante
Compensation and salaries, employee complaints, **Labor 98**
Employee rights, complaint, **Labor 98.7**
Injunction, workplace violence safety, **CCP 527.8**

LABOR

LABOR AND EMPLOYMENT—Cont'd
Hearings—Cont'd
Rehearings, working conditions, **Labor 1188**
Rules and regulations, petitions, **Labor 1176.3**
Wage board, **Labor 1178.5, 1182**
Working conditions, **Labor 517, 1178**
Notice of hearing, **Labor 1181**
High hazard industries list, establishment, occupational safety and health, **Labor 6401.7**
High Schools or Secondary Schools, this index
Hiring without notice of unpaid claims, larceny by fraud, **Pen 484**
Homework. Industrial Homework, generally, this index
Hospital benefits,
Discontinuance, notice, **Labor 2806**
Notice, **Labor 2807**
Hours of labor, **Labor 500 et seq.**
Administration and enforcement of laws, **Labor 1193.5**
Agricultural Labor and Employment, this index
Alternative workweek schedule, **Labor 500 et seq.**
Application of law, **Labor 556**
Camps and camping, student employees, **Labor 1182.4**
Children and minors, ante
Cities and counties, application of law, **Labor 555**
Collective bargaining, **Labor 514, 554, 750.5**
Commission, **Labor 1182**
Company vehicles, calculation of days work, **Labor 510**
Computation, **Labor 510**
Computers, software, overtime, **Labor 515.5**
Continuously operating manufacturing facilities, **Labor 1182.6**
County officers and employees, **Labor 1205**
Crimes and offenses, **Labor 553, 1198**
Druggists, **Labor 853**
Lumber industries, midday meal period, **Labor 801**
Maximum, **Labor 1198**
Mines, **Labor 752**
Smelters and underground workings, **Labor 752**
Day of rest, **Labor 550 et seq.**
Druggists, **Labor 852**
Days off, mandatory orders, exemptions, **Labor 1198.3**
Days work, **Labor 510**
Definitions, **Labor 500, 515**
Districts, officers and employees, **Labor 1205**
Drug stores, **Labor 850 et seq.**
Elections, smelters and underground workers, **Labor 750.5**
Emergencies, **Labor 554, 751**

LABOR AND EMPLOYMENT—Cont'd
Hours of labor—Cont'd
Emergencies—Cont'd
Druggists, **Labor 854**
Smelters, mines, **Labor 751.5**
Exemptions, **Labor 515, 554**
Computers, software, overtime, **Labor 515.5**
Days off, mandatory orders, **Labor 1198.3**
Thirty hour week and six hour day, **Labor 556**
Fines and penalties, **Labor 558**
Druggists, **Labor 853**
Lumber industries, midday meal period, **Labor 801**
Mines, **Labor 752**
Smelters and underground workings, **Labor 752**
Injunction to prevent violations, **Labor 1194.5**
Labor statistics and research division, collection and compilation of information, **Labor 150**
Laboratories, **Labor 850 et seq.**
Local agencies, officers and employees, **Labor 1205**
Lumber industries, midday meal period, **Labor 800, 801**
Lunch hour, lumber industries, **Labor 800, 801**
Makeup work time, **Labor 513**
Manufacturing facilities, continuous operation, **Labor 1182.6**
Maximum, **Labor 1198**
Commission, **Labor 1182**
Discharge, refusal to work, hours exceeding mandatory order, discrimination, **Labor 1198.3**
Working days, **Labor 552**
Mines, **Labor 750 et seq.**
Municipal officers and employees, **Labor 1205**
Notice, smelters and underground workers, **Labor 750.5**
One days rest in seven, **Labor 551 et seq.**
Overtime, generally, this index
Physicians and surgeons, overtime, exemptions, **Labor 515.6**
Preexisting workweek arrangement, petition for modification, **Labor 1182.5**
Public Buildings and Works, this index
Public works, **Const. Art. 14, § 2**
Railroads, this index
Records, women, **Labor 1178.5**
Rest periods, generally, post
Rules and regulations, **Labor 1178**
Presumptions of lawfulness, **Labor 1200**
Six days in seven, **Labor 552**
Smelters, **Labor 750 et seq.**
Underground workings, **Labor 750 et seq.**
Wage board, **Labor 1178.5, 1182**

LABOR AND EMPLOYMENT—Cont'd
Hours of labor—Cont'd
Women, post
Work experience education programs, **Labor 1391.1**
Housing,
Labor Camps, generally, this index
Youthbuild program, **Un Ins 9800 et seq.**
Hypodermic Syringes and Needles, this index
Identity and identification, numbers and numbering, compensation and salaries, itemized statement, **Labor 226**
Illness, family care and medical leave, **Gov 12945.2**
Immigration, this index
Immunities. Privileges and immunities, generally, post
Impurities, definitions, hazardous substances information and training, **Labor 6371**
Incapacity, termination of employment, **Labor 2921, 2924**
Incidental expense accounts, assignments to commissioner, **Labor 96**
Income Tax—State, this index
Incumbrances. Liens and incumbrances, generally, post
Indemnification, employees expenses and losses in discharging duties, **Labor 2802**
Independent contractors, rebuttable presumption, **Labor 2750.5**
Indictment and information, records and recordation, copies, **CC 1786.53**
Indigent persons, earned income tax credit, notice, **Rev & T 19850 et seq.**
Industrial Homework, generally, this index
Industrial promotion fund, employers failure to make payments, **Labor 227**
Infants. Children and minors, generally, ante
Information,
Disbursement by labor law enforcement division, **Labor 94**
Employment or insurance purposes, investigative consumer reporting agencies, **CC 1786 et seq.**
Hazardous substances and waste, generally, ante
Refusal or neglect to supply, **Labor 90**
Sexual harassment, **Gov 12950**
Injunction,
Civil air patrol, **Labor 1507**
Conditions of employment, **Labor 1194.5**
Disputes with employers, **CCP 527.3**
Foreign labor contractors, **Bus & P 9998.8**
Occupational safety and health, post
Peace officer employment applicants, background investigations, disclosure by other employers, **Gov 1031.1**
Working conditions, **Labor 1194.5**

LABOR AND EMPLOYMENT—Cont'd
Injunction—Cont'd
  Workplace violence safety, **CCP 527.8**
Injuries. Personal injuries, generally, post
Inspection and inspectors,
  Carcinogens, **Labor 9050 et seq.**
  Children and minors, employers records, **Labor 1299**
  Construction elevators, **Labor 7204**
  Employee records, **Labor 1198.5**
  Employment investigations, consumer reporting agencies, files, **CC 1786 et seq.**
  Hazardous industries, priority basis, **Labor 6314.1**
  Occupational safety and health, post
  Personnel records, **Labor 1198.5**
  Records and recordation, **Labor 1174, 1198.5**
Instruments relating to obtaining or holding employment, copy to employee upon request, **Labor 432**
Insurance,
  Advertisements, **Labor 139.4 et seq.**
  Continuation coverage, accident, health, and disability insurance, **Labor 2800.2**
  Disability insurance, generally, ante
  Domestic partnership, disability insurance, **Ins 10121.7**
  Insurable interest, employer, **Ins 10110.1**
  Noncustodial parents, **Labor 2803.5**
  Third parties, **Labor 2803.5**
  Workers Compensation, this index
Interest,
  Cash bond of employee, **Labor 404**
  Compensation and salaries, nonpayment, **Labor 218.6**
  Indemnity, discharge of duties, **Labor 2802**
Interference, freedom from, public policy, **Labor 923**
Interoffice mail, workplace violence safety, **CCP 527.8**
Interpreters and Translators, this index
Intervention, labor commissioner, actions concerning employees complaints, **Labor 98.5**
Inventions, ownership rights, **Labor 2870 et seq.**
Investigations and investigators,
  Aggrieved employees, actions and proceedings, **Labor 2699.3**
  Conditions of labor, **Labor 1173, 1193.5**
  Discrimination against employees filing complaints, occupational safety and health, **Labor 6312**
  Discrimination complaints, **Labor 98.7**
  Employees, **Labor 2930**
    Complaints, **Labor 98 et seq.**
  Employment or insurance purposes, reporting agencies, **CC 1786 et seq.**
  Labor statistics and research division, **Labor 1202**
  Layoffs, powers and duties, **Labor 1406**

LABOR AND EMPLOYMENT—Cont'd
Investigations and investigators—Cont'd
  Occupational safety and health, post
  Safety in employment, post
  Working conditions, **Labor 1178**
Investments by employee, **Labor 406, 407**
Janitors, generally, this index
Job preparation and training services. Unemployment Compensation, this index
Job Training Programs, generally, this index
Jobs for California graduates program, **Un Ins 9900 et seq.**
Jobs tax credit,
  Corporation tax, **Rev & T 23621 et seq.**
  Income tax, **Rev & T 17053.7**
Joint services, performance by survivor, **Labor 2866**
Judgments and decrees,
  Enforcement, employee complaints, **Labor 98.2**
  Records and recordation, copies, **CC 1786.53**
Judicial proceedings. Actions and proceedings, generally, ante
Jurisdiction, occupational safety and health, **Labor 6316, 6632**
Jury, time off to serve as juror, **Labor 230**
Juvenile Delinquents and Dependents, this index
Labor Camps, generally, this index
Labor market information, **Un Ins 10530 et seq.**
Labor Organizations, generally, this index
Labor statistics and research division, collection and compilation of information, **Labor 150 et seq.**
Lactation, **Labor 1030 et seq.**
Language,
  Services, **Labor 105**
  Unlawful employment practices, **Gov 12951**
Law enforcement,
  Heart trouble, presumptions, **Gov 12940.1**
  Protective orders, workplace violence safety, **CCP 527.8**
Lead poisoning, occupational safety, prevention programs, **Health & S 105185 et seq.**
Lead related construction work, employee protection, standards, **Labor 6717**
Leaves of absence,
  Birth, **Gov 12945**
  Civil air patrol, **Labor 1503 et seq.**
  Family care and medical leave, **Gov 12945.2**
  Military forces, **Mil & V 394.5**
    Marriage, **Mil & V 395.10**
  National guard, marriage, **Mil & V 395.10**
  Pregnancy, **Gov 12945**
  Schools and school districts, parents of expelled or suspended students, **Labor 230.7**

LABOR AND EMPLOYMENT—Cont'd
Leaves of absence—Cont'd
  Victims of crime, judicial proceedings, **Labor 230.2**
  Volunteer firefighters and fire departments, training, **Labor 230.4**
Leisure sharing programs, **Un Ins 12100 et seq.**
Letters and other correspondence, truthful statement of reasons for termination of employment, **Labor 1053**
Letters of recommendation, personal information held by governmental agencies, Information Practices Act, **CC 1798.38**
Liability of employer for injuries, **Labor 3602**
Libel and slander,
  Employment references, privileged communications, **CC 47**
  Privileged communications, **CC 47**
Licensed supervisors, explosives, **Labor 6710**
  Avalanche blasters, **Labor 6711**
Licenses and permits,
  Children and minors, ante
  Conviction of crime, **Labor 26**
  Exemptions, political subdivisions, **Bus & P 16300**
  Minimum wages, **Labor 1191**
  Occupational safety and health, post
  Sheltered workshops or rehabilitation facilities, **Labor 1191.5**
Lie detector tests, requiring applicants or employees to take, **Labor 432.2**
Liens and incumbrances,
  Assignments to commissioner, **Labor 96**
  Filing for record before assignment to commissioner, necessity, **Labor 97**
  Joinder of claimants, **Labor 100**
  Mechanics Liens, generally, this index
Life, safety and health of employees, protection, responsibilities and duties of employers, **Labor 6400 et seq.**
Limitation of actions,
  Braceros, funds, **CCP 354.7**
  Victims of crime, absence and absentees, judicial proceedings, **Labor 230.2**
Limited English proficient persons, occupational safety and health,
  State agencies, access, **Labor 176**
  Worker safety bilingual investigative support, enforcement and training account, **Labor 6356**
Liquidating account, employer and employee, bond, **Labor 405**
Lists,
  Hazardous substances and waste, **Labor 6314.1, 6380 et seq.**
  Labor camps, licenses and permits, **Health & S 17035**
Literacy, employee illiteracy assistance, **Labor 1040 et seq.**
Local workforce investment boards, **Un Ins 14200 et seq.**

LABOR

LABOR AND EMPLOYMENT—Cont'd

Locker rooms, audio or video recordings, **Labor 435**

Lodging, compensation and salaries, **Labor 1182.13**

Longshoremen, safety, **Labor 7600 et seq.**

Losses, employees discharging duties, indemnification, **Labor 2802**

Low hazard industries lists, establishment, occupational safety and health, **Labor 6401.7**

Lunch hour, lumber industries, **Labor 800, 801**

Mail and mailing, **Labor 8**

    Citation, employment of minors, **Labor 1287**

    Hearings, rules and regulations, **Labor 1181**

    Orders, wages, hours and working conditions, **Labor 1183**

    Workplace violence safety, **CCP 527.8**

Makeup work time, **Labor 513**

Management companies, fingerprints and photographs, **Labor 1057**

Mandate writ, lawfulness of original orders or decisions, **Labor 6627 et seq.**

Mandatory days off, orders, exemptions, **Labor 1198.3**

Manpower planning system, **Un Ins 10510 et seq.**

Manufacturer, definitions, hazardous substances information and training, **Labor 6372**

Manufacturing facility, continuous operation, days and hours of labor, **Labor 1182.6**

Marital status, discrimination, **Labor 1735**

Marriage, this index

Mass layoffs, **Labor 1400 et seq.**

Maximum working days, exemptions, mandatory orders, **Labor 1198.3**

Meals,

    Compensation and salaries, **Labor 226.7, 1182.13**

    Records and recordation, women, **Labor 1178.5**

    Time, **Labor 512**

        Motor carriers, collective bargaining, **Labor 512.5**

Mechanics Liens, generally, this index

Medi Cal Program, this index

Medical Care and Treatment, this index

Medical evaluators, advertisements, **Labor 139.4, 139.45**

Medical examinations. Physical examinations, generally, post

Medical records, disclosure, **CC 56.20 et seq.**

Memorial Day for workers, **Labor 29.5**

Mentally Ill Persons, this index

Mentally Retarded and Developmentally Disabled Persons, this index

Mexican officials, providing taxation information to, **Un Ins 1095**

LABOR AND EMPLOYMENT—Cont'd

Migrant farmworkers, overcrowded housing, actions and proceedings, **Health & S 17043**

Military Forces, this index

Mines and minerals,

    Underground diesel engines, permits, **Labor 6500**

    Underground telephones, **Labor 7500, 7501**

Minimum wages. Compensation and Salaries, this index

Minors. Children and minors, generally, ante

Misappropriation of property put up as employees bond, **Labor 405**

Misdemeanors. Crimes and offenses, generally, ante

Misrepresentation. Fraud, generally, ante

Mixtures, definitions, hazardous substances information and training, **Labor 6373**

Mobile internal combustion engines, **Labor 6701 et seq.**

Motion Pictures, this index

Motions, orders, working conditions, **Labor 1184**

Moving expenses, unsafe premises, **Health & S 17062**

MSDS,

    Definitions, hazardous substances information and training, **Labor 6374**

    Hazardous substances and waste, ante

Municipal Officers and Employees, generally, this index

Musical instruments and equipment security, **Labor 2800.1**

Names,

    Businesses, investigations, **Labor 98**

    Records, **Labor 1174**

National guard,

    Leaves of absence, marriage, **Mil & V 395.10**

    Restoration, **Mil & V 395.06**

National origin, discrimination, **Labor 1735**

Necessaries, employer guaranteeing payment of employees bills, **Labor 213**

Necessary cost of proper living, wage board, **Labor 1178.5, 1182**

Needles, bloodborne pathogens, **Labor 144.7**

Negligence,

    Actions by personal representative of deceased employee, **Labor 2803**

    Assumption of risk, **Labor 2801**

    Comparative negligence of employee, **Labor 2801**

    Compensated service, degree of care, **Labor 2854**

    Defense, employer, **Labor 2801**

    Employee, **Labor 2865**

    Employer, **Labor 2800**

    Fellow servant rule, **Labor 2801**

    Gratuitous service, **Labor 2850**

LABOR AND EMPLOYMENT—Cont'd

Negligence—Cont'd

    Information or statistics, furnishing, **Labor 90**

    Presumptions, **Labor 2801**

    Service of employee at own request, degree of care, **Labor 2853**

    Substitute for employee, **Labor 2864**

    Termination of employment, **Labor 2924**

    Waiver of right of action, **Labor 2804**

    Wrongful death, actions, **Labor 2803**

Negotiation of terms and conditions, public policy, **Labor 923**

Networks, statewide young worker health and safety resource network, **Labor 6359**

Newsboys, generally, this index

Nontraditional occupations, women, training, **Un Ins 9602.5**

Notice,

    Aggrieved employees, actions and proceedings, **Labor 2699.3**

    Applications for employment, investigative consumer reports, **CC 1786.16**

    Asbestos, workplace, **Labor 6501.5, 6505.5**

    Children and minors, ante

    Civil air patrol, leaves of absence, **Labor 1503**

    Crimes and offenses, victims of crime, absence and absentees, judicial proceedings, **Labor 230.2**

    Criminal history, disclosure, human resource agency, **Pen 11105.3**

    Dangerous conditions, failure to give notice, **Pen 387**

    Deferred compensation plans, employer managed, financial risks, **Labor 2809**

    Discrimination, complaints, **Labor 98.7**

    Earned income tax credit, indigent persons, **Rev & T 19850 et seq.**

    Family care and medical leave, **Gov 12945.2**

    Hazardous substances and waste, ante

    Health benefits,

        Continued coverage rights, **Labor 2807**

        Discontinuance, **Labor 2806**

    Hearings, working conditions, **Labor 1181**

    Inventions, ownership rights, **Labor 2872**

    Janitors, discharge, **Labor 1061**

    Jury service by employee, **Labor 230**

    Language, unlawful employment practices, **Gov 12951**

    Layoffs, **Labor 1401 et seq.**

    Meetings held by administrative director, workers compensation division, **Labor 138.2**

    Occupational safety and health, post

    Power of attorney, notice of termination, **Labor 2852**

    Publication, generally, post

LABOR AND EMPLOYMENT—Cont'd
Notice—Cont'd
Rehearings, working conditions, **Labor 1188**
Rules and regulations, publication, industrial welfare commission, **Labor 1182.1**
Service, **Labor 95**
Termination at will, **Labor 2922**
Valid evidence indicating concentration higher than necessary, **Labor 6383**
Victims of crime, absence and absentees, judicial proceedings, **Labor 230.2**
Violations, **Labor 95**
Wage claim, intention to file, employee discharge for garnishment of earnings, **Labor 2929**
Whistle blowing, posting, **Labor 1102.8**
Workplace violence safety, hearings, **CCP 527.8**
Written notices, **Labor 8**
Oaths and affirmations,
Administration, **Labor 92**
Investigation of working conditions, **Labor 1176**
Obedience of employee, **Labor 2856**
Obligations, **Labor 2800 et seq., 2850 et seq.**
Occupational Carcinogens Control Act, **Labor 9000 et seq.**
Occupational safety and health, **Labor 6300 et seq.**
Abatement, **Labor 6317**
Failure to abate, additional penalty, **Labor 6430**
Incomplete abatement, hearings, **Labor 6319.5**
Violations, **Labor 6318**
Action orders,
Appeal and review, **Labor 6600 et seq.**
Posting, **Labor 6318**
Actions and proceedings, unsafe conditions,
Carcinogens, use, **Labor 9060**
Inspection requested by employer, **Labor 6355**
Unsafe conditions, **Labor 6327.5**
Advisory boards and commissions, education fund, **Labor 6354.7**
Affidavits, **Labor 6314**
Appeal and review, **Labor 6611**
Agreements, enforcement of standards, orders or rules, **Labor 144**
Analysis, lead related construction work, **Labor 6717**
Apparel manufacturers, fire or safety hazards, **Labor 6409.5**
Appeal and review, **Labor 6600 et seq.**
Admissions, employers express admissions, **Labor 6611**
Affidavits, **Labor 6611**
Citations and orders, **Labor 6319**
Contempt, jurisdiction, **Labor 6603**
Deposition of witnesses, **Labor 6613**

LABOR AND EMPLOYMENT—Cont'd
Occupational safety and health—Cont'd
Appeal and review—Cont'd
Evidence, **Labor 6611**
Exhaustion of remedies, **Labor 6650, 6651**
Findings and conclusions, **Labor 6630**
Good cause, reinstatement of appeal, **Labor 6611**
Hearing officers, **Labor 6604 et seq.**
Appointments, **Labor 6605**
Deposition of witnesses, **Labor 6613**
Duties, **Labor 6604, 6608**
Objection to selection of hearing officer, **Labor 6606**
Witnesses, depositions of, **Labor 6613**
High hazard industries list, **Labor 6401.7**
Jurisdiction, **Labor 6632**
Contempt, **Labor 6603**
License revocation, **Labor 6506**
Mandate writ, lawfulness of original orders or decisions, **Labor 6627 et seq.**
Notice, **Labor 6601**
De minimis violations, **Labor 6317**
Oaths and affirmations, hearing officers, **Labor 6607**
Orders, rules, **Labor 6308**
Pleadings, service, **Labor 6631**
Prior orders, reconsideration, **Labor 6614 et seq.**
Reinstatement of dismissed appeal, **Labor 6611**
Rules of practice and procedure, **Labor 6603**
Service,
Inspection requested by employer, **Labor 6355**
Notices, orders, decisions, **Labor 6610**
Pleadings, **Labor 6631**
Stay of revocation, **Labor 6505**
Suspension or stay, pendency of writ of mandate, **Labor 6633**
Temporary variances, **Labor 6455 et seq.**
Third persons, **Labor 6319, 6600**
Time, **Labor 6601, 6601.5**
Appeal, **Labor 6600**
Violations, **Labor 6317.5**
Witnesses, deposition of, **Labor 6613**
Appeals board.   Industrial Relations Department, this index
Application of law, **Labor 6304.5**
Applications, temporary variances, **Labor 6451**
Compliance, **Labor 6407**
Death of employee, **Labor 6425**
Enforcement, **Labor 6307.1, 6308**
Fines and penalties, **Labor 6427 et seq.**
Injunctions, unsafe working conditions, **Labor 6324**

LABOR AND EMPLOYMENT—Cont'd
Occupational safety and health—Cont'd
Applications, temporary variances —Cont'd
Violations, **Labor 6317**
Asbestos, generally, ante
Bilingual services,
State agencies, **Labor 176**
Worker safety bilingual investigative support, enforcement and training account, **Labor 6356**
Bloodborne pathogens, **Labor 144.7**
Boilers, reports, **Labor 7722**
Building standards, **Labor 142 et seq.**
Buildings, demolition, licenses and permits, **Labor 6500 et seq.**
Cancer causing substances, Occupational Carcinogens Control Act, **Labor 9000 et seq.**
Carcinogens, **Labor 9000 et seq.**
Carpal tunnel syndrome, **Labor 6719**
Centers, program development, **Labor 50.8**
Chemical plants, workers, **Labor 7850 et seq.**
Children and minors, statewide young worker health and safety resource network, **Labor 6359**
Citations, **Labor 6317 et seq., 6317.5**
Multiemployer worksites, **Labor 6400**
Posting, **Labor 6408**
Colleges and universities, fines and penalties, refunds, **Labor 6434**
Combustible material for installation, acceptance pressure tests, gas houseline or piping, **Labor 6700**
Committees, injury prevention, **Labor 6401.7**
Compensation and salaries, physicians and surgeons, pesticide poisoning, **Labor 6409**
Complaints, unsafe working conditions, **Labor 6309**
Compliance, standards, **Labor 6407**
Concealed danger, failure to disclose, **Pen 387**
Conduct of hearings, **Labor 6308.5**
Conferences, safety conference, licenses and permits, **Labor 6503**
Confidential or privileged information,
Injuries to employees, medical reports, **Labor 6412**
Trade secrets, **Labor 6322**
Construction,
Licenses and permits, **Labor 6500 et seq.**
Multiemployer worksites, citations, **Labor 6400**
Unsafe or unhealthy places, **Labor 6405**
Consulting services, **Labor 6354**
Actions and proceedings, unsafe conditions, **Labor 6355**
Contractor licensing board, fines and penalties, notice, **Labor 6652**
Correctional Institutions, this index

LABOR

LABOR AND EMPLOYMENT—Cont'd
Occupational safety and health—Cont'd
Corrective orders, **Labor 6313**
Cranes, tower cranes, regulation, **Labor 7370 et seq.**
Crawler and wheel cranes, **Labor 6704**
Crimes and offenses, **Labor 6317 et seq., 6423 et seq.**
Abatement, failure to abate, additional penalty, **Labor 6430**
Advance notice of inspections or investigations, **Labor 6321**
Citations, posting, **Labor 6318**
Dangerous conditions, failure to disclose, **Pen 387**
Death of employees, **Labor 6425**
False representations, **Labor 6426**
Injunctions, unsafe working conditions, **Labor 6326**
Injuries and fatalities, reports, **Labor 6413.5**
Licenses and permits, **Labor 6509**
Minor violations, **Labor 6427**
Notice, citations, **Labor 6319**
Obstructing or hampering investigations or inspections, **Labor 6314**
Posting of citations, **Labor 6318**
Referral, prosecution, **Labor 6315**
Serious violations, **Labor 6428, 6432**
Willful or repeated violations, **Labor 6429**
Wrongfully discharged employees, refusal to rehire, **Labor 6310 et seq.**
Data gaps, state repository, notice, **Health & S 105175**
Data repository, toxic materials of harmful physical agents, **Labor 147.2**
De minimis violations, notice, **Labor 6317**
Death, reports, **Labor 6409.1**
Definitions, **Labor 6301 et seq.**
Demolition of buildings,
Licenses and permits, **Labor 6500 et seq.**
Salvaging materials, **Labor 6401.5**
Depositions, **Labor 6314**
Directors, annual reports, **Labor 6330**
Discharge of employee for making complaint, **Labor 6310 et seq.**
Disclosure, dangerous conditions, **Pen 387**
Discrimination against employee for filing complaint, **Labor 6312**
Education and research, **Labor 6350 et seq.**
Emergency first aid treatment, **Labor 6708**
Enforcement of laws, **Labor 6307 et seq.**
Agreements, standards, orders or rules, **Labor 144**
Civil penalties, **Labor 6650, 6651**
Laws, **Labor 6307 et seq.**
Safety orders, **Labor 142**
Responsible entity, **Labor 50.7**

LABOR AND EMPLOYMENT—Cont'd
Occupational safety and health—Cont'd
Enforcement of laws—Cont'd
Standards, **Labor 142, 144.5, 6308**
Labor camps, **Health & S 17022**
Entry on premises, **Labor 6314**
Evaluations, proposed standards and variances, **Labor 147**
Evidence, **Labor 6314**
Appeal and review, **Labor 6611**
Corrective orders, **Labor 6313**
Reports, **Labor 6412**
Standards, and orders, rules, regulations, **Labor 6314, 6315.5**
Excavations, licenses and permits, **Labor 6500 et seq.**
Exemptions,
Carcinogens, **Labor 9015**
Licenses and permits, **Labor 6508**
Exhaust purifier devices, internal combustion engines, use inside buildings, **Labor 6702**
Facsimiles, pesticide poisoning, reports, **Labor 6409**
Federal concurrent jurisdiction, state jurisdiction limited, **Labor 6303.5**
Fees, licenses and permits, **Labor 6507**
Field sanitation, standards, **Labor 6712**
Final orders, reconsideration, **Labor 6614 et seq.**
Fines and penalties, **Labor 6314, 6317, 6319, 6423 et seq.**
Advance notice of inspections or investigations, **Labor 6321**
Asbestos spraying, **Labor 6427 et seq.**
Carcinogens, **Labor 9060 et seq.**
Dangerous conditions, failure to disclose, **Pen 387**
Death of employees, **Labor 6425**
Educational institutions, refunds, **Labor 6434**
False representations, **Labor 6426**
Firefighters and fire departments, **Labor 6434.5**
Injunctions, unsafe working conditions, **Labor 6326**
Injuries and fatalities, reports, **Labor 6413.5**
Investigations or inspections, obstructing or hampering, **Labor 6314**
Judgments, entry, **Labor 6650**
Limitation of actions, **Labor 6651**
Minor violations, **Labor 6427**
Notice, contractor licensing, **Labor 6652**
Police, **Labor 6434.5**
Posting requirements, **Labor 6431**
Records, **Labor 6431**
Refunds, police, firefighters and fire departments, **Labor 6434.5**
Repeated or willful violations, **Labor 6429**
Reports, **Labor 6409.1**

LABOR AND EMPLOYMENT—Cont'd
Occupational safety and health—Cont'd
Fines and penalties—Cont'd
Rescinding adjustment of penalty, failure to abate violation, **Labor 6430**
Serious violations, **Labor 6428, 6432**
Fire hazards, garment manufacturing, **Labor 6409.5**
Firefighters and fire departments, fines and penalties, **Labor 6434.5**
First aid, pesticide poisoning, exclusion, **Labor 6409**
Flammable or combustible material, installation, pressure tests of piping, **Labor 6700**
Forms,
Completion, **Labor 6411**
Reports, **Labor 6410**
Fraud, **Labor 6317.5**
Funds, education fund, **Labor 6354.7**
Garment manufacturers, fire or safety hazards, **Labor 6409.5**
Gas pipeline tests, unsafe place of employment, **Labor 6700**
Harmful physical agents, standards, **Labor 144.6**
Hazardous exposures, records, notice, **Labor 6408**
Hazardous industries, safety improvement programs, **Labor 6354**
Hazardous substances and waste, generally, ante
Hearings, **Labor 6308.5**
Incomplete abatement, **Labor 6319.5**
Special order or action order hearings, requested by employers, **Labor 6308**
High hazard industries lists, establishment, **Labor 6401.7**
Illness, investigations, **Labor 6313, 6314**
Immigration, limited English proficient persons, state agencies, access, **Labor 176**
Incomplete abatement, hearings, **Labor 6319.5**
Information,
Posting, **Labor 6408**
Statistics, **Labor 150**
Injunction,
Engaging in activity without permit, **Labor 6510**
Unsafe working conditions, **Labor 6323 et seq.**
Affidavits, **Labor 6324**
Asbestos spraying, **Labor 6324**
Bonds, **Labor 6324**
Crimes and offenses, **Labor 6326**
Fines and penalties, **Labor 6326**
Notice, **Labor 6325**
Injury prevention programs, **Labor 6401.7**
Consulting services, **Labor 6354**
New employers, exemption, **Labor 6319.3**
Operative status, **Labor 6428.5**

LABOR AND EMPLOYMENT—Cont'd
Occupational safety and health—Cont'd
Injury prevention programs—Cont'd
Scope of inspection, **Labor 6314.5**
Inspection and inspectors, places of employment, **Labor 6309 et seq.**
Advance notice, **Labor 6321**
Carcinogens, **Labor 9050 et seq.**
Employer request, **Labor 6354**
Actions and proceedings, unsafe conditions, **Labor 6355**
Enforcement of standards, **Labor 144.5**
Misdemeanors, obstructing or hampering inspections, **Labor 6314**
Records, **Labor 6412**
Reinspections, **Labor 6320**
Scope of inspection, **Labor 6314.5**
Inspection warrant, **Labor 6314**
Interest, judgments, **Labor 6650**
Interpreters and translators, **Labor 176**
Investigations and investigators, **Health & S 105175; Labor 1173, 1178, 6309**
Accidents or illness, **Labor 6313**
Advance notice, **Labor 6321**
Misdemeanors, obstructing or hampering investigations, **Labor 6314**
Reports, transmit copies of investigations, **Labor 6313.5**
Jurisdiction, **Labor 6316**
Appeal and review, **Labor 6632**
Investigations, **Labor 6314**
Labor camps, enforcement of standards, **Health & S 17022**
Lead related construction work,
Definitions, **Labor 6716**
Employee protection, standards, **Labor 6717**
Licenses and permits, **Labor 6500 et seq.**
Appeals, revocation, **Labor 6506**
Crimes and offenses, **Labor 6509**
Exemptions, **Labor 6508**
Fees, **Labor 6507**
Injunctions, **Labor 6510**
Posting, **Labor 6504**
Public works contracts, **Labor 6706**
Revocation of permit, **Labor 6505, 6506**
Appeals, **Labor 6506**
Supersedeas or stay, revocation, **Labor 6506**
Life, safety and health of employees, responsibilities and duties of employers, **Labor 6400 et seq.**
Limitation of actions, fines and penalties, collection, **Labor 6651**
Limited English proficient persons, State agencies, access, **Labor 176**
Worker safety bilingual investigative support, enforcement and training account, **Labor 6356**
Liquified petroleum gas, storage facilities construction, **Labor 175**

LABOR AND EMPLOYMENT—Cont'd
Occupational safety and health—Cont'd
Lists,
Hazardous industries, **Labor 6314.1**
Nonhigh hazard industries, **Labor 6401.7**
Local health officers, pesticide poisoning, reports, **Labor 6409**
Low hazard industries list, establishment, **Labor 6401.7**
Mandate writ, lawfulness of original orders or decisions, **Labor 6627 et seq.**
Medical examinations, carcinogens, **Labor 9040**
Medical records, personal injuries, death, **Labor 6409 et seq.**
Medical surveillance, neighbor related construction work, **Labor 6717**
Misdemeanors, obstructing or hampering investigations or inspections, **Labor 6314**
Mobile internal combustion engines, **Labor 6701 et seq.**
Model injury and illness prevention programs, **Labor 6401.7**
Modification of penalties, **Labor 6319**
Multiemployer worksites, citations, **Labor 6400**
New employers, injury prevention programs, exemption, labor violations, **Labor 6317.5, 6317.7**
Notice, **Labor 6409.2**
Abatement, **Labor 6318**
Appeal and review, **Labor 6601**
Citations or orders and right of appeal, **Labor 6319**
Dangerous conditions, failure to disclose, **Pen 387**
De minimis violations, **Labor 6317**
Exposure to toxic materials, **Labor 6408**
Injunctions, unsafe working conditions, **Labor 6325**
Injuries and fatalities, **Labor 6409 et seq.**
Judgments, **Labor 6650**
Meetings, standards board, **Labor 142.1**
Orders, preservation of materials or accident site, **Labor 6314**
Safety rules and regulations, **Labor 6328**
Violations, **Labor 6318**
Oaths and affirmations, administering, **Labor 6314**
Obstructing or hampering inspections and investigations, **Labor 6314**
Occupational health standards or variances, evaluation, **Labor 147**
Occupational safety and health standards board. Industrial Relations Department, this index
Orders, **Labor 6313**
Adopting, amending or repealing, standards, **Labor 142.3 et seq.**

LABOR AND EMPLOYMENT—Cont'd
Occupational safety and health—Cont'd
Orders—Cont'd
Appeal and review, **Labor 6319, 6600 et seq.**
Final orders, reconsideration, **Labor 6614 et seq.**
Mandate writ, lawfulness of original orders or decisions, **Labor 6627 et seq.**
Posting, **Labor 6318**
Preservation of physical materials or accident site, **Labor 6314**
Rules, **Labor 6308**
Temporary variances, **Labor 6450 et seq.**
Pesticide poisoning,
Compensation and salaries, physicians and surgeons, **Labor 6409**
Facsimiles, reports, local health officers, **Labor 6409**
First aid, exclusion, **Labor 6409**
Reports, local health officers, **Labor 6409**
Treatment classification, **Labor 6409.3**
Petition for reconsideration of final orders, **Labor 6614 et seq.**
Photography and pictures, investigations, **Labor 6314**
Physicians and surgeons, reports, **Labor 6409**
Police, fines and penalties, **Labor 6434.5**
Portable and mobile internal combustion engines, **Labor 6701 et seq.**
Posting,
Citations, **Labor 6318**
Findings of no violations, **Labor 6318**
Information, **Labor 6408**
Licenses and permits, **Labor 6504**
Orders, **Labor 6318**
Preventing entry, unsafe or unhealthy place, **Labor 6402**
Production of books and papers, **Labor 6314**
Programs, **Health & S 105175, 105180; Labor 6314**
Development, **Labor 50.8**
Protection of life, safety and health of employees, responsibilities and duties of employers, **Labor 6400 et seq.**
Public works contracts, **Labor 6705 et seq.**
Bids, **Labor 6707**
Boring and jacking pits, bids for construction, **Labor 6707**
Emergency first aid treatment, **Labor 6708**
Emergency repair work to underground facilities, **Labor 6706**
Excavations,
Bids for construction, **Labor 6707**
Permits, **Labor 6706**
Graves, construction, **Labor 6706**

LABOR

LABOR AND EMPLOYMENT—Cont'd
Occupational safety and health—Cont'd
Public works contracts—Cont'd
Jacking pits, bids for construction, **Labor 6707**
Permits, **Labor 6706**
Pipelines, bids for construction, **Labor 6707**
Sewage disposal systems, bids for construction, **Labor 6707**
Sewers, bids for construction, **Labor 6707**
Swimming pools, construction, **Labor 6706**
Tort liability, **Labor 6707**
Trenches,
Bids for construction, **Labor 6707**
Permits, **Labor 6706**
Underground facilities, emergency repair work, permits, **Labor 6706**
Railroad employees, **Labor 6800**
Records and recordation,
Access, employee exposure to hazards, **Labor 6408**
Accurate records of complaints, **Labor 6309**
Citations, **Labor 6317**
Refunds, fines and penalties, police, firefighters and fire departments, **Labor 6434.5**
Registration, asbestos, work related, **Labor 6501.5, 6505.5**
Reinspections, **Labor 6320**
Repeated violations, citations, **Labor 6317**
Repetitive motion injuries, **Labor 6719**
Reports, **Labor 6317, 6409 et seq.**
Boilers, **Labor 7722**
Carcinogens, use, **Labor 9030 et seq.**
Clinical and research findings, **Labor 50.8**
Confidential or privileged information, medical reports, injuries to employees, **Labor 6412**
Directors, **Labor 6330**
Fines and penalties, injuries and fatalities, failure to make reports, **Labor 6413.5**
Forms, occupational illness, responsibilities and duties of employers, **Labor 6410**
Fraud warnings, forms, **Labor 6410.5**
Injuries, fatalities, and accident rates, **Labor 6409**
Local health officers, pesticide poisoning, **Labor 6409**
Occupational illness, responsibilities and duties of employers, **Labor 6409 et seq.**
Pesticide poisoning, **Labor 6409**
Public access, **Labor 6412**
Safety, correctional institutions, **Labor 6413.2**
Statistics on work injuries, occupational diseases and fatalities, **Labor 156**

LABOR AND EMPLOYMENT—Cont'd
Occupational safety and health—Cont'd
Reports—Cont'd
Transmit copies of reports of investigations, **Labor 6313.5**
Research and education, **Labor 6350 et seq.**
Responsibilities and duties of employers and employees, **Labor 6400 et seq.**
Revocation of penalty adjustments, failure to abate violations, **Labor 6320**
Rules and regulations,
Civil penalties, **Labor 6319**
Compliance, **Labor 6407**
Notice, **Labor 6328**
Temporary variances, **Labor 6454**
Rules of practice and procedure, appeal and review, **Labor 6603**
Safety conference, asbestos, **Labor 6503.5**
Salvaging materials, demolition of buildings, **Labor 6401.5**
Schools and school districts, fines and penalties, refunds, **Labor 6434**
Serious concealed danger, failure to disclose, **Pen 387**
Serious injury or illness, reports, **Labor 6409.1**
Serious violations,
Citations, **Labor 6317**
Complaints, **Labor 6309**
Crimes and offenses, **Labor 6428, 6432**
Signature, notice, de minimis violations, agreement to conditions, **Labor 6317**
Special orders,
Appeal and review, **Labor 6600 et seq.**
Posting, **Labor 6318**
Standards,
Adopting, amending or repealing, **Labor 142.3 et seq.**
Carcinogens, **Labor 9020 et seq.**
Compliance, **Labor 6407**
Definitions, **Labor 6305**
Development and enforcement, responsible entity, **Labor 50.7**
Evaluation of proposals, **Labor 147**
Field sanitation, **Labor 6712**
Temporary variances, **Labor 6450**
Toxic materials, **Labor 144.6**
State jurisdiction, federal concurrent, limiting state jurisdiction, **Labor 6303.5**
State treasury, general fund, deposit of fees, standards, **Labor 6329**
Statewide young worker health and safety resource network, **Labor 6359**
Statistics, collection, **Labor 6314**
Subpoenas, **Labor 6314**
Temporary variances, **Labor 6450 et seq.**
Appeals, **Labor 6455 et seq.**
Applications, **Labor 6451**

LABOR AND EMPLOYMENT—Cont'd
Occupational safety and health—Cont'd
Temporary variances—Cont'd
Rules and regulations, **Labor 6454**
Tests, investigations, **Labor 6314**
Time, appeal and review, **Labor 6601, 6601.5**
Tower cranes, regulation, **Labor 7370 et seq.**
Toxic materials,
Data repository, **Labor 147.2**
Notice of exposure, **Labor 6408**
Standards, **Labor 144.6**
Toxicity requests, notice of data gap, **Health & S 105175**
Trade secrets, confidential information, **Labor 6322**
Training, **Labor 6354.7**
Health hazard recognition, **Labor 144.5**
Injury prevention, **Labor 6401.7**
Trenches,
Excavation projects, public contracts, **Labor 6705**
Licenses and permits, **Labor 6500 et seq.**
Unsafe conditions,
Actions and proceedings, **Labor 6327.5**
Complaints, **Labor 6309**
Injunctions, **Labor 6323**
Mandamus, **Labor 6327.5**
Variances,
Evaluation of proposed variances, **Labor 147**
Hearings, permanent variances, **Labor 146**
Permanent variance from standards, orders or special orders, **Labor 143 et seq.**
Temporary variances, **Labor 6450 et seq.**
Violations,
Complaints, **Labor 6309**
Safe provisions, **Labor 6314**
Washing facilities, lead related construction industry, **Labor 6717**
Wearing apparel manufacturers, fire or safety hazards, **Labor 6409.5**
Wheel cranes, **Labor 6704**
Willful violations, citation, **Labor 6317**
Witnesses, **Labor 6314**
Worker safety bilingual investigative support, enforcement and training account, **Labor 6356**
Working conditions, hearing, **Labor 1178**
Wrongful death, **Labor 6304.5**
Offenses. Crimes and offenses, generally, ante
Older workers, **Un Ins 2070 et seq.**
Olympic Games, this index
One stop career centers, **Un Ins 14230 et seq.**
Orders,
Asbestos, prohibiting use, **Labor 6325.5**

LABOR AND EMPLOYMENT—Cont'd
Orders—Cont'd
  Employers, contesting safety orders, **Labor 6327**
  Layoffs, **Labor 1401**
  Mail and mailing, wages, hours and working conditions, **Labor 1183**
  Occupational safety and health, ante
  Posting, wages, hours and working conditions, **Labor 1183**
  Prerequisite to effectiveness, **Labor 1204**
  Publication, working conditions, **Labor 1182**
  Safety in employment, post
  Sexual harassment, **Gov 12950**
  Summaries, wages, hours and working conditions, **Labor 1183**
  Working conditions, post
Orders of court, workplace violence safety, **CCP 527.8**
Overtime, generally, this index
Ownership of things acquired by virtue of employment, **Labor 2860**
Pants, discrimination, **Gov 12947.5**
Papers. Books and papers, generally, ante
Parents,
  Serious illness, family care and medical leave, **Gov 12945.2**
  Sick leave, **Labor 233, 234**
Parole and Probation, this index
Paycheck stubs, failure to provide, fines and penalties, **Labor 226.3**
Payroll, generally, this index
Peace Officers, this index
Penalties. Fines and penalties, generally, ante
Pending proceedings, **Labor 4**
Per diem, workforce investment board, **Un Ins 14015**
Performance review, privileged communications, **CC 47**
Perjury, layoffs, notice, **Labor 1402.5**
Permissible jobs for minors 14 and 15, **Labor 1294.3**
Permits. Licenses and permits, generally, ante
Personal injuries,
  Advertisements, benefits and services, **Labor 139.4 et seq.**
  Affecting ability to serve employer, **CC 49**
  Negligence, generally, ante
  Obligations of employer, **Labor 2801**
  Reports, **Labor 6409 et seq.**
  Waiver of right of action, **Labor 2804**
Personal liability, harassment, discrimination, unlawful practices, **Gov 12940**
Personal Services, generally, this index
Personnel records, inspection by employees, **Labor 1198.5**
Pesticide poisoning. Occupational safety and health, ante
Petitions,
  Injunction, workplace violence safety, **CCP 527.8**

LABOR AND EMPLOYMENT—Cont'd
Petitions—Cont'd
  Orders, working conditions, **Labor 1184**
  Reconsideration of final orders, **Labor 6614 et seq.**
  Rules and regulations, **Labor 1176.1, 1176.3**
Photography and pictures,
  Employees, **Labor 400 et seq.**
    Improper use by employer, **Labor 1051**
    Management companies, improper use by employer, **Labor 1057**
  Occupational safety and health, ante
Physical examinations,
  Carcinogens, **Labor 9040**
  Discrimination, unlawful practices, **Gov 12940**
  Medical records, release, **CC 56.10**
Physicians and Surgeons, this index
Place of employment, definitions, **Labor 6303**
Plans and specifications,
  Employment and training, **Un Ins 10510 et seq.**
  Local workforce investment boards, **Un Ins 14220 et seq.**
  Workforce investment board, **Un Ins 14020**
Pleadings, aggrieved employees, actions and proceedings, **Labor 2699.3**
Police, this index
Political activities of employees, **Labor 1101 et seq.**
Polygraph tests, requiring applicants or employees to take, **Labor 432.2**
Portable and mobile internal combustion engines, **Labor 6701 et seq.**
Posters, sexual harassment, **Gov 12950**
Posting,
  Occupational safety and health, ante
  Orders, wages, hours and working conditions, **Labor 1183**
  Whistle blowing, notice, **Labor 1102.8**
Posttrial or pretrial diversion programs, referrals or participation, job applicants, disclosure, **Labor 432.7**
Power of attorney, notice of termination, **Labor 2852**
Powers and duties, layoffs, investigations and investigators, **Labor 1406**
Preemployment medical or physical examination, payment of fees, condition of employment, **Labor 222.5, 225**
Preemployment physical examination, children and minors, release authorization of medical records, **CC 56.10**
Preexisting workweek arrangement, petition for modification, **Labor 1182.5**
Pregnancy, unlawful practices, **Gov 12945**
Premiums, benefits, family care and medical leave, **Gov 12945.2**
Presumptions,
  Licenses and permits, political subdivisions, **Bus & P 16300**
  Working conditions, **Labor 1200**

LABOR AND EMPLOYMENT—Cont'd
Preventing entry, unsafe or unhealthy place, **Labor 6402**
Priorities and preferences, employees obligation to perform employers business, **Labor 2863**
Prisons and prisoners. Correctional Institutions, this index
Private security services, contracts, **Labor 2810**
Privileged information. Confidential or privileged information, generally, ante
Privileges and immunities,
  Arrests for violations of laws, **Labor 95**
  Contracts against public policy, **Labor 920 et seq.**
  Disclosure by other employers, background check on peace officer applicants, **Gov 1031.1**
  Employment references, communications, **CC 47**
  Libel and slander, **CC 47**
Probate proceedings, claims against estate, personal services, **Labor 97.5**
Proceedings. Actions and proceedings, generally, ante
Process, service, **Labor 95**
Production of books and papers, **CCP 1985.6; Labor 92**
Productivity, collection and compilation of information, **Labor 150**
Profit sharing plans, unclaimed trust funds, escheat to state, **CCP 1510, 1521**
Promotions, support, earnings assignment orders, **Fam 5290**
Property,
  Bonds (officers and fiduciaries), **Labor 405**
  Employment contract, **Labor 406**
Protection, life, safety and health of employees, responsibilities and duties of employers, **Labor 6400 et seq.**
Protective orders, workplace violence safety, **CCP 527.8**
Psychological examinations, discrimination, unlawful practices, **Gov 12940**
Public benefit corporations, religious organizations and societies, education, **Gov 12926.2**
Public Buildings and Works, generally, this index
Public employment offices. Unemployment Compensation, this index
Public Officers and Employees, this index
Public policy,
  Contracts, **Labor 920 et seq.**
  Declaration, **Labor 923**
  Investments, sale of stock or interest in business in connection with securing position, **Labor 407**
  Older workers, **Un Ins 2070**
Public works contracts. Occupational safety and health, ante
Publication,
  Hearings, **Labor 1181**

LABOR

LABOR AND EMPLOYMENT—Cont'd
Publication—Cont'd
Orders, working conditions, **Labor 1182**
Rules and regulations, industrial welfare commission, **Labor 1182.1**
Punishment. Crimes and offenses, generally, ante
Purchases, employees, compelling or coercing, **Labor 450 et seq.**
Quitting,
Compensation for services rendered, **Labor 2927**
Direct deposit, compensation and salaries, **Labor 213**
Race discrimination, **Labor 1735**
Radio. Television and Radio, this index
Railroads, this index
Reading, employee literacy assistance, **Labor 1040 et seq.**
Rebuttable presumptions, retaliation, **Labor 98.6**
Reciprocity,
Employee disputes, enforcement, **Labor 103 et seq.**
Employment tax information, furnishing to Mexican officials, **Un Ins 1095**
Records and recordation,
Children and minors, ante
Compelling production of records, **Labor 92**
Compensating time off, **Labor 204.3**
Crimes and offenses, maintenance of records, **Labor 1175**
Disclosure, crimes, **Pen 11105.3**
Discovery, **CCP 1985.6**
Employment investigations, consumer reporting agencies, **CC 1786 et seq.**
Failure to maintain and preserve, **Gov 12946**
Inspection and inspectors, **Labor 1174, 1198.5**
Layoffs, **Labor 1406**
Low hazard industries employers, **Labor 6401.7**
Occupational safety and health, ante
Personnel records, inspection and inspectors, **Labor 1198.5**
Subpoenas, **CCP 1985.6**
Wage board proceedings, **Labor 1180**
Women, **Labor 1178.5**
Written records, **Labor 8**
Recreation and Park Districts, this index
Recruitment,
Foreign labor contractors, **Bus & P 9998 et seq.**
Posters, **Labor 973**
Solicitation of employees by misrepresentation, **Labor 970 et seq.**
Reemployment, generally, this index
References, privileged communications, **CC 47**
Referral and labor market information services, **Un Ins 9608**
Referral records, failure to retain, **Gov 12946**

LABOR AND EMPLOYMENT—Cont'd
Refusal, disclosure by other employers, peace officer employment applicants, **Gov 1031.1**
Registration,
Asbestos related work, employers, contractors, **Labor 6501.5, 6505.5**
Employers of door to door minor sellers, **Labor 1308.2 et seq.**
Supervisors of door to door minor sellers, **Labor 1308.2 et seq.**
Regulations. Rules and regulations, generally, post
Rehabilitation facilities, licenses, **Labor 1191.5**
Rehearings, working conditions, **Labor 1188**
Religion, discrimination, **Labor 1735**
Religious organizations and societies, **Gov 12922**
Workforce investments, grants, contracts, **Un Ins 14003, 14004**
Relocations, **Labor 1400 et seq.**
Benefits, unsafe premises, **Health & S 17062**
Repair of buildings. Safety in employment, generally, post
Repetitive motion injuries, occupational safety and health, **Labor 6719**
Reports,
Carcinogens, use, **Labor 9030 et seq.**
Children and minors, ante
Deferred compensation plans, employer managed, **Labor 2809**
Discrimination, **Labor 98.75**
Employers, **Labor 1174**
Employment investigations, consumer reporting agencies, **CC 1786 et seq.**
Green collar jobs, grants, **Un Ins 14022**
Injuries, fatalities, and accident rates, **Labor 6409 et seq.**
Local health officers, pesticide poisoning, **Labor 6409**
Medical reports, employment related injuries or fatalities, **Labor 6409 et seq.**
Occupational safety and health, ante
Pesticide poisoning, **Labor 6409**
Wage board, **Labor 1178, 1178.5, 1182**
Workforce investment board, **Un Ins 14011, 14013**
Written reports, **Labor 8**
Research and education, **Labor 6350 et seq.**
Responsibilities and duties of employers and employees, **Labor 6400 et seq.**
Rest periods,
Compensation and salaries, **Labor 226.7**
Motor carriers, collective bargaining, **Labor 512.5**
Records, women, **Labor 1178.5**
Restraint, freedom from, public policy, **Labor 923**
Retaliation,
Child support, assignment of medical insurance coverage, **Fam 3769**

LABOR AND EMPLOYMENT—Cont'd
Retaliation—Cont'd
Civil air patrol, **Labor 1506**
Crimes and offenses, victims of crime, absence and absentees, judicial proceedings, **Labor 230.2**
Domestic violence, time off, **Labor 230, 230.1**
Employers against employees, unemployment compensation, enforcing rights, **Un Ins 1237**
Health facilities, whistle blowing, **Health & S 1278.5**
Rebuttable presumptions, **Labor 98.6**
Sexual assault, time off, **Labor 230, 230.1**
Statutory or regulatory violations, disclosure, **Labor 1102.5**
Victims of crime, absence and absentees, judicial proceedings, **Labor 230.2**
Retirement and Pensions, generally, this index
Review. Appeal and review, generally, ante
Revocation, registration of employers or supervisors of door to door minor sellers, **Labor 1308.4**
Rules and regulations, **Labor 1178**
Asbestos related work, **Labor 6501.5, 9021.5**
Bloodborne pathogens, **Labor 144.7**
Industrial welfare commission, copies, **Labor 1198.4**
Notice of hearings, **Labor 1181**
Occupational safety and health, ante
Petitions, **Labor 1176.1, 1176.3**
Settling employee complaints, **Labor 98.8**
Wage board, **Labor 1178.5, 1182**
Whistle blowing, **Labor 1102.5**
Workplace smoking regulation, **Labor 6404.5**
Rules of practice and procedure, appeal and review, **Labor 6603**
Safe, definitions, **Labor 6306**
Safeguard, definitions, **Labor 6306**
Safety device, definitions, **Labor 6306**
Safety in employment,
Abatement period, commencement, occupational safety and health standard violations, **Labor 6317**
Administration and enforcement of provisions, **Labor 60.5**
Aerial passenger tramways, **Labor 7340 et seq.**
Air pressure tanks, **Labor 7620 et seq.**
Asbestos spraying, violations, **Labor 6317**
Bloodborne pathogens, **Labor 144.7**
Boilers, **Labor 7620 et seq.**
Building construction or repair, **Labor 7100 et seq.**
Beams,
Covering with flooring, **Labor 7101**
Intermediate beams, **Labor 7104**

LABOR AND EMPLOYMENT—Cont'd
Safety in employment—Cont'd
Building construction or repair—Cont'd
Belts, safety belts, **Labor 7108**
Structural steel framed buildings, **Labor 7253, 7262, 7265**
Building construction in sections, **Labor 7106, 7110**
Structural steel framed buildings, **Labor 7264**
Building defined, **Labor 7100, 7250**
Concrete building construction, installation of flooring or forms before beginning work on next floor, **Labor 7102**
Construction elevators, **Labor 7200 et seq., 7204**
Crimes and offenses, **Labor 7205**
Decking,
Derrick or working floor, structural steel framed buildings, **Labor 7252**
Metal decking, structural steel framed buildings, **Labor 7258**
Demolition, salvaging materials, **Labor 6401.5**
Enforcement of law, **Labor 7110**
Structural steel framed buildings, **Labor 7267**
Erection gang, distance from flooring, **Labor 7107**
Exemption, large span buildings enumerated, **Labor 7251**
Falling substances, protection against, **Labor 7101**
Fines and penalties, construction elevators, **Labor 7205**
Floors, **Labor 7100 et seq.**
Structural steel framed buildings, **Labor 7252 et seq.**
Girders, covering with flooring, **Labor 7101**
Intermediate beams, **Labor 7104, 7105**
Intermediate flooring, **Labor 7106**
Joists, beams or girders, covering with flooring, **Labor 7101**
Lead related construction work, employee protection, standards, **Labor 6717**
Metal decking, structural steel framed buildings, **Labor 7258**
Nets, safety nets, **Labor 7108, 7109**
Structural steel framed buildings, **Labor 7265**
Planked floors, construction, **Labor 7104, 7107**
Structural steel framed buildings, **Labor 7254 et seq.**
Planking, working without, **Labor 7109**
Plywood, covering openings adjacent to columns, structural steel framed buildings, **Labor 7257**

LABOR AND EMPLOYMENT—Cont'd
Safety in employment—Cont'd
Building construction or repair—Cont'd
Reinforced concrete construction, installation of flooring or forms before beginning work on next floor, **Labor 7102**
Replanking after suspension of operations, **Labor 7105, 7109**
Riveting gang, **Labor 7108**
Safety nets and belts, **Labor 7106, 7108**
Structural steel framed buildings, **Labor 7253, 7262, 7265**
Working without, **Labor 7266**
Scaffolds, generally, this index
Second floors, commencement of work, **Labor 7102**
Sections, building constructed in, **Labor 7106**
Sequence of erection, bolting, temporary guying, structural steel framed buildings, **Labor 7263**
Signal system, construction elevators, **Labor 7201 et seq.**
Steel painters, **Labor 7108**
Structural frames, **Labor 7104**
Structural steel framed buildings, **Labor 7250 et seq.**
Suspended operations, replanking, **Labor 7105, 7109**
Structural steel framed buildings, **Labor 7259 et seq.**
Temporary floors, structural steel framed buildings, **Labor 7253 et seq.**
Underflooring, **Labor 7103**
Walls, **Labor 7100 et seq.**
Wire mesh, covering openings adjacent to columns, structural steel framed buildings, **Labor 7257**
Wooden floors, **Labor 7103**
Underflooring, **Labor 7102**
Working on derrick floor, decking, structural steel framed buildings, **Labor 7252**
Working with planking or nets not in place, **Labor 7109**
Structural steel framed buildings, **Labor 7266**
Carcinogens, Occupational Carcinogens Control Act, **Labor 9000 et seq.**
Children and minors, statewide young worker health and safety resource network, **Labor 6359**
Combustible liquids, **Labor 7800 et seq.**
Construction of elevators, **Labor 7200 et seq.**
Crimes and offenses,
Building construction or repair, working without planking or nets, **Labor 7109**
Structural steel framed buildings, **Labor 7266**
Construction elevators, **Labor 7205**

LABOR AND EMPLOYMENT—Cont'd
Safety in employment—Cont'd
Crimes and offenses—Cont'd
Window cleaners, safety devices on buildings, **Labor 7328 et seq.**
Definitions, **Labor 6306**
Construction elevators, **Labor 7200**
Volatile flammable liquids, **Labor 7800, 7801**
Electric interurban railroads, **Labor 6800**
Excavations, bracing or sloping requirements, **Labor 6705.5**
Fines and penalties, construction elevators, **Labor 7205**
Flammable liquids, **Labor 7800 et seq.**
Hazardous substances and waste, generally, ante
Inspection, construction elevators, **Labor 7204**
Interurban railroads, **Labor 6800**
Investigations and investigators, conditions, **Labor 1173**
Lead related construction work, employment protection, standards, **Labor 6717**
Licenses and permits, **Labor 6500 et seq.**
Liquefied petroleum gas storage tanks, **Labor 7620 et seq.**
Longshoremen, **Labor 7600 et seq.**
Mines, underground telephones, **Labor 7500, 7501**
Orders,
Aerial passenger tramways, **Labor 7345 et seq.**
Construction elevators, **Labor 7203**
Railroads, **Labor 6800 et seq.**
Rapid transit rail systems, **Labor 6800**
Scaffolds, generally, this index
Ships and vessels, loading and unloading operations, **Labor 7600 et seq.**
Standards, lead related construction work, employee protection, **Labor 6717**
Statewide young worker health and safety resource network, **Labor 6359**
Steam boilers, **Labor 7620 et seq.**
Stevedore operations, **Labor 7600 et seq.**
Street railroads, **Labor 6800**
Swimming pools, excavation safety, **Labor 6705.5**
Volatile flammable liquids, **Labor 7800 et seq.**
Window cleaners, safety devices on buildings, **Labor 7325 et seq.**
Salaries. Compensation and Salaries, generally, this index
Sale of interest in business, consideration for securing position of employment, **Labor 407**
Samples, lead related construction work, employee protection, **Labor 6717**

LABOR

LABOR AND EMPLOYMENT—Cont'd

Sanitary working conditions, collection and compilation of information, **Labor 150**

Savings plan, trust funds, escheat to state, **CCP 1510, 1521**

Scaffolds, generally, this index

Schools and School Districts, this index

Second and subsequent offenses, asbestos related work, **Labor 6505.5**

Self employment assistance program, unemployment compensation, **Un Ins 1300 et seq.**

Sentence and punishment. Crimes and offenses, generally, ante

Serious violations, complaints, occupational safety and health, **Labor 6309**

Service citation, employment of minors, **Labor 1287**

Service of process,
Judgment debtor, asset report, **Labor 98.2**
Workplace violence safety, injunctions, **CCP 527.8**

Services rendered jointly, **Labor 2866**

Severance pay,
Claims, assignment to commissioner, **Labor 96**
Trust funds, escheat to state, **CCP 1510, 1521**

Sex discrimination, **Labor 1735**
Apprentices, **Labor 1777.6, 3095**
Pants, **Gov 12947.5**

Sex Offenders, this index

Sexual assault, time off, **Labor 230, 230.1**

Sexual Harassment, this index

Sharps prevention technology, bloodborne pathogens, **Labor 144.7**

Sheepherders, **Labor 2695.1 et seq.**

Sheltered workshops or rehabilitation facilities, licenses, **Labor 1191.5**

Sheriffs, this index

Shingle mills, midday meal period, **Labor 800, 801**

Ships and Shipping, this index

Shopping investigators report, employee discharge or discipline, **Labor 2930 et seq.**

Showering facilities, lead related construction work, **Labor 6717**

Sick leave,
Family care and medical leave, **Gov 12945.2**
Family members, **Labor 233, 234**

Skill of employee, **Labor 2858, 2859**

Small Businesses, generally, this index

Smoking, workplaces, regulation, **Labor 6404.5**

Social Services, this index

Soldiers and Sailors Relief Act, **Mil & V 395.1**

Solicitation of employees by misrepresentation, **Labor 970 et seq.**

Special order, definitions, **Labor 6305**

Specific performance, personal services, **CC 3390**

LABOR AND EMPLOYMENT—Cont'd

Specifications. Plans and specifications, generally, ante

Stalking, workplace violence safety, **CCP 527.8**

Standards, **Labor 1178**
Bloodborne pathogens, **Labor 144.7**
Carcinogens, **Labor 9020 et seq.**
Commission, order, **Labor 1182**
County officers and employees, **Labor 1205**
Districts, officers and employees, **Labor 1205**
Hazardous substances, duties to employees, **Labor 6398**
Lead related construction work, employee protection, **Labor 6717**
Local agencies, officers and employees, **Labor 1205**
Municipal officers and employees, **Labor 1205**
Occupational safety and health, ante

Standards board, definitions, **Labor 6302**

State manpower programs, **Un Ins 9604, 9606**
Community employment development centers, **Un Ins 9607**

State treasury, general fund, deposit of fees, standards, **Labor 6329**

Statements,
Tax deductions, crimes and offenses, **Labor 226.6**
Wage statements, failure to provide, fines and penalties, **Labor 226.3**

Statewide young worker health and safety resource network, **Labor 6359**

Statistics,
Refusal or neglect to supply, **Labor 90**
Reports, **Labor 150; Un Ins 320.5**

Statutory violations, whistle blowing, **Labor 1102.5**

Sterilization, condition of employment, unlawful practice, **Gov 12945.5**

Stevedore operations, safety, **Labor 7600 et seq.**
Employee benefit plan distributions, escheat to state, **CCP 1521**

Stock purchase plans, employee benefit trust distributions, escheat to state, **CCP 1510, 1521**

Stop orders for wages, claims, assignment to commissioner, **Labor 96**

Subpoenas, **Labor 92, 93**
Investigation of working conditions, **Labor 1176**
Records and recordation, **CCP 1985.6**
Workplace violence safety, fees, **CCP 527.8**

Suits. Actions and proceedings, generally, ante

Summaries, orders, wages, hours and working conditions, **Labor 1183**

Supersedeas or stay, discrimination, complaints, **Labor 98.7**

LABOR AND EMPLOYMENT—Cont'd

Supervisors, licensed supervisors, explosives, **Labor 6710**
Avalanche blasting, **Labor 6711**

Supply and demand, collection and compilation of information, **Labor 150**

Support, this index

Suspension,
Jury duty or witnesses, **Labor 230**
Registration of employers or supervisors of door to door minor sellers, **Labor 1308.4**

Talent Agencies, generally, this index

Tardiness deductions, **Labor 2928**

Tax liens, records and recordation, copies, **CC 1786.53**

Taxation,
Mexican officials, providing information to, **Un Ins 1095**
Unemployed hiring, credit, **Rev & T 23622.7, 23622.8**

Technical rules governing assignments to commissioner, validity, **Labor 97**

Technically qualified individuals, definitions, hazardous substances, laboratories, **Labor 6386**

Telecommunications, this index

Television and Radio, this index

Temporary Employment, generally, this index

Temporary restraining orders, workplace violence safety, **CCP 527.8**

Temporary variances. Occupational safety and health, ante

Termination of employment. Discharge, generally, ante

Terms of employment,
Negotiation, public policy, **Labor 923**
Requiring employee agreement to illegal terms, **Labor 432.5**

Theaters and shows, dangerous occupations, licenses and permits, **Labor 6500**

Theft,
Construction funds, diversion, **Pen 484b**
Hiring employees without notice of unpaid claims, **Pen 484**

Third persons liable to employer for occupational safety and health violations, appeal and review, **Labor 6319, 6600**

Threats,
Discharge or loss of employment for political activities, **Labor 1101 et seq.**
Workplace violence safety, **CCP 527.8**

Ticket to work program, handicapped persons, **Un Ins 18000 et seq.**

Time,
Hearings, notice, **Labor 1181**
Hours of labor, generally, ante
Meals, **Labor 512**
Motor carriers, collective bargaining, **Labor 512.5**
Rest periods, generally, ante

LABOR AND EMPLOYMENT—Cont'd
Time—Cont'd
Rules and regulations, effective date, industrial welfare commission, **Labor 1184**
Time off,
Compensation in place of overtime pay, **Labor 204.3**
Domestic violence, **Labor 230, 230.1**
Jury, **Labor 230**
Sexual assault, **Labor 230**
Witnesses, **Labor 230**
Tips. Compensation and Salaries, this index
Tobacco and tobacco products, workplace smoking, **Labor 6404.5**
Tools,
Crimes and offenses, possession, claims for return, assignments to commissioner, **Labor 96**
Employers guaranteeing payment, **Labor 213**
Tower cranes, regulation, **Labor 7370 et seq.**
Trade secrets,
Hazardous substances and waste, ante
Occupational safety and health, ante
Whistle blowing, disclosure, **Labor 1102.5**
Training, **Un Ins 9500 et seq.**
Contracts, **Un Ins 9610**
Economic opportunity programs, workers compensation and insurance, **Labor 4201 et seq.**
Green collar jobs, **Un Ins 15000 et seq.**
Hazardous substances and waste, generally, ante
Job Training Programs, generally, this index
Nontraditional occupations, women, **Un Ins 9602.5**
Occupational safety and health, ante
Plan, **Un Ins 10510 et seq.**
Public works employees, per diem wages, **Labor 1773.1**
Sexual harassment, **Gov 12950.1**
Statewide young worker health and safety resource network, **Labor 6359**
Women, nontraditional occupations, **Un Ins 9602.5**
Workforce investment, **Un Ins 14000 et seq.**
Transportation, residents personal property, unsafe premises, **Health & S 17062**
Traveling expenses,
Labor standards enforcement division, **Labor 101**
Witnesses, investigation of working conditions, **Labor 1176**
Workforce investment board, **Un Ins 14015**
Triple damages,
Arrest record, disclosure, **Labor 432.7**

LABOR AND EMPLOYMENT—Cont'd
Triple damages—Cont'd
Contract with employer without permanent and fixed place of business in state, **Labor 2752**
Diversion programs, referrals or participation, disclosure, **Labor 432.7**
Preventing reemployment, **Labor 1054**
Trust funds for employees benefits, escheat to state, **CCP 1510, 1521**
Tunnels, diesel engines, permits, **Labor 6500**
Unclaimed employee benefit plan distribution, escheat to state, **CCP 1521**
Unclaimed employee benefit trust distribution, escheat to state, **CCP 1510**
Unemployment, generally, this index
Unemployment Compensation, generally, this index
Unfair labor practices,
Access for infants and mothers program, health services, **Ins 12698.50 et seq.**
Agricultural Labor Relations Act of 1975, **Labor 1153 et seq.**
Uniforms to be worn by employees, prescribing, **Labor 452**
Union card, unlawful use to obtain, **Labor 1017**
Unlawful practices, **Gov 12940 et seq.**
Unreturned bond money of employees, claims, assignment to commissioner, **Labor 96**
Vacation funds,
Employee benefit trust distributions, escheat to state, **CCP 1510, 1521**
Statement of employer payments, **Labor 227.5**
Vacation time,
Family care and medical leave, substitution, **Gov 12945.2**
Payment at termination, **Labor 227.3**
Variances. Occupational safety and health, ante
Verification of written instruments, **Labor 92**
Vested vacation time, forfeiture upon termination of employment, **Labor 227.3**
Veterans, this index
Victims of crime, absence and absentees, judicial proceedings, **Labor 230.2**
Videotape, comfort stations and restrooms, **Labor 435**
Vietnam Veterans Employment Act, **Gov 7280 et seq.**
Violence, **CCP 527.8**
Violent felonies, records and recordation, disclosure, **Pen 11105.3**
Vocational Education, generally, this index
Vocational Rehabilitation, generally, this index
Volatile flammable liquids, **Labor 7800 et seq.**
Voluntary agreements, public policy, **Labor 923**

LABOR AND EMPLOYMENT—Cont'd
Voluntary service without pay, definitions, workers compensation, **Labor 3363.6**
Volunteer firemen and fire departments,
Emergency duties, discharge or discrimination, **Labor 230.3**
Leaves of absence, training, **Labor 230.4**
Wage board,
Duties, **Labor 1178 et seq.**
Necessary cost of proper living, **Labor 1178.5, 1182**
Proceedings, evidence, **Labor 1180**
Rules and regulations, hearings, **Labor 1178.5, 1182**
Wages. Compensation and Salaries, generally, this index
Waiver,
Right of action, employers negligence, **Labor 2804**
Right to disclose wages, **Labor 232**
Working conditions, disclosure, **Labor 232.5**
War and Civil Defense, this index
Washing facilities, lead related construction work, **Labor 6717**
Water supply, inspection and inspectors, **Labor 2441**
Weapons,
Injunction, workplace violence, **CCP 527.8**
Necessity for employment, possession by former convicts, **Pen 12021**
Wearing Apparel, this index
Welfare,
Funds, statement of employer payments, **Labor 227.5**
Investigations, **Labor 1173**
Wheel cranes, **Labor 6704**
Whistle blowing,
Health facilities, **Health & S 1278.5**
Protection, **Labor 1102.5**
Window cleaners, safety devices on buildings, **Labor 7325 et seq.**
Witnesses, **Labor 92**
Committees, coercion, **Gov 9414**
Investigation of working conditions, **Labor 1176**
Signature or subscription by mark, **Labor 17**
Time off, **Labor 230**
Women,
Administration and enforcement of laws, **Labor 61**
Hours of labor, administration and enforcement of laws, **Labor 61**
Lactation, **Labor 1030 et seq.**
Nontraditional occupations, training, **Un Ins 9602.5**
Work Incentive Programs, generally, this index
Work performed, preferred claims, **Labor 100.5**
Worker safety bilingual investigative support, enforcement and training account, **Labor 6356**

LABOR

LABOR AND EMPLOYMENT—Cont'd

Workers Compensation, generally, this index

Workers Memorial Day, **Labor 29.5**

Workforce investments, **Un Ins 14000 et seq.**

Workforce preparation, handicapped persons, **Un Ins 18000 et seq.**

Working conditions, **Labor 1178**
Appeal and review, **Labor 1190**
Disclosure, **Labor 232.5**
Drinking water, inspection, **Labor 2441**
Evidence, **Labor 1200**
Hearings, **Labor 517**
Hours of labor, generally, ante
Injunction, **Labor 1194.5**
Investigations and investigators, **Labor 1193.5**
Misrepresentation in soliciting employees, **Labor 970**
Claims for damages, assignment to labor commissioner, **Labor 96**
Orders, **Labor 516, 517**
Prerequisite to effectiveness, **Labor 1204**
Publication, **Labor 1182**
Public policy, **Labor 923**
Regulations, presumption of lawfulness, **Labor 1200**
Rehearings, **Labor 1188**
Requiring employee agreement to illegal conditions, **Labor 432.5**
Safety in employment, generally, ante
Working days,
Continuously operating manufacturing facilities, **Labor 1182.6**
Maximum, **Labor 552**
Exemptions, mandatory orders, **Labor 1198.3**

Workplace smoking, regulation, **Labor 6404.5**

Workplace Violence Safety Act, **CCP 527.8**

Writings, form of recorded message, **Labor 8**

Wrongful death,
Occupational safety and health, **Labor 6304.5**
Right of action, **Labor 2803**

Wrongful discharge actions, unemployment compensation, setoff, **Un Ins 1382**

Youth placement services, operation by state, **Un Ins 2054, 2058**

Youthbuild program, **Un Ins 9800 et seq.**

LABOR AND WORKFORCE DEVELOPMENT AGENCY

Agricultural labor relations board, **Labor 1141**

Employment development department, **Un Ins 301**

Industrial relations department, **Labor 50**

LABOR CAMPS

Generally, **Health & S 17000 et seq.**

LABOR CAMPS—Cont'd

Abatement, overcrowding, **Health & S 17043**

Actions and proceedings,
Eviction of tenant or employee, **Health & S 17031.5, 17031.6**
Notice, **Health & S 17060**
Nuisances, abatement, **Health & S 17060**
Relocation assistance, **Health & S 17060.2**
Transfer of property to third party, **Health & S 17060.5**
Violations, **Health & S 17055**

Administrative complaints, **Health & S 17055**

Agricultural land use designation, **Health & S 17021.6**

Alternate designs, materials or methods of construction, approval, **Health & S 17002**

Appeal and review, overcrowding, **Health & S 17043**

Application of law, **Health & S 17020**

Applications,
Improvements, **Health & S 17021**
Permits,
Facilities owned or operated by railroads, required information, **Health & S 17033**
Required information, **Health & S 17032**

Assessments,
Agricultural land use designation, **Health & S 17021.6**
Fines and penalties, failure to correct violations after orders, **Health & S 17061.9**

Attorney fees,
Actions by residents, **Health & S 17061**
Contempt, **Health & S 17061.5**
Enforcement actions, **Health & S 17062**
Relocation assistance, **Health & S 17060.2**
Residents civil action, **Health & S 17055**

Blacklisting, tenant or employers exercising rights, **Health & S 17031.5**

Building standards, **Health & S 17000 et seq.**

Business taxes, **Health & S 17021.5**

Cancellation of responsibility, enforcement agencies, **Health & S 17050**

Certificate of nonoperation, discontinuation of camp, **Health & S 17037.5**

Charges, agricultural land use designation, **Health & S 17021.6**

Community housing. Labor and Employment, this index

Complaints, telephone availability, **Health & S 17038**

Conditional use permits, **Health & S 17021.6**

Consolidated cities and counties, rules and regulations, enforcement, **Health & S 17050**

LABOR CAMPS—Cont'd

Construction, alternative designs, materials or methods of construction, approval, **Health & S 17002**

Contempt, house confinement, **Health & S 17061.7**

Copies, orders and notices of violations, **Health & S 17060.2**

Correction of defects, orders, **Health & S 17062**

Costs,
Actions by residents, **Health & S 17061**
Contempt, **Health & S 17061.5**
Enforcement actions, **Health & S 17062**
Relocation assistance, **Health & S 17060.2**
Residents civil action, **Health & S 17055**

Counties, rules and regulations, enforcement, **Health & S 17050**

Crimes and offenses, **Health & S 17061**
House confinement, **Health & S 17061.7**

Damages,
Residence, civil actions, **Health & S 17055**
Violations, disposition, **Health & S 17062.5**

Declaratory relief, civil actions, **Health & S 17055**

Decreasing services, operators exempted from permit to requirements, **Health & S 17031.5**

Defenses, eviction, retaliation, **Health & S 17031.5, 17031.6**

Deferral, abatement orders, **Health & S 17060.2**

Definitions, **Health & S 17003 et seq.**
Health regulations, **Health & S 17008**

Demolition, **Health & S 17060.2**

Discharging tenant or employee, exercise of rights of tenant or employee, **Health & S 17031.5**

Discontinuation, certificate of nonoperation, **Health & S 17037.5**

Duration of permit, **Health & S 17031**

Emergencies, telephone, **Health & S 17038**

Employee housing standards, **Health & S 17000 et seq.**

Endangerment, health or safety of residents, **Health & S 17062**

Enforcement agencies, **Health & S 17050**
Definitions, **Health & S 17007**
Fees for investigations, **Health & S 17062**
Reports, **Health & S 17031.8**
Service of process, **Health & S 17051**

Enforcement of laws and regulations, **Health & S 17050 et seq.**

Entry on property, inspection, **Health & S 17050, 17052**

Evaluation of enforcement, **Health & S 17050**

Eviction,
Exercise of rights, **Health & S 17031.5, 17031.6**

LABOR CAMPS—Cont'd

Eviction—Cont'd
  Operators exempted from permit requirements, **Health & S 17031**
Existing buildings and structures, application of construction regulations, **Health & S 17023**
Farmworker housing assistance program, grant fund, fines and damages, disposition, **Health & S 17062.5**
Fees, **Health & S 17036**
  Agricultural land use designation, **Health & S 17021.6**
  Local enforcement agencies, **Health & S 17050**
  Schedule, construction and operation, **Health & S 17041**
Fines and penalties, **Health & S 17061**
  Operating camp without permit, **Health & S 17037**
  Orders for correction, continuation of violations, **Health & S 17061.9**
  Second or subsequent offenses, **Health & S 17061.5**
  Violations, **Health & S 17034**
  Disposition, **Health & S 17062.5**
Fire zones, reserved to local jurisdiction, **Health & S 17021**
Forms, permit applications, required information, **Health & S 17032**
House confinement, **Health & S 17061.7**
Imminent peril to residents, shortened period for civil action, **Health & S 17055**
Improvements, applications, **Health & S 17021**
Injunction, **Health & S 17055**
  Fines and penalties, **Health & S 17061.5**
  House confinement, violations, **Health & S 17061.7**
Inspection and inspectors, **Health & S 17050, 17052**
Intimidation of employees or tenants, **Health & S 17031.5**
Investigations and investigators,
  Attorney general, **Health & S 17054**
  Costs, **Health & S 17061.5**
    Enforcement actions, **Health & S 17062**
Licenses and permits, **Health & S 17030 et seq.**
  Application, **Health & S 17032**
  Certificate of nonoperation, discontinuation of camp, **Health & S 17037.5**
  Duration of permits, **Health & S 17031**
    Extensions, **Health & S 17030.5**
  Exemption, **Health & S 17031**
    Terminating or modifying tenancy, rent increase, eviction, **Health & S 17031.5**
  Extension of permits, **Health & S 17030.5**
  Improvements, **Health & S 17021**
  Issuance, suspension, **Health & S 17036**
  Multiyear permits, **Health & S 17030.5**
  Operating camp without permit, **Health & S 17037**

LABOR CAMPS—Cont'd

Licenses and permits—Cont'd
  Railroads, applications, **Health & S 17033**
  Rosters, camps having valid permit, **Health & S 17035**
  Violations, **Health & S 17034**
Lists, camps with valid permits, **Health & S 17035**
Local enforcement of laws and regulations, **Health & S 17050 et seq.**
Local jurisdictions, application of local requirements, **Health & S 17021**
Local use zone requirements, reserve to local jurisdictions, **Health & S 17021**
Maintenance, occupants, **Health & S 17039**
Maintenance personnel, appointment, **Health & S 17038**
Mobilehomes and Mobilehome Parks, this index
Multiyear permits, **Health & S 17030.5**
Municipalities, rules and regulations, enforcement, **Health & S 17050**
Notice,
  Actions and proceedings, enforcement agencies, **Health & S 17060**
  Overcrowding, **Health & S 17043**
  Service, enforcement agencies, **Health & S 17051**
Nuisances, abatement, **Health & S 17060**
Occupancy after rehabilitation, **Health & S 17062**
Occupational safety and health standards, enforcement, **Health & S 17022**
Officers and employees, maintenance personnel, appointment, **Health & S 17038**
Orders of court,
  Correction of defects, **Health & S 17062**
  Failure, assessment of fines, **Health & S 17061.9**
  Temporary orders, nuisance abatement, **Health & S 17060**
Ordinances, compliance, **Health & S 17001**
  Overcrowding, **Health & S 17043**
Overcrowding, **Health & S 17043**
Penalties. Fines and penalties, generally, ante
Permanent housing, definitions, **Health & S 17010**
Permits. Licenses and permits, generally, ante
Plans and specifications, prototype housing plans, **Health & S 17022.5**
Process, service, enforcement agencies, **Health & S 17051**
Proper use, occupants, **Health & S 17039**
Property lines, reserved to local jurisdiction, **Health & S 17021**
Railroad owned or operated facilities, permit applications, required information, **Health & S 17033**
Rates and charges, agricultural land use designation, **Health & S 17021.6**

LABOR CAMPS—Cont'd

Receivers and receivership, correction of defects, failure to follow court orders, **Health & S 17062**
Reduction of fees, construction or rehabilitation, **Health & S 17041**
Registration fees, **Health & S 17021.5**
Regulations. Rules and regulations, generally, post
Relocation, tenants, orders vacating, **Health & S 17060.2**
Rent, increasing, operators exempted from permits, **Health & S 17031.5**
Repairs, **Health & S 17060.2**
  Unsafe premises, **Health & S 17062**
Reports,
  Availability to enforcement agencies, **Health & S 17052**
  Enforcement agencies, **Health & S 17031.8**
  Extension of permit, **Health & S 17030.5**
  File and information, availability to enforcement agencies, **Health & S 17053**
Residential land use designation, **Health & S 17021.5**
Residents civil actions, damages, **Health & S 17055**
Retaliatory evictions of tenants or employees, exercise of rights by tenant or employee, **Health & S 17031.5, 17031.6**
Roster, camps with valid permits, **Health & S 17035**
Rules and regulations, **Health & S 17036, 17040, 17041**
  Compliance, **Health & S 17001**
  Enforcement, **Health & S 17050 et seq.**
Sanitation, occupants, **Health & S 17039**
Scope of law, **Health & S 17020 et seq.**
Second and subsequent offenses,
  Fines and penalties, **Health & S 17061.5**
  Operating camp without permit, **Health & S 17037**
Sewage disposal, reserved to local jurisdiction, **Health & S 17021**
Single family structures, zoning classification, **Health & S 17021.5**
Sleeping place, definitions, **Health & S 17011**
Standards, housing, **Health & S 17000 et seq.**
State, enforcement, **Health & S 17050, 17056**
Tax deductions, **Health & S 17061.5**
Tax returns, franchise tax board, examination, **Health & S 17061.5**
Taxation, agricultural land use designation, **Health & S 17021.6**
Telephone, emergencies and complaints, **Health & S 17038**
Temporary orders, nuisance abatement, **Health & S 17060**
Termination of tenancy, increase in rent, evicting, **Health & S 17031.5**

LABOR

LABOR CAMPS—Cont'd
Threatening employees or tenants, tenants exercise of rights, **Health & S 17031.5**
Time,
Abatement of nuisances, **Health & S 17060**
Applications, improvements, **Health & S 17021**
Duration of permit, **Health & S 17031**
Residents civil action, imminent perils to residents, **Health & S 17055**
Transfer of property to third parties, actions and proceedings, **Health & S 17060.5**
Use permit fees, **Health & S 17021.5**
Vacation,
Cost, **Health & S 17060.2**
Overcrowding, **Health & S 17043**
Variances, **Health & S 17021.6**
Venue, nuisance abatement actions, **Health & S 17060**
Violations,
Fines and penalties, **Health & S 17034**
Residents civil action, **Health & S 17055**
Waiver, fees, construction or rehabilitation, **Health & S 17041**
Water supply, reserve to local jurisdiction, **Health & S 17021**
Zoning and planning, **Health & S 17021.5, 17021.6**
Agricultural land use, **Health & S 17021.6**
Reserve to local jurisdiction, **Health & S 17021**
Residential land use designation, **Health & S 17021.5**

LABOR CODE
Generally, **Labor 1 et seq.**
Actions and proceedings, pending actions, **Labor 4**
Amendments and additions incorporated by reference, **Labor 9**
Construction, **Labor 5 et seq.**
Continuation of existing law, **Labor 2**
Definitions, **Labor 10 et seq.**
Delegation of administrative powers and duties, **Labor 7**
Enactment as restatements and continuations, **Labor 2**
Headings, **Labor 6**
Mail and mailing, notice, **Labor 8**
Notice, mail and mailing, **Labor 8**
Penalty for misdemeanors, **Labor 23**
Pending proceedings, effect, **Labor 4**
Persons continued in office, **Labor 3**
Reference to statutes, **Labor 9**
Restatements of law, **Labor 2**
Savings clause, **Labor 4**
Severability of provisions, **Labor 24**
Terms of office, **Labor 3**
Title, **Labor 1**
Vested rights, **Labor 4**
Writing, **Labor 8**

LABOR CODE PRIVATE ATTORNEYS GENERAL ACT
Generally, **Labor 2698, 2699**

LABOR COMMISSIONER
Access to all places of labor, **Labor 90**
Acknowledgment of written instruments, taking, **Labor 92**
Affidavits, taking, **Labor 92**
Appeal and review, decisions covering employee complaints, **Labor 98.2**
Assignments,
Authority to take claims, **Labor 96**
Deputies and assistants, claims, taking, **Labor 96**
Wage claims, employee discharged for having earnings garnished, **Labor 2929**
Books, issuance of subpoenas to compel production, **Labor 92**
Claims, authority to take assignments, **Labor 96**
Collection, foreign states, judgments, **Labor 103**
Reciprocal agreements, **Labor 64**
Costs, settling employees complaints, **Labor 102**
Crimes and offenses, refusal of admission to place of labor, **Labor 90**
Definitions, **Labor 21**
Employment of children, **Labor 1286**
Delegation of powers and duties, **Labor 7**
Depositions, taking, **Labor 92**
Deputies and assistants,
Access to all places of labor, **Labor 90**
Assignments, written authority to take, **Labor 96**
Field enforcement unit, **Labor 90.5**
Information, neglecting or refusing to furnish, misdemeanor, **Labor 90**
Misdemeanors, refusal of admission to place of labor, **Labor 90**
Refusal of admission to place of labor, misdemeanor, **Labor 90**
Statistics, neglecting or refusing to furnish, misdemeanor, **Labor 90**
Subpoenas, issuance, **Labor 92**
Wilfully impeding or preventing performance of duties, **Labor 91**
Employee complaints,
Decision,
Appeal and review, **Labor 98.2**
Filing, **Labor 98.1**
Investigation, **Labor 98**
Prosecution, **Labor 98.3**
English language, services, **Labor 105**
Fees, books and papers filing, **Labor 101.5**
Field enforcement unit, **Labor 90.5**
Foreign states, prosecuting employee complaints, **Labor 103 et seq.**
Hearings, employee complaints, **Labor 98**
Information, neglecting or refusal to furnish, misdemeanor, **Labor 90**
Judgments and decrees,
Assignments, foreign states, **Labor 103**

LABOR COMMISSIONER—Cont'd
Judgments and decrees—Cont'd
Reciprocal agreements, collection of claims or judgments for wages, **Labor 64**
Language, services, **Labor 105**
Oaths and affirmations, administration, **Labor 92**
Papers, issuance of subpoenas to compel production, **Labor 92**
Proof of written instruments, taking, **Labor 92**
Reciprocal agreements, collections of claims or judgments for wages in other states, **Labor 64**
Records and recordation,
Filing fees, **Labor 101.5**
Issuance of subpoenas to compel production, **Labor 92**
Refusal of admission to place of labor, misdemeanor, **Labor 90**
Reports,
Discrimination complaints, **Labor 98.75**
Field enforcement unit, **Labor 90.5**
Rules and regulations, **Labor 98.8**
Seasonal labor wages payable in presence, **Labor 252**
Statistics, neglecting or refusing to furnish, **Labor 90**
Subpoenas, **Labor 92**
Obedience to subpoenas enforced by courts, **Labor 93**
Verification of written instruments, **Labor 92**
Wilfully impeding or preventing performance of duties, **Labor 91**
Witnesses,
Examination under oath, **Labor 92**
Subpenas to compel attendance, **Labor 92**

LABOR DISPUTES
Actions, jurisdictional strikes, recovery of damages, **Labor 1116**
Advertisements,
Injunction, **CCP 527.3**
Workers during, representation, **Labor 973**
Agreements, legality, **Labor 1110**
Agricultural employment, farm labor contractor, **Labor 1696**
Agricultural Labor Relations Act of 1975, **Labor 1140 et seq.**
Arbitration and award, **Labor 65**
Actions to compel, attorney fee awards, **Labor 1128**
Agreements, application to action for unpaid wages, **Labor 229**
Industrial relations department, **Labor 65**
Public records, **Labor 65**
Reimbursement, **Labor 67**
Attorney fees,
Injunction, **Labor 1138.1**
Nonpayment actions, **Labor 218.5**
Boards of arbitration, **Labor 65**

LABOR DISPUTES—Cont'd
Bonds (officers and fiduciaries),
   Injunction, **Labor 1138.1**
   Striking employee, return, **Labor 209**
Collective bargaining,
   Agricultural labor and employment, mediation, **Labor 1164 et seq.**
   Agricultural Labor Relations Act of 1975, **Labor 1140 et seq.**
   Apprentices,
      Age, maximum age, **Labor 3077.5**
      Standards, establishing, **Labor 3086**
   Arbitration and award, application to action for unpaid wages, **Labor 229**
   Assignment of claims for wages, bargaining representatives, **Labor 96.3**
   Compensation and salaries, payment, time, **Labor 204**
   Contracts, leisure sharing, **Un Ins 12100.5**
   Deductions from employees compensation for insurance, **Labor 224**
   Duty to disclose, successor clause, employer, **Labor 1127**
   Enforcement of agreement, **Labor 1126**
   Health, welfare, pension fund or vacation plans,
      Failure of employer to make agreed payments, **Labor 227**
      Statement of employer payments, **Labor 227.5**
   Horse racing, jockeys, **Labor 3201.81**
   Hours of labor, **Labor 514, 554, 750.5**
   Injunction, **CCP 527.3; Labor 1126**
   Jockeys, **Labor 3201.81**
   Mechanics liens, express trust funds, fringe benefits, **CC 3111**
   On the job training programs, **Labor 3093**
   Public buildings and works, **Labor 1773**
      Per diem wages, fees, **Labor 1773.1**
   Public policy, **Labor 923**
   Remedies for breach of agreement, **Labor 1126**
   Representative, assignment of claims for wages, **Labor 96.3**
   Successor clause, **Labor 1127**
   Unemployment compensation,
      Compulsory retirement, **Un Ins 1030**
         Termination status, **Un Ins 3701, 4701**
      Eligibility for benefits, **Un Ins 1256**
      Longshoring operations, **Un Ins 1253.2**
   Wages, assignment of claims, collective bargaining representatives, **Labor 96.3**
   Withholding any part agreed, **Labor 222, 225**
   Workers compensation, alternative dispute resolution, **Labor 3201.5**
Compensation and salaries, **Labor 98 et seq.**
   Collection of wages, prosecution of actions, **Labor 98 et seq.**

LABOR DISPUTES—Cont'd
Compensation and salaries—Cont'd
   Collective bargaining, representatives, assignment of claims, **Labor 96.3**
   Nonpayment of valid wage claim, damages, **Labor 206**
   Payment of unpaid wages to employees, **Labor 209**
Complaints, injunction, **Labor 1138.1**
Compromise and settlement, injunction, **Labor 1138.2**
Conciliation, mediation and conciliation service, **Labor 66**
Confidential records, **Labor 65**
Costs,
   Injunction, **Labor 1138.1**
   Nonpayment actions, **Labor 218.5**
Crimes and offenses,
   Professional strikebreakers, **Labor 1134 et seq.**
   Recruitment of employees, forfeited, **Labor 974**
Damages,
   Injunction, **Labor 1138.1**
   Jurisdictional strikes, **Labor 1116**
      Employer controlled organization, injuries, **Labor 1122**
Decisions, public records, **Labor 65**
Definitions,
   Agricultural labor relations, **Labor 1140.4**
   Injunction, **Labor 1138.4**
   Jurisdictional strikes, **Labor 1117, 1118**
Deposits, return to striking employees, **Labor 209**
Disability compensation, disqualification, **Un Ins 2677**
Employees group life or disability insurance, work cessation, continuance of coverage, **Ins 10116**
Evidence, injunction, **Labor 1138, 1138.1**
Exemptions, injunction, **Labor 1138.5**
Existence or nonexistence, misrepresentation and solicitation of employees, **Labor 970**
Farm labor contractors, **Labor 1696**
Findings of fact, injunction, **Labor 1138.3**
Fines and penalties, professional strikebreakers, **Labor 1136**
Fire department employees, right to strike, **Labor 1962**
Fraud, solicitation of employees, **Labor 970**
Freedom from violence, **CC 51.7**
   Fines and penalties, **CC 52**
Hearings, injunction, **Labor 1138.1**
Hiring during, advertising and solicitation, **Labor 973**
Horse racing, jockeys, collective bargaining, **Labor 3201.81**
Hours of labor. Collective bargaining, ante
Industrial welfare commission, arbitration board, **Labor 1201**
   Publicity, **CCP 527.3**

LABOR DISPUTES—Cont'd
Injunction, **CCP 527.3; Labor 1138 et seq.**
   Jurisdictional strikes, **Labor 1116**
   Transit district employees, **Labor 1137.4**
Intervention, **Labor 98.5**
Investigation and intervention by industrial relations department, **Labor 65**
Jockeys, collective bargaining, **Labor 3201.81**
Jurisdictional strikes, **Labor 1115 et seq.**
   Application of law, **Labor 1119**
   Damages, employer controlled organizations, **Labor 1122**
   Definitions, **Labor 1118**
   Injunctions, **Labor 1160**
   Labor organization and person, definitions, **Labor 1117**
   Public policy, **Labor 1115**
Juvenile delinquents and dependents, institutionalized youth, replacing striking or locked out workers, **Welf & I 1768.1**
Labor statistics and research, collection and compilation of information, **Labor 150**
Lockouts,
   Employment agencies, loss of job by customer, fees, **CC 1812.506**
   Solicitation of employees by misrepresentation, **Labor 970**
   Unemployment compensation, **Un Ins 1259**
   Youth authority, wards, replacement, **Welf & I 1768.1**
Mediation, **Labor 65, 66**
   Injunction, **Labor 1138.2**
Misrepresentation, solicitation of employees, **Labor 970**
Notice, injunction, **Labor 1138.1**
Peace Officers, this index
Picketing, injunction, **CCP 527.3**
Privileges and immunities, **Labor 1138**
Process, injunction, **Labor 1138.1**
Professional strikebreakers, **Labor 1130 et seq.**
   Definitions, **Labor 1132.6**
Promotion of sound union employer relationships, **Labor 65**
Public records, **Labor 65**
Railroads, this index
Recruitment of employees during, **Labor 973**
Reimbursement, arbitration and award, **Labor 67**
Solicitation of employees,
   During, representation, **Labor 973**
   Misrepresentation, **Labor 970**
Strikebreakers,
   Professional strikebreakers, **Labor 1130 et seq.**
   Youth authority wards, **Welf & I 1768.1**
Successor clause, collective bargaining agreements, **Labor 1127**
Talent agencies, **Labor 1700.38**
Transit Districts, this index

LABOR

LABOR DISPUTES—Cont'd
Unemployment compensation,
  Disability base period, **Un Ins 2658**
  Disability compensation, disqualification, **Un Ins 2677**
  Ineligibility for benefits, **Un Ins 1262, 1262.5**
  Investigations, findings, **Un Ins 1262.5**
  Refusal of new work during strike, **Un Ins 1259**
Unlawful acts. Injunction, generally, ante
Violence, freedom from, **CC 51.7**
  Fines and penalties, **CC 52**
Wage investigations, **Labor 98 et seq.**
Witnesses, injunction, **Labor 1138.1**
Youth authority inmates, contract labor, replacing striking or locked out workers, **Welf & I 1768.1**

LABOR DISTRICTS
Reports, labor disputes, threatened strike or lockout, **Labor 1137.2**

LABOR ENFORCEMENT AND COMPLIANCE FUND
Workers compensation, **Labor 62.5**

LABOR MARKET AREAS
Definitions, unemployment compensation, training or retraining, **Un Ins 1270**

LABOR ORGANIZATIONS
Advertising, unauthorized use of labels, trademarks or insignia, **Labor 1016**
Agricultural labor and employment, **Labor 1140 et seq.**
  Elections, **Labor 1156 et seq.**
Badges, emblems and insignia,
  Articles of merchandise, **Labor 1010 et seq.**
  Wearing, **Labor 1018**
Certificates and certification, agricultural laborers, **Labor 1156.3**
Contracts, public policy, **Labor 920 et seq.**
Definitions,
  Agricultural labor relations, **Labor 1140.4**
  Fair employment and housing department, **Gov 12926**
  Jurisdictions strikes, **Labor 1117**
  Label, use on articles of merchandise, **Labor 1010**
  Unemployment compensation, **Un Ins 2071**
Discrimination, older workers, **Un Ins 2070 et seq.**
Duress or coercion, agreement not to join or become member, **Labor 922**
Elections, this index
Electricity, apprentices, standards, discrimination, **Labor 3099**
Employee as witness before committee, misdemeanor to coerce, **Gov 9414**
Employment agencies,
  Application of law, **CC 1812.502**
  Membership in union as requirement, notice, **CC 1812.509**

LABOR ORGANIZATIONS—Cont'd
Fair employment and housing, training, **Gov 12940**
Firefighters and fire departments, **Labor 1960 et seq.**
Forgery, label or trademark, **Labor 1015**
Freedom of individual worker, **Labor 923**
Grants, promotion or deterrence, **Gov 16645.2**
Group legal insurance, **Labor 923**
Job preparation and training services. Unemployment Compensation, this index
Labels, articles of merchandise, **Labor 1010 et seq.**
Older workers, discrimination, **Un Ins 2070 et seq.**
On the job training programs, **Labor 3093**
One stop career centers, **Un Ins 14233**
Public buildings and works, promotion or deterrence, state funds, **Gov 16645 et seq.**
Public lands, promotion or deterrence, state funds, **Gov 16645 et seq.**
Public Officers and Employees, this index
Public policy, contracts, **Labor 920 et seq.**
Records and recordation, subpoenas, **CCP 1985.6**
Registration of labels and trademarks, **Labor 1014**
Representation, freedom of worker, **Labor 923**
Self organization, public policy, **Labor 923**
State contracts, promotion or deterrence, state funds, **Gov 16645 et seq.**
State treasury, promotion or deterrence, state contracts, **Gov 16645 et seq.**
Subpoenas, records and recordation, **CCP 1985.6**
Talent agencies, advance fees, exemptions, **Labor 1702.4**
Trademarks, articles of merchandise, **Labor 1010 et seq.**
Transit Districts, this index
Trespass, lawful labor activities, **Pen 602, 602.8**
Unemployment compensation,
  Refusal of new work because of requirements, **Un Ins 1259**
  Trade disputes, appeal, **Un Ins 1262.5**
Union card, unlawful use, **Labor 1017**
Workers compensation, appeals boards, members and membership, **Labor 112**

LABOR RELATIONS
Labor Disputes, generally, this index

LABOR RELATIONS BOARD
Agricultural Labor Relations Board, generally, this index

LABOR STANDARDS ENFORCEMENT DIVISION
Industrial Relations Department, this index

LABOR STATISTICS AND RESEARCH DIVISION
Generally, **Labor 150 et seq.**
Industrial Relations Department, this index

LABOR SUPPLY EMPLOYEE HOUSING
Definitions, **Health & S 17009**

LABOR UNIONS
Labor Organizations, generally, this index

LABORATORIES
Crimes and offenses, hours of labor, **Labor 853**
Fines and penalties, hours of labor, **Labor 853**
Hours of labor, **Labor 850 et seq.**
Industrial relations department, services and personnel, **Labor 60.9**
Nonprofit organizations, technicians, unemployment compensation, optional, **Un Ins 711**
Occupational safety and health division, services and personnel, **Labor 60.9**
Workers compensation, contested cases, medical legal expenses, **Labor 4620 et seq.**

LABORATORY TECHNOLOGISTS
Workers compensation, **Labor 3208.05**

LACTATION
Labor and employment, **Labor 1030 et seq.**

LADDERS
Building construction, unsafe ladders, **Labor 7156**

LAKE COUNTY
Agricultural labor and employment, children and minors, hours of labor, exemption, **Labor 1393.5**
Agricultural products, processors, children and minors, hours of labor, exemptions, **Labor 1393.5**

LAKES AND PONDS
Fish and Game, generally, this index

LAMBRA EXPIRATION DATE
Definitions, local agency military base recovery areas,
  Corporation taxes, credits, **Rev & T 23646**
  Income tax credits, **Rev & T 17053.46**

LAND
Real Estate, generally, this index

LAND LEVELING
Definitions, agricultural labor relations, **Labor 1140.4**

LAND SURVEYORS
Surveys and Surveyors, generally, this index

LAND USE PLANNING
Zoning and Planning, generally, this index

LANDING FIELDS
Airports and Landing Fields, generally, this index

LANDLORD AND TENANT
Consumer credit reporting agencies, **CC 1786 et seq.**
Use of information in hiring of dwelling, **CC 1785.1 et seq.**
Furnishing report, **CC 1785.11, 1785.12**
Unlawful detainer, use, **CC 1785.13, 1786.18**
Leases, generally, this index
Low and moderate income housing. Housing, this index
Notice, consumer credit reporting agencies, **CC 1786.16**
Records and recordation, discrimination, preservation of records, **Gov 12956**
Rent, generally, this index
Windows, cleaners, installation of safety devices on buildings, **Labor 7329 et seq.**
Written instruments. Leases, generally, this index

LANDSCAPES AND LANDSCAPING
Zoning and Planning, generally, this index

LANGUAGE
English Language, generally, this index
Foreign labor contractors, contracts, **Bus & P 9998.2**
Interpreters and Translators, generally, this index
Labor and employment,
Services, **Labor 105**
Unlawful employment practices, **Gov 12951**
Unemployment compensation, informational pamphlets, printing in English and Spanish, **Un Ins 316**

LANGUAGES
Language, generally, this index

LARCENY
Theft, generally, this index

LASCIVIOUSNESS
Lewdness and Obscenity, generally, this index

LAVATORIES
Comfort Stations and Rest Rooms, generally, this index

LAW
Legislature, generally, this index
Statutes, generally, this index

LAW ENFORCEMENT
Labor and employment, protective orders, workplace violence safety, **CCP 527.8**
Peace Officers, generally, this index
Police, generally, this index
Privileges and immunities, adult abuse reports, **Welf & I 15634**

LAW ENFORCEMENT—Cont'd
Sheriffs, generally, this index
Storage, weapons, injunction, **CCP 527.9**
Unemployment compensation, applicants, outstanding felony arrest warrants, furnishing information to agencies, **Un Ins 1095, 2714**
Weapons,
Disposition, transportation, **Pen 12021**
Storage, injunction, **CCP 527.9**

LAW GOVERNING
Conflict of Laws, generally, this index

LAWYERS
Attorneys, generally, this index

LAYOFFS
Generally, **Labor 1400 et seq.**
Unemployment Compensation, this index

LEAD
Employee protection, standards, lead related construction work, **Labor 6717**
Paint. Lead Base Paint, generally, this index
Poisons, occupational poisoning prevention program, fees, **Health & S 105190**
Exemption, **Health & S 105191**
Standards, lead related construction work, employee protection, **Labor 6717**

LEAD BASE PAINT
Hazards, reduction programs, **Health & S 105185 et seq.**
Programs, hazard reduction, **Health & S 105185 et seq.**
Residential lead based paint hazard reduction program, **Health & S 105197**

LEAD RELATED CONSTRUCTION WORK
Definitions, labor and employment, **Labor 6716**

LEAN TO SCAFFOLDS
Use as support for scaffolds, **Labor 7154.1**

LEARNERS
Apprentices, generally, this index

LEASES
Assumed or fictitious names, personal property, **Pen 484**
Evidence,
Presumptions, theft by fraud, **Pen 484**
Theft by fraud, **Pen 484**
False identification, theft, **Pen 484**
False statements, theft, **Pen 484**
Fictitious names, theft by fraud, **Pen 484**
Fraud, theft, **Pen 484**
Machinery and Equipment, this index
Mail and mailing, certified or registered mail, written demands for return of property, **Pen 484**
Motor Vehicles, this index
Presumptions. Evidence, ante
Public employment offices, **Un Ins 2054**
Rent, generally, this index

LEASES—Cont'd
Street railroads, window cleaners, installation of safety devices on buildings, **Labor 7329 et seq.**
Theft by fraud, **Pen 484**
Time, demand, return of property, **Pen 484**
Tools, theft by fraud, **Pen 484**
Trailers, this index
Window cleaners, installation of safety devices on buildings, **Labor 7329 et seq.**
Workers compensation, injury by defective products, **Labor 3602**

LEASING EMPLOYER
Definitions, unemployment compensation, **Un Ins 606.5**

LEAVES OF ABSENCE
Absence and Absentees, this index
National guard. Military Forces, this index

LEGACIES AND LEGATEES
Probate Proceedings, generally, this index

LEGAL ASSISTANCE
Attorneys, generally, this index

LEGAL DAYS WORK
Definitions, public buildings and works, **Labor 1810**

LEGAL HOLIDAYS
Holidays, generally, this index

LEGAL IMMIGRANTS
Aliens, generally, this index

LEGAL INVESTMENTS
Investments, generally, this index

LEGAL SEPARATION
Marriage, this index

LEGAL SERVICES
Attorney General, generally, this index
Attorneys, generally, this index
District Attorneys, generally, this index

LEGEND DRUGS
Drugs and Medicine, generally, this index

LEGISLATION
Statutes, generally, this index

LEGISLATIVE ANALYST
Legislature, this index

LEGISLATURE
Appropriations, generally, this index
Assembly, military service, reentry of office on discharge, **Mil & V 395.3**
Coercion, witnesses, **Gov 9414**
Crimes and offenses, coercion of witnesses, **Gov 9414**
Duress or coercion, witnesses, **Gov 9414**
Legislative analyst, reports, labor camps, **Health & S 17056**
Libel and slander, privileges and immunities, **CC 47**

LEGISLATURE—Cont'd

Members, unemployment compensation, excluded service, **Un Ins 634.5**

Military forces, Iraq Kuwait Crisis, benefits, **Mil & V 395.07**

Privileges and immunities, libel and slander, **CC 47**

Reports,
Labor and employment, discrimination complaints and actions, **Labor 98.75**
Legislative analyst, ante

Senate,
Advise and consent, industrial accidents division, administrative director, **Labor 138.1**
Industrial relations director, appointment with advice and consent, **Labor 51**
Military service, reentry of office on discharge, **Mil & V 395.3**

State senate. Senate, generally, ante

Statutes, generally, this index

Witnesses,
Duress or coercion, **Gov 9414**
Harassment, **Gov 9414**

LEGS

Workers compensation, subsequent injuries, **Labor 4751**

LEISURE SHARING

Definitions, employment opportunities creation, **Un Ins 12102**

Employment, **Un Ins 12100 et seq.**

LETTERS AND OTHER CORRESPONDENCE

Discovery, generally, this index

Employment agencies, misrepresentations, earnings of salesmen, **Labor 976**

Labor and employment, truthful statement by employer for reasons for termination, **Labor 1053**

Public utility corporations, employees leaving service, **Labor 1055, 1056**

Solicitation of employees, representation, **Labor 973**

LETTERS OF ATTORNEY

Power of Attorney, generally, this index

LETTERS OF CREDIT

Workers compensation, self insuring employers, deposit, **Labor 3701, 3701.5**

LEWDNESS AND OBSCENITY

Child pornography. Children and Minors, this index

Children and minors,
Identity of suppliers, records, retention and disclosure, **Labor 1309.5, 1309.6**
Sale or distribution of obscene material, suppliers, identity, records, retention and disclosure, **Labor 1309.5, 1309.6**

LEWDNESS AND OBSCENITY—Cont'd

Confidential or privileged information, identity of suppliers, **Labor 1309.5, 1309.6**

Fines and penalties, records and recordation, identity suppliers, failure to maintain, **Labor 1309.5, 1309.6**
Civil remedies, disposition of recovery, **Labor 1309.6**

Identity of suppliers, retention and disclosure, **Labor 1309.5, 1309.6**

Records and recordation, identity of suppliers, retention and disclosure, **Labor 1309.5, 1309.6**

LIABILITY INSURANCE

Insurance, this index

Motor Vehicle Insurance, generally, this index

LIBEL AND SLANDER

Complaints, warrants issued upon, privileged publication, **CC 47**

Consumer credit reporting agencies, investigations and investigators, **CC 1786.52**

Destruction of evidence, privileged communications, exceptions, **CC 47**

Dissolution of marriage, privileges and immunities, pleadings, **CC 47**

Divorce actions, affidavits, **CC 47**

Evidence, destruction of evidence, privileged communications, exceptions, **CC 47**

Exconvict seeking employment, **Pen 2947**

Immunities. Privileges and immunities, generally, post

Investigative consumer reporting agencies, **CC 1786.52**

Job performance or qualifications, privileged communications, **CC 47**

Judicial proceedings, **CC 47**

Labor and employment,
Employment references, privileged communications, **CC 47**
Privileged communications, **CC 47**

Legal separation, pleadings, privileges and immunities, **CC 47**

Legislature, this index

Meetings, public, privileged publications, **CC 47**

Privileges and immunities, **CC 47**
Employment references, **CC 47**
Publication or broadcast, **CC 47**

Public meetings, privileged publications, **CC 47**

Warrants, issuance upon complaint, privileged publication, **CC 47**

LIBRARIES

Unemployment compensation, excludable services, **Un Ins 711**

LICENSED VOCATIONAL NURSES

Vocational Nursing, generally, this index

LICENSES AND PERMITS

Aerial passenger tramways, **Labor 7340 et seq.**

Agricultural Labor and Employment, this index

Agriculture, this index

Air pressure tanks, **Labor 7620 et seq.**
Operation permits, **Labor 7683**

Amusement rides, safety, **Labor 7900 et seq.**

Applications, farm labor contractors, **Labor 1684**

Apprentices, special employment and compensation, **Labor 1192**

Boilers, **Labor 7680 et seq.**

Bungee jumping, **Labor 7901**

Business and Commerce, this index

Car washes, registration, **Labor 2055**

Chemical plants, workers, safety, **Labor 7865**

Cities and counties. Consolidated Cities and Counties, this index

Clinics, this index

Consolidated Cities and Counties, this index

Contractors, this index

Conviction of crime, **Labor 26**

Counties, this index

Cranes, tower cranes, **Labor 7370 et seq.**

Definitions,
Aerial passenger tramways, **Labor 7340**
Amusement rides, **Labor 7901**
Elevators, dumbwaiters and escalators, **Labor 7300.1**
Farm labor contractor, **Labor 1682**
Talent agencies, **Labor 1700.3**

Detectives. Private Investigators, this index

Discrimination, **Gov 12944**

Drivers licenses. Motor Vehicles, this index

Elevators, Dumbwaiters and Escalators, this index

Employee housing. Labor Camps, this index

Employment. Labor and Employment, this index

Employment Agencies, this index

Explosives, this index

Farm labor contractors special enforcement unit, **Labor 1682.8**

Farm labor contracts, **Labor 1682 et seq.**

Fees, farm labor contractors, **Labor 1684**

Finance Lenders, this index

Handicapped Persons, this index

Homework, industrial, **Labor 2650 et seq.**

Industrial Homework, this index

Investigators. Private Investigators, this index

Labor and Employment, this index

Labor Camps, this index

Learners, special employment and compensation, **Labor 1192**

LICENSES AND PERMITS—Cont'd

Letters of recommendation, personal information held by governmental agencies, Information Practices Act, **CC 1798.38**

Liquefied petroleum gas, storage tanks, **Labor 7620 et seq.**

Mentally Ill Persons, this index

Mentally Retarded and Developmentally Disabled Persons, this index

Mines and Minerals, this index

Motion Pictures, this index

Motor Carriers, this index

Motor Vehicles, this index

Municipalities, this index

Occupational safety and health. Labor and Employment, this index

Private Investigators, this index

Railroads, this index

Residential mortgage lenders. Mortgages, this index

Sales and Use Taxes, this index

Sheltered workshops or rehabilitation facilities, **Labor 1191.5**

Steam boilers, **Labor 7680 et seq.**

Supervisors, explosives, **Labor 6710**
  Avalanche blasters, **Labor 6711**

Talent Agencies, this index

Tanks,
  Air pressure tanks, operation permits, **Labor 7683**
  Storage of air pressure or liquefied petroleum gas, **Labor 7620 et seq.**

Telecommuting, exemptions, political subdivisions, **Bus & P 16300**

Television and Radio, this index

Theaters and Shows, this index

Tower cranes, **Labor 7370 et seq.**

Tunnels and mines, explosives, **Labor 7990 et seq.**

Use taxes. Sales and Use Taxes, this index

Women, labor and employment, mentally deficient or physically handicapped, minimum wages, unemployment insurance code, **Un Ins 8**

LICENSING BOARD

Definitions, discrimination, **Gov 12944**

LIE DETECTOR TESTS

Employees or applicants for employment, requiring, **Labor 432.2**

LIENS AND INCUMBRANCES

Attachment, this index

Compensation and salaries, **CCP 1204 et seq.**

Consumer credit reporting agencies, release, **CC 1785.135**

Debtors and Creditors, this index

Disability benefits, liens against workers compensation, **Labor 3865; Un Ins 2629.1, 2735.5, 2741**

Discrimination, good faith incumbrances, **Gov 12995**

LIENS AND INCUMBRANCES—Cont'd

Employment. Mechanics Liens, generally, this index

Filing,
  Labor standards enforcement division, **Labor 99**
  Record as prerequisite to assignment to labor commissioner, **Labor 97**

Garnishment, **CCP 706.029**

Judgment Liens, generally, this index

Labor and Employment, this index

Labor commissioner, taking assignments, **Labor 96**

Labor law enforcement division, filing, **Labor 99**

Labor standards enforcement division, Filing, **Labor 99**
  Joinder of claimants, **Labor 100**

Mechanics Liens, generally, this index

Mortgages, generally, this index

Priorities and preferences,
  Attachment, labor claims, **CCP 1206 et seq.**
  Execution, labor claims, **CCP 1206 et seq.**
  Salary and wages, **CCP 1204 et seq.**

Records and recordation, filing before assignment to labor commissioner, necessity, **Labor 97**

Salary and wages, **CCP 1204 et seq.**

Support, this index

Tax Liens, generally, this index

Unemployment Compensation, this index

Wages and salaries, **CCP 1204 et seq.**

Workers Compensation, this index

LIFE

Emergencies, hours of labor, smelters, mines, **Labor 751**

LIFE INSURANCE

Insurance, this index

LIFEGUARDS

Disability benefits, workers compensation, leaves of absence, **Labor 4850**

Leaves of absence, workers compensation, disability benefits, **Labor 4850**

Skin cancer, workers compensation, injury, **Labor 3212.11**

Workers compensation,
  Leaves of absence, disability benefits, **Labor 4850**
  Skin cancer, injury, **Labor 3212.11**

LIGHT AND POWER COMPANIES

Electricity, generally, this index

LIGHTS AND LIGHTING

Electricity, generally, this index

LIMITATION OF ACTIONS

Agricultural labor and employment, braceros, funds, **CCP 354.7**

Armenians, genocide, **CCP 354.45**

Art and Artists, this index

Asbestos, death benefits, **Labor 5406.5**

LIMITATION OF ACTIONS—Cont'd

Braceros, labor and employment, funds, **CCP 354.7**

Children and Minors, this index

Civil rights, fines and penalties, **CC 52**

Colleges and Universities, this index

Community Development and Housing, this index

Compensation and Salaries, this index

Disability compensation overpayment, action to recover, **Un Ins 2739**

Disability fund, claims for refunds, **Un Ins 3010**

Discrimination,
  Compensation and salaries, **Labor 1197.5**
  Fines and penalties, **CC 52**

Domestic Violence, this index

Employment investigations, consumer reporting agencies, **CC 1786.52**

Fair Employment and Housing, this index

Firefighters and fire departments, asbestosis, death benefits, **Labor 5406.5**

Force and violence, fines and penalties, **CC 52**

Gender violence, **CC 52.4**

Hate crimes, fines and penalties, **CC 52**

Infants. Children and Minors, this index

Labor and Employment, this index

Minors. Children and Minors, this index

Private patrol operators, retaliation, officers and employees, disclosure, **Bus & P 7583.46**

Public Buildings and Works, this index

Railroads, braceros, labor and employment, funds, **CCP 354.7**

Sex, force and violence, **CC 52.4**

Sexual assault, labor and employment, time off, **Labor 230, 230.1**

State Agencies, this index

Talent agencies, fee disputes, **Labor 1700.44**

Tolling, fair employment and housing, **Gov 12965**
  Children and minors, **Gov 12960**

Unemployment Compensation, this index

Whistle blowing, hotlines, attorney general, **Labor 1102.7**

Workers Compensation, this index

LIMITATION OF PROSECUTIONS

Workers Compensation, this index

LIMITED ENGLISH PROFICIENT

Definitions, occupational safety and health division, bilingual employees, **Labor 176**

LIMITED LIABILITY COMPANIES

Business activities, dangerous business practices, **Pen 387**

Contributions, unemployment compensation, withholding, **Un Ins 2110**

Crimes and offenses, dangerous business practices, **Pen 387**

Damages, managers and management, dangerous business practices, **Pen 387**

LIMITED LIABILITY COMPANIES—Cont'd
Dangerous business practices, **Pen 387**
Disclosure, dangerous business practices, **Pen 387**
Dissolution, unemployment compensation, final reports and returns, **Un Ins 1116, 1735**
Managers and management, dangerous business practices, **Pen 387**
Merger and consolidation, unemployment compensation, employing unit, **Un Ins 135, 135.1**
Officers and employees, definitions, workers compensation, **Labor 3351**
Practices, dangerous business practices, **Pen 387**
Unemployment Compensation, this index
Withholding, unemployment compensation, contributions, **Un Ins 2110**
Workers compensation, employees, definitions, **Labor 3351**

LIQUEFIED PETROLEUM GAS
Occupational safety and health, storage facilities construction, **Labor 175**
Storage tanks, inspection, permits and safety regulations, **Labor 7620 et seq.**
Tanks, inspections, **Labor 7681**
Vendor safety standards, **Labor 7655**

LIQUIDATED DAMAGES
Damages, this index

LIQUOR
Alcoholic Beverages, generally, this index

LIS PENDENS
Libel and slander, privileged publication, **CC 47**

LISTS
Car washes, registration, Internet, **Labor 2063**
Hazardous Substances and Waste, this index
Health Care Service Plans, this index
High hazard industries lists, establishment, occupational safety and health, **Labor 6401.7**
Janitors, discharge, **Labor 1061**
Labor and Employment, this index
Low hazard industries lists, establishment, occupational safety and health, **Labor 6401.7**
Public buildings and works, contractors, compensation and salaries, assessments, **Labor 1741**
Talent agencies, fees, **Labor 1701 et seq.**
Workers Compensation, this index

LITERACY
Employee illiteracy assistance, **Labor 1040 et seq.**

LIVE SCAN TECHNOLOGY
Fingerprints and Fingerprinting, this index

LIVESTOCK
Animals, generally, this index

LOANS
Finance Lenders, generally, this index
Military Forces, this index
Mortgages, generally, this index
Rates and charges, military forces, discrimination, **Mil & V 394**
Real Estate, this index
Residential mortgage lenders. Mortgages, this index
Savings Associations, this index
Student loans. Colleges and Universities, this index

LOBBY
Definitions, smoking, **Labor 6404.5**

LOBBYING
Unemployment compensation, eligibility for disability benefits, **Un Ins 2606**

LOCAL AGENCIES
Aliens, illegal aliens, employment services, ineligibility, **Un Ins 9601.5, 9601.7**
Bids and bidding. Public Contracts, this index
Cable Television, generally, this index
Cities and counties. Consolidated Cities and Counties, generally, this index
Consolidated Cities and Counties, generally, this index
Definitions, public transportation labor disputes, **Labor 1137**
Employment services, illegal aliens, ineligibility, **Un Ins 9601.5, 9601.7**
Illegal aliens, employment services, ineligibility, **Un Ins 9601.5, 9601.7**
Notice, employment services, illegal aliens, ineligibility, **Un Ins 9601.7**
Officers and employees,
    Compensation and salaries, minimum wages, **Labor 1205**
    Hours of labor, **Labor 1205**
    Minimum wages, **Labor 1205**
    Standards, labor and employment, **Labor 1205**
Sewers and Sewer Systems, generally, this index
Zoning and Planning, generally, this index

LOCAL AGENCY MILITARY BASE RECOVERY AREAS
Income tax—state, credits, **Rev & T 17053.46**

LOCAL CHILD SUPPORT AGENCIES
Child Support Services Department, this index

LOCAL CHILD SUPPORT ENFORCEMENT AGENCY
Definitions, consumer credit reporting agencies, **CC 1785.3**

LOCAL EDUCATIONAL AGENCIES
Schools and School Districts, generally, this index

LOCAL GOVERNMENT
Political Subdivisions, generally, this index

LOCAL HEALTH DEPARTMENTS
Health and Sanitation, this index

LOCAL PUBLIC ENTITIES
Public Entities, generally, this index
Unemployment Compensation, this index

LOCAL SAFETY MEMBERS
Public Employees Retirement System, this index

LOCAL WORKFORCE INVESTMENT BOARDS
Generally, **Un Ins 14200 et seq.**

LOCAL ZONING AND PLANNING
Zoning and Planning, generally, this index

LOCKER ROOMS
Labor and employment, audio or video recordings, **Labor 435**

LOCKOUTS
Definitions, professional strikebreakers, **Labor 1132.8**
Labor Disputes, this index

LOCKS AND LOCKING
Tampering, **Pen 602**

LOCKUPS
Jails, generally, this index

LOCOMOTIVES
Railroads, this index

LODGING
Compensation and salaries, **Labor 1182.13**

LOGOS
Trademarks, generally, this index

LOGS AND LOGGING
Timber and Lumber, generally, this index

LONG BEACH STATE COLLEGE
Colleges and Universities, generally, this index

LONG TERM HEALTH CARE FACILITIES
Nursing Homes, generally, this index

LONGSHOREMEN
Safety, loading or unloading ships and vessels, **Labor 7600 et seq.**
Unemployment compensation, benefits, **Un Ins 1253.2**
Workers Compensation, this index

LOS ANGELES
Labor commissioner, field enforcement unit, **Labor 90.5**
Officers and employees, disability retirement, advanced payments, **Labor 4850.3, 4850.4**
Public employment offices, **Un Ins 2055**
Revitalization zone. Los Angeles Revitalization Zone, generally, this index

LOS ANGELES COUNTY
Officers and employees,
County Officers and Employees Retirement Systems, generally, this index
Retirement and pensions. County Officers and Employees Retirement Systems, generally, this index
Public employment offices, **Un Ins 2055**
Retirement and pensions. County Officers and Employees Retirement Systems, generally, this index
Revitalization zone. Los Angeles Revitalization Zone, generally, this index

LOS ANGELES REVITALIZATION ZONE
Corporation taxes,
Carryovers, net operating losses, **Rev & T 24416.4**
Deductions, net operating losses, **Rev & T 24416.2**
Carrybacks, **Rev & T 24416.4**
Deductions, operating loss carryovers, **Rev & T 17276.2**
Income tax—state,
Carryovers, net operating losses, **Rev & T 17276.4**
Deductions, net operating losses, **Rev & T 17276.4**

LOS ANGELES STATE COLLEGE OF APPLIED ARTS AND SCIENCES
Colleges and Universities, generally, this index

LOSSES
Labor and employment, employees discharging duties, indemnification, **Labor 2802**

LOW AND MODERATE INCOME FAMILIES
Youthbuild program, **Un Ins 9800 et seq.**

LOW AND MODERATE INCOME HOUSING
Housing, this index

LOW INCOME HOUSING
Low and moderate income housing. Housing, this index

LOW INCOME PERSONS
Indigent Persons, generally, this index

LOWER EXPLOSIVE LIMIT
Definitions, tunnel and mine safety, **Labor 7951**

LP GAS
Liquefied Petroleum Gas, generally, this index

LUGS
Containers, generally, this index

LUMBER
Timber and Lumber, generally, this index

LUMBER LABORERS LUNCH HOUR LAW
Generally, **Labor 800, 801**

LUNCHEONETTES
Restaurants, generally, this index

LUNCHES
Food, generally, this index

LUNCHROOMS
Restaurants, generally, this index

LYME DISEASE
Workers compensation, presumptions, **Labor 3212.12**

LYRICISTS
Music and Musicians, generally, this index

MACHINERY AND EQUIPMENT
Boilers, generally, this index
Chemical plants, safety, procedures, **Labor 7864**
Children and minors, machine operation programs, certificates of completion, child labor laws applicability, **Labor 1295**
Construction, diversion of funds, **Pen 484b**
Cranes, generally, this index
Industrial relations department, **Labor 58**
Lead poisoning, occupational safety, programs, **Health & S 105185 et seq.**
Leases,
Mechanics Liens, generally, this index
Theft by fraud, **Pen 484**
Safety in employment. Labor and Employment, this index
Theft by fraud, **Pen 484**
Withholding tax on wages, **Un Ins 13011**

MACHINISTS
Mechanics Liens, generally, this index

MAGAZINES
Advertisements, generally, this index
Children and minors, sale or distribution, **Labor 1298**
Employment agencies, advertising, misrepresentations, earnings of salesman, brokers or agents, **Labor 976**
Independent contractors, workers compensation, elective coverage, **Labor 4157**
Lewdness and Obscenity, generally, this index
Publication, generally, this index
Unemployment compensation, delivery by minors, **Un Ins 649**
Workers compensation,
Advertisements, disclosures, **Labor 5432, 5433**
Independent contractors, elective coverage, **Labor 4157**

MAGNETIC TAPE
Computers, generally, this index

MAIDS
Domestic Service or Work, generally, this index

MAIL AND MAILING
Certified or registered mail,
Certified mail as compliance with mailing requirements, **Labor 8**

MAIL AND MAILING—Cont'd
Certified or registered mail—Cont'd
Industrial homeworker, removal of article or material for violation, **Labor 2664**
Notice, work order issued against not securing workers compensation payment, findings, **Labor 3710.1**
Requirements, **Labor 8**
Wearing apparel, manufacturers,
Notice, confiscation, **Labor 2680**
Penalty orders, **Labor 2678**
Workers compensation, notice, findings, stop order issued against employer not securing payment, **Labor 3710.1**
Written demand for return of leased or rented personal property, **Pen 484**
Colleges and Universities, this index
Compensation and salaries,
Employee quitting without 72 hour notice, **Labor 202**
Termination of seasonal employment, **Labor 201**
Computer e mail, workplace violence safety, **CCP 527.8**
Domestic partnership, termination, **Fam 299**
E mail, workplace violence safety, **CCP 527.8**
Employment. Labor and Employment, this index
Garnishment, this index
Interoffice mail, workplace violence safety, **CCP 527.8**
Labor and Employment, this index
Leases, this index
Notice,
Certified or registered mail, ante
Labor and employment, hearings, **Labor 1181**
Registered mail. Certified or registered mail, generally, ante
Requirements, **Labor 8**
Sheepherders, agricultural labor and employment, **Labor 2695.2**
Tax Collection, this index
Wearing apparel, manufacturers,
Notice, confiscation, **Labor 2680**
Penalty orders, **Labor 2678**
Workers Compensation, this index
Workplace violence safety, **CCP 527.8**

MAINTAIN
Definitions, Information Practices Act, **CC 1798.3**

MAINTENANCE
Amusement rides, reports, **Labor 7914**
Buildings, this index
Janitors, generally, this index

MAJOR LIFE ACTIVITIES
Definitions, fair employment and housing, **Gov 12926**

MAKEUP WORK TIME
Labor and employment, **Labor 513**

MALFEASANCE
Whistle Blowing, generally, this index

MALICE
Damages, labor and employment, **CC 3294**
Definitions, damages, **CC 3294**
Fair employment and housing, fines and penalties, **Gov 12987**
Labor and employment, damages, **CC 3294**

MALICIOUS MISCHIEF
Buildings, this index
Entry,
    Oyster lands, without permission, **Pen 602**
    Posted lands without permission, **Pen 602**
Fences, destroying, **Pen 602**
Fires, building without permission, **Pen 602**
Gates, opening, **Pen 602**
Motor Vehicles, this index
Oyster lands, entering upon without permission, **Pen 602**
Posted lands, entering upon without permission, **Pen 602**
Private property, refusal to leave upon request, **Pen 602**
Public buildings, refusal to leave at closing time, **Pen 602**
Signs and Signals, this index
Soil, removal without permission, **Pen 602**
Timber, cutting, destroying, or carrying away without permission, **Pen 602**
Trespasses, **Pen 602**

MAMMALS
Fish and Game, generally, this index

MAN
Construction of statutes, **Labor 12.1**

MANAGED HEALTH CARE DEPARTMENT
Medical records, fingerprints and fingerprinting, **Gov 1041**
Officers and employees, fingerprints and fingerprinting, **Gov 1041**

MANAGED HEALTH CARE PLAN
Health Care Service Plans, generally, this index

MANAGERS AND MANAGEMENT
Diseases, medical records, disclosure, **CC 56.10**
Limited Liability Companies, this index
Photographs of fingerprints, employees, **Labor 1057**

MANDAMUS
Compensation and salaries, minimum wages, **Labor 1197.1**
Disability compensation, review of denial of claim, **Un Ins 3264**
Labor and employment, occupational safety and health, lawfulness of original orders or decisions, **Labor 6627 et seq.**

MANDAMUS—Cont'd
Occupational safety and health, compelling action, **Labor 6327.5**
Public buildings and works, contractors, compensation and salaries, assessments, **Labor 1742**
Unemployment compensation,
    Issuance to prevent collection of contributions, **Un Ins 1851**
    Religious organizations and societies, **Un Ins 1241**
Workers Compensation, this index

MANPOWER PLANNING SYSTEM
Labor and Employment, this index

MANPOWER PROGRAMS
Handicapped clients of department of rehabilitation, **Un Ins 9003**

MANUFACTURE
Definitions, industrial homework, **Labor 2650**

MANUFACTURERS AND MANUFACTURING
    Generally, **Labor 2330 et seq.**
Air, sanitary conditions, **Labor 2350 et seq.**
California Industries for the Blind. Blind Persons, this index
Chemical plants, workers, safety, **Labor 7850 et seq.**
Class of labor employed, labels, **Labor 1010 et seq.**
Comfort stations and restrooms, **Labor 2330, 2350**
Condemnation, sanitation, use of facility, **Labor 2352**
Crimes and offenses, sanitation, **Labor 2354**
Definitions,
    Hazardous substance information and training, **Labor 6372**
    Hazardous substances, **Labor 6372**
    Laboratories, **Labor 6386**
    Workers compensation, power press workers, **Labor 4558**
Eminent domain, sanitation, use of facility, **Labor 2352**
Enterprise Zones, generally, this index
Fans, **Labor 2353**
Fines and penalties, sanitation, **Labor 2354**
First aid, equipment, **Labor 2440**
Food, this index
Hazardous substances and waste. Labor and Employment, this index
Homework. Industrial Homework, generally, this index
Industrial Homework, generally, this index
Labor union insignia, articles of merchandise, **Labor 1010 et seq.**
Lead, poisoning, occupational safety, prevention programs, **Health & S 105185 et seq.**
Medical care and treatment, first aid and services, **Labor 2440**
Sanitary conditions, **Labor 2330 et seq.**

MANUFACTURERS AND MANUFACTURING —Cont'd
Toilets, **Labor 2330, 2350**
Ventilation, **Labor 2351**
    Foundries and metal shops, **Labor 2331**
Wearing Apparel, this index

MANUFACTURING
Manufacturers and Manufacturing, generally, this index

MANUFACTURING ENHANCEMENT AREA EXPIRATION DATE
Definitions,
    Corporation taxes, credits, enterprise zones, **Rev & T 23622.8**
    Enterprise zones, income tax—state, credits, **Rev & T 17053.47**

MANUFACTURING ENHANCEMENT AREAS
Definitions,
    Corporation taxes, credits, enterprise zones, **Rev & T 23622.8**
    Enterprise zones, income tax—state, credits, **Rev & T 17053.47**
Enterprise Zones, this index

MARIN COUNTY
Transit Development Boards, generally, this index

MARINE CARRIERS
Ships and Shipping, generally, this index

MARINE CORPS
Military Forces, generally, this index

MARINE TERMINALS
Elevators, dumbwaiters and escalators, mechanics, certificates and certification, **Labor 7311.5**
Mechanics, elevators, dumbwaiters and escalators, certificates and certification, **Labor 7311.5**
Trespass, **Pen 602**

MARINES
Military Forces, generally, this index

MARKETS AND MARKETING
Labor union insignia, **Labor 1010 et seq.**

MARKS
Brands, Marks and Labels, generally, this index
Signatures, this index
Trademarks, generally, this index

MARRIAGE
Abuse. Domestic Violence, generally, this index
Annulment,
    Domestic partnership, **Fam 298.5, 299**
    Jurisdiction, **Fam 298**
    Support, generally, this index
Assignment of wages, written consent, **Labor 300**
Children and minors. Support, generally, this index

MARRIAGE—Cont'd

Consent,
Assignment of claim, labor commissioner, **Labor 97**
Assignment of wages, **Labor 300**
Dissolution of marriage,
Domestic partnership, **Fam 298.5, 299**
Jurisdiction, **Fam 298**
Libel and slander, privileges and immunities, **CC 47**
Pleadings, libel and slander, privileges and immunities, **CC 47**
Support, generally, this index
Divorce. Dissolution of marriage, generally, ante
Domestic Partnership, generally, this index
Domestic Violence, generally, this index
Employment. Labor and employment, generally, post
Fair Employment and Housing, generally, this index
Family care leave, serious health conditions, **Un Ins 3300 et seq.**
Garnishment, withholding orders against spouse, **CCP 706.109**
Homosexuality, **Fam 308.5**
Housing. Fair Employment and Housing, generally, this index
Illness, family care leave, **Un Ins 3300 et seq.**
Injuries, family care leave, **Un Ins 3300 et seq.**
Insurance, group disability insurance, continuation of benefits, **Ins 10116.5**
Labor and employment,
Consent as necessary to assignment, **Labor 97**
Discrimination, **Labor 1735**
Fair Employment and Housing, generally, this index
Serious illness, family care and medical leave, **Gov 12945.2**
Sick leave, **Labor 233**
Violations, **Labor 234**
Legal separation,
Domestic partnership, **Fam 298.5, 299**
Jurisdiction, **Fam 298**
Libel and slander, privileges and immunities, **CC 47**
Support, generally, this index
Military Forces, this index
Municipal officers and employees, sick leave, **Labor 233**
Violations, **Labor 234**
Nullity. Annulment, generally, ante
Orders of court. Support, this index
Paid family care leave, serious health conditions, **Un Ins 3300 et seq.**
Personal injuries, family care leave, **Un Ins 3300 et seq.**
Pleadings. Dissolution of marriage, ante
Pregnancy, generally, this index
Protective orders,
Domestic Violence, this index
Weapons, acquisition of firearms by restrainees, **Pen 12021**

MARRIAGE—Cont'd

Public Officers and Employees, this index
Same sex marriage, **Fam 308.5**
Separate maintenance. Legal separation, generally, ante
Separation. Legal separation, generally, ante
State Officers and Employees, this index
Support, generally, this index
Surviving Spouse, generally, this index
Unemployment Compensation, this index
Void or voidable marriages. Annulment, generally, ante

MARRIAGE AND FAMILY THERAPISTS

Health Care Service Plans, this index
Privileges and immunities, criminally related personal injuries, reports, **Pen 11161.9**
Workers compensation, treatment of condition arising out of injury, **Labor 3209.8**

MARSHALS

Municipal Courts, this index

MASS TRANSIT

Actions and proceedings, displaced workers, **Labor 1073**
Attorney fees, displaced workers, actions and proceedings, **Labor 1073**
Buses, generally, this index
Contracts, displaced workers, **Labor 1070 et seq.**
Costs, displaced workers, actions and proceedings, **Labor 1073**
Displaced workers, **Labor 1070 et seq.**
Districts. Transit Districts, generally, this index
High speed rail. Railroads, this index
Injunction, displaced workers, **Labor 1073**
Minimum number, employees on passenger trains, application of law, **Labor 6902**
Officers and employees,
Displaced workers, **Labor 1070 et seq.**
Minimum number on train, application of law, **Labor 6902**
Paratransit Vehicles, generally, this index
Railroads, generally, this index
Transit Development Boards, generally, this index
Transit Districts, generally, this index

MASSACHUSETTS TRUST

Corporation Taxes, generally, this index

MASTER AND SERVANT

Labor and Employment, generally, this index

MATCH GAMES

Gambling, generally, this index

MATERIALMAN

Mechanics Liens, generally, this index

MATERIALS

Construction funds, crimes and offenses, **Pen 484b**
Mechanics Liens, generally, this index

MCALISTER DUFFY GREENE UNEMPLOYMENT BENEFIT PENSION OFFSET REFUND ACT

Generally, **Un Ins 1255.3**

MDA

Drugs and Medicine, generally, this index

MEALS

Compensation and salaries, **Labor 1182.13**
Consolidated cities and counties, officers and employees, motor carriers, collective bargaining, **Labor 512.5**
County officers and employees, motor carriers, collective bargaining, **Labor 512.5**
Labor and Employment, this index
Municipal officers and employees,
Motor carriers, collective bargaining, **Labor 512.5**
Time off duty to procure, **Labor 1900, 1901**
Special districts, officers and employees, motor carriers, collective bargaining, **Labor 512.5**
State officers and employees, motor carriers, collective bargaining, **Labor 512.5**
Workers compensation,
Medical examinations, **Labor 4600**
Medical legal expenses, contested cases, **Labor 4621**

MEATS

Fish and Game, generally, this index
Game. Fish and Game, generally, this index

MECHANICAL ENGINEERS

Engineers, generally, this index

MECHANICS

Elevators, Dumbwaiters and Escalators, this index
Liens. Mechanics Liens, generally, this index
Marine terminals, elevators, dumbwaiters and escalators, certificates and certification, **Labor 7311.5**
Workers compensation, alternative dispute resolution system, **Labor 3201.5**

MECHANICS LIENS

Generally, **Const. Art. 14, § 3**
Assignments, **Labor 96**
Collective bargaining, express trust funds, fringe benefits, **CC 3111**
Express trust funds, fringe benefits, collective bargaining, **CC 3111**
Filing,
Labor law enforcement division, **Labor 99**
Necessity, filing before assignment to labor commissioner, **Labor 97**

MECHANICS LIENS—Cont'd
Fringe benefits,
Express trust funds, collective bargaining, **CC 3111**
Trust funds, labor agreements, **CC 3111**
Labor standards enforcement division, filing, **Labor 99**
Records and recordation, assignment to labor commissioner, **Labor 97**
Trust funds, fringe benefits, collective bargaining, **CC 3111**

MEDI CAL ACT
Medi Cal Program, generally, this index

MEDI CAL PROGRAM
Hospitals, pediatric subacute units, supplemental reimbursement, enforcement, **Labor 107**
Intermediate care facilities,
Reimbursement, enforcement, **Labor 107**
Supplemental reimbursement, enforcement, **Labor 107**
Labor and employment, personal care services, **Welf & I 14132.955**
Nursing homes,
Reimbursement, enforcement, **Labor 107**
Supplemental reimbursement, enforcement, **Labor 107**
Pediatric subacute units, supplemental reimbursement, enforcement, **Labor 107**
Reimbursement, pediatric subacute units, enforcement, **Labor 107**
Supplemental reimbursement,
Intermediate care facilities/developmentally disabled nursing facilities, enforcement, **Labor 107**
Nursing homes, enforcement, **Labor 107**
Pediatric subacute units, enforcement, **Labor 107**
Unemployment compensation, confidential or privileged information, disclosure, **Un Ins 1095**

MEDIATION
Agricultural labor and employment, **Labor 1164 et seq.**
Arbitration and Award, generally, this index
Fair employment and housing, boards and commissions, **Gov 12935**
Labor Disputes, this index
Military forces, national guard, state officers and employees, complaints, **Mil & V 395.6**
National guard, state officers and employees, complaints, **Mil & V 395.6**
State officers and employees, national guard, complaints, **Mil & V 395.6**

MEDICAID
Medi Cal Program, generally, this index

MEDICAL ASSISTANCE
Medi Cal Program, generally, this index

MEDICAL CARE AND TREATMENT
Acquired immune deficiency syndrome. AIDS, generally, this index
AIDS, generally, this index
Alcoholics and Alcoholism, this index
Assault and battery, community health care workers, records and recordation, **Labor 6332**
Cancer, generally, this index
Clinics, generally, this index
Confidential or privileged information. Medical Records, this index
Definitions, workers compensation, **Labor 3209.5**
Disability insurance. Insurance, this index
Diseases, generally, this index
Drug Addicts, generally, this index
Drugs and Medicine, generally, this index
Employment. Labor and employment, generally, post
Expenses and expenditures, contested claims, medical legal expenses, **Labor 4620 et seq.**
Fair Employment and Housing, generally, this index
Faith Healing, generally, this index
First Aid, generally, this index
Force and violence, community health care workers, records and recordation, **Labor 6332**
Group disability insurance. Insurance, this index
Health Care Providers, generally, this index
Health Care Service Plans, generally, this index
Health Facilities, generally, this index
Health insurance, disability insurance. Insurance, this index
Home Health Agencies, generally, this index
Hospitals, generally, this index
Housing. Fair Employment and Housing, generally, this index
Hypodermic Syringes and Needles, generally, this index
In home health care, assault and battery, records and recordation, **Labor 6332**
Information, definitions, investigative consumer reporting agencies, **CC 1786.2**
Labor and employment,
Lead related construction work, **Labor 6717**
Medical leave, **Gov 12945.2**
Notice, **Labor 2807**
Discontinuance, **Labor 2806**
Reports, employment related injuries or fatalities, **Labor 6409 et seq.**
Leave of absence, labor and employment, **Gov 12945.2**
Managed care. Health Care Service Plans, generally, this index
Manufacturers and manufacturing, first aid and services, **Labor 2440**
Narcotics. Drug Addicts, generally, this index

MEDICAL CARE AND TREATMENT—Cont'd
Physical Examinations, generally, this index
Prayer. Faith Healing, generally, this index
Primary care clinics. Clinics, this index
Public officers and employees, retraining and rehabilitation, **Labor 6206**
Records and recordation. Medical Records, generally, this index
Reports, employment related injuries or vitalities, **Labor 6409 et seq.**
Sterilization of persons. Birth Control, this index
Tissue Banks, generally, this index
Unemployment Compensation, this index
Workers Compensation, this index

MEDICAL CONDITION
Definitions, fair employment and housing department, **Gov 12926**

MEDICAL DIRECTOR
Definitions, workers compensation, **Labor 29**

MEDICAL EXAMINATIONS
Physical Examinations, generally, this index

MEDICAL EXAMINERS
Coroners, generally, this index

MEDICAL INSURANCE
Disability insurance. Insurance, this index

MEDICAL LEAVE
Definitions, **Gov 12945.2**
Labor and employment, **Gov 12945.2**

MEDICAL LEGAL EXPENSES
Definitions, workers compensation, contested claims, **Labor 4620**

MEDICAL PRACTICE ACT
Physicians and Surgeons, generally, this index

MEDICAL RECORDS
Actions and proceedings,
Disclosure, employers, **CC 56.20**
Negligence, release, **CC 56.36**
Arbitration, disclosure, **CC 56.10**
Attorney general, negligence, release, **CC 56.36**
Authorization. Release, post
Cancelling authorization, employers, **CC 56.24**
Children and Minors, this index
Comatose patients, information disclosure to government agencies, **CC 56.10**
Confidential or privileged information,
Consumer credit reporting agencies, **CC 1785.13**
Disability compensation, **Un Ins 2714**
Injuries to employees, **Labor 6412**
Mentally ill persons, outpatient psychotherapy, **CC 56.104**
Outpatient psychotherapy, **CC 56.104**

MEDICAL RECORDS—Cont'd
Conservators and Conservatorships, this
index
Coroners, disclosure, **CC 56.10**
Counties, attorneys, negligence, release,
CC 56.36
Crimes and offenses,
Disclosure, **CC 56.36**
Negligence, release, **CC 56.36**
Damages, negligence, release, **CC 56.36**
Destruction, **CC 56.101**
Disability insurance. Insurance, this index
Disaster relief organizations, disclosure,
CC 56.10
Disclosure, **CC 56.10 et seq.**
Employers, **CC 56.20 et seq.**
Mentally ill persons, outpatient psycho-
therapy, **CC 56.104**
Outpatient psychotherapy, **CC 56.104**
Diseases, this index
District attorneys, negligence, release, **CC
56.36**
Emergencies, disclosure, **CC 56.10**
Employee welfare benefit plans, disclo-
sure, **CC 56.10**
Employers, use and disclosure of medical
information, **CC 56.20 et seq.**
Evidence, disclosure, **CC 56.10**
Fines and penalties, negligence, release,
CC 56.36
Forms, release, employers, **CC 56.21**
Good faith compliance, unauthorized use,
CC 56.23
Employers, **CC 56.23**
Government agencies, information disclo-
sure, comatose patients, **CC 56.10**
Guardian and ward, determination of
need for guardianship, disclosure of
records, **CC 56.10**
Health Care Service Plans, this index
Insurance, this index
Labor and employment, disclosure, **CC
56.20 et seq.**
Mentally Ill Persons, this index
Modification, release authorization, em-
ployers, **CC 56.24**
Municipal attorneys, negligence, release,
CC 56.36
Negligence,
Disposal, **CC 56.101**
Release, **CC 56.36**
Nominal damages, negligence, release, **CC
56.36**
Notice, authorization, cancellation, **CC
56.24**
Orders of court, disclosure, **CC 56.10**
Outpatient psychotherapy, confidential or
privileged information, **CC 56.104**
Preemployment physical examination, mi-
nors, release, **CC 56.10**
Privileged information. Confidential or
privileged information, generally, ante
Privileges and immunities, release, **CC
56.36**
Production of books and papers, disclo-
sure, **CC 56.10**

MEDICAL RECORDS—Cont'd
Professional use, disclosure, **CC 56.10**
Psychotherapists and psychotherapy,
Confidential or privileged information,
CC 56.104
Disclosure, threats, **CC 56.10**
Release,
Authorization, **CC 56.10**
Disclosure to other persons, employ-
ers, **CC 56.245**
Cancelling, employers, **CC 56.24**
Disclosure to other parties, employers,
CC 56.23
Employers, **CC 56.20 et seq.**
Form, employers, **CC 56.21**
Mentally ill persons, outpatient psycho-
therapy, **CC 56.104**
Negligence, **CC 56.36**
Outpatient psychotherapy, **CC 56.104**
Search warrant, disclosure, **CC 56.10**
Subpoenas,
Disclosure, **CC 56.10**
Workers compensation, **Labor 4055.2**
Third parties, confidential or privileged
information, **CC 56.10**
Tissue banks, disclosure, **CC 56.10**
Workers Compensation, this index

MEDICINE
Drugs and Medicine, generally, this index

MEN
Construction of statutes, **Labor 12.1**

MENACE
Duress or Coercion, generally, this index

MENINGITIS
Workers Compensation, this index

MENTAL DISABILITY
Definitions, fair employment and housing,
Gov 12926

MENTAL EXAMINATIONS
Peace officers, weapons, surrender, exemptions, **CCP 527.9**

MENTAL HEALTH
Mentally Ill Persons, generally, this index

MENTAL INSTITUTION, ATASCADERO
Workers compensation, officers and employees, heart trouble, **Labor 3212.2**

MENTAL INSTITUTIONS
Mentally Ill Persons, generally, this index
Mentally Retarded and Developmentally
Disabled Persons, generally, this in-
dex

MENTALLY ILL PERSONS
Compensation and salaries, minimum
wages, **Labor 1191**
Confidential or privileged information,
medical records, **CC 56.104**
Definitions, mentally unable to make
claim, unemployment compensation,
Un Ins 2705.1

MENTALLY ILL PERSONS—Cont'd
Fair Employment and Housing, generally,
this index
Guardian and Ward, generally, this index
Health care service plans, confidential or
privileged information, records and
recordation, **CC 56.104**
Hospitals. State Hospitals, generally, this
index
Husband and wife, unemployment com-
pensation, claims, **Un Ins 2705.1**
Labor and employment, **Un Ins 9003**
Minimum wages, **Labor 1191**
Licenses and permits, labor and employ-
ment, minimum wages, **Labor 1191**
Medical records, confidential or privileged
information, **CC 56.104**
Minimum wages, **Labor 1191**
Outpatients, psychotherapy, medical rec-
ords, confidential or privileged infor-
mation, **CC 56.104**
Psychotherapists and Psychotherapy, gen-
erally, this index
Social Services, generally, this index
State Hospitals, generally, this index
Talent agencies, certificate of convenience
to conduct business, **Labor 1700.20a,
1700.20b**
Unemployment compensation,
Disability compensation, claims, **Un Ins
2705.1**
Payment, **Un Ins 1341**

**MENTALLY RETARDED AND DEVELOPMEN-
TALLY DISABLED PERSONS**
Committees, labor and employment, **Welf
& I 4868**
Compensation and salaries, minimum
wages, **Labor 1191**
Crimes and offenses. State Hospitals, this
index
Definitions, mentally unable to make a
claim, unemployment compensation,
disability benefits, **Un Ins 2705.1**
Employment, development, clients of de-
partment of rehabilitation, **Un Ins
9003**
Guardian and Ward, generally, this index
Hospitals. State Hospitals, generally, this
index
Labor and employment,
Committees, **Welf & I 4868**
Minimum wages, **Labor 1191**
Licenses and permits, labor and employ-
ment, minimum wages, **Labor 1191**
Minimum wages, **Labor 1191**
Motor vehicles. Paratransit Vehicles,
generally, this index
Paratransit Vehicles, generally, this index
Rates and charges,
Supported employment services, **Welf &
I 4865.1**
Work activity programs, post
Social Services, generally, this index
State Hospitals, generally, this index

MENTALLY RETARDED AND DEVELOPMENTALLY DISABLED PERSONS—Cont'd

Supported employment, work activity programs, rates and charges, **Welf & I 4865.1**

Talent agencies, certificate of convenience to conduct business, **Labor 1700.20a, 1700.20b**

Unemployment compensation benefits,
Disability compensation, claims, filing by spouse, **Un Ins 2705.1**
Payment, **Un Ins 1341**

Work activity programs,
Rates and charges, supported employment, **Welf & I 4865.1**
Supported employment, rates and charges, **Welf & I 4865.1**

Workers Compensation, this index

MERCHANDISE
Goods, Wares and Merchandise, generally, this index

MERCHANT MARINE
School officers and employees, noncertificated employees, restoration of position after service, **Mil & V 395.2**

MERCHANTS
Hawkers and Peddlers, generally, this index
Itinerant merchants. Hawkers and Peddlers, generally, this index
Stores, generally, this index

MERGER AND CONSOLIDATION
Corporations, this index
Limited Liability Companies, this index
Unemployment compensation, consolidation for hearing, **Un Ins 1951**

MERIT SYSTEM
Civil Service, generally, this index

MESSAGES
Telecommunications, generally, this index

MESSENGERS
Children and minors, employment, **Labor 1297**

METAL BARS
Weapons, generally, this index

METAL KNUCKLES
Weapons, generally, this index

METAL PIPES
Weapons, generally, this index

METAL PLATE WEAPONS
Weapons, generally, this index

METAL SHOPS
Health and sanitation, **Labor 2330, 2331**

METALS AND METAL PRODUCTS
Lead poisoning, occupational safety, programs, **Health & S 105185 et seq.**

METHYL CHLOROMETHYL ETHER
Occupational Carcinogens Control Act, **Labor 9000 et seq.**

MEXICO
Employment tax information, furnishing to Mexican officials, reciprocity, **Un Ins 1095**

MICHIGAN CALIFORNIA LUMBER COMPANY
Fire, unemployment caused by, extended benefits, **Un Ins 1281.7**

MIDWIVES
Unemployment compensation, certificates of disability, **Un Ins 2708**

MIGRANT AND SEASONAL FARMWORKER PROGRAMS
Housing, overcrowding, actions and proceedings, **Health & S 17043**

MILEAGE
Traveling Expenses, generally, this index

MILITARY BASES, RESERVATIONS AND AREAS
Closing, bank and corporations tax credit, **Rev & T 23622.7**
Corporation taxes,
Credits, **Rev & T 23645, 23646**
Deductions, **Rev & T 24416.2**
Firefighters and fire departments, workers compensation, cancer, **Labor 3212.1**
Workers compensation, firefighters and fire departments, cancer, **Labor 3212.1**

MILITARY DEPARTMENT
Military Forces, generally, this index

MILITARY FORCES
Absence and absentees, **Mil & V 395 et seq.**
Leaves of absence, generally, post
Air National Guard, unemployment compensation, excluded service, **Un Ins 634.5**
Attorney fees, employment discrimination actions, **Mil & V 394**
Bases. Military Bases, Reservations and Areas, generally, this index
Bosnia crisis, state officers and employees, compensation and benefits, **Mil & V 395.08**
Civil Service, this index
Closing. Military Bases, Reservations and Areas, this index
Crimes and offenses, discrimination, **Mil & V 394**
Damages, employment discrimination actions, **Mil & V 394**
Deductions, base recovery areas, net operating loss, **Rev & T 17276.2**
Definitions, withholding tax, wages, **Un Ins 13003**
Disability compensation, trainees in military service, **Un Ins 2765 et seq.**

MILITARY FORCES—Cont'd
Discharge, employee for membership, **Mil & V 394**
Discrimination, **Mil & V 394**
Drill instruction,
Hindering or preventing attendance, **Mil & V 394**
Leave of absence for military duty,
Private employees, **Mil & V 394.5**
Public employees, **Mil & V 395 et seq.**
Elected officers, resignation to enter military service, reentry into office on discharge, **Mil & V 395.3**
Employment. Labor and employment, generally, post
Encampments,
Hindering or preventing attendance, **Mil & V 394**
Leave of absence for military duty,
Private employees, **Mil & V 394.5**
Public employees, **Mil & V 395 et seq.**
Finance, discrimination, **Mil & V 394**
Firefighters and fire departments, workers compensation, **Labor 3365**
Hindering or preventing enlistment, **Mil & V 394**
Housing, discrimination, **Mil & V 394**
Husband and wife. Marriage, generally, post
Inactive duty training, leave of absence, public officers and employees, **Mil & V 395, 395.01**
Income tax—state,
Credits, **Rev & T 17053.46**
Definitions, withholding tax on wages, **Un Ins 13003**
Local agency military base recovery areas, credits, **Rev & T 17053.46**
Judges, this index
Labor and employment,
Discrimination, **Mil & V 394**
Leaves of absence, marriage, **Mil & V 395.10**
National guard, restoration, **Mil & V 395.06**
Leaves of absence,
Marriage, labor and employment, **Mil & V 395.10**
National guard, post
Private employees, **Mil & V 394.5**
Public employees, **Mil & V 395 et seq.**
Reserves, post
Legislators, resignation to enter military service, reentry into office on discharge, **Mil & V 395.3**
Loans, discrimination, **Mil & V 394**
Local agency military base recovery areas, income tax—state, credits, **Rev & T 17053.46**
Marriage,
Leaves of absence, labor and employment, **Mil & V 395.10**
National guard, leaves of absence, labor and employment, **Mil & V 395.10**
Reserves, leaves of absence, labor and employment, **Mil & V 395.10**

MILITARY FORCES—Cont'd

Mediation, national guard, state officers and employees, complaints, **Mil & V 395.6**

Municipal attorneys, national guard, labor and employment, restoration, **Mil & V 395.06**

National guard,
Absence, leave, **Mil & V 394 et seq.**
Bosnia crisis, state officers and employees, compensation and benefits, **Mil & V 395.08**
Civil Service, this index
Discrimination, **Mil & V 394**
Labor and employment,
Leaves of absence, husband and wife, **Mil & V 395.10**
Restoration, **Mil & V 395.06**
Leaves of absence, **Mil & V 394 et seq.**
Marriage, labor and employment, **Mil & V 395.10**
Marriage, leaves of absence, labor and employment, **Mil & V 395.10**
Mediation, state officers and employees, complaints, **Mil & V 395.6**
Municipal attorneys, labor and employment, restoration, **Mil & V 395.06**
State Officers and Employees, this index
Unemployment compensation, **Un Ins 1252, 1279**
Excluded service, **Un Ins 634.5**
Naval cruises, leave of absence for military duty,
Private employees, **Mil & V 394.5**
Public employees, **Mil & V 395 et seq.**
Naval militia,
Absence, leave, **Mil & V 394.5 et seq.**
Leaves of absence, **Mil & V 394.5**
Privileges and immunities,
Public officers, absence in military service, rights, **Mil & V 395.1 et seq.**
Reentry into public office or employment, **Mil & V 395.3**
Public Officers and Employees, this index
Public policy, labor and employment, civilian workforce, **Un Ins 2054**
Rates and charges, loans, discrimination, **Mil & V 394**
Reserves,
Bosnia crisis, state officers and employees, compensation and benefits, **Mil & V 395.08**
Labor and employment, leaves of absence, husband and wife, **Mil & V 395.10**
Leaves of absence, **Mil & V 394.5 et seq.**
Marriage, labor and employment, **Mil & V 395.10**
Marriage, leaves of absence, labor and employment, **Mil & V 395.10**
Mediation, state officers and employees, complaints, **Mil & V 395.6**
State military reserve, generally, post
State officers and employees, mediation, complaints, **Mil & V 395.6**

MILITARY FORCES—Cont'd

Reserves—Cont'd
Unemployment compensation, **Un Ins 1252, 1279**
School Officers and Employees, this index
Soldiers and Sailors Relief Act, **Mil & V 395.1**
Spouse. Marriage, generally, ante
State military reserve,
Absence, leave, **Mil & V 394.5 et seq.**
Labor and employment, leave of absence, military duty, **Mil & V 395.9**
Leaves of absence, regular employment, military training, **Mil & V 395.9**
State Officers and Employees, this index
Taxation. Income tax—state, generally, ante
Theaters and Shows, this index
Unemployment Compensation, this index
Veterans, generally, this index
Wife. Marriage, generally, ante
Workers compensation,
Fire suppressing, **Labor 3365**
Subsequent injuries after preexisting service disability or impairment, **Labor 4753**

MILITARY OR NAVAL FORCES

Definitions, withholding tax on wages, **Un Ins 13003**

MILITARY RESERVATIONS

Military Bases, Reservations and Areas, generally, this index

MILLER COLLIER ACT

Extended unemployment compensation, **Un Ins 3501 et seq.**

MILLS

Manufacturers and Manufacturing, generally, this index

MINE TELEPHONE LAW

Generally, **Labor 7500, 7501**

MINERAL, OIL AND GAS BROKERS

Unemployment compensation, **Un Ins 650**

MINES AND MINERALS

Access shaft, **Labor 7964**
Alternate escape routes, extrahazardous tunnels, **Labor 7981**
Asbestos, generally, this index
Chemists, **Labor 7954**
Children and minors, employment, **Labor 1294**
Classification, **Labor 7955**
Coal and Coal Mines, generally, this index
Communication systems, **Labor 7963**
Compensation, labor, payment, **Labor 270 et seq.**
Crimes and offenses,
Availability of funds, payment of wages, **Labor 270**
Explosives safety violations, **Labor 8003**
Hours of labor, **Labor 752**
Underground telephones, installation or maintenance, **Labor 7501**

MINES AND MINERALS—Cont'd

Cutoff, electrical equipment power, gassy tunnels, **Labor 7975**
Definitions, tunnel and mine safety, **Labor 7951**
Diesel engines, labor permits, **Labor 6500**
Electrical lighting and power, review of plans, gassy mines, **Labor 7969**
Escape chamber, extrahazardous tunnels, **Labor 7981**
Excess gas level, removal of men, **Labor 7972**
Explosives, licenses and permits, **Labor 7990 et seq.**
Extrahazardous tunnels, safety regulations, **Labor 7977 et seq.**
Fines and penalties, hours of labor, **Labor 752**
Fire extinguishers, gassy tunnels, **Labor 7976**
Gassy mines,
Excessive gas readings, **Labor 7961**
Testing prior to each shift, **Labor 7960**
Gassy tunnels, safety regulations, **Labor 7965 et seq.**
Geologists and Geophysicists, generally, this index
Hours of labor, **Labor 750 et seq.**
Ignition of gas or labor, **Labor 7971**
Industrial hygiene engineer, **Labor 7954**
Inspection and inspectors, **Labor 7953**
Labor, compensation, payment, **Labor 270, 272**
Laboratories, **Labor 7954**
Lead, generally, this index
Licenses and permits, explosives, **Labor 7990 et seq.**
Miners Eight Hour Day Law, **Labor 750 et seq.**
Notice, gassy mines, excess gas levels, **Labor 7967**
Oil and Gas, generally, this index
Posting, classifications, orders or rules, **Labor 7956**
Practice sessions, rescue, **Labor 7959**
Prejob safety conference, **Labor 7955**
Rescue, **Labor 7957 et seq.**
Safety in employment, underground telephones, **Labor 7500, 7501**
Safety regulations, **Labor 7950 et seq.**
Shutdown for testing, gassy mines, **Labor 7968**
Silicosis sufferers, workers compensation, **Labor 5500.5**
Smoking, gassy tunnels, **Labor 7970**
Special orders, gassy tunnels, **Labor 7973**
Telephones, underground telephones, **Labor 7500, 7501**
Tunnel and Mine Safety Act, **Labor 7950 et seq.**
Underground telephones, **Labor 7500, 7501**
Ventilation, gassy tunnels, **Labor 7974**
Workers compensation, silicosis sufferers, **Labor 5500.5**
Zoning and Planning, generally, this index

MINIMUM WAGES
Generally, **Const. Art. 14, § 1; Labor 1171 et seq.**
Compensation and Salaries, this index
Definitions,
Corporation taxes, enterprise zones, credits, **Rev & T 23634**
Enterprise zones, income tax—state, credits, **Rev & T 17053.34**
Manufacturing enhancement areas, **Rev & T 17053.47**
Local agency military base recovery areas, income tax credits, **Rev & T 17053.46**
Military base recovery areas, corporation taxes, credits, **Rev & T 23646**

MINISTERS
Clergy, generally, this index

MINORITY, WOMEN, OR DISABLED VETERAN BUSINESSES
Contracts, employment training programs, **Un Ins 10205**

MINORITY GROUPS
Apprentices, **Labor 3071**
Participation, **Labor 3073.3**

MINORS
Children and Minors, generally, this index

MISBRANDED
Brands, Marks and Labels, generally, this index

MISCELLANEOUS PAYROLL PERIOD
Definitions, withholding tax on wages, **Un Ins 13007**

MISCREANT CHILDREN
Juvenile Delinquents and Dependents, generally, this index

MISDEMEANORS
Crimes and Offenses, generally, this index

MISREPRESENTATION
Fraud, generally, this index

MIXTURES
Definitions, hazardous substances information and training, **Labor 6373**

MOBILE DWELLINGS
Mobilehomes and Mobilehome Parks, generally, this index

MOBILE INTERNAL COMBUSTION ENGINES
Generally, **Labor 6701 et seq.**

MOBILE TOWER CRANE
Definitions, regulation, **Labor 7371**

MOBILE VANS
Outpatient settings. Clinics, this index

MOBILEHOMES AND MOBILEHOME PARKS
Agricultural labor and employment, **Health & S 17021.7**
Sheepherders, **Labor 2695.2**

MOBILEHOMES AND MOBILEHOME PARKS—Cont'd
Employee housing, **Health & S 17000 et seq.**
Labor camps, employee housing, **Health & S 17000 et seq.**
Sheepherders, housing, **Labor 2695.2**

MODELS
Advance fees, talent services, **Labor 1702 et seq.**
Children and minors, employment, **Labor 1294.3**
Talent services, fees, **Labor 1701 et seq.**

MODERATE INCOME HOUSING
Low and moderate income housing. Housing, this index

MODIFICATION OR CHANGE
Workers compensation, medical care and treatment, authorization, **Labor 4610.3**

MONEY
Construction funds, wrongful diversion, **Pen 484b**
Executions, this index
Larceny by fraud, **Pen 484**

MONOPOLIES AND UNFAIR TRADE
Access for infants and mothers program, health services, **Ins 12698.50 et seq.**
Employment agencies, **CC 1812.5095**
Insurance, this index

MOORE BROWN ROBERTI FAMILY RIGHTS ACT
Generally, **Gov 12945.1, 12945.2**

MORALS
Labor and employment, hours and working conditions, **Labor 1178**
Lewdness and Obscenity, generally, this index

MORPHINE
Drug Addicts, generally, this index

MORTGAGE BROKERS AND LENDERS
Originators. Mortgages, this index
Residential mortgage lenders. Mortgages, this index

MORTGAGES
Brokers. Originators, generally, post
Credit scores, notice, **CC 1785.15.1, 1785.15.2**
Discrimination, **Gov 12955 et seq.**
Good faith purchasers, discriminatory clauses or covenants, **Gov 12995**
Fraud,
Originators, post
Residential mortgage lenders, post
Licenses and permits,
Originators, post
Residential mortgage lenders, post
Notice,
Credit scores, **CC 1785.15.1, 1785.15.2**
Risk scores, **CC 1785.15.1, 1785.15.2**

MORTGAGES—Cont'd
Originators,
Fraud, licenses and permits, revocation or suspension, **Fin 22168**
Licenses and permits, revocation or suspension, fraud, **Fin 22168**
Revocation or suspension, licenses and permits, fraud, **Fin 22168**
Real estate brokers and salespersons. Originators, generally, ante
Residential mortgage lenders,
Fraud, licenses and permits, revocation or suspension, **Fin 50511**
Licenses and permits, revocation or suspension, fraud, **Fin 50511**
Originators, generally, ante
Revocation or suspension. Originators, ante
Risk scores, notice, **CC 1785.15.1, 1785.15.2**

MOSQUES
Religious Organizations and Societies, generally, this index

MOTELS AND MOTOR COURTS
Civil Rights Act, **CC 51 et seq.**
Employee housing, **Health & S 17000 et seq.**
Exemptions, workplace smoking regulation, **Labor 6404.5**
Rules and regulations, workplace smoking regulation, exemptions, **Labor 6404.5**
Sex discrimination, **CC 51 et seq.**
Smoking in workplace regulation, exemptions, **Labor 6404.5**
Trespass, **Pen 602**
Workplace smoking regulation, exemptions, **Labor 6404.5**

MOTHER AND CHILD
Children and Minors, generally, this index

MOTION PICTURE ENGAGEMENT
Definitions, talent agencies, **Labor 1700.1**

MOTION PICTURES
Advance fees, talent services, **Labor 1702 et seq.**
Business and commerce, reports, **Un Ins 335**
Certificates and certification, children and minors, labor and employment, **Labor 1308.8**
Child labor, hours of employment, **Labor 1308.7**
Children and minors,
Employment contracts, **Labor 1700.37**
Labor and employment, **Labor 1308.8**
Compensation and salaries,
Discharge or layoff, payment, **Labor 201.5**
Payment, **Labor 201.5**
Talent services, **Labor 1701 et seq.**
Termination, payment, **Labor 201.5**
Contracts, talent services, fees, **Labor 1701 et seq.**

MOTION PICTURES—Cont'd

Crimes and offenses, child labor, **Labor 1308.8**

Hours, **Labor 1308.7**

Directors, talent services, fees, **Labor 1701 et seq.**

Discharge, labor and employment, compensation and salaries, payment, **Labor 201.5**

Employment. Labor and employment, generally, post

Exemptions, labor and employment, meals, time, **Labor 512**

Fees, talent services, **Labor 1701 et seq.**

Fines and penalties, child labor, **Labor 1308.8**

Labor and employment,
Children and minors, **Labor 1308.8**
Compensation and salaries, generally, ante
Dangerous occupations, licenses and permits, **Labor 6500**
Exemptions, meals, time, **Labor 512**
Reports, **Un Ins 335**

Layoffs, compensation and salaries, payment, **Labor 201.5**

Lewdness and Obscenity, generally, this index

Licenses and permits, dangerous occupations, **Labor 6500**

Obscenity. Lewdness and Obscenity, generally, this index

Physicians and surgeons, children and minors, labor and employment, certificates, **Labor 1308.8**

Pornography. Lewdness and Obscenity, generally, this index

Reports, labor and employment, **Un Ins 335**

Resignation, labor and employment, compensation and salaries, payment, **Labor 201.5**

Sanitary standards, **Labor 2260**

Talent Agencies, generally, this index

Termination, labor and employment, compensation and salaries, payment, **Labor 201.5**

Unemployment Compensation, this index

MOTIONS

Discovery, this index

Garnishment, equitable division, **CCP 706.052**

Labor and employment, orders, working conditions, **Labor 1184**

Support, this index

MOTOR CARRIERS

Air pressure tanks, inspection and safety regulation, **Labor 7624**

Boilers, inspection and safety regulation, **Labor 7624**

Buses, generally, this index

Cabs of trucks, workplace smoking regulation, exemption, **Labor 6404.5**

MOTOR CARRIERS—Cont'd

Cargo tanks,
Gasoline, vapor emission tests, climbing upon tank, **Labor 6718**
Vapor emission tests, climbing upon tank, **Labor 6718**

Consolidated cities and counties, officers and employees, meals, collective bargaining, **Labor 512.5**

County officers and employees, meals, collective bargaining, **Labor 512.5**

Explosives, generally, this index

Gasoline cargo vehicles, vapor controls, climbing upon tank, **Labor 6718**

Licenses and permits, farm labor contractors, **Labor 1696.2**

Liquefied petroleum gas storage tanks, inspection and safety regulation, **Labor 7624**

Municipal officers and employees, meals, collective bargaining, **Labor 512.5**

Officers and employees,
Meals, time, collective bargaining, **Labor 512.5**
Rest periods, collective bargaining, **Labor 512.5**

Rules and regulations, workplace smoking regulation, exemption, truck cabs, **Labor 6404.5**

Smoking, exemptions, **Labor 6404.5**

Special districts, officers and employees, meals, collective bargaining, **Labor 512.5**

State officers and employees, meals, collective bargaining, **Labor 512.5**

Tests, cargo tank vehicles, vapor emission tests, climbing upon tank, **Labor 6718**

Vapor controls, gasoline cargo vehicles, climbing upon tank, **Labor 6718**

Workers compensation,
Judgments and decrees, **Labor 3716.4**
Stop orders, **Labor 3710.3**

Workplace smoking regulation, exemption, truck cabs, **Labor 6404.5**

MOTOR COURTS

Motels and Motor Courts, generally, this index

MOTOR VEHICLE INSURANCE

Agricultural employment, farm labor contractors, **Labor 1695**

Farm labor contractors, **Labor 1695, 1696.4**

MOTOR VEHICLE SERVICE STATIONS

Children and minors, employment, **Labor 1294, 1294.5**

Lead poisoning, occupational safety, programs, **Health & S 105185 et seq.**

Restrictions, work performable by children and minors, **Labor 1294.5**

MOTOR VEHICLES

Accidents, reports, disclosure, information practices, **CC 1798 et seq.**

Aged persons. Paratransit Vehicles, generally, this index

MOTOR VEHICLES—Cont'd

Agricultural Labor and Employment, this index

Air pressure tanks, inspection and safety regulation, **Labor 7624**

Appearance. Drivers licenses, post

Boilers, inspection and safety regulation, **Labor 7625**

Buses, generally, this index

Car Washes, generally, this index

Carriers. Motor Carriers, generally, this index

Chauffeurs licenses. Drivers licenses, generally, post

Children and minors, employment in operation, **Labor 1294**

Commercial vehicles,
Consolidated cities and counties, officers and employees, meals, collective bargaining, **Labor 512.5**
County officers and employees, meals, collective bargaining, **Labor 512.5**
Fines and penalties,
Out of service orders, **Veh 15311.1**
Railroad crossings, **Veh 15312.1**
Labor and employment, meals, time, collective bargaining, **Labor 512.5**
Municipal officers and employees, meals, collective bargaining, **Labor 512.5**
Officers and employees, meals, time, collective bargaining, **Labor 512.5**
Out of service orders, fines and penalties, **Veh 15311.1**
Railroad crossings, fines and penalties, **Veh 15312.1**
Special districts, officers and employees, meals, collective bargaining, **Labor 512.5**
State officers and employees, meals, collective bargaining, **Labor 512.5**

Common carriers. Motor Carriers, generally, this index

Dealers,
Commission wages of employees, payment, **Labor 204.1**
Employees, payment of commission wages, time, **Labor 204.1**

Drivers licenses,
Farm labor contractors, **Labor 1696.3**
Identity and identification, domestic partnership, **Fam 298.6**
Physical examination, condition of employment, expense, **Labor 231**

Evidence, presumptions, theft by fraud, **Pen 484**

Fines and penalties. Commercial vehicles, ante

Gas stations. Motor Vehicle Service Stations, generally, this index

Gasoline stations. Motor Vehicle Service Stations, generally, this index

Handicapped persons. Paratransit Vehicles, generally, this index

Identity and identification. Drivers licenses, ante

MOTOR VEHICLES—Cont'd

Insurance. Motor Vehicle Insurance, generally, this index

Leases, theft, fraud, **Pen 484**

Liability insurance. Motor Vehicle Insurance, generally, this index

Licenses and permits,
Agricultural employment, farm labor contractors, **Labor 1696.2**
Drivers licenses, generally, ante
Farm labor contractors, **Labor 1696.2**

Malicious mischief, trespass with vehicle, **Pen 602**

Motels and Motor Courts, generally, this index

Motor Vehicle Insurance, generally, this index

Operators licenses. Drivers licenses, generally, ante

Out of service orders, commercial vehicles, fines and penalties, **Veh 15311.1**

Paratransit Vehicles, generally, this index

Polishing. Car Washes, generally, this index

Presumptions. Evidence, ante

Process, service of process, trespass, exemptions, **Pen 602**

Railroad crossings. Commercial vehicles, ante

Real Estate, this index

Registration,
Agricultural employment, farm labor contractors, **Labor 1696.4**
Farm labor contractors, **Labor 1696.4**

Repair shops. Motor Vehicle Service Stations, generally, this index

Repairs, occupational lead poisoning, hazardous substances and waste, **Health & S 105185 et seq.**

Reports. Accidents, ante

Semitrailers. Motor Carriers, generally, this index

Service of process. Process, ante

Service stations. Motor Vehicle Service Stations, generally, this index

Theft. Leases, ante

Tractors, truck tractors. Motor Carriers, generally, this index

Trailers, generally, this index

Trespass, **Pen 602**

Washing. Car Washes, generally, this index

MOTORBOATS

Boats and Boating, generally, this index

MOTORS

Engines, generally, this index

MOVING PICTURES

Motion Pictures, generally, this index

MOVING WALKS

Elevators, Dumbwaiters and Escalators, generally, this index

MSDS

Definitions, hazardous substances information and training, **Labor 6374**

Labor and Employment, this index

MUCK

Definitions, tunnel and mine safety, **Labor 7951**

MULTIFAMILY HOUSING

Housing, this index

MULTIPLE DWELLINGS

Apartment Houses, generally, this index

Condominiums, generally, this index

MULTIPLE LISTINGS

Discrimination, **Gov 12955 et seq.**

MUNICIPAL AND JUSTICE COURT ACT

Municipal Courts, generally, this index

MUNICIPAL ATTORNEYS

Civil rights actions, **CC 52**

Medical records, negligence, release, **CC 56.36**

National guard, labor and employment, restoration, **Mil & V 395.06**

Workers compensation, actions, securing payment of compensation, **Labor 3712**

MUNICIPAL BONDS

Investments, unemployment insurance disability fund, **Un Ins 3003**

Unemployment insurance disability fund, investment, **Un Ins 3003**

MUNICIPAL BUILDINGS AND GROUNDS

Permits, workers compensation, certificates, **Labor 3800**

MUNICIPAL CLERKS

Deputies, workers compensation, exclusion, **Labor 3352**

Workers compensation, deputies, exclusion, **Labor 3352**

MUNICIPAL CORPORATIONS

Municipalities, generally, this index

MUNICIPAL COURTS

Claims courts. Small Claims Courts, generally, this index

Marshals,
Death in line of duty, dependents, scholarships, **Labor 4709**
Dependents, scholarships, **Labor 4709**
Handicapped persons, disability in line of duty, dependents, scholarships, **Labor 4709**
Scholarships, dependents, **Labor 4709**

Small Claims Courts, generally, this index

Subpoenas, generally, this index

MUNICIPAL EMPLOYEES

Municipal Officers and Employees, generally, this index

MUNICIPAL OFFICERS AND EMPLOYEES

Application of law, illegal acts, temporary appointments, absentee in military service, **Mil & V 395.8**

Attorneys. Municipal Attorneys, generally, this index

Children and minors, sick leave, **Labor 233**
Violations, **Labor 234**

Commercial vehicles, meals, collective bargaining, **Labor 512.5**

Compensation and salaries,
Application of law, **Labor 220**
Itemized statement, deductions, application of law, **Labor 226**
Leave of absence for military duty, **Mil & V 395.01 et seq.**
Minimum wages, **Labor 1205**
Unemployment compensation, voluntary plans, **Un Ins 710**

Crimes and offenses, meals, time off duty to procure, failure to provide for, **Labor 1901**

Elevator inspectors, **Labor 7310**

Family members, sick leave, **Labor 233**
Violations, **Labor 234**

Firefighters and Fire Departments, generally, this index

Food, meals, time off duty to procure, **Labor 1900, 1901**

Hours of labor, **Labor 1205**

Husband and wife, sick leave, **Labor 233**
Violations, **Labor 234**

Leave of absence, military duty, **Mil & V 395 et seq.**

Legal advisor. Municipal Attorneys, generally, this index

Lie detector tests, condition of employment, **Labor 432.2**

Lunches, time off duty to procure, **Labor 1900, 1901**

Marriage, sick leave, **Labor 233**
Violations, **Labor 234**

Marshals. Municipal Courts, this index

Meals,
Motor carriers, collective bargaining, **Labor 512.5**
Time off duty to procure, **Labor 1900, 1901**

Military forces, discrimination, **Mil & V 394**

Minimum wages, **Labor 1205**

Motor carriers, meals, collective bargaining, **Labor 512.5**

Parents, sick leave, **Labor 233**
Violations, **Labor 234**

Police, generally, this index

Polygraph tests, condition of employment, **Labor 432.2**

Resignations, military service entry, reentry into office or employment on discharge, **Mil & V 395.3**

Rest periods, motor carriers, collective bargaining, **Labor 512.5**

Salaries. Compensation and salaries, generally, ante

MUNICIPAL OFFICERS AND EMPLOYEES
—Cont'd
Sick leave, family members, **Labor 233**
Violations, **Labor 234**
Spouse, sick leave, **Labor 233**
Violations, **Labor 234**
Standards, labor and employment, **Labor 1205**
Temporary appointment, absentee in military service, **Mil & V 395.8**
Unemployment compensation,
Elective coverage, **Un Ins 709**
Voluntary plans, **Un Ins 709, 710**
Wages. Compensation and salaries, generally, ante
Workers compensation,
Rehabilitation plans, volunteering, **Labor 6208**
Self insurers, medical and related treatment and supplies, former employees, **Labor 4606**
Service of notices, orders, **Labor 5317**

MUNICIPALITIES
Airports and Landing Fields, generally, this index
Amusement rides, safety, **Labor 7900 et seq.**
Attorneys. Municipal Attorneys, generally, this index
Business and commerce, licenses and permits, exemptions, **Bus & P 16300**
Cable Television, generally, this index
Cemeteries and Dead Bodies, generally, this index
Chartered cities,
Business and commerce, licenses and permits, exemptions, **Bus & P 16300**
Licenses and permits, business and commerce, exemptions, **Bus & P 16300**
Civil defense. War and Civil Defense, generally, this index
Comfort Stations and Rest Rooms, generally, this index
Consolidated Cities and Counties, generally, this index
Courts. Municipal Courts, generally, this index
Definitions, unemployment insurance code, **Un Ins 13**
Docks. Wharves, Docks and Piers, generally, this index
Elevator inspection, **Labor 7310**
Employees. Municipal Officers and Employees, generally, this index
Employment compensation, employer, definitions, **Un Ins 677**
Enterprise Zones, generally, this index
Exemptions, business and commerce, licenses and permits, **Bus & P 16300**
Fair employment and housing department, liaison, powers and duties, **Gov 12933**
Fees, business and commerce, registration, exemptions, **Bus & P 16300**
Firefighters and Fire Departments, generally, this index

MUNICIPALITIES—Cont'd
Fires and Fire Protection, generally, this index
Health Facilities, generally, this index
Housing, generally, this index
Improvements, generally, this index
Indigent Persons, generally, this index
Inspection and inspectors, elevators, **Labor 7310**
Jails, generally, this index
Labor and employment. Municipal Officers and Employees, generally, this index
Labor camps,
Application of law, **Health & S 17024**
Enforcement of laws and regulations, **Health & S 17050**
Landing fields. Airports and Landing Fields, generally, this index
Licenses and permits, business and commerce, exemptions, **Bus & P 16300**
Local Agencies, generally, this index
Los Angeles, generally, this index
Low and moderate income housing. Housing, this index
Municipal Officers and Employees, generally, this index
National defense. War and Civil Defense, generally, this index
Officers and employees. Municipal Officers and Employees, generally, this index
Peace Officers, generally, this index
Piers. Wharves, Docks and Piers, generally, this index
Planning. Zoning and Planning, generally, this index
Police, generally, this index
Recreation and Park Districts, generally, this index
Registration, business and commerce, fees, exemptions, **Bus & P 16300**
Schools and School Districts, generally, this index
Screening, prospective concessionaires, application of law, **Labor 432.7**
Sewers and Sewer Systems, generally, this index
Tax Collection, generally, this index
Taxation, generally, this index
Tuberculosis, generally, this index
War and Civil Defense, generally, this index
Water Supply, generally, this index
Wharves, Docks and Piers, generally, this index
Zoning and Planning, generally, this index

MUNICIPALLY OWNED UTILITIES
Sewers and Sewer Systems, generally, this index
Water Supply, generally, this index

MURDER
Homicide, generally, this index

MUSIC AND MUSICIANS
Advance fees, talent services, **Labor 1702 et seq.**
Compensation and salaries, talent services, **Labor 1701 et seq.**
Contracts, talent services, fees, **Labor 1701 et seq.**
Equipment, employers, security, **Labor 2800.1**
Fees, talent services, **Labor 1701 et seq.**
Talent Agencies, generally, this index

MUSICAL INSTRUMENTS
Children and minors, encouraging playing, **Labor 1308**
Security, employers, **Labor 2800.1**

MUTE PERSONS
Deaf and Mute Persons, generally, this index

MUTUAL BENEFIT CORPORATIONS
Self insurers security fund, workers compensation, **Labor 3740 et seq.**

N NITROSODIMETHYLAMINE
Occupational Carcinogens Control Act, **Labor 9000 et seq.**

NAMES
Change of name. Domestic Partnership, this index
Domestic Partnership, this index
Earnings withholding orders, applications, **CCP 706.121**
Employment Agencies, this index
Garnishment, applications, **CCP 706.121 et seq.**
Labor and employment, records, **Labor 1174**
Signatures, generally, this index
Solicitation, employees, representation, **Labor 973**
Trademarks, generally, this index
Workers Compensation, this index
Youthbuild program, restrictions, **Un Ins 9808**

NARCOTIC ADDICTS
Drug Addicts, generally, this index

NARCOTICS
Drugs and Medicine, generally, this index

NARCOTICS ENFORCEMENT DIVISION
Justice Department, this index

NATIONAL DEFENSE
War and Civil Defense, generally, this index

NATIONAL GUARD
Military Forces, this index

NATIONALITY
Discrimination, generally, this index

NATURAL GAS
Oil and Gas, generally, this index

NATURAL RESOURCES AGENCY
Forestry and Fire Protection Department, generally, this index

NAVAL CRUISES
Military Forces, this index

NAVAL MILITIA
Military Forces, this index

NAVIGATION
Ships and Shipping, generally, this index

NAVY
Military Forces, generally, this index

NECESSARIES
Assignment of wages, **Labor 300**
Employer guaranteeing payment of employees bills, **Labor 213**

NEEDLES
Hypodermic Syringes and Needles, generally, this index

NEEDY CHILDREN
Social Services, generally, this index

NEGLECT OF DUTY
Termination of employment, **Labor 2924**

NEGLECTED CHILDREN
Juvenile Delinquents and Dependents, generally, this index

NEGLIGENCE
AIDS, blood tests, results disclosure, **Health & S 120980**
Boiler operation, **Labor 7770, 7771**
Contributory negligence,
  Obligations of employer, **Labor 2801**
  Presumption, action for injury or death of employee, **Labor 2801**
  Workers compensation, defense abolished, **Labor 3708**
Death. Wrongful Death, generally, this index
Gross negligence, steam boiler operation, **Labor 7770**
Health care service plans, medical records, **CC 56.36, 56.101**
Indemnity, generally, this index
Labor and Employment, this index
Medical records,
  Disposal, **CC 56.101**
  Release, **CC 56.36**
Steam boiler operation, **Labor 7770, 7771**
Workers Compensation, this index
Wrongful Death, generally, this index

NEGOTIABLE INSTRUMENTS
Bad checks,
  Building and construction industry, payment of wages or fringe benefits, **Labor 203.1**
  Wages, payment, **Labor 212**
Checks,
  Building and construction industry, payment of wages or fringe benefits with bad checks, **Labor 203.1**

NEGOTIABLE INSTRUMENTS—Cont'd
Checks—Cont'd
  Unemployment compensation, imprint, **Un Ins 1339**
  Workers compensation payments, **Labor 4651**
Compensation and salaries, issuance in payment to employees, **Labor 212**
Dishonor,
  Evidence, instrument issued in payment of wages, **Labor 212**
  Protests, instrument issued in payment of wages, evidence, **Labor 212**
Labor and employment,
  Compensation, payment, **Labor 212**
  Property put up by employee as part of employment contract, **Labor 406**
Workers compensation, payments, **Labor 4651**

NEGOTIATION
Labor, terms and conditions, public policy, **Labor 923**

NET BALANCE OF RESERVE
Definitions, unemployment compensation, **Un Ins 904**

NET LOSS
Definitions,
  Corporation taxes, net operating losses, **Rev & T 24416**
  Income tax—state, net operating losses, **Rev & T 17276**

NETWORKS
Labor and employment, statewide young worker health and safety resource network, **Labor 6359**
Statewide young worker health and safety resource network, **Labor 6359**
Telecommunications, generally, this index

NEW AND FURTHER DISABILITY ACT
Workers compensation, **Labor 5410**

NEW BUSINESS
Definitions, corporation taxes, net operating losses, **Rev & T 24416**

NEW HIRE TRAINING
Definitions, employment training panel, **Un Ins 10201**

NEW TRIAL
Evidence, newly discovered evidence, workers compensation, petition for reconsideration, **Labor 5903**
Wearing apparel, manufacturers,
  Arbitration, **Labor 2691**
  Penalties or confiscation, **Labor 2681**
Workers compensation, **Labor 5952**

NEWBORN CHILDREN
Children and Minors, generally, this index

NEWLY DISCOVERED EVIDENCE
New trial, workers compensation, petition for reconsideration, **Labor 5903**

NEWSBOYS
Children and minors, employment, **Labor 1294.4**
Sale or distribution of newspapers, **Labor 1298**
Unemployment compensation, **Un Ins 649**

NEWSPAPERS
Advertisements, generally, this index
Children and minors, sale or distribution, **Labor 1298**
Employment agencies, advertising, misrepresentations, earnings of salesmen, brokers or agents, **Labor 976**
Independent contractors, workers compensation, elective coverage, **Labor 4157**
Libel and Slander, generally, this index
Notice, generally, this index
Publication, generally, this index
Solicitation of employees, representation, **Labor 973**
Unemployment compensation, delivery by minors, **Un Ins 634.5, 649**
Workers compensation,
  Advertisements, disclosures, **Labor 5432, 5433**
  Independent contractors, elective coverage, **Labor 4157**

NIGHT SCHOOLS
Schoolteachers, retirement and pensions. Schoolteachers Retirement System, generally, this index

NITROGLYCERINE
Explosives, generally, this index

NOLO CONTENDERE
Unemployment Compensation, this index

NOMINAL DAMAGES
Damages, this index

NONCITIZENS
Aliens, generally, this index

NONCORE COVERAGE
Definitions, Cal COBRA, accident and health insurance, **Health & S 1366.21; Ins 10128.51**

NONPROFIT ASSOCIATIONS
Unemployment compensation, **Un Ins 608, 652, 702.1, 711 et seq.**
  Contributions, **Un Ins 801, 803**
  Definitions, **Un Ins 702.1**
  Elective coverage, **Un Ins 702.1**
  Eligibility, **Un Ins 1253.3**

NONPROFIT CHARITABLE ORGANIZATIONS
Charities, generally, this index
Nonprofit Organizations, generally, this index

NONPROFIT CORPORATIONS
Charities, generally, this index
Credit Unions, generally, this index

NONPROFIT CORPORATIONS—Cont'd
Employment agencies, application of law, **CC 1812.502**
Fair employment and housing, **Gov 12940**
Farm labor contractors, application of law, **Labor 1682.5**
Foundations, generally, this index
Religious Organizations and Societies, generally, this index
Self insurers security fund, workers compensation, **Labor 3740 et seq.**
Sponsor of sentenced person, workers compensation, **Labor 3301**
Talent agencies, advance fees, exemptions, **Labor 1702.4**
Unemployment Compensation, this index

NONPROFIT ORGANIZATIONS
Definitions, unemployment compensation, **Un Ins 711**
Housing discrimination, religious organizations or societies, **Gov 12955.4**
Religious Organizations and Societies, generally, this index
Sponsor of sentenced persons, workers compensation, **Labor 3301**
Unemployment Compensation, this index
Voluntary service without pay, definitions, workers compensation, **Labor 3363.6**
Volunteer employees, workers compensation, **Labor 3363.6**
    Exclusions, **Labor 3352**
Workers compensation, **Labor 3352**
    Amateur athletic officiating services, **Labor 3352, 3706.5**
    Sponsor of sentenced persons, **Labor 3301**
    Sports officials, exemption, **Labor 3352**
    Volunteer employees, coverage, **Labor 3363.6**
        Exclusion, **Labor 3352**

NONPROFIT RELIGIOUS CORPORATIONS
Religious Organizations and Societies, generally, this index

NONPUBLIC SCHOOLS
Private Schools, generally, this index

NONRESIDENTS
Definitions, withholding tax on wages, **Un Ins 13003**
Income Tax—State, this index
Workers compensation, commutation, **Labor 5100**

NONSUFFICIENT FUNDS CHECKS
Bad checks. Negotiable Instruments, this index

NONSUPPORT
Support, generally, this index

NONTRADITIONAL OCCUPATIONS
Definitions, employment training, women, **Un Ins 9602.5**

NORTH COUNTY TRANSIT DISTRICT
Application of law, railroad crew requirements, **Labor 6901**
Railroad crew requirements, application of law, **Labor 6901**

NORTHERN CALIFORNIA SCHOOL FOR THE DEAF
Schools for the Deaf, generally, this index

NOTARIES PUBLIC
Assignment of wages, authentication of statement of marital status, **Labor 300**
Domestic partnership, forms, **Fam 298**
Workers compensation, release or compromise agreements, **Labor 5003**

NOTES
Negotiable Instruments, generally, this index

NOTICE
Adoption of Children, this index
Agricultural Labor and Employment, this index
Amusement rides, construction, alterations, **Labor 7908**
Apprentices, disciplinary proceedings, **Labor 3076**
Apprenticeship council, training criteria, **Labor 3073.2**
Asbestos, this index
Attachment, this index
Buildings, this index
Certified or registered mail. Mail and Mailing, this index
Children and Minors, this index
Civil air patrol, labor and employment, leaves of absence, **Labor 1503**
Compensation and Salaries, this index
Constructive notice, unemployment compensation, assistants to individual employed by employing unit, **Un Ins 606**
Consumer Credit Reporting Agencies, this index
Contractors, this index
Deferred compensation plans, employer managed, financial risks, **Labor 2809**
Disability insurance. Insurance, this index
Domestic Partnership, this index
Elections, this index
Electricity, this index
Elevators, revocation of permit to operate, **Labor 7312**
Employees Earning Protection Law, labor claims, release, **CCP 1208**
Employer managed deferred compensation plans, financial risks, **Labor 2809**
Employment. Labor and Employment, this index
Employment Agencies, this index
Executions, this index
Extended unemployment compensation. Unemployment Compensation, this index
Fair Employment and Housing, this index
Farm labor contractors, licenses and permits, **Labor 1686**

NOTICE—Cont'd
Garnishment, this index
Handicapped Persons, this index
Hazardous Substances and Waste, this index
Health benefits, continuance, **Labor 2806, 2807**
Health Care Providers, this index
Health Care Service Plans, this index
Health Facilities, this index
Income Tax—State, this index
Industrial homework,
    Hearings, **Labor 2655**
    Removal of article or material for violation, **Labor 2664**
Industrial relations department, public officers, **Labor 95**
Infants. Children and Minors, this index
Insurance, this index
Inventions, ownership rights, employers and employees, **Labor 2872**
Janitors, discharge, **Labor 1061**
Labor and Employment, this index
Labor Camps, this index
Labor disputes, injunction, **Labor 1138.1**
Labor standards enforcement division, officers and employees, authority to serve, **Labor 95**
Landlord and Tenant, this index
Local Agencies, this index
Mail and Mailing, this index
Medical Records, this index
Mines and Minerals, this index
Minors. Children and Minors, this index
Mortgages, this index
National service programs, overtime, **Labor 1171**
Nurses, this index
Nursing Homes, this index
Occupational safety and health. Labor and Employment, this index
Overtime, national service programs, **Labor 1171**
Posting, generally, this index
Protective orders. Domestic Violence, this index
Public Buildings and Works, this index
Public Officers and Employees, this index
Publication, generally, this index
Residential Care Facilities for the Elderly, this index
Rules and regulations, publication, industrial welfare commission, **Labor 1182.1**
Salaries. Compensation and Salaries, this index
Scaffolds, unsafe equipment, destruction or removal of notice, **Labor 7156**
State, this index
State Contracts, this index
State Hospitals, this index
State Officers and Employees, this index
Support, this index
Talent Agencies, this index
Tax Collection, this index
Tenant. Landlord and Tenant, this index

NOTICE

NOTICE—Cont'd

Unemployment Compensation, this index

Victims of crime. Crimes and Offenses, this index

Volunteer firemen and fire departments, removal, hearing, **Labor 1964**

Wage claim, intention to file, employee discharged for garnishment of earnings, **Labor 2929**

Wages. Compensation and Salaries, this index

Weapons, this index

Whistle Blowing, this index

Window cleaners, safety violations, **Labor 7331**

Workers Compensation, this index

Workers compensation division, meetings, **Labor 138.2**

Writing, unemployment insurance, **Un Ins 8**

Written demands for return of leased or rented property, **Pen 484**

NOTIFICATION

Notice, generally, this index

NSF CHECKS

Bad checks. Negotiable Instruments, this index

NUISANCE

Abatement, labor camps, **Health & S 17060**

Labor camps, abatement actions, **Health & S 17060**

NURSE MIDWIVES

Compensation and salaries, hours of labor, **Labor 515**

Health care service plans, lists, **Health & S 1367.26**

NURSE PRACTITIONERS

Nurses, this index

NURSERIES AND NURSERY STOCK

Unemployment compensation, qualifications, **Un Ins 611 et seq.**

NURSERY SCHOOLS

Day Care and Nursery Schools, generally, this index

NURSES

Abuse,
  Long term health care facilities, temporary employment, **CC 1812.543**
  Patients, reports, **Pen 11161.8**
Assistants,
  Abuse, long term health care facilities, temporary employment, **CC 1812.543**
  Long term health care facilities, employment agencies, temporary employment, **CC 1812.509, 1812.540 et seq.**
Caregiver training initiative, **Un Ins 11020 et seq.**

NURSES—Cont'd

Certified nurse assistants, caregiver training initiative, **Un Ins 11020 et seq.**

Compensation and salaries, hours of labor, **Labor 515**

Contracts, registries, **CC 1812.526**

Criminal history information, long term health care facilities, temporary employment, **CC 1812.542**

Discipline, whistle blowing, **Health & S 1278.5**

Discrimination, whistle blowing, **Health & S 1278.5**

Education, regional nursing simulation laboratories, grants, **Un Ins 9619**

Employment. Nurses Registries, generally, this index

Employment agencies, long term health care facilities, temporary employment, **CC 1812.509, 1812.540 et seq.**

Grants, regional nursing simulation laboratories, **Un Ins 9619**

Home Health Agencies, generally, this index

Hours of labor, compensation and salaries, **Labor 515**

Hypodermic Syringes and Needles, generally, this index

Labor and employment. Nurses Registries, generally, this index

Licensed vocational nurses. Vocational Nursing, generally, this index

Notice, safety, whistleblowers, **Health & S 1278.5**

Nurse practitioners,
  Reports, workers compensation, **Labor 3209.10**
  Workers compensation, reports, **Labor 3209.10**

Nursing Homes, this index

Occupational health and medicine, program development, **Labor 50.8**

Practical nurses. Home Health Agencies, generally, this index

Privileges and immunities, criminally related personal injuries, reports, **Pen 11161.9**

Psychiatric Technicians, generally, this index

Public health nurses. Home Health Agencies, generally, this index

Referrals. Nurses Registries, generally, this index

Regional nursing simulation laboratories, grants, **Un Ins 9619**

Registries. Nurses Registries, generally, this index

Reports, nurse practitioners, **Labor 3209.10**

Retaliation, whistle blowing, **Health & S 1278.5**

Rural areas, regional nursing simulation laboratories, grants, **Un Ins 9619**

Students, unemployment compensation, exclusion, **Un Ins 645, 711**

NURSES—Cont'd

Training,
  Caregiver training initiative, **Un Ins 11020 et seq.**
  Regional nursing simulation laboratories, grants, **Un Ins 9619**

Unemployment Compensation, this index

Vocational Nursing, generally, this index

Whistle blowing, **Health & S 1278.5**

Workers compensation, **Labor 3208.05, 4600**

NURSES REGISTRIES

Generally, **CC 1812.524 et seq.**

Advertisements, **CC 1812.533**

Bonds (officers and fiduciaries), **CC 1812.525**

Contracts, **CC 1812.526**

Definitions, **CC 1812.524**
  Employment agency regulation, **CC 1812.501**

Deposits in lieu of bond, **CC 1812.525**

Experience and training, verification, **CC 1812.528**

Fees, **CC 1812.527**
  Prohibition,
    Registration fees, **CC 1812.530**
    Splitting, **CC 1812.531**

Fraud, **CC 1812.533**

Payment, assignments, **CC 1812.532**

Qualifications, verification, **CC 1812.528**

Records, **CC 1812.529**

Registration fees, prohibition, **CC 1812.530**

Schedules, fees schedules, **CC 1812.527**

Verification, claims as to experience and training, **CC 1812.528**

NURSING HOMES

Abuse,
  Nurses, temporary employment, **CC 1812.543**
  Reports, **Pen 11161.8**

Assisted living. Residential Care Facilities for the Elderly, generally, this index

Crimes and offenses, officers and employees, records, disclosure, **Pen 11105.3**

Criminal history information, nurses, temporary employment, **CC 1812.542**

Disclosure, crimes and offenses, employment, **Pen 11105.3**

Employment agencies, nurses, temporary employment, **CC 1812.509, 1812.540 et seq.**

Intermediate care facilities. Medi Cal Program, this index

Intermediate care facilities/developmentally disabled nursing facilities, Medi Cal program, supplemental reimbursement, enforcement, **Labor 107**

Labor and employment, crimes and offenses, disclosure, **Pen 11105.3**

Medi Cal Program, this index

Neglect, reports, **Pen 11161.8**

Notice, criminal history, disclosure, employment, **Pen 11105.3**

NURSING HOMES—Cont'd

Nurses, employment agencies, temporary employment, **CC 1812.509, 1812.540 et seq.**

Officers and employees, crimes and offenses, records, disclosure, **Pen 11105.3**

Psychiatric technicians, employment agencies, temporary employment, **CC 1812.540 et seq.**

Residential Care Facilities for the Elderly, generally, this index

Skilled nursing facilities, workers compensation, fees, **Labor 5307.1**

Temporary employment, nurses, employment agencies, **CC 1812.509, 1812.540 et seq.**

Vocational nursing, employment agencies, temporary employment, **CC 1812.540 et seq.**

NURSING SCHOOLS

Unemployment compensation, excluded services, option, **Un Ins 711**

OAKLAND

Public employment offices, **Un Ins 2055**

OATHS AND AFFIRMATIONS

Affidavits, generally, this index

Agricultural labor relations board investigations, witnesses, **Labor 1151**

Definitions, Labor Code, **Labor 16**

Employment. Labor and Employment, this index

Garnishment, **CCP 706.121 et seq.**

Labor and Employment, this index

Labor commissioner, deputies and assistants, administering, **Labor 92**

Labor standards enforcement division, **Labor 74**

Labor statistics and research division, chief and employees, administering, **Labor 152**

Occupational safety and health, administering oaths, **Labor 6314**

Perjury, generally, this index

Unemployment compensation, appeals board, power to administer, **Un Ins 1953**

Workers Compensation, this index

OATS

Agricultural Products, generally, this index

OBSCENITY

Lewdness and Obscenity, generally, this index

OCCUPATIONAL CARCINOGENS CONTROL ACT

Generally, **Labor 9000 et seq.**

OCCUPATIONAL DISEASES

Generally, **Health & S 105150**

Applications for benefits, diseases arising out of more than one employment, **Labor 5500.5**

OCCUPATIONAL DISEASES—Cont'd

Arising out of more than one employment,

Application for benefits, **Labor 5500.5**

Compromise and release agreements, **Labor 5005**

Asbestosis, **Labor 4401 et seq.**

Data gaps, state repository, notice, **Health & S 105175**

Date of injury, definitions, limitation of proceedings, **Labor 5412**

Definitions,

Material change in ownership, sale of business, self insured employers, **Labor 5500.5**

Medical records, **Labor 6409**

Occupational safety and health, **Labor 6409**

Work location, sale of business, self insured employers, **Labor 5500.5**

Health and sanitation programs, **Health & S 105175, 105180**

Investigations and investigators, **Health & S 105175**

Liability,

Determination or limitation, **Labor 5500.6**

Multiple employers, **Labor 5500.5**

Limitation of actions, **Labor 5412, 5500.5**

Multiple employers, liability of insurers, **Labor 5500.5**

Notice, repository data gaps, **Health & S 105175**

Programs, **Health & S 105175, 105180**

Sale of business, self insured employers, liability of buyer and seller, **Labor 5500.5**

Silicosis, disability or death from, apportionment of liability, **Labor 5500.5**

State funds, occupational diseases arising out of more than one employment, payment, **Labor 5500.5**

Statute of limitations, **Labor 5412, 5500.5**

Subrogation of insurer, multiple employers, primary uninsured, **Labor 5500.5**

Toxicity information request, notice of data gaps, **Health & S 105175**

OCCUPATIONAL HEALTH SERVICES

Health departments, promotion, **Health & S 105150**

Program development, **Labor 50.8**

OCCUPATIONAL ILLNESS

Occupational Diseases, generally, this index

OCCUPATIONAL LEAD POISONING

Hazardous Substances and Waste, this index

OCCUPATIONAL SAFETY AND HEALTH

Labor and Employment, this index

OCCUPATIONAL SAFETY AND HEALTH ACT OF 1973

Generally, **Labor 6300 et seq.**

OCCUPATIONAL SAFETY AND HEALTH APPEALS BOARD

Generally, **Labor 148 et seq.**

Industrial Relations Department, this index

OCCUPATIONAL SAFETY AND HEALTH DIVISION

Industrial Relations Department, this index

OCCUPATIONAL SAFETY AND HEALTH STANDARDS AND ORDERS

Definitions, occupational safety and health, **Labor 6305**

OCCUPATIONAL SAFETY AND HEALTH STANDARDS BOARD

Generally, **Labor 140 et seq.**

Industrial Relations Department, this index

OFF INDICATOR

Unemployment compensation, extended benefits, **Un Ins 4003**

OFFENSES

Crimes and Offenses, generally, this index

OFFICE WORK

Children and minors, employment, **Labor 1294.3**

OFFICERS AND EMPLOYEES

Associations and Societies, this index

Banks and Banking, this index

Computers, software, compensation and salaries, overtime, **Labor 515.5**

Corporation Taxes, this index

Correctional Institutions, this index

County Officers and Employees, generally, this index

Definitions,

Disclosure, violations, **Labor 1106**

Employment records, discovery, **CCP 1985.6**

Discovery, employment records, **CCP 1985.6**

Districts, this index

Employment Development Department, this index

Food and Agriculture Department, this index

Health Care Services Department, this index

Industrial Relations Department, this index

Juvenile Facilities Division, this index

Limited Liability Companies, this index

Motor Carriers, this index

Municipal Officers and Employees, generally, this index

Nursing Homes, this index

Partnership, this index

Political Subdivisions, this index

Private Security Services, this index

Production of books and papers, employment records, **CCP 1985.6**

OFFICERS AND EMPLOYEES—Cont'd
Public Officers and Employees, generally, this index
Railroads, this index
Records, employment, discovery, **CCP 1985.6**
Residential Care Facilities for the Elderly, this index
Savings and Loan Associations, this index
Savings Associations, this index
Special districts. Districts, this index
State Officers and Employees, generally, this index
Superior Courts, this index
Transportation, this index

OFFICIAL ADVERTISEMENTS
Advertisements, generally, this index

OFFICIAL BONDS
Bonds (Officers and Fiduciaries), generally, this index

OIL AND GAS
Analysis and analysts, used oil, **Health & S 25250.29**
Chemical plants, safety preparedness, workers, **Labor 7850 et seq.**
Compensation and salaries, drillers, layoffs, **Labor 201.7**
Contracts, used oil, foreign states, recycling, tests, reports, **Health & S 25250.30**
Drills and drilling, lay offs, wage payments, **Labor 201.7**
Foreign states, used oil, recycling, contracts, tests, reports, **Health & S 25250.30**
Gassy tunnels, safety, **Labor 7965 et seq.**
Hazardous substances and waste. Used oil, generally, post
Inspection and inspectors, liquefied petroleum gas tanks, **Labor 7620 et seq.**
Labor and employment,
  Occupational safety and health, gas pipeline tests, **Labor 6700**
  Safety in employment, **Labor 7800 et seq.**
Laying off employees, oil drilling industry, prompt compensation payment, **Labor 201.7**
Recycling, tests, used oil, foreign states, contracts, **Health & S 25250.30**
Reports. Used oil, post
Safety, employment, **Labor 7800 et seq.**
Standards, used oil, tests, **Health & S 25250.29**
Tests, used oil, **Health & S 25250.29**
  Foreign states, recycling, contracts, **Health & S 25250.30**
Time, laying off employees, oil drilling industry, compensation payment, **Labor 201.7**
Transportation. Used oil, post
Used oil,
  Contracts, foreign states, recycling, tests, reports, **Health & S 25250.30**

OIL AND GAS—Cont'd
Used oil—Cont'd
  Foreign states, recycling, contracts, tests, reports, **Health & S 25250.30**
  Reports, foreign states, recycling, contracts, **Health & S 25250.30**
  Tests, **Health & S 25250.29**
    Foreign states, recycling, contracts, **Health & S 25250.30**
  Transportation, tests, **Health & S 25250.29**
Volatile flammable liquids, safety in employment, **Labor 7800 et seq.**

OIL STATIONS
Motor Vehicle Service Stations, generally, this index

OLD AGE
Aged Persons, generally, this index

OLD AGE AND SURVIVORS INSURANCE
Social Security, generally, this index

OLD PERSONS
Aged Persons, generally, this index

OLYMPIC GAMES
Labor and employment, law enforcement recommendations, **Labor 432.7**

ON INDICATOR
Unemployment compensation, extended benefits, **Un Ins 4003**

ON THE JOB TRAINING
Definitions, apprenticeship, **Labor 3093**

ONE DAY IN SEVEN ACT
Generally, **Labor 551 et seq.**

ONE STOP CAREER CENTERS
Generally, **Un Ins 14230 et seq.**

OPEN SPACE LANDS
Districts. Recreation and Park Districts, generally, this index
Recreation and Park Districts, generally, this index

OPEN VIDEO SYSTEMS
Criminal history information,
  Franchises, **Pub U 5910**
    Officers and employees, **Pub U 7910**
Employees, criminal history information, **Pub U 7910**
Independent contractors, criminal history information, **Pub U 7910**
Officers and employees, criminal history information, **Pub U 7910**
Reports, franchises, **Pub U 5920**
Vendor and purchaser, criminal history information, **Pub U 7910**

OPERAS AND OPERETTAS
Compensation and salaries, deposits for security of payment, **Labor 271**

OPERATED
Definitions, workers compensation, health care providers, fraud, contracts, **Labor 3219**

OPERATORS
Definitions, permanent amusement rides, safety, inspection and inspectors, **Labor 7921**

OPERATORS LICENSE
Drivers licenses. Motor Vehicles, this index

OPINION AND EXPERT TESTIMONY
Witnesses, this index

OPPRESSION
Definitions, damages, **CC 3294**
Duress or Coercion, generally, this index

OPTOMETRISTS
Health Care Service Plans, this index
Privileges and immunities, criminally related personal injuries, reports, **Pen 11161.9**
Representation of optometrists as a physician, **Labor 3209.4**
Unemployment compensation, primary care clinics, **Un Ins 656**
Workers Compensation, this index

ORAL DEPOSITIONS
Depositions, generally, this index

ORANGE COUNTY STATE COLLEGE
Colleges and Universities, generally, this index

ORDERS
Garnishment, generally, this index
Insurance, this index
Labor and Employment, this index
Occupational safety and health standards board, adopting, amending or repealing, **Labor 142.3 et seq.**
Sexual harassment, workplace, **Gov 12950**
Wearing apparel, penalties, manufacturers, service, **Labor 2678**
Workers Compensation, this index

ORDERS OF COURT
Appeal and Review, generally, this index
Colleges and universities, force and violence, protective orders, **CCP 527.85**
Contempt, generally, this index
Earnings withholding order. Garnishment, this index
Fair employment and housing, **Gov 12973**
Injunction, generally, this index
Judgments and Decrees, generally, this index
Labor Camps, this index
Medical Records, this index
Nuisances, abatement, labor camps, temporary orders, **Health & S 17060**
Protective orders,
  Colleges and universities, force and violence, **CCP 527.85**

ORDERS OF COURT—Cont'd
Protective orders—Cont'd
Domestic Violence, this index
Family law, acquisition of firearms by restrainees, **Pen 12021**
Harassment, this index
Labor and employment, workplace violence safety, **CCP 527.8**
Marriage, this index
Weapons, this index
Service of process. Process, this index
Support, this index
Temporary restraining orders. Injunction, this index

ORDINANCES
Disaster council, establishment, **Labor 3211.9**
Labor camps, compliance, **Health & S 17001**

ORGANIZATIONS
Associations and Societies, generally, this index

ORGANIZED CAMP
Definitions, minimum wage, maximum hours, **Labor 1182.4**

ORGANIZED LABOR
Labor Organizations, generally, this index

ORPHANS AND ORPHANAGES
Foster homes. Social Services, this index

ORTHOTIC DEVICES
Workers compensation, **Labor 4600**

OSTEOPATHS
Contracts, preferred reimbursement rates, **Labor 4609**
Disclosure, preferred reimbursement rates, **Labor 4609**
Outpatient settings. Clinics, this index
Preferred reimbursement rates, **Labor 4609**
Rates and charges, preferred reimbursement rates, **Labor 4609**
Reimbursement, preferred reimbursement rates, **Labor 4609**
Unemployment compensation, primary care clinics, **Un Ins 656**
Workers Compensation, this index

OUT OF SERVICE ORDERS
Motor vehicles, commercial vehicles, fines and penalties, **Veh 15311.1**

OUTDOOR ADVERTISING
Mutilating or destroying, **Pen 602**

OUTHOUSES
Comfort Stations and Rest Rooms, generally, this index

OUTPATIENTS
Health Care Service Plans, this index
Hospitals, this index
Mentally Ill Persons, this index

OVERPAYMENTS
Disability compensation, **Un Ins 2735 et seq.**

OVERTIME
Generally, **Labor 500 et seq.**
Action to recover, **Labor 1193.6, 1194**
AmeriCorps, **Labor 1171**
Compensating time off, **Labor 204.3**
Computers, software, officers and employees, **Labor 515.5**
Daily overtime compensation petitions, review, **Labor 1182.5**
Discrimination, national service programs, **Labor 1171**
Industrial welfare division, recovery, **Labor 1193.5**
National service programs, **Labor 1171**
Notice, national service programs, **Labor 1171**
Payments, actions to recover, **Labor 1193.6, 1194**
Physicians and surgeons, exemptions, **Labor 515.6**
Preexisting workweek arrangements, review, **Labor 1182.5**
Private schools, schoolteachers, exemptions, **Labor 515.8**
Public buildings and works, **Const. Art. 14, § 2**
Schoolteachers, private schools, exemptions, **Labor 515.8**
Smelters, **Labor 751.8**
State Officers and Employees, this index
Time off in lieu of compensation, **Labor 204.3**
Underground workers, **Labor 751.8**
Wearing apparel, manufacturers and manufacturing, contractors, suretyship and guarantee, **Labor 2673.1**
Workers compensation, average weekly earnings, computation, **Labor 4454**

OWNERS AND OWNERSHIP
Title to Property, generally, this index

OYSTERS
Shellfish, this index

PACKAGES
Containers, generally, this index

PAID FAMILY CARE LEAVE
Generally, **Un Ins 3300 et seq.**

PAINTS AND PAINTING
Art and Artists, generally, this index
Building construction or repair, steel painters, safety, **Labor 7108**
Lead Base Paint, generally, this index
Lead poisoning, occupational safety, programs, **Health & S 105185 et seq.**

PANELS
Definitions, employment training panel, **Un Ins 10201**

PANTOPON
Drug Addicts, generally, this index

PAPERS
Books and Papers, generally, this index
Negotiable Instruments, generally, this index
Newspapers, generally, this index
Production of Books and Papers, generally, this index

PARALYSIS
Workers compensation, **Labor 4662**

PARAPLEGICS
Handicapped Persons, generally, this index

PARATRANSIT VEHICLES
Actions and proceedings, displaced workers, **Labor 1073**
Contracts, displaced workers, **Labor 1070 et seq.**
Costs, displaced workers, actions and proceedings, **Labor 1073**
Displaced workers, **Labor 1070 et seq.**
Injunction, displaced workers, **Labor 1073**
Officers and employees, displaced workers, **Labor 1070 et seq.**

PARENT AND CHILD RELATIONSHIP
Children and Minors, generally, this index

PARENTS
Children and Minors, generally, this index
Definitions,
Family care leave, **Gov 12945.2; Un Ins 3302**
Sick leave, **Labor 233**
Schools and School Districts, this index

PARKING LOTS AND FACILITIES
Mobilehomes and Mobilehome Parks, generally, this index
Zoning and Planning, generally, this index

PARKS
Districts. Recreation and Park Districts, generally, this index
Mobilehomes and Mobilehome Parks, generally, this index
Recreation and Park Districts, generally, this index
Zoning and Planning, generally, this index

PAROCHIAL SCHOOLS
Private Schools, generally, this index

PAROLE AND PROBATION
Adult probation officers. Probation officers, generally, post
Consumer credit reports, contents of records, **CC 1785.13**
Counselors and counseling, trespass, neonatal units, maternity wards, birthing centers, **Pen 602**
County probation officers. Probation officers, generally, post
Juvenile Delinquents and Dependents, this index

PAROLE AND PROBATION—Cont'd

Labor and employment, workers compensation, nonprofit organizations as sponsors of sentenced persons, **Labor 3301**

Medical records, disclosure to probation officers, **CC 56.10**

Nonprofit organizations, sponsors of sentenced persons, workers compensation, **Labor 3301**

Officers and employees. Probation officers, generally, post

Parole officers, workers compensation, injuries, presumptions, **Labor 3212.10**

Probation officers,
Leaves of absence, workers compensation, disability benefits, **Labor 4850, 4850.5**
San Luis Obispo County, leaves of absence, workers compensation, disability benefits, **Labor 4850.5**
Workers compensation,
Disability benefits, leaves of absence, **Labor 4850, 4850.5**
Injuries, presumptions, **Labor 3212.10**

Purchases, weapons, crimes and offenses, **Pen 12021**

San Luis Obispo County, probation officers, leaves of absence, workers compensation, disability benefits, **Labor 4850.5**

Setting aside plea or verdict, effect on unemployment compensation benefits, **Un Ins 1263**

Trespass, neonatal units, maternity wards, birthing centers, **Pen 602**

Unemployment compensation. Correctional Institutions, this index

Volunteer firemen, probation period, **Labor 1964**

Weapons, this index

Workers compensation,
Nonprofit organizations as sponsors of sentenced persons, **Labor 3301**
Probation officers, ante

PAROLE OFFICERS

Parole and Probation, this index

PART TIME QUALIFIED CARE PLAN

Definitions, child care, tax credit, **Rev & T 17052.18**

PART TIME SERVICE OR EMPLOYMENT

Unemployment Compensation, this index

PARTICIPANT

Definitions, youthbuild program, **Un Ins 9801**

PARTIES

Contempt, generally, this index

Depositions, generally, this index

Disability compensation appeals, director, **Un Ins 2737**

Fair employment and housing, complaints, **Gov 12965**

Intervention, generally, this index

PARTIES—Cont'd

Joinder of parties,
Labor standards enforcement division, **Labor 100**
Wage claims or liens, enforcement, **Labor 100**
Workers compensation, **Labor 5307.5, 5500.5**

Shareholders, uninsured employer actions, workers compensation, **Labor 3717.1**

Third Parties, generally, this index

Unemployment compensation,
Appeals, **Un Ins 1377, 2707.2, 3655**
Training contracts, **Un Ins 10209**

Witnesses, generally, this index

Workers Compensation, this index

PARTNER ABUSE

Domestic Violence, generally, this index

PARTNERSHIP

Compensation and salaries, work or service rendered or performed under partnership, **Labor 200**

Convict labor, **Const. Art. 14, § 5**

Definitions, withholding tax on wages, **Un Ins 13003**

Domestic Partnership, generally, this index

Foreign limited liability partnerships, unemployment compensation, withholdings, **Un Ins 1735**

Income Tax—State, this index

Joint Ventures, generally, this index

Limited Liability Companies, generally, this index

Limited partnership. Limited Liability Companies, generally, this index

Officers and employees, definitions, workers compensation, **Labor 3351**

One stop career centers, **Un Ins 14231, 14232**

Registered limited liability partnerships, unemployment compensation, withholdings, **Un Ins 1735**

Unemployment Compensation, this index

Workers Compensation, this index

PARTY

Parties, generally, this index

PARTY TO THE ARBITRATION

Definitions, **CCP 1280**

PASS THROUGH ENTITIES

Definitions, corporation taxes, enterprise zones, credits, **Rev & T 23634**

PASSENGER SERVICE

Railroads, this index

PASSENGERS

Aerial Passenger Tramways, generally, this index

Boats and Boating, this index

Ships and Shipping, this index

PASSING OFF

Fraud, generally, this index

PASTORS

Clergy, generally, this index

PATERNITY

Support, generally, this index

PATROL

Highway Patrol, generally, this index

PATROLMEN

Police, generally, this index

Private Investigators, generally, this index

PAUPERS

Indigent Persons, generally, this index

PAY

Compensation and Salaries, generally, this index

PAYMENT

Advances and Advancements, generally, this index

Compensation and Salaries, this index

Garnishment, this index

Public Buildings and Works, this index

Retirement and Pensions, this index

Salaries. Compensation and Salaries, this index

Support, this index

Trusts and Trustees, this index

Unemployment Compensation, this index

Wages. Compensation and Salaries, this index

Workers Compensation, this index

PAYROLL

Attorney fees, records and recordation, **Labor 226**

Copies, records and recordation, **Labor 226**

Inspection and inspectors, **Labor 1174**
Records and recordation, **Labor 226**

Records and recordation,
Copies, **Labor 226**
Farm labor contractors, production for agricultural grower, **Labor 1695.5**
Inspection and inspectors, **Labor 226**
Public buildings projects, contractors and subcontractors, **Labor 1776**

PAYROLL DEDUCTIONS

Compensation and Salaries, generally, this index

PAYROLL PERIOD

Definitions, withholding tax on wages, **Un Ins 13008**

PEACE OFFICERS

Accident and health insurance, death in line of duty, survivors health benefits, **Labor 4856**

Arrest, generally, this index

Biochemical substances, workers compensation, presumptions, **Labor 3212.85**

Burden of proof, weapons, exemptions, injunction, surrender, **CCP 527.9**

Cancer, workers compensation, **Labor 3212.1**

PEACE OFFICERS—Cont'd

Colleges and Universities, this index

Compensation and salaries. Workers compensation, generally, post

Confidential or privileged information, applicants for employment, information disclosed by other employers, **Gov 1031.1**

Costs, background investigations, employment applicants, disclosure by other employers, **Gov 1031.1**

Counselors and counseling, weapons, **Pen 12021**

Crimes and offenses,
  Disclosing suppliers identity, obscene materials, **Labor 1309.5**
  Reserves or auxiliaries, absence and absentees, labor and employment, emergency duties, **Labor 230.3**

Criminal history information, applicants, disclosure by other employers, **Gov 1031.1**

Damages, workers compensation claims, third parties, **Labor 3852**

Death, in line of duty,
  Dependents, scholarships, **Labor 4709**
  Workers compensation, survivors, health benefits, **Labor 4856**

Definitions, workers compensation, **Labor 3600.3**

Dependents, scholarships, **Labor 4709**

Discharge, reserves or auxiliaries, absence and absentees, labor and employment, emergency duties, **Labor 230.3**

Disclosure,
  Former employers, applicants for employment, **Gov 1031.1**
  Suppliers identity, obscene materials, crimes and offenses, **Labor 1309.5**

Discrimination,
  Heart trouble, employment, presumption, **Gov 12940.1**
  Reserves or auxiliaries, absence and absentees, labor and employment, emergency duties, **Labor 230.3**

Diversion programs, referral or participation, disclosure, **Labor 432.7**

Emergencies, reserves or auxiliaries, absence and absentees, labor and employment, **Labor 230.3**

Employment. Labor and employment, generally, post

Evidence, burden of proof, weapons, exemptions, injunction, surrender, **CCP 527.9**

Exemptions. Weapons, post

Firearms. Weapons, generally, post

Handicapped persons, disability in line of duty, dependents, scholarships, **Labor 4709**

Heart trouble, employment, discrimination, **Gov 12940.1**

Highway Patrol, generally, this index

In line of duty. Death, ante

Injunction,
  Labor disputes, **Labor 1138.5**

PEACE OFFICERS—Cont'd

Injunction—Cont'd
  Weapons, surrender, **CCP 527.9**

Insurance, death in line of duty, survivors, health benefits, **Labor 4856**

Investigations and investigators, applicants for employment as peace officers, background information, disclosure by other employers, **Gov 1031.1**

Labor and employment,
  Arrest record, disclosure, **Labor 432.7**
  Diversion programs, referral or participation, disclosure, **Labor 432.7**
  Heart trouble, discrimination, **Gov 12940.1**

Labor disputes, injunction, **Labor 1138.5**

Leaves of absence, workers compensation, disability benefits, **Labor 4850**

Lewdness and obscenity, disclosure, identity, suppliers of obscene materials, **Labor 1309.5**

Lower back impairment, workers compensation, **Labor 3213.2**

Lyme disease, workers compensation, presumptions, **Labor 3212.12**

Mental examinations, weapons, surrender, exemptions, **CCP 527.9**

Off duty, workers compensation, **Labor 3600.2, 3600.3**

Police, generally, this index

Presumptions, inability, heart trouble, employment, **Gov 12940.1**

Privileges and immunities,
  Other employers, disclosure, background check on employment applicant, **Gov 1031.1**
  Weapons, ban on possession, incorrect enforcement, **Pen 12021**

Records and recordation, arrest, labor and employment, disclosure on seeking employment, **Labor 432.7**

Reserves or auxiliaries,
  Discrimination, absence and absentees, labor and employment, emergency duties, **Labor 230.3**
  Workers compensation, **Labor 3362.5**

Scholarships, dependents, **Labor 4709**

School Officers and Employees, this index

Sheriffs, generally, this index

State police. Highway Patrol, generally, this index

Third parties,
  Actions against, workers compensation, **Labor 3852 et seq.**
  Damages, workers compensation claims, **Labor 3852**

Unemployment compensation, applicants with outstanding felony arrest warrants, furnishing information to peace officers, **Un Ins 1095**

Weapons,
  Ban on carrying, petition for relief from, **Pen 12021**
  Confiscation, persons formerly forbidden to possess, immunity, **Pen 12021**

PEACE OFFICERS—Cont'd

Weapons—Cont'd
  Exemptions, injunction, surrender, **CCP 527.9**
  Injunction, surrender, **CCP 527.9**
  Unlawful possession, relief from prohibition, **Pen 12021**

Workers compensation,
  Assisting officers, **Labor 3366, 4458.2**
  Biochemical substances, presumptions, **Labor 3212.85**
  Cancer, **Labor 3212.1**
  Death benefits, limitation of actions, AIDS, **Labor 5406.6**
  Death in line of duty, survivors, health benefits, **Labor 4856**
  Foreign states, deputies, **Labor 3352, 3366, 3367**
  Leaves of absence, disability benefits, **Labor 4850**
  Lower back impairment, **Labor 3213.2**
  Lyme disease, presumptions, **Labor 3212.12**
  Off duty officers performing services, **Labor 3600.2, 3600.3**
  Persons assisting officers, **Labor 4458.2**
  Reserves or auxiliaries, **Labor 3362.5**
  Scholarships, dependents, **Labor 4709**
  Third parties, actions against, **Labor 3852 et seq.**

PEAS

Vegetables, generally, this index

PECUNIARY INTEREST

Adverse or Pecuniary Interest, generally, this index

PEDDLERS

Hawkers and Peddlers, generally, this index

PEN GUNS

Weapons, generally, this index

PENAL INSTITUTIONS

Correctional Institutions, generally, this index

PENALTIES

Fines and Penalties, generally, this index

PENDING ACTIONS

Labor Code, **Labor 4**

Unemployment insurance code, **Un Ins 3**

PENITENTIARIES

Correctional Institutions, generally, this index

PENSIONS

Retirement and Pensions, generally, this index

PENSIONS, PROFIT SHARING AND STOCK BONUS PLANS

Income Tax—State, this index

PER

PER DIEM
Athletic officials, workers compensation, **Labor 3352**
Definitions, public works employees, **Labor 1773.1**
Employment development department, employment training panel, members, **Un Ins 10202.5**
Health and safety and workers compensation board, **Labor 75**
Labor and employment, workforce investment board, **Un Ins 14015**
Workforce investment board, **Un Ins 14015**
Youthbuild program, **Un Ins 9802**

PERCEIVE
Definitions, fair employment and housing, **Gov 12926**

PERFORMANCE BONDS
Bonds (Officers and Fiduciaries), generally, this index

PERIODICALS
Magazines, generally, this index

PERISHABLE PROPERTY
Seasonal employment termination, computation and payment of wages, **Labor 201**

PERJURY
State officers and employees, whistle blowing, **Gov 8547.8**
Support, this index
Unemployment compensation, **Un Ins 16**
Whistle blowing, state officers and employees, **Gov 8547.8**
Workers Compensation, this index

PERMANENT AMUSEMENT RIDE SAFETY INSPECTION PROGRAM
Generally, **Labor 7920 et seq.**

PERMANENT PARTIAL DISABILITY
Definitions, workers compensation, **Labor 4452.5**

PERMANENT TOTAL DISABILITY
Definitions, workers compensation, **Labor 4452.5**

PERMISSIBLE EQUIPMENT
Definitions, tunnel and mine safety, **Labor 7951**

PERMITS
Licenses and Permits, generally, this index

PERSONAL CARE SERVICES
Social Services, this index

PERSONAL INCOME TAX
Income Tax—State, generally, this index

PERSONAL INJURIES
Aerial passenger tramways, reports, **Labor 7356**
Amusement rides, reports, **Labor 7904, 7914**

PERSONAL INJURIES—Cont'd
Apprentices, **Labor 3078**
Assault and Battery, generally, this index
Children and minors, family care leave, **Un Ins 3300 et seq.**
Correctional Institutions, this index
Damages, generally, this index
Definitions,
   Lifeguards, skin cancer, workers compensation, **Labor 3212.11**
   Workers compensation, **Labor 3208, 3212.1**
      Biochemical substances, peace officers, firefighters and fire departments, presumptions, **Labor 3212.85**
      Correctional institutions, presumptions, **Labor 3212.10**
      Hepatitis, **Labor 3212.8**
      Lyme disease, presumptions, **Labor 3212.12**
      Meningitis, **Labor 3212.9**
Disability compensation. Unemployment Compensation, this index
Disability insurance. Insurance, this index
Domestic partnership, family care leave, **Un Ins 3300 et seq.**
Economic opportunity programs, enrollees, **Labor 4201 et seq.**
Employment. Labor and Employment, this index
Health insurance, disability insurance. Insurance, this index
Labor and Employment, this index
Marriage, this index
Negligence, generally, this index
Obligations of employer, **Labor 2801**
Prisons and prisoners. Correctional Institutions, this index
Reports, **Labor 6409 et seq.**
Workers Compensation, generally, this index

PERSONAL PHYSICIAN
Definitions, workers compensation, **Labor 4600**

PERSONAL PROPERTY
Abandoned or Unclaimed Property, generally, this index
Attachment, generally, this index
Diseases, generally, this index
Escheat, generally, this index
Executions, generally, this index
Forfeitures, generally, this index
Goods, Wares and Merchandise, generally, this index
Liens and Incumbrances, generally, this index
Sales, generally, this index
Theft, generally, this index
Title to Property, generally, this index
Unclaimed property. Abandoned or Unclaimed Property, generally, this index
Withholding tax on wages, **Un Ins 13011**

PERSONAL PROPERTY BROKERS
Finance Lenders, generally, this index

PERSONAL SERVICE
Service of process. Process, this index

PERSONAL SERVICES
Contracts, **Labor 2855**
   Specific performance, restrictions against, **CC 3390**
Preferred claims, **Labor 100.5**
Specific performance, restrictions against, **CC 3390**

PERSONNEL BOARDS AND COMMISSIONS
Civil Service, generally, this index
School Officers and Employees, this index

PERSONNEL SERVICES BUREAU
Consumer Affairs Department, generally, this index

PERSONNEL SYSTEM
Civil Service, generally, this index

PERSONS
Words and Phrases, this index

PERSONS WITH DISABILITIES
Handicapped Persons, generally, this index

PESTICIDE REGULATION DEPARTMENT
Pesticides, generally, this index

PESTICIDES
Agriculture labor contractors, safety examinations, **Labor 1684**
Examinations and examiners, safety, farm labor contractors, **Labor 1684**
Farm labor contractors, safety examination, **Labor 1684**
Poisoning, medical reports, **Labor 6409**
Poisons, **Labor 6409**
Reports, poisoning cases, **Labor 6409**
Safety, examinations and examiners, farm labor contractors, **Labor 1684**

PESTILENCE
Diseases, generally, this index

PETIT JURY
Jury, generally, this index

PETIT LARCENY
Theft, generally, this index

PETROLEUM
Oil and Gas, generally, this index

PETROLEUM ENGINEERS
Engineers, generally, this index

PETROLEUM PRODUCTS
Oil and Gas, generally, this index

PHARMACISTS
Alternative workweeks, **Labor 1186.5**
Compensation and salaries, exemptions, **Labor 1186**
Crimes and offenses, hours of labor, **Labor 853**
Emergencies, hours of labor, **Labor 854**

PHARMACISTS—Cont'd
Exemptions, compensation and salaries, **Labor 1186**
Hours of labor, **Labor 850 et seq.**
    Alternative workweeks, **Labor 1186.5**
Hypodermic Syringes and Needles, generally, this index

PHIALS
Containers, generally, this index
Drugs and Medicine, generally, this index

PHILANTHROPY
Charities, generally, this index

PHONORECORD CONTRACTS
Generally, **Labor 2855**

PHOTOGRAPHY AND PICTURES
Attorney fees, criminally related personal injury reports, frivolous actions, **Pen 11161.9**
Crimes and Offenses, this index
Labor and Employment, this index
Lewdness and Obscenity, generally, this index
Management companies, employees, **Labor 1057**
Motion Pictures, generally, this index
Obscenity. Lewdness and Obscenity, generally, this index
Occupational safety and health. Labor and Employment, this index
Pornography. Lewdness and Obscenity, generally, this index
Talent services, fees, **Labor 1703.4**

PHYSICAL DISABILITY
Definitions, fair employment and housing, **Gov 12926**

PHYSICAL EXAMINATIONS
Carcinogens, use in place of employment, **Labor 9040**
Drivers licenses, condition of employment, payment of expenses, **Labor 231**
Employment. Labor and Employment, this index
Family care leave, **Un Ins 3306**
Labor and Employment, this index
Occupational Carcinogens Control Act, **Labor 9040**
Occupational safety and health standards board, **Labor 142.3**
Preemployment examination, charging fee to employee, **Labor 222.5, 225**
Workers compensation, **Labor 4050 et seq.**

PHYSICAL THERAPISTS
Workers compensation,
    Treatment, **Labor 3209.5**
    Visits, numbers and numbering, **Labor 4604.5**

PHYSICALLY HANDICAPPED PERSONS
Handicapped Persons, generally, this index

PHYSICIAN ASSISTANTS
Reports, workers compensation, **Labor 3209.10**
Workers compensation, reports, **Labor 3209.10**

PHYSICIANS AND SURGEONS
Adverse or pecuniary interest, workers compensation, treatment, tests or studies, **Labor 139.3**
Advertisements, labor and employment, disability benefits and services, **Labor 139.4 et seq.**
Advocacy, appropriate health care, **Bus & P 2056**
Appropriate health care, advocacy, **Bus & P 2056**
Chiropractors, generally, this index
Clinics, generally, this index
Communications, appropriate health care, **Bus & P 2056**
Compulsory retirement, **Gov 12942**
Confidential or privileged information, forensic medical examinations, sexual assault, reports, **Pen 11160.1**
Contracts, preferred reimbursement rates, **Labor 4609**
Controlled substances. Drugs and Medicine, generally, this index
Definitions,
    Personal physician, workers compensation, **Labor 4600**
    Unemployment compensation, disability, **Un Ins 2708**
    Workers compensation, **Labor 3209.3**
Disability insurance. Insurance, this index
Discipline, application of law, **Bus & P 2056**
Disclosure, preferred reimbursement rates, **Labor 4609**
Drugs and Medicine, generally, this index
Evidence, presumptions, primary care clinics, independent contractors, **Labor 2750.6**
Forensic medical examinations, sexual assault, reports, **Pen 11160.1**
Gag rule, **Bus & P 2056**
Handicapped persons, certificate of disability, **Un Ins 2708**
Health Care Service Plans, this index
Health insurance, disability insurance. Insurance, this index
Hours of labor, overtime, exemptions, **Labor 515.6**
Hypodermic Syringes and Needles, generally, this index
Independent contractors, primary care clinics, presumptions, **Labor 2750.6**
Information, appropriate health care, **Bus & P 2056**
Labor and employment,
    Confidential or privileged information, whistle blowing, **Labor 1102.5**
    Occupational safety and health, reports, **Labor 6409**
    Overtime, exemptions, **Labor 515.6**
Medical Records, generally, this index

PHYSICIANS AND SURGEONS—Cont'd
Medically appropriate health care for patients, capability of advocating, **Bus & P 2056**
Medicine. Drugs and Medicine, generally, this index
Motion pictures, children and minors, labor and employment, certificates, **Labor 1308.8**
Narcotics. Drugs and Medicine, generally, this index
Occupational health and medicine, development and training, **Labor 50.8**
Osteopaths, generally, this index
Outpatient settings. Clinics, this index
Overtime, exemptions, **Labor 515.6**
Peer review, medical records, disclosure, **CC 56.10**
Personal services arrangements, referrals, workers compensation, **Labor 139.31**
Physical Examinations, generally, this index
Presumptions, primary care clinics, independent contractors, **Labor 2750.6**
Primary care clinics, presumptions, independent contractors, **Labor 2750.6**
Priorities and preferences, reimbursement rates, **Labor 4609**
Privilege of physician patient, whistle blowing, application of law, **Labor 1102.5**
Privileges and immunities,
    Criminally related personal injuries, reports, **Pen 11161.9**
    Forensic medical examinations, sexual assault, reports, **Pen 11160.1**
Psychiatric Technicians, generally, this index
Psychologists and Psychology, generally, this index
Psychotherapists and Psychotherapy, generally, this index
Public policy, advocating for medically appropriate health care for patients, **Bus & P 2056**
Rates and charges, preferred reimbursement rates, **Labor 4609**
Records and recordation. Medical Records, generally, this index
Reimbursement, preferred reimbursement rates, **Labor 4609**
Reports, personal injuries caused by abuse, patients received from another health facility, **Pen 11161.8**
Retaliation, advocacy for appropriate health care, **Bus & P 2056**
Sexual assault, forensic medical examinations, reports, **Pen 11160.1**
Sterilization of persons. Birth Control, this index
Unemployment Compensation, this index
Workers Compensation, this index

PICKETING
Injunction, **CCP 527.3**
Labor Disputes, this index

PICRIC ACID
Explosives, generally, this index

PICTURES
Photography and Pictures, generally, this index

PIERS
Wharves, Docks and Piers, generally, this index

PILOT PROGRAMS
Jails, reentry, assistance, indigent persons, inmate welfare fund, **Pen 4025.5**
Support, this index

PILOTS
Aircraft, generally, this index

PIPES AND PIPELINES
Labor and employment, occupational safety and health, bids for construction of pipelines, **Labor 6707**
Occupational safety and health, bids for construction, **Labor 6707**
Sewers and Sewer Systems, generally, this index
Tests, gas pipelines, on safe place of employment, **Labor 6700**

PISTOLS
Weapons, generally, this index

PLACE OF EMPLOYMENT
Definitions,
    Occupational safety and health, **Labor 6303**
    Smoking, **Labor 6404.5**

PLACE OF TRIAL
Venue, generally, this index

PLACEMENT
Unemployment compensation, workforce investment, **Un Ins 14000 et seq.**

PLAINTIFF
Parties, generally, this index

PLANES
Aircraft, generally, this index

PLANNING
Zoning and Planning, generally, this index

PLANS AND SPECIFICATIONS
Asbestos, management plans, buildings, **Health & S 25915.1**
Correctional Institutions, this index
Employment development department, automation, **Un Ins 4900 et seq.**
Employment training, **Un Ins 10205**
Health Care Service Plans, generally, this index
Health Care Services Department, this index
Labor and Employment, this index
Labor camps, prototype housing plans, **Health & S 17022.5**
Land use planning. Zoning and Planning, generally, this index

PLANS AND SPECIFICATIONS—Cont'd
Local workforce investment boards, **Un Ins 14220 et seq.**
Workers Compensation, this index
Workforce investment board, **Un Ins 14020**
Zoning and Planning, generally, this index

PLASMA CENTERS
Reports, AIDS, blood test results, **Health & S 120980**

PLASTICS
Lead poisoning, occupational safety, programs, **Health & S 105185 et seq.**

PLATFORM LIFTS
Elevators, Dumbwaiters and Escalators, generally, this index

PLAYS
Definitions, child labor, **Labor 1390**

PLEADINGS
Answer,
    Counterclaim. Setoff and Counterclaim, generally, this index
    Setoff and Counterclaim, generally, this index
Counterclaim. Setoff and Counterclaim, generally, this index
Dissolution of marriage. Marriage, this index
Injunction, generally, this index
Labor and employment, aggrieved employees, actions and proceedings, **Labor 2699.3**
Mandamus, generally, this index
Setoff and Counterclaim, generally, this index
Workers Compensation, this index

PLUMBERS AND PLUMBING
Comfort Stations and Rest Rooms, generally, this index
Foundries, **Labor 2330**
Metal shops and foundries, **Labor 2330**

PLUMS
Fruits, generally, this index

PNEUMONIA
District attorneys, workers compensation, **Labor 3212**
Firemen, workers compensation, **Labor 3212**
Fish and game wardens, workers compensation, **Labor 3212**
Highway patrol, workers compensation, **Labor 3212.5**
Police, workers compensation, **Labor 3212 et seq.**
Sheriffs, workers compensation, **Labor 3212, 3212.5**
University of California, police, workers compensation, **Labor 3213**
Workers Compensation, this index

PODIATRISTS (CHIROPODY)
Disability compensation, certificate of disability, **Un Ins 2708**
Health care service plans, lists, **Health & S 1367.26**
Hypodermic Syringes and Needles, generally, this index
Outpatient settings. Clinics, this index
Privileges and immunities, criminally related personal injuries, reports, **Pen 11161.9**
Unemployment compensation, primary care clinics, **Un Ins 656**

POISONS
Industrial homework, manufacturer, **Labor 2651**
Lead, this index
Pesticides, this index

POLICE
Airports and Landing Fields, this index
Arrest, generally, this index
Biochemical substances, workers compensation, presumptions, **Labor 3212.85**
Blood borne infectious diseases, workers compensation, presumptions, **Labor 3212.8**
Colleges and Universities, this index
Community colleges and districts. Colleges and Universities, this index
Confidential or privileged information, criminal history information, disclosure by former employers, applicants, **Gov 1031.1**
Costs, criminal history information, applicants, disclosure by other employers, **Gov 1031.1**
Counseling services, weapons ban removal, **Pen 12021**
County Officers and Employees Retirement Systems, generally, this index
Crimes and offenses, reserves or auxiliaries, absence and absentees, labor and employment, emergency duties, **Labor 230.3**
Criminal history information, applicants, disclosure by former employers, **Gov 1031.1**
Death, in line of duty, dependents, scholarships, **Labor 4709**
Dependents, scholarships, **Labor 4709**
Disability, workers compensation, **Labor 4702**
Discharge, reserves or auxiliaries, absence and absentees, labor and employment, emergency duties, **Labor 230.3**
Discrimination, reserves or auxiliaries, absence and absentees, labor and employment, emergency duties, **Labor 230.3**
Emergencies, reserves or auxiliaries, absence and absentees, labor and employment, **Labor 230.3**
Handicapped persons, disability in line of duty, dependents, scholarships, **Labor 4709**

POLICE—Cont'd
Harbors and Ports, this index
Heart trouble,
    Employment, discrimination, **Gov 12940.1**
    Workers compensation, **Labor 3211**
Hernias, workers compensation, **Labor 3212**
Highway Patrol, generally, this index
In line of duty. Death, ante
Investigations and investigators,
    Applicants for employment, disclosure by other employers, **Gov 1031.1**
    Industrial homework, powers, **Labor 2666**
Labor and employment, heart trouble, presumptions, **Gov 12940.1**
Leaves of absence, workers compensation, disability benefits, **Labor 4850**
Los Angeles unified school district, leaves of absence, disability benefits, **Labor 4850**
Lower back impairment, workers compensation, **Labor 3213.2**
Meningitis, workers compensation, presumptions, **Labor 3212.9**
Methicillin resistant staphylococcus aureus (MRSA) skin infections, workers compensation, presumptions, **Labor 3212.8**
Occupational safety and health, fines and penalties, **Labor 6434.5**
Pneumonia, workers compensation, **Labor 3212**
Ports. Harbors and Ports, this index
Privileges and immunities,
    Applicants for employment, disclosure by former employers, **Gov 1031.1**
    Weapons possession ban, incorrect enforcement, **Pen 12021**
Railroads, this index
Reserves or auxiliaries,
    Discrimination, absence and absentees, labor and employment, emergency duties, **Labor 230.3**
    Workers compensation, **Labor 3362.5**
Retirement and pensions. County Officers and Employees Retirement Systems, generally, this index
San Francisco Harbor, this index
Scholarships, dependents, **Labor 4709**
Searches and Seizures, generally, this index
Third parties, damages, workers compensation claims, **Labor 3852**
University of California. Colleges and Universities, this index
Weapons, incorrect enforcement, immunity, **Pen 12021**
    Petition for relief, **Pen 12021**
Workers compensation, **Labor 3362**
    Actions against third persons, **Labor 3852**
    Biochemical substances, presumptions, **Labor 3212.85**

POLICE—Cont'd
Workers compensation—Cont'd
    Blood borne infectious diseases, presumptions, **Labor 3212.8**
    Disability benefits, **Labor 4702**
    Hepatitis, presumptions, **Labor 3212.8**
    Hernia, heart trouble and pneumonia, **Labor 3212, 3212.5**
    Leaves of absence, disability benefits, **Labor 4850**
    Lower back impairment, **Labor 3213.2**
    Meningitis, presumptions, **Labor 3212.9**
    Off duty officer performing service, **Labor 3600.3**
    Pneumonia, **Labor 3212.5**
    Reserves or auxiliaries, **Labor 3362.5**
    Scholarships, dependents, **Labor 4709**
    Tuberculosis, **Labor 3212.6**
    University of California, **Labor 3213, 4806 et seq.**
    Volunteer police, **Labor 4458.2**

POLICE POWERS
Unemployment compensation, **Un Ins 100**
Workers compensation, **Labor 3201**

POLICEMAN
Police, generally, this index

POLICIES
Insurance, this index
Public Policy, generally, this index

POLITICAL SUBDIVISIONS
Airports and Landing Fields, generally, this index
Application of law, labor camps, **Health & S 17024**
Bids and bidding. Public Contracts, this index
Cable Television, generally, this index
Claims, false claims, **Gov 12650 et seq.**
Consolidated Cities and Counties, generally, this index
Contracts, bids and bidding. Public Contracts, this index
Counties, generally, this index
Definitions,
    False claims against state, **Gov 12650**
    Public works, **Labor 1721**
Districts, generally, this index
Employment compensation, employer, definitions, **Un Ins 677**
Health Facilities, generally, this index
Labor camps, application of state law, **Health & S 17024**
Landing fields. Airports and Landing Fields, generally, this index
Local Agencies, generally, this index
Municipalities, generally, this index
Officers and employees, unemployment compensation, excluded service, **Un Ins 634.5**
Public Buildings and Works, generally, this index
Public Entities, generally, this index
Schools and School Districts, generally, this index

POLITICAL SUBDIVISIONS—Cont'd
Sewers and Sewer Systems, generally, this index
Taxation, generally, this index
Unemployment compensation,
    Elective coverage, **Un Ins 709**
    Employees, excluded services, **Un Ins 634.5**
    Employing unit, **Un Ins 135**
    Public entity, definitions, **Un Ins 135, 605**

POLLUTION
Hazardous Substances and Waste, generally, this index

POOLED MONEY INVESTMENT BOARD
State Treasury, this index

POOR PERSONS
Indigent Persons, generally, this index

POPULAR NAME LAWS
Agricultural Labor Relations Act, **Labor 1140 et seq.**
Alatorre Zenovich Dunlap Berman Agricultural Labor Relations Act, **Labor 1140 et seq.**
Amusement rides safety, **Labor 7900 et seq.**
Antiblacklisting Act, **Labor 1050 et seq.**
Antiyellow Dog Act, **Labor 921**
Apprentice Labor Standards Act, **Labor 3070 et seq.**
Arbitration Act, **CCP 1280 et seq.**
Blacklisting Act, **Labor 1050 et seq.**
Boiler Inspection Law, **Labor 7680 et seq.**
Burton Stull Vietnam Veterans Employment Act, **Gov 7280 et seq.**
Business Establishments Act, equal rights, **CC 51, 52**
Cal COBRA, **Health & S 1366.20 et seq.; Ins 10128.50 et seq.**
California State University Investigation of Reported Improper Governmental Activities Act, **Educ 89570 et seq.**
Child Labor Law, **Labor 1290 et seq.**
Civil Air Patrol Employment Protection Act, **Labor 1500 et seq.**
Civil Rights Act, **CC 51 et seq.**
Collier Miller Act, **Un Ins 3501 et seq.**
Consumer Credit Reporting Agencies Act, **CC 1785.1 et seq.**
Continuation Benefits Replacement Act, **Health & S 1366.20 et seq.; Ins 10128.50 et seq.**
Corporate Criminal Liability Act, **Pen 387**
Credit, Consumer Credit Reporting Agencies Act, **CC 1785.1 et seq.**
Criminal Trespass Act, **Pen 602**
Days Rest Law, **Labor 550 et seq.**
Defense of Marriage Act, **Fam 308.5**
Disability Benefits Law (unemployment compensation), **Un Ins 2601 et seq.**
Displaced Janitor Opportunity Act, **Labor 1060 et seq.**
Drug Free Workplace Act, **Gov 8350 et seq.**

POPULAR

POPULAR NAME LAWS—Cont'd

Earned Income Tax Credit Information Act, **Rev & T 19850 et seq.**

Eight Hour Act, **Labor 500 et seq.**
Minors, **Labor 1390 et seq.**

Employee Housing Act, **Health & S 17000 et seq.**

Employee Illiteracy Education Assistance Act, **Labor 1040 et seq.**

Employees Bond Law, **Labor 400 et seq.**

Employees Drinking Water Law, **Labor 2441**

Employees Political Rights Law, **Labor 1101 et seq.**

Employees Purchase Law, **Labor 450 et seq.**

Employees Safety Act, **Labor 6300 et seq.**

Employers Liability Act, **Labor 2801**

Employment Agency, Employment Counseling and Job Listing Services Act, **CC 1812.500 et seq.**

Employment Contracts Law, **Labor 430 et seq.**

Employment Taxpayers Bill of Rights Act, **Un Ins 1231 et seq.**

Enforcement of Fair Labor Standards Act, **Labor 50.6**

Engine Cab Handrail Law (railroads), **Labor 6952**

Engine Tender Clearance Law, **Labor 6950, 6951**

Equal Pay Act, **Labor 1197.5**

Equal Rights Law, **CC 51, 52**

Extended unemployment compensation, **Un Ins 3501 et seq.**

Factory Medical Chest Law, **Labor 2440**

Factory Sanitation Law, **Labor 2350 et seq.**

Fair Employment and Housing Act, **Gov 12900 et seq.**

False Claims Act, **Gov 12650 et seq.**

False Pretenses Act, **Pen 484**

Foundry Sanitation Law, **Labor 2330, 2331**

Full Crew Law (railroads), **Labor 6901 et seq.**

Garnishment, Wage Garnishment Law, **CCP 706.010**

Green Collar Jobs Act, **Un Ins 15000 et seq.**

Hazardous Substances Information and Training Act, **Labor 6360 et seq.**

Health Facilities Whistleblowers Law, **Health & S 1278.5**

Health Insurance Access and Equity Act, **Labor 2808**

Homework Act, **Labor 2650 et seq.**

Industrial Compensation Law, **Labor 3201 et seq.**

Industrial Homework Act, **Labor 2650 et seq.**

Industrial welfare commission, **Labor 70 et seq.**

Information Practices Act, **CC 1798 et seq.**

POPULAR NAME LAWS—Cont'd

Investigative Consumer Reporting Agencies Act, consumer employment or insurance investigation, **CC 1786 et seq.**

Jobs Tax Credit Act, **Rev & T 23621**

Jurisdictional Strikes Act, **Labor 1115 et seq.**

Labor Code Private Attorneys General Act, **Labor 2698, 2699**

Literacy, Employee Illiteracy Education Assistance Act, **Labor 1040 et seq.**

Lumber Laborers Lunch Hour Law, **Labor 800, 801**

McAlister Duffy Greene Unemployment Benefit Pension Offset Refund Act, **Un Ins 1255.3**

Miller Collier Act, **Un Ins 3501 et seq.**

Mine Telephone Law, **Labor 7500, 7501**

Miners Eight Hour Day Law, **Labor 750 et seq.**

Miners Wages Law, **Labor 270**

Moore Brown Roberti Family Rights Act, **Gov 12945.1, 12945.2**

New and Further Disability Act (workers compensation), **Labor 5410**

Occupational Carcinogens Control Act, **Labor 9000 et seq.**

Occupational Safety and Health Act, **Labor 6300 et seq.**

One Day In Seven Act, **Labor 551 et seq.**

Permanent amusement ride safety inspection program, **Labor 7920 et seq.**

Prevailing Wage Rate Law, **Labor 1770 et seq.**

Public Accommodations Act, **CC 52**

Public Works Wage Rate Act, **Labor 1770 et seq.**

Railroad Antifeatherbedding Law, **Labor 6900.1, 6900.5**

Ralph Civil Rights Act, **CC 51.7, 52**

Refinery and Chemical Plant Workers Safety Act, **Labor 7850 et seq.**

Regular Pay Day Law, **Labor 200 et seq.**

Reporting by Community College Employees of Improper Governmental Activities Act, **Educ 87160 et seq.**

Reporting by School Employees of Improper Governmental Activities Act, **Educ 44110 et seq.**

Roseberry Act (employers liability), **Labor 2801**

Safety Act (employees), **Labor 6300 et seq.**

Scaffolding Act, **Labor 7150 et seq.**

Seasonal Labor Wages Law, **Labor 250 et seq.**

SemiMonthly Pay Day Law, **Labor 204**

Shelley Maloney Apprentice Labor Standards Act, **Labor 3070 et seq.**

Soldiers and Sailors Relief Act, **Mil & V 395.1**

Solicitation of Employees Law, **Labor 973, 974**

Steam Boiler Inspection Law, **Labor 7680 et seq.**

POPULAR NAME LAWS—Cont'd

Taxpayer Browsing Protection Act, **Un Ins 13018**

Tipping laws, **Labor 350 et seq.**

Tom Carrell Memorial Tunnel and Mine Safety Act, **Labor 7950 et seq.**

Train Employees Hours Law, **Labor 600 et seq.**

Train Manning Law, **Labor 6901 et seq.**

Trespass, Criminal Trespass Act, **Pen 602**

Unemployment Compensation Disability Benefits Law, **Un Ins 2601 et seq.**

Unemployment Relief Act, **Labor 2010 et seq.**

Unemployment Reserves Act, **Un Ins 1025 et seq.**

Unruh Civil Rights Act, **CC 51, 52**

Utility Employees Service Letter Law, **Labor 1055, 1056**

Victims Of Domestic Violence Employment Leave Act, **Labor 230**

Vietnam Veterans Employment Act, **Gov 7280 et seq.**

Voluntary Arbitration Law, **CCP 1280 et seq.**

Wage Garnishment Law, **CCP 706.010**

Wage Payment Law, **Labor 200 et seq.**

Willie L. Brown, Jr. Bill Lockyer Civil Liability Reform Act, **CC 3294**

Workers Compensation Law, **Labor 3201 et seq.**

Workers Compensation Truth in Advertising Act, **Labor 5430 et seq.**

Workforce Investment Act, **Un Ins 14000 et seq.**

Workplace Violence Safety Act, **CCP 527.8**

Young La Follette Self Insurers Security Act, **Labor 3740 et seq.**

Youthbuild Program Law, **Un Ins 9800 et seq.**

PORNOGRAPHY

Lewdness and Obscenity, generally, this index

PORT HUENEME

Municipalities, generally, this index

PORTABLE AND MOBILE INTERNAL COMBUSTION ENGINES

Generally, **Labor 6701 et seq.**

PORTABLE FIRE EXTINGUISHERS

Fire Extinguishers, generally, this index

POSSE COMITATUS

Workers compensation, **Labor 4458.2**

POSSESSION

Weapons, this index

POSTAL SERVICE

Mail and Mailing, generally, this index

POSTERS

Employment agencies, misrepresentations, earnings of salesmen, brokers or agents, **Labor 976**

POSTERS—Cont'd
Sexual harassment, workplace, **Gov 12950**
Solicitation of employees, representation, **Labor 973**

POSTING
Aerial passenger tramways, permits for operation, **Labor 7341**
Car washes, registration,
  Certificates and certification, **Labor 2057**
  Internet, **Labor 2063**
Citations, occupational safety and health, **Labor 6318**
Compensation and salaries,
  Failure to post notices, evidence of violations, **Labor 215**
  Posting notice of regular pay days, **Labor 207**
Elections, this index
Fish and Game, this index
Labor and Employment, this index
No smoking signs, workplaces, **Labor 6404.5**
Occupational safety and health citations, orders and findings of no violations, **Labor 6318**
Talent agencies, applicable laws, **Labor 1700.28**
Wearing apparel, manufacturers, registration forms, **Labor 2675**
Whistle blowing, notice, **Labor 1102.8**
Workplace no smoking signs, **Labor 6404.5**

POSTSECONDARY EDUCATION
Colleges and Universities, generally, this index

POTTERY
Lead poisoning, occupational safety, programs, **Health & S 105185 et seq.**

POTWS
Sewers and Sewer Systems, generally, this index

POULTRY AND POULTRY PRODUCTS
Labor, compensation, time due and payable, **Labor 205**

POVERTY
Indigent Persons, generally, this index

POWDER
Explosives, generally, this index

POWER BOATS
Boats and Boating, generally, this index

POWER COMPANIES
Electricity, generally, this index

POWER OF ATTORNEY
Assignment of wages, revocability, **Labor 300**
Gratuitous employee, **Labor 2852**
Revocation or suspension, assignment of wages, **Labor 300**

POWER PRESS
Definitions, workers compensation, **Labor 4558**

PRACTICE OF LAW
Attorneys, generally, this index

PRACTITIONERS
Definitions, unemployment compensation, disability, **Un Ins 2708**

PRAYER HEALING
Faith Healing, generally, this index

PREACHERS
Clergy, generally, this index

PRECINCTS
Election Precincts, generally, this index

PREEMPTION
Domestic partnership, **Fam 299.6**

PREEXISTING WORKWEEK ARRANGE-MENT
Definitions, hours of labor, **Labor 1182.6**

PREFERENCES
Priorities and Preferences, generally, this index

PREGNANCY
Disability compensation, **Un Ins 2626**
Fair employment and housing, unlawful practices, **Gov 12945**
Labor and employment, unlawful practices, **Gov 12945**
School Officers and Employees, this index

PREMIUMS
Health Care Service Plans, this index
Insurance, this index

PREPAID HEALTH PLANS
Health Care Service Plans, generally, this index

PREPONDERANCE OF THE EVIDENCE
Definitions, workers compensation, **Labor 3202.5**

PREQUALIFYING REPORT
Definitions, consumer credit reporting agencies, **CC 1785.3**

PRESIDENTIAL PRIMARY
Elections, this index

PRESS
Newspapers, generally, this index

PRESSURE VESSEL ACCOUNT
Generally, **Labor 7722**

PRESSURE VESSELS
Boilers, generally, this index

PRESUMPTIONS
Evidence, this index

PRETRIAL OR POSTTRIAL DIVERSION PROGRAM
Definitions, labor and employment, job applicants, disclosure of referrals or participation, **Labor 432.7**

PREVAILING WAGE RATE LAW
Generally, **Labor 1770 et seq.**

PRICES
Children and minors, price marking and tagging, employment, **Labor 1294.3**

PRIESTS
Clergy, generally, this index

PRIMARILY
Definitions, labor and employment, hours of labor, **Labor 515**

PRIMARY CARE CLINICS
Clinics, this index

PRIMARY ELECTIONS
Elections, this index

PRINCIPAL AND ACCESSORY
Accomplices and Accessories, generally, this index

PRINCIPAL AND AGENT
Agents, generally, this index

PRINTING
Lead poisoning, occupational safety, programs, **Health & S 105185 et seq.**
Lewdness and Obscenity, generally, this index
Libel and Slander, generally, this index
Obscenity. Lewdness and Obscenity, generally, this index
Pornography. Lewdness and Obscenity, generally, this index

PRIORITIES AND PREFERENCES
Actions and Proceedings, this index
Agricultural Labor and Employment, this index
Appeal and Review, this index
Assignment for Benefit of Creditors, this index
Assignment of wages, **Labor 300**
CalWORKs. Social Services, this index
Disability compensation, voluntary plans, funds, **Un Ins 3261**
Employment development, **Un Ins 9602**
  State department of, space, **Un Ins 3015**
Executions, this index
Garnishment, this index
Labor and Employment, this index
Leisure sharing program grants, employment opportunities creation, **Un Ins 12114**
Liens and Incumbrances, this index
Physicians and Surgeons, this index
Review. Appeal and Review, this index
Support, this index
Talent agencies, restitution, fees, **Labor 1704**
Trusts and Trustees, this index

PRIORITIES AND PREFERENCES—Cont'd
Unemployment Compensation, this index
Veterans, this index
Workers Compensation, this index

PRISONS AND PRISONERS
Correctional Institutions, generally, this index
Jails, generally, this index

PRIVACY
Alcoholics and alcoholism, voluntary rehabilitation program enrollment, employer safeguarding of privacy, **Labor 1026**
Harassment, injunctions, **CCP 527.6**
Information Practices Act, **CC 1798 et seq.**
Invasion of privacy,
Information Practices Act, **CC 1798 et seq.**
Investigative consumer reporting agencies, action for damages, **CC 1786.52**
Investigative consumer reporting agencies, action for damages, **CC 1786.52**

PRIVATE CEMETERIES
Cemeteries and Dead Bodies, generally, this index

PRIVATE CORPORATIONS
Corporations, generally, this index

PRIVATE DETECTIVES
Private Investigators, generally, this index

PRIVATE FOUNDATIONS
Foundations, generally, this index

PRIVATE INDUSTRY COUNCIL
Definitions, job training or employment training panel, **Un Ins 10201**

PRIVATE INVESTIGATORS
Labor and employment, investigations, **Labor 2930 et seq.**
Licenses and permits, **Labor 2930 et seq.**
Officers and employees, investigations, **Labor 2930 et seq.**

PRIVATE PATROL OPERATORS
Private Security Services, this index

PRIVATE SCHOOLS
Hours of labor, work experience education programs, **Labor 1391.1**
Overtime, schoolteachers, exemptions, **Labor 515.8**
Schoolteachers, overtime, exemptions, **Labor 515.8**
Unemployment compensation, excluded services, option, **Un Ins 711**
Vocational Education, this index
Work experience education programs, hours of labor, **Labor 1391.1**

PRIVATE SECURITY SERVICES
Actions and proceedings,
Contracts, labor and employment, **Labor 2810**

PRIVATE SECURITY SERVICES—Cont'd
Actions and proceedings—Cont'd
Private patrol operators, retaliation, officers and employees, disclosure, **Bus & P 7583.46**
Attorney fees, contracts, labor and employment, **Labor 2810**
Contracts, labor and employment, **Labor 2810**
Costs, contracts, labor and employment, **Labor 2810**
Crimes and offenses, officers and employees, records and recordation, disclosure, **Pen 11105.4**
Damages,
Contracts, labor and employment, **Labor 2810**
Private patrol operators, retaliation, officers and employees, disclosure, **Bus & P 7583.46**
Employees convicted of crime, disclosure, **Pen 11105.4**
Injunction, contracts, labor and employment, **Labor 2810**
Labor and employment, contracts, **Labor 2810**
Limitation of actions, private patrol operators, retaliation, officers and employees, disclosure, **Bus & P 7583.46**
Officers and employees,
Crimes and offenses, disclosure, **Pen 11105.4**
Criminal history, disclosure, **Pen 11105.4**
Private patrol operators,
Actions and proceedings, retaliation, officers and employees, disclosure, **Bus & P 7583.46**
Damages, retaliation, officers and employees, disclosure, **Bus & P 7583.46**
Limitation of actions, retaliation, officers and employees, disclosure, **Bus & P 7583.46**
Officers and employees, retaliation, disclosure, **Bus & P 7583.46**
Retaliation, officers and employees, disclosure, **Bus & P 7583.46**
Retaliation, private patrol operators, officers and employees, disclosure, **Bus & P 7583.46**
Statute of limitations, private patrol operators, retaliation, officers and employees, disclosure, **Bus & P 7583.46**

PRIVATE SELF INSURERS
Definitions, workers compensation self insurance, **Labor 3741**

PRIVATE SMOKERS LOUNGES
Definitions, workplaces, **Labor 6404.5**
Workplace smoking regulation, exemption, **Labor 6404.5**

PRIVIES
Comfort Stations and Rest Rooms, generally, this index

PRIVILEGED COMMUNICATIONS
Confidential or Privileged Information, generally, this index

PRIVILEGES AND IMMUNITIES
Adult abuse reports, **Welf & I 15634**
Banks and Banking, this index
Chiropractors, this index
Clinics, this index
Coroners, this index
Credit Unions, this index
Dentists and Dentistry, this index
Elections, this index
Emergency Medical Technicians, this index
Former employee, misrepresentation to prevent obtaining employment, **Labor 1050 et seq.**
Garnishment, this index
Health Care Providers, this index
Health care services department, forensic medical examinations, sexual assault, reports, **Pen 11160.1**
Health Facilities, this index
Hospitals, this index
Industrial relations department, officers and employees, civil liability for arrest or use of force, **Labor 95**
Insurance, this index
Judicial proceedings, libel and slander, **CC 47**
Labor and Employment, this index
Labor disputes, **Labor 1138**
Agreements in connection with, **Labor 1110**
Labor law enforcement division, officers and employees, civil liability, arrest or use of force, **Labor 95**
Law Enforcement, this index
Legislature, this index
Libel and Slander, this index
Local health departments, forensic medical examinations, sexual assault, reports, **Pen 11160.1**
Marriage and Family Therapists, this index
Medical records, release, **CC 56.36**
Military Forces, this index
Nurses, this index
Optometrists, this index
Peace Officers, this index
Physicians and Surgeons, this index
Podiatrists (Chiropody), this index
Police, this index
Political activities of employees, **Labor 1101 et seq.**
Psychologists and Psychology, this index
Public Officers and Employees, this index
Reemployment privileges, **Labor 1050 et seq.**
Religious Organizations and Societies, this index
Savings and Loan Associations, this index
Savings Associations, this index
Sheriffs, this index
Support, this index
Taxation, this index

PRIVILEGES AND IMMUNITIES—Cont'd
Unemployment compensation proceedings, immunity from criminal prosecution, **Un Ins 1955**
Workers Compensation, this index

PROBATE OF WILLS
Probate Proceedings, generally, this index

PROBATE PROCEEDINGS
Claims against estate,
Labor and personal services, **Labor 97.5**
Unemployment compensation, **Un Ins 1090**
Workers compensation, **Labor 5306**
Conservators and Conservatorships, generally, this index
Escheat, generally, this index
Executors and administrators. Unemployment Compensation, this index
Guardian and Ward, generally, this index
Labor and employment, claims against estate, personal services, **Labor 97.5**
Medical records, disclosure, conservators and conservatorships, **CC 56.10**
Talent agencies, certificate of convenience to conduct business, **Labor 1700.20a, 1700.20b**
Unemployment Compensation, this index
Workers compensation,
Death benefits, dependent beneficiaries, **Labor 4706**
Lump sum payment, deposits, **Labor 5102**
Presentation of claims, **Labor 5306**
Wrongful death, actions for, labor and employment, **Labor 2803**

PROBATION
Parole and Probation, generally, this index

PROBATION OFFICERS
Parole and Probation, this index

PROBATIONARY EMPLOYEES
School Officers and Employees, this index

PROCEEDINGS
Actions and Proceedings, generally, this index

PROCESS
Agent for service of process, farm labor contractors, license application, **Labor 1684**
Attachment, generally, this index
Compensation and salaries, failure to pay to employees, recovery of penalties, **Labor 211**
Contractors, this index
Exemptions,
Bonds, employees cash bond, **Labor 404**
Cash bond of employee, **Labor 404**
Door to door salesmen, money deposited as security for wages, **Labor 270.6**
Employees cash bond, **Labor 404**
Itinerant merchants, money deposited as security for wages, **Labor 270.6**

PROCESS—Cont'd
Exemptions—Cont'd
Telephone solicitors, money deposited as security for wages, **Labor 270.6**
Farm labor contracts, service, **Labor 1694**
Garnishment, generally, this index
Harassment, protective orders, service, **CCP 527.6**
Industrial relations department, public officers, **Labor 95**
Injunction, generally, this index
Labor disputes, injunction, **Labor 1138.1**
Labor standards enforcement division, officers and employees, service, **Labor 95**
Labor violations, **Labor 95**
Motor Vehicles, this index
Service of process,
Agricultural Labor and Employment, this index
Agricultural Labor Relations Act, **Labor 1165.3**
Agricultural labor relations board, **Labor 1151.4**
Colleges and Universities, this index
Enforcement agencies, labor camps, **Health & S 17051**
Fair employment and housing, **Gov 12986**
Harassment, protective orders, **CCP 527.6**
Industrial homework, searches and seizures, appeal and review, **Labor 2664**
Industrial relations department, public officers, **Labor 95**
Labor camps, enforcement agencies, **Health & S 17051**
Labor violations, **Labor 95**
Support, this index
Trespass, exemptions, motor vehicles, **Pen 602**
Unemployment Compensation, this index
Subpoenas, generally, this index
Summons,
Labor standards enforcement division, costs, **Labor 101**
Workers compensation, appeals board, power to issue, **Labor 134**
Support persons, appearance in court, domestic violence, **CCP 527.6**
Unemployment Compensation, this index
Workers Compensation, this index

PROCESS SERVERS
Earnings withholding orders, service, **CCP 706.108**

PROCESSORS
Agricultural Products, this index

PRODUCE
Agricultural Products, generally, this index

PRODUCERS
Agricultural Products, generally, this index

PRODUCTION OF BOOKS AND PAPERS
Contractors and subcontractors, payroll records, public works project, **Labor 1776**
Employment records, **CCP 1985.6**
Fair employment and housing department, **Gov 12930, 12963.4**
Farm labor contractors, payroll records, **Labor 1695.5**
Labor and employment, **CCP 1985.6**
Labor commissioner, deputies and assistants, issuance of subpoenas, **Labor 92**
Labor standards enforcement division, investigations, **Labor 74**
Labor statistics and research division, **Labor 152**
Medical Records, this index
Occupational safety and health, **Labor 6314**
Payroll records, contractors and subcontractors,
Farm labor contractors, **Labor 1695.5**
Public works projects, **Labor 1776**
Talent agencies, **Labor 1703.1**
Unemployment compensation, appeals board, powers, **Un Ins 1953**
Wearing apparel, manufacturers and manufacturing, arbitration, **Labor 2689**
Workers Compensation, this index

PRODUCTS LIABILITY
Crimes and offenses, dangerous conditions, failure to disclose, **Pen 387**

PROFESSIONAL AND VOCATIONAL STANDARDS DEPARTMENT
Consumer Affairs Department, generally, this index

PROFESSIONAL ENGINEERS
Engineers, generally, this index

PROFESSIONAL SPORTS
Athletics, generally, this index

PROFESSIONAL STRIKEBREAKERS
Generally, **Labor 1130 et seq.**
Definitions, labor disputes, **Labor 1133**

PROFESSIONS AND OCCUPATIONS
Attorneys, generally, this index
Chiropody. Podiatrists (Chiropody), generally, this index
Chiropractors, generally, this index
Clergy, generally, this index
Contractors, generally, this index
Dentists and Dentistry, generally, this index
Discrimination, **Const. Art. 1, § 8**
Engineers, generally, this index
Foresters, generally, this index
Jockeys, generally, this index
Notaries Public, generally, this index
Nurses, generally, this index
Optometrists, generally, this index
Osteopaths, generally, this index
Pharmacists, generally, this index

PROFESSIONS

PROFESSIONS AND OCCUPATIONS
—Cont'd
Physicians and Surgeons, generally, this index
Podiatrists (Chiropody), generally, this index
Private Investigators, generally, this index
Private Security Services, generally, this index
Psychiatric Technicians, generally, this index
Psychologists and Psychology, generally, this index
Psychotherapists and Psychotherapy, generally, this index
Receivers and Receivership, generally, this index
Talent Agencies, generally, this index
Vocational Nursing, generally, this index

PROMISSORY NOTES
Negotiable Instruments, generally, this index

PROOF
Evidence, generally, this index

PROPAGANDA
Unemployment compensation, employment activities, eligibility, **Un Ins 2606**

PROPER IDENTIFICATION
Definitions,
Consumer credit reporting, **CC 1785.15**
Investigative consumer reporting agencies, **CC 1786.22**

PROPERTY
Deeds and Conveyances, generally, this index
Escheat, generally, this index
Leases, generally, this index
Real Estate, generally, this index
Title to Property, generally, this index

PROPERTY DAMAGE
Damages, generally, this index

PROPERTY TAXES
Taxation, generally, this index

PROSECUTING ATTORNEYS
District Attorneys, generally, this index

PROSECUTORS
District Attorneys, generally, this index

PROSPECTIVE RELIEF
Definitions, fair employment and housing, **Gov 12926**

PROSTHETIC APPLIANCES
Workers compensation, **Labor 4600**

PROSTITUTION
Farm labor contractors,
Contracts for employment, **Labor 1698.4**
Frequenting prostitutes, **Labor 1698.6**

PROTECTED DISCLOSURE
Definitions, whistle blowing, **Gov 8547.2**

PROTECTIVE ORDERS
Orders of Court, this index

PROTESTS
Extended unemployment compensation, computation of benefits, **Un Ins 3656**
Unemployment Compensation, this index

PROXIMATE CAUSE
Workers compensation,
Injury, **Labor 3602**
Injury caused by employment, **Labor 3600**

PSYCHIATRIC TECHNICIANS
Abuse, long term health care facilities, temporary employment, **CC 1812.543**
Criminal history information, long term health care facilities, temporary employment, **CC 1812.542**
Employment agencies, long term health care facilities, temporary employment, **CC 1812.540 et seq.**
Long term health care facilities, employment agencies, temporary employment, **CC 1812.540 et seq.**

PSYCHIATRISTS AND PSYCHIATRY
Correctional Institutions, this index
Psychotherapist patient privilege, criminally related personal injury reports, **Pen 11161.9**
Technicians. Psychiatric Technicians, generally, this index
Workers compensation, **Labor 3208.3**

PSYCHOLOGISTS AND PSYCHOLOGY
Definitions, workers compensation, **Labor 3209.3**
Health Care Service Plans, this index
Privileges and immunities, criminally related personal injuries, reports, **Pen 11161.9**
Talent agencies, fees, exemptions, **Labor 1703.6**
Unemployment compensation, primary care clinics, **Un Ins 656**
Workers Compensation, this index

PSYCHOTHERAPISTS AND PSYCHOTHER-APY
Confidential or privileged information, medical records, **CC 56.104**
Definitions, medical records, confidential or privileged information, **CC 56.104**
Medical records,
Confidential or privileged information, **CC 56.104**
Disclosure, threats, **CC 56.10**
Records and recordation, confidential or privileged information, **CC 56.104**

PUBLIC ACCOMMODATIONS
Discrimination, **CC 51 et seq.**

PUBLIC AGENCIES
Civil Service, generally, this index
Confidential employees, disability compensation, **Un Ins 710.5**
Definitions, meals, motor carriers, collective bargaining, **Labor 512.5**
Employees. Public Officers and Employees, generally, this index
Federal agencies. United States Agencies and Institutions, generally, this index
Finance Department, generally, this index
Management employees, disability compensation, **Un Ins 710.5**
Officers and employees. Public Officers and Employees, generally, this index
Public Buildings and Works, generally, this index
Public Employees Retirement System, generally, this index
Retirement system. Public Employees Retirement System, generally, this index
Social Security, generally, this index
State Agencies, generally, this index
Unemployment compensation,
Elective coverage, **Un Ins 709**
Disability compensation, **Un Ins 710.5**
Public entity, definitions, **Un Ins 135, 605**
Workers Compensation, this index

PUBLIC AID
Federal Aid, generally, this index

PUBLIC ASSISTANCE
Social Services, generally, this index

PUBLIC BENEFIT CORPORATIONS
Education, religious organizations and societies, labor and employment, **Gov 12926.2**
Labor and employment, religious organizations and societies, education, **Gov 12926.2**
Religious Organizations and Societies, this index

PUBLIC BODIES
Political Subdivisions, generally, this index
Public Agencies, generally, this index

PUBLIC BUILDINGS AND WORKS
Generally, **Labor 1720 et seq.**
Actions and proceedings,
Contractors,
Action against subcontractor for forfeiture, **Labor 1729**
Second highest bidder, highest bidders failure to have unemployment compensation or workers compensation coverage, **Labor 1750**
Prevailing wage rate, **Labor 1726, 1771.2, 1776, 1781**
Advertisements, contractors, debarment, **Labor 1777.1**

I–156

PUBLIC BUILDINGS AND WORKS—Cont'd
Appeal and review,
  Apprentices, fines and penalties, **Labor 1777.7**
  Contractors, compensation and salaries,
    Assessments, **Labor 1742**
    Withholding, **Labor 1771.6**
  Wage rate determination, **Labor 1773.4**
Apprentices,
  Appeal and review, fines and penalties, **Labor 1777.7**
  Compensation and salaries, **Labor 1777.5**
  Debarment, **Labor 1777.7**
  Discrimination, **Labor 1777.5, 1777.6**
  Employment, **Labor 1777.5**
  Exemption, small contracts, **Labor 1777.5**
  Fines and penalties, **Labor 1777.7**
  Specialty contractors, small contracts, **Labor 1777.5**
  Training programs, per diem wages, **Labor 1773.1**
Assessments, contractors, compensation and salaries, **Labor 1741 et seq.**
Attorney fees,
  Action by second highest bidder, failure of winning bidder to have workers compensation or unemployment compensation, **Labor 1750**
  Prevailing wage rate, **Labor 1726, 1776**
Benefits, prevailing wage rate, credits, **Labor 1773.1**
Bids and bidding,
  Contracts, wage rates, **Labor 1773.2**
  Debarment, contractors and subcontractors, **Labor 1777.1, 1777.7**
  Prevailing wage rates, publication, **Labor 1773**
  Second lowest bidder, workers compensation and unemployment compensation coverage, failure of highest bidder, actions, **Labor 1750**
  Unemployment compensation or workers compensation coverage, action by second highest bidder, **Labor 1750**
  Wage rates, **Labor 1773.2**
Certificates and certification,
  Apprentices, **Labor 1777.5**
  Workers compensation, **Labor 1861**
Collective bargaining, per diem wages, fees, **Labor 1773.1**
Comfort Stations and Rest Rooms, generally, this index
Compensation and salaries, **Labor 1770 et seq.**
  Actions and proceedings, prevailing wage rate, **Labor 1726, 1771.2, 1776, 1781**
  Apprentices, **Labor 1777.5**
  Attorney fees, prevailing wage rate, **Labor 1726, 1776**
  Bidding on contracts, wage rates, **Labor 1773.2**

PUBLIC BUILDINGS AND WORKS—Cont'd
Compensation and salaries—Cont'd
  Change of prevailing wage rates, notice, **Labor 1773.3**
  Computers, records and recordation, **Labor 1776**
  Contractors, post
  Costs, prevailing wage rate, **Labor 1726, 1776**
  Credit, prevailing wage rate, benefits, **Labor 1773.1**
  Crimes and offenses,
    Officer of awarding body, taking employees wages for own use, **Labor 1778**
    Records, failure to maintain, **Labor 1777**
  Federal minimum wage schedules, application, **Labor 1740**
  Fines and penalties, payment of less than prevailing wage rate, **Labor 1775**
  Forfeiture, payment of less than prevailing wage rate, **Labor 1775**
  Holidays, **Labor 1771, 1773.9**
    Rates, **Labor 1773**
  Labor compliance program, **Labor 1771.5**
  Limitation of actions, prevailing wage rate, **Labor 1771.2, 1775**
  Maintenance workers, prevailing wage rate, **Labor 1771**
  Overtime, **Labor 1771, 1773.9, 1815**
    Rates, **Labor 1773**
  Per diem wages, **Labor 1773.1, 1773.9**
  Prevailing wage rate, **Labor 1770 et seq.**
    Actions and proceedings, **Labor 1726, 1771.2, 1776, 1781**
    Attorney fees, **Labor 1726, 1776**
    California State University, construction, **Labor 1771.7**
    Changes, **Labor 1773.6**
    Colleges and universities, construction, **Labor 1771.7**
    Community colleges and districts, construction, **Labor 1771.7**
    Confidential or privileged information, investigations and investigators, **Labor 1736**
    Costs, **Labor 1726, 1776**
    Credit, benefits, **Labor 1773.1**
    Determination, **Labor 1773.11**
    Fees, compliance, **Labor 1771.3, 1771.55, 1771.85**
    Filing, **Labor 1773.3**
    Fines and penalties, **Labor 1775**
    Homeless persons, shelters, **Labor 1720**
    Housing, indigent persons, **Labor 1720**
    Indigent persons, housing, **Labor 1720**
    Labor compliance program, **Labor 1771.5**
    Limitation of actions, **Labor 1771.2, 1775**

PUBLIC BUILDINGS AND WORKS—Cont'd
Compensation and salaries—Cont'd
  Prevailing wage rate—Cont'd
    Low and moderate income housing, **Labor 1720**
    Payment, **Labor 1771**
    Restitution, **Labor 1776**
    School buildings and grounds, construction or alteration, **Labor 1771.7**
    Solid waste, hauling, **Labor 1720.3**
    University of California, construction, **Labor 1771.7**
  Records, **Labor 1776, 1777**
  Restitution, prevailing wage rate, **Labor 1776**
  Review of determination of prevailing wages, **Labor 1773.4**
  Rules and regulations, wage rates, **Labor 1773.5**
  Subcontractors, post
Compromise and settlement, contractors, compensation and salaries, assessments, **Labor 1742.1**
Computers, compensation and salaries, records and recordation, **Labor 1776**
Confidential or privileged information, prevailing wage rate, investigations and investigators, **Labor 1736**
Conservation corps, application of law, **Labor 1720.4**
Construction, prevailing wage rate. Compensation and salaries, ante
Contractors,
  Appeal and review, compensation and salaries,
    Assessments, **Labor 1742**
    Withholding, **Labor 1771.6**
  Apprentices, employment, **Labor 1777.5, 1777.7**
  Assessments, compensation and salaries, **Labor 1741 et seq.**
  Bids and bidding, generally, ante
  Compensation and salaries,
    Assessments, **Labor 1741 et seq.**
    Wage and penalty assessments, **Labor 1727 et seq.**
  Compromise and settlement, compensation and salaries, assessments, **Labor 1742.1**
  Contributions to funds to administer apprenticeship programs, **Labor 1777.5**
  Damages, compensation and salaries, assessments, **Labor 1742.1**
  Debarment, **Labor 1777.1, 1777.7**
    Apprentices, **Labor 1777.7**
  Definitions, **Labor 1722.1**
  Employees, deemed to be employed upon public works, **Labor 1772**
  Fines and penalties, **Labor 1727 et seq.**
    Apprentices, **Labor 1777.7**
    Assessments, **Labor 1741 et seq.**
  Hearings, compensation and salaries, assessments, **Labor 1742**

PUBLIC BUILDINGS AND WORKS—Cont'd

Contractors—Cont'd

Interest, compensation and salaries, assessments, **Labor 1741**

Joint and several liability, compensation and salaries, assessments, **Labor 1743**

Judgments and decrees, compensation and salaries, assessments, **Labor 1742**

Limitation of actions, compensation and salaries, assessments, bonds (officers and fiduciaries), **Labor 1743**

Lists, debarment, **Labor 1777.1**

Mandamus, compensation and salaries, assessments, **Labor 1742**

Notice,

Compensation and salaries, withholding, **Labor 1771.6**

Production of payroll records, **Labor 1776**

Payment, wage and penalty assessments, **Labor 1727 et seq.**

Payroll records, **Labor 1776**

Service, compensation and salaries, Assessments, **Labor 1741, 1742**

Withholding, notice, **Labor 1771.6**

Subcontractors, generally, post

Time, compensation and salaries, assessments, service, **Labor 1741**

Unemployment compensation or workers compensation, noncoverage, bidding process, action by second highest bidder, **Labor 1750**

Contracts,

Bids and bidding, wage rates, **Labor 1773.2**

Compensation and salaries, **Labor 1773.9**

Rates, **Labor 1773**

Federal minimum wage schedules, applicability, **Labor 1740**

Notice, awarding agency, **Labor 1773.3**

Reports, violations, **Labor 1726**

State Contracts, generally, this index

Violations in execution, **Labor 1726**

Costs,

Advertisements, contractors, debarment, **Labor 1777.1**

Prevailing wage rate, **Labor 1726, 1776**

Credits, prevailing wage rate, benefits, **Labor 1773.1**

Crimes and offenses,

Compensation of employees,

Officer awarding body, taking or receiving for own use, **Labor 1778**

Records, failure to maintain, **Labor 1777**

Fees, registering or information as to securing employment, **Labor 1779, 1780**

Hours of labor, **Labor 1814**

Damages,

Contractors, compensation and salaries, assessments, **Labor 1742.1**

PUBLIC BUILDINGS AND WORKS—Cont'd

Damages—Cont'd

Subcontractors, compensation and salaries, assessments, **Labor 1742.1**

Debarment,

Contractors, ante

Subcontractors, post

Definitions, **Labor 1720**

Contractor, **Labor 1722.1**

Prevailing wage rate, **Labor 1720.2, 1720.3**

Subcontractor, **Labor 1722.1**

Wages, **Labor 1720.2**

Discrimination, **Labor 1735**

Apprentices, **Labor 1777.5, 1777.6**

Disposition of fines, penalties and forfeitures, **Labor 1734**

Emergencies, hours of labor, **Const. Art. 14, § 2**

Exemptions, **Labor 1720**

Fair employment practices, apprentices, **Labor 1777.5**

Federal aid, bids, federal minimum wage schedules, **Labor 1740**

Fees, registering or information to secure employment, **Labor 1779, 1780**

Fines and penalties,

Apprentices, **Labor 1777.7**

Compensation and salaries, payment of less than prevailing wage rate, **Labor 1775**

Contractors, ante

Discrimination, **Labor 1735**

Disposition, **Labor 1734**

Labor organizations, promotion or deterrence, state funds, **Gov 16645.5**

Subcontractors, assessments, **Labor 1741 et seq.**

Force account labor, prevailing wage rates, **Labor 1771**

Forfeitures,

Compensation and salaries, payment of less than prevailing wage rate, **Labor 1775**

Hours of labor, **Labor 1813**

Fraud, contractors, debarment, **Labor 1777.1**

Funds,

Apprenticeship programs, contributions, **Labor 1777.5**

Prevailing wage rates, **Labor 1773.6, 1773.7**

Hearings, contractors, compensation and salaries, assessments, **Labor 1742**

Holidays, compensation and salaries, **Labor 1771**

Hours of labor, **Const. Art. 14, § 2; Labor 1810 et seq.**

Crimes and offenses, **Labor 1814**

Forfeitures, **Labor 1813**

Legal days work, definitions, **Labor 1810**

Maximum, **Labor 1811**

Overtime, **Labor 1815**

Records, **Labor 1812**

PUBLIC BUILDINGS AND WORKS—Cont'd

Inspection and inspectors,

Compensation, payments, records, **Labor 1776, 1777**

Hours of labor, records, **Labor 1812**

Payroll records, **Labor 1776**

Records of wages paid, **Labor 1776**

Trespass, **Pen 602**

Interest, contractors, compensation and salaries, assessments, **Labor 1741**

Investigations, prevailing wage rate, confidential or privileged information, **Labor 1736**

Joint and several liability, contractors, compensation and salaries, assessments, **Labor 1743**

Judgments and decrees,

Apprentices, fines and penalties, **Labor 1777.7**

Contractors, compensation and salaries, assessments, **Labor 1742**

Labor compliance program, compensation and salaries, **Labor 1771.5**

Labor organizations, promotion or deterrence, state funds, **Gov 16645 et seq.**

Limitation of actions,

Contractors, compensation and salaries, assessments, bonds (officers and fiduciaries), **Labor 1743**

Prevailing wage rate, **Labor 1771.2, 1775**

Lists, contractors,

Compensation and salaries, assessments, **Labor 1741**

Debarment, **Labor 1777.1**

Maintenance workers, prevailing wage rate, **Labor 1771**

Mandamus, contractors, compensation and salaries, assessments, **Labor 1742**

Notice,

Change of prevailing wage rates, **Labor 1773.3**

Contractors, compensation and salaries, withholding, **Labor 1771.6**

Contracts, apprenticeship standards, **Labor 1773.3**

Production of payroll records, **Labor 1776**

Review, prevailing wage rate determination, **Labor 1773.4**

Subcontractors, post

Occupational safety and health, public works contracts, **Labor 6705 et seq.**

Offenses. Crimes and offenses, generally, ante

Overtime work, **Const. Art. 14, § 2; Labor 1770, 1771, 1815**

Payment,

Contractors, wage and penalty assessments, **Labor 1727 et seq.**

Subcontractors, post

Payroll records, **Labor 1776**

Penalties. Fines and penalties, generally, ante

Per diem wages, definitions, **Labor 1773.1**

PUBLIC BUILDINGS AND WORKS—Cont'd

Petition, compensation and salaries, prevailing wage rate determination, review of determination, **Labor 1773.4**

Prevailing wage rate. Compensation and salaries, ante

Proceedings. Actions and proceedings, generally, ante

Publication, prevailing wage rates, contract awards, **Labor 1773, 1773.4**

Rates and charges, compensation and salaries, fines and penalties, prevailing wage rate, **Labor 1775**

Ratio of apprentices to journeymen, **Labor 1777.5**

Records and recordation,
Compensation, payments, **Labor 1776, 1777**
Hours of labor, **Labor 1812**

Refusal to leave building at closing time, **Pen 602**

Reimbursement, disclosure of payroll records, **Labor 1776**

Reports,
Contracts, violations, **Labor 1726**
Hours of labor, violations, **Labor 1813**
Volunteers, **Labor 1720.4**

Restitution, prevailing wage rate, **Labor 1776**

Review. Appeal and review, generally, ante

Rules and regulations, wage rate, **Labor 1773.5**

Screening, trespass, **Pen 602**

Section, hours of labor, records, **Labor 1812**

Service, contractors, compensation and salaries,
Assessments, **Labor 1741, 1742**
Withholding, notice, **Labor 1771.6**

Solid waste, hauling, prevailing wage rate, **Labor 1720.3**

Specialty contractors, small contracts, employment of apprentices, **Labor 1777.5**

State Contracts, generally, this index

Statute of limitations. Limitation of actions, generally, ante

Subcontractors,
Appeal and review, compensation and salaries,
Assessments, **Labor 1742**
Withholding, **Labor 1771.6**
Apprentices, **Labor 1777.5, 1777.7**
Assessments, compensation and salaries, **Labor 1741 et seq.**
Compensation and salaries,
Assessments, **Labor 1741 et seq.**
Labor performed for subcontractor, **Labor 200**
Wage and penalty assessments, **Labor 1727 et seq.**
Compromise and settlement, compensation and salaries, assessments, **Labor 1742.1**

PUBLIC BUILDINGS AND WORKS—Cont'd

Subcontractors—Cont'd

Contractor withholding sums due, **Labor 1729**

Damages, compensation and salaries, assessments, **Labor 1742.1**

Debarment, **Labor 1777.1**
Apprentices, **Labor 1777.7**

Definitions, **Labor 1722.1**

Employees, deemed to be employed upon public works, **Labor 1772**

Fines and penalties,
Apprentices, **Labor 1777.7**
Assessments, **Labor 1741 et seq.**

Hearings, compensation and salaries, assessments, **Labor 1742**

Interest, compensation and salaries, assessments, **Labor 1741**

Joint and several liability, compensation and salaries, assessments, **Labor 1743**

Judgments and decrees, compensation and salaries, assessments, **Labor 1742**

Liens. Mechanics Liens, generally, this index

Limitation of actions, compensation and salaries, assessments, bonds (officers and fiduciaries), **Labor 1743**

Mandamus, compensation and salaries, assessments, **Labor 1742**

Notice,
Compensation and salaries, withholding, **Labor 1771.6**
Production of payroll records, **Labor 1776**

Payment, wage and penalty assessments, **Labor 1727 et seq.**

Payroll records, **Labor 1776**

Service, compensation and salaries,
Assessments, **Labor 1741, 1742**
Withholding, notice, **Labor 1771.6**

Time, compensation and salaries, assessments, service, **Labor 1741**

Training programs, apprentices, per diem wages, **Labor 1773.1**

Trespass, **Pen 602**

Unemployment, leave, **Labor 2010 et seq.**

Unemployment compensation, contractors, winning bidder failure to carry, action by second highest bidder, **Labor 1750**

Volunteers, application of law, **Labor 1720.4**

Wages. Compensation and salaries, generally, ante

War and civil defense, hours of labor, **Const. Art. 14, § 2**

Workers compensation, contractors, winning bidder failure to carry, action by second highest bidder, **Labor 1750**

PUBLIC CONTRACTS

Bids and bidding, public works project, winning bidder failure to carry unemployment compensation or workers compensation, action by second highest bidder, **Labor 1750**

State Contracts, generally, this index

PUBLIC CORPORATIONS

Unemployment compensation,
Elective coverage, **Un Ins 709**
Public entity, definitions, **Un Ins 135, 605**

Workers compensation,
Self insurers, medical and related treatment and supplies, former employees, **Labor 4606**
Service of notices, orders, **Labor 5317**

PUBLIC EATING PLACES

Restaurants, generally, this index

PUBLIC EMPLOYEES RETIREMENT SYSTEM

Accumulated contributions, mandatory furloughs, **Gov 20969**

Advanced disability payments, **Labor 4850.3, 4850.4**

Allowances. Disability retirement, post

Benefits,
Mandatory furloughs, **Gov 20969**
Unemployment compensation, information, **Un Ins 1095**

Compensation and salaries,
Advanced disability payments, **Labor 4850.3, 4850.4**
School members, post

Confidential or privileged information, earnings information, members receiving disability allowance, **Un Ins 1095**

Contributions, basis, **Labor 220.2**

Death benefits, **Labor 4707**

Deductions, **Labor 4707**

Dependents, workers compensation, death benefits, **Labor 4703.6**

Disability retirement,
Advanced payments, **Labor 4850.3, 4850.4**
Allowances, earnings information, access, **Un Ins 1095**
Earnings information, access, **Un Ins 1095**
School members, post

Earnings information, members receiving disability allowance, **Un Ins 1094, 1095**

Final compensation,
Career executive assignments, **Gov 20037.13**
Definitions, **Gov 20037.8**

Funds transfers, **Un Ins 1094, 1095**

Hybrid contempt, workers compensation hearings, **Labor 5309**

Incapacitation. Disability retirement, generally, ante

PUBLIC

**PUBLIC EMPLOYEES RETIREMENT SYS-
TEM—Cont'd**
Local safety members,
  Dependents, workers compensation,
    death benefits, **Labor 4703.6**
  Workers compensation, dependents,
    death benefits, **Labor 4703.6**
Patrol members,
  Dependents, workers compensation,
    death benefits, **Labor 4703.6**
  Workers compensation, dependents,
    death benefits, **Labor 4703.6**
Reimbursement, advanced disability pay-
  ments, **Labor 4850.3**
Retired member. Disability retirement,
  generally, ante
School members,
  Compensation and salaries, final com-
    pensation, **Gov 20035.5**
  Final compensation, **Gov 20035.5**
Service credits,
  Mandatory furloughs, **Gov 20969**
  Superior courts, officers and employees,
    furloughs, **Gov 20969.1**
Superior courts, officers and employees,
  furloughs, service credits, **Gov 20969.1**
Unemployment compensation, benefits,
  information, **Un Ins 1095**
Workers compensation,
  Death benefits, **Labor 4707, 4708**
  Dependents, death benefits, **Labor
    4703.6**

PUBLIC EMPLOYMENT OFFICES
Generally, **Un Ins 2051 et seq.**
Unemployment Compensation, this index

PUBLIC ENTITIES
Correctional institutions, labor, contracts,
  Const. Art. 14, § 5
Definitions, **Un Ins 135, 605**
  Unemployment compensation, **Un Ins
    135, 605**
Officers and employees. Public Officers
  and Employees, generally, this index
Unemployment Compensation, this index

PUBLIC FUNDS
Funds, generally, this index

PUBLIC HEALTH
Health and Sanitation, generally, this index

PUBLIC HIGHWAYS
Highways and Roads, generally, this index

PUBLIC HOSPITALS
Hospitals, generally, this index

PUBLIC IMPROVEMENTS
Improvements, generally, this index

PUBLIC INSTRUCTION
Schools and School Districts, generally,
  this index

PUBLIC LANDS
Fines and penalties, labor organizations,
  promotion or deterrence, state funds,
  Gov 16645.5
Labor organizations, promotion or deter-
  rence, state funds, **Gov 16645 et seq.**

PUBLIC MEETINGS
Workers compensation division, **Labor
  138.2**

PUBLIC NOTICE
Advertisements, generally, this index
Notice, generally, this index

PUBLIC OFFICERS AND EMPLOYEES
Advisory position, unemployment com-
  pensation, excluded service, **Un Ins
    634.5**
Armed forces, reentry to office or posi-
  tion, **Mil & V 395.1**
Arrest, records, job applicants, obtaining,
  Labor 432.7
Assassination, elected public officials,
  death benefits, **Labor 4720 et seq.**
Assault against, disclosure of criminal rec-
  ord, employment, **Pen 11105.3**
Attempted murder against, disclosure of
  criminal record, employment, **Pen
    11105.3**
Bonds (Officers and Fiduciaries), general-
  ly, this index
Children and Minors, this index
Civil Service, generally, this index
College scholarships, dependents, elected
  officials killed in office, **Labor 4728**
Compensation and salaries. Unemploy-
  ment compensation, generally, post
Confidential or privileged information,
  privileged broadcasts and publica-
  tions, defamation, **CC 47**
Contributions,
  Health and welfare benefits, **Labor
    220.2**
  Vacation allowance, sick leave and re-
    tirement fund, **Labor 220.2**
County Officers and Employees, generally,
  this index
Death,
  Assassination, benefits, **Labor 4720 et
    seq.**
  College scholarships, dependents, elect-
    ed officials killed in office, **Labor
    4728**
  Dependents, officials killed in office, col-
    lege scholarships, **Labor 4728**
Disaster service workers. War and Civil
  Defense, this index
Diversion program, referrals or partic-
  ipation, job applicants, obtaining in-
  formation regarding, **Labor 432.7**
Elected officials,
  Death benefits, assassination, **Labor
    4720 et seq.**
  Killed in office, dependents, college
    scholarships, **Labor 4728**

**PUBLIC OFFICERS AND EMPLOYEES
—Cont'd**
Elected officials—Cont'd
  Unemployment compensation, excluded
    service, **Un Ins 634.5**
Elections, generally, this index
Employment development department, **Un
  Ins 9502**
Family, sick leave, **Labor 233, 234**
Fires and fire protection, workers compen-
  sation, **Labor 3365**
Handicapped persons, retraining and re-
  habilitation, **Labor 6200 et seq.**
Killed in office, dependents, college schol-
  arships, **Labor 4728**
Labor and employment,
  Job applicant, diversion program, refer-
    rals or participation, obtaining in-
    formation, **Labor 432.7**
  Obtaining arrest record, **Labor 432.7**
Labor organizations, promotion or deter-
  rence, state funds, **Gov 16645 et seq.**
Leaves of absence, military forces, **Mil &
  V 395**
Marriage, sick leave, **Labor 233, 234**
Memorandum of understanding, labor
  agreements, conflicts with statutes,
  military duty, **Mil & V 395 et seq.**
Military forces, leaves of absence, **Mil & V
  395**
Minors. Children and Minors, this index
Municipal Officers and Employees, gener-
  ally, this index
Notice, retraining and rehabilitation, in-
  jured employees, **Labor 6201**
Official bonds. Bonds (Officers and Fidu-
  ciaries), generally, this index
Parents, sick leave, **Labor 233, 234**
Pensions. Public Employees Retirement
  System, generally, this index
Personal injuries, retraining and rehabili-
  tation, **Labor 6200 et seq.**
Policy making positions, unemployment
  compensation, excluded service, **Un
  Ins 634.5**
Privileges and immunities, publication and
  broadcasts, **CC 47**
Rehabilitation, injured employees, **Labor
  6200 et seq.**
Retirement and pensions. Public Employ-
  ees Retirement System, generally, this
  index
Retraining and rehabilitation, **Labor 6200
  et seq.**
Scholarships, college, dependents, elected
  officials killed in office, **Labor 4728**
School Officers and Employees, generally,
  this index
Sick leave, family members, **Labor 233,
  234**
Social Security, generally, this index
State Officers and Employees, generally,
  this index

PUBLIC OFFICERS AND EMPLOYEES
—Cont'd
Subsistence allowance, injured employees, retraining and rehabilitation, **Labor 6203**
Suspension, **Labor 6204**
Temporary employees, unemployment compensation, excluded service, **Un Ins 634.5**
Unemployment compensation,
Elective coverage, **Un Ins 711**
Employing units, **Un Ins 135, 605**
Exclusion, **Un Ins 634.5**
Substitute employees, excluded services, **Un Ins 634.5**
Vacations, sick leave, contributions to funds for payment, **Labor 220.2**
Vocational rehabilitation, injured employees, **Labor 6200 et seq.**
Workers Compensation, this index

PUBLIC POLICY
Apprentices, state and local agencies, encouragement and utilization, **Labor 3075.1**
Consumer credit reporting agencies, **CC 1785.1**
Credit, **CC 1785.1**
Discrimination, employment, **Gov 12920.5**
Employment development, **Un Ins 9000**
Health facilities, whistleblowers, **Health & S 1278.5**
Investigative consumer reporting agencies, **CC 1786**
Investments, employees or applicants to secure position, **Labor 407**
Jobs for California graduates program, **Un Ins 9900**
Jurisdictional strikes, **Labor 1115**
Labor and Employment, this index
Military Forces, this index
Physicians and Surgeons, this index
Railroads, this index
Self insurers security fund, workers compensation, **Labor 3740**
Smoking, workplace, **Labor 6404.5**
Tips, private agreements contravening laws, **Labor 356**
Unemployment compensation, **Un Ins 100**
Vietnam Veterans Employment Act, **Gov 7280.1**
Workers compensation, **Labor 3200**
Workplace smoking, **Labor 6404.5**

PUBLIC PROSECUTORS
District Attorneys, generally, this index

PUBLIC RECORDS
Records and Recordation, generally, this index

PUBLIC ROADS
Highways and Roads, generally, this index

PUBLIC SAFETY
Safety, generally, this index

PUBLIC SAFETY OFFICERS
Peace Officers, generally, this index

PUBLIC SCHOOLS
Schools and School Districts, generally, this index

PUBLIC SCHOOLTEACHERS RETIREMENT LAW
Schoolteachers Retirement System, generally, this index

PUBLIC SERVICE CORPORATIONS
Public Utilities, generally, this index

PUBLIC SERVICE EMPLOYMENT
Work Incentive Programs, generally, this index

PUBLIC SOCIAL SERVICES
Social Services, generally, this index

PUBLIC STATUTES
Statutes, generally, this index

PUBLIC TRANSIT
Mass Transit, generally, this index

PUBLIC TRANSIT EMPLOYEE
Definitions, labor disputes, **Labor 1137**

PUBLIC UTILITIES
Commission. Public Utilities Commission, generally, this index
Crimes and offenses, letter of kind and period of service rendered by employee leaving service, failure to furnish, **Labor 1056**
Definitions, unclaimed property, **CCP 1501**
Electricity, generally, this index
Explosives, safety regulations, exemption, **Labor 8004**
Gas. Oil and Gas, generally, this index
Letter of kind and period of service rendered by employee leaving service, failure to furnish, **Labor 1056**
Natural gas. Oil and Gas, generally, this index
Officers and employees, leaving service, letter stating period and kind of service rendered, **Labor 1055, 1056**
Oil and Gas, generally, this index
Public Utilities Commission, generally, this index
Railroads, generally, this index
Telecommunications, generally, this index
Water Supply, generally, this index
Zoning and Planning, generally, this index

PUBLIC UTILITIES COMMISSION
Enforcement of law safeguarding railroad operation personnel, **Labor 6900**
Explosives, generally, this index
Jurisdiction, **Labor 6801**
Railroad employees, safety, enforcement, **Labor 6900**

PUBLIC UTILITY DISTRICTS
Sewers and Sewer Systems, generally, this index

PUBLIC WATER SUPPLY
Water Supply, generally, this index

PUBLIC WAYS
Highways and Roads, generally, this index

PUBLIC WELFARE
Social Services, generally, this index

PUBLIC WORKS
Public Buildings and Works, generally, this index

PUBLIC WORKS DEPARTMENT
Public Buildings and Works, generally, this index

PUBLIC WORKS WAGE RATE ACT
Generally, **Labor 1770 et seq.**

PUBLICATION
Fair employment and housing department, powers and duties, **Gov 12930**
Garnishment, instructions, **CCP 706.127**
Industrial accidents division, **Labor 127**
Industrial welfare commission, reports, **Labor 1203**
Labor and Employment, this index
Lewdness and Obscenity, generally, this index
Libel and Slander, generally, this index
Obscenity. Lewdness and Obscenity, generally, this index
Orders, working conditions, **Labor 1182**
Pornography. Lewdness and Obscenity, generally, this index
Public works, prevailing wage rates, contract awards, **Labor 1773, 1773.4**
Rules and regulations, industrial welfare commission, **Labor 1182.1**
Talent agencies, advance fees, exemptions, **Labor 1702.4**
Unemployment Compensation, this index
Workers Compensation, this index

PUBLICITY
Labor disputes, injunction, **CCP 527.3**

PUBLICLY OWNED TREATMENT WORKS
Sewers and Sewer Systems, generally, this index

PUERTO RICO
State, definitions, unemployment compensation, **Un Ins 139**

PUNISHMENT
Crimes and Offenses, generally, this index
Fines and Penalties, generally, this index

PUPILS
Schools and School Districts, generally, this index

PURCHASER
Vendor and Purchaser, generally, this index

PURCHASES

PURCHASES
Attempts, weapons, crimes and offenses, **Pen 12021**
Drug addicts, weapons, crimes and offenses, **Pen 12021**
Parole and probation, weapons, crimes and offenses, **Pen 12021**

PURE FOOD AND DRUG LAWS
Drugs and Medicine, generally, this index
Food, generally, this index

QUALIFIED BENEFICIARY
Definitions, Cal COBRA, accident and health insurance, **Health & S 1366.21; Ins 10128.51**

QUALIFIED CARE
Definitions, child care, tax credit, **Rev & T 17052.18**

QUALIFIED CARE PLAN
Definitions, child care, tax credit, **Rev & T 17052.18**

QUALIFIED DEPENDENT
Definitions, child care, tax credit, **Rev & T 17052.18**

QUALIFIED DISADVANTAGED INDIVIDUALS
Definitions,
Corporation taxes, credits, enterprise zones, **Rev & T 23622.8**
Enterprise zones, income tax—state, credits, **Rev & T 17053.47**
Local agency military base recovery areas,
Corporation taxes, credits, **Rev & T 23646**
Income tax credits, **Rev & T 17053.46**
Military base recovery areas, corporation taxes, credits, **Rev & T 23646**

QUALIFIED DISPLACED EMPLOYEE
Definitions, military base recovery areas,
Corporation taxes, credits, **Rev & T 23646**
Income tax credits, **Rev & T 17053.46**

QUALIFIED EMPLOYEE
Definitions,
Child care, tax credit, **Rev & T 17052.18**
Corporation taxes, enterprise zones, **Rev & T 23622.7, 23634**
Enterprise zones, income tax—state, credits, **Rev & T 17053.34**

QUALIFIED PROPERTY
Definitions, local agency military base recovery areas, corporation taxes, credits, **Rev & T 23645**

QUALIFIED TAXPAYER
Definitions,
Corporation taxes, credits, **Rev & T 23646**
Credits, enterprise zones, **Rev & T 23622.8**
Enterprise zones, **Rev & T 23634**

QUALIFIED TAXPAYER—Cont'd
Definitions—Cont'd
Enterprise zones, income tax—state, credits, **Rev & T 17053.34, 17053.47**
Military base recovery areas,
Corporation taxes, credits, **Rev & T 23646**
Income tax credits, **Rev & T 17053.46**

QUALIFIED WAGES
Credits, income tax credits, enterprise zones, **Rev & T 17053.74**
Definitions,
Bank and corporation tax credits, enterprise zones, **Rev & T 23622.7, 23622.8, 23634**
Enterprise zones,
Income tax—state, credits, **Rev & T 17053.34**
Manufacturing enhancement areas, **Rev & T 17053.47**
Tax credits, **Rev & T 17053.74**
Income tax credits, unemployed persons, **Rev & T 17053.74**
Military base recovery areas,
Corporation taxes, credits, **Rev & T 23646**
Income tax credits, **Rev & T 17053.46**

QUALIFIED YEARS ONE THROUGH FIVE WAGES
Definitions, military base recovery areas,
Corporation taxes, credits, **Rev & T 23646**
Income tax credits, **Rev & T 17053.46**

QUALIFYING EVENT
Definitions, Cal COBRA, accident and health insurance, **Health & S 1366.21; Ins 10128.51**

QUARRIES
Safety regulations, **Labor 7950 et seq.**
Workers compensation, alternative dispute resolution system, **Labor 3201.5**

QUITTING BUSINESS
Definitions, unemployment compensation, **Un Ins 1116**

RABBIS
Clergy, generally, this index

RACE
Affirmative action, actions and proceedings, challenges, **Gov 8315**
Discrimination, generally, this index
Evidence, affirmative action, **Gov 8315**
Fair Employment and Housing, generally, this index
Housing. Fair Employment and Housing, generally, this index
Labor and employment. Fair Employment and Housing, generally, this index
Preferential treatment, affirmative action, challenges, **Gov 8315**

RACE HORSES
Horse Racing, generally, this index

RACES AND RACING
Horse Racing, generally, this index

RACETRACKS
Horse Racing, generally, this index

RACIAL GROUPS
Apprentices, survey of ethnic derivation, division of labor statistics and research, **Labor 151**

RADIO
Television and Radio, generally, this index

RAIL TRANSIT SYSTEMS
Railroads, generally, this index

RAILINGS
Wharves, docks and piers, **Labor 7604**

RAILROAD ANTIFEATHERBEDDING LAW
Generally, **Labor 6900.1, 6900.5**

RAILROAD COMMISSION
Public Utilities Commission, generally, this index

RAILROAD CROSSINGS
Commercial vehicles. Motor Vehicles, this index
Fines and penalties, commercial vehicles, **Veh 15312.1**

RAILROAD RETIREMENT BOARD
Unemployment compensation, administration fund, contribution to, **Un Ins 1556**

RAILROADS
Generally, **Labor 6800 et seq.**
Accidents,
Crew members, hours of labor, **Labor 607**
Location of caboose, application of law, **Labor 7000**
Actions and proceedings,
Displaced workers, **Labor 1073**
Hours of labor violations, recovery of penalties, **Labor 605**
Acts of God, hours of labor, application of law, **Labor 607**
Antifeatherbedding Law, **Labor 6900.1, 6900.5**
Application of law, hours of labor, **Labor 607**
Attorney fees, displaced workers, actions and proceedings, **Labor 1073**
Baggage, baggagemen, necessity of presence on train, **Labor 6901**
Baggageman, necessity of presence, **Labor 6901**
Braceros, labor and employment, funds, limitation of actions, **CCP 354.7**
Brakemen, **Labor 6901**
Antifeatherbedding Law of 1964, **Labor 6900.5**
Qualifications, **Labor 6906**

RAILROADS—Cont'd
Caboose, **Labor 7000**
  Definitions, **Labor 7000**
  Pusher engine, placement ahead of caboose, **Labor 7000**
Cabs, locomotives, overhang, opening, **Labor 6950, 6951**
Cars. Caboose, generally, ante
Casualty cases, hours of labor, application of law, **Labor 607**
Children and minors, employment, **Labor 1294**
Commuter and intercity passenger rail service. Interurban Railroads, generally, this index
Conductors, **Labor 6901**
  Qualifications, **Labor 6906**
Contracts,
  Displaced workers, **Labor 1070 et seq.**
  Passenger service, minimum personnel requirements, **Labor 6902**
Corporation Taxes, generally, this index
Costs, displaced workers, actions and proceedings, **Labor 1073**
Crimes and offenses,
  Fines and penalties, generally, post
  Handrails and footboards on engine cabs, **Labor 6952**
  Hours of labor, **Labor 606**
  Laminated safety glass devices, **Labor 6956**
  Opening roof of engine cab, violations, **Labor 6951**
  Violation of safeguards, **Labor 6908**
Damages, officers and employees, retaliation, security, **Pub U 7666**
Definitions,
  Caboose, **Labor 7000**
  Hours of labor, **Labor 600**
  Laminated safety glass, **Labor 6955**
Dispatchers, period of duty, **Labor 604**
Displaced workers, **Labor 1070 et seq.**
Electric Railroads, generally, this index
Emergencies, hours of labor, **Labor 604, 607**
Employees. Officers and employees, generally, post
Enforcement, safety, operation personnel, **Labor 6900**
Engine tender clearance, **Labor 6950, 6951**
Engineers,
  Diesel locomotives, **Labor 6901**
  Firemen, locomotives without cars, **Labor 6904**
  Locomotive without cars, **Labor 6904**
  Qualifications, **Labor 6906**
Express train crews, **Labor 6901**
Featherbedding, **Labor 6900.1, 6900.5**
Fines and penalties,
  Handrails and footboards on engine cabs, **Labor 6952**
  Hours of labor, **Labor 605, 606**
  Laminated safety glass devices, **Labor 6956**
  Opening roof of engine cab, violations, **Labor 6951**

RAILROADS—Cont'd
Firefighters and fire departments, Antifeatherbedding Law of 1964, **Labor 6900.5**
  Diesel locomotive, **Labor 6901**
Footboards along engine cab, **Labor 6952**
Full Crew Law, **Labor 6901 et seq.**
Gasoline motor cars, safeguards, exceptions, **Labor 6910**
Handrails, engine cab, **Labor 6952**
High speed rail, compensation and salaries, prevailing wage rates, **Labor 1771.9**
Hours of labor, **Labor 554, 600 et seq.**
  Application of law, **Labor 607**
  Crimes and offenses, **Labor 606**
  Definitions, **Labor 600**
  Emergencies, **Labor 604, 607**
  Fines and penalties, **Labor 605, 606**
  Maximum aggregate hours of duty in 24 hour period, **Labor 603**
  Maximum consecutive hours on duty, **Labor 601**
  Maximum hours of persons handling orders affecting train movements, **Labor 604**
  Minimum consecutive hours off duty, **Labor 602, 603**
  Violations, action for penalties, **Labor 605**
Injunction, displaced workers, **Labor 1073**
Interurban Railroads, generally, this index
Jurisdiction, safeguards, **Labor 6800 et seq.**
Labor and employment,
  Applications for employment, exemptions, **Labor 434**
  Braceros, funds, limitation of actions, **CCP 354.7**
  Hours of labor, generally, ante
Labor Camps, generally, this index
Labor disputes,
  Featherbedding, **Labor 6900.5**
  Operation of railroad, **Labor 6909**
Laminated safety glass, **Labor 6953 et seq.**
Licenses and permits, labor camps, permit applications, **Health & S 17033**
Limitation of actions, braceros, labor and employment, funds, **CCP 354.7**
Local agency, definitions, employees, **Labor 6902**
Location of caboose, **Labor 7000**
Lockouts, operation during lockouts, **Labor 6909**
Locomotives, without cars, **Labor 6904**
Mail train crews, **Labor 6901**
Minimum number, employees on train, passenger service, **Labor 6902**
Misdemeanors. Crimes and offenses, generally, ante
Motor or power control man, necessity of presence on train, **Labor 6901**
Offenses. Crimes and offenses, generally, ante

RAILROADS—Cont'd
Officers and employees, **Labor 6900 et seq.**
  Antifeatherbedding Law of 1964, **Labor 6900.1, 6900.5**
  Damages, retaliation, security, **Pub U 7666**
  Displaced workers, **Labor 1070 et seq.**
  Featherbedding, **Labor 6900.1, 6900.5**
  Full Crew Law, **Labor 6901 et seq.**
  Hours of labor, generally, ante
  Minimum number on train, passenger service, **Labor 6902**
  Passenger service, minimum number on train, **Labor 6902**
  Required employees for passenger, mail and express trains, **Labor 6901**
  Retaliation, security, **Pub U 7666**
  Safety in employment, **Labor 6800 et seq.**
Operation,
  Locomotives at terminals, shops and engine houses, **Labor 6907**
  Personnel, **Labor 6900 et seq.**
Passenger service,
  Contracts, minimum personnel requirements, **Labor 6902**
  Minimum number of employees on train, **Labor 6902**
  Officers and employees, minimum number on train, **Labor 6902**
Passenger train crews, **Labor 6901**
Penalties. Fines and penalties, generally, ante
Police, leaves of absence, workers compensation, disability benefits, **Labor 4850**
Public policy, antifeatherbedding, **Labor 6900.5**
Public Utilities Commission, generally, this index
Pusher engine, placement ahead of caboose, **Labor 7000**
Qualifications of engineers, conductors and brakemen, **Labor 6906**
Rapid transit system, safety, employment, **Labor 6800**
Relief trains,
  Crew, **Labor 6905**
    Hours of labor, **Labor 607**
  Location of caboose, **Labor 7000**
Retaliation, officers and employees, security, **Pub U 7666**
Revenue service, definitions, employees, **Labor 6902**
Safeguards, **Labor 6800 et seq.**
Safety, **Labor 6800 et seq.**
  Devices, **Labor 6950 et seq.**
  Employment, **Labor 6800 et seq.**
Statute of limitations, braceros, labor and employment, funds, **CCP 354.7**
Taxation. Corporation Taxes, generally, this index
Tender, opening from cab engine permitting access, **Labor 6950, 6951**
Train Manning Law, **Labor 6901 et seq.**

RAILROADS—Cont'd
Unavoidable accidents, hours of labor, application of provision, **Labor 607**
Venue,
Hours of labor violations, recovery of penalties, **Labor 605**
Prosecution of officers or agents for hours of labor violations, **Labor 606**
Working hours. Hours of labor, generally, ante
Wrecks and wreckers,
Crews, **Labor 6905**
Hours of labor, **Labor 607**
Location of caboose, **Labor 7000**
Zoning and Planning, generally, this index

RANCHES
Unemployment compensation, qualifications, **Un Ins 611 et seq.**

RAPID TRANSIT
Mass Transit, generally, this index

RAPID TRANSIT DISTRICTS
Transit Districts, generally, this index

RATES AND CHARGES
Aerial passenger tramways, inspection, **Labor 7350 et seq.**
Chiropractors, this index
Health Care Service Plans, this index
Mentally Retarded and Developmentally Disabled Persons, this index
Physicians and Surgeons, this index
Public buildings and works, compensation and salaries, fines and penalties, prevailing wage rate, **Labor 1775**
Unemployment Compensation, this index
Workers Compensation, this index

RATES AND RATING ORGANIZATIONS
Insurance, this index

RATING PERIOD
Definitions, unemployment compensation, **Un Ins 903**

RAZORS
Weapons, generally, this index

REAL ESTATE
Abandoned or Unclaimed Property, generally, this index
Agents. Real Estate Brokers and Salespersons, generally, this index
Brokers. Real Estate Brokers and Salespersons, generally, this index
Construction funds, crimes and offenses, **Pen 484b**
Conveyances. Deeds and Conveyances, generally, this index
Covenants. Deeds and Conveyances, this index
Deeds and Conveyances, generally, this index
Discrimination, **Gov 12955 et seq.**
Domestic partnership, termination, **Fam 299**
Entry On Property, generally, this index

REAL ESTATE—Cont'd
Escheat, generally, this index
Executions, generally, this index
Funds, improvements, illegal disposition, **Pen 484**
Housing, generally, this index
Improvements, generally, this index
Industrial relations department, possession and control, **Labor 58**
Landlord and Tenant, generally, this index
Larceny by fraud, **Pen 484**
Leases, generally, this index
Liens and Incumbrances, generally, this index
Loans,
Credit scores, notice, **CC 1785.15.1, 1785.15.2**
Notice, credit scores, **CC 1785.15.1, 1785.15.2**
Risk scores, notice, **CC 1785.15.1, 1785.15.2**
Malicious mischief, trespass, **Pen 602**
Mortgages, generally, this index
Motor vehicles, trespass with vehicle, **Pen 602**
Public improvements. Improvements, generally, this index
Records and Recordation, generally, this index
Rent, generally, this index
Salesmen. Real Estate Brokers and Salespersons, generally, this index
School Buildings and Grounds, generally, this index
Surveys and Surveyors, generally, this index
Taxation, generally, this index
Title to Property, generally, this index
Transfers. Deeds and Conveyances, generally, this index
Trespass, **Pen 602, 602.8**
Unclaimed property. Abandoned or Unclaimed Property, generally, this index
Withholding tax on wages, **Un Ins 13011**
Workers compensation, attachment, levying preference, **Labor 5603**
Written instruments. Deeds and Conveyances, generally, this index
Zoning and Planning, generally, this index

REAL ESTATE BROKERS AND SALESPERSONS
Discrimination, **Gov 12955 et seq.**
Multiple listing service, discrimination, **Gov 12955**
Unemployment compensation, **Un Ins 650**

REAL ESTATE INVESTMENT TRUSTS
Corporation Taxes, generally, this index

REAL PROPERTY
Real Estate, generally, this index

REASONABLE ACCOMMODATION
Definitions, fair employment and housing, **Gov 12926**

REASONABLE ASSURANCE
Definitions, unemployment compensation, **Un Ins 1253.3**

REASONABLE STEPS
Definitions, smoking, workplaces, **Labor 6404.5**

REBATES
Workers Compensation, this index

RECEIPTS
Workers compensation, lump sum payments, **Labor 5105**

RECEIVERS AND RECEIVERSHIP
Compensation and salaries, priorities and preferences, **CCP 1204**
Disability compensation, voluntary plans, appointment, **Un Ins 3261**
Employee benefit plans, priorities and preferences, **CCP 1204**
Labor camps, correction of defects, failure to follow court orders, **Health & S 17062**
Priorities and preferences, compensation and salaries, **CCP 1204**
Unemployment Compensation, this index

RECEPTACLES
Containers, generally, this index

RECIDIVISTS
Second and subsequent offenses. Crimes and Offenses, this index

RECIPROCAL AGREEMENTS
Definitions, employment tax information, **Un Ins 1095**

RECIPROCAL INFORMATION EXCHANGE
Employment tax, **Un Ins 1095**

RECIPROCITY
Complaints, prosecution, **Labor 103 et seq.**
Employment tax information, furnishing to Mexican officials, **Un Ins 1095**
Labor and employment, complaints by employees, prosecution, **Labor 103 et seq.**

RECORDERS
Conveyances. Deeds and Conveyances, generally, this index
Deeds and Conveyances, generally, this index

RECORDING CONTRACTS
Generally, **Labor 2855**

RECORDS AND RECORDATION
Access, information practices, **CC 1798 et seq.**
Amusements, rides, safety, **Labor 7916**
Arrest, this index
Boards and Commissions, this index
Car washes, **Labor 2052**
Colleges and Universities, this index

RECORDS AND RECORDATION—Cont'd

Community health care workers, assault and battery, **Labor 6332**

Compensation and Salaries, this index

Consumer Credit Reporting Agencies, this index

Crimes and Offenses, this index

Criminal History Information, generally, this index

Definitions,
Information Practices Act, **CC 1798.3**
Labor and employment, copies, **CC 1786.53**

Disability compensation. Unemployment Compensation, this index

Disclosure, generally, this index

Diversion programs, referrals or participation, job applicants, **Labor 432.7**

Elevators, dumbwaiters and escalators, continuing education, **Labor 7311.3**

Employment. Labor and Employment, this index

Employment Agencies, this index

English language, **Un Ins 8**

Exemptions, access, information practices, **CC 1798.40**

Extended unemployment compensation, computation, **Un Ins 3504**

Fair Employment and Housing, this index

Fair Employment and Housing Department, this index

Financial Statements and Reports, generally, this index

Governmental entity, definitions, Information Practices Act, **CC 1798.3**

Grants, this index

Hazardous Substances and Waste, this index

Health Care Service Plans, this index

Health Facilities, this index

Health records. Medical Records, generally, this index

Housing, this index

Income Tax—State, this index

Industrial homework, **Labor 2665, 2666**

Industrial relations department, **Labor 58**
Labor disputes, **Labor 65**

Information Practices Act, personal information, disclosure, **CC 1798 et seq.**

Inspection and inspectors, industrial home work employer, **Labor 2666**

Insurance, this index

Investigative consumer reporting agencies, **CC 1786 et seq.**

Job listing services, **CC 1812.522**

Labor and Employment, this index

Labor organizations, subpoenas, **CCP 1985.6**

Labor statistics and research division, **Labor 152**

Landlord and Tenant, this index

Lead related construction work, employee protection, **Labor 6717**

Lewdness and obscenity, identity of suppliers, **Labor 1309.5, 1309.6**

Liens and Incumbrances, this index

RECORDS AND RECORDATION—Cont'd

Mechanics Liens, this index

Medical Records, generally, this index

Nurses registries, **CC 1812.529**

Occupational safety and health division, **Labor 60.7**

Payroll, this index

Peace Officers, this index

Personal information, disclosure, Information Practices Act, **CC 1798 et seq.**

Privacy, generally, this index

Production of Books and Papers, generally, this index

Public Buildings and Works, this index

Public employment offices, **Un Ins 2054**

Right to privacy, Information Practices Act, **CC 1798 et seq.**

Savings Associations, this index

State, this index

State Agencies, this index

State Contracts, this index

State Departments, this index

State Officers and Employees, this index

System of records, definitions, Information Practices Act, **CC 1798.3**

Talent Agencies, this index

Telecommunications, this index

Tips, employers, inspection, **Labor 353**

Unemployment Compensation, this index

Withholding tax on wages, **Un Ins 13011**

Workers Compensation, this index

RECOUPMENT

Setoff and Counterclaim, generally, this index

RECREATION AND PARK DISTRICTS

Labor and employment, volunteers, workers compensation, **Labor 3361.5**

Volunteers, workers compensation, **Labor 3361.5**

Workers compensation, volunteers, **Labor 3361.5**

RECREATION AND RECREATIONAL FACILITIES

Boats and Boating, generally, this index

Camps and Camping, generally, this index

Districts. Recreation and Park Districts, generally, this index

Licenses and permits, bungee jumping, **Labor 7901**

Recreation and Park Districts, generally, this index

Workers compensation, **Labor 3600**

Zoning and Planning, generally, this index

RECREATION DISTRICTS

Recreation and Park Districts, generally, this index

RECREATIONAL TRAILER PARKS

Mobilehomes and Mobilehome Parks, generally, this index

RECREATIONAL VESSELS

Boats and Boating, generally, this index

RECYCLING

Oil and Gas, this index

RED CROSS

Noncertificated school employees, restoration of position after service, **Mil & V 395.2**

Unemployment compensation, excludable services, **Un Ins 711**

RED WOLF

Fish and Game, generally, this index

REDUCED WORKTIME

Definitions, employment opportunities creation, **Un Ins 12102**

REDUCED WORKWEEK

Definitions, employment opportunities creation, **Un Ins 12102**

REDUCED WORKYEAR

Definitions, employment opportunities creation, **Un Ins 12102**

REEMPLOYMENT

Generally, **Labor 1050 et seq.**

Janitors, **Labor 1060 et seq.**

Unemployment compensation, studies, **Un Ins 325**

REFERENCE AND REFEREES

Workers Compensation, this index

REFERRALS

Workers Compensation, this index

REFINERY AND CHEMICAL PLANT WORKERS SAFETY ACT

Generally, **Labor 7850 et seq.**

REFORMATORIES

Correctional Institutions, generally, this index

REFUNDS

Income Tax—State, this index

Industrial relations department, director, money in payment of license fees, or other services, **Labor 63**

Unemployment Compensation, this index

Workers Compensation, this index

REGENTS

University of California. Colleges and Universities, this index

REGIONAL OCCUPATIONAL CENTERS

Vocational Education, this index

REGIONAL TRANSPORTATION PLANNING AGENCIES

Transit Development Boards, generally, this index

REGIONAL YOUTH EDUCATION FACILITIES

Juvenile Institutions and Schools, this index

REGISTERED LIMITED LIABILITY PARTNERSHIPS

Partnership, this index

REGISTERED MAIL
Certified or registered mail. Mail and Mailing, this index

REGISTERED NURSES
Nurses, generally, this index

REGISTERED STUDENT APPRENTICE
Definitions, workers compensation, **Labor 3368**

REGISTERS AND REGISTRIES
Lead poisoning, occupational safety, prevention programs, **Health & S 105185 et seq.**
Nurses Registries, generally, this index

REGISTRATION
Apprentices, electricity, **Labor 3099.4**
Asbestos related work, employers, contractors, **Labor 6501.5, 6505.5**
Car Washes, this index
Consolidated Cities and Counties, this index
Contractors, this index
Counties, this index
Domestic partnership, **Fam 297 et seq., 298, 298.5**
Electricity, this index
Garment manufacturers, **Labor 2676.7**
Labor organization labels and trademarks, **Labor 1014**
Motor Vehicles, this index
Municipalities, this index
Trademarks, this index
Unemployment Compensation, this index

REGISTRATION FEES
Definitions, employment agency regulation, **CC 1812.501**

REGULAR PAY DAY LAW
Generally, **Labor 200 et seq.**

REGULATED INVESTMENT COMPANIES
Corporation Taxes, generally, this index

REGULATIONS
See text preceding index

REGULATORY AGENCY
Definitions, Information Practices Act, **CC 1798.3**

REHABILITATION
Compensation and Salaries, this index
Drugs and Medicine, this index
Housing, this index
Juvenile Delinquents and Dependents, this index
Licenses, rehabilitation facilities, **Labor 1191.5**
Public employees, voluntary nature of plans, **Labor 6208**
Social Services, this index
Unemployment compensation, coverage, **Un Ins 634.5**
Vocational Rehabilitation, generally, this index
Workers Compensation, this index

REHABILITATION DEPARTMENT
Labor market information, **Un Ins 10530 et seq.**
Vocational Rehabilitation, generally, this index
Workers compensation, employment training, **Labor 3351.5**

REIMBURSEMENT
Labor disputes, arbitration and award, **Labor 67**
Medi Cal Program, this index
Physicians and Surgeons, this index
Public Employees Retirement System, this index
Support, this index
Workers Compensation, this index

RELATED PERSON
Definitions,
Corporation taxes, **Rev & T 24416**
Income tax—state, net operating losses, **Rev & T 17276**

RELATIVES
Domestic partnership, **Fam 297**
Unemployment compensation, services performed, **Un Ins 631**

RELEASE
Attachment, this index
Compensation and salaries, employer requiring without payment, **Labor 206.5**
Executions, this index
Health care service plans, medical records, negligence, **CC 56.36**
Jails, this index
Medical Records, this index
Unemployment compensation, benefits from supplemental plans established by employers, **Un Ins 1342**
Workers Compensation, this index

RELIGION
Definitions, fair employment and housing, **Gov 12926**
Disability compensation,
Certificate of disability, **Un Ins 2709**
Exemption, **Un Ins 2902**
Discrimination, generally, this index
Employment. Fair Employment and Housing, generally, this index
Fair Employment and Housing, generally, this index
Faith Healing, generally, this index
Housing. Fair Employment and Housing, generally, this index
Labor and employment. Fair Employment and Housing, generally, this index

RELIGIOUS ORGANIZATIONS AND SOCIETIES
Actions and proceedings,
Exemptions, unemployment insurance, **Un Ins 1241**
Unemployment compensation exemptions, **Un Ins 1241**

RELIGIOUS ORGANIZATIONS AND SOCIETIES—Cont'd
Children and minors, entertainment, hours, **Labor 1310**
Clergy, generally, this index
Contracts, workforce investments, **Un Ins 14003, 14004**
Definitions, labor and employment, **Gov 12926.2**
Discrimination, workforce investments, grants, contracts, **Un Ins 14003**
Employment, disability compensation, **Un Ins 2606**
Fair employment and housing, **Gov 12940**
Faith based organizations, unemployment compensation, job training and placement services, **Un Ins 9617**
Faith Healing, generally, this index
Grants,
Unemployment compensation, job training and placement services, **Un Ins 9617**
Workforce investments, **Un Ins 14003, 14004**
Housing discrimination, **Gov 12955.4**
Labor and employment, **Gov 12922**
Workforce investments, grants, contracts, **Un Ins 14003, 14004**
Privileges and immunities, criminally related personal injuries, reports, **Pen 11161.9**
Public benefit corporations, education, labor and employment, **Gov 12926.2**
Tax exemptions, unemployment insurance, **Un Ins 1241**
Unemployment compensation, **Un Ins 608, 641, 711 et seq.**
Disclaimers, **Un Ins 637.1**
Excluded services, **Un Ins 634.5**
Exemptions, **Un Ins 1241**
Job training and placement services, grants, **Un Ins 9617**
Workers compensation, exclusion, religious workers, **Labor 3352**
Workforce investments, grants, contracts, **Un Ins 14003, 14004**

RELIGIOUS PRACTITIONERS
Clergy, generally, this index

RELOCATION
Labor and employment, **Labor 1400 et seq.**

REMEDIES
Immigration, labor and employment, **CC 3339; Gov 7285**

REMOVAL OR TRANSFER OF CAUSES
Workers compensation, **Labor 5310**

REMUNERATION
Compensation and Salaries, generally, this index

RENT
Apartment houses, resident managers, credit, **Labor 1182.8**

RENT—Cont'd

Assumed or fictitious names, personal property, **Pen 484**

Employment development department, space, priority, **Un Ins 3015**

Housing, this index

Labor camps, increasing, operators exempted from permits, **Health & S 17031.5**

RENTAL CARS

Leases, Motor Vehicles, this index

RENTAL HOUSING

Apartment Houses, generally, this index

REPETITIVE MOTION INJURIES

Labor and employment, occupational safety and health, **Labor 6719**

REPORTING BY SCHOOL EMPLOYEES OF IMPROPER GOVERNMENTAL ACTIVITIES ACT

Generally, **Educ 44110 et seq.**

REPORTS

Accidents, this index

Aerial passenger tramways, personal injuries, **Labor 7356**

Agricultural Labor and Employment, this index

Air pressure tanks, inspection, **Labor 7654**

Apprentices, electricity, certificates and certification, **Labor 3099.3**

Apprenticeship council, **Labor 3071, 3073.5**

Asbestos, this index

Blood Banks, this index

Boards and Commissions, this index

Boilers,
  Inspection and inspectors, **Labor 7654**
  Safety, **Labor 7722**

Cable television, franchises, **Pub U 5920**

CalWORKs. Social Services, this index

Car washes, **Labor 2068**

Carcinogens, labor and employment, use, **Labor 9030 et seq.**

Civil Service, this index

Community colleges and districts. Colleges and Universities, this index

Compensation and salaries, employer managed deferred compensation plans, **Labor 2809**

Consumer Credit Reporting Agencies, generally, this index

Correctional Institutions, this index

Credit ratings. Consumer Credit Reporting Agencies, generally, this index

Day Care and Nursery Schools, this index

Deferred compensation plans, employer managed, **Labor 2809**

Electricity, this index

Elevators, dumbwaiters and escalators, **Labor 7316**
  Inspection and inspectors, **Labor 7313**

Employment. Labor and Employment, this index

REPORTS—Cont'd

Employment Development Department, this index

Employment development director, **Un Ins 320**

English language, **Un Ins 8**

Fair Employment and Housing, this index

Financial Statements and Reports, generally, this index

Food and Agriculture Department, this index

Green collar jobs, grants, **Un Ins 14022**

Health Facilities, this index

High Schools or Secondary Schools, this index

Hospitals, this index

Housing, this index

Income Tax—State, this index

Industrial accidents division, **Labor 127**

Industrial homework, employers, **Labor 2665**

Industrial relations department, apprenticeship status division, **Labor 3073.5**

Industrial welfare commission, **Labor 1203**

Injuries, fatalities and accident rates, **Labor 6409 et seq.**

Labor and Employment, this index

Labor Camps, this index

Labor market information, coordination, **Un Ins 10530 et seq.**

Labor statistics and research division, misuse, of names, **Labor 153**

Legislature, this index

Leisure sharing program, employment opportunities creation, **Un Ins 12141**

Liquefied petroleum gas storage tanks, inspection, **Labor 7654**

Medical Care and Treatment, this index

Motion Pictures, this index

Nurses, this index

Occupational Carcinogens Control Act, **Labor 9030 et seq.**

Occupational diseases, **Labor 156**

Occupational health and safety centers, clinical and research findings, **Labor 50.8**

Occupational safety and health. Labor and Employment, this index

Occupational safety and health division, evaluation of proposed variances and standards, **Labor 147**

Open video systems, franchises, **Pub U 5920**

Personal Injuries, this index

Pesticides, this index

Physician Assistants, this index

Physicians and Surgeons, this index

Plasma Centers, this index

Prisons and prisoners. Correctional Institutions, this index

Public Buildings and Works, this index

Safety,
  Boilers, **Labor 7722**
  Correctional institutions, **Labor 6413.2**

State Agencies, this index

Statistics, generally, this index

REPORTS—Cont'd

Steam boiler inspection, **Labor 7654**

Support, this index

Unemployment Compensation, this index

Veterans, this index

Video programming services, franchises, **Pub U 5920**

Vocational Education, this index

Wage board, **Labor 1178, 1178.5, 1182**

Wage reports, calendar week, **Un Ins 1088**

Warehouses and warehousemen, working warehouses, safety, **Labor 9104**

Withholding tax, **Un Ins 13050 et seq.**

Worker safety and health training and education program, **Labor 6354.7**

Workers Compensation, this index

Workforce investment board, **Un Ins 14011, 14013**

REPRESENTATION

Legislature, generally, this index

REPRESENTATIVES

Definitions, agricultural labor relations, **Labor 1140.4**

REQUESTS FOR ADMISSIONS

Admissions, generally, this index

RES JUDICATA

Unemployment compensation, decisions of appeals board, **Un Ins 410**

RESEARCH

Labor and employment, occupational safety and health, research programs, **Labor 6350 et seq.**

Occupational health and medicine, program development, **Labor 50.8**

Occupational safety and health, research programs, **Labor 6350**

Toxic materials and harmful physical agents, data repository, **Labor 147.2**

Workers compensation, individually identifiable information, **Labor 138.7**

RESERVES

Military Forces, this index

National guard. Military Forces, this index

RESIDENCE

Domicile and Residence, generally, this index

RESIDENTIAL BUILDINGS

Housing, generally, this index

RESIDENTIAL CARE FACILITIES FOR THE ELDERLY

Crimes and offenses, officers and employees, records, disclosure, **Pen 11105.3**

Disclosure, crimes and offenses, employment, **Pen 11105.3**

Labor and employment, crimes and offenses, disclosure, **Pen 11105.3**

Notice, criminal history, disclosure, employment, **Pen 11105.3**

RESIDENTIAL

RESIDENTIAL CARE FACILITIES FOR THE ELDERLY—Cont'd
Officers and employees, crimes and offenses, records, disclosure, **Pen 11105.3**

RESIDENTIAL FACILITIES
Aged persons. Residential Care Facilities for the Elderly, generally, this index
Residential Care Facilities for the Elderly, generally, this index

RESIDENTIAL MORTGAGE LENDERS
Mortgages, this index

RESIDENTS
Domicile and Residence, generally, this index

RESIDUALS
Definitions, Unclaimed Property Law, **CCP 1501**
Employee benefit plan distributions, escheat, **CCP 1521**

REST HOMES
Nursing Homes, generally, this index

RESTAURANTS
Children and minors, preparation and service, **Labor 1294.3**
Civil Rights Act, **CC 51 et seq.**
Sex discrimination, **CC 51 et seq.**

RESTITUTION
Battered womens shelters, trespass on, **Pen 602**
Car washes, labor and employment, funds, **Labor 2065**
Public buildings and works, prevailing wage rate, **Labor 1776**
Talent Agencies, this index
Unemployment Compensation, this index

RESTRAINING ORDER
Injunction, generally, this index

RESTRAINT
Labor contracts, public policy, **Labor 923**

RESTROOMS
Comfort Stations and Rest Rooms, generally, this index

RETAIL
Retailers, generally, this index

RETAIL FOOD FACILITIES
Restaurants, generally, this index

RETAIL OR WHOLESALE TOBACCO SHOP
Definitions, smoking, **Labor 6404.5**

RETAIL SALES
Sales, generally, this index

RETAIL SELLER
Retailers, generally, this index

RETAILERS
Grocery Stores, generally, this index

RETAILERS—Cont'd
Income tax—state, wages, withholding tax, **Un Ins 13025**
Safety, working warehouses, **Labor 9100 et seq.**
Working warehouses, safety, **Labor 9100 et seq.**

RETALIATION
Evictions, labor camps, **Health & S 17031.5, 17031.6**
Health care providers, whistle blowing, **Health & S 1278.5**
Health facilities, whistle blowing, **Health & S 1278.5**
Labor and Employment, this index
Nurses, whistle blowing, **Health & S 1278.5**
Private patrol operators, officers and employees, disclosure, **Bus & P 7583.46**
Railroads, officers and employees, security, **Pub U 7666**
State Officers and Employees, this index
Veterans, inspector general for veterans affairs, **Mil & V 73.7**
Whistle Blowing, generally, this index

RETARDATION
Mentally Retarded and Developmentally Disabled Persons, generally, this index

RETIREMENT AND PENSIONS
Age, compulsory retirement, **Gov 12942**
Collections, unpaid wages or benefits, **Labor 96.7**
Compensation and salaries,
  Employees deductions, contributions, **Labor 224**
  Unpaid wages or benefits, collection, deposit, payment, escheat, **Labor 96.7**
Compulsory retirement, age, **Gov 12942**
Contributions, family care and medical leave, **Gov 12945.2**
County Officers and Employees Retirement Systems, generally, this index
Death benefits, public officials, assassination, **Labor 4720 et seq.**
Elected public officials, death benefits, assassination, **Labor 4720 et seq.**
Employee benefit plan distribution,
  Definitions, Unclaimed Property Law, **CCP 1501**
  Escheat to state, **CCP 1521**
Employee benefit trust distribution, escheat to state, **CCP 1510**
Employers failure to make agreed payments to plan, **Labor 227**
Escheat,
  Unclaimed employee benefit trust distribution, **CCP 1510, 1521**
  Unpaid wages or benefits, **Labor 96.7**
Family care and medical leave, contributions, **Gov 12945.2**
Industrial relations unpaid wage fund, **Labor 96.7**

RETIREMENT AND PENSIONS—Cont'd
Medical leave, contributions, **Gov 12945.2**
Payment, unpaid wages or benefits, **Labor 96.7**
Public Employees Retirement System, generally, this index
Public officials, death benefits, assassination, **Labor 4720 et seq.**
Schoolteachers Retirement System, generally, this index
Social Security, generally, this index
State Officers and Employees, this index
Statement of payments made to plan by employer, **Labor 227.5**
Trust funds, escheat, employee benefit plan distribution,
  Definitions, Unclaimed Property Law, **CCP 1501**
  Escheat to state, **CCP 1521**
Trusts and trustees, employee benefit trust distribution, escheat to state, **CCP 1510**
Unclaimed employee benefit plan distribution, escheat to state, **CCP 1521**
Unemployment Compensation, this index
Unpaid wages or benefits, collections, payments, deposits, escheat, **Labor 96.7**

RETRAINING
Definitions, employment training panel, **Un Ins 10201**
Unemployment Compensation, this index

RETURN TO WORK PROGRAM
Workers Compensation, this index

RETURNS
Income Tax—State, this index
Unemployment Compensation, this index
Withholding tax on wages, **Un Ins 13021, 13050 et seq.**

REVENUE BONDS
Bonds, generally, this index

REVIEW
Appeal and Review, generally, this index

REVOLVERS
Weapons, generally, this index

REVOLVING FUNDS
Disability compensation, **Un Ins 3051**
Workers compensation insurance fund, subsequent injuries, **Labor 4755**

REWARDS
State Officers and Employees, this index

RIFLES
Weapons, generally, this index

RIGHT OF ENTRY
Entry On Property, generally, this index

RIGHT OF WAY
Zoning and Planning, generally, this index

RIGHT TO COUNSEL
Attorneys, this index

RIGHT TO PRIVACY
Privacy, generally, this index

RIOT GUNS
Weapons, generally, this index

RIOTS AND MOBS
Los Angeles Revitalization Zone, generally, this index

RIVERS AND STREAMS
Fish and Game, generally, this index

RIVETS
Building construction or repair, riveting gang, safety, **Labor 7108**

ROADS
Highways and Roads, generally, this index

RODEOS
Children and minors, employment, **Labor 1308**

ROOMS
Board and Room, generally, this index

ROSEBERRY ACT
Employers liability, **Labor 2801**

ROUTE DEVIATED BUS SERVICE
Paratransit Vehicles, generally, this index

RUBBER
Lead poisoning, occupational safety, programs, **Health & S 105185 et seq.**

RULES AND REGULATIONS
See text preceding index

RULES OF NAVIGATION
Ships and Shipping, generally, this index

RUM
Alcoholic Beverages, generally, this index

RURAL AREAS
Nurses, regional nursing simulation laboratories, grants, **Un Ins 9619**

RYE
Agricultural Products, generally, this index

SABBATICAL LEAVE
Definitions, employment opportunities creation, **Un Ins 12102**

SACKS
Containers, generally, this index

SACRAMENTO CITY AND COUNTY
Labor commissioner, field enforcement unit, **Labor 90.5**
Public employment offices, **Un Ins 2055**

SAFE
Definitions, occupational safety and health, **Labor 6306**

SAFEGUARDS
Definitions, occupational safety and health, **Labor 6306**

SAFEGUARDS—Cont'd
Labor and employment, occupational safety and health, responsibilities and duties of employers, **Labor 6400 et seq.**

SAFETY
Aerial passenger tramways, **Labor 7340 et seq.**
Air pressure tanks, **Labor 7620 et seq.**
Amusement rides, **Labor 7900 et seq.**
Boilers, **Labor 7620 et seq.**
  Reports, **Labor 7722**
Bungee jumping,
  Inspection and inspectors, **Labor 7920 et seq.**
  Licenses and permits, **Labor 7901**
Chemical plants, workers, **Labor 7850 et seq.**
Colleges and Universities, this index
Correctional Institutions, this index
Definitions, occupational safety and health, **Labor 6306**
Electric railroads, **Labor 6800**
Elevators, Dumbwaiters and Escalators, this index
Employment. Labor and Employment, this index
Fires and Fire Protection, generally, this index
Flammable liquids, **Labor 7800 et seq.**
Gassy tunnels, **Labor 7965 et seq.**
Health Facilities, this index
Interurban railroads, **Labor 6800**
Labor and Employment, this index
Liquefied petroleum gas, storage tanks, **Labor 7620 et seq.**
Longshoremen, **Labor 7600 et seq.**
Mines and tunnels, **Labor 7950 et seq.**
Occupational safety and health appeals board, **Labor 148 et seq.**
Occupational safety and health standards board, **Labor 140 et seq.**
  Industrial Relations Department, this index
Oil and Gas, this index
Permanent amusement rides, inspection and inspectors, **Labor 7920 et seq.**
Railroads, this index
Rapid transit rail systems, **Labor 6800**
Reports, boilers, **Labor 7722**
Retailers, working warehouses, **Labor 9100 et seq.**
Scaffolds, generally, this index
Ships and Shipping, this index
Statistics, labor statistics and research division, **Labor 150**
Steam boilers, **Labor 7620 et seq.**
Stevedore operations, **Labor 7600 et seq.**
Stores, working warehouses, **Labor 9100 et seq.**
Street railroads, **Labor 6800**
Talent agencies, sending artist to unsafe environment, **Labor 1700.33**
Tanks, storage of air pressure or liquefied petroleum gas, **Labor 7620 et seq.**
Tunnels and mines, **Labor 7950 et seq.**

SAFETY—Cont'd
Unemployment compensation privilege, corporation testing for public safety, **Un Ins 711**
Volatile flammable liquids, **Labor 7800 et seq.**
Window cleaners, **Labor 7325 et seq.**
Worker safety and health training and education program, **Labor 6354.7**
Working warehouses, **Labor 9100 et seq.**

SAFETY BELTS
Window cleaners, **Labor 7325 et seq.**

SAFETY DEVICES
Definitions, occupational safety and health, **Labor 6306**
Labor and employment, occupational safety and health, responsibility and duty of employers, **Labor 6400 et seq.**

SAFETY GLASS
Electric railroads, cars and locomotives, laminated safety glass, **Labor 6953 et seq.**

SAFETY NETS
Building construction or repair, **Labor 7106**

SAILBOATS
Boats and Boating, generally, this index

SAILORS
Military Forces, generally, this index

SALARIES
Compensation and Salaries, generally, this index

SALARY CONTINUATION PLAN
Definitions, workers compensation, **Labor 4650**

SALES
Children and Minors, this index
Housing, this index
Investigations and investigators, employee discipline or discharge, **Labor 2930 et seq.**
Labor union insignia, **Labor 1010 et seq.**
Lewd or obscene material. Lewdness and Obscenity, generally, this index
Officers and employees, shopping investigators report, **Labor 2930 et seq.**
Retailers, generally, this index
Securities, generally, this index
Solicitation, generally, this index
Talent agencies, **Labor 1700.30**
Unemployment compensation,
  Door to door salespersons, **Un Ins 13004.1**
  Sale of business, withholding money or property to pay unpaid contributions, **Un Ins 1731 et seq.**
Weapons, this index
Workers compensation, injury by defective products, **Labor 3602**

SALES

SALES AND USE TAXES
Industrial relations department, licenses and permits, compliance, information, **Labor 64.5**
Licenses and permits, industrial relations department, compliance, information, **Labor 64.5**

SALESPERSONS
Compensation, minimum wages, exemption, outside salesmen, **Labor 1171**
Employment agencies, misrepresentations, **Labor 976**
Real Estate Brokers and Salespersons, generally, this index

SALOONS
Taverns and Saloons, generally, this index

SALVAGE
Demolition of buildings, safety in employment, **Labor 6401.5**

SAME SEX MARRIAGE
Generally, **Fam 308.5**

SAMPLES
Employment development department, census bureau contract, population survey, **Un Ins 327**
Lead related construction work, employee protection, **Labor 6717**

SAN BERNARDINO RIVERSIDE STATE COLLEGE
Colleges and Universities, generally, this index

SAN DIEGO
Biotechnology, training, **Un Ins 9700 et seq.**
Definitions, biotechnology, training, **Un Ins 9700**
Labor commissioner, field enforcement unit, **Labor 90.5**
Training, biotechnology, **Un Ins 9700 et seq.**

SAN DIEGO COUNTY
Transit Development Boards, this index

SAN DIEGO METROPOLITAN TRANSIT DEVELOPMENT BOARD
San Diego County. Transit Development Boards, this index

SAN DIEGO STATE COLLEGE
Colleges and Universities, generally, this index

SAN FERNANDO VALLEY STATE COLLEGE
Colleges and Universities, generally, this index

SAN FRANCISCO ADMINISTRATIVE CODE
See text preceding index

SAN FRANCISCO BAY AREA
Harbor. San Francisco Harbor, generally, this index

SAN FRANCISCO CITY AND COUNTY
Labor commissioner, field enforcement unit, **Labor 90.5**
Public employment offices, **Un Ins 2055**

SAN FRANCISCO HARBOR
Police,
    Leave of absence with pay in lieu of disability payments, **Labor 4800 et seq.**
    Medical care and treatment, workers compensation, **Labor 4802**
    Workers compensation, special payments, **Labor 4800 et seq.**

SAN FRANCISCO STATE COLLEGE
Colleges and Universities, generally, this index

SAN JOSE
Labor commissioner, field enforcement unit, **Labor 90.5**

SAN LUIS OBISPO COUNTY
Firemen, leave of absence, salary in lieu of temporary disability benefits, **Labor 4850.5**
Parole and probation, probation officers, leaves of absence, workers compensation, disability benefits, **Labor 4850.5**
Workers compensation, officers and employees, leaves of absence, disability benefits, **Labor 4850.5**

SAN MATEO COUNTY
Support, labor and employment, orders of court, pilot programs, **Fam 4505**

SAN MATEO COUNTY STATE COLLEGE
Colleges and Universities, generally, this index

SAN MATEO SANTA CLARA COUNTY STATE COLLEGE
Colleges and Universities, generally, this index

SAND AND GRAVEL
Workers compensation, alternative dispute resolution system, **Labor 3201.5**

SANDBAGS
Weapons, generally, this index

SANDCLUBS
Weapons, generally, this index

SANDWICH STANDS
Restaurants, generally, this index

SANITARIUMS
Mentally Retarded and Developmentally Disabled Persons, generally, this index

SANITARY SEWERS
Sewers and Sewer Systems, generally, this index

SANITATION
Health and Sanitation, generally, this index

SATELLITE TELEVISION
Television and Radio, this index

SATISFACTION
Accord and Satisfaction, generally, this index
Judgments and Decrees, this index

SATURDAY
Workers compensation, instruments and documents, filing, time, **Labor 3730**

SAVINGS
Employee savings plans, unclaimed trust funds, escheat to state, **CCP 1510, 1521**

SAVINGS AND LOAN ASSOCIATIONS
Aged persons, financial abuse, reports, **Welf & I 15630.1**
Compensation and salaries, deposit of wages by employer in employees account, **Labor 213**
Corporation Taxes, generally, this index
Dependent adults, financial abuse, reports, **Welf & I 15630.1**
Fines and penalties,
    Aged persons, financial abuse, reports, **Welf & I 15630.1**
    Dependent adults, financial abuse, reports, **Welf & I 15630.1**
Officers and employees,
    Aged persons, financial abuse, reports, **Welf & I 15630.1**
    Dependent adults, financial abuse, reports, **Welf & I 15630.1**
Privileges and immunities,
    Aged persons, financial abuse, reports, **Welf & I 15634**
    Dependent adults, financial abuse, reports, **Welf & I 15634**
Workers compensation, disability payments, employer deposits, **Labor 4651**

SAVINGS ASSOCIATIONS
Adverse or pecuniary interest, loans, mortgages, **Fin 6525**
Aged persons, financial abuse, reports, **Welf & I 15630.1**
Crimes and offenses, officers and employees, records, **Fin 6525**
Dependent adults, financial abuse, reports, **Welf & I 15630.1**
Employees. Officers and employees, generally, post
Fines and penalties,
    Aged persons, financial abuse, reports, **Welf & I 15630.1**
    Dependent adults, financial abuse, reports, **Welf & I 15630.1**
Fingerprints and fingerprinting, criminal history information, **Fin 6525**
Loans, fingerprints, applicants, **Fin 6525**

SAVINGS ASSOCIATIONS—Cont'd
Officers and employees,
Aged persons, financial abuse, reports, **Welf & I 15630.1**
Crimes and offenses, records and recordation, **Fin 6525**
Dependent adults, financial abuse, reports, **Welf & I 15630.1**
Fingerprints and fingerprinting, criminal history information, **Fin 6525**
Privileges and immunities,
Aged persons, financial abuse, reports, **Welf & I 15634**
Dependent adults, financial abuse, reports, **Welf & I 15634**
Records and recordation, crimes and offenses, loan applicants and employees, **Fin 6525**

SAVINGS BANKS
Bank Deposits and Collections, generally, this index
Collections. Bank Deposits and Collections, generally, this index
Deposits. Bank Deposits and Collections, generally, this index
Unclaimed property. Abandoned or Unclaimed Property, generally, this index
Workers compensation, deposit of lump sum payments, **Labor 5102, 5103**

SAWED OFF SHOTGUN
Weapons, generally, this index

SAWMILLS
Compensation, deposits, security for payment, **Labor 270.5**
Midday meal period, **Labor 800, 801**

SCAFFOLDS
Generally, **Labor 7150 et seq.**
Children and minors, employment, **Labor 1294**
Crimes and offenses, **Labor 7155, 7156**
Definitions, **Labor 7150**
Enforcement of law, **Labor 7158**
Enforcement of safety orders, **Labor 7157**
Erection or furnishing of unsafe scaffolding, **Labor 7156**
Hooks and hangers, safety lines, **Labor 7152**
Inspection, **Labor 7156**
Jack scaffolds, **Labor 7154.1**
Lean to scaffolds, **Labor 7154.1**
Notice, unsafe equipment, destruction or removal, **Labor 7156**
Platforms or floors, **Labor 7153**
Safety lines, **Labor 7152**
Safety orders, **Labor 7157**
Safety rail, **Labor 7151**
Strength of scaffolding, **Labor 7151**
Suspending scaffolding, **Labor 7151**
Use of scaffolding after declaration of unsafeness, **Labor 7156**
Width of platforms and floors, **Labor 7153**

SCHOLARSHIPS
Colleges and Universities, this index

SCHOLARSHIPS—Cont'd
Firefighters and fire departments, dependents, **Labor 4709**
Juvenile facilities division, dependents, **Labor 4709**
Peace officers, dependents, **Labor 4709**

SCHOOL BONDS
Investments, unemployment insurance disability fund, **Un Ins 3003**
Unemployment insurance disability fund, investment, **Un Ins 3003**

SCHOOL BUILDINGS AND GROUNDS
Community colleges and districts. Colleges and Universities, this index
Construction or alteration,
Compensation and salaries, prevailing wage rate, **Labor 1771.7**
Fees, compliance, **Labor 1771.75**
Prevailing wage rate, **Labor 1771.7**
Fees, compliance, **Labor 1771.75**

SCHOOL DISTRICTS
Schools and School Districts, generally, this index

SCHOOL EMPLOYEES FUND
School Funds, this index

SCHOOL EMPLOYER
Definitions, unemployment compensation, **Un Ins 821.4**

SCHOOL EMPLOYER ADVISORY COMMITTEE
Unemployment compensation, **Un Ins 831**

SCHOOL FOR THE BLIND
Compensation and salaries, unemployment compensation, nonprofessional employees, **Un Ins 1451 et seq.**
Nonprofessional employees, unemployment compensation, **Un Ins 1451 et seq.**
Officers and employees, unemployment compensation, nonprofessional employees, **Un Ins 1451 et seq.**
Unemployment compensation, nonprofessional employees, **Un Ins 1451 et seq.**

SCHOOL FUNDS
Scholarships, generally, this index
School employees fund, **Un Ins 822 et seq.**
Deposits, **Un Ins 823**
Experience relationships, benefits paid, **Un Ins 832**
Reimbursement, **Un Ins 829**
Transfers to unemployment insurance management system, **Un Ins 826**
Unemployment compensation, **Un Ins 822 et seq.**

SCHOOL MEMBERS
Public Employees Retirement System, this index

SCHOOL OFFICERS AND EMPLOYEES
Bribery and corruption, whistle blowing, **Educ 44110 et seq.**

SCHOOL OFFICERS AND EMPLOYEES—Cont'd
Classified employees,
Disability compensation, unemployment insurance, **Un Ins 710.4**
School employees fund, **Un Ins 822**
Unemployment compensation,
Disability compensation, **Un Ins 710.4**
Financing, **Un Ins 821 et seq.**
Local experience charge, **Un Ins 828**
Compensation and salaries,
Leaves of absence, military duty, **Mil & V 395.01 et seq.**
Unemployment compensation, generally, post
Crimes and offenses, whistle blowing, **Educ 44110 et seq.**
Disability insurance,
Leaves of absence, police, **Labor 4850**
Unemployment insurance, **Un Ins 710.4**
Disclosure, whistle blowing, **Educ 44110 et seq.**
Discrimination,
Temporary disability, unlawful employment practices, **Gov 12943**
Unlawful employment practice, pregnancy or temporary disability, **Gov 12943**
Duress or coercion, whistle blowing, **Educ 44110 et seq.**
Improper activity, whistle blowing, **Educ 44110 et seq.**
Leaves of absence,
Compensation and salaries, ante
Military duty, **Mil & V 395 et seq.**
Los Angeles unified school district, police, disability benefits, leaves of absence, **Labor 4850**
Merchant Marine, this index
Military forces, discrimination, **Mil & V 394**
Peace officers, disability benefits, leaves of absence, **Labor 4850**
Personnel commission, unemployment compensation, public entity, definitions, **Un Ins 135, 605**
Pregnancy, unlawful employment practices, **Gov 12943**
Probationary employees, investigations, places of child employment, **Labor 1302**
Reprisal actions, whistle blowing, **Educ 44110 et seq.**
School employees fund. School Funds, this index
Soldiers and Sailors Relief Act, **Mil & V 395.1**
State superintendent of public instruction. Schools and School Districts, this index
Threats, whistle blowing, **Educ 44110 et seq.**
Traveling expenses, excluded services, **Un Ins 634.5**

SCHOOL

SCHOOL OFFICERS AND EMPLOYEES
—Cont'd

Unemployment compensation,
  Classified employees, local experience charge, **Un Ins 828**
  Disability compensation, **Un Ins 710.4**
  Disability insurance, application of law, employment insurance, **Un Ins 710.5**
  Employees fund, contribution rates, **Un Ins 823**
  Employer advisory committee, **Un Ins 831**
  Funds, contribution rates, **Un Ins 823**
  Local experience charge, **Un Ins 828, 829**
  Qualifications, **Un Ins 605**
  School employees fund, **Un Ins 822, 823**
    Credits to accounts, school employers with positive balance in fund, **Un Ins 827**
    Experience relationships, benefits paid, **Un Ins 832**
    Reimbursements, **Un Ins 829**
    Transfers to unemployment insurance management system, **Un Ins 826**
Whistle blowing, **Educ 44110 et seq.**
Workers compensation,
  Disability benefits, leaves of absence, police, **Labor 4850**
  Self insurers, medical and related treatment and supplies, former employees, **Labor 4606**
  Service of notices, orders, **Labor 5317**
  Volunteer employees, **Labor 3364.5**

SCHOOL SUPERINTENDENTS

County superintendents of schools,
  Unemployment compensation,
    Elective coverage, **Un Ins 709**
    Public entity, definitions, **Un Ins 135, 605**
  Workers compensation, volunteers, **Labor 3364.5**
State superintendent of public instruction. Schools and School Districts, this index

SCHOOLS AND SCHOOL DISTRICTS

Apprentices,
  Instruction classes, **Labor 3074**
    Registration, prerequisite programs, **Labor 3074.3**
  Workers compensation, **Labor 3368**
At risk students, youthbuild program, **Un Ins 9801 et seq.**
Attendance, parents, classrooms, suspended or expelled child, **Labor 230.7**
Blind persons. School for the Blind, generally, this index
Boards and commissions. Governing boards, generally, post
Buildings and grounds. School Buildings and Grounds, generally, this index
Career counseling. Vocational Education, generally, this index
Career resource network, **Educ 53086**

SCHOOLS AND SCHOOL DISTRICTS
—Cont'd

Career technical education. Vocational Education, generally, this index
Classified employees. School Officers and Employees, this index
Colleges and Universities, generally, this index
Community colleges and districts. Colleges and Universities, this index
Compensation and salaries. School Officers and Employees, this index
Construction or alteration. School Buildings and Grounds, this index
County superintendents of schools. School Superintendents, this index
Courses of instruction or study, youthbuild program, **Un Ins 9801 et seq.**
Crimes and offenses,
  Officers and employees. School Officers and Employees, this index
  School Officers and Employees, this index
Deaf, school for. Schools for the Deaf, generally, this index
Dependent children. Juvenile Institutions and Schools, generally, this index
Discrimination. School Officers and Employees, this index
Dropouts. High Schools or Secondary Schools, this index
Employees. School Officers and Employees, generally, this index
Employment. Labor and employment, generally, post
Extended unemployment compensation, student employment during vacation period, **Un Ins 3701**
Facilities. School Buildings and Grounds, generally, this index
Finance. School Funds, generally, this index
Fines and penalties, occupational safety and health, refunds, **Labor 6434**
Funds. School Funds, generally, this index
Governing boards,
  Public entity, definitions, unemployment compensation, **Un Ins 135, 605**
  Unemployment compensation, elective coverage, **Un Ins 709**
    Public entity, definitions, **Un Ins 135, 605**
Graduation, youthbuild program, **Un Ins 9801 et seq.**
Grants, youthbuild program, **Un Ins 9801 et seq.**
Grounds. School Buildings and Grounds, generally, this index
High Schools or Secondary Schools, generally, this index
Housing, youthbuild program, **Un Ins 9801 et seq.**
Indigent persons, youthbuild program, **Un Ins 9801 et seq.**

SCHOOLS AND SCHOOL DISTRICTS
—Cont'd

Juvenile Institutions and Schools, generally, this index
Labor and employment,
  Parents, attendance in classrooms, suspended or expelled children, **Labor 230.7**
  Statewide young worker health and safety resource network, **Labor 6359**
  Suspended or expelled children, attendance of parents in classrooms, **Labor 230.7**
  Visits, discharge or discrimination, **Labor 230.8**
Labor camps, application of law, **Health & S 17024**
Nonpublic schools. Private Schools, generally, this index
Occupational safety and health, fines and penalties, refunds, **Labor 6434**
Officers and employees. School Officers and Employees, generally, this index
Parents, attendance, classrooms, suspended or expelled child, **Labor 230.7**
Parochial schools. Private Schools, generally, this index
Private Schools, generally, this index
Public entity, unemployment compensation, **Un Ins 135, 605**
Regional occupational centers. Vocational Education, this index
Regional youth education facilities. Juvenile Institutions and Schools, this index
Restrictions, **Labor 1394**
Scholarships, generally, this index
School Buildings and Grounds, generally, this index
School for the Blind, generally, this index
School Funds, generally, this index
Schools for the Deaf, generally, this index
Schoolteachers Retirement System, generally, this index
Secondary schools. High Schools or Secondary Schools, generally, this index
State superintendent of public instruction, apprenticeship council member, **Labor 3070**
Superintendents. School Superintendents, generally, this index
Suspension or expulsion of students,
  Attendance of parents, classrooms, **Labor 230.7**
  Parents, attendance, classrooms, **Labor 230.7**
Teachers retirement system. Schoolteachers Retirement System, generally, this index
Technical schools. Vocational Education, generally, this index
Unemployment compensation,
  Governing boards, elective coverage, **Un Ins 709**

SCHOOLS AND SCHOOL DISTRICTS
—Cont'd
Unemployment compensation—Cont'd
Public entity, definitions, **Un Ins 135, 605**
Qualifications, **Un Ins 605**
School Officers and Employees, this index
Student services, **Un Ins 642**
Temporary employment, students, **Un Ins 4701**
Unified schools and districts. Schoolteachers Retirement System, generally, this index
Union schools and districts. Schoolteachers Retirement System, generally, this index
Vocational Education, generally, this index
Volunteers, workers compensation, **Labor 3364.5**
Work experience education. High Schools or Secondary Schools, this index
Workers compensation. School Officers and Employees, this index

SCHOOLS FOR THE DEAF
Compensation and salaries, unemployment compensation, nonprofessional employees, **Un Ins 1451 et seq.**
Nonprofessional employees, unemployment compensation, **Un Ins 1451 et seq.**
Officers and employees, nonprofessional employees, unemployment compensation, **Un Ins 1451 et seq.**
Unemployment compensation, nonprofessional employees, **Un Ins 1451 et seq.**

SCHOOLTEACHERS
Overtime, private schools, exemptions, **Labor 515.8**
Pensions. Schoolteachers Retirement System, generally, this index
Private Schools, this index
Retirement and pensions. Schoolteachers Retirement System, generally, this index
Unemployment compensation, optional exclusion, **Un Ins 711**

SCHOOLTEACHERS RETIREMENT SYSTEM
Confidential or privileged information, earnings, members receiving disability allowance, **Un Ins 1095**
Disability retirement, earnings information, access, **Un Ins 1095**
Earnings information, access, disability allowance, **Un Ins 1095**
Unemployment compensation benefits, access to information, members receiving disability allowance, **Un Ins 1095**

SCIENTISTS
Unemployment compensation, independent contractors status, presumption, **Un Ins 656**

SCOREKEEPERS
Athletics, workers compensation, exemption, **Labor 3352**

SCOWS
Ships and Shipping, generally, this index

SCRAP METAL AND SALVAGE MATERIAL
Lead poisoning, occupational safety, programs, **Health & S 105185 et seq.**

SCRIP
Labor, compensation, issuance in payment, **Labor 212**

SEALS
Labor organizations, unauthorized use, **Labor 1016**
Workers compensation appeals board, **Labor 116**

SEAMEN
Compensation and salaries, seasonal labor, application of law, **Labor 251**
Seasonal labor, application of law, **Labor 251**

SEARCHES AND SEIZURES
Industrial Homework, this index
Warrants,
Industrial homework, **Labor 2656**
Medical records, **CC 56.10**
Unemployment compensation, applicant information, **Un Ins 1095**
Wearing Apparel, this index

SEASONAL LABOR
Agricultural Labor and Employment, this index
Compensation and Salaries, this index

SEASONAL LABOR WAGE LAW
Generally, **Labor 250 et seq.**

SEATS
Elevator operators, **Labor 7319**

SECONDARY SCHOOLS
High Schools or Secondary Schools, generally, this index

SECRETARIES
Definitions, labor and workforce development agency, **Labor 19.5**
Health and Human Services Agency, this index

SECRETARY OF STATE
Domestic Partnership, this index
Elections, generally, this index
Filing, domestic partnership, termination, **Fam 299**
Water Districts, generally, this index

SECRETS AND SECRECY
Confidential or Privileged Information, generally, this index

SECTARIAN SCHOOLS
Private Schools, generally, this index

SECURED TRANSACTIONS
Workers compensation, self insurers, security interest in assets, **Labor 3701**

SECURITIES
Agents. Security Agents and Broker Dealers, generally, this index
Brokers. Security Agents and Broker Dealers, generally, this index
Dealers. Security Agents and Broker Dealers, generally, this index
Pensions. Retirement and Pensions, generally, this index
Retirement and Pensions, generally, this index
Support, liquidation, instructions, **Fam 17522.5**
Workers compensation, deposit, self insuring employers, **Labor 3701, 3701.5**

SECURITIES AGENTS AND BROKER DEALERS
Security Agents and Broker Dealers, generally, this index

SECURITY
Airports and Landing Fields, this index
Workers compensation, security for payment of compensation, **Labor 3700**

SECURITY AGENTS AND BROKER DEALERS
Crimes and offenses, fingerprints and fingerprinting, **Corp 25221**
Fingerprints and fingerprinting, **Corp 25221**
Live scan technology, fingerprints and fingerprinting, **Corp 25221**

SECURITY DEPOSITS
Sheepherders, agricultural labor and employment, **Labor 2695.2**

SECURITY GUARDS
Private Security Services, generally, this index

SEDUCTION
Children and minors, **CC 49**

SEGREGATION
Discrimination, generally, this index

SEIZURES
Searches and Seizures, generally, this index

SELF EMPLOYMENT
Unemployment Compensation, this index

SELF INCRIMINATION
Agricultural labor relations board proceedings, witnesses, **Labor 1151.2**
Unemployment compensation, subpoena for production of records, effect, **Un Ins 1955**

SELF INSURANCE
Insurance, this index

SELF INSURANCE PLANS FUND
Workers compensation, **Labor 3702.5**

SEMICONDUCTORS
Lead poisoning, occupational safety, programs, **Health & S 105185 et seq.**

SEMIMONTHLY PAY DAY LAW
Generally, **Labor 204**

SEMINARIES
Colleges and Universities, generally, this index

SEMITRAILERS
Motor Carriers, generally, this index

SENATE
Legislature, this index

SENIOR CITIZENS
Aged Persons, generally, this index

SENIORITY
Hazardous substances, discrimination, **Labor 6399.7**

SENTENCE AND PUNISHMENT
Crimes and Offenses, generally, this index
Fines and Penalties, generally, this index

SEPARATION
Legal separation. Marriage, this index

SERIOUS CONCEALED DANGERS
Definitions, consumer products or business practices, **Pen 387**

SERIOUS EXPOSURE
Definitions, dangerous business practices, **Pen 387**

SERIOUS HEALTH CONDITION
Definitions, family care and medical leave, **Gov 12945.2**

SERIOUS VIOLATION
Definitions,
  Agricultural labor and employment, judgments, **Labor 1691**
  Occupational safety and health, penalties, **Labor 6432**

SERVANTS
Domestic Service or Work, generally, this index

SERVICE CONTRACTS
Janitors, discharge, **Labor 1060 et seq.**

SERVICE CREDITS
Public Employees Retirement System, this index

SERVICE MARKS
Trademarks, generally, this index

SERVICE OF PROCESS
Process, this index

SERVICE PROVIDERS
Definitions, unemployment compensation, support, reports, **Un Ins 1088.8**

SERVICE RECIPIENT
Definitions, unemployment compensation, support, reports, **Un Ins 1088.8**

SERVICE STATIONS
Motor Vehicle Service Stations, generally, this index

SETBACK LINES
Zoning and Planning, generally, this index

SETOFF AND COUNTERCLAIM
Disability compensation, overpayments, **Un Ins 2739**
  Extended unemployment compensation benefits, **Un Ins 3751**
Extended unemployment compensation overpayments, **Un Ins 3751**
Unemployment Compensation, this index
Wrongful discharge actions, unemployment insurance, benefits, **Un Ins 1382**

SETTLEMENT
Compromise and Settlement, generally, this index

SEVERANCE
Compensation and Salaries, this index

SEVERELY HEARING IMPAIRED PERSONS
Deaf and Mute Persons, generally, this index

SEWAGE
Sewers and Sewer Systems, generally, this index

SEWERS AND SEWER SYSTEMS
Labor and employment, occupational safety and health, bids for construction of sewers, **Labor 6707**
Labor camps, reserved to local jurisdictions, **Health & S 17021**
Occupational safety and health, bids for construction of sewers, **Labor 6707**
Zoning and Planning, generally, this index

SEX
Actions and proceedings, force and violence, **CC 52.4**
Apprentices, discrimination, **Labor 1777.6, 3095**
Attorney fees, force and violence, actions and proceedings, **CC 52.4**
Costs, force and violence, actions and proceedings, **CC 52.4**
Crimes and offenses, force and violence, actions and proceedings, **CC 52.4**
Damages, force and violence, **CC 52.4**
Definitions, fair employment and housing, **Gov 12926**
Discrimination, generally, this index
Exemplary damages, force and violence, **CC 52.4**
Fair Employment and Housing, generally, this index
Force and violence, actions and proceedings, **CC 52.4**

SEX—Cont'd
Gender identity, labor and employment, wearing apparel, **Gov 12949**
Housing. Fair Employment and Housing, generally, this index
Injunction, force and violence, **CC 52.4**
Labor and employment. Fair Employment and Housing, generally, this index
Limitation of actions, force and violence, **CC 52.4**
Statute of limitations, force and violence, **CC 52.4**
Violence, actions and proceedings, **CC 52.4**
Women, generally, this index

SEX DISCRIMINATION
Discrimination, generally, this index

SEX OFFENDERS
Children and minors, criminal record, disclosure, employment, **Pen 11105.3**
Disability, compensation, disqualification, **Un Ins 2678**
Disclosure, records and recordation, employment, **Pen 11105.3**
Foreign states, employment records, **Pen 11105.3**
Labor and employment, disclosure, records and recordation, **Pen 11105.3**
Sexual Assault, generally, this index

SEX OFFENSES
Lewdness and Obscenity, generally, this index

SEXUAL ASSAULT
Children and Minors, this index
Clinics, forensic medical examinations, reports, **Pen 11160.1**
Definitions,
  Labor and employment, time off, **Labor 230, 230.1**
  Protective orders, service of process, fees, **CCP 527.6**
Discovery, **CCP 2017.220**
Forensic medical examinations, health care providers, reports, **Pen 11160.1**
Health care providers, forensic medical examinations, reports, **Pen 11160.1**
Health care services department, forensic medical examinations, reports, **Pen 11160.1**
Health Facilities, this index
Hospitals, this index
Labor and employment, time off, **Labor 230, 230.1**
Limitation of actions, labor and employment, time off, **Labor 230, 230.1**
Local health departments, forensic medical examinations, reports, **Pen 11160.1**
Physicians and Surgeons, this index
Statute of limitations, labor and employment, time off, **Labor 230, 230.1**
Time off, labor and employment, **Labor 230.1**

SEXUAL BATTERY
Discovery, **CCP 2017.220**

SEXUAL EXPLOITATION
Children and Minors, this index

SEXUAL HARASSMENT
Actions and proceedings, discovery, **CCP 2017.220**
Attorney fees, **CC 52**
Damages, **CC 52**
Discovery, **CCP 2017.220**
Fair employment and housing, **Gov 12940**
Fines and penalties, **CC 52**
Labor and employment, **Gov 12940, 12950**
Training, **Gov 12950.1**
Punitive damages, **CC 52**
Training, labor and employment, **Gov 12950.1**
Unemployment compensation, good cause, **Un Ins 1256.5**

SEXUAL ORIENTATION
Civil rights, **CC 51.7**
Definitions,
Civil rights, **CC 51.7**
Fair employment and housing, **Gov 12926**
Discrimination, **CC 51.7**
Civil rights, **CC 51**
Fair employment and housing, **Gov 12920, 12921, 12926, 12940 et seq., 12955, 12955.8**
Fair Employment and Housing, this index

SEXUAL PSYCHOPATHS
Sex Offenders, generally, this index

SEXUAL RELATIONS
Sex Offenders, generally, this index

SEXUALLY TRANSMITTED DISEASES
AIDS, generally, this index

SHAKEMILLS
Labor and employment, midday meal period, **Labor 800, 801**

SHARES AND SHAREHOLDERS
Corporations, this index
Liabilities, income tax—state, withholding, **Un Ins 1735**
Unemployment Compensation, this index

SHARPS
Hypodermic Syringes and Needles, generally, this index

SHEEP
Herders, **Labor 2695.1 et seq.**

SHEEPHERDERS
Generally, **Labor 2695.1 et seq.**

SHELLEY MALONEY ALSA OF 1939
Generally, **Labor 3070 et seq.**

SHELLFISH
Oysters, trespasses, acts constituting, **Pen 602**

SHELTERS
Homeless Persons, this index
Social Services, this index

SHERIFFS
Arrest, generally, this index
Attachment, generally, this index
Auxiliaries. Reserves or auxiliaries, generally, post
Blood borne infectious diseases, workers compensation, presumptions, **Labor 3212.8**
Confidential or privileged information, background investigation of employment applicants, disclosure by other employers, **Gov 1031.1**
Costs, background investigation, employment applicants, disclosure by other employers, **Gov 1031.1**
Crimes and offenses, reserves or auxiliaries, absence and absentees, labor and employment, emergency duties, **Labor 230.3**
Criminal history information, applicants, disclosure by other employers, **Gov 1031.1**
Death, line of duty, dependents, scholarships, **Labor 4709**
Definitions, Labor Code, **Labor 25**
Dependents, scholarships, **Labor 4709**
Discharge, reserves or auxiliaries, absence and absentees, labor and employment, emergency duties, **Labor 230.3**
Discrimination, reserves or auxiliaries, absence and absentees, labor and employment, emergency duties, **Labor 230.3**
Emergencies, reserves or auxiliaries, absence and absentees, labor and employment, **Labor 230.3**
Employment Security Law, collection of delinquent contributions, **Un Ins 1785 et seq.**
Executions, generally, this index
Fees,
Labor commissioner, actions, **Labor 102**
Labor standards enforcement division, service of process, **Labor 101**
Handicapped persons, disability in line of duty, dependents, scholarships, **Labor 4709**
Heart trouble,
Employment, discrimination, **Gov 12940.1**
Workers compensation, **Labor 3212.5**
Hernias, workers compensation, **Labor 3212.5**
Investigations and investigators, applicants for employment, disclosure by other employers, **Gov 1031.1**
Jails, generally, this index
Labor and employment,
Definitions, **Labor 25**
Heart trouble, presumptions, **Gov 12940.1**
Labor standards enforcement division, costs, **Labor 101**

SHERIFFS—Cont'd
Line of duty. Death, ante
Lower back impairment, workers compensation, **Labor 3213.2**
Meningitis, workers compensation, presumptions, **Labor 3212.9**
Methicillin resistant staphylococcus aureus (MRSA) skin infections, workers compensation, presumptions, **Labor 3212.8**
Pneumonia, workers compensation, **Labor 3212.5**
Presumptions, heart trouble, employment, **Gov 12940.1**
Prisons and prisoners. Jails, generally, this index
Privileges and immunities, criminal history information, disclosure by other employers, **Gov 1031.1**
Process, generally, this index
Reserves or auxiliaries,
Discrimination, absence and absentees, labor and employment, emergency duties, **Labor 230.3**
Workers compensation, **Labor 3362.5, 3364**
Scholarships, dependents, **Labor 4709**
Searches and Seizures, generally, this index
Workers compensation, **Labor 3352, 3362.5**
Blood borne infectious diseases, presumptions, **Labor 3212.8**
Deputies and assistants, **Labor 3362.5**
Exclusion, deputies and assistants, **Labor 3352**
Hepatitis, presumptions, **Labor 3212.8**
Hernia, heart trouble and pneumonia, **Labor 3212, 3212.5**
Leaves of absence, disability benefits, **Labor 4850**
Lower back impairment, **Labor 3213.2**
Meningitis, presumptions, **Labor 3212.9**
Pneumonia, **Labor 3212, 3212.5**
Reserves or auxiliaries, **Labor 3362.5, 3364**
San Luis Obispo County, leave of absence, salary in lieu of temporary disability benefits, **Labor 4850.5**
Scholarships, dependents, **Labor 4709**
Tuberculosis, **Labor 3212.6**

SHIPS AND SHIPPING
Age, signalman, loading or unloading operations, **Labor 7600**
Children and minors, employment, **Labor 1294**
Contracts, loading or unloading ship, signalman or hatch tender, **Labor 7600**
Crimes and offenses,
Loading or unloading, safety violations, **Labor 7608**
Safety, loading or unloading operations, **Labor 7608**
Signalmen, employment, loading and unloading operations, **Labor 7600, 7608**

SHIPS

SHIPS AND SHIPPING—Cont'd
Definitions, American vessel, **Un Ins 125.5**
Hatch tenders, loading and unloading operations, **Labor 7600, 7608**
Labor and employment, loading and unloading operations, safety, **Labor 7600 et seq.**
Loading and unloading operations, safety, **Labor 7600 et seq.**
Longshoremen, safety, **Labor 7600 et seq.**
Offenses. Crimes and offenses, generally, ante
Passengers, terminals, trespass, **Pen 602**
Safety, loading and unloading operations, **Labor 7600 et seq.**
Signalmen, loading and unloading operations, **Labor 7600, 7608**
Stevedore operations, safety, **Labor 7600 et seq.**
Terminals, passengers, trespass, **Pen 602**
Trespass, passengers, terminals, **Pen 602**
Unemployment compensation,
    Coverage, **Un Ins 609**
    Excluded services, **Un Ins 648**

SHOPPING INVESTIGATOR
Definitions, reports, **Labor 2930**
Report, employee discharge or discipline, **Labor 2930 et seq.**

SHOPS
Stores, generally, this index

SHORT ORDER CAFES
Restaurants, generally, this index

SHORT TITLES
Popular Name Laws, generally, this index

SHOTGUNS
Weapons, generally, this index

SHOWS
Motion Pictures, generally, this index
Theaters and Shows, generally, this index

SICK LEAVE
Alcoholics and alcoholism, voluntary treatment program enrollment, employers duties, **Labor 1027**
Definitions, family members, **Labor 233**
Domestic partnership, **Labor 233**
    Violations, **Labor 234**
Family members, **Labor 233**
    Violations, **Labor 234**
Income tax—state, unemployment compensation, **Un Ins 13028.6**
Labor and employment, family members, **Labor 233**
    Violations, **Labor 234**
Municipal officers and employees, family members, **Labor 233**
    Violations, **Labor 234**
Public Officers and Employees, this index
State Officers and Employees, this index
Unemployment compensation, **Un Ins 13028.6**
Violations, family members, **Labor 234**

SICK PAY
Definitions, unemployment compensation, **Un Ins 13028.6**
Unemployment Compensation, this index

SICKNESS
Disability insurance. Insurance, this index
Illness, generally, this index

SIGNALS
Signs and Signals, generally, this index

SIGNATURES
Assignment of wages, **Labor 300**
Bank Deposits and Collections, this index
Definitions, Labor Code, **Labor 17**
Marks, writing signature by mark, unemployment insurance code, **Un Ins 17**
Workers Compensation, this index

SIGNS AND SIGNALS
Agricultural land, trespass, **Pen 602**
Construction elevators, signals and signalling devices, **Labor 7201 et seq.**
Malicious mischief, altering, masking, **Pen 602**
No smoking signs, workplaces, **Labor 6404.5**
Trespass, this index
Workplace no smoking signs, **Labor 6404.5**

SILICOSIS
Workers compensation, apportionment, **Labor 5500.5**

SINGLE FAMILY DWELLINGS
Housing, generally, this index

SINGLE FAMILY RESIDENTIAL HOUSING
Housing, generally, this index

SINGLE TARGETED TAX AREA
Enterprise Zones, this index

SKIING
Lift operators, off duty employees, workers compensation, exclusion, **Labor 3352**
Lifts. Aerial Passenger Tramways, generally, this index
Trespass, **Pen 602**

SKILLED NURSING FACILITIES
Nursing Homes, this index

SKIN CANCER
Lifeguards, workers compensation, injury, **Labor 3212.11**

SKINS
Tissue Banks, generally, this index

SLANDER
Libel and Slander, generally, this index

SLEEPING PLACE
Definitions, employee housing, **Health & S 17011**

SLIDES
Photography and Pictures, generally, this index

SLINGS
Building construction, repair, furnishing unsafe equipment, **Labor 7156**

SLINGSHOTS
Weapons, generally, this index

SMALL BUSINESSES
Corporation Taxes, this index
Education, unemployment compensation, **Un Ins 1231**
Training, **Un Ins 10203**
Unemployment compensation,
    Education, **Un Ins 1231**
    Employment training panel, plans and specifications, **Un Ins 10205**

SMALL CLAIMS COURTS
Civil rights, jurisdiction, **CC 52.2**
Discrimination, jurisdiction, **CC 52.2**
Jurisdiction, civil rights, **CC 52.2**

SMALL EMPLOYERS
Small Businesses, generally, this index

SMELTERS
Hours of labor, **Labor 750 et seq.**

SMOKING
Infractions, workplaces, **Labor 6404.5**
Motor Carriers, this index
Places of employment, regulation, **Labor 6404.5**
Workplaces, rules and regulations, **Labor 6404.5**

SOCIAL ACTIVITIES
Workers compensation, **Labor 3600**

SOCIAL SECURITY
Disability compensation, nonconformity with provisions of Security Act, **Un Ins 2605**
Earnings withholding orders, applications, social security number, **CCP 706.121**
Garnishment, application, **CCP 706.121 et seq.**
Numbers and numbering, compensation and salaries, itemized statement, **Labor 226**
Unemployment compensation,
    Administration fund, contributions, **Un Ins 1556**
    Money credited to unemployment trust fund, **Un Ins 1528.5**
    Reduction of benefits, **Un Ins 1255.3**
    Social security taxes paid, exclusion from wages, **Un Ins 935**

SOCIAL SERVICES
Abuse, patients, reports, **Pen 11161.8**
Actions and proceedings,
    County aid and relief, post
    Unemployment compensation, disclosure of confidential information, **Un Ins 1095**

SOCIAL SERVICES—Cont'd

AFDC. CalWORKs, generally, post

Aid to families with dependent children. CalWORKs, generally, post

Aliens,
Domestic violence,
Labor and employment, **Welf & I 13283**
Money, **Welf & I 13283**
Human trafficking,
Labor and employment, **Welf & I 13283**
Money, **Welf & I 13283**

Appropriations, CalWORKs, employment training fund, **Un Ins 1611.5**

California work opportunity and responsibility to kids program. CalWORKs, generally, post

CalWORKs,
Clearinghouse, job creation, **Un Ins 17002**
Corporation taxes, credit, hiring, **Rev & T 23622.7**
Councils, job creation, **Un Ins 17002**
Information, unemployment compensation reports, **Un Ins 1088.5**
Job training programs, funds, **Un Ins 10214.7**
Labor and employment,
Job creation, **Un Ins 17000 et seq.**
Job training programs. CalWORKs, ante
Training fund, appropriations, **Un Ins 1611.5**
Medi Cal Program, generally, this index
Priorities and preferences, unemployment compensation, **Un Ins 9615**
Reports, unemployment compensation information, **Un Ins 1088.5**
Training, funds, **Un Ins 10214.7**
Unemployment compensation,
Information and reports, **Un Ins 1088.5**
Priorities, **Un Ins 9615**

Certified homes of foster family agencies. Foster homes, generally, post

Clearinghouse, CalWORKs, job creation, **Un Ins 17002**

Compensation and salaries, sheltered workshops and rehabilitation facilities, **Labor 1191.5**

Confidential or privileged information, unemployment compensation, disclosure of confidential information, **Un Ins 1094**

Councils, CalWORKs, job creation, **Un Ins 17002**

Counties. County aid and relief, generally, post

County aid and relief,
Actions and proceedings, confidential or privileged information, unemployment compensation, disclosure of confidential information, **Un Ins 1094, 1095**

SOCIAL SERVICES—Cont'd

County aid and relief—Cont'd
Confidential or privileged information, unemployment compensation, disclosure of confidential information, **Un Ins 1094, 1095**
Crimes and offenses, unemployment compensation, confidential or privileged information, **Un Ins 1094**
Evidence, unemployment compensation, confidential information, **Un Ins 1094, 1095**
In home supportive services program, domestic employees, unemployment compensation, **Un Ins 683**
Unemployment compensation, disclosure of confidential information, **Un Ins 1094, 1095**
Vouchers, unlawful use, workers compensation coverage, **Labor 3351.5**

Crimes and offenses,
County aid and relief, unemployment compensation, confidential or privileged information, **Un Ins 1094**
Foster homes, post

Criminal history information, in home supportive services, **Welf & I 12301.8, 15660**

Disclosure. Foster homes, post

District attorneys, unemployment compensation, confidential information furnished to, **Un Ins 1095**

Domestic violence. Aliens, ante

Employment. Labor and employment, generally, post

Employment Development, generally, this index

Evidence, county aid and relief, unemployment compensation, confidential information, **Un Ins 1095**

Family homes. Foster homes, generally, post

Fees,
Criminal history information, care facilities, **Welf & I 15660**
In home supportive services, criminal history information, **Welf & I 15660**

Food stamps,
Information, unemployment compensation, reports, **Un Ins 1088.5**
Unemployment compensation, information and reports, **Un Ins 1088.5**

Foreign countries. Aliens, generally, ante

Foster homes,
Crimes and offenses, disclosure, **Pen 11105.3**
Disclosure, crimes and offenses, foster parents, **Pen 11105.3**
Family care leave, **Un Ins 3300 et seq.**
Notice, criminal history, disclosure, employment, **Pen 11105.3**
Paid family care leave, **Un Ins 3300 et seq.**
Unemployment compensation, family care leave, **Un Ins 3300 et seq.**

SOCIAL SERVICES—Cont'd

General assistance. County aid and relief, generally, ante

Greater avenues for independence (GAIN), enterprise zones, tax credits, **Rev & T 23622.7**

Handicapped persons,
Labor and employment, personal care services, **Welf & I 14132.955**
Personal care services, labor and employment, **Welf & I 14132.955**

Health care and services. Medi Cal Program, generally, this index

Human trafficking. Aliens, ante

In home supportive services,
Criminal history information, **Welf & I 12301.8, 15660**
Domestic employees unemployment compensation coverage, **Un Ins 683**
Fees, criminal history information, **Welf & I 15660**
Notice, criminal history information, employees, **Welf & I 15660**
Unemployment compensation coverage, **Un Ins 683**
Workers compensation, **Labor 3351.5**

Information,
Aid to families with dependent children (CalWORKs) applicants and recipients, unemployment compensation information, **Un Ins 1088.5**
Employment development department, **Un Ins 1094, 1095**
Food stamp program applicants and recipients, unemployment compensation information, **Un Ins 1088.5**

Interstate commerce, **Labor 3203**

Job preparation and training services. Unemployment Compensation, this index

Job training programs,
CalWORKs, ante
Handicapped clients, **Un Ins 9003**

Jobs. Labor and employment, generally, post

Labor and employment,
Application of law, **Labor 2700**
CalWORKs, ante
Handicapped persons, personal care services, **Welf & I 14132.955**
Health care and services, personal care services, **Welf & I 14132.955**
Job creation, CalWORKs, **Un Ins 17000 et seq.**
Personal care services, **Welf & I 14132.955**
Rehabilitation facilities, licenses, **Labor 1191.5**
Sheltered workshops, licenses, **Labor 1191.5**
Work Incentive Programs, generally, this index

Local child support agencies. Child Support Services Department, this index

Medi Cal Program, generally, this index

SOCIAL

SOCIAL SERVICES—Cont'd

Medical assistance. Medi Cal Program, generally, this index

Misdemeanors. Crimes and offenses, generally, ante

Noncitizens. Aliens, generally, ante

Notice,
  Foster homes, ante
  In home supportive services, ante

Offenses. Crimes and offenses, generally, ante

Personal care services, labor and employment, **Welf & I 14132.955**

Priorities and preferences. CalWORKs, ante

Rehabilitation, licenses, rehabilitation facilities, **Labor 1191.5**

Reports. CalWORKs, ante

Residential Care Facilities for the Elderly, generally, this index

Shelters,
  Licenses, **Labor 1191.5**
  Rehabilitation facilities, licenses, **Labor 1191.5**

Social Security, generally, this index

Support, local child support agencies.
  Child Support Services Department, this index

Supportive services. In home supportive services, generally, ante

Temporary assistance for needy families. CalWORKs, generally, ante

Training,
  CalWORKs, ante
  Employment, **Un Ins 2059**
  Work Incentive Programs, generally, this index

Unemployment compensation,
  Actions and proceedings, confidential information, disclosure, **Un Ins 1095**
  Disclosure of confidential information, **Un Ins 1094**
  In home supportive services, domestic employees, **Un Ins 683**

Welfare to work. CalWORKs, generally, ante

Work Incentive Programs, generally, this index

Work opportunity and responsibility to kids program. CalWORKs, generally, ante

Workers compensation,
  Exclusion, religious, charitable or relief workers, **Labor 3352**
  Payments, preexisting disability, subsequent injury compensation reduction, **Labor 4753**
  Subsequent injuries, reduction in payments, **Labor 4753**

SOCIAL SERVICES DEPARTMENT

Food stamps. Social Services, this index

Labor market information, **Un Ins 10530 et seq.**

SOCIAL WORKERS

Clinical social workers,
  Health Care Service Plans, this index
  Workers compensation, treatment of condition arising out of injury, **Labor 3209.8**

SOCIETIES

Associations and Societies, generally, this index

SOFTWARE

Computers, this index

SOIL CONSERVATION

Removal of soil without permission, **Pen 602**

SOLAR ENERGY

Unemployment compensation, job preparation and training services, **Un Ins 9618**

SOLDIERS, SAILORS AND MARINES

Military Forces, generally, this index

Veterans, generally, this index

SOLE CORPORATIONS

Religious Organizations and Societies, generally, this index

SOLE PROPRIETORSHIPS

Limited Liability Companies, generally, this index

SOLICITATION

Attorneys, this index

Credit Cards, this index

Employment agencies, misrepresentations, earnings of salesmen, brokers or agents, **Labor 976**

Fines and penalties, officers and employees, misrepresentation, **Labor 971**

Fraud, this index

Labor and employment,
  Employees, representation, labor dispute, **Labor 974**
  Misrepresentation, **Labor 971, 972**

Talent agencies,
  Advance fees, **Labor 1702**
  Notice, **Labor 1703.1**

Telecommunications, this index

SOLICITATION OF EMPLOYEES LAW

Generally, **Labor 973, 974**

SOLICITOR GENERAL

Attorney General, generally, this index

SOLID WASTE

Hazardous Substances and Waste, generally, this index

Public buildings and works, hauling, prevailing wage rate, **Labor 1720.3**

Sewers and Sewer Systems, generally, this index

State agencies, hauling, prevailing wage rate, **Labor 1720.3**

Zoning and Planning, generally, this index

SONGS

Music and Musicians, generally, this index

SORORITIES

Colleges and Universities, this index

Unemployment compensation, domestic service, **Un Ins 639**

SOUND RECORDINGS

Personal service contracts, performers, **Labor 2855**

SOUTHERN CALIFORNIA SCHOOL FOR THE DEAF

Schools for the Deaf, generally, this index

SPACE

Priorities and preferences, **Un Ins 3015**

SPANISH LANGUAGE

Farm labor contractors, information posted, **Labor 1695**

Unemployment compensation, publication of information, **Un Ins 316**

Workers Compensation, this index

SPECIAL DISTRICTS

Districts, this index

SPECIAL EDUCATION

Mentally Retarded and Developmentally Disabled Persons, generally, this index

SPECIAL FIRE PROTECTION ZONES

Fires and Fire Protection, generally, this index

SPECIAL ORDERS

Definitions, occupational safety and health, **Labor 6305**

SPECIAL PROCEEDINGS

Definitions, enforcement of arbitration agreements, **CCP 1281.2**

SPECIAL PRORATERS

Debtors and Creditors, generally, this index

SPECIFIC INJURIES

Definitions, workers compensation, **Labor 3208.1**

SPECIFIC PERFORMANCE

Labor contracts, personal service, **CC 3390**

Obligations not specifically enforceable, **CC 3390**

Personal service obligations, **CC 3390**

SPECIFICALLY AUTHORIZED

Definitions, workers compensation, power press workers, **Labor 4558**

SPECIFICATIONS

Plans and Specifications, generally, this index

SPERM

Tissue Banks, generally, this index

SPIRITOUS LIQUORS
Alcoholic Beverages, generally, this index

SPIRITUAL HEALING
Faith Healing, generally, this index

SPORTING EVENTS
Athletics, generally, this index

SPORTS
Athletics, generally, this index

SPORTS OFFICIALS
Definitions, workers compensation, **Labor 3352**

SPOUSAL ABUSE
Domestic Violence, generally, this index

SPOUSE
Definitions, family care leave, **Un Ins 3302**
Marriage, generally, this index
Support, generally, this index

SPRAYING
Asbestos, this index

STAGING
Scaffolds, generally, this index

STAIRWAY CHAIR LIFTS
Elevators, Dumbwaiters and Escalators, generally, this index

STALKING
Colleges and universities, injunction, **CCP 527.85**
Labor and employment, workplace violence safety, **CCP 527.8**
Weapons, prior convictions, possession, **Pen 12021**
Workplace violence safety, **CCP 527.8**

STAMPS
Food stamps. Social Services, this index
Labor union insignia, articles of merchandise, **Labor 1010 et seq.**

STANDARDS
Breathing apparatus, positive pressure closed circuit apparatus for use in fires, **Labor 6331**
Building Standards, generally, this index
Carcinogens, Occupational Carcinogens Control Act, **Labor 9020 et seq.**
Chemical plants, process safety management, **Labor 7855 et seq.**
Definitions, Occupational Carcinogens Control Act, **Labor 9007**
Electricity, this index
Fires and Fire Protection, this index
Hazardous Substances and Waste, this index
Labor and Employment, this index
Occupational Carcinogens Control Act, **Labor 9020 et seq.**
Occupational safety and health standards board. Industrial Relations Department, this index
Oil and Gas, this index

STANDARDS—Cont'd
Workers Compensation, this index
Workplace smoking regulation, statewide uniformity, **Labor 6404.5**

STANDARDS BOARD
Definitions,
    Occupational Carcinogens Control Act, **Labor 9008**
    Occupational safety and health, **Labor 6302**

STAR PERFORMER CONTRACTS
Generally, **Labor 2855**

STATE
Actions and proceedings. Claims, post
Agencies. Public Agencies, generally, this index
Aliens, illegal aliens, employment services, ineligibility, **Un Ins 9601.5, 9601.7**
Application of law, state operated labor camps, **Health & S 17024**
Appropriations, generally, this index
Boards and Commissions, generally, this index
Buildings. Public Buildings and Works, generally, this index
Civil defense. War and Civil Defense, generally, this index
Civil Service, generally, this index
Claims,
    Actions and proceedings,
      False claims, **Gov 12650 et seq.**
      Personal information, maintenance and disclosure, violations, **CC 1798.45 et seq.**
    False claims actions, **Gov 12650 et seq.**
    Fines and penalties, false claims against state, **Gov 12650 et seq.**
    Fraud, **Gov 12650 et seq.**
    Information, personal information, maintenance and disclosure, **CC 1798.45 et seq.**
Comfort Stations and Rest Rooms, generally, this index
Commissions and commissioners. Boards and Commissions, generally, this index
Confidential or privileged information, personal information, requirements to maintain or disclosure, **CC 1798 et seq.**
Contracts. State Contracts, generally, this index
Convicts, working for benefit of state, **Const. Art. 14, § 5**
Damages, personal information in agency records, disclosure, **CC 1798.45 et seq.**
Definitions,
    Garnishment, **CCP 706.070**
    Virgin Islands, unemployment insurance code, **Un Ins 139, 142.5**
    Withholding tax on wages, **Un Ins 13003**
Departments. State Departments, generally, this index

STATE—Cont'd
Drug free workplaces, state contractors and grantees, **Gov 8350 et seq.**
Elections, generally, this index
Employees. State Officers and Employees, generally, this index
Employment services, illegal aliens, ineligibility, **Un Ins 9601.5, 9601.7**
Escheat, generally, this index
Funds. State Treasury, generally, this index
Grants, drug free workplaces, state grantees, **Gov 8350 et seq.**
Highways and Roads, this index
Holidays, generally, this index
Illegal aliens, employment services, ineligibility, **Un Ins 9601.5, 9601.7**
Improvements, generally, this index
Income Tax—State, generally, this index
Information Practices Act, **CC 1798 et seq.**
Injunction, records, personal information, disclosure, **CC 1798.46, 1798.47**
Labor camps,
    Application of law to state camps, **Health & S 17024**
    Enforcement, **Health & S 17050, 17056**
Legislature, generally, this index
Liens and incumbrances. Tax Liens, generally, this index
National defense. War and Civil Defense, generally, this index
Notice, employment services, illegal aliens, ineligibility, posting, **Un Ins 9601.7**
Officers and employees. State Officers and Employees, generally, this index
Pensions. Public Employees Retirement System, generally, this index
Personal information, requirements to maintain or disclosure, **CC 1798 et seq.**
Personnel. State Officers and Employees, generally, this index
Privacy, Information Practices Act, **CC 1798 et seq.**
Property. Escheat, generally, this index
Public Buildings and Works, generally, this index
Public employment offices, **Un Ins 2051 et seq.**
Public Policy, generally, this index
Records and recordation,
    Disclosure, Information Practices Act, **CC 1798 et seq.**
    Information Practices Act, **CC 1798 et seq.**
    Personal information, disclosure, **CC 1798 et seq.**
Retirement system. Public Employees Retirement System, generally, this index
Roads. Highways and Roads, this index
Tax Liens, generally, this index
Taxation, generally, this index
Treasurer. State Treasurer, generally, this index
Unemployment Compensation, this index

STATE

STATE—Cont'd
War and Civil Defense, generally, this index

STATE AGENCIES
Actions and proceedings, personal information, maintenance and disclosure, violations, **CC 1798.45 et seq.**
Administrative Law and Procedure, generally, this index
Affirmative action, **Const. Art. 1, § 31**
Agricultural labor relations board, cooperation with, **Labor 1151.5**
Application of law, agency operated labor camps, **Health & S 17024**
Attorney fees, personal information in agency records, disclosure, **CC 1798.46, 1798.48, 1798.53**
Attorneys, fees. Attorney fees, generally, ante
Buildings. Public Buildings and Works, generally, this index
Civil Service, generally, this index
Claims, personal information, maintenance and disclosure, violations, **CC 1798.45 et seq.**
Comatose patients, medical information disclosure, **CC 56.10**
Comfort Stations and Rest Rooms, generally, this index
Compensation and salaries. State Officers and Employees, this index
Confidential or privileged information,
   Information Practices Act, **CC 1798 et seq.**
   Personal information, disclosure, **CC 1798 et seq.**
Contracts. State Contracts, generally, this index
Costs, personal information in agency records, disclosure, **CC 1798.46, 1798.48, 1798.53**
Damages, personal information in agency records, disclosure, **CC 1798.45 et seq.**
Definitions,
   Administrative law and procedure, **Gov 11346.3**
   Labor and employment, standards, **Labor 1205**
   State employees, workmens compensation and insurance, **Labor 6101**
   Unemployment relief, **Labor 2010**
   Whistle blowing, **Gov 8547.2**
   Information, **Gov 8548 et seq.**
Disclosure,
   Personal information, Information Practices Act, **CC 1798 et seq.**
   Records and recordation, post
Employees. State Officers and Employees, generally, this index
Information Practices Act, **CC 1798 et seq.**
Injunction, records, personal information, disclosure, **CC 1798.46, 1798.47**
Judgments and decrees, personal information in agency records, disclosure, **CC 1798.47**

STATE AGENCIES—Cont'd
Labor and Workforce Development Agency, generally, this index
Labor camps, application of law to state agency camps, **Health & S 17024**
Limitation of actions, personal information in agency records, disclosure, **CC 1798.49**
Medical records, comatose patients, information disclosure to agency, **CC 56.10**
Officers and employees. State Officers and Employees, generally, this index
Orders, generally, this index
Personal information on individuals, requirements to maintain, **CC 1798 et seq.**
Privacy, Information Practices Act, **CC 1798 et seq.**
Records and recordation,
   Actions and proceedings, personal information, maintenance and disclosure, **CC 1798.45 et seq.**
   Disclosure, Information Practices Act, **CC 1798 et seq.**
   Information Practices Act, **CC 1798 et seq.**
   Injunction, personal information, disclosure, **CC 1798.46, 1798.47**
   Personal information, requirements, **CC 1798 et seq.**
Reports,
   Disclosure, Information Practices Act, **CC 1798 et seq.**
   Information Practices Act, **CC 1798 et seq.**
Solid Waste, this index
State Contracts, generally, this index
State Officers and Employees, generally, this index
Unemployment compensation, exchange of information, **Un Ins 322**
   Employment development department, **Un Ins 322**

STATE AID
Employment development, **Un Ins 9001**
Job training and placement services, **Un Ins 9001**

STATE AVERAGE HOURLY WAGE
Definitions, employment training panel, **Un Ins 10201**

STATE BANKS
Banks and Banking, generally, this index

STATE BOARDS AND COMMISSIONS
Boards and Commissions, generally, this index

STATE BONDS
Investments, unemployment insurance disability fund, **Un Ins 3003**
Unemployment insurance disability fund, investment, **Un Ins 3003**

STATE BUILDINGS AND GROUNDS
Public Buildings and Works, generally, this index

STATE CANDIDATES
Elections, generally, this index

STATE CIVIL SERVICE ACT
Civil Service, generally, this index

STATE COLLEGES
Colleges and Universities, generally, this index

STATE COMMISSIONS AND COMMISSIONERS
Boards and Commissions, generally, this index

STATE COMMITTEES
Committees, generally, this index

STATE COMPENSATION INSURANCE FUND
Generally, **Labor 55 et seq.**
Workers Compensation, this index

STATE CONSTITUTION
Constitution of California, generally, this index

STATE CONTRACTS
Actions and proceedings, labor organizations, promotion or deterrence, state funds, **Gov 16645.8**
Attorney fees, labor organizations, promotion or deterrence, state funds, **Gov 16645.8**
Bonds (officers and fiduciaries), bonded company, failure to pay verified claim for wages, **Labor 203.5**
Certificates and certification, drug free workplaces, **Gov 8355**
Costs, labor organizations, promotion or deterrence, state funds, **Gov 16645.8**
Damages, labor organizations, promotion or deterrence, state funds, **Gov 16645.8**
Discrimination, **Gov 12966**
Drug free workplaces, contractors, **Gov 8350 et seq.**
Fair employment and housing, state contractor or supplier of goods and services to state, **Gov 12966**
Fines and penalties,
   Failure of surety or bonding company to pay verified claim for wages, **Labor 203.5**
   Labor organizations, promotion or deterrence, state funds, **Gov 16645.1 et seq.**
Injunction, labor organizations, promotion or deterrence, state funds, **Gov 16645.8**
Labor organizations, promotion or deterrence, state funds, **Gov 16645 et seq.**
Leisure sharing program evaluation, **Un Ins 12130, 12131**

STATE CONTRACTS—Cont'd

Letters of recommendation, personal information held by governmental agencies, Information Practices Act, **CC 1798.38**

Notice,
Drug free workplaces, **Gov 8355**
Labor organizations, promotion or deterrence, state funds, **Gov 16645.8**

Records and recordation, labor organizations, promotion or deterrence, state funds, **Gov 16645.1, 16645.4, 16645.7**

Termination, drug free workplaces, failure, **Gov 8356**

Wage payments, failure of surety or bonding company to pay verified claim for wages, **Labor 203.5**

STATE CONTROLLER

Human resource management system, **Gov 12432**

State Treasurer, generally, this index

Twenty first century project, human resource management system, **Gov 12432**

STATE DEPARTMENTS

Administrative Law and Procedure, generally, this index

Agricultural labor relations board proceedings, cooperation, **Labor 1151.5**

Benefit Payments Department, generally, this index

Buildings. Public Buildings and Works, generally, this index

Civil Service, generally, this index

Confidential or privileged information, Information Practices Act, **CC 1798 et seq.**
Personal information, disclosure, **CC 1798 et seq.**

Consumer Affairs Department, generally, this index

Contracts. State Contracts, generally, this index

Corrections and Rehabilitation Department, generally, this index

Disclosure, personal information, Information Practices Act, **CC 1798 et seq.**

Employees. State Officers and Employees, generally, this index

Employment Development Department, generally, this index

Fair Employment and Housing, generally, this index

Finance Department, generally, this index

Forestry and Fire Protection Department, generally, this index

Health Care Services Department, generally, this index

Highway patrol department. Highway Patrol, generally, this index

Industrial Relations Department, generally, this index

Information Practices Act, **CC 1798 et seq.**

Juvenile Facilities Division, generally, this index

STATE DEPARTMENTS—Cont'd

Officers and employees. State Officers and Employees, generally, this index

Personal information on individuals, requirements to maintain, **CC 1798 et seq.**

Privacy, Information Practices Act, **CC 1798 et seq.**

Public Buildings and Works, generally, this index

Records and recordation,
Information Practices Act, **CC 1798 et seq.**
Personal information, requirements, **CC 1798 et seq.**

State Contracts, generally, this index

STATE EMPLOYEES

State Officers and Employees, generally, this index

STATE EMPLOYEES RETIREMENT SYSTEM

Public Employees Retirement System, generally, this index

STATE FIRE MARSHAL

Explosives, generally, this index

Fire Extinguishers, generally, this index

STATE FUNDS

State Treasury, generally, this index

STATE HEALTH FACILITIES

Health Facilities, generally, this index

STATE HIGHWAY PATROL

Highway Patrol, generally, this index

STATE HIGHWAYS

Highways and Roads, this index

STATE HOSPITALS

Crimes and offenses, officers and employees, records, disclosure, **Pen 11105.3**

Disclosure, crimes and offenses, employment, **Pen 11105.3**

Labor and employment, crimes and offenses, disclosure, **Pen 11105.3**

Notice, criminal history, disclosure, employment, **Pen 11105.3**

Officers and employees, crimes and offenses, records, disclosure, **Pen 11105.3**

STATE HOUSING LAW

Housing, generally, this index

STATE INSTITUTIONS

Labor and employment, children and minors, courses of training, exception to employment, **Labor 1295**

STATE MANPOWER PROGRAMS

Labor and Employment, this index

STATE MILITARY RESERVE

Military Forces, this index

STATE OFFICERS AND EMPLOYEES

Actions and proceedings,
Against state for negligence, credit for benefits paid under workers compensation provisions, **Labor 6147, 6148**
Negligence, workers compensation, **Labor 6147, 6148**
Veterans, disclosure, improper activities, **Mil & V 73.7**
Whistle blowing, **Gov 8547.8**
Workers compensation, negligence, **Labor 6147, 6148**

Administrative law and procedure, whistle blowing, **Gov 8547.8**

Attorney fees,
Veterans, disclosure, improper activities, **Mil & V 73.7**
Whistle blowing, **Gov 8547.8**

Attorney General, generally, this index

Bosnia crisis, compensation and benefits, **Mil & V 395.08**

Burden of proof, whistle blowing, **Gov 8547.8**

Children and minors, sick leave, **Labor 233**
Violations, **Labor 234**

Civil Service, generally, this index

Commercial vehicles, meals, collective bargaining, **Labor 512.5**

Compensation and salaries, **Gov 19825.5**
Application of law, **Labor 220**
Dismissal, **Labor 201**
Final compensation, retirement and pensions, **Gov 20037.9**
Human resource management system, **Gov 12432**
Leave of absence for military duty, **Mil & V 395.01 et seq.**
Resignation, **Labor 202**
Sick leave, generally, post
Twenty first century project, human resource management system, **Gov 12432**

Complaints, whistle blowing, **Gov 8547.8**

Crimes and offenses, injuries from criminal violence, workers compensation, waiting period, **Labor 4650.5**

Damages,
Veterans, disclosure, improper activities, **Mil & V 73.7**
Whistle blowing, **Gov 8547.3, 8547.8**

Definitions, whistle blowing, **Gov 8547.3**

Discipline, whistle blowing, **Gov 8547.8**

Disclosure, Information Practices Act, **CC 1798 et seq.**

Dismissal, compensation and salaries, **Labor 201**

Duress or coercion, inspector general for veterans affairs, **Mil & V 73.7**

Elections,
Dismissal, compensation and salaries, **Labor 201**
Resignation, compensation and salaries, **Labor 202**

Evidence, whistle blowing, **Gov 8547.8**

STATE

STATE OFFICERS AND EMPLOYEES
—Cont'd

Family members, sick leave, **Labor 233**
Violations, **Labor 234**
Final compensation, retirement and pensions, **Gov 20037.9**
Fines and penalties, whistle blowing, **Gov 8547.8**
Franchise Tax Board, generally, this index
Garnishment, service of process, **CCP 706.101**
Governor, generally, this index
Health and safety and workers compensation board, **Labor 76**
Highway Patrol, generally, this index
Holidays,
    Dismissal, compensation and salaries, **Labor 201**
    Resignation, compensation and salaries, **Labor 202**
Human resource management system, **Gov 12432**
Information, whistle blowing, **Gov 8548 et seq.**
Information Practices Act, **CC 1798 et seq.**
Insurance, nonindustrial disability insurance, **Un Ins 2781 et seq.**
Iraq Kuwait Crisis, active duty, benefits, **Mil & V 395.07**
Juvenile Facilities Division, generally, this index
Leaves of absence,
    Dismissal, compensation and salaries, **Labor 201**
    Military forces, post
    Resignation, compensation and salaries, **Labor 202**
    Sick leave, generally, post
Lie detector tests, condition of employment, **Labor 432.2**
Marriage, sick leave, **Labor 233**
Violations, **Labor 234**
Meals, motor carriers, collective bargaining, **Labor 512.5**
Mediation, national guard, complaints, **Mil & V 395.6**
Military forces,
    Bosnia crisis, compensation and benefits, **Mil & V 395.08**
    Civil Service, this index
    Discrimination, **Mil & V 394**
    Leaves of absence, **Mil & V 395 et seq.**
Motor carriers, meals, collective bargaining, **Labor 512.5**
National guard,
    Bosnia crisis, compensation and benefits, **Mil & V 395.08**
    Mediation, complaints, **Mil & V 395.6**
Nonindustrial disability insurance, **Un Ins 2781 et seq.**
Notice, whistle blowing, information, **Gov 8548.2**
Overtime, computation of compensation, **Gov 19844.1**
Parents, sick leave, **Labor 233**
Violations, **Labor 234**

STATE OFFICERS AND EMPLOYEES
—Cont'd

Payroll. Compensation and salaries, generally, ante
Pensions. Public Employees Retirement System, generally, this index
Perjury, whistle blowing, **Gov 8547.8**
Polygraph tests, condition of employment, **Labor 432.2**
Public Agencies, generally, this index
Public Employees Retirement System, generally, this index
Public employment offices, **Un Ins 2054**
Public Utilities Commission, generally, this index
Records and recordation,
    Disclosure, Information Practices Act, **CC 1798 et seq.**
    Information Practices Act, **CC 1798 et seq.**
Reports. Civil Service, this index
Resignation,
    Compensation and salaries, **Labor 202**
    Military service entry, reentry into office or employment on discharge, **Mil & V 395.3**
Rest periods, motor carriers, collective bargaining, **Labor 512.5**
Retaliation, inspector general for veterans affairs, **Mil & V 73.7**
Retirement and pensions,
    Public Employees Retirement System, generally, this index
    Supplemental retirement accounts,
        Dismissal, compensation and salaries, **Labor 201**
        Resignation, compensation and salaries, **Labor 202**
Rewards, contributions to fund, **Labor 220.2**
Right to privacy, Information Practices Act, **CC 1798 et seq.**
Sick leave,
    Accumulated sick leave, family members, **Labor 233**
    Family members, **Labor 233**
        Violations, **Labor 234**
Social Security, generally, this index
Soldiers and Sailors Relief Act, **Mil & V 395.1**
State Treasurer, generally, this index
Suits. Actions and proceedings, generally, ante
Supplemental retirement accounts,
    Dismissal, compensation and salaries, **Labor 201**
    Resignation, compensation and salaries, **Labor 202**
Threats, inspector general for veterans affairs, **Mil & V 73.7**
Treasurer. State Treasurer, generally, this index
Trophy, distinguished service award,
    Elective coverage, **Un Ins 709**
    Excluded service, **Un Ins 634.5**

STATE OFFICERS AND EMPLOYEES
—Cont'd

Trophy, distinguished service award
—Cont'd
    Nonindustrial disability insurance, **Un Ins 2781 et seq.**
Twenty first century project, human resource management system, **Gov 12432**
Unemployment compensation,
    Excluded services, **Un Ins 634.5**
    Nonindustrial disability insurance, **Un Ins 2781 et seq.**
Vacancies, contributions to fund, **Labor 220.2**
Vacations, accumulated vacation,
    Dismissal, compensation and salaries, **Labor 201**
    Resignation, compensation and salaries, **Labor 202**
Vanpooling, workers compensation, course of employment, **Labor 3600.8**
Veterans, this index
Wages. Compensation and salaries, generally, ante
Workers compensation, **Labor 6100 et seq.**
    Actions against,
        State by employee, credit for benefits paid, **Labor 6147, 6148**
        Third persons, **Labor 6115**
    Adjustment and disposition of claims, **Labor 6111**
    Agreement to arbitrate controversies, **Labor 6144**
    Application of law, **Labor 6141, 6142**
    Arbitration of controversies, **Labor 6144 et seq.**
    Benefits and procedure, **Labor 6140 et seq.**
    Claims, adjustment or settlement, **Labor 6113**
    Compromise of claims against third persons, **Labor 6115**
    Controversies, jurisdiction to try and determine, **Labor 6144**
    Death benefits, **Labor 6110 et seq., 6140**
    Direct payments, **Labor 6110 et seq.**
    Disputes, jurisdiction, **Labor 6143**
    Fee or cost for arbitrator, **Labor 6146**
    Findings, **Labor 6146**
    Hospitalization, medical treatment and indemnity, **Labor 6110, 6140**
    Insurance, **Labor 6130, 6131**
    Judges, **Labor 123.5**
    Jurisdiction, **Labor 6143**
    Limitation of proceedings, **Labor 6141**
    Master agreement for adjustment and disposition of claims, **Labor 6111**
    Powers of appeals board, **Labor 6143**
    Premiums for insurance, **Labor 6131**
    Procedure, **Labor 6140 et seq.**
    Rehabilitation plans, voluntary, **Labor 6208**
    Reimbursement of insurance fund by state agency, **Labor 6114**
    Request for arbitration, **Labor 6144**

STATE OFFICERS AND EMPLOYEES
—Cont'd
Workers compensation—Cont'd
Service of notices, orders, **Labor 5317**
Services at uniform rate to all state
agencies, **Labor 6112**
Vanpooling, course of employment, **Labor 3600.8**
Waiting period, **Labor 4650.5**
Working conditions, civil service rules,
written agreement of claimant, **Labor 6147 et seq.**

STATE OFFICERS AND EMPLOYEES RETIREMENT SYSTEM
Public Employees Retirement System,
generally, this index

STATE OR LOCAL CHILD SUPPORT ENFORCEMENT AGENCY
Definitions, consumer credit reporting, **CC 1785.3**

STATE PATROL
Highway Patrol, generally, this index

STATE POLICE
Highway Patrol, generally, this index

STATE POLICY
Public Policy, generally, this index

STATE PRISONS
Correctional Institutions, generally, this
index

STATE RETIREMENT SYSTEM
Public Employees Retirement System,
generally, this index

STATE SCHOOL FOR THE BLIND
School for the Blind, generally, this index

STATE SUPERINTENDENT OF PUBLIC INSTRUCTION
Schools and School Districts, this index

STATE TAX LIABILITY
Definitions, garnishment, **CCP 706.070**

STATE TEACHERS RETIREMENT SYSTEM
Schoolteachers Retirement System, generally, this index

STATE TREASURER
Bonds (officers and fiduciaries),
Disability compensation fund, **Un Ins 3002**
Unemployment compensation fund, **Un Ins 1524, 1561**
Unclaimed property. Abandoned or Unclaimed Property, generally, this index
Unemployment compensation disability
fund, placed under provisions of surplus money investment fund, **Un Ins 3002**

STATE TREASURY
Agricultural employee relief fund, **Labor 1161**

STATE TREASURY—Cont'd
Apprenticeship training contribution fund,
Labor 1777.5
Appropriations, generally, this index
Asbestos workers account, uninsured employers fund, **Labor 4401 et seq.**
Back wages and taxes account, wearing
apparel, manufacturers and manufacturing, **Labor 2680**
Car wash worker fund, **Labor 2065**
Car wash worker restitution fund, **Labor 2065**
Contingent funds, deposits, **Un Ins 1526.3**
Department of employment development
contingent fund, **Un Ins 1585**
Deposits, workers compensation managed
care fund, **Labor 4600.7**
Disability compensation fund, **Un Ins 3001, 3002**
Deposits, **Un Ins 1526.2**
Electrician certification fund, **Labor 3099.5**
Employment development, contingent
fund, augmentation of appropriations,
Un Ins 1586.5
Employment development department
benefit audit fund, **Un Ins 1595 et seq.**
Employment Training Fund, generally,
this index
General fund,
Children and minors, fines for improper
employment, crediting, **Labor 1305**
Compensation and salaries, failure of
employer to pay, disposition of
penalties, **Labor 210, 225.5**
Employment training fund, loans, **Un Ins 1611**
Industrial accidents division, fees deposited in, **Labor 127**
Occupational safety and health, deposit
of fees, standards, **Labor 6329**
Public works, penalties and forfeitures,
disposition, **Labor 1734**
School employees fund, loans, **Un Ins 822**
Tips, fines collected, **Labor 355**
Transfers, unemployment compensation
disability fund, **Un Ins 1176**
Unemployment compensation disability
fund, loans, **Un Ins 3001**
Workers compensation, collection of
award from uninsured employer,
Labor 3715
Industrial homework, license fees, **Labor 2658**
Industrial relations unpaid wage fund, **Labor 96.6, 96.7**
Payment, unpaid wages or benefits, **Labor 96.7**
Labor enforcement and compliance fund,
workers compensation, **Labor 62.5**
Labor organizations, promotion or deterrence, state contracts, **Gov 16645 et seq.**

STATE TREASURY—Cont'd
Personal income tax fund, deposits, **Un Ins 1526.1, 1585.5**
Pooled money investment board, retransfer of surplus money to special funds,
Un Ins 3002
Return to work fund, workers compensation, **Labor 139.48**
School employees fund, contribution rates,
Un Ins 823
Special funds. Industrial relations unpaid
wage fund, generally, ante
State general fund. General fund, generally, ante
State public works enforcement fund, **Labor 1771.3**
Transfers. General fund, ante
Unemployment compensation,
Administration fund, bonds (officers
and employees), **Un Ins 1561**
Custodians, **Un Ins 1501, 1524**
Deposits, **Un Ins 1526.4**
Records and recordation, **Un Ins 1528.5**
Uninsured employers benefits trust fund.
Workers Compensation, this index
Uninsured employers fund, asbestos workers account, **Labor 4401 et seq.**
Wagner Peyser Act, moneys received by
state under provisions, disposition,
Un Ins 2053
Worker safety bilingual investigative support, enforcement and training account, **Labor 6356**
Workers compensation managed care
fund, **Labor 4600.7**
Workers occupational safety and health
education fund, **Labor 6354.7**

STATE UNIVERSITY
California State University. Colleges and
Universities, this index

STATE WARRANTS
Workers compensation insurance fund,
subsequent injuries, **Labor 4755**

STATEMENTS
Aged person caretaker employees, abuse
reporting, statutory knowledge, **Welf & I 15659**
Compensation and Salaries, this index
Definitions, workers compensation, misrepresentations, **Labor 3820**
Dependent adult caretaker employees,
abuse reporting, statutory knowledge,
Welf & I 15659
Family care leave, claims, **Un Ins 3306**
Financial Statements and Reports, generally, this index
Officers and employees, reasons for leaving employment furnished to prospective employer, **Labor 1053**
Unemployment Compensation, this index
Workers Compensation, this index

STATEWIDE YOUNG WORKER HEALTH AND SAFETY RESOURCE NETWORK
Generally, **Labor 6359**

STATISTICIANS
Industrial accidents division, employment, **Labor 123**
Occupational safety and health, **Labor 6314**

STATISTICS
Labor and employment, **Labor 150; Un Ins 320.5**
Occupational safety and health, collection of statistics, **Labor 6314**
Safety in employment, collection, **Labor 6314**
Occupational health, local health departments promoting, **Health & S 105150**

STATUTE OF LIMITATIONS
Limitation of Actions, generally, this index

STATUTES
Choice of law. Conflict of Laws, generally, this index
Conflict of Laws, generally, this index
Construction of statutes,
    Employment relations, effect of statutes upon workmens compensation and insurance provisions, **Labor 2700**
    Masculine gender, **Labor 12.1**
    Person, masculine gender, **Labor 12.1**
    Talent agencies, fees, **Labor 1705 et seq.**
    Workers compensation,
        Application of laws to employment relations, **Labor 2700**
        Medical care and treatment, authorization, rescission, modification or change, **Labor 4610.3**
    Workplace Violence Safety Act, **CCP 527.8**
Popular Name Laws, generally, this index

STAY OF PROCEEDINGS
Supersedeas or Stay, generally, this index

STEALING
Theft, generally, this index

STEAM BOILERS
Boilers, generally, this index

STEAMBOATS AND STEAMSHIPS
Ships and Shipping, generally, this index

STERILIZATION
Birth Control, this index

STIPENDS
Compensation and Salaries, generally, this index

STIPULATIONS
Fines and penalties, **CC 52**
Workers compensation hearings, **Labor 5702**

STOCK
Animals, generally, this index

STOCK AND STOCKHOLDERS
Shares and shareholders. Corporations, this index

STOCK BROKERS AND DEALERS
Security Agents and Broker Dealers, generally, this index

STOCK CORPORATIONS
Corporations, generally, this index

STOCKHOLDERS
Shares and shareholders. Corporations, this index

STOLEN PROPERTY
Theft, generally, this index

STOP ORDERS
Workers Compensation, this index

STORAGE
Liquefied petroleum gas, safety regulations, **Labor 7655**
Tissue Banks, generally, this index
Weapons, this index

STORES
Children and minors, price marking and tagging, employment, **Labor 1294.3**
Grocery Stores, generally, this index
Investigations, shopping investigators report, **Labor 2930 et seq.**
Officers and employees, shopping investigators report, discipline or discharge, **Labor 2930 et seq.**
Price marking and tagging, minors, employment, **Labor 1294.3**
Safety, working warehouses, **Labor 9100 et seq.**
Shopping investigators report, **Labor 2930 et seq.**
Working warehouses, safety, **Labor 9100 et seq.**

STORM SEWERS
Sewers and Sewer Systems, generally, this index

STORMS
Temporary public employees, unemployment compensation, excluded service, **Un Ins 634.5**
Unemployment compensation, temporary public employees, excluded service, **Un Ins 634.5**

STP
Drugs and Medicine, generally, this index

STREET RAILWAYS
Air pressure tanks, inspection and safety regulation, **Labor 7624**
Safeguards, **Labor 6800**
Zoning and Planning, generally, this index

STREETS AND ALLEYS
Sewers and Sewer Systems, generally, this index
Zoning and Planning, generally, this index

STRIKES
Definitions, professional strike breakers, **Labor 1132.6**

STRIKES—Cont'd
Labor Disputes, generally, this index

STRINGER RAILS
Wharves, docks and piers, **Labor 7604**

STRUCTURAL ENGINEERS
Engineers, generally, this index

STRUCTURES
Buildings, generally, this index

STUDENT LOANS
Colleges and Universities, this index

STUDENTS
Colleges and Universities, generally, this index
Schools and School Districts, generally, this index
Unemployment Compensation, this index

STUDIES
Fair employment and housing, **Gov 12940.3**
Workers Compensation, this index

SUBCONTRACTORS
Definitions,
    Public buildings, **Labor 1722.1**
    Public transit, displaced workers, **Labor 1071**
Mechanics Liens, generally, this index
Public Buildings and Works, this index

SUBPOENA DUCES TECUM
Production of Books and Papers, generally, this index

SUBPOENAING PARTY
Definitions, employment records, **CCP 1985.6**

SUBPOENAS
Affirmative defenses, consumers, records and recordation, **CCP 1985.6**
Agricultural labor relations board investigation proceedings, **Labor 1151 et seq.**
Consumer credit reporting agencies, inspection of records, **CC 1785.11**
Contempt, generally, this index
Employment. Labor and Employment, this index
Fair Employment and Housing, this index
Labor and Employment, this index
Labor commissioner deputies and assistants, issuance, **Labor 92, 93**
Labor organizations, records and recordation, **CCP 1985.6**
Labor standards enforcement division, investigations, **Labor 74**
Labor statistics and research division, **Labor 152**
Medical Records, this index
Occupational safety and health, **Labor 6314**
Production of Books and Papers, generally, this index

SUBPOENAS—Cont'd
Quashing, employment records, **CCP 1985.6**
Unemployment Compensation, this index
Wearing apparel, manufacturers and manufacturing, arbitration, **Labor 2689**
Workers Compensation, this index

SUBROGATION
Workers Compensation, this index

SUBSTANCE ABUSE
Alcoholics and Alcoholism, generally, this index
Drug Addicts, generally, this index

SUBSTANTIAL CAUSE
Definitions, workers compensation, psychiatric injuries, **Labor 3208.3**

SUCCESSION
Workers compensation,
   Death benefits, dependent beneficiaries, **Labor 4706**
   Lump sum payment, deposits, **Labor 5102**

SUCCESSOR EMPLOYER
Definitions, collective bargaining agreements, **Labor 1127**

SUFFRAGE
Elections, generally, this index

SUICIDE
Investigation. Coroners, generally, this index
Workers compensation, **Labor 3600**

SUITABLE EMPLOYMENT
Definitions, unemployment compensation, **Un Ins 1258, 1258.5**

SUITS
Actions and Proceedings, generally, this index

SUMMARY JUDGMENT
Unemployment Compensation, this index

SUMMONS
Process, this index

SUNDAY
Workers compensation, instruments and documents, filing, time, **Labor 3730**

SUPERINTENDENT OF PUBLIC INSTRUCTION
State superintendent of public instruction. Schools and School Districts, this index

SUPERINTENDENTS
State superintendent of public instruction. Schools and School Districts, this index

SUPERINTENDENTS OF SCHOOLS
School Superintendents, generally, this index

SUPERIOR COURT JUDGES
Military service, reentry of office after discharge, **Mil & V 395.3**

SUPERIOR COURTS
Adoption of Children, generally, this index
Contempt, generally, this index
Fair employment and housing department, discovery, jurisdiction, **Gov 12963.5**
Furloughs, public employees retirement system, service credits, **Gov 20969.1**
Interpreters and Translators, generally, this index
Judgments and Decrees, generally, this index
Jurisdiction,
   Fair employment and housing, unlawful practices complaints, **Gov 12965**
   Housing discrimination actions, **Gov 12980**
Jury, generally, this index
Officers and employees,
   Furloughs, public employees retirement system, service credits, **Gov 20969.1**
   Public employees retirement system, furloughs, service credits, **Gov 20969.1**
Probate Proceedings, generally, this index
Small Claims Courts, generally, this index
Subpoenas, generally, this index

SUPERMARKETS
Grocery Stores, generally, this index

SUPERSEDEAS OR STAY
Arbitration and Award, this index
Bonds (officers and fiduciaries), workers compensation, **Labor 6000 et seq.**
Labor and employment, discrimination, complaints, **Labor 98.7**
Talent agencies, money awards, **Labor 1700.44**
Workers Compensation, this index

SUPERVISORIAL PERSONNEL
Definitions, professional strikebreakers, **Labor 1133**

SUPERVISORS
Definitions,
   Agricultural labor relations, **Labor 1140.4**
   Fair employment and housing, **Gov 12926**

SUPPLEMENTAL UNEMPLOYMENT COMPENSATION BENEFITS
Definitions, withholding tax on wages, **Un Ins 13028**

SUPPORT
Accomplices and accessories, arrearages, evasion, treble damages, **CC 1714.41**
Agency, local child support agencies. Child Support Services Department, this index
Appeal and review, withholding orders for support, **CCP 706.030**

SUPPORT—Cont'd
Arrearages,
   Accomplices and accessories, evasion, treble damages, **CC 1714.41**
   Assets, transfers, accomplices and accessories, treble damages, **CC 1714.41**
   Assignments, generally, post
   Avoidance, accomplices and accessories, treble damages, **CC 1714.41**
   Damages, evasion, accomplices and accessories, **CC 1714.41**
   Definitions, enforcement, **Fam 5201**
   Earnings assignment orders, **Fam 5200 et seq.**
   Escape, accomplices and accessories, treble damages, **CC 1714.41**
   Evasion, accomplices and accessories, treble damages, **CC 1714.41**
   Income, withholding, **Fam 5246**
   Notice, assignment, **Fam 5246**
   Specification of amount, perjury, **Fam 5230.5**
   Treble damages, evasion, accomplices and accessories, **CC 1714.41**
Assets, transfers, arrearages, accomplices and accessories, treble damages, **CC 1714.41**
Assigned obligees, definitions, **Fam 5214**
Assignments, **Fam 5200 et seq.**
   Earnings assignment orders, **Fam 5200 et seq.**
   Family support, **Labor 300**
   Garnishment, application of law, **CCP 706.031**
   Health insurance,
      Notice, service, Title IV D cases, **Fam 3773**
      Orders, **Fam 3760 et seq.**
   Notice, **Fam 5246**
   Privileges and immunities, **Fam 5247**
Attachment, this index
Changes, address, notice, earning assignment orders, **Fam 5237**
Compensation and salaries,
   Assignments, generally, ante
   Definitions, support enforcement, **Fam 5206**
Consolidation, earnings assignment order withholdings, **Fam 5236**
Contempt,
   Accident and health insurance, assignment of rights, **Fam 3768**
   Labor and employment, assignment of wages, **Fam 5241**
Copies, health insurance coverage assignment orders, **Fam 3764**
Counties, local child support agencies. Child Support Services Department, this index
Damages, arrearages, evasion, accomplices and accessories, **CC 1714.41**
Declarations, income and expenses, requests for production, **Fam 3664**
Default, unemployment, **Fam 4505**
Delinquency. Arrearages, generally, ante

SUPPORT

SUPPORT—Cont'd
Disability insurance, assignments,
  Notice, service, Title IV D cases, **Fam 3773**
  Orders, **Fam 3760 et seq.**
Disclosure, unemployment compensation, **Un Ins 1088.8**
Discrimination, health insurance coverage assignments, hiring practices, **Fam 3769**
Domestic partnership, termination, waiver, **Fam 299**
Due date of support payments, definitions, **Fam 5204**
Earnings. Assignments, generally, ante
Enforcement,
  Earnings assignment orders, **Fam 5200 et seq.**
  Local child support agencies. Child Support Services Department, this index
  Substitution of payee, employer duties, **Fam 5235**
Evidence, employer income and benefit information, modification or termination of orders, **Evid 1567**
Expenses and expenditures, discovery, **Fam 3664**
Fees, earnings assignment orders, **Fam 5232**
  Employer deduction, **Fam 5235**
Fines and penalties,
  Accident and health insurance, assignments, coverage, retaliation against employee, **Fam 3769**
  Labor and employment, **CCP 706.030; Fam 5241**
  Unemployment compensation, reports, **Un Ins 1088.8**
Foreign states, earnings assignments, income withholding orders, binding employer, **Fam 5230.1**
Forms,
  Employer income and benefit information, **Evid 1567; Fam 3664**
  Health insurance coverage assignments, **Fam 3772**
IV D case, definitions, **Fam 5212**
Funds transfers, labor and employment, **Fam 5241**
Garnishment, this index
Grounds, health insurance coverage assignment, motion to quash, **Fam 3765**
Hearings,
  Assignment of wages, **Fam 5246**
  Labor and employment, **Fam 5241**
Income,
  Declaration, discovery, **Fam 3664**
  Employer income and benefit information, **Fam 3664**
    Modification or termination of support, **Evid 1567**
  Withholding, arrearages, **Fam 5246**
Information,
  Address of obligor, **Fam 5280 et seq.**

SUPPORT—Cont'd
Information—Cont'd
  Employment of obligor, **Fam 5280 et seq.**
  Health insurance coverage assignment orders, **Fam 3764**
Instructions, financial assets, liquidation, **Fam 17522.5**
Interest, labor and employment, **Fam 5241**
Labor and employment,
  Contempt, assignment of wages, **Fam 5241**
  Definitions, **Fam 5210**
  Discharge, earnings assignment orders, **Fam 5290**
  Discipline, earnings assignment orders, **Fam 5290**
  Earnings assignment orders, **Fam 5200 et seq.**
  Fines and penalties, **Fam 5241**
    Earnings assignment orders, **Fam 5290**
  Funds transfers, **Fam 5241**
  Hearings, **Fam 5241**
  Income and benefit information, **Evid 1567; Fam 3664**
  Interest, **Fam 5241**
  Modification or termination of support, **Evid 1567**
  Notice, **Fam 5241**
  Orders of court, San Mateo County, pilot programs, **Fam 4505**
  Promotions, earnings assignment orders, **Fam 5290**
Liens and incumbrances, wage assignment, service, **Fam 5242**
Liquidation, financial assets, instructions, **Fam 17522.5**
Lists, unemployed spouse, default, list of employment application locations, **Fam 4505**
Local child support agencies. Child Support Services Department, this index
Modification of support orders,
  Employer income and benefit information, admissibility of evidence, **Evid 1567**
  Health insurance coverage assignment order, **Fam 3763**
Motions, quashing, health insurance coverage assignments, **Fam 3765**
Notice,
  Arrearages, ante
  Assignment of wages, **Fam 5246**
  Change of address, earnings assignment orders, **Fam 5237**
  Income, withholding, **Fam 5246**
  Labor and employment, **Fam 5241**
  Withholding, appeal and review, **CCP 706.030**
Obligee, definitions, **Fam 5214**
Obligor, definitions, **Fam 5216**
Orders of court,
  Contempt, health insurance assignment of rights, **Fam 3768**

SUPPORT—Cont'd
Orders of court—Cont'd
  Earnings assignment orders, **Fam 5200 et seq.**
  Income, withholding, **Fam 5246**
  Local child support agencies. Child Support Services Department, this index
Payment,
  Arrearages, generally, ante
  Local child support agencies. Child Support Services Department, this index
  State disbursement unit, **Fam 5235**
  Timely payment, definitions, **Fam 5220**
  Undeliverable payments, reimbursement, **Fam 5237**
Penalties. Fines and penalties, generally, ante
Perjury, arrearages, specification of amount, **Fam 5230.5**
Pilot programs, labor and employment, orders of court, San Mateo County, **Fam 4505**
Priorities and preferences, assignment of wages, **Fam 5238, 5243**
Privileges and immunities, assignment of wages, **Fam 5247**
Process. Service of process, generally, post
Reimbursement, undeliverable payments, **Fam 5237**
Reports, unemployment compensation, **Un Ins 1088.8**
Retaliation against employees, assignment orders, accident and health insurance, **Fam 3769**
San Mateo County, labor and employment, orders of court, pilot programs, **Fam 4505**
Securities, liquidation, instructions, **Fam 17522.5**
Service of process,
  Earnings assignment orders, **Fam 5232**
  Health care assignment orders, mail service, **Fam 3764**
  Withholding order for support, **CCP 706.030**
State disbursement unit, payment, **Fam 5235**
Termination,
  Assignment of earnings, **Fam 5240**
  Employer income and benefit information, admissibility of evidence, **Evid 1567**
  Health insurance coverage assignment orders, **Fam 3770**
Time, health insurance coverage assignment order, **Fam 3763**
  Effective date, **Fam 3764**
Timely payment, definitions, **Fam 5220**
Transfers, financial assets, liquidation, instructions, **Fam 17522.5**
Treble damages, arrearages, evasion, accomplices and accessories, **CC 1714.41**

SUPPORT—Cont'd
Undeliverable payments, reimbursement, **Fam 5237**
Unemployment, default in payments, **Fam 4505**
Unemployment compensation,
Child support obligations, deductions and withholding, **Un Ins 1255.7**
Fines and penalties, reports, **Un Ins 1088.8**
Information, enforcement program, **Un Ins 1095**
Notice, judgments, **Un Ins 2630**
Records and recordation, **Un Ins 2630**
Reports, **Un Ins 1088.5, 1088.8**
Wages. Assignments, generally, ante
Withholding,
Earnings assignment orders, **Fam 5233**
Employer duties, **Fam 5235**
Income, arrearages, **Fam 5246**
Notice, ante
Workers compensation, notification project, **Labor 138.5**

SUPPORTIVE SERVICES
Domestic employees, unemployment compensation coverage, **Un Ins 683**
Workers compensation coverage, domestic employees, **Labor 3351.5**

SUPREME COURT
Appeal and Review, generally, this index
Jurisdiction, workers compensation, review, **Labor 5955**
Occupational safety and health orders, rules, review of, **Labor 6308**
Workers compensation, jurisdiction to review, **Labor 5955**

SUPREME COURT JUSTICES
Military service, reentry of office after discharge, **Mil & V 395.3**

SURCHARGE
Workers Compensation, this index

SURETY BONDS
Bonds (Officers and Fiduciaries), generally, this index

SURETYSHIP AND GUARANTY
Bonds (Officers and Fiduciaries), generally, this index
Wearing apparel, manufacturers and manufacturing, compensation and salaries, contractors, **Labor 2673.1**

SURGEONS
Physicians and Surgeons, generally, this index

SURGICAL TREATMENT
Definitions, workers compensation, **Labor 3209.5**
Officers compensation, employer employee agreements, **Labor 3209.7**

SURVEYS AND SURVEYORS
Employment development department, contract with census bureau, population survey, **Un Ins 327**
Liens and incumbrances. Mechanics Liens, generally, this index
Mechanics Liens, generally, this index
Trespass, exemptions, **Pen 602.8**
Workers compensation, alternative dispute resolution system, **Labor 3201.5**

SURVIVING SPOUSE
Death benefits, elected public officials, assassination, **Labor 4720 et seq.**
Elected public officials, death benefits, assassination, **Labor 4720 et seq.**
Veterans,
Fair employment and housing, **Gov 12940**
Preference, fair employment and housing, **Gov 12940**
Workers compensation, dependents, presumptions, **Labor 3501**

SWIMMING POOLS
Excavation, safety, **Labor 6705.5**

SYRINGES
Hypodermic Syringes and Needles, generally, this index

SYSTEM OF RECORDS
Definitions, Information Practices Act, **CC 1798.3**

TABLES
Disability compensation, **Un Ins 2655**
Unemployment compensation contribution rates, **Un Ins 977**

TAGS
Labor union insignia, articles of merchandise, **Labor 1010 et seq.**
Licenses and Permits, generally, this index

TAKING
Fish and Game, generally, this index

TALENT AGENCIES
Generally, **Labor 1700 et seq.**
Accounts and accounting, trust funds, **Labor 1700.25**
Actions and proceedings, fees, **Labor 1703.3, 1704.1 et seq.**
Advance fees, **Labor 1702 et seq.**
Adverse or pecuniary interest, **Labor 1700.40**
Fees, **Labor 1703.4**
Licenses, corporations, **Labor 1700.6**
Advertisements,
Advance fees, **Labor 1702**
Fees, **Labor 1703.4**
Fraud, **Labor 1700.32**
Notice, **Labor 1703.1**
Alcoholic beverages, **Labor 1700.34**
Application of law, advance fees, **Labor 1702.3**
Arbitration and award, **Labor 1700.45**
Assignment, licenses, **Labor 1700.13**

TALENT AGENCIES—Cont'd
Attorney fees, **Labor 1704.2**
Advance fees, **Labor 1701.16**
Retention of artist funds, **Labor 1700.25**
Banks and banking, trust funds, **Labor 1700.25**
Bonds (officers and fiduciaries), **Labor 1703.3**
Contracts, **Labor 1703**
Damages,
Fees, **Labor 1704.3**
Fraud, **Labor 1700.16**
Licenses and permits, **Labor 1700.15 et seq.**
Supersedeas or stay of money award, **Labor 1700.44**
Books and papers, **Labor 1703.1**
Branch office, licenses and permits, application, **Labor 1700.10**
Cancellation, contracts, **Labor 1703**
Certificate of convenience to conduct business, death of licensee, **Labor 1700.20a, 1700.20b**
Children and minors,
Contracts, **Labor 1700.37**
On sale liquor establishments, **Labor 1700.34**
Talent agencies, **Labor 1700.36 et seq.**
Claims, deposits, **Labor 1703.3**
Compensation and salaries, **Labor 1701 et seq.**
Conflict of interest. Adverse or pecuniary interest, generally, ante
Construction of statutes, fees, **Labor 1705 et seq.**
Contracts,
Children and minors, **Labor 1700.37**
Fees, **Labor 1701 et seq.**
Form, **Labor 1700.23**
Judicially improved contracts, children and minors, **Labor 1700.37**
Unlawful provisions, **Labor 1700.31**
Corporations, licenses, **Labor 1700.6**
Costs, fees, **Labor 1704.2**
Crimes and offenses,
Fees, **Labor 1704**
Transfer of interest, **Labor 1700.30**
Damages, fees, **Labor 1704.2**
Bonds (officers and fiduciaries), **Labor 1704.3**
Death, certificate of convenience to conduct business, **Labor 1700.20a, 1700.20b**
Definitions, **Labor 1700 et seq.**
Deposits, bonds (officers and fiduciaries), **Labor 1703.3**
Disbursement of artist funds, **Labor 1700.25**
Disclosure, contracts, **Labor 1703**
Discrimination, **Labor 1700.47**
Education, exemptions,
Advance fees, **Labor 1702.4**
Fees, **Labor 1703.6**
Employment contracts, children and minors, **Labor 1700.37**
Evidence, fees, **Labor 1703.4**

TALENT AGENCIES—Cont'd
Exemplary damages, fees, **Labor 1704.2**
Exemptions,
  Advance fees, **Labor 1702.4**
  Fees, **Labor 1703.6**
Expenses and expenditures, reimbursement, **Labor 1700.41**
Fees, **Labor 1700.24, 1701 et seq.**
  Adverse or pecuniary interest, **Labor 1700.40**
  Definitions, **Labor 1700.2**
  Division with employer, prohibition, **Labor 1700.39**
  Licenses and permits, **Labor 1700.12**
  Refund, **Labor 1700.40**
  Registration fees, **Labor 1700.40**
  Transfer of license, **Labor 1700.13**
Fines and penalties,
  Disposition, **Labor 1700.18**
  Fees, **Labor 1704**
Fingerprints and fingerprinting, licenses and permits, applications, **Labor 1700.6**
Forms, contracts, **Labor 1703**
Fraud,
  Advertising, **Labor 1700.32**
  Fees, **Labor 1703.4**
  License revocation or suspension, **Labor 1700.21**
Funds, artists, trusts and trustees, **Labor 1700.25**
Health and sanitation, sending artist to unhealthy environment, **Labor 1700.33**
Hearings, **Labor 1700.44**
Injunction, fees, **Labor 1704.1, 1704.2**
Interest, retention of artist funds, **Labor 1700.25**
Internet,
  Contracts, **Labor 1703**
  Fees, **Labor 1703.4**
Investigations and investigators, licenses and permits, **Labor 1700.7**
Judicially improved contracts, children and minors, **Labor 1700.37**
Labor disputes, **Labor 1700.38**
Labor organizations, advance fees, exemptions, **Labor 1702.4**
Licenses and permits, **Labor 1700.5 et seq.**
  Affidavits, **Labor 1700.6**
  Application, **Labor 1700.6**
  Assignment, **Labor 1700.13**
  Bonds (officers and fiduciaries), **Labor 1700.15 et seq.**
  Branch offices, **Labor 1700.10**
  Certificate of convenience, **Labor 1700.20a et seq.**
  Contents, **Labor 1700.19**
  Corporations, **Labor 1700.6**
  Fees, **Labor 1700.12**
  Hearings, **Labor 1700.22**
  Investigations, **Labor 1700.7**
  Nonlicensed persons, negotiation of employment contracts, **Labor 1700.44**
  Provisional licenses, **Labor 1700.14**
  Refusal to grant, **Labor 1700.8, 1700.9**

TALENT AGENCIES—Cont'd
Licenses and permits—Cont'd
  Renewal, **Labor 1700.10**
    Application, **Labor 1700.11**
  Revocation or suspension, grounds, **Labor 1700.21**
  Temporary licenses, **Labor 1700.14**
  Transferability, **Labor 1700.20**
    Fees, **Labor 1700.13**
Limitation of actions, **Labor 1700.44**
Lists, fees, **Labor 1701 et seq.**
Money awards, supersedeas or stay, **Labor 1700.44**
Nonlicensed personnel, action in conjunction with licensees, **Labor 1700.44**
Nonprofit corporations, advance fees, exemptions, **Labor 1702.4**
Notice,
  Advertisements, **Labor 1703.1**
  Contracts, **Labor 1703**
Persons of bad character, **Labor 1700.35**
Posting,
  Applicable laws, **Labor 1700.28**
  Fees, **Labor 1700.24**
Priorities and preferences, restitution, fees, **Labor 1704**
Production of books and papers, **Labor 1703.1**
Psychologists and psychology, fees, exemptions, **Labor 1703.6**
Publication, advance fees, exemptions, **Labor 1702.4**
Records and recordation, **Labor 1700.26 et seq., 1703.1**
  Artist funds, **Labor 1700.25**
Referral fees, **Labor 1703.4**
  Adverse or pecuniary interest, **Labor 1700.40**
Refunds, fees, **Labor 1700.40**
Registration fees, **Labor 1700.40**
Reimbursement, expenses, **Labor 1700.41**
Restitution, fees, **Labor 1704**
  Bonds (officers and fiduciaries), **Labor 1704.3**
Retention of artist funds, **Labor 1700.25**
Rules and regulations, **Labor 1700.29**
Safety, sending artist to unsafe environment, **Labor 1700.33**
Sales, **Labor 1700.30**
Solicitation,
  Advance fees, **Labor 1702**
  Notice, **Labor 1703.1**
Statute of limitations, **Labor 1700.44**
Supersedeas or stay, money awards, **Labor 1700.44**
Time, contracts, **Labor 1703**
Trademarks and trade names, fees, **Labor 1703.5**
Training, fees, **Labor 1701 et seq.**
Transfer,
  Interest, **Labor 1700.30**
  Licenses, **Labor 1700.13**
Trusts and trustees, artist funds, **Labor 1700.25**
Waiver, fees, construction of statutes, **Labor 1705.2**

TALENT AGENCIES—Cont'd
Withholding of artist funds, **Labor 1700.25**

TANKS
Air pressure tanks,
  Inspection, **Labor 7681**
  Operation permits, **Labor 7683**
    Permits and safety regulations, **Labor 7620 et seq.**
Liquified petroleum gas, inspections, **Labor 7681**
  Permits and safety regulations, **Labor 7620 et seq.**

TAPE RECORDINGS
Audiotapes, generally, this index

TARGETED TAX AREA
Definitions,
  Corporation taxes, deductions, **Rev & T 24416.2**
  Income tax—state, deductions, **Rev & T 17276.2**
Enterprise Zones, this index

TARGETED TAX AREA EXPIRATION DATE
Definitions,
  Corporation taxes,
    Deductions, **Rev & T 24416.2**
    Enterprise zones, credits, **Rev & T 23634**
  Enterprise zones, income tax—state, credits, **Rev & T 17053.34**
  Income tax—state, deductions, **Rev & T 17276.2**

TAVERNS AND SALOONS
Definitions, smoking, **Labor 6404.5**
Exemptions, workplace smoking regulation, **Labor 6404.5**
Place of employment, smoking regulation, exemption, **Labor 6404.5**
Rules and regulations, workplace smoking regulation, exemptions, **Labor 6404.5**
Workplace smoking regulation, exemption, **Labor 6404.5**

TAX ASSESSMENT ROLLS, LISTS AND BOOKS
Collection. Tax Collection, generally, this index

TAX ASSESSMENTS
Jeopardy Assessments, generally, this index

TAX ASSESSMENTS—SPECIAL
Collection. Tax Collection, generally, this index

TAX COLLECTION
Mail and mailing, withholding tax on wages, **Un Ins 13072**
Notice, withholding tax on wages, **Un Ins 13072**
Service, withholding tax on wages, **Un Ins 13072**
Withholding tax on wages, **Un Ins 13070 et seq.**

TAX COLLECTORS
Tax Collection, generally, this index

TAX CREDITS
Correctional institutions, inmate labor, joint venture programs, **Rev & T 23624**

TAX EXEMPTIONS
Business license tax, **Bus & P 16300**
Churches. Religious Organizations and Societies, this index
Religious Organizations and Societies, this index

TAX LIENS
Consumer credit reporting agencies, **CC 1786.18**
Contents of records, **CC 1785.13**
Labor and employment, records and recordation, copies, **CC 1786.53**
Unemployment compensation, liens for unpaid contributions, interest and penalties, **Un Ins 1701 et seq.**

TAX PREPARERS
Confidential or privileged information, **Un Ins 13019**

TAX RETURNS AND REPORTS
Labor camp owners, examination, **Health & S 17061.5**

TAX WARRANTS
Unemployment compensation, collection of delinquent contributions, **Un Ins 1785 et seq.**

TAXABLE YEAR
Definitions, withholding tax on wages, **Un Ins 13003**

TAXATION
Business license taxes, exemptions, **Bus & P 16300**
Collection. Tax Collection, generally, this index
Corporation Taxes, generally, this index
Crimes and offenses, employers statements, tax deductions, **Labor 226.6**
Deductions, employers statements, crimes and offenses, **Labor 226.6**
Employer statements, crimes and offenses, **Labor 226.6**
Enterprise Zones, generally, this index
Equalization state board, joint enforcement strike force on the underground economy, **Un Ins 329**
Federal Unemployment Tax Act, generally, this index
Fines and penalties,
Employers statements, tax deductions, **Labor 226.6**
Income Tax—State, this index
Motor Vehicles, this index
Franchise Tax Board, generally, this index
Income Tax—Federal, generally, this index
Income Tax—State, generally, this index

TAXATION—Cont'd
Incumbrances. Tax Liens, generally, this index
Labor and Employment, this index
Labor camps, agricultural land use designation, **Health & S 17021.6**
Liens. Tax Liens, generally, this index
Privileges and immunities, preparers, **Un Ins 13019**
Records and recordation. Income Tax—State, this index
Refunds. Income Tax—State, this index
Tax Collection, generally, this index
Unemployment Compensation, this index
Withholding Tax, generally, this index

TAXING AGENCIES
Taxation, generally, this index

TAXPAYER BROWSING PROTECTION ACT
Generally, **Un Ins 13018**

TAXPAYERS
Definitions,
Bank and corporation tax credits, **Rev & T 23622.7**
Corporation taxes, deductions, military base recovery areas, **Rev & T 24416.2**
Income tax credits, **Rev & T 17053.74**
Local agency military base recovery areas,
Corporation taxes, credits, **Rev & T 23645**
Income tax deductions, **Rev & T 17276.2**
Unemployment compensation, disability insurance, refunds and overpayments, **Un Ins 1185**
Withholding tax on wages, **Un Ins 13003**

TEACHERS RETIREMENT SYSTEM
Schoolteachers Retirement System, generally, this index

TEAMSTERS
Mechanics Liens, generally, this index

TECHNICAL SCHOOLS
Vocational Education, generally, this index

TECHNICALLY QUALIFIED INDIVIDUALS
Definitions, hazardous substances, **Labor 6386**

TECHNOLOGY
Information technologies. Telecommunications, generally, this index
Live scan technology. Fingerprints and Fingerprinting, this index

TELECOMMUNICATIONS
Agricultural labor relations board, 24 hour telephone, information and counseling, **Labor 1142.5**
Children and minors, messengers, **Labor 1297**

TELECOMMUNICATIONS—Cont'd
Coal mines, underground telephones, **Labor 7500, 7501**
Colleges and Universities, this index
Computers, generally, this index
Consumer Credit Reporting Agencies, this index
Crimes and offenses,
Calling patterns, records and recordation, **Pen 638**
Mines and mining, underground telephones, installation and maintenance, **Labor 7501**
Records and recordation, calling patterns, **Pen 638**
Telephone solicitors, security for wages, **Labor 270.6**
Criminal history information, officers and employees, **Pub U 7910**
Databases. Computers, generally, this index
Facsimile machines. Fax Machines, generally, this index
Fax Machines, generally, this index
Fines and penalties,
Calling patterns, records and recordation, **Pen 638**
Records and recordation, calling patterns, **Pen 638**
Fraud, calling patterns, records and recordation, **Pen 638**
Hotlines, whistle blowing, attorney general, **Labor 1102.7**
Independent contractors, criminal history information, **Pub U 7910**
Labor and employment,
Criminal history information, **Pub U 7910**
Workplace violence safety, **CCP 527.8**
Lead poisoning, occupational safety, programs, **Health & S 105185 et seq.**
Messengers, employment, **Labor 1297**
Mines and mining, underground telephones, **Labor 7500, 7501**
Misdemeanors. Crimes and offenses, generally, ante
Numbers and numbering, consumer credit reporting agencies, disclosure, **CC 1785.10**
Offenses. Crimes and offenses, generally, ante
Officers and employees, criminal history information, **Pub U 7910**
Public Utilities Commission, generally, this index
Records and recordation, calling patterns, crimes and offenses, **Pen 638**
Sheepherders, agricultural labor and employment, **Labor 2695.2**
Solicitation, deposit, security for payment of wages, **Labor 270.6**
Toll free telephone number, whistle blowing, attorney general, **Labor 1102.7**
Unemployment Compensation, this index
Vendor and purchaser, criminal history information, **Pub U 7910**

TELECOMMUNICATIONS

TELECOMMUNICATIONS—Cont'd
Workplace violence safety, **CCP 527.8**

TELECOMMUTING
Licenses and permits, exemptions, political
 subdivisions, **Bus & P 16300**

TELEGRAMS
Telecommunications, generally, this index

TELEPHONES
Telecommunications, generally, this index

TELEVISION AND RADIO
Advance fees, talent services, **Labor 1702
 et seq.**
Cable Television, generally, this index
Children and minors,
 Appearance on entertainment, hours of
  labor, **Labor 1310**
 Employment contracts, **Labor 1700.31**
Compensation and salaries,
 Payment, **Labor 271**
 Talent services, **Labor 1701 et seq.**
 Termination, labor and employment,
  payment, **Labor 201.5**
Completion, labor and employment, com-
 pensation and salaries, payment, **La-
 bor 201.5**
Contracts, talent services, fees, **Labor 1701
 et seq.**
Directors, talent services, fees, **Labor 1701
 et seq.**
Discharge, labor and employment, com-
 pensation and salaries, payment, **La-
 bor 201.5**
Employment. Labor and employment,
 generally, post
Exemptions, labor and employment,
 meals, time, **Labor 512**
Fees, talent services, **Labor 1701 et seq.**
Labor and employment,
 Dangerous occupations, licenses and
  permits, **Labor 6500**
 Exemptions, meals, time, **Labor 512**
 Termination, compensation and salaries,
  payment, **Labor 201.5**
Layoffs, compensation and salaries, pay-
 ment, **Labor 201.5**
Lead poisoning, occupational safety, pro-
 grams, **Health & S 105185 et seq.**
Libel and Slander, generally, this index
Licenses and permits, dangerous occupa-
 tions, **Labor 6500**
Master antenna television, criminal history
 information, officers and employees,
 Pub U 7910
Multipoint distribution services, criminal
 history information, officers and em-
 ployees, **Pub U 7910**
Resignation, labor and employment, com-
 pensation and salaries, payment, **Labor 201.5**
Salaries. Compensation and salaries, generally, ante
Satellite television, criminal history information, officers and employees, **Pub
 U 7910**

TELEVISION AND RADIO—Cont'd
Talent Agencies, generally, this index
Termination, labor and employment, compensation and salaries, payment, **Labor 201.5**
Unemployment compensation, service in
 artistic or literary capacity, **Un Ins
 601.5**
Videotape, generally, this index
Workers compensation, advertisements,
 disclosures, **Labor 5432, 5433**

TEMPLES
Religious Organizations and Societies,
 generally, this index

TEMPORARY EMPLOYMENT
Compensation and salaries, **Labor 201.3**
Fines and penalties, compensation and sal-
 aries, **Labor 201.3**
Public officers and employees, unemploy-
 ment compensation, excluded service,
 Un Ins 634.5

TEMPORARY INCAPACITATION
Definitions, military forces, collateral ben-
 efits, restriction or termination, **Mil &
 V 394**

TEMPORARY INJUNCTIONS
Injunction, this index

TEMPORARY RESTRAINING ORDERS
Injunction, this index

TEMPORARY SERVICES EMPLOYER
Definitions, unemployment compensation,
 Un Ins 606.5

TENANTS
Landlord and Tenant, generally, this index

TENT CAMPS
Mobilehomes and Mobilehome Parks,
 generally, this index

TERMINALS
Marine Terminals, generally, this index

TESTIMONY
Evidence, generally, this index
Witnesses, generally, this index

TESTS
Breathing apparatus for use in fires, devel-
 opment of safety standards, **Labor
 6331**
Electricity, this index
Laboratories, generally, this index
Motor Carriers, this index
Occupational safety and health, investiga-
 tions, **Labor 6314**
Oil and Gas, this index

THEATERS AND SHOWS
Advance fees, talent services, **Labor 1702
 et seq.**
Children and minors,
 Hours of employment, **Labor 1308.7,
 1310**

THEATERS AND SHOWS—Cont'd
Children and minors—Cont'd
 Illegal employment, **Labor 1308**
Circus, generally, this index
Collective bargaining, discharge or layoff,
 compensation and salaries, payment,
 Labor 201.9
Compensation and salaries,
 Discharge or layoff, payment, collective
  bargaining, **Labor 201.9**
 Payment, **Labor 271**
 Talent services, **Labor 1701 et seq.**
Contracts, talent services, fees, **Labor 1701
 et seq.**
Directors, talent services, fees, **Labor 1701
 et seq.**
Discharge or layoff, compensation and sal-
 aries, payment, collective bargaining,
 Labor 201.9
Discrimination, **CC 51 et seq.**
Exemptions, workplace smoking regula-
 tion, **Labor 6404.5**
Fees, talent services, **Labor 1701 et seq.**
Infants. Children and minors, generally,
 ante
Labor and employment, dangerous occu-
 pations, licenses and permits, **Labor
 6500**
Licenses and permits,
 Artists managers, **Labor 1700.5 et seq.**
 Dangerous occupations, **Labor 6500**
Military forces, refusing admission, **Mil &
 V 394**
Minors. Children and minors, generally,
 ante
Motion Pictures, generally, this index
Place of employment, smoking regulation,
 exemption, **Labor 6404.5**
Rules and regulations, workplace smoking
 regulation, exemptions, **Labor 6404.5**
Salaries. Compensation and salaries, gen-
 erally, ante
Sanitary standards, **Labor 2260**
Talent Agencies, generally, this index
Workplace smoking regulation, exemp-
 tion, **Labor 6404.5**

THEATRICAL ENGAGEMENT
Definitions, talent agencies, **Labor 1700.1**

THEFT
 Generally, **Pen 484 et seq.**
Bond of employee, property put up as,
 misappropriation by employer, **Labor
 405**
Construction, this index
Consumer Credit Reporting Agencies, this
 index
Credit, obtaining falsely, **Pen 484**
Definitions, Penal Code, **Pen 484**
Employment. Labor and Employment,
 this index
False representations, **Pen 484**
Indictment and information, contents, lar-
 ceny by fraud, **Pen 484**
Intent, theft by fraud, rented property,
 Pen 484

THEFT—Cont'd
Labor and Employment, this index
Motor Vehicles, this index
Musical instruments and equipment, security, employers, **Labor 2800.1**
Trailers, this index
Value, determination, **Pen 484**

THERAPISTS AND THERAPY
Psychotherapists and Psychotherapy, generally, this index

THIRD PARTIES
Firefighters and fire departments, actions against, workers compensation, **Labor 3852 et seq.**
Medical records, confidential or privileged information, **CC 56.10**
Peace officers, actions against, workers compensation, **Labor 3852 et seq.**
Unemployment Compensation, this index
Workers Compensation, this index

THREATS
Civil rights, violation, injunction, **CC 52**
Colleges and Universities, this index
Discharged prisoners seeking employment, **Pen 2947**
Duress or Coercion, generally, this index
Employees, discharge or loss of employment for political affiliations, **Labor 1101 et seq.**
Handicapped persons, housing rights, **Gov 12955.7**
Injunctions, violation of civil rights, **CC 52**
Labor and employment, exconvict, **Pen 2947**
Labor camps, tenants or employees, exercise of rights by tenant or employees, **Health & S 17031.5**
Labor disputes, agreements, **Labor 1110**
School Officers and Employees, this index
State Officers and Employees, this index
Workers compensation, threatening employee testifying or making application, **Labor 132a**

THREE, THREE DICHLOROBENZIDINE
Occupational Carcinogens Control Act, **Labor 9000 et seq.**

THROUGH HIGHWAY
Highways and Roads, generally, this index

TIMBER AND LUMBER
Compensation and salaries, executions, cash and securities on deposit to insure wage payments, **Labor 270.5**
Deposit, security for payment of logging wages, **Labor 270.5**
Executions, compensation, cash and securities on deposit to insure wage payments, **Labor 270.5**
Exemptions, executions, cash and securities on deposit to insure wage payments, **Labor 270.5**
Labor and employment, midday meal period, **Labor 800, 801**

TIMBER AND LUMBER—Cont'd
Logging contractor, deposits, security for payment of wages, **Labor 270.5**
Trespass, **Pen 602**

TIMBER WOLF
Fish and Game, generally, this index

TIME
Compensation and Salaries, this index
Earnings withholding orders, filings, **CCP 706.108**
Elections, this index
Electricity, this index
Family care leave, claims, **Un Ins 3301**
Garnishment, this index
Health Care Service Plans, this index
Income Tax—State, this index
Industrial welfare commission, rules and regulations, effective date, **Labor 1184**
Insurance, this index
Labor and Employment, this index
Labor Camps, this index
Leases, this index
Limitation of Actions, generally, this index
Nonpayment of wages, second and subsequent offenses, **Labor 243**
Occupational safety and health, appeal and review, orders, **Labor 6601, 6601.5**
Oil and Gas, this index
Payment. Compensation and Salaries, this index
Rental agreements, written demand for return of property, **Pen 484**
Support, this index
Unemployment Compensation, this index
Wearing apparel, manufacturers, arbitration award, **Labor 2690**
Workers Compensation, this index

TIME OFF
Labor and Employment, this index

TIMEKEEPERS
Athletics, workers compensation, exemption, **Labor 3352**

TIPPING LAWS
Generally, **Labor 350 et seq.**

TIPS
Compensation and Salaries, this index

TISSUE BANKS
Disclosure, medical records, **CC 56.10**
Medical records, disclosure, **CC 56.10**
Records and recordation, medical records, disclosure, **CC 56.10**

TITLE
Geologists and Geophysicists, this index

TITLE TO PROPERTY
Abandoned or Unclaimed Property, generally, this index

TITLE TO PROPERTY—Cont'd
Definitions,
    Fair employment and housing department, **Gov 12927**
    Permanent amusement rides, safety, inspection and inspectors, **Labor 7921**
    Unclaimed property, **CCP 1501**
Good faith purchasers, discriminatory provisions, **Gov 12995**
Industrial relations department, property held for use and benefit of state, transfer to state, **Labor 58**
Unclaimed property. Abandoned or Unclaimed Property, generally, this index

TITLE 11 OR SIMILAR CASE
Definitions, corporation taxes, net operating losses, **Rev & T 24416**

TITLES OF ACTS
Popular Name Laws, generally, this index

TOBACCO AND TOBACCO PRODUCTS
Industrial homework, manufacturer, **Labor 2651**
Labor and employment, workplace smoking, **Labor 6404.5**
Workplace smoking regulation, exemption, **Labor 6404.5**

TOILETS
Comfort Stations and Rest Rooms, generally, this index

TOLL FREE TELEPHONE NUMBER
Telecommunications, this index

TOLLING
Limitation of Actions, this index

TOM CARRELL MEMORIAL TUNNEL AND MINE SAFETY ACT
Generally, **Labor 7950 et seq.**

TOOLS
Labor and employment,
    Claims for return, assignment to labor commissioner, **Labor 96**
    Employer guaranteeing payment by employees, **Labor 213**
Leases, theft by fraud, **Pen 484**
Presumption, theft by fraud, **Pen 484**
Ships and vessels, loading or unloading, safety, **Labor 7602**

TORPEDOES
Explosives, generally, this index

TORTS
Hospitals, reports of physical abuse of patients received from health facilities, **Pen 11161.8**
Invasion of privacy. Privacy, this index
Negligence, generally, this index
Personal Injuries, generally, this index
Physicians and surgeons, reports, abuse of patients by another health facility, **Pen 11161.8**
Wrongful Death, generally, this index

TOWER CRANES
Definitions, regulation, **Labor 7371**

TOWNS
Fire companies. Firefighters and Fire Departments, generally, this index
Health Facilities, generally, this index

TOWNSHIP OFFICERS AND EMPLOYEES
Resignation, military service entry, reentry into office or employment on discharge, **Mil & V 395.3**

TOWNSHIPS
Health Facilities, generally, this index

TOXIC MATERIALS
Hazardous Substances and Waste, generally, this index

TOXIC SUBSTANCES
Hazardous Substances and Waste, generally, this index

TOXIC WASTE
Hazardous Substances and Waste, generally, this index

TOXICOLOGY
Occupational health and medicine, program development, **Labor 50.8**

TOYS
Industrial homework, manufacturer, **Labor 2651**

TRACKLESS TROLLEYS
Buses, generally, this index

TRACKS
Railroads, generally, this index

TRACTORS
Motor Carriers, generally, this index

TRADE, BUSINESS, PROFESSION OR OCCUPATION
Definitions, workers compensation, **Labor 3356**

TRADE AND BUSINESS
Business and Commerce, generally, this index

TRADE NAMES
Talent agencies, fees, **Labor 1703.5**

TRADE SCHOOLS
Vocational Education, generally, this index

TRADE SECRETS
Labor and Employment, this index
Occupational safety and health. Labor and Employment, this index
Workers compensation, insurance, studies, insolvency, **Labor 77.7**

TRADE UNIONS
Labor Organizations, generally, this index

TRADEMARKS
Crimes and offenses, forgery, labor organizations, **Labor 1015**
Forgery, labor organizations, **Labor 1015**
Labor union insignia, **Labor 1010 et seq.**
Registration, labor organizations, **Labor 1014**
Talent agencies, fees, **Labor 1703.5**

TRAFFIC RULES AND REGULATIONS
Juvenile delinquents and dependents, public works projects, workers compensation, **Labor 3364.6**

TRAILER COACHES
Mobilehomes and Mobilehome Parks, generally, this index

TRAILER PARKS
Mobilehomes and Mobilehome Parks, generally, this index

TRAILERS
Leases, theft by fraud, **Pen 484**
Mobilehomes and Mobilehome Parks, generally, this index
Motor Carriers, generally, this index
Presumption, theft by fraud, **Pen 484**
Theft, fraud, **Pen 484**

TRAIN EMPLOYEES HOURS LAW
Generally, **Labor 600 et seq.**

TRAIN MANNING LAW
Generally, **Labor 6901 et seq.**

TRAINED NURSES
Nurses, generally, this index

TRAINEES
Definitions, employment training panel, **Un Ins 10201**

TRAINING
Generally, **Un Ins 9500 et seq.**
Agencies, definitions, employment training panel, **Un Ins 10201**
Amusements, rides, safety, **Labor 7916**
Apprentices, generally, this index
Asbestos training and consultant certification fund, **Labor 9021.7**
Biotechnology, **Un Ins 9700 et seq.**
CalWORKS. Social Services, this index
Career resource network, **Educ 53086**
Caregiver training initiative, **Un Ins 11020 et seq.**
Chemical plant workers, safety, **Labor 7850 et seq.**
Contracts, **Un Ins 9610**
Employment Training Fund, generally, this index
Firefighters and Fire Departments, this index
Funds. Employment Training Fund, generally, this index
Geologists and geophysicists, certificates and certification, **Bus & P 7843**
Green collar jobs, **Un Ins 15000 et seq.**
Handicapped Persons, this index

TRAINING—Cont'd
Health care providers, caregiver training initiative, **Un Ins 11020 et seq.**
High Schools or Secondary Schools, this index
Job preparation and training services. Unemployment Compensation, this index
Juvenile Delinquents and Dependents, this index
Labor and Employment, this index
Nontraditional occupations, women, **Un Ins 9602.5**
Nurses, this index
Occupational safety and health, **Labor 144.5**
One stop career centers, **Un Ins 14230 et seq.**
Sexual harassment, labor and employment, **Gov 12950.1**
Social Services, this index
Talent agencies, fees, **Labor 1701 et seq.**
Unemployment Compensation, this index
Vietnam Veterans Employment Act, **Gov 7280 et seq.**
Vouchers, workers compensation, **Labor 4658.5**
    Liability, **Labor 4658.6**
Women, nontraditional occupations, **Un Ins 9602.5**
Workers Compensation, this index
Workforce investment, **Un Ins 14000 et seq.**

TRAINS
Railroads, generally, this index

TRAMWAYS
Aerial Passenger Tramways, generally, this index

TRANSCRIPT OF RECORD
Administrative Law and Procedure, generally, this index

TRANSFER OF POWERS AND DUTIES
Benefit Payments Department, this index
Employment development department, benefit payments department, **Un Ins 301**
Industrial relations department, occupational safety and health division, transfer from industrial safety division, **Labor 60.5**
Industrial safety division, transfer to occupational safety and health division, **Labor 60.5 et seq.**
Industrial welfare division, transfer to labor standards enforcement division, **Labor 83**
Labor standards enforcement division, transfer from division of labor law enforcement, **Labor 82**
Occupational safety and health division, transfer from industrial safety division, **Labor 60.5**
Unemployment compensation, **Un Ins 20**

TRANSFER OF PROPERTY
Deeds and Conveyances, generally, this index

TRANSIT DEVELOPMENT BOARDS
San Diego County,
Application of law, railroad crew requirements, **Labor 6901**
Labor requirements, railroad crews, application of law, **Labor 6901**
Railroads, minimum crew requirements, application of law, **Labor 6901**

TRANSIT DISTRICTS
Arbitration and award, labor disputes, **Labor 1137 et seq.**
Boards and commissions, labor disputes, threatened strike or lockout, board of investigation, **Labor 1137.2 et seq.**
Conciliation, state conciliation service, labor disputes, **Labor 1137.1**
Contracts, labor disputes, **Labor 1137 et seq.**
Injunction, labor disputes, **Labor 1137.4**
Labor disputes, **Labor 1137 et seq.**
Labor organizations, **Labor 1137 et seq.**
Lockouts, labor disputes, **Labor 1137 et seq.**
Officers and employees, labor dispute, **Labor 1137 et seq.**
Strikes, labor disputes, **Labor 1137.2**

TRANSIT SYSTEMS
Labor disputes, **Labor 1137 et seq.**
Officers and employees, labor disputes, **Labor 1137 et seq.**
Paratransit Vehicles, generally, this index
Transit Development Boards, generally, this index

TRANSLATORS
Interpreters and Translators, generally, this index

TRANSPLANTS
Tissue Banks, generally, this index

TRANSPORTATION
Actions and proceedings, displaced workers, **Labor 1073**
Aerial passenger tramways, **Labor 7340 et seq.**
Alcoholics and alcoholism, volunteers, criminal history information, **Pen 11105.3**
Attorney fees, displaced workers, actions and proceedings, **Labor 1073**
Buses, generally, this index
Contracts, displaced workers, **Labor 1070 et seq.**
Costs, displaced workers, actions and proceedings, **Labor 1073**
Displaced workers, **Labor 1070 et seq.**
Drug addicts, volunteers, criminal history information, **Pen 11105.3**
Foreign labor contractors, inducement, **Bus & P 9998.5**
High speed rail. Railroads, this index

TRANSPORTATION—Cont'd
Highways and Roads, generally, this index
Injunction, displaced workers, **Labor 1073**
Labor and Employment, this index
Labor disputes, **Labor 1137 et seq.**
Mass Transit, generally, this index
Officers and employees,
Displaced workers, **Labor 1070 et seq.**
Labor disputes, **Labor 1137**
Paratransit Vehicles, generally, this index
Railroads, generally, this index
Rapid transit districts. Transit Districts, generally, this index
State highways. Highways and Roads, this index
Transit Development Boards, generally, this index
Transit Districts, generally, this index
Weapons, this index

TRANSPORTATION DISTRICTS
Transit Districts, generally, this index

TRANSPORTATION PLANNING AGENCIES
Transit Development Boards, generally, this index

TRAVEL TRAILERS
Mobilehomes and Mobilehome Parks, generally, this index

TRAVELING EXPENSES
Apprenticeship council members, **Labor 3070**
Disability compensation, revolving fund, **Un Ins 3051**
Health and safety and workers compensation board, **Labor 75**
Industrial welfare commission, wage board, **Labor 1179**
Labor and Employment, this index
Occupational safety and health standards board, **Labor 141**
Public officers and employees, injured employees, retraining and rehabilitation, **Labor 6203**
School Officers and Employees, this index
Talent agencies, reimbursements, **Labor 1700.41**
Wage board, industrial welfare commission, **Labor 1179**
Witnesses, this index
Workers Compensation, this index
Workforce investment board, **Un Ins 14015**

TREASURERS
State Treasurer, generally, this index

TREASURY
State Treasury, generally, this index

TREBLE DAMAGES
Damages, this index

TREES
Products. Timber and Lumber, generally, this index

TREMOLITE
Occupational Carcinogens Control Act, **Labor 9000 et seq.**

TRENCHES
Construction, licenses and permits, **Labor 6500 et seq.**
Licenses and permits, **Labor 6500 et seq.**

TRESPASS
Generally, **Pen 602, 602.8**
Acts constituting, **Pen 602**
Agricultural land, **Pen 602, 602.8**
Airports and landing fields, **Pen 602**
Animals, **Pen 602**
Battered womens shelters, **Pen 602**
Birthing centers, **Pen 602**
Boats and boating, passengers, terminals, **Pen 602**
Brands, marks and labels, agricultural land, **Pen 602**
Counselors and counseling, neonatal units, maternity wards, birthing centers, parole and probation, **Pen 602**
Exemptions, **Pen 602.8**
Service of process, motor vehicles, **Pen 602**
Fences, **Pen 602, 602.8**
Agricultural land, **Pen 602**
Fines and penalties, **Pen 602.8**
Battered womens shelters, **Pen 602**
Neonatal units, maternity wards, birthing centers, **Pen 602**
Fires, hazardous fire area, **Pen 602**
Fish and Game, this index
Goats, **Pen 602**
Hazardous fire area, **Pen 602**
Hogs, **Pen 602**
Hotels, **Pen 602**
Infractions, **Pen 602.8**
Labor organizations, lawful labor activities, **Pen 602**
Marine terminals, **Pen 602**
Maternity wards, **Pen 602**
Motels and motor courts, **Pen 602**
Motor Vehicles, this index
Neonatal units, **Pen 602**
Parole and probation, neonatal units, maternity wards, birthing centers, **Pen 602**
Private property, refusal to leave upon request, **Pen 602**
Public buildings and works, refusal to leave at closing time, **Pen 602**
Restitution, battered womens shelters, **Pen 602**
Second and subsequent offenses, **Pen 602.8**
Ships and shipping, passengers, terminals, **Pen 602**
Signs and signals, agricultural land, **Pen 602**
Ski areas or trails, **Pen 602**
Sterile areas, airports and landing fields, **Pen 602**
Surveys and surveyors, exemptions, **Pen 602.8**

TRIAL
Costs, generally, this index
Jury, generally, this index
New Trial, generally, this index
Process, generally, this index
Venue, generally, this index
Witnesses, generally, this index
Workers compensation insurance, uninsured employers fund awards, **Labor 3717 et seq.**
Workers compensation proceedings, trial by judges, **Labor 5309**

TRIAL DE NOVO
New Trial, generally, this index

TRUCK TRACTORS
Motor Carriers, generally, this index

TRUCKS
Motor Carriers, generally, this index

TRUST COMPANIES
Corporation Taxes, generally, this index
Wages, deposits to secure payment, special occupations, **Labor 270.5 et seq.**
Workers compensation, deposit of lump sum payments, **Labor 5102 et seq.**

TRUST FUNDS
Mechanics liens, fringe benefits, collective bargaining, **CC 3111**
Retirement and Pensions, this index
Subsequent injuries benefits trust fund, workers compensation, **Labor 62.5**
Uninsured employers benefits trust fund, workers compensation, **Labor 62.5**
Workers compensation,
    Subsequent injuries benefits trust fund, **Labor 62.5**
    Uninsured employers benefits trust fund, **Labor 62.5**

TRUSTS AND TRUSTEES
Bond put up by employee, commingling of property by employer, **Labor 405**
Collections, unpaid wages or benefits, **Labor 96.7**
Colleges and Universities, this index
Compensation and salaries,
    Priorities and preferences, **CCP 1204**
    Unpaid wages or benefits, collection, deposits, payment, escheat, **Labor 96.7**
Definitions, workers compensation, **Labor 3700.1**
    Self insurance, **Labor 3741**
Employee benefit plan distribution, definitions, Unclaimed Property Law, **CCP 1501**
Employee benefit plans,
    Escheat, **CCP 1510, 1521**
    Priorities and preferences, **CCP 1204**
Escheat, employee benefit plans, **CCP 1510, 1521**
Fringe benefits, unpaid wages or benefits, collection, deposits, payment, escheat, **Labor 96.7**

TRUSTS AND TRUSTEES—Cont'd
Industrial relations unpaid wage fund, **Labor 96.7**
Payment, unpaid wages or benefits, **Labor 96.7**
Pensions. Retirement and Pensions, this index
Priorities and preferences, compensation and salaries, **CCP 1204**
Retirement and Pensions, this index
Self insurers security fund, workers compensation, **Labor 3742**
Talent agencies, artist funds, **Labor 1700.25**
Trust Funds, generally, this index
Unclaimed employee trust benefit distribution, escheat to state, **CCP 1510**
Unemployment Compensation, this index
Unpaid wages or benefits, collections, deposits, payments, escheat, **Labor 96.7**
Workers Compensation, this index

TUBERCULOSIS
Correctional Institutions, this index
Correctional officers, workers compensation, **Labor 3212.6**
Criminal identification and investigation bureau, workers compensation, **Labor 3212.7**
Firefighters and fire departments, workers compensation, **Labor 3212.6**
Guards, jails or prisons, workers compensation, **Labor 3212.6**
Highway patrol, workers compensation, **Labor 3212.6**
Jails, this index
Juvenile Facilities Division, this index
Law enforcement officers, workers compensation, **Labor 3212.6**
Narcotic enforcement bureau, workers compensation, **Labor 3212.7**
Police, workers compensation, **Labor 3212.6**
Sheriffs, workers compensation, **Labor 3212.6**
State peace officer, workers compensation, **Labor 3212.7**
Workers Compensation, this index

TUNNEL AND MINE SAFETY ACT
Generally, **Labor 7950 et seq.**

TUNNELS
Access shaft, **Labor 7964**
Alternate escape route, extrahazardous tunnels, **Labor 7981**
Chemists, **Labor 7954**
Children and minors, working in tunnels, **Labor 1294**
Classification, **Labor 7955**
Communication systems, **Labor 7963**
Crimes and offenses, explosive safety violations, **Labor 8003**
Cutoff, electrical equipment power, gassy tunnels, **Labor 7975**
Definitions, tunnel and mine safety, **Labor 7951**

TUNNELS—Cont'd
Electrical lighting and power, review of plans, gassy tunnels, **Labor 7969**
Escape chamber, **Labor 7981**
Excess gas levels, removal of men, **Labor 7972**
Explosives, licenses and permits, **Labor 7990 et seq.**
Extrahazardous tunnels, safety regulations, **Labor 7977 et seq.**
Fire extinguishers, gassy tunnels, **Labor 7976**
Gassy tunnels,
    Excessive gas readings, **Labor 7961**
    Safety regulations, **Labor 7965 et seq.**
    Testing prior to each shift, **Labor 7960**
Ignition, gas or vapor, **Labor 7971**
Industrial hygiene engineer, **Labor 7954**
Inspection and inspectors, **Labor 7953**
Laboratories, **Labor 7954**
Licenses and permits, explosives, **Labor 7990 et seq.**
Notice, gassy tunnels, excess gas levels, **Labor 7967**
Posting, classifications, orders or rules, **Labor 7956**
Practice sessions, rescue and search equipment, **Labor 7959**
Prejob safety conference, **Labor 7955**
Rescue, **Labor 7957 et seq.**
Safety regulations, **Labor 7950 et seq.**
Shutdown for testing, gassy tunnels, **Labor 7968**
Smoking, gassy tunnels, **Labor 7970**
Special orders, gassy tunnels, **Labor 7973**
Tunnel and Mine Safety Act, **Labor 7950 et seq.**
Ventilation, gassy tunnels, **Labor 7974**

TURKISH EMPIRE
Genocide. Armenians, this index

TWINNING
Definitions, employment opportunities creation, **Un Ins 12102**

TWO ACETYLAMINOFLUORENE
Occupational Carcinogens Control Act, **Labor 9000 et seq.**

TYPHOID FEVER
Diseases, generally, this index

UMPIRES
Amateur sporting events, workers compensation, **Labor 3352**
Workers compensation, amateur sporting events, **Labor 3352**

UNCLAIMED EMPLOYEE BENEFIT PLAN DISTRIBUTIONS
Escheat to state, **CCP 1521**

UNCLAIMED PROPERTY
Abandoned or Unclaimed Property, generally, this index

UNDERGROUND MINE
Definitions, tunnel and mine safety, **Labor 7951**

UNDERTAKINGS
Bonds (Officers and Fiduciaries), generally, this index

UNDUE HARDSHIP
Definitions, fair employment and housing, **Gov 12926**

UNDUE INFLUENCE
Whistle Blowing, this index

UNEMPLOYMENT
Corporation taxes, credit, **Rev & T 23622.7, 23622.8**
Deaf, hearing impaired persons, employment services, **Un Ins 11000 et seq.**
Definitions, unemployment compensation, **Un Ins 1252**
Disability insurance, premiums, waiver, **Ins 10110.5**
Employment Development, generally, this index
Hearing impaired persons, employment services, **Un Ins 11000 et seq.**
Labor statistics and research division, collection and compilation of information, **Labor 150**
Life insurance, premiums, waiver, **Ins 10110.5**
Public Buildings and Works, this index
Small Businesses, generally, this index
Support, this index
Workers compensation, injury to unemployment work relief employee, disability benefits, **Labor 4456**

UNEMPLOYMENT COMPENSATION
Generally, **Labor 2010 et seq.; Un Ins 1 et seq.**
Absence and absentees, alcoholics and alcoholism, disqualifications, **Un Ins 1256.4**
Abstracts of judgment, disability compensation, **Un Ins 2739.1, 2739.2**
Accomplices and accessories, benefits, fraud, **Un Ins 2107, 2121**
Accounts and accounting,
  Administration fund, **Un Ins 1559**
  Disability compensation, post
  Independent contractors status, presumption, **Un Ins 656**
  Reserve accounts, generally, post
  Unemployment fund, **Un Ins 1525 et seq.**
Acknowledgment of satisfaction of judgment, **Un Ins 1379.6**
  Disability compensation, **Un Ins 2739.2**
Acquisition,
  Computation, wages, **Un Ins 930.5**
  Contributions, post
  Coverage, **Un Ins 803.1**
  Reserve accounts, transfer, **Un Ins 1051 et seq.**
  Successors, liability, **Un Ins 1731 et seq.**

UNEMPLOYMENT COMPENSATION
—Cont'd
Actions and proceedings, **Un Ins 1326 et seq.**
  Collection,
    Additional remedies, **Un Ins 1860**
    Contributions due, bulk transfers, **Un Ins 1734**
    Delinquent contributions, interest or penalties, **Un Ins 1785 et seq.**
    Unpaid contributions, **Un Ins 1734**
  Disability compensation, post
  Extended compensation, **Un Ins 3651 et seq., 4651 et seq.**
  Injunctions, inducement to violate code, **Un Ins 1855**
  Limitation of actions, generally, post
  Notice, filing of new or additional claims, **Un Ins 1030**
  Overpayment, recovery, **Un Ins 1379, 1381**
    Disability compensation, **Un Ins 2739**
    Statute of limitations, **Un Ins 1379**
  Personal liability of assignee, receiver, enforcement, **Un Ins 1736**
  Precedent decisions of appeals board, determination of validity, **Un Ins 409.2**
  Preference on calendar, collection of delinquent contributions, **Un Ins 1853**
  Primary claim, definitions, **Un Ins 3503**
  Process to prevent collection of contributions, **Un Ins 1851**
  Reciprocity, **Un Ins 453**
  Summary judgment, delinquent contributions, penalties or interest, **Un Ins 1815 et seq.**
  Unclaimed contributions erroneously paid, **Un Ins 1536**
  Wrongful discharge actions, benefits, **Un Ins 1382**
Acute drug induced illness, disability, definitions, **Un Ins 2626**
Additional withholding, withholding tax on wages, **Un Ins 13024**
Addresses, withholding tax on wages, **Un Ins 13016**
Administration fund, **Un Ins 1522, 1528.5, 1555 et seq.**
  Accounting, **Un Ins 1559**
  Appropriations, **Un Ins 1555, 1556**
  Balances, use, **Un Ins 1555**
  Budget report by governor for replacement, **Un Ins 1562**
  Commingling with other state funds prohibited, **Un Ins 1557**
  Composition, **Un Ins 1556**
  Contingent fund, transfers, **Un Ins 1588**
  Continued in existence, **Un Ins 1555**
  Deposit, **Un Ins 1526.4, 1557, 1559, 1560**
  Disbursements, procedure, **Un Ins 1559**
  Employment service of United States, contribution to, **Un Ins 1556**
  Expenditures, **Un Ins 1558.5**

UNEMPLOYMENT COMPENSATION
—Cont'd
Administration fund—Cont'd
  Investments, **Un Ins 1560**
  Matching money, **Un Ins 1562**
  Procedure for administration, **Un Ins 1559**
  Purposes, **Un Ins 1558**
  Railroad retirement board, contribution to, **Un Ins 1556**
  Refunds and overpayments, collection costs, deposit, **Un Ins 1384**
  Replacements of federal monies, **Un Ins 1562**
  Reports, **Un Ins 1562**
  Revolving fund, creation, **Un Ins 1559**
  Secretary of Labor,
    Expenditures from, **Un Ins 1558**
    Moneys received from, **Un Ins 1556**
  Separate accounts, **Un Ins 1557**
  Social Security Administration, contribution to, **Un Ins 1556**
  Treasurer, state, liability on bond, **Un Ins 1561**
  United States, contributions to, **Un Ins 1556**
  Vouchers, necessity, **Un Ins 1559**
  Wagner Peyser Act, money granted pursuant to, **Un Ins 1562**
  Warrants, unclaimed, **Un Ins 1537**
  Withdrawals, **Un Ins 1558, 1559**
Administration of Act, use of moneys credited from Social Security Act, **Un Ins 1528.5**
Administrative appellate review, **Un Ins 1221 et seq.**
  Offers in compromise, **Un Ins 1872**
Administrative law judges, **Un Ins 404 et seq.**
  Appeal and review, generally, post
  Appeals division, **Un Ins 315**
  Appointment, **Un Ins 404**
  Chief administrative law judge,
    Appointment, qualifications, **Un Ins 405**
    Duties, **Un Ins 406**
  Claims, denial review, **Un Ins 1180**
  Compensation, **Un Ins 404**
  Conflict of interest, **Un Ins 404**
  Consolidation of cases for hearing, **Un Ins 1951**
  Decision, review by appeals board, **Un Ins 412**
  Delegation of power by appeals board, **Un Ins 1959**
  Finality of decision, **Un Ins 1224**
    Good cause, extension of time, **Un Ins 1334**
  Petitions, **Un Ins 1035, 1055, 1180**
  Precedent decisions, controlling effect, **Un Ins 409**
  Recovery of overpayments, **Un Ins 1379**
    Disability compensation, **Un Ins 2739**
Administrators. Executors and administrators, generally, post

UNEMPLOYMENT

UNEMPLOYMENT COMPENSATION
—Cont'd

Adoption of children, family care leave, **Un Ins 3300 et seq.**

Advanced payments, balances, exclusions, **Un Ins 980**

Advances to unemployment fund, application, **Un Ins 323**

Adverse or pecuniary interest, administrative law judges, **Un Ins 404**

Advertising, injunctions, inducing to violate law, **Un Ins 1855**

Advisory committees, school employer advisory committee, **Un Ins 831**

Advisory councils, caregiver training initiative, **Un Ins 11020**

Advisory position, public officers and employees, excluded services, **Un Ins 634.5**

Affidavits,
Disability compensation, claims, mentally deficient claimants, **Un Ins 2705.1**
Payment, **Un Ins 1341**

Agency for payment, **Un Ins 1339**

Agents,
Appearance before appeals board, **Un Ins 1957**
Records, several employers, preparation, **Un Ins 1096 et seq.**
Violations, **Un Ins 2103 et seq.**

Agreements, elective coverage, **Un Ins 705**

Agricultural corporations, officers and directors, **Un Ins 637**

Agricultural labor and employment, **Un Ins 611 et seq., 935**
Contributions,
License denial, **Labor 1690.1**
Notice, **Labor 1690.1; Un Ins 1141**
Employer defined, **Un Ins 676**
Included as employment, **Un Ins 611**

Air National Guard, excluded services, **Un Ins 634.5**

Aircraft,
Excluded services, **Un Ins 648**
Operating aircraft, **Un Ins 609**

Alcoholics and alcoholism,
Disability, definitions, **Un Ins 2626**
Disqualifications, **Un Ins 1256.4**
Reasons for leaving employment, **Un Ins 1030**
Payments charged against employer, **Un Ins 1032**
Recovery home residents, disability benefits, **Un Ins 2626.1**

Aliens,
Exclusion from benefits, **Un Ins 1264**
Foreign professional athletes, **Un Ins 655**
Temporary residence status applied for, **Un Ins 1264**

Allowances,
Expenses, exclusion from wages, **Un Ins 929**
Self employment assistance program, **Un Ins 1300 et seq.**

UNEMPLOYMENT COMPENSATION
—Cont'd

Amendment, rights, privileges conferred subject to, **Un Ins 102**

American aircraft, definitions, **Un Ins 125.3**

American employer, definitions, **Un Ins 125.4**

American vessel, definitions, **Un Ins 125.5**

Amount of benefits, **Un Ins 1280, 1281**
Available for work, **Un Ins 1253.5**
Computation, **Un Ins 301**
Determination, **Un Ins 1093**
Reduction, amount equal to pension or similar periodic payment, **Un Ins 1255.3**
Retroactive application of law, pensions or similar periodic payments, reduction of benefits, **Un Ins 1255.3**

Annuities,
Definitions, withholding tax on wages, **Un Ins 13028**
Payments under, exclusion from wages, **Un Ins 931, 934**
Withholding tax on wages, **Un Ins 13028**

Appeal and review, **Un Ins 1221 et seq., 1328 et seq., 1951 et seq.**
Administrative appellate review, **Un Ins 1221 et seq.**
Assessments, **Un Ins 1241 et seq.**
Administrative appellate review, **Un Ins 1221 et seq.**
Computation of benefits, **Un Ins 1330 et seq.**
Continuous review of cases, chief administrative law judge, **Un Ins 406**
Contributions, administrative appellate review, **Un Ins 1221 et seq.**
Conviction of offense, reason for termination of employment, **Un Ins 1256.1**
Correct employer determination, **Un Ins 1127.5**
Costs, **Un Ins 1958**
Decision on appeal, **Un Ins 1334**
Modification, **Un Ins 1336**
Director, interested party, **Un Ins 1377, 2707.2**
Director of employment development, **Un Ins 410**
Disability compensation, post
Eligibility,
Detained individual, **Un Ins 1253.1**
Determination, **Un Ins 1328**
Extended unemployment compensation, post
Finality, administrative law judges decision, **Un Ins 1224, 1334**
Fines and penalties, **Un Ins 1241 et seq.**
Incarceration for offense, reason for termination of employment, **Un Ins 1256.1**
Jeopardy assessment, administrative appellate review, **Un Ins 1221 et seq.**

UNEMPLOYMENT COMPENSATION
—Cont'd

Appeal and review—Cont'd
Joint enforcement strike force on the underground economy, citations, penalty assessment orders, **Labor 106**
Judgments and decrees, **Un Ins 1241 et seq.**
Judicial review of decisions of appeals board, **Un Ins 410**
Offers in compromise, **Un Ins 1872**
Overpayments, **Un Ins 1241 et seq., 1377, 1378**
Good cause, extension of time, **Un Ins 1377**
Part time employment, receiving less than weekly benefit amount, **Un Ins 1032.5**
Payment, **Un Ins 1335**
Pending decision or appeal, **Un Ins 1179.5**
Protest, decision on, **Un Ins 1035**
Recomputation of benefits, **Un Ins 1332**
Refunds and overpayments, **Un Ins 1178, 1241 et seq.**
Removal of proceedings, **Un Ins 412, 413**
Representation of claimant by counsel or agent, authorization forms, **Un Ins 1957.5**
Reserve accounts, post
Termination of employment, reasons, ruling, **Un Ins 1030**
Time, refunds and overpayments, **Un Ins 1241**
Trade dispute determination, **Un Ins 1262.5**
Transfer of proceedings, **Un Ins 1336**
Transfer or removal, **Un Ins 412, 413**

Appeals boards, **Un Ins 1334 et seq., 1951**
Administrative law judges, **Un Ins 404**
Affirming, modifying or reversing preliminary determination of trade dispute, **Un Ins 1262.5**
Agent, appearance before, **Un Ins 1957**
Appeals division, **Un Ins 315, 401**
Appointment of chief administrative law judge, **Un Ins 405**
Assignment of cases, **Un Ins 409**
Attorney appearing before, **Un Ins 1957**
Books and records, production, power to compel, **Un Ins 1953**
Budget, **Un Ins 403**
Certification, powers, **Un Ins 1953**
Chairman, **Un Ins 401**
Compensation and salaries, **Un Ins 401**
Compromise and settlement, tax disputes, **Un Ins 1236**
Costs, **Un Ins 1958**
Crimes and offenses, divulging confidential information, **Un Ins 2111**
Decisions and orders,
Content, stating facts and reasons, **Un Ins 409**
Index, **Un Ins 409**

UNEMPLOYMENT COMPENSATION
—Cont'd

Appeals boards—Cont'd

Decisions and orders—Cont'd

Majority vote, when required, **Un Ins 409**

Number of members deciding, **Un Ins 409**

Precedent decisions, modification by board, **Un Ins 409.1**

Publication, **Un Ins 409**

Writing, necessity, **Un Ins 408**

Definitions, **Un Ins 126**

Delegation of power, **Un Ins 1959**

Depositions, authority to take, **Un Ins 1953**

Director of employment development, **Un Ins 410**

Disability compensation, post

Divulging confidential information, **Un Ins 2111**

Evidence, delegation of authority to take and hear, **Un Ins 407**

Fees of witnesses, **Un Ins 1956**

Finality of decision, **Un Ins 410**

Impasse, **Un Ins 409**

Judicial review of board decisions, **Un Ins 410**

Meeting or acting as whole, **Un Ins 409, 411**

Oaths, administration, **Un Ins 1953**

Overpayment, review, **Un Ins 1378**

Personnel of appeals division, appointment, direction, **Un Ins 403**

Powers as department head, **Un Ins 407**

Precedent decisions, designation, **Un Ins 409**

Qualifications of members, **Un Ins 401**

Reporter for proceedings, **Un Ins 1952**

Rules of procedure, **Un Ins 1952**
Appeals, **Un Ins 411**

Settlement, tax disputes, **Un Ins 1236**

Subpoenas, **Un Ins 1953 et seq.**

Tax disputes, compromise and settlement, **Un Ins 1236**

Terms of members, vacancies, **Un Ins 402**

Transfer of reserve account, decision on application, **Un Ins 1055**

Vacancy in office, **Un Ins 402**

Witnesses, power to compel attendance, **Un Ins 1953**

Appeals division, **Un Ins 315, 401**

Personnel, appointment, **Un Ins 403**

Appearance,

Before appeals board by agent, **Un Ins 1957**

Failure to appear at hearings, **Un Ins 2104**

Application for determination of potential eligibility during retraining, **Un Ins 1268**

Appointments,

Administrative law judges, **Un Ins 404**

Appeals board, **Un Ins 401**

Appropriations, **Un Ins 1521, 1535, 1586**

UNEMPLOYMENT COMPENSATION
—Cont'd

Approximation of deductions, withholding tax on wages, **Un Ins 13022**

Architects, presumption of independent contractors status, **Un Ins 656**

Armed forces. Military forces, generally, post

Arrest,

Eligibility for benefits, **Un Ins 1253.1**

Warrants, applicants accused of felonies, furnishing information to law enforcement agencies, **Un Ins 1095**

Assessments, **Un Ins 301, 1126 et seq.**

Administrative appellate review, **Un Ins 1221 et seq.**

Agricultural labor and employment, unpaid contributions,

License denial, **Labor 1690.1**

Notice, **Labor 1690.1; Un Ins 1141**

Appeals, **Un Ins 1241 et seq.**

Associations and societies, shareholders, officers and others, personal liability for nonpayment, **Un Ins 1735**

Offers in compromise, **Un Ins 1870 et seq.**

Bill of rights, **Un Ins 1231 et seq.**

Cancellation, erroneous assessment, **Un Ins 1136**

Computation,

Failure to make return, **Un Ins 1126**

Unsatisfactory return, **Un Ins 1127**

Corporations, shareholders, liability for nonpayments, **Un Ins 1735**

Deficiency, **Un Ins 1127, 1135**

Fraud, **Un Ins 1128**

Disability compensation, post

Election by employer that his services constitute employment, **Un Ins 708**

Erroneous, cancellation, **Un Ins 1136**

Estimate on failure to make return, **Un Ins 1126**

Fines and penalties, post

Indians, delinquency, notice, **Un Ins 1141.1**

Information, disclosure, **Un Ins 1095**

Interest, **Un Ins 1129**

Jeopardy assessments, **Un Ins 991, 1137, 1137.1**

Administrative appellate review, **Un Ins 1221 et seq.**

Notice, **Un Ins 1131**

Correction of errors, **Un Ins 1036**

Limitations, **Un Ins 1132**

Waiver of limitations, **Un Ins 1132**

Number, **Un Ins 1130**

Offset of overpayments against underpayments, **Un Ins 1130**

Overpayment of benefits, **Un Ins 1375.1**

Incorrect employer, **Un Ins 1127.5**

Notice, **Un Ins 1376**

Perishable goods, security deposit, **Un Ins 1137**

Reassessment,

Claim for refund, **Un Ins 1179.5**

UNEMPLOYMENT COMPENSATION
—Cont'd

Assessments—Cont'd

Reassessment—Cont'd

Payment before decision, **Un Ins 1179.5**

Reemployment activities, participation, eligibility, **Un Ins 1253**

Refunds, erroneous, **Un Ins 1184**

Returns,

Failure to make, **Un Ins 1126, 1128**

Unsatisfactory, **Un Ins 1127**

Security deposit, **Un Ins 1137**

Taxpayers Bill of Rights, **Un Ins 1231 et seq.**

Waiver, limitation period for notice, **Un Ins 1132**

Assignments,

Employing unit, information regarding, **Un Ins 1090**

Lien for unpaid contributions, interest and penalties, **Un Ins 1701**

Personal liability of assignee, **Un Ins 1736**

Under supplemental plans established by employer, **Un Ins 1342**

Assistants to individual employed by employing unit, **Un Ins 606**

Associations and Societies, this index

Athletics, this index

Attachment,

Benefits, supplemental plans established by employer, **Un Ins 1342**

Contributions, exemption, **Un Ins 988**

Fees, **Un Ins 1559**

Attorney general, actions to enforce liabilities, interstate cooperation, **Un Ins 453**

Attorneys,

Appearing before appeals board, **Un Ins 1957**

Authorization forms, representation before appeals board by counsel or agent, **Un Ins 1957.5**

Contributions to qualified group legal services, exclusions, **Un Ins 938.1**

Independent contractors, presumption, **Un Ins 656**

Presumption of independent contractor status, **Un Ins 656**

Representation of claimant by counsel or agent, authorization forms, **Un Ins 1957.5**

Audits and auditors,

Offers in compromise, **Un Ins 1873**

Underreported payroll, **Labor 90.7**

Authorized regulations, definitions, **Un Ins 127**

Average base pay roll, definitions, **Un Ins 905**

Average of wages, withholding tax on wages, **Un Ins 13023**

Balance. Funds, post

Bankruptcy, this index

Banks, deposit of money, **Un Ins 1501**

UNEMPLOYMENT COMPENSATION
—Cont'd

Base period,
Definitions, **Un Ins 1275**
Determination of quarter for which wages were highest, **Un Ins 1280**
Disability compensation, post
Employers, notice of computation, **Un Ins 1030**
Minimum earnings, **Un Ins 1281**
Baseball players, **Un Ins 653, 1253.4**
Benefit account. Funds, post
Benefit audit fund, **Un Ins 1595 et seq.**
Benefit Payments Department, generally, this index
Benefit year, definitions, **Un Ins 1276**
Benefits, **Un Ins 1251 et seq.**
Amount of benefits, generally, ante
Charges against employers account, voluntarily leaving employment or discharge by reason of misconduct, **Un Ins 1032**
Definitions, **Un Ins 128, 130.5, 140**
Deposit, **Un Ins 1375.1**
Extended benefits, training or retraining, **Un Ins 1271, 1271.5**
Reimbursement of benefits, generally, post
Retraining, generally, post
Wrongful discharge actions, setoff, **Un Ins 1382**
Better job, termination of employment, charges against employer, **Un Ins 1032**
Bids and bidding, training, contracts, **Un Ins 10205**
Bill of rights, taxpayers, **Un Ins 1231 et seq.**
Biologists, independent contractor status, presumption, **Un Ins 656**
Birth,
Disability, **Un Ins 2626**
Family care leave, **Un Ins 3300 et seq.**
Blind Persons, this index
Bond purchase plans, payments under or to not included as wages, **Un Ins 934**
Bonuses as wages, **Un Ins 926**
Books and papers,
Compelling production, **Un Ins 1953**
Failure to produce, **Un Ins 2104**
Offers in compromise, rescission, **Un Ins 1875**
Subpoena for production, **Un Ins 1953 et seq.**
Withholding tax on wages, **Un Ins 13011**
Bulk transfers,
Action against successor, contributions due, **Un Ins 1734**
Successor liability, **Un Ins 1731 et seq.**
Bulletins, providing upon request, **Un Ins 307**
Business, acquisition of business, successor liability, **Un Ins 1731 et seq.**
Business opportunity broker or salesman, **Un Ins 650**
Calendar quarter, definitions, **Un Ins 129**

UNEMPLOYMENT COMPENSATION
—Cont'd

Calendar week, definitions, wage reports, **Un Ins 1088**
California State University, disability compensation, elective coverage, **Un Ins 710.8**
CalWORKs. Social Services, this index
Camps, students, exclusions, **Un Ins 642.1**
Canada, performance of services, **Un Ins 603.5**
Cancellation of wage credits, **Un Ins 1260.1**
Career centers,
Handicapped persons, **Un Ins 18000 et seq.**
Job order sharing, **Un Ins 2061**
Caregiver training initiative, **Un Ins 11020 et seq.**
Cash remuneration, withholding tax on wages, **Un Ins 13025**
Cemetery broker or salesman, **Un Ins 650**
Certificates and certification,
Appeals board, powers, **Un Ins 1953**
Contribution due, certificate of bulk transfers, successors liability, **Un Ins 1732**
Delinquent contributions, evidence, **Un Ins 1854**
Disability compensation, post
Exemptions, withholding tax on wages, **Un Ins 13040 et seq.**
Family care leave, **Un Ins 2708**
Fraud,
Crimes and offenses, **Un Ins 2116**
Fines and penalties, **Un Ins 1143**
Judgment liens, release or subordination, **Un Ins 1817**
Lien for unpaid contributions, interest and penalties, **Un Ins 1703**
Payment of contributions, sale of business, **Un Ins 1731 et seq.**
Release or subordination or judgment lien, **Un Ins 1817**
Returns, failure to file, evidence, **Un Ins 2123**
Summary judgment, delinquent contributions, penalties, or interest, **Un Ins 1815 et seq.**
Certified nurse assistants, caregiver training initiative, **Un Ins 11020 et seq.**
Charging benefits to employers account, **Un Ins 4702**
Charitable and religious organizations, **Un Ins 641**
Excludable services for nonprofit organizations, **Un Ins 711**
Chemists, independent contractors status, presumption, **Un Ins 656**
Chief administrative law judge. Administrative law judges, ante
Child support. Support, this index
Childbirth, disability, definitions, **Un Ins 2626**
Children and minors,
Disclaimer of rights, **Un Ins 637.1**

UNEMPLOYMENT COMPENSATION
—Cont'd

Children and minors—Cont'd
Distribution of newspapers and magazines, **Un Ins 634.5, 649**
Employment of parents, coverage, **Un Ins 631, 702.5**
Family care leave, serious health conditions, **Un Ins 3300 et seq.**
Services performed for parents, **Un Ins 631**
Youthbuild program, **Un Ins 9800 et seq.**
Chiropractors, independent contractors, **Un Ins 656**
Citations, joint enforcement strike force on the underground economy, **Labor 106**
Cities,
Elective coverage, **Un Ins 709**
Voluntary plans, employee classifications, **Un Ins 709, 710**
Claims,
Actions and proceedings, generally, ante
Extended compensation, **Un Ins 3651 et seq., 4651 et seq.**
Family care leave, time, **Un Ins 3301**
Filing, new claims, **Un Ins 1342.1**
Fraud, penalties, **Un Ins 1144**
Notice of filing new or additional claim, **Un Ins 1030**
Primary claim, definitions, **Un Ins 3503**
Refunds and overpayments, post
Clearing account. Funds, post
Clergymen, **Un Ins 711**
Excluded services, **Un Ins 634.5**
Clinics, primary care clinics, health care practitioners, **Un Ins 656**
Clubs, domestic servants, **Un Ins 682**
Collection,
Actions and proceedings, ante
Bill of rights, **Un Ins 1231 et seq.**
Contributions, **Un Ins 301**
Additional remedies, **Un Ins 1860**
Bulk transfers, successor liability, **Un Ins 1734**
Delinquent contributions, interest and penalties, **Un Ins 1785 et seq., 1851 et seq.**
Jeopardy, **Un Ins 991, 1115**
Offers in compromise, **Un Ins 1870 et seq.**
Appeal and review, **Un Ins 1872**
Approval, **Un Ins 1871**
Claims for refunds, **Un Ins 1180.1**
Conditions, **Un Ins 1870**
Joint and several liability, **Un Ins 1874**
Notice, **Un Ins 1870**
Release, **Un Ins 1873**
Rescission, **Un Ins 1875**
Liens and incumbrances, **Un Ins 1703**
Satisfaction, **Un Ins 1873**
Statement, **Un Ins 1873**
Overpayment, **Un Ins 333, 334**

UNEMPLOYMENT COMPENSATION
—Cont'd

Collection—Cont'd

Overpayment—Cont'd

Disability compensation, **Un Ins 2735.1**

Refunds and overpayments, post

Taxpayers Bill of Rights, **Un Ins 1231 et seq.**

Withholding tax on wages, **Un Ins 13070 et seq.**

Collective bargaining. Labor Disputes, this index

Colleges and universities, **Un Ins 100 et seq., 711**

Clubs, domestic service, **Un Ins 639**

Community colleges and districts,

Chancellor, job preparation and training services, coordination, services and resources,

Elective coverage, governing boards, **Un Ins 709**

Public entity, definitions, **Un Ins 135, 605**

Disability compensation, elective coverage, **Un Ins 710.9**

Elective coverage, disability compensation, **Un Ins 710.9**

Governing boards, elective coverage, **Un Ins 709**

Information, disclosure, **Un Ins 1095**

Personnel commission, public entity, definitions, **Un Ins 135, 605**

Disability compensation, community colleges and districts, elective coverage, **Un Ins 710.9**

Elections for financing, **Un Ins 802, 803**

Elective coverage, **Un Ins 709**

Community colleges and districts, disability compensation, **Un Ins 710.9**

Eligibility, **Un Ins 1253.3**

Employer, definitions, **Un Ins 677**

Employing unit, **Un Ins 135**

Excludable services for nonprofit organizations, **Un Ins 711**

Fines and penalties, termination, reports, false statements, **Un Ins 1142.1**

Fraternities and sororities, domestic service, wages, **Un Ins 639**

Fraud, termination, reports, **Un Ins 1142.1**

Intermittent or adjunct instructor, application of law, **Un Ins 633**

Qualifications, **Un Ins 605**

Reports, false reports by employer, **Un Ins 1142.1**

Students, generally, post

Termination, employment, reports, false statements, **Un Ins 1142.1**

Comity, **Un Ins 451 et seq.**

Commercial fishermen, **Un Ins 1252.1, 1252.2**

Commissions,

Wages, **Un Ins 926**

UNEMPLOYMENT COMPENSATION
—Cont'd

Commissions—Cont'd

Warrant for collection of delinquent contributions, **Un Ins 1786, 1787**

Committees, joint enforcement strike force on the underground economy, **Un Ins 329**

Community chest, elections for financing, **Un Ins 801, 803**

Community colleges and districts. Colleges and universities, ante

Commutation, plans established by employers, **Un Ins 1342**

Compromise and settlement,

Definitions, tax disputes, **Un Ins 1236**

Penalties for violations, **Un Ins 2127**

Tax disputes, **Un Ins 1236**

Compulsory retirement, collective bargaining agreement,

Termination status, extended benefit purposes, **Un Ins 4701**

Voluntariness of employment termination, **Un Ins 3701**

Computations, **Un Ins 1275 et seq., 1329 et seq.**

Extended unemployment compensation, post

Withholding tax on wages, **Un Ins 13020**

Concealed wages, fines and penalties, **Un Ins 1128.1, 1735.1**

Concealment. Fraud, generally, post

Conditions of labor, refusal of new work, **Un Ins 1259**

Confidential or privileged information,

Contributions, **Un Ins 989**

Disclosure, **Un Ins 1094, 2111**

Felony arrest warrants issued for applicants, furnishing information to law enforcement agencies, **Un Ins 1095**

Preparers, withholding, **Un Ins 13019**

Tax paid, **Un Ins 989**

Withholding taxes, **Un Ins 13018**

Conflict of interest, administrative law judges, **Un Ins 404**

Consolidation of cases for hearing, **Un Ins 1951**

Conspiracy to obtain benefits, **Un Ins 2107**

Construction of law, **Un Ins 2, 4, 5, 125**

Contingent effect of certain statutes, **Un Ins 638**

Employers plan for supplemental payment of benefits, **Un Ins 1265**

Constructive knowledge, assistants to individual employed by employing unit, **Un Ins 606**

Consultants, qualifications, **Un Ins 656**

Contingent funds, **Un Ins 1585 et seq.**

Acquisition of trade or business, successors liability, **Un Ins 1731 et seq.**

Administration, **Un Ins 301**

Transfers, **Un Ins 1588**

Agricultural labor and employment, failure to remit,

License denial, **Labor 1690.1**

Notice, **Labor 1690.1; Un Ins 1141**

UNEMPLOYMENT COMPENSATION
—Cont'd

Contingent funds—Cont'd

Allocation of funds, augmentation of appropriations, **Un Ins 1586.5**

Allocation of payments, **Un Ins 1110.1**

Amount, **Un Ins 984**

Appropriations, **Un Ins 1586**

Continued in existence, **Un Ins 1585**

Controller, state, filing claim for refund with, **Un Ins 1589**

Definitions, **Un Ins 130**

Deposits, **Un Ins 1526.3**

Interest and penalties, **Un Ins 1585**

Expenditures, **Un Ins 1588**

Interest, **Un Ins 1536**

Deposit in, **Un Ins 1585**

Penalties, **Un Ins 1536**

Deposit in, **Un Ins 1585**

Refunds, **Un Ins 1589**

Rental payments deposited in, **Un Ins 1585**

Transfers, **Un Ins 1588, 1590**

Warrants, **Un Ins 1589**

Unclaimed, effect, **Un Ins 1537**

Continuous employment, elective coverage, approval, **Un Ins 704 et seq.**

Continuous review of decisions, chief administrative law judge, **Un Ins 406**

Contracts. Training, post

Contributions, **Un Ins 901 et seq., 1241 et seq.**

Accrual, **Un Ins 976**

Acquisition, **Un Ins 930.5**

Rates and charges, **Un Ins 336**

Successors, liability, **Un Ins 1731 et seq.**

Additional, **Un Ins 992 et seq.**

Administration, **Un Ins 301**

Administrative appellate review, **Un Ins 1221 et seq.**

Agricultural labor and employment, ante

Amount, **Un Ins 984**

Appeals, **Un Ins 1241 et seq.**

Application of definitions, **Un Ins 901**

Assessments, contributions on tips and gratuities in excess of other wages, reports, **Un Ins 1088.6**

Attachment, exemption from, **Un Ins 988**

Average base payroll, definitions, **Un Ins 905**

Bankruptcy of employer,

Effect, **Un Ins 988**

Employing unit, information regarding, **Un Ins 1090**

Bill of rights, **Un Ins 1231 et seq.**

Bonuses, **Un Ins 926**

Bulk transfers, successor liability, **Un Ins 1731 et seq.**

Business expenses or allowance, **Un Ins 929**

California Industries for the Blind, elections for financing, **Un Ins 802, 803**

UNEMPLOYMENT

UNEMPLOYMENT COMPENSATION
—Cont'd
Contributions—Cont'd
  Choice, table and schedule used, statement, **Un Ins 979**
  Collection, **Un Ins 301**
    Additional remedies, **Un Ins 1860**
    Bulk transfers, successor liability, **Un Ins 1734**
    Offers in compromise, **Un Ins 1870 et seq.**
    Taxpayers Bill of Rights, **Un Ins 1231 et seq.**
  Colleges and universities, elections for financing, **Un Ins 802, 803**
  Commissions, **Un Ins 926**
  Community chest, elections for financing, **Un Ins 801, 803**
  Compromise and settlement, tax disputes, **Un Ins 1236**
  Computation date, definitions, **Un Ins 902**
  Concealed wages, fines and penalties, **Un Ins 1128.1, 1735.1**
  Contributions paid on his own behalf, definitions, **Un Ins 906**
  Corporation with sole stockholder, exemption, **Un Ins 637.1**
  Credits,
    Excess employee contributions, **Un Ins 1176.5**
    Training projects, funding, **Un Ins 10215**
  Crimes and offenses, **Un Ins 1145, 2101 et seq.**
    Failure to withhold or pay, **Un Ins 2118, 2118.5**
  Deductions greater than required, **Un Ins 2103**
  Definitions, **Un Ins 131**
  Delinquency, **Un Ins 1110, 1115, 1703**
    Agricultural labor and employment,
    License denial, **Labor 1690.1**
    Notice, **Labor 1690.1; Un Ins 1141**
    Garnishment, **Un Ins 1755 et seq.**
    Indians, finance, elections, **Un Ins 803**
    Judgment liens, release or subordination, **Un Ins 1817**
    Liability by contract, **Un Ins 1110.6**
    Notices of levy, **Un Ins 1755 et seq.**
  Deposit, clearing account, **Un Ins 1526**
  Disability compensation, post
  Due date, quitting business, **Un Ins 1116**
  Election by employer that his services constitute employment, **Un Ins 708, 984.5**
  Emergency solvency surcharge rate, **Un Ins 977.5**
  Employee contributions, **Un Ins 984 et seq.**
  Employment training fund,
    Employer, **Un Ins 976.6**
    Negative reserve account balance, **Un Ins 976.8**

UNEMPLOYMENT COMPENSATION
—Cont'd
Contributions—Cont'd
  Erroneous payment to other state or federal agency, **Un Ins 991**
  Evading, injunctions, **Un Ins 1855**
  Excess employee contributions,
    Credits and refunds, **Un Ins 1176.5**
    State income tax credit or refund, **Rev & T 17061; Un Ins 1176, 1185**
  Exchange of money, concealment of wages, fines and penalties, **Un Ins 1128.1, 1735.1**
  Exclusion from wages of certain amounts paid to employee, **Un Ins 931 et seq.**
  Execution, exemption from, **Un Ins 988**
  Exemptions,
    Judicial process, **Un Ins 988**
    Sole stockholder and his corporation, **Un Ins 637.1**
  Extension of time for payment, **Un Ins 1111**
  Failure or refusal to make, **Un Ins 2108, 2110**
    Elective coverage, **Un Ins 704, 704.1**
    Liability of corporation and association officers, **Un Ins 1735**
      Offers in compromise, **Un Ins 1870 et seq.**
  Final return, **Un Ins 1116**
  Fines and penalties, post
  Fraud, rates and charges, **Un Ins 977, 1036, 2101.6**
  Funds transfers, payment, **Un Ins 1110**
  Garnishment, exemption from, **Un Ins 988**
  Governmental entity, election to become employer, **Un Ins 710**
  Gratuities as wages, **Un Ins 927**
  Hospital, elections for financing, **Un Ins 802, 803**
  Indians,
    Delinquency, notice, **Un Ins 1119**
    Finance, elections, **Un Ins 802, 803**
  Injunction, inducing violations, **Un Ins 1855**
  Insolvency, **Un Ins 1115**
    Effect, **Un Ins 988**
  Interest, **Un Ins 1111, 1113**
    Collection, **Un Ins 301**
    Deposit in contingent fund, **Un Ins 1585**
  Jeopardy assessment and collection, **Un Ins 991, 1115**
    Administrative appellate review, **Un Ins 1221 et seq.**
  Joint accounts,
    Elective financing, **Un Ins 802**
    Two or more nonprofit organizations, **Un Ins 711**
  Liability,
    Corporation and association officers, shareholders and others, nonpayment, **Un Ins 1735, 1735.1**

UNEMPLOYMENT COMPENSATION
—Cont'd
Contributions—Cont'd
  Liability—Cont'd
    Corporation and association officers, shareholders and others, nonpayment—Cont'd
      Offers in compromise, **Un Ins 1870 et seq.**
    Employee contributions withheld, **Un Ins 987**
    Lien for unpaid contributions, **Un Ins 1701 et seq.**
    Maximum wages considered, **Un Ins 930, 930.1**
    Multiple employees, overpayment, refunds, **Un Ins 1176.5**
    Net balance of reserve, definitions, **Un Ins 904**
    New employers, rates and charges, **Un Ins 982**
    Nonprofit organizations,
      Credit for prior contributions, **Un Ins 712**
      Elected coverage, **Un Ins 702.1**
      Selection of method, **Un Ins 711**
      Elections for financing, **Un Ins 801, 803**
    Other states, erroneous payments to, **Un Ins 991**
    Out of state remuneration, **Un Ins 930.1**
    Overdeductions from employees, **Un Ins 2103**
    Payment, **Un Ins 976, 1110 et seq.**
      Allocation, **Un Ins 1110.1**
        License denial, **Labor 1690.1**
        Notice, **Labor 1690.1; Un Ins 1141**
      Bill of rights, **Un Ins 1231 et seq.**
      Erroneous payments to other state or federal agency, **Un Ins 991**
      Failure to pay, crimes, **Un Ins 2118, 2118.5**
      Fractions of cent, **Un Ins 990**
      Liability of corporation and association officers, shareholders and others, **Un Ins 1735, 1735.1**
        Offers in compromise, **Un Ins 1870 et seq.**
      Reported contributions, **Un Ins 1110 et seq.**
      Taxpayers Bill of Rights, **Un Ins 1231 et seq.**
    Payroll records, employee contributions, **Un Ins 986**
    Personal liability, corporation and association officers, shareholders and others, nonpayment, **Un Ins 1735, 1735.1**
      Offers in compromise, **Un Ins 1870 et seq.**
    Pooling, **Un Ins 1025**
    Priority, lien for unpaid contributions, **Un Ins 1701 et seq.**
    Protests, **Un Ins 1034, 1037**
      Referees, **Un Ins 1035**

UNEMPLOYMENT COMPENSATION
—Cont'd—
Contributions—Cont'd
Public housing administration agency, elections for financing, **Un Ins 802, 803**
Rates and charges, **Un Ins 976 et seq.**
Acquisition, **Un Ins 336**
New employers, **Un Ins 982**
Balance in fund, determination, **Un Ins 980**
Bill of rights, **Un Ins 1231 et seq.**
Choice, table and schedule used, statement, **Un Ins 979**
Compromise and settlement, tax disputes, **Un Ins 1236**
Correction of errors, **Un Ins 1036**
Determination, **Un Ins 301, 984**
Emergency solvency surcharge rate, **Un Ins 977.5**
Employee contributions, **Un Ins 984 et seq.**
Fraud, **Un Ins 977, 1036, 2101.6**
Fund balance, under or over specified percentage, **Un Ins 977**
Increase or decrease, worker contributions, **Un Ins 984**
Inspection, **Un Ins 989**
Minimum, **Un Ins 982**
Motion picture payroll services company, employer or employing unit, **Un Ins 679**
Net balance of reserve, effect, **Un Ins 977**
New employers, **Un Ins 982**
Notification or statement of rate, **Un Ins 1033**
Protest, **Un Ins 1034, 1037**
Publication, **Un Ins 989**
Reduced rates, eligibility, **Un Ins 982**
Self employment, **Un Ins 984.5**
Settlement, tax disputes, **Un Ins 1236**
Tables, **Un Ins 977**
Taxpayers Bill of Rights, **Un Ins 1231 et seq.**
Transfer of reserve account, effect, **Un Ins 1060**
Rating period, definitions, **Un Ins 903**
Reciprocity, **Un Ins 456**
Records and recordation, amount, **Un Ins 984, 984.5**
Refunds,
Erroneous or illegal collection, **Un Ins 1177**
Several employers, **Un Ins 1176, 1176.5**
Reimbursement financing, reserve accounts, **Un Ins 801.5, 1051.5**
Remuneration paid in another state, **Un Ins 930.1**
Reports,
Crimes and offenses, **Un Ins 1145**
Employers, **Un Ins 1088**
Errors, excusable neglect, **Un Ins 1113.1**
Periods, **Un Ins 1115**

UNEMPLOYMENT COMPENSATION
—Cont'd—
Contributions—Cont'd
School employees funds, **Un Ins 823**
Self employment, rate, **Un Ins 984.5**
Settlement, tax disputes, **Un Ins 1236**
Sole stockholder, exemption, **Un Ins 637.1**
Statements, table and schedule used, **Un Ins 979**
Summary judgment, delinquent contributions, **Un Ins 1815 et seq.**
Taxpayers Bill of Rights, **Un Ins 1231 et seq.**
Time for payment, **Un Ins 1110**
Contract, **Un Ins 1110.6**
Tips, **Un Ins 927**
Transmission, **Un Ins 986**
Underpayments, penalty, **Un Ins 1113.1**
Unpaid contributions, **Un Ins 2108, 2110**
Liens and incumbrances, post
Warrant for collection of delinquent contributions, **Un Ins 1785 et seq.**
Willful failure or refusal to pay contributions, **Un Ins 2108**
Withholding,
Bill of rights, **Un Ins 1231 et seq.**
Bulk transfers, successor liability, **Un Ins 1731 et seq.**
Disability compensation, post
Employee contributions, **Un Ins 986**
Failure to withhold, crimes, **Un Ins 2118, 2118.5**
Money or property, unpaid contributions, **Un Ins 1731 et seq.**
Nonprofit organization, **Un Ins 711**
Taxpayers Bill of Rights, **Un Ins 1231 et seq.**
Workers, or employees, definitions, **Un Ins 144**
Conviction of offense, **Un Ins 1030.1, 1256.1**
Election coverage,
Approval, **Un Ins 704**
Termination, **Un Ins 704.1**
False statements or concealment, disqualification, duration, **Un Ins 1263**
Cooperation, interstate and federal, **Un Ins 451 et seq.**
Copies, records and recordation, **Un Ins 1095**
Corporate officers and directors, **Un Ins 622, 637**
Corporations,
Contributions, nonpayment, liability of officers, shareholders and others, **Un Ins 1735**
Definitions, withholding tax on wages, **Un Ins 13003**
Directors, **Un Ins 637, 637.1**
Dissolution, final return, **Un Ins 1116**
Employing unit, **Un Ins 135**
Exemption from contributions, corporation with sole stockholder, **Un Ins 637.1**

UNEMPLOYMENT COMPENSATION
—Cont'd—
Corporations—Cont'd
Officers and employees,
Contributions, liability for nonpayment, **Un Ins 1735**
Final return, liability for failure to file, **Un Ins 1735**
Sole shareholders and agricultural corporations, **Un Ins 637**
Sole shareholders, **Un Ins 637**
Correct employer, determination, **Un Ins 1127.5**
Correctional Institutions, this index
Costs,
Appeal, **Un Ins 1958**
Reciprocity, **Un Ins 453**
Disclosure, applicant information, **Un Ins 1095**
Investigations, persons convicted of violation of chapter, **Un Ins 2126**
Counterclaim. Setoff and counterclaim, generally, post
Counties,
Domestic employees, **Un Ins 683**
Elective coverage, **Un Ins 709**
Employing unit, **Un Ins 135**
In home supportive services program, domestic employees, coverage, **Un Ins 683**
Job preparation and training services, generally, post
Public entity, definitions, **Un Ins 135, 605**
County Officers and Employees, this index
County superintendent of schools, elective coverage, **Un Ins 709**
Court reporters, transcription performed away from office, **Un Ins 630**
Coverage. Elective coverage, generally, post
Credit cards, domestic service employers, contributions, payment, **Un Ins 1118**
Creditors, exemption of benefits from plans established by employers, **Un Ins 1342**
Credits,
Administration, **Un Ins 301**
Allowance, **Un Ins 1178**
Contributions, employers, training project funding, **Un Ins 10215**
Employing unit overpayment, **Un Ins 1177.5**
Excess employee contributions, **Un Ins 1176.5**
Notice of denial, **Un Ins 1180**
Waiver, **Un Ins 1179**
Crimes and offenses, **Un Ins 2101 et seq.**
Applicants accused of felonies, furnishing information to law enforcement agencies, **Un Ins 1095**
Benefit information, failure to post, **Un Ins 1089**
Confidential or privileged information, Disclosure, **Un Ins 1094, 1095**
Withholding taxes, **Un Ins 13018**

UNEMPLOYMENT

UNEMPLOYMENT COMPENSATION
—Cont'd

Crimes and offenses—Cont'd
Contributions, **Un Ins 1145**
Failure to pay or withhold, **Un Ins 2118, 2118.5**
Conviction constituting voluntary leaving of work, **Un Ins 1030.1, 1256.1**
Divulging confidential information, **Un Ins 2111**
Elective coverage,
Approval, conviction, **Un Ins 704**
Termination, **Un Ins 704.1**
Employers or employing units, false reports, **Un Ins 2115**
Fictitious employers, employees or wages, **Un Ins 2114**
Fraud, generally, post
Information requirements, **Un Ins 1089**
Offers in compromise, **Un Ins 1870 et seq.**
Restitution for overpayment of benefits in lieu of criminal proceeding, **Un Ins 2113**
Victims, restitution, information, **Un Ins 1095**
Violations, sentencing and fines, **Un Ins 2122**
Custodial institution inmates, excluded services, **Un Ins 634.5**
Data, joint enforcement strike force on the underground economy, **Un Ins 329**
Deaf,
Hearing impaired persons, employment services, **Un Ins 11000 et seq.**
School for the deaf, nonprofessional employees, **Un Ins 1451 et seq.**
Death benefits,
Due deceased persons, payment, **Un Ins 1341**
Wages, exclusion, **Un Ins 938**
Death in immediate family, **Un Ins 1253.1, 1253.12**
Decedents estates,
Notice of claims, **Un Ins 1090**
Payment, **Un Ins 1341**
Deceit. Fraud, generally, post
Decisions and orders. Appeals boards, ante
Declaratory judgments, appeals board, **Un Ins 409.1, 409.2**
Decrees. Judgments and decrees, generally, post
Deductions,
Child support obligations of claimants, **Un Ins 1255.7**
Compensation and salaries, **Un Ins 3260, 3260.5**
Withholding tax, **Un Ins 13021**
Notice, **Un Ins 1342.1**
Default, restitution arrangement, overpayment of benefits, **Un Ins 2113**
Deferred compensation plans,
Exempt governmental deferred compensation plans, **Un Ins 934**

UNEMPLOYMENT COMPENSATION
—Cont'd

Deferred compensation plans—Cont'd
Income tax, application of law, **Un Ins 13003**
Rules and regulations, **Un Ins 928**
Definitions, **Un Ins 8 et seq., 125 et seq., 1252 et seq.**
American aircraft, **Un Ins 125.3**
American employer, **Un Ins 125.4**
American vessel, **Un Ins 125.5**
Benefit audit fund, **Un Ins 130.5**
Calendar week, wage reports, **Un Ins 1088**
Child support obligations, deductions and withholding, **Un Ins 1255.7**
Demand occupations, training and retraining, **Un Ins 1270**
Department, **Un Ins 133**
Employment training panel, **Un Ins 10201**
Director, **Un Ins 134**
Disability benefits, **Un Ins 140.5**
Disability compensation, post
Eligible participants, employment training panel, **Un Ins 10201**
Employee, **Un Ins 621, 622**
Contractors, **Un Ins 621.5**
Employee contributions, **Un Ins 144**
Employer, **Un Ins 675 et seq.**
Domestic service, **Un Ins 684**
Employment training panel, **Un Ins 10201**
In home supportive services, **Un Ins 685**
Transfer of accounts, **Un Ins 1057, 1058**
Employing unit, **Un Ins 135**
Agricultural labor, **Un Ins 676**
Employment, **Un Ins 601 et seq., 2606.5**
Entity, **Un Ins 803**
Exhaustee, extended compensation, **Un Ins 3503**
Extended benefit period, **Un Ins 3503**
Extended duration award, **Un Ins 3503**
Extended duration benefits, **Un Ins 3503**
Extended duration period, extended compensation, **Un Ins 3503**
Federal Unemployment Tax Act, **Un Ins 136**
Fund, employment training fund, **Un Ins 10201**
Good cause, leaving employment, **Un Ins 1256**
Insured unemployment rate, extended benefits, **Un Ins 3503**
Joint venture, transfer of accounts, **Un Ins 1058**
Labor market areas, training or retraining, **Un Ins 1270**
Most recent work, **Un Ins 1256.3**
Nonprofit organization, **Un Ins 702.1, 711**
Contributions, **Un Ins 801**

UNEMPLOYMENT COMPENSATION
—Cont'd

Definitions—Cont'd
Nonqualified deferred compensation plan, **Un Ins 928.5**
Normal benefits, extended compensation, **Un Ins 3503**
Panel, employment training panel, **Un Ins 10201**
Parent benefit year, extended compensation, **Un Ins 3503**
Parent unemployment compensation claim, training, extended benefits, **Un Ins 1271**
Pay period, **Un Ins 607**
Payment, wages, **Un Ins 931**
Performance based, training or retraining, demand occupations, **Un Ins 1270**
Primary claim, extended compensation, **Un Ins 3503**
Public employment office, **Un Ins 137**
Public entity, **Un Ins 135, 605**
Rating period, **Un Ins 903**
Regulations, **Un Ins 127**
Remuneration, out of state remuneration, **Un Ins 930.1**
Services in his capacity as a director, **Un Ins 622**
State, **Un Ins 139**
Third parties, payers, wages, reports, **Un Ins 13009.5**
Training agencies, employment training panel, **Un Ins 10201**
Training or retraining benefits, allowances, or stipends, demand occupations, **Un Ins 1273**
Unemployed, **Un Ins 1252**
Unemployed individual, **Un Ins 1252**
Unemployment insurance, **Un Ins 141**
United States, **Un Ins 142.5**
Valid claim, **Un Ins 1276**
Wages, **Un Ins 926 et seq., 1277 et seq.**
Deferred compensation plans, **Un Ins 928.5**
Week, **Un Ins 143**
Worker contributions, **Un Ins 144**
Delegation of powers, **Un Ins 6**
Delinquency,
Contributions, ante
Indians,
Finance, elections, **Un Ins 803**
Notice, **Un Ins 804, 1119, 1141.1**
Demand occupations, training or retraining, **Un Ins 1266 et seq.**
Denial of claim, **Un Ins 1326**
Dentists, presumption of independent contractor status, **Un Ins 656**
Department of employment development contingent fund, **Un Ins 1585**
Departments,
Benefit Payments Department, generally, this index
Definitions, **Un Ins 133**
Employment training panel, **Un Ins 10201**

UNEMPLOYMENT COMPENSATION
—Cont'd
Departments—Cont'd
Employment Development Department, generally, this index
Dependent care assistance, exclusion, **Un Ins 938.3**
Deposit account, **Un Ins 1501**
Deposit of funds in state treasury, **Un Ins 1526.1 et seq.**
Depositions, **Un Ins 1953**
Determination,
Disability compensation, post
Potential eligibility, training, demand occupations, **Un Ins 1268**
Developmental services department, furnishing information, **Un Ins 1095**
Directors,
Corporations and associations, **Un Ins 622, 637, 637.1**
Definitions, **Un Ins 134**
Economically disadvantaged areas, designation, **Un Ins 9602**
Interested party to all appeals, **Un Ins 1377, 2707.2, 2737, 3655**
Tax disputes, settlement, **Un Ins 1236**
Disability base period, trade disputes, computation, **Un Ins 2658**
Disability compensation, **Un Ins 1277, 2601 et seq.**
Accounts and accounting,
Administration account, **Un Ins 3051**
Benefit payment account, **Un Ins 3075**
Voluntary plans, **Un Ins 3261**
Actions and proceedings, recovery of overpayment, **Un Ins 2739**
Enforcement, **Un Ins 2742**
Administration account, **Un Ins 3051**
Administrative expenses, **Un Ins 3012, 3013**
Voluntary plans, **Un Ins 3269**
Affidavits,
Claims, filing by spouse, mentally deficient claimant, **Un Ins 2705.1**
Trainees, military service, establishing benefit balance, **Un Ins 2768**
Alcoholic recovery home residents, **Un Ins 2626.1**
Appeal and review,
Computation of benefits, **Un Ins 2707.4, 2707.5**
Protests, extension of time, good cause, **Un Ins 2707.4**
Determination as to eligibility for benefits, **Un Ins 2707.2**
Director, interested party, **Un Ins 1377, 2707.2, 2737, 3655**
Eligibility determination, good cause, extension of time, **Un Ins 2707.2**
Interested parties, **Un Ins 2707.5**
Liability, benefits received pending appeal, **Un Ins 2740**
Overpayments, **Un Ins 2737, 2738**
Determinations, good cause, extension of time, **Un Ins 2737**

UNEMPLOYMENT COMPENSATION
—Cont'd
Disability compensation—Cont'd
Appeal and review—Cont'd
Voluntary plans, **Un Ins 3264**
Appeals boards,
Dispute as to fund from which benefits payable, **Un Ins 2712**
Overpayments, review, **Un Ins 2737, 2738**
Voluntary plans, **Un Ins 3264**
Application of law, **Un Ins 2602**
Armenians, genocide, reduction of benefits, **Un Ins 2629.5**
Assessments, **Un Ins 3265**
Administrative expenses, **Un Ins 3269**
Insured, **Un Ins 3259**
Overpayment, **Un Ins 2735.1**
Refunds of excess contributions, **Un Ins 3266**
Reimbursement of disability fund, **Un Ins 2712.5**
Tips and gratuities in excess of other wages, **Un Ins 987.7**
Reports, **Un Ins 1088.6**
Assignment of claims to state, military service of United States, **Un Ins 2772**
Audits and auditors, fund, **Un Ins 3051**
Base period,
Determination after military service, **Un Ins 2768**
Extension of benefits, **Un Ins 2612**
Industrial disability, **Un Ins 2775 et seq.**
Quarter in which wages were highest, determination, **Un Ins 2655**
Bonds,
Custodian of fund, **Un Ins 3002**
Voluntary plans, **Un Ins 3258**
California State University, elective coverage, **Un Ins 710.8**
Certificates and certification,
Filing, **Un Ins 2627**
Fraud, **Un Ins 1143**
Supporting claim, **Un Ins 2708 et seq.**
Continued medical certification, filing, time, **Un Ins 2706.2**
Change in contribution rate or disability benefit amounts to protect solvency of disability fund, **Un Ins 984, 2604**
Charge against employers account, **Un Ins 2603**
Child support obligations, deduction and withholding from claimants, **Un Ins 1255.7**
Children, payments to, **Un Ins 2702**
Chiropodist, certificate of disability, **Un Ins 2708 et seq.**
Cities, voluntary plans, **Un Ins 710**
Claims, **Un Ins 2701 et seq.**
Excess contributions, payment, **Un Ins 3009**
Filing by spouse, mentally deficient claimant, **Un Ins 2705.1**
Necessity of filing, **Un Ins 2627**

UNEMPLOYMENT COMPENSATION
—Cont'd
Disability compensation—Cont'd
Collection,
Contributions, **Un Ins 2903**
Overpayments, **Un Ins 2735.1**
Colleges and universities, community colleges and districts, elective coverage, **Un Ins 710.9**
Compromise and release agreement, discharge of claim of lien, **Un Ins 2741**
Computation of benefits, **Un Ins 2707.3 et seq.**
Protests, appeals, extension of time, good cause, **Un Ins 2707.4**
Confidential medical records, **Un Ins 2714**
Conflicts with unemployment compensation provisions, **Un Ins 2602**
Construction of law, **Un Ins 2601**
Continued medical certification, filing, time, **Un Ins 2706.2**
Contributions, **Un Ins 2901 et seq.**
Assessment, contributions on tips and gratuities in excess of other wages, **Un Ins 987.7**
Collection, **Un Ins 2903**
Elective coverage, employee contributions, **Un Ins 984.5**
Employee contributions, deposit in disability fund, **Un Ins 3008**
Employees, **Un Ins 984, 2901 et seq.**
Excess employee contributions, refunds, **Un Ins 1185**
Fund, **Un Ins 984, 3004**
Payment, **Un Ins 2903**
Rate,
Change, **Un Ins 984, 2604**
Determination, **Un Ins 984**
Religious beliefs, exemption, **Un Ins 2902**
Self employment, election, **Un Ins 708.5, 984.5**
Tips and gratuities as wages, withholding, **Un Ins 987.7**
Reports, **Un Ins 1088.6**
Voluntary plans, **Un Ins 3252**
Counties, voluntary plans, **Un Ins 710**
Credits, income tax—state, overpayments, **Un Ins 1185**
Criminal violations, incarceration, eligibility, **Un Ins 2680, 2681**
Death before making claim, **Un Ins 2705**
Deductions,
Child support obligations of claimants, **Un Ins 1255.7**
Notice, **Un Ins 1342.1**
Definitions, **Un Ins 140.5, 2602, 2626**
Disability base period, **Un Ins 2610, 2611**
Disability benefit period, **Un Ins 2608**
Disability benefits, **Un Ins 140.5**
Disability or disabled, **Un Ins 2626**
Eligible persons, **Un Ins 3012**

UNEMPLOYMENT

UNEMPLOYMENT COMPENSATION
—Cont'd
Disability compensation—Cont'd
Definitions—Cont'd
Employees, voluntary plans, **Un Ins 3254**
Employer, **Un Ins 676**
Employment, **Un Ins 2606**
Mentally unable to make a claim, **Un Ins 2705.1**
Military service, **Un Ins 2766**
Trainees, **Un Ins 2767**
Valid claim, **Un Ins 2609**
Dentist, certificate of disability, **Un Ins 2708 et seq.**
Determination,
Eligibility, **Un Ins 2707.2**
Overpayment, **Un Ins 2736**
Weekly wage, irregular payment of wages, **Un Ins 2657**
Dipsomaniacs, **Un Ins 2678**
Director, interested party to all appeals, **Un Ins 2707.2, 2737**
Disability administration account, **Un Ins 3051**
Disability base period, definitions, **Un Ins 2610, 2611**
Disability benefit payment account, **Un Ins 3075**
Disability benefit period,
Definitions, **Un Ins 2608**
Establishment, effect as to unemployment compensation, **Un Ins 2703**
Disability of disabled, definitions, **Un Ins 2626**
Dispute as to fund from which payable, **Un Ins 2712**
Disqualifications for benefits, **Un Ins 2675 et seq.**
Domestic or marital duties causing resignation, **Un Ins 1264**
Domestic partnership, filing, claims, **Un Ins 2705.1**
Domestic service, application of law, **Un Ins 684**
Drug addicts, **Un Ins 2678**
Drug free residential facility residents, **Un Ins 2626.2**
Education, benefits and rights, **Un Ins 2613**
Elective coverage,
Approval, **Un Ins 704 et seq.**
California State University, **Un Ins 710.8**
Contributions, **Un Ins 984.5**
Indians, **Un Ins 709, 710.6**
Self employment, **Un Ins 708.5**
State, **Un Ins 710.7**
State residents covered under laws of another state lacking disability program, **Un Ins 702.6**
Eligibility, **Un Ins 2625 et seq.**
Alcoholic recovery home residents, **Un Ins 2626.1**
Cities, **Un Ins 710**
Counties, **Un Ins 710**

UNEMPLOYMENT COMPENSATION
—Cont'd
Disability compensation—Cont'd
Eligibility—Cont'd
Criminal conduct, incarceration, **Un Ins 2680, 2681**
Disqualification for unemployment compensation, **Un Ins 1253.5, 1255.5**
Holocaust, restitution, **Un Ins 2629.5**
Voluntary plans, **Un Ins 3253**
Eligible persons, definitions, **Un Ins 3012**
Employees, definitions, voluntary plans, **Un Ins 3254**
Employers Liability Law, receiving benefits from, effect, **Un Ins 2629**
Employment,
Definitions, **Un Ins 2606 et seq.**
Self employment, elective coverage, **Un Ins 708.5**
Establishment of claim after disqualification, **Un Ins 2676, 2677**
Exclusion from wages, **Un Ins 931, 933**
Extension of time, **Un Ins 2612**
Appeals, good cause,
Computation protests, **Un Ins 2707.4**
Eligibility determinations, **Un Ins 2707.2**
Filing claim, **Un Ins 2706.1**
False claims, foreign physicians and surgeons, procedures, **Un Ins 2708**
Family care leave, **Un Ins 3300 et seq.**
Federal claims arising from military service, assignment to state, **Un Ins 2772**
Federal Unemployment Tax Act, nonconformity with provisions, **Un Ins 2605**
Filing benefit claims, **Un Ins 2701 et seq.**
Spouse, mentally deficient claimant, **Un Ins 2705.1**
Findings, requisites, **Un Ins 2627**
Fines and penalties, fraud, **Un Ins 1143**
First benefit payment, time, **Un Ins 2701.5**
First claim, time for filing, **Un Ins 2706.1**
Foreign physicians and surgeons, false claims investigations, procedures, **Un Ins 2708**
Foreign states,
Alcohol recovery home residents, **Un Ins 2626.1**
Drug free residential facility residents, **Un Ins 2626.2**
Form, filing claim, **Un Ins 2706.1**
Fraud, **Un Ins 1143, 2116, 2675**
Assessments, **Un Ins 2735.1**
Overpayments, **Un Ins 2735, 2736**
Funds, **Un Ins 3001 et seq.**
Administration, **Un Ins 3001**
Account, **Un Ins 3051**
Expenses, **Un Ins 3012, 3013**

UNEMPLOYMENT COMPENSATION
—Cont'd
Disability compensation—Cont'd
Funds—Cont'd
Appropriation, **Un Ins 3012**
Audit, **Un Ins 3051**
Benefit payment account, **Un Ins 3075**
Bond of custodian, **Un Ins 3002**
Change in rate or benefits, **Un Ins 2604**
Composition, **Un Ins 3004**
Continued in existence, **Un Ins 3001**
Contributions, **Un Ins 2110.3 et seq., 3004**
Custodian, **Un Ins 3002**
Definitions, **Un Ins 134.5**
Depositary, **Un Ins 3075**
Deposits, **Un Ins 1526.2**
Disability administration account, **Un Ins 3051**
Disability benefit payment account, **Un Ins 3075**
Dispute as to fund from which benefits payable, **Un Ins 2712**
Employees, contributions, **Un Ins 2901 et seq.**
Failure to reimburse fund, **Un Ins 2712.5**
Finance department, investments, **Un Ins 3002**
Interest, **Un Ins 3003**
Payment, **Un Ins 3009, 3012**
Investment, **Un Ins 3002, 3003**
Judgments, payment, **Un Ins 3009, 3012**
Liability of officer of corporate employee, **Un Ins 1735**
Limitation of actions, **Un Ins 3010**
Notice, election to come under provisions of surplus money investment fund, **Un Ins 3002**
Payment,
Credits, erroneously collected contributions, **Un Ins 3009**
Refunds or judgments, **Un Ins 3012**
Protection of solvency, **Un Ins 2604**
Refunds,
Limitation of actions, **Un Ins 3010**
Payments, **Un Ins 3009, 3012**
Reports, **Un Ins 995**
Revolving fund, **Un Ins 3051**
State treasurer, duties, **Un Ins 3002**
Surplus money investment fund, **Un Ins 3002**
Transfers,
General fund, **Un Ins 1176**
Surplus money in investment fund, **Un Ins 3002**
Unemployment trust fund, **Un Ins 3006**
Unencumbered balance, **Un Ins 1590**
Trust, **Un Ins 3001**
Unclaimed, warrants, **Un Ins 3011**

UNEMPLOYMENT COMPENSATION
—Cont'd
Disability compensation—Cont'd
Funds—Cont'd
Unemployed disabled account, **Un Ins 3012**
Unemployment trust fund, requisition, **Un Ins 3006**
United States, money received from, **Un Ins 3004, 3005**
Voluntary plans,
Coverage, **Un Ins 3253**
Employees covered, **Un Ins 3253**
Payments from, **Un Ins 3252**
Vouchers, administration account, **Un Ins 3051**
Warrants, **Un Ins 3075**
Payment of refunds or judgments, **Un Ins 3009**
Withdrawals, **Un Ins 3014**
Garnishment, refunds and overpayments, service of process, **CCP 706.101**
Governor, notice of change in rate of contributions or benefits, **Un Ins 2604**
Hearings,
Appeal of overpayment, **Un Ins 2737**
Closed, **Un Ins 2713**
Holocaust, restitution, **Un Ins 2629.5**
In home supportive services, application of law, **Un Ins 685**
Income tax—state, credits, overpayments, **Un Ins 1185**
Indians, elective coverage, **Un Ins 709, 710.6**
Industrial disability, **Un Ins 2775 et seq.**
Information,
Claims,
Procedure, posting by employer, **Un Ins 2706**
Submission of notices, protests and information, **Un Ins 2707.6**
Furnished by employer, **Un Ins 2707.1**
Inspection of medical records, **Un Ins 2714**
Interest,
Overpayments, **Un Ins 1185**
Payment, **Un Ins 3009, 3012**
Interested parties, appeals, **Un Ins 2707.5**
Investments, **Un Ins 3002, 3003**
Judgments, payment, **Un Ins 3009, 3012**
Labor disputes, **Un Ins 2677**
Liability for overpayments, **Un Ins 2735**
Liens,
Discharge, **Un Ins 2741**
Workers compensation, **Labor 3865; Un Ins 2629.1, 2735.5, 2741**
Limitation of actions,
Recovery of overpayments, **Un Ins 2739**
Refunds, **Un Ins 3010**
Mandamus, review of denial of claim, **Un Ins 3264**
Manner of making claims, **Un Ins 2706**

UNEMPLOYMENT COMPENSATION
—Cont'd
Disability compensation—Cont'd
Marriage, leaving employment, **Un Ins 1264**
Maximum amount, **Un Ins 2653, 2656**
Medical examinations, **Un Ins 2677, 2708 et seq.**
Continued medical certification, filing, time, **Un Ins 2706**
Records, confidential, **Un Ins 2714**
Mental or physical injury or illness, **Un Ins 1253.5, 2626**
Midwives, certificates of disability, **Un Ins 2708**
Military service,
Disqualification for acts prior to service, **Un Ins 2771**
Trainees, **Un Ins 2765 et seq.**
Minimum wages for eligibility, **Un Ins 2652**
Modification of benefit scale in emergency, **Un Ins 2604**
Motion pictures, payroll services companies, employer or employing unit, **Un Ins 680**
Notice,
Benefits and rights, **Un Ins 2613**
Change in contributions rate or benefits, **Un Ins 2604**
Claims for benefits, **Un Ins 2707 et seq.**
Computation of benefits, **Un Ins 2707.3**
Deductions, withholding, **Un Ins 1342.1**
Eligibility determined, **Un Ins 2707.2**
Overpayments, **Un Ins 2736**
Submission, methods, **Un Ins 2707.6**
Offset,
Extended unemployment compensation benefits, **Un Ins 3751**
Uncollected assessments, contributions on tips and gratuities in excess of other wages, **Un Ins 987.7**
Overpayment, **Un Ins 1185, 2735 et seq.**
Appeals, good cause, extension of time, **Un Ins 2737**
Collection, **Un Ins 2735.1**
Offset against extended unemployment compensation benefits, **Un Ins 3751**
Paid family care leave, **Un Ins 3300 et seq.**
Payment, **Un Ins 3009 et seq.**
Benefits, **Un Ins 2701 et seq.**
Contributions, **Un Ins 2903**
Disability fund payments, **Un Ins 3009 et seq.**
Judgments, **Un Ins 3012**
Refunds, **Un Ins 3012, 3075**
Voluntary plans, **Un Ins 3252**
Wages,
Employer during disability, **Un Ins 2656**

UNEMPLOYMENT COMPENSATION
—Cont'd
Disability compensation—Cont'd
Payment—Cont'd
Wages—Cont'd
Irregular intervals, **Un Ins 2657**
Payroll deductions, **Un Ins 3260, 3260.5**
Physical examinations, **Un Ins 2708 et seq.**
Physicians, certificate of disability, **Un Ins 2708 et seq.**
Posting information by employer, procedure for making claims, **Un Ins 2706**
Prayer healing, ineligibility for benefits, **Un Ins 2902**
Pregnancy, **Un Ins 2626**
Presumptions, disqualifications, **Un Ins 2676, 2677**
Protests,
Computation of benefits, **Un Ins 2707.4**
Appeals, good cause, extension of time, **Un Ins 2707.4**
Submission, methods, **Un Ins 2707.6**
Public employment offices, payment of benefits, **Un Ins 2701**
Purpose of law, **Un Ins 2601**
Rates and charges, reimbursement, voluntary plans, **Un Ins 3252**
Reconsideration of computation, **Un Ins 2707.5**
Records and recordation,
Destruction, establishment of unexpended balance after military service, **Un Ins 2768**
Medical records, confidential, **Un Ins 2714**
Military service trainees, unexpended balance of benefits, reestablishment of lost records, **Un Ins 2768**
Voluntary plans, **Un Ins 3267**
Recovery of overpayments, **Un Ins 2739**
Enforcement, **Un Ins 2742**
Reduction,
Genocide, **Un Ins 2629.5**
Receiving other benefits, **Un Ins 2629**
Refunds and overpayments, **Un Ins 1185**
Garnishment, service of process, **CCP 706.101**
Limitation of actions, **Un Ins 3010**
Payment, **Un Ins 3009, 3012, 3075**
Service of process, garnishment, **CCP 706.101**
Reimbursement of disability fund, **Un Ins 2712.5**
Religious beliefs, healing by prayer, ineligibility for benefits, **Un Ins 2902**
Religious practitioners, certificate of disability, **Un Ins 2709**
Repayments to state, disability suffered in federal military service, **Un Ins 2772**
Reports, funds, **Un Ins 995**
Revolving fund, **Un Ins 3051**

UNEMPLOYMENT

UNEMPLOYMENT COMPENSATION
—Cont'd

Disability compensation—Cont'd

Rules and regulations,

Claims, method of submission of notices, protests and information, **Un Ins 2707.6**

Dispute as to funds from which benefits payable, **Un Ins 2712**

Individuals simultaneously covered by voluntary plan and disability fund, **Un Ins 3253**

Payment of benefits, **Un Ins 3075**

Self employment, elective coverage, **Un Ins 708.5**

Service of process, refunds and overpayments, garnishment, **CCP 706.101**

Sexual psychopaths, **Un Ins 2678**

Social Security Act, nonconformity with provisions, **Un Ins 2605**

Sole stockholder of corporation, disclaiming rights, **Un Ins 637.1**

Spouse of mentally deficient claimant, filing claims, **Un Ins 2705.1**

State, elective coverage, **Un Ins 710.7**

State residents covered under laws of another state lacking disability program, **Un Ins 702.6**

Subsequent claims, wages used to establish prior claim, **Un Ins 2703**

Tables, weekly benefit amount, **Un Ins 2655**

Time,

Action for recovery of overpayment, **Un Ins 2739**

Appeal,

Determination as to eligibility for benefits, **Un Ins 2707.2**

Overpayment, **Un Ins 2737**

Claims,

Filing first claim, **Un Ins 2706.1**

Refund, **Un Ins 3010**

Continued medical certification, filing, **Un Ins 2706.2**

Contributions, payment, **Un Ins 2903**

Day of death, disqualification, **Un Ins 2679**

Disqualification period, **Un Ins 2675**

Employer to furnish information, **Un Ins 2707.1**

Extension of time for filing claim, **Un Ins 2706.1**

First benefit payment, **Un Ins 2701.5**

Notice of overpayment, **Un Ins 2736**

Presumptions of ineligibility for benefits, **Un Ins 2676, 2677**

Reconsideration, computation or recomputations, **Un Ins 2707.5**

Tips, assessment, contributions in excess of other wages, **Un Ins 987.7**

Reports, **Un Ins 1088.6**

Trade dispute, disqualification, **Un Ins 2677**

Trainees, military service, **Un Ins 2765 et seq.**

UNEMPLOYMENT COMPENSATION
—Cont'd

Disability compensation—Cont'd

Unemployment compensation, effect of receiving, **Un Ins 2628**

United States, certificate of disability from medical facility, **Un Ins 2708**

United States Postal Service, employees, **Un Ins 2606.4**

Vacation pay as wages, eligibility determination, **Un Ins 2656**

Valid claim, definitions, **Un Ins 2609**

Voluntary plans, **Un Ins 3251 et seq.**

Accounting for funds, **Un Ins 3261**

Adjustment of future benefits, approval of amendment, **Un Ins 3271**

Administrative expenses, **Un Ins 3269**

Refunds and overpayments, **Un Ins 3272**

Admitted disability insurer, **Un Ins 3254**

Adoption for all employees not rejecting, **Un Ins 3257**

Amendment adjusting future benefits, approval, **Un Ins 3271**

Appeal and review, **Un Ins 3264**

Termination, **Un Ins 3262**

Application for approval, **Un Ins 3251**

Approval, **Un Ins 3254**

Assessments, **Un Ins 3252, 3259, 3265, 3266**

Termination, **Un Ins 3262**

Bankruptcy, **Un Ins 3261**

Benefits, redirecting, **Un Ins 1345**

Bond, **Un Ins 3258**

Cities, **Un Ins 710**

Commingling of funds, **Un Ins 3261**

Conforming to change in law, **Un Ins 3254.5**

Consent of employees, **Un Ins 3254**

Contributions, **Un Ins 3252**

Exemptions, **Un Ins 3252**

Refunds and overpayments, **Un Ins 3272**

Several employers in same industry, **Un Ins 3255**

Costs, assumption by employer, **Un Ins 3260**

Refunds and overpayments, **Un Ins 3272**

Counties, **Un Ins 710**

Credits, excess contributions, **Un Ins 3266**

Deductions, **Un Ins 3260, 3260.5**

Denial of liability, **Un Ins 3264**

Deposit of securities in lieu of bond, **Un Ins 3258**

Disability fund, **Un Ins 3252**

Rights of employees covered by voluntary plan, **Un Ins 3253**

Dispute as to fund from which benefits payable, **Un Ins 2712**

Disqualification, **Un Ins 3253**

Duration, **Un Ins 3254**

Employees, definitions, **Un Ins 3254**

UNEMPLOYMENT COMPENSATION
—Cont'd

Disability compensation—Cont'd

Voluntary plans—Cont'd

Exemptions from contributions, **Un Ins 3252**

Failure to make payment after decision on appeal, **Un Ins 3265**

Funds,

Accounting, **Un Ins 3261**

Commingling, **Un Ins 3261**

Future employees, **Un Ins 3254**

Increased benefits, **Un Ins 3254.5, 3265**

Refunds and overpayments, **Un Ins 3272**

Individuals simultaneously covered by voluntary plan and disability fund, **Un Ins 3253**

Information, furnishing, **Un Ins 3267, 3268**

Insolvency, **Un Ins 3261**

Insurance, **Un Ins 3254**

Noninsured plans, **Un Ins 3258**

Notice, **Un Ins 3255, 3257**

Contributions, assessment, **Un Ins 3252**

Determination of employees rights to benefits, **Un Ins 3265**

Termination, **Un Ins 3262**

Payroll deductions, **Un Ins 3255, 3256, 3260, 3260.5**

Preferences, funds, **Un Ins 3261**

Receiver, appointment, **Un Ins 3261**

Records, **Un Ins 3267**

Redirecting benefits, employee paid benefits cost, **Un Ins 1345**

Refunds, excess contributions, **Un Ins 3266, 3272**

Rejection by employee, **Un Ins 3257**

Reports, **Un Ins 3267**

Review by appeals board, **Un Ins 3264**

Risks adverse to disability fund, selection, **Un Ins 3270**

Rotational workers, **Un Ins 3255**

Security requirements, noninsured plans, **Un Ins 3258**

Several employers, **Un Ins 3255**

Statement of benefits, in plan, **Un Ins 3251**

Substantial selection of risks adverse to disability fund, **Un Ins 3254**

Successor employing units, **Un Ins 3254.5**

Termination, **Un Ins 3262**

Coverage, **Un Ins 3263**

Successor employing units, **Un Ins 3254.5**

Time,

Amendment adjusting future benefits, approval, **Un Ins 3271**

Notice of adoption for all employees not rejecting, posting, **Un Ins 3257**

UNEMPLOYMENT COMPENSATION
—Cont'd
Disability compensation—Cont'd
Voluntary plans—Cont'd
Time—Cont'd
Payment of benefits by employer or insured, **Un Ins 3265**
Workers engaged for several employers in same industry, **Un Ins 3255**
Trust funds, **Un Ins 3261**
Wage deductions, increase, **Un Ins 3254**
Withdrawal by employee, **Un Ins 3257**
Vouchers, administration account, **Un Ins 3051**
Wages,
Due and unpaid, **Un Ins 2654**
Exclusion, **Un Ins 938**
Waiting period, **Un Ins 2627**
Increase during emergency, **Un Ins 2604**
Warrants,
Fund, **Un Ins 3075**
Payment,
Benefits, **Un Ins 3075**
From disability fund, **Un Ins 3009 et seq.**
Weekly amount, **Un Ins 2655**
Withholding,
Assessment, contributions on tips and gratuities in excess of other wages, **Un Ins 987.7**
Reports, **Un Ins 1088.6**
Child support obligations, **Un Ins 1255.7**
Notice, **Un Ins 1342.1**
Tips and gratuities as wages, withholding employee contributions, contributions in excess of other wages, **Un Ins 987.7**
Reports, **Un Ins 1088.6**
Workers Compensation, this index
Discharge,
Military personnel, unexpired leave time, compensation eligibility, **Un Ins 1253.15**
Misconduct, **Un Ins 1256**
Retaliatory actions against employees for enforcing rights, **Un Ins 1237**
Disclaimer of rights, sole stockholder and corporation, contributions, exemption, **Un Ins 637.1**
Disclosure,
Confidential information, **Un Ins 2111**
Confidential or privileged information, ante
Employers, avoiding charges to reserve accounts, **Un Ins 1030**
Income tax, application of law, **Un Ins 13003**
Support, **Un Ins 1088.8**
Discrimination by employer,
Retaliatory actions against employees for enforcing rights, **Un Ins 1237**

UNEMPLOYMENT COMPENSATION
—Cont'd
Discrimination by employer—Cont'd
Termination of employment, eligibility for benefits, **Un Ins 1256.2**
Disputed claims, **Un Ins 1951 et seq.**
Disqualifications, **Un Ins 1251 et seq.**
Alcoholics and alcoholism, **Un Ins 1256.4**
Claimant, **Un Ins 1031**
Conviction for false statement or concealment, dismissal of complaint, **Un Ins 1263**
False statement or concealment, **Un Ins 1263**
Federal state extended benefits, **Un Ins 4553 et seq.**
Income, receipt, **Un Ins 1260.1**
Physical or mental illness or injury, **Un Ins 1253.5**
Successive periods, extended duration, **Un Ins 1261**
Time, **Un Ins 1260**
Extension, **Un Ins 1261**
False statement or concealment, **Un Ins 1263**
Dissolution of employing unit, jeopardy assessments, **Un Ins 1137.1**
Districts, this index
Divisions, **Un Ins 304**
Domestic or marital duties causing resignation, **Un Ins 1264**
Domestic partnership,
Disability compensation, filing, claims, **Un Ins 2705.1**
Family care leave, serious health conditions, **Un Ins 3300 et seq.**
Domestic Service or Work, this index
Domestic violence, termination of employment, **Un Ins 1030, 1032, 1256**
Domicile and residence, foreign state, effect on eligibility, **Un Ins 455.7**
Door to door salespersons, **Un Ins 13004.1**
Drug addicts, reasons for leaving employment, **Un Ins 1030**
Payments charged to employers, **Un Ins 1032**
Drugs and medicine,
Acute drug induced illness, disability, definitions, **Un Ins 2626**
Drug free residential facility residents, disability benefits, **Un Ins 2626.2**
Foreign states, residential facility residents, disability benefits, **Un Ins 2626.2**
Earthquakes, temporary public employees, excluded services, **Un Ins 634.5**
Education,
Officers and employees, **Un Ins 1253.3**
Pamphlets, **Un Ins 316**
Taxpayers rights, **Un Ins 1231**
Educational assistance program, exclusion, **Un Ins 938.3**
Elected officials, excluded services, **Un Ins 634.5**

UNEMPLOYMENT COMPENSATION
—Cont'd
Elections, nonprofit corporations, reimbursement financing, **Un Ins 801, 801.5, 1051.5**
Elective coverage, **Un Ins 701 et seq.**
Agreements, **Un Ins 705**
Approval, **Un Ins 301, 704 et seq.**
Requisites for, nonprofit organization, **Un Ins 711**
Balance in fund, determination, **Un Ins 980.5**
California State University, disability compensation, **Un Ins 710.8**
Community colleges and districts, disability compensation, **Un Ins 710.9**
Contributions,
Elective financing, **Un Ins 803**
Employer services deemed employment, **Un Ins 984.5**
Time payable, **Un Ins 708**
Counties, **Un Ins 709**
Disability compensation, ante
Employer, **Un Ins 708**
Employer services deemed employment for employer, **Un Ins 708**
Employing unit, effect, **Un Ins 701**
Exclusions, wages, **Un Ins 981**
Filing election, **Un Ins 702**
Governmental entity, **Un Ins 710**
Hearings, **Un Ins 707**
Indians, **Un Ins 709, 710, 710.6**
Individual working for parents, son, daughter or spouse, **Un Ins 631, 702.5**
Local public entities, **Un Ins 709 et seq.**
Nonprofit organizations, **Un Ins 702.1, 711 et seq.**
Notice,
Employee contributions, rates, **Un Ins 984.5**
Hearing, **Un Ins 707**
Objections and hearing, **Un Ins 707**
Termination of agreement, **Un Ins 704.1 et seq.**
Petition, review of termination, **Un Ins 1222**
Political subdivisions, termination, **Un Ins 705 et seq.**
Self employment, disability compensation, **Un Ins 708.5**
Services performed without state, **Un Ins 703**
State,
Department or unit, **Un Ins 709**
Disability compensation, **Un Ins 710.7**
Termination of agreement, **Un Ins 704.1 et seq.**
Wages, basis of contributions, determination, **Un Ins 981**
Waiver of requisites for termination, **Un Ins 706**
Electronic funds transfers. Funds transfers, generally, post
Eligibility, **Un Ins 1251 et seq.**
Ability and availability, **Un Ins 1253**

UNEMPLOYMENT

UNEMPLOYMENT COMPENSATION
—Cont'd
Eligibility—Cont'd
Colleges and universities, **Un Ins 1253.3**
Computation of wages, **Un Ins 1277.5**
Days off and holidays, **Un Ins 1253.2**
Death in family, **Un Ins 1253.1, 1253.12**
Detention, **Un Ins 1253.1**
Disability compensation, ante
Discharge,
  Military personnel, unexpired leave
    time, **Un Ins 1253.15**
  Misconduct, **Un Ins 1256**
Education, officers and employees, **Un Ins 1253.3**
Family care leave, **Un Ins 3303, 3303.1**
Federally operated school, **Un Ins 1253.3**
Nonprofit corporations, officers and
  employees, **Un Ins 1253.3**
Nonprofit organizations, **Un Ins 1253.3**
Part time employment, **Un Ins 1253.8**
Physical or mental illness or injury,
  work availability, **Un Ins 1253.5**
Public entity, **Un Ins 1253.3**
Reason for termination of employment,
  Un Ins 1256
Reemployment activities, participation,
  Un Ins 1253
Refusal to work, grounds, **Un Ins 1259**
Registration for employment, **Un Ins 1253**
Retirement under collective bargaining
  agreement, **Un Ins 1256**
Retraining benefits, **Un Ins 1269**
Suitable employment, **Un Ins 1253, 1258.5**
Waiting period, **Un Ins 1253, 1254**
Eligible participants, definitions, employ-
  ment training panel, **Un Ins 10201**
Emergencies,
  Solvency surcharge rate, **Un Ins 977.5**
  Temporary public employees, excluded
    services, **Un Ins 634.5**
  Time extension, returns reports, **Un Ins 1111.5**
Emergency medical care, qualification for
  benefits, **Un Ins 1253.7**
Employee, definitions, **Un Ins 621, 622**
  Withholding tax on wages, **Un Ins 13004**
Employee benefit plan distribution,
  Definitions, Unclaimed Property Law,
    CCP 1501
  Escheat to state, **CCP 1521**
Employee contributions, definitions, **Un Ins 144**
Employer or employing unit, **Un Ins 135**
  Acquisitions, merger, consolidation,
    Change in organization, **Un Ins 135.1, 135.2**
    New employer unit, **Un Ins 982**
  Agricultural labor, **Un Ins 676**
  Assistance in performing work of indi-
    vidual employed by, **Un Ins 606**
  Bill of rights, **Un Ins 1231 et seq.**

UNEMPLOYMENT COMPENSATION
—Cont'd
Employer or employing unit—Cont'd
  Control of enterprise, new employing
    unit created, **Un Ins 135.1, 135.2**
  Correct employer, determination, **Un Ins 1127.5**
  Crimes and offenses, fraud, reports, **Un Ins 2115**
  Death, duty of representative, **Un Ins 1090**
  Definitions, **Un Ins 678, 682, 821.4**
    Employment training panel, **Un Ins 10201**
  Determination, **Un Ins 606.5**
  Election,
    Covered employer, **Un Ins 701 et seq.**
    Qualify for benefits, **Un Ins 708**
      Employer and individual working
        for son, daughter, or spouse,
        Un Ins 631, 702.5
  Failure to register, **Un Ins 2109**
  Final return, **Un Ins 1116**
  Fines and penalties, fraudulent reports,
    Un Ins 1128, 2115
  Fraud, reports on wages or time peri-
    ods, **Un Ins 2115**
  Governmental entity, election to be-
    come, **Un Ins 710**
  Information returns, fines and penalties,
    Un Ins 1128
  Insolvency, **Un Ins 1090**
    Contributions, **Un Ins 988**
  Motion pictures, payroll services compa-
    nies, **Un Ins 679**
    Disability compensation, **Un Ins 680**
  Recipients of in home supportive ser-
    vices, **Un Ins 683**
  Registration, **Un Ins 1086, 1126.1**
    Agents authorized to accept, **Un Ins 1087**
    Failure to register, **Un Ins 2109**
    Liability for failure to register, **Un Ins 2109**
    Penalties, **Un Ins 1126.1**
  Reports, fraud, **Un Ins 2115**
  Reserves, rates and charges, **Un Ins 982**
  Retaliatory actions against employees,
    Un Ins 1237
  Service not in course of trade or busi-
    ness, **Un Ins 640**
  Several employers,
    Agents, **Un Ins 1096 et seq.**
    Benefits paid pursuant to election,
      additional cost, **Un Ins 713**
    Failure of one or more to keep or
      furnish records or reports, **Un Ins 1093**
    Refund of excessive worker contribu-
      tions, **Un Ins 1176**
  Takeovers, new employing unit, **Un Ins 135.1, 135.2**
  Taxpayers Bill of Rights, **Un Ins 1231 et seq.**
  Withholding tax and wages, **Un Ins 13005**

UNEMPLOYMENT COMPENSATION
—Cont'd
Employer or employing unit—Cont'd
  Work records, **Un Ins 1085**
Employers Liability Law, wages paid, **Un Ins 1277.5**
Employment Development, generally, this
  index
Employment Development Department,
  generally, this index
Employment services board, divulging
  confidential information, **Un Ins 2111**
Employment Training Fund, generally,
  this index
Employment training panel. Employment
  Development Department, this index
Encumbrances. Liens and incumbrances,
  generally, post
Engineers, presumption of independent
  contractors status, **Un Ins 656**
Entity, definitions, **Un Ins 803**
Equipment, withholding tax on wages, **Un Ins 13011**
Errors,
  Assessments, cancellation, **Un Ins 1136**
  Claim for refund or overpayment, erro-
    neous denial, **Un Ins 1180.5**
  Payments, contributions, **Un Ins 991**
  Refunds erroneously made, **Un Ins 1184**
  Statement of account, notice of correc-
    tion, **Un Ins 1036**
  Underpayment of contributions, **Un Ins 1113.1**
Escheat, trust funds, **CCP 1510, 1521**
Estimate,
  Contributions, **Un Ins 1127**
  Wages, withholding tax on wages, **Un Ins 13023**
Evidence, **Un Ins 1952**
  Certificate, delinquent contributions, **Un Ins 1854**
  Family care leave, claims, **Un Ins 3306**
  Findings, subsequent proceedings, **Un Ins 1960**
  Hearings, **Un Ins 407**
  Independent contractors status, **Un Ins 656**
  Judgment liens, certificate of release or
    subordination, conclusiveness, **Un Ins 1817**
  Presumptions,
    Discharge, **Un Ins 1256**
    Pensions or similar periodic pay-
      ments, reduction of benefits, divi-
      sion of contributions, **Un Ins 1255.3**
    Professional services consultant, pre-
      sumption of independent con-
      tractor status, **Un Ins 656**
    Termination of employment, **Un Ins 1256**
      Reason for termination, **Un Ins 1030**
  Voluntary leaving of employment
    without notification to employer,
    Un Ins 3701

UNEMPLOYMENT COMPENSATION
—Cont'd

Evidence—Cont'd

Returns, failure to file, certificate of department, **Un Ins 2123**

Exchange of money, concealment of wages, fines and penalties, **Un Ins 1128.1, 1735.1**

Excluded services,

Full time students organized camps, **Un Ins 642.1**

Optional, nonprofit organization, **Un Ins 711**

Exclusion from wages or other benefits paid employee, **Un Ins 931 et seq.**

Executions,

Benefits, supplementary plans established by employer, **Un Ins 1342**

Contributions, exemption, **Un Ins 988**

Exemptions, **Un Ins 988**

Fees, levy of writ, **Un Ins 1559**

Overpayments, judgment liens, **Un Ins 1379.5**

Summary judgment for delinquent contributions, **Un Ins 1816**

Unemployment administration funds, fees, levy of writs, **Un Ins 1559**

Executors and administrators,

Employing unit, information regarding, **Un Ins 1090**

Lien for unpaid contributions, interest and penalties, **Un Ins 1701**

Personal liability, **Un Ins 1736**

Exemptions,

Benefits from supplemental plan established by employer, **Un Ins 1342**

Contributions from legal process, **Un Ins 988**

Corporations with sole stockholder, **Un Ins 637.1**

Disability compensation, contributions, **Un Ins 2902**

Election to include employment, **Un Ins 702**

Wage exclusions, amounts paid to employees, **Un Ins 931 et seq.**

Withholding tax on wages, **Un Ins 13040 et seq.**

Exercise boys, **Un Ins 654**

Exhaustee, definitions, extended compensation, **Un Ins 3503**

Expenses and expenditures,

Administration, **Un Ins 324**

Allowances, exclusion from wages, **Un Ins 929**

Extended unemployment compensation, **Un Ins 1253.3, 3501 et seq., 4001 et seq.**

Accounts, extended compensation account, **Un Ins 4004**

Amount of benefits, computation, **Un Ins 4601**

Appeal and review, **Un Ins 3654.4, 4701**

Computation protests, good cause, extension of time, **Un Ins 3656**

UNEMPLOYMENT COMPENSATION
—Cont'd

Extended unemployment compensation
—Cont'd

Appeal and review—Cont'd

Denial of recomputation of benefits, **Un Ins 3656**

Determination and eligibility, **Un Ins 4655, 4656**

Determination as to eligibility, **Un Ins 3655**

Federal state extended benefits, computation protests, extension of time, good cause, **Un Ins 4656**

Good cause, extension of time, **Un Ins 3654.4 et seq.**

Ruling, cause for termination of employment, **Un Ins 3701, 4701**

Application for federal state extended benefits, **Un Ins 4652 et seq.**

Application of law, **Un Ins 3502**

Base period, wages received, **Un Ins 3552**

Information required, **Un Ins 3654.1**

Charging benefits to employers account, **Un Ins 3702**

Claims, **Un Ins 3651 et seq., 4651 et seq.**

Computations, **Un Ins 3601 et seq., 3656**

Amount and duration of federal state extended benefits, **Un Ins 4601**

Protests, good cause, extension of time, appeals, **Un Ins 3656**

Public records, **Un Ins 3504**

Rate, **Un Ins 3504**

Suitable work, definitions, **Un Ins 4553**

Definitions, **Un Ins 3503**

Determination of eligibility, **Un Ins 3654.1 et seq., 3654.2 et seq.**

Disqualifications, **Un Ins 4551, 4552**

Duration of benefits, **Un Ins 3602, 3603**

Computation, **Un Ins 4601**

Eligibility, **Un Ins 3505 et seq., 4551, 4552**

Information required, **Un Ins 3654.1**

Federal Act, definitions, **Un Ins 3503**

Federal state extended benefits, **Un Ins 4001 et seq.**

Appeals, extension of time, eligibility determination, **Un Ins 4655**

Charging benefits to employers account, **Un Ins 4702**

Definitions, **Un Ins 4003**

Disqualification, **Un Ins 4553 et seq.**

Eligibility determination, extension of time, good cause, **Un Ins 4655**

Extension of time, appeals, computation protest, **Un Ins 4656**

Pensions or similar periodic payments, offsets, reduction of benefits, **Un Ins 1255.3**

State on or off indicator, **Un Ins 4003**

Suitable work, definitions, **Un Ins 4553**

Suspension, **Un Ins 3506, 4003**

UNEMPLOYMENT COMPENSATION
—Cont'd

Extended unemployment compensation
—Cont'd

Filing claims, **Un Ins 3651 et seq., 4651 et seq.**

Fines and penalties, failure to furnish information, **Un Ins 3654.1, 3654.2**

Indians, **Un Ins 710**

Information required, **Un Ins 3654.1 et seq.**

Michigan California lumber company fire, unemployment caused by, **Un Ins 1281.7**

Monthly computation of rate, **Un Ins 3504**

Notice,

Computation of benefits, **Un Ins 3656**

Determination as to eligibility, **Un Ins 3655**

Filing of claim, **Un Ins 3654, 4655**

Overpayments, **Un Ins 3751, 4751**

Recomputation or denial of recomputation of benefits, **Un Ins 3656**

Ruling as to cause of termination of employment, **Un Ins 3701**

Offset, overpayments, **Un Ins 3751, 4751**

Overpayments, **Un Ins 3751, 4751**

Payment from unemployment fund, **Un Ins 3551**

Pensions or similar periodic payments, offsets, reduction of benefits, retroactive application of law, **Un Ins 1255.3**

Primary claim,

Definitions, **Un Ins 3503**

Necessity of filing, **Un Ins 3652**

Protests, determination of benefits, **Un Ins 4656**

Purpose of law, **Un Ins 3501**

Rates and charges, computation, **Un Ins 3504**

Recomputation or denial of recomputation of benefits, **Un Ins 3656**

Ruling as to cause of termination of employment, **Un Ins 3701**

State on or off indicator, **Un Ins 4003**

Students,

Employment during vacation period, **Un Ins 3701**

Leaving employment to return to school, **Un Ins 4701**

Submission of facts affecting exhaustees eligibility, **Un Ins 3654 et seq.**

Training or retraining, **Un Ins 1271, 1271.5**

Unemployment compensation benefits, receiving, **Un Ins 3505**

Wage information required, **Un Ins 3654.1 et seq.**

Wages, definitions, base period, **Un Ins 3552**

Weekly benefit amount, **Un Ins 3601**

Fairs and Expositions, this index

UNEMPLOYMENT

UNEMPLOYMENT COMPENSATION
—Cont'd

Faith based organizations, job training and placement services, grants, **Un Ins 9617**

False statement or concealment. Fraud, generally, post

Family care leave, **Gov 12945.2; Un Ins 3300 et seq.**

Fraud, **Un Ins 2116, 3305**

Family economic security. Job preparation and training services, generally, post

Family employment, **Un Ins 631**

Farm labor. Agricultural labor and employment, generally, ante

Federal aid, workforce recovery training, **Un Ins 10214.6**

Federal cooperation, **Un Ins 451 et seq.**

Federal Employers Liability Law, wages paid, **Un Ins 1277.5**

Federal service, **Un Ins 632**

Federal unemployment compensation system, service under, **Un Ins 635**

Federal state extended benefits. Extended unemployment compensation, ante

Federal Unemployment Tax Act, generally, this index

Fees,

Attachment or execution, levy of writs, **Un Ins 1559**

Providing rules, regulations, guidelines, upon request, **Un Ins 307**

Warrant for collection of delinquent contributions, **Un Ins 1786, 1787**

Witnesses, **Un Ins 1956**

Fictitious employer, employees or wages, fraudulent reports, **Un Ins 2114**

Fiduciary, definitions, withholding tax on wages, **Un Ins 13003**

Finance, **Un Ins 1501 et seq.**

Approval, **Un Ins 301**

Coverage, **Un Ins 801 et seq.**

Indians, elections, **Un Ins 802, 803**

Finance department,

Accounts and accounting, administration fund, **Un Ins 1559**

Investments, disability compensation fund, **Un Ins 3002**

Financial statements and reports,

Confidential information, **Un Ins 1092**

Excess worker contributions, tips, gratuities, **Un Ins 1088.6**

Withholding tax on wages, **Un Ins 13050 et seq.**

Findings, evidentiary effect, other proceedings, **Un Ins 1960**

Fines and penalties,

Appeal and review, **Un Ins 1241 et seq.**

Bad faith, **Un Ins 1958**

Appearance before appeals board by agent or attorney, charging more than approved fee, **Un Ins 1957**

Assessments,

Deficiency, **Un Ins 1127**

Delinquency, **Un Ins 1135**

UNEMPLOYMENT COMPENSATION
—Cont'd

Fines and penalties—Cont'd

Assessments—Cont'd

Joint enforcement strike force on the underground economy, **Labor 106**

Return not filed, **Un Ins 1126**

Collection,

Additional remedies, **Un Ins 1860**

Delinquent penalties, **Un Ins 1851 et seq.**

Compromise and settlement, violations, **Un Ins 2127**

Concealed wages, **Un Ins 1128.1, 1735.1**

Contributions,

Collections, **Un Ins 301**

Concealed wages, **Un Ins 1128.1, 1735.1**

Delinquent payments, **Un Ins 1110.6**

Exchange of money, concealment of wages, **Un Ins 1128.1, 1735.1**

Failure to pay, **Un Ins 1112, 2118, 2118.5**

Reports on file, **Un Ins 1114**

Underpayment, **Un Ins 1113.1**

Deposit of penalties, contingent fund, **Un Ins 1585**

Disability compensation, fraud, **Un Ins 1143**

Electronic funds transfers, remitting payments, employers, **Un Ins 1112**

Employing units, failure to register, **Un Ins 1126.1**

Exchange of money, concealment of wages, **Un Ins 1128.1, 1735.1**

Extended in compensation, failure to provide information, **Un Ins 3654.2**

Family care leave, fraud, **Un Ins 3305**

Fraud, **Un Ins 1143, 3654.2**

Claims, **Un Ins 1144**

Employer or employing unit, **Un Ins 2115**

Fictitious employers, employees or wages, **Un Ins 2114**

Statement, withholding tax on wages, **Un Ins 13052**

Identity and identification, withholding tax on wages, **Un Ins 13057**

Indians, concealed wages, **Un Ins 1128.1, 1735.1**

Information,

Collection of criminal penalties, **Un Ins 1095**

Disclosure, **Un Ins 1095**

Insurance, employing unit failure to file, **Un Ins 1128**

Judgment liens, release and subordination, **Un Ins 1817**

Liens for unpaid penalties, **Un Ins 1701 et seq.**

Misstatements, **Un Ins 13101**

New hires, reports, **Un Ins 1088.5**

Personal liability for failure to file notice, **Un Ins 1736**

Prosecutors, payment, **Un Ins 2122.5**

UNEMPLOYMENT COMPENSATION
—Cont'd

Fines and penalties—Cont'd

Reciprocity, **Un Ins 453**

Reconciliation returns, delinquency, **Un Ins 1117**

Refunds, **Un Ins 1177**

Reports,

Employing unit,

Failure to file, **Un Ins 1128**

Fraud, **Un Ins 2115**

Fictitious employers, employees or wages, **Un Ins 2114**

New hires, **Un Ins 1088.5**

Support, **Un Ins 1088.8**

Wages after demand, failure to file, **Un Ins 1114**

Returns, fraudulent or failure to file, **Un Ins 2117, 2117.5**

Summary judgment, unpaid penalties, **Un Ins 1815 et seq.**

Support, reports, **Un Ins 1088.8**

Termination, reports, false statements, **Un Ins 1142**

Colleges and universities, **Un Ins 1142.1**

Violations of law, **Un Ins 2122**

Fires, temporary public employees, excluded services, **Un Ins 634.5**

Fiscal year, definitions, withholding tax on wages, **Un Ins 13003**

Floods, temporary public employees, excluded services, **Un Ins 634.5**

Foreign Corporations, this index

Foreign Countries, this index

Foreign government,

Cooperation, **Un Ins 452**

Employment, **Un Ins 643, 644**

Foreign limited liability partnerships, withholdings, **Un Ins 1735**

Foreign states,

Benefits from, effect upon eligibility, **Un Ins 1255**

Claims, eligibility, **Un Ins 455.7**

Elective coverage, **Un Ins 703**

False statements or representations, **Un Ins 2102**

Mutual payment, **Un Ins 455.5**

Officers and employees, **Un Ins 632**

Performance of services, **Un Ins 603.5**

Residence, effect upon eligibility, **Un Ins 455.7**

Services performed in, **Un Ins 602 et seq.**

Elective coverage, **Un Ins 703**

Forfeitures, benefits, forfeiture of rights, **Un Ins 1263**

Foster homes, family care leave, **Un Ins 3300 et seq.**

Foundations, elections for financing, **Un Ins 801, 803**

Franchise tax board, definitions, withholding tax on wages, **Un Ins 13003**

Fraternal association officials, **Un Ins 652**

Fraternities, domestic service, **Un Ins 639, 682**

UNEMPLOYMENT COMPENSATION
—Cont'd
Fraud, **Un Ins 1143, 2101 et seq., 2121**
  Aiding or assisting in fraudulent claim, violations, **Un Ins 2121**
  Applying for benefits, **Un Ins 1257 et seq., 2114**
  Assessment, **Un Ins 1128, 1375.1**
  Claims, penalties, **Un Ins 1144**
  Contributions, rates and charges, **Un Ins 977, 1036, 2101.6**
  Denial of benefits, **Un Ins 1260.1**
  Disability compensation, ante
  Disqualification, duration, **Un Ins 1263**
  Employer or employing unit, reports, **Un Ins 2115**
  Family care leave, **Un Ins 2116, 3305**
  Fictitious employer, employees or wages, **Un Ins 2114**
  Fines and penalties, ante
  Medical condition, crimes and offenses, **Un Ins 2116**
  Motion picture payroll services company, employer or employing unit, **Un Ins 679**
  Offers in compromise, rescission, **Un Ins 1875**
  Overpayments, **Un Ins 1375**
    Recovery,
      Disability benefits, **Un Ins 2739**
      Statute of limitations, **Un Ins 1379**
  Reconsideration, benefits, time limits, **Un Ins 1332.5**
  Reports, deterrence and detection activity, **Un Ins 2614**
  Returns, crimes, **Un Ins 2117, 2117.5**
  Statement, withholding tax on wages, **Un Ins 13052**
  Termination, reports, **Un Ins 1142**
    Colleges and universities, **Un Ins 1142.1**
Full time students, organized camps, exclusions, **Un Ins 642.1**
Funds, **Un Ins 1521 et seq.**
  Accounts, **Un Ins 1525 et seq.**
  Administration fund, generally, ante
  Advances to, **Un Ins 323**
  Appeal in bad faith, deposit of penalty, **Un Ins 1958**
  Appropriation, **Un Ins 1521, 1535**
  Balance,
    Computation, summary of data used, **Un Ins 979**
    Determination, **Un Ins 980, 980.5**
    Unemployment fund under specified percentage, **Un Ins 977**
  Balancing account, cancellation of employer reserve account, **Un Ins 1027.1**
  Benefit account, **Un Ins 1525, 1528**
    Commingling with other state funds prohibited, **Un Ins 1533**
    Deposit of money, **Un Ins 1533**
    Source, **Un Ins 1529**
    Insurance premiums, payment for protection, **Un Ins 1531, 1533**

UNEMPLOYMENT COMPENSATION
—Cont'd
Funds—Cont'd
  Benefit account—Cont'd
    Money credited pursuant to Social Security Act, **Un Ins 1532**
    Purposes and use, **Un Ins 1532**
    Refunds, payment from, **Un Ins 1532, 1534**
    Unclaimed or unpaid balances, **Un Ins 1532**
    Warrants, unclaimed, **Un Ins 1537**
    Withdrawals, **Un Ins 1531**
  Benefits, available for payment, **Un Ins 1251**
  Bond of custodian, **Un Ins 1524**
  Clearing account, **Un Ins 1525, 1526**
    Commingling with other state funds prohibited, **Un Ins 1533**
    Deposit of money, **Un Ins 1533**
    Insurance premiums, payment for protection, **Un Ins 1533**
    Investment of moneys from, **Un Ins 1527**
    Refunds or judgments, payment, **Un Ins 1534**
    Warrants, unclaimed, **Un Ins 1537**
  Composition, **Un Ins 1521**
  Contingent funds, generally, ante
  Continued in existence, **Un Ins 1521**
  Contributions, determination of balance, **Un Ins 980.5**
  Controller, payment on warrants, **Un Ins 1534**
  Custodian, **Un Ins 1524**
  Definitions, employment training fund, **Un Ins 10201**
  Deposits, **Un Ins 1501**
  Disability compensation, ante
  Employment Training Fund, generally, this index
  Extended compensation, penalties for not providing information, **Un Ins 3654.2**
  Governmental entity as employer, **Un Ins 710**
  Investment, **Un Ins 1527**
  Pooling of contributions, **Un Ins 1025**
  Purposes, **Un Ins 1522**
  Refunds, contributions erroneously paid, unclaimed, inclusion, **Un Ins 1536**
  Rights of employer and employees, **Un Ins 1025**
  Separate accounts, **Un Ins 1525**
  Social Security Act,
    Credits, **Un Ins 1521**
    Use of money credited to unemployment trust fund, **Un Ins 1528.5**
  State liability, **Un Ins 1522**
  Treasurer, state, custodian, **Un Ins 1524**
  Trust fund account, **Un Ins 1525**
    Credit from Social Security Act, **Un Ins 980**
    Duration, **Un Ins 1530**
    Escheat to state, **CCP 1510, 1521**

UNEMPLOYMENT COMPENSATION
—Cont'd
Funds—Cont'd
  Trust fund account—Cont'd
    Investment, moneys or property on cessation, **Un Ins 1530**
    Transfer of money or property on cessation, **Un Ins 1530, 1590**
    Warrants, unclaimed, **Un Ins 1537**
  Unclaimed or unpaid,
    Balances, **Un Ins 1529**
      Benefit account, **Un Ins 1532**
      Refundable contributions, **Un Ins 1536**
    Warrants, **Un Ins 1537**
  Unemployment administration fund.
    Administration fund, generally, ante
  Unemployment trust fund,
    Account, **Un Ins 1527**
      Balances, disposition, **Un Ins 1529**
      Investment, **Un Ins 1530**
      Requisitions on, purposes, **Un Ins 1529**
    Definitions, **Un Ins 142**
    Requisition or use of money, **Un Ins 1528.5**
    Transfer of moneys, **Un Ins 1528, 1590**
  Warrants, unclaimed, **Un Ins 1537**
  Withdrawals, **Un Ins 1523**
    Benefit account, **Un Ins 1531, 3075**
Funds transfers,
  Contributions, payment, **Un Ins 1110**
  Withholding tax on wages, **Un Ins 13021, 13021.5**
Garnishment, this index
Golf caddies, **Un Ins 651**
Good cause,
  Leaving employment, **Un Ins 1256**
  Sexual harassment, **Un Ins 1256.5**
Governmental entity, election to become employer, approval, **Un Ins 710**
Grand jurors, eligibility, **Un Ins 1253.6**
Grants,
  Green collar jobs, **Un Ins 14022**
  Job training and placement services, faith based organizations, **Un Ins 9617**
  Training projects, **Un Ins 10215**
Gratuities as wages, **Un Ins 927**
Green collar jobs,
  Grants, **Un Ins 14022**
  Training, **Un Ins 15000 et seq.**
Gross income, definitions, withholding tax on wages, **Un Ins 13006**
Guidelines, providing upon request, **Un Ins 307**
Handicapped persons, **Un Ins 18000 et seq.**
  Disability benefits, **Un Ins 2606**
  Job preparation and training services, post
  Neurologically handicapped, nonprofessional employees, **Un Ins 1451 et seq.**

UNEMPLOYMENT

UNEMPLOYMENT COMPENSATION
—Cont'd

Handicapped persons—Cont'd
Qualifications, **Un Ins 605**

Hazard, degree, **Un Ins 326**

Health care providers, caregiver training initiative, **Un Ins 11020 et seq.**

Health facilities, family care leave, claims, statements, **Un Ins 3306**

Hearing impaired persons, employment services, **Un Ins 11000 et seq.**

Hearings, **Un Ins 1951 et seq.**
Elective coverage, objections, **Un Ins 707**
Evidence, **Un Ins 407**
Failure to appear or testify or produce records, **Un Ins 2104**
Telecommunications, **Un Ins 1953.5**

History, training projects participants, employment, wages, and benefits, **Un Ins 10214**

Holiday pay,
Construing as wages for personal services, **Un Ins 1265.5**
Delayed payment, **Un Ins 1265.6**

Holocaust, disability compensation, restitution, **Un Ins 2629.5**

Horse racing, **Un Ins 654**

Horticultural labor, **Un Ins 611 et seq.**

Hospitals, this index

Hotlines, joint enforcement strike force on the underground economy, **Un Ins 329**

Hours of labor, refusal of new work, **Un Ins 1259**

Husband and wife,
Definitions, withholding tax on wages, **Un Ins 13003**
Disability compensation, claims, mentally deficient claimants, **Un Ins 2705.1**
Disclaimer of rights, **Un Ins 637.1**
Employment of spouse, **Un Ins 631**
Family care leave, serious health conditions, **Un Ins 3300 et seq.**
Joining husband beyond commuting area as reason for leaving employment, **Un Ins 1030**
Mentally deficient claimant, **Un Ins 2705.1**
Paid family care leave, serious health conditions, **Un Ins 3300 et seq.**
Reserve accounts, leaving employment to join spouse beyond commuting area, charges, **Un Ins 1032**

Identity and identification, persons, withholding tax on wages, **Un Ins 13015, 13057**

Immigration, undocumented workers, liability of employers providing wage statements, **Un Ins 2128**

Immunity from prosecution, **Un Ins 1955**

Impasse, appeals board, **Un Ins 409**

In home supportive services,
Application of law, **Un Ins 685**

UNEMPLOYMENT COMPENSATION
—Cont'd

In home supportive services—Cont'd
Domestic employees, coverage, **Un Ins 683**

Inactive out of business accounts, offers in compromise, **Un Ins 1870 et seq.**

Incarceration, **Un Ins 1030.1, 1256.1**

Income Tax—State, this index

Incorrect employer, underpayment or overpayment, **Un Ins 1127.5**

Incumbrances. Liens and incumbrances, generally, post

Independent contractors,
Fees for services, eligibility, **Un Ins 1252**
Professional services, presumption, **Un Ins 656**

Index, decisions of appeals board, **Un Ins 409**

Indians,
Assessments, delinquency, notice, **Un Ins 1141.1**
Concealed wages, fines and penalties, **Un Ins 1128.1, 1735.1**
Contributions,
Delinquency, notice, **Un Ins 1119**
Finance, elections, **Un Ins 802, 803**
Delinquency,
Finance, elections, **Un Ins 803**
Notice, **Un Ins 804, 1119, 1141.1**
Disability compensation, elective coverage, **Un Ins 709, 710.6**
Elective coverage, **Un Ins 709, 710, 710.6**
Employing unit, **Un Ins 135**
Exclusions, **Un Ins 634.5**
Extended unemployment compensation, **Un Ins 710**
Finance, elections, **Un Ins 802, 803**
Fines and penalties, concealed wages, **Un Ins 1128.1, 1735.1**
Notice, delinquency, **Un Ins 804, 1119, 1141.1**
Registration, **Un Ins 1086**
Tribal councils, exclusions, **Un Ins 634.5**

Industrial disability, **Un Ins 2775 et seq.**

Infants. Children and minors, generally, ante

Information, **Un Ins 1088 et seq.**
Aid to families with dependent children (CalWORKs) applicants and recipients, **Un Ins 1088.5**
Applicants and recipients, **Un Ins 1088.5**
Benefit rights and claims, duty of employer, **Un Ins 1089**
Confidential or privileged information, generally, post
Disability compensation, ante
Disclosure of confidential information, **Un Ins 2111**
Employment development department, **Un Ins 322**
Exchanges, **Un Ins 322**

UNEMPLOYMENT COMPENSATION
—Cont'd

Information—Cont'd
Felony arrest warrant issued for applicant, furnishing information to law enforcement agencies, **Un Ins 1095**
Furnishing to federal agencies, **Un Ins 321**
Governmental entity as employer, filing, **Un Ins 710**
New hirees and rehirees, **Un Ins 1088.5**
Public instruction, employee pamphlets, **Un Ins 316**
Sharing, joint enforcement strike force on the underground economy, **Un Ins 329**
Submission, method, **Un Ins 1333**
Taxpayers rights, **Un Ins 1231**
Use, permission by director, **Un Ins 1095**
Work records, **Un Ins 1085**
Workforce and economic information program, **Un Ins 10529**

Informing employers and workers of rights and responsibilities, **Un Ins 316**

Injunction,
Inducing violation, **Un Ins 1855**
Issuance to prevent collection of contributions, **Un Ins 1851**

Inmates, excluded services, **Un Ins 634.5**

Insane persons, payment, **Un Ins 1341**

Insolvency,
Contributions,
Effect, **Un Ins 988**
Payment, **Un Ins 1115**
Employing unit, information regarding, **Un Ins 1090**
Failure to give notice, personal liability of successor or representative, **Un Ins 1736**
Jeopardy assessments, **Un Ins 1137.1**
Personal liability of representative, **Un Ins 1736**
Priority of lien for unpaid contributions, interest and penalties, **Un Ins 1701**

Inspection and inspectors,
Confidential or privileged information, withholding taxes, browsing, **Un Ins 13018**
Offers in compromise, records, **Un Ins 1873**

Installment payments, offers in compromise, **Un Ins 1870**

Institution of higher education, definitions, **Un Ins 1253.3**

Interest,
Assessments, **Un Ins 1129**
Collection,
Additional remedies, **Un Ins 1860**
Delinquent contributions, interest, **Un Ins 1851 et seq.**
Contributions, ante
Deposit in contingent fund, **Un Ins 1585**
Erroneous refunds, assessments, **Un Ins 1184**

UNEMPLOYMENT COMPENSATION
—Cont'd
Interest—Cont'd
Judgment liens, release or subordination, **Un Ins 1817**
Liens for unpaid interest, **Un Ins 1701 et seq.**
Obligations, withholding tax on wages, **Un Ins 13014**
Reciprocity, **Un Ins 453**
Refunds and overpayment, **Un Ins 1177, 1178, 1179.5, 1181 et seq., 1242**
Summary judgment, delinquent contributions, interest, **Un Ins 1815 et seq.**
Intergovernmental cooperation, joint enforcement strike force on the underground economy, **Un Ins 329**
Internal Revenue Service Schedule SE, definitions, elective coverage, **Un Ins 704, 704.1, 708, 708.5**
Interns, **Un Ins 645, 711**
Interstate cooperation, **Un Ins 451 et seq.**
Intoxicated persons. Alcoholics and alcoholism, generally, ante
Intrastate services, **Un Ins 602 et seq.**
Investigations and investigators,
Persons convicted of violations, payment of costs, **Un Ins 2126**
Research, **Un Ins 325, 326**
Field investigating staff, authorization for and functions, **Un Ins 317**
Investments,
Administration fund, **Un Ins 1560**
Disability compensation, **Un Ins 3002, 3003**
Irregular payment of wages, computation of benefits, **Un Ins 1282**
Jeopardy assessments, administrative appellate review, **Un Ins 1221 et seq.**
Job preparation and training services, **Un Ins 10200 et seq.**
Caregiver training initiative, **Un Ins 11020 et seq.**
Compensation and salaries, minimum wages, waiver, **Un Ins 10201.5**
Economically disadvantaged areas, **Un Ins 9602**
Faith based organizations, grants, **Un Ins 9617**
Grants, faith based organizations, **Un Ins 9617**
Handicapped persons, **Un Ins 18000 et seq.**
Screens and screening, **Un Ins 14002**
Housing programs, youthbuild program, **Un Ins 9800 et seq.**
Learning disabilities, screens and screening, **Un Ins 14002**
Local plans, **Un Ins 9616.1**
Minimum wages, waiver, **Un Ins 10201.5**
Religious organizations and societies, grants, **Un Ins 9617**
Solar energy, **Un Ins 9618**
Statewide plan, **Un Ins 9600**

UNEMPLOYMENT COMPENSATION
—Cont'd
Job preparation and training services
—Cont'd
Workforce and economic information program, **Un Ins 10529**
Youthbuild program, **Un Ins 9800 et seq.**
Jockeys, **Un Ins 654**
Joint accounts,
Elective financing, **Un Ins 803**
Nonprofit corporations, elective coverage, **Un Ins 711**
Joint and several liability, offers in compromise, **Un Ins 1874**
Joint enforcement strike force on the underground economy, **Un Ins 329**
Citations, penalty assessment orders, **Labor 106**
Judges,
Administrative law judges, generally, ante
Excluded service, **Un Ins 634.5**
Judgment liens,
Overpayments, **Un Ins 1379.5**
Release and subordination, **Un Ins 1817**
Relief and subordination, **Un Ins 1817**
Judgments and decrees,
Appeals, **Un Ins 1241 et seq.**
Appeals board precedent decisions, reversal or invalidity, **Un Ins 409.1**
Contingent fund, appropriations for interest, **Un Ins 1586**
Overpayment recovery, enforcement, **Un Ins 1379, 1381**
Disability compensation, **Un Ins 2739**
Payment, **Un Ins 1534**
Summary judgment, generally, post
Jury,
Eligibility, **Un Ins 1252, 1253.6, 1253.7**
Fees as wages, **Un Ins 1252**
Qualification for benefits, **Un Ins 1253.7**
Weekly benefit amount, **Un Ins 1279**
Juvenile facilities division, wards, excluded services, **Un Ins 633.1, 634.5**
Labor Disputes, this index
Labor organizations, refusal of new work because of requirements, **Un Ins 1259**
Laboratory technicians, **Un Ins 711**
Law enforcement agencies, information exchanges, applicants with outstanding felony arrest warrants, **Un Ins 1095**
Layoffs,
Election in place of employee with less seniority, **Un Ins 1256**
Record, **Un Ins 1085**
Learning disabilities, job preparation and training services, screens and screening, **Un Ins 14002**
Leasing of employees, determination of employer, **Un Ins 606.5**
Leave of absence, record, **Un Ins 1085**
Legislature, members, excluded services, **Un Ins 634.5**
Leisure sharing, **Un Ins 12100 et seq.**

UNEMPLOYMENT COMPENSATION
—Cont'd
Liability,
Nonpayment of contributions, corporation and association officers, shareholders and others, **Un Ins 1735, 1735.1**
Offers in compromise, **Un Ins 1870 et seq.**
Overpayment, **Un Ins 1380**
Libraries, **Un Ins 711**
Licensed vocational nurses, caregiver training initiative, **Un Ins 11020 et seq.**
Licenses and permits,
Denial, agricultural labor, failure to remit contributions, **Labor 1690.1**
Employer failing to have proper license, refusing employment, **Un Ins 1259**
Liens and incumbrances,
Abstracts of judgment, disability compensation, **Un Ins 2739.1, 2739.2**
Disability compensation, **Un Ins 2739.1**
Filing and releasing, **Un Ins 301**
Judgment liens, generally, ante
Offers in compromise, rescission, **Un Ins 1703, 1875**
Overpayment of benefits, **Un Ins 1375.3 et seq.**
Release,
Judgment liens, **Un Ins 1817**
Offers in compromise, **Un Ins 1873**
Rescission, offers in compromise, **Un Ins 1703**
Satisfaction of judgment, **Un Ins 1379.6**
Subordination, judgment liens, **Un Ins 1817**
Unpaid contributions, interest and penalties, **Un Ins 1701 et seq.**
After acquired property, **Un Ins 1703**
Enforcement, **Un Ins 1785**
Notices of levy, **Un Ins 1755 et seq.**
Priorities and preferences, **Un Ins 1703**
Summary judgment, **Un Ins 1816**
Warrant for collection, **Un Ins 1785 et seq.**
Workers compensation,
Discharge, **Un Ins 1375.5**
Overpayment of benefits, **Un Ins 1375.3**
Limitation of actions,
Bulk transfers, contributions due, action against successor, **Un Ins 1734**
Collection of delinquent contributions, **Un Ins 1785, 1852**
Obligation for contributions, enforcement, **Un Ins 1734**
Overpayments, recovery, **Un Ins 1379, 1383, 2113**
Disability compensation, **Un Ins 2739**
Refunds of contributions, **Un Ins 1536**
Violations of chapter, **Un Ins 2125**
Limited liability companies,
Contributions, withholding, **Un Ins 2110**

UNEMPLOYMENT

UNEMPLOYMENT COMPENSATION
—Cont'd

Limited liability companies—Cont'd

Dissolution, final return, **Un Ins 1116, 1735**

Loans of employees, determination of employer, **Un Ins 606.5**

Local experience charge, school districts, **Un Ins 828**

Local plans, job development, **Un Ins 9616.1**

Local public entities, elective coverage, **Un Ins 709**

Localized service, **Un Ins 603**

Lockouts, refusal of new work during, **Un Ins 1259**

Longshoring operations, **Un Ins 1253.2**

Magazines, distribution by minors, **Un Ins 649**

Mailing notice, **Un Ins 1206**

Erroneous payments to other state or federal agency, **Un Ins 991**

Mandamus,

Issuance to prevent collection of contributions, **Un Ins 1851**

Religious organizations and societies, **Un Ins 1241**

Manuals, providing upon request, **Un Ins 307**

Marriage,

Husband and wife, generally, ante

Leaving employment for purpose, **Un Ins 1264**

Maximum benefits, **Un Ins 1281**

Medical care and treatment,

Condition, fraud, offenses, **Un Ins 2116**

Emergencies, qualification for benefits, **Un Ins 1253.7**

Expenses and expenditures, **Un Ins 931, 933**

Medical examinations,

Disability compensation, ante

Family care leave, **Un Ins 3306**

Medical leave, **Gov 12945.2**

Medicine. Drugs and medicine, generally, ante

Mentally ill persons,

Benefits, payment, **Un Ins 1341**

Eligibility, **Un Ins 1253.5**

Mentally retarded and developmentally disabled persons,

Benefits, payment, **Un Ins 1341**

Eligibility, **Un Ins 1253.5**

Merger and consolidation, employer unit, effect, **Un Ins 135.1, 135.2**

Michigan California lumber company fire, unemployment caused by, extended benefits, **Un Ins 1281.7**

Midwives, certificates of disability, **Un Ins 2708**

Military forces, **Un Ins 1252, 1279**

Definitions, withholding tax on wages, **Un Ins 13003**

Disability compensation,

Disqualification for acts prior to service, **Un Ins 2771**

UNEMPLOYMENT COMPENSATION
—Cont'd

Military forces—Cont'd

Disability compensation—Cont'd

Trainees, **Un Ins 2765 et seq.**

Discharged personnel, unexpired leave time, compensation eligibility, **Un Ins 1253.15**

Income tax, application of law, **Un Ins 13003**

National guard, excluded service, **Un Ins 634.5**

Wages, exclusion of payments, **Un Ins 938.5**

Mineral broker or salesman, **Un Ins 650**

Minimum wages, **Un Ins 1281**

Computation, **Un Ins 1277.5**

Job preparation and training services, waiver, **Un Ins 10201.5**

Minorities, economically disadvantaged areas, **Un Ins 9602**

Minors. Children and minors, generally, ante

Miscellaneous payroll period, definitions, withholding tax on wages, **Un Ins 13007**

Misconduct, **Un Ins 1030, 1030.1, 1032**

Charges against employers account, **Un Ins 1032**

Conviction of offense, **Un Ins 1030.1, 1256.1**

Denial of benefits, **Un Ins 1260.1**

Discharge, **Un Ins 1256**

Misrepresentation. Fraud, generally, ante

Mistakes. Errors, generally, ante

Moneys of department, withholding tax on wages, **Un Ins 13011**

Most recent work, eligibility, **Un Ins 1256.3**

Motion pictures, **Un Ins 601.5**

Payroll services companies, employer or employing unit, **Un Ins 679**

Disability compensation, **Un Ins 680**

Moving expenses, **Un Ins 937**

Deductions, income tax, application of law, **Un Ins 13003**

Municipal Officers and Employees, this index

National guard, **Un Ins 1252, 1279**

Excluded services, **Un Ins 634.5**

National plan, policy, **Un Ins 101**

National service programs, excluded services, **Un Ins 634.5**

Neglect of duty, alcoholics and alcoholism, disqualifications, **Un Ins 1256.4**

Net balance of reserve, definitions, **Un Ins 904**

Neurologically handicapped students, nonprofessional employees, **Un Ins 1451 et seq.**

New claims, computations, **Un Ins 1277, 1277.1**

New employers, rates and charges, **Un Ins 982**

New hires, reports, **Un Ins 1088.5**

UNEMPLOYMENT COMPENSATION
—Cont'd

Newsboys, delivery, excluded services, **Un Ins 634.5**

Newspapers, distribution by minors, **Un Ins 649**

Nolo contendere, conviction of crime,

Elective coverage, **Un Ins 704, 704.1**

Qualification for benefits, **Un Ins 1263**

Voluntarily leaving work, **Un Ins 1256.1**

Nonparticipating employer, eligibility, **Un Ins 1259**

Nonprofit Associations, this index

Nonprofit corporations, **Un Ins 641**

Contributions, credits, **Un Ins 713**

Officers and employees, **Un Ins 1253.3**

Nonprofit organizations,

Contributions, generally, ante

Definitions, **Un Ins 711**

Elective coverage, **Un Ins 711 et seq.**

Excludable services, **Un Ins 711**

Officers and employees, **Un Ins 1253.3**

Officials, **Un Ins 652**

Previously accumulated favorable reserve account, reimbursement of benefits, **Un Ins 803.2**

Proportionate share of cost, **Un Ins 711**

Reimbursement financing, **Un Ins 805**

Nonqualified deferred compensation plans, definitions, **Un Ins 928.5**

Nonresident,

Definitions, withholding tax on wages, **Un Ins 13003**

Foreign state and political subdivisions employees, **Un Ins 632**

Taxpayers, income tax, application of law, **Un Ins 13003**

Notice, **Un Ins 1206, 1333, 1334**

Agricultural labor, failure to remit contributions, **Labor 1690.1; Un Ins 1141**

Assessments, ante

Assistants to individual employed by employing unit, **Un Ins 606**

Change of relationship to employer, employers duty, **Un Ins 1089**

Child support obligations owed by claimants, **Un Ins 1255.7**

Claim for benefit,

Filing, determinations, **Un Ins 1327 et seq.**

New or additional, **Un Ins 1030**

Public entities, election of method of financing, **Un Ins 806**

Collections,

Offers in compromise, **Un Ins 1870**

Withholding tax on wages, **Un Ins 13072**

Computations, **Un Ins 1329**

Contributions,

Agricultural labor, failure to remit, **Labor 1690.1; Un Ins 1141**

Jeopardy collection, **Un Ins 1115**

Correct employer, determination, **Un Ins 1127.5**

Demand for wage report, **Un Ins 1114**

UNEMPLOYMENT COMPENSATION
—Cont'd
Notice—Cont'd
Disability compensation, ante
Discharge for misconduct, **Un Ins 1256**
Elective coverage, ante
Employing unit, insolvency, information, **Un Ins 1090**
Erroneous payments to other state or federal agency, **Un Ins 991**
Erroneously collected contributions, **Un Ins 1177**
Extended unemployment compensation, ante
Garnishment for delinquent contributions, **Un Ins 1755 et seq.**
Indians, delinquency, **Un Ins 804, 1119, 1141.1**
Jeopardy collection, contributions, **Un Ins 1115**
Levy, notices of, **Un Ins 1755 et seq.**
Mail and mailing, **Un Ins 1206**
Modified precedent decisions, duty of appeals board, **Un Ins 409.1**
Motion picture payroll services company, employer or employing unit, **Un Ins 679**
Offers in compromise, rescissions, **Un Ins 1875**
Overpayment, **Un Ins 1376**
Part time employment, **Un Ins 1032.5**
Personal liability for failure to file, **Un Ins 1736**
Presumptions, reason for termination, **Un Ins 1256**
Protest, decision on, **Un Ins 1035**
Public entities, method of financing, **Un Ins 806**
Publication, generally, post
Reasons for termination of employment, time, **Un Ins 1030**
Recomputation of benefits, **Un Ins 1332**
Records or reports, furnishing, **Un Ins 1093**
Refunds and overpayments, post
Rescission, offers in compromise, **Un Ins 1875**
Reserve accounts, post
Submission, regulations, **Un Ins 1333**
Support, **Un Ins 2630**
Termination of employment,
Employer report, **Un Ins 1030**
Reasons, employer reports, **Un Ins 1030**
Third party payors, **Un Ins 931.5**
Training and retraining benefits, **Un Ins 1271, 1271.5**
Transfer of reserve account, ruling on application, **Un Ins 1055**
Withhold notices, delinquent contributions, **Un Ins 1755 et seq.**
Number of unreported employees, definitions, **Un Ins 1126.1**
Nurses,
Caregiver training initiative, **Un Ins 11020 et seq.**

UNEMPLOYMENT COMPENSATION
—Cont'd
Nurses—Cont'd
Student nurses, **Un Ins 645**
Training, **Un Ins 10214.9**
Oaths and affirmations, **Un Ins 16, 1953**
Statements, withholding tax on wages, **Un Ins 13058**
Off indicator, federal state extended benefits for week, **Un Ins 4003**
Offenses. Crimes and offenses, generally, ante
Offers in compromise. Collection, ante
Officers of corporation, **Un Ins 637**
Liability, nonpayment of contributions, **Un Ins 1735**
Offset,
Overpayments, **Un Ins 1379**
Disability compensation, **Un Ins 2739**
Extended unemployment compensation benefits, **Un Ins 3751**
Pensions or similar periodic payments, **Un Ins 1255.3**
Oil and gas broker or salesman, **Un Ins 650**
On indicator, federal state extended benefits for week, **Un Ins 4003**
Optometrists, primary care clinics, **Un Ins 656**
Organized camps, full time students, exclusion, **Un Ins 642.1**
Orientation, reemployment activities, participation, eligibility, **Un Ins 1253**
Osteopaths, primary care clinics, **Un Ins 656**
Other benefits, definitions, **Un Ins 2629**
Other proceedings, evidence, **Un Ins 1960**
Out of business accounts, offers in compromise, **Un Ins 1870 et seq.**
Out of state,
Remuneration, **Un Ins 930.1**
Service, **Un Ins 602 et seq.**
Elective coverage, **Un Ins 703**
Overpayments. Refunds and overpayments, generally, post
Paid family care leave, **Un Ins 3300 et seq.**
Pamphlets, informational, printing in English, **Un Ins 316**
Papers. Books and papers, generally, ante
Parent benefit year, definitions, extended compensation, **Un Ins 3503**
Parents employed by son or daughter, coverage, **Un Ins 631, 702.5**
Part time service or employment, **Un Ins 1252**
Computation of benefits, **Un Ins 1279**
Eligibility, **Un Ins 1253.8**
Receiving less than weekly benefit amount, **Un Ins 1032.5**
Parties, training contracts, **Un Ins 10209**
Partnership,
Definitions, withholding tax on wages, **Un Ins 13003**
Delinquent contributions, offers in compromise, **Un Ins 1870 et seq.**

UNEMPLOYMENT COMPENSATION
—Cont'd
Partnership—Cont'd
Foreign limited liability partnerships, withholdings, **Un Ins 1735**
Income tax, application of law, **Un Ins 13003**
Registered limited liability partnerships, withholdings, **Un Ins 1735**
Violations, **Un Ins 2110**
Workforce recovery training, **Un Ins 10214.6**
Pay period,
Definitions, **Un Ins 607**
Services performed during half or more of pay period, effect, **Un Ins 607**
Payment, **Un Ins 1326**
Agency, **Un Ins 1339**
Appeal pending, **Un Ins 1335**
Appeals board decision, **Un Ins 1338**
Child support obligations of claimants, **Un Ins 1255.7**
Children and minors, **Un Ins 1340**
Confidential or privileged information, disclosure, **Un Ins 1095**
Contracts, training contracts, **Un Ins 10209**
Contributions, ante
Deceased persons, **Un Ins 1341**
Definitions, wages, **Un Ins 931**
Disability compensation, ante
Eligible days, disqualification, **Un Ins 1253.5**
Incompetent persons, **Un Ins 1341**
Multistate coverage, **Un Ins 455.5**
Overpayments. Refunds and overpayments, generally, post
Reciprocal arrangements, **Un Ins 455**
Refunds and overpayments, generally, post
Supplemental plan of employer, **Un Ins 1265**
Third parties, wages, reports, **Un Ins 13009.5**
Payroll period,
Definitions, withholding tax on wages, **Un Ins 13008**
Withholding tax on wages, **Un Ins 13020, 13021**
Payroll underreporting, audits, **Labor 90.7**
Peace officers, applicants with felony arrest warrants outstanding, information exchange with law enforcement agencies, **Un Ins 1095**
Penal institution inmates, excluded services, **Un Ins 634.5**
Penalties. Fines and penalties, generally, ante
Pensions. Retirement and pensions, generally, post
Perjury, **Un Ins 16**
Personal income tax fund,
Deposits, **Un Ins 1526.1, 1585.5**
Transfer of funds, **Un Ins 1589**
Personal injuries, eligibility, **Un Ins 1253.5**

UNEMPLOYMENT

UNEMPLOYMENT COMPENSATION
—Cont'd

Personal liability,
  Officers and shareholders, contributions, withholding, penalties and interest, **Un Ins 1735.1**
  Successors, unpaid contributions, interest and penalties, **Un Ins 1732, 1733**
Persons, definitions, withholding tax on wages, **Un Ins 13003**
Petitions, **Un Ins 1951 et seq.**
Physicians and surgeons,
  Family care leave, claims, statements, **Un Ins 3306**
  Independent contractors, presumption as, **Un Ins 656**
  Presumption of independent contractor status, **Un Ins 656**
  Primary care clinics, **Un Ins 656**
Place of rendition of services, **Un Ins 602 et seq.**
Placement, workforce investment, **Un Ins 14000 et seq.**
Plea of guilty deemed conviction, **Un Ins 1030.1, 1256.1**
Podiatrists (chiropody), primary care clinics, **Un Ins 656**
Policy making positions, public officers and employees, excluded services, **Un Ins 634.5**
Political campaign workers, **Un Ins 636**
Political Subdivisions, this index
Population surveys, **Un Ins 327**
Postal service authorities, disability compensation, definitions, **Un Ins 2606.4**
Posting information as to benefits, **Un Ins 1089**
Powers and duties,
  Department, **Un Ins 325**
  Joint enforcement strike force on the underground economy, **Un Ins 329**
Prayer healing, disability benefits, certificate of disability, **Un Ins 2709**
Preferences. Priorities and preferences, generally, post
Presumptions. Evidence, ante
Primary care clinics, health care practitioners, **Un Ins 656**
Primary claim, definitions, extended compensation, **Un Ins 3503**
Priorities and preferences,
  Actions to collect delinquent contributions, **Un Ins 1853**
  Aid to families with dependent children (CalWORKs), **Un Ins 9615**
  Automation, benefit payment control program, **Un Ins 333**
  Liens for contributions, **Un Ins 1701 et seq.**
  Public works, **Labor 2015**
Private industry councils, **Un Ins 3503**
Privileged information. Confidential or privileged information, generally, ante
Probate proceedings,
  Benefits, payment, **Un Ins 1341**

UNEMPLOYMENT COMPENSATION
—Cont'd

Probate proceedings—Cont'd
  Executors and administrators, generally, ante
Probationary period, employment training contracts, **Un Ins 10209**
Proceedings. Actions and proceedings, generally, ante
Process,
  Exemption of benefits from supplemental plans, **Un Ins 1342**
  Issuance to prevent collection of contributions, **Un Ins 1851**
  Service of process, generally, post
Production of books and records,
  Failure, **Un Ins 2104**
  Power to compel, **Un Ins 1953**
Prompt payment of benefits, **Un Ins 1326**
Property affected by liens for contributions, **Un Ins 1703**
Protests,
  Computation of benefits, **Un Ins 1330**
  Disability compensation, ante
  Statement of account or rate, **Un Ins 1034**
  Submission, method, **Un Ins 1333**
Psychology and psychologists, primary care clinics, **Un Ins 656**
Public Agencies, this index
Public buildings and works, winning bidder failure to carry, action by second highest bidder, **Labor 1750**
Public corporations, elective coverage, **Un Ins 709**
Public Employees Retirement System, this index
Public employment offices, **Un Ins 2051 et seq.**
  Benefits, payment, **Un Ins 1339**
  Definitions, **Un Ins 137**
  Disability compensation, **Un Ins 2701**
  Payment, benefits, **Un Ins 1339**
  Registration, **Un Ins 1253**
  Reports, **Un Ins 1260**
Public entities,
  Definitions, **Un Ins 135, 605**
  Elective coverage, **Un Ins 709, 711**
  Eligibility, **Un Ins 1253.3**
  Employing units, **Un Ins 135, 605**
  Financing coverage, **Un Ins 802, 803**
Public housing administration agency,
  Elections for financing, **Un Ins 802, 803**
  Services performed for, **Un Ins 605**
Public Officers and Employees, this index
Public policy, **Un Ins 100**
Public records. Records and recordation, generally, post
Public safety, corporation testing for, elective coverage, **Un Ins 711**
Public service employment. Work Incentive Programs, generally, this index
Publication,
  Determination of trade dispute, **Un Ins 1262.5**

UNEMPLOYMENT COMPENSATION
—Cont'd

Publication—Cont'd
  Information by director, governmental entity as employer, **Un Ins 710**
  Rate, annual tax or contribution, **Un Ins 989**
Purchaser of business, withholding money or property, unpaid contributions, **Un Ins 1731 et seq.**
Quitting business, **Un Ins 1116**
Radio and television, employer, definitions, **Un Ins 678**
Rates and charges, **Un Ins 982**
  Contributions, ante
  Disability compensation, voluntary plans, reimbursement, **Un Ins 3252**
  Emergency solvency surcharge rate, **Un Ins 977.5**
  Extended unemployment compensation, computations, **Un Ins 3504**
  School employees fund, contribution rate, **Un Ins 823**
Rating period, definitions, **Un Ins 903**
Real estate, department, withholding tax on wages, **Un Ins 13011**
Real estate broker or salesman, **Un Ins 650**
Reasonable assurance, definitions, **Un Ins 1253.3**
Reasonable cash value, remuneration payable in medium other than cash, **Un Ins 926**
Reassessment. Assessments, ante
Receivers and receivership,
  Employing unit, **Un Ins 135**
  Information regarding, **Un Ins 1090**
  Personal liability, **Un Ins 1736**
Reciprocity, **Un Ins 451 et seq.**
Recomputation of benefits, **Un Ins 1330, 1332**
Reconciliation returns. Returns, post
Records and recordation, **Un Ins 1085 et seq.**
  Acknowledgment of satisfaction of judgment, disability compensation, **Un Ins 2739.2**
  Agents, several employers, preparation, **Un Ins 1096 et seq.**
  Confidential or privileged information, disclosure, **Un Ins 1095**
  Copying of employer records, **Un Ins 1092**
  Decisions of appeals board, public inspection, **Un Ins 409**
  Disability compensation, ante
  Employee contributions, **Un Ins 984, 984.5**
  Employment records, duty to keep, **Un Ins 1085**
  Erroneously collected contributions, **Un Ins 1177**
  Extended unemployment compensation, computation, **Un Ins 3504**
  Failure to produce, **Un Ins 2104, 2105**

UNEMPLOYMENT COMPENSATION
—Cont'd

Records and recordation—Cont'd
Governmental entity as employer, work records, **Un Ins 710**
Hearing proceedings, **Un Ins 1952**
Information, employer furnishing from, **Un Ins 1092**
Inspection of employer records, **Un Ins 1092**
Liens and incumbrances,
Disability compensation, **Un Ins 2739.1**
Unpaid contributions, interest and penalties, **Un Ins 1702 et seq.**
Offers in compromise, **Un Ins 1873**
Rescission, **Un Ins 1875**
Pay roll records, employee contributions, **Un Ins 986**
Power to compel production, **Un Ins 1953**
Presumption on failure to keep or furnish, **Un Ins 1093**
Public inspection of records, **Un Ins 2111**
Statement of employer tax schedules, **Un Ins 979**
Satisfaction of judgment, acknowledgment, **Un Ins 1379.6**
Statement of employer tax schedules, **Un Ins 979**
Subpoena for production, **Un Ins 1953 et seq.**
Summary judgment, delinquent contributions, interest or penalties, **Un Ins 1815, 1816**
Sworn statements of matters contained in, **Un Ins 1092**
Tax disputes, compromise and settlement, **Un Ins 1236**
Withholding tax on wages, **Un Ins 13011**
Work record of employing unit, **Un Ins 1085**
Recovery, workforce recovery training, **Un Ins 10214.6**
Recurrence of disqualification, **Un Ins 2675**
Reduction, **Un Ins 1260.1**
Genocide, disability compensation, **Un Ins 2629.5**
Retirement and pensions, **Un Ins 1255.3**
Redwood Park expansion, severance or terminal pay, application of law, **Un Ins 1265.9**
Reemployment activities, participation, eligibility, **Un Ins 1253**
Referees. Administrative law judges, generally, ante
Refunds and overpayments, **Un Ins 1176 et seq., 1375 et seq., 1534, 3751**
Administration, **Un Ins 301**
Amounts collected by setoffs against income tax refunds, deposit, **Un Ins 1384**
Appeals, **Un Ins 1178, 1241 et seq., 1377**

UNEMPLOYMENT COMPENSATION
—Cont'd

Refunds and overpayments—Cont'd
Appeals—Cont'd
Determination by appeals board, **Un Ins 1378**
Assessments, **Un Ins 1375.1**
Erroneous refunds, **Un Ins 1184**
Claims,
Denial, reversal, **Un Ins 1180.5**
Necessity, **Un Ins 1179**
Offers in compromise, **Un Ins 1180.1**
Payments pending decision on assessments or reassessment, **Un Ins 1179.5**
Requisites, **Un Ins 1179**
Review of denial, **Un Ins 1180**
Time for, **Un Ins 1178**
Collection,
Automation, **Un Ins 333, 334**
Offers in compromise, **Un Ins 1180.1**
Conditions precedent to allowance, **Un Ins 1178**
Contingent fund, appropriations, **Un Ins 1586**
Contributions, **Un Ins 1176.5, 1177, 1178**
Correction of errors, **Un Ins 1037**
Correction of errors, **Un Ins 1036**
Decision on appeal, **Un Ins 1377, 1378**
Determination of amount, **Un Ins 1376**
Disability compensation, ante
Employee contributions, several employers, **Un Ins 1176**
Employing units, **Un Ins 1177.5**
Enforcement of recovery, **Un Ins 1381**
Erroneously collected contributions, **Un Ins 1177**
Executions, judgment liens, **Un Ins 1379.5**
Garnishment, service of process, **CCP 706.101**
Illegally collected contributions, **Un Ins 1177**
Incorrect employer, **Un Ins 1127.5**
Interest, **Un Ins 1177, 1178, 1179.5, 1181 et seq., 1242**
Judgment liens, **Un Ins 1379.5**
Liability for overpayment, **Un Ins 1375**
Liens and incumbrances, judgment liens, **Un Ins 1379.5**
Notice,
Assessment for erroneous refunds, **Un Ins 1184**
Denial, **Un Ins 1180**
Overpayment, **Un Ins 1376**
Reversal of denied claim, **Un Ins 1180.5**
Offset,
Extended unemployment compensation benefits, **Un Ins 3751**
Overpayment, **Un Ins 1379**
Disability compensation, **Un Ins 2739**
Penalties, **Un Ins 1177, 1178**

UNEMPLOYMENT COMPENSATION
—Cont'd

Refunds and overpayments—Cont'd
Petition for review, failure to file, effect, **Un Ins 1179**
Reciprocity, **Un Ins 453**
Recovery of overpayment, **Un Ins 1379**
Disability compensation, **Un Ins 2739**
Disposition, **Un Ins 1381**
Enforcement, **Un Ins 1381**
Restitution, overpayment of benefits, **Un Ins 2113**
School employees fund, **Un Ins 1177.5**
Service of process, garnishment, **CCP 706.101**
Summary judgments, **Un Ins 1379**
Disability compensation, **Un Ins 2739**
Time, **Un Ins 1036**
Action on claim, recovery of overpayment, **Un Ins 1379, 1383**
Claim, **Un Ins 1176, 1178**
Notice of overpayment, **Un Ins 1377**
Petition for review, **Un Ins 1180**
Restitution for overpayment of benefits, **Un Ins 2113**
Various funds, **Un Ins 1589**
Waiver, **Un Ins 1179, 1241**
Workers compensation, disallowance of lien, **Un Ins 1375.3**
Refusal,
Grounds, **Un Ins 1259**
New work, conditions authorizing, **Un Ins 1259**
Suitable employment, **Un Ins 1257 et seq.**
Regents, University of California elective coverage, **Un Ins 709**
Registered limited liability partnerships, withholdings, **Un Ins 1735**
Registration,
Employer or employing unit, ante
Indians, **Un Ins 1086**
Public employment office, **Un Ins 1253**
Regular or customary work, definitions, **Un Ins 2626**
Regulations. Rules and regulations, generally, post
Rehabilitation program, excluded services, **Un Ins 634.5**
Rehired employees, reports, **Un Ins 1088.5**
Reimbursement financing, nonprofit corporations, reserve accounts, **Un Ins 801, 801.5, 1051.5**
Reimbursement of benefits,
Acquiring entity, **Un Ins 803.1**
Disability benefits and administrative costs, voluntary plans, **Un Ins 3252**
Nonprofit organizations, **Un Ins 805**
Accumulating favorable reserve account, **Un Ins 803.2**
Relatives, services performed by, **Un Ins 631**
Release,
Benefits from supplemental plans, **Un Ins 1342**
Offers in compromise, **Un Ins 1873**

UNEMPLOYMENT

UNEMPLOYMENT COMPENSATION
—Cont'd

Religious Organizations and Societies, this index

Remuneration,
Other than cash, withholding tax on wages, **Un Ins 13025**
Out of state remuneration, definitions, **Un Ins 930.1**

Rental payment deposited in contingent fund, **Un Ins 1585**

Repeals, rights, privileges, conferred, **Un Ins 102**

Reports, **Un Ins 1085 et seq., 1951**
Administration fund, **Un Ins 1562**
Agents, several employers, preparation, **Un Ins 1096 et seq.**
Contributions, ante
Crimes and offenses, **Un Ins 1145**
Employer fraud, **Un Ins 2115**
Delinquency, wage reports, **Un Ins 1114**
Director of employment development, **Un Ins 320**
Domestic service employees, wages, telephone filing, **Un Ins 1118**
Employer report,
Employee claim for benefits, **Un Ins 1327**
Fraud, **Un Ins 2115**
Evidence, failure to file, certification, **Un Ins 2123**
Excess worker contribution, tips, gratuities, **Un Ins 1088.6**
Failure to file, **Un Ins 1093, 2106, 2109**
Crimes and offenses, **Un Ins 2117, 2117.5**
Fines and penalties, **Un Ins 1128**
Report of wages after demand, penalty, **Un Ins 1114**
False reports by employer, **Un Ins 1142, 2115**
Colleges and universities, **Un Ins 1142.1**
Final, **Un Ins 1116**
Financial statements and reports, generally, ante
Fines and penalties, ante
Fraud deterrence and detection activity, **Un Ins 2614**
Funds, **Un Ins 995**
Governmental entity, filing, **Un Ins 710**
Green collar jobs, grants, **Un Ins 14022**
Hazards, various industries and occupations and cost to fund, **Un Ins 326**
Joint enforcement strike force on the underground economy, **Un Ins 329**
Motion picture payroll services company, employer or employing unit, **Un Ins 679**
New hirees, **Un Ins 1088.5**
Payroll underreporting, audits, **Labor 90.7**
Presumption on failure to keep or furnish, **Un Ins 1093**
Receivers, **Un Ins 1090**
Regulations, **Un Ins 320.5**

UNEMPLOYMENT COMPENSATION
—Cont'd

Reports—Cont'd
Rehired employees, **Un Ins 1088.5**
Returns, generally, post
Support, **Un Ins 1088.8**
Support obligors, **Un Ins 1088.5**
Training, expenses and expenditures, **Un Ins 9600.5**
Wages, post
Withholding tax on wages, **Un Ins 13050 et seq.**
Emergencies, time extension, **Un Ins 13059**

Representation before appeals board, authorization forms, **Un Ins 1957.5**

Rescission, offers in compromise, **Un Ins 1875**

Reserve accounts, **Un Ins 1025 et seq.**
Administration, **Un Ins 301**
Appeal and review,
Decision on protest, **Un Ins 1035**
Payments, **Un Ins 1335**
Transfer, ruling on application, **Un Ins 1055**
Balancing account,
Negative reserve balance, cancellation, **Un Ins 1027.5, 1027.6**
Negative reserve balances transferred, **Un Ins 1027.1**
Cancellation, **Un Ins 1027.1, 1027.5, 1027.6, 1029**
Charges against employer, **Un Ins 1025 et seq., 1032**
Credits to employer, **Un Ins 1025, 1026**
Disability benefits not to be charged, **Un Ins 2603**
Disclosures, avoiding charges, **Un Ins 1030**
Employers, rates and charges, **Un Ins 982**
Establishment, **Un Ins 301**
Funds, availability to pay benefits, **Un Ins 1025**
Inactive accounts, cancellation, **Un Ins 1029**
Joint account, **Un Ins 1056**
Joint venture, **Un Ins 1057, 1058**
Nonprofit corporations, reimbursement financing, **Un Ins 801, 801.5, 1051.5**
Nonprofit organizations, reimbursement of benefits, **Un Ins 803.2**
Notice,
Correction of error, **Un Ins 1036**
Decision on protest, **Un Ins 1035**
Transfer, ruling on application, **Un Ins 1055**
Pooling of contributions, **Un Ins 1025**
Protest of statement, **Un Ins 1034**
Rate of contribution pending protest, **Un Ins 1037**
Separate records, duty to keep, **Un Ins 1025, 1026**
Several employers, charging benefits paid, **Un Ins 1026**

UNEMPLOYMENT COMPENSATION
—Cont'd

Reserve accounts—Cont'd
Statements,
Furnishing to employer, **Un Ins 1033**
Notice of error, **Un Ins 1036**
Protest, **Un Ins 1034**
Successor employer, transfer, **Un Ins 1052**
Time,
Appeals, decision on protest, **Un Ins 1035**
Application for transfer, **Un Ins 1051, 1053**
Contribution rate, change on transfer, **Un Ins 1060**
Protest of statement, **Un Ins 1034**
Transfer, **Un Ins 1061**
Review, **Un Ins 1055**
Transfer, **Un Ins 301, 1051 et seq.**
Applicability of provision for transfer, **Un Ins 1052**
Application, **Un Ins 1051, 1055**
Time, contents, **Un Ins 1051**
Contribution rate, effect, **Un Ins 1060**
Employer, definitions, **Un Ins 1057, 1058**
Joint venture, **Un Ins 1057, 1058**
Notice of ruling on application, **Un Ins 1055**
Predecessor employer to successor nonprofit organization, **Un Ins 1051.5**
Reports in lieu of application for transfer, **Un Ins 1054**
Time, **Un Ins 1061**
Reserve of military forces, **Un Ins 1252, 1279**
Resident, definitions, withholding tax on wages, **Un Ins 13003**
Restitution,
Crime victims, wage and claim information, **Un Ins 1095**
Information, **Un Ins 1095**
Overpayment of benefits, **Un Ins 2113**
Retaliatory actions against employees, **Un Ins 1237**
Retirement and pensions,
Amount of pension or similar periodic payments, reduction of compensation benefits, **Un Ins 1255.3**
Payments, **Un Ins 931**
Presumptions, division of contributions, reduction of benefits, **Un Ins 1255.3**
Under collective bargaining agreement, Eligibility for benefits, **Un Ins 1256**
New or additional claims, **Un Ins 1030**
Withholding tax and wages, **Un Ins 13028.1**
Retirement savings, deductions, income tax, application of law, **Un Ins 13003**
Retraining, **Un Ins 1266 et seq.**
Eligibility, **Un Ins 1269**
Notice, **Un Ins 1271.5**

UNEMPLOYMENT COMPENSATION
—Cont'd

Retroactive benefits, eligibility, **Un Ins 1253.3**

Retroactive effect of rules and regulations, **Un Ins 310**

Pensions or similar periodic payments, reduction of benefits, **Un Ins 1255.3**

Returns,

Agents, several employers, preparation, **Un Ins 1096 et seq.**

Bill of rights, **Un Ins 1231 et seq.**

Corporate officers, personal liability for failure to file return, **Un Ins 1735**

Evidence, failure to file, certificate of department, **Un Ins 2123**

Extension of time, **Un Ins 1111, 1116**

Failure to file returns, **Un Ins 2109**

Crimes, **Un Ins 2117, 2117.5**

Elective coverage, **Un Ins 704, 704.1**

Fines and penalties, **Un Ins 1128**

Motion picture payroll services company, employer or employing unit, **Un Ins 679**

Personal liability of corporate officer, **Un Ins 1735**

Offers in compromise, **Un Ins 1870 et seq.**

Reconciliation returns, **Un Ins 13021**

Delinquency, penalties, **Un Ins 1117**

Employers, **Un Ins 1088**

Taxpayers Bill of Rights, **Un Ins 1231 et seq.**

Wages of workers, contributions due, duty of employer to file, **Un Ins 1088**

Emergencies, time extension, **Un Ins 1111.5**

Waiver, withholding tax on wages, **Un Ins 13021**

Withholding tax on wages, **Un Ins 13021, 13050 et seq.**

Review. Appeal and review, generally, ante

Rules and regulations,

Adoption, amendment or repeal, **Un Ins 305, 306**

Amateur athletic officials, **Un Ins 657**

Appeals, board of appeals, **Un Ins 411**

Definitions, **Un Ins 127**

Disability compensation, ante

Evidence or procedure, **Un Ins 1952**

Joint enforcement strike force on the underground economy, **Un Ins 329**

Necessary regulations, adoption, **Un Ins 306**

Prior regulation to remain in effect, **Un Ins 305.6**

Providing upon request, **Un Ins 307**

Reports, **Un Ins 320.5**

Retroactive effect, **Un Ins 310**

Violations, **Un Ins 2112**

Wages at irregular intervals, computation of benefits, **Un Ins 1282**

Withholding tax on wages, **Un Ins 13013**

UNEMPLOYMENT COMPENSATION
—Cont'd

Sale of business, withholding money or property, unpaid contributions, **Un Ins 1731 et seq.**

Sales, door to door salespersons, **Un Ins 13004.1**

Sanctions, joint enforcement strike force on the underground economy, **Un Ins 329**

Satisfaction, offers in compromise, **Un Ins 1873**

School employer, definitions, **Un Ins 821.4**

School employer advisory committee, **Un Ins 831**

School for the blind, nonprofessional employees, **Un Ins 1451 et seq.**

School for the deaf, nonprofessional employees, **Un Ins 1451 et seq.**

School Officers and Employees, this index

Schools and School Districts, this index

Schoolteachers retirement system, access to information, members receiving disability allowance, **Un Ins 1095**

Scientists, presumption of independent contractor status, **Un Ins 656**

Governing boards, elective coverage, **Un Ins 709**

Student services, **Un Ins 642**

Seasonal labor, elective coverage, approval, **Un Ins 704 et seq.**

Secretary of Labor, administration fund, **Un Ins 1558**

Self employment,

Approval of elective coverage, **Un Ins 704**

Assistance program, **Un Ins 1300 et seq.**

Contributions, rate, **Un Ins 708.5, 984.5**

Election for disability coverage, **Un Ins 708.5**

Self employment assistance program, **Un Ins 1300 et seq.**

Self incrimination, subpoena for production of records, effect, **Un Ins 1955**

Service not in course of employing unit trade or business, **Un Ins 640**

Remuneration paid in medium other than cash, exclusion from wages, **Un Ins 936**

Service of process,

Refunds and overpayments, garnishment, **CCP 706.101**

Satisfaction of judgment, acknowledgment, **Un Ins 1379.6**

Disability compensation, **Un Ins 2739.2**

Services,

Economically disadvantaged areas, minorities, **Un Ins 9602**

Performed during half or more of pay period, **Un Ins 607**

Setoff and counterclaim,

Extended overpayments, **Un Ins 3751**

Shares and shareholders, liability, nonpayment of contributions, offers in compromise, **Un Ins 1870 et seq.**

UNEMPLOYMENT COMPENSATION
—Cont'd

Setoff and counterclaim—Cont'd

Wrongful discharge actions, benefits, **Un Ins 1382**

Settlement. Compromise and settlement, generally, ante

Several employers. Employer or employing unit, ante

Sexual harassment, good cause, **Un Ins 1256.5**

Shares and shareholders,

Distributions, income tax, application of law, **Un Ins 13003**

Liability, contributions, withholding, penalties and interest, **Un Ins 1735, 1735.1**

Officers and directors, sole shareholders, **Un Ins 637, 637.1**

Ships and shipping,

Excluded services, **Un Ins 648**

Operating ships on navigable waters, **Un Ins 609**

Sick pay, **Un Ins 931, 933**

Wages for personal services, **Un Ins 1265.7**

Withholding tax, **Un Ins 13050**

Signatures, **Un Ins 17**

Small Businesses, this index

Snow, temporary public employees, excluded services, **Un Ins 634.5**

Social Security, this index

Social Services, this index

Solar energy, job preparation and training services, **Un Ins 9618**

Sole stockholder of corporation, exemption, contributions, **Un Ins 637.1**

Solicitation, violations, injunction, **Un Ins 1855**

Solvency, emergency solvency surcharge rate, contributions, **Un Ins 977.5**

Sororities, domestic service, **Un Ins 639, 682**

Special examiners, evidence, taking on hearing, **Un Ins 407**

Sports participants, exclusion from benefits, **Un Ins 1253.4**

Spouse employed by spouse, coverage, **Un Ins 631, 702.5**

Standard, general application, providing upon request, **Un Ins 307**

State,

Definitions, **Un Ins 139, 13003**

Disability compensation, **Un Ins 710.7**

Employing units, **Un Ins 135**

Qualifications, **Un Ins 605**

Withholding tax, **Un Ins 13003**

State agencies, exchange of information, **Un Ins 322**

State college auxiliary organizations, exclusion from coverage, **Un Ins 711**

State contracts, contracts. Training, post

State officers and employees,

Excluded services, **Un Ins 634.5**

Nonindustrial disability insurance, **Un Ins 2781 et seq.**

UNEMPLOYMENT

UNEMPLOYMENT COMPENSATION
—Cont'd

State tax liens, unpaid contributions, **Un Ins 1703**

State Treasury, this index

Statements,
Failure to file or fraudulent statements, violations, **Un Ins 2119**
Family care leave, claims, **Un Ins 3306**
Fines and penalties, **Un Ins 13101**
Motion picture payroll services company, employer or employing unit, **Un Ins 679**
Offers in compromise, **Un Ins 1873**
Reserve accounts, ante
Tax schedule used, **Un Ins 979**
Withholding tax on wages, **Un Ins 13050 et seq.**

Status of workers, record, **Un Ins 1085**

Statute of limitations. Limitation of actions, generally, ante

Statutes, references to division 1 as including other divisions, **Un Ins 304**

Stockholders. Shares and shareholders, generally, ante

Storms, temporary public employees, excluded services, **Un Ins 634.5**

Strike force on the underground economy, **Un Ins 329**

Strikes, **Un Ins 1262, 1262.5**
Refusal of new work during, **Un Ins 1259**

Students, **Un Ins 1253.3, 1253.9, 4701**
Employed during vacation period, **Un Ins 1030**
Loans, default, **Un Ins 1095**
Nurses, **Un Ins 645, 711**
Organized camps, employment by, exclusion, **Un Ins 642.1**
Part time employment, eligibility, **Un Ins 1253.8**
Services, **Un Ins 642**
Temporary employment, leaving to return to school, **Un Ins 4701**
Vacation period employment, **Un Ins 1032**

Studies and recommendations, **Un Ins 325**

Subpoenas, **Un Ins 1252, 1953 et seq.**
Person answering subpoena, eligibility, **Un Ins 1253.6**

Substantially better job, termination of employment, charges against employers account, **Un Ins 1032**

Substitute employees, excluded services, **Un Ins 634.5**

Succession of employers, **Un Ins 1051 et seq.**

Successor entity, financing coverage, **Un Ins 803.1**

Suitable employment,
Definitions, **Un Ins 1258**
Eligibility, **Un Ins 1253**
Failure to apply, **Un Ins 1257 et seq.**
Refusal to accept, **Un Ins 1257 et seq.**

Suits. Actions and proceedings, generally, ante

UNEMPLOYMENT COMPENSATION
—Cont'd

Summary judgment,
Delinquent contributions, penalties or interest, **Un Ins 1815 et seq.**
Overpayments, **Un Ins 1379**
Disability compensation, **Un Ins 2739**

Supplemental plan of employer, **Un Ins 1265, 1342**
Exemption from judicial process, **Un Ins 1342**

Supplemental unemployment compensation benefits, withholding tax, **Un Ins 13028.5**

Supplies, withholding tax on wages, **Un Ins 13011**

Supplying information, wilful failure to supply or fraudulent information, violations, **Un Ins 2120**

Support, this index

Supportive services program, domestic employees, coverage, **Un Ins 683**

Suspension of benefits, complaint, **Un Ins 1263**

Tables,
Contribution rates, **Un Ins 977**
Weekly benefit amounts, **Un Ins 1280**

Tabulation of wages, revision, **Un Ins 979**

Takeovers, employing unit, effect, **Un Ins 135.1, 135.2**

Tax liens, unpaid contributions, **Un Ins 1703**
Collection, offers in compromise, **Un Ins 1870 et seq.**

Taxation,
Exempt wages, **Un Ins 940**
Joint enforcement strike force on the underground economy, **Un Ins 329**
Schedules, **Un Ins 979**
Withholding, **Un Ins 13000 et seq.**

Taxpayer, definitions, withholding tax on wages, **Un Ins 13003**

Taxpayers Bill of Rights, **Un Ins 1231 et seq.**

Teachers, **Un Ins 711**

Telecommunications,
Domestic service employees, wage reports, telephone filing, **Un Ins 1118**
Filing, wage reports, domestic service employees, **Un Ins 1118**
Hearings, **Un Ins 1953.5**
Hotlines, joint enforcement strike force on the underground economy, **Un Ins 329**

Television and radio, employer, definitions, **Un Ins 678**

Temporary employment, students, return to school, **Un Ins 4701**

Temporary public employees, excluded services, **Un Ins 634.5**

Temporary residence status, aliens application for, **Un Ins 1264**

Temporary services employers, determination of employer, **Un Ins 606.5**

Termination,
Elective coverage, **Un Ins 704.1 et seq.**

UNEMPLOYMENT COMPENSATION
—Cont'd

Termination—Cont'd
Employment,
Conviction of crime, **Un Ins 1030.1, 1256.1**
Discrimination, eligibility for benefits, **Un Ins 1256.2**
Reports, false statements, **Un Ins 1142**
Colleges and universities, **Un Ins 1142.1**
Substantially better job, charges against employers account, **Un Ins 1032**

Third parties, payers, wages, reports, **Un Ins 13009.5**

Third party payors, **Un Ins 931.5**

Ticket to work program, handicapped persons, **Un Ins 18000 et seq.**

Time,
Appeal and review, **Un Ins 1328**
Refunds and overpayments, **Un Ins 1241**
Base period, generally, ante
Benefits, **Un Ins 1275 et seq.**
Certificate of contributions,
Interest and penalties due, **Un Ins 1732, 1733**
Lien for unpaid contributions, filing, **Un Ins 1703**
Computation, **Un Ins 301**
Contributions, payment, **Un Ins 1110**
Liability by contract, **Un Ins 1110.6**
Decision on appeal, **Un Ins 1337**
Disability compensation, ante
Disqualifications, ante
Enforcement, liability of successor employer for contributions, **Un Ins 1734**
Extension for return or payment of contributions, **Un Ins 1111, 1111.5**
Extension of period of ineligibility for benefits for successive disqualifications, **Un Ins 1261**
Extension of time. Disability compensation, ante
Family care leave, claims, **Un Ins 3301**
Jeopardy assessment, immediately due, finality, **Un Ins 1137**
Jeopardy collection, contributions, procedure, **Un Ins 1115**
Judicial review of decisions of appeals board, **Un Ins 410**
Liens for contributions, creation and duration, **Un Ins 1703**
Notice, generally, ante
Payment of benefits, **Un Ins 1326**
Reconciliation reports, delinquency, penalties, **Un Ins 1117**
Refunds and overpayments, ante
Reports and returns, wages and contributions, employers filing, **Un Ins 1088**
Reserve accounts, ante

UNEMPLOYMENT COMPENSATION
—Cont'd
Time—Cont'd
Wages of workers, contributions due, duty of employer to file, emergencics, time extension, **Un Ins 1111.5**
Warrant for collection of delinquent contributions, **Un Ins 1785**
Withhold notices, delinquent contributions, **Un Ins 1755**
Withholding returns, emergencies, extension, **Un Ins 13059**
Tips,
Disability compensation, ante
Wages, **Un Ins 927**
Withholding tax on wages, **Un Ins 13027, 13055**
Trade disputes,
Benefits, effect, **Un Ins 1259, 1262**
Computation of disability base period, **Un Ins 2658**
Investigation by department, **Un Ins 1262.5**
Trade or business, definitions, withholding tax on wages, **Un Ins 13003**
Training, **Un Ins 10200 et seq.**
Contracts,
Construction of law, **Un Ins 10208**
Fixed fee performance contracts, **Un Ins 10205**
Minority and women owned businesses, **Un Ins 10205**
Officers and employees, **Un Ins 1253.3**
Parties, **Un Ins 10209**
Payments, **Un Ins 10209**
Training agencies, **Un Ins 10210**
Demand occupations, **Un Ins 1266 et seq.**
Funding, individual projects grants, **Un Ins 10215**
Green collar jobs, **Un Ins 15000 et seq.**
Handicapped persons, screens and screening, **Un Ins 14002**
History, program participants, employment, wages, and benefits, **Un Ins 10214**
Job preparation and training services, generally, ante
Learning disabilities, screens and screening, **Un Ins 14002**
Notice, **Un Ins 1271.5**
Nurses, **Un Ins 10214.9**
Plan, **Un Ins 10205**
Reports, expenses and expenditures, **Un Ins 9600.5**
Retraining, generally, ante
Self employment assistance program, **Un Ins 1300 et seq.**
Workforce investment, **Un Ins 14000 et seq.**
Workforce recovery training, **Un Ins 10214.6**
Youthbuild program, **Un Ins 9800 et seq.**

UNEMPLOYMENT COMPENSATION
—Cont'd
Training agencies, definitions, employment training panel, **Un Ins 10201**
Training or retraining benefits, allowances, or stipends, definitions, demand occupations, **Un Ins 1273**
Training programs. Job preparation and training services, generally, ante
Transcription, court reporters, performance away from office, **Un Ins 630**
Transcripts, hearings, **Un Ins 1952**
Transfer. Reserve accounts, ante
Treasury, state, deposit of money, **Un Ins 1501, 1526.1 et seq.**
Tribal councils, Indians, exclusions, **Un Ins 634.5**
Trust fund account. Funds, ante
Trusts and trustees,
California state colleges, elective coverage, **Un Ins 709**
Payments from or to, exclusion from wages, **Un Ins 934**
Unclaimed or unpaid. Funds, ante
Unemployed, definitions, **Un Ins 1252**
Unemployment administration fund. Administration fund, generally, ante
Unemployment fund,
Advances to, **Un Ins 323**
Interest, payment, employment training fund, **Un Ins 1611**
Reports, **Un Ins 995**
Transfer of monies, **Un Ins 1590**
Unemployment insurance appeals boards. Appeals boards, generally, ante
Unemployment insurance management system, transfer from school employees fund, **Un Ins 826**
Unemployment trust fund. Funds, ante
Uninsured employers, disclosure, **Un Ins 1095**
United States, this index
Universities. Colleges and universities, generally, ante
University of California, **Un Ins 100 et seq.**
Unlawful detention, eligibility, **Un Ins 1253.1**
Vacations,
Employment, students, **Un Ins 1030, 1032**
Family care leave, **Un Ins 3303.1**
Pay, construing to be wages for personal services, **Un Ins 1265.5**
Vacation pay, construing as wages for personal services, **Un Ins 1265.5**
Valid claim, definitions, **Un Ins 1276**
Venue,
Injunctions, actions for, **Un Ins 1855**
Trials of violations of chapter, **Un Ins 2124**
Vested rights, repeals or amendment, **Un Ins 102**
Veterans, this index
Vietnam veterans, discrimination, **Gov 12940**

UNEMPLOYMENT COMPENSATION
—Cont'd
Virgin Islands, defined as part of United States, **Un Ins 139, 142.5**
Vocational education. Training, generally, ante
Voluntarily leaving work without good cause, **Un Ins 1256**
Charges against employers account, **Un Ins 1032**
Conviction of offense, **Un Ins 1030.1, 1256.1**
Voluntary plans. Disability compensation, ante
Wages,
Basis of contributions. Contributions, generally, ante
Benefits paid, exclusion from wages, **Un Ins 931, 933**
Concealed wages, fines and penalties, **Un Ins 1128.1, 1735.1**
Definitions, **Un Ins 926 et seq., 1277 et seq.**
Withholding tax on wages, **Un Ins 13009**
Exchange of money, concealment of wages, fines and penalties, **Un Ins 1128.1, 1735.1**
Fines and penalties, concealed wages, **Un Ins 1128.1, 1735.1**
For employment for employers, **Un Ins 1278**
Holiday pay,
Construing as wages for personal services, **Un Ins 1265.5**
Delayed payment, **Un Ins 1265.6**
Military forces, exclusion of payments, **Un Ins 938.5**
Payment, definitions, **Un Ins 931**
Reciprocity, **Un Ins 455**
Reports,
Delinquency, **Un Ins 1114**
Domestic service employees, telephone filing, **Un Ins 1118**
Duty of employer to file, **Un Ins 1088**
Third parties, payers, **Un Ins 13009.5**
Sick pay, generally, ante
Vacation pay, construing to be wages for personal services, **Un Ins 1265.5**
WARN payments, **Un Ins 1265.1**
Wagner Peyser Act, money granted pursuant to, **Un Ins 1562**
Waiting period, **Un Ins 1253, 1254**
Disability compensation, ante
Waiver, **Un Ins 1342**
Elective coverage, requisites for termination, **Un Ins 706**
Notice of assessment, limitation period, **Un Ins 1132**
Penalty, **Un Ins 13101**
Refunds and overpayments, **Un Ins 1179, 1241**
Returns, withholding tax on wages, **Un Ins 13021**
WARN payments, wages, **Un Ins 1265.1**

UNEMPLOYMENT

UNEMPLOYMENT COMPENSATION
—Cont'd
Warrants,
Applicants accused of felonies, furnishing information to law enforcement agencies, **Un Ins 1095**
Collection of unpaid contributions, **Un Ins 1785 et seq.**
Contingent fund, **Un Ins 1589**
Disability compensation, ante
Payment from fund, **Un Ins 1534**
Unclaimed, **Un Ins 1537**
Week, definitions, **Un Ins 143**
Weekly benefit amounts, **Un Ins 1280**
Jurors and witnesses, **Un Ins 1279**
Wife. Husband and wife, generally, ante
Withholding,
Agent, definitions, withholding tax, wages, **Un Ins 13010**
Bill of rights, **Un Ins 1231 et seq.**
Child support obligations of claimants, **Un Ins 1255.7**
Confidential or privileged information,
Browsing, **Un Ins 13018**
Preparers, **Un Ins 13019**
Contributions, ante
Disability compensation, ante
Election, **Un Ins 13028**
Emergencies, returns, time extension, **Un Ins 13059**
Employee contributions, **Un Ins 986, 2110**
Exemption certificate, withholding tax on wages, **Un Ins 13026**
Information to aid individual to obtain benefits, **Un Ins 2107**
Money or property, unpaid contributions, **Un Ins 1731 et seq.**
Notice, **Un Ins 1342.1**
Delinquent contributions, **Un Ins 1755 et seq.**
Returns, withholding tax on wages, **Un Ins 13021**
Emergencies, time extension, **Un Ins 13059**
Tax on wages, **Un Ins 13000 et seq.**
Taxpayers Bill of Rights, **Un Ins 1231 et seq.**
Withholding agent, definitions, withholding tax on wages, **Un Ins 13010**
Witnesses, **Un Ins 1953 et seq.**
Failure of witness to appear, **Un Ins 2104**
Fees as wages, **Un Ins 1252**
Responding to subpoenas, **Un Ins 1253.6**
Subpoenaed witnesses as unemployed, **Un Ins 1252**
Weekly benefit amount, **Un Ins 1279**
Women, economically disadvantaged areas, **Un Ins 9602**
Work experience education programs, excluded services, **Un Ins 646**
Work Incentive Programs, generally, this index

UNEMPLOYMENT COMPENSATION
—Cont'd
Work search. Suitable employment, generally, ante
Worker contributions, definitions, **Un Ins 144**
Workers Compensation, this index
Workforce and economic information program, **Un Ins 10529**
Workforce investment, **Un Ins 14000 et seq.**
Workforce preparation, handicapped persons, **Un Ins 18000 et seq.**
Workforce recovery training, **Un Ins 10214.6**
Writing, decisions and orders, necessity, **Un Ins 408**
Wrongful discharge, actions, benefits, **Un Ins 1382**
Youthbuild program, **Un Ins 9800 et seq.**

UNEMPLOYMENT COMPENSATION DISABILITY BENEFITS LAW
Generally, **Un Ins 2601 et seq.**
Disability compensation. Unemployment Compensation, this index

UNEMPLOYMENT DEVELOPMENT
Contracts, conformance, **Un Ins 9002**
Economically disadvantaged areas, **Un Ins 9602**

UNEMPLOYMENT INSURANCE
Definitions, panel, employment training panel, **Un Ins 10201**

UNEMPLOYMENT INSURANCE ACT
Generally, **Un Ins 1 et seq.**

UNEMPLOYMENT INSURANCE CODE
Generally, **Un Ins 1 et seq.**
Accrued rights, **Un Ins 3**
Actions pending, **Un Ins 3**
Additions, references, **Un Ins 7**
Amendments, references, **Un Ins 7**
Citation, **Un Ins 1**
Construction, **Un Ins 2 et seq.**
Continuation of existing law, **Un Ins 2**
Definitions, **Un Ins 8 et seq.**
Delegation of powers, **Un Ins 6**
Deputies, duties and powers, **Un Ins 6**
English language, notices, **Un Ins 8**
Headings, division, part, **Un Ins 5**
Pending actions, **Un Ins 3**
References to, **Un Ins 7**
Restatements of law, **Un Ins 2**
Severability, **Un Ins 18**
Tenure of office, **Un Ins 19**
Title, **Un Ins 1**
Transfer of powers and duties, reference to person, officer, **Un Ins 20**
Vested rights, **Un Ins 3**
Written instruments, English language, **Un Ins 8**

UNEMPLOYMENT RELIEF
Generally, **Labor 2010 et seq.**

UNEMPLOYMENT RESERVES ACT
Generally, **Un Ins 1025 et seq.**

UNFAIR DISCRIMINATION
Discrimination, generally, this index

UNFAIR LABOR PRACTICES
Labor and Employment, this index

UNIFORMS
Employees required to wear, prescribing, **Labor 452**

UNINCORPORATED ASSOCIATIONS
Associations and Societies, generally, this index

UNINSURED EMPLOYERS BENEFITS TRUST FUND
Workers Compensation, this index

UNIONS
Labor Organizations, generally, this index

UNITED STATES
Agencies. United States Agencies and Institutions, generally, this index
Air pressure tanks, exemption from state inspection or safety regulation, **Labor 7624**
Application of law, federally operated labor camps, **Health & S 17024**
Boilers, exemption from state inspection or safety regulation, **Labor 7625**
Bonds, unemployment insurance disability fund, investment, **Un Ins 3003**
Childrens Bureau, assistance and cooperation of department of industrial relations, **Labor 50.6**
Correctional Institutions, this index
Criminal history information, **Pen 11105.3**
Definitions,
Unemployment insurance code, **Un Ins 142.5**
Virgin Islands, unemployment insurance code, **Un Ins 139, 142.5**
Withholding tax on wages, **Un Ins 13003**
Disability compensation fund, money received, **Un Ins 3004, 3005**
Elevators under jurisdiction, exemptions, inspection, **Labor 7317**
Employment compensation, employer, definitions, **Un Ins 677**
Federal Aid, generally, this index
Income Tax—Federal, generally, this index
Income Tax—State, this index
Labor camps, application of law, federally operated camps, **Health & S 17024**
Liquefied petroleum gas storage tanks, exemption from state inspection or safety regulation, **Labor 7624**
Longshoremens and Harbor Workers Compensation Act,
Delegation of authority to industrial accidents division, **Labor 128**
Workers compensation, appeals board, deputy commissioner, **Labor 128**
Military Forces, generally, this index

UNITED STATES—Cont'd

Officers and employees, lie detector test, **Labor 432.2**

Prisoners of state department of corrections, suppressing fire in service of United States, reimbursement for service, **Labor 3365**

Steam boilers, exemption from state inspection or safety regulation, **Labor 7625**

Tax collection, withholding tax on wages, **Un Ins 13076**

Unemployment compensation,
  Agencies, exchange of information, **Un Ins 322**
  Definitions, **Un Ins 142.5**
    Withholding tax on wages, **Un Ins 13003**
  Employment, **Un Ins 632**
  Federal Unemployment Tax Act, generally, this index
  Information available, director of employment development, **Un Ins 321**
  Postal Service, employees, disability compensation, **Un Ins 2606.4**

Wage and hour division, assistance and cooperation of department of industrial relations, **Labor 50.6**

Wagner Peyser Act, state cooperation under provisions of Act, **Un Ins 2052**

Workers compensation, benefits, setoff and counterclaim, **Labor 4355**

UNITED STATES AGENCIES AND INSTITUTIONS

Comatose patients, medical information disclosure, **CC 56.10**

Employing unit, unemployment compensation, **Un Ins 135**

Medical records, comatose patients, information disclosure, **CC 56.10**

Unemployment compensation, exchange of information, **Un Ins 322**

UNITED STATES DEPARTMENT OF LABOR

Unemployment compensation, administration fund, **Un Ins 1558**
  Moneys received from, **Un Ins 1556**

UNITED STATES POSTAL SERVICE

Employees, disability compensation, unemployment insurance, **Un Ins 2606.4**

Unemployment insurance, disability compensation, employees, **Un Ins 2606.4**

UNIVERSITIES

Colleges and Universities, generally, this index

UNIVERSITY OF CALIFORNIA

Colleges and Universities, this index

UNLAWFUL VIOLENCE

Definitions, harassment, **CCP 527.6**

UNRUH CIVIL RIGHTS ACT

Generally, **CC 51**

URBAN RENEWAL

Housing, youthbuild program, **Un Ins 9800 et seq.**

Youthbuild program, **Un Ins 9800 et seq.**

URINALS

Comfort Stations and Rest Rooms, generally, this index

USE

Definitions, Occupational Carcinogens Control Act, **Labor 9009**

USED OIL

Oil and Gas, this index

USES AND TRUSTS

Trusts and Trustees, generally, this index

UTILITIES

Public Utilities, generally, this index

UTILITY EMPLOYEES SERVICE LETTER LAW

Generally, **Labor 1055, 1056**

UTILITY TRAILERS

Trailers, generally, this index

VACATING OR SETTING ASIDE

Domestic partnership, termination, **Fam 299**

VACATIONS

Agreed payments to plan, employer failure to make, **Labor 227**

Employee benefit plan distribution,
  Definitions, Unclaimed Property Law, **CCP 1501**
  Escheat to state, **CCP 1521**

Family care leave, **Un Ins 3303.1**

Labor and employment, termination, payment of vacation time, **Labor 227.3**

Pay, claims, assignment to labor commissioner, **Labor 96**

State Officers and Employees, this index

Statement of employers payments made to plan, **Labor 227.5**

Unemployment Compensation, this index

Vested vacation time, forfeiture upon termination of employment, **Labor 227.3**

VACUUM CLEANERS

Children and minors, employment, **Labor 1294.3**

VALID CLAIM

Definitions,
  Disability compensation, **Un Ins 2609**
  Unemployment compensation, **Un Ins 1276**

VANDALISM

Malicious Mischief, generally, this index

VANPOOLING

Workers compensation, course of employment, **Labor 3600.8**

VANS

Paratransit Vehicles, generally, this index

VAUDEVILLE

Theaters and Shows, generally, this index

VEGETABLES

Children and minors, permissible employment, **Labor 1294.3**

Handlers, children and minors, employment, **Labor 1294.3**

Labor and employment, termination of seasonal employment, payment of wages, **Labor 201**

VEHICLES

Motor Vehicles, generally, this index

VENDOR AND PURCHASER

Cable television, criminal history information, **Pub U 7910**

Open video systems, criminal history information, **Pub U 7910**

Telecommunications, criminal history information, **Pub U 7910**

Video programming services, criminal history information, **Pub U 7910**

VENEER MILLS

Labor and employment, midday meal period, **Labor 800, 801**

VENIRE

Jury, generally, this index

VENTILATION

Foundries and metal shops, **Labor 2331**

Manufacturing establishments, sanitary conditions, **Labor 2331, 2351**

VENTURA COUNTY STATE COLLEGE

Colleges and Universities, generally, this index

VENUE

Agricultural labor and employment, labor organizations, **Labor 1165**

Compensation and salaries, prosecution for illegal form of payment, **Labor 214**

Fair employment and housing, actions, **Gov 12965**

Labor camps, nuisance abatement actions, **Health & S 17060**

Railroads, this index

Unemployment compensation, place of trial for violations, **Un Ins 2124**

VESSELS

Boats and Boating, generally, this index

Ships and Shipping, generally, this index

VESTED RIGHTS

Labor Code, **Labor 4**

Unemployment insurance code, **Un Ins 3**

VETERANS

Apprenticeships, selection standards, **Labor 3076.5**

VETERANS—Cont'd

Burton Stull Vietnam Veterans Employment Act, **Gov 7280 et seq.**

Definitions,
   Apprenticeship programs, **Labor 3076.5**
   Vietnam veterans, **Gov 7280.2**

Disclosure, inspector general for veterans affairs, **Mil & V 73.7**

Discrimination, fair employment housing, **Gov 12940**

Employment. Labor and employment, generally, post

Fair employment and housing, discrimination, **Gov 12940**

Housing, fair employment and housing, veterans preference, **Gov 12940**

Labor and employment,
   Apprenticeships, **Labor 3076.5**
   Discrimination, **Gov 12940**
   Fair employment, **Gov 12940**
   Placement service, **Un Ins 2054**
   Training, **Un Ins 325.5**
     Reports, **Un Ins 325.6**
   Vietnam Veterans Employment Act, **Gov 7280 et seq.**

Plans and specifications, employment, training, **Un Ins 325.5**
   Reports, **Un Ins 325.6**

Priorities and preferences, fair employment and housing, **Gov 12940**

Reports, labor and employment, training, **Un Ins 325.6**

Retaliation, inspector general for veterans affairs, **Mil & V 73.7**

State officers and employees, retaliation, inspector general for veterans affairs, **Mil & V 73.7**

Surviving Spouse, this index

Unemployment compensation,
   Eligibility, discharged veterans with unexpired leave time, **Un Ins 1253.15**
   Employment, training, **Un Ins 325.5**
   Reports, **Un Ins 325.6**

Vietnam War, this index

Widows and widowers. Surviving Spouse, this index

VETERINARIANS

Drugs and Medicine, generally, this index

Hypodermic Syringes and Needles, generally, this index

Medicine. Drugs and Medicine, generally, this index

VIALS

Containers, generally, this index

VICTIMS

Definitions, fair employment and housing, **Gov 12926**

Victims of crime. Crimes and Offenses, this index

VICTIMS OF CRIME

Crimes and Offenses, this index

VICTIMS OF DOMESTIC VIOLENCE EMPLOYMENT LEAVE ACT

Generally, **Labor 230**

VIDEO PROGRAMMING SERVICES

Criminal history information,
   Franchises, **Pub U 5910**
     Officers and employees, **Pub U 7910**

Employees, criminal history information, **Pub U 7910**

Independent contractors, criminal history information, **Pub U 7910**

Officers and employees, criminal history information, **Pub U 7910**

Reports, franchises, **Pub U 5920**

VIDEOTAPE

Comfort stations and rest rooms, labor and employment, **Labor 435**

Labor and employment, comfort stations and rest rooms, **Labor 435**

Lewdness and Obscenity, generally, this index

Obscenity. Lewdness and Obscenity, generally, this index

Pornography. Lewdness and Obscenity, generally, this index

Talent services, fees, **Labor 1703.4**

VIETNAM VETERANS EMPLOYMENT ACT

Generally, **Gov 7280 et seq.**

VIETNAM WAR

Veterans, Agent Orange, tumor registry, plans and options,
   Burton Stull Vietnam Veterans Employment Act, **Gov 7280 et seq.**
   Fair employment and housing, discrimination, **Gov 12940**

VILLAGES

Health Facilities, generally, this index

VINYL CHLORIDE

Occupational Carcinogens Control Act, **Labor 9000 et seq.**

Reports, labor and employment, use, **Labor 9030 et seq.**

VIOLENCE

Force and Violence, generally, this index

VIOLENT CRIMES

Force and Violence, generally, this index

VIOLENT FELONIES

Crimes and Offenses, this index

VIRGIN ISLANDS

United States, defined as part of, unemployment compensation, **Un Ins 139, 142.5**

VISION

Blind Persons, generally, this index

VISUAL ARTS

Art and Artists, generally, this index

VISUALLY IMPAIRED PERSONS

Blind Persons, generally, this index

VITICULTURE

Labor, compensation, time due and payable, **Labor 205**

VOCATIONAL COURSES

Vocational Education, generally, this index

VOCATIONAL EDUCATION

Apprentices, this index

Career resource network, **Educ 53086**

Children and minors, courses of training, exception to employment, **Labor 1295**

Family economic security, job preparation and training services. Unemployment Compensation, this index

Handicapped persons, **Un Ins 9003**

Housing, youthbuild program, **Un Ins 9800 et seq.**

Job preparation and training services. Unemployment Compensation, this index

Juvenile Delinquents and Dependents, this index

Private schools, credit, apprentices, **Labor 3092**

Regional occupational centers,
   Credit towards term of apprenticeship, **Labor 3092**
   Occupational training programs, workers compensation, **Labor 3368**
   Work experience education, workers compensation, **Labor 3368**

Reports, youthbuild program, **Un Ins 9809, 9809.5**

Work Incentive Programs, generally, this index

Workers compensation, **Labor 3368**

Workforce investment, **Un Ins 14000 et seq.**

Youthbuild program, **Un Ins 9800 et seq.**

VOCATIONAL NURSING

Abuse, long term health care facilities, temporary employment, **CC 1812.543**

Caregiver training initiative, **Un Ins 11020 et seq.**

Criminal history information, long term health care facilities, temporary employment, **CC 1812.542**

Employment agencies, long term health care facilities, temporary employment, **CC 1812.540 et seq.**

Long term health care facilities, employment agencies, temporary employment, **CC 1812.540 et seq.**

Psychiatric Technicians, generally, this index

VOCATIONAL REHABILITATION

California Industries for the Blind. Blind Persons, this index

Public officers and employees, injured employees, **Labor 6206**

Vouchers, workers compensation, **Labor 4658.5**
   Liability, **Labor 4658.6**

Workers Compensation, this index

VODKA
Alcoholic Beverages, generally, this index

VOLATILE FLAMMABLE LIQUIDS
Safety in employment, **Labor 7800 et seq.**

VOLUNTARY ARBITRATION LAW
Generally, **CCP 1280 et seq.**

VOLUNTARY SERVICE WITHOUT PAY
Definitions, workers compensation, **Labor 3363.6**

VOLUNTEER FIREFIGHTERS AND FIRE DEPARTMENTS
Firefighters and Fire Departments, this index

VOLUNTEER POLICE DEPARTMENTS
Workers compensation, **Labor 4458.2**

VOLUNTEERS
Alcoholics and alcoholism, transportation, criminal history information, **Pen 11105.3**
Definitions,
Fair employment and housing, **Gov 12940**
Public buildings and works, **Labor 1720.4**
Drug addicts, transportation, criminal history information, **Pen 11105.3**
Public buildings and works, application of law, **Labor 1720.4**
Schools and School Districts, this index
Workers Compensation, this index

VOTERS AND VOTING
Elections, generally, this index

VOUCHERS
Building and construction industry, payment of wages or fringe benefits, insufficient funds, **Labor 203.1**
Training, workers compensation, **Labor 4658.5**
Liability, **Labor 4658.6**
Vocational rehabilitation, workers compensation, **Labor 4658.5**
Liability, **Labor 4658.6**
Workers compensation, vocational rehabilitation, **Labor 4658.5**
Liability, **Labor 4658.6**

WAGE ASSIGNMENT FOR SUPPORT
Definitions, garnishment, **CCP 706.011**

WAGE ASSIGNMENTS
Compensation and Salaries, this index

WAGE BOARD
Industrial welfare commission, powers and duties, **Labor 1178 et seq.**
Labor and Employment, this index

WAGE PAYMENT LAW
Generally, **Labor 200 et seq.**

WAGERS AND WAGERING
Gambling, generally, this index

WAGES
Generally, **Labor 200 et seq.**
Compensation and Salaries, generally, this index

WAGES AND HOURS LAW
Generally, **Labor 1171 et seq.**

WAGES SUBJECT TO PERSONAL INCOME TAX
Definitions, unemployment compensation, **Un Ins 13009.5**

WAGNER PEYSER ACT
Generally, **Un Ins 2051 et seq.**

WALKATHONS
Compensation and salaries, deposits for security of payment, **Labor 271**

WALKOUTS
Labor Disputes, generally, this index

WALLET GUN
Weapons, generally, this index

WALLPAPER
Lead poisoning, occupational safety, programs, **Health & S 105185 et seq.**

WALLS
Safety in employment, building construction or repair, **Labor 7100 et seq.**

WAR AND CIVIL DEFENSE
Disaster council, definitions, **Labor 3211.9**
Disaster service workers, definitions, **Labor 3211.92**
Labor and employment, definitions, **Labor 3211.92**
Public buildings and works, hours of labor, **Const. Art. 14, § 2**
Veterans, generally, this index

WARDENS
Fish and Game, this index

WARDS
Guardian and Ward, generally, this index
Juvenile Facilities Division, this index

WAREHOUSES AND WAREHOUSEMEN
Accidents, working warehouses, **Labor 9100 et seq.**
Definitions, smoking, **Labor 6404.5**
Investigations and investigators, shopping investigators report, **Labor 2930 et seq.**
Officers and employees, shopping investigators report, **Labor 2930 et seq.**
Reports, working warehouses, safety, **Labor 9104**
Rules and regulations, workplace smoking regulation, exemptions, **Labor 6404.5**
Safety, working warehouses, **Labor 9100 et seq.**
Smoking in workplace, regulation, exemption, **Labor 6404.5**
Working warehouses, safety, **Labor 9100 et seq.**

WAREHOUSES AND WAREHOUSEMEN —Cont'd
Workplace smoking regulation, exemption, **Labor 6404.5**

WARNING SIGNALS AND DEVICES
Signs and Signals, generally, this index

WARNINGS
Buildings, this index
Workers compensation, fraud, **Labor 3822**

WARRANTS
Arrest, this index
Attachment, this index
Searches and Seizures, this index
Unemployment Compensation, this index
Workers Compensation, this index

WARRANTS FOR PAYMENT OF MONEY
Disability compensation,
Benefits, **Un Ins 3075**
Fund, **Un Ins 3009 et seq.**

WASHROOMS
Comfort Stations and Rest Rooms, generally, this index

WASTE
Hazardous Substances and Waste, generally, this index
Sewers and Sewer Systems, generally, this index
Water. Sewers and Sewer Systems, generally, this index

WASTE WATER
Sewers and Sewer Systems, generally, this index

WATCHMEN
Workers compensation, exclusion, **Labor 3358**

WATER APPROPRIATION
Irrigation and Irrigation Districts, generally, this index

WATER CARRIERS
Ships and Shipping, generally, this index

WATER CLOSETS
Comfort Stations and Rest Rooms, generally, this index

WATER COMPANIES
Public Utilities Commission, generally, this index

WATER DISTRICTS
Officers and employees,
Compensation, leave of absence for military duty, **Mil & V 395.01 et seq.**
Leave of absence for military duty, **Mil & V 395 et seq.**
Military personnel, discrimination, **Mil & V 394**

WATER

WATER DISTRICTS—Cont'd
Officers and employees—Cont'd
  Soldiers and Sailors Relief Act, **Mil & V 395.1**

WATER QUALITY
Sewers and Sewer Systems, generally, this index

WATER SUPPLY
Agricultural labor and employment, drinking water facilities, field sanitation standards, **Labor 6712**
Field sanitation standards, drinking water facilities, **Labor 6712**
Labor camps, reserved to local jurisdiction, **Health & S 17021**

WATERCRAFT
Boats and Boating, generally, this index
Ships and Shipping, generally, this index

WATERFOWL
Fish and Game, generally, this index

WATERS AND WATER COURSES
Boats and Boating, generally, this index
Fish and Game, generally, this index
Irrigation and Irrigation Districts, generally, this index
Public Policy, generally, this index
Waste water. Sewers and Sewer Systems, generally, this index
Zoning and Planning, generally, this index

WATERWORKS
Water Supply, generally, this index

WAYS
Highways and Roads, generally, this index

WEAPONS
Actions and proceedings. Injunction, generally, post
Colleges and Universities, this index
Community property, change of possession, ex convicts, **Pen 12021**
Crimes and offenses,
  Acquisition of firearms by restrainees, **Pen 12021**
  Drug addicts, **Pen 12021**
  Protective orders, **Pen 12021**
Delivery,
  Law enforcement agencies, disposition, **Pen 12021**
  Prior convictions, possession, exemption, **Pen 12021**
Discharging, on private land, misdemeanor, **Pen 602**
Disposition, law enforcement agencies, transportation, **Pen 12021**
Domestic Violence, this index
Drug addicts, possession, **Pen 12021**
Drugs and medicine, prior convictions, possession, **Pen 12021**
Ex convict, possession, **Pen 12021**
Exemptions,
  Injunction, surrender, **CCP 527.9**
  Possession, prior convictions, **Pen 12021**

WEAPONS—Cont'd
Exhibition, threatening manner, **Pen 12021**
Fines and penalties,
  Acquisition of firearms by restrainees, **Pen 12021**
  Drug addicts, possession, **Pen 12021**
  Possession, **Pen 12021**
  Protective orders, **Pen 12021**
Former convicts, possession, **Pen 12021**
Harassment, protective orders, **CCP 527.6**
Injunction,
  Acquisition of firearms by restrainees, **Pen 12021**
  Fines and penalties, **Pen 12021**
  Surrender, **CCP 527.6 et seq.**
Juvenile Delinquents and Dependents, this index
Labor and employment,
  Injunction, workplace violence, **CCP 527.8**
  Weapon necessary for employment, possession by former convicts, **Pen 12021**
Law Enforcement, this index
Notice,
  Ineligibility to possess, restraining order, **Pen 12021**
  Law enforcement agencies, disposition, transportation, **Pen 12021**
Offenses. Crimes and offenses, generally, ante
Parole and probation, possession, **Pen 12021**
Peace Officers, this index
Penalties. Fines and penalties, generally, ante
Petitions, prior convictions, relief from prohibition on possession, **Pen 12021**
Police, this index
Possession, protective orders, crimes and offenses, **Pen 12021**
Protective orders,
  Acquisition of firearms by restrainees, **Pen 12021**
  Crimes and offenses, **Pen 12021**
  Fines and penalties, **Pen 12021**
  Surrender, **CCP 527.6 et seq.**
Relief from order, ineligibility to possess weapons, **Pen 12021**
Restraining orders. Injunction, generally, ante
Sales,
  Crimes and offenses, **Pen 12021**
  Protective orders, crimes and offenses, **Pen 12021**
Stalking, prior convictions, possession, **Pen 12021**
Storage, law enforcement, injunction, **CCP 527.9**
Surrender, injunction, **CCP 527.6 et seq.**
Transportation,
  Law enforcement agencies, disposition, **Pen 12021**
  Prior convictions, possession, exemption, **Pen 12021**
Workplace violence, injunction, **CCP 527.8**

WEARING APPAREL
Actions and proceedings,
  Contracts, labor and employment, **Labor 2810**
  Manufacturers and manufacturing, post
Advisory committees, manufacturing industry, **Labor 2674.1**
Appeal and review. Manufacturers and manufacturing, post
Arbitration and award. Manufacturers and manufacturing, post
Assembly, successor employers, compensation and salaries, liability, **Labor 2684**
Attorney fees,
  Contracts, labor and employment, **Labor 2810**
  Manufacturers and manufacturing, post
Attorneys, manufacturers, arbitration, **Labor 2689**
Bonds (officers and fiduciaries) manufacturers, wage and benefit payments, **Labor 2679**
Budgets, manufacturers and manufacturing, budgets submitted to legislature, **Labor 2674.2**
Certificates and certification, manufacturers, registration, **Labor 2675**
Claims, manufacturers and manufacturing, compensation and salaries, contractors, suretyship and guarantee, **Labor 2673.1**
Compensation and salaries. Manufacturers and manufacturing, post
Contractors, manufacturers and manufacturing, compensation and salaries, suretyship and guarantee, **Labor 2673.1**
Contracts,
  Labor and employment, **Labor 2810**
  Manufacturers and contractors, pricing and quality disputes, investigation and mediation, **Labor 2680.5**
Costs,
  Contracts, labor and employment, **Labor 2810**
  Manufacturers, arbitration, **Labor 2688, 2692**
Crimes and offenses, manufacturers, engaging in business without registering, **Labor 2676**
Damages,
  Contracts, labor and employment, **Labor 2810**
  Manufacturers and manufacturing, post
Discretion, confiscation or disposal, **Labor 2672**
Discrimination, labor and employment, **Gov 12947.5**
Evidence, manufacturers, arbitration, **Labor 2689**
Fees, manufacturers, registration, **Labor 2675**
Financial security, manufacturers wages, payment guaranty, evidence, deposit, **Labor 2679**

WEARING APPAREL—Cont'd
Fines and penalties. Manufacturers and manufacturing, post
Garment manufacturers. Manufacturers and manufacturing, generally, post
Gender identity, labor and employment, fair employment and housing, **Gov 12949**
Hearings. Manufacturers and manufacturing, post
Industrial homework, manufacturer, **Labor 2651**
Injunction, contracts, labor and employment, **Labor 2810**
Investigations and investigators. Manufacturers and manufacturing, post
Joint and several liability, manufacturers, contracts with unregistered or unbonded manufacturers, **Labor 2677**
Judgments and decrees, manufacturers and manufacturing,
  Compensation and salaries, satisfaction, **Labor 273**
  Confiscation, **Labor 2681**
Labor and employment,
  Changing rooms, audio or video recordings, **Labor 435**
  Contracts, **Labor 2810**
  Discrimination, pants, **Gov 12947.5**
  Gender identity, **Gov 12949**
  Manufacturers and manufacturing, generally, post
Mail and mailing, certified or registered mail, manufacturers, penalty orders, **Labor 2678**
Manufacturers and manufacturing, **Labor 2670 et seq.**
  Actions and proceedings,
    Compensation and salaries, contractors, suretyship and guarantee, **Labor 2673.1**
    Registration, **Labor 2677**
  Advisory committee, **Labor 2674.1**
  Appeal and review,
    Arbitration, **Labor 2691**
    Compensation and salaries, contractors, suretyship and guarantee, **Labor 2673.1**
    Confiscation, **Labor 2681**
  Arbitration and award, pricing and quality disputes with contractors, **Labor 2685 et seq.**
  Assembly, successor employers, compensation and salaries, liability, **Labor 2684**
  Attorney fees,
    Arbitration, **Labor 2688, 2692**
    Compensation and salaries, contractors, suretyship and guarantee, **Labor 2673.1**
  Attorneys, arbitration, **Labor 2689**
  Bonds (officers and fiduciaries),
    Persons penalized within prior three years, **Labor 2675**
    Wage and benefit payments, **Labor 2679**

WEARING APPAREL—Cont'd
Manufacturers and manufacturing —Cont'd
  Budgets submitted to legislature, **Labor 2674.2**
  Certificates, registration, **Labor 2675**
  Claims, compensation and salaries, contractors, suretyship and guarantee, **Labor 2673.1**
  Compensation and salaries,
    Contractors, suretyship and guarantee, **Labor 2673.1**
    Judgments and decrees, satisfaction, **Labor 273**
    Sewing or assembly, successor employers, liability, **Labor 2684**
  Contractors, compensation and salaries, suretyship and guarantee, **Labor 2673.1**
  Contracts, manufacturers and contractors,
    Investigation and mediation of pricing and quality disputes, **Labor 2680.5**
    Registered manufacturers, illegal business practices, **Labor 2677.5**
  Costs, arbitration, **Labor 2688, 2692**
  Crimes and offenses, manufacturing without registering, **Labor 2676**
  Damages,
    Amounts exceeding registrant bond, separate account, **Labor 2675.5**
    Compensation and salaries, contractors, suretyship and guarantee, **Labor 2673.1**
  Evidence, arbitration, **Labor 2689**
  Examiners and examinations, registration, **Labor 2675**
  Fees, registration, **Labor 2675, 2675.5**
    Damages account, deposit of part of fee, **Labor 2675.5**
  Financial security sufficient to guaranty wages, evidence, deposit, **Labor 2679**
  Fines and penalties,
    Appeal and review, **Labor 2681**
    Judgment, **Labor 2681**
      Failure to comply timely, **Labor 2678**
    Nonregistration, **Labor 2676, 2678**
    Objections, **Labor 2681**
    Records and recordation, **Labor 2678**
    Terms, discretion, **Labor 2672**
  Fire hazards, **Labor 6409.5**
  Hearings,
    Arbitration, **Labor 2688**
    Compensation and salaries, contractors, suretyship and guarantee, **Labor 2673.1**
    Penalties or confiscation, objections, **Labor 2681**
  Investigations and investigators,
    Compensation and salaries, contractors, suretyship and guarantee, **Labor 2673.1**

WEARING APPAREL—Cont'd
Manufacturers and manufacturing —Cont'd
  Investigations and investigators—Cont'd
    Pricing and quality disputes between manufacturers and contractors, **Labor 2680.5**
  Joint liability, contracts with unregistered or unbonded manufacturers, **Labor 2677**
  Judgments and decrees,
    Compensation and salaries, satisfaction, **Labor 273**
    Confiscation, **Labor 2681**
  Mail and mailing, certified or registered mail,
    Confiscation, notice, **Labor 2680**
    Penalty orders, **Labor 2678**
  Minimum wages, contractors, suretyship and guarantee, **Labor 2673.1**
  Names, display, registration as garment manufacturer, **Labor 2676.5**
  Notice,
    Arbitration,
      Hearing, **Labor 2687**
      Requests for arbitration, **Labor 2686**
    Confiscation, **Labor 2680**
    Renewal, registration, **Labor 2675**
  Oaths and affirmations, arbitration, witnesses, **Labor 2689**
  Objections, penalties or confiscation, **Labor 2681**
  Order imposing penalty, **Labor 2678**
  Overtime, contractors, suretyship and guarantee, **Labor 2673.1**
  Petitions, objections, penalties or confiscation, **Labor 2681**
  Posting, registration form, **Labor 2675**
  Priorities and preferences,
    Moneys recovered under statute, application, **Labor 2682**
    Penalty or confiscation judgments, enforcement, **Labor 2681**
  Production of books and papers, arbitration, **Labor 2689**
  Records and recordation, **Labor 2673**
    Arbitration, **Labor 2689**
    Enforcement, statutes, **Labor 2674**
  Registration, **Labor 2675 et seq.**
    Actions and proceedings, **Labor 2677**
    Bonds (officers and fiduciaries), wage and benefit payments, **Labor 2679**
    Certificates, **Labor 2675**
    Confiscation, **Labor 2680**
    Crimes and offenses, manufacturing without registering, **Labor 2676**
    Display, **Labor 2676.5**
    Examinations, **Labor 2675**
    Fees, **Labor 2675, 2675.5**
      Damages account, deposit of part of fee, **Labor 2675.5**
    Fines and penalties, **Labor 2678**
    Licenses and permits, **Labor 2676.7**

WEARING APPAREL—Cont'd
Manufacturers and manufacturing
—Cont'd
Registration—Cont'd
Posting, registration forms, **Labor
2675**
Revocation or suspension,
Compensation and salaries, **Labor
2673.1**
Discretion, **Labor 2672**
Minimum wage, child labor, or
maximum hours violations, **Labor 2679**
Renewal, registration, **Labor 2675,
2675.2**
Requirements for registration, **Labor
2675**
Safety hazards, **Labor 6409.5**
Searches and seizures,
Appeal and review, **Labor 2681**
Discretion, **Labor 2672**
Judgment, **Labor 2681**
Minimum wage, child labor, or maxi-
mum hours violations, **Labor
2679**
Objections, **Labor 2681**
Registration, **Labor 2680**
Sewing, successor employers, compensa-
tion and salaries, liability, **Labor
2684**
Subpoenas, arbitration, **Labor 2689**
Successor employers, sewing or assem-
bly, compensation and salaries, lia-
bility, **Labor 2684**
Suretyship and guarantee, compensation
and salaries, contractors, **Labor
2673.1**
Time, arbitration award, **Labor 2690**
Trial de novo, penalties or confiscation,
Labor 2681
Verification, petitions, objections, pen-
alties or confiscation, **Labor 2681**
Workers compensation, evidence of, application for registration, **Labor
2675**
Minimum wages, manufacturers and manufacturing, contractors, suretyship and
guarantee, **Labor 2673.1**
Notice. Manufacturers and manufactur-
ing, ante
Oaths and affirmations, manufacturers, ar-
bitration, witnesses, **Labor 2689**
Objections, manufacturers, penalties or
confiscation, **Labor 2681**
Orders, penalties, manufacturers, service,
Labor 2678
Overtime, manufacturers and manufactur-
ing, contractors, suretyship and guar-
antee, **Labor 2673.1**
Petitions, manufacturers, objections, pen-
alties or confiscation, **Labor 2681**
Posting, manufacturers, registration forms,
Labor 2675
Priorities and preferences, manufacturers,
Moneys recovered under statute, appli-
cation, **Labor 2682**

WEARING APPAREL—Cont'd
Priorities and preferences, manufacturers
—Cont'd
Penalty or confiscation judgments, en-
forcement, **Labor 2681**
Production of books and papers, manufac-
turers and manufacturing, arbitration,
Labor 2689
Records and recordation. Manufacturers
and manufacturing, ante
Registration. Manufacturers and manu-
facturing, ante
Requirements for registration, manufac-
turers, **Labor 2675**
Searches and seizures,
Discretion, **Labor 2672**
Manufacturers and manufacturing, ante
Sewing, successor employers, compensa-
tion and salaries, liability, **Labor 2684**
Subpoenas, manufacturers and manufac-
turing, arbitration, **Labor 2689**
Successor employers, sewing or assembly,
compensation and salaries, liability,
Labor 2684
Suretyship and guarantee, manufacturers
and manufacturing, compensation
and salaries, contractors, **Labor
2673.1**
Time, manufacturers, arbitration award,
Labor 2690
Trial de novo, manufacturers,
Arbitration, **Labor 2691**
Penalties or confiscation, **Labor 2681**

WEIGHTS AND MEASURES
Wharves, docks and piers, maximum
weight of stored material, **Labor 7603**

WELFARE
Social Services, generally, this index

WHARVES, DOCKS AND PIERS
Bull rails, stringer rails or curbs, **Labor
7604**
Crimes and offenses, safety violations, **La-
bor 7608**
Dock plates, construction and mainte-
nance, **Labor 7606**
Hand tools, safe condition, **Labor 7602**
Hand trucks, safe condition, **Labor 7601**
Hatch tenders, employment, **Labor 7600,
7608**
Inspection and inspectors, machinery and
equipment, **Labor 7605**
Internal combustion engine operation, **La-
bor 7607**
Plates, dock plates, construction and main-
tenance, **Labor 7606**
Safety, loading and unloading ships and
vessels, **Labor 7600 et seq.**
San Francisco Harbor, generally, this in-
dex
Signalmen, employment, **Labor 7600, 7608**
Stored material, weight limits, **Labor 7603**
Tools, safe condition, **Labor 7602**

WHEEL CRANES
Generally, **Labor 6704**

WHISKEY
Alcoholic Beverages, generally, this index

WHISTLE BLOWING
Actions and proceedings, health facilities,
Health & S 1278.5
Attorney fees, health facilities, **Health & S
1278.5**
Attorney general, hotlines, **Labor 1102.7**
Bribery and Corruption, this index
Burden of proof, labor and employment,
Labor 1102.6
California State University, **Educ 89570 et
seq.**
Colleges and Universities, this index
Community colleges and districts, **Educ
87160 et seq.**
Costs, health facilities, **Health & S 1278.5**
Crimes and offenses,
Community colleges and districts, **Educ
87160 et seq.**
Health facilities, **Health & S 1278.5**
School officers and employees, **Educ
44110 et seq.**
Disclosure,
Community colleges and districts, **Educ
87160 et seq.**
School officers and employees, **Educ
44110 et seq.**
Duress or coercion,
Community colleges and districts, **Educ
87160 et seq.**
School officers and employees, **Educ
44110 et seq.**
Evidence, burden of proof, labor and em-
ployment, **Labor 1102.6**
Exemptions, health facilities, **Health & S
1278.5**
Fines and penalties,
Community colleges and districts, **Educ
87160 et seq.**
Health facilities, **Health & S 1278.5**
Labor and employment, **Labor 1102.5**
School officers and employees, **Educ
44110 et seq.**
Health care providers, **Health & S 1278.5**
Health facilities, **Health & S 1278.5**
Hotlines, attorney general, **Labor 1102.7**
Information, state officers and employees,
Gov 8548 et seq.
Labor and employment, **Labor 1102.5**
Limitation of actions, hotlines, attorney
general, **Labor 1102.7**
Notice,
Posting, **Labor 1102.8**
State officers and employees, informa-
tion, **Gov 8548.2**
Nurses, **Health & S 1278.5**
Posting, notice, **Labor 1102.8**
School officers and employees, **Educ
44110 et seq.**
State officers and employees, information,
Gov 8548 et seq.
Statute of limitations, hotlines, attorney
general, **Labor 1102.7**

WHISTLE BLOWING—Cont'd
Undue influence,
> Community colleges and districts, **Educ 87160 et seq.**
> School officers and employees, **Educ 44110 et seq.**

WIDOWS AND WIDOWERS
Surviving Spouse, generally, this index

WIDTH
Scaffold platforms and floors, **Labor 7153**

WILD ANIMALS AND BIRDS
Fish and Game, generally, this index

WILDLIFE
Fish and Game, generally, this index

WILLIE L. BROWN, JR. BILL LOCKYER CIVIL LIABILITY REFORM ACT
Generally, **CC 3294**

WILLS
Probate Proceedings, generally, this index

WINDOWS
Children and minors, window trimming, employment, **Labor 1294.3**
Cleaners, **Labor 7325 et seq.**
> Safety devices on buildings, **Labor 7325 et seq.**
Window trimming, minors, employment, **Labor 1294.3**

WITHHOLDING
Income Tax—State, this index
Support, this index
Unemployment Compensation, this index

WITHHOLDING AGENT
Definitions, withholding tax on wages, **Un Ins 13010**

WITHHOLDING ORDER FOR SUPPORT
Definitions, garnishment, **CCP 706.030**

WITHHOLDING ORDER FOR TAXES
Definitions, garnishment, **CCP 706.072**

WITHHOLDING ORDERS
Garnishment, generally, this index

WITHHOLDING PERIOD
Definitions, garnishment, **CCP 706.022**

WITHHOLDING TAX
> Generally, **Un Ins 13000 et seq.**
Fines and penalties, **Un Ins 13052**
Income Tax—State, this index
Unauthorized tax, **Labor 224**
Unemployment Compensation, this index

WITNESSES
Agricultural labor relations board investigation proceedings, **Labor 1151 et seq.**
Compensation and salaries. Fees, generally, post
Costs. Fees, generally, post
Depositions, generally, this index

WITNESSES—Cont'd
Discrimination, time off from employment, **Labor 230**
Employment. Labor and Employment, this index
Expert testimony. Opinion and expert testimony, generally, post
Fair employment and housing department, subpoenas, **Gov 12963.1**
Fees,
> Agricultural labor relations board proceedings, **Labor 1151.4**
> Expert witnesses. Opinion and expert testimony, post
> Labor and employment, investigation of working conditions, **Labor 1176**
> Occupational safety and health appeals board, award to employers, **Labor 149.5**
> Opinion and expert testimony, post
> Traveling expenses, generally, post
> Wages, unemployment compensation, **Un Ins 1252**
> Workers compensation, **Labor 131**
Intimidation,
> Legislative committees, witnesses testifying before, **Gov 9414**
> Misdemeanor, **Gov 9414**
Labor and Employment, this index
Labor commissioner, deputies and assistants, examination under oath, **Labor 92**
Labor disputes, injunction, **Labor 1138.1**
Labor standards enforcement division, **Labor 74**
Labor statistics and research, compelling attendance, **Labor 152**
Legislature, this index
Mileage. Traveling expenses, generally, post
Occupational safety and health, **Labor 6314**
Opinion and expert testimony,
> Fair employment and housing, cease and desist orders, fees, **Gov 12987**
> Fees, fair employment and housing, **Gov 12989.2, 12989.3**
>> Cease and desist orders, **Gov 12987**
> Industrial accidents division, employment, **Labor 123**
Per diem. Fees, generally, ante
Perjury, generally, this index
Privileges and Immunities, generally, this index
Subpoenas, generally, this index
Traveling expenses,
> Agricultural labor relations board proceedings, **Labor 1151.4**
> Labor and employment, investigation of working conditions, **Labor 1176**
> Workers compensation appeals boards, **Labor 131**
Unemployment Compensation, this index
Workers Compensation, this index

WOMEN
Apprentices, **Labor 3071**
> Participation, **Labor 3073.3**
Breastfeeding. Children and Minors, this index
Civil rights. Discrimination, generally, this index
Discrimination, generally, this index
Domestic Violence, generally, this index
Fair Employment and Housing, generally, this index
Housing. Fair Employment and Housing, generally, this index
Labor and Employment, this index
Lactation, labor and employment, **Labor 1030 et seq.**
Minority designation, economically disadvantaged areas, **Un Ins 9602**
Nontraditional occupations, training, **Un Ins 9602.5**
Pregnancy, generally, this index
Support, generally, this index
Training, nontraditional occupations, **Un Ins 9602.5**
Unemployment Compensation, this index

WOOD
Timber and Lumber, generally, this index

WORDS AND PHRASES
Access shaft, tunnel and mine safety, **Labor 7951**
Accredited disaster council, workers compensation, **Labor 3211.91**
Acquire,
> Corporation taxes, net operating losses, **Rev & T 24416**
> Income tax—state, net operating losses, **Rev & T 17276**
Acquired, corporation taxes, credits, labor and employment, hiring, **Rev & T 23623**
Actual cost, storage, weapons, injunction, **CCP 527.9**
Actual damages,
> Fair employment and housing, **Gov 12970**
> Hate crimes, **CC 52**
Actual knowledge, dangerous business practices, **Pen 387**
Acupuncturist, workers compensation, **Labor 3209.3**
Administrative director, workers compensation, **Labor 110, 3206**
Advance fee talent representation service, **Labor 1702.1**
Adverse action,
> Consumer credit reporting, **CC 1785.3**
> Labor and employment, records and recordation, copies, **CC 1786.53**
Advertisement, workers compensation, attorneys and others, **Labor 5433**
Advertiser, workers compensation, crimes and offenses, **Labor 5434**
Aerial passenger tramways, **Labor 7340**

WORDS

WORDS AND PHRASES—Cont'd

Affiliate,
  Criminal history information disclosure, concessionaire application purposes, **Labor 432.7**
  Savings associations, fingerprints, criminal history information, **Fin 6525**
Affirmative action, fair employment and housing department, **Gov 12927**
Affirmative relief, fair employment and housing, **Gov 12926**
Age, fair employment and housing department, **Gov 12926**
Agency,
  Employment agency, **CC 1812.501**
  Information Practices Act, **CC 1798.3**
  Labor and workforce development agency, **Labor 18.5**
  Workforce investment, **Un Ins 14005**
Agent,
  Asbestos hazard, disclosure, **Health & S 25919.6**
  Gratuities or tips, **Labor 350**
Aggrieved employee, fines and penalties, actions and proceedings, **Labor 2699**
Aggrieved person, fair employment and housing department, **Gov 12927**
Agreements, arbitration, **CCP 1280**
Agricultural employee, Agricultural Labor Relations Act of 1975, **Labor 1140.4**
Agricultural employer,
  Agricultural Labor Relations Act of 1975, **Labor 1140.4**
  Mediation, **Labor 1164**
Agricultural production, processing and handling facilities, manlifts, **Labor 7311.25**
Agricultural zone of danger, employment of minors, **Labor 1293.1**
Agriculture, Agricultural Labor Relations Act of 1975, **Labor 1140.4**
Airport, trespass, **Pen 602**
Airport operations area, trespass, **Pen 602**
Aliens, public works, **Labor 1725**
Alternative work, workers compensation, permanent disability, payment, **Labor 4658.1**
Alternative workweek schedule, hours, **Labor 500**
American aircraft, **Un Ins 125.3**
American employer, unemployment compensation, **Un Ins 125.4**
American vessel, **Un Ins 125.5**
Amusement rides, safety, **Labor 7901**
Annual full time equivalent, labor and employment, hiring, credits, corporation taxes, **Rev & T 23623**
Any interest, public buildings and works, contractors, debarment, **Labor 1777.1**
Any party affected thereby, workers compensation, award, **Labor 5806**
Apparent owner, Unclaimed Property Law, **CCP 1501**
Appeals board,
  Occupational safety and health, **Labor 6302**

WORDS AND PHRASES—Cont'd

Appeals board—Cont'd
  State employees, workers compensation, **Labor 6101**
  Unemployment compensation, **Un Ins 126**
  Workers compensation, **Labor 110, 3205.5**
Applicable current group rate, group disability insurance, continuation benefits, **Ins 10116.5**
Applicable elevator safety orders, manlifts, **Labor 7311.25**
Applicant,
  Bonds and photographs, applicant for employment, **Labor 400**
  Employment, **Labor 430**
  Youthbuild program, **Un Ins 9801**
Applicant for employment, California State University, whistle blowing, **Educ 89572**
Apprentice, **Labor 3077**
Apprenticeable craft or trade, public buildings and works, **Labor 1777.5**
Appropriate government agency, dangerous business practices, **Pen 387**
Approved curriculum of classroom instruction, electricity, apprentices, certificates and certification, **Labor 3099.4**
Aquaculture, occupational safety and health, **Labor 6302**
Armenian genocide victim, limitation of actions, **CCP 354.45**
Arrearage, support enforcement, **Fam 5201**
Artists, **Labor 1700.4**
  Talent agencies, **Labor 1700.4**
  Talent services, fees, **Labor 1701**
Asbestos,
  Building owners, disclosure, **Health & S 25918**
  Workplace, registration, **Labor 6501.7**
Asbestos consultant, **Labor 6509.5**
Asbestos containing construction material, building owners disclosure, **Health & S 25919**
Asbestos related work, registration, **Labor 6501.8**
Asbestos workers, workers compensation, **Labor 4402**
Asbestos workers benefits, workers compensation, **Labor 4402**
Asbestosis, workers compensation, **Labor 4402**
ASCE 21, elevators, dumbwaiters and escalators, **Labor 7300.1**
ASME A17.1, elevators, dumbwaiters and escalators, **Labor 7300.1**
ASME A17.3, elevators, dumbwaiters and escalators, **Labor 7300.1**
ASME A18.1, elevators, dumbwaiters and escalators, **Labor 7300.1**
Assassination, public officials, death benefits, **Labor 4720**
Assigned obligee, earnings assignment orders, support enforcement, **Fam 5214**

WORDS AND PHRASES—Cont'd

Assignment order,
  Child health care insurance, **Fam 3760**
  Support, **Fam 5202**
Assist, promote or deter union organizing, state contracts, funds, **Gov 16645**
Associate, criminal history information disclosure, concessionaire application purposes, **Labor 432.7**
Association, asbestos, notice, **Health & S 25915.2, 25915.5**
Attributable income,
  Corporation taxes,
    Enterprise zones,
      Credits, **Rev & T 23622.7, 23622.8, 23634**
      Deductions, **Rev & T 24416.2**
    Military base recovery areas, **Rev & T 23645, 24416.5**
  Enterprise zones, income tax—state, credits, **Rev & T 17053.34**
  Manufacturing enhancement areas, **Rev & T 17053.47**
  Income tax—state, enterprise zones,
    Credits, **Rev & T 17053.74**
    Deductions, **Rev & T 17276.2**
Audition, talent agencies, fees, **Labor 1701**
Authorized personnel,
  Airports and landing fields, trespass, **Pen 602**
  Trespass on airport property, **Pen 602**
Authorized regulations, unemployment compensation, **Un Ins 127**
Automated clearinghouse, unemployment compensation, electronic funds transfers, withholding tax on wages, **Un Ins 13021.5**
Automated clearinghouse credits, unemployment compensation, electronic funds transfers, withholding tax on wages, **Un Ins 13021.5**
Automated clearinghouse debits, unemployment compensation, electronic funds transfers, withholding tax on wages, **Un Ins 13021.5**
Average base pay roll, unemployment compensation, **Un Ins 905**
Award, arbitration, **CCP 1280**
Awarding authority,
  Janitors, displaced workers, **Labor 1060**
  Public transit, displaced workers, **Labor 1071**
Awarding body,
  Public buildings and works, actions and proceedings, prevailing wage rate, **Labor 1781**
  Public works, **Labor 1722**
Bank, Armenians, genocide, limitation of actions, **CCP 354.45**
Banking day, unemployment compensation, funds transfers, withholding tax on wages, **Un Ins 13021.5**
Banking organization, Unclaimed Property Law, **CCP 1501**
Bar, workplace smoking regulation, **Labor 6404.5**

WORDS AND PHRASES—Cont'd

Base period, unemployment compensation, **Un Ins 1275**

Beneficiary, health care providers, preferred reimbursement rates, **Labor 4609**

Benefit audit fund, unemployment compensation, **Un Ins 130.5**

Benefit year, unemployment compensation, **Un Ins 1276**

Benefits, unemployment compensation, **Un Ins 128, 140**

Bidder, public transit, displaced workers, **Labor 1071**

Biochemical substance, workers compensation, peace officers, firefighters and fire departments, presumptions, **Labor 3212.85**

Biopharmaceutical activities,
  Corporation taxes, net operating losses, **Rev & T 24416**
  Income tax—state, net operating losses, **Rev & T 17276**

Blood borne infectious disease, workers compensation, presumptions, **Labor 3212.8**

Board,
  Agricultural Labor Relations Act of 1975, **Labor 1140.4**
  Elevators, dumbwaiters and escalators, **Labor 7300.1**
  Occupational safety and health standards board, **Labor 140**
  Tunnel and mine safety, **Labor 7951**
  Workforce investment, **Un Ins 14005**

Board certified, medical evaluators, workers compensation, **Labor 139.2**

Board qualified, medical evaluators, workers compensation, **Labor 139.2**

Body awarding the contract, public works, **Labor 1722**

Bracero, limitation of actions, labor and employment, funds, **CCP 354.7**

Building,
  Asbestos hazard, disclosure, **Health & S 25919.2**
  Construction elevators, safety, **Labor 7200**
  Safety in employment, building construction and repair, **Labor 7100**
  Structural steel frames, safety, **Labor 7250**
  Window cleaners, safety devices, **Labor 7325**

Business, gratuities or tips of employees, **Labor 350**

Business association, Unclaimed Property Law, **CCP 1501**

Business day, farm labor contractors, licenses and permits, **Labor 1695.7**

Business entity, unemployment compensation, **Un Ins 1145**
  Concealed wages, fines and penalties, **Un Ins 1128.1, 1735.1**

WORDS AND PHRASES—Cont'd

Business necessity, labor and employment, language, unlawful employment practices, **Gov 12951**

Caboose, railroads, **Labor 7000**

Calendar quarter, unemployment insurance code, **Un Ins 129**

Campus, workers compensation, University of California police, **Labor 3213**

Campus department, workers compensation, University of California police, **Labor 3213**

Car washing and polishing, **Labor 2051**

Carcinogen, Occupational Carcinogens Control Act, **Labor 9004**

Care provider, family care leave, **Un Ins 3302**

Care recipient, family care leave, **Un Ins 3302**

CAS number, hazardous substances information and training, **Labor 6366**

Case services, employment development, **Un Ins 9608**

Center, biotechnology, training, **Un Ins 9700**

Certificating agency, tower crane regulation, **Labor 7371**

Certified competent conveyance mechanics, elevators, dumbwaiters and escalators, **Labor 7300.1**

Certified inspectors, boilers or tanks, **Labor 7650**

Certified qualified conveyance companies, elevators, dumbwaiters and escalators, **Labor 7300.1**

Certified trainee, Vietnam Veterans Employment Act, **Gov 7280.9**

Chemical name, hazardous substances information and training, **Labor 6367**

Chief administrative officer, colleges and universities, force and violence, injunction, **CCP 527.85**

Child,
  Family care and medical leave, **Gov 12945.2**
  Family care leave, **Un Ins 3302**
  Sick leave, **Labor 233**

City, unemployment insurance code, **Un Ins 13**

Civil air patrol leave, labor and employment, **Labor 1501**

Claim, fraudulent claims against state, **Gov 12650**

Claims administrator, workers compensation, **Labor 138.4**

Client, temporary employment, compensation and salaries, **Labor 201.3**

COBRA, group disability insurance, continuation benefits, **Ins 10116.5**

Collateral benefit, military forces, temporary incapacitation, restriction or termination, **Mil & V 394**

Commercial purposes, Information Practices Act, **CC 1798.3**

WORDS AND PHRASES—Cont'd

Commission,
  Employee housing and labor camps, **Health & S 17003**
  Fair employment and housing commission, **Gov 12925**

Commission wages, employees, motor vehicle dealers, **Labor 204.1**

Commissioner,
  Car washes, **Labor 2051**
  Fair employment and housing commission, **Gov 12925**
  Wearing apparel, manufacturing, **Labor 2671**

Common interest development, asbestos, notice, **Health & S 25915.2, 25915.5**

Common name, hazardous substances, information and training, **Labor 6368**

Community health care worker, assault and battery, records and recordation, **Labor 6332**

Compensating time, labor and employment, **Labor 204.3**

Compensating time off, labor and employment, **Labor 204.3**

Compensation,
  Approval of release or compromise of workers compensation claims, **Labor 5001**
  Foreign labor contractors, **Bus & P 9998.1**
  Workers compensation, **Labor 3207**

Complainant, California State University, whistle blowing, **Educ 89572**

Computation date, unemployment compensation, **Un Ins 902**

Conciliation council, fair employment and housing department, **Gov 12927**

Construction, public works, **Labor 1720**

Construction, farm labor, garment, janitorial or security guard contractor, labor and employment, **Labor 2810**

Construction elevators, safety, **Labor 7200**

Consumer credit report, **CC 1785.3**

Consumers,
  Credit reporting, **CC 1785.3**
  Investigative Consumer Reporting Agencies Act, **CC 1786.2**

Contested claim, workers compensation, **Labor 4620**

Contingent fund, unemployment insurance code, **Un Ins 130**

Continuation coverage, Cal COBRA, accident and health insurance, **Health & S 1366.21; Ins 10128.51**

Contract of employment, **Labor 2750**

Contract security organization, criminal history information, **Pen 11105.4**

Contracting agents, health care providers, preferred reimbursement rates, **Labor 4609**

Contractor or subcontractor, public buildings and works, debarment, **Labor 1777.1**

WORDS

WORDS AND PHRASES—Cont'd

Contractors,
  Apprentices, public buildings and works, **Labor 1777.5**
  Deaf and mute persons, **Un Ins 11000.5**
  Drug free workplaces, state contracts, **Gov 8351**
  Janitors, displaced workers, **Labor 1060**
  Public buildings and works, **Labor 1722.1**
  Public transit, displaced workers, **Labor 1071**
  Wearing apparel, manufacturers and manufacturing, **Labor 2671**
Contributions,
  Child care, tax credit, **Rev & T 17052.18**
  Unemployment compensation, **Un Ins 131**
  Workers or employees, unemployment compensation, **Un Ins 144**
Contributions paid on his own behalf, unemployment compensation, **Un Ins 906**
Control, criminal history information disclosure, concessionaire application purposes, **Labor 432.7**
Controlled group of corporations,
  Bank and corporation tax credits, **Rev & T 23622.7**
  Corporation taxes, enterprise zones, credits, **Rev & T 23634**
Controlled substance, drug free work places, state contractors and grantees, **Gov 8351**
Controversy, arbitration, **CCP 1280**
Conveyance, elevators, dumbwaiters and escalators, **Labor 7300.1**
Conveyance inspectors, elevators, dumbwaiters and escalators, **Labor 7300.1**
Core coverage, Cal COBRA, accident and health insurance, **Health & S 1366.21; Ins 10128.51**
Corporation,
  Withholding tax on wages, **Un Ins 13003**
  Workers compensation, uninsured employers fund, **Labor 3717**
County,
  Labor Code, **Labor 14**
  Unemployment insurance code, **Un Ins 14**
Course of conduct,
  Colleges and universities, force and violence, injunction, **CCP 527.85**
  Harassment, injunction, **CCP 527.6**
  Workplace violence safety, **CCP 527.8**
Course of trade, business, profession or occupation of employer, workers compensation, **Labor 3355**
Court administrator, workers compensation, **Labor 110**
Court of competent jurisdiction, civil rights, jurisdiction, **CC 52.2**
Covered establishment, layoffs, **Labor 1400**

WORDS AND PHRASES—Cont'd

Covered multifamily dwellings, handicapped persons, discrimination, **Gov 12955.1, 12955.1.1**
Crane, tower crane regulation, **Labor 7371**
Crane employer, tower crane regulation, **Labor 7371**
Credible threat of violence,
  Colleges and universities, injunction, **CCP 527.85**
  Harassment, **CCP 527.6**
  Workplace violence safety, **CCP 527.8**
Credit score, consumer credit reporting agencies, notice, **CC 1785.15.1**
Credit transaction that is not initiated by the consumer, consumer credit reporting, **CC 1785.3**
Creed, fair employment and housing, **Gov 12926**
Cumulative average payment, unemployment compensation, withholding tax on wages, **Un Ins 13021.5**
Cumulative injuries, workers compensation, **Labor 3208.1**
Cure, aggrieved employees, fines and penalties, actions and proceedings, **Labor 2699**
Customer, temporary employment, compensation and salaries, **Labor 201.3**
Daily or weekly call, motion pictures, termination, compensation and salaries, payment, **Labor 201.5**
Damages, workers compensation, **Labor 3209**
Date of injury, workers compensation, limitation of proceedings, **Labor 5411**
  Occupational diseases, **Labor 5412**
Day hauler, farm labor contractors, **Labor 1682.3**
Days rest, labor and employment, **Labor 550**
Defendant, fair employment and housing, **Gov 12926**
Demand occupations, unemployment compensation, training or retraining, **Un Ins 1270**
Department,
  Benefit payments, **Un Ins 133.5**
  CalWORKs, job creation, **Un Ins 17000**
  Children and minors, employment, **Labor 1286**
  Employee housing and labor camps, **Health & S 17004**
  Employment development, **Un Ins 133, 9101**
    Employment training panel, **Un Ins 10201**
  Employment development department, automation report, **Un Ins 4900**
  Fair employment and housing department, **Gov 12925**
  Labor Code, **Labor 19**
  Occupational safety and health, **Labor 6302**
  Unemployment compensation, **Un Ins 133**

WORDS AND PHRASES—Cont'd

Department of benefit payments, unemployment compensation, **Un Ins 133.5**
Dependents,
  Asbestos workers, workers compensation, **Labor 4402**
  Elected public officials killed in office, college scholarships, **Labor 4728**
  Workers compensation,
    Benefits, correctional institution inmates, **Labor 3370**
    Scholarships for dependents, **Labor 4709**
Deposit, employment agencies, **CC 1812.501**
Deposited assets, Armenians, genocide, limitation of actions, **CCP 354.45**
Deposition officer, employment records, **CCP 1985.6**
Designated list of high hazard industries, occupational safety and health, **Labor 6401.7**
Diagnostic imaging, workers compensation, **Labor 139.3**
Direct care service, long term health care facilities, employment agencies, nurses, temporary employment, **CC 1812.540**
Director,
  Benefit payments, **Un Ins 134.1**
  Children and minors, employment, **Labor 1286**
  Employment development, **Un Ins 9102**
  Employment development department, automation report, **Un Ins 4900**
  Employment of minors, **Labor 1286**
  Fair employment and housing department, **Gov 12925**
  Labor Code, **Labor 20**
  Occupational safety and health, **Labor 6302**
  Unemployment compensation, **Un Ins 134**
  Workers compensation, **Labor 3700.1**
    Self insurance, **Labor 3741**
  Workers compensation enforcement, **Labor 3710**
Disability,
  Disability compensation, **Un Ins 2626**
  Discrimination, **CC 51**
  Housing discrimination, **Gov 12955.3**
Disability base period, disability compensation, **Un Ins 2610, 2611**
Disability benefit period,
  Disability compensation, **Un Ins 2608**
  Family care leave, **Un Ins 3302.1**
Disability benefits, unemployment compensation, **Un Ins 140.5**
Disability fund, unemployment compensation, **Un Ins 134.5**
Disabled, disability compensation, **Un Ins 2626**
Disaster council, workers compensation, **Labor 3211.9**
Disaster service, workers compensation, **Labor 3211.93**

WORDS AND PHRASES—Cont'd

Disclose, information practices, **CC 1798.3**

Disclosed, AIDS, blood tests results disclosure, **Health & S 120980**

Discrimination,
  Fair employment and housing department, **Gov 12927**
  Housing, disabled persons, **Gov 12955.1**

Discrimination on the basis of race, **Gov 8315**

Discriminatory treatment of an employee, health facilities, whistleblowers, **Health & S 1278.5**

Dispense, generic drugs, **Labor 4600.1**

Dispensing unit, liquified petroleum gas installations, inspections, **Labor 7681**

Division,
  Boilers, **Labor 7620**
  Elevators, dumbwaiters and escalators, **Labor 7300.1**
  Industrial homework, **Labor 2650**
  Occupational Carcinogens Control Act, **Labor 9005**
  Occupational safety and health, **Labor 6302**
  Tunnel and mine safety, **Labor 7951**

Domestic agency, employment, **CC 1812.501**

Domestic agency operating as a registry, employment agencies, **CC 1812.504**

Domestic violence, labor and employment, time off, **Labor 230, 230.1**

Door to door sales, employment of children, **Labor 1286**

Dormant elevator, dumbwaiter or escalator, **Labor 7300.1**

Drama, child labor, **Labor 1390**

Drug free workplace, state grantees and contractors, **Gov 8351**

Due date for support payments, support, **Fam 5204**

Duty belt, workers compensation, peace officers, **Labor 3213.2**

Earnings,
  Garnishment, **CCP 706.011**
  Support, **Fam 5206**

Earnings assignment order for support, Garnishment, **CCP 706.011**
  Support enforcement, **Fam 5208**

Earnings withholding order, garnishment, **CCP 706.125**

Economic deprivation, employment development, **Un Ins 9110**

Economic opportunity programs, injuries or death to enrollees, **Labor 4202**

Economic profiling, workers compensation, medical provider networks, **Labor 4616.1**

Economically disadvantaged area, employment development, **Un Ins 9111**

Economically displaced persons, employment development, **Un Ins 9115**

Educational service agency, unemployment compensation, **Un Ins 1253.3**

WORDS AND PHRASES—Cont'd

EITC (earned income tax credit), labor and employment, notice, **Rev & T 19852**

Elected public official, death benefits, **Labor 4720**

Electrician, apprentices, standards, **Labor 3099**

Electronic funds transfer, unemployment compensation, withholding tax on wages, **Un Ins 13021.5**

Elevator, **Labor 7300.1**
  Multistory dwelling units, handicapped persons, discrimination, **Gov 12955.1**

Eligible employee, unemployment compensation, disabilities, **Un Ins 702.6**

Eligible employers, workers compensation, return to work program, **Labor 139.48**

Eligible participant, employment training panel, **Un Ins 10201**

Eligible person,
  Disability compensation, **Un Ins 3012**
  Employment development, **Un Ins 9112**

Eligible small business,
  Corporation taxes, net operating losses, **Rev & T 24416**
  Income tax—state, net operating losses, **Rev & T 17276**

Emergency,
  Druggists, hours of labor, **Labor 854**
  Engagement, talent agencies, **Labor 1700.1**
  Hazardous substances information and training, **Labor 6362**

Emergency rescue personnel, labor and employment, discrimination, **Labor 230.3**

Emergency worker, elections, provisional ballots, **Elec 14313**

Employed as a teacher, private schools, overtime, exemptions, **Labor 515.8**

Employee benefit plan distribution, unclaimed property, **CCP 1501**

Employee benefits, civil air patrol, **Labor 1501**

Employee community housing, **Health & S 17005.5**

Employee engaged in the production or broadcasting of motion pictures, termination, compensation and salaries, payment, **Labor 201.5**

Employee housing, health regulation, **Health & S 17008**

Employees,
  Agricultural Labor Relations Act of 1975, **Labor 1140.4**
  Asbestos hazard, disclosure, **Health & S 25919.3**
  California State University, whistle blowing, **Educ 89572**
  Car washes, **Labor 2051**
  Child care, tax credit, **Rev & T 17052.18**
  Civil air patrol, **Labor 1501**
  Contributions, unemployment compensation, **Un Ins 144**

WORDS AND PHRASES—Cont'd

Employees—Cont'd
  Disability compensation, voluntary plans, **Un Ins 3254**
  Disclosure, violations, **Labor 1106**
  Discovery, employment records, **CCP 1985.6**
  Drug free workplaces, state contractors and grantees, **Gov 8351**
  Earned income tax credit, notice, **Rev & T 19852**
  Fair employment and housing department, **Gov 12926**
  Fire departments, **Labor 1961**
  Garnishment, **CCP 706.011**
  Health care providers, preferred reimbursement rates, **Labor 4609**
  Janitors, displaced workers, **Labor 1060**
  Labor camps and housing, **Health & S 17005**
  Layoffs, **Labor 1400**
  Military forces, leave of absence, compensation, **Mil & V 395.02**
  Musical instruments and equipment security, **Labor 2800.1**
  Occupational safety and health, **Labor 6304.1**
  Professional strike breakers, **Labor 1132.4**
  Public transit, displaced workers, **Labor 1071**
  State prisoners, occupational safety and health, **Labor 6304.2**
  Unemployment compensation, **Un Ins 621, 622, 2071**
    Contractors, **Un Ins 621.5**
  Whistle blowing, **Gov 8547.2**
    Community colleges and districts, **Educ 87162**
    School officers and employees, **Educ 44112**
  Withholding tax on wages, **Un Ins 13004**
  Workers compensation, **Labor 3352.94**
    Return to work program, **Labor 139.48**
    Subrogation, **Labor 3850**
  Workplace violence safety, **CCP 527.8**

Employees representative, asbestos hazard, disclosure, **Health & S 25919.4**

Employer,
  Artist, unemployment compensation, **Un Ins 686**
  Cal COBRA, accident and health insurance, **Health & S 1366.21; Ins 10128.51**
  Car washes, **Labor 2051**
  Care facilities, criminal history information, **Welf & I 15660**
  Children, health insurance, **Fam 3760**
  Civil air patrol, **Labor 1501**
  Community health care workers, assault and battery, records and recordation, **Labor 6332**
  Crimes, records, **Pen 11105.3**
  Earned income tax credit, notice, **Rev & T 19852**

WORDS

WORDS AND PHRASES—Cont'd

Employer—Cont'd

Employment agencies, **CC 1812.501**

Employment training panel, **Un Ins 10201**

Fair employment and housing, **Gov 12940**

Department of, **Gov 12926**

Family care and medical leave, **Gov 12945.2**

Garnishment, **CCP 706.011**

Gratuities or tips of employees, **Labor 350**

In home supportive services, criminal history information, **Welf & I 12301.8**

Industrial homework, **Labor 2650**

Layoffs, **Labor 1400**

Musical instruments and equipment security, **Labor 2800.1**

New hires, reports, **Un Ins 1088.5**

Occupational Carcinogens Control Act, **Labor 9006**

Occupational safety and health, **Labor 6304**

Professional strikebreakers, **Labor 1132.2**

Religious organizations and societies, labor and employment, **Gov 12926.2**

Sex crime, records, **Pen 11105.3**

Sexual harassment, training, **Gov 12950.1**

Sick leave, **Labor 233**

State contracts, labor organizations, promotion or deterrence, state funds, **Gov 16645**

State prisoners, occupational safety and health, **Labor 6304.2**

Support, enforcement, **Fam 5210**

Unemployment compensation, **Un Ins 675, 2071**

Domestic service, **Un Ins 684**

In home supportive services, **Un Ins 685**

Joint ventures, **Un Ins 1057, 1058**

Motion picture payroll services company, **Un Ins 679**

Withholding tax on wages, **Un Ins 13005**

Workers compensation, **Labor 3300**

Medical provider networks, **Labor 4616.5**

Power press workers, **Labor 4558**

Subrogation, **Labor 3850**

Workplace violence safety, **CCP 527.8**

Employing, gratuities or tips of employees, **Labor 350**

Unemployment compensation, **Un Ins 135, 821.4**

Employment,

Disability compensation, **Un Ins 2606**

Domestic service, unemployment compensation, **Un Ins 2606.5**

Occupational safety and health, **Labor 6303**

Professional strikebreakers, **Labor 1133**

WORDS AND PHRASES—Cont'd

Employment—Cont'd

Unemployment compensation, **Un Ins 601, 629, 632, 633, 633.1**

Domestic service, **Un Ins 2606.5**

Unemployment insurance, **Un Ins 642.1**

Employment agency,

Domestic service, **CC 1812.5095**

Fair employment and housing department, **Gov 12926**

Regulation, **CC 1812.501**

Unemployment compensation, **Un Ins 2071**

Employment counseling service, regulation, **CC 1812.501**

Employment for the duration of such strike or lockout, professional strikebreakers, **Labor 1133**

Employment in the same or a comparable position,

Family care and medical leave, **Gov 12945.2**

Family care leave, **Gov 12945.2**

Employment information, peace officer applicants, **Gov 1031.1**

Employment opportunity, talent agencies, fees, **Labor 1701**

Employment purposes,

Consumer credit reporting, **CC 1785.3**

Investigative Consumer Reporting Agencies Act, **CC 1786.2**

Employment records, discovery, **CCP 1985.6**

Employment services, foreign labor contractors, **Bus & P 9998.1**

Enclosed space, smoking, workplace, **Labor 6404.5**

Enforcement agency, employee housing and labor camps, **Health & S 17007**

Enrollee, economic opportunity programs, **Labor 4203**

Enterprise zone,

Corporation taxes, credits, **Rev & T 23622.7**

Income tax credits, **Rev & T 17053.74**

Enterprise zone expiration date,

Los Angeles revitalization zone, **Rev & T 17276.2, 24416.2**

Operating loss carryovers, **Rev & T 17276.2**

Entity,

Campaign contributions and expenditures, debarment, **Labor 1777.1**

Unemployment compensation, **Un Ins 803**

Escalator, **Labor 7300.1**

Essential functions, fair employment and housing, **Gov 12926**

Execution of a release, compensation and salaries, **Labor 206.5**

Executive director, employment training panel, **Un Ins 10201**

Exhaustee, extended unemployment compensation, **Un Ins 3503**

Existing installation, elevators, dumbwaiters and escalators, **Labor 7300.1**

WORDS AND PHRASES—Cont'd

Explosives, labor and employment, **Labor 6710**

Expose or exposure, hazardous substances information and training, **Labor 6370**

Extended benefit period, unemployment compensation, **Un Ins 3503**

Extended duration award, extended unemployment compensation, **Un Ins 3503**

Extended duration benefits, extended unemployment compensation, **Un Ins 3503**

Extended duration period, extended unemployment compensation, **Un Ins 3503**

Extended leave, employment opportunities creation, **Un Ins 12102**

Face, tunnel and mine safety, **Labor 7951**

Failure to install, workers compensation, power press workers, **Labor 4558**

Familial status, housing discrimination, **Gov 12955.2**

Family care and medical leave, **Gov 12945.2**

Family care leave, **Un Ins 3302**

Family members, family care leave, **Un Ins 3302**

Family of the judgment debtor, garnishment, **CCP 706.051**

Farm labor contractor, **Labor 1682, 1682.3**

Commercial packing house, **Labor 1682.4**

Federal acts, unemployment compensation, **Un Ins 3503**

Federal state extended benefits, unemployment compensation, **Un Ins 4003**

Federal Unemployment Tax Act, unemployment compensation, **Un Ins 136**

Federally authorized tax practitioners, confidential or privileged information, **Un Ins 13019**

Fedwire, unemployment compensation, electronic funds transfers, withholding tax on wages, **Un Ins 13021.5**

Fee,

Employment agencies, **CC 1812.501**

Farm labor contractors, **Labor 1682**

Talent agencies, **Labor 1700.2**

Talent services, **Labor 1701**

Fiduciary, withholding tax on wages, **Un Ins 13003**

Field inspection, tanks or boilers, **Labor 7725**

File,

Consumer credit reporting, **CC 1785.3**

Investigative Consumer Reporting Agencies Act, **CC 1786.2**

Final compensation,

Public employees retirement system, **Gov 20037.8, 20037.10**

Career executive assignments, **Gov 20037.13**

School members, **Gov 20035.5**

State officers and employees, retirement and pensions, **Gov 20037.9**

WORDS AND PHRASES—Cont'd

Final earnings withholding order for costs and interest, garnishment, **CCP 706.028**

Final judgment issued by a court, compensation and salaries, satisfaction, farm labor contractors, wearing apparel, manufacturers and manufacturing, **Labor 273**

Financial assets, support, liquidation, instructions, **Fam 17522.5**

Financial institution, financial abuse, aged persons, dependent adults, **Welf & I 15630.1**

Financial interest, workers compensation, physicians, **Labor 139.3**

Financial organization, Unclaimed Property Law, **CCP 1501**

Fire and rescue services coordinators, workers compensation, cancer, **Labor 3212.1**

Firefighter, workers compensation, **Labor 3211.5**

Firefighting member, workers compensation, **Labor 3211.5**

Firm offer of credit, consumer credit reporting, **CC 1785.3**

Fiscal year, withholding tax on wages, **Un Ins 13003**

FMLA, family care and medical leave, **Gov 12945.2**

Foreign country, withholding tax on wages, **Un Ins 13003**

Foreign labor contractor, **Bus & P 9998.1**

Foreign worker, foreign labor contractors, **Bus & P 9998.1**

Forge, labor union insignia, articles of merchandise, **Labor 1013**

Former spouse, group disability insurance, continuation of benefits, **Ins 10116.5**

IV D case, earnings assignment orders, support, **Fam 5212**

Franchise tax board, withholding tax on wages, **Un Ins 13003**

Fraud, damages, **CC 3294**

Full maintenance service contract, elevators, dumbwaiters and escalators, **Labor 7300.1**

Full time employment, hours of labor, exemptions, **Labor 515**

Full time student, unemployment insurance, **Un Ins 642.1**

Fund,
  Agricultural employee relief fund, **Labor 1161**
  Employment training fund, **Un Ins 10201**
  State employees, workers compensation, **Labor 6101**
  Workers compensation, **Labor 3700.1**
  Workers compensation self insurance, **Labor 3741**

Gaming clubs, workplace smoking regulation, **Labor 6404.5**

WORDS AND PHRASES—Cont'd

Garment manufacturer, compensation and salaries, judgments and decrees, satisfaction, **Labor 273**

Garment manufacturing, labor and employment, **Labor 2671**

Garnishment, **Labor 2929**

Gender,
  Labor Code, **Labor 12**
  Unemployment insurance code, **Un Ins 11**

Gender violence, actions and proceedings, **CC 52.4**

Genetic characteristic, fair employment and housing, **Gov 12926**

Good cause,
  Leaving employment, unemployment compensation, **Un Ins 1256**
  Unemployment compensation, extension of time, appeals,
    Computation protests, **Un Ins 1330**
    Disability compensation,
      Computation protests, **Un Ins 2707.4**
      Eligibility determination, **Un Ins 2707.2**
      Overpayments, **Un Ins 2737**
    Eligibility determination, **Un Ins 1328**
    Extended unemployment compensation, **Un Ins 3654.4, 3655**
      Computation protest, **Un Ins 3656**
      Federal state extended benefits,
        Computation protest, **Un Ins 4656**
        Eligibility determination, **Un Ins 4655**
    Extension of time, appeals, finality of administrative law judges decisions, **Un Ins 1334**
    Overpayment determinations, **Un Ins 1377**
  Workers compensation,
    Medical evaluations, time, **Labor 139.2**
    Self insurance, **Labor 3702.6**

Governmental entity,
  Information Practices Act, **CC 1798.3**
  Unemployment compensation, **Un Ins 710**
  Workers compensation, vanpooling, **Labor 3600.8**

Grantee, drug free workplaces, state grants, **Gov 8351**

Gratuity, employees, **Labor 350**

Great bodily harm, dangerous business practices, **Pen 387**

Gross income, withholding tax on wages, **Un Ins 13006**

Group benefit plan, Cal COBRA, accident and health insurance, **Health & S 1366.21; Ins 10128.51**

Group health coverage, access for infants and mothers program, unfair competition and labor practices, **Ins 12698.56**

WORDS AND PHRASES—Cont'd

Grower, farm labor contractors, licenses and permits, **Labor 1695.7**

Harassment,
  Fair employment and housing, **Gov 12940**
  Right to privacy, **CCP 527.6**

Have a common residence, domestic partnership, **Fam 297**

Hazardous substance removal work, **Labor 142.7**

Head of department, industrial relations department, **Labor 53**

Health care providers, family care and medical leave, **Gov 12945.2**

Health care services, child health care coverage, **Fam 3760**

Health care worker, workers compensation, **Labor 3208.05**
  Death benefits, limitation of actions, AIDS, **Labor 5406.6**

Health facilities, whistle blowing, **Health & S 1278.5**

Health insurance, child health care coverage, **Fam 3760**

Health insurance coverage, child health care coverage, **Fam 3760**

Health insurance coverage assignment, child health care coverage, **Fam 3760**

Health insurance plan, child health care coverage, **Fam 3760**

High unemployment period, unemployment compensation, extended unemployment compensation, **Un Ins 4004**

Holder, Unclaimed Property Law, **CCP 1501**

Home, industrial homework, **Labor 2650**

Horticultural, child labor, **Labor 1390**

Hospital market baskets, workers compensation, **Labor 5307.1**

Hospital market baskets for excluded hospitals, workers compensation, **Labor 5307.1**

Hospital treatment, workers compensation, **Labor 3209.5**

Housing accommodation, fair employment and housing department, **Gov 12927**

Human resource agency, crimes, records, **Pen 11105.3**

Husband and wife, income tax—state, withholding tax on wages, **Un Ins 13003**

Illegal order, whistle blowing, **Gov 8547.2**
  Community colleges and districts, **Educ 87162**
  School officers and employees, **Educ 44112**

Immediate family, workers compensation, **Labor 139.3**

Immediate family members, victims of crime, labor and employment, absence and absentees, judicial proceedings, **Labor 230.2**

WORDS

WORDS AND PHRASES—Cont'd

Improper governmental activity, whistle blowing, **Gov 8547.2**

Community colleges and districts, **Educ 87162**

School officers and employees, **Educ 44112**

Impurities, hazardous substances information and training, **Labor 6371**

Incarceration, unemployment compensation disability, **Un Ins 2680**

Income, business and commerce, licenses and permits, political subdivisions, **Bus & P 16300**

Increased costs, public buildings and works, actions and proceedings, prevailing wage rate, **Labor 1781**

Incurred liabilities for the payment of compensation, workers compensation, **Labor 3700.1**

Independent medical examiner, workers compensation, **Labor 28**

Indian tribe, unemployment compensation, **Un Ins 605**

Individual,
Information Practices Act, **CC 1798.3**
Unemployment compensation, training or retraining, demand occupations, **Un Ins 1267**
Withholding tax on wages, **Un Ins 13003**

Individually identifiable information, workers compensation, **Labor 138.7**

Industrial, homework, **Labor 2650**

Industrial disability, unemployment compensation, **Un Ins 2776**

Injury,
Lifeguards, skin cancer, workers compensation, **Labor 3212.11**
Workers compensation, **Labor 3208, 3208.05, 3212, 3212.1**
Biochemical substance, peace officers, firefighters and fire departments, presumptions, **Labor 3212.85**
Correctional institutions, presumptions, **Labor 3212.10**
Law enforcement personnel, hepatitis, **Labor 3212.8**
Lyme disease, presumptions, **Labor 3212.12**
Meningitis, **Labor 3212.9**
Peace officers, **Labor 3213.2**

Insolvent self insurers, workers compensation, **Labor 3700.1, 3741**

Inspect, farm labor contractors, licenses and permits, **Labor 1695.7**

Inspection, unemployment compensation, withholding taxes, confidential or privileged information, **Un Ins 13018**

Insured unemployment rate, extended unemployment compensation, **Un Ins 3503**

Insurer,
Occupational safety and health, **Labor 6302**
Workers compensation, **Labor 3211**

WORDS AND PHRASES—Cont'd

Integrated employment, mentally retarded and developmentally disabled persons, committees, **Welf & I 4868**

Internal Revenue Service Schedule SE, unemployment compensation, elective coverage, **Un Ins 704, 704.1, 708, 708.5**

Investigative consumer reporting agency, **CC 1786.2**

Investigative position, occupational safety and health division, bilingual employees, **Labor 176**

Involving unpaid wages, judgments and decrees, satisfaction, farm labor contractors, wearing apparel, manufacturers and manufacturing, **Labor 273**

Isolated apprentices, instructions, **Labor 3074**

Item of information, consumer credit reporting, **CC 1785.3**

Job, employment training panel, **Un Ins 10201**

Job listing service, regulation, **CC 1812.501**

Job order, employment agencies, **CC 1812.501**

Job pairing, employment opportunities creation, **Un Ins 12102**

Job sharing, employment opportunities creation, **Un Ins 12102**

Job training and placement services, employment development, **Un Ins 9107**

Jobseeker, employment agencies, **CC 1812.501**

Joint venture, unemployment compensation, **Un Ins 1058**

Journeyman, on the job training programs, **Labor 3093**

Judgment creditor, garnishment, **CCP 706.011**

Judgment debtor, garnishment, **CCP 706.011**

Jurisdictional strikes, **Labor 1118**

Key factors, consumer credit reporting agencies, credit score, notice, **CC 1785.15.1**

Knowing,
False claims against state, **Gov 12650**
Fraudulent claims against state, **Gov 12650**

Knows, contracts, labor and employment, **Labor 2810**

Label, labor union insignia, use on articles of merchandise, **Labor 1010**

Labor, payment of wages, **Labor 200**

Labor camps, health regulation, **Health & S 17008**

Labor commissioner, **Labor 21**
Employment of minors, **Labor 1286**

Labor compliance program, public buildings and works, compensation and salaries, **Labor 1771.5**

Labor dispute,
Agricultural Labor Relations Act of 1975, **Labor 1140.4**
Injunction, **CCP 527.3; Labor 1138.4**

WORDS AND PHRASES—Cont'd

Labor market areas, unemployment compensation, training or retraining, **Un Ins 1270**

Labor organizations,
Agricultural Labor Relations Act of 1975, **Labor 1140.4**
Fair employment and housing department, **Gov 12926**
Jurisdictional strikes, **Labor 1117**
Unemployment compensation, **Un Ins 2071**

Labor standards, local jurisdictions, **Labor 1205**

Labor supply employee housing, **Health & S 17009**

LAMBRA,
Corporation taxes,
Credits, military base recovery areas, **Rev & T 23645**
Deductions, enterprise zones, **Rev & T 24416.2**
Military base recovery areas, net operating losses, carrybacks, **Rev & T 24416.5**
Deductions, net operating loss, **Rev & T 17276.2**
Income tax—state, local agency military base recovery areas, credits, **Rev & T 17276.5**
Local agency military base recovery areas,
Income tax, credits, **Rev & T 17053.46**
Personal income taxes, credits, **Rev & T 17053.46**
Military base recovery areas, corporation taxes, credits, **Rev & T 23646**

LAMBRA expiration date, **Rev & T 17276.2**
Corporation taxes, local agency military base recovery areas, **Rev & T 24416.5**
Income tax—state, local agency military base recovery areas, credits, **Rev & T 17053.46, 17276.5**
Local agency military base recovery areas,
Corporation taxes, credits, **Rev & T 23646**
Income tax credits, **Rev & T 17053.46**
Los Angeles revitalization zone, **Rev & T 24416.2**

Laminated safety glass, railroads, **Labor 6955**

Land leveling, Agricultural Labor Relations Act of 1975, **Labor 1140.4**

Large tanks, inspection, air pressure or liquefied petroleum gas, **Labor 7725**

Layoffs, **Labor 1400**

Lead related construction industry, labor and employment, **Labor 6716**

Leasing employer, unemployment compensation, **Un Ins 606.5**

Legal days work, public works, **Labor 1810**

Leisure sharing, employment opportunities creation, **Un Ins 12102**

WORDS AND PHRASES—Cont'd

Levying officer, garnishment, **CCP 706.073**

License verification unit, farm labor contractors, **Labor 1695.7**

Licensed nursing staff, long term health care facilities, employment agencies, temporary employment, **CC 1812.540**

Licensee,
Farm labor contractors, **Labor 1682**
Talent agencies, **Labor 1700.3**

Licenses,
Farm labor contractors, **Labor 1682**
Fee, artists managers, **Labor 1700.3**
Talent agencies, **Labor 1700.3**

Licensing board, discrimination, **Gov 12944**

Life insurance corporation, Unclaimed Property Law, **CCP 1501**

Limited English proficient, occupational safety and health division, bilingual employees, **Labor 176**

Limits, fair employment and housing, **Gov 12926, 12926.1**

Lobby, smoking, **Labor 6404.5**

Local agencies,
Public transportation labor disputes, **Labor 1137**
Railroad employees, **Labor 6902**

Local child support enforcement agency, consumer credit reporting, **CC 1785.3**

Local jurisdiction, labor and employment, standards, **Labor 1205**

Local labor federation, workforce investment, **Un Ins 14005**

Locality in which public work is performed, public works, **Labor 1724**

Lockout, professional strikebreakers, **Labor 1132.8**

Long term health care facility, employment agencies, nurses, temporary employment, **CC 1812.540**

Looted assets, Armenians, genocide, limitation of actions, **CCP 354.45**

Los Angeles revitalization zone expiration date, **Rev & T 17276.2, 24416.2**
Corporation taxes, **Rev & T 24416.4**
Income tax—state, **Rev & T 17276.4**

Lower explosive limit, tunnel and mine safety, **Labor 7951**

Maintain, Information Practices Act, **CC 1798.3**

Major life activities, fair employment and housing, **Gov 12926, 12926.1**

Major mechanical failures, amusements, rides, reports, **Labor 7914**

Malice, damages, **CC 3294**

Managers, dangerous business practices, **Pen 387**

Mandated reporter of suspected financial abuse of an elder or dependent adult, financial institutions, **Welf & I 15630.1**

Mandatory furloughs, public employees retirement system, **Gov 20969**
Superior courts, service credits, **Gov 20969.1**

WORDS AND PHRASES—Cont'd

Manufacture, industrial homework, **Labor 2650**

Manufacturer,
Hazardous substances and waste, information and training, **Labor 6372**
Workers compensation, power press workers, **Labor 4558**

Manufacturing enhancement area,
Corporation taxes, credits, enterprise zones, **Rev & T 23622.8**
Enterprise zones, income tax—state, credits, **Rev & T 17053.47**

Manufacturing enhancement area expiration date,
Corporation taxes, credits, enterprise zones, **Rev & T 23622.8**
Enterprise zones, income tax—state, credits, **Rev & T 17053.47**

Mass layoffs, **Labor 1400**

Material, false claims against state, **Gov 12650**

Material alteration, elevators, dumbwaiters and escalators, **Labor 7300.1**

Material change in ownership, workers compensation, occupational diseases, multiple employers, **Labor 5500.5**

May,
Labor Code, **Labor 15**
Unemployment insurance code, **Un Ins 15**

Medical condition,
Discrimination, **CC 51**
Fair employment and housing department, **Gov 12926**

Medical director, workers compensation, **Labor 29, 110**

Medical information, Investigative Consumer Reporting Agencies Act, **CC 1786.2**

Medical leave, **Gov 12945.2**

Medical legal expenses, workers compensation, contested claims, **Labor 4620**

Medical surgical and hospital treatment, workers compensation, **Labor 3209.5**

Medical treatment, workers compensation, reports, **Labor 3209.10**

Medicare economic index, workers compensation, **Labor 5307.1**

Member, workers compensation, **Labor 3212.5, 3700.1**
Self insurance, **Labor 3741**
University of California, **Labor 3212.4**
University of California police, **Labor 3213**

Member of a fire department, workers compensation, **Labor 3211.5**
Biochemical substances, presumptions, **Labor 3212.85**

Mental disability, fair employment and housing, **Gov 12926, 12926.1**

Mentally unable to make a claim, unemployment compensation, disability benefits, **Un Ins 2705.1**

Military or naval forces, withholding tax on wages, **Un Ins 13003**

WORDS AND PHRASES—Cont'd

Military service, disability compensation, **Un Ins 2766**

Mine, tunnel and mine safety, **Labor 7951**

Minimum wage,
Corporation taxes, enterprise zones, **Rev & T 23622.7**
Credits, **Rev & T 23622.8, 23634**
Enterprise zones,
Income tax—state, credits, **Rev & T 17053.34**
Manufacturing enhancement areas, **Rev & T 17053.47**
Tax credits, **Rev & T 17053.74**
Local agency military base recovery areas, income tax credits, **Rev & T 17053.46**
Military base recovery areas, corporation taxes, credits, **Rev & T 23646**

Minors, employment, **Labor 1286**

Miscellaneous payroll period, withholding tax on wages, **Un Ins 13007**

Mixtures, hazardous substances information and training, **Labor 6373**

Mobile tower crane, tower crane regulation, **Labor 7371**

Modified work, workers compensation, permanent disability, payment, **Labor 4658.1**

Most recent work, unemployment compensation, **Un Ins 1256.3**

Motion picture engagement, talent agencies, **Labor 1700.1**

Motion picture production companies, unemployment compensation, motion picture payroll services company, employer or employing unit, **Un Ins 679**

Motion picture production workers, unemployment compensation, motion picture payroll services company, employer or employing unit, **Un Ins 679**

Moving walk, **Labor 7300.1**

MSDS, hazardous substances information and training, **Labor 6374**

Muck, tunnel and mine safety, **Labor 7951**

Multistory dwelling unit, handicapped persons, discrimination, **Gov 12955.1.1**

National medical support notice, child health care coverage, **Fam 3760**

Nature of the physical injury or disfigurement, workers compensation, permanent disability, **Labor 4660**

Necessary expenditures or losses, labor and employment, indemnity, discharge of duties, **Labor 2802**

Net balance of reserve, unemployment compensation, **Un Ins 904**

Net loss,
Corporation taxes, net operating losses, **Rev & T 24416**
Income tax—state, net operating losses, **Rev & T 17276**

Net operating loss,
Corporation taxes,
Local agency military base recovery areas, **Rev & T 24416.5**

WORDS

WORDS AND PHRASES—Cont'd
Net operating loss—Cont'd
  Corporation taxes—Cont'd
    Los Angeles revitalization zone, **Rev & T 24416.4**
    Net operating loss deduction, **Rev & T 24416.2**
    Targeted tax areas, **Rev & T 24416.6**
  Deductions, **Rev & T 17276.2**
  Income tax—state,
    Carrybacks, Los Angeles revitalization zone, **Rev & T 17276.4**
    Enterprise zones,
      Local agency military base recovery areas, credits, **Rev & T 17276.5**
      Targeted tax areas, carrybacks, **Rev & T 17276.6**
Net take home salary, state university police, **Labor 4816**
Neutral arbitrator, **CCP 1280**
New business,
  Corporation taxes, net operating losses, **Rev & T 24416**
  Net operating losses, deductions and carryovers, **Rev & T 17276**
New hire training, employment training panel, **Un Ins 10201**
Next regular payday, motion pictures, termination, compensation and salaries, payment, **Labor 201.5**
Noncore coverage, Cal COBRA, accident and health insurance, **Health & S 1366.21; Ins 10128.51**
Nonprofit, organization, unemployment compensation, **Un Ins 711**
Nonprofit organization, unemployment compensation, **Un Ins 702.1**
  Elections for financing, **Un Ins 801**
Nonqualified deferred compensation plan, unemployment compensation, **Un Ins 928.5**
Nonresident, withholding tax on wages, **Un Ins 13003**
Nontraditional occupations, training for women, **Un Ins 9602.5**
Normal benefits, extended unemployment compensation, **Un Ins 3503**
Normally and continuously engaged in a regular trade, business or occupation, unemployment compensation, elective coverage, **Un Ins 704.2**
Number,
  Labor Code, **Labor 13**
  Unemployment insurance code, **Un Ins 12**
Number of nonreported employees, unemployment compensation, **Un Ins 1126.1**
Nurses registry, employment agencies, **CC 1812.501, 1812.524**
Nursing service,
  Long term health care facilities, employment agencies, temporary employment, **CC 1812.540**
  Nurses registries, **CC 1812.524**

WORDS AND PHRASES—Cont'd
Oaths,
  Labor Code, **Labor 16**
  Unemployment insurance code, **Un Ins 16**
Obligee, earnings assignment orders, support enforcement, **Fam 5214**
Obligor, assignment of earnings, support enforcement, **Fam 5216**
Occupational illness, **Labor 6409**
  Medical records, **Labor 6409**
Occupational safety and health standards and orders, **Labor 6305**
Occupational safety and health standards board, safety in employment, **Labor 7801**
Office of a group practice, workers compensation, **Labor 139.3**
Officer, military forces, leave of absence, compensation, **Mil & V 395.02**
Official agent, whistle blowing, school officers and employees, **Educ 44112**
On the bases enumerated in this part, fair employment and housing department, **Gov 12926**
On the job training, **Labor 3093**
Operated, workers compensation, health care providers, fraud, contracts, **Labor 3219**
Operator,
  Amusement rides, safety, **Labor 7901**
  Permanent amusement rides, safety, inspection and inspectors, **Labor 7921**
Oppression, damages, **CC 3294**
Organizational provider, workers compensation, health care services, **Labor 4614**
Organized camp, minimum wages, maximum hours, **Labor 1182.4**
Other benefits, unemployment compensation, **Un Ins 2629**
Other biotechnology activities,
  Corporation taxes, net operating losses, **Rev & T 24416**
  Income tax—state, net operating losses, **Rev & T 17276**
Outpatient surgery, workers compensation, **Labor 139.3**
Owner,
  Amusement rides, safety, **Labor 7901**
  Asbestos hazard, building owners disclosure, **Health & S 25919.5**
  Fair employment and housing department, **Gov 12927**
  Labor camps, **Health & S 17062**
  Permanent amusement rides, safety, inspection and inspectors, **Labor 7921**
  Unclaimed Property Law, **CCP 1501**
Paid for in whole or in part out of public funds, public buildings and works, **Labor 1720**
Panels, employment training panel, **Un Ins 10201**

WORDS AND PHRASES—Cont'd
Parent,
  Family care and medical leave, **Gov 12945.2**
  Family care leave, **Un Ins 3302**
  Sick leave, **Labor 233**
Parent benefit year, extended unemployment compensation, **Un Ins 3503**
Parent unemployment compensation claim, training, extended benefits, **Un Ins 1271**
Partially unemployed individual, commercial fishermen, unemployment compensation, **Un Ins 1252.2**
Participant, youthbuild program, **Un Ins 9801**
Participating agency, economic opportunity programs, compensation for injuries or death to enrollees, **Labor 4205**
Partnership, withholding tax on wages, **Un Ins 13003**
Party to the arbitration, **CCP 1280**
Pass through entities, corporation taxes, credits, **Rev & T 23634**
Passenger vessel terminal, trespass, **Pen 602**
Pay period, unemployment compensation, **Un Ins 607**
Payment, wages, unemployment compensation, **Un Ins 931**
Payor, health care providers, preferred reimbursement rates, **Labor 4609**
Payor summary, health care providers, preferred reimbursement rates, **Labor 4609**
Payroll period, withholding tax on wages, **Un Ins 13008**
Peace officer,
  Off duty services, workers compensation, **Labor 3600.3**
  Workers compensation, **Labor 3600.3**
Pending court action, enforcement of arbitration agreement, **CCP 1281.2**
Per diem, public works employees, **Labor 1773.1**
Perceive, fair employment and housing, **Gov 12926**
Period of military conflict, labor and employment, leaves of absence, marriage, **Mil & V 395.10**
Permanent amusement ride, safety, inspection and inspectors, **Labor 7921**
Permanent employee housing, labor camps, **Health & S 17010**
Permanent partial disability, workers compensation, **Labor 4452.5**
Permanent single family employee housing, labor camps, **Health & S 17010**
Permanent total disability, workers compensation, **Labor 4452.5**
Permissible equipment, tunnel and mine safety, **Labor 7951**
Permits,
  Aerial passenger tramways, **Labor 7340**
  Amusement rides, **Labor 7901**

WORDS AND PHRASES—Cont'd

Permits—Cont'd

Elevators, dumbwaiters and escalators, **Labor 7300.1**

Person providing services pursuant to a contract, fair employment and housing, **Gov 12940**

Personal chiropractor, workers compensation, **Labor 4601**

Personal information, Information Practices Act, **CC 1798.3**

Personal physicians, workers compensation, **Labor 4600**

Persons,

Agricultural Labor Relations Act of 1975, **Labor 1140.4**

Consumer credit reporting, **CC 1785.3**

Employment agencies, **CC 1812.501**

Fair employment and housing, **Gov 12925, 12927**

False claims against state, **Gov 12650**

Farm labor contractors, **Labor 1682**

Foreign labor contractors, **Bus & P 9998.1**

Garnishment, **CCP 706.011**

Industrial homework, **Labor 2650**

Information Practices Act, **CC 1798.3**

Investigative Consumer Reporting Agencies Act, **CC 1786.2**

Janitors, displaced workers, **Labor 1060**

Jurisdictional strikes, **Labor 1117**

Labor and employment, fines and penalties, actions and proceedings, **Labor 2699**

Labor Code, **Labor 18**

Labor supply employee housing, **Health & S 17009.5**

Physicians and surgeons, **Bus & P 2056**

Public transit, displaced workers, **Labor 1071**

Talent agencies, **Labor 1700**

Talent services, fees, **Labor 1701**

Telecommunications, calling patterns, records and recordation, crimes and offenses, **Pen 638**

Unclaimed Property Law, **CCP 1501**

Unemployment compensation, **Un Ins 2071, 2129**

Withhold notices, delinquent contributions, **Un Ins 1758**

Wearing apparel, manufacturing, **Labor 2671**

Whistle blowing, **Gov 8547.2**

Community colleges and districts, **Educ 87162**

School officers and employees, **Educ 44112**

Withholding tax on wages, **Un Ins 13003**

Workers compensation, **Labor 3210**

Physical disability, fair employment and housing, **Gov 12926, 12926.1**

Physical evidence, destruction of evidence, privileged communications, exceptions, **CC 47**

WORDS AND PHRASES—Cont'd

Physician,

Unemployment compensation, disability, **Un Ins 2708**

Workers compensation, **Labor 3209.3**

Physicians office, workers compensation, **Labor 139.3**

Place of employment,

Occupational safety and health, **Labor 6303**

Workplace smoking regulation, **Labor 6404.5**

Play, child labor, **Labor 1390**

Political subdivision,

Fraudulent claims against state, **Gov 12650**

Public works, **Labor 1721**

Political subdivision funds, false claims against state, **Gov 12650**

Postsecondary educational institution, force and violence, injunction, **CCP 527.85**

Power press, workers compensation, **Labor 4558**

Practitioner, unemployment compensation, disability, **Un Ins 2708**

Preexisting workweek arrangement, labor and employment, **Labor 1182.6**

Preponderance of the evidence, workers compensation, **Labor 3202.5**

Prequalifying report, consumer credit reporting, **CC 1785.3**

Pretrial or posttrial diversion program, labor and employment, job applicants, disclosures of referrals or participation, **Labor 432.7**

Primarily, labor and employment, hours of labor, **Labor 515**

Primary claim, extended unemployment compensation, **Un Ins 3503**

Primary entry level entrance, multistory dwelling units, handicapped persons, discrimination, **Gov 12955.1**

Private duty nurses, nurses registries, **CC 1812.524**

Private industry council, employment training panel, **Un Ins 10201**

Private self insurer, workers compensation, **Labor 3700.1, 3741**

Private smokers lounge, workplace smoking regulation, **Labor 6404.5**

Privileged publication, libel and slander, **CC 47**

Product, dangerous concealed condition, **Pen 387**

Production or broadcasting of motion pictures, termination, compensation and salaries, payment, **Labor 201.5**

Professional strikebreaker, labor disputes, **Labor 1133**

Program, youthbuild program, **Un Ins 9801**

Promise, labor and employment, contracts, public policy, **Labor 920**

Proper identification,

Consumer credit reporting, **CC 1785.15**

WORDS AND PHRASES—Cont'd

Proper identification—Cont'd

Employment or insurance investigations, consumer reporting agencies, **CC 1786.22**

Proprietary security organization, criminal history information, **Pen 11105.4**

Prosecuting authority, false claims against state, **Gov 12650**

Prospective concessionaire, criminal history information disclosure, **Labor 432.7**

Prospective relief, fair employment and housing, **Gov 12926**

Protected disclosure,

California State University, whistle blowing, **Educ 89572**

Whistle blowing, **Gov 8547.2**

Community colleges and districts, **Educ 87162**

School officers and employees, **Educ 44112**

Provider,

Health care providers, preferred reimbursement rates, **Labor 4609**

In home supportive services, criminal history information, **Welf & I 12301.8**

Psychologists, workers compensation, **Labor 3209.3**

Psychotherapists, medical records, confidential or privileged information, **CC 56.104**

Public, employment office, unemployment compensation, **Un Ins 137**

Public agency, meals, motor carriers, collective bargaining, **Labor 512.5**

Public contact positions, occupational safety and health division, bilingual employees, **Labor 176**

Public entity, unemployment compensation, **Un Ins 135, 605**

Public records, labor and employment, copies, **CC 1786.53**

Public school employer, whistle blowing, **Educ 44112, 87162**

Public transit employee, labor disputes, **Labor 1137**

Public transit services, displaced workers, **Labor 1071**

Public work project, bidders workers and unemployment compensation coverage, **Labor 1750**

Public works, **Labor 1720, 1720.2**

Prevailing wage rate, **Labor 1720.2, 1720.3**

Purchase, telecommunications, calling patterns, records and recordation, crimes and offenses, **Pen 638**

Qualified beneficiary, Cal COBRA, accident and health insurance, **Health & S 1366.21; Ins 10128.51**

Qualified care, child care, tax credit, **Rev & T 17052.18**

Qualified care plan, child care, tax credit, **Rev & T 17052.18**

WORDS

WORDS AND PHRASES—Cont'd
Qualified dependent, child care, tax credit, **Rev & T 17052.18**
Qualified disadvantaged individual,
  Corporation taxes, credits, enterprise zones, **Rev & T 23622.8**
  Enterprise zones, income tax—state, credits, **Rev & T 17053.47**
  Income tax—state, local agency military base recovery areas, credits, **Rev & T 17053.46**
  Local agency military base recovery areas,
    Corporation taxes, credits, **Rev & T 23646**
    Income tax credits, **Rev & T 17053.46**
Qualified displaced employee,
  Local agency military base recovery areas, income tax credits, **Rev & T 17053.46**
  Military base recovery areas, corporation taxes, credits, **Rev & T 23646**
Qualified employees,
  Child care, tax credits, **Rev & T 17052.18**
  Corporation taxes, credits,
    Enterprise zones, **Rev & T 23622.7, 23634**
    Hiring, **Rev & T 23623**
  Income tax—state, credits, enterprise zones, **Rev & T 17053.34**
  Leaves of absence, military forces, marriage, **Mil & V 395.10**
Qualified employers,
  Hiring, credits, corporation taxes, **Rev & T 23623**
  Leaves of absence, military forces, marriage, **Mil & V 395.10**
Qualified full time employees, hiring, credits, corporation taxes, **Rev & T 23623**
Qualified interpreters, workers compensation, **Labor 4600**
Qualified leave periods, labor and employment, military forces, marriage, **Mil & V 395.10**
Qualified medical evaluator, workers compensation, **Labor 110**
Qualified members, labor and employment, leaves of absence, military forces, marriage, **Mil & V 395.10**
Qualified property, credits, corporation taxes, military base recovery areas, **Rev & T 23645**
Qualified safety engineer, boiler or tank inspections, **Labor 7650**
Qualified safety inspector, permanent amusement rides, **Labor 7921**
Qualified taxpayer,
  Corporation taxes,
    Credits, enterprise zones, **Rev & T 23622.8, 23634**
    Local agency military base recovery areas, **Rev & T 24416.5**
    Los Angeles revitalization zone, **Rev & T 24416.4**

WORDS AND PHRASES—Cont'd
Qualified taxpayer—Cont'd
  Corporation taxes—Cont'd
    Targeted tax areas, **Rev & T 24416.6**
  Enterprise zones,
    Income tax—state, credits, **Rev & T 17053.34, 17053.47**
    Net operating loss deduction, **Rev & T 24416.2**
  Income tax—state,
    Carrybacks, Los Angeles revitalization zone, **Rev & T 17276.4**
    Enterprise zones, net operating losses, carrybacks, **Rev & T 17276.6**
    Los Angeles revitalization zone, **Rev & T 17276.4**
  Local agency military base recovery areas, income tax credits, **Rev & T 17053.46, 17276.5**
  Military base recovery areas, corporation taxes, credits, **Rev & T 23646**
  Net operating loss carryback, income tax—state, **Rev & T 17276.2**
Qualified wages,
  Bank and corporation tax credits, enterprise zones, **Rev & T 23622.7, 23622.8, 23634**
  Corporation taxes, credits, labor and employment, hiring, **Rev & T 23623**
  Enterprise zones,
    Bank and corporation tax credits, **Rev & T 23622.7**
    Income tax—state, credits, **Rev & T 17053.34, 17053.74**
      Manufacturing enhancement areas, **Rev & T 17053.47**
  Local agency military base recovery areas, income tax credits, **Rev & T 17053.46**
  Military base recovery areas, corporation taxes, credits, **Rev & T 23646**
Qualifying event, Cal COBRA, accident and health insurance, **Health & S 1366.21; Ins 10128.51**
Quitting business, unemployment compensation, **Un Ins 1116**
Race, participation by minors, **Labor 1308**
Racial discrimination, **Gov 8315**
Railroad corporation, hours of labor, **Labor 600**
Railroads, hours of labor, **Labor 600**
Rating period, unemployment compensation, **Un Ins 903**
Real estate related transactions, fair employment and housing department, **Gov 12927**
Reasonable accommodation, fair employment and housing, **Gov 12926**
Reasonable assurance, unemployment compensation, **Un Ins 1253.3**
Reasonable expenses of transportation, workers compensation, **Labor 4600**
Reasonable monthly rental value, labor camps, **Health & S 17031.6**

WORDS AND PHRASES—Cont'd
Reasonable period of time, labor and employment, leaves of absence, pregnancy, **Gov 12945**
Reasonable steps, workplace smoking regulation, **Labor 6404.5**
Reciprocal agreements, employment tax information, **Un Ins 1095**
Records, information practices, **CC 1798.3**
Reduced workday, employment opportunities creation, **Un Ins 12102**
Reduced worktime, employment opportunities creation, **Un Ins 12102**
Reduced workweek, employment opportunities creation, **Un Ins 12102**
Reduced workyear, employment opportunities creation, **Un Ins 12102**
Registered domestic partner, victims of crime, labor and employment, absence and absentees, judicial proceedings, **Labor 230.2**
Registered student apprentice, workers compensation, **Labor 3368**
Registrant, compensation and salaries, judgments and decrees, satisfaction, farm labor contractors, wearing apparel, manufacturers and manufacturing, **Labor 273**
Registration fee,
  Employment agencies, **CC 1812.501**
  Talent agencies, **Labor 1700.2**
Regular or customary work, disability compensation, **Un Ins 2626**
Regular work, workers compensation, permanent disability, payment, **Labor 4658.1**
Regulation, unemployment compensation, **Un Ins 127**
Regulatory agency, Information Practices Act, **CC 1798.3**
Related person,
  Corporation taxes, net operating losses, **Rev & T 24416**
  Income tax—state, net operating losses, **Rev & T 17276**
Religion,
  Discrimination, **CC 51**
  Fair employment and housing, **Gov 12926**
Religious belief, fair employment and housing, **Gov 12926**
Religious corporation, labor and employment, **Gov 12926.2**
Religious creed, fair employment and housing, **Gov 12926**
Religious duties, labor and employment, **Gov 12926.2**
Religious employer,
  Disability insurance, birth control, coverage, **Ins 10123.196**
  Health care service plans, contraceptives, benefits and coverage, **Health & S 1367.25**
Religious observance, fair employment and housing, **Gov 12926**

WORDS AND PHRASES—Cont'd

Relocation, labor and employment, **Labor 1400**

Removal, workers compensation, power press workers, **Labor 4558**

Remuneration,
Unemployment compensation disability benefits, election of employer to qualify, **Un Ins 708**
Unemployment insurance contributions, **Un Ins 930.1, 930.5**

Repeated occasions, professional strike-breakers, **Labor 1133**

Representatives, Agricultural Labor Relations Act of 1975, **Labor 1140.4**

Resale inspection, tanks or boilers, **Labor 7725**

Resident, withholding tax on wages, **Un Ins 13003**

Resident employment housing, **Health & S 17006**

Residuals, Unclaimed Property Law, **CCP 1501**

Retail or wholesale tobacco shop, workplace smoking regulation, **Labor 6404.5**

Retraining, employment training panel, **Un Ins 10201**

Revenue service,
Railroad crew requirements, San Diego County transit district, **Labor 6901**
Railroad employees, **Labor 6902**

Rough stock rodeo event, participation by minors, **Labor 1308**

Sabbatical leave, employment opportunities creation, **Un Ins 12102**

Safe, occupational safety and health, **Labor 6306**

Safeguard, occupational safety and health, **Labor 6306**

Safety, occupational safety and health, **Labor 6306**

Safety device, occupational safety and health, **Labor 6306**

Salary continuation plan, workers compensation, **Labor 4650**

Sales floor, working warehouses, safety, **Labor 9100**

Savings funds, braceros, labor and employment, limitation of actions, **CCP 354.7**

Scaffolding, safety in employment, **Labor 7150**

School employer, unemployment compensation, **Un Ins 821.4**

Schoolday,
Child labor, **Labor 1308.7**
Hours of labor, **Labor 1391**

Screening, criminal history information, concessionaire applications, **Labor 432.7**

Seasonal employee housing, labor camps, **Health & S 17010**

Seasonal employment,
Corporation taxes,
Enterprise zones, **Rev & T 23622.7, 23622.8**

WORDS AND PHRASES—Cont'd

Seasonal employment—Cont'd
Corporation taxes—Cont'd
Single targeted tax area, **Rev & T 23634**
Income tax—state,
Enterprise zones, **Rev & T 17053.34, 17053.74**
Local agency military base recovery areas, credits, **Rev & T 17053.46**
Manufacturing enhancement areas, credits, **Rev & T 17053.46**

Seasonal in its operations, unemployment compensation, elective coverage, **Un Ins 704.2**

Seasonal labor, payment of wages, **Labor 250**

Second lowest bidder, public works, **Labor 1750**

Secretary, labor and workforce development agency, **Labor 19.5**

Section,
Labor Code, **Labor 10**
Unemployment insurance code, **Un Ins 9**

Sell, telecommunications, calling patterns, records and recordation, crimes and offenses, **Pen 638**

Serious concealed danger, product or business practice, **Pen 387**

Serious exposure,
Dangerous business practices, **Pen 387**
Occupational safety and health, **Labor 6302**

Serious health condition,
Family care and medical leave, **Gov 12945.2**
Family care leave, **Un Ins 3302**

Serious injury or illness, occupational health and safety, **Labor 6302**

Serious violation,
Agricultural labor and employment, judgments, **Labor 1691**
Occupational Carcinogens Control Act, **Labor 9061**
Occupational safety and health, penalties, **Labor 6432**

Service contract,
Janitors, displaced workers, **Labor 1060**
Public transit, displaced workers, **Labor 1071**

Service providers, unemployment compensation, support, reports, **Un Ins 1088.8**

Service recipient, unemployment compensation, support, reports, **Un Ins 1088.8**

Settlement, unemployment compensation, tax disputes, **Un Ins 1236**

Settlement date, unemployment compensation, withholding tax on wages, **Un Ins 13021.5**

Sex,
Discrimination, **CC 51**
Fair employment and housing, **Gov 12926**

WORDS AND PHRASES—Cont'd

Sexual assault,
Labor and employment, time off, **Labor 230, 230.1**
Protective orders, service of process, fees, **CCP 527.6**

Sexual orientation,
Civil rights, **CC 51.7**
Discrimination, **CC 51**
Fair employment and housing, **Gov 12926**

Shall, Labor Code, **Labor 15**

Sheriff, Labor Code, **Labor 25**

Shop inspection, tanks or boilers, **Labor 7725**

Shopping investigator, reports, **Labor 2930**

Should know, contracts, labor and employment, **Labor 2810**

Sick leave, family members, **Labor 233**

Sick pay, unemployment compensation, **Un Ins 13028.6**

Signature,
Labor Code, **Labor 17**
Unemployment insurance code, **Un Ins 17**

Sleeping place, employee housing, **Health & S 17011**

Small tanks, inspection, air pressure or liquefied petroleum gas, **Labor 7725**

Special order, occupational safety and health, **Labor 6305**

Special proceeding, enforcement of arbitration agreement, **CCP 1281.2**

Specialized center, income tax—state, child care, **Rev & T 17052.18**

Specific, injuries, workers compensation, **Labor 3208.1**

Specifically authorized, workers compensation, power press workers, **Labor 4558**

Sponsoring agency, economic opportunity programs, compensation for injuries or death of enrollees, **Labor 4204**

Sports official, workers compensation, **Labor 3352**

Spouse,
Family care leave, **Un Ins 3302**
Unemployment compensation, **Un Ins 1032, 1256, 3701, 4701**

Standards, Occupational Carcinogens Control Act, **Labor 9007**

Standards board,
Elevators, dumbwaiters and escalators, **Labor 7300.1**
Occupational Carcinogens Control Act, **Labor 9008**
Occupational safety and health, **Labor 6302**

State,
Affirmative action, proposed amendment, **Const. Art. 1, § 31**
Discrimination, proposed amendment, **Const. Art. 1, § 31**
Garnishment, **CCP 706.070**
Unemployment compensation, **Un Ins 139**

WORDS

WORDS AND PHRASES—Cont'd

State—Cont'd

Withholding tax on wages, **Un Ins 13003**

State agency,

Administrative law and procedure, **Gov 11346.3**

Employment development, **Un Ins 9105**

Labor and employment, standards, **Labor 1205**

Unemployment relief, **Labor 2010**

Whistle blowing, **Gov 8547.2**

Information, **Gov 8548 et seq.**

Workers compensation, **Labor 6101**

State average hourly wage, employment training panel, **Un Ins 10201**

State average weekly wage, workers compensation, **Labor 4453**

Permanent disability, **Labor 4659**

State contractor, labor organizations, promotion or deterrence, state funds, **Gov 16645**

State department, benefit payments, **Un Ins 133.5**

State fund,

False claims against state, **Gov 12650**

State contracts, labor organizations, promotion or deterrence, **Gov 16645**

State or local child support enforcement agency, consumer credit reporting, **CC 1785.3**

State property, state contracts, labor organizations, promotion or deterrence, **Gov 16645**

State tax liability, garnishment, **CCP 706.070**

Statements, evidence, misrepresentations, **Labor 3820**

Strike, professional strikebreakers, **Labor 1132.6**

Student, colleges and universities, force and violence, injunction, **CCP 527.85**

Subcontractors,

Janitors, displaced workers, **Labor 1060**

Public buildings and works, **Labor 1722.1**

Public transit, displaced workers, **Labor 1071**

Subpoenaing party, employment records, **CCP 1985.6**

Subscription,

Labor Code, **Labor 17**

Unemployment insurance code, **Un Ins 17**

Substantial cause, workers compensation, psychiatric injuries, **Labor 3208.3**

Substantial harm, health care service plans, medically necessary health care, powers and duties, **CC 3428**

Substantial probability, occupational safety and health, penalties, **Labor 6432**

Substantial shareholder, workers compensation, uninsured employers fund, **Labor 3717**

WORDS AND PHRASES—Cont'd

Successor employer, labor disputes, collective bargaining agreements, **Labor 1127**

Successor service contract, janitors, displaced workers, **Labor 1060**

Suitable employment, unemployment compensation, **Un Ins 1258, 1258.5**

Suitable work, federal state extended benefits, **Un Ins 4553**

Supervisor,

Agricultural Labor Relations Act of 1975, **Labor 1140.4**

Fair employment and housing, **Gov 12926**

Supervisorial personnel, professional strikebreakers, **Labor 1133**

Supplemental unemployment compensation benefits, tax withholding, **Un Ins 13028.5**

Support obligation, unemployment compensation, deductions and withholdings, **Un Ins 1255.7**

Support person, domestic violence, actions and proceedings, **CCP 527.6**

Surgical treatment, workers compensation, **Labor 3209.5**

Suspected financial abuse of an elder or dependent adult, financial institutions, **Welf & I 15630.1**

System of records, information practices, **CC 1798.3**

Talent agency, **Labor 1700.4**

Talent counseling service, fees, **Labor 1701**

Talent listing service, fees, **Labor 1701**

Talent scout, fees, **Labor 1701**

Talent service, fees, **Labor 1701**

Talent training service, fees, **Labor 1701**

Tank, boilers, inspection and safety regulations, **Labor 7622**

Targeted tax area,

Corporation taxes, deductions, **Rev & T 24416.2**

Income tax—state, **Rev & T 17276.2**

Targeted tax area expiration date,

Corporation taxes, **Rev & T 23634, 24416.2, 24416.6**

Enterprise zones, income tax—state, **Rev & T 17053.34**

Income tax—state, **Rev & T 17276.2, 17276.6**

Tavern, workplace smoking regulation, **Labor 6404.5**

Tax advice, confidential or privileged information, **Un Ins 13019**

Tax shelters, confidential or privileged information, **Un Ins 13019**

Taxable year, withholding tax on wages, **Un Ins 13003**

Taxpayer,

Corporation taxes,

Credits, **Rev & T 23622.7**

Military base recovery areas, **Rev & T 23645**

WORDS AND PHRASES—Cont'd

Taxpayer—Cont'd

Corporation taxes—Cont'd

Local agency military base recovery areas, **Rev & T 24416.5**

Deductions, military base recovery areas, **Rev & T 24416.2**

Enterprise zones, income tax credits, **Rev & T 17053.74**

Local agency military base recovery areas,

Credits, **Rev & T 17276.5**

Income tax deductions, **Rev & T 17276.2**

Unemployment compensation, disability insurance, refunds and overpayments, **Un Ins 1185**

Withholding tax on wages, **Un Ins 13003**

Technically qualified individuals, hazardous substances, **Labor 6386**

Telephone calling pattern record or list, crimes and offenses, **Pen 638**

Telephone companies, calling patterns, records and recordation, crimes and offenses, **Pen 638**

Temporarily dormant elevator, dumbwaiter or escalator, **Labor 7300.1**

Temporary employee housing, labor camps, **Health & S 17010**

Temporary incapacitation, military forces, collateral benefits, restriction or termination, **Mil & V 394**

Temporary permit, elevators, dumbwaiters and escalators, **Labor 7300.1**

Temporary services employers,

Compensation and salaries, **Labor 201.3**

Unemployment compensation, **Un Ins 606.5**

Tense,

Labor Code, **Labor 11**

Unemployment insurance code, **Un Ins 10**

Termination, labor and employment, **Labor 1400**

Theatrical engagement, talent agencies, **Labor 1700.1**

Theatrical enterprises, security for payment of wages, deposits, **Labor 271**

Theft, Penal Code, **Pen 484**

Timely payment, earnings assignment orders, support enforcement, **Fam 5220**

Title 11 or similar case,

Corporation taxes, net operating losses, **Rev & T 24416**

Income tax—state, net operating losses, **Rev & T 17276**

To advocate for medically appropriate health care, physicians and surgeons, **Bus & P 2056**

Totally unemployed individual, commercial fishermen, unemployment compensation, **Un Ins 1252.1**

Tower crane, regulation, **Labor 7371**

Trade, business, profession or occupation, workers compensation household employees, **Labor 3356**

I–242

WORDS AND PHRASES—Cont'd
Trade or business, withholding tax on wages, **Un Ins 13003**
Trainee,
Disability compensation, **Un Ins 2767**
Employment training fund, **Un Ins 10201**
Training agencies, employment training panel, **Un Ins 10201**
Training or retraining benefits, allowances, or stipends, unemployment compensation, demand occupations, **Un Ins 1273**
Trainman, hours of labor, **Labor 600**
Trial court employees, public employees retirement system, furloughs, service credits, **Gov 20969.1**
Trustees, workers compensation, **Labor 3700.1**
Self insurance, **Labor 3741**
Tunnel, tunnel and mine safety, **Labor 7951**
Twelve month period, family care leave, **Un Ins 3302**
Twinning, employment opportunities creation, **Un Ins 12102**
Underemployed person, employment development, **Un Ins 9109**
Underground mine, tunnel and mine safety, **Labor 7951**
Undue hardship, fair employment and housing, **Gov 12926**
Unemployed individual, unemployment compensation, **Un Ins 1252**
Unemployed person, employment development, **Un Ins 9108**
Unemployment compensation,
Child support obligations, deductions and withholding, **Un Ins 1255.7**
Extended unemployment compensation, **Un Ins 3503**
Wages paid, **Un Ins 1277.5**
Unemployment compensation disability benefits, **Un Ins 140.5**
Unemployment insurance, **Un Ins 141**
Unemployment trust fund, unemployment compensation, **Un Ins 142**
Unfair labor practice, Agricultural Labor Relations Act of 1975, **Labor 1140.4**
United States, **Un Ins 142.5**
Withholding tax on wages, **Un Ins 13003**
Unlawful subleasing of a motor vehicle, workplace violence safety, **CCP 527.8**
Unlawful violence, injunction,
Colleges and universities, **CCP 527.85**
Harassment, **CCP 527.6**
Use, Occupational Carcinogens Control Act, **Labor 9009**
Use of official authority or influence, whistle blowing, **Gov 8547.3**
Community colleges and districts, **Educ 87162**
School officers and employees, **Educ 44112**
Utilization review, workers compensation, **Labor 4610**

WORDS AND PHRASES—Cont'd
Valid claim,
Disability compensation, **Un Ins 2609**
Family care leave, **Un Ins 3302**
Unemployment compensation, **Un Ins 1276**
Verify, farm labor contractors, licenses and permits, **Labor 1695.7**
Veterans,
Apprenticeship programs, **Labor 3076.5**
Vietnam Veterans Employment Act, **Gov 7280.2**
Victim,
Crimes and offenses, labor and employment, absence and absentees, judicial proceedings, **Labor 230.2**
Fair employment and housing, **Gov 12926**
Violations, Labor Code, **Labor 22**
Violence, community health care workers, records and recordation, **Labor 6332**
Volatile flammable liquids, safety in employment, **Labor 7800**
Voluntary service without pay, workers compensation, **Labor 3363.6**
Volunteers, **Labor 3363.5**
Volunteer, public buildings and works, **Labor 1720.4**
Volunteer coordinator, public buildings and works, **Labor 1720.4**
Wages,
Corporation taxes, job incentive program, **Rev & T 23621**
Employment or employers, unemployment compensation, **Un Ins 1278**
Extended unemployment compensation, base period, **Un Ins 3552**
Garnishment, **Labor 2929**
Income tax—state, credit qualified employees, **Rev & T 17053.7**
Partial employment, unemployment compensation, **Un Ins 926, 1279**
Payment, **Labor 200**
Unemployment compensation, **Un Ins 938.7, 1252, 1277, 1277.1, 1281**
Deferred compensation plans, **Un Ins 928.5**
Motion picture payroll services company, employer or employing unit, **Un Ins 679**
Unemployment compensation contributions, **Un Ins 926**
Unemployment insurance, **Un Ins 927**
Withholding tax on wages, **Un Ins 13008**
Wages subject to personal income tax, unemployment compensation, **Un Ins 13009.5**
Warehouse facility, workplace smoking regulation, **Labor 6404.5**
Warn its affected employees, dangerous conditions, **Pen 387**
Warrants the participation of the employee, family care leave, certificates and certification, **Un Ins 2708**
Week, unemployment compensation, **Un Ins 143**

WORDS AND PHRASES—Cont'd
Wife, withholding tax on wages, **Un Ins 13003**
Withholding agents, income tax—state, withholding tax on wages, **Un Ins 13010**
Withholding order for support, garnishment, **CCP 706.030**
Withholding order for taxes, **CCP 706.072**
Withholding period, garnishment, **CCP 706.022**
Work location, workers compensation, occupational diseases, multiple employers, **Labor 5500.5**
Work responsibilities, workplace smoking regulation, **Labor 6404.5**
Work units, alternative workweek schedule, **Labor 511**
Workday, hours, **Labor 500**
Worker, public buildings and works, **Labor 1723**
Worker contributions, unemployment compensation, **Un Ins 144**
Workers compensation, **Labor 3200**
Workers compensation judge, **Labor 27**
Workforce Investment Act of 1998, **Un Ins 14005**
Working warehouse, safety, **Labor 9101**
Workweek, hours, **Labor 500**
Writings,
Labor Code, **Labor 8**
Unemployment insurance code, **Un Ins 8**
Written agreement, arbitration, **CCP 1280**
Written authorization, AIDS, blood test results disclosure, **Health & S 120980**
Youthbuild program, **Un Ins 9801**
Zone expiration date,
Corporation taxes, enterprise zones, credits, **Rev & T 23622.7**
Enterprise zones, tax credits, **Rev & T 17053.74**

WORK ACTIVITY PROGRAMS
Mentally Retarded and Developmentally Disabled Persons, this index

WORK EXPERIENCE EDUCATION
High Schools or Secondary Schools, this index
Unemployment compensation, excluded services, **Un Ins 646**

WORK INCENTIVE PROGRAMS
Corporation tax, credits, Jobs Tax Credit Act, **Rev & T 23621 et seq.**
Handicapped clients of department of rehabilitation, **Un Ins 9003**
Income tax—state, credits, Jobs Tax Credit Act, **Rev & T 17053.7**
Jobs tax credit,
Corporation tax, **Rev & T 23621 et seq.**
Income tax, **Rev & T 17053.7**

WORK RESPONSIBILITIES
Definitions, smoking, **Labor 6404.5**

WORKDAY
Definitions, hours, **Labor 500**

WORKER SAFETY AND HEALTH TRAINING AND EDUCATION PROGRAM
Generally, **Labor 6354.7**

WORKERS COMPENSATION
Generally, **Const. Art. 14, § 4; Labor 3201 et seq.**
Abatement of actions or proceedings,
Subrogation of employer, death caused by third person, **Labor 3851**
Substitution of insurer in place of employer, **Labor 3758**
Acceptance, election to be subject to compensation liability, **Labor 4150 et seq.**
Accounts and accounting,
Compelling production, **Labor 130, 132**
Insurance, post
Production, issuance of subpoenas, **Labor 130**
Accredited disaster council, definitions, **Labor 3211.91**
Accrued disability compensation unpaid at time of death, **Labor 4700**
Acknowledgments, release or compromise agreements, **Labor 5003**
Actions and proceedings, **Labor 5300**
Appeals board proceedings,
Application in lieu of, **Labor 3715 et seq.**
Uninsured employer, **Labor 3715 et seq.**
Application for adjudication of claim, **Labor 5501.5**
Assault by employer, **Labor 3602**
Attorney fees, reduction of disability payments, **Labor 4651.3, 5410.1**
Change of venue, **Labor 5501.6**
Compensation, recovery from employer and insurer, **Labor 3753**
Concealment of injury, employers fraudulent concealment, **Labor 3602**
Death of employee caused by acts, of another employee, remedies, **Labor 3601**
Defective products, third persons, **Labor 3602**
Discrimination against employee making application or testifying, **Labor 132a**
Employees rights against third persons, **Labor 3852**
Exclusive remedy, **Labor 3601, 3602**
Judgment or settlement, **Labor 3601**
Fraud, **Labor 3820**
Health care providers, fraud, contracts, **Labor 3219**
Insurance, post
Insurance carrier, encouragement of discrimination against employee making application or testifying, **Labor 132a**
Joinder,
Insurer, **Labor 3759**

WORKERS COMPENSATION—Cont'd
Actions and proceedings—Cont'd
Joinder—Cont'd
Uninsured employers fund, **Labor 3718**
Jurisdiction, generally, post
Limitation of actions, generally, post
Medical examination requirement, employee noncompliance, bar to action, **Labor 4053**
Objections, reference of proceedings, **Labor 5311**
Affidavits, examination of witnesses, **Labor 5311**
Order, employer relief from liability, **Labor 3759**
Payment of compensation, employers failure to secure, **Labor 3706, 3712**
Power press workers, **Labor 4558**
Product defects, third persons, **Labor 3602**
Reconsideration of award, order or decision as prerequisite to action, **Labor 5901**
Rights against third persons, employees, **Labor 3852 et seq.**
Self insurers security fund, **Labor 3744**
Party, **Labor 3743**
Single cause of action for each injury, **Labor 5303**
Subrogation of employer, injury or death caused by third person, **Labor 3850 et seq.**
Substitution, insurer in place of employer, **Labor 3755, 3757, 3758**
Suspension of right to maintain, noncompliance with request for medical examination, **Labor 4053**
Uninsured employer, appeals board proceedings, **Labor 3715 et seq.**
Uninsured employers fund, recovery of amount paid or payable, **Labor 3732**
Venue, change of venue, **Labor 5501.6**
Witnesses, fees and mileage, collection, **Labor 131**
Acupuncture,
Evaluation of participation, **Labor 3209.3**
Medical treatment, **Labor 3209.3, 3209.5, 3209.9, 4600 et seq.**
Fees, **Labor 5307.1**
Adjournment, hearing on application, **Labor 5700**
Adjudication of claim, filing of application, **Labor 5501.5**
Adjustment of claims, rebates or other consideration, adjusters, **Labor 3219**
Adjustment of state benefits, economic opportunity enrollees, **Labor 4226**
Administration of benefits, self insurers, **Labor 3703**
Administration revolving fund, **Labor 62.5**
Administrative assistance, **Labor 5450 et seq.**

WORKERS COMPENSATION—Cont'd
Administrative law judges. Judges, generally, post
Administrative penalties, assessment, **Labor 129.5**
Admissions of employee, receipt of payment, allowance, or benefit, **Labor 4909**
Advance on temporary disability and medical benefits, asbestosis, **Labor 4401 et seq.**
Adverse or pecuniary interest,
Medical evaluators, **Labor 139.2**
Physicians and surgeons, post
Advertisements, **Labor 139.4 et seq.**
Attorneys and others, **Labor 5430 et seq.**
Advisory boards and commissions, worker safety and health training and education program, **Labor 6354.7**
Affirmative defenses,
Burden of proof, **Labor 5705**
Limitation of proceedings, **Labor 5409**
Age, disability payment, computation, **Labor 4660**
Agents, payment of compensation to, **Labor 4902**
Aggravation, disability, employees unreasonable conduct as defense, burden of proof, **Labor 5705**
AIDS,
Death benefits, limitation of actions, **Labor 5406.6**
Medical records, disclosure, **CC 56.31**
Alcoholics and alcoholism, **Labor 3600**
Burden of proof, **Labor 5705**
Economic opportunity program enrollees, **Labor 4207**
Aliens, **Labor 3351**
Alteration, order, decision or award, **Labor 5803 et seq.**
Altercation by injured employee, **Labor 3600**
Alternate commute programs, course of employment, **Labor 3600.8**
Alternative dispute resolution,
Collective bargaining, **Labor 3201.5**
Labor and management agreements, **Labor 3201.7**
Alternative work, permanent disability, payment, **Labor 4658, 4658.1**
Ambulatory surgical centers, fees, **Labor 5307.1**
Amendment, order, decision or award, **Labor 5803 et seq.**
Amount of payment, **Labor 5801**
Change in amount or type of benefits, notice, **Labor 138.4**
Annual earnings, computation of average, **Labor 4453**
Answer. Pleadings, post
Appeal and review, **Const. Art. 14, § 4; Labor 5301, 5302**
Arbitration and award, labor and management agreements, **Labor 3201.7**
Fines and penalties, **Labor 129.5**

WORKERS COMPENSATION—Cont'd
Appeal and review—Cont'd
Fraud convictions, reconsideration, **Labor 5803.5**
Insurance, post
Medical care and treatment, billing, **Labor 4603.2**
Physicians and surgeons, billing, **Labor 4603.2**
Self insurance, self insurers security fund, composite deposits, assessments, **Labor 3701.8**
Self insurers security fund, party, **Labor 3743**
Uninsured employers, penalty assessment, **Labor 3725**
Appeals boards, **Labor 111 et seq.**
Adoption, modification or vacation, **Labor 5315**
Affixation of seal to writs and authentications of copies of records and other instruments, **Labor 116**
Appointment, qualifications and salary, **Labor 112**
Arbitrator, acting as, **Labor 5308**
Assignment, reassignment of cases, **Labor 115**
Attorneys, **Labor 119**
Correctional institutions, **Labor 3371**
Membership, **Labor 112**
Attorneys fees, **Labor 5801**
Bad faith actions, payment of costs, expenses or attorneys fees, **Labor 5813**
Certification of official acts, **Labor 130**
Chairman, **Labor 113**
Children and minors, appearance and representation, **Labor 5307**
Collateral estoppel, criminal prosecutions, **Labor 5006, 5413, 5816**
Contempt, **Labor 5309**
Copies of records, authentications, seal affixed, **Labor 116**
Correctional institutions, attorneys, **Labor 3371**
Criminal prosecutions, collateral estoppel, **Labor 5006, 5413, 5816**
Death benefit,
Dependent beneficiaries death without surviving dependent, **Labor 4706**
Public employees retirement system member, **Labor 4708**
Decision of two or three members, **Labor 115**
Definitions, **Labor 110**
Division of workers compensation, **Labor 3205.5**
Workers compensation division, **Labor 3205.5**
Deputy members, **Labor 121**
Evidence, prohibition of new and additional evidence on writ of review return day, **Labor 5951**

WORKERS COMPENSATION—Cont'd
Appeals boards—Cont'd
Expenses, performance of services under United States Longshoremens and Harbor Workers Compensation Act, **Labor 128**
Fact determinations, collateral estoppel, criminal prosecutions, **Labor 5006, 5413, 5816**
Files, destruction, **Labor 135**
Findings against substantial shareholders or parents, uninsured employers, **Labor 3717.2**
Fines and penalties, hearings, **Labor 129.5**
Forms, uniform, **Labor 5500.3**
Fraud convictions, reconsideration, **Labor 5803.5**
Fund, uninsured employers fund, **Labor 3716 et seq.**
Inscription, seal, **Labor 116**
Judgment, entry, **Labor 5953**
Judicial review, scope, **Labor 5952**
Jurisdiction, **Labor 5300 et seq.**
Limited to supreme court and court of appeal, **Labor 5955**
Labor organizations, members and membership, **Labor 112**
Medical legal expenses,
Contested claims, **Labor 4620 et seq.**
Reasonableness of charges, **Labor 4625**
Members, **Labor 112, 130**
Oaths, administration, **Labor 130**
Orders, rules, findings, decisions and awards,
Judicial review, **Labor 5810**
Presumption of lawfulness, **Labor 5302**
Reconsideration, petition, **Labor 5900**
Writ of review, appeal to supreme court or court of appeal, **Labor 5950**
Uninsured employers, **Labor 3715 et seq.**
Powers, **Labor 111**
Practice and procedure, **Labor 5307**
Presumption, lawfulness of orders, rules, findings, decisions and awards, **Labor 5302**
Procedures, uniform, **Labor 5500.3**
Quorum, **Labor 115**
Reconsideration petition, **Labor 5900 et seq.**
Records,
Authentications of copies, seal affixed, **Labor 116**
Certification required on appeal, **Labor 5951**
Remand following court hearing, **Labor 5953**
Return day, writ of review, **Labor 5951**
Rules and regulations, **Labor 5307, 5307.3, 5307.4**
Scope, judicial review, **Labor 5952, 5953**
Seal, **Labor 116**

WORKERS COMPENSATION—Cont'd
Appeals boards—Cont'd
Secretary, **Labor 120**
Certification of official acts, **Labor 130**
Deputy board member, **Labor 121**
Oath, administration, **Labor 130**
Powers, **Labor 130**
Subpoenas, issuance, **Labor 130**
Service of pleadings, **Labor 5954**
Stay of proceedings, filing writ of review, **Labor 5956**
Subpoenas, **Labor 130, 132**
Time,
Application for writ of review, **Labor 5950**
Judicial review, **Labor 5810**
Unemployment disability benefits, liens, **Labor 3865; Un Ins 2629.1, 2735.5, 2741**
Uniform procedures and forms, **Labor 5500.3**
Uninsured employers fund, **Labor 3716 et seq.**
United States Longshoremens and Harbor Workers Compensation Act, deputy commissioner, **Labor 128**
Witness fees, **Labor 131**
Writ of review,
New or additional evidence, **Labor 5951**
Return day, **Labor 5951**
Appearance,
Children and minors, **Labor 5307**
Defendants nonappearance, **Labor 5506**
Mentally ill persons, **Labor 5307**
Suspension of privilege of appearing as representative of party to proceedings, **Labor 4907**
Application of division, **Labor 6304.5**
Application of law, labor and management agreements, **Labor 3201.7**
Applications, **Labor 5500 et seq.**
Compensation, filing, **Labor 5501**
Limitation of time for payment, **Labor 5404**
Designation of parties, **Labor 5503**
Dismissal application, **Labor 5507**
Forms, **Labor 5500**
Hearings, generally, post
Medical provider networks, independent medical reviewers, **Labor 4616.4**
Timely filing, requesting partial compensation, effect, **Labor 5404**
Writ of review, **Labor 5950**
Appointments,
Deputy commissioner under Longshoremens and Harbor Workers Compensation Act, **Labor 128**
Guardian ad litem, **Labor 5307.5**
Judges, **Labor 5310**
Asbestosis claims, **Labor 4409.5**
Medical evaluators, **Labor 139.2**
Trustee, **Labor 5307.5**
Lump sum deposit, **Labor 5104**
Apportionment. Benefits, post

WORKERS COMPENSATION—Cont'd

Apprentices, students, **Labor 3368**

Approval of court, release or settlement of claim against third person causing injury or death, **Labor 3859**

Arbitration and award, **Const. Art. 14, § 4; Labor 5270 et seq., 5308**

Labor and management agreements, **Labor 3201.7**

Liens and incumbrances, reimbursement, **Labor 4903.1**

Armed forces, disabilities incurred in service, subsequent injuries, **Labor 4753**

Arms and artificial members, **Labor 3208**

Subsequent injuries, **Labor 4751**

Artist, work upon commission projects, **Labor 3351.5**

Asbestos related work, registration, **Labor 6501.5, 6505.5**

Asbestos workers benefits, definitions, **Labor 4402**

Asbestosis, **Labor 4401 et seq.**

Assault and battery, **Labor 3600, 3602**

Assessments,

Administration revolving fund, **Labor 62.5**

Administrative penalties, **Labor 129.5**

Cal OSHA targeted inspection and consultation fund, **Labor 62.7, 62.9**

Self insurers security fund members, **Labor 3745**

State fraud investigation and prosecution surcharge, **Labor 62.6**

Subsequent injuries benefits trust fund, **Labor 62.5**

Uninsured employers benefits trust fund, **Labor 62.5**

Assignments,

Claims, **Labor 4900**

Investigative services, **Labor 3716.1**

Unpaid awards, assignment to labor commissioner, **Labor 96**

Assumption of risk by employee, defense abolished, **Labor 3708**

Atascadero State Hospital, officers and employees, heart trouble, **Labor 3212.2**

Athletics, this index

Attachment, **Labor 5600 et seq.**

Employers property, securing payment of judgment, **Labor 3707**

Proceedings, **Labor 5600 et seq.**

Securing payment for judgment, **Labor 3707**

Warrants, power to issue, **Labor 134**

Attendance of witnesses, issuance of subpoenas, **Labor 130**

Attorney fees,

Action against third party causing injury or death, **Labor 3856**

Actions against uninsured employers fund, **Labor 3717**

Bad faith actions, payment, **Labor 5813**

Decrease or termination, **Labor 4651.3, 5410.1**

WORKERS COMPENSATION—Cont'd

Attorney fees—Cont'd

Deductibility from disability benefits award, notice, **Labor 4061**

Delay or refusal of award, **Labor 5814.5**

Depositions, **Labor 5710**

Employer failing to secure payment of compensation, **Labor 3709, 4555**

Health care providers, fraud, contracts, **Labor 3219**

Judgment and decree, payment, **Labor 3709.5**

Liens and incumbrances, **Labor 4903**

Medical evaluations, ex parte communications, **Labor 4062.3**

Medical legal expenses, **Labor 4620 et seq.**

Medical treatment, termination proceeding, successful defense against, **Labor 4607**

Notice, fee deductibility from disability benefits award, **Labor 4061**

Partition alleging decrease or termination of disability, **Labor 4651.3**

Petition, decrease or termination of payments, **Labor 4651.3, 5410.1**

Petition for writ of review, **Labor 5801**

Preexisting disability, **Labor 4753**

Reasonableness of claim for legal services, **Labor 4906**

Reimbursed lien claimants, award to applicants attorney, **Labor 4903.2**

Release or settlement of claim against third person causing injury or death, **Labor 3860**

Self insurers security fund, compensation obligations, **Labor 3744**

Uninsured employers fund, recovery of amounts paid, **Labor 3732**

Unreasonably delayed or refused awards, **Labor 5814.5**

Attorney general,

Action against employer, failure to secure compensation payment, **Labor 3712**

Asbestosis proceedings, **Labor 4415**

Hearings, subsequent injuries, **Labor 4753.5**

Prosecution of criminal violations, **Labor 3710**

Representation of state, **Labor 3716.1**

Subsequent injuries,

Compromise or release of claim, **Labor 4754.5**

Hearings, **Labor 4753.5**

Attorneys, **Labor 5700**

Administrative law judges, honoraria, traveling expenses, **Labor 123.6**

Advertisements, **Labor 5430 et seq.**

Appeals boards, ante

Asbestosis proceedings, **Labor 4415**

Division of workers compensation, **Labor 119**

Performing legal services for industrial relations department, **Labor 54.5**

WORKERS COMPENSATION—Cont'd

Attorneys—Cont'd

Employers and others, statements, **Labor 4906**

Judges, **Labor 123.5, 123.7**

Medical evaluations, **Labor 4060**

Payments to, **Labor 4902**

Proceeding to reduce or terminate payments, **Labor 4651.3, 5410.1**

Right to hire attorney, notice, alternatives, **Labor 4061 et seq.**

Self insurers, **Labor 3702.6**

Solicitation of business, referral of clients, exemptions, **Labor 3217**

Subsequent injuries, **Labor 4755**

Audits and auditors, **Labor 129**

Insurance, post

Self insurers, **Labor 3702.5, 3702.6**

Suspension of privilege of appearing as representative, **Labor 4907**

Security fund, **Labor 3746**

Authorization, medical care and treatment, rescission, modification or change, **Labor 4610.3**

Autopsy, **Labor 5706, 5707**

Average earnings, computation, **Labor 4451 et seq.**

Awards, **Const. Art. 14, § 4; Labor 5800 et seq.**

Insurance, post

Liens, reimbursement, **Labor 4903.1**

Nominal disability indemnity, **Labor 5802**

Uninsured employers, **Labor 3715 et seq.**

Unpaid, assignment to labor commissioner, **Labor 96**

Bad faith actions, costs, expenses or attorneys fees, payment, **Labor 5813**

Bank deposits and collections, disability benefits, employers deposit directly into employees bank account, **Labor 4651**

Benefits,

Apportionment,

Death benefits, **Labor 4703**

Permanent disability, **Labor 4663**

Two or more injuries, **Labor 3208.2**

Asbestos workers account, **Labor 4412**

Continuing information program, **Labor 139.6**

Correctional institution inmates, **Labor 3370**

Death benefits, generally, post

Information, **Labor 5450 et seq.**

Information system, **Labor 138.6**

Liens and incumbrances, reimbursement, **Labor 4903.1**

Posttermination benefits, **Labor 3208.3, 3600**

Statutory change in amounts payable subsequent to injuries, **Labor 4453.5**

United States, setoff and counterclaim, **Labor 4355**

WORKERS COMPENSATION—Cont'd

Benefits in addition to compensation insurance, **Labor 3750**

Best interest of applicant, commutation of compensation payable, **Labor 5100**

Biochemical substances, peace officers, firefighters and fire departments, presumptions, **Labor 3212.85**

Boards and commissions, health and safety and workers compensation board, **Labor 75 et seq.**

Bonds, voluntary technical assistance to public entity, **Labor 3367**

Bonds (officers and fiduciaries),
 Appeals board proceedings, uninsured employers, **Labor 3715 et seq.**
 Self insuring employers, **Labor 3701, 3701.5, 3705**
 Stay order, **Labor 6000 et seq.**
 Trustee or guardian ad litem, **Labor 5307.5**
 Uninsured employers, appeals board award, **Labor 3715 et seq.**

Books and papers,
 Compelling production, **Labor 132**
 Production, issuance of subpoenas, **Labor 130**

Bowling team sponsor, **Labor 3301**

Braces, **Labor 3208**

Brain injury resulting in mental illness, **Labor 4662**

Burden of proof. Evidence, post

Burial expenses. Funeral expenses, generally, post

Burns, medical care and treatment, fees, **Labor 5307.1**

Cal OSHA targeted inspection and consultation fund, **Labor 62.7, 62.9**

Camp volunteers, exclusion, **Labor 3352**

Cancer, **Labor 3212.1**

Car washes, registration, **Labor 2055**

Cash revolving fund, uninsured employers benefits trust fund, **Labor 3728**

Casual employment, exclusion, **Labor 3352**

Causation,
 Permanent disability, apportionment of benefits, **Labor 4663, 4664**
 Third parties, discrimination, **Labor 3600**

Certificate of consent. Self insurance, post

Certificates and certification,
 Competency of physicians, **Labor 4602**
 Construction permits, filing certificates of insurance coverage, **Labor 3800**
 Lump sum payments, **Labor 5105**
 Out of state employer insured, **Labor 3600.5**
 Undertaking on stay order, **Labor 6002**

Certified copies, fees and costs, transcripts, **Labor 5811**

Certified mail, notice, findings, stop order issued against employer not securing compensation payment, **Labor 3710.1**

Change in amount or type of benefits, notice, **Labor 138.4**

WORKERS COMPENSATION—Cont'd

Change in amounts payable subsequent to injuries, **Labor 4453.5**

Change of designation, **Un Ins 21**

Change of physician or chiropractor, **Labor 4600 et seq.**

Change of venue, **Labor 5501.6**

Charitable workers, exclusion, **Labor 3352**

Checks, payment of benefits, **Labor 4651**

Children and minors, **Labor 3351**
 Appearance and representation before appeals board, **Labor 5307**
 Appointment of trustee or guardian ad litem, **Labor 5307.5**
 Child employed by parent, exclusion from coverage, **Labor 3352**
 Counselors, treatment of condition arising out of injury, **Labor 3209.8**
 Employment, by parent, exclusion form coverage, **Labor 3352**
 Illegally employed minor under 16, **Labor 4557**
 Limitation of proceedings, **Labor 5408**
 Misconduct of minor employee, **Labor 4551**
 Payments to minor, **Labor 3605**
 Permanent injury to minor employee, determination of average weekly earnings, **Labor 4455**
 Presumption of dependency, **Labor 3501**
 Support, notification project, **Labor 138.5**

Chiropractors, **Labor 3209.6**
 Change, **Labor 4600 et seq.**
 Health care provider organizations, care disputes, **Labor 4600.5**
 Medical evaluators, **Labor 139.2**
 Treatment provided by employer, **Labor 4600**
 Visits, numbers and numbering, **Labor 4604.5**

Claims,
 Adjusters, **Labor 3219**
  Subsequent injuries, **Labor 4755**
 Advertisements, attorneys and others, **Labor 5430 et seq.**
 Asbestosis claims, investigations, **Labor 4409**
 Dismissal, old claims, after notice, **Labor 5404.5**
 Insurance, post
 Medical evaluations, compensability of claims, disputes, **Labor 4061 et seq.**

Clerks of courts, fees, **Labor 5811**

Clinical social workers, treatment of condition arising out of injury, **Labor 3209.8**

Clinics, advertisements, **Labor 5430 et seq.**

Code of judicial ethics, administrative law judges, **Labor 123.6**

Collateral estoppel, criminal prosecutions, **Labor 5006, 5413, 5816**

Collections, asbestos workers account, benefits and costs, **Labor 4412 et seq.**

Collective bargaining, **Labor 3201.5**

Colleges and Universities, this index

WORKERS COMPENSATION—Cont'd

Combined permanent partial disabilities, prior injury, **Labor 4751**
 Subsequent injuries, commutation of compensation, **Labor 5100.5**

Commercial paper, payment of disability benefits, **Labor 4651**

Commission,
 Finding, order, decision or award, appeals board members, **Labor 115**
 Subpoenas, **Labor 130**

Commitment warrants, power to issue, **Labor 134**

Commutation of compensation, **Labor 5100 et seq.**
 Lump sum payments, generally, post

Compelling attendance of witnesses, **Labor 132**

Compensation insurance fund. State compensation insurance fund, generally, post

Complaints,
 Actions against third parties, copies, **Labor 3853**
 Copy, uninsured employers fund, **Labor 3708.5**

Compromise and settlement, **Const. Art. 14, § 4; Labor 5000 et seq.**
 Approval, **Labor 5001**
 Awards, reimbursement, liens against compensation, **Labor 4903.1, 5005**
 Claim against third person causing injury or death, **Labor 3859, 3860**
  Notice, **Labor 3860**
 Compensation, definitions, **Labor 5001**
 Death benefits, **Labor 5004**
 Exclusive remedy, **Labor 3600**
 Execution of agreement, **Labor 5003**
 Filing copy, **Labor 5002**
 Form, **Labor 5003**
  Death benefits, **Labor 5004**
 Liens against compensation payments, **Labor 3865, 4904**
 Limitation of proceedings, **Labor 5005**
 Multiple employers, occupational disease or cumulative injury cases, **Labor 5005**
 Notice, **Labor 3715**
 Offers of settlement, disclosure, **Labor 5278**
 Subsequent injuries benefits trust fund, conference settlement, **Labor 3714**
 Subsequent injuries claim, **Labor 4754.5**
 Uninsured employers benefits trust fund, conferences, **Labor 3714**
 Uninsured employers fund, **Labor 3719, 3732**

Computation, **Labor 4451 et seq.**
 Combined permanent partial disabilities, prior injury, **Labor 4751**
 Death benefits, **Labor 4702**
 Lump sum payments, **Labor 5101**
 Permanent disability benefits, **Labor 4659**

WORKERS

WORKERS COMPENSATION—Cont'd

Computation—Cont'd

Temporary and permanent disability arising out of same injury, **Labor 4661**

Temporary disability benefits, injuries existing in excess of two years, **Labor 4661.5**

Temporary partial disability, weekly loss of wages, **Labor 4657**

Computers, information system, **Labor 138.6**

Conditions of liability, **Labor 3600 et seq.**

Conduct of business without full compensation security, **Labor 3712**

Conduct of employee,

Aggravation of disability, burden of proof, **Labor 5705**

Children and minors, **Labor 4551**

Intoxication, **Labor 3600**

Medical examination, failure to comply, suspension of right to maintain action, **Labor 4053**

Misconduct, burden of proof, **Labor 5705**

Serious and willful misconduct, **Labor 4551 et seq.**

Reduction of compensation, limitation of proceedings, **Labor 5407.5**

Confidential or privileged information,

Collective bargaining, **Labor 3201.5, 3201.9**

Individually identifiable information, **Labor 138.7**

Insurance, post

Labor and management agreements, **Labor 3201.7**

Medical care and treatment, electronic claims, payment, **Labor 4603.4**

Self insurers, security fund, trustees, **Labor 3742**

Consent, employer and employee, release or settlement of claim against third person causing injury or death, **Labor 3859**

Conservation corps, Lyme disease, presumptions, **Labor 3212.12**

Conservation department, forestry division, peace officers, **Labor 3600.3**

Conservators and conservatorships, minor employee injured, **Labor 5408**

Consolidation of actions by employer and employee against third person causing injury or death, **Labor 3853**

Construction of statutes, **Labor 3202, 3204**

Medical care and treatment, authorization, rescission, modification or change, **Labor 4610.3**

Construction permits, insurance coverage, filing certificates, **Labor 3800**

Consultation,

Loss control services, insurers, **Labor 6354.5**

Physicians and surgeons, **Labor 4601**

Conflict of interest, **Labor 139.3**

WORKERS COMPENSATION—Cont'd

Contempt, **Labor 132, 5309**

Appeals board, **Labor 132, 134**

Cumulative remedies, **Labor 132**

Injury report, order directing submission, **Labor 3760**

Medical evaluations, ex parte communications, **Labor 4062.3**

Process, power to issue, **Labor 134**

Referee, **Labor 132**

Contested claims, medical legal expenses, **Labor 4620 et seq.**

Definitions, **Labor 4620**

Continuance,

Conferences and hearings, **Labor 5502.5**

Hearing on application, **Labor 5700**

Continuance of benefits, statutory change in amounts payable subsequent to injury, **Labor 4453.5**

Continuity of care policies, medical provider networks, **Labor 4616.2**

Contractors, this index

Contracts,

Drugs and medicine, **Labor 4600.2**

Employer employee, treatment of injuries, **Labor 3209.7**

Exempting employer from compensation liability, **Labor 5000**

Fraud, generally, post

Health care provider organizations, post

Medical fee schedules, **Labor 5307.1, 5307.11**

Medical provider networks, **Labor 4616.4**

Payment, **Labor 3700.5**

Other employers, **Labor 3602**

Physicians and surgeons, medical provider networks, **Labor 4616.4**

Contributing to injury, **Labor 3600**

Contribution, employer, power press workers, **Labor 4558**

Contributions of employee to cost of compensation, **Labor 3751**

Contributory negligence of employee, defense abolished, **Labor 3708**

Convict labor. Correctional Institutions, this index

Cooperative vocational education, **Labor 3368**

Copies,

Collective bargaining agreements, **Labor 3201.5**

Complaint, uninsured employers, fund, **Labor 3708.5**

Copy of release or compromise agreement, filing, **Labor 5002**

Corporate directors and officers, **Labor 3351**

Corporations,

Definitions, uninsured employers fund awards, **Labor 3717**

Parties, substantial shareholders and parents, uninsured employers, **Labor 3717.1**

Correctional Institutions, this index

WORKERS COMPENSATION—Cont'd

Corrections and Rehabilitation Department, this index

Costs, **Labor 5811**

Action against third party causing injury or death, **Labor 3856**

Action against uninsured employers fund, **Labor 3717**

Bad faith actions, payment, **Labor 5813**

Drugs and medicine, **Labor 4600.2**

Execution, employer subrogation lien, **Labor 3862**

Investigations and investigators, **Labor 3700.5**

Medical evaluations, ex parte communications, **Labor 4062.3**

Medical legal expenses, contested claims, **Labor 4620 et seq.**

Medical treatment, termination proceeding, successful defense against, attorney fees, **Labor 4607**

Payment, attorneys fees, **Labor 3709.5**

Permanent disability rating denial, order of payment, **Labor 4555.5**

Release or settlement of claim against third person causing injury or death, **Labor 3860**

Self procured medical costs, liens, reimbursement, **Labor 4903.1**

Undertaking on stay order, **Labor 6001**

Counties, domestic employees, **Labor 3351.5**

County construction permits, filing certificates as to insurance coverage, **Labor 3800**

County in home supportive service programs, domestic employees, coverage, **Labor 3351.5**

County Officers and Employees, this index

Course of employment, **Labor 3355, 3600**

Alternative commute programs, **Labor 3600.8**

Court reporters, proceedings, hearings and investigations, **Labor 5708**

Courts. Judges, generally, post

Courts of appeal, review of decisions, **Labor 5955**

Coverage,

Evidence, designated business license applicants, **Labor 3711**

Verification declaration, perjury, **Labor 3800**

Credit union deposits, disability benefits, employers deposit directly into employees account, **Labor 4651**

Credits against employer liability for compensation, recovery against third person causing injury or death, **Labor 3861**

Crimes and offenses,

Advertisements, attorneys and others, **Labor 5434**

Appeals board, fact determinations, collateral estoppel, **Labor 5006, 5413, 5816**

WORKERS COMPENSATION—Cont'd

Crimes and offenses—Cont'd

Claims adjusters, rebates or other consideration, **Labor 3219**

Conviction of crime, injured employee, exclusion, **Labor 3600**

Discrimination against employee testifying or making application, **Labor 132a**

Fraud, generally, post

Injured employee, exclusion, **Labor 3600**

Injuries from criminal violence, public employees, waiting period, **Labor 4650.5**

Insurance, post

Insurance carrier, encouragement of discrimination against employee making application or testifying, **Labor 132a**

Notice,

Failure to post, **Labor 3550, 6431**

Victims of crime, eligibility, **Labor 3553**

Physicians, referrals, conflict of interest, **Labor 139.3**

Receiving contributions from employees for cost of compensation, **Labor 3751**

Referral or solicitation of business, **Labor 3215 et seq.**

Securing payment of compensation, employers failure, **Labor 3710, 3710.2**

Solicitation of business, referral of clients, **Labor 3215 et seq.**

Uninsured employers, prima facie case, **Labor 3715**

Victims of crime, notice, eligibility, **Labor 3553**

Criminal labor, state highways or roads, exclusion, **Labor 3352**

Cumulative injuries, **Labor 5303**

Claims, multiple employers, compromise and release agreement, **Labor 5005**

Definitions, **Labor 3208.1**

Liability, **Labor 5500.5**

Determination or limitation, **Labor 5500.6**

Limitation of actions, **Labor 5500.5**

Curriculum vitae, physicians, **Labor 4628**

Damages,

Actions against third persons causing death or injury, **Labor 3852 et seq.**

Actions on behalf of insured employers fund, **Labor 3717 et seq.**

Awards, amounts, **Labor 3716.2**

Awards paid by uninsured employers fund, **Labor 3717 et seq.**

Definitions, **Labor 3209**

Exclusive remedy, awards and judgments or settlements, **Labor 3600**

Securing payment of compensation, employers failure, **Labor 3706**

WORKERS COMPENSATION—Cont'd

Damages—Cont'd

Subrogation of employer, injuries or death caused by third person, **Labor 3850 et seq.**

Uninsured employers fund awards, **Labor 3717 et seq.**

Date of injury, definitions, limitation of proceedings, **Labor 5411**

Occupational diseases, **Labor 5412**

Death,

Action against third person causing death, **Labor 3852 et seq.**

Additional remedy against another employee causing, **Labor 3601**

Application of law, occupational safety and health, **Labor 6304.5**

Caused by unreasonable refusal to submit to medical or surgical treatment, **Labor 4056**

Deliberately caused by employee, **Labor 3600**

Disability terminated by death, **Labor 4700**

Economic opportunity programs, **Labor 4201 et seq.**

Employers, subsequent to injury, **Labor 5306**

Misconduct of employee, **Labor 4551 et seq.**

Subrogation of employer, death caused by third person, **Labor 3850 et seq.**

Death benefits, **Labor 4700 et seq.**

Accrued disability compensation unpaid at time of death, **Labor 4700**

AIDS, limitation of actions, **Labor 5406.6**

Application for use of several beneficiaries, **Labor 4705**

Apportionment, **Labor 4703**

Asbestosis, **Labor 4401 et seq.**

Limitation of proceedings, **Labor 5406.5**

Assassination of elected public officials, **Labor 4720 et seq.**

Burial expenses, **Labor 4701**

Children and minors, assassination of elected public officials, **Labor 4720 et seq.**

Compromise of claim, **Labor 5004**

Computation of compensation, **Labor 5101**

Correctional institutions, officers and employees, limitation of actions, AIDS, **Labor 5406.6**

Cumulative injuries, **Labor 5303**

Dependent beneficiary, death without surviving dependent, **Labor 4706, 4706.5**

Conference settlement, **Labor 3714**

Disability indemnity, payment in addition to death benefits, **Labor 4702**

Economic opportunity program enrollees, **Labor 4212**

Elected public officials, assassination, **Labor 4720 et seq.**

WORKERS COMPENSATION—Cont'd

Death benefits—Cont'd

Equitable distribution, **Labor 4704**

Form, release or compromise agreement, **Labor 5004**

Grandchildren, **Labor 3503**

Health care providers, limitation of actions, AIDS, **Labor 5406.6**

Installment payments, **Labor 4702**

Interest on awards, **Labor 5800**

Joinder of all claims arising out of same injury, **Labor 5303**

Liability of employer, **Labor 4701**

Limitation of actions, **Labor 5406**

AIDS, **Labor 5406.6**

Limitation of proceedings for collection, asbestosis, **Labor 5406.5**

Maximum amounts, **Labor 4702**

Medical legal expenses, contested cases, reimbursement, **Labor 4621**

Partial dependency, **Labor 4702**

Payments, industrial relations fund, recovery, surviving dependent found, **Labor 4706.5**

Peace officers, limitation of actions, AIDS, **Labor 5406.6**

Public elected officials, assassination, **Labor 4720 et seq.**

Recovery of payments by employer or insurer, surviving dependent found, **Labor 4706.5**

Release of claim, **Labor 5004**

Scholarships, public safety officers, dependents, **Labor 4709**

Setting apart or reassigning, **Labor 4704**

State employees retirement system member, **Labor 4707, 4708**

Survival to estate, **Labor 4706**

Termination, death of dependent beneficiary without surviving dependent, **Labor 4706, 4706.5**

Total dependency, **Labor 4702**

Trustee, payment to, **Labor 4704**

Debts of party, liability, **Labor 4901**

Decisions, **Labor 5313**

Amendment, **Labor 5803 et seq.**

Determination of all issues raised, **Labor 5815**

Forms, **Labor 5815**

Petition for reconsideration, **Labor 5908.5**

Petition for reconsideration, **Labor 5906 et seq.**

Presumptions of lawfulness, **Labor 5302**

Reconsideration without petition, **Labor 5911**

Service of decisions, **Labor 5316**

Public officers, **Labor 5317**

Declarations, **Labor 3711**

Medical evaluations, **Labor 4628**

Decrease of compensation, misconduct of employee, **Labor 4551**

Default judgment, **Labor 5506**

Defective products, **Labor 3602**

Defects, notice of injury or death, **Labor 5403**

WORKERS

WORKERS COMPENSATION—Cont'd

Defenses, public employment in violation of law, **Labor 3604**

Defined to mean workers compensation, **Labor 3200**

Definitions, **Labor 3204 et seq., 3350 et seq.**

  Administrative director, **Labor 3206**

  Approval of release or compromise of claim, **Labor 5001**

  Asbestosis, **Labor 4402**

  Board certified, medical evaluators, **Labor 139.2**

  Board qualified, medical evaluators, **Labor 139.2**

  Compensation, **Labor 3207**

  Date of injury, limitation of proceedings, **Labor 5411**

    Occupational diseases, **Labor 5412**

  Economical opportunity programs, enrollees, **Labor 4202 et seq.**

  Independent medical examiner, **Labor 28**

  Labor Code, **Labor 3200**

  Medical director, **Labor 29**

  Personal physician, **Labor 4600**

  Psychologists, **Labor 3209.3**

  Self insurers security fund, **Labor 3741**

  State average weekly wage, **Labor 4453**

  Subrogation of employer for injuries or death caused by third person, **Labor 3850**

Delay. Payment, post

Demolition experts, voluntary technical assistance to public entity, **Labor 3367**

Denial of petition for consideration by inaction, **Labor 5909**

Dentures, **Labor 3208**

Dependents,

  Death benefits, generally, ante

  Definitions, asbestos workers, **Labor 4402**

  Presumptions, **Labor 3501**

Depositions, **Labor 5710**

Deposits,

  Lump sum payments, **Labor 5102 et seq.**

  Self insurance plans fund, **Labor 3702.5**

Deputies for own convenience, exclusion, **Labor 3352**

Descent and distribution,

  Death benefits, death of dependent beneficiary without surviving dependent, **Labor 4706**

  Lump sum payment deposits, **Labor 5102**

Destruction of files, **Labor 135**

Determination of questions, **Labor 5300**

  Controversy between employer and employee, **Labor 4604**

  Dependency questions, **Labor 3502**

Diagnostic imaging, physicians and surgeons, conflict of interest, **Labor 139.3, 139.31**

Diagnostic tests, medical legal expenses, contested claims, **Labor 4620 et seq.**

Dialysis, fees, **Labor 5307.1**

WORKERS COMPENSATION—Cont'd

Diminishing compensation awarded, **Labor 5803 et seq.**

Disability,

  Permanent disability, generally, post

  Permanent partial disability, generally, post

  Temporary disability, generally, post

  Total disability, generally, post

Disability benefits, **Const. Art. 14, § 4; Labor 4650 et seq.**

  Additional benefits, **Un Ins 2629**

  Bar of right to payments, failure or refusal of employee to submit to medical examination, **Labor 4054**

  Child support enforcement, **Labor 138.5**

  Cumulative injuries, **Labor 5303**

  Death,

    Payment after death, **Labor 4700**

    Payment of disability benefits in addition to death benefits, **Labor 4702, 4706.5**

  Delinquent payments, penalties, **Labor 4650**

  Disability caused by unreasonable refusal to submit to medical or surgical treatment, **Labor 4056**

  Economic opportunity program enrollees, **Labor 4213**

  Electronic deposits, **Labor 4651**

  Highway patrol, **Labor 4800.5 et seq.**

  Joinder of all claims arising out of same injury, **Labor 5303**

  Late payment, penalty, **Labor 4650**

  Lifeguards, leaves of absence, **Labor 4850**

  Los Angeles unified school district, police, leaves of absence, **Labor 4850**

  Negotiable instruments tendered for disability payments, **Labor 4651**

  Nominal award, likelihood of future disability, **Labor 5802**

  Orders, **Labor 4651**

  San Francisco Harbor police, **Labor 4800 et seq.**

  Temporary disability, generally, post

  Time of payment, **Labor 4650 et seq.**

  Unemployment work relief employee, **Labor 4456**

Disability evaluation report writing, medical evaluators, courses of instruction or study, **Labor 139.2**

Disaster council, definitions, **Labor 3211.9**

Disaster service, definitions, **Labor 3211.93, 3211.93a**

Disaster service workers, **Labor 3352.94, 4350 et seq.**

  Average weekly earnings, **Labor 4353**

  Definitions, **Labor 3211.92**

  Exclusive remedy, **Labor 4352**

  Percentage of disability, determination, **Labor 4354**

  Permanent disability, **Labor 4354**

  Right to compensation, **Labor 4351**

  Temporary and permanent disability indemnity, **Labor 4353**

WORKERS COMPENSATION—Cont'd

Discharge from liability, employer, payment of lump sum, **Labor 5105**

Discharge of claims, **Labor 3603**

Discharge of employee making application or testifying, **Labor 132a**

Disclosure,

  Advertisements, attorneys and others, **Labor 5432, 5433**

  AIDS, medical records, **CC 56.31**

  Health care provider organizations, post

  Individually identifiable information, **Labor 138.7**

  Insurance, post

  Medical evaluations, time and location, **Labor 4628**

Discounts,

  Attorneys, employers and others, **Labor 4906**

  Claims adjusters, **Labor 3219**

Discovery,

  Medical evaluations, **Labor 4062.3**

  Sexual harassment, assault or battery, prior sexual conduct, admissibility, **Labor 3208.4**

Discrimination,

  Against employee making application or testifying, **Labor 132a**

  Employees testifying or making application, **Labor 132a**

  Health care provider organizations, **Labor 4600.6**

  Return to work program, **Labor 139.48**

  Third parties, causation, **Labor 3600**

Disfigurement, disability payment, computation, **Labor 4660**

Dismissal and nonsuit,

  Application, **Labor 5507**

  Employer as party, substitution of insurer, **Labor 3755 et seq.**

  Old claims, notice, **Labor 5404.5**

Disposition, files, **Labor 135**

District Attorneys, this index

Dividends, claims adjusters, **Labor 3219**

Divisions,

  Definitions, **Labor 3205**

  Occupational safety and health, **Labor 6304.5**

  Workers compensation division. Industrial Relations Department, this index

Documents,

  Compelling production, **Labor 132**

  Production, issuance of subpoenas, **Labor 130**

Domestic Service or Work, this index

Drugs and medicine, **Labor 4600 et seq.**

  Fees, schedules, **Labor 5307.1, 5307.2**

  Generic drugs, **Labor 4600.1**

Dual coverage, workmens compensation and other statutes, **Labor 3369**

Duty of employee to submit to medical examination, **Labor 4050**

WORKERS COMPENSATION—Cont'd
Early intervention programs, rehabilitation, corrections and rehabilitation department, youth authority department, **Labor 3214**
Economic opportunity programs, enrollees, **Labor 4201 et seq.**
Economic profiling, medical provider networks, **Labor 4616.1**
Education,
Physicians and surgeons, **Labor 4062.8**
Return to work program, **Labor 139.47 et seq.**
Worker safety and health training and education program, **Labor 6354.7**
Election to be subject to compensation liability, **Labor 4150 et seq.**
Elective coverage, independent contractors, newspapers or magazines, **Labor 4157**
Electronic claims, medical care and treatment, payment, **Labor 4603.4**
Electronic deposits, disability benefits, **Labor 4651**
Elevators, dumbwaiters and escalators, insurance,
Licenses and permits, **Labor 7301**
Qualified elevator company, **Labor 7311.1**
Employer, definitions, **Labor 3300**
Employment agencies, contractors, **Labor 3302**
Employment trainees, state department of rehabilitation, **Labor 3351.5**
Encumbrances. Liens and incumbrances, generally, post
Enforcement of laws, **Labor 5300**
Securing payment of compensation, employers failure, **Labor 3710**
English language,
NonEnglish speaking persons, medical evaluations, interpreters, appointment, **Labor 4600**
Required forms, **Labor 124**
Entry of award based upon release or compromise agreement, **Labor 5002**
Errors, notice of injury or death, **Labor 5403**
Estate of employer, employee proceeding against, **Labor 5306**
Ethics, judges, **Labor 123.6**
Evidence, **Labor 5700, 5703**
Action by employee against third person causing injury, **Labor 3855**
Action by employer against third person causing injury or death, compensation payments and liability of employer, **Labor 3854**
Application of law, occupational safety and health, **Labor 6304.5**
Autopsy reports, **Labor 5706**
Burden of proof, **Labor 3202.5, 5705**
Aggravation of injury, fraudulent concealment, **Labor 3602**
Employee aggravation of disability, defense, **Labor 5705**

WORKERS COMPENSATION—Cont'd
Evidence—Cont'd
Burden of proof—Cont'd
Failure of employer to furnish statement showing security for payment of compensation, **Labor 3711**
Presumption of employers negligence, household employees, exclusion, **Labor 3708**
Psychiatric injuries, **Labor 3208.3**
Rebutting presumption of employers negligence, **Labor 3708**
Court reporters, **Labor 5708**
Fee schedule, medical legal expenses, prima facie, **Labor 5307.6**
Informality in admission of evidence, **Labor 5709**
Interpreters, liability for fees, **Labor 3600**
Judicial review, **Labor 5951 et seq.**
Matters not pleaded by answer, **Labor 5505**
Medical care and treatment, post
Medical evaluations,
Additional evaluations, **Labor 4062**
Reports, **Labor 4061**
Occupational disease or cumulative injuries, determination or limitation of liability, **Labor 5500.6**
Occupational safety and health, application of law, **Labor 6304.5**
Payment and acceptance, amount not due or pending dispute of right to compensation, **Labor 4909**
Permanent disability percentages schedule, **Labor 4660**
Petition for reconsideration, **Labor 5902, 5906, 5908**
Grounds, **Labor 5903**
Physician present at medical examinations, **Labor 4055**
Power of appeals board to procure evidence, **Labor 5701**
Presumptions, generally, post
Prima facie evidence, fee schedule, medical legal expenses, **Labor 5307.6**
Production, issuance of subpoenas, **Labor 130**
Production of books and papers, **Labor 5710**
Psychiatric injuries, **Labor 3208.3**
Records and reports, **Labor 5703**
Rules of evidence, **Labor 5307, 5708**
Securing payment of compensation, employers failure, **Labor 3710.2, 4554**
Service of transcripts of testimony and other matters added to record outside open hearing, **Labor 5704**
Sexual harassment, assault or battery cases, prior sexual conduct, admissibility, **Labor 3208.4**
Silicotic hazard, **Labor 5500.5**
Stipulations, **Labor 5702**
Summary, **Labor 5313**

WORKERS COMPENSATION—Cont'd
Evidence—Cont'd
Temporary partial disability, weekly loss in wages, **Labor 4657**
Treating physician reports, **Labor 4061**
Uninsured employers, **Labor 3715 et seq.**
Valid insurance coverage, **Labor 3711**
Ex parte communications, medical evaluations, **Labor 4062.3**
Examiners and examinations,
Health care provider organizations, **Labor 4600.6**
Medical evaluators, **Labor 139.2**
Physical examinations, **Labor 4050 et seq.**
Exclusions, **Labor 3352, 3352.94**
Household employees, **Labor 3352**
Liability, **Labor 3600**
Ski lift operators, off duty employees, **Labor 3352**
Volunteer employees, private nonprofit organizations, **Labor 3352**
Exclusive remedy, **Labor 3601**
Award and judgment or settlement, **Labor 3600**
Disaster service workers, **Labor 4352**
Economic opportunity programs, enrollees, **Labor 4208**
Executions,
Employer subrogation claim, **Labor 3862**
Subrogation lien, **Labor 3862**
Exemptions, **Labor 3352, 3352.94**
Bowling team sponsor, **Labor 3301**
Debts, **Labor 4901**
Liability for compensation, **Labor 4156, 5000**
Person afforded benefits under other statutes, **Labor 3369**
Physicians and surgeons, referrals, conflict of interest, no alternative providers, **Labor 139.31**
Verification declaration, perjury, **Labor 3800**
Exhumation of bodies, **Labor 5707**
Expenses and expenditures,
Bad faith actions, payment, **Labor 5813**
Medical legal expenses,
Contested claims, **Labor 4620 et seq.**
Fee schedule, **Labor 5307.6**
Payment, attorneys fees, **Labor 3709.5**
Personal physician, **Labor 4605**
State reimbursement, **Labor 3716.1**
Expert testimony, **Labor 5703**
Experts, fire and explosions, voluntary technical assistance to public entity, **Labor 3367**
Explosions, voluntary technical assistance to public entity, **Labor 3367**
Extended duration benefits, workmens compensation temporary partial disability, reduction of benefits, **Labor 4654**
Extension of time, payment, asbestos workers account lien, **Labor 4416**

WORKERS

WORKERS COMPENSATION—Cont'd
Extraterritorial provisions, **Labor 3600.5**
Eyeglasses, **Labor 3208**
Eyes,
  Loss of both eyes, **Labor 4662**
  Subsequent injuries, **Labor 4751**
Family care leave, liens and incumbrances, **Labor 4903, 4904**
Family counselors, treatment of condition arising out of injury, **Labor 3209.8**
Family relationship, dependents, **Labor 3503**
Federal longshore and harbor workers compensation, self insurance, joint security deposits, **Labor 3701, 3702.2**
Fees,
  Arbitrating controversies, **Labor 5308**
  Autopsy, **Labor 5706**
  Certificate fees, self insurers, **Labor 3702.5**
  Clerk of courts, **Labor 5811**
  Drugs and medicine, schedules, **Labor 5307.2**
  Excessive fees, **Labor 5307.1**
  Inflation, medical care and treatment, **Labor 5307.1**
  Insurance, post
  Interpreters and translators, post
  Medical evaluators, appointments, **Labor 139.2**
  Medical fee schedules, **Labor 5307.1, 5307.11**
  Persons executing process, **Labor 134**
  Physicians and surgeons, referrals, conflict of interest, **Labor 139.3**
  Schedule, medical legal expenses, **Labor 5307.6**
  Self insurers, certificate fees, **Labor 3702.5**
  Special audit costs, self insurers, **Labor 3702.5**
  Subsequent injuries, hearings, **Labor 4753.5**
  Witnesses, **Labor 131**
  Workers occupational safety and health education fund, **Labor 6354.7**
Feet, subsequent injuries, **Labor 4751**
Fellow servant, injury caused by negligence of, defense abolished, **Labor 3708**
Fictitious names, advertisements, attorneys and others, **Labor 5433**
Files, disposition, **Labor 135**
Filing,
  Liens and incumbrances, medical care and treatment, time, **Labor 4903.6**
  Pleadings, orders and papers, **Labor 5807**
Financial statements and reports, health care provider organizations, **Labor 4600.6**
Findings of fact, **Labor 5800 et seq.**
  Adoption, modification or vacation, **Labor 5315**
  Appeal and review, **Labor 115**
  Conclusiveness, **Labor 5953**

WORKERS COMPENSATION—Cont'd
Findings of fact—Cont'd
  Making and filing, **Labor 5313**
  Time, **Labor 5800.5**
  Misconduct of employer, **Labor 4553.1**
  Petition for reconsideration, grounds, **Labor 5903**
  Presumption of lawfulness, **Labor 5302**
  Scope of review, **Labor 5952**
  Stipulations, **Labor 5702**
Fines and penalties,
  Administrative penalties, assessment, **Labor 129.5**
  Claims adjusters, rebates or other consideration, **Labor 3219**
  Delay, payment, **Labor 4650, 5814, 5814.1, 5814.6**
  Employers,
    Failure to furnish statements, **Labor 3711**
    Failure to secure payment of compensation, **Labor 3710.1, 3710.2**
    Household employees, **Labor 3354**
  Fraud, generally, post
  Health and safety and workers compensation board, **Labor 78**
  Household employees, failure to secure payment, **Labor 3354**
  Injunctive relief, uninsured employers, **Labor 3710.2**
  Insurance, post
  Medical legal expenses, failure to pay within time period, **Labor 4622**
  Notice, failure to post, **Labor 6431**
  Payment, **Labor 3700.5**
    Delay, **Labor 4650, 5814, 5814.6**
  Physicians and surgeons, **Labor 4628**
    Referrals, conflict of interest, **Labor 139.3**
  Process, orders, uninsured employees, **Labor 3731**
  Referral of clients, solicitation of business, **Labor 3218**
  Reports, self insurers, failure to submit, **Labor 3702.3**
  Self insurance,
    Reports, failure to submit, **Labor 3702.3**
    Self insurers security fund, composite deposits, assessments, **Labor 3701.8**
  Stop orders,
    Employers failure to observe, **Labor 3710.2**
    Injunctive relief, **Labor 3710.2**
  Uninsured employers, **Labor 3718, 3722 et seq.**
  Utilization review, medical care and treatment, **Labor 4610**
  Withdrawal, employers securing payment of compensation, **Labor 3727.1**
Firefighters and Fire Departments, this index
Fires and Fire Protection, this index

WORKERS COMPENSATION—Cont'd
Fish and game, wardens, hernia, heart trouble and pneumonia, **Labor 3212**
  Reserve program, **Labor 3363**
Foreign employment, injury within state, **Labor 3600.5**
Foreign injury, domestic employment, **Labor 3600.5**
Foreign jurisdiction, injuries sustained in, jurisdiction of controversies, **Labor 5305**
Foreign states,
  Domestic injury, **Labor 3600.5**
  Injury occurring in, **Labor 3600.5**
  Jurisdiction of injuries sustained in foreign states, **Labor 5305**
  Peace officers, deputies, **Labor 3352, 3366, 3367**
Foresters, this index
Forestry division,
  Conservation department, peace officers, **Labor 3600.3**
  Fire fighting members, **Labor 3212**
Forms, **Labor 125**
  Answers, **Labor 5505**
  Applications and answers, **Labor 5500, 5505**
  Attorney fee deductibility from benefits notice, **Labor 4061**
  Awards, **Labor 5815**
  Bond of guardian or trustee representing minor or incompetent, **Labor 5307.5**
  Claims, **Labor 138.4**
  Decisions, **Labor 5815**
  Declaration, **Labor 3711**
  Fraud warning, **Labor 5401.7**
  Health care provider organizations, post
  Languages of required forms, **Labor 124**
  Medical care and treatment, payment, **Labor 4603.4**
  Notice of injury or death, **Labor 5401**
  Orders, **Labor 5815**
  Petition for reconsideration,
    Award, order or decision of appeals board, **Labor 5902**
    Determination and disposition by appeals board, **Labor 5908.5**
  Release or compromise agreements, **Labor 5003**
    Death benefits, **Labor 5004**
  Undertaking on stay order, **Labor 6001**
  Writ of review, **Labor 5951**
Fraud, **Labor 125, 3820**
  Advertisements, attorneys and others, **Labor 5432, 5433**
  Concealment of injury, **Labor 3602**
  Forms, warning, **Labor 5401.7**
  Health care provider organizations, post
  Health care providers, contracts, **Labor 3219**
  Insurance, post
  Judicial review, **Labor 5952**
  Notice, warnings, **Labor 3822**
  Petition for reconsideration, **Labor 5903**
  Reports, **Labor 3823**

WORKERS COMPENSATION—Cont'd
Fraud—Cont'd
  Representation of employee, **Labor 4906**
  Revocation of certificate of consent to self insure, **Labor 3702**
  State fraud investigation and prosecution surcharge, **Labor 62.6**
  Warnings, **Labor 3822**
Fringe benefits, exclusion, determination of average weekly earnings, **Labor 4454**
Frivolous actions, **Labor 5813**
Full compliance audits, **Labor 129**
  Fines and penalties, **Labor 129.5**
Funds,
  Administration revolving fund, **Labor 62.5**
  Cal OSHA targeted inspection and consultation fund, **Labor 62.7, 62.9**
  Labor enforcement and compliance fund, **Labor 62.5**
  Occupational safety and health fund, **Labor 62.5**
  Return to work fund, **Labor 139.48**
  Self insurers security fund, **Labor 3740 et seq.**
  Subsequent injuries benefits trust fund, **Labor 62.5**
  Trust funds,
    Subsequent injuries benefits trust fund, **Labor 62.5**
    Uninsured employers benefits trust fund, **Labor 62.5**
  Uninsured employers benefits trust fund, generally, post
  Workers compensation administration revolving fund, **Labor 78**
  Workers compensation managed care fund, **Labor 4600.7**
  Workers occupational safety and health education fund, **Labor 6354.7**
Funeral expenses, **Labor 4701**
  Death of dependent, beneficiary without surviving dependent, **Labor 4706, 4706.5**
  Economic opportunity program enrollees, **Labor 4214**
  Joinder of all claims arising out of same injury, **Labor 5303**
  Liens against compensation payments, **Labor 4903**
  State employees retirement system member, **Labor 4707**
Future disability likely, award of nominal disability, **Labor 5802**
Gardeners, part time gardeners, exclusion, **Labor 3352**
Generic drugs, **Labor 4600.1**
Grandchildren, death benefits, dependency, **Labor 3503**
Grievances, health care provider organizations, **Labor 4600.6**
Grounds for reconsideration, **Labor 5903**
Group insurance. Insurance, post

WORKERS COMPENSATION—Cont'd
Guardian ad litem, appointment, **Labor 5307.5, 5408**
Guardian and ward,
  Minor employees injured, **Labor 5408**
  Payment of minors compensation, **Labor 3605**
Guidelines,
  Medical evaluators, performance of duties, **Labor 139.2**
  Rights and benefits, **Labor 139.6**
  Utilization review, **Labor 4610**
  Utilization schedules, medical care and treatment, **Labor 4604.5**
Hands,
  Loss of both hands or use thereof, **Labor 4662**
  Subsequent injuries, **Labor 4751**
Harbor police, San Francisco, **Labor 4800 et seq.**
Hardship, commutation of compensation, **Labor 5100**
Head of department, definitions, **Labor 53**
Health and safety and workers compensation board, **Labor 75 et seq.**
Health care provider organizations,
  Certificates and certification, **Labor 4600.3, 4600.5, 4600.6**
  Chiropractic care, disputes, guidelines, **Labor 4600.5**
  Choice, right of choice, employees, **Labor 4600.3**
  Contracts, **Labor 4600.3, 4600.5, 4600.6**
    Fraud, **Labor 3219**
  Disclosure, **Labor 4600.6**
  Discrimination, **Labor 4600.6**
  Examiners and examinations, **Labor 4600.6**
  Fees,
    Schedules, alternative fees, discounted rates, **Labor 4614**
    Workers compensation managed care fund deposits, **Labor 4600.7**
  Financial statements and reports, **Labor 4600.6**
  Forms, disclosure forms, **Labor 4600.6**
  Fraud, **Labor 3219**
  Grievances, **Labor 4600.6**
  Labor organizations, contracts, negotiation, **Labor 4600.3**
  Licenses and permits, reimbursement, **Labor 4600.35**
  Occupational medicine, provision, contracts, **Labor 4600.5**
  Payment, work related occurrence or illness payment same as nonwork related, **Labor 4614**
  Physicians and surgeons, compensation levels, **Labor 4614**
  Privileges and immunities, **Labor 4600.6**
  Reimbursement, licenses and permits, **Labor 4600.35**
  Reports, **Labor 4600.6**
  Right of choice, employees, **Labor 4600.3**

WORKERS COMPENSATION—Cont'd
Health care provider organizations —Cont'd
  Schedules, fees and revenues, workers compensation managed care fund deposits, **Labor 4600.7**
  Self insurance, **Labor 4600.3**
  Standards, certificates and certification, **Labor 4600.3**
  Surveys, **Labor 4600.6**
Health care providers, **Labor 3208.05**
  Death benefits, limitation of actions, AIDS, **Labor 5406.6**
  Medical fee schedules, **Labor 5307.11**
  Preferred reimbursement rates, **Labor 4609**
Health care service plans,
  Coordination with health care provider organizations, **Labor 4600.3, 4614.1**
  Liens against compensation award, reimbursement, **Labor 4903.1**
  Medical provider networks, **Labor 4616.7**
Health care workers, **Labor 3208.05**
Health facilities, referrals, physicians, conflict of interest, **Labor 139.31**
Health insurers, security deposit, **Labor 3701**
Hearing aids, **Labor 3208**
Hearings, **Labor 5502, 5700 et seq.**
  Appeals board members, number, **Labor 115**
  Attorney general, representation of state, **Labor 3716.1**
  Changes in rules or regulations, **Labor 5307**
  Continuance, **Labor 5502.5**
  Depositions, **Labor 5710**
  Employer threatening to discharge or discharging employee for testifying, **Labor 132a**
  Fines and penalties, **Labor 129.5**
  Individually identifiable information, disclosure, **Labor 138.7**
  Informal proceedings, **Labor 5709**
  Judges, **Labor 5309**
  Medical evaluators, suspension or termination, **Labor 139.2**
  Medical fee schedules, **Labor 5307.1**
  Notice, **Labor 5504**
    Petition for reconsideration, **Labor 5906**
    Publication, **Labor 5316**
    Rules and regulations, **Labor 5307.4**
    Stop orders, issuance against employers not securing compensation payment, **Labor 3710.1**
  Objections to reference of proceeding, **Labor 5311**
  Petition for reconsideration, **Labor 5906, 5907**
  Powers of appeals board members, **Labor 130**
  Presence of parties, **Labor 5700**
  Publication of notice, **Labor 5316**
  Representation of parties, **Labor 5700**

WORKERS

WORKERS COMPENSATION—Cont'd
Hearings—Cont'd
  Rules and regulations, **Labor 5307.4**
    Adoption, amendment or rescission,
      Labor 5307, 5307.3
  Rules of practice and procedure, **Labor
    5708**
  Service of notice, **Labor 5504**
  Service of transcripts of testimony and
    other matters added to record out-
    side open hearing, **Labor 5704**
  Stop order, issuance against employer
    not securing compensation pay-
    ment, **Labor 3710.2**
  Subsequent injuries, **Labor 4753.5**
  Summary hearings, coverage, fines and
    penalties, **Labor 3722**
  Suspension of privilege of appearing as
    representative of party to proceed-
    ings, **Labor 4907**
  Uninsured employer, penalty assess-
    ment objection, **Labor 3725**
Heart disease,
  Correctional institutions, presumptions,
    Labor 3212.10
  Firefighters and fire departments, **Labor
    3212 et seq.**
  Juvenile facilities division, presump-
    tions, **Labor 3212.10**
  Parole officers, presumptions, **Labor
    3212.10**
  Police, **Labor 3212 et seq.**
  Probation officers, presumptions, **Labor
    3212.10**
  State police, **Labor 3212.3**
  University of California police, **Labor
    3213**
Hepatitis, presumptions, law enforcement
    personnel, **Labor 3212.8**
Hernias,
  Correctional institutions, presumptions,
    Labor 3212.10
  Firemen, **Labor 3212 et seq.**
  Juvenile facilities division, presump-
    tions, **Labor 3212.10**
  Parole officers, presumptions, **Labor
    3212.10**
  Police, **Labor 3212 et seq.**
  Probation officers, presumptions, **Labor
    3212.10**
  University of California, **Labor 3212**
    Firemen, **Labor 3212.4**
High schools, occupational training, **Labor
    3368**
Highway Patrol, this index
Hold harmless, third person causing injury
    or death, **Labor 3864**
Holidays, instruments and documents, fil-
    ing, time, **Labor 3730**
Home health agencies, fees, **Labor 5307.1**
Honoraria, administrative law judges, **La-
    bor 123.6**
Hospitals, **Labor 4600 et seq.**
  Contracts, liens and incumbrances, re-
    imbursement, **Labor 4903.1**
  Definitions, **Labor 3209.5**

WORKERS COMPENSATION—Cont'd
Hospitals—Cont'd
  Fees, **Labor 5307.1**
  Notice, **Labor 4603.5**
  Outpatient clinics, fees, **Labor 5307.1**
Household employees, **Labor 3352, 3354**
  Exclusion, **Labor 3352**
  Failure of employer to secure payment
    of compensation, **Labor 3354**
Housing, mutual self help housing, exemp-
    tions, **Labor 3352**
Hybrid contempt, definitions, **Labor 5309**
Identity and identification, employer re-
    sponsible, asbestosis, **Labor 4405**
Implantable medical devices, costs, reim-
    bursement, **Labor 5318**
In home supportive services, domestic em-
    ployees, coverage, **Labor 3351.5**
Incidental to employment, **Labor 3600**
Incompetents, limitations, **Labor 5408**
Increase of compensation,
  Employer failure to secure payment of
    compensation, **Labor 4554**
  Illegally employed minor under 16, **La-
    bor 4557**
  Misconduct of employer, **Labor 4553**
Increasing compensation awarded, **Labor
    5803 et seq.**
Incumbrances. Liens and incumbrances,
    generally, post
Indemnity,
  Employer, power press workers, **Labor
    4558**
  Statutory change in amount payable
    subsequent to injury, **Labor 4453.5**
Independent contractors,
  Burden of proof, **Labor 5705**
  Definitions, **Labor 3353**
  Newspapers or magazines, elective cov-
    erage, **Labor 4157**
Independent medical reviewers, medical
    provider networks, **Labor 4616.4**
Individually identifiable information, **La-
    bor 138.7**
Industrial accident commission, **Const.
    Art. 14, § 4**
Industrial medical council, **Labor 129 et
    seq.**
Inequity, commutation of awards avoiding,
    Labor 5100
Infants. Children and minors, generally,
    ante
Inflation, medical care and treatment,
    fees, **Labor 5307.1**
Informality in proceedings, **Labor 5709**
Information, rights and benefits, **Labor
    139.6**
  Administrative assistance, **Labor 5450 et
    seq.**
  Notice, posting, **Labor 3550**
Information system, development, **Labor
    138.6**
Injunction, health care providers, fraud,
    contracts, **Labor 3219**
Injunctive relief, failure of employers to
    observe stop orders, **Labor 3710.2**

WORKERS COMPENSATION—Cont'd
Injury prevention, reports, **Labor 6401.7**
Inquiries, powers of board, members, **La-
    bor 130**
Revocation of certificate of consent to
    self insure, **Labor 3702**
Insolvency. Insurance, post
Inspection and inspectors,
  Cal OSHA targeted inspection and con-
    sultation fund, **Labor 62.7, 62.9**
  Permanent disability percentage sched-
    ule, **Labor 4660**
  Place of injury, **Labor 5701**
  Premises or records, **Labor 5701**
Installments,
  Death benefits, **Labor 4702**
    Asbestos workers, **Labor 4407.3,
      4407.5**
  Liens against compensation payments,
    Labor 4904
  Uninsured employer, payments into
    state compensation insurance fund,
    Labor 5106
Institution of proceedings, **Labor 5300**
Insurance, **Const. Art. 14, § 4; Labor
    3700 et seq., 3750 et seq.**
  Accounts and accounting, liquidation,
    Labor 130, 132
  Actions and proceedings,
    Appeals board proceeding, uninsured
      employers, **Labor 3715 et seq.**
    Awards, uninsured employers, **Labor
      3715 et seq.**
    Unemployed insurers, application to
      appeals board, award, **Labor
      3715 et seq.**
    Uninsured employers, **Labor 3715 et
      seq.**
  Adjusters, rebates or other consider-
    ation, **Labor 3219**
  Appeal and review, writs of review,
    uninsured employers, penalty as-
    sessments, **Labor 3725**
  Application of law, insurance rights and
    privileges, **Labor 3750**
  Arbitration and award, **Labor 5270 et
    seq.**
  Asbestos related work, registration, **La-
    bor 6501.5**
  Assumption of liability, **Labor 3755**
    Relief of employer from liability to
      claimant, **Labor 3757**
  Audits and auditors, **Labor 129**
  Awards, uninsured employers, **Labor
    3715 et seq.**
  Bonds, appeals board proceedings,
    uninsured employers, **Labor 3715 et
    seq.**
  Building permits, **Labor 3800**
  Car washes, registration, **Labor 2055**
  Certificates, out of state employer in-
    sured, **Labor 3600.5**
  Claims, employer, discussion of claim
    elements that affect premium, **La-
    bor 3762**

WORKERS COMPENSATION—Cont'd
Insurance—Cont'd

Compensation insurance fund. State compensation insurance fund, generally, post

Compromise and settlement, unemployed insurers fund, **Labor 3719**

Confidential or privileged information, studies, insolvency, **Labor 77.7**

Construction permit, **Labor 3800**

Consultation, loss control services, **Labor 6354.5**

Contributions of employees, **Labor 3751**

Crimes and offenses, discrimination against employee making application or testifying, encouragement by insurance carrier, **Labor 132a**

Damages, uninsured employers fund, **Labor 3717 et seq.**

Declaration, **Labor 3711**

Definitions, **Labor 3211**

Disclosure, medical records, **Labor 3762**

Effect of payment of compensation by employer or insurer, **Labor 3754**

Election to be subject to compensation liability, **Labor 4150 et seq.**

Elevators, dumbwaiters and escalators, Licenses and permits, **Labor 7301**
Qualified elevator company, **Labor 7311.1**

Employee benefits in addition to insurance, **Labor 3750**

Encouragement of discrimination against employee making application or testifying, **Labor 132a**

Failure to pay, self insuring employers, **Labor 3701.5**

Fees,
Loss control consultation services, **Labor 6354.5**
Workers occupational safety and health education fund, **Labor 6354.7**

Fines and penalties, **Labor 129.5**
Uninsured employers fund, **Labor 3718 et seq.**

Forms, declarations, **Labor 3711**

Fraud, **Labor 129.5, 3820**
Health care providers, contracts, **Labor 3219**

Group insurance,
Disability insurance, liens and incumbrances, awards, reimbursement, **Labor 4903.1**
Medical provider networks, **Labor 4616.7**

Insolvency, studies, **Labor 77.7**

Judgments, uninsured employers fund, **Labor 3718 et seq.**

Liability insurers deemed admitted to transact workers compensation insurance, liens and incumbrances, uninsured employers fund, **Labor 3720 et seq.**

Liability not to be reduced by other benefits, **Labor 3752**

WORKERS COMPENSATION—Cont'd
Insurance—Cont'd

Licenses and permits, filing certificate, issuance of construction permits, **Labor 3800**

Liens and incumbrances, uninsured employers fund, damages action award, **Labor 3709**
Damages action award, **Labor 3709**

Loss control, consultation services, **Labor 6354.5**

Loss control services coordinator, **Labor 6354.5**

Mandamus, insured employers, penalty assessments, **Labor 3725**

Medical provider networks, generally, post

Medical records, disclosure, **Labor 3762**

Mutual insurer, **Labor 3750**

Name of carrier, notice to employees, **Labor 3550, 3551**

Name of insurer, employer required to furnish written statement, **Labor 3711**

Notice,
Assumption of liability, **Labor 3755**
Claims filed directly with insurers, **Labor 3761**
Demanding compliance with law requiring employer to secure payment of compensation, **Labor 3710.1**
Insurer agreement to pay compensation, **Labor 3756**
Liability, **Labor 3755**
Payment, **Labor 3756**

Order relieving employer from liability, insurer joined as party, **Labor 3759**

Out of state employer insured, certificates, **Labor 3600.5**

Paid in capital, reimbursement from employer, penalty due to late payment, **Labor 4650**

Payment, bar to recover against insurer or employer for amount paid, **Labor 3754**

Plans, health and safety loss control, **Labor 6354.5**

Premiums,
Discounts, **Labor 3217**
Return to work program, reimbursement, **Labor 139.48**

Priority of compensation claim over debts of insurer, **Labor 4908**

Provider networks. Medical provider networks, generally, post

Rates and charges,
Collective bargaining, **Labor 3201.5**
Discussion of claims that affect premiums, **Labor 3762**
Premium discounts, **Labor 3217**
Studies, **Labor 138.65**

Recovery of compensation from insurer, **Labor 3753**

Rehabilitation plans, voluntary, public employees, **Labor 6208**

WORKERS COMPENSATION—Cont'd
Insurance—Cont'd

Reimbursement, penalty due to late payment, **Labor 4650**

Relief of employer from liability, **Labor 3757**
Assumption of liability by insurer, **Labor 3755**

Reports, injuries, **Labor 3760**

Return to work program, reimbursement, **Labor 139.48**

Right of employer to insure, **Labor 3750**

Rights and privileges, **Labor 3750 et seq.**

Self employed persons, jurisdiction of controversies over insurance policies, **Labor 5308**

Self insurance, generally, post

Self insurers security fund, **Labor 3740 et seq.**

Special excess policies, termination of self insurance, **Labor 3702.8**

State assistance, collection of award from uninsured employer, **Labor 3715**

State compensation insurance fund, generally, post

State treasury, self insuring employer, **Labor 3701**

Statement of insurance, furnishing, employers failure to, **Labor 3711**

Studies,
Insolvency, **Labor 77.7**
Rates and charges, **Labor 138.65**

Subrogation, injury or death caused by third person, **Labor 3850 et seq.**

Subsequent injuries benefits trust fund, conference settlement, **Labor 3714**

Substitution of an insurer for an employer, **Labor 3755**

Trade secrets, studies, insolvency, **Labor 77.7**

Trust companies, redeposit of securities or cash in lieu of bond, state compensation insurance fund to guarantee future installment payments, **Labor 5106**

Uninsured employers, generally, post

Uninsured employers benefits trust fund, generally, post

Worker safety and health training and education program, **Labor 6354.7**

Writ of mandate, insured employers, penalty assessments, **Labor 3725**

Writs of review, uninsured employers, penalty assessments, **Labor 3725**

Insurance fund. State compensation insurance fund, generally, post

Interest,
Asbestos workers account lien payments, **Labor 4416**
Awards, **Labor 5800**
Deposit of lump sum payments, **Labor 5102**
Lump sum payments, computation of amount, **Labor 5101**

WORKERS

WORKERS COMPENSATION—Cont'd
Interest—Cont'd
  Penalties, payment delay, **Labor 5814.1**
  Uninsured employers, payments into
    state compensation insurance fund,
    Labor 5106
  Uninsured employers fund,
    Liability for, **Labor 3716.2**
    Recovery of amounts paid, **Labor 3732**
Interpreters and translators, **Labor 5811**
Fees,
  Depositions, **Labor 5710**
  Medical evaluations, **Labor 4600**
  Medical legal expenses, contested
    cases, **Labor 4620 et seq.**
Intoxicating liquors. Alcoholics and alco-
  holism, generally, ante
Investigations and investigators, **Labor 5708**
  Asbestosis claim, **Labor 4409**
  Assignment of services, **Labor 3716.1**
  Attorney general, representation of
    state, **Labor 3716.1**
  Costs, **Labor 3700.5**
  Discharge of employees by employers
    for testimony, **Labor 132a**
  Powers, **Labor 130**
  Rules of practice and procedure, **Labor 5708**
  Subsequent injuries, **Labor 4753.5**
Investments, self insurance, self insurers
  security fund, **Labor 3701.8**
Joinder of claims, **Labor 5303**
  Uninsured employers fund, **Labor 3718**
Joinder of parties, **Labor 5307.5**
Joint election of employer and employee
  to be subject to compensation liabili-
  ty, **Labor 4150 et seq.**
Judges, **Labor 123 et seq., 5309**
  Adjournment of hearings, **Labor 5700**
  Adoption, modification or vacation, **La-
    bor 5315**
  Asbestosis claims, **Labor 4409.5**
  Attorneys, **Labor 123.7**
  Certification, official acts, **Labor 130**
  Code of judicial ethics, **Labor 123.6**
  Definitions, **Labor 27**
  Employment qualifications, **Labor 123.5**
  Ethics, **Labor 123.6**
  Finding, time for filing, **Labor 5313**
  Honoraria, **Labor 123.6**
  Oaths and affirmations, **Labor 5312**
    Administration, **Labor 130**
  Official acts, certification, **Labor 130**
  Salary payments, **Labor 123.5**
  Subpoenas, **Labor 130**
    Enforcement, **Labor 132**
Judgment roll, **Labor 5807**
Judgments and decrees,
  Actions against third party causing inju-
    ry or death, **Labor 3856 et seq.**
  Attachment, employer property, secure
    payment of judgment, **Labor 3707**
  Award, **Labor 5806**

WORKERS COMPENSATION—Cont'd
Judgments and decrees—Cont'd
  Contribution, employers comparative
    share, **Labor 4558**
  Credit against judgment, employer fail-
    ing to secure payment of compen-
    sation, **Labor 3709**
  Docketing of awards as judgments, fees,
    Labor 5811
  Entry on judicial review, **Labor 5953**
  Exclusive remedy, **Labor 3600**
  Order, entry of satisfaction, **Labor 5809**
  Payment, attorneys fees, **Labor 3709.5**
  Priority of judgment over debts of em-
    ployer, **Labor 4908**
  Receipt for payment of lump sum as
    satisfaction, **Labor 5105**
  Satisfaction, **Labor 5809**
  Special judgments for uninsured em-
    ployers fund, **Labor 3726**
  Stay of execution, **Labor 5808**
  Undertaking on stay order, **Labor 6001**
  Uninsured employers, **Labor 3718, 3719**
    Penalty assessment, **Labor 3726**
Judicial review. Appeal and review, gen-
  erally, ante
Jurisdiction, **Labor 5300 et seq., 5501.5**
  Change of venue, **Labor 5501.6**
  Continuing jurisdiction, **Labor 5410,
    5803**
  Judicial review, **Labor 5955**
  Lack of jurisdiction, petition for recon-
    sideration, **Labor 5903**
  Mandamus, findings, stop orders, issued
    against employer not securing com-
    pensation payment, **Labor 3710.1**
Justice department, **Labor 3212.7, 4800 et
  seq.**
Juvenile court ward engaged in rehabilita-
  tive work, **Labor 3364.55**
Juvenile Delinquents and Dependents, this
  index
Juvenile Facilities Division, this index
Juvenile institutions and schools, regional
  youth educational facilities, **Labor
  3364.7**
Juvenile traffic offenders or probationers,
  rehabilitative work on public work
  projects, **Labor 3364.6**
Labor and management agreements, **La-
  bor 3201.7**
Labor enforcement and compliance fund,
  Labor 62.5
Labor organizations, appeals boards,
  members and membership, **Labor 112**
Laboratories, fraud, contracts, **Labor 3219**
Laboratory fees, medical legal expenses,
  Labor 4620 et seq.
Language assistance, medical examina-
  tions, **Labor 4600**
Law enforcement officers,
  Leaves of absence, disability benefits,
    Labor 4850
  Lower back impairment, **Labor 3213.2**
Leases, defective products, **Labor 3602**

WORKERS COMPENSATION—Cont'd
Legal expenses, medical legal expenses,
  Labor 4620 et seq.
Legs, subsequent injuries, **Labor 4751**
Letters of credit, self insuring employers,
  Labor 3701, 3701.5
Liability,
  Cumulative injuries, **Labor 5500.5**
  Exclusions, **Labor 3600**
  Occupational diseases, **Labor 5500.5**
  Vouchers, vocational rehabilitation, **La-
    bor 4658.6**
Licenses and permits,
  Health care provider organizations, re-
    imbursement, **Labor 4600.35**
  Insurance, ante
Liens and incumbrances, **Labor 4903 et
  seq.**
  Asbestos workers account, **Labor 4414**
  Awards, reimbursement, prior benefits
    or services, **Labor 4903.1**
  Employer, judgment against third per-
    son causing injury or death, **Labor
    3856 et seq.**
  Insurance, ante
  Priorities and preferences, uninsured
    employers fund, settlement pro-
    ceeds, **Labor 3709**
  Time, medical care and treatment, **La-
    bor 4903.5**
    Filing, **Labor 4903.6**
  Unemployment disability benefits, **La-
    bor 3865; Un Ins 2629.1, 2735.5,
    2741**
    Overpayments, **Un Ins 1375.3**
Life pensions,
  Permanent disability, **Labor 4658**
  Self insurers, payments into state com-
    pensation insurance fund, **Labor
    3703**
Lifeguards, skin cancer, injury, **Labor
  3212.11**
Light duty program,
  Collective bargaining agreements, **Labor
    3201.5**
  Labor and management agreements,
    Labor 3201.7
Limitation of actions, **Labor 5400 et seq.**
  Administrative assistance to claimants,
    Labor 5454
  Affirmative defense, **Labor 5409**
  Asbestos workers account, reimburse-
    ment, benefits and costs paid, **La-
    bor 4413**
  Children and minors, **Labor 5408**
  Cumulative injury, **Labor 5500.5**
  Date of injury, definitions, **Labor 5411**
  Death benefits, ante
  Delay, payment, fines and penalties, **La-
    bor 5814**
  Disability benefits, **Labor 5405**
  Discrimination against employee mak-
    ing application or testifying, **Labor
    132a**
  Employer serious and wilful misconduct,
    Labor 5407

WORKERS COMPENSATION—Cont'd
Limitation of actions—Cont'd
Employer serious and wilful misconduct
—Cont'd
Reduction of compensation, **Labor 5407.5**
Failure to institute proceedings within the proper time, **Labor 5404**
Failure to serve notice of injury or death, **Labor 5400**
Fines and penalties, payment, delay, **Labor 5814**
Hospital benefits, **Labor 5405**
Medical care and treatment, **Labor 5405**
Mentally ill persons, **Labor 5408**
New and further disability caused by original injury, **Labor 5410**
Occupational diseases, **Labor 5412, 5500.5**
Payment, delay, fines and penalties, **Labor 5814**
Surgical benefits, **Labor 5405**
Uninsured employers fund, recovery of amounts paid, **Labor 3732**
Waiver of defense, **Labor 5409**
Limitation of prosecutions, **Labor 3710.2**
Limitations, incompetents and minors, **Labor 5408**
Limited liability companies, employees, definitions, **Labor 3351**
Lists,
Medical evaluators, **Labor 139.2**
Labor and management agreements, **Labor 3201.7**
Medical treatment providers, collective bargaining agreements, **Labor 3201.5**
Living expenses,
Benefits paid by group disability policy, liens, **Labor 4903.1**
Liens, **Labor 4903**
Local agencies, self insurers, medical and related treatment and supplies, former employees, **Labor 4606**
Location, medical evaluation, disclosure, **Labor 4628**
Lodging expenses,
Medical examinations, **Labor 4600**
Medical legal expenses, contested cases, **Labor 4621**
Longshoremen and harbor workers, Longshoremens and Harbor Workers Compensation Act, enforcement, **Labor 128**
Loss control consultation services, insurers, **Labor 6354.5**
Loss control services coordinator, **Labor 6354.5**
Loss of earning capacity, determination of percentage of permanent disability, **Labor 4660**
Loss of time injuries, **Labor 138.4**
Loss of wages, deposition attendance, **Labor 5710**

WORKERS COMPENSATION—Cont'd
Lump sum payments, **Labor 5100 et seq.**
Asbestos workers benefits, installments commutation, **Labor 4407.5**
Certificate of appeals board, **Labor 5105**
Combined permanent partial disabilities, **Labor 5100.5**
Computation of amount, **Labor 5101**
Conditions, **Labor 5100**
Employee under rehabilitation, **Labor 5100.6**
Interest, computation of amount, **Labor 5101**
Liens against compensation payments, **Labor 4904**
Manner of payment, **Labor 5102**
Notice, **Labor 5100**
Payments by trustee from lump sum deposit, **Labor 5103**
Receipts, **Labor 5105**
Restrictions, **Labor 5100.5**
Time of commutation, **Labor 5100**
Trust deposits, **Labor 5102 et seq.**
Lyme disease, presumptions, **Labor 3212.12**
Magazines, advertisements, disclosures, **Labor 5432, 5433**
Magazines sales or delivery, exclusion, **Labor 3352**
Mail and mailing,
Complaint, uninsured employers fund, **Labor 3708.5**
Notice, hearing, stop orders, issuance against employers not securing compensation payment, **Labor 3710.1**
Stop orders or penalty assessment orders, uninsured employers, **Labor 3731**
Maintenance of assets or credit line, self insurers security fund, **Labor 3745**
Majority decision, **Labor 115**
Managed care fund, **Labor 4600.7**
Mandamus, **Labor 5955**
Findings, stop orders, **Labor 3710.1**
Insurance, ante
Penalty assessments, insured employers, **Labor 3725**
Manner of payment, award, **Labor 5801**
Marriage counselors, treatment of condition arising out of injury, **Labor 3209.8**
Marshals, scholarships for dependents, **Labor 4709**
Maximum aggregate temporary disability payments, **Labor 4656**
Maximum earnings, **Labor 4451 et seq.**
Meals, expenses,
Incident to medical examination, **Labor 4600**
Medical legal expenses, contested cases, **Labor 4621**
Mediation, labor and management agreements, **Labor 3201.7**
Medical braces, **Labor 3208**

WORKERS COMPENSATION—Cont'd
Medical care and treatment, **Const. Art. 14, § 4; Labor 4600 et seq.**
Access, studies, **Labor 5307.2**
Acupuncturists, **Labor 3209.3, 3209.9**
Advertisements, **Labor 5430 et seq.**
Appeal and review, billing, **Labor 4603.2**
Authorization, rescission, modification or change, **Labor 4610.3**
Change of physician or chiropractor, **Labor 4600 et seq.**
Collective bargaining, **Labor 3201.5**
Confidential or privileged information, electronic claims, payment, **Labor 4603.4**
Construction of statutes, authorization, rescission, modification or change, **Labor 4610.3**
Cumulative injuries, **Labor 5303**
Death or disability caused by unreasonable refusal to submit to medical or surgical treatment, **Labor 4056**
Definitions, **Labor 3209.5**
Reports, **Labor 3209.10**
Delay, utilization review, **Labor 4610.1**
Economic opportunity program enrollees, **Labor 4227, 4228**
Electronic claims, payment, **Labor 4603.4**
Employer employee agreements, **Labor 3209.7**
Employer's failure to provide, **Labor 4600**
Evidence,
Liability for expenses, **Labor 4600**
Medical legal expenses,
Contested claims, **Labor 4620 et seq.**
Prima facie evidence, fees, **Labor 5307.6**
Order to pay cost, denial of permanent disability rating, **Labor 4555.5**
Fees, **Labor 5307.1, 5307.11**
Subsequent injuries, hearings, **Labor 4753.5**
Fines and penalties, utilization review, **Labor 4610**
Firemen, **Labor 4852**
Forms, payment, **Labor 4603.4**
Fraud, reports, **Labor 3823**
Generic drugs, **Labor 4600.1**
Health care provider organizations, generally, ante
Highway patrol, **Labor 4802**
Hospitals, generally, ante
Hours, prior authorization services, **Labor 4600.4**
Independent medical review, evaluation, **Labor 77.5**
Joinder of all claims arising out of same injury, **Labor 5303**
Jurisdiction over controversies relating to treatment, **Labor 5304**
Labor and management agreements, **Labor 3201.7**

WORKERS

WORKERS COMPENSATION—Cont'd
Medical care and treatment—Cont'd
Law enforcement officers, **Labor 4852**
Liens and incumbrances, **Labor 4903**
Time, **Labor 4903.5, 4903.6**
Limitation of proceedings for collection of benefits, **Labor 5405**
Local public entities, self insurers, former employees, **Labor 4606**
Medical directors, utilization review, **Labor 4610**
Medical legal expenses, **Labor 4620 et seq.**
Medical provider networks, generally, post
Modification or change, authorization, **Labor 4610.3**
Notice, **Labor 4603.5**
Incomplete billing, **Labor 4603.2**
Objections and exceptions, **Labor 4062**
Objections and exceptions, medical evaluations, **Labor 4062**
Physicians and surgeons, generally, post
Police, **Labor 4852**
Provider networks. Medical provider networks, generally, post
Psychologists, medical collaboration, **Labor 3209.3**
Reasonableness of claim for medical services, **Labor 4906**
Reports, **Labor 3209.10**
Medical legal expenses, contested claims, **Labor 4620 et seq.**
Physicians, evidence, **Labor 5703**
Spinal surgery, second opinions, **Labor 4062**
Utilization standards, comparisons, **Labor 77.5**
Rescission, authorization, **Labor 4610.3**
San Francisco Harbor police, **Labor 4802**
Second opinions, spinal surgery, objections and exceptions, **Labor 4062**
Self procured medical costs, awards, liens, reimbursement, **Labor 4903.1**
Signatures, reports, **Labor 3209.10**
Specialties, protocols, evidence, **Labor 5703**
Spinal surgery, objections and exceptions, **Labor 4062**
Standards, evaluation, **Labor 77.5**
Studies, **Labor 127.6**
Access, **Labor 5307.2**
Termination proceedings, costs for successful defense against, **Labor 4607**
Time, **Labor 5402**
Utilization review, **Labor 4610**
United States, **Labor 4355**
Utilization review, **Labor 4610, 4610.1**
Utilization schedules, **Labor 4604.5, 5307.27**
Utilization standards, evaluation, **Labor 77.5**
Medical clinics, fraud, contracts, **Labor 3219**

WORKERS COMPENSATION—Cont'd
Medical directors, utilization review, **Labor 4610**
Medical evaluations, **Labor 4060 et seq.**
Additional evaluations, **Labor 4062**
Advertisements, **Labor 139.4, 139.45**
Eligibility, **Labor 4061.5 et seq.**
Medical provider networks, **Labor 4616.3**
Performance, notice, time limits, expenses, **Labor 4621**
Reports, evidence, **Labor 4061**
Scope, **Labor 4061**
Specialties, appointments, **Labor 139.2**
Suspension or termination, **Labor 139.2**
Medical examinations,
Admissible evidence, **Labor 5703.5**
Authority to require submission to, **Labor 5701**
Costs, **Labor 5703.5**
Duty to submit to, **Labor 4050 et seq.**
Expenses, contested cases, **Labor 4620 et seq.**
Independent medical reviewers, medical provider networks, **Labor 4616.4**
Language assistance, **Labor 4600**
Medical provider networks, independent medical reviewers, **Labor 4616.4**
Psychologists, medical collaboration, **Labor 3209.3**
Right of employee to receive expenses of transportation, **Labor 4600**
Submission to, employee failure or refusal, **Labor 4053, 4054**
Medical provider networks, **Labor 4616 et seq.**
Applications, independent medical reviewers, **Labor 4616.4**
Continuity of care policies, **Labor 4616.2**
Contracts, **Labor 4616.4**
Economic profiling, **Labor 4616.1**
Group insurance, **Labor 4616.7**
Health care service plans, **Labor 4616.7**
Independent medical reviewers, **Labor 4616.4**
Medical evaluations, **Labor 4616.3**
Medical examinations, independent medical reviewers, **Labor 4616.4**
Notice, **Labor 4616.3**
Plans and specifications, **Labor 4616**
Reports, independent medical reviewers, **Labor 4616.4**
Rules and regulations, **Labor 4616**
Second opinions, **Labor 4616.3**
Specialists, **Labor 4616.3**
Termination, **Labor 4616.2**
Medical records,
AIDS, disclosure, **CC 56.31**
Insurance, disclosure, **Labor 3762**
Subpoenas, **Labor 4055.2**
Medical treatment. Medical care and treatment, generally, ante
Medicine. Drugs and medicine, generally, ante

WORKERS COMPENSATION—Cont'd
Meningitis, presumptions, **Labor 3212.9, 3212.10**
Mentally retarded and developmentally disabled persons,
Appearance and representation before appeals board, **Labor 5307**
Appointment of trustee or guardian ad litem, **Labor 5307.5**
Brain injuries resulting in mental illness, **Labor 4662**
Limitation of proceedings, **Labor 5408**
Merger of injuries, **Labor 5303**
Methicillin resistant staphylococcus aureus (MRSA) skin infections, presumptions, **Labor 3212.8**
Military bases, reservations and areas, firefighters and fire departments, cancer, **Labor 3212.1**
Military Forces, this index
Minimum and maximum average earnings, **Labor 4451 et seq.**
Minors. Children and minors, generally, ante
Misconduct,
Employee, **Labor 4551 et seq.**
Burden of proof, **Labor 5705**
Employer, **Labor 4553, 4553.1**
Evidence, **Labor 5705**
Injured employee, **Labor 4551 et seq.**
Limitation of proceedings, **Labor 5407, 5407.5**
Misdemeanors. Crimes and offenses, generally, ante
Modification or change, medical care and treatment, authorization, **Labor 4610.3**
Modified job program, collective bargaining agreements, **Labor 3201.5, 3201.7**
Modified work, permanent disability, payment, **Labor 4658, 4658.1**
Motor Carriers, this index
Municipal construction permits, filing certificates as to insurance coverage, **Labor 3800**
Municipal corporations, service of notice, order, **Labor 5317**
Municipal Officers and Employees, this index
Names, notice of injury or death, **Labor 5401**
Narcotics enforcement bureau, **Labor 3212.7**
Negligence, **Labor 3602**
Conditions of liability, **Labor 3600**
Uninsured employers fund, recovery of amounts paid, **Labor 3732**
Negotiable instruments, payment of disability benefits, **Labor 4651**
New and further disability caused by original injury, limitation of proceedings, **Labor 5410**
Newly discovered evidence, petition for reconsideration, **Labor 5903**
Newspaper and magazine sales or delivery, exclusion, **Labor 3352**

WORKERS COMPENSATION—Cont'd

Newspapers, advertisements, disclosures, **Labor 5432, 5433**

Nominal disability indemnity, **Labor 5802**

Nonparticipation, refusal to work for non-participating employer, unemployment benefits, eligibility, **Un Ins 1259**

Nonprofit corporations, sponsor of sentenced person, **Labor 3301**

Nonprofit Organizations, this index

Nonresident employers, commutation of compensation, **Labor 5100**

Notice, **Labor 138.4, 3550, 3551, 5307**

    Action against third person causing injury or death, **Labor 3853**

    Asbestos workers account lien, amount necessary to satisfy fully, **Labor 4416**

    Claims, old claims, dismissal, **Labor 5404.5**

    Commutation of compensation, **Labor 5100**

    Crimes and offenses, ante

    Death, **Labor 5400 et seq.**

    Discharge or threatening to discharge employees for testifying, **Labor 132a**

    Entitlement to benefits,

        Knowledge of injury, **Labor 5402**

        Rules and regulations, **Labor 138.3**

    Failure of employer to secure payment of compensation, **Labor 3710.1**

    Failure to post, penalty, **Labor 3550, 6431**

    Fraud, ante

    Hearings, ante

    Individually identifiable information, disclosure, **Labor 138.7**

    Injuries, **Labor 5400 et seq.**

    Insurance, ante

    Liability exclusion, voluntary participation in off duty recreational, activities, **Labor 3600**

    Liens against compensation claims, **Labor 3865, 4904**

    Medical care and treatment, ante

    Medical evaluations, **Labor 4060 et seq.**

    Medical provider networks, **Labor 4616.3**

    Name and address of physician, **Labor 4603.2**

    Old claims, dismissal, **Labor 5404.5**

    Payment of compensation to minor, **Labor 3605**

    Petition for reconsideration, hearing on, **Labor 5906**

    Release or settlement of claim against third party causing injury or death, **Labor 3860**

    Rights and benefits, posting, **Labor 3550**

    Rules and regulations, hearings on adoption, **Labor 5307.3**

    Satisfaction of judgment against third party causing injury or death, **Labor 3858**

    Service, **Labor 5316**

WORKERS COMPENSATION—Cont'd

Notice—Cont'd

    Service—Cont'd

        Public officers, **Labor 5317**

    Substitution of insurer in place of employer in proceedings, **Labor 3757**

    Temporary disability, post

    Testimony, taking at hearings, **Labor 5701**

    Victims of crime, eligibility, **Labor 3553**

    Withdrawal of election to be subject to compensation liability, **Labor 4152**

Notification project, child support enforcements, **Labor 138.5**

Nurse practitioners, reports, **Labor 3209.10**

Nursing expenses, **Labor 4600**

Oaths and affirmations,

    Administration, **Labor 130**

    Appeals board, **Labor 130**

    Judges, **Labor 5312**

    Petition for reconsideration, **Labor 5902**

Objections and exceptions,

    Medical evaluations for claims, **Labor 4062**

    Petition for reconsideration, waiver, **Labor 5904**

    Reference of proceeding, **Labor 5311**

    Spinal surgery, **Labor 4062**

    Uninsured employers, petition objecting to penalty assessment, **Labor 3725 et seq.**

Occupational Diseases, generally, this index

Occupational safety and health, application of division or law, **Labor 6304.5**

Occupational safety and health fund, **Labor 62.5**

Occupational training, high schools or regional occupational centers, **Labor 3368**

Off duty recreational, activities, liability for injuries, **Labor 3600**

Offenses. Crimes and offenses, generally, ante

Official acts, certification, **Labor 130**

Opinions and decisions. Decisions, generally, ante

Optometrists, **Labor 3209.4**

Orders, **Labor 5300 et seq.**

    Amendment, **Labor 5803 et seq.**

    Attachment, issuance of writ, **Labor 5600**

    Decision or award, determination of, **Labor 5815**

    Failure of employer to comply, misconduct of employee, **Labor 4551**

    Forms, **Labor 5815**

    Medical examination, **Labor 4051**

    Payment of lien claim without notice of lien, **Labor 4905**

    Petition for reconsideration, **Labor 5906 et seq.**

    Presumption of lawfulness, **Labor 5302**

    Reconsideration without petition, **Labor 5911**

WORKERS COMPENSATION—Cont'd

Orders—Cont'd

    Report of injury, directing submission by employer to insurer, **Labor 3760**

    Rescission, alteration or amendment, **Labor 5805**

    Service, **Labor 5316**

        Public officers, **Labor 5317**

    Stop orders,

        Employers failure to secure payment of compensation, **Labor 3710.1**

        Failure to observe, fines and penalties, **Labor 3710.2**

    Uninsured employers, appeals board awards, **Labor 3715 et seq.**

    Violation, serious and wilful misconduct by employer, **Labor 4553.1**

Organizations. Health care provider organizations, generally, ante

Orthotic devices and services, **Labor 4600**

Osteopaths, medical evaluators, **Labor 139.2**

Outpatient surgery facilities,

    Physicians and surgeons, referrals, adverse or pecuniary interest, **Labor 139.3**

    Referrals, **Labor 139.31**

Outside state, injuries arising, **Labor 3600.5**

Overtime, average earnings, computation, **Labor 4454**

Paid in capital requirement, industrial accidents division, publication and distribution, **Labor 127**

Paralysis resulting from injury, **Labor 4662**

Parent and child relationship,

    Employed by child, exclusion from coverage, **Labor 3352**

    Uninsured employers, **Labor 3717.1, 3720.1**

    Liens and incumbrances, **Labor 3720**

Parents, dependents, presumptions, **Labor 3501**

Parole officers, injuries, presumptions, **Labor 3212.10**

Part time gardeners, exclusion, **Labor 3352**

Partial dependency, death benefits, **Labor 4702**

Parties,

    Action against third person causing injury or death, **Labor 3853**

    Designation of parties, **Labor 5503**

    Joinder of parties, **Labor 5307.5, 5500.5**

    Medical legal expenses, contested claims, **Labor 4620 et seq.**

    Objection to reference of proceedings, particular referee, **Labor 5311**

    Order relieving employer from liability, insurer joined as party, **Labor 3759**

    Recovery of compensation from employer and insurer, **Labor 3753**

    Self insurers security fund, **Labor 3743, 3744**

    Substitution of insurer for employer, **Labor 3755 et seq.**

    Third parties, generally, post

WORKERS

WORKERS COMPENSATION—Cont'd
Parties—Cont'd
Uninsured employer actions, shareholders and parents, **Labor 3717.1**
Partnership,
Employee, definitions, **Labor 3351**
Unascertainable weekly earnings of workmen associates, **Labor 4457**
Workmen associated in partnership, **Labor 3360**
Patronage,
Claims adjusters, **Labor 3219**
Dividends, attorneys, employers and others, **Labor 4906**
Payment,
Accrued disability compensation unpaid at time of death, **Labor 4700**
Allowance or benefit not due, payable or disputed, **Labor 4909**
Amount and manner of payments, **Labor 5801**
Benefits, statutory change in amounts payable subsequent to injury, **Labor 4453.5**
Compensation,
Discharge of claims, **Labor 3603**
Minors, **Labor 3605**
Compromise and settlement, generally, ante
Costs, investigations and investigators, **Labor 3700.5**
Crimes and offenses, **Labor 3700.5**
Death benefits, **Labor 4702**
Recovery by employer of insurer from industrial relations fund, surviving dependent found, **Labor 4706.5**
Delay, **Labor 5814**
Attorney fees, **Labor 5814.5**
Fines and penalties, **Labor 4650, 5814, 5814.1, 5814.6**
Notice, employees, **Labor 138.4**
Utilization review, **Labor 4610.1**
Direct payment to claimant, **Labor 4902**
Disability benefits, **Labor 4650 et seq.**
Effect, employer or insurer, **Labor 3754**
Employers failure to secure, **Labor 3706, 3710.2, 3712**
Attorneys fees, **Labor 4555**
Increase in amount of compensation recoverable, **Labor 4554**
Fines and penalties, ante
Installments, generally, ante
Insurance, ante
Interest on awards, **Labor 5800**
Investigations and investigators, costs, **Labor 3700.5**
Liens against compensation awards, reimbursement, **Labor 4903.1**
Liens against compensation payments, **Labor 4904, 4904.1**
Life payment, permanent disability, **Labor 4658**
Lump sum payments, generally, ante
Permanent disability, **Labor 4650 et seq.**

WORKERS COMPENSATION—Cont'd
Payment—Cont'd
Receipt before accrued or payable, admission, **Labor 4909**
Reduction of payments, preexisting disability, **Labor 4753**
Subsequent injuries, **Labor 4755**
Temporary and permanent disabilities arising out of same injury, **Labor 4661**
Temporary and total partial disability, **Labor 4655**
Temporary disability benefits, **Labor 4650 et seq.**
Temporary partial disability, **Labor 4654**
Temporary total disability, **Labor 4653**
Trustee, payments from lump sum deposit, **Labor 5103**
Uninsured employer, **Labor 5106**
Waiting period, **Labor 4652**
Peace Officers, this index
Penalties. Fines and penalties, generally, ante
Per diem, health and safety and workers compensation board, **Labor 75**
Percentage, permanent disability, determination, **Labor 4658, 4660**
Perjury,
Alternative dispute resolution system, construction industry, **Labor 3201.5**
Coverage or exemption verification declaration, **Labor 3800**
Examination or evaluation referral statements, **Labor 4906**
Medical evaluations, declaration, **Labor 4628**
Permanent disability, **Labor 4650 et seq.**
Alternative work, payment, **Labor 4658, 4658.1**
Apportionment of benefits, **Labor 4663**
Causation, apportionment of benefits, **Labor 4663, 4664**
Child support enforcement, **Labor 138.5**
Combined permanent partial disabilities, prior injury, **Labor 4751**
Computation, **Labor 4659**
Average annual earnings, **Labor 4453**
Compensation, **Labor 5101**
Death, payment of benefits, **Labor 4700**
Denial of petition to reduce award, payment of costs, **Labor 4555.5**
Determination of percentage, **Labor 4658, 4660**
Employee under 21 years of age, determination of average weekly earnings, **Labor 4455**
Formulas, payment, **Labor 4658**
Juvenile court ward engaged in rehabilitative work, **Labor 3364.55**
Life payment, **Labor 4658**
Manner of payment, **Labor 4651**
Medical evaluations, **Labor 4061 et seq.**
Misconduct of employee, **Labor 4551 et seq.**
Modified work, payment, **Labor 4658, 4658.1**

WORKERS COMPENSATION—Cont'd
Permanent disability—Cont'd
Payment, **Labor 4650 et seq.**
Percentage of disability, payments, **Labor 4658**
Presumptions,
Prior injuries, **Labor 4664**
Total disability, **Labor 4662**
Prior injuries, presumptions, **Labor 4664**
Regular work, payment, **Labor 4658, 4658.1**
Schedules, **Labor 4658, 4660**
Temporary and permanent disability arising out of same injury, **Labor 4661**
Time of payment, **Labor 4650 et seq.**
Vocational rehabilitation, generally, post
Permanent partial disability,
Additional permanent partial disability, subsequent injury, **Labor 4751**
Combined disability,
Prior injuries, **Labor 4751**
Subsequent injuries, commutation of compensation, **Labor 5100.5**
Vocational rehabilitation, vouchers, **Labor 4658.5, 4658.6**
Person, definitions, **Labor 3210**
Personal services arrangements, physicians and surgeons, referrals, **Labor 139.31**
Petitions,
Labor and management agreements, **Labor 3201.7**
Reconsideration of order, decision or award, **Labor 5900 et seq.**
Rescission, alteration or amendment of award, **Labor 5804**
Temporary disability, decrease or termination, **Labor 4651.1**
Attorneys fees, petition denied, **Labor 4651.3**
Injured workman pursuing rehabilitation plan, **Labor 4651.2**
Uninsured employers,
Objection to penalty assessments, **Labor 3725 et seq.**
Payment of compensation, **Labor 3715 et seq.**
Physical examinations. Medical examinations, generally, ante
Physical therapists,
Treatment, **Labor 3209.5**
Visits, numbers and numbering, **Labor 4604.5**
Physical therapy, physicians and surgeons, adverse or pecuniary interest, **Labor 139.3**
Physician assistants, reports, **Labor 3209.10**
Physicians and surgeons, **Labor 3208.05**
Adverse or pecuniary interest, **Labor 139.3**
Exemption from application of law, **Labor 139.31**
Spinal surgery, second opinions, **Labor 4062**

WORKERS COMPENSATION—Cont'd
Physicians and surgeons—Cont'd
Appeal and review, billing, **Labor 4603.2**
Bills for services, evidence, **Labor 5703**
Change, **Labor 4600 et seq.**
Collaboration, treatment or evaluation by psychologists, **Labor 3209.3**
Conflict of interest, alternative providers, rural areas, none available, exemption to referral restrictions, **Labor 139.31**
Contracts,
Fraud, **Labor 3219**
Medical provider networks, **Labor 4616.4**
Curriculum vitae, **Labor 4628**
Definitions, **Labor 3209.3**
Education, **Labor 4062.8**
Employee personal physician, treatment covered due to failure of employer notice, **Labor 3550**
Fees, **Labor 5307.1**
Fines and penalties, **Labor 4628**
Health care provider organizations, compensation levels, **Labor 4614**
Hours, prior authorization services, **Labor 4600.4**
Independent medical reviewers, medical provider networks, **Labor 4616.4**
Medical evaluators, **Labor 139.2**
Medical legal expenses, contested claims, **Labor 4620 et seq.**
Medical provider networks, generally, ante
Notice, incomplete billing, **Labor 4603.2**
Personal physician,
Expenses, **Labor 4605**
Treatment by, **Labor 4600**
Personal services arrangements, referrals, **Labor 139.31**
Provider networks. Medical provider networks, generally, ante
Qualified medical evaluators, **Labor 139.2**
Reports, **Labor 3209.10, 4603.2**
Treating physician reports, evidence, **Labor 4061**
Selection to examine employee, **Labor 4050**
Signatures, reports, **Labor 3209.10**
Solicitation of business, referral of patients, exemptions, **Labor 3217**
Specialists, medical provider networks, **Labor 4616.3**
Suspension or termination, medical evaluators, **Labor 139.2**
Plans and specifications, health and safety loss control, **Labor 6354.5**
Pleadings, **Labor 5500 et seq.**
Answer, **Labor 5500 et seq.**
Application for compensation, filing, **Labor 5505**
Designation of parties, **Labor 5503**
Failure to answer, **Labor 5506**
Form, **Labor 5500, 5505**

WORKERS COMPENSATION—Cont'd
Pleadings—Cont'd
Answer—Cont'd
Matters not pleaded by answer, evidence, **Labor 5505**
Petition for reconsideration, **Labor 5905**
Service, **Labor 5505**
Time for filing, **Labor 5505**
Applications, generally, ante
Service, **Labor 5954**
Pneumonia, **Labor 3212 et seq.**
Firemen, University of California, **Labor 3212.4**
Presumptions, **Labor 3212.10**
State police, **Labor 3212.3**
University of California police, **Labor 3213**
Police, this index
Police power, **Labor 3201**
Political subdivisions,
Reports, self insurers, **Labor 3702.3**
Self insurance, certificates, **Labor 3700**
Posse comitatus, persons serving as, **Labor 3366**
Postsurgical services, utilization schedules, medical care and treatment, **Labor 4604.5**
Posttermination benefits, **Labor 3208.3, 3600**
Practice and procedure, appeals board, **Labor 5307**
Preferences. Priorities and preferences, generally, post
Preferred reimbursement rates, health care providers, **Labor 4609**
Prejudice,
Failure to give notice of injury or death, **Labor 5403**
Notice of injury or death, burden of proof, **Labor 5705**
Premiums. Insurance, ante
Presence of employees physician at medical examination, **Labor 4052**
Presumptions,
Adverse decision, issues not determined, **Labor 5815**
Autopsy, refusal to allow, **Labor 5707**
Blood borne infectious diseases, **Labor 3212.8**
Cancer, **Labor 3212.1**
Dependents, **Labor 3501**
Employee status, **Labor 3357**
Employer negligence, **Labor 3708**
Failure of employer to furnish statement showing security for payment of compensation, **Labor 3711**
Firefighters and fire departments, hepatitis, **Labor 3212.8**
Foresters, hepatitis, **Labor 3212.8**
Hepatitis, law enforcement personnel, **Labor 3212.8**
Hernia, heart trouble or pneumonia, **Labor 3212, 3212.5**
Highway patrol, meningitis, **Labor 3212.9**

WORKERS COMPENSATION—Cont'd
Presumptions—Cont'd
Lawfulness of acts of appeals board, **Labor 5302**
Lyme disease, **Labor 3212.12**
Medical legal expenses, **Labor 4622**
Medical legal fees, reasonableness, rebuttable presumption, **Labor 4625**
Meningitis, **Labor 3212.9**
Methicillin resistant staphylococcus aureus (MRSA) skin infections, **Labor 3212.8**
Negligence of employer, **Labor 3708**
Permanent disability, prior injuries, **Labor 4664**
Police, hepatitis, **Labor 3212.8**
Public employment, election to be subject to compensation liability, **Labor 4155**
Rebuttable presumptions, medical legal charges, reasonableness, **Labor 4625**
Self insurance disputes, resolutions, **Labor 3701.5**
Sheriffs, hepatitis, **Labor 3212.8**
Silicotic exposure, **Labor 5500.5**
State peace officer, heart trouble, hernia, pneumonia or tuberculosis, **Labor 3212.7**
Temporary disability, continuance, **Labor 4651.1**
Time, hepatitis, **Labor 3212.8**
Total permanent disability, **Labor 4662**
Tuberculosis, police or sheriffs, **Labor 3212.6**
Utilization schedules, medical care and treatment, **Labor 4604.5**
Wilful uninsurance, **Labor 3710.2**
Previous disability, average earnings, computation, **Labor 4459**
Prima facie evidence, fee schedule, medical legal expenses, **Labor 5307.6**
Prior injuries, permanent disability, presumptions, **Labor 4664**
Priorities and preferences,
Administration revolving fund, **Labor 62.5**
Appointment of trustee, lump sum deposits, **Labor 5104**
Asbestosis claims, **Labor 4409.5, 4410**
Asbestos workers account, **Labor 4416**
Attachment, preference to real property of employer, **Labor 5603**
Attorneys, employers and others, compensation, **Labor 4906**
Claims, priority over debts of employer, **Labor 4908**
Claims adjusters, **Labor 3219**
Liens and incumbrances,
Asbestos workers account, **Labor 4416**
Compensation awards, **Labor 4903.1**
Subrogation rights of surety, self insurers, **Labor 3705**

WORKERS

WORKERS COMPENSATION—Cont'd

Prisons and prisoners. Correctional Institutions, this index

Privileges and immunities,
Fraud, reports, **Labor 3823**
Health care provider organizations, **Labor 4600.6**

Probate Proceedings, this index

Probation officers,
Injuries, presumptions, **Labor 3212.10**
Leaves of absence, disability benefits, **Labor 4850, 4850.5**

Proceedings. Actions and proceedings, generally, ante

Process,
Answers, service, **Labor 5505**
Contempt proceedings, power to issue, **Labor 134**
Service, generally, post
Stop orders or penalty assessment orders, uninsured employers, **Labor 3731**

Product defects, **Labor 3602**

Production of books and papers,
Compelling, **Labor 5710**
Cumulative remedies, **Labor 132**
Issuance of subpoenas, **Labor 130**

Profile audit reviews, **Labor 129**
Fines and penalties, **Labor 129.5**

Prosthetic devices and services, **Labor 4600**

Protest, stop order issued against employer not securing compensation payment, **Labor 3710.1**

Provider networks. Medical provider networks, generally, ante

Proximate cause of injury, **Labor 3600, 3602**

Psychiatric injuries, **Labor 3208.3**

Psychologists and psychology,
Medical evaluators, **Labor 139.2**
Treatment or evaluation, medical collaboration, **Labor 3209.3**

Public agencies,
Amateur athletic officiating services, **Labor 3352**
Application of law, **Labor 3706.5**
Employees, volunteers, coverage, **Labor 3363.5**
Student athletes, coverage, **Labor 3352**

Public buildings and works, winning bidder failure to carry, action by second highest bidder, **Labor 1750**

Public corporations, service of notices, orders, **Labor 5317**

Public Employees Retirement System, this index

Public officers and employees, **Labor 3351**
Election to be subject to compensation liability, presumption, **Labor 4155**
Fire suppression, **Labor 3365**
Public employment in violation of law, **Labor 3604**
Self insurance, reports, disclosure, **Labor 3702.2**

WORKERS COMPENSATION—Cont'd

Public officers and employees—Cont'd
Service of notices, orders or decisions, **Labor 5317**
Termination of employment, injuries, indemnity, **Labor 4458.5**
Volunteers, coverage, **Labor 3363.5**

Public works contracts, **Labor 1860, 1861**

Publication,
Evidence, **Labor 5703**
Notice of hearings, **Labor 5316**

Qualified medical evaluators, appointments, specialties, **Labor 139.2**

Questions of fact,
Conclusiveness of findings, **Labor 5953**
Two or more injuries, separate determination, **Labor 3208.2**

Radiation treatments, physicians, referrals, adverse or pecuniary interest, **Labor 139.3**

Rates and charges,
Insurance, ante
Preferred reimbursement rates, health care providers, **Labor 4609**

Reasonable amount, claim for legal and medical services, **Labor 4906**

Rebates,
Adjusters, **Labor 3219**
Statements, attorneys, employers and others, **Labor 4906**

Rebuttable presumptions, medical legal charges, reasonableness, **Labor 4625**

Receipt of employees contribution to cost of compensation, **Labor 3751**

Receipt of payment, allowance or benefit, **Labor 4909**
Lump sum payments, **Labor 5105**

Recommendations, information and assistance officer, **Labor 5453**

Reconsideration of award, order or decision, **Labor 5900 et seq.**
Appeals board, three members, **Labor 115**
Prerequisite to court action, **Labor 5901**
Time, **Labor 5900**

Record on appeal, **Labor 5951**

Records and recordation,
Disposal, **Labor 135**
Division of workers compensation, **Labor 126**
Evidence, **Labor 5703**
Individually identifiable information, **Labor 138.7**
Industrial relations department, death without surviving dependent, payment, **Labor 4706.5**
Inspection, **Labor 5701**
Service, transcripts of testimony and other matters added to record outside open hearing, **Labor 5704**
Subpoenas, **Labor 4055.2**

Recovery of compensation, **Labor 5300**
Employer and insurer, **Labor 3753**

Recreation and park district volunteers, **Labor 3361.5**

WORKERS COMPENSATION—Cont'd

Recreational activities, voluntary participation, liability for injuries, **Labor 3600**

Reduction of benefits,
Preexisting disability, **Labor 4753**
Unemployment compensation benefits, receiving, temporary partial disability, **Labor 4654**

Referees,
Athletics, exemption, **Labor 3352**
Judges, generally, ante

Referrals, **Labor 4600**
Physicians and surgeons, adverse or pecuniary interest, **Labor 139.3**
Exemptions, **Labor 139.31**
Solicitation of business, crimes and offenses, **Labor 3215 et seq.**

Refunds,
Claims adjusters, **Labor 3219**
Statements, attorneys, employers and others, **Labor 4906**

Refusal of employee to submit to medical or surgical treatment, **Labor 4056**

Refusal to allow autopsy, **Labor 5707**

Refusal to pay award, attorney fees, **Labor 5814.5**

Regional occupational centers, work experience education or educational training classes, **Labor 3368**

Regional youth educational facilities, juvenile institutions and schools, **Labor 3364.7**

Registered mail, notice, findings, stop order issued against employer not securing compensation payment, **Labor 3710.1**

Registered student apprentices, **Labor 3368**

Regular work, permanent disability, payment, **Labor 4658, 4658.1**

Regulations. Rules and regulations, generally, post

Rehabilitation,
Collective bargaining, **Labor 3201.5**
Commutation or settlement of compensation, **Labor 5100.6**
Corrections and rehabilitation department, early intervention, **Labor 3214**
Disability decreased or terminated, **Labor 4651.2**
Employee under, commutation or settlement of compensation, **Labor 5100.6**
Juvenile traffic offenders or probationers, work on public works or projects, **Labor 3364.6**
Labor and management agreements, **Labor 3201.7**
Notice, employees, **Labor 138.4**
Physicians and surgeons, referrals, adverse or pecuniary interest, **Labor 139.3**
Temporary disability benefits, **Labor 4651.2**

WORKERS COMPENSATION—Cont'd
Rehabilitation—Cont'd
  Vocational rehabilitation, generally, post
  Voluntary, public employees, **Labor 6208**
  Youth authority department, early intervention program, **Labor 3214**
Rehabilitation work, juvenile traffic offenders or probationers, public work projects, **Labor 3364.6**
Reimbursement,
  Deposition attendance, loss of wages, **Labor 5710**
  Employee expenses, medical examinations, **Labor 4600**
  Employer, judgment against third party causing injury or death, **Labor 3856 et seq., 3864**
  Health care provider organizations, licenses and permits, **Labor 4600.35**
  Liens and incumbrances, **Labor 4903.1**
    Attorney fees, **Labor 4903.2**
  Medical fee schedules, **Labor 5307.11**
  Medical legal expenses, contested claims, **Labor 4621**
  Preferred reimbursement rates, health care providers, **Labor 4609**
  Return to work program, **Labor 139.48**
Relationship, dependents, **Labor 3503**
Release, **Labor 5000 et seq.**
  Approval of release, **Labor 5001**
  Claim against third party causing injury or death, **Labor 3859**
  Claims against multiple employers, occupational disease or cumulative injury cases, **Labor 5005**
  Compensation defined, **Labor 5001**
  Copy filed with board, **Labor 5002**
  Death benefits, **Labor 5004**
  Execution of release, **Labor 5003**
  Form, **Labor 5003**
    Death benefits, **Labor 5004**
  Payment of compensation to minor, **Labor 3605**
  Subsequent injuries claim, **Labor 4754.5**
Relief of employer from liability,
  Payment of employer lien, **Labor 3858**
  Substitution of insurer, **Labor 3757**
Relief workers, exclusion, **Labor 3352**
Religious workers, exclusion, **Labor 3352**
Remand,
  Attorney fees, determination, supplemental award, **Labor 5801**
  Commission fact findings and conclusions, **Labor 5953**
Remuneration in other than money, average earnings, computation, **Labor 4454**
Reports,
  Added to record outside open hearing, **Labor 5704**
  Audits and auditors, **Labor 129**
  Autopsies, **Labor 5706**
  Cal OSHA targeted inspection and consultation fund, **Labor 62.9**

WORKERS COMPENSATION—Cont'd
Reports—Cont'd
  Collective bargaining, **Labor 3201.5, 3201.9**
  Disobedience to subpoena, **Labor 132**
  Evidence, **Labor 5703**
  Fines and penalties, self insurers, failure to submit, **Labor 3702.3**
  Fraud, ante
  Health and safety and workers compensation board, **Labor 77**
  Health care provider organizations, **Labor 4600.6**
  Illness, **Labor 6409.1**
  Independent medical reviewers, **Labor 77.5**
    Medical provider networks, **Labor 4616.4**
  Information system, **Labor 138.6**
  Injuries, **Labor 3760, 6409.1**
    Prevention, **Labor 6401.7**
  Insurance, ante
  Labor and management agreements, **Labor 3201.7**
  Medical care and treatment, ante
  Medical evaluations, evidence, **Labor 4061**
  Medical examinations, appeals board, **Labor 5703.5**
  Medical provider networks, independent medical reviewers, **Labor 4616.4**
  Nurse practitioners, **Labor 3209.10**
  Physician assistants, **Labor 3209.10**
  Physicians and surgeons, **Labor 3209.10, 4055, 4603.2**
  Political subdivisions, self insurers, **Labor 3702.3**
  Self insurance, post
  Standards of care, comparisons, **Labor 77.5**
  Subsequent injuries, **Labor 4755**
  Treating physician reports, evidence, **Labor 4061**
  Uninsured employers, **Labor 90.3**
  Uninsured employers benefits trust fund, **Labor 3716.1, 3716.5**
  Utilization standards, medical care and treatment, comparisons, **Labor 77.5**
  Worker safety and health training and education program, **Labor 6354.7**
Representation of state, attorney general, **Labor 3716.1**
Request for medical examination, **Labor 4051**
Rescission,
  Medical care and treatment, authorization, **Labor 4610.3**
  Order, decision or award, **Labor 5803 et seq.**
Research, individually identifiable information, **Labor 138.7**
Reserve fish and game wardens, **Labor 3363**
Reserve public safety employees, leaves of absence in lieu of disability payments, **Labor 4855**

WORKERS COMPENSATION—Cont'd
Retraining, labor and management agreements, **Labor 3201.7**
Return day, writ of review, **Labor 5951**
Return to work program, **Labor 139.47 et seq.**
  Collective bargaining, **Labor 3201.5**
  Labor and management agreements, **Labor 3201.7**
Review. Appeal and review, generally, ante
Rights and benefits, continuing information program, **Labor 139.6**
Risk of medical or surgical treatment, **Labor 4056**
Rules and regulations, **Labor 5307, 5307.3**
  Appeals board, **Labor 5307**
  Applications and answers, **Labor 5500**
  Claims, old claims, dismissal, notice, **Labor 5404.5**
  Exemption of employer from liability for compensation, **Labor 5000**
  Fines and penalties, **Labor 129.5**
  Individually identifiable information, **Labor 138.7**
  Information system, **Labor 138.6**
  Medical legal expenses, **Labor 4627**
    Time for payment, **Labor 4622**
  Medical provider networks, **Labor 4616**
  Notice, entitlement to benefit, **Labor 138.3**
  Presumption of lawfulness, **Labor 5302**
Safety, worker safety and health training and education program, **Labor 6354.7**
Safety committees, labor and management agreements, **Labor 3201.7**
Salary continuation plan, definitions, **Labor 4650**
Sales, defective products, **Labor 3602**
San Francisco Harbor police, special payments, **Labor 4800 et seq.**
San Luis Obispo County, officers and employees, leaves of absence, disability benefits, **Labor 4850.5**
Saturday, instruments and documents, filing, time, **Labor 3730**
Savings and loan association deposits, disability benefits, employers deposit directly into employees account, **Labor 4651**
Savings banks, deposits of lump sum payments, **Labor 5102, 5103**
Schedules, **Labor 4550 et seq.**
  Drugs and medicine, fees, **Labor 5307.2**
  Medical care and treatment, fees, **Labor 5307.1**
  Permanent disability, **Labor 4658, 4660**
School Officers and Employees, this index
Scope of employment. Course of employment, generally, ante
Scorekeepers, athletics, exemption, **Labor 3352**
Seal, **Labor 116**
Second opinions,
  Medical provider networks, **Labor 4616.3**

WORKERS

WORKERS COMPENSATION—Cont'd

Second opinions—Cont'd

Spinal surgery, objections and exceptions, **Labor 4062**

Securities, this index

Security for payment of compensation, **Labor 3700**

Economic opportunity programs, enrollees, **Labor 4207**

Self employed persons, jurisdiction of controversies over insurance policies, **Labor 5308**

Self inflicted injury, **Labor 3600**

Self insurance,

Administration expenses, certificate fees, **Labor 3702.5**

Administration of claims, certificates of consent, **Labor 3702.1, 3702.7**

Administration of compensation benefits, **Labor 3703**

Alternative security system, **Labor 3701.8**

Appeal and review, self insurers security fund, composite deposits, assessments, **Labor 3701.8**

Assessments,

Self insurers security fund, composite deposits, **Labor 3701.8**

State fraud investigation and prosecution surcharge, **Labor 62.6**

Audits and auditing, **Labor 3702.6**

Failure to pay, **Labor 3701.5**

Fees, **Labor 3702.5**

Bad faith failure to pay assessment, fines and penalties, **Labor 3702.9**

Certificate of consent, **Labor 3700, 3702.1**

Fees, **Labor 3702.5**

Revocation, **Labor 3702, 3702.7**

Third party administrators, **Labor 3702.1**

Construction industry, alternative dispute resolution system, **Labor 3201.5**

Construction permits, filing certificates, **Labor 3800**

Deposit of bond or securities, **Labor 3701**

Dispute resolution, **Labor 3701.5**

Failure to pay, **Labor 3701.5**

Fines and penalties, failure to deposit, **Labor 3702.9**

Presumption of validity, dispute resolutions, **Labor 3701.5**

Termination of self insurance, **Labor 3702.8**

Failure of employers to secure payment of compensation, **Labor 3706**

Failure to pay, **Labor 3701.5**

Federal longshore and harbor workers compensation, joint security deposit, **Labor 3701, 3702.2**

Fees, certificate fees, **Labor 3702.5**

Fines and penalties,

Reports, failure to submit, **Labor 3702.3**

WORKERS COMPENSATION—Cont'd

Self insurance—Cont'd

Fines and penalties—Cont'd

Self insurers security fund, composite deposits, assessments, **Labor 3701.8**

Fraud,

Assessments, payment, fines and penalties, **Labor 3702.9**

State fraud investigation and prosecution surcharge, **Labor 62.6**

Health care provider organizations, **Labor 4600.3**

Investments, **Labor 3702.5**

Self insurers security fund, **Labor 3701.8**

Labor and management agreements, **Labor 3201.7**

Letters of credit, deposit, **Labor 3701, 3701.5**

Life pensions, payments into state compensation insurance fund, **Labor 3703**

Liquidated damages, failure to pay assessment, malice or fraud, **Labor 3702.9**

Local public entities, medical and related treatment and supplies, former employees, **Labor 4606**

Malicious failure to pay assessment, fines and penalties, **Labor 3702.9**

Political subdivisions,

Certificates, **Labor 3700**

Reports, **Labor 3702.3**

Possession of security, states assumption, **Labor 3701.5**

Public officers and employees, reports, disclosure, **Labor 3702.2**

Repeated failure to pay assessments, fines and penalties, **Labor 3702.9**

Reports, **Labor 3702.2**

Failure to file, fines and penalties, **Labor 3702.9**

Injuries, illness, **Labor 6409.1**

Termination of self insurance, **Labor 3702.8**

Return to insurer of excess security, **Labor 3701.3**

Revocation, certificate of consent, **Labor 3702, 3702.7**

Rules and regulations, **Labor 3702.10**

Secured transactions, security interest on self insurers assets, **Labor 3701**

Security, **Labor 3701.8**

Self insurers security fund, **Labor 3740 et seq.**

Composite deposits, **Labor 3701.8**

Special audits, public self insured employers, **Labor 3702.6**

Special excess policies, termination of self insurance, **Labor 3702.8**

State compensation insurance fund, self insurers, exemption from payment, **Labor 3703**

State fraud investigation and prosecution surcharge, **Labor 62.6**

WORKERS COMPENSATION—Cont'd

Self insurance—Cont'd

Subrogation, payments by surety on bond, preferred subrogation rights of surety, **Labor 3705**

Summaries, reports, **Labor 3702.2**

Surcharge, state fraud investigation and prosecution surcharge, **Labor 62.6**

Termination, **Labor 3702.8**

Fines and penalties, **Labor 3702.9**

Third party administrators, **Labor 3702.1**

Total accrued liability, report, **Labor 3702.1**

Waiver, fines and penalties, **Labor 3702.9**

Withdrawal of securities deposited, **Labor 3701**

Young La Follette Self Insurers Security Act, **Labor 3740 et seq.**

Self insurance plans fund, **Labor 3702.5**

Self insurers security fund, subrogation, **Labor 3705**

Self procured medical costs, liens, reimbursement, **Labor 4903.1**

Self procured treatment, reimbursement, employer referral approval prerequisite, **Labor 3209.8**

Separate determinations, questions of law and fact, two or more injuries, **Labor 3208.2**

Serious and willful misconduct,

Employee, **Labor 4551 et seq.**

Reduction of compensation, limitation of proceedings, **Labor 5407.5**

Employer, **Labor 4553, 4553.1**

Limitation of proceedings for collection of compensation, **Labor 5407**

Service, **Labor 134, 5504**

Answers, **Labor 5505**

Complaint, uninsured employers fund, **Labor 3708.5**

Copy of petition, decrease or termination of temporary disability, **Labor 4651.1**

Medical evaluations, **Labor 4062.3**

Notice, order or decision, **Labor 5316**

Public officers, **Labor 5317**

Notice of hearing, **Labor 5504**

Notice of injury or death, **Labor 5400**

Petition for reconsideration, **Labor 5905**

Pleadings, **Labor 5954**

Transcripts of testimony and other matters added to record outside of open hearing, **Labor 5704**

Settlement of claims. Compromise and settlement, generally, ante

Sexual assault or battery cases, evidence, prior sexual conduct, admissibility, **Labor 3208.4**

Sexual harassment, injuries, evidence of prior sexual conduct, admissibility, **Labor 3208.4**

Sheriffs, this index

WORKERS COMPENSATION—Cont'd

Signatures,
Decision on reconsideration of order, decision or award, **Labor 5908.5**
Medical care and treatment, reports, **Labor 3209.10**
Medical evaluations, declarations, **Labor 4628**
Physicians and surgeons, reports, **Labor 3209.10**
Release or compromise agreements, **Labor 5003**
Silicosis, disability or death from, apportionment of liability, **Labor 5500.5**
Single cause of action for each injury, **Labor 5303**
Ski lift operators, off duty employees, exclusion, **Labor 3352**
Ski patrolmen, voluntary service, exclusion, **Labor 3352**
Skilled nursing facilities, fees, **Labor 5307.1**
Social activities, voluntary participation, liability for injuries, **Labor 3600**
Social security number, claims forms, **Labor 5401**
Social Services, this index
Solicitation of business, referral of clients, crimes and offenses, **Labor 3215 et seq.**
Spanish language,
Notice,
Injury or death, **Labor 5401**
Rights and benefits, **Labor 3550, 3551**
Required forms, **Labor 124**
Special additional compensation, fixing and awarding, subsequent injuries, **Labor 4754**
Special judgments, uninsured employers fund, **Labor 3726**
Specialists, medical provider networks, **Labor 4616.3**
Specific injuries, definitions, **Labor 3208.1**
Spinal surgery, objections and exceptions, **Labor 4062**
Sports officials, exemption, **Labor 3352**
Sports participants, exclusion, **Labor 3352**
Spouses, person employed by spouse, exclusion from coverage, **Labor 3352**
Standards,
Drugs and medicine, **Labor 4600.2**
Health care provider organizations, ante
Medical evaluators, time, **Labor 139.2**
State, service of notices, orders, decisions, **Labor 5317**
State assistance, collection of award from uninsured employer, **Labor 3715**
State compensation insurance fund, **Const. Art. 14, § 4; Labor 55 et seq.**
Arbitration of controversies, **Labor 5308**
Cash revolving fund, **Labor 4755**
Subsequent injury payments, **Labor 4755**
Claims adjustment services, contract, **Labor 3716.1**

WORKERS COMPENSATION—Cont'd

State compensation insurance fund —Cont'd
Contracts, investigative and claims adjustment services, **Labor 3716.1**
Investigations, contracts, **Labor 3716.1**
Lump sum payments, deposits in fund, **Labor 5102**
State employees, **Labor 6101**
Subsequent injuries, additional payments, **Labor 4754**
Uninsured employer, deposit of future compensation payments, **Labor 5106**
State Officers and Employees, this index
State police. Highway Patrol, this index
Statements,
Employers failure to furnish, fines and penalties, **Labor 3711**
Misrepresentations, **Labor 3820**
Rebates or other consideration, attorneys, employers and others, **Labor 4906**
Statute of limitations. Limitation of actions, generally, ante
Statutory change in benefits payable following injury, **Labor 4453.5**
Stay. Supersedeas or stay, generally, post
Stipulated findings, notice, **Labor 3715**
Stipulation,
Filing, **Labor 5702**
Uninsured employer fund, amounts paid or payable, recovery, **Labor 3732**
Stop orders,
Employers failure to secure payment of compensation, **Labor 3710.1**
Failure of employers to observe, fines and penalties, **Labor 3710.2**
Withdrawal, **Labor 3727.1**
Student apprenticeship programs, **Labor 3368**
Student athletes, exclusion, **Labor 3352**
Studies,
Insurance,
Insolvency, **Labor 77.7**
Rates and charges, **Labor 138.65**
Medical care and treatment, **Labor 127.6**
Subpoenas, **Labor 130, 132**
Medical records, **Labor 4055.2**
Records and recordation, **Labor 4055.2**
Subrogation,
Abatement of action, death of employee or other person, **Labor 3851**
Injury or death caused by third person, **Labor 3850 et seq.**
Self insurers, payment by surety on bond, preferred subrogation rights of surety, **Labor 3705**
Subsequent injuries benefits trust fund, **Labor 62.5**
Conference settlement, **Labor 3714**
Subsequent proceedings, prior failure of employer to secure payment of compensation, effect, **Labor 3712**

WORKERS COMPENSATION—Cont'd

Substantial cause, psychiatric injuries, **Labor 3208.3**
Substantial shareholder,
Definitions, uninsured employers fund awards, **Labor 3717**
Uninsured employers, **Labor 3717.1, 3720, 3720.1**
Substitution of insurer for employer, **Labor 3755, 3757, 3758**
Suicide, **Labor 3600**
Summaries, self insurance, reports, **Labor 3702.2**
Summary hearings, coverage, fines and penalties, **Labor 3722**
Summons, **Labor 134**
Sunday, instruments and documents, filing, time, **Labor 3730**
Supersedeas or stay,
Execution of judgment, **Labor 5808**
Filing writ of review, **Labor 5956**
Judgments, **Labor 5808**
Order, undertaking, **Labor 6000 et seq.**
Petition for reconsideration, filing, **Labor 5910**
Reconsideration petition, **Labor 5910**
Undertaking on order, **Labor 6000 et seq.**
Writ of review, filing, **Labor 5956**
Supplemental award, **Labor 5801**
Supportive services, domestic employees, coverage, **Labor 3351.5**
Supreme court, review of decisions, **Labor 5955**
Surcharge,
Managed care fund, **Labor 4600.7**
State fraud investigation and prosecution surcharge, **Labor 62.6**
Sureties, self insurers, **Labor 3701**
Surgical treatment, **Labor 4600 et seq.**
Definitions, **Labor 3209.5**
Survival of action, subrogation of employer, injuries or death caused by third person, **Labor 3851**
Survival of claims, **Labor 4900**
Survival to estate, death benefits, **Labor 4706**
Surviving spouse, dependents, presumptions, **Labor 3501**
Suspension, medical evaluators, **Labor 139.2**
Targeted inspection and consultation fund, **Labor 62.7, 62.9**
Targeted profile audit reviews, **Labor 129**
Television and radio, advertisements, disclosures, **Labor 5432, 5433**
Temporary and total partial disability, **Labor 4655**
Temporary disability, **Labor 4650 et seq.**
Asbestosis, **Labor 4401 et seq.**
Attorney fees, petition alleging decrease or termination of disability, **Labor 4651.3**
Awards, liens, **Labor 4903.1**
Computation,
Average annual earnings, **Labor 4453**

WORKERS

WORKERS COMPENSATION—Cont'd
Temporary disability—Cont'd
Computation—Cont'd
Compensation, **Labor 5101**
Injuries existing in excess of two
years, **Labor 4661.5**
Death, payment of benefits, **Labor 4700**
Economic opportunity program enroll-
ees, **Labor 4212**
Firemen, leaves of absence in lieu of
payments, **Labor 4850**
Highway patrol, **Labor 4800.5 et seq.**
Indemnity, awards, liens, **Labor 4903.1**
Juvenile court ward engaged in rehabili-
tative work, **Labor 3364.55**
Law enforcement officers, leaves of ab-
sence in lieu of payments, **Labor
4850**
Lifeguards, leaves of absence in lieu of
benefits, **Labor 4850**
Los Angeles unified school district, po-
lice, leaves of absence, **Labor 4850**
Manner of payment, **Labor 4651**
Maximum aggregate payments, **Labor
4656**
Notice, permanent disability payment
possibilities, **Labor 4061**
Partial disability, **Labor 4654**
Weekly loss of wages, computation of
probable earnings, **Labor 4657**
Payment for temporary and permanent
disability arising out of same injury,
Labor 4661
Petition alleging decrease or termi-
nation of disability, **Labor 4651.1,
4651.2**
Attorney fees, **Labor 4651.3**
Police,
Leaves of absence in lieu of pay-
ments, **Labor 4850**
Los Angeles unified school district,
leaves of absence, **Labor 4850**
Presumption of continuance of tempo-
rary disability, **Labor 4651.1**
Return to work program, **Labor 139.47
et seq.**
San Francisco Harbor police, **Labor
4800 et seq.**
Time of payment, **Labor 4650 et seq.**
Total disability, **Labor 4653**
Termination, **Labor 5803 et seq.**
Employment, injuries, indemnity, **Labor
4458, 4458.5**
Medical evaluators, **Labor 139.2**
Medical provider networks, **Labor
4616.2**
Notice, employees, **Labor 138.4**
Territorial limits injuries suffered without
by resident employee, **Labor 5305**
Testimony, compelling giving of, **Labor
132**
Third parties,
Actions against, injuries or death caused
by, **Labor 3852 et seq.**
Causation, discrimination, **Labor 3600**

WORKERS COMPENSATION—Cont'd
Third parties—Cont'd
Self insurance, administration of claims,
Labor 3702.1
Service, notice of injury or death, **Labor
5400**
Subrogation of employer, **Labor 3850 et
seq.**
Time,
Adoption, modification or vacation, **La-
bor 5315**
Amendment of award, **Labor 5804**
Answers, filing, **Labor 5505**
Appeals, **Labor 5810**
Application for writ of review, **Labor
5950**
Asbestos workers account lien, payment,
Labor 4416
Asbestosis, benefits claims, **Labor 4408**
Attachments, **Labor 5600**
Commutation of compensation, **Labor
5100**
Continuances, conferences and hear-
ings, **Labor 5502.5**
Dependency status, determination, **La-
bor 3502**
Disability payments, commencing, **La-
bor 4650 et seq.**
Failure to institute proceedings within
proper time, **Labor 5404**
Findings, filing, **Labor 5313, 5800.5**
Hearings, **Labor 5502**
Rules and regulations, **Labor 5307.4**
Instruments or documents, filing, **Labor
3730**
Interest starting to run on awards, **La-
bor 5800**
Liens and incumbrances, medical care
and treatment, **Labor 4903.5**
Filing, **Labor 4903.6**
Limitation of actions, generally, ante
Medical care and treatment, **Labor 5402**
Medical evaluations, **Labor 139.2**
Disclosure, **Labor 4628**
Medical legal expenses, payment, **Labor
4622**
Notice, eligibility, benefits, **Labor 138.4**
Notice of injury or death, **Labor 5400,
5401**
Reconsideration of award, order or de-
cision, **Labor 5900, 5909**
Report of injuries to insurer, **Labor
3760**
Utilization review, medical care and
treatment, **Labor 4610**
Timekeepers, athletics, exemption, **Labor
3352**
Total amount, determination, **Labor 5801**
Total dependency, death benefits, **Labor
4702**
Total disability,
Computation of payments, **Labor 4659**
Permanent disability, **Labor 4658, 4662**
Temporary disability, **Labor 4653**
Trade, business, profession or occupation
of employer, definitions, **Labor 3356**

WORKERS COMPENSATION—Cont'd
Trade secrets, insurance, studies, insolven-
cy, **Labor 77.7**
Training,
Return to work program, **Labor 139.47
et seq.**
State department of rehabilitation, **La-
bor 3351.5**
Vocational rehabilitation, generally,
post
Vouchers, **Labor 4658.5, 4658.6**
Worker safety and health training and
education program, **Labor 6354.7**
Transcripts, **Labor 5704**
Certified copies, fees and costs, **Labor
5811**
Translators. Interpreters and translators,
generally, ante
Traveling expenses,
Administrative law judges, **Labor 123.6**
Depositions, **Labor 5710**
Health and safety and workers compen-
sation board, **Labor 75**
Medical examinations, **Labor 4600**
Medical legal expenses, contested cases,
reimbursement, **Labor 4621**
Treatment. Medical care and treatment,
generally, ante
Trial, **Labor 5309**
Uninsured employers fund awards, **La-
bor 3717 et seq.**
Trial de novo, **Labor 5952**
Trust funds,
Subsequent injuries benefits trust fund,
Labor 62.5
Uninsured employers benefits trust
fund, **Labor 62.5**
Trusts and trustees,
Appointment, **Labor 5307.5, 5408**
Payment,
Death benefits, **Labor 4704**
Lump sum payments, **Labor 5102 et
seq.**
Tuberculosis,
Law enforcement officers, **Labor 3212.6**
Presumptions, **Labor 3212.10**
Two or more injuries, separate determina-
tion of questions of fact and law,
Labor 3208.2
Umpires, exemption, **Labor 3352**
Undertaking on stay order, **Labor 6000 et
seq.**
Undue expense, commutation of compen-
sation, **Labor 5100**
Unemployment compensation,
Application of law, **Un Ins 21**
Disability compensation,
Certificate of disability, **Un Ins 2708.1**
Effect of receiving, **Un Ins 2629**
Lien against, discharged, **Un Ins 2741**
Eligibility for benefits, **Un Ins 1255.5**
Liens, disability benefits, **Labor 3865,
4903, 4904**
Overpayment of benefits, **Un Ins 1375.3**
Reduction of benefits, **Un Ins 2629**

WORKERS COMPENSATION—Cont'd
Unemployment compensation—Cont'd
Temporary partial disability, reduction of benefits, **Labor 4654**
Unemployment work relief program, average earnings, computation, **Labor 4456**
Uninsured employers, **Labor 90.3**
Awards, payment or bond, **Labor 3715 et seq.**
Bonds (officers and fiduciaries), appeals boards, **Labor 3715 et seq.**
Fines and penalties, **Labor 3722 et seq.**
Injunction, **Labor 3710.2**
Payment, state compensation insurance fund, installments, **Labor 5106**
Stop orders, **Labor 3710.1**
Uninsured employers benefits trust fund, **Labor 62.5, 3716 et seq.**
Payment, **Labor 4903.3**
United States, benefits, setoff and counterclaim, **Labor 4355**
University of California,
Firemen, **Labor 3212.4, 4804.1 et seq.**
Police, **Labor 3213, 4806 et seq.**
Unreasonable delay or refusal of award, attorney fees, **Labor 5814.5**
Utilization review, medical care and treatment, **Labor 4610**
Utilization schedules, medical care and treatment, **Labor 4604.5, 5307.27**
Vanpooling, course of employment, **Labor 3600.8**
Venue, change of venue, **Labor 5501.6**
Verification, petition for reconsideration of award, order or decision, **Labor 5902, 5905**
Victims of crime, notice, eligibility, **Labor 3553**
Vocational education, **Labor 3368**
Vocational rehabilitation,
Collective bargaining, **Labor 3201.5**
Correctional institutions, direct placement services, **Labor 3370**
Included in term compensation, **Labor 3207**
Inmates, direct placement services, **Labor 3370**
Labor and management agreements, **Labor 3201.7**
Vouchers, **Labor 4658.5, 4658.6**
Voluntary off duty recreational activities, liability for injuries, **Labor 3600**
Volunteer firefighters and fire departments. Firefighters and Fire Departments, this index
Volunteer sheriffs reserve members, **Labor 3364**
Volunteers,
Nonprofit organizations, employees, coverage, **Labor 3363.6**
Private nonprofit corporations, exclusion, **Labor 3352**
Public officers and employees, **Labor 3363.5**

WORKERS COMPENSATION—Cont'd
Volunteers—Cont'd
Recreation and park workers, **Labor 3361.5**
Vouchers, vocational rehabilitation, **Labor 4658.5, 4658.6**
Waiting period,
Disability payment, **Labor 4652**
Waiver by employer, **Labor 3750**
Waiver,
Acceptance of benefits, **Labor 4909**
Limitation of proceedings, **Labor 5409**
Matters other than set forth in petition for reconsideration, **Labor 5904**
Warnings, fraud, **Labor 3822**
Warrants,
Attachment, power to issue, **Labor 134**
Cash revolving fund, uninsured employers benefits trust fund, **Labor 3728**
Commitment, power to issue, **Labor 134**
Subsequent injury payments, insurance fund, **Labor 4755**
Watchmen, exclusion, **Labor 3358**
Wearing apparel manufacturers, documentation of coverage, application for manufacturer registration, **Labor 2675**
Weekly loss of wages during temporary partial disability, computation of probable earnings, **Labor 4657**
Welfare benefit plans,
Employees, liens against compensation payments, reimbursement, **Labor 4903.1**
Liens and incumbrances, compensation award, reimbursement, **Labor 4903.1**
Wilful misconduct,
Employee, **Labor 4551 et seq.**
Employer, **Labor 4553, 4553.1**
Withdrawal, stop orders or penalty assessments, employers security payment compensation, **Labor 3727.1**
Witnesses,
Compelling attendance, **Labor 132**
Contempt proceedings, **Labor 132**
Depositions, **Labor 5710**
Fees and mileage, **Labor 131**
Subsequent injuries, hearings, **Labor 4753.5**
Objections to reference of proceedings, **Labor 5311**
Release or compromise agreements, **Labor 5003**
Subpoenas for attendance, **Labor 130**
Work experience education, high schools or regional occupational centers, **Labor 3368**
Work relief program, average earnings, computation, **Labor 4456**
Worker safety and health training and education program, **Labor 6354.7**
Workers compensation administration revolving fund, **Labor 78**
Workers compensation appeals boards.
Appeals boards, generally, ante

WORKERS COMPENSATION—Cont'd
Workers compensation division. Industrial Relations Department, this index
Workmen associated in partnership, **Labor 3360**
Writ of review, **Labor 5950, 5951, 5954**
Writs, power to issue, **Labor 134**
Written instruments,
Applications and answers, **Labor 5500**
Decision on reconsideration of order, decision or award, **Labor 5908.5**
Release or compromise agreements, **Labor 5003**
X rays,
Laboratory services, denial of petition to reduce award, liability for expenses, **Labor 4555.5**
Medical legal expenses, contested claims, **Labor 4620 et seq.**
Physicians and surgeons, referrals, conflict of interest, **Labor 139.3, 139.31**
Young La Follette Self Insurers Security Act, **Labor 3740 et seq.**

WORKERS COMPENSATION ADMINISTRATION REVOLVING FUND
Generally, **Labor 78**

WORKERS COMPENSATION HEALTH CARE PROVIDER ORGANIZATION ACT
Health care provider organizations. Workers Compensation, this index

WORKERS COMPENSATION TRUTH IN ADVERTISING ACT
Generally, **Labor 5430 et seq.**

WORKERS MEMORIAL DAY
Generally, **Labor 29.5**

WORKERS OCCUPATIONAL SAFETY AND HEALTH EDUCATION FUND
Generally, **Labor 6354.7**

WORKFORCE INVESTMENT ACT
Generally, **Un Ins 14000 et seq.**

WORKING CONDITIONS
Labor and Employment, this index

WORKING DAYS
Maximum, **Labor 552**
Exemptions, mandatory orders, **Labor 1198.3**

WORKMENS SAFETY ACT
Safety in employment. Labor and Employment, this index

WORKPLACE VIOLENCE SAFETY ACT
Generally, **CCP 527.8**

WORKS OF ART
Art and Artists, generally, this index

WORKSHOPS
Manufacturers and Manufacturing, generally, this index

WORKWEEK
Definitions, hours, **Labor 500**

WORLD

WORLD WAR II
Veterans, generally, this index

WORLD WAR VETERANS
Veterans, generally, this index

WORSHIP
Religion, generally, this index

WRECKS AND WRECKERS
Railroads, this index

WRIT OF ERROR
Appeal and Review, generally, this index

WRIT OF MANDATE
Mandamus, generally, this index

WRITING
Definitions,
　　Labor Code, **Labor 8**
　　Unemployment insurance code, **Un Ins 8**

WRITS
Attachment, generally, this index
Injunction, generally, this index
Mandamus, generally, this index
Workers compensation, appeals board, power to issue, **Labor 134**

WRITTEN AGREEMENT
Definitions, arbitration, **CCP 1280**

WRITTEN INSTRUMENTS
Assignment, wages, **Labor 300**
Cash bond of employee, **Labor 403**
Workers Compensation, this index

WRONGFUL DEATH
Boilers, negligent operation, **Labor 7771**
Distribution of claim recovery, priorities and preferences, **Labor 2803**
Exemplary damages, homicide, **CC 3294**
Homicide, exemplary damages, **CC 3294**
Labor and employment, occupational safety and health, **Labor 6304.5**
Occupational safety and health, **Labor 6304.5**
Priorities and preferences, proceeds of claim, **Labor 2803**
Probate Proceedings, this index

X RAYS
Workers Compensation, this index

YOUTH AUTHORITY
Juvenile Facilities Division, generally, this index

YOUTH CONSERVATION CORPS
Conservation Corps, generally, this index

YOUTH COUNCILS
Workforce investment, **Un Ins 14208 et seq.**

YOUTH EDUCATIONAL FACILITIES
Regional youth education facilities. Juvenile Institutions and Schools, this index

YOUTHBUILD PROGRAM
Generally, **Un Ins 9800 et seq.**

ZONE EXPIRATION DATE
Definitions,
　　Corporation taxes, enterprise zones, credits, **Rev & T 23622.7**
　　Income tax credits, enterprise zones, **Rev & T 17053.74**

ZONING AND PLANNING
Agricultural use designation, labor camps, **Health & S 17021.6**
Enterprise Zones, generally, this index
Fair employment and housing, referral of case to attorney general, **Gov 12981**
Housing, this index
Labor Camps, this index
Residential use of property, labor camps, **Health & S 17021.5**

†